BECKETT®

Baseball Card PRICE GUIDE

NUMBER 20

Edited By

Dr. James Beckett, Rich Klein & Grant Sandground

with the Price Guide staff of

BECKETT BASEBALL CARD MONTHLY

BECKETT PUBLICATIONS • DALLAS, TEXAS

Prices in this guide reflect current retail rates determined just prior to printing. They do not reflect for-sale prices by the author, publisher, distributors, advertisers, or any card dealers associated with this guide. Every effort has been made to eliminate errors. Readers are invited to write us noting any errors which may be researched and corrected in subsequent printings. The publisher will not be held responsible for losses which may occur in the sale or purchase of cards because of information contained herein.

BECKETT PUBLICATIONS
DALLAS, TEXAS

Manufactured in the United States of America
First Printing
ISBN 1-887432-37-X

Beckett Baseball Card Price Guide
Table of Contents

Baseball

Index to Advertisers

About the Author

Jim Beckett, the leading authority on sport card values in the United States, maintains a wide range of activities in the world of sports. He possesses one of the finest collections of sports cards and autographs in the world, has made numerous appearances on radio and television, and has been frequently cited in many national publications. He was awarded the first "Special Achievement Award" for Contributions to the Hobby by the National Sports Collectors Convention in 1980, the "Jock-Jaspersen Award" for Hobby Dedication in 1983, and the "Buck Barker, Spirit of the Hobby" Award in 1991.

Dr. Beckett is the author of *Beckett Baseball Card Price Guide, The Official Price Guide to Baseball Cards, Price Guide to Baseball Collectibles, The Sport Americana Baseball Memorabilia and Autograph Price Guide, Beckett Almanac of Baseball Cards and Collectibles, Beckett Football Card Price Guide, The Official Price Guide to Football Cards, Beckett Hockey Card Price Guide, The Official Price Guide to Hockey Cards, Beckett Basketball Card Price Guide, The Official Price Guide to Basketball Cards, and The Sport Americana Baseball Card Alphabetical Checklist.* In addition, he is the founder, publisher, and editor of *Beckett Baseball Card Monthly, Beckett Basketball Monthly, Beckett Football Card Monthly, Beckett Hockey Monthly, Beckett Sports Collectibles and Autograph, Beckett Racing Monthly.*

Jim Beckett received his Ph.D. in Statistics from Southern Methodist University in 1975. Prior to starting Beckett Publications in 1984, Dr. Beckett served as an Associate Professor of Statistics at Bowling Green State University and as a vice president of a consulting firm in Dallas, Texas. He currently resides in Dallas with his wife, Patti, and their daughters, Christina, Rebecca, and Melissa.

How To Use This Book

Isn't it great? Every year this book gets bigger and bigger with all the new sets coming out. But even more exciting is that every year there are more collectors, more shows, more stores, and more interest in the cards we love so much. This edition has been enhanced and expanded from the previous edition. The cards you collect — who appears on them, what they look like, where they are from, and (most important to most of you) what their current values are — are enumerated within. Many of the features contained in the other *Beckett Price Guides* have been incorporated into this volume since condition grading, terminology, and many other aspects of collecting are common to the card hobby in general. We hope you find the book both interesting and useful in your collecting pursuits.

The *Beckett Guide* has been successful where other attempts have failed because it is complete, current, and valid. This Price Guide contains not just one, but three prices by condition for all the baseball cards listed. The prices were added to the card lists just prior to printing and reflect not the author's opinions or desires but the going retail prices for each card, based on the marketplace (sports memorabilia conventions and shows, sports card shops, hobby papers, current mail-order catalogs, local club meetings, auction results, and other firsthand reportings of actually realized prices).

What is the best price guide available on the market today? Of course, card sellers prefer the price guide with the highest prices, while card buyers naturally prefer the one with the lowest prices. Accuracy, however, is the true test. Use the price guide trusted by more collectors and dealers than all the others combined. Look for the *Beckett®* name. I won't put my name on anything I won't stake my reputation on. Not the lowest and not the highest — but the most accurate, with integrity.

To facilitate your use of this book, read the complete introductory section on the following pages before going to the pricing pages. Every collectible field has its own terminology; we've tried to capture most of these terms and definitions in our glossary. Please read carefully the section on grading and the condition of your cards, as you cannot determine which price column is appropriate for a given card without first knowing its condition.

Welcome to the world of baseball cards.

Jim Beckett

Introduction

Welcome to the exciting world of baseball card collecting, America's fastest-growing avocation. You have made a good choice in buying this book, since it will open up to you the entire panorama of this field in the simplest, most concise way.

The growth of *Beckett Baseball Card Monthly, Beckett Basketball Monthly, Beckett Football Card Monthly, Beckett Hockey Monthly, Beckett Sports Collectibles and Autographs and Beckett Racing Monthly* is an indication of the unprecedented popularity of sports cards. Founded in 1984 by Dr. James Beckett, the author of this Price Guide, *Beckett Baseball Card Monthly* contains the most extensive and accepted monthly Price Guide, collectible glossy superstar covers, colorful feature articles, "Short Prints," Convention Calendar, tips for beginners, "Readers Write" letters to and responses from the editor, information on errors and varieties, autograph collecting tips and profiles of the sport's Hottest stars. Published every month, *BBCM* is the hobby's largest paid circulation periodical. The other five magazines were built on the success of *BBCM*.

So collecting baseball cards — while still pursued as a hobby with youthful exuberance by kids in the neighborhood — has also taken on the trappings of an industry, with thousands of full- and part-time card dealers, as well as vendors of supplies, clubs and conventions. In fact, each year since 1980 thousands of hobbyists have assembled for a National Sports Collectors Convention, at which hundreds of dealers have displayed their wares, seminars have been conducted, autographs penned by sports notables, and millions of cards changed hands. The Beckett Guide is the best annual guide available to the exciting world of baseball cards. Read it and use it. May your enjoyment and your card collection increase in the coming months and years.

How to Collect

Each collection is personal and reflects the individuality of its owner. There are no set rules on how to collect cards. Since card collecting is a hobby or leisure pastime, what you collect, how much you collect, and how much time and money you spend collecting are entirely up to you. The funds you have available for collecting and your own personal taste should determine how you collect. Information and ideas presented here are intended to help you get the most enjoyment from this hobby.

It is impossible to collect every card ever produced. Therefore, beginners as well as intermediate and advanced collectors usually specialize in some way. One of the reasons this hobby is popular is that individual collectors can define and tailor their collecting methods to match their own tastes. To give you some ideas of the various approaches to collecting, we will list some of the more popular areas of specialization.

Many collectors select complete sets from particular years. For example, they may concentrate on assembling complete sets from all the years since their birth or since they became avid sports fans. They may try to collect a card for every player during that specified period of time.

Many others wish to acquire only certain players. Usually such players are the superstars of the sport, but occasionally collectors will specialize in all the cards of players who attended a particular college or came from a certain town. Some collectors are only interested in the first cards or Rookie Cards of certain players. A handy guide for collectors interested in pursuing the hobby this way is the *Sport Americana Baseball Card Alphabetical Checklist*.

Another fun way to collect cards is by team. Most fans have a favorite team, and it is natural for that loyalty to be translated into a desire for cards of the players on that favorite team. For most of the recent years, team sets (all the cards from a given team for that year) are readily available at a reasonable price. *The Sport Americana Team Baseball Card Checklist* will open up this field to the collector.

Obtaining Cards

Several avenues are open to card collectors. Cards still can be purchased in the traditional way: by the pack at the local candy, grocery, drug or major discount stores.

But there are also thousands of card shops across the country that specialize in selling cards individually or by the pack, box, or set. Another alternative is the thousands of card shows held each month around the country, which feature any-

where from eight to 800 tables of sports cards and memorabilia for sale.

For many years, it has been possible to purchase complete sets of baseball cards through mail-order advertisers found in traditional sports media publications, such as *The Sporting News, Baseball Digest, Street & Smith* yearbooks, and others. These sets also are advertised in the card collecting periodicals. Many collectors will begin by subscribing to at least one of the hobby periodicals, all with good up-to-date information. In fact, subscription offers can be found in the advertising section of this book.

Most serious card collectors obtain old (and new) cards from one or more of several main sources: (1) trading or buying from other collectors or dealers; (2) responding to sale or auction ads in the hobby publications; (3) buying at a local hobby store; and/or (4) attending sports collectibles shows or conventions.

We advise that you try all four methods since each has its own distinct advantages: (1) trading is a great way to make new friends; (2) hobby periodicals help you keep up with what's going on in the hobby (including when and where the conventions are happening); (3) stores provide the opportunity to enjoy personalized service and consider a great diversity of material in a relaxed sports-oriented atmosphere; and (4) shows allow you to choose from multiple dealers and thousands of cards under one roof in a competitive situation.

Preserving Your Cards

Cards are fragile. They must be handled properly in order to retain their value. Careless handling can easily result in creased or bent cards. It is, however, not recommended that tweezers or tongs be used to pick up your cards since such utensils might mar or indent card surfaces and thus reduce those cards' conditions and values.

In general, your cards should be handled directly as little as possible. This is sometimes easier to say than to do.

Although there are still many who use custom boxes, storage trays, or even shoe boxes, plastic sheets are the preferred method of many collectors for storing cards.

A collection stored in plastic pages in a three-ring album allows you to view your collection at any time without the need to touch the card itself. Cards can also be kept in single holders (of various types and thickness) designed for the enjoyment of each card individually.

For a large collection, some collectors may use a combination of the above methods. When purchasing plastic sheets for your cards, be sure that you find the pocket size that fits the cards snugly. Don't put your 1951 Bowman in a sheet designed to fit 1981 Topps.

Most hobby and collectibles shops and virtually all collectors' conventions will have these plastic pages available in quantity for the various sizes offered, or you can purchase them directly from the advertisers in this book.

Also, remember that pocket size isn't the only factor to consider when looking for plastic sheets. Other factors such as safety, economy, appearance, availability, or personal preference also may indicate which types of sheets a collector may want to buy.

Damp, sunny and/or hot conditions — no, this is not a weather forecast — are three elements to avoid in extremes if you are interested in preserving your collection. Too much (or too little) humidity can cause the gradual deterioration of a card. Direct, bright sun (or fluorescent light) over time will bleach out the color of a card. Extreme heat accelerates the decomposition of the card. On the other hand, many cards have lasted more than 75 years without much scientific intervention. So be cautious, even if the above factors typically present a problem only when present in the extreme. It never hurts to be prudent.

Collecting vs. Investing

Collecting individual players and collecting complete sets are both popular vehicles for investment and speculation.

Most investors and speculators stock up on complete sets or on quantities of players they think have good investment potential.

There is obviously no guarantee in this book, or anywhere else for that matter, that cards will outperform the stock market or other investment alternatives in the future. After all, baseball cards do not pay quarterly dividends and cards cannot be sold at their "current values" as easily as stocks or bonds.

Nevertheless, investors have noticed a favorable long-term trend in the past performance of baseball and other sports collectibles, and certain cards and sets have outperformed just about any other investment in some years.

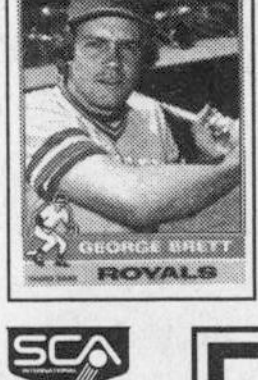

Many hobbyists maintain that the best investment is and always will be the building of a collection, which traditionally has held up better than outright speculation.

Some of the obvious questions are: Which cards? When to buy? When to sell? The best investment you can make is in your own education.

The more you know about your collection and the hobby, the more informed the decisions you will be able to make. We're not selling investment tips. We're selling information about the current value of baseball cards. It's up to you to use that information to your best advantage.

Terminology

Each hobby has its own language to describe its area of interest. The nomenclature traditionally used for trading cards is derived from the *American Card Catalog*, published in 1960 by Nostalgia Press. That catalog, written by Jefferson Burdick (who is called the "Father of Card Collecting" for his pioneering work), uses letter and number designations for each separate set of cards. The letter used in the ACC designation refers to the generic type of card. While both sport and non-sport issues are classified in the ACC, we shall confine ourselves to the sport issues. The following list defines the letters and their meanings as used by the *American Card Catalog.*

(none) or N - 19th Century U.S. Tobacco
B - Blankets
D - Bakery Inserts Including Bread
E - Early Candy and Gum
F - Food Inserts
H - Advertising
M - Periodicals
PC - Postcards
R - Candy and Gum since 1930

Following the letter prefix and an optional hyphen are one-, two-, or three-digit numbers, R(-)999. These typically represent the company or entity issuing the cards. In several cases, the ACC number is extended by an additional hyphen and another one- or two-digit numerical suffix. For example, the 1957 Topps regular-series baseball card issue carries an ACC designation of R414-11. The "R" indicates a Candy or Gum card produced since 1930. The "414" is the ACC designation for Topps Chewing Gum baseball card issues, and the "11" is the ACC designation for the 1957 regular issue (Topps' eleventh baseball set). Like other traditional methods of identification, this system provides order to the process of cataloging cards; however, most serious collectors learn the ACC designation of the popular sets by repetition and familiarity, rather than by attempting to "figure out" what they might or should be. From 1948 forward, collectors and dealers commonly refer to all sets by their year, maker, type of issue, and any other distinguishing characteristic. For example, such a characteristic could be an unusual issue or one of several regular issues put out by a specific maker in a single year. Regional issues are usually referred to by year, maker, and sometimes by title or theme of the set.

Glossary/Legend

Our glossary defines terms used in the card collecting hobby and in this book. Many of these terms are also common to other types of sports memorabilia collecting. Some terms may have several meanings depending on use and context.

ACC - Acronym for American Card Catalog.

ACETATE - A transparent plastic.

ANN- Announcer.

AS - All-Star card. A card portraying an All-Star Player of the previous year that says "All-Star" on its face.

ATG - All-Time Great card.

ATL - All-Time Leaders card.

AU(TO) - Autographed card.

BC - Bonus Card.

BL - Blue letters.

BLANKET - A felt square (normally 5 to 6 inches) portraying a baseball player.

BOX CARD - Card issued on a box (i.e., 1987 Topps Box Bottoms).

BRICK - A group of 50 or more cards having common characteristics that is intended to be bought, sold or traded as a unit.

CABINETS - Popular and highly valuable photographs on thick card stock produced in the 19th and early 20th century.

CHECKLIST - A list of the cards contained in a particular set. The list is always in numerical order if the cards are numbered. Some unnumbered sets are artificially numbered in alphabetical order, by team and alphabetically within the team, or by uniform number for convenience.

CL - Checklist card. A card that lists in order the cards and players in the set or series. Older

checklist cards in Mint condition that have not been marked are very desirable and command premiums.

CO - Coach.

COIN - A small disc of metal or plastic portraying a player in its center.

COLLECTOR ISSUE - A set produced for the sake of the card itself with no product or service sponsor. It derives its name from the fact that most of these sets are produced for sale directly to the hobby market.

COM - Card issued by the Post Cereal Company through their mail-in offer.

COMM - Commissioner.

COMMON CARD - The typical card of any set; it has no premium value accruing from subject matter, numerical scarcity, popular demand, or anomaly.

CONVENTION - A gathering of dealers and collectors at a single location for the purpose of buying, selling, and trading sports memorabilia items. Conventions are open to the public and sometimes feature autograph guests, door prizes, contests, seminars, etc. They are frequently referred to simply as "shows."

COOP - Cooperstown.

COR - Corrected card.

COUPON - See Tab.

CY - Cy Young Award.

DEALER - A person who engages in buying, selling, and trading sports collectibles or supplies. A dealer may also be a collector, but as a dealer, his main goal is to earn a profit.

DIE-CUT - A card with part of its stock partially cut, allowing one or more parts to be folded or removed. After removal or appropriate folding, the remaining part of the card can frequently be made to stand up.

DISC - A circular-shaped card.

DISPLAY CARD - A sheet, usually containing three to nine cards, that is printed and used by the manufacturer to advertise and/or display the packages containing his products and cards. The backs of display cards are blank or contain advertisements.

DK - Diamond King.

DL - Division Leaders.

DP - Double Print (a card that was printed in double the quantity compared to the other cards in the same series) or a Draft Pick card.

DUFEX - A method of card manufacturing technology patented by Pinnacle Brands, Inc. It involves a refractive quality to a card with a foil coating.

EMBOSSED - A raised surface; features of a card that are projected from a flat background.

ERA - Earned Run Average.

ERR - Error card. A card with erroneous information, spelling, or depiction on either side of the card. Most errors are not corrected by the producing card company.

ETCHED - Impressions within the surface of a card.

EXHIBIT - The generic name given to thick-stock, postcard-size cards with single color obverse pictures. The name is derived from the Exhibit Supply Co. of Chicago, the principal manufacturer of this type of card. These also are known as Arcade cards since they were found in many arcades.

FDP - First or First Round Draft Pick.

FOIL - Foil embossed stamp on card.

FOLD - Foldout.

FS - Father/son card.

FULL BLEED - A borderless card; a card containing a photo that encompasses the entire card.

FULL SHEET - A complete sheet of cards that has not been cut up into individual cards by the manufacturer. Also called an uncut sheet.

FUN - Fun Cards.

GL - Green letters.

GLOSS - A card with luster; a shiny finish as in a card with UV coating.

HIGH NUMBER - The cards in the last series of numbers in a year in which such higher-numbered cards were printed or distributed in significantly lesser amounts than the lower-numbered cards. The high-number designation refers to a scarcity of the high-numbered cards. Not all years have high numbers in terms of this definition.

HL - Highlight card.

HOF - Hall of Fame, or a card that portrays a Hall of Famer (HOFer).

HOLOGRAM - A three-dimensional photographic image.

HOR - Horizontal pose on card as opposed to the standard vertical orientation found on most cards.

IA - In Action card.

IF - Infielder.

INSERT - A card of a different type or any other

sports collectible (typically a poster or sticker) contained and sold in the same package along with a card or cards of a major set. An insert card is either unnumbered or not numbered in the same sequence as the major set. Sometimes the inserts are randomly distributed and are not found in every pack.

INTERACTIVE - A concept that involves collector participation.

ISSUE - Synonymous with set, but usually used in conjunction with a manufacturer, e.g., a Topps issue.

KARAT - A unit of measure for the fineness of gold; i.e. 24K.

LAYERING - The separation or peeling of one or more layers of the card stock, usually at the corner of the card.

LEGITIMATE ISSUE - A set produced to promote or boost sales of a product or service, e.g., bubblegum, cereal, cigarettes, etc. Most collector issues are not legitimate issues in this sense.

LHP - Lefthanded pitcher.

LID - A circular-shaped card (possibly with tab) that forms the top of the container for the product being promoted.

LL - League leaders or large letters on card.

MAJOR SET - A set produced by a national manufacturer of cards containing a large number of cards. Usually 100 or more different cards comprise a major set.

MEM - Memorial card. For example, the 1990 Donruss and Topps Bart Giamatti cards.

METALLIC - A glossy design method that enhances card features.

MG - Manager.

MINI - A small card; for example, a 1975 Topps card of identical design but smaller dimensions than the regular Topps issue of 1975.

ML - Major League.

MULTI-PLAYER CARD - A single card depicting two or more players (but not a team card).

MVP - Most Valuable Player.

NAU - No autograph on card.

NH - No-Hitter.

NNOF - No Name on Front.

NOF - Name on Front.

NON-SPORT CARD - A card from a set whose major theme is a subject other than a sports subject. A card of a sports figure or event that is part of a non-sport set is still a non-sport card, e.g., while the "Look 'N' See" non-sport card set contains a card of Babe Ruth, a sports figure; that card is a non-sport card.

NOTCHING - The grooving of the card, usually caused by fingernails, rubber bands, or bumping card edges against other objects.

OF - Outfield or Outfielder.

OLY - Olympics Card.

ORG - Organist.

P - Pitcher or Pitching pose.

P1 - First Printing.

P2 - Second Printing.

P3 - Third Printing.

PACKS - A means with which cards are issued in terms of pack type (wax, cello, foil, rack, etc.) and channels of distribution (hobby, retail, etc.).

PANEL - An extended card that is composed of two or more individual cards. Often the panel forms the back part of the container for the product being promoted, e.g., a Hostess panel, a Bazooka panel, an Esskay Meat panel.

PARALLEL- A card that is similar in design to its counterpart from a basic set, but offers a distinguishing quality.

PCL - Pacific Coast League.

PF - Profiles.

PLASTIC SHEET - A clear, plastic page that is punched for insertion into a binder (with standard three-ring spacing) containing pockets for displaying cards. Many different styles of sheets exist with pockets of varying sizes to hold the many differing card formats. Also called a display sheet or storage sheet.

PLATINUM - A metallic element used in the process of creating a glossy card.

PR - Printed name on back.

PREMIUM - A card, sometimes on photographic stock, that is purchased or obtained in conjunction with, or redemption for, another card or product. The premium is not packaged in the same unit as the primary item.

PRES - President.

PRISMATIC/PRISM - A glossy or bright design that refracts or disperses light.

PUZZLE CARD - A card whose back contains a part of a picture which, when joined correctly with other puzzle cards, forms the completed picture.

PUZZLE PIECE - A die-cut piece designed to interlock with similar pieces (e.g., early 1980's Donruss).

PVC - Polyvinyl Chloride, a substance used to make many of the popular card display protective sheets. Non-PVC sheets are considered preferable for long-term storage of cards by many.

RARE - A card or series of cards of very limited availability. Unfortunately, "rare" is a subjective term frequently used indiscriminately to hype value. "Rare" cards are harder to obtain than "scarce" cards.

RB - Record Breaker.

REDEMPTION- A program established by multiple card manufacturers that allows collectors to mail in a special card (usually a random insert) in return for special cards, sets or other prizes not available through conventional channels.

REFRACTORS - A card that features a design element which enhances (distorts) its color/appearance through deflecting light.

REGIONAL - A card or set of cards issued and distributed only in a limited geographical area of the country.

REPLICA - An identical copy or reproduction.

REV NEG - Reversed or flopped photo side of the card. This is a major type of error card, but only some are corrected.

RHP - Righthanded pitcher.

ROY - Rookie of the Year.

RP - Relief pitcher.

SA - Super Action card.

SASE - Self-Addressed, Stamped Envelope.

SB - Stolen Bases.

SCARCE - A card or series of cards of limited availability. This subjective term is sometimes used indiscriminately to hype value. "Scarce" cards are not as difficult to obtain as "rare" cards.

SCR - Script name on back.

SD - San Diego Padres.

SEMI-HIGH - A card from the next to last series of a sequentially issued set. It has more value than an average card and generally less value than a high number. A card is not called a semi-high unless the next to last series in which it exists has an additional premium attached to it.

SERIES - The entire set of cards issued by a particular producer in a particular year; e.g., the 1971 Topps series. Also, within a particular set, series can refer to a group of (consecutively numbered) cards printed at the same time; e.g., the first series of the 1957 Topps issue (#1 through #88).

SET - One each of the entire run of cards of the same type produced by a particular manufacturer during a single year. In other words, if you have a complete set of 1976 Topps then you have every card from #1 up to and including #660, i.e., all the different cards that were produced.

SF - Starflics.

SHEEN - Brightness or luster emitted by a card.

SKIP-NUMBERED - A set that has many unissued card numbers between the lowest number in the set and the highest number in the set; e.g., the 1948 Leaf baseball set contains 98 cards skip-numbered from #1 to #168. A major set in which a few numbers were not printed is not considered to be skip-numbered.

SP - Single or Short Print (a card which was printed in lesser quantity compared to the other cards in the same series; see also DP and TP).

SPECIAL CARD - A card that portrays something other than a single player or team; for example, a card that portrays the previous year's statistical leaders or the results from the previous year's World Series.

SS - Shortstop.

STAMP - Adhesive-backed papers depicting a player. The stamp may be individual or in a sheet of many stamps. Moisture must be applied to the adhesive in order for the stamp to be attached to another surface.

STANDARD SIZE - Most modern sports cards measure 2-1/2 by 3-1/2 inches. Exceptions are noted in card descriptions throughout this book.

STAR CARD - A card that portrays a player of some repute, usually determined by his ability, however, sometimes referring to sheer popularity.

STICKER - A card with a removable layer that can be affixed to (stuck onto) another surface.

STOCK - The cardboard or paper on which the card is printed.

STRIP CARDS - A sheet or strip of cards, particularly popular in the 1920s and 1930s, with the individual cards usually separated by broken or dotted lines.

SUPERIMPOSED - To be affixed on top of some-

thing, i.e., a player photo over a solid background.

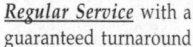

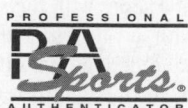

SUPERSTAR CARD - A card that portrays a superstar; e.g., a Hall of Famer or player with strong Hall of Fame potential.

TAB - A card portion set off from the rest of the card, usually with perforations, that may be removed without damaging the central character or event depicted by the card.

TC - Team Checklist.

TEAM CARD - A card that depicts an entire team.

TEST SET - A set, usually containing a small number of cards, issued by a national card producer and distributed in a limited section or sections of the country. Presumably, the purpose of a test set is to test market appeal for a particular type of card.

THREE-DIMENSIONAL (3D) - A visual image that provides an illusion of depth and perspective.

TOPICAL - a subset or group of cards that have a common theme (e.g., MVP award winners).

TP - Triple Print (a card that was printed in triple the quantity compared to the other cards in the same series).

TRANSPARENT - Clear, see through.

TR - Trade reference on card.

TRIMMED - A card cut down from its original size. Trimmed cards are undesirable to most collectors.

UDCA - Upper Deck Classic Alumni.

UER - Uncorrected Error.

UMP - Umpire.

USA - Team USA.

UV - Ultraviolet, a glossy coating used in producing cards.

VAR - Variation card. One of two or more cards from the same series with the same number (or player with identical pose if the series is unnumbered) differing from one another by some aspect, the different feature stemming from the printing or stock of the card. This can be caused when the manufacturer of the cards notices an error in one or more of the cards, makes the changes, and then resumes the print run. In this case there will be two versions or variations of the same card. Sometimes one of the variations is relatively scarce.

VERT - Vertical pose on card.

WAS - Washington National League (1974 Topps).

WC - What's the Call?

WL - White letter on front.

WS - World Series card.

YL - Yellow letters on front

YT - Yellow team name on front.

***** - to denote multi-sport sets.

Understanding Card Values

Determining Value

Why are some cards more valuable than others? Obviously, the economic laws of supply and demand are applicable to card collecting just as they are to any other field where a commodity is bought, sold or traded in a free, unregulated market.

Supply (the number of cards available on the market) is less than the total number of cards originally produced since attrition diminishes that original quantity. Each year a percentage of cards is typically thrown away, destroyed or otherwise lost to collectors. This percentage is much, much smaller today than it was in the past because more and more people have become increasingly aware of the value of their cards.

For those who collect only Mint condition cards, the supply of older cards can be quite small indeed. Until recently, collectors were not so conscious of the need to preserve the condition of their cards. For this reason, it is difficult to know exactly how many 1953 Topps are currently available, Mint or otherwise. It is generally accepted that there are fewer 1953 Topps available than 1963, 1973 or 1983 Topps cards. If demand were equal for each of these sets, the law of supply and demand would increase the price for the least available sets. Demand, however, is never equal for all sets, so price correlations can be complicated. The demand for a card is influenced by many factors. These include: (1) the age of the card; (2) the number of cards printed; (3) the player(s) portrayed on the card; (4) the attractiveness and popularity of the set; and (5) the physical condition of the card.

In general, (1) the older the card, (2) the fewer the number of the cards printed, (3) the more famous, popular and talented the player, (4) the more attractive and popular the set, and (5) the better the condition of the card, the higher the value of the card will be. There are exceptions to all but one of these factors: the condition of the card.

Given two cards similar in all respects except condition, the one in the best condition will always be valued higher.

While those guidelines help to establish the value of a card, the countless exceptions and peculiarities make any simple, direct mathematical formula to determine card values impossible.

Regional Variation

Since the market varies from region to region, card prices of local players may be higher. This is known as a regional premium. How significant the premium is — and if there is any premium at all — depends on the local popularity of the team and the player.

The largest regional premiums usually do not apply to superstars, who often are so well-known nationwide that the prices of their key cards are too high for local dealers to realize a premium.

Lesser stars often command the strongest premiums. Their popularity is concentrated in their home region, creating local demand that greatly exceeds overall demand.

Regional premiums can apply to popular retired players and sometimes can be found in the areas where the players grew up or starred in college.

A regional discount is the converse of a regional premium. Regional discounts occur when a player has been so popular in his region for so long that local collectors and dealers have accumulated quantities of his key cards. The abundant supply may make the cards available in that area at the lowest prices anywhere.

Set Prices

A somewhat paradoxical situation exists in the price of a complete set vs. the combined cost of the individual cards in the set. In nearly every case, the sum of the prices for the individual cards is higher than the cost for the complete set. This is prevalent especially in the cards of the last few years. The reasons for this apparent anomaly stem from the habits of collectors and from the carrying costs to dealers. Today, each card in a set normally is produced in the same quantity as all other cards in its set.

Many collectors pick up only stars, superstars and particular teams. As a result, the dealer is left with a shortage of certain player cards and an abundance of others. He therefore incurs an expense in simply "carrying" these less desirable cards in stock. On the other hand, if he sells a complete set, he gets rid of large numbers of cards at one time. For this reason, he generally is willing to receive less money for a complete set. By doing this, he recovers all of his costs and also makes a profit.

The disparity between the price of the complete set and the sum of the individual cards also has been influenced by the fact that some of the major manufacturers now are pre-collating card sets. Since "pulling" individual cards from the sets involves a specific type of labor (and cost), the singles or star card market is not affected significantly by pre-collation.

Set prices also do not include rare card varieties, unless specifically stated. Of course, the prices for sets do include one example of each type for the given set, but this is the least expensive variety.

Scarce Series

Scarce series occur because cards issued before 1974 were made available to the public each year in several series of finite numbers of cards, rather than all cards of the set being available for purchase at one time. At some point during the year, usually toward the end of the baseball season, interest in current year baseball cards waned. Consequently, the manufacturers produced smaller numbers of these later-series cards.

Nearly all nationwide issues from post-World War II manufacturers (1948 to 1973) exhibit these series variations. In the past, Topps, for example, may have issued series consisting of many different numbers of cards, including 55, 66, 80, 88 and others. Recently, Topps has settled on what is now its standard sheet size of 132 cards, six of which comprise its 792-card set.

While the number of cards within a given series is usually the same as the number of cards on one printed sheet, this is not always the case. For example, Bowman used 36 cards on its standard printed sheets, but in 1948 substituted 12 cards during later print runs of that year's baseball cards. Twelve of the cards from the initial sheet of 36 cards were removed and replaced by 12 different cards giving, in effect, a first series of 36 cards and a second series of 12 new cards. This replacement produced a scarcity of 24 cards — the 12 cards removed from the original sheet and the 12 new cards added to the sheet. A full sheet of 1948

Bowman cards (second printing) shows that card numbers 37 through 48 have replaced 12 of the cards on the first printing sheet.

The Topps Company also has created scarcities and/or excesses of certain cards in many of its sets. Topps, however, has most frequently gone the other direction by double printing some of the cards. Double printing causes an abundance of cards of the players who are on the same sheet more than one time. During the years from 1978 to 1981, Topps double printed 66 cards out of their large 726-card set. The Topps practice of double printing cards in earlier years is the most logical explanation for the known scarcities of particular cards in some of these Topps sets.

From 1988 through 1990, Donruss short printed and double printed certain cards in its major sets. Ostensibly this was because of its addition of bonus team MVP cards in its regular-issue wax packs.

We are always looking for information or photographs of printing sheets of cards for research. Each year, we try to update the hobby's knowledge of distribution anomalies. Please let us know at the address in this book if you have first-hand knowledge that would be helpful in this pursuit.

Grading Your Cards

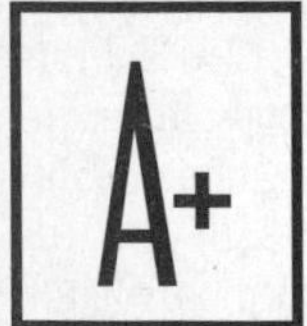

Each hobby has its own grading terminology — stamps, coins, comic books, record collecting, etc. Collectors of sports cards are no exception. The one invariable criterion for determining the value of a card is its condition: The better the condition of the card, the more valuable it is. Condition grading, however, is subjective. Individual card dealers and collectors differ in the strictness of their grading, but the stated condition of a card should be determined without regard to whether it is being bought or sold.

No allowance is made for age. A 1952 card is judged by the same standards as a 1992 card. But there are specific sets and cards that are condition sensitive (marked with "!" in the Price Guide) because of their border color, consistently poor centering, etc. Such cards and sets sometimes command premiums above the listed percentages in Mint condition.

Centering

Current centering terminology uses numbers representing the percentage of border on either side of the main design. Obviously, centering is diminished in importance for borderless cards such as Stadium Club.

Slightly Off-Center (60/40): A slightly off-center card is one that, upon close inspection, is found to have one border bigger than the opposite border. This degree once was offensive to only purists, but now some hobbyists try to avoid cards that are anything other than perfectly centered.

Off-Center (70/30): An off-center card has one border that is noticeably more than twice as wide as the opposite border.

Badly Off-Center (80/20 or worse): A badly off-center card has virtually no border on one side of the card.

Miscut: A miscut card actually shows part of the adjacent card in its larger border and consequently a corresponding amount of its card is cut off.

Corner Wear

Corner wear is the most scrutinized grading criteria in the hobby. These are the major categories of corner wear:

Corner with a slight touch of wear: The corner still is sharp, but there is a slight touch of wear showing. On a dark-bordered card, this shows as a dot of white.

Fuzzy corner: The corner still comes to a point, but the point has just begun to fray. A slightly "dinged" corner is considered the same as a fuzzy corner.

Slightly rounded corner: The fraying of the corner has increased to where there is only a hint of a point. Mild layering may be evident. A "dinged" corner is considered the same as a slightly rounded corner.

Rounded corner: The point is completely gone. Some layering is noticeable.

Badly rounded corner: The corner is completely round and rough. Severe layering is evident.

Creases

A third common defect is the crease. The degree of creasing in a card is difficult to show in a drawing or picture. On giving the specific condition of an expensive card for sale, the seller should note any creases additionally. Creases can be cate-

Centering

Well-centered

Slightly Off-centered

Off-centered

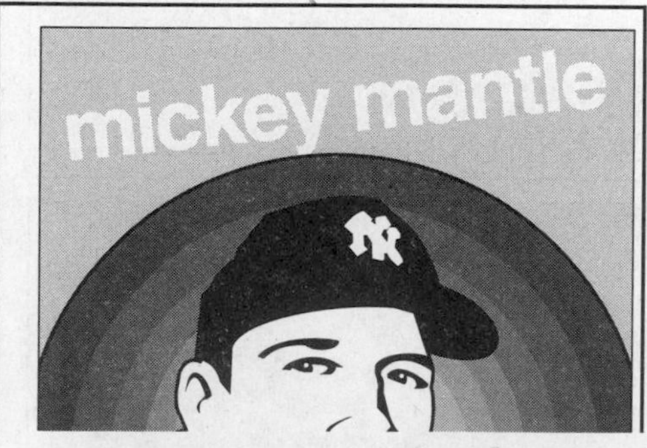

Badly Off-centered

Miscut

Corner Wear

The partial cards shown at right have been photographed at 300%. This was done in order to magnify each card's corner wear to such a degree that differences could be shown on a printed page.

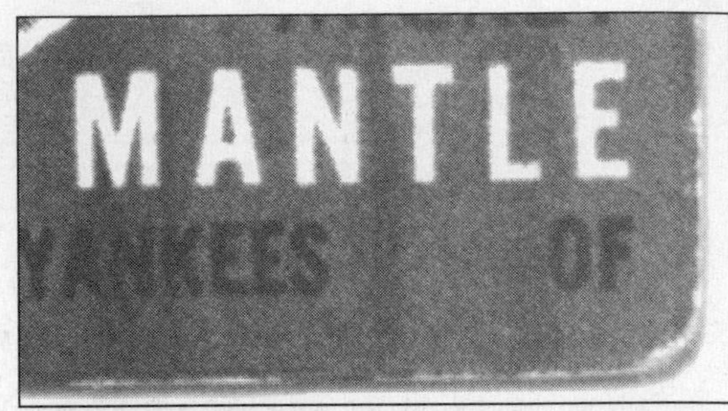

The 1962 Topps Mickey Mantle card definitely has a rounded corner. Some may say that this card is badly rounded, but that is a judgment call.

The 1962 Topps Hank Aaron card has a slighly rounded corner. Note that there is definite corner wear evident by the fraying and that the corner no longer sports a sharp point.

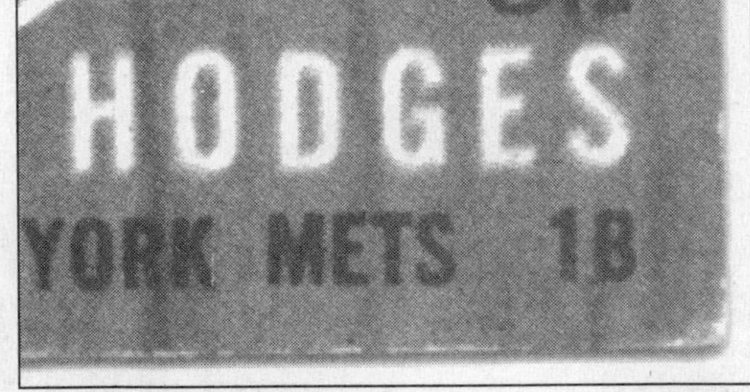

The 1962 Topps Gil Hodges card has corner wear; it is slightly better than the Aaron card above. Nevertheless, some collectors might classify this Hodges corner as slightly rounded.

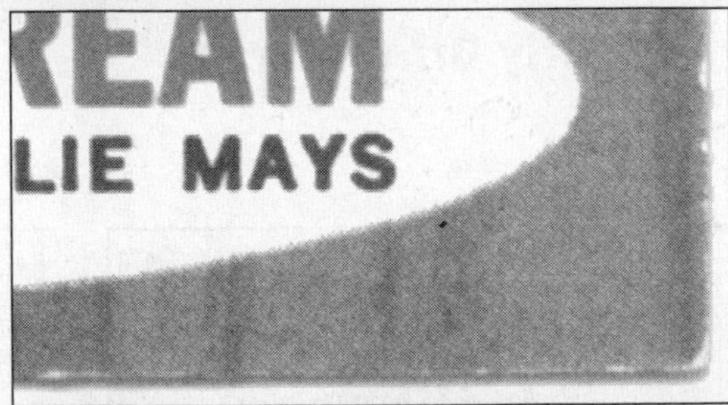

The 1962 Topps Manager's Dream card showing Mantle and Mays has slight corner wear. This is not a fuzzy corner as very slight wear is noticeable on the card's photo surface.

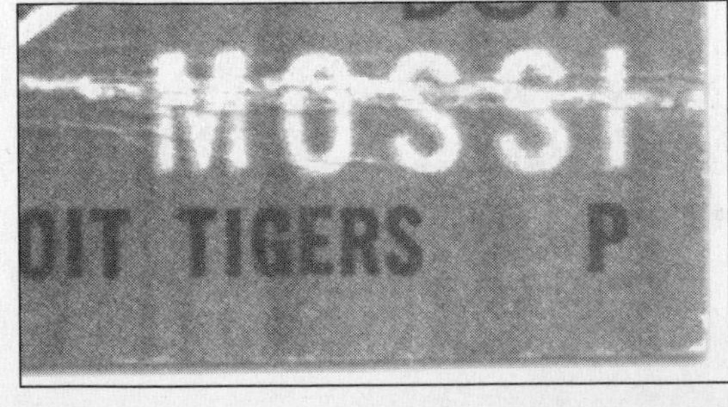

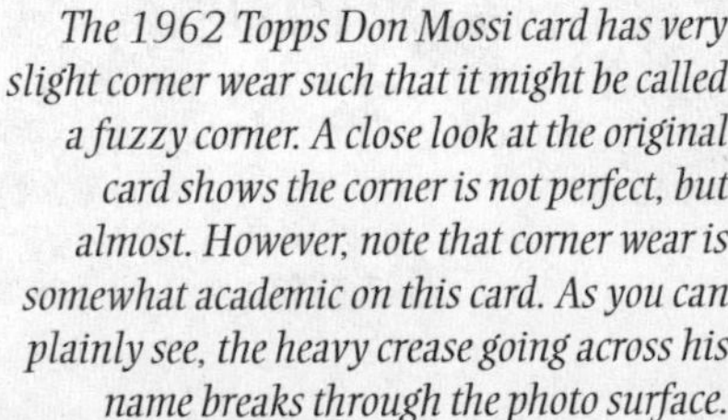

The 1962 Topps Don Mossi card has very slight corner wear such that it might be called a fuzzy corner. A close look at the original card shows the corner is not perfect, but almost. However, note that corner wear is somewhat academic on this card. As you can plainly see, the heavy crease going across his name breaks through the photo surface.

gorized as to severity according to the following scale:

Light Crease: A light crease is a crease that is barely noticeable upon close inspection. In fact, when cards are in plastic sheets or holders, a light crease may not be seen (until the card is taken out of the holder). A light crease on the front is much more serious than a light crease on the card back only.

Medium Crease: A medium crease is noticeable when held and studied at arm's length by the naked eye, but does not overly detract from the appearance of the card. It is an obvious crease, but not one that breaks the picture surface of the card.

Heavy Crease: A heavy crease is one that has torn or broken through the card's picture surface, e.g., puts a tear in the photo surface.

Alterations

Deceptive Trimming: This occurs when someone alters the card in order (1) to shave off edge wear, (2) to improve the sharpness of the corners, or (3) to improve centering — obviously their objective is to falsely increase the perceived value of the card to an unsuspecting buyer. The shrinkage usually is evident only if the trimmed card is compared to an adjacent full-sized card or if the trimmed card is itself measured.

Obvious Trimming: Obvious trimming is noticeable and unfortunate. It is usually performed by non-collectors who give no thought to the present or future value of their cards.

Deceptively Retouched Borders: This occurs when the borders (especially on those cards with dark borders) are touched up on the edges and corners with magic marker or crayons of appropriate color in order to make the card appear Mint.

Categorization of Defects

Miscellaneous Flaws

The following are common minor flaws that, depending on severity, lower a card's condition by one to four grades and often render it no better than Excellent-Mint: bubbles (lumps in surface), gum and wax stains, diamond cutting (slanted borders), notching, off-centered backs, paper wrinkles, scratched-off cartoons or puzzles on back, rubber band marks, scratches, surface impressions and warping.

The following are common serious flaws that, depending on severity, lower a card's condition at least four grades and often render it no better than Good: chemical or sun fading, erasure marks, mildew, miscutting (severe off-centering), holes, bleached or re-touched borders, tape marks, tears, trimming, water or coffee stains and writing.

Condition Guide

Grades

Mint (Mt) - A card with no flaws or wear. The card has four perfect corners, 60/40 or better centering from top to bottom and from left to right, original gloss, smooth edges and original color borders. A Mint card does not have print spots, color or focus imperfections.

Near Mint-Mint (NrMt-Mt) - A card with one minor flaw. Any one of the following would lower a Mint card to Near Mint-Mint: one corner with a slight touch of wear, barely noticeable print spots, color or focus imperfections. The card must have 60/40 or better centering in both directions, original gloss, smooth edges and original color borders.

Near Mint (NrMt) - A card with one minor flaw. Any one of the following would lower a Mint card to Near Mint: one fuzzy corner or two to four corners with slight touches of wear, 70/30 to 60/40 centering, slightly rough edges, minor print spots, color or focus imperfections. The card must have original gloss and original color borders.

Excellent-Mint (ExMt) - A card with two or three fuzzy, but not rounded, corners and centering no worse than 80/20. The card may have no more than two of the following: slightly rough edges, very slightly discolored borders, minor print spots, color or focus imperfections. The card must have original gloss.

Excellent (Ex) - A card with four fuzzy but definitely not rounded corners and centering no worse than 80/20. The card may have a small amount of original gloss lost, rough edges, slightly discolored borders and minor print spots, color or focus imperfections.

Very Good (Vg) - A card that has been handled but not abused: slightly rounded corners with slight layering, slight notching on edges, a significant amount of gloss lost from the surface but no scuffing and moderate discoloration of borders. The card may have a few light creases.

Good (G), Fair (F), Poor (P) - A well-worn, mishandled or abused card: badly rounded and layered corners, scuffing, most or all original gloss missing, seriously discolored borders, moderate or heavy creases, and one or more serious flaws. The grade of Good, Fair or Poor depends on the severity of wear and flaws. Good, Fair and Poor cards generally are used only as fillers.

The most widely used grades are defined above. Obviously, many cards will not perfectly fit one of the definitions.

Therefore, categories between the major grades known as in-between grades are used, such as Good to Very Good (G-Vg), Very Good to Excellent (VgEx), and Excellent-Mint to Near Mint (ExMt-NrMt). Such grades indicate a card with all qualities of the lower category but with at least a few qualities of the higher category.

Beckett Baseball Card Price Guide lists each card and set in three grades, with the middle grade valued at about 40-45% of the top grade, and the bottom grade valued at about 10-15% of the top grade.

The value of cards that fall between the listed columns can also be calculated using a percentage of the top grade. For example, a card that falls between the top and middle grades (Ex, ExMt or NrMt in most cases) will generally be valued at anywhere from 50% to 90% of the top grade.

Similarly, a card that falls between the middle and bottom grades (G-Vg, Vg or VgEx in most cases) will generally be valued at anywhere from 20% to 40% of the top grade.

There are also cases where cards are in better condition than the top grade or worse than the bottom grade. Cards that grade worse than the lowest grade are generally valued at 5-10% of the top grade.

When a card exceeds the top grade by one — such as NrMt-Mt when the top grade is NrMt, or Mint when the top grade is NrMt-Mt — a premium of up to 50% is possible, with 10-20% the usual norm.

When a card exceeds the top grade by two — such as Mint when the top grade is NrMt, or NrMt-Mt when the top grade is ExMt — a premium of 25-50% is the usual norm. But certain condition sensitive cards or sets, particularly those from the pre-war era, can bring premiums of up to 100% or even more.

Unopened packs, boxes and factory-collated sets are considered Mint in their unknown (and presumed perfect) state. Once opened, however, each card can be graded (and valued) in its own right by taking into account any defects that may be present in spite of the fact that the card has never been handled.

Selling Your Cards

Just about every collector sells cards or will sell cards eventually. Someday you may be interested in selling your duplicates or maybe even your whole collection. You may sell to other collectors, friends or dealers. You may even sell cards you purchased from a certain dealer back to that same dealer. In any event, it helps to know some of the mechanics of the typical transaction between buyer and seller.

Dealers will buy cards in order to resell them to other collectors who are interested in the cards. Dealers will always pay a higher percentage for items that (in their opinion) can be resold quickly, and a much lower percentage for those items that are perceived as having low demand and hence are slow moving. In either case, dealers must buy at a price that allows for the expense of doing business and a margin for profit.

If you have cards for sale, the best advice we can give is that you get several offers for your cards — either from card shops or at a card show — and take the best offer, all things considered. Note, the "best" offer may not be the one for the highest amount. And remember, if a dealer really wants your cards, he won't let you get away without making his best competitive offer. Another alternative is to place your cards in an auction as one or several lots.

Many people think nothing of going into a department store and paying $15 for an item of clothing for which the store paid $5. But if you were selling your $15 card to a dealer and he offered you $5 for it, you might consider his markup unreasonable. To complete the analogy: Most department stores (and card dealers) that consistently pay $10 for $15 items eventually go out of business. An exception is when the dealer has lined up a willing buyer for the item(s) you are attempting to sell, or if the cards are so Hot that it's likely he'll likely have to hold the cards for just a short period of time.

In those cases, an offer of up to 75 percent of book value still will allow the dealer to make a reasonable profit considering the short time he will need to hold the merchandise. In general, however, most cards and collections will bring offers in the range of 25 to 50 percent of retail price. Also consider that most material from the last five to 10 years is plentiful. If that's what you're selling, don't be surprised if your best offer is well below that range.

Interesting Notes

The first card numerically of an issue is the single card most likely to obtain excessive wear.

Consequently, you typically will find the price on the #1 card (in NrMt or Mint condition) somewhat higher than might otherwise be the case.

Similarly, but to a lesser extent (because normally the less important, reverse side of the card is the one exposed), the last card numerically in an issue also is prone to abnormal wear. This extra wear and tear occurs because the first and last cards are exposed to the elements (human element included) more than any of the other cards. They are generally end cards in any brick formations, rubber bandings, stackings on wet surfaces and like activities.

Sports cards have no intrinsic value. The value of a card, like the value of other collectibles, can be determined only by you and your enjoyment in viewing and possessing these cardboard treasures.

Remember, the buyer ultimately determines the price of each baseball card. You are the determining price factor because you have the ability to say "No" to the price of any card by not exchanging your hard-earned money for a given issue. When the cost of a trading card exceeds the enjoyment you will receive from it, your answer should be "No." We assess and report the prices. You set them!

We are always interested in receiving the price input of collectors and dealers. We happily credit major contributors.

We welcome your opinions, since your contributions assist us in ensuring a better guide each year.

If you would like to join our survey list for the next editions of this book and others authored by Dr. Beckett, please send your name and address to Dr. James Beckett, 15850 Dallas Parkway, Dallas, TX 75248.

History of Baseball Cards

Today's version of the baseball card, with its colorful and oft times high-tech fronts and backs, is a far cry from its earliest predecessors. The issue remains cloudy as to which was the very first baseball card ever produced, but the institution of baseball cards dates from the latter half of the 19th century, more than 100 years ago. Early issues, generally printed on heavy cardboard, were of poor quality, with photographs, drawings, and printing far short of today's standards.

Goodwin & Co., of New York, makers of Gypsy Queen, Old Judge, and other cigarette brands, is considered by many to be the first issuer of baseball and other sports cards. Its issues, predominantly sized 1-1/2 by 2-1/2 inches, generally consisted of photographs of baseball players, boxers, wrestlers, and other subjects mounted on stiff cardboard. More than 2,000 different photos of baseball players alone have been identified. These "Old Judges," a collective name commonly used for the Goodwin & Co. cards, were issued from 1886 to 1890 and are treasured parts of many collections today.

Among the other cigarette companies that issued baseball cards still attracting attention today are Allen & Ginter, D. Buchner & Co. (Gold Coin Chewing Tobacco), and P.H. Mayo & Brother. Cards from the first two companies bear colored line drawings, while the Mayos are sepia photographs on black cardboard. In addition to the small-size cards from this era, several tobacco companies issued cabinet-size baseball cards. These "cabinets" were considerably larger than the small cards, usually about 4-1/4 by 6-1/2 inches, and were printed on heavy stock. Goodwin & Co.'s Old Judge cabinets and the National Tobacco Works' "Newsboy" baseball photos are two that remain popular today.

By 1895, the American Tobacco Company began to dominate its competition. They discontinued baseball card inserts in their cigarette packages (actually slide boxes in those days). The lack of competition in the cigarette market had made these inserts unnecessary. This marked the end of the first era of baseball cards. At the dawn of the 20th century, few baseball cards were being issued. But

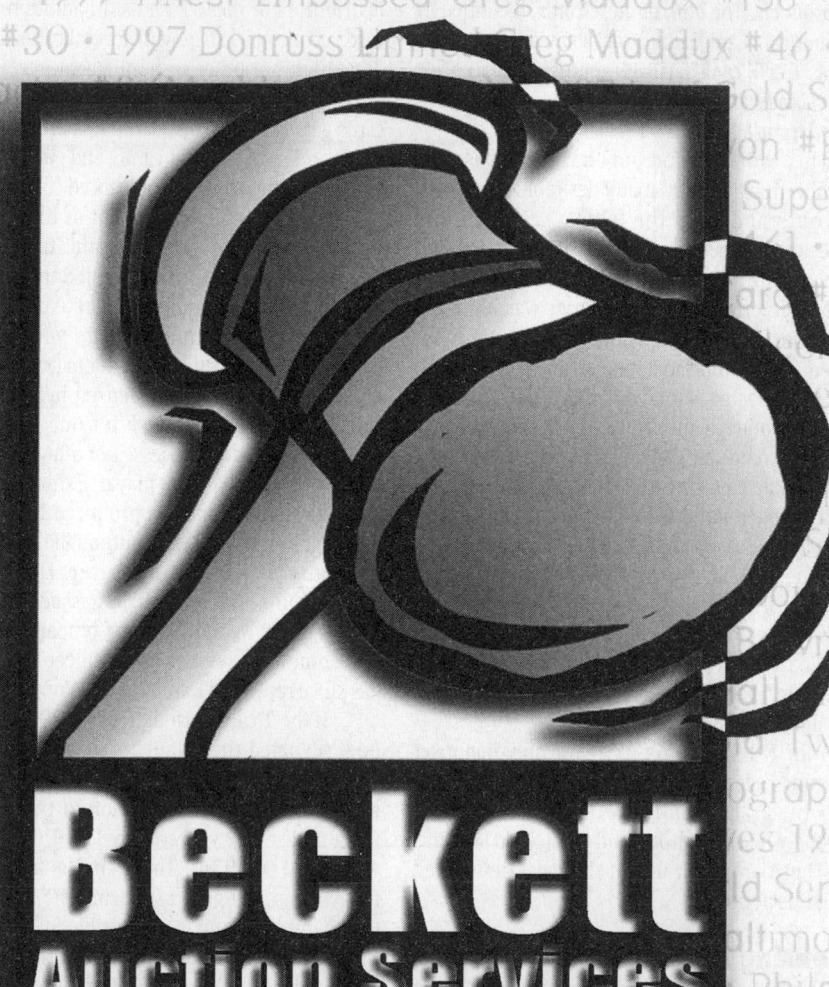

once again, it was the cigarette companies — particularly, the American Tobacco Company — followed to a lesser extent by the candy and gum makers that revived the practice of including baseball cards with their products. The bulk of these cards, identified in the American Card Catalog (designated hereafter as ACC) as T or E cards for 20th century "Tobacco" or "Early Candy and Gum" issues, respectively, were released from 1909 to 1915.

This romantic and popular era of baseball card collecting produced many desirable items. The most outstanding is the fabled T-206 Honus Wagner card. Other perennial favorites among collectors are the T-206 Eddie Plank card, and the T-206 Magee error card. The former was once the second most valuable card and only recently relinquished that position to a more distinctive and aesthetically pleasing Napoleon Lajoie card from the 1933-34 Goudey Gum series. The latter misspells the player's name as "Magie," the most famous and most valuable blooper card.

The ingenuity and distinctiveness of this era has yet to be surpassed. Highlights include:

• the T-202 Hassan triple-folders, one of the best looking and the most distinctive cards ever issued;

• the durable T-201 Mecca double-folders, one of the first sets with players' records on the reverse;

• the T-3 Turkey Reds, the hobby's most popular cabinet card;

• the E-145 Cracker Jacks, the only major set containing Federal League player cards;

• the T-204 Ramlys, with their distinctive black-and-white oval photos and ornate gold borders.

These are but a few of the varieties issued during this period.

Increasing Popularity

While the American Tobacco Company dominated the field, several other tobacco companies, as well as clothing manufacturers, newspapers and periodicals, game makers, and companies whose identities remain anonymous, also issued cards during this period. In fact, the Collins-McCarthy Candy Company, makers of Zeenuts Pacific Coast League baseball cards, issued cards yearly from 1911 to 1938. Its record for continuous annual card production has been exceeded only by the Topps Chewing Gum Company. The era of the tobacco card issues closed with the onset of World War I, with the exception of the Red Man chewing tobacco sets produced from 1952 to 1955.

The next flurry of card issues broke out in the roaring and prosperous 1920s, the era of the E card. The caramel companies (National Caramel, American Caramel, York Caramel) were the leading distributors of these E cards. In addition, the strip card, a continous strip with several cards divided by dotted lines or other sectioning features, flourished during this time. While the E cards and the strip cards generally are considered less imaginative than the T cards or the recent candy and gum issues, they still are pursued by many advanced collectors.

Another significant event of the 1920s was the introduction of the arcade card. Taking its designation from its issuer, the Exhibit Supply Company of Chicago, it is usually known as the "Exhibit" card. Once a trademark of the penny arcades, amusement parks and county fairs across the country, Exhibit machines dispensed nearly postcard-size photos on thick stock for one penny. These picture cards bore likenesses of a favorite cowboy, actor, actress or baseball player. Exhibit Supply and its associated companies produced baseball cards during a longer time span, although discontinuous, than any other manufacturer. Its first cards appeared in 1921, while its last issue was in 1966. In 1979, the Exhibit Supply Company was bought and somewhat revived by a collector/dealer who has since reprinted Exhibit photos of the past.

If the T card period, from 1909 to 1915, can be designated the "Golden Age" of baseball card collecting, then perhaps the "Silver Age" commenced with the introduction of the Big League Gum series of 239 cards in 1933 (a 240th card was added in 1934). These are the forerunners of today's baseball gum cards, and the Goudey Gum Company of Boston is responsible for their success. This era spanned the period from the Depression days of 1933 to America's formal involvement in World War II in 1941.

Goudey's attractive designs, with full-color line drawings on thick card stock, greatly influenced other cards being issued at that time. As a result, the most attractive and popular vintage cards in history were produced in this "Silver Age." The 1933 Goudey Big League Gum series also owes its popularity to the more than 40 Hall of Fame players in the set. These include four cards of Babe Ruth and two of Lou Gehrig. Goudey's reign continued in 1934, when it issued a 96-card set in color, together with the single remaining card from the 1933 series, #106, the Napoleon Lajoie card.

In addition to Goudey, several other bubblegum manufacturers issued baseball cards during this era. DeLong Gum Company issued an extremely attractive set in 1933. National Chicle Company's 192-card "Batter-Up" series of 1934-1936 became the largest die-cut set in card history. In addition, that company offered the popular "Diamond Stars" series during the same period. Other popular sets included the "Tattoo Orbit" set of 60 color cards issued in 1933 and Gum Products' 75-card "Double Play" set, featuring sepia depictions of two players per card.

In 1939, Gum Inc., which later became Bowman Gum, replaced Goudey Gum as the leading baseball card producer. In 1939 and the following year, it issued two important sets of black-and-white cards. In 1939, its "Play Ball America" set consisted of 162 cards. The larger, 240-card "Play Ball" set of 1940 still is considered by many to be the most attractive black-and-white cards ever produced. That firm introduced its only color set in 1941, consisting of 72 cards titled "Play Ball Sports Hall of Fame." Many of these were colored repeats of poses from the black-and-white 1940 series.

In addition to regular gum cards, many manufacturers distributed premium issues during the 1930s. These premiums were printed on paper or photographic stock, rather than card stock. They were much larger than the regular cards and were sold for a penny across the counter with gum (which was packaged separately from the premium). They often were redeemed at the store or through the mail in exchange for the wrappers of previously purchased gum cards, like proof-of-purchase box-top premiums today. The gum premiums are scarcer than the card issues of the 1930s and in most cases no manufacturer's name is present.

World War II brought an end to this popular era of card collecting when paper and rubber shortages curtailed the production of bubblegum baseball cards. They were resurrected again in 1948 by the Bowman Gum Company (the direct descendent of Gum, Inc.). This marked the beginning of the modern era of card collecting.

In 1948, Bowman Gum issued a 48-card set in black and white consisting of one card and one slab of gum in every 1 cent pack. That same year, the Leaf Gum Company also issued a set of cards. Although rather poor in quality, these cards were issued in color. A squabble over the rights to use players' pictures developed between Bowman and Leaf. Eventually Leaf dropped out of the card market, but not before it had left a lasting heritage to the hobby by issuing some of the rarest cards now in existence. Leaf's baseball card series of 1948-49 contained 98 cards, skip numbered to #168 (not all numbers were printed). Of these 98 cards, 49 are relatively plentiful; the other 49, however, are rare and quite valuable.

Bowman continued its production of cards in 1949 with a color series of 240 cards. Because there are many scarce "high numbers," this series remains the most difficult Bowman regular issue to complete. Although the set was printed in color and commands great interest due to its scarcity, it is considered aesthetically inferior to the Goudey and National Chicle issues of the 1930s. In addition to the regular issue of 1949, Bowman also produced a set of 36 Pacific Coast League players. While this was not a regular issue, it still is prized by collectors. In fact, it has become the most valuable Bowman series.

In 1950 (representing Bowman's one-year monopoly of the baseball card market), the company began a string of top quality cards that continued until its demise in 1955. The 1950 series was itself something of an oddity because the low numbers, rather than the traditional high numbers, were the more difficult cards to obtain.

The year 1951 marked the beginning of the most competitive and perhaps the highest quality period of baseball card production. In that year, Topps Chewing Gum Company of Brooklyn entered the market. Topps' 1951 series consisted of two sets of 52 cards each, one set with red backs and the other with blue backs. In addition, Topps also issued 31 insert cards, three of which remain the rarest Topps cards ("Current All-Stars" Konstanty, Roberts and Stanky). The 1951 Topps cards were unattractive and paled in comparison to the 1951 Bowman issues. They were successful, however, and Topps has continued to produce cards ever since.

Intensified Competition

Topps issued a larger and more attractive card set in 1952. This larger size became standard for the next five years. (Bowman followed with larger-size baseball cards in 1953.) This 1952 Topps set has become, like the 1933 Goudey series and the T-206 white border series, the classic set of its era. The 407-card set is a collector's dream of scarcities, rarities, errors and variations. It also contains the first Topps issues of Mickey Mantle and Willie Mays.

As with Bowman and Leaf in the late 1940s, competition over player rights arose. Ensuing court battles occurred between Topps and Bowman. The market split due to stiff competition, and in January 1956, Topps bought out Bowman. (Topps, using the Bowman name, resurrected Bowman as a later label in 1989.) Topps remained essentially unchallenged as the primary producer of baseball cards through 1980. So, the story of major baseball card sets from 1956 through 1980 is by and large the story of Topps' issues. Notable exceptions include the small sets produced by Fleer Gum in 1959, 1960, 1961 and 1963, and the Kellogg's Cereal and Hostess Cakes baseball cards issued to promote their products.

A court decision in 1980 paved the way for two other large gum companies to enter (or reenter, in Fleer's case) the baseball card arena. Fleer, which had last made photo cards in 1963, and the Donruss Company (then a division of General Mills) secured rights to produce baseball cards of current players, thus breaking Topps' monopoly. Each company issued major card sets in 1981 with bubblegum products.

Then a higher court decision in that year overturned the lower court ruling against Topps. It appeared that Topps had regained its sole position as a producer of baseball cards. Undaunted by the revocation ruling, Fleer and Donruss continued to issue cards in 1982 but without bubblegum or any other edible product. Fleer issued its current player baseball cards with "team logo stickers," while Donruss issued its cards with a piece of a baseball jigsaw puzzle.

Sharing the Pie

Since 1981, these three major baseball card producers all have thrived, sharing relatively equal recognition. Each has steadily increased its involvement in terms of numbers of issues per year. To the delight of collectors, their competition has generated novel, and in some cases exceptional, issues of current Major League Baseball players. Collectors also eagerly accepted the debut efforts of Score (1988) and Upper Deck (1989), the newest companies to enter the baseball card producing derby.

Upper Deck's successful entry into the market turned out to be very important. The company's card stock, photography, packaging and marketing gave baseball cards a new standard for quality, and began the "premium card" trend that continues today. The second premium baseball card set to be issued was the 1990 Leaf set, named for and issued by the parent company of Donruss. To gauge the significance of the premium card trend, one need only note that two of the most valuable post-1986 regular-issue cards in the hobby are the 1989 Upper Deck Ken Griffey Jr. and 1990 Leaf Frank Thomas Rookie Cards.

The impressive debut of Leaf in 1990 was followed by Studio, Ultra, and Stadium Club in 1991. Of those, Stadium Club made the biggest impact. In 1992, Bowman, and Pinnacle joined the premium fray. In 1992, Donruss and Fleer abandoned the traditional 50-cent pack market and instead produced premium sets comparable to (and presumably designed to compete against) Upper Deck's set. Those moves, combined with the almost instantaneous spread of premium cards to the other major team sports cards, serve as strong indicators that premium cards were here to stay. Bowman had been a lower-level product from 1989 to '91.

In 1993, Fleer, Topps and Upper Deck produced the first "super premium" cards with Flair, Finest and SP, respectively. The success of all three products was an indication the baseball card market was headed toward even higher price levels, and that turned out to be the case in 1994 with the introduction of Topps' Bowman's Best (a hybrid of prospect-oriented Bowman and the superpremium Finest) and Leaf Limited. Other 1994 debuts included Upper Deck's entry-level Collector's Choice and Pinnacle's hobby-only Select.

Overall, inserts continued to dominate the hobby scene. Specifically, the parallel chase cards first introduced in 1992 with Topps Gold became the latest major hobby trend. Topps Gold was followed by 1993 Finest Refractors (at the time the scarcest insert ever produced and still a landmark set), and the one-per-box Stadium Club First Day Issue.

Of course, the biggest on-field news of 1994 was the owner-provoked players strike that halted the season prematurely. While the baseball card hobby suffered noticeably from the strike, there was no catastrophic market crash as some had feared. In fact, the Vintage market was revitalized by that unfortunate event. However, the strike pulled the plug on a market that was both strong and growing, and contributed to a serious hobby contraction that continues to this day.

By 1995, parallel insert sets were commonplace and had taken on a new complexion: the most popular ones were those that had announced (or at least suspected) print runs of 500 or less, such as Finest Refractors and Select Artist's Proofs.

This trend continued in 1996, with several parallel inserts that were printed in quantities of 250 or less such as Finest Gold Refractors, Fleer Circa Rave, Studio Silver Press Proofs and three of the six Select Certified parallels. It could be argued that the high price tags on these extremely limited parallel cards (many exceeded the $1000 plateau) were driving many single-player collectors to frustration, and even completely out of the hobby. At the same time, average pack prices soared while average number of cards per pack dropped, making the baseball card hobby increasingly more expensive.

On the positive side, two trends from 1996 clearly brought in new collectors: Topps' Mickey Mantle retrospective inserts in both series of Topps and Stadium Club; and Leaf's Signature Series, which included one certified autograph per pack. While the Mantle craze following his passing seemed to be a short-term phenomenon, the inclusion of autographs in packs seemed to have more long-term significance.

In 1997 the print runs in selected sets got even lower. Both Fleer/SkyBox and Pinnacle brands issued cards of which only one exists.

The grouth in popularity of autographs also continued. Many products had autographed cards in their packs. A very positive trend was a return to basics. Many collectors bought Rockie Cards as they understood that concept and worked on finishing sets.

There was also an increase in international players collecting. Hideo Nomo was incredibly popular in Japan while Chan Ho Park was in demand in Korea. This Godes wall for an international grouth in the hobby.

Unfortunately, such positives were clearly overshadowed by the industry's overriding problem: too many products costing too much money, with fewer and fewer buyers willing to ante up. The result? Many dealers going out of business, and a buyer's market in which new products usually were available cheaper to the consumer than original dealer cost from the factory. The hobby still faces this very complex problem with no easy solutions in sight.

Finding Out More

The above has been a thumbnail sketch of card collecting from its inception in the 1880s to the present. It is difficult to tell the whole story in just a few pages — there are several other good sources of information. Serious collectors should subscribe to at least one of the excellent hobby periodicals. We also suggest that collectors visit their local card shop(s) and also attend a sports collectibles show in their area. Card collecting is still a young and informal hobby. You can learn more about it in either place. After all, smart dealers realize that spending a few minutes teaching beginners about the hobby often pays off in the long run.

Additional Reading

Each year Beckett Publications produces comprehensive annual price guides for each of the four major sports: *Beckett Baseball Card Price Guide, Beckett Football Card Price Guide, Beckett Basketball Card Price Guide*, and *Beckett Hockey Card Price Guide.* The aim of these annual guides is to provide information and accurate pricing on a wide array of sports cards, ranging from main issues by the major card manufacturers to various regional, promotional, and food issues. Also alphabetical checklists, such as *Sport Americana Baseball Card Alphabetical Checklist #6*, are published to assist the collector in identifying all the cards of any particular player. The seasoned collector will find these tools valuable sources of information that will enable him to pursue his hobby interests.

In addition, abridged editions of the Beckett Price Guides have been published for each of the four major sports as part of the House of Collectibles series: *The Official Price Guide to Baseball Cards, The Official Price Guide to Football Cards, The Official Price Guide to Basketball Cards,* and *The Official Price Guide to Hockey Cards.* Published in a convenient mass-market paperback format, these price guides provide information and accurate pricing on all the main issues by the major card manufacturers.

Advertising

Within this Price Guide you will find advertisements for sports memorabilia material, mail order, and retail sports collectibles establishments. All advertisements were accepted in good faith based on the reputation of the advertiser; however, neither the author, the publisher, the distributors, nor the other advertisers in this Price Guide accept any responsibility for any particular advertiser not complying with the terms of his or her ad.

Readers also should be aware that prices in advertisements are subject to change over the annual period before a new edition of this volume is issued each spring. When replying to an advertisement late in the baseball year, the reader should take this into account, and contact the dealer by phone or in writing for up-to-date price information. Should you come into contact with any of the advertisers in this guide as a result of their advertisement herein, please mention this source as your contact.

Prices in this Guide

Prices found in this guide reflect current retail rates just prior to the printing of this book. They do not reflect the FOR SALE prices of the author, the publisher, the distributors, the advertisers, or any card dealers associated with this guide. No one is obligated in any way to buy, sell or trade his or her cards based on these prices. The price listings were compiled by the author from actual buy/sell transactions at sports conventions, sports card shops, buy/sell advertisements in the hobby papers, for sale prices from dealer catalogs and price lists, and discussions with leading hobbyists in the U.S. and Canada. All prices are in U.S. dollars.

Acknowledgments

A great deal of diligence, hard work, and dedicated effort went into this year's volume. However, the high standards to which we hold ourselves could not have been met without the expert input and generous amount of time contributed by many people. Our sincere thanks are extended to each and every one of you.

A complete list of these invaluable contributors appears after the Price Guide section.

1984 A's Mother's

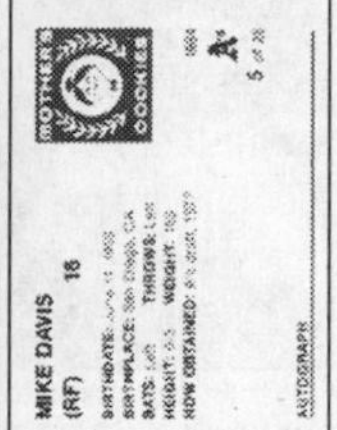

he cards in this 28-card set measure 2 1/2" by 3 1/2". In 984, the Los Angeles based Mother's Cookies Co. issued ve sets of cards featuring players from major league eams. The Oakland A's set features current players epicted by photos. Similar to the Mother's Cookies 1952 nd 1953 issues, the cards have rounded corners. The acks of the cards contain the Mother's Cookies logo. The ards were distributed in partial sets to fans at the espective stadiums of the teams involved. Whereas 20 ards were given to each patron, a redemption card, edeemable for eight more cards was included. Infortunately, the eight cards received by redeeming the oupon were not necessarily the eight needed to complete set. Hobbyist Barry Colla was involved in the production f these sets.

	NRMT	VG-E
OMPLETE SET (28)	12.50	5.50
OMMON CARD (1-28)	.25	.11
☐ 1 Steve Boros MG	.25	.11
☐ 2 Rickey Henderson	5.00	2.20
☐ 3 Joe Morgan	3.00	1.35
☐ 4 Dwayne Murphy	.25	.11
☐ 5 Mike Davis	.25	.11
☐ 6 Bruce Bochte	.25	.11
☐ 7 Carney Lansford	.75	.35
☐ 8 Steve McCatty	.25	.11
☐ 9 Mike Heath	.25	.11
☐ 10 Chris Codiroli	.25	.11
☐ 11 Bill Almon	.25	.11
☐ 12 Bill Caudill	.25	.11
☐ 13 Donnie Hill	.25	.11
☐ 14 Lary Sorensen	.25	.11
☐ 15 Dave Kingman	.75	.35
☐ 16 Garry Hancock	.25	.11
☐ 17 Jeff Burroughs	.25	.11
☐ 18 Tom Burgmeier	.25	.11
☐ 19 Jim Essian	.25	.11
☐ 20 Mike Warren	.25	.11
☐ 21 Davey Lopes	.75	.35
☐ 22 Ray Burris	.25	.11
☐ 23 Tony Phillips	1.50	.70
☐ 24 Tim Conroy	.25	.11
☐ 25 Jeff Bettendorf	.25	.11
☐ 26 Keith Atherton	.25	.11
☐ 27 A's Coaches Ron Schueler Billy Williams Clete Boyer Jackie Moore Bob Didier	.50	.23
☐ 28 A's Checklist Oakland Coliseum	.25	.11

1985 A's Mother's

The cards in this 28-card set measure 2 1/2" by 3 1/2". In 1985, the Los Angeles based Mother's Cookies Co. again issued five sets of cards featuring players from major league teams. The Oakland A's set features current players depicted by photos on cards with rounded corners. The backs of the cards contain the Mother's Cookies logo. Cards were passed out at the stadium on July 6.

	NRMT	VG-E
COMPLETE SET (28)	10.00	4.50
COMMON CARD (1-28)	.25	.11
☐ 1 Jackie Moore MG	.25	.11
☐ 2 Dave Kingman	.75	.35
☐ 3 Don Sutton	1.50	.70
☐ 4 Mike Heath	.25	.11
☐ 5 Alfredo Griffin	.25	.11
☐ 6 Dwayne Murphy	.25	.11
☐ 7 Mike Davis	.25	.11
☐ 8 Carney Lansford	.75	.35
☐ 9 Chris Codiroli	.25	.11
☐ 10 Bruce Bochte	.25	.11
☐ 11 Mickey Tettleton	1.50	.70
☐ 12 Donnie Hill	.25	.11
☐ 13 Rob Picciolo	.25	.11
☐ 14 Dave Collins	.25	.11
☐ 15 Dusty Baker	1.00	.45
☐ 16 Tim Conroy	.25	.11
☐ 17 Keith Atherton	.25	.11
☐ 18 Jay Howell	.25	.11
☐ 19 Mike Warren	.25	.11
☐ 20 Steve McCatty	.25	.11
☐ 21 Bill Krueger	.25	.11
☐ 22 Curt Young	.25	.11
☐ 23 Dan Meyer	.25	.11
☐ 24 Mike Gallego	.25	.11
☐ 25 Jeff Kaiser	.25	.11
☐ 26 Steve Henderson	.25	.11
☐ 27 A's Coaches Clete Boyer Bob Didier Dave McKay Wes Stock Billy Williams	.50	.23
☐ 28 A's Checklist Oakland Stadium	.25	.11

1986 A's Mother's

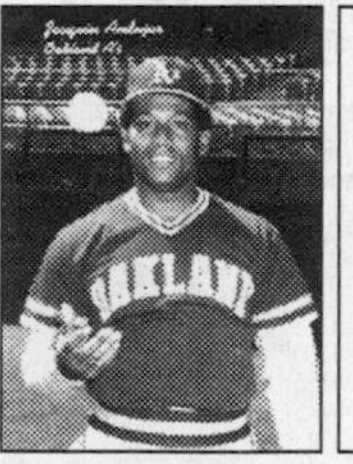

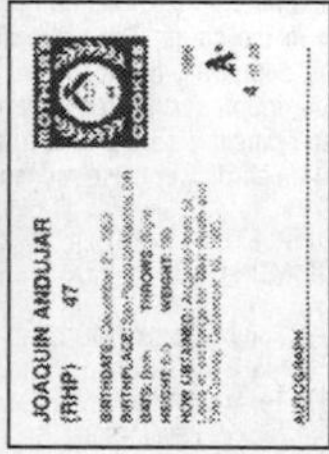

This set consists of 28 full-color, rounded-corner cards each measuring the standard size. Starter sets (only 20 cards but also including a certificate for eight more cards) were given out at the ballpark and collectors were encouraged to trade to fill in the rest of their set. The cards were originally given away on July 20th at Oakland Coliseum. Jose Canseco is featured in his rookie season.

	MINT	NRMT
COMPLETE SET (28)	18.00	8.00
COMMON CARD (1-28)	.25	.11
☐ 1 Jackie Moore MG	.25	.11
☐ 2 Dave Kingman	.75	.35
☐ 3 Dusty Baker	1.00	.45
☐ 4 Joaquin Andujar	.25	.11
☐ 5 Alfredo Griffin	.25	.11
☐ 6 Dwayne Murphy	.25	.11
☐ 7 Mike Davis	.25	.11
☐ 8 Carney Lansford	.75	.35
☐ 9 Jose Canseco	10.00	4.50
☐ 10 Bruce Bochte	.25	.11
☐ 11 Mickey Tettleton	1.25	.55
☐ 12 Donnie Hill	.25	.11
☐ 13 Jose Rijo	.25	.11
☐ 14 Rick Langford	.25	.11
☐ 15 Chris Codiroli	.25	.11
☐ 16 Moose Haas	.25	.11
☐ 17 Keith Atherton	.25	.11
☐ 18 Jay Howell	.25	.11
☐ 19 Tony Phillips	.75	.35
☐ 20 Steve Henderson	.25	.11
☐ 21 Bill Krueger	.25	.11
☐ 22 Steve Ontiveros	.25	.11
☐ 23 Bill Bathe	.25	.11
☐ 24 Ricky Peters	.25	.11
☐ 25 Tim Birtsas	.25	.11
☐ 26 A's Trainers and Equipment Managers Frank Ciensczyk Steve Vucinich Barry Weinberg Larry Davis	.25	.11
☐ 27 A's Coaches Bob Didier Dave McKay Jeff Newman Ron Plaza Wes Stock Bob Watson	.50	.23
☐ 28 A's Checklist Card Oakland Coliseum	.25	.11

1987 A's Mother's

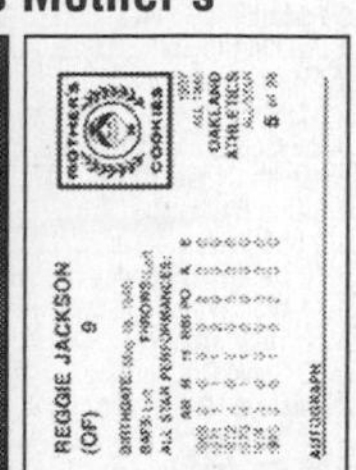

This set consists of 28 full-color, rounded-corner cards each measuring the standard size. Starter sets (only 20 cards but also including a certificate for eight more cards) were given out at the ballpark and collectors were encouraged to trade to fill in the rest of their set. The cards were originally given away on July 5th at Oakland Coliseum during a game against the Boston Red Sox. This set is actually an All-Time All-Star set including every A's All-Star player since 1968 (when the franchise moved to Oakland). The vintage photos (each shot during the year of All-Star appearance) were taken from the collection of Doug McWilliams. The set is sequenced by what year the player first made the All-Star team. The sets were reportedly given out free to the first 25,000 paid admissions at the game.

	MINT	NRMT
COMPLETE SET (28)	20.00	9.00
COMMON CARD (1-28)	.25	.11
☐ 1 Bert Campaneris	.50	.23
☐ 2 Rick Monday	.50	.23
☐ 3 John Odom	.25	.11
☐ 4 Sal Bando	.50	.23
☐ 5 Reggie Jackson	3.00	1.35
☐ 6 Jim Hunter	1.50	.70
☐ 7 Vida Blue	.75	.35
☐ 8 Dave Duncan	.50	.23
☐ 9 Joe Rudi	.75	.35
☐ 10 Rollie Fingers	1.25	.55
☐ 11 Ken Holtzman	.50	.23
☐ 12 Dick Williams MG	.25	.11
☐ 13 Alvin Dark MG	.25	.11
☐ 14 Gene Tenace	.50	.23
☐ 15 Claudell Washington	.25	.11
☐ 16 Phil Garner	.50	.23
☐ 17 Wayne Gross	.25	.11
☐ 18 Matt Keough	.25	.11
☐ 19 Jeff Newman	.25	.11
☐ 20 Rickey Henderson	3.00	1.35
☐ 21 Tony Armas	.25	.11
☐ 22 Mike Norris	.25	.11
☐ 23 Billy Martin MG	1.00	.45
☐ 24 Bill Caudill	.25	.11
☐ 25 Jay Howell	.25	.11
☐ 26 Jose Canseco	4.00	1.80
☐ 27 Jose Canseco Reggie Jackson	3.00	1.35
☐ 28 Checklist Card A's Logo	.25	.11

1988 A's Mother's

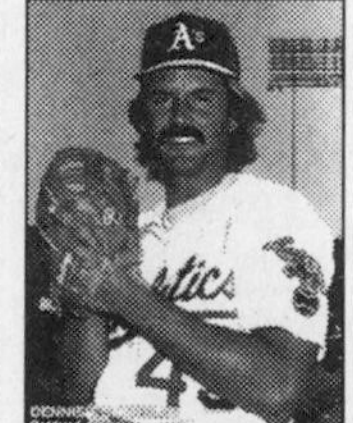

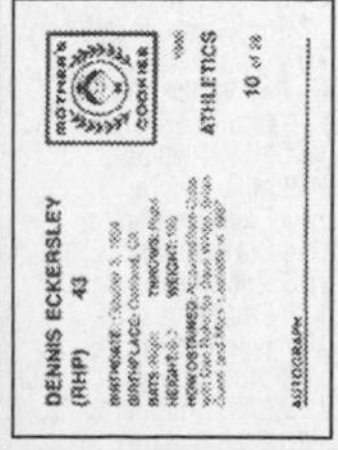

This set consists of 28 full-color, rounded-corner cards each measuring the standard-size. Starter sets (only 20 cards but also including a certificate for eight more cards)

were given out at the ballpark and collectors were encouraged to trade to fill in the rest of their set. The cards were originally given away on July 23rd at Oakland Coliseum during a game. Short sets (20 cards plus certificate) were reportedly given out free to the first 35,000 paid admissions at the game.

	MINT	NRMT
COMPLETE SET (28)	15.00	6.75
COMMON CARD (1-28)	.25	.11
☐ 1 Tony LaRussa MG	1.00	.45
☐ 2 Mark McGwire	6.00	2.70
☐ 3 Dave Stewart	.75	.35
☐ 4 Terry Steinbach	.75	.35
☐ 5 Dave Parker	1.00	.45
☐ 6 Carney Lansford	.75	.35
☐ 7 Jose Canseco	3.00	1.35
☐ 8 Don Baylor	.75	.35
☐ 9 Bob Welch	.50	.23
☐ 10 Dennis Eckersley	2.00	.90
☐ 11 Walt Weiss	1.00	.45
☐ 12 Tony Phillips	.50	.23
☐ 13 Steve Ontiveros	.25	.11
☐ 14 Dave Henderson	.25	.11
☐ 15 Stan Javier	.25	.11
☐ 16 Ron Hassey	.25	.11
☐ 17 Curt Young	.25	.11
☐ 18 Glenn Hubbard	.25	.11
☐ 19 Storm Davis	.25	.11
☐ 20 Eric Plunk	.25	.11
☐ 21 Matt Young	.25	.11
☐ 22 Mike Gallego	.25	.11
☐ 23 Rick Honeycutt	.25	.11
☐ 24 Doug Jennings	.25	.11
☐ 25 Gene Nelson	.25	.11
☐ 26 Greg Cadaret	.25	.11
☐ 27 A's Coaches Dave Duncan Rene Lachemann Jim Lefebvre Dave McKay Mike Paul Bob Watson	.50	.23
☐ 28 Checklist Card Jose Canseco Mark McGwire	1.50	.70

1989 A's Mother's

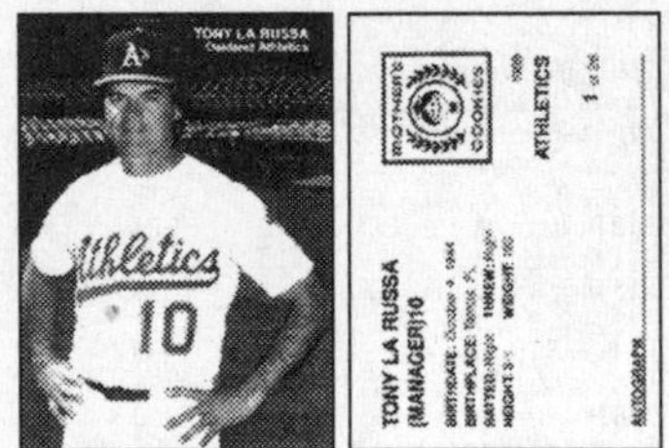

The 1989 Mother's Cookies Oakland A's set contains 28 standard-size cards with rounded corners. The fronts have borderless color photos, and the horizontally oriented backs have biographical information. Starter sets containing 20 of these cards were given away at an A's home game during the 1989 season.

	MINT	NRMT
COMPLETE SET (28)	15.00	6.75
COMMON CARD (1-28)	.25	.11
☐ 1 Tony LaRussa MG	1.00	.45
☐ 2 Mark McGwire	5.00	2.20
☐ 3 Terry Steinbach	.75	.35
☐ 4 Dave Parker	1.00	.45
☐ 5 Carney Lansford	.75	.35
☐ 6 Dave Stewart	.75	.35
☐ 7 Jose Canseco	2.50	1.10
☐ 8 Walt Weiss	.50	.23
☐ 9 Bob Welch	.50	.23
☐ 10 Dennis Eckersley	1.50	.70
☐ 11 Tony Phillips	.50	.23
☐ 12 Mike Moore	.25	.11
☐ 13 Dave Henderson	.25	.11
☐ 14 Curt Young	.25	.11
☐ 15 Ron Hassey	.25	.11
☐ 16 Eric Plunk	.25	.11
☐ 17 Luis Polonia	.50	.23
☐ 18 Storm Davis	.25	.11
☐ 19 Glenn Hubbard	.25	.11
☐ 20 Greg Cadaret	.25	.11
☐ 21 Stan Javier	.25	.11
☐ 22 Felix Jose	.25	.11
☐ 23 Mike Gallego	.25	.11
☐ 24 Todd Burns	.25	.11
☐ 25 Rick Honeycutt	.25	.11
☐ 26 Gene Nelson	.25	.11
☐ 27 A's Coaches Dave Duncan Rene Lachemann Art Kusnyer Dave McKay Tommie Reynolds Merv Rettenmund	.50	.23
☐ 28 Checklist Card Walt Weiss Mark McGwire Jose Canseco	1.50	.70

1990 A's Mother's

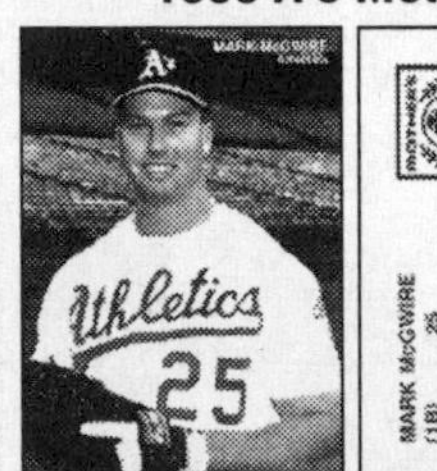

1990 Mother's Cookies Oakland Athletics set contains 28 standard-size cards with rounded corners. The envelope containing the cards honors the 1989 World Championship Oakland Athletics. The A's cards were released at the July 22nd game to the first 35,000 fans to walk through the gates. They were distributed in 20-card random packets at the game and eight more at the redemption booths. However, both groups of cards were random and there was no guarantee of getting a complete set in the cards. The promotional idea was that the only way one could finish the set was to trade for them. The redemption certificates were to be used at the Labor Day San Francisco card show. In addition to this the Mother's Giants cards were also redeemable at that show.

	MINT	NRMT
COMPLETE SET (28)	11.00	4.90
COMMON CARD (1-28)	.25	.11
☐ 1 Tony LaRussa MG	.75	.35
☐ 2 Mark McGwire	4.00	1.80
☐ 3 Terry Steinbach	.50	.23
☐ 4 Rickey Henderson	1.50	.70
☐ 5 Dave Stewart	.50	.23
☐ 6 Jose Canseco	1.50	.70
☐ 7 Dennis Eckersley	1.25	.55
☐ 8 Carney Lansford	.75	.35
☐ 9 Mike Moore	.25	.11
☐ 10 Walt Weiss	.50	.23
☐ 11 Scott Sanderson	.25	.11
☐ 12 Ron Hassey	.25	.11
☐ 13 Rick Honeycutt	.25	.11
☐ 14 Ken Phelps	.25	.11
☐ 15 Jamie Quirk	.25	.11
☐ 16 Bob Welch	.50	.23
☐ 17 Felix Jose	.25	.11
☐ 18 Dave Henderson	.25	.11
☐ 19 Mike Norris	.25	.11
☐ 20 Todd Burns	.25	.11
☐ 21 Lance Blankenship	.25	.11
☐ 22 Gene Nelson	.25	.11
☐ 23 Stan Javier	.25	.11
☐ 24 Curt Young	.25	.11
☐ 25 Mike Gallego	.25	.11
☐ 26 Joe Klink	.25	.11
☐ 27 A's Coaches Rene Lachemann Dave Duncan Merv Rettenmund Tommie Reynolds Art Kusnyer Dave McKay	.50	.23
☐ 28 Checklist Card A's Personnel Larry Davis, TR Steve Vuchinch, Visiting Club Mgr. Frank Cienscyk, Equipment Mgr. Barry Weinberg, TR	.25	.11

1991 A's Mother's

The 1991 Mother's Cookies Oakland Athletics set contains 28 standard-size cards with rounded corners. The set

includes an additional card advertising a trading card collectors album. The front design has borderless glossy color player photos from the waist up. The horizontally oriented backs are printed in red and purple, present biographical information, and have blank slots for player autographs.

	MINT	NRMT
COMPLETE SET (28)	12.00	5.50
COMMON CARD (1-28)	.25	.11
☐ 1 Tony LaRussa MG	.75	.35
☐ 2 Mark McGwire	3.00	1.35
☐ 3 Terry Steinbach	.75	.35
☐ 4 Rickey Henderson	1.50	.70
☐ 5 Dave Stewart	.75	.35
☐ 6 Jose Canseco	1.50	.70
☐ 7 Dennis Eckersley	1.25	.55
☐ 8 Carney Lansford	.75	.35
☐ 9 Bob Welch	.50	.23
☐ 10 Walt Weiss	.50	.23
☐ 11 Mike Moore	.25	.11
☐ 12 Vance Law	.25	.11
☐ 13 Rick Honeycutt	.25	.11
☐ 14 Harold Baines	.75	.35
☐ 15 Jamie Quirk	.25	.11
☐ 16 Ernest Riles	.25	.11
☐ 17 Willie Wilson	.50	.23
☐ 18 Dave Henderson	.25	.11
☐ 19 Kirk Dressendorfer	.25	.11
☐ 20 Todd Burns	.25	.11
☐ 21 Lance Blankenship	.25	.11
☐ 22 Gene Nelson	.25	.11
☐ 23 Eric Show	.25	.11
☐ 24 Curt Young	.25	.11
☐ 25 Mike Gallego	.25	.11
☐ 26 Joe Klink	.25	.11
☐ 27 Steve Chitren	.25	.11
☐ 28 Checklist Card Tommie Reynolds CO Art Kusnyer CO Reggie Jackson CO Rick Burleson CO Rene Lachemann CO Dave Duncan CO Dave McKay CO	.50	.23

1992 A's Mother's

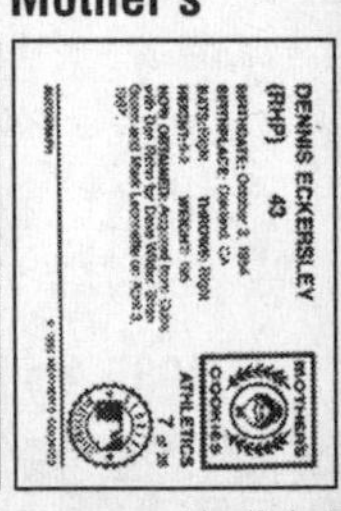

This 28-card standard-size set, sponsored by Mother's Cookies, contains borderless posed color player photos of the Oakland Athletics team. The cards have rounded corners. The red and purple backs include biographical information. The set also includes an order-form card for a Mother's Cookies Oakland Athletics collectors album. The album was available for 3.95.

	MINT	NRMT
COMPLETE SET (28)	10.00	4.50
COMMON CARD (1-28)	.25	.11
☐ 1 Tony LaRussa MG	.75	.35
☐ 2 Mark McGwire	3.00	1.35
☐ 3 Terry Steinbach	.75	.35
☐ 4 Rickey Henderson	1.50	.70
☐ 5 Dave Stewart	.75	.35
☐ 6 Jose Canseco	1.50	.70
☐ 7 Dennis Eckersley	1.25	.55
☐ 8 Carney Lansford	.75	.35
☐ 9 Bob Welch	.50	.23

	MINT	NRMT
☐ 10 Walt Weiss	.50	.23
☐ 11 Mike Moore	.25	.11
☐ 12 Goose Gossage	.75	.35
☐ 13 Rick Honeycutt	.25	.11
☐ 14 Harold Baines	.75	.35
☐ 15 Jamie Quirk	.25	.11
☐ 16 Jeff Parrett	.25	.11
☐ 17 Willie Wilson	.25	.11
☐ 18 Dave Henderson	.25	.11
☐ 19 Joe Slusarski	.25	.11
☐ 20 Mike Bordick	.25	.11
☐ 21 Lance Blankenship	.25	.11
☐ 22 Gene Nelson	.25	.11
☐ 23 Vince Horsman	.25	.11
☐ 24 Ron Darling	.25	.11
☐ 25 Randy Ready	.25	.11
☐ 26 Scott Hemond	.25	.11
☐ 27 Scott Brosius	.50	.23
☐ 28 Checklist Rene Lachemann CO Art Kusnyer CO Dave McKay CO Tommie Reynolds CO Dave Duncan CO Doug Rader CO	.50	.23

1993 A's Mother's

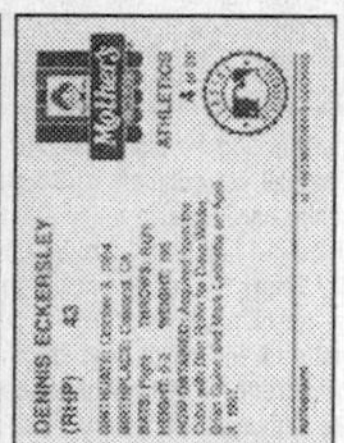

The 1993 Mother's Cookies Athletics set consists of 28 standard-size cards with rounded corners. The fronts display full-bleed color player portraits shot from the waist up in stadium settings. The player's name and team name appear in one of the corners. On a white background in red and purple print, the horizontal backs carry biographical information and the sponsor's logo. A blank slot for the player's autograph rounds out the back.

	MINT	NRMT
COMPLETE SET (28)	10.00	4.50
COMMON CARD (1-28)	.25	.11
☐ 1 Tony LaRussa MG	.75	.35
☐ 2 Mark McGwire	3.00	1.35
☐ 3 Terry Steinbach	.75	.35
☐ 4 Dennis Eckersley	1.25	.55
☐ 5 Ruben Sierra	.50	.23
☐ 6 Rickey Henderson	1.50	.70
☐ 7 Mike Bordick	.25	.11
☐ 8 Rick Honeycutt	.25	.11
☐ 9 Dave Henderson	.25	.11
☐ 10 Bob Welch	.50	.23
☐ 11 Dale Sveum	.25	.11
☐ 12 Ron Darling	.25	.11
☐ 13 Jerry Browne	.25	.11
☐ 14 Bobby Witt	.25	.11
☐ 15 Troy Neel	.25	.11
☐ 16 Goose Gossage	.75	.35
☐ 17 Brent Gates	.25	.11
☐ 18 Storm Davis	.25	.11
☐ 19 Scott Hemond	.25	.11
☐ 20 Kelly Downs	.25	.11
☐ 21 Kevin Seitzer	.25	.11
☐ 22 Lance Blankenship	.25	.11
☐ 23 Mike Mohler	.25	.11
☐ 24 Edwin Nunez	.25	.11
☐ 25 Joe Boever	.25	.11
☐ 26 Shawn Hillegas	.25	.11
☐ 27 Coaches Card Dave McKay Dave Duncan Tommie Reynolds Art Kusnyer Greg Luzinski	.50	.23
☐ 28 Checklist Card Frank Cienscyzk EQ MG	.25	.11

1994 A's Mother's

The 1994 Mother's Cookies Athletics set consists of 28 standard-size cards with rounded corners. The fronts display full-bleed color player portraits shot from the waist up against a stadium background. The player's name and team name appear in one of the corners. On a

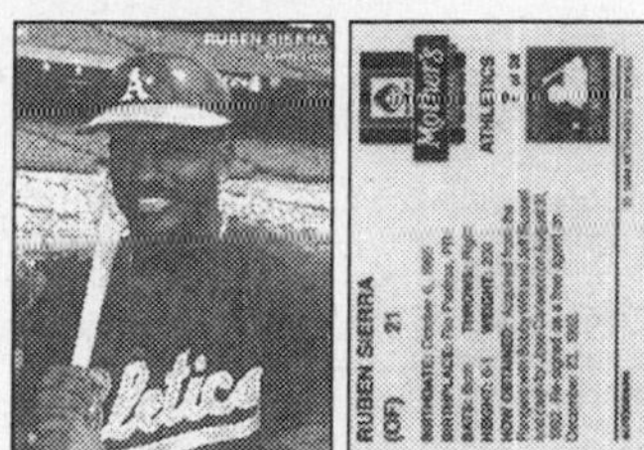

white background in red and purple print, the horizontal backs carry biographical information and the sponsor's logo. A blank slot for the player's autograph rounds out the back.

	MINT	NRMT
COMPLETE SET (28)	10.00	4.50
COMMON CARD (1-28)	.25	.11
☐ 1 Tony LaRussa MG	.75	.35
☐ 2 Mark McGwire	3.00	1.35
☐ 3 Terry Steinbach	.75	.35
☐ 4 Dennis Eckersley	1.25	55
☐ 5 Mike Bordick	.25	.11
☐ 6 Rickey Henderson	1.50	.70
☐ 7 Ruben Sierra	.25	.11
☐ 8 Stan Javier	.25	.11
☐ 9 Todd Van Poppel	.25	.11
☐ 10 Bob Welch	.50	.23
☐ 11 Miguel Jimenez	.25	.11
☐ 12 Steve Karsay	.25	.11
☐ 13 Geronimo Berroa	.50	.23
☐ 14 Bobby Witt	.25	.11
☐ 15 Troy Neel	.25	.11
☐ 16 Ron Darling	.25	.11
☐ 17 Scott Hemond	.25	.11
☐ 18 Steve Ontiveros	.25	.11
☐ 19 Mike Aldrete	.25	.11
☐ 20 Carlos Reyes	.25	.11
☐ 21 Brent Gates	.25	.11
☐ 22 Mark Acre	.25	.11
☐ 23 Eric Helfand	.25	.11
☐ 24 Vince Horsman	.25	.11
☐ 25 Bill Taylor	.25	.11
☐ 26 Scott Brosius	.50	.23
☐ 27 John Briscoe	.25	.11
☐ 28 Checklist/Coaches Dave Duncan Jim Lefebvre Carney Lansford Tommie Reynolds Art Kusnyer Dave McKay	.50	.23

1995 A's Mother's

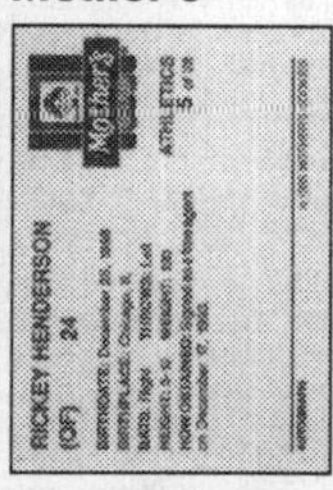

The 1995 Mother's Cookies Oakland A's set consists of 30 standard-size cards with rounded corners. The fronts display posed color player portraits in stadium settings. The player's name and team name appear in one of the top corners. The backs carry biographical information and the sponsor's logo on a white background in red and purple print. A blank slot for the player's autograph rounds out the back. A special card of Ariel Prieto, as well as a special coupon card, was issued in September as part of Hispanic-American night. The complete set includes the Prieto SP card.

	MINT	NRMT
COMPLETE SET (30)	20.00	9.00
COMMON CARD (1-30)	.25	.11
☐ 1 Tony LaRussa MG	.75	.35
☐ 2 Mark McGwire	3.00	1.35
☐ 3 Terry Steinbach	.50	.23
☐ 4 Dennis Eckersley	1.25	.55
☐ 5 Rickey Henderson	1.50	.70
☐ 6 Ron Darling	.25	.11
☐ 7 Ruben Sierra	.50	.23
☐ 8 Mike Aldrete	.25	.11
☐ 9 Stan Javier	.25	.11
☐ 10 Mike Bordick	.25	.11
☐ 11 Dave Stewart	.75	.35
☐ 12 Geronimo Berroa	.50	.23
☐ 13 Todd Van Poppel	.25	.11
☐ 14 Todd Stottlemyre	.50	.23
☐ 15 Eric Helfand	.25	.11
☐ 16 Dave Leiper	.25	.11
☐ 17 Rick Honeycutt	.25	.11
☐ 18 Steve Ontiveros	.25	.11
☐ 19 Mike Gallego	.25	.11
☐ 20 Carlos Reyes	.25	.11
☐ 21 Brent Gates	.25	.11
☐ 22 Craig Paquette	.25	.11
☐ 23 Mike Harkey	.25	.11
☐ 24 Andy Tomberlin	.25	.11
☐ 25 Jim Corsi	.25	.11
☐ 26 Mark Acre	.25	.11
☐ 27 Scott Brosius	.50	.23
☐ 28 Coaches/Checklist Jim Lefebvre Tommie Reynolds Carney Lansford Dave Duncan Art Kusnyer Dave McKay	.50	.23
☐ 29 Ariel Prieto SP	10.00	4.50
☐ 30 Coupon Card	.25	.11

1996 A's Mother's

This 28-card set consists of borderless posed color player portraits in stadium settings. The player's and team's names appear in one of the top rounded corners. The backs carry biographical information and the sponsor's logo on a white background in red and purple print. A blank slot for the player's autograph rounds out the back.

	MINT	NRMT
COMPLETE SET (28)	8.00	3.60
COMMON CARD (1-28)	.25	.11
☐ 1 Art Howe MG	.25	.11
☐ 2 Mark McGwire	3.00	1.35
☐ 3 Jason Giambi	1.00	.45
☐ 4 Terry Steinbach	.75	.35
☐ 5 Mike Bordick	.25	.11
☐ 6 Brent Gates	.25	.11
☐ 7 Scott Brosius	.50	.23
☐ 8 Doug Johns	.25	.11
☐ 9 Jose Herrera	.50	.23
☐ 10 John Wasdin	.50	.23
☐ 11 Ernie Young	.25	.11
☐ 12 Pedro Munoz	.25	.11
☐ 13 Steve Wojciechowski	.25	.11
☐ 14 Geronimo Berroa	.50	.23
☐ 15 Phil Plantier	.25	.11
☐ 16 Bobby Chouinard	.25	.11
☐ 17 George Williams	.25	.11
☐ 18 Jim Corsi	.25	.11
☐ 19 Mike Mohler	.25	.11
☐ 20 Torey Lovullo	.25	.11
☐ 21 Carlos Reyes	.25	.11
☐ 22 Buddy Groom	.25	.11
☐ 23 Don Wengert	.25	.11
☐ 24 Bill Taylor	.25	.11
☐ 25 Todd Van Poppel	.25	.11
☐ 26 Rafael Bournigal	.25	.11
☐ 27 Damon Mashore	.25	.11
☐ 28 Coaches Card CL Bob Cluck Brad Fischer Duffy Dyer Ron Washington Bob Alejo Denny Walling	.25	.11

1997 A's Mothers

This 28-card set of the Oakland Athletics sponsored by Mother's Cookies consists of posed color player photos with rounded corners. The backs carry biographical information and the sponsor's logo on a white

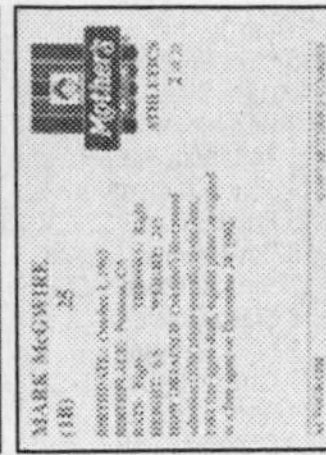

background in red and purple print. A blank slot for the player's autograph rounds out the back.

	MINT	NRMT
COMPLETE SET (28)	12.00	5.50
COMMON CARD (1-28)	.25	.11
☐ 1 Art Howe MG	.25	.11
☐ 2 Mark McGwire	3.00	1.35
☐ 3 Jose Canseco	1.50	.70
☐ 4 Jason Giambi	1.00	.45
☐ 5 Geronimo Berroa	.50	.23
☐ 6 Ernie Young	.25	.11
☐ 7 Scott Brosius	.50	.23
☐ 8 Dave Magadan	.25	.11
☐ 9 Mike Mohler	.25	.11
☐ 10 George Williams	.25	.11
☐ 11 Tony Batista	.50	.23
☐ 12 Steve Karsay	.25	.11
☐ 13 Rafael Bournigal	.25	.11
☐ 14 Ariel Prieto	.25	.11
☐ 15 Buddy Groom	.25	.11
☐ 16 Matt Stairs	.50	.23
☐ 17 Brent Mayne	.25	.11
☐ 18 Bill Taylor	.25	.11
☐ 19 Scott Spiezio	1.25	.55
☐ 20 Richie Lewis	.25	.11
☐ 21 Mark Acre	.25	.11
☐ 22 Dave Telgheder	.25	.11
☐ 23 Willie Adams	.25	.11
☐ 24 Izzy Molina	.25	.11
☐ 25 Don Wengert	.25	.11
☐ 26 Damon Mashore	.25	.11
☐ 27 Aaron Small	.25	.11
☐ 28 Coaches Card CL Bob Alejo Bob Cluck Duffy Dyer Brad Fischer Denny Walling Ron Washington	.25	.11

1992 Action Packed ASG

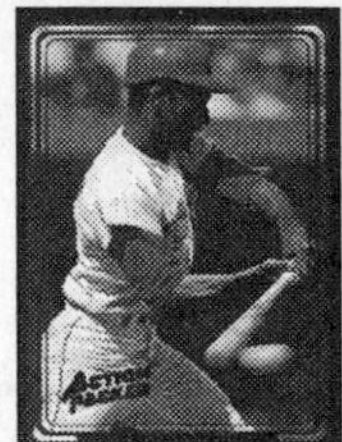

The 1992 Action Packed All-Star Gallery consists of 84 player standard-size cards and pays tribute to former greats of baseball. With the exception of Joe Garagiola, all the players represented appeared in at least one All-Star game. The first 18 cards feature Hall of Famers, and Action Packed guaranteed one Hall of Famer card in each seven-card foil pack. Also 24K gold leaf stamped versions of these Hall of Famer cards were randomly inserted into foil packs. The fronts feature embossed action player photos framed by inner gold border stripes and a black outer border. Most of the photos are color; 13 of them, however, are sepia-toned that have been converted to black and white. On a gray background, the horizontally oriented backs carry biography, career statistics, and a special career highlight section that lists memorable highlights that spanned the players' career.

	MINT	NRMT
COMPLETE SET (84)	18.00	8.00
COMMON CARD (1-84)	.25	.11
☐ 1 Yogi Berra	1.25	.55
☐ 2 Lou Brock	1.00	.45
☐ 3 Bob Gibson	1.00	.45
☐ 4 Ferguson Jenkins	.75	.35
☐ 5 Ralph Kiner	.75	.35
☐ 6 Al Kaline	1.00	.45
☐ 7 Lou Boudreau	.50	.23
☐ 8 Bobby Doerr	.50	.23
☐ 9 Billy Herman	.50	.23
☐ 10 Monte Irvin	.50	.23
☐ 11 George Kell	.50	.23
☐ 12 Robin Roberts	.75	.35
☐ 13 Johnny Mize	.75	.35
☐ 14 Willie Mays	2.50	1.10
☐ 15 Enos Slaughter	.50	.23
☐ 16 Warren Spahn	.75	.35
☐ 17 Willie Stargell	.75	.35
☐ 18 Billy Williams	.35	.16
☐ 19 Vernon Law	.25	.11
☐ 20 Virgil Trucks	.25	.11
☐ 21 Mel Parnell	.25	.11
☐ 22 Wally Moon	.25	.11
☐ 23 Gene Woodling	.25	.11
☐ 24 Richie Ashburn	1.00	.45
☐ 25 Mark Fidrych	.35	.16
☐ 26 Elroy Face	.25	.11
☐ 27 Larry Doby	.35	.16
☐ 28 Dick Groat	.25	.11
☐ 29 Cesar Cedeno	.25	.11
☐ 30 Bob Horner	.25	.11
☐ 31 Bobby Richardson	.35	.16
☐ 32 Bobby Murcer	.35	.16
☐ 33 Gil McDougald	.25	.11
☐ 34 Roy White	.25	.11
☐ 35 Bill Skowron	.35	.16
☐ 36 Mickey Lolich	.35	.16
☐ 37 Minnie Minoso	.35	.16
☐ 38 Bill Pierce	.35	.16
☐ 39 Ron Santo	.35	.16
☐ 40 Sal Bando	.35	.16
☐ 41 Ralph Branca	.35	.16
☐ 42 Bert Campaneris	.25	.11
☐ 43 Joe Garagiola	.50	.23
☐ 44 Vida Blue	.35	.16
☐ 45 Frank Crosetti	.50	.23
☐ 46 Luis Tiant	.25	.11
☐ 47 Maury Wills	.35	.16
☐ 48 Sam McDowell	.25	.11
☐ 49 Jimmy Piersall	.35	.16
☐ 50 Jim Lonborg	.25	.11
☐ 51 Don Newcombe	.35	.16
☐ 52 Bobby Thomson	.35	.16
☐ 53 Wilbur Wood	.25	.11
☐ 54 Carl Erskine	.35	.16
☐ 55 Chris Chambliss	.25	.11
☐ 56 Dave Kingman	.25	.11
☐ 57 Ken Holtzman	.25	.11
☐ 58 Bud Harrelson	.25	.11
☐ 59 Clem Labine	.35	.16
☐ 60 Tony Oliva	.35	.16
☐ 61 George Foster	.35	.16
☐ 62 Bobby Bonds	.35	.16
☐ 63 Harvey Haddix	.25	.11
☐ 64 Steve Garvey	.35	.16
☐ 65 Rocky Colavito	.50	.23
☐ 66 Orlando Cepeda	.50	.23
☐ 67 Ed Lopat	.35	.16
☐ 68 Al Oliver	.35	.16
☐ 69 Bill Mazeroski	.35	.16
☐ 70 Al Rosen	.35	.16
☐ 71 Bob Grich	.35	.16
☐ 72 Curt Flood	.35	.16
☐ 73 Willie Horton	.35	.16
☐ 74 Rico Carty	.25	.11
☐ 75 Davey Johnson	.35	.16
☐ 76 Don Kessinger	.25	.11
☐ 77 Frank Thomas	.25	.11
☐ 78 Bobby Shantz	.25	.11
☐ 79 Herb Score	.35	.16
☐ 80 Boog Powell	.35	.16
☐ 81 Rusty Staub	.35	.16
☐ 82 Bill Madlock	.35	.16
☐ 83 Manny Mota	.25	.11
☐ 84 Bill White	.35	.16

1992 Action Packed ASG 24K

The first 18 cards of the 1992 Action Packed All-Star Gallery feature Hall of Famers and were also produced in a 24K version on a limited basis. These 24K gold-leaf stamped versions of these Hall of Famer cards were randomly inserted into foil packs.

	MINT	NRMT
COMPLETE SET (18)	300.00	135.00
COMMON CARD (1G-18G)	15.00	6.75
☐ 1G Yogi Berra	40.00	18.00
☐ 2G Lou Brock	25.00	11.00
☐ 3G Bob Gibson	25.00	11.00
☐ 4G Ferguson Jenkins	15.00	6.75
☐ 5G Ralph Kiner	20.00	9.00
☐ 6G Al Kaline	25.00	11.00
☐ 7G Lou Boudreau	15.00	6.75
☐ 8G Bobby Doerr	15.00	6.75
☐ 9G Billy Herman	15.00	6.75
☐ 10G Monte Irvin	15.00	6.75
☐ 11G George Kell	15.00	6.75
☐ 12G Robin Roberts	20.00	9.00
☐ 13G Johnny Mize	20.00	9.00
☐ 14G Willie Mays	50.00	22.00
☐ 15G Enos Slaughter	15.00	6.75
☐ 16G Warren Spahn	20.00	9.00
☐ 17G Willie Stargell	20.00	9.00
☐ 18G Billy Williams	15.00	6.75

1993 Action Packed ASG

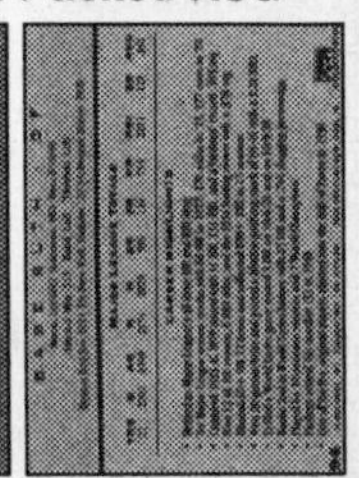

The second series of the Action Packed All-Star Gallery baseball set consists of 84 standard-size cards. Fifty two of the cards are in color, 31 are sepia-tone, and one is a colorized black-and-white. Action Packed included 46 Hall of Famers in the series and guaranteed one of these cards in every pack. Moreover, series II includes randomly inserted 24K cards of these Hall of Famers and contains a card honoring Bud Abbott and Lou Costello, creators of the famous "Who's on First" comedy routine. And as a special bonus for hobby dealers only, each box of cards included two free "Chiptopper" prototype cards of forthcoming Action Packed cards. The fronts feature embossed player photos with gold foil inner border stripes and red outer borders. On a gray background, the horizontal backs carry a biography and career summary.

	MINT	NRMT
COMPLETE SET (84)	18.00	8.00
COMMON CARD (85-130)	.50	.23
COMMON CARD (131-168)	.25	.11
☐ 85 Cy Young	.75	.35
☐ 86 Honus Wagner	1.00	.45
☐ 87 Christy Mathewson	1.00	.45
☐ 88 Ty Cobb	1.50	.70
☐ 89 Eddie Collins	.50	.23
☐ 90 Walter Johnson	1.00	.45
☐ 91 Tris Speaker	.75	.35
☐ 92 Grover Alexander	.75	.35
☐ 93 Edd Roush	.50	.23
☐ 94 Babe Ruth	2.00	.90
☐ 95 Rogers Hornsby	1.00	.45
☐ 96 Pie Traynor	.50	.23
☐ 97 Lou Gehrig	1.50	.70
☐ 98 Mickey Cochrane	.75	.35
☐ 99 Lefty Grove	.75	.35
☐ 100 Jimmie Foxx	1.00	.45
☐ 101 Tony Lazzeri	.50	.23
☐ 102 Mel Ott	.75	.35
☐ 103 Carl Hubbell	.50	.23
☐ 104 Al Lopez	.50	.23
☐ 105 Lefty Gomez	.75	.35
☐ 106 Dizzy Dean	1.00	.45
☐ 107 Hank Greenberg	1.00	.45
☐ 108 Joe Medwick	.50	.23
☐ 109 Arky Vaughan	.50	.23
☐ 110 Bob Feller	.75	.35
☐ 111 Hal Newhouser	.50	.23
☐ 112 Early Wynn	.50	.23
☐ 113 Bob Lemon	.50	.23
☐ 114 Red Schoendienst	.50	.23
☐ 115 Satchel Paige	1.00	.45
☐ 116 Whitey Ford	.75	.35
☐ 117 Eddie Mathews	.75	.35
☐ 118 Harmon Killebrew	.75	.35
☐ 119 Roberto Clemente	2.00	.90
☐ 120 Brooks Robinson	.75	.35
☐ 121 Don Drysdale	.75	.35
☐ 122 Luis Aparicio	.50	.23
☐ 123 Willie McCovey	.75	.35
☐ 124 Juan Marichal	.50	.23
☐ 125 Gaylord Perry	.50	.23
☐ 126 Catfish Hunter	.50	.23
☐ 127 Jim Palmer	.75	.35
☐ 128 Rod Carew	.75	.35

☐ 129 Tom Seaver	.75	.35
☐ 130 Rollie Fingers	.50	.23
☐ 131 Joe Jackson	1.50	.70
☐ 132 Pepper Martin	.25	.11
☐ 133 Joe Gordon	.35	.16
☐ 134 Marty Marion	.25	.11
☐ 135 Allie Reynolds	.35	.16
☐ 136 Johnny Sain	.35	.16
☐ 137 Gil Hodges	.75	.35
☐ 138 Ted Kluszewski	.35	.16
☐ 139 Nellie Fox	.75	.35
☐ 140 Billy Martin	.50	.23
☐ 141 Smoky Burgess	.25	.11
☐ 142 Lew Burdette	.35	.16
☐ 143 Joe Black	.25	.11
☐ 144 Don Larsen	.35	.16
☐ 145 Ken Boyer	.35	.16
☐ 146 Johnny Callison	.25	.11
☐ 147 Norm Cash	.35	.16
☐ 148 Keith Hernandez	.25	.11
☐ 149 Jim Kaat	.35	.16
☐ 150 Bill Freehan	.25	.11
☐ 151 Joe Torre	.35	.16
☐ 152 Bob Uecker	.35	.16
☐ 153 Dave McNally	.25	.11
☐ 154 Denny McLain	.35	.16
☐ 155 Dick Allen	.35	.16
☐ 156 Jimmy Wynn	.25	.11
☐ 157 Tommy John	.35	.16
☐ 158 Paul Blair	.25	.11
☐ 159 Reggie Smith	.25	.11
☐ 160 Jerry Koosman	.25	.11
☐ 161 Thurman Munson	.50	.23
☐ 162 Graig Nettles	.35	.16
☐ 163 Ron Cey	.25	.11
☐ 164 Cecil Cooper	.25	.11
☐ 165 Dave Parker	.35	.16
☐ 166 Jim Rice	.35	.16
☐ 167 Kent Tekulve	.25	.11
☐ 168 Who's On First Bud Abbott Lou Costello	.75	.35

1993 Action Packed ASG 24K

The second series of the 1993 Action Packed All-Star Gallery baseball set included 46 Hall of Famers and a special card honoring Bud Abbott and Lou Costello. Action Packed produced 24K gold leaf versions of all these cards and randomly inserted them throughout the foil packs.

	MINT	NRMT
COMPLETE SET (47)	800.00	350.00
COMMON CARD (19G-65G)	15.00	6.75
☐ 19G Cy Young	25.00	11.00
☐ 20G Honus Wagner	35.00	16.00
☐ 21G Christy Mathewson	35.00	16.00
☐ 22G Ty Cobb	50.00	22.00
☐ 23G Eddie Collins	15.00	6.75
☐ 24G Walter Johnson	35.00	16.00
☐ 25G Tris Speaker	25.00	11.00
☐ 26G Grover Alexander	25.00	11.00
☐ 27G Ed Roush	15.00	6.75
☐ 28G Babe Ruth	75.00	34.00
☐ 29G Rogers Hornsby	35.00	16.00
☐ 30G Pie Traynor	15.00	6.75
☐ 31G Lou Gehrig	50.00	22.00
☐ 32G Mickey Cochrane	25.00	11.00
☐ 33G Lefty Grove	25.00	11.00
☐ 34G Jimmie Foxx	35.00	16.00
☐ 35G Tony Lazzeri	15.00	6.75
☐ 36G Mel Ott	25.00	11.00
☐ 37G Carl Hubbell	20.00	9.00
☐ 38G Al Lopez	15.00	6.75
☐ 39G Lefty Gomez	25.00	11.00
☐ 40G Dizzy Dean	35.00	16.00
☐ 41G Hank Greenberg	35.00	16.00
☐ 42G Joe Medwick	15.00	6.75
☐ 43G Arky Vaughan	15.00	6.75
☐ 44G Bob Feller	35.00	16.00
☐ 45G Hal Newhouser	15.00	6.75
☐ 46G Early Wynn	15.00	6.75
☐ 47G Bob Lemon	15.00	6.75
☐ 48G Red Schoendienst	15.00	6.75
☐ 49G Satchel Paige	35.00	16.00
☐ 50G Whitey Ford	25.00	11.00
☐ 51G Eddie Mathews	25.00	11.00
☐ 52G Harmon Killebrew	25.00	11.00
☐ 53G Roberto Clemente	50.00	22.00
☐ 54G Brooks Robinson	35.00	16.00
☐ 55G Don Drysdale	25.00	11.00
☐ 56G Luis Aparicio	15.00	6.75
☐ 57G Willie McCovey	20.00	9.00
☐ 58G Juan Marichal	15.00	6.75
☐ 59G Gaylord Perry	15.00	6.75
☐ 60G Catfish Hunter	15.00	6.75
☐ 61G Jim Palmer	20.00	9.00
☐ 62G Rod Carew	20.00	9.00
☐ 63G Tom Seaver	35.00	16.00
☐ 64G Rollie Fingers	15.00	6.75
☐ 65G Who's On First	20.00	9.00

1993 Action Packed ASG Coke/Amoco

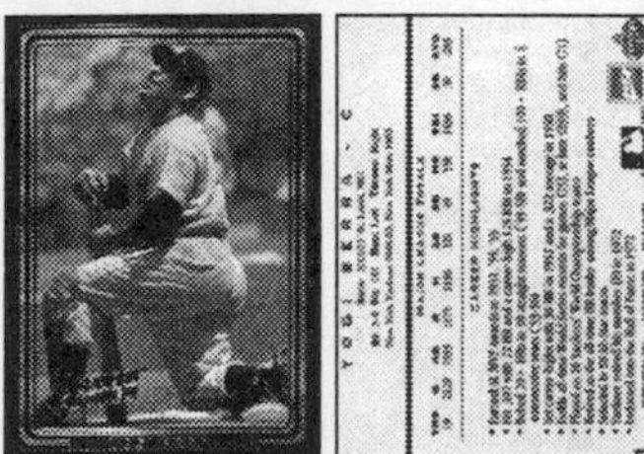

This 18-card standard-size set pays tribute to former greats of baseball. The cards feature Hall of Fame players and were sponsored by Coca Cola and Amoco. The fronts feature embossed action photos framed by inner gold-border stripes and a black outer border. Most of the photos are color; however five of them are sepia-toned. On a gray background, the horizontal back carries biography, career statistics, and special career highlights that list memorable events that spanned the player's career. The cards are numbered on the back. With the purchase of four multi-packs of Coca-Cola products at participating Amoco gas stations, collectors could send in through the mail for a complete set plus a 1.00 off coupon good toward the purchase of Amoco Ultimate gasoline. There was also a pre-promotion set with a red header card, with reportedly only 3000 sets produced, which was not distributed to the public. The red header version was indistinguishable from the gray header set listed below with the exception that Ferguson Jenkins and Billy Herman were replaced in the gray set by Red Schoendienst and Gaylord Perry; Jenkins and Herman were both members of the original 1992 Action Packed ASG set.

	MINT	NRMT
COMPLETE SET (18)	5.00	2.20
COMMON CARD (1-18)	.25	.11
☐ 1 Yogi Berra	.60	.25
☐ 2 Lou Brock	.35	.16
☐ 3 Bob Gibson	.35	.16
☐ 4 Red Schoendienst	.25	.11
☐ 5 Ralph Kiner	.35	.16
☐ 6 Al Kaline	.50	.23
☐ 7 Lou Boudreau	.25	.11
☐ 8 Bobby Doerr	.25	.11
☐ 9 Gaylord Perry	.25	.11
☐ 10 Monte Irvin	.25	.11
☐ 11 George Kell	.25	.11
☐ 12 Robin Roberts	.35	.16
☐ 13 Johnny Mize	.25	.11
☐ 14 Willie Mays	1.00	.45
☐ 15 Enos Slaughter	.25	.11
☐ 16 Warren Spahn	.35	.16
☐ 17 Willie Stargell	.35	.16
☐ 18 Billy Williams	.25	.11

1990 AGFA

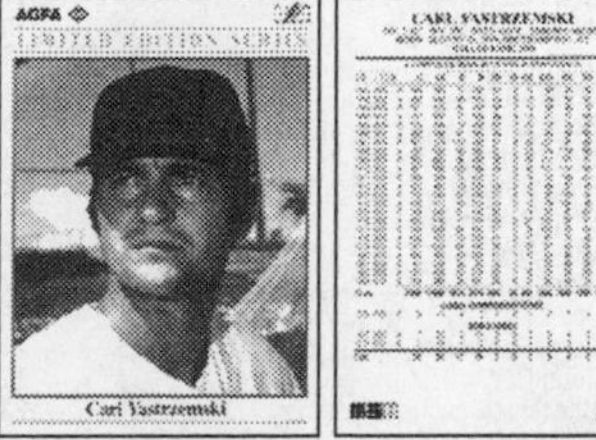

This 22-card standard-size set was issued by MSA (Michael Schechter Associates) for AGFA. The fronts display color head and shoulders shots, with a thin red border on a white card face. In turquoise lettering, the words "Limited Edition Series" appear above the pictures; the player's name is given below the pictures. In black on white, the backs present complete year by year major league statistics. The promotion reportedly consisted of a three-card pack of these cards given away with any purchase of a three-pack of AGFA film.

	MINT	NRMT
COMPLETE SET (22)	15.00	6.75
COMMON CARD (1-22)	.25	.11
☐ 1 Willie Mays	1.50	.70
☐ 2 Carl Yastrzemski	1.00	.45
☐ 3 Harmon Killebrew	1.00	.45
☐ 4 Joe Torre	.35	.16
☐ 5 Al Kaline	1.00	.45
☐ 6 Hank Aaron	1.50	.70
☐ 7 Rod Carew	1.00	.45
☐ 8 Roberto Clemente	2.00	.90
☐ 9 Luis Aparicio	.35	.16
☐ 10 Roger Maris	.75	.35
☐ 11 Joe Morgan	.75	.35
☐ 12 Maury Wills	.35	.16
☐ 13 Brooks Robinson	1.00	.45
☐ 14 Tom Seaver	1.00	.45
☐ 15 Steve Carlton	.75	.35
☐ 16 Whitey Ford	1.00	.45
☐ 17 Jim Palmer	1.00	.45
☐ 18 Rollie Fingers	.35	.16
☐ 19 Bruce Sutter	.25	.11
☐ 20 Willie McCovey	1.00	.45
☐ 21 Mike Schmidt	1.00	.45
☐ 22 Yogi Berra	1.00	.45

1990 All-American Baseball Team

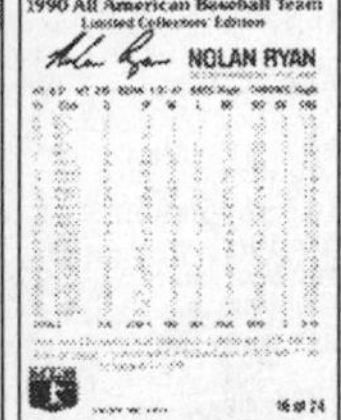

This 24-card, standard-size set was issued by MSA (Michael Schechter Associates) for 7/11, Squirt, and Dr. Pepper, and other carbonated beverages (but there are no markings on the cards whatsoever to indicate who sponsored the set other than MSA). These cards were distributed and issued inside 12-packs of sodas. The 12-packs included a checklist on one panel, and the cards themselves were glued on the inside of the pack so that it was difficult to remove a card without damaging it. The fronts feature a red-white and blue design framing the players photos while the back has major league career statistics and a sentence of career highlights. The back also has a fascimile autograph of the player on the back. Like many of the sets sponsored by MSA there are no team logos on the cards as they have been airbrushed away.

	MINT	NRMT
COMPLETE SET (24)	25.00	11.00
COMMON CARD (1-24)	.50	.23
☐ 1 George Brett	2.00	.90
☐ 2 Mark McGwire	3.00	1.35
☐ 3 Wade Boggs	1.25	.55
☐ 4 Cal Ripken	6.00	2.70
☐ 5 Rickey Henderson	1.00	.45
☐ 6 Dwight Gooden	.75	.35
☐ 7 Bo Jackson	.75	.35
☐ 8 Roger Clemens	2.50	1.10
☐ 9 Orel Hershiser	.75	.35
☐ 10 Ozzie Smith	2.00	.90
☐ 11 Don Mattingly	2.50	1.10
☐ 12 Kirby Puckett	3.00	1.35
☐ 13 Robin Yount	1.00	.45
☐ 14 Tony Gwynn	3.00	1.35
☐ 15 Jose Canseco	1.00	.45
☐ 16 Nolan Ryan	5.00	2.20
☐ 17 Ken Griffey Jr.	6.00	2.70
☐ 18 Will Clark	1.25	.55
☐ 19 Ryne Sandberg	2.00	.90
☐ 20 Kent Hrbek	.50	.23
☐ 21 Carlton Fisk	1.00	.45
☐ 22 Paul Molitor	1.25	.55
☐ 23 Dave Winfield	1.00	.45
☐ 24 Andre Dawson	1.00	.45

1987 Angels Grich Sheet

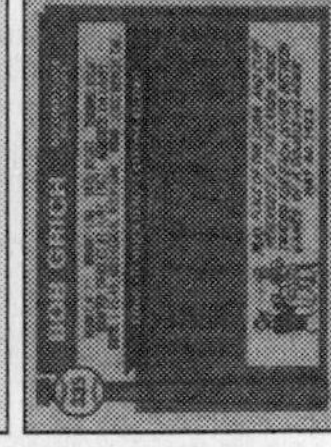

Issued to pay tribute to Bobby Grich's last season, this sheet was issued to fans at Bobby Grich Night, May 1, 1987. The perforated sheet measures approximately 10" by 17 1/2" and features 17 different Topps cards of Grich, from his 1971 Rookie Card (#193) through his 1987 Topps card (#677). When perforated, each card measured the standard size.

	MINT	NRMT
COMPLETE SET	7.50	3.40
COMMON CARD	.50	.23
☐ 1 Bobby Grich 1971	.50	.23
☐ 2 Bobby Grich 1972	.50	.23
☐ 3 Bobby Grich 1973	.50	.23
☐ 4 Bobby Grich 1974	.50	.23
☐ 5 Bobby Grich 1975	.50	.23
☐ 6 Bobby Grich 1976	.50	.23
☐ 7 Bobby Grich 1977	.50	.23
☐ 8 Bobby Grich 1978	.50	.23
☐ 9 Bobby Grich 1979	.50	.23
☐ 10 Bobby Grich 1980	.50	.23
☐ 11 Bobby Grich 1981	.50	.23
☐ 12 Bobby Grich 1982	.50	.23
☐ 13 Bobby Grich 1983	.50	.23
☐ 14 Bobby Grich 1984	.50	.23
☐ 15 Bobby Grich 1985	.50	.23
☐ 16 Bobby Grich 1986	.50	.23
☐ 17 Bobby Grich 1987	.50	.23

1993 Angels Mother's

The 1993 Mother's Cookies Angels set consists of 28 standard-size cards with rounded corners. The fronts display full-bleed color player portraits shot from the waist up in stadium settings. The player's name and team name appear in one of the corners. On a white background in red and purple print, the horizontal backs carry biographical information and the sponsor's logo.

	MINT	NRMT
COMPLETE SET (28)	12.50	5.50
COMMON CARD (1-28)	.25	.11
☐ 1 Buck Rodgers MG	.25	.11
☐ 2 Gary DiSarcina	.25	.11
☐ 3 Chuck Finley	.75	.35
☐ 4 J.T. Snow	1.50	.70
☐ 5 Gary Gaetti	.50	.23
☐ 6 Chili Davis	1.00	.45
☐ 7 Tim Salmon	3.00	1.35
☐ 8 Mark Langston	.50	.23
☐ 9 Scott Sanderson	.25	.11
☐ 10 John Orton	.25	.11
☐ 11 Julio Valera	.25	.11
☐ 12 Chad Curtis	1.00	.45
☐ 13 Kelly Gruber	.25	.11
☐ 14 Rene Gonzales	.25	.11
☐ 15 Luis Polonia	.25	.11
☐ 16 Greg Myers	.25	.11
☐ 17 Gene Nelson	.25	.11
☐ 18 Torey Lovullo	.25	.11
☐ 19 Scott Lewis	.25	.11
☐ 20 Chuck Crim	.25	.11
☐ 21 John Farrell	.25	.11
☐ 22 Steve Frey	.25	.11
☐ 23 Stan Javier	.25	.11
☐ 24 Ken Patterson	.25	.11
☐ 25 Ron Tingley	.25	.11
☐ 26 Damion Easley	.25	.11
☐ 27 Joe Grahe	.25	.11
☐ 28 Checklist/Coaches Chuck Hernandez Jimmie Reese Ken Macha Rod Carew John Wathan Bobby Knoop Rick Turner	.75	.35

1994 Angels Mother's

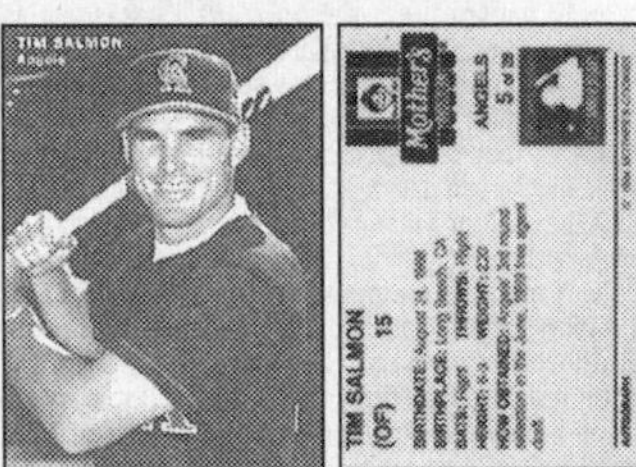

The 1994 Mother's Cookies Angels set consists of 28 standard-size cards with rounded corners. The fronts display full-bleed color player portraits shot from the waist up against a stadium background. The player's name and team name appear in one of the corners. On a white background in red and purple print, the horizontal backs carry biographical information and the sponsor's logo. A blank slot for the player's autograph rounds out the back.

	MINT	NRMT
COMPLETE SET (28)	12.50	5.50
COMMON CARD (1-28)	.25	.11
☐ 1 Marcel Lachemann MG	.25	.11
☐ 2 Mark Langston	.75	.35
☐ 3 J.T. Snow	1.00	.45
☐ 4 Chad Curtis	.75	.35
☐ 5 Tim Salmon	4.00	1.80
☐ 6 Gary DiSarcina	.25	.11
☐ 7 Bo Jackson	.75	.35
☐ 8 Dwight Smith	.25	.11
☐ 9 Chuck Finley	.75	.35
☐ 10- Rod Correia	.25	.11
☐ 11 Spike Owen	.25	.11
☐ 12 Harold Reynolds	.50	.23
☐ 13 Chris Turner	.25	.11
☐ 14 Chili Davis	.75	.35
☐ 15 Bob Patterson	.25	.11
☐ 16 Jim Edmonds	3.00	1.35
☐ 17 Joe Magrane	.25	.11
☐ 18 Craig Lefferts	.25	.11
☐ 19 Scott Lewis	.25	.11
☐ 20 Rex Hudler	.25	.11
☐ 21 Mike Butcher	.25	.11
☐ 22 Brian Anderson	.25	.11
☐ 23 Greg Myers	.25	.11
☐ 24 Mark Leiter	.25	.11
☐ 25 Joe Grahe	.25	.11
☐ 26 Jorge Fabregas	.25	.11
☐ 27 John Dopson	.25	.11
☐ 28 Checklist/Coaches Chuck Hernandez Ken Macha Bobby Knoop Joe Maddon Rod Carew Max Oliveras	.50	.23

1995 Angels Mother's

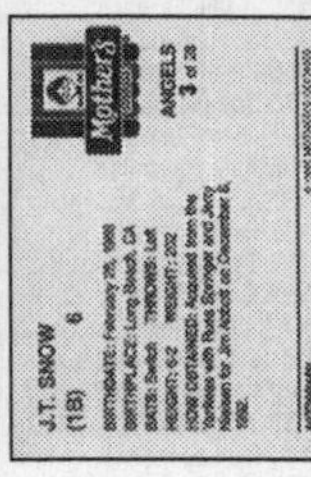

This 1995 Mother's Cookies California Angels set consists of 28 standard-size cards with rounded corners. The fronts display posed color player portraits. The player's name and team name appear in one of the top corners. The horizontal backs carry biographical information and the sponsor's logo on a white background in red and purple print. A blank slot at the bottom for the player's autograph rounds out the back.

	MINT	NRMT
COMPLETE SET (28)	12.50	5.50
COMMON CARD (1-28)	.25	.11
☐ 1 Marcel Lachemann MG	.25	.11
☐ 2 Mark Langston	.75	.35
☐ 3 J.T. Snow	1.00	.45
☐ 4 Tim Salmon	3.00	1.35
☐ 5 Chili Davis	.75	.35
☐ 6 Gary DiSarcina	.25	.11
☐ 7 Tony Phillips	.50	.23
☐ 8 Jim Edmonds	1.50	.70
☐ 9 Chuck Finley	.75	.35
☐ 10 Mark Dalesandro	.25	.11
☐ 11 Greg Myers	.25	.11
☐ 12 Spike Owen	.25	.11
☐ 13 Lee Smith	.50	.23
☐ 14 Eduardo Perez	.25	.11
☐ 15 Bob Patterson	.25	.11
☐ 16 Mitch Williams	.50	.23
☐ 17 Garret Anderson	1.50	.70
☐ 18 Mike Bielecki	.25	.11
☐ 19 Shawn Boskie	.25	.11
☐ 20 Damion Easley	.25	.11
☐ 21 Mike Butcher	.25	.11
☐ 22 Brian Anderson	.25	.11
☐ 23 Andy Allanson	.25	.11
☐ 24 Scott Sanderson	.25	.11
☐ 25 Troy Percival	.50	.23
☐ 26 Rex Hudler	.25	.11
☐ 27 Mike James	.25	.11
☐ 28 Coaches/Checklist Rod Carew Chuck Hernandez Rick Burleson Bobby Knoop Bill Lachemann Mick Billmeyer Joe Maddon	.75	.35

1996 Angels Mother's

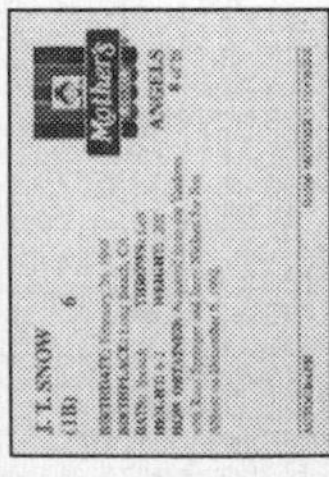

This 28-card set consists of borderless posed color player portraits in stadium settings. The player's and team's names appear in one of the top rounded corners. The backs carry biographical information and the sponsor's logo on a white background in red and purple print. A blank slot for the player's autograph rounds out the back.

	MINT	NRMT
COMPLETE SET (28)	10.00	4.50
COMMON CARD (1-28)	.25	.11
☐ 1 Marcel Lachemann MG	.25	.11
☐ 2 Chili Davis	.75	.35
☐ 3 Mark Langston	.75	.35
☐ 4 Tim Salmon	2.00	.90
☐ 5 Jim Abbott	.25	.11

☐ 6 Jim Edmonds 1.25 .55
☐ 7 Gary DiSarcina .25 .11
☐ 8 J.T. Snow .75 .35
☐ 9 Chuck Finley .75 .35
☐ 10 Tim Wallach .25 .11
☐ 11 Lee Smith .50 .23
☐ 12 George Arias .25 .11
☐ 13 Troy Percival .50 .23
☐ 14 Randy Velarde .25 .11
☐ 15 Garret Anderson 1.00 .45
☐ 16 Jorge Fabregas .25 .11
☐ 17 Shawn Boskie .25 .11
☐ 18 Mark Eichhorn .25 .11
☐ 19 Jack Howell .25 .11
☐ 20 Jason Grimsley .25 .11
☐ 21 Rex Hudler .25 .11
☐ 22 Mike Aldrete .25 .11
☐ 23 Mike James .25 .11
☐ 24 Scott Sanderson .25 .11
☐ 25 Don Slaught .25 .11
☐ 26 Mark Holzemer .25 .11
☐ 27 Dick Schofield .25 .11
☐ 28 Coaches Card CL .75 .35
Mick Billmeyer
Rick Burleson
Rod Carew
Chuck Hernandez
Bobby Knoop
Bill Lachemann
Joe Maddon

1997 Angels Mothers

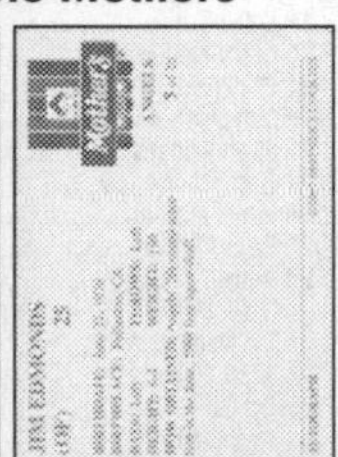

This 28-card set of the Anaheim Angels sponsored by Mother's Cookies consists of posed color player photos with rounded corners. The backs carry biographical information and the sponsor's logo on a white background in red and purple print. A blank slot for the player's autograph rounds out the back.

	MINT	NRMT
COMPLETE SET (28)	12.00	5.50
COMMON CARD (1-28)	.25	.11

☐ 1 Terry Collins MG .25 .11
☐ 2 Tim Salmon 2.50 1.10
☐ 3 Eddie Murray 1.25 .55
☐ 4 Mark Langston .75 .35
☐ 5 Jim Edmonds 1.25 .55
☐ 6 Tony Phillips .25 .11
☐ 7 Gary DiSarcina .25 .11
☐ 8 Garret Anderson 1.00 .45
☐ 9 Chuck Finley .75 .35
☐ 10 Darin Erstad 2.50 1.10
☐ 11 Jim Leyritz .25 .11
☐ 12 Shigetoshi Hasegawa 1.25 .55
☐ 13 Luis Alicea .25 .11
☐ 14 Troy Percival .50 .23
☐ 15 Allen Watson .25 .11
☐ 16 Craig Grebeck .25 .11
☐ 17 Mike Holtz .25 .11
☐ 18 Chad Kreuter .25 .11
☐ 19 Dennis Springer .25 .11
☐ 20 Jason Dickson .50 .23
☐ 21 Mike James .25 .11
☐ 22 Orlando Palmeiro .25 .11
☐ 23 Dave Hollins .25 .11
☐ 24 Mark Gubicza .25 .11
☐ 25 Pep Harris .25 .11
☐ 26 Jack Howell .25 .11
☐ 27 Rich DeLucia .25 .11
☐ 28 Coaches Card CL .25 .11
Larry Bowa
Rod Carew
Joe Coleman
Marcel Lachemann
Joe Maddon
Dave Parker

1978 Astros Burger King

The cards in this 23-card set measure 2 1/2" by 3 1/2". Released in local Houston Burger King outlets during the

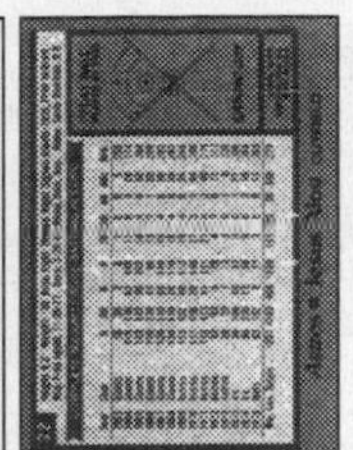

1978 season, this Houston Astros series contains the standard 22 numbered player cards and one unnumbered checklist. The player poses found to differ from the regular Topps issue are marked with asterisks.

	NRMT	VG-E
COMPLETE SET (23)	16.00	7.25
COMMON CARD (1-22)	.50	.23

☐ 1 Bill Virdon MG .75 .35
☐ 2 Joe Ferguson .50 .23
☐ 3 Ed Herrmann .50 .23
☐ 4 J.R. Richard 1.25 .55
☐ 5 Joe Niekro 1.25 .55
☐ 6 Floyd Bannister .75 .35
☐ 7 Joaquin Andujar 1.25 .55
☐ 8 Ken Forsch .50 .23
☐ 9 Mark Lemongello .50 .23
☐ 10 Joe Sambito .50 .23
☐ 11 Gene Pentz .50 .23
☐ 12 Bob Watson 1.50 .70
☐ 13 Julio Gonzalez .50 .23
☐ 14 Enos Cabell .60 .25
☐ 15 Roger Metzger .50 .23
☐ 16 Art Howe .75 .35
☐ 17 Jose Cruz 1.50 .70
☐ 18 Cesar Cedeno 1.25 .55
☐ 19 Terry Puhl .75 .35
☐ 20 Wilbur Howard .50 .23
☐ 21 Dave Bergman * .60 .25
☐ 22 Jesus Alou * .75 .35
☐ NNO Checklist Card TP .25 .11

1984 Astros Mother's

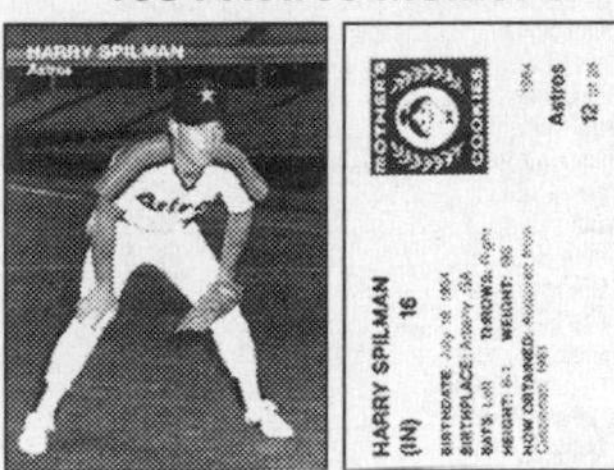

The cards in this 28-card set measure 2 1/2" by 3 1/2". In 1984, the Los Angeles based Mother's Cookies Co. issued five sets of cards featuring players from major league teams. The Houston Astros set features current players depicted by photos. Similar to their 1952 and 1953 issues, the cards have rounded corners. The backs of the cards contain the Mother's Cookies logo. The cards were distributed in partial sets to fans at the respective stadiums of the teams involved. Whereas 20 cards were given to each patron, a redemption card, redeemable for eight more cards was included. Unfortunately, the eight cards received by redeeming the coupon were not necessarily the eight needed to complete a set. Hobbyist Barry Colla was involved in the production of these sets.

	NRMT	VG-E
COMPLETE SET (28)	18.00	8.00
COMMON CARD (1-28)	.25	.11

☐ 1 Nolan Ryan 10.00 4.50
☐ 2 Joe Niekro .75 .35
☐ 3 Alan Ashby .25 .11
☐ 4 Bill Doran .75 .35
☐ 5 Phil Garner 1.00 .45
☐ 6 Ray Knight .75 .35
☐ 7 Dickie Thon .25 .11
☐ 8 Jose Cruz 1.00 .45
☐ 9 Jerry Mumphrey .25 .11
☐ 10 Terry Puhl .50 .23
☐ 11 Enos Cabell .25 .11
☐ 12 Harry Spilman .25 .11
☐ 13 Dave Smith .50 .23
☐ 14 Mike Scott 1.00 .45
☐ 15 Bob Lillis MG .25 .11
☐ 16 Bob Knepper .25 .11
☐ 17 Frank DiPino .25 .11
☐ 18 Tom Wieghaus .25 .11
☐ 19 Denny Walling .25 .11
☐ 20 Tony Scott .25 .11
☐ 21 Alan Bannister .25 .11
☐ 22 Bill Dawley .25 .11
☐ 23 Vern Ruhle .25 .11
☐ 24 Mike LaCoss .25 .11
☐ 25 Mike Madden .25 .11
☐ 26 Craig Reynolds .25 .11
☐ 27 Astros' Coaches .50 .23
Cot Deal
Don Leppert
Denis Menke
Les Moss
Jerry Walker
☐ 28 Astros' Checklist .25 .11
Astros Logo

1985 Astros Mother's

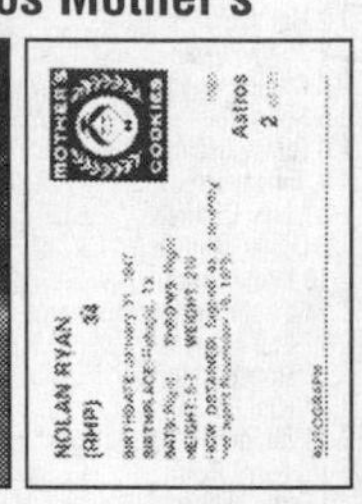

The cards in this 28-card set measure 2 1/2" by 3 1/2". In 1985, the Los Angeles-based Mother's Cookies Co. again issued five sets of cards featuring players from major league teams. The Houston Astros set features current players depicted by photos on cards with rounded corners. The backs of the cards contain the Mother's Cookies logo. Cards were passed out at the stadium on July 13. The checklist card features the Astros logo on the obverse.

	NRMT	VG-E
COMPLETE SET (28)	12.50	5.50
COMMON CARD (1-28)	.25	.11

☐ 1 Bob Lillis MG .25 .11
☐ 2 Nolan Ryan 7.50 3.40
☐ 3 Phil Garner .75 .35
☐ 4 Jose Cruz 1.00 .45
☐ 5 Denny Walling .25 .11
☐ 6 Joe Niekro .75 .35
☐ 7 Terry Puhl .50 .23
☐ 8 Bill Doran .25 .11
☐ 9 Dickie Thon .25 .11
☐ 10 Enos Cabell .25 .11
☐ 11 Frank DiPino .25 .11
☐ 12 Julio Solano .25 .11
☐ 13 Alan Ashby .25 .11
☐ 14 Craig Reynolds .25 .11
☐ 15 Jerry Mumphrey .25 .11
☐ 16 Bill Dawley .25 .11
☐ 17 Mark Bailey .25 .11
☐ 18 Mike Scott 1.00 .45
☐ 19 Harry Spilman .25 .11
☐ 20 Bob Knepper .25 .11
☐ 21 Dave Smith .50 .23
☐ 22 Kevin Bass .25 .11
☐ 23 Tim Tolman .25 .11
☐ 24 Jeff Calhoun .25 .11
☐ 25 Jim Pankovits .25 .11
☐ 26 Ron Mathis .25 .11
☐ 27 Astros' Coaches .50 .23
Cot Deal
Matt Galante
Don Leppert
Denis Menke
Jerry Walker
☐ 28 Astros' Checklist .25 .11
Astros Logo

1986 Astros Mother's

This set consists of 28 full-color, rounded-corner standard-size cards. Starter sets (only 20 cards but also including a certificate for eight more cards) were given out at the ballpark and collectors were encouraged to trade to fill in the rest of their set. Cards were originally given out at the Astrodome on July 10th. Since the 1986 All-Star Game was held in Houston, the set features Astro All-Stars since 1962 as painted by artist Richard Wallich. The set numbering is essentially chronological according

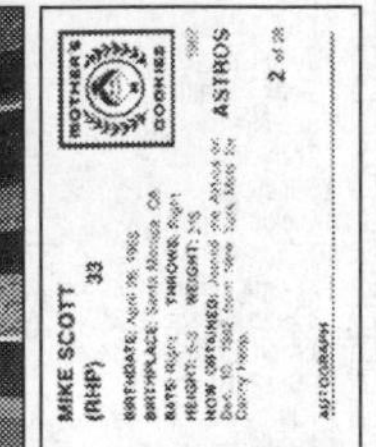

to when each player was selected for the All-Star Game as an Astro.

	MINT	NRMT
COMPLETE SET (28)	12.00	5.50
COMMON CARD (1-28)	.25	.11

	MINT	NRMT
☐ 1 Dick Farrell	.25	.11
☐ 2 Hal Woodeshick	.25	.11
☐ 3 Joe Morgan	2.00	.90
☐ 4 Claude Raymond	.25	.11
☐ 5 Mike Cuellar	.50	.23
☐ 6 Rusty Staub	1.00	.45
☐ 7 Jimmy Wynn	.75	.35
☐ 8 Larry Dierker	.75	.35
☐ 9 Denis Menke	.25	.11
☐ 10 Don Wilson	.25	.11
☐ 11 Cesar Cedeno	.50	.23
☐ 12 Lee May	.50	.23
☐ 13 Bob Watson	1.00	.45
☐ 14 Ken Forsch	.25	.11
☐ 15 Joaquin Andujar	.25	.11
☐ 16 Terry Puhl	.25	.11
☐ 17 Joe Niekro	.75	.35
☐ 18 Craig Reynolds	.25	.11
☐ 19 Joe Sambito	.25	.11
☐ 20 Jose Cruz	1.00	.45
☐ 21 J.R. Richard	.75	.35
☐ 22 Bob Knepper	.25	.11
☐ 23 Nolan Ryan	7.50	3.40
☐ 24 Ray Knight	.75	.35
☐ 25 Bill Dawley	.25	.11
☐ 26 Dickie Thon	.25	.11
☐ 27 Jerry Mumphrey	.25	.11
☐ 28 Checklist Card Astros' A-S Logo	.25	.11

1987 Astros Mother's

This set consists of 28 full-color, rounded-corner standard-size cards. Starter sets (only 20 cards but also including a certificate for eight more cards) were given out at the ballpark and collectors were encouraged to trade to fill in the rest of their set. Cards were originally given out at the Astrodome on July 17th during a game against the Phillies. Photos were taken by Barry Colla. The sets were reportedly given out free to the first 25,000 paid admissions at the game.

	MINT	NRMT
COMPLETE SET (28)	12.00	5.50
COMMON CARD (1-28)	.25	.11

	MINT	NRMT
☐ 1 Hal Lanier MG	.25	.11
☐ 2 Mike Scott	.75	.35
☐ 3 Jose Cruz	1.00	.45
☐ 4 Bill Doran	.25	.11
☐ 5 Bob Knepper	.25	.11
☐ 6 Phil Garner	.75	.35
☐ 7 Terry Puhl	.50	.23
☐ 8 Nolan Ryan	6.00	2.70
☐ 9 Kevin Bass	.25	.11
☐ 10 Glenn Davis	.50	.23
☐ 11 Alan Ashby	.25	.11
☐ 12 Charlie Kerfeld	.25	.11
☐ 13 Denny Walling	.25	.11
☐ 14 Danny Darwin	.50	.23
☐ 15 Mark Bailey	.25	.11
☐ 16 Davey Lopes	.75	.35
☐ 17 Dave Meads	.25	.11
☐ 18 Aurelio Lopez	.25	.11
☐ 19 Craig Reynolds	.25	.11
☐ 20 Dave Smith	.50	.23
☐ 21 Larry Andersen	.25	.11
☐ 22 Jim Pankovits	.25	.11
☐ 23 Jim Deshaies	.25	.11
☐ 24 Bert Pena	.25	.11
☐ 25 Dickie Thon	.25	.11
☐ 26 Billy Hatcher	.25	.11
☐ 27 Astros' Coaches Yogi Berra Denis Menke Gene Tenace Matt Galante Les Moss	1.00	.45
☐ 28 Checklist Card Astrodome	.25	.11

1988 Astros Mother's

This set consists of 28 full-color, rounded-corner standard-size cards. Starter sets (only 20 cards but also including a certificate for eight more cards) were given out at the ballpark and collectors were encouraged to trade to fill in the rest of their set. Cards were originally given out at the Astrodome on August 26th during a game. The sets were reportedly given out free to the first 25,000 paid admissions at the game.

	MINT	NRMT
COMPLETE SET (28)	12.00	5.50
COMMON CARD (1-28)	.25	.11

	MINT	NRMT
☐ 1 Hal Lanier MG	.25	.11
☐ 2 Mike Scott	.75	.35
☐ 3 Gerald Young	.25	.11
☐ 4 Bill Doran	.25	.11
☐ 5 Bob Knepper	.25	.11
☐ 6 Billy Hatcher	.25	.11
☐ 7 Terry Puhl	.50	.23
☐ 8 Nolan Ryan	6.00	2.70
☐ 9 Kevin Bass	.25	.11
☐ 10 Glenn Davis	.50	.23
☐ 11 Alan Ashby	.25	.11
☐ 12 Steve Henderson	.25	.11
☐ 13 Denny Walling	.25	.11
☐ 14 Danny Darwin	.50	.23
☐ 15 Mark Bailey	.25	.11
☐ 16 Ernie Camacho	.25	.11
☐ 17 Rafael Ramirez	.25	.11
☐ 18 Jeff Heathcock	.25	.11
☐ 19 Craig Reynolds	.25	.11
☐ 20 Dave Smith	.50	.23
☐ 21 Larry Andersen	.25	.11
☐ 22 Jim Pankovits	.25	.11
☐ 23 Jim Deshaies	.25	.11
☐ 24 Juan Agosto	.25	.11
☐ 25 Chuck Jackson	.25	.11
☐ 26 Joaquin Andujar	.25	.11
☐ 27 Astros' Coaches Yogi Berra Gene Clines Matt Galante Marc Hill Denis Menke Les Moss	1.00	.45
☐ 28 Checklist Card Dave Labossiere TR Dennis Liborio EQMG Doc Ewell TR	.25	.11

1989 Astros Mother's

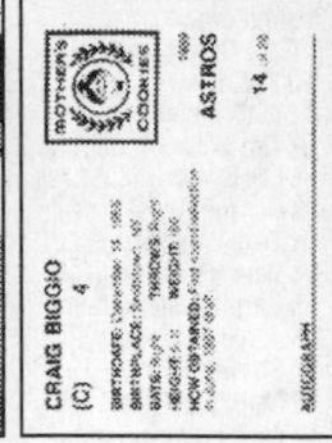

The 1989 Mother's Cookies Houston Astros set contains 28 standard-size cards with rounded corners. The fronts have borderless color photos, and the horizontally oriented backs have biographical information. Starter sets containing 20 of these cards were given away at an Astros home game during the 1989 season.

	MINT	NRMT
COMPLETE SET (28)	10.00	4.50
COMMON CARD (1-28)	.25	.11

	MINT	NRMT
☐ 1 Art Howe MG	.25	.11
☐ 2 Mike Scott	.75	.35
☐ 3 Gerald Young	.25	.11
☐ 4 Bill Doran	.25	.11
☐ 5 Billy Hatcher	.25	.11
☐ 6 Terry Puhl	.50	.23
☐ 7 Bob Knepper	.25	.11
☐ 8 Kevin Bass	.25	.11
☐ 9 Glenn Davis	.50	.23
☐ 10 Alan Ashby	.25	.11
☐ 11 Bob Forsch	.25	.11
☐ 12 Greg Gross	.25	.11
☐ 13 Danny Darwin	.50	.23
☐ 14 Craig Biggio	4.00	1.80
☐ 15 Jim Clancy	.25	.11
☐ 16 Rafael Ramirez	.25	.11
☐ 17 Alex Trevino	.25	.11
☐ 18 Craig Reynolds	.25	.11
☐ 19 Dave Smith	.50	.23
☐ 20 Larry Andersen	.25	.11
☐ 21 Eric Yelding	.25	.11
☐ 22 Jim Deshaies	.25	.11
☐ 23 Juan Agosto	.25	.11
☐ 24 Rick Rhoden	.25	.11
☐ 25 Ken Caminiti	3.00	1.35
☐ 26 Dave Meads	.25	.11
☐ 27 Astros Coaches Yogi Berra Ed Napoleon Matt Galante Ed Ott Phil Garner Les Moss	1.00	.45
☐ 28 Checklist Card Dave Labossiere TR Doc Ewell TR Dennis Liborio EQMG	.25	.11

1990 Astros Mother's

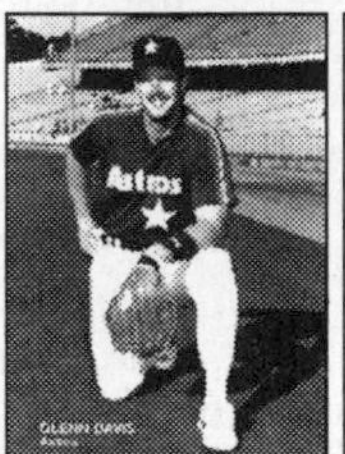

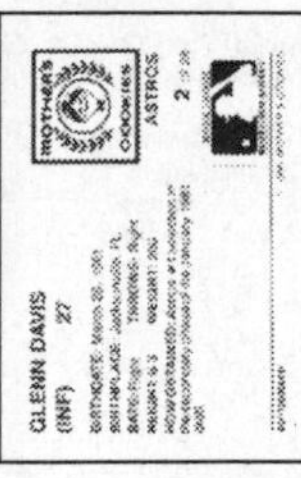

This 28-card standard-size set features members of the 1990 Houston Astros. This set features the traditional rounded corners and has biographical information about each player on the back. These Astros cards were given away on July 15th to the first 25,000 fans at the Astrodome. They were distributed in 20 card random packets at the game and eight more at the redemption booths. However, both groups of cards were random and there was no guarantee of getting a complete set in the cards. The promotional idea was that the only way one could finish the set was to trade for them. The certificates of redemption for eight were redeemable at the major card show at the AstroArena on August 24-26, 1990.

	MINT	NRMT
COMPLETE SET (28)	8.00	3.60
COMMON CARD (1-28)	.25	.11

	MINT	NRMT
☐ 1 Art Howe MG	.25	.11
☐ 2 Glenn Davis	.50	.23
☐ 3 Eric Anthony	.25	.11
☐ 4 Mike Scott	.75	.35
☐ 5 Craig Biggio	2.00	.90
☐ 6 Ken Caminiti	1.50	.70
☐ 7 Bill Doran	.25	.11
☐ 8 Gerald Young	.25	.11
☐ 9 Terry Puhl	.50	.23
☐ 10 Mark Portugal	.25	.11

Card	MINT	NRMT
☐ 11 Mark Davidson	.25	.11
☐ 12 Jim Deshaies	.25	.11
☐ 13 Bill Gullickson	.25	.11
☐ 14 Franklin Stubbs	.25	.11
☐ 15 Danny Darwin	.50	.23
☐ 16 Ken Oberkfell	.25	.11
☐ 17 Dave Smith	.50	.23
☐ 18 Dan Schatzeder	.25	.11
☐ 19 Rafael Ramirez	.25	.11
☐ 20 Larry Andersen	.25	.11
☐ 21 Alex Trevino	.25	.11
☐ 22 Glenn Wilson	.25	.11
☐ 23 Jim Clancy	.25	.11
☐ 24 Eric Yelding	.25	.11
☐ 25 Casey Candaele	.25	.11
☐ 26 Juan Agosto	.25	.11
☐ 27 Coaches Card Billy Bowman Bob Cluck Phil Garner Matt Galante Ed Napoleon Rudy Jaramillo	.50	.23
☐ 28 Personnel Card Dave Labossiere TR Dennis Liborio EQ.MG Doc Ewell TR	.25	.11

1991 Astros Mother's

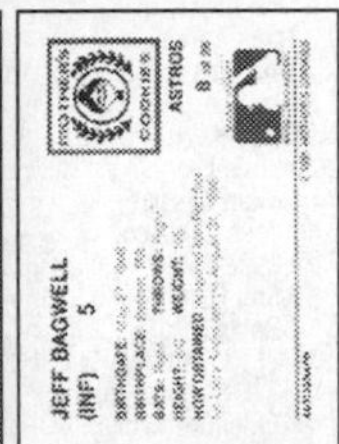

The 1991 Mother's Cookies Houston Astros set contains 28 standard-size cards with rounded corners. The front design has borderless glossy color player photos from the waist up. The horizontally oriented backs are printed in red and purple, present biographical information, and have blank slots for player autographs.

	MINT	NRMT
COMPLETE SET (28)	12.00	5.50
COMMON CARD (1-28)	.25	.11
☐ 1 Art Howe MG	.25	.11
☐ 2 Steve Finley	1.00	.45
☐ 3 Pete Harnisch	.25	.11
☐ 4 Mike Scott	.75	.35
☐ 5 Craig Biggio	2.00	.90
☐ 6 Ken Caminiti	1.50	.70
☐ 7 Eric Yelding	.25	.11
☐ 8 Jeff Bagwell	6.00	2.70
☐ 9 Jim Deshaies	.25	.11
☐ 10 Mark Portugal	.25	.11
☐ 11 Mark Davidson	.25	.11
☐ 12 Jimmy Jones	.25	.11
☐ 13 Luis Gonzalez	1.00	.45
☐ 14 Karl Rhodes	.25	.11
☐ 15 Curt Schilling	1.50	.70
☐ 16 Ken Oberkfell	.25	.11
☐ 17 Mark McLemore	.25	.11
☐ 18 Dave Rohde	.25	.11
☐ 19 Rafael Ramirez	.25	.11
☐ 20 Al Osuna	.25	.11
☐ 21 Jim Corsi	.25	.11
☐ 22 Carl Nichols	.25	.11
☐ 23 Jim Clancy	.25	.11
☐ 24 Dwayne Henry	.25	.11
☐ 25 Casey Candaele	.25	.11
☐ 26 Xavier Hernandez	.25	.11
☐ 27 Darryl Kile	1.50	.70
☐ 28 Checklist Card Phil Garner CO Bob Cluck CO Ed Ott CO Matt Galante CO Rudy Jaramillo CO	.50	.23

1992 Astros Mother's

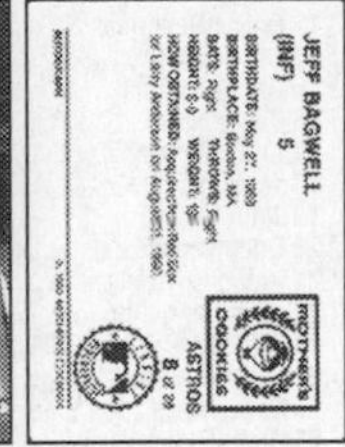

The 1992 Mother's Cookies Astros set contains 28 standard-size cards with rounded corners. The front design has borderless glossy color player photos in which the players are posed with either their glove or a bat. The player's name and team name appear in the upper right corner. The horizontal backs are printed in red and purple, and present biography and a "how obtained" remark where appropriate. A blank slot for the player's autograph rounds out the back.

	MINT	NRMT
COMPLETE SET (28)	10.00	4.50
COMMON CARD (1-28)	.25	.11
☐ 1 Art Howe MG	.25	.11
☐ 2 Steve Finley	1.00	.45
☐ 3 Pete Harnisch	.25	.11
☐ 4 Pete Incaviglia	.25	.11
☐ 5 Craig Biggio	2.00	.90
☐ 6 Ken Caminiti	1.50	.70
☐ 7 Eric Anthony	.25	.11
☐ 8 Jeff Bagwell	5.00	2.20
☐ 9 Andujar Cedeno	.25	.11
☐ 10 Mark Portugal	.25	.11
☐ 11 Eddie Taubensee	.50	.23
☐ 12 Jimmy Jones	.25	.11
☐ 13 Joe Boever	.25	.11
☐ 14 Benny Distefano	.25	.11
☐ 15 Juan Guerrero	.25	.11
☐ 16 Doug Jones	.25	.11
☐ 17 Scott Servais	.25	.11
☐ 18 Butch Henry	.25	.11
☐ 19 Rafael Ramirez	.25	.11
☐ 20 Al Osuna	.25	.11
☐ 21 Rob Murphy	.25	.11
☐ 22 Chris Jones	.25	.11
☐ 23 Rob Mallicoat	.25	.11
☐ 24 Darryl Kile	1.00	.45
☐ 25 Casey Candaele	.25	.11
☐ 26 Xavier Hernandez	.25	.11
☐ 27 Coaches Rudy Jaramillo Ed Ott Matt Galante Bob Cluck Tom Spencer	.50	.23
☐ 28 Checklist Dennis Liborio EQMG Dave Labossiere TR Doc Ewell TR	.25	.11

1993 Astros Mother's

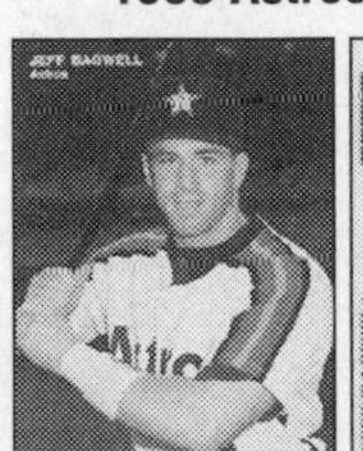
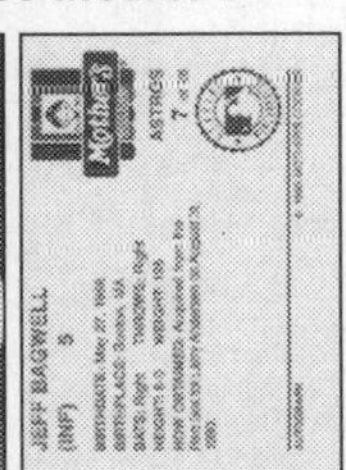

The 1993 Mother's Cookies Astros set consists of 28 standard-size cards with rounded corners. The fronts display full-bleed color player portraits shot from the waist up in stadium settings. The player's name and team name appear in one of the corners. On a white background in red and purple print, the horizontal backs carry biographical information and the sponsor's logo. A blank slot for the player's autograph rounds out the back.

	MINT	NRMT
COMPLETE SET (28)	10.00	4.50
COMMON CARD (1-28)	.25	.11
☐ 1 Art Howe MG	.25	.11
☐ 2 Steve Finley	.50	.23
☐ 3 Pete Harnisch	.25	.11
☐ 4 Craig Biggio	2.00	.90
☐ 5 Doug Drabek	.50	.23
☐ 6 Scott Servais	.25	.11
☐ 7 Jeff Bagwell	4.00	1.80
☐ 8 Eric Anthony	.25	.11
☐ 9 Ken Caminiti	1.50	.70
☐ 10 Andujar Cedeno	.25	.11
☐ 11 Mark Portugal	.25	.11
☐ 12 Jose Uribe	.25	.11
☐ 13 Rick Parker	.25	.11
☐ 14 Doug Jones	.25	.11
☐ 15 Luis Gonzalez	.50	.23
☐ 16 Kevin Bass	.25	.11
☐ 17 Greg Swindell	.25	.11
☐ 18 Eddie Taubensee	.25	.11
☐ 19 Darryl Kile	1.00	.45
☐ 20 Brian Williams	.25	.11
☐ 21 Chris James	.25	.11
☐ 22 Chris Donnels	.25	.11
☐ 23 Xavier Hernandez	.25	.11
☐ 24 Casey Candaele	.25	.11
☐ 25 Eric Bell	.25	.11
☐ 26 Mark Grant	.25	.11
☐ 27 Tom Edens	.25	.11
☐ 28 Checklist/Coaches Ed Ott Bob Cluck Matt Galante Billy Joe Bowman Rudy Jaramillo Tom Spencer	.50	.23

1994 Astros Mother's

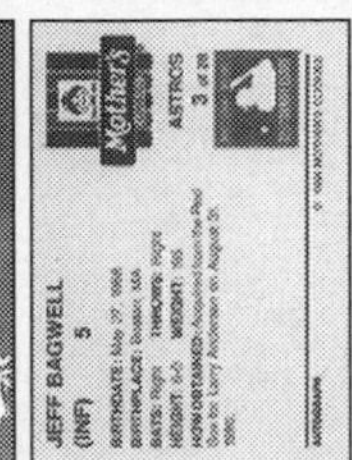

The 1994 Mother's Cookies Astros set consists of 28 standard-size cards with rounded corners. The fronts display full-bleed color player portraits shot from the waist up against a stadium background. The player's name and team name appear in one of the corners. On a white background in red and purple print, the horizontal backs carry biographical information and the sponsor's logo. A blank slot for the player's autograph rounds out the back.

	MINT	NRMT
COMPLETE SET (28)	10.00	4.50
COMMON CARD (1-28)	.25	.11
☐ 1 Terry Collins MG	.25	.11
☐ 2 Mitch Williams	.25	.11
☐ 3 Jeff Bagwell	3.00	1.35
☐ 4 Luis Gonzalez	.50	.23
☐ 5 Craig Biggio	1.50	.70
☐ 6 Darryl Kile	1.00	.45
☐ 7 Ken Caminiti	1.50	.70
☐ 8 Steve Finley	1.00	.45
☐ 9 Pete Harnisch	.25	.11
☐ 10 Sid Bream	.25	.11
☐ 11 Mike Felder	.25	.11
☐ 12 Tom Edens	.25	.11
☐ 13 James Mouton	.25	.11
☐ 14 Doug Drabek	.25	.11
☐ 15 Greg Swindell	.25	.11
☐ 16 Chris Donnels	.25	.11
☐ 17 John Hudek	.25	.11
☐ 18 Andujar Cedeno	.25	.11
☐ 19 Scott Servais	.25	.11
☐ 20 Todd Jones	.25	.11
☐ 21 Kevin Bass	.25	.11
☐ 22 Shane Reynolds	.50	.23
☐ 23 Brian Williams	.25	.11
☐ 24 Tony Eusebio	.25	.11
☐ 25 Mike Hampton	.50	.23
☐ 26 Andy Stankiewicz	.25	.11
☐ 27 Astros Coaches Matt Galante Steve Henderson Ben Hines Julio Linares Mel Stottlemyre	.50	.23
☐ 28 Checklist Dennis Liborio EQMG Dave Labossiere TR Rex Jones TR	.25	.11

1995 Astros Mother's

This 1995 Mother's Cookies Houston Astros set consists of 28 standard-size cards with rounded corners. The

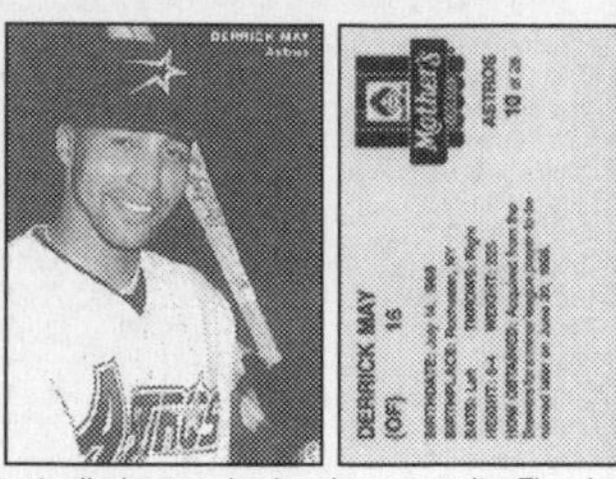

fronts display posed color player portraits. The player's name and team name appear in one of the top corners. The horizontal backs carry biographical information and the sponsor's logo on a white background in red and purple print. A blank slot at the bottom for the player's autograph rounds out the back.

	MINT	NRMT
COMPLETE SET (28)	10.00	4.50
COMMON CARD (1-28)	.25	.11
☐ 1 Terry Collins MG	.25	.11
☐ 2 Jeff Bagwell	3.00	1.35
☐ 3 Luis Gonzalez	.50	.23
☐ 4 Darryl Kile	.75	.35
☐ 5 Derek Bell	.50	.23
☐ 6 Scott Servais	.25	.11
☐ 7 Craig Biggio	1.50	.70
☐ 8 Dave Magadan	.25	.11
☐ 9 Milt Thompson	.25	.11
☐ 10 Derrick May	.25	.11
☐ 11 Doug Drabek	.50	.23
☐ 12 Tony Eusebio	.25	.11
☐ 13 Phil Nevin	.25	.11
☐ 14 James Mouton	.25	.11
☐ 15 Phil Plantier	.25	.11
☐ 16 Pedro Martinez	.25	.11
☐ 17 Orlando Miller	.25	.11
☐ 18 John Hudek	.25	.11
☐ 19 Doug Brocail	.25	.11
☐ 20 Craig Shipley	.25	.11
☐ 21 Shane Reynolds	.50	.23
☐ 22 Mike Hampton	.50	.23
☐ 23 Todd Jones	.50	.23
☐ 24 Greg Swindell	.25	.11
☐ 25 Jim Dougherty	.25	.11
☐ 26 Brian Hunter	1.50	.70
☐ 27 Dave Veres	.25	.11
☐ 28 Coaches/Checklist Julio Linares Matt Galante Jesse Barfield Mel Stottlemyre Steve Henderson	.50	.23

1996 Astros Mother's

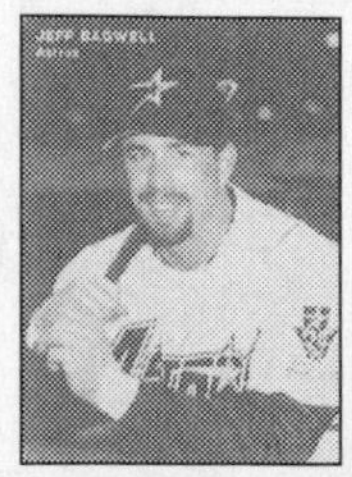

This 28-card set consists of borderless posed color player portraits in stadium settings. The player's and team's names appear in one of the top rounded corners. The backs carry biographical information and the sponsor's logo on a white background in red and purple print. A blank slot for the player's autograph rounds out the back.

	MINT	NRMT
COMPLETE SET (28)	8.00	3.60
COMMON CARD (1-28)	.25	.11
☐ 1 Terry Collins MG	.25	.11
☐ 2 Jeff Bagwell	3.00	1.35
☐ 3 Craig Biggio	1.50	.70
☐ 4 Derek Bell	.50	.23
☐ 5 Darryl Kile	.75	.35
☐ 6 Sean Berry	.25	.11
☐ 7 Doug Drabek	.50	.23
☐ 8 Derrick May	.25	.11
☐ 9 Orlando Miller	.25	.11
☐ 10 Mike Hampton	.50	.23
☐ 11 Rick Wilkins	.25	.11
☐ 12 Brian Hunter	1.00	.45
☐ 13 Shane Reynolds	.50	.23
☐ 14 James Mouton	.25	.11
☐ 15 Greg Swindell	.25	.11
☐ 16 Bill Spiers	.25	.11
☐ 17 Alvin Morman	.25	.11
☐ 18 Tony Eusebio	.25	.11
☐ 19 John Hudek	.25	.11
☐ 20 Doug Brocail	.25	.11
☐ 21 Anthony Young	.25	.11
☐ 22 John Cangelosi	.25	.11
☐ 23 Jeff Tabaka	.25	.11
☐ 24 Mike Simms	.25	.11
☐ 25 Todd Jones	.50	.23
☐ 26 Ricky Gutierrez	.25	.11
☐ 27 Mark Small	.25	.11
☐ 28 Coaches Card CL Matt Galante Julio Linares Rick Sweet Brent Strom Steve Henderson	.25	.11

1997 Astros Mothers

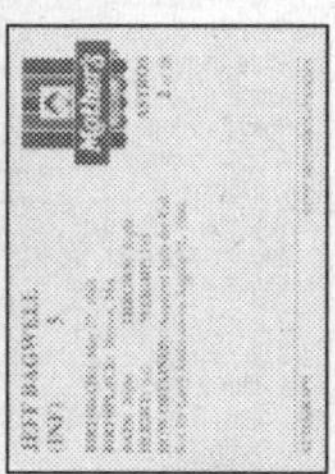

This 28-card set of the Houston Astros sponsored by Mother's Cookies consists of posed color player photos with rounded corners. The backs carry biographical information and the sponsor's logo on a white background in red and purple print. A blank slot for the player's autograph rounds out the back.

	MINT	NRMT
COMPLETE SET (28)	12.00	5.50
COMMON CARD (1-28)	.25	.11
☐ 1 Larry Dierker MG	.50	.23
☐ 2 Jeff Bagwell	3.00	1.35
☐ 3 Craig Biggio	1.50	.70
☐ 4 Darryl Kile	.75	.35
☐ 5 Luis Gonzalez	.50	.23
☐ 6 Shane Reynolds	.50	.23
☐ 7 James Mouton	.25	.11
☐ 8 Sean Berry	.25	.11
☐ 9 Billy Wagner	1.50	.70
☐ 10 Ricky Gutierrez	.25	.11
☐ 11 Mike Hampton	.50	.23
☐ 12 Tony Eusebio	.25	.11
☐ 13 Derek Bell	.50	.23
☐ 14 Ray Montgomery	.25	.11
☐ 15 Bill Spiers	.25	.11
☐ 16 Sid Fernandez	.25	.11
☐ 17 Brad Ausmus	.25	.11
☐ 18 John Hudek	.25	.11
☐ 19 Bob Abreu	.50	.23
☐ 20 Russ Springer	.25	.11
☐ 21 Chris Holt	.25	.11
☐ 22 Tom Martin	.25	.11
☐ 23 Donne Wall	.25	.11
☐ 24 Thomas Howard	.25	.11
☐ 25 Jose Lima	.25	.11
☐ 26 Pat Listach	.25	.11
☐ 27 Ramon Garcia	.25	.11
☐ 28 Coaches Card CL Alan Ashby Jose Cruz Mike Cubbage Tom McCraw Vern Ruhle Bill Virdon	.50	.23

1990 Baseball Wit

The 1990 Baseball Wit set was issued in complete set form only. This set was dedicated to and featured several ex-members of the Little Leagues. This 108-card, standard-size set was available primarily in retail and chain outlets. Most of the older (retired) players in the set are shown in black and white. The card backs typically give three trivia questions with answers following. The object of the game is to collect points by correctly answering any one of the questions on the back of each

card or identifying the picture on the front. The firs printing of 10,000 sets had several errors, and the card were not numbered. The second printing corrected thes errors and numbered the cards. The number on the fron of the card is used when playing the game and is not to be confused with the card number, which is found on the back of all cards.

	MINT	NRMT
COMPLETE SET (108)	8.00	3.60
COMMON CARD (1-108)	.05	.02
☐ 1 Orel Hershiser	.10	.05
☐ 2 Tony Gwynn	.75	.35
☐ 3 Mickey Mantle	1.50	.70
☐ 4 Willie Stargell	.15	.07
☐ 5 Don Baylor	.10	.05
☐ 6 Hank Aaron	.75	.35
☐ 7 Don Larsen	.10	.05
☐ 8 Lee Mazzilli	.05	.02
☐ 9 Boog Powell	.10	.05
☐ 10 Little League World Series	.05	.02
☐ 11 Jose Canseco	.25	.11
☐ 12 Mike Scott	.05	.02
☐ 13 Bob Feller	.15	.07
☐ 14 Ron Santo	.10	.05
☐ 15A Mel Stottlemyer ERR sic, Stottlemyre	.10	.05
☐ 15B Mel Stottlemyre COR	.10	.05
☐ 16 Shea Stadium	.05	.02
☐ 17 Brooks Robinson	.15	.07
☐ 18 Willie Mays	.75	.35
☐ 19 Ernie Banks	.25	.11
☐ 20 Keith Hernandez	.10	.05
☐ 21 Bret Saberhagen	.10	.05
☐ 22 Baseball Hall of Fame	.05	.02
☐ 23 Luis Aparicio	.15	.07
☐ 24 Yogi Berra	.25	.11
☐ 25 Manny Mota	.10	.05
☐ 26 Steve Garvey	.10	.05
☐ 27 Bill Shea	.05	.02
☐ 28 Fred Lynn	.05	.02
☐ 29 Todd Worrell	.05	.02
☐ 30 Roy Campanella	.30	.14
☐ 31 Bob Gibson	.15	.07
☐ 32 Gary Carter	.10	.05
☐ 33 Jim Palmer	.15	.07
☐ 34 Carl Yastrzemski	.15	.07
☐ 35 Dwight Gooden	.10	.05
☐ 36 Stan Musial	.50	.23
☐ 37 Rickey Henderson	.25	.11
☐ 38 Dale Murphy	.15	.07
☐ 39 Mike Schmidt	.25	.11
☐ 40 Gaylord Perry	.15	.07
☐ 41 Ozzie Smith	.50	.23
☐ 42 Reggie Jackson	.25	.11
☐ 43 Steve Carlton	.15	.07
☐ 44 Jim Perry	.05	.02
☐ 45 Vince Coleman	.05	.02
☐ 46 Tom Seaver	.25	.11
☐ 47 Marty Marion	.05	.02
☐ 48 Frank Robinson	.15	.07
☐ 49 Joe DiMaggio	1.00	.45
☐ 50 Ted Williams	1.00	.45
☐ 51 Rollie Fingers	.10	.05
☐ 52 Jackie Robinson	.75	.35
☐ 53 Vic Raschi	.05	.02
☐ 54 Johnny Bench	.25	.11
☐ 55 Nolan Ryan	1.00	.45
☐ 56 Ty Cobb	.75	.35
☐ 57 Harry Steinfeldt	.05	.02
☐ 58 James O'Rourke	.05	.02
☐ 59 John McGraw	.15	.07
☐ 60 Candy Cummings	.10	.05
☐ 61 Jimmie Foxx	.15	.07
☐ 62 Walter Johnson	.15	.07
☐ 63 1903 World Series	.05	.02
☐ 64 Satchel Paige	.25	.11
☐ 65 Bobby Wallace	.10	.05
☐ 66 Cap Anson	.15	.07
☐ 67 Hugh Duffy	.10	.05
☐ 68 William(Buck) Ewing	.10	.05
☐ 69 Bobo Holloman	.05	.02

☐ 70 Ed Delahanty	.10	.05
☐ 71 Dizzy Dean	.15	.07
☐ 72 Tris Speaker	.15	.07
☐ 73 Lou Gehrig	1.00	.45
☐ 74 Wee Willie Keeler	.10	.05
☐ 75 Cal Hubbard	.10	.05
☐ 76 Eddie Collins	.15	.07
☐ 77 Chris Von Der Ahe	.05	.02
☐ 78 Sam Crawford	.15	.07
☐ 79 Cy Young	.15	.07
☐ 80 Johnny Vander Meer	.10	.05
☐ 81 Joey Jay	.05	.02
☐ 82 Zack Wheat	.10	.05
☐ 83 Jim Bottomley	.10	.05
☐ 84 Honus Wagner	.30	.14
☐ 85 Casey Stengel	.25	.11
☐ 86 Babe Ruth	1.50	.70
☐ 87 John Lindemuth Carl Stotz	.05	.02
☐ 88 Max Carey	.10	.05
☐ 89 Mordecai Brown	.10	.05
☐ 90 Cincinnati Red Stockings 1869	.05	.02
☐ 91 Rube Marquard	.10	.05
☐ 92 Charles Radbourne Horse	.10	.05
☐ 93 Hack Wilson	.10	.05
☐ 94 Lefty Grove	.15	.07
☐ 95 Carl Hubbell	.15	.07
☐ 96 A.J. Cartwright	.05	.02
☐ 97 Rogers Hornsby	.15	.07
☐ 98 Ernest Thayer	.05	.02
☐ 99 Connie Mack	.10	.05
☐ 100 Centennial Celebration 1939	.05	.02
☐ 101 Branch Rickey	.10	.05
☐ 102 Dan Brouthers	.10	.05
☐ 103 1st Baseball Uniform	.05	.02
☐ 104 Christy Mathewson	.15	.07
☐ 105 Joe Nuxhall	.05	.02
☐ 106 Centennial Celebration 1939	.05	.02
☐ 107 William H. Taft PRES	.15	.07
☐ 108 Abner Doubleday	.05	.02

1934-36 Batter-Up R318

The 1934-36 Batter-Up set, issued by National Chicle, contains 192 blank-backed die-cut cards. Numbers 1 to 80 are approximately 2 3/8" by 3 1/4" in size while 81 to 192 are 2 3/8" by 3". The latter are more difficult to find than the former. The pictures come in basic black and white or in tints of blue, brown, green, purple, red, or sepia. There are three combination cards (each featuring two players per card) in the high series (98, 111, and 115). Cards with the die-cut backing removed are graded fair at best.

	EX-MT	VG-E
COMPLETE SET (192)	18000.00	8100.00
COMMON CARD (1-80)	40.00	18.00
COMMON CARD (81-192)	80.00	36.00
WRAPPER (1-CENT, CATCHER)	200.00	90.00
WRAPPER (1-CENT, BAT)	600.00	275.00

☐ 1 Wally Berger	100.00	45.00
☐ 2 Ed Brandt	40.00	18.00
☐ 3 Al Lopez	90.00	40.00
☐ 4 Dick Bartell	50.00	22.00
☐ 5 Carl Hubbell	125.00	55.00
☐ 6 Bill Terry	150.00	70.00
☐ 7 Pepper Martin	60.00	27.00
☐ 8 Jim Bottomley	100.00	45.00
☐ 9 Tommy Bridges	50.00	22.00
☐ 10 Rick Ferrell	90.00	40.00
☐ 11 Ray Benge	40.00	18.00
☐ 12 Wes Ferrell	50.00	22.00
☐ 13 Chalmer Cissell	40.00	18.00
☐ 14 Pie Traynor	125.00	55.00
☐ 15 Leroy Mahaffey	40.00	18.00
☐ 16 Chick Hafey	90.00	40.00
☐ 17 Lloyd Waner	90.00	40.00
☐ 18 Jack Burns	40.00	18.00
☐ 19 Buddy Myer	50.00	22.00
☐ 20 Bob Johnson	50.00	22.00
☐ 21 Arky Vaughan	90.00	40.00
☐ 22 Red Rolfe	50.00	22.00
☐ 23 Lefty Gomez	150.00	70.00
☐ 24 Earl Averill	125.00	55.00
☐ 25 Mickey Cochrane	150.00	70.00
☐ 26 Van Lingle Mungo	60.00	27.00
☐ 27 Mel Ott	200.00	90.00
☐ 28 Jimmie Foxx	250.00	110.00
☐ 29 Jimmy Dykes	50.00	22.00
☐ 30 Bill Dickey	200.00	90.00
☐ 31 Lefty Grove	200.00	90.00
☐ 32 Joe Cronin	150.00	70.00
☐ 33 Frankie Frisch	125.00	55.00
☐ 34 Al Simmons	125.00	55.00
☐ 35 Rogers Hornsby	250.00	110.00
☐ 36 Ted Lyons	90.00	40.00
☐ 37 Rabbit Maranville	90.00	40.00
☐ 38 Jimmy Wilson	50.00	22.00
☐ 39 Willie Kamm	40.00	18.00
☐ 40 Bill Hallahan	40.00	18.00
☐ 41 Gus Suhr	40.00	18.00
☐ 42 Charley Gehringer	125.00	55.00
☐ 43 Joe Heving	40.00	18.00
☐ 44 Adam Comorosky	40.00	18.00
☐ 45 Tony Lazzeri	125.00	55.00
☐ 46 Sam Leslie	40.00	18.00
☐ 47 Bob Smith	40.00	18.00
☐ 48 Willis Hudlin	40.00	18.00
☐ 49 Carl Reynolds	40.00	18.00
☐ 50 Fred Schulte	40.00	18.00
☐ 51 Cookie Lavagetto	60.00	27.00
☐ 52 Hal Schumacher	50.00	22.00
☐ 53 Roger Cramer	50.00	22.00
☐ 54 Sylvester Johnson	40.00	18.00
☐ 55 Ollie Bejma	40.00	18.00
☐ 56 Sam Byrd	40.00	18.00
☐ 57 Hank Greenberg	250.00	110.00
☐ 58 Bill Knickerbocker	40.00	18.00
☐ 59 Bill Urbanski	40.00	18.00
☐ 60 Eddie Morgan	40.00	18.00
☐ 61 Rabbit McNair	40.00	18.00
☐ 62 Ben Chapman	50.00	22.00
☐ 63 Roy Johnson	40.00	18.00
☐ 64 Dizzy Dean	400.00	180.00
☐ 65 Zeke Bonura	40.00	18.00
☐ 66 Fred Marberry	40.00	18.00
☐ 67 Gus Mancuso	40.00	18.00
☐ 68 Joe Vosmik	40.00	18.00
☐ 69 Earl Grace	40.00	18.00
☐ 70 Tony Piet	40.00	18.00
☐ 71 Rollie Hemsley	40.00	18.00
☐ 72 Fred Fitzsimmons	50.00	22.00
☐ 73 Hack Wilson	150.00	70.00
☐ 74 Chick Fullis	40.00	18.00
☐ 75 Fred Frankhouse	40.00	18.00
☐ 76 Ethan Allen	40.00	18.00
☐ 77 Heinie Manush	90.00	40.00
☐ 78 Rip Collins	40.00	18.00
☐ 79 Tony Cuccinello	40.00	18.00
☐ 80 Joe Kuhel	40.00	18.00
☐ 81 Tommy Bridges	90.00	40.00
☐ 82 Clint Brown	80.00	36.00
☐ 83 Albert Blanche	80.00	36.00
☐ 84 Boze Berger	80.00	36.00
☐ 85 Goose Goslin	175.00	80.00
☐ 86 Lefty Gomez	225.00	100.00
☐ 87 Joe Glenn	80.00	36.00
☐ 88 Cy Blanton	80.00	36.00
☐ 89 Tom Carey	80.00	36.00
☐ 90 Ralph Birkofer	80.00	36.00
☐ 91 Fred Gabler	80.00	36.00
☐ 92 Dick Coffman	80.00	36.00
☐ 93 Ollie Bejma	80.00	36.00
☐ 94 Leroy Parmelee	80.00	36.00
☐ 95 Carl Reynolds	80.00	36.00
☐ 96 Ben Cantwell	80.00	36.00
☐ 97 Curtis Davis	80.00	36.00
☐ 98 Earl Webb and Wally Moses	125.00	55.00
☐ 99 Ray Benge	80.00	36.00
☐ 100 Pie Traynor	200.00	90.00
☐ 101 Phil Cavarretta	100.00	45.00
☐ 102 Pep Young	80.00	36.00
☐ 103 Willis Hudlin	80.00	36.00
☐ 104 Mickey Haslin	80.00	36.00
☐ 105 Ossie Bluege	90.00	40.00
☐ 106 Paul Andrews	80.00	36.00
☐ 107 Ed Brandt	80.00	36.00
☐ 108 Don Taylor	80.00	36.00
☐ 109 Thornton Lee	90.00	40.00
☐ 110 Hal Schumacher	90.00	40.00
☐ 111 Hayes and Ted Lyons	150.00	70.00
☐ 112 Odell Hale	80.00	36.00
☐ 113 Earl Averill	175.00	80.00
☐ 114 Italo Chelini	80.00	36.00
☐ 115 Ivy Andrews and Jim Bottomley	150.00	70.00
☐ 116 Bill Walker	80.00	36.00
☐ 117 Bill Dickey	300.00	135.00
☐ 118 Gerald Walker	80.00	36.00
☐ 119 Ted Lyons	176.00	00.00
☐ 120 Eldon Auker	80.00	36.00
☐ 121 Bill Hallahan	90.00	40.00
☐ 122 Fred Lindstrom	175.00	80.00
☐ 123 Oral Hildebrand	80.00	36.00
☐ 124 Luke Appling	225.00	100.00
☐ 125 Pepper Martin	100.00	45.00
☐ 126 Rick Ferrell	175.00	80.00
☐ 127 Ival Goodman	80.00	36.00
☐ 128 Joe Kuhel	80.00	36.00
☐ 129 Ernie Lombardi	175.00	80.00
☐ 130 Charley Gehringer	225.00	100.00
☐ 131 Van Lingle Mungo	90.00	40.00
☐ 132 Larry French	80.00	36.00
☐ 133 Buddy Myer	90.00	40.00
☐ 134 Mel Harder	100.00	45.00
☐ 135 Augie Galan	80.00	36.00
☐ 136 Gabby Hartnett	175.00	80.00
☐ 137 Stan Hack	90.00	40.00
☐ 138 Billy Herman	175.00	80.00
☐ 139 Bill Jurges	80.00	36.00
☐ 140 Bill Lee	90.00	40.00
☐ 141 Zeke Bonura	80.00	36.00
☐ 142 Tony Piet	80.00	36.00
☐ 143 Paul Dean	100.00	45.00
☐ 144 Jimmie Foxx	400.00	180.00
☐ 145 Joe Medwick	225.00	100.00
☐ 146 Rip Collins	80.00	36.00
☐ 147 Mel Almada	80.00	36.00
☐ 148 Allan Cooke	80.00	36.00
☐ 149 Moe Berg	400.00	180.00
☐ 150 Dolph Camilli	90.00	40.00
☐ 151 Oscar Melillo	80.00	36.00
☐ 152 Bruce Campbell	80.00	36.00
☐ 153 Lefty Grove	300.00	135.00
☐ 154 Johnny Murphy	100.00	45.00
☐ 155 Luke Sewell	90.00	40.00
☐ 156 Leo Durocher	250.00	110.00
☐ 157 Lloyd Waner	175.00	80.00
☐ 158 Guy Bush	80.00	36.00
☐ 159 Jimmy Dykes	90.00	40.00
☐ 160 Steve O'Neill	90.00	40.00
☐ 161 General Crowder	90.00	40.00
☐ 162 Joe Cascarella	90.00	40.00
☐ 163 Daniel(Bud) Hafey	90.00	40.00
☐ 164 Gilly Campbell	80.00	36.00
☐ 165 Ray Hayworth	80.00	36.00
☐ 166 Frank Demaree	80.00	36.00
☐ 167 John Babich	80.00	36.00
☐ 168 Marvin Owen	80.00	36.00
☐ 169 Ralph Kress	80.00	36.00
☐ 170 Mule Haas	80.00	36.00
☐ 171 Frank Higgins	90.00	40.00
☐ 172 Wally Berger	100.00	45.00
☐ 173 Frankie Frisch	225.00	100.00
☐ 174 Wes Ferrell	90.00	40.00
☐ 175 Pete Fox	80.00	36.00
☐ 176 John Vergez	80.00	36.00
☐ 177 Billy Rogell	80.00	36.00
☐ 178 Don Brennan	80.00	36.00
☐ 179 Jim Bottomley	175.00	80.00
☐ 180 Travis Jackson	175.00	80.00
☐ 181 Red Rolfe	100.00	45.00
☐ 182 Frank Crosetti	125.00	55.00
☐ 183 Joe Cronin	175.00	80.00
☐ 184 Schoolboy Rowe	100.00	45.00
☐ 185 Chuck Klein	225.00	100.00
☐ 186 Lon Warneke	90.00	40.00
☐ 187 Gus Suhr	80.00	36.00
☐ 188 Ben Chapman	90.00	40.00
☐ 189 Clint Brown	80.00	36.00
☐ 190 Paul Derringer	100.00	45.00
☐ 191 John Burns	80.00	36.00
☐ 192 John Broaca	125.00	55.00

1959 Bazooka

The 23 full-color, unnumbered cards comprising the 1959 Bazooka set were cut from the bottom of the boxes of gum marketed nationally that year by Topps. Bazooka was the brand name which Topps had been using to sell its one cent bubblegum; this year Topps decided to distribute 25 pieces of Bazooka gum in a box. The cards themselves measure 2 13/16" by 4 15/16". Only nine cards were originally issued; 14 more were added to the set at a later date (these are marked with SP in the checklist). The latter are less plentiful and hence more valuable than the original nine. All the cards are blank backed and the catalog designation is R414-15. The prices below are for the cards cut from the box; complete boxes intact would be worth about 50 percent more.

	NRMT	VG-E
COMPLETE SET (23)	7000.00	3200.00
COMMON CARD (1-23)	50.00	22.00
COMMON CARD SP	200.00	90.00
☐ 1 Hank Aaron	550.00	250.00
☐ 2 Richie Ashburn SP	400.00	180.00
☐ 3 Ernie Banks SP	600.00	275.00
☐ 4 Ken Boyer SP	300.00	135.00
☐ 5 Orlando Cepeda	100.00	45.00
☐ 6 Bob Cerv SP	200.00	90.00
☐ 7 Rocky Colavito SP	400.00	180.00
☐ 8 Del Crandall	50.00	22.00
☐ 9 Jim Davenport	50.00	22.00
☐ 10 Don Drysdale SP	500.00	220.00
☐ 11 Nellie Fox SP	400.00	180.00
☐ 12 Jackie Jensen SP	300.00	135.00
☐ 13 Harvey Kuenn SP	250.00	110.00
☐ 14 Mickey Mantle	1750.00	800.00
☐ 15 Willie Mays	600.00	275.00
☐ 16 Bill Mazeroski	100.00	45.00
☐ 17 Roy McMillan	50.00	22.00
☐ 18 Billy Pierce SP	200.00	90.00
☐ 19 Roy Sievers SP	200.00	90.00
☐ 20 Duke Snider SP	750.00	350.00
☐ 21 Gus Triandos SP	200.00	90.00
☐ 22 Bob Turley	50.00	22.00
☐ 23 Vic Wertz SP	200.00	90.00

1960 Bazooka

In 1960, Topps introduced a 36-card baseball player set in three card panels on the bottom of Bazooka gum boxes. The cards measure 1 13/16" by 2 3/4" and the panels measure 2 3/4" by 5 1/2". The cards carried full color pictures and were numbered at the bottom underneath the team position. The checklist below contains prices for individual cards. Complete panels of three would have a 50 percent more than the sum of the indiviudal cards (prices) on the panel and complete boxes would command a premium of another 50 percent above those prices.

	NRMT	VG-E
COMPLETE INDIV.SET	1000.00	450.00
COMMON CARD (1-36)	12.00	5.50
☐ 1 Ernie Banks	50.00	22.00
☐ 2 Bud Daley	12.00	5.50
☐ 3 Wally Moon	12.00	5.50
☐ 4 Hank Aaron	100.00	45.00
☐ 5 Milt Pappas	12.00	5.50
☐ 6 Dick Stuart	12.00	5.50
☐ 7 Roberto Clemente	150.00	70.00
☐ 8 Yogi Berra	75.00	34.00
☐ 9 Ken Boyer	15.00	6.75
☐ 10 Orlando Cepeda	20.00	9.00
☐ 11 Gus Triandos	12.00	5.50
☐ 12 Frank Malzone	12.00	5.50
☐ 13 Willie Mays	110.00	50.00
☐ 14 Camilo Pascual	12.00	5.50
☐ 15 Bob Cerv	12.00	5.50
☐ 16 Vic Power	12.00	5.50
☐ 17 Larry Sherry	12.00	5.50
☐ 18 Al Kaline	50.00	22.00
☐ 19 Warren Spahn	50.00	22.00
☐ 20 Harmon Killebrew	50.00	22.00
☐ 21 Jackie Jensen	15.00	6.75
☐ 22 Luis Aparicio	30.00	13.50
☐ 23 Gil Hodges	30.00	13.50
☐ 24 Richie Ashburn	40.00	18.00
☐ 25 Nellie Fox	40.00	18.00
☐ 26 Robin Roberts	40.00	18.00
☐ 27 Joe Cunningham	12.00	5.50
☐ 28 Early Wynn	30.00	13.50
☐ 29 Frank Robinson	50.00	22.00
☐ 30 Rocky Colavito	30.00	13.50
☐ 31 Mickey Mantle	275.00	125.00
☐ 32 Glen Hobbie	12.00	5.50
☐ 33 Roy McMillan	12.00	5.50
☐ 34 Harvey Kuenn	12.00	5.50
☐ 35 Johnny Antonelli	12.00	5.50
☐ 36 Del Crandall	12.00	5.50

1961 Bazooka

The 36 card set issued by Bazooka in 1961 follows the format established in 1960; three full color, numbered cards to each panel found on a Bazooka gum box. The individual cards measure 1 13/16" by 2 3/4" whereas the panels measure 2 3/4" by 5 1/2". The cards of 1960 and 1961 are similar in design but are easily distinguished from one another by their numbers. Complete panels of three would have a value of 40 percent more than the sum of the individual cards (prices) on the panel and complete boxes would command a premium of another 40 percent above those prices.

	NRMT	VG-E
COMPLETE INDIV. SET	800.00	350.00
COMMON CARD (1-36)	12.00	5.50
☐ 1 Art Mahaffey	12.00	5.50
☐ 2 Mickey Mantle	275.00	125.00
☐ 3 Ron Santo	15.00	6.75
☐ 4 Bud Daley	12.00	5.50
☐ 5 Roger Maris	75.00	34.00
☐ 6 Eddie Yost	12.00	5.50
☐ 7 Minnie Minoso	15.00	6.75
☐ 8 Dick Groat	12.00	5.50
☐ 9 Frank Malzone	12.00	5.50
☐ 10 Dick Donovan	12.00	5.50
☐ 11 Eddie Mathews	50.00	22.00
☐ 12 Jim Lemon	12.00	5.50
☐ 13 Chuck Estrada	12.00	5.50
☐ 14 Ken Boyer	15.00	6.75
☐ 15 Harvey Kuenn	12.00	5.50
☐ 16 Ernie Broglio	12.00	5.50
☐ 17 Rocky Colavito	30.00	13.50
☐ 18 Ted Kluszewski	30.00	13.50
☐ 19 Ernie Banks	50.00	22.00
☐ 20 Al Kaline	50.00	22.00
☐ 21 Ed Bailey	12.00	5.50
☐ 22 Jim Perry	12.00	5.50
☐ 23 Willie Mays	100.00	45.00
☐ 24 Bill Mazeroski	25.00	11.00
☐ 25 Gus Triandos	12.00	5.50
☐ 26 Don Drysdale	30.00	13.50
☐ 27 Frank Herrera	12.00	5.50
☐ 28 Earl Battey	12.00	5.50
☐ 29 Warren Spahn	50.00	22.00
☐ 30 Gene Woodling	12.00	5.50
☐ 31 Frank Robinson	50.00	22.00
☐ 32 Pete Runnels	12.00	5.50
☐ 33 Woodie Held	12.00	5.50
☐ 34 Norm Larker	12.00	5.50
☐ 35 Luis Aparicio	30.00	13.50
☐ 36 Bill Tuttle	12.00	5.50

1962 Bazooka

The 1962 Bazooka set of 45 full color, blank backed, unnumbered cards was issued in panels of three on Bazooka bubble gum. The individual cards measure 1 13/16" by 2 3/4" whereas the panels measure 2 3/4" by 5 1/2". The cards below are numbered by panel alphabetically based on the last name of the player pictured on the far left card of the panel. The cards with SP in the checklist below are more difficult to obtain. Complete panels would have a value of 40 percent more

than the sum of the individual cards (prices) on the panel and complete boxes would command a premium of another 40 percent above those prices.

	NRMT	VG-E
COMPLETE INDIV. SET	3000.00	1350.00
COMMON CARD (1-45)	12.00	5.50
☐ 1 Bob Allison SP	75.00	34.00
☐ 2 Eddie Mathews SP	500.00	220.00
☐ 3 Vada Pinson SP	75.00	34.00
☐ 4 Earl Battey	12.00	5.50
☐ 5 Warren Spahn	50.00	22.00
☐ 6 Lee Thomas	12.00	5.50
☐ 7 Orlando Cepeda	20.00	9.00
☐ 8 Woodie Held	12.00	5.50
☐ 9 Bob Aspromonte	12.00	5.50
☐ 10 Dick Howser	12.00	5.50
☐ 11 Roberto Clemente	150.00	70.00
☐ 12 Al Kaline	50.00	22.00
☐ 13 Joe Jay	12.00	5.50
☐ 14 Roger Maris	75.00	34.00
☐ 15 Frank Howard	15.00	6.75
☐ 16 Sandy Koufax	75.00	34.00
☐ 17 Jim Gentile	12.00	5.50
☐ 18 Johnny Callison	12.00	5.50
☐ 19 Jim Landis	12.00	5.50
☐ 20 Ken Boyer	15.00	6.75
☐ 21 Chuck Schilling	12.00	5.50
☐ 22 Art Mahaffey	12.00	5.50
☐ 23 Mickey Mantle	275.00	125.00
☐ 24 Dick Stuart	12.00	5.50
☐ 25 Ken McBride	12.00	5.50
☐ 26 Frank Robinson	50.00	22.00
☐ 27 Gil Hodges	40.00	18.00
☐ 28 Milt Pappas	12.00	5.50
☐ 29 Hank Aaron	100.00	45.00
☐ 30 Luis Aparicio	30.00	13.50
☐ 31 Johnny Romano SP	75.00	34.00
☐ 32 Ernie Banks SP	500.00	220.00
☐ 33 Norm Siebern SP	75.00	34.00
☐ 34 Ron Santo	20.00	9.00
☐ 35 Norm Cash	15.00	6.75
☐ 36 Jim Piersall	15.00	6.75
☐ 37 Don Schwall	12.00	5.50
☐ 38 Willie Mays	110.00	50.00
☐ 39 Norm Larker	12.00	5.50
☐ 40 Bill White	15.00	6.75
☐ 41 Whitey Ford	50.00	22.00
☐ 42 Rocky Colavito	30.00	13.50
☐ 43 Don Zimmer SP	75.00	34.00
☐ 44 Harmon Killebrew SP	500.00	220.00
☐ 45 Gene Woodling SP	75.00	34.00

1963 Bazooka

The 1963 Bazooka set of 36 full color, blank backed numbered cards was issued on Bazooka bubble gum boxes. This year marked a change in format from previous Bazooka issues with a smaller sized card being issued. The individual cards measure 1 9/16" by 2 1/2" whereas the panels measure 2 1/2" by 4 11/16". The card features a white strip with the player's name printed in black on the card. The number appears in the white border on the bottom of the card. Three cards were issued per panel. Complete panels of three would have a value of 15 percent more thant he sum of the individual cards (prices) on the anel and complete boxes owuld command a premium of nother 30 percent above those prices.

	NRMT	VG-E
OMPLETE INDIV.SET	800.00	350.00
OMMON CARD (1-36)	7.50	3.40
☐ 1 Mickey Mantle	225.00	100.00
☐ 2 Bob Rodgers	7.50	3.40
☐ 3 Ernie Banks	50.00	22.00
☐ 4 Norm Siebern	7.50	3.40
☐ 5 Warren Spahn	40.00	18.00
☐ 6 Bill Mazeroski	15.00	6.75
☐ 7 Harmon Killebrew	40.00	18.00
☐ 8 Dick Farrell	7.50	3.40
☐ 9 Hank Aaron	75.00	34.00
☐ 10 Dick Donovan	7.50	3.40
☐ 11 Jim Gentile	7.50	3.40
☐ 12 Willie Mays	85.00	38.00
☐ 13 Camilo Pascual	7.50	3.40
☐ 14 Roberto Clemente	125.00	55.00
☐ 15 Johnny Callison	7.50	3.40
☐ 16 Carl Yastrzemski	40.00	18.00
☐ 17 Don Drysdale	35.00	16.00
☐ 18 Johnny Romano	7.50	3.40
☐ 19 Al Jackson	7.50	3.40
☐ 20 Ralph Terry	7.50	3.40
☐ 21 Bill Monbouquette	7.50	3.40
☐ 22 Orlando Cepeda	15.00	6.75
☐ 23 Stan Musial	50.00	22.00
☐ 24 Floyd Robinson	7.50	3.40
☐ 25 Chuck Hinton	7.50	3.40
☐ 26 Bob Purkey	7.50	3.40
☐ 27 Ken Hubbs	10.00	4.50
☐ 28 Bill White	10.00	4.50
☐ 29 Ray Herbert	7.50	3.40
☐ 30 Brooks Robinson	50.00	22.00
☐ 31 Frank Robinson	50.00	22.00
☐ 32 Lee Thomas	7.50	3.40
☐ 33 Rocky Colavito	20.00	9.00
☐ 34 Al Kaline	50.00	22.00
☐ 35 Art Mahaffey	7.50	3.40
☐ 36 Tommy Davis	7.50	3.40

1963 Bazooka ATG

The 1963 Bazooka All Time Greats set contains 41 black and white numbered cards issued as inserts in boxes of Bazooka Bubble gum. The cards feature bust shots with gold trim and measure 1 9/16" by 2 1/2". The backs are yellow with black print containing vital information and a biography of the player. Many of the players are pictured not as they looked during their playing careers but as they looked many years after their playing days were through. The cards also exist in a scarcer variety with silver trim instead of gold; the silver trim variety cards are worth approximately double the prices listed below. Cards are numbered on the back.

	NRMT	VG-E
COMPLETE SET (41)	350.00	160.00
COMMON CARD (1-41)	4.00	1.80
☐ 1 Joe Tinker	6.00	2.70
☐ 2 Harry Heilmann	6.00	2.70
☐ 3 Jack Chesbro	4.00	1.80
☐ 4 Christy Mathewson	15.00	6.75
☐ 5 Herb Pennock	6.00	2.70
☐ 6 Cy Young	10.00	4.50
☐ 7 Ed Walsh	6.00	2.70
☐ 8 Nap Lajoie	10.00	4.50
☐ 9 Eddie Plank	6.00	2.70
☐ 10 Honus Wagner	15.00	6.75
☐ 11 Chief Bender	6.00	2.70
☐ 12 Walter Johnson	15.00	6.75
☐ 13 Mordecai Brown	6.00	2.70
☐ 14 Rabbit Maranville	6.00	2.70
☐ 15 Lou Gehrig	50.00	22.00
☐ 16 Ban Johnson	4.00	1.80
☐ 17 Babe Ruth	75.00	34.00
☐ 18 Connie Mack	6.00	2.70
☐ 19 Hank Greenberg	6.00	2.70
☐ 20 John McGraw	6.00	2.70
☐ 21 Al Simmons	6.00	2.70
☐ 23 Jimmy Collins	6.00	2.70
☐ 24 Tris Speaker	8.00	3.60
☐ 25 Frank Chance	6.00	2.70
☐ 26 Fred Clarke	6.00	2.70
☐ 27 Wilbert Robinson	6.00	2.70
☐ 28 Dazzy Vance	6.00	2.70
☐ 29 Pete Alexander	8.00	3.60
☐ 30 Judge Landis	6.00	2.70
☐ 31 Willie Keeler	6.00	2.70
☐ 32 Rogers Hornsby	10.00	4.50
☐ 33 Hugh Duffy	6.00	2.70
☐ 34 Mickey Cochrane	6.00	2.70
☐ 35 Ty Cobb	50.00	22.00
☐ 36 Mel Ott	10.00	4.50
☐ 37 Clark Griffith	6.00	2.70
☐ 38 Ted Lyons	6.00	2.70
☐ 39 Cap Anson	6.00	2.70
☐ 40 Bill Dickey	6.00	2.70
☐ 41 Eddie Collins	6.00	2.70

1964 Bazooka

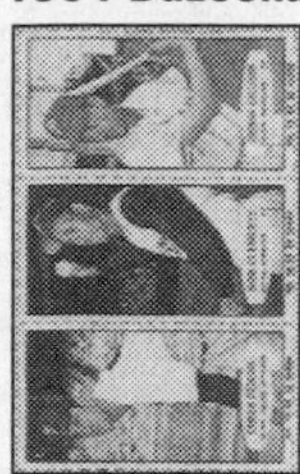

The 1964 Bazooka set of 36 full color, blank backed, numbered cards were issued in panels of three on the backs of Bazooka bubble gum boxes. The individual cards measure 1 9/16" by 2 1/2" whereas the panels measure 2 1/2" by 4 11/16". Many players from the 1963 set have the same numbers; however, the pictures are different. Complete panels of three would have a value of 15 percent more than the sum of the individual cards (prices) on the panel and complete boxes would command a premium of another 40 percent above those prices.

	NRMT	VG-E
COMPLETE INDIV. SET	1000.00	450.00
COMMON CARD (1-36)	10.00	4.50
☐ 1 Mickey Mantle	200.00	90.00
☐ 2 Dick Groat	10.00	4.50
☐ 3 Steve Barber	10.00	4.50
☐ 4 Ken McBride	10.00	4.50
☐ 5 Warren Spahn	40.00	18.00
☐ 6 Bob Friend	10.00	4.50
☐ 7 Harmon Killebrew	40.00	18.00
☐ 8 Dick Farrell	10.00	4.50
☐ 9 Hank Aaron	100.00	45.00
☐ 10 Rich Rollins	10.00	4.50
☐ 11 Jim Gentile	10.00	4.50
☐ 12 Willie Mays	100.00	45.00
☐ 13 Camilo Pascual	10.00	4.50
☐ 14 Roberto Clemente	125.00	55.00
☐ 15 Johnny Callison	10.00	4.50
☐ 16 Carl Yastrzemski	50.00	22.00
☐ 17 Billy Williams	30.00	13.50
☐ 18 Johnny Romano	10.00	4.50
☐ 19 Jim Maloney	10.00	4.50
☐ 20 Norm Cash	15.00	6.75
☐ 21 Willie McCovey	30.00	13.50
☐ 22 Jim Fregosi	10.00	4.50
☐ 23 George Altman	10.00	4.50
☐ 24 Floyd Robinson	10.00	4.50
☐ 25 Chuck Hinton	10.00	4.50
☐ 26 Ron Hunt	10.00	4.50
☐ 27 Gary Peters	10.00	4.50
☐ 28 Dick Ellsworth	10.00	4.50
☐ 29 Elston Howard	15.00	6.75
☐ 30 Brooks Robinson	50.00	22.00
☐ 31 Frank Robinson	50.00	22.00
☐ 32 Sandy Koufax	75.00	34.00
☐ 33 Rocky Colavito	20.00	9.00
☐ 34 Al Kaline	50.00	22.00
☐ 35 Ken Boyer	15.00	6.75
☐ 36 Tommy Davis	10.00	4.50

1965 Bazooka

The 1965 Bazooka set of 36 full color, blank backed, numbered cards was issued in panels of three on the backs of Bazooka bubble gum boxes. The individual cards measure 1 9/16" by 2 1/2" whereas the panels measure 2 1/2" by 4 11/16". As in the previous two years some of the

players have the same numbers on their cards; however all pictures are different from the previous two years. Complete panels of three would have a value of 15 percent more than the sum of the individual cards (prices) on the panel and complete boxes would command a premium of another 40 percent above those prices.

	NRMT	VG-E
COMPLETE INDIV. SET	750.00	350.00
COMMON CARD (1-36)	7.50	3.40
☐ 1 Mickey Mantle	150.00	70.00
☐ 2 Larry Jackson	7.50	3.40
☐ 3 Chuck Hinton	7.50	3.40
☐ 4 Tony Oliva	10.00	4.50
☐ 5 Dean Chance	7.50	3.40
☐ 6 Jim O'Toole	7.50	3.40
☐ 7 Harmon Killebrew	30.00	13.50
☐ 8 Pete Ward	7.50	3.40
☐ 9 Hank Aaron	75.00	34.00
☐ 10 Dick Radatz	7.50	3.40
☐ 11 Boog Powell	10.00	4.50
☐ 12 Willie Mays	75.00	34.00
☐ 13 Bob Veale	7.50	3.40
☐ 14 Roberto Clemente	100.00	45.00
☐ 15 Johnny Callison	7.50	3.40
☐ 16 Joe Torre	10.00	4.50
☐ 17 Billy Williams	20.00	9.00
☐ 18 Bob Chance	7.50	3.40
☐ 19 Bob Aspromonte	7.50	3.40
☐ 20 Joe Christopher	7.50	3.40
☐ 21 Jim Bunning	20.00	9.00
☐ 22 Jim Fregosi	7.50	3.40
☐ 23 Bob Gibson	30.00	13.50
☐ 24 Juan Marichal	30.00	13.50
☐ 25 Dave Wickersham	7.50	3.40
☐ 26 Ron Hunt	7.50	3.40
☐ 27 Gary Peters	7.50	3.40
☐ 28 Ron Santo	15.00	6.75
☐ 29 Elston Howard	10.00	4.50
☐ 30 Brooks Robinson	35.00	16.00
☐ 31 Frank Robinson	35.00	16.00
☐ 32 Sandy Koufax	50.00	22.00
☐ 33 Rocky Colavito	15.00	6.75
☐ 34 Al Kaline	35.00	16.00
☐ 35 Ken Boyer	10.00	4.50
☐ 36 Tommy Davis	7.50	3.40

1966 Bazooka

The 1966 Bazooka set of 48 full color, blank backed, numbered cards was issued in panels of three on the backs of Bazooka bubble gum boxes. The individual cardsd measure 1 9/16" by 2 1/2" whereas the complete panels measure 2 1/2" by 4 11/16". The set is distinguishable from the previous years by mention of "48 card set" at the bottom of the card. Complete panels of three would have a value of 15 percent more than the sum of the individual cards (prices) on the panel and complete boxes would command a premium of another 40 percent above those prices.

	NRMT	VG-E
COMPLETE INDIV. SET	800.00	350.00
COMMON CARD (1-48)	7.50	3.40
☐ 1 Sandy Koufax	50.00	22.00
☐ 2 Willie Horton	7.50	3.40
☐ 3 Frank Howard	10.00	4.50

Card	NRMT	VG-E
☐ 4 Richie Allen	10.00	4.50
☐ 5 Mel Stottlemyre	7.50	3.40
☐ 6 Tony Conigliaro	12.50	5.50
☐ 7 Mickey Mantle	150.00	70.00
☐ 8 Leon Wagner	7.50	3.40
☐ 9 Ed Kranepool	7.50	3.40
☐ 10 Juan Marichal	30.00	13.50
☐ 11 Harmon Killebrew	30.00	13.50
☐ 12 Johnny Callison	7.50	3.40
☐ 13 Roy McMillan	7.50	3.40
☐ 14 Willie McCovey	30.00	13.50
☐ 15 Rocky Colavito	12.50	5.50
☐ 16 Willie Mays	75.00	34.00
☐ 17 Sam McDowell	7.50	3.40
☐ 18 Vern Law	7.50	3.40
☐ 19 Jim Fregosi	7.50	3.40
☐ 20 Ron Fairly	7.50	3.40
☐ 21 Bob Gibson	30.00	13.50
☐ 22 Carl Yastrzemski	40.00	18.00
☐ 23 Bill White	10.00	4.50
☐ 24 Bob Aspromonte	7.50	3.40
☐ 25 Dean Chance	7.50	3.40
☐ 26 Roberto Clemente	100.00	45.00
☐ 27 Tony Cloninger	7.50	3.40
☐ 28 Curt Blefary	7.50	3.40
☐ 29 Milt Pappas	7.50	3.40
☐ 30 Hank Aaron	75.00	34.00
☐ 31 Jim Bunning	15.00	6.75
☐ 32 Frank Robinson	30.00	13.50
☐ 33 Bill Skowron	10.00	4.50
☐ 34 Brooks Robinson	40.00	18.00
☐ 35 Jim Wynn	7.50	3.40
☐ 36 Joe Torre	10.00	4.50
☐ 37 Jim Grant	7.50	3.40
☐ 38 Pete Rose	75.00	34.00
☐ 39 Ron Santo	15.00	6.75
☐ 40 Tom Tresh	7.50	3.40
☐ 41 Tony Oliva	12.50	5.50
☐ 42 Don Drysdale	25.00	11.00
☐ 43 Pete Richert	7.50	3.40
☐ 44 Bert Campaneris	7.50	3.40
☐ 45 Jim Maloney	7.50	3.40
☐ 46 Al Kaline	35.00	16.00
☐ 47 Eddie Fisher	7.50	3.40
☐ 48 Billy Williams	25.00	11.00

1967 Bazooka

The 1967 Bazooka set of 48 full color, blank backed, numbered cards was issued in panels of three on the backs of Bazooka bubble gum boxes. The individual cards measure 1 9/16" by 2 1/2" whereas the complete panels measure 2 1/2" by 4 11/16". This set is virtually identical to the 1966 set with the exception of ten new cards as replacements for ten 1966 cards. The remaining 38 cards are identical in pose and number. The replacement cards are listed in the checklist below with an asterisk. Complete panels of three would have a value of 15 percent more than the sum of the individual cards (prices) on the panel and complete boxes would command a premium of another 40 percent above those prices.

	NRMT	VG-E
COMPLETE INDIV. SET	800.00	350.00
COMMON CARD (1-48)	7.50	3.40

Card	NRMT	VG-E
☐ 1 Rick Reichardt	7.50	3.40
☐ 2 Tommie Agee	7.50	3.40
☐ 3 Frank Howard	10.00	4.50
☐ 4 Richie Allen	10.00	4.50
☐ 5 Mel Stottlemyre	7.50	3.40
☐ 6 Tony Conigliaro	12.50	5.50
☐ 7 Mickey Mantle	175.00	80.00
☐ 8 Leon Wagner	7.50	3.40
☐ 9 Gary Peters	7.50	3.40
☐ 10 Juan Marichal	25.00	11.00
☐ 11 Harmon Killebrew	25.00	11.00
☐ 12 Johnny Callison	7.50	3.40
☐ 13 Denny McLain	12.50	5.50
☐ 14 Willie McCovey	20.00	9.00
☐ 15 Rocky Colavito	20.00	9.00
☐ 16 Willie Mays	85.00	38.00
☐ 17 Sam McDowell	7.50	3.40
☐ 18 Jim Kaat	12.50	5.50
☐ 19 Jim Fregosi	7.50	3.40
☐ 20 Ron Fairly	7.50	3.40
☐ 21 Bob Gibson	25.00	11.00
☐ 22 Carl Yastrzemski	40.00	18.00
☐ 23 Bill White	10.00	4.50
☐ 24 Bob Aspromonte	7.50	3.40
☐ 25 Dean Chance	7.50	3.40
☐ 26 Roberto Clemente	125.00	55.00
☐ 27 Tony Cloninger	7.50	3.40
☐ 28 Curt Blefary	7.50	3.40
☐ 29 Phil Regan	7.50	3.40
☐ 30 Hank Aaron	75.00	34.00
☐ 31 Jim Bunning	20.00	9.00
☐ 32 Frank Robinson	30.00	13.50
☐ 33 Ken Boyer	10.00	4.50
☐ 34 Brooks Robinson	30.00	13.50
☐ 35 Jim Wynn	7.50	3.40
☐ 36 Joe Torre	10.00	4.50
☐ 37 Tommy Davis	7.50	3.40
☐ 38 Pete Rose	75.00	34.00
☐ 39 Ron Santo	12.50	5.50
☐ 40 Tom Tresh	7.50	3.40
☐ 41 Tony Oliva	12.50	5.50
☐ 42 Don Drysdale	25.00	11.00
☐ 43 Pete Richert	7.50	3.40
☐ 44 Bert Campaneris	7.50	3.40
☐ 45 Jim Maloney	7.50	3.40
☐ 46 Al Kaline	30.00	13.50
☐ 47 Matty Alou	7.50	3.40
☐ 48 Billy Williams	20.00	9.00

1968 Bazooka

The 1968 Bazooka Tipps from the Topps is a set of 15 numbered boxes (measuring 5 1/2" by 6 1/4" when detached). each containing on the back panel (measuring 3" by 6 1/4") a baseball playing tip from a star, and on the side panels four mini cards, two per side, in full color, measuring 1 1/4" by 3 1/8". Although the set contains a total of 60 of these small cards, 4 are repeated; therefore there are only 56 different small cards. Some collectors cut the panels into individual card; however most collectors retain entire panels or boxes. The prices in the checklist therfore reflect only the values of the complete boxes.

	NRMT	VG-E
COMPLETE BOX SET	1250.00	550.00
COMMON BOX	60.00	27.00
COMMON INDIV. PLAYER	3.00	1.35

Box	NRMT	VG-E
☐ 1 Maury Wills: Bunting	150.00	70.00
Al Kaline		
Paul Casanova		
Clete Boyer		
Tom Seaver		
☐ 2 C.Yastrzemski: Batting	100.00	45.00
Jim Hunter		
Bill Freehan		
Matty Alou		
Jim Lefebvre		
☐ 3 B.Campaneris: Stealing	60.00	27.00
Tim McCarver		
Bob Veale		
Frank Robinson		
Bobby Knoop		
☐ 4 Maury Wills: Sliding	60.00	27.00
Ken Holtzman		
Jose Azcue		
Tony Conigliaro		
Bill White		
☐ 5 J.Javier: Double Play	150.00	70.00
Juan Marichal		
Rico Petrocelli		
Joe Pepitone		
Hank Aaron		
☐ 6 O.Cepeda: 1st Base	100.00	45.00
Ron Santo		
Don Drysdale		
Pete Rose		
Tommie Agee		
☐ 7 B.Mazeroski: 2nd Base	60.00	27.00
John Roseboro		
Jim Bunning		
Frank Howard		
George Scott		
☐ 8 B.Robinson: 3rd Base	75.00	34.00
Tony Gonzalez		
Jim McGlothlin		
Wille Horton		
Harmon Killebrew		
☐ 9 Jim Fregosi: Shortstop	60.00	27.00
Max Alvis		
Bob Gibson		
Tony Oliva		
Vada Pinson		
☐ 10 Joe Torre: Catching	60.00	27.00
Dean Chance		
Fergie Jenkins		
Tommy Davis		
Rick Monday		
☐ 11 Jim Lonborg: Pitching	250.00	110.00
Joel Horlen		
Jim Wynn		
Curt Flood		
Mickey Mantle		
☐ 12 Mike McCormick:	60.00	27.00
Fielding Pitcher		
Don Mincher		
Tony Perez		
Roberto Clemente		
Al Downing		
☐ 13 F.Crosetti: Coaching	60.00	27.00
Rod Carew		
Don Wilson		
Ron Swoboda		
Willie McCovey		
☐ 14 Willie Mays: Outfield	150.00	70.00
Richie Allen		
Gary Peters		
Billy Williams		
Rusty Staub		
☐ 15 L.Brock: Base Running	150.00	70.00
Tommie Agee		
Pete Rose		
Ron Santo		
Don Drysdale		

1969-70 Bazooka

The 1969-70 Bazooka Baseball Extra News set contains 12 complete panels, each comprising a large action shot of a significant event in baseball history and four small cards, comparable to those in the Tipps from the Topps set of 1968, of Hall of Famers. Although some collectors cut the panels into individual cards (measuring 3" by 6 1/4" or 1 1/4" by 3 1/8"), most collectors retain the entire panel, or box (measuring 5 1/2" by 6 1/4"). The prices in the checklist below reflect the value for the entire box, as these cards are more widely seen and collected as complete panels or boxes.

	NRMT	VG-E
COMPLETE PANEL SET	500.00	220.00
COMMON PANEL (1-12)	35.00	16.00
COMMON INDIV. PLAYER	.50	.23

Panel	NRMT	VG-E
☐ 1 No-Hit Duel by	50.00	22.00
Fred Toney		
Hippo Vaughn:		
Ty Cobb		
Willie Keeler		
Mordecai Brown		
Eddie Plank		
☐ 2 Alexander Conquers	35.00	16.00
Yankees:		
Al Simmons		
Ban Johnson		
Walter Johnson		
Rogers Hornsby		
☐ 3 Yanks' Lazzeri Sets	35.00	16.00
AL Record:		
Christy Mathewson		
Chief Bender		
Grover Alexander		

Cy Young		
☐ 4 Homerun Almost Hit	50.00	22.00
Out of Stadium:		
Lou Gehrig		
Hugh Duffy		
Tris Speaker		
Joe Tinker		
☐ 5 Four Consecutive	100.00	45.00
Homers by Lou:		
John McGraw		
Frank Chance		
Babe Ruth		
Mickey Cochrane		
☐ 6 No-Hit Game by	35.00	16.00
Walter Johnson:		
Cy Young		
Walter Johnson		
Johnny Evers		
John McGraw		
☐ 7 Twelve RBIs by	60.00	27.00
Jim Bottomley:		
Johnny Evers		
Eddie Collins		
Lou Gehrig		
Ty Cobb		
☐ 8 Ty Cobb Ties Record:	50.00	22.00
Honus Wagner		
Mickey Cochrane		
Eddie Collins		
Mel Ott		
☐ 9 Babe Ruth Hits Three	60.00	27.00
Homers in Game:		
Cap Anson		
Tris Speaker		
Jack Chesbro		
Al Simmons		
☐ 10 Babe Ruth Calls Shot	60.00	27.00
in Series Game:		
Rabbit Maranville		
Ed Walsh		
Nap Lajoie		
Connie Mack		
☐ 11 Babe Ruth's 60th Homer	60.00	27.00
Sets New Record:		
Joe Tinker		
Nap Lajoie		
Mel Ott		
Frank Chance		
☐ 12 Double Shutout by	35.00	16.00
Ed Reulbach:		
Rogers Hornsby		
Rabbit Maranville		
Christy Mathewson		
Honus Wagner		

1971 Bazooka Numbered Test

This was supposedly a test issue which was different from the more common unnumbered set and much more difficult to find. There are 48 cards (16 panels) in this numbered set whereas the unnumbered set had only 12 panels or 36 individual cards. Individual cards measure approximately 2" by 2 5/8" whereas the panels measure 2 5/8" by 5 15/16". Complete panels of three would have a value of 10 percent more than the sum of the individual cards (prices) on the panel and complete boxes would command a premium of another 30 percent above those prices.

	NRMT	VG-E
COMPLETE SET (48)	600.00	275.00
COMMON CARD (1-48)	4.00	1.80
☐ 1 Tim McCarver	10.00	4.50
☐ 2 Frank Robinson	35.00	16.00
☐ 3 Bill Mazeroski	10.00	4.50
☐ 4 Willie McCovey	20.00	9.00
☐ 5 Carl Yastrzemski	30.00	13.50
☐ 6 Clyde Wright	4.00	1.80
☐ 7 Jim Merritt	4.00	1.80
☐ 8 Luis Aparicio	20.00	9.00
☐ 9 Bobby Murcer	6.00	2.70
☐ 10 Rico Petrocelli	4.00	1.80
☐ 11 Sam McDowell	4.00	1.80
☐ 12 Clarence Gaston	4.00	1.80
☐ 13 Fergie Jenkins	15.00	6.75
☐ 14 Al Kaline	35.00	16.00
☐ 15 Ken Harrelson	4.00	1.80
☐ 16 Tommie Agee	4.00	1.80
☐ 17 Harmon Killebrew	15.00	6.75
☐ 18 Reggie Jackson	45.00	20.00
☐ 19 Juan Marichal	20.00	9.00
☐ 20 Frank Howard	6.00	2.70
☐ 21 Bill Melton	4.00	1.80
☐ 22 Brooks Robinson	35.00	16.00
☐ 23 Hank Aaron	45.00	20.00
☐ 24 Larry Dierker	4.00	1.80
☐ 25 Jim Fregosi	4.00	1.80
☐ 26 Billy Williams	20.00	9.00
☐ 27 Dave McNally	4.00	1.80
☐ 28 Rico Carty	4.00	1.80
☐ 29 Johnny Bench	40.00	18.00
☐ 30 Tommy Harper	4.00	1.80
☐ 31 Bert Campaneris	4.00	1.80
☐ 32 Pete Rose	50.00	22.00
☐ 33 Orlando Cepeda	6.00	2.70
☐ 34 Maury Wills	6.00	2.70
☐ 35 Tom Seaver	40.00	18.00
☐ 36 Tony Oliva	10.00	4.50
☐ 37 Bill Freehan	4.00	1.80
☐ 38 Roberto Clemente	85.00	38.00
☐ 39 Claude Osteen	4.00	1.80
☐ 40 Rusty Staub	6.00	2.70
☐ 41 Bob Gibson	20.00	9.00
☐ 42 Amos Otis	4.00	1.80
☐ 43 Jim Wynn	10.00	4.50
☐ 44 Rich Allen	15.00	6.75
☐ 45 Tony Conigliaro	15.00	6.75
☐ 46 Randy Hundley	4.00	1.80
☐ 47 Willie Mays	50.00	22.00
☐ 48 Jim Hunter	20.00	9.00

1971 Bazooka Unnumbered

The 1971 Bazooka set of 36 full-color, unnumbered cards was issued in 12 panels of three cards each on the backs of boxes containing one cent Bazooka bubble gum. Individual cards measure approximately 2" by 2 5/8" whereas the panels measure 2 5/8" by 5 15/16". The panels are numbered in the checklist alphabetically by the player's last name on the left most card of the panel. Complete panels of three would have a value of 10 percent more than the sum of the individual cards (prices) on the panel and complete boxes would command a premium of another 30 percent above those prices.

	NRMT	VG-E
COMPLETE INDIV.SET	350.00	160.00
COMMON CARD (1-36)	3.00	1.35
☐ 1 Tommie Agee	3.00	1.35
☐ 2 Harmon Killebrew	15.00	6.75
☐ 3 Reggie Jackson	30.00	13.50
☐ 4 Bert Campaneris	3.00	1.35
☐ 5 Pete Rose	30.00	13.50
☐ 6 Orlando Cepeda	5.00	2.20
☐ 7 Rico Carty	3.00	1.35
☐ 8 Johnny Bench	25.00	11.00
☐ 9 Tommy Harper	3.00	1.35
☐ 10 Bill Freehan	3.00	1.35
☐ 11 Roberto Clemente	60.00	27.00
☐ 12 Claude Osteen	3.00	1.35
☐ 13 Jim Fregosi	3.00	1.35
☐ 14 Billy Williams	15.00	6.75
☐ 15 Dave McNally	3.00	1.35
☐ 16 Randy Hundley	3.00	1.35
☐ 17 Willie Mays	35.00	16.00
☐ 18 Jim Hunter	15.00	6.75
☐ 19 Juan Marichal	20.00	9.00
☐ 20 Frank Howard	5.00	2.20
☐ 21 Bill Melton	3.00	1.35
☐ 22 Willie McCovey	20.00	9.00
☐ 23 Carl Yastrzemski	25.00	11.00
☐ 24 Clyde Wright	3.00	1.35
☐ 25 Jim Merritt	3.00	1.35
☐ 26 Luis Aparicio	15.00	6.75
☐ 27 Bobby Murcer	5.00	2.20
☐ 28 Rico Petrocelli	3.00	1.35
☐ 29 Sam McDowell	3.00	1.35
☐ 30 Clarence Gaston	3.00	1.35
☐ 31 Brooks Robinson	20.00	9.00
☐ 32 Hank Aaron	30.00	13.50
☐ 33 Larry Dierker	3.00	1.35
☐ 34 Rusty Staub	5.00	2.20
☐ 35 Bob Gibson	20.00	9.00
☐ 36 Amos Otis	3.00	1.35

1988 Bazooka

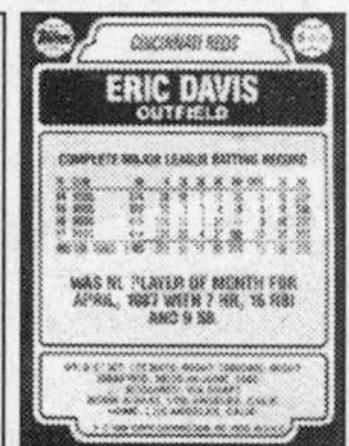

There are 22 standard-size cards in the set. The cards have extra thick white borders. Card backs are printed in blue and red on white card stock. Some sets can also be found with gray backs; these gray backs carry no additional value premium. Cards are numbered on the back; they were numbered by Topps alphabetically. The word "Bazooka" only appears faintly as background for the statistics on the back of the card. Cards were available inside specially marked boxes of Bazooka gum retailing between 59 cents and 99 cents. The emphasis in the player selection for this set is on young stars of baseball.

	MINT	NRMT
COMPLETE SET (22)	8.00	3.60
COMMON CARD (1-22)	.20	.09
☐ 1 George Bell	.20	.09
☐ 2 Wade Boggs	.50	.23
☐ 3 Jose Canseco	.75	.35
☐ 4 Roger Clemens	1.00	.45
☐ 5 Vince Coleman	.20	.09
☐ 6 Eric Davis	.20	.09
☐ 7 Tony Fernandez	.20	.09
☐ 8 Dwight Gooden	.40	.18
☐ 9 Tony Gwynn	1.00	.45
☐ 10 Wally Joyner	.40	.18
☐ 11 Don Mattingly	1.00	.45
☐ 12 Willie McGee	.20	.09
☐ 13 Mark McGwire	1.50	.70
☐ 14 Kirby Puckett	1.00	.45
☐ 15 Tim Raines	.40	.18
☐ 16 Dave Righetti	.20	.09
☐ 17 Cal Ripken	2.00	.90
☐ 18 Juan Samuel	.20	.09
☐ 19 Ryne Sandberg	.75	.35
☐ 20 Benito Santiago	.20	.09
☐ 21 Darryl Strawberry	.40	.18
☐ 22 Todd Worrell	.20	.09

1989 Bazooka

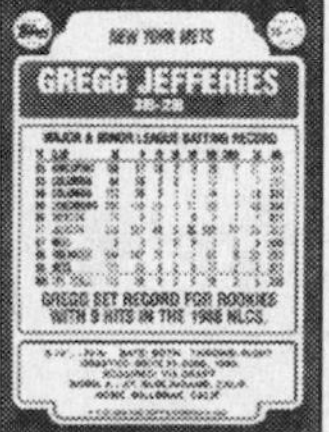

The 1989 Bazooka Shining Stars set contains 22 standard-size cards. The fronts have white borders and a large yellow stripe; the vertically oriented backs are pink, red and white and have career stats. The cards were inserted one per box of Bazooka Gum. The set is sequenced in alphabetical order.

	MINT	NRMT
COMPLETE SET (22)	8.00	3.60
COMMON CARD (1-22)	.20	.09
☐ 1 Tim Belcher	.20	.09
☐ 2 Damon Berryhill	.20	.09
☐ 3 Wade Boggs	.50	.23
☐ 4 Jay Buhner	.50	.23

☐ 5 Jose Canseco	.50	.23
☐ 6 Vince Coleman	.20	.09
☐ 7 Cecil Espy	.20	.09
☐ 8 Dave Gallagher	.20	.09
☐ 9 Ron Gant	.50	.23
☐ 10 Kirk Gibson	.40	.18
☐ 11 Paul Gibson	.20	.09
☐ 12 Mark Grace	.75	.35
☐ 13 Tony Gwynn	1.00	.45
☐ 14 Rickey Henderson	.50	.23
☐ 15 Orel Hershiser	.40	.18
☐ 16 Gregg Jefferies	.50	.23
☐ 17 Ricky Jordan	.20	.09
☐ 18 Chris Sabo	.20	.09
☐ 19 Gary Sheffield	1.00	.45
☐ 20 Darryl Strawberry	.40	.18
☐ 21 Frank Viola	.20	.09
☐ 22 Walt Weiss	.20	.09

1990 Bazooka

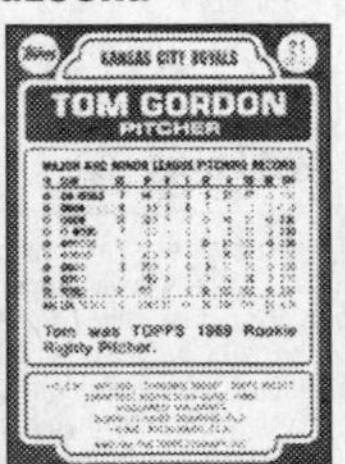

The 1990 Bazooka Shining Stars set contains 22 standard-size cards with a mix of award winners, league leaders, and young stars. This set was issued by Topps using the Bazooka name. Card backs were printed in blue and red on white card stock. The word "Bazooka" appears faintly as background for the statistics on the back of the card as well as appearing prominently on the front of each card.

	MINT	NRMT
COMPLETE SET (22)	8.00	3.60
COMMON CARD (1-22)	.15	.07
☐ 1 Kevin Mitchell	.25	.11
☐ 2 Robin Yount	.50	.23
☐ 3 Mark Davis	.15	.07
☐ 4 Bret Saberhagen	.25	.11
☐ 5 Fred McGriff	.75	.35
☐ 6 Tony Gwynn	1.50	.70
☐ 7 Kirby Puckett	1.25	.55
☐ 8 Vince Coleman	.15	.07
☐ 9 Rickey Henderson	.75	.35
☐ 10 Ben McDonald	.15	.07
☐ 11 Gregg Olson	.15	.07
☐ 12 Todd Zeile	.25	.11
☐ 13 Carlos Martinez	.15	.07
☐ 14 Gregg Jefferies	.25	.11
☐ 15 Craig Worthington	.15	.07
☐ 16 Gary Sheffield	.75	.35
☐ 17 Greg Briley	.15	.07
☐ 18 Ken Griffey Jr.	5.00	2.20
☐ 19 Jerome Walton	.15	.07
☐ 20 Bob Geren	.15	.07
☐ 21 Tom Gordon	.15	.07
☐ 22 Jim Abbott	.25	.11

1991 Bazooka

The 1991 Bazooka Shining Stars set contains 22 standard-size cards featuring league leaders and rookie sensations. The set was produced by Topps for Bazooka. One card was inserted in each box of Bazooka Bubble Gum. The fronts are similar to the Topps regular issue, only that the "Shining Star" emblem appears at the card top and the Bazooka logo overlays the lower right corner of the picture. In a blue and red design on white card stock, the backs have statistics and biography.

	MINT	NRMT
COMPLETE SET (22)	8.00	3.60
COMMON CARD (1-22)	.15	.07
☐ 1 Barry Bonds	.75	.35
☐ 2 Rickey Henderson	.50	.23
☐ 3 Bob Welch	.15	.07
☐ 4 Doug Drabek	.15	.07
☐ 5 Alex Fernandez	.30	.14
☐ 6 Jose Offerman	.15	.07
☐ 7 Frank Thomas	2.50	1.10
☐ 8 Cecil Fielder	.30	.14
☐ 9 Ryne Sandberg	1.25	.55
☐ 10 George Brett	1.25	.55
☐ 11 Willie McGee	.30	.14
☐ 12 Vince Coleman	.15	.07
☐ 13 Hal Morris	.15	.07
☐ 14 Delino DeShields	.15	.07
☐ 15 Robin Ventura	.30	.14
☐ 16 Jeff Huson	.15	.07
☐ 17 Felix Jose	.15	.07
☐ 18 Dave Justice	.75	.35
☐ 19 Larry Walker	.75	.35
☐ 20 Sandy Alomar Jr.	.30	.14
☐ 21 Kevin Appier	.30	.14
☐ 22 Scott Radinsky	.15	.07

1992 Bazooka Quadracard '53 Archives

This 22-card set was produced by Topps for Bazooka, and the set is subtitled "Topps Archives Quadracard" on the top of the backs. Each standard-size card features four micro-reproductions of 1953 Topps baseball cards. These front and back borders of the cards are blue.

	MINT	NRMT
COMPLETE SET (22)	12.00	5.50
COMMON CARD (1-22)	.35	.16
☐ 1 Joe Adcock	1.00	.45
Bob Lemon		
Willie Mays		
Vic Wertz		
☐ 2 Carl Furillo	.50	.23
Don Newcombe		
Phil Rizzuto		
Hank Sauer		
☐ 3 Ferris Fain	.50	.23
John Logan		
Ed Mathews		
Bobby Shantz		
☐ 4 Yogi Berra	.75	.35
Del Crandall		
Howie Pollet		
Gene Woodling		
☐ 5 Richie Ashburn	1.00	.45
Leo Durocher MG		
Allie Reynolds		
Early Wynn		
☐ 6 Hank Aaron	1.50	.70
Ray Boone		
Luke Easter		
Dick Williams		
☐ 7 Ralph Branca	.75	.35
Bob Feller		
Rogers Hornsby		
Bobby Thomson		
☐ 8 Jim Gilliam	.50	.23
Billy Martin		
Minnie Minoso		
Hal Newhouser		
☐ 9 Smoky Burgess	.50	.23
John Mize		
Preacher Roe		
Warren Spahn		
☐ 10 Monte Irvin	.75	.35
Bobo Newsom		
Duke Snider		
Wes Westrum		
☐ 11 Carl Erskine	.50	.23
Jackie Jensen		
George Kell		
Red Schoendienst		
☐ 12 Bill Bruton	.50	.23
Whitey Ford		
Ed Lopat		
Mickey Vernon		
☐ 13 Joe Black	.35	.16
Lew Burdette		
Johnny Pesky		
Enos Slaughter		
☐ 14 Gus Bell	.75	.35
Mike Garcia		
Mel Parnell		
Jackie Robinson		
☐ 15 Alvin Dark	.50	.23
Dick Groat		
Pee Wee Reese		
John Sain		
☐ 16 Gil Hodges	.50	.23
Sal Maglie		
Wilmer Mizell		
Billy Pierce		
☐ 17 Nellie Fox	.50	.23
Ralph Kiner		
Ted Kluszewski		
Eddie Stanky		
☐ 18 Ewell Blackwell	.50	.23
Vern Law		
Satchel Paige		
Jim Wilson		
☐ 19 Lou Boudreau MG	.35	.16
Roy Face		
Harvey Haddix		
Bill Rigney		
☐ 20 Roy Campanella	.50	.23
Walt Dropo		
Harvey Kuenn		
Al Rosen		
☐ 21 Joe Garagiola	1.00	.45
Robin Roberts		
Casey Stengel MG		
Hoyt Wilhelm		
☐ 22 John Antonelli	1.00	.45
Bob Friend		
Dixie Walker CO		
Ted Williams		

1993 Bazooka Team USA

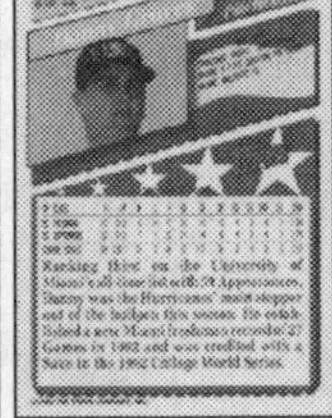

Originally available only in a special Bazooka collector's box, these 22 standard-size cards were produced by Topps and feature the 1993 Team USA players. The card design is similar to that of the '93 Topps series. The white-bordered fronts feature posed color player photos. The player's name appears in a blue stripe near the bottom; the Bazooka logo appears at the upper right. The colorful white-bordered backs carry a color head shot, biography, statistics, and career highlights. The cards are numbered on the back as "X of 22."

	MINT	NRMT
COMPLETE SET (22)	10.00	4.50
COMMON CARD (1-22)	.15	.07
☐ 1 Terry Harvey	.15	.07
☐ 2 Dante Powell	1.00	.45
☐ 3 Andy Barkett	.15	.07
☐ 4 Steve Reich	.15	.07
☐ 5 Charlie Nelson	.30	.14
☐ 6 Todd Walker	1.25	.55
☐ 7 Dustin Hermanson	.50	.23
☐ 8 Pat Clougherty	.15	.07
☐ 9 Danny Graves	.15	.07
☐ 10 Paul Wilson	.50	.23
☐ 11 Todd Helton	5.00	2.20
☐ 12 Russ Johnson	.75	.35
☐ 13 Darren Grass	.30	.14
☐ 14 A.J. Hinch	2.00	.90
☐ 15 Mark Merila	.15	.07
☐ 16 John Powell	.30	.14
☐ 17 Bob Scafa	.15	.07
☐ 18 Matt Beaumont	.50	.23
☐ 19 Todd Dunn	.15	.07
☐ 20 Mike Martin	.30	.14

☐ 21 Carlton Loewer	.50	.23
☐ 22 Bret Wagner	.50	.23

1995 Bazooka

This 132-card standard-size set was issued by Topps. For the previous 35 years, Topps had used the Bazooka label to issue various cards, but this was the first time a mainstream set was issued in pack form. The five-card packs, with a suggested retail price of 50 cents, included an info card as well as a piece of bubble gum. The fronts have an action photo surrounded by white borders. The "Bazooka" label is in the upper left corner, while the player's name and team are on the bottom of the card. The player's position is identified on the right. The backs have a game as well as his previous season and career stats. There are no Rookie Cards in this set. Factory sets included five Red Hots.

	MINT	NRMT
COMPLETE SET (132)	10.00	4.50
COMPLETE FACT.SET (137)	15.00	6.75
COMMON CARD (1-132)	.05	.02
☐ 1 Greg Maddux	1.25	.55
☐ 2 Cal Ripken Jr.	1.50	.70
☐ 3 Lee Smith	.15	.07
☐ 4 Sammy Sosa	.50	.23
☐ 5 Jason Bere	.05	.02
☐ 6 David Justice	.50	.23
☐ 7 Kevin Mitchell	.05	.02
☐ 8 Ozzie Guillen	.05	.02
☐ 9 Roger Clemens	1.00	.45
☐ 10 Mike Mussina	.50	.23
☐ 11 Sandy Alomar Jr.	.15	.07
☐ 12 Cecil Fielder	.15	.07
☐ 13 Dennis Martinez	.15	.07
☐ 14 Randy Myers	.15	.07
☐ 15 Jay Buhner	.30	.14
☐ 16 Ivan Rodriguez	.50	.23
☐ 17 Mo Vaughn	.50	.23
☐ 18 Ryan Klesko	.30	.14
☐ 19 Chuck Finley	.05	.02
☐ 20 Barry Bonds	.60	.25
☐ 21 Dennis Eckersley	.30	.14
☐ 22 Kenny Lofton	.60	.25
☐ 23 Rafael Palmeiro	.30	.14
☐ 24 Mike Stanley	.05	.02
☐ 25 Gregg Jefferies	.05	.02
☐ 26 Robin Ventura	.15	.07
☐ 27 Mark McGwire	.75	.35
☐ 28 Ozzie Smith	.60	.25
☐ 29 Troy Neel	.05	.02
☐ 30 Tony Gwynn	1.00	.45
☐ 31 Ken Griffey Jr.	2.00	.90
☐ 32 Will Clark	.30	.14
☐ 33 Craig Biggio	.30	.14
☐ 34 Shawon Dunston	.05	.02
☐ 35 Wilson Alvarez	.05	.02
☐ 36 Bobby Bonilla	.15	.07
☐ 37 Marquis Grissom	.15	.07
☐ 38 Ben McDonald	.05	.02
☐ 39 Delino DeShields	.05	.02
☐ 40 Barry Larkin	.30	.14
☐ 41 John Olerud	.05	.02
☐ 42 Jose Canseco	.30	.14
☐ 43 Greg Vaughn	.05	.02
☐ 44 Gary Sheffield	.50	.23
☐ 45 Paul O'Neill	.15	.07
☐ 46 Bob Hamelin	.05	.02
☐ 47 Don Mattingly	.75	.35
☐ 48 John Franco	.15	.07
☐ 49 Bret Boone	.05	.02
☐ 50 Rick Aguilera	.15	.07
☐ 51 Tim Wallach	.05	.02
☐ 52 Roberto Kelly	.05	.02
☐ 53 Danny Tartabull	.05	.02
☐ 54 Randy Johnson	.50	.23
☐ 55 Greg McMichael	.05	.02
☐ 56 Bip Roberts	.05	.02
☐ 57 David Cone	.15	.07
☐ 58 Raul Mondesi	.50	.23
☐ 59 Travis Fryman	.30	.14
☐ 60 Jeff Conine	.15	.07
☐ 61 Jeff Bagwell	.75	.35
☐ 62 Rickey Henderson	.30	.14
☐ 63 Fred McGriff	.30	.14
☐ 64 Matt Williams	.30	.14
☐ 65 Rick Wilkins	.05	.02
☐ 66 Eric Karros	.15	.07
☐ 67 Mel Rojas	.05	.02
☐ 68 Juan Gonzalez	1.00	.45
☐ 69 Chuck Carr	.05	.02
☐ 70 Moises Alou	.15	.07
☐ 71 Mark Grace	.30	.14
☐ 72 Alex Fernandez	.15	.07
☐ 73 Rod Beck	.05	.02
☐ 74 Ray Lankford	.15	.07
☐ 75 Dean Palmer	.05	.02
☐ 76 Joe Carter	.15	.07
☐ 77 Mike Piazza	1.25	.55
☐ 78 Eddie Murray	.50	.23
☐ 79 Dave Nilsson	.05	.02
☐ 80 Brett Butler	.15	.07
☐ 81 Roberto Alomar	.50	.23
☐ 82 Jeff Kent	.05	.02
☐ 83 Andres Galarraga	.50	.23
☐ 84 Brady Anderson	.30	.14
☐ 85 Jimmy Key	.05	.02
☐ 86 Bret Saberhagen	.05	.02
☐ 87 Chili Davis	.05	.02
☐ 88 Jose Rijo	.05	.02
☐ 89 Wade Boggs	.30	.14
☐ 90 Len Dykstra	.15	.07
☐ 91 Steve Howe	.05	.02
☐ 92 Hal Morris	.05	.02
☐ 93 Larry Walker	.50	.23
☐ 94 Jeff Montgomery	.15	.07
☐ 95 Wil Cordero	.05	.02
☐ 96 Jay Bell	.05	.02
☐ 97 Tom Glavine	.30	.14
☐ 98 Chris Hoiles	.05	.02
☐ 99 Steve Avery	.05	.02
☐ 100 Ruben Sierra	.05	.02
☐ 101 Mickey Tettleton	.05	.02
☐ 102 Paul Molitor	.50	.23
☐ 103 Carlos Baerga	.15	.07
☐ 104 Walt Weiss	.05	.02
☐ 105 Darren Daulton	.15	.07
☐ 106 Jack McDowell	.05	.02
☐ 107 Doug Drabek	.05	.02
☐ 108 Mark Langston	.05	.02
☐ 109 Manny Ramirez	.50	.23
☐ 110 Kevin Appier	.15	.07
☐ 111 Andy Benes	.05	.02
☐ 112 Chuck Knoblauch	.50	.23
☐ 113 Kirby Puckett	.75	.35
☐ 114 Dante Bichette	.30	.14
☐ 115 Deion Sanders	.50	.23
☐ 116 Albert Belle	.75	.35
☐ 117 Todd Zeile	.05	.02
☐ 118 Devon White	.15	.07
☐ 119 Tim Salmon	.50	.23
☐ 120 Frank Thomas	2.00	.90
☐ 121 John Wetteland	.15	.07
☐ 122 James Mouton	.05	.02
☐ 123 Javier Lopez	.30	.14
☐ 124 Carlos Delgado	.15	.07
☐ 125 Cliff Floyd	.05	.02
☐ 126 Alex Gonzalez	.05	.02
☐ 127 Billy Ashley	.05	.02
☐ 128 Rondell White	.15	.07
☐ 129 Rico Brogna	.05	.02
☐ 130 Melvin Nieves	.15	.07
☐ 131 Jose Oliva	.05	.02
☐ 132 J.R. Phillips	.05	.02

1995 Bazooka Red Hot

This 22-card standard-size set, featuring some of the most popular players, is similar to the regular issue. Differences between these cards and the regular issue include the photo being shaded in a red background, the position is also in red and the player's name is stamped in gold foil. The backs are numbered with an "RH" prefix.

	MINT	NRMT
COMPLETE SET (22)	20.00	9.00
COMMON CARD (1-22)	.15	.07
☐ RH1 Greg Maddux	2.50	1.10
☐ RH2 Cal Ripken Jr.	3.00	1.35
☐ RH3 Barry Bonds	1.00	.45
☐ RH4 Kenny Lofton	1.00	.45
☐ RH5 Mike Stanley	.15	.07
☐ RH6 Tony Gwynn	2.00	.90
☐ RH7 Ken Griffey Jr.	4.00	1.80
☐ RH8 Barry Larkin	.75	.35
☐ RH9 Jose Canseco	.75	.35
☐ RH10 Paul O'Neill	.60	.25
☐ RH11 Randy Johnson	1.00	.45
☐ RH12 David Cone	.60	.25
☐ RH13 Jeff Bagwell	2.00	.90
☐ RH14 Matt Williams	.75	.35
☐ RH15 Mike Piazza	2.50	1.10
☐ RH16 Roberto Alomar	1.00	.45
☐ RH17 Jimmy Key	.15	.07
☐ RH18 Wade Boggs	.75	.35
☐ RH19 Paul Molitor	1.00	.45
☐ RH20 Carlos Baerga	.60	.25
☐ RH21 Albert Belle	1.25	.55
☐ RH22 Frank Thomas	3.00	1.35

1996 Bazooka

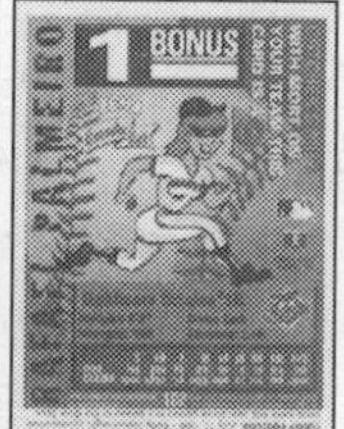

The 1996 Bazooka standard-size set was issued in one series totalling 132 cards. The 5-card packs retail for $.50 each. The set contains baseball's best rookies, rising stars and veterans. The card fronts feature an exciting full-color photo of the player. The back of each card contains one of five different Bazooka Joe characters, along with the Bazooka Ball flipping game, the player's biographical data and 1995 career statistics. Additionally, every card contains a Funny Fortune, which predicts the fate of each player on a particular date. Packs contain five cards plus one chunk of Bazooka gum. Finally, each factory set also included a reprint of Mickey Mantle's 1959 Bazooka card.

	MINT	NRMT
COMP.FACT.SET (133)	12.00	5.50
COMPLETE SET (132)	10.00	4.50
COMMON CARD (1-132)	.05	.02
☐ 1 Ken Griffey, Jr.	2.00	.90
☐ 2 J.T. Snow	.15	.07
☐ 3 Rondell White	.15	.07
☐ 4 Reggie Sanders	.05	.02
☐ 5 Jeff Montgomery	.05	.02
☐ 6 Mike Stanley	.05	.02
☐ 7 Bernie Williams	.40	.18
☐ 8 Mike Piazza	1.25	.55
☐ 9 Brian L.Hunter	.15	.07
☐ 10 Len Dykstra	.15	.07
☐ 11 Ray Lankford	.15	.07
☐ 12 Kenny Lofton	.50	.23
☐ 13 Robin Ventura	.15	.07
☐ 14 Devon White	.05	.02
☐ 15 Cal Ripken	1.50	.70
☐ 16 Heathcliff Slocumb	.05	.02
☐ 17 Ryan Klesko	.30	.14
☐ 18 Terry Steinbach	.05	.02
☐ 19 Travis Fryman	.15	.07
☐ 20 Sammy Sosa	.40	.18
☐ 21 Jim Thome	.40	.18
☐ 22 Kenny Rogers	.05	.02
☐ 23 Don Mattingly	1.00	.45
☐ 24 Kirby Puckett	.75	.35
☐ 25 Matt Williams	.30	.14
☐ 26 Larry Walker	.40	.18
☐ 27 Tim Wakefield	.05	.02
☐ 28 Greg Vaughn	.05	.02
☐ 29 Denny Neagle	.05	.02
☐ 30 Ken Caminiti	.40	.18
☐ 31 Garret Anderson	.15	.07
☐ 32 Brady Anderson	.30	.14
☐ 33 Carlos Baerga	.15	.07
☐ 34 Wade Boggs	.40	.18

☐ 35 Roberto Alomar	.40	.18
☐ 36 Eric Karros	.15	.07
☐ 37 Jay Buhner	.30	.14
☐ 38 Dante Bichette	.30	.14
☐ 39 Darren Daulton	.15	.07
☐ 40 Jeff Bagwell	.75	.35
☐ 41 Jay Bell	.05	.02
☐ 42 Dennis Eckersley	.30	.14
☐ 43 Will Clark	.40	.18
☐ 44 Tom Glavine	.30	.14
☐ 45 Rick Aguilera	.15	.07
☐ 46 Kevin Seitzer	.05	.02
☐ 47 Bret Boone	.05	.02
☐ 48 Mark Grace	.30	.14
☐ 49 Ray Durham	.15	.07
☐ 50 Rico Brogna	.05	.02
☐ 51 Kevin Appier	.15	.07
☐ 52 Moises Alou	.15	.07
☐ 53 Jeff Conine	.15	.07
☐ 54 Marty Cordova	.05	.02
☐ 55 Jose Mesa	.05	.02
☐ 56 Rod Beck	.05	.02
☐ 57 Marquis Grissom	.15	.07
☐ 58 David Cone	.15	.07
☐ 59 Albert Belle	.75	.35
☐ 60 Lee Smith	.15	.07
☐ 61 Frank Thomas	2.00	.90
☐ 62 Roger Clemens	.40	.18
☐ 63 Bobby Bonilla	.15	.07
☐ 64 Paul Molitor	.40	.18
☐ 65 Chuck Knoblauch	.40	.18
☐ 66 Steve Finley	.05	.02
☐ 67 Craig Biggio	.30	.14
☐ 68 Ramon Martinez	.15	.07
☐ 69 Jason Isringhausen	.05	.02
☐ 70 Mark Wohlers	.15	.07
☐ 71 Vinny Castilla	.15	.07
☐ 72 Ron Gant	.15	.07
☐ 73 Juan Gonzalez	1.00	.45
☐ 74 Mark McGwire	.60	.25
☐ 75 Jeff King	.05	.02
☐ 76 Pedro Martinez	.40	.18
☐ 77 Chad Curtis	.05	.02
☐ 78 John Olerud	.15	.07
☐ 79 Greg Maddux	1.25	.55
☐ 80 Derek Jeter	1.25	.55
☐ 81 Mike Mussina	.30	.14
☐ 82 Gregg Jefferies	.05	.02
☐ 83 Jim Edmonds	.30	.14
☐ 84 Carlos Perez	.05	.02
☐ 85 Mo Vaughn	.50	.23
☐ 86 Todd Hundley	.15	.07
☐ 87 Roberto Hernandez	.05	.02
☐ 88 Derek Bell	.15	.07
☐ 89 Andres Galarraga	.30	.14
☐ 90 Brian McRae	.05	.02
☐ 91 Joe Carter	.30	.14
☐ 92 Orlando Merced	.05	.02
☐ 93 Cecil Fielder	.15	.07
☐ 94 Dean Palmer	.05	.02
☐ 95 Randy Johnson	.40	.18
☐ 96 Chipper Jones	1.25	.55
☐ 97 Barry Larkin	.30	.14
☐ 98 Hideo Nomo	.50	.23
☐ 99 Gary Gaetti	.05	.02
☐ 100 Edgar Martinez	.30	.14
☐ 101 John Wetteland	.15	.07
☐ 102 Rafael Palmeiro	.30	.14
☐ 103 Chuck Finley	.05	.02
☐ 104 Ivan Rodriguez	.50	.23
☐ 105 Shawn Green	.05	.02
☐ 106 Manny Ramirez	.40	.18
☐ 107 Lance Johnson	.05	.02
☐ 108 Jose Canseco	.30	.14
☐ 109 Fred McGriff	.30	.14
☐ 110 David Segui	.05	.02
☐ 111 Tim Salmon	.40	.18
☐ 112 Hal Morris	.05	.02
☐ 113 Tino Martinez	.40	.18
☐ 114 Bret Saberhagen	.05	.02
☐ 115 Brian Jordan	.15	.07
☐ 116 David Justice	.40	.18
☐ 117 Jack McDowell	.05	.02
☐ 118 Barry Bonds	.50	.23
☐ 119 Mark Langston	.05	.02
☐ 120 John Valentin	.05	.02
☐ 121 Raul Mondesi	.30	.14
☐ 122 Quilvio Veras	.05	.02
☐ 123 Randy Myers	.05	.02
☐ 124 Tony Gwynn	.75	.35
☐ 125 Johnny Damon	.15	.07
☐ 126 Doug Drabek	.05	.02
☐ 127 Bill Pulsipher	.05	.02
☐ 128 Paul O'Neill	.05	.02
☐ 129 Rickey Henderson	.30	.14
☐ 130 Deion Sanders	.30	.14
☐ 131 Orel Hershiser	.15	.07
☐ 132 Gary Sheffield	.40	.18
☐ NNO 59 Bazooka Mantle	4.00	1.80

1951 Berk Ross *

The 1951 Berk Ross set consists of 72 cards (each measuring approximately 2 1/16" by 2 1/2") with tinted photographs, divided evenly into four series (designated in the checklist as A, B, C and D). The cards were marketed in boxes containing two card panels, without gum, and the set includes stars of other sports as well as baseball players. The set is sometimes still found in the original packaging. Intact panels are worth 25 percent more than the sum of the individual cards. The catalog designation for this set is W532-1. In every series the first ten cards are baseball players; the set has a heavy emphasis on Yankees and Phillies players as they were in the World Series the year before. The set includes the first card of Bob Cousy as well as a card of Whitey Ford in his Rookie Card year. For the Baseball Book, only the Baseball players are listed.

	NRMT	VG-E
COMPLETE SET (72)	1200.00	550.00
COMMON BASEBALL	10.00	4.50
COMMON FOOTBALL	10.00	4.50
COMMON OTHERS	5.00	2.20
☐ A1 Al Rosen	12.00	5.50
☐ A2 Bob Lemon	20.00	9.00
☐ A3 Phil Rizzuto	25.00	11.00
☐ A4 Hank Bauer	15.00	6.75
☐ A5 Billy Johnson	10.00	4.50
☐ A6 Jerry Coleman	10.00	4.50
☐ A7 Johnny Mize	20.00	9.00
☐ A8 Dom DiMaggio	15.00	6.75
☐ A9 Richie Ashburn	25.00	11.00
☐ A10 Del Ennis	10.00	4.50
☐ B1 Stan Musial	125.00	55.00
☐ B2 Warren Spahn	30.00	13.50
☐ B3 Tom Henrich	12.00	5.50
☐ B4 Yogi Berra	75.00	34.00
☐ B5 Joe DiMaggio	175.00	80.00
☐ B6 Bobby Brown	12.00	5.50
☐ B7 Granny Hamner	10.00	4.50
☐ B8 Willie Jones	10.00	4.50
☐ B9 Stan Lopata	10.00	4.50
☐ B10 Mike Goliat	10.00	4.50
☐ C1 Ralph Kiner	20.00	9.00
☐ C2 Bill Goodman	10.00	4.50
☐ C3 Allie Reynolds	15.00	6.75
☐ C4 Vic Raschi	12.00	5.50
☐ C5 Joe Page	12.00	5.50
☐ C6 Eddie Lopat	15.00	6.75
☐ C7 Andy Seminick	10.00	4.50
☐ C8 Dick Sisler	10.00	4.50
☐ C9 Eddie Waitkus	10.00	4.50
☐ C10 Ken Heintzelman	10.00	4.50
☐ D1 Gene Woodling	12.00	5.50
☐ D2 Cliff Mapes	10.00	4.50
☐ D3 Fred Sanford	10.00	4.50
☐ D4 Tommy Byrne	10.00	4.50
☐ D5 Whitey Ford	75.00	34.00
☐ D6 Jim Konstanty	10.00	4.50
☐ D7 Russ Meyer	12.00	5.50
☐ D8 Robin Roberts	25.00	11.00
☐ D9 Curt Simmons	12.00	5.50
☐ D10 Sam Jethroe	12.00	5.50

1952 Berk Ross

The 1952 Berk Ross set of 72 unnumbered, tinted photocards, each measuring approximately 2" by 3", seems to have been patterned after the highly successful 1951 Bowman set. The reverses of Ewell Blackwell and Nellie Fox are transposed while Phil Rizzuto comes with two different poses. The complete set below includes both poses of Rizzuto. There is a card of Joe DiMaggio even though he retired after the 1951 season. The catalog designation for this set is W532-2, and the cards have been assigned numbers in the alphabetical checklist below.

	NRMT	VG-E
COMPLETE SET (72)	5500.00	2500.00
COMMON CARD (1-71)	20.00	9.00
☐ 1 Richie Ashburn	60.00	27.00
☐ 2 Hank Bauer	25.00	11.00
☐ 3 Yogi Berra	150.00	70.00
☐ 4 Ewell Blackwell UER (photo actually Nellie Fox)	30.00	13.50
☐ 5 Bobby Brown	25.00	11.00
☐ 6 Jim Busby	20.00	9.00
☐ 7 Roy Campanella	150.00	70.00
☐ 8 Chico Carrasquel	25.00	11.00
☐ 9 Jerry Coleman	25.00	11.00
☐ 10 Joe Collins	20.00	9.00
☐ 11 Alvin Dark	25.00	11.00
☐ 12 Dom DiMaggio	30.00	13.50
☐ 13 Joe DiMaggio	1250.00	550.00
☐ 14 Larry Doby	30.00	13.50
☐ 15 Bobby Doerr	40.00	18.00
☐ 16 Bob Elliott	20.00	9.00
☐ 17 Del Ennis	20.00	9.00
☐ 18 Ferris Fain	20.00	9.00
☐ 19 Bob Feller	100.00	45.00
☐ 20 Nellie Fox UER (photo actually Ewell Blackwell)	60.00	27.00
☐ 21 Ned Garver	20.00	9.00
☐ 22 Clint Hartung	20.00	9.00
☐ 23 Jim Hearn	20.00	9.00
☐ 24 Gil Hodges	60.00	27.00
☐ 25 Monte Irvin	40.00	18.00
☐ 26 Larry Jansen	20.00	9.00
☐ 27 Sheldon Jones	20.00	9.00
☐ 28 George Kell	40.00	18.00
☐ 29 Monte Kennedy	20.00	9.00
☐ 30 Ralph Kiner	60.00	27.00
☐ 31 Dave Koslo	20.00	9.00
☐ 32 Bob Kuzava	20.00	9.00
☐ 33 Bob Lemon	40.00	18.00
☐ 34 Whitey Lockman	20.00	9.00
☐ 35 Ed Lopat	25.00	11.00
☐ 36 Sal Maglie	25.00	11.00
☐ 37 Mickey Mantle	1800.00	800.00
☐ 38 Billy Martin	60.00	27.00
☐ 39 Willie Mays	600.00	275.00
☐ 40 Gil McDougald	25.00	11.00
☐ 41 Minnie Minoso	30.00	13.50
☐ 42 Johnny Mize	60.00	27.00
☐ 43 Tom Morgan	20.00	9.00
☐ 44 Don Mueller	20.00	9.00
☐ 45 Stan Musial	300.00	135.00
☐ 46 Don Newcombe	30.00	13.50
☐ 47 Ray Noble	20.00	9.00
☐ 48 Joe Ostrowski	20.00	9.00
☐ 49 Mel Parnell	25.00	11.00
☐ 50 Vic Raschi	25.00	11.00
☐ 51 Pee Wee Reese	75.00	34.00
☐ 52 Allie Reynolds	25.00	11.00
☐ 53 Bill Rigney	20.00	9.00
☐ 54A Phil Rizzuto (bunting)	60.00	27.00
☐ 54B Phil Rizzuto (swinging)	60.00	27.00
☐ 55 Robin Roberts	50.00	22.00
☐ 56 Eddie Robinson UER White Cox on Back	20.00	9.00
☐ 57 Jackie Robinson	400.00	180.00
☐ 58 Preacher Roe	25.00	11.00
☐ 59 Johnny Sain	25.00	11.00
☐ 60 Red Schoendienst	40.00	18.00
☐ 61 Duke Snider	150.00	70.00
☐ 62 George Spencer	20.00	9.00
☐ 63 Eddie Stanky	25.00	11.00
☐ 64 Hank Thompson	25.00	11.00
☐ 65 Bobby Thomson	30.00	13.50
☐ 66 Vic Wertz	20.00	9.00
☐ 67 Wally Westlake	20.00	9.00
☐ 68 Wes Westrum	20.00	9.00
☐ 69 Ted Williams	400.00	180.00
☐ 70 Gene Woodling	25.00	11.00
☐ 71 Gus Zernial	25.00	11.00

1986 Big League Chew

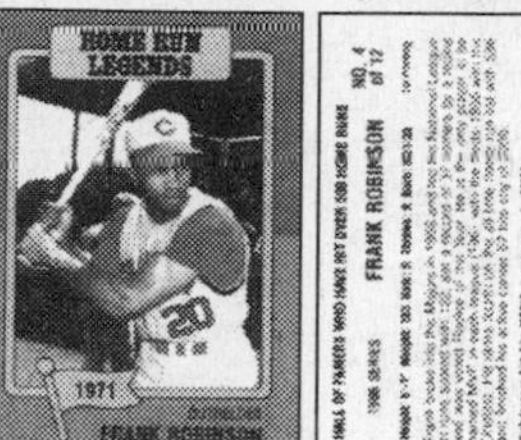

his 12-card standard-size set was produced by Big eague Chew and was inserted in with their packages of g League Chew gum, which were shaped and styled ter a pouch of chewing tobacco. The cards were found ne per pouch of shredded gum or were available through mail-in offer of two coupons and $2.00 for a complete et. The cards in the packs often were damaged in the ackaging process. The players featured are members of e 500 career home run club. The backs are printed in ue ink on white card stock. The set is subtitled "Home un Legends". The front of each card shows a year inside small flag; the year is the year that player passed 500 omers.

	MINT	NRMT
OMPLETE SET (12)	6.00	2.70
OMMON CARD (1-12)	.25	.11
☐ 1 Hank Aaron	1.50	.70
☐ 2 Babe Ruth	2.00	.90
☐ 3 Willie Mays	1.50	.70
☐ 4 Frank Robinson	.50	.23
☐ 5 Harmon Killebrew	.50	.23
☐ 6 Mickey Mantle	2.00	.90
☐ 7 Jimmie Foxx	.50	.23
☐ 8 Ted Williams	1.50	.70
☐ 9 Ernie Banks	.50	.23
☐ 10 Eddie Mathews	.50	.23
☐ 11 Mel Ott	.50	.23
☐ 12 500 HR Members	.25	.11

1991 Blue Jays Score

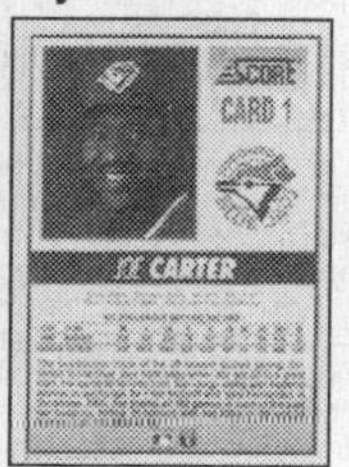

he 1991 Score Toronto Blue Jays set contains 40 player ards plus five magic motion trivia cards. The standard-ze cards feature on the fronts glossy color action photos ith white borders. The bottom corners of the pictures are ut off by aqua-shaped triangles such that home plate is sembled. The player's name and position appear in an qua stripe above the picture. The producer's name and e team logo at the bottom round out the card face. The acks have a color head shot of the player, biography, ajor League statistics, and a player profile.

	MINT	NRMT
OMPLETE SET (40)	14.00	6.25
OMMON CARD (1-40)	.25	.11
☐ 1 Joe Carter	1.50	.70
☐ 2 Tom Henke	.75	.35
☐ 3 Jimmy Key	.75	.35
☐ 4 Al Leiter	1.00	.45
☐ 5 Dave Stieb	.75	.35
☐ 6 Todd Stottlemyre	1.00	.45
☐ 7 Mike Timlin	.50	.23
☐ 8 Duane Ward	.50	.23
☐ 9 David Wells	.50	.23
☐ 10 Frank Wills	.25	.11
☐ 11 Pat Borders	.25	.11
☐ 12 Greg Myers	.25	.11
☐ 13 Roberto Alomar	2.50	1.10
☐ 14 Rene Gonzales	.25	.11
☐ 15 Kelly Gruber	.50	.23
☐ 16 Manny Lee	.25	.11
☐ 17 Rance Mulliniks	.25	.11
☐ 18 John Olerud	1.50	.70
☐ 19 Pat Tabler	.25	.11
☐ 20 Derek Bell	1.25	.55
☐ 21 Jim Acker	.25	.11
☐ 22 Rob Ducey	.25	.11
☐ 23 Devon White	.75	.35
☐ 24 Mookie Wilson	.50	.23
☐ 25 Juan Guzman	2.00	.90
☐ 26 Ed Sprague	.75	.35
☐ 27 Ken Dayley	.25	.11
☐ 28 Tom Candiotti	.25	.11
☐ 29 Candy Maldonado	.25	.11
☐ 30 Eddie Zosky	.25	.11
☐ 31 Steve Karsay	1.25	.55
☐ 32 Bob MacDonald	.25	.11
☐ 33 Ray Giannelli	.25	.11
☐ 34 Jerry Schunk	.25	.11
☐ 35 Dave Weathers	.50	.23
☐ 36 Cito Gaston MG	1.00	.45
☐ 37 Joe Carter AS	.50	.23
☐ 38 Jimmy Key AS	.50	.23
☐ 39 Roberto Alomar AS	1.25	.55
☐ 40 1991 All-Star Game	.25	.11

1993 Blue Jays Donruss 45

This standard-size 45-card gold-boxed set showcases the 1992 Blue Jays with full-bleed action color photos. The words "Commemorative Set Toronto Blue Jays" appear on a team color-coded logo in the lower right. The player's name is displayed in white lettering along a blue bar at the bottom. The top half of each back carries a color player photo with his name printed on a blue bar at the top. The bottom portion contains biography as well as 1992 and World Series statistics.

	MINT	NRMT
COMPLETE SET (45)	15.00	6.75
COMMON CARD (1-45)	.25	.11
☐ 1 Checklist Card	.25	.11
☐ 2 Roberto Alomar	1.50	.70
☐ 3 Derek Bell	.25	.11
☐ 4 Pat Borders	.25	.11
☐ 5 Joe Carter	1.25	.55
☐ 6 Alfredo Griffin	.25	.11
☐ 7 Kelly Gruber	.25	.11
☐ 8 Manny Lee	.25	.11
☐ 9 Candy Maldonado	.25	.11
☐ 10 John Olerud	1.00	.45
☐ 11 Ed Sprague	.50	.23
☐ 12 Pat Tabler	.25	.11
☐ 13 Devon White	.50	.23
☐ 14 Dave Winfield	1.50	.70
☐ 15 David Cone	.50	.23
☐ 16 Mark Eichhorn	.25	.11
☐ 17 Juan Guzman	.50	.23
☐ 18 Tom Henke	.75	.35
☐ 19 Jimmy Key	1.00	.45
☐ 20 Jack Morris	1.00	.45
☐ 21 Todd Stottlemyre	.75	.35
☐ 22 Mike Timlin	.50	.23
☐ 23 Duane Ward	.25	.11
☐ 24 David Wells	.50	.23
☐ 25 Randy Knorr	.25	.11
☐ 26 Rance Mulliniks	.25	.11
☐ 27 Tom Quinlan	.25	.11
☐ 28 Cito Gaston MG	.50	.23
☐ 29 Dave Stieb	.50	.23
☐ 30 Ken Dayley	.25	.11
☐ 31 Turner Ward	.25	.11
☐ 32 Eddie Zosky	.25	.11
☐ 33 Pat Hentgen	2.00	.90
☐ 34 Al Leiter	.75	.35
☐ 35 Doug Linton	.25	.11
☐ 36 Bob MacDonald	.25	.11
☐ 37 Rick Trlicek	.25	.11
☐ 38 Domingo Martinez	.25	.11
☐ 39 Mike Maksudian	.25	.11
☐ 40 Rob Ducey	.25	.11
☐ 41 Jeff Kent	1.50	.70
☐ 42 Greg Myers	.25	.11
☐ 43 Dave Weathers	.25	.11
☐ 44 Skydome	.25	.11
☐ 45 Trophy Presentation	.25	.11

1993 Blue Jays Donruss McDonald's

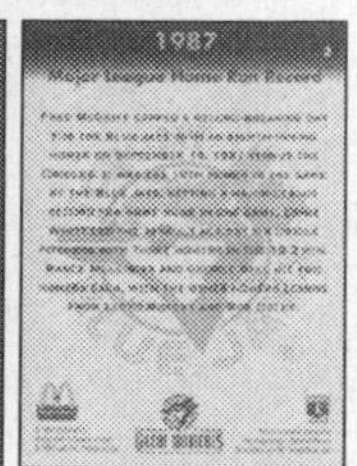

This 36-card standard-size set was produced by Donruss for McDonald's and recognizes "Great Moments" of the Blue Jays. Foil packs sold for 45 cents Canadian with purchase of fries or hash browns. In terms of design, the set subdivides into three sections: 1985-92 Team Highlights (1-13); 1992 World Series (14-26); and regular-issue player cards (27-35). The cards have fronts depicting significant plays and players from 1985 to 1992 in action photos. The McDonald's logo is located in the top left. On cards 1-26, the gold-foil stamped "Great Moments" appears near the bottom with the name of the great moment listed below, while the back describes the event pictured on the front and is superimposed on a ghosted logo of the Blue Jays, with the date in gold lettering across the top. The cards are numbered on the back and are arranged in date sequence.

	MINT	NRMT
COMPLETE SET (36)	15.00	6.75
COMMON CARD (1-36)	.25	.11
☐ 1 Willie Upshaw 1985-First Title	.50	.23
☐ 2 Jesse Barfield 1986-Home Run King	.75	.35
☐ 3 Fred McGriff 1987-Home Run King	2.50	1.10
☐ 4 George Bell 1988-Opening Bell	.75	.35
☐ 5 Kelly Gruber 1989-First Cycle	.50	.23
☐ 6 Ernie Whitt 1989-Comeback	.25	.11
☐ 7 Tom Henke 1989-Winners Again	.75	.35
☐ 8 Dave Stieb 1990-1st No-Hitter	.50	.23
☐ 9 Jack Morris 1992-1st 20-Gamer	.75	.35
☐ 10 Team salutes fans 1992-FANtastic	.25	.11
☐ 11 Pat Borders Mark McGwire 1992-Sudden Impact	1.00	.45
☐ 12 Roberto Alomar 1992-Turning Point	2.00	.90
☐ 13 Candy Maldonado 1992-On to Atlanta	.25	.11
☐ 14 Ed Sprague 1992-WS Instant Hero	.50	.23
☐ 15 Bobby Cox MG Cito Gaston MG 1992-WS Old Friends	.50	.23
☐ 16 Devon White 1992-WS The Catch	.75	.35
☐ 17 Kelly Gruber Deion Sanders 1992-WS Near Triple Play	2.00	.90
☐ 18A Roberto Alomar ERR Winning Welcome missing from front) Kelly Gruber 1992-Winning Welcome	2.00	.90
☐ 18B Roberto Alomar COR Kelly Gruber 1992-Winning Welcome	2.00	.90
☐ 19 Kelly Gruber Damon Berryhill 1992-WS Winning slide	.25	.11
☐ 20 Jimmy Key 1992-WS Final Farewell	.75	.35
☐ 21 Devon White Candy Maldonado 1992-WS Winning RBI	.50	.23
☐ 22 Joe Carter	.75	.35

Otis Nixon; Clincher 1992-WS Clincher		
☐ 23 Blue Jays COR 1992-World Champions	.75	.35
☐ 23A Blue Jays ERR 1992-World Champions (Front is Jimmy Key photo from card 20)	.75	.35
☐ 24 Paul Beeston PR Cito Gaston MG 1992-WS Trophy	.25	.11
☐ 25 Pat Borders 1992-WS MVP	.25	.11
☐ 26 SkyDome victory parade 1992-WS Heroes	.25	.11
☐ 27 John Olerud	1.00	.45
☐ 28 Roberto Alomar	2.00	.90
☐ 29 Ed Sprague	.50	.23
☐ 30 Dick Schofield	.25	.11
☐ 31 Devon White	.50	.23
☐ 32 Joe Carter	1.50	.70
☐ 33 Darrin Jackson	.25	.11
☐ 34 Pat Borders	.25	.11
☐ 35 Paul Molitor	2.00	.90
☐ 36 Checklist 1-36	.25	.11

1993 Blue Jays Donruss World Series

This nine-card horizontally oriented set captures highlights from the 1992 World Series. The standard-size cards feature full-bleed action color pictures with red, white, and blue bunting draped along the top edge. The World Series gold-stamped logo appears below the photo. The backs carry the box score and statistics for each game overlaid on a ghosted Blue Jays' logo. The red, white, and blue bunting design appears at the top with the number of the game and the World Series logo. The cards are numbered on the back with a "WS" prefix.

	MINT	NRMT
COMPLETE SET (9)	6.00	2.70
COMMON CARD (1-9)	.50	.23
☐ 1 Series Opener (Blue Jays-Braves)	.50	.23
☐ 2 Joe Carter (Home run, Game 1)	1.00	.45
☐ 3 Ed Sprague Derek Bell (Sprague homer, Game 2)	.75	.35
☐ 4 Candy Maldonado (Game-winning RBI, Game 3)	.50	.23
☐ 5 Jimmy Key (Key wins Game 4)	1.00	.45
☐ 6 John Olerud (Scoring run, Game 5)	1.00	.45
☐ 7 Dave Winfield Derek Bell (Winfield's Series-winning double, Game 6)	1.50	.70
☐ 8 Pat Borders (Series MVP)	.75	.35
☐ 9 Blue Jays celebrate	.75	.35

1987 Boardwalk and Baseball

This 33-card standard-size set was produced by Topps for distribution by the "Boardwalk and Baseball" Theme Park which was located in Haines City, Florida. The set comes in a custom blue collector box. The full-color fronts are surrounded by a pink and black frame border. The card backs are printed in pink and black on white card stock. The set is subtitled "Top Run Makers." Hence no pitchers are included in the set. The checklist for the set is given on the back panel of the box.

	MINT	NRMT
COMPLETE SET (33)	5.00	2.20
COMMON CARD (1-33)	.05	.02

☐ 1 Mike Schmidt	.60	.25
☐ 2 Eddie Murray	.50	.23
☐ 3 Dale Murphy	.20	.09
☐ 4 Dave Winfield	.20	.09
☐ 5 Jim Rice	.10	.05
☐ 6 Cecil Cooper	.05	.02
☐ 7 Dwight Evans	.05	.02
☐ 8 Rickey Henderson	.30	.14
☐ 9 Robin Yount	.20	.09
☐ 10 Andre Dawson	.20	.09
☐ 11 Gary Carter	.20	.09
☐ 12 Keith Hernandez	.10	.05
☐ 13 George Brett	1.00	.45
☐ 14 Bill Buckner	.05	.02
☐ 15 Tony Armas	.05	.02
☐ 16 Harold Baines	.10	.05
☐ 17 Don Baylor	.10	.05
☐ 18 Steve Garvey	.10	.05
☐ 19 Lance Parrish	.05	.02
☐ 20 Dave Parker	.10	.05
☐ 21 Buddy Bell	.05	.02
☐ 22 Cal Ripken	2.50	1.10
☐ 23 Bob Horner	.05	.02
☐ 24 Tim Raines	.10	.05
☐ 25 Jack Clark	.05	.02
☐ 26 Leon Durham	.05	.02
☐ 27 Pedro Guerrero	.05	.02
☐ 28 Kent Hrbek	.10	.05
☐ 29 Kirk Gibson	.10	.05
☐ 30 Ryne Sandberg	.75	.35
☐ 31 Wade Boggs	.30	.14
☐ 32 Don Mattingly	1.00	.45
☐ 33 Darryl Strawberry	.20	.09

1948 Bowman

The 48-card Bowman set of 1948 was the first major set of the post-war period. Each 2 1/16" by 2 1/2" card had a black and white photo of a current player, with his biographical information printed in black ink on a gray back. Due to the printing process and the 36-card sheet size upon which Bowman was then printing, the 12 cards marked with an SP in the checklist are scarcer numerically, as they were removed from the printing sheet in order to make room for the 12 high numbers (37-48). Cards were issued in one-card penny packs. Many cards are found with over-printed, transposed, or blank backs. The set features the Rookie Cards of Hall of Famers Yogi Berra, Ralph Kiner, Stan Musial, Red Schoendienst, and Warren Spahn. Half of the cards in the set feature New York players (Yankees or Giants).

	NRMT	VG-E
COMPLETE SET (48)	3400.00	1500.00
COMMON CARD (1-36)	20.00	9.00
COMMON CARD (37-48)	30.00	13.50
WRAPPER (5-CENT)	700.00	325.00
☐ 1 Bob Elliott	80.00	12.00
☐ 2 Ewell Blackwell	40.00	18.00
☐ 3 Ralph Kiner	150.00	70.00
☐ 4 Johnny Mize	100.00	45.00
☐ 5 Bob Feller	225.00	100.00
☐ 6 Yogi Berra	450.00	200.00
☐ 7 Pete Reiser SP	120.00	55.00
☐ 8 Phil Rizzuto SP	300.00	135.00
☐ 9 Walker Cooper	20.00	9.00
☐ 10 Buddy Rosar	20.00	9.00
☐ 11 Johnny Lindell	25.00	11.00
☐ 12 Johnny Sain	50.00	22.00
☐ 13 Willard Marshall SP	40.00	18.00
☐ 14 Allie Reynolds	50.00	22.00
☐ 15 Eddie Joost	20.00	9.00
☐ 16 Jack Lohrke SP	40.00	18.00
☐ 17 Enos Slaughter	100.00	45.00
☐ 18 Warren Spahn	350.00	160.00
☐ 19 Tommy Henrich	50.00	22.00
☐ 20 Buddy Kerr SP	40.00	18.00
☐ 21 Ferris Fain	40.00	18.00
☐ 22 Floyd Bevens SP	50.00	22.00
☐ 23 Larry Jansen	25.00	11.00
☐ 24 Dutch Leonard SP	40.00	18.00
☐ 25 Barney McCosky	20.00	9.00
☐ 26 Frank Shea SP	50.00	22.00
☐ 27 Sid Gordon	22.50	10.00
☐ 28 Emil Verban SP	40.00	18.00
☐ 29 Joe Page SP	75.00	34.00
☐ 30 Whitey Lockman SP	50.00	22.00
☐ 31 Bill McCahan	20.00	9.00
☐ 32 Bill Rigney	20.00	9.00
☐ 33 Bill Johnson	25.00	11.00
☐ 34 Sheldon Jones SP	40.00	18.00
☐ 35 Snuffy Stirnweiss	40.00	18.00
☐ 36 Stan Musial	800.00	350.00
☐ 37 Clint Hartung	30.00	13.50
☐ 38 Red Schoendienst	150.00	70.00
☐ 39 Augie Galan	30.00	13.50
☐ 40 Marty Marion	75.00	34.00
☐ 41 Rex Barney	60.00	27.00
☐ 42 Ray Poat	30.00	13.50
☐ 43 Bruce Edwards	30.00	13.50
☐ 44 Johnny Wyrostek	30.00	13.50
☐ 45 Hank Sauer	60.00	27.00
☐ 46 Herman Wehmeier	30.00	13.50
☐ 47 Bobby Thomson	100.00	45.00
☐ 48 Dave Koslo	80.00	19.50

1949 Bowman

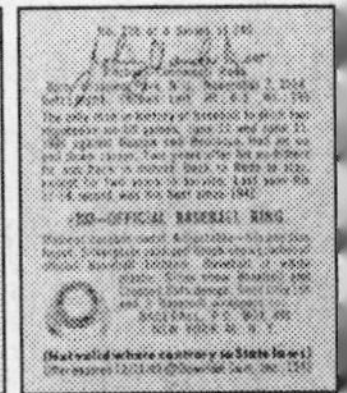

The cards in this 240-card set measure approximately 2 1/16" by 2 1/2". In 1949 Bowman took an intermediate step between black and white and full color with this set of tinted photos on colored backgrounds. Collectors should note the series price variations, which reflect some inconsistencies in the printing process. There are four major varieties in name printing, which are noted in the checklist below: NOF: name on front; NNOF: no name on front; PR: printed name on back; and SCR: script name on back. Cards were issued in five card nickle packs. These variations resulted when Bowman used twelve of the lower numbers to fill out the last press sheet of 36 cards adding to numbers 217-240. Cards 1-3 and 5-73 can be found with either gray or white backs. The set features the Rookie Cards of Hall of Famers Roy Campanella, Bob Lemon, Robin Roberts, Duke Snider, and Early Wynn as well as Rookie Cards of Richie Ashburn and Gil Hodges.

	NRMT	VG-E
COMPLETE SET (240)	13000.00	5800.00
COMMON CARD (1-144)	15.00	6.75
COMMON CARD (145-240)	50.00	22.00
WRAPPER (5-cent, green)	250.00	110.00
WRAPPER (5-cent, blue)	200.00	90.00
☐ 1 Vern Bickford	80.00	16.00
☐ 2 Whitey Lockman	40.00	18.00
☐ 3 Bob Porterfield	15.00	6.75
☐ 4A Jerry Priddy NNOF	15.00	6.75
☐ 4B Jerry Priddy NOF	40.00	18.00
☐ 5 Hank Sauer	40.00	18.00
☐ 6 Phil Cavarretta	40.00	18.00
☐ 7 Joe Dobson	15.00	6.75
☐ 8 Murry Dickson	15.00	6.75
☐ 9 Ferris Fain	40.00	18.00
☐ 10 Ted Gray	15.00	6.75
☐ 11 Lou Boudreau	60.00	27.00
☐ 12 Cass Michaels	15.00	6.75
☐ 13 Bob Chesnes	15.00	6.75
☐ 14 Curt Simmons	35.00	16.00
☐ 15 Ned Garver	15.00	6.75
☐ 16 Al Kozar	15.00	6.75
☐ 17 Earl Torgeson	15.00	6.75

Card	NRMT	VG-E
18 Bobby Thomson	35.00	16.00
19 Bobby Brown	35.00	16.00
20 Gene Hermanski	15.00	6.75
21 Frank Baumholtz	40.00	18.00
22 Peanuts Lowrey	15.00	6.75
23 Bobby Doerr	60.00	27.00
24 Stan Musial	500.00	220.00
25 Carl Scheib	15.00	6.75
26 George Kell	60.00	27.00
27 Bob Feller	175.00	80.00
28 Don Kolloway	15.00	6.75
29 Ralph Kiner	125.00	55.00
30 Andy Seminick	40.00	18.00
31 Dick Kokos	15.00	6.75
32 Eddie Yost	60.00	27.00
33 Warren Spahn	175.00	80.00
34 Dave Koslo	15.00	6.75
35 Vic Raschi	55.00	25.00
36 Pee Wee Reese	175.00	80.00
37 Johnny Wyrostek	15.00	6.75
38 Emil Verban	15.00	6.75
39 Billy Goodman	15.00	6.75
40 Red Munger	15.00	6.75
41 Lou Brissie	15.00	6.75
42 Hoot Evers	15.00	6.75
43 Dale Mitchell	40.00	18.00
44 Dave Philley	15.00	6.75
45 Wally Westlake	15.00	6.75
46 Robin Roberts	200.00	90.00
47 Johnny Sain	25.00	11.00
48 Willard Marshall	15.00	6.75
49 Frank Shea	25.00	11.00
50 Jackie Robinson	1000.00	450.00
51 Herman Wehmeier	15.00	6.75
52 Johnny Schmitz	15.00	6.75
53 Jack Kramer	15.00	6.75
54 Marty Marion	60.00	27.00
55 Eddie Joost	15.00	6.75
56 Pat Mullin	15.00	6.75
57 Gene Bearden	40.00	18.00
58 Bob Elliott	40.00	18.00
59 Jack Lohrke	15.00	6.75
60 Yogi Berra	275.00	125.00
61 Rex Barney	40.00	18.00
62 Grady Hatton	15.00	6.75
63 Andy Pafko	40.00	18.00
64 Dom DiMaggio	35.00	16.00
65 Enos Slaughter	70.00	32.00
66 Elmer Valo	15.00	6.75
67 Alvin Dark	35.00	16.00
68 Sheldon Jones	15.00	6.75
69 Tommy Henrich	35.00	16.00
70 Carl Furillo	100.00	45.00
71 Vern Stephens	15.00	6.75
72 Tommy Holmes	40.00	18.00
73 Billy Cox	35.00	16.00
74 Tom McBride	15.00	6.75
75 Eddie Mayo	15.00	6.75
76 Bill Nicholson	25.00	11.00
77 Ernie Bonham	15.00	6.75
78A Sam Zoldak NNOF	15.00	6.75
78B Sam Zoldak NOF	40.00	18.00
79 Ron Northey	15.00	6.75
80 Bill McCahan	15.00	6.75
81 Virgil Stallcup	15.00	6.75
82 Joe Page	60.00	27.00
83A Bob Scheffing NNOF	15.00	6.75
83B Bob Scheffing NOF	40.00	18.00
84 Roy Campanella	700.00	325.00
85A Johnny Mize NNOF	80.00	36.00
85B Johnny Mize NOF	150.00	70.00
86 Johnny Pesky	60.00	27.00
87 Randy Gumpert	15.00	6.75
88A Bill Salkeld NNOF	15.00	6.75
88B Bill Salkeld NOF	40.00	18.00
89 Mizell Platt	15.00	6.75
90 Gil Coan	15.00	6.75
91 Dick Wakefield	15.00	6.75
92 Willie Jones	40.00	18.00
93 Ed Stevens	15.00	6.75
94 Mickey Vernon	35.00	16.00
95 Howie Pollet	15.00	6.75
96 Taft Wright	15.00	6.75
97 Danny Litwhiler	15.00	6.75
98A Phil Rizzuto NNOF	125.00	55.00
98B Phil Rizzuto NOF	200.00	90.00
99 Frank Gustine	15.00	6.75
100 Gil Hodges	250.00	110.00
101 Sid Gordon	15.00	6.75
102 Stan Spence	15.00	6.75
103 Joe Tipton	15.00	6.75
104 Eddie Stanky	35.00	16.00
105 Bill Kennedy	15.00	6.75
106 Jake Early	15.00	6.75
107 Eddie Lake	15.00	6.75
108 Ken Heintzelman	15.00	6.75
109A Ed Fitzgerald SCR	15.00	6.75
109B Ed Fitzgerald PR	40.00	18.00
110 Early Wynn	125.00	55.00
111 Red Schoendienst	70.00	32.00
112 Sam Chapman	60.00	27.00
113 Ray LaManno	15.00	6.75
114 Allie Reynolds	40.00	18.00
115 Dutch Leonard	15.00	6.75
116 Joe Hatton	15.00	6.75
117 Walker Cooper	15.00	6.75
118 Sam Mele	15.00	6.75
119 Floyd Baker	15.00	6.75
120 Cliff Fannin	15.00	6.75
121 Mark Christman	15.00	6.75
122 George Vico	15.00	6.75
123 Johnny Blatnick	15.00	6.75
124A Danny Murtaugh SCR	60.00	27.00
124B Danny Murtaugh PR	45.00	20.00
125 Ken Keltner	40.00	18.00
126A Al Brazle SCR	15.00	6.75
126B Al Brazle PR	40.00	18.00
127A Hank Majeski SCR	15.00	6.75
127B Hank Majeski PR	40.00	18.00
128 Johnny VanderMeer	60.00	27.00
129 Bill Johnson	40.00	18.00
130 Harry Walker	15.00	6.75
131 Paul Lehner	15.00	6.75
132A Al Evans SCR	15.00	6.75
132B Al Evans PR	40.00	18.00
133 Aaron Robinson	15.00	6.75
134 Hank Borowy	15.00	6.75
135 Stan Rojek	15.00	6.75
136 Hank Edwards	15.00	6.75
137 Ted Wilks	15.00	6.75
138 Buddy Rosar	15.00	6.75
139 Hank Arft	15.00	6.75
140 Ray Scarborough	15.00	6.75
141 Tony Lupien	15.00	6.75
142 Eddie Waitkus	40.00	18.00
143A Bob Dillinger SCR	25.00	11.00
143B Bob Dillinger PR	75.00	34.00
144 Mickey Haefner	15.00	6.75
145 Sylvester Donnelly	50.00	22.00
146 Mike McCormick	80.00	36.00
147 Bert Singleton	50.00	22.00
148 Bob Swift	50.00	22.00
149 Roy Partee	50.00	22.00
150 Allie Clark	50.00	22.00
151 Mickey Harris	50.00	22.00
152 Clarence Maddern	50.00	22.00
153 Phil Masi	50.00	22.00
154 Clint Hartung	75.00	34.00
155 Mickey Guerra	50.00	22.00
156 Al Zarilla	50.00	22.00
157 Walt Masterson	50.00	22.00
158 Harry Brecheen	75.00	34.00
159 Glen Moulder	50.00	22.00
160 Jim Blackburn	50.00	22.00
161 Jocko Thompson	50.00	22.00
162 Preacher Roe	125.00	55.00
163 Clyde McCullough	50.00	22.00
164 Vic Wertz	75.00	34.00
165 Snuffy Stirnweiss	75.00	34.00
166 Mike Tresh	50.00	22.00
167 Babe Martin	50.00	22.00
168 Doyle Lade	50.00	22.00
169 Jeff Heath	80.00	36.00
170 Bill Rigney	80.00	36.00
171 Dick Fowler	50.00	22.00
172 Eddie Pellagrini	50.00	22.00
173 Eddie Stewart	50.00	22.00
174 Terry Moore	100.00	45.00
175 Luke Appling	125.00	55.00
176 Ken Raffensberger	50.00	22.00
177 Stan Lopata	80.00	36.00
178 Tom Brown	80.00	36.00
179 Hugh Casey	75.00	34.00
180 Connie Berry	50.00	22.00
181 Gus Niarhos	50.00	22.00
182 Hal Peck	50.00	22.00
183 Lou Stringer	50.00	22.00
184 Bob Chipman	50.00	22.00
185 Pete Reiser	100.00	45.00
186 Buddy Kerr	50.00	22.00
187 Phil Marchildon	50.00	22.00
188 Karl Drews	50.00	22.00
189 Earl Wooten	50.00	22.00
190 Jim Hearn	50.00	22.00
191 Joe Haynes	50.00	22.00
192 Harry Gumbert	50.00	22.00
193 Ken Trinkle	50.00	22.00
194 Ralph Branca	100.00	45.00
195 Eddie Bockman	50.00	22.00
196 Fred Hutchinson	75.00	34.00
197 Johnny Lindell	75.00	34.00
198 Steve Gromek	50.00	22.00
199 Tex Hughson	50.00	22.00
200 Jess Dobernic	50.00	22.00
201 Sibby Sisti	50.00	22.00
202 Larry Jansen	75.00	34.00
203 Barney McCosky	50.00	22.00
204 Bob Savage	50.00	22.00
205 Dick Sisler	80.00	36.00
206 Bruce Edwards	50.00	22.00
207 Johnny Hopp	50.00	22.00
208 Dizzy Trout	75.00	34.00
209 Charlie Keller	100.00	45.00
210 Joe Gordon	100.00	45.00
211 Boo Ferriss	50.00	22.00
212 Ralph Hamner	50.00	22.00
213 Red Barrett	50.00	22.00
214 Richie Ashburn	550.00	250.00
215 Kirby Higbe	50.00	22.00
216 Schoolboy Rowe	75.00	34.00
217 Marino Pieretti	50.00	22.00
218 Dick Kryhoski	50.00	22.00
219 Virgil Fire Trucks	80.00	36.00
220 Johnny McCarthy	50.00	22.00
221 Bob Muncrief	50.00	22.00
222 Alex Kellner	50.00	22.00
223 Bobby Hofman	50.00	22.00
224 Satchell Paige	1000.00	450.00
225 Jerry Coleman	100.00	45.00
226 Duke Snider	850.00	375.00
227 Fritz Ostermueller	50.00	22.00
228 Jackie Mayo	50.00	22.00
229 Ed Lopat	125.00	55.00
230 Augie Galan	80.00	36.00
231 Earl Johnson	50.00	22.00
232 George McQuinn	80.00	36.00
233 Larry Doby	150.00	70.00
234 Rip Sewell	50.00	22.00
235 Jim Russell	50.00	22.00
236 Fred Sanford	50.00	22.00
237 Monte Kennedy	50.00	22.00
238 Bob Lemon	200.00	90.00
239 Frank McCormick	50.00	22.00
240 Babe Young UER (Photo actually Bobby Young)	100.00	25.00

1950 Bowman

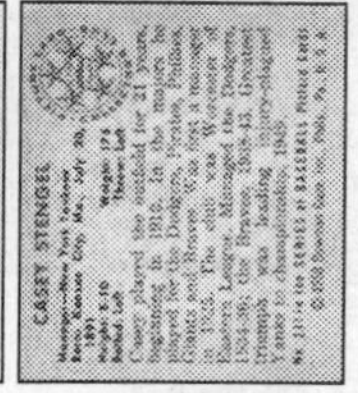

The cards in this 252-card set measure approximately 2 1/16" by 2 1/2". This set, marketed in 1950 by Bowman, represented a major improvement in terms of quality over their previous efforts. Each card was a beautifully colored line drawing developed from a simple photograph. The first 72 cards are the scarcest in the set, while the final 72 cards may be found with or without the copyright line. This was the only Bowman sports set to carry the famous "5-Star" logo. Cards were issued in five-card nickle packs. Key rookies in this set are Hank Bauer, Don Newcombe, and Al Rosen.

	NRMT	VG-E
COMPLETE SET (252)	8500.00	3800.00
COMMON CARD (1-72)	50.00	22.00
COMMON CARD (73-252)	15.00	6.75
WRAPPER (1-cent)	250.00	110.00
WRAPPER (5-cent)	250.00	110.00
1 Mel Parnell	150.00	30.00
2 Vern Stephens	65.00	29.00
3 Dom DiMaggio	70.00	32.00
4 Gus Zernial	65.00	29.00
5 Bob Kuzava	50.00	22.00
6 Bob Feller	225.00	100.00
7 Jim Hegan	60.00	27.00
8 George Kell	75.00	34.00
9 Vic Wertz	65.00	29.00
10 Tommy Henrich	80.00	36.00
11 Phil Rizzuto	225.00	100.00
12 Joe Page	75.00	34.00
13 Ferris Fain	65.00	29.00
14 Alex Kellner	50.00	22.00
15 Al Kozar	50.00	22.00
16 Roy Sievers	80.00	36.00
17 Sid Hudson	50.00	22.00
18 Eddie Robinson	50.00	22.00
19 Warren Spahn	225.00	100.00
20 Bob Elliott	65.00	29.00

☐ 21 Pee Wee Reese 225.00 100.00
☐ 22 Jackie Robinson 750.00 350.00
☐ 23 Don Newcombe 150.00 70.00
☐ 24 Johnny Schmitz 50.00 22.00
☐ 25 Hank Sauer 65.00 29.00
☐ 26 Grady Hatton 50.00 22.00
☐ 27 Herman Wehmeier 50.00 22.00
☐ 28 Bobby Thomson 70.00 32.00
☐ 29 Eddie Stanky 65.00 29.00
☐ 30 Eddie Waitkus 65.00 29.00
☐ 31 Del Ennis 80.00 36.00
☐ 32 Robin Roberts 150.00 70.00
☐ 33 Ralph Kiner 100.00 45.00
☐ 34 Murry Dickson 50.00 22.00
☐ 35 Enos Slaughter 100.00 45.00
☐ 36 Eddie Kazak 55.00 25.00
☐ 37 Luke Appling 75.00 34.00
☐ 38 Bill Wight 50.00 22.00
☐ 39 Larry Doby 75.00 34.00
☐ 40 Bob Lemon 75.00 34.00
☐ 41 Hoot Evers 50.00 22.00
☐ 42 Art Houtteman 50.00 22.00
☐ 43 Bobby Doerr 75.00 34.00
☐ 44 Joe Dobson 50.00 22.00
☐ 45 Al Zarilla 50.00 22.00
☐ 46 Yogi Berra 325.00 145.00
☐ 47 Jerry Coleman 75.00 34.00
☐ 48 Lou Brissie 50.00 22.00
☐ 49 Elmer Valo 50.00 22.00
☐ 50 Dick Kokos 50.00 22.00
☐ 51 Ned Garver 65.00 29.00
☐ 52 Sam Mele 50.00 22.00
☐ 53 Clyde Vollmer 50.00 22.00
☐ 54 Gil Coan 50.00 22.00
☐ 55 Buddy Kerr 50.00 22.00
☐ 56 Del Crandall 65.00 29.00
☐ 57 Vern Bickford 50.00 22.00
☐ 58 Carl Furillo 80.00 36.00
☐ 59 Ralph Branca 75.00 34.00
☐ 60 Andy Pafko 65.00 29.00
☐ 61 Bob Rush 50.00 22.00
☐ 62 Ted Kluszewski 100.00 45.00
☐ 63 Ewell Blackwell 65.00 29.00
☐ 64 Alvin Dark 65.00 29.00
☐ 65 Dave Koslo 50.00 22.00
☐ 66 Larry Jansen 65.00 29.00
☐ 67 Willie Jones 60.00 27.00
☐ 68 Curt Simmons 65.00 29.00
☐ 69 Wally Westlake 50.00 22.00
☐ 70 Bob Chesnes 50.00 22.00
☐ 71 Red Schoendienst 75.00 34.00
☐ 72 Howie Pollet 50.00 22.00
☐ 73 Willard Marshall 15.00 6.75
☐ 74 Johnny Antonelli 60.00 27.00
☐ 75 Roy Campanella 275.00 125.00
☐ 76 Rex Barney 40.00 18.00
☐ 77 Duke Snider 275.00 125.00
☐ 78 Mickey Owen 25.00 11.00
☐ 79 Johnny VanderMeer 40.00 18.00
☐ 80 Howard Fox 15.00 6.75
☐ 81 Ron Northey 15.00 6.75
☐ 82 Whitey Lockman 25.00 11.00
☐ 83 Sheldon Jones 15.00 6.75
☐ 84 Richie Ashburn 100.00 45.00
☐ 85 Ken Heintzelman 15.00 6.75
☐ 86 Stan Rojek 15.00 6.75
☐ 87 Bill Werle 15.00 6.75
☐ 88 Marty Marion 40.00 18.00
☐ 89 Red Munger 15.00 6.75
☐ 90 Harry Brecheen 40.00 18.00
☐ 91 Cass Michaels 15.00 6.75
☐ 92 Hank Majeski 15.00 6.75
☐ 93 Gene Bearden 40.00 18.00
☐ 94 Lou Boudreau 60.00 27.00
☐ 95 Aaron Robinson 15.00 6.75
☐ 96 Virgil Trucks 25.00 11.00
☐ 97 Maurice McDermott 15.00 6.75
☐ 98 Ted Williams 825.00 375.00
☐ 99 Billy Goodman 25.00 11.00
☐ 100 Vic Raschi 60.00 27.00
☐ 101 Bobby Brown 60.00 27.00
☐ 102 Billy Johnson 25.00 11.00
☐ 103 Eddie Joost 15.00 6.75
☐ 104 Sam Chapman 15.00 6.75
☐ 105 Bob Dillinger 15.00 6.75
☐ 106 Cliff Fannin 15.00 6.75
☐ 107 Sam Dente 15.00 6.75
☐ 108 Ray Scarborough 15.00 6.75
☐ 109 Sid Gordon 15.00 6.75
☐ 110 Tommy Holmes 25.00 11.00
☐ 111 Walker Cooper 15.00 6.75
☐ 112 Gil Hodges 100.00 45.00
☐ 113 Gene Hermanski 15.00 6.75
☐ 114 Wayne Terwilliger 15.00 6.75
☐ 115 Roy Smalley 15.00 6.75
☐ 116 Virgil Stallcup 15.00 6.75
☐ 117 Bill Rigney 15.00 6.75
☐ 118 Clint Hartung 15.00 6.75
☐ 119 Dick Sisler 25.00 11.00
☐ 120 John Thompson 15.00 6.75
☐ 121 Andy Seminick 25.00 11.00
☐ 122 Johnny Hopp 25.00 11.00
☐ 123 Dino Restelli 15.00 6.75
☐ 124 Clyde McCullough 15.00 6.75
☐ 125 Del Rice 15.00 6.75
☐ 126 Al Brazle 15.00 6.75
☐ 127 Dave Philley 15.00 6.75
☐ 128 Phil Masi 15.00 6.75
☐ 129 Joe Gordon 25.00 11.00
☐ 130 Dale Mitchell 25.00 11.00
☐ 131 Steve Gromek 15.00 6.75
☐ 132 Mickey Vernon 25.00 11.00
☐ 133 Don Kolloway 15.00 6.75
☐ 134 Paul Trout 15.00 6.75
☐ 135 Pat Mullin 15.00 6.75
☐ 136 Warren Rosar 15.00 6.75
☐ 137 Johnny Pesky 25.00 11.00
☐ 138 Allie Reynolds 60.00 27.00
☐ 139 Johnny Mize 75.00 34.00
☐ 140 Pete Suder 15.00 6.75
☐ 141 Joe Coleman 25.00 11.00
☐ 142 Sherman Lollar 40.00 18.00
☐ 143 Eddie Stewart 15.00 6.75
☐ 144 Al Evans 15.00 6.75
☐ 145 Jack Graham 15.00 6.75
☐ 146 Floyd Baker 15.00 6.75
☐ 147 Mike Garcia 40.00 18.00
☐ 148 Early Wynn 75.00 34.00
☐ 149 Bob Swift 15.00 6.75
☐ 150 George Vico 15.00 6.75
☐ 151 Fred Hutchinson 25.00 11.00
☐ 152 Ellis Kinder 15.00 6.75
☐ 153 Walt Masterson 15.00 6.75
☐ 154 Gus Niarhos 15.00 6.75
☐ 155 Frank Shea 25.00 11.00
☐ 156 Fred Sanford 25.00 11.00
☐ 157 Mike Guerra 15.00 6.75
☐ 158 Paul Lehner 15.00 6.75
☐ 159 Joe Tipton 15.00 6.75
☐ 160 Mickey Harris 15.00 6.75
☐ 161 Sherry Robertson 15.00 6.75
☐ 162 Eddie Yost 25.00 11.00
☐ 163 Earl Torgeson 15.00 6.75
☐ 164 Sibby Sisti 15.00 6.75
☐ 165 Bruce Edwards 15.00 6.75
☐ 166 Joe Hatton 15.00 6.75
☐ 167 Preacher Roe 60.00 27.00
☐ 168 Bob Scheffing 15.00 6.75
☐ 169 Hank Edwards 15.00 6.75
☐ 170 Dutch Leonard 15.00 6.75
☐ 171 Harry Gumbert 15.00 6.75
☐ 172 Peanuts Lowrey 15.00 6.75
☐ 173 Lloyd Merriman 15.00 6.75
☐ 174 Hank Thompson 40.00 18.00
☐ 175 Monte Kennedy 15.00 6.75
☐ 176 Sylvester Donnelly 15.00 6.75
☐ 177 Hank Borowy 15.00 6.75
☐ 178 Ed Fitzgerald 15.00 6.75
☐ 179 Chuck Diering 15.00 6.75
☐ 180 Harry Walker 15.00 6.75
☐ 181 Marino Pieretti 15.00 6.75
☐ 182 Sam Zoldak 15.00 6.75
☐ 183 Mickey Haefner 15.00 6.75
☐ 184 Randy Gumpert 15.00 6.75
☐ 185 Howie Judson 15.00 6.75
☐ 186 Ken Keltner 25.00 11.00
☐ 187 Lou Stringer 15.00 6.75
☐ 188 Earl Johnson 15.00 6.75
☐ 189 Owen Friend 15.00 6.75
☐ 190 Ken Wood 15.00 6.75
☐ 191 Dick Starr 15.00 6.75
☐ 192 Bob Chipman 15.00 6.75
☐ 193 Pete Reiser 40.00 18.00
☐ 194 Billy Cox 60.00 27.00
☐ 195 Phil Cavarretta 40.00 18.00
☐ 196 Doyle Lade 15.00 6.75
☐ 197 Johnny Wyrostek 15.00 6.75
☐ 198 Danny Litwhiler 15.00 6.75
☐ 199 Jack Kramer 15.00 6.75
☐ 200 Kirby Higbe 25.00 11.00
☐ 201 Pete Castiglione 15.00 6.75
☐ 202 Cliff Chambers 15.00 6.75
☐ 203 Danny Murtaugh 25.00 11.00
☐ 204 Granny Hamner 40.00 18.00
☐ 205 Mike Goliat 15.00 6.75
☐ 206 Stan Lopata 25.00 11.00
☐ 207 Max Lanier 15.00 6.75
☐ 208 Jim Hearn 15.00 6.75
☐ 209 Johnny Lindell 15.00 6.75
☐ 210 Ted Gray 15.00 6.75
☐ 211 Charlie Keller 25.00 11.00
☐ 212 Jerry Priddy 15.00 6.75
☐ 213 Carl Scheib 15.00 6.75
☐ 214 Dick Fowler 15.00 6.75
☐ 215 Ed Lopat 60.00 27.0
☐ 216 Bob Porterfield 25.00 11.0
☐ 217 Casey Stengel MG 125.00 55.0
☐ 218 Cliff Mapes 25.00 11.0
☐ 219 Hank Bauer 75.00 34.0
☐ 220 Leo Durocher MG 60.00 27.0
☐ 221 Don Mueller 40.00 18.0
☐ 222 Bobby Morgan 15.00 6.7
☐ 223 Jim Russell 15.00 6.7
☐ 224 Jack Banta 15.00 6.7
☐ 225 Eddie Sawyer MG 25.00 11.0
☐ 226 Jim Konstanty 60.00 27.0
☐ 227 Bob Miller 15.00 6.7
☐ 228 Bill Nicholson 25.00 11.0
☐ 229 Frank Frisch MG 60.00 27.0
☐ 230 Bill Serena 15.00 6.7
☐ 231 Preston Ward 15.00 6.7
☐ 232 Al Rosen 60.00 27.0
☐ 233 Allie Clark 15.00 6.7
☐ 234 Bobby Shantz 60.00 27.0
☐ 235 Harold Gilbert 15.00 6.7
☐ 236 Bob Cain 15.00 6.7
☐ 237 Bill Salkeld 15.00 6.7
☐ 238 Nippy Jones 15.00 6.7
☐ 239 Bill Howerton 15.00 6.7
☐ 240 Eddie Lake 15.00 6.7
☐ 241 Neil Berry 15.00 6.7
☐ 242 Dick Kryhoski 15.00 6.7
☐ 243 Johnny Groth 15.00 6.7
☐ 244 Dale Coogan 15.00 6.7
☐ 245 Al Papai 15.00 6.7
☐ 246 Walt Dropo 40.00 18.0
☐ 247 Irv Noren 25.00 11.0
☐ 248 Sam Jethroe 60.00 27.0
☐ 249 Snuffy Stirnweiss 25.00 11.0
☐ 250 Ray Coleman 15.00 6.7
☐ 251 Les Moss 15.00 6.7
☐ 252 Billy DeMars 60.00 16.5

1951 Bowman

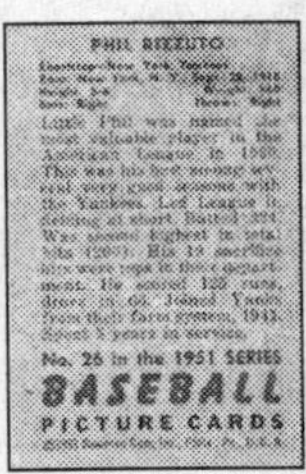

The cards in this 324-card set measure approximately 1/16" by 3 1/8". Many of the obverses of the card appearing in the 1951 Bowman set are enlargements c those appearing in the previous year. The high numbe series (253-324) is highly valued and contains the tru "Rookie" cards of Mickey Mantle and Willie Mays. Car number 195 depicts Paul Richards in caricature. Georg Kell's card (number 46) incorrectly lists him as being i the "1941" Bowman series. Cards were issued either i one card penny packs or in five card nickle packs. Playe names are found printed in a panel on the front of th card. These cards were supposedly also sold in sheets i variety stores in the Philadelphia area.

	NRMT	VG-
COMPLETE SET (324)	16000.00	7200.0
COMMON CARD (1-252)	18.00	8.0
COMMON CARD (253-324)	50.00	22.0
WRAPPER (1-cent)	200.00	90.0
WRAPPER (5-cent)	250.00	110.0

☐ 1 Whitey Ford 800.00 200.0
☐ 2 Yogi Berra 275.00 125.0
☐ 3 Robin Roberts 75.00 34.0
☐ 4 Del Ennis 25.00 11.0
☐ 5 Dale Mitchell 25.00 11.0
☐ 6 Don Newcombe 50.00 22.0
☐ 7 Gil Hodges 90.00 40.0
☐ 8 Paul Lehner 18.00 8.0
☐ 9 Sam Chapman 18.00 8.0
☐ 10 Red Schoendienst 55.00 25.0
☐ 11 Red Munger 18.00 8.0
☐ 12 Hank Majeski 18.00 8.0
☐ 13 Eddie Stanky 25.00 11.0
☐ 14 Alvin Dark 40.00 18.0
☐ 15 Johnny Pesky 25.00 11.0
☐ 16 Maurice McDermott 18.00 8.0
☐ 17 Pete Castiglione 18.00 8.0
☐ 18 Gil Coan 18.00 8.0
☐ 19 Sid Gordon 18.00 8.0
☐ 20 Del Crandall UER 25.00 11.0

(Misspelled Crandell on card)
21 Snuffy Stirnweiss 25.00 11.00
22 Hank Sauer 25.00 11.00
23 Hoot Evers 18.00 8.00
24 Ewell Blackwell 40.00 18.00
25 Vic Raschi 60.00 27.00
26 Phil Rizzuto 125.00 55.00
27 Jim Konstanty 25.00 11.00
28 Eddie Waitkus 18.00 8.00
29 Allie Clark 18.00 8.00
30 Bob Feller 125.00 55.00
31 Roy Campanella 225.00 100.00
32 Duke Snider 225.00 100.00
33 Bob Hooper 18.00 8.00
34 Marty Marion 40.00 18.00
35 Al Zarilla 18.00 8.00
36 Joe Dobson 18.00 8.00
37 Whitey Lockman 40.00 18.00
38 Al Evans 18.00 8.00
39 Ray Scarborough 18.00 8.00
40 Gus Bell 60.00 27.00
41 Eddie Yost 25.00 11.00
42 Vern Bickford 18.00 8.00
43 Billy DeMars 18.00 8.00
44 Roy Smalley 18.00 8.00
45 Art Houtteman 18.00 8.00
46 George Kell 1941 UER 55.00 25.00
47 Grady Hatton 18.00 8.00
48 Ken Raffensberger 18.00 8.00
49 Jerry Coleman 30.00 13.50
50 Johnny Mize 55.00 25.00
51 Andy Seminick 18.00 8.00
52 Dick Sisler 40.00 18.00
53 Bob Lemon 55.00 25.00
54 Ray Boone 35.00 16.00
55 Gene Hermanski 18.00 8.00
56 Ralph Branca 60.00 27.00
57 Alex Kellner 18.00 8.00
58 Enos Slaughter 55.00 25.00
59 Randy Gumpert 18.00 8.00
60 Chico Carrasquel 60.00 27.00
61 Jim Hearn 22.00 10.00
62 Lou Boudreau 55.00 25.00
63 Bob Dillinger 18.00 8.00
64 Bill Werle 18.00 8.00
65 Mickey Vernon 40.00 18.00
66 Bob Elliott 25.00 11.00
67 Roy Sievers 25.00 11.00
68 Dick Kokos 18.00 8.00
69 Johnny Schmitz 18.00 8.00
70 Ron Northey 18.00 8.00
71 Jerry Priddy 18.00 8.00
72 Lloyd Merriman 18.00 8.00
73 Tommy Byrne 18.00 8.00
74 Billy Johnson 25.00 11.00
75 Russ Meyer 25.00 11.00
76 Stan Lopata 25.00 11.00
77 Mike Goliat 18.00 8.00
78 Early Wynn 55.00 25.00
79 Jim Hegan 25.00 11.00
80 Pee Wee Reese 125.00 55.00
81 Carl Furillo 50.00 22.00
82 Joe Tipton 18.00 8.00
83 Carl Scheib 18.00 8.00
84 Barney McCosky 18.00 8.00
85 Eddie Kazak 18.00 8.00
86 Harry Brecheen 25.00 11.00
87 Floyd Baker 18.00 8.00
88 Eddie Robinson 18.00 8.00
89 Hank Thompson 25.00 11.00
90 Dave Koslo 25.00 11.00
91 Clyde Vollmer 18.00 8.00
92 Vern Stephens 25.00 11.00
93 Danny O'Connell 18.00 8.00
94 Clyde McCullough 18.00 8.00
95 Sherry Robertson 18.00 8.00
96 Sandy Consuegra 18.00 8.00
97 Bob Kuzava 18.00 8.00
98 Willard Marshall 18.00 8.00
99 Earl Torgeson 18.00 8.00
100 Sherm Lollar 25.00 11.00
101 Owen Friend 18.00 8.00
102 Dutch Leonard 18.00 8.00
103 Andy Pafko 40.00 18.00
104 Virgil Trucks 25.00 11.00
105 Don Kolloway 18.00 8.00
106 Pat Mullin 18.00 8.00
107 Johnny Wyrostek 18.00 8.00
108 Virgil Stallcup 18.00 8.00
109 Allie Reynolds 60.00 27.00
110 Bobby Brown 40.00 18.00
111 Curt Simmons 18.00 8.00
112 Willie Jones 18.00 8.00
113 Bill Nicholson 25.00 11.00
114 Sam Zoldak 18.00 8.00
115 Steve Gromek 18.00 8.00
116 Bruce Edwards 18.00 8.00

☐ 117 Eddie Miksis 18.00 8.00
☐ 118 Preacher Roe 60.00 27.00
☐ 119 Eddie Joost 18.00 8.00
☐ 120 Joe Coleman 25.00 11.00
☐ 121 Jerry Staley 18.00 8.00
☐ 122 Joe Garagiola 75.00 34.00
☐ 123 Howie Judson 18.00 8.00
☐ 124 Gus Niarhos 18.00 8.00
☐ 125 Bill Rigney 25.00 11.00
☐ 126 Bobby Thomson 60.00 27.00
☐ 127 Sal Maglie 55.00 25.00
☐ 128 Ellis Kinder 18.00 8.00
☐ 129 Matt Batts 18.00 8.00
☐ 130 Tom Saffell 18.00 8.00
☐ 131 Cliff Chambers 18.00 8.00
☐ 132 Cass Michaels 18.00 8.00
☐ 133 Sam Dente 18.00 8.00
☐ 134 Warren Spahn 125.00 55.00
☐ 135 Walker Cooper 18.00 8.00
☐ 136 Ray Coleman 18.00 8.00
☐ 137 Dick Starr 18.00 8.00
☐ 138 Phil Cavarretta 25.00 11.00
☐ 139 Doyle Lade 18.00 8.00
☐ 140 Eddie Lake 18.00 8.00
☐ 141 Fred Hutchinson 25.00 11.00
☐ 142 Aaron Robinson 18.00 8.00
☐ 143 Ted Kluszewski 60.00 27.00
☐ 144 Herman Wehmeier 18.00 8.00
☐ 145 Fred Sanford 25.00 11.00
☐ 146 Johnny Hopp 25.00 11.00
☐ 147 Ken Heintzelman 18.00 8.00
☐ 148 Granny Hamner 18.00 8.00
☐ 149 Bubba Church 18.00 8.00
☐ 150 Mike Garcia 25.00 11.00
☐ 151 Larry Doby 60.00 27.00
☐ 152 Cal Abrams 18.00 8.00
☐ 153 Rex Barney 25.00 11.00
☐ 154 Pete Suder 18.00 8.00
☐ 155 Lou Brissie 18.00 8.00
☐ 156 Del Rice 18.00 8.00
☐ 157 Al Brazle 18.00 8.00
☐ 158 Chuck Diering 18.00 8.00
☐ 159 Eddie Stewart 18.00 8.00
☐ 160 Phil Masi 18.00 8.00
☐ 161 Wes Westrum 18.00 8.00
☐ 162 Larry Jansen 25.00 11.00
☐ 163 Monte Kennedy 18.00 8.00
☐ 164 Bill Wight 18.00 8.00
☐ 165 Ted Williams 700.00 325.00
☐ 166 Stan Rojek 18.00 8.00
☐ 167 Murry Dickson 18.00 8.00
☐ 168 Sam Mele 18.00 8.00
☐ 169 Sid Hudson 18.00 8.00
☐ 170 Sibby Sisti 18.00 8.00
☐ 171 Buddy Kerr 18.00 8.00
☐ 172 Ned Garver 18.00 8.00
☐ 173 Hank Arft 18.00 8.00
☐ 174 Mickey Owen 25.00 11.00
☐ 175 Wayne Terwilliger 18.00 8.00
☐ 176 Vic Wertz 40.00 18.00
☐ 177 Charlie Keller 25.00 11.00
☐ 178 Ted Gray 18.00 8.00
☐ 179 Danny Litwhiler 18.00 8.00
☐ 180 Howie Fox 18.00 8.00
☐ 181 Casey Stengel MG 75.00 34.00
☐ 182 Tom Ferrick 18.00 8.00
☐ 183 Hank Bauer 60.00 27.00
☐ 184 Eddie Sawyer MG 40.00 18.00
☐ 185 Jimmy Bloodworth 18.00 8.00
☐ 186 Richie Ashburn 90.00 40.00
☐ 187 Al Rosen 40.00 18.00
☐ 188 Bobby Avila 25.00 11.00
☐ 189 Erv Palica 18.00 8.00
☐ 190 Joe Hatten 18.00 8.00
☐ 191 Billy Hitchcock 18.00 8.00
☐ 192 Hank Wyse 18.00 8.00
☐ 193 Ted Wilks 18.00 8.00
☐ 194 Peanuts Lowrey 18.00 8.00
☐ 195 Paul Richards MG 25.00 11.00
(Caricature)
☐ 196 Billy Pierce 60.00 27.00
☐ 197 Bob Cain 18.00 8.00
☐ 198 Monte Irvin 100.00 45.00
☐ 199 Sheldon Jones 18.00 8.00
☐ 200 Jack Kramer 18.00 8.00
☐ 201 Steve O'Neill MG 18.00 8.00
☐ 202 Mike Guerra 18.00 8.00
☐ 203 Vernon Law 60.00 27.00
☐ 204 Vic Lombardi 18.00 8.00
☐ 205 Mickey Grasso 18.00 8.00
☐ 206 Conrado Marrero 18.00 8.00
☐ 207 Billy Southworth MG 18.00 8.00
☐ 208 Blix Donnelly 18.00 8.00
☐ 209 Ken Wood 18.00 8.00
☐ 210 Les Moss 18.00 8.00
☐ 211 Hal Jeffcoat 18.00 8.00
☐ 212 Bob Rush 18.00 8.00

☐ 213 Neil Berry 18.00 8.00
☐ 214 Bob Swift 18.00 8.00
☐ 215 Ken Peterson 18.00 8.00
☐ 216 Connie Ryan 18.00 8.00
☐ 217 Joe Page 25.00 11.00
☐ 218 Ed Lopat 60.00 27.00
☐ 219 Gene Woodling 60.00 27.00
☐ 220 Bob Miller 18.00 8.00
☐ 221 Dick Whitman 18.00 8.00
☐ 222 Thurman Tucker 18.00 8.00
☐ 223 Johnny VanderMeer 40.00 18.00
☐ 224 Billy Cox 30.00 13.50
☐ 225 Dan Bankhead 40.00 18.00
☐ 226 Jimmy Dykes MG 25.00 11.00
☐ 227 Bobby Schantz UER 25.00 11.00
(Sic, Shantz)
☐ 228 Cloyd Boyer 25.00 11.00
☐ 229 Bill Howerton 18.00 8.00
☐ 230 Max Lanier 18.00 8.00
☐ 231 Luis Aloma 18.00 8.00
☐ 232 Nelson Fox 225.00 100.00
☐ 233 Leo Durocher MG 60.00 27.00
☐ 234 Clint Hartung 25.00 11.00
☐ 235 Jack Lohrke 18.00 8.00
☐ 236 Warren Rosar 18.00 8.00
☐ 237 Billy Goodman 25.00 11.00
☐ 238 Pete Reiser 40.00 18.00
☐ 239 Bill MacDonald 18.00 8.00
☐ 240 Joe Haynes 18.00 8.00
☐ 241 Irv Noren 25.00 11.00
☐ 242 Sam Jethroe 25.00 11.00
☐ 243 Johnny Antonelli 25.00 11.00
☐ 244 Cliff Fannin 18.00 8.00
☐ 245 John Berardino 60.00 27.00
☐ 246 Bill Serena 18.00 8.00
☐ 247 Bob Ramazzotti 18.00 8.00
☐ 248 Johnny Klippstein 18.00 8.00
☐ 249 Johnny Groth 18.00 8.00
☐ 250 Hank Borowy 18.00 8.00
☐ 251 Willard Ramsdell 18.00 8.00
☐ 252 Dixie Howell 18.00 8.00
☐ 253 Mickey Mantle 8000.00 3600.00
☐ 254 Jackie Jensen 100.00 45.00
☐ 255 Milo Candini 50.00 22.00
☐ 256 Ken Sylvestri 50.00 22.00
☐ 257 Birdie Tebbetts 65.00 29.00
☐ 258 Luke Easter 65.00 29.00
☐ 259 Chuck Dressen MG 75.00 34.00
☐ 260 Carl Erskine 100.00 45.00
☐ 261 Wally Moses 60.00 27.00
☐ 262 Gus Zernial 60.00 27.00
☐ 263 Howie Pollet 60.00 27.00
☐ 264 Don Richmond 50.00 22.00
☐ 265 Steve Bilko 60.00 27.00
☐ 266 Harry Dorish 50.00 22.00
☐ 267 Ken Holcombe 50.00 22.00
☐ 268 Don Mueller 60.00 27.00
☐ 269 Ray Noble 50.00 22.00
☐ 270 Willard Nixon 50.00 22.00
☐ 271 Tommy Wright 50.00 22.00
☐ 272 Billy Meyer MG 50.00 22.00
☐ 273 Danny Murtaugh 65.00 29.00
☐ 274 George Metkovich 50.00 22.00
☐ 275 Bucky Harris MG 65.00 29.00
☐ 276 Frank Quinn 50.00 22.00
☐ 277 Roy Hartsfield 50.00 22.00
☐ 278 Norman Roy 50.00 22.00
☐ 279 Jim Delsing 50.00 22.00
☐ 280 Frank Overmire 50.00 22.00
☐ 281 Al Widmar 50.00 22.00
☐ 282 Frank Frisch MG 90.00 40.00
☐ 283 Walt Dubiel 50.00 22.00
☐ 284 Gene Bearden 60.00 27.00
☐ 285 Johnny Lipon 50.00 22.00
☐ 286 Bob Usher 50.00 22.00
☐ 287 Jim Blackburn 50.00 22.00
☐ 288 Bobby Adams 50.00 22.00
☐ 289 Cliff Mapes 60.00 27.00
☐ 290 Bill Dickey CO 100.00 45.00
☐ 291 Tommy Henrich CO 90.00 40.00
☐ 292 Eddie Pellegrini 50.00 22.00
☐ 293 Ken Johnson 50.00 22.00
☐ 294 Jocko Thompson 50.00 22.00
☐ 295 Al Lopez MG 120.00 55.00
☐ 296 Bob Kennedy 60.00 27.00
☐ 297 Dave Philley 50.00 22.00
☐ 298 Joe Astroth 50.00 22.00
☐ 299 Clyde King 50.00 22.00
☐ 300 Hal Rice 50.00 22.00
☐ 301 Tommy Glaviano 50.00 22.00
☐ 302 Jim Busby 50.00 22.00
☐ 303 Marv Rotblatt 50.00 22.00
☐ 304 Al Gettell 50.00 22.00
☐ 305 Willie Mays 3200.00 1450.00
☐ 306 Jim Piersall 100.00 45.00
☐ 307 Walt Masterson 50.00 22.00
☐ 308 Ted Beard 50.00 22.00

☐ 309 Mel Queen	50.00	22.00
☐ 310 Erv Dusak	50.00	22.00
☐ 311 Mickey Harris	50.00	22.00
☐ 312 Gene Mauch	65.00	29.00
☐ 313 Ray Mueller	50.00	22.00
☐ 314 Johnny Sain	65.00	29.00
☐ 315 Zack Taylor MG	50.00	22.00
☐ 316 Duane Pillette	50.00	22.00
☐ 317 Smoky Burgess	75.00	34.00
☐ 318 Warren Hacker	50.00	22.00
☐ 319 Red Rolfe MG	65.00	29.00
☐ 320 Hal White	50.00	22.00
☐ 321 Earl Johnson	50.00	22.00
☐ 322 Luke Sewell MG	65.00	29.00
☐ 323 Joe Adcock	75.00	34.00
☐ 324 Johnny Pramesa	80.00	24.00

1952 Bowman

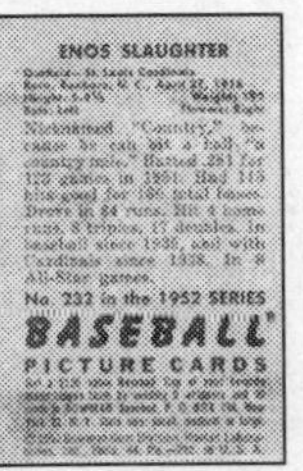

The cards in this 252-card set measure approximately 2 1/16" by 3 1/8". While the Bowman set of 1952 retained the card size introduced in 1951, it employed a modification of color tones from the two preceding years. The cards also appeared with a facsimile autograph on the front and, for the first time since 1949, premium advertising on the back. The 1952 set was apparently sold in sheets as well as in gum packs. Artwork for 15 cards that were never issued was discovered in the early 1980s. Cards were issued in one card penny packs or five card nickle packs. Notable Rookie Cards in this set are Lew Burdette, Gil McDougald, and Minnie Minoso.

	NRMT	VG-E
COMPLETE SET (252)	7500.00	3400.00
COMMON CARD (1-216)	15.00	6.75
COMMON CARD (217-252)	40.00	18.00
WRAPPER (1-cent)	200.00	90.00
WRAPPER (5-cent)	100.00	45.00

☐ 1 Yogi Berra	400.00	125.00
☐ 2 Bobby Thomson	40.00	18.00
☐ 3 Fred Hutchinson	25.00	11.00
☐ 4 Robin Roberts	60.00	27.00
☐ 5 Minnie Minoso	125.00	55.00
☐ 6 Virgil Stallcup	15.00	6.75
☐ 7 Mike Garcia	25.00	11.00
☐ 8 Pee Wee Reese	125.00	55.00
☐ 9 Vern Stephens	25.00	11.00
☐ 10 Bob Hooper	15.00	6.75
☐ 11 Ralph Kiner	50.00	22.00
☐ 12 Max Surkont	15.00	6.75
☐ 13 Cliff Mapes	15.00	6.75
☐ 14 Cliff Chambers	15.00	6.75
☐ 15 Sam Mele	15.00	6.75
☐ 16 Turk Lown	15.00	6.75
☐ 17 Ed Lopat	40.00	18.00
☐ 18 Don Mueller	25.00	11.00
☐ 19 Bob Cain	15.00	6.75
☐ 20 Willie Jones	15.00	6.75
☐ 21 Nellie Fox	90.00	40.00
☐ 22 Willard Ramsdell	15.00	6.75
☐ 23 Bob Lemon	50.00	22.00
☐ 24 Carl Furillo	40.00	18.00
☐ 25 Mickey McDermott	15.00	6.75
☐ 26 Eddie Joost	15.00	6.75
☐ 27 Joe Garagiola	50.00	22.00
☐ 28 Roy Hartsfield	15.00	6.75
☐ 29 Ned Garver	15.00	6.75
☐ 30 Red Schoendienst	50.00	22.00
☐ 31 Eddie Yost	25.00	11.00
☐ 32 Eddie Miksis	15.00	6.75
☐ 33 Gil McDougald	80.00	36.00
☐ 34 Alvin Dark	25.00	11.00
☐ 35 Granny Hamner	15.00	6.75
☐ 36 Cass Michaels	15.00	6.75
☐ 37 Vic Raschi	25.00	11.00
☐ 38 Whitey Lockman	25.00	11.00
☐ 39 Vic Wertz	25.00	11.00
☐ 40 Bubba Church	15.00	6.75
☐ 41 Chico Carrasquel	25.00	11.00
☐ 42 Johnny Wyrostek	15.00	6.75
☐ 43 Bob Feller	125.00	55.00
☐ 44 Roy Campanella	225.00	100.00
☐ 45 Johnny Pesky	25.00	11.00
☐ 46 Carl Scheib	15.00	6.75
☐ 47 Pete Castiglione	15.00	6.75
☐ 48 Vern Bickford	15.00	6.75
☐ 49 Jim Hearn	15.00	6.75
☐ 50 Jerry Staley	15.00	6.75
☐ 51 Gil Coan	15.00	6.75
☐ 52 Phil Rizzuto	125.00	55.00
☐ 53 Richie Ashburn	90.00	40.00
☐ 54 Billy Pierce	25.00	11.00
☐ 55 Ken Raffensberger	15.00	6.75
☐ 56 Clyde King	25.00	11.00
☐ 57 Clyde Vollmer	15.00	6.75
☐ 58 Hank Majeski	15.00	6.75
☐ 59 Murry Dickson	15.00	6.75
☐ 60 Sid Gordon	20.00	9.00
☐ 61 Tommy Byrne	15.00	6.75
☐ 62 Joe Presko	15.00	6.75
☐ 63 Irv Noren	20.00	9.00
☐ 64 Roy Smalley	15.00	6.75
☐ 65 Hank Bauer	25.00	11.00
☐ 66 Sal Maglie	25.00	11.00
☐ 67 Johnny Groth	15.00	6.75
☐ 68 Jim Busby	15.00	6.75
☐ 69 Joe Adcock	25.00	11.00
☐ 70 Carl Erskine	35.00	16.00
☐ 71 Vernon Law	25.00	11.00
☐ 72 Earl Torgeson	15.00	6.75
☐ 73 Jerry Coleman	25.00	11.00
☐ 74 Wes Westrum	22.00	10.00
☐ 75 George Kell	50.00	22.00
☐ 76 Del Ennis	25.00	11.00
☐ 77 Eddie Robinson	15.00	6.75
☐ 78 Lloyd Merriman	15.00	6.75
☐ 79 Lou Brissie	15.00	6.75
☐ 80 Gil Hodges	90.00	40.00
☐ 81 Billy Goodman	20.00	9.00
☐ 82 Gus Zernial	20.00	9.00
☐ 83 Howie Pollet	15.00	6.75
☐ 84 Sam Jethroe	25.00	11.00
☐ 85 Marty Marion CO	25.00	11.00
☐ 86 Cal Abrams	20.00	9.00
☐ 87 Mickey Vernon	25.00	11.00
☐ 88 Bruce Edwards	15.00	6.75
☐ 89 Billy Hitchcock	15.00	6.75
☐ 90 Larry Jansen	25.00	11.00
☐ 91 Don Kolloway	15.00	6.75
☐ 92 Eddie Waitkus	20.00	9.00
☐ 93 Paul Richards MG	20.00	9.00
☐ 94 Luke Sewell MG	20.00	9.00
☐ 95 Luke Easter	25.00	11.00
☐ 96 Ralph Branca	25.00	11.00
☐ 97 Willard Marshall	15.00	6.75
☐ 98 Jimmy Dykes MG	25.00	11.00
☐ 99 Clyde McCullough	15.00	6.75
☐ 100 Sibby Sisti	15.00	6.75
☐ 101 Mickey Mantle	2500.00	1100.00
☐ 102 Peanuts Lowrey	15.00	6.75
☐ 103 Joe Haynes	15.00	6.75
☐ 104 Hal Jeffcoat	15.00	6.75
☐ 105 Bobby Brown	25.00	11.00
☐ 106 Randy Gumpert	15.00	6.75
☐ 107 Del Rice	15.00	6.75
☐ 108 George Metkovich	20.00	9.00
☐ 109 Tom Morgan	20.00	9.00
☐ 110 Max Lanier	15.00	6.75
☐ 111 Hoot Evers	15.00	6.75
☐ 112 Smoky Burgess	25.00	11.00
☐ 113 Al Zarilla	15.00	6.75
☐ 114 Frank Hiller	15.00	6.75
☐ 115 Larry Doby	40.00	18.00
☐ 116 Duke Snider	200.00	90.00
☐ 117 Bill Wight	15.00	6.75
☐ 118 Ray Murray	15.00	6.75
☐ 119 Bill Howerton	15.00	6.75
☐ 120 Chet Nichols	15.00	6.75
☐ 121 Al Corwin	15.00	6.75
☐ 122 Billy Johnson	15.00	6.75
☐ 123 Sid Hudson	15.00	6.75
☐ 124 Birdie Tebbetts	25.00	11.00
☐ 125 Howie Fox	15.00	6.75
☐ 126 Phil Cavarretta	25.00	11.00
☐ 127 Dick Sisler	15.00	6.75
☐ 128 Don Newcombe	35.00	16.00
☐ 129 Gus Niarhos	15.00	6.75
☐ 130 Allie Clark	15.00	6.75
☐ 131 Bob Swift	15.00	6.75
☐ 132 Dave Cole	15.00	6.75
☐ 133 Dick Kryhoski	15.00	6.75
☐ 134 Al Brazle	15.00	6.75
☐ 135 Mickey Harris	15.00	6.75
☐ 136 Gene Hermanski	15.00	6.75
☐ 137 Stan Rojek	15.00	6.75
☐ 138 Ted Wilks	15.00	6.75
☐ 139 Jerry Priddy	15.00	6.75
☐ 140 Ray Scarborough	15.00	6.75
☐ 141 Hank Edwards	15.00	6.7
☐ 142 Early Wynn	50.00	22.
☐ 143 Sandy Consuegra	15.00	6.7
☐ 144 Joe Hatton	15.00	6.7
☐ 145 Johnny Mize	50.00	22.
☐ 146 Leo Durocher MG	50.00	22.
☐ 147 Marlin Stuart	15.00	6.7
☐ 148 Ken Heintzelman	15.00	6.7
☐ 149 Howie Judson	15.00	6.7
☐ 150 Herman Wehmeier	15.00	6.7
☐ 151 Al Rosen	25.00	11.
☐ 152 Billy Cox	15.00	6.7
☐ 153 Fred Hatfield	15.00	6.7
☐ 154 Ferris Fain	20.00	9.
☐ 155 Billy Meyer MG	15.00	6.7
☐ 156 Warren Spahn	125.00	55.
☐ 157 Jim Delsing	15.00	6.7
☐ 158 Bucky Harris MG	25.00	11.
☐ 159 Dutch Leonard	15.00	6.7
☐ 160 Eddie Stanky	25.00	11.
☐ 161 Jackie Jensen	35.00	16.
☐ 162 Monte Irvin	50.00	22.
☐ 163 Johnny Lipon	15.00	6.7
☐ 164 Connie Ryan	15.00	6.7
☐ 165 Saul Rogovin	15.00	6.7
☐ 166 Bobby Adams	15.00	6.7
☐ 167 Bobby Avila	25.00	11.
☐ 168 Preacher Roe	25.00	11.
☐ 169 Walt Dropo	20.00	9.
☐ 170 Joe Astroth	15.00	6.7
☐ 171 Mel Queen	15.00	6.7
☐ 172 Ebba St.Claire	15.00	6.7
☐ 173 Gene Bearden	15.00	6.7
☐ 174 Mickey Grasso	15.00	6.7
☐ 175 Randy Jackson	15.00	6.7
☐ 176 Harry Brecheen	20.00	9.
☐ 177 Gene Woodling	25.00	11.
☐ 178 Dave Williams	20.00	9.
☐ 179 Pete Suder	15.00	6.7
☐ 180 Ed Fitzgerald	15.00	6.7
☐ 181 Joe Collins	25.00	11.
☐ 182 Dave Koslo	15.00	6.7
☐ 183 Pat Mullin	15.00	6.7
☐ 184 Curt Simmons	25.00	11.
☐ 185 Eddie Stewart	15.00	6.7
☐ 186 Frank Smith	15.00	6.7
☐ 187 Jim Hegan	20.00	9.
☐ 188 Chuck Dressen MG	25.00	11.
☐ 189 Jimmy Piersall	25.00	11.
☐ 190 Dick Fowler	15.00	6.7
☐ 191 Bob Friend	40.00	18.
☐ 192 John Cusick	15.00	6.7
☐ 193 Bobby Young	15.00	6.7
☐ 194 Bob Porterfield	15.00	6.7
☐ 195 Frank Baumholtz	15.00	6.7
☐ 196 Stan Musial	600.00	275.
☐ 197 Charlie Silvera	15.00	6.7
☐ 198 Chuck Diering	15.00	6.7
☐ 199 Ted Gray	15.00	6.7
☐ 200 Ken Silvestri	15.00	6.7
☐ 201 Ray Coleman	15.00	6.7
☐ 202 Harry Perkowski	15.00	6.7
☐ 203 Steve Gromek	15.00	6.7
☐ 204 Andy Pafko	25.00	11.
☐ 205 Walt Masterson	15.00	6.7
☐ 206 Elmer Valo	15.00	6.7
☐ 207 George Strickland	15.00	6.7
☐ 208 Walker Cooper	15.00	6.7
☐ 209 Dick Littlefield	15.00	6.7
☐ 210 Archie Wilson	15.00	6.7
☐ 211 Paul Minner	15.00	6.7
☐ 212 Solly Hemus	15.00	6.7
☐ 213 Monte Kennedy	15.00	6.7
☐ 214 Ray Boone	25.00	11.
☐ 215 Sheldon Jones	15.00	6.7
☐ 216 Matt Batts	15.00	6.7
☐ 217 Casey Stengel MG	150.00	70.
☐ 218 Willie Mays	1200.00	550.
☐ 219 Neil Berry	40.00	18.
☐ 220 Russ Meyer	40.00	18.
☐ 221 Lou Kretlow	40.00	18.
☐ 222 Dixie Howell	40.00	18.
☐ 223 Harry Simpson	40.00	18.
☐ 224 Johnny Schmitz	40.00	18.
☐ 225 Del Wilber	40.00	18.
☐ 226 Alex Kellner	40.00	18.
☐ 227 Clyde Sukeforth CO	40.00	18.
☐ 228 Bob Chipman	40.00	18.
☐ 229 Hank Arft	40.00	18.
☐ 230 Frank Shea	40.00	18.
☐ 231 Dee Fondy	40.00	18.
☐ 232 Enos Slaughter	90.00	40.
☐ 233 Bob Kuzava	40.00	18.
☐ 234 Fred Fitzsimmons CO	50.00	22.
☐ 235 Steve Souchock	40.00	18.
☐ 236 Tommy Brown	40.00	18.
☐ 237 Sherm Lollar	50.00	22.

☐ 238 Roy McMillan	50.00	22.00
☐ 239 Dale Mitchell	50.00	22.00
☐ 240 Billy Loes	50.00	22.00
☐ 241 Mel Parnell	50.00	22.00
☐ 242 Everett Kell	40.00	18.00
☐ 243 Red Munger	40.00	18.00
☐ 244 Lew Burdette	50.00	22.00
☐ 245 George Schmees	40.00	18.00
☐ 246 Jerry Snyder	40.00	18.00
☐ 247 Johnny Pramesa	40.00	18.00
☐ 248 Bill Werle	40.00	18.00
☐ 249 Hank Thompson	50.00	22.00
☐ 250 Ike Delock	40.00	18.00
☐ 251 Jack Lohrke	40.00	18.00
☐ 252 Frank Crosetti CO	100.00	25.00

1953 Bowman B/W

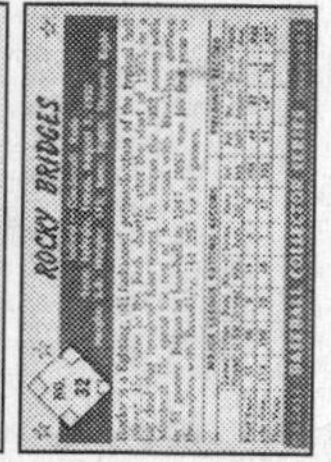

The cards in this 64-card set measure approximately 2 1/2" by 3 3/4". Some collectors believe that the high cost of producing the 1953 color series forced Bowman to issue this set in black and white, since the two sets are identical in design except for the element of color. This set was also produced in fewer numbers than its color counterpart, and is popular among collectors for the challenge involved in completing it. Cards were issued in five-card nickle packs. There are no key Rookie Cards in this set.

	NRMT	VG-E
COMPLETE SET (64)	2400.00	1100.00
COMMON CARD (1-64)	35.00	16.00
WRAPPER (1-CENT)	350.00	160.00
☐ 1 Gus Bell	120.00	24.00
☐ 2 Willard Nixon	35.00	16.00
☐ 3 Bill Rigney	35.00	16.00
☐ 4 Pat Mullin	35.00	16.00
☐ 5 Dee Fondy	35.00	16.00
☐ 6 Ray Murray	35.00	16.00
☐ 7 Andy Seminick	35.00	16.00
☐ 8 Pete Suder	35.00	16.00
☐ 9 Walt Masterson	35.00	16.00
☐ 10 Dick Sisler	60.00	27.00
☐ 11 Dick Gernert	35.00	16.00
☐ 12 Randy Jackson	35.00	16.00
☐ 13 Joe Tipton	35.00	16.00
☐ 14 Bill Nicholson	60.00	27.00
☐ 15 Johnny Mize	125.00	55.00
☐ 16 Stu Miller	60.00	27.00
☐ 17 Virgil Trucks	60.00	27.00
☐ 18 Billy Hoeft	35.00	16.00
☐ 19 Paul LaPalme	35.00	16.00
☐ 20 Eddie Robinson	35.00	16.00
☐ 21 Clarence Podbielan	35.00	16.00
☐ 22 Matt Batts	35.00	16.00
☐ 23 Wilmer Mizell	60.00	27.00
☐ 24 Del Wilber	35.00	16.00
☐ 25 Johnny Sain	60.00	27.00
☐ 26 Preacher Roe	60.00	27.00
☐ 27 Bob Lemon	125.00	55.00
☐ 28 Hoyt Wilhelm	125.00	55.00
☐ 29 Sid Hudson	35.00	16.00
☐ 30 Walker Cooper	35.00	16.00
☐ 31 Gene Woodling	60.00	27.00
☐ 32 Rocky Bridges	35.00	16.00
☐ 33 Bob Kuzava	35.00	16.00
☐ 34 Ebba St.Claire	35.00	16.00
☐ 35 Johnny Wyrostek	35.00	16.00
☐ 36 Jimmy Piersall	60.00	27.00
☐ 37 Hal Jeffcoat	35.00	16.00
☐ 38 Dave Cole	35.00	16.00
☐ 39 Casey Stengel MG	325.00	145.00
☐ 40 Larry Jansen	60.00	27.00
☐ 41 Bob Ramazzotti	35.00	16.00
☐ 42 Howie Judson	35.00	16.00
☐ 43 Hal Bevan	35.00	16.00
☐ 44 Jim Delsing	35.00	16.00
☐ 45 Irv Noren	60.00	27.00
☐ 46 Bucky Harris MG	60.00	27.00
☐ 47 Jack Lohrke	35.00	16.00
☐ 48 Steve Ridzik	35.00	16.00
☐ 49 Floyd Baker	35.00	16.00
☐ 50 Dutch Leonard	35.00	16.00
☐ 51 Lou Burdette	60.00	27.00
☐ 52 Ralph Branca	60.00	27.00
☐ 53 Morrie Martin	35.00	16.00
☐ 54 Bill Miller	35.00	16.00
☐ 55 Don Johnson	35.00	16.00
☐ 56 Roy Smalley	35.00	16.00
☐ 57 Andy Pafko	60.00	27.00
☐ 58 Jim Konstanty	60.00	27.00
☐ 59 Duane Pillette	35.00	16.00
☐ 60 Billy Cox	60.00	27.00
☐ 61 Tom Gorman	35.00	16.00
☐ 62 Keith Thomas	35.00	16.00
☐ 63 Steve Gromek	35.00	16.00
☐ 64 Andy Hansen	60.00	19.00

1953 Bowman Color

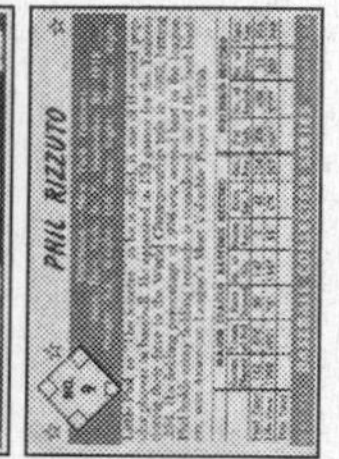

The cards in this 160-card set measure approximately 2 1/2" by 3 3/4". The 1953 Bowman Color set, considered by many to be the best looking set of the modern era, contains Kodachrome photographs with no names or facsimile autographs on the face. Cards were issued in five-card nickle packs. Numbers 113 to 160 are somewhat more difficult to obtain, with numbers 113 to 128 being the most difficult. There are two cards of Al Corwin (126 and 149). There are no key Rookie Cards in this set.

	NRMT	VG-E
COMPLETE SET (160)	12000.00	5400.00
COMMON CARD (1-112)	40.00	18.00
COMMON CARD (113-128)	80.00	36.00
COMMON CARD (129-160)	60.00	27.00
WRAPPER (1-cent)	400.00	180.00
WRAPPER (5-CENT)	300.00	135.00
☐ 1 Dave Williams	100.00	20.00
☐ 2 Vic Wertz	50.00	22.00
☐ 3 Sam Jethroe	50.00	22.00
☐ 4 Art Houtteman	40.00	18.00
☐ 5 Sid Gordon	40.00	18.00
☐ 6 Joe Ginsberg	40.00	18.00
☐ 7 Harry Chiti	40.00	18.00
☐ 8 Al Rosen	50.00	22.00
☐ 9 Phil Rizzuto	175.00	80.00
☐ 10 Richie Ashburn	140.00	65.00
☐ 11 Bobby Shantz	45.00	20.00
☐ 12 Carl Erskine	50.00	22.00
☐ 13 Gus Zernial	50.00	22.00
☐ 14 Billy Loes	50.00	22.00
☐ 15 Jim Busby	40.00	18.00
☐ 16 Bob Friend	45.00	20.00
☐ 17 Gerry Staley	40.00	18.00
☐ 18 Nellie Fox	140.00	65.00
☐ 19 Alvin Dark	45.00	20.00
☐ 20 Don Lenhardt	40.00	18.00
☐ 21 Joe Garagiola	60.00	27.00
☐ 22 Bob Porterfield	40.00	18.00
☐ 23 Herman Wehmeier	40.00	18.00
☐ 24 Jackie Jensen	50.00	22.00
☐ 25 Hoot Evers	40.00	18.00
☐ 26 Roy McMillan	50.00	22.00
☐ 27 Vic Raschi	50.00	22.00
☐ 28 Smoky Burgess	45.00	20.00
☐ 29 Bobby Avila	45.00	20.00
☐ 30 Phil Cavarretta	45.00	20.00
☐ 31 Jimmy Dykes MG	45.00	20.00
☐ 32 Stan Musial	700.00	325.00
☐ 33 Pee Wee Reese	850.00	375.00
☐ 34 Gil Coan	40.00	18.00
☐ 35 Maurice McDermott	40.00	18.00
☐ 36 Minnie Minoso	60.00	27.00
☐ 37 Jim Wilson	40.00	18.00
☐ 38 Harry Byrd	40.00	18.00
☐ 39 Paul Richards MG	45.00	20.00
☐ 40 Larry Doby	60.00	27.00
☐ 41 Sammy White	40.00	18.00
☐ 42 Tommy Brown	40.00	18.00
☐ 43 Mike Garcia	50.00	22.00
☐ 44 Yogi Berra Hank Bauer Mickey Mantle	675.00	300.00
☐ 45 Walt Dropo	50.00	22.00
☐ 46 Roy Campanella	275.00	125.00
☐ 47 Ned Garver	40.00	18.00
☐ 48 Hank Sauer	45.00	20.00
☐ 49 Eddie Stanky MG	45.00	20.00
☐ 50 Lou Kretlow	40.00	18.00
☐ 51 Monte Irvin	60.00	27.00
☐ 52 Marty Marion MG	50.00	22.00
☐ 53 Del Rice	40.00	18.00
☐ 54 Chico Carrasquel	40.00	18.00
☐ 55 Leo Durocher MG	70.00	32.00
☐ 56 Bob Cain	40.00	18.00
☐ 57 Lou Boudreau MG	60.00	27.00
☐ 58 Willard Marshall	40.00	18.00
☐ 59 Mickey Mantle	3000.00	1350.00
☐ 60 Granny Hamner	40.00	18.00
☐ 61 George Kell	70.00	32.00
☐ 62 Ted Kluszewski	60.00	27.00
☐ 63 Gil McDougald	60.00	27.00
☐ 64 Curt Simmons	45.00	20.00
☐ 65 Robin Roberts	100.00	45.00
☐ 66 Mel Parnell	50.00	22.00
☐ 67 Mel Clark	40.00	18.00
☐ 68 Allie Reynolds	50.00	22.00
☐ 69 Charlie Grimm MG	45.00	20.00
☐ 70 Clint Courtney	40.00	18.00
☐ 71 Paul Minner	40.00	18.00
☐ 72 Ted Gray	40.00	18.00
☐ 73 Billy Pierce	45.00	20.00
☐ 74 Don Mueller	50.00	22.00
☐ 75 Saul Rogovin	40.00	18.00
☐ 76 Jim Hearn	40.00	18.00
☐ 77 Mickey Grasso	40.00	18.00
☐ 78 Carl Furillo	50.00	22.00
☐ 79 Ray Boone	45.00	20.00
☐ 80 Ralph Kiner	70.00	32.00
☐ 81 Enos Slaughter	60.00	27.00
☐ 82 Joe Astroth	40.00	18.00
☐ 83 Jack Daniels	40.00	18.00
☐ 84 Hank Bauer	50.00	22.00
☐ 85 Solly Hemus	40.00	18.00
☐ 86 Harry Simpson	40.00	18.00
☐ 87 Harry Perkowski	40.00	18.00
☐ 88 Joe Dobson	40.00	18.00
☐ 89 Sandy Consuegra	40.00	18.00
☐ 90 Joe Nuxhall	45.00	20.00
☐ 91 Steve Souchock	40.00	18.00
☐ 92 Gil Hodges	175.00	80.00
☐ 93 Phil Rizzuto and Billy Martin	250.00	110.00
☐ 94 Bob Addis	40.00	18.00
☐ 95 Wally Moses CO	50.00	22.00
☐ 96 Sal Maglie	50.00	22.00
☐ 97 Eddie Mathews	275.00	125.00
☐ 98 Hector Rodriguez	40.00	18.00
☐ 99 Warren Spahn	225.00	100.00
☐ 100 Bill Wight	40.00	18.00
☐ 101 Red Schoendienst	60.00	27.00
☐ 102 Jim Hegan	50.00	22.00
☐ 103 Del Ennis	45.00	20.00
☐ 104 Luke Easter	50.00	22.00
☐ 105 Eddie Joost	40.00	18.00
☐ 106 Ken Raffensberger	40.00	18.00
☐ 107 Alex Kellner	40.00	18.00
☐ 108 Bobby Adams	40.00	18.00
☐ 109 Ken Wood	40.00	18.00
☐ 110 Bob Rush	40.00	18.00
☐ 111 Jim Dyck	40.00	18.00
☐ 112 Toby Atwell	40.00	18.00
☐ 113 Karl Drews	80.00	36.00
☐ 114 Bob Feller	300.00	135.00
☐ 115 Cloyd Boyer	80.00	36.00
☐ 116 Eddie Yost	100.00	45.00
☐ 117 Duke Snider	550.00	250.00
☐ 118 Billy Martin	300.00	135.00
☐ 119 Dale Mitchell	75.00	34.00
☐ 120 Marlin Stuart	80.00	36.00
☐ 121 Yogi Berra	575.00	250.00
☐ 122 Bill Serena	80.00	36.00
☐ 123 Johnny Lipon	80.00	36.00
☐ 124 Charlie Dressen MG	90.00	40.00
☐ 125 Fred Hatfield	80.00	36.00
☐ 126 Al Corwin	80.00	36.00
☐ 127 Dick Kryhoski	80.00	36.00
☐ 128 Whitey Lockman	100.00	45.00
☐ 129 Russ Meyer	60.00	27.00
☐ 130 Cass Michaels	60.00	27.00
☐ 131 Connie Ryan	60.00	27.00
☐ 132 Fred Hutchinson	80.00	36.00
☐ 133 Willie Jones	60.00	27.00
☐ 134 Johnny Pesky	75.00	34.00
☐ 135 Bobby Morgan	60.00	27.00
☐ 136 Jim Brideweser	60.00	27.00
☐ 137 Sam Dente	60.00	27.00
☐ 138 Bubba Church	60.00	27.00
☐ 139 Pete Runnels	75.00	34.00
☐ 140 Al Brazle	60.00	27.00

	NRMT	VG-E
☐ 141 Frank Shea	60.00	27.00
☐ 142 Larry Miggins	60.00	27.00
☐ 143 Al Lopez MG	75.00	34.00
☐ 144 Warren Hacker	60.00	27.00
☐ 145 George Shuba	80.00	36.00
☐ 146 Early Wynn	125.00	55.00
☐ 147 Clem Koshorek	60.00	27.00
☐ 148 Billy Goodman	80.00	36.00
☐ 149 Al Corwin	60.00	27.00
☐ 150 Carl Scheib	60.00	27.00
☐ 151 Joe Adcock	75.00	34.00
☐ 152 Clyde Vollmer	60.00	27.00
☐ 153 Whitey Ford	500.00	220.00
☐ 154 Turk Lown	60.00	27.00
☐ 155 Allie Clark	60.00	27.00
☐ 156 Max Surkont	60.00	27.00
☐ 157 Sherm Lollar	80.00	36.00
☐ 158 Howard Fox	60.00	27.00
☐ 159 Mickey Vernon UER (Photo actually Floyd Baker)	75.00	34.00
☐ 160 Cal Abrams	100.00	34.00

1954 Bowman

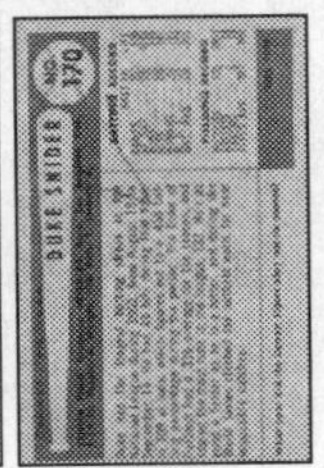

The cards in this 224-card set measure approximately 2 1/2" by 3 3/4". The set was distributed in two separate series: 1-128 in first series and 129-224 in second series. A contractual problem apparently resulted in the deletion of the number 66 Ted Williams card from this Bowman set, thereby creating a scarcity that is highly valued among collectors. The set price below does NOT include number 66 Williams but does include number 66 Jim Piersall, the apparent replacement for Williams in spite of the fact that Piersall was already number 210 to appear later in the set. Many errors in players' statistics exist (and some were corrected) while a few players' names were printed on the front, instead of appearing as a facsimile autograph. Most of these differences are so minor that there is no price differential for either card. The cards which changes were made on are #'s 12, 22,25,26,35,38, 41, 43, 47, 53, 61, 67, 80, 81, 82, 85, 93, 94, 99, 103, 105, 124, 138, 139, 140, 145, 153, 156, 174, 179, 185, 212, 216 and 217. The set was issued in seven-card nickle packs. The notable Rookie Cards in this set are Harvey Kuenn and Don Larsen.

	NRMT	VG-E
COMPLETE SET (224)	4000.00	1800.00
COMMON CARD (1-224)	12.00	5.50
WRAPPER (1-CENT, DATED)	150.00	70.00
WRAPPER (1-CENT, UNDATED)	200.00	90.00
WRAPPER (5-CENT, DATED)	150.00	70.00
WRAPPER (5-CENT, UNDATED)	60.00	27.00

	NRMT	VG-E
☐ 1 Phil Rizzuto	150.00	45.00
☐ 2 Jackie Jensen	20.00	9.00
☐ 3 Marion Fricano	12.00	5.50
☐ 4 Bob Hooper	12.00	5.50
☐ 5 Billy Hunter	12.00	5.50
☐ 6 Nellie Fox	75.00	34.00
☐ 7 Walt Dropo	20.00	9.00
☐ 8 Jim Busby	12.00	5.50
☐ 9 Dave Williams	12.00	5.50
☐ 10 Carl Erskine	20.00	9.00
☐ 11 Sid Gordon	12.00	5.50
☐ 12 Roy McMillan	20.00	9.00
☐ 13 Paul Minner	12.00	5.50
☐ 14 Jerry Staley	12.00	5.50
☐ 15 Richie Ashburn	75.00	34.00
☐ 16 Jim Wilson	12.00	5.50
☐ 17 Tom Gorman	12.00	5.50
☐ 18 Hoot Evers	12.00	5.50
☐ 19 Bobby Shantz	20.00	9.00
☐ 20 Art Houtteman	12.00	5.50
☐ 21 Vic Wertz	20.00	9.00
☐ 22 Sam Mele	12.00	5.50
☐ 23 Harvey Kuenn	35.00	16.00
☐ 24 Bob Porterfield	12.00	5.50
☐ 25 Wes Westrum	20.00	9.00
☐ 26 Billy Cox	20.00	9.00
☐ 27 Dick Cole	12.00	5.50
☐ 28 Jim Greengrass	12.00	5.50
☐ 29 Johnny Klippstein	12.00	5.50
☐ 30 Del Rice	12.00	5.50
☐ 31 Smoky Burgess	20.00	9.00
☐ 32 Del Crandall	20.00	9.00
☐ 33A Vic Raschi (No mention of trade on back)	20.00	9.00
☐ 33B Vic Raschi (Traded to St.Louis)	35.00	16.00
☐ 34 Sammy White	12.00	5.50
☐ 35 Eddie Joost	12.00	5.50
☐ 36 George Strickland	12.00	5.50
☐ 37 Dick Kokos	12.00	5.50
☐ 38 Minnie Minoso	25.00	11.00
☐ 39 Ned Garver	12.00	5.50
☐ 40 Gil Coan	12.00	5.50
☐ 41 Alvin Dark	20.00	9.00
☐ 42 Billy Loes	20.00	9.00
☐ 43 Bob Friend	20.00	9.00
☐ 44 Harry Perkowski	12.00	5.50
☐ 45 Ralph Kiner	40.00	18.00
☐ 46 Rip Repulski	12.00	5.50
☐ 47 Granny Hamner	12.00	5.50
☐ 48 Jack Dittmer	12.00	5.50
☐ 49 Harry Byrd	12.00	5.50
☐ 50 George Kell	40.00	18.00
☐ 51 Alex Kellner	12.00	5.50
☐ 52 Joe Ginsberg	12.00	5.50
☐ 53 Don Lenhardt	12.00	5.50
☐ 54 Chico Carrasquel	12.00	5.50
☐ 55 Jim Delsing	12.00	5.50
☐ 56 Maurice McDermott	12.00	5.50
☐ 57 Hoyt Wilhelm	35.00	16.00
☐ 58 Pee Wee Reese	75.00	34.00
☐ 59 Bob Schultz	12.00	5.50
☐ 60 Fred Baczewski	12.00	5.50
☐ 61 Eddie Miksis	12.00	5.50
☐ 62 Enos Slaughter	40.00	18.00
☐ 63 Earl Torgeson	12.00	5.50
☐ 64 Eddie Mathews	60.00	27.00
☐ 65 Mickey Mantle	1300.00	575.00
☐ 66A Ted Williams	4600.00	2100.00
☐ 66B Jimmy Piersall	75.00	34.00
☐ 67 Carl Scheib	12.00	5.50
☐ 68 Bobby Avila	20.00	9.00
☐ 69 Clint Courtney	12.00	5.50
☐ 70 Willard Marshall	12.00	5.50
☐ 71 Ted Gray	12.00	5.50
☐ 72 Eddie Yost	20.00	9.00
☐ 73 Don Mueller	20.00	9.00
☐ 74 Jim Gilliam	30.00	13.50
☐ 75 Max Surkont	12.00	5.50
☐ 76 Joe Nuxhall	20.00	9.00
☐ 77 Bob Rush	12.00	5.50
☐ 78 Sal Yvars	12.00	5.50
☐ 79 Curt Simmons	20.00	9.00
☐ 80 Johnny Logan	12.00	5.50
☐ 81 Jerry Coleman	20.00	9.00
☐ 82 Billy Goodman	20.00	9.00
☐ 83 Ray Murray	12.00	5.50
☐ 84 Larry Doby	25.00	11.00
☐ 85 Jim Dyck	12.00	5.50
☐ 86 Harry Dorish	12.00	5.50
☐ 87 Don Lund	12.00	5.50
☐ 88 Tom Umphlett	12.00	5.50
☐ 89 Willie Mays	400.00	180.00
☐ 90 Roy Campanella	175.00	80.00
☐ 91 Cal Abrams	12.00	5.50
☐ 92 Ken Raffensberger	12.00	5.50
☐ 93 Bill Serena	12.00	5.50
☐ 94 Solly Hemus	12.00	5.50
☐ 95 Robin Roberts	50.00	22.00
☐ 96 Joe Adcock	20.00	9.00
☐ 97 Gil McDougald	20.00	9.00
☐ 98 Ellis Kinder	12.00	5.50
☐ 99 Pete Suder	12.00	5.50
☐ 100 Mike Garcia	20.00	9.00
☐ 101 Don Larsen	60.00	27.00
☐ 102 Billy Pierce	20.00	9.00
☐ 103 Steve Souchock	12.00	5.50
☐ 104 Frank Shea	12.00	5.50
☐ 105 Sal Maglie	20.00	9.00
☐ 106 Clem Labine	20.00	9.00
☐ 107 Paul LaPalme	12.00	5.50
☐ 108 Bobby Adams	12.00	5.50
☐ 109 Roy Smalley	12.00	5.50
☐ 110 Red Schoendienst	35.00	16.00
☐ 111 Murry Dickson	12.00	5.50
☐ 112 Andy Pafko	20.00	9.00
☐ 113 Allie Reynolds	20.00	9.00
☐ 114 Willard Nixon	12.00	5.50
☐ 115 Don Bollweg	12.00	5.50
☐ 116 Luke Easter	20.00	9.00
☐ 117 Dick Kryhoski	12.00	5.50
☐ 118 Bob Boyd	12.00	5.50
☐ 119 Fred Hatfield	12.00	5.50
☐ 120 Mel Hoderlein	12.00	5.50
☐ 121 Ray Katt	12.00	5.50
☐ 122 Carl Furillo	25.00	11.00
☐ 123 Toby Atwell	12.00	5.50
☐ 124 Gus Bell	20.00	9.00
☐ 125 Warren Hacker	12.00	5.50
☐ 126 Cliff Chambers	12.00	5.50
☐ 127 Del Ennis	20.00	9.00
☐ 128 Ebba St.Claire	12.00	5.50
☐ 129 Hank Bauer	20.00	9.00
☐ 130 Milt Bolling	12.00	5.50
☐ 131 Joe Astroth	12.00	5.50
☐ 132 Bob Feller	75.00	34.00
☐ 133 Duane Pillette	12.00	5.50
☐ 134 Luis Aloma	12.00	5.50
☐ 135 Johnny Pesky	20.00	9.00
☐ 136 Clyde Vollmer	12.00	5.50
☐ 137 Al Corwin	12.00	5.50
☐ 138 Gil Hodges	75.00	34.00
☐ 139 Preston Ward	12.00	5.50
☐ 140 Saul Rogovin	12.00	5.50
☐ 141 Joe Garagiola	30.00	13.50
☐ 142 Al Brazle	12.00	5.50
☐ 143 Willie Jones	12.00	5.50
☐ 144 Ernie Johnson	25.00	11.00
☐ 145 Billy Martin	75.00	34.00
☐ 146 Dick Gernert	12.00	5.50
☐ 147 Joe DeMaestri	12.00	5.50
☐ 148 Dale Mitchell	20.00	9.00
☐ 149 Bob Young	12.00	5.50
☐ 150 Cass Michaels	12.00	5.50
☐ 151 Pat Mullin	12.00	5.50
☐ 152 Mickey Vernon	20.00	9.00
☐ 153 Whitey Lockman	20.00	9.00
☐ 154 Don Newcombe	30.00	13.50
☐ 155 Frank Thomas	20.00	9.00
☐ 156 Rocky Bridges	12.00	5.50
☐ 157 Turk Lown	12.00	5.50
☐ 158 Stu Miller	20.00	9.00
☐ 159 Johnny Lindell	12.00	5.50
☐ 160 Danny O'Connell	12.00	5.50
☐ 161 Yogi Berra	175.00	80.00
☐ 162 Ted Lepcio	12.00	5.50
☐ 163A Dave Philley (No mention of trade on back)	20.00	9.00
☐ 163B Dave Philley (Traded to Cleveland)	36.00	16.00
☐ 164 Early Wynn	50.00	22.00
☐ 165 Johnny Groth	12.00	5.50
☐ 166 Sandy Consuegra	12.00	5.50
☐ 167 Billy Hoeft	12.00	5.50
☐ 168 Ed Fitzgerald	12.00	5.50
☐ 169 Larry Jansen	20.00	9.00
☐ 170 Duke Snider	125.00	55.00
☐ 171 Carlos Bernier	12.00	5.50
☐ 172 Andy Seminick	12.00	5.50
☐ 173 Dee Fondy	12.00	5.50
☐ 174 Pete Castiglione	12.00	5.50
☐ 175 Mel Clark	12.00	5.50
☐ 176 Vern Bickford	12.00	5.50
☐ 177 Whitey Ford	100.00	45.00
☐ 178 Del Wilber	12.00	5.50
☐ 179 Morrie Martin	12.00	5.50
☐ 180 Joe Tipton	12.00	5.50
☐ 181 Les Moss	12.00	5.50
☐ 182 Sherm Lollar	20.00	9.00
☐ 183 Matt Batts	12.00	5.50
☐ 184 Mickey Grasso	12.00	5.50
☐ 185 Daryl Spencer	12.00	5.50
☐ 186 Russ Meyer	12.00	5.50
☐ 187 Vern Law	20.00	9.00
☐ 188 Frank Smith	12.00	5.50
☐ 189 Randy Jackson	12.00	5.50
☐ 190 Joe Presko	12.00	5.50
☐ 191 Karl Drews	12.00	5.50
☐ 192 Lou Burdette	20.00	9.00
☐ 193 Eddie Robinson	12.00	5.50
☐ 194 Sid Hudson	12.00	5.50
☐ 195 Bob Cain	12.00	5.50
☐ 196 Bob Lemon	40.00	18.00
☐ 197 Lou Kretlow	12.00	5.50
☐ 198 Virgil Trucks	12.00	5.50
☐ 199 Steve Gromek	12.00	5.50
☐ 200 Conrado Marrero	12.00	5.50
☐ 201 Bobby Thomson	25.00	11.00
☐ 202 George Shuba	20.00	9.00
☐ 203 Vic Janowicz	20.00	9.00
☐ 204 Jack Collum	12.00	5.50
☐ 205 Hal Jeffcoat	12.00	5.50
☐ 206 Steve Bilko	12.00	5.50
☐ 207 Stan Lopata	12.00	5.50
☐ 208 Johnny Antonelli	20.00	9.00
☐ 209 Gene Woodling	12.00	5.50
☐ 210 Jimmy Piersall	20.00	9.00
☐ 211 Al Robertson	12.00	5.50

☐ 212 Owen Friend	12.00	5.50
☐ 213 Dick Littlefield	12.00	5.50
☐ 214 Ferris Fain	20.00	9.00
☐ 215 Johnny Bucha	12.00	5.50
☐ 216 Jerry Snyder	12.00	5.50
☐ 217 Hank Thompson	20.00	0.00
☐ 218 Preacher Roe	25.00	11.00
☐ 219 Hal Rice	12.00	5.50
☐ 220 Hobie Landrith	12.00	5.50
☐ 221 Frank Baumholtz	12.00	5.50
☐ 222 Memo Luna	12.00	5.50
☐ 223 Steve Ridzik	12.00	5.50
☐ 224 Bill Bruton	40.00	10.00

1955 Bowman

'he cards in this 320-card set measure approximately 2 /2" by 3 3/4". The Bowman set of 1955 is known as the TV set" because each player photograph is cleverly shown within a television set design. The set contains umpire ards, some transposed pictures (e.g., Johnsons and ollings), an incorrect spelling for Harvey Kuenn, and a raded line for Palica (all of which are noted in the hecklist below). Some three-card advertising strips exist, he backs of these panels contain advertising for Bowman roducts. Advertising panels seen include Nellie Fox/Carl urillo/Carl Erskine, Hank Aaron/Johnny Logan/Eddie Miksis, and a panel including Early Wynn and Pee Wee Reese. Cards were issued either in 9-card nickel packs or ne card penny packs. The notable Rookie Cards in this et are Elston Howard and Don Zimmer. Hall of Fame mpires pictured in the set are Al Barlick, Jocko Conlon nd Cal Hubbard.

	NRMT	VG-E
OMPLETE SET (320)	4600.00	2100.00
OMMON CARD (1-96)	12.00	5.50
OMMON CARD (97-224)	10.00	4.50
OMMON CARD (225-320)	15.00	6.75
OMMON UMPIRE 225-320	30.00	13.50
VRAPPER (1-CENT)	60.00	27.00
VRAPPER (5-CENT)	60.00	27.00

☐ 1 Hoyt Wilhelm	100.00	22.00
☐ 2 Alvin Dark	15.00	6.75
☐ 3 Joe Coleman	15.00	6.75
☐ 4 Eddie Waitkus	15.00	6.75
☐ 5 Jim Robertson	12.00	5.50
☐ 6 Pete Suder	12.00	5.50
☐ 7 Gene Baker	12.00	5.50
☐ 8 Warren Hacker	12.00	5.50
☐ 9 Gil McDougald	20.00	9.00
☐ 10 Phil Rizzuto	65.00	29.00
☐ 11 Bill Bruton	15.00	6.75
☐ 12 Andy Pafko	15.00	6.75
☐ 13 Clyde Vollmer	12.00	5.50
☐ 14 Gus Keriazakos	12.00	5.50
☐ 15 Frank Sullivan	12.00	5.50
☐ 16 Jimmy Piersall	15.00	6.75
☐ 17 Del Ennis	15.00	6.75
☐ 18 Stan Lopata	12.00	5.50
☐ 19 Bobby Avila	15.00	6.75
☐ 20 Al Smith	15.00	6.75
☐ 21 Don Hoak	12.00	5.50
☐ 22 Roy Campanella	125.00	55.00
☐ 23 Al Kaline	150.00	70.00
☐ 24 Al Aber	12.00	5.50
☐ 25 Minnie Minoso	25.00	11.00
☐ 26 Virgil Trucks	15.00	6.75
☐ 27 Preston Ward	12.00	5.50
☐ 28 Dick Cole	12.00	5.50
☐ 29 Red Schoendienst	30.00	13.50
☐ 30 Bill Sarni	12.00	5.50
☐ 31 Johnny Temple	15.00	6.75
☐ 32 Wally Post	15.00	6.75
☐ 33 Nellie Fox	45.00	20.00
☐ 34 Clint Courtney	12.00	5.50
☐ 35 Bill Tuttle	12.00	5.50
☐ 36 Wayne Belardi	12.00	5.50
☐ 37 Pee Wee Reese	65.00	29.00
☐ 38 Early Wynn	30.00	13.50
☐ 39 Bob Darnell	15.00	6.75
☐ 40 Vic Wertz	15.00	6.75
☐ 41 Mel Clark	12.00	5.50
☐ 42 Bob Greenwood	12.00	5.50
☐ 43 Bob Buhl	15.00	6.75
☐ 44 Danny O'Connell	12.00	5.50
☐ 45 Tom Umphlett	12.00	5.50
☐ 46 Mickey Vernon	15.00	6.75
☐ 47 Sammy White	12.00	5.50
☐ 48A Milt Bolling ERR	30.00	13.50
(Name on back is Frank Bolling)		
☐ 48B Milt Bolling COR	15.00	6.75
☐ 49 Jim Greengrass	12.00	5.50
☐ 50 Hobie Landrith	12.00	5.50
☐ 51 Elvin Tappe	12.00	5.50
☐ 52 Hal Rice	12.00	5.50
☐ 53 Alex Kellner	12.00	5.50
☐ 54 Don Bollweg	12.00	5.50
☐ 55 Cal Abrams	12.00	5.50
☐ 56 Billy Cox	15.00	6.75
☐ 57 Bob Friend	15.00	6.75
☐ 58 Frank Thomas	15.00	6.75
☐ 59 Whitey Ford	75.00	34.00
☐ 60 Enos Slaughter	30.00	13.50
☐ 61 Paul LaPalme	12.00	5.50
☐ 62 Royce Lint	12.00	5.50
☐ 63 Irv Noren	15.00	6.75
☐ 64 Curt Simmons	15.00	6.75
☐ 65 Don Zimmer	25.00	11.00
☐ 66 George Shuba	20.00	9.00
☐ 67 Don Larsen	20.00	9.00
☐ 68 Elston Howard	75.00	34.00
☐ 69 Billy Hunter	12.00	5.50
☐ 70 Lou Burdette	15.00	6.75
☐ 71 Dave Jolly	12.00	5.50
☐ 72 Chet Nichols	12.00	5.50
☐ 73 Eddie Yost	15.00	6.75
☐ 74 Jerry Snyder	12.00	5.50
☐ 75 Brooks Lawrence	12.00	5.50
☐ 76 Tom Poholsky	12.00	5.50
☐ 77 Jim McDonald	12.00	5.50
☐ 78 Gil Coan	12.00	5.50
☐ 79 Willie Miranda	12.00	5.50
☐ 80 Lou Limmer	12.00	5.50
☐ 81 Bobby Morgan	12.00	5.50
☐ 82 Lee Walls	12.00	5.50
☐ 83 Max Surkont	12.00	5.50
☐ 84 George Freese	12.00	5.50
☐ 85 Cass Michaels	12.00	5.50
☐ 86 Ted Gray	12.00	5.50
☐ 87 Randy Jackson	12.00	5.50
☐ 88 Steve Bilko	12.00	5.50
☐ 89 Lou Boudreau MG	30.00	13.50
☐ 90 Art Ditmar	12.00	5.50
☐ 91 Dick Marlowe	12.00	5.50
☐ 92 George Zuverink	12.00	5.50
☐ 93 Andy Seminick	12.00	5.50
☐ 94 Hank Thompson	15.00	6.75
☐ 95 Sal Maglie	15.00	6.75
☐ 96 Ray Narleski	12.00	5.50
☐ 97 Johnny Podres	25.00	11.00
☐ 98 Jim Gilliam	25.00	11.00
☐ 99 Jerry Coleman	18.00	8.00
☐ 100 Tom Morgan	10.00	4.50
☐ 101A Don Johnson ERR	15.00	6.75
(Photo actually Ernie Johnson)		
☐ 101B Don Johnson COR	30.00	13.50
☐ 102 Bobby Thomson	15.00	6.75
☐ 103 Eddie Mathews	50.00	22.00
☐ 104 Bob Porterfield	10.00	4.50
☐ 105 Johnny Schmitz	10.00	4.50
☐ 106 Del Rice	10.00	4.50
☐ 107 Solly Hemus	10.00	4.50
☐ 108 Lou Kretlow	10.00	4.50
☐ 109 Vern Stephens	15.00	6.75
☐ 110 Bob Miller	10.00	4.50
☐ 111 Steve Ridzik	10.00	4.50
☐ 112 Granny Hamner	10.00	4.50
☐ 113 Bob Hall	10.00	4.50
☐ 114 Vic Janowicz	15.00	6.75
☐ 115 Roger Bowman	10.00	4.50
☐ 116 Sandy Consuegra	10.00	4.50
☐ 117 Johnny Groth	10.00	4.50
☐ 118 Bobby Adams	10.00	4.50
☐ 119 Joe Astroth	10.00	4.50
☐ 120 Ed Burtschy	10.00	4.50
☐ 121 Rufus Crawford	10.00	4.50
☐ 122 Al Corwin	10.00	4.50
☐ 123 Marv Grissom	10.00	4.50
☐ 124 Johnny Antonelli	15.00	6.75
☐ 125 Paul Giel	15.00	6.75
☐ 126 Billy Goodman	15.00	6.75
☐ 127 Hank Majeski	10.00	4.50
☐ 128 Mike Garcia	15.00	6.75
☐ 129 Hal Naragon	10.00	4.50
☐ 130 Richie Ashburn	45.00	20.00
☐ 131 Willard Marshall	10.00	4.50
☐ 132A Harvey Kueen ERR	20.00	9.00
(Sic, Kuenn)		
☐ 132B Harvey Kuenn COR	30.00	13.50
☐ 133 Charles King	10.00	4.50
☐ 134 Bob Feller	70.00	32.00
☐ 135 Lloyd Merriman	10.00	4.50
☐ 136 Rocky Bridges	10.00	4.50
☐ 137 Bob Talbot	10.00	4.50
☐ 138 Davey Williams	20.00	9.00
☐ 139 Shantz Brothers	15.00	6.75
Wilmer Shantz		
Bobby Shantz		
☐ 140 Bobby Shantz	20.00	9.00
☐ 141 Wes Westrum	20.00	9.00
☐ 142 Rudy Regalado	10.00	4.50
☐ 143 Don Newcombe	25.00	11.00
☐ 144 Art Houtteman	10.00	4.50
☐ 145 Bob Nieman	10.00	4.50
☐ 146 Don Liddle	10.00	4.50
☐ 147 Sam Mele	10.00	4.50
☐ 148 Bob Chakales	10.00	4.50
☐ 149 Cloyd Boyer	10.00	4.50
☐ 150 Billy Klaus	10.00	4.50
☐ 151 Jim Brideweser	10.00	4.50
☐ 152 Johnny Klippstein	10.00	4.50
☐ 153 Eddie Robinson	10.00	4.50
☐ 154 Frank Lary	15.00	6.75
☐ 155 Gerry Staley	10.00	4.50
☐ 156 Jim Hughes	15.00	6.75
☐ 157A Ernie Johnson ERR	20.00	9.00
(Photo actually Don Johnson)		
☐ 157B Ernie Johnson COR	30.00	13.50
☐ 158 Gil Hodges	45.00	20.00
☐ 159 Harry Byrd	10.00	4.50
☐ 160 Bill Skowron	25.00	11.00
☐ 161 Matt Batts	10.00	4.50
☐ 162 Charlie Maxwell	10.00	4.50
☐ 163 Sid Gordon	15.00	6.75
☐ 164 Toby Atwell	10.00	4.50
☐ 165 Maurice McDermott	10.00	4.50
☐ 166 Jim Busby	10.00	4.50
☐ 167 Bob Grim	25.00	11.00
☐ 168 Yogi Berra	90.00	40.00
☐ 169 Carl Furillo	25.00	11.00
☐ 170 Carl Erskine	25.00	11.00
☐ 171 Robin Roberts	35.00	16.00
☐ 172 Willie Jones	10.00	4.50
☐ 173 Chico Carrasquel	10.00	4.50
☐ 174 Sherm Lollar	15.00	6.75
☐ 175 Wilmer Shantz	10.00	4.50
☐ 176 Joe DeMaestri	10.00	4.50
☐ 177 Willard Nixon	10.00	4.50
☐ 178 Tom Brewer	10.00	4.50
☐ 179 Hank Aaron	200.00	90.00
☐ 180 Johnny Logan	15.00	6.75
☐ 181 Eddie Miksis	10.00	4.50
☐ 182 Bob Rush	10.00	4.50
☐ 183 Ray Katt	10.00	4.50
☐ 184 Willie Mays	225.00	100.00
☐ 185 Vic Raschi	10.00	4.50
☐ 186 Alex Grammas	10.00	4.50
☐ 187 Fred Hatfield	10.00	4.50
☐ 188 Ned Garver	10.00	4.50
☐ 189 Jack Collum	10.00	4.50
☐ 190 Fred Baczewski	10.00	4.50
☐ 191 Bob Lemon	30.00	13.50
☐ 192 George Strickland	10.00	4.50
☐ 193 Howie Judson	10.00	4.50
☐ 194 Joe Nuxhall	15.00	6.75
☐ 195A Erv Palica	15.00	6.75
(Without trade)		
☐ 195B Erv Palica	30.00	13.50
(With trade)		
☐ 196 Russ Meyer	15.00	6.75
☐ 197 Ralph Kiner	30.00	13.50
☐ 198 Dave Pope	10.00	4.50
☐ 199 Vern Law	15.00	6.75
☐ 200 Dick Littlefield	10.00	4.50
☐ 201 Allie Reynolds	18.00	8.00
☐ 202 Mickey Mantle UER	900.00	400.00
Birthdate listed as 10/30/31		
Should be 10/20/31		
☐ 203 Steve Gromek	10.00	4.50
☐ 204A Frank Bolling ERR	20.00	9.00
(Name on back is Milt Bolling)		
☐ 204B Frank Bolling COR	20.00	9.00
☐ 205 Rip Repulski	10.00	4.50
☐ 206 Ralph Beard	10.00	4.50
☐ 207 Frank Shea	10.00	4.50
☐ 208 Ed Fitzgerald	10.00	4.50
☐ 209 Smoky Burgess	15.00	6.75
☐ 210 Earl Torgeson	10.00	4.50
☐ 211 Sonny Dixon	10.00	4.50
☐ 212 Jack Dittmer	10.00	4.50

☐ 213 George Kell 30.00 13.50
☐ 214 Billy Pierce 15.00 6.75
☐ 215 Bob Kuzava 10.00 4.50
☐ 216 Preacher Roe 15.00 6.75
☐ 217 Del Crandall 15.00 6.75
☐ 218 Joe Adcock 15.00 6.75
☐ 219 Whitey Lockman 15.00 6.75
☐ 220 Jim Hearn 10.00 4.50
☐ 221 Hector Brown 10.00 4.50
☐ 222 Russ Kemmerer 10.00 4.50
☐ 223 Hal Jeffcoat 10.00 4.50
☐ 224 Dee Fondy 10.00 4.50
☐ 225 Paul Richards MG 15.00 6.75
☐ 226 Bill McKinley UMP 30.00 13.50
☐ 227 Frank Baumholtz 15.00 6.75
☐ 228 John Phillips 15.00 6.75
☐ 229 Jim Brosnan 20.00 9.00
☐ 230 Al Brazle 15.00 6.75
☐ 231 Jim Konstanty 20.00 9.00
☐ 232 Birdie Tebbetts MG 22.00 10.00
☐ 233 Bill Serena 15.00 6.75
☐ 234 Dick Bartell CO 20.00 9.00
☐ 235 Joe Paparella UMP 30.00 13.50
☐ 236 Murry Dickson 15.00 6.75
☐ 237 Johnny Wyrostek 15.00 6.75
☐ 238 Eddie Stanky MG 20.00 9.00
☐ 239 Edwin Rommel UMP 40.00 18.00
☐ 240 Billy Loes 20.00 9.00
☐ 241 Johnny Pesky CO 20.00 9.00
☐ 242 Ernie Banks 350.00 160.00
☐ 243 Gus Bell 20.00 9.00
☐ 244 Duane Pillette 15.00 6.75
☐ 245 Bill Miller 15.00 6.75
☐ 246 Hank Bauer 25.00 11.00
☐ 247 Dutch Leonard CO 15.00 6.75
☐ 248 Harry Dorish 15.00 6.75
☐ 249 Billy Gardner 20.00 9.00
☐ 250 Larry Napp UMP 30.00 13.50
☐ 251 Stan Jok 15.00 6.75
☐ 252 Roy Smalley 15.00 6.75
☐ 253 Jim Wilson 15.00 6.75
☐ 254 Bennett Flowers 15.00 6.75
☐ 255 Pete Runnels 20.00 9.00
☐ 256 Owen Friend 15.00 6.75
☐ 257 Tom Alston 15.00 6.75
☐ 258 John Stevens UMP 30.00 13.50
☐ 259 Don Mossi 25.00 11.00
☐ 260 Edwin Hurley UMP 30.00 13.50
☐ 261 Walt Moryn 20.00 9.00
☐ 262 Jim Lemon 15.00 6.75
☐ 263 Eddie Joost 15.00 6.75
☐ 264 Bill Henry 15.00 6.75
☐ 265 Albert Barlick UMP 75.00 34.00
☐ 266 Mike Fornieles 15.00 6.75
☐ 267 Jim Honochick UMP 75.00 34.00
☐ 268 Roy Lee Hawes 15.00 6.75
☐ 269 Joe Amalfitano 22.00 10.00
☐ 270 Chico Fernandez 20.00 9.00
☐ 271 Bob Hooper 15.00 6.75
☐ 272 John Flaherty UMP 30.00 13.50
☐ 273 Bubba Church 15.00 6.75
☐ 274 Jim Delsing 15.00 6.75
☐ 275 William Grieve UMP 30.00 13.50
☐ 276 Ike Delock 15.00 6.75
☐ 277 Ed Runge UMP 30.00 13.50
☐ 278 Charlie Neal 35.00 16.00
☐ 279 Hank Soar UMP 40.00 18.00
☐ 280 Clyde McCullough 15.00 6.75
☐ 281 Charles Berry UMP 40.00 18.00
☐ 282 Phil Cavarretta 22.00 10.00
☐ 283 Nestor Chylak UMP 30.00 13.50
☐ 284 Bill Jackowski UMP 30.00 13.50
☐ 285 Walt Dropo 20.00 9.00
☐ 286 Frank Secory UMP 30.00 13.50
☐ 287 Ron Mrozinski 15.00 6.75
☐ 288 Dick Smith 15.00 6.75
☐ 289 Arthur Gore UMP 30.00 13.50
☐ 290 Hershell Freeman 15.00 6.75
☐ 291 Frank Dascoli UMP 30.00 13.50
☐ 292 Marv Blaylock 15.00 6.75
☐ 293 Thomas Gorman UMP 40.00 18.00
☐ 294 Wally Moses CO 15.00 6.75
☐ 295 Lee Ballanfant UMP 30.00 13.50
☐ 296 Bill Virdon 35.00 16.00
☐ 297 Dusty Boggess UMP 30.00 13.50
☐ 298 Charlie Grimm MG 22.00 10.00
☐ 299 Lon Warneke UMP 40.00 18.00
☐ 300 Tommy Byrne 20.00 9.00
☐ 301 William Engeln UMP 30.00 13.50
☐ 302 Frank Malzone 30.00 13.50
☐ 303 Jocko Conlan UMP 75.00 34.00
☐ 304 Harry Chiti 15.00 6.75
☐ 305 Frank Umont UMP 30.00 13.50
☐ 306 Bob Cerv 22.00 10.00
☐ 307 Babe Pinelli UMP 40.00 18.00
☐ 308 Al Lopez MG 50.00 22.00
☐ 309 Hal Dixon UMP 30.00 13.50
☐ 310 Ken Lehman 15.00 6.75
☐ 311 Lawrence Goetz UMP 30.00 13.50
☐ 312 Bill Wight 15.00 6.75
☐ 313 Augie Donatelli UMP 50.00 22.00
☐ 314 Dale Mitchell 22.00 10.00
☐ 315 Cal Hubbard UMP 75.00 34.00
☐ 316 Marion Fricano 15.00 6.75
☐ 317 William Summers UMP 20.00 9.00
☐ 318 Sid Hudson 15.00 6.75
☐ 319 Al Schroll 15.00 6.75
☐ 320 George Susce Jr. 45.00 9.00

1989 Bowman

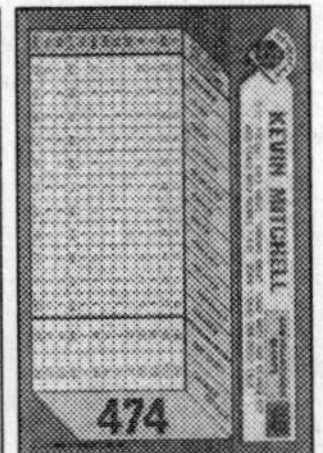

The 1989 Bowman set, produced by Topps, contains 484 slightly oversized cards (measuring 2 1/2" by 3 3/4"). The cards were released in midseason 1989 in wax, rack, cello and factory set formats. The fronts have white-bordered color photos with facsimile autographs and small Bowman logos. The backs feature charts detailing 1988 player performances vs. each team. The cards are ordered alphabetically according to teams in the AL and NL. Cards 258-261 form a father/son subset. Rookie Cards in this set include Andy Benes, Ken Griffey Jr., Tino Martinez, Charles Nagy, Gary Sheffield, John Smoltz and Robin Ventura.

	MINT	NRMT
COMPLETE SET (484)	12.00	5.50
COMPLETE FACT.SET (484)	12.00	5.50
COMMON CARD (1-484)	.05	.02

☐ 1 Oswald Peraza .05 .02
☐ 2 Brian Holton .05 .02
☐ 3 Jose Bautista .05 .02
☐ 4 Pete Harnisch .10 .05
☐ 5 Dave Schmidt .05 .02
☐ 6 Gregg Olson .10 .05
☐ 7 Jeff Ballard .05 .02
☐ 8 Bob Melvin .05 .02
☐ 9 Cal Ripken .75 .35
☐ 10 Randy Milligan .05 .02
☐ 11 Juan Bell .05 .02
☐ 12 Billy Ripken .05 .02
☐ 13 Jim Traber .05 .02
☐ 14 Pete Stanicek .05 .02
☐ 15 Steve Finley .25 .11
☐ 16 Larry Sheets .05 .02
☐ 17 Phil Bradley .05 .02
☐ 18 Brady Anderson .50 .23
☐ 19 Lee Smith .10 .05
☐ 20 Tom Fischer .05 .02
☐ 21 Mike Boddicker .05 .02
☐ 22 Rob Murphy .05 .02
☐ 23 Wes Gardner .05 .02
☐ 24 John Dopson .05 .02
☐ 25 Bob Stanley .05 .02
☐ 26 Roger Clemens .40 .18
☐ 27 Rich Gedman .05 .02
☐ 28 Marty Barrett .05 .02
☐ 29 Luis Rivera .05 .02
☐ 30 Jody Reed .05 .02
☐ 31 Nick Esasky .05 .02
☐ 32 Wade Boggs .20 .09
☐ 33 Jim Rice .10 .05
☐ 34 Mike Greenwell .05 .02
☐ 35 Dwight Evans .10 .05
☐ 36 Ellis Burks .10 .05
☐ 37 Chuck Finley .10 .05
☐ 38 Kirk McCaskill .05 .02
☐ 39 Jim Abbott .20 .09
☐ 40 Bryan Harvey .10 .05
☐ 41 Bert Blyleven .10 .05
☐ 42 Mike Witt .05 .02
☐ 43 Bob McClure .05 .02
☐ 44 Bill Schroeder .05 .02
☐ 45 Lance Parrish .05 .02
☐ 46 Dick Schofield .05 .02
☐ 47 Wally Joyner .10 .05
☐ 48 Jack Howell .05 .02
☐ 49 Johnny Ray .05 .02
☐ 50 Chili Davis .10 .05
☐ 51 Tony Armas .05 .02
☐ 52 Claudell Washington .05 .02
☐ 53 Brian Downing .05 .02
☐ 54 Devon White .10 .05
☐ 55 Bobby Thigpen .05 .02
☐ 56 Bill Long .05 .02
☐ 57 Jerry Reuss .05 .02
☐ 58 Shawn Hillegas .05 .02
☐ 59 Melido Perez .05 .02
☐ 60 Jeff Bittiger .05 .02
☐ 61 Jack McDowell .10 .05
☐ 62 Carlton Fisk .20 .09
☐ 63 Steve Lyons .05 .02
☐ 64 Ozzie Guillen .05 .02
☐ 65 Robin Ventura .40 .18
☐ 66 Fred Manrique .05 .02
☐ 67 Dan Pasqua .05 .02
☐ 68 Ivan Calderon .05 .02
☐ 69 Ron Kittle .05 .02
☐ 70 Daryl Boston .05 .02
☐ 71 Dave Gallagher .05 .02
☐ 72 Harold Baines .10 .05
☐ 73 Charles Nagy .25 .11
☐ 74 John Farrell .05 .02
☐ 75 Kevin Wickander .05 .02
☐ 76 Greg Swindell .05 .02
☐ 77 Mike Walker .05 .02
☐ 78 Doug Jones .05 .02
☐ 79 Rich Yett .05 .02
☐ 80 Tom Candiotti .05 .02
☐ 81 Jesse Orosco .05 .02
☐ 82 Bud Black .05 .02
☐ 83 Andy Allanson .05 .02
☐ 84 Pete O'Brien .05 .02
☐ 85 Jerry Browne .05 .02
☐ 86 Brook Jacoby .05 .02
☐ 87 Mark Lewis .20 .09
☐ 88 Luis Aguayo .05 .02
☐ 89 Cory Snyder .05 .02
☐ 90 Oddibe McDowell .05 .02
☐ 91 Joe Carter .20 .09
☐ 92 Frank Tanana .05 .02
☐ 93 Jack Morris .10 .05
☐ 94 Doyle Alexander .05 .02
☐ 95 Steve Searcy .05 .02
☐ 96 Randy Bockus .05 .02
☐ 97 Jeff M. Robinson .05 .02
☐ 98 Mike Henneman .05 .02
☐ 99 Paul Gibson .05 .02
☐ 100 Frank Williams .05 .02
☐ 101 Matt Nokes .05 .02
☐ 102 Rico Brogna UER .20 .09
(Misspelled Ricco on card back)
☐ 103 Lou Whitaker .10 .05
☐ 104 Al Pedrique .05 .02
☐ 105 Alan Trammell .10 .05
☐ 106 Chris Brown .05 .02
☐ 107 Pat Sheridan .05 .02
☐ 108 Chet Lemon .05 .02
☐ 109 Keith Moreland .05 .02
☐ 110 Mel Stottlemyre Jr. .05 .02
☐ 111 Bret Saberhagen .05 .02
☐ 112 Floyd Bannister .05 .02
☐ 113 Jeff Montgomery .10 .05
☐ 114 Steve Farr .05 .02
☐ 115 Tom Gordon UER .20 .09
(Front shows autograph of Don Gordon)
☐ 116 Charlie Leibrandt .05 .02
☐ 117 Mark Gubicza .05 .02
☐ 118 Mike Macfarlane .10 .05
☐ 119 Bob Boone .10 .05
☐ 120 Kurt Stillwell .05 .02
☐ 121 George Brett .40 .18
☐ 122 Frank White .10 .05
☐ 123 Kevin Seitzer .05 .02
☐ 124 Willie Wilson .05 .02
☐ 125 Pat Tabler .05 .02
☐ 126 Bo Jackson .20 .09
☐ 127 Hugh Walker .05 .02
☐ 128 Danny Tartabull .05 .02
☐ 129 Teddy Higuera .05 .02
☐ 130 Don August .05 .02
☐ 131 Juan Nieves .05 .02
☐ 132 Mike Birkbeck .05 .02
☐ 133 Dan Plesac .05 .02
☐ 134 Chris Bosio .05 .02
☐ 135 Bill Wegman .05 .02
☐ 136 Chuck Crim .05 .02
☐ 137 B.J. Surhoff .20 .09
☐ 138 Joey Meyer .05 .02
☐ 139 Dale Sveum .05 .02
☐ 140 Paul Molitor .20 .09
☐ 141 Jim Gantner .05 .02
☐ 142 Gary Sheffield .75 .35
☐ 143 Greg Brock .05 .02

144 Robin Yount	.20	.09
145 Glenn Braggs	.05	.02
146 Rob Deer	.05	.02
147 Fred Toliver	.05	.02
148 Jeff Reardon	.10	.05
149 Allan Anderson	.05	.02
150 Frank Viola	.05	.02
151 Shane Rawley	.05	.02
152 Juan Berenguer	.05	.02
153 Johnny Ard	.05	.02
154 Tim Laudner	.05	.02
155 Brian Harper	.05	.02
156 Al Newman	.05	.02
157 Kent Hrbek	.10	.05
158 Gary Gaetti	.05	.02
159 Wally Backman	.05	.02
160 Gene Larkin	.05	.02
161 Greg Gagne	.05	.02
162 Kirby Puckett	.40	.18
163 Dan Gladden	.05	.02
164 Randy Bush	.05	.02
165 Dave LaPoint	.05	.02
166 Andy Hawkins	.05	.02
167 Dave Righetti	.05	.02
168 Lance McCullers	.05	.02
169 Jimmy Jones	.05	.02
170 Al Leiter	.10	.05
171 John Candelaria	.05	.02
172 Don Slaught	.05	.02
173 Jamie Quirk	.05	.02
174 Rafael Santana	.05	.02
175 Mike Pagliarulo	.05	.02
176 Don Mattingly	.30	.14
177 Ken Phelps	.05	.02
178 Steve Sax	.05	.02
179 Dave Winfield	.20	.09
180 Stan Jefferson	.05	.02
181 Rickey Henderson	.20	.09
182 Bob Brower	.05	.02
183 Roberto Kelly	.10	.05
184 Curt Young	.05	.02
185 Gene Nelson	.05	.02
186 Bob Welch	.05	.02
187 Rick Honeycutt	.05	.02
188 Dave Stewart	.10	.05
189 Mike Moore	.05	.02
190 Dennis Eckersley	.20	.09
191 Eric Plunk	.05	.02
192 Storm Davis	.05	.02
193 Terry Steinbach	.10	.05
194 Ron Hassey	.05	.02
195 Stan Royer	.05	.02
196 Walt Weiss	.05	.02
197 Mark McGwire	.40	.18
198 Carney Lansford	.10	.05
199 Glenn Hubbard	.05	.02
200 Dave Henderson	.05	.02
201 Jose Canseco	.10	.05
202 Dave Parker	.10	.05
203 Scott Bankhead	.05	.02
204 Tom Niedenfuer	.05	.02
205 Mark Langston	.05	.02
206 Erik Hanson	.10	.05
207 Mike Jackson	.05	.02
208 Dave Valle	.05	.02
209 Scott Bradley	.05	.02
210 Harold Reynolds	.05	.02
211 Tino Martinez	1.00	.45
212 Rich Renteria	.05	.02
213 Rey Quinones	.05	.02
214 Jim Presley	.05	.02
215 Alvin Davis	.05	.02
216 Edgar Martinez	.20	.09
217 Darnell Coles	.05	.02
218 Jeffrey Leonard	.05	.02
219 Jay Buhner	.25	.11
220 Ken Griffey Jr.	6.00	2.70
221 Drew Hall	.05	.02
222 Bobby Witt	.05	.02
223 Jamie Moyer	.05	.02
224 Charlie Hough	.10	.05
225 Nolan Ryan	.75	.35
226 Jeff Russell	.05	.02
227 Jim Sundberg	.05	.02
228 Julio Franco	.10	.05
229 Buddy Bell	.10	.05
230 Scott Fletcher	.05	.02
231 Jeff Kunkel	.05	.02
232 Steve Buechele	.05	.02
233 Monty Fariss	.05	.02
234 Rick Leach	.05	.02
235 Ruben Sierra	.05	.02
236 Cecil Espy	.05	.02
237 Rafael Palmeiro	.20	.09
238 Pete Incaviglia	.10	.05
239 Dave Stieb	.05	.02
240 Jeff Musselman	.05	.02
241 Mike Flanagan	.05	.02
242 Todd Stottlemyre	.10	.05
243 Jimmy Key	.10	.05
244 Tony Castillo	.05	.02
245 Alex Sanchez	.05	.02
246 Tom Henke	.05	.02
247 John Cerutti	.05	.02
248 Ernie Whitt	.05	.02
249 Bob Brenly	.05	.02
250 Rance Mulliniks	.05	.02
251 Kelly Gruber	.05	.02
252 Ed Sprague	.25	.11
253 Fred McGriff	.20	.09
254 Tony Fernandez	.05	.02
255 Tom Lawless	.05	.02
256 George Bell	.05	.02
257 Jesse Barfield	.05	.02
258 Roberto Alomar Sandy Alomar	.20	.09
259 Ken Griffey Jr. Ken Griffey Sr.	1.00	.45
260 Cal Ripken Jr. Cal Ripken Sr.	.30	.14
261 Mel Stottlemyre Jr. Mel Stottlemyre Sr.	.05	.02
262 Zane Smith	.05	.02
263 Charlie Puleo	.05	.02
264 Derek Lilliquist	.05	.02
265 Paul Assenmacher	.05	.02
266 John Smoltz	.50	.23
267 Tom Glavine	.25	.11
268 Steve Avery	.10	.05
269 Pete Smith	.05	.02
270 Jody Davis	.05	.02
271 Bruce Benedict	.05	.02
272 Andres Thomas	.05	.02
273 Gerald Perry	.05	.02
274 Ron Gant	.20	.09
275 Darrell Evans	.10	.05
276 Dale Murphy	.20	.09
277 Dion James	.05	.02
278 Lonnie Smith	.05	.02
279 Geronimo Berroa	.10	.05
280 Steve Wilson	.05	.02
281 Rick Sutcliffe	.05	.02
282 Kevin Coffman	.05	.02
283 Mitch Williams	.05	.02
284 Greg Maddux	.75	.35
285 Paul Kilgus	.05	.02
286 Mike Harkey	.05	.02
287 Lloyd McClendon	.05	.02
288 Damon Berryhill	.05	.02
289 Ty Griffin	.05	.02
290 Ryne Sandberg	.25	.11
291 Mark Grace	.20	.09
292 Curt Wilkerson	.05	.02
293 Vance Law	.05	.02
294 Shawon Dunston	.05	.02
295 Jerome Walton	.10	.05
296 Mitch Webster	.05	.02
297 Dwight Smith	.10	.05
298 Andre Dawson	.20	.09
299 Jeff Sellers	.05	.02
300 Jose Rijo	.05	.02
301 John Franco	.10	.05
302 Rick Mahler	.05	.02
303 Ron Robinson	.05	.02
304 Danny Jackson	.05	.02
305 Rob Dibble	.10	.05
306 Tom Browning	.05	.02
307 Bo Diaz	.05	.02
308 Manny Trillo	.05	.02
309 Chris Sabo	.05	.02
310 Ron Oester	.05	.02
311 Barry Larkin	.20	.09
312 Todd Benzinger	.05	.02
313 Paul O'Neill	.10	.05
314 Kal Daniels	.05	.02
315 Joel Youngblood	.05	.02
316 Eric Davis	.10	.05
317 Dave Smith	.05	.02
318 Mark Portugal	.05	.02
319 Brian Meyer	.05	.02
320 Jim Deshaies	.05	.02
321 Juan Agosto	.05	.02
322 Mike Scott	.05	.02
323 Rick Rhoden	.05	.02
324 Jim Clancy	.05	.02
325 Larry Andersen	.05	.02
326 Alex Trevino	.05	.02
327 Alan Ashby	.05	.02
328 Craig Reynolds	.05	.02
329 Bill Doran	.05	.02
330 Rafael Ramirez	.05	.02
331 Glenn Davis	.05	.02
332 Willie Ansley	.05	.02
333 Gerald Young	.05	.02
334 Cameron Drew	.05	.02
335 Jay Howell	.05	.02
336 Tim Belcher	.05	.02
337 Fernando Valenzuela	.10	.05
338 Ricky Horton	.05	.02
339 Tim Leary	.05	.02
340 Bill Bene	.05	.02
341 Orel Hershiser	.10	.05
342 Mike Scioscia	.05	.02
343 Rick Dempsey	.05	.02
344 Willie Randolph	.10	.05
345 Alfredo Griffin	.05	.02
346 Eddie Murray	.20	.09
347 Mickey Hatcher	.05	.02
348 Mike Sharperson	.05	.02
349 John Shelby	.05	.02
350 Mike Marshall	.05	.02
351 Kirk Gibson	.10	.05
352 Mike Davis	.05	.02
353 Bryn Smith	.05	.02
354 Pascual Perez	.05	.02
355 Kevin Gross	.05	.02
356 Andy McGaffigan	.05	.02
357 Brian Holman	.05	.02
358 Dave Wainhouse	.05	.02
359 Dennis Martinez	.10	.05
360 Tim Burke	.05	.02
361 Nelson Santovenia	.05	.02
362 Tim Wallach	.05	.02
363 Spike Owen	.05	.02
364 Rex Hudler	.05	.02
365 Andres Galarraga	.20	.09
366 Otis Nixon	.05	.02
367 Hubie Brooks	.05	.02
368 Mike Aldrete	.05	.02
369 Tim Raines	.10	.05
370 Dave Martinez	.05	.02
371 Bob Ojeda	.05	.02
372 Ron Darling	.05	.02
373 Wally Whitehurst	.05	.02
374 Randy Myers	.10	.05
375 David Cone	.20	.09
376 Dwight Gooden	.10	.05
377 Sid Fernandez	.05	.02
378 Dave Proctor	.05	.02
379 Gary Carter	.20	.09
380 Keith Miller	.05	.02
381 Gregg Jefferies	.20	.09
382 Tim Teufel	.05	.02
383 Kevin Elster	.10	.05
384 Dave Magadan	.05	.02
385 Keith Hernandez	.10	.05
386 Mookie Wilson	.10	.05
387 Darryl Strawberry	.10	.05
388 Kevin McReynolds	.05	.02
389 Mark Carreon	.05	.02
390 Jeff Parrett	.05	.02
391 Mike Maddux	.05	.02
392 Don Carman	.05	.02
393 Bruce Ruffin	.05	.02
394 Ken Howell	.05	.02
395 Steve Bedrosian	.05	.02
396 Floyd Youmans	.05	.02
397 Larry McWilliams	.05	.02
398 Pat Combs	.05	.02
399 Steve Lake	.05	.02
400 Dickie Thon	.05	.02
401 Ricky Jordan	.05	.02
402 Mike Schmidt	.25	.11
403 Tom Herr	.05	.02
404 Chris James	.05	.02
405 Juan Samuel	.05	.02
406 Von Hayes	.05	.02
407 Ron Jones	.05	.02
408 Curt Ford	.05	.02
409 Bob Walk	.05	.02
410 Jeff D. Robinson	.05	.02
411 Jim Gott	.05	.02
412 Scott Medvin	.05	.02
413 John Smiley	.05	.02
414 Bob Kipper	.05	.02
415 Brian Fisher	.05	.02
416 Doug Drabek	.10	.05
417 Mike LaValliere	.05	.02
418 Ken Oberkfell	.05	.02
419 Sid Bream	.05	.02
420 Austin Manahan	.05	.02
421 Jose Lind	.05	.02
422 Bobby Bonilla	.10	.05
423 Glenn Wilson	.05	.02
424 Andy Van Slyke	.10	.05
425 Gary Redus	.05	.02
426 Barry Bonds	.40	.18
427 Don Heinkel	.05	.02
428 Ken Dayley	.05	.02
429 Todd Worrell	.05	.02
430 Brad DuVall	.05	.02

	MINT	NRMT
☐ 431 Jose DeLeon	.05	.02
☐ 432 Joe Magrane	.05	.02
☐ 433 John Ericks	.05	.02
☐ 434 Frank DiPino	.05	.02
☐ 435 Tony Pena	.05	.02
☐ 436 Ozzie Smith	.25	.11
☐ 437 Terry Pendleton	.10	.05
☐ 438 Jose Oquendo	.05	.02
☐ 439 Tim Jones	.05	.02
☐ 440 Pedro Guerrero	.10	.05
☐ 441 Milt Thompson	.05	.02
☐ 442 Willie McGee	.05	.02
☐ 443 Vince Coleman	.05	.02
☐ 444 Tom Brunansky	.05	.02
☐ 445 Walt Terrell	.05	.02
☐ 446 Eric Show	.05	.02
☐ 447 Mark Davis	.05	.02
☐ 448 Andy Benes	.20	.09
☐ 449 Ed Whitson	.05	.02
☐ 450 Dennis Rasmussen	.05	.02
☐ 451 Bruce Hurst	.05	.02
☐ 452 Pat Clements	.05	.02
☐ 453 Benito Santiago	.10	.05
☐ 454 Sandy Alomar Jr.	.50	.23
☐ 455 Garry Templeton	.05	.02
☐ 456 Jack Clark	.10	.05
☐ 457 Tim Flannery	.05	.02
☐ 458 Roberto Alomar	.30	.14
☐ 459 Carmelo Martinez	.05	.02
☐ 460 John Kruk	.10	.05
☐ 461 Tony Gwynn	.50	.23
☐ 462 Jerald Clark	.05	.02
☐ 463 Don Robinson	.05	.02
☐ 464 Craig Lefferts	.05	.02
☐ 465 Kelly Downs	.05	.02
☐ 466 Rick Reuschel	.05	.02
☐ 467 Scott Garrelts	.05	.02
☐ 468 Wil Tejada	.05	.02
☐ 469 Kirt Manwaring	.05	.02
☐ 470 Terry Kennedy	.05	.02
☐ 471 Jose Uribe	.05	.02
☐ 472 Royce Clayton	.20	.09
☐ 473 Robby Thompson	.05	.02
☐ 474 Kevin Mitchell	.10	.05
☐ 475 Ernie Riles	.05	.02
☐ 476 Will Clark	.20	.09
☐ 477 Donell Nixon	.05	.02
☐ 478 Candy Maldonado	.05	.02
☐ 479 Tracy Jones	.05	.02
☐ 480 Brett Butler	.10	.05
☐ 481 Checklist 1-121	.05	.02
☐ 482 Checklist 122-242	.05	.02
☐ 483 Checklist 243-363	.05	.02
☐ 484 Checklist 364-484	.05	.02

1989 Bowman Tiffany

This is a parallel to the regular 1989 Bowman set. This set was issued with a glossy front and clear back, thus joining other Bowman sets known in the Topps family as "Tiffany" sets. The set measure 2 1/2" by 3 3/4" and was issued in factory set form only. In addition to the 484 regular cards, the 11 Reprint inserts were also included in the factory set. Reportedly, only 6,000 factory sets were printed.

	MINT	NRMT
COMPLETE FACT.SET (495)	80.00	36.00
COMMON CARD (1-484)	.10	.05
COMMON REPRINT (R1-R11)	.30	.14
*STARS: 2X to 4X BASIC CARDS		

1989 Bowman Reprint Inserts

The 1989 Bowman Reprint Inserts set contains 11 cards measuring approximately 2 1/2" by 3 3/4". The fronts depict reproduced actual size "classic" Bowman cards, which are noted as reprints. The backs are devoted to a sweepstakes entry form. One of these reprint cards was included in each 1989 Bowman wax pack thus making these "reprints" quite easy to find. Since the cards are unnumbered, they are ordered below in alphabetical order by player's name and year within player.

	MINT	NRMT
COMPLETE SET (11)	2.00	.90
COMMON CARD (1-11)	.15	.07
☐ 1 Richie Ashburn '49	.15	.07
☐ 2 Yogi Berra '48	.25	.11
☐ 3 Whitey Ford '51	.25	.11
☐ 4 Gil Hodges '49	.15	.07
☐ 5 Mickey Mantle '51	.75	.35
☐ 6 Mickey Mantle '53	.50	.23
☐ 7 Willie Mays '51	.40	.18
☐ 8 Satchel Paige '49	.25	.11
☐ 9 Jackie Robinson '50	.40	.18
☐ 10 Duke Snider '49	.25	.11
☐ 11 Ted Williams '54	.40	.18

1990 Bowman

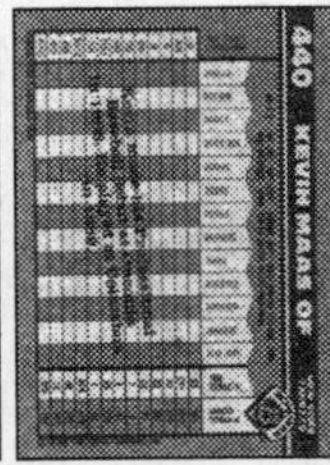

The 1990 Bowman set (produced by Topps) consists of 528 standard-size cards. The cards were issued in wax packs and factory sets. Each wax pack contained one of 11 different 1950's retro art cards. Unlike most sets, player selection focused primarily on rookies instead of proven major leaguers. The cards feature a white border with the player's photo inside and the Bowman logo on top. The card numbering is in team order with the teams themselves being ordered alphabetically within each league. Notable Rookie Cards include Moises Alou, Carlos Baerga, Travis Fryman, Juan Gonzalez, Marquis Grissom, Chuck Knoblauch, Ray Lankford, Ben McDonald, Sammy Sosa, Frank Thomas, Mo Vaughn, Larry Walker, and Bernie Williams.

	MINT	NRMT
COMPLETE SET (528)	10.00	4.50
COMP.FACT.SET (528)	10.00	4.50
COMMON CARD (1-528)	.05	.02
☐ 1 Tommy Greene	.05	.02
☐ 2 Tom Glavine	.20	.09
☐ 3 Andy Nezelek	.05	.02
☐ 4 Mike Stanton	.10	.05
☐ 5 Rick Luecken	.05	.02
☐ 6 Kent Mercker	.10	.05
☐ 7 Derek Lilliquist	.05	.02
☐ 8 Charlie Leibrandt	.05	.02
☐ 9 Steve Avery	.05	.02
☐ 10 John Smoltz	.20	.09
☐ 11 Mark Lemke	.05	.02
☐ 12 Lonnie Smith	.05	.02
☐ 13 Oddibe McDowell	.05	.02
☐ 14 Tyler Houston	.20	.09
☐ 15 Jeff Blauser	.10	.05
☐ 16 Ernie Whitt	.05	.02
☐ 17 Alexis Infante	.05	.02
☐ 18 Jim Presley	.05	.02
☐ 19 Dale Murphy	.20	.09
☐ 20 Nick Esasky	.05	.02
☐ 21 Rick Sutcliffe	.05	.02
☐ 22 Mike Bielecki	.05	.02
☐ 23 Steve Wilson	.05	.02
☐ 24 Kevin Blankenship	.05	.02
☐ 25 Mitch Williams	.05	.02
☐ 26 Dean Wilkins	.05	.02
☐ 27 Greg Maddux	.60	.25
☐ 28 Mike Harkey	.05	.02
☐ 29 Mark Grace	.20	.09
☐ 30 Ryne Sandberg	.25	.11
☐ 31 Greg Smith	.05	.02
☐ 32 Dwight Smith	.05	.02
☐ 33 Damon Berryhill	.05	.02
☐ 34 Earl Cunningham UER (Errant * by the word "in")	.05	.02
☐ 35 Jerome Walton	.05	.02
☐ 36 Lloyd McClendon	.05	.02
☐ 37 Ty Griffin	.05	.02
☐ 38 Shawon Dunston	.05	.02
☐ 39 Andre Dawson	.20	.09
☐ 40 Luis Salazar	.05	.02
☐ 41 Tim Layana	.05	.02
☐ 42 Rob Dibble	.05	.02
☐ 43 Tom Browning	.05	.02
☐ 44 Danny Jackson	.05	.02
☐ 45 Jose Rijo	.05	.02
☐ 46 Scott Scudder	.05	.02
☐ 47 Randy Myers UER (Career ERA .274, should be 2.74)	.10	.0
☐ 48 Brian Lane	.05	.0
☐ 49 Paul O'Neill	.10	.05
☐ 50 Barry Larkin	.20	.09
☐ 51 Reggie Jefferson	.20	.09
☐ 52 Jeff Branson	.05	.02
☐ 53 Chris Sabo	.05	.02
☐ 54 Joe Oliver	.05	.02
☐ 55 Todd Benzinger	.05	.02
☐ 56 Rolando Roomes	.05	.02
☐ 57 Hal Morris	.10	.05
☐ 58 Eric Davis	.10	.05
☐ 59 Scott Bryant	.05	.02
☐ 60 Ken Griffey Sr.	.05	.02
☐ 61 Darryl Kile	.40	.18
☐ 62 Dave Smith	.05	.02
☐ 63 Mark Portugal	.05	.02
☐ 64 Jeff Juden	.05	.02
☐ 65 Bill Gullickson	.05	.02
☐ 66 Danny Darwin	.05	.02
☐ 67 Larry Andersen	.05	.02
☐ 68 Jose Cano	.05	.02
☐ 69 Dan Schatzeder	.05	.02
☐ 70 Jim Deshaies	.05	.02
☐ 71 Mike Scott	.05	.02
☐ 72 Gerald Young	.05	.02
☐ 73 Ken Caminiti	.20	.09
☐ 74 Ken Oberkfell	.05	.02
☐ 75 Dave Rohde	.05	.02
☐ 76 Bill Doran	.05	.02
☐ 77 Andujar Cedeno	.05	.02
☐ 78 Craig Biggio	.20	.09
☐ 79 Karl Rhodes	.05	.02
☐ 80 Glenn Davis	.05	.02
☐ 81 Eric Anthony	.10	.05
☐ 82 John Wetteland	.20	.09
☐ 83 Jay Howell	.05	.02
☐ 84 Orel Hershiser	.10	.05
☐ 85 Tim Belcher	.05	.02
☐ 86 Kiki Jones	.05	.02
☐ 87 Mike Hartley	.05	.02
☐ 88 Ramon Martinez	.20	.09
☐ 89 Mike Scioscia	.05	.02
☐ 90 Willie Randolph	.10	.05
☐ 91 Juan Samuel	.05	.02
☐ 92 Jose Offerman	.20	.09
☐ 93 Dave Hansen	.05	.02
☐ 94 Jeff Hamilton	.05	.02
☐ 95 Alfredo Griffin	.05	.02
☐ 96 Tom Goodwin	.20	.09
☐ 97 Kirk Gibson	.10	.05
☐ 98 Jose Vizcaino	.20	.09
☐ 99 Kal Daniels	.05	.02
☐ 100 Hubie Brooks	.05	.02
☐ 101 Eddie Murray	.20	.09
☐ 102 Dennis Boyd	.05	.02
☐ 103 Tim Burke	.05	.02
☐ 104 Bill Sampen	.05	.02
☐ 105 Brett Gideon	.05	.02
☐ 106 Mark Gardner	.05	.02
☐ 107 Howard Farmer	.05	.02
☐ 108 Mel Rojas	.20	.09
☐ 109 Kevin Gross	.05	.02
☐ 110 Dave Schmidt	.05	.02
☐ 111 Denny Martinez	.10	.05
☐ 112 Jerry Goff	.05	.02
☐ 113 Andres Galarraga	.20	.09
☐ 114 Tim Wallach	.05	.02
☐ 115 Marquis Grissom	.40	.18
☐ 116 Spike Owen	.05	.02
☐ 117 Larry Walker	1.00	.45
☐ 118 Tim Raines	.10	.05
☐ 119 Delino DeShields	.20	.09
☐ 120 Tom Foley	.05	.02
☐ 121 Dave Martinez	.05	.02
☐ 122 Frank Viola UER (Career ERA .384 should be 3.84)	.05	.02
☐ 123 Julio Valera	.05	.02
☐ 124 Alejandro Pena	.05	.02
☐ 125 David Cone	.20	.09
☐ 126 Dwight Gooden	.10	.05
☐ 127 Kevin D. Brown	.05	.02
☐ 128 John Franco	.10	.05
☐ 129 Terry Bross	.05	.02
☐ 130 Blaine Beatty	.05	.02
☐ 131 Sid Fernandez	.05	.02
☐ 132 Mike Marshall	.05	.02
☐ 133 Howard Johnson	.05	.02
☐ 134 Jaime Roseboro	.05	.02
☐ 135 Alan Zinter	.05	.02

☐ 136 Keith Miller .05 .02
☐ 137 Kevin Elster .05 .02
☐ 138 Kevin McReynolds .05 .02
☐ 139 Barry Lyons .05 .02
☐ 140 Gregg Jefferies .10 .05
☐ 141 Darryl Strawberry .10 .05
☐ 142 Todd Hundley .40 .18
☐ 143 Scott Service .05 .02
☐ 144 Chuck Malone .05 .02
☐ 145 Steve Ontiveros .05 .02
☐ 146 Roger McDowell .05 .02
☐ 147 Ken Howell .05 .02
☐ 148 Pat Combs .05 .02
☐ 149 Jeff Parrett .05 .02
☐ 150 Chuck McElroy .05 .02
☐ 151 Jason Grimsley .05 .02
☐ 152 Len Dykstra .10 .05
☐ 153 Mickey Morandini .20 .09
☐ 154 John Kruk .10 .05
☐ 155 Dickie Thon .05 .02
☐ 156 Ricky Jordan .05 .02
☐ 157 Jeff Jackson .05 .02
☐ 158 Darren Daulton .10 .05
☐ 159 Tom Herr .05 .02
☐ 160 Von Hayes .05 .02
☐ 161 Dave Hollins .20 .09
☐ 162 Carmelo Martinez .05 .02
☐ 163 Bob Walk .05 .02
☐ 164 Doug Drabek .05 .02
☐ 165 Walt Terrell .05 .02
☐ 166 Bill Landrum .05 .02
☐ 167 Scott Ruskin .05 .02
☐ 168 Bob Patterson .05 .02
☐ 169 Bobby Bonilla .10 .05
☐ 170 Jose Lind .05 .02
☐ 171 Andy Van Slyke .10 .05
☐ 172 Mike LaValliere .05 .02
☐ 173 Willie Greene .20 .09
☐ 174 Jay Bell .10 .05
☐ 175 Sid Bream .05 .02
☐ 176 Tom Prince .05 .02
☐ 177 Wally Backman .05 .02
☐ 178 Moises Alou .50 .23
☐ 179 Steve Carter .05 .02
☐ 180 Gary Redus .05 .02
☐ 181 Barry Bonds .25 .11
☐ 182 Don Slaught UER .05 .02
(Card back shows headings for a pitcher)
☐ 183 Joe Magrane .05 .02
☐ 184 Bryn Smith .05 .02
☐ 185 Todd Worrell .05 .02
☐ 186 Jose DeLeon .05 .02
☐ 187 Frank DiPino .05 .02
☐ 188 John Tudor .05 .02
☐ 189 Howard Hilton .05 .02
☐ 190 John Ericks .05 .02
☐ 191 Ken Dayley .05 .02
☐ 192 Ray Lankford .50 .23
☐ 193 Todd Zeile .10 .05
☐ 194 Willie McGee .05 .02
☐ 195 Ozzie Smith .25 .11
☐ 196 Milt Thompson .05 .02
☐ 197 Terry Pendleton .10 .05
☐ 198 Vince Coleman .05 .02
☐ 199 Paul Coleman .05 .02
☐ 200 Jose Oquendo .05 .02
☐ 201 Pedro Guerrero .05 .02
☐ 202 Tom Brunansky .05 .02
☐ 203 Roger Smithberg .05 .02
☐ 204 Eddie Whitson .05 .02
☐ 205 Dennis Rasmussen .05 .02
☐ 206 Craig Lefferts .05 .02
☐ 207 Andy Benes .20 .09
☐ 208 Bruce Hurst .05 .02
☐ 209 Eric Show .05 .02
☐ 210 Rafael Valdez .05 .02
☐ 211 Joey Cora .20 .09
☐ 212 Thomas Howard .05 .02
☐ 213 Rob Nelson .05 .02
☐ 214 Jack Clark .10 .05
☐ 215 Garry Templeton .05 .02
☐ 216 Fred Lynn .05 .02
☐ 217 Tony Gwynn .50 .23
☐ 218 Benito Santiago .05 .02
☐ 219 Mike Pagliarulo .05 .02
☐ 220 Joe Carter .10 .05
☐ 221 Roberto Alomar .25 .11
☐ 222 Bip Roberts .05 .02
☐ 223 Rick Reuschel .05 .02
☐ 224 Russ Swan .05 .02
☐ 225 Eric Gunderson .05 .02
☐ 226 Steve Bedrosian .05 .02
☐ 227 Mike Remlinger .05 .02
☐ 228 Scott Garrelts .05 .02
☐ 229 Ernie Camacho .05 .02
☐ 230 Andres Santana .05 .02
☐ 231 Will Clark .20 .09
☐ 232 Kevin Mitchell .10 .05
☐ 233 Robby Thompson .05 .02
☐ 234 Bill Bathe .05 .02
☐ 235 Tony Perezchica .05 .02
☐ 236 Gary Carter .20 .09
☐ 237 Brett Butler .10 .05
☐ 238 Matt Williams .20 .09
☐ 239 Earnie Riles .05 .02
☐ 240 Kevin Bass .05 .02
☐ 241 Terry Kennedy .05 .02
☐ 242 Steve Hosey .05 .02
☐ 243 Ben McDonald .20 .09
☐ 244 Jeff Ballard .05 .02
☐ 245 Joe Price .05 .02
☐ 246 Curt Schilling .05 .02
☐ 247 Pete Harnisch .05 .02
☐ 248 Mark Williamson .05 .02
☐ 249 Gregg Olson .05 .02
☐ 250 Chris Myers .05 .02
☐ 251A David Segui ERR .20 .09
(Missing vital stats at top of card back under name)
☐ 251B David Segui COR .20 .09
☐ 252 Joe Orsulak .05 .02
☐ 253 Craig Worthington .05 .02
☐ 254 Mickey Tettleton .10 .05
☐ 255 Cal Ripken .75 .35
☐ 256 Billy Ripken .05 .02
☐ 257 Randy Milligan .05 .02
☐ 258 Brady Anderson .20 .09
☐ 259 Chris Hoiles UER .20 .09
Baltimore is spelled Balitmore
☐ 260 Mike Devereaux .05 .02
☐ 261 Phil Bradley .05 .02
☐ 262 Leo Gomez .05 .02
☐ 263 Lee Smith .20 .09
☐ 264 Mike Rochford .05 .02
☐ 265 Jeff Reardon .10 .05
☐ 266 Wes Gardner .05 .02
☐ 267 Mike Boddicker .05 .02
☐ 268 Roger Clemens .40 .18
☐ 269 Rob Murphy .05 .02
☐ 270 Mickey Pina .05 .02
☐ 271 Tony Pena .05 .02
☐ 272 Jody Reed .05 .02
☐ 273 Kevin Romine .05 .02
☐ 274 Mike Greenwell .05 .02
☐ 275 Maurice Vaughn 1.25 .55
☐ 276 Danny Heep .05 .02
☐ 277 Scott Cooper .05 .02
☐ 278 Greg Blosser .05 .02
☐ 279 Dwight Evans UER .10 .05
(* by "1990 Team Breakdown")
☐ 280 Ellis Burks .20 .09
☐ 281 Wade Boggs .20 .09
☐ 282 Marty Barrett .05 .02
☐ 283 Kirk McCaskill .05 .02
☐ 284 Mark Langston .05 .02
☐ 285 Bert Blyleven .10 .05
☐ 286 Mike Fetters .05 .02
☐ 287 Kyle Abbott .05 .02
☐ 288 Jim Abbott .10 .05
☐ 289 Chuck Finley .10 .05
☐ 290 Gary DiSarcina .20 .09
☐ 291 Dick Schofield .05 .02
☐ 292 Devon White .05 .02
☐ 293 Bobby Rose .05 .02
☐ 294 Brian Downing .05 .02
☐ 295 Lance Parrish .05 .02
☐ 296 Jack Howell .05 .02
☐ 297 Claudell Washington .05 .02
☐ 298 John Orton .05 .02
☐ 299 Wally Joyner .10 .05
☐ 300 Lee Stevens .05 .02
☐ 301 Chili Davis .15 .07
☐ 302 Johnny Ray .05 .02
☐ 303 Greg Hibbard .05 .02
☐ 304 Eric King .05 .02
☐ 305 Jack McDowell .05 .02
☐ 306 Bobby Thigpen .05 .02
☐ 307 Adam Peterson .05 .02
☐ 308 Scott Radinsky .05 .02
☐ 309 Wayne Edwards .05 .02
☐ 310 Melido Perez .05 .02
☐ 311 Robin Ventura .20 .09
☐ 312 Sammy Sosa .75 .35
☐ 313 Dan Pasqua .05 .02
☐ 314 Carlton Fisk .20 .09
☐ 315 Ozzie Guillen .05 .02
☐ 316 Ivan Calderon .05 .02
☐ 317 Daryl Boston .05 .02
☐ 318 Craig Grebeck .05 .02
☐ 319 Scott Fletcher .05 .02
☐ 320 Frank Thomas 4.00 1.80
☐ 321 Steve Lyons .05 .02
☐ 322 Carlos Martinez .05 .02
☐ 323 Joe Skalski .05 .02
☐ 324 Tom Candiotti .05 .02
☐ 325 Greg Swindell .05 .02
☐ 326 Steve Olin .10 .05
☐ 327 Kevin Wickander .05 .02
☐ 328 Doug Jones .05 .02
☐ 329 Jeff Shaw .05 .02
☐ 330 Kevin Bearse .05 .02
☐ 331 Dion James .05 .02
☐ 332 Jerry Browne .05 .02
☐ 333 Joey Belle .50 .23
☐ 334 Felix Fermin .05 .02
☐ 335 Candy Maldonado .05 .02
☐ 336 Cory Snyder .05 .02
☐ 337 Sandy Alomar Jr. .20 .09
☐ 338 Mark Lewis .10 .05
☐ 339 Carlos Baerga .25 .11
☐ 340 Chris James .05 .02
☐ 341 Brook Jacoby .05 .02
☐ 342 Keith Hernandez .10 .05
☐ 343 Frank Tanana .05 .02
☐ 344 Scott Aldred .05 .02
☐ 345 Mike Henneman .05 .02
☐ 346 Steve Wapnick .05 .02
☐ 347 Greg Gohr .05 .02
☐ 348 Eric Stone .05 .02
☐ 349 Brian DuBois .05 .02
☐ 350 Kevin Ritz .05 .02
☐ 351 Rico Brogna .20 .09
☐ 352 Mike Heath .05 .02
☐ 353 Alan Trammell .15 .07
☐ 354 Chet Lemon .05 .02
☐ 355 Dave Bergman .05 .02
☐ 356 Lou Whitaker .10 .05
☐ 357 Cecil Fielder UER .10 .05
(* by "1990 Team Breakdown")
☐ 358 Milt Cuyler .05 .02
☐ 359 Tony Phillips .05 .02
☐ 360 Travis Fryman .40 .18
☐ 361 Ed Romero .05 .02
☐ 362 Lloyd Moseby .05 .02
☐ 363 Mark Gubicza .05 .02
☐ 364 Bret Saberhagen .05 .02
☐ 365 Tom Gordon .05 .02
☐ 366 Steve Farr .05 .02
☐ 367 Kevin Appier .20 .09
☐ 368 Storm Davis .05 .02
☐ 369 Mark Davis .05 .02
☐ 370 Jeff Montgomery .10 .05
☐ 371 Frank White .10 .05
☐ 372 Brent Mayne .05 .02
☐ 373 Bob Boone .10 .05
☐ 374 Jim Eisenreich .10 .05
☐ 375 Danny Tartabull .05 .02
☐ 376 Kurt Stillwell .05 .02
☐ 377 Bill Pecota .05 .02
☐ 378 Bo Jackson .20 .09
☐ 379 Bob Hamelin .20 .09
☐ 380 Kevin Seitzer .05 .02
☐ 381 Rey Palacios .05 .02
☐ 382 George Brett .40 .18
☐ 383 Gerald Perry .05 .02
☐ 384 Teddy Higuera .05 .02
☐ 385 Tom Filer .05 .02
☐ 386 Dan Plesac .05 .02
☐ 387 Cal Eldred .20 .09
☐ 388 Jaime Navarro .05 .02
☐ 389 Chris Bosio .05 .02
☐ 390 Randy Veres .05 .02
☐ 391 Gary Sheffield .25 .11
☐ 392 George Canale .05 .02
☐ 393 B.J. Surhoff .10 .05
☐ 394 Tim McIntosh .05 .02
☐ 395 Greg Brock .05 .02
☐ 396 Greg Vaughn .10 .05
☐ 397 Darryl Hamilton .05 .02
☐ 398 Dave Parker .10 .05
☐ 399 Paul Molitor .20 .09
☐ 400 Jim Gantner .05 .02
☐ 401 Rob Deer .05 .02
☐ 402 Billy Spiers .05 .02
☐ 403 Glenn Braggs .05 .02
☐ 404 Robin Yount .20 .09
☐ 405 Rick Aguilera .10 .05
☐ 406 Johnny Ard .05 .02
☐ 407 Kevin Tapani .10 .05
☐ 408 Park Pittman .05 .02
☐ 409 Allan Anderson .05 .02
☐ 410 Juan Berenguer .05 .02
☐ 411 Willie Banks .05 .02
☐ 412 Rich Yett .05 .02
☐ 413 Dave West .05 .02
☐ 414 Greg Gagne .05 .02
☐ 415 Chuck Knoblauch .75 .35

☐ 416 Randy Bush	.05	.02
☐ 417 Gary Gaetti	.10	.05
☐ 418 Kent Hrbek	.10	.05
☐ 419 Al Newman	.05	.02
☐ 420 Danny Gladden	.05	.02
☐ 421 Paul Sorrento	.20	.09
☐ 422 Derek Parks	.05	.02
☐ 423 Scott Leius	.05	.02
☐ 424 Kirby Puckett	.40	.18
☐ 425 Willie Smith	.05	.02
☐ 426 Dave Righetti	.05	.02
☐ 427 Jeff D. Robinson	.05	.02
☐ 428 Alan Mills	.05	.02
☐ 429 Tim Leary	.05	.02
☐ 430 Pascual Perez	.05	.02
☐ 431 Alvaro Espinoza	.05	.02
☐ 432 Dave Winfield	.20	.09
☐ 433 Jesse Barfield	.05	.02
☐ 434 Randy Velarde	.05	.02
☐ 435 Rick Cerone	.05	.02
☐ 436 Steve Balboni	.05	.02
☐ 437 Mel Hall	.05	.02
☐ 438 Bob Geren	.05	.02
☐ 439 Bernie Williams	.75	.35
☐ 440 Kevin Maas	.05	.02
☐ 441 Mike Blowers	.20	.09
☐ 442 Steve Sax	.05	.02
☐ 443 Don Mattingly	.30	.14
☐ 444 Roberto Kelly	.05	.02
☐ 445 Mike Moore	.05	.02
☐ 446 Reggie Harris	.05	.02
☐ 447 Scott Sanderson	.05	.02
☐ 448 Dave Otto	.05	.02
☐ 449 Dave Stewart	.10	.05
☐ 450 Rick Honeycutt	.05	.02
☐ 451 Dennis Eckersley	.20	.09
☐ 452 Carney Lansford	.05	.02
☐ 453 Scott Hemond	.05	.02
☐ 454 Mark McGwire	.40	.18
☐ 455 Felix Jose	.05	.02
☐ 456 Terry Steinbach	.10	.05
☐ 457 Rickey Henderson	.20	.09
☐ 458 Dave Henderson	.05	.02
☐ 459 Mike Gallego	.05	.02
☐ 460 Jose Canseco	.20	.09
☐ 461 Walt Weiss	.05	.02
☐ 462 Ken Phelps	.05	.02
☐ 463 Darren Lewis	.05	.02
☐ 464 Ron Hassey	.05	.02
☐ 465 Roger Salkeld	.05	.02
☐ 466 Scott Bankhead	.05	.02
☐ 467 Keith Comstock	.05	.02
☐ 468 Randy Johnson	.30	.14
☐ 469 Erik Hanson	.05	.02
☐ 470 Mike Schooler	.05	.02
☐ 471 Gary Eave	.05	.02
☐ 472 Jeffrey Leonard	.05	.02
☐ 473 Dave Valle	.05	.02
☐ 474 Omar Vizquel	.20	.09
☐ 475 Pete O'Brien	.05	.02
☐ 476 Henry Cotto	.05	.02
☐ 477 Jay Buhner	.20	.09
☐ 478 Harold Reynolds	.05	.02
☐ 479 Alvin Davis	.05	.02
☐ 480 Darnell Coles	.05	.02
☐ 481 Ken Griffey Jr.	1.50	.70
☐ 482 Greg Briley	.05	.02
☐ 483 Scott Bradley	.05	.02
☐ 484 Tino Martinez	.20	.09
☐ 485 Jeff Russell	.05	.02
☐ 486 Nolan Ryan	.75	.35
☐ 487 Robb Nen	.20	.09
☐ 488 Kevin Brown	.20	.09
☐ 489 Brian Bohanon	.05	.02
☐ 490 Ruben Sierra	.05	.02
☐ 491 Pete Incaviglia	.05	.02
☐ 492 Juan Gonzalez	2.00	.90
☐ 493 Steve Buechele	.05	.02
☐ 494 Scott Coolbaugh	.05	.02
☐ 495 Geno Petralli	.05	.02
☐ 496 Rafael Palmeiro	.20	.09
☐ 497 Julio Franco	.10	.05
☐ 498 Gary Pettis	.05	.02
☐ 499 Donald Harris	.05	.02
☐ 500 Monty Fariss	.05	.02
☐ 501 Harold Baines	.10	.05
☐ 502 Cecil Espy	.05	.02
☐ 503 Jack Daugherty	.05	.02
☐ 504 Willie Blair	.05	.02
☐ 505 Dave Stieb	.05	.02
☐ 506 Tom Henke	.05	.02
☐ 507 John Cerutti	.05	.02
☐ 508 Paul Kilgus	.05	.02
☐ 509 Jimmy Key	.15	.07
☐ 510 John Olerud	.20	.09
☐ 511 Ed Sprague	.10	.05
☐ 512 Manuel Lee	.05	.02
☐ 513 Fred McGriff	.20	.09
☐ 514 Glenallen Hill	.05	.02
☐ 515 George Bell	.05	.02
☐ 516 Mookie Wilson	.05	.02
☐ 517 Luis Sojo	.05	.02
☐ 518 Nelson Liriano	.05	.02
☐ 519 Kelly Gruber	.05	.02
☐ 520 Greg Myers	.05	.02
☐ 521 Pat Borders	.05	.02
☐ 522 Junior Felix	.05	.02
☐ 523 Eddie Zosky	.05	.02
☐ 524 Tony Fernandez	.05	.02
☐ 525 Checklist 1-132 UER (No copyright mark on the back)	.05	.02
☐ 526 Checklist 133-264	.05	.02
☐ 527 Checklist 265-396	.05	.02
☐ 528 Checklist 397-528	.05	.02

1990 Bowman Tiffany

These 528 standard-size cards were issued as a factory set by Topps. These cards parallel the regular Bowman issue except they have glossy fronts and a very easy to read back. In addition to the 528 basic cards, the 11 insert art cards were also included in the factory set.

	MINT	NRMT
COMPLETE FACT.SET (539)	125.00	55.00
COMMON CARD (1-528)	.10	.05
COMMON ART CARD (A1-A11)	.20	.09

*STARS: 2.5X to 5X BASIC CARDS ....
*YOUNG STARS: 2.5X to 5X BASIC CARDS

1990 Bowman Inserts

These standard-size cards were included as an insert in every 1990 Bowman pack. This set, which consists of 11 superstars, depicts drawings by Craig Pursley with the backs being descriptions of the 1990 Bowman sweepstakes. We have checklisted the set alphabetically by player. All the cards in this set can be found with either one asterisk or two on the back.

	MINT	NRMT
COMPLETE SET (11)	2.00	.90
COMMON CARD (1-11)	.10	.05
☐ 1 Will Clark	.25	.11
☐ 2 Mark Davis	.10	.05
☐ 3 Dwight Gooden	.15	.07
☐ 4 Bo Jackson	.15	.07
☐ 5 Don Mattingly	.40	.18
☐ 6 Kevin Mitchell	.10	.05
☐ 7 Gregg Olson	.10	.05
☐ 8 Nolan Ryan	.75	.35
☐ 9 Bret Saberhagen	.10	.05
☐ 10 Jerome Walton	.10	.05
☐ 11 Robin Yount	.25	.11

1991 Bowman

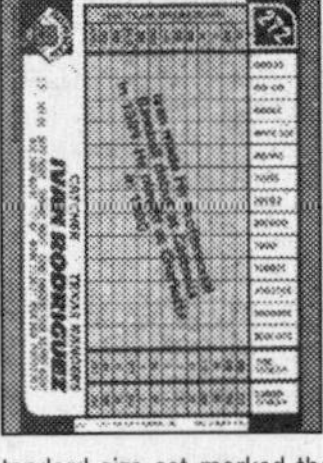

This single-series 704-card standard-size set marked the third straight year that Topps issued a set weighted towards prospects using the Bowman name. Cards were issued in wax packs and factory sets. The cards share a design very similar to the 1990 Bowman set with white borders enframing a color photo. The player name, however, is more prominent than in the previous year set. The cards are arranged in team order by division as follows: AL East, AL West, NL East, and NL West. Subsets include Rod Carew Tribute (1-5), Minor League MVP's (180-185/693-698), AL Silver Sluggers (367-375), NL Silver Sluggers (376-384) and checklists (699-704). Rookie Cards in this set include Jeff Bagwell, Jeff Conine, Carlos Garcia, Pat Hentgen, Chipper Jones, Eric Karros, Ryan Klesko, Kenny Lofton, Javier Lopez, Brian McRae, Raul Mondesi, Mike Mussina, Ivan "Pudge" Rodriguez, Tim Salmon, Reggie Sanders, Jim Thome, Rondell White and Mark Wohlers. There are two instances of misnumbering in the set; Ken Griffey (should be 255) and Ken Griffey Jr. are both numbered 246 and Donovan Osborne (should be 406) and Thomson/Branca share number 410.

	MINT	NRMT
COMPLETE SET (704)	30.00	13.50
COMP.FACT.SET (704)	30.00	13.50
COMMON CARD (1-704)	.05	.02
☐ 1 Rod Carew I	.20	.09
☐ 2 Rod Carew II	.20	.09
☐ 3 Rod Carew III	.20	.09
☐ 4 Rod Carew IV	.20	.09
☐ 5 Rod Carew V	.20	.09
☐ 6 Willie Fraser	.05	.02
☐ 7 John Olerud	.10	.05
☐ 8 William Suero	.05	.02
☐ 9 Roberto Alomar	.20	.09
☐ 10 Todd Stottlemyre	.10	.05
☐ 11 Joe Carter	.20	.09
☐ 12 Steve Karsay	.10	.05
☐ 13 Mark Whiten	.05	.02
☐ 14 Pat Borders	.05	.02
☐ 15 Mike Timlin	.05	.02
☐ 16 Tom Henke	.05	.02
☐ 17 Eddie Zosky	.05	.02
☐ 18 Kelly Gruber	.05	.02
☐ 19 Jimmy Key	.10	.05
☐ 20 Jerry Schunk	.05	.02
☐ 21 Manuel Lee	.05	.02
☐ 22 Dave Stieb	.05	.02
☐ 23 Pat Hentgen	.50	.23
☐ 24 Glenallen Hill	.05	.02
☐ 25 Rene Gonzales	.05	.02
☐ 26 Ed Sprague	.05	.02
☐ 27 Ken Dayley	.05	.02
☐ 28 Pat Tabler	.05	.02
☐ 29 Denis Boucher	.05	.02
☐ 30 Devon White	.05	.02
☐ 31 Dante Bichette	.10	.05
☐ 32 Paul Molitor	.10	.05
☐ 33 Greg Vaughn	.05	.02
☐ 34 Dan Plesac	.05	.02
☐ 35 Chris George	.05	.02
☐ 36 Tim McIntosh	.05	.02
☐ 37 Franklin Stubbs	.05	.02
☐ 38 Bo Dodson	.05	.02
☐ 39 Ron Robinson	.05	.02
☐ 40 Ed Nunez	.05	.02
☐ 41 Greg Brock	.05	.02
☐ 42 Jaime Navarro	.05	.02
☐ 43 Chris Bosio	.05	.02
☐ 44 B.J. Surhoff	.10	.05
☐ 45 Chris Johnson	.05	.02
☐ 46 Willie Randolph	.10	.05
☐ 47 Narciso Elvira	.05	.02
☐ 48 Jim Gantner	.05	.02
☐ 49 Kevin Brown	.10	.05
☐ 50 Julio Machado	.05	.02
☐ 51 Chuck Crim	.05	.02
☐ 52 Gary Sheffield	.20	.09
☐ 53 Angel Miranda	.05	.02
☐ 54 Teddy Higuera	.05	.02
☐ 55 Robin Yount	.20	.09
☐ 56 Cal Eldred	.05	.02
☐ 57 Sandy Alomar Jr.	.10	.05
☐ 58 Greg Swindell	.05	.02
☐ 59 Brook Jacoby	.05	.02
☐ 60 Efrain Valdez	.05	.02
☐ 61 Ever Magallanes	.05	.02
☐ 62 Tom Candiotti	.05	.02
☐ 63 Eric King	.05	.02
☐ 64 Alex Cole	.05	.02
☐ 65 Charles Nagy	.20	.09
☐ 66 Mitch Webster	.05	.02
☐ 67 Chris James	.05	.02
☐ 68 Jim Thome	1.50	.70
☐ 69 Carlos Baerga	.10	.05
☐ 70 Mark Lewis	.05	.02
☐ 71 Jerry Browne	.05	.02
☐ 72 Jesse Orosco	.05	.02
☐ 73 Mike Huff	.05	.02
☐ 74 Jose Escobar	.05	.02
☐ 75 Jeff Manto	.05	.02

76 Turner Ward .05 .02
77 Doug Jones .05 .02
78 Bruce Egloff .05 .02
79 Tim Costo .05 .02
80 Beau Allred .05 .02
81 Albert Belle .30 .14
82 John Farrell .05 .02
83 Glenn Davis .05 .02
84 Joe Orsulak .05 .02
85 Mark Williamson .05 .02
86 Ben McDonald .10 .05
87 Billy Ripken .05 .02
88 Leo Gomez UER .05 .02
Baltimore is spelled Baltimore
89 Bob Melvin .05 .02
90 Jeff M. Robinson .05 .02
91 Jose Mesa .10 .05
92 Gregg Olson .05 .02
93 Mike Devereaux .05 .02
94 Luis Mercedes .05 .02
95 Arthur Rhodes .10 .05
96 Juan Bell .05 .02
97 Mike Mussina 1.25 .55
98 Jeff Ballard .05 .02
99 Chris Hoiles .05 .02
100 Brady Anderson .20 .09
101 Bob Milacki .05 .02
102 David Segui .10 .05
103 Dwight Evans .10 .05
104 Cal Ripken .75 .35
105 Mike Linskey .05 .02
106 Jeff Tackett .05 .02
107 Jeff Reardon .10 .05
108 Dana Kiecker .05 .02
109 Ellis Burks .10 .05
110 Dave Owen .05 .02
111 Danny Darwin .05 .02
112 Mo Vaughn .40 .18
113 Jeff McNeely .05 .02
114 Tom Bolton .05 .02
115 Greg Blosser .05 .02
116 Mike Greenwell .05 .02
117 Phil Plantier .20 .09
118 Roger Clemens .40 .18
119 John Marzano .05 .02
120 Jody Reed .05 .02
121 Scott Taylor .05 .02
122 Jack Clark .10 .05
123 Derek Livernois .05 .02
124 Tony Pena .05 .02
125 Tom Brunansky .05 .02
126 Carlos Quintana .05 .02
127 Tim Naehring .10 .05
128 Matt Young .05 .02
129 Wade Boggs .20 .09
130 Kevin Morton .05 .02
131 Pete Incaviglia .05 .02
132 Rob Deer .05 .02
133 Bill Gullickson .05 .02
134 Rico Brogna .20 .09
135 Lloyd Moseby .05 .02
136 Cecil Fielder .10 .05
137 Tony Phillips .05 .02
138 Mark Leiter .05 .02
139 John Cerutti .05 .02
140 Mickey Tettleton .10 .05
141 Milt Cuyler .05 .02
142 Greg Gohr .05 .02
143 Tony Bernazard .05 .02
144 Dan Gakeler .05 .02
145 Travis Fryman .20 .09
146 Dan Petry .05 .02
147 Scott Aldred .05 .02
148 John DeSilva .05 .02
149 Rusty Meacham .05 .02
150 Lou Whitaker .10 .05
151 Dave Haas .05 .02
152 Luis de los Santos .05 .02
153 Ivan Cruz .05 .02
154 Alan Trammell .10 .05
155 Pat Kelly .05 .02
156 Carl Everett .15 .07
157 Greg Cadaret .05 .02
158 Kevin Maas .05 .02
159 Jeff Johnson .05 .02
160 Willie Smith .05 .02
161 Gerald Williams .05 .02
162 Mike Humphreys .05 .02
163 Alvaro Espinoza .05 .02
164 Matt Nokes .05 .02
165 Wade Taylor .05 .02
166 Roberto Kelly .05 .02
167 John Habyan .05 .02
168 Steve Farr .05 .02
169 Jesse Barfield .05 .02
170 Steve Sax .05 .02
171 Jim Leyritz .10 .05
172 Robert Eenhoorn .05 .02
173 Bernie Williams .25 .11
174 Scott Lusader .05 .02
175 Torey Lovullo .05 .02
176 Chuck Cary .05 .02
177 Scott Sanderson .05 .02
178 Don Mattingly .30 .14
179 Mel Hall .05 .02
180 Juan Gonzalez .75 .35
181 Hensley Meulens .05 .02
182 Jose Offerman .05 .02
183 Jeff Bagwell 2.50 1.10
184 Jeff Conine .25 .11
185 Henry Rodriguez .40 .18
186 Jimmie Reese CO .10 .05
187 Kyle Abbott .05 .02
188 Lance Parrish .05 .02
189 Rafael Montalvo .05 .02
190 Floyd Bannister .05 .02
191 Dick Schofield .05 .02
192 Scott Lewis .05 .02
193 Jeff D. Robinson .05 .02
194 Kent Anderson .05 .02
195 Wally Joyner .10 .05
196 Chuck Finley .10 .05
197 Luis Sojo .05 .02
198 Jeff Richardson .05 .02
199 Dave Parker .10 .05
200 Jim Abbott .10 .05
201 Junior Felix .05 .02
202 Mark Langston .05 .02
203 Tim Salmon 1.25 .55
204 Cliff Young .05 .02
205 Scott Bailes .05 .02
206 Bobby Rose .05 .02
207 Gary Gaetti .10 .05
208 Ruben Amaro .05 .02
209 Luis Polonia .05 .02
210 Dave Winfield .20 .09
211 Bryan Harvey .05 .02
212 Mike Moore .05 .02
213 Rickey Henderson .20 .09
214 Steve Chitren .05 .02
215 Bob Welch .05 .02
216 Terry Steinbach .10 .05
217 Earnest Riles .05 .02
218 Todd Van Poppel .05 .02
219 Mike Gallego .05 .02
220 Curt Young .05 .02
221 Todd Burns .05 .02
222 Vance Law .05 .02
223 Eric Show .05 .02
224 Don Peters .05 .02
225 Dave Stewart .10 .05
226 Dave Henderson .05 .02
227 Jose Canseco .20 .09
228 Walt Weiss .05 .02
229 Dann Howitt .05 .02
230 Willie Wilson .05 .02
231 Harold Baines .10 .05
232 Scott Hemond .05 .02
233 Joe Slusarski .05 .02
234 Mark McGwire .40 .18
235 Kirk Dressendorfer .05 .02
236 Craig Paquette .05 .02
237 Dennis Eckersley .10 .05
238 Dana Allison .05 .02
239 Scott Bradley .05 .02
240 Brian Holman .05 .02
241 Mike Schooler .05 .02
242 Rich DeLucia .05 .02
243 Edgar Martinez .20 .09
244 Henry Cotto .05 .02
245 Omar Vizquel .20 .09
246 Ken Griffey Jr. 1.50 .70
(See also 255)
247 Jay Buhner .20 .09
248 Bill Krueger .05 .02
249 Dave Fleming .05 .02
250 Patrick Lennon .05 .02
251 Dave Valle .05 .02
252 Harold Reynolds .05 .02
253 Randy Johnson .25 .11
254 Scott Bankhead .05 .02
255 Ken Griffey Sr. UER .05 .02
(Card number is 246)
256 Greg Briley .05 .02
257 Tino Martinez .20 .09
258 Alvin Davis .05 .02
259 Pete O'Brien .05 .02
260 Erik Hanson .05 .02
261 Bret Boone .10 .05
262 Roger Salkeld .05 .02
263 Dave Burba .05 .02
264 Kerry Woodson .05 .02
265 Julio Franco .10 .05
266 Dan Peltier .05 .02
267 Jeff Russell .05 .02
268 Steve Buechele .05 .02
269 Donald Harris .05 .02
270 Robb Nen .20 .09
271 Rich Gossage .10 .05
272 Ivan Rodriguez 1.50 .70
273 Jeff Huson .05 .02
274 Kevin Brown .10 .05
275 Dan Smith .05 .02
276 Gary Pettis .05 .02
277 Jack Daugherty .05 .02
278 Mike Jeffcoat .05 .02
279 Brad Arnsberg .05 .02
280 Nolan Ryan .75 .35
281 Eric McCray .05 .02
282 Scott Chiamparino .05 .02
283 Ruben Sierra .05 .02
284 Geno Petralli .05 .02
285 Monty Fariss .05 .02
286 Rafael Palmeiro .20 .09
287 Bobby Witt .05 .02
288 Dean Palmer UER .10 .05
Photo is Dan Peltier
289 Tony Scruggs .05 .02
290 Kenny Rogers .05 .02
291 Bret Saberhagen .05 .02
292 Brian McRae .25 .11
293 Storm Davis .05 .02
294 Danny Tartabull .05 .02
295 David Howard .05 .02
296 Mike Boddicker .05 .02
297 Joel Johnston .05 .02
298 Tim Spehr .05 .02
299 Hector Wagner .05 .02
300 George Brett .40 .18
301 Mike Macfarlane .05 .02
302 Kirk Gibson .10 .05
303 Harvey Pulliam .05 .02
304 Jim Eisenreich .10 .05
305 Kevin Seitzer .05 .02
306 Mark Davis .05 .02
307 Kurt Stillwell .05 .02
308 Jeff Montgomery .10 .05
309 Kevin Appier .20 .09
310 Bob Hamelin .05 .02
311 Tom Gordon .05 .02
312 Kerwin Moore .05 .02
313 Hugh Walker .05 .02
314 Terry Shumpert .05 .02
315 Warren Cromartie .05 .02
316 Gary Thurman .05 .02
317 Steve Bedrosian .05 .02
318 Danny Gladden .05 .02
319 Jack Morris .10 .05
320 Kirby Puckett .40 .18
321 Kent Hrbek .10 .05
322 Kevin Tapani .05 .02
323 Denny Neagle .60 .25
324 Rich Garces .05 .02
325 Larry Casian .05 .02
326 Shane Mack .05 .02
327 Allan Anderson .05 .02
328 Junior Ortiz .05 .02
329 Paul Abbott .05 .02
330 Chuck Knoblauch .25 .11
331 Chili Davis .10 .05
332 Todd Ritchie .05 .02
333 Brian Harper .05 .02
334 Rick Aguilera .10 .05
335 Scott Erickson .10 .05
336 Pedro Munoz .05 .02
337 Scott Leius .05 .02
338 Greg Gagne .05 .02
339 Mike Pagliarulo .05 .02
340 Terry Leach .05 .02
341 Willie Banks .05 .02
342 Bobby Thigpen .05 .02
343 Roberto Hernandez .20 .09
344 Melido Perez .05 .02
345 Carlton Fisk .20 .09
346 Norberto Martin .05 .02
347 Johnny Ruffin .05 .02
348 Jeff Carter .05 .02
349 Lance Johnson .10 .05
350 Sammy Sosa .25 .11
351 Alex Fernandez .20 .09
352 Jack McDowell .05 .02
353 Bob Wickman .05 .02
354 Wilson Alvarez .20 .09
355 Charlie Hough .05 .02
356 Ozzie Guillen .05 .02
357 Cory Snyder .05 .02
358 Robin Ventura .20 .09
359 Scott Fletcher .05 .02
360 Cesar Bernhardt .05 .02
361 Dan Pasqua .05 .02
362 Tim Raines .10 .05

☐ 363 Brian Drahman	.05	.02
☐ 364 Wayne Edwards	.05	.02
☐ 365 Scott Radinsky	.05	.02
☐ 366 Frank Thomas	1.50	.70
☐ 367 Cecil Fielder SLUG	.10	.05
☐ 368 Julio Franco SLUG	.05	.02
☐ 369 Kelly Gruber SLUG	.05	.02
☐ 370 Alan Trammell SLUG	.10	.05
☐ 371 Rickey Henderson SLUG	.20	.09
☐ 372 Jose Canseco SLUG	.20	.09
☐ 373 Ellis Burks SLUG	.10	.05
☐ 374 Lance Parrish SLUG	.05	.02
☐ 375 Dave Parker SLUG	.10	.05
☐ 376 Eddie Murray SLUG	.20	.09
☐ 377 Ryne Sandberg SLUG	.20	.09
☐ 378 Matt Williams SLUG	.20	.09
☐ 379 Barry Larkin SLUG	.20	.09
☐ 380 Barry Bonds SLUG	.20	.09
☐ 381 Bobby Bonilla SLUG	.10	.05
☐ 382 Darryl Strawberry SLUG	.10	.05
☐ 383 Benny Santiago SLUG	.05	.02
☐ 384 Don Robinson SLUG	.05	.02
☐ 385 Paul Coleman	.05	.02
☐ 386 Milt Thompson	.05	.02
☐ 387 Lee Smith	.20	.09
☐ 388 Ray Lankford	.20	.09
☐ 389 Tom Pagnozzi	.05	.02
☐ 390 Ken Hill	.10	.05
☐ 391 Jamie Moyer	.05	.02
☐ 392 Greg Carmona	.05	.02
☐ 393 John Ericks	.05	.02
☐ 394 Bob Tewksbury	.05	.02
☐ 395 Jose Oquendo	.05	.02
☐ 396 Rheal Cormier	.05	.02
☐ 397 Mike Milchin	.05	.02
☐ 398 Ozzie Smith	.25	.11
☐ 399 Aaron Holbert	.05	.02
☐ 400 Jose DeLeon	.05	.02
☐ 401 Felix Jose	.05	.02
☐ 402 Juan Agosto	.05	.02
☐ 403 Pedro Guerrero	.05	.02
☐ 404 Todd Zeile	.10	.05
☐ 405 Gerald Perry	.05	.02
☐ 406 Donovan Osborne UER Card number is 410	.05	.02
☐ 407 Bryn Smith	.05	.02
☐ 408 Bernard Gilkey	.10	.05
☐ 409 Rex Hudler	.05	.02
☐ 410 Thomson/Branca Shot Bobby Thomson Ralph Branca (See also 406)	.20	.09
☐ 411 Lance Dickson	.05	.02
☐ 412 Danny Jackson	.05	.02
☐ 413 Jerome Walton	.05	.02
☐ 414 Sean Cheetham	.05	.02
☐ 415 Joe Girardi	.10	.05
☐ 416 Ryne Sandberg	.25	.11
☐ 417 Mike Harkey	.05	.02
☐ 418 George Bell	.05	.02
☐ 419 Rick Wilkins	.05	.02
☐ 420 Earl Cunningham	.05	.02
☐ 421 Heathcliff Slocumb	.20	.09
☐ 422 Mike Bielecki	.05	.02
☐ 423 Jessie Hollins	.05	.02
☐ 424 Shawon Dunston	.05	.02
☐ 425 Dave Smith	.05	.02
☐ 426 Greg Maddux	.60	.25
☐ 427 Jose Vizcaino	.05	.02
☐ 428 Luis Salazar	.05	.02
☐ 429 Andre Dawson	.20	.09
☐ 430 Rick Sutcliffe	.05	.02
☐ 431 Paul Assenmacher	.05	.02
☐ 432 Erik Pappas	.05	.02
☐ 433 Mark Grace	.20	.09
☐ 434 Dennis Martinez	.10	.05
☐ 435 Marquis Grissom	.10	.05
☐ 436 Wil Cordero	.05	.02
☐ 437 Tim Wallach	.05	.02
☐ 438 Brian Barnes	.05	.02
☐ 439 Barry Jones	.05	.02
☐ 440 Ivan Calderon	.05	.02
☐ 441 Stan Spencer	.05	.02
☐ 442 Larry Walker	.30	.14
☐ 443 Chris Haney	.05	.02
☐ 444 Hector Rivera	.05	.02
☐ 445 Delino DeShields	.05	.02
☐ 446 Andres Galarraga	.20	.09
☐ 447 Gilberto Reyes	.05	.02
☐ 448 Willie Greene	.10	.05
☐ 449 Greg Colbrunn	.05	.02
☐ 450 Rondell White	.40	.18
☐ 451 Steve Frey	.05	.02
☐ 452 Shane Andrews	.05	.02
☐ 453 Mike Fitzgerald	.05	.02
☐ 454 Spike Owen	.05	.02
☐ 455 Dave Martinez	.05	.02

☐ 456 Dennis Boyd	.05	.02
☐ 457 Eric Bullock	.05	.02
☐ 458 Reid Cornelius	.05	.02
☐ 459 Chris Nabholz	.05	.02
☐ 460 David Cone	.10	.05
☐ 461 Hubie Brooks	.05	.02
☐ 462 Sid Fernandez	.05	.02
☐ 463 Doug Simons	.05	.02
☐ 464 Howard Johnson	.05	.02
☐ 465 Chris Donnels	.05	.02
☐ 466 Anthony Young	.05	.02
☐ 467 Todd Hundley	.20	.09
☐ 468 Rick Cerone	.05	.02
☐ 469 Kevin Elster	.05	.02
☐ 470 Wally Whitehurst	.05	.02
☐ 471 Vince Coleman	.05	.02
☐ 472 Dwight Gooden	.10	.05
☐ 473 Charlie O'Brien	.05	.02
☐ 474 Jeromy Burnitz	.20	.09
☐ 475 John Franco	.05	.02
☐ 476 Daryl Boston	.05	.02
☐ 477 Frank Viola	.05	.02
☐ 478 D.J. Dozier	.05	.02
☐ 479 Kevin McReynolds	.05	.02
☐ 480 Tom Herr	.05	.02
☐ 481 Gregg Jefferies	.10	.05
☐ 482 Pete Schourek	.10	.05
☐ 483 Ron Darling	.05	.02
☐ 484 Dave Magadan	.05	.02
☐ 485 Andy Ashby	.20	.09
☐ 486 Dale Murphy	.20	.09
☐ 487 Von Hayes	.05	.02
☐ 488 Kim Batiste	.05	.02
☐ 489 Tony Longmire	.05	.02
☐ 490 Wally Backman	.05	.02
☐ 491 Jeff Jackson	.05	.02
☐ 492 Mickey Morandini	.05	.02
☐ 493 Darrel Akerfelds	.05	.02
☐ 494 Ricky Jordan	.05	.02
☐ 495 Randy Ready	.05	.02
☐ 496 Darrin Fletcher	.05	.02
☐ 497 Chuck Malone	.05	.02
☐ 498 Pat Combs	.05	.02
☐ 499 Dickie Thon	.05	.02
☐ 500 Roger McDowell	.05	.02
☐ 501 Len Dykstra	.10	.05
☐ 502 Joe Boever	.05	.02
☐ 503 John Kruk	.10	.05
☐ 504 Terry Mulholland	.05	.02
☐ 505 Wes Chamberlain	.05	.02
☐ 506 Mike Lieberthal	.15	.07
☐ 507 Darren Daulton	.10	.05
☐ 508 Charlie Hayes	.05	.02
☐ 509 John Smiley	.05	.02
☐ 510 Gary Varsho	.05	.02
☐ 511 Curt Wilkerson	.05	.02
☐ 512 Orlando Merced	.10	.05
☐ 513 Barry Bonds	.25	.11
☐ 514 Mike LaValliere	.05	.02
☐ 515 Doug Drabek	.05	.02
☐ 516 Gary Redus	.05	.02
☐ 517 William Pennyfeather	.05	.02
☐ 518 Randy Tomlin	.05	.02
☐ 519 Mike Zimmerman	.05	.02
☐ 520 Jeff King	.10	.05
☐ 521 Kurt Miller	.05	.02
☐ 522 Jay Bell	.10	.05
☐ 523 Bill Landrum	.05	.02
☐ 524 Zane Smith	.05	.02
☐ 525 Bobby Bonilla	.10	.05
☐ 526 Bob Walk	.05	.02
☐ 527 Austin Manahan	.05	.02
☐ 528 Joe Ausanio	.05	.02
☐ 529 Andy Van Slyke	.10	.05
☐ 530 Jose Lind	.05	.02
☐ 531 Carlos Garcia	.05	.02
☐ 532 Don Slaught	.05	.02
☐ 533 Gen.Colin Powell	.75	.35
☐ 534 Frank Bolick	.05	.02
☐ 535 Gary Scott	.05	.02
☐ 536 Nikco Riesgo	.05	.02
☐ 537 Reggie Sanders	.25	.11
☐ 538 Tim Howard	.05	.02
☐ 539 Ryan Bowen	.05	.02
☐ 540 Eric Anthony	.05	.02
☐ 541 Jim Deshaies	.05	.02
☐ 542 Tom Nevers	.05	.02
☐ 543 Ken Caminiti	.20	.09
☐ 544 Karl Rhodes	.05	.02
☐ 545 Xavier Hernandez	.05	.02
☐ 546 Mike Scott	.05	.02
☐ 547 Jeff Juden	.05	.02
☐ 548 Darryl Kile	.20	.09
☐ 549 Willie Ansley	.05	.02
☐ 550 Luis Gonzalez	.10	.05
☐ 551 Mike Simms	.05	.02
☐ 552 Mark Portugal	.05	.02

☐ 553 Jimmy Jones	.05	.02
☐ 554 Jim Clancy	.05	.02
☐ 555 Pete Harnisch	.05	.02
☐ 556 Craig Biggio	.20	.09
☐ 557 Eric Yelding	.05	.02
☐ 558 Dave Rohde	.05	.02
☐ 559 Casey Candaele	.05	.02
☐ 560 Curt Schilling	.20	.09
☐ 561 Steve Finley	.10	.05
☐ 562 Javier Ortiz	.05	.02
☐ 563 Andujar Cedeno	.05	.02
☐ 564 Rafael Ramirez	.05	.02
☐ 565 Kenny Lofton	1.50	.70
☐ 566 Steve Avery	.10	.05
☐ 567 Lonnie Smith	.05	.02
☐ 568 Kent Mercker	.05	.02
☐ 569 Chipper Jones	4.00	1.80
☐ 570 Terry Pendleton	.10	.05
☐ 571 Otis Nixon	.05	.02
☐ 572 Juan Berenguer	.05	.02
☐ 573 Charlie Leibrandt	.05	.02
☐ 574 David Justice	.25	.11
☐ 575 Keith Mitchell	.05	.02
☐ 576 Tom Glavine	.20	.09
☐ 577 Greg Olson	.05	.02
☐ 578 Rafael Belliard	.05	.02
☐ 579 Ben Rivera	.05	.02
☐ 580 John Smoltz	.20	.09
☐ 581 Tyler Houston	.05	.02
☐ 582 Mark Wohlers	.15	.07
☐ 583 Ron Gant	.10	.05
☐ 584 Ramon Caraballo	.05	.02
☐ 585 Sid Bream	.05	.02
☐ 586 Jeff Treadway	.05	.02
☐ 587 Javier Lopez	.75	.35
☐ 588 Deion Sanders	.20	.09
☐ 589 Mike Heath	.05	.02
☐ 590 Ryan Klesko	1.00	.45
☐ 591 Bob Ojeda	.05	.02
☐ 592 Alfredo Griffin	.05	.02
☐ 593 Raul Mondesi	1.00	.45
☐ 594 Greg Smith	.05	.02
☐ 595 Orel Hershiser	.10	.05
☐ 596 Juan Samuel	.05	.02
☐ 597 Brett Butler	.10	.05
☐ 598 Gary Carter	.20	.09
☐ 599 Stan Javier	.05	.02
☐ 600 Kal Daniels	.05	.02
☐ 601 Jamie McAndrew	.05	.02
☐ 602 Mike Sharperson	.05	.02
☐ 603 Jay Howell	.05	.02
☐ 604 Eric Karros	.50	.23
☐ 605 Tim Belcher	.05	.02
☐ 606 Dan Opperman	.05	.02
☐ 607 Lenny Harris	.05	.02
☐ 608 Tom Goodwin	.10	.05
☐ 609 Darryl Strawberry	.10	.05
☐ 610 Ramon Martinez	.10	.05
☐ 611 Kevin Gross	.05	.02
☐ 612 Zakary Shinall	.05	.02
☐ 613 Mike Scioscia	.05	.02
☐ 614 Eddie Murray	.20	.09
☐ 615 Ronnie Walden	.05	.02
☐ 616 Will Clark	.20	.09
☐ 617 Adam Hyzdu	.05	.02
☐ 618 Matt Williams	.20	.09
☐ 619 Don Robinson	.05	.02
☐ 620 Jeff Brantley	.05	.02
☐ 621 Greg Litton	.05	.02
☐ 622 Steve Decker	.05	.02
☐ 623 Robby Thompson	.05	.02
☐ 624 Mark Leonard	.05	.02
☐ 625 Kevin Bass	.05	.02
☐ 626 Scott Garrelts	.05	.02
☐ 627 Jose Uribe	.05	.02
☐ 628 Eric Gunderson	.05	.02
☐ 629 Steve Hosey	.05	.02
☐ 630 Trevor Wilson	.05	.02
☐ 631 Terry Kennedy	.05	.02
☐ 632 Dave Righetti	.05	.02
☐ 633 Kelly Downs	.05	.02
☐ 634 Johnny Ard	.05	.02
☐ 635 Eric Christopherson	.05	.02
☐ 636 Kevin Mitchell	.10	.05
☐ 637 John Burkett	.10	.05
☐ 638 Kevin Rogers	.05	.02
☐ 639 Bud Black	.05	.02
☐ 640 Willie McGee	.05	.02
☐ 641 Royce Clayton	.10	.05
☐ 642 Tony Fernandez	.05	.02
☐ 643 Ricky Bones	.05	.02
☐ 644 Thomas Howard	.05	.02
☐ 645 Dave Staton	.05	.02
☐ 646 Jim Presley	.05	.02
☐ 647 Tony Gwynn	.50	.23
☐ 648 Marty Barrett	.05	.02
☐ 649 Scott Coolbaugh	.05	.02

☐ 650 Craig Lefferts	.05	.02
☐ 651 Eddie Whitson	.05	.02
☐ 652 Oscar Azocar	.05	.02
☐ 653 Wes Gardner	.05	.02
☐ 654 Bip Roberts	.05	.02
☐ 655 Robbie Beckett	.05	.02
☐ 656 Benito Santiago	.05	.02
☐ 657 Greg W.Harris	.05	.02
☐ 658 Jerald Clark	.05	.02
☐ 659 Fred McGriff	.20	.09
☐ 660 Larry Andersen	.05	.02
☐ 661 Bruce Hurst	.05	.02
☐ 662 Steve Martin UER Card said he pitched at Waterloo He's an outfielder	.05	.02
☐ 663 Rafael Valdez	.05	.02
☐ 664 Paul Faries	.05	.02
☐ 665 Andy Benes	.10	.05
☐ 666 Randy Myers	.10	.05
☐ 667 Rob Dibble	.05	.02
☐ 668 Glenn Sutko	.05	.02
☐ 669 Glenn Braggs	.05	.02
☐ 670 Billy Hatcher	.05	.02
☐ 671 Joe Oliver	.05	.02
☐ 672 Freddy Benavides	.05	.02
☐ 673 Barry Larkin	.20	.09
☐ 674 Chris Sabo	.05	.02
☐ 675 Mariano Duncan	.05	.02
☐ 676 Chris Jones	.05	.02
☐ 677 Gino Minutelli	.05	.02
☐ 678 Reggie Jefferson	.20	.09
☐ 679 Jack Armstrong	.05	.02
☐ 680 Chris Hammond	.05	.02
☐ 681 Jose Rijo	.05	.02
☐ 682 Bill Doran	.05	.02
☐ 683 Terry Lee	.05	.02
☐ 684 Tom Browning	.05	.02
☐ 685 Paul O'Neill	.10	.05
☐ 686 Eric Davis	.10	.05
☐ 687 Dan Wilson	.25	.11
☐ 688 Ted Power	.05	.02
☐ 689 Tim Layana	.05	.02
☐ 690 Norm Charlton	.05	.02
☐ 691 Hal Morris	.05	.02
☐ 692 Rickey Henderson	.20	.09
☐ 693 Sam Militello	.05	.02
☐ 694 Matt Mieske	.20	.09
☐ 695 Paul Russo	.05	.02
☐ 696 Domingo Mota	.05	.02
☐ 697 Todd Guggiana	.05	.02
☐ 698 Marc Newfield	.15	.07
☐ 699 Checklist 1-122	.05	.02
☐ 700 Checklist 123-244	.05	.02
☐ 701 Checklist 245-366	.05	.02
☐ 702 Checklist 367-471	.05	.02
☐ 703 Checklist 472-593	.05	.02
☐ 704 Checklist 594-704	.05	.02

1992 Bowman

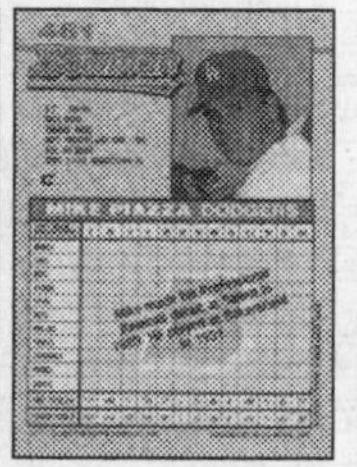

This 705-card standard-size set was issued in one comprehensive series. Unlike the previous Bowman issues, the 1992 set was radically upgraded to slick stock with gold foil subset cards in an attempt to reposition the brand as a premium level product. It initially stumbled out of the gate, but it's superior selection of prospects enabled it to eventually gain acceptance in the hobby and now stands as one of the more important issues of the 1990's. Cards were distributed in plastic wrap packs, retail jumbo packs and special 80-card retail carton packs. Card fronts feature posed and action color player photos on a UV-coated white card face. A gradated orange bar accented with black diagonal stripes carries the player's name at the bottom right corner. Interspersed throughout the set are 45 special cards with an identical front design except for a textured gold-foil border. The foil cards were inserted one per wax pack and two per jumbo (23 regular cards) pack. These foil cards feature past and present Team USA players and minor league POY Award winners. Each foil card has an extremely slight variation in that the photos are cropped differently. There is no additional value to either version. Some of the regular and special cards picture players in civilian clothing who are still in the farm system. Rookie Cards in this set include Garret Anderson, Carlos Delgado, Alex Gonzalez, Butch Huskey, Brian Jordan, Mike Piazza, Manny Ramirez, Mariano Rivera and Michael Tucker.

	MINT	NRMT
COMPLETE SET (705)	300.00	135.00
COMMON CARD (1-705)	.25	.11
☐ 1 Ivan Rodriguez	3.00	1.35
☐ 2 Kirk McCaskill	.25	.11
☐ 3 Scott Livingstone	.25	.11
☐ 4 Salomon Torres	.25	.11
☐ 5 Carlos Hernandez	.25	.11
☐ 6 Dave Hollins	.25	.11
☐ 7 Scott Fletcher	.25	.11
☐ 8 Jorge Fabregas	.25	.11
☐ 9 Andujar Cedeno	.25	.11
☐ 10 Howard Johnson	.25	.11
☐ 11 Trevor Hoffman	1.00	.45
☐ 12 Roberto Kelly	.25	.11
☐ 13 Gregg Jefferies	.25	.11
☐ 14 Marquis Grissom	.50	.23
☐ 15 Mike Ignasiak	.25	.11
☐ 16 Jack Morris	.50	.23
☐ 17 William Pennyfeather	.25	.11
☐ 18 Todd Stottlemyre	.50	.23
☐ 19 Chito Martinez	.25	.11
☐ 20 Roberto Alomar	1.50	.70
☐ 21 Sam Militello	.25	.11
☐ 22 Hector Fajardo	.25	.11
☐ 23 Paul Quantrill	.25	.11
☐ 24 Chuck Knoblauch	1.50	.70
☐ 25 Reggie Jefferson	1.00	.45
☐ 26 Jeremy McGarity	.25	.11
☐ 27 Jerome Walton	.25	.11
☐ 28 Chipper Jones	40.00	18.00
☐ 29 Brian Barber	.25	.11
☐ 30 Ron Darling	.25	.11
☐ 31 Roberto Petagine	.25	.11
☐ 32 Chuck Finley	.25	.11
☐ 33 Edgar Martinez	1.50	.70
☐ 34 Napoleon Robinson	.25	.11
☐ 35 Andy Van Slyke	.50	.23
☐ 36 Bobby Thigpen	.25	.11
☐ 37 Travis Fryman	.50	.23
☐ 38 Eric Christopherson	.25	.11
☐ 39 Terry Mulholland	.25	.11
☐ 40 Darryl Strawberry	.50	.23
☐ 41 Manny Alexander	.50	.23
☐ 42 Tracy Sanders	.50	.23
☐ 43 Pete Incaviglia	.25	.11
☐ 44 Kim Batiste	.25	.11
☐ 45 Frank Rodriguez	.50	.23
☐ 46 Greg Swindell	.25	.11
☐ 47 Delino DeShields	.25	.11
☐ 48 John Ericks	.25	.11
☐ 49 Franklin Stubbs	.25	.11
☐ 50 Tony Gwynn	4.00	1.80
☐ 51 Clifton Garrett	.25	.11
☐ 52 Mike Gardella	.25	.11
☐ 53 Scott Erickson	.50	.23
☐ 54 Gary Caraballo	.25	.11
☐ 55 Jose Oliva	.25	.11
☐ 56 Brook Fordyce	.25	.11
☐ 57 Mark Whiten	.25	.11
☐ 58 Joe Slusarski	.25	.11
☐ 59 J.R. Phillips	.25	.11
☐ 60 Barry Bonds	2.00	.90
☐ 61 Bob Milacki	.25	.11
☐ 62 Keith Mitchell	.25	.11
☐ 63 Angel Miranda	.25	.11
☐ 64 Raul Mondesi	10.00	4.50
☐ 65 Brian Koelling	.25	.11
☐ 66 Brian McRae	.25	.11
☐ 67 John Patterson	.25	.11
☐ 68 John Wetteland	.50	.23
☐ 69 Wilson Alvarez	.50	.23
☐ 70 Wade Boggs	1.50	.70
☐ 71 Darryl Ratliff	.25	.11
☐ 72 Jeff Jackson	.25	.11
☐ 73 Jeremy Hernandez	.25	.11
☐ 74 Darryl Hamilton	.25	.11
☐ 75 Rafael Belliard	.25	.11
☐ 76 Rick Trlicek	.25	.11
☐ 77 Felipe Crespo	.50	.23
☐ 78 Carney Lansford	.25	.11
☐ 79 Ryan Long	.25	.11
☐ 80 Kirby Puckett	3.00	1.35
☐ 81 Earl Cunningham	.25	.11
☐ 82 Pedro Martinez	8.00	3.60
☐ 83 Scott Hatteberg	.25	.11
☐ 84 Juan Gonzalez UER (65 doubles vs. Tigers)	5.00	2.20
☐ 85 Robert Nutting	.25	.11
☐ 86 Calvin Reese	1.00	.45
☐ 87 Dave Silvestri	.25	.11
☐ 88 Scott Ruffcorn	.25	.11
☐ 89 Rick Aguilera	.25	.11
☐ 90 Cecil Fielder	.50	.23
☐ 91 Kirk Dressendorfer	.25	.11
☐ 92 Jerry DiPoto	.25	.11
☐ 93 Mike Felder	.25	.11
☐ 94 Craig Paquette	.25	.11
☐ 95 Elvin Paulino	.25	.11
☐ 96 Donovan Osborne	.25	.11
☐ 97 Hubie Brooks	.25	.11
☐ 98 Derek Lowe	.50	.23
☐ 99 David Zancanaro	.25	.11
☐ 100 Ken Griffey Jr.	10.00	4.50
☐ 101 Todd Hundley	1.50	.70
☐ 102 Mike Trombley	.25	.11
☐ 103 Ricky Gutierrez	.25	.11
☐ 104 Braulio Castillo	.25	.11
☐ 105 Craig Lefferts	.25	.11
☐ 106 Rick Sutcliffe	.25	.11
☐ 107 Dean Palmer	.50	.23
☐ 108 Henry Rodriguez	2.00	.90
☐ 109 Mark Clark	.50	.23
☐ 110 Kenny Lofton	10.00	4.50
☐ 111 Mark Carreon	.25	.11
☐ 112 J.T. Bruett	.25	.11
☐ 113 Gerald Williams	.25	.11
☐ 114 Frank Thomas	8.00	3.60
☐ 115 Kevin Reimer	.25	.11
☐ 116 Sammy Sosa	1.50	.70
☐ 117 Mickey Tettleton	.25	.11
☐ 118 Reggie Sanders	.50	.23
☐ 119 Trevor Wilson	.25	.11
☐ 120 Cliff Brantley	.25	.11
☐ 121 Spike Owen	.25	.11
☐ 122 Jeff Montgomery	.50	.23
☐ 123 Alex Sutherland	.25	.11
☐ 124 Brien Taylor	.25	.11
☐ 125 Brian Williams	.25	.11
☐ 126 Kevin Seitzer	.25	.11
☐ 127 Carlos Delgado	10.00	4.50
☐ 128 Gary Scott	.25	.11
☐ 129 Scott Cooper	.25	.11
☐ 130 Domingo Jean	.25	.11
☐ 131 Pat Mahomes	.25	.11
☐ 132 Mike Boddicker	.25	.11
☐ 133 Roberto Hernandez	1.50	.70
☐ 134 Dave Valle	.25	.11
☐ 135 Kurt Stillwell	.25	.11
☐ 136 Brad Pennington	.25	.11
☐ 137 Jermaine Swinton	.25	.11
☐ 138 Ryan Hawblitzel	.25	.11
☐ 139 Tito Navarro	.25	.11
☐ 140 Sandy Alomar	.50	.23
☐ 141 Todd Benzinger	.25	.11
☐ 142 Danny Jackson	.25	.11
☐ 143 Melvin Nieves	1.50	.70
☐ 144 Jim Campanis	.25	.11
☐ 145 Luis Gonzalez	.25	.11
☐ 146 Dave Doorneweerd	.25	.11
☐ 147 Charlie Hayes	.25	.11
☐ 148 Greg Maddux	5.00	2.20
☐ 149 Brian Harper	.25	.11
☐ 150 Brent Miller	.25	.11
☐ 151 Shawn Estes	5.00	2.20
☐ 152 Mike Williams	.25	.11
☐ 153 Charlie Hough	.25	.11
☐ 154 Randy Myers	.50	.23
☐ 155 Kevin Young	.25	.11
☐ 156 Rick Wilkins	.25	.11
☐ 157 Terry Shumpert	.25	.11
☐ 158 Steve Karsay	.50	.23
☐ 159 Gary DiSarcina	.25	.11
☐ 160 Deion Sanders	1.50	.70
☐ 161 Tom Browning	.25	.11
☐ 162 Dickie Thon	.25	.11
☐ 163 Luis Mercedes	.25	.11
☐ 164 Riccardo Ingram	.25	.11
☐ 165 Tavo Alvarez	.25	.11
☐ 166 Rickey Henderson	1.50	.70
☐ 167 Jaime Navarro	.25	.11
☐ 168 Billy Ashley	1.00	.45
☐ 169 Phil Dauphin	.25	.11
☐ 170 Ivan Cruz	.25	.11
☐ 171 Harold Baines	.50	.23
☐ 172 Bryan Harvey	.25	.11
☐ 173 Alex Cole	.25	.11
☐ 174 Curtis Shaw	.25	.11
☐ 175 Matt Williams	1.50	.70
☐ 176 Felix Jose	.25	.11
☐ 177 Sam Horn	.25	.11
☐ 178 Randy Johnson	1.50	.70
☐ 179 Ivan Calderon	.25	.11
☐ 180 Steve Avery	.25	.11
☐ 181 William Suero	.25	.11
☐ 182 Bill Swift	.25	.11

☐ 183 Howard Battle .25 .11
☐ 184 Ruben Amaro .25 .11
☐ 185 Jim Abbott .25 .11
☐ 186 Mike Fitzgerald .25 .11
☐ 187 Bruce Hurst .25 .11
☐ 188 Jeff Juden .25 .11
☐ 189 Jeromy Burnitz 1.00 .45
☐ 190 Dave Burba .25 .11
☐ 191 Kevin Brown .50 .23
☐ 192 Patrick Lennon .25 .11
☐ 193 Jeff McNeely .25 .11
☐ 194 Wil Cordero .25 .11
☐ 195 Chili Davis .50 .23
☐ 196 Milt Cuyler .25 .11
☐ 197 Von Hayes .25 .11
☐ 198 Todd Revenig .25 .11
☐ 199 Joel Johnston .25 .11
☐ 200 Jeff Bagwell 5.00 2.20
☐ 201 Alex Fernandez .50 .23
☐ 202 Todd Jones 1.00 .45
☐ 203 Charles Nagy .50 .23
☐ 204 Tim Raines .50 .23
☐ 205 Kevin Maas .25 .11
☐ 206 Julio Franco .50 .23
☐ 207 Randy Velarde .25 .11
☐ 208 Lance Johnson .50 .23
☐ 209 Scott Leius .25 .11
☐ 210 Derek Lee .25 .11
☐ 211 Joe Sondrini .25 .11
☐ 212 Royce Clayton .50 .23
☐ 213 Chris George .25 .11
☐ 214 Gary Sheffield 1.50 .70
☐ 215 Mark Gubicza .25 .11
☐ 216 Mike Moore .25 .11
☐ 217 Rick Huisman .25 .11
☐ 218 Jeff Russell .25 .11
☐ 219 D.J. Dozier .25 .11
☐ 220 Dave Martinez .25 .11
☐ 221 Alan Newman .25 .11
☐ 222 Nolan Ryan 6.00 2.70
☐ 223 Teddy Higuera .25 .11
☐ 224 Damon Buford .25 .11
☐ 225 Ruben Sierra .25 .11
☐ 226 Tom Nevers .25 .11
☐ 227 Tommy Greene .25 .11
☐ 228 Nigel Wilson .25 .11
☐ 229 John DeSilva .25 .11
☐ 230 Bobby Witt .25 .11
☐ 231 Greg Cadaret .25 .11
☐ 232 John Vander Wal .25 .11
☐ 233 Jack Clark .50 .23
☐ 234 Bill Doran .25 .11
☐ 235 Bobby Bonilla .50 .23
☐ 236 Steve Olin .25 .11
☐ 237 Derek Bell 1.00 .45
☐ 238 David Cone .50 .23
☐ 239 Victor Cole .25 .11
☐ 240 Rod Bolton .25 .11
☐ 241 Tom Pagnozzi .25 .11
☐ 242 Rob Dibble .25 .11
☐ 243 Michael Carter .25 .11
☐ 244 Don Peters .25 .11
☐ 245 Mike LaValliere .25 .11
☐ 246 Joe Perona .25 .11
☐ 247 Mitch Williams .25 .11
☐ 248 Jay Buhner 1.00 .45
☐ 249 Andy Benes .50 .23
☐ 250 Alex Ochoa 1.50 .70
☐ 251 Greg Blosser .25 .11
☐ 252 Jack Armstrong .25 .11
☐ 253 Juan Samuel .25 .11
☐ 254 Terry Pendleton .50 .23
☐ 255 Ramon Martinez .25 .11
☐ 256 Rico Brogna .50 .23
☐ 257 John Smiley .25 .11
☐ 258 Carl Everett .50 .23
☐ 259 Tim Salmon 6.00 2.70
☐ 260 Will Clark 1.00 .45
☐ 261 Ugueth Urbina 1.00 .45
☐ 262 Jason Wood .25 .11
☐ 263 Dave Magadan .25 .11
☐ 264 Dante Bichette 1.00 .45
☐ 265 Jose DeLeon .25 .11
☐ 266 Mike Neill .25 .11
☐ 267 Paul O'Neill .50 .23
☐ 268 Anthony Young .25 .11
☐ 269 Greg W. Harris .25 .11
☐ 270 Todd Van Poppel .25 .11
☐ 271 Pedro Castellano .25 .11
☐ 272 Tony Phillips .25 .11
☐ 273 Mike Gallego .25 .11
☐ 274 Steve Cooke .25 .11
☐ 275 Robin Ventura .50 .23
☐ 276 Kevin Mitchell .25 .11
☐ 277 Doug Linton .25 .11
☐ 278 Robert Eenhoorn .25 .11
☐ 279 Gabe White .25 .11
☐ 280 Dave Stewart .25 .11
☐ 281 Mo Sanford .25 .11
☐ 282 Greg Perschke .25 .11
☐ 283 Kevin Flora .25 .11
☐ 284 Jeff Williams .25 .11
☐ 285 Keith Miller .25 .11
☐ 286 Andy Ashby .25 .11
☐ 287 Doug Dascenzo .25 .11
☐ 288 Eric Karros 2.00 .90
☐ 289 Glenn Murray .25 .11
☐ 290 Troy Percival 1.00 .45
☐ 291 Orlando Merced .25 .11
☐ 292 Peter Hoy .25 .11
☐ 293 Tony Fernandez .25 .11
☐ 294 Juan Guzman .25 .11
☐ 295 Jesse Barfield .25 .11
☐ 296 Sid Fernandez .25 .11
☐ 297 Scott Cepicky .25 .11
☐ 298 Garret Anderson 4.00 1.80
☐ 299 Cal Eldred .25 .11
☐ 300 Ryne Sandberg 2.00 .90
☐ 301 Jim Gantner .25 .11
☐ 302 Mariano Rivera 5.00 2.20
☐ 303 Ron Lockett .25 .11
☐ 304 Jose Offerman .25 .11
☐ 305 Denny Martinez .50 .23
☐ 306 Luis Ortiz .25 .11
☐ 307 David Howard .25 .11
☐ 308 Russ Springer .25 .11
☐ 309 Chris Howard .25 .11
☐ 310 Kyle Abbott .25 .11
☐ 311 Aaron Sele 1.00 .45
☐ 312 David Justice 1.50 .70
☐ 313 Pete O'Brien .25 .11
☐ 314 Greg Hansell .25 .11
☐ 315 Dave Winfield 1.50 .70
☐ 316 Lance Dickson .25 .11
☐ 317 Eric King .25 .11
☐ 318 Vaughn Eshelman .25 .11
☐ 319 Tim Belcher .25 .11
☐ 320 Andres Galarraga 1.00 .45
☐ 321 Scott Bullett .25 .11
☐ 322 Doug Strange .25 .11
☐ 323 Jerald Clark .25 .11
☐ 324 Dave Righetti .25 .11
☐ 325 Greg Hibbard .25 .11
☐ 326 Eric Hillman .25 .11
☐ 327 Shane Reynolds 2.00 .90
☐ 328 Chris Hammond .25 .11
☐ 329 Albert Belle 2.00 .90
☐ 330 Rich Becker 1.00 .45
☐ 331 Eddie Williams .25 .11
☐ 332 Donald Harris .25 .11
☐ 333 Dave Smith .25 .11
☐ 334 Steve Fireovid .25 .11
☐ 335 Steve Buechele .25 .11
☐ 336 Mike Schooler .25 .11
☐ 337 Kevin McReynolds .25 .11
☐ 338 Hensley Meulens .25 .11
☐ 339 Benji Gil 1.00 .45
☐ 340 Don Mattingly 2.50 1.10
☐ 341 Alvin Davis .25 .11
☐ 342 Alan Mills .25 .11
☐ 343 Kelly Downs .25 .11
☐ 344 Leo Gomez .25 .11
☐ 345 Tarrik Brock .25 .11
☐ 346 Ryan Turner .25 .11
☐ 347 John Smoltz 1.00 .45
☐ 348 Bill Sampen .25 .11
☐ 349 Paul Byrd .25 .11
☐ 350 Mike Bordick .25 .11
☐ 351 Jose Lind .25 .11
☐ 352 David Wells .25 .11
☐ 353 Barry Larkin 1.00 .45
☐ 354 Bruce Ruffin .25 .11
☐ 355 Luis Rivera .25 .11
☐ 356 Sid Bream .25 .11
☐ 357 Julian Vasquez .25 .11
☐ 358 Jason Bere .50 .23
☐ 359 Ben McDonald .25 .11
☐ 360 Scott Stahoviak .50 .23
☐ 361 Kirt Manwaring .25 .11
☐ 362 Jeff Johnson .25 .11
☐ 363 Rob Deer .25 .11
☐ 364 Tony Pena .25 .11
☐ 365 Melido Perez .25 .11
☐ 366 Clay Parker .25 .11
☐ 367 Dale Sveum .25 .11
☐ 368 Mike Scioscia .25 .11
☐ 369 Roger Salkeld .25 .11
☐ 370 Mike Stanley .25 .11
☐ 371 Jack McDowell .25 .11
☐ 372 Tim Wallach .25 .11
☐ 373 Billy Ripken .25 .11
☐ 374 Mike Christopher .25 .11
☐ 375 Paul Molitor 1.50 .70
☐ 376 Dave Stieb .25 .11
☐ 377 Pedro Guerrero .25 .11
☐ 378 Russ Swan .25 .11
☐ 379 Bob Ojeda .25 .11
☐ 380 Donn Pall .25 .11
☐ 381 Eddie Zosky .25 .11
☐ 382 Darnell Coles .25 .11
☐ 383 Tom Smith .25 .11
☐ 384 Mark McGwire 3.00 1.35
☐ 385 Gary Carter 1.50 .70
☐ 386 Rich Amaral .25 .11
☐ 387 Alan Embree .25 .11
☐ 388 Jonathan Hurst .25 .11
☐ 389 Bobby Jones 2.50 1.10
☐ 390 Rico Rossy .25 .11
☐ 391 Dan Smith .25 .11
☐ 392 Terry Steinbach .50 .23
☐ 393 Jon Farrell .25 .11
☐ 394 Dave Anderson .25 .11
☐ 395 Benny Santiago .25 .11
☐ 396 Mark Wohlers 1.50 .70
☐ 397 Mo Vaughn 2.50 1.10
☐ 398 Randy Kramer .25 .11
☐ 399 John Jaha 1.00 .45
☐ 400 Cal Ripken 6.00 2.70
☐ 401 Ryan Bowen .25 .11
☐ 402 Tim McIntosh .25 .11
☐ 403 Bernard Gilkey .50 .23
☐ 404 Junior Felix .25 .11
☐ 405 Cris Colon .25 .11
☐ 406 Marc Newfield 1.50 .70
☐ 407 Bernie Williams 1.50 .70
☐ 408 Jay Howell .25 .11
☐ 409 Zane Smith .25 .11
☐ 410 Jeff Shaw .25 .11
☐ 411 Kerry Woodson .25 .11
☐ 412 Wes Chamberlain .25 .11
☐ 413 Dave Mlicki .25 .11
☐ 414 Benny Distefano .25 .11
☐ 415 Kevin Rogers .25 .11
☐ 416 Tim Naehring .50 .23
☐ 417 Clemente Nunez 1.00 .45
☐ 418 Luis Sojo .25 .11
☐ 419 Kevin Ritz .25 .11
☐ 420 Omar Olivares .25 .11
☐ 421 Manuel Lee .25 .11
☐ 422 Julio Valera .25 .11
☐ 423 Omar Vizquel 1.00 .45
☐ 424 Darren Burton .25 .11
☐ 425 Mel Hall .25 .11
☐ 426 Dennis Powell .25 .11
☐ 427 Lee Stevens .25 .11
☐ 428 Glenn Davis .25 .11
☐ 429 Willie Greene .50 .23
☐ 430 Kevin Wickander .25 .11
☐ 431 Dennis Eckersley 1.50 .70
☐ 432 Joe Orsulak .25 .11
☐ 433 Eddie Murray 1.50 .70
☐ 434 Matt Stairs .25 .11
☐ 435 Wally Joyner .50 .23
☐ 436 Rondell White 4.00 1.80
☐ 437 Rob Maurer .25 .11
☐ 438 Joe Redfield .25 .11
☐ 439 Mark Lewis .25 .11
☐ 440 Darren Daulton .50 .23
☐ 441 Mike Henneman .25 .11
☐ 442 John Cangelosi .25 .11
☐ 443 Vince Moore .25 .11
☐ 444 John Wehner .25 .11
☐ 445 Kent Hrbek .50 .23
☐ 446 Mark McLemore .25 .11
☐ 447 Bill Wegman .25 .11
☐ 448 Robby Thompson .25 .11
☐ 449 Mark Anthony .25 .11
☐ 450 Archi Cianfrocco .25 .11
☐ 451 Johnny Ruffin .25 .11
☐ 452 Javier Lopez 8.00 3.60
☐ 453 Greg Gohr .25 .11
☐ 454 Tim Scott .25 .11
☐ 455 Stan Belinda .25 .11
☐ 456 Darrin Jackson .25 .11
☐ 457 Chris Gardner .25 .11
☐ 458 Esteban Beltre .25 .11
☐ 459 Phil Plantier .25 .11
☐ 460 Jim Thome 15.00 6.75
☐ 461 Mike Piazza 60.00 27.00
☐ 462 Matt Sinatro .25 .11
☐ 463 Scott Servais .25 .11
☐ 464 Brian Jordan 4.00 1.80
☐ 465 Doug Drabek .25 .11
☐ 466 Carl Willis .25 .11
☐ 467 Bret Barberie .25 .11
☐ 468 Hal Morris .25 .11
☐ 469 Steve Sax .25 .11
☐ 470 Jerry Willard .25 .11
☐ 471 Dan Wilson .50 .23
☐ 472 Chris Hoiles .25 .11
☐ 473 Rheal Cormier .25 .11

☐ 474 John Morris .25 .11
☐ 475 Jeff Reardon .50 .23
☐ 476 Mark Leiter .25 .11
☐ 477 Tom Gordon .25 .11
☐ 478 Kent Bottenfield .25 .11
☐ 479 Gene Larkin .25 .11
☐ 480 Dwight Gooden .50 .23
☐ 481 B.J. Surhoff .50 .23
☐ 482 Andy Stankiewicz .25 .11
☐ 483 Tino Martinez 1.50 .70
☐ 484 Craig Biggio 1.00 .45
☐ 485 Denny Neagle 3.00 1.35
☐ 486 Rusty Meacham .25 .11
☐ 487 Kal Daniels .25 .11
☐ 488 Dave Henderson .25 .11
☐ 489 Tim Costo .25 .11
☐ 490 Doug Davis .25 .11
☐ 491 Frank Viola .25 .11
☐ 492 Cory Snyder .25 .11
☐ 493 Chris Martin .25 .11
☐ 494 Dion James .25 .11
☐ 495 Randy Tomlin .25 .11
☐ 496 Greg Vaughn .25 .11
☐ 497 Dennis Cook .25 .11
☐ 498 Rosario Rodriguez .25 .11
☐ 499 Dave Staton .25 .11
☐ 500 George Brett 3.00 1.35
☐ 501 Brian Barnes .25 .11
☐ 502 Butch Henry .25 .11
☐ 503 Harold Reynolds .25 .11
☐ 504 David Nied .25 .11
☐ 505 Lee Smith .50 .23
☐ 506 Steve Chitren .25 .11
☐ 507 Ken Hill .25 .11
☐ 508 Robbie Beckett .25 .11
☐ 509 Troy Afenir .25 .11
☐ 510 Kelly Gruber .25 .11
☐ 511 Bret Boone .50 .23
☐ 512 Jeff Branson .25 .11
☐ 513 Mike Jackson .25 .11
☐ 514 Pete Harnisch .25 .11
☐ 515 Chad Kreuter .25 .11
☐ 516 Joe Vitko .25 .11
☐ 517 Orel Hershiser .50 .23
☐ 518 John Doherty .25 .11
☐ 519 Jay Bell .50 .23
☐ 520 Mark Langston .25 .11
☐ 521 Dann Howitt .25 .11
☐ 522 Bobby Reed .25 .11
☐ 523 Roberto Munoz .25 .11
☐ 524 Todd Ritchie .25 .11
☐ 525 Bip Roberts .25 .11
☐ 526 Pat Listach .25 .11
☐ 527 Scott Brosius .25 .11
☐ 528 John Roper .25 .11
☐ 529 Phil Hiatt .25 .11
☐ 530 Denny Walling .25 .11
☐ 531 Carlos Baerga .50 .23
☐ 532 Manny Ramirez 20.00 9.00
☐ 533 Pat Clements UER .25 .11
(Mistakenly numbered 553)
☐ 534 Ron Gant .50 .23
☐ 535 Pat Kelly .25 .11
☐ 536 Billy Spiers .25 .11
☐ 537 Darren Reed .25 .11
☐ 538 Ken Caminiti 1.50 .70
☐ 539 Butch Huskey 3.00 1.35
☐ 540 Matt Nokes .25 .11
☐ 541 John Kruk .50 .23
☐ 542 John Jaha FOIL .50 .23
☐ 543 Justin Thompson 5.00 2.20
☐ 544 Steve Hosey .25 .11
☐ 545 Joe Kmak .25 .11
☐ 546 John Franco .25 .11
☐ 547 Devon White .25 .11
☐ 548 Elston Hansen FOIL .25 .11
☐ 549 Ryan Klesko 10.00 4.50
☐ 550 Danny Tartabull .25 .11
☐ 551 Frank Thomas FOIL 10.00 4.50
☐ 552 Kevin Tapani .25 .11
☐ 553 Willie Banks .25 .11
(See also 533)
☐ 554 B.J. Wallace FOIL .25 .11
☐ 555 Orlando Miller .25 .11
☐ 556 Mark Smith .25 .11
☐ 557 Tim Wallach FOIL .25 .11
☐ 558 Bill Gullickson .25 .11
☐ 559 Derek Bell FOIL .50 .23
☐ 560 Joe Randa FOIL .50 .23
☐ 561 Frank Seminara .25 .11
☐ 562 Mark Gardner .25 .11
☐ 563 Rick Greene FOIL .25 .11
☐ 564 Gary Gaetti .50 .23
☐ 565 Ozzie Guillen .25 .11
☐ 566 Charles Nagy FOIL .50 .23
☐ 567 Mike Milchin .25 .11
☐ 568 Ben Shelton .25 .11
☐ 569 Chris Roberts FOIL .25 .11
☐ 570 Ellis Burks .50 .23
☐ 571 Scott Scudder .25 .11
☐ 572 Jim Abbott FOIL .25 .11
☐ 573 Joe Carter 1.00 .45
☐ 574 Steve Finley .50 .23
☐ 575 Jim Olander FOIL .25 .11
☐ 576 Carlos Garcia .25 .11
☐ 577 Gregg Olson .25 .11
☐ 578 Greg Swindell FOIL .25 .11
☐ 579 Matt Williams FOIL 1.00 .45
☐ 580 Mark Grace 1.00 .45
☐ 581 Howard House FOIL .25 .11
☐ 582 Luis Polonia .25 .11
☐ 583 Erik Hanson .25 .11
☐ 584 Salomon Torres FOIL .25 .11
☐ 585 Carlton Fisk 1.50 .70
☐ 586 Bret Saberhagen .25 .11
☐ 587 Chad McConnell FOIL .25 .11
☐ 588 Jimmy Key .50 .23
☐ 589 Mike Macfarlane .25 .11
☐ 590 Barry Bonds FOIL 2.00 .90
☐ 591 Jamie McAndrew .25 .11
☐ 592 Shane Mack .25 .11
☐ 593 Kerwin Moore .25 .11
☐ 594 Joe Oliver .25 .11
☐ 595 Chris Sabo .25 .11
☐ 596 Alex Gonzalez 1.50 .70
☐ 597 Brett Butler .50 .23
☐ 598 Mark Hutton .25 .11
☐ 599 Andy Benes FOIL .50 .23
☐ 600 Jose Canseco 1.00 .45
☐ 601 Darryl Kile .50 .23
☐ 602 Matt Stairs FOIL .25 .11
☐ 603 Robert Butler FOIL .25 .11
☐ 604 Willie McGee .25 .11
☐ 605 Jack McDowell FOIL .25 .11
☐ 606 Tom Candiotti .25 .11
☐ 607 Ed Martel .25 .11
☐ 608 Matt Mieske FOIL .50 .23
☐ 609 Darrin Fletcher .25 .11
☐ 610 Rafael Palmeiro 1.00 .45
☐ 611 Bill Swift FOIL .25 .11
☐ 612 Mike Mussina 2.50 1.10
☐ 613 Vince Coleman .25 .11
☐ 614 Scott Cepicky FOIL UER .25 .11
(Bats: LEFLT)
☐ 615 Mike Greenwell .25 .11
☐ 616 Kevin McGehee .25 .11
☐ 617 Jeffrey Hammonds FOIL 1.50 .70
☐ 618 Scott Taylor .25 .11
☐ 619 Dave Otto .25 .11
☐ 620 Mark McGwire FOIL 3.00 1.35
☐ 621 Kevin Tatar .25 .11
☐ 622 Steve Farr .25 .11
☐ 623 Ryan Klesko FOIL 2.00 .90
☐ 624 Dave Fleming .25 .11
☐ 625 Andre Dawson 1.00 .45
☐ 626 Tino Martinez FOIL 1.50 .70
☐ 627 Chad Curtis 1.50 .70
☐ 628 Mickey Morandini .25 .11
☐ 629 Gregg Olson FOIL .25 .11
☐ 630 Lou Whitaker .50 .23
☐ 631 Arthur Rhodes .25 .11
☐ 632 Brandon Wilson .25 .11
☐ 633 Lance Jennings .25 .11
☐ 634 Allen Watson .25 .11
☐ 635 Len Dykstra .50 .23
☐ 636 Joe Girardi .25 .11
☐ 637 Kiki Hernandez FOIL .25 .11
☐ 638 Mike Hampton 2.00 .90
☐ 639 Al Osuna .25 .11
☐ 640 Kevin Appier .50 .23
☐ 641 Rick Helling FOIL .25 .11
☐ 642 Jody Reed .25 .11
☐ 643 Ray Lankford 1.50 .70
☐ 644 John Olerud .50 .23
☐ 645 Paul Molitor FOIL 1.50 .70
☐ 646 Pat Borders .25 .11
☐ 647 Mike Morgan .25 .11
☐ 648 Larry Walker 1.50 .70
☐ 649 Pedro Castellano FOIL .25 .11
☐ 650 Fred McGriff 1.00 .45
☐ 651 Walt Weiss .25 .11
☐ 652 Calvin Murray FOIL .25 .11
☐ 653 Dave Nilsson .50 .23
☐ 654 Greg Pirkl .25 .11
☐ 655 Robin Ventura FOIL .50 .23
☐ 656 Mark Portugal .25 .11
☐ 657 Roger McDowell .25 .11
☐ 658 Rick Hirtensteiner FOIL .25 .11
☐ 659 Glenallen Hill .25 .11
☐ 660 Greg Gagne .25 .11
☐ 661 Charles Johnson FOIL 8.00 3.60
☐ 662 Brian Hunter .25 .11
☐ 663 Mark Lemke .25 .11
☐ 664 Tim Belcher FOIL .25 .11
☐ 665 Rich DeLucia .25 .11
☐ 666 Bob Walk .25 .11
☐ 667 Joe Carter FOIL 1.00 .45
☐ 668 Jose Guzman .25 .11
☐ 669 Otis Nixon .50 .23
☐ 670 Phil Nevin FOIL .50 .23
☐ 671 Eric Davis .50 .23
☐ 672 Damion Easley 1.00 .45
☐ 673 Will Clark FOIL 1.00 .45
☐ 674 Mark Kiefer .25 .11
☐ 675 Ozzie Smith 2.00 .90
☐ 676 Manny Ramirez FOIL 4.00 1.80
☐ 677 Gregg Olson .25 .11
☐ 678 Cliff Floyd 2.00 .90
☐ 679 Duane Singleton .25 .11
☐ 680 Jose Rijo .25 .11
☐ 681 Willie Randolph .50 .23
☐ 682 Michael Tucker FOIL 4.00 1.80
☐ 683 Darren Lewis .25 .11
☐ 684 Dale Murphy 1.50 .70
☐ 685 Mike Pagliarulo .25 .11
☐ 686 Paul Miller .25 .11
☐ 687 Mike Robertson .25 .11
☐ 688 Mike Devereaux .25 .11
☐ 689 Pedro Astacio .50 .23
☐ 690 Alan Trammell 1.00 .45
☐ 691 Roger Clemens 3.00 1.35
☐ 692 Bud Black .25 .11
☐ 693 Turk Wendell .50 .23
☐ 694 Barry Larkin FOIL 1.00 .45
☐ 695 Todd Zeile .25 .11
☐ 696 Pat Hentgen 3.00 1.35
☐ 697 Eddie Taubensee .25 .11
☐ 698 Guillermo Velasquez .25 .11
☐ 699 Tom Glavine 1.50 .70
☐ 700 Robin Yount 1.00 .45
☐ 701 Checklist 1-141 .25 .11
☐ 702 Checklist 142-282 .25 .11
☐ 703 Checklist 283-423 .25 .11
☐ 704 Checklist 424-564 .25 .11
☐ 705 Checklist 565-705 .25 .11

1993 Bowman

This 708-card standard-size set was issued in one series and features one of the more comprehensive selection of prospects and rookies available that year. Cards were distributed in 14-card plastic wrapped packs and jumbo packs. Each 14-card pack contained one silver foil bordered subset card. The basic issue card fronts feature white-bordered color action player photos. The player's name appears in white lettering at the bottom right, with his last name printed on an ocher rectangle. The 48 foil subset cards (339-374 and 693-704) feature sixteen 1992 MVPs of the Minor Leagues, top prospects and a few father/son combinations. Rookie Cards in this set include James Baldwin, Roger Cedeno, Marty Cordova, Brian L. Hunter, Derek Jeter, Jason Kendall, Andy Pettite and Preston Wilson.

	MINT	NRMT
COMPLETE SET (708)	70.00	32.00
COMMON CARD (1-708)	.15	.07

☐ 1 Glenn Davis .15 .07
☐ 2 Hector Roa .15 .07
☐ 3 Ken Ryan .15 .07
☐ 4 Derek Wallace .15 .07
☐ 5 Jorge Fabregas .15 .07
☐ 6 Joe Oliver .15 .07
☐ 7 Brandon Wilson .15 .07
☐ 8 Mark Thompson .30 .14
☐ 9 Tracy Sanders .15 .07
☐ 10 Rich Renteria .15 .07
☐ 11 Lou Whitaker .30 .14
☐ 12 Brian Hunter 2.00 .90
☐ 13 Joe Vitiello .15 .07
☐ 14 Eric Karros .30 .14
☐ 15 Joe Kmak .15 .07
☐ 16 Tavo Alvarez .15 .07
☐ 17 Steve Dunn .15 .07

☐ 18 Tony Fernandez .15 .07
☐ 19 Melido Perez .15 .07
☐ 20 Mike Lieberthal .15 .07
☐ 21 Terry Steinbach .30 .14
☐ 22 Stan Belinda .15 .07
☐ 23 Jay Buhner .40 .18
☐ 24 Allen Watson .15 .07
☐ 25 Daryl Henderson .15 .07
☐ 26 Ray McDavid .15 .07
☐ 27 Shawn Green .75 .35
☐ 28 Bud Black .15 .07
☐ 29 Sherman Obando .15 .07
☐ 30 Mike Hostetler .15 .07
☐ 31 Nate Minchey .15 .07
☐ 32 Randy Myers .30 .14
☐ 33 Brian Grebeck .15 .07
☐ 34 John Roper .15 .07
☐ 35 Larry Thomas .15 .07
☐ 36 Alex Cole .15 .07
☐ 37 Tom Kramer .15 .07
☐ 38 Matt Whisenant .15 .07
☐ 39 Chris Gomez .40 .18
☐ 40 Luis Gonzalez .15 .07
☐ 41 Kevin Appier .30 .14
☐ 42 Omar Daal .30 .14
☐ 43 Duane Singleton .15 .07
☐ 44 Bill Risley .15 .07
☐ 45 Pat Meares .30 .14
☐ 46 Butch Huskey .60 .25
☐ 47 Bobby Munoz .15 .07
☐ 48 Juan Bell .15 .07
☐ 49 Scott Lydy .15 .07
☐ 50 Dennis Moeller .15 .07
☐ 51 Marc Newfield .30 .14
☐ 52 Tripp Cromer .15 .07
☐ 53 Kurt Miller .15 .07
☐ 54 Jim Pena .15 .07
☐ 55 Juan Guzman .15 .07
☐ 56 Matt Williams .40 .18
☐ 57 Harold Reynolds .15 .07
☐ 58 Donnie Elliott .15 .07
☐ 59 Jon Shave .15 .07
☐ 60 Kevin Roberson .15 .07
☐ 61 Hilly Hathaway .15 .07
☐ 62 Jose Rijo .15 .07
☐ 63 Kerry Taylor .15 .07
☐ 64 Ryan Hawblitzel .15 .07
☐ 65 Glenallen Hill .15 .07
☐ 66 Ramon Martinez .30 .14
☐ 67 Travis Fryman .30 .14
☐ 68 Tom Nevers .15 .07
☐ 69 Phil Hiatt .15 .07
☐ 70 Tim Wallach .15 .07
☐ 71 B.J. Surhoff .30 .14
☐ 72 Rondell White .40 .18
☐ 73 Denny Hocking .30 .14
☐ 74 Mike Oquist .15 .07
☐ 75 Paul O'Neill .30 .14
☐ 76 Willie Banks .15 .07
☐ 77 Bob Welch .15 .07
☐ 78 Jose Sandoval .15 .07
☐ 79 Bill Haselman .15 .07
☐ 80 Rheal Cormier .15 .07
☐ 81 Dean Palmer .30 .14
☐ 82 Pat Gomez .15 .07
☐ 83 Steve Karsay .30 .14
☐ 84 Carl Hanselman .15 .07
☐ 85 T.R. Lewis .15 .07
☐ 86 Chipper Jones 3.00 1.35
☐ 87 Scott Hatteberg .15 .07
☐ 88 Greg Hibbard .15 .07
☐ 89 Lance Painter .15 .07
☐ 90 Chad Mottola .30 .14
☐ 91 Jason Bere .30 .14
☐ 92 Dante Bichette .40 .18
☐ 93 Sandy Alomar Jr. .30 .14
☐ 94 Carl Everett .40 .18
☐ 95 Danny Bautista .30 .14
☐ 96 Steve Finley .30 .14
☐ 97 David Cone .30 .14
☐ 98 Todd Hollandsworth .75 .35
☐ 99 Matt Mieske .30 .14
☐ 100 Larry Walker .60 .25
☐ 101 Shane Mack .15 .07
☐ 102 Aaron Ledesma .15 .07
☐ 103 Andy Pettitte 5.00 2.20
☐ 104 Kevin Stocker .15 .07
☐ 105 Mike Mohler .15 .07
☐ 106 Tony Menendez .15 .07
☐ 107 Derek Lowe .30 .14
☐ 108 Basil Shabazz .15 .07
☐ 109 Dan Smith .15 .07
☐ 110 Scott Sanders .15 .07
☐ 111 Todd Stottlemyre .15 .07
☐ 112 Benji Simonton .15 .07
☐ 113 Rick Sutcliffe .15 .07
☐ 114 Lee Heath .15 .07
☐ 115 Jeff Russell .15 .07
☐ 116 Dave Stevens .15 .07
☐ 117 Mark Holzemer .15 .07
☐ 118 Tim Belcher .15 .07
☐ 119 Bobby Thigpen .15 .07
☐ 120 Roger Bailey .15 .07
☐ 121 Tony Mitchell .15 .07
☐ 122 Junior Felix .15 .07
☐ 123 Rich Robertson .15 .07
☐ 124 Andy Cook .15 .07
☐ 125 Brian Bevil .30 .14
☐ 126 Darryl Strawberry .30 .14
☐ 127 Cal Eldred .15 .07
☐ 128 Cliff Floyd .30 .14
☐ 129 Alan Newman .15 .07
☐ 130 Howard Johnson .15 .07
☐ 131 Jim Abbott .15 .07
☐ 132 Chad McConnell .15 .07
☐ 133 Miguel Jimenez .30 .14
☐ 134 Brett Backlund .15 .07
☐ 135 John Cummings .15 .07
☐ 136 Brian Barber .15 .07
☐ 137 Rafael Palmeiro .40 .18
☐ 138 Tim Worrell .15 .07
☐ 139 Jose Pett .50 .23
☐ 140 Barry Bonds .60 .25
☐ 141 Damon Buford .15 .07
☐ 142 Jeff Blauser .15 .07
☐ 143 Frankie Rodriguez .15 .07
☐ 144 Mike Morgan .15 .07
☐ 145 Gary DiSarcina .15 .07
☐ 146 Calvin Reese .30 .14
☐ 147 Johnny Ruffin .15 .07
☐ 148 David Nied .15 .07
☐ 149 Charles Nagy .30 .14
☐ 150 Mike Myers .15 .07
☐ 151 Kenny Carlyle .15 .07
☐ 152 Eric Anthony .15 .07
☐ 153 Jose Lind .15 .07
☐ 154 Pedro Martinez .60 .25
☐ 155 Mark Kiefer .15 .07
☐ 156 Tim Laker .15 .07
☐ 157 Pat Mahomes .15 .07
☐ 158 Bobby Bonilla .30 .14
☐ 159 Domingo Jean .15 .07
☐ 160 Darren Daulton .30 .14
☐ 161 Mark McGwire 1.25 .55
☐ 162 Jason Kendall 2.00 .90
☐ 163 Desi Relaford .30 .14
☐ 164 Ozzie Canseco .15 .07
☐ 165 Rick Helling .15 .07
☐ 166 Steve Pegues .15 .07
☐ 167 Paul Molitor .60 .25
☐ 168 Larry Carter .15 .07
☐ 169 Arthur Rhodes .15 .07
☐ 170 Damon Hollins .50 .23
☐ 171 Frank Viola .15 .07
☐ 172 Steve Trachsel .30 .14
☐ 173 J.T. Snow 1.50 .70
☐ 174 Keith Gordon .15 .07
☐ 175 Carlton Fisk .60 .25
☐ 176 Jason Bates .30 .14
☐ 177 Mike Crosby .15 .07
☐ 178 Benny Santiago .15 .07
☐ 179 Mike Moore .15 .07
☐ 180 Jeff Juden .15 .07
☐ 181 Darren Burton .15 .07
☐ 182 Todd Williams .15 .07
☐ 183 John Jaha .30 .14
☐ 184 Mike Lansing .30 .14
☐ 185 Pedro Grifol .15 .07
☐ 186 Vince Coleman .15 .07
☐ 187 Pat Kelly .15 .07
☐ 188 Clemente Alvarez .15 .07
☐ 189 Ron Darling .15 .07
☐ 190 Orlando Merced .30 .14
☐ 191 Chris Bosio .15 .07
☐ 192 Steve Dixon .15 .07
☐ 193 Doug Dascenzo .15 .07
☐ 194 Ray Holbert .15 .07
☐ 195 Howard Battle .15 .07
☐ 196 Willie McGee .15 .07
☐ 197 John O'Donoghue .15 .07
☐ 198 Steve Avery .15 .07
☐ 199 Greg Blosser .15 .07
☐ 200 Ryne Sandberg .75 .35
☐ 201 Joe Grahe .15 .07
☐ 202 Dan Wilson .30 .14
☐ 203 Domingo Martinez .15 .07
☐ 204 Andres Galarraga .40 .18
☐ 205 Jamie Taylor .15 .07
☐ 206 Darrell Whitmore .15 .07
☐ 207 Ben Blomdahl .15 .07
☐ 208 Doug Drabek .15 .07
☐ 209 Keith Miller .15 .07
☐ 210 Billy Ashley .15 .07
☐ 211 Mike Farrell .15 .07
☐ 212 John Wetteland .30 .14
☐ 213 Randy Tomlin .15 .07
☐ 214 Sid Fernandez .15 .07
☐ 215 Quilvio Veras .75 .35
☐ 216 Dave Hollins .15 .07
☐ 217 Mike Neill .15 .07
☐ 218 Andy Van Slyke .30 .14
☐ 219 Bret Boone .30 .14
☐ 220 Tom Pagnozzi .15 .07
☐ 221 Mike Welch .15 .07
☐ 222 Frank Seminara .15 .07
☐ 223 Ron Villone .15 .07
☐ 224 D.J. Thielen .15 .07
☐ 225 Cal Ripken 2.50 1.10
☐ 226 Pedro Borbon Jr. .15 .07
☐ 227 Carlos Quintana .15 .07
☐ 228 Tommy Shields .15 .07
☐ 229 Tim Salmon .75 .35
☐ 230 John Smiley .15 .07
☐ 231 Ellis Burks .30 .14
☐ 232 Pedro Castellano .15 .07
☐ 233 Paul Byrd .15 .07
☐ 234 Bryan Harvey .15 .07
☐ 235 Scott Livingstone .15 .07
☐ 236 James Mouton .30 .14
☐ 237 Joe Randa .15 .07
☐ 238 Pedro Astacio .15 .07
☐ 239 Darryl Hamilton .15 .07
☐ 240 Joey Eischen .30 .14
☐ 241 Edgar Herrera .15 .07
☐ 242 Dwight Gooden .30 .14
☐ 243 Sam Militello .15 .07
☐ 244 Ron Blazier .15 .07
☐ 245 Ruben Sierra .15 .07
☐ 246 Al Martin .30 .14
☐ 247 Mike Felder .15 .07
☐ 248 Bob Tewksbury .15 .07
☐ 249 Craig Lefferts .15 .07
☐ 250 Luis Lopez .15 .07
☐ 251 Devon White .15 .07
☐ 252 Will Clark .40 .18
☐ 253 Mark Smith .15 .07
☐ 254 Terry Pendleton .30 .14
☐ 255 Aaron Sele .30 .14
☐ 256 Jose Viera .15 .07
☐ 257 Damion Easley .15 .07
☐ 258 Rod Lofton .15 .07
☐ 259 Chris Snopek .50 .23
☐ 260 Quinton McCracken .30 .14
☐ 261 Mike Matthews .15 .07
☐ 262 Hector Carrasco .15 .07
☐ 263 Rick Greene .15 .07
☐ 264 Chris Holt .15 .07
☐ 265 George Brett 1.25 .55
☐ 266 Rick Gorecki .15 .07
☐ 267 Francisco Gamez .15 .07
☐ 268 Marquis Grissom .30 .14
☐ 269 Kevin Tapani UER .15 .07
(Misspelled Tapan
on card front)
☐ 270 Ryan Thompson .15 .07
☐ 271 Gerald Williams .15 .07
☐ 272 Paul Fletcher .15 .07
☐ 273 Lance Blankenship .15 .07
☐ 274 Marty Neff .15 .07
☐ 275 Shawn Estes .75 .35
☐ 276 Rene Arocha .15 .07
☐ 277 Scott Eyre .15 .07
☐ 278 Phil Plantier .15 .07
☐ 279 Paul Spoljaric .15 .07
☐ 280 Chris Gambs .15 .07
☐ 281 Harold Baines .30 .14
☐ 282 Jose Oliva .15 .07
☐ 283 Matt Whiteside .15 .07
☐ 284 Brant Brown .50 .23
☐ 285 Russ Springer .15 .07
☐ 286 Chris Sabo .15 .07
☐ 287 Ozzie Guillen .15 .07
☐ 288 Marcus Moore .15 .07
☐ 289 Chad Ogea .30 .14
☐ 290 Walt Weiss .15 .07
☐ 291 Brian Edmondson .15 .07
☐ 292 Jimmy Gonzalez .15 .07
☐ 293 Danny Miceli .30 .14
☐ 294 Jose Offerman .15 .07
☐ 295 Greg Vaughn .15 .07
☐ 296 Frank Bolick .15 .07
☐ 297 Mike Maksudian .15 .07
☐ 298 John Franco .15 .07
☐ 299 Danny Tartabull .15 .07
☐ 300 Len Dykstra .30 .14
☐ 301 Bobby Witt .15 .07
☐ 302 Trey Beamon .50 .23
☐ 303 Tino Martinez .60 .25
☐ 304 Aaron Holbert .15 .07
☐ 305 Juan Gonzalez 1.50 .70
☐ 306 Billy Hall .15 .07

☐ 307 Duane Ward	.15	.07
☐ 308 Rod Beck	.30	.14
☐ 309 Jose Mercedes	.15	.07
☐ 310 Otis Nixon	.15	.07
☐ 311 Gettys Glaze	.15	.07
☐ 312 Candy Maldonado	.15	.07
☐ 313 Chad Curtis	.30	.14
☐ 314 Tim Costo	.15	.07
☐ 315 Mike Robertson	.15	.07
☐ 316 Nigel Wilson	.15	.07
☐ 317 Greg McMichael	.15	.07
☐ 318 Scott Pose	.15	.07
☐ 319 Ivan Cruz	.15	.07
☐ 320 Greg Swindell	.15	.07
☐ 321 Kevin McReynolds	.15	.07
☐ 322 Tom Candiotti	.15	.07
☐ 323 Rob Wishnevski	.15	.07
☐ 324 Ken Hill	.30	.14
☐ 325 Kirby Puckett	1.25	.55
☐ 326 Tim Bogar	.15	.07
☐ 327 Mariano Rivera	.75	.35
☐ 328 Mitch Williams	.15	.07
☐ 329 Craig Paquette	.15	.07
☐ 330 Jay Bell	.30	.14
☐ 331 Jose Martinez	.15	.07
☐ 332 Rob Deer	.15	.07
☐ 333 Brook Fordyce	.15	.07
☐ 334 Matt Nokes	.15	.07
☐ 335 Derek Lee	.15	.07
☐ 336 Paul Ellis	.15	.07
☐ 337 Desi Wilson	.15	.07
☐ 338 Roberto Alomar	.60	.25
☐ 339 Jim Tatum FOIL	.15	.07
☐ 340 J.T. Snow FOIL	.60	.25
☐ 341 Tim Salmon FOIL	.75	.35
☐ 342 Russ Davis FOIL	1.00	.45
☐ 343 Javier Lopez FOIL	.60	.25
☐ 344 Troy O'Leary FOIL	.40	.18
☐ 345 Marty Cordova FOIL	1.50	.70
☐ 346 Bubba Smith FOIL	.15	.07
☐ 347 Chipper Jones FOIL	3.00	1.35
☐ 348 Jessie Hollins FOIL	.15	.07
☐ 349 Willie Greene FOIL	.30	.14
☐ 350 Mark Thompson FOIL	.30	.14
☐ 351 Nigel Wilson FOIL	.15	.07
☐ 352 Todd Jones FOIL	.30	.14
☐ 353 Raul Mondesi FOIL	.75	.35
☐ 354 Cliff Floyd FOIL	.30	.14
☐ 355 Bobby Jones FOIL	.30	.14
☐ 356 Kevin Stocker FOIL	.15	.07
☐ 357 Midre Cummings FOIL	.30	.14
☐ 358 Allen Watson FOIL	.15	.07
☐ 359 Ray McDavid FOIL	.15	.07
☐ 360 Steve Hosey FOIL	.15	.07
☐ 361 Brad Pennington FOIL	.15	.07
☐ 362 Frankie Rodriguez FOIL	.15	.07
☐ 363 Troy Percival FOIL	.30	.14
☐ 364 Jason Bere FOIL	.30	.14
☐ 365 Manny Ramirez FOIL	1.25	.55
☐ 366 Justin Thompson FOIL	.75	.35
☐ 367 Joe Vitiello FOIL	.15	.07
☐ 368 Tyrone Hill FOIL	.15	.07
☐ 369 David McCarty FOIL	.15	.07
☐ 370 Brien Taylor FOIL	.15	.07
☐ 371 Todd Van Poppel FOIL	.15	.07
☐ 372 Marc Newfield FOIL	.30	.14
☐ 373 Terrell Lowery FOIL	.15	.07
☐ 374 Alex Gonzalez FOIL	.40	.18
☐ 375 Ken Griffey Jr.	3.00	1.35
☐ 376 Donovan Osborne	.15	.07
☐ 377 Ritchie Moody	.15	.07
☐ 378 Shane Andrews	.15	.07
☐ 379 Carlos Delgado	.60	.25
☐ 380 Bill Swift	.15	.07
☐ 381 Leo Gomez	.15	.07
☐ 382 Ron Gant	.30	.14
☐ 383 Scott Fletcher	.15	.07
☐ 384 Matt Walbeck	.15	.07
☐ 385 Chuck Finley	.15	.07
☐ 386 Kevin Mitchell	.30	.14
☐ 387 Wilson Alvarez UER (Misspelled Alverez on card front)	.30	.14
☐ 388 John Burke	.15	.07
☐ 389 Alan Embree	.15	.07
☐ 390 Trevor Hoffman	.60	.25
☐ 391 Alan Trammell	.40	.18
☐ 392 Todd Jones	.30	.14
☐ 393 Felix Jose	.15	.07
☐ 394 Orel Hershiser	.30	.14
☐ 395 Pat Listach	.15	.07
☐ 396 Gabe White	.15	.07
☐ 397 Dan Serafini	.50	.23
☐ 398 Todd Hundley	.40	.18
☐ 399 Wade Boggs	.40	.18
☐ 400 Tyler Green	.15	.07
☐ 401 Mike Bordick	.15	.07
☐ 402 Scott Bullett	.15	.07
☐ 403 LaGrande Russell	.15	.07
☐ 404 Ray Lankford	.40	.18
☐ 405 Nolan Ryan	2.50	1.10
☐ 406 Robbie Beckett	.15	.07
☐ 407 Brent Bowers	.30	.14
☐ 408 Adell Davenport	.15	.07
☐ 409 Brady Anderson	.40	.18
☐ 410 Tom Glavine	.40	.18
☐ 411 Doug Hecker	.15	.07
☐ 412 Jose Guzman	.15	.07
☐ 413 Luis Polonia	.15	.07
☐ 414 Brian Williams	.15	.07
☐ 415 Bo Jackson	.30	.14
☐ 416 Eric Young	.60	.25
☐ 417 Kenny Lofton	1.25	.55
☐ 418 Orestes Destrade	.15	.07
☐ 419 Tony Phillips	.15	.07
☐ 420 Jeff Bagwell	1.25	.55
☐ 421 Mark Gardner	.15	.07
☐ 422 Brett Butler	.30	.14
☐ 423 Graeme Lloyd	.15	.07
☐ 424 Delino DeShields	.15	.07
☐ 425 Scott Erickson	.15	.07
☐ 426 Jeff Kent	.30	.14
☐ 427 Jimmy Key	.30	.14
☐ 428 Mickey Morandini	.15	.07
☐ 429 Marcos Armas	.15	.07
☐ 430 Don Slaught	.15	.07
☐ 431 Randy Johnson	.60	.25
☐ 432 Omar Olivares	.15	.07
☐ 433 Charlie Leibrandt	.15	.07
☐ 434 Kurt Stillwell	.15	.07
☐ 435 Scott Brow	.15	.07
☐ 436 Robby Thompson	.15	.07
☐ 437 Ben McDonald	.15	.07
☐ 438 Deion Sanders	.60	.25
☐ 439 Tony Pena	.15	.07
☐ 440 Mark Grace	.60	.25
☐ 441 Eduardo Perez	.15	.07
☐ 442 Tim Pugh	.15	.07
☐ 443 Scott Ruffcorn	.15	.07
☐ 444 Jay Gainer	.15	.07
☐ 445 Albert Belle	.75	.35
☐ 446 Bret Barberie	.15	.07
☐ 447 Justin Mashore	.15	.07
☐ 448 Pete Harnisch	.15	.07
☐ 449 Greg Gagne	.15	.07
☐ 450 Eric Davis	.30	.14
☐ 451 Dave Mlicki	.15	.07
☐ 452 Moises Alou	.30	.14
☐ 453 Rick Aguilera	.15	.07
☐ 454 Eddie Murray	.60	.25
☐ 455 Bob Wickman	.15	.07
☐ 456 Wes Chamberlain	.15	.07
☐ 457 Brent Gates	.15	.07
☐ 458 Paul Wagner	.15	.07
☐ 459 Mike Hampton	.40	.18
☐ 460 Ozzie Smith	.75	.35
☐ 461 Tom Henke	.15	.07
☐ 462 Ricky Gutierrez	.15	.07
☐ 463 Jack Morris	.30	.14
☐ 464 Joel Chimelis	.15	.07
☐ 465 Gregg Olson	.15	.07
☐ 466 Javier Lopez	.60	.25
☐ 467 Scott Cooper	.15	.07
☐ 468 Willie Wilson	.15	.07
☐ 469 Mark Langston	.15	.07
☐ 470 Barry Larkin	.40	.18
☐ 471 Rod Bolton	.15	.07
☐ 472 Freddie Benavides	.15	.07
☐ 473 Ken Ramos	.15	.07
☐ 474 Chuck Carr	.15	.07
☐ 475 Cecil Fielder	.30	.14
☐ 476 Eddie Taubensee	.15	.07
☐ 477 Chris Eddy	.15	.07
☐ 478 Greg Hansell	.15	.07
☐ 479 Kevin Reimer	.15	.07
☐ 480 Denny Martinez	.30	.14
☐ 481 Chuck Knoblauch	.60	.25
☐ 482 Mike Draper	.15	.07
☐ 483 Spike Owen	.15	.07
☐ 484 Terry Mulholland	.15	.07
☐ 485 Dennis Eckersley	.40	.18
☐ 486 Blas Minor	.15	.07
☐ 487 Dave Fleming	.15	.07
☐ 488 Dan Cholowsky	.15	.07
☐ 489 Ivan Rodriguez	.75	.35
☐ 490 Gary Sheffield	.60	.25
☐ 491 Ed Sprague	.15	.07
☐ 492 Steve Hosey	.15	.07
☐ 493 Jimmy Haynes	.60	.25
☐ 494 John Smoltz	.40	.18
☐ 495 Andre Dawson	.40	.18
☐ 496 Rey Sanchez	.15	.07
☐ 497 Ty Van Burkleo	.15	.07
☐ 498 Bobby Ayala	.30	.14
☐ 499 Tim Raines	.30	.14
☐ 500 Charlie Hayes	.15	.07
☐ 501 Paul Sorrento	.15	.07
☐ 502 Richie Lewis	.15	.07
☐ 503 Jason Pfaff	.15	.07
☐ 504 Ken Caminiti	.60	.25
☐ 505 Mike Macfarlane	.15	.07
☐ 506 Jody Reed	.15	.07
☐ 507 Bobby Hughes	.15	.07
☐ 508 Wil Cordero	.15	.07
☐ 509 George Tsamis	.15	.07
☐ 510 Bret Saberhagen	.15	.07
☐ 511 Derek Jeter	8.00	3.60
☐ 512 Gene Schall	.15	.07
☐ 513 Curtis Shaw	.15	.07
☐ 514 Steve Cooke	.15	.07
☐ 515 Edgar Martinez	.40	.18
☐ 516 Mike Milchin	.15	.07
☐ 517 Billy Ripken	.15	.07
☐ 518 Andy Benes	.30	.14
☐ 519 Juan de la Rosa	.15	.07
☐ 520 John Burkett	.15	.07
☐ 521 Alex Ochoa	.15	.07
☐ 522 Tony Tarasco	.15	.07
☐ 523 Luis Ortiz	.15	.07
☐ 524 Rick Wilkins	.15	.07
☐ 525 Chris Turner	.15	.07
☐ 526 Rob Dibble	.15	.07
☐ 527 Jack McDowell	.15	.07
☐ 528 Daryl Boston	.15	.07
☐ 529 Bill Wertz	.15	.07
☐ 530 Charlie Hough	.15	.07
☐ 531 Sean Bergman	.15	.07
☐ 532 Doug Jones	.15	.07
☐ 533 Jeff Montgomery	.30	.14
☐ 534 Roger Cedeno	.50	.23
☐ 535 Robin Yount	.40	.18
☐ 536 Mo Vaughn	.75	.35
☐ 537 Brian Harper	.15	.07
☐ 538 Juan Castillo	.15	.07
☐ 539 Steve Farr	.15	.07
☐ 540 John Kruk	.30	.14
☐ 541 Troy Neel	.15	.07
☐ 542 Danny Clyburn	1.25	.55
☐ 543 Jim Converse	.15	.07
☐ 544 Gregg Jefferies	.30	.14
☐ 545 Jose Canseco	.40	.18
☐ 546 Julio Bruno	.15	.07
☐ 547 Rob Butler	.15	.07
☐ 548 Royce Clayton	.30	.14
☐ 549 Chris Hoiles	.15	.07
☐ 550 Greg Maddux	2.00	.90
☐ 551 Joe Ciccarella	.15	.07
☐ 552 Ozzie Timmons	.30	.14
☐ 553 Chili Davis	.30	.14
☐ 554 Brian Koelling	.15	.07
☐ 555 Frank Thomas	2.50	1.10
☐ 556 Vinny Castilla	.60	.25
☐ 557 Reggie Jefferson	.30	.14
☐ 558 Rob Natal	.15	.07
☐ 559 Mike Henneman	.15	.07
☐ 560 Craig Biggio	.40	.18
☐ 561 Billy Brewer	.15	.07
☐ 562 Dan Melendez	.15	.07
☐ 563 Kenny Felder	.15	.07
☐ 564 Miguel Batista	.30	.14
☐ 565 Dave Winfield	.40	.18
☐ 566 Al Shirley	.30	.14
☐ 567 Robert Eenhoorn	.15	.07
☐ 568 Mike Williams	.15	.07
☐ 569 Tanyon Sturtze	.30	.14
☐ 570 Tim Wakefield	.30	.14
☐ 571 Greg Pirkl	.15	.07
☐ 572 Sean Lowe	.30	.14
☐ 573 Terry Burrows	.15	.07
☐ 574 Kevin Higgins	.15	.07
☐ 575 Joe Carter	.40	.18
☐ 576 Kevin Rogers	.15	.07
☐ 577 Manny Alexander	.15	.07
☐ 578 David Justice	.60	.25
☐ 579 Brian Conroy	.15	.07
☐ 580 Jessie Hollins	.15	.07
☐ 581 Ron Watson	.15	.07
☐ 582 Bip Roberts	.15	.07
☐ 583 Tom Urbani	.15	.07
☐ 584 Jason Hutchins	.15	.07
☐ 585 Carlos Baerga	.30	.14
☐ 586 Jeff Mutis	.15	.07
☐ 587 Justin Thompson	.75	.35
☐ 588 Orlando Miller	.30	.14
☐ 589 Brian McRae	.15	.07
☐ 590 Ramon Martinez	.30	.14
☐ 591 Dave Nilsson	.30	.14
☐ 592 Jose Vidro	.50	.23
☐ 593 Rich Becker	.30	.14
☐ 594 Preston Wilson	1.50	.70
☐ 595 Don Mattingly	1.00	.45

☐ 596 Tony Longmire .15 .07
☐ 597 Kevin Seitzer .15 .07
☐ 598 Midre Cummings .30 .14
☐ 599 Omar Vizquel .30 .14
☐ 600 Lee Smith .30 .14
☐ 601 David Hulse .15 .07
☐ 602 Darrell Sherman .15 .07
☐ 603 Alex Gonzalez .40 .18
☐ 604 Geronimo Pena .15 .07
☐ 605 Mike Devereaux .15 .07
☐ 606 Sterling Hitchcock .60 .25
☐ 607 Mike Greenwell .15 .07
☐ 608 Steve Buechele .15 .07
☐ 609 Troy Percival .40 .18
☐ 610 Roberto Kelly .15 .07
☐ 611 James Baldwin 1.00 .45
☐ 612 Jerald Clark .15 .07
☐ 613 Albie Lopez .30 .14
☐ 614 Dave Magadan .15 .07
☐ 615 Mickey Tettleton .15 .07
☐ 616 Sean Runyan .15 .07
☐ 617 Bob Hamelin .15 .07
☐ 618 Raul Mondesi .75 .35
☐ 619 Tyrone Hill .15 .07
☐ 620 Darrin Fletcher .15 .07
☐ 621 Mike Trombley .15 .07
☐ 622 Jeromy Burnitz .15 .07
☐ 623 Bernie Williams .40 .18
☐ 624 Mike Farmer .15 .07
☐ 625 Rickey Henderson .40 .18
☐ 626 Carlos Garcia .15 .07
☐ 627 Jeff Darwin .15 .07
☐ 628 Todd Zeile .15 .07
☐ 629 Benji Gil .15 .07
☐ 630 Tony Gwynn 1.50 .70
☐ 631 Aaron Small .15 .07
☐ 632 Joe Rosselli .15 .07
☐ 633 Mike Mussina .60 .25
☐ 634 Ryan Klesko .75 .35
☐ 635 Roger Clemens 1.25 .55
☐ 636 Sammy Sosa .60 .25
☐ 637 Orlando Palmeiro .15 .07
☐ 638 Willie Greene .30 .14
☐ 639 George Bell .15 .07
☐ 640 Garvin Alston .15 .07
☐ 641 Pete Janicki .15 .07
☐ 642 Chris Sheff .15 .07
☐ 643 Felipe Lira .30 .14
☐ 644 Roberto Petagine .30 .14
☐ 645 Wally Joyner .30 .14
☐ 646 Mike Piazza 3.00 1.35
☐ 647 Jaime Navarro .15 .07
☐ 648 Jeff Hartsock .15 .07
☐ 649 David McCarty .15 .07
☐ 650 Bobby Jones .30 .14
☐ 651 Mark Hutton .15 .07
☐ 652 Kyle Abbott .15 .07
☐ 653 Steve Cox .50 .23
☐ 654 Jeff King .30 .14
☐ 655 Norm Charlton .15 .07
☐ 656 Mike Gulan .15 .07
☐ 657 Julio Franco .30 .14
☐ 658 Cameron Cairncross .15 .07
☐ 659 John Olerud .15 .07
☐ 660 Salomon Torres .15 .07
☐ 661 Brad Pennington .15 .07
☐ 662 Melvin Nieves .40 .18
☐ 663 Ivan Calderon .15 .07
☐ 664 Turk Wendell .15 .07
☐ 665 Chris Pritchett .15 .07
☐ 666 Reggie Sanders .40 .18
☐ 667 Robin Ventura .30 .14
☐ 668 Joe Girardi .15 .07
☐ 669 Manny Ramirez 1.25 .55
☐ 670 Jeff Conine .30 .14
☐ 671 Greg Gohr .15 .07
☐ 672 Andujar Cedeno .15 .07
☐ 673 Les Norman .15 .07
☐ 674 Mike James .15 .07
☐ 675 Marshall Boze .15 .07
☐ 676 B.J. Wallace .15 .07
☐ 677 Kent Hrbek .30 .14
☐ 678 Jack Voigt .15 .07
☐ 679 Brien Taylor .15 .07
☐ 680 Curt Schilling .15 .07
☐ 681 Todd Van Poppel .15 .07
☐ 682 Kevin Young .15 .07
☐ 683 Tommy Adams .15 .07
☐ 684 Bernard Gilkey .30 .14
☐ 685 Kevin Brown .30 .14
☐ 686 Fred McGriff .40 .18
☐ 687 Pat Borders .15 .07
☐ 688 Kirt Manwaring .15 .07
☐ 689 Sid Bream .15 .07
☐ 690 John Valentin .30 .14
☐ 691 Steve Olsen .15 .07
☐ 692 Roberto Mejia .15 .07
☐ 693 Carlos Delgado FOIL .60 .25
☐ 694 Steve Gibralter FOIL .30 .14
☐ 695 Gary Mota FOIL .15 .07
☐ 696 Jose Malave FOIL .15 .07
☐ 697 Larry Sutton FOIL .15 .07
☐ 698 Dan Frye FOIL .15 .07
☐ 699 Tim Clark FOIL .15 .07
☐ 700 Brian Rupp FOIL .15 .07
☐ 701 Felipe Alou FOIL .30 .14
Moises Alou
☐ 702 Barry Bonds FOIL .60 .25
Bobby Bonds
☐ 703 Ken Griffey Sr. FOIL 1.00 .45
Ken Griffey Jr.
☐ 704 Brian McRae FOIL .15 .07
Hal McRae
☐ 705 Checklist 1 .15 .07
☐ 706 Checklist 2 .15 .07
☐ 707 Checklist 3 .15 .07
☐ 708 Checklist 4 .15 .07

1994 Bowman Previews

This 10-card standard-size set served as a preview to the 1994 Bowman set. The cards were randomly inserted one in every 24 1994 Stadium Club second series packs. Card fronts are similar to the full-bleed basic issue. The differences are a multi-colored foil stripe up the left-hand border with a red stripe at bottom. Red foil also surrounds the Bowman logo. In the upper right-hand corner is a blue foil Bowman Preview logo.The backs are identical to the basic issue with a horizontal layout containing a player photo, text and statistics.

	MINT	NRMT
COMPLETE SET (10)	40.00	18.00
COMMON CARD (1-10)	1.00	.45
☐ 1 Frank Thomas	15.00	6.75
☐ 2 Mike Piazza	12.00	5.50
☐ 3 Albert Belle	5.00	2.20
☐ 4 Javier Lopez	2.50	1.10
☐ 5 Cliff Floyd	1.00	.45
☐ 6 Alex Gonzalez	1.00	.45
☐ 7 Ricky Bottalico	1.00	.45
☐ 8 Tony Clark	10.00	4.50
☐ 9 Mac Suzuki	1.00	.45
☐ 10 James Mouton Foil	1.00	.45

1994 Bowman

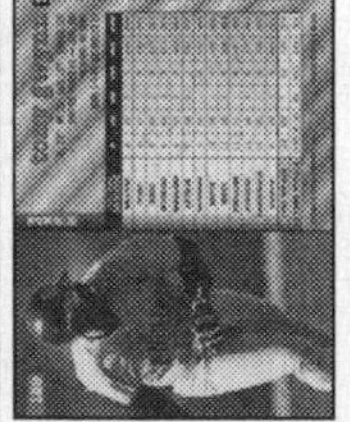

The 1994 Bowman set consists of 682 standard-size, full-bleed cards primarily distributed in plastic wrap packs and jumbo packs. In addition to a color photo on the front, there is a line of gold foil that runs up the far left side and across the bottom of the card. The player's name is also in gold foil at bottom and the Bowman logo at bottom left is enclosed in gold foil. Horizontal backs contain a player photo on the left and statistics and highlights on the right. There are 51 Foil cards (337-388) that include a number of top young stars and prospects. These foil cards were issued one per foil pack and two per jumbo. Rookie Cards of note include Alan Benes, Tony Clark, Brad Fullmer, Derrek Lee, Chan Ho Park, Edgar Renteria and Ruben Rivera.

	MINT	NRMT
COMPLETE SET (682)	125.00	55.00
COMMON CARD (1-682)	.20	.09
☐ 1 Joe Carter	.20	.09
☐ 2 Marcus Moore	.20	.09
☐ 3 Doug Creek	.20	.09
☐ 4 Pedro Martinez	.75	.35
☐ 5 Ken Griffey Jr.	4.00	1.80
☐ 6 Greg Swindell	.20	.09
☐ 7 J.J. Johnson	.40	.18
☐ 8 Homer Bush	.40	.18
☐ 9 Arquimedez Pozo	.40	.18
☐ 10 Bryan Harvey	.20	.09
☐ 11 J.T. Snow	.40	.18
☐ 12 Alan Benes	4.00	1.80
☐ 13 Chad Kreuter	.20	.09
☐ 14 Eric Karros	.40	.18
☐ 15 Frank Thomas	3.00	1.35
☐ 16 Bret Saberhagen	.20	.09
☐ 17 Terrell Lowery	.20	.09
☐ 18 Rod Bolton	.20	.09
☐ 19 Harold Baines	.40	.18
☐ 20 Matt Walbeck	.20	.09
☐ 21 Tom Glavine	.20	.09
☐ 22 Todd Jones	.20	.09
☐ 23 Alberto Castillo	.40	.18
☐ 24 Ruben Sierra	.20	.09
☐ 25 Don Mattingly	1.25	.55
☐ 26 Mike Morgan	.20	.09
☐ 27 Jim Musselwhite	.40	.18
☐ 28 Matt Brunson	.40	.18
☐ 29 Adam Meinershagen	.20	.09
☐ 30 Joe Girardi	.20	.09
☐ 31 Shane Halter	.20	.09
☐ 32 Jose Paniagua	.40	.18
☐ 33 Paul Perkins	.20	.09
☐ 34 John Hudek	.20	.09
☐ 35 Frank Viola	.20	.09
☐ 36 David Lamb	.20	.09
☐ 37 Marshall Boze	.20	.09
☐ 38 Jorge Posada	.40	.18
☐ 39 Brian Anderson	1.00	.45
☐ 40 Mark Whiten	.20	.09
☐ 41 Sean Bergman	.40	.18
☐ 42 Jose Parra	.40	.18
☐ 43 Mike Robertson	.20	.09
☐ 44 Pete Walker	.20	.09
☐ 45 Juan Gonzalez	2.00	.90
☐ 46 Cleveland Ladell	.40	.18
☐ 47 Mark Smith	.20	.09
☐ 48 Kevin Jarvis UER (team listed as Yankees on back)	.20	.09
☐ 49 Amaury Telemaco	1.00	.45
☐ 50 Andy Van Slyke	.40	.18
☐ 51 Rikkert Faneyte	.20	.09
☐ 52 Curtis Shaw	.20	.09
☐ 53 Matt Drews	.50	.23
☐ 54 Wilson Alvarez	.40	.18
☐ 55 Manny Ramirez	1.00	.45
☐ 56 Bobby Munoz	.20	.09
☐ 57 Ed Sprague	.20	.09
☐ 58 Jamey Wright	1.50	.70
☐ 59 Jeff Montgomery	.20	.09
☐ 60 Kirk Rueter	.20	.09
☐ 61 Edgar Martinez	.20	.09
☐ 62 Luis Gonzalez	.20	.09
☐ 63 Tim Vanegmond	.20	.09
☐ 64 Bip Roberts	.20	.09
☐ 65 John Jaha	.20	.09
☐ 66 Chuck Carr	.20	.09
☐ 67 Chuck Finley	.20	.09
☐ 68 Aaron Holbert	.20	.09
☐ 69 Cecil Fielder	.40	.18
☐ 70 Tom Engle	.20	.09
☐ 71 Ron Karkovice	.20	.09
☐ 72 Joe Orsulak	.20	.09
☐ 73 Duff Brumley	.20	.09
☐ 74 Craig Clayton	.20	.09
☐ 75 Cal Ripken	3.00	1.35
☐ 76 Brad Fulimer	4.00	1.80
☐ 77 Tony Tarasco	.20	.09
☐ 78 Terry Farrar	.20	.09
☐ 79 Matt Williams	.20	.09
☐ 80 Rickey Henderson	.20	.09
☐ 81 Terry Mulholland	.20	.09
☐ 82 Sammy Sosa	.75	.35
☐ 83 Paul Sorrento	.20	.09
☐ 84 Pete Incaviglia	.20	.09
☐ 85 Darren Hall	.20	.09
☐ 86 Scott Klingenbeck	.20	.09
☐ 87 Dario Perez	.20	.09
☐ 88 Ugueth Urbina	.40	.18
☐ 89 Dave Vanhof	.20	.09
☐ 90 Domingo Jean	.20	.09
☐ 91 Otis Nixon	.20	.09
☐ 92 Andres Berumen	.20	.09

93 Jose Valentin	.40	.18
94 Edgar Renteria	4.00	1.80
95 Chris Turner	.20	.09
96 Ray Lankford	.40	.18
97 Danny Bautista	.20	.09
98 Chan Ho Park	6.00	2.70
99 Glenn DiSarcina	.40	.18
100 Butch Huckey	.40	.18
☐ 101 Ivan Rodriguez	1.00	.45
☐ 102 Johnny Ruffin	.20	.09
☐ 103 Alex Ochoa	.20	.09
☐ 104 Torii Hunter	.75	.35
☐ 105 Ryan Klesko	.20	.09
☐ 106 Jay Bell	.40	.18
☐ 107 Kurt Peltzer	.20	.09
☐ 108 Miguel Jimenez	.20	.09
☐ 109 Russ Davis	.40	.18
☐ 110 Derek Wallace	.20	.09
☐ 111 Keith Lockhart	.20	.09
☐ 112 Mike Lieberthal	.20	.09
☐ 113 Dave Stewart	.40	.18
☐ 114 Tom Schmidt	.20	.09
☐ 115 Brian McRae	.20	.09
☐ 116 Moises Alou	.40	.18
☐ 117 Dave Fleming	.20	.09
☐ 118 Jeff Bagwell	1.50	.70
☐ 119 Luis Ortiz	.20	.09
☐ 120 Tony Gwynn	2.00	.90
☐ 121 Jaime Navarro	.20	.09
☐ 122 Benny Santiago	.20	.09
☐ 123 Darrell Whitmore	.20	.09
☐ 124 John Mabry	.75	.35
☐ 125 Mickey Tettleton	.20	.09
☐ 126 Tom Candiotti	.20	.09
☐ 127 Tim Raines	.20	.09
☐ 128 Bobby Bonilla	.40	.18
☐ 129 John Dettmer	.20	.09
☐ 130 Hector Carrasco	.20	.09
☐ 131 Chris Hoiles	.20	.09
☐ 132 Rick Aguilera	.20	.09
☐ 133 David Justice	.75	.35
☐ 134 Esteban Loaiza	1.00	.45
☐ 135 Barry Bonds	1.00	.45
☐ 136 Bob Welch	.20	.09
☐ 137 Mike Stanley	.20	.09
☐ 138 Roberto Hernandez	.40	.18
☐ 139 Sandy Alomar	.40	.18
☐ 140 Darren Daulton	.40	.18
☐ 141 Angel Martinez	.40	.18
☐ 142 Howard Johnson	.20	.09
☐ 143 Bob Hamelin UER	.20	.09
(name and card number colors don't match)		
☐ 144 J.J. Thobe	.20	.09
☐ 145 Roger Salkeld	.20	.09
☐ 146 Orlando Miller	.20	.09
☐ 147 Dmitri Young	.75	.35
☐ 148 Tim Hyers	.20	.09
☐ 149 Mark Loretta	.20	.09
☐ 150 Chris Hammond	.20	.09
☐ 151 Joel Moore	.20	.09
☐ 152 Todd Zeile	.20	.09
☐ 153 Wil Cordero	.20	.09
☐ 154 Chris Smith	.20	.09
☐ 155 James Baldwin	.20	.09
☐ 156 Edgardo Alfonzo	2.50	1.10
☐ 157 Kym Ashworth	.40	.18
☐ 158 Paul Bako	.20	.09
☐ 159 Rick Krivda	.20	.09
☐ 160 Pat Mahomes	.20	.09
☐ 161 Damon Hollins	.40	.18
☐ 162 Felix Martinez	.50	.23
☐ 163 Jason Myers	.40	.18
☐ 164 Izzy Molina	.40	.18
☐ 165 Brien Taylor	.20	.09
☐ 166 Kevin Orie	3.00	1.35
☐ 167 Casey Whitten	.40	.18
☐ 168 Tony Longmire	.20	.09
☐ 169 John Olerud	.40	.18
☐ 170 Mark Thompson	.20	.09
☐ 171 Jorge Fabregas	.20	.09
☐ 172 John Wetteland	.40	.18
☐ 173 Dan Wilson	.40	.18
☐ 174 Doug Drabek	.20	.09
☐ 175 Jeffrey McNeely	.20	.09
☐ 176 Melvin Nieves	.40	.18
☐ 177 Doug Glanville	.40	.18
☐ 178 Javier De La Hoya	.20	.09
☐ 179 Chad Curtis	.20	.09
☐ 180 Brian Barber	.20	.09
☐ 181 Mike Henneman	.20	.09
☐ 182 Jose Offerman	.20	.09
☐ 183 Robert Ellis	.20	.09
☐ 184 John Franco	.20	.09
☐ 185 Benji Gil	.20	.09
☐ 186 Hal Morris	.20	.09
☐ 187 Chris Sabo	.20	.09
☐ 188 Blaise Ilsley	.20	.09
☐ 189 Steve Avery	.20	.09
☐ 190 Rick White	.20	.09
☐ 191 Rod Beck	.40	.18
☐ 192 Mark McGwire UER	1.50	.70
(No card number on back)		
☐ 193 Jim Abbott	.20	.09
☐ 194 Randy Myers	.20	.09
☐ 195 Kenny Lofton	1.00	.45
☐ 196 Mariano Duncan	.20	.09
☐ 197 Lee Daniels	.20	.09
☐ 198 Armando Reynoso	.20	.09
☐ 199 Joe Randa	.20	.09
☐ 200 Cliff Floyd	.20	.09
☐ 201 Tim Harkrider	.20	.09
☐ 202 Kevin Gallaher	.20	.09
☐ 203 Scott Cooper	.20	.09
☐ 204 Phil Stidham	.20	.09
☐ 205 Jeff D'Amico	1.50	.70
☐ 206 Matt Whisenant	.20	.09
☐ 207 De Shawn Warren	.40	.18
☐ 208 Rene Arocha	.20	.09
☐ 209 Tony Clark	15.00	6.75
☐ 210 Jason Jacome	.20	.09
☐ 211 Scott Christman	.40	.18
☐ 212 Bill Pulsipher	.40	.18
☐ 213 Dean Palmer	.40	.18
☐ 214 Chad Mottola	.20	.09
☐ 215 Manny Alexander	.20	.09
☐ 216 Rich Becker	.40	.18
☐ 217 Andre King	.20	.09
☐ 218 Carlos Garcia	.20	.09
☐ 219 Ron Pezzoni	.20	.09
☐ 220 Steve Karsay	.20	.09
☐ 221 Jose Musset	.20	.09
☐ 222 Karl Rhodes	.20	.09
☐ 223 Frank Cimorelli	.20	.09
☐ 224 Kevin Jordan	.20	.09
☐ 225 Duane Ward	.20	.09
☐ 226 John Burke	.20	.09
☐ 227 Mike Macfarlane	.20	.09
☐ 228 Mike Lansing	.40	.18
☐ 229 Chuck Knoblauch	.75	.35
☐ 230 Ken Caminiti	.75	.35
☐ 231 Gar Finnvold	.20	.09
☐ 232 Derrek Lee	10.00	4.50
☐ 233 Brady Anderson	.75	.35
☐ 234 Vic Darensbourg	.40	.18
☐ 235 Mark Langston	.20	.09
☐ 236 T.J. Mathews	.40	.18
☐ 237 Lou Whitaker	.20	.09
☐ 238 Roger Cedeno	.40	.18
☐ 239 Alex Fernandez	.20	.09
☐ 240 Ryan Thompson	.20	.09
☐ 241 Kerry Lacy	.20	.09
☐ 242 Reggie Sanders	.40	.18
☐ 243 Brad Pennington	.20	.09
☐ 244 Bryan Eversgerd	.20	.09
☐ 245 Greg Maddux	2.50	1.10
☐ 246 Jason Kendall	.75	.35
☐ 247 J.R. Phillips	.20	.09
☐ 248 Bobby Witt	.20	.09
☐ 249 Paul O'Neill	.40	.18
☐ 250 Ryne Sandberg	1.00	.45
☐ 251 Charles Nagy	.40	.18
☐ 252 Kevin Stocker	.20	.09
☐ 253 Shawn Green	.40	.18
☐ 254 Charlie Hayes	.20	.09
☐ 255 Donnie Elliott	.20	.09
☐ 256 Rob Fitzpatrick	.20	.09
☐ 257 Tim Davis	.20	.09
☐ 258 James Mouton	.20	.09
☐ 259 Mike Greenwell	.20	.09
☐ 260 Ray McDavid	.20	.09
☐ 261 Mike Kelly	.20	.09
☐ 262 Andy Larkin	.40	.18
☐ 263 Marquis Riley UER	.20	.09
(No card number on back)		
☐ 264 Bob Tewksbury	.20	.09
☐ 265 Brian Edmondson	.20	.09
☐ 266 Eduardo Lantigua	.40	.18
☐ 267 Brandon Wilson	.20	.09
☐ 268 Mike Welch	.20	.09
☐ 269 Tom Henke	.20	.09
☐ 270 Calvin Reese	.40	.18
☐ 271 Greg Zaun	.20	.09
☐ 272 Todd Ritchie	.20	.09
☐ 273 Javier Lopez	.20	.09
☐ 274 Kevin Young	.20	.09
☐ 275 Kirt Manwaring	.20	.09
☐ 276 Bill Taylor	.20	.09
☐ 277 Robert Eenhoorn	.20	.09
☐ 278 Jessie Hollins	.20	.09
☐ 279 Julian Tavarez	.40	.18
☐ 280 Gene Schall	.20	.09
☐ 281 Paul Molitor	.75	.35
☐ 282 Neifi Perez	3.00	1.35
☐ 283 Greg Gagne	.20	.09
☐ 284 Marquis Grissom	.40	.18
☐ 285 Randy Johnson	.75	.35
☐ 286 Pete Harnisch	.20	.09
☐ 287 Joel Bennett	.20	.09
☐ 288 Derek Bell	.20	.09
☐ 289 Darryl Hamilton	.20	.09
☐ 290 Gary Sheffield	.75	.35
☐ 291 Eduardo Perez	.20	.09
☐ 292 Basil Shabazz	.20	.09
☐ 293 Eric Davis	.40	.18
☐ 294 Pedro Astacio	.20	.09
☐ 295 Robin Ventura	.40	.18
☐ 296 Jeff Kent	.20	.09
☐ 297 Rick Helling	.20	.09
☐ 298 Joe Oliver	.20	.09
☐ 299 Lee Smith	.40	.18
☐ 300 Dave Winfield	.20	.09
☐ 301 Deion Sanders	.75	.35
☐ 302 Ravelo Manzanillo	.20	.09
☐ 303 Mark Portugal	.20	.09
☐ 304 Brent Gates	.20	.09
☐ 305 Wade Boggs	.75	.35
☐ 306 Rick Wilkins	.20	.09
☐ 307 Carlos Baerga	.40	.18
☐ 308 Curt Schilling	.20	.09
☐ 309 Shannon Stewart	1.00	.45
☐ 310 Darren Holmes	.20	.09
☐ 311 Robert Toth	.40	.18
☐ 312 Gabe White	.20	.09
☐ 313 Mac Suzuki	.20	.09
☐ 314 Alvin Morman	.20	.09
☐ 315 Mo Vaughn	1.00	.45
☐ 316 Bryce Florie	.20	.09
☐ 317 Gabby Martinez	.50	.23
☐ 318 Carl Everett	.20	.09
☐ 319 Kerwin Moore	.20	.09
☐ 320 Tom Pagnozzi	.20	.09
☐ 321 Chris Gomez	.20	.09
☐ 322 Todd Williams	.20	.09
☐ 323 Pat Hentgen	.40	.18
☐ 324 Kirk Presley	.20	.09
☐ 325 Kevin Brown	.40	.18
☐ 326 Jason Isringhausen	2.00	.90
☐ 327 Rick Forney	.20	.09
☐ 328 Carlos Pulido	.20	.09
☐ 329 Terrell Wade	.20	.09
☐ 330 Al Martin	.20	.09
☐ 331 Dan Carlson	.20	.09
☐ 332 Mark Acre	.20	.09
☐ 333 Sterling Hitchcock	.40	.18
☐ 334 Jon Ratliff	.40	.18
☐ 335 Alex Ramirez	1.50	.70
☐ 336 Phil Geisler	.20	.09
☐ 337 Eddie Zambrano FOIL	.20	.09
☐ 338 Jim Thome FOIL	1.00	.45
☐ 339 James Mouton FOIL	.40	.18
☐ 340 Cliff Floyd FOIL	.20	.09
☐ 341 Carlos Delgado FOIL	.20	.09
☐ 342 Roberto Petagine FOIL	.20	.09
☐ 343 Tim Clark FOIL	.20	.09
☐ 344 Bubba Smith FOIL	.20	.09
☐ 345 Randy Curtis FOIL	.20	.09
☐ 346 Joe Biasucci FOIL	.20	.09
☐ 347 D.J. Boston FOIL	.40	.18
☐ 348 Ruben Rivera FOIL	6.00	2.70
☐ 349 Bryan Link FOIL	.20	.09
☐ 350 Mike Bell FOIL	.75	.35
☐ 351 Marty Watson FOIL	.20	.09
☐ 352 Jason Myers FOIL	.40	.18
☐ 353 Chipper Jones FOIL	2.50	1.10
☐ 354 Brooks Kieschnick FOIL	1.00	.45
☐ 355 Calvin Reese FOIL	.40	.18
☐ 356 John Burke FOIL	.20	.09
☐ 357 Kurt Miller FOIL	.20	.09
☐ 358 Orlando Miller FOIL	.20	.09
☐ 359 Todd Hollandsworth FOIL	.75	.35
☐ 360 Rondell White FOIL	.75	.35
☐ 361 Bill Pulsipher FOIL	.40	.18
☐ 362 Tyler Green FOIL	.20	.09
☐ 363 Midre Cummings FOIL	.20	.09
☐ 364 Brian Barber FOIL	.20	.09
☐ 365 Melvin Nieves FOIL	.40	.18
☐ 366 Salomon Torres FOIL	.20	.09
☐ 367 Alex Ochoa FOIL	.20	.09
☐ 368 Frankie Rodriguez FOIL	.20	.09
☐ 369 Brian Anderson FOIL	1.00	.45
☐ 370 James Baldwin FOIL	.20	.09
☐ 371 Manny Ramirez FOIL	1.00	.45
☐ 372 Justin Thompson FOIL	1.00	.45
☐ 373 Johnny Damon FOIL	.75	.35
☐ 374 Jeff D'Amico FOIL	1.50	.70
☐ 375 Rich Becker FOIL	.40	.18
☐ 376 Derek Jeter FOIL	3.00	1.35
☐ 377 Steve Karsay FOIL	.20	.09
☐ 378 Mac Suzuki FOIL	.20	.09
☐ 379 Benji Gil FOIL	.20	.09
☐ 380 Alex Gonzalez FOIL	.40	.18

☐ 381 Jason Bere FOIL	.40	.18
☐ 382 Brett Butler FOIL	.40	.18
☐ 383 Jeff Conine FOIL	.40	.18
☐ 384 Darren Daulton FOIL	.40	.18
☐ 385 Jeff Kent FOIL	.20	.09
☐ 386 Don Mattingly FOIL	1.25	.55
☐ 387 Mike Piazza FOIL	2.50	1.10
☐ 388 Ryne Sandberg FOIL	1.00	.45
☐ 389 Rich Amaral	.20	.09
☐ 390 Craig Biggio	.20	.09
☐ 391 Jeff Suppan	2.00	.90
☐ 392 Andy Benes	.40	.18
☐ 393 Cal Eldred	.20	.09
☐ 394 Jeff Conine	.40	.18
☐ 395 Tim Salmon	.75	.35
☐ 396 Ray Suplee	.20	.09
☐ 397 Tony Phillips	.20	.09
☐ 398 Ramon Martinez	.20	.09
☐ 399 Julio Franco	.40	.18
☐ 400 Dwight Gooden	.40	.18
☐ 401 Kevin Lomon	.20	.09
☐ 402 Jose Rijo	.20	.09
☐ 403 Mike Devereaux	.20	.09
☐ 404 Mike Zolecki	.20	.09
☐ 405 Fred McGriff	.20	.09
☐ 406 Danny Clyburn	.40	.18
☐ 407 Robby Thompson	.20	.09
☐ 408 Terry Steinbach	.40	.18
☐ 409 Luis Polonia	.20	.09
☐ 410 Mark Grace	.75	.35
☐ 411 Albert Belle	1.00	.45
☐ 412 John Kruk	.40	.18
☐ 413 Scott Spiezio	2.50	1.10
☐ 414 Ellis Burks UER	.40	.18
(Name spelled Elkis on front)		
☐ 415 Joe Vitiello	.20	.09
☐ 416 Tim Costo	.20	.09
☐ 417 Marc Newfield	.40	.18
☐ 418 Oscar Henriquez	.50	.23
☐ 419 Matt Perisho	1.00	.45
☐ 420 Julio Bruno	.20	.09
☐ 421 Kenny Felder	.20	.09
☐ 422 Tyler Green	.20	.09
☐ 423 Jim Edmonds	.75	.35
☐ 424 Ozzie Smith	1.00	.45
☐ 425 Rick Greene	.20	.09
☐ 426 Todd Hollandsworth	.75	.35
☐ 427 Eddie Pearson	.20	.09
☐ 428 Quilvio Veras	.40	.18
☐ 429 Kenny Rogers	.20	.09
☐ 430 Willie Greene	.40	.18
☐ 431 Vaughn Eshelman	.20	.09
☐ 432 Pat Meares	.20	.09
☐ 433 Jermaine Dye	2.00	.90
☐ 434 Steve Cooke	.20	.09
☐ 435 Bill Swift	.20	.09
☐ 436 Fausto Cruz	.20	.09
☐ 437 Mark Hutton	.20	.09
☐ 438 Brooks Kieschnick	1.00	.45
☐ 439 Yorkis Perez	.20	.09
☐ 440 Len Dykstra	.40	.18
☐ 441 Pat Borders	.20	.09
☐ 442 Doug Walls	.20	.09
☐ 443 Wally Joyner	.40	.18
☐ 444 Ken Hill	.20	.09
☐ 445 Eric Anthony	.20	.09
☐ 446 Mitch Williams	.20	.09
☐ 447 Cory Bailey	.20	.09
☐ 448 Dave Staton	.20	.09
☐ 449 Greg Vaughn	.20	.09
☐ 450 Dave Magadan	.20	.09
☐ 451 Chili Davis	.40	.18
☐ 452 Gerald Santos	.20	.09
☐ 453 Joe Perona	.20	.09
☐ 454 Delino DeShields	.20	.09
☐ 455 Jack McDowell	.20	.09
☐ 456 Todd Hundley	.40	.18
☐ 457 Ritchie Moody	.20	.09
☐ 458 Bret Boone	.40	.18
☐ 459 Ben McDonald	.20	.09
☐ 460 Kirby Puckett	1.50	.70
☐ 461 Gregg Olson	.20	.09
☐ 462 Rich Aude	.20	.09
☐ 463 John Burkett	.20	.09
☐ 464 Troy Neel	.20	.09
☐ 465 Jimmy Key	.40	.18
☐ 466 Ozzie Timmons	.20	.09
☐ 467 Eddie Murray	.75	.35
☐ 468 Mark Tranberg	.20	.09
☐ 469 Alex Gonzalez	.40	.18
☐ 470 David Nied	.20	.09
☐ 471 Barry Larkin	.75	.35
☐ 472 Brian Looney	.20	.09
☐ 473 Shawn Estes	1.00	.45
☐ 474 A.J. Sager	.20	.09
☐ 475 Roger Clemens	1.50	.70
☐ 476 Vince Moore	.20	.09
☐ 477 Scott Karl	.40	.18
☐ 478 Kurt Miller	.20	.09
☐ 479 Garret Anderson	.75	.35
☐ 480 Allen Watson	.20	.09
☐ 481 Jose Lima	.40	.18
☐ 482 Rick Gorecki	.20	.09
☐ 483 Jimmy Hurst	.40	.18
☐ 484 Preston Wilson	.40	.18
☐ 485 Will Clark	.75	.35
☐ 486 Mike Ferry	.20	.09
☐ 487 Curtis Goodwin	.40	.18
☐ 488 Mike Myers	.20	.09
☐ 489 Chipper Jones	2.50	1.10
☐ 490 Jeff King	.40	.18
☐ 491 William VanLandingham	.20	.09
☐ 492 Carlos Reyes	.20	.09
☐ 493 Andy Pettitte	1.50	.70
☐ 494 Brant Brown	.20	.09
☐ 495 Daron Kirkreit	.20	.09
☐ 496 Ricky Bottalico	1.00	.45
☐ 497 Devon White	.20	.09
☐ 498 Jason Johnson	.20	.09
☐ 499 Vince Coleman	.20	.09
☐ 500 Larry Walker	.75	.35
☐ 501 Bobby Ayala	.20	.09
☐ 502 Steve Finley	.20	.09
☐ 503 Scott Fletcher	.20	.09
☐ 504 Brad Ausmus	.20	.09
☐ 505 Scott Talanoa	.20	.09
☐ 506 Orestes Destrade	.20	.09
☐ 507 Gary DiSarcina	.20	.09
☐ 508 Willie Smith	.20	.09
☐ 509 Alan Trammell	.20	.09
☐ 510 Mike Piazza	2.50	1.10
☐ 511 Ozzie Guillen	.20	.09
☐ 512 Jeromy Burnitz	.20	.09
☐ 513 Darren Oliver	1.00	.45
☐ 514 Kevin Mitchell	.40	.18
☐ 515 Rafael Palmeiro	.20	.09
☐ 516 David McCarty	.20	.09
☐ 517 Jeff Blauser	.20	.09
☐ 518 Trey Beamon	.40	.18
☐ 519 Royce Clayton	.40	.18
☐ 520 Dennis Eckersley	.20	.09
☐ 521 Bernie Williams	.75	.35
☐ 522 Steve Buechele	.20	.09
☐ 523 Denny Martinez	.40	.18
☐ 524 Dave Hollins	.20	.09
☐ 525 Joey Hamilton	.75	.35
☐ 526 Andres Galarraga	.75	.35
☐ 527 Jeff Granger	.20	.09
☐ 528 Joey Eischen	.20	.09
☐ 529 Desi Relaford	.20	.09
☐ 530 Roberto Petagine	.40	.18
☐ 531 Andre Dawson	.20	.09
☐ 532 Ray Holbert	.20	.09
☐ 533 Duane Singleton	.20	.09
☐ 534 Kurt Abbott	.20	.09
☐ 535 Bo Jackson	.40	.18
☐ 536 Gregg Jefferies	.40	.18
☐ 537 David Mysel	.20	.09
☐ 538 Raul Mondesi	.75	.35
☐ 539 Chris Snopek	.20	.09
☐ 540 Brook Fordyce	.20	.09
☐ 541 Ron Frazier	.20	.09
☐ 542 Brian Koelling	.20	.09
☐ 543 Jimmy Haynes	.40	.18
☐ 544 Marty Cordova	.40	.18
☐ 545 Jason Green	.40	.18
☐ 546 Orlando Merced	.20	.09
☐ 547 Lou Pote	.20	.09
☐ 548 Todd Van Poppel	.20	.09
☐ 549 Pat Kelly	.20	.09
☐ 550 Turk Wendell	.20	.09
☐ 551 Herbert Perry	.20	.09
☐ 552 Ryan Karp	.40	.18
☐ 553 Juan Guzman	.20	.09
☐ 554 Bryan Rekar	.40	.18
☐ 555 Kevin Appier	.40	.18
☐ 556 Chris Schwab	.20	.09
☐ 557 Jay Buhner	.20	.09
☐ 558 Andujar Cedeno	.20	.09
☐ 559 Ryan McGuire	.40	.18
☐ 560 Ricky Gutierrez	.20	.09
☐ 561 Keith Kimsey	.20	.09
☐ 562 Tim Clark	.20	.09
☐ 563 Damion Easley	.20	.09
☐ 564 Clint Davis	.20	.09
☐ 565 Mike Moore	.20	.09
☐ 566 Orel Hershiser	.40	.18
☐ 567 Jason Bere	.20	.09
☐ 568 Kevin McReynolds	.20	.09
☐ 569 Leland Macon	.40	.18
☐ 570 John Courtright	.20	.09
☐ 571 Sid Fernandez	.20	.09
☐ 572 Chad Roper	.20	.09
☐ 573 Terry Pendleton	.40	.18
☐ 574 Danny Miceli	.20	.0
☐ 575 Joe Rosselli	.20	.0
☐ 576 Mike Bordick	.20	.0
☐ 577 Danny Tartabull	.20	.0
☐ 578 Jose Guzman	.20	.0
☐ 579 Omar Vizquel	.40	.1
☐ 580 Tommy Greene	.20	.0
☐ 581 Paul Spoljaric	.20	.0
☐ 582 Walt Weiss	.20	.0
☐ 583 Oscar Jimenez	.20	.0
☐ 584 Rod Henderson	.20	.09
☐ 585 Derek Lowe	.20	.09
☐ 586 Richard Hidalgo	6.00	2.70
☐ 587 Shayne Bennett	.40	.18
☐ 588 Tim Belk	.20	.09
☐ 589 Matt Mieske	.20	.09
☐ 590 Nigel Wilson	.20	.09
☐ 591 Jeff Knox	.40	.18
☐ 592 Bernard Gilkey	.40	.18
☐ 593 David Cone	.40	.18
☐ 594 Paul LoDuca	.40	.18
☐ 595 Scott Ruffcorn	.20	.09
☐ 596 Chris Roberts	.40	.18
☐ 597 Oscar Munoz	.20	.09
☐ 598 Scott Sullivan	.40	.18
☐ 599 Matt Jarvis	.20	.09
☐ 600 Jose Canseco	.20	.09
☐ 601 Tony Graffanino	.40	.18
☐ 602 Don Slaught	.20	.09
☐ 603 Brett King	.40	.18
☐ 604 Jose Herrera	.20	.09
☐ 605 Melido Perez	.20	.09
☐ 606 Mike Hubbard	.20	.09
☐ 607 Chad Ogea	.40	.18
☐ 608 Wayne Gomes	.40	.18
☐ 609 Roberto Alomar	.75	.35
☐ 610 Angel Echevarria	.50	.23
☐ 611 Jose Lind	.20	.09
☐ 612 Darrin Fletcher	.20	.09
☐ 613 Chris Bosio	.20	.09
☐ 614 Darryl Kile	.20	.09
☐ 615 Frankie Rodriguez	.40	.18
☐ 616 Phil Plantier	.20	.09
☐ 617 Pat Listach	.20	.09
☐ 618 Charlie Hough	.20	.09
☐ 619 Ryan Hancock	.40	.18
☐ 620 Darrel Deak	.20	.09
☐ 621 Travis Fryman	.40	.18
☐ 622 Brett Butler	.40	.18
☐ 623 Lance Johnson	.20	.09
☐ 624 Pete Smith	.20	.09
☐ 625 James Hurst	.20	.09
☐ 626 Roberto Kelly	.20	.09
☐ 627 Mike Mussina	.75	.35
☐ 628 Kevin Tapani	.20	.09
☐ 629 John Smoltz	.20	.09
☐ 630 Midre Cummings	.20	.09
☐ 631 Salomon Torres	.20	.09
☐ 632 Willie Adams	.20	.09
☐ 633 Derek Jeter	3.00	1.35
☐ 634 Steve Trachsel	.40	.18
☐ 635 Albie Lopez	.40	.18
☐ 636 Jason Moler	.20	.09
☐ 637 Carlos Delgado	.20	.09
☐ 638 Roberto Mejia	.20	.09
☐ 639 Darren Burton	.20	.09
☐ 640 B.J. Wallace	.20	.09
☐ 641 Brad Clontz	.20	.09
☐ 642 Billy Wagner	3.00	1.35
☐ 643 Aaron Sele	.40	.18
☐ 644 Cameron Cairncross	.20	.09
☐ 645 Brian Harper	.20	.09
☐ 646 Marc Valdes UER	.40	.18
(No card number on back)		
☐ 647 Mark Ratekin	.20	.09
☐ 648 Terry Bradshaw	.20	.09
☐ 649 Justin Thompson	1.00	.45
☐ 650 Mike Busch	.40	.18
☐ 651 Joe Hall	.20	.09
☐ 652 Bobby Jones	.40	.18
☐ 653 Kelly Stinnett	.20	.09
☐ 654 Rod Steph	.20	.09
☐ 655 Jay Powell	.40	.18
☐ 656 Keith Garagozzo UER	.20	.09
(No card number on back)		
☐ 657 Todd Dunn	.20	.09
☐ 658 Charles Peterson	.50	.23
☐ 659 Darren Lewis	.20	.09
☐ 660 John Wasdin	.20	.09
☐ 661 Tate Seefried	.40	.18
☐ 662 Hector Trinidad	.40	.18
☐ 663 John Carter	.20	.09
☐ 664 Larry Mitchell	.20	.09
☐ 665 David Catlett	.40	.18
☐ 666 Dante Bichette	.20	.09
☐ 667 Felix Jose	.20	.09
☐ 668 Rondell White	.40	.18

Card	MINT	NRMT
☐ 669 Tino Martinez	.75	.35
☐ 670 Brian L. Hunter	.75	.35
☐ 671 Jose Malave	.40	.18
☐ 672 Archi Cianfrocco	.20	.09
☐ 673 Mike Matheny	.20	.09
☐ 674 Bret Barberie	.20	.09
☐ 675 Andrew Lorraine	.20	.09
☐ 676 Brian Jordan	.40	.18
☐ 677 Tim Belcher	.20	.09
☐ 678 Antonio Osuna	.40	.18
☐ 679 Checklist	.20	.09
☐ 680 Checklist	.20	.09
☐ 681 Checklist	.20	.09
☐ 682 Checklist	.20	.09

1995 Bowman

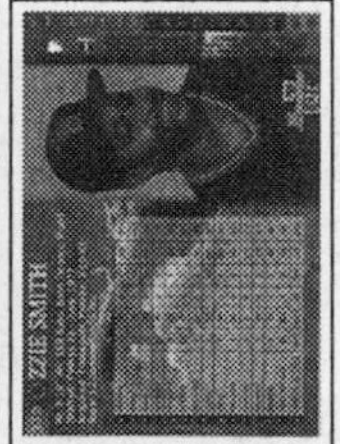

Cards from this 439-card standard-size prsopect-oriented set were primarily issued in plastic wrapped packs and jumbo packs. Card fronts feature white broders enframing full color photos. The left border is a reversed negative of the photo. The set includes 54 silver foil subset cards (221-274). The foil subset, largely comprising of minor league stars, have embossed borders and are found one per pack and two per jumbo pack. Rookie Cards of note include Bartolo Colon, Karim Garcia, Derrick Gibson, Vladmir Guerrero, Andruw Jones, Eli Marrero, Hideo Nomo and Scott Rolen.

	MINT	NRMT
COMPLETE SET (439)	225.00	100.00
COMMON CARD (1-439)	.25	.11

Card	MINT	NRMT
☐ 1 Billy Wagner	.75	.35
☐ 2 Chris Widger	.25	.11
☐ 3 Brent Bowers	.25	.11
☐ 4 Bob Abreu	3.00	1.35
☐ 5 Lou Collier	1.00	.45
☐ 6 Juan Acevedo	.25	.11
☐ 7 Jason Kelley	.25	.11
☐ 8 Brian Sackinsky	.25	.11
☐ 9 Scott Christman	.25	.11
☐ 10 Damon Hollins	.50	.23
☐ 11 Willis Otanez	.50	.23
☐ 12 Jason Ryan	.50	.23
☐ 13 Jason Giambi	1.00	.45
☐ 14 Andy Taulbee	.25	.11
☐ 15 Mark Thompson	.25	.11
☐ 16 Hugo Pivaral	.50	.23
☐ 17 Brien Taylor	.25	.11
☐ 18 Antonio Osuna	.25	.11
☐ 19 Edgardo Alfonzo	1.00	.45
☐ 20 Carl Everett	.50	.23
☐ 21 Matt Drews	.50	.23
☐ 22 Bartolo Colon	3.00	1.35
☐ 23 Andruw Jones	30.00	13.50
☐ 24 Robert Person	.25	.11
☐ 25 Derrek Lee	2.00	.90
☐ 26 John Ambrose	.50	.23
☐ 27 Eric Knowles	.50	.23
☐ 28 Chris Roberts	.25	.11
☐ 29 Don Wengert	.25	.11
☐ 30 Marcus Jensen	.50	.23
☐ 31 Brian Barber	.25	.11
☐ 32 Kevin Brown C	.50	.23
☐ 33 Benji Gil	.25	.11
☐ 34 Mike Hubbard	.25	.11
☐ 35 Bart Evans	.25	.11
☐ 36 Enrique Wilson	2.00	.90
☐ 37 Brian Buchanan	1.50	.70
☐ 38 Ken Ray	.25	.11
☐ 39 Micah Franklin	.25	.11
☐ 40 Ricky Otero	.25	.11
☐ 41 Jason Kendall	1.00	.45
☐ 42 Jimmy Hurst	.50	.23
☐ 43 Jerry Wolak	.25	.11
☐ 44 Jayson Peterson	.50	.23
☐ 45 Allen Battle	.25	.11
☐ 46 Scott Stahoviak	.25	.11
☐ 47 Steve Schrenk	.25	.11
☐ 48 Travis Miller	.50	.23
☐ 49 Eddie Rios	.25	.11
☐ 50 Mike Hampton	.25	.11
☐ 51 Chad Frontera	.25	.11
☐ 52 Tom Evans	.25	.11
☐ 53 C.J. Nitkowski	.25	.11
☐ 54 Clay Caruthers	.50	.23
☐ 55 Shannon Stewart	.50	.23
☐ 56 Jorge Posada	.50	.23
☐ 57 Aaron Holbert	.25	.11
☐ 58 Harry Berrios	.25	.11
☐ 59 Steve Rodriguez	.25	.11
☐ 60 Shane Andrews	.25	.11
☐ 61 Will Cunnane	.50	.23
☐ 62 Richard Hidalgo	2.00	.90
☐ 63 Bill Selby	.25	.11
☐ 64 Jay Cranford	.25	.11
☐ 65 Jeff Suppan	.50	.23
☐ 66 Curtis Goodwin	.25	.11
☐ 67 John Thomson	1.00	.45
☐ 68 Justin Thompson	1.00	.45
☐ 69 Troy Percival	.50	.23
☐ 70 Matt Wagner	.50	.23
☐ 71 Terry Bradshaw	.25	.11
☐ 72 Greg Hansell	.25	.11
☐ 73 John Burke	.25	.11
☐ 74 Jeff D'Amico	1.00	.45
☐ 75 Ernie Young	.25	.11
☐ 76 Jason Bates	.25	.11
☐ 77 Chris Stynes	.25	.11
☐ 78 Cade Gaspar	.50	.23
☐ 79 Melvin Nieves	.50	.23
☐ 80 Rick Gorecki	.25	.11
☐ 81 Felix Rodriguez	.50	.23
☐ 82 Ryan Hancock	.25	.11
☐ 83 Chris Carpenter	2.00	.90
☐ 84 Ray McDavid	.25	.11
☐ 85 Chris Wimmer	.25	.11
☐ 86 Doug Glanville	.25	.11
☐ 87 DeShawn Warren	.25	.11
☐ 88 Damian Moss	1.00	.45
☐ 89 Rafael Orellano	.50	.23
☐ 90 Vladimir Guerrero	25.00	11.00
☐ 91 Raul Casanova	2.00	.90
☐ 92 Karim Garcia	8.00	3.60
☐ 93 Bryce Florie	.25	.11
☐ 94 Kevin Orie	1.00	.45
☐ 95 Ryan Nye	.50	.23
☐ 96 Matt Sachse	.50	.23
☐ 97 Ivan Arteaga	.25	.11
☐ 98 Glenn Murray	.25	.11
☐ 99 Stacy Hollins	.25	.11
☐ 100 Jim Pittsley	.75	.35
☐ 101 Craig Mattson	.25	.11
☐ 102 Neifi Perez	.75	.35
☐ 103 Keith Williams	.25	.11
☐ 104 Roger Cedeno	.50	.23
☐ 105 Tony Terry	.50	.23
☐ 106 Jose Malave	.25	.11
☐ 107 Joe Rosselli	.25	.11
☐ 108 Kevin Jordan	.25	.11
☐ 109 Sid Roberson	.25	.11
☐ 110 Alan Embree	.25	.11
☐ 111 Terrell Wade	.25	.11
☐ 112 Bob Wolcott	.50	.23
☐ 113 Carlos Perez	.50	.23
☐ 114 Mike Bovee	.50	.23
☐ 115 Tommy Davis	.50	.23
☐ 116 Jeremey Kendall	.25	.11
☐ 117 Rich Aude	.25	.11
☐ 118 Rick Huisman	.25	.11
☐ 119 Tim Belk	.25	.11
☐ 120 Edgar Renteria	1.00	.45
☐ 121 Calvin Maduro	.50	.23
☐ 122 Jerry Martin	.25	.11
☐ 123 Ramon Fermin	.25	.11
☐ 124 Kimera Bartee	.50	.23
☐ 125 Mark Farris	.50	.23
☐ 126 Frank Rodriguez	.50	.23
☐ 127 Bobby Higginson	4.00	1.80
☐ 128 Bret Wagner	.50	.23
☐ 129 Edwin Diaz	1.00	.45
☐ 130 Jimmy Haynes	.50	.23
☐ 131 Chris Weinke	.25	.11
☐ 132 Damian Jackson	1.00	.45
☐ 133 Felix Martinez	.25	.11
☐ 134 Edwin Hurtado	.25	.11
☐ 135 Matt Raleigh	.25	.11
☐ 136 Paul Wilson	1.25	.55
☐ 137 Ron Villone	.25	.11
☐ 138 Eric Stuckenschneider	.25	.11
☐ 139 Tate Seefried	.25	.11
☐ 140 Rey Ordonez	2.50	1.10
☐ 141 Eddie Pearson	.25	.11
☐ 142 Kevin Gallaher	.25	.11
☐ 143 Torii Hunter	.75	.35
☐ 144 Daron Kirkreit	.25	.11
☐ 145 Craig Wilson	.25	.11
☐ 146 Ugueth Urbina	.25	.11
☐ 147 Chris Snopek	.25	.11
☐ 148 Kym Ashworth	.50	.23
☐ 149 Wayne Gomes	.25	.11
☐ 150 Mark Loretta	.25	.11
☐ 151 Ramon Morel	.50	.23
☐ 152 Trot Nixon	.50	.23
☐ 153 Desi Relaford	.50	.23
☐ 154 Scott Sullivan	.25	.11
☐ 155 Marc Barcelo	.25	.11
☐ 156 Willie Adams	.25	.11
☐ 157 Derrick Gibson	10.00	4.50
☐ 158 Brian Meadows	.50	.23
☐ 159 Julian Tavarez	.25	.11
☐ 160 Bryan Rekar	.25	.11
☐ 161 Steve Gibralter	.50	.23
☐ 162 Esteban Loaiza	.50	.23
☐ 163 John Wasdin	.25	.11
☐ 164 Kirk Presley	.50	.23
☐ 165 Mariano Rivera	1.00	.45
☐ 166 Andy Larkin	.25	.11
☐ 167 Sean Whiteside	.25	.11
☐ 168 Matt Apana	.25	.11
☐ 169 Shawn Senior	.25	.11
☐ 170 Scott Gentile	.25	.11
☐ 171 Quilvio Veras	.25	.11
☐ 172 Eli Marrero	5.00	2.20
☐ 173 Mendy Lopez	.50	.23
☐ 174 Homer Bush	.25	.11
☐ 175 Brian Stephenson	.50	.23
☐ 176 Jon Nunnally	.50	.23
☐ 177 Jose Herrera	.25	.11
☐ 178 Corey Avrard	.50	.23
☐ 179 David Bell	.25	.11
☐ 180 Jason Isringhausen	.50	.23
☐ 181 Jamey Wright	.75	.35
☐ 182 Lonell Roberts	.25	.11
☐ 183 Marty Cordova	.75	.35
☐ 184 Amaury Telemaco	.50	.23
☐ 185 John Mabry	.75	.35
☐ 186 Andrew Vessel	.50	.23
☐ 187 Jim Cole	.25	.11
☐ 188 Marquis Riley	.25	.11
☐ 189 Todd Dunn	.50	.23
☐ 190 John Carter	.25	.11
☐ 191 Donnie Sadler	2.00	.90
☐ 192 Mike Bell	.75	.35
☐ 193 Chris Cumberland	.50	.23
☐ 194 Jason Schmidt	1.00	.45
☐ 195 Matt Brunson	.25	.11
☐ 196 James Baldwin	.25	.11
☐ 197 Bill Simas	.25	.11
☐ 198 Gus Gandarillas	.25	.11
☐ 199 Mac Suzuki	.75	.35
☐ 200 Rick Holifield	.25	.11
☐ 201 Fernando Lunar	.50	.23
☐ 202 Kevin Jarvis	.25	.11
☐ 203 Everett Stull	.25	.11
☐ 204 Steve Wojciechowski	.25	.11
☐ 205 Shawn Estes	1.00	.45
☐ 206 Jermaine Dye	.50	.23
☐ 207 Marc Kroon	.25	.11
☐ 208 Peter Munro	.50	.23
☐ 209 Pat Watkins	.50	.23
☐ 210 Matt Smith	.50	.23
☐ 211 Joe Vitiello	.25	.11
☐ 212 Gerald Witasick Jr.	.25	.11
☐ 213 Freddy Garcia	1.00	.45
☐ 214 Glenn Dishman	.50	.23
☐ 215 Jay Canizaro	.50	.23
☐ 216 Angel Martinez	.25	.11
☐ 217 Yamil Benitez	.75	.35
☐ 218 Fausto Macey	.50	.23
☐ 219 Eric Owens	.50	.23
☐ 220 Checklist	.25	.11
☐ 221 Dwayne Hosey FOIL	.50	.23
☐ 222 Brad Woodall FOIL	.40	.18
☐ 223 Billy Ashley FOIL	.40	.18
☐ 224 Mark Grudzielanek FOIL	2.00	.90
☐ 225 Mark Johnson FOIL	.40	.18
☐ 226 Tim Unroe FOIL	.40	.18
☐ 227 Todd Greene FOIL	3.00	1.35
☐ 228 Larry Sutton FOIL	.40	.18
☐ 229 Derek Jeter FOIL	4.00	1.80
☐ 230 Sal Fasano FOIL	.40	.18
☐ 231 Ruben Rivera FOIL	2.00	.90
☐ 232 Chris Truby FOIL	.40	.18
☐ 233 John Donati FOIL	.40	.18
☐ 234 Decomba Conner FOIL	.50	.23
☐ 235 Sergio Nunez FOIL	.75	.35
☐ 236 Ray Brown FOIL	.40	.18
☐ 237 Juan Melo FOIL	2.00	.90
☐ 238 Hideo Nomo FOIL	12.00	5.50
☐ 239 Jamie Bluma FOIL	.40	.18
☐ 240 Jay Payton FOIL	1.00	.45
☐ 241 Paul Konerko FOIL	20.00	9.00
☐ 242 Scott Elarton FOIL	3.00	1.35
☐ 243 Jeff Abbott FOIL	1.50	.70

Card	MINT	NRMT
☐ 244 Jim Brower FOIL	.40	.18
☐ 245 Geoff Blum FOIL	.50	.23
☐ 246 Aaron Boone FOIL	2.00	.90
☐ 247 J.R. Phillips FOIL	.40	.18
☐ 248 Alex Ochoa FOIL	.40	.18
☐ 249 Nomar Garciaparra FOIL	25.00	11.00
☐ 250 Garret Anderson FOIL	1.00	.45
☐ 251 Ray Durham FOIL	.50	.23
☐ 252 Paul Shuey FOIL	.40	.18
☐ 253 Tony Clark FOIL	2.50	1.10
☐ 254 Johnny Damon FOIL	.40	.18
☐ 255 Duane Singleton FOIL	.40	.18
☐ 256 LaTroy Hawkins FOIL	.25	.11
☐ 257 Andy Pettitte FOIL	1.50	.70
☐ 258 Ben Grieve FOIL	20.00	9.00
☐ 259 Marc Newfield FOIL	.50	.23
☐ 260 Terrell Lowery FOIL	.40	.18
☐ 261 Shawn Green FOIL	.50	.23
☐ 262 Chipper Jones FOIL	3.00	1.35
☐ 263 Brooks Kieschnick FOIL	.50	.23
☐ 264 Calvin Reese FOIL	.40	.18
☐ 265 Doug Million FOIL	.40	.18
☐ 266 Marc Valdes FOIL	.40	.18
☐ 267 Brian L.Hunter FOIL	.50	.23
☐ 268 Todd Hollandsworth FOIL	.50	.23
☐ 269 Rod Henderson FOIL	.40	.18
☐ 270 Bill Pulsipher FOIL	.40	.18
☐ 271 Scott Rolen FOIL	25.00	11.00
☐ 272 Trey Beamon FOIL	.40	.18
☐ 273 Alan Benes FOIL	.60	.25
☐ 274 Dustin Hermanson FOIL	.40	.18
☐ 275 Ricky Bottalico	.50	.23
☐ 276 Albert Belle	1.25	.55
☐ 277 Deion Sanders	1.00	.45
☐ 278 Matt Williams	.75	.35
☐ 279 Jeff Bagwell	2.00	.90
☐ 280 Kirby Puckett	2.00	.90
☐ 281 Dave Hollins	.25	.11
☐ 282 Don Mattingly	1.50	.70
☐ 283 Joey Hamilton	.50	.23
☐ 284 Bobby Bonilla	.50	.23
☐ 285 Moises Alou	.50	.23
☐ 286 Tom Glavine	.75	.35
☐ 287 Brett Butler	.50	.23
☐ 288 Chris Hoiles	.25	.11
☐ 289 Kenny Rogers	.25	.11
☐ 290 Larry Walker	1.00	.45
☐ 291 Tim Raines	.25	.11
☐ 292 Kevin Appier	.50	.23
☐ 293 Roger Clemens	2.00	.90
☐ 294 Chuck Carr	.25	.11
☐ 295 Randy Myers	.50	.23
☐ 296 Dave Nilsson	.50	.23
☐ 297 Joe Carter	.75	.35
☐ 298 Chuck Finley	.50	.23
☐ 299 Ray Lankford	.75	.35
☐ 300 Roberto Kelly	.25	.11
☐ 301 Jon Lieber	.25	.11
☐ 302 Travis Fryman	.50	.23
☐ 303 Mark McGwire	2.00	.90
☐ 304 Tony Gwynn	2.50	1.10
☐ 305 Kenny Lofton	1.25	.55
☐ 306 Mark Whiten	.25	.11
☐ 307 Doug Drabek	.25	.11
☐ 308 Terry Steinbach	.50	.23
☐ 309 Ryan Klesko	.75	.35
☐ 310 Mike Piazza	3.00	1.35
☐ 311 Ben McDonald	.25	.11
☐ 312 Reggie Sanders	.25	.11
☐ 313 Alex Fernandez	.25	.11
☐ 314 Aaron Sele	.25	.11
☐ 315 Gregg Jefferies	.50	.23
☐ 316 Rickey Henderson	.75	.35
☐ 317 Brian Anderson	.25	.11
☐ 318 Jose Valentin	.50	.23
☐ 319 Rod Beck	.25	.11
☐ 320 Marquis Grissom	.50	.23
☐ 321 Ken Griffey Jr.	5.00	2.20
☐ 322 Bret Saberhagen	.25	.11
☐ 323 Juan Gonzalez	2.50	1.10
☐ 324 Paul Molitor	1.00	.45
☐ 325 Gary Sheffield	1.00	.45
☐ 326 Darren Daulton	.50	.23
☐ 327 Bill Swift	.25	.11
☐ 328 Brian McRae	.25	.11
☐ 329 Robin Ventura	.50	.23
☐ 330 Lee Smith	.50	.23
☐ 331 Fred McGriff	.75	.35
☐ 332 Delino DeShields	.25	.11
☐ 333 Edgar Martinez	.75	.35
☐ 334 Mike Mussina	1.00	.45
☐ 335 Orlando Merced	.25	.11
☐ 336 Carlos Baerga	.50	.23
☐ 337 Wil Cordero	.25	.11
☐ 338 Tom Pagnozzi	.25	.11
☐ 339 Pat Hentgen	.75	.35
☐ 340 Chad Curtis	.25	.11
☐ 341 Darren Lewis	.25	.11
☐ 342 Jeff Kent	.25	.11
☐ 343 Bip Roberts	.25	.11
☐ 344 Ivan Rodriguez	1.25	.55
☐ 345 Jeff Montgomery	.50	.23
☐ 346 Hal Morris	.25	.11
☐ 347 Danny Tartabull	.25	.11
☐ 348 Raul Mondesi	.75	.35
☐ 349 Ken Hill	.25	.11
☐ 350 Pedro Martinez	1.00	.45
☐ 351 Frank Thomas	4.00	1.80
☐ 352 Manny Ramirez	1.00	.45
☐ 353 Tim Salmon	1.00	.45
☐ 354 W. VanLandingham	.25	.11
☐ 355 Andres Galarraga	.75	.35
☐ 356 Paul O'Neill	.50	.23
☐ 357 Brady Anderson	.75	.35
☐ 358 Ramon Martinez	.50	.23
☐ 359 John Olerud	.50	.23
☐ 360 Ruben Sierra	.25	.11
☐ 361 Cal Eldred	.25	.11
☐ 362 Jay Buhner	.75	.35
☐ 363 Jay Bell	.50	.23
☐ 364 Wally Joyner	.50	.23
☐ 365 Chuck Knoblauch	1.00	.45
☐ 366 Len Dykstra	.50	.23
☐ 367 John Wetteland	.50	.23
☐ 368 Roberto Alomar	1.00	.45
☐ 369 Craig Biggio	.75	.35
☐ 370 Ozzie Smith	1.25	.55
☐ 371 Terry Pendleton	.50	.23
☐ 372 Sammy Sosa	1.00	.45
☐ 373 Carlos Garcia	.25	.11
☐ 374 Jose Rijo	.25	.11
☐ 375 Chris Gomez	.25	.11
☐ 376 Barry Bonds	1.25	.55
☐ 377 Steve Avery	.25	.11
☐ 378 Rick Wilkins	.25	.11
☐ 379 Pete Harnisch	.25	.11
☐ 380 Dean Palmer	.50	.23
☐ 381 Bob Hamelin	.25	.11
☐ 382 Jason Bere	.25	.11
☐ 383 Jimmy Key	.50	.23
☐ 384 Dante Bichette	.75	.35
☐ 385 Rafael Palmeiro	.75	.35
☐ 386 David Justice	1.00	.45
☐ 387 Chili Davis	.50	.23
☐ 388 Mike Greenwell	.25	.11
☐ 389 Todd Zeile	.25	.11
☐ 390 Jeff Conine	.50	.23
☐ 391 Rick Aguilera	.25	.11
☐ 392 Eddie Murray	1.00	.45
☐ 393 Mike Stanley	.25	.11
☐ 394 Cliff Floyd UER (numbered 294)	.50	.23
☐ 395 Randy Johnson	1.00	.45
☐ 396 David Nied	.25	.11
☐ 397 Devon White	.25	.11
☐ 398 Royce Clayton	.25	.11
☐ 399 Andy Benes	.25	.11
☐ 400 John Hudek	.25	.11
☐ 401 Bobby Jones	.50	.23
☐ 402 Eric Karros	.50	.23
☐ 403 Will Clark	.75	.35
☐ 404 Mark Langston	.25	.11
☐ 405 Kevin Brown	.50	.23
☐ 406 Greg Maddux	3.00	1.35
☐ 407 David Cone	.50	.23
☐ 408 Wade Boggs	1.00	.45
☐ 409 Steve Trachsel	.25	.11
☐ 410 Greg Vaughn	.25	.11
☐ 411 Mo Vaughn	1.25	.55
☐ 412 Wilson Alvarez	.50	.23
☐ 413 Cal Ripken	4.00	1.80
☐ 414 Rico Brogna	.25	.11
☐ 415 Barry Larkin	.75	.35
☐ 416 Cecil Fielder	.50	.23
☐ 417 Jose Canseco	.75	.35
☐ 418 Jack McDowell	.25	.11
☐ 419 Mike Lieberthal	.25	.11
☐ 420 Andrew Lorraine	.25	.11
☐ 421 Rich Becker	.25	.11
☐ 422 Tony Phillips	.25	.11
☐ 423 Scott Ruffcorn	.25	.11
☐ 424 Jeff Granger	.25	.11
☐ 425 Greg Pirkl	.25	.11
☐ 426 Dennis Eckersley	.75	.35
☐ 427 Jose Lima	.25	.11
☐ 428 Russ Davis	.25	.11
☐ 429 Armando Benitez	.25	.11
☐ 430 Alex Gonzalez	.25	.11
☐ 431 Carlos Delgado	.75	.35
☐ 432 Chan Ho Park	1.00	.45
☐ 433 Mickey Tettleton	.25	.11
☐ 434 Dave Winfield	.75	.35
☐ 435 John Burkett	.50	.23
☐ 436 Orlando Miller	.25	.11
☐ 437 Rondell White	.75	.35
☐ 438 Jose Oliva	.25	.11
☐ 439 Checklist	.25	.11

1995 Bowman Gold Foil

Numbered 221-274, this 54-card standard-size set is the gold insert parallel version of the silver foil subset found in the basic issue. The odds of finding a gold foil version are one in six packs.

	MINT	NRMT
COMPLETE SET (54)	180.00	80.00
COMMON CARD (221-274)	2.00	.90
SEMISTARS	4.00	1.80
UNLISTED STARS	6.00	2.70
*GOLD: 3X TO 6X BASIC CARDS		
☐ 229 Derek Jeter	12.00	5.50
☐ 238 Hideo Nomo	15.00	6.75
☐ 241 Paul Konerko	25.00	11.00
☐ 249 Nomar Garciaparra	30.00	13.50
☐ 253 Tony Clark	8.00	3.60
☐ 257 Andy Pettitte	8.00	3.60
☐ 258 Ben Grieve	25.00	11.00
☐ 262 Chipper Jones	12.00	5.50
☐ 271 Scott Rolen	30.00	13.50

1996 Bowman

The 1996 Bowman set was issued in one series totalling 385 cards. The 11-card packs retail for $2.50 each. The fronts feature color action player photos in a tan-checkered frame with the player's name printed in silver foil at the bottom. The backs carry another color player photo with player information, 1995 and career player statistics. Each pack contained 10 regular issue cards plus either one foil parallel or an insert card. In a special promotional program, Topps offered collector's a $100 guarantee on complete sets. To get the guarantee, collectors had to mail in a Guaranteed Value Certificate request form, found in packs, along with a $5 processing and registration fee before the December 31st, 1996 deadline. Collectors would then receive a $100 Guaranteed Value Certificate, of which they could mail back to Topps between August 31st, 1999 and December 31st, 1999, along with their complete set, to receive $100. A reprint version of the 1952 Bowman Mickey Mantle card was randomly inserted into packs. Rookie Cards in this set include Russell Branyan, Mike Cameron, Jose Guillen, Livan Hernandez, Carl Pavano, Brian Rose and Ron Wright

	MINT	NRMT
COMPLETE SET (385)	125.00	55.00
COMMON CARD (1-385)	.20	.09
☐ 1 Cal Ripken	3.00	1.35
☐ 2 Ray Durham	.40	.18
☐ 3 Ivan Rodriguez	1.00	.45
☐ 4 Fred McGriff	.50	.23
☐ 5 Hideo Nomo	2.00	.90
☐ 6 Troy Percival	.40	.18
☐ 7 Moises Alou	.40	.18
☐ 8 Mike Stanley	.20	.09
☐ 9 Jay Buhner	.50	.23
☐ 10 Shawn Green	.20	.09
☐ 11 Ryan Klesko	.50	.23
☐ 12 Andres Galarraga	.50	.23
☐ 13 Dean Palmer	.20	.09
☐ 14 Jeff Conine	.40	.18
☐ 15 Brian L.Hunter	.40	.18
☐ 16 J.T. Snow	.20	.09
☐ 17 Larry Walker	.50	.23
☐ 18 Barry Larkin	.40	.18
☐ 19 Alex Gonzalez	.20	.09
☐ 20 Edgar Martinez	.50	.23
☐ 21 Mo Vaughn	1.00	.45
☐ 22 Mark McGwire	1.50	.70
☐ 23 Jose Canseco	.50	.23
☐ 24 Jack McDowell	.20	.09
☐ 25 Dante Bichette	.50	.23
☐ 26 Wade Boggs	.50	.23

☐ 27 Mike Piazza	2.50	1.10
☐ 28 Ray Lankford	.40	.18
☐ 29 Craig Biggio	.50	.23
☐ 30 Rafael Palmeiro	.50	.23
☐ 31 Ron Gant	.40	.18
☐ 32 Javy Lopez	.40	.18
☐ 33 Brian Jordan	.40	.18
☐ 34 Paul O'Neill	.20	.09
☐ 35 Mark Grace	.50	.23
☐ 36 Matt Williams	.50	.23
☐ 37 Pedro Martinez	.75	.35
☐ 38 Rickey Henderson	.50	.23
☐ 39 Bobby Bonilla	.40	.18
☐ 40 Todd Hollandsworth	.40	.18
☐ 41 Jim Thome	.75	.35
☐ 42 Gary Sheffield	.75	.35
☐ 43 Tim Salmon	.75	.35
☐ 44 Gregg Jefferies	.20	.09
☐ 45 Roberto Alomar	.75	.35
☐ 46 Carlos Baerga	.40	.18
☐ 47 Mark Grudzielanek	.40	.18
☐ 48 Randy Johnson	.75	.35
☐ 49 Tino Martinez	.75	.35
☐ 50 Robin Ventura	.40	.18
☐ 51 Ryne Sandberg	1.00	.45
☐ 52 Jay Bell	.20	.09
☐ 53 Jason Schmidt	.50	.23
☐ 54 Frank Thomas	3.00	1.35
☐ 55 Kenny Lofton	1.00	.45
☐ 56 Ariel Prieto	.20	.09
☐ 57 David Cone	.40	.18
☐ 58 Reggie Sanders	.20	.09
☐ 59 Michael Tucker	.40	.18
☐ 60 Vinny Castilla	.40	.18
☐ 61 Len Dykstra	.40	.18
☐ 62 Todd Hundley	.40	.18
☐ 63 Brian McRae	.20	.09
☐ 64 Dennis Eckersley	.50	.23
☐ 65 Rondell White	.40	.18
☐ 66 Eric Karros	.40	.18
☐ 67 Greg Maddux	2.50	1.10
☐ 68 Kevin Appier	.40	.18
☐ 69 Eddie Murray	.75	.35
☐ 70 John Olerud	.20	.09
☐ 71 Tony Gwynn	2.00	.90
☐ 72 David Justice	.75	.35
☐ 73 Ken Caminiti	.75	.35
☐ 74 Terry Steinbach	.20	.09
☐ 75 Alan Benes	.40	.18
☐ 76 Chipper Jones	2.50	1.10
☐ 77 Jeff Bagwell	1.50	.70
☐ 78 Barry Bonds	1.00	.45
☐ 79 Ken Griffey Jr.	4.00	1.80
☐ 80 Roger Cedeno	.20	.09
☐ 81 Joe Carter	.40	.18
☐ 82 Henry Rodriguez	.20	.09
☐ 83 Jason Isringhausen	.20	.09
☐ 84 Chuck Knoblauch	.75	.35
☐ 85 Manny Ramirez	.75	.35
☐ 86 Tom Glavine	.50	.23
☐ 87 Jeffrey Hammonds	.40	.18
☐ 88 Paul Molitor	.75	.35
☐ 89 Roger Clemens	1.50	.70
☐ 90 Greg Vaughn	.20	.09
☐ 91 Marty Cordova	.20	.09
☐ 92 Albert Belle	1.00	.45
☐ 93 Mike Mussina	.75	.35
☐ 94 Garret Anderson	.40	.18
☐ 95 Juan Gonzalez	2.00	.90
☐ 96 John Valentin	.20	.09
☐ 97 Jason Giambi	.50	.23
☐ 98 Kirby Puckett	1.50	.70
☐ 99 Jim Edmonds	.75	.35
☐ 100 Cecil Fielder	.40	.18
☐ 101 Mike Aldrete	.20	.09
☐ 102 Marquis Grissom	.40	.18
☐ 103 Derek Bell	.40	.18
☐ 104 Raul Mondesi	.50	.23
☐ 105 Sammy Sosa	.75	.35
☐ 106 Travis Fryman	.40	.18
☐ 107 Rico Brogna	.20	.09
☐ 108 Will Clark	.50	.23
☐ 109 Bernie Williams	.75	.35
☐ 110 Brady Anderson	.50	.23
☐ 111 Torii Hunter	.40	.18
☐ 112 Derek Jeter	2.50	1.10
☐ 113 Mike Kusiewicz	.50	.23
☐ 114 Scott Rolen	4.00	1.80
☐ 115 Ramon Castro	.40	.18
☐ 116 Jose Guillen	10.00	4.50
☐ 117 Wade Walker	.20	.09
☐ 118 Shawn Senior	.20	.09
☐ 119 Onan Masaoka	1.00	.45
☐ 120 Marlon Anderson	.75	.35
☐ 121 Katsuhiro Maeda	2.00	.90
☐ 122 Garrett Stephenson	.20	.09
☐ 123 Butch Huskey	.20	.09
☐ 124 D'Angelo Jimenez	3.00	1.35
☐ 125 Tony Mounce	.50	.23
☐ 126 Jay Canizaro	.20	.09
☐ 127 Juan Melo	.40	.18
☐ 128 Steve Gibralter	.20	.09
☐ 129 Freddy Garcia	.40	.18
☐ 130 Julio Santana UER Card has him born in 1993	.20	.09
☐ 131 Richard Hidalgo	.75	.35
☐ 132 Jermaine Dye	.20	.09
☐ 133 Willie Adams	.20	.09
☐ 134 Everett Stull	.20	.09
☐ 135 Ramon Morel	.40	.18
☐ 136 Chan Ho Park	.75	.35
☐ 137 Jamey Wright	.50	.23
☐ 138 Luis Garcia	.20	.09
☐ 139 Dan Serafini	.40	.18
☐ 140 Ryan Dempster	1.00	.45
☐ 141 Tate Seefried	.20	.09
☐ 142 Jimmy Hurst	.20	.09
☐ 143 Travis Miller	.20	.09
☐ 144 Curtis Goodwin	.20	.09
☐ 145 Rocky Coppinger	.75	.35
☐ 146 Enrique Wilson	.50	.23
☐ 147 Jaime Bluma	.20	.09
☐ 148 Andrew Vessel	.40	.18
☐ 149 Damian Moss	.50	.23
☐ 150 Shawn Gallagher	1.00	.45
☐ 151 Pat Watkins	.40	.18
☐ 152 Jose Paniagua	.40	.18
☐ 153 Danny Graves	.40	.18
☐ 154 Bryon Gainey	.75	.35
☐ 155 Steve Soderstrom	.20	.09
☐ 156 Cliff Brumbaugh	.20	.09
☐ 157 Eugene Kingsale	1.00	.45
☐ 158 Lou Collier	.40	.18
☐ 159 Todd Walker	3.00	1.35
☐ 160 Kris Detmers	1.00	.45
☐ 161 Josh Booty	2.00	.90
☐ 162 Greg Whiteman	.20	.09
☐ 163 Damian Jackson	.40	.18
☐ 164 Tony Clark	1.00	.45
☐ 165 Jeff D'Amico	.75	.35
☐ 166 Johnny Damon	.40	.18
☐ 167 Rafael Orellano	.40	.18
☐ 168 Ruben Rivera	.75	.35
☐ 169 Alex Ochoa	.20	.09
☐ 170 Jay Powell	.20	.09
☐ 171 Tom Evans	.20	.09
☐ 172 Ron Villone	.20	.09
☐ 173 Shawn Estes	.40	.18
☐ 174 John Wasdin	.20	.09
☐ 175 Bill Simas	.20	.09
☐ 176 Kevin Brown	.40	.18
☐ 177 Shannon Stewart	.20	.09
☐ 178 Todd Greene	.50	.23
☐ 179 Bob Wolcott	.20	.09
☐ 180 Chris Snopek	.20	.09
☐ 181 Nomar Garciaparra	4.00	1.80
☐ 182 Cameron Smith	.20	.09
☐ 183 Matt Drews	.40	.18
☐ 184 Jimmy Haynes	.20	.09
☐ 185 Chris Carpenter	.50	.23
☐ 186 Desi Relaford	.20	.09
☐ 187 Ben Grieve	3.00	1.35
☐ 188 Mike Bell	.50	.23
☐ 189 Luis Castillo	1.00	.45
☐ 190 Ugueth Urbina	.40	.18
☐ 191 Paul Wilson	.40	.18
☐ 192 Andruw Jones	4.00	1.80
☐ 193 Wayne Gomes	.20	.09
☐ 194 Craig Counsell	.50	.23
☐ 195 Jim Cole	.20	.09
☐ 196 Brooks Kieschnick	.40	.18
☐ 197 Trey Beamon	.40	.18
☐ 198 Marino Santana	.20	.09
☐ 199 Bob Abreu	.40	.18
☐ 200 Calvin Reese	.20	.09
☐ 201 Dante Powell	2.00	.90
☐ 202 George Arias	.40	.18
☐ 203 Jorge Velandia	.20	.09
☐ 204 George Lombard	3.00	1.35
☐ 205 Byron Browne	.20	.09
☐ 206 John Frascatore	.20	.09
☐ 207 Terry Adams	.20	.09
☐ 208 Wilson Delgado	.20	.09
☐ 209 Billy McMillon	.20	.09
☐ 210 Jeff Abbott	.40	.18
☐ 211 Trot Nixon	.20	.09
☐ 212 Amaury Telemaco	.40	.18
☐ 213 Scott Sullivan	.20	.09
☐ 214 Justin Thompson	.40	.18
☐ 215 Decomba Conner	.40	.18
☐ 216 Ryan McGuire	.20	.09
☐ 217 Matt Luke	.20	.09
☐ 218 Doug Million	.20	.09
☐ 219 Jason Dickson	4.00	1.80
☐ 220 Ramon Hernandez	4.00	1.80
☐ 221 Mark Bellhorn	2.00	.90
☐ 222 Eric Ludwick	.20	.09
☐ 223 Luke Wilcox	.20	.09
☐ 224 Marty Malloy	.50	.23
☐ 225 Gary Coffee	.50	.23
☐ 226 Wendell Magee	.50	.23
☐ 227 Brett Tomko	2.00	.90
☐ 228 Derek Lowe	.20	.09
☐ 229 Jose Rosado	2.50	1.10
☐ 230 Steve Bourgeois	.20	.09
☐ 231 Neil Weber	.20	.09
☐ 232 Jeff Ware	.20	.09
☐ 233 Edwin Diaz	.40	.18
☐ 234 Greg Norton	.20	.09
☐ 235 Aaron Boone	.75	.35
☐ 236 Jeff Suppan	.50	.23
☐ 237 Bret Wagner	.20	.09
☐ 238 Elieser Marrero	.50	.23
☐ 239 Will Cunnane	.40	.18
☐ 240 Brian Barkley	.50	.23
☐ 241 Jay Payton	.40	.18
☐ 242 Marcus Jensen	.20	.09
☐ 243 Ryan Nye	.20	.09
☐ 244 Chad Mottola	.20	.09
☐ 245 Scott McClain	.20	.09
☐ 246 Jessie Ibarra	.40	.18
☐ 247 Mike Darr	1.00	.45
☐ 248 Bobby Estalella	3.00	1.35
☐ 249 Michael Barrett	.30	.14
☐ 250 Jamie Lopiccolo	.50	.23
☐ 251 Shane Spencer	.20	.09
☐ 252 Ben Petrick	1.25	.55
☐ 253 Jason Bell	1.00	.45
☐ 254 Arnold Gooch	.50	.23
☐ 255 T.J. Mathews	.20	.09
☐ 256 Jason Ryan	.20	.09
☐ 257 Pat Cline	1.00	.45
☐ 258 Rafael Carmona	.20	.09
☐ 259 Carl Pavano	6.00	2.70
☐ 260 Ben Davis	.50	.23
☐ 261 Matt Lawton	.50	.23
☐ 262 Kevin Sefcik	.20	.09
☐ 263 Chris Fussell	.75	.35
☐ 264 Mike Cameron	5.00	2.20
☐ 265 Marty Janzen	.50	.23
☐ 266 Livan Hernandez	6.00	2.70
☐ 267 Raul Ibanez	1.00	.45
☐ 268 Juan Encarnacion	1.50	.70
☐ 269 David Yocum	.50	.23
☐ 270 Jonathan Johnson	.50	.23
☐ 271 Reggie Taylor	.40	.18
☐ 272 Danny Buxbaum	.75	.35
☐ 273 Jacob Cruz	.40	.18
☐ 274 Bobby Morris	.20	.09
☐ 275 Andy Fox	.20	.09
☐ 276 Greg Keagle	.20	.09
☐ 277 Charles Peterson	.20	.09
☐ 278 Derrek Lee	.20	.09
☐ 279 Bryant Nelson	.50	.23
☐ 280 Antone Williamson	.75	.35
☐ 281 Scott Elarton	.40	.18
☐ 282 Shad Williams	.20	.09
☐ 283 Rich Hunter	.20	.09
☐ 284 Chris Sheff	.20	.09
☐ 285 Derrick Gibson	1.50	.70
☐ 286 Felix Rodriguez	.20	.09
☐ 287 Brian Banks	.20	.09
☐ 288 Jason McDonald	.20	.09
☐ 289 Glendon Rusch	1.00	.45
☐ 290 Gary Rath	.20	.09
☐ 291 Peter Munro	.40	.18
☐ 292 Tom Fordham	.40	.18
☐ 293 Jason Kendall	.50	.23
☐ 294 Russ Johnson	.20	.09
☐ 295 Joe Long	.20	.09
☐ 296 Robert Smith	1.00	.45
☐ 297 Jarrod Washburn	1.00	.45
☐ 298 Dave Coggin	.50	.23
☐ 299 Jeff Yoder	.50	.23
☐ 300 Jed Hansen	.20	.09
☐ 301 Matt Morris	3.00	1.35
☐ 302 Josh Bishop	.50	.23
☐ 303 Dustin Hermanson	.20	.09
☐ 304 Mike Gulan	.20	.09
☐ 305 Felipe Crespo	.20	.09
☐ 306 Quinton McCracken	.20	.09
☐ 307 Jim Bonnici	.20	.09
☐ 308 Sal Fasano	.20	.09
☐ 309 Gabe Alvarez	1.25	.55
☐ 310 Heath Murray	.50	.23
☐ 311 Jose Valentin	1.50	.70
☐ 312 Bartolo Colon	.75	.35
☐ 313 Olmedo Saenz	.20	.09
☐ 314 Norm Hutchins	2.00	.90
☐ 315 Chris Holt	.20	.09
☐ 316 David Doster	.20	.09

☐ 317 Robert Person	.20	.09
☐ 318 Donne Wall	.20	.09
☐ 319 Adam Riggs	.40	.18
☐ 320 Homer Bush	.20	.09
☐ 321 Brad Rigby	.20	.09
☐ 322 Lou Merloni	.20	.09
☐ 323 Neifi Perez	.50	.23
☐ 324 Chris Cumberland	.20	.09
☐ 325 Alvie Shepherd	.50	.23
☐ 326 Jarrod Patterson	.20	.09
☐ 327 Ray Ricken	.20	.09
☐ 328 Danny Klassen	.75	.35
☐ 329 David Miller	.50	.23
☐ 330 Chad Alexander	.75	.35
☐ 331 Matt Beaumont	.40	.18
☐ 332 Damon Hollins	.20	.09
☐ 333 Todd Dunn	.20	.09
☐ 334 Mike Sweeney	2.00	.90
☐ 335 Richie Sexson	.50	.23
☐ 336 Billy Wagner	.75	.35
☐ 337 Ron Wright	5.00	2.20
☐ 338 Paul Konerko	2.50	1.10
☐ 339 Tommy Phelps	.50	.23
☐ 340 Karim Garcia	.20	.09
☐ 341 Mike Grace	.20	.09
☐ 342 Russell Branyan	8.00	3.60
☐ 343 Randy Winn	.50	.23
☐ 344 A.J. Pierzynski	1.00	.45
☐ 345 Mike Busby	.20	.09
☐ 346 Matt Beech	.50	.23
☐ 347 Jose Cepeda	.50	.23
☐ 348 Brian Stephenson	.20	.09
☐ 349 Rey Ordonez	.20	.09
☐ 350 Rich Aurilla	.20	.09
☐ 351 Edgard Velazquez	2.00	.90
☐ 352 Raul Casanova	.40	.18
☐ 353 Carlos Guillen	.75	.35
☐ 354 Bruce Aven	.20	.09
☐ 355 Ryan Jones	1.00	.45
☐ 356 Derek Aucoin	.20	.09
☐ 357 Brian Rose	6.00	2.70
☐ 358 Richard Almanzar	.50	.23
☐ 359 Fletcher Bates	.75	.35
☐ 360 Russ Ortiz	.20	.09
☐ 361 Wilton Guerrero	2.00	.90
☐ 362 Geoff Jenkins	2.00	.90
☐ 363 Pete Janicki	.20	.09
☐ 364 Yamil Benitez	.40	.18
☐ 365 Aaron Holbert	.20	.09
☐ 366 Tim Belk	.20	.09
☐ 367 Terrell Wade	.20	.09
☐ 368 Terrence Long	.75	.35
☐ 369 Brad Fullmer	.75	.35
☐ 370 Matt Wagner	.20	.09
☐ 371 Craig Wilson	.20	.09
☐ 372 Mark Loretta	.20	.09
☐ 373 Eric Owens	.20	.09
☐ 374 Vladimir Guerrero	3.00	1.35
☐ 375 Tommy Davis	.20	.09
☐ 376 Donnie Sadler	.40	.18
☐ 377 Edgar Renteria	.50	.23
☐ 378 Todd Helton	8.00	3.60
☐ 379 Ralph Milliard	.20	.09
☐ 380 Darin Blood	1.50	.70
☐ 381 Shayne Bennett	.20	.09
☐ 382 Mark Redman	.40	.18
☐ 383 Felix Martinez	.20	.09
☐ 384 Sean Watkins	.75	.35
☐ 385 Oscar Henriquez	.20	.09
☐ M20 1952 Bowman Mantle Reprint	10.00	4.50
☐ NNO Unnumbered Checklists	.20	.09

1996 Bowman Foil

These parallel foil cards were seeded at an approximate rate of one per pack. Packs that did not contain a Foil card had a Bowman's Best Preview or Minor League Player of the Year insert card instead. The striking silver foil card fronts differ them from the base 1996 Bowman cards. Please refer to the multipliers provided below to ascertain value for Foil singles.

	MINT	NRMT
COMPLETE SET (385)	300.00	135.00
COMMON CARD (1-385)	.50	.23

*STARS: 1.5X TO 3X BASIC CARDS
*ROOKIES: 1.25X TO 2.5X BASIC CARDS

1996 Bowman Minor League POY

Randomly inserted in packs at a rate of one in 12, this 15-card set features top minor league prospects for Player of the Year Candidates. The fronts carry a color player photo with red-and-silver foil printing. The backs display player information including his career bests.

	MINT	NRMT
COMPLETE SET (15)	40.00	18.00
COMMON CARD (1-15)	1.50	.70
☐ 1 Andruw Jones	12.00	5.50
☐ 2 Derrick Gibson	4.00	1.80
☐ 3 Bob Abreu	1.75	.80
☐ 4 Todd Walker	4.00	1.80
☐ 5 Jamey Wright	1.75	.80
☐ 6 Wes Helms	6.00	2.70
☐ 7 Karim Garcia	2.00	.90
☐ 8 Bartolo Colon	2.50	1.10
☐ 9 Alex Ochoa	1.50	.70
☐ 10 Mike Sweeney	2.00	.90
☐ 11 Ruben Rivera	2.50	1.10
☐ 12 Gabe Alvarez	1.50	.70
☐ 13 Billy Wagner	2.50	1.10
☐ 14 Vladimir Guerrero	10.00	4.50
☐ 15 Edgard Velazquez	3.00	1.35

1997 Bowman

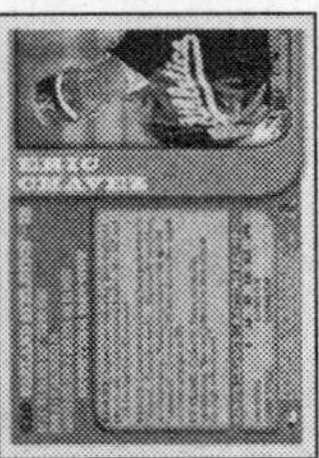

The 1997 Bowman set was issued in two series (series one #'s 1-221, series two #'s 222-441) and was distributed in 10 card packs with a suggested retail price of $2.50. The 441-card set features color photos of 300 top prospects with silver and blue foil stamping and 140 veteran stars designated by silver and red foil stamping. An unannounced Hideki Irabu red bordered card (#441) was also included in series 2 packs. Players that were featured for the first time on a Bowman card also carried a blue foil "1st Bowman Card" logo on the card front. Topps offered collectors a $125 guarantee on complete sets. To get the guarantee, collectors had to mail in the Guaranteed Certificate Request Form which was found in every three packs of both series 1 and series 2 along with a $5 registration and processing fee. To redeem the guarantee, collectors had to send a complete set of Bowman regular cards (440 cards in both series) along with the certificate to Topps between August 31 and December 31 in the year 2000. Notable Rookie Cards in this set include Adrian Beltre, Jose Cruz Jr, Hideki Irabu, Travis Lee, Aramis Ramirez, Miguel Tejada and Jaret Wright. Please note that cards 155 and 158 don't exist. Calvin "Pokey" Reese and George Arias are both numbered 156 (Reese is an uncorrected error - should be numbered 155). Chris Carpenter and Eric Milton are both numbered 159 (Carpenter is an uncorrected error - should be numbered 158).

	MINT	NRMT
COMPLETE SET (441)	150.00	70.00
COMPLETE SERIES 1 (221)	90.00	40.00
COMPLETE SERIES 2 (220)	60.00	27.00
COMMON CARD (1-441)	.20	.09
☐ 1 Derek Jeter	2.50	1.10
☐ 2 Edgar Renteria	.40	.18
☐ 3 Chipper Jones	2.50	1.10
☐ 4 Hideo Nomo	2.00	.90
☐ 5 Tim Salmon	.75	.35
☐ 6 Jason Giambi	.40	.18
☐ 7 Robin Ventura	.40	.18
☐ 8 Tony Clark	.75	.35
☐ 9 Barry Larkin	.50	.23
☐ 10 Paul Molitor	.75	.35
☐ 11 Bernard Gilkey	.20	.09
☐ 12 Jack McDowell	.20	.09
☐ 13 Andy Benes	.20	.09
☐ 14 Ryan Klesko	.50	.23
☐ 15 Mark McGwire	1.50	.70
☐ 16 Ken Griffey Jr.	4.00	1.80
☐ 17 Robb Nen	.20	.09
☐ 18 Cal Ripken	3.00	1.35
☐ 19 John Valentin	.20	.09
☐ 20 Ricky Bottalico	.40	.18
☐ 21 Mike Lansing	.20	.09
☐ 22 Ryne Sandberg	1.00	.45
☐ 23 Carlos Delgado	.40	.18
☐ 24 Craig Biggio	.50	.23
☐ 25 Eric Karros	.40	.18
☐ 26 Kevin Appier	.20	.09
☐ 27 Mariano Rivera	.75	.35
☐ 28 Vinny Castilla	.40	.18
☐ 29 Juan Gonzalez	2.00	.90
☐ 30 Al Martin	.20	.09
☐ 31 Jeff Cirillo	.40	.18
☐ 32 Eddie Murray	.75	.35
☐ 33 Ray Lankford	.40	.18
☐ 34 Manny Ramirez	.75	.35
☐ 35 Roberto Alomar	.75	.35
☐ 36 Will Clark	.50	.23
☐ 37 Chuck Knoblauch	.75	.35
☐ 38 Harold Baines	.40	.18
☐ 39 Trevor Hoffman	.40	.18
☐ 40 Edgar Martinez	.50	.23
☐ 41 Geronimo Berroa	.20	.09
☐ 42 Rey Ordonez	.20	.09
☐ 43 Mike Stanley	.20	.09
☐ 44 Mike Mussina	.75	.35
☐ 45 Kevin Brown	.20	.09
☐ 46 Dennis Eckersley	.50	.23
☐ 47 Henry Rodriguez	.20	.09
☐ 48 Tino Martinez	.75	.35
☐ 49 Eric Young	.20	.09
☐ 50 Bret Boone	.20	.09
☐ 51 Raul Mondesi	.50	.23
☐ 52 Sammy Sosa	.75	.35
☐ 53 John Smoltz	.40	.18
☐ 54 Billy Wagner	.40	.18
☐ 55 Jeff D'Amico	.20	.09
☐ 56 Ken Caminiti	.75	.35
☐ 57 Jason Kendall	.40	.18
☐ 58 Wade Boggs	.75	.35
☐ 59 Andres Galarraga	.75	.35
☐ 60 Jeff Brantley	.20	.09
☐ 61 Mel Rojas	.20	.09
☐ 62 Brian L. Hunter	.40	.18
☐ 63 Bobby Bonilla	.40	.18
☐ 64 Roger Clemens	1.50	.70
☐ 65 Jeff Kent	.20	.09
☐ 66 Matt Williams	.50	.23
☐ 67 Albert Belle	1.00	.45
☐ 68 Jeff King	.20	.09
☐ 69 John Wetteland	.20	.09
☐ 70 Deion Sanders	.75	.35
☐ 71 Bubba Trammell	2.00	.90
☐ 72 Felix Heredia	.75	.35
☐ 73 Billy Koch	.50	.23
☐ 74 Sidney Ponson	.75	.35
☐ 75 Ricky Ledee	4.00	1.80
☐ 76 Brett Tomko	.20	.09
☐ 77 Braden Looper	.75	.35
☐ 78 Damian Jackson	.20	.09
☐ 79 Jason Dickson	.20	.09
☐ 80 Chad Green	1.25	.55
☐ 81 R.A. Dickey	.50	.23
☐ 82 Jeff Liefer	.20	.09
☐ 83 Matt Wagner	.20	.09
☐ 84 Richard Hidalgo	.75	.35
☐ 85 Adam Riggs	.20	.09
☐ 86 Robert Smith	.20	.09
☐ 87 Chad Hermansen	6.00	2.70
☐ 88 Felix Martinez	.20	.09
☐ 89 J.J. Johnson	.20	.09
☐ 90 Todd Dunwoody	1.00	.45
☐ 91 Katsuhiro Maeda	.75	.35
☐ 92 Darin Erstad	1.25	.55
☐ 93 Elieser Marrero	.40	.18
☐ 94 Bartolo Colon	.50	.23
☐ 95 Chris Fussell	.20	.09
☐ 96 Ugueth Urbina	.40	.18
☐ 97 Josh Paul	1.00	.45
☐ 98 Jaime Bluma	.20	.09
☐ 99 Seth Greisinger	.75	.35
☐ 100 Jose Cruz Jr.	20.00	9.00
☐ 101 Todd Dunn	.20	.09
☐ 102 Joe Young	.50	.23
☐ 103 Jonathan Johnson	.40	.18
☐ 104 Justin Towle	1.50	.70
☐ 105 Brian Rose	1.00	.45
☐ 106 Jose Guillen	1.00	.45
☐ 107 Andruw Jones	2.00	.90
☐ 108 Mark Kotsay	5.00	2.20

☐ 109 Wilton Guerrero	.40	.18
☐ 110 Jacob Cruz	.20	.09
☐ 111 Mike Sweeney	.20	.09
☐ 112 Julio Mosquera	.20	.09
☐ 113 Matt Morris	.20	.09
☐ 114 Wendell Magee	.20	.09
☐ 115 John Thomson	.20	.09
☐ 116 Javier (Jose) Valentin	.20	.09
☐ 117 Tom Fordham	.20	.09
☐ 118 Ruben Rivera	.20	.09
☐ 119 Mike Drumright	1.00	.45
☐ 120 Chris Holt	.20	.09
☐ 121 Sean Maloney	.20	.09
☐ 122 Michael Barrett	.20	.09
☐ 123 Tony Saunders	1.25	.55
☐ 124 Kevin Brown C	.20	.09
☐ 125 Richard Almanzar	.20	.09
☐ 126 Mark Redman	.20	.09
☐ 127 Anthony Sanders	1.50	.70
☐ 128 Jeff Abbott	.20	.09
☐ 129 Eugene Kingsale	.20	.09
☐ 130 Paul Konerko	1.25	.55
☐ 131 Randall Simon	4.00	1.80
☐ 132 Andy Larkin	.20	.09
☐ 133 Rafael Medina	.20	.09
☐ 134 Mendy Lopez	.20	.09
☐ 135 Freddy Garcia	.20	.09
☐ 136 Karim Garcia	.20	.09
☐ 137 Larry Rodriguez	.50	.23
☐ 138 Carlos Guillen	.20	.09
☐ 139 Aaron Boone	.40	.18
☐ 140 Donnie Sadler	.20	.09
☐ 141 Brooks Kieschnick	.40	.18
☐ 142 Scott Spiezio	.40	.18
☐ 143 Everett Stull	.20	.09
☐ 144 Enrique Wilson	.20	.09
☐ 145 Milton Bradley	2.00	.90
☐ 146 Kevin Orie	.40	.18
☐ 147 Derek Wallace	.20	.09
☐ 148 Russ Johnson	.20	.09
☐ 149 Joe Lagarde	.50	.23
☐ 150 Luis Castillo	.20	.09
☐ 151 Jay Payton	.20	.09
☐ 152 Joe Long	.20	.09
☐ 153 Livan Hernandez	1.00	.45
☐ 154 Vladimir Nunez	1.00	.45
☐ 155 Calvin Reese UER	.20	.09
Card actually numbered 156		
☐ 156 George Arias	.20	.09
☐ 157 Homer Bush	.20	.09
☐ 158 Chris Carpenter UER	.20	.09
Card numbered 159		
☐ 159 Eric Milton	2.00	.90
☐ 160 Richie Sexson	.20	.09
☐ 161 Carl Pavano	1.00	.45
☐ 162 Chris Gissell	.50	.23
☐ 163 Mac Suzuki	.40	.18
☐ 164 Pat Cline	.20	.09
☐ 165 Ron Wright	.20	.09
☐ 166 Dante Powell	.20	.09
☐ 167 Mark Bellhorn	.20	.09
☐ 168 George Lombard	.20	.09
☐ 169 Pee Wee Lopez	1.00	.45
☐ 170 Paul Wilder	2.50	1.10
☐ 171 Brad Fullmer	.20	.09
☐ 172 Willie Martinez	1.25	.55
☐ 173 Dario Veras	.50	.23
☐ 174 Dave Coggin	.20	.09
☐ 175 Kris Benson	4.00	1.80
☐ 176 Torii Hunter	.20	.09
☐ 177 D.T. Cromer	.20	.09
☐ 178 Nelson Figueroa	.50	.23
☐ 179 Hiram Bocachica	1.50	.70
☐ 180 Shane Monahan	.20	.09
☐ 181 Jimmy Anderson	.75	.35
☐ 182 Juan Melo	.20	.09
☐ 183 Pablo Ortega	.75	.35
☐ 184 Calvin Pickering	4.00	1.80
☐ 185 Reggie Taylor	.20	.09
☐ 186 Jeff Farnsworth	.50	.23
☐ 187 Terrence Long	.40	.18
☐ 188 Geoff Jenkins	.20	.09
☐ 189 Steve Rain	.50	.23
☐ 190 Nerio Rodriguez	.75	.35
☐ 191 Derrick Gibson	1.00	.45
☐ 192 Darin Blood	.20	.09
☐ 193 Ben Davis	.20	.09
☐ 194 Adrian Beltre	10.00	4.50
☐ 195 Damian Sapp UER	2.00	.90
☐ 196 Kerry Wood	5.00	2.20
☐ 197 Nate Rolison	2.00	.90
☐ 198 Fernando Tatis	5.00	2.20
☐ 199 Brad Penny	.75	.35
☐ 200 Jake Westbrook	1.50	.70
☐ 201 Edwin Diaz	.20	.09
☐ 202 Joe Fontenot	.75	.35
☐ 203 Matt Halloran	.75	.35
☐ 204 Blake Stein	.50	.23
☐ 205 Onan Masaoka	.20	.09
☐ 206 Ben Petrick	.20	.09
☐ 207 Matt Clement	1.50	.70
☐ 208 Todd Greene	.40	.18
☐ 209 Ray Ricken	.20	.09
☐ 210 Eric Chavez	6.00	2.70
☐ 211 Edgard Velazquez	.20	.09
☐ 212 Bruce Chen	2.00	.90
☐ 213 Danny Patterson	.20	.09
☐ 214 Jeff Yoder	.20	.09
☐ 215 Luis Ordaz	.50	.23
☐ 216 Chris Widger	.20	.09
☐ 217 Jason Brester	.20	.09
☐ 218 Carlton Loewer	.20	.09
☐ 219 Chris Reitsma	.50	.23
☐ 220 Neifi Perez	.20	.09
☐ 221 Hideki Irabu	2.50	1.10
☐ 222 Ellis Burks	.40	.18
☐ 223 Pedro Martinez	.75	.35
☐ 224 Kenny Lofton	1.00	.45
☐ 225 Randy Johnson	.75	.35
☐ 226 Terry Steinbach	.40	.18
☐ 227 Bernie Williams	.75	.35
☐ 228 Dean Palmer	.40	.18
☐ 229 Alan Benes	.40	.18
☐ 230 Marquis Grissom	.40	.18
☐ 231 Gary Sheffield	.75	.35
☐ 232 Curt Schilling	.40	.18
☐ 233 Reggie Sanders	.20	.09
☐ 234 Bobby Higginson	.40	.18
☐ 235 Moises Alou	.40	.18
☐ 236 Tom Glavine	.40	.18
☐ 237 Mark Grace	.50	.23
☐ 238 Ramon Martinez	.40	.18
☐ 239 Rafael Palmeiro	.50	.23
☐ 240 John Olerud	.40	.18
☐ 241 Dante Bichette	.40	.18
☐ 242 Greg Vaughn	.20	.09
☐ 243 Jeff Bagwell	1.50	.70
☐ 244 Barry Bonds	1.00	.45
☐ 245 Pat Hentgen	.40	.18
☐ 246 Jim Thome	.75	.35
☐ 247 Jermaine Allensworth	.20	.09
☐ 248 Andy Pettitte	.75	.35
☐ 249 Jay Bell	.20	.09
☐ 250 John Jaha	.20	.09
☐ 251 Jim Edmonds	.75	.35
☐ 252 Ron Gant	.40	.18
☐ 253 David Cone	.40	.18
☐ 254 Jose Canseco	.50	.23
☐ 255 Jay Buhner	.50	.23
☐ 256 Greg Maddux	2.50	1.10
☐ 257 Brian McRae	.20	.09
☐ 258 Lance Johnson	.20	.09
☐ 259 Travis Fryman	.40	.18
☐ 260 Paul O'Neill	.40	.18
☐ 261 Ivan Rodriguez	1.00	.45
☐ 262 Gregg Jefferies	.40	.18
☐ 263 Fred McGriff	.50	.23
☐ 264 Derek Bell	.20	.09
☐ 265 Jeff Conine	.20	.09
☐ 266 Mike Piazza	2.50	1.10
☐ 267 Mark Grudzielanek	.20	.09
☐ 268 Brady Anderson	.50	.23
☐ 269 Marty Cordova	.20	.09
☐ 270 Ray Durham	.20	.09
☐ 271 Joe Carter	.50	.23
☐ 272 Brian Jordan	.20	.09
☐ 273 David Justice	.75	.35
☐ 274 Tony Gwynn	2.00	.90
☐ 275 Larry Walker	.75	.35
☐ 276 Cecil Fielder	.40	.18
☐ 277 Mo Vaughn	1.00	.45
☐ 278 Alex Fernandez	.20	.09
☐ 279 Michael Tucker	.40	.18
☐ 280 Jose Valentin	.20	.09
☐ 281 Sandy Alomar	.40	.18
☐ 282 Todd Hollandsworth	.20	.09
☐ 283 Rico Brogna	.20	.09
☐ 284 Rusty Greer	.40	.18
☐ 285 Roberto Hernandez	.20	.09
☐ 286 Hal Morris	.20	.09
☐ 287 Johnny Damon	.20	.09
☐ 288 Todd Hundley	.40	.18
☐ 289 Rondell White	.40	.18
☐ 290 Frank Thomas	3.00	1.35
☐ 291 Don Denbow	.50	.23
☐ 292 Derrek Lee	.40	.18
☐ 293 Todd Walker	.20	.09
☐ 294 Scott Rolen	2.50	1.10
☐ 295 Wes Helms	.20	.09
☐ 296 Bob Abreu	.75	.35
☐ 297 John Patterson	1.50	.70
☐ 298 Alex Gonzalez	1.50	.70
☐ 299 Grant Roberts	1.50	.70
☐ 300 Jeff Suppan	.20	.09
☐ 301 Luke Wilcox	.20	.09
☐ 302 Marlon Anderson	.20	.09
☐ 303 Ray Brown	.20	.09
☐ 304 Mike Caruso	1.25	.55
☐ 305 Sam Marsonek	.50	.23
☐ 306 Brady Raggio	.20	.00
☐ 307 Kevin McGlinchy	1.00	.45
☐ 308 Roy Halladay	1.00	.45
☐ 309 Jeremi Gonzalez	1.50	.70
☐ 310 Aramis Ramirez	8.00	3.60
☐ 311 Dermal Brown	4.00	1.80
☐ 312 Justin Thompson	.20	.09
☐ 313 Jay Tessmer	.20	.09
☐ 314 Mike Johnson	.50	.23
☐ 315 Danny Clyburn	.20	.09
☐ 316 Bruce Aven	.20	.09
☐ 317 Keith Foulke	.20	.09
☐ 318 Jimmy Osting	.50	.23
☐ 319 Valerio De Los Santos	.75	.35
☐ 320 Shannon Stewart	.40	.18
☐ 321 Willie Adams	.20	.09
☐ 322 Larry Barnes	.20	.09
☐ 323 Mark Johnson	.50	.23
☐ 324 Chris Stowers	.50	.23
☐ 325 Brandon Reed	.50	.23
☐ 326 Randy Winn	.20	.09
☐ 327 Steve Chavez	.75	.35
☐ 328 Nomar Garciaparra	2.50	1.10
☐ 329 Jacque Jones	2.50	1.10
☐ 330 Chris Clemons	.20	.09
☐ 331 Todd Helton	1.25	.55
☐ 332 Ryan Brannan	.50	.23
☐ 333 Alex Sanchez	1.50	.70
☐ 334 Arnold Gooch	.20	.09
☐ 335 Russell Branyan	1.25	.55
☐ 336 Daryle Ward	2.00	.90
☐ 337 John LeRoy	.50	.23
☐ 338 Steve Cox	.20	.09
☐ 339 Kevin Witt	2.50	1.10
☐ 340 Norm Hutchins	.20	.09
☐ 341 Gabby Martinez	.20	.09
☐ 342 Kris Detmers	.20	.09
☐ 343 Mike Villano	.20	.09
☐ 344 Preston Wilson	.40	.18
☐ 345 James Manias	.50	.23
☐ 346 Deivi Cruz	1.00	.45
☐ 347 Donzell McDonald	.50	.23
☐ 348 Rod Myers	.75	.35
☐ 349 Shawn Chacon	1.00	.45
☐ 350 Elvin Hernandez	.50	.23
☐ 351 Orlando Cabrera	.75	.35
☐ 352 Brian Banks	.20	.09
☐ 353 Robbie Bell	1.00	.45
☐ 354 Brad Rigby	.20	.09
☐ 355 Scott Elarton	.20	.09
☐ 356 Kevin Sweeney	.50	.23
☐ 357 Steve Soderstrom	.20	.09
☐ 358 Ryan Nye	.20	.09
☐ 359 Marlon Allen	.50	.23
☐ 360 Donny Leon	.50	.23
☐ 361 Garrett Neubart	.75	.35
☐ 362 Abraham Nunez	1.50	.70
☐ 363 Adam Eaton	.50	.23
☐ 364 Octavio Dotel	.50	.23
☐ 365 Dean Crow	.20	.09
☐ 366 Jason Baker	.50	.23
☐ 367 Sean Casey	3.00	1.35
☐ 368 Joe Lawrence	.50	.23
☐ 369 Adam Johnson	1.25	.55
☐ 370 Scott Schoeneweis	.75	.35
☐ 371 Gerald Witasick Jr.	.20	.09
☐ 372 Ronnie Belliard	.50	.23
☐ 373 Russ Ortiz	.20	.09
☐ 374 Robert Stratton	.75	.35
☐ 375 Bobby Estalella	.40	.18
☐ 376 Corey Lee	1.00	.45
☐ 377 Carlos Beltran	1.00	.45
☐ 378 Mike Cameron	.40	.18
☐ 379 Scott Randall	.50	.23
☐ 380 Corey Erickson	.75	.35
☐ 381 Jay Canizaro	.20	.09
☐ 382 Kerry Robinson	.50	.23
☐ 383 Todd Noel	1.00	.45
☐ 384 A.J. Zapp	4.00	1.80
☐ 385 Jarrod Washburn	.20	.09
☐ 386 Ben Grieve	1.50	.70
☐ 387 Javier Vazquez	1.00	.45
☐ 388 Tony Graffanino	.20	.09
☐ 389 Travis Lee	15.00	6.75
☐ 390 DaRond Stovall	.20	.09
☐ 391 Dennis Reyes	1.50	.70
☐ 392 Danny Buxbaum	.20	.09
☐ 393 Marc Lewis	1.00	.45
☐ 394 Kelvim Escobar	.75	.35
☐ 395 Danny Klassen	.20	.09
☐ 396 Ken Cloude	2.50	1.10
☐ 397 Gabe Alvarez	.20	.09

Card	MINT	NRMT
☐ 398 Jaret Wright	10.00	4.50
☐ 399 Raul Casanova	.20	.09
☐ 400 Clayton Bruner	1.00	.45
☐ 401 Jason Marquis	1.00	.45
☐ 402 Marc Kroon	.20	.09
☐ 403 Jamey Wright	.40	.18
☐ 404 Matt Snyder	.50	.23
☐ 405 Josh Garrett	.75	.35
☐ 406 Juan Encarnacion	1.00	.45
☐ 407 Heath Murray	.20	.09
☐ 408 Brett Herbison	.50	.23
☐ 409 Brent Butler	3.00	1.35
☐ 410 Danny Peoples	2.00	.90
☐ 411 Miguel Tejada	6.00	2.70
☐ 412 Damian Moss	.20	.09
☐ 413 Jim Pittsley	.20	.09
☐ 414 Dmitri Young	.40	.18
☐ 415 Glendon Rusch	.20	.09
☐ 416 Vladimir Guerrero	1.50	.70
☐ 417 Cole Liniak	2.50	1.10
☐ 418 Ramon Hernandez UER Card back says 1st Bowman card is 1997 He had a 1996 Bowman	.20	.09
☐ 419 Cliff Politte	.75	.35
☐ 420 Mel Rosario	.50	.23
☐ 421 Jorge Carrion	.50	.23
☐ 422 John Barnes	1.00	.45
☐ 423 Chris Stowe	.75	.35
☐ 424 Vernon Wells	4.00	1.80
☐ 425 Brett Caradonna	1.50	.70
☐ 426 Scott Hodges	1.25	.55
☐ 427 Jon Garland	1.50	.70
☐ 428 Nathan Haynes	1.00	.45
☐ 429 Geoff Goetz	.75	.35
☐ 430 Adam Kennedy	1.25	.55
☐ 431 T.J. Tucker	.50	.23
☐ 432 Aaron Akin	.75	.35
☐ 433 Jayson Werth	2.50	1.10
☐ 434 Glenn Davis	1.25	.55
☐ 435 Mark Mangum	.50	.23
☐ 436 Troy Cameron	3.00	1.35
☐ 437 J.J. Davis	2.50	1.10
☐ 438 Lance Berkman	5.00	2.20
☐ 439 Jason Standridge	.75	.35
☐ 440 Jason Dellaero	1.25	.55
☐ 441 Hideki Irabu	1.25	.55

1997 Bowman International

Inserted one in every pack, this 441-card set is parallel to the regular Bowman set. The difference is found in the flag in the background of each card that tells in what country the pictured player was born.

	MINT	NRMT
COMPLETE SET (441)	300.00	135.00
COMPLETE SERIES 1 (221)	180.00	80.00
COMPLETE SERIES 2 (220)	120.00	55.00
COMMON CARD (1-441)	.50	.23

*STARS: 1.25X TO 2.5X BASE CARDS
*ROOKIES: .75X TO 1.5X BASIC CARDS

1997 Bowman 1998 ROY Favorites

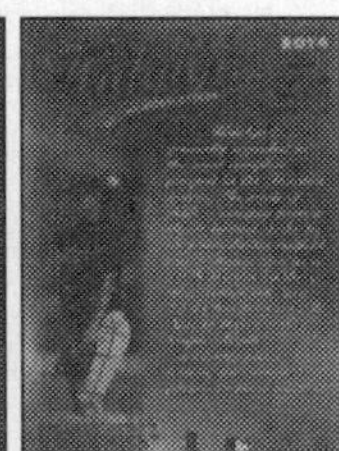

Randomly inserted in 1997 Bowman Series two packs at the rate of one in 12, this 15-card set features color photos of prospective 1998 Rookie of the Year candidates.

	MINT	NRMT
COMPLETE SET (15)	40.00	18.00
COMMON CARD (1-15)	1.00	.45

Card	MINT	NRMT
☐ ROY1 Jeff Abbott	1.00	.45
☐ ROY2 Karim Garcia	1.00	.45
☐ ROY3 Todd Helton	3.00	1.35
☐ ROY4 Richard Hidalgo	1.00	.45
☐ ROY5 Geoff Jenkins	1.00	.45
☐ ROY6 Russ Johnson	1.00	.45
☐ ROY7 Paul Konerko	3.00	1.35
☐ ROY8 Mark Kotsay	5.00	2.20
☐ ROY9 Ricky Ledee	4.00	1.80
☐ ROY10 Travis Lee	15.00	6.75
☐ ROY11 Derrek Lee	1.25	.55
☐ ROY12 Elieser Marrero	1.25	.55
☐ ROY13 Juan Melo	1.00	.45
☐ ROY14 Brian Rose	2.50	1.10
☐ ROY15 Fernando Tatis	5.00	2.20

1997 Bowman Certified Blue Ink Autographs

Randomly inserted in first and second series packs at a rate of one in 96, this 90-card set features color player photos of top prospects with blue ink autographs and printed on sturdy 16 pt. card stock with the Topps Certified Autograph Issue Stamp. The Derek Jeter blue ink and green ink versions are seeded in every 1,928 packs.

	MINT	NRMT
COMPLETE SET (90)	2200.00	1000.00
COMMON BLUE INK (1-90)	12.00	5.50
COMMON BLACK INK (1-90)	25.00	11.00
*BLACK INK: 1X TO 2X BASIC CARDS		
COMMON GOLD INK (1-90)	60.00	27.00
*GOLD INK: 2.5X TO 5X BASE CARDS		

Card	MINT	NRMT
☐ CA1 Jeff Abbott	12.00	5.50
☐ CA2 Bob Abreu	20.00	9.00
☐ CA3 Willie Adams	12.00	5.50
☐ CA4 Brian Banks	12.00	5.50
☐ CA5 Kris Benson	50.00	22.00
☐ CA6 Darin Blood	15.00	6.75
☐ CA7 Jaime Bluma	12.00	5.50
☐ CA8 Kevin Brown	15.00	6.75
☐ CA9 Ray Brown	12.00	5.50
☐ CA10 Homer Bush	12.00	5.50
☐ CA11 Mike Cameron	30.00	13.50
☐ CA12 Jay Canizaro	12.00	5.50
☐ CA13 Luis Castillo	12.00	5.50
☐ CA14 Dave Coggin	15.00	6.75
☐ CA15 Bartolo Colon	25.00	11.00
☐ CA16 Rocky Coppinger	12.00	5.50
☐ CA17 Jacob Cruz	25.00	11.00
☐ CA18 Jose Cruz Jr.	150.00	70.00
☐ CA19 Jeff D'Amico	15.00	6.75
☐ CA20 Ben Davis	25.00	11.00
☐ CA21 Mike Drumright	15.00	6.75
☐ CA22 Scott Elarton	15.00	6.75
☐ CA23 Darin Erstad	50.00	22.00
☐ CA24 Bobby Estalella	20.00	9.00
☐ CA25 Joe Fontenot	15.00	6.75
☐ CA26 Tom Fordham	12.00	5.50
☐ CA27 Brad Fullmer	25.00	11.00
☐ CA28 Chris Fussell	12.00	5.50
☐ CA29 Karim Garcia	25.00	11.00
☐ CA30 Kris Detmers	15.00	6.75
☐ CA31 Todd Greene	25.00	11.00
☐ CA32 Ben Grieve	60.00	27.00
☐ CA33 Vladimir Guerrero	60.00	27.00
☐ CA34 Jose Guillen	40.00	18.00
☐ CA35 Roy Halladay	15.00	6.75
☐ CA36 Wes Helms	30.00	13.50
☐ CA37 Chad Hermansen	60.00	27.00
☐ CA38 Richard Hidalgo	25.00	11.00
☐ CA39 Todd Hollandsworth	15.00	6.75
☐ CA40 Damian Jackson	12.00	5.50
☐ CA41 Derek Jeter Blue DP	100.00	45.00
☐ CA41B Derek Jeter Green	100.00	45.00
☐ CA42 Andruw Jones	80.00	36.00
☐ CA43 Brooks Kieschnick	15.00	6.75
☐ CA44 Eugene Kingsale	12.00	5.50
☐ CA45 Paul Konerko	50.00	22.00
☐ CA46 Marc Kroon	12.00	5.50
☐ CA47 Derrek Lee	40.00	18.00
☐ CA48 Travis Lee	120.00	55.00
☐ CA49 Terrence Long	15.00	6.75
☐ CA50 Curt Lyons	12.00	5.50
☐ CA51 Elieser Marrero	25.00	11.00
☐ CA52 Rafael Medina	12.00	5.50
☐ CA53 Juan Melo	15.00	6.75
☐ CA54 Shane Monahan	15.00	6.75
☐ CA55 Julio Mosquera	12.00	5.50
☐ CA56 Heath Murray	12.00	5.50
☐ CA57 Ryan Nye	12.00	5.50
☐ CA58 Kevin Orie	30.00	13.50
☐ CA59 Russ Ortiz	12.00	5.50
☐ CA60 Carl Pavano	40.00	18.00
☐ CA61 Jay Payton	12.00	5.50
☐ CA62 Neifi Perez	20.00	9.00
☐ CA63 Sidney Ponson	12.00	5.50
☐ CA64 Calvin Reese	12.00	5.50
☐ CA65 Ray Ricken	12.00	5.50
☐ CA66 Brad Rigby	12.00	5.50
☐ CA67 Adam Riggs	12.00	5.50
☐ CA68 Ruben Rivera	25.00	11.00
☐ CA69 J.J. Johnson	15.00	6.75
☐ CA70 Scott Rolen	80.00	36.00
☐ CA71 Tony Saunders	25.00	11.00
☐ CA72 Donnie Sadler	12.00	5.50
☐ CA73 Richie Sexson	25.00	11.00
☐ CA74 Scott Spiezio	25.00	11.00
☐ CA75 Everett Stull	12.00	5.50
☐ CA76 Mike Sweeney	15.00	6.75
☐ CA77 Fernando Tatis	50.00	22.00
☐ CA78 Miguel Tejada	60.00	27.00
☐ CA79 Justin Thompson	30.00	13.50
☐ CA80 Justin Towle	25.00	11.00
☐ CA81 Billy Wagner	20.00	9.00
☐ CA82 Todd Walker	25.00	11.00
☐ CA83 Luke Wilcox	12.00	5.50
☐ CA84 Paul Wilder	30.00	13.50
☐ CA85 Enrique Wilson	12.00	5.50
☐ CA86 Kerry Wood	50.00	22.00
☐ CA87 Jamey Wright	15.00	6.75
☐ CA88 Ron Wright	30.00	13.50
☐ CA89 Dmitri Young	15.00	6.75
☐ CA90 Nelson Figueroa	12.00	5.50

1997 Bowman International Best

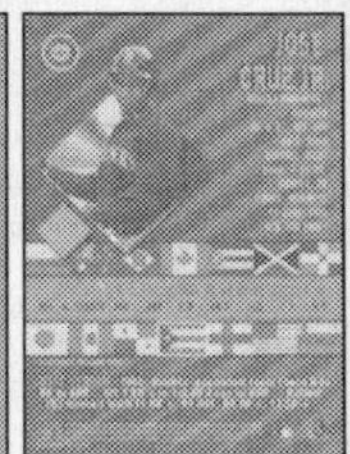

Randomly inserted in series two packs at the rate of one in 12, this 20-card set features color photos of both prospects and veterans from far and wide who have made an impact on the game.

	MINT	NRMT
COMPLETE SET (20)	100.00	45.00
COMMON CARD (1-20)	1.50	.70
COMP.ATOMIC SET (20)	400.00	180.00
COMMON ATOMIC (1-20)	6.00	2.70
*ATOMIC: 2X TO 4X BASIC CARDS		
COMP.REF.SET (20)	200.00	90.00
COMMON REF. (1-20)	3.00	1.35
*REFRACTORS: 1X TO 2X BASIC CARDS		

Card	MINT	NRMT
☐ BBI1 Frank Thomas	12.00	5.50
☐ BBI2 Ken Griffey Jr.	15.00	6.75
☐ BBI3 Juan Gonzalez	8.00	3.60
☐ BBI4 Bernie Williams	3.00	1.35
☐ BBI5 Hideo Nomo	8.00	3.60
☐ BBI6 Sammy Sosa	3.00	1.35
☐ BBI7 Larry Walker	3.00	1.35
☐ BBI8 Vinny Castilla	2.00	.90
☐ BBI9 Mariano Rivera	3.00	1.35
☐ BBI10 Rafael Palmeiro	2.50	1.10
☐ BBI11 Nomar Garciaparra	10.00	4.50
☐ BBI12 Todd Walker	1.50	.70
☐ BBI13 Andruw Jones	8.00	3.60
☐ BBI14 Vladimir Guerrero	6.00	2.70
☐ BBI15 Ruben Rivera	2.00	.90
☐ BBI16 Bob Abreu	3.00	1.35
☐ BBI17 Karim Garcia	1.50	.70
☐ BBI18 Katsuhiro Maeda	2.00	.90
☐ BBI19 Jose Cruz Jr.	20.00	9.00
☐ BBI20 Damian Moss	1.50	.70

1997 Bowman Scout's Honor Roll

Randomly inserted in first series packs at a rate of one in 12, this 15-card set features color photos of top prospects and rookies printed on double-etched foil cards.

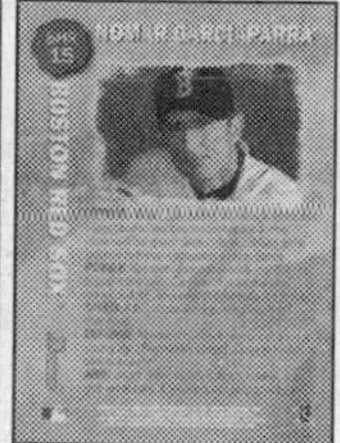

	MINT	NRMT
OMPLETE SET (15)	50.00	22.00
OMMON CARD (1-15)	1.25	.55
☐ 1 Dmitri Young	1.25	.55
☐ 2 Bob Abreu	1.50	.70
☐ 3 Vladimir Guerrero	4.00	1.80
☐ 4 Paul Konerko	3.00	1.35
☐ 5 Kevin Orie	2.00	.90
☐ 6 Todd Walker	1.25	.55
☐ 7 Ben Grieve	4.00	1.80
☐ 8 Darin Erstad	3.00	1.35
☐ 9 Derrek Lee	2.00	.90
☐ 10 Jose Cruz Jr.	20.00	9.00
☐ 11 Scott Rolen	5.00	2.20
☐ 12 Travis Lee	15.00	6.75
☐ 13 Andruw Jones	5.00	2.20
☐ 14 Wilton Guerrero	1.25	.55
☐ 15 Nomar Garciaparra	6.00	2.70

1997 Bowman Chrome

he 1997 Bowman Chrome set was issued in one series otalling 300 cards and was distributed in four-card packs vith a suggested retail price of $3.00. The product was eleased in the winter, after the end of the 1997 season. he fronts feature color action player photos printed on azzling chromium cards. The backs carry player nformation. Key Rookie Cards in this set include Adrian eltre, Jose Cruz Jr., Travis Lee, Aramis Ramirez and liguel Tejada.

	MINT	NRMT
OMPLETE SET (300)	325.00	145.00
OMMON RED (1-100)	.40	.18
OMMON BLUE (101-300)	.60	.25
☐ 1 Derek Jeter	5.00	2.20
☐ 2 Chipper Jones	5.00	2.20
☐ 3 Hideo Nomo	4.00	1.80
☐ 4 Tim Salmon	1.50	.70
☐ 5 Robin Ventura	.75	.35
☐ 6 Tony Clark	1.50	.70
☐ 7 Barry Larkin	1.00	.45
☐ 8 Paul Molitor	1.50	.70
☐ 9 Andy Benes	.40	.18
☐ 10 Ryan Klesko	1.00	.45
☐ 11 Mark McGwire	3.00	1.35
☐ 12 Ken Griffey Jr.	8.00	3.60
☐ 13 Robb Nen	.40	.18
☐ 14 Cal Ripken	6.00	2.70
☐ 15 John Valentin	.40	.18
☐ 16 Ricky Bottalico	.75	.35
☐ 17 Mike Lansing	.40	.18
☐ 18 Ryne Sandberg	2.00	.90
☐ 19 Carlos Delgado	.75	.35
☐ 20 Craig Biggio	1.00	.45
☐ 21 Eric Karros	.75	.35
☐ 22 Kevin Appier	.75	.35
☐ 23 Mariano Rivera	.75	.35
☐ 24 Vinny Castilla	.75	.35
☐ 25 Juan Gonzalez	4.00	1.80
☐ 26 Al Martin	.40	.18
☐ 27 Jeff Cirillo	.75	.35
☐ 28 Ray Lankford	.75	.35
☐ 29 Manny Ramirez	1.50	.70
☐ 30 Roberto Alomar	1.50	.70
☐ 31 Will Clark	1.00	.45
☐ 32 Chuck Knoblauch	1.50	.70
☐ 33 Harold Baines	.75	.35
☐ 34 Edgar Martinez	1.00	.45
☐ 35 Mike Mussina	1.50	.70
☐ 36 Kevin Brown	.40	.18
☐ 37 Dennis Eckersley	1.00	.45
☐ 38 Tino Martinez	1.50	.70
☐ 39 Raul Mondesi	1.00	.45
☐ 40 Sammy Sosa	1.50	.70
☐ 41 John Smoltz	.75	.35
☐ 42 Billy Wagner	1.00	.45
☐ 43 Ken Caminiti	1.50	.70
☐ 44 Wade Boggs	1.50	.70
☐ 45 Andres Galarraga	1.00	.45
☐ 46 Roger Clemens	3.00	1.35
☐ 47 Matt Williams	1.00	.45
☐ 48 Albert Belle	2.00	.90
☐ 49 Jeff King	.40	.18
☐ 50 John Wetteland	.75	.35
☐ 51 Deion Sanders	1.50	.70
☐ 52 Ellis Burks	.75	.35
☐ 53 Pedro Martinez	1.50	.70
☐ 54 Kenny Lofton	2.00	.90
☐ 55 Randy Johnson	1.50	.70
☐ 56 Bernie Williams	1.50	.70
☐ 57 Marquis Grissom	.75	.35
☐ 58 Gary Sheffield	1.50	.70
☐ 59 Curt Schilling	.75	.35
☐ 60 Reggie Sanders	.40	.18
☐ 61 Bobby Higginson	.75	.35
☐ 62 Moises Alou	.75	.35
☐ 63 Tom Glavine	.75	.35
☐ 64 Mark Grace	1.00	.45
☐ 65 Rafael Palmeiro	1.00	.45
☐ 66 John Olerud	.75	.35
☐ 67 Dante Bichette	.75	.35
☐ 68 Jeff Bagwell	3.00	1.35
☐ 69 Barry Bonds	2.00	.90
☐ 70 Pat Hentgen	.75	.35
☐ 71 Jim Thome	1.50	.70
☐ 72 Andy Pettitte	1.50	.70
☐ 73 Jay Bell	.40	.18
☐ 74 Jim Edmonds	1.50	.70
☐ 75 Ron Gant	.75	.35
☐ 76 David Cone	.75	.35
☐ 77 Jose Canseco	1.00	.45
☐ 78 Jay Buhner	1.00	.45
☐ 79 Greg Maddux	5.00	2.20
☐ 80 Lance Johnson	.40	.18
☐ 81 Travis Fryman	.75	.35
☐ 82 Paul O'Neill	.75	.35
☐ 83 Ivan Rodriguez	2.00	.90
☐ 84 Fred McGriff	1.00	.45
☐ 85 Mike Piazza	5.00	2.20
☐ 86 Brady Anderson	1.00	.45
☐ 87 Marty Cordova	.40	.18
☐ 88 Joe Carter	.75	.35
☐ 89 Brian Jordan	.75	.35
☐ 90 David Justice	1.50	.70
☐ 91 Tony Gwynn	2.50	1.10
☐ 92 Larry Walker	1.50	.70
☐ 93 Mo Vaughn	2.00	.90
☐ 94 Sandy Alomar	.75	.35
☐ 95 Rusty Greer	.75	.35
☐ 96 Roberto Hernandez	.40	.18
☐ 97 Hal Morris	.40	.18
☐ 98 Todd Hundley	.75	.35
☐ 99 Rondell White	.40	.18
☐ 100 Frank Thomas	6.00	2.70
☐ 101 Bubba Trammell	4.00	1.80
☐ 102 Sidney Ponson	1.50	.70
☐ 103 Ricky Ledee	8.00	3.60
☐ 104 Brett Tomko	.40	.18
☐ 105 Braden Looper	1.50	.70
☐ 106 Jason Dickson	.40	.18
☐ 107 Chad Green	2.50	1.10
☐ 108 R.A. Dickey	1.00	.45
☐ 109 Jeff Liefer	.40	.18
☐ 110 Richard Hidalgo	.40	.18
☐ 111 Chad Hermansen	12.00	5.50
☐ 112 Felix Martinez	.40	.18
☐ 113 J.J. Johnson	.40	.18
☐ 114 Todd Dunwoody	1.50	.70
☐ 115 Katsuhiro Maeda	.75	.35
☐ 116 Darin Erstad	2.50	1.10
☐ 117 Elieser Marrero	.75	.35
☐ 118 Bartolo Colon	.75	.35
☐ 119 Ugueth Urbina	.75	.35
☐ 120 Jaime Bluma	.40	.18
☐ 121 Seth Greisinger	1.50	.70
☐ 122 Jose Cruz Jr.	35.00	16.00
☐ 123 Todd Dunn	.40	.18
☐ 124 Justin Towle	3.00	1.35
☐ 125 Brian Rose	2.00	.90
☐ 126 Jose Guillen	2.00	.90
☐ 127 Andruw Jones	4.00	1.80
☐ 128 Mark Kotsay	10.00	4.50
☐ 129 Wilton Guerrero	.40	.18
☐ 130 Jacob Cruz	.40	.18
☐ 131 Mike Sweeney	.40	.18
☐ 132 Matt Morris	.40	.18
☐ 133 John Thomson	.40	.18
☐ 134 Javier Valentin	.40	.18
☐ 135 Mike Drumright	2.00	.90
☐ 136 Michael Barrett	.40	.18
☐ 137 Tony Saunders	2.50	1.10
☐ 138 Kevin Brown	.40	.18
☐ 139 Anthony Sanders	3.00	1.35
☐ 140 Jeff Abbott	.40	.18
☐ 141 Eugene Kingsale	.40	.18
☐ 142 Paul Konerko	2.50	1.10
☐ 143 Randall Simon	8.00	3.60
☐ 144 Freddy Garcia	.40	.18
☐ 145 Karim Garcia	.40	.18
☐ 146 Carlos Guillen	.40	.18
☐ 147 Aaron Boone	.75	.35
☐ 148 Donnie Sadler	.40	.18
☐ 149 Brooks Kieschnick	.75	.35
☐ 150 Scott Spiezio	.75	.35
☐ 151 Kevin Orie	.75	.35
☐ 152 Russ Johnson	.40	.18
☐ 153 Livan Hernandez	1.00	.45
☐ 154 Vladimir Nunez	2.00	.90
☐ 155 Calvin Reese	.40	.18
☐ 156 Chris Carpenter	.40	.18
☐ 157 Eric Milton	4.00	1.80
☐ 158 Richie Sexson	.40	.18
☐ 159 Carl Pavano	2.00	.90
☐ 160 Pat Cline	.40	.18
☐ 161 Ron Wright	.40	.18
☐ 162 Dante Powell	.40	.18
☐ 163 Mark Bellhorn	.40	.18
☐ 164 George Lombard	.40	.18
☐ 165 Paul Wilder	5.00	2.20
☐ 166 Brad Fullmer	.40	.18
☐ 167 Kris Benson	8.00	3.60
☐ 168 Torii Hunter	.40	.18
☐ 169 D.T. Cromer	.40	.18
☐ 170 Nelson Figueroa	1.00	.45
☐ 171 Hiram Bocachica	3.00	1.35
☐ 172 Shane Monahan	.40	.18
☐ 173 Juan Melo	.40	.18
☐ 174 Calvin Pickering	8.00	3.60
☐ 175 Reggie Taylor	.40	.18
☐ 176 Geoff Jenkins	.40	.18
☐ 177 Steve Rain	1.00	.45
☐ 178 Nerio Rodriguez	1.50	.70
☐ 179 Derrick Gibson	1.50	.70
☐ 180 Darin Blood	.40	.18
☐ 181 Ben Davis	.40	.18
☐ 182 Adrian Beltre	20.00	9.00
☐ 183 Kerry Wood	10.00	4.50
☐ 184 Nate Rolison	4.00	1.80
☐ 185 Fernando Tatis	10.00	4.50
☐ 186 Jake Westbrook	3.00	1.35
☐ 187 Edwin Diaz	.40	.18
☐ 188 Joe Fontenot	1.50	.70
☐ 189 Matt Halloran	1.50	.70
☐ 190 Matt Clement	3.00	1.35
☐ 191 Todd Greene	1.50	.70
☐ 192 Eric Chavez	12.00	5.50
☐ 193 Edgard Velazquez	.40	.18
☐ 194 Bruce Chen	4.00	1.80
☐ 195 Jason Brester	.40	.18
☐ 196 Chris Reitsma	1.00	.45
☐ 197 Neifi Perez	.40	.18
☐ 198 Hideki Irabu	5.00	2.20
☐ 199 Don Denbow	.40	.18
☐ 200 Derrek Lee	.40	.18
☐ 201 Todd Walker	.40	.18
☐ 202 Scott Rolen	4.00	1.80
☐ 203 Wes Helms	.40	.18
☐ 204 Bob Abreu	1.50	.70
☐ 205 John Patterson	3.00	1.35
☐ 206 Alex Gonzalez	3.00	1.35
☐ 207 Grant Roberts	3.00	1.35
☐ 208 Jeff Suppan	.40	.18
☐ 209 Luke Wilcox	.40	.18
☐ 210 Marlon Anderson	.40	.18
☐ 211 Mike Caruso	2.50	1.10
☐ 212 Roy Halladay	2.00	.90
☐ 213 Jeremi Gonzalez	3.00	1.35
☐ 214 Aramis Ramirez	15.00	6.75
☐ 215 Dermal Brown	8.00	3.60
☐ 216 Justin Thompson	.40	.18
☐ 217 Danny Clyburn	.40	.18
☐ 218 Bruce Aven	.40	.18
☐ 219 Keith Foulke	.40	.18
☐ 220 Shannon Stewart	.40	.18
☐ 221 Larry Barnes	.40	.18
☐ 222 Mark Johnson	1.00	.45
☐ 223 Randy Winn	.40	.18
☐ 224 Nomar Garciaparra	5.00	2.20
☐ 225 Jacque Jones	5.00	2.20

☐ 226 Chris Clemons	.40	.18
☐ 227 Todd Helton	2.50	1.10
☐ 228 Ryan Brannan	1.00	.45
☐ 229 Alex Sanchez	3.00	1.35
☐ 230 Russell Branyan	2.50	1.10
☐ 231 Daryle Ward	4.00	1.80
☐ 232 Kevin Witt	5.00	2.20
☐ 233 Gabby Martinez	.40	.18
☐ 234 Preston Wilson	.40	.18
☐ 235 Donzell McDonald	1.00	.45
☐ 236 Orlando Cabrera	1.50	.70
☐ 237 Brian Banks	.40	.18
☐ 238 Robbie Bell	2.00	.90
☐ 239 Brad Rigby	.40	.18
☐ 240 Scott Elarton	.40	.18
☐ 241 Donny Leon	1.00	.45
☐ 242 Abraham Nunez	3.00	1.35
☐ 243 Adam Eaton	1.00	.45
☐ 244 Octavio Dotel	1.00	.45
☐ 245 Sean Casey	6.00	2.70
☐ 246 Joe Lawrence	1.00	.45
☐ 247 Adam Johnson	2.50	1.10
☐ 248 Ronnie Belliard	1.00	.45
☐ 249 Bobby Estalella	.40	.18
☐ 250 Corey Lee	2.00	.90
☐ 251 Mike Cameron	.40	.18
☐ 252 Kerry Robinson	1.00	.45
☐ 253 A.J. Zapp	8.00	3.60
☐ 254 Jarrod Washburn	.40	.18
☐ 255 Ben Grieve	3.00	1.35
☐ 256 Javier Vazquez	2.00	.90
☐ 257 Travis Lee	30.00	13.50
☐ 258 Dennis Reyes	3.00	1.35
☐ 259 Danny Buxbaum	.40	.18
☐ 260 Kelvim Escobar	1.50	.70
☐ 261 Danny Klassen	.40	.18
☐ 262 Ken Cloude	5.00	2.20
☐ 263 Gabe Alvarez	.40	.18
☐ 264 Clayton Bruner	2.00	.90
☐ 265 Jason Marquis	2.00	.90
☐ 266 Jamey Wright	.40	.18
☐ 267 Matt Snyder	1.00	.45
☐ 268 Josh Garrett	1.50	.70
☐ 269 Juan Encarnacion	1.50	.70
☐ 270 Heath Murray	.40	.18
☐ 271 Brent Butler	6.00	2.70
☐ 272 Danny Peoples	4.00	1.80
☐ 273 Miguel Tejada	12.00	5.50
☐ 274 Jim Pittsley	.40	.18
☐ 275 Dmitri Young	.40	.18
☐ 276 Vladimir Guerrero	3.00	1.35
☐ 277 Cole Liniak	5.00	2.20
☐ 278 Ramon Hernandez	.40	.18
☐ 279 Cliff Politte	1.50	.70
☐ 280 Mel Rosario	1.00	.45
☐ 281 Jorge Carrion	1.00	.45
☐ 282 John Barnes	2.00	.90
☐ 283 Chris Stowe	1.50	.70
☐ 284 Vernon Wells	8.00	3.60
☐ 285 Brett Caradonna	3.00	1.35
☐ 286 Scott Hodges	2.50	1.10
☐ 287 Jon Garland	3.00	1.35
☐ 288 Nathan Haynes	2.00	.90
☐ 289 Geoff Goetz	1.50	.70
☐ 290 Adam Kennedy	2.50	1.10
☐ 291 T.J. Tucker	1.00	.45
☐ 292 Aaron Akin	1.50	.70
☐ 293 Jayson Werth	5.00	2.20
☐ 294 Glenn Davis	2.50	1.10
☐ 295 Mark Mangum	1.00	.45
☐ 296 Troy Cameron	6.00	2.70
☐ 297 J.J. Davis	5.00	2.20
☐ 298 Lance Berkman	10.00	4.50
☐ 299 Jason Standridge	1.50	.70
☐ 300 Jason Dellaero	2.50	1.10

1997 Bowman Chrome International

Randomly inserted in packs at the rate of one in four, this 300-card set is parallel to the base set and is distinguished by the flag on the background of each card front identifying the country where that player was born.

	MINT	NRMT
COMPLETE SET (300)	800.00	350.00
COMMON CARD (1-300)	1.00	.45

*STARS: 1.5X TO 3X BASIC CARDS ...
*ROOKIES: 1X TO 2X BASIC CARDS ..

1997 Bowman Chrome International Refractor

Randomly inserted in packs at the rate of one in 24, this 300-card set is a parallel version of the Bowman Chrome International set and is similar in design. The difference is found in the refractive quality of the card.

	MINT	NRMT
COMPLETE SET (300)	5000.00	2200.00
COMMON CARD (1-300)	8.00	3.60

*STARS: 10X TO 20X BASIC CARDS ..
*ROOKIES: 6X TO 12X BASIC CARDS

1997 Bowman Chrome Refractors

Randomly inserted in packs at the rate of one in 12, this 300-card set is parallel to the base set and is similar in design. The difference can be found in the refractive quality of the cards.

	MINT	NRMT
COMPLETE SET (300)	3000.00	1350.00
COMMON CARD (1-300)	4.00	1.80
MINOR STARS	6.00	2.70
SEMISTARS	10.00	4.50
UNLISTED STARS	15.00	6.75

*STARS: 5X TO 10X BASIC CARDS ....
*YOUNG STARS: 4X TO 8X BASIC CARDS
*ROOKIES: 2.5X TO 5X BASIC CARDS

☐ 1 Derek Jeter	40.00	18.00
☐ 2 Chipper Jones	50.00	22.00
☐ 3 Hideo Nomo	50.00	22.00
☐ 11 Mark McGwire	30.00	13.50
☐ 12 Ken Griffey Jr.	80.00	36.00
☐ 14 Cal Ripken	60.00	27.00
☐ 18 Ryne Sandberg	20.00	9.00
☐ 46 Roger Clemens	30.00	13.50
☐ 48 Albert Belle	20.00	9.00
☐ 54 Kenny Lofton	20.00	9.00
☐ 68 Jeff Bagwell	30.00	13.50
☐ 69 Barry Bonds	20.00	9.00
☐ 79 Greg Maddux	50.00	22.00
☐ 83 Ivan Rodriguez	20.00	9.00
☐ 85 Mike Piazza	50.00	22.00
☐ 91 Tony Gwynn	40.00	18.00
☐ 93 Mo Vaughn	20.00	9.00
☐ 100 Frank Thomas	60.00	27.00
☐ 101 Bubba Trammell	15.00	6.75
☐ 103 Ricky Ledee	40.00	18.00
☐ 111 Chad Hermansen	60.00	27.00
☐ 116 Darin Erstad	20.00	9.00
☐ 122 Jose Cruz Jr.	175.00	80.00
☐ 127 Andruw Jones	30.00	13.50
☐ 128 Mark Kotsay	50.00	22.00
☐ 142 Paul Konerko	20.00	9.00
☐ 143 Randall Simon	40.00	18.00
☐ 157 Eric Milton	20.00	9.00
☐ 165 Paul Wilder	25.00	11.00
☐ 167 Kris Benson	40.00	18.00
☐ 174 Calvin Pickering	40.00	18.00
☐ 182 Adrian Beltre	100.00	45.00
☐ 183 Kerry Wood	50.00	22.00
☐ 184 Nate Rolison	20.00	9.00
☐ 185 Fernando Tatis	50.00	22.00
☐ 192 Eric Chavez	60.00	27.00
☐ 194 Bruce Chen	20.00	9.00
☐ 198 Hideki Irabu	25.00	11.00
☐ 202 Scott Rolen	30.00	13.50
☐ 214 Aramis Ramirez	70.00	32.00
☐ 215 Dermal Brown	40.00	18.00
☐ 224 Nomar Garciaparra	40.00	18.00
☐ 225 Jacque Jones	25.00	11.00
☐ 227 Todd Helton	20.00	9.00
☐ 231 Daryle Ward	20.00	9.00
☐ 232 Kevin Witt	25.00	11.00
☐ 242 Abraham Nunez	4.00	1.80
☐ 245 Sean Casey	30.00	13.50
☐ 253 A.J. Zapp	40.00	18.00
☐ 255 Ben Grieve	25.00	11.00
☐ 257 Travis Lee	135.00	60.00
☐ 262 Ken Cloude	25.00	11.00
☐ 271 Brent Butler	30.00	13.50
☐ 272 Danny Peoples	20.00	9.00
☐ 273 Miguel Tejada	60.00	27.00
☐ 276 Vladimir Guerrero	25.00	11.00
☐ 277 Cole Liniak	25.00	11.00
☐ 284 Vernon Wells	40.00	18.00
☐ 293 Jayson Werth	25.00	11.00
☐ 296 Troy Cameron	30.00	13.50
☐ 297 J.J. Davis	25.00	11.00
☐ 298 Lance Berkman	50.00	22.00

1997 Bowman Chrome 1998 ROY Favorites

Randomly inserted in packs at the rate of one in 24, cards from this 15-card set features color action photos of 1998 Rookie of the Year prospective candidtates printed on chromium cards. The backs carry player information.

	MINT	NRMT
COMPLETE SET (15)	60.00	27.00
COMMON CARD (1-15)	1.50	.70
COMP.REF.SET (15)	120.00	55.00
COMMON REF. (1-15)	3.00	1.35

*REFRACTORS: 1X TO 2X BASIC CARDS

☐ ROY1 Jeff Abbott	1.50	.70
☐ ROY2 Karim Garcia	2.50	1.10
☐ ROY3 Todd Helton	5.00	2.20
☐ ROY4 Richard Hidalgo	3.00	1.35
☐ ROY5 Geoff Jenkins	1.50	.70
☐ ROY6 Russ Johnson	1.50	.70
☐ ROY7 Paul Konerko	5.00	2.20
☐ ROY8 Mark Kotsay	8.00	3.60
☐ ROY9 Ricky Ledee	6.00	2.70
☐ ROY10 Travis Lee	25.00	11.00
☐ ROY11 Derrek Lee	2.00	.90
☐ ROY12 Elieser Marrero	2.00	.90
☐ ROY13 Juan Melo	1.50	.70
☐ ROY14 Brian Rose	4.00	1.80
☐ ROY15 Fernando Tatis	8.00	3.60

1997 Bowman Chrome Scout's Honor Roll

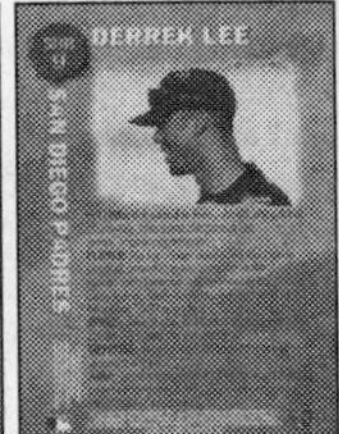

Randomly inserted in packs at a rate of one in 12, this 15-card set features color photos of top prospects and rookies printed on chromium cards. The backs carry player information.

	MINT	NRMT
COMPLETE SET (15)	60.00	27.00
COMMON CARD (1-15)	1.50	.70
COMP.REF.SET (15)	120.00	55.00
COMMON REF. (1-15)	3.00	1.35

REFRACTORS: 1X TO 2X BASIC CARDS

☐ SHR1 Dmitri Young	2.00	.90
☐ SHR2 Bob Abreu	2.50	1.10
☐ SHR3 Vladimir Guerrero	5.00	2.20
☐ SHR4 Paul Konerko	4.00	1.80
☐ SHR5 Kevin Orie	2.00	.90
☐ SHR6 Todd Walker	1.50	.70
☐ SHR7 Ben Grieve	5.00	2.20
☐ SHR8 Darin Erstad	4.00	1.80
☐ SHR9 Derrek Lee	1.50	.70
☐ SHR10 Jose Cruz Jr.	25.00	11.00
☐ SHR11 Scott Rolen	6.00	2.70
☐ SHR12 Travis Lee	20.00	9.00
☐ SHR13 Andruw Jones	6.00	2.70
☐ SHR14 Wilton Guerrero	1.50	.70
☐ SHR15 Nomar Garciaparra	8.00	3.60

1994 Bowman's Best

This 200-card standard-size set consists of 90 veteran stars, 90 rookies and prospects and 20 Mirror Image cards. The veteran cards have red backs and are designated 1R-90R. The rookies and prospects cards have blue backs and are designated 1B-90B. The Mirror Image cards feature a veteran star and a prospect matched by position. These cards are numbered 91-110. Subsets featured are Super Vet (1R-6R), Super Rookie (82R-90R), and Blue Chip (1B-11B). Rookie Cards include Alan Benes, Tony Clark, Brad Fullmer, Chan Ho Park, Edgar Renteria and Ruben Rivera.

	MINT	NRMT
OMPLETE SET (200)	80.00	36.00
OMMON CARD (B1-X110)	.30	.14
B1 Chipper Jones	4.00	1.80
B2 Derek Jeter	5.00	2.20
B3 Bill Pulsipher	.60	.25
B4 James Baldwin	1.00	.45
B5 Brooks Kieschnick	1.00	.45
B6 Justin Thompson	2.00	.90
B7 Midre Cummings	.30	.14
B8 Joey Hamilton	.60	.25
B9 Calvin Reese	.30	.14
B10 Brian Barber	.30	.14
B11 John Burke	.30	.14
B12 DeShawn Warren	.30	.14
B13 Edgardo Alfonzo	2.50	1.10
B14 Eddie Pearson	1.00	.45
B15 Jimmy Haynes	.60	.25
B16 Danny Bautista	.30	.14
B17 Roger Cedeno	.60	.25
B18 Jon Lieber	.30	.14
B19 Billy Wagner	3.00	1.35
B20 Tate Seefried	.60	.25
B21 Chad Mottola	.30	.14
B22 Jose Malave	.60	.25
B23 Terrell Wade	1.00	.45
B24 Shane Andrews	.30	.14
B25 Chan Ho Park	6.00	2.70
B26 Kirk Presley	1.00	.45
B27 Robbie Beckett	.30	.14
B28 Orlando Miller	.30	.14
B29 Jorge Posada	.30	.14
B30 Frankie Rodriguez	.60	.25
B31 Brian L.Hunter	1.25	.55
B32 Billy Ashley	.30	.14
B33 Rondell White	1.25	.55
B34 John Roper	.30	.14
B35 Marc Valdes	.60	.25
B36 Scott Ruffcorn	.30	.14
B37 Rod Henderson	.30	.14
B38 Curtis Goodwin	.30	.14
B39 Russ Davis	1.00	.45
B40 Rick Gorecki	.30	.14
B41 Johnny Damon	1.25	.55
B42 Roberto Petagine	.30	.14
B43 Chris Snopek	.30	.14
B44 Mark Acre	.30	.14
B45 Todd Hollandsworth	1.25	.55
B46 Shawn Green	1.00	.45
B47 John Carter	.30	.14
B48 Jim Pittsley	1.25	.55
B49 John Wasdin	1.25	.55
B50 D.J.Boston	.30	.14
B51 Tim Clark	.30	.14
B52 Alex Ochoa	.30	.14
B53 Chad Roper	.30	.14
B54 Mike Kelly	.30	.14
B55 Brad Fullmer	4.00	1.80
B56 Carl Everett	.30	.14
B57 Tim Belk	.30	.14
B58 Jimmy Hurst	.60	.25
B59 Mac Suzuki	1.25	.55
B60 Michael Moore	.30	.14
B61 Alan Benes	4.00	1.80
B62 Tony Clark	15.00	6.75
B63 Edgar Renteria	4.00	1.80
B64 Trey Beamon	.60	.25
B65 LaTroy Hawkins	.60	.25
B66 Wayne Gomes	.30	.14
B67 Ray McDavid	.30	.14
B68 John Dettmer	.30	.14
B69 Willie Greene	1.00	.45
B70 Dave Stevens	.30	.14
B71 Kevin Orie	3.00	1.35
B72 Chad Ogea	.60	.25
B73 Ben Van Ryn	.30	.14
B74 Kym Ashworth	.60	.25
B75 Dmitri Young	1.50	.70
B76 Herbert Perry	.60	.25
B77 Joey Eischen	.30	.14
B78 Arquimedez Pozo	1.00	.45
B79 Ugueth Urbina	.60	.25
B80 Keith Williams	.60	.25
B81 John Frascatore	.30	.14
B82 Garey Ingram	.30	.14
B83 Aaron Small	.30	.14
B84 Olmedo Saenz	.30	.14
B85 Jesus Tavarez	.30	.14
B86 Jose Silva	.60	.25
B87 Jay Witasick	.60	.25
B88 Jay Maldonado	.30	.14
B89 Keith Heberling	.30	.14
B90 Rusty Greer	6.00	2.70
R1 Paul Molitor	1.25	.55
R2 Eddie Murray	1.25	.55
R3 Ozzie Smith	1.50	.70
R4 Rickey Henderson	1.00	.45
R5 Lee Smith	.60	.25
R6 Dave Winfield	1.00	.45
R7 Roberto Alomar	1.25	.55
R8 Matt Williams	1.00	.45
R9 Mark Grace	1.00	.45
R10 Lance Johnson	.30	.14
R11 Darren Daulton	.60	.25
R12 Tom Glavine	1.25	.55
R13 Gary Sheffield	1.25	.55
R14 Rod Beck	.60	.25
R15 Fred McGriff	1.00	.45
R16 Joe Carter	1.00	.45
R17 Dante Bichette	1.25	.55
R18 Danny Tartabull	.30	.14
R19 Juan Gonzalez	3.00	1.35
R20 Steve Avery	.30	.14
R21 John Wetteland	.60	.25
R22 Ben McDonald	.30	.14
R23 Jack McDowell	.30	.14
R24 Jose Canseco	1.25	.55
R25 Tim Salmon	1.25	.55
R26 Wilson Alvarez	.60	.25
R27 Gregg Jefferies	.60	.25
R28 John Burkett	.30	.14
R29 Greg Vaughn	.30	.14
R30 Robin Ventura	.60	.25
R31 Paul O'Neill	.60	.25
R32 Cecil Fielder	.60	.25
R33 Kevin Mitchell	.60	.25
R34 Jeff Conine	.60	.25
R35 Carlos Baerga	.60	.25
R36 Greg Maddux	4.00	1.80
R37 Roger Clemens	2.50	1.10
R38 Deion Sanders	1.25	.55
R39 Delino DeShields	.60	.25
R40 Ken Griffey Jr.	6.00	2.70
R41 Albert Belle	1.50	.70
R42 Wade Boggs	1.25	.55
R43 Andres Galarraga	1.25	.55
R44 Aaron Sele	.30	.14
R45 Don Mattingly	2.00	.90
R46 David Cone	.60	.25
R47 Len Dykstra	.60	.25
R48 Brett Butler	.60	.25
R49 Bill Swift	.30	.14
R50 Bobby Bonilla	.60	.25
R51 Rafael Palmeiro	1.25	.55
R52 Moises Alou	.60	.25
R53 Jeff Bagwell	2.50	1.10
R54 Mike Mussina	1.25	.55
R55 Frank Thomas	5.00	2.20
R56 Jose Rijo	.30	.14
R57 Ruben Sierra	.30	.14
R58 Randy Myers	.60	.25
R59 Barry Bonds	1.50	.70
R60 Jimmy Key	.60	.25
R61 Travis Fryman	.60	.25
R62 John Olerud	.60	.25
R63 David Justice	1.25	.55
R64 Ray Lankford	1.00	.45
R65 Bob Tewksbury	.30	.14
R66 Chuck Carr	.30	.14
R67 Jay Buhner	1.00	.45
R68 Kenny Lofton	1.50	.70
R69 Marquis Grissom	.60	.25
R70 Sammy Sosa	1.25	.55
R71 Cal Ripken	5.00	2.20
R72 Ellis Burks	.60	.25
R73 Jeff Montgomery	.60	.25
R74 Julio Franco	.60	.25
R75 Kirby Puckett	2.50	1.10
R76 Larry Walker	1.25	.55
R77 Andy Van Slyke	.60	.25
R78 Tony Gwynn	3.00	1.35
R79 Will Clark	1.25	.55
R80 Mo Vaughn	1.50	.70
R81 Mike Piazza	4.00	1.80
R82 James Mouton	.60	.25
R83 Carlos Delgado	1.00	.45
R84 Ryan Klesko	1.00	.45
R85 Javier Lopez	1.00	.45
R86 Raul Mondesi	1.00	.45
R87 Cliff Floyd	.60	.25
R88 Manny Ramirez	1.50	.70
R89 Hector Carrasco	.60	.25
R90 Jeff Granger	.30	.14
X91 Frank Thomas	2.50	1.10
Dmitri Young		
X92 Fred McGriff	1.25	.55
Brooks Kieschnick		
X93 Matt Williams	.30	.14
Shane Andrews		
X94 Cal Ripken	2.50	1.10
Kevin Orie		
X95 Barry Larkin	2.50	1.10
Derek Jeter		
X96 Ken Griffey Jr.	3.00	1.35
Johnny Damon		
X97 Barry Bonds	1.25	.55
Rondell White		
X98 Albert Belle	1.25	.55
Jimmy Hurst		
X99 Raul Mondesi	6.00	2.70
Ruben Rivera		
X100 Roger Clemens	1.00	.45
Scott Ruffcorn		
X101 Greg Maddux	2.00	.90
John Wasdin		
X102 Tim Salmon	1.00	.45
Chad Mottola		
X103 Carlos Baerga	.60	.25
Arquimedez Pozo		
X104 Mike Piazza	2.00	.90
Bobby Hughes		
X105 Carlos Delgado	1.25	.55
Melvin Nieves		
X106 Javier Lopez	.60	.25
Jorge Posada		
X107 Manny Ramirez	1.25	.55
Jose Malave		
X108 Travis Fryman	2.00	.90
Chipper Jones		
X109 Steve Avery	.30	.14
Bill Pulsipher		
X110 John Olerud	.60	.25
Shawn Green		

1994 Bowman's Best Refractors

This 200-card standard-size set is a parallel to the basic Bowman's Best issue. The cards were randomly inserted in packs at a rate of one in nine Bowman's Best packs. The only difference is the refractive coating that allows for a brighter, shinier appearance.

	MINT	NRMT
COMPLETE SET (200)	1300.00	575.00
COMMON CARD	3.00	1.35
SEMISTARS	6.00	2.70
UNLISTED STARS	12.00	5.50

*RED STARS: 5X TO 10X BASIC CARDS
*BLUE STARS: 4X TO 8X BASIC CARDS
*MIRROR IMAGE STARS: 3X TO 6X BASIC CARDS

	MINT	NRMT
B1 Chipper Jones	60.00	27.00
B2 Derek Jeter	60.00	27.00
B6 Justin Thompson	25.00	11.00
B13 Edgardo Alfonzo	15.00	6.75
B19 Billy Wagner	20.00	9.00
B25 Chan Ho Park	30.00	13.50
B55 Brad Fullmer	20.00	9.00
B61 Alan Benes	25.00	11.00
B62 Tony Clark	70.00	32.00
B63 Edgar Renteria	25.00	11.00
B71 Kevin Orie	20.00	9.00
B90 Rusty Greer	30.00	13.50
X91 Frank Thomas	15.00	6.75
Dmitri Young		
X94 Cal Ripken	15.00	6.75
Kevin Orie		
X96 Ken Griffey Jr.	20.00	9.00
Johnny Damon		
X99 Ruben Rivera	30.00	13.50
Raul Mondesi		

1995 Bowman's Best

This 195 card standard-size set consists of 90 veteran stars, 90 rookies and prospects and 15 Mirror Image cards. The packs contain seven cards and the suggested retail price was $5. The veteran cards have red backs and are designated R1-R90. Cards of rookies and prospects have blue backs and are designated B1-B90. The Mirror Image cards feature a veteran star and a prospect matched by position. These cards are numbered X1-X15. The fronts have an action photo with the background in silver-foil with the team names at the top and red or blue at the bottom corresponding to the back. The backs have a head shot along with player statistics and information. Rookie Cards include Bartolo Colon, Juan Encarnacion, Karim Garcia, Vladimir Guerrero, Andruw Jones, Hideo Nomo, Jay Payton and Scott Rolen.

	MINT	NRMT
COMPLETE SET (195)	225.00	100.00
COMMON CARD (B1-R90)	.40	.18
COMMON CARD (X1-X15)	.50	.23

	MINT	NRMT
☐ B1 Derek Jeter	5.00	2.20
☐ B2 Vladimir Guerrero	30.00	13.50
☐ B3 Bob Abreu	4.00	1.80
☐ B4 Chan Ho Park	1.50	.70
☐ B5 Paul Wilson	1.50	.70
☐ B6 Chad Ogea	.40	.18
☐ B7 Andruw Jones	35.00	16.00
☐ B8 Brian Barber	.40	.18
☐ B9 Andy Larkin	.40	.18
☐ B10 Richie Sexson	4.00	1.80
☐ B11 Everett Stull	.40	.18
☐ B12 Brooks Kieschnick	.75	.35
☐ B13 Matt Murray	.40	.18
☐ B14 John Wasdin	.40	.18
☐ B15 Shannon Stewart	.75	.35
☐ B16 Luis Ortiz	.40	.18
☐ B17 Marc Kroon	.40	.18
☐ B18 Todd Greene	4.00	1.80
☐ B19 Juan Acevedo	.40	.18
☐ B20 Tony Clark	3.00	1.35
☐ B21 Jermaine Dye	.75	.35
☐ B22 Derrek Lee	2.50	1.10
☐ B23 Pat Watkins	.75	.35
☐ B24 Calvin Reese	.40	.18
☐ B25 Ben Grieve	25.00	11.00
☐ B26 Julio Santana	.40	.18
☐ B27 Felix Rodriguez	.75	.35
☐ B28 Paul Konerko	25.00	11.00
☐ B29 Nomar Garciaparra	30.00	13.50
☐ B30 Pat Ahearne	.40	.18
☐ B31 Jason Schmidt	1.00	.45
☐ B32 Billy Wagner	1.00	.45
☐ B33 Rey Ordonez RC	3.00	1.35
☐ B34 Curtis Goodwin	.75	.35
☐ B35 Sergio Nunez	1.00	.45
☐ B36 Tim Belk	.40	.18
☐ B37 Scott Elarton	4.00	1.80
☐ B38 Jason Isringhausen	1.00	.45
☐ B39 Trot Nixon	.75	.35
☐ B40 Sid Roberson	.40	.18
☐ B41 Ron Villone	.40	.18
☐ B42 Ruben Rivera	2.50	1.10
☐ B43 Rick Huisman	.40	.18
☐ B44 Todd Hollandsworth	.75	.35
☐ B45 Johnny Damon	.75	.35
☐ B46 Garret Anderson	.75	.35
☐ B47 Jeff D'Amico	1.00	.45
☐ B48 Dustin Hermanson	.75	.35
☐ B49 Juan Encarnacion	12.00	5.50
☐ B50 Andy Pettitte	2.50	1.10
☐ B51 Chris Stynes	.40	.18
☐ B52 Troy Percival	.40	.18
☐ B53 LaTroy Hawkins	.40	.18
☐ B54 Roger Cedeno	.75	.35
☐ B55 Alan Benes	1.50	.70
☐ B56 Karim Garcia	10.00	4.50
☐ B57 Andrew Lorraine	.40	.18
☐ B58 Gary Rath	.40	.18
☐ B59 Bret Wagner	.75	.35
☐ B60 Jeff Suppan	1.00	.45
☐ B61 Bill Pulsipher	.40	.18
☐ B62 Jay Payton	1.25	.55
☐ B63 Alex Ochoa	.40	.18
☐ B64 Ugueth Urbina	.40	.18
☐ B65 Armando Benitez	.40	.18
☐ B66 George Arias	1.00	.45
☐ B67 Raul Casanova	2.50	1.10
☐ B68 Matt Drews	.75	.35
☐ B69 Jimmy Haynes	.75	.35
☐ B70 Jimmy Hurst	.75	.35
☐ B71 C.J. Nitkowski	.40	.18
☐ B72 Tommy Davis	.75	.35
☐ B73 Bartolo Colon	4.00	1.80
☐ B74 Chris Carpenter	2.50	1.10
☐ B75 Trey Beamon	.75	.35
☐ B76 Bryan Rekar	.40	.18
☐ B77 James Baldwin	.75	.35
☐ B78 Marc Valdes	.40	.18
☐ B79 Tom Fordham	.75	.35
☐ B80 Marc Newfield	.40	.18
☐ B81 Angel Martinez	.40	.18
☐ B82 Brian L. Hunter	1.00	.45
☐ B83 Jose Herrera	.40	.18
☐ B84 Glenn Dishman	.75	.35
☐ B85 Jacob Cruz	5.00	2.20
☐ B86 Paul Shuey	.40	.18
☐ B87 Scott Rolen	30.00	13.50
☐ B88 Doug Million	.40	.18
☐ B89 Desi Relaford	.75	.35
☐ B90 Michael Tucker	1.00	.45
☐ R1 Randy Johnson	1.50	.70
☐ R2 Joe Carter	1.00	.45
☐ R3 Chili Davis	.75	.35
☐ R4 Moises Alou	.75	.35
☐ R5 Gary Sheffield	1.50	.70
☐ R6 Kevin Appier	.75	.35
☐ R7 Denny Neagle	.75	.35
☐ R8 Ruben Sierra	.40	.18
☐ R9 Darren Daulton	.75	.35
☐ R10 Cal Ripken	6.00	2.70
☐ R11 Bobby Bonilla	.75	.35
☐ R12 Manny Ramirez	1.50	.70
☐ R13 Barry Bonds	2.00	.90
☐ R14 Eric Karros	.75	.35
☐ R15 Greg Maddux	5.00	2.20
☐ R16 Jeff Bagwell	3.00	1.35
☐ R17 Paul Molitor	1.50	.70
☐ R18 Ray Lankford	.75	.35
☐ R19 Mark Grace	1.00	.45
☐ R20 Kenny Lofton	2.00	.90
☐ R21 Tony Gwynn	4.00	1.80
☐ R22 Will Clark	1.00	.45
☐ R23 Roger Clemens	3.00	1.35
☐ R24 Dante Bichette	1.00	.45
☐ R25 Barry Larkin	1.00	.45
☐ R26 Wade Boggs	1.50	.70
☐ R27 Kirby Puckett	3.00	1.35
☐ R28 Cecil Fielder	.75	.35
☐ R29 Jose Canseco	1.00	.45
☐ R30 Juan Gonzalez	4.00	1.80
☐ R31 David Cone	.75	.35
☐ R32 Craig Biggio	1.00	.45
☐ R33 Tim Salmon	1.50	.70
☐ R34 David Justice	1.50	.70
☐ R35 Sammy Sosa	1.50	.70
☐ R36 Mike Piazza	5.00	2.20
☐ R37 Carlos Baerga	.75	.35
☐ R38 Jeff Conine	.75	.35
☐ R39 Rafael Palmeiro	1.00	.45
☐ R40 Bret Saberhagen	.40	.18
☐ R41 Len Dykstra	.75	.35
☐ R42 Mo Vaughn	2.00	.90
☐ R43 Wally Joyner	.75	.35
☐ R44 Chuck Knoblauch	1.50	.70
☐ R45 Robin Ventura	.75	.35
☐ R46 Don Mattingly	2.50	1.10
☐ R47 Dave Hollins	.75	.35
☐ R48 Andy Benes	.40	.18
☐ R49 Ken Griffey Jr.	8.00	3.60
☐ R50 Albert Belle	2.00	.90
☐ R51 Matt Williams	1.00	.45
☐ R52 Rondell White	.75	.35
☐ R53 Raul Mondesi	1.00	.45
☐ R54 Brian Jordan	.75	.35
☐ R55 Greg Vaughn	.40	.18
☐ R56 Fred McGriff	1.00	.45
☐ R57 Roberto Alomar	1.50	.70
☐ R58 Dennis Eckersley	1.00	.45
☐ R59 Lee Smith	.75	.35
☐ R60 Eddie Murray	1.50	.70
☐ R61 Kenny Rogers	.75	.35
☐ R62 Ron Gant	.75	.35
☐ R63 Larry Walker	1.50	.70
☐ R64 Chad Curtis	.75	.35
☐ R65 Frank Thomas	6.00	2.70
☐ R66 Paul O'Neill	.75	.35
☐ R67 Kevin Seitzer	.40	.18
☐ R68 Marquis Grissom	.75	.35
☐ R69 Mark McGwire	3.00	1.35
☐ R70 Travis Fryman	.75	.35
☐ R71 Andres Galarraga	1.00	.45
☐ R72 Carlos Perez	.75	.35
☐ R73 Tyler Green	.75	.35
☐ R74 Marty Cordova	1.00	.45
☐ R75 Shawn Green	.75	.35
☐ R76 Vaughn Eshelman	.40	.18
☐ R77 John Mabry	1.00	.45
☐ R78 Jason Bates	.40	.18
☐ R79 Jon Nunnally	.40	.18
☐ R80 Ray Durham	.75	.35
☐ R81 Edgardo Alfonzo	1.50	.70
☐ R82 Esteban Loaiza	.75	.35
☐ R83 Hideo Nomo	15.00	6.75
☐ R84 Orlando Miller	.40	.18
☐ R85 Alex Gonzalez	.75	.35
☐ R86 Mark Grudzielanek	2.50	1.10
☐ R87 Julian Tavarez	.40	.18
☐ R88 Benji Gil	.40	.18
☐ R89 Quilvio Veras	.75	.35
☐ R90 Ricky Bottalico	.75	.35
☐ X1 Ben Davis Ivan Rodriguez	3.00	1.35
☐ X2 Mark Redman Manny Ramirez	1.00	.45
☐ X3 Reggie Taylor Deion Sanders	1.25	.55
☐ X4 Ryan Jaroncyk Shawn Green	1.25	.55
☐ X5 Juan LeBron Juan Gonzalez	2.50	1.10
☐ X6 Toby McKnight Craig Biggio	1.25	.55
☐ X7 Michael Barrett Travis Fryman	1.25	.55
☐ X8 Corey Jenkins Mo Vaughn	2.50	1.10
☐ X9 Ruben Rivera Frank Thomas	3.00	1.35
☐ X10 Curtis Goodwin Kenny Lofton	.50	.23
☐ X11 Brian L. Hunter Tony Gwynn	2.00	.90
☐ X12 Todd Greene Ken Griffey Jr.	4.00	1.80
☐ X13 Karim Garcia Matt Williams	2.00	.90
☐ X14 Billy Wagner Randy Johnson	.50	.23
☐ X15 Pat Watkins Jeff Bagwell	1.50	.70

1995 Bowman's Best Refractors

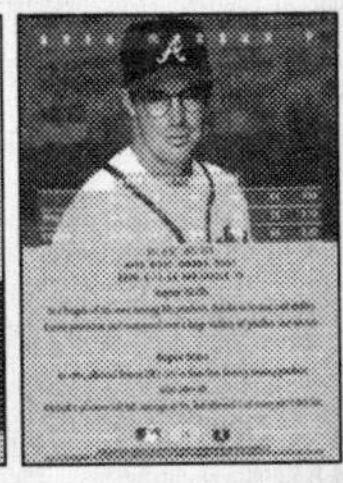

Randomly inserted at a rate of one in six packs, this set is a parallel to the basic Bowman's Best issue. As far as the refractive qualities, the final 15 Mirror Image cards (X1-X15) are considered diffractors which reflects light in a different manner than the typical refractor. The veteran refractor cards have been seen with or without the word refractor on the back. These cards without the word refractors are currently valued the same as the regular refractors.

	MINT	NRMT
COMPLETE SET (195)	2500.00	1100.00
COMMON BLUE (B1-B90)	5.00	2.20
COMMON RED (R1-R90)	4.00	1.80
COMMON MIR.IMAGE (X1-X15)	5.00	2.20
MINOR STARS	6.00	2.70
SEMISTARS	10.00	4.50
STARS	15.00	6.75

*STARS: 5X TO 10X BASIC CARDS
*YOUNG STARS: 6X TO 12X BASIC CARDS
*RCs: 4X TO 8X BASIC CARDS
*MIRROR IMAGE: 2.5X TO 5X BASIC CARDS

	MINT	NRMT
☐ B1 Derek Jeter	60.00	27.00
☐ B2 Vladimir Guerrero	150.00	70.00

] B3 Bob Abreu	25.00	11.00
] B7 Andruw Jones	200.00	90.00
] B10 Richie Sexson	25.00	11.00
] B18 Todd Greene	25.00	11.00
] B20 Tony Clark	40.00	18.00
] B22 Derrek Lee	40.00	18.00
] B25 Ben Grieve	110.00	50.00
] B28 Paul Konerko	110.00	50.00
] B29 Nomar Garciaparra	120.00	55.00
] B33 Rey Ordonez	20.00	9.00
] B37 Scott Elarton	25.00	11.00
] B42 Ruben Rivera	30.00	13.50
] B49 Juan Encarnacion	60.00	27.00
] B50 Andy Pettitte	40.00	18.00
] B56 Karim Garcia	50.00	22.00
] B73 Bartolo Colon	25.00	11.00
] B85 Jacob Cruz	30.00	13.50
] B87 Scott Rolen	150.00	70.00
] R83 Hideo Nomo	100.00	45.00
] X1 Ben Davis Ivan Rodriguez	20.00	9.00

1995 Bowman's Best Jumbo Refractors

is ten-card set was produced for various retail outlets. ne card was inserted into each specially marked retail opps box. According to Treat, Inc. there are no more an 9,000 of each card issued. Each over-sized card easures approximately 4" by 6". The most available of ese cards are Albert Belle and Greg Maddux since they ere distributed nationally. The other eight players were sued on a more regional basis. The cards are an exact arallel of the standard-size Refractor inserts except for eir larger size.

	MINT	NRMT
OMPLETE SET (10)	160.00	70.00
OMMON CARD (1-10)	8.00	3.60
] 1 Albert Belle DP	8.00	3.60
] 2 Ken Griffey Jr	35.00	16.00
] 3 Tony Gwynn	15.00	6.75
] 4 Greg Maddux DP	10.00	4.50
] 5 Hideo Nomo	20.00	9.00
] 6 Mike Piazza	30.00	13.50
] 7 Cal Ripken	30.00	13.50
] 8 Sammy Sosa	8.00	3.60
] 9 Frank Thomas	30.00	13.50
] 10 Mo Vaughn	10.00	4.50

1996 Bowman's Best Previews

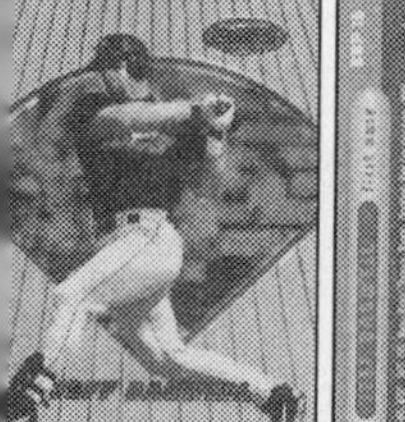

inted with Finest technology, this 30-card set features e hottest 15 top prospects and 15 veterans and was ndomly inserted in 1996 Bowman packs at the rate of e in 12. The fronts display a color action player photo. e backs carry player information.

	MINT	NRMT
OMPLETE SET (30)	120.00	55.00
OMMON CARD (BBP1-BBP30)	1.50	.70
EFRACTORS: 1X TO 2X BASIC CARD		
TOMIC REFRACTORS: 2X TO 4X BASIC CARD		
] BBP1 Chipper Jones	10.00	4.50
] BBP2 Alan Benes	2.50	1.10
☐ BBP3 Brooks Kieschnick	1.50	.70
☐ BBP4 Barry Bonds	4.00	1.80
☐ BBP5 Rey Ordonez	1.50	.70
☐ BBP6 Tim Salmon	3.00	1.35
☐ BBP7 Mike Piazza	10.00	4.50
☐ BBP8 Billy Wagner	2.50	1.10
☐ BBP9 Andruw Jones	10.00	4.50
☐ BBP10 Tony Gwynn	8.00	3.60
☐ BBP11 Paul Wilson	1.50	.70
☐ BBP12 Calvin Reese	1.50	.70
☐ BBP13 Frank Thomas	12.00	5.50
☐ BBP14 Greg Maddux	10.00	4.50
☐ BBP15 Derek Jeter	8.00	3.60
☐ BBP16 Jeff Bagwell	6.00	2.70
☐ BBP17 Barry Larkin	2.00	.90
☐ BBP18 Todd Greene	2.00	.90
☐ BBP19 Ruben Rivera	2.00	.90
☐ BBP20 Richard Hidalgo	3.00	1.35
☐ BBP21 Larry Walker	3.00	1.35
☐ BBP22 Carlos Baerga	2.00	.90
☐ BBP23 Derrick Gibson	3.00	1.35
☐ BBP24 Richie Sexson	3.00	1.35
☐ BBP25 Mo Vaughn	4.00	1.80
☐ BBP26 Hideo Nomo	8.00	3.60
☐ BBP27 Nomar Garciaparra	10.00	4.50
☐ BBP28 Cal Ripken	12.00	5.50
☐ BBP29 Karim Garcia	2.50	1.10
☐ BBP30 Ken Griffey Jr.	15.00	6.75

1996 Bowman's Best

This 180-card set was issued in packs of six cards at the cost of $4.99 per pack. The fronts feature a color action player cutout of 90 outstanding veteran players on a chromium classic gold background design and 90 up and coming prospects and rookies on a silver design. The backs carry a color player portrait, player information and statistics. Card number 33 was never actually issued. Instead, both Roger Clemens and Rafael Palmeiro are erroneously numbered 32. A chrome reprint of the 1952 Bowman Mickey Mantle was inserted at the rate of one in 24 packs. A Refractor version of the Mantle was seeded at 1:96 packs and an Atomic Refractor version was seeded at 1:192. Notable Rookie Cards include Todd Dunwoody, Jose Guillen and Wes Helms.

	MINT	NRMT
COMPLETE SET (180)	100.00	45.00
COMMON GOLD (1-90)	.25	.11
COMMON SILVER (91-180)	.25	.11
☐ 1 Hideo Nomo	3.00	1.35
☐ 2 Edgar Martinez	.75	.35
☐ 3 Cal Ripken	5.00	2.20
☐ 4 Wade Boggs	1.25	.55
☐ 5 Cecil Fielder	.60	.25
☐ 6 Albert Belle	1.50	.70
☐ 7 Chipper Jones	4.00	1.80
☐ 8 Ryne Sandberg	1.50	.70
☐ 9 Tim Salmon	1.25	.55
☐ 10 Barry Bonds	1.50	.70
☐ 11 Ken Caminiti	1.25	.55
☐ 12 Ron Gant	.60	.25
☐ 13 Frank Thomas	5.00	2.20
☐ 14 Dante Bichette	.75	.35
☐ 15 Jason Kendall	.75	.35
☐ 16 Mo Vaughn	1.50	.70
☐ 17 Rey Ordonez	.25	.11
☐ 18 Henry Rodriguez	.25	.11
☐ 19 Ryan Klesko	.75	.35
☐ 20 Jeff Bagwell	2.50	1.10
☐ 21 Randy Johnson	1.25	.55
☐ 22 Jim Edmonds	1.25	.55
☐ 23 Kenny Lofton	1.50	.70
☐ 24 Andy Pettitte	1.50	.70
☐ 25 Brady Anderson	.75	.35
☐ 26 Mike Piazza	4.00	1.80
☐ 27 Greg Vaughn	.25	.11
☐ 28 Joe Carter	.60	.25
☐ 29 Jason Giambi	.60	.25
☐ 30 Ivan Rodriguez	1.50	.70
☐ 31 Jeff Conine	.60	.25
☐ 32 Rafael Palmeiro	.75	.35
☐ 33 Roger Clemens	2.50	1.10
☐ 34 Chuck Knoblauch	1.25	.55
☐ 35 Reggie Sanders	.25	.11
☐ 36 Andres Galarraga	.75	.35
☐ 37 Paul O'Neill	.25	.11
☐ 38 Tony Gwynn	3.00	1.35
☐ 39 Paul Wilson	.60	.25
☐ 40 Garret Anderson	.60	.25
☐ 41 David Justice	1.25	.55
☐ 42 Eddie Murray	1.25	.55
☐ 43 Mike Grace	.25	.11
☐ 44 Marty Cordova	.25	.11
☐ 45 Kevin Appier	.60	.25
☐ 46 Raul Mondesi	.75	.35
☐ 47 Jim Thome	1.25	.55
☐ 48 Sammy Sosa	1.25	.55
☐ 49 Craig Biggio	.75	.35
☐ 50 Marquis Grissom	.60	.25
☐ 51 Alan Benes	.60	.25
☐ 52 Manny Ramirez	1.25	.55
☐ 53 Gary Sheffield	1.25	.55
☐ 54 Mike Mussina	1.25	.55
☐ 55 Robin Ventura	.60	.25
☐ 56 Johnny Damon	.60	.25
☐ 57 Jose Canseco	.75	.35
☐ 58 Juan Gonzalez	3.00	1.35
☐ 59 Tino Martinez	1.25	.55
☐ 60 Brian Hunter	.60	.25
☐ 61 Fred McGriff	.75	.35
☐ 62 Jay Buhner	.75	.35
☐ 63 Carlos Delgado	.60	.25
☐ 64 Moises Alou	.60	.25
☐ 65 Roberto Alomar	1.25	.55
☐ 66 Barry Larkin	.60	.25
☐ 67 Vinny Castilla	.75	.35
☐ 68 Ray Durham	.25	.11
☐ 69 Travis Fryman	.60	.25
☐ 70 Jason Isringhausen	.25	.11
☐ 71 Ken Griffey Jr.	6.00	2.70
☐ 72 John Smoltz	.60	.25
☐ 73 Matt Williams	.75	.35
☐ 74 Chan Ho Park	1.25	.55
☐ 75 Mark McGwire	2.50	1.10
☐ 76 Jeffrey Hammonds	.60	.25
☐ 77 Will Clark	.75	.35
☐ 78 Kirby Puckett	2.50	1.10
☐ 79 Derek Jeter	4.00	1.80
☐ 80 Derek Bell	.60	.25
☐ 81 Eric Karros	.60	.25
☐ 82 Len Dykstra	.60	.25
☐ 83 Larry Walker	1.25	.55
☐ 84 Mark Grudzielanek	.60	.25
☐ 85 Greg Maddux	4.00	1.80
☐ 86 Carlos Baerga	.60	.25
☐ 87 Paul Molitor	1.25	.55
☐ 88 John Valentin	.25	.11
☐ 89 Mark Grace	.75	.35
☐ 90 Ray Lankford	.60	.25
☐ 91 Andruw Jones	5.00	2.20
☐ 92 Nomar Garciaparra	5.00	2.20
☐ 93 Alex Ochoa	.25	.11
☐ 94 Derrick Gibson	2.00	.90
☐ 95 Jeff D'Amico	.75	.35
☐ 96 Ruben Rivera	1.25	.55
☐ 97 Vladimir Guerrero	4.00	1.80
☐ 98 Calvin Reese	.25	.11
☐ 99 Richard Hidalgo	.75	.35
☐ 100 Bartolo Colon	.60	.25
☐ 101 Karim Garcia	.25	.11
☐ 102 Ben Davis	1.25	.55
☐ 103 Jay Powell	.25	.11
☐ 104 Chris Snopek	.25	.11
☐ 105 Glendon Rusch	1.25	.55
☐ 106 Enrique Wilson	.75	.35
☐ 107 Antonio Alfonseca	.25	.11
☐ 108 Wilton Guerrero	2.50	1.10
☐ 109 Jose Guillen	12.00	5.50
☐ 110 Miguel Mejia	.25	.11
☐ 111 Jay Payton	.75	.35
☐ 112 Scott Elarton	.60	.25
☐ 113 Brooks Kieschnick	.60	.25
☐ 114 Dustin Hermanson	.25	.11
☐ 115 Roger Cedeno	.60	.25
☐ 116 Matt Wagner	.25	.11
☐ 117 Lee Daniels	.25	.11
☐ 118 Ben Grieve	4.00	1.80
☐ 119 Ugueth Urbina	.60	.25
☐ 120 Danny Graves	.60	.25
☐ 121 Dan Donato	.25	.11
☐ 122 Matt Ruebel	.25	.11
☐ 123 Mark Sievert	.25	.11
☐ 124 Chris Stynes	.25	.11
☐ 125 Jeff Abbott	.60	.25
☐ 126 Rocky Coppinger	1.00	.45
☐ 127 Jermaine Dye	.25	.11
☐ 128 Todd Greene	.60	.25

Card	MINT	NRMT
☐ 129 Chris Carpenter	.75	.35
☐ 130 Edgar Renteria	.75	.35
☐ 131 Matt Drews	.25	.11
☐ 132 Edgard Velazquez	2.50	1.10
☐ 133 Casey Whitten	.25	.11
☐ 134 Ryan Jones	1.25	.55
☐ 135 Todd Walker	4.00	1.80
☐ 136 Geoff Jenkins	2.50	1.10
☐ 137 Matt Morris	4.00	1.80
☐ 138 Richie Sexson	.75	.35
☐ 139 Todd Dunwoody	6.00	2.70
☐ 140 Gabe Alvarez	1.50	.70
☐ 141 J.J. Johnson	.25	.11
☐ 142 Shannon Stewart	.25	.11
☐ 143 Brad Fullmer	.75	.35
☐ 144 Julio Santana	.25	.11
☐ 145 Scott Rolen	5.00	2.20
☐ 146 Amaury Telemaco	.60	.25
☐ 147 Trey Beamon	.25	.11
☐ 148 Billy Wagner	.75	.35
☐ 149 Todd Hollandsworth	.60	.25
☐ 150 Doug Million	.25	.11
☐ 151 Jose Valentin	2.00	.90
☐ 152 Wes Helms	5.00	2.20
☐ 153 Jeff Suppan	.75	.35
☐ 154 Luis Castillo	1.25	.55
☐ 155 Bob Abreu	.75	.35
☐ 156 Paul Konerko	3.00	1.35
☐ 157 Jamey Wright	.75	.35
☐ 158 Eddie Pearson	.25	.11
☐ 159 Jimmy Haynes	.25	.11
☐ 160 Derrek Lee	.25	.11
☐ 161 Damian Moss	.75	.35
☐ 162 Carlos Guillen	1.00	.45
☐ 163 Chris Fussell	1.00	.45
☐ 164 Mike Sweeney	2.50	1.10
☐ 165 Donnie Sadler	.60	.25
☐ 166 Desi Relaford	.25	.11
☐ 167 Steve Gibralter	.25	.11
☐ 168 Neifi Perez	.75	.35
☐ 169 Antone Williamson	.75	.35
☐ 170 Marty Janzen	.25	.11
☐ 171 Todd Helton	10.00	4.50
☐ 172 Raul Ibanez	1.25	.55
☐ 173 Bill Selby	.25	.11
☐ 174 Shane Monahan	1.50	.70
☐ 175 Robin Jennings	.25	.11
☐ 176 Bobby Chouinard	.25	.11
☐ 177 Einar Diaz	.25	.11
☐ 178 Jason Thompson	.25	.11
☐ 179 Rafael Medina	1.50	.70
☐ 180 Kevin Orie	.75	.35
☐ NNO 1952 Mantle Refractor	15.00	6.75
☐ NNO 1952 Mantle Atomic Refractor	30.00	13.50
☐ NNO 1952 Mantle Chrome	8.00	3.60

1996 Bowman's Best Atomic Refractors

Inserted one in every 48 packs, this 180-card set is parallel to the 1996 Bowman's Best set. It is similar in design to the regular set but was printed with the newest sparkling refractor technology.

	MINT	NRMT
COMMON GOLD (1-90)	10.00	4.50
COMMON SILVER (91-180)	15.00	6.75
MINOR STARS	20.00	9.00
SEMISTARS	30.00	13.50
STARS	50.00	22.00

*STARS: 20X TO 40X BASIC CARDS
*YOUNG STARS: 18X TO 30X BASIC CARDS
*ROOKIES: 9X TO 15X BASIC CARDS

Card	MINT	NRMT
☐ 1 Hideo Nomo	150.00	70.00
☐ 3 Cal Ripken	200.00	90.00
☐ 6 Albert Belle	60.00	27.00
☐ 7 Chipper Jones	120.00	55.00
☐ 8 Ryne Sandberg	60.00	27.00
☐ 10 Barry Bonds	60.00	27.00
☐ 13 Frank Thomas	200.00	90.00
☐ 16 Mo Vaughn	60.00	27.00
☐ 20 Jeff Bagwell	100.00	45.00
☐ 23 Kenny Lofton	60.00	27.00
☐ 24 Andy Pettitte	60.00	27.00
☐ 26 Mike Piazza	150.00	70.00
☐ 30 Ivan Rodriguez	60.00	27.00
☐ 33 Roger Clemens	100.00	45.00
☐ 38 Tony Gwynn	120.00	55.00
☐ 58 Juan Gonzalez	120.00	55.00
☐ 71 Ken Griffey Jr.	250.00	110.00
☐ 75 Mark McGwire	100.00	45.00
☐ 78 Kirby Puckett	100.00	45.00
☐ 79 Derek Jeter	120.00	55.00
☐ 85 Greg Maddux	150.00	70.00
☐ 91 Andruw Jones	150.00	70.00
☐ 92 Nomar Garciaparra	150.00	70.00
☐ 94 Derrick Gibson	80.00	36.00
☐ 96 Ruben Rivera	40.00	18.00
☐ 97 Vladimir Guerrero	125.00	55.00
☐ 99 Richard Hidalgo	50.00	22.00
☐ 101 Karim Garcia	40.00	18.00
☐ 102 Ben Davis	40.00	18.00
☐ 108 Wilton Guerrero	40.00	18.00
☐ 109 Jose Guillen	160.00	70.00
☐ 118 Ben Grieve	125.00	55.00
☐ 132 Edgard Velazquez	40.00	18.00
☐ 135 Todd Walker	60.00	27.00
☐ 136 Geoff Jenkins	40.00	18.00
☐ 137 Matt Morris	60.00	27.00
☐ 139 Todd Dunwoody	100.00	45.00
☐ 145 Scott Rolen	150.00	70.00
☐ 151 Jose Valentin	40.00	18.00
☐ 152 Wes Helms	80.00	36.00
☐ 156 Paul Konerko	125.00	55.00
☐ 160 Derrek Lee	60.00	27.00
☐ 164 Mike Sweeney	40.00	18.00
☐ 171 Todd Helton	160.00	70.00

1996 Bowman's Best Refractors

This 180-card set is parallel to the regular 1996 Bowman Best set and is similar in design. The difference is in the refractive quality of the cards. The cards were inserted at the rate of one in every 12 packs.

	MINT	NRMT
COMPLETE SET (180)	1500.00	700.00
COMMON CARD (1-180)	2.50	1.10

*STARS: 5X TO 10X BASIC CARDS
*YOUNG STARS: 4X TO 8X BASIC CARDS
*ROOKIES: 2.5X TO 5X HI BASIC CARDS

Card	MINT	NRMT
☐ 1 Hideo Nomo	40.00	18.00
☐ 3 Cal Ripken	60.00	27.00
☐ 7 Chipper Jones	40.00	18.00
☐ 13 Frank Thomas	60.00	27.00
☐ 20 Jeff Bagwell	30.00	13.50
☐ 26 Mike Piazza	50.00	22.00
☐ 33 Roger Clemens	30.00	13.50
☐ 38 Tony Gwynn	40.00	18.00
☐ 58 Juan Gonzalez	40.00	18.00
☐ 71 Ken Griffey Jr.	80.00	36.00
☐ 75 Mark McGwire	30.00	13.50
☐ 78 Kirby Puckett	30.00	13.50
☐ 79 Derek Jeter	40.00	18.00
☐ 85 Greg Maddux	50.00	22.00
☐ 91 Andruw Jones	50.00	22.00
☐ 92 Nomar Garciaparra	50.00	22.00
☐ 97 Vladimir Guerrero	40.00	18.00
☐ 109 Jose Guillen	50.00	22.00
☐ 118 Ben Grieve	40.00	18.00
☐ 139 Todd Dunwoody	30.00	13.50
☐ 145 Scott Rolen	50.00	22.00
☐ 156 Paul Konerko	30.00	13.50
☐ 171 Todd Helton	60.00	27.00

1996 Bowman's Best Cuts

Randomly inserted in packs at a rate of one in 24, this chromium card die-cut set features 15 top hobby stars. The fronts display color action player cutouts over the team name and a background of swinging bars. The backs carry player information.

	MINT	NRMT
COMPLETE SET (15)	200.00	90.00
COMMON CARD (1-15)	1.50	.70

*REFRACTORS: .75X TO 2X BASIC CUTS
*ATOMIC REF: 1.5X TO 4X BASIC CUTS

Card	MINT	NRMT
☐ 1 Ken Griffey Jr.	30.00	13.50
☐ 2 Jason Isringhausen	1.50	.70
☐ 3 Derek Jeter	15.00	6.75
☐ 4 Andruw Jones	20.00	9.00
☐ 5 Chipper Jones	20.00	9.00
☐ 6 Ryan Klesko	3.00	1.35
☐ 7 Raul Mondesi	3.00	1.3
☐ 8 Hideo Nomo	15.00	6.7
☐ 9 Mike Piazza	20.00	9.0
☐ 10 Manny Ramirez	8.00	3.6
☐ 11 Cal Ripken	25.00	11.0
☐ 12 Ruben Rivera	3.00	1.3
☐ 13 Tim Salmon	6.00	2.7
☐ 14 Frank Thomas	25.00	11.0
☐ 15 Jim Thome	6.00	2.7

1996 Bowman's Best Mirror Image

Randomly inserted in packs at a rate of one in 48, this 1C card set features four top players on a single card at on of ten different positions. The fronts display a color phot of an AL verteran with a semicircle containing a colo portrait of a prospect who plays the same position. Th backs carry a color photo of a NL veteran with semicircle color portrait of a prospect.

	MINT	NRM
COMPLETE SET (10)	150.00	70.0
COMMON CARD (1-10)	8.00	3.6

*REFRACTORS: .75X TO 2X BASIC CARDS
*ATOMIC REFRACTORS: 1.5X TO 4X BASIC CARDS

Card	MINT	NRMT
☐ 1 Jeff Bagwell Todd Helton Frank Thomas Richie Sexson	25.00	11.0
☐ 2 Craig Biggio Luis Castillo Roberto Alomar Desi Relaford	8.00	3.6
☐ 3 Chipper Jones Scott Rolen Wade Boggs George Arias	25.00	11.0
☐ 4 Barry Larkin Neifi Perez Cal Ripken Mark Bellhorn	20.00	9.0
☐ 5 Larry Walker Karim Garcia Albert Belle Ruben Rivera	10.00	4.5
☐ 6 Barry Bonds Andruw Jones Kenny Lofton Donnie Sadler	20.00	9.0
☐ 7 Tony Gwynn Vladimir Guerrero Ken Griffey Ben Grieve	30.00	13.5
☐ 8 Mike Piazza Ben Davis Ivan Rodriguez Jose Valentin	15.00	6.7
☐ 9 Greg Maddux Jamey Wright Mike Mussina Bartolo Colon	15.00	6.7
☐ 10 Tom Glavine Billy Wagner Randy Johnson Jarrod Washburn	8.00	3.6

1997 Bowman's Best Previews

Randomly inserted in packs at a rate of one in 12, this 20 card set features color photos of 10 rookies and 1 veterans that would be appearing in the 1997 Bowman' Best set.

	MINT	NRM
COMPLETE SET (20)	100.00	45.0
COMMON CARD (1-20)	1.50	.7

Card	MINT	NRMT
☐ 1 Frank Thomas	12.00	5.5
☐ 2 Ken Griffey Jr.	15.00	6.7

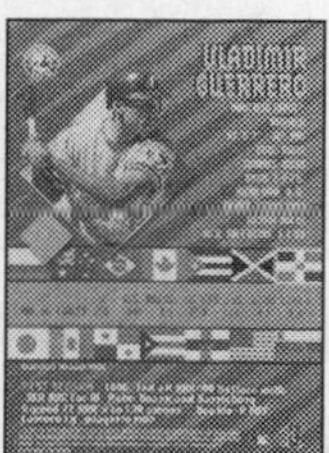

3 Barry Bonds	4.00	1.80
4 Derek Jeter	8.00	3.60
5 Chipper Jones	10.00	4.50
6 Mark McGwire	5.00	2.20
7 Cal Ripken	12.00	5.50
8 Kenny Lofton	4.00	1.80
9 Gary Sheffield	2.50	1.10
10 Jeff Bagwell	6.00	2.70
11 Wilton Guerrero	1.50	.70
12 Scott Rolen	6.00	2.70
13 Todd Walker	1.50	.70
14 Ruben Rivera	2.25	1.00
15 Andruw Jones	6.00	2.70
16 Nomar Garciaparra	8.00	3.60
17 Vladimir Guerrero	5.00	2.20
18 Miguel Tejada	6.00	2.70
19 Bartolo Colon	2.25	1.00
20 Katsuhiro Maeda	2.25	1.00

1997 Bowman's Best

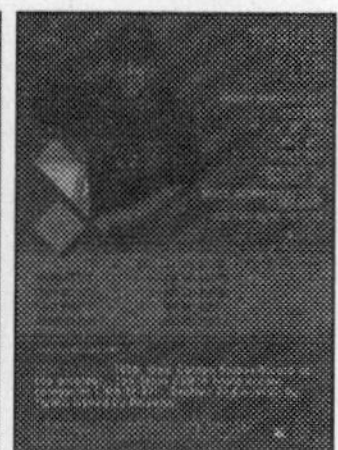

e 1997 Bowman's Best set was issued in one series alling 200 cards and was distributed in six-card packs RP $4.99). The fronts feature borderless color player otos printed on chromium card stock. The cards of the) current superstars display a classic gold design while cards of the 100 top prospects carry a sleek silver sign. Key Rookie Cards include Adrian Beltre, Jose Cruz Travis Lee and Miguel Tejada.

	MINT	NRMT
MPLETE SET (200)	110.00	50.00
MMON CARD (1-200)	.25	.11
1 Ken Griffey Jr.	5.00	2.20
2 Cecil Fielder	.50	.23
3 Albert Belle	1.25	.55
4 Todd Hundley	.50	.23
5 Mike Piazza	3.00	1.35
6 Matt Williams	1.00	.45
7 Mo Vaughn	1.25	.55
8 Ryne Sandberg	1.25	.55
9 Chipper Jones	3.00	1.35
10 Edgar Martinez	1.00	.45
11 Kenny Lofton	1.25	.55
12 Ron Gant	.50	.23
13 Moises Alou	.50	.23
14 Pat Hentgen	.50	.23
15 Steve Finley	.50	.23
16 Mark Grace	1.00	.45
17 Jay Buhner	1.00	.45
18 Jeff Conine	.50	.23
19 Jim Edmonds	1.00	.45
20 Todd Hollandsworth	.25	.11
21 Andy Pettitte	1.00	.45
22 Jim Thome	1.00	.45
23 Eric Young	.25	.11
24 Ray Lankford	.50	.23
25 Marquis Grissom	.50	.23
26 Tony Clark	1.00	.45
27 Jermaine Allensworth	.25	.11
28 Ellis Burks	.50	.23
29 Tony Gwynn	2.50	1.10
30 Barry Larkin	1.00	.45
31 John Olerud	.50	.23
32 Mariano Rivera	.50	.23
33 Paul Molitor	1.00	.45
34 Ken Caminiti	1.00	.45
35 Gary Sheffield	1.00	.45
☐ 36 Al Martin	.25	.11
☐ 37 John Valentin	.25	.11
☐ 38 Frank Thomas	4.00	1.80
☐ 39 John Jaha	.25	.11
☐ 40 Greg Maddux	3.00	1.35
☐ 41 Alex Fernandez	.25	.11
☐ 42 Dean Palmer	.25	.11
☐ 43 Bernie Williams	1.00	.45
☐ 44 Deion Sanders	1.00	.45
☐ 45 Mark McGwire	2.00	.90
☐ 46 Brian Jordan	.25	.11
☐ 47 Bernard Gilkey	.25	.11
☐ 48 Will Clark	1.00	.45
☐ 49 Kevin Appier	.50	.23
☐ 50 Tom Glavine	.50	.23
☐ 51 Chuck Knoblauch	1.00	.45
☐ 52 Rondell White	.50	.23
☐ 53 Greg Vaughn	.25	.11
☐ 54 Mike Mussina	1.00	.45
☐ 55 Brian McRae	.25	.11
☐ 56 Chili Davis	.50	.23
☐ 57 Wade Boggs	1.00	.45
☐ 58 Jeff Bagwell	2.00	.90
☐ 59 Roberto Alomar	1.00	.45
☐ 60 Dennis Eckersley	1.00	.45
☐ 61 Ryan Klesko	1.00	.45
☐ 62 Manny Ramirez	1.00	.45
☐ 63 John Wetteland	.50	.23
☐ 64 Cal Ripken	4.00	1.80
☐ 65 Edgar Renteria	.50	.23
☐ 66 Tino Martinez	1.00	.45
☐ 67 Larry Walker	1.00	.45
☐ 68 Gregg Jefferies	.50	.23
☐ 69 Lance Johnson	.25	.11
☐ 70 Carlos Delgado	.50	.23
☐ 71 Craig Biggio	1.00	.45
☐ 72 Jose Canseco	1.00	.45
☐ 73 Barry Bonds	1.25	.55
☐ 74 Juan Gonzalez	2.50	1.10
☐ 75 Eric Karros	.50	.23
☐ 76 Reggie Sanders	.25	.11
☐ 77 Robin Ventura	.50	.23
☐ 78 Hideo Nomo	2.50	1.10
☐ 79 David Justice	1.00	.45
☐ 80 Vinny Castilla	.50	.23
☐ 81 Travis Fryman	.50	.23
☐ 82 Derek Jeter	3.00	1.35
☐ 83 Sammy Sosa	1.00	.45
☐ 84 Ivan Rodriguez	1.25	.55
☐ 85 Rafael Palmeiro	1.00	.45
☐ 86 Roger Clemens	2.00	.90
☐ 87 Jason Giambi	.50	.23
☐ 88 Andres Galarraga	1.00	.45
☐ 89 Jermaine Dye	.25	.11
☐ 90 Joe Carter	.50	.23
☐ 91 Brady Anderson	1.00	.45
☐ 92 Derek Bell	.25	.11
☐ 93 Randy Johnson	1.00	.45
☐ 94 Fred McGriff	1.00	.45
☐ 95 John Smoltz	.50	.23
☐ 96 Harold Baines	.50	.23
☐ 97 Raul Mondesi	1.00	.45
☐ 98 Tim Salmon	1.00	.45
☐ 99 Carlos Baerga	.50	.23
☐ 100 Dante Bichette	.50	.23
☐ 101 Vladimir Guerrero	2.00	.90
☐ 102 Richard Hidalgo	1.00	.45
☐ 103 Paul Konerko	1.50	.70
☐ 104 Alex Gonzalez	2.00	.90
☐ 105 Jason Dickson	1.00	.45
☐ 106 Jose Rosado	.25	.11
☐ 107 Todd Walker	.25	.11
☐ 108 Seth Greisinger	1.00	.45
☐ 109 Todd Helton	1.50	.70
☐ 110 Ben Davis	.25	.11
☐ 111 Bartolo Colon	.50	.23
☐ 112 Elieser Marrero	.50	.23
☐ 113 Jeff D'Amico	.25	.11
☐ 114 Miguel Tejada	8.00	3.60
☐ 115 Darin Erstad	1.50	.70
☐ 116 Kris Benson	5.00	2.20
☐ 117 Adrian Beltre	12.00	5.50
☐ 118 Neifi Perez	.25	.11
☐ 119 Calvin Reese	.25	.11
☐ 120 Carl Pavano	1.25	.55
☐ 121 Juan Melo	.25	.11
☐ 122 Kevin McGlinchy	1.25	.55
☐ 123 Pat Cline	.25	.11
☐ 124 Felix Heredia	1.00	.45
☐ 125 Aaron Boone	.50	.23
☐ 126 Glendon Rusch	.25	.11
☐ 127 Mike Cameron	.50	.23
☐ 128 Justin Thompson	.50	.23
☐ 129 Chad Hermansen	8.00	3.60
☐ 130 Sidney Ponson	1.00	.45
☐ 131 Willie Martinez	1.50	.70
☐ 132 Paul Wilder	3.00	1.35
☐ 133 Geoff Jenkins	.25	.11
☐ 134 Roy Halladay	1.25	.55
☐ 135 Carlos Guillen	.25	.11
☐ 136 Tony Batista	.25	.11
☐ 137 Todd Greene	.50	.23
☐ 138 Luis Castillo	.25	.11
☐ 139 Jimmy Anderson	1.00	.45
☐ 140 Edgard Velazquez	.25	.11
☐ 141 Chris Snopek	.25	.11
☐ 142 Ruben Rivera	.50	.23
☐ 143 Javier Valentin	.25	.11
☐ 144 Brian Rose	1.25	.55
☐ 145 Fernando Tatis	6.00	2.70
☐ 146 Dean Crow	.25	.11
☐ 147 Karim Garcia	.25	.11
☐ 148 Dante Powell	.25	.11
☐ 149 Hideki Irabu	3.00	1.35
☐ 150 Matt Morris	.25	.11
☐ 151 Wes Helms	.25	.11
☐ 152 Russ Johnson	.25	.11
☐ 153 Jarrod Washburn	.25	.11
☐ 154 Kerry Wood	6.00	2.70
☐ 155 Joe Fontenot	1.00	.45
☐ 156 Eugene Kingsale	.25	.11
☐ 157 Terrence Long	.50	.23
☐ 158 Calvin Maduro	.25	.11
☐ 159 Jeff Suppan	.50	.23
☐ 160 DaRond Stovall	.25	.11
☐ 161 Mark Redman	.25	.11
☐ 162 Ken Cloude	3.00	1.35
☐ 163 Bobby Estalella	.50	.23
☐ 164 Abraham Nunez	2.00	.90
☐ 165 Derrick Gibson	1.00	.45
☐ 166 Mike Drumright	1.25	.55
☐ 167 Katsuhiro Maeda	.50	.23
☐ 168 Jeff Liefer	.25	.11
☐ 169 Ben Grieve	2.00	.90
☐ 170 Bob Abreu	1.00	.45
☐ 171 Shannon Stewart	.50	.23
☐ 172 Braden Looper	1.00	.45
☐ 173 Brant Brown	.25	.11
☐ 174 Marlon Anderson	.25	.11
☐ 175 Brad Fullmer	.25	.11
☐ 176 Carlos Beltran	1.25	.55
☐ 177 Nomar Garciaparra	3.00	1.35
☐ 178 Derrek Lee	.50	.23
☐ 179 Valerio De Los Santos	1.00	.45
☐ 180 Dmitri Young	.50	.23
☐ 181 Jamey Wright	.50	.23
☐ 182 Hiram Bocachica	2.00	.90
☐ 183 Wilton Guerrero	.25	.11
☐ 184 Chris Carpenter	.25	.11
☐ 185 Scott Spiezio	.50	.23
☐ 186 Andruw Jones	2.50	1.10
☐ 187 Travis Lee	20.00	9.00
☐ 188 Jose Cruz Jr.	25.00	11.00
☐ 189 Jose Guillen	1.25	.55
☐ 190 Jeff Abbott	.25	.11
☐ 191 Ricky Ledee	5.00	2.20
☐ 192 Mike Sweeney	.25	.11
☐ 193 Donnie Sadler	.25	.11
☐ 194 Scott Rolen	2.50	1.10
☐ 195 Kevin Orie	.50	.23
☐ 196 Jason Conti	1.50	.70
☐ 197 Mark Kotsay	6.00	2.70
☐ 198 Eric Milton	2.50	1.10
☐ 199 Russell Branyan	1.50	.70
☐ 200 Alex Sanchez	2.00	.90

1997 Bowman's Best Atomic Refractor

Randomly inserted in packs at a rate of one in 24, cards from this 200 card set parallel the regular Bowman's Best set and were printed with the sparkling cross-weave refractor technology.

	MINT	NRMT
COMPLETE SET (200)	3000.00	1350.00
COMMON CARD (1-200)	6.00	2.70

*STARS: 12.5X TO 25X BASIC CARDS
*YOUNG STARS: 10X TO 20X BASIC CARDS
*ROOKIES: 5X TO 10X BASIC CARDS

☐ 1 Ken Griffey Jr.	120.00	55.00
☐ 3 Albert Belle	30.00	13.50
☐ 5 Mike Piazza	80.00	36.00
☐ 7 Mo Vaughn	30.00	13.50
☐ 8 Ryne Sandberg	30.00	13.50
☐ 9 Chipper Jones	80.00	36.00
☐ 11 Kenny Lofton	30.00	13.50
☐ 29 Tony Gwynn	60.00	27.00
☐ 38 Frank Thomas	100.00	45.00
☐ 40 Greg Maddux	80.00	36.00
☐ 45 Mark McGwire	50.00	22.00
☐ 58 Jeff Bagwell	50.00	22.00
☐ 64 Cal Ripken	100.00	45.00

☐ 73 Barry Bonds	30.00	13.50
☐ 74 Juan Gonzalez	80.00	36.00
☐ 78 Hideo Nomo	80.00	36.00
☐ 82 Derek Jeter	60.00	27.00
☐ 84 Ivan Rodriguez	30.00	13.50
☐ 86 Roger Clemens	50.00	22.00
☐ 101 Vladimir Guerrero	40.00	18.00
☐ 103 Paul Konerko	30.00	13.50
☐ 109 Todd Helton	30.00	13.50
☐ 114 Miguel Tejada	80.00	36.00
☐ 115 Darin Erstad	30.00	13.50
☐ 116 Kris Benson	50.00	22.00
☐ 117 Adrian Beltre	120.00	55.00
☐ 129 Chad Hermansen	80.00	36.00
☐ 145 Fernando Tatis	60.00	27.00
☐ 154 Kerry Wood	60.00	27.00
☐ 169 Ben Grieve	40.00	18.00
☐ 177 Nomar Garciaparra	60.00	27.00
☐ 186 Andruw Jones	50.00	22.00
☐ 187 Travis Lee	200.00	90.00
☐ 188 Jose Cruz Jr.	250.00	110.00
☐ 191 Ricky Ledee	50.00	22.00
☐ 194 Scott Rolen	50.00	22.00
☐ 197 Mark Kotsay	60.00	27.00

1997 Bowman's Best Refractor

Randomly inserted in packs at a rate of one in 12, this 200 card set is parallel to the regular set and is similar in design. The difference is found in the refractive quality of the cards.

	MINT	NRMT
COMPLETE SET (200)	1500.00	700.00
COMMON CARD (1-200)	4.00	1.80

*STARS: 6X TO 12X BASIC CARDS ....
*YOUNG STARS: 5X TO 10X BASIC CARDS
*ROOKIES: 2.5X TO 5X BASIC CARDS

1997 Bowman's Best Autographs

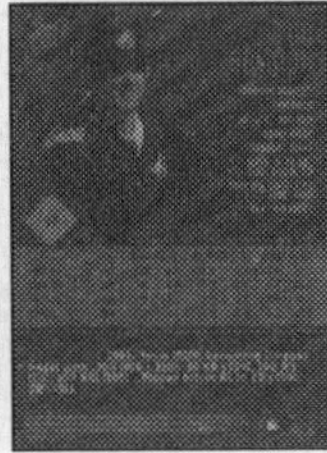

Randomly inserted in packs at a rate of 1:170, this 10-card set features five silver rookie cards and five gold veteran cards with authentic autographs and a "Certified Autograph Issue" stamp.

	MINT	NRMT
COMPLETE SET (10)	600.00	275.00
COMMON CARD	15.00	6.75

*REF.STARS: 1.25X TO 3X BASIC CARDS
*REF.YOUNG STARS: 1X TO 2.5X BASIC CARDS
*ATOMIC STARS: 3X TO 8X BASIC CARDS
*ATOMIC YOUNG STARS: 2.5X TO 6X BASIC CARDS

☐ 29 Tony Gwynn	120.00	55.00
☐ 33 Paul Molitor	50.00	22.00
☐ 82 Derek Jeter	120.00	55.00
☐ 91 Brady Anderson	30.00	13.50
☐ 98 Tim Salmon	40.00	18.00
☐ 107 Todd Walker	25.00	11.00
☐ 183 Wilton Guerrero	15.00	6.75
☐ 185 Scott Spiezio	20.00	9.00
☐ 188 Jose Cruz Jr.	150.00	70.00
☐ 194 Scott Rolen	80.00	36.00

1997 Bowman's Best Best Cuts

Randomly inserted in packs at a rate of one in 24, this 20-card set features color player photos printed on intricate, Laser Cut Chromium card stock.

	MINT	NRMT
COMPLETE SET (20)	200.00	90.00
COMMON CARD (BC1-BC20)	3.00	1.35

*REFRACTORS: .75X TO 1.5X BASIC CARDS
*ATOMIC REFRACTORS: 1.5X TO 3X BASIC CARDS

☐ BC1 Derek Jeter	12.00	5.50
☐ BC2 Chipper Jones	15.00	6.75
☐ BC3 Frank Thomas	20.00	9.00
☐ BC4 Cal Ripken	20.00	9.00
☐ BC5 Mark McGwire	10.00	4.50
☐ BC6 Ken Griffey Jr.	25.00	11.00
☐ BC7 Jeff Bagwell	10.00	4.50

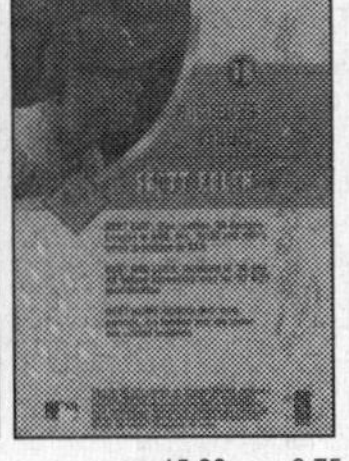

☐ BC8 Mike Piazza	15.00	6.75
☐ BC9 Ken Caminiti	5.00	2.20
☐ BC10 Albert Belle	6.00	2.70
☐ BC11 Jose Cruz Jr.	25.00	11.00
☐ BC12 Wilton Guerrero	3.00	1.35
☐ BC13 Darin Erstad	8.00	3.60
☐ BC14 Andruw Jones	12.00	5.50
☐ BC15 Scott Rolen	12.00	5.50
☐ BC16 Jose Guillen	6.00	2.70
☐ BC17 Bob Abreu	3.00	1.35
☐ BC18 Vladimir Guerrero	10.00	4.50
☐ BC19 Todd Walker	3.00	1.35
☐ BC20 Nomar Garciaparra	15.00	6.75

1997 Bowman's Best Mirror Image

Randomly inserted in packs at a rate of one in 48, this 10-card set features color photos of four of the best players in the same position printed on double-sided chromium card stock. Two veterans and two rookies appear on each card. The veteran players are displayed in the larger photos with the rookies appearing in smaller corner photos.

	MINT	NRMT
COMPLETE SET (10)	150.00	70.00
COMMON CARD (MI1-MI10)	5.00	2.20

*REFRACTORS: 1X TO 2X BASIC CARDS
*ATOMIC REFRACTORS: 2X TO 4X BASIC CARDS
*INVERTED: 1X TO 2X NON-INVERTED

☐ MI1 Nomar Garciaparra Derek Jeter Hiram Bocachica Barry Larkin	20.00	9.00
☐ MI2 Travis Lee Frank Thomas Derrick Lee Jeff Bagwell	30.00	13.50
☐ MI3 Kerry Wood Greg Maddux Kris Benson John Smoltz	15.00	6.75
☐ MI4 Kevin Brown Ivan Rodriguez Eli Marrero Mike Piazza	12.00	5.50
☐ MI5 Jose Cruz Jr. Ken Griffey Jr. Andruw Jones Barry Bonds	40.00	18.00
☐ MI6 Jose Guillen Juan Gonzalez Richard Hidalgo Gary Sheffield	10.00	4.50
☐ MI7 Paul Konerko Mark McGwire Todd Helton Rafael Palmeiro	15.00	6.75
☐ MI8 Wilton Guerrero Craig Biggio Donnie Sadler Chuck Knoblauch	5.00	2.20
☐ MI9 Russell Branyan Matt Williams Adrian Beltre Chipper Jones	20.00	9.00
☐ MI10 Bob Abreu Kenny Lofton Vladimir Guerrero Albert Belle	10.00	4.

1997 Bowman's Best Jumbo

This 16-card set features selected cards from the 19 regular Bowman's Best set in a 4" by 6" jumbo versi available to Stadium Club members only by mail. Only 6 of each of the 16 cards were produced for this jum version. The cards are checklisted below according their number in the regular size set.

	MINT	NRM
COMPLETE SET (16)	100.00	45.(
COMMON CARD	2.50	1.

*REFRACTORS: 2X TO 4X BASIC CARDS
*ATOMIC REFRACTORS: 4X TO 8X BASIC CARDS

☐ 1 Ken Griffey Jr.	12.50	5.
☐ 5 Mike Piazza	7.50	3.
☐ 9 Chipper Jones	7.50	3.
☐ 11 Kenny Lofton	2.50	1.
☐ 29 Tony Gwynn	7.50	3.
☐ 33 Paul Molitor	2.50	1.
☐ 38 Frank Thomas	10.00	4.
☐ 45 Mark McGwire	6.00	2.
☐ 64 Cal Ripken Jr.	10.00	4.
☐ 73 Barry Bonds	5.00	2.
☐ 74 Juan Gonzalez	6.00	2.
☐ 82 Derek Jeter	7.50	3.
☐ 101 Vladimir Guerrero	4.00	1.
☐ 177 Nomar Garciaparra	7.50	3.
☐ 186 Andruw Jones	5.00	2.
☐ 188 Jose Cruz Jr.	10.00	4.

1985 Braves Hostess

The cards in this 22-card set measure 2 1/2" by 3 1/2" a feature players of the Atlanta Braves. Cards we produced by Topps for Hostess (Continental Baking C and are quite attractive. The card backs are similar design to the 1985 Topps regular issue; however photos are different from those that Topps used as the were apparently taken during Spring Training. Cards we available in boxes of Hostess products in packs of fo (three players and a contest card). Other than t manager card, the rest of the set is ordered and number alphabetically.

	NRMT	VG
COMPLETE SET (22)	8.00	3.
COMMON CARD (1-22)	.25	.

☐ 1 Eddie Haas MG	.25	.
☐ 2 Len Barker	.25	.
☐ 3 Steve Bedrosian	.50	.
☐ 4 Bruce Benedict	.25	.
☐ 5 Rick Camp	.25	.
☐ 6 Rick Cerone	.25	.
☐ 7 Chris Chambliss	.50	.
☐ 8 Terry Forster	.25	.
☐ 9 Gene Garber	.50	.
☐ 10 Albert Hall	.25	.
☐ 11 Bob Horner	.50	.
☐ 12 Glenn Hubbard	.25	.
☐ 13 Brad Komminsk	.25	.

] 14 Rick Mahler	.25	.11
] 15 Craig McMurtry	.25	.11
] 16 Dale Murphy	1.00	.45
] 17 Ken Oberkfell	.25	.11
] 18 Pascual Perez	.25	.11
] 19 Gerald Perry	.25	.11
] 20 Rafael Ramirez	.25	.11
] 21 Bruce Sutter	.75	.35
] 22 Claudell Washington	.50	.23

1983 Brewers Gardner's

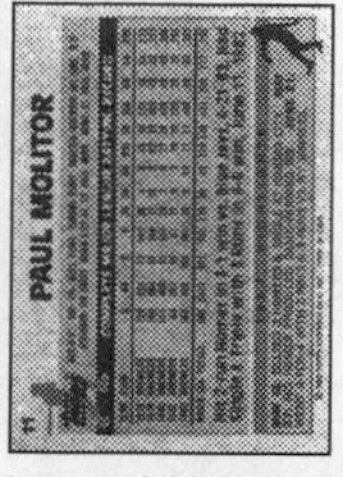

ne cards in this 22-card set measure 2 1/2" by 3 1/2". ne 1983 Gardner's Brewers set features Milwaukee rewer players and manager Harvey Kuenn. Topps printed e set for the Madison (Wisconsin) bakery, hence, the acks are identical to the 1983 Topps backs except for the ard number. The fronts of the cards, however, feature all ew photos and include the Gardner's logo and the rewers' logo. Many of the cards are grease laden, as ey were issued with packages of bread and hamburger nd hot-dog buns. The card numbering for this set is ssentially in alphabetical order by player's name (after e manager is listed first).

	NRMT	VG-E
OMPLETE SET (22)	25.00	11.00
OMMON CARD (1-22)	.75	.35
] 1 Harvey Kuenn MG	1.50	.70
] 2 Dwight Bernard	.75	.35
] 3 Mark Brouhard	.75	.35
] 4 Mike Caldwell	1.00	.45
] 5 Cecil Cooper	1.50	.70
] 6 Marshall Edwards	.75	.35
] 7 Rollie Fingers	3.00	1.35
] 8 Jim Gantner	1.25	.55
] 9 Moose Haas	.75	.35
] 10 Bob McClure	.75	.35
] 11 Paul Molitor	8.00	3.60
] 12 Don Money	1.00	.45
] 13 Charlie Moore	1.00	.45
] 14 Ben Oglivie	1.25	.55
] 15 Ed Romero	.75	.35
] 16 Ted Simmons	2.00	.90
] 17 Jim Slaton	.75	.35
] 18 Don Sutton	3.00	1.35
] 19 Gorman Thomas	1.50	.70
] 20 Pete Vuckovich	1.25	.55
] 21 Ned Yost	.75	.35
] 22 Robin Yount	6.00	2.70

1984 Brewers Gardner's

ne cards in this 22-card set measure 2 1/2" by 3 1/2". For e second year in a row, the Gardner Bakery Company sued a set of cards available in packages of Gardner akery products. The set was manufactured by Topps, nd the backs of the cards are identical to the Topps cards this year except for the numbers. The Gardner logo pears on the fronts of the cards with the player's name, osition abbreviation, the name Brewers, and the words 984 Series II. The card numbering for this set is ssentially in alphabetical order by player's name (after e manager is listed first).

	NRMT	VG-E
COMPLETE SET (22)	12.00	5.50
COMMON CARD (1-22)	.25	.11
☐ 1 Rene Lachemann MG	.25	.11
☐ 2 Mark Brouhard	.25	.11
☐ 3 Mike Caldwell	.50	.23
☐ 4 Bobby Clark	.25	.11
☐ 5 Cecil Cooper	1.00	.45
☐ 6 Rollie Fingers	2.00	.90
☐ 7 Jim Gantner	.75	.35
☐ 8 Moose Haas	.25	.11
☐ 9 Roy Howell	.25	.11
☐ 10 Pete Ladd	.25	.11
☐ 11 Rick Manning	.25	.11
☐ 12 Bob McClure	.25	.11
☐ 13 Paul Molitor	4.00	1.80
☐ 14 Charlie Moore	.50	.23
☐ 15 Ben Oglivie	.75	.35
☐ 16 Ed Romero	.25	.11
☐ 17 Ted Simmons	1.00	.45
☐ 18 Jim Sundberg	.50	.23
☐ 19 Don Sutton	2.00	.90
☐ 20 Tom Tellmann	.25	.11
☐ 21 Pete Vuckovich	.75	.35
☐ 22 Robin Yount	3.00	1.35

1985 Brewers Gardner's

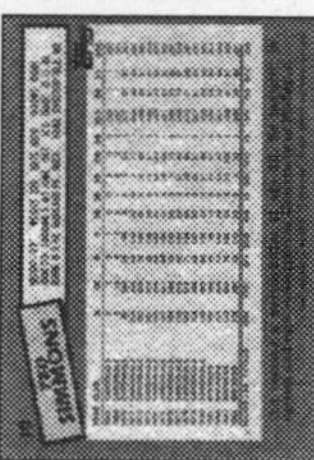

The cards in this 22-card set measure 2 1/2" by 3 1/2". For the third year in a row, the Gardner Bakery Company issued a set of cards available in packages of Gardner Bakery products. The set was manufactured by Topps, and the backs of the cards are identical to the Topps cards of this year except for the card numbers and copyright information. The Gardner logo appears on the fronts of the cards with the player's name, position abbreviation, and the name Brewers. The card numbering for this set is essentially in alphabetical order.

	NRMT	VG-E
COMPLETE SET (22)	10.00	4.50
COMMON CARD (1-22)	.25	.11
☐ 1 George Bamberger MG	.50	.23
☐ 2 Mark Brouhard	.25	.11
☐ 3 Bobby Clark	.25	.11
☐ 4 Jaime Cocanower	.25	.11
☐ 5 Cecil Cooper	1.00	.45
☐ 6 Rollie Fingers	1.50	.70
☐ 7 Jim Gantner	.75	.35
☐ 8 Moose Haas	.25	.11
☐ 9 Dion James	.25	.11
☐ 10 Pete Ladd	.25	.11
☐ 11 Rick Manning	.25	.11
☐ 12 Bob McClure	.25	.11
☐ 13 Paul Molitor	4.00	1.80
☐ 14 Charlie Moore	.50	.23
☐ 15 Ben Oglivie	.75	.35
☐ 16 Chuck Porter	.25	.11
☐ 17 Ed Romero	.25	.11
☐ 18 Bill Schroeder	.25	.11
☐ 19 Ted Simmons	1.00	.45
☐ 20 Tom Tellmann	.25	.11
☐ 21 Pete Vuckovich	.75	.35
☐ 22 Robin Yount	3.00	1.35

1887 Buchner N284

The baseball players found in this Buchner set are a part of a larger group of cards portraying policemen, jockeys and actors, all of which were issued with the tobacco brand "Gold Coin." The set is comprised of three major groupings or types. In the first type, nine players from eight teams, plus three Brooklyn players, are all portrayed in identical poses according to position. In the second type, St. Louis has 14 players depicted in poses which are not repeated. The last group contains 53 additional cards which vary according to pose, team change, spelling, etc. These third type cards are indicated in the checklist below by an asterisk. In all, there are 116 individuals portrayed on 142 cards. The existence of an additional player in the

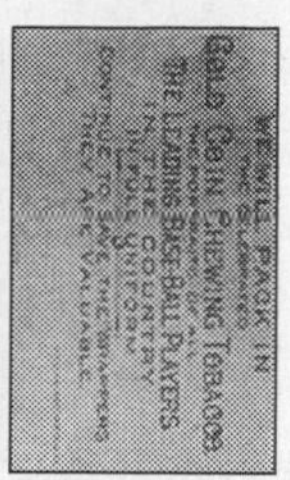

set, McClellan of Brooklyn, has never been verified and the card probably doesn't exist. The set was issued circa 1887. The cards are numbered below in alphabetical order within team with teams themselves listed in alphabetical order: Baltimore (1-4), Boston (5-13), Brooklyn (14-17), Chicago (18-26), Detroit (27-35), Indianapolis (36-47), LaCrosse (48-51), Milwaukee (52-55), New York Mets (56-63), New York (64-73), Philadelphia (74-83), Pittsburg (84-92), St. Louis (93-106), and Washington (107-117).

	EX-MT	VG-E
COMPLETE SET (152)	17500.00	7900.00
COMMON CARD	100.00	45.00
COMMON ST. LOUIS	150.00	70.00
COMMON CARD *	125.00	55.00
☐ 1 Tommy(Oyster) Burns: Baltimore *	125.00	55.00
☐ 2 Chris Fulmer: Baltimore *	125.00	55.00
☐ 3 Matt Kilroy: Baltimore *	125.00	55.00
☐ 4 Blondie Purcell: Baltimore *	125.00	55.00
☐ 5 John Burdock: Boston	100.00	45.00
☐ 6 Bill Daley: Boston	100.00	45.00
☐ 7 Joe Hornung: Boston	100.00	45.00
☐ 8 Dick Johnston: Boston	100.00	45.00
☐ 9A King Kelly: Boston (Right field)	250.00	110.00
☐ 9B King Kelly: Boston (Catcher) *	300.00	135.00
☐ 10A John Morrell: Boston (Both hands out-stretched face high)	100.00	45.00
☐ 10B John Morrell: Boston * (Hands clasped near chin)	125.00	55.00
☐ 11A Hoss Radbourn: Boston (Sic, Radbourne)	200.00	90.00
☐ 11B Hoss Radbourn: Boston * (Sic, Radbourne; hands together above waist)	250.00	110.00
☐ 12 Ezra Sutton: Boston	100.00	45.00
☐ 13 Sam Wise: Boston	100.00	45.00
☐ 14 Bill McClellan: Brooklyn (Never confirmed)		
☐ 15 Jimmy Peoples: Brooklyn	100.00	45.00
☐ 16 Bill Phillips: Brooklyn	100.00	45.00
☐ 17 Henry Porter: Brooklyn	100.00	45.00
☐ 18A Adrian Anson: Chicago Both hands out-stretched face high)	400.00	180.00
☐ 18B Adrian Anson: Chicago * (Left hand on hip right hand down	600.00	275.00
☐ 19 Tom Burns: Chicago	100.00	45.00
☐ 20A John Clarkson: Chicago	200.00	90.00
☐ 20B John Clarkson: Chicago * (Right arm extended, left arm near side)	250.00	110.00
☐ 21 Silver Flint: Chicago	100.00	45.00
☐ 22 Fred Pfeffer: Chicago	100.00	45.00
☐ 23 Jimmy Ryan: Chicago	125.00	55.00
☐ 24 Billy Sullivan: Chicago	125.00	55.00
☐ 25 Billy Sunday: Chicago	250.00	110.00
☐ 26A Ned Williamson: Chicago	100.00	45.00

(Shortstop)
☐ 26B Ned Williamson: 125.00 55.00
Chicago
(Second base) *
☐ 27 Charlie Bennett: 100.00 45.00
Detroit
☐ 28A Dan Brouthers: 200.00 90.00
Detroit (Fielding)
☐ 28B Dan Brouthers: 250.00 110.00
Detroit * (Batting)
☐ 29 Fred Dunlap: Detroit........ 100.00 45.00
☐ 30 Charlie Getzien: 100.00 45.00
Detroit
☐ 31 Ned Hanlon: Detroit 125.00 55.00
☐ 32 Jim Manning: Detoit 100.00 45.00
☐ 33A Hardy Richardson: 100.00 45.00
Detroit
(Hands together in front of chest)
☐ 33B Hardy Richardson: 125.00 55.00
Detroit *
(Right hand holding ball above head)
☐ 34A Sam Thompson: 200.00 90.00
Detroit
(Looking up with hands at waist)
☐ 34B Sam Thompson: 250.00 110.00
Detroit *
(Hands chest high)
☐ 35 Deacon White: Detroit........ 125.00 55.00
☐ 36 Tug Arundel: 100.00 45.00
Indianapolis
☐ 37 Charley Bassett: 100.00 45.00
Indianapolis
☐ 38 Henry Boyle: 125.00 55.00
Indianapolis *
☐ 39 John Cahill: 125.00 55.00
Indianapolis *
☐ 40A Jerry Denny: 100.00 45.00
Indianapolis
(Hands on knees, legs bent)
☐ 40B Jerry Denny: 125.00 55.00
Indianapolis *
(Hands on knees, legs not bent)
☐ 41A Jack Glasscock: 125.00 55.00
Indianapolis
(Crouching, catching a grounder)
☐ 41B Jack Glasscock: 150.00 70.00
Indianapolis *
(Hands on knees)
☐ 42 John Healy: 100.00 45.00
Indianapolis
☐ 43 George Meyers: 125.00 55.00
Indianapolis *
☐ 44 Jack McGeachy: 100.00 45.00
Indianapolis
☐ 45 Mark Polhemus: 100.00 45.00
Indianapolis
☐ 46A Emmett Seery: 100.00 45.00
Indianapolis
(Hands together in front of chest)
☐ 46B Emmett Seery: 125.00 55.00
Indianapolis *
(Hands outstretched head high)
☐ 47 Shomberg: 100.00 45.00
Indianapolis
☐ 48 Corbett: LaCrosse * 125.00 55.00
☐ 49 Crowley: LaCrosse * 125.00 55.00
☐ 50 Kennedy: LaCrosse * 125.00 55.00
☐ 51 Rooks: LaCrosse * 125.00 55.00
☐ 52 Forster: Milwaukee * 125.00 55.00
☐ 53 Hart: Milwaukee * 125.00 55.00
☐ 54 Morrissy: 125.00 55.00
Milwaukee *
☐ 55 Strauss: Milwaukee * 125.00 55.00
☐ 56 Ed Cushmann: 125.00 55.00
NY Mets *
☐ 57 Jim Donohue: 125.00 55.00
NY Mets *
☐ 58 Dude Esterbrooke 125.00 55.00
(Sic):
NY Mets *
☐ 59 Joe Gerhardt: 125.00 55.00
NY Mets *
☐ 60 Frank Hankinson: 125.00 55.00
NY Mets *
☐ 61 Jack Nelson: 125.00 55.00
NY Mets *
☐ 62 Dave Orr: NY Mets * 125.00 55.00
☐ 63 James Rosemann: 125.00 55.00
NY Mets *
☐ 64A Roger Connor: 200.00 90.00
New York
(Both hands outstretched face high)
☐ 64B Roger Connor: 250.00 110.00
New York *
(Hands outstretched, palms up)
☐ 65 Pat Deasley: 125.00 55.00
New York *
☐ 66A Mike Dorgan: 100.00 45.00
New York: Fielding
☐ 66B Mike Dorgan: 125.00 55.00
New York: Batting *
☐ 67A Buck Ewing: 200.00 90.00
New York (Ball in left hand, right arm out shoulder high)
☐ 67B Buck Ewing: 250.00 110.00
New York *
Appears ready to clap
☐ 68A Pete Gillespie: 100.00 45.00
New York: Fielding
☐ 68B Pete Gillespie: 125.00 55.00
New York: Batting *
☐ 69 George Gore: 100.00 45.00
New York
☐ 70A Tim Keefe: 200.00 90.00
New York
☐ 70B Tim Keefe: 250.00 110.00
New York *
Ball just released from right hand
☐ 71A Jim O'Rourke: 200.00 90.00
New York
Hands cupped in front, thigh high
☐ 71B Jim O'Rourke: 250.00 110.00
New York *
(Hands on knees, looking right)
☐ 72A Danny Richardson: 100.00 45.00
New York
(Third base)
☐ 72B Danny Richardson: 125.00 55.00
New York
(Second base) *
☐ 73A John M. Ward: 200.00 90.00
New York
(Crouching, catching a grounder)
☐ 73B John M. Ward: 250.00 110.00
New York *
(Hands by left knee)
☐ 73C John M. Ward: 250.00 110.00
New York *
(Hands on knees)
☐ 74A Ed Andrews: 100.00 45.00
Philadelphia
(Hands together in front of neck)
☐ 74B Ed Andrews: 125.00 55.00
Philadelphia *
(Catching, hands waist high)
☐ 75 Charlie Bastian: 100.00 45.00
Philadelphia
☐ 76 Dan Casey: 125.00 55.00
Philadelphia *
☐ 77 Jack Clements: 100.00 45.00
Philadelphia
☐ 78 Sid Farrar: 125.00 55.00
Philadelphia
☐ 79 Charlie Ferguson: 100.00 45.00
Philadelphia
☐ 80 Jim Fogarty: 100.00 45.00
Philadelphia
☐ 81 Arthur Irwin: 100.00 45.00
Philadelphia
☐ 82A Joel Mulvey: 100.00 45.00
Philadelphia
(Hands on knees)
☐ 82B Joel Mulvey: 125.00 55.00
Philadelphia *
(Hands together above head)
☐ 83A Pete Wood: Philadelphia (Fielding) 100.00 45.00
☐ 83B Pete Wood: Philadelphia HOR (Stealing a Base) * 125.00 55.00
☐ 84 Sam Barkley: 100.00 45.00
Pittsburg
☐ 85 Ed Beecher: 100.00 45.00
☐ 86 Tom Brown: 100.00 45.00
☐ 87 Fred Carroll: 100.00 45.00
☐ 88 John Coleman: 100.00 45.00
☐ 89 Jim McCormick: 100.00 45.00
☐ 90 Doggie Miller: 100.00 45.00
☐ 91 Pop Smith: 100.00 45.00
☐ 92 Art Whitney: 100.00 45.00
☐ 93 Sam Barkley: 150.00 70.00
St. Louis
☐ 94 Doc Bushong: 150.00 70.00
St. Louis
☐ 95 Bob Carruthers 175.00 80.00
(Sic): St. Louis
☐ 96 Charles Comiskey: 300.00 135.00
St. Louis
☐ 97 Dave Foutz: 150.00 70.00
St. Louis
☐ 98 William Gleason: 175.00 80.00
St. Louis
☐ 99 Arlie Latham: 200.00 90.00
St. Louis
☐ 100 Jumbo McGinnis: 150.00 70.00
St. Louis
☐ 101 Hugh Nicol: 150.00 70.00
St. Louis
☐ 102 James O'Neil: 150.00 70.00
St. Louis
☐ 103 Yank Robinson: 150.00 70.00
St. Louis
☐ 104 Sullivan: St. Louis 150.00 70.00
☐ 105 Chris Von Der Ahe OWN 300.00 135.00
St. Louis
Actually a photo rather than drawing
☐ 106 Curt Welch: 150.00 70.00
St. Louis
☐ 107 Cliff Carroll: 100.00 45.00
Washington
☐ 108 Craig: Washington * 125.00 55.00
☐ 109 Sam Crane: 125.00 55.00
Washington *
☐ 110 Ed Dailey: Washington 100.00 45.00
☐ 111 Jim Donnelly: 100.00 45.00
Washington
☐ 112A Jack Farrell: 100.00 45.00
Washington
Ball in left hand right arm out shoulder high)
☐ 112B Jack Farrell: 125.00 55.00
Washington *
(Ball in hands near right knee)
☐ 113 Barney Gilligan: 100.00 45.00
Washington
☐ 114A Paul Hines: 100.00 45.00
Washington
Fielding
☐ 114B Paul Hines: 125.00 55.00
Washington *
(Batting)
☐ 115 Al Myers: Washington 100.00 45.00
☐ 116 Billy O'Brien: 100.00 45.00
Washington
☐ 117 Jim Whitney: 100.00 45.00
Washington

1980 Burger King Pitch/Hit/Run

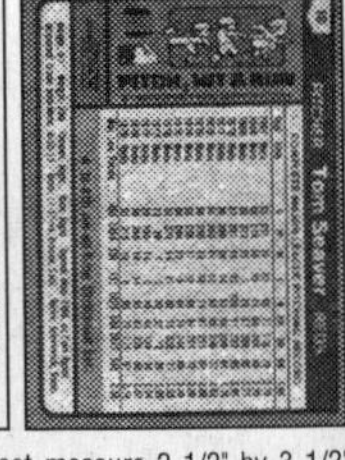

The cards in this 34-card set measure 2 1/2" by 3 1/2". The "Pitch, Hit, and Run" set was a promotion introduced by Burger King in 1980. The cards carry a Burger King logo on the front and those marked by an asterisk in the checklist contain a different photo from that found in the regularly issued Topps series. For example, Nolan Ryan was shown as a California Angel and Joe Morgan was a Cincinnati Red in the 1980 Topps regular set. Cards 1-11 are pitchers, 12-22 are hitters, and 23-33 are speedsters. Within each subgroup, the players are numbered corresponding to the alphabetical order of their names. The unnumbered checklist card was triple printed and is the least valuable card in the set.

	NRMT	VG-E
COMPLETE SET (34)	20.00	9.00
COMMON CARD (1-33)	.10	.05

	MINT	NRMT
☐ 1 Vida Blue *	.50	.23
☐ 2 Steve Carlton	1.50	.70
☐ 3 Rollie Fingers	1.00	.45
☐ 4 Ron Guidry *	.25	.11
☐ 5 Jerry Koosman *	.25	.11
☐ 6 Phil Niekro	1.00	.45
☐ 7 Jim Palmer	2.00	.90
☐ 8 J.R. Richard	.25	.11
☐ 9 Nolan Ryan *	15.00	6.75
Houston Astros		
☐ 10 Tom Seaver *	2.00	.90
☐ 11 Bruce Sutter	.25	.11
☐ 12 Don Baylor	.50	.23
☐ 13 George Brett	6.00	2.70
☐ 14 Rod Carew	1.50	.70
☐ 15 George Foster	.25	.11
☐ 16 Keith Hernandez *	.25	.11
☐ 17 Reggie Jackson *	3.00	1.35
☐ 18 Fred Lynn *	.25	.11
☐ 19 Dave Parker	.25	.11
☐ 20 Jim Rice	.25	.11
☐ 21 Pete Rose	4.00	1.80
☐ 22 Dave Winfield *	3.00	1.35
☐ 23 Bobby Bonds *	.50	.23
☐ 24 Enos Cabell	.10	.05
☐ 25 Cesar Cedeno	.25	.11
☐ 26 Julio Cruz	.10	.05
☐ 27 Ron LeFlore *	.25	.11
☐ 28 Dave Lopes *	.25	.11
☐ 29 Omar Moreno *	.25	.11
☐ 30 Joe Morgan *	2.00	.90
Houston Astros		
☐ 31 Bill North	.10	.05
☐ 32 Frank Taveras	.10	.05
☐ 33 Willie Wilson	.25	.11
☐ NNO Checklist Card TP	.10	.05

1986 Burger King All-Pro

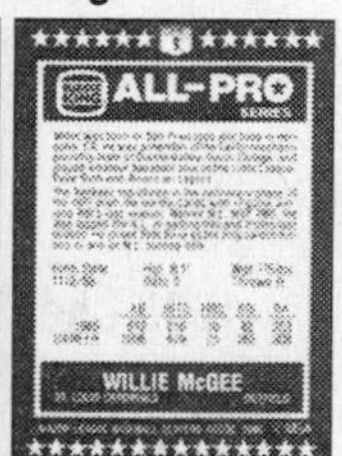

his 20-card standard-size set was distributed in Burger ing restaurants across the country. They were produced s panels of three where the middle card was actually a pecial discount coupon card. The folded panel was given ith the purchase of a Whopper. Each individual card easures 2 1/2" by 3 1/2". The team logos have been rbrushed from the pictures. The cards are numbered on e front at the top.

	MINT	NRMT
OMPLETE SET (20)	10.00	4.50
OMMON CARD (1-20)	.10	.05
☐ 1 Tony Pena	.10	.05
☐ 2 Dave Winfield	.50	.23
☐ 3 Fernando Valenzuela	.25	.11
☐ 4 Pete Rose	1.00	.45
☐ 5 Mike Schmidt	1.00	.45
☐ 6 Steve Carlton	.50	.23
☐ 7 Glenn Wilson	.10	.05
☐ 8 Jim Rice	.25	.11
☐ 9 Wade Boggs	1.00	.45
☐ 10 Juan Samuel	.10	.05
☐ 11 Dale Murphy	.50	.23
☐ 12 Reggie Jackson	.75	.35
☐ 13 Kirk Gibson	.25	.11
☐ 14 Eddie Murray	1.25	.55
☐ 15 Cal Ripken	4.00	1.80
☐ 16 Willie McGee	.25	.11
☐ 17 Dwight Gooden	.50	.23
☐ 18 Steve Garvey	.25	.11
☐ 19 Don Mattingly	2.00	.90
☐ 20 George Brett	2.00	.90

1987 Burger King All-Pro

his 20-card set consists of ten panels of two cards each oined together along with a promotional coupon. ndividual cards measure 2 1/2" by 3 1/2" whereas the anels measure approximately 3 1/2" by 7 5/8". MSA Mike Schechter Associates produced the cards for urger King; there are no Major League logos on the ards. The cards are numbered on the front. The set card numbering is almost (but not quite) in alphabetical order by player's name.

	MINT	NRMT
COMPLETE SET (20)	4.00	1.80
COMMON CARD (1-20)	.10	.05
☐ 1 Wade Boggs	.40	.18
☐ 2 Gary Carter	.30	.14
☐ 3 Will Clark	.50	.23
☐ 4 Roger Clemens	.75	.35
☐ 5 Steve Garvey	.30	.14
☐ 6 Ron Darling	.10	.05
☐ 7 Pedro Guerrero	.10	.05
☐ 8 Von Hayes	.10	.05
☐ 9 Rickey Henderson	.40	.18
☐ 10 Keith Hernandez	.20	.09
☐ 11 Wally Joyner	.30	.14
☐ 12 Mike Krukow	.10	.05
☐ 13 Don Mattingly	1.00	.45
☐ 14 Ozzie Smith	.75	.35
☐ 15 Tony Pena	.10	.05
☐ 16 Jim Rice	.20	.09
☐ 17 Mike Schmidt	.50	.23
☐ 18 Ryne Sandberg	.75	.35
☐ 19 Darryl Strawberry	.20	.09
☐ 20 Fernando Valenzuela	.20	.09

1994 Burger King Ripken

Co-sponsored by Coca-Cola and Burger King, this nine-card standard-size set was produced by Pinnacle to honor Baltimore Orioles star shortstop, Cal Ripken Jr. Three-card packs were available for 25 cents with the purchase of a large soft drink at Baltimore and Washington, D.C. Burger Kings, beginning May 22. The cards were available until June 19, or while supplies lasted. Each card was issued in two versions: standard and gold-foil, with the three-card packs containing two standard and one gold foil card. Ripken autographed several hundred cards, which were awarded in a drawing held after the promotion to collectors who had mailed in entry forms. The cards feature color photos of Ripken, with the lone black parabolic border on the left carrying his name in white (or gold-foil) lettering at the lower left. A similarly unusual curved border design continues on the back, which carries another color photo and career highlights in white lettering. The cards are numbered on the back as "X of 9." The gold-foil versions are valued at two times the regular cards.

	MINT	NRMT
COMPLETE SET (9)	5.00	2.20
COMMON CARD (1-9)	.75	.35
☐ 1 Cal Ripken	.75	.35
Double Honors		
☐ 2 Cal Ripken	.75	.35
Perennial All-Star		
☐ 3 Cal Ripken	.75	.35
Peerless Power		
☐ 4 Cal Ripken	.75	.35
Fitness Fan		
☐ 5 Cal Ripken	.75	.35
Prime Concerns		
☐ 6 Cal Ripken	.75	.35
Home Run Club		
☐ 7 Cal Ripken	.75	.35
The Ironman		
☐ 8 Cal Ripken	.75	.35
Heavy Hitter		
☐ 9 Cal Ripken	.75	.35
Gold Glover		

1997 Burger King Ripken

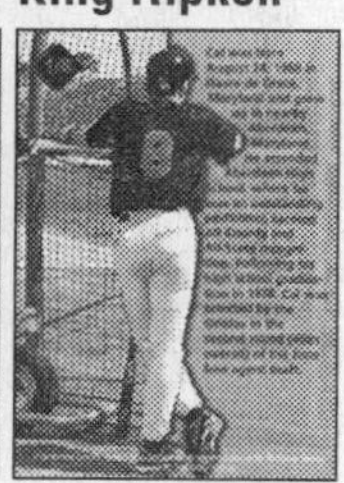

This eight-card set features borderless color action photos of Cal Ripken Jr. and was sponsored by Burger King. The backs carry another photo and a paragraph about an event in the life of Cal Ripken Jr. The set was available in three-card packs beginning August 4, and running through September 13, 1997 at participating Burger Kings for 99 cents a pack with the purchase of a Value Meal. The cards were also available in limited quantities to be purchased separately for $1.15 per pack. Each pack contained a game piece which gave the collector a chance to win a Ripken watch or autographed Ripken balls or jerseys. All proceeds from this promotion benefited the Ripken Charities. Gold cards, which were also inserted into packs, are valued at 2X the regular cards.

	MINT	NRMT
COMPLETE SET (8)	6.00	2.70
COMMON CARD (1-8)	1.00	.45
☐ 1 Cal Ripken Jr.	1.00	.45
(Batting)		
☐ 2 Cal Ripken Jr.	1.00	.45
(Bunting)		
☐ 3 Cal Ripken Jr.	1.00	.45
(Ready to throw)		
☐ 4 Cal Ripken Jr.	1.00	.45
(At end of swing after hitting the ball)		
☐ 5 Cal Ripken Jr.	1.00	.45
(After throwing the ball)		
☐ 6 Cal Ripken Jr.	1.00	.45
(Pointing)		
☐ 7 Cal Ripken Jr.	1.00	.45
(Running after the ball)		
☐ 8 Cal Ripken Jr.	1.00	.45
(Waving)		
☐ NNO Game Card	1.00	.45

1950-56 Callahan HOF W576

The cards in this 82-card set measure approximately 1 3/4" by 2 1/2". The 1950-56 Callahan Hall of Fame set was issued over a number of years at the Baseball Hall of Fame museum in Cooperstown, New York. New cards were added to the set each year when new members were inducted into the Hall of Fame. The cards with (2) in the checklist exist with two different biographies. The year of each card's first inclusion in the set is also given in parentheses; those not listed parenthetically below were issued in 1950 as well as in all the succeeding years and are hence the most common. Naturally the supply of cards is directly related to how many years a player was included in the set; cards that were not issued until 1955 are much scarcer than those printed all the years between 1950 and 1956. The catalog designation is W576. One frequently finds "complete" sets in the original box; take care to investigate the year of issue, the set may be complete in the sense of all the cards issued up to a certain year, but not all 82 cards below. The box is priced below. For example, a "complete" 1950 set would obviously not include any of the cards marked below with ('52), ('54), or ('55) as none of those cards existed in 1950 since those respective players had not yet been inducted. The complete set price below refers to a set including all 83 cards below. Since the cards are unnumbered, they are numbered below for reference alphabetically by player's name.

	NRMT	VG-E
COMPLETE SET (83)	750.00	350.00
COMMON CARD '50	3.00	1.35
COMMON CARD '52	4.00	1.80
COMMON CARD '54	5.00	2.20
COMMON CARD '55	6.00	2.70
☐ 1 Grover Alexander	5.00	2.20
☐ 2 Cap Anson	4.00	1.80
☐ 3 Frank Baker '55	6.00	2.70
☐ 4 Edward Barrow '54	5.00	2.20
☐ 5 Chief Bender (2) '54	5.00	2.20
☐ 6 Roger Bresnahan	3.00	1.35
☐ 7 Dan Brouthers	3.00	1.35
☐ 8 Mordecai Brown	3.00	1.35
☐ 9 Morgan Bulkeley	3.00	1.35
☐ 10 Jesse Burkett	3.00	1.35
☐ 11 Alexander Cartwright	3.00	1.35
☐ 12 Henry Chadwick	3.00	1.35
☐ 13 Frank Chance	3.00	1.35
☐ 14 Happy Chandler '52	50.00	22.00
☐ 15 Jack Chesbro	3.00	1.35
☐ 16 Fred Clarke	3.00	1.35
☐ 17 Ty Cobb	75.00	34.00
☐ 18A Mickey Cochrane ERR Name spelled Cochran	6.00	2.70
☐ 18B Mickey Cochrane COR	30.00	13.50
☐ 19 Eddie Collins (2)	3.00	1.35
☐ 20 Jimmie Collins	3.00	1.35
☐ 21 Charles Comiskey	3.00	1.35
☐ 22 Tom Connolly '54	5.00	2.20
☐ 23 Candy Cummings	3.00	1.35
☐ 24 Dizzy Dean '54	25.00	11.00
☐ 25 Ed Delahanty	3.00	1.35
☐ 26 Bill Dickey '54 (2)	10.00	4.50
☐ 27 Joe DiMaggio '55	200.00	90.00
☐ 28 Hugh Duffy	3.00	1.35
☐ 29 Johnny Evers	3.00	1.35
☐ 30 Buck Ewing	3.00	1.35
☐ 31 Jimmie Foxx	6.00	2.70
☐ 32 Frank Frisch	3.00	1.35
☐ 33 Lou Gehrig	100.00	45.00
☐ 34 Charles Gehringer	5.00	2.20
☐ 35 Clark Griffith	3.00	1.35
☐ 36 Lefty Grove	6.00	2.70
☐ 37 Gabby Hartnett '55	6.00	2.70
☐ 38 Harry Heilmann '52	4.00	1.80
☐ 39 Rogers Hornsby	6.00	2.70
☐ 40 Carl Hubbell	4.00	1.80
☐ 41 Hughie Jennings	3.00	1.35
☐ 42 Ban Johnson	3.00	1.35
☐ 43 Walter Johnson	12.00	5.50
☐ 44 Willie Keeler	3.00	1.35
☐ 45 Mike Kelly	3.00	1.35
☐ 46 Bill Klem '54	5.00	2.20
☐ 47 Napoleon Lajoie	5.00	2.20
☐ 48 Kenesaw Landis	3.00	1.35
☐ 49 Ted Lyons '55	6.00	2.70
☐ 50 Connie Mack	3.00	1.35
☐ 51 Rabbit Maranville '54	5.00	2.20
☐ 52 Christy Mathewson	12.00	5.50
☐ 53 Tommy McCarthy	3.00	1.35
☐ 54 Joe McGinnity	3.00	1.35
☐ 55 John McGraw	4.00	1.80
☐ 56 Kid Nichols	3.00	1.35
☐ 57 Jim O'Rourke	3.00	1.35
☐ 58 Mel Ott	5.00	2.20
☐ 59 Herb Pennock	3.00	1.35
☐ 60 Eddie Plank	3.00	1.35
☐ 61 Charles Radbourne	3.00	1.35
☐ 62 Wilbert Robinson	3.00	1.35
☐ 63 Babe Ruth	150.00	70.00
☐ 64 Ray Schalk '55	6.00	2.70
☐ 65 Al Simmons '54	5.00	2.20
☐ 66 George Sisler (2)	3.00	1.35
☐ 67 Albert G. Spalding	3.00	1.35
☐ 68 Tris Speaker	5.00	2.20
☐ 69 Bill Terry '54	6.00	2.70
☐ 70 Joe Tinker	3.00	1.35
☐ 71 Pie Traynor	3.00	1.35
☐ 72 Dazzy Vance '55	6.00	2.70
☐ 73 Rube Waddell	3.00	1.35
☐ 74 Hans Wagner	12.00	5.50
☐ 75 Bobby Wallace '54	5.00	2.20
☐ 76 Ed Walsh	3.00	1.35
☐ 77 Paul Waner '52	6.00	2.70
☐ 78 George Wright	3.00	1.35
☐ 79 Harry Wright '54	5.00	2.20
☐ 80 Cy Young	7.50	3.40
☐ 81 Museum Interior '54 (2)	5.00	2.20
☐ 82 Museum Exterior '54 (2)	5.00	2.20
☐ XX Presentation Box	3.00	1.35

1992 Cardinals McDonald's/Pacific

Produced by Pacific, this 55-card standard-size set commemorates the 100th anniversary of the St. Louis Cardinals. The collection was available at McDonald's restaurants in the greater St. Louis area for 1.49 with a purchase, and was distributed to raise money for Ronald McDonald Children's Charities. The set features black-and-white and color action player photos of players throughout Cardinals' history. The pictures are bordered in gold and include the player's name, the Cardinals 100th anniversary logo, and the McDonald's logo. The back design consists of a posed player photo, biographical and statistical information, and a career summary. There was also an album issued to go with this set. The album is not widely available at this time.

	MINT	NRMT
COMPLETE SET (55)	40.00	18.00
COMMON CARD (1-55)	.25	.11
☐ 1 Jim Bottomley	1.00	.45
☐ 2 Rip Collins	.25	.11
☐ 3 Johnny Mize	1.50	.70
☐ 4 Rogers Hornsby	3.00	1.35
☐ 5 Miller Huggins	1.00	.45
☐ 6 Marty Marion	.75	.35
☐ 7 Frank Frisch	1.00	.45
☐ 8 Whitey Kurowski	.25	.11
☐ 9 Joe Medwick	1.00	.45
☐ 10 Terry Moore	.75	.35
☐ 11 Chick Hafey	1.00	.45
☐ 12 Pepper Martin	.75	.35
☐ 13 Bob O'Farrell	.25	.11
☐ 14 Walker Cooper	.25	.11
☐ 15 Dizzy Dean	2.00	.90
☐ 16 Grover C. Alexander	1.50	.70
☐ 17 Jesse Haines	1.00	.45
☐ 18 Bill Hallahan	.25	.11
☐ 19 Mort Cooper	.50	.23
☐ 20 Burleigh Grimes	1.00	.45
☐ 21 Red Schoendienst	1.50	.70
☐ 22 Stan Musial	7.50	3.40
☐ 23 Enos Slaughter	1.50	.70
☐ 24 Keith Hernandez	.75	.35
☐ 25 Bill White	.75	.35
☐ 26 Orlando Cepeda	1.00	.45
☐ 27 Julian Javier	.50	.23
☐ 28 Dick Groat	.50	.23
☐ 29 Ken Boyer	.75	.35
☐ 30 Lou Brock	1.50	.70
☐ 31 Mike Shannon	.50	.23
☐ 32 Curt Flood	.75	.35
☐ 33 Joe Cunningham	.25	.11
☐ 34 Reggie Smith	.50	.23
☐ 35 Ted Simmons	.75	.35
☐ 36 Tim McCarver	.75	.35
☐ 37 Tom Herr	.25	.11
☐ 38 Ozzie Smith	5.00	2.20
☐ 39 Joe Torre	1.00	.45
☐ 40 Terry Pendleton	.75	.35
☐ 41 Ken Reitz	.25	.11
☐ 42 Vince Coleman	.25	.11
☐ 43 Willie McGee	.75	.35
☐ 44 Bake McBride	.25	.11
☐ 45 George Hendrick	.25	.11
☐ 46 Bob Gibson	1.50	.70
☐ 47 Whitey Herzog MG	.75	.35
☐ 48 Harry Brecheen	.50	.23
☐ 49 Howard Pollet	.25	.11
☐ 50 John Tudor	.25	.11
☐ 51 Bob Forsch	.25	.11
☐ 52 Bruce Sutter	.75	.35
☐ 53 Lee Smith	.50	.23
☐ 54 Todd Worrell	.75	.35
☐ 55 Al Hrabosky	.50	.23

1989 Cereal Superstars

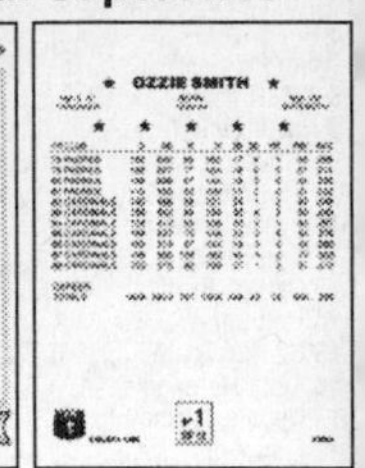

This 12-card, standard-size set was issued by MSA (Michael Schechter Associates) and celebrates some of the baseball's best players as of 1989. The sets have an attractive design of stars in each of the front corners with the word Superstars on the top of the card and players name, team, and position underneath the full color photo of the player. Like most of the MSA sets there are no team logos used. The vertically oriented backs show career statistics. Reportedly two cards were included in each specially marked Ralston Purina cereal box.

	MINT	NRMT
COMPLETE SET (12)	6.00	2.70
COMMON CARD (1-12)	.25	.11
☐ 1 Ozzie Smith	1.50	.70
☐ 2 Andre Dawson	.50	.23
☐ 3 Darryl Strawberry	.25	.11
☐ 4 Mike Schmidt	1.00	.45
☐ 5 Orel Hershiser	.25	.11
☐ 6 Tim Raines	.50	.23
☐ 7 Roger Clemens	2.00	.90
☐ 8 Kirby Puckett	1.50	.70
☐ 9 George Brett	1.50	.70
☐ 10 Alan Trammell	.75	.35
☐ 11 Don Mattingly	1.50	.70
☐ 12 Jose Canseco	.75	.35

1988 Chef Boyardee

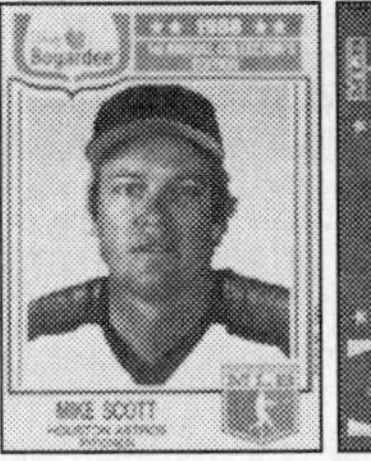

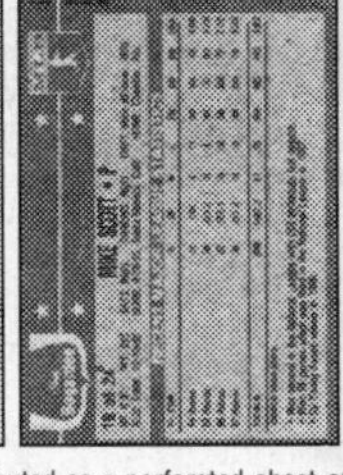

This 24-card set was distributed as a perforated sheet of four rows and six columns of cards in return for ten proofs of purchase of Chef Boyardeee products and 1.50 for postage and handling. The card photos on the fronts are in full color with a light blue border but are not shown with team logos. The card backs are numbered and printed in red and blue on gray card stock. Individual cards measure approximately 2 1/2" by 3 1/2" and show the Chef Boyardee logo in the upper right corner of the obverse. Card backs feature year-by-year season statistics since 1984. There is no additional premium for having the sheet intact as opposed to having individual cards neatly cut.

	MINT	NRMT
COMPLETE SET (24)	10.00	4.50
COMMON CARD (1-24)	.25	.11
☐ 1 Mark McGwire	2.50	1.10
☐ 2 Eric Davis	.50	.23
☐ 3 Jack Morris	.50	.23
☐ 4 George Bell	.25	.11
☐ 5 Ozzie Smith	2.00	.90
☐ 6 Tony Gwynn	2.50	1.10
☐ 7 Cal Ripken	4.00	1.80
☐ 8 Todd Worrell	.25	.11
☐ 9 Larry Parrish	.25	.11
☐ 10 Gary Carter	.75	.35
☐ 11 Ryne Sandberg	1.50	.70
☐ 12 Keith Hernandez	.50	.23
☐ 13 Kirby Puckett	2.00	.90
☐ 14 Mike Schmidt	1.00	.45
☐ 15 Frank Viola	.25	.11

] 16 Don Mattingly	2.00	.90
] 17 Dale Murphy	.75	.35
] 18 Andre Dawson	.50	.23
] 19 Mike Scott	.25	.11
] 20 Rickey Henderson	1.00	.45
] 21 Jim Rice	.50	.23
] 22 Wade Boggs	1.00	.45
] 23 Roger Clemens	2.00	.90
] 24 Fernando Valenzuela	.50	.23

1994 Church's Hometown Stars

pack containing four standard-size cards from the 28-ard Hometown Stars set produced by Pinnacle was ffered to consumers who bought a nine-piece family eal at Church's Chicken during April and May. Packs ere also sold separately for 69 cents each. Each pack ontained three regular cards and one gold foil-stamped ard from the set. The gold foil cards are valued at two mes the regular cards. A portion of the proceeds from ard sales went to Habitat for Humanity, a national olunteer organization that helps families build their own omes. The cards, which are subtitled "Hometown Stars," eature on their fronts borderless color player action shots ith team logos airbrushed away. The player's name ppears in white lettering (or gold foil for the special ards) at the lower right. The back carries a color player ead shot on the left; career highlights appear on the ght. The player's name and team are shown near the top; tatistics appear near the bottom. The cards are umbered on the back as "X of 28."

	MINT	NRMT
OMPLETE SET (28)	12.00	5.50
OMMON CARD (1-28)	.10	.05
] 1 Brian McRae	.10	.05
] 2 Dwight Gooden	.25	.11
] 3 Ruben Sierra	.10	.05
] 4 Greg Maddux	3.00	1.35
] 5 Kirby Puckett	2.00	.90
] 6 Jeff Bagwell	2.00	.90
] 7 Cal Ripken	4.00	1.80
] 8 Lenny Dykstra	.25	.11
] 9 Tim Salmon	.60	.25
] 10 Matt Williams	.40	.18
] 11 Roberto Alomar	.60	.25
] 12 Barry Larkin	.40	.18
] 13 Roger Clemens	1.50	.70
] 14 Mike Piazza	2.50	1.10
] 15 Travis Fryman	.25	.11
] 16 Ryne Sandberg	1.00	.45
] 17 Robin Ventura	.25	.11
] 18 Gary Sheffield	.60	.25
] 19 Carlos Baerga	.25	.11
] 20 Jay Bell	.10	.05
] 21 Edgar Martinez	.40	.18
] 22 Phil Plantier	.10	.05
] 23 Danny Tartabull	.10	.05
] 24 Marquis Grissom	.25	.11
] 25 Robin Yount	.40	.18
] 26 Ozzie Smith	1.00	.45
] 27 Ivan Rodriguez	1.00	.45
] 28 Dante Bichette	.40	.18

1994 Church's Show Stoppers

ne of ten Show Stoppers cards was inserted in every ourth pack of 1994 Church's Chicken Stars of the iamond four-card packs. The standard-size inserts were roduced by Pinnacle using the "Dufex" printing process nd highlight the major leagues' top home run hitters. The olorful metallic fronts feature color player action shots hat appear to project from within home plate icons. Team ogos are airbrushed away. The player's name appears at ne lower right. The light blue back carries a color player ead shot on the right, with the player's name, team, and areer highlights shown alongside. Statistics for home uns, slugging percentage, and at bat/home run ratio

appear near the bottom. The cards are numbered on the back as "X of 10."

	MINT	NRMT
COMPLETE SET (10)	40.00	18.00
COMMON CARD (1-10)	1.00	.45
☐ 1 Juan Gonzalez	6.00	2.70
☐ 2 Barry Bonds	3.00	1.35
☐ 3 Ken Griffey Jr.	12.00	5.50
☐ 4 David Justice	1.50	.70
☐ 5 Frank Thomas	12.00	5.50
☐ 6 Fred McGriff	2.50	1.10
☐ 7 Albert Belle	6.00	2.70
☐ 8 Joe Carter	1.50	.70
☐ 9 Cecil Fielder	1.50	.70
☐ 10 Mickey Tettleton	1.00	.45

1996 Circa

The 1996 Circa set was issued in one series totalling 200 cards. The eight-card packs retail for $1.99 each. The cards feature color action player photos on one of 28 different background designs and colors indicating the player's major league team. The backs carry player information and statistics. The only notable Rookie Card is Darin Erstad.

	MINT	NRMT
COMPLETE SET (200)	25.00	11.00
COMMON CARD (1-200)	.15	.07
☐ 1 Roberto Alomar	.60	.25
☐ 2 Brady Anderson	.40	.18
☐ 3 Rocky Coppinger	.60	.25
☐ 4 Eddie Murray	.60	.25
☐ 5 Mike Mussina	.60	.25
☐ 6 Randy Myers	.15	.07
☐ 7 Rafael Palmeiro	.40	.18
☐ 8 Cal Ripken	2.50	1.10
☐ 9 Jose Canseco	.40	.18
☐ 10 Roger Clemens	1.25	.55
☐ 11 Mike Greenwell	.15	.07
☐ 12 Tim Naehring	.15	.07
☐ 13 John Valentin	.15	.07
☐ 14 Mo Vaughn	.75	.35
☐ 15 Tim Wakefield	.15	.07
☐ 16 Jim Abbott	.15	.07
☐ 17 Garret Anderson	.40	.18
☐ 18 Jim Edmonds	.60	.25
☐ 19 Darin Erstad	3.00	1.35
☐ 20 Chuck Finley	.15	.07
☐ 21 Troy Percival	.30	.14
☐ 22 Tim Salmon	.60	.25
☐ 23 J.T. Snow	.30	.14
☐ 24 Wilson Alvarez	.30	.14
☐ 25 Harold Baines	.30	.14
☐ 26 Ray Durham	.30	.14
☐ 27 Alex Fernandez	.30	.14
☐ 28 Tony Phillips	.15	.07
☐ 29 Frank Thomas	2.50	1.10
☐ 30 Robin Ventura	.30	.14
☐ 31 Sandy Alomar Jr.	.30	.14
☐ 32 Albert Belle	.75	.35
☐ 33 Kenny Lofton	.75	.35
☐ 34 Dennis Martinez	.30	.14
☐ 35 Jose Mesa	.30	.14
☐ 36 Charles Nagy	.30	.14
☐ 37 Manny Ramirez	.60	.25
☐ 38 Jim Thome	.60	.25
☐ 39 Travis Fryman	.30	.14
☐ 40 Bob Higginson	.40	.18
☐ 41 Melvin Nieves	.15	.07
☐ 42 Alan Trammell	.40	.18
☐ 43 Kevin Appier	.30	.14
☐ 44 Johnny Damon	.30	.14
☐ 45 Keith Lockhart	.15	.07
☐ 46 Jeff Montgomery	.15	.07
☐ 47 Joe Randa	.15	.07
☐ 48 Bip Roberts	.15	.07
☐ 49 Ricky Bones	.15	.07
☐ 50 Jeff Cirillo	.30	.14
☐ 51 Marc Newfield	.30	.14
☐ 52 Dave Nilsson	.30	.14
☐ 53 Kevin Seitzer	.15	.07
☐ 54 Ron Coomer	.15	.07
☐ 55 Marty Cordova	.30	.14
☐ 56 Roberto Kelly	.15	.07
☐ 57 Chuck Knoblauch	.60	.25
☐ 58 Paul Molitor	.60	.25
☐ 59 Kirby Puckett	1.25	.55
☐ 60 Scott Stahoviak	.15	.07
☐ 61 Wade Boggs	.60	.25
☐ 62 David Cone	.30	.14
☐ 63 Cecil Fielder	.30	.14
☐ 64 Dwight Gooden	.30	.14
☐ 65 Derek Jeter	2.00	.90
☐ 66 Tino Martinez	.60	.25
☐ 67 Paul O'Neill	.15	.07
☐ 68 Andy Pettitte	.75	.35
☐ 69 Ruben Rivera	.40	.18
☐ 70 Bernie Williams	.60	.25
☐ 71 Geronimo Berroa	.15	.07
☐ 72 Jason Giambi	.40	.18
☐ 73 Mark McGwire	1.25	.55
☐ 74 Terry Steinbach	.30	.14
☐ 75 Todd Van Poppel	.15	.07
☐ 76 Jay Buhner	.40	.18
☐ 77 Norm Charlton	.15	.07
☐ 78 Ken Griffey Jr.	3.00	1.35
☐ 79 Randy Johnson	.60	.25
☐ 80 Edgar Martinez	.40	.18
☐ 81 Alex Rodriguez	2.50	1.10
☐ 82 Paul Sorrento	.15	.07
☐ 83 Dan Wilson	.15	.07
☐ 84 Will Clark	.40	.18
☐ 85 Kevin Elster	.15	.07
☐ 86 Juan Gonzalez	1.50	.70
☐ 87 Rusty Greer	.40	.18
☐ 88 Ken Hill	.15	.07
☐ 89 Mark McLemore	.15	.07
☐ 90 Dean Palmer	.30	.14
☐ 91 Roger Pavlik	.15	.07
☐ 92 Ivan Rodriguez	.75	.35
☐ 93 Joe Carter	.30	.14
☐ 94 Carlos Delgado	.30	.14
☐ 95 Juan Guzman	.15	.07
☐ 96 John Olerud	.15	.07
☐ 97 Ed Sprague	.15	.07
☐ 98 Jermaine Dye	.15	.07
☐ 99 Tom Glavine	.40	.18
☐ 100 Marquis Grissom	.30	.14
☐ 101 Andruw Jones	2.50	1.10
☐ 102 Chipper Jones	2.00	.90
☐ 103 David Justice	.60	.25
☐ 104 Ryan Klesko	.40	.18
☐ 105 Greg Maddux	2.00	.90
☐ 106 Fred McGriff	.40	.18
☐ 107 John Smoltz	.40	.18
☐ 108 Brant Brown	.15	.07
☐ 109 Mark Grace	.40	.18
☐ 110 Brian McRae	.15	.07
☐ 111 Ryne Sandberg	.75	.35
☐ 112 Sammy Sosa	.60	.25
☐ 113 Steve Trachsel	.15	.07
☐ 114 Bret Boone	.15	.07
☐ 115 Eric Davis	.30	.14
☐ 116 Steve Gibralter	.15	.07
☐ 117 Barry Larkin	.15	.07
☐ 118 Reggie Sanders	.15	.07
☐ 119 John Smiley	.15	.07
☐ 120 Dante Bichette	.40	.18
☐ 121 Ellis Burks	.30	.14
☐ 122 Vinny Castilla	.30	.14
☐ 123 Andres Galarraga	.40	.18
☐ 124 Larry Walker	.60	.25
☐ 125 Eric Young	.30	.14
☐ 126 Kevin Brown	.30	.14
☐ 127 Greg Colbrunn	.15	.07
☐ 128 Jeff Conine	.30	.14
☐ 129 Charles Johnson	.30	.14
☐ 130 Al Leiter	.15	.07
☐ 131 Gary Sheffield	.60	.25
☐ 132 Devon White	.15	.07
☐ 133 Jeff Bagwell	1.25	.55
☐ 134 Derek Bell	.30	.14
☐ 135 Craig Biggio	.40	.18

☐ 136 Doug Drabek	.15	.07
☐ 137 Brian L.Hunter	.30	.14
☐ 138 Darryl Kile	.30	.14
☐ 139 Shane Reynolds	.15	.07
☐ 140 Brett Butler	.15	.07
☐ 141 Eric Karros	.30	.14
☐ 142 Ramon Martinez	.30	.14
☐ 143 Raul Mondesi	.40	.18
☐ 144 Hideo Nomo	1.50	.70
☐ 145 Chan Ho Park	.60	.25
☐ 146 Mike Piazza	2.00	.90
☐ 147 Moises Alou	.30	.14
☐ 148 Yamil Benitez	.30	.14
☐ 149 Mark Grudzielanek	.30	.14
☐ 150 Pedro Martinez	.60	.25
☐ 151 Henry Rodriguez	.15	.07
☐ 152 David Segui	.15	.07
☐ 153 Rondell White	.30	.14
☐ 154 Carlos Baerga	.30	.14
☐ 155 John Franco	.30	.14
☐ 156 Bernard Gilkey	.15	.07
☐ 157 Todd Hundley	.30	.14
☐ 158 Jason Isringhausen	.15	.07
☐ 159 Lance Johnson	.15	.07
☐ 160 Alex Ochoa	.15	.07
☐ 161 Rey Ordonez	.15	.07
☐ 162 Paul Wilson	.15	.07
☐ 163 Ron Blazier	.15	.07
☐ 164 Ricky Bottalico	.15	.07
☐ 165 Jim Eisenreich	.30	.14
☐ 166 Pete Incaviglia	.15	.07
☐ 167 Mickey Morandini	.15	.07
☐ 168 Ricky Otero	.15	.07
☐ 169 Curt Schilling	.30	.14
☐ 170 Jay Bell	.30	.14
☐ 171 Charlie Hayes	.15	.07
☐ 172 Jason Kendall	.30	.14
☐ 173 Jeff King	.30	.14
☐ 174 Al Martin	.15	.07
☐ 175 Alan Benes	.30	.14
☐ 176 Royce Clayton	.15	.07
☐ 177 Brian Jordan	.30	.14
☐ 178 Ray Lankford	.30	.14
☐ 179 John Mabry	.30	.14
☐ 180 Willie McGee	.15	.07
☐ 181 Ozzie Smith	.75	.35
☐ 182 Todd Stottlemyre	.15	.07
☐ 183 Andy Ashby	.15	.07
☐ 184 Ken Caminiti	.60	.25
☐ 185 Steve Finley	.30	.14
☐ 186 Tony Gwynn	1.50	.70
☐ 187 Rickey Henderson	.40	.18
☐ 188 Wally Joyner	.15	.07
☐ 189 Fernando Valenzuela	.30	.14
☐ 190 Greg Vaughn	.15	.07
☐ 191 Rod Beck	.15	.07
☐ 192 Barry Bonds	.75	.35
☐ 193 Shawon Dunston	.15	.07
☐ 194 Chris Singleton	.15	.07
☐ 195 Robby Thompson	.15	.07
☐ 196 Matt Williams	.40	.18
☐ 197 Barry Bonds CL	.60	.25
☐ 198 Ken Griffey Jr. CL	1.50	.70
☐ 199 Cal Ripken CL	1.25	.55
☐ 200 Frank Thomas CL	1.50	.70

1996 Circa Rave

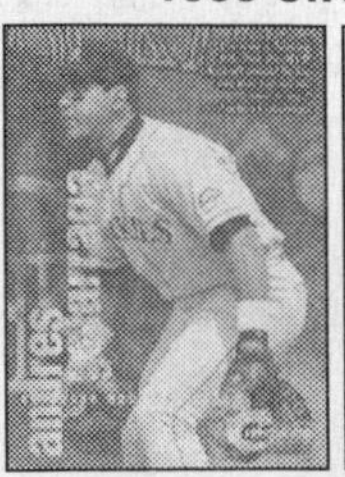
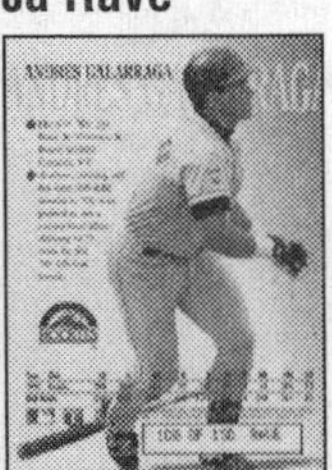

Randomly inserted in packs at a rate of one in 60, this 200-card set is parallel and similar in design to the regular set except for sparkling foil lettering on front. Each card is individually numbered on back with 150 of each card produced.

	MINT	NRMT
COMPLETE SET (200)	8000.00	3600.00
COMMON CARD (1-200)	15.00	6.75
MINOR STARS	25.00	11.00
SEMISTARS	40.00	18.00
UNLISTED STARS	60.00	27.00

☐ 4 Eddie Murray	100.00	45.00
☐ 8 Cal Ripken	250.00	110.00
☐ 10 Roger Clemens	150.00	70.00
☐ 14 Mo Vaughn	80.00	36.00
☐ 19 Darin Erstad	120.00	55.00
☐ 29 Frank Thomas	300.00	135.00
☐ 32 Albert Belle	80.00	36.00
☐ 33 Kenny Lofton	80.00	36.00
☐ 58 Paul Molitor	90.00	40.00
☐ 59 Kirby Puckett	120.00	55.00
☐ 65 Derek Jeter	150.00	70.00
☐ 73 Mark McGwire	150.00	70.00
☐ 78 Ken Griffey Jr.	350.00	160.00
☐ 81 Alex Rodriguez	250.00	110.00
☐ 86 Juan Gonzalez	150.00	70.00
☐ 92 Ivan Rodriguez	80.00	36.00
☐ 101 Andruw Jones	150.00	70.00
☐ 102 Chipper Jones	150.00	70.00
☐ 105 Greg Maddux	200.00	90.00
☐ 111 Ryne Sandberg	100.00	45.00
☐ 133 Jeff Bagwell	120.00	55.00
☐ 144 Hideo Nomo	200.00	90.00
☐ 146 Mike Piazza	200.00	90.00
☐ 181 Ozzie Smith	100.00	45.00
☐ 186 Tony Gwynn	150.00	70.00
☐ 192 Barry Bonds	100.00	45.00
☐ 198 Ken Griffey Jr. CL	150.00	70.00
☐ 199 Cal Ripken CL	120.00	55.00
☐ 200 Frank Thomas CL	120.00	55.00

1996 Circa Access

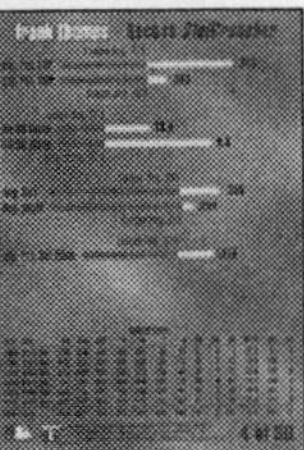

Randomly inserted in packs at a rate of one in 12, this 30-card limited edition set features a fold-out, three-panel card showcasing some of the hottest superstars of the game. The panels display color player photos, player statistics and personal information on team-colored backgrounds. A promotional card featuring Matt Williams was issued to dealers. The card is similar to the basic Access Williams except for the words "Promotional Sample" written across the card front.

	MINT	NRMT
COMPLETE SET (30)	120.00	55.00
COMMON CARD (1-30)	2.00	.90

☐ 1 Cal Ripken	15.00	6.75
☐ 2 Mo Vaughn	5.00	2.20
☐ 3 Tim Salmon	4.00	1.80
☐ 4 Frank Thomas	20.00	9.00
☐ 5 Albert Belle	8.00	3.60
☐ 6 Kenny Lofton	5.00	2.20
☐ 7 Manny Ramirez	4.00	1.80
☐ 8 Paul Molitor	4.00	1.80
☐ 9 Kirby Puckett	8.00	3.60
☐ 10 Paul O'Neill	2.50	1.10
☐ 11 Mark McGwire	6.00	2.70
☐ 12 Ken Griffey Jr.	20.00	9.00
☐ 13 Randy Johnson	4.00	1.80
☐ 14 Greg Maddux	12.00	5.50
☐ 15 John Smoltz	4.00	1.80
☐ 16 Sammy Sosa	4.00	1.80
☐ 17 Barry Larkin	2.50	1.10
☐ 18 Gary Sheffield	4.00	1.80
☐ 19 Jeff Bagwell	8.00	3.60
☐ 20 Hideo Nomo	5.00	2.20
☐ 21 Mike Piazza	12.00	5.50
☐ 22 Moises Alou	2.50	1.10
☐ 23 Henry Rodriguez	2.00	.90
☐ 24 Rey Ordonez	2.00	.90
☐ 25 Jay Bell	2.00	.90
☐ 26 Ozzie Smith	5.00	2.20
☐ 27 Tony Gwynn	8.00	3.60
☐ 28 Rickey Henderson	3.00	1.35
☐ 29 Barry Bonds	5.00	2.20
☐ 30 Matt Williams	3.00	1.35
☐ P30 Matt Williams Promo	1.00	.45

1996 Circa Boss

Randomly inserted in packs at a rate of one in six, this 50-card set features a sculpted embossed player image on a team-colored background containing the team logo. The

backs carry a information about the player's career. A promotional card featuring Cal Ripken was issued to dealers. The card is similar to the basic Boss Ripken except for the words "Promotional Sample" written across the card front.

	MINT	NRMT
COMPLETE SET (50)	100.00	45.00
COMMON CARD (1-50)	1.50	.70

☐ 1 Roberto Alomar	3.00	1.35
☐ 2 Cal Ripken	12.00	5.50
☐ 3 Jose Canseco	2.50	1.10
☐ 4 Mo Vaughn	4.00	1.80
☐ 5 Tim Salmon	2.50	1.10
☐ 6 Frank Thomas	15.00	6.75
☐ 7 Robin Ventura	2.00	.90
☐ 8 Albert Belle	6.00	2.70
☐ 9 Kenny Lofton	4.00	1.80
☐ 10 Manny Ramirez	4.00	1.80
☐ 11 Dave Nilsson	1.50	.70
☐ 12 Chuck Knoblauch	2.50	1.10
☐ 13 Paul Molitor	3.00	1.35
☐ 14 Kirby Puckett	6.00	2.70
☐ 15 Wade Boggs	2.50	1.10
☐ 16 Dwight Gooden	2.00	.90
☐ 17 Paul O'Neill	1.50	.70
☐ 18 Mark McGwire	5.00	2.20
☐ 19 Jay Buhner	2.50	1.10
☐ 20 Ken Griffey Jr.	15.00	6.75
☐ 21 Randy Johnson	2.50	1.10
☐ 22 Will Clark	2.50	1.10
☐ 23 Juan Gonzalez	8.00	3.60
☐ 24 Joe Carter	2.00	.90
☐ 25 Tom Glavine	2.50	1.10
☐ 26 Ryan Klesko	2.50	1.10
☐ 27 Greg Maddux	10.00	4.50
☐ 28 John Smoltz	2.50	1.10
☐ 29 Ryne Sandberg	4.00	1.80
☐ 30 Sammy Sosa	2.50	1.10
☐ 31 Barry Larkin	2.00	.90
☐ 32 Reggie Sanders	2.00	.90
☐ 33 Dante Bichette	2.50	1.10
☐ 34 Andres Galarraga	2.50	1.10
☐ 35 Charles Johnson	2.00	.90
☐ 36 Gary Sheffield	2.50	1.10
☐ 37 Jeff Bagwell	6.00	2.70
☐ 38 Hideo Nomo	4.00	1.80
☐ 39 Mike Piazza	10.00	4.50
☐ 40 Moises Alou	2.00	.90
☐ 41 Henry Rodriguez	2.00	.90
☐ 42 Rey Ordonez	2.50	1.10
☐ 43 Ricky Otero	1.50	.70
☐ 44 Jay Bell	1.50	.70
☐ 45 Royce Clayton	1.50	.70
☐ 46 Ozzie Smith	4.00	1.80
☐ 47 Tony Gwynn	6.00	2.70
☐ 48 Rickey Henderson	2.50	1.10
☐ 49 Barry Bonds	4.00	1.80
☐ 50 Matt Williams	2.50	1.10
☐ P2 Cal Ripken Promo	2.00	.90

1997 Circa

The 1997 Circa set was issued in one series totalling 400 cards and was distributed in eight-card foil packs with a suggested retail price of $1.49. The set contains 393 player cards and seven checklist cards. The fronts feature olor player photos with new in-your-face graphics that ft the player off the card. The backs carry in-depth player tatistics and "Did you know" information. An Alex odriguez promo card (P100) was distributed to dealers ith their ordering papers.

	MINT	NRMT
OMPLETE SET (400)	40.00	18.00
OMMON CARD (1-400)	.15	.07
☐ 1 Kenny Lofton	.75	.35
☐ 2 Ray Durham	.15	.07
☐ 3 Mariano Rivera	.30	.14
☐ 4 Jon Lieber	.15	.07
☐ 5 Tim Salmon	.60	.25
☐ 6 Mark Grudzielanek	.30	.14
☐ 7 Neifi Perez	.15	.07
☐ 8 Cal Ripken	2.50	1.10
☐ 9 John Olerud	.30	.14
☐ 10 Edgar Renteria	.30	.14
☐ 11 Jose Rosado	.15	.07
☐ 12 Mickey Morandini	.15	.07
☐ 13 Orlando Miller	.15	.07
☐ 14 Ben McDonald	.15	.07
☐ 15 Hideo Nomo	1.50	.70
☐ 16 Fred McGriff	.40	.18
☐ 17 Sean Berry	.15	.07
☐ 18 Roger Pavlik	.15	.07
☐ 19 Aaron Sele	.15	.07
☐ 20 Joey Hamilton	.15	.07
☐ 21 Roger Clemens	1.25	.55
☐ 22 Jose Herrera	.15	.07
☐ 23 Ryne Sandberg	.75	.35
☐ 24 Ken Griffey Jr.	3.00	1.35
☐ 25 Barry Bonds	.75	.35
☐ 26 Dan Naulty	.15	.07
☐ 27 Wade Boggs	.60	.25
☐ 28 Ray Lankford	.30	.14
☐ 29 Rico Brogna	.15	.07
☐ 30 Wally Joyner	.15	.07
☐ 31 F.P. Santangelo	.15	.07
☐ 32 Vinny Castilla	.30	.14
☐ 33 Eddie Murray	.60	.25
☐ 34 Kevin Elster	.15	.07
☐ 35 Mike Macfarlane	.15	.07
☐ 36 Jeff Kent	.15	.07
☐ 37 Orlando Merced	.15	.07
☐ 38 Jason Isringhausen	.15	.07
☐ 39 Chad Ogea	.15	.07
☐ 40 Greg Gagne	.15	.07
☐ 41 Curt Lyons	.15	.07
☐ 42 Mo Vaughn	.75	.35
☐ 43 Rusty Greer	.30	.14
☐ 44 Shane Reynolds	.15	.07
☐ 45 Frank Thomas	2.50	1.10
☐ 46 Chris Hoiles	.15	.07
☐ 47 Scott Sanders	.15	.07
☐ 48 Mark Lemke	.15	.07
☐ 49 Fernando Vina	.15	.07
☐ 50 Mark McGwire	1.25	.55
☐ 51 Bernie Williams	.60	.25
☐ 52 Bobby Higginson	.30	.14
☐ 53 Kevin Tapani	.15	.07
☐ 54 Rich Becker	.15	.07
☐ 55 Felix Heredia	.15	.07
☐ 56 Delino DeShields	.15	.07
☐ 57 Rick Wilkins	.15	.07
☐ 58 Edgardo Alfonzo	.30	.14
☐ 59 Brett Butler	.30	.14
☐ 60 Ed Sprague	.15	.07
☐ 61 Joe Randa	.15	.07
☐ 62 Ugueth Urbina	.30	.14
☐ 63 Todd Greene	.30	.14
☐ 64 Devon White	.15	.07
☐ 65 Bruce Ruffin	.15	.07
☐ 66 Mark Gardner	.15	.07
☐ 67 Omar Vizquel	.15	.07
☐ 68 Luis Gonzalez	.15	.07
☐ 69 Tom Glavine	.30	.14
☐ 70 Cal Eldred	.15	.07
☐ 71 Wm. VanLandingham	.15	.07
☐ 72 Jay Buhner	.40	.18
☐ 73 James Baldwin	.15	.07
☐ 74 Robin Jennings	.15	.07
☐ 75 Terry Steinbach	.15	.07
☐ 76 Billy Taylor	.15	.07
☐ 77 Armando Benitez	.15	.07
☐ 78 Joe Girardi	.15	.07
☐ 79 Jay Bell	.15	.07
☐ 80 Damon Buford	.15	.07
☐ 81 Deion Sanders	.60	.25
☐ 82 Bill Haselman	.15	.07
☐ 83 John Flaherty	.15	.07
☐ 84 Todd Stottlemyre	.15	.07
☐ 85 J.T. Snow	.15	.07
☐ 86 Felipe Lira	.15	.07
☐ 87 Steve Avery	.15	.07
☐ 88 Trey Beamon	.15	.07

Card	MINT	NRMT
☐ 89 Alex Gonzalez	.15	.07
☐ 90 Mark Clark	.15	.07
☐ 91 Shane Andrews	.15	.07
☐ 92 Randy Myers	.30	.14
☐ 93 Gary Gaetti	.30	.14
☐ 94 Jeff Blauser	.15	.07
☐ 95 Tony Batista	.15	.07
☐ 96 Todd Worrell	.15	.07
☐ 97 Jim Edmonds	.60	.25
☐ 98 Eric Young	.15	.07
☐ 99 Roberto Kelly	.15	.07
☐ 100 Alex Rodriguez	2.50	1.10
☐ 101 Julio Franco	.30	.14
☐ 102 Jeff Bagwell	1.25	.55
☐ 103 Bobby Witt	.15	.07
☐ 104 Tino Martinez	.60	.25
☐ 105 Shannon Stewart	.15	.07
☐ 106 Brian Banks	.15	.07
☐ 107 Eddie Taubensee	.15	.07
☐ 108 Terry Mulholland	.15	.07
☐ 109 Lyle Mouton	.15	.07
☐ 110 Jeff Conine	.15	.07
☐ 111 Johnny Damon	.15	.07
☐ 112 Quilvio Veras	.15	.07
☐ 113 Wilton Guerrero	.15	.07
☐ 114 Dmitri Young	.15	.07
☐ 115 Garret Anderson	.30	.14
☐ 116 Bill Pulsipher	.15	.07
☐ 117 Jacob Brumfield	.15	.07
☐ 118 Mike Lansing	.15	.07
☐ 119 Jose Canseco	.40	.18
☐ 120 Mike Bordick	.15	.07
☐ 121 Kevin Stocker	.15	.07
☐ 122 Frankie Rodriguez	.15	.07
☐ 123 Mike Cameron	.15	.07
☐ 124 Tony Womack	.50	.23
☐ 125 Bret Boone	.15	.07
☐ 126 Moises Alou	.30	.14
☐ 127 Tim Naehring	.15	.07
☐ 128 Brant Brown	.15	.07
☐ 129 Todd Zeile	.15	.07
☐ 130 Dave Nilsson	.15	.07
☐ 131 Donne Wall	.15	.07
☐ 132 Jose Mesa	.30	.14
☐ 133 Mark McLemore	.15	.07
☐ 134 Mike Stanton	.15	.07
☐ 135 Dan Wilson	.15	.07
☐ 136 Jose Offerman	.15	.07
☐ 137 David Justice	.60	.25
☐ 138 Kirt Manwaring	.15	.07
☐ 139 Raul Casanova	.15	.07
☐ 140 Ron Coomer	.15	.07
☐ 141 Dave Hollins	.15	.07
☐ 142 Shawn Estes	.15	.07
☐ 143 Darren Daulton	.30	.14
☐ 144 Turk Wendell	.15	.07
☐ 145 Darrin Fletcher	.15	.07
☐ 146 Marquis Grissom	.30	.14
☐ 147 Andy Benes	.15	.07
☐ 148 Nomar Garciaparra	2.00	.90
☐ 149 Andy Pettitte	.60	.25
☐ 150 Tony Gwynn	1.50	.70
☐ 151 Robb Nen	.30	.14
☐ 152 Kevin Seitzer	.15	.07
☐ 153 Ariel Prieto	.15	.07
☐ 154 Scott Karl	.15	.07
☐ 155 Carlos Baerga	.30	.14
☐ 156 Wilson Alvarez	.30	.14
☐ 157 Thomas Howard	.15	.07
☐ 158 Kevin Appier	.15	.07
☐ 159 Russ Davis	.15	.07
☐ 160 Justin Thompson	.30	.14
☐ 161 Pete Schourek	.15	.07
☐ 162 John Burkett	.15	.07
☐ 163 Roberto Alomar	.60	.25
☐ 164 Darren Holmes	.15	.07
☐ 165 Travis Miller	.15	.07
☐ 166 Mark Langston	.15	.07
☐ 167 Juan Guzman	.15	.07
☐ 168 Pedro Astacio	.15	.07
☐ 169 Mark Johnson	.15	.07
☐ 170 Mark Leiter	.15	.07
☐ 171 Heathcliff Slocumb	.15	.07
☐ 172 Dante Bichette	.30	.14
☐ 173 Brian Giles	.15	.07
☐ 174 Paul Wilson	.15	.07
☐ 175 Eric Davis	.15	.07
☐ 176 Charles Johnson	.15	.07
☐ 177 Willie Greene	.30	.14
☐ 178 Geronimo Berroa	.15	.07
☐ 179 Mariano Duncan	.15	.07
☐ 180 Robert Person	.15	.07
☐ 181 David Segui	.15	.07
☐ 182 Ozzie Guillen	.15	.07
☐ 183 Osvaldo Fernandez	.15	.07
☐ 184 Dean Palmer	.15	.07
☐ 185 Bob Wickman	.15	.07

Card	MINT	NRMT
☐ 186 Eric Karros	.15	.07
☐ 187 Travis Fryman	.30	.14
☐ 188 Andy Ashby	.15	.07
☐ 189 Scott Stahoviak	.15	.07
☐ 190 Norm Charlton	.15	.07
☐ 191 Craig Paquette	.15	.07
☐ 192 John Smoltz UER	.30	.14
Name spelled "Smotlz" on back		
☐ 193 Orel Hershiser	.30	.14
☐ 194 Glenallen Hill	.15	.07
☐ 195 George Arias	.15	.07
☐ 196 Brian Jordan	.15	.07
☐ 197 Greg Vaughn	.15	.07
☐ 198 Rafael Palmeiro	.40	.18
☐ 199 Darryl Kile	.30	.14
☐ 200 Derek Jeter	2.00	.90
☐ 201 Jose Vizcaino	.15	.07
☐ 202 Rick Aguilera	.30	.14
☐ 203 Jason Schmidt	.15	.07
☐ 204 Trot Nixon	.15	.07
☐ 205 Tom Pagnozzi	.15	.07
☐ 206 Mark Wohlers	.15	.07
☐ 207 Lance Johnson	.15	.07
☐ 208 Carlos Delgado	.15	.07
☐ 209 Cliff Floyd	.15	.07
☐ 210 Kent Mercker	.15	.07
☐ 211 Matt Mieske	.15	.07
☐ 212 Ismael Valdes	.15	.07
☐ 213 Shawon Dunston	.15	.07
☐ 214 Melvin Nieves	.15	.07
☐ 215 Tony Phillips	.15	.07
☐ 216 Scott Spiezio	.15	.07
☐ 217 Michael Tucker	.30	.14
☐ 218 Matt Williams	.40	.18
☐ 219 Ricky Otero	.15	.07
☐ 220 Kevin Ritz	.15	.07
☐ 221 Darryl Strawberry	.30	.14
☐ 222 Troy Percival	.30	.14
☐ 223 Eugene Kingsale	.15	.07
☐ 224 Julian Tavarez	.15	.07
☐ 225 Jermaine Dye	.15	.07
☐ 226 Jason Kendall	.30	.14
☐ 227 Sterling Hitchcock	.15	.07
☐ 228 Jeff Cirillo	.30	.14
☐ 229 Roberto Hernandez	.15	.07
☐ 230 Ricky Bottalico	.30	.14
☐ 231 Bobby Bonilla	.30	.14
☐ 232 Edgar Martinez	.40	.18
☐ 233 John Valentin	.15	.07
☐ 234 Ellis Burks	.15	.07
☐ 235 Benito Santiago	.15	.07
☐ 236 Terrell Wade	.15	.07
☐ 237 Armando Reynoso	.15	.07
☐ 238 Danny Graves	.15	.07
☐ 239 Ken Hill	.15	.07
☐ 240 Dennis Eckersley	.40	.18
☐ 241 Darin Erstad	1.00	.45
☐ 242 Lee Smith UER	.30	.14
Position 2b		
☐ 243 Cecil Fielder	.30	.14
☐ 244 Tony Clark	.60	.25
☐ 245 Scott Erickson	.15	.07
☐ 246 Bob Abreu	.60	.25
☐ 247 Ruben Sierra	.15	.07
☐ 248 Chili Davis	.30	.14
☐ 249 Darryl Hamilton	.15	.07
☐ 250 Albert Belle	.75	.35
☐ 251 Todd Hollandsworth	.15	.07
☐ 252 Terry Adams	.15	.07
☐ 253 Rey Ordonez	.15	.07
☐ 254 Steve Finley	.30	.14
☐ 255 Jose Valentin	.15	.07
☐ 256 Royce Clayton	.15	.07
☐ 257 Sandy Alomar	.30	.14
☐ 258 Mike Lieberthal	.15	.07
☐ 259 Ivan Rodriguez	.75	.35
☐ 260 Rod Beck	.30	.14
☐ 261 Ron Karkovice	.15	.07
☐ 262 Mark Gubicza	.15	.07
☐ 263 Chris Holt	.15	.07
☐ 264 Jaime Bluma UER	.15	.07
Name spelled "Jamie" on front and back		
☐ 265 Francisco Cordova	.15	.07
☐ 266 Javy Lopez	.30	.14
☐ 267 Reggie Jefferson	.30	.14
☐ 268 Kevin Brown	.30	.14
☐ 269 Scott Brosius	.15	.07
☐ 270 Dwight Gooden	.30	.14
☐ 271 Marty Cordova	.15	.07
☐ 272 Jeff Brantley	.15	.07
☐ 273 Joe Carter	.30	.14
☐ 274 Todd Jones	.15	.07
☐ 275 Sammy Sosa	.60	.25
☐ 276 Randy Johnson	.60	.25
☐ 277 B.J. Surhoff	.30	.14
☐ 278 Chan Ho Park	.60	.25
☐ 279 Jamey Wright	.15	.07

☐ 280 Manny Ramirez	.60	.25
☐ 281 John Franco	.30	.14
☐ 282 Tim Worrell	.15	.07
☐ 283 Scott Rolen	1.50	.70
☐ 284 Reggie Sanders	.15	.07
☐ 285 Mike Fetters	.15	.07
☐ 286 Tim Wakefield	.15	.07
☐ 287 Trevor Hoffman	.30	.14
☐ 288 Donovan Osborne	.15	.07
☐ 289 Phil Nevin	.15	.07
☐ 290 Jermaine Allensworth	.15	.07
☐ 291 Rocky Coppinger	.15	.07
☐ 292 Tim Raines	.15	.07
☐ 293 Henry Rodriguez	.15	.07
☐ 294 Paul Sorrento	.15	.07
☐ 295 Tom Goodwin	.15	.07
☐ 296 Raul Mondesi	.40	.18
☐ 297 Allen Watson	.15	.07
☐ 298 Derek Bell	.15	.07
☐ 299 Gary Sheffield	.60	.25
☐ 300 Paul Molitor	.60	.25
☐ 301 Shawn Green	.30	.14
☐ 302 Darren Oliver	.15	.07
☐ 303 Jack McDowell	.15	.07
☐ 304 Denny Neagle	.30	.14
☐ 305 Doug Drabek	.15	.07
☐ 306 Mel Rojas	.15	.07
☐ 307 Andres Galarraga	.60	.25
☐ 308 Alex Ochoa	.15	.07
☐ 309 Gary DiSarcina	.15	.07
☐ 310 Ron Gant	.30	.14
☐ 311 Gregg Jefferies	.30	.14
☐ 312 Ruben Rivera	.15	.07
☐ 313 Vladimir Guerrero	1.25	.55
☐ 314 Willie Adams	.15	.07
☐ 315 Bip Roberts	.15	.07
☐ 316 Mark Grace	.40	.18
☐ 317 Bernard Gilkey	.15	.07
☐ 318 Marc Newfield	.15	.07
☐ 319 Al Leiter	.15	.07
☐ 320 Otis Nixon	.15	.07
☐ 321 Tom Candiotti	.15	.07
☐ 322 Mike Stanley	.15	.07
☐ 323 Jeff Fassero	.15	.07
☐ 324 Billy Wagner	.15	.07
☐ 325 Todd Walker	.15	.07
☐ 326 Chad Curtis	.15	.07
☐ 327 Quinton McCracken	.15	.07
☐ 328 Will Clark	.40	.18
☐ 329 Andruw Jones	1.50	.70
☐ 330 Robin Ventura	.15	.07
☐ 331 Curtis Pride	.15	.07
☐ 332 Barry Larkin	.40	.18
☐ 333 Jimmy Key	.30	.14
☐ 334 David Wells	.15	.07
☐ 335 Mike Holtz	.15	.07
☐ 336 Paul Wagner	.15	.07
☐ 337 Greg Maddux	2.00	.90
☐ 338 Curt Schilling	.30	.14
☐ 339 Steve Trachsel	.15	.07
☐ 340 John Wetteland	.15	.07
☐ 341 Rickey Henderson	.40	.18
☐ 342 Ernie Young	.15	.07
☐ 343 Harold Baines	.30	.14
☐ 344 Bobby Jones	.15	.07
☐ 345 Jeff D'Amico	.15	.07
☐ 346 John Mabry	.15	.07
☐ 347 Pedro Martinez	.60	.25
☐ 348 Mark Lewis	.15	.07
☐ 349 Dan Miceli	.15	.07
☐ 350 Chuck Knoblauch	.60	.25
☐ 351 John Smiley	.15	.07
☐ 352 Brady Anderson	.40	.18
☐ 353 Jim Leyritz	.15	.07
☐ 354 Al Martin	.15	.07
☐ 355 Pat Hentgen	.15	.07
☐ 356 Mike Piazza	2.00	.90
☐ 357 Charles Nagy	.15	.07
☐ 358 Luis Castillo	.15	.07
☐ 359 Paul O'Neill	.30	.14
☐ 360 Steve Reed	.15	.07
☐ 361 Tom Gordon	.15	.07
☐ 362 Craig Biggio	.40	.18
☐ 363 Jeff Montgomery	.15	.07
☐ 364 Jamie Moyer	.15	.07
☐ 365 Ryan Klesko	.40	.18
☐ 366 Todd Hundley	.30	.14
☐ 367 Bobby Estalella	.15	.07
☐ 368 Jason Giambi	.30	.14
☐ 369 Brian Hunter	.30	.14
☐ 370 Ramon Martinez	.30	.14
☐ 371 Carlos Garcia	.15	.07
☐ 372 Hal Morris	.15	.07
☐ 373 Juan Gonzalez	1.50	.70
☐ 374 Brian McRae	.15	.07
☐ 375 Mike Mussina	.60	.25
☐ 376 John Ericks	.15	.07
☐ 377 Larry Walker	.60	.25
☐ 378 Chris Gomez	.15	.07
☐ 379 John Jaha	.15	.07
☐ 380 Rondell White	.30	.14
☐ 381 Chipper Jones	2.00	.90
☐ 382 David Cone	.30	.14
☐ 383 Alan Benes	.15	.07
☐ 384 Troy O'Leary	.15	.07
☐ 385 Ken Caminiti	.60	.25
☐ 386 Jeff King	.15	.07
☐ 387 Mike Hampton	.15	.07
☐ 388 Jaime Navarro	.15	.07
☐ 389 Brad Radke	.30	.14
☐ 390 Joey Cora	.30	.14
☐ 391 Jim Thome	.60	.25
☐ 392 Alex Fernandez	.15	.07
☐ 393 Chuck Finley	.15	.07
☐ 394 Andruw Jones CL	1.00	.45
☐ 395 Ken Griffey Jr. CL	1.50	.70
☐ 396 Frank Thomas CL	1.25	.55
☐ 397 Alex Rodriguez CL	1.25	.55
☐ 398 Cal Ripken CL	1.25	.55
☐ 399 Mike Piazza CL	1.00	.45
☐ 400 Greg Maddux CL	1.00	.45
☐ P100 Alex Rodriguez Promo	3.00	1.35

1997 Circa Rave

Randomly inserted in packs at a rate of one in 30, this hobby exclusive set is a parallel version of the regular set and is similar in design. 150 of this limited edition set were produced and are sequentially numbered.

	MINT	NRMT
COMMON CARD (1-400)	12.00	5.50
MINOR STARS	20.00	9.00
SEMISTARS	30.00	13.50
UNLISTED STARS	50.00	22.00
☐ 1 Kenny Lofton	60.00	27.00
☐ 8 Cal Ripken	200.00	90.00
☐ 15 Hideo Nomo	120.00	55.00
☐ 21 Roger Clemens	100.00	45.00
☐ 23 Ryne Sandberg	60.00	27.00
☐ 24 Ken Griffey Jr.	300.00	135.00
☐ 25 Barry Bonds	60.00	27.00
☐ 42 Mo Vaughn	60.00	27.00
☐ 45 Frank Thomas	200.00	90.00
☐ 50 Mark McGwire	100.00	45.00
☐ 100 Alex Rodriguez	150.00	70.00
☐ 102 Jeff Bagwell	100.00	45.00
☐ 148 Nomar Garciaparra	120.00	55.00
☐ 150 Tony Gwynn	120.00	55.00
☐ 200 Derek Jeter	120.00	55.00
☐ 241 Darin Erstad	60.00	27.00
☐ 250 Albert Belle	60.00	27.00
☐ 259 Ivan Rodriguez	60.00	27.00
☐ 283 Scott Rolen	100.00	45.00
☐ 313 Vladimir Guerrero	80.00	36.00
☐ 329 Andruw Jones	100.00	45.00
☐ 337 Greg Maddux	150.00	70.00
☐ 356 Mike Piazza	150.00	70.00
☐ 373 Juan Gonzalez	120.00	55.00
☐ 381 Chipper Jones	120.00	55.00
☐ 395 Ken Griffey Jr. CL	150.00	70.00
☐ 396 Frank Thomas CL	100.00	45.00
☐ 397 Alex Rodriguez CL	80.00	36.00
☐ 398 Cal Ripken CL	80.00	36.00
☐ 399 Mike Piazza CL	60.00	27.00
☐ 400 Greg Maddux CL	60.00	27.00

1997 Circa Boss

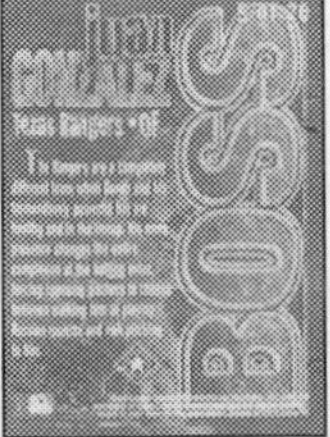

Randomly inserted in packs at a rate of one in six, this 20-card set features color player photos of Baseball's leading men on the field and at bat and are printed on sculpted, embossed cards. The backs carry player information.

	MINT	NRMT
COMPLETE SET (20)	40.00	18.00
COMMON CARD (1-20)	.25	.11
COMP.SUPER BOSS SET (20)	150.00	70.00
COMMON SUPER BOSS (1-20)	2.00	.90
*SUPER BOSS: 3X TO 8X BASIC BOSS		
☐ 1 Jeff Bagwell	2.50	1.10
☐ 2 Albert Belle	1.50	.70
☐ 3 Barry Bonds	1.50	.70
☐ 4 Ken Caminiti	1.00	.45
☐ 5 Juan Gonzalez	3.00	1.35
☐ 6 Ken Griffey Jr.	6.00	2.70
☐ 7 Tony Gwynn	3.00	1.35
☐ 8 Derek Jeter	4.00	1.80
☐ 9 Andruw Jones	3.00	1.35
☐ 10 Chipper Jones	4.00	1.80
☐ 11 Greg Maddux	4.00	1.80
☐ 12 Mark McGwire	2.50	1.10
☐ 13 Mike Piazza	4.00	1.80
☐ 14 Manny Ramirez	1.00	.45
☐ 15 Cal Ripken	5.00	2.20
☐ 16 Alex Rodriguez	5.00	2.20
☐ 17 John Smoltz	.50	.23
☐ 18 Frank Thomas	5.00	2.20
☐ 19 Mo Vaughn	1.50	.70
☐ 20 Bernie Williams	1.00	.45

1997 Circa Emerald Autographs

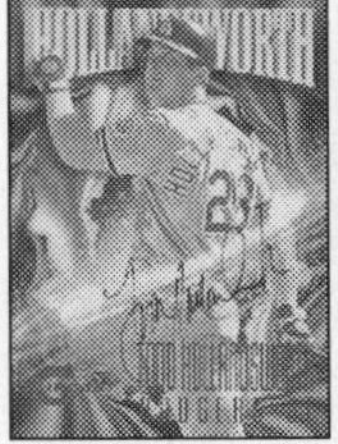

These autographed cards were made available only to those collectors lucky enough to pull one of the scarce Circa Emerald Autograph Redemption cards (randomly seeded into 1:1000 1997 Circa packs). These cards are identical to the regular issue Circa cards except, of course, for the player's autograph on the card front and an embossed Fleer seal for authenticity. The deadline to redeem these cards was May 1st, 1998. In addition, an Emerald Autograph Redemption program entitled "Collect and Win" was featured in 1997 Fleer 2 packs. One in every 4 packs contained one of ten different redemption cards. The object was for collectors to piece together all ten cards and then mail them in to receive a complete set of the Circa Emerald Autographs. The catch was that card #7 was extremely shortprinted (official numbers were not released but speculation is that only a handful of #7 cards made their way into packs). The exchange deadline on this "collect and win" promotion was August 1st, 1998.

	MINT	NRMT
COMPLETE SET (6)	300.00	135.00
COMMON CARD	12.00	5.50
☐ 100 Alex Rodriguez AU	150.00	70.00
☐ 241 Darin Erstad AU	60.00	27.00
☐ 251 Todd Hollandsworth AU	15.00	6.75
☐ 283 Scott Rolen AU	80.00	36.00
☐ 308 Alex Ochoa AU	12.00	5.50
☐ 325 Todd Walker AU	25.00	11.00

1997 Circa Fast Track

Randomly inserted in packs at a rate of one in 24, this 10-card set features color player photos of young stars and rookies who will carry baseball into the 21st century. The fronts display the player's image on a flocked background design which shows grass as raised fabric.

	MINT	NRMT
COMPLETE SET (10)	50.00	22.00

☐ 1 Vladimir Guerrero	8.00	3.60
☐ 2 Todd Hollandsworth	1.50	.70
☐ 3 Derek Jeter	10.00	4.50
☐ 4 Andruw Jones	10.00	4.50
☐ 5 Chipper Jones	10.00	4.50
☐ 6 Andy Pettitte	4.00	1.80
☐ 7 Mariano Rivera	2.00	.90
☐ 8 Alex Rodriguez	12.00	5.50
☐ 9 Scott Rolen	8.00	3.60
☐ 10 Todd Walker	1.50	.70

1997 Circa Icons

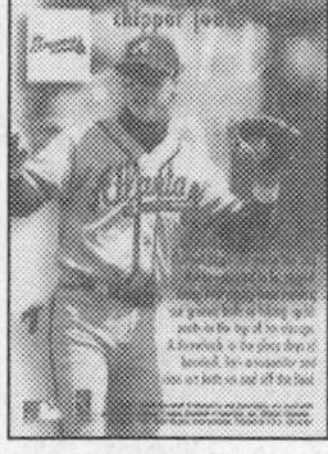

Randomly inserted in packs at a rate of one in 36, this 12-card set features color player images of twelve legendary players printed on 100% holofoil with the word "icon" running across the background. The backs carry player information.

	MINT	NRMT
COMPLETE SET (12)	100.00	45.00
COMMON CARD (1-12)	2.50	1.10
☐ 1 Juan Gonzalez	10.00	4.50
☐ 2 Ken Griffey Jr.	20.00	9.00
☐ 3 Tony Gwynn	10.00	4.50
☐ 4 Derek Jeter	10.00	4.50
☐ 5 Chipper Jones	12.00	5.50
☐ 6 Greg Maddux	12.00	5.50
☐ 7 Mark McGwire	8.00	3.60
☐ 8 Mike Piazza	12.00	5.50
☐ 9 Cal Ripken	15.00	6.75
☐ 10 Alex Rodriguez	12.00	5.50
☐ 11 Frank Thomas	15.00	6.75
☐ 12 Matt Williams	2.50	1.10

1997 Circa Limited Access

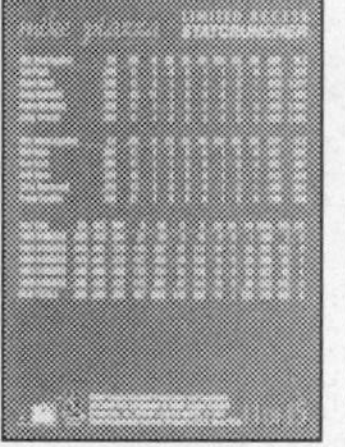

Randomly inserted in retail packs only at a rate of one in 18, this 15-card set features color player photos on die-cut, bi-fold cards which track the players from their youth to the present with in-depth statistical analysis.

	MINT	NRMT
COMPLETE SET (15)	180.00	80.00
COMMON CARD (1-15)	6.00	2.70
☐ 1 Jeff Bagwell	10.00	4.50
☐ 2 Albert Belle	6.00	2.70
☐ 3 Barry Bonds	6.00	2.70
☐ 4 Juan Gonzalez	12.00	5.50
☐ 5 Ken Griffey Jr.	25.00	11.00
☐ 6 Tony Gwynn	12.00	5.50
☐ 7 Derek Jeter	12.00	5.50
☐ 8 Chipper Jones	15.00	6.75
☐ 9 Greg Maddux	15.00	6.75
☐ 10 Mark McGwire	10.00	4.50
☐ 11 Mike Piazza	15.00	6.75
☐ 12 Cal Ripken	20.00	9.00
☐ 13 Alex Rodriguez	15.00	6.75
☐ 14 Frank Thomas	20.00	9.00
☐ 15 Mo Vaughn	6.00	2.70

1997 Circa Rave Reviews

Randomly inserted in packs at a rate of one in 288, this 12-card set features color photos of twelve players who generate incredible numbers off the bat and are printed on 100% holofoil. The backs carry player information.

	MINT	NRMT
COMPLETE SET (12)	500.00	220.00
COMMON CARD (1-12)	15.00	6.75
☐ 1 Albert Belle	20.00	9.00
☐ 2 Barry Bonds	20.00	9.00
☐ 3 Juan Gonzalez	40.00	18.00
☐ 4 Ken Griffey Jr.	80.00	36.00
☐ 5 Tony Gwynn	40.00	18.00
☐ 6 Greg Maddux	50.00	22.00
☐ 7 Mark McGwire	30.00	13.50
☐ 8 Eddie Murray	15.00	6.75
☐ 9 Mike Piazza	50.00	22.00
☐ 10 Cal Ripken	60.00	27.00
☐ 11 Alex Rodriguez	60.00	27.00
☐ 12 Frank Thomas	60.00	27.00

1985 Circle K

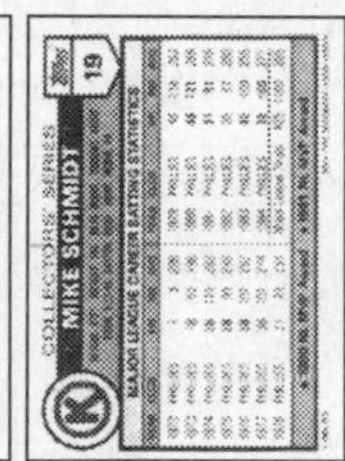

The cards in this 33-card set measure 2 1/2" by 3 1/2" and were issued with an accompanying custom box. In 1985, Topps produced this set for Circle K; cards were printed in Ireland. Cards are numbered on the back according to each player's rank on the all-time career Home Run list. The backs are printed in blue and red on white card stock. The card fronts are glossy and each player is named in the lower left corner. Most of the obverses are in color, although the older vintage players are pictured in black and white. Joe DiMaggio was not included in the set; card number 31 does not exist. It was intended to be DiMaggio but he apparently would not consent to be included in the set.

	MINT	NRMT
COMPLETE SET (33)	5.00	2.20
COMMON CARD (1-34)	.10	.05
☐ 1 Hank Aaron	.75	.35
☐ 2 Babe Ruth	1.00	.45
☐ 3 Willie Mays	.75	.35
☐ 4 Frank Robinson	.25	.11
☐ 5 Harmon Killebrew	.25	.11
☐ 6 Mickey Mantle	1.00	.45
☐ 7 Jimmie Foxx	.25	.11
☐ 8 Willie McCovey	.25	.11
☐ 9 Ted Williams	.75	.35
☐ 10 Ernie Banks	.25	.11
☐ 11 Eddie Mathews	.25	.11
☐ 12 Mel Ott	.25	.11
☐ 13 Reggie Jackson	.50	.23
☐ 14 Lou Gehrig	.75	.35
☐ 15 Stan Musial	.50	.23
☐ 16 Willie Stargell	.25	.11
☐ 17 Carl Yastrzemski	.25	.11
☐ 18 Billy Williams	.15	.07
☐ 19 Mike Schmidt	.50	.23
☐ 20 Duke Snider	.25	.11
☐ 21 Al Kaline	.25	.11
☐ 22 Johnny Bench	.25	.11
☐ 23 Frank Howard	.10	.05
☐ 24 Orlando Cepeda	.15	.07
☐ 25 Norm Cash	.10	.05
☐ 26 Dave Kingman	.10	.05
☐ 27 Rocky Colavito	.15	.07
☐ 28 Tony Perez	.15	.07
☐ 29 Gil Hodges	.15	.07
☐ 30 Ralph Kiner	.15	.07
☐ 31 Joe DiMaggio (card does not exist)		
☐ 32 Johnny Mize	.15	.07
☐ 33 Yogi Berra	.25	.11
☐ 34 Lee May	.10	.05

1987 Classic Game

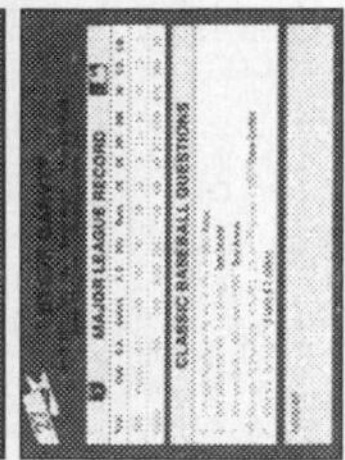

This 100-card standard-size set was actually distributed as part of a trivia board game. The card backs contain several trivia questions (and answers) which are used to play the game. A dark green border frames the full-color photo. The games were produced by Game Time, Ltd. and were available in toy stores as well as from card dealers. According to the producers of this game, only 75,000 sets were distributed. The set features Bo Jackson, Wally Joyner, and Barry Larkin in their Rookie Card year.

	MINT	NRMT
COMPLETE SET (100)	75.00	34.00
COMMON CARD (1-100)	.15	.07
☐ 1 Pete Rose	3.00	1.35
☐ 2 Len Dykstra	.25	.11
☐ 3 Darryl Strawberry	.50	.23
☐ 4 Keith Hernandez	.25	.11
☐ 5 Gary Carter	.25	.11
☐ 6 Wally Joyner	.75	.35
☐ 7 Andres Thomas	.15	.07
☐ 8 Pat Dodson	.15	.07
☐ 9 Kirk Gibson	.25	.11
☐ 10 Don Mattingly	5.00	2.20
☐ 11 Dave Winfield	.50	.23
☐ 12 Rickey Henderson	2.00	.90
☐ 13 Dan Pasqua	.15	.07
☐ 14 Don Baylor	.25	.11
☐ 15 Bo Jackson (Swinging bat in Auburn FB uniform)	5.00	2.20
☐ 16 Pete Incaviglia	.25	.11
☐ 17 Kevin Bass	.15	.07
☐ 18 Barry Larkin	4.00	1.80
☐ 19 Dave Magadan	.25	.11
☐ 20 Steve Sax	.15	.07
☐ 21 Eric Davis	.75	.35
☐ 22 Mike Pagliarulo	.15	.07
☐ 23 Fred Lynn	.25	.11
☐ 24 Reggie Jackson	2.00	.90
☐ 25 Larry Parrish	.15	.07
☐ 26 Tony Gwynn	5.00	2.20
☐ 27 Steve Garvey	.50	.23
☐ 28 Glenn Davis	.15	.07
☐ 29 Tim Raines	.25	.11
☐ 30 Vince Coleman	.15	.07
☐ 31 Willie McGee	.25	.11
☐ 32 Ozzie Smith	4.00	1.80
☐ 33 Dave Parker	.25	.11
☐ 34 Tony Pena	.15	.07
☐ 35 Ryne Sandberg	4.00	1.80
☐ 36 Brett Butler	.25	.11
☐ 37 Dale Murphy	.50	.23
☐ 38 Bob Horner	.15	.07
☐ 39 Pedro Guerrero	.15	.07
☐ 40 Brook Jacoby	.15	.07
☐ 41 Carlton Fisk	1.50	.70
☐ 42 Harold Baines	.15	.07
☐ 43 Rob Deer	.15	.07
☐ 44 Robin Yount	2.00	.90
☐ 45 Paul Molitor	2.50	1.10
☐ 46 Jose Canseco	4.00	1.80
☐ 47 George Brett	4.00	1.80
☐ 48 Jim Presley	.15	.07
☐ 49 Rich Gedman	.15	.07
☐ 50 Lance Parrish	.15	.07
☐ 51 Eddie Murray	2.50	1.10
☐ 52 Cal Ripken	8.00	3.60
☐ 53 Kent Hrbek	.15	.07
☐ 54 Gary Gaetti	.15	.07
☐ 55 Kirby Puckett	6.00	2.70
☐ 56 George Bell	.15	.07
☐ 57 Tony Fernandez	.15	.07
☐ 58 Jesse Barfield	.15	.07
☐ 59 Jim Rice	.25	.11
☐ 60 Wade Boggs	2.00	.90

☐ 61 Marty Barrett	.15	.07
☐ 62 Mike Schmidt	3.00	1.35
☐ 63 Von Hayes	.15	.07
☐ 64 Jeff Leonard	.15	.07
☐ 65 Chris Brown	.15	.07
☐ 66 Dave Smith	.15	.07
☐ 67 Mike Krukow	.15	.07
☐ 68 Ron Guidry	.25	.11
☐ 69 Rob Woodward	.15	.07
☐ 70 Rob Murphy	.15	.07
☐ 71 Andres Galarraga	3.00	1.35
☐ 72 Dwight Gooden	.50	.23
☐ 73 Bob Ojeda	.15	.07
☐ 74 Sid Fernandez	.15	.07
☐ 75 Jesse Orosco	.15	.07
☐ 76 Roger McDowell	.15	.07
☐ 77 John Tudor UER (Misspelled Tutor)	.15	.07
☐ 78 Tom Browning	.15	.07
☐ 79 Rick Aguilera	.25	.11
☐ 80 Lance McCullers	.15	.07
☐ 81 Mike Scott	.15	.07
☐ 82 Nolan Ryan	8.00	3.60
☐ 83 Bruce Hurst	.15	.07
☐ 84 Roger Clemens	5.00	2.20
☐ 85 Dennis Boyd	.15	.07
☐ 86 Dave Righetti	.15	.07
☐ 87 Dennis Rasmussen	.15	.07
☐ 88 Bret Saberhagen	.50	.23
☐ 89 Mark Langston	.15	.07
☐ 90 Jack Morris	.25	.11
☐ 91 Fernando Valenzuela	.25	.11
☐ 92 Orel Hershiser	.25	.11
☐ 93 Rick Honeycutt	.15	.07
☐ 94 Jeff Reardon	.15	.07
☐ 95 John Habyan	.15	.07
☐ 96 Goose Gossage	.25	.11
☐ 97 Todd Worrell	.25	.11
☐ 98 Floyd Youmans	.15	.07
☐ 99 Don Aase	.15	.07
☐ 100 John Franco	.25	.11

1987 Classic Update Yellow

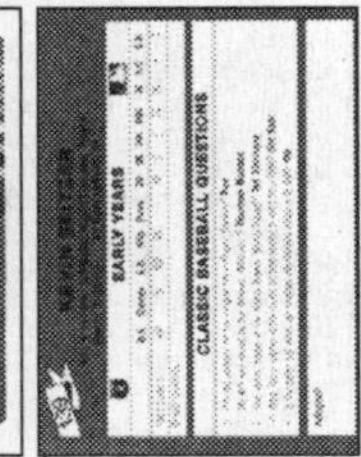

This 50-card standard-size set was actually distributed as part of an update to a trivia board game, but (unlike the original Classic game) was sold without the game. The set is sometimes referred to as the "Travel Edition" of the game. The card backs contain several trivia questions (and answers) which are used to play the game. A yellow border frames the full-color photo. The games were produced by Game Time, Ltd. and were available in toy stores as well as from card dealers. Cards are numbered beginning with 101, as they are an extension of the original set. According to the set's producers, reportedly about 1/3 of the 150,000 sets printed were error sets in that they had green backs instead of yellow backs. This "green back" variation/error set is valued at approximately double the prices listed below.

	MINT	NRMT
COMPLETE SET (50)	15.00	6.75
COMMON CARD (101-150)	.10	.05

☐ 101 Mike Schmidt	1.00	.45
☐ 102 Eric Davis	.40	.18
☐ 103 Pete Rose	1.00	.45
☐ 104 Don Mattingly	2.50	1.10
☐ 105 Wade Boggs	1.25	.55
☐ 106 Dale Murphy	.40	.18
☐ 107 Glenn Davis	.10	.05
☐ 108 Wally Joyner	.40	.18
☐ 109 Bo Jackson	.60	.25
☐ 110 Cory Snyder	.10	.05
☐ 111 Jim Lindeman	.10	.05
☐ 112 Kirby Puckett	3.00	1.35
☐ 113 Barry Bonds	3.00	1.35
☐ 114 Roger Clemens	2.50	1.10
☐ 115 Oddibe McDowell	.10	.05
☐ 116 Bret Saberhagen	.20	.09
☐ 117 Joe Magrane	.10	.05
☐ 118 Scott Fletcher	.10	.05
☐ 119 Mark McLemore	.10	.05
☐ 120 Joe Niekro Who Me	.20	.09
☐ 121 Mark McGwire	1.50	.70
☐ 122 Darryl Strawberry	.40	.18
☐ 123 Mike Scott	.10	.05
☐ 124 Andre Dawson	.60	.25
☐ 125 Jose Canseco	2.00	.90
☐ 126 Kevin McReynolds	.10	.05
☐ 127 Joe Carter	1.25	.55
☐ 128 Casey Candaele	.10	.05
☐ 129 Matt Nokes	.10	.05
☐ 130 Kal Daniels	.10	.05
☐ 131 Pete Incaviglia	.20	.09
☐ 132 Benito Santiago	.10	.05
☐ 133 Barry Larkin	2.00	.90
☐ 134 Gary Pettis	.10	.05
☐ 135 B.J. Surhoff	.20	.09
☐ 136 Juan Nieves	.10	.05
☐ 137 Jim Deshaies	.10	.05
☐ 138 Pete O'Brien	.10	.05
☐ 139 Kevin Seitzer	.20	.09
☐ 140 Devon White	.40	.18
☐ 141 Rob Deer	.10	.05
☐ 142 Kurt Stillwell	.10	.05
☐ 143 Edwin Correa	.10	.05
☐ 144 Dion James	.10	.05
☐ 145 Danny Tartabull	.20	.09
☐ 146 Jerry Browne	.10	.05
☐ 147 Ted Higuera	.10	.05
☐ 148 Jack Clark	.10	.05
☐ 149 Ruben Sierra	.20	.09
☐ 150 Mark McGwire and Eric Davis	.75	.35

1988 Classic Blue

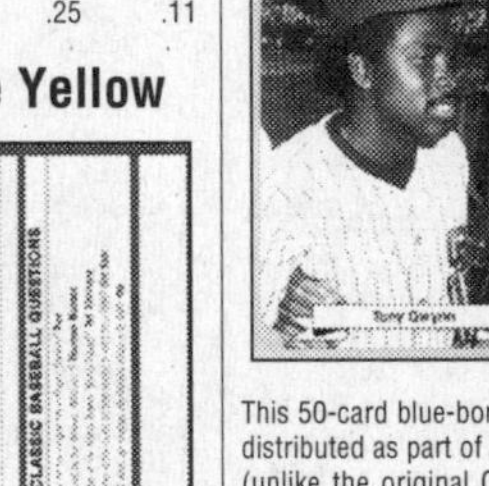

This 50-card blue-bordered standard-size set was actually distributed as part of an update to a trivia board game, but (unlike the original Classic game) was sold without the game. The card backs contain several trivia questions (and answers) which are used to play the game. A blue border frames the full color photo. The games were produced by Game Time, Ltd. and were available in toy stores as well as from card dealers. Cards are numbered beginning with 201 as they are an extension of the original sets.

	MINT	NRMT
COMPLETE SET (50)	10.00	4.50
COMMON CARD (201-250)	.10	.05

☐ 201 Eric Davis and Dale Murphy	.20	.09
☐ 202 B.J. Surhoff	.10	.05
☐ 203 John Kruk	.20	.09
☐ 204 Sam Horn	.10	.05
☐ 205 Jack Clark	.20	.09
☐ 206 Wally Joyner	.20	.09
☐ 207 Matt Nokes	.10	.05
☐ 208 Bo Jackson	.40	.18
☐ 209 Darryl Strawberry	.20	.09
☐ 210 Ozzie Smith	1.50	.70
☐ 211 Don Mattingly	1.25	.55
☐ 212 Mark McGwire	1.50	.70
☐ 213 Eric Davis	.20	.09
☐ 214 Wade Boggs	.60	.25
☐ 215 Dale Murphy	.40	.18
☐ 216 Andre Dawson	.40	.18
☐ 217 Roger Clemens	1.25	.55
☐ 218 Kevin Seitzer	.20	.09
☐ 219 Benito Santiago	.10	.05
☐ 220 Tony Gwynn	2.00	.90
☐ 221 Mike Scott	.10	.05
☐ 222 Steve Bedrosian	.10	.05
☐ 223 Vince Coleman	.10	.05
☐ 224 Rick Sutcliffe	.10	.05
☐ 225 Will Clark	1.00	.45
☐ 226 Pete Rose	.75	.35
☐ 227 Mike Greenwell	.20	.09
☐ 228 Ken Caminiti	1.00	.45
☐ 229 Ellis Burks	.60	.25
☐ 230 Dave Magadan	.10	.05
☐ 231 Alan Trammell	.40	.18
☐ 232 Paul Molitor	.75	.35
☐ 233 Gary Gaetti	.10	.05
☐ 234 Rickey Henderson	.60	.25
☐ 235 Danny Tartabull UER (Photo actually Hal McRae)	.10	.05
☐ 236 Bobby Bonilla	.40	.18
☐ 237 Mike Dunne	.10	.05
☐ 238 Al Leiter	.40	.18
☐ 239 John Farrell	.10	.05
☐ 240 Joe Magrane	.10	.05
☐ 241 Mike Henneman	.10	.05
☐ 242 George Bell	.10	.05
☐ 243 Gregg Jefferies	.20	.09
☐ 244 Jay Buhner	1.00	.45
☐ 245 Todd Benzinger	.10	.05
☐ 246 Matt Williams	1.00	.45
☐ 247 Mark McGwire and Don Mattingly (Unnumbered; game instructions on back)	1.25	.55
☐ 248 George Brett	1.25	.55
☐ 249 Jimmy Key	.20	.09
☐ 250 Mark Langston	.10	.05

1988 Classic Red

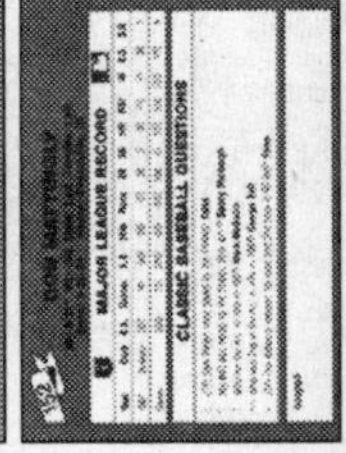

This 50-card red-bordered standard-size set was actually distributed as part of an update to a trivia board game, but (unlike the original Classic game) was sold without the game. The card backs contain several trivia questions (and answers) which are used to play the game. A red border frames the full color photo. The games were produced by Game Time, Ltd. and were available in toy stores as well as from card dealers. Cards are numbered beginning with 151 as they are an extension of the original sets.

	MINT	NRMT
COMPLETE SET (50)	10.00	4.50
COMMON CARD (151-200)	.10	.05

☐ 151 Mark McGwire and Don Mattingly	1.25	.55
☐ 152 Don Mattingly	1.50	.70
☐ 153 Mark McGwire	1.25	.55
☐ 154 Eric Davis	.20	.09
☐ 155 Wade Boggs	.60	.25
☐ 156 Dale Murphy	.40	.18
☐ 157 Andre Dawson	.40	.18
☐ 158 Roger Clemens	1.25	.55
☐ 159 Kevin Seitzer	.20	.09
☐ 160 Benito Santiago	.10	.05
☐ 161 Kal Daniels	.10	.05
☐ 162 John Kruk	.20	.09
☐ 163 Bill Ripken	.10	.05
☐ 164 Kirby Puckett	1.50	.70
☐ 165 Jose Canseco	.60	.25
☐ 166 Matt Nokes	.10	.05
☐ 167 Mike Schmidt	.75	.35
☐ 168 Tim Raines	.20	.09
☐ 169 Ryne Sandberg	1.25	.55
☐ 170 Dave Winfield	.60	.25
☐ 171 Dwight Gooden	.20	.09
☐ 172 Bret Saberhagen	.20	.09
☐ 173 Willie McGee	.20	.09
☐ 174 Jack Morris	.20	.09
☐ 175 Jeff Leonard	.10	.05
☐ 176 Cal Ripken	3.00	1.35
☐ 177 Pete Incaviglia	.10	.05
☐ 178 Devon White	.20	.09
☐ 179 Nolan Ryan	3.00	1.35
☐ 180 Ruben Sierra	.20	.09
☐ 181 Todd Worrell	.10	.05
☐ 182 Glenn Davis	.10	.05
☐ 183 Frank Viola	.10	.05
☐ 184 Cory Snyder	.10	.05
☐ 185 Tracy Jones	.10	.05
☐ 186 Terry Steinbach	.20	.09
☐ 187 Julio Franco	.20	.09

Card	MINT	NRMT
☐ 188 Larry Sheets	.10	.05
☐ 189 John Marzano	.10	.05
☐ 190 Kevin Elster	.10	.05
☐ 191 Vicente Palacios	.10	.05
☐ 192 Kent Hrbek	.10	.05
☐ 193 Eric Bell	.10	.05
☐ 194 Kelly Downs	.10	.05
☐ 195 Jose Lind	.10	.05
☐ 196 Dave Stewart	.10	.05
☐ 197 Mark McGwire and Jose Canseco	.60	.25
☐ 198 Phil Niekro Cleveland Indians	.40	.18
☐ 199 Phil Niekro Toronto Blue Jays	.40	.18
☐ 200 Phil Niekro Atlanta Braves	.40	.18

1989 Classic Light Blue

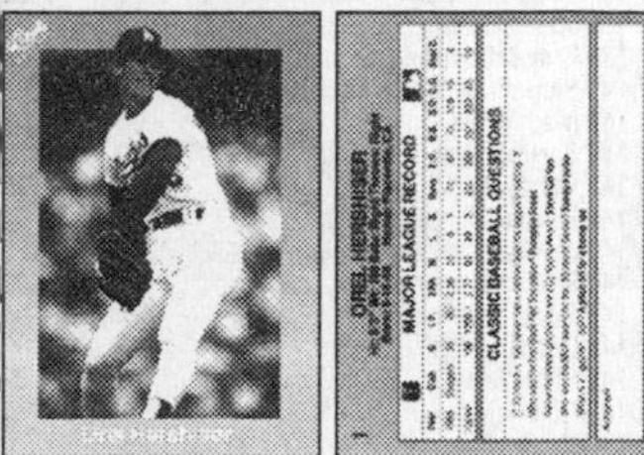

The 1989 Classic set contains 100 standard-size cards. The fronts of these cards have light blue borders. The backs feature 1988 and lifetime stats. The cards were distributed with a baseball boardgame. Reportedly there were 150,000 sets produced.

	MINT	NRMT
COMPLETE SET (100)	15.00	6.75
COMMON CARD (1-100)	.10	.05
☐ 1 Orel Hershiser	.20	.09
☐ 2 Wade Boggs	.60	.25
☐ 3 Jose Canseco	.40	.18
☐ 4 Mark McGwire	1.50	.70
☐ 5 Don Mattingly	1.50	.70
☐ 6 Gregg Jefferies	.20	.09
☐ 7 Dwight Gooden	.20	.09
☐ 8 Darryl Strawberry	.20	.09
☐ 9 Eric Davis	.20	.09
☐ 10 Joey Meyer	.10	.05
☐ 11 Joe Carter	.40	.18
☐ 12 Paul Molitor	.75	.35
☐ 13 Mark Grace	.75	.35
☐ 14 Kurt Stillwell	.10	.05
☐ 15 Kirby Puckett	1.50	.70
☐ 16 Keith Miller	.10	.05
☐ 17 Glenn Davis	.10	.05
☐ 18 Will Clark	.40	.18
☐ 19 Cory Snyder	.10	.05
☐ 20 Jose Lind	.10	.05
☐ 21 Andres Thomas	.10	.05
☐ 22 Dave Smith	.10	.05
☐ 23 Mike Scott	.10	.05
☐ 24 Kevin McReynolds	.10	.05
☐ 25 B.J. Surhoff	.20	.09
☐ 26 Mackey Sasser	.10	.05
☐ 27 Chad Kreuter	.10	.05
☐ 28 Hal Morris	.10	.05
☐ 29 Wally Joyner	.20	.09
☐ 30 Tony Gwynn	2.00	.90
☐ 31 Kevin Mitchell	.10	.05
☐ 32 Dave Winfield	.40	.18
☐ 33 Billy Bean	.10	.05
☐ 34 Steve Bedrosian	.10	.05
☐ 35 Ron Gant	.20	.09
☐ 36 Len Dykstra	.20	.09
☐ 37 Andre Dawson	.40	.18
☐ 38 Brett Butler	.20	.09
☐ 39 Rob Deer	.10	.05
☐ 40 Tommy John	.20	.09
☐ 41 Gary Gaetti	.20	.09
☐ 42 Tim Raines	.20	.09
☐ 43 George Bell	.10	.05
☐ 44 Dwight Evans	.20	.09
☐ 45 Dennis Martinez	.10	.05
☐ 46 Andres Galarraga	.75	.35
☐ 47 George Brett	1.50	.70
☐ 48 Mike Schmidt	.75	.35
☐ 49 Dave Stieb	.10	.05
☐ 50 Rickey Henderson	.60	.25
☐ 51 Craig Biggio	1.25	.55
☐ 52 Mark Lemke	.10	.05
☐ 53 Chris Sabo	.10	.05
☐ 54 Jeff Treadway	.10	.05
☐ 55 Kent Hrbek	.10	.05
☐ 56 Cal Ripken	4.00	1.80
☐ 57 Tim Belcher	.10	.05
☐ 58 Ozzie Smith	1.00	.45
☐ 59 Keith Hernandez	.10	.05
☐ 60 Pedro Guerrero	.10	.05
☐ 61 Greg Swindell	.10	.05
☐ 62 Bret Saberhagen	.10	.05
☐ 63 John Tudor	.10	.05
☐ 64 Gary Carter	.20	.09
☐ 65 Kevin Seitzer	.10	.05
☐ 66 Jesse Barfield	.10	.05
☐ 67 Luis Medina	.10	.05
☐ 68 Walt Weiss	.10	.05
☐ 69 Terry Steinbach	.20	.09
☐ 70 Barry Larkin	.60	.25
☐ 71 Pete Rose	.75	.35
☐ 72 Luis Salazar	.10	.05
☐ 73 Benito Santiago	.10	.05
☐ 74 Kal Daniels	.10	.05
☐ 75 Kevin Elster	.10	.05
☐ 76 Rob Dibble	.20	.09
☐ 77 Bobby Witt	.10	.05
☐ 78 Steve Searcy	.10	.05
☐ 79 Sandy Alomar Jr.	1.00	.45
☐ 80 Chili Davis	.10	.05
☐ 81 Alvin Davis	.10	.05
☐ 82 Charlie Leibrandt	.10	.05
☐ 83 Robin Yount	.60	.25
☐ 84 Mark Carreon	.10	.05
☐ 85 Pascual Perez	.10	.05
☐ 86 Dennis Rasmussen	.10	.05
☐ 87 Ernie Riles	.10	.05
☐ 88 Melido Perez	.10	.05
☐ 89 Doug Jones	.10	.05
☐ 90 Dennis Eckersley	.40	.18
☐ 91 Bob Welch	.10	.05
☐ 92 Bob Milacki	.10	.05
☐ 93 Jeff Robinson	.10	.05
☐ 94 Mike Henneman	.10	.05
☐ 95 Randy Johnson	2.00	.90
☐ 96 Ron Jones	.10	.05
☐ 97 Jack Armstrong	.10	.05
☐ 98 Willie McGee	.20	.09
☐ 99 Ryne Sandberg	.75	.35
☐ 100 David Cone and Danny Jackson	.10	.05

1989 Classic Travel Orange

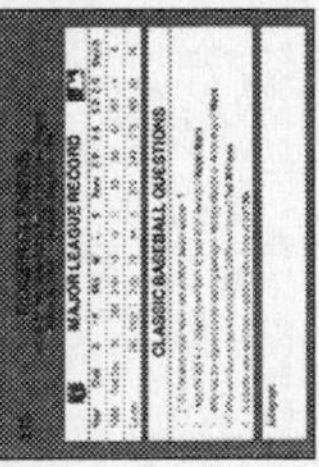

The 1989 Classic Travel Orange set contains 50 standard-size cards. The fronts of the cards have orange borders. The backs feature 1988 and lifetime stats. This subset of cards were distributed as a set in blister packs as "Travel Update I" subsets. Reportedly there were 150,000 sets produced.

	MINT	NRMT
COMPLETE SET (50)	8.00	3.60
COMMON CARD (101-150)	.10	.05
☐ 101 Gary Sheffield	.75	.35
☐ 102 Wade Boggs	.40	.18
☐ 103 Jose Canseco	.40	.18
☐ 104 Mark McGwire	1.25	.55
☐ 105 Orel Hershiser	.20	.09
☐ 106 Don Mattingly	2.00	.90
☐ 107 Dwight Gooden	.20	.09
☐ 108 Darryl Strawberry	.20	.09
☐ 109 Eric Davis	.20	.09
☐ 110 Hensley Meulens UER (Listed on card as Bam Bam Muelens)	.10	.05
☐ 111 Andy Van Slyke	.20	.09
☐ 112 Al Leiter	.20	.09
☐ 113 Matt Nokes	.10	.05
☐ 114 Mike Krukow	.10	.05
☐ 115 Tony Fernandez	.10	.05
☐ 116 Fred McGriff	.30	.14
☐ 117 Barry Bonds	1.00	.45
☐ 118 Gerald Perry	.10	.05
☐ 119 Roger Clemens	1.00	.45
☐ 120 Kirk Gibson	.30	.14
☐ 121 Greg Maddux	2.00	.90
☐ 122 Bo Jackson	.20	.09
☐ 123 Danny Jackson	.10	.05
☐ 124 Dale Murphy	.30	.14
☐ 125 David Cone	.20	.09
☐ 126 Tom Browning	.10	.05
☐ 127 Roberto Alomar	1.00	.45
☐ 128 Alan Trammell	.30	.14
☐ 129 Ricky Jordan UER (Misspelled Jordon on card back)	.10	.05
☐ 130 Ramon Martinez	.50	.23
☐ 131 Ken Griffey Jr.	5.00	2.20
☐ 132 Gregg Olson	.10	.05
☐ 133 Carlos Quintana	.10	.05
☐ 134 Dave West	.10	.05
☐ 135 Cameron Drew	.10	.05
☐ 136 Teddy Higuera	.10	.05
☐ 137 Sil Campusano	.10	.05
☐ 138 Mark Gubicza	.10	.05
☐ 139 Mike Boddicker	.10	.05
☐ 140 Paul Gibson	.10	.05
☐ 141 Jose Rijo	.10	.05
☐ 142 John Costello	.10	.05
☐ 143 Cecil Espy	.10	.05
☐ 144 Frank Viola	.10	.05
☐ 145 Erik Hanson	.10	.05
☐ 146 Juan Samuel	.10	.05
☐ 147 Harold Reynolds	.10	.05
☐ 148 Joe Magrane	.10	.05
☐ 149 Mike Greenwell	.10	.05
☐ 150 Darryl Strawberry and Will Clark	.20	.09

1989 Classic Travel Purple

The 1989 Classic "Travel Update II" set contains 50 standard-size cards. The fronts have purple (and gray) borders. The set features "two sport" cards of Bo Jackson and Deion Sanders. The cards were distributed as a set in blister packs.

	MINT	NRMT
COMPLETE SET (50)	8.00	3.60
COMMON CARD (151-200)	.10	.05
☐ 151 Jim Abbott	.20	.09
☐ 152 Ellis Burks	.20	.09
☐ 153 Mike Schmidt	.50	.23
☐ 154 Gregg Jefferies	.20	.09
☐ 155 Mark Grace	.75	.35
☐ 156 Jerome Walton	.20	.09
☐ 157 Bo Jackson	.30	.14
☐ 158 Jack Clark	.10	.05
☐ 159 Tom Glavine	.75	.35
☐ 160 Eddie Murray	.75	.35
☐ 161 John Dopson	.10	.05
☐ 162 Ruben Sierra	.20	.09
☐ 163 Rafael Palmeiro	.30	.14
☐ 164 Nolan Ryan	2.00	.90
☐ 165 Barry Larkin	.40	.18
☐ 166 Tommy Herr	.10	.05
☐ 167 Roberto Kelly	.10	.05
☐ 168 Glenn Davis	.10	.05
☐ 169 Glenn Braggs	.10	.05
☐ 170 Juan Bell	.10	.05
☐ 171 Todd Burns	.10	.05
☐ 172 Derek Lilliquist	.10	.05
☐ 173 Orel Hershiser	.20	.09
☐ 174 John Smoltz	.75	.35
☐ 175 Ozzie Guillen and Ellis Burks	.10	.05
☐ 176 Kirby Puckett	1.25	.55
☐ 177 Robin Ventura	.50	.23
☐ 178 Allan Anderson	.10	.05
☐ 179 Steve Sax	.10	.05
☐ 180 Will Clark	.60	.25
☐ 181 Mike Devereaux	.10	.05
☐ 182 Tom Gordon	.20	.09
☐ 183 Rob Murphy	.10	.05
☐ 184 Pete O'Brien	.10	.05
☐ 185 Cris Carpenter	.10	.05

	MINT	NRMT
☐ 186 Tom Brunansky	.10	.05
☐ 187 Bob Boone	.20	.09
☐ 188 Lou Whitaker	.20	.09
☐ 189 Dwight Gooden	.20	.09
☐ 190 Mark McGwire	1.50	.70
☐ 191 John Smiley	.10	.05
☐ 192 Tommy Gregg	.10	.05
☐ 193 Ken Griffey Jr.	4.00	1.80
☐ 194 Bruce Hurst	.10	.05
☐ 195 Greg Swindell	.10	.05
☐ 196 Nelson Liriano	.10	.05
☐ 197 Randy Myers	.20	.09
☐ 198 Kevin Mitchell	.10	.05
☐ 199 Dante Bichette	.60	.25
☐ 200 Deion Sanders	1.00	.45

1990 Classic Blue

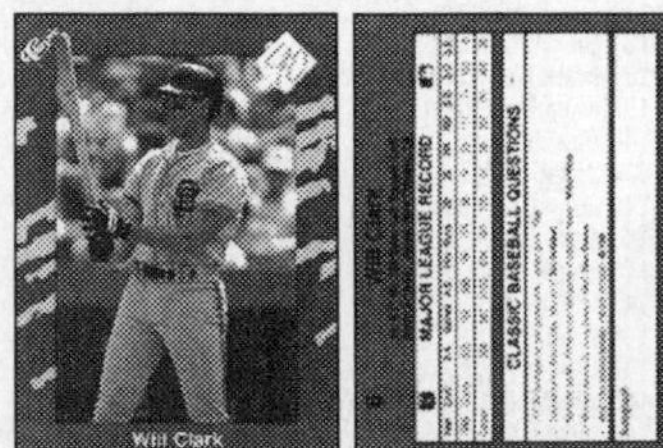

The 1990 Classic Blue (Game) set contains 150 standard-size cards, the largest Classic set to date in terms of player selection. The front borders are blue with magenta splotches. The backs feature 1989 and career total stats. The cards were distributed as a set in blister packs. According to distributors of the set, reportedly there were 200,000 sets produced. Reportedly the Sanders "correction" was made at Sanders own request; less than 10 percent of the sets contain the first version and hence it has the higher value in the checklist below. The complete set price below does not include any of the more difficult variation cards.

	MINT	NRMT
COMPLETE SET (150)	12.50	5.50
COMMON CARD (1-150)	.05	.02

	MINT	NRMT
☐ 1 Nolan Ryan	1.50	.70
☐ 2 Bo Jackson	.20	.09
☐ 3 Gregg Olson	.05	.02
☐ 4 Tom Gordon	.10	.05
☐ 5 Robin Ventura	.20	.09
☐ 6 Will Clark	.40	.18
☐ 7 Ruben Sierra	.10	.05
☐ 8 Mark Grace	.40	.18
☐ 9 Luis DeLosSantos	.05	.02
☐ 10 Bernie Williams	1.00	.45
☐ 11 Eric Davis	.10	.05
☐ 12 Carney Lansford	.10	.05
☐ 13 John Smoltz	.30	.14
☐ 14 Gary Sheffield	.30	.14
☐ 15 Kent Mercker	.05	.02
☐ 16 Don Mattingly	.75	.35
☐ 17 Tony Gwynn	1.00	.45
☐ 18 Ozzie Smith	.75	.35
☐ 19 Fred McGriff	.30	.14
☐ 20 Ken Griffey Jr.	2.00	.90
☐ 21A Deion Sanders Identified only as Prime Time on front	4.00	1.80
☐ 21B Deion Sanders Identified as Deion Prime Time Sanders on front of card	1.00	.45
☐ 22 Jose Canseco	.20	.09
☐ 23 Mitch Williams	.05	.02
☐ 24 Cal Ripken UER Misspelled Ripkin on back	1.50	.70
☐ 25 Bob Geren	.05	.02
☐ 26 Wade Boggs	.20	.09
☐ 27 Ryne Sandberg	.60	.25
☐ 28 Kirby Puckett	.75	.35
☐ 29 Mike Scott	.05	.02
☐ 30 Dwight Smith	.05	.02
☐ 31 Craig Worthington	.05	.02
☐ 32A Ricky Jordan ERR Misspelled Jordon on back	1.00	.45
☐ 32B Ricky Jordan COR	.05	.02
☐ 33 Darryl Strawberry	.10	.05
☐ 34 Jerome Walton	.05	.02
☐ 35 John Olerud	.50	.23
☐ 36 Tom Glavine	.30	.14
☐ 37 Rickey Henderson	.30	.14
☐ 38 Rolando Roomes	.05	.02
☐ 39 Mickey Tettleton	.10	.05
☐ 40 Jim Abbott	.10	.05
☐ 41 Dave Righetti	.05	.02
☐ 42 Mike LaValliere	.05	.02
☐ 43 Rob Dibble	.05	.02
☐ 44 Pete Harnisch	.05	.02
☐ 45 Jose Offerman	.10	.05
☐ 46 Walt Weiss	.05	.02
☐ 47 Mike Greenwell	.10	.05
☐ 48 Barry Larkin	.30	.14
☐ 49 Dave Gallagher	.05	.02
☐ 50 Junior Felix	.05	.02
☐ 51 Roger Clemens	1.00	.45
☐ 52 Lonnie Smith	.05	.02
☐ 53 Jerry Browne	.05	.02
☐ 54 Greg Briley	.05	.02
☐ 55 Delino DeShields	.20	.09
☐ 56 Carmelo Martinez	.05	.02
☐ 57 Craig Biggio	.40	.18
☐ 58 Dwight Gooden	.10	.05
☐ 59A Bo/Rubin/Mark Bo Jackson Ruben Sierra Mark McGwire	3.00	1.35
☐ 59B A.L. Fence Busters Bo Jackson Ruben Sierra Mark McGwire	1.00	.45
☐ 60 Greg Vaughn	.10	.05
☐ 61 Roberto Alomar	.50	.23
☐ 62 Steve Bedrosian	.05	.02
☐ 63 Devon White	.05	.02
☐ 64 Kevin Mitchell	.10	.05
☐ 65 Marquis Grissom	.50	.23
☐ 66 Brian Holman	.05	.02
☐ 67 Julio Franco	.10	.05
☐ 68 Dave West	.05	.02
☐ 69 Harold Baines	.10	.05
☐ 70 Eric Anthony	.05	.02
☐ 71 Glenn Davis	.05	.02
☐ 72 Mark Langston	.05	.02
☐ 73 Matt Williams	.40	.18
☐ 74 Rafael Palmeiro	.20	.09
☐ 75 Pete Rose Jr.	.10	.05
☐ 76 Ramon Martinez	.30	.14
☐ 77 Dwight Evans	.10	.05
☐ 78 Mackey Sasser	.05	.02
☐ 79 Mike Schooler	.05	.02
☐ 80 Dennis Cook	.05	.02
☐ 81 Orel Hershiser	.10	.05
☐ 82 Barry Bonds	.50	.23
☐ 83 Geronimo Berroa	.05	.02
☐ 84 George Bell	.05	.02
☐ 85 Andre Dawson	.20	.09
☐ 86 John Franco	.10	.05
☐ 87A Clark/Gwynn Will Clark Tony Gwynn	3.00	1.35
☐ 87B N.L. Hit Kings Will Clark Tony Gwynn	1.00	.45
☐ 88 Glenallen Hill	.05	.02
☐ 89 Jeff Ballard	.05	.02
☐ 90 Todd Zeile	.10	.05
☐ 91 Frank Viola	.05	.02
☐ 92 Ozzie Guillen	.05	.02
☐ 93 Jeffrey Leonard	.05	.02
☐ 94 Dave Smith	.05	.02
☐ 95 Dave Parker	.10	.05
☐ 96 Jose Gonzalez	.05	.02
☐ 97 Dave Stieb	.05	.02
☐ 98 Charlie Hayes	.05	.02
☐ 99 Jesse Barfield	.05	.02
☐ 100 Joey Belle	1.00	.45
☐ 101 Jeff Reardon	.10	.05
☐ 102 Bruce Hurst	.05	.02
☐ 103 Luis Medina	.05	.02
☐ 104 Mike Moore	.05	.02
☐ 105 Vince Coleman	.05	.02
☐ 106 Alan Trammell	.20	.09
☐ 107 Randy Myers	.10	.05
☐ 108 Frank Tanana	.05	.02
☐ 109 Craig Lefferts	.05	.02
☐ 110 John Wetteland	.40	.18
☐ 111 Chris Gwynn	.05	.02
☐ 112 Mark Carreon	.05	.02
☐ 113 Von Hayes	.05	.02
☐ 114 Doug Jones	.05	.02
☐ 115 Andres Galarraga	.30	.14
☐ 116 Carlton Fisk UER Bellows Falls misspelled as Bellow Falls on back	.50	.23
☐ 117 Paul O'Neill	.10	.05
☐ 118 Tim Raines	.10	.05
☐ 119 Tom Brunansky	.05	.02
☐ 120 Andy Benes	.30	.14
☐ 121 Mark Portugal	.05	.02
☐ 122 Willie Randolph	.10	.05
☐ 123 Jeff Blauser	.05	.02
☐ 124 Don August	.05	.02
☐ 125 Chuck Cary	.05	.02
☐ 126 John Smiley	.05	.02
☐ 127 Terry Mulholland	.05	.02
☐ 128 Harold Reynolds	.05	.02
☐ 129 Hubie Brooks	.05	.02
☐ 130 Ben McDonald	.10	.05
☐ 131 Kevin Ritz	.05	.02
☐ 132 Luis Quinones	.05	.02
☐ 133A Hensley Meulens ERR Misspelled Muelens on front	.75	.35
☐ 133B Hensley Meulens COR	.05	.02
☐ 134 Bill Spiers UER Orangeburg misspelled as Orangburg on back	.05	.02
☐ 135 Andy Hawkins	.05	.02
☐ 136 Alvin Davis	.05	.02
☐ 137 Lee Smith	.10	.05
☐ 138 Joe Carter	.30	.14
☐ 139 Bret Saberhagen	.10	.05
☐ 140 Sammy Sosa	.75	.35
☐ 141 Matt Nokes	.05	.02
☐ 142 Bert Blyleven	.10	.05
☐ 143 Bobby Bonilla	.10	.05
☐ 144 Howard Johnson	.05	.02
☐ 145 Joe Magrane	.05	.02
☐ 146 Pedro Guerrero	.10	.05
☐ 147 Robin Yount	.30	.14
☐ 148 Dan Gladden	.05	.02
☐ 149 Steve Sax	.05	.02
☐ 150A Clark/Mitchell Will Clark Kevin Mitchell	1.50	.70
☐ 150B Bay Bombers Will Clark Kevin Mitchell	.30	.14

1990 Classic Update

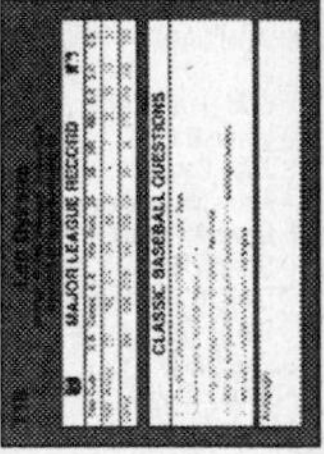

The 1990 Classic Update set was the second set issued by the Classic Game company in 1990. Sometimes referenced as Classic Pink or Red, this set includes a Juan Gonzalez card. This 50-card, standard-size set was issued in late June of 1990. With a few exceptions, the set numbering is in alphabetical order by player's name.

	MINT	NRMT
COMPLETE SET (50)	6.00	2.70
COMMON CARD (T1-T49)	.10	.05

	MINT	NRMT
☐ T1 Gregg Jefferies	.20	.09
☐ T2 Steve Adkins	.10	.05
☐ T3 Sandy Alomar Jr.	.30	.14
☐ T4 Steve Avery	.10	.05
☐ T5 Mike Blowers	.10	.05
☐ T6 George Brett	.60	.25
☐ T7 Tom Browning	.10	.05
☐ T8 Ellis Burks	.30	.14
☐ T9 Joe Carter	.40	.18
☐ T10 Jerald Clark	.10	.05
☐ T11 Hot Corners HOR Matt Williams Will Clark	.50	.23
☐ T12 Pat Combs	.10	.05
☐ T13 Scott Cooper	.10	.05
☐ T14 Mark Davis	.10	.05
☐ T15 Storm Davis	.10	.05
☐ T16 Larry Walker	1.50	.70
☐ T17 Brian DuBois	.10	.05
☐ T18 Len Dykstra	.20	.09
☐ T19 John Franco	.10	.05
☐ T20 Kirk Gibson	.20	.09
☐ T21 Juan Gonzalez	2.00	.90
☐ T22 Tommy Greene	.10	.05
☐ T23 Kent Hrbek	.10	.05
☐ T24 Mike Huff	.10	.05
☐ T25 Bo Jackson	.20	.09
☐ T26 Nolan Ryan Nolan Knows Bo	2.00	.90
☐ T27 Roberto Kelly	.10	.05
☐ T28 Mark Langston	.10	.05

Card	MINT	NRMT
☐ T29 Ray Lankford	.75	.35
☐ T30 Kevin Maas	.10	.05
☐ T31 Julio Machado	.10	.05
☐ T32 Greg Maddux	1.50	.70
☐ T33 Mark McGwire	1.00	.45
☐ T34 Paul Molitor	.50	.23
☐ T35 Hal Morris	.20	.09
☐ T36 Dale Murphy	.40	.18
☐ T37 Eddie Murray	.40	.18
☐ T38 Jaime Navarro	.10	.05
☐ T39 Dean Palmer	.50	.23
☐ T40 Derek Parks	.10	.05
☐ T41 Bobby Rose	.10	.05
☐ T42 Wally Joyner	.20	.09
☐ T43 Chris Sabo	.10	.05
☐ T44 Benito Santiago	.10	.05
☐ T45 Mike Stanton	.10	.05
☐ T46 Terry Steinbach UER	.20	.09
Career BA .725		
☐ T47 Dave Stewart	.10	.05
☐ T48 Greg Swindell	.10	.05
☐ T49 Jose Vizcaino	.10	.05
☐ NNO Royal Flush		
Mark Davis		
Bret Saberhagen		
(Instructions on back)		

1990 Classic Yellow

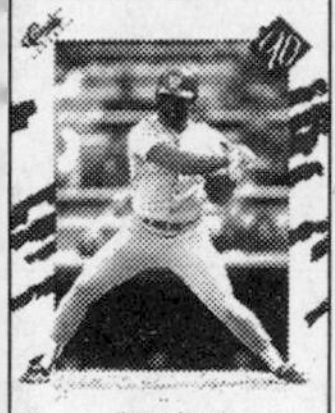

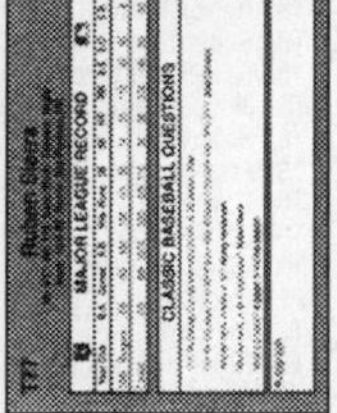

The 1990 Classic III set is also referenced as Classic Yellow. This set also featured number one draft picks of the current year mixed with the other Classic cards. This 100-card standard-size set also contained a special Nolan Ryan commemorative card, Texas Heat. A very early card of Chipper Jones is included in this set. Card T51 was never issued.

	MINT	NRMT
COMPLETE SET (100)	8.00	3.60
COMMON CARD (T1-T100)	.05	.02
☐ T1 Ken Griffey Jr.	2.50	1.10
☐ T2 John Tudor	.05	.02
☐ T3 John Kruk	.10	.05
☐ T4 Mark Gardner	.05	.02
☐ T5 Scott Radinsky	.05	.02
☐ T6 John Burkett	.05	.02
☐ T7 Will Clark	.40	.18
☐ T8 Gary Carter	.20	.09
☐ T9 Ted Higuera	.05	.02
☐ T10 Dave Parker	.05	.02
☐ T11 Dante Bichette	.40	.18
☐ T12 Don Mattingly	.75	.35
☐ T13 Greg Harris	.05	.02
☐ T14 Dave Hollins	.05	.02
☐ T15 Matt Nokes	.05	.02
☐ T16 Kevin Tapani	.05	.02
☐ T17 Shane Mack	.05	.02
☐ T18 Randy Myers	.05	.02
☐ T19 Greg Olson	.05	.02
☐ T20 Shawn Abner	.05	.02
☐ T21 Jim Presley	.05	.02
☐ T22 Randy Johnson	.60	.25
☐ T23 Edgar Martinez	.50	.23
☐ T24 Scott Coolbaugh	.05	.02
☐ T25 Jeff Treadway	.05	.02
☐ T26 Joe Klink	.05	.02
☐ T27 Rickey Henderson	.30	.14
☐ T28 Sam Horn	.05	.02
☐ T29 Kurt Stillwell	.05	.02
☐ T30 Andy Van Slyke	.05	.02
☐ T31 Willie Banks	.05	.02
☐ T32 Jose Canseco	.30	.14
☐ T33 Felix Jose	.05	.02
☐ T34 Candy Maldonado	.05	.02
☐ T35 Carlos Baerga	.50	.23
☐ T36 Keith Hernandez	.10	.05
☐ T37 Frank Viola	.05	.02
☐ T38 Pete O'Brien	.05	.02
☐ T39 Pat Borders	.05	.02
☐ T40 Mike Heath	.05	.02
☐ T41 Kevin Brown	.20	.09
☐ T42 Chris Bosio	.05	.02
☐ T43 Shawn Boskie	.05	.02
☐ T44 Carlos Quintana	.05	.02
☐ T45 Juan Samuel	.05	.02
☐ T46 Tim Layana	.05	.02
☐ T47 Mike Harkey	.05	.02
☐ T48 Gerald Perry	.05	.02
☐ T49 Mike Witt	.05	.02
☐ T50 Joe Orsulak	.05	.02
☐ T52 Willie Blair	.05	.02
☐ T53 Gene Larkin	.05	.02
☐ T54 Jody Reed	.05	.02
☐ T55 Jeff Reardon	.05	.02
☐ T56 Kevin McReynolds	.05	.02
☐ T57 Mike Marshall	.05	.02
Unnumbered		
game instructions on back		
☐ T58 Eric Yelding	.05	.02
☐ T59 Fred Lynn	.05	.02
☐ T60 Jim Leyritz	.30	.14
☐ T61 John Orton	.05	.02
☐ T62 Mike Lieberthal	.05	.02
☐ T63 Mike Hartley	.05	.02
☐ T64 Kal Daniels	.05	.02
☐ T65 Terry Shumpert	.05	.02
☐ T66 Sil Campusano	.05	.02
☐ T67 Tony Pena	.05	.02
☐ T68 Barry Bonds	.50	.23
☐ T69 Roger McDowell	.05	.02
☐ T70 Kelly Gruber	.05	.02
☐ T71 Willie Randolph	.05	.02
☐ T72 Rick Parker	.05	.02
☐ T73 Bobby Bonilla	.10	.05
☐ T74 Jack Armstrong	.05	.02
☐ T75 Hubie Brooks	.05	.02
☐ T76 Sandy Alomar Jr.	.20	.09
☐ T77 Ruben Sierra	.05	.02
☐ T78 Erik Hanson	.05	.02
☐ T79 Tony Phillips	.05	.02
☐ T80 Rondell White	.75	.35
☐ T81 Bobby Thigpen	.05	.02
☐ T82 Ron Walden	.05	.02
☐ T83 Don Peters	.05	.02
☐ T84 Nolan Ryan 6th	1.50	.70
☐ T85 Lance Dickson	.05	.02
☐ T86 Ryne Sandberg	.60	.25
☐ T87 Eric Christopherson	.05	.02
☐ T88 Shane Andrews	.10	.05
☐ T89 Marc Newfield	.40	.18
☐ T90 Adam Hyzdu	.05	.02
☐ T91 Texas Heat	1.00	.45
Nolan Ryan		
Reid Ryan		
☐ T92 Chipper Jones	3.00	1.35
☐ T93 Frank Thomas	2.50	1.10
☐ T94 Cecil Fielder	.10	.05
☐ T95 Delino DeShields	.40	.18
☐ T96 John Olerud	.40	.18
☐ T97 Dave Justice	1.00	.45
☐ T98 Joe Oliver	.05	.02
☐ T99 Alex Fernandez	.30	.14
☐ T100 Todd Hundley	.30	.14
☐ NNO0 Micro Players	.40	.18
Frank Viola		
Texas Heat		
Don Mattingly		
Chipper Jones		
(Blue blank back)		

1991 Classic Game

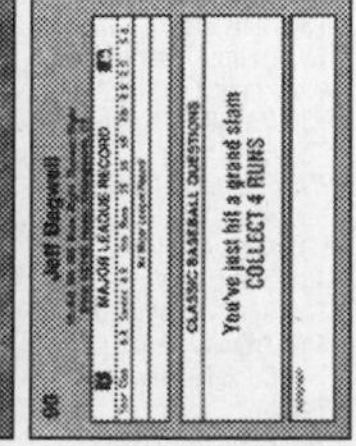

The 1991 Classic Baseball Collector's Edition board game is Classic's first Big Game issue since the 1989 Big Game. 100,000 games were produced, and each one included a board game, action spinner, eight stand-up baseball player pieces, action scoreboard, eight-page picture book with tips from five great baseball players (Carew, Spahn, Schmidt, Brock, and Aaron), 200 player cards, and a certificate of limited edition. The standard-size cards have on the fronts glossy color action photos bordered in purple. The backs are purple and white and have biography, statistics, five trivia questions, and an autograph slot.

	MINT	NRMT
COMPLETE SET (200)	20.00	9.00
COMMON CARD (1-200)	.05	.02
☐ 1 Frank Viola	.05	.02
☐ 2 Tim Wallach	.05	.02
☐ 3 Lou Whitaker	.10	.05
☐ 4 Brett Butler	.10	.05
☐ 5 Jim Abbott	.10	.05
☐ 6 Jack Armstrong	.05	.02
☐ 7 Craig Biggio	.40	.18
☐ 8 Brian Barnes	.05	.02
☐ 9 Dennis(Oil Can) Boyd	.05	.02
☐ 10 Tom Browning	.05	.02
☐ 11 Tom Brunansky	.05	.02
☐ 12 Ellis Burks	.20	.09
☐ 13 Harold Baines	.05	.02
☐ 14 Kal Daniels	.05	.02
☐ 15 Mark Davis	.05	.02
☐ 16 Storm Davis	.05	.02
☐ 17 Tom Glavine	.30	.14
☐ 18 Mike Greenwell	.05	.02
☐ 19 Kelly Gruber	.05	.02
☐ 20 Mark Gubicza	.05	.02
☐ 21 Pedro Guerrero	.05	.02
☐ 22 Mike Harkey	.05	.02
☐ 23 Orel Hershiser	.10	.05
☐ 24 Ted Higuera	.05	.02
☐ 25 Von Hayes	.05	.02
☐ 26 Andre Dawson	.20	.09
☐ 27 Shawon Dunston	.05	.02
☐ 28 Roberto Kelly	.05	.02
☐ 29 Joe Magrane	.05	.02
☐ 30 Dennis Martinez	.10	.05
☐ 31 Kevin McReynolds	.05	.02
☐ 32 Matt Nokes	.05	.02
☐ 33 Dan Plesac	.05	.02
☐ 34 Dave Parker	.10	.05
☐ 35 Randy Johnson	.75	.35
☐ 36 Bret Saberhagen	.05	.02
☐ 37 Mackey Sasser	.05	.02
☐ 38 Mike Scott	.05	.02
☐ 39 Ozzie Smith	.75	.35
☐ 40 Kevin Seitzer	.05	.02
☐ 41 Ruben Sierra	.05	.02
☐ 42 Kevin Tapani	.05	.02
☐ 43 Danny Tartabull	.05	.02
☐ 44 Robby Thompson	.05	.02
☐ 45 Andy Van Slyke	.05	.02
☐ 46 Greg Vaughn	.05	.02
☐ 47 Harold Reynolds	.10	.05
☐ 48 Will Clark	.40	.18
☐ 49 Gary Gaetti	.10	.05
☐ 50 Joe Grahe	.05	.02
☐ 51 Carlton Fisk	.40	.18
☐ 52 Robin Ventura	.30	.14
☐ 53 Ozzie Guillen	.05	.02
☐ 54 Tom Candiotti	.05	.02
☐ 55 Doug Jones	.05	.02
☐ 56 Eric King	.05	.02
☐ 57 Kirk Gibson	.10	.05
☐ 58 Tim Costo	.05	.02
☐ 59 Robin Yount	.30	.14
☐ 60 Sammy Sosa	.75	.35
☐ 61 Jesse Barfield	.05	.02
☐ 62 Marc Newfield	.20	.09
☐ 63 Jimmy Key	.05	.02
☐ 64 Felix Jose	.05	.02
☐ 65 Mark Whiten	.05	.02
☐ 66 Tommy Greene	.05	.02
☐ 67 Kent Mercker	.05	.02
☐ 68 Greg Maddux	2.00	.90
☐ 69 Danny Jackson	.05	.02
☐ 70 Reggie Sanders	.30	.14
☐ 71 Eric Yelding	.05	.02
☐ 72 Karl Rhodes	.05	.02
☐ 73 Fernando Valenzuela	.10	.05
☐ 74 Chris Nabholz	.05	.02
☐ 75 Andres Galarraga	.30	.14
☐ 76 Howard Johnson	.05	.02
☐ 77 Hubie Brooks	.05	.02
☐ 78 Terry Mulholland	.05	.02
☐ 79 Paul Molitor	.40	.18
☐ 80 Roger McDowell	.05	.02
☐ 81 Darren Daulton	.10	.05
☐ 82 Zane Smith	.05	.02
☐ 83 Ray Lankford	.30	.14
☐ 84 Bruce Hurst	.05	.02
☐ 85 Andy Benes	.10	.05
☐ 86 John Burkett	.05	.02
☐ 87 Dave Righetti	.05	.02
☐ 88 Steve Karsay	.10	.05
☐ 89 D.J. Dozier	.05	.02
☐ 90 Jeff Bagwell	2.00	.90
☐ 91 Joe Carter	.20	.09
☐ 92 Wes Chamberlain	.05	.02
☐ 93 Vince Coleman	.05	.02

☐ 94 Pat Combs .05 .02
☐ 95 Jerome Walton .05 .02
☐ 96 Jeff Conine .50 .23
☐ 97 Alan Trammell .20 .09
☐ 98 Don Mattingly 1.50 .70
☐ 99 Ramon Martinez .10 .05
☐ 100 Dave Magadan .05 .02
☐ 101 Greg Swindell UER .05 .02
Misnumbered as T10
☐ 102 Dave Stewart .05 .02
☐ 103 Gary Sheffield .30 .14
☐ 104 George Bell .05 .02
☐ 105 Mark Grace .40 .18
☐ 106 Steve Sax .05 .02
☐ 107 Ryne Sandberg 1.00 .45
☐ 108 Chris Sabo .05 .02
☐ 109 Jose Rijo .05 .02
☐ 110 Cal Ripken 2.00 .90
☐ 111 Kirby Puckett 1.25 .55
☐ 112 Eddie Murray .75 .35
☐ 113 Roberto Alomar .60 .25
☐ 114 Randy Myers .05 .02
☐ 115 Rafael Palmeiro .20 .09
☐ 116 John Olerud .10 .05
☐ 117 Gregg Jefferies .10 .05
☐ 118 Kent Hrbek .05 .02
☐ 119 Marquis Grissom .20 .09
☐ 120 Ken Griffey Jr. 3.00 1.35
☐ 121 Dwight Gooden .10 .05
☐ 122 Juan Gonzalez 1.50 .70
☐ 123 Ron Gant .10 .05
☐ 124 Travis Fryman .10 .05
☐ 125 John Franco .05 .02
☐ 126 Dennis Eckersley .20 .09
☐ 127 Cecil Fielder .10 .05
☐ 128 Phil Plantier .05 .02
☐ 129 Kevin Mitchell .05 .02
☐ 130 Kevin Maas .05 .02
☐ 131 Mark McGwire 1.50 .70
☐ 132 Ben McDonald .05 .02
☐ 133 Len Dykstra .10 .05
☐ 134 Delino DeShields .10 .05
☐ 135 Jose Canseco .40 .18
☐ 136 Eric Davis .05 .02
☐ 137 George Brett 1.50 .70
☐ 138 Steve Avery .05 .02
☐ 139 Eric Anthony .05 .02
☐ 140 Bobby Thigpen .05 .02
☐ 141 Ken Griffey Sr. .10 .05
☐ 142 Barry Larkin .40 .18
☐ 143 Jeff Brantley .05 .02
☐ 144 Bobby Bonilla .10 .05
☐ 145 Jose Offerman .05 .02
☐ 146 Mike Mussina 1.00 .45
☐ 147 Erik Hanson .05 .02
☐ 148 Dale Murphy .40 .18
☐ 149 Roger Clemens 1.00 .45
☐ 150 Tino Martinez .75 .35
☐ 151 Todd Van Poppel .05 .02
☐ 152 Mo Vaughn 1.00 .45
☐ 153 Derrick May .10 .05
☐ 154 Jack Clark .05 .02
☐ 155 Dave Hansen .05 .02
☐ 156 Tony Gwynn 1.50 .70
☐ 157 Brian McRae .40 .18
☐ 158 Matt Williams .30 .14
☐ 159 Kirk Dressendorfer .05 .02
☐ 160 Scott Erickson .05 .02
☐ 161 Tony Fernandez .05 .02
☐ 162 Willie McGee .10 .05
☐ 163 Fred McGriff .20 .09
☐ 164 Leo Gomez .05 .02
☐ 165 Bernard Gilkey .10 .05
☐ 166 Bobby Witt .05 .02
☐ 167 Doug Drabek .05 .02
☐ 168 Rob Dibble .05 .02
☐ 169 Glenn Davis .05 .02
☐ 170 Danny Darwin .05 .02
☐ 171 Eric Karros .75 .35
☐ 172 Eddie Zosky .05 .02
☐ 173 Todd Zeile .05 .02
☐ 174 Tim Raines .10 .05
☐ 175 Benito Santiago .05 .02
☐ 176 Dan Peltier .05 .02
☐ 177 Darryl Strawberry .10 .05
☐ 178 Hal Morris .10 .05
☐ 179 Hensley Meulens .05 .02
☐ 180 John Smoltz .60 .25
☐ 181 Frank Thomas 3.00 1.35
☐ 182 Dave Staton .05 .02
☐ 183 Scott Chiamparino .05 .02
☐ 184 Alex Fernandez .10 .05
☐ 185 Mark Lewis .05 .02
☐ 186 Bo Jackson .10 .05
☐ 187 Mickey Morandini UER .10 .05
Photo is Darren Daulton
☐ 188 Cory Snyder .05 .02
☐ 189 Rickey Henderson .30 .14
☐ 190 Junior Felix .05 .02
☐ 191 Milt Cuyler .05 .02
☐ 192 Wade Boggs .30 .14
☐ 193 Dave Justice .40 .18
Justice Prevails
☐ 194 Sandy Alomar Jr. .20 .09
☐ 195 Barry Bonds .75 .35
☐ 196 Nolan Ryan 2.50 1.10
☐ 197 Rico Brogna .10 .05
☐ 198 Steve Decker .05 .02
☐ 199 Bob Welch .05 .02
☐ 200 Andujar Cedeno .05 .02

1991 Classic I

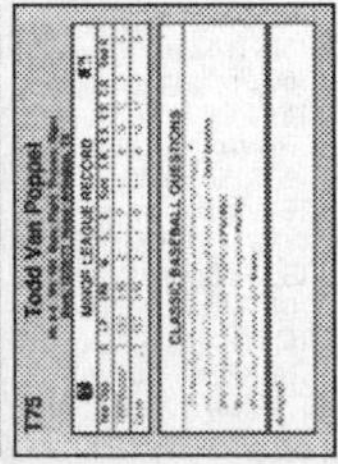

This 100-card standard-size set features many of the most popular players in the game of baseball as well as some of the more exciting prospects. The set includes trivia questions on the backs of the cards. For the most part the set is arranged alphabetically by team and then alphabetically by players within that team.

	MINT	NRMT
COMPLETE SET (100)	7.50	3.40
COMMON CARD (T1-T99)	.05	.02

☐ T1 John Olerud .20 .09
☐ T2 Tino Martinez .40 .18
☐ T3 Ken Griffey Jr. 2.00 .90
☐ T4 Jeromy Burnitz .50 .23
☐ T5 Ron Gant .10 .05
☐ T6 Mike Benjamin .05 .02
☐ T7 Steve Decker .05 .02
☐ T8 Matt Williams .30 .14
☐ T9 Rafael Novoa .05 .02
☐ T10 Kevin Mitchell .05 .02
☐ T11 Dave Justice .30 .14
☐ T12 Leo Gomez .05 .02
☐ T13 Chris Hoiles .10 .05
☐ T14 Ben McDonald .05 .02
☐ T15 David Segui .10 .05
☐ T16 Anthony Telford .05 .02
☐ T17 Mike Mussina .75 .35
☐ T18 Roger Clemens 1.00 .45
☐ T19 Wade Boggs .50 .23
☐ T20 Tim Naehring .10 .05
☐ T21 Joe Carter .20 .09
☐ T22 Phil Plantier .10 .05
☐ T23 Rob Dibble .05 .02
☐ T24 Mo Vaughn .75 .35
☐ T25 Lee Stevens .05 .02
☐ T26 Chris Sabo .05 .02
☐ T27 Mark Grace .30 .14
☐ T28 Derrick May .05 .02
☐ T29 Ryne Sandberg .50 .23
☐ T30 Matt Stark .05 .02
☐ T31 Bobby Thigpen .05 .02
☐ T32 Frank Thomas 2.00 .90
☐ T33 Don Mattingly .75 .35
☐ T34 Eric Davis .05 .02
☐ T35 Reggie Jefferson .40 .18
☐ T36 Alex Cole .05 .02
☐ T37 Mark Lewis .10 .05
☐ T38 Tim Costo .05 .02
☐ T39 Sandy Alomar Jr. .10 .05
☐ T40 Travis Fryman .20 .09
☐ T41 Cecil Fielder .10 .05
☐ T42 Milt Cuyler .05 .02
☐ T43 Andujar Cedeno .05 .02
☐ T44 Danny Darwin .05 .02
☐ T45 Randy Hennis .05 .02
☐ T46 George Brett .50 .23
☐ T47 Jeff Conine .40 .18
☐ T48 Bo Jackson .10 .05
☐ T49 Brian McRae .30 .14
☐ T50 Brent Mayne .05 .02
☐ T51 Eddie Murray .40 .18
☐ T52 Ramon Martinez .20 .09
☐ T53 Jim Neidlinger .05 .02
☐ T54 Jim Poole .05 .02
☐ T55 Tim McIntosh .05 .02
☐ T56 Randy Veres .05 .02
☐ T57 Kirby Puckett .75 .35
☐ T58 Todd Ritchie .05 .02
☐ T59 Rich Garces .05 .02
☐ T60 Moises Alou .50 .23
☐ T61 Delino DeShields .10 .05
☐ T62 Oscar Azocar .05 .02
☐ T63 Kevin Maas .05 .02
☐ T64 Alan Mills .05 .02
☐ T65 John Franco .10 .05
☐ T66 Chris Jelic .05 .02
☐ T67 Dave Magadan .05 .02
☐ T68 Darryl Strawberry .10 .05
☐ T69 Hensley Meulens .05 .02
☐ T70 Juan Gonzalez 1.00 .45
☐ T71 Reggie Harris .05 .02
☐ T72 Rickey Henderson .30 .14
☐ T73 Mark McGwire .75 .35
☐ T74 Willie McGee .10 .05
☐ T75 Todd Van Poppel .05 .02
☐ T76 Bob Welch .05 .02
☐ T77 Future Aces .05 .02
Todd Van Poppel
Don Peters
David Zancanaro
Kirk Dressendorfer
☐ T78 Len Dykstra .10 .05
☐ T79 Mickey Morandini .05 .02
☐ T80 Wes Chamberlain .05 .02
☐ T81 Barry Bonds .40 .18
☐ T82 Doug Drabek .05 .02
☐ T83 Randy Tomlin .05 .02
☐ T84 Scott Chiamparino .05 .02
☐ T85 Rafael Palmeiro .20 .09
☐ T86 Nolan Ryan 1.50 .70
☐ T87 Bobby Witt .05 .02
☐ T88 Fred McGriff .20 .09
☐ T89 Dave Stieb .05 .02
☐ T90 Ed Sprague .05 .02
☐ T91 Vince Coleman .05 .02
☐ T92 Rod Brewer .05 .02
☐ T93 Bernard Gilkey .10 .05
☐ T94 Roberto Alomar .40 .18
☐ T95 Chuck Finley .05 .02
☐ T96 Dale Murphy .30 .14
☐ T97 Jose Rijo .05 .02
☐ T98 Hal Morris .05 .02
☐ T99 Friendly Foes .10 .05
Darryl Strawberry
Dwight Gooden
Instructions on back
☐ NNO Todd Van Poppel .10 .05
Dave Justice
Ryne Sandberg
Kevin Maas
(Blank back)

1991 Classic II

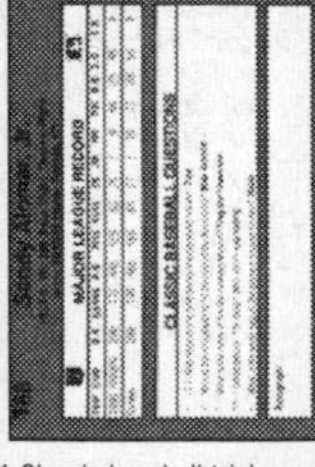

This second issue of the 1991 Classic baseball trivia game contains a small gameboard, accessories, 99 player cards with trivia questions on the backs, and one "4-in-1" micro player card. The cards measure the standard size and have on the fronts glossy color action photos with cranberry red borders. The backs are cranberry and white and have biography, statistics, five trivia questions, and an autograph slot.

	MINT	NRMT
COMPLETE SET (100)	7.50	3.40
COMMON CARD (T1-T100)	.05	.02

☐ T1 Ken Griffey Jr. 2.50 1.10
☐ T2 Wil Cordero .05 .02
☐ T3 Cal Ripken 1.50 .70
☐ T4 D.J. Dozier .05 .02
☐ T5 Darrin Fletcher .05 .02
☐ T6 Glenn Davis .05 .02
☐ T7 Alex Fernandez .10 .05
☐ T8 Cory Snyder .05 .02
☐ T9 Tim Raines .05 .02
☐ T10 Greg Swindell .05 .02
☐ T11 Mark Lewis .10 .05
☐ T12 Rico Brogna .10 .05

☐ T13 Gary Sheffield .40 .18
☐ T14 Paul Molitor .40 .18
☐ T15 Kent Hrbek .05 .02
☐ T16 Scott Erickson .05 .02
☐ T17 Steve Sax .05 .02
☐ T18 Dennis Eckersley .20 .09
☐ T19 Jose Canseco .30 .14
☐ T20 Kirk Dressendorfer .05 .02
☐ T21 Ken Griffey Sr. .05 .02
☐ T22 Erik Hanson .05 .02
☐ T23 Dan Peltier .05 .02
☐ T24 John Olerud .10 .05
☐ T25 Eddie Zosky .05 .02
☐ T26 Steve Avery .05 .02
☐ T27 John Smoltz .40 .18
☐ T28 Frank Thomas 2.00 .90
☐ T29 Jerome Walton .05 .02
☐ T30 George Bell .05 .02
☐ T31 Jose Rijo .05 .02
☐ T32 Randy Myers .05 .02
☐ T33 Barry Larkin .30 .14
☐ T34 Eric Anthony .05 .02
☐ T35 Dave Hansen .05 .02
☐ T36 Eric Karros .35 .16
☐ T37 Jose Offerman .05 .02
☐ T38 Marquis Grissom .10 .05
☐ T39 Dwight Gooden .10 .05
☐ T40 Gregg Jefferies .10 .05
☐ T41 Pat Combs .05 .02
☐ T42 Todd Zeile .05 .02
☐ T43 Benito Santiago .05 .02
☐ T44 Dave Staton .05 .02
☐ T45 Tony Fernandez .05 .02
☐ T46 Fred McGriff .30 .14
☐ T47 Jeff Brantley .05 .02
☐ T48 Junior Felix .05 .02
☐ T49 Jack Morris .05 .02
☐ T50 Chris George .05 .02
☐ T51 Henry Rodriguez .10 .05
☐ T52 Paul Marak .05 .02
☐ T53 Ryan Klesko 1.00 .45
☐ T54 Darren Lewis .05 .02
☐ T55 Lance Dickson .05 .02
☐ T56 Anthony Young .05 .02
☐ T57 Willie Banks .05 .02
☐ T58 Mike Bordick .10 .05
☐ T59 Roger Salkeld .05 .02
☐ T60 Steve Karsay .10 .05
☐ T61 Bernie Williams .40 .18
☐ T62 Mickey Tettleton .05 .02
☐ T63 Dave Justice .30 .14
☐ T64 Steve Decker .05 .02
☐ T65 Roger Clemens .75 .35
☐ T66 Phil Plantier .10 .05
☐ T67 Ryne Sandberg .50 .23
☐ T68 Sandy Alomar Jr. .10 .05
☐ T69 Cecil Fielder .10 .05
☐ T70 George Brett .75 .35
☐ T71 Delino DeShields .10 .05
☐ T72 Dave Magadan .05 .02
☐ T73 Darryl Strawberry .10 .05
☐ T74 Juan Gonzalez .75 .35
☐ T75 Rickey Henderson .30 .14
☐ T76 Willie McGee .10 .05
☐ T77 Todd Van Poppel .05 .02
☐ T78 Barry Bonds .50 .23
☐ T79 Doug Drabek .05 .02
☐ T80 Nolan Ryan .75 .35
300 Game Winner
☐ T81 Roberto Alomar .40 .18
☐ T82 Ivan Rodriguez .75 .35
☐ T83 Dan Opperman .05 .02
☐ T84 Jeff Bagwell 1.50 .70
☐ T85 Braulio Castillo .05 .02
☐ T86 Doug Simons .05 .02
☐ T87 Wade Taylor .05 .02
☐ T88 Gary Scott .05 .02
☐ T89 Dave Stewart .05 .02
☐ T90 Mike Simms .05 .02
☐ T91 Luis Gonzalez .30 .14
☐ T92 Bobby Bonilla .10 .05
☐ T93 Tony Gwynn .75 .35
☐ T94 Will Clark .40 .18
☐ T95 Rich Rowland .05 .02
☐ T96 Alan Trammell .20 .09
☐ T97 Strikeout Kings .60 .25
Nolan Ryan
Roger Clemens
☐ T98 Joe Carter .10 .05
☐ T99 Jack Clark .05 .02
☐ T100 Steve Decker .05 .02

1991 Classic III

The third issue of the 1991 Classic baseball trivia game contains a small gameboard, accessories, 99 player cards with trivia questions on the backs, and one "4-in-1" micro

player card. The cards measure the standard size and have on the fronts glossy color action photos with grayish-green borders. In a horizontal format, the backs feature biography, statistics, and five trivia questions. This information is superimposed over the team logo. The card numbers on the back appear in a green stripe. With few exceptions, the cards are arranged in alphabetical order.

	MINT	NRMT
COMPLETE SET (100)	10.00	4.50
COMMON CARD (T1-T99)	.05	.02

☐ T1 Jim Abbott .10 .05
☐ T2 Craig Biggio .40 .18
☐ T3 Wade Boggs .30 .14
☐ T4 Bobby Bonilla .10 .05
☐ T5 Ivan Calderon .05 .02
☐ T6 Jose Canseco .30 .14
☐ T7 Andy Benes .10 .05
☐ T8 Wes Chamberlain .05 .02
☐ T9 Will Clark .40 .18
☐ T10 Royce Clayton .10 .05
☐ T11 Gerald Alexander .05 .02
☐ T12 Chili Davis .10 .05
☐ T13 Eric Davis .10 .05
☐ T14 Andre Dawson .20 .09
☐ T15 Rob Dibble .05 .02
☐ T16 Chris Donnels .05 .02
☐ T17 Scott Erickson .05 .02
☐ T18 Monty Fariss .05 .02
☐ T19 Ruben Amaro Jr. .05 .02
☐ T20 Chuck Finley .05 .02
☐ T21 Carlton Fisk .30 .14
☐ T22 Carlos Baerga .10 .05
☐ T23 Ron Gant .10 .05
☐ T24 Dave Justice .10 .05
and Ron Gant
☐ T25 Mike Gardiner .05 .02
☐ T26 Tom Glavine .30 .14
☐ T27 Joe Grahe .05 .02
☐ T28 Derek Bell .20 .09
☐ T29 Mike Greenwell .05 .02
☐ T30 Ken Griffey Jr. 2.50 1.10
☐ T31 Leo Gomez .05 .02
☐ T32 Tom Goodwin .05 .02
☐ T33 Tony Gwynn 1.00 .45
☐ T34 Mel Hall .05 .02
☐ T35 Brian Harper .05 .02
☐ T36 Dave Henderson .05 .02
☐ T37 Albert Belle .75 .35
☐ T38 Orel Hershiser .10 .05
☐ T39 Brian Hunter .05 .02
☐ T40 Howard Johnson .05 .02
☐ T41 Felix Jose .05 .02
☐ T42 Wally Joyner .10 .05
☐ T43 Jeff Juden .05 .02
☐ T44 Pat Kelly .05 .02
☐ T45 Jimmy Key .10 .05
☐ T46 Chuck Knoblauch .60 .25
☐ T47 John Kruk .10 .05
☐ T48 Ray Lankford .30 .14
☐ T49 Ced Landrum .05 .02
☐ T50 Scott Livingstone .05 .02
☐ T51 Kevin Maas .05 .02
☐ T52 Greg Maddux 1.50 .70
☐ T53 Dennis Martinez .05 .02
☐ T54 Edgar Martinez .20 .09
☐ T55 Pedro Martinez 1.00 .45
☐ T56 Don Mattingly 1.00 .45
☐ T57 Orlando Merced .05 .02
☐ T58 Keith Mitchell .05 .02
☐ T59 Kevin Mitchell .05 .02
☐ T60 Paul Molitor .40 .18
☐ T61 Jack Morris .10 .05
☐ T62 Hal Morris .05 .02
☐ T63 Kevin Morton .05 .02
☐ T64 Pedro Munoz .05 .02
☐ T65 Eddie Murray .40 .18
☐ T66 Jack McDowell .05 .02
☐ T67 Jeff McNeely .05 .02
☐ T68 Brian McRae .30 .14
☐ T69 Kevin McReynolds .05 .02
☐ T70 Gregg Olson .05 .02
☐ T71 Rafael Palmeiro .20 .09
☐ T72 Dean Palmer .10 .05
☐ T73 Tony Phillips .05 .02
☐ T74 Kirby Puckett .75 .35
☐ T75 Carlos Quintana .05 .02
☐ T76 Pat Rice .05 .02
☐ T77 Cal Ripken 1.50 .70
☐ T78 Ivan Rodriguez 1.25 .55
☐ T79 Nolan Ryan Number 7 1.00 .45
☐ T80 Bret Saberhagen .05 .02
☐ T81 Tim Salmon 1.00 .45
☐ T82 Juan Samuel .05 .02
☐ T83 Ruben Sierra .05 .02
☐ T84 Heathcliff Slocumb .10 .05
☐ T85 Joe Slusarski .05 .02
☐ T86 John Smiley .05 .02
☐ T87 Dave Smith .05 .02
☐ T88 Ed Sprague .05 .02
☐ T89 Todd Stottlemyre .05 .02
☐ T90 Mike Timlin .10 .05
☐ T91 Greg Vaughn .05 .02
☐ T92 Frank Viola .05 .02
☐ T93 Chico Walker .05 .02
☐ T94 Devon White .05 .02
☐ T95 Matt Williams .30 .14
☐ T96 Rick Wilkins .05 .02
☐ T97 Bernie Williams .40 .18
☐ T98 Starter and Stopper .75 .35
Nolan Ryan
Goose Gossage
☐ T99 Gerald Williams .05 .02
☐ NNO 4-in-1 Card .50 .23
Bobby Bonilla
Will Clark
Cal Ripken
Scott Erickson

1992 Classic Game

The 1992 Classic Baseball Collector's Edition game contains 200 standard-size cards. The cards were issued in two boxes labeled "Trivia Cards A" and "Trivia Cards B." The game also included an official Major League Action Spinner, eight stand-up baseball hero player pieces, an action scoreboard, a hand-illustrated game board, and a collectible book featuring tips from a new group of baseball legends. According to Classic, production has been limited to 125,000 games. The fronts display glossy color action photos bordered in dark purple. The Classic logo and the year "1992" appear in the top border, while the player's name is given in white lettering in the bottom border. The horizontally oriented backs present biography, statistics (1991 and career), and five baseball trivia questions.

	MINT	NRMT
COMPLETE SET (200)	18.00	8.00
COMMON CARD (1-200)	.10	.05

☐ 1 Chuck Finley .10 .05
☐ 2 Craig Biggio .40 .18
☐ 3 Luis Gonzalez .10 .05
☐ 4 Pete Harnisch .10 .05
☐ 5 Jeff Juden .10 .05
☐ 6 Harold Baines .10 .05
☐ 7 Kirk Dressendorfer .10 .05
☐ 8 Dennis Eckersley .30 .14
☐ 9 Dave Henderson .10 .05
☐ 10 Dave Stewart .10 .05
☐ 11 Joe Carter .20 .09
☐ 12 Juan Guzman .10 .05
☐ 13 Dave Stieb .10 .05
☐ 14 Todd Stottlemyre .10 .05
☐ 15 Ron Gant .20 .09
☐ 16 Brian Hunter .10 .05
☐ 17 Dave Justice .40 .18
☐ 18 John Smoltz .30 .14
☐ 19 Mike Stanton .10 .05
☐ 20 Chris George .10 .05
☐ 21 Paul Molitor .40 .18
☐ 22 Omar Olivares .10 .05
☐ 23 Lee Smith .10 .05
☐ 24 Ozzie Smith .50 .23

☐ 25 Todd Zeile	.10	.05
☐ 26 George Bell	.10	.05
☐ 27 Andre Dawson	.30	.14
☐ 28 Shawon Dunston	.10	.05
☐ 29 Mark Grace	.30	.14
☐ 30 Greg Maddux	1.50	.70
☐ 31 Dave Smith	.10	.05
☐ 32 Brett Butler	.20	.09
☐ 33 Orel Hershiser	.20	.09
☐ 34 Eric Karros	.40	.18
☐ 35 Ramon Martinez	.20	.09
☐ 36 Jose Offerman	.10	.05
☐ 37 Juan Samuel	.10	.05
☐ 38 Delino DeShields	.10	.05
☐ 39 Marquis Grissom	.20	.09
☐ 40 Tim Wallach	.10	.05
☐ 41 Eric Gunderson	.10	.05
☐ 42 Willie McGee	.20	.09
☐ 43 Dave Righetti	.10	.05
☐ 44 Robby Thompson	.10	.05
☐ 45 Matt Williams	.30	.14
☐ 46 Sandy Alomar Jr.	.20	.09
☐ 47 Reggie Jefferson	.10	.05
☐ 48 Mark Lewis	.10	.05
☐ 49 Robin Ventura	.20	.09
☐ 50 Tino Martinez	.40	.18
☐ 51 Roberto Kelly	.10	.05
☐ 52 Vince Coleman	.10	.05
☐ 53 Dwight Gooden	.20	.09
☐ 54 Todd Hundley	.20	.09
☐ 55 Kevin Maas	.10	.05
☐ 56 Wade Taylor	.10	.05
☐ 57 Bryan Harvey	.10	.05
☐ 58 Leo Gomez	.10	.05
☐ 59 Ben McDonald	.10	.05
☐ 60 Ricky Bones	.10	.05
☐ 61 Tony Gwynn	.75	.35
☐ 62 Benito Santiago	.10	.05
☐ 63 Wes Chamberlain	.10	.05
☐ 64 Tommy Greene	.10	.05
☐ 65 Dale Murphy	.40	.18
☐ 66 Steve Buechele	.10	.05
☐ 67 Doug Drabek	.10	.05
☐ 68 Joe Grahe	.10	.05
☐ 69 Rafael Palmeiro	.30	.14
☐ 70 Wade Boggs	.40	.18
☐ 71 Ellis Burks	.20	.09
☐ 72 Mike Greenwell	.10	.05
☐ 73 Mo Vaughn	.60	.25
☐ 74 Derek Bell	.20	.09
☐ 75 Rob Dibble	.10	.05
☐ 76 Barry Larkin	.30	.14
☐ 77 Jose Rijo	.10	.05
☐ 78 Doug Henry	.10	.05
☐ 79 Chris Sabo	.10	.05
☐ 80 Pedro Guerrero	.10	.05
☐ 81 George Brett	.75	.35
☐ 82 Tom Gordon	.10	.05
☐ 83 Mark Gubicza	.10	.05
☐ 84 Mark Whiten	.10	.05
☐ 85 Brian McRae	.10	.05
☐ 86 Danny Jackson	.10	.05
☐ 87 Milt Cuyler	.10	.05
☐ 88 Travis Fryman	.20	.09
☐ 89 Mickey Tettleton	.10	.05
☐ 90 Alan Trammell	.30	.14
☐ 91 Lou Whitaker	.20	.09
☐ 92 Chili Davis	.20	.09
☐ 93 Scott Erickson	.10	.05
☐ 94 Kent Hrbek	.10	.05
☐ 95 Alex Fernandez	.20	.09
☐ 96 Carlton Fisk	.40	.18
☐ 97 Ramon Garcia	.10	.05
☐ 98 Ozzie Guillen	.10	.05
☐ 99 Tim Raines	.20	.09
☐ 100 Bobby Thigpen	.10	.05
☐ 101 Kirby Puckett	.75	.35
☐ 102 Bernie Williams	.40	.18
☐ 103 Dave Hansen	.10	.05
☐ 104 Kevin Tapani	.10	.05
☐ 105 Don Mattingly	1.00	.45
☐ 106 Frank Thomas	2.00	.90
☐ 107 Monty Fariss	.10	.05
☐ 108 Bo Jackson	.20	.09
☐ 109 Jim Abbott	.20	.09
☐ 110 Jose Canseco	.40	.18
☐ 111 Phil Plantier	.10	.05
☐ 112 Brian Williams	.10	.05
☐ 113 Mark Langston	.10	.05
☐ 114 Wilson Alvarez	.20	.09
☐ 115 Roberto Hernandez	.40	.18
☐ 116 Darryl Kile	.20	.09
☐ 117 Ryan Bowen	.10	.05
☐ 118 Rickey Henderson	.40	.18
☐ 119 Mark McGwire	1.00	.45
☐ 120 Devon White	.10	.05
☐ 121 Roberto Alomar	.40	.18
☐ 122 Kelly Gruber	.10	.05
☐ 123 Eddie Zosky	.10	.05
☐ 124 Tom Glavine	.30	.14
☐ 125 Kal Daniels	.10	.05
☐ 126 Cal Eldred	.10	.05
☐ 127 Deion Sanders	.40	.18
☐ 128 Robin Yount	.40	.18
☐ 129 Cecil Fielder	.20	.09
☐ 130 Ray Lankford	.30	.14
☐ 131 Ryne Sandberg	.50	.23
☐ 132 Darryl Strawberry	.20	.09
☐ 133 Chris Haney	.10	.05
☐ 134 Dennis Martinez	.20	.09
☐ 135 Bryan Hickerson	.10	.05
☐ 136 Will Clark	.30	.14
☐ 137 Hal Morris	.10	.05
☐ 138 Charles Nagy	.20	.09
☐ 139 Jim Thome	.75	.35
☐ 140 Albert Belle	.60	.25
☐ 141 Reggie Sanders	.20	.09
☐ 142 Scott Cooper	.10	.05
☐ 143 David Cone	.20	.09
☐ 144 Anthony Young	.10	.05
☐ 145 Howard Johnson	.10	.05
☐ 146 Arthur Rhodes	.10	.05
☐ 147 Scott Aldred	.10	.05
☐ 148 Mike Mussina	.75	.35
☐ 149 Fred McGriff	.30	.14
☐ 150 Andy Benes	.20	.09
☐ 151 Ruben Sierra	.10	.05
☐ 152 Len Dykstra	.20	.09
☐ 153 Andy Van Slyke	.10	.05
☐ 154 Orlando Merced	.10	.05
☐ 155 Barry Bonds	.50	.23
☐ 156 John Smiley	.10	.05
☐ 157 Julio Franco	.20	.09
☐ 158 Juan Gonzalez	1.25	.55
☐ 159 Ivan Rodriguez	.75	.35
☐ 160 Willie Banks	.10	.05
☐ 161 Eric Davis	.10	.05
☐ 162 Eddie Murray	.40	.18
☐ 163 Dave Fleming	.10	.05
☐ 164 Wally Joyner	.10	.05
☐ 165 Kevin Mitchell	.10	.05
☐ 166 Ed Taubensee	.10	.05
☐ 167 Danny Tartabull	.10	.05
☐ 168 Ken Hill	.10	.05
☐ 169 Willie Randolph	.10	.05
☐ 170 Kevin McReynolds	.10	.05
☐ 171 Gregg Jefferies	.20	.09
☐ 172 Patrick Lennon	.10	.05
☐ 173 Luis Mercedes	.10	.05
☐ 174 Glenn Davis	.10	.05
☐ 175 Bret Saberhagen	.10	.05
☐ 176 Bobby Bonilla	.20	.09
☐ 177 Kenny Lofton	1.25	.55
☐ 178 Jose Lind	.10	.05
☐ 179 Royce Clayton	.20	.09
☐ 180 Scott Scudder	.10	.05
☐ 181 Chuck Knoblauch	.50	.23
☐ 182 Terry Pendleton	.10	.05
☐ 183 Nolan Ryan	2.00	.90
☐ 184 Rob Maurer	.10	.05
☐ 185 Brian Bohanon	.10	.05
☐ 186 Ken Griffey Jr.	2.50	1.10
☐ 187 Jeff Bagwell	1.50	.70
☐ 188 Steve Avery	.10	.05
☐ 189 Roger Clemens	.75	.35
☐ 190 Cal Ripken	2.00	.90
☐ 191 Kim Batiste	.10	.05
☐ 192 Bip Roberts	.10	.05
☐ 193 Greg Swindell	.10	.05
☐ 194 Dave Winfield	.40	.18
☐ 195 Steve Sax	.10	.05
☐ 196 Frank Viola	.10	.05
☐ 197 Mo Sanford	.10	.05
☐ 198 Kyle Abbott	.10	.05
☐ 199 Jack Morris	.20	.09
☐ 200 Andy Ashby	.10	.05

1992 Classic I

The first issue of the 1992 Classic baseball trivia game contains a small gameboard, accessories, 99 player standard-size cards with trivia questions on the backs, one "4-in-1" micro player card, and four micro player pieces. The cards have on the fronts glossy color action photos bordered in white. A red, gray, and purple stripe with the year "1992" traverses the top of the card. In a horizontal format, the backs feature biography, statistics, and five trivia questions, printed on a ghosted image of the 26 major league city skylines. The cards are numbered on the back and basically arranged in alphabetical order.

	MINT	NRMT
COMPLETE SET (100)	7.50	3.40
COMMON CARD (T1-T99)	.05	.02

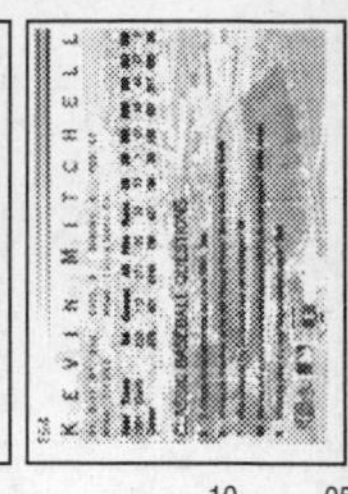

☐ T1 Jim Abbott	.10	.05
☐ T2 Kyle Abbott	.05	.02
☐ T3 Scott Aldred	.05	.02
☐ T4 Roberto Alomar	.40	.18
☐ T5 Wilson Alvarez	.10	.05
☐ T6 Andy Ashby	.05	.02
☐ T7 Steve Avery	.05	.02
☐ T8 Jeff Bagwell	1.50	.70
☐ T9 Bret Barberie	.05	.02
☐ T10 Kim Batiste	.05	.02
☐ T11 Derek Bell	.10	.05
☐ T12 Jay Bell	.05	.02
☐ T13 Albert Belle	.75	.35
☐ T14 Andy Benes	.10	.05
☐ T15 Sean Berry	.05	.02
☐ T16 Barry Bonds	.40	.18
☐ T17 Ryan Bowen	.05	.02
☐ T18 Trifecta Alejandro Pena Mark Wohlers Kent Mercker	.05	.02
☐ T19 Scott Brosius	.05	.02
☐ T20 Jay Buhner	.40	.18
☐ T21 David Burba	.05	.02
☐ T22 Jose Canseco	.30	.14
☐ T23 Andujar Cedeno	.05	.02
☐ T24 Will Clark	.40	.18
☐ T25 Royce Clayton	.05	.02
☐ T26 Roger Clemens	.75	.35
☐ T27 David Cone	.10	.05
☐ T28 Scott Cooper	.05	.02
☐ T29 Chris Cron	.05	.02
☐ T30 Len Dykstra	.10	.05
☐ T31 Cal Eldred	.05	.02
☐ T32 Hector Fajardo	.05	.02
☐ T33 Cecil Fielder	.10	.05
☐ T34 Dave Fleming	.05	.02
☐ T35 Steve Foster	.05	.02
☐ T36 Julio Franco	.10	.05
☐ T37 Carlos Garcia	.05	.02
☐ T38 Tom Glavine	.20	.09
☐ T39 Tom Goodwin	.05	.02
☐ T40 Ken Griffey Jr.	2.50	1.10
☐ T41 Chris Haney	.05	.02
☐ T42 Bryan Harvey	.05	.02
☐ T43 Rickey Henderson 939	.40	.18
☐ T44 Carlos Hernandez	.05	.02
☐ T45 Roberto Hernandez	.10	.05
☐ T46 Brook Jacoby	.05	.02
☐ T47 Howard Johnson	.05	.02
☐ T48 Pat Kelly	.05	.02
☐ T49 Darryl Kile	.10	.05
☐ T50 Chuck Knoblauch	.40	.18
☐ T51 Ray Lankford With Ozzie Smith	.40	.18
☐ T52 Mark Leiter	.05	.02
☐ T53 Darren Lewis	.05	.02
☐ T54 Scott Livingstone	.05	.02
☐ T55 Shane Mack	.05	.02
☐ T56 Chito Martinez	.05	.02
☐ T57 Dennis Martinez The Perfect Game	.10	.05
☐ T58 Don Mattingly	1.00	.45
☐ T59 Paul McClellan	.05	.02
☐ T60 Chuck McElroy	.05	.02
☐ T61 Fred McGriff	.20	.09
☐ T62 Orlando Merced	.05	.02
☐ T63 Luis Mercedes	.05	.02
☐ T64 Kevin Mitchell	.05	.02
☐ T65 Hal Morris	.05	.02
☐ T66 Jack Morris	.05	.02
☐ T67 Mike Mussina	.50	.23
☐ T68 Denny Neagle	.10	.05
☐ T69 Tom Pagnozzi	.05	.02
☐ T70 Terry Pendleton	.05	.02
☐ T71 Phil Plantier	.05	.02
☐ T72 Kirby Puckett	.75	.35
☐ T73 Carlos Quintana	.05	.02
☐ T74 Willie Randolph	.05	.02
☐ T75 Arthur Rhodes	.05	.02
☐ T76 Cal Ripken	1.50	.70
☐ T77 Ivan Rodriguez	.75	.35
☐ T78 Nolan Ryan	1.50	.70

Card	MINT	NRMT
☐ T79 Ryne Sandberg	.50	.23
☐ T80 Deion Sanders Deion Drops In	.40	.18
☐ T81 Reggie Sanders	.10	.05
☐ T82 Mo Sanford	.05	.02
☐ T83 Terry Shumpert	.05	.02
☐ T84 Tim Spehr	.05	.02
☐ T85 Lee Stevens	.05	.02
☐ T86 Darryl Strawberry	.10	.05
☐ T87 Kevin Tapani	.05	.02
☐ T88 Danny Tartabull	.05	.02
☐ T89 Frank Thomas	2.00	.90
☐ T90 Jim Thome	.50	.23
☐ T91 Todd Van Poppel	.05	.02
☐ T92 Andy Van Slyke	.05	.02
☐ T93 John Wehner	.05	.02
☐ T94 John Wetteland	.10	.05
☐ T95 Devon White	.05	.02
☐ T96 Brian Williams	.05	.02
☐ T97 Mark Wohlers	.10	.05
☐ T98 Robin Yount	.30	.14
☐ T99 Eddie Zosky	.05	.02
☐ NNO 4-in-1 Card Barry Bonds Roger Clemens Steve Avery Nolan Ryan	.75	.35

1992 Classic II

The 1992 Series II baseball trivia board game features 99 new player trivia standard-size cards, one "4-in-1" micro player card, a gameboard, and a spinner. The cards display color action player photos on the fronts. The side borders are either red or blue, shading to white as they merge with the top and bottom borders. The player's name appears in a blue stripe at the bottom of the picture. In a horizontal format, the backs have biography, statistics (1991 and career), five trivia questions, and a color drawing of the team's uniform. According to Classic, the production run was 175,000 games.

	MINT	NRMT
COMPLETE SET (100)	7.50	3.40
COMMON CARD (T1-T99)	.05	.02
☐ T1 Jim Abbott	.10	.05
☐ T2 Jeff Bagwell	1.50	.70
☐ T3 Jose Canseco	.30	.14
☐ T4 Julio Valera	.05	.02
☐ T5 Scott Brosius	.05	.02
☐ T6 Mark Langston	.05	.02
☐ T7 Andy Stankiewicz	.05	.02
☐ T8 Gary DiSarcina	.05	.02
☐ T9 Pete Harnisch	.05	.02
☐ T10 Mark McGwire	.75	.35
☐ T11 Ricky Bones	.05	.02
☐ T12 Steve Avery	.05	.02
☐ T13 Deion Sanders	.40	.18
☐ T14 Mike Mussina	.40	.18
☐ T15 Dave Justice	.30	.14
☐ T16 Pat Hentgen	.50	.23
☐ T17 Tom Glavine	.20	.09
☐ T18 Juan Guzman	.05	.02
☐ T19 Ron Gant	.10	.05
☐ T20 Kelly Gruber	.05	.02
☐ T21 Eric Karros	.20	.09
☐ T22 Derrick May	.05	.02
☐ T23 Dave Hansen	.05	.02
☐ T24 Andre Dawson	.20	.09
☐ T25 Eric Davis	.10	.05
☐ T26 Ozzie Smith	.75	.35
☐ T27 Sammy Sosa	.30	.14
☐ T28 Lee Smith	.10	.05
☐ T29 Ryne Sandberg	.50	.23
☐ T30 Robin Yount	.30	.14
☐ T31 Matt Williams	.30	.14
☐ T32 John Vander Wal	.05	.02
☐ T33 Bill Swift	.05	.02
☐ T34 Delino DeShields	.10	.05
☐ T35 Royce Clayton	.05	.02
☐ T36 Moises Alou	.20	.09
☐ T37 Will Clark	.40	.18
☐ T38 Darryl Strawberry	.10	.05
☐ T39 Larry Walker	.40	.18
☐ T40 Ramon Martinez	.10	.05
☐ T41 Howard Johnson	.05	.02
☐ T42 Tino Martinez	.40	.18
☐ T43 Dwight Gooden	.10	.05
☐ T44 Ken Griffey Jr.	2.50	1.10
☐ T45 David Cone	.10	.05
☐ T46 Kenny Lofton	.75	.35
☐ T47 Bobby Bonilla	.10	.05
☐ T48 Carlos Baerga	.10	.05
☐ T49 Don Mattingly	1.00	.45
☐ T50 Sandy Alomar Jr.	.10	.05
☐ T51 Lenny Dykstra	.10	.05
☐ T52 Tony Gwynn	1.00	.45
☐ T53 Felix Jose	.05	.02
☐ T54 Rick Sutcliffe	.05	.02
☐ T55 Wes Chamberlain	.05	.02
☐ T56 Cal Ripken	1.50	.70
☐ T57 Kyle Abbott	.05	.02
☐ T58 Leo Gomez	.05	.02
☐ T59 Gary Sheffield	.30	.14
☐ T60 Anthony Young	.05	.02
☐ T61 Roger Clemens	.75	.35
☐ T62 Rafael Palmeiro	.20	.09
☐ T63 Wade Boggs	.30	.14
☐ T64 Andy Van Slyke	.10	.05
☐ T65 Ruben Sierra	.05	.02
☐ T66 Denny Neagle	.10	.05
☐ T67 Nolan Ryan	1.50	.70
☐ T68 Doug Drabek	.05	.02
☐ T69 Ivan Rodriguez	.75	.35
☐ T70 Barry Bonds	.40	.18
☐ T71 Chuck Knoblauch	.50	.23
☐ T72 Reggie Sanders	.10	.05
☐ T73 Cecil Fielder	.10	.05
☐ T74 Barry Larkin	.20	.09
☐ T75 Scott Aldred	.05	.02
☐ T76 Rob Dibble	.05	.02
☐ T77 Brian McRae	.05	.02
☐ T78 Tim Belcher	.05	.02
☐ T79 George Brett	.75	.35
☐ T80 Frank Viola	.05	.02
☐ T81 Roberto Kelly	.05	.02
☐ T82 Jack McDowell	.05	.02
☐ T83 Mel Hall	.05	.02
☐ T84 Esteban Beltre	.05	.02
☐ T85 Robin Ventura	.10	.05
☐ T86 George Bell	.05	.02
☐ T87 Frank Thomas	2.50	1.10
☐ T88 John Smiley	.05	.02
☐ T89 Bobby Thigpen	.05	.02
☐ T90 Kirby Puckett	.75	.35
☐ T91 Kevin Mitchell	.05	.02
☐ T92 Peter Hoy	.05	.02
☐ T93 Russ Springer	.05	.02
☐ T94 Donovan Osborne	.05	.02
☐ T95 Dave Silvestri	.05	.02
☐ T96 Chad Curtis	.30	.14
☐ T97 Pat Mahomes	.05	.02
☐ T98 Danny Tartabull	.05	.02
☐ T99 John Doherty	.05	.02
☐ NNO 4-in-1 Card Ryne Sandberg Mike Mussina Reggie Sanders Jose Canseco	.40	.18

1993 Classic Game

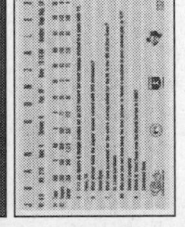

The 1993 Classic Game contains 99 trivia standard-size cards, a micro player card, four micro piece stands, a color game board, and a reusable plastic carrying case. As a special bonus, Classic included highlight trivia cards of George Brett and Robin Yount commemorating their 3,000 hits this past season. The cards feature color action player photos with navy blue borders. The player's name appears in the bottom border. A "1993 Series" logo is superimposed over the photo in the upper left corner. The backs display biographical information, statistics, and trivia questions against a two-tone gray striped background.

	MINT	NRMT
COMPLETE SET (100)	8.00	3.60
COMMON CARD (1-99)	.05	.02
☐ 1 Jim Abbott	.10	.05
☐ 2 Roberto Alomar	.40	.18
☐ 3 Moises Alou	.20	.09
☐ 4 Brady Anderson	.30	.14
☐ 5 Eric Anthony	.05	.02
☐ 6 Alex Arias	.05	.02
☐ 7 Pedro Astacio	.05	.02
☐ 8 Steve Avery	.05	.02
☐ 9 Carlos Baerga	.10	.05
☐ 10 Jeff Bagwell	1.00	.45
☐ 11 George Bell	.05	.02
☐ 12 Albert Belle	.75	.35
☐ 13 Craig Biggio	.40	.18
☐ 14 Barry Bonds	.50	.23
☐ 15 Bobby Bonilla	.10	.05
☐ 16 Mike Bordick	.05	.02
☐ 17 George Brett	.75	.35
☐ 18 Jose Canseco	.30	.14
☐ 19 Joe Carter	.10	.05
☐ 20 Royce Clayton	.05	.02
☐ 21 Roger Clemens	.75	.35
☐ 22 Greg Colbrunn	.05	.02
☐ 23 David Cone	.10	.05
☐ 24 Darren Daulton	.10	.05
☐ 25 Delino DeShields	.05	.02
☐ 26 Rob Dibble	.05	.02
☐ 27 Dennis Eckersley	.20	.09
☐ 28 Cal Eldred	.05	.02
☐ 29 Scott Erickson	.05	.02
☐ 30 Junior Felix	.05	.02
☐ 31 Tony Fernandez	.05	.02
☐ 32 Cecil Fielder	.10	.05
☐ 33 Steve Finley	.20	.09
☐ 34 Dave Fleming	.05	.02
☐ 35 Travis Fryman	.10	.05
☐ 36 Tom Glavine	.20	.09
☐ 37 Juan Gonzalez	1.25	.55
☐ 38 Ken Griffey Jr.	2.50	1.10
☐ 39 Marquis Grissom	.10	.05
☐ 40 Juan Guzman	.05	.02
☐ 41 Tony Gwynn	.75	.35
☐ 42 Rickey Henderson	.30	.14
☐ 43 Felix Jose	.05	.02
☐ 44 Wally Joyner	.05	.02
☐ 45 David Justice	.30	.14
☐ 46 Eric Karros	.20	.09
☐ 47 Roberto Kelly	.05	.02
☐ 48 Ryan Klesko	.75	.35
☐ 49 Chuck Knoblauch	.40	.18
☐ 50 John Kruk	.10	.05
☐ 51 Ray Lankford	.10	.05
☐ 52 Barry Larkin	.20	.09
☐ 53 Pat Listach	.05	.02
☐ 54 Kenny Lofton	.75	.35
☐ 55 Shane Mack	.05	.02
☐ 56 Greg Maddux	1.50	.70
☐ 57 Dave Magadan	.05	.02
☐ 58 Edgar Martinez	.30	.14
☐ 59 Don Mattingly	1.00	.45
☐ 60 Ben McDonald	.05	.02
☐ 61 Jack McDowell	.05	.02
☐ 62 Fred McGriff	.20	.09
☐ 63 Mark McGwire	.75	.35
☐ 64 Kevin McReynolds	.05	.02
☐ 65 Sam Militello	.05	.02
☐ 66 Paul Molitor	.40	.18
☐ 67 Jeff Montgomery	.10	.05
☐ 68 Jack Morris	.10	.05
☐ 69 Eddie Murray	.40	.18
☐ 70 Mike Mussina	.50	.23
☐ 71 Otis Nixon	.10	.05
☐ 72 Donovan Osborne	.05	.02
☐ 73 Terry Pendleton	.05	.02
☐ 74 Mike Piazza	2.00	.90
☐ 75 Kirby Puckett	.75	.35
☐ 76 Cal Ripken Jr.	1.50	.70
☐ 77 Bip Roberts	.05	.02
☐ 78 Ivan Rodriguez	.75	.35
☐ 79 Nolan Ryan	1.50	.70
☐ 80 Ryne Sandberg	.50	.23
☐ 81 Deion Sanders	.40	.18
☐ 82 Reggie Sanders	.05	.02
☐ 83 Frank Seminara	.05	.02
☐ 84 Gary Sheffield	.30	.14
☐ 85 Ruben Sierra	.05	.02
☐ 86 John Smiley	.05	.02
☐ 87 Lee Smith	.10	.05
☐ 88 Ozzie Smith	.50	.23
☐ 89 John Smoltz	.10	.05
☐ 90 Danny Tartabull	.05	.02
☐ 91 Bob Tewksbury	.05	.02
☐ 92 Frank Thomas	2.00	.90
☐ 93 Andy Van Slyke	.05	.02
☐ 94 Mo Vaughn	.50	.23

☐ 95 Robin Ventura	.10	.05
☐ 96 Tim Wakefield	.05	.02
☐ 97 Larry Walker	.40	.18
☐ 98 Dave Winfield	.30	.14
☐ 99 Robin Yount	.20	.09
☐ NNO 4-in-1 Card Mark McGwire Sam Militello Ryan Klesko Greg Maddux	.50	.23

1981 Coke Team Sets

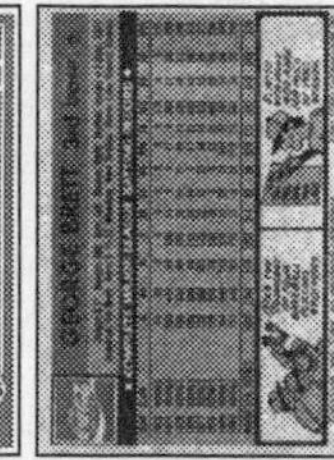

The cards in this 132-card set measure 2 1/2" by 3 1/2". In 1981, Topps produced 11 sets of 12 cards each for the Coca-Cola Company. Each set features 11 star players for a particular team plus an advertising card with the team name on the front. Although the cards are numbered in the upper right corner of the back from 1 to 11, they are re-numbered below within team, i.e., Boston Red Sox (1-12), Chicago Cubs (13-24), Chicago White Sox (25-36), Cincinnati Reds (37-48), Detroit Tigers (49-60), Houston Astros (61-72), Kansas City Royals (73-84), New York Mets (85-96), Philadelphia Phillies (97-108), Pittsburgh Pirates (109-120), and St. Louis Cardinals (121-132). Within each team the player actually numbered number 1 (on the card back) is the first player below and the player numbered number 11 is the last in that team's list. These player cards are quite similar to the 1981 Topps issue but feature a Coca-Cola logo on both the front and the back. The advertising card for each team features, on its back, an offer for obtaining an uncut sheet of 1981 Topps cards. These promotional cards were actually issued by Coke in only a few of the cities, and most of these cards have reached collectors hands through dealers who have purchased the cards through suppliers. Recently, cards of the following New York Yankees have been discovered: Rick Cerone, Rich Gossage and Reggie Jackson. Since these cards are so infrequently found, we have not yet placed a value on them.

	MINT	NRMT
COMPLETE SET (132)	40.00	18.00
COMMON CARD (1-132)	.20	.09
COMMON AD CARD	.10	.05

☐ 1 Tom Burgmeier	.20	.09
☐ 2 Dennis Eckersley	2.00	.90
☐ 3 Dwight Evans	.75	.35
☐ 4 Bob Stanley	.20	.09
☐ 5 Glenn Hoffman	.20	.09
☐ 6 Carney Lansford	.30	.14
☐ 7 Frank Tanana	.40	.18
☐ 8 Tony Perez	1.25	.55
☐ 9 Jim Rice	.30	.14
☐ 10 Dave Stapleton	.20	.09
☐ 11 Carl Yastrzemski	3.50	1.55
☐ 12 Red Sox Ad Card (Unnumbered)	.10	.05
☐ 13 Tim Blackwell	.20	.09
☐ 14 Bill Buckner	.30	.14
☐ 15 Ivan DeJesus	.20	.09
☐ 16 Leon Durham	.30	.14
☐ 17 Steve Henderson	.20	.09
☐ 18 Mike Krukow	.20	.09
☐ 19 Ken Reitz	.20	.09
☐ 20 Rick Reuschel	.30	.14
☐ 21 Scot Thompson	.20	.09
☐ 22 Dick Tidrow	.20	.09
☐ 23 Mike Tyson	.20	.09
☐ 24 Cubs Ad Card (Unnumbered)	.10	.05
☐ 25 Britt Burns	.20	.09
☐ 26 Todd Cruz	.20	.09
☐ 27 Rich Dotson	.20	.09
☐ 28 Jim Essian	.20	.09
☐ 29 Ed Farmer	.20	.09
☐ 30 Lamar Johnson	.20	.09
☐ 31 Ron LeFlore	.20	.09
☐ 32 Chet Lemon	.20	.09
☐ 33 Bob Molinaro	.20	.09
☐ 34 Jim Morrison	.20	.09
☐ 35 Wayne Nordhagen	.20	.09
☐ 36 White Sox Ad Card (Unnumbered)	.10	.05
☐ 37 Johnny Bench	4.00	1.80
☐ 38 Dave Collins	.20	.09
☐ 39 Dave Concepcion	.30	.14
☐ 40 Dan Driessen	.20	.09
☐ 41 George Foster	.50	.23
☐ 42 Ken Griffey	.30	.14
☐ 43 Tom Hume	.20	.09
☐ 44 Ray Knight	.50	.23
☐ 45 Ron Oester	.20	.09
☐ 46 Tom Seaver	4.00	1.80
☐ 47 Mario Soto	.20	.09
☐ 48 Reds Ad Card (Unnumbered)	.10	.05
☐ 49 Champ Summers	.20	.09
☐ 50 Al Cowens	.20	.09
☐ 51 Rich Hebner	.30	.14
☐ 52 Steve Kemp	.30	.14
☐ 53 Aurelio Lopez	.20	.09
☐ 54 Jack Morris	1.50	.70
☐ 55 Lance Parrish	.75	.35
☐ 56 Johnny Wockenfuss	.20	.09
☐ 57 Alan Trammell	3.00	1.35
☐ 58 Lou Whitaker	2.00	.90
☐ 59 Kirk Gibson	3.00	1.35
☐ 60 Tigers Ad Card (Unnumbered)	.10	.05
☐ 61 Alan Ashby	.20	.09
☐ 62 Cesar Cedeno	.30	.14
☐ 63 Jose Cruz	.30	.14
☐ 64 Art Howe	.20	.09
☐ 65 Rafael Landestoy	.20	.09
☐ 66 Joe Niekro	.30	.14
☐ 67 Terry Puhl	.30	.14
☐ 68 J.R. Richard	.30	.14
☐ 69 Nolan Ryan	8.00	3.60
☐ 70 Joe Sambito	.30	.14
☐ 71 Don Sutton	2.00	.90
☐ 72 Astros Ad Card (Unnumbered)	.10	.05
☐ 73 Willie Aikens	.20	.09
☐ 74 George Brett	7.50	3.40
☐ 75 Larry Gura	.20	.09
☐ 76 Dennis Leonard	.30	.14
☐ 77 Hal McRae	.50	.23
☐ 78 Amos Otis	.30	.14
☐ 79 Dan Quisenberry	.30	.14
☐ 80 U.L. Washington	.20	.09
☐ 81 John Wathan	.20	.09
☐ 82 Frank White	.30	.14
☐ 83 Willie Wilson	.30	.14
☐ 84 Royals Ad Card (Unnumbered)	.10	.05
☐ 85 Neil Allen	.20	.09
☐ 86 Doug Flynn	.20	.09
☐ 87 Dave Kingman	.30	.14
☐ 88 Randy Jones	.20	.09
☐ 89 Pat Zachry	.20	.09
☐ 90 Lee Mazzilli	.20	.09
☐ 91 Rusty Staub	.30	.14
☐ 92 Craig Swan	.20	.09
☐ 93 Frank Taveras	.20	.09
☐ 94 Alex Trevino	.20	.09
☐ 95 Joel Youngblood	.20	.09
☐ 96 Mets Ad Card (Unnumbered)	.10	.05
☐ 97 Bob Boone	.30	.14
☐ 98 Larry Bowa	.30	.14
☐ 99 Steve Carlton	2.00	.90
☐ 100 Greg Luzinski	.50	.23
☐ 101 Garry Maddox	.30	.14
☐ 102 Bake McBride	.20	.09
☐ 103 Tug McGraw	.30	.14
☐ 104 Pete Rose	4.00	1.80
☐ 105 Mike Schmidt	4.00	1.80
☐ 106 Lonnie Smith	.30	.14
☐ 107 Manny Trillo	.30	.14
☐ 108 Phillies Ad Card (Unnumbered)	.10	.05
☐ 109 Jim Bibby	.20	.09
☐ 110 John Candelaria	.30	.14
☐ 111 Mike Easler	.30	.14
☐ 112 Tim Foli	.20	.09
☐ 113 Phil Garner	.30	.14
☐ 114 Bill Madlock	.30	.14
☐ 115 Omar Moreno	.20	.09
☐ 116 Ed Ott	.20	.09
☐ 117 Dave Parker	.75	.35
☐ 118 Willie Stargell	1.50	.70
☐ 119 Kent Tekulve	.30	.14
☐ 120 Pirates Ad Card (Unnumbered)	.10	.05
☐ 121 Bob Forsch	.20	.09
☐ 122 George Hendrick	.30	.14
☐ 123 Keith Hernandez	.30	.14
☐ 124 Tom Herr	.30	.14
☐ 125 Sixto Lezcano	.20	.09
☐ 126 Ken Oberkfell	.20	.09
☐ 127 Darrell Porter	.30	.14
☐ 128 Tony Scott	.20	.09
☐ 129 Lary Sorensen	.20	.09
☐ 130 Bruce Sutter	.30	.14
☐ 131 Garry Templeton	.20	.09
☐ 132 Cardinals Ad Card (Unnumbered)	.10	.05

1992 Colla All-Star Game

This 24-card standard-size set was made available at the 1992 All-Star game in San Diego. The cards feature 24 All-Stars from the National and American League. Randomly inserted throughout the sets were 200 numbered and autographed Roberto Alomar cards. The production run was limited to 25,000 sets, and the first card (McGwire) of each set bears the set serial number ("X of 25,000"). The fronts display full-bleed glossy color player photos. The All-Star Game logo and the player's name are superimposed across the bottom of the picture. The backs carry a close-up color photo and All-Star statistics. The cards are numbered in a diamond in the upper left corner.

	MINT	NRMT
COMPLETE SET (24)	12.50	5.50
COMMON CARD (1-24)	.25	.11

☐ 1 Mark McGwire	1.50	.70
☐ 2 Will Clark	.50	.23
☐ 3 Roberto Alomar	.75	.35
☐ 4 Ryne Sandberg	1.00	.45
☐ 5 Cal Ripken	3.00	1.35
☐ 6 Ozzie Smith	1.00	.45
☐ 7 Wade Boggs	.75	.35
☐ 8 Terry Pendleton	.25	.11
☐ 9 Kirby Puckett	1.25	.55
☐ 10 Chuck Knoblauch	.75	.35
☐ 11 Ken Griffey Jr.	3.00	1.35
☐ 12 Joe Carter	.35	.16
☐ 13 Sandy Alomar Jr.	.35	.16
☐ 14 Benito Santiago	.25	.11
☐ 15 Mike Mussina	.75	.35
☐ 16 Fred McGriff	.50	.23
☐ 17 Dennis Eckersley	.50	.23
☐ 18 Tony Gwynn	1.50	.70
☐ 19 Roger Clemens	1.25	.55
☐ 20 Gary Sheffield	.75	.35
☐ 21 Jose Canseco	.50	.23
☐ 22 Barry Bonds	1.00	.45
☐ 23 Ivan Rodriguez	1.00	.45
☐ 24 Tony Fernandez	.25	.11

1993 Colla All-Star Game

Issued by noted photographer Barry Colla, this 24-card boxed set was made available at the 1993 All-Star game in Baltimore. The standard-size cards feature 24 All-Stars from the National and American Leagues. The fronts display high-gloss, full-action photos framed by variously colored borders with a black outer border. The set's title, "The Colla Collection", appears at the top and the player's name, team logo, and position are printed at the bottom.

The backs carry close-up color pictures on a black background with All-Star statistics appearing at the bottom.

	MINT	NRMT
COMPLETE SET (25)	15.00	6.75
COMMON CARD (1-24)	.25	.11
☐ 1 Roberto Alomar	1.00	.45
☐ 2 Barry Bonds	1.25	.55
☐ 3 Ken Griffey Jr.	4.00	1.80
☐ 4 John Kruk	.50	.23
☐ 5 Kirby Puckett	1.50	.70
☐ 6 Darren Daulton	.50	.23
☐ 7 Wade Boggs	1.00	.45
☐ 8 Matt Williams	.75	.35
☐ 9 Cal Ripken	3.00	1.35
☐ 10 Ryne Sandberg	1.25	.55
☐ 11 Ivan Rodriguez	1.25	.55
☐ 12 Andy Van Slyke	.25	.11
☐ 13 John Olerud	.50	.23
☐ 14 Tom Glavine	.50	.23
☐ 15 Juan Gonzalez	2.00	.90
☐ 16 David Justice	1.00	.45
☐ 17 Mike Mussina	1.00	.45
☐ 18 Tony Gwynn	2.00	.90
☐ 19 Joe Carter	.50	.23
☐ 20 Barry Larkin	.75	.35
☐ 21 Brian Harper	.25	.11
☐ 22 Ozzie Smith	1.25	.55
☐ 23 Mark McGwire	1.50	.70
☐ 24 Mike Piazza	3.00	1.35
☐ NNO Checklist Card	.25	.11

1990 Collect-A-Books

The 1990 Collect-A-Books set was issued by CMC (Collectors Marketing Corp.) in three different sets (boxes) of 12 players apiece. The sets (boxes) were distinguishable by color, red, yellow, or green. The Collect-A-Books were in the style of the 1970 Topps Comic Book inserts but were much more profesionally made. The cards all fit into a nine-pocket sheet (since they are standard size) even though they can be expanded. The set contains an interesting mixture of retired and current players.

	MINT	NRMT
COMPLETE SET (36)	7.00	3.10
COMMON CARD (1-36)	.10	.05
☐ 1 Bo Jackson	.20	.09
☐ 2 Dwight Gooden	.20	.09
☐ 3 Ken Griffey Jr.	1.50	.70
☐ 4 Will Clark	.30	.14
☐ 5 Ozzie Smith	.75	.35
☐ 6 Orel Hershiser	.20	.09
☐ 7 Ruben Sierra	.10	.05
☐ 8 Rickey Henderson	.30	.14
☐ 9 Robin Yount	.30	.14
☐ 10 Babe Ruth	1.50	.70
☐ 11 Ernie Banks	.40	.18
☐ 12 Carl Yastrzemski	.40	.18
☐ 13 Don Mattingly	1.00	.45
☐ 14 Nolan Ryan	1.25	.55
☐ 15 Jerome Walton	.10	.05
☐ 16 Kevin Mitchell	.10	.05
☐ 17 Tony Gwynn	1.00	.45
☐ 18 Dave Stewart	.10	.05
☐ 19 Roger Clemens	1.00	.45
☐ 20 Darryl Strawberry	.20	.09
☐ 21 George Brett	.75	.35
☐ 22 Hank Aaron	1.00	.45
☐ 23 Ted Williams	1.00	.45
☐ 24 Warren Spahn	.40	.18
☐ 25 Jose Canseco	.30	.14
☐ 26 Wade Boggs	.30	.14
☐ 27 Jim Abbott	.20	.09
☐ 28 Eric Davis	.20	.09
☐ 29 Ryne Sandberg	.75	.35
☐ 30 Bret Saberhagen	.10	.05
☐ 31 Mark Grace	.30	.14
☐ 32 Gregg Olson	.10	.05
☐ 33 Kirby Puckett	.75	.35
☐ 34 Lou Gehrig	1.25	.55
☐ 35 Roberto Clemente	1.25	.55
☐ 36 Bob Feller	.40	.18

1991 Collect-A-Books

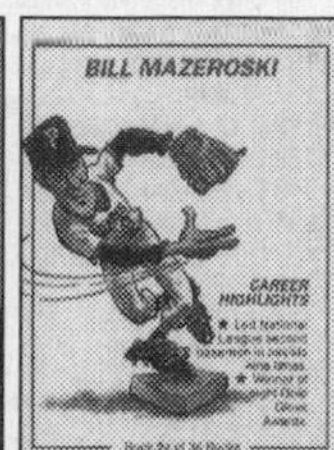

This 36-card set, which measures the standard size, was issued by Impel for the second consecutive year. Collectors Marketing Corp., the 1990 Collect-a-Book producer, was a division within the Impel Corporation. This 1991 set was issued under Impel's Line Drive brand. Each book consists of eight pages and fits into a standard size plastic sheet. The set features 27 active stars and nine famous retired stars. An action shot of the player is pictured on the first two pages. The next four pages has textual information broken down into biographical information, two pages of more detailed personal information and a page of statistics. The inside back cover has a quote from the player pictured while the back cover has an attractive drawing of the player. Unlike the 1990 issue, the Collect-A-Books were issued in random packs.

	MINT	NRMT
COMPLETE SET (36)	8.00	3.60
COMMON CARD (1-36)	.10	.05
☐ 1 Roger Clemens	1.00	.45
☐ 2 Cal Ripken	1.25	.55
☐ 3 Nolan Ryan	1.25	.55
☐ 4 Ken Griffey Jr.	1.50	.70
☐ 5 Bob Welch	.10	.05
☐ 6 Kevin Mitchell	.10	.05
☐ 7 Kirby Puckett	.75	.35
☐ 8 Len Dykstra	.20	.09
☐ 9 Ben McDonald	.10	.05
☐ 10 Don Drysdale	.40	.18
☐ 11 Lou Brock	.40	.18
☐ 12 Ralph Kiner	.40	.18
☐ 13 Jose Canseco	.30	.14
☐ 14 Cecil Fielder	.20	.09
☐ 15 Ryne Sandberg	.60	.25
☐ 16 Wade Boggs	.30	.14
☐ 17 Dwight Gooden	.20	.09
☐ 18 Ramon Martinez	.20	.09
☐ 19 Tony Gwynn	.75	.35
☐ 20 Mark Grace	.30	.14
☐ 21 Kevin Maas	.10	.05
☐ 22 Thurman Munson	.30	.14
☐ 23 Bob Gibson	.40	.18
☐ 24 Bill Mazeroski	.30	.14
☐ 25 Rickey Henderson	.50	.23
☐ 26 Barry Bonds	.40	.18
☐ 27 Jose Rijo	.10	.05
☐ 28 George Brett	.60	.25
☐ 29 Doug Drabek	.10	.05
☐ 30 Matt Williams	.30	.14
☐ 31 Barry Larkin	.30	.14
☐ 32 Dave Stewart	.10	.05
☐ 33 Dave Justice	.40	.18
☐ 34 Harmon Killebrew	.40	.18
☐ 35 Yogi Berra	.40	.18
☐ 36 Billy Williams	.40	.18

1994 Collector's Choice

Issued by Upper Deck, this 670 standard-size card set was issued in two series of 320 and 350. Cards were issued in foil-wrapped 12-card packs and factory sets (of which contained five Gold Signature cards for a total of 675 cards). Basic card fronts feature color player action photos with white borders that are highlighted by vertical gray pinstripes. Subsets include Rookie Class (1-20), First Draft Picks (21-30), Top Performers (306-315), Up Close (631-640) and Future Foundation (641-650). Notable Rookie Cards include Michael Jordan, Derrek Lee and Alex Rodriguez.

	MINT	NRMT
COMPLETE SET (670)	25.00	11.00
COMP.FACT.SET (675)	30.00	13.50
COMPLETE SERIES 1 (320)	10.00	4.50
COMPLETE SERIES 2 (350)	15.00	6.75
COMMON CARD (1-670)	.10	.05
☐ 1 Rich Becker	.20	.09
☐ 2 Greg Blosser	.10	.05
☐ 3 Midre Cummings	.10	.05
☐ 4 Carlos Delgado	.10	.05
☐ 5 Steve Dreyer	.10	.05
☐ 6 Carl Everett	.10	.05
☐ 7 Cliff Floyd	.20	.09
☐ 8 Alex Gonzalez	.20	.09
☐ 9 Shawn Green	.20	.09
☐ 10 Butch Huskey	.10	.05
☐ 11 Mark Hutton	.10	.05
☐ 12 Miguel Jimenez	.10	.05
☐ 13 Steve Karsay	.10	.05
☐ 14 Marc Newfield	.20	.09
☐ 15 Luis Ortiz	.10	.05
☐ 16 Manny Ramirez	.50	.23
☐ 17 Johnny Ruffin	.10	.05
☐ 18 Scott Stahoviak	.10	.05
☐ 19 Salomon Torres	.10	.05
☐ 20 Gabe White	.10	.05
☐ 21 Brian Anderson	.20	.09
☐ 22 Wayne Gomes	.10	.05
☐ 23 Jeff Granger	.10	.05
☐ 24 Steve Soderstrom	.10	.05
☐ 25 Trot Nixon	.10	.05
☐ 26 Kirk Presley	.20	.09
☐ 27 Matt Brunson	.20	.09
☐ 28 Brooks Kieschnick	.20	.09
☐ 29 Billy Wagner	.75	.35
☐ 30 Matt Drews	.40	.18
☐ 31 Kurt Abbott	.10	.05
☐ 32 Luis Alicea	.10	.05
☐ 33 Roberto Alomar	.40	.18
☐ 34 Sandy Alomar Jr.	.20	.09
☐ 35 Moises Alou	.10	.05
☐ 36 Wilson Alvarez	.20	.09
☐ 37 Rich Amaral	.10	.05
☐ 38 Eric Anthony	.10	.05
☐ 39 Luis Aquino	.10	.05
☐ 40 Jack Armstrong	.10	.05
☐ 41 Rene Arocha	.10	.05
☐ 42 Rich Aude	.10	.05
☐ 43 Brad Ausmus	.10	.05
☐ 44 Steve Avery	.10	.05
☐ 45 Bob Ayrault	.10	.05
☐ 46 Willie Banks	.10	.05
☐ 47 Bret Barberie	.10	.05
☐ 48 Kim Batiste	.10	.05
☐ 49 Rod Beck	.20	.09
☐ 50 Jason Bere	.10	.05
☐ 51 Sean Berry	.10	.05
☐ 52 Dante Bichette	.10	.05
☐ 53 Jeff Blauser	.10	.05
☐ 54 Mike Blowers	.10	.05
☐ 55 Tim Bogar	.10	.05
☐ 56 Tom Bolton	.10	.05
☐ 57 Ricky Bones	.10	.05
☐ 58 Bobby Bonilla	.20	.09
☐ 59 Bret Boone	.20	.09
☐ 60 Pat Borders	.10	.05
☐ 61 Mike Bordick	.10	.05
☐ 62 Daryl Boston	.10	.05
☐ 63 Ryan Bowen	.10	.05
☐ 64 Jeff Branson	.10	.05
☐ 65 George Brett	.75	.35
☐ 66 Steve Buechele	.10	.05
☐ 67 Dave Burba	.10	.05
☐ 68 John Burkett	.10	.05
☐ 69 Jeromy Burnitz	.10	.05
☐ 70 Brett Butler	.20	.09
☐ 71 Rob Butler	.10	.05
☐ 72 Ken Caminiti	.40	.18
☐ 73 Cris Carpenter	.10	.05
☐ 74 Vinny Castilla	.40	.18
☐ 75 Andujar Cedeno	.10	.05
☐ 76 Wes Chamberlain	.10	.05
☐ 77 Archi Cianfrocco	.10	.05
☐ 78 Dave Clark	.10	.05
☐ 79 Jerald Clark	.10	.05
☐ 80 Royce Clayton	.10	.05
☐ 81 David Cone	.10	.05

☐ 82 Jeff Conine	.20	.09
☐ 83 Steve Cooke	.10	.05
☐ 84 Scott Cooper	.10	.05
☐ 85 Joey Cora	.20	.09
☐ 86 Tim Costo	.10	.05
☐ 87 Chad Curtis	.10	.05
☐ 88 Ron Darling	.10	.05
☐ 89 Danny Darwin	.10	.05
☐ 90 Rob Deer	.10	.05
☐ 91 Jim Deshaies	.10	.05
☐ 92 Delino DeShields	.10	.05
☐ 93 Rob Dibble	.10	.05
☐ 94 Gary DiSarcina	.10	.05
☐ 95 Doug Drabek	.10	.05
☐ 96 Scott Erickson	.10	.05
☐ 97 Rikkert Faneyte	.10	.05
☐ 98 Jeff Fassero	.10	.05
☐ 99 Alex Fernandez	.10	.05
☐ 100 Cecil Fielder	.20	.09
☐ 101 Dave Fleming	.10	.05
☐ 102 Darrin Fletcher	.10	.05
☐ 103 Scott Fletcher	.10	.05
☐ 104 Mike Gallego	.10	.05
☐ 105 Carlos Garcia	.10	.05
☐ 106 Jeff Gardner	.10	.05
☐ 107 Brent Gates	.10	.05
☐ 108 Benji Gil	.10	.05
☐ 109 Bernard Gilkey	.20	.09
☐ 110 Chris Gomez	.10	.05
☐ 111 Luis Gonzalez	.10	.05
☐ 112 Tom Gordon	.10	.05
☐ 113 Jim Gott	.10	.05
☐ 114 Mark Grace	.20	.09
☐ 115 Tommy Greene	.10	.05
☐ 116 Willie Greene	.20	.09
☐ 117 Ken Griffey Jr.	2.00	.90
☐ 118 Bill Gullickson	.10	.05
☐ 119 Ricky Gutierrez	.10	.05
☐ 120 Juan Guzman	.10	.05
☐ 121 Chris Gwynn	.10	.05
☐ 122 Tony Gwynn	1.00	.45
☐ 123 Jeffrey Hammonds	.20	.09
☐ 124 Erik Hanson	.10	.05
☐ 125 Gene Harris	.10	.05
☐ 126 Greg W. Harris	.10	.05
☐ 127 Bryan Harvey	.10	.05
☐ 128 Billy Hatcher	.10	.05
☐ 129 Hilly Hathaway	.10	.05
☐ 130 Charlie Hayes	.10	.05
☐ 131 Rickey Henderson	.10	.05
☐ 132 Mike Henneman	.10	.05
☐ 133 Pat Hentgen	.20	.09
☐ 134 Roberto Hernandez	.20	.09
☐ 135 Orel Hershiser	.20	.09
☐ 136 Phil Hiatt	.10	.05
☐ 137 Glenallen Hill	.10	.05
☐ 138 Ken Hill	.10	.05
☐ 139 Eric Hillman	.10	.05
☐ 140 Chris Hoiles	.10	.05
☐ 141 Dave Hollins	.10	.05
☐ 142 David Hulse	.10	.05
☐ 143 Todd Hundley	.20	.09
☐ 144 Pete Incaviglia	.10	.05
☐ 145 Danny Jackson	.10	.05
☐ 146 John Jaha	.10	.05
☐ 147 Domingo Jean	.10	.05
☐ 148 Gregg Jefferies	.20	.09
☐ 149 Reggie Jefferson	.20	.09
☐ 150 Lance Johnson	.10	.05
☐ 151 Bobby Jones	.20	.09
☐ 152 Chipper Jones	1.25	.55
☐ 153 Todd Jones	.10	.05
☐ 154 Brian Jordan	.20	.09
☐ 155 Wally Joyner	.20	.09
☐ 156 David Justice	.40	.18
☐ 157 Ron Karkovice	.10	.05
☐ 158 Eric Karros	.20	.09
☐ 159 Jeff Kent	.10	.05
☐ 160 Jimmy Key	.20	.09
☐ 161 Mark Kiefer	.10	.05
☐ 162 Darryl Kile	.20	.09
☐ 163 Jeff King	.20	.09
☐ 164 Wayne Kirby	.10	.05
☐ 165 Ryan Klesko	.40	.18
☐ 166 Chuck Knoblauch	.40	.18
☐ 167 Chad Kreuter	.10	.05
☐ 168 John Kruk	.20	.09
☐ 169 Mark Langston	.10	.05
☐ 170 Mike Lansing	.10	.05
☐ 171 Barry Larkin	.40	.18
☐ 172 Manuel Lee	.10	.05
☐ 173 Phil Leftwich	.10	.05
☐ 174 Darren Lewis	.10	.05
☐ 175 Derek Lilliquist	.10	.05
☐ 176 Jose Lind	.10	.05
☐ 177 Albie Lopez	.20	.09
☐ 178 Javier Lopez	.40	.18
☐ 179 Torey Lovullo	.10	.05
☐ 180 Scott Lydy	.10	.05
☐ 181 Mike Macfarlane	.10	.05
☐ 182 Shane Mack	.10	.05
☐ 183 Greg Maddux	1.25	.55
☐ 184 Dave Magadan	.10	.05
☐ 185 Joe Magrane	.10	.05
☐ 186 Kirk Manwaring	.10	.05
☐ 187 Al Martin	.10	.05
☐ 188 Pedro A. Martinez	.10	.05
☐ 189 Pedro J. Martinez	.40	.18
☐ 190 Ramon Martinez	.10	.05
☐ 191 Tino Martinez	.40	.18
☐ 192 Don Mattingly	.60	.25
☐ 193 Derrick May	.10	.05
☐ 194 David McCarty	.10	.05
☐ 195 Ben McDonald	.10	.05
☐ 196 Roger McDowell	.10	.05
☐ 197 Fred McGriff UER (Stats on back have 73 stolen bases for 1989; should be 7)	.10	.05
☐ 198 Mark McLemore	.10	.05
☐ 199 Greg McMichael	.10	.05
☐ 200 Jeff McNeely	.10	.05
☐ 201 Brian McRae	.10	.05
☐ 202 Pat Meares	.10	.05
☐ 203 Roberto Mejia	.10	.05
☐ 204 Orlando Merced	.10	.05
☐ 205 Jose Mesa	.20	.09
☐ 206 Blas Minor	.10	.05
☐ 207 Angel Miranda	.10	.05
☐ 208 Paul Molitor	.40	.18
☐ 209 Raul Mondesi	.10	.05
☐ 210 Jeff Montgomery	.10	.05
☐ 211 Mickey Morandini	.10	.05
☐ 212 Mike Morgan	.10	.05
☐ 213 Jamie Moyer	.10	.05
☐ 214 Bobby Munoz	.10	.05
☐ 215 Troy Neel	.10	.05
☐ 216 Dave Nilsson	.20	.09
☐ 217 John O'Donoghue	.10	.05
☐ 218 Paul O'Neill	.20	.09
☐ 219 Jose Offerman	.10	.05
☐ 220 Joe Oliver	.10	.05
☐ 221 Greg Olson	.10	.05
☐ 222 Donovan Osborne	.10	.05
☐ 223 J. Owens	.10	.05
☐ 224 Mike Pagliarulo	.10	.05
☐ 225 Craig Paquette	.10	.05
☐ 226 Roger Pavlik	.10	.05
☐ 227 Brad Pennington	.10	.05
☐ 228 Eduardo Perez	.10	.05
☐ 229 Mike Perez	.10	.05
☐ 230 Tony Phillips	.10	.05
☐ 231 Hipolito Pichardo	.10	.05
☐ 232 Phil Plantier	.10	.05
☐ 233 Curtis Pride	.20	.09
☐ 234 Tim Pugh	.10	.05
☐ 235 Scott Radinsky	.10	.05
☐ 236 Pat Rapp	.10	.05
☐ 237 Kevin Reimer	.10	.05
☐ 238 Armando Reynoso	.10	.05
☐ 239 Jose Rijo	.10	.05
☐ 240 Cal Ripken	1.50	.70
☐ 241 Kevin Roberson	.10	.05
☐ 242 Kenny Rogers	.10	.05
☐ 243 Kevin Rogers	.10	.05
☐ 244 Mel Rojas	.10	.05
☐ 245 John Roper	.10	.05
☐ 246 Kirk Rueter	.10	.05
☐ 247 Scott Ruffcorn	.10	.05
☐ 248 Ken Ryan	.10	.05
☐ 249 Nolan Ryan	1.50	.70
☐ 250 Bret Saberhagen	.10	.05
☐ 251 Tim Salmon	.40	.18
☐ 252 Reggie Sanders	.10	.05
☐ 253 Curt Schilling	.20	.09
☐ 254 David Segui	.10	.05
☐ 255 Aaron Sele	.10	.05
☐ 256 Scott Servais	.10	.05
☐ 257 Gary Sheffield	.40	.18
☐ 258 Ruben Sierra	.10	.05
☐ 259 Don Slaught	.10	.05
☐ 260 Lee Smith	.20	.09
☐ 261 Cory Snyder	.10	.05
☐ 262 Paul Sorrento	.10	.05
☐ 263 Sammy Sosa	.40	.18
☐ 264 Bill Spiers	.10	.05
☐ 265 Mike Stanley	.10	.05
☐ 266 Dave Staton	.10	.05
☐ 267 Terry Steinbach	.20	.09
☐ 268 Kevin Stocker	.10	.05
☐ 269 Todd Stottlemyre	.10	.05
☐ 270 Doug Strange	.10	.05
☐ 271 Bill Swift	.10	.05
☐ 272 Kevin Tapani	.10	.05
☐ 273 Tony Tarasco	.10	.05
☐ 274 Julian Tavarez	.20	.09
☐ 275 Mickey Tettleton	.10	.05
☐ 276 Ryan Thompson	.10	.05
☐ 277 Chris Turner	.10	.05
☐ 278 John Valentin	.20	.09
☐ 279 Todd Van Poppel	.10	.05
☐ 280 Andy Van Slyke	.20	.09
☐ 281 Mo Vaughn	.50	.23
☐ 282 Robin Ventura	.20	.09
☐ 283 Frank Viola	.10	.05
☐ 284 Jose Vizcaino	.10	.05
☐ 285 Omar Vizquel	.20	.09
☐ 286 Larry Walker	.40	.18
☐ 287 Duane Ward	.10	.05
☐ 288 Allen Watson	.10	.05
☐ 289 Bill Wegman	.10	.05
☐ 290 Turk Wendell	.10	.05
☐ 291 Lou Whitaker	.20	.09
☐ 292 Devon White	.10	.05
☐ 293 Rondell White	.20	.09
☐ 294 Mark Whiten	.10	.05
☐ 295 Darrel Whitmore	.10	.05
☐ 296 Bob Wickman	.10	.05
☐ 297 Rick Wilkins	.10	.05
☐ 298 Bernie Williams	.40	.18
☐ 299 Matt Williams	.10	.05
☐ 300 Woody Williams	.10	.05
☐ 301 Nigel Wilson	.10	.05
☐ 302 Dave Winfield	.10	.05
☐ 303 Anthony Young	.10	.05
☐ 304 Eric Young	.20	.09
☐ 305 Todd Zeile	.10	.05
☐ 306 Jack McDowell TP John Burkett Tom Glavine	.10	.05
☐ 307 Randy Johnson TP	.10	.05
☐ 308 Randy Myers TP	.10	.05
☐ 309 Jack McDowell TP	.10	.05
☐ 310 Mike Piazza TP	.60	.25
☐ 311 Barry Bonds TP	.40	.18
☐ 312 Andres Galarraga TP	.10	.05
☐ 313 Juan Gonzalez TP Barry Bonds	.40	.18
☐ 314 Albert Belle TP	.40	.18
☐ 315 Kenny Lofton TP	.10	.05
☐ 316 Barry Bonds CL	.10	.05
☐ 317 Ken Griffey Jr. CL	.40	.18
☐ 318 Mike Piazza CL	.40	.18
☐ 319 Kirby Puckett CL	.40	.18
☐ 320 Nolan Ryan CL	.40	.18
☐ 321 Roberto Alomar CL	.20	.09
☐ 322 Roger Clemens CL	.40	.18
☐ 323 Juan Gonzalez CL	.40	.18
☐ 324 Ken Griffey Jr. CL	.40	.18
☐ 325 David Justice CL	.20	.09
☐ 326 John Kruk CL	.10	.05
☐ 327 Frank Thomas CL	.40	.18
☐ 328 Tim Salmon TC	.10	.05
☐ 329 Jeff Bagwell TC	.40	.18
☐ 330 Mark McGwire TC	.40	.18
☐ 331 Roberto Alomar TC	.20	.09
☐ 332 David Justice TC	.20	.09
☐ 333 Pat Listach TC	.10	.05
☐ 334 Ozzie Smith TC	.40	.18
☐ 335 Ryne Sandberg TC	.10	.05
☐ 336 Mike Piazza TC	.60	.25
☐ 337 Cliff Floyd TC	.10	.05
☐ 338 Barry Bonds TC	.40	.18
☐ 339 Albert Belle TC	.40	.18
☐ 340 Ken Griffey Jr. TC	1.00	.45
☐ 341 Gary Sheffield TC	.20	.09
☐ 342 Dwight Gooden TC	.10	.05
☐ 343 Cal Ripken TC	.75	.35
☐ 344 Tony Gwynn TC	.40	.18
☐ 345 Lenny Dykstra TC	.10	.05
☐ 346 Andy Van Slyke TC	.10	.05
☐ 347 Juan Gonzalez TC	.40	.18
☐ 348 Roger Clemens TC	.40	.18
☐ 349 Barry Larkin TC	.20	.09
☐ 350 Andres Galarraga TC	.20	.09
☐ 351 Kevin Appier TC	.10	.05
☐ 352 Cecil Fielder TC	.10	.05
☐ 353 Kirby Puckett TC	.40	.18
☐ 354 Frank Thomas TC	1.00	.45
☐ 355 Don Mattingly TC	.40	.18
☐ 356 Bo Jackson	.20	.09
☐ 357 Randy Johnson	.40	.18
☐ 358 Darren Daulton	.20	.09
☐ 359 Charlie Hough	.10	.05
☐ 360 Andres Galarraga	.10	.05
☐ 361 Mike Felder	.10	.05
☐ 362 Chris Hammond	.10	.05
☐ 363 Shawon Dunston	.10	.05
☐ 364 Junior Felix	.10	.05
☐ 365 Ray Lankford	.10	.05
☐ 366 Darryl Strawberry	.20	.09

☐ 367 Dave Magadan	.10	.05
☐ 368 Gregg Olson	.10	.05
☐ 369 Lenny Dykstra	.20	.09
☐ 370 Darrin Jackson	.10	.05
☐ 371 Dave Stewart	.20	.09
☐ 372 Terry Pendleton	.10	.05
☐ 373 Arthur Rhodes	.10	.05
☐ 374 Benito Santiago	.10	.05
☐ 375 Travis Fryman	.20	.09
☐ 376 Scott Brosius	.10	.05
☐ 377 Stan Belinda	.10	.05
☐ 378 Derek Parks	.10	.05
☐ 379 Kevin Seitzer	.10	.05
☐ 380 Wade Boggs	.40	.18
☐ 381 Wally Whitehurst	.10	.05
☐ 382 Scott Leius	.10	.05
☐ 383 Danny Tartabull	.10	.05
☐ 384 Harold Reynolds	.10	.05
☐ 385 Tim Raines	.10	.05
☐ 386 Darryl Hamilton	.10	.05
☐ 387 Felix Fermin	.10	.05
☐ 388 Jim Eisenreich	.20	.09
☐ 389 Kurt Abbott	.10	.05
☐ 390 Kevin Appier	.10	.05
☐ 391 Chris Bosio	.10	.05
☐ 392 Randy Tomlin	.10	.05
☐ 393 Bob Hamelin	.10	.05
☐ 394 Kevin Gross	.10	.05
☐ 395 Wil Cordero	.10	.05
☐ 396 Joe Girardi	.10	.05
☐ 397 Orestes Destrade	.10	.05
☐ 398 Chris Haney	.10	.05
☐ 399 Xavier Hernandez	.10	.05
☐ 400 Mike Piazza	1.25	.55
☐ 401 Alex Arias	.10	.05
☐ 402 Tom Candiotti	.10	.05
☐ 403 Kirk Gibson	.20	.09
☐ 404 Chuck Carr	.10	.05
☐ 405 Brady Anderson	.10	.05
☐ 406 Greg Gagne	.10	.05
☐ 407 Bruce Ruffin	.10	.05
☐ 408 Scott Hemond	.10	.05
☐ 409 Keith Miller	.10	.05
☐ 410 John Wetteland	.20	.09
☐ 411 Eric Anthony	.10	.05
☐ 412 Andre Dawson	.10	.05
☐ 413 Doug Henry	.10	.05
☐ 414 John Franco	.10	.05
☐ 415 Julio Franco	.20	.09
☐ 416 Dave Hansen	.10	.05
☐ 417 Mike Harkey	.10	.05
☐ 418 Jack Armstrong	.10	.05
☐ 419 Joe Orsulak	.10	.05
☐ 420 John Smoltz	.10	.05
☐ 421 Scott Livingstone	.10	.05
☐ 422 Darren Holmes	.10	.05
☐ 423 Ed Sprague	.10	.05
☐ 424 Jay Buhner	.10	.05
☐ 425 Kirby Puckett	.75	.35
☐ 426 Phil Clark	.10	.05
☐ 427 Anthony Young	.10	.05
☐ 428 Reggie Jefferson	.10	.05
☐ 429 Mariano Duncan	.10	.05
☐ 430 Tom Glavine	.10	.05
☐ 431 Dave Henderson	.10	.05
☐ 432 Melido Perez	.10	.05
☐ 433 Paul Wagner	.10	.05
☐ 434 Tim Worrell	.10	.05
☐ 435 Ozzie Guillen	.10	.05
☐ 436 Mike Butcher	.10	.05
☐ 437 Jim Deshaies	.10	.05
☐ 438 Kevin Young	.10	.05
☐ 439 Tom Browning	.10	.05
☐ 440 Mike Greenwell	.10	.05
☐ 441 Mike Stanton	.10	.05
☐ 442 John Doherty	.10	.05
☐ 443 John Dopson	.10	.05
☐ 444 Carlos Baerga	.20	.09
☐ 445 Jack McDowell	.10	.05
☐ 446 Kent Mercker	.10	.05
☐ 447 Ricky Jordan	.10	.05
☐ 448 Jerry Browne	.10	.05
☐ 449 Fernando Vina	.10	.05
☐ 450 Jim Abbott	.10	.05
☐ 451 Teddy Higuera	.10	.05
☐ 452 Tim Naehring	.10	.05
☐ 453 Jim Leyritz	.10	.05
☐ 454 Frank Castillo	.10	.05
☐ 455 Joe Carter	.10	.05
☐ 456 Craig Biggio	.10	.05
☐ 457 Geronimo Pena	.10	.05
☐ 458 Alejandro Pena	.10	.05
☐ 459 Mike Moore	.10	.05
☐ 460 Randy Myers	.10	.05
☐ 461 Greg Myers	.10	.05
☐ 462 Greg Hibbard	.10	.05
☐ 463 Jose Guzman	.10	.05
☐ 464 Tom Pagnozzi	.10	.05
☐ 465 Marquis Grissom	.20	.09
☐ 466 Tim Wallach	.10	.05
☐ 467 Joe Grahe	.10	.05
☐ 468 Bob Tewksbury	.10	.05
☐ 469 B.J. Surhoff	.10	.05
☐ 470 Kevin Mitchell	.20	.09
☐ 471 Bobby Witt	.10	.05
☐ 472 Milt Thompson	.10	.05
☐ 473 John Smiley	.10	.05
☐ 474 Alan Trammell	.10	.05
☐ 475 Mike Mussina	.40	.18
☐ 476 Rick Aguilera	.10	.05
☐ 477 Jose Valentin	.10	.05
☐ 478 Harold Baines	.20	.09
☐ 479 Bip Roberts	.10	.05
☐ 480 Edgar Martinez	.10	.05
☐ 481 Rheal Cormier	.10	.05
☐ 482 Hal Morris	.10	.05
☐ 483 Pat Kelly	.10	.05
☐ 484 Roberto Kelly	.10	.05
☐ 485 Chris Sabo	.10	.05
☐ 486 Kent Hrbek	.20	.09
☐ 487 Scott Kamieniecki	.10	.05
☐ 488 Walt Weiss	.10	.05
☐ 489 Karl Rhodes	.10	.05
☐ 490 Derek Bell	.20	.09
☐ 491 Chili Davis	.20	.09
☐ 492 Brian Harper	.10	.05
☐ 493 Felix Jose	.10	.05
☐ 494 Trevor Hoffman	.20	.09
☐ 495 Dennis Eckersley	.10	.05
☐ 496 Pedro Astacio	.10	.05
☐ 497 Jay Bell	.20	.09
☐ 498 Randy Velarde	.10	.05
☐ 499 David Wells	.10	.05
☐ 500 Frank Thomas	1.50	.70
☐ 501 Mark Lemke	.10	.05
☐ 502 Mike Devereaux	.10	.05
☐ 503 Chuck McElroy	.10	.05
☐ 504 Luis Polonia	.10	.05
☐ 505 Damion Easley	.10	.05
☐ 506 Greg A. Harris	.10	.05
☐ 507 Chris James	.10	.05
☐ 508 Terry Mulholland	.10	.05
☐ 509 Pete Smith	.10	.05
☐ 510 Rickey Henderson	.10	.05
☐ 511 Sid Fernandez	.10	.05
☐ 512 Al Leiter	.10	.05
☐ 513 Doug Jones	.10	.05
☐ 514 Steve Farr	.10	.05
☐ 515 Chuck Finley	.10	.05
☐ 516 Bobby Thigpen	.10	.05
☐ 517 Jim Edmonds	.40	.18
☐ 518 Graeme Lloyd	.10	.05
☐ 519 Dwight Gooden	.20	.09
☐ 520 Pat Listach	.10	.05
☐ 521 Kevin Bass	.10	.05
☐ 522 Willie Banks	.10	.05
☐ 523 Steve Finley	.20	.09
☐ 524 Delino DeShields	.10	.05
☐ 525 Mark McGwire	.75	.35
☐ 526 Greg Swindell	.10	.05
☐ 527 Chris Nabholz	.10	.05
☐ 528 Scott Sanders	.10	.05
☐ 529 David Segui	.10	.05
☐ 530 Howard Johnson	.10	.05
☐ 531 Jaime Navarro	.10	.05
☐ 532 Jose Vizcaino	.10	.05
☐ 533 Mark Lewis	.10	.05
☐ 534 Pete Harnisch	.10	.05
☐ 535 Robby Thompson	.10	.05
☐ 536 Marcus Moore	.10	.05
☐ 537 Kevin Brown	.20	.09
☐ 538 Mark Clark	.10	.05
☐ 539 Sterling Hitchcock	.20	.09
☐ 540 Will Clark	.20	.09
☐ 541 Denis Boucher	.10	.05
☐ 542 Jack Morris	.20	.09
☐ 543 Pedro Munoz	.10	.05
☐ 544 Bret Boone	.10	.05
☐ 545 Ozzie Smith	.50	.23
☐ 546 Dennis Martinez	.20	.09
☐ 547 Dan Wilson	.20	.09
☐ 548 Rick Sutcliffe	.10	.05
☐ 549 Kevin McReynolds	.10	.05
☐ 550 Roger Clemens	.75	.35
☐ 551 Todd Benzinger	.10	.05
☐ 552 Bill Haselman	.10	.05
☐ 553 Bobby Munoz	.10	.05
☐ 554 Ellis Burks	.20	.09
☐ 555 Ryne Sandberg	.50	.23
☐ 556 Lee Smith	.20	.09
☐ 557 Danny Bautista	.10	.05
☐ 558 Rey Sanchez	.10	.05
☐ 559 Norm Charlton	.10	.05
☐ 560 Jose Canseco	.10	.05
☐ 561 Tim Belcher	.10	.05
☐ 562 Denny Neagle	.20	.09
☐ 563 Eric Davis	.20	.09
☐ 564 Jody Reed	.10	.05
☐ 565 Kenny Lofton	.50	.23
☐ 566 Gary Gaetti	.20	.09
☐ 567 Todd Worrell	.10	.05
☐ 568 Mark Portugal	.10	.05
☐ 569 Dick Schofield	.10	.05
☐ 570 Andy Benes	.20	.09
☐ 571 Zane Smith	.10	.05
☐ 572 Bobby Ayala	.10	.05
☐ 573 Chip Hale	.10	.05
☐ 574 Bob Welch	.10	.05
☐ 575 Deion Sanders	.40	.18
☐ 576 Dave Nied	.10	.05
☐ 577 Pat Mahomes	.10	.05
☐ 578 Charles Nagy	.20	.09
☐ 579 Otis Nixon	.20	.09
☐ 580 Dean Palmer	.20	.09
☐ 581 Roberto Petagine	.10	.05
☐ 582 Dwight Smith	.10	.05
☐ 583 Jeff Russell	.10	.05
☐ 584 Mark Dewey	.10	.05
☐ 585 Greg Vaughn	.10	.05
☐ 586 Brian Hunter	.10	.05
☐ 587 Willie McGee	.10	.05
☐ 588 Pedro J. Martinez	.40	.18
☐ 589 Roger Salkeld	.10	.05
☐ 590 Jeff Bagwell	.75	.35
☐ 591 Spike Owen	.10	.05
☐ 592 Jeff Reardon	.20	.09
☐ 593 Erik Pappas	.10	.05
☐ 594 Brian Williams	.10	.05
☐ 595 Eddie Murray	.40	.18
☐ 596 Henry Rodriguez	.10	.05
☐ 597 Erik Hanson	.10	.05
☐ 598 Stan Javier	.10	.05
☐ 599 Mitch Williams	.10	.05
☐ 600 John Olerud	.10	.05
☐ 601 Vince Coleman	.10	.05
☐ 602 Damon Berryhill	.10	.05
☐ 603 Tom Brunansky	.10	.05
☐ 604 Robb Nen	.20	.09
☐ 605 Rafael Palmeiro	.10	.05
☐ 606 Cal Eldred	.10	.05
☐ 607 Jeff Brantley	.10	.05
☐ 608 Alan Mills	.10	.05
☐ 609 Jeff Nelson	.10	.05
☐ 610 Barry Bonds	.50	.23
☐ 611 Carlos Pulido	.10	.05
☐ 612 Tim Hyers	.10	.05
☐ 613 Steve Howe	.10	.05
☐ 614 Brian Turang	.10	.05
☐ 615 Leo Gomez	.10	.05
☐ 616 Jesse Orosco	.10	.05
☐ 617 Dan Pasqua	.10	.05
☐ 618 Marvin Freeman	.10	.05
☐ 619 Tony Fernandez	.10	.05
☐ 620 Albert Belle	.50	.23
☐ 621 Eddie Taubensee	.10	.05
☐ 622 Mike Jackson	.10	.05
☐ 623 Jose Bautista	.10	.05
☐ 624 Jim Thome	.50	.23
☐ 625 Ivan Rodriguez	.50	.23
☐ 626 Ben Rivera	.10	.05
☐ 627 Dave Valle	.10	.05
☐ 628 Tom Henke	.10	.05
☐ 629 Omar Vizquel	.20	.09
☐ 630 Juan Gonzalez	1.00	.45
☐ 631 Roberto Alomar UP	.20	.09
☐ 632 Barry Bonds UP	.40	.18
☐ 633 Juan Gonzalez UP	.50	.23
☐ 634 Ken Griffey Jr. UP	1.00	.45
☐ 635 Michael Jordan UP	2.50	1.10
☐ 636 David Justice UP	.20	.09
☐ 637 Mike Piazza UP	.60	.25
☐ 638 Kirby Puckett UP	.40	.18
☐ 639 Tim Salmon UP	.10	.05
☐ 640 Frank Thomas UP	1.00	.45
☐ 641 Alan Benes FF	1.00	.45
☐ 642 Johnny Damon FF	.20	.09
☐ 643 Brad Fullmer FF	1.00	.45
☐ 644 Derek Jeter FF	1.50	.70
☐ 645 Derrek Lee FF	1.25	.55
☐ 646 Alex Ochoa FF	.10	.05
☐ 647 Alex Rodriguez FF	5.00	2.20
☐ 648 Jose Silva FF	.10	.05
☐ 649 Terrell Wade FF	.40	.18
☐ 650 Preston Wilson FF	.20	.09
☐ 651 Shane Andrews	.10	.05
☐ 652 James Baldwin	.20	.09
☐ 653 Ricky Bottalico	.20	.09
☐ 654 Tavo Alvarez	.10	.05
☐ 655 Donnie Elliott	.10	.05
☐ 656 Joey Eischen	.10	.05
☐ 657 Jason Giambi	.40	.18

	MINT	NRMT
☐ 658 Todd Hollandsworth	.40	.18
☐ 659 Brian L. Hunter	.10	.05
☐ 660 Charles Johnson	.10	.05
☐ 661 Michael Jordan	6.00	2.70
☐ 662 Jeff Juden	.10	.05
☐ 663 Mike Kelly	.10	.05
☐ 664 James Mouton	.20	.09
☐ 665 Ray Holbert	.10	.05
☐ 666 Pokey Reese	.10	.05
☐ 667 Ruben Santana	.10	.05
☐ 668 Paul Spoljaric	.10	.05
☐ 669 Luis Lopez	.10	.05
☐ 670 Matt Walbeck	.10	.05
☐ P50 Ken Griffey Jr. Promo	1.00	.45

1994 Collector's Choice Gold Signature

This 670-card Gold Signature set is a parallel to the basic Collector's Choice issue. These cards were randomly inserted into first and second series packs at a rate of one in 36. Gold cards were also issued five per factory set. These cards are identical to the basic issue except for gold foil fronts and a facsimile gold foil player's signature. Some subset cards feature borderless designs (unlike the basic player cards), thus their corresponding borderless Gold Foil Signature cards differ only by the gold foil replica autograph. The Jeffrey Hammonds card has the signature of Orioles General Manager Roland Hemond.

	MINT	NRMT
COMPLETE SET (670)	2400.00	1100.00
COMPLETE SERIES 1 (320)	1200.00	550.00
COMPLETE SERIES 2 (350)	1200.00	550.00
COMMON CARD (1-670)	1.50	.70

*STARS: 20X TO 40X BASIC CARDS ..
*YOUNG STARS: 15X TO 30X BASIC CARDS
*ROOKIES: 10X to 20X BASIC CARDS

1994 Collector's Choice Silver Signature

This 670-card set is a parallel to the basic Collector's Choice set. One card was inserted into every first and second series pack. Silver cards were also inserted at different rates in other pack forms. Each Silver Foil Signature card is identical in design to its corresponding regular issue card except for the silver borders and silver replica autograph. As with the gold set, the Jeffrey Hammonds card has the signature of Orioles General Manager Roland Hemond.

	MINT	NRMT
COMPLETE SET (670)	200.00	90.00
COMPLETE SERIES 1 (320)	90.00	40.00
COMPLETE SERIES 2 (350)	110.00	50.00
COMMON CARD (1-670)	.10	.05

*STARS: 2X to 4X BASIC CARDS ....
*YOUNG STARS: 1.5X to 3X BASIC CARDS

1994 Collector's Choice Home Run All-Stars

This 15-card standard-size set served as the eighth place prize in the Crash the Game contest, which was a promotion in both series of Collector's Choice. The series 1 expiration was May 18, 1994; series 2 was Oct. 31, 1994. Horizontal fronts feature holographic images of the player that breaks through a brick wall. A small color photo of the player appears at left or right. The backs, outlined with bricks, features a small photo and text that appears over a stadium background. The cards are numbered with an "HA" prefix.

	MINT	NRMT
COMPLETE SET (8)	4.00	1.80
COMMON CARD (HA1-HA8)	.25	.11
☐ HA1 Juan Gonzalez	1.50	.70
☐ HA2 Ken Griffey Jr.	3.00	1.35
☐ HA3 Barry Bonds	.75	.35
☐ HA4 Bobby Bonilla	.35	.16
☐ HA5 Cecil Fielder UER (Card number is HA4)	.25	.11
☐ HA6 Albert Belle	.75	.35
☐ HA7 David Justice	.60	.25
☐ HA8 Mike Piazza	2.00	.90

1994 Collector's Choice Team vs. Team

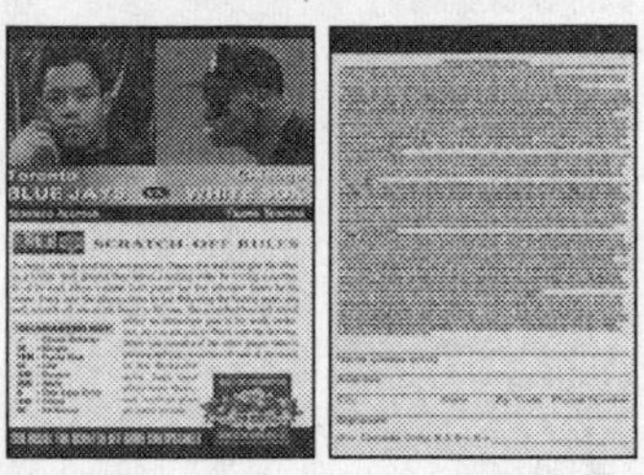

Issued one per second series pack, these 15 foldout, scratch-off game cards feature one team's lineup against the other. Various prizes were available through these game cards. The most plentiful was the eighth place Home Run All-Stars hologram set. Prizes were redeemable through October 31, 1994. Scratch-off rules and two small player photos are on the front with complete rules and provisions on the back. The cards fold out to expose the game portion. Cards that are scratched are half the values below.

	MINT	NRMT
COMPLETE SET (15)	5.00	2.20
COMMON FOLDOUT (1-15)	.25	.11
☐ 1 Roberto Alomar / Frank Thomas	1.00	.45
☐ 2 Barry Bonds / Ken Griffey Jr.	1.00	.45
☐ 3 Roger Clemens / Don Mattingly	.50	.23
☐ 4 Lenny Dykstra / David Justice	.25	.11
☐ 5 Andres Galarraga / Tony Gwynn	.40	.18
☐ 6 Dwight Gooden / Gary Sheffield	.40	.18
☐ 7 Ken Griffey Jr. / Juan Gonzalez	1.00	.45
☐ 8 Barry Larkin / Jeff Bagwell	.40	.18
☐ 9 Pat Listach / Albert Belle	.25	.11
☐ 10 Mark McGwire / Tim Salmon	.40	.18
☐ 11 Mike Piazza / Barry Bonds	.60	.25
☐ 12 Kirby Puckett / Brian McRae	.40	.18
☐ 13 Cal Ripken / Cecil Fielder	.75	.35
☐ 14 Ryne Sandberg / Ozzie Smith	.50	23
☐ 15 Andy Van Slyke / Cliff Floyd	.25	.11

1995 Collector's Choice

This set contains 530 standard-size cards issued in 12-card foil hobby and retail packs for a suggested price of 99 cents. The fronts have a color photo with a white border and the player's last name at the bottom in his team's color. The backs have an action photo at the to with statistics and information at the bottom with a silve Upper Deck hologram below that. Subsets featured ar Rookie Class (1-27), Future Foundation (28-45), Best c the '90s (51-65) and Whatís the Call? (86-90). Key Rooki Cards in this set include Karim Garcia and Hideo Nomo The 55-card Trade set represents the cards a collecto received when the five randomly inserted trade cards wer redeemed. They are numbered in continuation of th regular Collector's Choice cards but have a "T" suffix. Th cards numbered 542-552 were also issued as a bonus t dealers who ordered collector's choice factory sets. Th trade cards offer expired on February 1, 1996.

	MINT	NRMT
COMPLETE SET (530)	20.00	9.00
COMP.FACT.SET (545)	25.00	11.00
COMMON CARD (1-530)	.10	.05
COMP.TRADE SET (55)	10.00	4.50
COMMON TRADE (531-585)	.15	.07
COMMON TRADE DP (542-552)	.05	.02
COMP.TRADE EXCH.SET (5)	4.00	1.80
COMMON TRD.EXCH. (TC1-TC5)	1.00	.45
☐ 1 Charles Johnson	.20	.09
☐ 2 Scott Ruffcorn	.10	.05
☐ 3 Ray Durham	.20	.09
☐ 4 Armando Benitez	.10	.05
☐ 5 Alex Rodriguez	1.50	.70
☐ 6 Julian Tavarez	.10	.05
☐ 7 Chad Ogea	.10	.05
☐ 8 Quilvio Veras	.10	.05
☐ 9 Phil Nevin	.10	.05
☐ 10 Michael Tucker	.30	.14
☐ 11 Mark Thompson	.20	.09
☐ 12 Rod Henderson	.10	.05
☐ 13 Andrew Lorraine	.20	.09
☐ 14 Joe Randa	.10	.05
☐ 15 Derek Jeter	1.25	.55
☐ 16 Tony Clark	.50	.23
☐ 17 Juan Castillo	.10	.05
☐ 18 Mark Acre	.10	.05
☐ 19 Orlando Miller	.10	.05
☐ 20 Paul Wilson	.20	.09
☐ 21 John Mabry	.30	.14
☐ 22 Garey Ingram	.10	.05
☐ 23 Garret Anderson	.30	.14
☐ 24 Dave Stevens	.10	.05
☐ 25 Dustin Hermanson	.10	.05
☐ 26 Paul Shuey	.10	.05
☐ 27 J.R. Phillips	.10	.05
☐ 28 Ruben Rivera FF	.40	.18
☐ 29 Nomar Garciaparra FF	2.50	1.10
☐ 30 John Wasdin FF	.20	.09
☐ 31 Jim Pittsley FF	.30	.14
☐ 32 Scott Elarton FF	.50	.23
☐ 33 Raul Casanova FF	.30	.14
☐ 34 Todd Greene FF	.40	.18
☐ 35 Bill Pulsipher FF	.20	.09
☐ 36 Trey Beamon FF	.20	.09
☐ 37 Curtis Goodwin FF	.10	.05
☐ 38 Doug Million FF	.10	.05
☐ 39 Karim Garcia FF	1.00	.45
☐ 40 Ben Grieve FF	2.00	.90
☐ 41 Mark Farris FF	.20	.09
☐ 42 Juan Acevedo FF	.10	.05
☐ 43 C.J. Nitkowski FF	.10	.05
☐ 44 Travis Miller FF	.20	.09
☐ 45 Reid Ryan FF	.40	.18
☐ 46 Nolan Ryan	1.50	.70
☐ 47 Robin Yount	.30	.14
☐ 48 Ryne Sandberg	.50	.23
☐ 49 George Brett	.75	.35
☐ 50 Mike Schmidt	.50	.23
☐ 51 Cecil Fielder B90	.20	.09
☐ 52 Nolan Ryan B90	.60	.25
☐ 53 Rickey Henderson B90	.30	.14
☐ 54 George Brett B90 / Robin Yount / Dave Winfield	.40	.18
☐ 55 Sid Bream B90	.10	.05
☐ 56 Carlos Baerga B90	.20	.09
☐ 57 Lee Smith B90	.20	.09
☐ 58 Mark Whiten B90	.10	.05
☐ 59 Joe Carter B90	.30	.14
☐ 60 Barry Bonds B90	.40	.18
☐ 61 Tony Gwynn B90	.40	.18
☐ 62 Ken Griffey Jr. B90	1.00	.45
☐ 63 Greg Maddux B90	.60	.25
☐ 64 Frank Thomas B90	1.00	.45
☐ 65 Dennis Martinez B90 / Kenny Rogers	.10	.05
☐ 66 David Cone	.20	.09
☐ 67 Greg Maddux	1.25	.55
☐ 68 Jimmy Key	.20	.09
☐ 69 Fred McGriff	.30	.14
☐ 70 Ken Griffey Jr.	2.00	.90
☐ 71 Matt Williams	.30	.14

☐ 72 Paul O'Neill	.20	.09
☐ 73 Tony Gwynn	1.00	.45
☐ 74 Randy Johnson	.40	.18
☐ 75 Frank Thomas	1.50	.70
☐ 76 Jeff Bagwell	.75	.35
☐ 77 Kirby Puckett	.75	.35
☐ 78 Bob Hamelin	.10	.05
☐ 79 Raul Mondesi	.30	.14
☐ 80 Mike Piazza	1.25	.55
☐ 81 Kenny Lofton	.50	.23
☐ 82 Barry Bonds	.50	.23
☐ 83 Albert Belle	.50	.23
☐ 84 Juan Gonzalez	1.00	.45
☐ 85 Cal Ripken Jr.	1.50	.70
☐ 86 Barry Bonds WC	.40	.18
☐ 87 Mike Piazza WC	.60	.25
☐ 88 Ken Griffey Jr. WC	1.00	.45
☐ 89 Frank Thomas WC	1.00	.45
☐ 90 Juan Gonzalez WC	.50	.23
☐ 91 Jorge Fabregas	.10	.05
☐ 92 J.T. Snow	.20	.09
☐ 93 Spike Owen	.10	.05
☐ 94 Eduardo Perez	.10	.05
☐ 95 Bo Jackson	.20	.09
☐ 96 Damion Easley	.10	.05
☐ 97 Gary DiSarcina	.10	.05
☐ 98 Jim Edmonds	.30	.14
☐ 99 Chad Curtis	.10	.05
☐ 100 Tim Salmon	.30	.14
☐ 101 Chili Davis	.20	.09
☐ 102 Chuck Finley	.20	.09
☐ 103 Mark Langston	.10	.05
☐ 104 Brian Anderson	.10	.05
☐ 105 Lee Smith	.20	.09
☐ 106 Phil Leftwich	.10	.05
☐ 107 Chris Donnels	.10	.05
☐ 108 John Hudek	.10	.05
☐ 109 Craig Biggio	.30	.14
☐ 110 Luis Gonzalez	.10	.05
☐ 111 Brian L. Hunter	.20	.09
☐ 112 James Mouton	.10	.05
☐ 113 Scott Servais	.10	.05
☐ 114 Tony Eusebio	.10	.05
☐ 115 Derek Bell	.20	.09
☐ 116 Doug Drabek	.10	.05
☐ 117 Shane Reynolds	.10	.05
☐ 118 Darryl Kile	.20	.09
☐ 119 Greg Swindell	.10	.05
☐ 120 Phil Plantier	.10	.05
☐ 121 Todd Jones	.10	.05
☐ 122 Steve Ontiveros	.10	.05
☐ 123 Bobby Witt	.10	.05
☐ 124 Brent Gates	.10	.05
☐ 125 Rickey Henderson	.30	.14
☐ 126 Scott Brosius	.10	.05
☐ 127 Mike Bordick	.10	.05
☐ 128 Fausto Cruz	.10	.05
☐ 129 Stan Javier	.10	.05
☐ 130 Mark McGwire	.75	.35
☐ 131 Geronimo Berroa	.10	.05
☐ 132 Terry Steinbach	.20	.09
☐ 133 Steve Karsay	.10	.05
☐ 134 Dennis Eckersley	.30	.14
☐ 135 Ruben Sierra	.10	.05
☐ 136 Ron Darling	.10	.05
☐ 137 Todd Van Poppel	.10	.05
☐ 138 Alex Gonzalez	.10	.05
☐ 139 John Olerud	.10	.05
☐ 140 Roberto Alomar	.40	.18
☐ 141 Darren Hall	.10	.05
☐ 142 Ed Sprague	.10	.05
☐ 143 Devon White	.20	.09
☐ 144 Shawn Green	.20	.09
☐ 145 Paul Molitor	.40	.18
☐ 146 Pat Borders	.10	.05
☐ 147 Carlos Delgado	.30	.14
☐ 148 Juan Guzman	.10	.05
☐ 149 Pat Hentgen	.20	.09
☐ 150 Joe Carter	.30	.14
☐ 151 Dave Stewart	.20	.09
☐ 152 Todd Stottlemyre	.10	.05
☐ 153 Dick Schofield	.10	.05
☐ 154 Chipper Jones	1.25	.55
☐ 155 Ryan Klesko	.30	.14
☐ 156 David Justice	.40	.18
☐ 157 Mike Kelly	.10	.05
☐ 158 Roberto Kelly	.10	.05
☐ 159 Tony Tarasco	.10	.05
☐ 160 Javier Lopez	.30	.14
☐ 161 Steve Avery	.10	.05
☐ 162 Greg McMichael	.10	.05
☐ 163 Kent Mercker	.10	.05
☐ 164 Mark Lemke	.10	.05
☐ 165 Tom Glavine	.30	.14
☐ 166 Jose Oliva	.10	.05
☐ 167 John Smoltz	.30	.14
☐ 168 Jeff Blauser	.10	.05
☐ 169 Troy O'Leary	.10	.05
☐ 170 Greg Vaughn	.10	.05
☐ 171 Jody Reed	.10	.05
☐ 172 Kevin Seitzer	.10	.05
☐ 173 Jeff Cirillo	.20	.09
☐ 174 B.J. Surhoff	.20	.09
☐ 175 Cal Eldred	.10	.05
☐ 176 Jose Valentin	.20	.09
☐ 177 Turner Ward	.10	.05
☐ 178 Darryl Hamilton	.10	.05
☐ 179 Pat Listach	.10	.05
☐ 180 Matt Mieske	.20	.09
☐ 181 Brian Harper	.10	.05
☐ 182 Dave Nilsson	.20	.09
☐ 183 Mike Fetters	.10	.05
☐ 184 John Jaha	.10	.05
☐ 185 Ricky Bones	.10	.05
☐ 186 Geronimo Pena	.10	.05
☐ 187 Bob Tewksbury	.10	.05
☐ 188 Todd Zeile	.10	.05
☐ 189 Danny Jackson	.10	.05
☐ 190 Ray Lankford	.30	.14
☐ 191 Bernard Gilkey	.10	.05
☐ 192 Brian Jordan	.20	.09
☐ 193 Tom Pagnozzi	.10	.05
☐ 194 Rick Sutcliffe	.10	.05
☐ 195 Mark Whiten	.10	.05
☐ 196 Tom Henke	.10	.05
☐ 197 Rene Arocha	.10	.05
☐ 198 Allen Watson	.10	.05
☐ 199 Mike Perez	.10	.05
☐ 200 Ozzie Smith	.50	.23
☐ 201 Anthony Young	.10	.05
☐ 202 Rey Sanchez	.10	.05
☐ 203 Steve Buechele	.10	.05
☐ 204 Shawon Dunston	.10	.05
☐ 205 Mark Grace	.30	.14
☐ 206 Glenallen Hill	.10	.05
☐ 207 Eddie Zambrano	.10	.05
☐ 208 Rick Wilkins	.10	.05
☐ 209 Derrick May	.10	.05
☐ 210 Sammy Sosa	.40	.18
☐ 211 Kevin Roberson	.10	.05
☐ 212 Steve Trachsel	.10	.05
☐ 213 Willie Banks	.10	.05
☐ 214 Kevin Foster	.10	.05
☐ 215 Randy Myers	.10	.05
☐ 216 Mike Morgan	.10	.05
☐ 217 Rafael Bournigal	.10	.05
☐ 218 Delino DeShields	.10	.05
☐ 219 Tim Wallach	.10	.05
☐ 220 Eric Karros	.20	.09
☐ 221 Jose Offerman	.10	.05
☐ 222 Tom Candiotti	.10	.05
☐ 223 Ismael Valdes	.20	.09
☐ 224 Henry Rodriguez	.10	.05
☐ 225 Billy Ashley	.10	.05
☐ 226 Darren Dreifort	.10	.05
☐ 227 Ramon Martinez	.20	.09
☐ 228 Pedro Astacio	.10	.05
☐ 229 Orel Hershiser	.20	.09
☐ 230 Brett Butler	.20	.09
☐ 231 Todd Hollandsworth	.20	.09
☐ 232 Chan Ho Park	.40	.18
☐ 233 Mike Lansing	.10	.05
☐ 234 Sean Berry	.10	.05
☐ 235 Rondell White	.30	.14
☐ 236 Ken Hill	.10	.05
☐ 237 Marquis Grissom	.20	.09
☐ 238 Larry Walker	.40	.18
☐ 239 John Wetteland	.20	.09
☐ 240 Cliff Floyd	.20	.09
☐ 241 Joey Eischen	.10	.05
☐ 242 Lou Frazier	.10	.05
☐ 243 Darrin Fletcher	.10	.05
☐ 244 Pedro J. Martinez	.40	.18
☐ 245 Wil Cordero	.10	.05
☐ 246 Jeff Fassero	.10	.05
☐ 247 Butch Henry	.10	.05
☐ 248 Mel Rojas	.10	.05
☐ 249 Kirk Rueter	.10	.05
☐ 250 Moises Alou	.20	.09
☐ 251 Rod Beck	.10	.05
☐ 252 John Patterson	.10	.05
☐ 253 Robby Thompson	.10	.05
☐ 254 Royce Clayton	.10	.05
☐ 255 Wm. VanLandingham	.10	.05
☐ 256 Darren Lewis	.10	.05
☐ 257 Kirt Manwaring	.10	.05
☐ 258 Mark Portugal	.10	.05
☐ 259 Bill Swift	.10	.05
☐ 260 Rikkert Faneyte	.10	.05
☐ 261 Mike Jackson	.10	.05
☐ 262 Todd Benzinger	.10	.05
☐ 263 Bud Black	.10	.05
☐ 264 Salomon Torres	.10	.05
☐ 265 Eddie Murray	.40	.18
☐ 266 Mark Clark	.10	.05
☐ 267 Paul Sorrento	.10	.05
☐ 268 Jim Thome	.40	.18
☐ 269 Omar Vizquel	.20	.09
☐ 270 Carlos Baerga	.20	.09
☐ 271 Jeff Russell	.10	.05
☐ 272 Herbert Perry	.10	.05
☐ 273 Sandy Alomar Jr.	.10	.05
☐ 274 Dennis Martinez	.20	.09
☐ 275 Manny Ramirez	.40	.18
☐ 276 Wayne Kirby	.10	.05
☐ 277 Charles Nagy	.20	.09
☐ 278 Albie Lopez	.10	.05
☐ 279 Jeromy Burnitz	.10	.05
☐ 280 Dave Winfield	.30	.14
☐ 281 Tim Davis	.10	.05
☐ 282 Marc Newfield	.20	.09
☐ 283 Tino Martinez	.40	.18
☐ 284 Mike Blowers	.10	.05
☐ 285 Goose Gossage	.20	.09
☐ 286 Luis Sojo	.10	.05
☐ 287 Edgar Martinez	.30	.14
☐ 288 Rich Amaral	.10	.05
☐ 289 Felix Fermin	.10	.05
☐ 290 Jay Buhner	.30	.14
☐ 291 Dan Wilson	.20	.09
☐ 292 Bobby Ayala	.10	.05
☐ 293 Dave Fleming	.10	.05
☐ 294 Greg Pirkl	.10	.05
☐ 295 Reggie Jefferson	.20	.09
☐ 296 Greg Hibbard	.10	.05
☐ 297 Yorkis Perez	.10	.05
☐ 298 Kurt Miller	.10	.05
☐ 299 Chuck Carr	.10	.05
☐ 300 Gary Sheffield	.40	.18
☐ 301 Jerry Browne	.10	.05
☐ 302 Dave Magadan	.10	.05
☐ 303 Kurt Abbott	.10	.05
☐ 304 Pat Rapp	.10	.05
☐ 305 Jeff Conine	.20	.09
☐ 306 Benito Santiago	.10	.05
☐ 307 Dave Weathers	.10	.05
☐ 308 Robb Nen	.10	.05
☐ 309 Chris Hammond	.10	.05
☐ 310 Bryan Harvey	.10	.05
☐ 311 Charlie Hough	.10	.05
☐ 312 Greg Colbrunn	.10	.05
☐ 313 David Segui	.10	.05
☐ 314 Rico Brogna	.10	.05
☐ 315 Jeff Kent	.10	.05
☐ 316 Jose Vizcaino	.10	.05
☐ 317 Jim Lindeman	.10	.05
☐ 318 Carl Everett	.10	.05
☐ 319 Ryan Thompson	.10	.05
☐ 320 Bobby Bonilla	.20	.09
☐ 321 Joe Orsulak	.10	.05
☐ 322 Pete Harnisch	.10	.05
☐ 323 Doug Linton	.10	.05
☐ 324 Todd Hundley	.20	.09
☐ 325 Bret Saberhagen	.10	.05
☐ 326 Kelly Stinnett	.10	.05
☐ 327 Jason Jacome	.10	.05
☐ 328 Bobby Jones	.20	.09
☐ 329 John Franco	.20	.09
☐ 330 Rafael Palmeiro	.30	.14
☐ 331 Chris Hoiles	.10	.05
☐ 332 Leo Gomez	.10	.05
☐ 333 Chris Sabo	.10	.05
☐ 334 Brady Anderson	.30	.14
☐ 335 Jeffrey Hammonds	.20	.09
☐ 336 Dwight Smith	.10	.05
☐ 337 Jack Voigt	.10	.05
☐ 338 Harold Baines	.20	.09
☐ 339 Ben McDonald	.10	.05
☐ 340 Mike Mussina	.40	.18
☐ 341 Bret Barberie	.10	.05
☐ 342 Jamie Moyer	.10	.05
☐ 343 Mike Oquist	.10	.05
☐ 344 Sid Fernandez	.10	.05
☐ 345 Eddie Williams	.10	.05
☐ 346 Joey Hamilton	.30	.14
☐ 347 Brian Williams	.10	.05
☐ 348 Luis Lopez	.10	.05
☐ 349 Steve Finley	.20	.09
☐ 350 Andy Benes	.10	.05
☐ 351 Andujar Cedeno	.10	.05
☐ 352 Bip Roberts	.10	.05
☐ 353 Ray McDavid	.10	.05
☐ 354 Ken Caminiti	.40	.18
☐ 355 Trevor Hoffman	.20	.09
☐ 356 Mel Nieves	.20	.09
☐ 357 Brad Ausmus	.10	.05
☐ 358 Andy Ashby	.10	.05
☐ 359 Scott Sanders	.10	.05
☐ 360 Gregg Jefferies	.20	.09
☐ 361 Mariano Duncan	.10	.05
☐ 362 Dave Hollins	.10	.05

☐ 363 Kevin Stocker .10 .05
☐ 364 Fernando Valenzuela .20 .09
☐ 365 Lenny Dykstra .20 .09
☐ 366 Jim Eisenreich .20 .09
☐ 367 Ricky Bottalico .20 .09
☐ 368 Doug Jones .10 .05
☐ 369 Ricky Jordan .10 .05
☐ 370 Darren Daulton .20 .09
☐ 371 Mike Lieberthal .10 .05
☐ 372 Bobby Munoz .10 .05
☐ 373 John Kruk .20 .09
☐ 374 Curt Schilling .20 .09
☐ 375 Orlando Merced .10 .05
☐ 376 Carlos Garcia .10 .05
☐ 377 Lance Parrish .10 .05
☐ 378 Steve Cooke .10 .05
☐ 379 Jeff King .20 .09
☐ 380 Jay Bell .20 .09
☐ 381 Al Martin .20 .09
☐ 382 Paul Wagner .10 .05
☐ 383 Rick White .10 .05
☐ 384 Midre Cummings .10 .05
☐ 385 Jon Lieber .10 .05
☐ 386 Dave Clark .10 .05
☐ 387 Don Slaught .10 .05
☐ 388 Denny Neagle .20 .09
☐ 389 Zane Smith .10 .05
☐ 390 Andy Van Slyke .20 .09
☐ 391 Ivan Rodriguez .50 .23
☐ 392 David Hulse .10 .05
☐ 393 John Burkett .10 .05
☐ 394 Kevin Brown .20 .09
☐ 395 Dean Palmer .20 .09
☐ 396 Otis Nixon .20 .09
☐ 397 Rick Helling .10 .05
☐ 398 Kenny Rogers .10 .05
☐ 399 Darren Oliver .30 .14
☐ 400 Will Clark .30 .14
☐ 401 Jeff Frye .10 .05
☐ 402 Kevin Gross .10 .05
☐ 403 John Dettmer .10 .05
☐ 404 Manny Lee .10 .05
☐ 405 Rusty Greer .40 .18
☐ 406 Aaron Sele .10 .05
☐ 407 Carlos Rodriguez .10 .05
☐ 408 Scott Cooper .10 .05
☐ 409 John Valentin .20 .09
☐ 410 Roger Clemens .75 .35
☐ 411 Mike Greenwell .10 .05
☐ 412 Tim Vanegmond .10 .05
☐ 413 Tom Brunansky .10 .05
☐ 414 Steve Farr .10 .05
☐ 415 Jose Canseco .30 .14
☐ 416 Joe Hesketh .10 .05
☐ 417 Ken Ryan .10 .05
☐ 418 Tim Naehring .10 .05
☐ 419 Frank Viola .10 .05
☐ 420 Andre Dawson .30 .14
☐ 421 Mo Vaughn .50 .23
☐ 422 Jeff Brantley .10 .05
☐ 423 Pete Schourek .10 .05
☐ 424 Hal Morris .10 .05
☐ 425 Deion Sanders .40 .18
☐ 426 Brian R. Hunter .10 .05
☐ 427 Bret Boone .20 .09
☐ 428 Willie Greene .10 .05
☐ 429 Ron Gant .20 .09
☐ 430 Barry Larkin .30 .14
☐ 431 Reggie Sanders .10 .05
☐ 432 Eddie Taubensee .10 .05
☐ 433 Jack Morris .20 .09
☐ 434 Jose Rijo .10 .05
☐ 435 Johnny Ruffin .10 .05
☐ 436 John Smiley .10 .05
☐ 437 John Roper .10 .05
☐ 438 Dave Nied .10 .05
☐ 439 Roberto Mejia .10 .05
☐ 440 Andres Galarraga .30 .14
☐ 441 Mike Kingery .10 .05
☐ 442 Curt Leskanic .10 .05
☐ 443 Walt Weiss .10 .05
☐ 444 Marvin Freeman .10 .05
☐ 445 Charlie Hayes .10 .05
☐ 446 Eric Young .20 .09
☐ 447 Ellis Burks .20 .09
☐ 448 Joe Girardi .10 .05
☐ 449 Lance Painter .10 .05
☐ 450 Dante Bichette .30 .14
☐ 451 Bruce Ruffin .10 .05
☐ 452 Jeff Granger .10 .05
☐ 453 Wally Joyner .20 .09
☐ 454 Jose Lind .10 .05
☐ 455 Jeff Montgomery .20 .09
☐ 456 Gary Gaetti .20 .09
☐ 457 Greg Gagne .10 .05
☐ 458 Vince Coleman .10 .05
☐ 459 Mike Macfarlane .10 .05
☐ 460 Brian McRae .10 .05
☐ 461 Tom Gordon .10 .05
☐ 462 Kevin Appier .20 .09
☐ 463 Billy Brewer .10 .05
☐ 464 Mark Gubicza .10 .05
☐ 465 Travis Fryman .20 .09
☐ 466 Danny Bautista .10 .05
☐ 467 Sean Bergman .10 .05
☐ 468 Mike Henneman .10 .05
☐ 469 Mike Moore .10 .05
☐ 470 Cecil Fielder .20 .09
☐ 471 Alan Trammell .30 .14
☐ 472 Kirk Gibson .20 .09
☐ 473 Tony Phillips .10 .05
☐ 474 Mickey Tettleton .10 .05
☐ 475 Lou Whitaker .20 .09
☐ 476 Chris Gomez .10 .05
☐ 477 John Doherty .10 .05
☐ 478 Greg Gohr .10 .05
☐ 479 Bill Gullickson .10 .05
☐ 480 Rick Aguilera .10 .05
☐ 481 Matt Walbeck .10 .05
☐ 482 Kevin Tapani .10 .05
☐ 483 Scott Erickson .10 .05
☐ 484 Steve Dunn .10 .05
☐ 485 David McCarty .10 .05
☐ 486 Scott Leius .10 .05
☐ 487 Pat Meares .10 .05
☐ 488 Jeff Reboulet .10 .05
☐ 489 Pedro Munoz .10 .05
☐ 490 Chuck Knoblauch .40 .18
☐ 491 Rich Becker .10 .05
☐ 492 Alex Cole .10 .05
☐ 493 Pat Mahomes .10 .05
☐ 494 Ozzie Guillen .10 .05
☐ 495 Tim Raines .10 .05
☐ 496 Kirk McCaskill .10 .05
☐ 497 Olmedo Saenz .10 .05
☐ 498 Scott Sanderson .10 .05
☐ 499 Lance Johnson .20 .09
☐ 500 Michael Jordan 2.50 1.10
☐ 501 Warren Newson .10 .05
☐ 502 Ron Karkovice .10 .05
☐ 503 Wilson Alvarez .20 .09
☐ 504 Jason Bere .10 .05
☐ 505 Robin Ventura .20 .09
☐ 506 Alex Fernandez .20 .09
☐ 507 Roberto Hernandez .10 .05
☐ 508 Norberto Martin .10 .05
☐ 509 Bob Wickman .10 .05
☐ 510 Don Mattingly .60 .25
☐ 511 Melido Perez .10 .05
☐ 512 Pat Kelly .10 .05
☐ 513 Randy Velarde .10 .05
☐ 514 Tony Fernandez .10 .05
☐ 515 Jack McDowell .20 .09
☐ 516 Luis Polonia .10 .05
☐ 517 Bernie Williams .40 .18
☐ 518 Danny Tartabull .10 .05
☐ 519 Mike Stanley .10 .05
☐ 520 Wade Boggs .40 .18
☐ 521 Jim Leyritz .10 .05
☐ 522 Steve Howe .10 .05
☐ 523 Scott Kamieniecki .10 .05
☐ 524 Russ Davis .10 .05
☐ 525 Jim Abbott .10 .05
☐ 526 Eddie Murray CL .40 .18
☐ 527 Alex Rodriguez CL 1.25 .55
☐ 528 Jeff Bagwell CL .40 .18
☐ 529 Joe Carter CL .30 .14
☐ 530 Fred McGriff CL .30 .14
☐ 531T Tony Phillips TRADE .15 .07
☐ 532T Dave Magadan TRADE .15 .07
☐ 533T Mike Gallego TRADE .15 .07
☐ 534T Dave Stewart TRADE .20 .09
☐ 535T Todd Stottlemyre TRADE .20 .09
☐ 536T David Cone TRADE .20 .09
☐ 537T Marquis Grissom TRADE .20 .09
☐ 538T Derrick May TRADE .15 .07
☐ 539T Joe Oliver TRADE .15 .07
☐ 540T Scott Cooper TRADE .15 .07
☐ 541T Ken Hill TRADE .15 .07
☐ 542T Howard Johnson TRADE DP .15 .07
☐ 543T Brian McRae TRADE DP .15 .07
☐ 544T Jaime Navarro TRADE DP .15 .07
☐ 545T Ozzie Timmons TRADE DP .15 .07
☐ 546T Roberto Kelly TRADE DP .15 .07
☐ 547T Hideo Nomo TRADE DP 5.00 2.20
☐ 548T Shane Andrews TRADE DP .15 .07
☐ 549T M.Grudzielanek TRADE DP .75 .35
☐ 550T Carlos Perez TRADE DP .15 .07
☐ 551T Henry Rodriguez TRADE DP .15 .07
☐ 552T Tony Tarasco TRADE DP .15 .07
☐ 553T Glenallen Hill TRADE .15 .07
☐ 554T Terry Mulholland TRADE .15 .07
☐ 555T Orel Hershiser TRADE .20 .09
☐ 556T Darren Bragg TRADE .15 .07
☐ 557T John Burkett TRADE .15 .0
☐ 558T Bobby Witt TRADE .15 .0
☐ 559T Terry Pendleton TRADE .15 .0
☐ 560T Andre Dawson TRADE .30 .1
☐ 561T Brett Butler TRADE .20 .0
☐ 562T Kevin Brown TRADE .15 .0
☐ 563T Doug Jones TRADE .15 .0
☐ 564T Andy Van Slyke TRADE .20 .0
☐ 565T Jody Reed TRADE .15 .0
☐ 566T Fernando Valenzuela TRADE .20 .0
☐ 567T Charlie Hayes TRADE .15 .0
☐ 568T Benji Gil TRADE .15 .0
☐ 569T Mark McLemore TRADE .15 .0
☐ 570T Mickey Tettleton TRADE .15 .0
☐ 571T Bob Tewksbury TRADE .15 .0
☐ 572T Rheal Cormier TRADE .15 .0
☐ 573T Vaughn Eshelman TRADE .15 .0
☐ 574T Mike Macfarlane TRADE .15 .0
☐ 575T Bill Swift TRADE .15 .0
☐ 576T Mark Whiten TRADE .15 .0
☐ 577T Benito Santiago TRADE .15 .0
☐ 578T Jason Bates TRADE .15 .0
☐ 579T Larry Walker TRADE .75 .3
☐ 580T Chad Curtis TRADE .15 .0
☐ 581T Bobby Higginson TRADE 1.50 .7
☐ 582T Marty Cordova TRADE .40 .1
☐ 583T Mike Devereaux TRADE .15 .0
☐ 584T John Kruk TRADE .20 .0
☐ 585T John Wetteland TRADE .20 .0
☐ TC1 Larry Walker 2.00 .9
☐ TC2 David Cone 1.00 .4
☐ TC3 Marquis Grissom 1.00 .4
☐ TC4 Terry Pendleton 1.00 .4
☐ TC5 Fernando Valenzuela 1.00 .4

1995 Collector's Choice Gold Signature

This set is a parallel of the 530 regular cards from the Collector's Choice set. Gold cards were inserted into one in every 35 packs, 12 per gold super pack and 15 pe factory set. Unlike regular issue cards, each Gold Signature card features a gold border (except for a selection of borderless subset cards) and gold facsimile signature on front.

	MINT	NRMT
COMPLETE SET (530)	1000.00	450.00
COMMON CARD (1-530)	1.00	.45

*STARS: 10X TO 20X BASIC CARDS
*YOUNG STARS: 7.5X TO 15X BASIC CARDS

1995 Collector's Choice Silver Signature

This set is a parallel of the 530 regular cards from the Collector's Choice set. Silver Signature cards were inserted at a rate of one per pack, two per mini jumbo and 12 per silver super pack. Unlike regular issue cards, Silver Signature cards feature silver borders and a silver facsimile signature on front.

	MINT	NRMT
COMPLETE SET (530)	80.00	36.00
COMMON CARD (1-530)	.15	.07

*STARS: 2X to 4X BASIC CARDS
*YOUNG STARS: 1.5X to 3X BASIC CARDS

1995 Collector's Choice Crash the Game

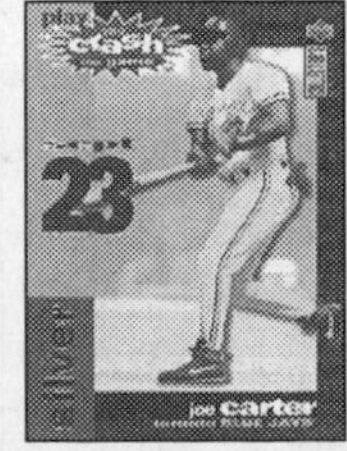

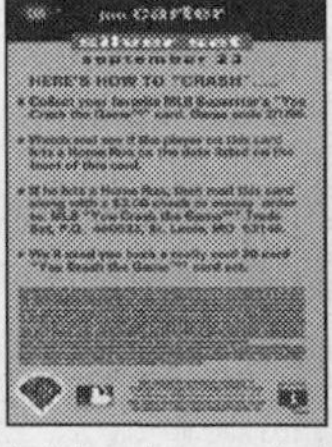

Cards from this 60-card standard-size set were randomly inserted in packs at a rate of one in five. The set is an interactive set in which all 20 players have three cards with a date on it. If the player hit a home run on that date, the collector could redeem the card for a complete nanced set of all 20 players. The fronts have a color-:ion photo with the game background in yellow and a ge date stamped in silver foil. The expiration date for eeming these cards was February 1, 1996. Winning rds eligible for redemption at the time have been ghlighted with a "W" in our listings below.

	MINT	NRMT
MPLETE SET (60)	50.00	22.00
MMON CARD (CG1-CG20)	.10	.05
OLD: 2.5X TO 5X BASIC CARDS		
XCHANGE: .25X TO .5X BASIC CARDS		
OLD EXCHANGE: 2X TO 4X BASIC CARDS		

CG1 Jeff Bagwell 7/30	.75	.35
CG1B Jeff Bagwell 8/13	.75	.35
CG1C Jeff Bagwell 9/28	.75	.35
CG2 Albert Belle 6/18	.50	.23
CG2B Albert Belle 8/26	.50	.23
CG2C Albert Belle 9/20	.50	.23
CG3 Barry Bonds 6/28	.50	.23
CG3B Barry Bonds 7/9	.50	.23
CG3C Barry Bonds 9/6	.50	.23
CG4 Jose Canseco 6/30 W	.35	.16
CG4B Jose Canseco 7/30 W	.35	.16
CG4C Jose Canseco 9/3	.35	.16
CG5 Joe Carter 7/14	.25	.11
CG5B Joe Carter 8/9	.25	.11
CG5C Joe Carter 9/23	.25	.11
CG6 Cecil Fielder 7/4	.25	.11
CG6B Cecil Fielder 8/2	.25	.11
CG6C Cecil Fielder 10/1	.25	.11
CG7 Juan Gonzalez 6/29	1.00	.45
CG7B Juan Gonzalez 8/13	1.00	.45
CG7C Juan Gonzalez 9/3 W	1.00	.45
CG8 Ken Griffey Jr. 7/2	2.00	.90
CG8B Ken Griffey Jr. 8/24 W	2.00	.90
CG8C Ken Griffey Jr. 9/15	2.00	.90
CG9 Bob Hamelin 7/23	.10	.05
CG9B Bob Hamelin 8/1	.10	.05
CG9C Bob Hamelin 9/29	.10	.05
CG10 David Justice 6/24	.25	.11
CG10B David Justice 7/25	.25	.11
CG10C David Justice 9/17	.25	.11
CG11 Ryan Klesko 7/13	.25	.11
CG11B Ryan Klesko 8/20	.25	.11
CG11C Ryan Klesko 9/10	.25	.11
CG12 Fred McGriff 8/25	.25	.11
CG12B Fred McGriff 9/8	.25	.11
CG12C Fred McGriff 9/24	.25	.11
CG13 Mark McGwire 7/23	.75	.35
CG13B Mark McGwire 8/3 W	.75	.35
CG13C Mark McGwire 9/27	.75	.35
CG14 Raul Mondesi 7/27 W	.25	.11
CG14B Raul Mondesi 8/13	.25	.11
CG14C Raul Mondesi 9/15 W	.25	.11
CG15 Mike Piazza 7/23 W	1.25	.55
CG15B Mike Piazza 8/27	1.25	.55
CG15C Mike Piazza 9/19	1.25	.55
CG16 Manny Ramirez 6/21	.40	.18
CG16B Manny Ramirez 8/13	.40	.18
CG16C Manny Ramirez 9/26	.40	.18
CG17 Alex Rodriguez 9/10	1.50	.70
CG17B Alex Rodriguez 9/18	1.50	.70
CG17C Alex Rodriguez 9/24	1.50	.70
CG18 Gary Sheffield	.25	.11
CG18B Gary Sheffield 8/13	.25	.11
CG18C Gary Sheffield 9/4 W	.25	.11
CG19 Frank Thomas 7/26	1.50	.70
CG19B Frank Thomas 8/17	1.50	.70
CG19C Frank Thomas 9/23	1.50	.70
CG20 Matt Williams 7/29	.35	.16
CG20B Matt Williams 8/12	.35	.16
CG20C Matt Williams 9/19	.35	.16

1995 Collector's Choice Crash the All-Star Game

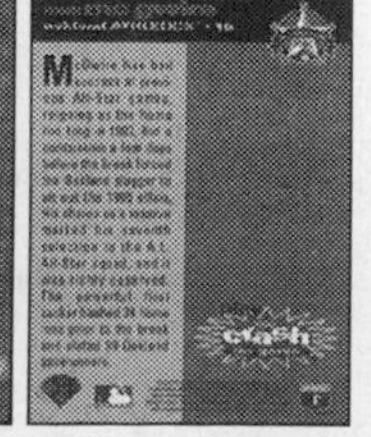

is eight card standard-size set measures the standard ze. The cards carry the names of players who rticipated in the 1995 All-Star game on July 11. The fronts feature color action player photos with a tri-colored border. The player's name and team name are printed in the bottom border. The backs contain the player's name, date of game, and the directions of how to claim a prize if the player hit a home run during the All-Star game. Winner cards could be mailed in, along with 2.00, and redeemed for a gold foil enhanced set. These enhanced cards are valued at the same value as the regular cards. The two winning cards were Mike Piazza and Frank Thomas. The cards are unnumbered and checklisted below in alphabetical order.

	MINT	NRMT
COMPLETE SET (8)	18.00	8.00
COMMON CARD (1-8)	1.00	.45
*REDEMPTION WINNERS: 3X VALUE		

☐ 1 Albert Belle	2.00	.90
☐ 2 Barry Bonds	2.00	.90
☐ 3 Fred McGriff	1.00	.45
☐ 4 Mark McGwire	3.00	1.35
☐ 5 Raul Mondesi	1.00	.45
☐ 6 Mike Piazza	5.00	2.20
☐ 7 Manny Ramirez	1.50	.70
☐ 8 Frank Thomas	6.00	2.70

1996 Collector's Choice

This 790-card standard-size set was issued in 12-card packs with 36 packs per box and 20 boxes per case. Suggested retail price on these packs was 99 cents. The fronts of the regular set feature a player photo, his name and team logo. The backs feature another photo, vital stats and a baseball quiz. The set includes the following subsets: 1995 Stat Leaders (2-9), Rookie Class (10-39), Traditional Threads (100-108), Fantasy Team (268-279), International Flavor (325-342), Series 1 Checklists (358-365), Team Checklists (396-423), First HOF Class (500-504), Award Winners (704-711) and Series 2 Checklists (753-760). Postseason Trade cards were inserted one every 11 packs. These cards had an ordering deadline of May 13 and were each redeemable for 10 cards depicting highlights from the playoffs and World Series, resulting in a 30-card redemption set. Finally, a 30-card Update set was included in each factory set and was also available through a Series 2 wrapper offer.

	MINT	NRMT
COMPLETE SET (730)	24.00	11.00
COMP.FACT.SET (790)	30.00	13.50
COMPLETE SERIES 1 (365)	12.00	5.50
COMPLETE SERIES 2 (365)	12.00	5.50
COMMON (1-365/396-760)	.10	.05
COMP.TRADE SET (30)	15.00	6.75
COMMON TRADE (366T-395T)	.15	.07
COMPLETE UPDATE SET (30)	6.00	2.70
COMMON UPDATE (761-790)	.25	.11

☐ 1 Cal Ripken	1.50	.70
☐ 2 Edgar Martinez SL Tony Gwynn	.40	.18
☐ 3 Albert Belle SL Dante Bichette	.20	.09
☐ 4 Albert Belle SL Mo Vaughn Dante Bichette	.20	.09
☐ 5 Kenny Lofton SL Quilvio Veras	.20	.09
☐ 6 Mike Mussina SL Greg Maddux	.50	.23
☐ 7 Randy Johnson SL Hideo Nomo	.40	.18
☐ 8 Randy Johnson SL Greg Maddux	.50	.23
☐ 9 Jose Mesa SL Randy Myers	.10	.05
☐ 10 Johnny Damon	.20	.09
☐ 11 Rick Krivda	.10	.05
☐ 12 Roger Cedeno	.10	.05
☐ 13 Angel Martinez	.10	.05
☐ 14 Ariel Prieto	.10	.05
☐ 15 John Wasdin	.20	.09
☐ 16 Edwin Hurtado	.10	.05
☐ 17 Lyle Mouton	.10	.05
☐ 18 Chris Snopek	.10	.05
☐ 19 Mariano Rivera	.40	.18
☐ 20 Ruben Rivera	.25	.11
☐ 21 Juan Castro	.40	.18
☐ 22 Jimmy Haynes	.20	.09
☐ 23 Bob Wolcott	.10	.05
☐ 24 Brian Barber	.10	.05
☐ 25 Frank Rodriguez	.10	.05
☐ 26 Jesus Tavarez	.20	.09
☐ 27 Glenn Dishman	.20	.09
☐ 28 Jose Herrera	.20	.09
☐ 29 Chan Ho Park	.40	.18
☐ 30 Jason Isringhausen	.10	.05
☐ 31 Doug Johns	.10	.05
☐ 32 Gene Schall	.10	.05
☐ 33 Kevin Jordan	.10	.05
☐ 34 Matt Lawton	.10	.05
☐ 35 Karim Garcia	.20	.09
☐ 36 George Williams	.10	.05
☐ 37 Orlando Palmeiro	.10	.05
☐ 38 Jamie Brewington	.10	.05
☐ 39 Robert Person	.10	.05
☐ 40 Greg Maddux	1.25	.55
☐ 41 Marquis Grissom	.20	.09
☐ 42 Chipper Jones	1.25	.55
☐ 43 David Justice	.25	.11
☐ 44 Mark Lemke	.10	.05
☐ 45 Fred McGriff	.25	.11
☐ 46 Javier Lopez	.20	.09
☐ 47 Mark Wohlers	.20	.09
☐ 48 Jason Schmidt	.20	.09
☐ 49 John Smoltz	.20	.09
☐ 50 Curtis Goodwin	.10	.05
☐ 51 Greg Zaun	.10	.05
☐ 52 Armando Benitez	.10	.05
☐ 53 Manny Alexander	.10	.05
☐ 54 Chris Hoiles	.10	.05
☐ 55 Harold Baines	.20	.09
☐ 56 Ben McDonald	.10	.05
☐ 57 Scott Erickson	.10	.05
☐ 58 Jeff Manto	.10	.05
☐ 59 Luis Alicea	.10	.05
☐ 60 Roger Clemens	.75	.35
☐ 61 Rheal Cormier	.10	.05
☐ 62 Vaughn Eshelman	.10	.05
☐ 63 Zane Smith	.10	.05
☐ 64 Mike Macfarlane	.10	.05
☐ 65 Erik Hanson	.10	.05
☐ 66 Tim Naehring	.20	.09
☐ 67 Lee Tinsley	.10	.05
☐ 68 Troy O'Leary	.20	.09
☐ 69 Garret Anderson	.25	.11
☐ 70 Chili Davis	.10	.05
☐ 71 Jim Edmonds	.40	.18
☐ 72 Troy Percival	.20	.09
☐ 73 Mark Langston	.10	.05
☐ 74 Spike Owen	.10	.05
☐ 75 Tim Salmon	.40	.18
☐ 76 Brian Anderson	.10	.05
☐ 77 Lee Smith	.20	.09
☐ 78 Jim Abbott	.20	.09
☐ 79 Jim Bullinger	.10	.05
☐ 80 Mark Grace	.25	.11
☐ 81 Todd Zeile	.20	.09
☐ 82 Kevin Foster	.10	.05
☐ 83 Howard Johnson	.10	.05
☐ 84 Brian McRae	.10	.05
☐ 85 Randy Myers	.10	.05
☐ 86 Jaime Navarro	.10	.05
☐ 87 Luis Gonzalez	.10	.05
☐ 88 Ozzie Timmons	.10	.05
☐ 89 Wilson Alvarez	.20	.09
☐ 90 Frank Thomas	1.50	.70
☐ 91 James Baldwin	.10	.05
☐ 92 Ray Durham	.20	.09
☐ 93 Alex Fernandez	.20	.09
☐ 94 Ozzie Guillen	.10	.05
☐ 95 Tim Raines	.10	.05
☐ 96 Roberto Hernandez	.20	.09
☐ 97 Lance Johnson	.10	.05
☐ 98 John Kruk	.20	.09
☐ 99 Mark Portugal	.10	.05
☐ 100 Don Mattingly TT	.40	.18
☐ 101 Roger Clemens TT	.40	.18
☐ 102 Raul Mondesi TT	.25	.11
☐ 103 Cecil Fielder TT	.20	.09
☐ 104 Ozzie Smith TT	.40	.18
☐ 105 Frank Thomas TT	1.00	.45
☐ 106 Sammy Sosa TT	.40	.18
☐ 107 Fred McGriff TT	.25	.11
☐ 108 Barry Bonds TT	.40	.18
☐ 109 Thomas Howard	.10	.05
☐ 110 Ron Gant	.20	.09
☐ 111 Eddie Taubensee	.10	.05

☐ 112 Hal Morris	.10	.05
☐ 113 Jose Rijo	.10	.05
☐ 114 Pete Schourek	.10	.05
☐ 115 Reggie Sanders	.10	.05
☐ 116 Benito Santiago	.10	.05
☐ 117 Jeff Brantley	.10	.05
☐ 118 Julian Tavarez	.10	.05
☐ 119 Carlos Baerga	.10	.05
☐ 120 Jim Thome	.40	.18
☐ 121 Jose Mesa	.20	.09
☐ 122 Dennis Martinez	.20	.09
☐ 123 Dave Winfield	.25	.11
☐ 124 Eddie Murray	.40	.18
☐ 125 Manny Ramirez	.40	.18
☐ 126 Paul Sorrento	.10	.05
☐ 127 Kenny Lofton	.50	.23
☐ 128 Eric Young	.20	.09
☐ 129 Jason Bates	.10	.05
☐ 130 Bret Saberhagen	.10	.05
☐ 131 Andres Galarraga	.25	.11
☐ 132 Joe Girardi	.10	.05
☐ 133 John VanderWal	.10	.05
☐ 134 David Nied	.10	.05
☐ 135 Dante Bichette	.25	.11
☐ 136 Vinny Castilla	.20	.09
☐ 137 Kevin Ritz	.10	.05
☐ 138 Felipe Lira	.10	.05
☐ 139 Joe Boever	.10	.05
☐ 140 Cecil Fielder	.20	.09
☐ 141 John Flaherty	.10	.05
☐ 142 Kirk Gibson	.20	.09
☐ 143 Brian Maxcy	.10	.05
☐ 144 Lou Whitaker	.20	.09
☐ 145 Alan Trammell	.25	.11
☐ 146 Bobby Higginson	.25	.11
☐ 147 Chad Curtis	.10	.05
☐ 148 Quilvio Veras	.10	.05
☐ 149 Jerry Browne	.10	.05
☐ 150 Andre Dawson	.25	.11
☐ 151 Robb Nen	.10	.05
☐ 152 Greg Colbrunn	.10	.05
☐ 153 Chris Hammond	.10	.05
☐ 154 Kurt Abbott	.10	.05
☐ 155 Charles Johnson	.20	.09
☐ 156 Terry Pendleton	.20	.09
☐ 157 Dave Weathers	.10	.05
☐ 158 Mike Hampton	.10	.05
☐ 159 Craig Biggio	.25	.11
☐ 160 Jeff Bagwell	.75	.35
☐ 161 Brian L.Hunter	.20	.09
☐ 162 Mike Henneman	.10	.05
☐ 163 Dave Magadan	.10	.05
☐ 164 Shane Reynolds	.20	.09
☐ 165 Derek Bell	.20	.09
☐ 166 Orlando Miller	.10	.05
☐ 167 James Mouton	.10	.05
☐ 168 Melvin Bunch	.10	.05
☐ 169 Tom Gordon	.10	.05
☐ 170 Kevin Appier	.20	.09
☐ 171 Tom Goodwin	.10	.05
☐ 172 Greg Gagne	.10	.05
☐ 173 Gary Gaetti	.20	.09
☐ 174 Jeff Montgomery	.10	.05
☐ 175 Jon Nunnally	.10	.05
☐ 176 Michael Tucker	.20	.09
☐ 177 Joe Vitiello	.10	.05
☐ 178 Billy Ashley	.10	.05
☐ 179 Tom Candiotti	.10	.05
☐ 180 Hideo Nomo	1.00	.45
☐ 181 Chad Fonville	.10	.05
☐ 182 Todd Hollandsworth	.10	.05
☐ 183 Eric Karros	.20	.09
☐ 184 Roberto Kelly	.10	.05
☐ 185 Mike Piazza	1.25	.55
☐ 186 Ramon Martinez	.20	.09
☐ 187 Tim Wallach	.10	.05
☐ 188 Jeff Cirillo	.20	.09
☐ 189 Sid Roberson	.10	.05
☐ 190 Kevin Seitzer	.10	.05
☐ 191 Mike Fetters	.10	.05
☐ 192 Steve Sparks	.10	.05
☐ 193 Matt Mieske	.10	.05
☐ 194 Joe Oliver	.10	.05
☐ 195 B.J. Surhoff	.10	.05
☐ 196 Alberto Reyes	.10	.05
☐ 197 Fernando Vina	.10	.05
☐ 198 LaTroy Hawkins	.10	.05
☐ 199 Marty Cordova	.10	.05
☐ 200 Kirby Puckett	.75	.35
☐ 201 Brad Radke	.20	.09
☐ 202 Pedro Munoz	.10	.05
☐ 203 Scott Klingenbeck	.10	.05
☐ 204 Pat Meares	.10	.05
☐ 205 Chuck Knoblauch	.40	.18
☐ 206 Scott Stahoviak	.10	.05
☐ 207 Dave Stevens	.10	.05
☐ 208 Shane Andrews	.10	.05
☐ 209 Moises Alou	.20	.09
☐ 210 David Segui	.10	.05
☐ 211 Cliff Floyd	.10	.05
☐ 212 Carlos Perez	.10	.05
☐ 213 Mark Grudzielanek	.10	.05
☐ 214 Butch Henry	.10	.05
☐ 215 Rondell White	.20	.09
☐ 216 Mel Rojas	.20	.09
☐ 217 Ugueth Urbina	.10	.05
☐ 218 Edgardo Alfonzo	.40	.18
☐ 219 Carl Everett	.10	.05
☐ 220 John Franco	.10	.05
☐ 221 Todd Hundley	.20	.09
☐ 222 Bobby Jones	.10	.05
☐ 223 Bill Pulsipher	.10	.05
☐ 224 Rico Brogna	.10	.05
☐ 225 Jeff Kent	.10	.05
☐ 226 Chris Jones	.10	.05
☐ 227 Butch Huskey	.20	.09
☐ 228 Robert Eenhoorn	.10	.05
☐ 229 Sterling Hitchcock	.10	.05
☐ 230 Wade Boggs	.40	.18
☐ 231 Derek Jeter	1.25	.55
☐ 232 Tony Fernandez	.10	.05
☐ 233 Jack McDowell	.10	.05
☐ 234 Andy Pettitte	.50	.23
☐ 235 David Cone	.20	.09
☐ 236 Mike Stanley	.10	.05
☐ 237 Don Mattingly	.60	.25
☐ 238 Geronimo Berroa	.10	.05
☐ 239 Scott Brosius	.10	.05
☐ 240 Rickey Henderson	.25	.11
☐ 241 Terry Steinbach	.20	.09
☐ 242 Mike Gallego	.10	.05
☐ 243 Jason Giambi	.20	.09
☐ 244 Steve Ontiveros	.10	.05
☐ 245 Dennis Eckersley	.25	.11
☐ 246 Dave Stewart	.20	.09
☐ 247 Don Wengert	.10	.05
☐ 248 Paul Quantrill	.10	.05
☐ 249 Ricky Bottalico	.10	.05
☐ 250 Kevin Stocker	.10	.05
☐ 251 Lenny Dykstra	.20	.09
☐ 252 Tony Longmire	.10	.05
☐ 253 Tyler Green	.10	.05
☐ 254 Mike Mimbs	.10	.05
☐ 255 Charlie Hayes	.10	.05
☐ 256 Mickey Morandini	.10	.05
☐ 257 Heathcliff Slocumb	.10	.05
☐ 258 Jeff King	.10	.05
☐ 259 Midre Cummings	.10	.05
☐ 260 Mark Johnson	.10	.05
☐ 261 Freddy Garcia	.10	.05
☐ 262 Jon Lieber	.10	.05
☐ 263 Esteban Loaiza	.10	.05
☐ 264 Dan Miceli	.10	.05
☐ 265 Orlando Merced	.10	.05
☐ 266 Denny Neagle	.20	.09
☐ 267 Steve Parris	.10	.05
☐ 268 Greg Maddux FT	.60	.25
☐ 269 Randy Johnson FT	.40	.18
☐ 270 Hideo Nomo FT	.30	.14
☐ 271 Jose Mesa FT	.10	.05
☐ 272 Mike Piazza FT	.60	.25
☐ 273 Mo Vaughn FT	.40	.18
☐ 274 Craig Biggio FT	.25	.11
☐ 275 Edgar Martinez FT	.25	.11
☐ 276 Barry Larkin FT	.25	.11
☐ 277 Sammy Sosa FT	.40	.18
☐ 278 Dante Bichette FT	.25	.11
☐ 279 Albert Belle FT	.40	.18
☐ 280 Ozzie Smith	.50	.23
☐ 281 Mark Sweeney	.10	.05
☐ 282 Terry Bradshaw	.10	.05
☐ 283 Allen Battle	.10	.05
☐ 284 Danny Jackson	.10	.05
☐ 285 Tom Henke	.20	.09
☐ 286 Scott Cooper	.10	.05
☐ 287 Tripp Cromer	.10	.05
☐ 288 Bernard Gilkey	.20	.09
☐ 289 Brian Jordan	.20	.09
☐ 290 Tony Gwynn	1.00	.45
☐ 291 Brad Ausmus	.10	.05
☐ 292 Bryce Florie	.10	.05
☐ 293 Andres Berumen	.10	.05
☐ 294 Ken Caminiti	.40	.18
☐ 295 Bip Roberts	.10	.05
☐ 296 Trevor Hoffman	.20	.09
☐ 297 Roberto Petagine	.10	.05
☐ 298 Jody Reed	.10	.05
☐ 299 Fernando Valenzuela	.20	.09
☐ 300 Barry Bonds	.50	.23
☐ 301 Mark Leiter	.10	.05
☐ 302 Mark Carreon	.10	.05
☐ 303 Royce Clayton	.10	.05
☐ 304 Kirt Manwaring	.10	.05
☐ 305 Glenallen Hill	.10	.05
☐ 306 Deion Sanders	.40	.1
☐ 307 Joe Rosselli	.10	.0
☐ 308 Robby Thompson	.10	.0
☐ 309 W. VanLandingham	.10	.0
☐ 310 Ken Griffey Jr.	2.00	.9
☐ 311 Bobby Ayala	.10	.0
☐ 312 Joey Cora	.20	.0
☐ 313 Mike Blowers	.10	.0
☐ 314 Darren Bragg	.10	.0
☐ 315 Randy Johnson	.40	.1
☐ 316 Alex Rodriguez	1.50	.7
☐ 317 Andy Benes	.10	.0
☐ 318 Tino Martinez	.40	.1
☐ 319 Dan Wilson	.10	.0
☐ 320 Will Clark	.25	.1
☐ 321 Jeff Frye	.10	.0
☐ 322 Benji Gil	.10	.0
☐ 323 Rick Helling	.10	.0
☐ 324 Mark McLemore	.10	.0
☐ 325 Dave Nilsson IF	.10	.0
☐ 326 Larry Walker IF	.40	.1
☐ 327 Jose Canseco IF	.25	.1
☐ 328 Raul Mondesi IF	.25	.1
☐ 329 Manny Ramirez IF	.40	.1
☐ 330 Robert Eenhoorn IF	.10	.0
☐ 331 Chili Davis IF	.20	.0
☐ 332 Hideo Nomo IF	.30	.1
☐ 333 Benji Gil IF	.10	.0
☐ 334 Fernando Valenzuela IF	.20	.0
☐ 335 Dennis Martinez IF	.20	.0
☐ 336 Roberto Kelly IF	.10	.0
☐ 337 Carlos Baerga IF	.20	.0
☐ 338 Juan Gonzalez IF	.50	.2
☐ 339 Roberto Alomar IF	.25	.1
☐ 340 Chan Ho Park IF	.40	.1
☐ 341 Andres Galarraga IF	.25	.1
☐ 342 Midre Cummings IF	.10	.0
☐ 343 Otis Nixon	.20	.0
☐ 344 Jeff Russell	.10	.0
☐ 345 Ivan Rodriguez	.50	.2
☐ 346 Mickey Tettleton	.10	.0
☐ 347 Bob Tewksbury	.10	.0
☐ 348 Domingo Cedeno	.10	.0
☐ 349 Lance Parrish	.20	.0
☐ 350 Joe Carter	.25	.1
☐ 351 Devon White	.10	.0
☐ 352 Carlos Delgado	.20	.0
☐ 353 Alex Gonzalez	.10	.0
☐ 354 Darren Hall	.10	.0
☐ 355 Paul Molitor	.40	.1
☐ 356 Al Leiter	.10	.0
☐ 357 Randy Knorr	.10	.0
☐ 358 Ken Caminiti CL	.10	.0
Steve Finley		
Brian Williams		
Roberto Petagine		
Andujar Cedeno		
Phil Plantier		
Derek Bell		
Pedro A. Martinez		
Doug Brocail		
Craig Shipley		
Ricky Gutierrez		
☐ 359 Hideo Nomo CL	.30	.1
☐ 360 Ramon A.Martinez CL	.10	.0
Ramon J.Martinez		
☐ 361 Robin Ventura CL	.20	.0
☐ 362 Cal Ripken CL	.75	.3
☐ 363 Ken Caminiti CL	.40	.1
☐ 364 Albert Belle CL	.40	.1
Eddie Murray		
☐ 365 Randy Johnson CL	.40	.1
☐ 366T Tony Pena TRADE	.15	.0
☐ 367T Jim Thome TRADE	.75	.3
☐ 368T Don Mattingly TRADE	1.25	.5
☐ 369T Jim Leyritz TRADE	.15	.0
☐ 370T Ken Griffey Jr. TRADE	4.00	1.8
☐ 371T Edgar Martinez TRADE	.50	.2
☐ 372T Pete Schourek TRADE	.15	.0
☐ 373T Mark Lewis TRADE	.15	.0
☐ 374T Chipper Jones TRADE	2.50	1.1
☐ 375T Fred McGriff TRADE	.50	.2
☐ 376T Javy Lopez TRADE	.50	.2
☐ 377T Fred McGriff TRADE	.50	.2
☐ 378T Charlie O'Brien TRADE	.15	.0
☐ 379T Mike Devereaux TRADE	.15	.0
☐ 380T Mark Wohlers TRADE	.30	.1
☐ 381T Bob Wolcott TRADE	.15	.0
☐ 382T Manny Ramirez TRADE	.75	.3
☐ 383T Jay Buhner TRADE	.30	.1
☐ 384T Orel Hershiser TRADE	.30	.1
☐ 385T Kenny Lofton TRADE	1.00	.4
☐ 386T Greg Maddux TRADE	2.50	1.1
☐ 387T Javier Lopez TRADE	.50	.2
☐ 388T Kenny Lofton TRADE	1.00	.4
☐ 389T Eddie Murray TRADE	.75	.3
☐ 390T Luis Polonia TRADE	.15	.0

391T Pedro Borbon TRADE	.15	.07
392T Jim Thome TRADE	.75	.35
393T Orel Hershiser TRADE	.15	.07
394T David Justice TRADE	.30	.14
395T Tom Glavine TRADE	.50	.23
396 Greg Maddux TC	.60	.25
397 Darren Daulton TC	.20	.09
398 Rico Brogna TC	.10	.05
399 Gary Sheffield TC	.40	.18
400 Moises Alou TC	.20	.09
401 Barry Larkin TC	.25	.11
402 Jeff Bagwell TC	.40	.18
403 Sammy Sosa TC	.40	.18
404 Ozzie Smith TC	.40	.18
405 Jay Bell TC	.10	.05
406 Mike Piazza TC	.60	.25
407 Dante Bichette TC	.25	.11
408 Tony Gwynn TC	.40	.18
409 Barry Bonds TC	.40	.18
410 Kenny Lofton TC	.40	.18
411 Johnny Damon TC	.20	.09
412 Frank Thomas TC	1.00	.45
413 Greg Vaughn TC	.10	.05
414 Paul Molitor TC	.40	.18
415 Ken Griffey Jr. TC	1.00	.45
416 Tim Salmon TC	.40	.18
417 Juan Gonzalez TC	.50	.23
418 Mark McGwire TC	.40	.18
419 Roger Clemens TC	.40	.18
420 Wade Boggs TC	.40	.18
421 Cal Ripken TC	.75	.35
422 Cecil Fielder TC	.20	.09
423 Joe Carter TC	.20	.09
424 Osvaldo Fernandez	.40	.18
425 Billy Wagner	.25	.11
426 George Arias	.10	.05
427 Mendy Lopez	.20	.09
428 Jeff Suppan	.20	.09
429 Rey Ordonez	.10	.05
430 Brooks Kieschnick	.10	.05
431 Raul Ibanez	.20	.09
432 Livan Hernandez	1.00	.45
433 Shannon Stewart	.10	.05
434 Steve Cox	.10	.05
435 Trey Beamon	.20	.09
436 Sergio Nunez	.20	.09
437 Jermaine Dye	.10	.05
438 Mike Sweeney	.40	.18
439 Richard Hidalgo	.40	.18
440 Todd Greene	.20	.09
441 Robert Smith	.40	.18
442 Rafael Orellano	.10	.05
443 Wilton Guerrero	.40	.18
444 David Doster	.10	.05
445 Jason Kendall	.40	.18
446 Edgar Renteria	.20	.09
447 Scott Spiezio	.20	.09
448 Jay Canizaro	.10	.05
449 Enrique Wilson	.20	.09
450 Bob Abreu	.40	.18
451 Dwight Smith	.10	.05
452 Jeff Blauser	.10	.05
453 Steve Avery	.10	.05
454 Brad Clontz	.10	.05
455 Tom Glavine	.25	.11
456 Mike Mordecai	.10	.05
457 Rafael Belliard	.10	.05
458 Greg McMichael	.10	.05
459 Pedro Borbon	.10	.05
460 Ryan Klesko	.25	.11
461 Terrell Wade	.10	.05
462 Brady Anderson	.25	.11
463 Roberto Alomar	.40	.18
464 Bobby Bonilla	.20	.09
465 Mike Mussina	.40	.18
466 Cesar Devarez	.10	.05
467 Jeffrey Hammonds	.10	.05
468 Mike Devereaux	.10	.05
469 B.J. Surhoff	.10	.05
470 Rafael Palmeiro	.25	.11
471 John Valentin	.20	.09
472 Mike Greenwell	.10	.05
473 Dwayne Hosey	.10	.05
474 Tim Wakefield	.10	.05
475 Jose Canseco	.25	.11
476 Aaron Sele	.10	.05
477 Stan Belinda	.10	.05
478 Mike Stanley	.10	.05
479 Jamie Moyer	.10	.05
480 Mo Vaughn	.50	.23
481 Randy Velarde	.10	.05
482 Gary DiSarcina	.10	.05
483 Jorge Fabregas	.10	.05
484 Rex Hudler	.10	.05
485 Chuck Finley	.10	.05
486 Tim Wallach	.10	.05
487 Eduardo Perez	.10	.05
☐ 488 Scott Sanderson	.10	.05
☐ 489 J.T. Snow	.20	.09
☐ 490 Sammy Sosa	.40	.18
☐ 491 Terry Adams	.10	.05
☐ 492 Matt Franco	.10	.05
☐ 493 Scott Servais	.10	.05
☐ 494 Frank Castillo	.10	.05
☐ 495 Ryne Sandberg	.50	.23
☐ 496 Rey Sanchez	.10	.05
☐ 497 Steve Trachsel	.10	.05
☐ 498 Jose Hernandez	.10	.05
☐ 499 Dave Martinez	.10	.05
☐ 500 Babe Ruth FC	.50	.23
☐ 501 Ty Cobb FC	.40	.18
☐ 502 Walter Johnson FC	.25	.11
☐ 503 Christy Mathewson FC	.25	.11
☐ 504 Honus Wagner FC	.25	.11
☐ 505 Robin Ventura	.20	.09
☐ 506 Jason Bere	.10	.05
☐ 507 Mike Cameron	1.00	.45
☐ 508 Ron Karkovice	.10	.05
☐ 509 Matt Karchner	.10	.05
☐ 510 Harold Baines	.20	.09
☐ 511 Kirk McCaskill	.10	.05
☐ 512 Larry Thomas	.10	.05
☐ 513 Danny Tartabull	.10	.05
☐ 514 Steve Gilbralter	.10	.05
☐ 515 Bret Boone	.10	.05
☐ 516 Jeff Branson	.10	.05
☐ 517 Kevin Jarvis	.10	.05
☐ 518 Xavier Hernandez	.10	.05
☐ 519 Eric Owens	.10	.05
☐ 520 Barry Larkin	.25	.11
☐ 521 Dave Burba	.10	.05
☐ 522 John Smiley	.10	.05
☐ 523 Paul Assenmacher	.10	.05
☐ 524 Chad Ogea	.10	.05
☐ 525 Orel Hershiser	.20	.09
☐ 526 Alan Embree	.10	.05
☐ 527 Tony Pena	.10	.05
☐ 528 Omar Vizquel	.20	.09
☐ 529 Mark Clark	.10	.05
☐ 530 Albert Belle	.50	.23
☐ 531 Charles Nagy	.20	.09
☐ 532 Herbert Perry	.10	.05
☐ 533 Darren Holmes	.10	.05
☐ 534 Ellis Burks	.20	.09
☐ 535 Billy Swift	.10	.05
☐ 536 Armando Reynoso	.10	.05
☐ 537 Curtis Leskanic	.10	.05
☐ 538 Quinton McCracken	.10	.05
☐ 539 Steve Reed	.10	.05
☐ 540 Larry Walker	.40	.18
☐ 541 Walt Weiss	.10	.05
☐ 542 Bryan Rekar	.10	.05
☐ 543 Tony Clark	.40	.18
☐ 544 Steve Rodriguez	.10	.05
☐ 545 C.J. Nitkowski	.10	.05
☐ 546 Todd Steverson	.10	.05
☐ 547 Jose Lima	.10	.05
☐ 548 Phil Nevin	.10	.05
☐ 549 Chris Gomez	.10	.05
☐ 550 Travis Fryman	.20	.09
☐ 551 Mark Lewis	.10	.05
☐ 552 Alex Arias	.10	.05
☐ 553 Marc Valdes	.10	.05
☐ 554 Kevin Brown	.20	.09
☐ 555 Jeff Conine	.20	.09
☐ 556 John Burkett	.10	.05
☐ 557 Devon White	.10	.05
☐ 558 Pat Rapp	.10	.05
☐ 559 Jay Powell	.10	.05
☐ 560 Gary Sheffield	.40	.18
☐ 561 Jim Dougherty	.10	.05
☐ 562 Todd Jones	.10	.05
☐ 563 Tony Eusebio	.10	.05
☐ 564 Darryl Kile	.20	.09
☐ 565 Doug Drabek	.10	.05
☐ 566 Mike Simms	.10	.05
☐ 567 Derrick May	.10	.05
☐ 568 Donne Wall	.10	.05
☐ 569 Greg Swindell	.10	.05
☐ 570 Jim Pittsley	.20	.09
☐ 571 Bob Hamelin	.10	.05
☐ 572 Mark Gubicza	.10	.05
☐ 573 Chris Haney	.10	.05
☐ 574 Keith Lockhart	.10	.05
☐ 575 Mike Macfarlane	.10	.05
☐ 576 Les Norman	.10	.05
☐ 577 Joe Randa	.10	.05
☐ 578 Chris Stynes	.10	.05
☐ 579 Greg Gagne	.10	.05
☐ 580 Raul Mondesi	.25	.11
☐ 581 Delino DeShields	.10	.05
☐ 582 Pedro Astacio	.10	.05
☐ 583 Antonio Osuna	.10	.05
☐ 584 Brett Butler	.20	.09
☐ 585 Todd Worrell	.20	.09
☐ 586 Mike Blowers	.10	.05
☐ 587 Felix Rodriguez	.10	.05
☐ 588 Ismael Valdes	.20	.09
☐ 589 Ricky Bones	.10	.05
☐ 590 Greg Vaughn	.10	.05
☐ 591 Mark Loretta	.10	.05
☐ 592 Cal Eldred	.10	.05
☐ 593 Chuck Carr	.10	.05
☐ 594 Dave Nilsson	.20	.09
☐ 595 John Jaha	.10	.05
☐ 596 Scott Karl	.10	.05
☐ 597 Pat Listach	.10	.05
☐ 598 Jose Valentin	.10	.05
☐ 599 Mike Trombley	.10	.05
☐ 600 Paul Molitor	.40	.18
☐ 601 Dave Hollins	.10	.05
☐ 602 Ron Coomer	.10	.05
☐ 603 Matt Walbeck	.10	.05
☐ 604 Roberto Kelly	.10	.05
☐ 605 Rick Aguilera	.10	.05
☐ 606 Pat Mahomes	.10	.05
☐ 607 Jeff Reboulet	.10	.05
☐ 608 Rich Becker	.20	.09
☐ 609 Tim Scott	.10	.05
☐ 610 Pedro J. Martinez	.40	.18
☐ 611 Kirk Rueter	.10	.05
☐ 612 Tavo Alvarez	.10	.05
☐ 613 Yamil Benitez	.20	.09
☐ 614 Darrin Fletcher	.10	.05
☐ 615 Mike Lansing	.10	.05
☐ 616 Henry Rodriguez	.10	.05
☐ 617 Tony Tarasco	.10	.05
☐ 618 Alex Ochoa	.10	.05
☐ 619 Tim Bogar	.10	.05
☐ 620 Bernard Gilkey	.20	.09
☐ 621 Dave Mlicki	.10	.05
☐ 622 Brent Mayne	.10	.05
☐ 623 Ryan Thompson	.10	.05
☐ 624 Pete Harnisch	.10	.05
☐ 625 Lance Johnson	.20	.09
☐ 626 Jose Vizcaino	.10	.05
☐ 627 Doug Henry	.10	.05
☐ 628 Scott Kamieniecki	.10	.05
☐ 629 Jim Leyritz	.10	.05
☐ 630 Ruben Sierra	.10	.05
☐ 631 Pat Kelly	.10	.05
☐ 632 Joe Girardi	.10	.05
☐ 633 John Wetteland	.20	.09
☐ 634 Melido Perez	.10	.05
☐ 635 Paul O'Neill	.10	.05
☐ 636 Jorge Posada	.10	.05
☐ 637 Bernie Williams	.40	.18
☐ 638 Mark Acre	.10	.05
☐ 639 Mike Bordick	.10	.05
☐ 640 Mark McGwire	.75	.35
☐ 641 Fausto Cruz	.10	.05
☐ 642 Ernie Young	.10	.05
☐ 643 Todd Van Poppel	.10	.05
☐ 644 Craig Paquette	.10	.05
☐ 645 Brent Gates	.10	.05
☐ 646 Pedro Munoz	.10	.05
☐ 647 Andrew Lorraine	.10	.05
☐ 648 Sid Fernandez	.10	.05
☐ 649 Jim Eisenreich	.20	.09
☐ 650 Johnny Damon	.20	.09
☐ 651 Dustin Hermanson	.10	.05
☐ 652 Joe Randa	.10	.05
☐ 653 Michael Tucker	.20	.09
☐ 654 Alan Benes	.25	.11
☐ 655 Chad Fonville	.10	.05
☐ 656 David Bell	.10	.05
☐ 657 Jon Nunnally	.10	.05
☐ 658 Chan Ho Park	.40	.18
☐ 659 LaTroy Hawkins	.10	.05
☐ 660 Jamie Brewington	.10	.05
☐ 661 Quinton McCracken	.10	.05
☐ 662 Tim Unroe	.10	.05
☐ 663 Jeff Ware	.10	.05
☐ 664 Todd Greene	.40	.18
☐ 665 Andrew Lorraine	.10	.05
☐ 666 Ernie Young	.10	.05
☐ 667 Toby Borland	.10	.05
☐ 668 Lenny Webster	.10	.05
☐ 669 Benito Santiago	.10	.05
☐ 670 Gregg Jefferies	.20	.09
☐ 671 Darren Daulton	.20	.09
☐ 672 Curt Schilling	.20	.09
☐ 673 Mark Whiten	.10	.05
☐ 674 Todd Zeile	.20	.09
☐ 675 Jay Bell	.10	.05
☐ 676 Paul Wagner	.10	.05
☐ 677 Dave Clark	.10	.05
☐ 678 Nelson Liriano	.10	.05
☐ 679 Ramon Morel	.10	.05
☐ 680 Charlie Hayes	.10	.05
☐ 681 Angelo Encarnacion	.10	.05

Card	MINT	NRMT
☐ 682 Al Martin	.10	.05
☐ 683 Jacob Brumfield	.10	.05
☐ 684 Mike Kingery	.10	.05
☐ 685 Carlos Garcia	.10	.05
☐ 686 Tom Pagnozzi	.10	.05
☐ 687 David Bell	.10	.05
☐ 688 Todd Stottleymyre	.10	.05
☐ 689 Jose Oliva	.10	.05
☐ 690 Ray Lankford	.20	.09
☐ 691 Mike Morgan	.10	.05
☐ 692 John Frascatore	.10	.05
☐ 693 John Mabry	.20	.09
☐ 694 Mark Petkovsek	.10	.05
☐ 695 Alan Benes	.20	.09
☐ 696 Steve Finley	.20	.09
☐ 697 Marc Newfield	.20	.09
☐ 698 Andy Ashby	.10	.05
☐ 699 Marc Kroon	.10	.05
☐ 700 Wally Joyner	.10	.05
☐ 701 Joey Hamilton	.20	.09
☐ 702 Dustin Hermanson	.10	.05
☐ 703 Scott Sanders	.10	.05
☐ 704 Marty Cordova ROY	.20	.09
☐ 705 Hideo Nomo ROY	.40	.18
☐ 706 Mo Vaughn MVP	.40	.18
☐ 707 Barry Larkin MVP	.25	.11
☐ 708 Randy Johnson CY	.40	.18
☐ 709 Greg Maddux CY	.60	.25
☐ 710 Mark McGwire CB	.40	.18
☐ 711 Ron Gant CB	.20	.09
☐ 712 Andujar Cedeno	.10	.05
☐ 713 Brian Johnson	.10	.05
☐ 714 J.R. Phillips	.10	.05
☐ 715 Rod Beck	.10	.05
☐ 716 Sergio Valdez	.10	.05
☐ 717 Marvin Benard	.10	.05
☐ 718 Steve Scarsone	.10	.05
☐ 719 Rich Aurilia	.10	.05
☐ 720 Matt Williams	.25	.11
☐ 721 John Patterson	.10	.05
☐ 722 Shawn Estes	.20	.09
☐ 723 Russ Davis	.10	.05
☐ 724 Rich Amaral	.10	.05
☐ 725 Edgar Martinez	.20	.09
☐ 726 Norm Charlton	.10	.05
☐ 727 Paul Sorrento	.10	.05
☐ 728 Luis Sojo	.10	.05
☐ 729 Arquimedez Pozo	.10	.05
☐ 730 Jay Buhner	.25	.11
☐ 731 Chris Bosio	.10	.05
☐ 732 Chris Widger	.10	.05
☐ 733 Kevin Gross	.10	.05
☐ 734 Darren Oliver	.10	.05
☐ 735 Dean Palmer	.20	.09
☐ 736 Matt Whiteside	.10	.05
☐ 737 Luis Ortiz	.10	.05
☐ 738 Roger Pavlik	.10	.05
☐ 739 Damon Buford	.10	.05
☐ 740 Juan Gonzalez	1.00	.45
☐ 741 Rusty Greer	.40	.18
☐ 742 Lou Frazier	.10	.05
☐ 743 Pat Hentgen	.20	.09
☐ 744 Tomas Perez	.10	.05
☐ 745 Juan Guzman	.10	.05
☐ 746 Otis Nixon	.20	.09
☐ 747 Robert Perez	.10	.05
☐ 748 Ed Sprague	.10	.05
☐ 749 Tony Castillo	.10	.05
☐ 750 John Olerud	.20	.09
☐ 751 Shawn Green	.20	.09
☐ 752 Jeff Ware	.10	.05
☐ 753 Dante Bichette CL Vinny Castilla Andres Galarraga Larry Walker	.20	.09
☐ 754 Greg Maddux CL	.60	.25
☐ 755 Marty Cordova CL	.10	.05
☐ 756 Ozzie Smith CL	.40	.18
☐ 757 John Vanderwal CL	.10	.05
☐ 758 Andres Galarraga CL	.25	.11
☐ 759 Frank Thomas CL	1.00	.45
☐ 760 Tony Gwynn CL	.40	.18
☐ 761 Randy Myers UPD	.35	.16
☐ 762 Kent Mercker UPD	.25	.11
☐ 763 David Wells UPD	.25	.11
☐ 764 Tom Gordon UPD	.25	.11
☐ 765 Wil Cordero UPD	.25	.11
☐ 766 Dave Magadan UPD	.25	.11
☐ 767 Doug Jones UPD	.25	.11
☐ 768 Kevin Tapani UPD	.35	.16
☐ 769 Curtis Goodwin UPD	.25	.11
☐ 770 Julio Franco UPD	.35	.16
☐ 771 Jack McDowell UPD	.25	.11
☐ 772 Al Leiter UPD	.25	.11
☐ 773 Sean Berry UPD	.25	.11
☐ 774 Bip Roberts UPD	.25	.11
☐ 775 Jose Offerman UPD	.25	.11
☐ 776 Ben McDonald UPD	.35	.16
☐ 777 Dan Serafini UPD	.25	.11
☐ 778 Ryan McGuire UPD	.35	.16
☐ 779 Tim Raines UPD	.25	.11
☐ 780 Tino Martinez UPD	.75	.35
☐ 781 Kenny Rogers UPD	.25	.11
☐ 782 Bob Tewksbury UPD	.25	.11
☐ 783 Rickey Henderson UPD	1.00	.45
☐ 784 Ron Gant UPD	.35	.16
☐ 785 Gary Gaetti UPD	.25	.11
☐ 786 Andy Benes UPD	.25	.11
☐ 787 Royce Clayton UPD	.25	.11
☐ 788 Darryl Hamilton UPD	.25	.11
☐ 789 Ken Hill UPD	.25	.11
☐ 790 Erik Hanson UPD	.25	.11
☐ P100 Ken Griffey Jr. Promo	3.00	1.35

1996 Collector's Choice Gold Signature

This 730-card set parallels the basic Collector's Choice issue. These cards were inserted approximately one every 35 packs. Cards 1-365 were issued in first series and 396-730 in second series. The cards are similar to the regular issue except they have gold borders and a gold facsimile player's signature on front.

	MINT	NRMT
COMPLETE SET (730)	1500.00	700.00
COMPLETE SERIES 1 (365)	800.00	350.00
COMPLETE SERIES 2 (365)	700.00	325.00
COMMON CARD (1-360/396-760)	1.00	.45

*STARS: 12.5X TO 25X BASIC CARDS
*YOUNG STARS: 10X TO 20X BASIC CARDS

1996 Collector's Choice Silver Signature

This 730-card set parallels the regular Collector's Choice set. These cards were inserted one per pack in both first and second series packs. The cards are similar to the regular issue except for silver borders and a silver foil facsimile player's signature on the card front. Cards 366-395 do not exist.

	MINT	NRMT
COMPLETE SET (730)	110.00	50.00
COMPLETE SERIES 1 (365)	60.00	27.00
COMPLETE SERIES 2 (365)	50.00	22.00
COMMON CARD (1-365/396-760)	.10	.05

*STARS: 1.5X TO 3X BASIC CARDS
*YOUNG STARS: 1.25X TO 2.5X BASIC CARDS

1996 Collector's Choice Crash the Game

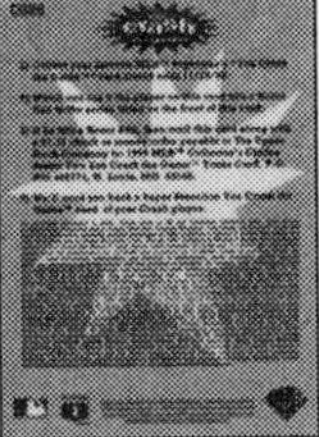

Randomly inserted into one in every five Series 2 packs, silver Crash the Game interactive cards feature a selection of thirty of baseball's top stars. If the featured player hit a home run during the series specified on the card, it was then eligible to be redeemed for a super premium Cell Card of the same player. Winning cards have been highlighted with a "W" in the listings below. The postmark expiration date for exchanging winning cards was November 18th, 1996.

	MINT	NRMT
COMPLETE SET (90)	50.00	22.00
COMMON CARD (CG1-CG30)	.40	.18
COMP.GOLD SET (90)	250.00	110.00

*GOLD: 2.5X TO 5X BASIC CARDS
*EXCHANGE: 2.5X TO 5X BASIC CARDS
*GOLD EXCHANGE: 7.5X TO 15X BASIC CARDS

Card	MINT	NRMT
☐ CG1 Chipper Jones 7/11 W	2.00	.90
☐ CG1B Chipper Jones 8/27 W	2.00	.90
☐ CG1C Chipper Jones 9/19	2.00	.90
☐ CG2 Fred McGriff 7/1	.60	.25
☐ CG2B Fred McGriff 8/30	.60	.25
☐ CG2C Fred McGriff 9/10 W	.60	.25
☐ CG3 Rafael Palmeiro 7/4 W	.60	.25
☐ CG3B Rafael Palmeiro 8/29	.60	.25
☐ CG3C Rafael Palmeiro 9/26	.60	.25
☐ CG4 Cal Ripken 6/27	2.50	1.10
☐ CG4B Cal Ripken 7/25 W	2.50	1.10
☐ CG4C Cal Ripken 9/2	2.50	1.10
☐ CG5 Jose Canseco 6/27	.60	.25
☐ CG5B Jose Canseco 7/11 W	.60	.25
☐ CG5C Jose Canseco 8/23	.60	.25
☐ CG6 Mo Vaughn 6/21 W	.75	.35
☐ CG6B Mo Vaughn 7/18 W	.75	.35
☐ CG6C Mo Vaughn 9/20	.75	.35
☐ CG7 Jim Edmonds 7/18 W	.75	.35
☐ CG7B Jim Edmonds 8/16 W	.75	.35
☐ CG7C Jim Edmonds 9/20	.75	.35
☐ CG8 Tim Salmon 6/20	.75	.35
☐ CG8B Tim Salmon 7/30	.75	.35
☐ CG8C Tim Salmon 9/9	.75	.35
☐ CG9 Sammy Sosa 7/4 W	.75	.35
☐ CG9B Sammy Sosa 8/1 W	.75	.35
☐ CG9C Sammy Sosa 9/2	.75	.35
☐ CG10 Frank Thomas 6/27	3.00	1.35
☐ CG10B Frank Thomas 7/4	2.50	1.10
☐ CG10C Frank Thomas 9/2 W	2.50	1.10
☐ CG11 Albert Belle 6/25	1.25	.55
☐ CG11B Albert Belle 8/2 W	.75	.35
☐ CG11C Albert Belle 9/6	.75	.35
☐ CG12 Manny Ramirez 7/18 W	.75	.35
☐ CG12B Manny Ramirez 8/26	.75	.35
☐ CG12C Manny Ramirez 9/9 W	.75	.35
☐ CG13 Jim Thome 6/27	.75	.35
☐ CG13B Jim Thome 7/4 W	.60	.25
☐ CG13C Jim Thome 9/23	.60	.25
☐ CG14 Dante Bichette 7/11 W	.60	.25
☐ CG14B Dante Bichette 8/9	.60	.25
☐ CG14C Dante Bichette 9/9	.60	.25
☐ CG15 Vinny Castilla 7/1	.40	.18
☐ CG15B Vinny Castilla 8/23 W	.40	.18
☐ CG15C Vinny Castilla 9/13 W	.40	.18
☐ CG16 Larry Walker 6/24	.75	.35
☐ CG16B Larry Walker 7/18	.75	.35
☐ CG16C Larry Walker 9/27	.75	.35
☐ CG17 Cecil Fielder 6/27	.50	.23
☐ CG17B Cecil Fielder 7/30 W	.50	.23
☐ CG17C Cecil Fielder 9/17 W	.50	.23
☐ CG18 Gary Sheffield 7/4	.75	.35
☐ CG18B Gary Sheffield 8/2	.75	.35
☐ CG18C Gary Sheffield 9/5 W	.75	.35
☐ CG19 Jeff Bagwell 7/4 W	1.25	.55
☐ CG19B Jeff Bagwell 8/16	1.25	.55
☐ CG19C Jeff Bagwell 9/13	1.25	.55
☐ CG20 Eric Karros 7/4 W	.40	.18
☐ CG20B Eric Karros 8/13 W	.40	.18
☐ CG20C Eric Karros 9/16	.40	.18
☐ CG21 Mike Piazza 6/27 W	2.00	.90
☐ CG21B Mike Piazza 7/26	2.00	.90
☐ CG21C Mike Piazza 9/12 W	2.00	.90
☐ CG22 Ken Caminiti 7/11 W	.75	.35
☐ CG22B Ken Caminiti 8/16 W	.75	.35
☐ CG22C Ken Caminiti 9/19 W	.75	.35
☐ CG23 Barry Bonds 6/27 W	.75	.35
☐ CG23B Barry Bonds 7/22	.75	.35
☐ CG23C Barry Bonds 9/24	.75	.35
☐ CG24 Matt Williams 7/11 W	.60	.25
☐ CG24B Matt Williams 8/19	.60	.25
☐ CG24C Matt Williams 9/27	.60	.25
☐ CG25 Jay Buhner 6/20	.60	.25
☐ CG25B Jay Buhner 7/25	.60	.25
☐ CG25C Jay Buhner 8/29 W	.60	.25
☐ CG26 Ken Griffey Jr. 7/18 W	3.00	1.35
☐ CG26B Ken Griffey Jr. 8/16 W	3.00	1.35
☐ CG26C Ken Griffey Jr. 9/20 W	3.00	1.35
☐ CG27 Ron Gant 6/24 W	.40	.18
☐ CG27B Ron Gant 7/11 W	.40	.18
☐ CG27C Ron Gant 9/27 W	.40	.18
☐ CG28 Juan Gonzalez 6/28 W	1.50	.70
☐ CG28B Juan Gonzalez 7/15 W	1.50	.70
☐ CG28C Juan Gonzalez 8/6	1.50	.70
☐ CG29 Mickey Tettleton 7/4 W	.40	.18
☐ CG29B Mickey Tettleton 8/6	.40	.18
☐ CG29C Mickey Tettleton 9/6 W	.40	.18
☐ CG30 Joe Carter 6/25	.50	.23
☐ CG30B Joe Carter 8/5	.50	.23
☐ CG30C Joe Carter 9/23	.50	.23

1996 Collector's Choice Griffey A Cut Above

These ten cards focus on Seattle Mariners superstar Ken Griffey Jr. The cards were inserted at a rate of one per pack in special six-card retail packs (five basic CC cards

us one Griffey ACA insert). The packs were sold at Wal-art's nationwide and carried a suggested retail price of $0.97.

	MINT	NRMT
MPLETE SET (10)	8.00	3.60
MMON CARD (CA1-CA10)	1.00	.45
CA1 Ken Griffey Jr.	1.00	.45
CA2 Ken Griffey Jr.	1.00	.45
CA3 Ken Griffey Jr.	1.00	.45
CA4 Ken Griffey Jr.	1.00	.45
CA5 Ken Griffey Jr.	1.00	.45
CA6 Ken Griffey Jr.	1.00	.45
CA7 Ken Griffey Jr.	1.00	.45
CA8 Ken Griffey Jr.	1.00	.45
CA9 Ken Griffey Jr.	1.00	.45
CA10 Ken Griffey Jr.	1.00	.45

1996 Collector's Choice Nomo Scrapbook

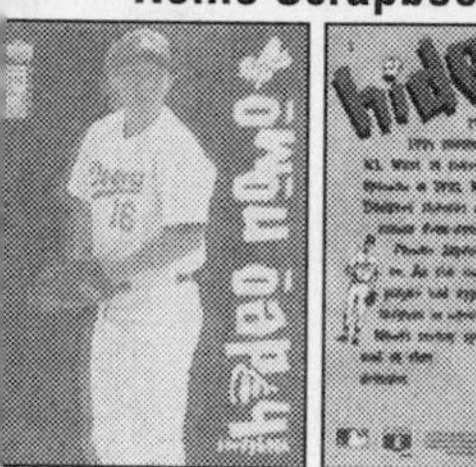

is five-card set was randomly inserted one in every 17 cond series packs and features season highlights from okie of the Year, Hideo Nomo's first year in the Majors. e fronts display color action player cut-outs with yellow d red shadows on a metallic background. The backs rry a career fact about Nomo.

	MINT	NRMT
MPLETE SET (5)	6.00	2.70
MMON NOMO (1-5)	1.50	.70
1 Hideo Nomo	1.50	.70
2 Hideo Nomo Releasing ball	1.50	.70
3 Hideo Nomo Back turned to batter	1.50	.70
4 Hideo Nomo Hands over head	1.50	.70
5 Hideo Nomo Glove at side	1.50	.70

1996 Collector's Choice You Make the Play

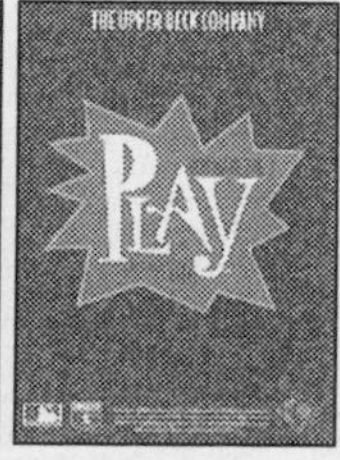

rds from this 90-card set were inserted one per first ries pack. Forty-five players are featured and each ayer is given two outcomes. The cards measure just out the standard-size but have rounded corners. In dition to being inserted into packs, dealers also were fered extra You Make the Play cards depending on how any cases ordered. A dealer who ordered one case ceived two 12-card packs of these cards for a total of 24 rds. Meanwhile, a dealer who ordered two cases received six 12-card packs for a total of 72 packs. Customers could also receive 12 of these cards by sending 10 wrappers and $2 to an a mail-in order. This offer expired on May 15, 1996.

	MINT	NRMT
COMPLETE SET (90)	15.00	6.75
COMMON CARD (1-45)	.15	.07
COMP GOLD SET (90)	200.00	90.00
GOLD STARS: 7.5X TO 15X BASIC CARDS		
☐ 1 Kevin Appier	.20	.09
☐ 1A Kevin Appier	.20	.09
☐ 2 Carlos Baerga	.15	.07
☐ 2A Carlos Baerga	.15	.07
☐ 3 Jeff Bagwell	.75	.35
☐ 3A Jeff Bagwell	.75	.35
☐ 4 Jay Bell	.15	.07
☐ 4A Jay Bell	.15	.07
☐ 5 Albert Belle	.75	.35
☐ 5A Albert Belle	.50	.23
☐ 6 Craig Biggio	.30	.14
☐ 6A Craig Biggio	.30	.14
☐ 7 Wade Boggs	.40	.18
☐ 7A Wade Boggs	.40	.18
☐ 8 Barry Bonds	.50	.23
☐ 8A Barry Bonds	.50	.23
☐ 9 Bobby Bonilla	.20	.09
☐ 9A Bobby Bonilla	.20	.09
☐ 10 Jose Canseco	.30	.14
☐ 10A Jose Canseco	.30	.14
☐ 11 Joe Carter	.20	.09
☐ 11A Joe Carter	.20	.09
☐ 12 Darren Daulton	.15	.07
☐ 12A Darren Daulton	.15	.07
☐ 13 Cecil Fielder	.20	.09
☐ 13A Cecil Fielder	.20	.09
☐ 14 Ron Gant	.15	.07
☐ 14A Ron Gant	.15	.07
☐ 15 Juan Gonzalez	1.00	.45
☐ 15A Juan Gonzalez	1.00	.45
☐ 16 Ken Griffey Jr.	2.00	.90
☐ 16A Ken Griffey Jr.	2.00	.90
☐ 17 Tony Gwynn	.75	.35
☐ 17A Tony Gwynn	1.00	.45
☐ 18 Randy Johnson	.50	.23
☐ 18A Randy Johnson	.50	.23
☐ 19 Chipper Jones	1.25	.55
☐ 19A Chipper Jones	1.25	.55
☐ 20 Barry Larkin	.30	.14
☐ 20A Barry Larkin	.30	.14
☐ 21 Kenny Lofton	.50	.23
☐ 21A Kenny Lofton	.50	.23
☐ 22 Greg Maddux	1.25	.55
☐ 22A Greg Maddux	1.25	.55
☐ 23 Don Mattingly	1.00	.45
☐ 23A Don Mattingly	.60	.25
☐ 24 Fred McGriff	.30	.14
☐ 24A Fred McGriff	.30	.14
☐ 25 Mark McGwire	.60	.25
☐ 25A Mark McGwire	.75	.35
☐ 26 Paul Molitor	.40	.18
☐ 26A Paul Molitor	.40	.18
☐ 27 Raul Mondesi	.30	.14
☐ 27A Raul Mondesi	.30	.14
☐ 28 Eddie Murray	.40	.18
☐ 28A Eddie Murray	.40	.18
☐ 29 Hideo Nomo	.50	.23
☐ 29A Hideo Nomo	1.00	.45
☐ 30 Jon Nunnally	.15	.07
☐ 30A Jon Nunnally	.15	.07
☐ 31 Mike Piazza	1.25	.55
☐ 31A Mike Piazza	1.25	.55
☐ 32 Kirby Puckett	.75	.35
☐ 32A Kirby Puckett	.75	.35
☐ 33 Cal Ripken	1.50	.70
☐ 33A Cal Ripken	1.50	.70
☐ 34 Alex Rodriguez	2.00	.90
☐ 34A Alex Rodriguez	1.50	.70
☐ 35 Tim Salmon	.40	.18
☐ 35A Tim Salmon	.40	.18
☐ 36 Gary Sheffield	.40	.18
☐ 36A Gary Sheffield	.40	.18
☐ 37 Lee Smith	.20	.09
☐ 37A Lee Smith	.20	.09
☐ 38 Ozzie Smith	.50	.23
☐ 38A Ozzie Smith	.50	.23
☐ 39 Sammy Sosa	.40	.18
☐ 39A Sammy Sosa	.40	.18
☐ 40 Frank Thomas	2.00	.90
☐ 40A Frank Thomas	1.50	.70
☐ 41 Greg Vaughn	.15	.07
☐ 41A Greg Vaughn	.15	.07
☐ 42 Mo Vaughn	.50	.23
☐ 42A Mo Vaughn	.50	.23
☐ 43 Larry Walker	.40	.18
☐ 43A Larry Walker	.40	.18
☐ 44 Rondell White	.20	.09
☐ 44A Rondell White	.20	.09
☐ 45 Matt Williams	.30	.14
☐ 45A Matt Williams	.30	.14

1997 Collector's Choice

This 506-card set was distributed in 12-card packs with a suggested retail price of $.99. The fronts feature color action player photos while the backs carry player statistics. The set contains the following subsets: Rookie Class (1-27), League Leaders (56-63), Postseason (218-224) which recaps action from the 1996 playoffs and World Series Games and Ken Griffey Jr. Checklist (244-246) which also carry collecting tips. The 260-card second series set was distributed in 14-card packs with a suggested retail price of $1.29 and features color player photos in white borders. The backs carry player statistics. The set contains the following: 199 regular player cards, 10 Ken Griffey Jr.'s Hot List (325-334), 18 Rookie Class, 3 Collecting 101 Set checklists, and 30 full-bleed All-Star cards.

	MINT	NRMT
COMPLETE SET (506)	30.00	13.50
COMP.FACT.SET (516)	40.00	18.00
COMPLETE SERIES 1 (246)	15.00	6.75
COMPLETE SERIES 2 (260)	15.00	6.75
COMMON CARD (1-506)	.10	.05
☐ 1 Andruw Jones	1.00	.45
☐ 2 Rocky Coppinger	.20	.09
☐ 3 Jeff D'Amico	.20	.09
☐ 4 Dmitri Young	.20	.09
☐ 5 Darin Erstad	.60	.25
☐ 6 Jermaine Allensworth	.10	.05
☐ 7 Damian Jackson	.10	.05
☐ 8 Bill Mueller	.20	.09
☐ 9 Jacob Cruz	.10	.05
☐ 10 Vladimir Guerrero	.75	.35
☐ 11 Marty Janzen	.10	.05
☐ 12 Kevin L. Brown	.20	.09
☐ 13 Willie Adams	.10	.05
☐ 14 Wendell Magee	.10	.05
☐ 15 Scott Rolen	1.00	.45
☐ 16 Matt Beech	.10	.05
☐ 17 Neifi Perez	.20	.09
☐ 18 Jamey Wright	.20	.09
☐ 19 Jose Paniagua	.10	.05
☐ 20 Todd Walker	.10	.05
☐ 21 Justin Thompson	.20	.09
☐ 22 Robin Jennings	.10	.05
☐ 23 Dario Veras	.25	.11
☐ 24 Brian Lesher	.10	.05
☐ 25 Nomar Garciaparra	1.25	.55
☐ 26 Luis Castillo	.10	.05
☐ 27 Brian Giles	.10	.05
☐ 28 Jermaine Dye	.10	.05
☐ 29 Terrell Wade	.10	.05
☐ 30 Fred McGriff	.30	.14
☐ 31 Marquis Grissom	.20	.09
☐ 32 Ryan Klesko	.30	.14
☐ 33 Javier Lopez	.20	.09
☐ 34 Mark Wohlers	.10	.05
☐ 35 Tom Glavine	.20	.09
☐ 36 Denny Neagle	.10	.05
☐ 37 Scott Erickson	.10	.05
☐ 38 Chris Hoiles	.10	.05
☐ 39 Roberto Alomar	.40	.18
☐ 40 Eddie Murray	.40	.18
☐ 41 Cal Ripken	1.50	.70
☐ 42 Randy Myers	.10	.05
☐ 43 B.J. Surhoff	.10	.05
☐ 44 Rick Krivda	.10	.05
☐ 45 Jose Canseco	.30	.14
☐ 46 Heathcliff Slocumb	.10	.05
☐ 47 Jeff Suppan	.20	.09
☐ 48 Tom Gordon	.10	.05
☐ 49 Aaron Sele	.10	.05
☐ 50 Mo Vaughn	.50	.23
☐ 51 Darren Bragg	.10	.05
☐ 52 Wil Cordero	.10	.05
☐ 53 Scott Bullett	.10	.05

☐ 54 Terry Adams .10 .05
☐ 55 Jackie Robinson 1.00 .45
☐ 56 Tony Gwynn LL .50 .23
Alex Rodriguez
☐ 57 Andres Galarraga LL .20 .09
Mark McGwire
☐ 58 Andres Galarraga LL .20 .09
Albert Belle
☐ 59 Eric Young LL .20 .09
Kenny Lofton
☐ 60 John Smoltz LL .20 .09
Andy Pettitte
☐ 61 John Smoltz LL .20 .09
Roger Clemens
☐ 62 Kevin Brown LL .10 .05
Juan Guzman
☐ 63 John Wetteland LL .10 .05
Todd Worrell
Jeff Brantley
☐ 64 Scott Servais .10 .05
☐ 65 Sammy Sosa .40 .18
☐ 66 Ryne Sandberg .50 .23
☐ 67 Frank Castillo .10 .05
☐ 68 Rey Sanchez .10 .05
☐ 69 Steve Trachsel .10 .05
☐ 70 Robin Ventura .20 .09
☐ 71 Wilson Alvarez .10 .05
☐ 72 Tony Phillips .10 .05
☐ 73 Lyle Mouton .10 .05
☐ 74 Mike Cameron .20 .09
☐ 75 Harold Baines .20 .09
☐ 76 Albert Belle .50 .23
☐ 77 Chris Snopek .10 .05
☐ 78 Reggie Sanders .10 .05
☐ 79 Jeff Brantley .10 .05
☐ 80 Barry Larkin .30 .14
☐ 81 Kevin Jarvis .10 .05
☐ 82 John Smiley .10 .05
☐ 83 Pete Schourek .10 .05
☐ 84 Thomas Howard .10 .05
☐ 85 Lee Smith .20 .09
☐ 86 Omar Vizquel .20 .09
☐ 87 Julio Franco .20 .09
☐ 88 Orel Hershiser .20 .09
☐ 89 Charles Nagy .20 .09
☐ 90 Matt Williams .30 .14
☐ 91 Dennis Martinez .20 .09
☐ 92 Jose Mesa .20 .09
☐ 93 Sandy Alomar Jr. .20 .09
☐ 94 Jim Thome .40 .18
☐ 95 Vinny Castilla .20 .09
☐ 96 Armando Reynoso .10 .05
☐ 97 Kevin Ritz .10 .05
☐ 98 Larry Walker .40 .18
☐ 99 Eric Young .20 .09
☐ 100 Dante Bichette .20 .09
☐ 101 Quinton McCracken .10 .05
☐ 102 John Vander Wal .10 .05
☐ 103 Phil Nevin .10 .05
☐ 104 Tony Clark .40 .18
☐ 105 Alan Trammell .30 .14
☐ 106 Felipe Lira .10 .05
☐ 107 Curtis Pride .10 .05
☐ 108 Bobby Higginson .20 .09
☐ 109 Mark Lewis .10 .05
☐ 110 Travis Fryman .20 .09
☐ 111 Al Leiter .10 .05
☐ 112 Devon White .10 .05
☐ 113 Jeff Conine .20 .09
☐ 114 Charles Johnson .10 .05
☐ 115 Andre Dawson .30 .14
☐ 116 Edgar Renteria .20 .09
☐ 117 Robb Nen .10 .05
☐ 118 Kevin Brown .20 .09
☐ 119 Derek Bell .10 .05
☐ 120 Bob Abreu .40 .18
☐ 121 Mike Hampton .10 .05
☐ 122 Todd Jones .10 .05
☐ 123 Billy Wagner .20 .09
☐ 124 Shane Reynolds .10 .05
☐ 125 Jeff Bagwell .75 .35
☐ 126 Brian L. Hunter .20 .09
☐ 127 Jeff Montgomery .10 .05
☐ 128 Rod Myers .30 .14
☐ 129 Tim Belcher .10 .05
☐ 130 Kevin Appier .20 .09
☐ 131 Mike Sweeney .10 .05
☐ 132 Craig Paquette .10 .05
☐ 133 Joe Randa .10 .05
☐ 134 Michael Tucker .20 .09
☐ 135 Raul Mondesi .30 .14
☐ 136 Tim Wallach .10 .05
☐ 137 Brett Butler .20 .09
☐ 138 Karim Garcia .10 .05
☐ 139 Todd Hollandsworth .10 .05
☐ 140 Eric Karros .20 .09
☐ 141 Hideo Nomo 1.00 .45
☐ 142 Ismael Valdes .20 .09
☐ 143 Cal Eldred .10 .05
☐ 144 Scott Karl .10 .05
☐ 145 Matt Mieske .10 .05
☐ 146 Mike Fetters .10 .05
☐ 147 Mark Loretta .10 .05
☐ 148 Fernando Vina .10 .05
☐ 149 Jeff Cirillo .20 .09
☐ 150 Dave Nilsson .10 .05
☐ 151 Kirby Puckett .75 .35
☐ 152 Rich Becker .10 .05
☐ 153 Chuck Knoblauch .40 .18
☐ 154 Marty Cordova .20 .09
☐ 155 Paul Molitor .40 .18
☐ 156 Rick Aguilera .20 .09
☐ 157 Pat Meares .10 .05
☐ 158 Frank Rodriguez .10 .05
☐ 159 David Segui .10 .05
☐ 160 Henry Rodriguez .10 .05
☐ 161 Shane Andrews .10 .05
☐ 162 Pedro Martinez .40 .18
☐ 163 Mark Grudzielanek .10 .05
☐ 164 Mike Lansing .10 .05
☐ 165 Rondell White .10 .05
☐ 166 Ugueth Urbina .20 .09
☐ 167 Rey Ordonez .10 .05
☐ 168 Robert Person .10 .05
☐ 169 Carlos Baerga .20 .09
☐ 170 Bernard Gilkey .10 .05
☐ 171 John Franco .20 .09
☐ 172 Pete Harnisch .10 .05
☐ 173 Butch Huskey .10 .05
☐ 174 Paul Wilson .10 .05
☐ 175 Bernie Williams .40 .18
☐ 175 Dwight Gooden ERR .20 .09
incorrectly numbered 175
☐ 177 Wade Boggs .40 .18
☐ 178 Ruben Rivera .20 .09
☐ 179 Jim Leyritz .10 .05
☐ 180 Derek Jeter 1.25 .55
☐ 181 Tino Martinez .40 .18
☐ 182 Tim Raines .10 .05
☐ 183 Scott Brosius .10 .05
☐ 184 Jason Giambi .20 .09
☐ 185 Geronimo Berroa .10 .05
☐ 186 Ariel Prieto .10 .05
☐ 187 Scott Spiezio .20 .09
☐ 188 John Wasdin .10 .05
☐ 189 Ernie Young .10 .05
☐ 190 Mark McGwire .75 .35
☐ 191 Jim Eisenreich .20 .09
☐ 192 Ricky Bottalico .20 .09
☐ 193 Darren Daulton .20 .09
☐ 194 David Doster .10 .05
☐ 195 Gregg Jefferies .20 .09
☐ 196 Lenny Dykstra .20 .09
☐ 197 Curt Schilling .20 .09
☐ 198 Todd Stottlemyre .10 .05
☐ 199 Willie McGee .10 .05
☐ 200 Ozzie Smith .50 .23
☐ 201 Dennis Eckersley .30 .14
☐ 202 Ray Lankford .20 .09
☐ 203 John Mabry .20 .09
☐ 204 Alan Benes .20 .09
☐ 205 Ron Gant .20 .09
☐ 206 Archi Cianfrocco .10 .05
☐ 207 Fernando Valenzuela .20 .09
☐ 208 Greg Vaughn .10 .05
☐ 209 Steve Finley .20 .09
☐ 210 Tony Gwynn 1.00 .45
☐ 211 Rickey Henderson .30 .14
☐ 212 Trevor Hoffman .20 .09
☐ 213 Jason Thompson .10 .05
☐ 214 Osvaldo Fernandez .10 .05
☐ 215 Glenallen Hill .10 .05
☐ 216 William VanLandingham .10 .05
☐ 217 Marvin Benard .10 .05
☐ 218 Juan Gonzalez POST .50 .23
☐ 219 Roberto Alomar POST .40 .18
☐ 220 Brian Jordan POST .10 .05
☐ 221 John Smoltz POST .20 .09
☐ 222 Javy Lopez POST .20 .09
☐ 223 Bernie Williams POST .40 .18
☐ 224 Jim Leyritz POST .10 .05
John Wetteland
☐ 225 Barry Bonds .50 .23
☐ 226 Rich Aurilia .10 .05
☐ 227 Jay Canizaro .10 .05
☐ 228 Dan Wilson .10 .05
☐ 229 Bob Wolcott .10 .05
☐ 230 Ken Griffey Jr. 2.00 .90
☐ 231 Sterling Hitchcock .10 .05
☐ 232 Edgar Martinez .30 .14
☐ 233 Joey Cora .20 .09
☐ 234 Norm Charlton .10 .05
☐ 235 Alex Rodriguez 1.50 .70
☐ 236 Bobby Witt .10 .05
☐ 237 Darren Oliver .10 .05
☐ 238 Kevin Elster .10 .05
☐ 239 Rusty Greer .20 .09
☐ 240 Juan Gonzalez 1.00 .45
☐ 241 Will Clark .30 .14
☐ 242 Dean Palmer .10 .05
☐ 243 Ivan Rodriguez .50 .23
☐ 244 Ken Griffey Jr. CL .25 .11
☐ 245 Ken Griffey Jr. CL .25 .11
☐ 246 Ken Griffey Jr. CL .25 .11
☐ 247 Ken Griffey Jr. CL .25 .11
☐ 248 Ken Griffey Jr. CL .25 .11
☐ 249 Ken Griffey Jr. CL .25 .11
☐ 250 Eddie Murray .40 .18
☐ 251 Troy Percival .10 .05
☐ 252 Garret Anderson .20 .09
☐ 253 Allen Watson .10 .05
☐ 254 Jason Dickson .10 .05
☐ 255 Jim Edmonds .40 .18
☐ 256 Chuck Finley .10 .05
☐ 257 Randy Velarde .10 .05
☐ 258 Shigetoshi Hasegawa .25 .11
☐ 259 Todd Greene .20 .09
☐ 260 Tim Salmon .40 .18
☐ 261 Mark Langston .10 .05
☐ 262 Dave Hollins .10 .05
☐ 263 Gary DiSarcina .10 .05
☐ 264 Kenny Lofton .50 .23
☐ 265 John Smoltz .20 .09
☐ 266 Greg Maddux 1.25 .55
☐ 267 Jeff Blauser .10 .05
☐ 268 Alan Embree .10 .05
☐ 269 Mark Lemke .10 .05
☐ 270 Chipper Jones 1.25 .55
☐ 271 Mike Mussina .40 .18
☐ 272 Rafael Palmeiro .30 .14
☐ 273 Jimmy Key .10 .05
☐ 274 Mike Bordick .10 .05
☐ 275 Brady Anderson .30 .14
☐ 276 Eric Davis .10 .05
☐ 277 Jeffrey Hammonds .10 .05
☐ 278 Reggie Jefferson .20 .09
☐ 279 Tim Naehring .10 .05
☐ 280 John Valentin .10 .05
☐ 281 Troy O'Leary .10 .05
☐ 282 Shane Mack .10 .05
☐ 283 Mike Stanley .10 .05
☐ 284 Tim Wakefield .10 .05
☐ 285 Brian McRae .10 .05
☐ 286 Brooks Kieschnick .10 .05
☐ 287 Shawon Dunston .10 .05
☐ 288 Kevin Foster .10 .05
☐ 289 Mel Rojas .10 .05
☐ 290 Mark Grace .30 .14
☐ 291 Brant Brown .10 .05
☐ 292 Amaury Telemaco .10 .05
☐ 293 Dave Martinez .10 .05
☐ 294 Jaime Navarro .10 .05
☐ 295 Ray Durham .10 .05
☐ 296 Ozzie Guillen .10 .05
☐ 297 Roberto Hernandez .20 .09
☐ 298 Ron Karkovice .10 .05
☐ 299 James Baldwin .10 .05
☐ 300 Frank Thomas 1.50 .70
☐ 301 Eddie Taubensee .10 .05
☐ 302 Bret Boone .10 .05
☐ 303 Willie Greene .10 .05
☐ 304 Dave Burba .10 .05
☐ 305 Deion Sanders .40 .18
☐ 306 Reggie Sanders .10 .05
☐ 307 Hal Morris .20 .09
☐ 308 Pokey Reese .10 .05
☐ 309 Tony Fernandez .10 .05
☐ 310 Manny Ramirez .40 .18
☐ 311 Chad Ogea .10 .05
☐ 312 Jack McDowell .10 .05
☐ 313 Kevin Mitchell .10 .05
☐ 314 Chad Curtis .10 .05
☐ 315 Steve Kline .10 .05
☐ 316 Kevin Seitzer .10 .05
☐ 317 Kirt Manwaring .10 .05
☐ 318 Billy Swift .10 .05
☐ 319 Ellis Burks .10 .05
☐ 320 Andres Galarraga .40 .18
☐ 321 Bruce Ruffin .10 .05
☐ 322 Mark Thompson .10 .05
☐ 323 Walt Weiss .10 .05
☐ 324 Todd Jones .10 .05
☐ 325 Andruw Jones GHL .05 .02
☐ 326 Chipper Jones GHL .05 .02
☐ 327 Mo Vaughn GHL .40 .18
☐ 328 Frank Thomas GHL .05 .02
☐ 329 Albert Belle GHL .40 .18
☐ 330 Mark McGwire GHL .40 .18
☐ 331 Derek Jeter GHL .05 .02
☐ 332 Alex Rodriguez GHL .05 .02
☐ 333 Jay Buhner GHL .40 .18

with Ken Griffey Jr.
334 Ken Griffey Jr. GHL .05 .02
335 Brian L. Hunter .20 .09
336 Brian Johnson .10 .05
337 Omar Olivares .10 .05
338 Deivi Cruz .25 .11
339 Damion Easley .10 .05
340 Melvin Nieves .10 .05
341 Moises Alou .20 .09
342 Jim Eisenreich .20 .09
343 Mark Hutton .10 .05
344 Alex Fernandez .20 .09
345 Gary Sheffield .40 .18
346 Pat Rapp .10 .05
347 Brad Ausmus .10 .05
348 Sean Berry .10 .05
349 Darryl Kile .20 .09
350 Craig Biggio .30 .14
351 Chris Holt .10 .05
352 Luis Gonzalez .10 .05
353 Pat Listach .10 .05
354 Jose Rosado .10 .05
355 Mike Macfarlane .10 .05
356 Tom Goodwin .10 .05
357 Chris Haney .10 .05
358 Chili Davis .10 .05
359 Jose Offerman .10 .05
360 Johnny Damon .10 .05
361 Bip Roberts .10 .05
362 Ramon Martinez .20 .09
363 Pedro Astacio .10 .05
364 Todd Zeile .10 .05
365 Mike Piazza 1.25 .55
366 Greg Gagne .10 .05
367 Chan Ho Park .40 .18
368 Wilton Guerrero .10 .05
369 Todd Worrell .20 .09
370 John Jaha .10 .05
371 Steve Sparks .10 .05
372 Mike Matheny .10 .05
373 Marc Newfield .10 .05
374 Jeromy Burnitz .20 .09
375 Jose Valentin .10 .05
376 Ben McDonald .10 .05
377 Roberto Kelly .10 .05
378 Bob Tewksbury .10 .05
379 Ron Coomer .10 .05
380 Brad Radke .20 .09
381 Matt Lawton .10 .05
382 Dan Naulty .10 .05
383 Scott Stahoviak .10 .05
384 Matt Wagner .10 .05
385 Jim Bullinger .10 .05
386 Carlos Perez .10 .05
387 Darrin Fletcher .10 .05
388 Chris Widger .10 .05
389 F.P. Santangelo .10 .05
390 Lee Smith .20 .09
391 Bobby Jones .10 .05
392 John Olerud .20 .09
393 Mark Clark .10 .05
394 Jason Isringhausen .10 .05
395 Todd Hundley .20 .09
396 Lance Johnson .10 .05
397 Edgardo Alfonzo .20 .09
398 Alex Ochoa .10 .05
399 Darryl Strawberry .20 .09
400 David Cone .20 .09
401 Paul O'Neill .20 .09
402 Joe Girardi .10 .05
403 Charlie Hayes .10 .05
404 Andy Pettitte .40 .18
405 Mariano Rivera .20 .09
406 Mariano Duncan .10 .05
407 Kenny Rogers .10 .05
408 Cecil Fielder .20 .09
409 George Williams .10 .05
410 Jose Canseco .10 .05
411 Tony Batista .20 .09
412 Steve Karsay .10 .05
413 Dave Telgheder .10 .05
414 Billy Taylor .10 .05
415 Mickey Morandini .10 .05
416 Calvin Maduro .10 .05
417 Mark Leiter .10 .05
418 Kevin Stocker .10 .05
419 Mike Lieberthal .10 .05
420 Rico Brogna .10 .05
421 Mark Portugal .10 .05
422 Rex Hudler .10 .05
423 Mark Johnson .10 .05
424 Esteban Loaiza .10 .05
425 Lou Collier .10 .05
426 Kevin Elster .10 .05
427 Francisco Cordova .10 .05
428 Marc Wilkins .10 .05
429 Joe Randa .10 .05
430 Jason Kendall .20 .09
☐ 431 Jon Lieber .10 .05
☐ 432 Steve Cooke .10 .05
☐ 433 Emil Brown .10 .05
☐ 434 Tony Womack .30 .14
☐ 435 Al Martin .10 .05
☐ 436 Jason Schmidt .10 .05
☐ 437 Andy Benes .20 .09
☐ 438 Delino DeShields .10 .05
☐ 439 Royce Clayton .10 .05
☐ 440 Brian Jordan .20 .09
☐ 441 Donovan Osborne .10 .05
☐ 442 Gary Gaetti .20 .09
☐ 443 Tom Pagnozzi .10 .05
☐ 444 Joey Hamilton .10 .05
☐ 445 Wally Joyner .20 .09
☐ 446 John Flaherty .10 .05
☐ 447 Chris Gomez .10 .05
☐ 448 Sterling Hitchcock .10 .05
☐ 449 Andy Ashby .10 .05
☐ 450 Ken Caminiti .40 .18
☐ 451 Tim Worrell .10 .05
☐ 452 Jose Vizcaino .10 .05
☐ 453 Rod Beck .10 .05
☐ 454 Wilson Delgado .10 .05
☐ 455 Darryl Hamilton .10 .05
☐ 456 Mark Lewis .10 .05
☐ 457 Mark Gardner .10 .05
☐ 458 Rick Wilkins .10 .05
☐ 459 Scott Sanders .10 .05
☐ 460 Kevin Orie .10 .05
☐ 461 Glendon Rusch .10 .05
☐ 462 Juan Melo .10 .05
☐ 463 Richie Sexson .20 .09
☐ 464 Bartolo Colon .20 .09
☐ 465 Jose Guillen .50 .23
☐ 466 Heath Murray .10 .05
☐ 467 Aaron Boone .10 .05
☐ 468 Bubba Trammell RC .40 .18
☐ 469 Jeff Abbott .10 .05
☐ 470 Derrick Gibson .40 .18
☐ 471 Matt Morris .20 .09
☐ 472 Ryan Jones .10 .05
☐ 473 Pat Cline .10 .05
☐ 474 Adam Riggs .10 .05
☐ 475 Jay Payton .10 .05
☐ 476 Derrek Lee .20 .09
☐ 477 Eli Marrero .20 .09
☐ 478 Lee Tinsley .10 .05
☐ 479 Jamie Moyer .10 .05
☐ 480 Jay Buhner .30 .14
☐ 481 Bob Wells .10 .05
☐ 482 Jeff Fassero .10 .05
☐ 483 Paul Sorrento .10 .05
☐ 484 Russ Davis .10 .05
☐ 485 Randy Johnson .40 .18
☐ 486 Roger Pavlik .10 .05
☐ 487 Damon Buford .10 .05
☐ 488 Julio Santana .10 .05
☐ 489 Mark McLemore .10 .05
☐ 490 Mickey Tettleton .10 .05
☐ 491 Ken Hill .10 .05
☐ 492 Benji Gil .10 .05
☐ 493 Ed Sprague .10 .05
☐ 494 Mike Timlin .10 .05
☐ 495 Pat Hentgen .20 .09
☐ 496 Orlando Merced .10 .05
☐ 497 Carlos Garcia .10 .05
☐ 498 Carlos Delgado .10 .05
☐ 499 Juan Guzman .10 .05
☐ 500 Roger Clemens .75 .35
☐ 501 Erik Hanson .10 .05
☐ 502 Otis Nixon .10 .05
☐ 503 Shawn Green .20 .09
☐ 504 Charlie O'Brien .10 .05
☐ 505 Joe Carter .20 .09
☐ 506 Alex Gonzalez .10 .05

1997 Collector's Choice All-Star Connection

Inserted one in every series two packs, this 45-card set celebrates the unique history of Baseball's All Star Game and highlights the League's top All-Star caliber players. The fronts feature color player cut-outs on a big star background.

	MINT	NRMT
COMPLETE SET (45)	12.00	5.50
COMMON CARD (1-45)	.10	.05
☐ 1 Mark McGwire	.75	.35
☐ 2 Chuck Knoblauch	.40	.18
☐ 3 Jim Thome	.40	.18
☐ 4 Alex Rodriguez	1.50	.70
☐ 5 Ken Griffey Jr.	2.00	.90
☐ 6 Brady Anderson	.30	.14
☐ 7 Albert Belle	.50	.23
☐ 8 Ivan Rodriguez	.50	.23
☐ 9 Pat Hentgen	.20	.09
☐ 10 Frank Thomas	1.50	.70
☐ 11 Roberto Alomar	.40	.18
☐ 12 Robin Ventura	.20	.09
☐ 13 Cal Ripken	1.50	.70
☐ 14 Juan Gonzalez	1.00	.45
☐ 15 Manny Ramirez	.40	.18
☐ 16 Bernie Williams	.40	.18
☐ 17 Terry Steinbach	.10	.05
☐ 18 Andy Pettitte	.40	.18
☐ 19 Jeff Bagwell	.75	.35
☐ 20 Craig Biggio	.30	.14
☐ 21 Ken Caminiti	.40	.18
☐ 22 Barry Larkin	.30	.14
☐ 23 Tony Gwynn	1.00	.45
☐ 24 Barry Bonds	.50	.23
☐ 25 Kenny Lofton	.50	.23
☐ 26 Mike Piazza	1.25	.55
☐ 27 John Smoltz	.20	.09
☐ 28 Andres Galarraga	.40	.18
☐ 29 Ryne Sandberg	.50	.23
☐ 30 Chipper Jones	1.25	.55
☐ 31 Mark Grudzielanek	.10	.05
☐ 32 Sammy Sosa	.40	.18
☐ 33 Steve Finley	.20	.09
☐ 34 Gary Sheffield	.40	.18
☐ 35 Todd Hundley	.20	.09
☐ 36 Greg Maddux	1.25	.55
☐ 37 Mo Vaughn	.40	.18
☐ 38 Eric Young	.10	.05
☐ 39 Vinny Castilla	.20	.09
☐ 40 Derek Jeter	1.25	.55
☐ 41 Lance Johnson	.10	.05
☐ 42 Ellis Burks	.10	.05
☐ 43 Dante Bichette	.20	.09
☐ 44 Javy Lopez	.20	.09
☐ 45 Hideo Nomo	1.00	.45

1997 Collector's Choice Big Shots

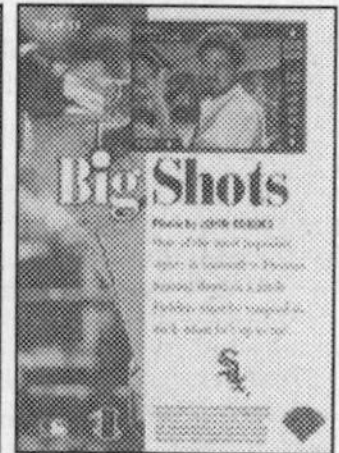

Randomly inserted in series two packs at the rate of one in 12, this 19-card set features unique and exciting photos depicting some of the game's most recognized players.

	MINT	NRMT
COMPLETE SET (19)	60.00	27.00
COMMON CARD (1-19)	1.00	.45
COMP.GOLD SET (20)	250.00	110.00
*GOLD CARDS: 15X TO 25X BASIC CARDS		
☐ 1 Ken Griffey Jr.	10.00	4.50
☐ 2 Nomar Garciaparra	6.00	2.70
☐ 3 Brian Jordan	1.00	.45
☐ 4 Scott Rolen	5.00	2.20
☐ 5 Alex Rodriguez	8.00	3.60
☐ 6 Larry Walker	2.00	.90
☐ 7 Mariano Rivera	1.25	.55
☐ 8 Cal Ripken	8.00	3.60
☐ 9 Deion Sanders	2.00	.90
☐ 10 Frank Thomas	8.00	3.60
☐ 11 Dean Palmer	1.00	.45
☐ 12 Ken Caminiti	2.00	.90
☐ 13 Derek Jeter	6.00	2.70
☐ 14 Barry Bonds	2.50	1.10
☐ 15 Chipper Jones	6.00	2.70
☐ 16 Mo Vaughn	2.50	1.10
☐ 17 Jay Buhner	1.50	.70

Card	MINT	NRMT
☐ 18 Mike Piazza	6.00	2.70
☐ 19 Tony Gwynn	5.00	2.20

1997 Collector's Choice The Big Show

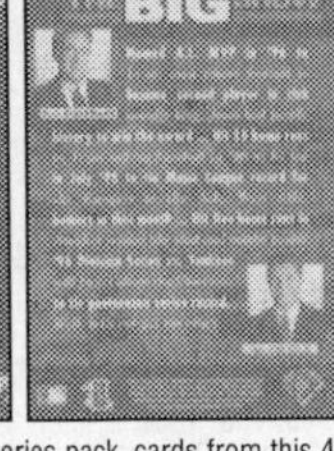

Inserted one in every first series pack, cards from this 45-card set feature color photos of some of the hottest players in baseball. The backs carry comments about the pictured player by ESPN SportsCenter television sportscasters, Keith Olbermann and Dan Patrick.

	MINT	NRMT
COMPLETE SET (45)	10.00	4.50
COMMON CARD (1-45)	.10	.05
COMP.WORLD HEADQUATER SET(45)	250.00	110.00

*WHQ STARS 12.5X TO 25X BASIC SHOW

Card	MINT	NRMT
☐ 1 Greg Maddux	1.25	.55
☐ 2 Chipper Jones	1.25	.55
☐ 3 Andruw Jones	1.25	.55
☐ 4 John Smoltz	.20	.09
☐ 5 Cal Ripken	1.50	.70
☐ 6 Roberto Alomar	.40	.18
☐ 7 Rafael Palmeiro	.30	.14
☐ 8 Eddie Murray	.40	.18
☐ 9 Jose Canseco	.30	.14
☐ 10 Roger Clemens	.75	.35
☐ 11 Mo Vaughn	.50	.23
☐ 12 Jim Edmonds	.40	.18
☐ 13 Tim Salmon	.40	.18
☐ 14 Sammy Sosa	.40	.18
☐ 15 Albert Belle	.50	.23
☐ 16 Frank Thomas	1.50	.70
☐ 17 Barry Larkin	.30	.14
☐ 18 Kenny Lofton	.50	.23
☐ 19 Manny Ramirez	.40	.18
☐ 20 Matt Williams	.30	.14
☐ 21 Dante Bichette	.20	.09
☐ 22 Gary Sheffield	.40	.18
☐ 23 Craig Biggio	.30	.14
☐ 24 Jeff Bagwell	.75	.35
☐ 25 Todd Hollandsworth	.10	.05
☐ 26 Raul Mondesi	.30	.14
☐ 27 Hideo Nomo	1.00	.45
☐ 28 Mike Piazza	1.25	.55
☐ 29 Paul Molitor	.40	.18
☐ 30 Kirby Puckett	.75	.35
☐ 31 Rondell White	.20	.09
☐ 32 Rey Ordonez	.10	.05
☐ 33 Paul Wilson	.10	.05
☐ 34 Derek Jeter	1.25	.55
☐ 35 Andy Pettitte	.40	.18
☐ 36 Mark McGwire	.75	.35
☐ 37 Jason Kendall	.20	.09
☐ 38 Ozzie Smith	.50	.23
☐ 39 Tony Gwynn	.75	.35
☐ 40 Barry Bonds	.50	.23
☐ 41 Alex Rodriguez	1.25	.55
☐ 42 Jay Buhner	.30	.14
☐ 43 Ken Griffey Jr.	2.00	.90
☐ 44 Randy Johnson	.40	.18
☐ 45 Juan Gonzalez	1.00	.45

1997 Collector's Choice Crash the Game

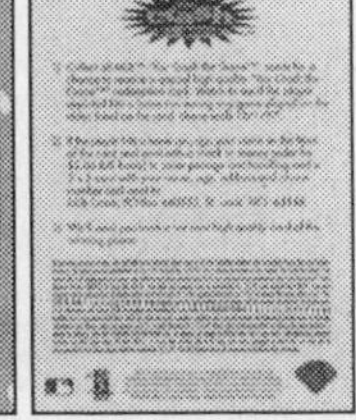

Inserted in series two packs at the rate of one in five, cards from this interactive game set features three separate cards each of 30 top home run hitters. If the featured player hit a home run during the series specified on the card, the card could than have been redeemed for a special card of the same player. The postmark expiration date for exchanging winning cards was December 1, 1997.

	MINT	NRMT
COMPLETE SET (90)	60.00	27.00
COMMON CARD (CG1-CG30)	.20	.09

*INSTANT WIN: 10X TO 20X BASIC CARDS.

Card	MINT	NRMT
☐ 1A R.Klesko July 28-30 L	.40	.18
☐ 1B R.Klesko Aug 8-11 L	.40	.18
☐ 1C R.Klesko Sept 19-21 L	.40	.18
☐ 2A C.Jones Aug 15-17 L	2.50	1.10
☐ 2B C.Jones Aug 29-31 L	2.50	1.10
☐ 2C C.Jones Sept 12-14 L	2.50	1.10
☐ 3A Andruw Jones Aug 22-24 W	2.50	1.10
☐ 3B Andruw Jones Sept 1-3	2.50	1.10
☐ 3C A.Jones Sept 19-22 L	2.50	1.10
☐ 4A B.Anderson July 31-Aug 3 W	.40	.18
☐ 4B B.Anderson Sept 4-7 L	.40	.18
☐ 4C B.Anderson Sept 19-22 L	.40	.18
☐ 5A R.Palmeiro July 29-30 L	.40	.18
☐ 5B R.Palmeiro Aug 29-31 L	.40	.18
☐ 5C R.Palmeiro Sept 26-28 L	.40	.18
☐ 6A Cal Ripken Aug 8-10	3.00	1.35
☐ 6B C.Ripken Sept 1-3 W	3.00	1.35
☐ 6C C.Ripken Sept 11-14 L	3.00	1.35
☐ 7A M.Vaughn Aug 14-17 L	1.00	.45
☐ 7B M.Vaughn Aug 29-31 W	1.00	.45
☐ 7C M.Vaughn Sept 23-25 W	1.00	.45
☐ 8A S.Sosa Aug 1-3 W	.50	.23
☐ 8B S.Sosa Aug 29-31 L	.50	.23
☐ 8C S.Sosa Sept 19-21 W	.50	.23
☐ 9A A.Belle Aug 7-10 L	1.00	.45
☐ 9B A.Belle Sept 11-14 L	1.00	.45
☐ 9C A.Belle Sept 19-21 W	1.00	.45
☐ 10A F.Thomas Aug 29-31 L	3.00	1.35
☐ 10B F.Thomas Sept 1-3 L	3.00	1.35
☐ 10C F.Thomas Sept 23-25 W	3.00	1.35
☐ 11A M.Ramirez Aug 12-14 W	.50	.23
☐ 11B M.Ramirez Aug 29-31 L	.50	.23
☐ 11C M.Ramirez Sept 11-14 W	.50	.23
☐ 12A J.Thome July 28-30 L	.50	.23
☐ 12B J.Thome Aug 15-18 W	.50	.23
☐ 12C J.Thome Sept 19-22 L	.50	.23
☐ 13A M.Williams Aug 4-5 L	.40	.18
☐ 13B M.Williams Sept 1-3 W	.40	.18
☐ 13C M.Williams Sept 23-25 L	.40	.18
☐ 14A D.Bichette July 24-27 W	.30	.14
☐ 14B D.Bichette Aug 28-29 L	.30	.14
☐ 14C D.Bichette Sept 26-28 W	.30	.14
☐ 15A V.Castilla Aug 12-13 L	.30	.14
☐ 15B V.Castilla Sept 4-7 W	.30	.14
☐ 15C V.Castilla Sept 19-21 L	.30	.14
☐ 16A A.Galarraga Aug 8-10 W	.50	.23
☐ 16B A.Galarraga Aug 30-31 L	.50	.23
☐ 16C A.Galarraga Sept 12-14 L	.50	.23
☐ 17A G.Sheffield Aug 1-3 W	.50	.23
☐ 17B G.Sheffield Sept 1-3 W	.50	.23
☐ 17C G.Sheffield Sept 12-14 W	.50	.23
☐ 18A J.Bagwell Sept 9-10 L	1.50	.70
☐ 18B J.Bagwell Sept 19-22 W	1.50	.70
☐ 18C J.Bagwell Sept 23-25 W	1.50	.70
☐ 19A E.Karros Aug 1-3 L	.30	.14
☐ 19B E.Karros Aug 15-17 L	.30	.14
☐ 19C E.Karros Sept 25-28 W	.30	.14
☐ 20A M.Piazza Aug 11-12 L	2.50	1.10
☐ 20B M.Piazza Sept 5-8 W	2.50	1.10
☐ 20C M.Piazza Sept 19-21 W	2.50	1.10
☐ 21A V.Guerrero Aug 22-24 L	1.00	.45
☐ 21B V.Guerrero Aug 29-31 L	1.00	.45
☐ 21C V.Guerrero Sept 19-22 L	1.00	.45
☐ 22A C.Fielder Aug 29-31 L	.20	.09
☐ 22B C.Fielder Sept 4-7 L	.20	.09
☐ 22C C.Fielder Sept 26-28 L	.20	.09
☐ 23A J.Canseco Sept 12-14 L	.40	.18
☐ 23B J.Canseco Sept 22-24 L	.40	.18
☐ 23C J.Canseco Sept 26-28 L	.40	.18
☐ 24A M.McGwire July 31-Aug 3 L	1.50	.70
☐ 24B M.McGwire Aug 30-31 L	1.50	.70
☐ 24C M.McGwire Sept 19-22 W	1.50	.70
☐ 25A K.Caminiti Aug 8-10 L	.50	.23
☐ 25B K.Caminiti Sept 4-7 W	.50	.23
☐ 25C K.Caminiti Sept 17-18 W	.50	.23
☐ 26A B.Bonds Aug 5-7 L	1.00	.45
☐ 26B B.Bonds Sept 4-7 L	1.00	.45
☐ 26C B.Bonds Sept 23-24 W	1.00	.45
☐ 27A J.Buhner Aug 7-10 L	.40	.18
☐ 27B J.Buhner Aug 28-29 L	.40	.18
☐ 27C J.Buhner Sept 1-3 L	.40	.18
☐ 28A K.Griffey Jr. Aug 22-24 W	4.00	1.80
☐ 28B K.Griffey Jr. Aug 28-29 L	4.00	1.80
☐ 28C K.Griffey Jr. Sept 19-22 W	4.00	1.80
☐ 29A A.Rodriguez July 29-31 L	3.00	1.35
☐ 29B A.Rodriguez Aug 30-31 L	3.00	1.35
☐ 29C A.Rodriguez Sept 12-15 L	3.00	1.35
☐ 30A J.Gonzalez Aug 11-13 W	2.00	.9
☐ 30B J.Gonzalez Aug 30-31 L	2.00	.9
☐ 30C J.Gonzalez Sept 19-21 W	2.00	.9

1997 Collector's Choice Griffey Clearly Dominant

Randomly inserted in first series packs at a rate of one i 144, this five-card set highlights superstar Ken Griffey J with different color photos and information on each card.

	MINT	NRM
COMPLETE SET (5)	80.00	36.0
COMMON GRIFFEY (CD1-CD5)	20.00	9.0

Card	MINT	NRMT
☐ CD1 Ken Griffey Jr.	20.00	9.0
☐ CD2 Ken Griffey Jr.	20.00	9.0
☐ CD3 Ken Griffey Jr.	20.00	9.0
☐ CD4 Ken Griffey Jr.	20.00	9.0
☐ CD5 Ken Griffey Jr.	20.00	9.0

1997 Collector's Choice New Frontier

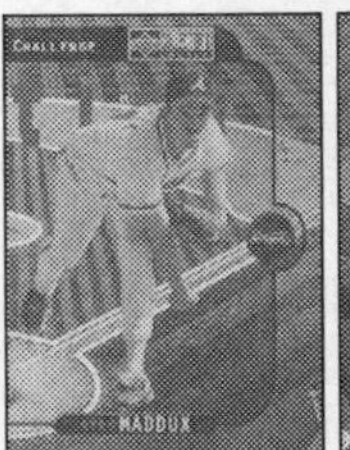

Randomly inserted one in every 69 series two packs, thi 40-card set showcases the most anticipated InterLeagu match-ups. Each card features a color player cut-out of great player from either the American or National Leagu on half of a baseball diamond background and is designe to fit with another card displaying a great player match-u from the opposite league to complete the diamond.

	MINT	NRM
COMPLETE SET (40)	450.00	200.0
COMMON CARD (NF1-NF40)	4.00	1.8

Card	MINT	NRMT
☐ NF1 Alex Rodriguez	25.00	11.0
☐ NF2 Tony Gwynn	20.00	9.0
☐ NF3 Jose Canseco	6.00	2.7
☐ NF4 Hideo Nomo	20.00	9.0
☐ NF5 Mark McGwire	15.00	6.7
☐ NF6 Barry Bonds	10.00	4.5
☐ NF7 Juan Gonzalez	20.00	9.0
☐ NF8 Ken Caminiti	8.00	3.6
☐ NF9 Tim Salmon	8.00	3.6
☐ NF10 Mike Piazza	25.00	11.0
☐ NF11 Ken Griffey Jr.	40.00	18.0
☐ NF12 Andres Galarraga	8.00	3.6
☐ NF13 Jay Buhner	6.00	2.7
☐ NF14 Dante Bichette	5.00	2.2
☐ NF15 Frank Thomas	30.00	13.5
☐ NF16 Ryne Sandberg	10.00	4.5
☐ NF17 Roger Clemens	15.00	6.7
☐ NF18 Andruw Jones	20.00	9.0
☐ NF19 Jim Thome	8.00	3.6
☐ NF20 Sammy Sosa	8.00	3.6
☐ NF21 Dave Justice	8.00	3.6
☐ NF22 Deion Sanders	8.00	3.6
☐ NF23 Todd Walker	4.00	1.8
☐ NF24 Kevin Orie	5.00	2.2
☐ NF25 Albert Belle	10.00	4.5
☐ NF26 Jeff Bagwell	15.00	6.7
☐ NF27 Manny Ramirez	8.00	3.6
☐ NF28 Brian Jordan	5.00	2.2
☐ NF29 Derek Jeter	20.00	9.0
☐ NF30 Chipper Jones	25.00	11.0
☐ NF31 Mo Vaughn	10.00	4.5

☐ NF32 Gary Sheffield	8.00	3.60
☐ NF33 Carlos Delgado	5.00	2.20
☐ NF34 Vladimir Guerrero	15.00	6.75
☐ NF35 Cal Ripken	30.00	13.50
☐ NF36 Greg Maddux	25.00	11.00
☐ NF37 Cecil Fielder	5.00	2.20
☐ NF38 Todd Hundley	5.00	2.20
☐ NF39 Mike Mussina	8.00	3.60
☐ NF40 Scott Rolen	20.00	9.00

1997 Collector's Choice Premier Power

andomly inserted in first series packs at a rate of one in 5, this silver version 20-card set features borderless olor action player photos and information about the 20 p Major League Home Run hitters.

	MINT	NRMT
OMPLETE SET (20)	40.00	18.00
OMMON CARD (PP1-PP20)	1.00	.45
OMP.GOLD SET (20)	150.00	70.00
GOLD STARS 1.5X TO 3X BASIC POWER.		

☐ PP1 Mark McGwire	3.00	1.35
☐ PP2 Brady Anderson	1.50	.70
☐ PP3 Ken Griffey Jr.	10.00	4.50
☐ PP4 Albert Belle	2.50	1.10
☐ PP5 Juan Gonzalez	5.00	2.20
☐ PP6 Andres Galarraga	2.00	.90
☐ PP7 Jay Buhner	1.50	.70
☐ PP8 Mo Vaughn	2.50	1.10
☐ PP9 Barry Bonds	2.50	1.10
☐ PP10 Gary Sheffield	2.00	.90
☐ PP11 Todd Hundley	1.25	.55
☐ PP12 Frank Thomas	8.00	3.60
☐ PP13 Sammy Sosa	2.00	.90
☐ PP14 Ken Caminiti	2.00	.90
☐ PP15 Vinny Castilla	1.25	.55
☐ PP16 Ellis Burks	1.00	.45
☐ PP17 Rafael Palmeiro	1.50	.70
☐ PP18 Alex Rodriguez	8.00	3.60
☐ PP19 Mike Piazza	6.00	2.70
☐ PP20 Eddie Murray	2.00	.90

1997 Collector's Choice Stick'Ums

andomly inserted in first series packs at a rate of one in ree, cards from this 30-card set features color sticker ages of star players. These interactive reusable stickers uld be used to create mini baseball scenes.

	MINT	NRMT
OMPLETE SET (30)	15.00	6.75
OMMON CARD (1-30)	.25	.11

☐ 1 Ozzie Smith	.75	.35
☐ 2 Andruw Jones	2.00	.90
☐ 3 Alex Rodriguez	2.50	1.10
☐ 4 Paul Molitor	.50	.23
☐ 5 Jeff Bagwell	1.25	.55
☐ 6 Manny Ramirez	.50	.23
☐ 7 Kenny Lofton	.75	.35
☐ 8 Albert Belle	.75	.35
☐ 9 Jay Buhner	.40	.18
☐ 10 Chipper Jones	2.00	.90
☐ 11 Barry Larkin	.40	.18
☐ 12 Dante Bichette	.30	.14
☐ 13 Mike Piazza	2.00	.90
☐ 14 Andres Galarraga	.50	.23
☐ 15 Barry Bonds	.75	.35
☐ 16 Brady Anderson	.25	.11
☐ 17 Gary Sheffield	.50	.23
☐ 18 Jim Thome	.50	.23
☐ 19 Tony Gwynn	1.25	.55
☐ 20 Cal Ripken	2.50	1.10
☐ 21 Sammy Sosa	.50	.23
☐ 22 Juan Gonzalez	1.50	.70
☐ 23 Greg Maddux	2.00	.90
☐ 24 Ken Griffey Jr.	3.00	1.35
☐ 25 Mark McGwire	1.00	.45
☐ 26 Kirby Puckett	1.25	.55
☐ 27 Mo Vaughn	.75	.35
☐ 28 Vladimir Guerrero	1.50	.70
☐ 29 Ken Caminiti	.50	.23
☐ 30 Frank Thomas	2.50	1.10

1997 Collector's Choice Toast of the Town

Randomly inserted in series two packs at the rate of one in 35, this 30-card set features color photos of some of the best Major League players printed on premium, foil enhanced card stock.

	MINT	NRMT
COMPLETE SET (30)	250.00	110.00
COMMON CARD (T1-T30)	2.50	1.10

☐ T1 Andruw Jones	12.00	5.50
☐ T2 Chipper Jones	15.00	6.75
☐ T3 Greg Maddux	15.00	6.75
☐ T4 John Smoltz	2.50	1.10
☐ T5 Kenny Lofton	6.00	2.70
☐ T6 Brady Anderson	4.00	1.80
☐ T7 Cal Ripken	20.00	9.00
☐ T8 Mo Vaughn	6.00	2.70
☐ T9 Sammy Sosa	5.00	2.20
☐ T10 Albert Belle	6.00	2.70
☐ T11 Frank Thomas	20.00	9.00
☐ T12 Barry Larkin	4.00	1.80
☐ T13 Manny Ramirez	5.00	2.20
☐ T14 Jeff Bagwell	10.00	4.50
☐ T15 Mike Piazza	15.00	6.75
☐ T16 Paul Molitor	5.00	2.20
☐ T17 Vladimir Guerrero	10.00	4.50
☐ T18 Todd Hundley	3.00	1.35
☐ T19 Derek Jeter	12.00	5.50
☐ T20 Andy Pettitte	5.00	2.20
☐ T21 Bernie Williams	5.00	2.20
☐ T22 Mark McGwire	10.00	4.50
☐ T23 Scott Rolen	12.00	5.50
☐ T24 Ken Caminiti	5.00	2.20
☐ T25 Tony Gwynn	12.00	5.50
☐ T26 Barry Bonds	6.00	2.70
☐ T27 Ken Griffey Jr.	25.00	11.00
☐ T28 Alex Rodriguez	15.00	6.75
☐ T29 Juan Gonzalez	12.00	5.50
☐ T30 Roger Clemens	10.00	4.50

1997 Collector's Choice Update

This 30-card Update set was made available to collectors who mailed in 10 series two wrappers (plus a check or money order for $3 to cover postage and handling) prior to the December 1st, 1997 deadline. The cards share the same design as the basic issue 1997 Collector's Choice set and content focuses on traded veterans pictured in their new uniforms and a handful of prospects called up during the season (including Jose Cruz Jr. and Hideki Irabu).

	MINT	NRMT
COMPLETE SET (30)	6.00	2.70
COMMON CARD (U1-U30)	.10	.05

☐ U1 Jim Leyritz	.10	.05
☐ U2 Matt Perisho	.10	.05
☐ U3 Michael Tucker	.20	.09
☐ U4 Mike Johnson	.10	.05
☐ U5 Jaime Navarro	.10	.05
☐ U6 Doug Drabek	.10	.05
☐ U7 Terry Mulholland	.10	.05
☐ U8 Brett Tomko	.10	.05
☐ U9 Marquis Grissom	.20	.09
☐ U10 David Justice	.40	.18
☐ U11 Brian Moehler	.10	.05
☐ U12 Bobby Bonilla	.20	.09
☐ U13 Todd Dunwoody	.40	.18
☐ U14 Tony Saunders	.20	.09
☐ U15 Jay Bell	.10	.05
☐ U16 Jeff King	.10	.05
☐ U17 Terry Steinbach	.10	.05
☐ U18 Steve Bieser	.10	.05
☐ U19 Takashi Kashiwada	.25	.11
☐ U20 Hideki Irabu	.50	.23
☐ U21 Damon Mashore	.10	.05
☐ U22 Quilvio Veras	.10	.05
☐ U23 Will Cunnane	.10	.05
☐ U24 Jeff Kent	.10	.05
☐ U25 J.T. Snow	.20	.09
☐ U26 Dante Powell	.10	.05
☐ U27 Jose Cruz Jr.	4.00	1.80
☐ U28 John Burkett	.10	.05
☐ U29 John Wetteland	.20	.09
☐ U30 Benito Santiago	.10	.05

1997 Collector's Choice Stick'Ums Retail

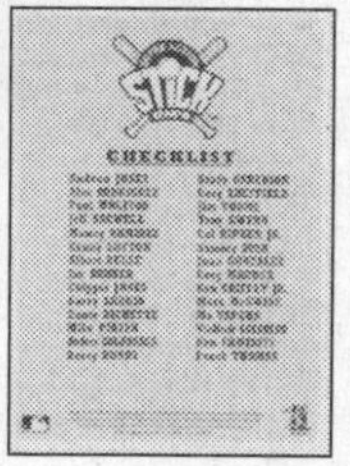

This 28-card set features color sticker images of star players. These interactive reusable stickers could be used to create mini baseball scenes. The back of each sticker displays the checklist for the set. The set was distributed in packs of 15 stickers plus three regular Collector's Choice cards. The stickers are unnumbered and checklisted below in alphabetical order.

	MINT	NRMT
COMPLETE SET (28)	10.00	4.50
COMMON CARD	.10	.05

☐ 1 Brady Anderson	.20	.09
☐ 2 Jeff Bagwell	1.25	.55
☐ 3 Albert Belle	.50	.23
☐ 4 Dante Bichette	.10	.05
☐ 5 Barry Bonds	.50	.23
☐ 6 Jay Buhner	.20	.09
☐ 7 Ken Caminiti	.30	.14
☐ 8 Andres Galarraga	.30	.14
☐ 9 Juan Gonzalez	1.00	.45
☐ 10 Ken Griffey Jr.	2.00	.90
☐ 11 Vladimir Guerrero	.75	.35
☐ 12 Tony Gwynn	1.00	.45
☐ 13 Andruw Jones	1.00	.45
☐ 14 Chipper Jones	1.25	.55
☐ 15 Barry Larkin	.20	.09
☐ 16 Kenny Lofton	.50	.23
☐ 17 Greg Maddux	1.25	.55
☐ 18 Mark McGwire	1.00	.45
☐ 19 Paul Molitor	.30	.14
☐ 20 Mike Piazza	1.25	.55
☐ 21 Manny Ramirez	.30	.14
☐ 22 Cal Ripken Jr.	1.50	.70
☐ 23 Alex Rodriguez	1.50	.70
☐ 24 Gary Sheffield	.30	.14
☐ 25 Sammy Sosa	.30	.14

	MINT	NRMT
☐ 26 Frank Thomas	1.50	.70
☐ 27 Jim Thome	.50	.23
☐ 28 Mo Vaughn	.50	.23

1997 Collector's Choice Teams

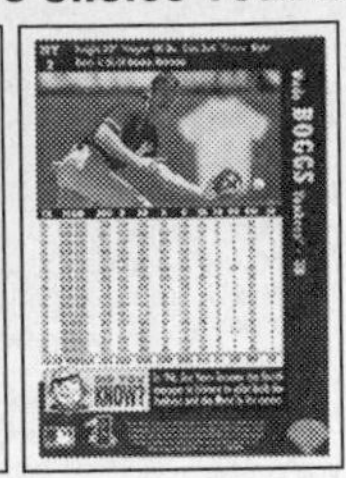

This set features color action and posed player photos either borderless or in white borders of 13 players each of selected major league baseball teams. The backs carry player information and career statistics. Each set was distributed in a special package along with a foil enhanced die cut 3 1/2" by 5" Home Team Heroes card displaying two star players of that team. The cards are checklisted below by teams with the Home Team Heroes cards, which was also issued seperately, priced as a Upper Deck set.

	MINT	NRMT
COMPLETE SET	100.00	45.00
COMMON CARD	.25	.11
☐ AB Atlanta Braves Logo CL	.25	.11
☐ AB1 Andruw Jones	2.00	.90
☐ AB2 Kenny Lofton	1.25	.55
☐ AB3 Fred McGriff	.75	.35
☐ AB4 Michael Tucker	.50	.23
☐ AB5 Ryan Klesko	.75	.35
☐ AB6 Javier Lopez	.50	.23
☐ AB7 Mark Wohlers	.50	.23
☐ AB8 Tom Glavine	.50	.23
☐ AB9 Denny Neagle	.50	.23
☐ AB10 Chipper Jones	3.00	1.35
☐ AB11 Jeff Blauser	.50	.23
☐ AB12 Greg Maddux	3.00	1.35
☐ AB13 John Smoltz	.50	.23
☐ BO Baltimore Orioles Logo CL	.25	.11
☐ BO1 Rocky Coppinger	.25	.11
☐ BO2 Scott Erickson	.25	.11
☐ BO3 Chris Hoiles	.25	.11
☐ BO4 Roberto Alomar	1.00	.45
☐ BO5 Cal Ripken Jr.	4.00	1.80
☐ BO6 Randy Myers	.50	.23
☐ BO7 B.J. Surhoff	.50	.23
☐ BO8 Mike Mussina	1.00	.45
☐ BO9 Rafael Palmeiro	.75	.35
☐ BO10 Jimmy Key	.50	.23
☐ BO11 Mike Bordick	.25	.11
☐ BO12 Brady Anderson	.75	.35
☐ BO13 Eric Davis	.50	.23
☐ CI Cleveland Indians Logo CL	.25	.11
☐ CI1 Brian Giles	.25	.11
☐ CI2 Omar Vizquel	.50	.23
☐ CI3 Julio Franco	.50	.23
☐ CI4 Orel Hershiser	.50	.23
☐ CI5 Charles Nagy	.50	.23
☐ CI6 Matt Williams	.75	.35
☐ CI7 Jose Mesa	.50	.23
☐ CI8 Sandy Alomar Jr.	.50	.23
☐ CI9 Jim Thome	1.25	.55
☐ CI10 David Justice	1.00	.45
☐ CI11 Marquis Grissom	.50	.23
☐ CI12 Chad Ogea	.25	.11
☐ CI13 Manny Ramirez	1.00	.45
☐ CR Colorado Rockies Logo CL	.25	.11
☐ CR1 Dante Bichette	.50	.23
☐ CR2 Vinny Castilla	.50	.23
☐ CR3 Kevin Ritz	.25	.11
☐ CR4 Larry Walker	1.25	.55
☐ CR5 Eric Young	.25	.11
☐ CR6 Quinton McCracken	.25	.11
☐ CR7 John Vander Wal	.25	.11
☐ CR8 Jamey Wright	.25	.11
☐ CR9 Mark Thompson	.25	.11
☐ CR10 Andres Galarraga	1.00	.45
☐ CR11 Ellis Burks	.50	.23
☐ CR12 Kirt Manwaring	.25	.11
☐ CR13 Walt Weiss	.25	.11
☐ CW Chicago White Sox Logo CL	.25	.11
☐ CW1 Robin Ventura	.50	.23
☐ CW2 Wilson Alvarez	.50	.23
☐ CW3 Tony Phillips	.25	.11
☐ CW4 Lyle Mouton	.25	.11
☐ CW5 James Baldwin	.25	.11
☐ CW6 Harold Baines	.50	.23
☐ CW7 Albert Belle	1.25	.55
☐ CW8 Chris Snopek	.25	.11
☐ CW9 Ray Durham	.25	.11
☐ CW10 Frank Thomas	4.00	1.80
☐ CW11 Ozzie Guillen	.25	.11
☐ CW12 Roberto Hernandez	.50	.23
☐ CW13 Jaime Navarro	.25	.11
☐ FM Florida Marlins Logo CL	.25	.11
☐ FM1 Luis Castillo	.25	.11
☐ FM2 Al Leiter	.25	.11
☐ FM3 Devon White	.25	.11
☐ FM4 Jeff Conine	.25	.11
☐ FM5 Charles Johnson	.75	.35
☐ FM6 Edgar Renteria	.50	.23
☐ FM7 Robb Nen	.50	.23
☐ FM8 Kevin Brown	.50	.23
☐ FM9 Gary Sheffield	1.00	.45
☐ FM10 Alex Fernandez	.25	.11
☐ FM11 Pat Rapp	.25	.11
☐ FM12 Moises Alou	.50	.23
☐ FM13 Bobby Bonilla	.50	.23
☐ LA Los Angles Dodgers Logo CL	.25	.11
☐ LA1 Raul Mondesi	1.00	.45
☐ LA2 Brett Butler	.50	.23
☐ LA3 Todd Hollandsworth	.25	.11
☐ LA4 Eric Karros	.50	.23
☐ LA5 Hideo Nomo	2.50	1.10
☐ LA6 Ismael Valdes	.25	.11
☐ LA7 Wilton Guerrero	.25	.11
☐ LA8 Ramon Martinez	.50	.23
☐ LA9 Greg Gagne	.25	.11
☐ LA10 Mike Piazza	3.00	1.35
☐ LA11 Chan Ho Park	1.50	.70
☐ LA12 Todd Worrell	.50	.23
☐ LA13 Todd Zeile	.25	.11
☐ NY New York Yankees Logo CL	.25	.11
☐ NY1 Bernie Williams	1.00	.45
☐ NY2 Dwight Gooden	.50	.23
☐ NY3 Wade Boggs	1.00	.45
☐ NY4 Ruben Rivera	.50	.23
☐ NY5 Derek Jeter	3.00	1.35
☐ NY6 Tino Martinez	1.00	.45
☐ NY7 Tim Raines	.50	.23
☐ NY8 Joe Girardi	.25	.11
☐ NY9 Charlie Hayes	.25	.11
☐ NY10 Andy Pettitte	1.00	.45
☐ NY11 Cecil Fielder	.50	.23
☐ NY12 Paul O'Neill	.50	.23
☐ NY13 David Cone	.50	.23
☐ SM Seattle Mariners Logo CL	.25	.11
☐ SM1 Dan Wilson	.25	.11
☐ SM2 Ken Griffey Jr.	5.00	2.20
☐ SM3 Edgar Martinez	.75	.35
☐ SM4 Joey Cora	.50	.23
☐ SM5 Norm Charlton	.25	.11
☐ SM6 Alex Rodriguez	4.00	1.80
☐ SM7 Randy Johnson	1.25	.55
☐ SM8 Paul Sorrento	.25	.11
☐ SM9 Jamie Moyer	.25	.11
☐ SM10 Jay Buhner	.75	.35
☐ SM11 Russ Davis	.25	.11
☐ SM12 Jeff Fassero	.25	.11
☐ SM13 Bob Wells	.25	.11
☐ TR Texas Rangers Logo CL	.25	.11
☐ TR1 Bobby Witt	.25	.11
☐ TR2 Darren Oliver	.25	.11
☐ TR3 Rusty Greer	.50	.23
☐ TR4 Juan Gonzalez	2.50	1.10
☐ TR5 Will Clark	.75	.35
☐ TR6 Dean Palmer	.50	.23
☐ TR7 Ivan Rodriguez	1.25	.55
☐ TR8 John Wetteland	.50	.23
☐ TR9 Mark McLemore	.25	.11
☐ TR10 John Burkett	.25	.11
☐ TR11 Benji Gil	.25	.11
☐ TR12 Ken Hill	.25	.11
☐ TR13 Mickey Tettleton	.25	.11

1995 Collector's Choice SE

The 1995 Collector's Choice SE set consists of 265 standard-size cards issued in foil packs. The fronts feature color action player photos with blue borders. The player's name, position and the team name are printed on th bottom of the photo. The SE logo in blue-foil appears in top corner. On a white background, the backs carr another color player photo with a short player biography career stats and 1994 highlights. Subsets featured includ Rookie Class (1-25), Record Pace (26-30), Stat Leader (137-144), Fantasy Team (249-260). There are no Rooki Cards in this set.

	MINT	NRMT
COMPLETE SET (265)	20.00	9.0
COMMON CARD (1-265)	.15	.07
☐ 1 Alex Rodriguez	2.50	1.1
☐ 2 Derek Jeter	2.00	.9
☐ 3 Dustin Hermanson	.15	.07
☐ 4 Bill Pulsipher	.15	.07
☐ 5 Terrell Wade	.15	.07
☐ 6 Darren Dreifort	.15	.07
☐ 7 LaTroy Hawkins	.15	.07
☐ 8 Alex Ochoa	.15	.07
☐ 9 Paul Wilson	.30	.14
☐ 10 Rod Henderson	.15	.07
☐ 11 Alan Benes	.30	.14
☐ 12 Garret Anderson	.30	.14
☐ 13 Armando Benitez	.15	.07
☐ 14 Mark Thompson	.30	.14
☐ 15 Herbert Perry	.15	.07
☐ 16 Jose Silva	.15	.07
☐ 17 Orlando Miller	.15	.07
☐ 18 Russ Davis	.15	.07
☐ 19 Jason Isringhausen	.30	.14
☐ 20 Ray McDavid	.15	.07
☐ 21 Tim VanEgmond	.15	.07
☐ 22 Paul Shuey	.15	.07
☐ 23 Steve Dunn	.15	.07
☐ 24 Mike Lieberthal	.15	.07
☐ 25 Chan Ho Park	.60	.25
☐ 26 Ken Griffey Jr. RP	1.50	.70
☐ 27 Tony Gwynn RP	.60	.25
☐ 28 Chuck Knoblauch RP	.60	.25
☐ 29 Frank Thomas RP	1.50	.70
☐ 30 Matt Williams RP	.40	.18
☐ 31 Chili Davis	.30	.14
☐ 32 Chad Curtis	.15	.07
☐ 33 Brian Anderson	.15	.07
☐ 34 Chuck Finley	.30	.14
☐ 35 Tim Salmon	.60	.2
☐ 36 Bo Jackson	.30	.14
☐ 37 Doug Drabek	.15	.07
☐ 38 Craig Biggio	.40	.1
☐ 39 Ken Caminiti	.60	.25
☐ 40 Jeff Bagwell	1.25	.55
☐ 41 Darryl Kile	.15	.07
☐ 42 John Hudek	.15	.0
☐ 43 Brian L. Hunter	.30	.14
☐ 44 Dennis Eckersley	.40	.18
☐ 45 Mark McGwire	1.25	.55
☐ 46 Brent Gates	.15	.07
☐ 47 Steve Karsay	.15	.07
☐ 48 Rickey Henderson	.40	.18
☐ 49 Terry Steinbach	.30	.14
☐ 50 Ruben Sierra	.15	.0
☐ 51 Roberto Alomar	.60	.2
☐ 52 Carlos Delgado	.30	.1
☐ 53 Alex Gonzalez	.30	.1
☐ 54 Joe Carter	.40	.18
☐ 55 Paul Molitor	.60	.25
☐ 56 Juan Guzman	.15	.0
☐ 57 John Olerud	.30	.1
☐ 58 Shawn Green	.30	.1
☐ 59 Tom Glavine	.40	.18
☐ 60 Greg Maddux	2.00	.9
☐ 61 Roberto Kelly	.15	.0
☐ 62 Ryan Klesko	.40	.18
☐ 63 Javier Lopez	.40	.18
☐ 64 Jose Oliva	.15	.07
☐ 65 Fred McGriff	.40	.18
☐ 66 Steve Avery	.15	.07
☐ 67 David Justice	.60	.25
☐ 68 Ricky Bones	.15	.07
☐ 69 Cal Eldred	.15	.07
☐ 70 Greg Vaughn	.15	.0
☐ 71 Dave Nilsson	.30	.1
☐ 72 Jose Valentin	.30	.1
☐ 73 Matt Mieske	.30	.1
☐ 74 Todd Zeile	.15	.0
☐ 75 Ozzie Smith	.75	.3
☐ 76 Bernard Gilkey	.30	.1
☐ 77 Ray Lankford	.40	.1
☐ 78 Bob Tewksbury	.15	.0
☐ 79 Mark Whiten	.15	.0
☐ 80 Gregg Jefferies	.30	.1
☐ 81 Randy Myers	.15	.0
☐ 82 Shawon Dunston	.15	.0
☐ 83 Mark Grace	.40	.1
☐ 84 Derrick May	.15	.0

Card	MINT	NRMT
☐ 85 Sammy Sosa	.60	.25
☐ 86 Steve Trachsel	.15	.07
☐ 87 Brett Butler	.30	.14
☐ 88 Delino DeShields	.15	.07
☐ 89 Orel Hershiser	.30	.14
☐ 90 Mike Piazza	2.00	.90
☐ 91 Todd Hollandsworth	.30	.14
☐ 92 Eric Karros	.30	.14
☐ 93 Ramon Martinez	.30	.14
☐ 94 Tim Wallach	.15	.07
☐ 95 Raul Mondesi	.40	.18
☐ 96 Larry Walker	.60	.25
☐ 97 Wil Cordero	.15	.07
☐ 98 Marquis Grissom	.30	.14
☐ 99 Ken Hill	.15	.07
☐ 100 Cliff Floyd	.30	.14
☐ 101 Pedro J. Martinez	.60	.25
☐ 102 John Wetteland	.30	.14
☐ 103 Rondell White	.40	.18
☐ 104 Moises Alou	.30	.14
☐ 105 Barry Bonds	.75	.35
☐ 106 Darren Lewis	.15	.07
☐ 107 Mark Portugal	.15	.07
☐ 108 Matt Williams	.40	.18
☐ 109 William VanLandingham	.15	.07
☐ 110 Bill Swift	.15	.07
☐ 111 Robby Thompson	.15	.07
☐ 112 Rod Beck	.15	.07
☐ 113 Darryl Strawberry	.30	.14
☐ 114 Jim Thome	.60	.25
☐ 115 Dave Winfield	.40	.18
☐ 116 Eddie Murray	.60	.25
☐ 117 Manny Ramirez	.60	.25
☐ 118 Carlos Baerga	.30	.14
☐ 119 Kenny Lofton	.75	.35
☐ 120 Albert Belle	.75	.35
☐ 121 Mark Clark	.15	.07
☐ 122 Dennis Martinez	.30	.14
☐ 123 Randy Johnson	.60	.25
☐ 124 Jay Buhner	.40	.18
☐ 125 Ken Griffey Jr.	3.00	1.35
☐ 126 Goose Gossage	.30	.14
☐ 127 Tino Martinez	.60	.25
☐ 128 Reggie Jefferson	.30	.14
☐ 129 Edgar Martinez	.40	.18
☐ 130 Gary Sheffield	.60	.25
☐ 131 Pat Rapp	.15	.07
☐ 132 Bret Barberie	.15	.07
☐ 133 Chuck Carr	.15	.07
☐ 134 Jeff Conine	.30	.14
☐ 135 Charles Johnson	.30	.14
☐ 136 Benito Santiago	.15	.07
☐ 137 Matt Williams STL	.40	.18
☐ 138 Jeff Bagwell STL	.60	.25
☐ 139 Kenny Lofton STL	.40	.18
☐ 140 Tony Gwynn STL	.60	.25
☐ 141 Jimmy Key STL	.15	.07
☐ 142 Greg Maddux STL	1.00	.45
☐ 143 Randy Johnson STL	.60	.25
☐ 144 Lee Smith STL	.30	.14
☐ 145 Bobby Bonilla	.30	.14
☐ 146 Jason Jacome	.15	.07
☐ 147 Jeff Kent	.15	.07
☐ 148 Ryan Thompson	.15	.07
☐ 149 Bobby Jones	.30	.14
☐ 150 Bret Saberhagen	.15	.07
☐ 151 John Franco	.15	.07
☐ 152 Lee Smith	.30	.14
☐ 153 Rafael Palmeiro	.40	.18
☐ 154 Brady Anderson	.40	.18
☐ 155 Cal Ripken Jr.	2.50	1.10
☐ 156 Jeffrey Hammonds	.30	.14
☐ 157 Mike Mussina	.60	.25
☐ 158 Chris Hoiles	.15	.07
☐ 159 Ben McDonald	.15	.07
☐ 160 Tony Gwynn	1.50	.70
☐ 161 Joey Hamilton	.30	.14
☐ 162 Andy Benes	.15	.07
☐ 163 Trevor Hoffman	.30	.14
☐ 164 Phil Plantier	.15	.07
☐ 165 Derek Bell	.30	.14
☐ 166 Bip Roberts	.15	.07
☐ 167 Eddie Williams	.15	.07
☐ 168 Fernando Valenzuela	.30	.14
☐ 169 Mariano Duncan	.15	.07
☐ 170 Lenny Dykstra	.30	.14
☐ 171 Darren Daulton	.30	.14
☐ 172 Danny Jackson	.15	.07
☐ 173 Bobby Munoz	.15	.07
☐ 174 Doug Jones	.15	.07
☐ 175 Jay Bell	.30	.14
☐ 176 Zane Smith	.15	.07
☐ 177 Jon Lieber	.15	.07
☐ 178 Carlos Garcia	.15	.07
☐ 179 Orlando Merced	.15	.07
☐ 180 Andy Van Slyke	.30	.14
☐ 181 Rick Helling	.15	.07
☐ 182 Rusty Greer	.60	.25
☐ 183 Kenny Rogers UER (shows 110 wins in 1990)	.15	.07
☐ 184 Will Clark	.40	.18
☐ 185 Jose Canseco	.40	.18
☐ 186 Juan Gonzalez	1.50	.70
☐ 187 Dean Palmer	.30	.14
☐ 188 Ivan Rodriguez	.75	.35
☐ 189 John Valentin	.30	.14
☐ 190 Roger Clemens	1.25	.55
☐ 191 Aaron Sele	.15	.07
☐ 192 Scott Cooper	.15	.07
☐ 193 Mike Greenwell	.15	.07
☐ 194 Mo Vaughn	.75	.35
☐ 195 Andre Dawson	.40	.18
☐ 196 Ron Gant	.30	.14
☐ 197 Jose Rijo	.15	.07
☐ 198 Bret Boone	.15	.07
☐ 199 Deion Sanders	.60	.25
☐ 200 Barry Larkin	.30	.14
☐ 201 Hal Morris	.15	.07
☐ 202 Reggie Sanders	.15	.07
☐ 203 Kevin Mitchell	.15	.07
☐ 204 Marvin Freeman	.15	.07
☐ 205 Andres Galarraga	.40	.18
☐ 206 Walt Weiss	.15	.07
☐ 207 Charlie Hayes	.15	.07
☐ 208 Dave Nied	.15	.07
☐ 209 Dante Bichette	.40	.18
☐ 210 David Cone	.30	.14
☐ 211 Jeff Montgomery	.30	.14
☐ 212 Felix Jose	.15	.07
☐ 213 Mike Macfarlane	.15	.07
☐ 214 Wally Joyner	.30	.14
☐ 215 Bob Hamelin	.15	.07
☐ 216 Brian McRae	.15	.07
☐ 217 Kirk Gibson	.30	.14
☐ 218 Lou Whitaker	.30	.14
☐ 219 Chris Gomez	.15	.07
☐ 220 Cecil Fielder	.30	.14
☐ 221 Mickey Tettleton	.15	.07
☐ 222 Travis Fryman	.30	.14
☐ 223 Tony Phillips	.15	.07
☐ 224 Rick Aguilera	.15	.07
☐ 225 Scott Erickson	.15	.07
☐ 226 Chuck Knoblauch	.60	.25
☐ 227 Kent Hrbek	.30	.14
☐ 228 Shane Mack	.15	.07
☐ 229 Kevin Tapani	.15	.07
☐ 230 Kirby Puckett	1.25	.55
☐ 231 Julio Franco	.30	.14
☐ 232 Jack McDowell	.15	.07
☐ 233 Jason Bere	.15	.07
☐ 234 Alex Fernandez	.30	.14
☐ 235 Frank Thomas	2.50	1.10
☐ 236 Ozzie Guillen	.15	.07
☐ 237 Robin Ventura	.30	.14
☐ 238 Michael Jordan	4.00	1.80
☐ 239 Wilson Alvarez	.30	.14
☐ 240 Don Mattingly	1.00	.45
☐ 241 Jim Abbott	.15	.07
☐ 242 Jim Leyritz	.15	.07
☐ 243 Paul O'Neill	.30	.14
☐ 244 Melido Perez	.15	.07
☐ 245 Wade Boggs	.60	.25
☐ 246 Mike Stanley	.15	.07
☐ 247 Danny Tartabull	.15	.07
☐ 248 Jimmy Key	.30	.14
☐ 249 Greg Maddux FT	1.00	.45
☐ 250 Randy Johnson FT	.60	.25
☐ 251 Bret Saberhagen FT	.15	.07
☐ 252 John Wetteland FT	.30	.14
☐ 253 Mike Piazza FT	1.00	.45
☐ 254 Jeff Bagwell FT	.60	.25
☐ 255 Craig Biggio FT	.40	.18
☐ 256 Matt Williams FT	.40	.18
☐ 257 Wil Cordero FT	.15	.07
☐ 258 Kenny Lofton FT	.40	.18
☐ 259 Barry Bonds FT	.30	.14
☐ 260 Dante Bichette FT	.40	.18
☐ 261 Ken Griffey Jr. CL	1.00	.45
☐ 262 Goose Gossage CL	.30	.14
☐ 263 Cal Ripken CL	1.00	.45
☐ 264 Kenny Rogers CL	.15	.07
☐ 265 John Valentin CL	.30	.14
☐ P125 Ken Griffey Jr. Promo	3.00	1.35

1995 Collector's Choice SE Gold Signature

A parallel to the basic 265-card Collector's Choice SE set, each card features a gold-foil replica signature on it. Inserted one in 35 packs, the fronts feature color action player photos with blue borders. Super packs inserted 1:720 contained 12 gold signature cards.

	MINT	NRMT
COMPLETE SET (265)	1500.00	700.00
COMMON CARD (1-265)	2.50	1.10
*STARS: 15X TO 30X BASIC CARDS ..		
*YOUNG STARS: 15X TO 25X BASIC CARDS		

1995 Collector's Choice SE Silver Signature

A parallel to the basic 265-card Collector's Choice issue, each card has a silver-foil replica signature on the front. These cards were inserted one in every pack, two per mini jumbo and 12 per super pack (inserted 1:216).

	MINT	NRMT
COMPLETE SET (265)	60.00	27.00
COMMON CARD (1-265)	.25	.11
*STARS: 2X to 4X BASIC CARDS		
*YOUNG STARS: 1.5X to 3X BASIC CARDS		

1992 Conlon TSN

This 330-card standard-size set is numbered in continuation of the previous year's issue and again features the photography of Charles Conlon. The fronts have either posed or action black and white player photos, enframed by a white line on a black card face. A caption in a diagonal stripe cuts across the upper right corner of the picture. The player's name, team, position, and year the photos were taken appear below the pictures in white lettering. The back has biography, statistics, and career summary. The cards are numbered on the back. Special subsets include No-Hitters (331-372), Two Sports (393-407), Great Stories (421-440), Why Not in Hall of Fame (441-450), Hall of Fame (459-474), 75 Years Ago Highlights (483-492), Triple Crown Winners (525-537), Everyday Heroes (538-550), Nicknames (551-566), Trivia (581-601), and St. Louis Cardinals 1892-1992 (618-657). The set was available in packs as well as in a factory set. Four special gold-border cards previewing the 1993 Conlon Sporting News set were available exclusively in the factory sets. Also randomly inserted in the wax packs were a limited number of personally autographed (but not certified) cards of Bobby Doerr, Bob Feller, Marty Marion, Johnny Mize, Enos Slaughter, and Johnny Vander Meer. These autographed cards range in value from 15.00 to 30.00.

	MINT	NRMT
COMPLETE SET (330)	18.00	8.00
COMMON CARD (331-660)	.05	.02
☐ 331 Christy Mathewson	.40	.18
☐ 332 Hooks Wiltse	.05	.02
☐ 333 Nap Rucker	.05	.02
☐ 334 Red Ames	.05	.02
☐ 335 Chief Bender	.20	.09
☐ 336 Joe Wood	.10	.05
☐ 337 Ed Walsh	.20	.09
☐ 338 George Mullin	.05	.02
☐ 339 Earl Hamilton	.05	.02
☐ 340 Jeff Tesreau	.05	.02
☐ 341 Jim Scott	.05	.02
☐ 342 Rube Marquard	.20	.09
☐ 343 Claude Hendrix	.05	.02
☐ 344 Jimmy Lavender	.05	.02
☐ 345 Joe Bush	.10	.05
☐ 346 Dutch Leonard	.10	.05
☐ 347 Fred Toney	.05	.02
☐ 348 Hippo Vaughn	.05	.02
☐ 349 Ernie Koob	.05	.02
☐ 350 Bob Groom	.05	.02
☐ 351 Ernie Shore	.10	.05
☐ 352 Hod Eller	.05	.02
☐ 353 Walter Johnson	.40	.18
☐ 354 Charles Robertson	.05	.02
☐ 355 Jesse Barnes	.05	.02
☐ 356 Sad Sam Jones	.10	.05
☐ 357 Howard Ehmke	.05	.02
☐ 358 Jesse Haines	.20	.09
☐ 359 Ted Lyons	.20	.09
☐ 360 Carl Hubbell	.25	.11

☐ 361 Wes Ferrell	.15	.07
☐ 362 Bobby Burke	.05	.02
☐ 363 Daffy Dean	.10	.05
☐ 364 Bobo Newsom	.15	.07
☐ 365 Vern Kennedy	.05	.02
☐ 366 Bill Dietrich	.05	.02
☐ 367 Johnny VanderMeer	.15	.07
☐ 368 Johnny VanderMeer	.15	.07
☐ 369 Monte Pearson	.05	.02
☐ 370 Bob Feller	.30	.14
☐ 371 Lon Warneke	.10	.05
☐ 372 Jim Tobin	.05	.02
☐ 373 Earl Moore	.05	.02
☐ 374 Bill Dineen	.05	.02
☐ 375 Mal Eason	.05	.02
☐ 376 George Mogridge	.05	.02
☐ 377 Dazzy Vance	.20	.09
☐ 378 Tex Carleton	.05	.02
☐ 379 Clyde Shoun	.05	.02
☐ 380 Frankie Hayes	.05	.02
☐ 381 Benny Frey	.05	.02
☐ 382 Hank Johnson	.05	.02
☐ 383 Red Kress	.05	.02
☐ 384 Johnny Allen	.05	.02
☐ 385 Hal Trosky	.10	.05
☐ 386 Gene Robertson	.05	.02
☐ 387 Pep Young	.05	.02
☐ 388 George Selkirk	.10	.05
☐ 389 Ed Wells	.05	.02
☐ 390 Jim Weaver	.05	.02
☐ 391 George McQuinn	.05	.02
☐ 392 Hans Lobert	.05	.02
☐ 393 Evar Swanson	.05	.02
☐ 394 Ernie Nevers	.25	.11
☐ 395 Jim Levey	.05	.02
☐ 396 Hugo Bezdek	.05	.02
☐ 397 Walt French	.05	.02
☐ 398 Charlie Berry	.10	.05
☐ 399 Frank Grube	.05	.02
☐ 400 Chuck Dressen	.10	.05
☐ 401 Greasy Neale	.10	.05
☐ 402 Ernie Vick	.05	.02
☐ 403 Jim Thorpe	1.00	.45
☐ 404 Wally Gilbert	.05	.02
☐ 405 Luke Urban	.05	.02
☐ 406 Pid Purdy	.05	.02
☐ 407 Ab Wright	.05	.02
☐ 408 Billy Urbanski	.05	.02
☐ 409 Carl Fischer	.05	.02
☐ 410 Jack Warner	.05	.02
☐ 411 Bill Cissell	.05	.02
☐ 412 Merv Shea	.05	.02
☐ 413 Dolf Luque	.10	.05
☐ 414 Johnny Bassler	.05	.02
☐ 415 Odell Hale	.05	.02
☐ 416 Larry French	.05	.02
☐ 417 Curt Walker	.05	.02
☐ 418 Dusty Cooke	.05	.02
☐ 419 Phil Todt	.05	.02
☐ 420 Poison Andrews	.05	.02
☐ 421 Billy Herman	.20	.09
☐ 422 Tris Speaker	.25	.11
☐ 423 Al Simmons	.20	.09
☐ 424 Hack Wilson	.25	.11
☐ 425 Ty Cobb	.75	.35
☐ 426 Babe Ruth	1.00	.45
☐ 427 Ernie Lombardi	.20	.09
☐ 428 Dizzy Dean	.40	.18
☐ 429 Lloyd Waner	.20	.09
☐ 430 Hank Greenberg	.30	.14
☐ 431 Lefty Grove	.30	.14
☐ 432 Mickey Cochrane	.25	.11
☐ 433 Burleigh Grimes	.20	.09
☐ 434 Pie Traynor	.20	.09
☐ 435 Johnny Mize	.25	.11
☐ 436 Sam Rice	.20	.09
☐ 437 Goose Goslin	.20	.09
☐ 438 Chuck Klein	.20	.09
☐ 439 Connie Mack	.25	.11
☐ 440 Jim Bottomley	.20	.09
☐ 441 Riggs Stephenson	.15	.07
☐ 442 Ken Williams	.15	.07
☐ 443 Babe Adams	.10	.05
☐ 444 Joe Jackson	1.00	.45
☐ 445 Hal Newhouser	.20	.09
☐ 446 Wes Ferrell	.15	.07
☐ 447 Lefty O'Doul	.10	.05
☐ 448 Wally Schang	.10	.05
☐ 449 Sherry Magee	.05	.02
☐ 450 Mike Donlin	.10	.05
☐ 451 Doc Cramer	.10	.05
☐ 452 Dick Bartell	.05	.02
☐ 453 Earle Mack	.05	.02
☐ 454 Jumbo Brown	.05	.02
☐ 455 Johnnie Heving	.05	.02
☐ 456 Percy Jones	.05	.02
☐ 457 Ted Blankenship	.05	.02
☐ 458 Al Wingo	.05	.02
☐ 459 Roger Bresnahan	.20	.09
☐ 460 Bill Klem	.25	.11
☐ 461 Charlie Gehringer	.25	.11
☐ 462 Stan Coveleski	.20	.09
☐ 463 Eddie Plank	.20	.09
☐ 464 Clark Griffith	.20	.09
☐ 465 Herb Pennock	.20	.09
☐ 466 Earle Combs	.20	.09
☐ 467 Bobby Doerr	.20	.09
☐ 468 Waite Hoyt	.20	.09
☐ 469 Tommy Connolly	.20	.09
☐ 470 Harry Hooper	.20	.09
☐ 471 Rick Ferrell	.20	.09
☐ 472 Billy Evans	.15	.07
☐ 473 Billy Herman	.20	.09
☐ 474 Bill Dickey	.25	.11
☐ 475 Luke Appling	.20	.09
☐ 476 Babe Pinelli	.10	.05
☐ 477 Eric McNair	.05	.02
☐ 478 Sherriff Blake	.05	.02
☐ 479 Val Picinich	.05	.02
☐ 480 Fred Heimach	.05	.02
☐ 481 Jack Graney	.05	.02
☐ 482 Reb Russell	.05	.02
☐ 483 Red Faber	.20	.09
☐ 484 Benny Kauff	.10	.05
☐ 485 Pants Rowland	.05	.02
☐ 486 Bobby Veach	.05	.02
☐ 487 Jim Bagby Sr.	.05	.02
☐ 488 Pol Perritt	.05	.02
☐ 489 Buck Herzog	.05	.02
☐ 490 Art Fletcher	.05	.02
☐ 491 Walter Holke	.05	.02
☐ 492 Art Nehf	.10	.05
☐ 493 Fresco Thompson	.05	.02
☐ 494 Jimmy Welsh	.05	.02
☐ 495 Ossie Vitt	.05	.02
☐ 496 Ownie Carroll	.05	.02
☐ 497 Ken O'Dea	.05	.02
☐ 498 Fred Frankhouse	.05	.02
☐ 499 Jewel Ens	.05	.02
☐ 500 Morrie Arnovich	.05	.02
☐ 501 Wally Gerber	.05	.02
☐ 502 Kiddo Davis	.05	.02
☐ 503 Buddy Myer	.05	.02
☐ 504 Sam Leslie	.05	.02
☐ 505 Cliff Bolton	.05	.02
☐ 506 Dixie Walker	.10	.05
☐ 507 Jack Smith	.05	.02
☐ 508 Bump Hadley	.05	.02
☐ 509 Buck Crouse	.05	.02
☐ 510 Joe Glenn	.05	.02
☐ 511 Chad Kimsey	.05	.02
☐ 512 Lou Finney	.05	.02
☐ 513 Roxie Lawson	.05	.02
☐ 514 Chuck Fullis	.05	.02
☐ 515 Earl Sheely	.05	.02
☐ 516 George Gibson	.05	.02
☐ 517 Johnny Broaca	.05	.02
☐ 518 Bibb Falk	.05	.02
☐ 519 Don Hurst	.05	.02
☐ 520 Grover Hartley	.05	.02
☐ 521 Don Heffner	.05	.02
☐ 522 Harvey Hendrick	.05	.02
☐ 523 Allen Sothoron	.05	.02
☐ 524 Tony Piet	.05	.02
☐ 525 Ty Cobb	.75	.35
☐ 526 Jimmie Foxx	.35	.16
☐ 527 Rogers Hornsby	.35	.16
☐ 528 Nap Lajoie	.35	.16
☐ 529 Lou Gehrig	.75	.35
☐ 530 Heinie Zimmerman	.05	.02
☐ 531 Chuck Klein	.20	.09
☐ 532 Hugh Duffy	.20	.09
☐ 533 Lefty Grove	.30	.14
☐ 534 Grover C. Alexander	.30	.14
☐ 535 Amos Rusie	.20	.09
☐ 536 Lefty Gomez	.25	.11
☐ 537 Bucky Walters	.15	.07
☐ 538 Johnny Hodapp	.05	.02
☐ 539 Bruce Campbell	.05	.02
☐ 540 Hod Lisenbee	.05	.02
☐ 541 Jack Fournier	.05	.02
☐ 542 Jim Tabor	.05	.02
☐ 543 Johnny Burnett	.05	.02
☐ 544 Roy Hartzell	.05	.02
☐ 545 Doc Gautreau	.05	.02
☐ 546 Emil Yde	.05	.02
☐ 547 Bob Johnson	.10	.05
☐ 548 Joe Hauser	.05	.02
☐ 549 Ed Reulbach	.05	.02
☐ 550 Mel Almada	.05	.02
☐ 551 Mickey Cochrane	.25	.11
☐ 552 Carl Hubbell	.25	.11
☐ 553 Charlie Gehringer	.25	.11
☐ 554 Al Simmons	.20	.09
☐ 555 Mordecai Brown	.20	.09
☐ 556 Hugh Jennings	.20	.09
☐ 557 Kid Elberfeld	.05	.02
☐ 558 Casey Stengel	.30	.14
☐ 559 Al Schacht	.15	.07
☐ 560 Jimmie Foxx	.35	.16
☐ 561 George Kelly	.20	.09
☐ 562 Lloyd Waner	.20	.09
☐ 563 Paul Waner	.20	.09
☐ 564 Walter Johnson	.40	.18
☐ 565 Home Run Baker	.20	.09
☐ 566 Roy Hughes	.05	.02
☐ 567 Lew Riggs	.05	.02
☐ 568 John Whitehead	.05	.02
☐ 569 Elam Vangilder	.05	.02
☐ 570 Billy Zitzmann	.05	.02
☐ 571 Walter Schmidt	.05	.02
☐ 572 Jackie Tavener	.05	.02
☐ 573 Joe Genewich	.05	.02
☐ 574 Johnny Marcum	.05	.02
☐ 575 Fred Hoffmann	.05	.02
☐ 576 Red Rolfe	.10	.05
☐ 577 Vic Sorrell	.05	.02
☐ 578 Pete Scott	.05	.02
☐ 579 Tommy Thomas	.05	.02
☐ 580 Al Smith	.05	.02
☐ 581 Butch Henline	.05	.02
☐ 582 Eddie Collins	.20	.09
☐ 583 Earle Combs	.20	.09
☐ 584 John McGraw	.25	.11
☐ 585 Hack Wilson	.25	.11
☐ 586 Gabby Hartnett	.20	.09
☐ 587 Kiki Cuyler	.20	.09
☐ 588 Bill Terry	.25	.11
☐ 589 Joe McCarthy	.20	.09
☐ 590 Hank Greenberg	.30	.14
☐ 591 Tris Speaker	.25	.11
☐ 592 Bill McKechnie	.20	.09
☐ 593 Bucky Harris	.20	.09
☐ 594 Herb Pennock	.20	.09
☐ 595 George Sisler	.20	.09
☐ 596 Fred Lindstrom	.20	.09
☐ 597 Earl Averill	.20	.09
☐ 598 Dave Bancroft	.20	.09
☐ 599 Connie Mack	.25	.11
☐ 600 Joe Cronin	.20	.09
☐ 601 Ken Ash	.05	.02
☐ 602 Al Spohrer	.05	.02
☐ 603 Roy Mahaffey	.05	.02
☐ 604 Frank O'Rourke	.05	.02
☐ 605 Lil Stoner	.05	.02
☐ 606 Frank Gabler	.05	.02
☐ 607 Tom Padden	.05	.02
☐ 608 Art Shires	.05	.02
☐ 609 Sherry Smith	.05	.02
☐ 610 Phil Weintraub	.05	.02
☐ 611 Russ Van Atta	.05	.02
☐ 612 Jo Jo White	.05	.02
☐ 613 Cliff Melton	.05	.02
☐ 614 Jimmy Ring	.05	.02
☐ 615 Heinie Sand	.05	.02
☐ 616 Dale Alexander	.05	.02
☐ 617 Kent Greenfield	.05	.02
☐ 618 Eddie Dyer	.05	.02
☐ 619 Bill Sherdel	.05	.02
☐ 620 Max Lanier	.05	.02
☐ 621 Bob O'Farrell	.05	.02
☐ 622 Rogers Hornsby	.35	.16
☐ 623 Bill Beckman	.05	.02
☐ 624 Mort Cooper	.05	.02
☐ 625 Bill DeLancey	.05	.02
☐ 626 Marty Marion	.10	.05
☐ 627 Billy Southworth	.05	.02
☐ 628 Johnny Mize	.25	.11
☐ 629 Joe Medwick	.20	.09
☐ 630 Grover C. Alexander	.30	.14
☐ 631 Daffy Dean	.10	.05
☐ 632 Hi Bell	.05	.02
☐ 633 Walker Cooper	.05	.02
☐ 634 Frank Frisch	.20	.09
☐ 635 Dizzy Dean	.40	.18
☐ 636 Don Gutteridge	.05	.02
☐ 637 Pepper Martin	.15	.07
☐ 638 Ed Konetchy	.05	.02
☐ 639 Bill Hallahan	.05	.02
☐ 640 Lon Warneke	.10	.05
☐ 641 Terry Moore	.10	.05
☐ 642 Enos Slaughter	.20	.09
☐ 643 Heinie Mueller	.05	.02
☐ 644 Specs Toporcer	.05	.02
☐ 645 Jim Bottomley	.20	.09
☐ 646 Ray Blades	.05	.02
☐ 647 Jesse Haines	.20	.09
☐ 648 Andy High	.05	.02
☐ 649 Miller Huggins	.20	.09
☐ 650 Ernie Orsatti	.05	.02
☐ 651 Les Bell	.05	.02

☐ 652 Gabby Street	.05	.02
☐ 653 Wally Roettger	.05	.02
☐ 654 Syl Johnson	.05	.02
☐ 655 Mike Gonzalez	.05	.02
☐ 656 Ripper Collins	.05	.02
☐ 657 Chick Hafey	.20	.09
☐ 658 Checklist 331-440	.05	.02
☐ 659 Checklist 441-550	.05	.02
☐ 660 Checklist 551-660	.05	.02

1992-93 Conlon TSN Color Inserts

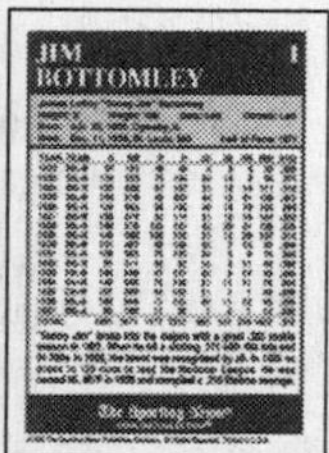

All the cards in this 22-card standard-size set were previously released in black and white in the 1991 or 1992 Conlon regular issue sets. Released on two different occasions, cards 1-6 and 7-12 were issued exclusively as a bonus to collectors who purchased Megacards' hobby accessory products (plastic sheets, card frames, and card sleeves) through retail outlets. The announced production figures for cards 1-6 were 250,000 of each card. For cards 7-12, the announced production run was 252,000 of each card. Cards 13-20 were randomly inserted in 1993 Conlon counter packs and blister packs, with an announced production run of 100,000 of each card. Cards 21-22 were available only through a special send-away offer on the backs of Conlon counter packs and blister packs; 75,000 of each card were produced. There were 60,000 cards of Bob Feller (23) produced exclusively for the Sports Collectors Digest 1993 Price Guide and bound inside copies of that book. The fronts display color player portraits inside a white picture frame on a navy blue card face. A diagonal graphic across the upper right corner of the picture gives the year the player was inducted into the Hall of Fame. The black and white backs are accented in navy blue and provide biography, career statistics, and career summary. The corresponding card number of the black and white regular issue card is given on the line after each player's name.

	MINT	NRMT
COMPLETE SET (23)	50.00	22.00
COMMON CARD (1-6)	1.00	.45
COMMON CARD (6-12)	1.00	.45
COMMON CARD (13-20)	2.00	.90
COMMON CARD (21-22)	6.00	2.70
COMMON CARD (23)	5.00	2.20

☐ 1 Jim Bottomley Card 22	1.00	.45
☐ 2 Lefty Grove Card 23	2.00	.90
☐ 3 Lou Gehrig Card 111	4.00	1.80
☐ 4 Babe Ruth Card 145	6.00	2.70
☐ 5 Casey Stengel Card 37	2.00	.90
☐ 6 Rube Marquard Card 252	1.00	.45
☐ 7 Walter Johnson Card 353	2.00	.90
☐ 8 Lou Gehrig Card 310	4.00	1.80
☐ 9 Christy Mathewson Card 331	2.00	.90
☐ 10 Ty Cobb Card 250	4.00	1.80
☐ 11 Mel Ott Card 225	2.00	.90
☐ 12 Carl Hubbell Card 253	1.00	.45
☐ 13 Al Simmons Card 49	2.00	.90
☐ 14 Connie Mack Card 47	3.00	1.35
☐ 15 Grover C. Alexander Card 32	3.00	1.35
☐ 16 Jimmie Foxx Card 303	3.00	1.35
☐ 17 Lloyd Waner Card 6	2.00	.90
☐ 18 Tris Speaker Card 422	3.00	1.35
☐ 19 Dizzy Dean Card 3	4.00	1.80
☐ 20 Rogers Hornsby Card 1	4.00	1.80
☐ 21 Joe Jackson Card 444	6.00	2.70
☐ 22 Jim Thorpe Card 403	6.00	2.70
☐ 23 Bob Feller	5.00	2.20

1993 Conlon TSN

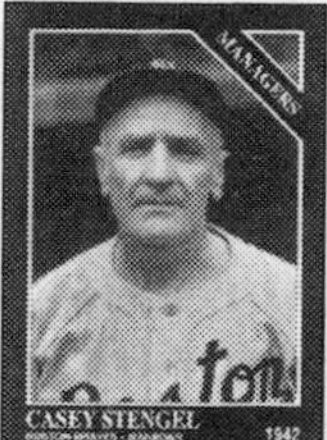

The third 330-card standard-size set of The Sporting News Conlon Collection again features turn-of-the-century to World War II-era players photographed by Charles Conlon, including more than 100 cards of Hall of Famers. Cards from a subset displaying computer color-enhanced photos were randomly inserted in the counter box packs and blister packs. The standard-size cards feature a mix of black-and-white vintage player photos inside a white frame on a black card face. Topical subset titles are printed on a diagonal bar at the upper right corner of the pictures. The backs carry biography, statistics, and extended career summary and highlights. The set contains several subsets continuing from last year's issue and some new subsets unique to this year's set: Game of the Century: 1933 All-Star Game (661-689), Spitballers (702-712), Accused Spitballers (717-725), Nicknames (730-741), Great Stories (751-770), Native Americans: American Indians who played big-league ball (771-777), League Leaders (795-798 and 801-805), Great Managers (817-848), Great Backstops (861-880), Against All Odds (881-894), Trivia (905-918), Nolan Ryan: compares eight Hall of Famers to Ryan (928-935), and First Cards: players for whom cards have never been done before (945-987). The set closes with checklist cards (988-990). The set was also available as a factory set in a special commemorative tin and in the form of three 110-card uncut sheets.

	MINT	NRMT
COMPLETE SET (330)	18.00	8.00
COMMON CARD (661-990)	.05	.02

☐ 661 Bill Terry	.25	.11
☐ 662 Lefty Gomez	.25	.11
☐ 663 Babe Ruth	1.00	.45
☐ 664 Frank Frisch	.20	.09
☐ 665 Carl Hubbell	.25	.11
☐ 666 Al Simmons	.20	.09
☐ 667 Charlie Gehringer	.25	.11
☐ 668 Earl Averill	.20	.09
☐ 669 Lefty Grove	.30	.14
☐ 670 Pie Traynor	.20	.09
☐ 671 Chuck Klein	.20	.09
☐ 672 Paul Waner	.20	.09
☐ 673 Lou Gehrig	.75	.35
☐ 674 Rick Ferrell	.20	.09
☐ 675 Gabby Hartnett	.20	.09
☐ 676 Joe Cronin	.20	.09
☐ 677 Chick Hafey	.20	.09
☐ 678 Jimmy Dykes	.10	.05
☐ 679 Sammy West	.05	.02
☐ 680 Pepper Martin	.15	.07
☐ 681 Lefty O'Doul	.10	.05
☐ 682 General Crowder	.05	.02
☐ 683 Jimmie Wilson	.05	.02
☐ 684 Dick Bartell	.05	.02
☐ 685 Bill Hallahan	.05	.02
☐ 686 Wally Berger	.10	.05
☐ 687 Lon Warneke	.10	.05
☐ 688 Ben Chapman	.05	.02
☐ 689 Woody English	.05	.02
☐ 690 Jimmy Reese	.10	.05
☐ 691 Wattie Holm	.05	.02
☐ 692 Charlie Jamieson	.05	.02
☐ 693 Tom Zachary	.05	.02
☐ 694 Blondy Ryan	.05	.02
☐ 695 Sparky Adams	.05	.02
☐ 696 Bill Hunnefield	.05	.02
☐ 697 Lee Meadows	.05	.02
☐ 698 Tom Carey	.05	.02
☐ 699 Johnny Rawlings	.05	.02
☐ 700 Ken Holloway	.05	.02
☐ 701 Lance Richbourg	.05	.02
☐ 702 Ray Fisher	.05	.02
☐ 703 Ed Walsh	.20	.09
☐ 704 Dick Rudolph	.05	.02
☐ 705 Ray Caldwell	.05	.02
☐ 706 Burleigh Grimes	.20	.09
☐ 707 Stan Coveleski	.20	.09
☐ 708 George Hildebrand	.05	.02
☐ 709 Jack Quinn	.10	.05
☐ 710 Red Faber	.20	.09
☐ 711 Urban Shocker	.10	.05
☐ 712 Dutch Leonard	.10	.05
☐ 713 Lou Koupal	.05	.02
☐ 714 Jimmy Wasdell	.05	.02
☐ 715 Johnny Lindell	.05	.02
☐ 716 Don Padgett	.05	.02
☐ 717 Nelson Potter	.05	.02
☐ 718 Schoolboy Rowe	.10	.05
☐ 719 Dave Danforth	.05	.02
☐ 720 Claude Passeau	.05	.02
☐ 721 Harry Kelley	.05	.02
☐ 722 Johnny Allen	.05	.02
☐ 723 Tommy Bridges	.10	.05
☐ 724 Bill Lee	.05	.02
☐ 725 Fred Frankhouse	.05	.02
☐ 726 Johnny McCarthy	.05	.02
☐ 727 Rip Russell	.05	.02
☐ 728 Emory(Topper) Rigney	.05	.02
☐ 729 Howie Shanks	.05	.02
☐ 730 Luke Appling	.20	.09
☐ 731 Bill Byron UMP	.05	.02
☐ 732 Earle Combs	.20	.09
☐ 733 Hank Greenberg	.30	.14
☐ 734 Walter(Boom Boom) Beck	.05	.02
☐ 735 Sloppy Thurston	.05	.02
☐ 736 Hack Wilson	.25	.11
☐ 737 Bill McGowan UMP	.20	.09
☐ 738 Zeke Bonura	.10	.05
☐ 739 Tom Baker	.05	.02
☐ 740 Bill(Baby Doll) Jacobson	.05	.02
☐ 741 Kiki Cuyler	.20	.09
☐ 742 George Blaeholder	.05	.02
☐ 743 Dee Miles	.05	.02
☐ 744 Lee Handley	.05	.02
☐ 745 Shano Collins	.05	.02
☐ 746 Rosy Ryan	.05	.02
☐ 747 Aaron Ward	.05	.02
☐ 748 Monte Pearson	.05	.02
☐ 749 Jake Early	.05	.02
☐ 750 Bill Atwood	.05	.02
☐ 751 Mark Koenig	.10	.05
☐ 752 Buddy Hassett	.05	.02
☐ 753 Davy Jones	.05	.02
☐ 754 Honus Wagner	.40	.18
☐ 755 Bill Dickey	.25	.11
☐ 756 Max Butcher	.05	.02
☐ 757 Waite Hoyt	.20	.09
☐ 758 Walter Johnson	.40	.18
☐ 759 Howard Ehmke	.05	.02
☐ 760 Bobo Newsom	.15	.07
☐ 761 Tony Lazzeri	.20	.09
☐ 762 Tony Lazzeri	.20	.09
☐ 763 Spud Chandler	.10	.05
☐ 764 Kirby Higbe	.05	.02
☐ 765 Paul Richards	.10	.05
☐ 766 Rogers Hornsby	.35	.16
☐ 767 Joe Vosmik	.05	.02
☐ 768 Jesse Haines	.20	.09
☐ 769 Bucky Walters	.15	.07
☐ 770 Tommy Henrich	.15	.07
☐ 771 Jim Thorpe	1.00	.45
☐ 772 Euel Moore	.05	.02
☐ 773 Rudy York	.10	.05
☐ 774 Chief Bender	.20	.09
☐ 775 Chief Meyers	.05	.02
☐ 776 Bob Johnson	.10	.05
☐ 777 Roy Johnson	.05	.02
☐ 778 Dick Porter	.05	.02
☐ 779 Ethan Allen	.10	.05
☐ 780 Slim Sallee	.05	.02
☐ 781 Beau Bell	.05	.02
☐ 782 Jigger Statz	.05	.02
☐ 783 Dutch Henry	.05	.02
☐ 784 Larry Woodall	.05	.02
☐ 785 Phil Collins	.05	.02
☐ 786 Joe Sewell	.20	.09
☐ 787 Billy Herman	.20	.09
☐ 788 Rube Oldring	.05	.02

☐ 789 Bill Walker	.05	.02
☐ 790 Joe Schultz	.05	.02
☐ 791 Fred Maguire	.05	.02
☐ 792 Claude Willoughby	.05	.02
☐ 793 Alex Ferguson	.05	.02
☐ 794 Johnny Morrison	.05	.02
☐ 795 Tris Speaker	.25	.11
☐ 796 Ty Cobb	.75	.35
☐ 797 Max Carey	.20	.09
☐ 798 George Sisler	.20	.09
☐ 799 Charlie Hollocher	.05	.02
☐ 800 Hippo Vaughn	.05	.02
☐ 801 Sad Sam Jones	.10	.05
☐ 802 Harry Hooper	.20	.09
☐ 803 Gavvy Cravath	.10	.05
☐ 804 Walter Johnson	.20	.09
☐ 805 Jake Daubert	.10	.05
☐ 806 Clyde Milan	.10	.05
☐ 807 Hugh McQuillan	.05	.02
☐ 808 Fred Brickell	.05	.02
☐ 809 Joe Stripp	.05	.02
☐ 810 Johnny Hodapp	.05	.02
☐ 811 Johnny Vergez	.05	.02
☐ 812 Lonny Frey	.05	.02
☐ 813 Bill Regan	.05	.02
☐ 814 Babe Young	.05	.02
☐ 815 Charlie Robertson	.05	.02
☐ 816 Walt Judnich	.05	.02
☐ 817 Joe Tinker	.20	.09
☐ 818 Johnny Evers	.20	.09
☐ 819 Frank Chance	.20	.09
☐ 820 John McGraw	.25	.11
☐ 821 Charlie Grimm	.15	.07
☐ 822 Ted Lyons	.20	.09
☐ 823 Joe McCarthy MG	.20	.09
☐ 824 Connie Mack MG	.25	.11
☐ 825 George Gibson	.05	.02
☐ 826 Steve O'Neill	.05	.02
☐ 827 Tris Speaker	.25	.11
☐ 828 Bill Carrigan	.05	.02
☐ 829 Casey Stengel	.30	.14
☐ 830 Miller Huggins	.20	.09
☐ 831 Bill McKechnie MG	.20	.09
☐ 832 Chuck Dressen	.10	.05
☐ 833 Gabby Street	.05	.02
☐ 834 Mel Ott	.30	.14
☐ 835 Frank Frisch	.20	.09
☐ 836 George Sisler	.20	.09
☐ 837 Nap Lajoie	.35	.16
☐ 838 Ty Cobb	.75	.35
☐ 839 Billy Southworth MG	.05	.02
☐ 840 Clark Griffith	.20	.09
☐ 841 Bill Terry	.25	.11
☐ 842 Rogers Hornsby	.35	.16
☐ 843 Joe Cronin	.20	.09
☐ 844 Al Lopez	.20	.09
☐ 845 Bucky Harris MG	.20	.09
☐ 846 Wilbert Robinson MG	.20	.09
☐ 847 Hughie Jennings	.20	.09
☐ 848 Jimmie Dykes	.10	.05
☐ 849 Roy Cullenbine	.05	.02
☐ 850 Eddie Moore	.05	.02
☐ 851 Jack Rothrock	.05	.02
☐ 852 Bill Lamar	.05	.02
☐ 853 Monte Weaver	.05	.02
☐ 854 Ival Goodman	.05	.02
☐ 855 Hank Severeid	.05	.02
☐ 856 Fred Haney	.05	.02
☐ 857 Joe Shaute	.05	.02
☐ 858 Smead Jolley	.05	.02
☐ 859 Dib Williams	.05	.02
☐ 860 Benny Bengough	.10	.05
☐ 861 Rick Ferrell	.20	.09
☐ 862 Bob O'Farrell	.05	.02
☐ 863 Spud Davis	.05	.02
☐ 864 Frankie Hayes	.05	.02
☐ 865 Muddy Ruel	.05	.02
☐ 866 Mickey Cochrane	.25	.11
☐ 867 Johnny Kling	.05	.02
☐ 868 Ivey Wingo	.05	.02
☐ 869 Bill Dickey	.25	.11
☐ 870 Frank Snyder	.05	.02
☐ 871 Roger Bresnahan	.20	.09
☐ 872 Wally Schang	.10	.05
☐ 873 Al Lopez	.20	.09
☐ 874 Jimmie Wilson	.05	.02
☐ 875 Val Picinich	.05	.02
☐ 876 Steve O'Neill	.05	.02
☐ 877 Ernie Lombardi	.20	.09
☐ 878 Johnny Bassler	.05	.02
☐ 879 Ray Schalk	.20	.09
☐ 880 Gabby Hartnett	.20	.09
☐ 881 Bruce Campbell	.05	.02
☐ 882 Red Ruffing	.20	.09
☐ 883 Mordecai Brown	.20	.09
☐ 884 Jimmy Archer	.05	.02
☐ 885 Dave Keefe	.05	.02
☐ 886 Nate Andrews	.05	.02
☐ 887 Sam Rice	.20	.09
☐ 888 Babe Ruth	1.00	.45
☐ 889 Chick Hafey	.20	.09
☐ 890 Oscar Melillo	.05	.02
☐ 891 Joe Wood	.10	.05
☐ 892 Johnny Evers	.20	.09
☐ 893 Specs Toporcer	.05	.02
☐ 894 Myril Hoag	.05	.02
☐ 895 Bob Weiland	.05	.02
☐ 896 Joe Marty	.05	.02
☐ 897 Sherry Magee	.05	.02
☐ 898 Danny Taylor	.05	.02
☐ 899 Willie Kamm	.05	.02
☐ 900 Jimmy Sheckard	.05	.02
☐ 901 Syl Johnson	.05	.02
☐ 902 Steve Sundra	.05	.02
☐ 903 Doc Cramer	.10	.05
☐ 904 Hub Pruett	.05	.02
☐ 905 Lena Blackburne	.05	.02
☐ 906 Eppa Rixey	.20	.09
☐ 907 Goose Goslin	.20	.09
☐ 908 George Kelly	.20	.09
☐ 909 Jim Bottomley	.20	.09
☐ 910 Christy Mathewson	.40	.18
☐ 911 Tony Lazzeri	.20	.09
☐ 912 Johnny Mostil	.05	.02
☐ 913 Bobby Doerr	.20	.09
☐ 914 Rabbit Maranville	.20	.09
☐ 915 Harry Heilmann	.20	.09
☐ 916 Bobby Wallace	.20	.09
☐ 917 Jimmie Foxx	.35	.16
☐ 918 Johnny Mize	.25	.11
☐ 919 Jack Bentley	.05	.02
☐ 920 Al Schacht	.15	.07
☐ 921 Ed Coleman	.05	.02
☐ 922 Dode Paskert	.05	.02
☐ 923 Hod Ford	.05	.02
☐ 924 Randy Moore	.05	.02
☐ 925 Milt Shoffner	.05	.02
☐ 926 Dick Siebert	.05	.02
☐ 927 Tony Kaufmann	.05	.02
☐ 928 Dizzy Dean with Nolan Ryan	1.00	.45
☐ 929 Dazzy Vance with Nolan Ryan	.60	.25
☐ 930 Lefty Grove with Nolan Ryan	.75	.35
☐ 931 Rube Waddell with Nolan Ryan	.75	.35
☐ 932 Grover C. Alexander with Nolan Ryan	.75	.35
☐ 933 Bob Feller with Nolan Ryan	.75	.35
☐ 934 Walter Johnson with Nolan Ryan	1.50	.70
☐ 935 Ted Lyons with Nolan Ryan	.75	.35
☐ 936 Jim Bagby Jr.	.05	.02
☐ 937 Joe Sugden CO	.05	.02
☐ 938 Earl Grace	.05	.02
☐ 939 Jeff Heath	.05	.02
☐ 940 Ken Williams	.15	.07
☐ 941 Marv Owen	.05	.02
☐ 942 Roy Weatherly	.05	.02
☐ 943 Ed Morgan	.05	.02
☐ 944 Johnny Rizzo	.05	.02
☐ 945 Archie McKain	.05	.02
☐ 946 Bob Garbark	.05	.02
☐ 947 Bob Osborn	.05	.02
☐ 948 Johnny Podgajny	.05	.02
☐ 949 Joe Evans	.05	.02
☐ 950 Tony Rensa	.05	.02
☐ 951 John Humphries	.05	.02
☐ 952 Merritt(Sugar) Cain	.05	.02
☐ 953 Roy(Snipe) Hansen	.05	.02
☐ 954 Johnny Niggeling	.05	.02
☐ 955 Hal Wiltse	.05	.02
☐ 956 Alex Carrasquel	.10	.05
☐ 957 George Grant	.05	.02
☐ 958 Lefty Weinert	.05	.02
☐ 959 Erv Brame	.05	.02
☐ 960 Ray Harrell	.05	.02
☐ 961 Ed Linke	.05	.02
☐ 962 Sam Gibson	.05	.02
☐ 963 Johnny Watwood	.05	.02
☐ 964 Doc Prothro	.05	.02
☐ 965 Julio Bonetti	.05	.02
☐ 966 Lefty Mills	.05	.02
☐ 967 Chick Galloway	.05	.02
☐ 968 Hal Kelleher	.05	.02
☐ 969 Chief Hogsett	.05	.02
☐ 970 Ed Heusser	.05	.02
☐ 971 Ed Baecht	.05	.02
☐ 972 Jack Saltzgaver	.05	.02
☐ 973 Leroy Herrmann	.05	.02
☐ 974 Belve Bean	.05	.02
☐ 975 Harry(Socks) Seibold	.05	.02
☐ 976 Vic Keen	.05	.02
☐ 977 Bill Barrett	.05	.02
☐ 978 Pat McNulty	.05	.02
☐ 979 George Turbeville	.05	.02
☐ 980 Eddie Phillips	.05	.02
☐ 981 Garland Buckeye	.05	.02
☐ 982 Vic Frasier	.05	.02
☐ 983 Gordon Rhodes	.05	.02
☐ 984 Red Barnes	.05	.02
☐ 985 Jim Joe Edwards	.05	.02
☐ 986 Herschel Bennett	.05	.02
☐ 987 Carmen Hill	.05	.02
☐ 988 Checklist 661-770	.05	.02
☐ 989 Checklist 771-880	.05	.02
☐ 990 Checklist 881-990	.05	.02

1994 Conlon TSN

This fourth 330-card standard-size set of The Sporting News Conlon Collection again features the work of noted sports photographer Charles Conlon. The fronts feature black-and-white vintage player photos inside a white frame on a black card face. Subset cards are marked by their title in a black diagonal that cuts across the top right corner. The backs carry biography, statistics, and extended career summary and highlights. Topical subsets featured are Great Stories (991-1007), Hall of Fame (1008-1018), Black Sox Scandal (1019-1042), Nicknames (1050-1066), 1934 All-Star Game (1075-1113), In Memoriam (1121-1128), 1929 Athletics (1135-1159), Double Play Combo (1164-1166), Brothers (1169-1180), Umpires (1185-1212), All-Time Leaders (1217-1223), Switch-Hitters (1229-1237), Trivia (1247-1257), Action (1266-1274), First Card (1282-1317), and Checklists (1318-1320). The cards are numbered on the back in continuation of the previous year's issue. Card 1000 is the famous photo of Ty Cobb sliding. The 1994 Conlon set was issued in 12-card foil packs instead of the 15-card foil packs used in previous years. Reportedly 10,000 gold-bordered burgundy cards were produced for every card in the set. Each foil pack contained one of these cards, while two were inserted in each blister pack. According to Megacards, no more than 200,000 of each card were produced. The set was also available in factory set form.

	MINT	NRMT
COMPLETE SET (330)	18.00	8.00
COMPLETE FACT.SET (330)	18.00	8.00
COMMON CARD (991-1320)	.05	.02

☐ 991 Pepper Martin	.15	.07
☐ 992 Joe Sewell	.20	.09
☐ 993 Edd Roush	.20	.09
☐ 994 Rick Ferrell	.20	.09
☐ 995 Johnny Broaca	.05	.02
☐ 996 Luke Sewell	.10	.05
☐ 997 Burleigh Grimes	.20	.09
☐ 998 Hack Wilson	.25	.11
☐ 999 Lefty Grove	.30	.14
☐ 1000 Ty Cobb	.75	.35
☐ 1001 John McGraw	.25	.11
☐ 1002 Eddie Plank	.20	.09
☐ 1003 Sad Sam Jones	.10	.05
☐ 1004 Jim Bottomley	.20	.09
☐ 1005 Hank Greenberg	.30	.14
☐ 1006 Lloyd Waner	.20	.09
☐ 1007 Wilcy Moore	.05	.02
☐ 1008 Luke Appling	.20	.09
☐ 1009 Hal Newhouser	.20	.09
☐ 1010 Al Lopez	.20	.09
☐ 1011 Ty Cobb	.75	.35
☐ 1012 Kid Nichols	.20	.09
☐ 1013 Ed Walsh	.20	.09
☐ 1014 Hugh Duffy	.20	.09
☐ 1015 Rube Marquard	.20	.09
☐ 1016 Addie Joss	.20	.09
☐ 1017 Bobby Wallace	.20	.09
☐ 1018 Willie Keeler	.25	.11
☐ 1019 Jake Daubert	.10	.05
☐ 1020 Slim Sallee	.05	.02

☐ 1021 Dolf Luque	.10	.05
☐ 1022 Ivey Wingo	.05	.02
☐ 1023 Edd Roush	.20	.09
☐ 1024 Bill Rariden	.05	.02
☐ 1025 Sherry Magee	.05	.02
☐ 1026 Pat Duncan	.05	.02
☐ 1027 Hod Eller	.05	.02
☐ 1028 Greasy Neale	.10	.05
☐ 1029 Buck Weaver	.20	.09
☐ 1030 Joe Jackson	1.00	.45
☐ 1031 Chick Gandil	.25	.11
☐ 1032 Swede Risberg	.20	.09
☐ 1033 Ray Schalk	.20	.09
☐ 1034 Eddie Cicotte	.15	.07
☐ 1035 Bill James	.05	.02
☐ 1036 Nemo Leibold	.05	.02
☐ 1037 Dickie Kerr	.15	.07
☐ 1038 Kid Gleason MG	.10	.05
☐ 1039 Fred McMullin	.05	.02
☐ 1040 Eddie Collins	.20	.09
☐ 1041 Sox Pitchers	.15	.07
Lefty Williams		
Bill James		
Ed Cicotte		
Dickie Kerr		
☐ 1042 Sox Outfielders	.25	.11
Nemo Leibold		
Happy Felsch		
Shano Collins		
Joe Jackson		
☐ 1043 Ken Keltner	.10	.05
☐ 1044 Charlie Berry	.10	.05
☐ 1045 Rube Lutzke	.05	.02
☐ 1046 Johnny Schulte	.05	.02
☐ 1047 Johnny Welch	.05	.02
☐ 1048 Jack Russell	.05	.02
☐ 1049 Red Murray	.05	.02
☐ 1050 Pie Traynor	.20	.09
☐ 1051 Mike Donlin	.10	.05
☐ 1052 Gabby Hartnett	.20	.09
☐ 1053 Tony Lazzeri	.20	.09
☐ 1054 Hack Miller	.05	.02
☐ 1055 Dazzy Vance	.20	.09
☐ 1056 Bill Carrigan	.05	.02
☐ 1057 Johnny Murphy	.10	.05
☐ 1058 Cliff Heathcote	.05	.02
☐ 1059 Joe Dugan	.10	.05
☐ 1060 Rabbit Maranville	.20	.09
☐ 1061 Tommy Henrich	.15	.07
☐ 1062 Roy Parmelee	.05	.02
☐ 1063 Lefty Gomez	.25	.11
☐ 1064 Ernie Lombardi	.20	.09
☐ 1065 Dave Bancroft	.20	.09
☐ 1066 Bill McKechnie MG	.20	.09
☐ 1067 Buddy Hassett	.05	.02
☐ 1068 Spud Chandler	.10	.05
☐ 1069 Roy Hughes	.05	.02
☐ 1070 Hooks Dauss	.05	.02
☐ 1071 Joe Hauser	.05	.02
☐ 1072 Spud Davis	.05	.02
☐ 1073 Max Butcher	.05	.02
☐ 1074 Lou Chiozza	.05	.02
☐ 1075 Polo Grounds	.05	.02
1934 All-Star Game		
☐ 1076 Charlie Gehringer	.25	.11
☐ 1077 Heinie Manush	.20	.09
☐ 1078 Red Ruffing	.20	.09
☐ 1079 Mel Harder	.10	.05
☐ 1080 Babe Ruth	1.00	.45
☐ 1081 Ben Chapman	.05	.02
☐ 1082 Lou Gehrig	.75	.35
☐ 1083 Jimmie Foxx	.35	.16
☐ 1084 Al Simmons	.20	.09
☐ 1085 Joe Cronin	.20	.09
☐ 1086 Bill Dickey	.25	.11
☐ 1087 Mickey Cochrane	.25	.11
☐ 1088 Lefty Gomez	.25	.11
☐ 1089 Earl Averill Sr.	.20	.09
☐ 1090 Sammy West	.05	.02
☐ 1091 Frank Frisch P/MG	.20	.09
☐ 1092 Billy Herman	.20	.09
☐ 1093 Pie Traynor	.20	.09
☐ 1094 Joe Medwick	.20	.09
☐ 1095 Chuck Klein	.20	.09
☐ 1096 Kiki Cuyler	.20	.09
☐ 1097 Mel Ott	.30	.14
☐ 1098 Wally Berger	.10	.05
☐ 1099 Paul Waner	.20	.09
☐ 1100 Bill Terry	.25	.11
☐ 1101 Travis Jackson	.20	.09
☐ 1102 Arky Vaughan	.20	.09
☐ 1103 Gabby Hartnett	.20	.09
☐ 1104 Al Lopez	.20	.09
☐ 1105 Carl Hubbell	.25	.11
☐ 1106 Lon Warneke	.10	.05
☐ 1107 Van Lingle Mungo	.10	.05
☐ 1108 Pepper Martin	.15	.07
☐ 1109 Dizzy Dean	.40	.18
☐ 1110 Fred Frankhouse	.05	.02
☐ 1111 Bob Quinn	.05	.02
J.G. Taylor Spink		
Mrs. J.G. Taylor Spink		
☐ 1112 Joseph Gilleaudeau	.05	.02
Mrs. Joseph Gilleaudeau		
Mrs. J.G. Taylor Spink		
J.G. Taylor Spink		
Mrs. John Heydler		
John Heydler		
☐ 1113 Bill Hinchman	.05	.02
Edward Keller		
☐ 1114 Vic Aldridge	.05	.02
☐ 1115 Pinky Higgins	.05	.02
☐ 1116 Hal Carlson	.05	.02
☐ 1117 Fred Fitzsimmons	.10	.05
☐ 1118 Bucky Walters	.15	.07
☐ 1119 Nick Altrock	.05	.02
☐ 1120 Chuck Dressen	.10	.05
☐ 1121 Mark Koenig	.10	.05
☐ 1122 Charlie Gehringer	.25	.11
☐ 1123 Vern Kennedy	.05	.02
☐ 1124 Harlond Clift	.05	.02
☐ 1125 Babe Phelps	.05	.02
☐ 1126 Johnny Mize	.25	.11
☐ 1127 Hal Schumacher	.10	.05
☐ 1128 Ethan Allen	.10	.05
☐ 1129 Bill Wambsganss	.05	.02
☐ 1130 Freddy Leach	.05	.02
☐ 1131 Bud Clancy	.05	.02
☐ 1132 Stuffy Stewart	.05	.02
☐ 1133 Bill Brubaker	.05	.02
☐ 1134 Les Mann	.05	.02
☐ 1135 Howard Ehmke	.05	.02
☐ 1136 Al Simmons	.20	.09
☐ 1137 George Earnshaw	.10	.05
☐ 1138 Mule Haas	.05	.02
☐ 1139 Bing Miller	.05	.02
☐ 1140 Lefty Grove	.30	.14
☐ 1141 Joe Boley	.05	.02
☐ 1142 Eddie Collins	.20	.09
☐ 1143 Walter French	.05	.02
☐ 1144 Eric McNair	.05	.02
☐ 1145 Bill Shores	.05	.02
☐ 1146 Mickey Cochrane	.25	.11
☐ 1147 Homer Summa	.05	.02
☐ 1148 Jack Quinn	.10	.05
☐ 1149 Max Bishop	.05	.02
☐ 1150 Jimmy Dykes	.10	.05
☐ 1151 Rube Walberg	.05	.02
☐ 1152 Jimmie Foxx	.35	.16
☐ 1153 George H. Burns	.05	.02
☐ 1154 Doc Cramer	.10	.05
☐ 1155 Sammy Hale	.05	.02
☐ 1156 Eddie Rommel	.05	.02
☐ 1157 Cy Perkins	.05	.02
☐ 1158 Jim Cronin	.05	.02
☐ 1159 Connie Mack MG	.25	.11
☐ 1160 Ray Kolp	.05	.02
☐ 1161 Clyde Manion	.05	.02
☐ 1162 Frank Grube	.05	.02
☐ 1163 Steve Swetonic	.05	.02
☐ 1164 Joe Tinker	.20	.09
☐ 1165 Johnny Evers	.20	.09
☐ 1166 Frank Chance	.20	.09
☐ 1167 Emerson Dickman	.05	.02
☐ 1168 Jack Tobin	.05	.02
☐ 1169 Wes Ferrell	.15	.07
Rick Ferrell		
☐ 1170 Dizzy Dean	.20	.09
Daffy Dean		
☐ 1171 Tony Cuccinello	.05	.02
Al Cuccinello		
☐ 1172 Harry Coveleski	.10	.05
Stan Coveleski		
☐ 1173 Bob Johnson	.05	.02
Roy Johnson		
☐ 1174 Andy High	.05	.02
Hugh High		
☐ 1175 Luke Sewell	.15	.07
Joe Sewell		
☐ 1176 Johnnie Heving	.05	.02
Joe Heving		
☐ 1177 Al Wingo	.05	.02
Ivy Wingo		
☐ 1178 Red Killefer	.05	.02
Bill Killefer		
☐ 1179 Bubbles Hargrave	.05	.02
Pinky Hargrave		
☐ 1180 Paul Waner	.15	.07
Lloyd Waner		
☐ 1181 Johnny VanderMeer	.15	.07
☐ 1182 Jo Jo Moore	.05	.02
☐ 1183 Bobby Burke	.05	.02
☐ 1184 Johnny Moore	.05	.02
☐ 1185 Jack Egan UMP	.05	.02
☐ 1186 Tommy Connolly UMP	.20	.09
☐ 1187 Silk O'Loughlin UMP	.05	.02
☐ 1188 Beans Reardon UMP	.10	.05
☐ 1189 Charles Moran UMP	.05	.02
☐ 1190 Bill Klem UMP	.25	.11
☐ 1191 Dolly Stark UMP	.10	.05
☐ 1192 Albert Orth UMP	.05	.02
☐ 1193 Kitty Bransfield UMP	.05	.02
☐ 1194 Roy Van Graflan UMP	.05	.02
☐ 1195 Bob Hart UMP	.05	.02
☐ 1196 Jocko Conlan UMP	.20	.09
☐ 1197 Babe Pinelli UMP	.10	.05
☐ 1198 John Sheridan UMP	.05	.02
☐ 1199 Dick Nallin UMP	.05	.02
☐ 1200 Bill Dineen UMP	.05	.02
☐ 1201 Hank O'Day UMP	.10	.05
☐ 1202 Cy Rigler UMP	.05	.02
☐ 1203 Bob Emslie UMP	.05	.02
☐ 1204 Charles Pfirman UMP	.05	.02
☐ 1205 Harry Geisel UMP	.05	.02
☐ 1206 Ernest Quigley UMP	.05	.02
☐ 1207 Red Ormsby UMP	.05	.02
☐ 1208 George Hildebrand UMP	.05	.02
☐ 1209 George Moriarty UMP	.10	.05
☐ 1210 Billy Evans UMP	.15	.07
☐ 1211 Brick Owens UMP	.05	.02
☐ 1212 Bill McGowan UMP	.20	.09
☐ 1213 Kirby Higbe	.05	.02
☐ 1214 Taylor Douthit	.05	.02
☐ 1215 Del Baker	.05	.02
☐ 1216 Al Demaree	.05	.02
☐ 1217 Connie Mack MG	.25	.11
☐ 1218 Nap Lajoie	.35	.16
☐ 1219 Honus Wagner	.40	.18
☐ 1220 Christy Mathewson	.40	.18
☐ 1221 Sam Crawford	.20	.09
☐ 1222 Tris Speaker	.25	.11
☐ 1223 Grover C. Alexander	.30	.14
☐ 1224 Joe Bowman	.05	.02
☐ 1225 Johnny Rigney	.05	.02
☐ 1226 Earl Webb	.10	.05
☐ 1227 Whitey Moore	.05	.02
☐ 1228 Bruce Campbell	.05	.02
☐ 1229 Lu Blue	.05	.02
☐ 1230 Mark Koenig	.10	.05
☐ 1231 Wally Schang	.10	.05
☐ 1232 Max Carey	.20	.09
☐ 1233 Frank Frisch	.20	.09
☐ 1234 Donie Bush	.05	.02
☐ 1235 George Davis	.05	.02
☐ 1236 Billy Rogell	.05	.02
☐ 1237 Ripper Collins	.05	.02
☐ 1238 Dick Burrus	.05	.02
☐ 1239 Evar Swanson	.05	.02
☐ 1240 Woody English	.05	.02
☐ 1241 Joe Harris	.05	.02
☐ 1242 Harry McCurdy	.05	.02
☐ 1243 Dick Bartell	.05	.02
☐ 1244 Tommy Thompson	.05	.02
☐ 1245 Babe Adams	.10	.05
☐ 1246 Art Nehf	.10	.05
☐ 1247 Jack Graney	.05	.02
☐ 1248 Ted Lyons	.20	.09
☐ 1249 Lou Gehrig	.75	.35
☐ 1250 Mickey Welch	.20	.09
☐ 1251 Red Faber	.20	.09
☐ 1252 Joe McGinnity	.20	.09
☐ 1253 Rogers Hornsby	.35	.16
☐ 1254 Mel Ott	.30	.14
☐ 1255 Walter Johnson	.40	.18
☐ 1256 Sam Rice	.20	.09
☐ 1257 Jim Tobin	.05	.02
☐ 1258 Roger Peckinpaugh	.10	.05
☐ 1259 George Stovall	.05	.02
☐ 1260 Fred Merkle	.10	.05
☐ 1261 Rip Collins	.05	.02
☐ 1262 Carl Lind	.05	.02
☐ 1263 Nap Rucker	.05	.02
☐ 1264 Sloppy Thurston	.05	.02
☐ 1265 Alex Metzler	.05	.02
☐ 1266 Charles Conlon	.05	.02
☐ 1267 Lew McCarty IA	.05	.02
Sherry Magee		
☐ 1268 B.A. Daniels IA	.05	.02
☐ 1269 Benny Kauff IA	.10	.05
☐ 1270 Heinie Groh IA	.10	.05
☐ 1271 Fritz Mollwitz IA	.05	.02
☐ 1272 George H. Burns IA	.05	.02
☐ 1273 Lee Magee IA	.05	.02
☐ 1274 Bill Killefer IA	.05	.02
☐ 1275 Jack Warhop	.05	.02
☐ 1276 Dutch Leonard	.10	.05
☐ 1277 General Crowder	.05	.02
☐ 1278 Chet Laabs	.05	.02
☐ 1279 Joe Bush	.10	.05
☐ 1280 Rube Bressler	.05	.02
☐ 1281 Bob Brown	.05	.02

Card	MINT	NRMT
☐ 1282 Bernie DeViveiros	.05	.02
☐ 1283 Les Tietje	.05	.02
☐ 1284 Charlie Devens	.05	.02
☐ 1285 Elliott Bigelow	.05	.02
☐ 1286 Johnny Dickshot	.05	.02
☐ 1287 Buster Chatham	.05	.02
☐ 1288 Walter Beall	.05	.02
☐ 1289 Dick Attreau	.05	.02
☐ 1290 Bunny Brief	.05	.02
☐ 1291 Jim Gleeson	.05	.02
☐ 1292 Wally Shaner	.05	.02
☐ 1293 Pat Crawford	.05	.02
☐ 1294 Manny Salvo	.05	.02
☐ 1295 Cal Dorsett	.05	.02
☐ 1296 Rusty Peters	.05	.02
☐ 1297 Johnny Couch	.05	.02
☐ 1298 Dutch Ulrich	.05	.02
☐ 1299 Jim Bivin	.05	.02
☐ 1300 Paul Strand	.05	.02
☐ 1301 Johnny Lanning	.05	.02
☐ 1302 Bill Brenzel	.05	.02
☐ 1303 Don Songer	.05	.02
☐ 1304 Dutch Levsen	.05	.02
☐ 1305 Otto Bluege	.05	.02
☐ 1306 Fabian Gaffke	.05	.02
☐ 1307 Flash Archdeacon	.05	.02
☐ 1308 Tiny Chaplin	.05	.02
☐ 1309 Larry Rosenthal	.05	.02
☐ 1310 Bill Bagwell	.05	.02
☐ 1311 Joe Dawson	.05	.02
☐ 1312 Johnny Sturm	.05	.02
☐ 1313 Haskell Billings	.05	.02
☐ 1314 Whitey Wilshere	.05	.02
☐ 1315 Asby Asbjornson	.05	.02
☐ 1316 Hank Steinbacher	.05	.02
☐ 1317 Stan Baumgartner	.05	.02
☐ 1318 Checklist 991-1100	.05	.02
☐ 1319 Checklist 1101-1210	.05	.02
☐ 1320 Checklist 1211-1320	.05	.02

1994 Conlon TSN Burgundy

This set is a parallel to the regular 1994 Conlon issue. Instead of the black and white borders, the borders had a burgundy color. One of these cards were inserted in each 1994 Conlon pack.

	MINT	NRMT
COMPLETE SET (330)	50.00	22.00
COMMON CARD (991-1320)	.10	.05
*STARS: 2X TO 4X BASIC CARDS		

1994 Conlon TSN Color Inserts

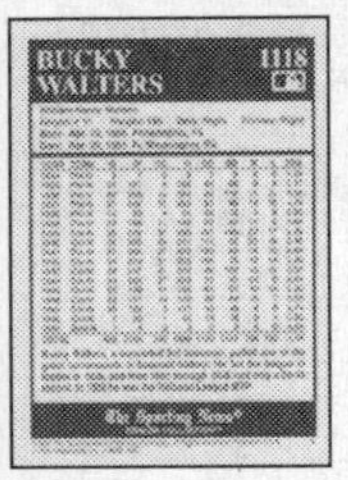

All the cards in this 16-card standard-size set were previously released in black and white in the Conlon regular issue sets. The cards are numbered on the back. The corresponding card number of the black and white regular issue card is given on the line after each player's name. Insert cards 24-39 were issued in 1994. Of these, cards 29-30 were available through a send-away offer, while cards 31-33 were inserted exclusively in hobby foil packs. The production figures for cards 24-39 were as follows: 84,000 for card numbers 24-28; 12,000 for card numbers 29-33; 48,000 for card numbers 34-37; and 12,000 for card numbers 38-39. Cards 34-37 were only available with accessory items purchased at Toys'R'Us. Cards 38-39 were available through special offers to be announced. Finally, 24,000 more of card number 28 were printed and have "Conlon Collection Day, Sept. 11, 1994" printed diagonally across their backs. These cards are specially numbered "28CCD" and were to be given out at a Cardinals game against the Dodgers in St. Louis.

	MINT	NRMT
COMPLETE SET (16)	40.00	18.00
COMMON CARD (24-28)	1.50	.70
COMMON CARD (29-33)	2.00	.90
COMMON CARD (34-37)	1.50	.70
COMMON CARD (38-39)	3.00	1.35

Card	MINT	NRMT
☐ 24 Hal Newhouser Card 445	2.00	.90
☐ 25 Hugh Jennings Card 556	1.50	.70
☐ 26 Red Faber	1.50	.70
☐ 27 Enos Slaughter Card 710	2.00	.90
☐ 28 Johnny Mize Card 56	2.00	.90
☐ 29 Pie Traynor Card 628	3.00	1.35
☐ 30 Walter Johnson Nolan Ryan Card 268	6.00	2.70
☐ 31 Lou Gehrig Card 529	6.00	2.70
☐ 32 Benny Bengough Card 860	2.00	.90
☐ 33 Babe Ruth Card 888	7.50	3.40
☐ 34 Charlie Gehringer Card 667	2.00	.90
☐ 35 Babe Ruth Card 426	6.00	2.70
☐ 36 Bill Dickey Card 869	2.50	1.10
☐ 37 Three Finger Brown Card 883	1.50	.70
☐ 38 Ray Schalk Card 48	3.00	1.35
☐ 39 Homerun Baker Card 565	4.00	1.80

1995 Conlon TSN

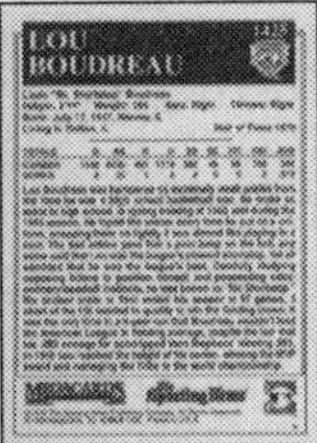

The 1995 Conlon Collection set consists of 110 standard-size cards. This continuation of the Conlon Collection set was supposed to be released in two 110-card series (February and August respectively), but the second series was never released because of the baseball strike. This was the first year that the Conlon Collection did not consist of 330 cards. The set continues to feature the work of noted sports photographer Charles Conlon. No more than 50,000 sets were printed, with a suggested retail price of $19.95 per series. As a special tribute to Conlon and the 100th Anniversary of Babe Ruth's birth, Megacards teamed with Topps to produce a 100th Birthday Card. The card was issued in two forms: a sepia-tone version for 1995 Topps regular series (#3) and an color-enhanced version (#3C) inserted in each 1995 Conlon complete set. On the fronts, each black-and-white photo has a gold foil inner border and a forest green outer border. Topical subsets featured are Veterans of World War I and II (1321-1350), '75 Champs (1354-1367), Great Stories (1371-1378), Nicknames (1382-1390), Behind the Scenes (1394-1400), Great Games (1404-1412), and Beating the Odds (1416-1429). Also groups of three "Generic" cards are scattered throughout the set (1351-1352, 1368-1370, 1379-1381, 1391-1393, 1401-1403, 1413-1415).

	MINT	NRMT
COMPLETE FACT. SET (110)	15.00	6.75
COMMON CARD (1321-1430)	.15	.07

Card	MINT	NRMT
☐ 1321 Grover C. Alexander	.60	.25
☐ 1322 Christy Mathewson	.60	.25
☐ 1323 Eddie Grant	.15	.07
☐ 1324 Gabby Street	.15	.07
☐ 1325 Hank Gowdy	.15	.07
☐ 1326 Jack Bentley	.15	.07
☐ 1327 Eppa Rixey	.40	.18
☐ 1328 Bob Shawkey	.25	.11
☐ 1329 Rabbit Maranville	.40	.18
☐ 1330 Casey Stengel	.60	.25
☐ 1331 Herb Pennock	.40	.18
☐ 1332 Eddie Collins Sr.	.40	.18
☐ 1333 Buddy Hassett	.15	.07
☐ 1334 Andy Cohen	.15	.07
☐ 1335 Hank Greenberg	.75	.35
☐ 1336 Andy High	.15	.07
☐ 1337 Bob Feller	.60	.25
☐ 1338 George Earnshaw	.25	.11
☐ 1339 Jack Knott	.15	.07
☐ 1340 Larry French	.15	.07
☐ 1341 Skippy Roberge	.15	.07
☐ 1342 Boze Berger	.15	.07
☐ 1343 Bill Posedel	.15	.07
☐ 1344 Kirby Higbe	.15	.07
☐ 1345 Bob Neighbors	.15	.07
☐ 1346 Hugh Mulcahy	.15	.07
☐ 1347 Harry Walker	.15	.07
☐ 1348 Buddy Lewis	.15	.07
☐ 1349 Cecil Travis	.15	.07
☐ 1350 Moe Berg	1.25	.55
☐ 1351 Nixey Callahan	.15	.07
☐ 1352 Heinie Peitz	.15	.07
☐ 1353 Doc White	.15	.07
☐ 1354 Joe Wood	.40	.18
☐ 1355 Larry Gardner	.15	.07
☐ 1356 Steve O'Neill	.15	.07
☐ 1357 Tris Speaker	.60	.25
☐ 1358 Bill Wambsganss	.15	.07
☐ 1359 George H. Burns	.15	.07
☐ 1360 Charlie Jamieson	.15	.07
☐ 1361 Les Nunamaker	.15	.07
☐ 1362 Stan Coveleski	.40	.18
☐ 1363 Joe Sewell	.40	.18
☐ 1364 Jim Bagby Sr.	.15	.07
☐ 1365 Duster Mails	.15	.07
☐ 1366 Jack Graney	.15	.07
☐ 1367 Elmer Smith	.15	.07
☐ 1368 Tommy Leach	.15	.07
☐ 1369 Russ Ford	.15	.07
☐ 1370 Harry M. Wolter	.15	.07
☐ 1371 Dazzy Vance	.40	.18
☐ 1372 Germany Schaefer	.25	.11
☐ 1373 Elbie Fletcher	.15	.07
☐ 1374 Clark Griffith	.40	.18
☐ 1375 Al Simmons	.40	.18
☐ 1376 Billy Jurges	.15	.07
☐ 1377 Earl Averill Sr.	.40	.18
☐ 1378 Bill Klem	.40	.18
☐ 1379 Armando Marsans	.15	.07
☐ 1380 Mike Gonzalez	.15	.07
☐ 1381 Jack Fournier	.15	.07
☐ 1382 Burleigh Grimes	.40	.18
☐ 1383 Arlie Latham	.15	.07
☐ 1384 Ray Schalk	.40	.18
☐ 1385 Goose Goslin	.40	.18
☐ 1386 Joe Hauser	.15	.07
☐ 1387 Dixie Walker	.25	.11
☐ 1388 Jesse Burkett	.15	.07
☐ 1389 Cliff Melton	.15	.07
☐ 1390 Gee Walker	.15	.07
☐ 1391 Tony Cuccinello	.15	.07
☐ 1392 Vern Kennedy	.15	.07
☐ 1393 Tuck Stainback	.15	.07
☐ 1394 Ed Barrow	.25	.11
☐ 1395 Ford C. Frick	.25	.11
☐ 1396 Ban Johnson August Herrmann	.25	.11
☐ 1397 Charles Comiskey	.25	.11
☐ 1398 Jacob Ruppert Joe McCarthy	.25	.11
☐ 1399 Branch Rickey	.40	.18
☐ 1400 Jack Kieran Moe Berg	.40	.18
☐ 1401 Mike Ryba	.15	.07
☐ 1402 Stan Spence	.15	.07
☐ 1403 Red Barrett	.15	.07
☐ 1404 Gabby Hartnett	.40	.18
☐ 1405 Babe Ruth	2.00	.90
☐ 1406 Fred Merkle	.25	.11
☐ 1407 Claude Passeau	.15	.07
☐ 1408 Joe Wood	.40	.18
☐ 1409 Cliff Heathcote	.15	.07
☐ 1410 Walt Cruise	.15	.07
☐ 1411 Cookie Lavagetto	.15	.07
☐ 1412 Tony Lazzeri	.40	.18
☐ 1413 Atley Donald	.15	.07
☐ 1414 Ken Raffensberger	.15	.07
☐ 1415 Dizzy Trout	.15	.07
☐ 1416 Augie Galan	.15	.07
☐ 1417 Monty Stratton	.15	.07
☐ 1418 Claude Passeau	.15	.07
☐ 1419 Oscar Grimes	.15	.07
☐ 1420 Rollie Hemsley	.15	.07
☐ 1421 Lou Gehrig	1.50	.70
☐ 1422 Tom Sunkel	.15	.07
☐ 1423 Tris Speaker	.40	.18
☐ 1424 Chick Fewster	.15	.07
☐ 1425 Lou Boudreau	.40	.18
☐ 1426 Hank Leiber	.15	.07
☐ 1427 Eddie Mayo	.15	.07
☐ 1428 Charley Gelbert	.15	.07
☐ 1429 Jackie Hayes	.15	.07
☐ 1430 Checklist	.15	.07
☐ NNO Babe Ruth 100th Birthday	2.00	.90

1995 Conlon TSN Griffey Jr.

Titled "In the Zone," this eight-card standard-size set commemorates legends of the game from different eras by comparing Ken Griffey, Jr. to eight players from the Conlon era. No more than 50,000 sets were printed. Six cards were in each 110-card clamshell package, three were inserted in the 55-card clamshell, and there is one per 22-card clamshell. The other two cards were available through a mail-in offer. The fronts feature a color action cut-out of Ken Griffey superimposed over a color photo of the player mentioned on the card. Both players' names, along with the set logo, also appear on the fronts. On a ghosted color action Ken Griffey photo, the backs carry a small, black-and-white photo of the past player, along with a description of how those two players are alike.

	MINT	NRMT
COMPLETE SET (8)	12.50	5.50
COMMON CARD (1-8)	1.00	.45
☐ 1 Ken Griffey Jr.	3.00	1.35
Babe Ruth		
☐ 2 Ken Griffey Jr.	2.50	1.10
Lou Gehrig		
☐ 3 Ken Griffey Jr.	2.00	.90
Ty Cobb		
☐ 4 Ken Griffey Jr.	1.50	.70
Jimmie Foxx		
☐ 5 Ken Griffey Jr.	1.50	.70
Mel Ott		
☐ 6 Ken Griffey Jr.	2.50	1.10
Shoeless Joe Jackson		
☐ 7 Ken Griffey Jr.	1.50	.70
Tris Speaker		
☐ 8 Ken Griffey Jr.	1.00	.45
Jim(Sunny) Bottomley		

1914 Cracker Jack E145-1

The cards in this 144-card set measure approximately 2 1/4" by 3". This "Series of colored pictures of Famous Ball Players and Managers" was issued in packages of Cracker Jack in 1914. The cards have tinted photos set against red backgrounds and many are found with caramel stains. The set also contains Federal League players. The company claims to have printed 15 million cards. The 1914 series can be distinguished from the 1915 issue by the advertising found on the back of the cards. Team names are included for some players to show differences between the 1914 and 1915 issue.

	EX-MT	VG-E
COMPLETE SET (144)	45000.00	20200.00
COMMON CARD (1-144)	150.00	70.00
☐ 1 Otto Knabe	200.00	90.00
☐ 2 Frank Baker	350.00	160.00
☐ 3 Joe Tinker	350.00	160.00
☐ 4 Larry Doyle	150.00	70.00
☐ 5 Ward Miller	150.00	70.00
☐ 6 Eddie Plank	600.00	275.00
Phila. AL		
☐ 7 Eddie Collins	450.00	200.00
Phila. AL		
☐ 8 Rube Oldring	150.00	70.00
☐ 9 Artie Hoffman	150.00	70.00
☐ 10 John McInnis	150.00	70.00
☐ 11 George Stovall	150.00	70.00
☐ 12 Connie Mack MG	500.00	220.00
☐ 13 Art Wilson	150.00	70.00
☐ 14 Sam Crawford	300.00	135.00
☐ 15 Reb Russell	150.00	70.00
☐ 16 Howie Camnitz	150.00	70.00
☐ 17 Roger Bresnahan	350.00	160.00
Catcher		
☐ 18 Johnny Evers	350.00	160.00
☐ 19 Chief Bender	450.00	200.00
Phila. AL		
☐ 20 Cy Falkenberg	150.00	70.00
☐ 21 Heinie Zimmerman	150.00	70.00
☐ 22 Joe Wood	300.00	135.00
☐ 23 Charles Comiskey OWN	300.00	135.00
☐ 24 George Mullen	150.00	70.00
☐ 25 Michael Simon	150.00	70.00
☐ 26 James Scott	150.00	70.00
☐ 27 Bill Carrigan	150.00	70.00
☐ 28 Jack Barry	150.00	70.00
☐ 29 Vean Gregg	175.00	80.00
Cleveland		
☐ 30 Ty Cobb	6000.00	2700.00
☐ 31 Heinie Wagner	150.00	70.00
☐ 32 Mordecai Brown	300.00	135.00
☐ 33 Amos Strunk	150.00	70.00
☐ 34 Ira Thomas	150.00	70.00
☐ 35 Harry Hooper	300.00	135.00
☐ 36 Ed Walsh	300.00	135.00
☐ 37 Grover C. Alexander	800.00	350.00
☐ 38 Red Dooin	175.00	80.00
Phila. NL		
☐ 39 Chick Gandil	325.00	145.00
☐ 40 Jimmy Austin	175.00	80.00
St.L. AL		
☐ 41 Tommy Leach	150.00	70.00
☐ 42 Al Bridwell	150.00	70.00
☐ 43 Rube Marquard	350.00	160.00
NY NL		
☐ 44 Charles Tesreau	150.00	70.00
☐ 45 Fred Luderus	150.00	70.00
☐ 46 Bob Groom	150.00	70.00
☐ 47 Josh Devore	175.00	80.00
Phila. NL		
☐ 48 Harry Lord	250.00	110.00
☐ 49 John Miller	150.00	70.00
☐ 50 John Hummell	150.00	70.00
☐ 51 Nap Rucker	150.00	70.00
☐ 52 Zach Wheat	350.00	160.00
☐ 53 Otto Miller	150.00	70.00
☐ 54 Marty O'Toole	150.00	70.00
☐ 55 Dick Hoblitzel	175.00	80.00
Cinc.		
☐ 56 Clyde Milan	150.00	70.00
☐ 57 Walter Johnson	1600.00	700.00
☐ 58 Wally Schang	150.00	70.00
☐ 59 Harry Gessler	150.00	70.00
☐ 60 Rollie Zeider	250.00	110.00
☐ 61 Ray Schalk	300.00	135.00
☐ 62 Jay Cashion	300.00	135.00
☐ 63 Babe Adams	150.00	70.00
☐ 64 Jimmy Archer	150.00	70.00
☐ 65 Tris Speaker	700.00	325.00
☐ 66 Napoleon Lajoie	800.00	350.00
Cleve.		
☐ 67 Otis Crandall	150.00	70.00
☐ 68 Honus Wagner	1800.00	800.00
☐ 69 John McGraw	450.00	200.00
☐ 70 Fred Clarke	300.00	135.00
☐ 71 Chief Meyers	150.00	70.00
☐ 72 John Boehling	150.00	70.00
☐ 73 Max Carey	300.00	135.00
☐ 74 Frank Owens	150.00	70.00
☐ 75 Miller Huggins	300.00	135.00
☐ 76 Claude Hendrix	150.00	70.00
☐ 77 Hughie Jennings MG	300.00	135.00
☐ 78 Fred Merkle	175.00	80.00
☐ 79 Ping Bodie	150.00	70.00
☐ 80 Ed Ruelbach	150.00	70.00
☐ 81 Jim C. Delehanty	150.00	70.00
☐ 82 Gavvy Cravath	175.00	80.00
☐ 83 Russ Ford	150.00	70.00
☐ 84 Elmer E. Knetzer	150.00	70.00
☐ 85 Buck Herzog	150.00	70.00
☐ 86 Burt Shotton	150.00	70.00
☐ 87 Forrest Cady	150.00	70.00
☐ 88 Christy Mathewson	3000.00	1350.00
Pitching		
☐ 89 Lawrence Cheney	150.00	70.00
☐ 90 Frank Smith	150.00	70.00
☐ 91 Roger Peckinpaugh	150.00	70.00
☐ 92 Al Demaree N.Y. NL	175.00	80.00
☐ 93 Del Pratt	250.00	110.00
Throwing		
☐ 94 Eddie Cicotte	300.00	135.00
☐ 95 Ray Keating	150.00	70.00
☐ 96 Beals Becker	150.00	70.00
☐ 97 John(Rube) Benton	150.00	70.00
☐ 98 Frank LaPorte	150.00	70.00
☐ 99 Frank Chance	1500.00	700.00
☐ 100 Thomas Seaton	150.00	70.00
☐ 101 Frank Schulte	150.00	70.00
☐ 102 Ray Fisher	150.00	70.00
☐ 103 Joe Jackson	8000.00	3600.00
☐ 104 Vic Saier	150.00	70.00
☐ 105 James Lavender	150.00	70.00
☐ 106 Joe Birmingham	150.00	70.00
☐ 107 Tom Downey	150.00	70.00
☐ 108 Sherry Magee	175.00	80.00
Phila. NL		
☐ 109 Fred Blanding	150.00	70.00
☐ 110 Bob Bescher	150.00	70.00
☐ 111 Jim Callahan	250.00	110.00
☐ 112 Ed Sweeney	150.00	70.00
☐ 113 George Suggs	150.00	70.00
☐ 114 Geo.J. Moriarty	150.00	70.00
☐ 115 Addison Brennan	150.00	70.00
☐ 116 Rollie Zeider	150.00	70.00
☐ 117 Ted Easterly	150.00	70.00
☐ 118 Ed Konetchy	175.00	80.00
Pittsburgh		
☐ 119 George Perring	150.00	70.00
☐ 120 Mike Doolan	150.00	70.00
☐ 121 Hub Perdue	175.00	80.00
Boston NL		
☐ 122 Owen Bush	150.00	70.00
☐ 123 Slim Sallee	150.00	70.00
☐ 124 Earl Moore	150.00	70.00
☐ 125 Bert Niehoff	175.00	80.00
☐ 126 Walter Blair	150.00	70.00
☐ 127 Butch Schmidt	150.00	70.00
☐ 128 Steve Evans	150.00	70.00
☐ 129 Ray Caldwell	150.00	70.00
☐ 130 Ivy Wingo	150.00	70.00
☐ 131 George Baumgardner	150.00	70.00
☐ 132 Les Nunamaker	150.00	70.00
☐ 133 Branch Rickey	450.00	200.00
☐ 134 Armando Marsans	175.00	80.00
Cincinnati		
☐ 135 Bill Killefer	150.00	70.00
☐ 136 Rabbit Maranville	300.00	135.00
☐ 137 William Rariden	150.00	70.00
☐ 138 Hank Gowdy	150.00	70.00
☐ 139 Rebel Oakes	150.00	70.00
☐ 140 Danny Murphy	150.00	70.00
☐ 141 Cy Barger	150.00	70.00
☐ 142 Eugene Packard	150.00	70.00
☐ 143 Jake Daubert	150.00	70.00
☐ 144 James C. Walsh	175.00	80.00

1915 Cracker Jack E145-2

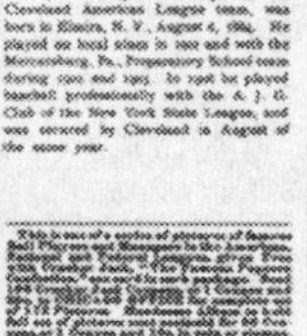

The cards in this 176-card set measure approximately 2 1/4" by 3". When turned over in a lateral motion, a 1915 "series of 176" Cracker Jack card shows the back printing upside-down. Cards were available in boxes of Cracker Jack or from the company for "100 Cracker Jack coupons, or one coupon and 25 cents." An album was available for "50 coupons or one coupon and 10 cents." Because of this send-in offer, the 1915 Cracker Jack cards are noticeably easier to find than the 1914 Cracker Jack cards, although obviously neither set is plentiful. The set essentially duplicates E145-1 (1914 Cracker Jack) except for some additional cards and new poses. Players in the Federal League are indicated by FED in the checklist below.

	EX-MT	VG-E
COMPLETE SET (176)	35000.00	15800.00
COMMON CARD (1-144)	100.00	45.00
COMMON CARD (145-176)	125.00	55.00
☐ 1 Otto Knabe	175.00	80.00
☐ 2 Frank Baker	300.00	135.00
☐ 3 Joe Tinker	300.00	135.00
☐ 4 Larry Doyle	110.00	50.00
☐ 5 Ward Miller	100.00	45.00
☐ 6 Eddie Plank	450.00	200.00
St.L. FED		
☐ 7 Eddie Collins	350.00	160.00

Chicago AL
☐ 8 Rube Oldring 100.00 45.00
☐ 9 Artie Hoffman 100.00 45.00
☐ 10 John McInnis 110.00 50.00
☐ 11 George Stovall 100.00 45.00
☐ 12 Connie Mack MG 350.00 160.00
☐ 13 Art Wilson 100.00 45.00
☐ 14 Sam Crawford 250.00 110.00
☐ 15 Reb Russell 100.00 45.00
☐ 16 Howie Camnitz 100.00 45.00
☐ 17 Roger Bresnahan 250.00 110.00
☐ 18 Johnny Evers 300.00 135.00
☐ 19 Chief Bender 350.00 160.00
Baltimore FED
☐ 20 Cy Falkenberg 100.00 45.00
☐ 21 Heinie Zimmerman 100.00 45.00
☐ 22 Joe Wood 250.00 110.00
☐ 23 Charles Comiskey OWN 250.00 110.00
☐ 24 George Mullen 100.00 45.00
☐ 25 Michael Simon 100.00 45.00
☐ 26 James Scott 100.00 45.00
☐ 27 Bill Carrigan 100.00 45.00
☐ 28 Jack Barry 100.00 45.00
☐ 29 Vean Gregg 110.00 50.00
Boston AL
☐ 30 Ty Cobb 4500.00 2000.00
☐ 31 Heinie Wagner 100.00 45.00
☐ 32 Mordecai Brown 250.00 110.00
☐ 33 Amos Strunk 100.00 45.00
☐ 34 Ira Thomas 100.00 45.00
☐ 35 Harry Hooper 250.00 110.00
☐ 36 Ed Walsh 250.00 110.00
☐ 37 Grover C. Alexander 600.00 275.00
☐ 38 Red Dooin 110.00 50.00
Cincinnati
☐ 39 Chick Gandil 275.00 125.00
☐ 40 Jimmy Austin 110.00 50.00
Pitts. FED
☐ 41 Tommy Leach 100.00 45.00
☐ 42 Al Bridwell 100.00 45.00
☐ 43 Rube Marquard 350.00 160.00
Brooklyn FED
☐ 44 Charles(Jeff) Tesreau 100.00 45.00
☐ 45 Fred Luderus 100.00 45.00
☐ 46 Bob Groom 100.00 45.00
☐ 47 Josh Devore 110.00 50.00
Boston NL
☐ 48 Steve O'Neill 110.00 50.00
☐ 49 John Miller 100.00 45.00
☐ 50 John Hummell 100.00 45.00
☐ 51 Nap Rucker 110.00 50.00
☐ 52 Zach Wheat 300.00 135.00
☐ 53 Otto Miller 100.00 45.00
☐ 54 Marty O'Toole 100.00 45.00
☐ 55 Dick Hoblitzel 110.00 50.00
Boston AL
☐ 56 Clyde Milan 110.00 50.00
☐ 57 Walter Johnson 1200.00 550.00
☐ 58 Wally Schang 110.00 50.00
☐ 59 Harry Gessler 110.00 50.00
☐ 60 Oscar Dugey 110.00 50.00
☐ 61 Ray Schalk 250.00 110.00
☐ 62 Willie Mitchell 110.00 50.00
☐ 63 Babe Adams 110.00 50.00
☐ 64 Jimmy Archer 110.00 50.00
☐ 65 Tris Speaker 500.00 220.00
☐ 66 Napoleon Lajoie 600.00 275.00
Phila. AL
☐ 67 Otis Crandall 110.00 50.00
☐ 68 Honus Wagner 1400.00 650.00
☐ 69 John McGraw MG 300.00 135.00
☐ 70 Fred Clarke 250.00 110.00
☐ 71 Chief Meyers 110.00 50.00
☐ 72 John Boehling 100.00 45.00
☐ 73 Max Carey 250.00 110.00
☐ 74 Frank Owens 100.00 45.00
☐ 75 Miller Huggins 250.00 110.00
☐ 76 Claude Hendrix 100.00 45.00
☐ 77 Hughie Jennings MG 250.00 110.00
☐ 78 Fred Merkle 110.00 50.00
☐ 79 Ping Bodie 110.00 50.00
☐ 80 Ed Ruelbach 110.00 50.00
☐ 81 Jim C. Delehanty 110.00 50.00
☐ 82 Gavvy Cravath 110.00 50.00
☐ 83 Russ Ford 100.00 45.00
☐ 84 Elmer E. Knetzer 100.00 45.00
☐ 85 Buck Herzog 100.00 45.00
☐ 86 Burt Shotton 100.00 45.00
☐ 87 Forrest Cady 100.00 45.00
☐ 88 Christy Mathewson 1500.00 700.00
Portrait
☐ 89 Lawrence Cheney 100.00 45.00
☐ 90 Frank Smith 100.00 45.00
☐ 91 Roger Peckinpaugh 110.00 50.00
☐ 92 Al Demaree 110.00 50.00
Phila. NL
☐ 93 Del Pratt 175.00 80.00
Portrait
☐ 94 Eddie Cicotte 250.00 110.00
☐ 95 Ray Keating 100.00 45.00
☐ 96 Beals Becker 100.00 45.00
☐ 97 John(Rube) Benton 100.00 45.00
☐ 98 Frank LaPorte 100.00 45.00
☐ 99 Hal Chase 300.00 135.00
☐ 100 Thomas Seaton 100.00 45.00
☐ 101 Frank Schulte 100.00 45.00
☐ 102 Ray Fisher 100.00 45.00
☐ 103 Joe Jackson 6500.00 2900.00
☐ 104 Vic Saier 100.00 45.00
☐ 105 James Lavender 100.00 45.00
☐ 106 Joe Birmingham 100.00 45.00
☐ 107 Thomas Downey 100.00 45.00
☐ 108 Sherry Magee 110.00 50.00
Boston NL
☐ 109 Fred Blanding 100.00 45.00
☐ 110 Bob Bescher 100.00 45.00
☐ 111 Herbie Moran 110.00 50.00
☐ 112 Ed Sweeney 100.00 45.00
☐ 113 George Suggs 100.00 45.00
☐ 114 Geo.J. Moriarty 110.00 50.00
☐ 115 Addison Brennan 100.00 45.00
☐ 116 Rollie Zeider 100.00 45.00
☐ 117 Ted Easterly 100.00 45.00
☐ 118 Ed Konetchy 110.00 50.00
Pitts. FED
☐ 119 George Perring 100.00 45.00
☐ 120 Mike Doolan 100.00 45.00
☐ 121 Hub Perdue 110.00 50.00
St. Louis NL
☐ 122 Owen Bush 100.00 45.00
☐ 123 Slim Sallee 100.00 45.00
☐ 124 Earl Moore 100.00 45.00
☐ 125 Bert Niehoff 110.00 50.00
Phila. NL
☐ 126 Walter Blair 100.00 45.00
☐ 127 Butch Schmidt 100.00 45.00
☐ 128 Steve Evans 100.00 45.00
☐ 129 Ray Caldwell 100.00 45.00
☐ 130 Ivy Wingo 100.00 45.00
☐ 131 Geo. Baumgardner 100.00 45.00
☐ 132 Les Nunamaker 100.00 45.00
☐ 133 Branch Rickey 300.00 135.00
☐ 134 Armando Marsans 110.00 50.00
St.L. FED
☐ 135 William Killefer 100.00 45.00
☐ 136 Rabbit Maranville 250.00 110.00
☐ 137 William Rariden 100.00 45.00
☐ 138 Hank Gowdy 110.00 50.00
☐ 139 Rebel Oakes 100.00 45.00
☐ 140 Danny Murphy 100.00 45.00
☐ 141 Cy Barger 100.00 45.00
☐ 142 Eugene Packard 100.00 45.00
☐ 143 Jake Daubert 110.00 50.00
☐ 144 James C. Walsh 100.00 45.00
☐ 145 Ted Cather 125.00 55.00
☐ 146 George Tyler 125.00 55.00
☐ 147 Lee Magee 125.00 55.00
☐ 148 Owen Wilson 125.00 55.00
☐ 149 Hal Janvrin 125.00 55.00
☐ 150 Doc Johnston 125.00 55.00
☐ 151 George Whitted 125.00 55.00
☐ 152 George McQuillen 125.00 55.00
☐ 153 Bill James 125.00 55.00
☐ 154 Dick Rudolph 125.00 55.00
☐ 155 Joe Connolly 125.00 55.00
☐ 156 Jean Dubuc 125.00 55.00
☐ 157 George Kaiserling 125.00 55.00
☐ 158 Fritz Maisel 125.00 55.00
☐ 159 Heinie Groh 125.00 55.00
☐ 160 Benny Kauff 125.00 55.00
☐ 161 Edd Roush 300.00 135.00
☐ 162 George Stallings MG 125.00 55.00
☐ 163 Bert Whaling 125.00 55.00
☐ 164 Bob Shawkey 125.00 55.00
☐ 165 Eddie Murphy 125.00 55.00
☐ 166 Joe Bush 125.00 55.00
☐ 167 Clark Griffith 300.00 135.00
☐ 168 Vin Campbell 125.00 55.00
☐ 169 Raymond Collins 125.00 55.00
☐ 170 Hans Lobert 125.00 55.00
☐ 171 Earl Hamilton 125.00 55.00
☐ 172 Erskine Mayer 125.00 55.00
☐ 173 Tilly Walker 125.00 55.00
☐ 174 Robert Veach 125.00 55.00
☐ 175 Joseph Benz 125.00 55.00
☐ 176 Hippo Vaughn 175.00 80.00

1982 Cracker Jack

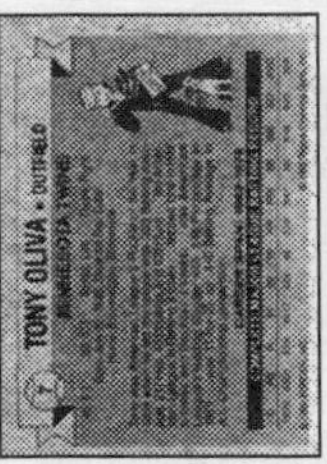

The cards in this 16-card set measure 2 1/2" by 3 1/2"; cards came in two sheets of eight cards, plus an advertising card with a title in the center, which measured approximately 7 1/2" by 10 1/2". Cracker Jack reentered the baseball card market for the first time since 1915 to promote the first "Old Timers Baseball Classic" held July 19, 1982. The color player photos have a Cracker Jack border and have either green (NL) or red (AL) frame lines and name panels. The Cracker Jack logo appears on both sides of each card, with AL players numbered 1-8 and NL players numbered 9-16. Of the 16 ballplayers pictured, five did not appear at the game. At first, the two sheets were available only through the mail but are now commonly found in hobby circles. The set was prepared for Cracker Jack by Topps. The prices below reflect individual card prices; the price for complete panels would be about the same as the sum of the card prices for those players on the panel due to the easy availability of uncut sheets.

	NRMT	VG-E
COMPLETE SET (16)	10.00	4.50
COMMON CARD (1-16)	.25	.11

☐ 1 Larry Doby .25 .11
☐ 2 Bob Feller .75 .35
☐ 3 Whitey Ford 1.00 .45
☐ 4 Al Kaline 1.00 .45
☐ 5 Harmon Killebrew .50 .23
☐ 6 Mickey Mantle 5.00 2.20
☐ 7 Tony Oliva .25 .11
☐ 8 Brooks Robinson 1.00 .45
☐ 9 Hank Aaron 3.00 1.35
☐ 10 Ernie Banks 1.50 .70
☐ 11 Ralph Kiner .50 .23
☐ 12 Ed Mathews .50 .23
☐ 13 Willie Mays 3.00 1.35
☐ 14 Robin Roberts .75 .35
☐ 15 Duke Snider 1.50 .70
☐ 16 Warren Spahn .75 .35

1993 Cracker Jack

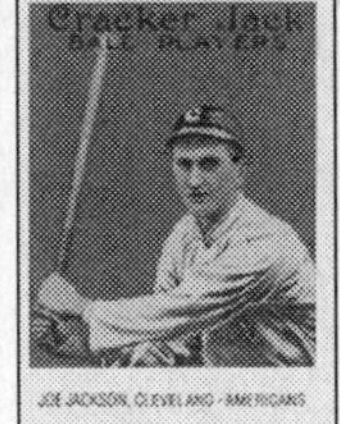

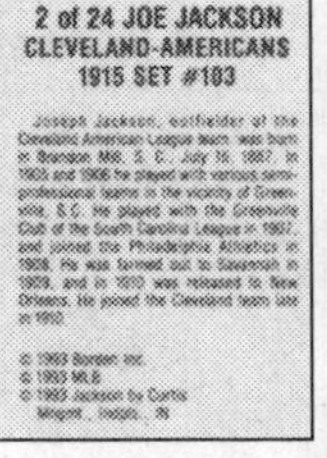

2 of 24 JOE JACKSON
CLEVELAND-AMERICANS
1915 SET #103

To commemorate its 100th anniversary, Cracker Jack issued a 24-card set of miniature replicas of its 1915 set. One mini-card was inserted into each specially marked single, triple, and value-pack box. A mini-card holder album and a fact booklet that includes each player's lifetime stats were available for 6.95 through a mail-in offer. The album features room for 72 cards implying that Cracker Jack would like to continue this series into future years as well. Each minicard measures approximately 1 1/4" by 1 3/4" and features on its front a white-bordered color portrait of the player on a brick-colored background. The player's name, team, and league appear in the white margin below the picture and "Cracker Jack Ball Players" appears at the top. The white back displays the player's name, team, and league at the top, along with his card number from the 1915 set, followed below by a biography.

	MINT	NRMT
COMPLETE SET (24)	15.00	6.75
COMMON CARD (1-24)	.25	.11

☐ 1 Ty Cobb 3.00 1.35
☐ 2 Joe Jackson 3.00 1.35
☐ 3 Honus Wagner 1.50 .70
☐ 4 Christy Mathewson 1.25 .55
☐ 5 Walter Johnson 1.50 .70
☐ 6 Tris Speaker 1.00 .45
☐ 7 Grover Alexander 1.00 .45
☐ 8 Nap Lajoie 1.00 .45
☐ 9 Rube Marquard .50 .23

☐ 10 Connie Mack MG	.75	.35
☐ 11 Johnny Evers	.75	.35
☐ 12 Branch Rickey	.50	.23
☐ 13 Fred Clarke MG	.50	.23
☐ 14 Harry Hooper	.50	.23
☐ 15 Zack Wheat	.50	.23
☐ 16 Joe Tinker	.50	.20
☐ 17 Eddie Collins	1.00	.45
☐ 18 Mordecai Brown	.50	.23
☐ 19 Eddie Plank	.50	.23
☐ 20 Rabbit Maranville	.50	.23
☐ 21 John McGraw MG	.75	.35
☐ 22 Miller Huggins	.50	.23
☐ 23 Ed Walsh	.50	.23
☐ 24 Joe Bush	.25	.11

1997 Cracker Jack

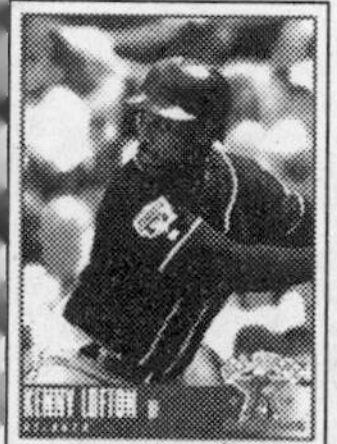
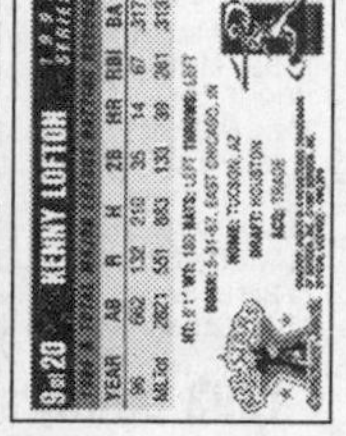

This 20-card set was distributed in Cracker Jack boxes and measures approximately 1 5/16" by 1 3/4". The fronts feature color action player photos in white borders. The backs carry player information and statistics.

	MINT	NRMT
COMPLETE SET (20)	20.00	9.00
COMMON CARD (1-20)	.50	.23
☐ 1 Jeff Bagwell	2.00	.90
☐ 2 Chuck Knoblauch	1.00	.45
☐ 3 Cal Ripken	4.00	1.80
☐ 4 Chipper Jones	3.00	1.35
☐ 5 Derek Jeter	3.00	1.35
☐ 6 Barry Larkin	.50	.23
☐ 7 Bernie Williams	1.00	.45
☐ 8 Barry Bonds	1.25	.55
☐ 9 Kenny Lofton	1.25	.55
☐ 10 Gary Sheffield	.75	.35
☐ 11 Sammy Sosa	.75	.35
☐ 12 Paul Molitor	1.00	.45
☐ 13 Andres Galarraga	1.00	.45
☐ 14 Ivan Rodriguez	1.25	.55
☐ 15 Mike Piazza	3.00	1.35
☐ 16 Andy Pettitte	1.00	.45
☐ 17 Tom Glavine	.50	.23
☐ 18 Albert Belle	1.25	.55
☐ 19 Mark McGwire	2.00	.90
☐ 20 Mo Vaughn	1.25	.55

1995 D3

Manufactured by Topps, this set consists of 59 three-dimension standard-size cards of better players. Utilizing uncluttered fronts, the player's name is at the top with the set logo toward bottom right. The backs offer a small photo with statistical breakdowns in areas such as Home, Away, Day, Night, etc. A second series was planned for this issue but was never issued due to consumer disinterest.

	MINT	NRMT
COMPLETE SET (59)	15.00	6.75
COMMON CARD (1-59)	.10	.05
☐ 1 David Justice	.75	.35
☐ 2 Cal Ripken	4.00	1.80
☐ 3 Ruben Sierra	.10	.05
☐ 4 Roberto Alomar	.75	.35
☐ 5 Denny Martinez	.10	.05
☐ 6 Todd Zeile	.10	.05
☐ 7 Albert Belle	1.25	.55
☐ 8 Chuck Knoblauch	.75	.35
☐ 9 Roger Clemens	2.00	.90
☐ 10 Cal Eldred	.10	.05
☐ 11 Dennis Eckersley	.25	.11
☐ 12 Andy Benes	.25	.11
☐ 13 Moises Alou	.25	.11
☐ 14 Andres Galarraga	.75	.35
☐ 15 Jim Thome	1.00	.45
☐ 16 Tim Salmon	.75	.35
☐ 17 Carlos Garcia	.10	.05
☐ 18 Scott Leius	.10	.05
☐ 19 Jeff Montgomery	.10	.05
☐ 20 Brian Anderson	.10	.05
☐ 21 Will Clark	.50	.23
☐ 22 Bobby Bonilla	.25	.11
☐ 23 Mike Stanley	.10	.05
☐ 24 Barry Bonds	1.25	.55
☐ 25 Jeff Conine	.25	.11
☐ 26 Paul O'Neill	.25	.11
☐ 27 Mike Piazza	3.00	1.35
☐ 28 Tom Glavine	.25	.11
☐ 29 Jim Edmonds	.75	.35
☐ 30 Lou Whitaker	.25	.11
☐ 31 Jeff Frye	.10	.05
☐ 32 Ivan Rodriguez	1.25	.55
☐ 33 Bret Boone	.10	.05
☐ 34 Mike Greenwell	.10	.05
☐ 35 Mark Grace	.50	.23
☐ 36 Darren Lewis	.10	.05
☐ 37 Don Mattingly	1.50	.70
☐ 38 Jose Rijo	.10	.05
☐ 39 Robin Ventura	.25	.11
☐ 40 Bob Hamelin	.10	.05
☐ 41 Tim Wallach	.10	.05
☐ 42 Tony Gwynn	2.50	1.10
☐ 43 Ken Griffey Jr.	5.00	2.20
☐ 44 Doug Drabek	.10	.05
☐ 45 Rafael Palmeiro	.50	.23
☐ 46 Dean Palmer	.25	.11
☐ 47 Bip Roberts	.10	.05
☐ 48 Barry Larkin	.50	.23
☐ 49 Dave Nilsson	.10	.05
☐ 50 Wil Cordero	.10	.05
☐ 51 Travis Fryman	.25	.11
☐ 52 Chuck Carr	.10	.05
☐ 53 Rey Sanchez	.10	.05
☐ 54 Walt Weiss	.10	.05
☐ 55 Joe Carter	.25	.11
☐ 56 Len Dykstra	.25	.11
☐ 57 Orlando Merced	.10	.05
☐ 58 Ozzie Smith	1.25	.55
☐ 59 Chris Gomez	.10	.05
☐ PB1 Greg Gagne Baseball Promo	1.00	.45

1995 D3 Zone

This three-dimensional, six-card set was inserted in Topps D3 packs. They were inserted one in three hobby packs and one in six retail packs. The 3D front has a player photo surrounded by baseballs. The player's name is at the top with the set logo at the bottom. Horizontal backs offer a small player photo and a synopsis of various hot streaks in 1994. Cards are numbered with a "DIII" prefix.

	MINT	NRMT
COMPLETE SET (6)	15.00	6.75
COMMON CARD (1-6)	1.00	.45
☐ 1 Frank Thomas	8.00	3.60
☐ 2 Kirby Puckett	4.00	1.80
☐ 3 Jeff Bagwell	4.00	1.80
☐ 4 Fred McGriff	1.00	.45
☐ 5 Raul Mondesi	1.50	.70
☐ 6 Kenny Lofton	2.00	.90

1994 Dairy Queen Griffey Jr.

The 1994 Dairy Queen Ken Griffey Jr. set consists of ten standard-size cards. The cards were distributed in 5-card

packs at the restaurants, with the gold cards randomly inserted. The fronts feature color action shots of Griffey with the set title's logo appearing in the upper left corner of the picture. Ken Griffey's name is printed below the photo in gold block lettering beside the Dairy Queen logo. The photo is bordered in gold on some sets, and in green on others. The production run on the green-border sets was 90,000, while that of the gold-bordered sets was 10,000. The gold versions are valued at double the values listed below. Except for card number 2, the backs are in a horizontal format, with a posed or action photo on the left side. The right side has a ghosted set logo on a gray marbleized background. The card title and a brief narrative appears on the right side. According to the information on the back, Ken Griffey Jr. personally authorized the set. The cards are numbered on the back.

	MINT	NRMT
COMPLETE SET (10)	10.00	4.50
COMMON CARD (1-10)	1.25	.55
☐ 1 Ken Griffey Jr. The Spider Man Catch	1.25	.55
☐ 2 Ken Griffey Jr. Back to Back Home Runs	1.25	.55
☐ 3 Ken Griffey Jr. Hit .327 in 1991	1.25	.55
☐ 4 Ken Griffey Jr. 1992 All-Star MVP	1.25	.55
☐ 5 Ken Griffey Jr. Dialing Long Distance	1.25	.55
☐ 6 Ken Griffey Jr. 8 Straight Home Runs	1.25	.55
☐ 7 Ken Griffey Jr. 4-Time Gold Glove Winner	1.25	.55
☐ 8 Ken Griffey Jr. 45 Home Runs in 1993	1.25	.55
☐ 9 Ken Griffey Jr. Major League Career Hitting Record	1.25	.55
☐ 10 Ken Griffey Jr. Looking to 1994	1.25	.55

1954 Dan Dee

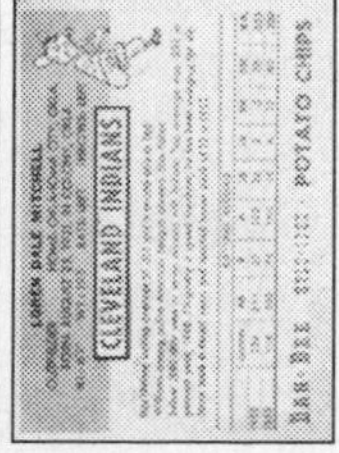

The cards in this 29-card set measure approximately 2 1/2" by 3 5/8". Most of the cards marketed by Dan Dee in bags of potato chips in 1954 depict players from the Cleveland Indians or Pittsburgh Pirates. The Pitttsburgh Pirates players in the set are much tougher to find than the Cleveland Indians players. The pictures used for New York Yankees players were also employed in the Briggs and Stahl-Meyer sets. Dan Dee cards have a waxed surface, but are commonly found with product stains. Paul Smith and Walker Cooper are considered the known scarcities. The catalog designation for this set is F342. These unnumbered cards are listed below in alphabetical order.

	NRMT	VG-E
COMPLETE SET (29)	4500.00	2000.00
COMMON CARD (1-29)	50.00	22.00
COMMON PIRATE CARD	65.00	29.00
☐ 1 Bobby Avila	50.00	22.00
☐ 2 Hank Bauer	60.00	27.00
☐ 3 Walker Cooper SP Pittsburgh Pirates	300.00	135.00
☐ 4 Larry Doby	75.00	34.00

☐ 5 Luke Easter	60.00	27.00
☐ 6 Bob Feller	200.00	90.00
☐ 7 Bob Friend	90.00	40.00
Pittsburgh Pirates		
☐ 8 Mike Garcia	50.00	22.00
☐ 9 Sid Gordon	65.00	29.00
Pittsburgh Pirates		
☐ 10 Jim Hegan	50.00	22.00
☐ 11 Gil Hodges	125.00	55.00
☐ 12 Art Houtteman	50.00	22.00
☐ 13 Monte Irvin	100.00	45.00
☐ 14 Paul LaPalme	65.00	29.00
Pittsburgh Pirates		
☐ 15 Bob Lemon	100.00	45.00
☐ 16 Al Lopez MG	100.00	45.00
☐ 17 Mickey Mantle	1800.00	800.00
☐ 18 Dale Mitchell	50.00	22.00
☐ 19 Phil Rizzuto	200.00	90.00
☐ 20 Curt Roberts	65.00	29.00
Pittsburgh Pirates		
☐ 21 Al Rosen	60.00	27.00
☐ 22 Red Schoendienst	100.00	45.00
☐ 23 Paul Smith SP	500.00	220.00
Pittsburgh Pirates		
☐ 24 Duke Snider	225.00	100.00
☐ 25 George Strickland	50.00	22.00
☐ 26 Max Surkont	65.00	29.00
Pittsburgh Pirates		
☐ 27 Frank Thomas	150.00	70.00
Pittsburgh Pirates		
☐ 28 Wally Westlake	50.00	22.00
☐ 29 Early Wynn	100.00	45.00

1933 Delong R333

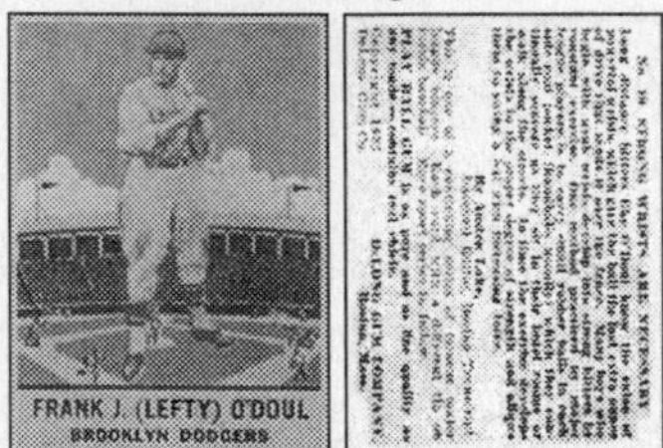

The cards in this 24-card set measure approximately 2" by 3". The 1933 Delong Gum set of 24 multi-colored cards was, along with the 1933 Goudey Big League series, one of the first baseball card sets issued with chewing gum. It was the only card set issued by this company. The reverse text was written by Austen Lake, who also wrote the sports tips found on the Diamond Stars series which began in 1934, leading to speculation that Delong was bought out by National Chicle.

	EX-MT	VG-E
COMPLETE SET (24)	8000.00	3600.00
COMMON CARD (1-24)	150.00	70.00
☐ 1 Marty McManus	165.00	75.00
☐ 2 Al Simmons	350.00	160.00
☐ 3 Oscar Melillo	150.00	70.00
☐ 4 Bill Terry	300.00	135.00
☐ 5 Charlie Gehringer	300.00	135.00
☐ 6 Mickey Cochrane	350.00	160.00
☐ 7 Lou Gehrig	3200.00	1450.00
☐ 8 Kiki Cuyler	275.00	125.00
☐ 9 Bill Urbanski	150.00	70.00
☐ 10 Lefty O'Doul	165.00	75.00
☐ 11 Fred Lindstrom	275.00	125.00
☐ 12 Pie Traynor	300.00	135.00
☐ 13 Rabbit Maranville	275.00	125.00
☐ 14 Lefty Gomez	300.00	135.00
☐ 15 Riggs Stephenson	165.00	75.00
☐ 16 Lon Warneke	150.00	70.00
☐ 17 Pepper Martin	165.00	75.00
☐ 18 Jimmy Dykes	165.00	75.00
☐ 19 Chick Hafey	275.00	125.00
☐ 20 Joe Vosmik	150.00	70.00
☐ 21 Jimmie Foxx	500.00	220.00
☐ 22 Chuck Klein	300.00	135.00
☐ 23 Lefty Grove	450.00	200.00
☐ 24 Goose Goslin	275.00	125.00

1991 Denny's Holograms

The 1991 Denny's Grand Slam hologram baseball card set was produced by Upper Deck. The 26-card standard-size set contains one player from each major league team, who was selected on the basis of the number and circumstances of his grand slam home runs. These cards were available at Denny's only with the purchase of a meal

from the restaurant's Grand Slam menu; each card came sealed in a plastic bag that prevents prior identification. It is estimated that two million cards were printed. The 3-D cards alternate between silver and full color, and the player appears to stand apart from a background of exploding fireworks. A stripe at the top of the card has the player's name and team, while the Upper Deck and Denny's logos appear toward the bottom of the card face. The back has a descriptive account of the player's grand slams. In 1991, if the contest card was a winner, the collector was entitled to a free meal. By the end of the contest, almost half the teams had hit grand slams during the length of the contest. So many teams hit grand slams that that part of the promotion was never repeated. The cards are numbered on the front.

	MINT	NRMT
COMPLETE SET (26)	35.00	16.00
COMMON CARD (1-26)	.75	.35
☐ 1 Ellis Burks	1.00	.45
☐ 2 Cecil Fielder	1.00	.45
☐ 3 Will Clark	2.00	.90
☐ 4 Eric Davis	.75	.35
☐ 5 Dave Parker	1.00	.45
☐ 6 Kelly Gruber	.75	.35
☐ 7 Kent Hrbek	1.00	.45
☐ 8 Don Mattingly	5.00	2.20
☐ 9 Brook Jacoby	.75	.35
☐ 10 Mark McGwire	5.00	2.20
☐ 11 Howard Johnson	.75	.35
☐ 12 Tim Wallach	.75	.35
☐ 13 Ricky Jordan	.75	.35
☐ 14 Andre Dawson	1.50	.70
☐ 15 Eddie Murray	3.00	1.35
☐ 16 Danny Tartabull	.75	.35
☐ 17 Bobby Bonilla	1.00	.45
☐ 18 Benito Santiago	.75	.35
☐ 19 Alvin Davis	.75	.35
☐ 20 Cal Ripken	10.00	4.50
☐ 21 Ruben Sierra	.75	.35
☐ 22 Pedro Guerrero	.75	.35
☐ 23 Wally Joyner	.75	.35
☐ 24 Craig Biggio	2.00	.90
☐ 25 Dave Justice	2.00	.90
☐ 26 Tim Raines	1.00	.45

1992 Denny's Holograms

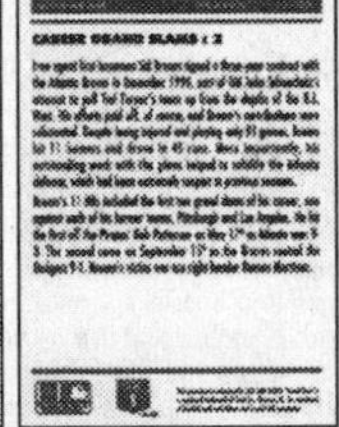

This 26-card standard-size set of holographic cards was produced by Upper Deck for Denny's. The set features one player from each major league team, who was selected on the basis of the number and circumstances of his grand slam home runs. With each order of a Grand Slam meal, the customer received one hologram card. Each hologram shows a cut-out player photo superimposed over a scene from the city in which the team resides. A bar with the words "limited edition" runs along the top of the card, and the words "collector series" run vertically down the right edge. The "1992 Grand Slam" insignia appears in the lower left corner, with the player's name in a bar extending to the right. The backs feature a blue stripe with the player's name across the top. Two red stripes border the top and bottom of a career summary printed in black on a white background.

	MINT	NRMT
COMPLETE SET (26)	30.00	13.50
COMMON CARD (1-26)	.50	.23
☐ 1 Marquis Grissom	.75	.35
☐ 2 Ken Caminiti	1.50	.70
☐ 3 Fred McGriff	1.00	.45
☐ 4 Felix Jose	.50	.23
☐ 5 Jack Clark	.50	.23
☐ 6 Albert Belle	5.00	2.20
☐ 7 Sid Bream	.50	.23
☐ 8 Robin Ventura	.75	.35
☐ 9 Cal Ripken	10.00	4.50
☐ 10 Ryne Sandberg	4.00	1.80
☐ 11 Paul O'Neill	.75	.35
☐ 12 Luis Polonia	.50	.23
☐ 13 Cecil Fielder	.75	.35
☐ 14 Kal Daniels	.50	.23
☐ 15 Brian McRae	.50	.23
☐ 16 Howard Johnson	.50	.23
☐ 17 Greg Vaughn	.75	.35
☐ 18 Dale Murphy	1.50	.70
☐ 19 Kent Hrbek	.75	.35
☐ 20 Barry Bonds	3.00	1.35
☐ 21 Matt Nokes	.50	.23
☐ 22 Jose Canseco	1.50	.70
☐ 23 Jay Buhner	1.00	.45
☐ 24 Will Clark	1.50	.70
☐ 25 Ruben Sierra	.50	.23
☐ 26 Joe Carter	.75	.35

1993 Denny's Holograms

This 28-card standard-size set of holographic cards was produced by Upper Deck for Denny's. The set features one player from each major league team who was selected on the basis of the number and circumstances of his grand slam home runs. With each order of a Grand Slam meal and a Coca-Cola Classic, the customer received one lithogram card. A lithogram card represents the combination of lithography with a hologram. Each hologram shows a cutout player photo superimposed over an action photo. The words "Collector's Series" and the Upper Deck logo are shown along the top. The words "Limited Edition" appear vertically down the left edge. The top, left, and bottom edges are various shades of blue, with the player's name displayed on a team color-coded bar and the Grand Slam insignia in the lower right. The back carries a team color-coded bar with the player's name and team printed across the top. A red box displays the player's career grand slam statistics in the upper left, with a descriptive career summary printed on a light blue background. The cards are numbered on the front. The set ordering follows alphabetical order of team nicknames.

	MINT	NRMT
COMPLETE SET (28)	30.00	13.50
COMMON CARD (1-28)	.50	.23
☐ 1 Chili Davis	.75	.35
☐ 2 Eric Anthony	.50	.23
☐ 3 Rickey Henderson	1.50	.70
☐ 4 Joe Carter	.75	.35
☐ 5 Terry Pendleton	.75	.35
☐ 6 Robin Yount	1.00	.45
☐ 7 Ray Lankford	.75	.35
☐ 8 Ryne Sandberg	3.00	1.35
☐ 9 Darryl Strawberry	.75	.35
☐ 10 Marquis Grissom	.75	.35
☐ 11 Will Clark	1.00	.45
☐ 12 Albert Belle	4.00	1.80
☐ 13 Edgar Martinez	1.00	.45
☐ 14 Benito Santiago	.50	.23
☐ 15 Eddie Murray	2.50	1.10
☐ 16 Cal Ripken	8.00	3.60
☐ 17 Gary Sheffield	1.50	.70
☐ 18 Dave Hollins	.50	.23
☐ 19 Andy Van Slyke	.50	.23
☐ 20 Juan Gonzalez	6.00	2.70
☐ 21 John Valentin	.75	.35
☐ 22 Joe Oliver	.50	.23
☐ 23 Dante Bichette	.75	.35

	MINT	NRMT
☐ 24 Wally Joyner	.50	.23
☐ 25 Cecil Fielder	.75	.35
☐ 26 Kirby Puckett	4.00	1.80
☐ 27 Robin Ventura	.75	.35
☐ 28 Danny Tartabull	.50	.23

1994 Denny's Holograms

This 28-card standard-size set of holographic cards was produced by Upper Deck for Denny's and features a star player from each of the 28 Major League baseball teams. With each order of any "Classic Hits" entree, the customer received one hologram card in a blue poly pack. The fronts feature a full-bleed design that is highlighted by a "multi-level" hologram, with a portrait-style hologram at the forefront and an action photo that appears to be "behind" the other photo. The player's name and Major League Baseball's 125th Anniversary logo round out the fronts. The backs carry the player's color photograph and a brief biography. The cards are arranged alphabetically according to player's last name. There was also a Reggie Jackson Hologram printed. The Jackson card was a contest giveaway for each participating Denny's. The Jackson card is currently valued at between $20-30.

	MINT	NRMT
COMPLETE SET (28)	35.00	16.00
COMMON CARD (1-28)	.25	.11
☐ 1 Jim Abbott	.25	.11
☐ 2 Roberto Alomar	1.00	.45
☐ 3 Kevin Appier	.50	.23
☐ 4 Jeff Bagwell	2.50	1.10
☐ 5 Albert Belle	1.50	.70
☐ 6 Barry Bonds	1.25	.55
☐ 7 Bobby Bonilla	.50	.23
☐ 8 Lenny Dykstra	.25	.11
☐ 9 Cal Eldred	.25	.11
☐ 10 Cecil Fielder	.50	.23
☐ 11 Andres Galarraga	1.00	.45
☐ 12 Ken Griffey Jr.	5.00	2.20
☐ 13 Juan Gonzalez	3.00	1.35
☐ 14 Tony Gwynn	3.00	1.35
☐ 15 Rickey Henderson	.75	.35
☐ 16 Kent Hrbek	.25	.11
☐ 17 David Justice	1.00	.45
☐ 18 Mike Piazza	3.00	1.35
☐ 19 Jose Rijo	.25	.11
☐ 20 Cal Ripken	4.00	1.80
☐ 21 Tim Salmon	1.00	.45
☐ 22 Ryne Sandberg	2.00	.90
☐ 23 Gary Sheffield	1.00	.45
☐ 24 Ozzie Smith	2.00	.90
☐ 25 Frank Thomas	4.00	1.80
☐ 26 Andy Van Slyke	.25	.11
☐ 27 Mo Vaughn	1.00	.45
☐ 28 Larry Walker	1.00	.45

1995 Denny's Holograms

This 28-card standard-size set of holographic cards was produced by Upper Deck for Denny's and features a star player from each of the 28 Major League baseball teams. With each order of an "Classic Hits" entree and a non-alcoholic beverage, the customer received one hologram card in a blue poly pack. Also guests at the restaurants could enter a sweepstakes drawing for a complete set of cards, to be given away by each participating restaurant at the end of the promotion after September 30. The fronts feature a "multilevel" hologram with a portrait-style hologram at the forefront and an action photo that appears to be in front of the rest of the hologram. The player's name, team name and sponsor logos round out the fronts. The backs carry the player's color photograph, a brief biography and statistics.

	MINT	NRMT
COMPLETE SET (28)	30.00	13.50
COMMON CARD (1-28)	.50	.23
☐ 1 Roberto Alomar	1.25	.55
☐ 2 Moises Alou	.75	.35
☐ 3 Jeff Bagwell	2.50	1.10
☐ 4 Albert Belle	1.50	.70
☐ 5 Jason Bere	.50	.23
☐ 6 Roger Clemens	2.00	.90
☐ 7 Darren Daulton	.75	.35
☐ 8 Cecil Fielder	.75	.35
☐ 9 Andres Galarraga	1.25	.55
☐ 10 Juan Gonzalez	3.00	1.35
☐ 11 Ken Griffey Jr.	5.00	2.20
☐ 12 Tony Gwynn	3.00	1.35
☐ 13 Barry Larkin	1.00	.45
☐ 14 Greg Maddux	3.00	1.35
☐ 15 Don Mattingly	2.00	.90
☐ 16 Mark McGwire	3.00	1.35
☐ 17 Orlando Merced	.50	.23
☐ 18 Jeff Montgomery	.50	.23
☐ 19 Rafael Palmeiro	1.00	.45
☐ 20 Mike Piazza	3.00	1.35
☐ 21 Kirby Puckett	2.50	1.10
☐ 22 Bret Saberhagen	.50	.23
☐ 23 Tim Salmon	1.25	.55
☐ 24 Gary Sheffield	1.25	.55
☐ 25 Ozzie Smith	2.00	.90
☐ 26 Sammy Sosa	1.25	.55
☐ 27 Greg Vaughn	.50	.23
☐ 28 Matt Williams	1.00	.45

1996 Denny's Holograms

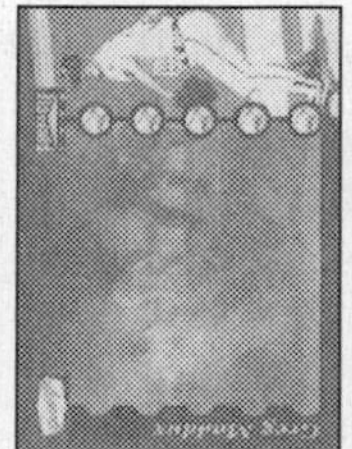

This 28-card set was produced by Pinnacle for Denny's and features a star player from each of the Major League baseball teams. The fronts feature a full motion hologram player image. The backs carry player information. By ordering anything on the menu, a customer could buy two packs. Each Denny's also sponsored a drawing to win all 48 cards (the regular set and both insert sets).

	MINT	NRMT
COMPLETE SET (28)	15.00	6.75
COMMON CARD (1-28)	.15	.07
☐ 1 Greg Maddux	1.50	.70
☐ 2 Cal Ripken	2.00	.90
☐ 3 Frank Thomas	3.00	1.35
☐ 4 Albert Belle	1.00	.45
☐ 5 Mo Vaughn	.75	.35
☐ 6 Jeff Bagwell	1.25	.55
☐ 7 Jay Buhner	.40	.18
☐ 8 Barry Bonds	.75	.35
☐ 9 Ryne Sandberg	1.00	.45
☐ 10 Hideo Nomo	1.25	.55
☐ 11 Kirby Puckett	1.50	.70
☐ 12 Gary Sheffield	.60	.25
☐ 13 Barry Larkin	.40	.18
☐ 14 Wade Boggs	.60	.25
☐ 15 Tony Gwynn	1.25	.55
☐ 16 Tim Salmon	.60	.25
☐ 17 Jason Isringhausen	.15	.07
☐ 18 Cecil Fielder	.25	.11
☐ 19 Dante Bichette	.40	.18
☐ 20 Ozzie Smith	1.00	.45
☐ 21 Ivan Rodriguez	1.00	.45
☐ 22 Kevin Appier	.25	.11
☐ 23 Joe Carter	.25	.11
☐ 24 Moises Alou	.25	.11
☐ 25 Mark McGwire	1.50	.70
☐ 26 Kevin Seitzer	.15	.07
☐ 27 Darren Daulton	.25	.11
☐ 28 Jay Bell	.15	.07

1996 Denny's Holograms Grand Slam

Randomly inserted in packs, this 10-card set features star players from several of the Major League baseball teams. The fronts display a holographic player image with bursting fireworks in the background, while the backs carry player information.

	MINT	NRMT
COMPLETE SET (10)	50.00	22.00
COMMON CARD (1-10)	2.00	.90
*ARTIST PROOFS: 5X BASIC CARDS .	2.00	.90
☐ 1 Cal Ripken	10.00	4.50
☐ 2 Frank Thomas	10.00	4.50
☐ 3 Mike Piazza	7.50	3.40
☐ 4 Tony Gwynn	6.00	2.70
☐ 5 Sammy Sosa	2.00	.90
☐ 6 Barry Bonds	3.00	1.35
☐ 7 Jeff Bagwell	5.00	2.20
☐ 8 Albert Belle	4.00	1.80
☐ 9 Mo Vaughn	2.00	.90
☐ 10 Kirby Puckett	4.00	1.80

1997 Denny's Holograms

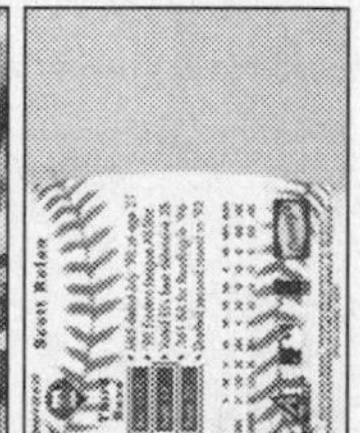

This 29-card set was produced by Pinnacle for Denny's Restaurants and features a star player from each of the Major League baseball teams. Card #29 is a commemorative Jackie Robinson card and card #30 was only distributed in the Cleveland area. The fronts feature 3-D lenticular color player photos. The backs carry a 3-D hologram and player statistics. By purchasing any entree and non-alcoholic beverage, a collector could purchase a card for 59 cents. A significant portion of the proceeds went to support Denny's national charity, Save the Children. The complete set price does not include the regional Larry Doby card

	MINT	NRMT
COMPLETE SET (29)	35.00	16.00
COMMON CARD (1-30)	.50	.23
☐ 1 Tim Salmon	1.25	.55
☐ 2 Rafael Palmeiro	1.00	.45
☐ 3 Mo Vaughn	1.25	.55
☐ 4 Frank Thomas	4.00	1.80
☐ 5 Dave Justice	1.25	.55
☐ 6 Travis Fryman	.50	.23
☐ 7 Johnny Damon	.50	.23
☐ 8 John Jaha	.50	.23
☐ 9 Chuck Knoblauch	1.25	.55
☐ 10 Mark McGwire	3.00	1.35
☐ 11 Alex Rodriguez	4.00	1.80
☐ 12 Juan Gonzalez	2.50	1.10
☐ 13 Roger Clemens	2.50	1.10
☐ 14 Derek Jeter	2.50	1.10
☐ 15 Andruw Jones	2.00	.90
☐ 16 Sammy Sosa	1.25	.55
☐ 17 Barry Larkin	1.00	.45
☐ 18 Dante Bichette	.75	.35
☐ 19 Jeff Bagwell	2.50	1.10
☐ 20 Mike Piazza	3.00	1.35
☐ 21 Gary Sheffield	1.25	.55
☐ 22 Vladimir Guerrero	.75	.35
☐ 23 Todd Hundley	.75	.35
☐ 24 Jason Kendall	.75	.35

☐ 25 Ray Lankford	.75	.35
☐ 26 Ken Caminiti	1.25	.55
☐ 27 Barry Bonds	1.50	.70
☐ 28 Scott Rolen	.75	.35
☐ 29 Jackie Robinson 50th Anniversary Commemorative	5.00	2.20
☐ 30 Larry Doby 50th Anniversary	5.00	2.20

1993 Diamond Marks

This 120-card bookmark set was a collaboration of Barry Colla and Terry Smith. Ten bookmarks and an ad card came in each cello pack. A total production run of only 2,500 cases were produced, and no factory sets were issued. The bookmarks measure approximately 2 1/2" by 5" and feature black-bordered color player shots, some action. others posed, on their fronts. Each photo is framed by a team color-coded line. The player's name appears in white lettering within the black border above the picture. His team's name and logo are printed over three team-colored stripes beneath the the picture. The black-bordered horizontal back is designed to resemble an open book. On the left "page" appears a color closeup of the player. On the right "page" is a smaller color player photo and, appearing alongside, a personal profile or career highlight. The bookmarks are unnumbered and checklisted below in alphabetical order.

	MINT	NRMT
COMPLETE SET (120)	20.00	9.00
COMMON CARD (1-120)	.10	.05
☐ 1 Roberto Alomar	.75	.35
☐ 2 Sandy Alomar Jr.	.25	.11
☐ 3 Moises Alou	.25	.11
☐ 4 Brady Anderson	.40	.18
☐ 5 Steve Avery	.10	.05
☐ 6 Carlos Baerga	.25	.11
☐ 7 Jeff Bagwell	2.00	.90
☐ 8 Derek Bell	.10	.05
☐ 9 Jay Bell	.10	.05
☐ 10 Albert Belle	1.00	.45
☐ 11 Dante Bichette	.25	.11
☐ 12 Craig Biggio	.40	.18
☐ 13 Wade Boggs	.60	.25
☐ 14 Barry Bonds	.75	.35
☐ 15 Bobby Bonilla	.25	.11
☐ 16 Pat Borders	.10	.05
☐ 17 Daryl Boston	.10	.05
☐ 18 George Brett	1.50	.70
☐ 19 John Burkett	.10	.05
☐ 20 Brett Butler	.25	.11
☐ 21 Ken Caminiti	.60	.25
☐ 22 Jose Canseco	.40	.18
☐ 23 Joe Carter	.25	.11
☐ 24 Will Clark	.40	.18
☐ 25 Roger Clemens	1.00	.45
☐ 26 Chad Curtis	.10	.05
☐ 27 Darren Daulton	.25	.11
☐ 28 Eric Davis	.25	.11
☐ 29 Andre Dawson	.40	.18
☐ 30 Delino DeShields	.25	.11
☐ 31 Orestes Destrade	.10	.05
☐ 32 Gary DiSarcina	.10	.05
☐ 33 Len Dykstra	.25	.11
☐ 34 Dennis Eckersley	.40	.18
☐ 35 Cecil Fielder	.25	.11
☐ 36 Andres Galarraga	.60	.25
☐ 37 Ron Gant	.25	.11
☐ 38 Tom Glavine	.25	.11
☐ 39 Luis Gonzalez	.10	.05
☐ 40 Juan Gonzalez	2.00	.90
☐ 41 Dwight Gooden	.25	.11
☐ 42 Mark Grace	.40	.18
☐ 43 Mike Greenwell	.10	.05
☐ 44 Ken Griffey Jr.	4.00	1.80
☐ 45 Marquis Grissom	.25	.11
☐ 46 Juan Guzman	.10	.05
☐ 47 Tony Gwynn	2.00	.90
☐ 48 Darryl Hamilton	.10	.05
☐ 49 Charlie Hayes	.10	.05
☐ 50 Rickey Henderson	.60	.25
☐ 51 Orel Hershiser	.25	.11
☐ 52 Dave Hollins	.10	.05
☐ 53 Kent Hrbek	.10	.05
☐ 54 Bo Jackson	.25	.11
☐ 55 Gregg Jefferies	.25	.11
☐ 56 Howard Johnson	.10	.05
☐ 57 Wally Joyner	.25	.11
☐ 58 David Justice	.60	.25
☐ 59 Eric Karros	.40	.18
☐ 60 Roberto Kelly	.10	.05
☐ 61 Chuck Knoblauch	.60	.25
☐ 62 John Kruk	.25	.11
☐ 63 Barry Larkin	.40	.18
☐ 64 Pat Listach	.10	.05
☐ 65 Kenny Lofton	1.00	.45
☐ 66 Mike Macfarlane	.10	.05
☐ 67 Al Martin	.10	.05
☐ 68 Dennis Martinez	.25	.11
☐ 69 Edgar Martinez	.40	.18
☐ 70 Ramon Martinez	.25	.11
☐ 71 Don Mattingly	1.50	.70
☐ 72 Fred McGriff	.40	.18
☐ 73 Mark McGwire	2.00	.90
☐ 74 Brian McRae	.10	.05
☐ 75 Orlando Merced	.10	.05
☐ 76 Kevin Mitchell	.25	.11
☐ 77 Paul Molitor	.60	.25
☐ 78 Eddie Murray	.60	.25
☐ 79 Mike Mussina	.60	.25
☐ 80 Randy Myers	.10	.05
☐ 81 Pete O'Brien	.10	.05
☐ 82 John Olerud	.25	.11
☐ 83 Tom Pagnozzi	.10	.05
☐ 84 Terry Pendleton	.10	.05
☐ 85 Tony Phillips	.10	.05
☐ 86 Mike Piazza	2.50	1.10
☐ 87 Kirby Puckett	2.00	.90
☐ 88 Jose Rijo	.10	.05
☐ 89 Cal Ripken	3.00	1.35
☐ 90 Ivan Rodriguez	1.25	.55
☐ 91 Nolan Ryan	3.00	1.35
☐ 92 Tim Salmon	.60	.25
☐ 93 Ryne Sandberg	1.50	.70
☐ 94 Deion Sanders	.60	.25
☐ 95 Reggie Sanders	.25	.11
☐ 96 Benito Santiago	.10	.05
☐ 97 Gary Sheffield	.60	.25
☐ 98 Ruben Sierra	.10	.05
☐ 99 Ozzie Smith	1.50	.70
☐ 100 John Smoltz	.25	.11
☐ 101 J.T. Snow	.75	.35
☐ 102 Terry Steinbach	.10	.05
☐ 103 Dave Stewart	.10	.05
☐ 104 Darryl Strawberry	.25	.11
☐ 105 B.J. Surhoff	.25	.11
☐ 106 Danny Tartabull	.10	.05
☐ 107 Mickey Tettleton	.10	.05
☐ 108 Frank Thomas	3.00	1.35
☐ 109 Alan Trammell	.40	.18
☐ 110 David Valle	.10	.05
☐ 111 Andy Van Slyke	.10	.05
☐ 112 Mo Vaughn	.75	.35
☐ 113 Robin Ventura	.25	.11
☐ 114 Jose Vizcaino	.10	.05
☐ 115 Larry Walker	.60	.25
☐ 116 Walt Weiss	.10	.05
☐ 117 Matt Williams	.40	.18
☐ 118 Dave Winfield	.60	.25
☐ 119 Robin Yount	.40	.18
☐ 120 Todd Zeile	.10	.05

1993 Diamond Marks Art

Complimenting the 120-card bookmark set, this eight-bookmark art card set was a collaboration of Barry Colla and Terry Smith. One of the special art cards is included in each 48-pack carton. The bookmark art cards measure approximately 2 1/2" by 5" and feature black-bordered fanciful color player paintings by Terry Smith on their fronts. The player's name appears in grayish lettering within the black border below the painting. The black-bordered horizontal back is designed to resemble an open book. On the right "page" appears a color closeup player photo. On the left "page" is a personal profile or career highlight. The bookmarks are unnumbered and checklisted below in alphabetical order. There are reports in the hobby that no more than 3,000 of each card were produced.

	MINT	NRMT
COMPLETE SET (8)	125.00	55.00
COMMON CARD (1-8)	5.00	2.20
☐ 1 Roberto Alomar	10.00	4.50
☐ 2 Barry Bonds	20.00	9.00
☐ 3 Ken Griffey Jr.	50.00	22.00
☐ 4 David Justice	5.00	2.20
☐ 5 John Olerud	5.00	2.20
☐ 6 Nolan Ryan	40.00	18.00
☐ 7 Frank Thomas	40.00	18.00
☐ 8 Robin Yount	15.00	6.75

1934-36 Diamond Stars R327

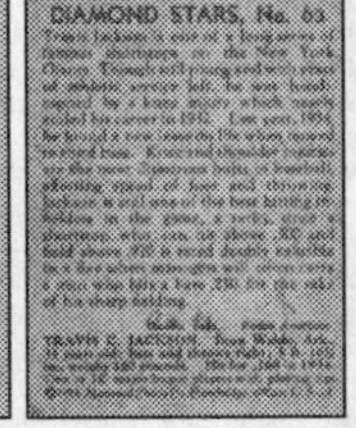

The cards in this 108-card set measure approximately 2 3/8" by 2 7/8". The Diamond Stars set, produced by National Chicle from 1934-36, is also commonly known by its catalog designation, R327. The year of production can be determined by the statistics contained on the back of the card. There are at least 168 possible front/back combinations counting blue (B) and green (G) backs over all three years. The last twelve cards are repeat players and are quite scarce. The checklist below lists the year(s) and back color(s) for the cards. Cards 32 through 72 were issued only in 1935 with green ink on back. Cards 73 through 84 were issued three ways: 35B, 35G, and 36B. Card numbers 85 through 108 were issued only in 1936 with blue ink on back. The complete set price below refers to the set of all variations listed explicitly below. A blank-backed proof sheet of 12 additional (never-issued) cards was discovered in 1980.

	EX-MT	VG-E
COMPLETE SET (119)	15000.00	6800.00
COMMON CARD (1-31)	45.00	20.00
COMMON CARD (32-84)	55.00	25.00
COMMON CARD (85-96)	110.00	50.00
COMMON CARD (97-108)	225.00	100.00
WRAPPER (1-CENT, BLUE)	250.00	110.00
WRAPPER (1-CENT, YELLOW)	200.00	90.00
WRAPPER (1-CENT, CLEAR)	200.00	90.00
☐ 1 Lefty Grove (34G, 35G)	750.00	350.00
☐ 2A Al Simmons (34G, 35G) (Sox on uniform)	125.00	55.00
☐ 2B Al Simmons (36B) (No name on uniform)	200.00	90.00
☐ 3 Rabbit Maranville (34G, 35G)	125.00	55.00
☐ 4 Buddy Myer (34G, 35G, 36B)	55.00	25.00
☐ 5 Tommy Bridges (34G, 35G, 36B)	55.00	25.00
☐ 6 Max Bishop (34G, 35G)	45.00	20.00
☐ 7 Lew Fonseca (34G, 35G)	45.00	20.00
☐ 8 Joe Vosmik (34G, 35G, 36B)	45.00	20.00
☐ 9 Mickey Cochrane (34G, 35G, 36B)	175.00	80.00
☐ 10A Leroy Mahaffey (34G, 35G) (A's on uniform)	45.00	20.00
☐ 10B Leroy Mahaffey (36B) (No name on uniform)	75.00	34.00
☐ 11 Bill Dickey (34G, 35G)	225.00	100.00
☐ 12A Fred Walker (34G) (Ruth retires	75.00	34.00

mentioned on back)
☐ 12B Fred Walker (35G) 55.00 25.00
(Ruth to Boston
mentioned on back)
☐ 12C Fred Walker (36B) 90.00 40.00
☐ 13 George Blaeholder 45.00 20.00
(34G, 35G)
☐ 14 Bill Terry 175.00 80.00
(34G, 35G)
☐ 15A Dick Bartell (34G) 75.00 34.00
(Philadelphia Phillies
on card back)
☐ 15B Dick Bartell (35G) 55.00 25.00
(New York Giants
on card back)
☐ 16 Lloyd Waner 125.00 55.00
(34G, 35G, 36B)
☐ 17 Frankie Frisch 125.00 55.00
(34G, 35G)
☐ 18 Chick Hafey 125.00 55.00
(34G, 35G)
☐ 19 Van Lingle Mungo 55.00 25.00
(34G, 35G)
☐ 20 Frank Hogan 45.00 20.00
(34G, 35G)
☐ 21A Johnny Vergez (34G) 75.00 34.00
(New York Giants
on card back)
☐ 21B Johnny Vergez (35G) 55.00 25.00
(Philadelphia Phillies
on card back)
☐ 22 Jimmy Wilson 45.00 20.00
(34G, 35G, 36B)
☐ 23 Bill Hallahan 45.00 20.00
(34G, 35G)
☐ 24 Earl Adams 45.00 20.00
(34G, 35G)
☐ 25 Wally Berger 60.00 27.00
(35G)
☐ 26 Pepper Martin 75.00 34.00
35G, 36B)
☐ 27 Pie Traynor (35G) 150.00 70.00
☐ 28 Al Lopez (35G) 100.00 45.00
☐ 29 Red Rolfe (35G) 75.00 34.00
☐ 30A Heinie Manush 150.00 70.00
(35G)
(W on sleeve)
☐ 30B Heinie Manush 200.00 90.00
(36B)
(No W on sleeve)
☐ 31A Kiki Cuyler (35G) 125.00 55.00
(Chicago Cubs)
☐ 31B Kiki Cuyler (36B) 175.00 80.00
(Cincinnati Reds)
☐ 32 Sam Rice 125.00 55.00
☐ 33 Schoolboy Rowe 75.00 34.00
☐ 34 Stan Hack 75.00 34.00
☐ 35 Earl Averill 125.00 55.00
☐ 36A Earnie Lombardi 300.00 135.00
(Sic, Ernie)
☐ 36B Ernie Lombardi 150.00 70.00
☐ 37 Billy Urbanski 55.00 25.00
☐ 38 Ben Chapman 75.00 34.00
☐ 39 Carl Hubbell 150.00 70.00
☐ 40 Blondy Ryan 55.00 25.00
☐ 41 Harvey Hendrick 55.00 25.00
☐ 42 Jimmy Dykes 75.00 34.00
☐ 43 Ted Lyons 125.00 55.00
☐ 44 Rogers Hornsby 325.00 145.00
☐ 45 Jo Jo White 55.00 25.00
☐ 46 Red Lucas 55.00 25.00
☐ 47 Bob Bolton 55.00 25.00
☐ 48 Rick Ferrell 125.00 55.00
☐ 49 Buck Jordan 55.00 25.00
☐ 50 Mel Ott 275.00 125.00
☐ 51 Burgess Whitehead 55.00 25.00
☐ 52 Tuck Stainback 55.00 25.00
☐ 53 Oscar Melillo 55.00 25.00
☐ 54A Hank Greenburg 550.00 250.00
(Sic, Greenberg)
☐ 54B Hank Greenberg 300.00 135.00
☐ 55 Tony Cuccinello 55.00 25.00
☐ 56 Gus Suhr 55.00 25.00
☐ 57 Cy Blanton 55.00 25.00
☐ 58 Glenn Myatt 55.00 25.00
☐ 59 Jim Bottomley 125.00 55.00
☐ 60 Red Ruffing 150.00 70.00
☐ 61 Bill Werber 55.00 25.00
☐ 62 Fred Frankhouse 55.00 25.00
☐ 63 Travis Jackson 125.00 55.00
☐ 64 Jimmie Foxx 450.00 200.00
☐ 65 Zeke Bonura 55.00 25.00
☐ 66 Ducky Medwick 150.00 70.00
☐ 67 Marvin Owen 55.00 25.00
☐ 68 Sam Leslie 55.00 25.00
☐ 69 Earl Grace 55.00 25.00
☐ 70 Hal Trosky 75.00 34.00
☐ 71 Ossie Bluege 75.00 34.00
☐ 72 Tony Piet 55.00 25.00
☐ 73 Fritz Ostermueller 55.00 25.00
☐ 74 Tony Lazzeri 175.00 80.00
☐ 75 Jack Burns 55.00 25.00
☐ 76 Billy Rogell 55.00 25.00
☐ 77 Charley Gehringer 165.00 75.00
☐ 78 Joe Kuhel 55.00 25.00
☐ 79 Willis Hudlin 55.00 25.00
☐ 80 Lou Chiozza 55.00 25.00
☐ 81 Bill Delancey 55.00 25.00
☐ 82A Johnny Babich 55.00 25.00
(Dodgers on uni-
form; 35G, 35B)
☐ 82B Johnny Babich 125.00 55.00
(No name on
uniform; 36B)
☐ 83 Paul Waner 150.00 70.00
☐ 84 Sam Byrd 55.00 25.00
☐ 85 Moose Solters 110.00 50.00
☐ 86 Frank Crosetti 125.00 55.00
☐ 87 Steve O'Neill MG 110.00 50.00
☐ 88 George Selkirk 125.00 55.00
☐ 89 Joe Stripp 110.00 50.00
☐ 90 Ray Hayworth 110.00 50.00
☐ 91 Bucky Harris MG 225.00 100.00
☐ 92 Ethan Allen 110.00 50.00
☐ 93 General Crowder 110.00 50.00
☐ 94 Wes Ferrell 125.00 55.00
☐ 95 Luke Appling 275.00 125.00
☐ 96 Lew Riggs 110.00 50.00
☐ 97 Al Lopez 450.00 200.00
☐ 98 Schoolboy Rowe 225.00 100.00
☐ 99 Pie Traynor 550.00 250.00
☐ 100 Earl Averill 450.00 200.00
☐ 101 Dick Bartell 225.00 100.00
☐ 102 Van Lingle Mungo 225.00 100.00
☐ 103 Bill Dickey 700.00 325.00
☐ 104 Red Rolfe 225.00 100.00
☐ 105 Ernie Lombardi 450.00 200.00
☐ 106 Red Lucas 225.00 100.00
☐ 107 Stan Hack 225.00 100.00
☐ 108 Wally Berger 275.00 125.00

1987 Dodgers Mother's

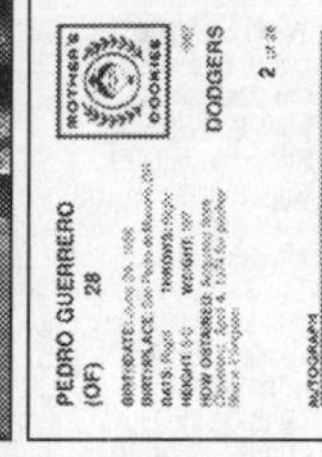

This set consists of 28 full-color, rounded-corner cards each measuring 2 1/2" by 3 1/2". Starter sets (only 20 cards but also including a certificate for eight more cards) were given out at the ballpark and collectors were encouraged to trade to fill in the rest of their set. Cards were originally given out at Dodger Stadium on August 9th. Photos were taken by Barry Colla. The sets were reportedly given out free to all game attendees 14 years of age and under.

	MINT	NRMT
COMPLETE SET (28)	8.00	3.60
COMMON CARD (1-28)	.25	.11

☐ 1 Tom Lasorda MG .... 1.00 .45
☐ 2 Pedro Guerrero .... .75 .35
☐ 3 Steve Sax .... .75 .35
☐ 4 Fernando Valenzuela .... .75 .35
☐ 5 Mike Marshall .... .25 .11
☐ 6 Orel Hershiser .... 1.00 .45
☐ 7 Mariano Duncan .... .50 .23
☐ 8 Bill Madlock .... .50 .23
☐ 9 Bob Welch .... .50 .23
☐ 10 Mike Scioscia .... .50 .23
☐ 11 Mike Ramsey .... .25 .11
☐ 12 Matt Young .... .25 .11
☐ 13 Franklin Stubbs .... .25 .11
☐ 14 Tom Niedenfuer .... .25 .11
☐ 15 Reggie Williams .... .25 .11
☐ 16 Rick Honeycutt .... .25 .11
☐ 17 Dave Anderson .... .25 .11
☐ 18 Alejandro Pena .... .25 .11
☐ 19 Ken Howell .... .25 .11
☐ 20 Len Matuszek .... .25 .11
☐ 21 Tim Leary .... .25 .11
☐ 22 Tracy Woodson .... .25 .11
☐ 23 Alex Trevino .... .25 .11
☐ 24 Ken Landreaux .... .25 .11
☐ 25 Mickey Hatcher .... .25 .11
☐ 26 Brian Holton .... .25 .11
☐ 27 Ron Perranoski .... .50 .23
Manny Mota
Don McMahon
Joe Amalfitano
Mark Cresse
Bill Russell
Dodger Coaches
☐ 28 Checklist Card .... .25 .11

1988 Dodgers Mother's

This set consists of 28 full-color, rounded-corner cards each measuring 2 1/2" by 3 1/2". Starter sets (only 20 cards but also including a certificate for eight more cards) were given out at the ballpark and collectors were encouraged to trade to fill in the rest of their set. Cards were originally given out at Dodger Stadium on July 31st. Photos were taken by Barry Colla. The sets were reportedly given out free to the first 25,000 game attendees 14 years of age and under.

	MINT	NRMT
COMPLETE SET (28)	10.00	4.50
COMMON CARD (1-28)	.25	.11

☐ 1 Tom Lasorda MG .... 1.00 .45
☐ 2 Pedro Guerrero .... .75 .35
☐ 3 Steve Sax .... .75 .35
☐ 4 Fernando Valenzuela .... .75 .35
☐ 5 Mike Marshall .... .25 .11
☐ 6 Orel Hershiser .... .75 .35
☐ 7 Alfredo Griffin .... .25 .11
☐ 8 Kirk Gibson .... .50 .23
☐ 9 Don Sutton .... 1.25 .55
☐ 10 Mike Scioscia .... .50 .23
☐ 11 Franklin Stubbs .... .25 .11
☐ 12 Mike Davis .... .25 .11
☐ 13 Jesse Orosco .... .25 .11
☐ 14 John Shelby .... .25 .11
☐ 15 Rick Dempsey .... .50 .23
☐ 16 Jay Howell .... .25 .11
☐ 17 Dave Anderson .... .25 .11
☐ 18 Alejandro Pena .... .25 .11
☐ 19 Jeff Hamilton .... .25 .11
☐ 20 Danny Heep .... .25 .11
☐ 21 Tim Leary .... .25 .11
☐ 22 Brad Havens .... .25 .11
☐ 23 Tim Belcher .... .50 .23
☐ 24 Ken Howell .... .25 .11
☐ 25 Mickey Hatcher .... .25 .11
☐ 26 Brian Holton .... .25 .11
☐ 27 Mike Devereaux .... .50 .23
☐ 28 Checklist Card .... .50 .23
Joe Ferguson CO
Mark Cresse CO
Ron Perranoski CO
Bill Russell CO
Joe Amalfitano CO
Manny Mota CO
Ben Hines CO

1989 Dodgers Mother's

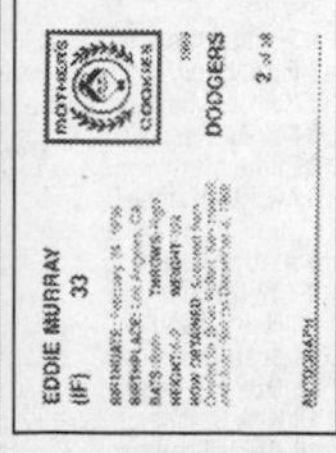

The 1989 Mother's Los Angeles Dodgers set contains 28 standard-size cards with rounded corners. The fronts have borderless color photos, and the horizontally oriented backs have biographical information. Starter sets containing 20 of these cards were given away at a Dodgers home game during the 1989 season.

	MINT	NRMT
COMPLETE SET (28)	8.00	3.60
COMMON CARD (1-28)	.25	.11

	MINT	NRMT
☐ 1 Tom Lasorda MG	1.00	.45
☐ 2 Eddie Murray	1.25	.55
☐ 3 Mike Scioscia	.50	.23
☐ 4 Fernando Valenzuela	.75	.35
☐ 5 Mike Marshall	.25	.11
☐ 6 Orel Hershiser	.75	.35
☐ 7 Alfredo Griffin	.25	.11
☐ 8 Kirk Gibson	.75	.35
☐ 9 John Tudor	.25	.11
☐ 10 Willie Randolph	.50	.23
☐ 11 Franklin Stubbs	.25	.11
☐ 12 Mike Davis	.25	.11
☐ 13 Mike Morgan	.25	.11
☐ 14 John Shelby	.25	.11
☐ 15 Rick Dempsey	.50	.23
☐ 16 Jay Howell	.25	.11
☐ 17 Dave Anderson	.25	.11
☐ 18 Alejandro Pena	.25	.11
☐ 19 Jeff Hamilton	.25	.11
☐ 20 Ricky Horton	.25	.11
☐ 21 Tim Leary	.25	.11
☐ 22 Ray Searage	.25	.11
☐ 23 Tim Belcher	.50	.23
☐ 24 Tim Crews	.25	.11
☐ 25 Mickey Hatcher	.25	.11
☐ 26 Mariano Duncan	.50	.23
☐ 27 Dodgers Coaches Joe Amalfitano Manny Mota Joe Ferguson Ron Perranoski Bill Russell Mark Cresse Ben Hines	.50	.23
☐ 28 Checklist Card World Championship Trophy	.50	.23

1990 Dodgers Mother's

The 1990 Mother's Cookies Los Angeles Dodgers set contains 28 standard-size cards issued with rounded corners and beautiful full color fronts with biographical information on the back. These Dodgers cards were given away at Chavez Ravine to all fans fourteen and under at the August 19th game. They were distributed in 20-card random packets at the game and eight more at the redemption booths. However, both groups of cards were random and there was no guarantee of getting a complete set in the cards. The promotional idea was that the only way one could finish the set was to trade for them. The redemption for eight more cards was done at the 22nd Annual Labor Day card show at the Anaheim Convention Center.

	MINT	NRMT
COMPLETE SET (28)	8.00	3.60
COMMON CARD (1-28)	.25	.11

	MINT	NRMT
☐ 1 Tom Lasorda MG	1.00	.45
☐ 2 Fernando Valenzuela	.75	.35
☐ 3 Kal Daniels	.25	.11
☐ 4 Mike Scioscia	.50	.23
☐ 5 Eddie Murray	1.50	.70
☐ 6 Mickey Hatcher	.25	.11
☐ 7 Juan Samuel	.25	.11
☐ 8 Alfredo Griffin	.25	.11
☐ 9 Tim Belcher	.50	.23
☐ 10 Hubie Brooks	.25	.11
☐ 11 Jose Gonzalez	.25	.11
☐ 12 Orel Hershiser	.75	.35
☐ 13 Kirk Gibson	.75	.35
☐ 14 Chris Gwynn	.25	.11
☐ 15 Jay Howell	.25	.11
☐ 16 Rick Dempsey	.50	.23
☐ 17 Ramon Martinez	1.50	.70
☐ 18 Lenny Harris	.25	.11
☐ 19 John Wetteland	1.50	.70
☐ 20 Mike Sharperson	.25	.11
☐ 21 Mike Morgan	.25	.11
☐ 22 Ray Searage	.25	.11
☐ 23 Jeff Hamilton	.25	.11
☐ 24 Jim Gott	.25	.11
☐ 25 John Shelby	.25	.11
☐ 26 Tim Crews	.25	.11
☐ 27 Don Aase	.25	.11
☐ 28 Dodger Coaches Joe Ferguson Ron Perranoski Mark Cresse Ben Hines Joe Amalfitano Bill Russell Manny Mota	.25	.11

1991 Dodgers Mother's

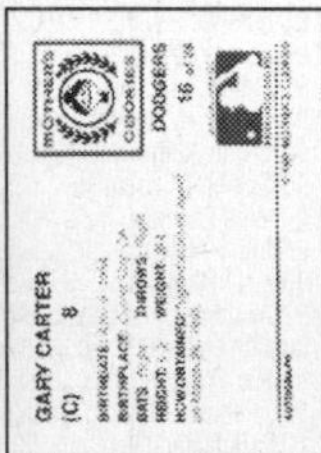

The 1991 Mother's Cookies Los Angeles Dodgers set contains 28 standard-size cards with rounded corners. The front design has borderless glossy color player photos. The horizontally oriented backs are printed in red and purple, present biographical information, and have blank slots for player autographs.

	MINT	NRMT
COMPLETE SET (28)	8.00	3.60
COMMON CARD (1-28)	.25	.11

	MINT	NRMT
☐ 1 Tom Lasorda MG	1.00	.45
☐ 2 Darryl Strawberry	.50	.23
☐ 3 Kal Daniels	.25	.11
☐ 4 Mike Scioscia	.50	.23
☐ 5 Eddie Murray	1.25	.55
☐ 6 Brett Butler	1.00	.45
☐ 7 Juan Samuel	.25	.11
☐ 8 Alfredo Griffin	.25	.11
☐ 9 Tim Belcher	.50	.23
☐ 10 Ramon Martinez	.75	.35
☐ 11 Jose Gonzalez	.25	.11
☐ 12 Orel Hershiser	.75	.35
☐ 13 Bob Ojeda	.25	.11
☐ 14 Chris Gwynn	.25	.11
☐ 15 Jay Howell	.25	.11
☐ 16 Gary Carter	.75	.35
☐ 17 Kevin Gross	.25	.11
☐ 18 Lenny Harris	.25	.11
☐ 19 Mike Hartley	.25	.11
☐ 20 Mike Sharperson	.25	.11
☐ 21 Mike Morgan	.25	.11
☐ 22 John Candelaria	.25	.11
☐ 23 Jeff Hamilton	.25	.11
☐ 24 Jim Gott	.25	.11
☐ 25 Barry Lyons	.25	.11
☐ 26 Tim Crews	.25	.11
☐ 27 Stan Javier	.25	.11
☐ 28 Checklist Card Joe Ferguson CO Ben Hines CO Mark Cresse CO Joe Amalfitano CO Ron Perranoski CO Manny Mota CO Bill Russell CO	.50	.23

1992 Dodgers Mother's

The 1992 Mother's Cookies Los Angeles Dodgers set contains 28 standard size cards with rounded corners. The front design features borderless color player photos with the baseball stadium as the background. The horizontally oriented backs display biographical information printed in purple and red.

	MINT	NRMT
COMPLETE SET (28)	10.00	4.50
COMMON CARD (1-28)	.25	.11

	MINT	NRMT
☐ 1 Tom Lasorda MG	1.00	.45
☐ 2 Brett Butler	.75	.35
☐ 3 Tom Candiotti	.25	.11
☐ 4 Eric Davis	.75	.35
☐ 5 Lenny Harris	.25	.11
☐ 6 Orel Hershiser	.75	.35
☐ 7 Ramon Martinez	.75	.35
☐ 8 Jose Offerman	.25	.11
☐ 9 Mike Scioscia	.50	.23
☐ 10 Darryl Strawberry	.50	.23
☐ 11 Todd Benzinger	.25	.11
☐ 12 John Candelaria	.25	.11
☐ 13 Tim Crews	.25	.11
☐ 14 Kal Daniels	.25	.11
☐ 15 Jim Gott	.25	.11
☐ 16 Kevin Gross	.25	.11
☐ 17 Dave Hansen	.25	.11
☐ 18 Carlos Hernandez	.25	.11
☐ 19 Jay Howell	.25	.11
☐ 20 Stan Javier	.25	.11
☐ 21 Eric Karros	3.00	1.35
☐ 22 Roger McDowell	.25	.11
☐ 23 Bob Ojeda	.25	.11
☐ 24 Juan Samuel	.25	.11
☐ 25 Mike Sharperson	.25	.11
☐ 26 Mitch Webster	.25	.11
☐ 27 Steve Wilson	.25	.11
☐ 28 Checklist Card Mark Cresse CO Ron Perranoski CO Ben Hines CO Manny Mota CO Joe Amalfitano CO Joe Ferguson CO Ron Roenicke CO	.50	.23

1993 Dodgers Mother's

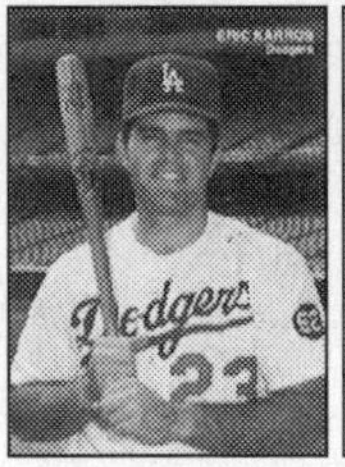

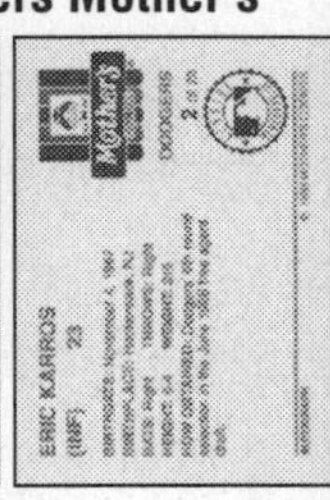

The 1993 Mother's Cookies Dodgers set consists of 28 standard-size cards with rounded corners. The fronts display full-bleed color player portraits shot from the waist up. The player's name and team name appear in one of the corners. On a white background in red and purple print, the horizontal backs carry biographical information and the sponsor's logo. A blank slot for the player's autograph rounds out the back.

	MINT	NRMT
COMPLETE SET (28)	15.00	6.75
COMMON CARD (1-28)	.25	.11

	MINT	NRMT
☐ 1 Tommy Lasorda MG	1.00	.45
☐ 2 Eric Karros	1.50	.70
☐ 3 Brett Butler	.75	.35
☐ 4 Mike Piazza	7.50	3.40
☐ 5 Jose Offerman	.25	.11
☐ 6 Tim Wallach	.50	.23
☐ 7 Eric Davis	.50	.23
☐ 8 Darryl Strawberry	.50	.23
☐ 9 Jody Reed	.25	.11
☐ 10 Orel Hershiser	.50	.23
☐ 11 Tom Candiotti	.25	.11
☐ 12 Ramon Martinez	.75	.35
☐ 13 Lenny Harris	.25	.11
☐ 14 Mike Sharperson	.25	.11
☐ 15 Omar Daal	.25	.11
☐ 16 Pedro Martinez	1.50	.70
☐ 17 Jim Gott	.25	.11
☐ 18 Carlos Hernandez	.25	.11
☐ 19 Kevin Gross	.25	.11
☐ 20 Cory Snyder	.25	.11
☐ 21 Todd Worrell	.75	.35

☐ 22 Mitch Webster	.25	.11
☐ 23 Steve Wilson	.25	.11
☐ 24 Dave Hansen	.25	.11
☐ 25 Roger McDowell	.25	.11
☐ 26 Pedro Astacio	.75	.35
☐ 27 Rick Trlicek	.25	.11
☐ 28 Checklist/Coaches	.50	.20

Joe Ferguson
Ben Hines
Manny Mota
Mark Cresse
Ron Perranoski
Joe Amalfitano
Ron Roenicke

1994 Dodgers Mother's

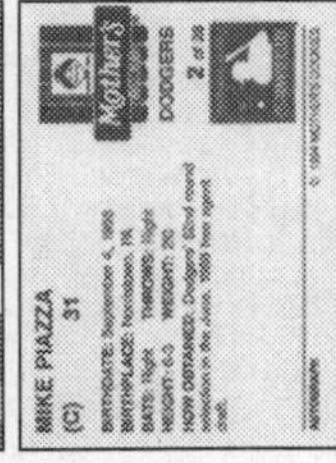

The 1994 Mother's Cookies Dodgers set consists of 28 standard-size cards with rounded corners. The fronts display full-bleed color player portraits shot from the waist up against a stadium background. The player's name and team name appear in one of the corners. On a white background in red and purple print, the horizontal backs carry biographical information and the sponsor's logo. A blank slot for the player's autograph rounds out the back.

	MINT	NRMT
COMPLETE SET (28)	15.00	6.75
COMMON CARD (1-28)	.25	.11

Card	MINT	NRMT
☐ 1 Tommy Lasorda MG	1.00	.45
☐ 2 Mike Piazza	6.00	2.70
☐ 3 Delino DeShields	.50	.23
☐ 4 Eric Karros	1.50	.70
☐ 5 Jose Offerman	.25	.11
☐ 6 Brett Butler	.75	.35
☐ 7 Orel Hershiser	.50	.23
☐ 8 Henry Rodriguez	.50	.23
☐ 9 Raul Mondesi	4.00	1.80
☐ 10 Tim Wallach	.50	.23
☐ 11 Ramon Martinez	.75	.35
☐ 12 Mitch Webster	.25	.11
☐ 13 Todd Worrell	.75	.35
☐ 14 Jeff Treadway	.25	.11
☐ 15 Tom Candiotti	.25	.11
☐ 16 Pedro Astacio	.50	.23
☐ 17 Chris Gwynn	.25	.11
☐ 18 Jim Gott	.25	.11
☐ 19 Omar Daal	.25	.11
☐ 20 Cory Snyder	.25	.11
☐ 21 Kevin Gross	.25	.11
☐ 22 Dave Hansen	.25	.11
☐ 23 Al Osuna	.25	.11
☐ 24 Darren Dreifort	.25	.11
☐ 25 Roger McDowell	.25	.11
☐ 26 Carlos Hernandez	.25	.11
☐ 27 Gary Wayne	.25	.11
☐ 28 Checklist/Coaches	.50	.23

Ron Perranoski
Joe Amalfitano
Reggie Smith
Joe Ferguson
Bill Russell
Mark Cresse

1995 Dodgers Mother's

The 1995 Mother's Cookies Los Angeles Dodgers set consists of 28 standard-size cards with rounded corners. The fronts display posed color player portraits in stadium settings. The player's name and team name appear in one of the top corners. The backs carry biographical information and the sponsor's logo on a white background in red and purple print. A blank slot for the player's autograph rounds out the back. A rookie year card of Hideo Nomo is in this set.

	MINT	NRMT
COMPLETE SET (28)	15.00	6.75
COMMON CARD (1-28)	.25	.11

Card	MINT	NRMT
☐ 1 Tommy Lasorda MG	1.00	.45
☐ 2 Mike Piazza	3.00	1.35
☐ 3 Raul Mondesi	1.50	.70
☐ 4 Ramon Martinez	.75	.35
☐ 5 Eric Karros	1.00	.45
☐ 6 Roberto Kelly	.25	.11
☐ 7 Tim Wallach	.50	.23
☐ 8 Jose Offerman	.25	.11
☐ 9 Delino DeShields	.50	.23
☐ 10 Dave Hansen	.25	.11
☐ 11 Pedro Astacio	.50	.23
☐ 12 Mitch Webster	.25	.11
☐ 13 Hideo Nomo	7.50	3.40
☐ 14 Billy Ashley	.25	.11
☐ 15 Chris Gwynn	.25	.11
☐ 16 Todd Hollandsworth	.75	.35
☐ 17 Omar Daal	.25	.11
☐ 18 Todd Worrell	.75	.35
☐ 19 Todd Williams	.25	.11
☐ 20 Carlos Hernandez	.25	.11
☐ 21 Tom Candiotti	.25	.11
☐ 22 Antonio Osuna	.50	.23
☐ 23 Ismael Valdes	.75	.35
☐ 24 Rudy Seanez	.25	.11
☐ 25 Joey Eischen	.25	.11
☐ 26 Greg Hansell	.25	.11
☐ 27 Rick Parker	.25	.11
☐ 28 Coaches/Checklist	.50	.23

Dave Wallace
Bill Russell
Reggie Smith
Joe Amalfitano
Manny Mota
Mark Cresse

1996 Dodgers Mother's

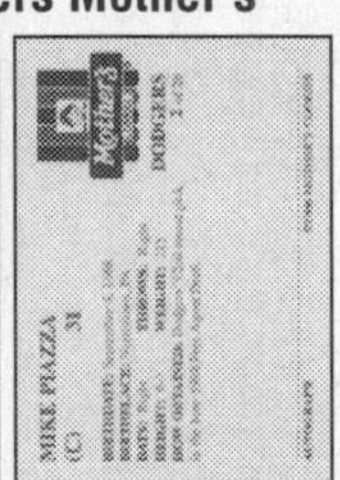

This 28-card set consists of borderless posed color player portraits in stadium settings. The player's and team's names appear in one of the top rounded corners. The backs carry biographical information and the sponsor's logo on a white background in red and purple print. A blank slot for the player's autograph rounds out the back.

	MINT	NRMT
COMPLETE SET (28)	12.00	5.50
COMMON CARD (1-28)	.25	.11

Card	MINT	NRMT
☐ 1 Tommy Lasorda MG	1.00	.45
☐ 2 Mike Piazza	3.00	1.35
☐ 3 Hideo Nomo	3.00	1.35
☐ 4 Raul Mondesi	1.00	.45
☐ 5 Eric Karros	.75	.35
☐ 6 Delino DeShields	.50	.23
☐ 7 Greg Gagne	.25	.11
☐ 8 Brett Butler	.75	.35
☐ 9 Todd Hollandsworth	.50	.23
☐ 10 Mike Blowers	.25	.11
☐ 11 Ismael Valdes	.75	.35
☐ 12 Pedro Astacio	.50	.23
☐ 13 Billy Ashley	.25	.11
☐ 14 Tom Candiotti	.25	.11
☐ 15 Dave Hansen	.25	.11
☐ 16 Joey Eischen	.25	.11
☐ 17 Milt Thompson	.25	.11
☐ 18 Chan Ho Park	1.50	.70
☐ 19 Antonio Osuna	.25	.11
☐ 20 Carlos Hernandez	.25	.11
☐ 21 Ramon Martinez	.50	.23
☐ 22 Scott Radinsky	.25	.11
☐ 23 Chad Fonville	.25	.11
☐ 24 Darren Hall	.25	.11
☐ 25 Todd Worrell	.75	.35
☐ 26 Mark Guthrie	.25	.11
☐ 27 Roger Cedeno	.25	.11
☐ 28 Coaches Card CL	.50	.23

Joe Amalfitano
Mark Cresse
Manny Mota
Bill Russell
Dave Wallace
Reggie Smith

1997 Dodgers Mothers

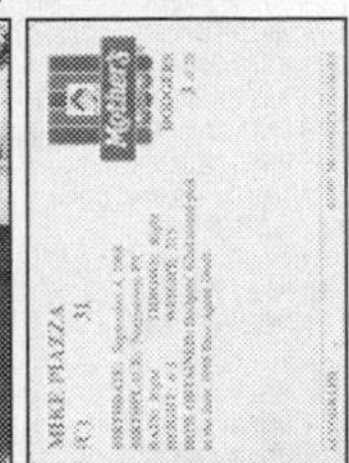

This 28-card set of the Los Angeles Dodgers sponsored by Mother's Cookies consists of posed color player photos with rounded corners. The backs carry biographical information and the sponsor's logo on a white background in red and purple print. A blank slot for the player's autograph rounds out the back.

	MINT	NRMT
COMPLETE SET (28)	12.50	5.50
COMMON CARD (1-28)	.25	.11

Card	MINT	NRMT
☐ 1 Bill Russell MG	.50	.23
☐ 2 Eric Karros	1.00	.45
☐ 3 Mike Piazza	2.50	1.10
☐ 4 Raul Mondesi	1.00	.45
☐ 5 Hideo Nomo	2.50	1.10
☐ 6 Todd Hollandsworth	.50	.23
☐ 7 Greg Gagne	.25	.11
☐ 8 Brett Butler	.75	.35
☐ 9 Ramon Martinez	.50	.23
☐ 10 Todd Zeile	.25	.11
☐ 11 Ismael Valdes	.50	.23
☐ 12 Chip Hale	.25	.11
☐ 13 Tom Candiotti	.25	.11
☐ 14 Billy Ashley	.25	.11
☐ 15 Chan Ho Park	1.50	.70
☐ 16 Wayne Kirby	.25	.11
☐ 17 Mark Guthrie	.25	.11
☐ 18 Juan Castro	.25	.11
☐ 19 Todd Worrell	.75	.35
☐ 20 Tom Prince	.25	.11
☐ 21 Scott Radinsky	.25	.11
☐ 22 Pedro Astacio	.50	.23
☐ 23 Wilton Guerrero	.50	.23
☐ 24 Darren Hall	.25	.11
☐ 25 Darren Dreifort	.25	.11
☐ 26 Nelson Liriano	.25	.11
☐ 27 Coaches Card	.50	.23

Joe Amalfitano
Mark Cresse
Manny Moto
Mike Scioscia
Reggie Smith
Dave Wallace

Card	MINT	NRMT
☐ 28 Checklist	.25	.11

1981 Donruss

In 1981 Donruss launched itself into the baseball card market with a 600-card set. Wax packs contained 15 cards as well as a piece of gum. This would be the only year that Donruss was allowed to have any confectionary product in their packs. The standard-size cards are printed on thin stock and more than one pose exists for several popular players. Numerous errors of the first print run were later corrected by the company. These are marked P1 and P2 in the checklist below. The key Rookie Cards in this set are Danny Ainge, Tim Raines, and Jeff Reardon.

	NRMT	VG-E
COMPLETE SET (605)	30.00	13.50
COMMON CARD (1-605)	.10	.05
☐ 1 Ozzie Smith	4.00	1.80
☐ 2 Rollie Fingers	.50	.23
☐ 3 Rick Wise	.10	.05
☐ 4 Gene Richards	.10	.05
☐ 5 Alan Trammell	1.25	.55
☐ 6 Tom Brookens	.10	.05
☐ 7A Duffy Dyer P1	.25	.11
1980 batting average		
has decimal point		
☐ 7B Duffy Dyer P2	.10	.05
1980 batting average		
has no decimal point		
☐ 8 Mark Fidrych	1.00	.45
☐ 9 Dave Rozema	.10	.05
☐ 10 Ricky Peters	.10	.05
☐ 11 Mike Schmidt	1.25	.55
☐ 12 Willie Stargell	1.00	.45
☐ 13 Tim Foli	.10	.05
☐ 14 Manny Sanguillen	.25	.11
☐ 15 Grant Jackson	.10	.05
☐ 16 Eddie Solomon	.10	.05
☐ 17 Omar Moreno	.10	.05
☐ 18 Joe Morgan	1.00	.45
☐ 19 Rafael Landestoy	.10	.05
☐ 20 Bruce Bochy	.10	.05
☐ 21 Joe Sambito	.10	.05
☐ 22 Manny Trillo	.10	.05
☐ 23A Dave Smith P1	.25	.11
Line box around stats		
is not complete		
☐ 23B Dave Smith P2	.25	.11
Box totally encloses		
stats at top		
☐ 24 Terry Puhl	.10	.05
☐ 25 Bump Wills	.10	.05
☐ 26A John Ellis P1 ERR	.50	.23
Danny Walton photo on front		
☐ 26B John Ellis P2 COR	.25	.11
☐ 27 Jim Kern	.10	.05
☐ 28 Richie Zisk	.10	.05
☐ 29 John Mayberry	.10	.05
☐ 30 Bob Davis	.10	.05
☐ 31 Jackson Todd	.10	.05
☐ 32 Alvis Woods	.10	.05
☐ 33 Steve Carlton	1.00	.45
☐ 34 Lee Mazzilli	.10	.05
☐ 35 John Stearns	.10	.05
☐ 36 Roy Lee Jackson	.10	.05
☐ 37 Mike Scott	.25	.11
☐ 38 Lamar Johnson	.10	.05
☐ 39 Kevin Bell	.10	.05
☐ 40 Ed Farmer	.10	.05
☐ 41 Ross Baumgarten	.10	.05
☐ 42 Leo Sutherland	.10	.05
☐ 43 Dan Meyer	.10	.05
☐ 44 Ron Reed	.10	.05
☐ 45 Mario Mendoza	.10	.05
☐ 46 Rick Honeycutt	.10	.05
☐ 47 Glenn Abbott	.10	.05
☐ 48 Leon Roberts	.10	.05
☐ 49 Rod Carew	.75	.35
☐ 50 Bert Campaneris	.25	.11
☐ 51A Tom Donahue P1 ERR	.25	.11
Name on front		
misspelled Donahue		
☐ 51B Tom Donohue	.10	.05
P2 COR		
☐ 52 Dave Frost	.10	.05
☐ 53 Ed Halicki	.10	.05
☐ 54 Dan Ford	.10	.05
☐ 55 Garry Maddox	.10	.05
☐ 56A Steve Garvey P1	1.00	.45
Surpassed 25 HR		
☐ 56B Steve Garvey P2	1.00	.45
Surpassed 21 HR		
☐ 57 Bill Russell	.25	.11
☐ 58 Don Sutton	1.00	.45
☐ 59 Reggie Smith	.25	.11
☐ 60 Rick Monday	.25	.11
☐ 61 Ray Knight	.25	.11
☐ 62 Johnny Bench	1.25	.55
☐ 63 Mario Soto	.10	.05
☐ 64 Doug Bair	.10	.05
☐ 65 George Foster	.25	.11
☐ 66 Jeff Burroughs	.10	.05
☐ 67 Keith Hernandez	.25	.11
☐ 68 Tom Herr	.25	.11
☐ 69 Bob Forsch	.10	.05
☐ 70 John Fulgham	.10	.05
☐ 71A Bobby Bonds P1 ERR	1.00	.45
986 lifetime HR		
☐ 71B Bobby Bonds P2 COR	.50	.23
326 lifetime HR		
☐ 72A Rennie Stennett P1	.25	.11
Breaking broke leg		
☐ 72B Rennie Stennett P2	.10	.05
Word "broke" deleted		
☐ 73 Joe Strain	.10	.05
☐ 74 Ed Whitson	.10	.05
☐ 75 Tom Griffin	.10	.05
☐ 76 Billy North	.10	.05
☐ 77 Gene Garber	.10	.05
☐ 78 Mike Hargrove	.25	.11
☐ 79 Dave Rosello	.10	.05
☐ 80 Ron Hassey	.10	.05
☐ 81 Sid Monge	.10	.05
☐ 82A Joe Charboneau P1	1.00	.45
'78 highlights		
For some reason		
☐ 82B Joe Charboneau P2	1.00	.45
Phrase "For some reason" deleted		
☐ 83 Cecil Cooper	.25	.11
☐ 84 Sal Bando	.25	.11
☐ 85 Moose Haas	.10	.05
☐ 86 Mike Caldwell	.10	.05
☐ 87A Larry Hisle P1	.25	.11
'77 highlights		
line ends with "28 RBI"		
☐ 87B Larry Hisle P2	.10	.05
Correct line "28 HR"		
☐ 88 Luis Gomez	.10	.05
☐ 89 Larry Parrish	.10	.05
☐ 90 Gary Carter	1.00	.45
☐ 91 Bill Gullickson	.50	.23
☐ 92 Fred Norman	.10	.05
☐ 93 Tommy Hutton	.10	.05
☐ 94 Carl Yastrzemski	1.00	.45
☐ 95 Glenn Hoffman	.10	.05
☐ 96 Dennis Eckersley	1.00	.45
☐ 97A Tom Burgmeier P1	.25	.11
ERR Throws: Right		
☐ 97B Tom Burgmeier P2	.10	.05
COR Throws: Left		
☐ 98 Win Remmerswaal	.10	.05
☐ 99 Bob Horner	.25	.11
☐ 100 George Brett	2.50	1.10
☐ 101 Dave Chalk	.10	.05
☐ 102 Dennis Leonard	.10	.05
☐ 103 Renie Martin	.10	.05
☐ 104 Amos Otis	.25	.11
☐ 105 Graig Nettles	.25	.11
☐ 106 Eric Soderholm	.10	.05
☐ 107 Tommy John	.50	.23
☐ 108 Tom Underwood	.10	.05
☐ 109 Lou Piniella	.25	.11
☐ 110 Mickey Klutts	.10	.05
☐ 111 Bobby Murcer	.25	.11
☐ 112 Eddie Murray	2.00	.90
☐ 113 Rick Dempsey	.25	.11
☐ 114 Scott McGregor	.10	.05
☐ 115 Ken Singleton	.25	.11
☐ 116 Gary Roenicke	.10	.05
☐ 117 Dave Revering	.10	.05
☐ 118 Mike Norris	.10	.05
☐ 119 Rickey Henderson	2.50	1.10
☐ 120 Mike Heath	.10	.05
☐ 121 Dave Cash	.10	.05
☐ 122 Randy Jones	.10	.05
☐ 123 Eric Rasmussen	.10	.05
☐ 124 Jerry Mumphrey	.10	.05
☐ 125 Richie Hebner	.10	.05
☐ 126 Mark Wagner	.10	.05
☐ 127 Jack Morris	1.00	.45
☐ 128 Dan Petry	.10	.05
☐ 129 Bruce Robbins	.10	.05
☐ 130 Champ Summers	.10	.05
☐ 131 Pete Rose P1	1.25	.55
Last line ends with		
see card 251		
☐ 131B Pete Rose P2	1.50	.70
Last line corrected		
see card 371		
☐ 132 Willie Stargell	1.00	.45
☐ 133 Ed Ott	.10	.05
☐ 134 Jim Bibby	.10	.05
☐ 135 Bert Blyleven	.50	.23
☐ 136 Dave Parker	.25	.11
☐ 137 Bill Robinson	.25	.11
☐ 138 Enos Cabell	.10	.05
☐ 139 Dave Bergman	.10	.05
☐ 140 J.R. Richard	.25	.11
☐ 141 Ken Forsch	.10	.05
☐ 142 Larry Bowa UER	.25	.11
Shortshop on front		
☐ 143 Frank LaCorte UER	.10	.05
Photo actually Randy Niemann		
☐ 144 Denny Walling	.10	.05
☐ 145 Buddy Bell	.25	.11
☐ 146 Ferguson Jenkins	1.00	.45
☐ 147 Dannny Darwin	.25	.11
☐ 148 John Grubb	.10	.05
☐ 149 Alfredo Griffin	.10	.05
☐ 150 Jerry Garvin	.10	.05
☐ 151 Paul Mirabella	.10	.05
☐ 152 Rick Bosetti	.10	.05
☐ 153 Dick Ruthven	.10	.05
☐ 154 Frank Taveras	.10	.05
☐ 155 Craig Swan	.10	.05
☐ 156 Jeff Reardon	1.00	.45
☐ 157 Steve Henderson	.10	.05
☐ 158 Jim Morrison	.10	.05
☐ 159 Glenn Borgmann	.10	.05
☐ 160 LaMarr Hoyt	.25	.11
☐ 161 Rich Wortham	.10	.05
☐ 162 Thad Bosley	.10	.05
☐ 163 Julio Cruz	.10	.05
☐ 164A Del Unser P1	.25	.11
No "3B" heading		
☐ 164B Del Unser P2	.10	.05
Batting record on back		
corrected "3B"		
☐ 165 Jim Anderson	.10	.05
☐ 166 Jim Beattie	.10	.05
☐ 167 Shane Rawley	.10	.05
☐ 168 Joe Simpson	.10	.05
☐ 169 Rod Carew	.75	.35
☐ 170 Fred Patek	.10	.05
☐ 171 Frank Tanana	.25	.11
☐ 172 Alfredo Martinez	.10	.05
☐ 173 Chris Knapp	.10	.05
☐ 174 Joe Rudi	.25	.11
☐ 175 Greg Luzinski	.25	.11
☐ 176 Steve Garvey	.50	.23
☐ 177 Joe Ferguson	.10	.05
☐ 178 Bob Welch	.25	.11
☐ 179 Dusty Baker	.50	.23
☐ 180 Rudy Law	.10	.05
☐ 181 Dave Concepcion	.25	.11
☐ 182 Johnny Bench	1.25	.55
☐ 183 Mike LaCoss	.10	.05
☐ 184 Ken Griffey	.50	.23
☐ 185 Dave Collins	.10	.05
☐ 186 Brian Asselstine	.10	.05
☐ 187 Garry Templeton	.10	.05
☐ 188 Mike Phillips	.10	.05
☐ 189 Pete Vuckovich	.25	.11
☐ 190 John Urrea	.10	.05
☐ 191 Tony Scott	.10	.05
☐ 192 Darrell Evans	.25	.11
☐ 193 Milt May	.10	.05
☐ 194 Bob Knepper	.10	.05
☐ 195 Randy Moffitt	.10	.05
☐ 196 Larry Herndon	.10	.05
☐ 197 Rick Camp	.10	.05
☐ 198 Andre Thornton	.25	.11
☐ 199 Tom Veryzer	.10	.05
☐ 200 Gary Alexander	.10	.05
☐ 201 Rick Waits	.10	.05
☐ 202 Rick Manning	.10	.05
☐ 203 Paul Molitor	2.00	.90
☐ 204 Jim Gantner	.25	.11
☐ 205 Paul Mitchell	.10	.05
☐ 206 Reggie Cleveland	.10	.05
☐ 207 Sixto Lezcano	.10	.05
☐ 208 Bruce Benedict	.10	.05
☐ 209 Rodney Scott	.10	.05
☐ 210 John Tamargo	.10	.05
☐ 211 Bill Lee	.25	.11
☐ 212 Andre Dawson UER	1.25	.55
Middle name Fernando		
should be Nolan		
☐ 213 Rowland Office	.10	.05
☐ 214 Carl Yastrzemski	1.00	.45
☐ 215 Jerry Remy	.10	.05
☐ 216 Mike Torrez	.10	.05
☐ 217 Skip Lockwood	.10	.05
☐ 218 Fred Lynn	.25	.11
☐ 219 Chris Chambliss	.25	.11
☐ 220 Willie Aikens	.10	.05
☐ 221 John Wathan	.10	.05
☐ 222 Dan Quisenberry	.25	.11
☐ 223 Willie Wilson	.25	.11
☐ 224 Clint Hurdle	.10	.05
☐ 225 Bob Watson	.25	.11
☐ 226 Jim Spencer	.10	.05
☐ 227 Ron Guidry	.25	.11
☐ 228 Reggie Jackson	1.25	.55
☐ 229 Oscar Gamble	.10	.05
☐ 230 Jeff Cox	.10	.05
☐ 231 Luis Tiant	.25	.11
☐ 232 Rich Dauer	.10	.05

233 Dan Graham	.10	.05
234 Mike Flanagan	.25	.11
235 John Lowenstein	.10	.05
236 Benny Ayala	.10	.05
237 Wayne Gross	.10	.05
238 Rick Langford	.10	.05
239 Tony Armas	.25	.11
240A Bob Lacey P1 ERR	.50	.23
Name misspelled Lacy		
240B Bob Lacey P2 COR	.10	.05
241 Gene Tenace	.25	.11
242 Bob Shirley	.10	.05
243 Gary Lucas	.10	.05
244 Jerry Turner	.10	.05
245 John Wockenfuss	.10	.05
246 Stan Papi	.10	.05
247 Milt Wilcox	.10	.05
248 Dan Schatzeder	.10	.05
249 Steve Kemp	.10	.05
250 Jim Lentine	.10	.05
251 Pete Rose	1.25	.55
252 Bill Madlock	.25	.11
253 Dale Berra	.10	.05
254 Kent Tekulve	.25	.11
255 Enrique Romo	.10	.05
256 Mike Easler	.10	.05
257 Chuck Tanner MG	.25	.11
258 Art Howe	.10	.05
259 Alan Ashby	.10	.05
260 Nolan Ryan	5.00	2.20
261A Vern Ruhle P1 ERR	.50	.23
Ken Forsch photo on front		
261B Vern Ruhle P2 COR	.25	.11
262 Bob Boone	.25	.11
263 Cesar Cedeno	.25	.11
264 Jeff Leonard	.25	.11
265 Pat Putnam	.10	.05
266 Jon Matlack	.10	.05
267 Dave Rajsich	.10	.05
268 Billy Sample	.10	.05
269 Damaso Garcia	.10	.05
270 Tom Buskey	.10	.05
271 Joey McLaughlin	.10	.05
272 Barry Bonnell	.10	.05
273 Tug McGraw	.25	.11
274 Mike Jorgensen	.10	.05
275 Pat Zachry	.10	.05
276 Neil Allen	.10	.05
277 Joel Youngblood	.10	.05
278 Greg Pryor	.10	.05
279 Britt Burns	.10	.05
280 Rich Dotson	.10	.05
281 Chet Lemon	.10	.05
282 Rusty Kuntz	.10	.05
283 Ted Cox	.10	.05
284 Sparky Lyle	.25	.11
285 Larry Cox	.10	.05
286 Floyd Bannister	.10	.05
287 Byron McLaughlin	.10	.05
288 Rodney Craig	.10	.05
289 Bobby Grich	.25	.11
290 Dickie Thon	.25	.11
291 Mark Clear	.10	.05
292 Dave Lemanczyk	.10	.05
293 Jason Thompson	.10	.05
294 Rick Miller	.10	.05
295 Lonnie Smith	.25	.11
296 Ron Cey	.25	.11
297 Steve Yeager	.10	.05
298 Bobby Castillo	.10	.05
299 Manny Mota	.25	.11
300 Jay Johnstone	.25	.11
301 Dan Driessen	.10	.05
302 Joe Nolan	.10	.05
303 Paul Householder	.10	.05
304 Harry Spilman	.10	.05
305 Cesar Geronimo	.10	.05
306A Gary Mathews P1 ERR	.50	.23
Name misspelled		
306B Gary Matthews P2 COR	.25	.11
307 Ken Reitz	.10	.05
308 Ted Simmons	.25	.11
309 John Littlefield	.10	.05
310 George Frazier	.10	.05
311 Dane Iorg	.10	.05
312 Mike Ivie	.10	.05
313 Dennis Littlejohn	.10	.05
314 Gary Lavelle	.10	.05
315 Jack Clark	.25	.11
316 Jim Wohlford	.10	.05
317 Rick Matula	.10	.05
318 Toby Harrah	.25	.11
319A Dwane Kuiper P1 ERR	.25	.11
Name misspelled		
319B Duane Kuiper P2 COR	.10	.05
320 Len Barker	.10	.05
321 Victor Cruz	.10	.05
322 Dell Alston	.10	.05
323 Robin Yount	1.25	.55
324 Charlie Moore	.10	.05
325 Lary Sorensen	.10	.05
326A Gorman Thomas P1	.50	.23
2nd line on back:		
"30 HR mark 4th"		
326B Gorman Thomas P2	.25	.11
30 HR mark 3rd		
327 Bob Rodgers MG	.10	.05
328 Phil Niekro	1.00	.45
329 Chris Speier	.10	.05
330A Steve Rodgers P1	.25	.11
ERR Name misspelled		
330B Steve Rogers P2 COR	.10	.05
331 Woodie Fryman	.10	.05
332 Warren Cromartie	.10	.05
333 Jerry White	.10	.05
334 Tony Perez	1.00	.45
335 Carlton Fisk	1.25	.55
336 Dick Drago	.10	.05
337 Steve Renko	.10	.05
338 Jim Rice	.25	.11
339 Jerry Royster	.10	.05
340 Frank White	.25	.11
341 Jamie Quirk	.10	.05
342A Paul Spittorff P1 ERR	.25	.11
Name misspelled		
342B Paul Splittorff P2 COR	.10	.05
343 Marty Pattin	.10	.05
344 Pete LaCock	.10	.05
345 Willie Randolph	.25	.11
346 Rick Cerone	.10	.05
347 Rich Gossage	1.00	.45
348 Reggie Jackson	1.25	.55
349 Ruppert Jones	.10	.05
350 Dave McKay	.10	.05
351 Yogi Berra CO	1.00	.45
352 Doug DeCinces	.25	.11
353 Jim Palmer	.60	.25
354 Tippy Martinez	.10	.05
355 Al Bumbry	.25	.11
356 Earl Weaver MG	1.00	.45
357A Bob Picciolo P1 ERR	.25	.11
Name misspelled		
357B Rob Picciolo P2 COR	.10	.05
358 Matt Keough	.10	.05
359 Dwayne Murphy	.10	.05
360 Brian Kingman	.10	.05
361 Bill Fahey	.10	.05
362 Steve Mura	.10	.05
363 Dennis Kinney	.10	.05
364 Dave Winfield	1.50	.70
365 Lou Whitaker	1.00	.45
366 Lance Parrish	.25	.11
367 Tim Corcoran	.10	.05
368 Pat Underwood	.10	.05
369 Al Cowens	.10	.05
370 Sparky Anderson MG	.25	.11
371 Pete Rose	1.25	.55
372 Phil Garner	.25	.11
373 Steve Nicosia	.10	.05
374 John Candelaria	.25	.11
375 Don Robinson	.10	.05
376 Lee Lacy	.10	.05
377 John Milner	.10	.05
378 Craig Reynolds	.10	.05
379A Luis Pujols P1 ERR	.25	.11
Name misspelled Pujois		
379B Luis Pujols P2 COR	.10	.05
380 Joe Niekro	.25	.11
381 Joaquin Andujar	.25	.11
382 Keith Moreland	.25	.11
383 Jose Cruz	.25	.11
384 Bill Virdon MG	.10	.05
385 Jim Sundberg	.25	.11
386 Doc Medich	.10	.05
387 Al Oliver	.25	.11
388 Jim Norris	.10	.05
389 Bob Bailor	.10	.05
390 Ernie Whitt	.10	.05
391 Otto Velez	.10	.05
392 Roy Howell	.10	.05
393 Bob Walk	.25	.11
394 Doug Flynn	.10	.05
395 Pete Falcone	.10	.05
396 Tom Hausman	.10	.05
397 Elliott Maddox	.10	.05
398 Mike Squires	.10	.05
399 Marvis Foley	.10	.05
400 Steve Trout	.10	.05
401 Wayne Nordhagen	.10	.05
402 Tony LaRussa MG	.25	.11
403 Bruce Bochte	.10	.05
404 Bake McBride	.10	.05
405 Jerry Narron	.10	.05
406 Rob Dressler	.10	.05
407 Dave Heaverlo	.10	.05
408 Tom Paciorek	.10	.05
409 Carney Lansford	.25	.11
410 Brian Downing	.10	.05
411 Don Aase	.10	.05
412 Jim Barr	.10	.05
413 Don Baylor	.50	.23
414 Jim Fregosi MG	.10	.05
415 Dallas Green MG	.10	.05
416 Dave Lopes	.25	.11
417 Jerry Reuss	.25	.11
418 Rick Sutcliffe	.25	.11
419 Derrel Thomas	.10	.05
420 Tom Lasorda MG	1.00	.45
421 Charlie Leibrandt	.50	.23
422 Tom Seaver	1.25	.55
423 Ron Oester	.10	.05
424 Junior Kennedy	.10	.05
425 Tom Seaver	1.25	.55
426 Bobby Cox MG	.25	.11
427 Leon Durham	.25	.11
428 Terry Kennedy	.10	.05
429 Silvio Martinez	.10	.05
430 George Hendrick	.10	.05
431 Red Schoendienst MG	1.00	.45
432 Johnnie LeMaster	.10	.05
433 Vida Blue	.25	.11
434 John Montefusco	.10	.05
435 Terry Whitfield	.10	.05
436 Dave Bristol MG	.10	.05
437 Dale Murphy	1.00	.45
438 Jerry Dybzinski	.10	.05
439 Jorge Orta	.10	.05
440 Wayne Garland	.10	.05
441 Miguel Dilone	.10	.05
442 Dave Garcia MG	.10	.05
443 Don Money	.10	.05
444A Buck Martinez P1 ERR	.25	.11
Reverse negative		
444B Buck Martinez P2 COR	.10	.05
445 Jerry Augustine	.10	.05
446 Ben Oglivie	.25	.11
447 Jim Slaton	.10	.05
448 Doyle Alexander	.10	.05
449 Tony Bernazard	.10	.05
450 Scott Sanderson	.10	.05
451 David Palmer	.10	.05
452 Stan Bahnsen	.10	.05
453 Dick Williams MG	.10	.05
454 Rick Burleson	.10	.05
455 Gary Allenson	.10	.05
456 Bob Stanley	.10	.05
457A John Tudor P1 ERR	.25	.11
Lifetime W-L 9.7		
457B John Tudor P2 COR	.25	.11
Lifetime W-L 9-7		
458 Dwight Evans	.50	.23
459 Glenn Hubbard	.10	.05
460 U.L. Washington	.10	.05
461 Larry Gura	.10	.05
462 Rich Gale	.10	.05
463 Hal McRae	.50	.23
464 Jim Frey MG	.10	.05
465 Bucky Dent	.25	.11
466 Dennis Werth	.10	.05
467 Ron Davis	.10	.05
468 Reggie Jackson UER	1.25	.55
32 HR in 1970		
should be 23		
469 Bobby Brown	.10	.05
470 Mike Davis	.10	.05
471 Gaylord Perry	1.00	.45
472 Mark Belanger	.25	.11
473 Jim Palmer	.60	.25
474 Sammy Stewart	.10	.05
475 Tim Stoddard	.10	.05
476 Steve Stone	.25	.11
477 Jeff Newman	.10	.05
478 Steve McCatty	.10	.05
479 Billy Martin MG	.50	.23
480 Mitchell Page	.10	.05
481 Steve Carlton CY	1.00	.45
482 Bill Buckner	.25	.11
483A Ivan DeJesus P1 ERR	.25	.11
Lifetime hits 702		
483B Ivan DeJesus P2 COR	.10	.05
Lifetime hits 642		
484 Cliff Johnson	.10	.05
485 Lenny Randle	.10	.05
486 Larry Milbourne	.10	.05
487 Roy Smalley	.10	.05
488 John Castino	.10	.05
489 Ron Jackson	.10	.05
490A Dave Roberts P1	.25	.11

Career Highlights
Showed pop in
☐ 490B Dave Roberts P2 .10 .05
Declared himself
☐ 491 George Brett MVP 1.25 .55
☐ 492 Mike Cubbage .10 .05
☐ 493 Rob Wilfong .10 .05
☐ 494 Danny Goodwin .10 .05
☐ 495 Jose Morales .10 .05
☐ 496 Mickey Rivers .25 .11
☐ 497 Mike Edwards .10 .05
☐ 498 Mike Sadek .10 .05
☐ 499 Lenn Sakata .10 .05
☐ 500 Gene Michael MG .10 .05
☐ 501 Dave Roberts .10 .05
☐ 502 Steve Dillard .10 .05
☐ 503 Jim Essian .10 .05
☐ 504 Rance Mulliniks .10 .05
☐ 505 Darrell Porter .10 .05
☐ 506 Joe Torre MG .25 .11
☐ 507 Terry Crowley .10 .05
☐ 508 Bill Travers .10 .05
☐ 509 Nelson Norman .10 .05
☐ 510 Bob McClure .10 .05
☐ 511 Steve Howe .25 .11
☐ 512 Dave Rader .10 .05
☐ 513 Mick Kelleher .10 .05
☐ 514 Kiko Garcia .10 .05
☐ 515 Larry Biittner .10 .05
☐ 516A Willie Norwood P1 .25 .11
Career Highlights
Spent most of
☐ 516B Willie Norwood P2 .10 .05
Traded to Seattle
☐ 517 Bo Diaz .10 .05
☐ 518 Juan Beniquez .10 .05
☐ 519 Scot Thompson .10 .05
☐ 520 Jim Tracy .10 .05
☐ 521 Carlos Lezcano .10 .05
☐ 522 Joe Amalfitano MG .10 .05
☐ 523 Preston Hanna .10 .05
☐ 524A Ray Burris P1 .25 .11
Career Highlights
Went on Ö
☐ 524B Ray Burris P2 .10 .05
Drafted by Ö
☐ 525 Broderick Perkins .10 .05
☐ 526 Mickey Hatcher .25 .11
☐ 527 John Goryl MG .10 .05
☐ 528 Dick Davis .10 .05
☐ 529 Butch Wynegar .10 .05
☐ 530 Sal Butera .10 .05
☐ 531 Jerry Koosman .25 .11
☐ 532A Geoff Zahn P1 .25 .11
(Career Highlights
Was 2nd in
☐ 532B Geoff Zahn P2 .10 .05
Signed a 3 year
☐ 533 Dennis Martinez .50 .23
☐ 534 Gary Thomasson .10 .05
☐ 535 Steve Macko .10 .05
☐ 536 Jim Kaat .50 .23
☐ 537 Best Hitters 1.50 .70
George Brett
Rod Carew
☐ 538 Tim Raines 2.00 .90
☐ 539 Keith Smith .10 .05
☐ 540 Ken Macha .10 .05
☐ 541 Burt Hooton .10 .05
☐ 542 Butch Hobson .10 .05
☐ 543 Bill Stein .10 .05
☐ 544 Dave Stapleton .10 .05
☐ 545 Bob Pate .10 .05
☐ 546 Doug Corbett .10 .05
☐ 547 Darrell Jackson .10 .05
☐ 548 Pete Redfern .10 .05
☐ 549 Roger Erickson .10 .05
☐ 550 Al Hrabosky .10 .05
☐ 551 Dick Tidrow .10 .05
☐ 552 Dave Ford .10 .05
☐ 553 Dave Kingman .50 .23
☐ 554A Mike Vail P1 .25 .11
Career Highlights
After two
☐ 554B Mike Vail P2 .10 .05
Traded to
☐ 555A Jerry Martin P1 .25 .11
Career Highlights
Overcame a
☐ 555B Jerry Martin P2 .10 .05
Traded to
☐ 556A Jesus Figueroa P1 .25 .11
Career Highlights
Had an
☐ 556B Jesus Figueroa P2 .10 .05
Traded to
☐ 557 Don Stanhouse .10 .05
☐ 558 Barry Foote .10 .05
☐ 559 Tim Blackwell .10 .05
☐ 560 Bruce Sutter .25 .11
☐ 561 Rick Reuschel .25 .11
☐ 562 Lynn McGlothen .10 .05
☐ 563A Bob Owchinko P1 .25 .11
Career Highlights
Traded to
☐ 563B Bob Owchinko P2 .10 .05
Involved in a
☐ 564 John Verhoeven .10 .05
☐ 565 Ken Landreaux .10 .05
☐ 566A Glen Adams P1 ERR .25 .11
Name misspelled
☐ 566B Glenn Adams P2 COR .10 .05
☐ 567 Hosken Powell .10 .05
☐ 568 Dick Noles .10 .05
☐ 569 Danny Ainge 2.00 .90
☐ 570 Bobby Mattick MG .10 .05
☐ 571 Joe Lefebvre .10 .05
☐ 572 Bobby Clark .10 .05
☐ 573 Dennis Lamp .10 .05
☐ 574 Randy Lerch .10 .05
☐ 575 Mookie Wilson .50 .23
☐ 576 Ron LeFlore .25 .11
☐ 577 Jim Dwyer .10 .05
☐ 578 Bill Castro .10 .05
☐ 579 Greg Minton .10 .05
☐ 580 Mark Littell .10 .05
☐ 581 Andy Hassler .10 .05
☐ 582 Dave Stieb .25 .11
☐ 583 Ken Oberkfell .10 .05
☐ 584 Larry Bradford .10 .05
☐ 585 Fred Stanley .10 .05
☐ 586 Bill Caudill .10 .05
☐ 587 Doug Capilla .10 .05
☐ 588 George Riley .10 .05
☐ 589 Willie Hernandez .25 .11
☐ 590 Mike Schmidt MVP 1.25 .55
☐ 591 Steve Stone CY .10 .05
☐ 592 Rick Sofield .10 .05
☐ 593 Bombo Rivera .10 .05
☐ 594 Gary Ward .10 .05
☐ 595A Dave Edwards P1 .25 .11
Career Highlights
Sidelined the
☐ 595B Dave Edwards P2 .10 .05
Traded to
☐ 596 Mike Proly .10 .05
☐ 597 Tommy Boggs .10 .05
☐ 598 Greg Gross .10 .05
☐ 599 Elias Sosa .10 .05
☐ 600 Pat Kelly .10 .05
☐ 601A Checklist 1-120 P1 .25 .11
ERR Unnumbered
51 Donahue
☐ 601B Checklist 1-120 P2 .50 .23
COR Unnumbered
51 Donohue
☐ 602 Checklist 121-240 .25 .11
Unnumbered
☐ 603A Checklist 241-360 P1 .25 .11
ERR Unnumbered
306 Mathews
☐ 603B Checklist 241-360 P2 .25 .11
COR Unnumbered
306 Matthews
☐ 604A Checklist 361-480 P1 .25 .11
ERR Unnumbered
379 Pujois
☐ 604B Checklist 361-480 P2 .25 .11
COR Unnumbered
379 Pujols
☐ 605A Checklist 481-600 P1 .25 .11
ERR Unnumbered
566 Glen Adams
☐ 605B Checklist 481-600 P2 .25 .11
COR Unnumbered
566 Glenn Adams

1982 Donruss

The 1982 Donruss set contains 653 numbered standard-size cards and seven unnumbered checklists. The first 26 cards of this set are entitled Diamond Kings (DK) and feature the artwork of Dick Perez of Perez-Steele Galleries. The set was marketed with puzzle pieces in 15-card packs rather than with bubble gum. There are 63 pieces to the puzzle, which, when put together, make a collage of Babe Ruth entitled "Hall of Fame Diamond King." The card stock in this year's Donruss cards is considerably thicker than the 1981 cards. The seven unnumbered checklist cards are arbitrarily assigned numbers 654 through 660 and are listed at the end of the list below. Notable Rookie Cards in this set include Brett Butler, Cal Ripken Jr., Lee Smith and Dave Stewart.

	NRMT	VG-E
COMPLETE SET (660)	70.00	32.00
COMP.FACT.SET (660)	75.00	34.00
COMMON CARD (1-660)	.10	.05
COMPLETE RUTH PUZZLE (63)	10.00	4.50

☐ 1 Pete Rose DK 2.00 .90
☐ 2 Gary Carter DK .20 .09
☐ 3 Steve Garvey DK .40 .18
☐ 4 Vida Blue DK .20 .09
☐ 5 Alan Trammell DK .40 .18
COR
☐ 5A Alan Trammel DK ERR .75 .35
(Name misspelled)
☐ 6 Len Barker DK .20 .09
☐ 7 Dwight Evans DK .40 .18
☐ 8 Rod Carew DK .75 .35
☐ 9 George Hendrick DK .20 .09
☐ 10 Phil Niekro DK .40 .18
☐ 11 Richie Zisk DK .20 .09
☐ 12 Dave Parker DK .20 .09
☐ 13 Nolan Ryan DK 4.00 1.80
☐ 14 Ivan DeJesus DK .20 .09
☐ 15 George Brett DK 2.00 .90
☐ 16 Tom Seaver DK 1.00 .45
☐ 17 Dave Kingman DK .40 .18
☐ 18 Dave Winfield DK 1.50 .70
☐ 19 Mike Norris DK .20 .09
☐ 20 Carlton Fisk DK .40 .18
☐ 21 Ozzie Smith DK 1.25 .55
☐ 22 Roy Smalley DK .20 .09
☐ 23 Buddy Bell DK .20 .09
☐ 24 Ken Singleton DK .20 .09
☐ 25 John Mayberry DK .20 .09
☐ 26 Gorman Thomas DK .20 .09
☐ 27 Earl Weaver MG .40 .18
☐ 28 Rollie Fingers .75 .35
☐ 29 Sparky Anderson MG .20 .09
☐ 30 Dennis Eckersley .75 .35
☐ 31 Dave Winfield 1.50 .70
☐ 32 Burt Hooton .10 .05
☐ 33 Rick Waits .10 .05
☐ 34 George Brett 1.50 .70
☐ 35 Steve McCatty .10 .05
☐ 36 Steve Rogers .10 .05
☐ 37 Bill Stein .10 .05
☐ 38 Steve Renko .10 .05
☐ 39 Mike Squires .10 .05
☐ 40 George Hendrick .10 .05
☐ 41 Bob Knepper .10 .05
☐ 42 Steve Carlton .75 .35
☐ 43 Larry Biittner .10 .05
☐ 44 Chris Welsh .10 .05
☐ 45 Steve Nicosia .10 .05
☐ 46 Jack Clark .20 .09
☐ 47 Chris Chambliss .20 .09
☐ 48 Ivan DeJesus .10 .05
☐ 49 Lee Mazzilli .10 .05
☐ 50 Julio Cruz .10 .05
☐ 51 Pete Redfern .10 .05
☐ 52 Dave Stieb .20 .09
☐ 53 Doug Corbett .10 .05
☐ 54 Jorge Bell .75 .35
☐ 55 Joe Simpson .10 .05
☐ 56 Rusty Staub .20 .09
☐ 57 Hector Cruz .10 .05
☐ 58 Claudell Washington .10 .05
☐ 59 Enrique Romo .10 .05
☐ 60 Gary Lavelle .10 .05
☐ 61 Tim Flannery .10 .05
☐ 62 Joe Nolan .10 .05
☐ 63 Larry Bowa .20 .09
☐ 64 Sixto Lezcano .10 .05
☐ 65 Joe Sambito .10 .05
☐ 66 Bruce Kison .10 .05
☐ 67 Wayne Nordhagen .10 .05
☐ 68 Woodie Fryman .10 .05
☐ 69 Billy Sample .10 .05
☐ 70 Amos Otis .20 .09
☐ 71 Matt Keough .10 .05
☐ 72 Toby Harrah .20 .09
☐ 73 Dave Righetti .75 .35
☐ 74 Carl Yastrzemski .75 .35
☐ 75 Bob Welch .20 .09
☐ 76 Alan Trammell COR .40 .18

76A	Alan Trammel ERR (Name misspelled)	1.00	.45
77	Rick Dempsey	.20	.09
78	Paul Molitor	1.25	.55
79	Dennis Martinez	.40	.18
80	Jim Slaton	.10	.05
81	Champ Summers	.10	.05
82	Carney Lansford	.20	.09
83	Barry Foote	.10	.05
84	Steve Garvey	.40	.18
85	Rick Manning	.10	.05
86	John Wathan	.10	.05
87	Brian Kingman	.10	.05
88	Andre Dawson UER (Middle name Fernando should be Nolan)	.75	.35
89	Jim Kern	.10	.05
90	Bobby Grich	.20	.09
91	Bob Forsch	.10	.05
92	Art Howe	.10	.05
93	Marty Bystrom	.10	.05
94	Ozzie Smith	2.00	.90
95	Dave Parker	.20	.09
96	Doyle Alexander	.10	.05
97	Al Hrabosky	.10	.05
98	Frank Taveras	.10	.05
99	Tim Blackwell	.10	.05
100	Floyd Bannister	.10	.05
101	Alfredo Griffin	.10	.05
102	Dave Engle	.10	.05
103	Mario Soto	.10	.05
104	Ross Baumgarten	.10	.05
105	Ken Singleton	.20	.09
106	Ted Simmons	.20	.09
107	Jack Morris	.20	.09
108	Bob Watson	.20	.09
109	Dwight Evans	.40	.18
110	Tom Lasorda MG	.40	.18
111	Bert Blyleven	.40	.18
112	Dan Quisenberry	.20	.09
113	Rickey Henderson	1.50	.70
114	Gary Carter	.75	.35
115	Brian Downing	.10	.05
116	Al Oliver	.20	.09
117	LaMarr Hoyt	.10	.05
118	Cesar Cedeno	.20	.09
119	Keith Moreland	.10	.05
120	Bob Shirley	.10	.05
121	Terry Kennedy	.10	.05
122	Frank Pastore	.10	.05
123	Gene Garber	.10	.05
124	Tony Pena	.10	.05
125	Allen Ripley	.10	.05
126	Randy Martz	.10	.05
127	Richie Zisk	.10	.05
128	Mike Scott	.20	.09
129	Lloyd Moseby	.10	.05
130	Rob Wilfong	.10	.05
131	Tim Stoddard	.10	.05
132	Gorman Thomas	.20	.09
133	Dan Petry	.10	.05
134	Bob Stanley	.10	.05
135	Lou Piniella	.20	.09
136	Pedro Guerrero	.20	.09
137	Len Barker	.10	.05
138	Rich Gale	.10	.05
139	Wayne Gross	.10	.05
140	Tim Wallach	.40	.18
141	Gene Mauch MG	.10	.05
142	Doc Medich	.10	.05
143	Tony Bernazard	.10	.05
144	Bill Virdon MG	.10	.05
145	John Littlefield	.10	.05
146	Dave Bergman	.10	.05
147	Dick Davis	.10	.05
148	Tom Seaver	1.00	.45
149	Matt Sinatro	.10	.05
150	Chuck Tanner MG	.10	.05
151	Leon Durham	.10	.05
152	Gene Tenace	.20	.09
153	Al Bumbry	.20	.09
154	Mark Brouhard	.10	.05
155	Rick Peters	.10	.05
156	Jerry Remy	.10	.05
157	Rick Reuschel	.20	.09
158	Steve Howe	.10	.05
159	Alan Bannister	.10	.05
160	U.L. Washington	.10	.05
161	Rick Langford	.10	.05
162	Bill Gullickson	.10	.05
163	Mark Wagner	.10	.05
164	Geoff Zahn	.10	.05
165	Ron LeFlore	.20	.09
166	Dane Iorg	.10	.05
167	Joe Niekro	.20	.09
168	Pete Rose	1.00	.45
169	Dave Collins	.10	.05
170	Rick Wise	.10	.05
171	Jim Bibby	.10	.05
172	Larry Herndon	.10	.05
173	Bob Horner	.20	.09
174	Steve Dillard	.10	.05
175	Mookie Wilson	.20	.09
176	Dan Meyer	.10	.05
177	Fernando Arroyo	.10	.05
178	Jackson Todd	.10	.05
179	Darrell Jackson	.10	.05
180	Alvis Woods	.10	.05
181	Jim Anderson	.10	.05
182	Dave Kingman	.40	.18
183	Steve Henderson	.10	.05
184	Brian Asselstine	.10	.05
185	Rod Scurry	.10	.05
186	Fred Breining	.10	.05
187	Danny Boone	.10	.05
188	Junior Kennedy	.10	.05
189	Sparky Lyle	.20	.09
190	Whitey Herzog MG	.20	.09
191	Dave Smith	.10	.05
192	Ed Ott	.10	.05
193	Greg Luzinski	.20	.09
194	Bill Lee	.20	.09
195	Don Zimmer MG	.10	.05
196	Hal McRae	.20	.09
197	Mike Norris	.10	.05
198	Duane Kuiper	.10	.05
199	Rick Cerone	.10	.05
200	Jim Rice	.20	.09
201	Steve Yeager	.10	.05
202	Tom Brookens	.10	.05
203	Jose Morales	.10	.05
204	Roy Howell	.10	.05
205	Tippy Martinez	.10	.05
206	Moose Haas	.10	.05
207	Al Cowens	.10	.05
208	Dave Stapleton	.10	.05
209	Bucky Dent	.20	.09
210	Ron Cey	.20	.09
211	Jorge Orta	.10	.05
212	Jamie Quirk	.10	.05
213	Jeff Jones	.10	.05
214	Tim Raines	.75	.35
215	Jon Matlack	.10	.05
216	Rod Carew	.75	.35
217	Jim Kaat	.20	.09
218	Joe Pittman	.10	.05
219	Larry Christenson	.10	.05
220	Juan Bonilla	.10	.05
221	Mike Easler	.10	.05
222	Vida Blue	.20	.09
223	Rick Camp	.10	.05
224	Mike Jorgensen	.10	.05
225	Jody Davis	.10	.05
226	Mike Parrott	.10	.05
227	Jim Clancy	.10	.05
228	Hosken Powell	.10	.05
229	Tom Hume	.10	.05
230	Britt Burns	.10	.05
231	Jim Palmer	.75	.35
232	Bob Rodgers MG	.10	.05
233	Milt Wilcox	.10	.05
234	Dave Revering	.10	.05
235	Mike Torrez	.10	.05
236	Robert Castillo	.10	.05
237	Von Hayes	.20	.09
238	Renie Martin	.10	.05
239	Dwayne Murphy	.10	.05
240	Rodney Scott	.10	.05
241	Fred Patek	.10	.05
242	Mickey Rivers	.10	.05
243	Steve Trout	.10	.05
244	Jose Cruz	.20	.09
245	Manny Trillo	.10	.05
246	Lary Sorensen	.10	.05
247	Dave Edwards	.10	.05
248	Dan Driessen	.10	.05
249	Tommy Boggs	.10	.05
250	Dale Berra	.10	.05
251	Ed Whitson	.10	.05
252	Lee Smith	2.50	1.10
253	Tom Paciorek	.10	.05
254	Pat Zachry	.10	.05
255	Luis Leal	.10	.05
256	John Castino	.10	.05
257	Rich Dauer	.10	.05
258	Cecil Cooper	.20	.09
259	Dave Rozema	.10	.05
260	John Tudor	.10	.05
261	Jerry Mumphrey	.10	.05
262	Jay Johnstone	.20	.09
263	Bo Diaz	.10	.05
264	Dennis Leonard	.10	.05
265	Jim Spencer	.10	.05
266	John Milner	.10	.05
267	Don Aase	.10	.05
268	Jim Sundberg	.20	.09
269	Lamar Johnson	.10	.05
270	Frank LaCorte	.10	.05
271	Barry Evans	.10	.05
272	Enos Cabell	.10	.05
273	Del Unser	.10	.05
274	George Foster	.20	.09
275	Brett Butler	1.25	.55
276	Lee Lacy	.10	.05
277	Ken Reitz	.10	.05
278	Keith Hernandez	.20	.09
279	Doug DeCinces	.20	.09
280	Charlie Moore	.10	.05
281	Lance Parrish	.40	.18
282	Ralph Houk MG	.20	.09
283	Rich Gossage	.40	.18
284	Jerry Reuss	.20	.09
285	Mike Stanton	.10	.05
286	Frank White	.20	.09
287	Bob Owchinko	.10	.05
288	Scott Sanderson	.10	.05
289	Bump Wills	.10	.05
290	Dave Frost	.10	.05
291	Chet Lemon	.10	.05
292	Tito Landrum	.10	.05
293	Vern Ruhle	.10	.05
294	Mike Schmidt	1.00	.45
295	Sam Mejias	.10	.05
296	Gary Lucas	.10	.05
297	John Candelaria	.10	.05
298	Jerry Martin	.10	.05
299	Dale Murphy	.75	.35
300	Mike Lum	.10	.05
301	Tom Hausman	.10	.05
302	Glenn Abbott	.10	.05
303	Roger Erickson	.10	.05
304	Otto Velez	.10	.05
305	Danny Goodwin	.10	.05
306	John Mayberry	.10	.05
307	Lenny Randle	.10	.05
308	Bob Bailor	.10	.05
309	Jerry Morales	.10	.05
310	Rufino Linares	.10	.05
311	Kent Tekulve	.20	.09
312	Joe Morgan	.75	.35
313	John Urrea	.10	.05
314	Paul Householder	.10	.05
315	Garry Maddox	.10	.05
316	Mike Ramsey	.10	.05
317	Alan Ashby	.10	.05
318	Bob Clark	.10	.05
319	Tony LaRussa MG	.20	.09
320	Charlie Lea	.10	.05
321	Danny Darwin	.10	.05
322	Cesar Geronimo	.10	.05
323	Tom Underwood	.10	.05
324	Andre Thornton	.10	.05
325	Rudy May	.10	.05
326	Frank Tanana	.20	.09
327	Dave Lopes	.20	.09
328	Richie Hebner	.20	.09
329	Mike Flanagan	.20	.09
330	Mike Caldwell	.10	.05
331	Scott McGregor	.10	.05
332	Jerry Augustine	.10	.05
333	Stan Papi	.10	.05
334	Rick Miller	.10	.05
335	Graig Nettles	.20	.09
336	Dusty Baker	.40	.18
337	Dave Garcia MG	.10	.05
338	Larry Gura	.10	.05
339	Cliff Johnson	.10	.05
340	Warren Cromartie	.10	.05
341	Steve Comer	.10	.05
342	Rick Burleson	.10	.05
343	John Martin	.10	.05
344	Craig Reynolds	.10	.05
345	Mike Proly	.10	.05
346	Ruppert Jones	.10	.05
347	Omar Moreno	.10	.05
348	Greg Minton	.10	.05
349	Rick Mahler	.10	.05
350	Alex Trevino	.10	.05
351	Mike Krukow	.10	.05
352A	Shane Rawley ERR (Photo actually Jim Anderson)	.40	.18
352B	Shane Rawley COR	.10	.05
353	Garth Iorg	.10	.05
354	Pete Mackanin	.10	.05
355	Paul Moskau	.10	.05
356	Richard Dotson	.10	.05
357	Steve Stone	.20	.09
358	Larry Hisle	.10	.05
359	Aurelio Lopez	.10	.05
360	Oscar Gamble	.10	.05

☐ 361 Tom Burgmeier .10 .05
☐ 362 Terry Forster .10 .05
☐ 363 Joe Charboneau .20 .09
☐ 364 Ken Brett .10 .05
☐ 365 Tony Armas .10 .05
☐ 366 Chris Speier .10 .05
☐ 367 Fred Lynn .20 .09
☐ 368 Buddy Bell .20 .09
☐ 369 Jim Essian .10 .05
☐ 370 Terry Puhl .10 .05
☐ 371 Greg Gross .10 .05
☐ 372 Bruce Sutter .20 .09
☐ 373 Joe Lefebvre .10 .05
☐ 374 Ray Knight .20 .09
☐ 375 Bruce Benedict .10 .05
☐ 376 Tim Foli .10 .05
☐ 377 Al Holland .10 .05
☐ 378 Ken Kravec .10 .05
☐ 379 Jeff Burroughs .10 .05
☐ 380 Pete Falcone .10 .05
☐ 381 Ernie Whitt .10 .05
☐ 382 Brad Havens .10 .05
☐ 383 Terry Crowley .10 .05
☐ 384 Don Money .10 .05
☐ 385 Dan Schatzeder .10 .05
☐ 386 Gary Allenson .10 .05
☐ 387 Yogi Berra CO .75 .35
☐ 388 Ken Landreaux .10 .05
☐ 389 Mike Hargrove .20 .09
☐ 390 Darryl Motley .10 .05
☐ 391 Dave McKay .10 .05
☐ 392 Stan Bahnsen .10 .05
☐ 393 Ken Forsch .10 .05
☐ 394 Mario Mendoza .10 .05
☐ 395 Jim Morrison .10 .05
☐ 396 Mike Ivie .10 .05
☐ 397 Broderick Perkins .10 .05
☐ 398 Darrell Evans .20 .09
☐ 399 Ron Reed .10 .05
☐ 400 Johnny Bench 1.00 .45
☐ 401 Steve Bedrosian .20 .09
☐ 402 Bill Robinson .10 .05
☐ 403 Bill Buckner .20 .09
☐ 404 Ken Oberkfell .10 .05
☐ 405 Cal Ripken 40.00 18.00
☐ 406 Jim Gantner .20 .09
☐ 407 Kirk Gibson .75 .35
☐ 408 Tony Perez .75 .35
☐ 409 Tommy John UER .40 .18
(Text says 52-56 as Yankee, should be 52-26)
☐ 410 Dave Stewart 1.00 .45
☐ 411 Dan Spillner .10 .05
☐ 412 Willie Aikens .10 .05
☐ 413 Mike Heath .10 .05
☐ 414 Ray Burris .10 .05
☐ 415 Leon Roberts .10 .05
☐ 416 Mike Witt .20 .09
☐ 417 Bob Molinaro .10 .05
☐ 418 Steve Braun .10 .05
☐ 419 Nolan Ryan UER 5.00 2.20
(Nisnumbering of Nolan's no-hitters on card back)
☐ 420 Tug McGraw .20 .09
☐ 421 Dave Concepcion .20 .09
☐ 422A Juan Eichelberger ERR (Photo actually Gary Lucas) .40 .18
☐ 422B Juan Eichelberger COR .10 .05
☐ 423 Rick Rhoden .10 .05
☐ 424 Frank Robinson MG .40 .18
☐ 425 Eddie Miller .10 .05
☐ 426 Bill Caudill .10 .05
☐ 427 Doug Flynn .10 .05
☐ 428 Larry Andersen UER .10 .05
(Misspelled Anderson on card front)
☐ 429 Al Williams .10 .05
☐ 430 Jerry Garvin .10 .05
☐ 431 Glenn Adams .10 .05
☐ 432 Barry Bonnell .10 .05
☐ 433 Jerry Narron .10 .05
☐ 434 John Stearns .10 .05
☐ 435 Mike Tyson .10 .05
☐ 436 Glenn Hubbard .10 .05
☐ 437 Eddie Solomon .10 .05
☐ 438 Jeff Leonard .10 .05
☐ 439 Randy Bass .10 .05
☐ 440 Mike LaCoss .10 .05
☐ 441 Gary Matthews .20 .09
☐ 442 Mark Littell .10 .05
☐ 443 Don Sutton .75 .35
☐ 444 John Harris .10 .05
☐ 445 Vada Pinson CO .20 .09
☐ 446 Elias Sosa .10 .05
☐ 447 Charlie Hough .20 .09
☐ 448 Willie Wilson .20 .09
☐ 449 Fred Stanley .10 .05
☐ 450 Tom Veryzer .10 .05
☐ 451 Ron Davis .10 .05
☐ 452 Mark Clear .10 .05
☐ 453 Bill Russell .20 .09
☐ 454 Lou Whitaker .75 .35
☐ 455 Dan Graham .10 .05
☐ 456 Reggie Cleveland .10 .05
☐ 457 Sammy Stewart .10 .05
☐ 458 Pete Vuckovich .10 .05
☐ 459 John Wockenfuss .10 .05
☐ 460 Glenn Hoffman .10 .05
☐ 461 Willie Randolph .20 .09
☐ 462 Fernando Valenzuela .75 .35
☐ 463 Ron Hassey .10 .05
☐ 464 Paul Splittorff .10 .05
☐ 465 Rob Picciolo .10 .05
☐ 466 Larry Parrish .10 .05
☐ 467 Johnny Grubb .10 .05
☐ 468 Dan Ford .10 .05
☐ 469 Silvio Martinez .10 .05
☐ 470 Kiko Garcia .10 .05
☐ 471 Bob Boone .20 .09
☐ 472 Luis Salazar .10 .05
☐ 473 Randy Niemann .10 .05
☐ 474 Tom Griffin .10 .05
☐ 475 Phil Niekro .75 .35
☐ 476 Hubie Brooks .20 .09
☐ 477 Dick Tidrow .10 .05
☐ 478 Jim Beattie .10 .05
☐ 479 Damaso Garcia .10 .05
☐ 480 Mickey Hatcher .10 .05
☐ 481 Joe Price .10 .05
☐ 482 Ed Farmer .10 .05
☐ 483 Eddie Murray 1.25 .55
☐ 484 Ben Oglivie .20 .09
☐ 485 Kevin Saucier .10 .05
☐ 486 Bobby Murcer .20 .09
☐ 487 Bill Campbell .10 .05
☐ 488 Reggie Smith .20 .09
☐ 489 Wayne Garland .10 .05
☐ 490 Jim Wright .10 .05
☐ 491 Billy Martin MG .20 .09
☐ 492 Jim Fanning MG .10 .05
☐ 493 Don Baylor .40 .18
☐ 494 Rick Honeycutt .10 .05
☐ 495 Carlton Fisk .75 .35
☐ 496 Denny Walling .10 .05
☐ 497 Bake McBride .10 .05
☐ 498 Darrell Porter .20 .09
☐ 499 Gene Richards .10 .05
☐ 500 Ron Oester .10 .05
☐ 501 Ken Dayley .10 .05
☐ 502 Jason Thompson .10 .05
☐ 503 Milt May .10 .05
☐ 504 Doug Bird .10 .05
☐ 505 Bruce Bochte .10 .05
☐ 506 Neil Allen .10 .05
☐ 507 Joey McLaughlin .10 .05
☐ 508 Butch Wynegar .10 .05
☐ 509 Gary Roenicke .10 .05
☐ 510 Robin Yount 1.50 .70
☐ 511 Dave Tobik .10 .05
☐ 512 Rich Gedman .20 .09
☐ 513 Gene Nelson .10 .05
☐ 514 Rick Monday .10 .05
☐ 515 Miguel Dilone .10 .05
☐ 516 Clint Hurdle .10 .05
☐ 517 Jeff Newman .10 .05
☐ 518 Grant Jackson .10 .05
☐ 519 Andy Hassler .10 .05
☐ 520 Pat Putnam .10 .05
☐ 521 Greg Pryor .10 .05
☐ 522 Tony Scott .10 .05
☐ 523 Steve Mura .10 .05
☐ 524 Johnnie LeMaster .10 .05
☐ 525 Dick Ruthven .10 .05
☐ 526 John McNamara MG .10 .05
☐ 527 Larry McWilliams .10 .05
☐ 528 Johnny Ray .20 .09
☐ 529 Pat Tabler .20 .09
☐ 530 Tom Herr .20 .09
☐ 531A San Diego Chicken ERR (Without TM) .75 .35
☐ 531B San Diego Chicken COR (With TM) .75 .35
☐ 532 Sal Butera .10 .05
☐ 533 Mike Griffin .10 .05
☐ 534 Kelvin Moore .10 .05
☐ 535 Reggie Jackson 1.00 .45
☐ 536 Ed Romero .10 .05
☐ 537 Derrel Thomas .10 .05
☐ 538 Mike O'Berry .10 .05
☐ 539 Jack O'Connor .10 .05
☐ 540 Bob Ojeda .40 .18
☐ 541 Roy Lee Jackson .10 .05
☐ 542 Lynn Jones .10 .05
☐ 543 Gaylord Perry .75 .35
☐ 544A Phil Garner ERR (Reverse negative) .40 .18
☐ 544B Phil Garner COR .20 .09
☐ 545 Garry Templeton .10 .05
☐ 546 Rafael Ramirez .10 .05
☐ 547 Jeff Reardon .40 .18
☐ 548 Ron Guidry .20 .09
☐ 549 Tim Laudner .10 .05
☐ 550 John Henry Johnson .10 .05
☐ 551 Chris Bando .10 .05
☐ 552 Bobby Brown .10 .05
☐ 553 Larry Bradford .10 .05
☐ 554 Scott Fletcher .20 .09
☐ 555 Jerry Royster .10 .05
☐ 556 Shooty Babitt UER .10 .05
(Spelled Babbitt on front)
☐ 557 Kent Hrbek 1.00 .45
☐ 558 Yankee Winners .20 .09
Ron Guidry
Tommy John
☐ 559 Mark Bomback .10 .05
☐ 560 Julio Valdez .10 .05
☐ 561 Buck Martinez .10 .05
☐ 562 Mike A. Marshall .20 .09
☐ 563 Rennie Stennett .10 .05
☐ 564 Steve Crawford .10 .05
☐ 565 Bob Babcock .10 .05
☐ 566 Johnny Podres CO .20 .09
☐ 567 Paul Serna .10 .05
☐ 568 Harold Baines .40 .18
☐ 569 Dave LaRoche .10 .05
☐ 570 Lee May .20 .09
☐ 571 Gary Ward .10 .05
☐ 572 John Denny .10 .05
☐ 573 Roy Smalley .10 .05
☐ 574 Bob Brenly .10 .05
☐ 575 Bronx Bombers 1.50 .70
Reggie Jackson
Dave Winfield
☐ 576 Luis Pujols .10 .05
☐ 577 Butch Hobson .10 .05
☐ 578 Harvey Kuenn MG .20 .09
☐ 579 Cal Ripken Sr. CO .20 .09
☐ 580 Juan Berenguer .10 .05
☐ 581 Benny Ayala .10 .05
☐ 582 Vance Law .10 .05
☐ 583 Rick Leach .10 .05
☐ 584 George Frazier .10 .05
☐ 585 Phillies Finest 1.00 .45
Pete Rose
Mike Schmidt
☐ 586 Joe Rudi .10 .05
☐ 587 Juan Beniquez .10 .05
☐ 588 Luis DeLeon .10 .05
☐ 589 Craig Swan .10 .05
☐ 590 Dave Chalk .10 .05
☐ 591 Billy Gardner MG .10 .05
☐ 592 Sal Bando .20 .09
☐ 593 Bert Campaneris .20 .09
☐ 594 Steve Kemp .10 .05
☐ 595A Randy Lerch ERR (Braves) .40 .18
☐ 595B Randy Lerch COR (Brewers) .10 .05
☐ 596 Bryan Clark .10 .05
☐ 597 Dave Ford .10 .05
☐ 598 Mike Scioscia .20 .09
☐ 599 John Lowenstein .10 .05
☐ 600 Rene Lachemann MG .10 .05
☐ 601 Mick Kelleher .10 .05
☐ 602 Ron Jackson .10 .05
☐ 603 Jerry Koosman .20 .09
☐ 604 Dave Goltz .10 .05
☐ 605 Ellis Valentine .10 .05
☐ 606 Lonnie Smith .20 .09
☐ 607 Joaquin Andujar .20 .09
☐ 608 Garry Hancock .10 .05
☐ 609 Jerry Turner .10 .05
☐ 610 Bob Bonner .10 .05
☐ 611 Jim Dwyer .10 .05
☐ 612 Terry Bulling .10 .05
☐ 613 Joel Youngblood .10 .05
☐ 614 Larry Milbourne .10 .05
☐ 615 Gene Roof UER .10 .05
(Name on front is Phil Roof)
☐ 616 Keith Drumwright .10 .05
☐ 617 Dave Rosello .10 .05
☐ 618 Rickey Keeton .10 .05
☐ 619 Dennis Lamp .10 .05
☐ 620 Sid Monge .10 .05
☐ 621 Jerry White .10 .05

Card	NRMT	VG-E
622 Luis Aguayo	.10	.05
623 Jamie Easterly	.10	.05
624 Steve Sax	.75	.35
625 Dave Roberts	.10	.05
626 Rick Bosetti	.10	.05
627 Terry Francona	.10	.05
628 Pride of Reds Tom Seaver Johnny Bench	1.00	.45
629 Paul Mirabella	.10	.05
630 Rance Mulliniks	.10	.05
631 Kevin Hickey	.10	.05
632 Reid Nichols	.10	.05
633 Dave Geisel	.10	.05
634 Ken Griffey	.20	.09
635 Bob Lemon MG	.75	.35
636 Orlando Sanchez	.10	.05
637 Bill Almon	.10	.05
638 Danny Ainge	1.00	.45
639 Willie Stargell	.75	.35
640 Bob Sykes	.10	.05
641 Ed Lynch	.10	.05
642 John Ellis	.10	.05
643 Ferguson Jenkins	.75	.35
644 Lenn Sakata	.10	.05
645 Julio Gonzalez	.10	.05
646 Jesse Orosco	.10	.05
647 Jerry Dybzinski	.10	.05
648 Tommy Davis CO	.20	.09
649 Ron Gardenhire	.10	.05
650 Felipe Alou CO	.20	.09
651 Harvey Haddix CO	.20	.09
652 Willie Upshaw	.10	.05
653 Bill Madlock	.20	.09
654A DK Checklist 1-26 ERR (Unnumbered) (With Trammel)	.75	.35
654B DK Checklist 1-26 COR (Unnumbered) (With Trammell)	.20	.09
655 Checklist 27-130 (Unnumbered)	.20	.09
656 Checklist 131-234 (Unnumbered)	.20	.09
657 Checklist 235-338 (Unnumbered)	.20	.09
658 Checklist 339-442 (Unnumbered)	.20	.09
659 Checklist 443-544 (Unnumbered)	.20	.09
660 Checklist 545-653 (Unnumbered)	.20	.09

1983 Donruss

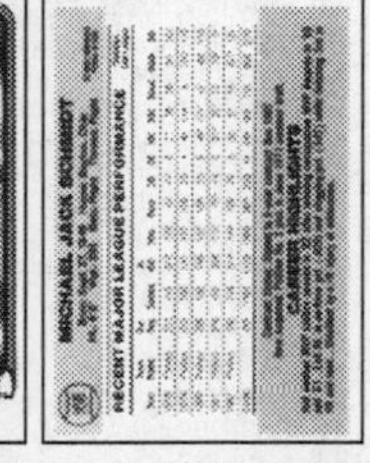

he 1983 Donruss baseball set leads off with a 26-card iamond Kings (DK) series. Of the remaining 634 tandard-size cards, two are combination cards, one ortrays the San Diego Chicken, one shows the completed y Cobb puzzle, and seven are unnumbered checklist ards. The seven unnumbered checklist cards are rbitrarily assigned numbers 654 through 660 and are sted at the end of the list below. All cards measure the tandard size. Card fronts feature full color photos around framed white broder. Several printing variations are vailable but the complete set price below includes only he more common of each variation pair. Cards were sued in 15-card packs which included a three-piece Ty obb puzzle panel (21 different panels were needed to omplete the puzzle). Notable Rookie Cards include Wade oggs, Tony Gwynn and Ryne Sandberg.

	NRMT	VG-E
OMPLETE SET (660)	80.00	36.00
OMPLETE FACT.SET (660)	90.00	40.00
OMMON CARD (1-660)	.10	.05
COMPLETE COBB PUZZLE	5.00	2.20

Card	NRMT	VG-E
1 Fernando Valenzuela DK	.75	.35
2 Rollie Fingers DK	.75	.35
3 Reggie Jackson DK	.75	.35
4 Jim Palmer DK	.75	.35
5 Jack Morris DK	.20	.09
6 George Foster DK	.20	.09
7 Jim Sundberg DK	.20	.09
8 Willie Stargell DK	.40	.18
9 Dave Stieb DK	.20	.09
10 Joe Niekro DK	.20	.09
11 Rickey Henderson DK	1.25	.55
12 Dale Murphy DK	.75	.35
13 Toby Harrah DK	.20	.09
14 Bill Buckner DK	.20	.09
15 Willie Wilson DK	.20	.09
16 Steve Carlton DK	.40	.18
17 Ron Guidry DK	.20	.09
18 Steve Rogers DK	.20	.09
19 Kent Hrbek DK	.20	.09
20 Keith Hernandez DK	.20	.09
21 Floyd Bannister DK	.20	.09
22 Johnny Bench DK	.40	.18
23 Britt Burns DK	.20	.09
24 Joe Morgan DK	.40	.18
25 Carl Yastrzemski DK	.40	.18
26 Terry Kennedy DK	.20	.09
27 Gary Roenicke	.10	.05
28 Dwight Bernard	.10	.05
29 Pat Underwood	.10	.05
30 Gary Allenson	.10	.05
31 Ron Guidry	.20	.09
32 Burt Hooton	.10	.05
33 Chris Bando	.10	.05
34 Vida Blue	.20	.09
35 Rickey Henderson	1.00	.45
36 Ray Burris	.10	.05
37 John Butcher	.10	.05
38 Don Aase	.10	.05
39 Jerry Koosman	.20	.09
40 Bruce Sutter	.20	.09
41 Jose Cruz	.20	.09
42 Pete Rose	1.00	.45
43 Cesar Cedeno	.20	.09
44 Floyd Chiffer	.10	.05
45 Larry McWilliams	.10	.05
46 Alan Fowlkes	.10	.05
47 Dale Murphy	.75	.35
48 Doug Bird	.10	.05
49 Hubie Brooks	.20	.09
50 Floyd Bannister	.10	.05
51 Jack O'Connor	.10	.05
52 Steve Senteney	.10	.05
53 Gary Gaetti	.75	.35
54 Damaso Garcia	.10	.05
55 Gene Nelson	.10	.05
56 Mookie Wilson	.20	.09
57 Allen Ripley	.10	.05
58 Bob Horner	.10	.05
59 Tony Pena	.10	.05
60 Gary Lavelle	.10	.05
61 Tim Lollar	.10	.05
62 Frank Pastore	.10	.05
63 Garry Maddox	.10	.05
64 Bob Forsch	.10	.05
65 Harry Spilman	.10	.05
66 Geoff Zahn	.10	.05
67 Salome Barojas	.10	.05
68 David Palmer	.10	.05
69 Charlie Hough	.20	.09
70 Dan Quisenberry	.20	.09
71 Tony Armas	.10	.05
72 Rick Sutcliffe	.20	.09
73 Steve Balboni	.10	.05
74 Jerry Remy	.10	.05
75 Mike Scioscia	.10	.05
76 John Wockenfuss	.10	.05
77 Jim Palmer	.75	.35
78 Rollie Fingers	.75	.35
79 Joe Nolan	.10	.05
80 Pete Vuckovich	.10	.05
81 Rick Leach	.10	.05
82 Rick Miller	.10	.05
83 Graig Nettles	.20	.09
84 Ron Cey	.20	.09
85 Miguel Dilone	.10	.05
86 John Wathan	.10	.05
87 Kelvin Moore	.10	.05
88A Byrn Smith ERR (Sic, Bryn)	.20	.09
88B Bryn Smith COR	.40	.18
89 Dave Hostetler	.10	.05
90 Rod Carew	.60	.25
91 Lonnie Smith	.10	.05
92 Bob Knepper	.10	.05
93 Marty Bystrom	.10	.05
94 Chris Welsh	.10	.05
95 Jason Thompson	.10	.05
96 Tom O'Malley	.10	.05
97 Phil Niekro	.75	.35
98 Neil Allen	.10	.05
99 Bill Buckner	.20	.09
100 Ed VandeBerg	.10	.05
101 Jim Clancy	.10	.05
102 Robert Castillo	.10	.05
103 Bruce Berenyi	.10	.05
104 Carlton Fisk	.75	.35
105 Mike Flanagan	.20	.09
106 Cecil Cooper	.20	.09
107 Jack Morris	.20	.09
108 Mike Morgan	.10	.05
109 Luis Aponte	.10	.05
110 Pedro Guerrero	.20	.09
111 Len Barker	.10	.05
112 Willie Wilson	.20	.09
113 Dave Beard	.10	.05
114 Mike Gates	.10	.05
115 Reggie Jackson	1.00	.45
116 George Wright	.10	.05
117 Vance Law	.10	.05
118 Nolan Ryan	4.00	1.80
119 Mike Krukow	.10	.05
120 Ozzie Smith	1.50	.70
121 Broderick Perkins	.10	.05
122 Tom Seaver	1.00	.45
123 Chris Chambliss	.20	.09
124 Chuck Tanner MG	.10	.05
125 Johnnie LeMaster	.10	.05
126 Mel Hall	.20	.09
127 Bruce Bochte	.10	.05
128 Charlie Puleo	.10	.05
129 Luis Leal	.10	.05
130 John Pacella	.10	.05
131 Glenn Gulliver	.10	.05
132 Don Money	.10	.05
133 Dave Rozema	.10	.05
134 Bruce Hurst	.20	.09
135 Rudy May	.10	.05
136 Tom Lasorda MG	.40	.18
137 Dan Spillner UER (Photo actually Ed Whitson)	.10	.05
138 Jerry Martin	.10	.05
139 Mike Norris	.10	.05
140 Al Oliver	.20	.09
141 Daryl Sconiers	.10	.05
142 Lamar Johnson	.10	.05
143 Harold Baines	.40	.18
144 Alan Ashby	.10	.05
145 Garry Templeton	.10	.05
146 Al Holland	.10	.05
147 Bo Diaz	.10	.05
148 Dave Concepcion	.20	.09
149 Rick Camp	.10	.05
150 Jim Morrison	.10	.05
151 Randy Martz	.10	.05
152 Keith Hernandez	.20	.09
153 John Lowenstein	.10	.05
154 Mike Caldwell	.10	.05
155 Milt Wilcox	.10	.05
156 Rich Gedman	.10	.05
157 Rich Gossage	.40	.18
158 Jerry Reuss	.20	.09
159 Ron Hassey	.10	.05
160 Larry Gura	.10	.05
161 Dwayne Murphy	.10	.05
162 Woodie Fryman	.10	.05
163 Steve Comer	.10	.05
164 Ken Forsch	.10	.05
165 Dennis Lamp	.10	.05
166 David Green	.10	.05
167 Terry Puhl	.10	.05
168 Mike Schmidt (Wearing 37 rather than 20)	1.00	.45
169 Eddie Milner	.10	.05
170 John Curtis	.10	.05
171 Don Robinson	.10	.05
172 Rich Gale	.10	.05
173 Steve Bedrosian	.20	.09
174 Willie Hernandez	.20	.09
175 Ron Gardenhire	.10	.05
176 Jim Beattie	.10	.05
177 Tim Laudner	.10	.05
178 Buck Martinez	.10	.05
179 Kent Hrbek	.20	.09
180 Alfredo Griffin	.10	.05
181 Larry Andersen	.10	.05
182 Pete Falcone	.10	.05
183 Jody Davis	.10	.05
184 Glenn Hubbard	.10	.05
185 Dale Berra	.10	.05
186 Greg Minton	.10	.05
187 Gary Lucas	.10	.05
188 Dave Van Gorder	.10	.05
189 Bob Dernier	.10	.05
190 Willie McGee	.75	.35
191 Dickie Thon	.10	.05
192 Bob Boone	.20	.09

☐ 193 Britt Burns .10 .05
☐ 194 Jeff Reardon .20 .09
☐ 195 Jon Matlack .10 .05
☐ 196 Don Slaught .40 .18
☐ 197 Fred Stanley .10 .05
☐ 198 Rick Manning .10 .05
☐ 199 Dave Righetti .20 .09
☐ 200 Dave Stapleton .10 .05
☐ 201 Steve Yeager .10 .05
☐ 202 Enos Cabell .10 .05
☐ 203 Sammy Stewart .10 .05
☐ 204 Moose Haas .10 .05
☐ 205 Lenn Sakata .10 .05
☐ 206 Charlie Moore .10 .05
☐ 207 Alan Trammell .75 .35
☐ 208 Jim Rice .40 .18
☐ 209 Roy Smalley .10 .05
☐ 210 Bill Russell .20 .09
☐ 211 Andre Thornton .10 .05
☐ 212 Willie Aikens .10 .05
☐ 213 Dave McKay .10 .05
☐ 214 Tim Blackwell .10 .05
☐ 215 Buddy Bell .20 .09
☐ 216 Doug DeCinces .20 .09
☐ 217 Tom Herr .20 .09
☐ 218 Frank LaCorte .10 .05
☐ 219 Steve Carlton .75 .35
☐ 220 Terry Kennedy .10 .05
☐ 221 Mike Easler .10 .05
☐ 222 Jack Clark .20 .09
☐ 223 Gene Garber .10 .05
☐ 224 Scott Holman .10 .05
☐ 225 Mike Proly .10 .05
☐ 226 Terry Bulling .10 .05
☐ 227 Jerry Garvin .10 .05
☐ 228 Ron Davis .10 .05
☐ 229 Tom Hume .10 .05
☐ 230 Marc Hill .10 .05
☐ 231 Dennis Martinez .20 .09
☐ 232 Jim Gantner .20 .09
☐ 233 Larry Pashnick .10 .05
☐ 234 Dave Collins .10 .05
☐ 235 Tom Burgmeier .10 .05
☐ 236 Ken Landreaux .10 .05
☐ 237 John Denny .10 .05
☐ 238 Hal McRae .20 .09
☐ 239 Matt Keough .10 .05
☐ 240 Doug Flynn .10 .05
☐ 241 Fred Lynn .20 .09
☐ 242 Billy Sample .10 .05
☐ 243 Tom Paciorek .20 .09
☐ 244 Joe Sambito .10 .05
☐ 245 Sid Monge .10 .05
☐ 246 Ken Oberkfell .10 .05
☐ 247 Joe Pittman UER .10 .05
(Photo actually
Juan Eichelberger)
☐ 248 Mario Soto .10 .05
☐ 249 Claudell Washington .10 .05
☐ 250 Rick Rhoden .10 .05
☐ 251 Darrell Evans .20 .09
☐ 252 Steve Henderson .10 .05
☐ 253 Manny Castillo .10 .05
☐ 254 Craig Swan .10 .05
☐ 255 Joey McLaughlin .10 .05
☐ 256 Pete Redfern .10 .05
☐ 257 Ken Singleton .10 .05
☐ 258 Robin Yount 1.25 .55
☐ 259 Elias Sosa .10 .05
☐ 260 Bob Ojeda .10 .05
☐ 261 Bobby Murcer .20 .09
☐ 262 Candy Maldonado .20 .09
☐ 263 Rick Waits .10 .05
☐ 264 Greg Pryor .10 .05
☐ 265 Bob Owchinko .10 .05
☐ 266 Chris Speier .10 .05
☐ 267 Bruce Kison .10 .05
☐ 268 Mark Wagner .10 .05
☐ 269 Steve Kemp .10 .05
☐ 270 Phil Garner .20 .09
☐ 271 Gene Richards .10 .05
☐ 272 Renie Martin .10 .05
☐ 273 Dave Roberts .10 .05
☐ 274 Dan Driessen .10 .05
☐ 275 Rufino Linares .10 .05
☐ 276 Lee Lacy .10 .05
☐ 277 Ryne Sandberg 12.00 5.50
☐ 278 Darrell Porter .10 .05
☐ 279 Cal Ripken 10.00 4.50
☐ 280 Jamie Easterly .10 .05
☐ 281 Bill Fahey .10 .05
☐ 282 Glenn Hoffman .10 .05
☐ 283 Willie Randolph .20 .09
☐ 284 Fernando Valenzuela .40 .18
☐ 285 Alan Bannister .10 .05
☐ 286 Paul Splittorff .10 .05
☐ 287 Joe Rudi .10 .05
☐ 288 Bill Gullickson .20 .09
☐ 289 Danny Darwin .10 .05
☐ 290 Andy Hassler .10 .05
☐ 291 Ernesto Escarrega .10 .05
☐ 292 Steve Mura .10 .05
☐ 293 Tony Scott .10 .05
☐ 294 Manny Trillo .10 .05
☐ 295 Greg Harris .10 .05
☐ 296 Luis DeLeon .10 .05
☐ 297 Kent Tekulve .20 .09
☐ 298 Atlee Hammaker .10 .05
☐ 299 Bruce Benedict .10 .05
☐ 300 Fergie Jenkins .75 .35
☐ 301 Dave Kingman .40 .18
☐ 302 Bill Caudill .10 .05
☐ 303 John Castino .10 .05
☐ 304 Ernie Whitt .10 .05
☐ 305 Randy Johnson .10 .05
☐ 306 Garth Iorg .10 .05
☐ 307 Gaylord Perry .75 .35
☐ 308 Ed Lynch .10 .05
☐ 309 Keith Moreland .10 .05
☐ 310 Rafael Ramirez .10 .05
☐ 311 Bill Madlock .20 .09
☐ 312 Milt May .10 .05
☐ 313 John Montefusco .10 .05
☐ 314 Wayne Krenchicki .10 .05
☐ 315 George Vukovich .10 .05
☐ 316 Joaquin Andujar .10 .05
☐ 317 Craig Reynolds .10 .05
☐ 318 Rick Burleson .10 .05
☐ 319 Richard Dotson .10 .05
☐ 320 Steve Rogers .10 .05
☐ 321 Dave Schmidt .10 .05
☐ 322 Bud Black .20 .09
☐ 323 Jeff Burroughs .10 .05
☐ 324 Von Hayes .20 .09
☐ 325 Butch Wynegar .10 .05
☐ 326 Carl Yastrzemski .75 .35
☐ 327 Ron Roenicke .10 .05
☐ 328 Howard Johnson .75 .35
☐ 329 Rick Dempsey UER .20 .09
(Posing as a left-
handed batter)
☐ 330A Jim Slaton .10 .05
(Bio printed
black on white)
☐ 330B Jim Slaton .20 .09
(Bio printed
black on yellow)
☐ 331 Benny Ayala .10 .05
☐ 332 Ted Simmons .20 .09
☐ 333 Lou Whitaker .20 .09
☐ 334 Chuck Rainey .10 .05
☐ 335 Lou Piniella .20 .09
☐ 336 Steve Sax .20 .09
☐ 337 Toby Harrah .10 .05
☐ 338 George Brett 1.50 .70
☐ 339 Dave Lopes .20 .09
☐ 340 Gary Carter .75 .35
☐ 341 John Grubb .10 .05
☐ 342 Tim Foli .10 .05
☐ 343 Jim Kaat .20 .09
☐ 344 Mike LaCoss .10 .05
☐ 345 Larry Christenson .10 .05
☐ 346 Juan Bonilla .10 .05
☐ 347 Omar Moreno .10 .05
☐ 348 Chili Davis .20 .09
☐ 349 Tommy Boggs .10 .05
☐ 350 Rusty Staub .20 .09
☐ 351 Bump Wills .10 .05
☐ 352 Rick Sweet .10 .05
☐ 353 Jim Gott .10 .05
☐ 354 Terry Felton .10 .05
☐ 355 Jim Kern .10 .05
☐ 356 Bill Almon UER .10 .05
(Expos/Mets in 1983,
not Padres/Mets)
☐ 357 Tippy Martinez .10 .05
☐ 358 Roy Howell .10 .05
☐ 359 Dan Petry .10 .05
☐ 360 Jerry Mumphrey .10 .05
☐ 361 Mark Clear .10 .05
☐ 362 Mike Marshall .10 .05
☐ 363 Lary Sorensen .10 .05
☐ 364 Amos Otis .20 .09
☐ 365 Rick Langford .10 .05
☐ 366 Brad Mills .10 .05
☐ 367 Brian Downing .10 .05
☐ 368 Mike Richardt .10 .05
☐ 369 Aurelio Rodriguez .10 .05
☐ 370 Dave Smith .10 .05
☐ 371 Tug McGraw .20 .09
☐ 372 Doug Bair .10 .05
☐ 373 Ruppert Jones .10 .05
☐ 374 Alex Trevino .10 .05
☐ 375 Ken Dayley .10 .05
☐ 376 Rod Scurry .10 .0
☐ 377 Bob Brenly .10 .0
☐ 378 Scot Thompson .10 .0
☐ 379 Julio Cruz .10 .0
☐ 380 John Stearns .10 .0
☐ 381 Dale Murray .10 .0
☐ 382 Frank Viola .75 .3
☐ 383 Al Bumbry .10 .0
☐ 384 Ben Oglivie .10 .0
☐ 385 Dave Tobik .10 .0
☐ 386 Bob Stanley .10 .0
☐ 387 Andre Robertson .10 .0
☐ 388 Jorge Orta .10 .0
☐ 389 Ed Whitson .10 .0
☐ 390 Don Hood .10 .0
☐ 391 Tom Underwood .10 .0
☐ 392 Tim Wallach .10 .0
☐ 393 Steve Renko .10 .0
☐ 394 Mickey Rivers .10 .0
☐ 395 Greg Luzinski .20 .0
☐ 396 Art Howe .10 .0
☐ 397 Alan Wiggins .10 .0
☐ 398 Jim Barr .10 .0
☐ 399 Ivan DeJesus .10 .0
☐ 400 Tom Lawless .10 .0
☐ 401 Bob Walk .10 .0
☐ 402 Jimmy Smith .10 .0
☐ 403 Lee Smith 2.00 .9
☐ 404 George Hendrick .10 .0
☐ 405 Eddie Murray 1.00 .4
☐ 406 Marshall Edwards .10 .0
☐ 407 Lance Parrish .20 .0
☐ 408 Carney Lansford .20 .0
☐ 409 Dave Winfield 1.25 .5
☐ 410 Bob Welch .20 .0
☐ 411 Larry Milbourne .10 .05
☐ 412 Dennis Leonard .10 .05
☐ 413 Dan Meyer .10 .05
☐ 414 Charlie Lea .10 .05
☐ 415 Rick Honeycutt .10 .05
☐ 416 Mike Witt .10 .05
☐ 417 Steve Trout .10 .05
☐ 418 Glenn Brummer .10 .05
☐ 419 Denny Walling .10 .05
☐ 420 Gary Matthews .20 .09
☐ 421 Charlie Leibrandt UER .10 .05
(Liebrandt on
front of card)
☐ 422 Juan Eichelberger UER .10 .05
(Photo actually
Joe Pittman)
☐ 423 Cecilio Guante UER .10 .05
(Listed as Matt
on card)
☐ 424 Bill Laskey .10 .05
☐ 425 Jerry Royster .10 .05
☐ 426 Dickie Noles .10 .05
☐ 427 George Foster .20 .09
☐ 428 Mike Moore .20 .09
☐ 429 Gary Ward .10 .05
☐ 430 Barry Bonnell .10 .05
☐ 431 Ron Washington .10 .05
☐ 432 Rance Mulliniks .10 .05
☐ 433 Mike Stanton .10 .05
☐ 434 Jesse Orosco .10 .05
☐ 435 Larry Bowa .20 .09
☐ 436 Biff Pocoroba .10 .05
☐ 437 Johnny Ray .10 .05
☐ 438 Joe Morgan .75 .35
☐ 439 Eric Show .10 .05
☐ 440 Larry Biittner .10 .05
☐ 441 Greg Gross .10 .05
☐ 442 Gene Tenace .20 .09
☐ 443 Danny Heep .10 .05
☐ 444 Bobby Clark .10 .05
☐ 445 Kevin Hickey .10 .05
☐ 446 Scott Sanderson .10 .05
☐ 447 Frank Tanana .20 .09
☐ 448 Cesar Geronimo .10 .05
☐ 449 Jimmy Sexton .10 .05
☐ 450 Mike Hargrove .20 .09
☐ 451 Doyle Alexander .10 .05
☐ 452 Dwight Evans .20 .09
☐ 453 Terry Forster .10 .05
☐ 454 Tom Brookens .10 .05
☐ 455 Rich Dauer .10 .05
☐ 456 Rob Picciolo .10 .05
☐ 457 Terry Crowley .10 .05
☐ 458 Ned Yost .10 .05
☐ 459 Kirk Gibson .75 .35
☐ 460 Reid Nichols .10 .05
☐ 461 Oscar Gamble .10 .05
☐ 462 Dusty Baker .20 .09
☐ 463 Jack Perconte .10 .05
☐ 464 Frank White .20 .09
☐ 465 Mickey Klutts .10 .05
☐ 466 Warren Cromartie .10 .05

467 Larry Parrish .10 .05
468 Bobby Grich .20 .09
469 Dane Iorg .10 .05
470 Joe Niekro .20 .09
471 Ed Farmer .10 .05
472 Tim Flannery .10 .05
473 Dave Parker .20 .09
474 Jeff Leonard .10 .05
475 Al Hrabosky .10 .05
476 Ron Hodges .10 .05
477 Leon Durham .10 .05
478 Jim Essian .10 .05
479 Roy Lee Jackson .10 .05
480 Brad Havens .10 .05
481 Joe Price .10 .05
482 Tony Bernazard .10 .05
483 Scott McGregor .10 .05
484 Paul Molitor 1.00 .45
485 Mike Ivie .10 .05
486 Ken Griffey .20 .09
487 Dennis Eckersley .75 .35
488 Steve Garvey .40 .18
489 Mike Fischlin .10 .05
490 U.L. Washington .10 .05
491 Steve McCatty .10 .05
492 Roy Johnson .10 .05
493 Don Baylor .40 .18
494 Bobby Johnson .10 .05
495 Mike Squires .10 .05
496 Bert Roberge .10 .05
497 Dick Ruthven .10 .05
498 Tito Landrum .10 .05
499 Sixto Lezcano .10 .05
500 Johnny Bench 1.00 .45
501 Larry Whisenton .10 .05
502 Manny Sarmiento .10 .05
503 Fred Breining .10 .05
504 Bill Campbell .10 .05
505 Todd Cruz .10 .05
506 Bob Bailor .10 .05
507 Dave Stieb .20 .09
508 Al Williams .10 .05
509 Dan Ford .10 .05
510 Gorman Thomas .10 .05
511 Chet Lemon .10 .05
512 Mike Torrez .10 .05
513 Shane Rawley .10 .05
514 Mark Belanger .10 .05
515 Rodney Craig .10 .05
516 Onix Concepcion .10 .05
517 Mike Heath .10 .05
518 Andre Dawson UER .75 .35
(Middle name Fernando, should be Nolan)
519 Luis Sanchez .10 .05
520 Terry Bogener .10 .05
521 Rudy Law .10 .05
522 Ray Knight .20 .09
523 Joe Lefebvre .10 .05
524 Jim Wohlford .10 .05
525 Julio Franco 1.00 .45
526 Ron Oester .10 .05
527 Rick Mahler .10 .05
528 Steve Nicosia .10 .05
529 Junior Kennedy .10 .05
530A Whitey Herzog MG .20 .09
(Bio printed black on white)
530B Whitey Herzog MG .20 .09
(Bio printed black on yellow)
531A Don Sutton .75 .35
(Blue border on photo)
531B Don Sutton .75 .35
(Green border on photo)
532 Mark Brouhard .10 .05
533A Sparky Anderson MG .20 .09
(Bio printed black on white)
533B Sparky Anderson MG .20 .09
(Bio printed black on yellow)
534 Roger LaFrancois .10 .05
535 George Frazier .10 .05
536 Tom Niedenfuer .10 .05
537 Ed Glynn .10 .05
538 Lee May .20 .09
539 Bob Kearney .10 .05
540 Tim Raines .75 .35
541 Paul Mirabella .10 .05
542 Luis Tiant .20 .09
543 Ron LeFlore .10 .05
544 Dave LaPoint .10 .05
545 Randy Moffitt .10 .05
546 Luis Aguayo .10 .05

☐ 547 Brad Lesley .20 .09
☐ 548 Luis Salazar .10 .05
☐ 549 John Candelaria .10 .05
☐ 550 Dave Bergman .10 .05
☐ 551 Bob Watson .20 .09
☐ 552 Pat Tabler .10 .05
☐ 553 Brent Gaff .10 .05
☐ 554 Al Cowens .10 .05
☐ 555 Tom Brunansky .20 .09
☐ 556 Lloyd Moseby .10 .05
☐ 557A Pascual Perez ERR 2.00 .90
(Twins in glove)
☐ 557B Pascual Perez COR .20 .09
(Braves in glove)
☐ 558 Willie Upshaw .10 .05
☐ 559 Richie Zisk .10 .05
☐ 560 Pat Zachry .10 .05
☐ 561 Jay Johnstone .20 .09
☐ 562 Carlos Diaz .10 .05
☐ 563 John Tudor .10 .05
☐ 564 Frank Robinson MG .40 .18
☐ 565 Dave Edwards .10 .05
☐ 566 Paul Householder .10 .05
☐ 567 Ron Reed .10 .05
☐ 568 Mike Ramsey .10 .05
☐ 569 Kiko Garcia .10 .05
☐ 570 Tommy John .40 .18
☐ 571 Tony LaRussa MG .20 .09
☐ 572 Joel Youngblood .10 .05
☐ 573 Wayne Tolleson .10 .05
☐ 574 Keith Creel .10 .05
☐ 575 Billy Martin MG .20 .09
☐ 576 Jerry Dybzinski .10 .05
☐ 577 Rick Cerone .10 .05
☐ 578 Tony Perez .75 .35
☐ 579 Greg Brock .10 .05
☐ 580 Glenn Wilson .10 .05
☐ 581 Tim Stoddard .10 .05
☐ 582 Bob McClure .10 .05
☐ 583 Jim Dwyer .10 .05
☐ 584 Ed Romero .10 .05
☐ 585 Larry Herndon .10 .05
☐ 586 Wade Boggs 8.00 3.60
☐ 587 Jay Howell .10 .05
☐ 588 Dave Stewart .20 .09
☐ 589 Bert Blyleven .40 .18
☐ 590 Dick Howser MG .10 .05
☐ 591 Wayne Gross .10 .05
☐ 592 Terry Francona .10 .05
☐ 593 Don Werner .10 .05
☐ 594 Bill Stein .10 .05
☐ 595 Jesse Barfield .20 .09
☐ 596 Bob Molinaro .10 .05
☐ 597 Mike Vail .10 .05
☐ 598 Tony Gwynn 20.00 9.00
☐ 599 Gary Rajsich .10 .05
☐ 600 Jerry Ujdur .10 .05
☐ 601 Cliff Johnson .10 .05
☐ 602 Jerry White .10 .05
☐ 603 Bryan Clark .10 .05
☐ 604 Joe Ferguson .10 .05
☐ 605 Guy Sularz .10 .05
☐ 606A Ozzie Virgil .20 .09
(Green border on photo)
☐ 606B Ozzie Virgil .20 .09
(Orange border on photo)
☐ 607 Terry Harper .10 .05
☐ 608 Harvey Kuenn MG .20 .09
☐ 609 Jim Sundberg .20 .09
☐ 610 Willie Stargell .75 .35
☐ 611 Reggie Smith .20 .09
☐ 612 Rob Wilfong .10 .05
☐ 613 The Niekro Brothers .40 .18
Joe Niekro
Phil Niekro
☐ 614 Lee Elia MG .10 .05
☐ 615 Mickey Hatcher .10 .05
☐ 616 Jerry Hairston .10 .05
☐ 617 John Martin .10 .05
☐ 618 Wally Backman .10 .05
☐ 619 Storm Davis .10 .05
☐ 620 Alan Knicely .10 .05
☐ 621 John Stuper .10 .05
☐ 622 Matt Sinatro .10 .05
☐ 623 Geno Petralli .40 .18
☐ 624 Duane Walker .10 .05
☐ 625 Dick Williams MG .10 .05
☐ 626 Pat Corrales MG .10 .05
☐ 627 Vern Ruhle .10 .05
☐ 628 Joe Torre MG .40 .18
☐ 629 Anthony Johnson .10 .05
☐ 630 Steve Howe .10 .05
☐ 631 Gary Woods .10 .05
☐ 632 LaMarr Hoyt .20 .09
☐ 633 Steve Swisher .10 .05

☐ 634 Terry Leach .10 .05
☐ 635 Jeff Newman .10 .05
☐ 636 Brett Butler .40 .18
☐ 637 Gary Gray .10 .05
☐ 638 Lee Mazzilli .10 .05
☐ 639A Ron Jackson ERR 5.00 2.20
(A's in glove)
☐ 639B Ron Jackson COR .10 .05
(Angels in glove, red border on photo)
☐ 639C Ron Jackson COR .75 .35
(Angels in glove, green border on photo)
☐ 640 Juan Beniquez .10 .05
☐ 641 Dave Rucker .10 .05
☐ 642 Luis Pujols .10 .05
☐ 643 Rick Monday .10 .05
☐ 644 Hosken Powell .10 .05
☐ 645 The Chicken .75 .35
☐ 646 Dave Engle .10 .05
☐ 647 Dick Davis .10 .05
☐ 648 Frank Robinson .20 .09
Vida Blue
Joe Morgan
☐ 649 Al Chambers .10 .05
☐ 650 Jesus Vega .10 .05
☐ 651 Jeff Jones .10 .05
☐ 652 Marvis Foley .10 .05
☐ 653 Ty Cobb Puzzle Card .75 .35
☐ 654A Dick Perez/Diamond .75 .35
King Checklist 1-26 (Unnumbered) ERR (Word "checklist" omitted from back)
☐ 654B Dick Perez/Diamond .75 .35
King Checklist 1-26 (Unnumbered) COR (Word "checklist" is on back)
☐ 655 Checklist 27-130 .10 .05
(Unnumbered)
☐ 656 Checklist 131-234 .10 .05
(Unnumbered)
☐ 657 Checklist 235-338 .10 .05
(Unnumbered)
☐ 658 Checklist 339-442 .10 .05
(Unnumbered)
☐ 659 Checklist 443-544 .10 .05
(Unnumbered)
☐ 660 Checklist 545-653 .10 .05
(Unnumbered)

1983 Donruss Action All-Stars

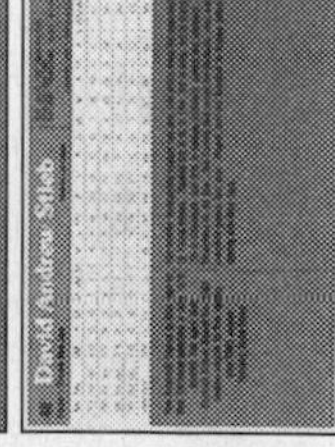

The cards in this 60-card set measure approximately 3 1/2" by 5". The 1983 Action All-Stars series depicts 60 major leagers in a distinctive new style. Each card contains a large close-up on the left and an action photo on the right. Team affiliations appear as part of the background design, and the cards have cranberry color borders. The backs contain the card number, the player's major league line record, and biographical material. A 63-piece Mickey Mantle puzzle (three pieces on one card per pack) was marketed as an insert premium; the complete puzzle card set is one of the more difficult of the Donruss insert puzzles and is currently valued at 20.00.

	NRMT	VG-E
COMPLETE SET (60)	6.00	2.70
COMMON CARD (1-60)	.05	.02

☐ 1 Eddie Murray .60 .25
☐ 2 Dwight Evans .10 .05
☐ 3A Reggie Jackson ERR 3.00 1.35
(Red screen on back covers some stats)
☐ 3B Reggie Jackson COR .50 .23
☐ 4 Greg Luzinski .10 .05
☐ 5 Larry Herndon .05 .02
☐ 6 Al Oliver .10 .05

Card	NRMT	VG-E
☐ 7 Bill Buckner	.10	.05
☐ 8 Jason Thompson	.05	.02
☐ 9 Andre Dawson	.40	.18
☐ 10 Greg Minton	.05	.02
☐ 11 Terry Kennedy	.05	.02
☐ 12 Phil Niekro	.40	.18
☐ 13 Willie Wilson	.05	.02
☐ 14 Johnny Bench	.50	.23
☐ 15 Ron Guidry	.10	.05
☐ 16 Hal McRae	.05	.02
☐ 17 Damaso Garcia	.05	.02
☐ 18 Gary Ward	.05	.02
☐ 19 Cecil Cooper	.10	.05
☐ 20 Keith Hernandez	.10	.05
☐ 21 Ron Cey	.10	.05
☐ 22 Rickey Henderson	.50	.23
☐ 23 Nolan Ryan	2.00	.90
☐ 24 Steve Carlton	.40	.18
☐ 25 John Stearns	.05	.02
☐ 26 Jim Sundberg	.05	.02
☐ 27 Joaquin Andujar	.05	.02
☐ 28 Gaylord Perry	.30	.14
☐ 29 Jack Clark	.10	.05
☐ 30 Bill Madlock	.10	.05
☐ 31 Pete Rose	.75	.35
☐ 32 Mookie Wilson	.10	.05
☐ 33 Rollie Fingers	.30	.14
☐ 34 Lonnie Smith	.05	.02
☐ 35 Tony Pena	.05	.02
☐ 36 Dave Winfield	.40	.18
☐ 37 Tim Lollar	.05	.02
☐ 38 Rod Carew	.40	.18
☐ 39 Toby Harrah	.05	.02
☐ 40 Buddy Bell	.10	.05
☐ 41 Bruce Sutter	.10	.05
☐ 42 George Brett	1.25	.55
☐ 43 Carlton Fisk	.50	.23
☐ 44 Carl Yastrzemski	.50	.23
☐ 45 Dale Murphy	.30	.14
☐ 46 Bob Horner	.05	.02
☐ 47 Dave Concepcion	.10	.05
☐ 48 Dave Stieb	.05	.02
☐ 49 Kent Hrbek	.10	.05
☐ 50 Lance Parrish	.10	.05
☐ 51 Joe Niekro	.05	.02
☐ 52 Cal Ripken	3.00	1.35
☐ 53 Fernando Valenzuela	.20	.09
☐ 54 Richie Zisk	.05	.02
☐ 55 Leon Durham	.05	.02
☐ 56 Robin Yount	.50	.23
☐ 57 Mike Schmidt	.75	.35
☐ 58 Gary Carter	.20	.09
☐ 59 Fred Lynn	.10	.05
☐ 60 Checklist Card	.05	.02

1983 Donruss HOF Heroes

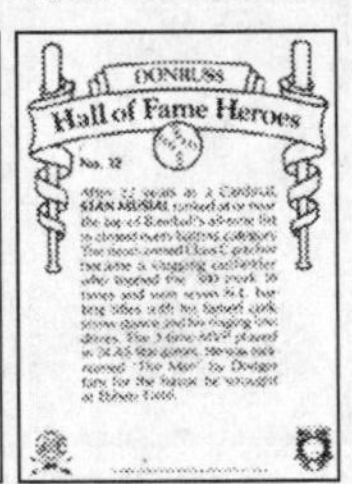

The cards in this 44-card set measure 2 1/2" by 3 1/2". Although it was issued with the same Mantle puzzle as the Action All Stars set, the Donruss Hall of Fame Heroes set is completely different in content and design. Of the 44 cards in the set, 42 are Dick Perez artwork portraying Hall of Fame members, while one card depicts the completed Mantle puzzle and the last card is a checklist. The red, white, and blue backs contain the card number and a short player biography. The cards were packaged eight cards plus one puzzle card (three pieces) for 30 cents in the summer of 1983.

	NRMT	VG-E
COMPLETE SET (44)	7.50	3.40
COMMON CARD (1-44)	.05	.02

Card	NRMT	VG-E
☐ 1 Ty Cobb	1.00	.45
☐ 2 Walter Johnson	.50	.23
☐ 3 Christy Mathewson	.50	.23
☐ 4 Josh Gibson	.50	.23
☐ 5 Honus Wagner	.75	.35
☐ 6 Jackie Robinson	.75	.35
☐ 7 Mickey Mantle	2.00	.90
☐ 8 Luke Appling	.05	.02
☐ 9 Ted Williams	1.00	.45
☐ 10 Johnny Mize	.20	.09
☐ 11 Satchel Paige	.50	.23
☐ 12 Lou Boudreau	.05	.02
☐ 13 Jimmie Foxx	.20	.09
☐ 14 Duke Snider	.30	.14
☐ 15 Monte Irvin	.20	.09
☐ 16 Hank Greenberg	.20	.09
☐ 17 Roberto Clemente	1.00	.45
☐ 18 Al Kaline	.30	.14
☐ 19 Frank Robinson	.30	.14
☐ 20 Joe Cronin	.20	.09
☐ 21 Burleigh Grimes	.05	.02
☐ 22 The Waner Brothers Paul Waner Lloyd Waner	.05	.02
☐ 23 Grover Alexander	.20	.09
☐ 24 Yogi Berra	.30	.14
☐ 25 Cool Papa Bell	.20	.09
☐ 26 Bill Dickey	.20	.09
☐ 27 Cy Young	.30	.14
☐ 28 Charlie Gehringer	.05	.02
☐ 29 Dizzy Dean	.30	.14
☐ 30 Bob Lemon	.20	.09
☐ 31 Red Ruffing	.05	.02
☐ 32 Stan Musial	.75	.35
☐ 33 Carl Hubbell	.20	.09
☐ 34 Hank Aaron	.75	.35
☐ 35 John McGraw	.05	.02
☐ 36 Bob Feller	.30	.14
☐ 37 Casey Stengel	.30	.14
☐ 38 Ralph Kiner	.20	.09
☐ 39 Roy Campanella	.50	.23
☐ 40 Mel Ott	.20	.09
☐ 41 Robin Roberts	.20	.09
☐ 42 Early Wynn	.05	.02
☐ 43 Mantle Puzzle Card	2.00	.90
☐ 44 Checklist Card	.05	.02

1984 Donruss

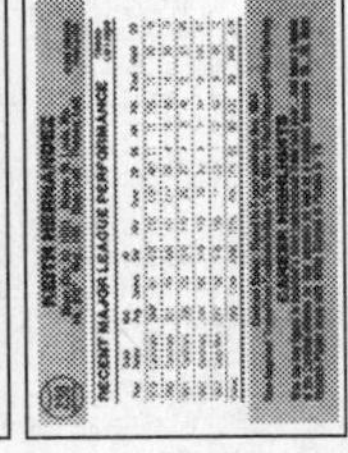

The 1984 Donruss set contains a total of 660 standard-size cards; however, only 658 are numbered. The first 26 cards in the set are again Diamond Kings (DK). A new feature, Rated Rookies (RR), was introduced with this set with Bill Madden's 20 selections comprising numbers 27 through 46. Two "Living Legend" cards designated A (featuring Gaylord Perry and Rollie Fingers) and B (featuring Johnny Bench and Carl Yastrzemski) were issued as bonus cards in wax packs, but were not issued in the factory sets sold to hobby dealers. The seven unnumbered checklist cards are arbitrarily assigned numbers 652 through 658 and are listed at the end of the list below. The attractive card front designs changed considerably from the previous two years. The backs contain statistics and are printed in green and black ink. The cards were distributed with a 3-piece puzzle panel of Duke Snider. There are no extra variation cards included in the complete set price below. The variation cards apparently resulted from a different printing for the factory sets as the Darling and Stenhouse no number variations as well as the Perez-Steele errors were corrected in the factory sets which were released later in the year. The Diamond King cards found in packs spelled Perez-Steele as Perez-Steel. Notable Rookie Cards in this set include Joe Carter, Don Mattingly, Tony Phillips, Darryl Strawberry, and Andy Van Slyke. The Joe Carter card is almost never found well centered.

	NRMT	VG-E
COMPLETE SET (660)	200.00	90.00
COMP.FACT.SET (658)	200.00	90.00
COMMON CARD (1-658)	.25	.11
COMPLETE SNIDER PUZZLE	5.00	2.20

Card	NRMT	VG-E
☐ 1 Robin Yount DK COR	5.00	2.20
☐ 1A Robin Yount DK ERR	1.50	.70
☐ 2 Dave Concepcion DK COR	1.50	.70
☐ 2A Dave Concepcion DK ERR	.75	.35
☐ 3 Dwayne Murphy DK COR	.75	.35
☐ 3A Dwayne Murphy DK ERR	.25	.1
☐ 4 John Castino DK COR	.75	.3
☐ 4A John Castino DK ERR	.25	.1
☐ 5 Leon Durham DK COR	.75	.3
☐ 5A Leon Durham DK ERR	.25	.1
☐ 6 Rusty Staub DK COR	.75	.3
☐ 6A Rusty Staub DK ERR	.75	.3
☐ 7 Jack Clark DK COR	.75	.3
☐ 7A Jack Clark DK ERR	.75	.3
☐ 8 Dave Dravecky DK COR	.75	.3
☐ 8A Dave Dravecky DK ERR	.75	.3
☐ 9 Al Oliver DK COR	.75	.3
☐ 9A Al Oliver DK ERR	.75	.3
☐ 10 Dave Righetti DK COR	.75	.3
☐ 10A Dave Righetti DK ERR	.75	.3
☐ 11 Hal McRae DK COR	.75	.3
☐ 11A Hal McRae DK ERR	.75	.3
☐ 12 Ray Knight DK COR	.75	.3
☐ 12A Ray Knight DK ERR	.75	.3
☐ 13 Bruce Sutter DK COR	.75	.3
☐ 13A Bruce Sutter DK ERR	.75	.3
☐ 14 Bob Horner DK COR	.75	.3
☐ 14A Bob Horner DK ERR	.75	.3
☐ 15 Lance Parrish DK COR	.75	.3
☐ 15A Lance Parrish DK ERR	.75	.3
☐ 16 Matt Young DK COR	.75	.3
☐ 16A Matt Young DK ERR	.25	.1
☐ 17 Fred Lynn DK COR	.75	.3
☐ 17A Fred Lynn DK ERR	.25	.1
☐ 18 Ron Kittle DK COR	.75	.3
☐ 18A Ron Kittle DK ERR	.25	.1
☐ 19 Jim Clancy DK COR	.75	.3
☐ 19A Jim Clancy DK ERR	.25	.1
☐ 20 Bill Madlock DK COR	.75	.3
☐ 20A Bill Madlock DK ERR	.75	.3
☐ 21 Larry Parrish DK COR	.75	.3
☐ 21A Larry Parrish DK ERR	.25	.1
☐ 22 Eddie Murray DK COR	3.00	1.3
☐ 22A Eddie Murray DK ERR	1.50	.7
☐ 23 Mike Schmidt DK COR	5.00	2.2
☐ 23A Mike Schmidt DK ERR	3.00	1.3
☐ 24 Pedro Guerrero DK COR	.75	.3
☐ 24A Pedro Guerrero DK ERR	.75	.3
☐ 25 Andre Thornton DK COR	.75	.3
☐ 25A Andre Thornton DK ERR	.75	.3
☐ 26 Wade Boggs DK COR	3.50	1.5
☐ 26A Wade Boggs DK ERR	2.50	1.1
☐ 27 Joel Skinner RR	.25	.1
☐ 28 Tommy Dunbar RR	.25	.1
☐ 29A Mike Stenhouse RR ERR No number on back	.25	.1
☐ 29B Mike Stenhouse RR COR Numbered on back	3.00	1.3
☐ 30A Ron Darling RR ERR (No number on back)	.75	.3
☐ 30B Ron Darling RR COR (Numbered on back)	3.00	1.3
☐ 31 Dion James RR	.75	.3
☐ 32 Tony Fernandez RR	1.50	.7
☐ 33 Angel Salazar RR	.25	.1
☐ 34 Kevin McReynolds RR	1.50	.7
☐ 35 Dick Schofield RR	.75	.3
☐ 36 Brad Komminsk RR	.25	.1
☐ 37 Tim Teufel RR	.25	.1
☐ 38 Doug Frobel RR	.25	.1
☐ 39 Greg Gagne RR	.75	.3
☐ 40 Mike Fuentes RR	.25	.1
☐ 41 Joe Carter RR	25.00	11.0
☐ 42 Mike Brown RR (Angels OF)	.25	.1
☐ 43 Mike Jeffcoat RR	.25	.1
☐ 44 Sid Fernandez RR	1.50	.7
☐ 45 Brian Dayett RR	.25	.1
☐ 46 Chris Smith RR	.25	.1
☐ 47 Eddie Murray	4.00	1.8
☐ 48 Robin Yount	4.00	1.8
☐ 49 Lance Parrish	.75	.3
☐ 50 Jim Rice	.75	.3
☐ 51 Dave Winfield	5.00	2.2
☐ 52 Fernando Valenzuela	.75	.3
☐ 53 George Brett	8.00	3.6
☐ 54 Rickey Henderson	4.00	1.8
☐ 55 Gary Carter	3.00	1.3
☐ 56 Buddy Bell	.75	.3

57 Reggie Jackson	5.00	2.20
58 Harold Baines	1.50	.70
59 Ozzie Smith	6.00	2.70
60 Nolan Ryan UER	20.00	9.00
(Text on back refers to 1972 as the year he struck out 383; the year was 1973)		
61 Pete Rose	5.00	2.20
62 Ron Oester	.25	.11
63 Steve Garvey	1.50	.70
64 Jason Thompson	.25	.11
65 Jack Clark	.75	.35
66 Dale Murphy	3.00	1.35
67 Leon Durham	.25	.11
68 Darryl Strawberry	10.00	4.50
69 Richie Zisk	.25	.11
70 Kent Hrbek	.75	.35
71 Dave Stieb	.25	.11
72 Ken Schrom	.25	.11
73 George Bell	.75	.35
74 John Moses	.25	.11
75 Ed Lynch	.25	.11
76 Chuck Rainey	.25	.11
77 Biff Pocoroba	.25	.11
78 Cecilio Guante	.25	.11
79 Jim Barr	.25	.11
80 Kurt Bevacqua	.25	.11
81 Tom Foley	.25	.11
82 Joe Lefebvre	.25	.11
83 Andy Van Slyke	2.50	1.10
84 Bob Lillis MG	.25	.11
85 Ricky Adams	.25	.11
86 Jerry Hairston	.25	.11
87 Bob James	.25	.11
88 Joe Altobelli MG	.25	.11
89 Ed Romero	.25	.11
90 John Grubb	.25	.11
91 John Henry Johnson	.25	.11
92 Juan Espino	.25	.11
93 Candy Maldonado	.25	.11
94 Andre Thornton	.25	.11
95 Onix Concepcion	.25	.11
96 Donnie Hill UER	.25	.11
(Listed as P, should be 2B)		
97 Andre Dawson UER	3.00	1.35
(Wrong middle name, should be Nolan)		
98 Frank Tanana	.75	.35
99 Curt Wilkerson	.25	.11
100 Larry Gura	.25	.11
101 Dwayne Murphy	.25	.11
102 Tom Brennan	.25	.11
103 Dave Righetti	.75	.35
104 Steve Sax	.75	.35
105 Dan Petry	.75	.35
106 Cal Ripken	30.00	13.50
107 Paul Molitor UER	4.00	1.80
('83 stats should say .270 BA, 608 AB, and 164 hits)		
108 Fred Lynn	.75	.35
109 Neil Allen	.25	.11
110 Joe Niekro	.75	.35
111 Steve Carlton	4.00	1.80
112 Terry Kennedy	.25	.11
113 Bill Madlock	.25	.11
114 Chili Davis	1.50	.70
115 Jim Gantner	.75	.35
116 Tom Seaver	5.00	2.20
117 Bill Buckner	.75	.35
118 Bill Caudill	.25	.11
119 Jim Clancy	.25	.11
120 John Castino	.25	.11
121 Dave Concepcion	.75	.35
122 Greg Luzinski	.75	.35
123 Mike Boddicker	.25	.11
124 Pete Ladd	.25	.11
125 Juan Berenguer	.25	.11
126 John Montefusco	.25	.11
127 Ed Jurak	.25	.11
128 Tom Niedenfuer	.25	.11
129 Bert Blyleven	.75	.35
130 Bud Black	.25	.11
131 Gorman Heimueller	.25	.11
132 Dan Schatzeder	.25	.11
133 Ron Jackson	.25	.11
134 Tom Henke	1.50	.70
135 Kevin Hickey	.25	.11
136 Mike Scott	.75	.35
137 Bo Diaz	.25	.11
138 Glenn Brummer	.25	.11
139 Sid Monge	.25	.11
140 Rich Gale	.25	.11
141 Brett Butler	1.50	.70
142 Brian Harper	.75	.35
143 John Rabb	.25	.11

☐ 144 Gary Woods	.25	.11
☐ 145 Pat Putnam	.25	.11
☐ 146 Jim Acker	.25	.11
☐ 147 Mickey Hatcher	.25	.11
☐ 148 Todd Cruz	.25	.11
☐ 149 Tom Tellmann	.25	.11
☐ 150 John Wockenfuss	.25	.11
☐ 151 Wade Boggs UER	8.00	3.60
1983 runs 10; should be 100		
☐ 152 Don Baylor	1.50	.70
☐ 153 Bob Welch	.25	.11
☐ 154 Alan Bannister	.25	.11
☐ 155 Willie Aikens	.25	.11
☐ 156 Jeff Burroughs	.25	.11
☐ 157 Bryan Little	.25	.11
☐ 158 Bob Boone	.75	.35
☐ 159 Dave Hostetler	.25	.11
☐ 160 Jerry Dybzinski	.25	.11
☐ 161 Mike Madden	.25	.11
☐ 162 Luis DeLeon	.25	.11
☐ 163 Willie Hernandez	.75	.35
☐ 164 Frank Pastore	.25	.11
☐ 165 Rick Camp	.25	.11
☐ 166 Lee Mazzilli	.25	.11
☐ 167 Scot Thompson	.25	.11
☐ 168 Bob Forsch	.25	.11
☐ 169 Mike Flanagan	.25	.11
☐ 170 Rick Manning	.25	.11
☐ 171 Chet Lemon	.75	.35
☐ 172 Jerry Remy	.25	.11
☐ 173 Ron Guidry	.75	.35
☐ 174 Pedro Guerrero	.75	.35
☐ 175 Willie Wilson	.25	.11
☐ 176 Carney Lansford	.75	.35
☐ 177 Al Oliver	.75	.35
☐ 178 Jim Sundberg	.75	.35
☐ 179 Bobby Grich	.75	.35
☐ 180 Rich Dotson	.25	.11
☐ 181 Joaquin Andujar	.25	.11
☐ 182 Jose Cruz	.75	.35
☐ 183 Mike Schmidt	5.00	2.20
☐ 184 Gary Redus	.25	.11
☐ 185 Garry Templeton	.25	.11
☐ 186 Tony Pena	.25	.11
☐ 187 Greg Minton	.25	.11
☐ 188 Phil Niekro	3.00	1.35
☐ 189 Ferguson Jenkins	3.00	1.35
☐ 190 Mookie Wilson	.75	.35
☐ 191 Jim Beattie	.25	.11
☐ 192 Gary Ward	.25	.11
☐ 193 Jesse Barfield	.75	.35
☐ 194 Pete Filson	.25	.11
☐ 195 Roy Lee Jackson	.25	.11
☐ 196 Rick Sweet	.25	.11
☐ 197 Jesse Orosco	.25	.11
☐ 198 Steve Lake	.25	.11
☐ 199 Ken Dayley	.25	.11
☐ 200 Manny Sarmiento	.25	.11
☐ 201 Mark Davis	.25	.11
☐ 202 Tim Flannery	.25	.11
☐ 203 Bill Scherrer	.25	.11
☐ 204 Al Holland	.25	.11
☐ 205 Dave Von Ohlen	.25	.11
☐ 206 Mike LaCoss	.25	.11
☐ 207 Juan Beniquez	.25	.11
☐ 208 Juan Agosto	.25	.11
☐ 209 Bobby Ramos	.25	.11
☐ 210 Al Bumbry	.75	.35
☐ 211 Mark Brouhard	.25	.11
☐ 212 Howard Bailey	.25	.11
☐ 213 Bruce Hurst	.25	.11
☐ 214 Bob Shirley	.25	.11
☐ 215 Pat Zachry	.25	.11
☐ 216 Julio Franco	1.50	.70
☐ 217 Mike Armstrong	.25	.11
☐ 218 Dave Beard	.25	.11
☐ 219 Steve Rogers	.25	.11
☐ 220 John Butcher	.25	.11
☐ 221 Mike Smithson	.25	.11
☐ 222 Frank White	.75	.35
☐ 223 Mike Heath	.25	.11
☐ 224 Chris Bando	.25	.11
☐ 225 Roy Smalley	.25	.11
☐ 226 Dusty Baker	1.50	.70
☐ 227 Lou Whitaker	3.00	1.35
☐ 228 John Lowenstein	.25	.11
☐ 229 Ben Oglivie	.25	.11
☐ 230 Doug DeCinces	.25	.11
☐ 231 Lonnie Smith	.25	.11
☐ 232 Ray Knight	.75	.35
☐ 233 Gary Matthews	.75	.35
☐ 234 Juan Bonilla	.25	.11
☐ 235 Rod Scurry	.25	.11
☐ 236 Atlee Hammaker	.25	.11
☐ 237 Mike Caldwell	.25	.11
☐ 238 Keith Hernandez	.75	.35
☐ 239 Larry Bowa	.75	.35

☐ 240 Tony Bernazard	.25	.11
☐ 241 Damaso Garcia	.25	.11
☐ 242 Tom Brunansky	.75	.35
☐ 243 Dan Driessen	.25	.11
☐ 244 Ron Kittle	.25	.11
☐ 245 Tim Stoddard	.25	.11
☐ 246 Bob L. Gibson	.25	.11
(Brewers Pitcher)		
☐ 247 Marty Castillo	.25	.11
☐ 248 Don Mattingly UER	40.00	18.00
("Traiing" on back)		
☐ 249 Jeff Newman	.25	.11
☐ 250 Alejandro Pena	.75	.35
☐ 251 Toby Harrah	.75	.35
☐ 252 Cesar Geronimo	.25	.11
☐ 253 Tom Underwood	.25	.11
☐ 254 Doug Flynn	.25	.11
☐ 255 Andy Hassler	.25	.11
☐ 256 Odell Jones	.25	.11
☐ 257 Rudy Law	.25	.11
☐ 258 Harry Spilman	.25	.11
☐ 259 Marty Bystrom	.25	.11
☐ 260 Dave Rucker	.25	.11
☐ 261 Ruppert Jones	.25	.11
☐ 262 Jeff R. Jones	.25	.11
(Reds OF)		
☐ 263 Gerald Perry	.75	.35
☐ 264 Gene Tenace	.75	.35
☐ 265 Brad Wellman	.25	.11
☐ 266 Dickie Noles	.25	.11
☐ 267 Jamie Allen	.25	.11
☐ 268 Jim Gott	.25	.11
☐ 269 Ron Davis	.25	.11
☐ 270 Benny Ayala	.25	.11
☐ 271 Ned Yost	.25	.11
☐ 272 Dave Rozema	.25	.11
☐ 273 Dave Stapleton	.25	.11
☐ 274 Lou Piniella	.75	.35
☐ 275 Jose Morales	.25	.11
☐ 276 Broderick Perkins	.25	.11
☐ 277 Butch Davis	.25	.11
☐ 278 Tony Phillips	4.00	1.80
☐ 279 Jeff Reardon	.75	.35
☐ 280 Ken Forsch	.25	.11
☐ 281 Pete O'Brien	.75	.35
☐ 282 Tom Paciorek	.25	.11
☐ 283 Frank LaCorte	.25	.11
☐ 284 Tim Lollar	.25	.11
☐ 285 Greg Gross	.25	.11
☐ 286 Alex Trevino	.25	.11
☐ 287 Gene Garber	.25	.11
☐ 288 Dave Parker	.75	.35
☐ 289 Lee Smith	3.00	1.35
☐ 290 Dave LaPoint	.25	.11
☐ 291 John Shelby	.25	.11
☐ 292 Charlie Moore	.25	.11
☐ 293 Alan Trammell	3.00	1.35
☐ 294 Tony Armas	.25	.11
☐ 295 Shane Rawley	.25	.11
☐ 296 Greg Brock	.25	.11
☐ 297 Hal McRae	.75	.35
☐ 298 Mike Davis	.25	.11
☐ 299 Tim Raines	1.50	.70
☐ 300 Bucky Dent	.75	.35
☐ 301 Tommy John	1.50	.70
☐ 302 Carlton Fisk	3.00	1.35
☐ 303 Darrell Porter	.25	.11
☐ 304 Dickie Thon	.25	.11
☐ 305 Garry Maddox	.25	.11
☐ 306 Cesar Cedeno	.75	.35
☐ 307 Gary Lucas	.25	.11
☐ 308 Johnny Ray	.25	.11
☐ 309 Andy McGaffigan	.25	.11
☐ 310 Claudell Washington	.25	.11
☐ 311 Ryne Sandberg	12.00	5.50
☐ 312 George Foster	.75	.35
☐ 313 Spike Owen	.75	.35
☐ 314 Gary Gaetti	1.50	.70
☐ 315 Willie Upshaw	.25	.11
☐ 316 Al Williams	.25	.11
☐ 317 Jorge Orta	.25	.11
☐ 318 Orlando Mercado	.25	.11
☐ 319 Junior Ortiz	.25	.11
☐ 320 Mike Proly	.25	.11
☐ 321 Randy Johnson UER	.25	.11
('72-'82 stats are from Twins' Randy Johnson, '83 stats are from Braves' Randy Johnson)		
☐ 322 Jim Morrison	.25	.11
☐ 323 Max Venable	.25	.11
☐ 324 Tony Gwynn	25.00	11.00
☐ 325 Duane Walker	.25	.11
☐ 326 Ozzie Virgil	.25	.11
☐ 327 Jeff Lahti	.25	.11
☐ 328 Bill Dawley	.25	.11
☐ 329 Rob Wilfong	.25	.11

☐ 330 Marc Hill .25 .11
☐ 331 Ray Burris .25 .11
☐ 332 Allan Ramirez .25 .11
☐ 333 Chuck Porter .25 .11
☐ 334 Wayne Krenchicki .25 .11
☐ 335 Gary Allenson .25 .11
☐ 336 Bobby Meacham .25 .11
☐ 337 Joe Beckwith .25 .11
☐ 338 Rick Sutcliffe .75 .35
☐ 339 Mark Huismann .25 .11
☐ 340 Tim Conroy .25 .11
☐ 341 Scott Sanderson .25 .11
☐ 342 Larry Biittner .25 .11
☐ 343 Dave Stewart .75 .35
☐ 344 Darryl Motley .25 .11
☐ 345 Chris Codiroli .25 .11
☐ 346 Rich Behenna .25 .11
☐ 347 Andre Robertson .25 .11
☐ 348 Mike Marshall .25 .11
☐ 349 Larry Herndon .75 .35
☐ 350 Rich Dauer .25 .11
☐ 351 Cecil Cooper .75 .35
☐ 352 Rod Carew 4.00 1.80
☐ 353 Willie McGee 1.50 .70
☐ 354 Phil Garner .75 .35
☐ 355 Joe Morgan 3.00 1.35
☐ 356 Luis Salazar .25 .11
☐ 357 John Candelaria .25 .11
☐ 358 Bill Laskey .25 .11
☐ 359 Bob McClure .25 .11
☐ 360 Dave Kingman .75 .35
☐ 361 Ron Cey .75 .35
☐ 362 Matt Young .25 .11
☐ 363 Lloyd Moseby .25 .11
☐ 364 Frank Viola 1.50 .70
☐ 365 Eddie Milner .25 .11
☐ 366 Floyd Bannister .25 .11
☐ 367 Dan Ford .25 .11
☐ 368 Moose Haas .25 .11
☐ 369 Doug Bair .25 .11
☐ 370 Ray Fontenot .25 .11
☐ 371 Luis Aponte .25 .11
☐ 372 Jack Fimple .25 .11
☐ 373 Neal Heaton .25 .11
☐ 374 Greg Pryor .25 .11
☐ 375 Wayne Gross .25 .11
☐ 376 Charlie Lea .25 .11
☐ 377 Steve Lubratich .25 .11
☐ 378 Jon Matlack .25 .11
☐ 379 Julio Cruz .25 .11
☐ 380 John Mizerock .25 .11
☐ 381 Kevin Gross .75 .35
☐ 382 Mike Ramsey .25 .11
☐ 383 Doug Gwosdz .25 .11
☐ 384 Kelly Paris .25 .11
☐ 385 Pete Falcone .25 .11
☐ 386 Milt May .25 .11
☐ 387 Fred Breining .25 .11
☐ 388 Craig Lefferts .25 .11
☐ 389 Steve Henderson .25 .11
☐ 390 Randy Moffitt .25 .11
☐ 391 Ron Washington .25 .11
☐ 392 Gary Roenicke .25 .11
☐ 393 Tom Candiotti 3.00 1.35
☐ 394 Larry Pashnick .25 .11
☐ 395 Dwight Evans .75 .35
☐ 396 Goose Gossage 1.50 .70
☐ 397 Derrel Thomas .25 .11
☐ 398 Juan Eichelberger .25 .11
☐ 399 Leon Roberts .25 .11
☐ 400 Dave Lopes .75 .35
☐ 401 Bill Gullickson .25 .11
☐ 402 Geoff Zahn .25 .11
☐ 403 Billy Sample .25 .11
☐ 404 Mike Squires .25 .11
☐ 405 Craig Reynolds .25 .11
☐ 406 Eric Show .25 .11
☐ 407 John Denny .25 .11
☐ 408 Dann Bilardello .25 .11
☐ 409 Bruce Benedict .25 .11
☐ 410 Kent Tekulve .75 .35
☐ 411 Mel Hall .75 .35
☐ 412 John Stuper .25 .11
☐ 413 Rick Dempsey .25 .11
☐ 414 Don Sutton 3.00 1.35
☐ 415 Jack Morris 3.00 1.35
☐ 416 John Tudor .25 .11
☐ 417 Willie Randolph .75 .35
☐ 418 Jerry Reuss .25 .11
☐ 419 Don Slaught .75 .35
☐ 420 Steve McCatty .25 .11
☐ 421 Tim Wallach .75 .35
☐ 422 Larry Parrish .25 .11
☐ 423 Brian Downing .25 .11
☐ 424 Britt Burns .25 .11
☐ 425 David Green .25 .11
☐ 426 Jerry Mumphrey .25 .11
☐ 427 Ivan DeJesus .25 .11
☐ 428 Mario Soto .25 .11
☐ 429 Gene Richards .25 .11
☐ 430 Dale Berra .25 .11
☐ 431 Darrell Evans .75 .35
☐ 432 Glenn Hubbard .25 .11
☐ 433 Jody Davis .25 .11
☐ 434 Danny Heep .25 .11
☐ 435 Ed Nunez .25 .11
☐ 436 Bobby Castillo .25 .11
☐ 437 Ernie Whitt .25 .11
☐ 438 Scott Ullger .25 .11
☐ 439 Doyle Alexander .25 .11
☐ 440 Domingo Ramos .25 .11
☐ 441 Craig Swan .25 .11
☐ 442 Warren Brusstar .25 .11
☐ 443 Len Barker .25 .11
☐ 444 Mike Easler .25 .11
☐ 445 Renie Martin .25 .11
☐ 446 Dennis Rasmussen .25 .11
☐ 447 Ted Power .25 .11
☐ 448 Charles Hudson .25 .11
☐ 449 Danny Cox .25 .11
☐ 450 Kevin Bass .25 .11
☐ 451 Daryl Sconiers .25 .11
☐ 452 Scott Fletcher .25 .11
☐ 453 Bryn Smith .25 .11
☐ 454 Jim Dwyer .25 .11
☐ 455 Rob Picciolo .25 .11
☐ 456 Enos Cabell .25 .11
☐ 457 Dennis Boyd .75 .35
☐ 458 Butch Wynegar .25 .11
☐ 459 Burt Hooton .25 .11
☐ 460 Ron Hassey .25 .11
☐ 461 Danny Jackson 1.50 .70
☐ 462 Bob Kearney .25 .11
☐ 463 Terry Francona .25 .11
☐ 464 Wayne Tolleson .25 .11
☐ 465 Mickey Rivers .25 .11
☐ 466 John Wathan .25 .11
☐ 467 Bill Almon .25 .11
☐ 468 George Vukovich .25 .11
☐ 469 Steve Kemp .25 .11
☐ 470 Ken Landreaux .25 .11
☐ 471 Milt Wilcox .25 .11
☐ 472 Tippy Martinez .25 .11
☐ 473 Ted Simmons .75 .35
☐ 474 Tim Foli .25 .11
☐ 475 George Hendrick .25 .11
☐ 476 Terry Puhl .25 .11
☐ 477 Von Hayes .25 .11
☐ 478 Bobby Brown .25 .11
☐ 479 Lee Lacy .25 .11
☐ 480 Joel Youngblood .25 .11
☐ 481 Jim Slaton .25 .11
☐ 482 Mike Fitzgerald .25 .11
☐ 483 Keith Moreland .25 .11
☐ 484 Ron Roenicke .25 .11
☐ 485 Luis Leal .25 .11
☐ 486 Bryan Oelkers .25 .11
☐ 487 Bruce Berenyi .25 .11
☐ 488 LaMarr Hoyt .25 .11
☐ 489 Joe Nolan .25 .11
☐ 490 Marshall Edwards .25 .11
☐ 491 Mike Laga .75 .35
☐ 492 Rick Cerone .25 .11
☐ 493 Rick Miller UER .25 .11
(Listed as Mike
on card front)
☐ 494 Rick Honeycutt .25 .11
☐ 495 Mike Hargrove .75 .35
☐ 496 Joe Simpson .25 .11
☐ 497 Keith Atherton .25 .11
☐ 498 Chris Welsh .25 .11
☐ 499 Bruce Kison .25 .11
☐ 500 Bobby Johnson .25 .11
☐ 501 Jerry Koosman .75 .35
☐ 502 Frank DiPino .25 .11
☐ 503 Tony Perez 3.00 1.35
☐ 504 Ken Oberkfell .25 .11
☐ 505 Mark Thurmond .25 .11
☐ 506 Joe Price .25 .11
☐ 507 Pascual Perez .25 .11
☐ 508 Marvell Wynne .25 .11
☐ 509 Mike Krukow .25 .11
☐ 510 Dick Ruthven .25 .11
☐ 511 Al Cowens .25 .11
☐ 512 Cliff Johnson .25 .11
☐ 513 Randy Bush .25 .11
☐ 514 Sammy Stewart .25 .11
☐ 515 Bill Schroeder .25 .11
☐ 516 Aurelio Lopez .75 .35
☐ 517 Mike G. Brown .25 .11
☐ 518 Graig Nettles .75 .35
☐ 519 Dave Sax .25 .11
☐ 520 Jerry Willard .25 .11
☐ 521 Paul Splittorff .25 .11
☐ 522 Tom Burgmeier .25 .11
☐ 523 Chris Speier .25 .11
☐ 524 Bobby Clark .25 .11
☐ 525 George Wright .25 .11
☐ 526 Dennis Lamp .25 .11
☐ 527 Tony Scott .25 .11
☐ 528 Ed Whitson .25 .11
☐ 529 Ron Reed .25 .11
☐ 530 Charlie Puleo .25 .11
☐ 531 Jerry Royster .25 .11
☐ 532 Don Robinson .25 .11
☐ 533 Steve Trout .25 .11
☐ 534 Bruce Sutter .75 .35
☐ 535 Bob Horner .25 .11
☐ 536 Pat Tabler .25 .11
☐ 537 Chris Chambliss .25 .11
☐ 538 Bob Ojeda .25 .11
☐ 539 Alan Ashby .25 .11
☐ 540 Jay Johnstone .75 .35
☐ 541 Bob Dernier .25 .11
☐ 542 Brook Jacoby .75 .35
☐ 543 U.L. Washington .25 .11
☐ 544 Danny Darwin .75 .35
☐ 545 Kiko Garcia .25 .11
☐ 546 Vance Law UER .25 .11
(Listed as P
on card front)
☐ 547 Tug McGraw .75 .35
☐ 548 Dave Smith .25 .11
☐ 549 Len Matuszek .25 .11
☐ 550 Tom Hume .25 .11
☐ 551 Dave Dravecky .75 .35
☐ 552 Rick Rhoden .25 .11
☐ 553 Duane Kuiper .25 .11
☐ 554 Rusty Staub .75 .35
☐ 555 Bill Campbell .25 .11
☐ 556 Mike Torrez .25 .11
☐ 557 Dave Henderson .75 .35
☐ 558 Len Whitehouse .25 .11
☐ 559 Barry Bonnell .25 .11
☐ 560 Rick Lysander .25 .11
☐ 561 Garth Iorg .25 .11
☐ 562 Bryan Clark .25 .11
☐ 563 Brian Giles .25 .11
☐ 564 Vern Ruhle .25 .11
☐ 565 Steve Bedrosian .25 .11
☐ 566 Larry McWilliams .25 .11
☐ 567 Jeff Leonard UER .25 .11
(Listed as P
on card front)
☐ 568 Alan Wiggins .25 .11
☐ 569 Jeff Russell .75 .35
☐ 570 Salome Barojas .25 .11
☐ 571 Dane Iorg .25 .11
☐ 572 Bob Knepper .25 .11
☐ 573 Gary Lavelle .25 .11
☐ 574 Gorman Thomas .25 .11
☐ 575 Manny Trillo .25 .11
☐ 576 Jim Palmer 4.00 1.80
☐ 577 Dale Murray .25 .11
☐ 578 Tom Brookens .75 .35
☐ 579 Rich Gedman .25 .11
☐ 580 Bill Doran .75 .35
☐ 581 Steve Yeager .25 .11
☐ 582 Dan Spillner .25 .11
☐ 583 Dan Quisenberry .25 .11
☐ 584 Rance Mulliniks .25 .11
☐ 585 Storm Davis .25 .11
☐ 586 Dave Schmidt .25 .11
☐ 587 Bill Russell .75 .35
☐ 588 Pat Sheridan .25 .11
☐ 589 Rafael Ramirez .25 .11
UER (A's on front)
☐ 590 Bud Anderson .25 .11
☐ 591 George Frazier .25 .11
☐ 592 Lee Tunnell .25 .11
☐ 593 Kirk Gibson 3.00 1.35
☐ 594 Scott McGregor .25 .11
☐ 595 Bob Bailor .25 .11
☐ 596 Tommy Herr .75 .35
☐ 597 Luis Sanchez .25 .11
☐ 598 Dave Engle .25 .11
☐ 599 Craig McMurtry .25 .11
☐ 600 Carlos Diaz .25 .11
☐ 601 Tom O'Malley .25 .11
☐ 602 Nick Esasky .25 .11
☐ 603 Ron Hodges .25 .11
☐ 604 Ed VandeBerg .25 .11
☐ 605 Alfredo Griffin .25 .11
☐ 606 Glenn Hoffman .25 .11
☐ 607 Hubie Brooks .25 .11
☐ 608 Richard Barnes UER .25 .11
(Photo actually
Neal Heaton)
☐ 609 Greg Walker .75 .35
☐ 610 Ken Singleton .25 .11
☐ 611 Mark Clear .25 .11

612 Buck Martinez	.25	.11
613 Ken Griffey	.75	.35
614 Reid Nichols	.25	.11
615 Doug Sisk	.25	.11
616 Bob Brenly	.25	.11
617 Joey McLaughlin	.25	.11
618 Glenn Wilson	.75	.35
619 Bob Stoddard	.25	.11
620 Lenn Sakata UER (Listed as Len on card front)	.25	.11
621 Mike Young	.25	.11
622 John Stefero	.25	.11
623 Carmelo Martinez	.25	.11
624 Dave Bergman	.25	.11
625 Runnin' Reds UER (Sic, Redbirds) David Green Willie McGee Lonnie Smith Ozzie Smith	3.00	1.35
626 Rudy May	.25	.11
627 Matt Keough	.25	.11
628 Jose DeLeon	.25	.11
629 Jim Essian	.25	.11
630 Darnell Coles	.25	.11
631 Mike Warren	.25	.11
632 Del Crandall MG	.25	.11
633 Dennis Martinez	.75	.35
634 Mike Moore	.75	.35
635 Lary Sorensen	.25	.11
636 Ricky Nelson	.25	.11
637 Omar Moreno	.25	.11
638 Charlie Hough	.75	.35
639 Dennis Eckersley	3.00	1.35
640 Walt Terrell	.25	.11
641 Denny Walling	.25	.11
642 Dave Anderson	.25	.11
643 Jose Oquendo	.75	.35
644 Bob Stanley	.25	.11
645 Dave Geisel	.25	.11
646 Scott Garrelts	.25	.11
647 Gary Pettis	.25	.11
648 Duke Snider Puzzle Card	1.50	.70
649 Johnnie LeMaster	.25	.11
650 Dave Collins	.25	.11
651 The Chicken	1.50	.70
652 DK Checklist 1-26 (Unnumbered)	.75	.35
653 Checklist 27-130 (Unnumbered)	.25	.11
654 Checklist 131-234 (Unnumbered)	.25	.11
655 Checklist 235-338 (Unnumbered)	.25	.11
656 Checklist 339-442 (Unnumbered)	.25	.11
657 Checklist 443-546 (Unnumbered)	.25	.11
658 Checklist 547-651 (Unnumbered)	.25	.11
A Living Legends A Gaylord Perry Rollie Fingers	2.50	1.10
B Living Legends B Carl Yastrzemski Johnny Bench	5.00	2.20

1984 Donruss Action All-Stars

The cards in this 60-card set measure approximately 3 1/2" by 5". For the second year in a row, Donruss issued a postcard-size card set. The set was distributed with a 63-piece Ted Williams puzzle. Unlike last year, when the fronts of the cards contained both an action and a portrait shot of the player, the fronts of this year's cards contain only an action photo. On the backs, the top section contains the card number and a full-color portrait of the player pictured on the front. The bottom half features the player's career statistics.

	NRMT	VG-E
COMPLETE SET (60)	6.00	2.70
COMMON CARD (1-60)	.05	.02
☐ 1 Gary Lavelle	.05	.02
☐ 2 Willie McGee	.30	.14
☐ 3 Tony Pena	.05	.02
☐ 4 Lou Whitaker	.20	.09
☐ 5 Robin Yount	.40	.18
☐ 6 Doug DeCinces	.05	.02
☐ 7 John Castino	.05	.02
☐ 8 Terry Kennedy	.05	.02
☐ 9 Rickey Henderson	.50	.23
☐ 10 Bob Horner	.05	.02
☐ 11 Harold Baines	.10	.05
☐ 12 Buddy Bell	.10	.05
☐ 13 Fernando Valenzuela	.10	.05
☐ 14 Nolan Ryan	2.50	1.10
☐ 15 Andre Thornton	.05	.02
☐ 16 Gary Redus	.05	.02
☐ 17 Pedro Guerrero	.10	.05
☐ 18 Andre Dawson	.40	.18
☐ 19 Dave Stieb	.05	.02
☐ 20 Cal Ripken	2.50	1.10
☐ 21 Ken Griffey	.10	.05
☐ 22 Wade Boggs	.75	.35
☐ 23 Keith Hernandez	.10	.05
☐ 24 Steve Carlton	.50	.23
☐ 25 Hal McRae	.05	.02
☐ 26 John Lowenstein	.05	.02
☐ 27 Fred Lynn	.10	.05
☐ 28 Bill Buckner	.10	.05
☐ 29 Chris Chambliss	.05	.02
☐ 30 Richie Zisk	.05	.02
☐ 31 Jack Clark	.10	.05
☐ 32 George Hendrick	.05	.02
☐ 33 Bill Madlock	.05	.02
☐ 34 Lance Parrish	.20	.09
☐ 35 Paul Molitor	.50	.23
☐ 36 Reggie Jackson	.50	.23
☐ 37 Kent Hrbek	.10	.05
☐ 38 Steve Garvey	.10	.05
☐ 39 Carney Lansford	.10	.05
☐ 40 Dale Murphy	.30	.14
☐ 41 Greg Luzinski	.10	.05
☐ 42 Larry Parrish	.05	.02
☐ 43 Ryne Sandberg	1.25	.55
☐ 44 Dickie Thon	.05	.02
☐ 45 Bert Blyleven	.10	.05
☐ 46 Ron Oester	.05	.02
☐ 47 Dusty Baker	.10	.05
☐ 48 Steve Rogers	.05	.02
☐ 49 Jim Clancy	.05	.02
☐ 50 Eddie Murray	.60	.25
☐ 51 Ron Guidry	.10	.05
☐ 52 Jim Rice	.10	.05
☐ 53 Tom Seaver	.50	.23
☐ 54 Pete Rose	.75	.35
☐ 55 George Brett	1.25	.55
☐ 56 Dan Quisenberry	.05	.02
☐ 57 Mike Schmidt	.60	.25
☐ 58 Ted Simmons	.10	.05
☐ 59 Dave Righetti	.05	.02
☐ 60 Checklist Card	.05	.02

1984 Donruss Champions

The cards in this 60-card set measure approximately 3 1/2" by 5". The 1984 Donruss Champions set is a hybrid photo/artwork issue. Grand Champions, listed GC in the checklist below, feature the artwork of Dick Perez of Perez-Steele Galleries. Current players in the set feature photographs. The theme of this postcard-size set features a Grand Champion and those current players that are directly behind him in a baseball statistical category, for example, Season Home Runs (1-7), Career Home Runs (8-13), Season Batting Average (14-19), Career Batting Average (20-25), Career Hits (26-30), Career Victories (31-36), Career Strikeouts (37-42), Most Valuable Players (43-49), World Series stars (50-54), and All-Star heroes (55-59). The cards were issued in cello packs with pieces of the Duke Snider puzzle.

	NRMT	VG-E
COMPLETE SET (60)	10.00	4.50
COMMON CARD (1-60)	.05	.02
☐ 1 Babe Ruth GC	2.00	.90
☐ 2 George Foster	.10	.05
☐ 3 Dave Kingman	.10	.05
☐ 4 Jim Rice	.10	.05
☐ 5 Gorman Thomas	.05	.02
☐ 6 Ben Oglivie	.05	.02
☐ 7 Jeff Burroughs	.05	.02
☐ 8 Hank Aaron GC	.75	.35
☐ 9 Reggie Jackson	.50	.23
☐ 10 Carl Yastrzemski	.50	.23
☐ 11 Mike Schmidt	.60	.25
☐ 12 Graig Nettles	.10	.05
☐ 13 Greg Luzinski	.10	.05
☐ 14 Ted Williams GC	1.50	.70
☐ 15 George Brett	1.25	.55
☐ 16 Wade Boggs	.50	.23
☐ 17 Hal McRae	.05	.02
☐ 18 Bill Buckner	.10	.05
☐ 19 Eddie Murray	.60	.25
☐ 20 Rogers Hornsby GC	.50	.23
☐ 21 Rod Carew	.40	.18
☐ 22 Bill Madlock	.10	.05
☐ 23 Lonnie Smith	.05	.02
☐ 24 Cecil Cooper	.10	.05
☐ 25 Ken Griffey	.10	.05
☐ 26 Ty Cobb GC	1.00	.45
☐ 27 Pete Rose	.75	.35
☐ 28 Rusty Staub	.10	.05
☐ 29 Tony Perez	.10	.05
☐ 30 Al Oliver	.10	.05
☐ 31 Cy Young GC	.50	.23
☐ 32 Gaylord Perry	.40	.18
☐ 33 Ferguson Jenkins	.40	.18
☐ 34 Phil Niekro	.40	.18
☐ 35 Jim Palmer	.40	.18
☐ 36 Tommy John	.10	.05
☐ 37 Walter Johnson GC	.50	.23
☐ 38 Steve Carlton	.40	.18
☐ 39 Nolan Ryan	2.50	1.10
☐ 40 Tom Seaver	.40	.18
☐ 41 Don Sutton	.40	.18
☐ 42 Bert Blyleven	.10	.05
☐ 43 Frank Robinson GC	.40	.18
☐ 44 Joe Morgan	.40	.18
☐ 45 Rollie Fingers	.30	.14
☐ 46 Keith Hernandez	.10	.05
☐ 47 Robin Yount	.30	.14
☐ 48 Cal Ripken	2.50	1.10
☐ 49 Dale Murphy	.30	.14
☐ 50 Mickey Mantle GC	3.00	1.35
☐ 51 Johnny Bench	.50	.23
☐ 52 Carlton Fisk	.50	.23
☐ 53 Tug McGraw	.10	.05
☐ 54 Paul Molitor	.50	.23
☐ 55 Carl Hubbell GC	.30	.14
☐ 56 Steve Garvey	.10	.05
☐ 57 Dave Parker	.10	.05
☐ 58 Gary Carter	.20	.09
☐ 59 Fred Lynn	.10	.05
☐ 60 Checklist Card	.05	.02

1985 Donruss

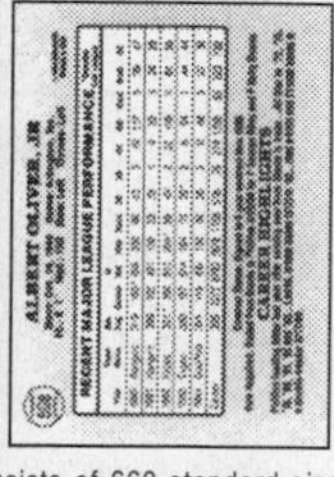

The 1985 Donruss set consists of 660 standard-size cards. Wax packs contained 15 cards and a Lou Gehrig puzzle panel. The fronts feature full color photos framed by jet black borders (making the cards condition sensitive). The first 26 cards of the set feature Diamond Kings (DK), for the fourth year in a row; the artwork on the Diamond Kings was again produced by the Perez-Steele Galleries. Cards 27-46 feature Rated Rookies (RR). The unnumbered checklist cards are arbitrarily numbered below as numbers 654 through 660. Rookie Cards in this set include Roger Clemens, Eric Davis, Shawon Dunston, Dwight Gooden, Orel Hershiser, Jimmy Key, Mark Langston, Terry Pendleton, Kirby Puckett, Jose Rijo, Bret Saberhagen, and Danny Tartabull.

	NRMT	VG-E
COMPLETE SET (660)	100.00	45.00
COMP.FACT.SET (660)	120.00	55.00
COMMON CARD (1-660)	.15	.07
COMPLETE GEHRIG PUZZLE	4.00	1.80
☐ 1 Ryne Sandberg DK	2.00	.90
☐ 2 Doug DeCinces DK	.15	.07
☐ 3 Richard Dotson DK	.15	.07
☐ 4 Bert Blyleven DK	.40	.18
☐ 5 Lou Whitaker DK	.75	.35
☐ 6 Dan Quisenberry DK	.15	.07
☐ 7 Don Mattingly DK	2.50	1.10
☐ 8 Carney Lansford DK	.40	.18
☐ 9 Frank Tanana DK	.40	.18
☐ 10 Willie Upshaw DK	.15	.07
☐ 11 Claudell Washington DK	.15	.07
☐ 12 Mike Marshall DK	.15	.07
☐ 13 Joaquin Andujar DK	.15	.07
☐ 14 Cal Ripken DK	4.00	1.80
☐ 15 Jim Rice DK	.40	.18
☐ 16 Don Sutton DK	.75	.35
☐ 17 Frank Viola DK	.40	.18
☐ 18 Alvin Davis DK	.15	.07
☐ 19 Mario Soto DK	.15	.07
☐ 20 Jose Cruz DK	.40	.18
☐ 21 Charlie Lea DK	.15	.07
☐ 22 Jesse Orosco DK	.15	.07
☐ 23 Juan Samuel DK	.15	.07
☐ 24 Tony Pena DK	.15	.07
☐ 25 Tony Gwynn DK	3.00	1.35
☐ 26 Bob Brenly DK	.15	.07
☐ 27 Danny Tartabull RR	1.50	.70
☐ 28 Mike Bielecki RR	.15	.07
☐ 29 Steve Lyons RR	.40	.18
☐ 30 Jeff Reed RR	.15	.07
☐ 31 Tony Brewer RR	.15	.07
☐ 32 John Morris RR	.15	.07
☐ 33 Daryl Boston RR	.15	.07
☐ 34 Al Pulido RR	.15	.07
☐ 35 Steve Kiefer RR	.15	.07
☐ 36 Larry Sheets RR	.15	.07
☐ 37 Scott Bradley RR	.15	.07
☐ 38 Calvin Schiraldi RR	.15	.07
☐ 39 Shawon Dunston RR	1.50	.70
☐ 40 Charlie Mitchell RR	.15	.07
☐ 41 Billy Hatcher RR	.75	.35
☐ 42 Russ Stephans RR	.15	.07
☐ 43 Alejandro Sanchez RR	.15	.07
☐ 44 Steve Jeltz RR	.15	.07
☐ 45 Jim Traber RR	.15	.07
☐ 46 Doug Loman RR	.15	.07
☐ 47 Eddie Murray	2.50	1.10
☐ 48 Robin Yount	2.00	.90
☐ 49 Lance Parrish	.40	.18
☐ 50 Jim Rice	.40	.18
☐ 51 Dave Winfield	1.50	.70
☐ 52 Fernando Valenzuela	.40	.18
☐ 53 George Brett	3.00	1.35
☐ 54 Dave Kingman	.40	.18
☐ 55 Gary Carter	1.50	.70
☐ 56 Buddy Bell	.40	.18
☐ 57 Reggie Jackson	2.00	.90
☐ 58 Harold Baines	.40	.18
☐ 59 Ozzie Smith	2.00	.90
☐ 60 Nolan Ryan UER (Set strikeout record in 1973, not 1972)	8.00	3.60
☐ 61 Mike Schmidt	2.00	.90
☐ 62 Dave Parker	.40	.18
☐ 63 Tony Gwynn	6.00	2.70
☐ 64 Tony Pena	.15	.07
☐ 65 Jack Clark	.40	.18
☐ 66 Dale Murphy	1.50	.70
☐ 67 Ryne Sandberg	3.00	1.35
☐ 68 Keith Hernandez	.40	.18
☐ 69 Alvin Davis	.40	.18
☐ 70 Kent Hrbek	.40	.18
☐ 71 Willie Upshaw	.15	.07
☐ 72 Dave Engle	.15	.07
☐ 73 Alfredo Griffin	.15	.07
☐ 74A Jack Perconte (Career Highlights takes four lines)	.15	.07
☐ 74B Jack Perconte (Career Highlights takes three lines)	.15	.07
☐ 75 Jesse Orosco	.15	.07
☐ 76 Jody Davis	.15	.07
☐ 77 Bob Horner	.15	.07
☐ 78 Larry McWilliams	.15	.07
☐ 79 Joel Youngblood	.15	.07
☐ 80 Alan Wiggins	.15	.07
☐ 81 Ron Oester	.15	.07
☐ 82 Ozzie Virgil	.15	.07
☐ 83 Ricky Horton	.15	.07
☐ 84 Bill Doran	.15	.07
☐ 85 Rod Carew	1.50	.70
☐ 86 LaMarr Hoyt	.15	.07
☐ 87 Tim Wallach	.40	.18
☐ 88 Mike Flanagan	.15	.07
☐ 89 Jim Sundberg	.15	.07
☐ 90 Chet Lemon	.15	.07
☐ 91 Bob Stanley	.15	.07
☐ 92 Willie Randolph	.40	.18
☐ 93 Bill Russell	.15	.07
☐ 94 Julio Franco	.75	.35
☐ 95 Dan Quisenberry	.40	.18
☐ 96 Bill Caudill	.15	.07
☐ 97 Bill Gullickson	.15	.07
☐ 98 Danny Darwin	.15	.07
☐ 99 Curtis Wilkerson	.15	.07
☐ 100 Bud Black	.15	.07
☐ 101 Tony Phillips	.40	.18
☐ 102 Tony Bernazard	.15	.07
☐ 103 Jay Howell	.15	.07
☐ 104 Burt Hooton	.15	.07
☐ 105 Milt Wilcox	.15	.07
☐ 106 Rich Dauer	.15	.07
☐ 107 Don Sutton	1.50	.70
☐ 108 Mike Witt	.15	.07
☐ 109 Bruce Sutter	.40	.18
☐ 110 Enos Cabell	.15	.07
☐ 111 John Denny	.15	.07
☐ 112 Dave Dravecky	.40	.18
☐ 113 Marvell Wynne	.15	.07
☐ 114 Johnnie LeMaster	.15	.07
☐ 115 Chuck Porter	.15	.07
☐ 116 John Gibbons	.15	.07
☐ 117 Keith Moreland	.15	.07
☐ 118 Darnell Coles	.15	.07
☐ 119 Dennis Lamp	.15	.07
☐ 120 Ron Davis	.15	.07
☐ 121 Nick Esasky	.15	.07
☐ 122 Vance Law	.15	.07
☐ 123 Gary Roenicke	.15	.07
☐ 124 Bill Schroeder	.15	.07
☐ 125 Dave Rozema	.15	.07
☐ 126 Bobby Meacham	.15	.07
☐ 127 Marty Barrett	.15	.07
☐ 128 R.J. Reynolds	.15	.07
☐ 129 Ernie Camacho UER (Photo actually Rich Thompson)	.15	.07
☐ 130 Jorge Orta	.15	.07
☐ 131 Lary Sorensen	.15	.07
☐ 132 Terry Francona	.15	.07
☐ 133 Fred Lynn	.40	.18
☐ 134 Bob Jones	.15	.07
☐ 135 Jerry Hairston	.15	.07
☐ 136 Kevin Bass	.15	.07
☐ 137 Garry Maddox	.15	.07
☐ 138 Dave LaPoint	.15	.07
☐ 139 Kevin McReynolds	.40	.18
☐ 140 Wayne Krenchicki	.15	.07
☐ 141 Rafael Ramirez	.15	.07
☐ 142 Rod Scurry	.15	.07
☐ 143 Greg Minton	.15	.07
☐ 144 Tim Stoddard	.15	.07
☐ 145 Steve Henderson	.15	.07
☐ 146 George Bell	.40	.18
☐ 147 Dave Meier	.15	.07
☐ 148 Sammy Stewart	.15	.07
☐ 149 Mark Brouhard	.15	.07
☐ 150 Larry Herndon	.15	.07
☐ 151 Oil Can Boyd	.15	.07
☐ 152 Brian Dayett	.15	.07
☐ 153 Tom Niedenfuer	.15	.07
☐ 154 Brook Jacoby	.15	.07
☐ 155 Onix Concepcion	.15	.07
☐ 156 Tim Conroy	.15	.07
☐ 157 Joe Hesketh	.15	.07
☐ 158 Brian Downing	.15	.07
☐ 159 Tommy Dunbar	.15	.07
☐ 160 Marc Hill	.15	.07
☐ 161 Phil Garner	.15	.07
☐ 162 Jerry Davis	.15	.07
☐ 163 Bill Campbell	.15	.07
☐ 164 John Franco	1.00	.45
☐ 165 Len Barker	.15	.07
☐ 166 Benny Distefano	.15	.07
☐ 167 George Frazier	.15	.07
☐ 168 Tito Landrum	.15	.07
☐ 169 Cal Ripken	8.00	3.60
☐ 170 Cecil Cooper	.40	.18
☐ 171 Alan Trammell	.75	.35
☐ 172 Wade Boggs	2.00	.90
☐ 173 Don Baylor	.75	.35
☐ 174 Pedro Guerrero	.40	.18
☐ 175 Frank White	.40	.18
☐ 176 Rickey Henderson	1.50	.70
☐ 177 Charlie Lea	.15	.07
☐ 178 Pete O'Brien	.15	.07
☐ 179 Doug DeCinces	.15	.07
☐ 180 Ron Kittle	.15	.0
☐ 181 George Hendrick	.15	.0
☐ 182 Joe Niekro	.15	.0
☐ 183 Juan Samuel	.15	.0
☐ 184 Mario Soto	.15	.0
☐ 185 Goose Gossage	.40	.1
☐ 186 Johnny Ray	.15	.0
☐ 187 Bob Brenly	.15	.0
☐ 188 Craig McMurtry	.15	.0
☐ 189 Leon Durham	.15	.0
☐ 190 Dwight Gooden	4.00	1.8
☐ 191 Barry Bonnell	.15	.0
☐ 192 Tim Teufel	.15	.0
☐ 193 Dave Stieb	.40	.1
☐ 194 Mickey Hatcher	.15	.0
☐ 195 Jesse Barfield	.15	.0
☐ 196 Al Cowens	.15	.0
☐ 197 Hubie Brooks	.15	.0
☐ 198 Steve Trout	.15	.0
☐ 199 Glenn Hubbard	.15	.0
☐ 200 Bill Madlock	.40	.1
☐ 201 Jeff D. Robinson	.15	.0
☐ 202 Eric Show	.15	.0
☐ 203 Dave Concepcion	.40	.1
☐ 204 Ivan DeJesus	.15	.0
☐ 205 Neil Allen	.15	.0
☐ 206 Jerry Mumphrey	.15	.0
☐ 207 Mike C. Brown	.15	.0
☐ 208 Carlton Fisk	1.50	.7
☐ 209 Bryn Smith	.15	.0
☐ 210 Tippy Martinez	.15	.0
☐ 211 Dion James	.15	.0
☐ 212 Willie Hernandez	.15	.0
☐ 213 Mike Easler	.15	.0
☐ 214 Ron Guidry	.40	.1
☐ 215 Rick Honeycutt	.15	.0
☐ 216 Brett Butler	.40	.1
☐ 217 Larry Gura	.15	.0
☐ 218 Ray Burris	.15	.0
☐ 219 Steve Rogers	.15	.0
☐ 220 Frank Tanana UER (Bats Left listed twice on card back)	.15	.0
☐ 221 Ned Yost	.15	.0
☐ 222 Bret Saberhagen UER (18 career IP on back)	1.50	.7
☐ 223 Mike Davis	.15	.0
☐ 224 Bert Blyleven	.75	.3
☐ 225 Steve Kemp	.15	.0
☐ 226 Jerry Reuss	.15	.0
☐ 227 Darrell Evans UER (80 homers in 1980)	.40	.1
☐ 228 Wayne Gross	.15	.0
☐ 229 Jim Gantner	.15	.0
☐ 230 Bob Boone	.40	.1
☐ 231 Lonnie Smith	.15	.0
☐ 232 Frank DiPino	.15	.07
☐ 233 Jerry Koosman	.15	.0
☐ 234 Graig Nettles	.40	.1
☐ 235 John Tudor	.15	.07
☐ 236 John Rabb	.15	.07
☐ 237 Rick Manning	.15	.0
☐ 238 Mike Fitzgerald	.15	.0
☐ 239 Gary Matthews	.15	.0
☐ 240 Jim Presley	.40	.1
☐ 241 Dave Collins	.15	.0
☐ 242 Gary Gaetti	.40	.1
☐ 243 Dann Bilardello	.15	.07
☐ 244 Rudy Law	.15	.07
☐ 245 John Lowenstein	.15	.07
☐ 246 Tom Tellmann	.15	.0
☐ 247 Howard Johnson	.40	.1
☐ 248 Ray Fontenot	.15	.07
☐ 249 Tony Armas	.15	.07
☐ 250 Candy Maldonado	.15	.07
☐ 251 Mike Jeffcoat	.15	.07
☐ 252 Dane Iorg	.15	.07
☐ 253 Bruce Bochte	.15	.07
☐ 254 Pete Rose	2.00	.9
☐ 255 Don Aase	.15	.07
☐ 256 George Wright	.15	.07
☐ 257 Britt Burns	.15	.07
☐ 258 Mike Scott	.15	.07
☐ 259 Len Matuszek	.15	.07
☐ 260 Dave Rucker	.15	.07
☐ 261 Craig Lefferts	.15	.07
☐ 262 Jay Tibbs	.15	.07
☐ 263 Bruce Benedict	.15	.07
☐ 264 Don Robinson	.15	.07
☐ 265 Gary Lavelle	.15	.07
☐ 266 Scott Sanderson	.15	.07
☐ 267 Matt Young	.15	.07
☐ 268 Ernie Whitt	.15	.07
☐ 269 Houston Jimenez	.15	.07
☐ 270 Ken Dixon	.15	.07
☐ 271 Pete Ladd	.15	.07
☐ 272 Juan Berenguer	.15	.07

☐ 273 Roger Clemens 25.00 11.00
☐ 274 Rick Cerone .15 .07
☐ 275 Dave Anderson .15 .07
☐ 276 George Vukovich .15 .07
☐ 277 Greg Pryor .15 .07
☐ 278 Mike Warren .15 .07
☐ 279 Bob James .15 .07
☐ 280 Bobby Grich .40 .18
☐ 281 Mike Mason .15 .07
☐ 282 Ron Reed .15 .07
☐ 283 Alan Ashby .15 .07
☐ 284 Mark Thurmond .15 .07
☐ 285 Joe Lefebvre .15 .07
☐ 286 Ted Power .15 .07
☐ 287 Chris Chambliss .15 .07
☐ 288 Lee Tunnell .15 .07
☐ 289 Rich Bordi .15 .07
☐ 290 Glenn Brummer .15 .07
☐ 291 Mike Boddicker .15 .07
☐ 292 Rollie Fingers 1.50 .70
☐ 293 Lou Whitaker .75 .35
☐ 294 Dwight Evans .40 .18
☐ 295 Don Mattingly 5.00 2.20
☐ 296 Mike Marshall .15 .07
☐ 297 Willie Wilson .15 .07
☐ 298 Mike Heath .15 .07
☐ 299 Tim Raines .40 .18
☐ 300 Larry Parrish .15 .07
☐ 301 Geoff Zahn .15 .07
☐ 302 Rich Dotson .15 .07
☐ 303 David Green .15 .07
☐ 304 Jose Cruz .40 .18
☐ 305 Steve Carlton .75 .35
☐ 306 Gary Redus .15 .07
☐ 307 Steve Garvey .75 .35
☐ 308 Jose DeLeon .15 .07
☐ 309 Randy Lerch .15 .07
☐ 310 Claudell Washington .15 .07
☐ 311 Lee Smith .75 .35
☐ 312 Darryl Strawberry 1.50 .70
☐ 313 Jim Beattie .15 .07
☐ 314 John Butcher .15 .07
☐ 315 Damaso Garcia .15 .07
☐ 316 Mike Smithson .15 .07
☐ 317 Luis Leal .15 .07
☐ 318 Ken Phelps .15 .07
☐ 319 Wally Backman .15 .07
☐ 320 Ron Cey .40 .18
☐ 321 Brad Komminsk .15 .07
☐ 322 Jason Thompson .15 .07
☐ 323 Frank Williams .15 .07
☐ 324 Tim Lollar .15 .07
☐ 325 Eric Davis 2.00 .90
☐ 326 Von Hayes .15 .07
☐ 327 Andy Van Slyke .75 .35
☐ 328 Craig Reynolds .15 .07
☐ 329 Dick Schofield .15 .07
☐ 330 Scott Fletcher .15 .07
☐ 331 Jeff Reardon .40 .18
☐ 332 Rick Dempsey .15 .07
☐ 333 Ben Oglivie .15 .07
☐ 334 Dan Petry .15 .07
☐ 335 Jackie Gutierrez .15 .07
☐ 336 Dave Righetti .40 .18
☐ 337 Alejandro Pena .15 .07
☐ 338 Mel Hall .15 .07
☐ 339 Pat Sheridan .15 .07
☐ 340 Keith Atherton .15 .07
☐ 341 David Palmer .15 .07
☐ 342 Gary Ward .15 .07
☐ 343 Dave Stewart .40 .18
☐ 344 Mark Gubicza .40 .18
☐ 345 Carney Lansford .40 .18
☐ 346 Jerry Willard .15 .07
☐ 347 Ken Griffey .40 .18
☐ 348 Franklin Stubbs .15 .07
☐ 349 Aurelio Lopez .15 .07
☐ 350 Al Bumbry .15 .07
☐ 351 Charlie Moore .15 .07
☐ 352 Luis Sanchez .15 .07
☐ 353 Darrell Porter .15 .07
☐ 354 Bill Dawley .15 .07
☐ 355 Charles Hudson .15 .07
☐ 356 Garry Templeton .15 .07
☐ 357 Cecilio Guante .15 .07
☐ 358 Jeff Leonard .15 .07
☐ 359 Paul Molitor 2.00 .90
☐ 360 Ron Gardenhire .15 .07
☐ 361 Larry Bowa .40 .18
☐ 362 Bob Kearney .15 .07
☐ 363 Garth Iorg .15 .07
☐ 364 Tom Brunansky .40 .18
☐ 365 Brad Gulden .15 .07
☐ 366 Greg Walker .15 .07
☐ 367 Mike Young .15 .07
☐ 368 Rick Waits .15 .07
☐ 369 Doug Bair .15 .07
☐ 370 Bob Shirley .15 .07
☐ 371 Bob Ojeda .15 .07
☐ 372 Bob Welch .15 .07
☐ 373 Neal Heaton .15 .07
☐ 374 Danny Jackson UER .15 .07
(Photo actually
Frank Willo)
☐ 375 Donnie Hill .15 .07
☐ 376 Mike Stenhouse .15 .07
☐ 377 Bruce Kison .15 .07
☐ 378 Wayne Tolleson .15 .07
☐ 379 Floyd Bannister .15 .07
☐ 380 Vern Ruhle .15 .07
☐ 381 Tim Corcoran .15 .07
☐ 382 Kurt Kepshire .15 .07
☐ 383 Bobby Brown .15 .07
☐ 384 Dave Van Gorder .15 .07
☐ 385 Rick Mahler .15 .07
☐ 386 Lee Mazzilli .15 .07
☐ 387 Bill Laskey .15 .07
☐ 388 Thad Bosley .15 .07
☐ 389 Al Chambers .15 .07
☐ 390 Tony Fernandez .40 .18
☐ 391 Ron Washington .15 .07
☐ 392 Bill Swaggerty .15 .07
☐ 393 Bob L. Gibson .15 .07
☐ 394 Marty Castillo .15 .07
☐ 395 Steve Crawford .15 .07
☐ 396 Clay Christiansen .15 .07
☐ 397 Bob Bailor .15 .07
☐ 398 Mike Hargrove .40 .18
☐ 399 Charlie Leibrandt .15 .07
☐ 400 Tom Burgmeier .15 .07
☐ 401 Razor Shines .15 .07
☐ 402 Rob Wilfong .15 .07
☐ 403 Tom Henke .40 .18
☐ 404 Al Jones .15 .07
☐ 405 Mike LaCoss .15 .07
☐ 406 Luis DeLeon .15 .07
☐ 407 Greg Gross .15 .07
☐ 408 Tom Hume .15 .07
☐ 409 Rick Camp .15 .07
☐ 410 Milt May .15 .07
☐ 411 Henry Cotto .15 .07
☐ 412 David Von Ohlen .15 .07
☐ 413 Scott McGregor .15 .07
☐ 414 Ted Simmons .40 .18
☐ 415 Jack Morris .75 .35
☐ 416 Bill Buckner .40 .18
☐ 417 Butch Wynegar .15 .07
☐ 418 Steve Sax .40 .18
☐ 419 Steve Balboni .15 .07
☐ 420 Dwayne Murphy .15 .07
☐ 421 Andre Dawson 1.50 .70
☐ 422 Charlie Hough .40 .18
☐ 423 Tommy John .75 .35
☐ 424A Tom Seaver ERR 2.00 .90
(Photo actually
Floyd Bannister)
☐ 424B Tom Seaver COR 25.00 11.00
☐ 425 Tommy Herr .40 .18
☐ 426 Terry Puhl .15 .07
☐ 427 Al Holland .15 .07
☐ 428 Eddie Milner .15 .07
☐ 429 Terry Kennedy .15 .07
☐ 430 John Candelaria .15 .07
☐ 431 Manny Trillo .15 .07
☐ 432 Ken Oberkfell .15 .07
☐ 433 Rick Sutcliffe .15 .07
☐ 434 Ron Darling .40 .18
☐ 435 Spike Owen .15 .07
☐ 436 Frank Viola .40 .18
☐ 437 Lloyd Moseby .15 .07
☐ 438 Kirby Puckett 25.00 11.00
☐ 439 Jim Clancy .15 .07
☐ 440 Mike Moore .15 .07
☐ 441 Doug Sisk .15 .07
☐ 442 Dennis Eckersley 1.50 .70
☐ 443 Gerald Perry .15 .07
☐ 444 Dale Berra .15 .07
☐ 445 Dusty Baker .40 .18
☐ 446 Ed Whitson .15 .07
☐ 447 Cesar Cedeno .40 .18
☐ 448 Rick Schu .15 .07
☐ 449 Joaquin Andujar .15 .07
☐ 450 Mark Bailey .15 .07
☐ 451 Ron Romanick .15 .07
☐ 452 Julio Cruz .15 .07
☐ 453 Miguel Dilone .15 .07
☐ 454 Storm Davis .15 .07
☐ 455 Jaime Cocanower .15 .07
☐ 456 Barbaro Garbey .15 .07
☐ 457 Rich Gedman .15 .07
☐ 458 Phil Niekro 1.50 .70
☐ 459 Mike Scioscia .15 .07
☐ 460 Pat Tabler .15 .07
☐ 461 Darryl Motley .15 .07
☐ 462 Chris Codiroli .15 .07
☐ 463 Doug Flynn .15 .07
☐ 464 Billy Sample .15 .07
☐ 465 Mickey Rivers .15 .07
☐ 466 John Wathan .15 .07
☐ 467 Bill Krueger .15 .07
☐ 468 Andre Thornton .15 .07
☐ 469 Rex Hudler .15 .07
☐ 470 Sid Bream .40 .18
☐ 471 Kirk Gibson .75 .35
☐ 472 John Shelby .15 .07
☐ 473 Moose Haas .15 .07
☐ 474 Doug Corbett .15 .07
☐ 475 Willie McGee .40 .18
☐ 476 Bob Knepper .15 .07
☐ 477 Kevin Gross .15 .07
☐ 478 Carmelo Martinez .15 .07
☐ 479 Kent Tekulve .15 .07
☐ 480 Chili Davis .40 .18
☐ 481 Bobby Clark .15 .07
☐ 482 Mookie Wilson .40 .18
☐ 483 Dave Owen .15 .07
☐ 484 Ed Nunez .15 .07
☐ 485 Rance Mulliniks .15 .07
☐ 486 Ken Schrom .15 .07
☐ 487 Jeff Russell .15 .07
☐ 488 Tom Paciorek .15 .07
☐ 489 Dan Ford .15 .07
☐ 490 Mike Caldwell .15 .07
☐ 491 Scottie Earl .15 .07
☐ 492 Jose Rijo 1.50 .70
☐ 493 Bruce Hurst .15 .07
☐ 494 Ken Landreaux .15 .07
☐ 495 Mike Fischlin .15 .07
☐ 496 Don Slaught .15 .07
☐ 497 Steve McCatty .15 .07
☐ 498 Gary Lucas .15 .07
☐ 499 Gary Pettis .15 .07
☐ 500 Marvis Foley .15 .07
☐ 501 Mike Squires .15 .07
☐ 502 Jim Pankovits .15 .07
☐ 503 Luis Aguayo .15 .07
☐ 504 Ralph Citarella .15 .07
☐ 505 Bruce Bochy .15 .07
☐ 506 Bob Owchinko .15 .07
☐ 507 Pascual Perez .15 .07
☐ 508 Lee Lacy .15 .07
☐ 509 Atlee Hammaker .15 .07
☐ 510 Bob Dernier .15 .07
☐ 511 Ed VandeBerg .15 .07
☐ 512 Cliff Johnson .15 .07
☐ 513 Len Whitehouse .15 .07
☐ 514 Dennis Martinez .40 .18
☐ 515 Ed Romero .15 .07
☐ 516 Rusty Kuntz .15 .07
☐ 517 Rick Miller .15 .07
☐ 518 Dennis Rasmussen .15 .07
☐ 519 Steve Yeager .15 .07
☐ 520 Chris Bando .15 .07
☐ 521 U.L. Washington .15 .07
☐ 522 Curt Young .15 .07
☐ 523 Angel Salazar .15 .07
☐ 524 Curt Kaufman .15 .07
☐ 525 Odell Jones .15 .07
☐ 526 Juan Agosto .15 .07
☐ 527 Denny Walling .15 .07
☐ 528 Andy Hawkins .15 .07
☐ 529 Sixto Lezcano .15 .07
☐ 530 Skeeter Barnes .15 .07
☐ 531 Randy Johnson .15 .07
☐ 532 Jim Morrison .15 .07
☐ 533 Warren Brusstar .15 .07
☐ 534A Jeff Pendleton ERR 1.50 .70
(Wrong first name)
☐ 534B Terry Pendleton COR 5.00 2.20
☐ 535 Vic Rodriguez .15 .07
☐ 536 Bob McClure .15 .07
☐ 537 Dave Bergman .15 .07
☐ 538 Mark Clear .15 .07
☐ 539 Mike Pagliarulo .15 .07
☐ 540 Terry Whitfield .15 .07
☐ 541 Joe Beckwith .15 .07
☐ 542 Jeff Burroughs .15 .07
☐ 543 Dan Schatzeder .15 .07
☐ 544 Donnie Scott .15 .07
☐ 545 Jim Slaton .15 .07
☐ 546 Greg Luzinski .40 .18
☐ 547 Mark Salas .15 .07
☐ 548 Dave Smith .15 .07
☐ 549 John Wockenfuss .15 .07
☐ 550 Frank Pastore .15 .07
☐ 551 Tim Flannery .15 .07
☐ 552 Rick Rhoden .15 .07
☐ 553 Mark Davis .15 .07
☐ 554 Jeff Dedmon .15 .07
☐ 555 Gary Woods .15 .07
☐ 556 Danny Heep .15 .07

☐ 557 Mark Langston	1.25	.55
☐ 558 Darrell Brown	.15	.07
☐ 559 Jimmy Key	2.00	.90
☐ 560 Rick Lysander	.15	.07
☐ 561 Doyle Alexander	.15	.07
☐ 562 Mike Stanton	.15	.07
☐ 563 Sid Fernandez	.40	.18
☐ 564 Richie Hebner	.15	.07
☐ 565 Alex Trevino	.15	.07
☐ 566 Brian Harper	.15	.07
☐ 567 Dan Gladden	.40	.18
☐ 568 Luis Salazar	.15	.07
☐ 569 Tom Foley	.15	.07
☐ 570 Larry Andersen	.15	.07
☐ 571 Danny Cox	.15	.07
☐ 572 Joe Sambito	.15	.07
☐ 573 Juan Beniquez	.15	.07
☐ 574 Joel Skinner	.15	.07
☐ 575 Randy St.Claire	.15	.07
☐ 576 Floyd Rayford	.15	.07
☐ 577 Roy Howell	.15	.07
☐ 578 John Grubb	.15	.07
☐ 579 Ed Jurak	.15	.07
☐ 580 John Montefusco	.15	.07
☐ 581 Orel Hershiser	2.00	.90
☐ 582 Tom Waddell	.15	.07
☐ 583 Mark Huismann	.15	.07
☐ 584 Joe Morgan	1.50	.70
☐ 585 Jim Wohlford	.15	.07
☐ 586 Dave Schmidt	.15	.07
☐ 587 Jeff Kunkel	.15	.07
☐ 588 Hal McRae	.40	.18
☐ 589 Bill Almon	.15	.07
☐ 590 Carmen Castillo	.15	.07
☐ 591 Omar Moreno	.15	.07
☐ 592 Ken Howell	.15	.07
☐ 593 Tom Brookens	.15	.07
☐ 594 Joe Nolan	.15	.07
☐ 595 Willie Lozado	.15	.07
☐ 596 Tom Nieto	.15	.07
☐ 597 Walt Terrell	.15	.07
☐ 598 Al Oliver	.40	.18
☐ 599 Shane Rawley	.15	.07
☐ 600 Denny Gonzalez	.15	.07
☐ 601 Mark Grant	.15	.07
☐ 602 Mike Armstrong	.15	.07
☐ 603 George Foster	.40	.18
☐ 604 Dave Lopes	.40	.18
☐ 605 Salome Barojas	.15	.07
☐ 606 Roy Lee Jackson	.15	.07
☐ 607 Pete Filson	.15	.07
☐ 608 Duane Walker	.15	.07
☐ 609 Glenn Wilson	.15	.07
☐ 610 Rafael Santana	.15	.07
☐ 611 Roy Smith	.15	.07
☐ 612 Ruppert Jones	.15	.07
☐ 613 Joe Cowley	.15	.07
☐ 614 Al Nipper UER (Photo actually Mike Brown)	.15	.07
☐ 615 Gene Nelson	.15	.07
☐ 616 Joe Carter	5.00	2.20
☐ 617 Ray Knight	.40	.18
☐ 618 Chuck Rainey	.15	.07
☐ 619 Dan Driessen	.15	.07
☐ 620 Daryl Sconiers	.15	.07
☐ 621 Bill Stein	.15	.07
☐ 622 Roy Smalley	.15	.07
☐ 623 Ed Lynch	.15	.07
☐ 624 Jeff Stone	.15	.07
☐ 625 Bruce Berenyi	.15	.07
☐ 626 Kelvin Chapman	.15	.07
☐ 627 Joe Price	.15	.07
☐ 628 Steve Bedrosian	.15	.07
☐ 629 Vic Mata	.15	.07
☐ 630 Mike Krukow	.15	.07
☐ 631 Phil Bradley	.40	.18
☐ 632 Jim Gott	.15	.07
☐ 633 Randy Bush	.15	.07
☐ 634 Tom Browning	.75	.35
☐ 635 Lou Gehrig Puzzle Card	1.50	.70
☐ 636 Reid Nichols	.15	.07
☐ 637 Dan Pasqua	.40	.18
☐ 638 German Rivera	.15	.07
☐ 639 Don Schulze	.15	.07
☐ 640A Mike Jones (Career Highlights, takes five lines)	.15	.07
☐ 640B Mike Jones (Career Highlights, takes four lines)	.15	.07
☐ 641 Pete Rose	2.00	.90
☐ 642 Wade Rowdon	.15	.07
☐ 643 Jerry Narron	.15	.07
☐ 644 Darrell Miller	.15	.07
☐ 645 Tim Hulett	.15	.07
☐ 646 Andy McGaffigan	.15	.07
☐ 647 Kurt Bevacqua	.15	.07
☐ 648 John Russell	.15	.07
☐ 649 Ron Robinson	.15	.07
☐ 650 Donnie Moore	.15	.07
☐ 651A Two for the Title Dave Winfield Don Mattingly (Yellow letters)	2.00	.90
☐ 651B Two for the Title Dave Winfield Don Mattingly (White letters)	5.00	2.20
☐ 652 Tim Laudner	.15	.07
☐ 653 Steve Farr	.40	.18
☐ 654 DK Checklist 1-26 (Unnumbered)	.15	.07
☐ 655 Checklist 27-130 (Unnumbered)	.15	.07
☐ 656 Checklist 131-234 (Unnumbered)	.15	.07
☐ 657 Checklist 235-338 (Unnumbered)	.15	.07
☐ 658 Checklist 339-442 (Unnumbered)	.15	.07
☐ 659 Checklist 443-546 (Unnumbered)	.15	.07
☐ 660 Checklist 547-653 (Unnumbered)	.15	.07

1985 Donruss Wax Box Cards

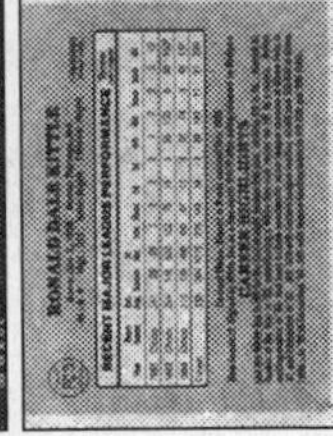

The boxes of the 1985 Donruss regular issue baseball cards, in which the wax packs were contained, featured four standard-size cards, with backs. The complete set price of the regular issue set does not include these cards; they are considered a separate set. The cards and are styled the same as the regular Donruss cards. The cards are numbered but with the prefix PC before the number. The value of the panel uncut is slightly greater, perhaps by 25 percent greater, than the value of the individual cards cut up carefully.

	NRMT	VG-E
COMPLETE SET (4)	4.00	1.80
COMMON CARD	.25	.11
☐ PC1 Dwight Gooden	1.25	.55
☐ PC2 Ryne Sandberg	2.00	.90
☐ PC3 Ron Kittle	.25	.11
☐ PUZ Lou Gehrig Puzzle Card	.75	.35

1985 Donruss Action All-Stars

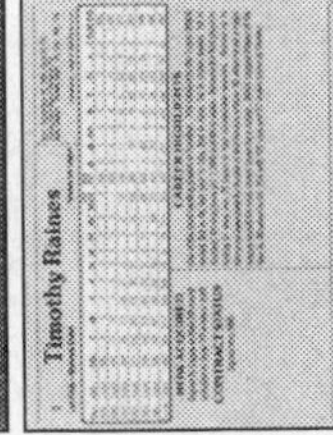

The cards in this 60-card set measure approximately 3 1/2" by 5". For the third year in a row, Donruss issued a set of Action All-Stars. This set features action photos on the obverse which also contains a portrait inset of the player. The backs, unlike the year before, do not contain a full color picture of the player but list, if space is available, full statistical data, biographical data, career highlights, and acquisition and contract status. The cards were issued with a Lou Gehrig puzzle card.

	NRMT	VG-E
COMPLETE SET (60)	6.00	2.70
COMMON CARD (1-60)	.05	.02
☐ 1 Tim Raines	.10	.0
☐ 2 Jim Gantner	.05	.02
☐ 3 Mario Soto	.05	.02
☐ 4 Spike Owen	.05	.02
☐ 5 Lloyd Moseby	.05	.02
☐ 6 Damaso Garcia	.05	.02
☐ 7 Cal Ripken	3.00	1.35
☐ 8 Dan Quisenberry	.05	.02
☐ 9 Eddie Murray	.60	.25
☐ 10 Tony Pena	.05	.02
☐ 11 Buddy Bell	.10	.05
☐ 12 Dave Winfield	.40	.18
☐ 13 Ron Kittle	.05	.02
☐ 14 Rich Gossage	.10	.05
☐ 15 Dwight Evans	.10	.05
☐ 16 Alvin Davis	.05	.02
☐ 17 Mike Schmidt	.60	.25
☐ 18 Pascual Perez	.05	.02
☐ 19 Tony Gwynn	1.50	.70
☐ 20 Nolan Ryan	2.50	1.10
☐ 21 Robin Yount	.40	.18
☐ 22 Mike Marshall	.05	.02
☐ 23 Brett Butler	.10	.05
☐ 24 Ryne Sandberg	.75	.35
☐ 25 Dale Murphy	.30	.14
☐ 26 George Brett	1.25	.55
☐ 27 Jim Rice	.10	.05
☐ 28 Ozzie Smith	1.00	.45
☐ 29 Larry Parrish	.05	.02
☐ 30 Jack Clark	.10	.05
☐ 31 Manny Trillo	.05	.02
☐ 32 Dave Kingman	.10	.05
☐ 33 Geoff Zahn	.05	.02
☐ 34 Pedro Guerrero	.10	.05
☐ 35 Dave Parker	.10	.05
☐ 36 Rollie Fingers	.30	.14
☐ 37 Fernando Valenzuela	.20	.09
☐ 38 Wade Boggs	.40	.18
☐ 39 Reggie Jackson	.50	.23
☐ 40 Kent Hrbek	.10	.05
☐ 41 Keith Hernandez	.10	.05
☐ 42 Lou Whitaker	.20	.09
☐ 43 Tom Herr	.05	.02
☐ 44 Alan Trammell	.20	.09
☐ 45 Butch Wynegar	.05	.02
☐ 46 Leon Durham	.05	.02
☐ 47 Dwight Gooden	.50	.23
☐ 48 Don Mattingly	1.50	.70
☐ 49 Phil Niekro	.40	.18
☐ 50 Johnny Ray	.05	.02
☐ 51 Doug DeCinces	.05	.02
☐ 52 Willie Upshaw	.05	.02
☐ 53 Lance Parrish	.10	.05
☐ 54 Jody Davis	.05	.02
☐ 55 Steve Carlton	.40	.18
☐ 56 Juan Samuel	.05	.02
☐ 57 Gary Carter	.20	.09
☐ 58 Harold Baines	.10	.05
☐ 59 Eric Show	.05	.02
☐ 60 Checklist Card	.05	.02

1985 Donruss Highlights

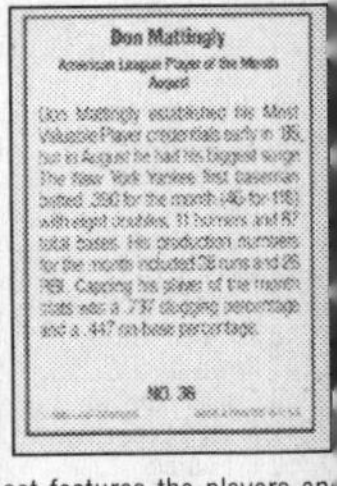

This 56-card standard-size set features the players an pitchers of the month for each league as well as a numbe of highlight cards commemorating the 1985 season. Th Donruss Company dedicated the last two cards to thei own selections for Rookies of the Year (ROY). This se proved to be more popular than the Donruss Compan had predicted, as their first and only print run was exhausted before card dealers' initial orders were filled.

	NRMT	VG-E
COMPLETE FACT. SET (56)	15.00	6.75
COMMON CARD (1-55)	.10	.05
☐ 1 Tom Seaver	.60	.25
☐ 2 Rollie Fingers	.50	.23
☐ 3 Mike Davis	.10	.05
☐ 4 Charlie Leibrandt	.10	.05
☐ 5 Dale Murphy	.50	.23
☐ 6 Fernando Valenzuela	.20	.09
☐ 7 Larry Bowa	.20	.09

] 8 Dave Concepcion	.20	.09
] 9 Tony Perez	.35	.16
] 10 Pete Rose	1.25	.55
] 11 George Brett	1.50	.70
] 12 Dave Stieb	.10	.05
] 13 Dave Parker	.20	.09
] 14 Andy Hawkins	.10	.05
] 15 Andy Hawkins	.10	.05
] 16 Von Hayes	.10	.05
] 17 Rickey Henderson	.60	.25
] 18 Jay Howell	.10	.05
] 19 Pedro Guerrero	.20	.09
] 20 John Tudor	.10	.05
] 21 Keith Hernandez Gary Carter	.20	.09
] 22 Nolan Ryan	5.00	2.20
] 23 LaMarr Hoyt	.10	.05
] 24 Oddibe McDowell	.10	.05
] 25 George Brett	1.50	.70
] 26 Bret Saberhagen	.20	.09
] 27 Keith Hernandez	.20	.09
] 28 Fernando Valenzuela	.20	.09
] 29 Willie McGee Vince Coleman	.20	.09
] 30 Tom Seaver	.60	.25
] 31 Rod Carew	.50	.23
] 32 Dwight Gooden	1.00	.45
] 33 Dwight Gooden	1.00	.45
] 34 Eddie Murray	1.00	.45
] 35 Don Baylor	.20	.09
] 36 Don Mattingly	2.50	1.10
] 37 Dave Righetti	.20	.09
] 38 Willie McGee	.20	.09
] 39 Shane Rawley	.10	.05
] 40 Pete Rose	1.50	.70
] 41 Andre Dawson	.50	.23
] 42 Rickey Henderson	.50	.23
] 43 Tom Browning	.20	.09
] 44 Don Mattingly	2.50	1.10
] 45 Don Mattingly	2.50	1.10
] 46 Charlie Leibrandt	.10	.05
] 47 Gary Carter	.35	.16
] 48 Dwight Gooden	1.00	.45
] 49 Wade Boggs	.50	.23
] 50 Phil Niekro	.60	.25
] 51 Darrell Evans	.20	.09
] 52 Willie McGee	.20	.09
] 53 Dave Winfield	.50	.23
] 54 Vince Coleman	.20	.09
] 55 Ozzie Guillen	.20	.09
] NNO Checklist Card	.10	.05

1985 Donruss HOF Sluggers

his eight-card set of Hall of Fame players features the rtwork of resident Donruss artist Dick Perez. These versized (3 1/2" by 6 1/2", blank backed cards actually rm part of a box of gum distributed by the Donruss ompany through supermarket type outlets. These cards e reminiscent of the Bazooka issues. The players in the t were ostensibly chosen based on their career slugging ercentage. The cards themselves are numbered by lugging percentage) rank. The boxes are also numbered n one of the white side tabs of the complete box; this mpletely different numbering system is not used.

	NRMT	VG-E
OMPLETE SET (8)	7.00	3.10
OMMON CARD (1-8)	.50	.23
] 1 Babe Ruth	2.00	.90
] 2 Ted Williams	1.50	.70
] 3 Lou Gehrig	1.50	.70
] 4 Johnny Mize	.50	.23
] 5 Stan Musial	.75	.35
] 6 Mickey Mantle	2.50	1.10
] 7 Hank Aaron	1.00	.45
] 8 Frank Robinson	.50	.23

1985 Donruss Super DK's

e cards in this 28-card set measure approximately 4 5/16 by 6 3/4". The 1985 Donruss Diamond Kings

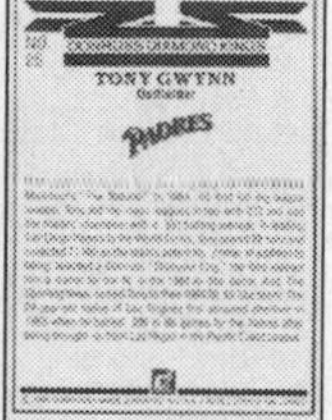

Supers set contains enlarged cards of the first 26 cards of the Donruss regular set of this year. In addition, the Diamond Kings checklist card, a card of artist Dick Perez and a Lou Gehrig puzzle card are included in the set. The set was the brain-child of the Perez-Steele Galleries and could be obtained via a write-in offer on the wrappers of the Donruss regular cards of this year. The Gehrig puzzle card is actually a 12-piece jigsaw puzzle. The back of the checklist card is blank; however, the Dick Perez card back gives a short history of Dick Perez and the Perez-Steele Galleries. The offer for obtaining this set was detailed on the wax pack wrappers; three wrappers plus $9.00 was required for this mail-in offer.

	NRMT	VG-E
COMPLETE SET (28)	15.00	6.75
COMMON CARD (1-28)	.50	.23
☐ 1 Ryne Sandberg	2.50	1.10
☐ 2 Doug DeCinces	.50	.23
☐ 3 Richard Dotson	.50	.23
☐ 4 Bert Blyleven	.75	.35
☐ 5 Lou Whitaker	1.00	.45
☐ 6 Dan Quisenberry	.50	.23
☐ 7 Don Mattingly	4.00	1.80
☐ 8 Carney Lansford	.75	.35
☐ 9 Frank Tanana	.50	.23
☐ 10 Willie Upshaw	.50	.23
☐ 11 Claudell Washington	.50	.23
☐ 12 Mike Marshall	.50	.23
☐ 13 Joaquin Andujar	.50	.23
☐ 14 Cal Ripken	6.00	2.70
☐ 15 Jim Rice	.75	.35
☐ 16 Don Sutton	2.00	.90
☐ 17 Frank Viola	.75	.35
☐ 18 Alvin Davis	.50	.23
☐ 19 Mario Soto	.50	.23
☐ 20 Jose Cruz	.50	.23
☐ 21 Charlie Lea	.50	.23
☐ 22 Jesse Orosco	.50	.23
☐ 23 Juan Samuel	.50	.23
☐ 24 Tony Pena	.50	.23
☐ 25 Tony Gwynn	4.00	1.80
☐ 26 Bob Brenly	.50	.23
☐ NNO Checklist Card	.50	.23
☐ NNO Dick Perez (History of DK's)	.50	.23

1986 Donruss

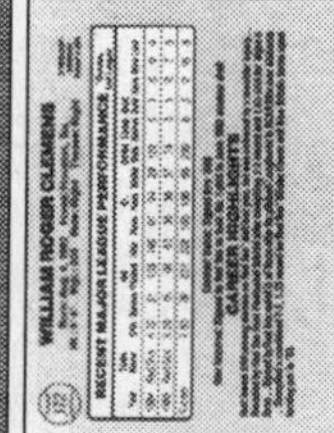

The 1986 Donruss set consists of 660 standard-size cards. Wax packs contained 15 cards plus a Hank Aaron puzzle panel. The card fronts feature blue borders, the standard team logo, player's name, position, and Donruss logo. The first 26 cards of the set are Diamond Kings (DK), for the fifth year in a row; the artwork on the Diamond Kings was again produced by the Perez-Steele Galleries. Cards 27-46 again feature Rated Rookies (RR). The unnumbered checklist cards are arbitrarily numbered below as numbers 654 through 660. Rookie Cards in this set include Jose Canseco, Darren Daulton, Len Dykstra, Cecil Fielder, Andres Galarraga, Fred McGriff, Paul O'Neill, and Mickey Tettleton.

	MINT	NRMT
COMPLETE SET (660)	40.00	18.00
COMP.FACT.SET (660)	50.00	22.00
COMMON CARD (1-660)	.10	.05
COMPLETE AARON PUZZLE	2.00	.90
☐ 1 Kirk Gibson DK	.50	.23
☐ 2 Goose Gossage DK	.50	.23
☐ 3 Willie McGee DK	.50	.23
☐ 4 George Bell DK	.10	.05
☐ 5 Tony Armas DK	.10	.05
☐ 6 Chili Davis DK	.50	.23
☐ 7 Cecil Cooper DK	.10	.05
☐ 8 Mike Boddicker DK	.10	.05
☐ 9 Dave Lopes DK	.10	.05
☐ 10 Bill Doran DK	.10	.05
☐ 11 Bret Saberhagen DK	.25	.11
☐ 12 Brett Butler DK	.25	.11
☐ 13 Harold Baines DK	.50	.23
☐ 14 Mike Davis DK	.10	.05
☐ 15 Tony Perez DK	.50	.23
☐ 16 Willie Randolph DK	.25	.11
☐ 17 Bob Boone DK	.25	.11
☐ 18 Orel Hershiser DK	.50	.23
☐ 19 Johnny Ray DK	.10	.05
☐ 20 Gary Ward DK	.10	.05
☐ 21 Rick Mahler DK	.10	.05
☐ 22 Phil Bradley DK	.10	.05
☐ 23 Jerry Koosman DK	.25	.11
☐ 24 Tom Brunansky DK	.10	.05
☐ 25 Andre Dawson DK	.50	.23
☐ 26 Dwight Gooden DK	.25	.11
☐ 27 Kal Daniels RR	.25	.11
☐ 28 Fred McGriff RR	6.00	2.70
☐ 29 Cory Snyder RR	.10	.05
☐ 30 Jose Guzman RR	.10	.05
☐ 31 Ty Gainey RR	.10	.05
☐ 32 Johnny Abrego RR	.10	.05
☐ 33 Andres Galarraga RR (No accent)	6.00	2.70
☐ 33B Andrés Galarraga RR (Accent over e)	6.00	2.70
☐ 34 Dave Shipanoff RR	.10	.05
☐ 35 Mark McLemore RR	.50	.23
☐ 36 Marty Clary RR	.10	.05
☐ 37 Paul O'Neill RR	2.00	.90
☐ 38 Danny Tartabull RR	.25	.11
☐ 39 Jose Canseco RR	8.00	3.60
☐ 40 Juan Nieves RR	.10	.05
☐ 41 Lance McCullers RR	.10	.05
☐ 42 Rick Surhoff RR	.10	.05
☐ 43 Todd Worrell RR	.50	.23
☐ 44 Bob Kipper RR	.10	.05
☐ 45 John Habyan RR	.10	.05
☐ 46 Mike Woodard RR	.10	.05
☐ 47 Mike Boddicker	.10	.05
☐ 48 Robin Yount	1.00	.45
☐ 49 Lou Whitaker	.25	.11
☐ 50 Oil Can Boyd	.10	.05
☐ 51 Rickey Henderson	1.00	.45
☐ 52 Mike Marshall	.10	.05
☐ 53 George Brett	2.00	.90
☐ 54 Dave Kingman	.25	.11
☐ 55 Hubie Brooks	.10	.05
☐ 56 Oddibe McDowell	.10	.05
☐ 57 Doug DeCinces	.10	.05
☐ 58 Britt Burns	.10	.05
☐ 59 Ozzie Smith	1.25	.55
☐ 60 Jose Cruz	.10	.05
☐ 61 Mike Schmidt	1.25	.55
☐ 62 Pete Rose	1.25	.55
☐ 63 Steve Garvey	.50	.23
☐ 64 Tony Pena	.10	.05
☐ 65 Chili Davis	.25	.11
☐ 66 Dale Murphy	1.00	.45
☐ 67 Ryne Sandberg	1.25	.55
☐ 68 Gary Carter	.25	.11
☐ 69 Alvin Davis	.10	.05
☐ 70 Kent Hrbek	.25	.11
☐ 71 George Bell	.25	.11
☐ 72 Kirby Puckett	4.00	1.80
☐ 73 Lloyd Moseby	.10	.05
☐ 74 Bob Kearney	.10	.05
☐ 75 Dwight Gooden	1.00	.45
☐ 76 Gary Matthews	.10	.05
☐ 77 Rick Mahler	.10	.05
☐ 78 Benny Distefano	.10	.05
☐ 79 Jeff Leonard	.10	.05
☐ 80 Kevin McReynolds	.25	.11
☐ 81 Ron Oester	.10	.05
☐ 82 John Russell	.10	.05
☐ 83 Tommy Herr	.10	.05
☐ 84 Jerry Mumphrey	.10	.05
☐ 85 Ron Romanick	.10	.05
☐ 86 Daryl Boston	.10	.05
☐ 87 Andre Dawson	1.00	.45
☐ 88 Eddie Murray	1.25	.55
☐ 89 Dion James	.10	.05
☐ 90 Chet Lemon	.10	.05
☐ 91 Bob Stanley	.10	.05
☐ 92 Willie Randolph	.25	.11
☐ 93 Mike Scioscia	.10	.05
☐ 94 Tom Waddell	.10	.05

☐ 95 Danny Jackson	.10	.05
☐ 96 Mike Davis	.10	.05
☐ 97 Mike Fitzgerald	.10	.05
☐ 98 Gary Ward	.10	.05
☐ 99 Pete O'Brien	.10	.05
☐ 100 Bret Saberhagen	.25	.11
☐ 101 Alfredo Griffin	.10	.05
☐ 102 Brett Butler	.25	.11
☐ 103 Ron Guidry	.25	.11
☐ 104 Jerry Reuss	.10	.05
☐ 105 Jack Morris	.25	.11
☐ 106 Rick Dempsey	.10	.05
☐ 107 Ray Burris	.10	.05
☐ 108 Brian Downing	.10	.05
☐ 109 Willie McGee	.25	.11
☐ 110 Bill Doran	.10	.05
☐ 111 Kent Tekulve	.10	.05
☐ 112 Tony Gwynn	2.50	1.10
☐ 113 Marvell Wynne	.10	.05
☐ 114 David Green	.10	.05
☐ 115 Jim Gantner	.10	.05
☐ 116 George Foster	.25	.11
☐ 117 Steve Trout	.10	.05
☐ 118 Mark Langston	.25	.11
☐ 119 Tony Fernandez	.10	.05
☐ 120 John Butcher	.10	.05
☐ 121 Ron Robinson	.10	.05
☐ 122 Dan Spillner	.10	.05
☐ 123 Mike Young	.10	.05
☐ 124 Paul Molitor	1.00	.45
☐ 125 Kirk Gibson	.25	.11
☐ 126 Ken Griffey	.25	.11
☐ 127 Tony Armas	.10	.05
☐ 128 Mariano Duncan	.50	.23
☐ 129 Pat Tabler	.10	.05
☐ 130 Frank White	.25	.11
☐ 131 Carney Lansford	.25	.11
☐ 132 Vance Law	.10	.05
☐ 133 Dick Schofield	.10	.05
☐ 134 Wayne Tolleson	.10	.05
☐ 135 Greg Walker	.10	.05
☐ 136 Denny Walling	.10	.05
☐ 137 Ozzie Virgil	.10	.05
☐ 138 Ricky Horton	.10	.05
☐ 139 LaMarr Hoyt	.10	.05
☐ 140 Wayne Krenchicki	.10	.05
☐ 141 Glenn Hubbard	.10	.05
☐ 142 Cecilio Guante	.10	.05
☐ 143 Mike Krukow	.10	.05
☐ 144 Lee Smith	.50	.23
☐ 145 Edwin Nunez	.10	.05
☐ 146 Dave Stieb	.10	.05
☐ 147 Mike Smithson	.10	.05
☐ 148 Ken Dixon	.10	.05
☐ 149 Danny Darwin	.10	.05
☐ 150 Chris Pittaro	.10	.05
☐ 151 Bill Buckner	.25	.11
☐ 152 Mike Pagliarulo	.10	.05
☐ 153 Bill Russell	.10	.05
☐ 154 Brook Jacoby	.10	.05
☐ 155 Pat Sheridan	.10	.05
☐ 156 Mike Gallego	.25	.11
☐ 157 Jim Wohlford	.10	.05
☐ 158 Gary Pettis	.10	.05
☐ 159 Toby Harrah	.10	.05
☐ 160 Richard Dotson	.10	.05
☐ 161 Bob Knepper	.10	.05
☐ 162 Dave Dravecky	.25	.11
☐ 163 Greg Gross	.10	.05
☐ 164 Eric Davis	.50	.23
☐ 165 Gerald Perry	.10	.05
☐ 166 Rick Rhoden	.10	.05
☐ 167 Keith Moreland	.10	.05
☐ 168 Jack Clark	.25	.11
☐ 169 Storm Davis	.10	.05
☐ 170 Cecil Cooper	.25	.11
☐ 171 Alan Trammell	.50	.23
☐ 172 Roger Clemens	4.00	1.80
☐ 173 Don Mattingly	1.50	.70
☐ 174 Pedro Guerrero	.25	.11
☐ 175 Willie Wilson	.10	.05
☐ 176 Dwayne Murphy	.10	.05
☐ 177 Tim Raines	.25	.11
☐ 178 Larry Parrish	.10	.05
☐ 179 Mike Witt	.10	.05
☐ 180 Harold Baines	.50	.23
☐ 181 Vince Coleman UER (BA 2.67 on back)	1.00	.45
☐ 182 Jeff Heathcock	.10	.05
☐ 183 Steve Carlton	.50	.23
☐ 184 Mario Soto	.10	.05
☐ 185 Goose Gossage	.25	.11
☐ 186 Johnny Ray	.10	.05
☐ 187 Dan Gladden	.10	.05
☐ 188 Bob Horner	.10	.05
☐ 189 Rick Sutcliffe	.10	.05
☐ 190 Keith Hernandez	.25	.11
☐ 191 Phil Bradley	.10	.05
☐ 192 Tom Brunansky	.10	.05
☐ 193 Jesse Barfield	.10	.05
☐ 194 Frank Viola	.25	.11
☐ 195 Willie Upshaw	.10	.05
☐ 196 Jim Beattie	.10	.05
☐ 197 Darryl Strawberry	.50	.23
☐ 198 Ron Cey	.25	.11
☐ 199 Steve Bedrosian	.10	.05
☐ 200 Steve Kemp	.10	.05
☐ 201 Manny Trillo	.10	.05
☐ 202 Garry Templeton	.10	.05
☐ 203 Dave Parker	.25	.11
☐ 204 John Denny	.10	.05
☐ 205 Terry Pendleton	.50	.23
☐ 206 Terry Puhl	.10	.05
☐ 207 Bobby Grich	.50	.23
☐ 208 Ozzie Guillen	.50	.23
☐ 209 Jeff Reardon	.25	.11
☐ 210 Cal Ripken	4.00	1.80
☐ 211 Bill Schroeder	.10	.05
☐ 212 Dan Petry	.10	.05
☐ 213 Jim Rice	.25	.11
☐ 214 Dave Righetti	.10	.05
☐ 215 Fernando Valenzuela	.25	.11
☐ 216 Julio Franco	.25	.11
☐ 217 Darryl Motley	.10	.05
☐ 218 Dave Collins	.10	.05
☐ 219 Tim Wallach	.10	.05
☐ 220 George Wright	.10	.05
☐ 221 Tommy Dunbar	.10	.05
☐ 222 Steve Balboni	.10	.05
☐ 223 Jay Howell	.10	.05
☐ 224 Joe Carter	2.00	.90
☐ 225 Ed Whitson	.10	.05
☐ 226 Orel Hershiser	.50	.23
☐ 227 Willie Hernandez	.10	.05
☐ 228 Lee Lacy	.10	.05
☐ 229 Rollie Fingers	1.00	.45
☐ 230 Bob Boone	.25	.11
☐ 231 Joaquin Andujar	.10	.05
☐ 232 Craig Reynolds	.10	.05
☐ 233 Shane Rawley	.10	.05
☐ 234 Eric Show	.10	.05
☐ 235 Jose DeLeon	.10	.05
☐ 236 Jose Uribe	.10	.05
☐ 237 Moose Haas	.10	.05
☐ 238 Wally Backman	.10	.05
☐ 239 Dennis Eckersley	1.00	.45
☐ 240 Mike Moore	.10	.05
☐ 241 Damaso Garcia	.10	.05
☐ 242 Tim Teufel	.10	.05
☐ 243 Dave Concepcion	.25	.11
☐ 244 Floyd Bannister	.10	.05
☐ 245 Fred Lynn	.25	.11
☐ 246 Charlie Moore	.10	.05
☐ 247 Walt Terrell	.10	.05
☐ 248 Dave Winfield	1.00	.45
☐ 249 Dwight Evans	.25	.11
☐ 250 Dennis Powell	.10	.05
☐ 251 Andre Thornton	.10	.05
☐ 252 Onix Concepcion	.10	.05
☐ 253 Mike Heath	.10	.05
☐ 254A David Palmer ERR (Position 2B)	.10	.05
☐ 254B David Palmer COR (Position P)	1.00	.45
☐ 255 Donnie Moore	.10	.05
☐ 256 Curtis Wilkerson	.10	.05
☐ 257 Julio Cruz	.10	.05
☐ 258 Nolan Ryan	4.00	1.80
☐ 259 Jeff Stone	.10	.05
☐ 260 John Tudor	.10	.05
☐ 261 Mark Thurmond	.10	.05
☐ 262 Jay Tibbs	.10	.05
☐ 263 Rafael Ramirez	.10	.05
☐ 264 Larry McWilliams	.10	.05
☐ 265 Mark Davis	.10	.05
☐ 266 Bob Dernier	.10	.05
☐ 267 Matt Young	.10	.05
☐ 268 Jim Clancy	.10	.05
☐ 269 Mickey Hatcher	.10	.05
☐ 270 Sammy Stewart	.10	.05
☐ 271 Bob L. Gibson	.10	.05
☐ 272 Nelson Simmons	.10	.05
☐ 273 Rich Gedman	.10	.05
☐ 274 Butch Wynegar	.10	.05
☐ 275 Ken Howell	.10	.05
☐ 276 Mel Hall	.10	.05
☐ 277 Jim Sundberg	.10	.05
☐ 278 Chris Codiroli	.10	.05
☐ 279 Herm Winningham	.10	.05
☐ 280 Rod Carew	1.00	.45
☐ 281 Don Slaught	.10	.05
☐ 282 Scott Fletcher	.10	.05
☐ 283 Bill Dawley	.10	.05
☐ 284 Andy Hawkins	.10	.05
☐ 285 Glenn Wilson	.10	.05
☐ 286 Nick Esasky	.10	.05
☐ 287 Claudell Washington	.10	.05
☐ 288 Lee Mazzilli	.10	.05
☐ 289 Jody Davis	.10	.05
☐ 290 Darrell Porter	.25	.11
☐ 291 Scott McGregor	.10	.05
☐ 292 Ted Simmons	.25	.11
☐ 293 Aurelio Lopez	.10	.05
☐ 294 Marty Barrett	.10	.05
☐ 295 Dale Berra	.10	.05
☐ 296 Greg Brock	.10	.05
☐ 297 Charlie Leibrandt	.10	.05
☐ 298 Bill Krueger	.10	.05
☐ 299 Bryn Smith	.10	.05
☐ 300 Burt Hooton	.10	.05
☐ 301 Stu Cliburn	.10	.05
☐ 302 Luis Salazar	.10	.05
☐ 303 Ken Dayley	.10	.05
☐ 304 Frank DiPino	.10	.05
☐ 305 Von Hayes	.10	.05
☐ 306 Gary Redus	.10	.05
☐ 307 Craig Lefferts	.10	.05
☐ 308 Sammy Khalifa	.10	.05
☐ 309 Scott Garrelts	.10	.05
☐ 310 Rick Cerone	.10	.05
☐ 311 Shawon Dunston	.25	.11
☐ 312 Howard Johnson	.25	.11
☐ 313 Jim Presley	.10	.05
☐ 314 Gary Gaetti	.25	.11
☐ 315 Luis Leal	.10	.05
☐ 316 Mark Salas	.10	.05
☐ 317 Bill Caudill	.10	.05
☐ 318 Dave Henderson	.10	.05
☐ 319 Rafael Santana	.10	.05
☐ 320 Leon Durham	.10	.05
☐ 321 Bruce Sutter	.25	.11
☐ 322 Jason Thompson	.10	.05
☐ 323 Bob Brenly	.10	.05
☐ 324 Carmelo Martinez	.10	.05
☐ 325 Eddie Milner	.10	.05
☐ 326 Juan Samuel	.10	.05
☐ 327 Tom Nieto	.10	.05
☐ 328 Dave Smith	.10	.05
☐ 329 Urbano Lugo	.10	.05
☐ 330 Joel Skinner	.10	.05
☐ 331 Bill Gullickson	.10	.05
☐ 332 Floyd Rayford	.10	.05
☐ 333 Ben Oglivie	.10	.05
☐ 334 Lance Parrish	.25	.11
☐ 335 Jackie Gutierrez	.10	.05
☐ 336 Dennis Rasmussen	.10	.05
☐ 337 Terry Whitfield	.10	.05
☐ 338 Neal Heaton	.10	.05
☐ 339 Jorge Orta	.10	.05
☐ 340 Donnie Hill	.10	.05
☐ 341 Joe Hesketh	.10	.05
☐ 342 Charlie Hough	.25	.11
☐ 343 Dave Rozema	.10	.05
☐ 344 Greg Pryor	.10	.05
☐ 345 Mickey Tettleton	2.00	.90
☐ 346 George Vukovich	.10	.05
☐ 347 Don Baylor	.50	.23
☐ 348 Carlos Diaz	.10	.05
☐ 349 Barbaro Garbey	.10	.05
☐ 350 Larry Sheets	.10	.05
☐ 351 Ted Higuera	.25	.11
☐ 352 Juan Beniquez	.10	.05
☐ 353 Bob Forsch	.10	.05
☐ 354 Mark Bailey	.10	.05
☐ 355 Larry Andersen	.10	.05
☐ 356 Terry Kennedy	.10	.05
☐ 357 Don Robinson	.10	.05
☐ 358 Jim Gott	.10	.05
☐ 359 Earnie Riles	.10	.05
☐ 360 John Christensen	.10	.05
☐ 361 Ray Fontenot	.10	.05
☐ 362 Spike Owen	.10	.05
☐ 363 Jim Acker	.10	.05
☐ 364 Ron Davis	.10	.05
☐ 365 Tom Hume	.10	.05
☐ 366 Carlton Fisk	1.00	.45
☐ 367 Nate Snell	.10	.05
☐ 368 Rick Manning	.10	.05
☐ 369 Darrell Evans	.25	.11
☐ 370 Ron Hassey	.10	.05
☐ 371 Wade Boggs	1.00	.45
☐ 372 Rick Honeycutt	.10	.05
☐ 373 Chris Bando	.10	.05
☐ 374 Bud Black	.10	.05
☐ 375 Steve Henderson	.10	.05
☐ 376 Charlie Lea	.10	.05
☐ 377 Reggie Jackson	1.25	.55
☐ 378 Dave Schmidt	.10	.05
☐ 379 Bob James	.10	.05
☐ 380 Glenn Davis	.25	.11
☐ 381 Tim Corcoran	.10	.05

☐ 382 Danny Cox	.10	.05
☐ 383 Tim Flannery	.10	.05
☐ 384 Tom Browning	.10	.05
☐ 385 Rick Camp	.10	.05
☐ 386 Jim Morrison	.10	.05
☐ 387 Dave LaPoint	.10	.05
☐ 388 Dave Lopes	.25	.11
☐ 389 Al Cowens	.10	.05
☐ 390 Doyle Alexander	.10	.05
☐ 391 Tim Laudner	.10	.05
☐ 392 Don Aase	.10	.05
☐ 393 Jaime Cocanower	.10	.05
☐ 394 Randy O'Neal	.10	.05
☐ 395 Mike Easler	.10	.05
☐ 396 Scott Bradley	.10	.05
☐ 397 Tom Niedenfuer	.10	.05
☐ 398 Jerry Willard	.10	.05
☐ 399 Lonnie Smith	.10	.05
☐ 400 Bruce Bochte	.10	.05
☐ 401 Terry Francona	.10	.05
☐ 402 Jim Slaton	.10	.05
☐ 403 Bill Stein	.10	.05
☐ 404 Tim Hulett	.10	.05
☐ 405 Alan Ashby	.10	.05
☐ 406 Tim Stoddard	.10	.05
☐ 407 Garry Maddox	.10	.05
☐ 408 Ted Power	.10	.05
☐ 409 Len Barker	.10	.05
☐ 410 Denny Gonzalez	.10	.05
☐ 411 George Frazier	.10	.05
☐ 412 Andy Van Slyke	.25	.11
☐ 413 Jim Dwyer	.10	.05
☐ 414 Paul Householder	.10	.05
☐ 415 Alejandro Sanchez	.10	.05
☐ 416 Steve Crawford	.10	.05
☐ 417 Dan Pasqua	.10	.05
☐ 418 Enos Cabell	.10	.05
☐ 419 Mike Jones	.10	.05
☐ 420 Steve Kiefer	.10	.05
☐ 421 Tim Burke	.10	.05
☐ 422 Mike Mason	.10	.05
☐ 423 Ruppert Jones	.10	.05
☐ 424 Jerry Hairston	.10	.05
☐ 425 Tito Landrum	.10	.05
☐ 426 Jeff Calhoun	.10	.05
☐ 427 Don Carman	.10	.05
☐ 428 Tony Perez	1.00	.45
☐ 429 Jerry Davis	.10	.05
☐ 430 Bob Walk	.10	.05
☐ 431 Brad Wellman	.10	.05
☐ 432 Terry Forster	.10	.05
☐ 433 Billy Hatcher	.10	.05
☐ 434 Clint Hurdle	.10	.05
☐ 435 Ivan Calderon	.25	.11
☐ 436 Pete Filson	.10	.05
☐ 437 Tom Henke	.25	.11
☐ 438 Dave Engle	.10	.05
☐ 439 Tom Filer	.10	.05
☐ 440 Gorman Thomas	.10	.05
☐ 441 Rick Aguilera	1.00	.45
☐ 442 Scott Sanderson	.10	.05
☐ 443 Jeff Dedmon	.10	.05
☐ 444 Joe Orsulak	.10	.05
☐ 445 Atlee Hammaker	.10	.05
☐ 446 Jerry Royster	.10	.05
☐ 447 Buddy Bell	.25	.11
☐ 448 Dave Rucker	.10	.05
☐ 449 Ivan DeJesus	.10	.05
☐ 450 Jim Pankovits	.10	.05
☐ 451 Jerry Narron	.10	.05
☐ 452 Bryan Little	.10	.05
☐ 453 Gary Lucas	.10	.05
☐ 454 Dennis Martinez	.25	.11
☐ 455 Ed Romero	.10	.05
☐ 456 Bob Melvin	.10	.05
☐ 457 Glenn Hoffman	.10	.05
☐ 458 Bob Shirley	.10	.05
☐ 459 Bob Welch	.10	.05
☐ 460 Carmen Castillo	.10	.05
☐ 461 Dave Leeper	.10	.05
☐ 462 Tim Birtsas	.10	.05
☐ 463 Randy St.Claire	.10	.05
☐ 464 Chris Welsh	.10	.05
☐ 465 Greg Harris	.10	.05
☐ 466 Lynn Jones	.10	.05
☐ 467 Dusty Baker	.25	.11
☐ 468 Roy Smith	.10	.05
☐ 469 Andre Robertson	.10	.05
☐ 470 Ken Landreaux	.10	.05
☐ 471 Dave Bergman	.10	.05
☐ 472 Gary Roenicke	.10	.05
☐ 473 Pete Vuckovich	.10	.05
☐ 474 Kirk McCaskill	.25	.11
☐ 475 Jeff Lahti	.10	.05
☐ 476 Mike Scott	.10	.05
☐ 477 Darren Daulton	2.00	.90
☐ 478 Graig Nettles	.25	.11
☐ 479 Bill Almon	.10	.05
☐ 480 Greg Minton	.10	.05
☐ 481 Randy Ready	.10	.05
☐ 482 Len Dykstra	2.00	.90
☐ 483 Thad Bosley	.10	.05
☐ 484 Harold Reynolds	1.00	.45
☐ 485 Al Oliver	.25	.11
☐ 486 Roy Smalley	.10	.05
☐ 487 John Franco	1.00	.45
☐ 488 Juan Agosto	.10	.05
☐ 489 Al Pardo	.10	.05
☐ 490 Bill Wegman	.10	.05
☐ 491 Frank Tanana	.10	.05
☐ 492 Brian Fisher	.10	.05
☐ 493 Mark Clear	.10	.05
☐ 494 Len Matuszek	.10	.05
☐ 495 Ramon Romero	.10	.05
☐ 496 John Wathan	.10	.05
☐ 497 Rob Picciolo	.10	.05
☐ 498 U.L. Washington	.10	.05
☐ 499 John Candelaria	.10	.05
☐ 500 Duane Walker	.10	.05
☐ 501 Gene Nelson	.10	.05
☐ 502 John Mizerock	.10	.05
☐ 503 Luis Aguayo	.10	.05
☐ 504 Kurt Kepshire	.10	.05
☐ 505 Ed Wojna	.10	.05
☐ 506 Joe Price	.10	.05
☐ 507 Milt Thompson	.25	.11
☐ 508 Junior Ortiz	.10	.05
☐ 509 Vida Blue	.25	.11
☐ 510 Steve Engel	.10	.05
☐ 511 Karl Best	.10	.05
☐ 512 Cecil Fielder	3.00	1.35
☐ 513 Frank Eufemia	.10	.05
☐ 514 Tippy Martinez	.10	.05
☐ 515 Billy Joe Robidoux	.10	.05
☐ 516 Bill Scherrer	.10	.05
☐ 517 Bruce Hurst	.10	.05
☐ 518 Rich Bordi	.10	.05
☐ 519 Steve Yeager	.10	.05
☐ 520 Tony Bernazard	.10	.05
☐ 521 Hal McRae	.25	.11
☐ 522 Jose Rijo	.10	.05
☐ 523 Mitch Webster	.10	.05
☐ 524 Jack Howell	.10	.05
☐ 525 Alan Bannister	.10	.05
☐ 526 Ron Kittle	.10	.05
☐ 527 Phil Garner	.10	.05
☐ 528 Kurt Bevacqua	.10	.05
☐ 529 Kevin Gross	.10	.05
☐ 530 Bo Diaz	.10	.05
☐ 531 Ken Oberkfell	.10	.05
☐ 532 Rick Reuschel	.10	.05
☐ 533 Ron Meridith	.10	.05
☐ 534 Steve Braun	.10	.05
☐ 535 Wayne Gross	.10	.05
☐ 536 Ray Searage	.10	.05
☐ 537 Tom Brookens	.10	.05
☐ 538 Al Nipper	.10	.05
☐ 539 Billy Sample	.10	.05
☐ 540 Steve Sax	.10	.05
☐ 541 Dan Quisenberry	.10	.05
☐ 542 Tony Phillips	.10	.05
☐ 543 Floyd Youmans	.10	.05
☐ 544 Steve Buechele	.25	.11
☐ 545 Craig Gerber	.10	.05
☐ 546 Joe DeSa	.10	.05
☐ 547 Brian Harper	.10	.05
☐ 548 Kevin Bass	.10	.05
☐ 549 Tom Foley	.10	.05
☐ 550 Dave Van Gorder	.10	.05
☐ 551 Bruce Bochy	.10	.05
☐ 552 R.J. Reynolds	.10	.05
☐ 553 Chris Brown	.10	.05
☐ 554 Bruce Benedict	.10	.05
☐ 555 Warren Brusstar	.10	.05
☐ 556 Danny Heep	.10	.05
☐ 557 Darnell Coles	.10	.05
☐ 558 Greg Gagne	.10	.05
☐ 559 Ernie Whitt	.10	.05
☐ 560 Ron Washington	.10	.05
☐ 561 Jimmy Key	1.00	.45
☐ 562 Billy Swift	.10	.05
☐ 563 Ron Darling	.10	.05
☐ 564 Dick Ruthven	.10	.05
☐ 565 Zane Smith	.10	.05
☐ 566 Sid Bream	.10	.05
☐ 567A Joel Youngblood ERR (Position P)	.10	.05
☐ 567B Joel Youngblood COR (Position IF)	1.00	.45
☐ 568 Mario Ramirez	.10	.05
☐ 569 Tom Runnells	.10	.05
☐ 570 Rick Schu	.10	.05
☐ 571 Bill Campbell	.10	.05
☐ 572 Dickie Thon	.10	.05
☐ 573 Al Holland	.10	.05
☐ 574 Reid Nichols	.10	.05
☐ 575 Bert Roberge	.10	.05
☐ 576 Mike Flanagan	.10	.05
☐ 577 Tim Leary	.10	.05
☐ 578 Mike Laga	.10	.05
☐ 579 Steve Lyons	.10	.05
☐ 580 Phil Niekro	1.00	.45
☐ 581 Gilberto Reyes	.10	.05
☐ 582 Jamie Easterly	.10	.05
☐ 583 Mark Gubicza	.10	.05
☐ 584 Stan Javier	.25	.11
☐ 585 Bill Laskey	.10	.05
☐ 586 Jeff Russell	.10	.05
☐ 587 Dickie Noles	.10	.05
☐ 588 Steve Farr	.10	.05
☐ 589 Steve Ontiveros	.25	.11
☐ 590 Mike Hargrove	.25	.11
☐ 591 Marty Bystrom	.10	.05
☐ 592 Franklin Stubbs	.10	.05
☐ 593 Larry Herndon	.10	.05
☐ 594 Bill Swaggerty	.10	.05
☐ 595 Carlos Ponce	.10	.05
☐ 596 Pat Perry	.10	.05
☐ 597 Ray Knight	.25	.11
☐ 598 Steve Lombardozzi	.10	.05
☐ 599 Brad Havens	.10	.05
☐ 600 Pat Clements	.10	.05
☐ 601 Joe Niekro	.10	.05
☐ 602 Hank Aaron Puzzle Card	1.00	.45
☐ 603 Dwayne Henry	.10	.05
☐ 604 Mookie Wilson	.25	.11
☐ 605 Buddy Biancalana	.10	.05
☐ 606 Rance Mulliniks	.10	.05
☐ 607 Alan Wiggins	.10	.05
☐ 608 Joe Cowley	.10	.05
☐ 609 Tom Seaver (Green borders on name)	1.25	.55
☐ 609B Tom Seaver (Yellow borders on name)	2.00	.90
☐ 610 Neil Allen	.10	.05
☐ 611 Don Sutton	1.00	.45
☐ 612 Fred Toliver	.10	.05
☐ 613 Jay Baller	.10	.05
☐ 614 Marc Sullivan	.10	.05
☐ 615 John Grubb	.10	.05
☐ 616 Bruce Kison	.10	.05
☐ 617 Bill Madlock	.10	.05
☐ 618 Chris Chambliss	.25	.11
☐ 619 Dave Stewart	.25	.11
☐ 620 Tim Lollar	.10	.05
☐ 621 Gary Lavelle	.10	.05
☐ 622 Charles Hudson	.10	.05
☐ 623 Joel Davis	.10	.05
☐ 624 Joe Johnson	.10	.05
☐ 625 Sid Fernandez	.25	.11
☐ 626 Dennis Lamp	.10	.05
☐ 627 Terry Harper	.10	.05
☐ 628 Jack Lazorko	.10	.05
☐ 629 Roger McDowell	.25	.11
☐ 630 Mark Funderburk	.10	.05
☐ 631 Ed Lynch	.10	.05
☐ 632 Rudy Law	.10	.05
☐ 633 Roger Mason	.10	.05
☐ 634 Mike Felder	.10	.05
☐ 635 Ken Schrom	.10	.05
☐ 636 Bob Ojeda	.10	.05
☐ 637 Ed VandeBerg	.10	.05
☐ 638 Bobby Meacham	.10	.05
☐ 639 Cliff Johnson	.10	.05
☐ 640 Garth Iorg	.10	.05
☐ 641 Dan Driessen	.10	.05
☐ 642 Mike Brown OF	.10	.05
☐ 643 John Shelby	.10	.05
☐ 644 Pete Rose (Ty-Breaking)	.60	.25
☐ 645 The Knuckle Brothers Phil Niekro Joe Niekro	.25	.11
☐ 646 Jesse Orosco	.10	.05
☐ 647 Billy Beane	.10	.05
☐ 648 Cesar Cedeno	.25	.11
☐ 649 Bert Blyleven	.50	.23
☐ 650 Max Venable	.10	.05
☐ 651 Fleet Feet Vince Coleman Willie McGee	.25	.11
☐ 652 Calvin Schiraldi	.10	.05
☐ 653 King of Kings (Pete Rose)	1.00	.45
☐ 654 Diamond Kings CL 1-26 (Unnumbered)	.10	.05
☐ 655A CL 1: 27-130 (Unnumbered)	.10	.05

	MINT	NRMT
(45 Beane ERR)		
☐ 655B CL 1: 27-130	.10	.05
(Unnumbered)		
(45 Habyan COR)		
☐ 656 CL 2: 131-234	.10	.05
(Unnumbered)		
☐ 657 CL 3: 235-338	.10	.05
(Unnumbered)		
☐ 658 CL 4: 339-442	.10	.05
(Unnumbered)		
☐ 659 CL 5: 443-546	.10	.05
(Unnumbered)		
☐ 660 CL 6: 547-653	.10	.05
(Unnumbered)		

1986 Donruss Wax Box Cards

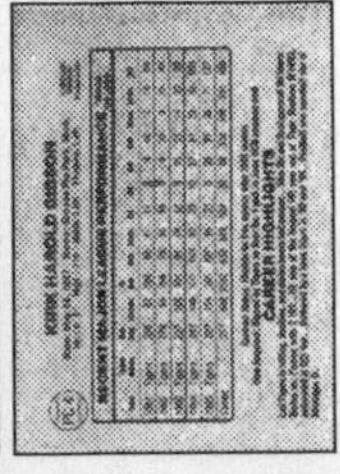

The cards in this four-card set measure the standard 2 1/2" by 3 1/2". Cards have essentially the same design as the 1986 Donruss regular issue set. The cards were printed on the bottoms of the regular issue wax pack boxes. The four cards (PC4 to PC6 plus a Hank Aaron puzzle card) are considered a separate set in their own right and are not typically included in a complete set of the regular issue 1986 Donruss cards. The value of the panel uncut is slightly greater, perhaps by 25 percent greater, than the value of the individual cards cut up carefully.

	MINT	NRMT
COMPLETE SET (4)	1.00	.45
COMMON CARD	.10	.05
☐ PC4 Kirk Gibson	.40	.18
☐ PC5 Willie Hernandez	.10	.05
☐ PC6 Doug DeCinces	.10	.05
☐ PUZ Hank Aaron Puzzle Card	.75	.35

1986 Donruss Rookies

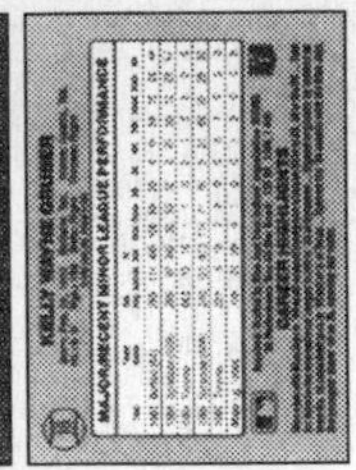

The 1986 Donruss "The Rookies" set features 56 full-color standard-size cards plus a 15-piece puzzle of Hank Aaron. The set was distributed through hobby dealers in a small green, cellophane wrapped factory box. Although the set was wrapped in cellophane, the top card was number 1 Joyner, resulting in a percentage of the Joyner cards arriving in less than perfect condition. Donruss fixed the problem after it was called to their attention and even went so far as to include a customer service phone number in their second printing. Card fronts are similar in design to the 1986 Donruss regular issue except for the presence of "The Rookies" logo in the lower left corner and a bluish green border instead of a blue border. The key extended Rookie Cards in this set are Barry Bonds, Bobby Bonilla, Will Clark, Bo Jackson, Wally Joyner, John Kruk, Kevin Mitchell, and Ruben Sierra.

	MINT	NRMT
COMP.FACT.SET (56)	25.00	11.00
COMMON CARD (1-56)	.10	.05
☐ 1 Wally Joyner	1.00	.45
☐ 2 Tracy Jones	.10	.05
☐ 3 Allan Anderson	.10	.05
☐ 4 Ed Correa	.10	.05
☐ 5 Reggie Williams	.10	.05
☐ 6 Charlie Kerfeld	.10	.05
☐ 7 Andres Galarraga	3.00	1.35
☐ 8 Bob Tewksbury	.25	.11
☐ 9 Al Newman	.25	.11
☐ 10 Andres Thomas	.10	.05
☐ 11 Barry Bonds	8.00	3.60
☐ 12 Juan Nieves	.10	.05
☐ 13 Mark Eichhorn	.10	.05
☐ 14 Dan Plesac	.10	.05
☐ 15 Cory Snyder	.10	.05
☐ 16 Kelly Gruber	.10	.05
☐ 17 Kevin Mitchell	1.00	.45
☐ 18 Steve Lombardozzi	.10	.05
☐ 19 Mitch Williams	.25	.11
☐ 20 John Cerutti	.10	.05
☐ 21 Todd Worrell	1.00	.45
☐ 22 Jose Canseco	3.00	1.35
☐ 23 Pete Incaviglia	1.00	.45
☐ 24 Jose Guzman	.10	.05
☐ 25 Scott Bailes	.10	.05
☐ 26 Greg Mathews	.10	.05
☐ 27 Eric King	.10	.05
☐ 28 Paul Assenmacher	.10	.05
☐ 29 Jeff Sellers	.10	.05
☐ 30 Bobby Bonilla	2.00	.90
☐ 31 Doug Drabek	1.00	.45
☐ 32 Will Clark UER (Listed as throwing right, should be left)	3.00	1.35
☐ 33 Bip Roberts	1.00	.45
☐ 34 Jim Deshaies	.10	.05
☐ 35 Mike LaValliere	.10	.05
☐ 36 Scott Bankhead	.10	.05
☐ 37 Dale Sveum	.10	.05
☐ 38 Bo Jackson	2.00	.90
☐ 39 Robby Thompson	.25	.11
☐ 40 Eric Plunk	.10	.05
☐ 41 Bill Bathe	.10	.05
☐ 42 John Kruk	1.00	.45
☐ 43 Andy Allanson	.10	.05
☐ 44 Mark Portugal	.25	.11
☐ 45 Danny Tartabull	.25	.11
☐ 46 Bob Kipper	.10	.05
☐ 47 Gene Walter	.10	.05
☐ 48 Rey Quinones UER (Misspelled Quinonez)	.10	.05
☐ 49 Bobby Witt	.25	.11
☐ 50 Bill Mooneyham	.10	.05
☐ 51 John Cangelosi	.10	.05
☐ 52 Ruben Sierra	2.00	.90
☐ 53 Rob Woodward	.10	.05
☐ 54 Ed Hearn	.10	.05
☐ 55 Joel McKeon	.10	.05
☐ 56 Checklist 1-56	.10	.05

1986 Donruss All-Stars

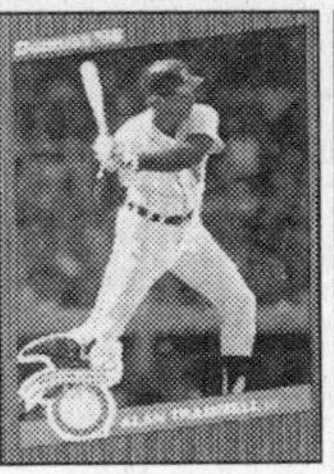

The cards in this 60-card set measure approximately 3 1/2" by 5". Players featured were involved in the 1985 All-Star game played in Minnesota. Cards are very similar in design to the 1986 Donruss regular issue set. The backs give each player's All-Star game statistics and have an orange-yellow border.

	MINT	NRMT
COMPLETE SET (60)	6.00	2.70
COMMON CARD (1-59)	.05	.02
☐ 1 Tony Gwynn	1.50	.70
☐ 2 Tommy Herr	.05	.02
☐ 3 Steve Garvey	.20	.09
☐ 4 Dale Murphy	.20	.09
☐ 5 Darryl Strawberry	.10	.05
☐ 6 Graig Nettles	.10	.05
☐ 7 Terry Kennedy	.05	.02
☐ 8 Ozzie Smith	1.00	.45
☐ 9 LaMarr Hoyt	.05	.02
☐ 10 Rickey Henderson	.40	.18
☐ 11 Lou Whitaker	.10	.05
☐ 12 George Brett	1.25	.55
☐ 13 Eddie Murray	.60	.25
☐ 14 Cal Ripken	2.00	.90
☐ 15 Dave Winfield	.40	.18
☐ 16 Jim Rice	.10	.05
☐ 17 Carlton Fisk	.40	.18
☐ 18 Jack Morris	.10	.05
☐ 19 Jose Cruz	.05	.02
☐ 20 Tim Raines	.10	.05
☐ 21 Nolan Ryan	2.50	1.10
☐ 22 Tony Pena	.05	.02
☐ 23 Jack Clark	.10	.05
☐ 24 Dave Parker	.10	.05
☐ 25 Tim Wallach	.05	.02
☐ 26 Ozzie Virgil	.05	.02
☐ 27 Fernando Valenzuela	.10	.05
☐ 28 Dwight Gooden	.20	.09
☐ 29 Glenn Wilson	.05	.02
☐ 30 Garry Templeton	.05	.02
☐ 31 Goose Gossage	.10	.05
☐ 32 Ryne Sandberg	.75	.35
☐ 33 Jeff Reardon	.05	.02
☐ 34 Pete Rose	.75	.35
☐ 35 Scott Garrelts	.05	.02
☐ 36 Willie McGee	.10	.05
☐ 37 Ron Darling	.05	.02
☐ 38 Dick Williams MG	.05	.02
☐ 39 Paul Molitor	.50	.23
☐ 40 Damaso Garcia	.05	.02
☐ 41 Phil Bradley	.05	.02
☐ 42 Dan Petry	.05	.02
☐ 43 Willie Hernandez	.05	.02
☐ 44 Tom Brunansky	.05	.02
☐ 45 Alan Trammell	.20	.09
☐ 46 Donnie Moore	.05	.02
☐ 47 Wade Boggs	.40	.18
☐ 48 Ernie Whitt	.05	.02
☐ 49 Harold Baines	.10	.05
☐ 50 Don Mattingly	1.00	.45
☐ 51 Gary Ward	.05	.02
☐ 52 Bert Blyleven	.10	.05
☐ 53 Jimmy Key	.20	.09
☐ 54 Cecil Cooper	.10	.05
☐ 55 Dave Stieb	.05	.02
☐ 56 Rich Gedman	.05	.02
☐ 57 Jay Howell	.05	.02
☐ 58 Sparky Anderson MG	.05	.02
☐ 59 Minneapolis Metrodome	.05	.02
☐ NNO Checklist Card	.05	.02

1986 Donruss All-Star Box

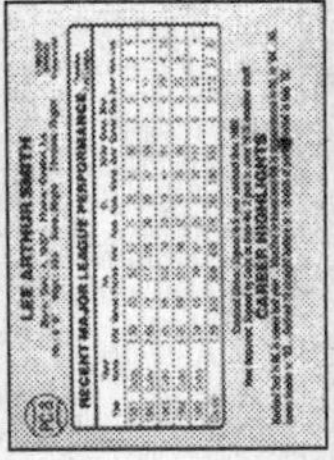

The cards in this four-card set measure the standard size in spite of the fact that they form the bottom of the wax pack box for the larger Donruss All-Star cards. These box cards have essentially the same design as the 1986 Donruss regular issue set. The cards were printed on the bottoms of the Donruss All-Star (3 1/2" by 5") wax pack boxes. The four cards (PC7 to PC9 plus a Hank Aaron puzzle card) are considered a separate set in their own right and are not typically included in a complete set of the regular issue 1986 Donruss All-Star (or regular) cards. The value of the panel uncut is slightly greater, perhaps by 25 percent greater, than the value of the individual cards cut up carefully.

	MINT	NRMT
COMPLETE SET (4)	2.00	.90
COMMON CARD	.25	.11
☐ PC7 Wade Boggs	1.00	.45
☐ PC8 Lee Smith	.50	.23
☐ PC9 Cecil Cooper	.25	.11
☐ PUZ Hank Aaron Puzzle Card	.75	.35

1986 Donruss Highlights

Donruss' second edition of Highlights was released late in 1986. These glossy-coated cards are standard size. Cards commemorate events during the 1986 season, as well as players and pitchers of the month from each league. The set was distributed in its own red, white, blue, and gold box along with a small Hank Aaron puzzle. Card fronts are similar to the regular 1986 Donruss issue except that the Highlights logo is positioned in the lower left-hand corner

...d the borders are in gold instead of blue. The backs are ...inted in black and gold on white card stock.

	MINT	NRMT
...OMPLETE FACT. SET (56)	3.00	1.35
...OMMON CARD (1-56)	.05	.02
1 Will Clark	.50	.23
2 Jose Rijo	.05	.02
3 George Brett	.50	.23
4 Mike Schmidt	.30	.14
5 Roger Clemens	.40	.18
6 Roger Clemens	.40	.18
7 Kirby Puckett	.60	.25
8 Dwight Gooden	.20	.09
9 Johnny Ray	.05	.02
10 Reggie Jackson Mickey Mantle	.75	.35
11 Wade Boggs	.30	.14
12 Don Aase	.05	.02
13 Wade Boggs	.30	.14
14 Jeff Reardon	.05	.02
15 Hubie Brooks	.05	.02
16 Don Sutton	.40	.18
17 Roger Clemens	.60	.25
18 Roger Clemens	.60	.25
19 Kent Hrbek	.10	.05
20 Rick Rhoden	.05	.02
21 Kevin Bass	.05	.02
22 Bob Horner	.05	.02
23 Wally Joyner	.30	.14
24 Darryl Strawberry	.20	.09
25 Fernando Valenzuela	.10	.05
26 Roger Clemens	.60	.25
27 Jack Morris	.10	.05
28 Scott Fletcher	.05	.02
29 Todd Worrell	.20	.09
30 Eric Davis	.10	.05
31 Bert Blyleven	.10	.05
32 Bobby Doerr	.10	.05
33 Ernie Lombardi	.10	.05
34 Willie McCovey	.30	.14
35 Steve Carlton	.40	.18
36 Mike Schmidt	.40	.18
37 Juan Samuel	.05	.02
38 Mike Witt	.05	.02
39 Doug DeCinces	.05	.02
40 Bill Gullickson	.05	.02
41 Dale Murphy	.30	.14
42 Joe Carter	.20	.09
43 Bo Jackson	.30	.14
44 Joe Cowley	.05	.02
45 Jim Deshaies	.05	.02
46 Mike Scott	.05	.02
47 Bruce Hurst	.05	.02
48 Don Mattingly	.60	.25
49 Mike Krukow	.05	.02
50 Steve Sax	.05	.02
51 John Cangelosi	.05	.02
52 Dave Righetti	.05	.02
53 Don Mattingly	.60	.25
54 Todd Worrell	.20	.09
55 Jose Canseco	.30	.14
56 Checklist Card	.05	.02

1986 Donruss Pop-Ups

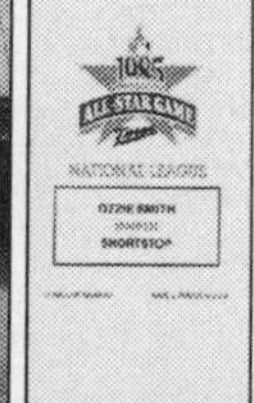

...his set is the companion of the 1986 Donruss All-Star ...60) set; as such it features the first 18 cards of that set (the All-Star starting line-ups) in a pop-up, die-cut type of card. These cards (measuring (2 1/2" X 5") can be "popped up" to feature a standing card showing the player in action in front of the Metrodome ballpark background. Although this set is unnumbered it is numbered in the same order as its companion set, presumably according to the respective batting orders of the starting line-ups. The first nine numbers below are National Leaguers and the last nine are American Leaguers. See also the Donruss All-Star checklist card which contains a checklist for the Pop-Ups as well.

	MINT	NRMT
COMPLETE SET (18)	5.00	2.20
COMMON CARD (1-18)	.05	.02
1 Tony Gwynn	1.25	.55
2 Tommy Herr	.05	.02
3 Steve Garvey	.20	.09
4 Dale Murphy	.30	.14
5 Darryl Strawberry	.10	.05
6 Graig Nettles	.10	.05
7 Terry Kennedy	.05	.02
8 Ozzie Smith	1.00	.45
9 LaMarr Hoyt	.05	.02
10 Rickey Henderson	.40	.18
11 Lou Whitaker	.10	.05
12 George Brett	1.25	.55
13 Eddie Murray	.60	.25
14 Cal Ripken	2.50	1.10
15 Dave Winfield	.40	.18
16 Jim Rice	.10	.05
17 Carlton Fisk	.40	.18
18 Jack Morris	.10	.05

1986 Donruss Super DK's

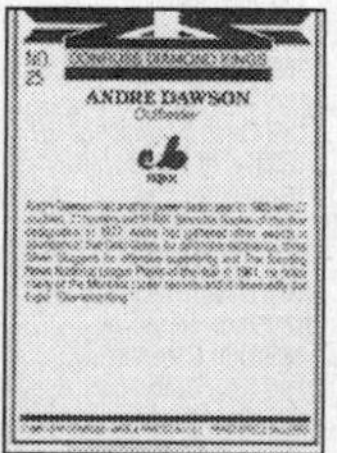

This 29-card set of large Diamond Kings features the full-color artwork of Dick Perez. The set could be obtained from Perez-Steele Galleries by sending three Donruss wrappers and $9.00. The cards measure 4 7/8" by 6 13/16" and are identical in design to the Diamond King cards in the Donruss regular issue.

	MINT	NRMT
COMPLETE SET (27)	12.50	5.50
COMMON CARD (1-27)	.50	.23
1 Kirk Gibson	.75	.35
2 Goose Gossage	.75	.35
3 Willie McGee	.75	.35
4 George Bell	.50	.23
5 Tony Armas	.50	.23
6 Chili Davis	.75	.35
7 Cecil Cooper	.75	.35
8 Mike Boddicker	.50	.23
9 Dave Lopes	.50	.23
10 Bill Doran	.50	.23
11 Bret Saberhagen	1.00	.45
12 Brett Butler	.75	.35
13 Harold Baines	.75	.35
14 Mike Davis	.50	.23
15 Tony Perez	1.50	.70
16 Willie Randolph	.75	.35
17 Bob Boone	.75	.35
18 Orel Hershiser	1.00	.45
19 Johnny Ray	.50	.23
20 Gary Ward	.50	.23
21 Rick Mahler	.50	.23
22 Phil Bradley	.50	.23
23 Jerry Koosman	.75	.35
24 Tom Brunansky	.50	.23
25 Andre Dawson	1.00	.45
26 Dwight Gooden	2.00	.90
27 Pete Rose King of Kings	3.00	1.35
NNO Checklist Card	.50	.23
NNO Aaron Large Puzzle	2.00	.90

1987 Donruss

This set consists of 660 standard-size cards. Cards were primarily distributed in 15-card wax packs, rack packs and

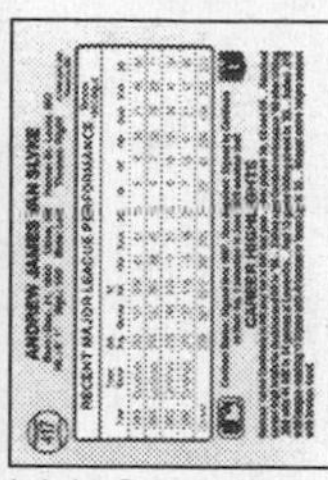

a factory set. All packs included a Roberto Clemente puzzle panel and the factory sets contained a complete puzzle.The regular-issue cards feature a black and gold border on the front. The backs of the cards in the factory sets are oriented differently than cards taken from wax packs, giving the appearance that one version or the other is upside down when sorting from the card backs. There are no premiums or discounts for either version. The popular Diamond King subset returns for the sixth consecutive year. Some of the Diamond King (1-26) selections are repeats from prior years; Perez-Steele Galleries had indicated in 1987 that a five-year rotation would be maintained in order to avoid depleting the pool of available worthy "kings" on some of the teams. Rookie Cards in this set include Barry Bonds, Bobby Bonilla, Kevin Brown, Will Clark, David Cone, Chuck Finley, Bo Jackson, Wally Joyner, Barry Larkin, Greg Maddux and Rafael Palmeiro. The Greg Maddux card has been noted to have a premium for perfectly centered copies.

	MINT	NRMT
COMPLETE SET (660)	30.00	13.50
COMPLETE FACT.SET (660)	30.00	13.50
COMMON CARD (1-660)	.10	.05
COMPLETE CLEMENTE PUZZLE	1.50	.70
1 Wally Joyner DK	.10	.05
2 Roger Clemens DK	.40	.18
3 Dale Murphy DK	.40	.18
4 Darryl Strawberry DK	.10	.05
5 Ozzie Smith DK	.40	.18
6 Jose Canseco DK	.40	.18
7 Charlie Hough DK	.10	.05
8 Brook Jacoby DK	.10	.05
9 Fred Lynn DK	.20	.09
10 Rick Rhoden DK	.10	.05
11 Chris Brown DK	.10	.05
12 Von Hayes DK	.10	.05
13 Jack Morris DK	.20	.09
14A Kevin McReynolds DK ERR (Yellow strip missing on back)	.40	.18
14B Kevin McReynolds DK COR	.10	.05
15 George Brett DK	.40	.18
16 Ted Higuera DK	.10	.05
17 Hubie Brooks DK	.10	.05
18 Mike Scott DK	.10	.05
19 Kirby Puckett DK	.50	.23
20 Dave Winfield DK	.10	.05
21 Lloyd Moseby DK	.10	.05
22A Eric Davis DK ERR (Yellow strip missing on back)	.40	.18
22B Eric Davis DK COR	.20	.09
23 Jim Presley DK	.10	.05
24 Keith Moreland DK	.10	.05
25A Greg Walker DK ERR (Yellow strip missing on back)	.40	.18
25B Greg Walker DK COR	.10	.05
26 Steve Sax DK	.10	.05
27 DK Checklist 1-26	.10	.05
28 B.J. Surhoff RR	.40	.18
29 Randy Myers RR	.40	.18
30 Ken Gerhart RR	.10	.05
31 Benito Santiago RR	.20	.09
32 Greg Swindell RR	.20	.09
33 Mike Birkbeck RR	.10	.05
34 Terry Steinbach RR	.40	.18
35 Bo Jackson RR	1.00	.45
36 Greg Maddux UER (middle name misspelled "Allen")	20.00	9.00
37 Jim Lindeman RR	.10	.05
38 Devon White RR	.40	.18
39 Eric Bell RR	.10	.05
40 Willie Fraser RR	.10	.05
41 Jerry Browne RR	.10	.05
42 Chris James RR	.10	.05
43 Rafael Palmeiro RR	2.00	.90
44 Pat Dodson RR	.10	.05
45 Duane Ward RR	.20	.09
46 Mark McGwire RR	4.00	1.80

☐ 47 Bruce Fields RR UER (Photo actually Darnell Coles)	.10	.05
☐ 48 Eddie Murray	.40	.18
☐ 49 Ted Higuera	.10	.05
☐ 50 Kirk Gibson	.20	.09
☐ 51 Oil Can Boyd	.10	.05
☐ 52 Don Mattingly	.60	.25
☐ 53 Pedro Guerrero	.20	.09
☐ 54 George Brett	.75	.35
☐ 55 Jose Rijo	.10	.05
☐ 56 Tim Raines	.20	.09
☐ 57 Ed Correa	.10	.05
☐ 58 Mike Witt	.10	.05
☐ 59 Greg Walker	.10	.05
☐ 60 Ozzie Smith	.50	.23
☐ 61 Glenn Davis	.10	.05
☐ 62 Glenn Wilson	.10	.05
☐ 63 Tom Browning	.10	.05
☐ 64 Tony Gwynn	1.00	.45
☐ 65 R.J. Reynolds	.10	.05
☐ 66 Will Clark	1.50	.70
☐ 67 Ozzie Virgil	.10	.05
☐ 68 Rick Sutcliffe	.10	.05
☐ 69 Gary Carter	.40	.18
☐ 70 Mike Moore	.10	.05
☐ 71 Bert Blyleven	.20	.09
☐ 72 Tony Fernandez	.10	.05
☐ 73 Kent Hrbek	.20	.09
☐ 74 Lloyd Moseby	.10	.05
☐ 75 Alvin Davis	.10	.05
☐ 76 Keith Hernandez	.20	.09
☐ 77 Ryne Sandberg	.50	.23
☐ 78 Dale Murphy	.40	.18
☐ 79 Sid Bream	.10	.05
☐ 80 Chris Brown	.10	.05
☐ 81 Steve Garvey	.20	.09
☐ 82 Mario Soto	.10	.05
☐ 83 Shane Rawley	.10	.05
☐ 84 Willie McGee	.10	.05
☐ 85 Jose Cruz	.20	.09
☐ 86 Brian Downing	.10	.05
☐ 87 Ozzie Guillen	.20	.09
☐ 88 Hubie Brooks	.10	.05
☐ 89 Cal Ripken	1.50	.70
☐ 90 Juan Nieves	.10	.05
☐ 91 Lance Parrish	.20	.09
☐ 92 Jim Rice	.20	.09
☐ 93 Ron Guidry	.20	.09
☐ 94 Fernando Valenzuela	.20	.09
☐ 95 Andy Allanson	.10	.05
☐ 96 Willie Wilson	.10	.05
☐ 97 Jose Canseco	.50	.23
☐ 98 Jeff Reardon	.20	.09
☐ 99 Bobby Witt	.20	.09
☐ 100 Checklist 28-133	.10	.05
☐ 101 Jose Guzman	.10	.05
☐ 102 Steve Balboni	.10	.05
☐ 103 Tony Phillips	.10	.05
☐ 104 Brook Jacoby	.10	.05
☐ 105 Dave Winfield	.40	.18
☐ 106 Orel Hershiser	.20	.09
☐ 107 Lou Whitaker	.20	.09
☐ 108 Fred Lynn	.20	.09
☐ 109 Bill Wegman	.10	.05
☐ 110 Donnie Moore	.10	.05
☐ 111 Jack Clark	.20	.09
☐ 112 Bob Knepper	.10	.05
☐ 113 Von Hayes	.10	.05
☐ 114 Bip Roberts	.10	.05
☐ 115 Tony Pena	.10	.05
☐ 116 Scott Garrelts	.10	.05
☐ 117 Paul Molitor	.40	.18
☐ 118 Darryl Strawberry	.20	.09
☐ 119 Shawon Dunston	.10	.05
☐ 120 Jim Presley	.10	.05
☐ 121 Jesse Barfield	.10	.05
☐ 122 Gary Gaetti	.10	.05
☐ 123 Kurt Stillwell	.10	.05
☐ 124 Joel Davis	.10	.05
☐ 125 Mike Boddicker	.10	.05
☐ 126 Robin Yount	.40	.18
☐ 127 Alan Trammell	.20	.05
☐ 128 Dave Righetti	.10	.05
☐ 129 Dwight Evans	.20	.09
☐ 130 Mike Scioscia	.10	.05
☐ 131 Julio Franco	.20	.09
☐ 132 Bret Saberhagen	.10	.05
☐ 133 Mike Davis	.10	.05
☐ 134 Joe Hesketh	.10	.05
☐ 135 Wally Joyner	.40	.18
☐ 136 Don Slaught	.10	.05
☐ 137 Daryl Boston	.10	.05
☐ 138 Nolan Ryan	1.50	.70
☐ 139 Mike Schmidt	.50	.23
☐ 140 Tommy Herr	.10	.05
☐ 141 Garry Templeton	.10	.05
☐ 142 Kal Daniels	.10	.05
☐ 143 Billy Sample	.10	.05
☐ 144 Johnny Ray	.10	.05
☐ 145 Rob Thompson	.20	.09
☐ 146 Bob Dernier	.10	.05
☐ 147 Danny Tartabull	.10	.05
☐ 148 Ernie Whitt	.10	.05
☐ 149 Kirby Puckett	1.00	.45
☐ 150 Mike Young	.10	.05
☐ 151 Ernest Riles	.10	.05
☐ 152 Frank Tanana	.10	.05
☐ 153 Rich Gedman	.10	.05
☐ 154 Willie Randolph	.20	.09
☐ 155 Bill Madlock	.20	.09
☐ 156 Joe Carter	.40	.18
☐ 157 Danny Jackson	.10	.05
☐ 158 Carney Lansford	.20	.09
☐ 159 Bryn Smith	.10	.05
☐ 160 Gary Pettis	.10	.05
☐ 161 Oddibe McDowell	.10	.05
☐ 162 John Cangelosi	.10	.05
☐ 163 Mike Scott	.10	.05
☐ 164 Eric Show	.10	.05
☐ 165 Juan Samuel	.10	.05
☐ 166 Nick Esasky	.10	.05
☐ 167 Zane Smith	.10	.05
☐ 168 Mike C. Brown OF	.10	.05
☐ 169 Keith Moreland	.10	.05
☐ 170 John Tudor	.10	.05
☐ 171 Ken Dixon	.10	.05
☐ 172 Jim Gantner	.10	.05
☐ 173 Jack Morris	.20	.09
☐ 174 Bruce Hurst	.10	.05
☐ 175 Dennis Rasmussen	.10	.05
☐ 176 Mike Marshall	.10	.05
☐ 177 Dan Quisenberry	.10	.05
☐ 178 Eric Plunk	.10	.05
☐ 179 Tim Wallach	.10	.05
☐ 180 Steve Buechele	.10	.05
☐ 181 Don Sutton	.40	.18
☐ 182 Dave Schmidt	.10	.05
☐ 183 Terry Pendleton	.20	.09
☐ 184 Jim Deshaies	.10	.05
☐ 185 Steve Bedrosian	.10	.05
☐ 186 Pete Rose	.50	.23
☐ 187 Dave Dravecky	.20	.09
☐ 188 Rick Reuschel	.10	.05
☐ 189 Dan Gladden	.10	.05
☐ 190 Rick Mahler	.10	.05
☐ 191 Thad Bosley	.10	.05
☐ 192 Ron Darling	.10	.05
☐ 193 Matt Young	.10	.05
☐ 194 Tom Brunansky	.10	.05
☐ 195 Dave Stieb	.10	.05
☐ 196 Frank Viola	.10	.05
☐ 197 Tom Henke	.10	.05
☐ 198 Karl Best	.10	.05
☐ 199 Dwight Gooden	.10	.05
☐ 200 Checklist 134-239	.10	.05
☐ 201 Steve Trout	.10	.05
☐ 202 Rafael Ramirez	.10	.05
☐ 203 Bob Walk	.10	.05
☐ 204 Roger Mason	.10	.05
☐ 205 Terry Kennedy	.10	.05
☐ 206 Ron Oester	.10	.05
☐ 207 John Russell	.10	.05
☐ 208 Greg Mathews	.10	.05
☐ 209 Charlie Kerfeld	.10	.05
☐ 210 Reggie Jackson	.50	.23
☐ 211 Floyd Bannister	.10	.05
☐ 212 Vance Law	.10	.05
☐ 213 Rich Bordi	.10	.05
☐ 214 Dan Plesac	.10	.05
☐ 215 Dave Collins	.10	.05
☐ 216 Bob Stanley	.10	.05
☐ 217 Joe Niekro	.10	.05
☐ 218 Tom Niedenfuer	.10	.05
☐ 219 Brett Butler	.10	.05
☐ 220 Charlie Leibrandt	.10	.05
☐ 221 Steve Ontiveros	.10	.05
☐ 222 Tim Burke	.10	.05
☐ 223 Curtis Wilkerson	.10	.05
☐ 224 Pete Incaviglia	.20	.09
☐ 225 Lonnie Smith	.10	.05
☐ 226 Chris Codiroli	.10	.05
☐ 227 Scott Bailes	.10	.05
☐ 228 Rickey Henderson	.40	.18
☐ 229 Ken Howell	.10	.05
☐ 230 Darnell Coles	.10	.05
☐ 231 Don Aase	.10	.05
☐ 232 Tim Leary	.10	.05
☐ 233 Bob Boone	.20	.09
☐ 234 Ricky Horton	.10	.05
☐ 235 Mark Bailey	.10	.05
☐ 236 Kevin Gross	.10	.05
☐ 237 Lance McCullers	.10	.05
☐ 238 Cecilio Guante	.10	.05
☐ 239 Bob Melvin	.10	.05
☐ 240 Billy Joe Robidoux	.10	.05
☐ 241 Roger McDowell	.10	.05
☐ 242 Leon Durham	.10	.05
☐ 243 Ed Nunez	.10	.05
☐ 244 Jimmy Key	.10	.05
☐ 245 Mike Smithson	.10	.05
☐ 246 Bo Diaz	.10	.05
☐ 247 Carlton Fisk	.40	.18
☐ 248 Larry Sheets	.10	.05
☐ 249 Juan Castillo	.10	.05
☐ 250 Eric King	.10	.05
☐ 251 Doug Drabek	.40	.18
☐ 252 Wade Boggs	.40	.18
☐ 253 Mariano Duncan	.10	.05
☐ 254 Pat Tabler	.10	.05
☐ 255 Frank White	.20	.09
☐ 256 Alfredo Griffin	.10	.05
☐ 257 Floyd Youmans	.10	.05
☐ 258 Rob Wilfong	.10	.05
☐ 259 Pete O'Brien	.10	.05
☐ 260 Tim Hulett	.10	.05
☐ 261 Dickie Thon	.10	.05
☐ 262 Darren Daulton	.10	.05
☐ 263 Vince Coleman	.10	.05
☐ 264 Andy Hawkins	.10	.05
☐ 265 Eric Davis	.10	.05
☐ 266 Andres Thomas	.10	.05
☐ 267 Mike Diaz	.10	.05
☐ 268 Chili Davis	.10	.05
☐ 269 Jody Davis	.10	.05
☐ 270 Phil Bradley	.10	.05
☐ 271 George Bell	.10	.05
☐ 272 Keith Atherton	.10	.05
☐ 273 Storm Davis	.10	.05
☐ 274 Rob Deer	.10	.05
☐ 275 Walt Terrell	.10	.05
☐ 276 Roger Clemens	1.00	.45
☐ 277 Mike Easler	.10	.05
☐ 278 Steve Sax	.10	.05
☐ 279 Andre Thornton	.10	.05
☐ 280 Jim Sundberg	.10	.05
☐ 281 Bill Bathe	.10	.05
☐ 282 Jay Tibbs	.10	.05
☐ 283 Dick Schofield	.10	.05
☐ 284 Mike Mason	.10	.05
☐ 285 Jerry Hairston	.10	.05
☐ 286 Bill Doran	.10	.05
☐ 287 Tim Flannery	.10	.05
☐ 288 Gary Redus	.10	.05
☐ 289 John Franco	.20	.09
☐ 290 Paul Assenmacher	.10	.05
☐ 291 Joe Orsulak	.10	.05
☐ 292 Lee Smith	.10	.05
☐ 293 Mike Laga	.10	.05
☐ 294 Rick Dempsey	.20	.09
☐ 295 Mike Felder	.10	.05
☐ 296 Tom Brookens	.10	.05
☐ 297 Al Nipper	.10	.05
☐ 298 Mike Pagliarulo	.10	.05
☐ 299 Franklin Stubbs	.10	.05
☐ 300 Checklist 240-345	.10	.05
☐ 301 Steve Farr	.10	.05
☐ 302 Bill Mooneyham	.10	.05
☐ 303 Andres Galarraga	.50	.23
☐ 304 Scott Fletcher	.10	.05
☐ 305 Jack Howell	.10	.05
☐ 306 Russ Morman	.10	.05
☐ 307 Todd Worrell	.20	.09
☐ 308 Dave Smith	.10	.05
☐ 309 Jeff Stone	.10	.05
☐ 310 Ron Robinson	.10	.05
☐ 311 Bruce Bochy	.10	.05
☐ 312 Jim Winn	.10	.05
☐ 313 Mark Davis	.10	.05
☐ 314 Jeff Dedmon	.10	.05
☐ 315 Jamie Moyer	.10	.05
☐ 316 Wally Backman	.10	.05
☐ 317 Ken Phelps	.10	.05
☐ 318 Steve Lombardozzi	.10	.05
☐ 319 Rance Mulliniks	.10	.05
☐ 320 Tim Laudner	.10	.05
☐ 321 Mark Eichhorn	.10	.05
☐ 322 Lee Guetterman	.10	.05
☐ 323 Sid Fernandez	.10	.05
☐ 324 Jerry Mumphrey	.10	.05
☐ 325 David Palmer	.10	.05
☐ 326 Bill Almon	.10	.05
☐ 327 Candy Maldonado	.10	.05
☐ 328 John Kruk	.40	.18
☐ 329 John Denny	.10	.05
☐ 330 Milt Thompson	.10	.05
☐ 331 Mike LaValliere	.10	.05
☐ 332 Alan Ashby	.10	.05
☐ 333 Doug Corbett	.10	.05
☐ 334 Ron Karkovice	.20	.09
☐ 335 Mitch Webster	.10	.05

☐ 336 Lee Lacy	.10	.05
☐ 337 Glenn Braggs	.10	.05
☐ 338 Dwight Lowry	.10	.05
☐ 339 Don Baylor	.10	.05
☐ 340 Brian Fisher	.10	.05
☐ 341 Reggie Williams	.10	.05
☐ 342 Tom Candiotti	.10	.05
☐ 343 Rudy Law	.10	.05
☐ 344 Curt Young	.10	.05
☐ 345 Mike Fitzgerald	.10	.05
☐ 346 Ruben Sierra	.40	.18
☐ 347 Mitch Williams	.20	.09
☐ 348 Jorge Orta	.10	.05
☐ 349 Mickey Tettleton	.20	.09
☐ 350 Ernie Camacho	.10	.05
☐ 351 Ron Kittle	.10	.05
☐ 352 Ken Landreaux	.10	.05
☐ 353 Chet Lemon	.10	.05
☐ 354 John Shelby	.10	.05
☐ 355 Mark Clear	.10	.05
☐ 356 Doug DeCinces	.10	.05
☐ 357 Ken Dayley	.10	.05
☐ 358 Phil Garner	.10	.05
☐ 359 Steve Jeltz	.10	.05
☐ 360 Ed Whitson	.10	.05
☐ 361 Barry Bonds	4.00	1.80
☐ 362 Vida Blue	.20	.09
☐ 363 Cecil Cooper	.20	.09
☐ 364 Bob Ojeda	.10	.05
☐ 365 Dennis Eckersley	.40	.18
☐ 366 Mike Morgan	.10	.05
☐ 367 Willie Upshaw	.10	.05
☐ 368 Allan Anderson	.10	.05
☐ 369 Bill Gullickson	.10	.05
☐ 370 Bobby Thigpen	.20	.09
☐ 371 Juan Beniquez	.10	.05
☐ 372 Charlie Moore	.10	.05
☐ 373 Dan Petry	.10	.05
☐ 374 Rod Scurry	.10	.05
☐ 375 Tom Seaver	.40	.18
☐ 376 Ed VandeBerg	.10	.05
☐ 377 Tony Bernazard	.10	.05
☐ 378 Greg Pryor	.10	.05
☐ 379 Dwayne Murphy	.10	.05
☐ 380 Andy McGaffigan	.10	.05
☐ 381 Kirk McCaskill	.10	.05
☐ 382 Greg Harris	.10	.05
☐ 383 Rich Dotson	.10	.05
☐ 384 Craig Reynolds	.10	.05
☐ 385 Greg Gross	.10	.05
☐ 386 Tito Landrum	.10	.05
☐ 387 Craig Lefferts	.10	.05
☐ 388 Dave Parker	.20	.09
☐ 389 Bob Horner	.10	.05
☐ 390 Pat Clements	.10	.05
☐ 391 Jeff Leonard	.10	.05
☐ 392 Chris Speier	.10	.05
☐ 393 John Moses	.10	.05
☐ 394 Garth Iorg	.10	.05
☐ 395 Greg Gagne	.10	.05
☐ 396 Nate Snell	.10	.05
☐ 397 Bryan Clutterbuck	.10	.05
☐ 398 Darrell Evans	.20	.09
☐ 399 Steve Crawford	.10	.05
☐ 400 Checklist 346-451	.10	.05
☐ 401 Phil Lombardi	.10	.05
☐ 402 Rick Honeycutt	.10	.05
☐ 403 Ken Schrom	.10	.05
☐ 404 Bud Black	.10	.05
☐ 405 Donnie Hill	.10	.05
☐ 406 Wayne Krenchicki	.10	.05
☐ 407 Chuck Finley	.40	.18
☐ 408 Toby Harrah	.10	.05
☐ 409 Steve Lyons	.10	.05
☐ 410 Kevin Bass	.10	.05
☐ 411 Marvell Wynne	.10	.05
☐ 412 Ron Roenicke	.10	.05
☐ 413 Tracy Jones	.10	.05
☐ 414 Gene Garber	.10	.05
☐ 415 Mike Bielecki	.10	.05
☐ 416 Frank DiPino	.10	.05
☐ 417 Andy Van Slyke	.20	.09
☐ 418 Jim Dwyer	.10	.05
☐ 419 Ben Oglivie	.10	.05
☐ 420 Dave Bergman	.10	.05
☐ 421 Joe Sambito	.10	.05
☐ 422 Bob Tewksbury	.20	.09
☐ 423 Len Matuszek	.10	.05
☐ 424 Mike Kingery	.20	.09
☐ 425 Dave Kingman	.20	.09
☐ 426 Al Newman	.10	.05
☐ 427 Gary Ward	.10	.05
☐ 428 Ruppert Jones	.10	.05
☐ 429 Harold Baines	.20	.09
☐ 430 Pat Perry	.10	.05
☐ 431 Terry Puhl	.10	.05
☐ 432 Don Carman	.10	.05
☐ 433 Eddie Milner	.10	.05
☐ 434 LaMarr Hoyt	.10	.05
☐ 435 Rick Rhoden	.10	.05
☐ 436 Jose Uribe	.10	.05
☐ 437 Ken Oberkfell	.10	.05
☐ 438 Ron Davis	.10	.05
☐ 439 Jesse Orosco	.10	.05
☐ 440 Scott Bradley	.10	.05
☐ 441 Randy Bush	.10	.05
☐ 442 John Cerutti	.10	.05
☐ 443 Roy Smalley	.10	.05
☐ 444 Kelly Gruber	.10	.05
☐ 445 Bob Kearney	.10	.05
☐ 446 Ed Hearn	.10	.05
☐ 447 Scott Sanderson	.10	.05
☐ 448 Bruce Benedict	.10	.05
☐ 449 Junior Ortiz	.10	.05
☐ 450 Mike Aldrete	.20	.09
☐ 451 Kevin McReynolds	.10	.05
☐ 452 Rob Murphy	.10	.05
☐ 453 Kent Tekulve	.10	.05
☐ 454 Curt Ford	.10	.05
☐ 455 Dave Lopes	.20	.09
☐ 456 Bob Grich	.20	.09
☐ 457 Jose DeLeon	.10	.05
☐ 458 Andre Dawson	.40	.18
☐ 459 Mike Flanagan	.10	.05
☐ 460 Joey Meyer	.10	.05
☐ 461 Chuck Cary	.10	.05
☐ 462 Bill Buckner	.20	.09
☐ 463 Bob Shirley	.10	.05
☐ 464 Jeff Hamilton	.10	.05
☐ 465 Phil Niekro	.40	.18
☐ 466 Mark Gubicza	.10	.05
☐ 467 Jerry Willard	.10	.05
☐ 468 Bob Sebra	.10	.05
☐ 469 Larry Parrish	.10	.05
☐ 470 Charlie Hough	.10	.05
☐ 471 Hal McRae	.20	.09
☐ 472 Dave Leiper	.10	.05
☐ 473 Mel Hall	.10	.05
☐ 474 Dan Pasqua	.10	.05
☐ 475 Bob Welch	.10	.05
☐ 476 Johnny Grubb	.10	.05
☐ 477 Jim Traber	.10	.05
☐ 478 Chris Bosio	.20	.09
☐ 479 Mark McLemore	.10	.05
☐ 480 John Morris	.10	.05
☐ 481 Billy Hatcher	.10	.05
☐ 482 Dan Schatzeder	.10	.05
☐ 483 Rich Gossage	.20	.09
☐ 484 Jim Morrison	.10	.05
☐ 485 Bob Brenly	.10	.05
☐ 486 Bill Schroeder	.10	.05
☐ 487 Mookie Wilson	.20	.09
☐ 488 Dave Martinez	.10	.05
☐ 489 Harold Reynolds	.10	.05
☐ 490 Jeff Hearron	.10	.05
☐ 491 Mickey Hatcher	.10	.05
☐ 492 Barry Larkin	2.00	.90
☐ 493 Bob James	.10	.05
☐ 494 John Habyan	.10	.05
☐ 495 Jim Adduci	.10	.05
☐ 496 Mike Heath	.10	.05
☐ 497 Tim Stoddard	.10	.05
☐ 498 Tony Armas	.10	.05
☐ 499 Dennis Powell	.10	.05
☐ 500 Checklist 452-557	.10	.05
☐ 501 Chris Bando	.10	.05
☐ 502 David Cone	1.50	.70
☐ 503 Jay Howell	.10	.05
☐ 504 Tom Foley	.10	.05
☐ 505 Ray Chadwick	.10	.05
☐ 506 Mike Loynd	.10	.05
☐ 507 Neil Allen	.10	.05
☐ 508 Danny Darwin	.10	.05
☐ 509 Rick Schu	.10	.05
☐ 510 Jose Oquendo	.10	.05
☐ 511 Gene Walter	.10	.05
☐ 512 Terry McGriff	.10	.05
☐ 513 Ken Griffey	.20	.09
☐ 514 Benny Distefano	.10	.05
☐ 515 Terry Mulholland	.20	.09
☐ 516 Ed Lynch	.10	.05
☐ 517 Bill Swift	.10	.05
☐ 518 Manny Lee	.10	.05
☐ 519 Andre David	.10	.05
☐ 520 Scott McGregor	.10	.05
☐ 521 Rick Manning	.10	.05
☐ 522 Willie Hernandez	.10	.05
☐ 523 Marty Barrett	.10	.05
☐ 524 Wayne Tolleson	.10	.05
☐ 525 Jose Gonzalez	.10	.05
☐ 526 Cory Snyder	.10	.05
☐ 527 Buddy Biancalana	.10	.05
☐ 528 Moose Haas	.10	.05
☐ 529 Wilfredo Tejada	.10	.05
☐ 530 Stu Cliburn	.10	.05
☐ 531 Dale Mohorcic	.10	.05
☐ 532 Ron Hassey	.10	.05
☐ 533 Ty Gainey	.10	.05
☐ 534 Jerry Royster	.10	.05
☐ 535 Mike Maddux	.10	.05
☐ 536 Ted Power	.10	.05
☐ 537 Ted Simmons	.20	.09
☐ 538 Rafael Belliard	.10	.05
☐ 539 Chico Walker	.10	.05
☐ 540 Bob Forsch	.10	.05
☐ 541 John Stefero	.10	.05
☐ 542 Dale Sveum	.10	.05
☐ 543 Mark Thurmond	.10	.05
☐ 544 Jeff Sellers	.10	.05
☐ 545 Joel Skinner	.10	.05
☐ 546 Alex Trevino	.10	.05
☐ 547 Randy Kutcher	.10	.05
☐ 548 Joaquin Andujar	.10	.05
☐ 549 Casey Candaele	.10	.05
☐ 550 Jeff Russell	.10	.05
☐ 551 John Candelaria	.10	.05
☐ 552 Joe Cowley	.10	.05
☐ 553 Danny Cox	.10	.05
☐ 554 Denny Walling	.10	.05
☐ 555 Bruce Ruffin	.10	.05
☐ 556 Buddy Bell	.20	.09
☐ 557 Jimmy Jones	.10	.05
☐ 558 Bobby Bonilla	1.00	.45
☐ 559 Jeff D. Robinson	.10	.05
☐ 560 Ed Olwine	.10	.05
☐ 561 Glenallen Hill	.40	.18
☐ 562 Lee Mazzilli	.10	.05
☐ 563 Mike G. Brown P	.10	.05
☐ 564 George Frazier	.10	.05
☐ 565 Mike Sharperson	.10	.05
☐ 566 Mark Portugal	.20	.09
☐ 567 Rick Leach	.10	.05
☐ 568 Mark Langston	.20	.09
☐ 569 Rafael Santana	.10	.05
☐ 570 Manny Trillo	.10	.05
☐ 571 Cliff Speck	.10	.05
☐ 572 Bob Kipper	.10	.05
☐ 573 Kelly Downs	.10	.05
☐ 574 Randy Asadoor	.10	.05
☐ 575 Dave Magadan	.20	.09
☐ 576 Marvin Freeman	.20	.09
☐ 577 Jeff Lahti	.10	.05
☐ 578 Jeff Calhoun	.10	.05
☐ 579 Gus Polidor	.10	.05
☐ 580 Gene Nelson	.10	.05
☐ 581 Tim Teufel	.10	.05
☐ 582 Odell Jones	.10	.05
☐ 583 Mark Ryal	.10	.05
☐ 584 Randy O'Neal	.10	.05
☐ 585 Mike Greenwell	.40	.18
☐ 586 Ray Knight	.20	.09
☐ 587 Ralph Bryant	.10	.05
☐ 588 Carmen Castillo	.10	.05
☐ 589 Ed Wojna	.10	.05
☐ 590 Stan Javier	.10	.05
☐ 591 Jeff Musselman	.10	.05
☐ 592 Mike Stanley	.40	.18
☐ 593 Darrell Porter	.10	.05
☐ 594 Drew Hall	.10	.05
☐ 595 Rob Nelson	.10	.05
☐ 596 Bryan Oelkers	.10	.05
☐ 597 Scott Nielsen	.10	.05
☐ 598 Brian Holton	.10	.05
☐ 599 Kevin Mitchell	.40	.18
☐ 600 Checklist 558-660	.10	.05
☐ 601 Jackie Gutierrez	.10	.05
☐ 602 Barry Jones	.10	.05
☐ 603 Jerry Narron	.10	.05
☐ 604 Steve Lake	.10	.05
☐ 605 Jim Pankovits	.10	.05
☐ 606 Ed Romero	.10	.05
☐ 607 Dave LaPoint	.10	.05
☐ 608 Don Robinson	.10	.05
☐ 609 Mike Krukow	.10	.05
☐ 610 Dave Valle	.10	.05
☐ 611 Len Dykstra	.40	.18
☐ 612 Roberto Clemente PUZ	.50	.23
☐ 613 Mike Trujillo	.10	.05
☐ 614 Damaso Garcia	.10	.05
☐ 615 Neal Heaton	.10	.05
☐ 616 Juan Berenguer	.10	.05
☐ 617 Steve Carlton	.40	.18
☐ 618 Gary Lucas	.10	.05
☐ 619 Geno Petralli	.10	.05
☐ 620 Rick Aguilera	.20	.09
☐ 621 Fred McGriff	.50	.23
☐ 622 Dave Henderson	.10	.05
☐ 623 Dave Clark	.20	.09
☐ 624 Angel Salazar	.10	.05
☐ 625 Randy Hunt	.10	.05
☐ 626 John Gibbons	.10	.05

Card	MINT	NRMT
☐ 627 Kevin Brown	1.50	.70
☐ 628 Bill Dawley	.10	.05
☐ 629 Aurelio Lopez	.10	.05
☐ 630 Charles Hudson	.10	.05
☐ 631 Ray Soff	.10	.05
☐ 632 Ray Hayward	.10	.05
☐ 633 Spike Owen	.10	.05
☐ 634 Glenn Hubbard	.10	.05
☐ 635 Kevin Elster	.40	.18
☐ 636 Mike LaCoss	.10	.05
☐ 637 Dwayne Henry	.10	.05
☐ 638 Rey Quinones	.10	.05
☐ 639 Jim Clancy	.10	.05
☐ 640 Larry Andersen	.10	.05
☐ 641 Calvin Schiraldi	.10	.05
☐ 642 Stan Jefferson	.10	.05
☐ 643 Marc Sullivan	.10	.05
☐ 644 Mark Grant	.10	.05
☐ 645 Cliff Johnson	.10	.05
☐ 646 Howard Johnson	.10	.05
☐ 647 Dave Sax	.10	.05
☐ 648 Dave Stewart	.20	.09
☐ 649 Danny Heep	.10	.05
☐ 650 Joe Johnson	.10	.05
☐ 651 Bob Brower	.10	.05
☐ 652 Rob Woodward	.10	.05
☐ 653 John Mizerock	.10	.05
☐ 654 Tim Pyznarski	.10	.05
☐ 655 Luis Aquino	.10	.05
☐ 656 Mickey Brantley	.10	.05
☐ 657 Doyle Alexander	.10	.05
☐ 658 Sammy Stewart	.10	.05
☐ 659 Jim Acker	.10	.05
☐ 660 Pete Ladd	.10	.05

1987 Donruss Wax Box Cards

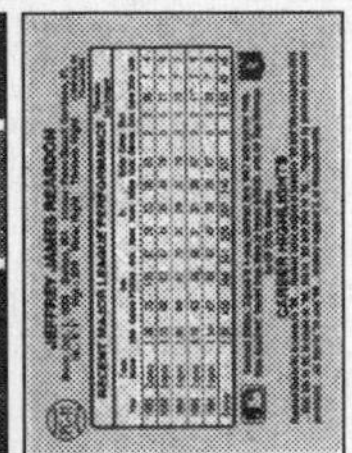

The cards in this four-card set measure the standard 2 1/2" by 3 1/2". Cards have essentially the same design as the 1987 Donruss regular issue set. The cards were printed on the bottoms of the regular issue wax pack boxes. The four cards (PC10 to PC12 plus a Roberto Clemente puzzle card) are considered a separate set in their own right and are not typically included in a complete set of the regular issue 1987 Donruss cards. The value of the panel uncut is slightly greater, perhaps by 25 percent greater, than the value of the individual cards cut up carefully.

	MINT	NRMT
COMPLETE SET (4)	2.00	.90
COMMON CARD	.25	.11
☐ PC10 Dale Murphy	.50	.23
☐ PC11 Jeff Reardon	.25	.11
☐ PC12 Jose Canseco	1.00	.45
☐ PUZ Roberto Clemente (Puzzle Card)	.75	.35

1987 Donruss Rookies

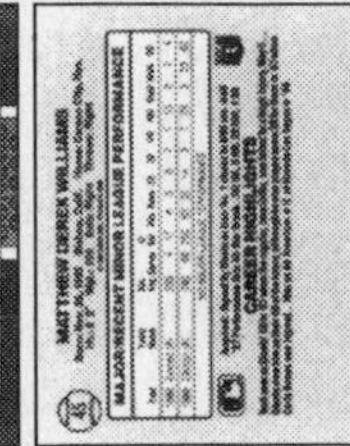

The 1987 Donruss "The Rookies" set features 56 full-color standard-size cards plus a 15-piece puzzle of Roberto Clemente. The set was distributed in factory set form packaged in a small green and black box through hobby dealers. Card fronts are similar in design to the 1987 Donruss regular issue except for the presence of "The Rookies" logo in the lower left corner and a green border instead of a black border. The key extended Rookie Cards in this set are Ellis Burks and Matt Williams. The second Donruss-issued cards of Greg Maddux and Rafael Palmeiro are also in this set.

	MINT	NRMT
COMP.FACT.SET (56)	20.00	9.00
COMMON CARD (1-56)	.10	.05
☐ 1 Mark McGwire	3.00	1.35
☐ 2 Eric Bell	.10	.05
☐ 3 Mark Williamson	.10	.05
☐ 4 Mike Greenwell	.50	.23
☐ 5 Ellis Burks	1.50	.70
☐ 6 DeWayne Buice	.10	.05
☐ 7 Mark McLemore	.10	.05
☐ 8 Devon White	.50	.23
☐ 9 Willie Fraser	.10	.05
☐ 10 Les Lancaster	.10	.05
☐ 11 Ken Williams	.10	.05
☐ 12 Matt Nokes	.25	.11
☐ 13 Jeff M. Robinson	.10	.05
☐ 14 Bo Jackson	1.00	.45
☐ 15 Kevin Seitzer	.75	.35
☐ 16 Billy Ripken	.10	.05
☐ 17 B.J. Surhoff	.75	.35
☐ 18 Chuck Crim	.10	.05
☐ 19 Mike Birkbeck	.10	.05
☐ 20 Chris Bosio	.25	.11
☐ 21 Les Straker	.10	.05
☐ 22 Mark Davidson	.10	.05
☐ 23 Gene Larkin	.25	.11
☐ 24 Ken Gerhart	.10	.05
☐ 25 Luis Polonia	.25	.11
☐ 26 Terry Steinbach	.75	.35
☐ 27 Mickey Brantley	.10	.05
☐ 28 Mike Stanley	.75	.35
☐ 29 Jerry Browne	.10	.05
☐ 30 Todd Benzinger	.10	.05
☐ 31 Fred McGriff	1.00	.45
☐ 32 Mike Henneman	.50	.23
☐ 33 Casey Candaele	.10	.05
☐ 34 Dave Magadan	.25	.11
☐ 35 David Cone	1.50	.70
☐ 36 Mike Jackson	.75	.35
☐ 37 John Mitchell	.10	.05
☐ 38 Mike Dunne	.10	.05
☐ 39 John Smiley	.25	.11
☐ 40 Joe Magrane	.10	.05
☐ 41 Jim Lindeman	.10	.05
☐ 42 Shane Mack	.25	.11
☐ 43 Stan Jefferson	.10	.05
☐ 44 Benito Santiago	.10	.05
☐ 45 Matt Williams	5.00	2.20
☐ 46 Dave Meads	.10	.05
☐ 47 Rafael Palmeiro	2.00	.90
☐ 48 Bill Long	.10	.05
☐ 49 Bob Brower	.10	.05
☐ 50 James Steels	.10	.05
☐ 51 Paul Noce	.10	.05
☐ 52 Greg Maddux	15.00	6.75
☐ 53 Jeff Musselman	.10	.05
☐ 54 Brian Holton	.10	.05
☐ 55 Chuck Jackson	.10	.05
☐ 56 Checklist 1-56	.10	.05

1987 Donruss All-Stars

This 60-card set features cards measuring approximately 3 1/2" by 5". Card fronts are in full color with a black border. The card backs are printed in black and blue on white card stock. Cards are numbered on the back. Card backs feature statistical information about the player's performance in past All-Star games. The set was distributed in packs which also contained a Pop-Up.

	MINT	NRMT
COMPLETE SET (60)	6.00	2.70
COMMON CARD (1-60)	.05	.02
☐ 1 Wally Joyner	.30	.14
☐ 2 Dave Winfield	.20	.09
☐ 3 Lou Whitaker	.10	.05
☐ 4 Kirby Puckett	1.25	.55
☐ 5 Cal Ripken	2.00	.90
☐ 6 Rickey Henderson	.40	.18
☐ 7 Wade Boggs	.40	.18
☐ 8 Roger Clemens	.75	.35
☐ 9 Lance Parrish	.10	.05
☐ 10 Dick Howser MG	.05	.02
☐ 11 Keith Hernandez	.10	.05
☐ 12 Darryl Strawberry	.10	.05
☐ 13 Ryne Sandberg	.75	.35
☐ 14 Dale Murphy	.10	.05
☐ 15 Ozzie Smith	1.00	.45
☐ 16 Tony Gwynn	1.50	.70
☐ 17 Mike Schmidt	.60	.25
☐ 18 Dwight Gooden	.20	.09
☐ 19 Gary Carter	.20	.09
☐ 20 Whitey Herzog MG	.05	.02
☐ 21 Jose Canseco	.50	.23
☐ 22 John Franco	.10	.05
☐ 23 Jesse Barfield	.05	.02
☐ 24 Rick Rhoden	.05	.02
☐ 25 Harold Baines	.10	.05
☐ 26 Sid Fernandez	.05	.02
☐ 27 George Brett	1.25	.55
☐ 28 Steve Sax	.05	.02
☐ 29 Jim Presley	.05	.02
☐ 30 Dave Smith	.05	.02
☐ 31 Eddie Murray	.60	.25
☐ 32 Mike Scott	.05	.02
☐ 33 Don Mattingly	1.00	.45
☐ 34 Dave Parker	.10	.05
☐ 35 Tony Fernandez	.05	.02
☐ 36 Tim Raines	.10	.05
☐ 37 Brook Jacoby	.05	.02
☐ 38 Chili Davis	.10	.05
☐ 39 Rich Gedman	.05	.02
☐ 40 Kevin Bass	.05	.02
☐ 41 Frank White	.10	.05
☐ 42 Glenn Davis	.05	.02
☐ 43 Willie Hernandez	.05	.02
☐ 44 Chris Brown	.05	.02
☐ 45 Jim Rice	.10	.05
☐ 46 Tony Pena	.05	.02
☐ 47 Don Aase	.05	.02
☐ 48 Hubie Brooks	.05	.02
☐ 49 Charlie Hough	.05	.02
☐ 50 Jody Davis	.05	.02
☐ 51 Mike Witt	.05	.02
☐ 52 Jeff Reardon	.05	.02
☐ 53 Ken Schrom	.05	.02
☐ 54 Fernando Valenzuela	.10	.05
☐ 55 Dave Righetti	.05	.02
☐ 56 Shane Rawley	.05	.02
☐ 57 Ted Higuera	.05	.02
☐ 58 Mike Krukow	.05	.02
☐ 59 Lloyd Moseby	.05	.02
☐ 60 Checklist Card	.05	.02

1987 Donruss All-Star Box

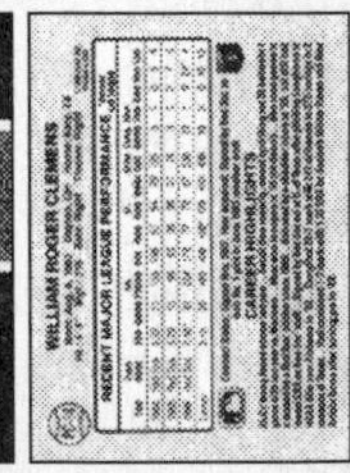

The cards in this four-card set measure the standard 2 1/2" by 3 1/2" in spite of the fact that they form the bottom of the wax pack box for the larger Donruss All-Star cards. These box cards have essentially the same design as the 1987 Donruss regular issue set. The cards were printed on the bottoms of the Donruss All-Star (3 1/2" by 5") wax pack boxes. The four cards (PC13 to PC15 plus a Roberto Clemente puzzle card) are considered a separate set in their own right and are not typically included in a complete set of the 1987 Donruss All-Star (or regular) cards. The value of the panel uncut is slightly greater, perhaps by 25 percent greater, than the value of the individual cards cut up carefully.

	MINT	NRMT
COMPLETE SET (4)	2.50	1.10
COMMON CARD	.25	.11
☐ PC13 Mike Scott	.25	.11
☐ PC14 Roger Clemens	1.00	.45
☐ PC15 Mike Krukow	.25	.11
☐ PUZ Roberto Clemente Puzzle Card	1.00	.45

1987 Donruss Highlights

Donruss' third (and last) edition of Highlights was released late in 1987. The cards are standard size and are glossy in appearance. Cards commemorate events during the 1987 season, as well as players and pitchers of the month from each league. The set was distributed in its own red, black, blue, and gold box along with a small Roberto Clemente puzzle. Card fronts are similar to the regular 1987 Donruss issue except that the Highlights logo is positioned in the lower right-hand corner and the borders are in blue instead of black. The backs are printed in black and gold on white card stock.

	MINT	NRMT
COMPLETE SET (56)	4.00	1.80
COMMON CARD (1-56)	.05	.02
☐ 1 Juan Nieves	.05	.02
☐ 2 Mike Schmidt	.25	.11
☐ 3 Eric Davis	.20	.09
☐ 4 Sid Fernandez	.05	.02
☐ 5 Brian Downing	.05	.02
☐ 6 Bret Saberhagen	.10	.05
☐ 7 Tim Raines	.10	.05
☐ 8 Eric Davis	.05	.02
☐ 9 Steve Bedrosian	.05	.02
☐ 10 Larry Parrish	.05	.02
☐ 11 Jim Clancy	.05	.02
☐ 12 Tony Gwynn UER	.50	.23
☐ 13 Orel Hershiser	.10	.05
☐ 14 Wade Boggs	.40	.18
☐ 15 Steve Ontiveros	.05	.02
☐ 16 Tim Raines	.10	.05
☐ 17 Don Mattingly	.50	.23
☐ 18 Ray Dandridge	.10	.05
☐ 19 Jim "Catfish" Hunter	.20	.09
☐ 20 Billy Williams	.20	.09
☐ 21 Bo Diaz	.05	.02
☐ 22 Floyd Youmans	.05	.02
☐ 23 Don Mattingly	.50	.23
☐ 24 Frank Viola	.05	.02
☐ 25 Bobby Witt	.10	.05
☐ 26 Kevin Seitzer	.10	.05
☐ 27 Mark McGwire	1.00	.45
☐ 28 Andre Dawson	.30	.14
☐ 29 Paul Molitor	.30	.14
☐ 30 Kirby Puckett	.50	.23
☐ 31 Andre Dawson	.30	.14
☐ 32 Doug Drabek	.10	.05
☐ 33 Dwight Evans	.10	.05
☐ 34 Mark Langston	.10	.05
☐ 35 Wally Joyner	.10	.05
☐ 36 Vince Coleman	.05	.02
☐ 37 Eddie Murray	.25	.11
☐ 38 Cal Ripken	1.00	.45
☐ 39 Fred McGriff Rob Ducey Ernie Whitt	.05	.02
☐ 40 Mark McGwire Jose Canseco	.50	.23
☐ 41 Bob Boone	.10	.05
☐ 42 Darryl Strawberry	.10	.05
☐ 43 Howard Johnson	.05	.02
☐ 44 Wade Boggs	.40	.18
☐ 45 Benito Santiago	.10	.05
☐ 46 Mark McGwire	1.00	.45
☐ 47 Kevin Seitzer	.20	.09
☐ 48 Don Mattingly	.50	.23
☐ 49 Darryl Strawberry	.10	.05
☐ 50 Pascual Perez	.05	.02
☐ 51 Alan Trammell	.20	.09
☐ 52 Doyle Alexander	.05	.02
☐ 53 Nolan Ryan	1.25	.55
☐ 54 Mark McGwire	.75	.35
☐ 55 Benito Santiago	.05	.02
☐ 56 Checklist 1-56	.05	.02

1987 Donruss Opening Day

This innovative set of 272 standard-size cards features a card for each of the players in the starting line-ups of all

the teams on Opening Day 1987. The set was packaged in a specially designed box. Cards are very similar in design to the 1987 regular Donruss issue except that these "OD" cards have a maroon border instead of a black border. Teams in the same city share a checklist card. A 15-piece puzzle of Roberto Clemente is also included with every complete set. The error on Barry Bonds (picturing Johnny Ray by mistake) was corrected very early in the press run; supposedly less than one percent of the sets have the error. Players in this set in their Rookie Card year include Will Clark, Bo Jackson, Wally Joyner and Barry Larkin.

	MINT	NRMT
COMPLETE FACT. SET (272)	10.00	4.50
COMMON CARD (1-248)	.05	.02
COMMON LOGO (249-272)	.05	.02
☐ 1 Doug DeCinces	.05	.02
☐ 2 Mike Witt	.05	.02
☐ 3 George Hendrick	.05	.02
☐ 4 Dick Schofield	.05	.02
☐ 5 Devon White	.10	.05
☐ 6 Butch Wynegar	.05	.02
☐ 7 Wally Joyner	.40	.18
☐ 8 Mark McLemore	.05	.02
☐ 9 Brian Downing	.05	.02
☐ 10 Gary Pettis	.05	.02
☐ 11 Bill Doran	.05	.02
☐ 12 Phil Garner	.05	.02
☐ 13 Jose Cruz	.05	.02
☐ 14 Kevin Bass	.05	.02
☐ 15 Mike Scott	.05	.02
☐ 16 Glenn Davis	.05	.02
☐ 17 Alan Ashby	.05	.02
☐ 18 Billy Hatcher	.05	.02
☐ 19 Craig Reynolds	.05	.02
☐ 20 Carney Lansford	.10	.05
☐ 21 Mike Davis	.05	.02
☐ 22 Reggie Jackson	.40	.18
☐ 23 Mickey Tettleton	.10	.05
☐ 24 Jose Canseco	.75	.35
☐ 25 Rob Nelson	.05	.02
☐ 26 Tony Phillips	.05	.02
☐ 27 Dwayne Murphy	.05	.02
☐ 28 Alfredo Griffin	.05	.02
☐ 29 Curt Young	.05	.02
☐ 30 Willie Upshaw	.05	.02
☐ 31 Mike Sharperson	.05	.02
☐ 32 Rance Mulliniks	.05	.02
☐ 33 Ernie Whitt	.05	.02
☐ 34 Jesse Barfield	.05	.02
☐ 35 Tony Fernandez	.05	.02
☐ 36 Lloyd Moseby	.05	.02
☐ 37 Jimmy Key	.10	.05
☐ 38 Fred McGriff	.75	.35
☐ 39 George Bell	.05	.02
☐ 40 Dale Murphy	.15	.07
☐ 41 Rick Mahler	.05	.02
☐ 42 Ken Griffey	.10	.05
☐ 43 Andres Thomas	.05	.02
☐ 44 Dion James	.05	.02
☐ 45 Ozzie Virgil	.05	.02
☐ 46 Ken Oberkfell	.05	.02
☐ 47 Gary Roenicke	.05	.02
☐ 48 Glenn Hubbard	.05	.02
☐ 49 Bill Schroeder	.05	.02
☐ 50 Greg Brock	.05	.02
☐ 51 Billy Joe Robidoux	.05	.02
☐ 52 Glenn Braggs	.05	.02
☐ 53 Jim Gantner	.05	.02
☐ 54 Paul Molitor	.50	.23
☐ 55 Dale Sveum	.05	.02
☐ 56 Ted Higuera	.05	.02
☐ 57 Rob Deer	.05	.02
☐ 58 Robin Yount	.40	.18
☐ 59 Jim Lindeman	.05	.02
☐ 60 Vince Coleman	.05	.02
☐ 61 Tommy Herr	.05	.02
☐ 62 Terry Pendleton	.10	.05
☐ 63 John Tudor	.05	.02
☐ 64 Tony Pena	.05	.02
☐ 65 Ozzie Smith	1.00	.45
☐ 66 Tito Landrum	.05	.02
☐ 67 Jack Clark	.10	.05
☐ 68 Bob Dernier	.05	.02
☐ 69 Rick Sutcliffe	.05	.02
☐ 70 Andre Dawson	.30	.14
☐ 71 Keith Moreland	.05	.02
☐ 72 Jody Davis	.05	.02
☐ 73 Brian Dayett	.05	.02
☐ 74 Leon Durham	.05	.02
☐ 75 Ryne Sandberg	1.25	.55
☐ 76 Shawon Dunston	.10	.05
☐ 77 Mike Marshall	.05	.02
☐ 78 Bill Madlock	.05	.02
☐ 79 Orel Hershiser	.10	.05
☐ 80 Mike Ramsey	.05	.02
☐ 81 Ken Landreaux	.05	.02
☐ 82 Mike Scioscia	.05	.02
☐ 83 Franklin Stubbs	.05	.02
☐ 84 Mariano Duncan	.05	.02
☐ 85 Steve Sax	.05	.02
☐ 86 Mitch Webster	.05	.02
☐ 87 Reid Nichols	.05	.02
☐ 88 Tim Wallach	.05	.02
☐ 89 Floyd Youmans	.05	.02
☐ 90 Andres Galarraga	.75	.35
☐ 91 Hubie Brooks	.05	.02
☐ 92 Jeff Reed	.05	.02
☐ 93 Alonzo Powell	.05	.02
☐ 94 Vance Law	.05	.02
☐ 95 Bob Brenly	.05	.02
☐ 96 Will Clark	1.50	.70
☐ 97 Chili Davis	.10	.05
☐ 98 Mike Krukow	.05	.02
☐ 99 Jose Uribe	.05	.02
☐ 100 Chris Brown	.05	.02
☐ 101 Robby Thompson	.05	.02
☐ 102 Candy Maldonado	.05	.02
☐ 103 Jeff Leonard	.05	.02
☐ 104 Tom Candiotti	.05	.02
☐ 105 Chris Bando	.05	.02
☐ 106 Cory Snyder	.05	.02
☐ 107 Pat Tabler	.05	.02
☐ 108 Andre Thornton	.05	.02
☐ 109 Joe Carter	.15	.07
☐ 110 Tony Bernazard	.05	.02
☐ 111 Julio Franco	.10	.05
☐ 112 Brook Jacoby	.05	.02
☐ 113 Brett Butler	.10	.05
☐ 114 Donell Nixon	.05	.02
☐ 115 Alvin Davis	.05	.02
☐ 116 Mark Langston	.05	.02
☐ 117 Harold Reynolds	.10	.05
☐ 118 Ken Phelps	.05	.02
☐ 119 Mike Kingery	.05	.02
☐ 120 Dave Valle	.05	.02
☐ 121 Rey Quinones	.05	.02
☐ 122 Phil Bradley	.05	.02
☐ 123 Jim Presley	.05	.02
☐ 124 Keith Hernandez	.10	.05
☐ 125 Kevin McReynolds	.05	.02
☐ 126 Rafael Santana	.05	.02
☐ 127 Bob Ojeda	.05	.02
☐ 128 Darryl Strawberry	.15	.07
☐ 129 Mookie Wilson	.10	.05
☐ 130 Gary Carter	.15	.07
☐ 131 Tim Teufel	.05	.02
☐ 132 Howard Johnson	.05	.02
☐ 133 Cal Ripken	2.50	1.10
☐ 134 Rick Burleson	.05	.02
☐ 135 Fred Lynn	.10	.05
☐ 136 Eddie Murray	.75	.35
☐ 137 Ray Knight	.05	.02
☐ 138 Alan Wiggins	.05	.02
☐ 139 John Shelby	.05	.02
☐ 140 Mike Boddicker	.05	.02
☐ 141 Ken Gerhart	.05	.02
☐ 142 Terry Kennedy	.05	.02
☐ 143 Steve Garvey	.10	.05
☐ 144 Marvell Wynne	.05	.02
☐ 145 Kevin Mitchell	.15	.07
☐ 146 Tony Gwynn	1.50	.70
☐ 147 Joey Cora	.20	.09
☐ 148 Benito Santiago	.10	.05
☐ 149 Eric Show	.05	.02
☐ 150 Garry Templeton	.05	.02
☐ 151 Carmelo Martinez	.05	.02
☐ 152 Von Hayes	.05	.02
☐ 153 Lance Parrish	.10	.05
☐ 154 Milt Thompson	.05	.02
☐ 155 Mike Easler	.05	.02
☐ 156 Juan Samuel	.05	.02
☐ 157 Steve Jeltz	.05	.02
☐ 158 Glenn Wilson	.05	.02
☐ 159 Shane Rawley	.05	.02
☐ 160 Mike Schmidt	.75	.35
☐ 161 Andy Van Slyke	.10	.05
☐ 162 Johnny Ray	.05	.02
☐ 163A Barry Bonds ERR	200.00	90.00

Card	MINT	NRMT
(Photo actually Johnny Ray wearing a black shirt)		
☐ 163B Barry Bonds COR	3.00	1.35
☐ 164 Junior Ortiz	.05	.02
☐ 165 Rafael Belliard	.05	.02
☐ 166 Bob Patterson	.05	.02
☐ 167 Bobby Bonilla	.75	.35
☐ 168 Sid Bream	.05	.02
☐ 169 Jim Morrison	.05	.02
☐ 170 Jerry Browne	.05	.02
☐ 171 Scott Fletcher	.05	.02
☐ 172 Ruben Sierra	.25	.11
☐ 173 Larry Parrish	.05	.02
☐ 174 Pete O'Brien	.05	.02
☐ 175 Pete Incaviglia	.10	.05
☐ 176 Don Slaught	.05	.02
☐ 177 Oddibe McDowell	.05	.02
☐ 178 Charlie Hough	.05	.02
☐ 179 Steve Buechele	.05	.02
☐ 180 Bob Stanley	.05	.02
☐ 181 Wade Boggs	.40	.18
☐ 182 Jim Rice	.10	.05
☐ 183 Bill Buckner	.10	.05
☐ 184 Dwight Evans	.10	.05
☐ 185 Spike Owen	.05	.02
☐ 186 Don Baylor	.10	.05
☐ 187 Marc Sullivan	.05	.02
☐ 188 Marty Barrett	.05	.02
☐ 189 Dave Henderson	.05	.02
☐ 190 Bo Diaz	.05	.02
☐ 191 Barry Larkin	1.50	.70
☐ 192 Kal Daniels	.05	.02
☐ 193 Terry Francona	.05	.02
☐ 194 Tom Browning	.05	.02
☐ 195 Ron Oester	.05	.02
☐ 196 Buddy Bell	.10	.05
☐ 197 Eric Davis	.15	.07
☐ 198 Dave Parker	.10	.05
☐ 199 Steve Balboni	.05	.02
☐ 200 Danny Tartabull	.10	.05
☐ 201 Ed Hearn	.05	.02
☐ 202 Buddy Biancalana	.05	.02
☐ 203 Danny Jackson	.05	.02
☐ 204 Frank White		
☐ 205 Bo Jackson	.25	.11
☐ 206 George Brett	1.50	.70
☐ 207 Kevin Seitzer	.15	.07
☐ 208 Willie Wilson	.05	.02
☐ 209 Orlando Mercado	.05	.02
☐ 210 Darrell Evans	.10	.05
☐ 211 Larry Herndon	.05	.02
☐ 212 Jack Morris	.10	.05
☐ 213 Chet Lemon	.05	.02
☐ 214 Mike Heath	.05	.02
☐ 215 Darnell Coles	.05	.02
☐ 216 Alan Trammell	.15	.07
☐ 217 Terry Harper	.05	.02
☐ 218 Lou Whitaker	.10	.05
☐ 219 Gary Gaetti	.10	.05
☐ 220 Tom Nieto	.05	.02
☐ 221 Kirby Puckett	1.50	.70
☐ 222 Tom Brunansky	.05	.02
☐ 223 Greg Gagne	.05	.02
☐ 224 Dan Gladden	.05	.02
☐ 225 Mark Davidson	.05	.02
☐ 226 Bert Blyleven	.10	.05
☐ 227 Steve Lombardozzi	.05	.02
☐ 228 Kent Hrbek	.10	.05
☐ 229 Gary Redus	.05	.02
☐ 230 Ivan Calderon	.05	.02
☐ 231 Tim Hulett	.05	.02
☐ 232 Carlton Fisk	.40	.18
☐ 233 Greg Walker	.05	.02
☐ 234 Ron Karkovice	.05	.02
☐ 235 Ozzie Guillen	.05	.02
☐ 236 Harold Baines	.10	.05
☐ 237 Donnie Hill	.05	.02
☐ 238 Rich Dotson	.05	.02
☐ 239 Mike Pagliarulo	.05	.02
☐ 240 Joel Skinner	.05	.02
☐ 241 Don Mattingly	1.25	.55
☐ 242 Gary Ward	.05	.02
☐ 243 Dave Winfield	.40	.18
☐ 244 Dan Pasqua	.05	.02
☐ 245 Wayne Tolleson	.05	.02
☐ 246 Willie Randolph	.10	.05
☐ 247 Dennis Rasmussen	.05	.02
☐ 248 Rickey Henderson	.40	.18
☐ 249 Angels Logo	.05	.02
☐ 250 Astros Logo	.05	.02
☐ 251 A's Logo	.05	.02
☐ 252 Blue Jays Logo	.05	.02
☐ 253 Braves Logo	.05	.02
☐ 254 Brewers Logo	.05	.02
☐ 255 Cardinals Logo	.05	.02
☐ 256 Dodgers Logo	.05	.02
☐ 257 Expos Logo	.05	.02
☐ 258 Giants Logo	.05	.02
☐ 259 Indians Logo	.05	.02
☐ 260 Mariners Logo	.05	.02
☐ 261 Orioles Logo	.05	.02
☐ 262 Padres Logo	.05	.02
☐ 263 Phillies Logo	.05	.02
☐ 264 Pirates Logo	.05	.02
☐ 265 Rangers Logo	.05	.02
☐ 266 Red Sox Logo	.05	.02
☐ 267 Reds Logo	.05	.02
☐ 268 Royals Logo	.05	.02
☐ 269 Tigers Logo	.05	.02
☐ 270 Twins Logo	.05	.02
☐ 271 Chicago Logos	.05	.02
☐ 272 New York Logos	.05	.02

1987 Donruss Pop-Ups

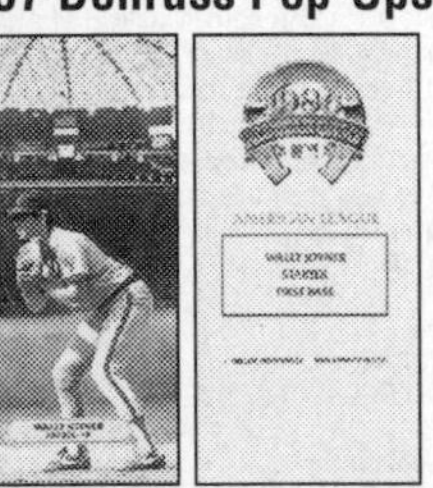

This 20-card set features "fold-out" cards measuring approximately 2 1/2" X 5". Card fronts are in full color. Cards are unnumbered but are listed in the same order as the Donruss All-Stars on the All-Star checklist card. Card backs present essentially no information about the player. The set was distributed in packs which also contained All-Star cards (3 1/2" by 5").

	MINT	NRMT
COMPLETE SET (20)	5.00	2.20
COMMON CARD (1-20)	.05	.02
☐ 1 Wally Joyner	.40	.18
☐ 2 Dave Winfield	.50	.23
☐ 3 Lou Whitaker	.10	.05
☐ 4 Kirby Puckett	1.25	.55
☐ 5 Cal Ripken	2.50	1.10
☐ 6 Rickey Henderson	.50	.23
☐ 7 Wade Boggs	.50	.23
☐ 8 Roger Clemens	.75	.35
☐ 9 Lance Parrish	.10	.05
☐ 10 Dick Howser MG	.05	.02
☐ 11 Keith Hernandez	.10	.05
☐ 12 Darryl Strawberry	.20	.09
☐ 13 Ryne Sandberg	.75	.35
☐ 14 Dale Murphy	.30	.14
☐ 15 Ozzie Smith	1.00	.45
☐ 16 Tony Gwynn	1.25	.55
☐ 17 Mike Schmidt	.75	.35
☐ 18 Dwight Gooden	.20	.09
☐ 19 Gary Carter	.20	.09
☐ 20 Whitey Herzog MG	.05	.02

1987 Donruss Super DK's

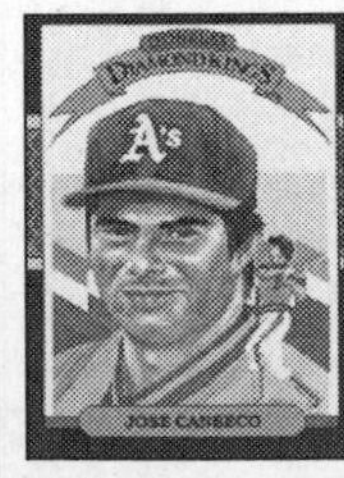

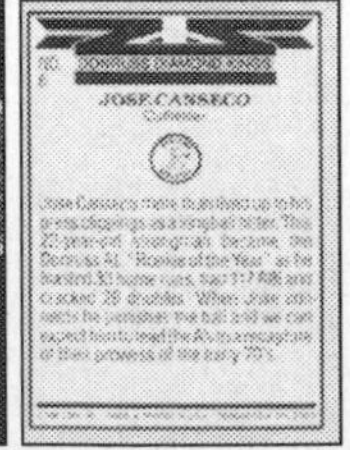

This 28-card set was available through a mail-in offer detailed on the wax packs. The set was sent in return for $8.00 and three wrappers plus $1.50 postage and handling. The set features the popular Diamond King subseries in large (approximately 4 7/8" X 6 13/16") form. Dick Perez of Perez-Steele Galleries did the original artwork from which these cards were taken. The cards are essentially a large version of the Donruss regular issue Diamond Kings.

	MINT	NRMT
COMPLETE SET (26)	12.00	5.50
COMMON CARD (1-26)	.50	.23
☐ 1 Wally Joyner	.75	.35
☐ 2 Roger Clemens	2.50	1.10
☐ 3 Dale Murphy	1.50	.70
☐ 4 Darryl Strawberry	.75	.35
☐ 5 Ozzie Smith	1.50	.70
☐ 6 Jose Canseco	1.50	.70
☐ 7 Charlie Hough	.50	.23
☐ 8 Brook Jacoby	.50	.23
☐ 9 Fred Lynn	.75	.35
☐ 10 Rick Rhoden	.50	.23
☐ 11 Chris Brown	.50	.23
☐ 12 Von Hayes	.50	.23
☐ 13 Jack Morris	.75	.35
☐ 14 Kevin McReynolds	.50	.23
☐ 15 George Brett	3.00	1.35
☐ 16 Ted Higuera	.50	.23
☐ 17 Hubie Brooks	.50	.23
☐ 18 Mike Scott	.50	.23
☐ 19 Kirby Puckett	3.00	1.35
☐ 20 Dave Winfield	1.50	.70
☐ 21 Lloyd Moseby	.50	.23
☐ 22 Eric Davis	.75	.35
☐ 23 Jim Presley	.50	.23
☐ 24 Keith Moreland	.50	.23
☐ 25 Greg Walker	.50	.23
☐ 26 Steve Sax	.50	.23
☐ NNO Roberto Clemente Large Puzzle	1.50	.70
☐ NNO DK Checklist 1-26	.50	.23

1988 Donruss

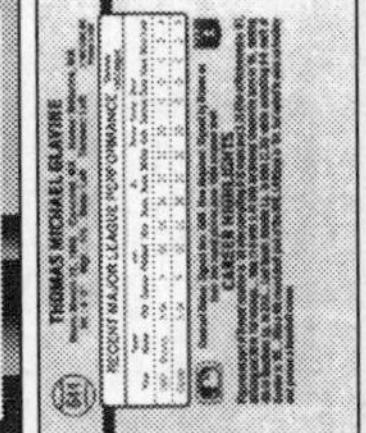

This set consists of 660 standard-size cards. For the seventh straight year, wax packs consisted of 15 cards plus a puzzle panel (featuring Stan Musial this time around). Cards were also distributed in rack packs and retail and hobby factory sets. Card fronts feature a distinctive black and blue border on the front. The card front border design pattern of the factory set card fronts is oriented differently from that of the regular wax pack cards. No premium or discount exists for either version. Subsets include Diamond Kings (1-27) and Rated Rookies (28-47). Cards marked as SP (short printed) from 648-660 are more difficult to find than the other 13 SP's in the lower 600s. These 26 cards listed as SP were apparently pulled from the printing sheet to make room for the 26 Bonus MVP cards. Numbered with the prefix "BC" for bonus card, this 26-card set featuring the most valuable player from each of the 26 teams was randomly inserted in the wax and rack packs. The cards are distinguished by the MVP logo in the upper left corner of the obverse, and cards BC14-BC26 are considered to be more difficult to find than cards BC1-BC13. Six of the checklist cards were done two different ways to reflect the inclusion or exclusion of the Bonus MVP cards in the wax packs. In the checklist below, the A variations (for the checklist cards) are from the wax packs and the B variations are from the factory-collated sets. The key Rookie Cards in this set are Roberto Alomar, Jay Bell, Jay Buhner, Ellis Burks, Ken Caminiti, Tom Glavine, Mark Grace, Gregg Jefferies and Matt Williams. There was also a Kirby Puckett card issued as the package back of Donruss blister packs; it uses a different photo from both of Kirby's regular and Bonus MVP cards and is unnumbered on the back.

	MINT	NRMT
COMPLETE SET (660)	8.00	3.60
COMPLETE FACT.SET (660)	8.00	3.60
COMMON CARD (1-660)	.05	.02
COMMON CARD SP (648-660)	.07	.03
COMPLETE MUSIAL PUZZLE	1.00	.45
☐ 1 Mark McGwire DK	.30	.14
☐ 2 Tim Raines DK	.07	.03
☐ 3 Benito Santiago DK	.05	.02
☐ 4 Alan Trammell DK	.10	.05
☐ 5 Danny Tartabull DK	.05	.02
☐ 6 Ron Darling DK	.05	.02
☐ 7 Paul Molitor DK	.20	.09
☐ 8 Devon White DK	.05	.02
☐ 9 Andre Dawson DK	.20	.09
☐ 10 Julio Franco DK	.05	.02

11 Scott Fletcher DK	.05	.02
12 Tony Fernandez DK	.05	.02
13 Shane Rawley DK	.05	.02
14 Kal Daniels DK	.05	.02
15 Jack Clark DK	.05	.02
16 Dwight Evans DK	.10	.05
17 Tommy John DK	.10	.05
18 Andy Van Slyke DK	.05	.02
19 Gary Gaetti DK	.05	.02
20 Mark Langston DK	.05	.02
21 Will Clark DK	.20	.09
22 Glenn Hubbard DK	.05	.02
23 Billy Hatcher DK	.05	.02
24 Bob Welch DK	.05	.02
25 Ivan Calderon DK	.05	.02
26 Cal Ripken DK	.40	.18
27 DK Checklist 1-26	.05	.02
28 Mackey Sasser RR	.05	.02
29 Jeff Treadway RR	.05	.02
30 Mike Campbell RR	.05	.02
31 Lance Johnson RR	.15	.07
32 Nelson Liriano RR	.05	.02
33 Shawn Abner RR	.05	.02
34 Roberto Alomar RR	1.00	.45
35 Shawn Hillegas RR	.05	.02
36 Joey Meyer RR	.05	.02
37 Kevin Elster RR	.10	.05
38 Jose Lind RR	.05	.02
39 Kirt Manwaring RR	.10	.05
40 Mark Grace RR	.60	.25
41 Jody Reed RR	.10	.05
42 John Farrell RR	.05	.02
43 Al Leiter RR	.20	.09
44 Gary Thurman RR	.05	.02
45 Vicente Palacios RR	.05	.02
46 Eddie Williams RR	.05	.02
47 Jack McDowell RR	.20	.09
48 Ken Dixon	.05	.02
49 Mike Birkbeck	.05	.02
50 Eric King	.05	.02
51 Roger Clemens	.40	.18
52 Pat Clements	.05	.02
53 Fernando Valenzuela	.10	.05
54 Mark Gubicza	.05	.02
55 Jay Howell	.05	.02
56 Floyd Youmans	.05	.02
57 Ed Correa	.05	.02
58 DeWayne Buice	.05	.02
59 Jose DeLeon	.05	.02
60 Danny Cox	.05	.02
61 Nolan Ryan	.75	.35
62 Steve Bedrosian	.05	.02
63 Tom Browning	.05	.02
64 Mark Davis	.05	.02
65 R.J. Reynolds	.05	.02
66 Kevin Mitchell	.10	.05
67 Ken Oberkfell	.05	.02
68 Rick Sutcliffe	.05	.02
69 Dwight Gooden	.10	.05
70 Scott Bankhead	.05	.02
71 Bert Blyleven	.10	.05
72 Jimmy Key	.10	.05
73 Les Straker	.05	.02
74 Jim Clancy	.05	.02
75 Mike Moore	.05	.02
76 Ron Darling	.05	.02
77 Ed Lynch	.05	.02
78 Dale Murphy	.20	.09
79 Doug Drabek	.05	.02
80 Scott Garrelts	.05	.02
81 Ed Whitson	.05	.02
82 Rob Murphy	.05	.02
83 Shane Rawley	.05	.02
84 Greg Mathews	.05	.02
85 Jim Deshaies	.05	.02
86 Mike Witt	.05	.02
87 Donnie Hill	.05	.02
88 Jeff Reed	.05	.02
89 Mike Boddicker	.05	.02
90 Ted Higuera	.05	.02
91 Walt Terrell	.05	.02
92 Bob Stanley	.05	.02
93 Dave Righetti	.05	.02
94 Orel Hershiser	.10	.05
95 Chris Bando	.05	.02
96 Bret Saberhagen	.05	.02
97 Curt Young	.05	.02
98 Tim Burke	.05	.02
99 Charlie Hough	.10	.05
100A Checklist 28-137	.05	.02
100B Checklist 28-133	.05	.02
101 Bobby Witt	.05	.02
102 George Brett	.40	.18
103 Mickey Tettleton	.10	.05
104 Scott Bailes	.05	.02
105 Mike Pagliarulo	.05	.02
106 Mike Scioscia	.05	.02
107 Tom Brookens	.05	.02
108 Ray Knight	.10	.05
109 Dan Plesac	.05	.02
110 Wally Joyner	.15	.07
111 Bob Forsch	.05	.02
112 Mike Scott	.05	.02
113 Kevin Gross	.05	.02
114 Benito Santiago	.05	.02
115 Bob Kipper	.05	.02
116 Mike Krukow	.05	.02
117 Chris Bosio	.05	.02
118 Sid Fernandez	.05	.02
119 Jody Davis	.05	.02
120 Mike Morgan	.05	.02
121 Mark Eichhorn	.05	.02
122 Jeff Reardon	.10	.05
123 John Franco	.15	.07
124 Richard Dotson	.05	.02
125 Eric Bell	.05	.02
126 Juan Nieves	.05	.02
127 Jack Morris	.15	.07
128 Rick Rhoden	.05	.02
129 Rich Gedman	.05	.02
130 Ken Howell	.05	.02
131 Brook Jacoby	.05	.02
132 Danny Jackson	.05	.02
133 Gene Nelson	.05	.02
134 Neal Heaton	.05	.02
135 Willie Fraser	.05	.02
136 Jose Guzman	.05	.02
137 Ozzie Guillen	.05	.02
138 Bob Knepper	.05	.02
139 Mike Jackson	.10	.05
140 Joe Magrane	.05	.02
141 Jimmy Jones	.05	.02
142 Ted Power	.05	.02
143 Ozzie Virgil	.05	.02
144 Felix Fermin	.05	.02
145 Kelly Downs	.05	.02
146 Shawon Dunston	.05	.02
147 Scott Bradley	.05	.02
148 Dave Stieb	.05	.02
149 Frank Viola	.05	.02
150 Terry Kennedy	.05	.02
151 Bill Wegman	.05	.02
152 Matt Nokes	.05	.02
153 Wade Boggs	.20	.09
154 Wayne Tolleson	.05	.02
155 Mariano Duncan	.05	.02
156 Julio Franco	.10	.05
157 Charlie Leibrandt	.05	.02
158 Terry Steinbach	.20	.09
159 Mike Fitzgerald	.05	.02
160 Jack Lazorko	.05	.02
161 Mitch Williams	.05	.02
162 Greg Walker	.05	.02
163 Alan Ashby	.05	.02
164 Tony Gwynn	.50	.23
165 Bruce Ruffin	.05	.02
166 Ron Robinson	.05	.02
167 Zane Smith	.05	.02
168 Junior Ortiz	.05	.02
169 Jamie Moyer	.05	.02
170 Tony Pena	.05	.02
171 Cal Ripken	.75	.35
172 B.J. Surhoff	.15	.07
173 Lou Whitaker	.10	.05
174 Ellis Burks	.30	.14
175 Ron Guidry	.05	.02
176 Steve Sax	.05	.02
177 Danny Tartabull	.05	.02
178 Carney Lansford	.10	.05
179 Casey Candaele	.05	.02
180 Scott Fletcher	.05	.02
181 Mark McLemore	.05	.02
182 Ivan Calderon	.05	.02
183 Jack Clark	.10	.05
184 Glenn Davis	.05	.02
185 Luis Aguayo	.05	.02
186 Bo Diaz	.05	.02
187 Stan Jefferson	.05	.02
188 Sid Bream	.05	.02
189 Bob Brenly	.05	.02
190 Dion James	.05	.02
191 Leon Durham	.05	.02
192 Jesse Orosco	.05	.02
193 Alvin Davis	.05	.02
194 Gary Gaetti	.05	.02
195 Fred McGriff	.20	.09
196 Steve Lombardozzi	.05	.02
197 Rance Mulliniks	.05	.02
198 Rey Quinones	.05	.02
199 Gary Carter	.15	.07
200A Checklist 138-247	.05	.02
200B Checklist 134-239	.05	.02
201 Keith Moreland	.05	.02
202 Ken Griffey	.05	.02
203 Tommy Gregg	.05	.02
204 Will Clark	.25	.11
205 John Kruk	.10	.05
206 Buddy Bell	.10	.05
207 Von Hayes	.05	.02
208 Tommy Herr	.05	.02
209 Craig Reynolds	.05	.02
210 Gary Pettis	.05	.02
211 Harold Baines	.15	.07
212 Vance Law	.05	.02
213 Ken Gerhart	.05	.02
214 Jim Gantner	.05	.02
215 Chet Lemon	.05	.02
216 Dwight Evans	.10	.05
217 Don Mattingly	.30	.14
218 Franklin Stubbs	.05	.02
219 Pat Tabler	.05	.02
220 Bo Jackson	.20	.09
221 Tony Phillips	.05	.02
222 Tim Wallach	.05	.02
223 Ruben Sierra	.05	.02
224 Steve Buechele	.05	.02
225 Frank White	.10	.05
226 Alfredo Griffin	.05	.02
227 Greg Swindell	.05	.02
228 Willie Randolph	.10	.05
229 Mike Marshall	.05	.02
230 Alan Trammell	.10	.05
231 Eddie Murray	.20	.09
232 Dale Sveum	.05	.02
233 Dick Schofield	.05	.02
234 Jose Oquendo	.05	.02
235 Bill Doran	.05	.02
236 Milt Thompson	.05	.02
237 Marvell Wynne	.05	.02
238 Bobby Bonilla	.20	.09
239 Chris Speier	.05	.02
240 Glenn Braggs	.05	.02
241 Wally Backman	.05	.02
242 Ryne Sandberg	.25	.11
243 Phil Bradley	.05	.02
244 Kelly Gruber	.05	.02
245 Tom Brunansky	.05	.02
246 Ron Oester	.05	.02
247 Bobby Thigpen	.05	.02
248 Fred Lynn	.05	.02
249 Paul Molitor	.20	.09
250 Darrell Evans	.10	.05
251 Gary Ward	.05	.02
252 Bruce Hurst	.05	.02
253 Bob Welch	.05	.02
254 Joe Carter	.20	.09
255 Willie Wilson	.05	.02
256 Mark McGwire	.60	.25
257 Mitch Webster	.05	.02
258 Brian Downing	.05	.02
259 Mike Stanley	.10	.05
260 Carlton Fisk	.20	.09
261 Billy Hatcher	.05	.02
262 Glenn Wilson	.05	.02
263 Ozzie Smith	.25	.11
264 Randy Ready	.05	.02
265 Kurt Stillwell	.05	.02
266 David Palmer	.05	.02
267 Mike Diaz	.05	.02
268 Robby Thompson	.05	.02
269 Andre Dawson	.10	.05
270 Lee Guetterman	.05	.02
271 Willie Upshaw	.05	.02
272 Randy Bush	.05	.02
273 Larry Sheets	.05	.02
274 Rob Deer	.05	.02
275 Kirk Gibson	.10	.05
276 Marty Barrett	.05	.02
277 Rickey Henderson	.20	.09
278 Pedro Guerrero	.10	.05
279 Brett Butler	.15	.07
280 Kevin Seitzer	.10	.05
281 Mike Davis	.05	.02
282 Andres Galarraga	.20	.09
283 Devon White	.15	.07
284 Pete O'Brien	.05	.02
285 Jerry Hairston	.05	.02
286 Kevin Bass	.05	.02
287 Carmelo Martinez	.05	.02
288 Juan Samuel	.05	.02
289 Kal Daniels	.05	.02
290 Albert Hall	.05	.02
291 Andy Van Slyke	.10	.05
292 Lee Smith	.10	.05
293 Vince Coleman	.05	.02
294 Tom Niedenfuer	.05	.02
295 Robin Yount	.20	.09
296 Jeff M. Robinson	.05	.02
297 Todd Benzinger	.10	.05
298 Dave Winfield	.20	.09
299 Mickey Hatcher	.05	.02

☐ 300A Checklist 248-357 .05 .02
☐ 300B Checklist 240-345 .05 .02
☐ 301 Bud Black .05 .02
☐ 302 Jose Canseco .20 .09
☐ 303 Tom Foley .05 .02
☐ 304 Pete Incaviglia .05 .02
☐ 305 Bob Boone .10 .05
☐ 306 Bill Long .05 .02
☐ 307 Willie McGee .05 .02
☐ 308 Ken Caminiti .75 .35
☐ 309 Darren Daulton .10 .05
☐ 310 Tracy Jones .05 .02
☐ 311 Greg Booker .05 .02
☐ 312 Mike LaValliere .05 .02
☐ 313 Chili Davis .20 .09
☐ 314 Glenn Hubbard .05 .02
☐ 315 Paul Noce .05 .02
☐ 316 Keith Hernandez .10 .05
☐ 317 Mark Langston .05 .02
☐ 318 Keith Atherton .05 .02
☐ 319 Tony Fernandez .05 .02
☐ 320 Kent Hrbek .10 .05
☐ 321 John Cerutti .05 .02
☐ 322 Mike Kingery .05 .02
☐ 323 Dave Magadan .05 .02
☐ 324 Rafael Palmeiro .20 .09
☐ 325 Jeff Dedmon .05 .02
☐ 326 Barry Bonds .50 .23
☐ 327 Jeffrey Leonard .05 .02
☐ 328 Tim Flannery .05 .02
☐ 329 Dave Concepcion .10 .05
☐ 330 Mike Schmidt .25 .11
☐ 331 Bill Dawley .05 .02
☐ 332 Larry Andersen .05 .02
☐ 333 Jack Howell .05 .02
☐ 334 Ken Williams .05 .02
☐ 335 Bryn Smith .05 .02
☐ 336 Billy Ripken .10 .05
☐ 337 Greg Brock .05 .02
☐ 338 Mike Heath .05 .02
☐ 339 Mike Greenwell .05 .02
☐ 340 Claudell Washington .05 .02
☐ 341 Jose Gonzalez .05 .02
☐ 342 Mel Hall .05 .02
☐ 343 Jim Eisenreich .20 .09
☐ 344 Tony Bernazard .05 .02
☐ 345 Tim Raines .10 .05
☐ 346 Bob Brower .05 .02
☐ 347 Larry Parrish .05 .02
☐ 348 Thad Bosley .05 .02
☐ 349 Dennis Eckersley .10 .05
☐ 350 Cory Snyder .05 .02
☐ 351 Rick Cerone .05 .02
☐ 352 John Shelby .05 .02
☐ 353 Larry Herndon .05 .02
☐ 354 John Habyan .05 .02
☐ 355 Chuck Crim .05 .02
☐ 356 Gus Polidor .05 .02
☐ 357 Ken Dayley .05 .02
☐ 358 Danny Darwin .05 .02
☐ 359 Lance Parrish .05 .02
☐ 360 James Steels .05 .02
☐ 361 Al Pedrique .05 .02
☐ 362 Mike Aldrete .05 .02
☐ 363 Juan Castillo .05 .02
☐ 364 Len Dykstra .10 .05
☐ 365 Luis Quinones .05 .02
☐ 366 Jim Presley .05 .02
☐ 367 Lloyd Moseby .05 .02
☐ 368 Kirby Puckett .40 .18
☐ 369 Eric Davis .10 .05
☐ 370 Gary Redus .05 .02
☐ 371 Dave Schmidt .05 .02
☐ 372 Mark Clear .05 .02
☐ 373 Dave Bergman .05 .02
☐ 374 Charles Hudson .05 .02
☐ 375 Calvin Schiraldi .05 .02
☐ 376 Alex Trevino .05 .02
☐ 377 Tom Candiotti .05 .02
☐ 378 Steve Farr .05 .02
☐ 379 Mike Gallego .05 .02
☐ 380 Andy McGaffigan .05 .02
☐ 381 Kirk McCaskill .05 .02
☐ 382 Oddibe McDowell .05 .02
☐ 383 Floyd Bannister .05 .02
☐ 384 Denny Walling .05 .02
☐ 385 Don Carman .05 .02
☐ 386 Todd Worrell .05 .02
☐ 387 Eric Show .05 .02
☐ 388 Dave Parker .15 .07
☐ 389 Rick Mahler .05 .02
☐ 390 Mike Dunne .05 .02
☐ 391 Candy Maldonado .05 .02
☐ 392 Bob Dernier .05 .02
☐ 393 Dave Valle .05 .02
☐ 394 Ernie Whitt .05 .02
☐ 395 Juan Berenguer .05 .02
☐ 396 Mike Young .05 .02
☐ 397 Mike Felder .05 .02
☐ 398 Willie Hernandez .05 .02
☐ 399 Jim Rice .10 .05
☐ 400A Checklist 358-467 .05 .02
☐ 400B Checklist 346-451 .05 .02
☐ 401 Tommy John .10 .05
☐ 402 Brian Holton .05 .02
☐ 403 Carmen Castillo .05 .02
☐ 404 Jamie Quirk .05 .02
☐ 405 Dwayne Murphy .05 .02
☐ 406 Jeff Parrett .05 .02
☐ 407 Don Sutton .20 .09
☐ 408 Jerry Browne .05 .02
☐ 409 Jim Winn .05 .02
☐ 410 Dave Smith .05 .02
☐ 411 Shane Mack .05 .02
☐ 412 Greg Gross .05 .02
☐ 413 Nick Esasky .05 .02
☐ 414 Damaso Garcia .05 .02
☐ 415 Brian Fisher .05 .02
☐ 416 Brian Dayett .05 .02
☐ 417 Curt Ford .05 .02
☐ 418 Mark Williamson .05 .02
☐ 419 Bill Schroeder .05 .02
☐ 420 Mike Henneman .10 .05
☐ 421 John Marzano .05 .02
☐ 422 Ron Kittle .05 .02
☐ 423 Matt Young .05 .02
☐ 424 Steve Balboni .05 .02
☐ 425 Luis Polonia .05 .02
☐ 426 Randy St.Claire .05 .02
☐ 427 Greg Harris .05 .02
☐ 428 Johnny Ray .05 .02
☐ 429 Ray Searage .05 .02
☐ 430 Ricky Horton .05 .02
☐ 431 Gerald Young .05 .02
☐ 432 Rick Schu .05 .02
☐ 433 Paul O'Neill .15 .07
☐ 434 Rich Gossage .10 .05
☐ 435 John Cangelosi .05 .02
☐ 436 Mike LaCoss .05 .02
☐ 437 Gerald Perry .05 .02
☐ 438 Dave Martinez .05 .02
☐ 439 Darryl Strawberry .10 .05
☐ 440 John Moses .05 .02
☐ 441 Greg Gagne .05 .02
☐ 442 Jesse Barfield .05 .02
☐ 443 George Frazier .05 .02
☐ 444 Garth Iorg .05 .02
☐ 445 Ed Nunez .05 .02
☐ 446 Rick Aguilera .10 .05
☐ 447 Jerry Mumphrey .05 .02
☐ 448 Rafael Ramirez .05 .02
☐ 449 John Smiley .10 .05
☐ 450 Atlee Hammaker .05 .02
☐ 451 Lance McCullers .05 .02
☐ 452 Guy Hoffman .05 .02
☐ 453 Chris James .05 .02
☐ 454 Terry Pendleton .10 .05
☐ 455 Dave Meads .05 .02
☐ 456 Bill Buckner .10 .05
☐ 457 John Pawlowski .05 .02
☐ 458 Bob Sebra .05 .02
☐ 459 Jim Dwyer .05 .02
☐ 460 Jay Aldrich .05 .02
☐ 461 Frank Tanana .05 .02
☐ 462 Oil Can Boyd .05 .02
☐ 463 Dan Pasqua .05 .02
☐ 464 Tim Crews .05 .02
☐ 465 Andy Allanson .05 .02
☐ 466 Bill Pecota .05 .02
☐ 467 Steve Ontiveros .05 .02
☐ 468 Hubie Brooks .05 .02
☐ 469 Paul Kilgus .05 .02
☐ 470 Dale Mohorcic .05 .02
☐ 471 Dan Quisenberry .05 .02
☐ 472 Dave Stewart .10 .05
☐ 473 Dave Clark .05 .02
☐ 474 Joel Skinner .05 .02
☐ 475 Dave Anderson .05 .02
☐ 476 Dan Petry .05 .02
☐ 477 Carl Nichols .05 .02
☐ 478 Ernest Riles .05 .02
☐ 479 George Hendrick .05 .02
☐ 480 John Morris .05 .02
☐ 481 Manny Hernandez .05 .02
☐ 482 Jeff Stone .05 .02
☐ 483 Chris Brown .05 .02
☐ 484 Mike Bielecki .05 .02
☐ 485 Dave Dravecky .10 .05
☐ 486 Rick Manning .05 .02
☐ 487 Bill Almon .05 .02
☐ 488 Jim Sundberg .05 .02
☐ 489 Ken Phelps .05 .02
☐ 490 Tom Henke .05 .02
☐ 491 Dan Gladden .05 .02
☐ 492 Barry Larkin .30 .1
☐ 493 Fred Manrique .05 .02
☐ 494 Mike Griffin .05 .02
☐ 495 Mark Knudson .05 .02
☐ 496 Bill Madlock .05 .02
☐ 497 Tim Stoddard .05 .02
☐ 498 Sam Horn .05 .02
☐ 499 Tracy Woodson .05 .0
☐ 500A Checklist 468-577 .05 .0
☐ 500B Checklist 452-557 .05 .0
☐ 501 Ken Schrom .05 .02
☐ 502 Angel Salazar .05 .02
☐ 503 Eric Plunk .05 .02
☐ 504 Joe Hesketh .05 .02
☐ 505 Greg Minton .05 .02
☐ 506 Geno Petralli .05 .02
☐ 507 Bob James .05 .02
☐ 508 Robbie Wine .05 .02
☐ 509 Jeff Calhoun .05 .02
☐ 510 Steve Lake .05 .02
☐ 511 Mark Grant .05 .02
☐ 512 Frank Williams .05 .02
☐ 513 Jeff Blauser .25 .1
☐ 514 Bob Walk .05 .02
☐ 515 Craig Lefferts .05 .02
☐ 516 Manny Trillo .05 .02
☐ 517 Jerry Reed .05 .02
☐ 518 Rick Leach .05 .02
☐ 519 Mark Davidson .05 .02
☐ 520 Jeff Ballard .05 .02
☐ 521 Dave Stapleton .05 .02
☐ 522 Pat Sheridan .05 .02
☐ 523 Al Nipper .05 .02
☐ 524 Steve Trout .05 .02
☐ 525 Jeff Hamilton .05 .02
☐ 526 Tommy Hinzo .05 .02
☐ 527 Lonnie Smith .05 .02
☐ 528 Greg Cadaret .05 .02
☐ 529 Bob McClure UER .05 .02
(Rob on front)
☐ 530 Chuck Finley .10 .05
☐ 531 Jeff Russell .05 .02
☐ 532 Steve Lyons .05 .02
☐ 533 Terry Puhl .05 .02
☐ 534 Eric Nolte .05 .02
☐ 535 Kent Tekulve .05 .02
☐ 536 Pat Pacillo .05 .02
☐ 537 Charlie Puleo .05 .02
☐ 538 Tom Prince .05 .02
☐ 539 Greg Maddux 1.25 .55
☐ 540 Jim Lindeman .05 .02
☐ 541 Pete Stanicek .05 .02
☐ 542 Steve Kiefer .05 .02
☐ 543A Jim Morrison ERR .20 .09
(No decimal before lifetime average)
☐ 543B Jim Morrison COR .05 .02
☐ 544 Spike Owen .05 .02
☐ 545 Jay Buhner .60 .25
☐ 546 Mike Devereaux .15 .07
☐ 547 Jerry Don Gleaton .05 .02
☐ 548 Jose Rijo .05 .02
☐ 549 Dennis Martinez .10 .05
☐ 550 Mike Loynd .05 .02
☐ 551 Darrell Miller .05 .02
☐ 552 Dave LaPoint .05 .02
☐ 553 John Tudor .05 .02
☐ 554 Rocky Childress .05 .02
☐ 555 Wally Ritchie .05 .02
☐ 556 Terry McGriff .05 .02
☐ 557 Dave Leiper .05 .02
☐ 558 Jeff D. Robinson .05 .02
☐ 559 Jose Uribe .05 .02
☐ 560 Ted Simmons .10 .05
☐ 561 Les Lancaster .05 .02
☐ 562 Keith A. Miller .05 .02
☐ 563 Harold Reynolds .05 .02
☐ 564 Gene Larkin .05 .02
☐ 565 Cecil Fielder .20 .09
☐ 566 Roy Smalley .05 .02
☐ 567 Duane Ward .05 .02
☐ 568 Bill Wilkinson .05 .02
☐ 569 Howard Johnson .05 .02
☐ 570 Frank DiPino .05 .02
☐ 571 Pete Smith .05 .02
☐ 572 Darnell Coles .05 .02
☐ 573 Don Robinson .05 .02
☐ 574 Rob Nelson UER .05 .02
(Career 0 RBI, but 1 RBI in '87)
☐ 575 Dennis Rasmussen .05 .02
☐ 576 Steve Jeltz UER .05 .02
(Photo actually Juan Samuel; Samuel noted for one batting glove and black bat)
☐ 577 Tom Pagnozzi .10 .05

☐ 578 Ty Gainey	.05	.02
☐ 579 Gary Lucas	.05	.02
☐ 580 Ron Hassey	.05	.02
☐ 581 Herm Winningham	.05	.02
☐ 582 Rene Gonzales	.05	.02
☐ 583 Brad Komminsk	.05	.02
☐ 584 Doyle Alexander	.05	.02
☐ 585 Jeff Sellers	.05	.02
☐ 586 Bill Gullickson	.05	.02
☐ 587 Tim Belcher	.05	.02
☐ 588 Doug Jones	.20	.09
☐ 589 Melido Perez	.10	.05
☐ 590 Rick Honeycutt	.05	.02
☐ 591 Pascual Perez	.05	.02
☐ 592 Curt Wilkerson	.05	.02
☐ 593 Steve Howe	.05	.02
☐ 594 John Davis	.05	.02
☐ 595 Storm Davis	.05	.02
☐ 596 Sammy Stewart	.05	.02
☐ 597 Neil Allen	.05	.02
☐ 598 Alejandro Pena	.05	.02
☐ 599 Mark Thurmond	.05	.02
☐ 600A Checklist 578-660/BC1-BC26	.05	02
☐ 600B Checklist 558-660	.05	.02
☐ 601 Jose Mesa	.20	.09
☐ 602 Don August	.05	.02
☐ 603 Terry Leach SP	.07	.03
☐ 604 Tom Newell	.05	.02
☐ 605 Randall Byers SP	.07	.03
☐ 606 Jim Gott	.05	.02
☐ 607 Harry Spilman	.05	.02
☐ 608 John Candelaria	.05	.02
☐ 609 Mike Brumley	.05	.02
☐ 610 Mickey Brantley	.05	.02
☐ 611 Jose Nunez SP	.07	.03
☐ 612 Tom Nieto	.05	.02
☐ 613 Rick Reuschel	.05	.02
☐ 614 Lee Mazzilli SP	.07	.03
☐ 615 Scott Lusader	.05	.02
☐ 616 Bobby Meacham	.05	.02
☐ 617 Kevin McReynolds SP	.07	.03
☐ 618 Gene Garber	.05	.02
☐ 619 Barry Lyons SP	.07	.03
☐ 620 Randy Myers	.15	.07
☐ 621 Donnie Moore	.05	.02
☐ 622 Domingo Ramos	.05	.02
☐ 623 Ed Romero	.05	.02
☐ 624 Greg Myers	.05	.02
☐ 625 Ripken Family Cal Ripken Sr. Cal Ripken Jr. Billy Ripken	.40	.18
☐ 626 Pat Perry	.05	.02
☐ 627 Andres Thomas SP	.07	.03
☐ 628 Matt Williams SP	.75	.35
☐ 629 Dave Hengel	.05	.02
☐ 630 Jeff Musselman SP	.07	.03
☐ 631 Tim Laudner	.05	.02
☐ 632 Bob Ojeda SP	.07	.03
☐ 633 Rafael Santana	.05	.02
☐ 634 Wes Gardner	.05	.02
☐ 635 Roberto Kelly SP	.20	.09
☐ 636 Mike Flanagan SP	.07	.03
☐ 637 Jay Bell	.25	.11
☐ 638 Bob Melvin	.05	.02
☐ 639 Damon Berryhill UER (Bats: Swithch)	.05	.02
☐ 640 David Wells SP	.07	.03
☐ 641 Stan Musial PUZ	.20	.09
☐ 642 Doug Sisk	.05	.02
☐ 643 Keith Hughes	.05	.02
☐ 644 Tom Glavine	.50	.23
☐ 645 Al Newman	.05	.02
☐ 646 Scott Sanderson	.05	.02
☐ 647 Scott Terry	.05	.02
☐ 648 Tim Teufel SP	.07	.03
☐ 649 Garry Templeton SP	.07	.03
☐ 650 Manny Lee SP	.07	.03
☐ 651 Roger McDowell SP	.07	.03
☐ 652 Mookie Wilson SP	.20	.09
☐ 653 David Cone SP	.30	.14
☐ 654 Ron Gant SP	.15	.07
☐ 655 Joe Price SP	.07	.03
☐ 656 George Bell SP	.10	.05
☐ 657 Gregg Jefferies SP	.25	.11
☐ 658 Todd Stottlemyre SP	.20	.09
☐ 659 Geronimo Berroa SP	.25	.11
☐ 660 Jerry Royster SP	.07	.03

1988 Donruss Bonus MVP's

Numbered with the prefix "BC" for bonus card, this 26-card set featuring the most valuable player from each major league team was randomly inserted in the wax and rack packs. The cards are distinguished by the MVP logo in the upper left corner of the obverse, and cards BC14-

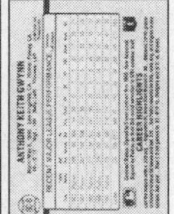

BC26 are considered to be more difficult to find than cards BC1-BC13.

	MINT	NRMT
COMPLETE SET (26)	3.00	1.35
COMMON CARD (BC1-BC13)	.05	.02
COMMON CARD (BC14-BC26)	.10	.05
☐ BC1 Cal Ripken	.50	.23
☐ BC2 Eric Davis	.10	.05
☐ BC3 Paul Molitor	.20	.09
☐ BC4 Mike Schmidt	.25	.11
☐ BC5 Ivan Calderon	.05	.02
☐ BC6 Tony Gwynn	.30	.14
☐ BC7 Wade Boggs	.15	.07
☐ BC8 Andy Van Slyke	.10	.05
☐ BC9 Joe Carter	.15	.07
☐ BC10 Andre Dawson	.10	.05
☐ BC11 Alan Trammell	.10	.05
☐ BC12 Mike Scott	.05	.02
☐ BC13 Wally Joyner	.15	.07
☐ BC14 Dale Murphy SP	.15	.07
☐ BC15 Kirby Puckett SP	.40	.18
☐ BC16 Pedro Guerrero SP	.10	.05
☐ BC17 Kevin Seitzer SP	.10	.05
☐ BC18 Tim Raines SP	.10	.05
☐ BC19 George Bell SP	.10	.05
☐ BC20 Darryl Strawberry SP	.10	.05
☐ BC21 Don Mattingly SP	.50	.23
☐ BC22 Ozzie Smith SP	.30	.14
☐ BC23 Mark McGwire SP	.60	.25
☐ BC24 Will Clark SP	.15	.07
☐ BC25 Alvin Davis SP	.10	.05
☐ BC26 Ruben Sierra SP	.15	.07

1988 Donruss Rookies

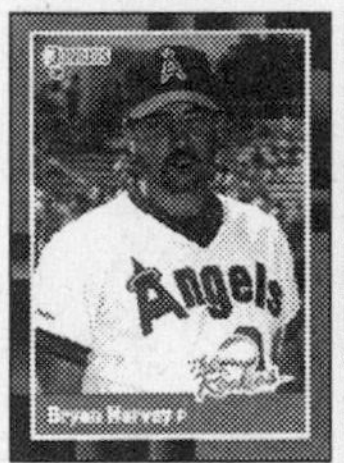

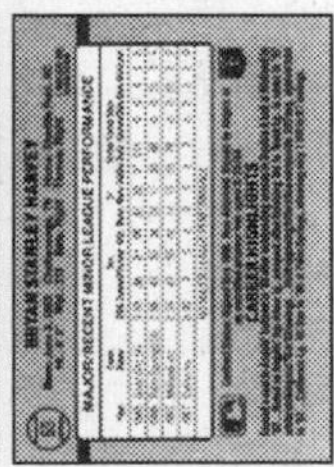

The 1988 Donruss "The Rookies" set features 56 standard-size full-color cards plus a 15-piece puzzle of Stan Musial. This set was distributed exclusively in factory set form in a small, cellophane-wrapped, green and black through hobby dealers. Card fronts are similar in design to the 1988 Donruss regular issue except for the presence of "The Rookies" logo in the lower right corner and a green and black border instead of a blue and black border on the fronts. Extended Rookie Cards in this set include Brady Anderson, Edgar Martinez, and Walt Weiss. Notable second cards were issued of Roberto Alomar and Jay Buhner.

	MINT	NRMT
COMP.FACT.SET (56)	12.00	5.50
COMMON CARD (1-56)	.15	.07
☐ 1 Mark Grace	2.00	.90
☐ 2 Mike Campbell	.15	.07
☐ 3 Todd Frohwirth	.15	.07
☐ 4 Dave Stapleton	.15	.07
☐ 5 Shawn Abner	.15	.07
☐ 6 Jose Cecena	.15	.07
☐ 7 Dave Gallagher	.15	.07
☐ 8 Mark Parent	.15	.07
☐ 9 Cecil Espy	.15	.07
☐ 10 Pete Smith	.15	.07
☐ 11 Jay Buhner	2.50	1.10
☐ 12 Pat Borders	.30	.14
☐ 13 Doug Jennings	.15	.07
☐ 14 Brady Anderson	2.50	1.10
☐ 15 Pete Stanicek	.15	.07
☐ 16 Roberto Kelly	.30	.14
☐ 17 Jeff Treadway	.15	.07
☐ 18 Walt Weiss	.30	.14
☐ 19 Paul Gibson	.15	.07
☐ 20 Tim Crews	.15	.07
☐ 21 Melido Perez	.15	.07
☐ 22 Steve Peters	.15	.07
☐ 23 Craig Worthington	.15	.07
☐ 24 John Trautwein	.15	.07
☐ 25 DeWayne Vaughn	.15	.07
☐ 26 David Wells	.30	.14
☐ 27 Al Leiter	.60	.25
☐ 28 Tim Belcher	.30	.14
☐ 29 Johnny Paredes	.15	.07
☐ 30 Chris Sabo	.30	.14
☐ 31 Damon Berryhill	.15	.07
☐ 32 Randy Milligan	.15	.07
☐ 33 Gary Thurman	.15	.07
☐ 34 Kevin Elster	.30	.14
☐ 35 Roberto Alomar	5.00	2.20
☐ 36 Edgar Martinez UER (Photo actually Edwin Nunez)	2.50	1.10
☐ 37 Todd Stottlemyre	.60	.25
☐ 38 Joey Meyer	.15	.07
☐ 39 Carl Nichols	.15	.07
☐ 40 Jack McDowell	.60	.25
☐ 41 Jose Bautista	.15	.07
☐ 42 Sil Campusano	.15	.07
☐ 43 John Dopson	.15	.07
☐ 44 Jody Reed	.30	.14
☐ 45 Darrin Jackson	.15	.07
☐ 46 Mike Capel	.15	.07
☐ 47 Ron Gant	.60	.25
☐ 48 John Davis	.15	.07
☐ 49 Kevin Coffman	.15	.07
☐ 50 Cris Carpenter	.15	.07
☐ 51 Mackey Sasser	.15	.07
☐ 52 Luis Alicea	.30	.14
☐ 53 Bryan Harvey	.30	.14
☐ 54 Steve Ellsworth	.15	.07
☐ 55 Mike Macfarlane	.30	.14
☐ 56 Checklist 1-56	.15	.07

1988 Donruss All-Stars

This 64-card set features cards measures the standard size. Card fronts are in full color with a solid blue and black border. The card backs are printed in black and blue on white card stock. Cards are numbered on the back inside a blue star in the upper right hand corner. Card backs feature statistical information about the player's performance in past All-Star games. The set was distributed in packs which also contained a Pop-Up. The AL Checklist card number 32 has two uncorrected errors on it, Wade Boggs is erroneously listed as the AL Leftfielder and Dan Plesac is erroneously listed as being on the Tigers.

	MINT	NRMT
COMPLETE SET (64)	8.00	3.60
COMMON CARD (1-64)	.05	.02
☐ 1 Don Mattingly	1.00	.45
☐ 2 Dave Winfield	.30	.14
☐ 3 Willie Randolph	.05	.02
☐ 4 Rickey Henderson	.30	.14
☐ 5 Cal Ripken	2.50	1.10
☐ 6 George Bell	.05	.02
☐ 7 Wade Boggs	.50	.23
☐ 8 Bret Saberhagen	.10	.05
☐ 9 Terry Kennedy	.05	.02
☐ 10 John McNamara MG	.05	.02
☐ 11 Jay Howell	.05	.02
☐ 12 Harold Baines	.10	.05
☐ 13 Harold Reynolds	.10	.05
☐ 14 Bruce Hurst	.05	.02
☐ 15 Kirby Puckett	1.50	.70
☐ 16 Matt Nokes	.05	.02
☐ 17 Pat Tabler	.05	.02
☐ 18 Dan Plesac	.05	.02
☐ 19 Mark McGwire	2.00	.90
☐ 20 Mike Witt	.05	.02
☐ 21 Larry Parrish	.05	.02

☐ 22 Alan Trammell .20 .09
☐ 23 Dwight Evans .10 .05
☐ 24 Jack Morris .10 .05
☐ 25 Tony Fernandez .05 .02
☐ 26 Mark Langston .05 .02
☐ 27 Kevin Seitzer .10 .05
☐ 28 Tom Henke .05 .02
☐ 29 Dave Righetti .05 .02
☐ 30 Oakland Stadium .05 .02
☐ 31 Wade Boggs .40 .18
(Top AL Vote Getter)
☐ 32 AL Checklist UER .05 .02
☐ 33 Jack Clark .10 .05
☐ 34 Darryl Strawberry .10 .05
☐ 35 Ryne Sandberg .75 .35
☐ 36 Andre Dawson .30 .14
☐ 37 Ozzie Smith 1.00 .45
☐ 38 Eric Davis .10 .05
☐ 39 Mike Schmidt .75 .35
☐ 40 Mike Scott .05 .02
☐ 41 Gary Carter .20 .09
☐ 42 Davey Johnson MG .05 .02
☐ 43 Rick Sutcliffe .05 .02
☐ 44 Willie McGee .10 .05
☐ 45 Hubie Brooks .05 .02
☐ 46 Dale Murphy .30 .14
☐ 47 Bo Diaz .05 .02
☐ 48 Pedro Guerrero .05 .02
☐ 49 Keith Hernandez .10 .05
☐ 50 Ozzie Virgil UER .05 .02
(Phillies logo
on card back,
wrong birth year)
☐ 51 Tony Gwynn 1.25 .55
☐ 52 Rick Reuschel UER .05 .02
(Pirates logo
on card back)
☐ 53 John Franco .10 .05
☐ 54 Jeffrey Leonard .05 .02
☐ 55 Juan Samuel .05 .02
☐ 56 Orel Hershiser .10 .05
☐ 57 Tim Raines .10 .05
☐ 58 Sid Fernandez .05 .02
☐ 59 Tim Wallach .05 .02
☐ 60 Lee Smith .10 .05
☐ 61 Steve Bedrosian .05 .02
☐ 62 Tim Raines .10 .05
☐ 63 Ozzie Smith 1.00 .45
(Top NL Vote Getter)
☐ 64 NL Checklist .05 .02

1988 Donruss Baseball's Best

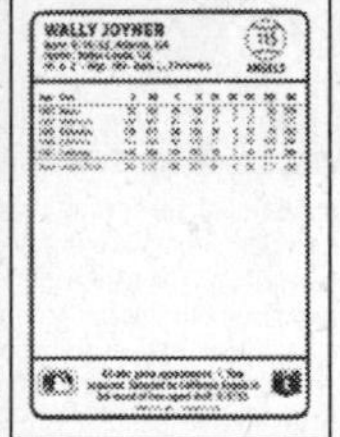

This innovative set of 336 standard-size cards was released by Donruss very late in the 1988 season to be sold in large national retail chains as a complete packaged set. The set was packaged in a specially designed box. Cards are very similar in design to the 1988 regular Donruss issue except that these cards have orange and black borders instead of blue and black borders. The set is also sometimes referred to as the Halloween set because of the orange box and design of the cards. Six (2 1/2" by 3 1/2") 15-piece puzzles of Stan Musial are also included with every complete set.

	MINT	NRMT
COMPLETE SET (336)	15.00	6.75
COMMON CARD (1-336)	.05	.02

☐ 1 Don Mattingly 1.00 .45
☐ 2 Ron Gant .50 .23
☐ 3 Bob Boone .10 .05
☐ 4 Mark Grace 1.50 .70
☐ 5 Andy Allanson .05 .02
☐ 6 Kal Daniels .05 .02
☐ 7 Floyd Bannister .05 .02
☐ 8 Alan Ashby .05 .02
☐ 9 Marty Barrett .05 .02
☐ 10 Tim Belcher .05 .02
☐ 11 Harold Baines .10 .05
☐ 12 Hubie Brooks .05 .02
☐ 13 Doyle Alexander .05 .02
☐ 14 Gary Carter .15 .07
☐ 15 Glenn Braggs .05 .02
☐ 16 Steve Bedrosian .05 .02
☐ 17 Barry Bonds 1.00 .45
☐ 18 Bert Blyleven .10 .05
☐ 19 Tom Brunansky .05 .02
☐ 20 John Candelaria .05 .02
☐ 21 Shawn Abner .05 .02
☐ 22 Jose Canseco .40 .18
☐ 23 Brett Butler .10 .05
☐ 24 Scott Bradley .05 .02
☐ 25 Ivan Calderon .05 .02
☐ 26 Rich Gossage .10 .05
☐ 27 Brian Downing .05 .02
☐ 28 Jim Rice .10 .05
☐ 29 Dion James .05 .02
☐ 30 Terry Kennedy .05 .02
☐ 31 George Bell .05 .02
☐ 32 Scott Fletcher .05 .02
☐ 33 Bobby Bonilla .15 .07
☐ 34 Tim Burke .05 .02
☐ 35 Darrell Evans .10 .05
☐ 36 Mike Davis .05 .02
☐ 37 Shawon Dunston .05 .02
☐ 38 Kevin Bass .05 .02
☐ 39 George Brett 1.25 .55
☐ 40 David Cone .35 .16
☐ 41 Ron Darling .05 .02
☐ 42 Roberto Alomar 2.00 .90
☐ 43 Dennis Eckersley .15 .07
☐ 44 Vince Coleman .05 .02
☐ 45 Sid Bream .05 .02
☐ 46 Gary Gaetti .10 .05
☐ 47 Phil Bradley .05 .02
☐ 48 Jim Clancy .05 .02
☐ 49 Jack Clark .10 .05
☐ 50 Mike Krukow .05 .02
☐ 51 Henry Cotto .05 .02
☐ 52 Rich Dotson .05 .02
☐ 53 Jim Gantner .05 .02
☐ 54 John Franco .10 .05
☐ 55 Pete Incaviglia .05 .02
☐ 56 Joe Carter .35 .16
☐ 57 Roger Clemens 1.00 .45
☐ 58 Gerald Perry .05 .02
☐ 59 Jack Howell .05 .02
☐ 60 Vance Law .05 .02
☐ 61 Jay Bell .25 .11
☐ 62 Eric Davis .10 .05
☐ 63 Gene Garber .10 .05
☐ 64 Glenn Davis .05 .02
☐ 65 Wade Boggs .40 .18
☐ 66 Kirk Gibson .10 .05
☐ 67 Carlton Fisk .40 .18
☐ 68 Casey Candaele .05 .02
☐ 69 Mike Heath .05 .02
☐ 70 Kevin Elster .15 .07
☐ 71 Greg Brock .05 .02
☐ 72 Don Carman .05 .02
☐ 73 Doug Drabek .10 .05
☐ 74 Greg Gagne .05 .02
☐ 75 Danny Cox .05 .02
☐ 76 Rickey Henderson .35 .16
☐ 77 Chris Brown .05 .02
☐ 78 Terry Steinbach .10 .05
☐ 79 Will Clark .40 .18
☐ 80 Mickey Brantley .05 .02
☐ 81 Ozzie Guillen .10 .05
☐ 82 Greg Maddux 2.50 1.10
☐ 83 Kirk McCaskill .05 .02
☐ 84 Dwight Evans .10 .05
☐ 85 Ozzie Virgil .05 .02
☐ 86 Mike Morgan .05 .02
☐ 87 Tony Fernandez .05 .02
☐ 88 Jose Guzman .05 .02
☐ 89 Mike Dunne .05 .02
☐ 90 Andres Galarraga .50 .23
☐ 91 Mike Henneman .10 .05
☐ 92 Alfredo Griffin .05 .02
☐ 93 Rafael Palmeiro .40 .18
☐ 94 Jim Deshaies .05 .02
☐ 95 Mark Gubicza .05 .02
☐ 96 Dwight Gooden .10 .05
☐ 97 Howard Johnson .05 .02
☐ 98 Mark Davis .05 .02
☐ 99 Dave Stewart .10 .05
☐ 100 Joe Magrane .05 .02
☐ 101 Brian Fisher .05 .02
☐ 102 Kent Hrbek .10 .05
☐ 103 Kevin Gross .05 .02
☐ 104 Tom Henke .05 .02
☐ 105 Mike Pagliarulo .05 .02
☐ 106 Kelly Downs .05 .02
☐ 107 Alvin Davis .05 .02
☐ 108 Willie Randolph .05 .02
☐ 109 Rob Deer .05 .02
☐ 110 Bo Diaz .05 .02
☐ 111 Paul Kilgus .05 .02
☐ 112 Tom Candiotti .05 .02
☐ 113 Dale Murphy .25 .11
☐ 114 Rick Mahler .05 .02
☐ 115 Wally Joyner .15 .07
☐ 116 Ryne Sandberg 1.00 .45
☐ 117 John Farrell .05 .02
☐ 118 Nick Esasky .05 .02
☐ 119 Bo Jackson .15 .07
☐ 120 Bill Doran .05 .02
☐ 121 Ellis Burks .40 .18
☐ 122 Pedro Guerrero .05 .02
☐ 123 Dave LaPoint .05 .02
☐ 124 Neal Heaton .05 .02
☐ 125 Willie Hernandez .05 .02
☐ 126 Roger McDowell .05 .02
☐ 127 Ted Higuera .05 .02
☐ 128 Von Hayes .05 .02
☐ 129 Mike LaValliere .05 .02
☐ 130 Dan Gladden .05 .02
☐ 131 Willie McGee .10 .05
☐ 132 Al Leiter .25 .11
☐ 133 Mark Grant .05 .02
☐ 134 Bob Welch .05 .02
☐ 135 Dave Dravecky .05 .02
☐ 136 Mark Langston .05 .02
☐ 137 Dan Pasqua .05 .02
☐ 138 Rick Sutcliffe .10 .05
☐ 139 Dan Petry .05 .02
☐ 140 Rich Gedman .05 .02
☐ 141 Ken Griffey Sr. .10 .05
☐ 142 Eddie Murray .50 .23
☐ 143 Jimmy Key .10 .05
☐ 144 Dale Mohorcic .05 .02
☐ 145 Jose Lind .05 .02
☐ 146 Dennis Martinez .10 .05
☐ 147 Chet Lemon .05 .02
☐ 148 Orel Hershiser .15 .07
☐ 149 Dave Martinez .05 .02
☐ 150 Billy Hatcher .05 .02
☐ 151 Charlie Leibrandt .05 .02
☐ 152 Keith Hernandez .10 .05
☐ 153 Kevin McReynolds .05 .02
☐ 154 Tony Gwynn 1.50 .70
☐ 155 Stan Javier .05 .02
☐ 156 Tony Pena .05 .02
☐ 157 Andy Van Slyke .10 .05
☐ 158 Gene Larkin .05 .02
☐ 159 Chris James .05 .02
☐ 160 Fred McGriff .40 .18
☐ 161 Rick Rhoden .05 .02
☐ 162 Scott Garrelts .05 .02
☐ 163 Mike Campbell .05 .02
☐ 164 Dave Righetti .05 .02
☐ 165 Paul Molitor .40 .18
☐ 166 Danny Jackson .05 .02
☐ 167 Pete O'Brien .05 .02
☐ 168 Julio Franco .10 .05
☐ 169 Mark McGwire 1.50 .70
☐ 170 Zane Smith .05 .02
☐ 171 Johnny Ray .05 .02
☐ 172 Les Lancaster .05 .02
☐ 173 Mel Hall .05 .02
☐ 174 Tracy Jones .05 .02
☐ 175 Kevin Seitzer .10 .05
☐ 176 Bob Knepper .05 .02
☐ 177 Mike Greenwell .10 .05
☐ 178 Mike Marshall .05 .02
☐ 179 Melido Perez .05 .02
☐ 180 Tim Raines .10 .05
☐ 181 Jack Morris .10 .05
☐ 182 Darryl Strawberry .10 .05
☐ 183 Robin Yount .25 .11
☐ 184 Lance Parrish .05 .02
☐ 185 Darnell Coles .05 .02
☐ 186 Kirby Puckett 1.00 .45
☐ 187 Terry Pendleton .10 .05
☐ 188 Don Slaught .05 .02
☐ 189 Jimmy Jones .05 .02
☐ 190 Dave Parker .10 .05
☐ 191 Mike Aldrete .05 .02
☐ 192 Mike Moore .05 .02
☐ 193 Greg Walker .05 .02
☐ 194 Calvin Schiraldi .05 .02
☐ 195 Dick Schofield .05 .02
☐ 196 Jody Reed .10 .05
☐ 197 Pete Smith .05 .02
☐ 198 Cal Ripken 2.50 1.10
☐ 199 Lloyd Moseby .05 .02
☐ 200 Ruben Sierra .10 .05
☐ 201 R.J. Reynolds .05 .02
☐ 202 Bryn Smith .05 .02
☐ 203 Gary Pettis .05 .02
☐ 204 Steve Sax .05 .02
☐ 205 Frank DiPino .05 .02
☐ 206 Mike Scott UER .05 .02
(1977 Jackson losses

say 1.10, should be 1)

☐ 207 Kurt Stillwell	.05	.02
☐ 208 Mookie Wilson	.10	.05
☐ 209 Lee Mazzilli	.05	.02
☐ 210 Lance McCullers	.05	.02
☐ 211 Rick Honeycutt	.05	.02
☐ 212 John Tudor	.05	.02
☐ 213 Jim Gott	.05	.02
☐ 214 Frank Viola	.05	.02
☐ 215 Juan Samuel	.05	.02
☐ 216 Jesse Barfield	.05	.02
☐ 217 Claudell Washington	.05	.02
☐ 218 Rick Reuschel	.05	.02
☐ 219 Jim Presley	.05	.02
☐ 220 Tommy John	.10	.05
☐ 221 Dan Plesac	.05	.02
☐ 222 Barry Larkin	.40	.18
☐ 223 Mike Stanley	.05	.02
☐ 224 Cory Snyder	.05	.02
☐ 225 Andre Dawson	.25	.11
☐ 226 Ken Oberkfell	.05	.02
☐ 227 Devon White	.10	.05
☐ 228 Jamie Moyer	.05	.02
☐ 229 Brook Jacoby	.05	.02
☐ 230 Rob Murphy	.05	.02
☐ 231 Bret Saberhagen	.10	.05
☐ 232 Nolan Ryan	2.00	.90
☐ 233 Bruce Hurst	.05	.02
☐ 234 Jesse Orosco	.05	.02
☐ 235 Bobby Thigpen	.05	.02
☐ 236 Pascual Perez	.05	.02
☐ 237 Matt Nokes	.05	.02
☐ 238 Bob Ojeda	.05	.02
☐ 239 Joey Meyer	.05	.02
☐ 240 Shane Rawley	.05	.02
☐ 241 Jeff Robinson	.05	.02
☐ 242 Jeff Reardon	.05	.02
☐ 243 Ozzie Smith	.75	.35
☐ 244 Dave Winfield	.40	.18
☐ 245 John Kruk	.15	.07
☐ 246 Carney Lansford	.10	.05
☐ 247 Candy Maldonado	.05	.02
☐ 248 Ken Phelps	.05	.02
☐ 249 Ken Williams	.05	.02
☐ 250 Al Nipper	.05	.02
☐ 251 Mark McLemore	.05	.02
☐ 252 Lee Smith	.10	.05
☐ 253 Albert Hall	.05	.02
☐ 254 Billy Ripken	.05	.02
☐ 255 Kelly Gruber	.05	.02
☐ 256 Charlie Hough	.05	.02
☐ 257 John Smiley	.10	.05
☐ 258 Tim Wallach	.05	.02
☐ 259 Frank Tanana	.05	.02
☐ 260 Mike Scioscia	.05	.02
☐ 261 Damon Berryhill	.05	.02
☐ 262 Dave Smith	.05	.02
☐ 263 Willie Wilson	.05	.02
☐ 264 Len Dykstra	.10	.05
☐ 265 Randy Myers	.10	.05
☐ 266 Keith Moreland	.05	.02
☐ 267 Eric Plunk	.05	.02
☐ 268 Todd Worrell	.05	.02
☐ 269 Bob Walk	.05	.02
☐ 270 Keith Atherton	.05	.02
☐ 271 Mike Schmidt	.50	.23
☐ 272 Mike Flanagan	.05	.02
☐ 273 Rafael Santana	.05	.02
☐ 274 Robby Thompson	.05	.02
☐ 275 Rey Quinones	.05	.02
☐ 276 Cecilio Guante	.05	.02
☐ 277 B.J. Surhoff	.15	.07
☐ 278 Chris Sabo	.10	.05
☐ 279 Mitch Williams	.05	.02
☐ 280 Greg Swindell	.05	.02
☐ 281 Alan Trammell	.15	.07
☐ 282 Storm Davis	.05	.02
☐ 283 Chuck Finley	.10	.05
☐ 284 Dave Stieb	.05	.02
☐ 285 Scott Bailes	.05	.02
☐ 286 Larry Sheets	.05	.02
☐ 287 Danny Tartabull	.05	.02
☐ 288 Checklist Card	.05	.02
☐ 289 Todd Benzinger	.05	.02
☐ 290 John Shelby	.05	.02
☐ 291 Steve Lyons	.05	.02
☐ 292 Mitch Webster	.05	.02
☐ 293 Walt Terrell	.05	.02
☐ 294 Pete Stanicek	.05	.02
☐ 295 Chris Bosio	.05	.02
☐ 296 Milt Thompson	.05	.02
☐ 297 Fred Lynn	.05	.02
☐ 298 Juan Berenguer	.05	.02
☐ 299 Ken Dayley	.05	.02
☐ 300 Joel Skinner	.05	.02
☐ 301 Benito Santiago	.05	.02
☐ 302 Ron Hassey	.05	.02
☐ 303 Jose Uribe	.05	.02
☐ 304 Harold Reynolds	.10	.05
☐ 305 Dale Sveum	.05	.02
☐ 306 Glenn Wilson	.05	.02
☐ 307 Mike Witt	.05	.02
☐ 308 Ron Robinson	.05	.02
☐ 309 Denny Walling	.05	.02
☐ 310 Joe Orsulak	.05	.02
☐ 311 David Wells	.05	.02
☐ 312 Steve Buechele	.05	.02
☐ 313 Jose Oquendo	.05	.02
☐ 314 Floyd Youmans	.05	.02
☐ 315 Lou Whitaker	.10	.05
☐ 316 Fernando Valenzuela	.10	.05
☐ 317 Mike Boddicker	.05	.02
☐ 318 Gerald Young	.05	.02
☐ 319 Frank White	.10	.05
☐ 320 Bill Wegman	.05	.02
☐ 321 Tom Niedenfuer	.05	.02
☐ 322 Ed Whitson	.05	.02
☐ 323 Curt Young	.05	.02
☐ 324 Greg Mathews	.05	.02
☐ 325 Doug Jones	.10	.05
☐ 326 Tommy Herr	.05	.02
☐ 327 Kent Tekulve	.05	.02
☐ 328 Rance Mulliniks	.05	.02
☐ 329 Checklist Card	.05	.02
☐ 330 Craig Lefferts	.05	.02
☐ 331 Franklin Stubbs	.05	.02
☐ 332 Rick Cerone	.05	.02
☐ 333 Dave Schmidt	.05	.02
☐ 334 Larry Parrish	.05	.02
☐ 335 Tom Browning	.05	.02
☐ 336 Checklist Card	.05	.02

1988 Donruss Pop-Ups

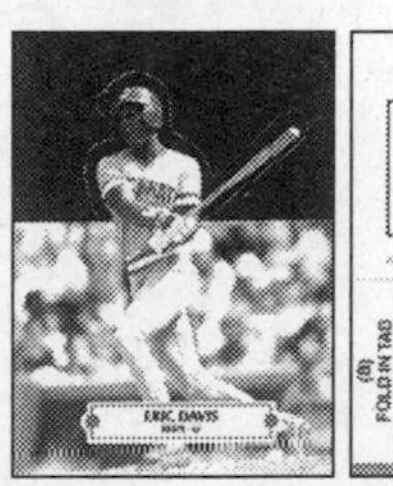

This 20-card set features "fold-out" cards measures the standard size. Card fronts are in full color. Cards are unnumbered but are listed in the same order as the Donruss All-Stars on the All-Star checklist card. Card backs present essentially no information about the player. The set was distributed in packs which also contained All-Star cards. In order to remain in mint condition, the cards should not be popped up.

	MINT	NRMT
COMPLETE SET (20)	5.00	2.20
COMMON CARD (1-20)	.05	.02
☐ 1 Don Mattingly	1.50	.70
☐ 2 Dave Winfield	.50	.23
☐ 3 Willie Randolph	.10	.05
☐ 4 Rickey Henderson	.50	.23
☐ 5 Cal Ripken	2.50	1.10
☐ 6 George Bell	.05	.02
☐ 7 Wade Boggs	.50	.23
☐ 8 Bret Saberhagen	.10	.05
☐ 9 Terry Kennedy	.05	.02
☐ 10 John McNamara MG	.05	.02
☐ 11 Jack Clark	.10	.05
☐ 12 Darryl Strawberry	.10	.05
☐ 13 Ryne Sandberg	.75	.35
☐ 14 Andre Dawson	.10	.05
☐ 15 Ozzie Smith	1.00	.45
☐ 16 Eric Davis	.10	.05
☐ 17 Mike Schmidt	.75	.35
☐ 18 Mike Scott	.05	.02
☐ 19 Gary Carter	.20	.09
☐ 20 Davey Johnson MG	.05	.02

1988 Donruss Super DK's

This 26-player card set was available through a mail-in offer detailed on the wax packs. The set was sent in return for 8.00 and three wrappers plus 1.50 postage and handling. The set features the popular Diamond King subseries in large (approximately 4 7/8" by 6 13/16") form. Dick Perez of Perez-Steele Galleries did another outstanding job on the artwork. The cards are essentially a large version of the Donruss regular issue Diamond Kings.

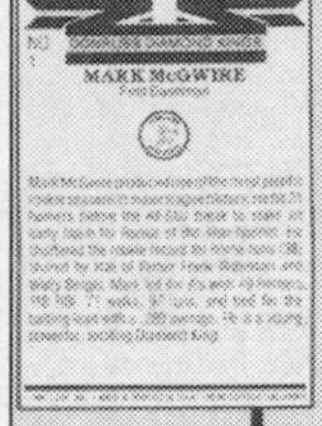

	MINT	NRMT
COMPLETE SET (26)	12.00	5.50
COMMON CARD (1-26)	.50	.23
☐ 1 Mark McGwire	3.00	1.35
☐ 2 Tim Raines	.75	.35
☐ 3 Benito Santiago	.50	.23
☐ 4 Alan Trammell	1.00	.45
☐ 5 Danny Tartabull	.50	.23
☐ 6 Ron Darling	.50	.23
☐ 7 Paul Molitor	1.50	.70
☐ 8 Devon White	.75	.35
☐ 9 Andre Dawson	1.00	.45
☐ 10 Julio Franco	.75	.35
☐ 11 Scott Fletcher	.50	.23
☐ 12 Tony Fernandez	.50	.23
☐ 13 Shane Rawley	.50	.23
☐ 14 Kal Daniels	.50	.23
☐ 15 Jack Clark	.75	.35
☐ 16 Dwight Evans	.75	.35
☐ 17 Tommy John	.75	.35
☐ 18 Andy Van Slyke	.75	.35
☐ 19 Gary Gaetti	.75	.35
☐ 20 Mark Langston	.50	.23
☐ 21 Will Clark	2.00	.90
☐ 22 Glenn Hubbard	.50	.23
☐ 23 Billy Hatcher	.50	.23
☐ 24 Bob Welch	.50	.23
☐ 25 Ivan Calderon	.50	.23
☐ 26 Cal Ripken	5.00	2.20

1988 Donruss Team Book Athletics

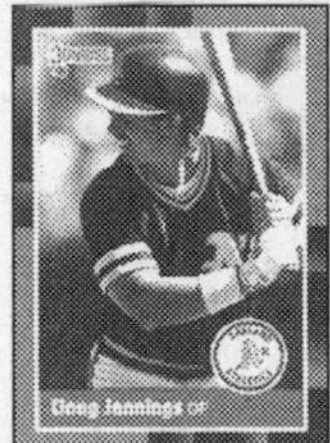

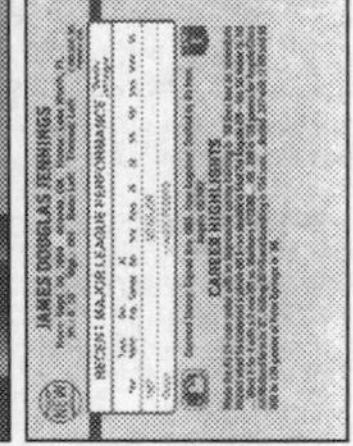

The 1988 Donruss Athletics Team Book set features 27 cards (three pages with nine cards on each page) plus a large full-page puzzle of Stan Musial. Cards are in full color and are standard size. The set was distributed as a four-page book; although the puzzle page was perforated, the card pages were not. The cover of the "Team Collection" book is primarily bright red. Card fronts are very similar in design to the 1988 Donruss regular issue. The card numbers on the backs are the same for those players that are the same as in the regular Donruss set; the new players pictured are numbered on the back as "NEW." In fact 1988 A.L. Rookie of the Year Walt Weiss makes his first Donruss appearance in this set as a "NEW" card. The book is usually sold intact. When cut from the book into individual cards, these cards are distinguishable from the regular 1988 Donruss cards since these have a 1988 copyright on the back whereas the regular issue has a 1987 copyright on the back.

	MINT	NRMT
COMPLETE SET (27)	4.00	1.80
COMMON CARD	.10	.05
COMMON NEW PLAYER	.15	.07
☐ 97 Curt Young	.10	.05
☐ 133 Gene Nelson	.10	.05
☐ 158 Terry Steinbach	.40	.18
☐ 178 Carney Lansford	.25	.11
☐ 221 Tony Phillips	.10	.05
☐ 256 Mark McGwire	1.25	.55
☐ 302 Jose Canseco	1.00	.45
☐ 349 Dennis Eckersley	.25	.11
☐ 379 Mike Gallego	.10	.05

	MINT	NRMT
☐ 425 Luis Polonia	.25	.11
☐ 467 Steve Ontiveros	.10	.05
☐ 472 Dave Stewart	.25	.11
☐ 503 Eric Plunk	.10	.05
☐ 528 Greg Cadaret	.10	.05
☐ 590 Rick Honeycutt	.10	.05
☐ 595 Storm Davis	.10	.05
☐ NEW Don Baylor UER (Career stats are incorrect)	.25	.11
☐ NEW Ron Hassey	.15	.07
☐ NEW Dave Henderson	.25	.11
☐ NEW Glenn Hubbard	.15	.07
☐ NEW Stan Javier	.15	.07
☐ NEW Doug Jennings	.15	.07
☐ NEW Ed Jurak	.15	.07
☐ NEW Dave Parker	.25	.11
☐ NEW Walt Weiss	.40	.18
☐ NEW Bob Welch	.25	.11
☐ NEW Matt Young	.15	.07

1988 Donruss Team Book Cubs

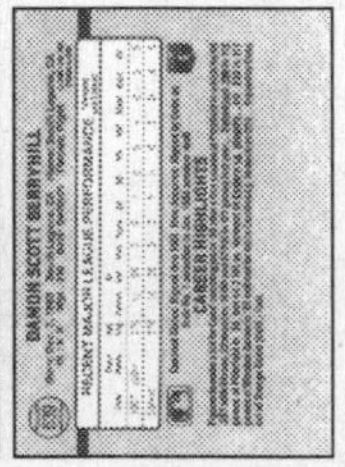

The 1988 Donruss Cubs Team Book set features 27 cards (three pages with nine cards on each page) plus a large full-page puzzle of Stan Musial. Cards are in full color and are standard size. The set was distributed as a four-page book; although the puzzle page was perforated, the card pages were not. The cover of the "Team Collection" book is primarily bright red. Card fronts are very similar in design to the 1988 Donruss regular issue. The card numbers on the backs are the same for those players that are the same as in the regular Donruss set; the new players pictured are numbered on the back as "NEW." The book is usually sold intact. When cut from the book into individual cards, these cards are distinguishable from the regular 1988 Donruss cards since these have a 1988 copyright on the back whereas the regular issue has a 1987 copyright on the back.

	MINT	NRMT
COMPLETE SET (27)	6.00	2.70
COMMON CARD	.10	.05
COMMON NEW PLAYER	.15	.07
☐ 40 Mark Grace RR	2.00	.90
☐ 68 Rick Sutcliffe	.10	.05
☐ 119 Jody Davis	.10	.05
☐ 146 Shawon Dunston	.25	.11
☐ 169 Jamie Moyer	.10	.05
☐ 191 Leon Durham	.10	.05
☐ 242 Ryne Sandberg	1.00	.45
☐ 269 Andre Dawson	.25	.11
☐ 315 Paul Noce	.10	.05
☐ 324 Rafael Palmeiro	1.00	.45
☐ 438 Dave Martinez	.10	.05
☐ 447 Jerry Mumphrey	.10	.05
☐ 488 Jim Sundberg	.25	.11
☐ 516 Manny Trillo	.10	.05
☐ 539 Greg Maddux	4.00	1.80
☐ 561 Les Lancaster	.10	.05
☐ 570 Frank DiPino	.10	.05
☐ 639 Damon Berryhill	.10	.05
☐ 646 Scott Sanderson	.10	.05
☐ NEW Mike Bielecki	.15	.07
☐ NEW Rich Gossage	.25	.11
☐ NEW Drew Hall	.15	.07
☐ NEW Darrin Jackson	.15	.07
☐ NEW Vance Law	.15	.07
☐ NEW Al Nipper	.15	.07
☐ NEW Angel Salazar	.15	.07
☐ NEW Calvin Schiraldi	.15	.07

1988 Donruss Team Book Mets

The 1988 Donruss Mets Team Book set features 27 cards (three pages with nine cards on each page) plus a large full-page puzzle of Stan Musial. Cards are in full color and are standard size. The set was distributed as a four-page book; although the puzzle page was perforated, the card pages were not. The cover of the "Team Collection" book

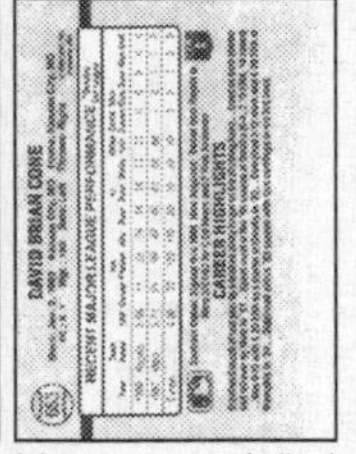

is primarily bright red. Card fronts are very similar in design to the 1988 Donruss regular issue. The card numbers on the backs are the same for those players that are the same as in the regular Donruss set; the new players pictured are numbered on the back as "NEW." The book is usually sold intact. When cut from the book into individual cards, these cards are distinguishable from the regular 1988 Donruss cards since these have a 1988 copyright on the back whereas the regular issue has a 1987 copyright on the back.

	MINT	NRMT
COMPLETE SET (27)	3.00	1.35
COMMON CARD	.10	.05
COMMON NEW PLAYER	.15	.07
☐ 37 Kevin Elster RR	.50	.23
☐ 69 Dwight Gooden	.25	.11
☐ 76 Ron Darling	.10	.05
☐ 118 Sid Fernandez	.10	.05
☐ 199 Gary Carter	.25	.11
☐ 241 Wally Backman	.10	.05
☐ 316 Keith Hernandez	.25	.11
☐ 323 Dave Magadan	.10	.05
☐ 364 Len Dykstra	.25	.11
☐ 439 Darryl Strawberry	.25	.11
☐ 446 Rick Aguilera	.25	.11
☐ 562 Keith Miller	.10	.05
☐ 569 Howard Johnson	.25	.11
☐ 603 Terry Leach	.10	.05
☐ 614 Lee Mazzilli	.10	.05
☐ 617 Kevin McReynolds	.10	.05
☐ 619 Barry Lyons	.10	.05
☐ 620 Randy Myers	.25	.11
☐ 632 Bob Ojeda	.10	.05
☐ 648 Tim Teufel	.10	.05
☐ 651 Roger McDowell	.10	.05
☐ 652 Mookie Wilson	.25	.11
☐ 653 David Cone	.75	.35
☐ 657 Gregg Jefferies	.75	.35
☐ NEW Jeff Innis	.15	.07
☐ NEW Mackey Sasser	.15	.07
☐ NEW Gene Walter	.15	.07

1988 Donruss Team Book Red Sox

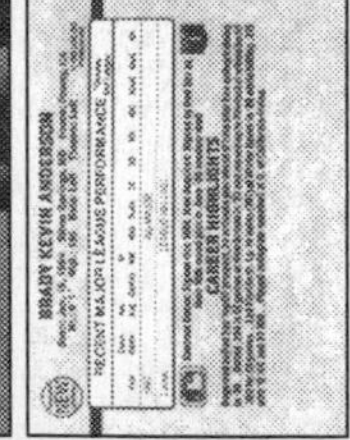

The 1988 Donruss Red Sox Team Book set features 27 cards (three pages with nine cards on each page) plus a large full-page puzzle of Stan Musial. Cards are in full color and are standard size. The set was distributed as a four-page book; although the puzzle page was perforated, the card pages were not. The cover of the "Team Collection" book is primarily bright red. Card fronts are very similar in design to the 1988 Donruss regular issue. The card numbers on the backs are the same for those players that are the same as in the regular Donruss set; the new players pictured are numbered on the back as "NEW." The book is usually sold intact. When cut from the book into individual cards, these cards are distinguishable from the regular 1988 Donruss cards since these have a 1988 copyright on the back whereas the regular issue has a 1987 copyright on the back.

	MINT	NRMT
COMPLETE SET (27)	4.00	1.80
COMMON CARD	.10	.05
COMMON NEW PLAYER	.15	.07
☐ 41 Jody Reed RR	.25	.11
☐ 51 Roger Clemens	1.00	.45
☐ 92 Bob Stanley	.10	.05
☐ 129 Rich Gedman	.10	.05
☐ 153 Wade Boggs	.75	.35
☐ 174 Ellis Burks	1.00	.45
☐ 216 Dwight Evans	.25	.11
☐ 252 Bruce Hurst	.10	.05
☐ 276 Marty Barrett	.10	.05
☐ 297 Todd Benzinger	.10	.05
☐ 339 Mike Greenwell	.25	.11
☐ 399 Jim Rice	.25	.11
☐ 421 John Marzano	.10	.05
☐ 462 Oil Can Boyd	.10	.05
☐ 498 Sam Horn	.10	.05
☐ 544 Spike Owen	.10	.05
☐ 585 Jeff Sellers	.10	.05
☐ 623 Ed Romero	.10	.05
☐ 634 Wes Gardner	.10	.05
☐ NEW Brady Anderson	2.00	.90
☐ NEW Rick Cerone	.15	.07
☐ NEW Steve Ellsworth	.15	.07
☐ NEW Dennis Lamp	.15	.07
☐ NEW Kevin Romine	.15	.07
☐ NEW Lee Smith	.50	.23
☐ NEW Mike Smithson	.15	.07
☐ NEW John Trautwein	.15	.07

1988 Donruss Team Book Yankees

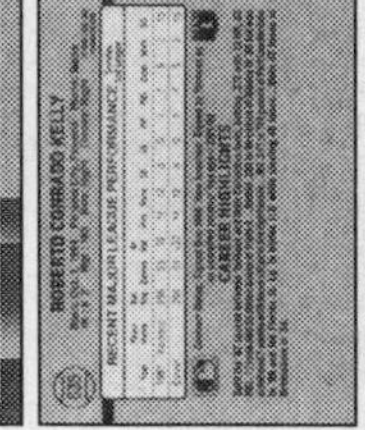

The 1988 Donruss Yankees Team Book set features 27 cards (three pages with nine cards on each page) plus a large full-page puzzle of Stan Musial. Cards are in full color and are standard size. The set was distributed as a four-page book; although the puzzle page was perforated, the card pages were not. The cover of the "Team Collection" book is primarily bright red. Card fronts are very similar in design to the 1988 Donruss regular issue. The card numbers on the backs are the same for those players that are the same as in the regular Donruss set; the new players pictured are numbered on the back as "NEW." The book is usually sold intact. When cut from the book into individual cards, these cards are distinguishable from the regular 1988 Donruss cards since these have a 1988 copyright on the back whereas the regular issue has a 1987 copyright on the back.

	MINT	NRMT
COMPLETE SET (27)	4.00	1.80
COMMON CARD	.10	.05
COMMON NEW PLAYER	.10	.05
☐ 43 Al Leiter RR	.50	.23
☐ 93 Dave Righetti	.10	.05
☐ 105 Mike Pagliarulo	.10	.05
☐ 128 Rick Rhoden	.10	.05
☐ 175 Ron Guidry	.25	.11
☐ 217 Don Mattingly	2.00	.90
☐ 228 Willie Randolph	.25	.11
☐ 251 Gary Ward	.10	.05
☐ 277 Rickey Henderson	.75	.35
☐ 278 Dave Winfield	.75	.35
☐ 340 Claudell Washington	.10	.05
☐ 374 Charles Hudson	.10	.05
☐ 401 Tommy John	.25	.11
☐ 474 Joel Skinner	.10	.05
☐ 497 Tim Stoddard	.10	.05
☐ 545 Jay Buhner	2.00	.90
☐ 616 Bobby Meacham	.10	.05
☐ 635 Roberto Kelly	.25	.11
☐ NEW John Candelaria	.10	.05
☐ NEW Jack Clark	.25	.11
☐ NEW Jose Cruz	.25	.11
☐ NEW Richard Dotson	.10	.05
☐ NEW Cecilio Guante	.10	.05
☐ NEW Lee Guetterman	.10	.05
☐ NEW Rafael Santana	.10	.05
☐ NEW Steve Shields	.10	.05
☐ NEW Don Slaught	.10	.05

1989 Donruss

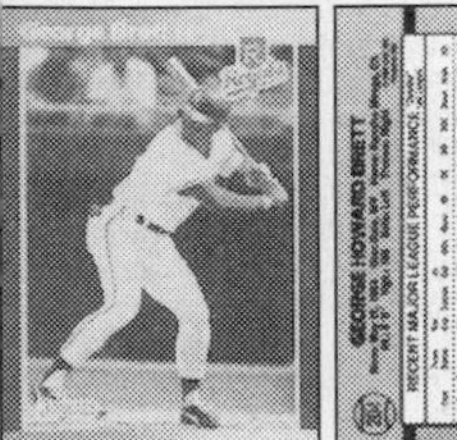

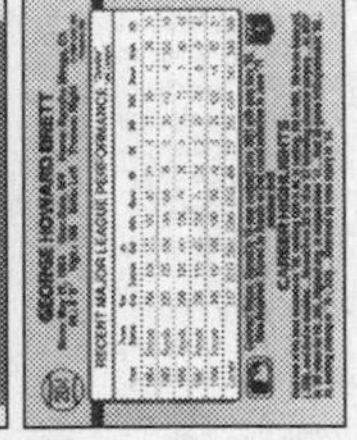

This set consists of 660 standard-size cards. The cards were primarily issued 15-card wax packs, rack packs and hobby and retail factory sets. Each wax pack also contained a puzzle panel (featuring Warren Spahn this year). The cards feature a distinctive black side border with an alternating coating. Subsets include Diamond Kings (1-27) and Rated Rookies (28-47). There are two variations that occur throughout most of the set. On the card backs "Denotes Led League" can be found with one asterisk to the left or with an asterisk on each side. On the card fronts the horizontal lines on the left and right borders can be glossy or non-glossy. Since both of these variation types are relatively minor and seem equally common, there is no premium value for either type. Rather than short-printing 26 cards in order to make room for printing the Bonus MVP's this year, Donruss apparently chose to double print 106 cards. These double prints are listed below by DP. Numbered with the prefix "BC" for bonus card, the 26-card set featuring the most valuable player from each of the 26 teams was randomly inserted in the wax and rack packs. These cards are distinguished by the bold MVP logo in the upper background of the obverse. Rookie Cards in this set include Sandy Alomar Jr., Brady Anderson, Dante Bichette, Craig Biggio, Ken Griffey Jr., Ken Hill, Randy Johnson, Ramon Martinez, Hal Morris, Gary Sheffield, and John Smoltz.

	MINT	NRMT
COMPLETE SET (660)	10.00	4.50
COMP.FACT.SET (672)	12.00	5.50
COMMON CARD (1-660)	.05	.02
COMPLETE SPAHN PUZZLE	1.00	.45

Card	MINT	NRMT
☐ 1 Mike Greenwell DK	.05	.02
☐ 2 Bobby Bonilla DK DP	.20	.09
☐ 3 Pete Incaviglia DK	.05	.02
☐ 4 Chris Sabo DK DP	.05	.02
☐ 5 Robin Yount DK	.20	.09
☐ 6 Tony Gwynn DK DP	.20	.09
☐ 7 Carlton Fisk DK UER (OF on back)	.20	.09
☐ 8 Cory Snyder DK	.05	.02
☐ 9 David Cone DK UER ("hurdlers")	.20	.09
☐ 10 Kevin Seitzer DK	.05	.02
☐ 11 Rick Reuschel DK	.05	.02
☐ 12 Johnny Ray DK	.05	.02
☐ 13 Dave Schmidt DK	.05	.02
☐ 14 Andres Galarraga DK	.20	.09
☐ 15 Kirk Gibson DK	.20	.09
☐ 16 Fred McGriff DK	.20	.09
☐ 17 Mark Grace DK	.20	.09
☐ 18 Jeff M. Robinson DK	.05	.02
☐ 19 Vince Coleman DK DP	.05	.02
☐ 20 Dave Henderson DK	.05	.02
☐ 21 Harold Reynolds DK	.05	.02
☐ 22 Gerald Perry DK	.05	.02
☐ 23 Frank Viola DK	.05	.02
☐ 24 Steve Bedrosian DK	.05	.02
☐ 25 Glenn Davis DK	.05	.02
☐ 26 Don Mattingly DK UER (Doesn't mention Don's previous DK in 1985)	.20	.09
☐ 27 DK Checklist 1-26 DP	.05	.02
☐ 28 Sandy Alomar Jr. RR	.50	.23
☐ 29 Steve Searcy RR	.05	.02
☐ 30 Cameron Drew RR	.05	.02
☐ 31 Gary Sheffield RR	.75	.35
☐ 32 Erik Hanson RR	.10	.05
☐ 33 Ken Griffey Jr. RR	6.00	2.70
☐ 34 Greg W. Harris RR	.05	.02
☐ 35 Gregg Jefferies RR	.10	.05
☐ 36 Luis Medina RR	.05	.02
☐ 37 Carlos Quintana RR	.05	.02
☐ 38 Felix Jose RR	.05	.02
☐ 39 Cris Carpenter RR	.05	.02
☐ 40 Ron Jones RR	.05	.02
☐ 41 Dave West RR	.05	.02
☐ 42 Randy Johnson RR UER Card says born in 1964 he was born in 1963	1.00	.45
☐ 43 Mike Harkey RR	.05	.02
☐ 44 Pete Harnisch RR DP	.10	.05
☐ 45 Tom Gordon RR DP	.20	.09
☐ 46 Gregg Olson RR DP	.10	.05
☐ 47 Alex Sanchez RR DP	.05	.02
☐ 48 Ruben Sierra	.05	.02
☐ 49 Rafael Palmeiro	.20	.09
☐ 50 Ron Gant	.10	.05
☐ 51 Cal Ripken	.75	.35
☐ 52 Wally Joyner	.10	.05
☐ 53 Gary Carter	.10	.05
☐ 54 Andy Van Slyke	.10	.05
☐ 55 Robin Yount	.20	.09
☐ 56 Pete Incaviglia	.10	.05
☐ 57 Greg Brock	.05	.02
☐ 58 Melido Perez	.05	.02
☐ 59 Craig Lefferts	.05	.02
☐ 60 Gary Pettis	.05	.02
☐ 61 Danny Tartabull	.05	.02
☐ 62 Guillermo Hernandez	.05	.02
☐ 63 Ozzie Smith	.25	.11
☐ 64 Gary Gaetti	.05	.02
☐ 65 Mark Davis	.05	.02
☐ 66 Lee Smith	.10	.05
☐ 67 Dennis Eckersley	.20	.09
☐ 68 Wade Boggs	.20	.09
☐ 69 Mike Scott	.05	.02
☐ 70 Fred McGriff	.20	.09
☐ 71 Tom Browning	.05	.02
☐ 72 Claudell Washington	.05	.02
☐ 73 Mel Hall	.05	.02
☐ 74 Don Mattingly	.30	.14
☐ 75 Steve Bedrosian	.05	.02
☐ 76 Juan Samuel	.05	.02
☐ 77 Mike Scioscia	.05	.02
☐ 78 Dave Righetti	.05	.02
☐ 79 Alfredo Griffin	.05	.02
☐ 80 Eric Davis UER (165 games in 1988, should be 135)	.10	.05
☐ 81 Juan Berenguer	.05	.02
☐ 82 Todd Worrell	.05	.02
☐ 83 Joe Carter	.20	.09
☐ 84 Steve Sax	.05	.02
☐ 85 Frank White	.10	.05
☐ 86 John Kruk	.10	.05
☐ 87 Rance Mulliniks	.05	.02
☐ 88 Alan Ashby	.05	.02
☐ 89 Charlie Leibrandt	.05	.02
☐ 90 Frank Tanana	.05	.02
☐ 91 Jose Canseco	.20	.09
☐ 92 Barry Bonds	.40	.18
☐ 93 Harold Reynolds	.05	.02
☐ 94 Mark McLemore	.05	.02
☐ 95 Mark McGwire	.40	.18
☐ 96 Eddie Murray	.20	.09
☐ 97 Tim Raines	.10	.05
☐ 98 Robby Thompson	.05	.02
☐ 99 Kevin McReynolds	.05	.02
☐ 100 Checklist 28-137	.05	.02
☐ 101 Carlton Fisk	.20	.09
☐ 102 Dave Martinez	.05	.02
☐ 103 Glenn Braggs	.05	.02
☐ 104 Dale Murphy	.20	.09
☐ 105 Ryne Sandberg	.25	.11
☐ 106 Dennis Martinez	.10	.05
☐ 107 Pete O'Brien	.05	.02
☐ 108 Dick Schofield	.05	.02
☐ 109 Henry Cotto	.05	.02
☐ 110 Mike Marshall	.05	.02
☐ 111 Keith Moreland	.05	.02
☐ 112 Tom Brunansky	.05	.02
☐ 113 Kelly Gruber UER (Wrong birthdate)	.05	.02
☐ 114 Brook Jacoby	.05	.02
☐ 115 Keith Brown	.05	.02
☐ 116 Matt Nokes	.05	.02
☐ 117 Keith Hernandez	.10	.05
☐ 118 Bob Forsch	.05	.02
☐ 119 Bert Blyleven UER (... 3000 strikeouts in 1987, should be 1986)	.10	.05
☐ 120 Willie Wilson	.05	.02
☐ 121 Tommy Gregg	.05	.02
☐ 122 Jim Rice	.10	.05
☐ 123 Bob Knepper	.05	.02
☐ 124 Danny Jackson	.05	.02
☐ 125 Eric Plunk	.05	.02
☐ 126 Brian Fisher	.05	.02
☐ 127 Mike Pagliarulo	.05	.02
☐ 128 Tony Gwynn	.50	.23
☐ 129 Lance McCullers	.05	.02
☐ 130 Andres Galarraga	.20	.09
☐ 131 Jose Uribe	.05	.02
☐ 132 Kirk Gibson UER (Wrong birthdate)	.10	.05
☐ 133 David Palmer	.05	.02
☐ 134 R.J. Reynolds	.05	.02
☐ 135 Greg Walker	.05	.02
☐ 136 Kirk McCaskill UER (Wrong birthdate)	.05	.02
☐ 137 Shawon Dunston	.05	.02
☐ 138 Andy Allanson	.05	.02
☐ 139 Rob Murphy	.05	.02
☐ 140 Mike Aldrete	.05	.02
☐ 141 Terry Kennedy	.05	.02
☐ 142 Scott Fletcher	.05	.02
☐ 143 Steve Balboni	.05	.02
☐ 144 Bret Saberhagen	.05	.02
☐ 145 Ozzie Virgil	.05	.02
☐ 146 Dale Sveum	.05	.02
☐ 147 Darryl Strawberry	.10	.05
☐ 148 Harold Baines	.10	.05
☐ 149 George Bell	.05	.02
☐ 150 Dave Parker	.10	.05
☐ 151 Bobby Bonilla	.10	.05
☐ 152 Mookie Wilson	.10	.05
☐ 153 Ted Power	.05	.02
☐ 154 Nolan Ryan	.75	.35
☐ 155 Jeff Reardon	.10	.05
☐ 156 Tim Wallach	.05	.02
☐ 157 Jamie Moyer	.05	.02
☐ 158 Rich Gossage	.10	.05
☐ 159 Dave Winfield	.20	.09
☐ 160 Von Hayes	.05	.02
☐ 161 Willie McGee	.05	.02
☐ 162 Rich Gedman	.05	.02
☐ 163 Tony Pena	.05	.02
☐ 164 Mike Morgan	.05	.02
☐ 165 Charlie Hough	.10	.05
☐ 166 Mike Stanley	.05	.02
☐ 167 Andre Dawson	.20	.09
☐ 168 Joe Boever	.05	.02
☐ 169 Pete Stanicek	.05	.02
☐ 170 Bob Boone	.10	.05
☐ 171 Ron Darling	.05	.02
☐ 172 Bob Walk	.05	.02
☐ 173 Rob Deer	.05	.02
☐ 174 Steve Buechele	.05	.02
☐ 175 Ted Higuera	.05	.02
☐ 176 Ozzie Guillen	.05	.02
☐ 177 Candy Maldonado	.05	.02
☐ 178 Doyle Alexander	.05	.02
☐ 179 Mark Gubicza	.05	.02
☐ 180 Alan Trammell	.10	.05
☐ 181 Vince Coleman	.05	.02
☐ 182 Kirby Puckett	.40	.18
☐ 183 Chris Brown	.05	.02
☐ 184 Marty Barrett	.05	.02
☐ 185 Stan Javier	.05	.02
☐ 186 Mike Greenwell	.05	.02
☐ 187 Billy Hatcher	.05	.02
☐ 188 Jimmy Key	.10	.05
☐ 189 Nick Esasky	.05	.02
☐ 190 Don Slaught	.05	.02
☐ 191 Cory Snyder	.05	.02
☐ 192 John Candelaria	.05	.02
☐ 193 Mike Schmidt	.25	.11
☐ 194 Kevin Gross	.05	.02
☐ 195 John Tudor	.05	.02
☐ 196 Neil Allen	.05	.02
☐ 197 Orel Hershiser	.10	.05
☐ 198 Kal Daniels	.05	.02
☐ 199 Kent Hrbek	.05	.02
☐ 200 Checklist 138-247	.05	.02
☐ 201 Joe Magrane	.05	.02
☐ 202 Scott Bailes	.05	.02
☐ 203 Tim Belcher	.05	.02
☐ 204 George Brett	.40	.18
☐ 205 Benito Santiago	.10	.05
☐ 206 Tony Fernandez	.05	.02
☐ 207 Gerald Young	.05	.02
☐ 208 Bo Jackson	.10	.05
☐ 209 Chet Lemon	.05	.02
☐ 210 Storm Davis	.05	.02
☐ 211 Doug Drabek	.05	.02
☐ 212 Mickey Brantley UER (Photo actually Nelson Simmons)	.05	.02
☐ 213 Devon White	.05	.02
☐ 214 Dave Stewart	.10	.05
☐ 215 Dave Schmidt	.05	.02
☐ 216 Bryn Smith	.05	.02
☐ 217 Brett Butler	.10	.05
☐ 218 Bob Ojeda	.05	.02
☐ 219 Steve Rosenberg	.05	.02
☐ 220 Hubie Brooks	.05	.02
☐ 221 B.J. Surhoff	.10	.05
☐ 222 Rick Mahler	.05	.02
☐ 223 Rick Sutcliffe	.05	.02
☐ 224 Neal Heaton	.05	.02

☐ 225 Mitch Williams .05 .02
☐ 226 Chuck Finley .10 .05
☐ 227 Mark Langston .05 .02
☐ 228 Jesse Orosco .05 .02
☐ 229 Ed Whitson .05 .02
☐ 230 Terry Pendleton .10 .05
☐ 231 Lloyd Moseby .05 .02
☐ 232 Greg Swindell .05 .02
☐ 233 John Franco .10 .05
☐ 234 Jack Morris .10 .05
☐ 235 Howard Johnson .05 .02
☐ 236 Glenn Davis .05 .02
☐ 237 Frank Viola .05 .02
☐ 238 Kevin Seitzer .05 .02
☐ 239 Gerald Perry .05 .02
☐ 240 Dwight Evans .10 .05
☐ 241 Jim Deshaies .05 .02
☐ 242 Bo Diaz .05 .02
☐ 243 Carney Lansford .10 .05
☐ 244 Mike LaValliere .05 .02
☐ 245 Rickey Henderson .20 .09
☐ 246 Roberto Alomar .30 .14
☐ 247 Jimmy Jones .05 .02
☐ 248 Pascual Perez .05 .02
☐ 249 Will Clark .20 .09
☐ 250 Fernando Valenzuela .10 .05
☐ 251 Shane Rawley .05 .02
☐ 252 Sid Bream .05 .02
☐ 253 Steve Lyons .05 .02
☐ 254 Brian Downing .05 .02
☐ 255 Mark Grace .20 .09
☐ 256 Tom Candiotti .05 .02
☐ 257 Barry Larkin .10 .05
☐ 258 Mike Krukow .05 .02
☐ 259 Billy Ripken .05 .02
☐ 260 Cecilio Guante .05 .02
☐ 261 Scott Bradley .05 .02
☐ 262 Floyd Bannister .05 .02
☐ 263 Pete Smith .05 .02
☐ 264 Jim Gantner UER .05 .02
(Wrong birthdate)
☐ 265 Roger McDowell .05 .02
☐ 266 Bobby Thigpen .05 .02
☐ 267 Jim Clancy .05 .02
☐ 268 Terry Steinbach .10 .05
☐ 269 Mike Dunne .05 .02
☐ 270 Dwight Gooden .10 .05
☐ 271 Mike Heath .05 .02
☐ 272 Dave Smith .05 .02
☐ 273 Keith Atherton .05 .02
☐ 274 Tim Burke .05 .02
☐ 275 Damon Berryhill .05 .02
☐ 276 Vance Law .05 .02
☐ 277 Rich Dotson .05 .02
☐ 278 Lance Parrish .05 .02
☐ 279 Denny Walling .05 .02
☐ 280 Roger Clemens .40 .18
☐ 281 Greg Mathews .05 .02
☐ 282 Tom Niedenfuer .05 .02
☐ 283 Paul Kilgus .05 .02
☐ 284 Jose Guzman .05 .02
☐ 285 Calvin Schiraldi .05 .02
☐ 286 Charlie Puleo UER .05 .02
(Career ERA 4.24,
should be 4.23)
☐ 287 Joe Orsulak .05 .02
☐ 288 Jack Howell .05 .02
☐ 289 Kevin Elster .05 .02
☐ 290 Jose Lind .05 .02
☐ 291 Paul Molitor .20 .09
☐ 292 Cecil Espy .05 .02
☐ 293 Bill Wegman .05 .02
☐ 294 Dan Pasqua .05 .02
☐ 295 Scott Garrelts UER .05 .02
(Wrong birthdate)
☐ 296 Walt Terrell .05 .02
☐ 297 Ed Hearn .05 .02
☐ 298 Lou Whitaker .10 .05
☐ 299 Ken Dayley .05 .02
☐ 300 Checklist 248-357 .05 .02
☐ 301 Tommy Herr .05 .02
☐ 302 Mike Brumley .05 .02
☐ 303 Ellis Burks .10 .05
☐ 304 Curt Young UER .05 .02
(Wrong birthdate)
☐ 305 Jody Reed .05 .02
☐ 306 Bill Doran .05 .02
☐ 307 David Wells .05 .02
☐ 308 Ron Robinson .05 .02
☐ 309 Rafael Santana .05 .02
☐ 310 Julio Franco .10 .05
☐ 311 Jack Clark .10 .05
☐ 312 Chris James .05 .02
☐ 313 Milt Thompson .05 .02
☐ 314 John Shelby .05 .02
☐ 315 Al Leiter .10 .05
☐ 316 Mike Davis .05 .02
☐ 317 Chris Sabo .05 .02
☐ 318 Greg Gagne .05 .02
☐ 319 Jose Oquendo .05 .02
☐ 320 John Farrell .05 .02
☐ 321 Franklin Stubbs .05 .02
☐ 322 Kurt Stillwell .05 .02
☐ 323 Shawn Abner .05 .02
☐ 324 Mike Flanagan .05 .02
☐ 325 Kevin Bass .05 .02
☐ 326 Pat Tabler .05 .02
☐ 327 Mike Henneman .05 .02
☐ 328 Rick Honeycutt .05 .02
☐ 329 John Smiley .05 .02
☐ 330 Rey Quinones .05 .02
☐ 331 Johnny Ray .05 .02
☐ 332 Bob Welch .05 .02
☐ 333 Larry Sheets .05 .02
☐ 334 Jeff Parrett .05 .02
☐ 335 Rick Reuschel UER .05 .02
(For Don Robinson,
should be Jeff)
☐ 336 Randy Myers .10 .05
☐ 337 Ken Williams .05 .02
☐ 338 Andy McGaffigan .05 .02
☐ 339 Joey Meyer .05 .02
☐ 340 Dion James .05 .02
☐ 341 Les Lancaster .05 .02
☐ 342 Tom Foley .05 .02
☐ 343 Geno Petralli .05 .02
☐ 344 Dan Petry .05 .02
☐ 345 Alvin Davis .05 .02
☐ 346 Mickey Hatcher .05 .02
☐ 347 Marvell Wynne .05 .02
☐ 348 Danny Cox .05 .02
☐ 349 Dave Stieb .05 .02
☐ 350 Jay Bell .10 .05
☐ 351 Jeff Treadway .05 .02
☐ 352 Luis Salazar .05 .02
☐ 353 Len Dykstra .10 .05
☐ 354 Juan Agosto .05 .02
☐ 355 Gene Larkin .05 .02
☐ 356 Steve Farr .05 .02
☐ 357 Paul Assenmacher .05 .02
☐ 358 Todd Benzinger .05 .02
☐ 359 Larry Andersen .05 .02
☐ 360 Paul O'Neill .10 .05
☐ 361 Ron Hassey .05 .02
☐ 362 Jim Gott .05 .02
☐ 363 Ken Phelps .05 .02
☐ 364 Tim Flannery .05 .02
☐ 365 Randy Ready .05 .02
☐ 366 Nelson Santovenia .05 .02
☐ 367 Kelly Downs .05 .02
☐ 368 Danny Heep .05 .02
☐ 369 Phil Bradley .05 .02
☐ 370 Jeff D. Robinson .05 .02
☐ 371 Ivan Calderon .05 .02
☐ 372 Mike Witt .05 .02
☐ 373 Greg Maddux .75 .35
☐ 374 Carmen Castillo .05 .02
☐ 375 Jose Rijo .05 .02
☐ 376 Joe Price .05 .02
☐ 377 Rene Gonzales .05 .02
☐ 378 Oddibe McDowell .05 .02
☐ 379 Jim Presley .05 .02
☐ 380 Brad Wellman .05 .02
☐ 381 Tom Glavine .25 .11
☐ 382 Dan Plesac .05 .02
☐ 383 Wally Backman .05 .02
☐ 384 Dave Gallagher .05 .02
☐ 385 Tom Henke .05 .02
☐ 386 Luis Polonia .10 .05
☐ 387 Junior Ortiz .05 .02
☐ 388 David Cone .20 .09
☐ 389 Dave Bergman .05 .02
☐ 390 Danny Darwin .05 .02
☐ 391 Dan Gladden .05 .02
☐ 392 John Dopson .05 .02
☐ 393 Frank DiPino .05 .02
☐ 394 Al Nipper .05 .02
☐ 395 Willie Randolph .10 .05
☐ 396 Don Carman .05 .02
☐ 397 Scott Terry .05 .02
☐ 398 Rick Cerone .05 .02
☐ 399 Tom Pagnozzi .05 .02
☐ 400 Checklist 358-467 .05 .02
☐ 401 Mickey Tettleton .10 .05
☐ 402 Curtis Wilkerson .05 .02
☐ 403 Jeff Russell .05 .02
☐ 404 Pat Perry .05 .02
☐ 405 Jose Alvarez .05 .02
☐ 406 Rick Schu .05 .02
☐ 407 Sherman Corbett .05 .02
☐ 408 Dave Magadan .05 .02
☐ 409 Bob Kipper .05 .02
☐ 410 Don August .05 .02
☐ 411 Bob Brower .05 .02
☐ 412 Chris Bosio .05 .02
☐ 413 Jerry Reuss .05 .02
☐ 414 Atlee Hammaker .05 .02
☐ 415 Jim Walewander .05 .02
☐ 416 Mike Macfarlane .10 .05
☐ 417 Pat Sheridan .05 .02
☐ 418 Pedro Guerrero .10 .05
☐ 419 Allan Anderson .05 .02
☐ 420 Mark Parent .05 .02
☐ 421 Bob Stanley .05 .02
☐ 422 Mike Gallego .05 .02
☐ 423 Bruce Hurst .05 .02
☐ 424 Dave Meads .05 .02
☐ 425 Jesse Barfield .05 .02
☐ 426 Rob Dibble .10 .05
☐ 427 Joel Skinner .05 .02
☐ 428 Ron Kittle .05 .02
☐ 429 Rick Rhoden .05 .02
☐ 430 Bob Dernier .05 .02
☐ 431 Steve Jeltz .05 .02
☐ 432 Rick Dempsey .05 .02
☐ 433 Roberto Kelly .05 .02
☐ 434 Dave Anderson .05 .02
☐ 435 Herm Winningham .05 .02
☐ 436 Al Newman .05 .02
☐ 437 Jose DeLeon .05 .02
☐ 438 Doug Jones .05 .02
☐ 439 Brian Holton .05 .02
☐ 440 Jeff Montgomery .10 .05
☐ 441 Dickie Thon .05 .02
☐ 442 Cecil Fielder .10 .05
☐ 443 John Fishel .05 .02
☐ 444 Jerry Don Gleaton .05 .02
☐ 445 Paul Gibson .05 .02
☐ 446 Walt Weiss .05 .02
☐ 447 Glenn Wilson .05 .02
☐ 448 Mike Moore .05 .02
☐ 449 Chili Davis .10 .05
☐ 450 Dave Henderson .05 .02
☐ 451 Jose Bautista .05 .02
☐ 452 Rex Hudler .05 .02
☐ 453 Bob Brenly .05 .02
☐ 454 Mackey Sasser .05 .02
☐ 455 Daryl Boston .05 .02
☐ 456 Mike R. Fitzgerald .05 .02
☐ 457 Jeffrey Leonard .05 .02
☐ 458 Bruce Sutter .05 .02
☐ 459 Mitch Webster .05 .02
☐ 460 Joe Hesketh .05 .02
☐ 461 Bobby Witt .05 .02
☐ 462 Stew Cliburn .05 .02
☐ 463 Scott Bankhead .05 .02
☐ 464 Ramon Martinez .25 .11
☐ 465 Dave Leiper .05 .02
☐ 466 Luis Alicea .05 .02
☐ 467 John Cerutti .05 .02
☐ 468 Ron Washington .05 .02
☐ 469 Jeff Reed .05 .02
☐ 470 Jeff M. Robinson .05 .02
☐ 471 Sid Fernandez .05 .02
☐ 472 Terry Puhl .05 .02
☐ 473 Charlie Lea .05 .02
☐ 474 Israel Sanchez .05 .02
☐ 475 Bruce Benedict .05 .02
☐ 476 Oil Can Boyd .05 .02
☐ 477 Craig Reynolds .05 .02
☐ 478 Frank Williams .05 .02
☐ 479 Greg Cadaret .05 .02
☐ 480 Randy Kramer .05 .02
☐ 481 Dave Eiland .05 .02
☐ 482 Eric Show .05 .02
☐ 483 Garry Templeton .05 .02
☐ 484 Wallace Johnson .05 .02
☐ 485 Kevin Mitchell .10 .05
☐ 486 Tim Crews .05 .02
☐ 487 Mike Maddux .05 .02
☐ 488 Dave LaPoint .05 .02
☐ 489 Fred Manrique .05 .02
☐ 490 Greg Minton .05 .02
☐ 491 Doug Dascenzo UER .05 .02
(Photo actually
Damon Berryhill)
☐ 492 Willie Upshaw .05 .02
☐ 493 Jack Armstrong .05 .02
☐ 494 Kirt Manwaring .05 .02
☐ 495 Jeff Ballard .05 .02
☐ 496 Jeff Kunkel .05 .02
☐ 497 Mike Campbell .05 .02
☐ 498 Gary Thurman .05 .02
☐ 499 Zane Smith .05 .02
☐ 500 Checklist 468-577 DP .05 .02
☐ 501 Mike Birkbeck .05 .02
☐ 502 Terry Leach .05 .02
☐ 503 Shawn Hillegas .05 .02
☐ 504 Manny Lee .05 .02
☐ 505 Doug Jennings .05 .02
☐ 506 Ken Oberkfell .05 .02

☐ 507 Tim Teufel .05 .02
☐ 508 Tom Brookens .05 .02
☐ 509 Rafael Ramirez .05 .02
☐ 510 Fred Toliver .05 .02
☐ 511 Brian Holman .05 .02
☐ 512 Mike Bielecki .05 .02
☐ 513 Jeff Pico .05 .02
☐ 514 Charles Hudson .05 .02
☐ 515 Bruce Ruffin .05 .02
☐ 516 Larry McWilliams UER .05 .02
(New Richland, should
be North Richland)
☐ 517 Jeff Sellers .05 .02
☐ 518 John Costello .05 .02
☐ 519 Brady Anderson .50 .23
☐ 520 Craig McMurtry .05 .02
☐ 521 Ray Hayward DP .05 .02
☐ 522 Drew Hall DP .05 .02
☐ 523 Mark Lemke DP .10 .05
☐ 524 Oswald Peraza DP .05 .02
☐ 525 Bryan Harvey DP .05 .02
☐ 526 Rick Aguilera DP .10 .05
☐ 527 Tom Prince DP .05 .02
☐ 528 Mark Clear DP .05 .02
☐ 529 Jerry Browne DP .05 .02
☐ 530 Juan Castillo DP .05 .02
☐ 531 Jack McDowell DP .05 .02
☐ 532 Chris Speier DP .05 .02
☐ 533 Darrell Evans DP .10 .05
☐ 534 Luis Aquino DP .05 .02
☐ 535 Eric King DP .05 .02
☐ 536 Ken Hill DP .40 .18
☐ 537 Randy Bush DP .05 .02
☐ 538 Shane Mack DP .05 .02
☐ 539 Tom Bolton DP .05 .02
☐ 540 Gene Nelson DP .05 .02
☐ 541 Wes Gardner DP .05 .02
☐ 542 Ken Caminiti DP .20 .09
☐ 543 Duane Ward DP .05 .02
☐ 544 Norm Charlton DP .10 .05
☐ 545 Hal Morris DP .10 .05
☐ 546 Rich Yett DP .05 .02
☐ 547 Hensley Meulens DP .05 .02
☐ 548 Greg A. Harris DP .05 .02
☐ 549 Darren Daulton DP .10 .05
(Posing as right-
handed hitter)
☐ 550 Jeff Hamilton DP .05 .02
☐ 551 Luis Aguayo DP .05 .02
☐ 552 Tim Leary DP .05 .02
(Resembles M.Marshall)
☐ 553 Ron Oester DP .05 .02
☐ 554 Steve Lombardozzi DP .05 .02
☐ 555 Tim Jones DP .05 .02
☐ 556 Bud Black DP .05 .02
☐ 557 Alejandro Pena DP .05 .02
☐ 558 Jose DeJesus DP .05 .02
☐ 559 Dennis Rasmussen DP .05 .02
☐ 560 Pat Borders DP .10 .05
☐ 561 Craig Biggio DP .50 .23
☐ 562 Luis DeLosSantos DP .05 .02
☐ 563 Fred Lynn DP .05 .02
☐ 564 Todd Burns DP .05 .02
☐ 565 Felix Fermin DP .05 .02
☐ 566 Darnell Coles DP .05 .02
☐ 567 Willie Fraser DP .05 .02
☐ 568 Glenn Hubbard DP .05 .02
☐ 569 Craig Worthington DP .05 .02
☐ 570 Johnny Paredes DP .05 .02
☐ 571 Don Robinson DP .05 .02
☐ 572 Barry Lyons DP .05 .02
☐ 573 Bill Long DP .05 .02
☐ 574 Tracy Jones DP .05 .02
☐ 575 Juan Nieves DP .05 .02
☐ 576 Andres Thomas DP .05 .02
☐ 577 Rolando Roomes DP .05 .02
☐ 578 Luis Rivera UER DP .05 .02
(Wrong birthdate)
☐ 579 Chad Kreuter DP .05 .02
☐ 580 Tony Armas DP .05 .02
☐ 581 Jay Buhner .25 .11
☐ 582 Ricky Horton DP .05 .02
☐ 583 Andy Hawkins DP .05 .02
☐ 584 Sil Campusano .05 .02
☐ 585 Dave Clark .05 .02
☐ 586 Van Snider DP .05 .02
☐ 587 Todd Frohwirth DP .05 .02
☐ 588 Warren Spahn DP PUZ .20 .09
☐ 589 William Brennan .05 .02
☐ 590 German Gonzalez .05 .02
☐ 591 Ernie Whitt DP .05 .02
☐ 592 Jeff Blauser .10 .05
☐ 593 Spike Owen DP .05 .02
☐ 594 Matt Williams .25 .11
☐ 595 Lloyd McClendon DP .05 .02
☐ 596 Steve Ontiveros .05 .02
☐ 597 Scott Medvin .05 .02
☐ 598 Hipolito Pena DP .05 .02
☐ 599 Jerald Clark DP .05 .02
☐ 600A Checklist 578-660 DP .05 .02
(635 Kurt Schilling)
☐ 600B Checklist 578-660 DP .05 .02
(635 Curt Schilling;
MVP's not listed
on checklist card)
☐ 600C Checklist 578-660 DP .05 .02
(635 Curt Schilling;
MVP's listed
following 660)
☐ 601 Carmelo Martinez DP .05 .02
☐ 602 Mike LaCoss .05 .02
☐ 603 Mike Devereaux .05 .02
☐ 604 Alex Madrid DP .05 .02
☐ 605 Gary Redus DP .05 .02
☐ 606 Lance Johnson .10 .05
☐ 607 Terry Clark DP .05 .02
☐ 608 Manny Trillo DP .05 .02
☐ 609 Scott Jordan .10 .05
☐ 610 Jay Howell DP .05 .02
☐ 611 Francisco Melendez .05 .02
☐ 612 Mike Boddicker .05 .02
☐ 613 Kevin Brown DP .10 .05
☐ 614 Dave Valle .05 .02
☐ 615 Tim Laudner DP .05 .02
☐ 616 Andy Nezelek UER .05 .02
(Wrong birthdate)
☐ 617 Chuck Crim .05 .02
☐ 618 Jack Savage DP .05 .02
☐ 619 Adam Peterson .05 .02
☐ 620 Todd Stottlemyre .10 .05
☐ 621 Lance Blankenship .05 .02
☐ 622 Miguel Garcia DP .05 .02
☐ 623 Keith A. Miller DP .05 .02
☐ 624 Ricky Jordan DP .10 .05
☐ 625 Ernest Riles DP .05 .02
☐ 626 John Moses DP .05 .02
☐ 627 Nelson Liriano DP .05 .02
☐ 628 Mike Smithson DP .05 .02
☐ 629 Scott Sanderson .05 .02
☐ 630 Dale Mohorcic .05 .02
☐ 631 Marvin Freeman DP .05 .02
☐ 632 Mike Young DP .05 .02
☐ 633 Dennis Lamp .05 .02
☐ 634 Dante Bichette DP .40 .18
☐ 635 Curt Schilling DP .50 .23
☐ 636 Scott May DP .05 .02
☐ 637 Mike Schooler .05 .02
☐ 638 Rick Leach .05 .02
☐ 639 Tom Lampkin UER .05 .02
(Throws Left, should
be Throws Right)
☐ 640 Brian Meyer .05 .02
☐ 641 Brian Harper .05 .02
☐ 642 John Smoltz .50 .23
☐ 643 Jose Canseco .20 .09
(40/40 Club)
☐ 644 Bill Schroeder .05 .02
☐ 645 Edgar Martinez .20 .09
☐ 646 Dennis Cook .05 .02
☐ 647 Barry Jones .05 .02
☐ 648 Orel Hershiser .10 .05
(59 and Counting)
☐ 649 Rod Nichols .05 .02
☐ 650 Jody Davis .05 .02
☐ 651 Bob Milacki .05 .02
☐ 652 Mike Jackson .05 .02
☐ 653 Derek Lilliquist .05 .02
☐ 654 Paul Mirabella .05 .02
☐ 655 Mike Diaz .05 .02
☐ 656 Jeff Musselman .05 .02
☐ 657 Jerry Reed .05 .02
☐ 658 Kevin Blankenship .05 .02
☐ 659 Wayne Tolleson .05 .02
☐ 660 Eric Hetzel .05 .02

1989 Donruss Bonus MVP's

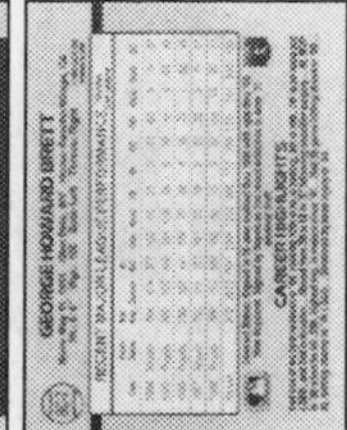

Rather than short-printing 26 cards in order to make room for printing the Bonus MVP's this year, Donruss apparently chose to double print 106 cards. Numbered with the prefix "BC" for bonus card, the 26-card set featuring the most valuable player from each of the 26 teams was randomly inserted in the wax and rack packs. These cards are distinguished by the bold MVP logo in the upper background of the obverse, and the four doubleprinted cards are denoted by "DP" in the checklist below.

	MINT	NRMT
COMPLETE SET (26)	1.50	.70
COMMON CARD (BC1-BC26)	.05	.02

☐ BC1 Kirby Puckett .40 .18
☐ BC2 Mike Scott .05 .02
☐ BC3 Joe Carter .10 .05
☐ BC4 Orel Hershiser .10 .05
☐ BC5 Jose Canseco .15 .07
☐ BC6 Darryl Strawberry .10 .05
☐ BC7 George Brett .40 .18
☐ BC8 Andre Dawson .15 .07
☐ BC9 Paul Molitor UER .20 .09
(Brewers logo missing
the word Milwaukee)
☐ BC10 Andy Van Slyke .05 .02
☐ BC11 Dave Winfield .20 .09
☐ BC12 Kevin Gross .05 .02
☐ BC13 Mike Greenwell .05 .02
☐ BC14 Ozzie Smith .30 .14
☐ BC15 Cal Ripken .75 .35
☐ BC16 Andres Galarraga .20 .09
☐ BC17 Alan Trammell .15 .07
☐ BC18 Kal Daniels .05 .02
☐ BC19 Fred McGriff .15 .07
☐ BC20 Tony Gwynn .40 .18
☐ BC21 Wally Joyner DP .05 .02
☐ BC22 Will Clark DP .10 .05
☐ BC23 Ozzie Guillen .05 .02
☐ BC24 Gerald Perry DP .05 .02
☐ BC25 Alvin Davis DP .05 .02
☐ BC26 Ruben Sierra .05 .02

1989 Donruss Grand Slammers

The 1989 Donruss Grand Slammers set contains 12 standard-size cards. Each card in the set can be found with five different colored border combinations, but no color combination of borders appears to be scarcer than any other. The set includes cards for each player who hit one or more grand slams in 1988. The backs detail the players' grand slams. The cards were distributed one per cello pack as well as an insert (complete) set in each factory set.

	MINT	NRMT
COMPLETE SET (12)	2.00	.90
COMMON CARD (1-12)	.05	.02

☐ 1 Jose Canseco .30 .14
☐ 2 Mike Marshall .05 .02
☐ 3 Walt Weiss .05 .02
☐ 4 Kevin McReynolds .05 .02
☐ 5 Mike Greenwell .05 .02
☐ 6 Dave Winfield .30 .14
☐ 7 Mark McGwire .60 .25
☐ 8 Keith Hernandez .10 .05
☐ 9 Franklin Stubbs .05 .02
☐ 10 Danny Tartabull .05 .02
☐ 11 Jesse Barfield .05 .02
☐ 12 Ellis Burks .15 .07

1989 Donruss Rookies

The 1989 Donruss Rookies set contains 56 standard-size cards. The cards were distributed exclusively in factory set form in small, emerald green, cellophane-wrapped boxes through hobby dealers. The cards are almost identical in design to geular 1989 Donruss except for the green borders. Rookie Cards in this set include Jim Abbott, Steve Finley, Kenny Rogers and Deion Sanders. Ken Griffey Jr. is also featured on a card within the set.

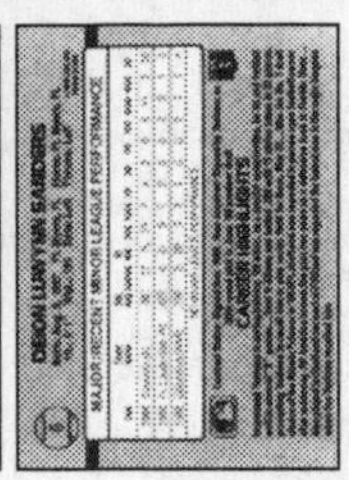

	MINT	NRMT
COMP.FACT.SET (56)	10.00	4.50
COMMON CARD (1-56)	.05	.02
☐ 1 Gary Sheffield	.75	.35
☐ 2 Gregg Jefferies	.10	.05
☐ 3 Ken Griffey Jr.	6.00	2.70
☐ 4 Tom Gordon	.20	.09
☐ 5 Billy Spiers	.05	.02
☐ 6 Deion Sanders	.75	.35
☐ 7 Donn Pall	.05	.02
☐ 8 Steve Carter	.05	.02
☐ 9 Francisco Oliveras	.05	.02
☐ 10 Steve Wilson	.05	.02
☐ 11 Bob Geren	.05	.02
☐ 12 Tony Castillo	.05	.02
☐ 13 Kenny Rogers	.10	.05
☐ 14 Carlos Martinez	.05	.02
☐ 15 Edgar Martinez	.20	.09
☐ 16 Jim Abbott	.20	.09
☐ 17 Torey Lovullo	.05	.02
☐ 18 Mark Carreon	.05	.02
☐ 19 Geronimo Berroa	.10	.05
☐ 20 Luis Medina	.05	.02
☐ 21 Sandy Alomar Jr.	.50	.23
☐ 22 Bob Milacki	.05	.02
☐ 23 Joe Girardi	.15	.07
☐ 24 German Gonzalez	.05	.02
☐ 25 Craig Worthington	.05	.02
☐ 26 Jerome Walton	.20	.09
☐ 27 Gary Wayne	.05	.02
☐ 28 Tim Jones	.05	.02
☐ 29 Dante Bichette	.40	.18
☐ 30 Alexis Infante	.05	.02
☐ 31 Ken Hill	.20	.09
☐ 32 Dwight Smith	.10	.05
☐ 33 Luis de los Santos	.05	.02
☐ 34 Eric Yelding	.05	.02
☐ 35 Gregg Olson	.10	.05
☐ 36 Phil Stephenson	.05	.02
☐ 37 Ken Patterson	.05	.02
☐ 38 Rick Wrona	.05	.02
☐ 39 Mike Brumley	.05	.02
☐ 40 Cris Carpenter	.05	.02
☐ 41 Jeff Brantley	.20	.09
☐ 42 Ron Jones	.05	.02
☐ 43 Randy Johnson	1.00	.45
☐ 44 Kevin Brown	.20	.09
☐ 45 Ramon Martinez	.20	.09
☐ 46 Greg W.Harris	.05	.02
☐ 47 Steve Finley	.25	.11
☐ 48 Randy Kramer	.05	.02
☐ 49 Erik Hanson	.10	.05
☐ 50 Matt Merullo	.05	.02
☐ 51 Mike Devereaux	.05	.02
☐ 52 Clay Parker	.05	.02
☐ 53 Omar Vizquel	.40	.18
☐ 54 Derek Lilliquist	.05	.02
☐ 55 Junior Felix	.05	.02
☐ 56 Checklist 1-56	.05	.02

1989 Donruss All-Stars

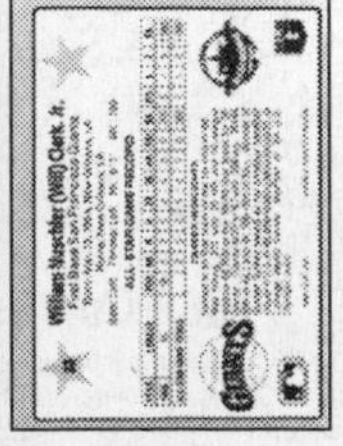

These All-Stars are standard size and very similar in design to the regular issue of 1989 Donruss. The set is distinguished by the presence of the respective League logos in the lower right corner of each obverse. The cards are numbered on the backs. The players chosen for the set are essentially the participants at the previous year's All-Star Game. Individual wax packs of All Stars (suggested retail price of 35 cents) contained one Pop-Up, five All-Star cards, and a Warren Spahn puzzle card.

	MINT	NRMT
COMPLETE SET (64)	8.00	3.60
COMMON CARD (1-64)	.05	.02
☐ 1 Mark McGwire	1.25	.55
☐ 2 Jose Canseco	.25	.11
☐ 3 Paul Molitor	.40	.18
☐ 4 Rickey Henderson	.25	.11
☐ 5 Cal Ripken	2.00	.90
☐ 6 Dave Winfield	.30	.14
☐ 7 Wade Boggs	.25	.11
☐ 8 Frank Viola	.05	.02
☐ 9 Terry Steinbach	.10	.05
☐ 10 Tom Kelly MG	.05	.02
☐ 11 George Brett	1.00	.45
☐ 12 Doyle Alexander	.05	.02
☐ 13 Gary Gaetti	.05	.02
☐ 14 Roger Clemens	.50	.23
☐ 15 Mike Greenwell	.05	.02
☐ 16 Dennis Eckersley	.10	.05
☐ 17 Carney Lansford	.15	.07
☐ 18 Mark Gubicza	.05	.02
☐ 19 Tim Laudner	.05	.02
☐ 20 Doug Jones	.05	.02
☐ 21 Don Mattingly	1.25	.55
☐ 22 Dan Plesac	.05	.02
☐ 23 Kirby Puckett	1.25	.55
☐ 24 Jeff Reardon	.10	.05
☐ 25 Johnny Ray	.05	.02
☐ 26 Jeff Russell	.05	.02
☐ 27 Harold Reynolds	.10	.05
☐ 28 Dave Stieb	.05	.02
☐ 29 Kurt Stillwell	.05	.02
☐ 30 Jose Canseco (Top AL Vote Getter)	.15	.07
☐ 31 Terry Steinbach (All-Star Game MVP)	.10	.05
☐ 32 AL Checklist 1-32	.05	.02
☐ 33 Will Clark	.30	.14
☐ 34 Darryl Strawberry	.10	.05
☐ 35 Ryne Sandberg	1.00	.45
☐ 36 Andre Dawson	.20	.09
☐ 37 Ozzie Smith	1.00	.45
☐ 38 Vince Coleman	.05	.02
☐ 39 Bobby Bonilla	.10	.05
☐ 40 Dwight Gooden	.10	.05
☐ 41 Gary Carter	.15	.07
☐ 42 Whitey Herzog MG	.05	.02
☐ 43 Shawon Dunston	.05	.02
☐ 44 David Cone	.15	.07
☐ 45 Andres Galarraga	.30	.14
☐ 46 Mark Davis	.05	.02
☐ 47 Barry Larkin	.15	.07
☐ 48 Kevin Gross	.05	.02
☐ 49 Vance Law	.05	.02
☐ 50 Orel Hershiser	.10	.05
☐ 51 Willie McGee	.05	.02
☐ 52 Danny Jackson	.05	.02
☐ 53 Rafael Palmeiro	.40	.18
☐ 54 Bob Knepper	.05	.02
☐ 55 Lance Parrish	.05	.02
☐ 56 Greg Maddux	2.00	.90
☐ 57 Gerald Perry	.05	.02
☐ 58 Bob Walk	.05	.02
☐ 59 Chris Sabo	.05	.02
☐ 60 Todd Worrell	.05	.02
☐ 61 Andy Van Slyke	.10	.05
☐ 62 Ozzie Smith (Top AL Vote Getter)	.75	.35
☐ 63 Riverfront Stadium	.05	.02
☐ 64 NL Checklist 33-64	.05	.02

1989 Donruss Baseball's Best

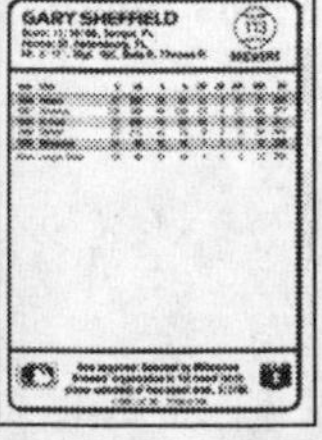

The 1989 Donruss Baseball's Best set contains 336 standard-size glossy cards. The fronts are green and yellow, and the backs feature career highlight information. The backs are green, and feature vertically oriented career stats. The cards were distributed as a set in a blister pac through various retail and department store chains. Th Sammy Sosa card in this set is the only card issued o him in 1989.

	MINT	NRMT
COMPLETE SET (336)	10.00	4.50
COMMON CARD (1-336)	.05	.02
☐ 1 Don Mattingly	1.00	.45
☐ 2 Tom Glavine	.50	.23
☐ 3 Bert Blyleven	.10	.05
☐ 4 Andre Dawson	.15	.07
☐ 5 Pete O'Brien	.05	.02
☐ 6 Eric Davis	.10	.05
☐ 7 George Brett	.75	.35
☐ 8 Glenn Davis	.05	.02
☐ 9 Ellis Burks	.10	.05
☐ 10 Kirk Gibson	.10	.05
☐ 11 Carlton Fisk	.25	.11
☐ 12 Andres Galarraga	.30	.14
☐ 13 Alan Trammell	.15	.07
☐ 14 Dwight Gooden	.10	.05
☐ 15 Paul Molitor	.40	.18
☐ 16 Roger McDowell	.05	.02
☐ 17 Doug Drabek	.05	.02
☐ 18 Kent Hrbek	.10	.05
☐ 19 Vince Coleman	.05	.02
☐ 20 Steve Sax	.05	.02
☐ 21 Roberto Alomar	.50	.23
☐ 22 Carney Lansford	.10	.05
☐ 23 Will Clark	.15	.07
☐ 24 Alvin Davis	.05	.02
☐ 25 Bobby Thigpen	.05	.02
☐ 26 Ryne Sandberg	.75	.35
☐ 27 Devon White	.10	.05
☐ 28 Mike Greenwell	.05	.02
☐ 29 Dale Murphy	.15	.07
☐ 30 Jeff Ballard	.05	.02
☐ 31 Kelly Gruber	.05	.02
☐ 32 Julio Franco	.10	.05
☐ 33 Bobby Bonilla	.15	.07
☐ 34 Tim Wallach	.05	.02
☐ 35 Lou Whitaker	.10	.05
☐ 36 Jay Howell	.05	.02
☐ 37 Greg Maddux	1.50	.70
☐ 38 Bill Doran	.05	.02
☐ 39 Danny Tartabull	.05	.02
☐ 40 Darryl Strawberry	.10	.05
☐ 41 Ron Darling	.05	.02
☐ 42 Tony Gwynn	1.00	.45
☐ 43 Mark McGwire	1.25	.55
☐ 44 Ozzie Smith	.60	.25
☐ 45 Andy Van Slyke	.10	.05
☐ 46 Juan Berenguer	.05	.02
☐ 47 Von Hayes	.05	.02
☐ 48 Tony Fernandez	.05	.02
☐ 49 Eric Plunk	.05	.02
☐ 50 Ernest Riles	.05	.02
☐ 51 Harold Reynolds	.10	.05
☐ 52 Andy Hawkins	.05	.02
☐ 53 Robin Yount	.20	.09
☐ 54 Danny Jackson	.05	.02
☐ 55 Nolan Ryan	1.50	.70
☐ 56 Joe Carter	.25	.11
☐ 57 Jose Canseco	.30	.14
☐ 58 Jody Davis	.05	.02
☐ 59 Lance Parrish	.05	.02
☐ 60 Mitch Williams	.05	.02
☐ 61 Brook Jacoby	.05	.02
☐ 62 Tom Browning	.05	.02
☐ 63 Kurt Stillwell	.05	.02
☐ 64 Rafael Ramirez	.05	.02
☐ 65 Roger Clemens	.50	.23
☐ 66 Mike Scioscia	.05	.02
☐ 67 Dave Gallagher	.05	.02
☐ 68 Mark Langston	.10	.05
☐ 69 Chet Lemon	.05	.02
☐ 70 Kevin McReynolds	.05	.02
☐ 71 Rob Deer	.05	.02
☐ 72 Tommy Herr	.05	.02
☐ 73 Barry Bonds	.40	.18
☐ 74 Frank Viola	.05	.02
☐ 75 Pedro Guerrero	.05	.02
☐ 76 Dave Righetti UER (ML total of 7 wins incorrect)	.05	.02
☐ 77 Bruce Hurst	.05	.02
☐ 78 Rickey Henderson	.25	.11
☐ 79 Robby Thompson	.05	.02
☐ 80 Randy Johnson	1.25	.55
☐ 81 Harold Baines	.10	.05
☐ 82 Calvin Schiraldi	.05	.02
☐ 83 Kirk McCaskill	.05	.02
☐ 84 Lee Smith	.10	.05
☐ 85 John Smoltz	1.00	.45
☐ 86 Mickey Tettleton	.05	.02
☐ 87 Jimmy Key	.10	.05

☐ 88 Rafael Palmeiro .30 .14
☐ 89 Sid Bream .05 .02
☐ 90 Dennis Martinez .10 .05
☐ 91 Frank Tanana .05 .02
☐ 92 Eddie Murray .40 .18
☐ 93 Shawon Dunston .05 .02
☐ 94 Mike Scott .05 .02
☐ 95 Bret Saberhagen .10 .05
☐ 96 David Cone .40 .18
☐ 97 Kevin Elster .05 .02
☐ 98 Jack Clark .10 .05
☐ 99 Dave Stewart .10 .05
☐ 100 Jose Oquendo .05 .02
☐ 101 Jose Lind .05 .02
☐ 102 Gary Gaetti .10 .05
☐ 103 Ricky Jordan .05 .02
☐ 104 Fred McGriff .40 .18
☐ 105 Don Slaught .05 .02
☐ 106 Jose Uribe .05 .02
☐ 107 Jeffrey Leonard .05 .02
☐ 108 Lee Guetterman .05 .02
☐ 109 Chris Bosio .05 .02
☐ 110 Barry Larkin .20 .09
☐ 111 Ruben Sierra .10 .05
☐ 112 Greg Swindell .05 .02
☐ 113 Gary Sheffield 1.00 .45
☐ 114 Lonnie Smith .05 .02
☐ 115 Chili Davis .10 .05
☐ 116 Damon Berryhill .05 .02
☐ 117 Tom Candiotti .05 .02
☐ 118 Kal Daniels .05 .02
☐ 119 Mark Gubicza .05 .02
☐ 120 Jim Deshaies .05 .02
☐ 121 Dwight Evans .10 .05
☐ 122 Mike Morgan .05 .02
☐ 123 Dan Pasqua .05 .02
☐ 124 Bryn Smith .05 .02
☐ 125 Doyle Alexander .05 .02
☐ 126 Howard Johnson .05 .02
☐ 127 Chuck Crim .05 .02
☐ 128 Darren Daulton .15 .07
☐ 129 Jeff Robinson .05 .02
☐ 130 Kirby Puckett 1.00 .45
☐ 131 Joe Magrane .05 .02
☐ 132 Jesse Barfield .05 .02
☐ 133 Mark Davis UER .05 .02
(Photo actually
Dave Leiper)
☐ 134 Dennis Eckersley .15 .07
☐ 135 Mike Krukow .05 .02
☐ 136 Jay Buhner .40 .18
☐ 137 Ozzie Guillen .05 .02
☐ 138 Rick Sutcliffe .05 .02
☐ 139 Wally Joyner .10 .05
☐ 140 Wade Boggs .25 .11
☐ 141 Jeff Treadway .05 .02
☐ 142 Cal Ripken 1.50 .70
☐ 143 Dave Stieb .05 .02
☐ 144 Pete Incaviglia .05 .02
☐ 145 Bob Walk .05 .02
☐ 146 Nelson Santovenia .05 .02
☐ 147 Mike Heath .05 .02
☐ 148 Willie Randolph .10 .05
☐ 149 Paul Kilgus .05 .02
☐ 150 Billy Hatcher .05 .02
☐ 151 Steve Farr .05 .02
☐ 152 Gregg Jefferies .20 .09
☐ 153 Randy Myers .10 .05
☐ 154 Garry Templeton .05 .02
☐ 155 Walt Weiss .05 .02
☐ 156 Terry Pendleton .10 .05
☐ 157 John Smiley .05 .02
☐ 158 Greg Gagne .05 .02
☐ 159 Len Dykstra .10 .05
☐ 160 Nelson Liriano .05 .02
☐ 161 Alvaro Espinoza .05 .02
☐ 162 Rick Reuschel .05 .02
☐ 163 Omar Vizquel UER .25 .11
(Photo actually
Darnell Coles)
☐ 164 Clay Parker .05 .02
☐ 165 Dan Plesac .05 .02
☐ 166 John Franco .10 .05
☐ 167 Scott Fletcher .05 .02
☐ 168 Cory Snyder .05 .02
☐ 169 Bo Jackson .10 .05
☐ 170 Tommy Gregg .05 .02
☐ 171 Jim Abbott .25 .11
☐ 172 Jerome Walton .10 .05
☐ 173 Doug Jones .05 .02
☐ 174 Todd Benzinger .05 .02
☐ 175 Frank White .10 .05
☐ 176 Craig Biggio .40 .18
☐ 177 John Dopson .05 .02
☐ 178 Alfredo Griffin .05 .02
☐ 179 Melido Perez .05 .02
☐ 180 Tim Burke .05 .02
☐ 181 Matt Nokes .05 .02
☐ 182 Gary Carter .15 .07
☐ 183 Ted Higuera .05 .02
☐ 184 Ken Howell .05 .02
☐ 185 Rey Quinones .05 .02
☐ 186 Wally Backman .05 .02
☐ 187 Tom Brunansky .05 .02
☐ 188 Steve Balboni .05 .02
☐ 189 Marvell Wynne .05 .02
☐ 190 Dave Henderson .05 .02
☐ 191 Don Robinson .05 .02
☐ 192 Ken Griffey Jr. 4.00 1.80
☐ 193 Ivan Calderon .05 .02
☐ 194 Mike Bielecki .05 .02
☐ 195 Johnny Ray .05 .02
☐ 196 Rob Murphy .05 .02
☐ 197 Andres Thomas .05 .02
☐ 198 Phil Bradley .05 .02
☐ 199 Junior Felix .05 .02
☐ 200 Jeff Russell .05 .02
☐ 201 Mike LaValliere .05 .02
☐ 202 Kevin Gross .05 .02
☐ 203 Keith Moreland .05 .02
☐ 204 Mike Marshall .05 .02
☐ 205 Dwight Smith .10 .05
☐ 206 Jim Clancy .05 .02
☐ 207 Kevin Seitzer .05 .02
☐ 208 Keith Hernandez .10 .05
☐ 209 Bob Ojeda .05 .02
☐ 210 Ed Whitson .05 .02
☐ 211 Tony Phillips .05 .02
☐ 212 Milt Thompson .05 .02
☐ 213 Randy Kramer .05 .02
☐ 214 Randy Bush .05 .02
☐ 215 Randy Ready .05 .02
☐ 216 Duane Ward .05 .02
☐ 217 Jimmy Jones .05 .02
☐ 218 Scott Garrelts .05 .02
☐ 219 Scott Bankhead .05 .02
☐ 220 Lance McCullers .05 .02
☐ 221 B.J. Surhoff .10 .05
☐ 222 Chris Sabo .05 .02
☐ 223 Steve Buechele .05 .02
☐ 224 Joel Skinner .05 .02
☐ 225 Orel Hershiser .10 .05
☐ 226 Derek Lilliquist .05 .02
☐ 227 Claudell Washington .05 .02
☐ 228 Lloyd McClendon .05 .02
☐ 229 Felix Fermin .05 .02
☐ 230 Paul O'Neill .10 .05
☐ 231 Charlie Leibrandt .05 .02
☐ 232 Dave Smith .05 .02
☐ 233 Bob Stanley .05 .02
☐ 234 Tim Belcher .05 .02
☐ 235 Eric King .05 .02
☐ 236 Spike Owen .05 .02
☐ 237 Mike Henneman .05 .02
☐ 238 Juan Samuel .05 .02
☐ 239 Greg Brock .05 .02
☐ 240 John Kruk .20 .09
☐ 241 Glenn Wilson .05 .02
☐ 242 Jeff Reardon .10 .05
☐ 243 Todd Worrell .05 .02
☐ 244 Dave LaPoint .05 .02
☐ 245 Walt Terrell .05 .02
☐ 246 Mike Moore .05 .02
☐ 247 Kelly Downs .05 .02
☐ 248 Dave Valle .05 .02
☐ 249 Ron Kittle .05 .02
☐ 250 Steve Wilson .05 .02
☐ 251 Dick Schofield .05 .02
☐ 252 Marty Barrett .05 .02
☐ 253 Dion James .05 .02
☐ 254 Bob Milacki .05 .02
☐ 255 Ernie Whitt .05 .02
☐ 256 Kevin Brown .20 .09
☐ 257 R.J. Reynolds .05 .02
☐ 258 Tim Raines .10 .05
☐ 259 Frank Williams .05 .02
☐ 260 Jose Gonzalez .05 .02
☐ 261 Mitch Webster .05 .02
☐ 262 Ken Caminiti .30 .14
☐ 263 Bob Boone .10 .05
☐ 264 Dave Magadan .05 .02
☐ 265 Rick Aguilera .10 .05
☐ 266 Chris James .05 .02
☐ 267 Bob Welch .05 .02
☐ 268 Ken Dayley .05 .02
☐ 269 Junior Ortiz .05 .02
☐ 270 Allan Anderson .05 .02
☐ 271 Steve Jeltz .05 .02
☐ 272 George Bell .05 .02
☐ 273 Roberto Kelly .05 .02
☐ 274 Brett Butler .10 .05
☐ 275 Mike Schooler .05 .02
☐ 276 Ken Phelps .05 .02
☐ 277 Glenn Braggs .05 .02
☐ 278 Jose Rijo .05 .02
☐ 279 Bobby Witt .05 .02
☐ 280 Jerry Browne .05 .02
☐ 281 Kevin Mitchell .10 .05
☐ 282 Craig Worthington .05 .02
☐ 283 Greg Minton .05 .02
☐ 284 Nick Esasky .05 .02
☐ 285 John Farrell .05 .02
☐ 286 Rick Mahler .05 .02
☐ 287 Tom Gordon .20 .09
☐ 288 Gerald Young .05 .02
☐ 289 Jody Reed .05 .02
☐ 290 Jeff Hamilton .05 .02
☐ 291 Gerald Perry .05 .02
☐ 292 Hubie Brooks .05 .02
☐ 293 Bo Diaz .05 .02
☐ 294 Terry Puhl .05 .02
☐ 295 Jim Gantner .05 .02
☐ 296 Jeff Parrett .05 .02
☐ 297 Mike Boddicker .05 .02
☐ 298 Dan Gladden .05 .02
☐ 299 Tony Pena .05 .02
☐ 300 Checklist Card .05 .02
☐ 301 Tom Henke .05 .02
☐ 302 Pascual Perez .05 .02
☐ 303 Steve Bedrosian .05 .02
☐ 304 Ken Hill .25 .11
☐ 305 Jerry Reuss .05 .02
☐ 306 Jim Eisenreich .20 .09
☐ 307 Jack Howell .05 .02
☐ 308 Rick Cerone .05 .02
☐ 309 Tim Leary .05 .02
☐ 310 Joe Orsulak .05 .02
☐ 311 Jim Dwyer .05 .02
☐ 312 Geno Petralli .05 .02
☐ 313 Rick Honeycutt .05 .02
☐ 314 Tom Foley .05 .02
☐ 315 Kenny Rogers .25 .11
☐ 316 Mike Flanagan .05 .02
☐ 317 Bryan Harvey .10 .05
☐ 318 Billy Ripken .05 .02
☐ 319 Jeff Montgomery .10 .05
☐ 320 Erik Hanson .20 .09
☐ 321 Brian Downing .05 .02
☐ 322 Gregg Olson .10 .05
☐ 323 Terry Steinbach .10 .05
☐ 324 Sammy Sosa 1.50 .70
☐ 325 Gene Harris .05 .02
☐ 326 Mike Devereaux .05 .02
☐ 327 Dennis Cook .05 .02
☐ 328 David Wells .05 .02
☐ 329 Checklist Card .05 .02
☐ 330 Kirt Manwaring .05 .02
☐ 331 Jim Presley .05 .02
☐ 332 Checklist Card .05 .02
☐ 333 Chuck Finley .10 .05
☐ 334 Rob Dibble .05 .02
☐ 335 Cecil Espy .05 .02
☐ 336 Dave Parker .15 .07

1989 Donruss Pop-Ups

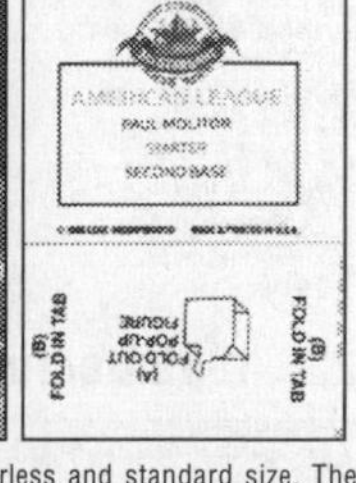

These Pop-Ups are borderless and standard size. The cards are unnumbered; however the All Star checklist card lists the same numbers as the All Star cards. Those numbers are used below for reference. The players chosen for the set are essentially the starting lineups for the previous year's All-Star Game. Individual wax packs of All Stars (suggested retail price of 35 cents) contained one Pop-Up, five All-Star cards and a puzzle card.

	MINT	NRMT
COMPLETE SET (20)	5.00	2.20
COMMON AL (1-10)	.10	.05
COMMON NL (33-42)	.10	.05

☐ 1 Mark McGwire 1.25 .55
☐ 2 Jose Canseco .50 .23
☐ 3 Paul Molitor .50 .23
☐ 4 Rickey Henderson .30 .14
☐ 5 Cal Ripken 2.50 1.10
☐ 6 Dave Winfield .30 .14
☐ 7 Wade Boggs .40 .18

☐ 8 Frank Viola	.10	.05
☐ 9 Terry Steinbach	.20	.09
☐ 10 Tom Kelly MG	.10	.05
☐ 33 Will Clark	.30	.14
☐ 34 Darryl Strawberry	.20	.09
☐ 35 Ryne Sandberg	1.00	.45
☐ 36 Andre Dawson	.20	.09
☐ 37 Ozzie Smith	1.00	.45
☐ 38 Vince Coleman	.10	.05
☐ 39 Bobby Bonilla	.30	.14
☐ 40 Dwight Gooden	.20	.09
☐ 41 Gary Carter	.20	.09
☐ 42 Whitey Herzog MG	.10	.05

1989 Donruss Super DK's

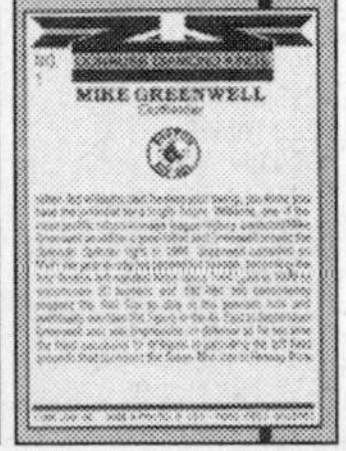

This 26-player card set was available through a mail-in offer detailed on the wax packs. The set was sent in return for $8.00 and three wrappers plus $2.00 postage and handling. The set features the popular Diamond King subseries in large (approximately 4 7/8" X 6 13/16") form. Dick Perez of Perez-Steele Galleries did another outstanding job on the artwork. The cards are essentially a large version of the Donruss regular issue Diamond Kings.

	MINT	NRMT
COMPLETE SET (26)	15.00	6.75
COMMON CARD (1-26)	.25	.11
☐ 1 Mike Greenwell	.25	.11
☐ 2 Bobby Bonilla	.75	.35
☐ 3 Pete Incaviglia	.25	.11
☐ 4 Chris Sabo	.25	.11
☐ 5 Robin Yount	.75	.35
☐ 6 Tony Gwynn	2.50	1.10
☐ 7 Carlton Fisk	1.25	.55
☐ 8 Cory Snyder	.25	.11
☐ 9 David Cone	1.25	.55
☐ 10 Kevin Seitzer	.25	.11
☐ 11 Rick Reuschel	.25	.11
☐ 12 Johnny Ray	.25	.11
☐ 13 Dave Schmidt	.25	.11
☐ 14 Andres Galarraga	1.00	.45
☐ 15 Kirk Gibson	.75	.35
☐ 16 Fred McGriff	2.00	.90
☐ 17 Mark Grace	2.00	.90
☐ 18 Jeff M. Robinson	.25	.11
☐ 19 Vince Coleman	.25	.11
☐ 20 Dave Henderson	.25	.11
☐ 21 Harold Reynolds	.50	.23
☐ 22 Gerald Perry	.25	.11
☐ 23 Frank Viola	.25	.11
☐ 24 Steve Bedrosian	.25	.11
☐ 25 Glenn Davis	.25	.11
☐ 26 Don Mattingly	3.00	1.35

1989 Donruss Traded

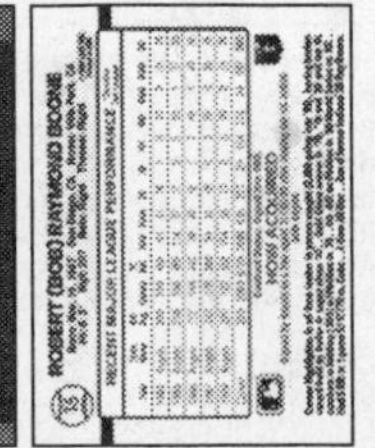

The 1989 Donruss Traded set contains 56 standard-size cards. The fronts have yellowish-orange borders; the backs are yellow and feature recent statistics. The cards were distributed as a boxed set. The set was never very popular with collectors since it included (as the name implies) only traded players rather than rookies. The cards are numbered with a "T" prefix.

	MINT	NRMT
COMPLETE SET (56)	4.00	1.80
COMMON CARD (1-56)	.05	.02
☐ 1 Jeffrey Leonard	.05	.02
☐ 2 Jack Clark	.10	.05
☐ 3 Kevin Gross	.05	.02
☐ 4 Tommy Herr	.05	.02
☐ 5 Bob Boone	.10	.05
☐ 6 Rafael Palmeiro	.75	.35
☐ 7 John Dopson	.05	.02
☐ 8 Willie Randolph	.10	.05
☐ 9 Chris Brown	.05	.02
☐ 10 Wally Backman	.05	.02
☐ 11 Steve Ontiveros	.05	.02
☐ 12 Eddie Murray	.75	.35
☐ 13 Lance McCullers	.05	.02
☐ 14 Spike Owen	.05	.02
☐ 15 Rob Murphy	.05	.02
☐ 16 Pete O'Brien	.05	.02
☐ 17 Ken Williams	.05	.02
☐ 18 Nick Esasky	.05	.02
☐ 19 Nolan Ryan	3.00	1.35
☐ 20 Brian Holton	.05	.02
☐ 21 Mike Moore	.05	.02
☐ 22 Joel Skinner	.05	.02
☐ 23 Steve Sax	.05	.02
☐ 24 Rick Mahler	.05	.02
☐ 25 Mike Aldrete	.05	.02
☐ 26 Jesse Orosco	.05	.02
☐ 27 Dave LaPoint	.05	.02
☐ 28 Walt Terrell	.05	.02
☐ 29 Eddie Williams	.05	.02
☐ 30 Mike Devereaux	.05	.02
☐ 31 Julio Franco	.10	.05
☐ 32 Jim Clancy	.05	.02
☐ 33 Felix Fermin	.05	.02
☐ 34 Curt Wilkerson	.05	.02
☐ 35 Bert Blyleven	.10	.05
☐ 36 Mel Hall	.05	.02
☐ 37 Eric King	.05	.02
☐ 38 Mitch Williams	.05	.02
☐ 39 Jamie Moyer	.05	.02
☐ 40 Rick Rhoden	.05	.02
☐ 41 Phil Bradley	.05	.02
☐ 42 Paul Kilgus	.05	.02
☐ 43 Milt Thompson	.05	.02
☐ 44 Jerry Browne	.05	.02
☐ 45 Bruce Hurst	.05	.02
☐ 46 Claudell Washington	.05	.02
☐ 47 Todd Benzinger	.05	.02
☐ 48 Steve Balboni	.05	.02
☐ 49 Oddibe McDowell	.05	.02
☐ 50 Charles Hudson	.05	.02
☐ 51 Ron Kittle	.05	.02
☐ 52 Andy Hawkins	.05	.02
☐ 53 Tom Brookens	.05	.02
☐ 54 Tom Niedenfuer	.05	.02
☐ 55 Jeff Parrett	.05	.02
☐ 56 Checklist Card	.05	.02

1990 Donruss Previews

The 1990 Donruss Previews set contains 12 standard-size cards. The bright red borders are exactly like the regular 1990 Donruss cards, but many of the photos are different. The horizontally oriented backs are plain white with career highlights in black lettering. Two cards were sent to each dealer in the Donruss dealer network thus making it quite difficult to put together a set.

	MINT	NRMT
COMPLETE SET (12)	400.00	180.00
COMMON CARD (1-12)	15.00	6.75
☐ 1 Todd Zeile (Not shown as Rated Rookie on front)	15.00	6.75
☐ 2 Ben McDonald	15.00	6.75
☐ 3 Bo Jackson	20.00	9.00
☐ 4 Will Clark	50.00	22.00
☐ 5 Dave Stewart	15.00	6.75
☐ 6 Kevin Mitchell	15.00	6.75
☐ 7 Nolan Ryan	200.00	90.00
☐ 8 Howard Johnson	15.00	6.75
☐ 9 Tony Gwynn	75.00	34.00
☐ 10 Jerome Walton (Shown ready to bunt)	20.00	9.00
☐ 11 Wade Boggs	50.00	22.00
☐ 12 Kirby Puckett	75.00	34.00

1990 Donruss

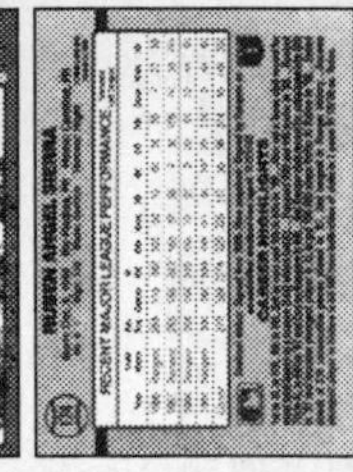

The 1990 Donruss set contains 716 standard-size cards. Cards were issued in wax packs and hobby and retail factory sets. The card fronts feature bright red borders. Subsets include Diamond Kings (1-27) and Rated Rookies (28-47). The set was the largest ever produced by Donruss, unfortunately it also had a large number of errors which were corrected after the cards were released. Most of these feature minor printing flaws and insignificant variations that collectors have found unworthy of price differentials. There are several double-printed cards within the set indicated in the checklists below with a "DP" coding. Rookie Cards of note include Juan Gonzalez, Marquis Grissom, Dave Justice, Ben McDonald, Dean Palmer, Sammy Sosa, Larry Walker and Bernie Williams. Numbered with the prefix "BC", Special Bonus Cards from a set featuring one most valuable player from each of the 26 teams were randomly inserted in all 1990 Donruss unopened pack formats. The factory sets were distributed without the Bonus Cards.

	MINT	NRMT
COMPLETE SET (716)	8.00	3.60
COMP.FACT.SET (728)	8.00	3.60
COMMON CARD (1-716)	.05	.02
COMPLETE YAZ PUZZLE	1.00	.45
☐ 1 Bo Jackson DK	.20	.09
☐ 2 Steve Sax DK	.05	.02
☐ 3A Ruben Sierra DK ERR (No small line on top border on card back)	.20	.09
☐ 3B Ruben Sierra DK COR	.10	.05
☐ 4 Ken Griffey Jr. DK	.75	.35
☐ 5 Mickey Tettleton DK	.05	.02
☐ 6 Dave Stewart DK	.10	.05
☐ 7 Jim Deshaies DK DP	.05	.02
☐ 8 John Smoltz DK	.20	.09
☐ 9 Mike Bielecki DK	.05	.02
☐ 10A Brian Downing DK ERR (Reverse negative on card front)	.20	.09
☐ 10B Brian Downing DK COR	.05	.02
☐ 11 Kevin Mitchell DK	.05	.02
☐ 12 Kelly Gruber DK	.05	.02
☐ 13 Joe Magrane DK	.05	.02
☐ 14 John Franco DK	.05	.02
☐ 15 Ozzie Guillen DK	.05	.02
☐ 16 Lou Whitaker DK	.10	.05
☐ 17 John Smiley DK	.05	.02
☐ 18 Howard Johnson DK	.05	.02
☐ 19 Willie Randolph DK	.10	.05
☐ 20 Chris Bosio DK	.05	.02
☐ 21 Tommy Herr DK DP	.05	.02
☐ 22 Dan Gladden DK	.05	.02
☐ 23 Ellis Burks DK	.20	.09
☐ 24 Pete O'Brien DK	.05	.02
☐ 25 Bryn Smith DK	.05	.02
☐ 26 Ed Whitson DK DP	.05	.02
☐ 27 DK Checklist 1-27 DP (Comments on Perez-Steele on back)	.05	.02
☐ 28 Robin Ventura RR	.20	.09
☐ 29 Todd Zeile RR	.10	.05
☐ 30 Sandy Alomar Jr. RR	.20	.09
☐ 31 Kent Mercker RR	.10	.05
☐ 32 Ben McDonald RR UER (Middle name Benard, not Benjamin)	.20	.09
☐ 33A Juan Gonzalez RR ERR (Reverse negative)	5.00	2.20
☐ 33B Juan Gonzalez RR COR	2.00	.90

☐ 34 Eric Anthony RR	.10	.05
☐ 35 Mike Fetters RR	.20	.09
☐ 36 Marquis Grissom RR	.40	.18
☐ 37 Greg Vaughn RR	.20	.09
☐ 38 Brian DuBois RR	.05	.02
☐ 39 Steve Avery RR UER	.20	.09
(Born in MI, not NJ)		
☐ 40 Mark Gardner RR	.05	.02
☐ 41 Andy Benes RR	.20	.09
☐ 42 Delino DeShields RR	.10	.05
☐ 43 Scott Coolbaugh RR	.05	.02
☐ 44 Pat Combs RR DP	.05	.02
☐ 45 Alex Sanchez RR DP	.05	.02
☐ 46 Kelly Mann RR DP	.05	.02
☐ 47 Julio Machado RR DP	.05	.02
☐ 48 Pete Incaviglia	.05	.02
☐ 49 Shawon Dunston	.05	.02
☐ 50 Jeff Treadway	.05	.02
☐ 51 Jeff Ballard	.05	.02
☐ 52 Claudell Washington	.05	.02
☐ 53 Juan Samuel	.05	.02
☐ 54 John Smiley	.10	.05
☐ 55 Rob Deer	.05	.02
☐ 56 Geno Petralli	.05	.02
☐ 57 Chris Bosio	.05	.02
☐ 58 Carlton Fisk	.20	.09
☐ 59 Kirt Manwaring	.05	.02
☐ 60 Chet Lemon	.05	.02
☐ 61 Bo Jackson	.20	.09
☐ 62 Doyle Alexander	.05	.02
☐ 63 Pedro Guerrero	.05	.02
☐ 64 Allan Anderson	.05	.02
☐ 65 Greg W. Harris	.05	.02
☐ 66 Mike Greenwell	.05	.02
☐ 67 Walt Weiss	.05	.02
☐ 68 Wade Boggs	.20	.09
☐ 69 Jim Clancy	.05	.02
☐ 70 Junior Felix	.05	.02
☐ 71 Barry Larkin	.20	.09
☐ 72 Dave LaPoint	.05	.02
☐ 73 Joel Skinner	.05	.02
☐ 74 Jesse Barfield	.05	.02
☐ 75 Tommy Herr	.05	.02
☐ 76 Ricky Jordan	.05	.02
☐ 77 Eddie Murray	.20	.09
☐ 78 Steve Sax	.05	.02
☐ 79 Tim Belcher	.05	.02
☐ 80 Danny Jackson	.05	.02
☐ 81 Kent Hrbek	.10	.05
☐ 82 Milt Thompson	.05	.02
☐ 83 Brook Jacoby	.05	.02
☐ 84 Mike Marshall	.05	.02
☐ 85 Kevin Seitzer	.05	.02
☐ 86 Tony Gwynn	.50	.23
☐ 87 Dave Stieb	.05	.02
☐ 88 Dave Smith	.05	.02
☐ 89 Bret Saberhagen	.05	.02
☐ 90 Alan Trammell	.10	.05
☐ 91 Tony Phillips	.05	.02
☐ 92 Doug Drabek	.05	.02
☐ 93 Jeffrey Leonard	.05	.02
☐ 94 Wally Joyner	.10	.05
☐ 95 Carney Lansford	.10	.05
☐ 96 Cal Ripken	.75	.35
☐ 97 Andres Galarraga	.20	.09
☐ 98 Kevin Mitchell	.10	.05
☐ 99 Howard Johnson	.05	.02
☐ 100A Checklist 28-129	.05	.02
☐ 100B Checklist 28-125	.05	.02
☐ 101 Melido Perez	.05	.02
☐ 102 Spike Owen	.05	.02
☐ 103 Paul Molitor	.20	.09
☐ 104 Geronimo Berroa	.10	.05
☐ 105 Ryne Sandberg	.25	.11
☐ 106 Bryn Smith	.05	.02
☐ 107 Steve Buechele	.05	.02
☐ 108 Jim Abbott	.10	.05
☐ 109 Alvin Davis	.05	.02
☐ 110 Lee Smith	.20	.09
☐ 111 Roberto Alomar	.25	.11
☐ 112 Rick Reuschel	.05	.02
☐ 113A Kelly Gruber ERR	.05	.02
(Born 2/22)		
☐ 113B Kelly Gruber COR	.05	.02
(Born 2/26; corrected in factory sets)		
☐ 114 Joe Carter	.20	.09
☐ 115 Jose Rijo	.05	.02
☐ 116 Greg Minton	.05	.02
☐ 117 Bob Ojeda	.05	.02
☐ 118 Glenn Davis	.05	.02
☐ 119 Jeff Reardon	.10	.05
☐ 120 Kurt Stillwell	.05	.02
☐ 121 John Smoltz	.20	.09
☐ 122 Dwight Evans	.10	.05
☐ 123 Eric Yelding	.05	.02
☐ 124 John Franco	.05	.02
☐ 125 Jose Canseco	.20	.09
☐ 126 Barry Bonds	.25	.11
☐ 127 Lee Guetterman	.05	.02
☐ 128 Jack Clark	.10	.05
☐ 129 Dave Valle	.05	.02
☐ 130 Hubie Brooks	.05	.02
☐ 131 Ernest Riles	.05	.02
☐ 132 Mike Morgan	.05	.02
☐ 133 Steve Jeltz	.05	.02
☐ 134 Jeff D. Robinson	.05	.02
☐ 135 Ozzie Guillen	.05	.02
☐ 136 Chili Davis	.10	.05
☐ 137 Mitch Webster	.05	.02
☐ 138 Jerry Browne	.05	.02
☐ 139 Bo Diaz	.05	.02
☐ 140 Robby Thompson	.05	.02
☐ 141 Craig Worthington	.05	.02
☐ 142 Julio Franco	.10	.05
☐ 143 Brian Holman	.05	.02
☐ 144 George Brett	.40	.18
☐ 145 Tom Glavine	.20	.09
☐ 146 Robin Yount	.20	.09
☐ 147 Gary Carter	.10	.05
☐ 148 Ron Kittle	.05	.02
☐ 149 Tony Fernandez	.05	.02
☐ 150 Dave Stewart	.10	.05
☐ 151 Gary Gaetti	.10	.05
☐ 152 Kevin Elster	.05	.02
☐ 153 Gerald Perry	.05	.02
☐ 154 Jesse Orosco	.05	.02
☐ 155 Wally Backman	.05	.02
☐ 156 Dennis Martinez	.10	.05
☐ 157 Rick Sutcliffe	.05	.02
☐ 158 Greg Maddux	.60	.25
☐ 159 Andy Hawkins	.05	.02
☐ 160 John Kruk	.10	.05
☐ 161 Jose Oquendo	.05	.02
☐ 162 John Dopson	.05	.02
☐ 163 Joe Magrane	.05	.02
☐ 164 Bill Ripken	.05	.02
☐ 165 Fred Manrique	.05	.02
☐ 166 Nolan Ryan UER	.75	.35
(Did not lead NL in K's in '89 as he was in AL in '89)		
☐ 167 Damon Berryhill	.05	.02
☐ 168 Dale Murphy	.20	.09
☐ 169 Mickey Tettleton	.10	.05
☐ 170A Kirk McCaskill ERR	.05	.02
(Born 4/19)		
☐ 170B Kirk McCaskill COR	.05	.02
(Born 4/9; corrected in factory sets)		
☐ 171 Dwight Gooden	.10	.05
☐ 172 Jose Lind	.05	.02
☐ 173 B.J. Surhoff	.10	.05
☐ 174 Ruben Sierra	.05	.02
☐ 175 Dan Plesac	.05	.02
☐ 176 Dan Pasqua	.05	.02
☐ 177 Kelly Downs	.05	.02
☐ 178 Matt Nokes	.05	.02
☐ 179 Luis Aquino	.05	.02
☐ 180 Frank Tanana	.05	.02
☐ 181 Tony Pena	.05	.02
☐ 182 Dan Gladden	.05	.02
☐ 183 Bruce Hurst	.05	.02
☐ 184 Roger Clemens	.40	.18
☐ 185 Mark McGwire	.40	.18
☐ 186 Rob Murphy	.05	.02
☐ 187 Jim Deshaies	.05	.02
☐ 188 Fred McGriff	.20	.09
☐ 189 Rob Dibble	.05	.02
☐ 190 Don Mattingly	.30	.14
☐ 191 Felix Fermin	.05	.02
☐ 192 Roberto Kelly	.05	.02
☐ 193 Dennis Cook	.05	.02
☐ 194 Darren Daulton	.10	.05
☐ 195 Alfredo Griffin	.05	.02
☐ 196 Eric Plunk	.05	.02
☐ 197 Orel Hershiser	.10	.05
☐ 198 Paul O'Neill	.10	.05
☐ 199 Randy Bush	.05	.02
☐ 200A Checklist 130-231	.05	.02
☐ 200B Checklist 126-223	.05	.02
☐ 201 Ozzie Smith	.25	.11
☐ 202 Pete O'Brien	.05	.02
☐ 203 Jay Howell	.05	.02
☐ 204 Mark Gubicza	.05	.02
☐ 205 Ed Whitson	.05	.02
☐ 206 George Bell	.05	.02
☐ 207 Mike Scott	.05	.02
☐ 208 Charlie Leibrandt	.05	.02
☐ 209 Mike Heath	.05	.02
☐ 210 Dennis Eckersley	.10	.05
☐ 211 Mike LaValliere	.05	.02
☐ 212 Darnell Coles	.05	.02
☐ 213 Lance Parrish	.05	.02
☐ 214 Mike Moore	.05	.02
☐ 215 Steve Finley	.20	.09
☐ 216 Tim Raines	.10	.05
☐ 217A Scott Garrelts ERR	.05	.02
(Born 10/20)		
☐ 217B Scott Garrelts COR	.05	.02
(Born 10/30; corrected in factory sets)		
☐ 218 Kevin McReynolds	.05	.02
☐ 219 Dave Gallagher	.05	.02
☐ 220 Tim Wallach	.05	.02
☐ 221 Chuck Crim	.05	.02
☐ 222 Lonnie Smith	.05	.02
☐ 223 Andre Dawson	.20	.09
☐ 224 Nelson Santovenia	.05	.02
☐ 225 Rafael Palmeiro	.20	.09
☐ 226 Devon White	.05	.02
☐ 227 Harold Reynolds	.05	.02
☐ 228 Ellis Burks	.20	.09
☐ 229 Mark Parent	.05	.02
☐ 230 Will Clark	.20	.09
☐ 231 Jimmy Key	.10	.05
☐ 232 John Farrell	.05	.02
☐ 233 Eric Davis	.10	.05
☐ 234 Johnny Ray	.05	.02
☐ 235 Darryl Strawberry	.10	.05
☐ 236 Bill Doran	.05	.02
☐ 237 Greg Gagne	.05	.02
☐ 238 Jim Eisenreich	.10	.05
☐ 239 Tommy Gregg	.05	.02
☐ 240 Marty Barrett	.05	.02
☐ 241 Rafael Ramirez	.05	.02
☐ 242 Chris Sabo	.05	.02
☐ 243 Dave Henderson	.05	.02
☐ 244 Andy Van Slyke	.10	.05
☐ 245 Alvaro Espinoza	.05	.02
☐ 246 Garry Templeton	.05	.02
☐ 247 Gene Harris	.05	.02
☐ 248 Kevin Gross	.05	.02
☐ 249 Brett Butler	.10	.05
☐ 250 Willie Randolph	.10	.05
☐ 251 Roger McDowell	.05	.02
☐ 252 Rafael Belliard	.05	.02
☐ 253 Steve Rosenberg	.05	.02
☐ 254 Jack Howell	.05	.02
☐ 255 Marvell Wynne	.05	.02
☐ 256 Tom Candiotti	.05	.02
☐ 257 Todd Benzinger	.05	.02
☐ 258 Don Robinson	.05	.02
☐ 259 Phil Bradley	.05	.02
☐ 260 Cecil Espy	.05	.02
☐ 261 Scott Bankhead	.05	.02
☐ 262 Frank White	.10	.05
☐ 263 Andres Thomas	.05	.02
☐ 264 Glenn Braggs	.05	.02
☐ 265 David Cone	.20	.09
☐ 266 Bobby Thigpen	.05	.02
☐ 267 Nelson Liriano	.05	.02
☐ 268 Terry Steinbach	.10	.05
☐ 269 Kirby Puckett UER	.40	.18
(Back doesn't consider Joe Torre's .363 in '71)		
☐ 270 Gregg Jefferies	.10	.05
☐ 271 Jeff Blauser	.10	.05
☐ 272 Cory Snyder	.05	.02
☐ 273 Roy Smith	.05	.02
☐ 274 Tom Foley	.05	.02
☐ 275 Mitch Williams	.05	.02
☐ 276 Paul Kilgus	.05	.02
☐ 277 Don Slaught	.05	.02
☐ 278 Von Hayes	.05	.02
☐ 279 Vince Coleman	.05	.02
☐ 280 Mike Boddicker	.05	.02
☐ 281 Ken Dayley	.05	.02
☐ 282 Mike Devereaux	.05	.02
☐ 283 Kenny Rogers	.10	.05
☐ 284 Jeff Russell	.05	.02
☐ 285 Jerome Walton	.05	.02
☐ 286 Derek Lilliquist	.05	.02
☐ 287 Joe Orsulak	.05	.02
☐ 288 Dick Schofield	.05	.02
☐ 289 Ron Darling	.05	.02
☐ 290 Bobby Bonilla	.10	.05
☐ 291 Jim Gantner	.05	.02
☐ 292 Bobby Witt	.05	.02
☐ 293 Greg Brock	.05	.02
☐ 294 Ivan Calderon	.05	.02
☐ 295 Steve Bedrosian	.05	.02
☐ 296 Mike Henneman	.05	.02
☐ 297 Tom Gordon	.10	.05
☐ 298 Lou Whitaker	.10	.05
☐ 299 Terry Pendleton	.10	.05
☐ 300A Checklist 232-333	.05	.02
☐ 300B Checklist 224-321	.05	.02
☐ 301 Juan Berenguer	.05	.02
☐ 302 Mark Davis	.05	.02
☐ 303 Nick Esasky	.05	.02

☐ 304 Rickey Henderson .20 .09
☐ 305 Rick Cerone .05 .02
☐ 306 Craig Biggio .20 .09
☐ 307 Duane Ward .05 .02
☐ 308 Tom Browning .05 .02
☐ 309 Walt Terrell .05 .02
☐ 310 Greg Swindell .05 .02
☐ 311 Dave Righetti .05 .02
☐ 312 Mike Maddux .05 .02
☐ 313 Len Dykstra .10 .05
☐ 314 Jose Gonzalez .05 .02
☐ 315 Steve Balboni .05 .02
☐ 316 Mike Scioscia .05 .02
☐ 317 Ron Oester .05 .02
☐ 318 Gary Wayne .05 .02
☐ 319 Todd Worrell .05 .02
☐ 320 Doug Jones .05 .02
☐ 321 Jeff Hamilton .05 .02
☐ 322 Danny Tartabull .05 .02
☐ 323 Chris James .05 .02
☐ 324 Mike Flanagan .05 .02
☐ 325 Gerald Young .05 .02
☐ 326 Bob Boone .10 .05
☐ 327 Frank Williams .05 .02
☐ 328 Dave Parker .10 .05
☐ 329 Sid Bream .05 .02
☐ 330 Mike Schooler .05 .02
☐ 331 Bert Blyleven .10 .05
☐ 332 Bob Welch .05 .02
☐ 333 Bob Milacki .05 .02
☐ 334 Tim Burke .05 .02
☐ 335 Jose Uribe .05 .02
☐ 336 Randy Myers .10 .05
☐ 337 Eric King .05 .02
☐ 338 Mark Langston .05 .02
☐ 339 Teddy Higuera .05 .02
☐ 340 Oddibe McDowell .05 .02
☐ 341 Lloyd McClendon .05 .02
☐ 342 Pascual Perez .05 .02
☐ 343 Kevin Brown UER .20 .09
(Signed is misspelled as signeed on back)
☐ 344 Chuck Finley .10 .05
☐ 345 Erik Hanson .05 .02
☐ 346 Rich Gedman .05 .02
☐ 347 Bip Roberts .05 .02
☐ 348 Matt Williams .20 .09
☐ 349 Tom Henke .05 .02
☐ 350 Brad Komminsk .05 .02
☐ 351 Jeff Reed .05 .02
☐ 352 Brian Downing .05 .02
☐ 353 Frank Viola .05 .02
☐ 354 Terry Puhl .05 .02
☐ 355 Brian Harper .05 .02
☐ 356 Steve Farr .05 .02
☐ 357 Joe Boever .05 .02
☐ 358 Danny Heep .05 .02
☐ 359 Larry Andersen .05 .02
☐ 360 Rolando Roomes .05 .02
☐ 361 Mike Gallego .05 .02
☐ 362 Bob Kipper .05 .02
☐ 363 Clay Parker .05 .02
☐ 364 Mike Pagliarulo .05 .02
☐ 365 Ken Griffey Jr. UER 1.50 .70
(Signed through 1990, should be 1991)
☐ 366 Rex Hudler .05 .02
☐ 367 Pat Sheridan .05 .02
☐ 368 Kirk Gibson .10 .05
☐ 369 Jeff Parrett .05 .02
☐ 370 Bob Walk .05 .02
☐ 371 Ken Patterson .05 .02
☐ 372 Bryan Harvey .05 .02
☐ 373 Mike Bielecki .05 .02
☐ 374 Tom Magrann .05 .02
☐ 375 Rick Mahler .05 .02
☐ 376 Craig Lefferts .05 .02
☐ 377 Gregg Olson .05 .02
☐ 378 Jamie Moyer .05 .02
☐ 379 Randy Johnson .30 .14
☐ 380 Jeff Montgomery .10 .05
☐ 381 Marty Clary .05 .02
☐ 382 Bill Spiers .05 .02
☐ 383 Dave Magadan .05 .02
☐ 384 Greg Hibbard .05 .02
☐ 385 Ernie Whitt .05 .02
☐ 386 Rick Honeycutt .05 .02
☐ 387 Dave West .05 .02
☐ 388 Keith Hernandez .10 .05
☐ 389 Jose Alvarez .05 .02
☐ 390 Joey Belle .50 .23
☐ 391 Rick Aguilera .10 .05
☐ 392 Mike Fitzgerald .05 .02
☐ 393 Dwight Smith .05 .02
☐ 394 Steve Wilson .05 .02
☐ 395 Bob Geren .05 .02
☐ 396 Randy Ready .05 .02
☐ 397 Ken Hill .20 .09
☐ 398 Jody Reed .05 .02
☐ 399 Tom Brunansky .05 .02
☐ 400A Checklist 334-435 .05 .02
☐ 400B Checklist 322-419 .05 .02
☐ 401 Rene Gonzales .05 .02
☐ 402 Harold Baines .10 .05
☐ 403 Cecilio Guante .05 .02
☐ 404 Joe Girardi .10 .05
☐ 405A Sergio Valdez ERR .05 .02
(Card front shows black line crossing S in Sergio)
☐ 405B Sergio Valdez COR .05 .02
☐ 406 Mark Williamson .05 .02
☐ 407 Glenn Hoffman .05 .02
☐ 408 Jeff Innis .05 .02
☐ 409 Randy Kramer .05 .02
☐ 410 Charlie O'Brien .05 .02
☐ 411 Charlie Hough .05 .02
☐ 412 Gus Polidor .05 .02
☐ 413 Ron Karkovice .05 .02
☐ 414 Trevor Wilson .05 .02
☐ 415 Kevin Ritz .05 .02
☐ 416 Gary Thurman .05 .02
☐ 417 Jeff M. Robinson .05 .02
☐ 418 Scott Terry .05 .02
☐ 419 Tim Laudner .05 .02
☐ 420 Dennis Rasmussen .05 .02
☐ 421 Luis Rivera .05 .02
☐ 422 Jim Corsi .05 .02
☐ 423 Dennis Lamp .05 .02
☐ 424 Ken Caminiti .20 .09
☐ 425 David Wells .05 .02
☐ 426 Norm Charlton .05 .02
☐ 427 Deion Sanders .20 .09
☐ 428 Dion James .05 .02
☐ 429 Chuck Cary .05 .02
☐ 430 Ken Howell .05 .02
☐ 431 Steve Lake .05 .02
☐ 432 Kal Daniels .05 .02
☐ 433 Lance McCullers .05 .02
☐ 434 Lenny Harris .05 .02
☐ 435 Scott Scudder .05 .02
☐ 436 Gene Larkin .05 .02
☐ 437 Dan Quisenberry .05 .02
☐ 438 Steve Olin .10 .05
☐ 439 Mickey Hatcher .05 .02
☐ 440 Willie Wilson .05 .02
☐ 441 Mark Grant .05 .02
☐ 442 Mookie Wilson .05 .02
☐ 443 Alex Trevino .05 .02
☐ 444 Pat Tabler .05 .02
☐ 445 Dave Bergman .05 .02
☐ 446 Todd Burns .05 .02
☐ 447 R.J. Reynolds .05 .02
☐ 448 Jay Buhner .20 .09
☐ 449 Lee Stevens .05 .02
☐ 450 Ron Hassey .05 .02
☐ 451 Bob Melvin .05 .02
☐ 452 Dave Martinez .05 .02
☐ 453 Greg Litton .05 .02
☐ 454 Mark Carreon .05 .02
☐ 455 Scott Fletcher .05 .02
☐ 456 Otis Nixon .10 .05
☐ 457 Tony Fossas .05 .02
☐ 458 John Russell .05 .02
☐ 459 Paul Assenmacher .05 .02
☐ 460 Zane Smith .05 .02
☐ 461 Jack Daugherty .05 .02
☐ 462 Rich Monteleone .05 .02
☐ 463 Greg Briley .05 .02
☐ 464 Mike Smithson .05 .02
☐ 465 Benito Santiago .05 .02
☐ 466 Jeff Brantley .10 .05
☐ 467 Jose Nunez .05 .02
☐ 468 Scott Bailes .05 .02
☐ 469 Ken Griffey Sr. .05 .02
☐ 470 Bob McClure .05 .02
☐ 471 Mackey Sasser .05 .02
☐ 472 Glenn Wilson .05 .02
☐ 473 Kevin Tapani .10 .05
☐ 474 Bill Buckner .05 .02
☐ 475 Ron Gant .10 .05
☐ 476 Kevin Romine .05 .02
☐ 477 Juan Agosto .05 .02
☐ 478 Herm Winningham .05 .02
☐ 479 Storm Davis .05 .02
☐ 480 Jeff King .20 .09
☐ 481 Kevin Mmahat .05 .02
☐ 482 Carmelo Martinez .05 .02
☐ 483 Omar Vizquel .20 .09
☐ 484 Jim Dwyer .05 .02
☐ 485 Bob Knepper .05 .02
☐ 486 Dave Anderson .05 .02
☐ 487 Ron Jones .05 .02
☐ 488 Jay Bell .10 .05
☐ 489 Sammy Sosa .75 .35
☐ 490 Kent Anderson .05 .02
☐ 491 Domingo Ramos .05 .02
☐ 492 Dave Clark .05 .02
☐ 493 Tim Birtsas .05 .02
☐ 494 Ken Oberkfell .05 .02
☐ 495 Larry Sheets .05 .02
☐ 496 Jeff Kunkel .05 .02
☐ 497 Jim Presley .05 .02
☐ 498 Mike Macfarlane .05 .02
☐ 499 Pete Smith .05 .02
☐ 500A Checklist 436-537 DP .05 .02
☐ 500B Checklist 420-517 .05 .02
☐ 501 Gary Sheffield .25 .11
☐ 502 Terry Bross .05 .02
☐ 503 Jerry Kutzler .05 .02
☐ 504 Lloyd Moseby .05 .02
☐ 505 Curt Young .05 .02
☐ 506 Al Newman .05 .02
☐ 507 Keith Miller .05 .02
☐ 508 Mike Stanton .10 .05
☐ 509 Rich Yett .05 .02
☐ 510 Tim Drummond .05 .02
☐ 511 Joe Hesketh .05 .02
☐ 512 Rick Wrona .05 .02
☐ 513 Luis Salazar .05 .02
☐ 514 Hal Morris .10 .05
☐ 515 Terry Mulholland .05 .02
☐ 516 John Morris .05 .02
☐ 517 Carlos Quintana .05 .02
☐ 518 Frank DiPino .05 .02
☐ 519 Randy Milligan .05 .02
☐ 520 Chad Kreuter .05 .02
☐ 521 Mike Jeffcoat .05 .02
☐ 522 Mike Harkey .05 .02
☐ 523A Andy Nezelek ERR .05 .02
(Wrong birth year)
☐ 523B Andy Nezelek COR .20 .09
(Finally corrected in factory sets)
☐ 524 Dave Schmidt .05 .02
☐ 525 Tony Armas .05 .02
☐ 526 Barry Lyons .05 .02
☐ 527 Rick Reed .05 .02
☐ 528 Jerry Reuss .05 .02
☐ 529 Dean Palmer .25 .11
☐ 530 Jeff Peterek .05 .02
☐ 531 Carlos Martinez .05 .02
☐ 532 Atlee Hammaker .05 .02
☐ 533 Mike Brumley .05 .02
☐ 534 Terry Leach .05 .02
☐ 535 Doug Strange .05 .02
☐ 536 Jose DeLeon .05 .02
☐ 537 Shane Rawley .05 .02
☐ 538 Joey Cora .20 .09
☐ 539 Eric Hetzel .05 .02
☐ 540 Gene Nelson .05 .02
☐ 541 Wes Gardner .05 .02
☐ 542 Mark Portugal .05 .02
☐ 543 Al Leiter .20 .09
☐ 544 Jack Armstrong .05 .02
☐ 545 Greg Cadaret .05 .02
☐ 546 Rod Nichols .05 .02
☐ 547 Luis Polonia .05 .02
☐ 548 Charlie Hayes .10 .05
☐ 549 Dickie Thon .05 .02
☐ 550 Tim Crews .05 .02
☐ 551 Dave Winfield .20 .09
☐ 552 Mike Davis .05 .02
☐ 553 Ron Robinson .05 .02
☐ 554 Carmen Castillo .05 .02
☐ 555 John Costello .05 .02
☐ 556 Bud Black .05 .02
☐ 557 Rick Dempsey .05 .02
☐ 558 Jim Acker .05 .02
☐ 559 Eric Show .05 .02
☐ 560 Pat Borders .05 .02
☐ 561 Danny Darwin .05 .02
☐ 562 Rick Luecken .05 .02
☐ 563 Edwin Nunez .05 .02
☐ 564 Felix Jose .05 .02
☐ 565 John Cangelosi .05 .02
☐ 566 Bill Swift .05 .02
☐ 567 Bill Schroeder .05 .02
☐ 568 Stan Javier .05 .02
☐ 569 Jim Traber .05 .02
☐ 570 Wallace Johnson .05 .02
☐ 571 Donell Nixon .05 .02
☐ 572 Sid Fernandez .05 .02
☐ 573 Lance Johnson .05 .02
☐ 574 Andy McGaffigan .05 .02
☐ 575 Mark Knudson .05 .02
☐ 576 Tommy Greene .05 .02
☐ 577 Mark Grace .20 .09
☐ 578 Larry Walker 1.00 .45
☐ 579 Mike Stanley .05 .02
☐ 580 Mike Witt DP .05 .02

☐ 581 Scott Bradley .05 .02
☐ 582 Greg A. Harris .05 .02
☐ 583A Kevin Hickey ERR .20 .09
☐ 583B Kevin Hickey COR .05 .02
☐ 584 Lee Mazzilli .05 .02
☐ 585 Jeff Pico .05 .02
☐ 586 Joe Oliver .05 .02
☐ 587 Willie Fraser DP .05 .02
☐ 588 Carl Yastrzemski .20 .09
Puzzle Card DP
☐ 589 Kevin Bass DP .05 .02
☐ 590 John Moses DP .05 .02
☐ 591 Tom Pagnozzi DP .05 .02
☐ 592 Tony Castillo DP .05 .02
☐ 593 Jerald Clark DP .05 .02
☐ 594 Dan Schatzeder .05 .02
☐ 595 Luis Quinones DP .05 .02
☐ 596 Pete Harnisch DP .05 .02
☐ 597 Gary Redus .05 .02
☐ 598 Mel Hall .05 .02
☐ 599 Rick Schu .05 .02
☐ 600A Checklist 538-639 .05 .02
☐ 600B Checklist 518-617 .05 .02
☐ 601 Mike Kingery DP .05 .02
☐ 602 Terry Kennedy DP .05 .02
☐ 603 Mike Sharperson DP .05 .02
☐ 604 Don Carman DP .05 .02
☐ 605 Jim Gott .05 .02
☐ 606 Donn Pall DP .05 .02
☐ 607 Rance Mulliniks .05 .02
☐ 608 Curt Wilkerson DP .05 .02
☐ 609 Mike Felder DP .05 .02
☐ 610 Guillermo Hernandez DP .05 .02
☐ 611 Candy Maldonado DP .05 .02
☐ 612 Mark Thurmond DP .05 .02
☐ 613 Rick Leach DP .05 .02
☐ 614 Jerry Reed DP .05 .02
☐ 615 Franklin Stubbs .05 .02
☐ 616 Billy Hatcher DP .05 .02
☐ 617 Don August DP .05 .02
☐ 618 Tim Teufel .05 .02
☐ 619 Shawn Hillegas DP .05 .02
☐ 620 Manny Lee .05 .02
☐ 621 Gary Ward DP .05 .02
☐ 622 Mark Guthrie DP .05 .02
☐ 623 Jeff Musselman DP .05 .02
☐ 624 Mark Lemke DP .10 .05
☐ 625 Fernando Valenzuela .10 .05
☐ 626 Paul Sorrento DP .20 .09
☐ 627 Glenallen Hill DP .10 .05
☐ 628 Les Lancaster DP .05 .02
☐ 629 Vance Law DP .05 .02
☐ 630 Randy Velarde DP .05 .02
☐ 631 Todd Frohwirth DP .05 .02
☐ 632 Willie McGee .05 .02
☐ 633 Dennis Boyd DP .05 .02
☐ 634 Cris Carpenter DP .05 .02
☐ 635 Brian Holton .05 .02
☐ 636 Tracy Jones DP .05 .02
☐ 637A Terry Steinbach AS .10 .05
(Recent Major
League Performance)
☐ 637B Terry Steinbach AS .10 .05
(All-Star Game
Performance)
☐ 638 Brady Anderson .20 .09
☐ 639A Jack Morris ERR .10 .05
(Card front shows
black line crossing
J in Jack)
☐ 639B Jack Morris COR .10 .05
☐ 640 Jaime Navarro .05 .02
☐ 641 Darrin Jackson .05 .02
☐ 642 Mike Dyer .05 .02
☐ 643 Mike Schmidt .25 .11
☐ 644 Henry Cotto .05 .02
☐ 645 John Cerutti .05 .02
☐ 646 Francisco Cabrera .05 .02
☐ 647 Scott Sanderson .05 .02
☐ 648 Brian Meyer .05 .02
☐ 649 Ray Searage .05 .02
☐ 650A Bo Jackson AS .10 .05
(Recent Major
League Performance)
☐ 650B Bo Jackson AS .10 .05
(All-Star Game
Performance)
☐ 651 Steve Lyons .05 .02
☐ 652 Mike LaCoss .05 .02
☐ 653 Ted Power .05 .02
☐ 654A Howard Johnson AS .10 .05
(Recent Major
League Performance)
☐ 654B Howard Johnson AS .05 .02
(All-Star Game
Performance)
☐ 655 Mauro Gozzo .05 .02
☐ 656 Mike Blowers .20 .09
☐ 657 Paul Gibson .05 .02
☐ 658 Neal Heaton .05 .02
☐ 659 Nolan Ryan 5000K .40 .18
COR (Still an error as
Ryan did not lead AL
in K's in '75)
☐ 659A Nolan Ryan 5000K 1.50 .70
(665 King of
Kings back) ERR
☐ 660A Harold Baines AS .75 .35
(Black line through
star on front;
Recent Major
League Performance)
☐ 660B Harold Baines AS 1.00 .45
(Black line through
star on front;
All-Star Game
Performance)
☐ 660C Harold Baines AS .20 .09
(Black line behind
star on front;
Recent Major
League Performance)
☐ 660D Harold Baines AS .05 .02
(Black line behind
star on front;
All-Star Game
Performance)
☐ 661 Gary Pettis .05 .02
☐ 662 Clint Zavaras .05 .02
☐ 663A Rick Reuschel AS .10 .05
(Recent Major
League Performance)
☐ 663B Rick Reuschel AS .05 .02
(All-Star Game
Performance)
☐ 664 Alejandro Pena .05 .02
☐ 665 Nolan Ryan KING COR .40 .18
☐ 665A Nolan Ryan KING 1.50 .70
(659 5000 K
back) ERR
☐ 665C Nolan Ryan KING ERR .75 .35
(No number on back;
in factory sets)
☐ 666 Ricky Horton .05 .02
☐ 667 Curt Schilling .20 .09
☐ 668 Bill Landrum .05 .02
☐ 669 Todd Stottlemyre .10 .05
☐ 670 Tim Leary .05 .02
☐ 671 John Wetteland .20 .09
☐ 672 Calvin Schiraldi .05 .02
☐ 673A Ruben Sierra AS .05 .02
(Recent Major
League Performance)
☐ 673B Ruben Sierra AS .05 .02
(All-Star Game
Performance)
☐ 674A Pedro Guerrero AS .10 .05
(Recent Major
League Performance)
☐ 674B Pedro Guerrero AS .05 .02
(All-Star Game
Performance)
☐ 675 Ken Phelps .05 .02
☐ 676 Cal Ripken AS .40 .18
(All-Star Game
Performance)
☐ 676A Cal Ripken AS .75 .35
(Recent Major
League Performance)
☐ 677 Denny Walling .05 .02
☐ 678 Goose Gossage .10 .05
☐ 679 Gary Mielke .05 .02
☐ 680 Bill Bathe .05 .02
☐ 681 Tom Lawless .05 .02
☐ 682 Xavier Hernandez .05 .02
☐ 683A Kirby Puckett AS .20 .09
(Recent Major
League Performance)
☐ 683B Kirby Puckett AS .20 .09
(All-Star Game
Performance)
☐ 684 Mariano Duncan .05 .02
☐ 685 Ramon Martinez .20 .09
☐ 686 Tim Jones .05 .02
☐ 687 Tom Filer .05 .02
☐ 688 Steve Lombardozzi .05 .02
☐ 689 Bernie Williams .75 .35
☐ 690 Chip Hale .05 .02
☐ 691 Beau Allred .05 .02
☐ 692A Ryne Sandberg AS .20 .09
(Recent Major
League Performance)
☐ 692B Ryne Sandberg AS .20 .09
(All-Star Game
Performance)
☐ 693 Jeff Huson .05 .02
☐ 694 Curt Ford .05 .02
☐ 695A Eric Davis AS .10 .05
(Recent Major
League Performance)
☐ 695B Eric Davis AS .10 .05
(All-Star Game
Performance)
☐ 696 Scott Lusader .05 .02
☐ 697A Mark McGwire AS .20 .09
(Recent Major
League Performance)
☐ 697B Mark McGwire AS .10 .05
(All-Star Game
Performance)
☐ 698 Steve Cummings .05 .02
☐ 699 George Canale .05 .02
☐ 700A Checklist 640-715 .20 .09
and BC1-BC26
☐ 700B Checklist 640-716 .10 .05
and BC1-BC26
☐ 700C Checklist 618-716 .05 .02
☐ 701A Julio Franco AS .10 .05
(Recent Major
League Performance)
☐ 701B Julio Franco AS .05 .02
(All-Star Game
Performance)
☐ 702 Dave Johnson (P) .05 .02
☐ 703A Dave Stewart AS .05 .02
(Recent Major
League Performance)
☐ 703B Dave Stewart AS .05 .02
(All-Star Game
Performance)
☐ 704 Dave Justice .75 .35
☐ 705 Tony Gwynn AS .20 .09
(All-Star Game
Performance)
☐ 705A Tony Gwynn AS .20 .09
(Recent Major
League Performance)
☐ 706 Greg Myers .05 .02
☐ 707A Will Clark AS .20 .09
(Recent Major
League Performance)
☐ 707B Will Clark AS .20 .09
(All-Star Game
Performance)
☐ 708A Benito Santiago AS .10 .05
(Recent Major
League Performance)
☐ 708B Benito Santiago AS .05 .02
(All-Star Game
Performance)
☐ 709 Larry McWilliams .05 .02
☐ 710A Ozzie Smith AS .20 .09
(Recent Major
League Performance)
☐ 710B Ozzie Smith AS .10 .05
(All-Star Game
Performance)
☐ 711 John Olerud .20 .09
☐ 712A Wade Boggs AS .20 .09
(Recent Major
League Performance)
☐ 712B Wade Boggs AS .20 .09
(All-Star Game
Performance)
☐ 713 Gary Eave .05 .02
☐ 714 Bob Tewksbury .05 .02
☐ 715A Kevin Mitchell AS .10 .05
(Recent Major
League Performance)
☐ 715B Kevin Mitchell AS .05 .02
(All-Star Game
Performance)
☐ 716 Bart Giamatti COMM .20 .09
(In Memoriam)

1990 Donruss Bonus MVP's

Numbered with the prefix "BC" for bonus card, a 26-card set featuring the most valuable player from each of the 26 teams was randomly inserted in all 1990 Donruss unopened pack formats. The factory sets were distributed without the Bonus Cards; thus there were again new checklist cards printed to reflect the exclusion of the Bonus Cards.

	MINT	NRMT
COMPLETE SET (26)	1.50	.70
COMMON CARD (BC1-BC26)	.05	.02

☐ BC1 Bo Jackson .10 .05
☐ BC2 Howard Johnson .05 .02
☐ BC3 Dave Stewart .10 .05

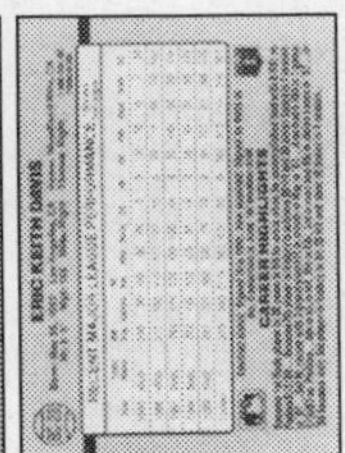

	MINT	NRMT
☐ BC4 Tony Gwynn	.40	.18
☐ BC5 Orel Hershiser	.10	.05
☐ BC6 Pedro Guerrero	.05	.02
☐ BC7 Tim Raines	.10	.05
☐ BC8 Kirby Puckett	.25	.11
☐ BC9 Alvin Davis	.05	.02
☐ BC10 Ryne Sandberg	.25	.11
☐ BC11 Kevin Mitchell	.10	.05
☐ BC12A John Smoltz ERR (Photo actually Tom Glavine)	.15	.07
☐ BC12B John Smoltz COR	.75	.35
☐ BC13 George Bell	.05	.02
☐ BC14 Julio Franco	.10	.05
☐ BC15 Paul Molitor	.20	.09
☐ BC16 Bobby Bonilla	.10	.05
☐ BC17 Mike Greenwell	.05	.02
☐ BC18 Cal Ripken	.60	.25
☐ BC19 Carlton Fisk	.15	.07
☐ BC20 Chili Davis	.10	.05
☐ BC21 Glenn Davis	.05	.02
☐ BC22 Steve Sax	.05	.02
☐ BC23 Eric Davis DP	.10	.05
☐ BC24 Greg Swindell DP	.05	.02
☐ BC25 Von Hayes DP	.05	.02
☐ BC26 Alan Trammell	.10	.05

1990 Donruss Grand Slammers

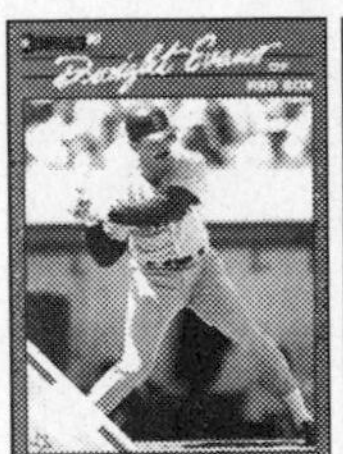

This 12-card standard size set was in the 1990 Donruss set as a special card deliniating each 55-card section of the 1990 Factory Set. This set honors those players who connected for grand slam homers during the 1989 season. The cards are in the 1990 Donruss design and the back describes the grand slam homer hit by each player.

	MINT	NRMT
COMPLETE SET (12)	1.50	.70
COMMON CARD (1-12)	.05	.02
☐ 1 Matt Williams	.20	.09
☐ 2 Jeffrey Leonard	.05	.02
☐ 3 Chris James	.05	.02
☐ 4 Mark McGwire	.75	.35
☐ 5 Dwight Evans	.10	.05
☐ 6 Will Clark	.15	.07
☐ 7 Mike Scioscia	.05	.02
☐ 8 Todd Benzinger	.05	.02
☐ 9 Fred McGriff	.15	.07
☐ 10 Kevin Bass	.05	.02
☐ 11 Jack Clark	.10	.05
☐ 12 Bo Jackson	.10	.05

1990 Donruss Rookies

The 1990 Donruss Rookies set marked the fifth consecutive year that Donruss issued a boxed set honoring the best rookies of the season. This set, which used the 1990 Donruss design but featured a green border, was issued exclusively through the Donruss dealer network to hobby dealers. This 56-card, standard size set came in its own box and the words "The Rookies" are featured prominently on the front of the cards. The only notable Rookie Card in this set is Carlos Baerga.

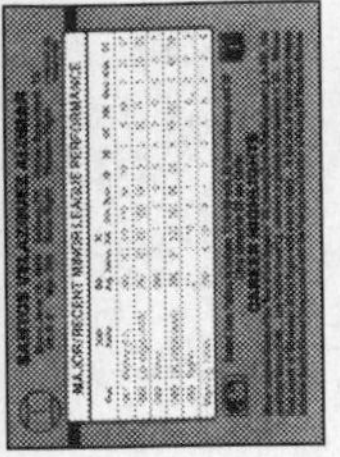

	MINT	NRMT
COMPLETE SET (56)	2.00	.90
COMMON CARD (1-56)	.05	.02
☐ 1 Sandy Alomar Jr. UER (No stitches on baseball on Donruss logo on card front)	.20	.09
☐ 2 John Olerud	.20	.09
☐ 3 Pat Combs	.05	.02
☐ 4 Brian DuBois	.05	.02
☐ 5 Felix Jose	.05	.02
☐ 6 Delino DeShields	.10	.05
☐ 7 Mike Stanton	.10	.05
☐ 8 Mike Munoz	.05	.02
☐ 9 Craig Grebeck	.05	.02
☐ 10 Joe Kraemer	.05	.02
☐ 11 Jeff Huson	.05	.02
☐ 12 Bill Sampen	.05	.02
☐ 13 Brian Bohanon	.05	.02
☐ 14 Dave Justice	.75	.35
☐ 15 Robin Ventura	.20	.09
☐ 16 Greg Vaughn	.10	.05
☐ 17 Wayne Edwards	.05	.02
☐ 18 Shawn Boskie	.05	.02
☐ 19 Carlos Baerga	.25	.11
☐ 20 Mark Gardner	.05	.02
☐ 21 Kevin Appier	.20	.09
☐ 22 Mike Harkey	.05	.02
☐ 23 Tim Layana	.05	.02
☐ 24 Glenallen Hill	.05	.02
☐ 25 Jerry Kutzler	.05	.02
☐ 26 Mike Blowers	.20	.09
☐ 27 Scott Ruskin	.05	.02
☐ 28 Dana Kiecker	.05	.02
☐ 29 Willie Blair	.05	.02
☐ 30 Ben McDonald	.20	.09
☐ 31 Todd Zeile	.10	.05
☐ 32 Scott Coolbaugh	.05	.02
☐ 33 Xavier Hernandez	.05	.02
☐ 34 Mike Hartley	.05	.02
☐ 35 Kevin Tapani	.10	.05
☐ 36 Kevin Wickander	.05	.02
☐ 37 Carlos Hernandez	.05	.02
☐ 38 Brian Traxler	.05	.02
☐ 39 Marty Brown	.05	.02
☐ 40 Scott Radinsky	.05	.02
☐ 41 Julio Machado	.05	.02
☐ 42 Steve Avery	.10	.05
☐ 43 Mark Lemke	.10	.05
☐ 44 Alan Mills	.05	.02
☐ 45 Marquis Grissom	.40	.18
☐ 46 Greg Olson	.05	.02
☐ 47 Dave Hollins	.20	.09
☐ 48 Jerald Clark	.05	.02
☐ 49 Eric Anthony	.10	.05
☐ 50 Tim Drummond	.05	.02
☐ 51 John Burkett	.20	.09
☐ 52 Brent Knackert	.05	.02
☐ 53 Jeff Shaw	.05	.02
☐ 54 John Orton	.05	.02
☐ 55 Terry Shumpert	.05	.02
☐ 56 Checklist 1-56	.05	.02

1990 Donruss Best AL

The 1990 Donruss Best of the American League set consists of 144 standard-size cards. This was Donruss' latest version of what had been titled the previous two years as Baseball's Best. In 1990, the sets were split into National and American League and marketed separately. The front design was similar to the regular issue Donruss set except for the front borders being blue while the backs have complete major and minor league statistics as compared to the regular Donruss cards which only cover the past five major-league seasons.

	MINT	NRMT
COMPLETE SET (144)	10.00	4.50
COMMON CARD (1-144)	.05	.02
☐ 1 Ken Griffey Jr.	3.00	1.35
☐ 2 Bob Milacki	.05	.02
☐ 3 Mike Boddicker	.05	.02
☐ 4 Bert Blyleven	.10	.05
☐ 5 Carlton Fisk	.40	.18
☐ 6 Greg Swindell	.05	.02
☐ 7 Alan Trammell	.15	.07
☐ 8 Mark Davis	.05	.02
☐ 9 Chris Bosio	.05	.02
☐ 10 Gary Gaetti	.05	.02
☐ 11 Matt Nokes	.05	.02
☐ 12 Dennis Eckersley	.15	.07
☐ 13 Kevin Brown	.20	.09
☐ 14 Tom Henke	.05	.02
☐ 15 Mickey Tettleton	.05	.02
☐ 16 Jody Reed	.05	.02
☐ 17 Mark Langston	.10	.05
☐ 18 Melido Perez UER (Listed as an Expo rather than White Sox)	.05	.02
☐ 19 John Farrell	.05	.02
☐ 20 Tony Phillips	.05	.02
☐ 21 Bret Saberhagen	.10	.05
☐ 22 Robin Yount	.20	.09
☐ 23 Kirby Puckett	1.25	.55
☐ 24 Steve Sax	.05	.02
☐ 25 Dave Stewart	.10	.05
☐ 26 Alvin Davis	.05	.02
☐ 27 Geno Petralli	.05	.02
☐ 28 Mookie Wilson	.05	.02
☐ 29 Jeff Ballard	.05	.02
☐ 30 Ellis Burks	.15	.07
☐ 31 Wally Joyner	.10	.05
☐ 32 Bobby Thigpen	.05	.02
☐ 33 Keith Hernandez	.10	.05
☐ 34 Jack Morris	.10	.05
☐ 35 George Brett	1.25	.55
☐ 36 Dan Plesac	.05	.02
☐ 37 Brian Harper	.05	.02
☐ 38 Don Mattingly	1.50	.70
☐ 39 Dave Henderson	.05	.02
☐ 40 Scott Bankhead UER (Asheboro misspelled as Ashboro on card)	.05	.02
☐ 41 Rafael Palmeiro	.25	.11
☐ 42 Jimmy Key	.10	.05
☐ 43 Gregg Olson	.05	.02
☐ 44 Tony Pena	.05	.02
☐ 45 Jack Howell	.05	.02
☐ 46 Eric King	.05	.02
☐ 47 Cory Snyder	.05	.02
☐ 48 Frank Tanana	.05	.02
☐ 49 Nolan Ryan	3.00	1.35
☐ 50 Bob Boone	.10	.05
☐ 51 Dave Parker	.10	.05
☐ 52 Allan Anderson	.05	.02
☐ 53 Tim Leary	.05	.02
☐ 54 Mark McGwire	1.50	.70
☐ 55 Dave Valle	.05	.02
☐ 56 Fred McGriff	.40	.18
☐ 57 Cal Ripken	2.00	.90
☐ 58 Roger Clemens	1.00	.45
☐ 59 Lance Parrish	.10	.05
☐ 60 Robin Ventura	.15	.07
☐ 61 Doug Jones	.05	.02
☐ 62 Lloyd Moseby	.05	.02
☐ 63 Bo Jackson	.10	.05
☐ 64 Paul Molitor	.40	.18
☐ 65 Kent Hrbek	.10	.05
☐ 66 Mel Hall	.05	.02
☐ 67 Bob Welch	.05	.02
☐ 68 Erik Hanson	.05	.02
☐ 69 Harold Baines	.10	.05
☐ 70 Junior Felix	.05	.02
☐ 71 Craig Worthington	.05	.02
☐ 72 Jeff Reardon	.05	.02
☐ 73 Johnny Ray	.05	.02
☐ 74 Ozzie Guillen	.05	.02
☐ 75 Brook Jacoby	.05	.02
☐ 76 Chet Lemon	.05	.02
☐ 77 Mark Gubicza	.05	.02
☐ 78 B.J. Surhoff	.05	.02
☐ 79 Rick Aguilera	.05	.02
☐ 80 Pascual Perez	.05	.02
☐ 81 Jose Canseco	.40	.18

☐ 82 Mike Schooler .05 .02
☐ 83 Jeff Huson .05 .02
☐ 84 Kelly Gruber .05 .02
☐ 85 Randy Milligan .05 .02
☐ 86 Wade Boggs .40 .18
☐ 87 Dave Winfield .15 .07
☐ 88 Scott Fletcher .05 .02
☐ 89 Tom Candiotti .05 .02
☐ 90 Mike Heath .05 .02
☐ 91 Kevin Seitzer .05 .02
☐ 92 Ted Higuera .05 .02
☐ 93 Kevin Tapani .10 .05
☐ 94 Roberto Kelly .05 .02
☐ 95 Walt Weiss .05 .02
☐ 96 Checklist Card .05 .02
☐ 97 Sandy Alomar Jr. .15 .07
☐ 98 Pete O'Brien .05 .02
☐ 99 Jeff Russell .05 .02
☐ 100 John Olerud .40 .18
☐ 101 Pete Harnisch .05 .02
☐ 102 Dwight Evans .10 .05
☐ 103 Chuck Finley .10 .05
☐ 104 Sammy Sosa 1.50 .70
☐ 105 Mike Henneman .05 .02
☐ 106 Kurt Stillwell .05 .02
☐ 107 Greg Vaughn .10 .05
☐ 108 Dan Gladden .05 .02
☐ 109 Jesse Barfield .05 .02
☐ 110 Willie Randolph .10 .05
☐ 111 Randy Johnson .75 .35
☐ 112 Julio Franco .10 .05
☐ 113 Tony Fernandez .05 .02
☐ 114 Ben McDonald .10 .05
☐ 115 Mike Greenwell .05 .02
☐ 116 Luis Polonia .05 .02
☐ 117 Carney Lansford .10 .05
☐ 118 Bud Black .05 .02
☐ 119 Lou Whitaker .10 .05
☐ 120 Jim Eisenreich .10 .05
☐ 121 Gary Sheffield .75 .35
☐ 122 Shane Mack .05 .02
☐ 123 Alvaro Espinoza .05 .02
☐ 124 Rickey Henderson .20 .09
☐ 125 Jeffrey Leonard .05 .02
☐ 126 Gary Pettis .05 .02
☐ 127 Dave Stieb .05 .02
☐ 128 Danny Tartabull .10 .05
☐ 129 Joe Orsulak .05 .02
☐ 130 Tom Brunansky .05 .02
☐ 131 Dick Schofield .05 .02
☐ 132 Candy Maldonado .05 .02
☐ 133 Cecil Fielder .10 .05
☐ 134 Terry Shumpert .05 .02
☐ 135 Greg Gagne .05 .02
☐ 136 Dave Righetti .05 .02
☐ 137 Terry Steinbach .10 .05
☐ 138 Harold Reynolds .10 .05
☐ 139 George Bell .05 .02
☐ 140 Carlos Quintana .05 .02
☐ 141 Ivan Calderon .05 .02
☐ 142 Greg Brock .05 .02
☐ 143 Ruben Sierra .05 .02
☐ 144 Checklist Card .05 .02

1990 Donruss Best NL

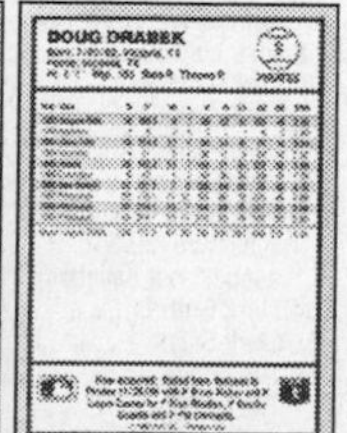

he 1990 Donruss Best of the National League set onsists of 144 standard-size cards. This was Donruss' atest version of what had been titled the previous two ears as Baseball's Best. In 1990, the sets were split into ational and American League and marketed separately. he front design was similar to the regular issue Donruss et except for the front borders being blue while the backs ave complete major and minor league statistics as ompared to the regular Donruss cards which only cover he past five major-league seasons.

	MINT	NRMT
OMPLETE SET (144)	8.00	3.60
OMMON CARD (1-144)	.05	.02

☐ 1 Eric Davis .10 .05
☐ 2 Tom Glavine .40 .18
☐ 3 Mike Bielecki .05 .02
☐ 4 Jim Deshaies .05 .02
☐ 5 Mike Scioscia .05 .02
☐ 6 Spike Owen .05 .02
☐ 7 Dwight Gooden .10 .05
☐ 8 Ricky Jordan .05 .02
☐ 9 Doug Drabek .05 .02
☐ 10 Bryn Smith .05 .02
☐ 11 Tony Gwynn 1.00 .45
☐ 12 John Burkett .05 .02
☐ 13 Nick Esasky .05 .02
☐ 14 Greg Maddux 1.50 .70
☐ 15 Joe Oliver .05 .02
☐ 16 Mike Scott .05 .02
☐ 17 Tim Belcher .05 .02
☐ 18 Kevin Gross .05 .02
☐ 19 Howard Johnson .05 .02
☐ 20 Darren Daulton .10 .05
☐ 21 John Smiley .05 .02
☐ 22 Ken Dayley .05 .02
☐ 23 Craig Lefferts .05 .02
☐ 24 Will Clark .15 .07
☐ 25 Greg Olson .05 .02
☐ 26 Ryne Sandberg .75 .35
☐ 27 Tom Browning .05 .02
☐ 28 Eric Anthony .05 .02
☐ 29 Juan Samuel .05 .02
☐ 30 Dennis Martinez .10 .05
☐ 31 Kevin Elster .05 .02
☐ 32 Tom Herr .05 .02
☐ 33 Sid Bream .05 .02
☐ 34 Terry Pendleton .10 .05
☐ 35 Roberto Alomar .75 .35
☐ 36 Kevin Bass .05 .02
☐ 37 Jim Presley .05 .02
☐ 38 Les Lancaster .05 .02
☐ 39 Paul O'Neill .10 .05
☐ 40 Dave Smith .05 .02
☐ 41 Kirk Gibson .10 .05
☐ 42 Tim Burke .05 .02
☐ 43 David Cone .15 .07
☐ 44 Ken Howell .05 .02
☐ 45 Barry Bonds .60 .25
☐ 46 Joe Magrane .05 .02
☐ 47 Andy Benes .10 .05
☐ 48 Gary Carter .15 .07
☐ 49 Pat Combs .05 .02
☐ 50 John Smoltz .40 .18
☐ 51 Mark Grace .20 .09
☐ 52 Barry Larkin .15 .07
☐ 53 Danny Darwin .05 .02
☐ 54 Orel Hershiser .10 .05
☐ 55 Tim Wallach .05 .02
☐ 56 Dave Magadan .05 .02
☐ 57 Roger McDowell .05 .02
☐ 58 Bill Landrum .05 .02
☐ 59 Jose DeLeon .05 .02
☐ 60 Bip Roberts .05 .02
☐ 61 Matt Williams .40 .18
☐ 62 Dale Murphy .15 .07
☐ 63 Dwight Smith .05 .02
☐ 64 Chris Sabo .05 .02
☐ 65 Glenn Davis .05 .02
☐ 66 Jay Howell .05 .02
☐ 67 Andres Galarraga .20 .09
☐ 68 Frank Viola .05 .02
☐ 69 John Kruk .10 .05
☐ 70 Bobby Bonilla .10 .05
☐ 71 Todd Zeile .05 .02
☐ 72 Joe Carter .15 .07
☐ 73 Robby Thompson .05 .02
☐ 74 Jeff Blauser .05 .02
☐ 75 Mitch Williams .05 .02
☐ 76 Rob Dibble .05 .02
☐ 77 Rafael Ramirez .05 .02
☐ 78 Eddie Murray .60 .25
☐ 79 Dave Martinez .05 .02
☐ 80 Darryl Strawberry .10 .05
☐ 81 Dickie Thon .05 .02
☐ 82 Jose Lind .05 .02
☐ 83 Ozzie Smith .75 .35
☐ 84 Bruce Hurst .05 .02
☐ 85 Kevin Mitchell .10 .05
☐ 86 Lonnie Smith .05 .02
☐ 87 Joe Girardi .05 .02
☐ 88 Randy Myers .05 .02
☐ 89 Craig Biggio .50 .23
☐ 90 Fernando Valenzuela .10 .05
☐ 91 Larry Walker 1.50 .70
☐ 92 John Franco .10 .05
☐ 93 Dennis Cook .05 .02
☐ 94 Bob Walk .05 .02
☐ 95 Pedro Guerrero .05 .02
☐ 96 Checklist Card .05 .02
☐ 97 Andre Dawson .20 .09
☐ 98 Ed Whitson .05 .02
☐ 99 Steve Bedrosian .05 .02
☐ 100 Oddibe McDowell .05 .02
☐ 101 Todd Benzinger .05 .02
☐ 102 Bill Doran .05 .02
☐ 103 Alfredo Griffin .05 .02
☐ 104 Tim Raines .10 .05
☐ 105 Sid Fernandez .05 .02
☐ 106 Charlie Hayes .05 .02
☐ 107 Mike LaValliere .05 .02
☐ 108 Jose Oquendo .05 .02
☐ 109 Jack Clark .10 .05
☐ 110 Scott Garrelts .05 .02
☐ 111 Ron Gant .15 .07
☐ 112 Shawon Dunston .05 .02
☐ 113 Mariano Duncan .05 .02
☐ 114 Eric Yelding .05 .02
☐ 115 Hubie Brooks .05 .02
☐ 116 Delino DeShields .20 .09
☐ 117 Gregg Jefferies .10 .05
☐ 118 Len Dykstra .10 .05
☐ 119 Andy Van Slyke .10 .05
☐ 120 Lee Smith .10 .05
☐ 121 Benito Santiago .05 .02
☐ 122 Jose Uribe .05 .02
☐ 123 Jeff Treadway .05 .02
☐ 124 Jerome Walton .05 .02
☐ 125 Billy Hatcher .05 .02
☐ 126 Ken Caminiti .25 .11
☐ 127 Kal Daniels .05 .02
☐ 128 Marquis Grissom .75 .35
☐ 129 Kevin McReynolds .05 .02
☐ 130 Wally Backman .05 .02
☐ 131 Willie McGee .10 .05
☐ 132 Terry Kennedy .05 .02
☐ 133 Garry Templeton .05 .02
☐ 134 Lloyd McClendon .05 .02
☐ 135 Daryl Boston .05 .02
☐ 136 Jay Bell .05 .02
☐ 137 Mike Pagliarulo .05 .02
☐ 138 Vince Coleman .05 .02
☐ 139 Brett Butler .10 .05
☐ 140 Von Hayes .05 .02
☐ 141 Ramon Martinez .15 .07
☐ 142 Jack Armstrong .05 .02
☐ 143 Franklin Stubbs .05 .02
☐ 144 Checklist Card .05 .02

1990 Donruss Learning Series

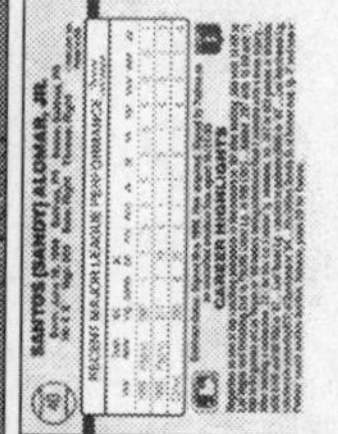

The 1990 Donruss Learning Series consists of 55 standard-size cards that served as part of an educational packet for elementary and middle school students. The cards were issued in two formats. Grades Three and Four received the cards, a historical timeline that relates events in baseball to major historical events, additional Donruss cards from wax packs, and a teacher's guide that focused on several academic subjects. Grades 5 through 8 received the cards, a teacher's guide designed for older students, and a 14-minute video shot at Chicago's Wrigley Field. The fronts feature color head shots of the players and bright red borders. The horizontally oriented backs are amber and present biography, statistics, and career highlights.

	MINT	NRMT
COMPLETE SET (55)	25.00	11.00
COMMON CARD (1-55)	.10	.05

☐ 1 George Brett DK 2.50 1.10
☐ 2 Kevin Mitchell .20 .09
☐ 3 Andy Van Slyke .20 .09
☐ 4 Benito Santiago .10 .05
☐ 5 Gary Carter .20 .09
☐ 6 Jose Canseco 1.00 .45
☐ 7 Rickey Henderson .75 .35
☐ 8 Ken Griffey Jr. 6.00 2.70
☐ 9 Ozzie Smith 2.50 1.10
☐ 10 Dwight Gooden .20 .09
☐ 11 Ryne Sandberg DK 2.50 1.10
☐ 12 Don Mattingly 3.00 1.35
☐ 13 Ozzie Guillen .10 .05
☐ 14 Dave Righetti .10 .05
☐ 15 Rick Dempsey .10 .05

	MINT	NRMT
☐ 16 Tom Herr	.10	.05
☐ 17 Julio Franco	.20	.09
☐ 18 Von Hayes	.10	.05
☐ 19 Cal Ripken	5.00	2.20
☐ 20 Alan Trammell	.75	.35
☐ 21 Wade Boggs	1.00	.45
☐ 22 Glenn Davis	.10	.05
☐ 23 Will Clark	1.25	.55
☐ 24 Nolan Ryan	6.00	2.70
☐ 25 George Bell	.10	.05
☐ 26 Cecil Fielder	.75	.35
☐ 27 Gregg Olson	.10	.05
☐ 28 Tim Wallach	.10	.05
☐ 29 Ron Darling	.10	.05
☐ 30 Kelly Gruber	.10	.05
☐ 31 Shawn Boskie	.10	.05
☐ 32 Mike Greenwell	.10	.05
☐ 33 Dave Parker	.20	.09
☐ 34 Joe Magrane	.10	.05
☐ 35 Dave Stewart	.20	.09
☐ 36 Kent Hrbek	.20	.09
☐ 37 Robin Yount	1.00	.45
☐ 38 Bo Jackson	.75	.35
☐ 39 Fernando Valenzuela	.20	.09
☐ 40 Sandy Alomar Jr.	.35	.16
☐ 41 Lance Parrish	.20	.09
☐ 42 Candy Maldonado	.10	.05
☐ 43 Mike LaValliere	.10	.05
☐ 44 Jim Abbott	.10	.05
☐ 45 Edgar Martinez	1.00	.45
☐ 46 Kirby Puckett	2.50	1.10
☐ 47 Delino DeShields	.60	.25
☐ 48 Tony Gwynn	3.00	1.35
☐ 49 Carlton Fisk	1.00	.45
☐ 50 Mike Scott	.10	.05
☐ 51 Barry Larkin	1.25	.55
☐ 52 Andre Dawson	.75	.35
☐ 53 Tom Glavine	1.50	.70
☐ 54 Tom Browning	.10	.05
☐ 55 Checklist Card	.10	.05

1990 Donruss Super DK's

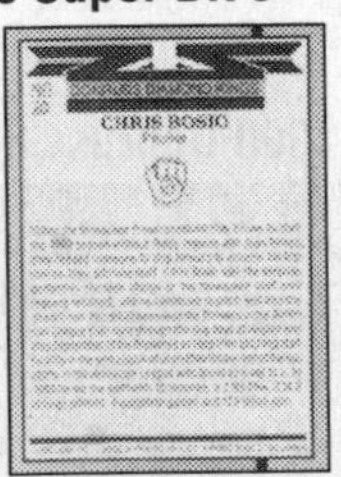

This 26-player card set was available through a mail-in offer detailed on the wax packs. The set was sent in return for 10.00 and three wrappers plus 2.00 postage and handling. The set features the popular Diamond King subseries in large (approximately 4 7/8" by 6 13/16") form. Dick Perez of Perez-Steele Galleries did another outstanding job on the artwork. The cards are essentially a large version of the Donruss regular issue Diamond Kings. There is also a jumbo sized Ryan King of Kings card. Although not listed with the regular set; it is heavily sought after by Ryan collectors.

	MINT	NRMT
COMPLETE SET (26)	12.00	5.50
COMMON CARD (1-26)	.50	.23

	MINT	NRMT
☐ 1 Bo Jackson	.75	.35
☐ 2 Steve Sax	.50	.23
☐ 3 Ruben Sierra	.50	.23
☐ 4 Ken Griffey Jr.	6.00	2.70
☐ 5 Mickey Tettleton	.50	.23
☐ 6 Dave Stewart	.75	.35
☐ 7 Jim Deshaies	.50	.23
☐ 8 John Smoltz	1.50	.70
☐ 9 Mike Bielecki	.50	.23
☐ 10 Brian Downing	.50	.23
☐ 11 Kevin Mitchell	.75	.35
☐ 12 Kelly Gruber	.50	.23
☐ 13 Joe Magrane	.50	.23
☐ 14 John Franco	.75	.35
☐ 15 Ozzie Guillen	.50	.23
☐ 16 Lou Whitaker	1.00	.45
☐ 17 John Smiley	.50	.23
☐ 18 Howard Johnson	.50	.23
☐ 19 Willie Randolph	.75	.35
☐ 20 Chris Bosio	.50	.23
☐ 21 Tommy Herr	.50	.23
☐ 22 Dan Gladden	.50	.23
☐ 23 Ellis Burks	1.00	.45
☐ 24 Pete O'Brien	.50	.23
☐ 25 Bryn Smith	.50	.23
☐ 26 Ed Whitson	.50	.23
☐ NNO Nolan Ryan King of Kings	12.00	5.50

1991 Donruss Previews

This 12-card standard-size set was issued by Donruss for hobby dealers as examples of what the 1991 Donruss cards would look like. This cards have the 1991 Donruss design on the front; the back merely says 1991 Preview card and identifies the player and the team.

	MINT	NRMT
COMPLETE SET (12)	400.00	180.00
COMMON CARD (1-12)	5.00	2.20

	MINT	NRMT
☐ 1 Dave Justice	25.00	11.00
☐ 2 Doug Drabek	8.00	3.60
☐ 3 Scott Chiamparino	5.00	2.20
☐ 4 Ken Griffey Jr.	125.00	55.00
☐ 5 Bob Welch	8.00	3.60
☐ 6 Tino Martinez	25.00	11.00
☐ 7 Nolan Ryan	125.00	55.00
☐ 8 Dwight Gooden	8.00	3.60
☐ 9 Ryne Sandberg	60.00	27.00
☐ 10 Barry Bonds	40.00	18.00
☐ 11 Jose Canseco	25.00	11.00
☐ 12 Eddie Murray	40.00	18.00

1991 Donruss

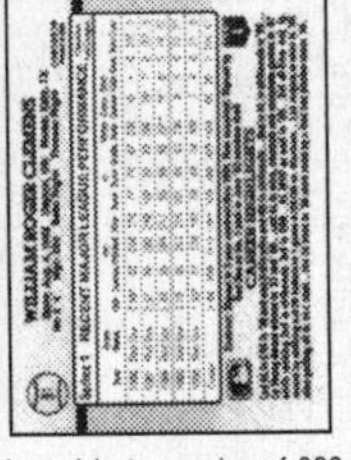

The 1991 Donruss set was issued in two series of 386 and 384 for a total of 770 standard-size cards. This set marked the first time Donruss issued cards in multiple series. The second series was issued approximately three months after the first series was issued. Cards were issued in wax packs and factory sets. As a separate promotion, wax packs were also given away with six and 12-packs of Coke and Diet Coke. First series cards feature blue borders and second series green borders with some stripes and the players name in white against a red background. Subsets include Diamond Kings (1-27), Rated Rookies (28-47/413-432), AL All-Stars (48-56), MVP's (387-412) and NL All-Stars (433-441). There were also special cards to honor the award winners and the heroes of the World Series. Rookie Cards in the set include Jeff Conine and Brian McRae. On cards 60, 70, 127, 182, 239, 294, 355, 368, and 377, the border stripes are red and yellow.

	MINT	NRMT
COMPLETE SET (770)	8.00	3.60
COMP.FACT.w/LEAF PREV	10.00	4.50
COMP.FACT.w/STUDIO PREV	10.00	4.50
COMMON CARD (1-770)	.05	.02
COMPLETE STARGELL PUZZLE	1.00	.45

	MINT	NRMT
☐ 1 Dave Stieb DK	.05	.02
☐ 2 Craig Biggio DK	.20	.09
☐ 3 Cecil Fielder DK	.10	.05
☐ 4 Barry Bonds DK	.20	.09
☐ 5 Barry Larkin DK	.20	.09
☐ 6 Dave Parker DK	.10	.05
☐ 7 Len Dykstra DK	.10	.05
☐ 8 Bobby Thigpen DK	.05	.02
☐ 9 Roger Clemens DK	.20	.09
☐ 10 Ron Gant DK UER (No trademark on team logo on back)	.10	.05
☐ 11 Delino DeShields DK	.05	.02
☐ 12 Roberto Alomar DK UER (No trademark on team logo on back)	.20	.09
☐ 13 Sandy Alomar Jr. DK	.10	.05
☐ 14 Ryne Sandberg DK UER (Was DK in '85, not '83 as shown)	.20	.09
☐ 15 Ramon Martinez DK	.10	.05
☐ 16 Edgar Martinez DK	.20	.09
☐ 17 Dave Magadan DK	.05	.02
☐ 18 Matt Williams DK	.20	.09
☐ 19 Rafael Palmeiro DK UER (No trademark on team logo on back)	.20	.09
☐ 20 Bob Welch DK	.05	.02
☐ 21 Dave Righetti DK	.05	.02
☐ 22 Brian Harper DK	.05	.02
☐ 23 Gregg Olson DK	.05	.02
☐ 24 Kurt Stillwell DK	.05	.02
☐ 25 Pedro Guerrero DK UER (No trademark on team logo on back)	.05	.02
☐ 26 Chuck Finley DK UER (No trademark on team logo on back)	.05	.02
☐ 27 DK Checklist 1-27	.05	.02
☐ 28 Tino Martinez RR	.20	.09
☐ 29 Mark Lewis RR	.05	.02
☐ 30 Bernard Gilkey RR	.10	.05
☐ 31 Hensley Meulens RR	.05	.02
☐ 32 Derek Bell RR	.20	.09
☐ 33 Jose Offerman RR	.05	.02
☐ 34 Terry Bross RR	.05	.02
☐ 35 Leo Gomez RR	.05	.02
☐ 36 Derrick May RR	.05	.02
☐ 37 Kevin Morton RR	.05	.02
☐ 38 Moises Alou RR	.10	.05
☐ 39 Julio Valera RR	.05	.02
☐ 40 Milt Cuyler RR	.05	.02
☐ 41 Phil Plantier RR	.20	.09
☐ 42 Scott Chiamparino RR	.05	.02
☐ 43 Ray Lankford RR	.20	.09
☐ 44 Mickey Morandini RR	.05	.02
☐ 45 Dave Hansen RR	.05	.02
☐ 46 Kevin Belcher RR	.05	.02
☐ 47 Darrin Fletcher RR	.05	.02
☐ 48 Steve Sax AS	.05	.02
☐ 49 Ken Griffey Jr. AS	.75	.35
☐ 50A Jose Canseco AS ERR (Team in stat box should be AL, not A's)	.20	.09
☐ 50B Jose Canseco AS COR	.75	.35
☐ 51 Sandy Alomar Jr. AS	.10	.05
☐ 52 Cal Ripken AS	.40	.18
☐ 53 Rickey Henderson AS	.20	.09
☐ 54 Bob Welch AS	.05	.02
☐ 55 Wade Boggs AS	.20	.09
☐ 56 Mark McGwire AS	.20	.09
☐ 57A Jack McDowell ERR (Career stats do not include 1990)	.20	.09
☐ 57B Jack McDowell COR (Career stats do not include 1990)	.25	.11
☐ 58 Jose Lind	.05	.02
☐ 59 Alex Fernandez	.10	.05
☐ 60 Pat Combs	.05	.02
☐ 61 Mike Walker	.05	.02
☐ 62 Juan Samuel	.05	.02
☐ 63 Mike Blowers UER (Last line has aseball, not baseball)	.05	.02
☐ 64 Mark Guthrie	.05	.02
☐ 65 Mark Salas	.05	.02
☐ 66 Tim Jones	.05	.02
☐ 67 Tim Leary	.05	.02
☐ 68 Andres Galarraga	.20	.09
☐ 69 Bob Milacki	.05	.02
☐ 70 Tim Belcher	.05	.02
☐ 71 Todd Zeile	.10	.05
☐ 72 Jerome Walton	.05	.02
☐ 73 Kevin Seitzer	.05	.02
☐ 74 Jerald Clark	.05	.02
☐ 75 John Smoltz UER (Born in Detroit, not Warren)	.20	.09
☐ 76 Mike Henneman	.05	.02
☐ 77 Ken Griffey Jr.	1.50	.70
☐ 78 Jim Abbott	.10	.05
☐ 79 Gregg Jefferies	.10	.05
☐ 80 Kevin Reimer	.05	.02
☐ 81 Roger Clemens	.40	.18
☐ 82 Mike Fitzgerald	.05	.02
☐ 83 Bruce Hurst UER (Middle name is	.05	.02

Lee, not Vee)
84 Eric Davis .10 .05
85 Paul Molitor .20 .09
86 Will Clark .20 .09
87 Mike Bielecki .05 .02
88 Bret Saberhagen .05 .02
89 Nolan Ryan .75 .35
90 Bobby Thigpen .05 .02
91 Dickie Thon .05 .02
92 Duane Ward .05 .02
93 Luis Polonia .05 .02
94 Terry Kennedy .05 .02
95 Kent Hrbek .10 .05
96 Danny Jackson .05 .02
97 Sid Fernandez .05 .02
98 Jimmy Key .10 .05
99 Franklin Stubbs .05 .02
100 Checklist 28-103 .05 .02
101 R.J. Reynolds .05 .02
102 Dave Stewart .10 .05
103 Dan Pasqua .05 .02
104 Dan Plesac .05 .02
105 Mark McGwire .40 .18
106 John Farrell .05 .02
107 Don Mattingly .30 .14
108 Carlton Fisk .20 .09
109 Ken Oberkfell .05 .02
110 Darrel Akerfelds .05 .02
111 Gregg Olson .05 .02
112 Mike Scioscia .05 .02
113 Bryn Smith .05 .02
114 Bob Geren .05 .02
115 Tom Candiotti .05 .02
116 Kevin Tapani .05 .02
117 Jeff Treadway .05 .02
118 Alan Trammell .10 .05
119 Pete O'Brien .05 .02
(Blue shading goes through stats)
120 Joel Skinner .05 .02
121 Mike LaValliere .05 .02
122 Dwight Evans .10 .05
123 Jody Reed .05 .02
124 Lee Guetterman .05 .02
125 Tim Burke .05 .02
126 Dave Johnson .05 .02
127 Fernando Valenzuela .10 .05
(Lower large stripe in yellow instead of blue) UER
128 Jose DeLeon .05 .02
129 Andre Dawson .20 .09
130 Gerald Perry .05 .02
131 Greg W. Harris .05 .02
132 Tom Glavine .20 .09
133 Lance McCullers .05 .02
134 Randy Johnson .25 .11
135 Lance Parrish UER .05 .02
(Born in McKeesport, not Clairton)
136 Mackey Sasser .05 .02
137 Geno Petralli .05 .02
138 Dennis Lamp .05 .02
139 Dennis Martinez .10 .05
140 Mike Pagliarulo .05 .02
141 Hal Morris .05 .02
142 Dave Parker .10 .05
143 Brett Butler .10 .05
144 Paul Assenmacher .05 .02
145 Mark Gubicza .05 .02
146 Charlie Hough .05 .02
147 Sammy Sosa .25 .11
148 Randy Ready .05 .02
149 Kelly Gruber .05 .02
150 Devon White .05 .02
151 Gary Carter .20 .09
152 Gene Larkin .05 .02
153 Chris Sabo .05 .02
154 David Cone .10 .05
155 Todd Stottlemyre .05 .02
156 Glenn Wilson .05 .02
157 Bob Walk .05 .02
158 Mike Gallego .05 .02
159 Greg Hibbard .05 .02
160 Chris Bosio .05 .02
161 Mike Moore .05 .02
162 Jerry Browne UER .05 .02
(Born Christiansted, should be St. Croix)
163 Steve Sax UER .05 .02
(No asterisk next to his 1989 At Bats)
164 Melido Perez .05 .02
165 Danny Darwin .05 .02
166 Roger McDowell .05 .02
167 Bill Ripken .05 .02
168 Mike Sharperson .05 .02
169 Lee Smith .10 .05

□ 170 Matt Nokes .05 .02
□ 171 Jesse Orosco .05 .02
□ 172 Rick Aguilera .10 .05
□ 173 Jim Presley .05 .02
□ 174 Lou Whitaker .10 .05
□ 175 Harold Reynolds .05 .02
□ 176 Brook Jacoby .05 .02
□ 177 Wally Backman .05 .02
□ 178 Wade Boggs .20 .09
□ 179 Chuck Cary .05 .02
(Comma after DOB, not on other cards)
□ 180 Tom Foley .05 .02
□ 181 Pete Harnisch .05 .02
□ 182 Mike Morgan .05 .02
□ 183 Bob Tewksbury .05 .02
□ 184 Joe Girardi .10 .05
□ 185 Storm Davis .05 .02
□ 186 Ed Whitson .05 .02
□ 187 Steve Avery UER .05 .02
(Born in New Jersey, should be Michigan)
□ 188 Lloyd Moseby .05 .02
□ 189 Scott Bankhead .05 .02
□ 190 Mark Langston .05 .02
□ 191 Kevin McReynolds .05 .02
□ 192 Julio Franco .10 .05
□ 193 John Dopson .05 .02
□ 194 Dennis Boyd .05 .02
□ 195 Bip Roberts .05 .02
□ 196 Billy Hatcher .05 .02
□ 197 Edgar Diaz .05 .02
□ 198 Greg Litton .05 .02
□ 199 Mark Grace .20 .09
□ 200 Checklist 104-179 .05 .02
□ 201 George Brett .40 .18
□ 202 Jeff Russell .05 .02
□ 203 Ivan Calderon .05 .02
□ 204 Ken Howell .05 .02
□ 205 Tom Henke .05 .02
□ 206 Bryan Harvey .05 .02
□ 207 Steve Bedrosian .05 .02
□ 208 Al Newman .05 .02
□ 209 Randy Myers .10 .05
□ 210 Daryl Boston .05 .02
□ 211 Manny Lee .05 .02
□ 212 Dave Smith .05 .02
□ 213 Don Slaught .05 .02
□ 214 Walt Weiss .05 .02
□ 215 Donn Pall .05 .02
□ 216 Jaime Navarro .05 .02
□ 217 Willie Randolph .10 .05
□ 218 Rudy Seanez .05 .02
□ 219 Jim Leyritz .05 .02
□ 220 Ron Karkovice .05 .02
□ 221 Ken Caminiti .20 .09
□ 222 Von Hayes .05 .02
□ 223 Cal Ripken .75 .35
□ 224 Lenny Harris .05 .02
□ 225 Milt Thompson .05 .02
□ 226 Alvaro Espinoza .05 .02
□ 227 Chris James .05 .02
□ 228 Dan Gladden .05 .02
□ 229 Jeff Blauser .05 .02
□ 230 Mike Heath .05 .02
□ 231 Omar Vizquel .20 .09
□ 232 Doug Jones .05 .02
□ 233 Jeff King .10 .05
□ 234 Luis Rivera .05 .02
□ 235 Ellis Burks .10 .05
□ 236 Greg Cadaret .05 .02
□ 237 Dave Martinez .05 .02
□ 238 Mark Williamson .05 .02
□ 239 Stan Javier .05 .02
□ 240 Ozzie Smith .25 .11
□ 241 Shawn Boskie .05 .02
□ 242 Tom Gordon .05 .02
□ 243 Tony Gwynn .50 .23
□ 244 Tommy Gregg .05 .02
□ 245 Jeff M. Robinson .05 .02
□ 246 Keith Comstock .05 .02
□ 247 Jack Howell .05 .02
□ 248 Keith Miller .05 .02
□ 249 Bobby Witt .05 .02
□ 250 Rob Murphy UER .05 .02
(Shown as on Reds in '89 in stats, should be Red Sox)
□ 251 Spike Owen .05 .02
□ 252 Garry Templeton .05 .02
□ 253 Glenn Braggs .05 .02
□ 254 Ron Robinson .05 .02
□ 255 Kevin Mitchell .05 .02
□ 256 Les Lancaster .05 .02
□ 257 Mel Stottlemyre Jr. .05 .02
□ 258 Kenny Rogers UER .05 .02
(IP listed as 171, should be 172)
□ 259 Lance Johnson .05 .02
□ 260 John Kruk .10 .05
□ 261 Fred McGriff .20 .09
□ 262 Dick Schofield .05 .02
□ 263 Trevor Wilson .05 .02
□ 264 David West .05 .02
□ 265 Scott Scudder .05 .02
□ 266 Dwight Gooden .10 .05
□ 267 Willie Blair .05 .02
□ 268 Mark Portugal .05 .02
□ 269 Doug Drabek .05 .02
□ 270 Dennis Eckersley .20 .09
□ 271 Eric King .05 .02
□ 272 Robin Yount .20 .09
□ 273 Carney Lansford .10 .05
□ 274 Carlos Baerga .10 .05
□ 275 Dave Righetti .05 .02
□ 276 Scott Fletcher .05 .02
□ 277 Eric Yelding .05 .02
□ 278 Charlie Hayes .05 .02
□ 279 Jeff Ballard .05 .02
□ 280 Orel Hershiser .10 .05
□ 281 Jose Oquendo .05 .02
□ 282 Mike Witt .05 .02
□ 283 Mitch Webster .05 .02
□ 284 Greg Gagne .05 .02
□ 285 Greg Olson .05 .02
□ 286 Tony Phillips UER .05 .02
(Born 4/15, should be 4/25)
□ 287 Scott Bradley .05 .02
□ 288 Cory Snyder UER .05 .02
(In text, led is repeated and Inglewood is misspelled as Englewood)
□ 289 Jay Bell UER .10 .05
(Born in Pensacola, not Eglin AFB)
□ 290 Kevin Romine .05 .02
□ 291 Jeff D. Robinson .05 .02
□ 292 Steve Frey UER .05 .02
(Bats left, should be right)
□ 293 Craig Worthington .05 .02
□ 294 Tim Crews .05 .02
□ 295 Joe Magrane .05 .02
□ 296 Hector Villanueva .05 .02
□ 297 Terry Shumpert .05 .02
□ 298 Joe Carter .20 .09
□ 299 Kent Mercker UER .05 .02
(IP listed as 53, should be 52)
□ 300 Checklist 180-255 .05 .02
□ 301 Chet Lemon .05 .02
□ 302 Mike Schooler .05 .02
□ 303 Dante Bichette .20 .09
□ 304 Kevin Elster .05 .02
□ 305 Jeff Huson .05 .02
□ 306 Greg A. Harris .05 .02
□ 307 Marquis Grissom UER .20 .09
(Middle name Deon, should be Dean)
□ 308 Calvin Schiraldi .05 .02
□ 309 Mariano Duncan .05 .02
□ 310 Bill Spiers .05 .02
□ 311 Scott Garrelts .05 .02
□ 312 Mitch Williams .05 .02
□ 313 Mike Macfarlane .05 .02
□ 314 Kevin Brown .10 .05
□ 315 Robin Ventura .20 .09
□ 316 Darren Daulton .10 .05
□ 317 Pat Borders .05 .02
□ 318 Mark Eichhorn .05 .02
□ 319 Jeff Brantley .05 .02
□ 320 Shane Mack .05 .02
□ 321 Rob Dibble .05 .02
□ 322 John Franco .05 .02
□ 323 Junior Felix .05 .02
□ 324 Casey Candaele .05 .02
□ 325 Bobby Bonilla .10 .05
□ 326 Dave Henderson .05 .02
□ 327 Wayne Edwards .05 .02
□ 328 Mark Knudson .05 .02
□ 329 Terry Steinbach .10 .05
□ 330 Colby Ward UER .05 .02
(No comma between city and state)
□ 331 Oscar Azocar .05 .02
□ 332 Scott Radinsky .05 .02
□ 333 Eric Anthony .05 .02
□ 334 Steve Lake .05 .02
□ 335 Bob Melvin .05 .02
□ 336 Kal Daniels .05 .02
□ 337 Tom Pagnozzi .05 .02
□ 338 Alan Mills .05 .02
□ 339 Steve Olin .05 .02
□ 340 Juan Berenguer .05 .02

☐ 341 Francisco Cabrera .05 .02
☐ 342 Dave Bergman .05 .02
☐ 343 Henry Cotto .05 .02
☐ 344 Sergio Valdez .05 .02
☐ 345 Bob Patterson .05 .02
☐ 346 John Marzano .05 .02
☐ 347 Dana Kiecker .05 .02
☐ 348 Dion James .05 .02
☐ 349 Hubie Brooks .05 .02
☐ 350 Bill Landrum .05 .02
☐ 351 Bill Sampen .05 .02
☐ 352 Greg Briley .05 .02
☐ 353 Paul Gibson .05 .02
☐ 354 Dave Eiland .05 .02
☐ 355 Steve Finley .10 .05
☐ 356 Bob Boone .10 .05
☐ 357 Steve Buechele .05 .02
☐ 358 Chris Hoiles .05 .02
☐ 359 Larry Walker .30 .14
☐ 360 Frank DiPino .05 .02
☐ 361 Mark Grant .05 .02
☐ 362 Dave Magadan .05 .02
☐ 363 Robby Thompson .05 .02
☐ 364 Lonnie Smith .05 .02
☐ 365 Steve Farr .05 .02
☐ 366 Dave Valle .05 .02
☐ 367 Tim Naehring .10 .05
☐ 368 Jim Acker .05 .02
☐ 369 Jeff Reardon UER .10 .05
(Born in Pittsfield, not Dalton)
☐ 370 Tim Teufel .05 .02
☐ 371 Juan Gonzalez .75 .35
☐ 372 Luis Salazar .05 .02
☐ 373 Rick Honeycutt .05 .02
☐ 374 Greg Maddux .60 .25
☐ 375 Jose Uribe UER .05 .02
(Middle name Elta, should be Alta)
☐ 376 Donnie Hill .05 .02
☐ 377 Don Carman .05 .02
☐ 378 Craig Grebeck .05 .02
☐ 379 Willie Fraser .05 .02
☐ 380 Glenallen Hill .05 .02
☐ 381 Joe Oliver .05 .02
☐ 382 Randy Bush .05 .02
☐ 383 Alex Cole .05 .02
☐ 384 Norm Charlton .05 .02
☐ 385 Gene Nelson .05 .02
☐ 386 Checklist 256-331 .05 .02
☐ 387 Rickey Henderson MVP .20 .09
☐ 388 Lance Parrish MVP .05 .02
☐ 389 Fred McGriff MVP .20 .09
☐ 390 Dave Parker MVP .10 .05
☐ 391 Candy Maldonado MVP .05 .02
☐ 392 Ken Griffey Jr. MVP .75 .35
☐ 393 Gregg Olson MVP .05 .02
☐ 394 Rafael Palmeiro MVP .20 .09
☐ 395 Roger Clemens MVP .20 .09
☐ 396 George Brett MVP .20 .09
☐ 397 Cecil Fielder MVP .10 .05
☐ 398 Brian Harper MVP .05 .02
UER (Major League Performance, should be Career)
☐ 399 Bobby Thigpen MVP .05 .02
☐ 400 Roberto Kelly MVP .05 .02
UER (Second Base on front and OF on back)
☐ 401 Danny Darwin MVP .05 .02
☐ 402 Dave Justice MVP .10 .05
☐ 403 Lee Smith MVP .10 .05
☐ 404 Ryne Sandberg MVP .20 .09
☐ 405 Eddie Murray MVP .20 .09
☐ 406 Tim Wallach MVP .05 .02
☐ 407 Kevin Mitchell MVP .05 .02
☐ 408 Darryl Strawberry MVP .10 .05
☐ 409 Joe Carter MVP .10 .05
☐ 410 Len Dykstra MVP .10 .05
☐ 411 Doug Drabek MVP .05 .02
☐ 412 Chris Sabo MVP .05 .02
☐ 413 Paul Marak RR .05 .02
☐ 414 Tim McIntosh RR .05 .02
☐ 415 Brian Barnes RR .05 .02
☐ 416 Eric Gunderson RR .05 .02
☐ 417 Mike Gardiner RR .05 .02
☐ 418 Steve Carter RR .05 .02
☐ 419 Gerald Alexander RR .05 .02
☐ 420 Rich Garces RR .05 .02
☐ 421 Chuck Knoblauch RR .25 .11
☐ 422 Scott Aldred RR .05 .02
☐ 423 Wes Chamberlain RR .05 .02
☐ 424 Lance Dickson RR .05 .02
☐ 425 Greg Colbrunn RR .05 .02
☐ 426 Rich DeLucia RR UER .05 .02
(Misspelled Delucia on card)
☐ 427 Jeff Conine RR .25 .11
☐ 428 Steve Decker RR .05 .02
☐ 429 Turner Ward RR .05 .02
☐ 430 Mo Vaughn RR .40 .18
☐ 431 Steve Chitren RR .05 .02
☐ 432 Mike Benjamin RR .05 .02
☐ 433 Ryne Sandberg AS .20 .09
☐ 434 Len Dykstra AS .10 .05
☐ 435 Andre Dawson AS .10 .05
☐ 436A Mike Scioscia AS .05 .02
(White star by name)
☐ 436B Mike Scioscia AS .05 .02
(Yellow star by name)
☐ 437 Ozzie Smith AS .20 .09
☐ 438 Kevin Mitchell AS .05 .02
☐ 439 Jack Armstrong AS .05 .02
☐ 440 Chris Sabo AS .05 .02
☐ 441 Will Clark AS .20 .09
☐ 442 Mel Hall .05 .02
☐ 443 Mark Gardner .05 .02
☐ 444 Mike Devereaux .05 .02
☐ 445 Kirk Gibson .10 .05
☐ 446 Terry Pendleton .10 .05
☐ 447 Mike Harkey .05 .02
☐ 448 Jim Eisenreich .10 .05
☐ 449 Benito Santiago .05 .02
☐ 450 Oddibe McDowell .05 .02
☐ 451 Cecil Fielder .10 .05
☐ 452 Ken Griffey Sr. .05 .02
☐ 453 Bert Blyleven .10 .05
☐ 454 Howard Johnson .05 .02
☐ 455 Monty Fariss UER .05 .02
(Misspelled Farris on card)
☐ 456 Tony Pena .05 .02
☐ 457 Tim Raines .10 .05
☐ 458 Dennis Rasmussen .05 .02
☐ 459 Luis Quinones .05 .02
☐ 460 B.J. Surhoff .10 .05
☐ 461 Ernest Riles .05 .02
☐ 462 Rick Sutcliffe .05 .02
☐ 463 Danny Tartabull .05 .02
☐ 464 Pete Incaviglia .05 .02
☐ 465 Carlos Martinez .05 .02
☐ 466 Ricky Jordan .05 .02
☐ 467 John Cerutti .05 .02
☐ 468 Dave Winfield .20 .09
☐ 469 Francisco Oliveras .05 .02
☐ 470 Roy Smith .05 .02
☐ 471 Barry Larkin .20 .09
☐ 472 Ron Darling .05 .02
☐ 473 David Wells .05 .02
☐ 474 Glenn Davis .05 .02
☐ 475 Neal Heaton .05 .02
☐ 476 Ron Hassey .05 .02
☐ 477 Frank Thomas 1.50 .70
☐ 478 Greg Vaughn .05 .02
☐ 479 Todd Burns .05 .02
☐ 480 Candy Maldonado .05 .02
☐ 481 Dave LaPoint .05 .02
☐ 482 Alvin Davis .05 .02
☐ 483 Mike Scott .05 .02
☐ 484 Dale Murphy .20 .09
☐ 485 Ben McDonald .05 .02
☐ 486 Jay Howell .05 .02
☐ 487 Vince Coleman .05 .02
☐ 488 Alfredo Griffin .05 .02
☐ 489 Sandy Alomar Jr. .10 .05
☐ 490 Kirby Puckett .40 .18
☐ 491 Andres Thomas .05 .02
☐ 492 Jack Morris .10 .05
☐ 493 Matt Young .05 .02
☐ 494 Greg Myers .05 .02
☐ 495 Barry Bonds .25 .11
☐ 496 Scott Cooper UER .05 .02
(No BA for 1990 and career)
☐ 497 Dan Schatzeder .05 .02
☐ 498 Jesse Barfield .05 .02
☐ 499 Jerry Goff .05 .02
☐ 500 Checklist 332-408 .05 .02
☐ 501 Anthony Telford .05 .02
☐ 502 Eddie Murray .20 .09
☐ 503 Omar Olivares .05 .02
☐ 504 Ryne Sandberg .25 .11
☐ 505 Jeff Montgomery .10 .05
☐ 506 Mark Parent .05 .02
☐ 507 Ron Gant .10 .05
☐ 508 Frank Tanana .05 .02
☐ 509 Jay Buhner .20 .09
☐ 510 Max Venable .05 .02
☐ 511 Wally Whitehurst .05 .02
☐ 512 Gary Pettis .05 .02
☐ 513 Tom Brunansky .05 .02
☐ 514 Tim Wallach .05 .02
☐ 515 Craig Lefferts .05 .02
☐ 516 Tim Layana .05 .02
☐ 517 Darryl Hamilton .05 .0
☐ 518 Rick Reuschel .05 .0
☐ 519 Steve Wilson .05 .0
☐ 520 Kurt Stillwell .05 .0
☐ 521 Rafael Palmeiro .20 .0
☐ 522 Ken Patterson .05 .0
☐ 523 Len Dykstra .10 .0
☐ 524 Tony Fernandez .05 .0
☐ 525 Kent Anderson .05 .0
☐ 526 Mark Leonard .05 .0
☐ 527 Allan Anderson .05 .0
☐ 528 Tom Browning .05 .0
☐ 529 Frank Viola .05 .0
☐ 530 John Olerud .05 .0
☐ 531 Juan Agosto .05 .0
☐ 532 Zane Smith .05 .0
☐ 533 Scott Sanderson .05 .0
☐ 534 Barry Jones .05 .0
☐ 535 Mike Felder .05 .0
☐ 536 Jose Canseco .20 .0
☐ 537 Felix Fermin .05 .0
☐ 538 Roberto Kelly .05 .0
☐ 539 Brian Holman .05 .0
☐ 540 Mark Davidson .05 .0
☐ 541 Terry Mulholland .05 .0
☐ 542 Randy Milligan .05 .0
☐ 543 Jose Gonzalez .05 .0
☐ 544 Craig Wilson .05 .0
☐ 545 Mike Hartley .05 .0
☐ 546 Greg Swindell .05 .0
☐ 547 Gary Gaetti .10 .0
☐ 548 Dave Justice .25 1
☐ 549 Steve Searcy .05 .0
☐ 550 Erik Hanson .05 .0
☐ 551 Dave Stieb .05 .0
☐ 552 Andy Van Slyke .10 .0
☐ 553 Mike Greenwell .05 .0
☐ 554 Kevin Maas .05 .0
☐ 555 Delino DeShields .05 .0
☐ 556 Curt Schilling .05 .0
☐ 557 Ramon Martinez .10 .0
☐ 558 Pedro Guerrero .05 .0
☐ 559 Dwight Smith .05 .0
☐ 560 Mark Davis .05 .0
☐ 561 Shawn Abner .05 .0
☐ 562 Charlie Leibrandt .05 .0
☐ 563 John Shelby .05 .0
☐ 564 Bill Swift .05 .0
☐ 565 Mike Fetters .05 .0
☐ 566 Alejandro Pena .05 .0
☐ 567 Ruben Sierra .05 .0
☐ 568 Carlos Quintana .05 .0
☐ 569 Kevin Gross .05 .0
☐ 570 Derek Lilliquist .05 .0
☐ 571 Jack Armstrong .05 .0
☐ 572 Greg Brock .05 .0
☐ 573 Mike Kingery .05 .0
☐ 574 Greg Smith .05 .0
☐ 575 Brian McRae .20 .0
☐ 576 Jack Daugherty .05 .0
☐ 577 Ozzie Guillen .05 .0
☐ 578 Joe Boever .05 .0
☐ 579 Luis Sojo .05 .0
☐ 580 Chili Davis .10 .0
☐ 581 Don Robinson .05 .0
☐ 582 Brian Harper .05 .0
☐ 583 Paul O'Neill .10 .0
☐ 584 Bob Ojeda .05 .0
☐ 585 Mookie Wilson .05 .0
☐ 586 Rafael Ramirez .05 .0
☐ 587 Gary Redus .05 .0
☐ 588 Jamie Quirk .05 .0
☐ 589 Shawn Hillegas .05 .0
☐ 590 Tom Edens .05 .0
☐ 591 Joe Klink .05 .0
☐ 592 Charles Nagy .20 .0
☐ 593 Eric Plunk .05 .0
☐ 594 Tracy Jones .05 .0
☐ 595 Craig Biggio .20 .0
☐ 596 Jose DeJesus .05 .0
☐ 597 Mickey Tettleton .10 .0
☐ 598 Chris Gwynn .05 .0
☐ 599 Rex Hudler .05 .0
☐ 600 Checklist 409-506 .05 .0
☐ 601 Jim Gott .05 .0
☐ 602 Jeff Manto .05 .0
☐ 603 Nelson Liriano .05 .0
☐ 604 Mark Lemke .05 .0
☐ 605 Clay Parker .05 .0
☐ 606 Edgar Martinez .20 .0
☐ 607 Mark Whiten .05 .0
☐ 608 Ted Power .05 .0
☐ 609 Tom Bolton .05 .0
☐ 610 Tom Herr .05 .0
☐ 611 Andy Hawkins UER .05 .0
(Pitched No-Hitter on 7/1, not 7/2)

Card	MINT	NRMT
☐ 612 Scott Ruskin	.05	.02
☐ 613 Ron Kittle	.05	.02
☐ 614 John Wetteland	.20	.09
☐ 615 Mike Perez	.05	.02
☐ 616 Dave Clark	.05	.02
☐ 617 Brent Mayne	.05	.02
☐ 618 Jack Clark	.10	.05
☐ 619 Marvin Freeman	.05	.02
☐ 620 Edwin Nunez	.05	.02
☐ 621 Russ Swan	.05	.02
☐ 622 Johnny Ray	.05	.02
☐ 623 Charlie O'Brien	.05	.02
☐ 624 Joe Bitker	.05	.02
☐ 625 Mike Marshall	.05	.02
☐ 626 Otis Nixon	.05	.02
☐ 627 Andy Benes	.10	.05
☐ 628 Ron Oester	.05	.02
☐ 629 Ted Higuera	.05	.02
☐ 630 Kevin Bass	.05	.02
☐ 631 Damon Berryhill	.05	.02
☐ 632 Bo Jackson	.20	.09
☐ 633 Brad Arnsberg	.05	.02
☐ 634 Jerry Willard	.05	.02
☐ 635 Tommy Greene	.05	.02
☐ 636 Bob MacDonald	.05	.02
☐ 637 Kirk McCaskill	.05	.02
☐ 638 John Burkett	.10	.05
☐ 639 Paul Abbott	.05	.02
☐ 640 Todd Benzinger	.05	.02
☐ 641 Todd Hundley	.20	.09
☐ 642 George Bell	.05	.02
☐ 643 Javier Ortiz	.05	.02
☐ 644 Sid Bream	.05	.02
☐ 645 Bob Welch	.05	.02
☐ 646 Phil Bradley	.05	.02
☐ 647 Bill Krueger	.05	.02
☐ 648 Rickey Henderson	.20	.09
☐ 649 Kevin Wickander	.05	.02
☐ 650 Steve Balboni	.05	.02
☐ 651 Gene Harris	.05	.02
☐ 652 Jim Deshaies	.05	.02
☐ 653 Jason Grimsley	.05	.02
☐ 654 Joe Orsulak	.05	.02
☐ 655 Jim Poole	.05	.02
☐ 656 Felix Jose	.05	.02
☐ 657 Denis Cook	.05	.02
☐ 658 Tom Brookens	.05	.02
☐ 659 Junior Ortiz	.05	.02
☐ 660 Jeff Parrett	.05	.02
☐ 661 Jerry Don Gleaton	.05	.02
☐ 662 Brent Knackert	.05	.02
☐ 663 Rance Mulliniks	.05	.02
☐ 664 John Smiley	.05	.02
☐ 665 Larry Andersen	.05	.02
☐ 666 Willie McGee	.05	.02
☐ 667 Chris Nabholz	.05	.02
☐ 668 Brady Anderson	.20	.09
☐ 669 Darren Holmes UER (19 CG's, should be 0)	.05	.02
☐ 670 Ken Hill	.10	.05
☐ 671 Gary Varsho	.05	.02
☐ 672 Bill Pecota	.05	.02
☐ 673 Fred Lynn	.05	.02
☐ 674 Kevin D. Brown	.05	.02
☐ 675 Dan Petry	.05	.02
☐ 676 Mike Jackson	.05	.02
☐ 677 Wally Joyner	.10	.05
☐ 678 Danny Jackson	.05	.02
☐ 679 Bill Haselman	.05	.02
☐ 680 Mike Boddicker	.05	.02
☐ 681 Mel Rojas	.20	.09
☐ 682 Roberto Alomar	.20	.09
☐ 683 Dave Justice ROY	.20	.09
☐ 684 Chuck Crim	.05	.02
☐ 685 Matt Williams	.20	.09
☐ 686 Shawon Dunston	.05	.02
☐ 687 Jeff Schulz	.05	.02
☐ 688 John Barfield	.05	.02
☐ 689 Gerald Young	.05	.02
☐ 690 Luis Gonzalez	.20	.09
☐ 691 Frank Wills	.05	.02
☐ 692 Chuck Finley	.10	.05
☐ 693 Sandy Alomar Jr. ROY	.10	.05
☐ 694 Tim Drummond	.05	.02
☐ 695 Herm Winningham	.05	.02
☐ 696 Darryl Strawberry	.10	.05
☐ 697 Al Leiter	.10	.05
☐ 698 Karl Rhodes	.05	.02
☐ 699 Stan Belinda	.05	.02
☐ 700 Checklist 507-604	.05	.02
☐ 701 Lance Blankenship	.05	.02
☐ 702 Willie Stargell PUZ	.20	.09
☐ 703 Jim Gantner	.05	.02
☐ 704 Reggie Harris	.05	.02
☐ 705 Rob Ducey	.05	.02
☐ 706 Tim Hulett	.05	.02
☐ 707 Atlee Hammaker	.05	.02
☐ 708 Xavier Hernandez	.05	.02
☐ 709 Chuck McElroy	.05	.02
☐ 710 John Mitchell	.05	.02
☐ 711 Carlos Hernandez	.05	.02
☐ 712 Geronimo Pena	.05	.02
☐ 713 Jim Neidlinger	.05	.02
☐ 714 John Orton	.05	.02
☐ 715 Terry Leach	.05	.02
☐ 716 Mike Stanton	.05	.02
☐ 717 Walt Terrell	.05	.02
☐ 718 Luis Aquino	.05	.02
☐ 719 Bud Black (Blue Jays uniform, but Giants logo)	.05	.02
☐ 720 Bob Kipper	.05	.02
☐ 721 Jeff Gray	.05	.02
☐ 722 Jose Rijo	.05	.02
☐ 723 Curt Young	.05	.02
☐ 724 Jose Vizcaino	.05	.02
☐ 725 Randy Tomlin	.05	.02
☐ 726 Junior Noboa	.05	.02
☐ 727 Bob Welch CY	.05	.02
☐ 728 Gary Ward	.05	.02
☐ 729 Rob Deer (Brewers uniform, but Tigers logo)	.05	.02
☐ 730 David Segui	.10	.05
☐ 731 Mark Carreon	.05	.02
☐ 732 Vicente Palacios	.05	.02
☐ 733 Sam Horn	.05	.02
☐ 734 Howard Farmer	.05	.02
☐ 735 Ken Dayley (Cardinals uniform, but Blue Jays logo)	.05	.02
☐ 736 Kelly Mann	.05	.02
☐ 737 Joe Grahe	.05	.02
☐ 738 Kelly Downs	.05	.02
☐ 739 Jimmy Kremers	.05	.02
☐ 740 Kevin Appier	.20	.09
☐ 741 Jeff Reed	.05	.02
☐ 742 Jose Rijo WS	.05	.02
☐ 743 Dave Rohde	.05	.02
☐ 744 Dr.Dirt/Mr.Clean Len Dykstra Dale Murphy UER (No '91 Donruss logo on card front)	.10	.05
☐ 745 Paul Sorrento	.05	.02
☐ 746 Thomas Howard	.05	.02
☐ 747 Matt Stark	.05	.02
☐ 748 Harold Baines	.10	.05
☐ 749 Doug Dascenzo	.05	.02
☐ 750 Doug Drabek CY	.05	.02
☐ 751 Gary Sheffield	.20	.09
☐ 752 Terry Lee	.05	.02
☐ 753 Jim Vatcher	.05	.02
☐ 754 Lee Stevens	.05	.02
☐ 755 Randy Veres	.05	.02
☐ 756 Bill Doran	.05	.02
☐ 757 Gary Wayne	.05	.02
☐ 758 Pedro Munoz	.05	.02
☐ 759 Chris Hammond	.05	.02
☐ 760 Checklist 605-702	.05	.02
☐ 761 Rickey Henderson MVP	.20	.09
☐ 762 Barry Bonds MVP	.20	.09
☐ 763 Billy Hatcher WS UER (Line 13, on should be one)	.05	.02
☐ 764 Julio Machado	.05	.02
☐ 765 Jose Mesa	.10	.05
☐ 766 Willie Randolph WS	.10	.05
☐ 767 Scott Erickson	.10	.05
☐ 768 Travis Fryman	.20	.09
☐ 769 Rich Rodriguez	.05	.02
☐ 770 Checklist 703-770 and BC1-BC22	.05	.02

1991 Donruss Bonus Cards

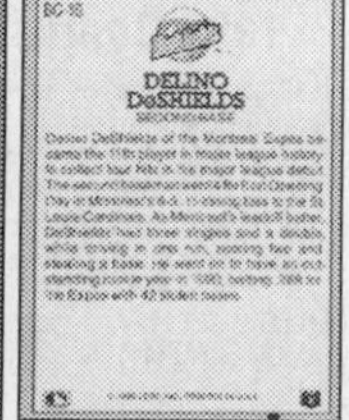

These bonus cards are standard size and were randomly inserted in Donruss packs and highlight outstanding player achievements, the first ten in the first series and the remaining 12 in the second series picking up in time beginning with Valenzuela's no-hitter and continuing until the end of the season.

	MINT	NRMT
COMPLETE SET (22)	1.50	.70
COMMON CARD (BC1-BC22)	.05	.02
☐ BC1 Mark Langston Mike Witt	.05	.02
☐ BC2 Randy Johnson	.25	.11
☐ BC3 Nolan Ryan No-Hitter	.50	.23
☐ BC4 Dave Stewart	.05	.02
☐ BC5 Cecil Fielder	.10	.05
☐ BC6 Carlton Fisk	.25	.11
☐ BC7 Ryne Sandberg	.25	.11
☐ BC8 Gary Carter	.15	.07
☐ BC9 Mark McGwire	.30	.14
☐ BC10 Bo Jackson	.10	.05
☐ BC11 Fernando Valenzuela	.10	.05
☐ BC12A Andy Hawkins ERR Pitcher	1.00	.45
☐ BC12B Andy Hawkins COR No Hits White Sox	.05	.02
☐ BC13 Melido Perez	.05	.02
☐ BC14 Terry Mulholland UER Charlie Hayes is called Chris Hayes	.05	.02
☐ BC15 Nolan Ryan 300th Win	.50	.23
☐ BC16 Delino DeShields	.05	.02
☐ BC17 Cal Ripken	.50	.23
☐ BC18 Eddie Murray	.25	.11
☐ BC19 George Brett	.30	.14
☐ BC20 Bobby Thigpen	.05	.02
☐ BC21 Dave Stieb	.05	.02
☐ BC22 Willie McGee	.05	.02

1991 Donruss Elite

These special cards were inserted in the 1991 Donruss first and second series wax packs. Production was limited to a maximum of 10,000 cards for each card in the Elite series, and lesser production for the Sandberg Signature (5,000) and Ryan Legend (7,500) cards. This was the first time that mainstream insert cards were ever numbered allowing for verifiable proof of print runs. The regular Elite cards are photos enclosed in a bronze marble borders which surround an evenly squared photo of the players. The Sandberg Signature card has a green marble border and is signed in a blue sharpie. The Nolan Ryan Legend card is a Dick Perez drawing with silver borders. The cards are all numbered on the back, 1 out of 10,000, etc.

	MINT	NRMT
COMPLETE SET (10)	1000.00	450.00
COMMON CARD (1-8)	20.00	9.00
☐ 1 Barry Bonds	80.00	36.00
☐ 2 George Brett	120.00	55.00
☐ 3 Jose Canseco	60.00	27.00
☐ 4 Andre Dawson	40.00	18.00
☐ 5 Doug Drabek	20.00	9.00
☐ 6 Cecil Fielder	30.00	13.50
☐ 7 Rickey Henderson	40.00	18.00
☐ 8 Matt Williams	60.00	27.00
☐ L1 Nolan Ryan (Legend)	200.00	90.00
☐ S1 Ryne Sandberg (Signature Series)	300.00	135.00

1991 Donruss Grand Slammers

This 14-card standard-size set commemorates players who hit grand slams in 1990. The cards feature on the fronts color player photos on a computer-generated background design, enframed by white borders on a green card face crisscrossed by different color diagonal

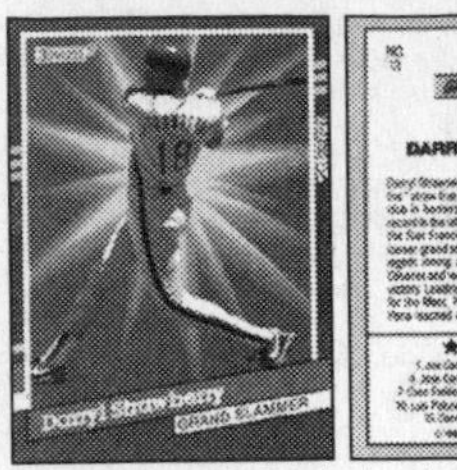
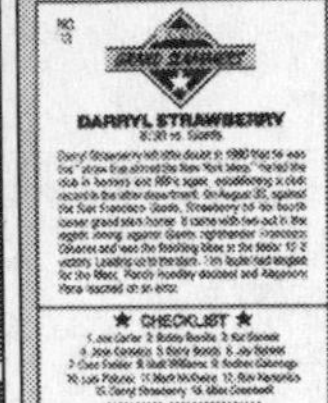

stripes. The player's name is given in a color stripe below the picture. Inside pale green borders, the back recounts grand slam homers by the player.

COMMON CARD (1-14)	.05	.02
COMPLETE SET (1-14)	.05	.90

☐ 1 Joe Carter	.10	.05
☐ 2 Bobby Bonilla	.10	.05
☐ 3 Kal Daniels	.05	.02
☐ 4 Jose Canseco	.25	.11
☐ 5 Barry Bonds	.40	.18
☐ 6 Jay Buhner	.25	.11
☐ 7 Cecil Fielder	.10	.05
☐ 8 Matt Williams	.15	.07
☐ 9 Andres Galarraga	.25	.11
☐ 10 Luis Polonia	.05	.02
☐ 11 Mark McGwire	.50	.23
☐ 12 Ron Karkovice	.05	.02
☐ 13 Darryl Strawberry UER (Todd Hundley is called Randy)	.10	.05
☐ 14 Mike Greenwell	.05	.02

1991 Donruss Rookies

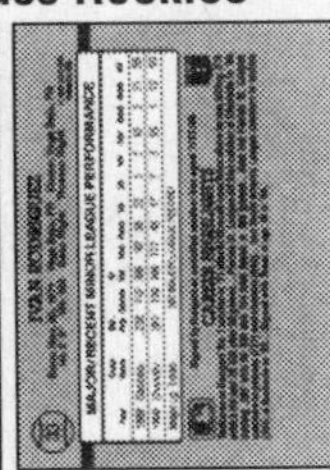

The 1991 Donruss Rookies set was issued exclusively in factory set form through hobby dealers. The cards measure the standard size and a mini puzzle featuring Hall of Famer Willie Stargell was included with the set. The fronts feature color action player photos, with white and red borders. Rookie Cards include Jeff Bagwell and Ivan Rodriguez.

	MINT	NRMT
COMPLETE SET (56)	4.00	1.80
COMMON CARD (1-56)	.05	.02

☐ 1 Pat Kelly	.05	.02
☐ 2 Rich DeLucia	.05	.02
☐ 3 Wes Chamberlain	.05	.02
☐ 4 Scott Leius	.05	.02
☐ 5 Darryl Kile	.20	.09
☐ 6 Milt Cuyler	.05	.02
☐ 7 Todd Van Poppel	.05	.02
☐ 8 Ray Lankford	.20	.09
☐ 9 Brian R. Hunter	.05	.02
☐ 10 Tony Perezchica	.05	.02
☐ 11 Ced Landrum	.05	.02
☐ 12 Dave Burba	.05	.02
☐ 13 Ramon Garcia	.05	.02
☐ 14 Ed Sprague	.05	.02
☐ 15 Warren Newson	.05	.02
☐ 16 Paul Faries	.05	.02
☐ 17 Luis Gonzalez	.10	.05
☐ 18 Charles Nagy	.10	.05
☐ 19 Chris Hammond	.05	.02
☐ 20 Frank Castillo	.05	.02
☐ 21 Pedro Munoz	.05	.02
☐ 22 Orlando Merced	.10	.05
☐ 23 Jose Melendez	.05	.02
☐ 24 Kirk Dressendorfer	.05	.02
☐ 25 Heathcliff Slocumb	.20	.09
☐ 26 Doug Simons	.05	.02
☐ 27 Mike Timlin	.05	.02
☐ 28 Jeff Fassero	.15	.07
☐ 29 Mark Leiter	.05	.02
☐ 30 Jeff Bagwell	2.50	1.10
☐ 31 Brian McRae	.20	.09
☐ 32 Mark Whiten	.05	.02
☐ 33 Ivan Rodriguez	1.50	.70
☐ 34 Wade Taylor	.05	.02
☐ 35 Darren Lewis	.05	.02
☐ 36 Mo Vaughn	.40	.18
☐ 37 Mike Remlinger	.05	.02
☐ 38 Rick Wilkins	.05	.02
☐ 39 Chuck Knoblauch	.25	.11
☐ 40 Kevin Morton	.05	.02
☐ 41 Carlos Rodriguez	.05	.02
☐ 42 Mark Lewis	.05	.02
☐ 43 Brent Mayne	.05	.02
☐ 44 Chris Haney	.05	.02
☐ 45 Denis Boucher	.05	.02
☐ 46 Mike Gardiner	.05	.02
☐ 47 Jeff Johnson	.05	.02
☐ 48 Dean Palmer	.10	.05
☐ 49 Chuck McElroy	.05	.02
☐ 50 Chris Jones	.05	.02
☐ 51 Scott Kamieniecki	.05	.02
☐ 52 Al Osuna	.05	.02
☐ 53 Rusty Meacham	.05	.02
☐ 54 Chito Martinez	.05	.02
☐ 55 Reggie Jefferson	.20	.09
☐ 56 Checklist 1-56	.05	.02

1991 Donruss Super DK's

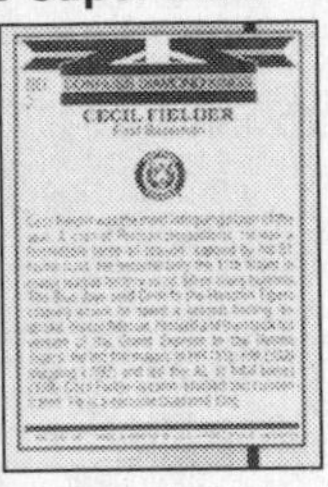

For the seventh consecutive year Donruss issued a card set featuring the players used in the current year's Diamond King subset in a larger size, approximately 5" X 7". The set again featured the art work of famed sports artist Dick Perez and was available through a postpaid mail-in offer detailed on the 1991 Donruss wax packs involving $14.00 and three wax wrappers.

	MINT	NRMT
COMPLETE SET (26)	15.00	6.75
COMMON CARD (1-26)	.50	.23

☐ 1 Dave Stieb	.50	.23
☐ 2 Craig Biggio	1.50	.70
☐ 3 Cecil Fielder	.75	.35
☐ 4 Barry Bonds	2.00	.90
☐ 5 Barry Larkin	1.50	.70
☐ 6 Dave Parker	.75	.35
☐ 7 Len Dykstra	.75	.35
☐ 8 Bobby Thigpen	.50	.23
☐ 9 Roger Clemens	3.00	1.35
☐ 10 Ron Gant	.75	.35
☐ 11 Delino DeShields	.50	.23
☐ 12 Roberto Alomar	1.50	.70
☐ 13 Sandy Alomar Jr.	1.00	.45
☐ 14 Ryne Sandberg	2.50	1.10
☐ 15 Ramon Martinez	.75	.35
☐ 16 Edgar Martinez	1.00	.45
☐ 17 Dave Magadan	.50	.23
☐ 18 Matt Williams	1.00	.45
☐ 19 Rafael Palmeiro	1.00	.45
☐ 20 Bob Welch	.50	.23
☐ 21 Dave Righetti	.50	.23
☐ 22 Brian Harper	.50	.23
☐ 23 Gregg Olson	.50	.23
☐ 24 Kurt Stillwell	.50	.23
☐ 25 Pedro Guerrero	.50	.23
☐ 26 Chuck Finley	.75	.35

1992 Donruss Previews

This 12-card preview set was available only to Donruss dealers. The standard-size cards feature the same glossy color player photos on the fronts and player information on the backs as the regular series issue. The statistics only go through the 1990 season. Only the numbering of the cards on the back is different.

	MINT	NRMT
COMPLETE SET (12)	225.00	100.00
COMMON CARD (1-12)	5.00	2.20

☐ 1 Wade Boggs	15.00	6.75
☐ 2 Barry Bonds	20.00	9.00
☐ 3 Will Clark	10.00	4.50
☐ 4 Andre Dawson	10.00	4.50
☐ 5 Dennis Eckersley	10.00	4.50
☐ 6 Robin Ventura	8.00	3.60
☐ 7 Ken Griffey Jr.	75.00	34.00
☐ 8 Kelly Gruber	5.00	2.20
☐ 9 Ryan Klesko	15.00	6.75
☐ 10 Cal Ripken	60.00	27.00
☐ 11 Nolan Ryan	60.00	27.00
☐ 12 Todd Van Poppel	5.00	2.20

1992 Donruss

The 1992 Donruss set contains 784 standard-size cards issued in two separate series of 396. Cards were issued i first and second series foil wrapped packs in addition t hobby and retail factory sets. One of 21 different puzzl panels featuring Hall of Famer Rod Carew was inserte into each pack. The basic card design features glossy color player photos with white borders. Two-toned blu stripes overlay the top and bottom of the picture. Subset include Rated Rookies (1-20, 397-421], All-Stars (21 30/422-431) and Highlights (33, 94, 154, 215, 276, 434 495, 555, 616, 677). The only notable Rookie Card in th set features John Jaha.

	MINT	NRMT
COMPLETE SET (784)	8.00	3.60
COMP.HOBBY SET (788)	15.00	6.75
COMP.RETAIL SET (788)	8.00	3.60
COMPLETE SERIES 1 (396)	4.00	1.80
COMPLETE SERIES 2 (388)	4.00	1.80
COMMON CARD (1-784)	.05	.02
COMPLETE CAREW PUZZLE	1.00	.45

☐ 1 Mark Wohlers RR	.20	.09
☐ 2 Wil Cordero RR	.05	.02
☐ 3 Kyle Abbott RR	.05	.02
☐ 4 Dave Nilsson RR	.10	.05
☐ 5 Kenny Lofton RR	.75	.35
☐ 6 Luis Mercedes RR	.05	.02
☐ 7 Roger Salkeld RR	.05	.02
☐ 8 Eddie Zosky RR	.05	.02
☐ 9 Todd Van Poppel RR	.05	.02
☐ 10 Frank Seminara RR	.05	.02
☐ 11 Andy Ashby RR	.05	.0
☐ 12 Reggie Jefferson RR	.05	.0
☐ 13 Ryan Klesko RR	.40	.1
☐ 14 Carlos Garcia RR	.05	.02
☐ 15 John Ramos RR	.05	.02
☐ 16 Eric Karros RR	.10	.05
☐ 17 Patrick Lennon RR	.05	.02
☐ 18 Eddie Taubensee RR	.05	.02
☐ 19 Roberto Hernandez RR	.20	.09
☐ 20 D.J. Dozier RR	.05	.02
☐ 21 Dave Henderson AS	.05	.02
☐ 22 Cal Ripken AS	.40	.18
☐ 23 Wade Boggs AS	.20	.09
☐ 24 Ken Griffey Jr. AS	.75	.3
☐ 25 Jack Morris AS	.05	.02
☐ 26 Danny Tartabull AS	.05	.02
☐ 27 Cecil Fielder AS	.10	.05
☐ 28 Roberto Alomar AS	.20	.09
☐ 29 Sandy Alomar Jr. AS	.10	.05
☐ 30 Rickey Henderson AS	.20	.0
☐ 31 Ken Hill	.10	.05
☐ 32 John Habyan	.05	.02
☐ 33 Otis Nixon HL	.10	.05
☐ 34 Tim Wallach	.05	.0

35 Cal Ripken .75 .35
36 Gary Carter .20 .09
37 Juan Agosto .05 .02
38 Doug Dascenzo .05 .02
39 Kirk Gibson .05 .02
40 Benito Santiago .05 .02
41 Otis Nixon .10 .05
42 Andy Allanson .05 .02
43 Brian Holman .05 .02
44 Dick Schofield .05 .02
45 Dave Magadan .05 .02
46 Rafael Palmeiro .05 .02
47 Jody Reed .05 .02
48 Ivan Calderon .05 .02
49 Greg W. Harris .05 .02
50 Chris Sabo .05 .02
51 Paul Molitor .20 .09
52 Robby Thompson .05 .02
53 Dave Smith .05 .02
54 Mark Davis .05 .02
55 Kevin Brown .10 .05
56 Donn Pall .05 .02
57 Len Dykstra .10 .05
58 Roberto Alomar .20 .09
59 Jeff D. Robinson .05 .02
60 Willie McGee .05 .02
61 Jay Buhner .05 .02
62 Mike Pagliarulo .05 .02
63 Paul O'Neill .10 .05
64 Hubie Brooks .05 .02
65 Kelly Gruber .05 .02
66 Ken Caminiti .20 .09
67 Gary Redus .05 .02
68 Harold Baines .10 .05
69 Charlie Hough .05 .02
70 B.J. Surhoff .10 .05
71 Walt Weiss .05 .02
72 Shawn Hillegas .05 .02
73 Roberto Kelly .05 .02
74 Jeff Ballard .05 .02
75 Craig Biggio .05 .02
76 Pat Combs .05 .02
77 Jeff M. Robinson .05 .02
78 Tim Belcher .05 .02
79 Cris Carpenter .05 .02
80 Checklist 1-79 .05 .02
81 Steve Avery .05 .02
82 Chris James .05 .02
83 Brian Harper .05 .02
84 Charlie Leibrandt .05 .02
85 Mickey Tettleton .05 .02
86 Pete O'Brien .05 .02
87 Danny Darwin .05 .02
88 Bob Walk .05 .02
89 Jeff Reardon .10 .05
90 Bobby Rose .05 .02
91 Danny Jackson .05 .02
92 John Morris .05 .02
93 Bud Black .05 .02
94 Tommy Greene HL .05 .02
95 Rick Aguilera .05 .02
96 Gary Gaetti .10 .05
97 David Cone .10 .05
98 John Olerud .10 .05
99 Joel Skinner .05 .02
100 Jay Bell .10 .05
101 Bob Milacki .05 .02
102 Norm Charlton .05 .02
103 Chuck Crim .05 .02
104 Terry Steinbach .10 .05
105 Juan Samuel .05 .02
106 Steve Howe .05 .02
107 Rafael Belliard .05 .02
108 Joey Cora .05 .02
109 Tommy Greene .05 .02
110 Gregg Olson .05 .02
111 Frank Tanana .05 .02
112 Lee Smith .10 .05
113 Greg A. Harris .05 .02
114 Dwayne Henry .05 .02
115 Chili Davis .10 .05
116 Kent Mercker .05 .02
117 Brian Barnes .05 .02
118 Rich DeLucia .05 .02
119 Andre Dawson .05 .02
120 Carlos Baerga .10 .05
121 Mike LaValliere .05 .02
122 Jeff Gray .05 .02
123 Bruce Hurst .05 .02
124 Alvin Davis .05 .02
125 John Candelaria .05 .02
126 Matt Nokes .05 .02
127 George Bell .05 .02
128 Bret Saberhagen .05 .02
129 Jeff Russell .05 .02
130 Jim Abbott .05 .02
131 Bill Gullickson .05 .02

☐ 132 Todd Zeile .05 .02
☐ 133 Dave Winfield .05 .02
☐ 134 Wally Whitehurst .05 .02
☐ 135 Matt Williams .05 .02
☐ 136 Tom Browning .05 .02
☐ 137 Marquis Grissom .10 .05
☐ 138 Erik Hanson .05 .02
☐ 139 Rob Dibble .05 .02
☐ 140 Don August .05 .02
☐ 141 Tom Henke .05 .02
☐ 142 Dan Pasqua .05 .02
☐ 143 George Brett .40 .18
☐ 144 Jerald Clark .05 .02
☐ 145 Robin Ventura .10 .05
☐ 146 Dale Murphy .20 .09
☐ 147 Dennis Eckersley .20 .09
☐ 148 Eric Yelding .05 .02
☐ 149 Mario Diaz .05 .02
☐ 150 Casey Candaele .05 .02
☐ 151 Steve Olin .05 .02
☐ 152 Luis Salazar .05 .02
☐ 153 Kevin Maas .05 .02
☐ 154 Nolan Ryan HL .40 .18
☐ 155 Barry Jones .05 .02
☐ 156 Chris Hoiles .05 .02
☐ 157 Bobby Ojeda .05 .02
☐ 158 Pedro Guerrero .05 .02
☐ 159 Paul Assenmacher .05 .02
☐ 160 Checklist 80-157 .05 .02
☐ 161 Mike Macfarlane .05 .02
☐ 162 Craig Lefferts .05 .02
☐ 163 Brian Hunter .05 .02
☐ 164 Alan Trammell .05 .02
☐ 165 Ken Griffey Jr. 1.25 .55
☐ 166 Lance Parrish .05 .02
☐ 167 Brian Downing .05 .02
☐ 168 John Barfield .05 .02
☐ 169 Jack Clark .10 .05
☐ 170 Chris Nabholz .05 .02
☐ 171 Tim Teufel .05 .02
☐ 172 Chris Hammond .05 .02
☐ 173 Robin Yount .05 .02
☐ 174 Dave Righetti .05 .02
☐ 175 Joe Girardi .05 .02
☐ 176 Mike Boddicker .05 .02
☐ 177 Dean Palmer .10 .05
☐ 178 Greg Hibbard .05 .02
☐ 179 Randy Ready .05 .02
☐ 180 Devon White .05 .02
☐ 181 Mark Eichhorn .05 .02
☐ 182 Mike Felder .05 .02
☐ 183 Joe Klink .05 .02
☐ 184 Steve Bedrosian .05 .02
☐ 185 Barry Larkin .05 .02
☐ 186 John Franco .05 .02
☐ 187 Ed Sprague .05 .02
☐ 188 Mark Portugal .05 .02
☐ 189 Jose Lind .05 .02
☐ 190 Bob Welch .05 .02
☐ 191 Alex Fernandez .10 .05
☐ 192 Gary Sheffield .20 .09
☐ 193 Rickey Henderson .05 .02
☐ 194 Rod Nichols .05 .02
☐ 195 Scott Kamieniecki .05 .02
☐ 196 Mike Flanagan .05 .02
☐ 197 Steve Finley .10 .05
☐ 198 Darren Daulton .10 .05
☐ 199 Leo Gomez .05 .02
☐ 200 Mike Morgan .05 .02
☐ 201 Bob Tewksbury .05 .02
☐ 202 Sid Bream .05 .02
☐ 203 Sandy Alomar Jr. .10 .05
☐ 204 Greg Gagne .05 .02
☐ 205 Juan Berenguer .05 .02
☐ 206 Cecil Fielder .10 .05
☐ 207 Randy Johnson .20 .09
☐ 208 Tony Pena .05 .02
☐ 209 Doug Drabek .05 .02
☐ 210 Wade Boggs .20 .09
☐ 211 Bryan Harvey .05 .02
☐ 212 Jose Vizcaino .05 .02
☐ 213 Alonzo Powell .05 .02
☐ 214 Will Clark .05 .02
☐ 215 Rickey Henderson HL .20 .09
☐ 216 Jack Morris .10 .05
☐ 217 Junior Felix .05 .02
☐ 218 Vince Coleman .05 .02
☐ 219 Jimmy Key .10 .05
☐ 220 Alex Cole .05 .02
☐ 221 Bill Landrum .05 .02
☐ 222 Randy Milligan .05 .02
☐ 223 Jose Rijo .05 .02
☐ 224 Greg Vaughn .05 .02
☐ 225 Dave Stewart .10 .05
☐ 226 Lenny Harris .05 .02
☐ 227 Scott Sanderson .05 .02
☐ 228 Jeff Blauser .05 .02

☐ 229 Ozzie Guillen .05 .02
☐ 230 John Kruk .10 .05
☐ 231 Bob Melvin .05 .02
☐ 232 Milt Cuyler .05 .02
☐ 233 Felix Jose .05 .02
☐ 234 Ellis Burks .10 .05
☐ 235 Pete Harnisch .05 .02
☐ 236 Kevin Tapani .05 .02
☐ 237 Terry Pendleton .05 .02
☐ 238 Mark Gardner .05 .02
☐ 239 Harold Reynolds .05 .02
☐ 240 Checklist 158-237 .05 .02
☐ 241 Mike Harkey .05 .02
☐ 242 Felix Fermin .05 .02
☐ 243 Barry Bonds .25 .11
☐ 244 Roger Clemens .40 .18
☐ 245 Dennis Rasmussen .05 .02
☐ 246 Jose DeLeon .05 .02
☐ 247 Orel Hershiser .10 .05
☐ 248 Mel Hall .05 .02
☐ 249 Rick Wilkins .05 .02
☐ 250 Tom Gordon .05 .02
☐ 251 Kevin Reimer .05 .02
☐ 252 Luis Polonia .05 .02
☐ 253 Mike Henneman .05 .02
☐ 254 Tom Pagnozzi .05 .02
☐ 255 Chuck Finley .05 .02
☐ 256 Mackey Sasser .05 .02
☐ 257 John Burkett .05 .02
☐ 258 Hal Morris .05 .02
☐ 259 Larry Walker .20 .09
☐ 260 Billy Swift .05 .02
☐ 261 Joe Oliver .05 .02
☐ 262 Julio Machado .05 .02
☐ 263 Todd Stottlemyre .05 .02
☐ 264 Matt Merullo .05 .02
☐ 265 Brent Mayne .05 .02
☐ 266 Thomas Howard .05 .02
☐ 267 Lance Johnson .05 .02
☐ 268 Terry Mulholland .05 .02
☐ 269 Rick Honeycutt .05 .02
☐ 270 Luis Gonzalez .05 .02
☐ 271 Jose Guzman .05 .02
☐ 272 Jimmy Jones .05 .02
☐ 273 Mark Lewis .05 .02
☐ 274 Rene Gonzales .05 .02
☐ 275 Jeff Johnson .05 .02
☐ 276 Dennis Martinez HL .05 .02
☐ 277 Delino DeShields .05 .02
☐ 278 Sam Horn .05 .02
☐ 279 Kevin Gross .05 .02
☐ 280 Jose Oquendo .05 .02
☐ 281 Mark Grace .10 .05
☐ 282 Mark Gubicza .05 .02
☐ 283 Fred McGriff .05 .02
☐ 284 Ron Gant .10 .05
☐ 285 Lou Whitaker .10 .05
☐ 286 Edgar Martinez .05 .02
☐ 287 Ron Tingley .05 .02
☐ 288 Kevin McReynolds .05 .02
☐ 289 Ivan Rodriguez .40 .18
☐ 290 Mike Gardiner .05 .02
☐ 291 Chris Haney .05 .02
☐ 292 Darrin Jackson .05 .02
☐ 293 Bill Doran .05 .02
☐ 294 Ted Higuera .05 .02
☐ 295 Jeff Brantley .05 .02
☐ 296 Les Lancaster .05 .02
☐ 297 Jim Eisenreich .10 .05
☐ 298 Ruben Sierra .05 .02
☐ 299 Scott Radinsky .05 .02
☐ 300 Jose DeJesus .05 .02
☐ 301 Mike Timlin .05 .02
☐ 302 Luis Sojo .05 .02
☐ 303 Kelly Downs .05 .02
☐ 304 Scott Bankhead .05 .02
☐ 305 Pedro Munoz .05 .02
☐ 306 Scott Scudder .05 .02
☐ 307 Kevin Elster .05 .02
☐ 308 Duane Ward .05 .02
☐ 309 Darryl Kile .10 .05
☐ 310 Orlando Merced .05 .02
☐ 311 Dave Henderson .05 .02
☐ 312 Tim Raines .10 .05
☐ 313 Mark Lee .05 .02
☐ 314 Mike Gallego .05 .02
☐ 315 Charles Nagy .10 .05
☐ 316 Jesse Barfield .05 .02
☐ 317 Todd Frohwirth .05 .02
☐ 318 Al Osuna .05 .02
☐ 319 Darrin Fletcher .05 .02
☐ 320 Checklist 238-316 .05 .02
☐ 321 David Segui .05 .02
☐ 322 Stan Javier .05 .02
☐ 323 Bryn Smith .05 .02
☐ 324 Jeff Treadway .05 .02
☐ 325 Mark Whiten .05 .02

☐ 326 Kent Hrbek	.10	.05
☐ 327 Dave Justice	.20	.09
☐ 328 Tony Phillips	.05	.02
☐ 329 Rob Murphy	.05	.02
☐ 330 Kevin Morton	.05	.02
☐ 331 John Smiley	.05	.02
☐ 332 Luis Rivera	.05	.02
☐ 333 Wally Joyner	.10	.05
☐ 334 Heathcliff Slocumb	.05	.02
☐ 335 Rick Cerone	.05	.02
☐ 336 Mike Remlinger	.05	.02
☐ 337 Mike Moore	.05	.02
☐ 338 Lloyd McClendon	.05	.02
☐ 339 Al Newman	.05	.02
☐ 340 Kirk McCaskill	.05	.02
☐ 341 Howard Johnson	.05	.02
☐ 342 Greg Myers	.05	.02
☐ 343 Kal Daniels	.05	.02
☐ 344 Bernie Williams	.20	.09
☐ 345 Shane Mack	.05	.02
☐ 346 Gary Thurman	.05	.02
☐ 347 Dante Bichette	.05	.02
☐ 348 Mark McGwire	.40	.18
☐ 349 Travis Fryman	.10	.05
☐ 350 Ray Lankford	.05	.02
☐ 351 Mike Jeffcoat	.05	.02
☐ 352 Jack McDowell	.05	.02
☐ 353 Mitch Williams	.05	.02
☐ 354 Mike Devereaux	.05	.02
☐ 355 Andres Galarraga	.05	.02
☐ 356 Henry Cotto	.05	.02
☐ 357 Scott Bailes	.05	.02
☐ 358 Jeff Bagwell	.60	.25
☐ 359 Scott Leius	.05	.02
☐ 360 Zane Smith	.05	.02
☐ 361 Bill Pecota	.05	.02
☐ 362 Tony Fernandez	.05	.02
☐ 363 Glenn Braggs	.05	.02
☐ 364 Bill Spiers	.05	.02
☐ 365 Vicente Palacios	.05	.02
☐ 366 Tim Burke	.05	.02
☐ 367 Randy Tomlin	.05	.02
☐ 368 Kenny Rogers	.05	.02
☐ 369 Brett Butler	.10	.05
☐ 370 Pat Kelly	.05	.02
☐ 371 Bip Roberts	.05	.02
☐ 372 Gregg Jefferies	.05	.02
☐ 373 Kevin Bass	.05	.02
☐ 374 Ron Karkovice	.05	.02
☐ 375 Paul Gibson	.05	.02
☐ 376 Bernard Gilkey	.10	.05
☐ 377 Dave Gallagher	.05	.02
☐ 378 Bill Wegman	.05	.02
☐ 379 Pat Borders	.05	.02
☐ 380 Ed Whitson	.05	.02
☐ 381 Gilberto Reyes	.05	.02
☐ 382 Russ Swan	.05	.02
☐ 383 Andy Van Slyke	.10	.05
☐ 384 Wes Chamberlain	.05	.02
☐ 385 Steve Chitren	.05	.02
☐ 386 Greg Olson	.05	.02
☐ 387 Brian McRae	.05	.02
☐ 388 Rich Rodriguez	.05	.02
☐ 389 Steve Decker	.05	.02
☐ 390 Chuck Knoblauch	.20	.09
☐ 391 Bobby Witt	.05	.02
☐ 392 Eddie Murray	.20	.09
☐ 393 Juan Gonzalez	.60	.25
☐ 394 Scott Ruskin	.05	.02
☐ 395 Jay Howell	.05	.02
☐ 396 Checklist 317-396	.05	.02
☐ 397 Royce Clayton RR	.10	.05
☐ 398 John Jaha RR	.20	.09
☐ 399 Dan Wilson RR	.10	.05
☐ 400 Archie Corbin RR	.05	.02
☐ 401 Barry Manuel RR	.05	.02
☐ 402 Kim Batiste RR	.05	.02
☐ 403 Pat Mahomes RR	.05	.02
☐ 404 Dave Fleming RR	.05	.02
☐ 405 Jeff Juden RR	.05	.02
☐ 406 Jim Thome RR	.60	.25
☐ 407 Sam Militello RR	.05	.02
☐ 408 Jeff Nelson RR	.05	.02
☐ 409 Anthony Young RR	.05	.02
☐ 410 Tino Martinez RR	.20	.09
☐ 411 Jeff Mutis RR	.05	.02
☐ 412 Rey Sanchez RR	.05	.02
☐ 413 Chris Gardner RR	.05	.02
☐ 414 John Vander Wal RR	.05	.02
☐ 415 Reggie Sanders RR	.05	.02
☐ 416 Brian Williams RR	.05	.02
☐ 417 Mo Sanford RR	.05	.02
☐ 418 David Weathers RR	.10	.05
☐ 419 Hector Fajardo RR	.05	.02
☐ 420 Steve Foster RR	.05	.02
☐ 421 Lance Dickson RR	.05	.02
☐ 422 Andre Dawson AS	.05	.02
☐ 423 Ozzie Smith AS	.20	.09
☐ 424 Chris Sabo AS	.05	.02
☐ 425 Tony Gwynn AS	.20	.09
☐ 426 Tom Glavine AS	.20	.09
☐ 427 Bobby Bonilla AS	.10	.05
☐ 428 Will Clark AS	.05	.02
☐ 429 Ryne Sandberg AS	.20	.09
☐ 430 Benito Santiago AS	.05	.02
☐ 431 Ivan Calderon AS	.05	.02
☐ 432 Ozzie Smith	.25	.11
☐ 433 Tim Leary	.05	.02
☐ 434 Bret Saberhagen HL	.05	.02
☐ 435 Mel Rojas	.10	.05
☐ 436 Ben McDonald	.05	.02
☐ 437 Tim Crews	.05	.02
☐ 438 Rex Hudler	.05	.02
☐ 439 Chico Walker	.05	.02
☐ 440 Kurt Stillwell	.05	.02
☐ 441 Tony Gwynn	.50	.23
☐ 442 John Smoltz	.20	.09
☐ 443 Lloyd Moseby	.05	.02
☐ 444 Mike Schooler	.05	.02
☐ 445 Joe Grahe	.05	.02
☐ 446 Dwight Gooden	.10	.05
☐ 447 Oil Can Boyd	.05	.02
☐ 448 John Marzano	.05	.02
☐ 449 Bret Barberie	.05	.02
☐ 450 Mike Maddux	.05	.02
☐ 451 Jeff Reed	.05	.02
☐ 452 Dale Sveum	.05	.02
☐ 453 Jose Uribe	.05	.02
☐ 454 Bob Scanlan	.05	.02
☐ 455 Kevin Appier	.10	.05
☐ 456 Jeff Huson	.05	.02
☐ 457 Ken Patterson	.05	.02
☐ 458 Ricky Jordan	.05	.02
☐ 459 Tom Candiotti	.05	.02
☐ 460 Lee Stevens	.05	.02
☐ 461 Rod Beck	.20	.09
☐ 462 Dave Valle	.05	.02
☐ 463 Scott Erickson	.10	.05
☐ 464 Chris Jones	.05	.02
☐ 465 Mark Carreon	.05	.02
☐ 466 Rob Ducey	.05	.02
☐ 467 Jim Corsi	.05	.02
☐ 468 Jeff King	.10	.05
☐ 469 Curt Young	.05	.02
☐ 470 Bo Jackson	.10	.05
☐ 471 Chris Bosio	.05	.02
☐ 472 Jamie Quirk	.05	.02
☐ 473 Jesse Orosco	.05	.02
☐ 474 Alvaro Espinoza	.05	.02
☐ 475 Joe Orsulak	.05	.02
☐ 476 Checklist 397-477	.05	.02
☐ 477 Gerald Young	.05	.02
☐ 478 Wally Backman	.05	.02
☐ 479 Juan Bell	.05	.02
☐ 480 Mike Scioscia	.05	.02
☐ 481 Omar Olivares	.05	.02
☐ 482 Francisco Cabrera	.05	.02
☐ 483 Greg Swindell UER	.05	.02
(Shown on Indians, but listed on Reds)		
☐ 484 Terry Leach	.05	.02
☐ 485 Tommy Gregg	.05	.02
☐ 486 Scott Aldred	.05	.02
☐ 487 Greg Briley	.05	.02
☐ 488 Phil Plantier	.05	.02
☐ 489 Curtis Wilkerson	.05	.02
☐ 490 Tom Brunansky	.05	.02
☐ 491 Mike Fetters	.05	.02
☐ 492 Frank Castillo	.05	.02
☐ 493 Joe Boever	.05	.02
☐ 494 Kirt Manwaring	.05	.02
☐ 495 Wilson Alvarez HL	.05	.02
☐ 496 Gene Larkin	.05	.02
☐ 497 Gary DiSarcina	.05	.02
☐ 498 Frank Viola	.05	.02
☐ 499 Manuel Lee	.05	.02
☐ 500 Albert Belle	.25	.11
☐ 501 Stan Belinda	.05	.02
☐ 502 Dwight Evans	.10	.05
☐ 503 Eric Davis	.10	.05
☐ 504 Darren Holmes	.05	.02
☐ 505 Mike Bordick	.05	.02
☐ 506 Dave Hansen	.05	.02
☐ 507 Lee Guetterman	.05	.02
☐ 508 Keith Mitchell	.05	.02
☐ 509 Melido Perez	.05	.02
☐ 510 Dickie Thon	.05	.02
☐ 511 Mark Williamson	.05	.02
☐ 512 Mark Salas	.05	.02
☐ 513 Milt Thompson	.05	.02
☐ 514 Mo Vaughn	.30	.14
☐ 515 Jim Deshaies	.05	.02
☐ 516 Rich Garces	.05	.02
☐ 517 Lonnie Smith	.05	.02
☐ 518 Spike Owen	.05	.0
☐ 519 Tracy Jones	.05	.0
☐ 520 Greg Maddux	.60	.2
☐ 521 Carlos Martinez	.05	.0
☐ 522 Neal Heaton	.05	.0
☐ 523 Mike Greenwell	.05	.0
☐ 524 Andy Benes	.05	.0
☐ 525 Jeff Schaefer UER	.05	.0
(Photo actually Tino Martinez)		
☐ 526 Mike Sharperson	.05	.0
☐ 527 Wade Taylor	.05	.0
☐ 528 Jerome Walton	.05	.0
☐ 529 Storm Davis	.05	.0
☐ 530 Jose Hernandez	.05	.0
☐ 531 Mark Langston	.05	.0
☐ 532 Rob Deer	.05	.0
☐ 533 Geronimo Pena	.05	.0
☐ 534 Juan Guzman	.05	.0
☐ 535 Pete Schourek	.05	.0
☐ 536 Todd Benzinger	.05	.0
☐ 537 Billy Hatcher	.05	.0
☐ 538 Tom Foley	.05	.0
☐ 539 Dave Cochrane	.05	.0
☐ 540 Mariano Duncan	.05	.0
☐ 541 Edwin Nunez	.05	.0
☐ 542 Rance Mulliniks	.05	.0
☐ 543 Carlton Fisk	.20	.0
☐ 544 Luis Aquino	.05	.0
☐ 545 Ricky Bones	.05	.0
☐ 546 Craig Grebeck	.05	.0
☐ 547 Charlie Hayes	.05	.0
☐ 548 Jose Canseco	.05	.0
☐ 549 Andujar Cedeno	.05	.0
☐ 550 Geno Petralli	.05	.0
☐ 551 Javier Ortiz	.05	.0
☐ 552 Rudy Seanez	.05	.0
☐ 553 Rich Gedman	.05	.0
☐ 554 Eric Plunk	.05	.0
☐ 555 Nolan Ryan HL	.25	.1
(With Rich Gossage)		
☐ 556 Checklist 478-555	.05	.0
☐ 557 Greg Colbrunn	.05	.0
☐ 558 Chito Martinez	.05	.0
☐ 559 Darryl Strawberry	.10	.0
☐ 560 Luis Alicea	.05	.0
☐ 561 Dwight Smith	.05	.0
☐ 562 Terry Shumpert	.05	.0
☐ 563 Jim Vatcher	.05	.0
☐ 564 Deion Sanders	.20	.0
☐ 565 Walt Terrell	.05	.0
☐ 566 Dave Burba	.05	.0
☐ 567 Dave Howard	.05	.0
☐ 568 Todd Hundley	.05	.0
☐ 569 Jack Daugherty	.05	.0
☐ 570 Scott Cooper	.05	.0
☐ 571 Bill Sampen	.05	.0
☐ 572 Jose Melendez	.05	.0
☐ 573 Freddie Benavides	.05	.0
☐ 574 Jim Gantner	.05	.0
☐ 575 Trevor Wilson	.05	.0
☐ 576 Ryne Sandberg	.25	.1
☐ 577 Kevin Seitzer	.05	.0
☐ 578 Gerald Alexander	.05	.0
☐ 579 Mike Huff	.05	.0
☐ 580 Von Hayes	.05	.0
☐ 581 Derek Bell	.10	.0
☐ 582 Mike Stanley	.05	.0
☐ 583 Kevin Mitchell	.10	.0
☐ 584 Mike Jackson	.05	.0
☐ 585 Dan Gladden	.05	.0
☐ 586 Ted Power UER	.05	.0
(Wrong year given for signing with Reds)		
☐ 587 Jeff Innis	.05	.0
☐ 588 Bob MacDonald	.05	.0
☐ 589 Jose Tolentino	.05	.0
☐ 590 Bob Patterson	.05	.0
☐ 591 Scott Brosius	.05	.0
☐ 592 Frank Thomas	1.00	.4
☐ 593 Darryl Hamilton	.05	.0
☐ 594 Kirk Dressendorfer	.05	.0
☐ 595 Jeff Shaw	.05	.0
☐ 596 Don Mattingly	.30	.1
☐ 597 Glenn Davis	.05	.0
☐ 598 Andy Mota	.05	.0
☐ 599 Jason Grimsley	.05	.0
☐ 600 Jimmy Poole	.05	.0
☐ 601 Jim Gott	.05	.0
☐ 602 Stan Royer	.05	.0
☐ 603 Marvin Freeman	.05	.0
☐ 604 Denis Boucher	.05	.0
☐ 605 Denny Neagle	.20	.0
☐ 606 Mark Lemke	.05	.0
☐ 607 Jerry Don Gleaton	.05	.0
☐ 608 Brent Knackert	.05	.0
☐ 609 Carlos Quintana	.05	.0

Card	MINT	NRMT
☐ 610 Bobby Bonilla	.10	.05
☐ 611 Joe Hesketh	.05	.02
☐ 612 Daryl Boston	.05	.02
☐ 613 Shawon Dunston	.05	.02
☐ 614 Danny Cox	.05	.02
☐ 615 Darren Lewis	.05	.02
☐ 616 Braves No-Hitter UER Kent Mercker (Misspelled Merker on card front) Alejandro Pena Mark Wohlers	.05	.02
☐ 617 Kirby Puckett	.40	.18
☐ 618 Franklin Stubbs	.05	.02
☐ 619 Chris Donnels	.05	.02
☐ 620 David Wells UER (Career Highlights in black not red)	.05	.02
☐ 621 Mike Aldrete	.05	.02
☐ 622 Bob Kipper	.05	.02
☐ 623 Anthony Telford	.05	.02
☐ 624 Randy Myers	.10	.05
☐ 625 Willie Randolph	.10	.05
☐ 626 Joe Slusarski	.05	.02
☐ 627 John Wetteland	.10	.05
☐ 628 Greg Cadaret	.05	.02
☐ 629 Tom Glavine	.05	.02
☐ 630 Wilson Alvarez	.10	.05
☐ 631 Wally Ritchie	.05	.02
☐ 632 Mike Mussina	.30	.14
☐ 633 Mark Leiter	.05	.02
☐ 634 Gerald Perry	.05	.02
☐ 635 Matt Young	.05	.02
☐ 636 Checklist 556-635	.05	.02
☐ 637 Scott Hemond	.05	.02
☐ 638 David West	.05	.02
☐ 639 Jim Clancy	.05	.02
☐ 640 Doug Piatt UER (Not born in 1955 as on card; incorrect info on How Acquired)	.05	.02
☐ 641 Omar Vizquel	.10	.05
☐ 642 Rick Sutcliffe	.05	.02
☐ 643 Glenallen Hill	.05	.02
☐ 644 Gary Varsho	.05	.02
☐ 645 Tony Fossas	.05	.02
☐ 646 Jack Howell	.05	.02
☐ 647 Jim Campanis	.05	.02
☐ 648 Chris Gwynn	.05	.02
☐ 649 Jim Leyritz	.05	.02
☐ 650 Chuck McElroy	.05	.02
☐ 651 Sean Berry	.05	.02
☐ 652 Donald Harris	.05	.02
☐ 653 Don Slaught	.05	.02
☐ 654 Rusty Meacham	.05	.02
☐ 655 Scott Terry	.05	.02
☐ 656 Ramon Martinez	.10	.05
☐ 657 Keith Miller	.05	.02
☐ 658 Ramon Garcia	.05	.02
☐ 659 Milt Hill	.05	.02
☐ 660 Steve Frey	.05	.02
☐ 661 Bob McClure	.05	.02
☐ 662 Ced Landrum	.05	.02
☐ 663 Doug Henry	.05	.02
☐ 664 Candy Maldonado	.05	.02
☐ 665 Carl Willis	.05	.02
☐ 666 Jeff Montgomery	.10	.05
☐ 667 Craig Shipley	.05	.02
☐ 668 Warren Newson	.05	.02
☐ 669 Mickey Morandini	.05	.02
☐ 670 Brook Jacoby	.05	.02
☐ 671 Ryan Bowen	.05	.02
☐ 672 Bill Krueger	.05	.02
☐ 673 Rob Mallicoat	.05	.02
☐ 674 Doug Jones	.05	.02
☐ 675 Scott Livingstone	.05	.02
☐ 676 Danny Tartabull	.05	.02
☐ 677 Joe Carter HL	.05	.02
☐ 678 Cecil Espy	.05	.02
☐ 679 Randy Velarde	.05	.02
☐ 680 Bruce Ruffin	.05	.02
☐ 681 Ted Wood	.05	.02
☐ 682 Dan Plesac	.05	.02
☐ 683 Eric Bullock	.05	.02
☐ 684 Junior Ortiz	.05	.02
☐ 685 Dave Hollins	.05	.02
☐ 686 Dennis Martinez	.10	.05
☐ 687 Larry Andersen	.05	.02
☐ 688 Doug Simons	.05	.02
☐ 689 Tim Spehr	.05	.02
☐ 690 Calvin Jones	.05	.02
☐ 691 Mark Guthrie	.05	.02
☐ 692 Alfredo Griffin	.05	.02
☐ 693 Joe Carter	.05	.02
☐ 694 Terry Mathews	.05	.02
☐ 695 Pascual Perez	.05	.02
☐ 696 Gene Nelson	.05	.02
☐ 697 Gerald Williams	.05	.02
☐ 698 Chris Cron	.05	.02
☐ 699 Steve Buechele	.05	.02
☐ 700 Paul McClellan	.05	.02
☐ 701 Jim Lindeman	.05	.02
☐ 702 Francisco Oliveras	.05	.02
☐ 703 Rob Maurer	.05	.02
☐ 704 Pat Hentgen	.05	.02
☐ 705 Jaime Navarro	.05	.02
☐ 706 Mike Magnante	.05	.02
☐ 707 Nolan Ryan	.75	.35
☐ 708 Bobby Thigpen	.05	.02
☐ 709 John Cerutti	.05	.02
☐ 710 Steve Wilson	.05	.02
☐ 711 Hensley Meulens	.05	.02
☐ 712 Rheal Cormier	.05	.02
☐ 713 Scott Bradley	.05	.02
☐ 714 Mitch Webster	.05	.02
☐ 715 Roger Mason	.05	.02
☐ 716 Checklist 636-716	.05	.02
☐ 717 Jeff Fassero	.05	.02
☐ 718 Cal Eldred	.05	.02
☐ 719 Sid Fernandez	.05	.02
☐ 720 Bob Zupcic	.05	.02
☐ 721 Jose Offerman	.05	.02
☐ 722 Cliff Brantley	.05	.02
☐ 723 Ron Darling	.05	.02
☐ 724 Dave Stieb	.05	.02
☐ 725 Hector Villanueva	.05	.02
☐ 726 Mike Hartley	.05	.02
☐ 727 Arthur Rhodes	.05	.02
☐ 728 Randy Bush	.05	.02
☐ 729 Steve Sax	.05	.02
☐ 730 Dave Otto	.05	.02
☐ 731 John Wehner	.05	.02
☐ 732 Dave Martinez	.05	.02
☐ 733 Ruben Amaro	.05	.02
☐ 734 Billy Ripken	.05	.02
☐ 735 Steve Farr	.05	.02
☐ 736 Shawn Abner	.05	.02
☐ 737 Gil Heredia	.05	.02
☐ 738 Ron Jones	.05	.02
☐ 739 Tony Castillo	.05	.02
☐ 740 Sammy Sosa	.20	.09
☐ 741 Julio Franco	.10	.05
☐ 742 Tim Naehring	.10	.05
☐ 743 Steve Wapnick	.05	.02
☐ 744 Craig Wilson	.05	.02
☐ 745 Darrin Chapin	.05	.02
☐ 746 Chris George	.05	.02
☐ 747 Mike Simms	.05	.02
☐ 748 Rosario Rodriguez	.05	.02
☐ 749 Skeeter Barnes	.05	.02
☐ 750 Roger McDowell	.05	.02
☐ 751 Dann Howitt	.05	.02
☐ 752 Paul Sorrento	.05	.02
☐ 753 Braulio Castillo	.05	.02
☐ 754 Yorkis Perez	.05	.02
☐ 755 Willie Fraser	.05	.02
☐ 756 Jeremy Hernandez	.05	.02
☐ 757 Curt Schilling	.05	.02
☐ 758 Steve Lyons	.05	.02
☐ 759 Dave Anderson	.05	.02
☐ 760 Willie Banks	.05	.02
☐ 761 Mark Leonard	.05	.02
☐ 762 Jack Armstrong (Listed on Indians, but shown on Reds)	.05	.02
☐ 763 Scott Servais	.05	.02
☐ 764 Ray Stephens	.05	.02
☐ 765 Junior Noboa	.05	.02
☐ 766 Jim Olander	.05	.02
☐ 767 Joe Magrane	.05	.02
☐ 768 Lance Blankenship	.05	.02
☐ 769 Mike Humphreys	.05	.02
☐ 770 Jarvis Brown	.05	.02
☐ 771 Damon Berryhill	.05	.02
☐ 772 Alejandro Pena	.05	.02
☐ 773 Jose Mesa	.10	.05
☐ 774 Gary Cooper	.05	.02
☐ 775 Carney Lansford	.10	.05
☐ 776 Mike Bielecki (Shown on Cubs, but listed on Braves)	.05	.02
☐ 777 Charlie O'Brien	.05	.02
☐ 778 Carlos Hernandez	.05	.02
☐ 779 Howard Farmer	.05	.02
☐ 780 Mike Stanton	.05	.02
☐ 781 Reggie Harris	.05	.02
☐ 782 Xavier Hernandez	.05	.02
☐ 783 Bryan Hickerson	.05	.02
☐ 784 Checklist 717-784 and BC1-BC8	.05	.02

1992 Donruss Bonus Cards

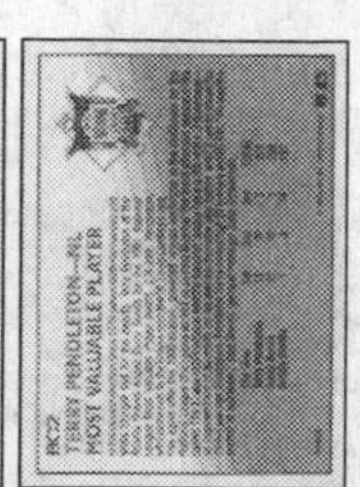

The 1992 Donruss Bonus Cards set contains eight standard-size. The cards are numbered on the back and checklisted below accordingly. The cards were randomly inserted in foil packs of 1992 Donruss baseball cards.

	MINT	NRMT
COMPLETE SET (8)	2.00	.90
COMMON CARD (BC1-BC8)	.10	.05
☐ BC1 Cal Ripken MVP	.75	.35
☐ BC2 Terry Pendleton MVP	.10	.05
☐ BC3 Roger Clemens CY	.50	.23
☐ BC4 Tom Glavine CY	.20	.09
☐ BC5 Chuck Knoblauch ROY	.30	.14
☐ BC6 Jeff Bagwell ROY	.60	.25
☐ BC7 Colorado Rockies	.20	.09
☐ BC8 Florida Marlins	.20	.09

1992 Donruss Diamond Kings

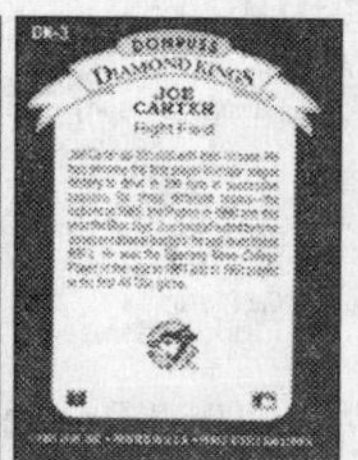

These standard-size cards were randomly inserted in 1992 Donruss I foil packs (cards 1-13 and the checklist only) and in 1992 Donruss II foil packs (cards 14-26). The fronts feature player portraits by noted sports artist Dick Perez. The words "Donruss Diamond Kings" are superimposed at the card top in a gold-trimmed blue and black banner, with the player's name in a similarly designed black stripe at the card bottom. A very limited amount of 5" by 7" cards were produced. These issues were never formally released but these cards were intended to be premiums in retail products. We are not valuing them currently since trading in these cards is very thin.

	MINT	NRMT
COMPLETE SET (27)	20.00	9.00
COMPLETE SERIES 1 (14)	16.00	7.25
COMPLETE SERIES 2 (13)	4.00	1.80
COMMON CARD (DK1-DK27)	.50	.23
☐ DK1 Paul Molitor	1.25	.55
☐ DK2 Will Clark	1.00	.45
☐ DK3 Joe Carter	1.00	.45
☐ DK4 Julio Franco	.75	.35
☐ DK5 Cal Ripken	8.00	3.60
☐ DK6 Dave Justice	1.25	.55
☐ DK7 George Bell	.50	.23
☐ DK8 Frank Thomas	8.00	3.60
☐ DK9 Wade Boggs	1.25	.55
☐ DK10 Scott Sanderson	.50	.23
☐ DK11 Jeff Bagwell	5.00	2.20
☐ DK12 John Kruk	.75	.35
☐ DK13 Felix Jose	.50	.23
☐ DK14 Harold Baines	.75	.35
☐ DK15 Dwight Gooden	.75	.35
☐ DK16 Brian McRae	.50	.23
☐ DK17 Jay Bell	.75	.35
☐ DK18 Brett Butler	1.00	.45
☐ DK19 Hal Morris	.50	.23
☐ DK20 Mark Langston	.50	.23
☐ DK21 Scott Erickson	.75	.35
☐ DK22 Randy Johnson	1.25	.55
☐ DK23 Greg Swindell	.50	.23
☐ DK24 Dennis Martinez	.75	.35
☐ DK25 Tony Phillips	.50	.23
☐ DK26 Fred McGriff	1.00	.45
☐ DK27 Checklist 1-26 DP (Dick Perez)	.50	.23

1992 Donruss Elite

These cards were random inserts in 1992 Donruss first and second series foil packs. Like the previous year, the cards were indidvidually numbered of 10,000. Card fronts feature dramatic prismatic borders encasing a full color action or posed shot of the player. The numbering of the set is essentially a continuation of the series started the year before. Only 5,000 Ripken Signature Series cards were printed and only 7,500 Henderson Legends cards were printed.

	MINT	NRMT
COMPLETE SET (12)	800.00	350.00
COMMON CARD (9-18)	15.00	6.75
☐ 9 Wade Boggs	25.00	11.00
☐ 10 Joe Carter	25.00	11.00
☐ 11 Will Clark	25.00	11.00
☐ 12 Dwight Gooden	20.00	9.00
☐ 13 Ken Griffey Jr.	150.00	70.00
☐ 14 Tony Gwynn	60.00	27.00
☐ 15 Howard Johnson	15.00	6.75
☐ 16 Terry Pendleton	15.00	6.75
☐ 17 Kirby Puckett	50.00	22.00
☐ 18 Frank Thomas	120.00	55.00
☐ L2 Rickey Henderson (Legend Series)	30.00	13.50
☐ S2 Cal Ripken (Signature Series)	400.00	180.00

1992 Donruss Update

Four cards from this 22-card standard-size set were included in each retail factory set. Card design is identical to regular issue 1992 Donruss cards except for the U-prefixed numbering on back. Card numbers U1-U6 are Rated Rookie cards, while card numbers U7-U9 are Highlights cards. A tough early Kenny Lofton card, his first as a member of the Cleveland Indians, highlights this set.

	MINT	NRMT
COMPLETE SET (22)	60.00	27.00
COMMON CARD (U1-U22)	1.00	.45
☐ U1 Pat Listach RR	1.00	.45
☐ U2 Andy Stankiewicz RR	1.00	.45
☐ U3 Brian Jordan RR	6.00	2.70
☐ U4 Dan Walters RR	1.00	.45
☐ U5 Chad Curtis RR	2.00	.90
☐ U6 Kenny Lofton RR	30.00	13.50
☐ U7 Mark McGwire HL	12.00	5.50
☐ U8 Eddie Murray HL	8.00	3.60
☐ U9 Jeff Reardon HL	2.00	.90
☐ U10 Frank Viola	1.00	.45
☐ U11 Gary Sheffield	6.00	2.70
☐ U12 George Bell	1.00	.45
☐ U13 Rick Sutcliffe	1.00	.45
☐ U14 Wally Joyner	2.00	.90
☐ U15 Kevin Seitzer	1.00	.45
☐ U16 Bill Krueger	1.00	.45
☐ U17 Danny Tartabull	1.00	.45
☐ U18 Dave Winfield	6.00	2.70
☐ U19 Gary Carter	6.00	2.70
☐ U20 Bobby Bonilla	2.00	.90
☐ U21 Cory Snyder	1.00	.45
☐ U22 Bill Swift	1.00	.45

1992 Donruss Rookies

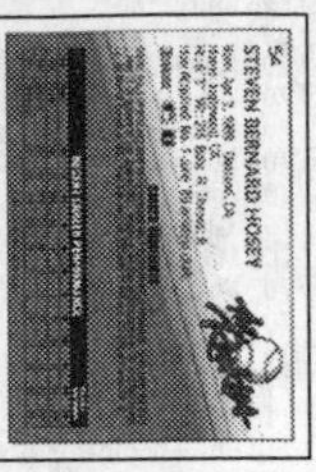

After six years of issuing "The Rookies" as a 56-card boxed set, Donruss expanded it to a 132-card standard-size set and distributed the cards exclusively in hobby and retail foil packs. The card design is the same as the 1992 Donruss regular issue except that the two-tone blue color bars have been replaced by green, as in the previous six Donruss Rookies sets. The cards are arranged in alphabetical order and numbered on the back. Rookie Cards in this set include Manny Ramirez, Shane Reynolds and Eric Young.

	MINT	NRMT
COMPLETE SET (132)	5.00	2.20
COMMON CARD (1-132)	.05	.02
☐ 1 Kyle Abbott	.05	.02
☐ 2 Troy Afenir	.05	.02
☐ 3 Rich Amaral	.05	.02
☐ 4 Ruben Amaro	.05	.02
☐ 5 Billy Ashley	.05	.02
☐ 6 Pedro Astacio	.10	.05
☐ 7 Jim Austin	.05	.02
☐ 8 Robert Ayrault	.05	.02
☐ 9 Kevin Baez	.05	.02
☐ 10 Esteban Beltre	.05	.02
☐ 11 Brian Bohanon	.05	.02
☐ 12 Kent Bottenfield	.05	.02
☐ 13 Jeff Branson	.05	.02
☐ 14 Brad Brink	.05	.02
☐ 15 John Briscoe	.05	.02
☐ 16 Doug Brocail	.05	.02
☐ 17 Rico Brogna	.10	.05
☐ 18 J.T. Bruett	.05	.02
☐ 19 Jacob Brumfield	.05	.02
☐ 20 Jim Bullinger	.05	.02
☐ 21 Kevin Campbell	.05	.02
☐ 22 Pedro Castellano	.05	.02
☐ 23 Mike Christopher	.05	.02
☐ 24 Archi Cianfrocco	.05	.02
☐ 25 Mark Clark	.05	.02
☐ 26 Craig Colbert	.05	.02
☐ 27 Victor Cole	.05	.02
☐ 28 Steve Cooke	.05	.02
☐ 29 Tim Costo	.05	.02
☐ 30 Chad Curtis	.10	.05
☐ 31 Doug Davis	.05	.02
☐ 32 Gary DiSarcina	.05	.02
☐ 33 John Doherty	.05	.02
☐ 34 Mike Draper	.05	.02
☐ 35 Monty Fariss	.05	.02
☐ 36 Bien Figueroa	.05	.02
☐ 37 John Flaherty	.05	.02
☐ 38 Tim Fortugno	.05	.02
☐ 39 Eric Fox	.05	.02
☐ 40 Jeff Frye	.05	.02
☐ 41 Ramon Garcia	.05	.02
☐ 42 Brent Gates	.10	.05
☐ 43 Tom Goodwin	.10	.05
☐ 44 Buddy Groom	.05	.02
☐ 45 Jeff Grotewold	.05	.02
☐ 46 Juan Guerrero	.05	.02
☐ 47 Johnny Guzman	.05	.02
☐ 48 Shawn Hare	.05	.02
☐ 49 Ryan Hawblitzel	.05	.02
☐ 50 Bert Hefferman	.05	.02
☐ 51 Butch Henry	.05	.02
☐ 52 Cesar Hernandez	.05	.02
☐ 53 Vince Horsman	.05	.02
☐ 54 Steve Hosey	.05	.02
☐ 55 Pat Howell	.05	.02
☐ 56 Peter Hoy	.05	.02
☐ 57 Jonathan Hurst	.05	.02
☐ 58 Mark Hutton	.05	.02
☐ 59 Shawn Jeter	.05	.02
☐ 60 Joel Johnston	.05	.02
☐ 61 Jeff Kent	.20	.09
☐ 62 Kurt Knudsen	.05	.02
☐ 63 Kevin Koslofski	.05	.02
☐ 64 Danny Leon	.05	.02
☐ 65 Jesse Levis	.05	.02
☐ 66 Tom Marsh	.05	.02
☐ 67 Ed Martel	.05	.02
☐ 68 Al Martin	.20	.09
☐ 69 Pedro Martinez	.40	.18
☐ 70 Derrick May	.05	.02
☐ 71 Matt Maysey	.05	.02
☐ 72 Russ McGinnis	.05	.02
☐ 73 Tim McIntosh	.05	.02
☐ 74 Jim McNamara	.05	.02
☐ 75 Jeff McNeely	.05	.02
☐ 76 Rusty Meacham	.05	.02
☐ 77 Tony Menendez	.05	.02
☐ 78 Henry Mercedes	.05	.02
☐ 79 Paul Miller	.05	.02
☐ 80 Joe Millette	.05	.02
☐ 81 Blas Minor	.05	.02
☐ 82 Dennis Moeller	.05	.02
☐ 83 Raul Mondesi	.40	.18
☐ 84 Rob Natal	.05	.02
☐ 85 Troy Neel	.05	.02
☐ 86 David Nied	.05	.02
☐ 87 Jerry Nielson	.05	.02
☐ 88 Donovan Osborne	.05	.02
☐ 89 John Patterson	.05	.02
☐ 90 Roger Pavlik	.10	.05
☐ 91 Dan Peltier	.05	.02
☐ 92 Jim Pena	.05	.02
☐ 93 William Pennyfeather	.05	.02
☐ 94 Mike Perez	.05	.02
☐ 95 Hipolito Pichardo	.05	.02
☐ 96 Greg Pirkl	.05	.02
☐ 97 Harvey Pulliam	.05	.02
☐ 98 Manny Ramirez	1.25	.55
☐ 99 Pat Rapp	.05	.02
☐ 100 Jeff Reboulet	.05	.02
☐ 101 Darren Reed	.05	.02
☐ 102 Shane Reynolds	.30	.14
☐ 103 Bill Risley	.05	.02
☐ 104 Ben Rivera	.05	.02
☐ 105 Henry Rodriguez	.20	.09
☐ 106 Rico Rossy	.05	.02
☐ 107 Johnny Ruffin	.05	.02
☐ 108 Steve Scarsone	.05	.02
☐ 109 Tim Scott	.05	.02
☐ 110 Steve Shifflett	.05	.02
☐ 111 Dave Silvestri	.05	.02
☐ 112 Matt Stairs	.05	.02
☐ 113 William Suero	.05	.02
☐ 114 Jeff Tackett	.05	.02
☐ 115 Eddie Taubensee	.05	.02
☐ 116 Rick Trlicek	.05	.02
☐ 117 Scooter Tucker	.05	.02
☐ 118 Shane Turner	.05	.02
☐ 119 Julio Valera	.05	.02
☐ 120 Paul Wagner	.05	.02
☐ 121 Tim Wakefield	.20	.09
☐ 122 Mike Walker	.05	.02
☐ 123 Bruce Walton	.05	.02
☐ 124 Lenny Webster	.05	.02
☐ 125 Bob Wickman	.05	.02
☐ 126 Mike Williams	.05	.02
☐ 127 Kerry Woodson	.05	.02
☐ 128 Eric Young	.25	.11
☐ 129 Kevin Young	.05	.02
☐ 130 Pete Young	.05	.02
☐ 131 Checklist 1-66	.05	.02
☐ 132 Checklist 67-132	.05	.02

1992 Donruss Rookies Phenoms

This 20-card standard size set features a selection young prospects. The first twelve cards were randomly inserted into 1992 Donruss The Rookies 12-card foil packs. The last eight were inserted one per 1992 Donruss Rookies 30-card jumbo pack. Each glossy card front features a black border surrounding a full color photo and gold foil type.

	MINT	NRMT
COMPLETE SET (20)	35.00	16.00
COMPLETE FOIL SET (12)	25.00	11.00
COMMON FOIL (BC1-BC12)	.50	.23

)MPLETE JUMBO SET (8)	10.00	4.50
)MMON JUMBO (BC13-BC20)	.50	.23

] BC1 Moises Alou	1.50	.70
] BC2 Bret Boone	.50	.23
] BC3 Jeff Conine	1.00	.45
] BC4 Dave Fleming	.50	.23
] BC5 Tyler Green	.50	.23
] BC6 Eric Karros	1.00	.45
] BC7 Pat Listach	.50	.23
] BC8 Kenny Lofton	8.00	3.60
] BC9 Mike Piazza	20.00	9.00
] BC10 Tim Salmon	5.00	2.20
] BC11 Andy Stankiewicz	.50	.23
] BC12 Dan Walters	.50	.23
] BC13 Ramon Caraballo	.50	.23
] BC14 Brian Jordan	1.50	.70
] BC15 Ryan Klesko	3.00	1.35
] BC16 Sam Militello	.50	.23
] BC17 Frank Seminara	.50	.23
] BC18 Salomon Torres	.50	.23
] BC19 John Valentin	1.50	.70
] BC20 Wil Cordero	.50	.23

1992 Donruss Coke Ryan

ıis 26-card standard-size set was produced by Donruss commemorate each year of Ryan's professional aseball career. Both sides of the card bear the Coca-Cola ›go, and four-card cello packs with one Ryan card and ree regular issue 1992 Donruss cards were inserted in 2-can packs of Coca-Cola classic, caffeine-free Coca-ola classic, diet Coke, caffeine-free diet Coke, Sprite, and et Sprite. An offer on the back panel of specially marked oca-Cola multi-packs (and the labels of two-liter bottles) ıade available boxed factory sets through a mail-in offer ›r 8.95 and UPC symbols from multi-pack wraps of oca-Cola products. The promotion ran from April to June ıd covered nearly 90 percent of the country. The andard-size (2 1/2" by 3 1/2") cards feature on the fronts olor player photos enclosed by a gold border. Blue ripes edge the pictures above and below, and in the ottom stripe appears the team name and year that the ard captures. The backs are aqua and white and present eason summary and statistics. The final card in the set ımmarizes his career and presents career statistics. The ards are numbered on the back in chronolgical order; ach year Nolan is pictured with his then-current team, ew York Mets (NYM), California Angels (CA), Houston stros (HA), Texas Rangers (TR).

	MINT	NRMT
OMPLETE SET (26)	10.00	4.50
OMMON CARD (1-26)	.50	.23

] 1 Nolan Ryan 1966 NYM	.50	.23
] 2 Nolan Ryan 1968 NYM	.50	.23
] 3 Nolan Ryan 1969 NYM	.50	.23
] 4 Nolan Ryan 1970 NYM	.50	.23
] 5 Nolan Ryan 1971 NYM	.50	.23
] 6 Nolan Ryan 1972 CA	.50	.23
] 7 Nolan Ryan 1973 CA	.50	.23
] 8 Nolan Ryan 1974 CA	.50	.23
] 9 Nolan Ryan 1975 CA	.50	.23
] 10 Nolan Ryan 1976 CA	.50	.23
] 11 Nolan Ryan 1977 CA	.50	.23
] 12 Nolan Ryan 1978 CA	.50	.23
] 13 Nolan Ryan 1979 CA	.50	.23
] 14 Nolan Ryan 1980 HA	.50	.23
☐ 15 Nolan Ryan 1981 HA	.50	.23
☐ 16 Nolan Ryan 1982 HA	.50	.23
☐ 17 Nolan Ryan 1983 HA	.50	.23
☐ 18 Nolan Ryan 1984 HA	.50	.23
☐ 19 Nolan Ryan 1985 HA	.50	.23
☐ 20 Nolan Ryan 1986 HA	.50	.23
☐ 21 Nolan Ryan 1987 HA	.50	.23
☐ 22 Nolan Ryan 1988 HA	.50	.23
☐ 23 Nolan Ryan 1989 TR	.50	.23
☐ 24 Nolan Ryan 1990 TR	.50	.23
☐ 25 Nolan Ryan 1991 TR	.50	.23
☐ 26 Nolan Ryan 1992 TR	.50	.23

1992 Donruss Cracker Jack I

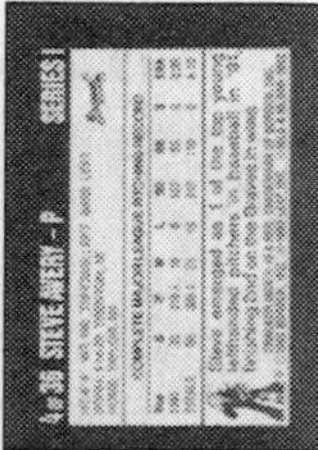

This 36-card set is the first of two series produced by Donruss for Cracker Jack, and the micro cards were protected by a paper sleeve and inserted into specially marked boxes of Cracker Jack. A side panel listed all 36 players in series I. The micro cards measure approximately 1 1/4" by 1 3/4". The front design is the same as the Donruss regular issue cards, only different color player photos are displayed. The backs, however, have a completely different design than the regular issue Donruss cards; they are horizontally oriented and present biography, major league pitching (or batting) record, and brief career summary inside navy blue borders. The cards are numbered on the back. On the paper sleeve was a mail-in offer for a mini card album with six top loading plastic pages for 4.95 per album.

	MINT	NRMT
COMPLETE SET (36)	12.00	5.50
COMMON CARD (1-36)	.05	.02

☐ 1 Dennis Eckersley	.20	.09
☐ 2 Jeff Bagwell	1.50	.70
☐ 3 Jim Abbott	.10	.05
☐ 4 Steve Avery	.05	.02
☐ 5 Kelly Gruber	.05	.02
☐ 6 Ozzie Smith	1.25	.55
☐ 7 Lance Dickson	.05	.02
☐ 8 Robin Yount	.20	.09
☐ 9 Brett Butler	.10	.05
☐ 10 Sandy Alomar Jr.	.10	.05
☐ 11 Travis Fryman	.10	.05
☐ 12 Ken Griffey Jr.	2.50	1.10
☐ 13 Cal Ripken	2.00	.90
☐ 14 Will Clark	.20	.09
☐ 15 Nolan Ryan	2.50	1.10
☐ 16 Tony Gwynn	1.50	.70
☐ 17 Roger Clemens	1.00	.45
☐ 18 Wes Chamberlain	.05	.02
☐ 19 Barry Larkin	.20	.09
☐ 20 Brian McRae	.05	.02
☐ 21 Marquis Grissom	.10	.05
☐ 22 Cecil Fielder	.10	.05
☐ 23 Dwight Gooden	.10	.05
☐ 24 Chuck Knoblauch	.50	.23
☐ 25 Jose Canseco	.40	.18
☐ 26 Terry Pendleton	.10	.05
☐ 27 Ivan Rodriguez	1.00	.45
☐ 28 Ryne Sandberg	.75	.35
☐ 29 Kent Hrbek	.10	.05
☐ 30 Ramon Martinez	.10	.05
☐ 31 Todd Zeile	.05	.02
☐ 32 Hal Morris	.05	.02
☐ 33 Robin Ventura	.10	.05
☐ 34 Doug Drabek	.05	.02
☐ 35 Frank Thomas	2.50	1.10
☐ 36 Don Mattingly	1.25	.55

1992 Donruss Cracker Jack II

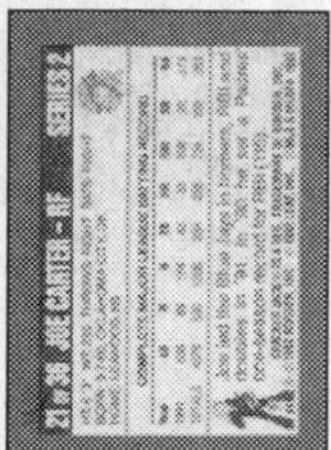

This 36-card set is the second of two series produced by Donruss for Cracker Jack. The mini cards were protected by a paper sleeve and inserted into specially marked boxes of Cracker Jacks. A side panel listed all 36 players in series II. The micro cards measure 1 1/4" by 1 3/4". The front design is the same as the Donruss regular issue cards, only different color player photos are displayed. The backs, however, have a completely different design than the regular issue Donruss cards; they are horizontally oriented and present biography, major league pitching (or batting) record, and brief career summary inside red borders. The cards are numbered on the back. On the paper sleeve was a mail-in offer for a mini card album with six top loading plastic pages for 4.95 per album.

	MINT	NRMT
COMPLETE SET (36)	7.50	3.40
COMMON CARD (1-36)	.10	.05

☐ 1 Craig Biggio	.50	.23
☐ 2 Tom Glavine	.20	.09
☐ 3 David Justice	.50	.23
☐ 4 Lee Smith	.20	.09
☐ 5 Mark Grace	.30	.14
☐ 6 George Bell	.10	.05
☐ 7 Darryl Strawberry	.20	.09
☐ 8 Eric Davis	.10	.05
☐ 9 Ivan Calderon	.10	.05
☐ 10 Royce Clayton	.10	.05
☐ 11 Matt Williams	.30	.14
☐ 12 Fred McGriff	.30	.14
☐ 13 Len Dykstra	.20	.09
☐ 14 Barry Bonds	.75	.35
☐ 15 Reggie Sanders	.20	.09
☐ 16 Chris Sabo	.10	.05
☐ 17 Howard Johnson	.10	.05
☐ 18 Bobby Bonilla	.20	.09
☐ 19 Rickey Henderson	.50	.23
☐ 20 Mark Langston	.10	.05
☐ 21 Joe Carter	.20	.09
☐ 22 Paul Molitor	.50	.23
☐ 23 Glenallen Hill	.10	.05
☐ 24 Edgar Martinez	.30	.14
☐ 25 Gregg Olson	.10	.05
☐ 26 Ruben Sierra	.10	.05
☐ 27 Julio Franco	.20	.09
☐ 28 Phil Plantier	.10	.05
☐ 29 Wade Boggs	.50	.23
☐ 30 George Brett	1.00	.45
☐ 31 Alan Trammell	.20	.09
☐ 32 Kirby Puckett	1.25	.55
☐ 33 Scott Erickson	.10	.05
☐ 34 Matt Nokes	.10	.05
☐ 35 Danny Tartabull	.20	.09
☐ 36 Jack McDowell	.10	.05

1992 Donruss McDonald's

This 33-card standard-size set was produced by Donruss for distribution by McDonald's Restaurants in the Toronto area. For 39 cents with the purchase of any sandwich or breakfast entree, the collector received a four-card pack featuring three cards from the MVP series and one card from the Blue Jays Gold series. A player from each MLB team is represented in the numbered 26-card MVP subset. Checklist cards were also randomly inserted throughout the foil packs. In addition, 1,000 packs included a randomly inserted prize card. By filling it out, answering the question and sending it to the address on the card, the winner received one of 1,000 numbered cards autographed by Roberto Alomar. The cards have the same design as the regular issue cards, with color action photos bordered in white and accented by blue stripes above and below the picture. One difference is an MVP logo with the McDonald's "Golden Arches" trademark on the front. The backs present a head shot, biography, recent major league performance statistics, career highlights and the card number ("X of 26"). Again, the McDonald's "Golden Arches" trademark appears on the back alongside the other logos. One card from the six-card gold subset (of Toronto Blue Jays) was included in each 1992 Donruss McDonald's MVP four-card foil pack. The gold card fronts feature full-bleed color player photos accented by goil foil stamping. The gold cards are listed below with a "G" prefix below for reference, although a "G" prefix does not appear anywhere on the cards. The player's name appears in a dark blue bar that overlays the bottom gold foil border stripe. In a horizontal format, the backs carry biography, contract status information, recent major league performance statistics and career highlights. As with the MVP series, the McDonald's "Golden Arches" trademark adorns both sides of the card.

	MINT	NRMT
COMPLETE SET (33)	15.00	6.75
COMMON CARD (1-26)	.15	.07
COMMON CARD (G1-G6)	.50	.23

	MINT	NRMT
☐ 1 Cal Ripken	2.00	.90
☐ 2 Frank Thomas	2.50	1.10
☐ 3 George Brett	.75	.35
☐ 4 Roberto Kelly	.15	.07
☐ 5 Nolan Ryan	2.00	.90
☐ 6 Ryne Sandberg	.75	.35
☐ 7 Darryl Strawberry	.25	.11
☐ 8 Len Dykstra	.25	.11
☐ 9 Fred McGriff	.50	.23
☐ 10 Roger Clemens	.60	.25
☐ 11 Sandy Alomar Jr.	.25	.11
☐ 12 Robin Yount	.50	.23
☐ 13 Jose Canseco	.50	.23
☐ 14 Jimmy Key	.25	.11
☐ 15 Barry Larkin	.50	.23
☐ 16 Dennis Martinez	.25	.11
☐ 17 Andy Van Slyke	.25	.11
☐ 18 Will Clark	.50	.23
☐ 19 Mark Langston	.25	.11
☐ 20 Cecil Fielder	.25	.11
☐ 21 Kirby Puckett	1.00	.45
☐ 22 Ken Griffey Jr.	2.50	1.10
☐ 23 David Justice	.50	.23
☐ 24 Jeff Bagwell	1.25	.55
☐ 25 Howard Johnson	.15	.07
☐ 26 Ozzie Smith	.75	.35
☐ G1 Roberto Alomar	2.50	1.10
☐ G2 Joe Carter	1.00	.45
☐ G3 Kelly Gruber	.50	.23
☐ G4 Jack Morris	.75	.35
☐ G5 Tom Henke	.50	.23
☐ G6 Devon White	.50	.23
☐ NNO Checklist Card SP	.25	.11

1993 Donruss Previews

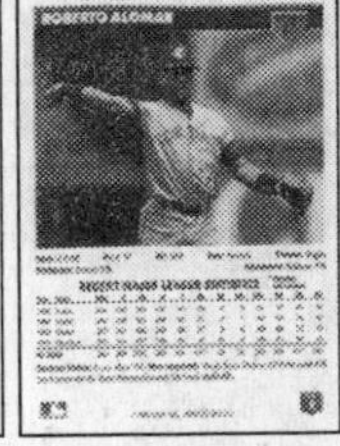

This 22-card standard-size set was issued by Donruss for hobby dealers to preview the 1993 Donruss regular issue series. The cards feature glossy color player photos with white borders on the fronts. The team logo appears in a diamond at the lower left corner, while the player's name appears in a bar that extends to the right. Both the diamond and bar are team-color coded. The top half of the back has a color close-up photo; the bottom half presents biography and recent major league statistics. In addition, one of these cards wer sent to each Donruss Club member. Also, George Brett has a card in this set but not in the 1993 regular Donruss set.

	MINT	NRMT
COMPLETE SET (22)	80.00	36.00
COMMON CARD (1-22)	1.50	.70

	MINT	NRMT
☐ 1 Tom Glavine	2.00	.90
☐ 2 Ryne Sandberg	6.00	2.70
☐ 3 Barry Larkin	3.00	1.35
☐ 4 Jeff Bagwell	10.00	4.50
☐ 5 Eric Karros	3.00	1.35
☐ 6 Larry Walker	5.00	2.20
☐ 7 Eddie Murray	5.00	2.20
☐ 8 Darren Daulton	2.00	.90
☐ 9 Andy Van Slyke	1.50	.70
☐ 10 Gary Sheffield	5.00	2.20
☐ 11 Will Clark	3.00	1.35
☐ 12 Cal Ripken	15.00	6.75
☐ 13 Roger Clemens	10.00	4.50
☐ 14 Frank Thomas	15.00	6.75
☐ 15 Cecil Fielder	2.00	.90
☐ 16 George Brett	10.00	4.50
☐ 17 Robin Yount	3.00	1.35
☐ 18 Don Mattingly	10.00	4.50
☐ 19 Dennis Eckersley	3.00	1.35
☐ 20 Ken Griffey Jr.	20.00	9.00
☐ 21 Jose Canseco	3.00	1.35
☐ 22 Roberto Alomar	5.00	2.20

1993 Donruss

The 792-card 1993 Donruss set was issued in two series, each with 396 standard-size cards. Cards were distributed in foil packs. The basic card fronts feature glossy color action photos with white borders. At the bottom of the picture, the team logo appears in a team color-coded diamond with the player's name in a color-coded bar extending to the right. A Rated Rookies (RR) subset , sprinkled throughout the set, spotlights 20 young prospects. There are no key Rookie Cards in this set.

	MINT	NRMT
COMPLETE SET (792)	30.00	13.50
COMPLETE SERIES 1 (396)	15.00	6.75
COMPLETE SERIES 2 (396)	15.00	6.75
COMMON CARD (1-792)	.10	.05

	MINT	NRMT
☐ 1 Craig Lefferts	.10	.05
☐ 2 Kent Mercker	.10	.05
☐ 3 Phil Plantier	.10	.05
☐ 4 Alex Arias	.10	.05
☐ 5 Julio Valera	.10	.05
☐ 6 Dan Wilson	.20	.09
☐ 7 Frank Thomas	1.50	.70
☐ 8 Eric Anthony	.10	.05
☐ 9 Derek Lilliquist	.10	.05
☐ 10 Rafael Bournigal	.10	.05
☐ 11 Manny Alexander RR	.10	.05
☐ 12 Bret Barberie	.10	.05
☐ 13 Mickey Tettleton	.10	.05
☐ 14 Anthony Young	.10	.05
☐ 15 Tim Spehr	.10	.05
☐ 16 Bob Ayrault	.10	.05
☐ 17 Bill Wegman	.10	.05
☐ 18 Jay Bell	.20	.09
☐ 19 Rick Aguilera	.10	.05
☐ 20 Todd Zeile	.10	.05
☐ 21 Steve Farr	.10	.05
☐ 22 Andy Benes	.20	.09
☐ 23 Lance Blankenship	.10	.05
☐ 24 Ted Wood	.10	.05
☐ 25 Omar Vizquel	.20	.09
☐ 26 Steve Avery	.10	.05
☐ 27 Brian Bohanon	.10	.05
☐ 28 Rick Wilkins	.10	.05
☐ 29 Devon White	.10	.05
☐ 30 Bobby Ayala	.10	.05
☐ 31 Leo Gomez	.10	.05
☐ 32 Mike Simms	.10	.05
☐ 33 Ellis Burks	.20	.09
☐ 34 Steve Wilson	.10	.05
☐ 35 Jim Abbott	.10	.05
☐ 36 Tim Wallach	.10	.05
☐ 37 Wilson Alvarez	.20	.09
☐ 38 Daryl Boston	.10	.05
☐ 39 Sandy Alomar Jr.	.20	.09
☐ 40 Mitch Williams	.10	.05
☐ 41 Rico Brogna	.20	.09
☐ 42 Gary Varsho	.10	.05
☐ 43 Kevin Appier	.20	.09
☐ 44 Eric Wedge RR	.10	.05
☐ 45 Dante Bichette	.10	.05
☐ 46 Jose Oquendo	.10	.05
☐ 47 Mike Trombley	.10	.05
☐ 48 Dan Walters	.10	.05
☐ 49 Gerald Williams	.10	.05
☐ 50 Bud Black	.10	.05
☐ 51 Bobby Witt	.10	.05
☐ 52 Mark Davis	.10	.05
☐ 53 Shawn Barton	.10	.05
☐ 54 Paul Assenmacher	.10	.05
☐ 55 Kevin Reimer	.10	.05
☐ 56 Billy Ashley RR	.10	.05
☐ 57 Eddie Zosky	.10	.05
☐ 58 Chris Sabo	.10	.05
☐ 59 Billy Ripken	.10	.05
☐ 60 Scooter Tucker	.10	.05
☐ 61 Tim Wakefield RR	.20	.09
☐ 62 Mitch Webster	.10	.05
☐ 63 Jack Clark	.10	.05
☐ 64 Mark Gardner	.10	.05
☐ 65 Lee Stevens	.10	.05
☐ 66 Todd Hundley	.10	.05
☐ 67 Bobby Thigpen	.10	.05
☐ 68 Dave Hollins	.10	.05
☐ 69 Jack Armstrong	.10	.05
☐ 70 Alex Cole	.10	.05
☐ 71 Mark Carreon	.10	.05
☐ 72 Todd Worrell	.10	.05
☐ 73 Steve Shifflett	.10	.05
☐ 74 Jerald Clark	.10	.05
☐ 75 Paul Molitor	.40	.18
☐ 76 Larry Carter	.10	.05
☐ 77 Rich Rowland RR	.10	.05
☐ 78 Damon Berryhill	.10	.05
☐ 79 Willie Banks	.10	.05
☐ 80 Hector Villanueva	.10	.05
☐ 81 Mike Gallego	.10	.05
☐ 82 Tim Belcher	.10	.05
☐ 83 Mike Bordick	.10	.05
☐ 84 Craig Biggio	.10	.05
☐ 85 Lance Parrish	.10	.05
☐ 86 Brett Butler	.20	.09
☐ 87 Mike Timlin	.10	.05
☐ 88 Brian Barnes	.10	.05
☐ 89 Brady Anderson	.10	.05
☐ 90 D.J. Dozier	.10	.05
☐ 91 Frank Viola	.10	.05
☐ 92 Darren Daulton	.20	.09
☐ 93 Chad Curtis	.20	.09
☐ 94 Zane Smith	.10	.05
☐ 95 George Bell	.10	.05
☐ 96 Rex Hudler	.10	.05
☐ 97 Mark Whiten	.10	.05
☐ 98 Tim Teufel	.10	.05
☐ 99 Kevin Ritz	.10	.05
☐ 100 Jeff Brantley	.10	.05
☐ 101 Jeff Conine	.20	.09
☐ 102 Vinny Castilla	.40	.18
☐ 103 Greg Vaughn	.10	.05
☐ 104 Steve Buechele	.10	.05
☐ 105 Darren Reed	.10	.05
☐ 106 Bip Roberts	.10	.05
☐ 107 John Habyan	.10	.05
☐ 108 Scott Servais	.10	.05
☐ 109 Walt Weiss	.10	.05
☐ 110 J.T. Snow RR	.50	.23
☐ 111 Jay Buhner	.10	.05
☐ 112 Darryl Strawberry	.20	.09
☐ 113 Roger Pavlik	.10	.05
☐ 114 Chris Nabholz	.10	.05
☐ 115 Pat Borders	.10	.05
☐ 116 Pat Howell	.10	.05
☐ 117 Gregg Olson	.10	.05
☐ 118 Curt Schilling	.20	.09
☐ 119 Roger Clemens	.75	.35
☐ 120 Victor Cole	.10	.05
☐ 121 Gary DiSarcina	.10	.05
☐ 122 Checklist 1-80 Gary Carter and Kirt Manwaring	.20	.09
☐ 123 Steve Sax	.10	.05
☐ 124 Chuck Carr	.10	.05
☐ 125 Mark Lewis	.10	.05
☐ 126 Tony Gwynn	1.00	.45
☐ 127 Travis Fryman	.20	.09
☐ 128 Dave Burba	.10	.05
☐ 129 Wally Joyner	.20	.09
☐ 130 John Smoltz	.10	.05

☐ 131 Cal Eldred	.10	.05
☐ 132 Checklist 81-159 Roberto Alomar and Devon White	.20	.09
☐ 133 Arthur Rhodes	.10	.05
☐ 134 Jeff Blauser	.10	.05
☐ 135 Scott Cooper	.10	.05
☐ 136 Doug Strange	.10	.05
☐ 137 Luis Sojo	.10	.05
☐ 138 Jeff Branson	.10	.05
☐ 139 Alex Fernandez	.20	.09
☐ 140 Ken Caminiti	.40	.18
☐ 141 Charles Nagy	.20	.09
☐ 142 Tom Candiotti	.10	.05
☐ 143 Willie Greene RR	.20	.09
☐ 144 John Vander Wal	.10	.05
☐ 145 Kurt Knudsen	.10	.05
☐ 146 John Franco	.10	.05
☐ 147 Eddie Pierce	.10	.05
☐ 148 Kim Batiste	.10	.05
☐ 149 Darren Holmes	.10	.05
☐ 150 Steve Cooke	.10	.05
☐ 151 Terry Jorgensen	.10	.05
☐ 152 Mark Clark	.10	.05
☐ 153 Randy Velarde	.10	.05
☐ 154 Greg W. Harris	.10	.05
☐ 155 Kevin Campbell	.10	.05
☐ 156 John Burkett	.10	.05
☐ 157 Kevin Mitchell	.20	.09
☐ 158 Deion Sanders	.10	.05
☐ 159 Jose Canseco	.10	.05
☐ 160 Jeff Hartsock	.10	.05
☐ 161 Tom Quinlan	.10	.05
☐ 162 Tim Pugh	.10	.05
☐ 163 Glenn Davis	.10	.05
☐ 164 Shane Reynolds	.40	.18
☐ 165 Jody Reed	.10	.05
☐ 166 Mike Sharperson	.10	.05
☐ 167 Scott Lewis	.10	.05
☐ 168 Dennis Martinez	.20	.09
☐ 169 Scott Radinsky	.10	.05
☐ 170 Dave Gallagher	.10	.05
☐ 171 Jim Thome	.75	.35
☐ 172 Terry Mulholland	.10	.05
☐ 173 Milt Cuyler	.10	.05
☐ 174 Bob Patterson	.10	.05
☐ 175 Jeff Montgomery	.20	.09
☐ 176 Tim Salmon RR	.50	.23
☐ 177 Franklin Stubbs	.10	.05
☐ 178 Donovan Osborne	.10	.05
☐ 179 Jeff Reboulet	.10	.05
☐ 180 Jeremy Hernandez	.10	.05
☐ 181 Charlie Hayes	.10	.05
☐ 182 Matt Williams	.10	.05
☐ 183 Mike Raczka	.10	.05
☐ 184 Francisco Cabrera	.10	.05
☐ 185 Rich DeLucia	.10	.05
☐ 186 Sammy Sosa	.40	.18
☐ 187 Ivan Rodriguez	.50	.23
☐ 188 Bret Boone RR	.20	.09
☐ 189 Juan Guzman	.20	.09
☐ 190 Tom Browning	.10	.05
☐ 191 Randy Milligan	.10	.05
☐ 192 Steve Finley	.20	.09
☐ 193 John Patterson RR	.10	.05
☐ 194 Kip Gross	.10	.05
☐ 195 Tony Fossas	.10	.05
☐ 196 Ivan Calderon	.10	.05
☐ 197 Junior Felix	.10	.05
☐ 198 Pete Schourek	.10	.05
☐ 199 Craig Grebeck	.10	.05
☐ 200 Juan Bell	.10	.05
☐ 201 Glenallen Hill	.10	.05
☐ 202 Danny Jackson	.10	.05
☐ 203 John Kiely	.10	.05
☐ 204 Bob Tewksbury	.10	.05
☐ 205 Kevin Koslofski	.10	.05
☐ 206 Craig Shipley	.10	.05
☐ 207 John Jaha	.20	.09
☐ 208 Royce Clayton	.10	.05
☐ 209 Mike Piazza RR	2.00	.90
☐ 210 Ron Gant	.20	.09
☐ 211 Scott Erickson	.10	.05
☐ 212 Doug Dascenzo	.10	.05
☐ 213 Andy Stankiewicz	.10	.05
☐ 214 Geronimo Berroa	.20	.09
☐ 215 Dennis Eckersley	.10	.05
☐ 216 Al Osuna	.10	.05
☐ 217 Tino Martinez	.40	.18
☐ 218 Henry Rodriguez	.20	.09
☐ 219 Ed Sprague	.20	.09
☐ 220 Ken Hill	.20	.09
☐ 221 Chito Martinez	.10	.05
☐ 222 Bret Saberhagen	.10	.05
☐ 223 Mike Greenwell	.10	.05
☐ 224 Mickey Morandini	.10	.05
☐ 225 Chuck Finley	.10	.05
☐ 226 Denny Neagle	.20	.09
☐ 227 Kirk McCaskill	.10	.05
☐ 228 Rheal Cormier	.10	.05
☐ 229 Paul Sorrento	.10	.05
☐ 230 Darrin Jackson	.10	.05
☐ 231 Rob Deer	.10	.05
☐ 232 Bill Swift	.10	.05
☐ 233 Kevin McReynolds	.10	.05
☐ 234 Terry Pendleton	.20	.09
☐ 235 Dave Nilsson	.20	.09
☐ 236 Chuck McElroy	.10	.05
☐ 237 Derek Parks	.10	.05
☐ 238 Norm Charlton	.10	.05
☐ 239 Matt Nokes	.10	.05
☐ 240 Juan Guerrero	.10	.05
☐ 241 Jeff Parrett	.10	.05
☐ 242 Ryan Thompson RR	.10	.05
☐ 243 Dave Fleming	.10	.05
☐ 244 Dave Hansen	.10	.05
☐ 245 Monty Fariss	.10	.05
☐ 246 Archi Cianfrocco	.10	.05
☐ 247 Pat Hentgen	.40	.18
☐ 248 Bill Pecota	.10	.05
☐ 249 Ben McDonald	.10	.05
☐ 250 Cliff Brantley	.10	.05
☐ 251 John Valentin	.20	.09
☐ 252 Jeff King	.20	.09
☐ 253 Reggie Williams	.10	.05
☐ 254 Checklist 160-238 (Damon Berryhill and Alex Arias)	.10	.05
☐ 255 Ozzie Guillen	.10	.05
☐ 256 Mike Perez	.10	.05
☐ 257 Thomas Howard	.10	.05
☐ 258 Kurt Stillwell	.10	.05
☐ 259 Mike Henneman	.10	.05
☐ 260 Steve Decker	.10	.05
☐ 261 Brent Mayne	.10	.05
☐ 262 Otis Nixon	.10	.05
☐ 263 Mark Kiefer	.10	.05
☐ 264 Checklist 239-317 (Don Mattingly and Mike Bordick)	.10	.05
☐ 265 Richie Lewis	.10	.05
☐ 266 Pat Gomez	.10	.05
☐ 267 Scott Taylor	.10	.05
☐ 268 Shawon Dunston	.10	.05
☐ 269 Greg Myers	.10	.05
☐ 270 Tim Costo	.10	.05
☐ 271 Greg Hibbard	.10	.05
☐ 272 Pete Harnisch	.10	.05
☐ 273 Dave Mlicki	.10	.05
☐ 274 Orel Hershiser	.20	.09
☐ 275 Sean Berry RR	.10	.05
☐ 276 Doug Simons	.10	.05
☐ 277 John Doherty	.10	.05
☐ 278 Eddie Murray	.40	.18
☐ 279 Chris Haney	.10	.05
☐ 280 Stan Javier	.10	.05
☐ 281 Jaime Navarro	.10	.05
☐ 282 Orlando Merced	.10	.05
☐ 283 Kent Hrbek	.20	.09
☐ 284 Bernard Gilkey	.20	.09
☐ 285 Russ Springer	.10	.05
☐ 286 Mike Maddux	.10	.05
☐ 287 Eric Fox	.10	.05
☐ 288 Mark Leonard	.10	.05
☐ 289 Tim Leary	.10	.05
☐ 290 Brian Hunter	.10	.05
☐ 291 Donald Harris	.10	.05
☐ 292 Bob Scanlan	.10	.05
☐ 293 Turner Ward	.10	.05
☐ 294 Hal Morris	.10	.05
☐ 295 Jimmy Poole	.10	.05
☐ 296 Doug Jones	.10	.05
☐ 297 Tony Pena	.10	.05
☐ 298 Ramon Martinez	.20	.09
☐ 299 Tim Fortugno	.10	.05
☐ 300 Marquis Grissom	.20	.09
☐ 301 Lance Johnson	.10	.05
☐ 302 Jeff Kent	.20	.09
☐ 303 Reggie Jefferson	.20	.09
☐ 304 Wes Chamberlain	.10	.05
☐ 305 Shawn Hare	.10	.05
☐ 306 Mike LaValliere	.10	.05
☐ 307 Gregg Jefferies	.20	.09
☐ 308 Troy Neel RR	.10	.05
☐ 309 Pat Listach	.10	.05
☐ 310 Geronimo Pena	.10	.05
☐ 311 Pedro Munoz	.10	.05
☐ 312 Guillermo Velasquez	.10	.05
☐ 313 Roberto Kelly	.10	.05
☐ 314 Mike Jackson	.10	.05
☐ 315 Rickey Henderson	.10	.05
☐ 316 Mark Lemke	.10	.05
☐ 317 Erik Hanson	.10	.05
☐ 318 Derrick May	.10	.05
☐ 319 Geno Petralli	.10	.05
☐ 320 Melvin Nieves RR	.20	.09
☐ 321 Doug Linton	.10	.05
☐ 322 Rob Dibble	.10	.05
☐ 323 Chris Hoiles	.10	.05
☐ 324 Jimmy Jones	.10	.05
☐ 325 Dave Staton RR	.10	.05
☐ 326 Pedro Martinez	.40	.18
☐ 327 Paul Quantrill	.10	.05
☐ 328 Greg Colbrunn	.10	.05
☐ 329 Hilly Hathaway	.10	.05
☐ 330 Jeff Innis	.10	.05
☐ 331 Ron Karkovice	.10	.05
☐ 332 Keith Shepherd	.10	.05
☐ 333 Alan Embree	.10	.05
☐ 334 Paul Wagner	.10	.05
☐ 335 Dave Haas	.10	.05
☐ 336 Ozzie Canseco	.10	.05
☐ 337 Bill Sampen	.10	.05
☐ 338 Rich Rodriguez	.10	.05
☐ 339 Dean Palmer	.20	.09
☐ 340 Greg Litton	.10	.05
☐ 341 Jim Tatum RR	.10	.05
☐ 342 Todd Haney	.10	.05
☐ 343 Larry Casian	.10	.05
☐ 344 Ryne Sandberg	.50	.23
☐ 345 Sterling Hitchcock	.20	.09
☐ 346 Chris Hammond	.10	.05
☐ 347 Vince Horsman	.10	.05
☐ 348 Butch Henry	.10	.05
☐ 349 Dann Howitt	.10	.05
☐ 350 Roger McDowell	.10	.05
☐ 351 Jack Morris	.20	.09
☐ 352 Bill Krueger	.10	.05
☐ 353 Cris Colon	.10	.05
☐ 354 Joe Vitko	.10	.05
☐ 355 Willie McGee	.10	.05
☐ 356 Jay Baller	.10	.05
☐ 357 Pat Mahomes	.10	.05
☐ 358 Roger Mason	.10	.05
☐ 359 Jerry Nielsen	.10	.05
☐ 360 Tom Pagnozzi	.10	.05
☐ 361 Kevin Baez	.10	.05
☐ 362 Tim Scott	.10	.05
☐ 363 Domingo Martinez	.10	.05
☐ 364 Kirt Manwaring	.10	.05
☐ 365 Rafael Palmeiro	.10	.05
☐ 366 Ray Lankford	.10	.05
☐ 367 Tim McIntosh	.10	.05
☐ 368 Jessie Hollins	.10	.05
☐ 369 Scott Leius	.10	.05
☐ 370 Bill Doran	.10	.05
☐ 371 Sam Militello	.10	.05
☐ 372 Ryan Bowen	.10	.05
☐ 373 Dave Henderson	.10	.05
☐ 374 Dan Smith RR	.10	.05
☐ 375 Steve Reed RR	.10	.05
☐ 376 Jose Offerman	.10	.05
☐ 377 Kevin Brown	.20	.09
☐ 378 Darrin Fletcher	.10	.05
☐ 379 Duane Ward	.10	.05
☐ 380 Wayne Kirby RR	.10	.05
☐ 381 Steve Scarsone	.10	.05
☐ 382 Mariano Duncan	.10	.05
☐ 383 Ken Ryan	.10	.05
☐ 384 Lloyd McClendon	.10	.05
☐ 385 Brian Holman	.10	.05
☐ 386 Braulio Castillo	.10	.05
☐ 387 Danny Leon	.10	.05
☐ 388 Omar Olivares	.10	.05
☐ 389 Kevin Wickander	.10	.05
☐ 390 Fred McGriff	.10	.05
☐ 391 Phil Clark	.10	.05
☐ 392 Darren Lewis	.10	.05
☐ 393 Phil Hiatt	.10	.05
☐ 394 Mike Morgan	.10	.05
☐ 395 Shane Mack	.10	.05
☐ 396 Checklist 318-396 (Dennis Eckersley and Art Kusnyer CO)	.20	.09
☐ 397 David Segui	.10	.05
☐ 398 Rafael Belliard	.10	.05
☐ 399 Tim Naehring	.10	.05
☐ 400 Frank Castillo	.10	.05
☐ 401 Joe Grahe	.10	.05
☐ 402 Reggie Sanders	.20	.09
☐ 403 Roberto Hernandez	.20	.09
☐ 404 Luis Gonzalez	.10	.05
☐ 405 Carlos Baerga	.20	.09
☐ 406 Carlos Hernandez	.10	.05
☐ 407 Pedro Astacio RR	.10	.05
☐ 408 Mel Rojas	.20	.09
☐ 409 Scott Livingstone	.10	.05
☐ 410 Chico Walker	.10	.05
☐ 411 Brian McRae	.10	.05
☐ 412 Ben Rivera	.10	.05
☐ 413 Ricky Bones	.10	.05

☐ 414 Andy Van Slyke .20 .09
☐ 415 Chuck Knoblauch .40 .18
☐ 416 Luis Alicea .10 .05
☐ 417 Bob Wickman .10 .05
☐ 418 Doug Brocail .10 .05
☐ 419 Scott Brosius .10 .05
☐ 420 Rod Beck .20 .09
☐ 421 Edgar Martinez .10 .05
☐ 422 Ryan Klesko .50 .23
☐ 423 Nolan Ryan 1.50 .70
☐ 424 Rey Sanchez .10 .05
☐ 425 Roberto Alomar .40 .18
☐ 426 Barry Larkin .10 .05
☐ 427 Mike Mussina .40 .18
☐ 428 Jeff Bagwell .75 .35
☐ 429 Mo Vaughn .50 .23
☐ 430 Eric Karros .20 .09
☐ 431 John Orton .10 .05
☐ 432 Wil Cordero .20 .09
☐ 433 Jack McDowell .10 .05
☐ 434 Howard Johnson .10 .05
☐ 435 Albert Belle .50 .23
☐ 436 John Kruk .20 .09
☐ 437 Skeeter Barnes .10 .05
☐ 438 Don Slaught .10 .05
☐ 439 Rusty Meacham .10 .05
☐ 440 Tim Laker RR .10 .05
☐ 441 Robin Yount .10 .05
☐ 442 Brian Jordan .20 .09
☐ 443 Kevin Tapani .10 .05
☐ 444 Gary Sheffield .40 .18
☐ 445 Rich Monteleone .10 .05
☐ 446 Will Clark .10 .05
☐ 447 Jerry Browne .10 .05
☐ 448 Jeff Treadway .10 .05
☐ 449 Mike Schooler .10 .05
☐ 450 Mike Harkey .10 .05
☐ 451 Julio Franco .20 .09
☐ 452 Kevin Young RR .10 .05
☐ 453 Kelly Gruber .10 .05
☐ 454 Jose Rijo .10 .05
☐ 455 Mike Devereaux .10 .05
☐ 456 Andujar Cedeno .10 .05
☐ 457 Damion Easley RR .10 .05
☐ 458 Kevin Gross .10 .05
☐ 459 Matt Young .10 .05
☐ 460 Matt Stairs .10 .05
☐ 461 Luis Polonia .10 .05
☐ 462 Dwight Gooden .20 .09
☐ 463 Warren Newson .10 .05
☐ 464 Jose DeLeon .10 .05
☐ 465 Jose Mesa .20 .09
☐ 466 Danny Cox .10 .05
☐ 467 Dan Gladden .10 .05
☐ 468 Gerald Perry .10 .05
☐ 469 Mike Boddicker .10 .05
☐ 470 Jeff Gardner .10 .05
☐ 471 Doug Henry .10 .05
☐ 472 Mike Benjamin .10 .05
☐ 473 Dan Peltier RR .10 .05
☐ 474 Mike Stanton .10 .05
☐ 475 John Smiley .10 .05
☐ 476 Dwight Smith .10 .05
☐ 477 Jim Leyritz .10 .05
☐ 478 Dwayne Henry .10 .05
☐ 479 Mark McGwire .75 .35
☐ 480 Pete Incaviglia .10 .05
☐ 481 Dave Cochrane .10 .05
☐ 482 Eric Davis .20 .09
☐ 483 John Olerud .10 .05
☐ 484 Kent Bottenfield .10 .05
☐ 485 Mark McLemore .10 .05
☐ 486 Dave Magadan .10 .05
☐ 487 John Marzano .10 .05
☐ 488 Ruben Amaro .10 .05
☐ 489 Rob Ducey .10 .05
☐ 490 Stan Belinda .10 .05
☐ 491 Dan Pasqua .10 .05
☐ 492 Joe Magrane .10 .05
☐ 493 Brook Jacoby .10 .05
☐ 494 Gene Harris .10 .05
☐ 495 Mark Leiter .10 .05
☐ 496 Bryan Hickerson .10 .05
☐ 497 Tom Gordon .10 .05
☐ 498 Pete Smith .10 .05
☐ 499 Chris Bosio .10 .05
☐ 500 Shawn Boskie .10 .05
☐ 501 Dave West .10 .05
☐ 502 Milt Hill .10 .05
☐ 503 Pat Kelly .10 .05
☐ 504 Joe Boever .10 .05
☐ 505 Terry Steinbach .20 .09
☐ 506 Butch Huskey RR .40 .18
☐ 507 David Valle .10 .05
☐ 508 Mike Scioscia .10 .05
☐ 509 Kenny Rogers .10 .05
☐ 510 Moises Alou .20 .09
☐ 511 David Wells .10 .05
☐ 512 Mackey Sasser .10 .05
☐ 513 Todd Frohwirth .10 .05
☐ 514 Ricky Jordan .10 .05
☐ 515 Mike Gardiner .10 .05
☐ 516 Gary Redus .10 .05
☐ 517 Gary Gaetti .20 .09
☐ 518 Checklist .10 .05
☐ 519 Carlton Fisk .40 .18
☐ 520 Ozzie Smith .50 .23
☐ 521 Rod Nichols .10 .05
☐ 522 Benito Santiago .10 .05
☐ 523 Bill Gullickson .10 .05
☐ 524 Robby Thompson .10 .05
☐ 525 Mike Macfarlane .10 .05
☐ 526 Sid Bream .10 .05
☐ 527 Darryl Hamilton .10 .05
☐ 528 Checklist .10 .05
☐ 529 Jeff Tackett .10 .05
☐ 530 Greg Olson .10 .05
☐ 531 Bob Zupcic .10 .05
☐ 532 Mark Grace .10 .05
☐ 533 Steve Frey .10 .05
☐ 534 Dave Martinez .10 .05
☐ 535 Robin Ventura .20 .09
☐ 536 Casey Candaele .10 .05
☐ 537 Kenny Lofton .75 .35
☐ 538 Jay Howell .10 .05
☐ 539 Fernando Ramsey RR .10 .05
☐ 540 Larry Walker .40 .18
☐ 541 Cecil Fielder .20 .09
☐ 542 Lee Guetterman .10 .05
☐ 543 Keith Miller .10 .05
☐ 544 Len Dykstra .20 .09
☐ 545 B.J. Surhoff .20 .09
☐ 546 Bob Walk .10 .05
☐ 547 Brian Harper .10 .05
☐ 548 Lee Smith .20 .09
☐ 549 Danny Tartabull .10 .05
☐ 550 Frank Seminara .10 .05
☐ 551 Henry Mercedes .10 .05
☐ 552 Dave Righetti .10 .05
☐ 553 Ken Griffey Jr. 2.00 .90
☐ 554 Tom Glavine .10 .05
☐ 555 Juan Gonzalez 1.00 .45
☐ 556 Jim Bullinger .10 .05
☐ 557 Derek Bell .20 .09
☐ 558 Cesar Hernandez .10 .05
☐ 559 Cal Ripken 1.50 .70
☐ 560 Eddie Taubensee .10 .05
☐ 561 John Flaherty .10 .05
☐ 562 Todd Benzinger .10 .05
☐ 563 Hubie Brooks .10 .05
☐ 564 Delino DeShields .10 .05
☐ 565 Tim Raines .20 .09
☐ 566 Sid Fernandez .10 .05
☐ 567 Steve Olin .10 .05
☐ 568 Tommy Greene .10 .05
☐ 569 Buddy Groom .10 .05
☐ 570 Randy Tomlin .10 .05
☐ 571 Hipolito Pichardo .10 .05
☐ 572 Rene Arocha RR .10 .05
☐ 573 Mike Fetters .10 .05
☐ 574 Felix Jose .10 .05
☐ 575 Gene Larkin .10 .05
☐ 576 Bruce Hurst .10 .05
☐ 577 Bernie Williams .10 .05
☐ 578 Trevor Wilson .10 .05
☐ 579 Bob Welch .10 .05
☐ 580 David Justice .40 .18
☐ 581 Randy Johnson .40 .18
☐ 582 Jose Vizcaino .10 .05
☐ 583 Jeff Huson .10 .05
☐ 584 Rob Maurer RR .10 .05
☐ 585 Todd Stottlemyre .10 .05
☐ 586 Joe Oliver .10 .05
☐ 587 Bob Milacki .10 .05
☐ 588 Rob Murphy .10 .05
☐ 589 Greg Pirkl RR .10 .05
☐ 590 Lenny Harris .10 .05
☐ 591 Luis Rivera .10 .05
☐ 592 John Wetteland .20 .09
☐ 593 Mark Langston .10 .05
☐ 594 Bobby Bonilla .20 .09
☐ 595 Esteban Beltre .10 .05
☐ 596 Mike Hartley .10 .05
☐ 597 Felix Fermin .10 .05
☐ 598 Carlos Garcia .10 .05
☐ 599 Frank Tanana .10 .05
☐ 600 Pedro Guerrero .10 .05
☐ 601 Terry Shumpert .10 .05
☐ 602 Wally Whitehurst .10 .05
☐ 603 Kevin Seitzer .10 .05
☐ 604 Chris James .10 .05
☐ 605 Greg Gohr RR .10 .05
☐ 606 Mark Wohlers .20 .09
☐ 607 Kirby Puckett .75 .35
☐ 608 Greg Maddux 1.25 .55
☐ 609 Don Mattingly .60 .25
☐ 610 Greg Cadaret .10 .05
☐ 611 Dave Stewart .20 .09
☐ 612 Mark Portugal .10 .05
☐ 613 Pete O'Brien .10 .05
☐ 614 Bobby Ojeda .10 .05
☐ 615 Joe Carter .10 .05
☐ 616 Pete Young .10 .05
☐ 617 Sam Horn .10 .05
☐ 618 Vince Coleman .10 .05
☐ 619 Wade Boggs .40 .18
☐ 620 Todd Pratt .10 .05
☐ 621 Ron Tingley .10 .05
☐ 622 Doug Drabek .10 .05
☐ 623 Scott Hemond .10 .05
☐ 624 Tim Jones .10 .05
☐ 625 Dennis Cook .10 .05
☐ 626 Jose Melendez .10 .05
☐ 627 Mike Munoz .10 .05
☐ 628 Jim Pena .10 .05
☐ 629 Gary Thurman .10 .05
☐ 630 Charlie Leibrandt .10 .05
☐ 631 Scott Fletcher .10 .05
☐ 632 Andre Dawson .10 .05
☐ 633 Greg Gagne .10 .05
☐ 634 Greg Swindell .10 .05
☐ 635 Kevin Maas .10 .05
☐ 636 Xavier Hernandez .10 .05
☐ 637 Ruben Sierra .10 .05
☐ 638 Dmitri Young RR .40 .18
☐ 639 Harold Reynolds .10 .05
☐ 640 Tom Goodwin .10 .05
☐ 641 Todd Burns .10 .05
☐ 642 Jeff Fassero .20 .09
☐ 643 Dave Winfield .10 .05
☐ 644 Willie Randolph .20 .09
☐ 645 Luis Mercedes .10 .05
☐ 646 Dale Murphy .10 .05
☐ 647 Danny Darwin .10 .05
☐ 648 Dennis Moeller .10 .05
☐ 649 Chuck Crim .10 .05
☐ 650 Checklist .10 .05
☐ 651 Shawn Abner .10 .05
☐ 652 Tracy Woodson .10 .05
☐ 653 Scott Scudder .10 .05
☐ 654 Tom Lampkin .10 .05
☐ 655 Alan Trammell .10 .05
☐ 656 Cory Snyder .10 .05
☐ 657 Chris Gwynn .10 .05
☐ 658 Lonnie Smith .10 .05
☐ 659 Jim Austin .10 .05
☐ 660 Checklist .10 .05
☐ 661 Tim Hulett .10 .05
☐ 662 Marvin Freeman .10 .05
☐ 663 Greg A. Harris .10 .05
☐ 664 Heathcliff Slocumb .10 .05
☐ 665 Mike Butcher .10 .05
☐ 666 Steve Foster .10 .05
☐ 667 Donn Pall .10 .05
☐ 668 Darryl Kile .10 .05
☐ 669 Jesse Levis .10 .05
☐ 670 Jim Gott .10 .05
☐ 671 Mark Hutton RR .10 .05
☐ 672 Brian Drahman .10 .05
☐ 673 Chad Kreuter .10 .05
☐ 674 Tony Fernandez .10 .05
☐ 675 Jose Lind .10 .05
☐ 676 Kyle Abbott .10 .05
☐ 677 Dan Plesac .10 .05
☐ 678 Barry Bonds .50 .23
☐ 679 Chili Davis .20 .09
☐ 680 Stan Royer .10 .05
☐ 681 Scott Kamieniecki .10 .05
☐ 682 Carlos Martinez .10 .05
☐ 683 Mike Moore .10 .05
☐ 684 Candy Maldonado .10 .05
☐ 685 Jeff Nelson .10 .05
☐ 686 Lou Whitaker .20 .09
☐ 687 Jose Guzman .10 .05
☐ 688 Manuel Lee .10 .05
☐ 689 Bob MacDonald .10 .05
☐ 690 Scott Bankhead .10 .05
☐ 691 Alan Mills .10 .05
☐ 692 Brian Williams .10 .05
☐ 693 Tom Brunansky .10 .05
☐ 694 Lenny Webster .10 .05
☐ 695 Greg Briley .10 .05
☐ 696 Paul O'Neill .20 .09
☐ 697 Joey Cora .20 .09
☐ 698 Charlie O'Brien .10 .05
☐ 699 Junior Ortiz .10 .05
☐ 700 Ron Darling .10 .05
☐ 701 Tony Phillips .10 .05
☐ 702 William Pennyfeather .10 .05
☐ 703 Mark Gubicza .10 .05
☐ 704 Steve Hosey RR .10 .05

☐ 705 Henry Cotto	.10	.05
☐ 706 David Hulse	.10	.05
☐ 707 Mike Pagliarulo	.10	.05
☐ 708 Dave Stieb	.10	.05
☐ 709 Melido Perez	.10	.05
☐ 710 Jimmy Key	.20	.09
☐ 711 Jeff Russell	.10	.05
☐ 712 David Cone	.20	.09
☐ 713 Russ Swan	.10	.05
☐ 714 Mark Guthrie	.10	.05
☐ 715 Checklist	.10	.05
☐ 716 Al Martin RR	.20	.09
☐ 717 Randy Knorr	.10	.05
☐ 718 Mike Stanley	.10	.05
☐ 719 Rick Sutcliffe	.10	.05
☐ 720 Terry Leach	.10	.05
☐ 721 Chipper Jones RR	2.00	.90
☐ 722 Jim Eisenreich	.20	.09
☐ 723 Tom Henke	.10	.05
☐ 724 Jeff Frye	.10	.05
☐ 725 Harold Baines	.20	.09
☐ 726 Scott Sanderson	.10	.05
☐ 727 Tom Foley	.10	.05
☐ 728 Bryan Harvey	.10	.05
☐ 729 Tom Edens	.10	.05
☐ 730 Eric Young	.40	.18
☐ 731 Dave Weathers	.10	.05
☐ 732 Spike Owen	.10	.05
☐ 733 Scott Aldred	.10	.05
☐ 734 Cris Carpenter	.10	.05
☐ 735 Dion James	.10	.05
☐ 736 Joe Girardi	.10	.05
☐ 737 Nigel Wilson RR	.10	.05
☐ 738 Scott Chiamparino	.10	.05
☐ 739 Jeff Reardon	.20	.09
☐ 740 Willie Blair	.10	.05
☐ 741 Jim Corsi	.10	.05
☐ 742 Ken Patterson	.10	.05
☐ 743 Andy Ashby	.10	.05
☐ 744 Rob Natal	.10	.05
☐ 745 Kevin Bass	.10	.05
☐ 746 Freddie Benavides	.10	.05
☐ 747 Chris Donnels	.10	.05
☐ 748 Kerry Woodson	.10	.05
☐ 749 Calvin Jones	.10	.05
☐ 750 Gary Scott	.10	.05
☐ 751 Joe Orsulak	.10	.05
☐ 752 Armando Reynoso	.10	.05
☐ 753 Monty Fariss	.10	.05
☐ 754 Billy Hatcher	.10	.05
☐ 755 Denis Boucher	.10	.05
☐ 756 Walt Weiss	.10	.05
☐ 757 Mike Fitzgerald	.10	.05
☐ 758 Rudy Seanez	.10	.05
☐ 759 Bret Barberie	.10	.05
☐ 760 Mo Sanford	.10	.05
☐ 761 Pedro Castellano	.10	.05
☐ 762 Chuck Carr	.10	.05
☐ 763 Steve Howe	.10	.05
☐ 764 Andres Galarraga	.10	.05
☐ 765 Jeff Conine	.20	.09
☐ 766 Ted Power	.10	.05
☐ 767 Butch Henry	.10	.05
☐ 768 Steve Decker	.10	.05
☐ 769 Storm Davis	.10	.05
☐ 770 Vinny Castilla	.40	.18
☐ 771 Junior Felix	.10	.05
☐ 772 Walt Terrell	.10	.05
☐ 773 Brad Ausmus	.10	.05
☐ 774 Jamie McAndrew	.10	.05
☐ 775 Milt Thompson	.10	.05
☐ 776 Charlie Hayes	.10	.05
☐ 777 Jack Armstrong	.10	.05
☐ 778 Dennis Rasmussen	.10	.05
☐ 779 Darren Holmes	.10	.05
☐ 780 Alex Arias	.10	.05
☐ 781 Randy Bush	.10	.05
☐ 782 Javier Lopez RR	.40	.18
☐ 783 Dante Bichette	.10	.05
☐ 784 John Johnstone	.10	.05
☐ 785 Rene Gonzales	.10	.05
☐ 786 Alex Cole	.10	.05
☐ 787 Jeromy Burnitz RR	.20	.09
☐ 788 Michael Huff	.10	.05
☐ 789 Anthony Telford	.10	.05
☐ 790 Jerald Clark	.10	.05
☐ 791 Joel Johnston	.10	.05
☐ 792 David Nied RR	.10	.05

1993 Donruss Diamond Kings

These standard-size cards, commemorating Donruss' annual selection of the games top players, were randomly inserted in 1993 Donruss packs. The first 15 cards were available in the first series of the 1993 Donruss and cards 16-31 were inserted with the second series. The cards are

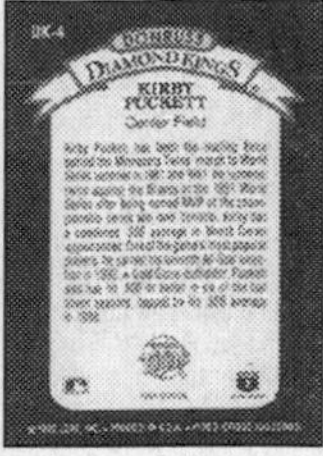

gold-foil stamped and feature player portraits by noted sports artist Dick Perez. Card numbers 27-28 honor the first draft picks of the new Florida Marlins and Colorado Rockies franchises. Collectors 16 years of age and younger could enter Donruss' Diamond King contest by writing an essay of 75 words or less explaining who their favorite Diamond King player was and why. Winners were awarded one of 30 framed watercolors at the National Convention, held in Chicago, July 22-25, 1993.

	MINT	NRMT
COMPLETE SET (31)	30.00	13.50
COMPLETE SERIES 1 (15)	20.00	9.00
COMPLETE SERIES 2 (16)	10.00	4.50
COMMON CARD (DK1-DK31)	.75	.35

☐ DK1 Ken Griffey Jr.	12.00	5.50
☐ DK2 Ryne Sandberg	3.00	1.35
☐ DK3 Roger Clemens	3.00	1.35
☐ DK4 Kirby Puckett	5.00	2.20
☐ DK5 Bill Swift	.75	.35
☐ DK6 Larry Walker	2.50	1.10
☐ DK7 Juan Gonzalez	6.00	2.70
☐ DK8 Wally Joyner	.75	.35
☐ DK9 Andy Van Slyke	.75	.35
☐ DK10 Robin Ventura	1.50	.70
☐ DK11 Bip Roberts	.75	.35
☐ DK12 Roberto Kelly	.75	.35
☐ DK13 Carlos Baerga	.75	.35
☐ DK14 Orel Hershiser	1.50	.70
☐ DK15 Cecil Fielder	1.50	.70
☐ DK16 Robin Yount	2.00	.90
☐ DK17 Darren Daulton	1.50	.70
☐ DK18 Mark McGwire	4.00	1.80
☐ DK19 Tom Glavine	2.00	.90
☐ DK20 Roberto Alomar	2.50	1.10
☐ DK21 Gary Sheffield	2.50	1.10
☐ DK22 Bob Tewksbury	.75	.35
☐ DK23 Brady Anderson	2.00	.90
☐ DK24 Craig Biggio	2.00	.90
☐ DK25 Eddie Murray	2.50	1.10
☐ DK26 Luis Polonia	.75	.35
☐ DK27 Nigel Wilson	.75	.35
☐ DK28 David Nied	.75	.35
☐ DK29 Pat Listach ROY	.75	.35
☐ DK30 Eric Karros ROY	1.50	.70
☐ DK31 Checklist 1-31	.75	.35

1993 Donruss Elite

Cards 19-27 were random inserts in 1993 Donruss series I foil packs while cards 28-36 were inserted in series II packs. The numbering on the 1993 Elite cards follows consecutively after that of the 1992 Elite series cards, and each of the 10,000 Elite cards is serially numbered. The backs of the Elite cards also carry the serial number ("X" of 10,000) as well as the card number. The Signature Series Will Clark card was randomly inserted in 1993 Donruss foil packs; he personally autographed 5,000 cards. Featuring a Dick Perez portrait, the ten thousand Legends Series cards honor Robin Yount for his 3,000th hit achievement. The front design of the Elite cards features a cutout color player photo superimposed on a neon-colored panel framed by a gray inner border and a variegated silver metallic outer border.

	MINT	NRMT
COMPLETE SET (20)	400.00	180.00
COMMON CARD (19-36)	10.00	4.50

☐ 19 Fred McGriff	15.00	6.75
☐ 20 Ryne Sandberg	30.00	13.50
☐ 21 Eddie Murray	25.00	11.00
☐ 22 Paul Molitor	25.00	11.00
☐ 23 Barry Larkin	20.00	9.00
☐ 24 Don Mattingly	40.00	18.00
☐ 25 Dennis Eckersley	15.00	6.75
☐ 26 Roberto Alomar	25.00	11.00
☐ 27 Edgar Martinez	15.00	6.75
☐ 28 Gary Sheffield	17.50	8.00
☐ 29 Darren Daulton	12.50	5.50
☐ 30 Larry Walker	25.00	11.00
☐ 31 Barry Bonds	30.00	13.50
☐ 32 Andy Van Slyke	10.00	4.50
☐ 33 Mark McGwire	50.00	22.00
☐ 34 Cecil Fielder	12.50	5.50
☐ 35 Dave Winfield	15.00	6.75
☐ 36 Juan Gonzalez	60.00	27.00
☐ L3 Robin Yount (Legend Series)	20.00	9.00
☐ S3 Will Clark AU (Signature Series)	150.00	70.00

1993 Donruss Long Ball Leaders

Randomly inserted in 26-card magazine distributor packs (1-9 in series I and 10-18 in series II), these standard-size cards feature some of MLB's outstanding sluggers. The fronts feature full-bleed color action player photos with a red and bright yellow stripe design across the bottom that carries the player's name and team. The Donruss Long Ball Leaders icon rests on the stripe at the lower left. The player's longest home run is printed in gold foil at the upper left.

	MINT	NRMT
COMPLETE SET (18)	60.00	27.00
COMPLETE SERIES 1 (9)	30.00	13.50
COMPLETE SERIES 2 (9)	30.00	13.50
COMMON CARD (LL1-LL18)	1.50	.70

☐ LL1 Rob Deer	1.50	.70
☐ LL2 Fred McGriff	3.00	1.35
☐ LL3 Albert Belle	8.00	3.60
☐ LL4 Mark McGwire	6.00	2.70
☐ LL5 David Justice	4.00	1.80
☐ LL6 Jose Canseco	3.00	1.35
☐ LL7 Kent Hrbek	1.50	.70
☐ LL8 Roberto Alomar	4.00	1.80
☐ LL9 Ken Griffey Jr.	20.00	9.00
☐ LL10 Frank Thomas	20.00	9.00
☐ LL11 Darryl Strawberry	2.00	.90
☐ LL12 Felix Jose	1.50	.70
☐ LL13 Cecil Fielder	2.00	.90
☐ LL14 Juan Gonzalez	10.00	4.50
☐ LL15 Ryne Sandberg	5.00	2.20
☐ LL16 Gary Sheffield	4.00	1.80
☐ LL17 Jeff Bagwell	8.00	3.60
☐ LL18 Larry Walker	4.00	1.80

1993 Donruss MVPs

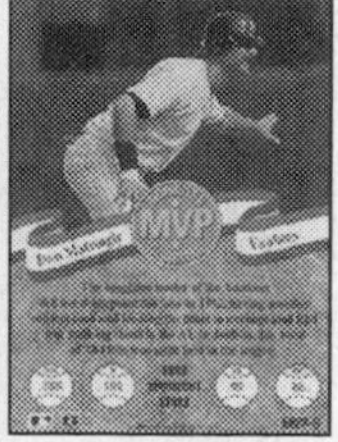

These twenty-six standard size MVP cards were issued 13 cards in each series, and they were inserted one per 23-card jumbo packs. The fronts feature full-bleed color action player photos with a red, white, and blue ribbon design across the bottom that contains the player's name and team. The Donruss MVP icon is gold-foil stamped over the ribbon.

	MINT	NRMT
COMPLETE SET (26)	30.00	13.50
COMPLETE SERIES 1 (13)	10.00	4.50
COMPLETE SERIES 2 (13)	20.00	9.00
COMMON CARD (1-26)	.50	.23

Card	MINT	NRMT
☐ 1 Luis Polonia	.50	.23
☐ 2 Frank Thomas	6.00	2.70
☐ 3 George Brett	3.00	1.35
☐ 4 Paul Molitor	1.00	.45
☐ 5 Don Mattingly	3.00	1.35
☐ 6 Roberto Alomar	1.00	.45
☐ 7 Terry Pendleton	.50	.23
☐ 8 Eric Karros	.60	.25
☐ 9 Larry Walker	1.00	.45
☐ 10 Eddie Murray	1.00	.45
☐ 11 Darren Daulton	.60	.25
☐ 12 Ray Lankford	.75	.35
☐ 13 Will Clark	.75	.35
☐ 14 Cal Ripken	6.00	2.70
☐ 15 Roger Clemens	2.50	1.10
☐ 16 Carlos Baerga	.50	.23
☐ 17 Cecil Fielder	.60	.25
☐ 18 Kirby Puckett	3.00	1.35
☐ 19 Mark McGwire	3.00	1.35
☐ 20 Ken Griffey Jr.	8.00	3.60
☐ 21 Juan Gonzalez	4.00	1.80
☐ 22 Ryne Sandberg	2.00	.90
☐ 23 Bip Roberts	.50	.23
☐ 24 Jeff Bagwell	3.00	1.35
☐ 25 Barry Bonds	2.00	.90
☐ 26 Gary Sheffield	1.00	.45

1993 Donruss Spirit of the Game

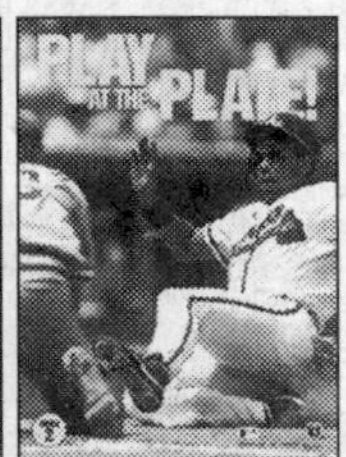

These 20 standard-size cards were randomly inserted in 1993 Donruss packs and packed approximately two per box. Cards 1-10 were first-series inserts, and cards 11-20 were second-series inserts. The fronts feature borderless glossy color action player photos. The set title, "Spirit of the Game," is stamped in gold foil script across the top or bottom of the picture.

	MINT	NRMT
COMPLETE SET (20)	20.00	9.00
COMPLETE SERIES 1 (10)	8.00	3.60
COMPLETE SERIES 2 (10)	12.00	5.50
COMMON CARD (SG1-SG20)	.50	.23

Card	MINT	NRMT
☐ SG1 Mike Bordick Turning Two	.50	.23
☐ SG2 Dave Justice Play at the Plate	1.50	.70
☐ SG3 Roberto Alomar In There	1.50	.70
☐ SG4 Dennis Eckersley Pumped	1.00	.45
☐ SG5 Juan Gonzalez and Jose Canseco Dynamic Duo	4.00	1.80
☐ SG6 George Bell and Frank Thomas ... Gone	1.50	.70
☐ SG7 Wade Boggs and Luis Polonia Safe or Out	1.50	.70
☐ SG8 Will Clark The Thrill	1.50	.70
☐ SG9 Bip Roberts Safe at Home	.50	.23
☐ SG10 Cecil Fielder Rob Deer Mickey Tettleton Thirty 3	.75	.35
☐ SG11 Kenny Lofton Bag Bandit	4.00	1.80
☐ SG12 Gary Sheffield Fred McGriff Back to Back	1.50	.70
☐ SG13 Greg Gagne Barry Larkin	.75	.35
☐ SG14 Ryne Sandberg The Ball Stops Here	2.50	1.10
☐ SG15 Carlos Baerga Gary Gaetti Over the Top	.75	.35
☐ SG16 Danny Tartabull At the Wall	.50	.23
☐ SG17 Brady Anderson Head First	1.00	.45
☐ SG18 Frank Thomas Big Hurt	10.00	4.50
☐ SG19 Kevin Gross No Hitter	.50	.23
☐ SG20 Robin Yount 3,000 Hits	1.50	.70

1993 Donruss Elite Dominators

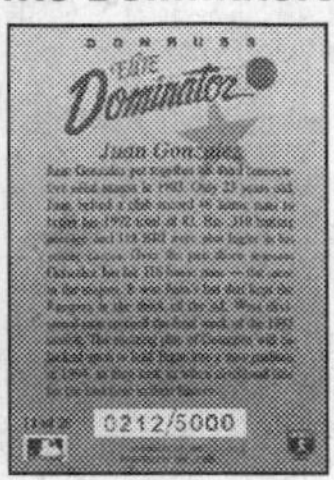

In a series of programs broadcast Dec. 8-13, 1993, on the Shop at Home cable network, viewers were offered the opportunity to purchase a factory-sealed box of either 1993 Donruss I or II, which included one Elite Dominator card produced especially for the promotion. The set retailed for 99.00 plus 6.00 for postage and handling. Just 5,000 of each card were produced, and Nolan Ryan, Juan Gonzalez, Paul Molitor, and Don Mattingly personally signed 2,500 of their cards. The entire print run of 100,000 cards were reportedly purchased by the Shop at Home network and were to be offered periodically over the network. The standard-size Dominator cards feature on their fronts color player action shots with green prismatic foil borders. The set's title appears at the top, along with a gold foil motion-streaked baseball icon at the upper right. The player's name appears near the bottom within a red bar. The tan back is highlighted by pink stars and carries the set's name at the top, followed by the player's name and career highlights. The production number, out of a total of 5,000 produced, is shown at the bottom.

	MINT	NRMT
COMP.UNSIGNED SET (20)	1200.00	550.00
COMMON CARD (1-20)	20.00	9.00

Card	MINT	NRMT
☐ 1 Ryne Sandberg	60.00	27.00
☐ 2 Fred McGriff	40.00	18.00
☐ 3 Greg Maddux	100.00	45.00
☐ 4 Ron Gant	30.00	13.50
☐ 5 David Justice	50.00	22.00
☐ 6 Don Mattingly	75.00	34.00
☐ 7 Tim Salmon	50.00	22.00
☐ 8 Mike Piazza	100.00	45.00
☐ 9 John Olerud	20.00	9.00
☐ 10 Nolan Ryan	125.00	55.00
☐ 11 Juan Gonzalez	60.00	27.00
☐ 12 Ken Griffey Jr.	150.00	70.00
☐ 13 Frank Thomas	100.00	45.00
☐ 14 Tom Glavine	30.00	13.50
☐ 15 George Brett	75.00	34.00
☐ 16 Barry Bonds	60.00	27.00
☐ 17 Albert Belle	60.00	27.00
☐ 18 Paul Molitor	50.00	22.00
☐ 19 Cal Ripken	125.00	55.00
☐ 20 Roberto Alomar	50.00	22.00
☐ AU6 Don Mattingly AU	175.00	80.00
☐ AU10 Nolan Ryan AU	250.00	110.00
☐ AU11 Juan Gonzalez AU	125.00	55.00
☐ AU18 Paul Molitor AU	125.00	55.00

1993 Donruss Elite Supers

Sequentially numbered one through 5,000, these 20 oversized cards measure approximately 3 1/2" by 5" and have wide prismatic foil borders with an inner gray borders. The front displays a color player photo cutout on a brightly colored background. The subset title is written above the photo and the player's name is printed in an oval under the photo. The backs have a two-toned outer border with a navy blue inner border. On a gray

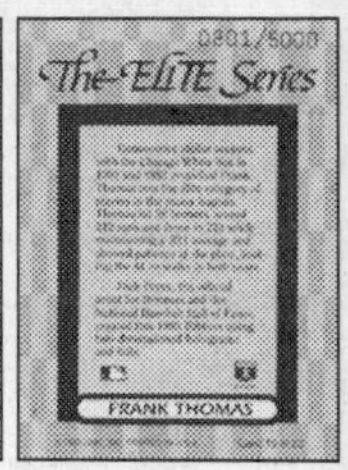

background the player's profile is printed in navy blue lettering. The Elite Update set features all the players found in the regular Elite set, plus Nolan Ryan and Frank Thomas, whose cards replace numbers 19 and 20 from the earlier release, and an updated card of Barry Bonds in his Giants uniform. The backs carry the production number and the card number. Bonds in his Giants uniform. The backs carry the production number and the card number.

	MINT	NRMT
COMPLETE SET (20)	225.00	100.00
COMMON CARD (1-20)	3.00	1.35

Card	MINT	NRMT
☐ 1 Fred McGriff	8.00	3.60
☐ 2 Ryne Sandberg	12.00	5.50
☐ 3 Eddie Murray	10.00	4.50
☐ 4 Paul Molitor	10.00	4.50
☐ 5 Barry Larkin	8.00	3.60
☐ 6 Don Mattingly	25.00	11.00
☐ 7 Dennis Eckersley	5.00	2.20
☐ 8 Roberto Alomar	10.00	4.50
☐ 9 Edgar Martinez	8.00	3.60
☐ 10 Gary Sheffield	10.00	4.50
☐ 11 Darren Daulton	5.00	2.20
☐ 12 Larry Walker	10.00	4.50
☐ 13 Barry Bonds	12.00	5.50
☐ 14 Andy Van Slyke	3.00	1.35
☐ 15 Mark McGwire	20.00	9.00
☐ 16 Cecil Fielder	5.00	2.20
☐ 17 Dave Winfield	8.00	3.60
☐ 18 Juan Gonzalez	25.00	11.00
☐ 19 Frank Thomas	40.00	18.00
☐ 20 Nolan Ryan	50.00	22.00

1993 Donruss Masters of the Game

These cards were issued in individual retail re-packs, and also were included in special 18-pack boxes of 1993 Donruss second series. The cards were originally available only at retail outlets such as WalMart along with a foil pack of 1993 Donruss. These 16 postcards measure approximately 3 1/2" by 5" and feature the work of artist Dick Perez on their fronts. The color paintings are trimmed and bordered in various colors. The player's name appears within an ellipse at the bottom. The back carries the player's name and career statistics at the bottom, and the upper right corner is reserved for a stamp. A faded team logo graces the middle. A few sentences describing Perez' art technique appear vertically on the left. The MLB and MLBPA logos round out the back on the bottom.

	MINT	NRMT
COMPLETE SET (16)	60.00	27.00
COMMON CARD (1-16)	1.00	.45

Card	MINT	NRMT
☐ 1 Frank Thomas	10.00	4.50
☐ 2 Nolan Ryan	12.00	5.50
☐ 3 Gary Sheffield	2.50	1.10
☐ 4 Fred McGriff	2.00	.90
☐ 5 Ryne Sandberg	4.00	1.80
☐ 6 Cal Ripken	12.00	5.50
☐ 7 Jose Canseco	2.00	.90
☐ 8 Ken Griffey Jr.	15.00	6.75
☐ 9 Will Clark	2.00	.90

Card	MINT	NRMT
☐ 10 Roberto Alomar	2.50	1.10
☐ 11 Juan Gonzalez	6.00	2.70
☐ 12 David Justice	2.50	1.10
☐ 13 Kirby Puckett	5.00	2.20
☐ 14 Barry Bonds	3.00	1.35
☐ 15 Robin Yount	2.00	.90
☐ 16 Deion Sanders	1.00	.45

1994 Donruss Promos

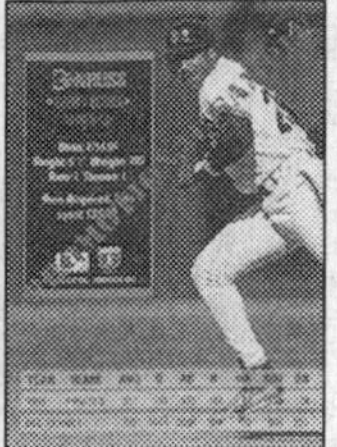

hese 12 standard-size promo cards feature borderless olor player action shots on their fronts. The player's ame and position appear in gold foil within a team color-oded stripe near the bottom. His team logo appears ithin a black rectangle framed by a team color near the ottom. The set name and year, stamped in gold foil, also ppear in this rectangle. Most of the backs are horizontal, nd feature another borderless color player action photo. black rectangle framed by a team color appears on one ide and carries the player's name, team, uniform umber, and biography. The player's 1992 stats appear ithin ghosted stripes near the bottom. The disclaimer Promotional Sample" is printed diagonally across both ides of the cards. The cards are numbered on the back. eportedly each of Leaf/Donruss" hobby accounts roughly 3,000) received one complete 11-card promo set ncluding one but not both Special Edition cards) with heir 1994 Donruss order form. Moreover, 42 different etail broker accounts also received five to ten complete 1-card promo sets for their presentations. From this nformation, it appears that approximately 3,500 11-card romo sets were printed. Each hobby account received ne of two Special Edition promos, either Barry Bonds or rank Thomas.

	MINT	NRMT
COMPLETE SET (12)	50.00	22.00
COMMON CARD (1-10)	1.00	.45
☐ 1 Barry Bonds	3.00	1.35
☐ 1SE Barry Bonds SP	6.00	2.70
☐ 2 Darren Daulton	1.50	.70
☐ 3 John Olerud	1.00	.45
☐ 4 Frank Thomas	7.50	3.40
☐ 4SE Frank Thomas SP	20.00	9.00
☐ 5 Mike Piazza	7.50	3.40
☐ 6 Tim Salmon	4.00	1.80
☐ 7 Ken Griffey Jr.	10.00	4.50
☐ 8 Fred McGriff	2.00	.90
☐ 9 Don Mattingly	5.00	2.20
☐ 10 Gary Sheffield	2.50	1.10

1994 Donruss

The 1994 Donruss set was issued in two separate series of 330 standard-size cards for a total of 660. The fronts feature borderless color player action photos on front. The player's name and position appear in gold foil within a team color-coded stripe near the bottom. The team logo appears within a black rectangle framed by a team color near the bottom. The set name and year, stamped in gold foil, also appear in this rectangle. Most of the backs are horizontal, and feature another borderless color player action photo. A black rectangle framed by a team color appears on one side and carries the player's name, team, uniform number, and biography. The player's stats appear within ghosted stripes near the bottom. Rookie Cards include Curtis Pride and Julian Tavarez.

	MINT	NRMT
COMPLETE SET (660)	40.00	18.00
COMPLETE SERIES 1 (330)	20.00	9.00
COMPLETE SERIES 2 (330)	20.00	9.00
COMMON CARD (1-660)	.15	.07
☐ 1 Nolan Ryan	3.00	1.35
☐ 2 Mike Piazza	2.00	.90
☐ 3 Moises Alou	.30	.14
☐ 4 Ken Griffey Jr.	3.00	1.35
☐ 5 Gary Sheffield	.60	.25
☐ 6 Roberto Alomar	.60	.25
☐ 7 John Kruk	.30	.14
☐ 8 Gregg Olson	.15	.07
☐ 9 Gregg Jefferies	.30	.14
☐ 10 Tony Gwynn	1.50	.70
☐ 11 Chad Curtis	.15	.07
☐ 12 Craig Biggio	.40	.18
☐ 13 John Burkett	.15	.07
☐ 14 Carlos Baerga	.30	.14
☐ 15 Robin Yount	.40	.18
☐ 16 Dennis Eckersley	.40	.18
☐ 17 Dwight Gooden	.30	.14
☐ 18 Ryne Sandberg	.75	.35
☐ 19 Rickey Henderson	.40	.18
☐ 20 Jack McDowell	.15	.07
☐ 21 Jay Bell	.30	.14
☐ 22 Kevin Brown	.30	.14
☐ 23 Robin Ventura	.30	.14
☐ 24 Paul Molitor	.60	.25
☐ 25 David Justice	.60	.25
☐ 26 Rafael Palmeiro	.40	.18
☐ 27 Cecil Fielder	.30	.14
☐ 28 Chuck Knoblauch	.60	.25
☐ 29 Dave Hollins	.15	.07
☐ 30 Jimmy Key	.30	.14
☐ 31 Mark Langston	.15	.07
☐ 32 Darryl Kile	.30	.14
☐ 33 Ruben Sierra	.15	.07
☐ 34 Ron Gant	.15	.07
☐ 35 Ozzie Smith	.75	.35
☐ 36 Wade Boggs	.60	.25
☐ 37 Marquis Grissom	.30	.14
☐ 38 Will Clark	.40	.18
☐ 39 Kenny Lofton	.75	.35
☐ 40 Cal Ripken	2.50	1.10
☐ 41 Steve Avery	.15	.07
☐ 42 Mo Vaughn	.75	.35
☐ 43 Brian McRae	.15	.07
☐ 44 Mickey Tettleton	.15	.07
☐ 45 Barry Larkin	.40	.18
☐ 46 Charlie Hayes	.15	.07
☐ 47 Kevin Appier	.30	.14
☐ 48 Robby Thompson	.15	.07
☐ 49 Juan Gonzalez	1.50	.70
☐ 50 Paul O'Neill	.30	.14
☐ 51 Marcos Armas	.15	.07
☐ 52 Mike Butcher	.15	.07
☐ 53 Ken Caminiti	.60	.25
☐ 54 Pat Borders	.15	.07
☐ 55 Pedro Munoz	.15	.07
☐ 56 Tim Belcher	.15	.07
☐ 57 Paul Assenmacher	.15	.07
☐ 58 Damon Berryhill	.15	.07
☐ 59 Ricky Bones	.15	.07
☐ 60 Rene Arocha	.15	.07
☐ 61 Shawn Boskie	.15	.07
☐ 62 Pedro Astacio	.15	.07
☐ 63 Frank Bolick	.15	.07
☐ 64 Bud Black	.15	.07
☐ 65 Sandy Alomar Jr.	.30	.14
☐ 66 Rich Amaral	.15	.07
☐ 67 Luis Aquino	.15	.07
☐ 68 Kevin Baez	.15	.07
☐ 69 Mike Devereaux	.15	.07
☐ 70 Andy Ashby	.15	.07
☐ 71 Larry Andersen	.15	.07
☐ 72 Steve Cooke	.15	.07
☐ 73 Mario Diaz	.15	.07
☐ 74 Rob Deer	.15	.07
☐ 75 Bobby Ayala	.15	.07
☐ 76 Freddie Benavides	.15	.07
☐ 77 Stan Belinda	.15	.07
☐ 78 John Doherty	.15	.07
☐ 79 Willie Banks	.15	.07
☐ 80 Spike Owen	.15	.07
☐ 81 Mike Bordick	.15	.07
☐ 82 Chili Davis	.30	.14
☐ 83 Luis Gonzalez	.15	.07
☐ 84 Ed Sprague	.15	.07
☐ 85 Jeff Reboulet	.15	.07
☐ 86 Jason Bere	.30	.14
☐ 87 Mark Hutton	.15	.07
☐ 88 Jeff Blauser	.15	.07
☐ 89 Cal Eldred	.15	.07
☐ 90 Bernard Gilkey	.30	.14
☐ 91 Frank Castillo	.15	.07
☐ 92 Jim Gott	.15	.07
☐ 93 Greg Colbrunn	.15	.07
☐ 94 Jeff Brantley	.15	.07
☐ 95 Jeremy Hernandez	.15	.07
☐ 96 Norm Charlton	.15	.07
☐ 97 Alex Arias	.15	.07
☐ 98 John Franco	.15	.07
☐ 99 Chris Hoiles	.15	.07
☐ 100 Brad Ausmus	.15	.07
☐ 101 Wes Chamberlain	.15	.07
☐ 102 Mark Dewey	.15	.07
☐ 103 Benji Gil	.15	.07
☐ 104 John Dopson	.15	.07
☐ 105 John Smiley	.15	.07
☐ 106 David Nied	.15	.07
☐ 107 George Brett	1.25	.55
☐ 108 Kirk Gibson	.30	.14
☐ 109 Larry Casian	.15	.07
☐ 110 Ryne Sandberg CL	.30	.14
☐ 111 Brent Gates	.15	.07
☐ 112 Damion Easley	.15	.07
☐ 113 Pete Harnisch	.15	.07
☐ 114 Danny Cox	.15	.07
☐ 115 Kevin Tapani	.15	.07
☐ 116 Roberto Hernandez	.30	.14
☐ 117 Domingo Jean	.15	.07
☐ 118 Sid Bream	.15	.07
☐ 119 Doug Henry	.15	.07
☐ 120 Omar Olivares	.15	.07
☐ 121 Mike Harkey	.15	.07
☐ 122 Carlos Hernandez	.15	.07
☐ 123 Jeff Fassero	.15	.07
☐ 124 Dave Burba	.15	.07
☐ 125 Wayne Kirby	.15	.07
☐ 126 John Cummings	.15	.07
☐ 127 Bret Barberie	.15	.07
☐ 128 Todd Hundley	.30	.14
☐ 129 Tim Hulett	.15	.07
☐ 130 Phil Clark	.15	.07
☐ 131 Danny Jackson	.15	.07
☐ 132 Tom Foley	.15	.07
☐ 133 Donald Harris	.15	.07
☐ 134 Scott Fletcher	.15	.07
☐ 135 Johnny Ruffin	.15	.07
☐ 136 Jerald Clark	.15	.07
☐ 137 Billy Brewer	.15	.07
☐ 138 Dan Gladden	.15	.07
☐ 139 Eddie Guardado	.15	.07
☐ 140 Cal Ripken CL	.60	.25
☐ 141 Scott Hemond	.15	.07
☐ 142 Steve Frey	.15	.07
☐ 143 Xavier Hernandez	.15	.07
☐ 144 Mark Eichhorn	.15	.07
☐ 145 Ellis Burks	.30	.14
☐ 146 Jim Leyritz	.15	.07
☐ 147 Mark Lemke	.15	.07
☐ 148 Pat Listach	.15	.07
☐ 149 Donovan Osborne	.15	.07
☐ 150 Glenallen Hill	.15	.07
☐ 151 Orel Hershiser	.30	.14
☐ 152 Darrin Fletcher	.15	.07
☐ 153 Royce Clayton	.15	.07
☐ 154 Derek Lilliquist	.15	.07
☐ 155 Mike Felder	.15	.07
☐ 156 Jeff Conine	.30	.14
☐ 157 Ryan Thompson	.15	.07
☐ 158 Ben McDonald	.15	.07
☐ 159 Ricky Gutierrez	.15	.07
☐ 160 Terry Mulholland	.15	.07
☐ 161 Carlos Garcia	.15	.07
☐ 162 Tom Henke	.15	.07
☐ 163 Mike Greenwell	.15	.07
☐ 164 Thomas Howard	.15	.07
☐ 165 Joe Girardi	.15	.07
☐ 166 Hubie Brooks	.15	.07
☐ 167 Greg Gohr	.15	.07
☐ 168 Chip Hale	.15	.07
☐ 169 Rick Honeycutt	.15	.07
☐ 170 Hilly Hathaway	.15	.07
☐ 171 Todd Jones	.15	.07
☐ 172 Tony Fernandez	.15	.07
☐ 173 Bo Jackson	.30	.14
☐ 174 Bobby Munoz	.15	.07
☐ 175 Greg McMichael	.15	.07
☐ 176 Graeme Lloyd	.15	.07
☐ 177 Tom Pagnozzi	.15	.07
☐ 178 Derrick May	.15	.07
☐ 179 Pedro Martinez	.60	.25
☐ 180 Ken Hill	.15	.07
☐ 181 Bryan Hickerson	.15	.07
☐ 182 Jose Mesa	.30	.14
☐ 183 Dave Fleming	.15	.07
☐ 184 Henry Cotto	.15	.07
☐ 185 Jeff Kent	.15	.07
☐ 186 Mark McLemore	.15	.07
☐ 187 Trevor Hoffman	.30	.14

☐ 188 Todd Pratt .15 .07
☐ 189 Blas Minor .15 .07
☐ 190 Charlie Leibrandt .15 .07
☐ 191 Tony Pena .15 .07
☐ 192 Larry Luebbers .15 .07
☐ 193 Greg W. Harris .15 .07
☐ 194 David Cone .30 .14
☐ 195 Bill Gullickson .15 .07
☐ 196 Brian Harper .15 .07
☐ 197 Steve Karsay .15 .07
☐ 198 Greg Myers .15 .07
☐ 199 Mark Portugal .15 .07
☐ 200 Pat Hentgen .30 .14
☐ 201 Mike LaValliere .15 .07
☐ 202 Mike Stanley .15 .07
☐ 203 Kent Mercker .15 .07
☐ 204 Dave Nilsson .30 .14
☐ 205 Erik Pappas .15 .07
☐ 206 Mike Morgan .15 .07
☐ 207 Roger McDowell .15 .07
☐ 208 Mike Lansing .30 .14
☐ 209 Kirt Manwaring .15 .07
☐ 210 Randy Milligan .15 .07
☐ 211 Erik Hanson .15 .07
☐ 212 Orestes Destrade .15 .07
☐ 213 Mike Maddux .15 .07
☐ 214 Alan Mills .15 .07
☐ 215 Tim Mauser .15 .07
☐ 216 Ben Rivera .15 .07
☐ 217 Don Slaught .15 .07
☐ 218 Bob Patterson .15 .07
☐ 219 Carlos Quintana .15 .07
☐ 220 Tim Raines CL .15 .07
☐ 221 Hal Morris .15 .07
☐ 222 Darren Holmes .15 .07
☐ 223 Chris Gwynn .15 .07
☐ 224 Chad Kreuter .15 .07
☐ 225 Mike Hartley .15 .07
☐ 226 Scott Lydy .15 .07
☐ 227 Eduardo Perez .15 .07
☐ 228 Greg Swindell .15 .07
☐ 229 Al Leiter .15 .07
☐ 230 Scott Radinsky .15 .07
☐ 231 Bob Wickman .15 .07
☐ 232 Otis Nixon .30 .14
☐ 233 Kevin Reimer .15 .07
☐ 234 Geronimo Pena .15 .07
☐ 235 Kevin Roberson .15 .07
☐ 236 Jody Reed .15 .07
☐ 237 Kirk Rueter .15 .07
☐ 238 Willie McGee .15 .07
☐ 239 Charles Nagy .30 .14
☐ 240 Tim Leary .15 .07
☐ 241 Carl Everett .15 .07
☐ 242 Charlie O'Brien .15 .07
☐ 243 Mike Pagliarulo .15 .07
☐ 244 Kerry Taylor .15 .07
☐ 245 Kevin Stocker .15 .07
☐ 246 Joel Johnston .15 .07
☐ 247 Geno Petralli .15 .07
☐ 248 Jeff Russell .15 .07
☐ 249 Joe Oliver .15 .07
☐ 250 Roberto Mejia .15 .07
☐ 251 Chris Haney .15 .07
☐ 252 Bill Krueger .15 .07
☐ 253 Shane Mack .15 .07
☐ 254 Terry Steinbach .30 .14
☐ 255 Luis Polonia .15 .07
☐ 256 Eddie Taubensee .15 .07
☐ 257 Dave Stewart .30 .14
☐ 258 Tim Raines .15 .07
☐ 259 Bernie Williams .60 .25
☐ 260 John Smoltz .40 .18
☐ 261 Kevin Seitzer .15 .07
☐ 262 Bob Tewksbury .15 .07
☐ 263 Bob Scanlan .15 .07
☐ 264 Henry Rodriguez .15 .07
☐ 265 Tim Scott .15 .07
☐ 266 Scott Sanderson .15 .07
☐ 267 Eric Plunk .15 .07
☐ 268 Edgar Martinez .40 .18
☐ 269 Charlie Hough .15 .07
☐ 270 Joe Orsulak .15 .07
☐ 271 Harold Reynolds .15 .07
☐ 272 Tim Teufel .15 .07
☐ 273 Bobby Thigpen .15 .07
☐ 274 Randy Tomlin .15 .07
☐ 275 Gary Redus .15 .07
☐ 276 Ken Ryan .15 .07
☐ 277 Tim Pugh .15 .07
☐ 278 J. Owens .15 .07
☐ 279 Phil Hiatt .15 .07
☐ 280 Alan Trammell .40 .18
☐ 281 Dave McCarty .15 .07
☐ 282 Bob Welch .15 .07
☐ 283 J.T. Snow .30 .14
☐ 284 Brian Williams .15 .07
☐ 285 Devon White .15 .07
☐ 286 Steve Sax .15 .07
☐ 287 Tony Tarasco .15 .07
☐ 288 Bill Spiers .15 .07
☐ 289 Allen Watson .15 .07
☐ 290 Rickey Henderson CL .30 .14
☐ 291 Jose Vizcaino .15 .07
☐ 292 Darryl Strawberry .30 .14
☐ 293 John Wetteland .30 .14
☐ 294 Bill Swift .15 .07
☐ 295 Jeff Treadway .15 .07
☐ 296 Tino Martinez .60 .25
☐ 297 Richie Lewis .15 .07
☐ 298 Bret Saberhagen .15 .07
☐ 299 Arthur Rhodes .15 .07
☐ 300 Guillermo Velasquez .15 .07
☐ 301 Milt Thompson .15 .07
☐ 302 Doug Strange .15 .07
☐ 303 Aaron Sele .30 .14
☐ 304 Bip Roberts .15 .07
☐ 305 Bruce Ruffin .15 .07
☐ 306 Jose Lind .15 .07
☐ 307 David Wells .15 .07
☐ 308 Bobby Witt .15 .07
☐ 309 Mark Wohlers .30 .14
☐ 310 B.J. Surhoff .15 .07
☐ 311 Mark Whiten .15 .07
☐ 312 Turk Wendell .15 .07
☐ 313 Raul Mondesi .40 .18
☐ 314 Brian Turang .15 .07
☐ 315 Chris Hammond .15 .07
☐ 316 Tim Bogar .15 .07
☐ 317 Brad Pennington .15 .07
☐ 318 Tim Worrell .15 .07
☐ 319 Mitch Williams .15 .07
☐ 320 Rondell White .40 .18
☐ 321 Frank Viola .15 .07
☐ 322 Manny Ramirez .75 .35
☐ 323 Gary Wayne .15 .07
☐ 324 Mike Macfarlane .15 .07
☐ 325 Russ Springer .15 .07
☐ 326 Tim Wallach .15 .07
☐ 327 Salomon Torres .15 .07
☐ 328 Omar Vizquel .30 .14
☐ 329 Andy Tomberlin .15 .07
☐ 330 Chris Sabo .15 .07
☐ 331 Mike Mussina .60 .25
☐ 332 Andy Benes .30 .14
☐ 333 Darren Daulton .30 .14
☐ 334 Orlando Merced .15 .07
☐ 335 Mark McGwire 1.25 .55
☐ 336 Dave Winfield .40 .18
☐ 337 Sammy Sosa .60 .25
☐ 338 Eric Karros .30 .14
☐ 339 Greg Vaughn .15 .07
☐ 340 Don Mattingly 1.00 .45
☐ 341 Frank Thomas 2.50 1.10
☐ 342 Fred McGriff .40 .18
☐ 343 Kirby Puckett 1.25 .55
☐ 344 Roberto Kelly .15 .07
☐ 345 Wally Joyner .30 .14
☐ 346 Andres Galarraga .40 .18
☐ 347 Bobby Bonilla .30 .14
☐ 348 Benito Santiago .15 .07
☐ 349 Barry Bonds .75 .35
☐ 350 Delino DeShields .15 .07
☐ 351 Albert Belle .75 .35
☐ 352 Randy Johnson .60 .25
☐ 353 Tim Salmon .60 .25
☐ 354 John Olerud .15 .07
☐ 355 Dean Palmer .30 .14
☐ 356 Roger Clemens 1.25 .55
☐ 357 Jim Abbott .15 .07
☐ 358 Mark Grace .40 .18
☐ 359 Ozzie Guillen .15 .07
☐ 360 Lou Whitaker .30 .14
☐ 361 Jose Rijo .15 .07
☐ 362 Jeff Montgomery .30 .14
☐ 363 Chuck Finley .15 .07
☐ 364 Tom Glavine .40 .18
☐ 365 Jeff Bagwell 1.25 .55
☐ 366 Joe Carter .40 .18
☐ 367 Ray Lankford .40 .18
☐ 368 Ramon Martinez .30 .14
☐ 369 Jay Buhner .40 .18
☐ 370 Matt Williams .40 .18
☐ 371 Larry Walker .60 .25
☐ 372 Jose Canseco .40 .18
☐ 373 Lenny Dykstra .30 .14
☐ 374 Bryan Harvey .15 .07
☐ 375 Andy Van Slyke .30 .14
☐ 376 Ivan Rodriguez .75 .35
☐ 377 Kevin Mitchell .15 .07
☐ 378 Travis Fryman .30 .14
☐ 379 Duane Ward .15 .07
☐ 380 Greg Maddux 2.00 .90
☐ 381 Scott Servais .15 .07
☐ 382 Greg Olson .15 .07
☐ 383 Rey Sanchez .15 .07
☐ 384 Tom Kramer .15 .07
☐ 385 David Valle .15 .07
☐ 386 Eddie Murray .60 .25
☐ 387 Kevin Higgins .15 .07
☐ 388 Dan Wilson .30 .14
☐ 389 Todd Frohwith .15 .07
☐ 390 Gerald Williams .15 .07
☐ 391 Hipolito Pichardo .15 .07
☐ 392 Pat Meares .15 .07
☐ 393 Luis Lopez .15 .07
☐ 394 Ricky Jordan .15 .07
☐ 395 Bob Walk .15 .07
☐ 396 Sid Fernandez .15 .07
☐ 397 Todd Worrell .15 .07
☐ 398 Darryl Hamilton .15 .07
☐ 399 Randy Myers .15 .07
☐ 400 Rod Brewer .15 .07
☐ 401 Lance Blankenship .15 .07
☐ 402 Steve Finley .30 .14
☐ 403 Phil Leftwich .15 .07
☐ 404 Juan Guzman .15 .07
☐ 405 Anthony Young .15 .07
☐ 406 Jeff Gardner .15 .07
☐ 407 Ryan Bowen .15 .07
☐ 408 Fernando Valenzuela .30 .14
☐ 409 David West .15 .07
☐ 410 Kenny Rogers .15 .07
☐ 411 Bob Zupcic .15 .07
☐ 412 Eric Young .30 .14
☐ 413 Bret Boone .15 .07
☐ 414 Danny Tartabull .15 .07
☐ 415 Bob MacDonald .15 .07
☐ 416 Ron Karkovice .15 .07
☐ 417 Scott Cooper .15 .07
☐ 418 Dante Bichette .40 .18
☐ 419 Tripp Cromer .15 .07
☐ 420 Billy Ashley .15 .07
☐ 421 Roger Smithberg .15 .07
☐ 422 Dennis Martinez .30 .14
☐ 423 Mike Blowers .15 .07
☐ 424 Darren Lewis .15 .07
☐ 425 Junior Ortiz .15 .07
☐ 426 Butch Huskey .30 .14
☐ 427 Jimmy Poole .15 .07
☐ 428 Walt Weiss .15 .07
☐ 429 Scott Bankhead .15 .07
☐ 430 Deion Sanders .60 .25
☐ 431 Scott Bullett .15 .07
☐ 432 Jeff Huson .15 .07
☐ 433 Tyler Green .15 .07
☐ 434 Billy Hatcher .15 .07
☐ 435 Bob Hamelin .15 .07
☐ 436 Reggie Sanders .30 .14
☐ 437 Scott Erickson .15 .07
☐ 438 Steve Reed .15 .07
☐ 439 Randy Velarde .15 .07
☐ 440 Tony Gwynn CL .60 .25
☐ 441 Terry Leach .15 .07
☐ 442 Danny Bautista .15 .07
☐ 443 Kent Hrbek .30 .14
☐ 444 Rick Wilkins .15 .07
☐ 445 Tony Phillips .15 .07
☐ 446 Dion James .15 .07
☐ 447 Joey Cora .15 .07
☐ 448 Andre Dawson .40 .18
☐ 449 Pedro Castellano .15 .07
☐ 450 Tom Gordon .15 .07
☐ 451 Rob Dibble .15 .07
☐ 452 Ron Darling .15 .07
☐ 453 Chipper Jones 2.00 .90
☐ 454 Joe Grahe .15 .07
☐ 455 Domingo Cedeno .15 .07
☐ 456 Tom Edens .15 .07
☐ 457 Mitch Webster .15 .07
☐ 458 Jose Bautista .15 .07
☐ 459 Troy O'Leary .15 .07
☐ 460 Todd Zeile .15 .07
☐ 461 Sean Berry .15 .07
☐ 462 Brad Holman .15 .07
☐ 463 Dave Martinez .15 .07
☐ 464 Mark Lewis .15 .07
☐ 465 Paul Carey .15 .07
☐ 466 Jack Armstrong .15 .07
☐ 467 David Telgheder .15 .07
☐ 468 Gene Harris .15 .07
☐ 469 Danny Darwin .15 .07
☐ 470 Kim Batiste .15 .07
☐ 471 Tim Wakefield .15 .07
☐ 472 Craig Lefferts .15 .07
☐ 473 Jacob Brumfield .15 .07
☐ 474 Lance Painter .15 .07
☐ 475 Milt Cuyler .15 .07
☐ 476 Melido Perez .15 .07
☐ 477 Derek Parks .15 .07
☐ 478 Gary DiSarcina .15 .07

Card	MINT	NRMT
☐ 479 Steve Bedrosian	.15	.07
☐ 480 Eric Anthony	.15	.07
☐ 481 Julio Franco	.30	.14
☐ 482 Tommy Greene	.15	.07
☐ 483 Pat Kelly	.15	.07
☐ 484 Nate Minchey	.15	.07
☐ 485 William Pennyfeather	.15	.07
☐ 486 Harold Baines	.30	.14
☐ 487 Howard Johnson	.15	.07
☐ 488 Angel Miranda	.15	.07
☐ 489 Scott Sanders	.15	.07
☐ 490 Shawon Dunston	.15	.07
☐ 491 Mel Rojas	.15	.07
☐ 492 Jeff Nelson	.15	.07
☐ 493 Archi Cianfrocco	.15	.07
☐ 494 Al Martin	.15	.07
☐ 495 Mike Gallego	.15	.07
☐ 496 Mike Henneman	.15	.07
☐ 497 Armando Reynoso	.15	.07
☐ 498 Mickey Morandini	.15	.07
☐ 499 Rick Renteria	.15	.07
☐ 500 Rick Sutcliffe	.15	.07
☐ 501 Bobby Jones	.30	.14
☐ 502 Gary Gaetti	.30	.14
☐ 503 Rick Aguilera	.15	.07
☐ 504 Todd Stottlemyre	.15	.07
☐ 505 Mike Mohler	.15	.07
☐ 506 Mike Stanton	.15	.07
☐ 507 Jose Guzman	.15	.07
☐ 508 Kevin Rogers	.15	.07
☐ 509 Chuck Carr	.15	.07
☐ 510 Chris Jones	.15	.07
☐ 511 Brent Mayne	.15	.07
☐ 512 Greg Harris	.15	.07
☐ 513 Dave Henderson	.15	.07
☐ 514 Eric Hillman	.15	.07
☐ 515 Dan Peltier	.15	.07
☐ 516 Craig Shipley	.15	.07
☐ 517 John Valentin	.30	.14
☐ 518 Wilson Alvarez	.30	.14
☐ 519 Andujar Cedeno	.15	.07
☐ 520 Troy Neel	.15	.07
☐ 521 Tom Candiotti	.15	.07
☐ 522 Matt Mieske	.15	.07
☐ 523 Jim Thome	.75	.35
☐ 524 Lou Frazier	.15	.07
☐ 525 Mike Jackson	.15	.07
☐ 526 Pedro Martinez	.60	.25
☐ 527 Roger Pavlik	.15	.07
☐ 528 Kent Bottenfield	.15	.07
☐ 529 Felix Jose	.15	.07
☐ 530 Mark Guthrie	.15	.07
☐ 531 Steve Farr	.15	.07
☐ 532 Craig Paquette	.15	.07
☐ 533 Doug Jones	.15	.07
☐ 534 Luis Alicea	.15	.07
☐ 535 Cory Snyder	.15	.07
☐ 536 Paul Sorrento	.15	.07
☐ 537 Nigel Wilson	.15	.07
☐ 538 Jeff King	.30	.14
☐ 539 Willie Greene	.30	.14
☐ 540 Kirk McCaskill	.15	.07
☐ 541 Al Osuna	.15	.07
☐ 542 Greg Hibbard	.15	.07
☐ 543 Brett Butler	.30	.14
☐ 544 Jose Valentin	.30	.14
☐ 545 Wil Cordero	.15	.07
☐ 546 Chris Bosio	.15	.07
☐ 547 Jamie Moyer	.15	.07
☐ 548 Jim Eisenreich	.30	.14
☐ 549 Vinny Castilla	.40	.18
☐ 550 Dave Winfield CL	.30	.14
☐ 551 John Roper	.15	.07
☐ 552 Lance Johnson	.15	.07
☐ 553 Scott Kamieniecki	.15	.07
☐ 554 Mike Moore	.15	.07
☐ 555 Steve Buechele	.15	.07
☐ 556 Terry Pendleton	.30	.14
☐ 557 Todd Van Poppel	.15	.07
☐ 558 Rob Butler	.15	.07
☐ 559 Zane Smith	.15	.07
☐ 560 David Hulse	.15	.07
☐ 561 Tim Costo	.15	.07
☐ 562 John Habyan	.15	.07
☐ 563 Terry Jorgensen	.15	.07
☐ 564 Matt Nokes	.15	.07
☐ 565 Kevin McReynolds	.15	.07
☐ 566 Phil Plantier	.15	.07
☐ 567 Chris Turner	.15	.07
☐ 568 Carlos Delgado	.40	.18
☐ 569 John Jaha	.15	.07
☐ 570 Dwight Smith	.15	.07
☐ 571 John Vander Wal	.15	.07
☐ 572 Trevor Wilson	.15	.07
☐ 573 Felix Fermin	.15	.07
☐ 574 Marc Newfield	.30	.14
☐ 575 Jeromy Burnitz	.15	.07
☐ 576 Leo Gomez	.15	.07
☐ 577 Curt Schilling	.30	.14
☐ 578 Kevin Young	.15	.07
☐ 579 Jerry Spradlin	.15	.07
☐ 580 Curt Leskanic	.15	.07
☐ 581 Carl Willis	.15	.07
☐ 582 Alex Fernandez	.15	.07
☐ 583 Mark Holzemer	.15	.07
☐ 584 Domingo Martinez	.15	.07
☐ 585 Pete Smith	.15	.07
☐ 586 Brian Jordan	.30	.14
☐ 587 Kevin Gross	.15	.07
☐ 588 J.R. Phillips	.15	.07
☐ 589 Chris Nabholz	.15	.07
☐ 590 Bill Wertz	.15	.07
☐ 591 Derek Bell	.30	.14
☐ 592 Brady Anderson	.40	.18
☐ 593 Matt Turner	.15	.07
☐ 594 Pete Incaviglia	.15	.07
☐ 595 Greg Gagne	.15	.07
☐ 596 John Flaherty	.15	.07
☐ 597 Scott Livingstone	.15	.07
☐ 598 Rod Bolton	.15	.07
☐ 599 Mike Perez	.15	.07
☐ 600 Roger Clemens CL	.60	.25
☐ 601 Tony Castillo	.15	.07
☐ 602 Henry Mercedes	.15	.07
☐ 603 Mike Fetters	.15	.07
☐ 604 Rod Beck	.30	.14
☐ 605 Damon Buford	.15	.07
☐ 606 Matt Whiteside	.15	.07
☐ 607 Shawn Green	.30	.14
☐ 608 Midre Cummings	.15	.07
☐ 609 Jeff McNeely	.15	.07
☐ 610 Danny Sheaffer	.15	.07
☐ 611 Paul Wagner	.15	.07
☐ 612 Torey Lovullo	.15	.07
☐ 613 Javier Lopez	.40	.18
☐ 614 Mariano Duncan	.15	.07
☐ 615 Doug Brocail	.15	.07
☐ 616 Dave Hansen	.15	.07
☐ 617 Ryan Klesko	.40	.18
☐ 618 Eric Davis	.30	.14
☐ 619 Scott Ruffcorn	.15	.07
☐ 620 Mike Trombley	.15	.07
☐ 621 Jaime Navarro	.15	.07
☐ 622 Rheal Cormier	.15	.07
☐ 623 Jose Offerman	.15	.07
☐ 624 David Segui	.15	.07
☐ 625 Robb Nen	.30	.14
☐ 626 Dave Gallagher	.15	.07
☐ 627 Julian Tavarez	.30	.14
☐ 628 Chris Gomez	.15	.07
☐ 629 Jeffrey Hammonds	.30	.14
☐ 630 Scott Brosius	.15	.07
☐ 631 Willie Blair	.15	.07
☐ 632 Doug Drabek	.15	.07
☐ 633 Bill Wegman	.15	.07
☐ 634 Jeff McKnight	.15	.07
☐ 635 Rich Rodriguez	.15	.07
☐ 636 Steve Trachsel	.30	.14
☐ 637 Buddy Groom	.15	.07
☐ 638 Sterling Hitchcock	.30	.14
☐ 639 Chuck McElroy	.15	.07
☐ 640 Rene Gonzales	.15	.07
☐ 641 Dan Plesac	.15	.07
☐ 642 Jeff Branson	.15	.07
☐ 643 Darrell Whitmore	.15	.07
☐ 644 Paul Quantrill	.15	.07
☐ 645 Rich Rowland	.15	.07
☐ 646 Curtis Pride	.30	.14
☐ 647 Erik Plantenberg	.15	.07
☐ 648 Albie Lopez	.30	.14
☐ 649 Rich Batchelor	.15	.07
☐ 650 Lee Smith	.30	.14
☐ 651 Cliff Floyd	.40	.18
☐ 652 Pete Schourek	.15	.07
☐ 653 Reggie Jefferson	.40	.18
☐ 654 Bill Haselman	.15	.07
☐ 655 Steve Hosey	.15	.07
☐ 656 Mark Clark	.15	.07
☐ 657 Mark Davis	.15	.07
☐ 658 Dave Magadan	.15	.07
☐ 659 Candy Maldonado	.15	.07
☐ 660 Mark Langston CL	.15	.07

1994 Donruss Special Edition

Issued in two series of 50 cards, this 100-card standard-size set of 1994 Donruss Special Edition represents a Gold edition parallel of the best players in the game. The first 50 cards correspond to cards 1-50 in the first series, while the second 50 cards correspond to cards 331-380 in the second series. The cards were issued one per pack or two per jumbo pack. The full-bleed fronts display glossy color action photos accented by a holographic embossed foil stripe across the bottom containing the player's name and position.

	MINT	NRMT
COMPLETE SET (100)	20.00	9.00
COMPLETE SERIES 1 (50)	10.00	4.50
COMPLETE SERIES 2 (50)	10.00	4.50
COMMON CARD (1-50/331-380)	.25	.11
*STARS: 1X to 2X BASIC CARDS		

1994 Donruss Anniversary '84

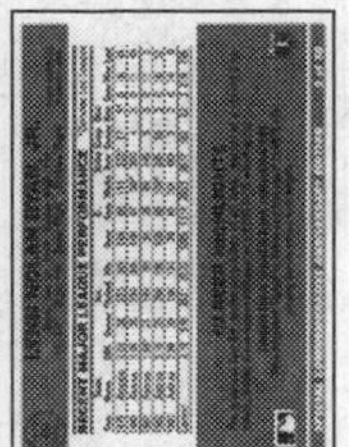

Randomly inserted in hobby foil packs at a rate of one in 12, this ten-card standard-size set reproduces selected cards from the 1984 Donruss baseball set. The cards feature white bordered color player photos on their fronts. The player's name appears in yellow lettering within a colored stripe at the bottom. The player's gold-foil team name is shown within wavy gold-foil lines near the bottom of the photo. The horizontal and white-bordered back carries the player's name and biography within a green-colored stripe across the top. A white area below contains the player's stats and, within a green panel further below, his career highlights. The cards are numbered on the back at the bottom right as "X of 10," and also carry the numbers from the original 1984 set at the upper left.

	MINT	NRMT
COMPLETE SET (10)	50.00	22.00
COMMON CARD (1-10)	2.00	.90
☐ 1 Joe Carter	2.00	.90
☐ 2 Robin Yount	3.00	1.35
☐ 3 George Brett	6.00	2.70
☐ 4 Rickey Henderson	3.00	1.35
☐ 5 Nolan Ryan	15.00	6.75
☐ 6 Cal Ripken	15.00	6.75
☐ 7 Wade Boggs UER 1983 runs 10, should be 100	4.00	1.80
☐ 8 Don Mattingly	10.00	4.50
☐ 9 Ryne Sandberg	5.00	2.20
☐ 10 Tony Gwynn	6.00	2.70

1994 Donruss Award Winner Jumbos

This 10-card set was issued one per jumbo foil and Canadian foil boxes and spotlights players that won various awards in 1993. Cards 1-5 were included in first series boxes and 6-10 with the second series. The cards measure approximately 3 1/2" by 5". Ten-thousand of each card were produced. Card fronts are full-bleed with a color player photo and the Award Winner logo at the top. The backs are individually numbered out of 10,000.

	MINT	NRMT
COMPLETE SET (10)	90.00	40.00
COMPLETE SERIES 1 (5)	50.00	22.00
COMPLETE SERIES 2 (5)	40.00	18.00
COMMON CARD (1-10)	3.00	1.35
☐ 1 Barry Bonds MVP	8.00	3.60
☐ 2 Greg Maddux CY	20.00	9.00
☐ 3 Mike Piazza ROY	20.00	9.00
☐ 4 Barry Bonds HR King	8.00	3.60
☐ 5 Kirby Puckett AS MVP	12.00	5.50
☐ 6 Frank Thomas MVP	30.00	13.50
☐ 7 Jack McDowell CY	3.00	1.35

☐ 8 Tim Salmon ROY	5.00	2.20
☐ 9 Juan Gonzalez HR King	15.00	6.75
☐ 10 Paul Molitor WS MVP	6.00	2.70

1994 Donruss Diamond Kings

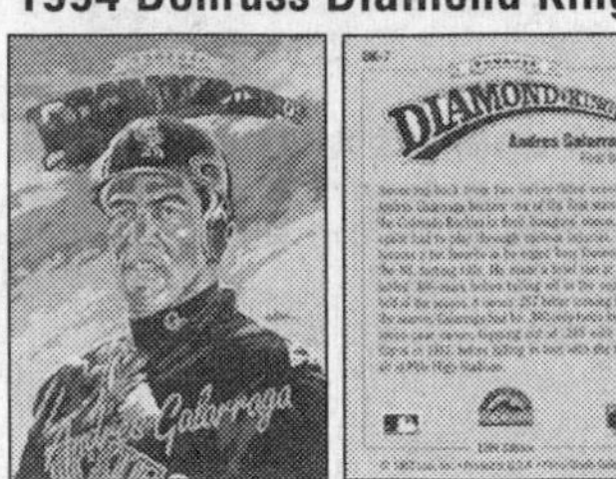

This 30-card standard-size set was split in two series. Cards 1-14 and 29 were randomly inserted in first series packs, while cards 15-28 and 30 were inserted in second series packs. With each series, the insertion rate was one in nine. The fronts feature full-bleed player portraits by noted sports artist Dick Perez. The cards are numbered on the back with the prefix DK. Jumbo versions of these cards were inserted one per retail box.

	MINT	NRMT
COMPLETE SET (30)	50.00	22.00
COMPLETE SERIES 1 (15)	25.00	11.00
COMPLETE SERIES 2 (15)	25.00	11.00
COMMON CARD (1-30)	.50	.23
*JUMBO DK's: 3X TO 6X BASIC CARDS		

☐ DK1 Barry Bonds	2.50	1.10
☐ DK2 Mo Vaughn	2.50	1.10
☐ DK3 Steve Avery	.50	.23
☐ DK4 Tim Salmon	1.50	.70
☐ DK5 Rick Wilkins	.50	.23
☐ DK6 Brian Harper	.50	.23
☐ DK7 Andres Galarraga	1.00	.45
☐ DK8 Albert Belle	4.00	1.80
☐ DK9 John Kruk	.75	.35
☐ DK10 Ivan Rodriguez	2.50	1.10
☐ DK11 Tony Gwynn	4.00	1.80
☐ DK12 Brian McRae	.50	.23
☐ DK13 Bobby Bonilla	.75	.35
☐ DK14 Ken Griffey Jr.	10.00	4.50
☐ DK15 Mike Piazza	6.00	2.70
☐ DK16 Don Mattingly	5.00	2.20
☐ DK17 Barry Larkin	1.00	.45
☐ DK18 Ruben Sierra	.50	.23
☐ DK19 Orlando Merced	.50	.23
☐ DK20 Greg Vaughn	.50	.23
☐ DK21 Gregg Jefferies	.75	.35
☐ DK22 Cecil Fielder	.75	.35
☐ DK23 Moises Alou	.75	.35
☐ DK24 John Olerud	.75	.35
☐ DK25 Gary Sheffield	1.50	.70
☐ DK26 Mike Mussina	1.50	.70
☐ DK27 Jeff Bagwell	4.00	1.80
☐ DK28 Frank Thomas	10.00	4.50
☐ DK29 Dave Winfield	1.00	.45
☐ DK30 Checklist	.50	.23

1994 Donruss Dominators

This 20-card, standard-size set was randomly inserted in all packs at a rate of one in 12. The 10 series 1 cards feature the top home run hitters of the '90s, while the 10 series 2 cards depict the decade's batting average leaders. The fronts displayed full-bleed color action shots with the set title printed along the bottom in gold and black lettering. Jumbo Dominators (3 1/2" by 5") were issued one per hobby box.

	MINT	NRMT
COMPLETE SET (20)	50.00	22.00
COMPLETE SER.1 SET (10)	20.00	9.00
COMPLETE SER.2 SET (10)	30.00	13.50
COMMON SER.1 CARD (A1-A10)	.60	.25
*JUMBOS: 3X TO 6X BASIC CARDS		

☐ A1 Cecil Fielder	.75	.35
☐ A2 Barry Bonds	2.50	1.10
☐ A3 Fred McGriff	1.25	.55
☐ A4 Matt Williams	1.25	.55
☐ A5 Joe Carter	.75	.35
☐ A6 Juan Gonzalez	5.00	2.20
☐ A7 Jose Canseco	1.25	.55
☐ A8 Ron Gant	.60	.25
☐ A9 Ken Griffey Jr.	10.00	4.50
☐ A10 Mark McGwire	3.00	1.35
☐ B1 Tony Gwynn	4.00	1.80
☐ B2 Frank Thomas	10.00	4.50
☐ B3 Paul Molitor	1.50	.70
☐ B4 Edgar Martinez	1.25	.55
☐ B5 Kirby Puckett	4.00	1.80
☐ B6 Ken Griffey Jr.	10.00	4.50
☐ B7 Barry Bonds	2.50	1.10
☐ B8 Willie McGee		
☐ B9 Lenny Dykstra	.75	.35
☐ B10 John Kruk		

1994 Donruss Elite

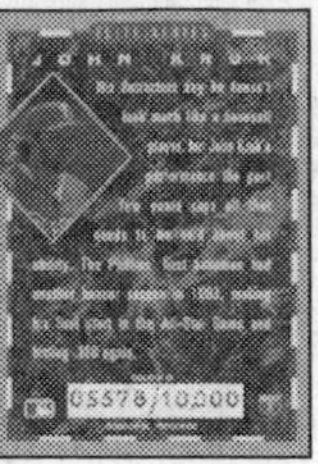

This 12-card set was issued in two series of six. Using a continued numbering system from previous years, cards 37-42 were randomly inserted in first series foil packs with cards 43-48 a second series offering. The cards measure the standard size. Only 10,000 of each card were produced. The color player photo inside a diamond design on the front rests on a marbleized panel framed by a red-and-white inner border and a silver foil outer border. Silver foil stripes radiate away from the edges of the picture. The player's name appears across the bottom of the front. The back design is similar, but with a color head shot in a small diamond and a player profile, both resting on a marbleized panel. The bottom carries the card number, the serial number, and the production run figure.

	MINT	NRMT
COMPLETE SET (12)	200.00	90.00
COMPLETE SERIES 1 (6)	110.00	50.00
COMPLETE SERIES 2 (6)	90.00	40.00
COMMON CARD (37-48)	8.00	3.60

☐ 37 Frank Thomas	40.00	18.00
☐ 38 Tony Gwynn	25.00	11.00
☐ 39 Tim Salmon	12.00	5.50
☐ 40 Albert Belle	12.00	5.50
☐ 41 John Kruk	10.00	4.50
☐ 42 Juan Gonzalez	25.00	11.00
☐ 43 John Olerud	8.00	3.60
☐ 44 Barry Bonds	12.00	5.50
☐ 45 Ken Griffey Jr.	50.00	22.00
☐ 46 Mike Piazza	30.00	13.50
☐ 47 Jack McDowell	8.00	3.60
☐ 48 Andres Galarraga	10.00	4.50

1994 Donruss Long Ball Leaders

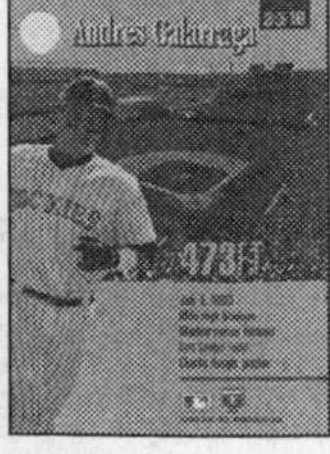

Inserted in second series hobby foil packs at a rate of one in 12, this 10-card standard-size set features some of top home run hitters and the distance of their longest home run of 1993. The card fronts have a color photo with a black right-hand border. Within the border is the Long Ball Leaders logo in silver foil. Also in silver foil at bottom, is the player's last name and the distance of the clout. Card backs contain a photo of the park with which the home run occurred as well as information such as the date, the pitcher and other particulars.

	MINT	NRMT
COMPLETE SET (10)	40.00	18.00
COMMON CARD (1-10)	1.00	.45

☐ 1 Cecil Fielder	1.25	.55
☐ 2 Dean Palmer	1.00	.45
☐ 3 Andres Galarraga	2.50	1.10
☐ 4 Bo Jackson	1.25	.55
☐ 5 Ken Griffey Jr.	15.00	6.75
☐ 6 David Justice	2.50	1.10
☐ 7 Mike Piazza	10.00	4.50
☐ 8 Frank Thomas	15.00	6.75
☐ 9 Barry Bonds	4.00	1.80
☐ 10 Juan Gonzalez	8.00	3.60

1994 Donruss MVPs

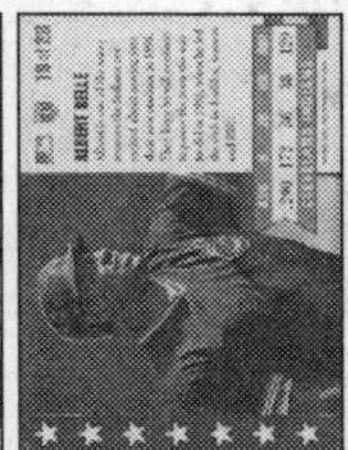

Inserted at a rate of one per first and second series jumbo pack, this 28-card standard-size set was split into two series of 14; one player for each team. The first 14 are of National League players with the latter group being American Leaguers. Full-bleed card fronts feature an action photo of the player with "MVP" in large red (American League) or blue (National) letters at the bottom. The player's name and, for Amercian League player cards only, team name are beneath the "MVP". A number of white stars stretches up the left border. The backs, which are horizontal, contain a photo, 1993 statistics, a short write-up and white stars within blue foil along the left border.

	MINT	NRMT
COMPLETE SET (28)	75.00	34.00
COMPLETE SERIES 1 (14)	15.00	6.75
COMPLETE SERIES 2 (14)	60.00	27.00
COMMON CARD (1-28)	.75	.35

☐ 1 David Justice	2.50	1.10
☐ 2 Mark Grace	1.00	.45
☐ 3 Jose Rijo	.75	.35
☐ 4 Andres Galarraga	1.00	.45
☐ 5 Bryan Harvey	.75	.35
☐ 6 Jeff Bagwell	6.00	2.70
☐ 7 Mike Piazza	10.00	4.50
☐ 8 Moises Alou	1.00	.45
☐ 9 Bobby Bonilla	1.00	.45
☐ 10 Len Dykstra	1.00	.45
☐ 11 Jeff King	.75	.35
☐ 12 Gregg Jefferies	.75	.35
☐ 13 Tony Gwynn	6.00	2.70
☐ 14 Barry Bonds	4.00	1.80
☐ 15 Cal Ripken Jr.	12.00	5.50
☐ 16 Mo Vaughn	4.00	1.80
☐ 17 Tim Salmon	2.50	1.10
☐ 18 Frank Thomas	12.00	5.50
☐ 19 Albert Belle	4.00	1.80
☐ 20 Cecil Fielder	1.00	.45
☐ 21 Wally Joyner	.75	.35
☐ 22 Greg Vaughn	.75	.35
☐ 23 Kirby Puckett	6.00	2.70
☐ 24 Don Mattingly	6.00	2.70
☐ 25 Ruben Sierra	.75	.35
☐ 26 Ken Griffey Jr.	15.00	6.75
☐ 27 Juan Gonzalez	8.00	3.60
☐ 28 John Olerud	.75	.35

1994 Donruss Spirit of the Game

This ten card set features a selction of the games top stars. Cards 1-5 were randomly inserted in first-series magazine jumbo packs and cards 6-10 in second series magazine jumbo packs. Card fronts feature borderless,

orizontal designs that have color action player photos uperposed upon triple exposure sepia-toned action hots. Jumbo sized Spirit of the Game cards, individually umbered out of 10,000, were issued one per magazine umbo box.

	MINT	NRMT
OMPLETE SET (10)	60.00	27.00
OMPLETE SERIES 1 (5)	30.00	13.50
OMPLETE SERIES 2 (5)	30.00	13.50
OMMON CARD (1-10)	1.00	.45
JUMBOS: 1X TO 2X BASIC SPIRIT OF THE GAME		
☐ 1 John Olerud	1.50	.70
☐ 2 Barry Bonds	5.00	2.20
☐ 3 Ken Griffey Jr.	20.00	9.00
☐ 4 Mike Piazza	12.00	5.50
☐ 5 Juan Gonzalez	10.00	4.50
☐ 6 Frank Thomas	20.00	9.00
☐ 7 Tim Salmon	3.00	1.35
☐ 8 David Justice	3.00	1.35
☐ 9 Don Mattingly	10.00	4.50
☐ 10 Lenny Dykstra	1.00	.45

1995 Donruss

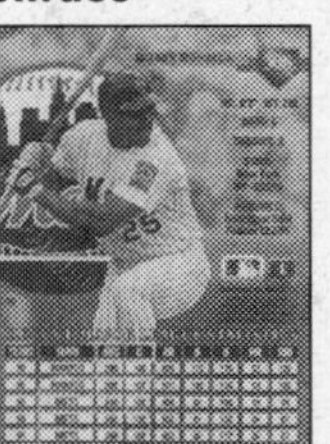

The 1995 Donruss set consists of 550 standard-size cards. The first series had 330 cards while 220 cards comprised the second series. The fronts feature borderless color action player photos. A second, smaller color player photo in a homeplate shape with team color-coded borders appears in the lower left corner. The player's position in silver-foil is above this smaller photo, while his name is printed in a silver-foil bar under the photo. The borderless backs carry a color action player cutout superimposed over the team logo, along with player biography and stats for the last five years. There are no key Rookie Cards in this set.

	MINT	NRMT
COMPLETE SET (550)	40.00	18.00
COMPLETE SERIES 1 (330)	25.00	11.00
COMPLETE SERIES 2 (220)	15.00	6.75
COMMON CARD (1-550)	.15	.07
☐ 1 David Justice	.60	.25
☐ 2 Rene Arocha	.15	.07
☐ 3 Sandy Alomar Jr.	.15	.07
☐ 4 Luis Lopez	.15	.07
☐ 5 Mike Piazza	2.00	.90
☐ 6 Bobby Jones	.30	.14
☐ 7 Damion Easley	.15	.07
☐ 8 Barry Bonds	.75	.35
☐ 9 Mike Mussina	.60	.25
☐ 10 Kevin Seitzer	.15	.07
☐ 11 John Smiley	.15	.07
☐ 12 Wm.VanLandingham	.15	.07
☐ 13 Ron Darling	.15	.07
☐ 14 Walt Weiss	.15	.07
☐ 15 Mike Lansing	.15	.07
☐ 16 Allen Watson	.15	.07
☐ 17 Aaron Sele	.15	.07
☐ 18 Randy Johnson	.40	.18
☐ 19 Dean Palmer	.30	.14
☐ 20 Jeff Bagwell	1.25	.55
☐ 21 Curt Schilling	.15	.07
☐ 22 Darrell Whitmore	.15	.07
☐ 23 Steve Trachsel	.15	.07
☐ 24 Dan Wilson	.30	.14
☐ 25 Steve Finley	.30	.14
☐ 26 Bret Boone	.15	.07
☐ 27 Charles Johnson	.30	.14
☐ 28 Mike Stanton	.15	.07
☐ 29 Ismael Valdes	.30	.14
☐ 30 Salomon Torres	.15	.07
☐ 31 Eric Anthony	.15	.07
☐ 32 Spike Owen	.15	.07
☐ 33 Joey Cora	.30	.14
☐ 34 Robert Eenhoorn	.15	.07
☐ 35 Rick White	.15	.07
☐ 36 Omar Vizquel	.30	.14
☐ 37 Carlos Delgado	.30	.14
☐ 38 Eddie Williams	.15	.07
☐ 39 Shawon Dunston	.15	.07
☐ 40 Darrin Fletcher	.15	.07
☐ 41 Leo Gomez	.15	.07
☐ 42 Juan Gonzalez	1.50	.70
☐ 43 Luis Alicea	.15	.07
☐ 44 Ken Ryan	.15	.07
☐ 45 Lou Whitaker	.30	.14
☐ 46 Mike Blowers	.15	.07
☐ 47 Willie Blair	.15	.07
☐ 48 Todd Van Poppel	.15	.07
☐ 49 Roberto Alomar	.60	.25
☐ 50 Ozzie Smith	.75	.35
☐ 51 Sterling Hitchcock	.30	.14
☐ 52 Mo Vaughn	.75	.35
☐ 53 Rick Aguilera	.15	.07
☐ 54 Kent Mercker	.15	.07
☐ 55 Don Mattingly	1.00	.45
☐ 56 Bob Scanlan	.15	.07
☐ 57 Wilson Alvarez	.30	.14
☐ 58 Jose Mesa	.30	.14
☐ 59 Scott Kamieniecki	.15	.07
☐ 60 Todd Jones	.15	.07
☐ 61 John Kruk	.30	.14
☐ 62 Mike Stanley	.15	.07
☐ 63 Tino Martinez	.60	.25
☐ 64 Eddie Zambrano	.15	.07
☐ 65 Todd Hundley	.30	.14
☐ 66 Jamie Moyer	.15	.07
☐ 67 Rich Amaral	.15	.07
☐ 68 Jose Valentin	.30	.14
☐ 69 Alex Gonzalez	.30	.14
☐ 70 Kurt Abbott	.15	.07
☐ 71 Delino DeShields	.15	.07
☐ 72 Brian Anderson	.15	.07
☐ 73 John Vander Wal	.15	.07
☐ 74 Turner Ward	.15	.07
☐ 75 Tim Raines	.15	.07
☐ 76 Mark Acre	.15	.07
☐ 77 Jose Offerman	.15	.07
☐ 78 Jimmy Key	.30	.14
☐ 79 Mark Whiten	.15	.07
☐ 80 Mark Gubicza	.15	.07
☐ 81 Darren Hall	.15	.07
☐ 82 Travis Fryman	.30	.14
☐ 83 Cal Ripken	2.50	1.10
☐ 84 Geronimo Berroa	.15	.07
☐ 85 Bret Barberie	.15	.07
☐ 86 Andy Ashby	.15	.07
☐ 87 Steve Avery	.15	.07
☐ 88 Rich Becker	.15	.07
☐ 89 John Valentin	.30	.14
☐ 90 Glenallen Hill	.15	.07
☐ 91 Carlos Garcia	.15	.07
☐ 92 Dennis Martinez	.30	.14
☐ 93 Pat Kelly	.15	.07
☐ 94 Orlando Miller	.15	.07
☐ 95 Felix Jose	.15	.07
☐ 96 Mike Kingery	.15	.07
☐ 97 Jeff Kent	.15	.07
☐ 98 Pete Incaviglia	.15	.07
☐ 99 Chad Curtis	.15	.07
☐ 100 Thomas Howard	.15	.07
☐ 101 Hector Carrasco	.15	.07
☐ 102 Tom Pagnozzi	.15	.07
☐ 103 Danny Tartabull	.15	.07
☐ 104 Donnie Elliott	.15	.07
☐ 105 Danny Jackson	.15	.07
☐ 106 Steve Dunn	.15	.07
☐ 107 Roger Salkeld	.15	.07
☐ 108 Jeff King	.30	.14
☐ 109 Cecil Fielder	.30	.14
☐ 110 Paul Molitor CL	.15	.07
☐ 111 Denny Neagle	.30	.14
☐ 112 Troy Neel	.15	.07
☐ 113 Rod Beck	.15	.07
☐ 114 Alex Rodriguez	2.50	1.10
☐ 115 Joey Eischen	.15	.07
☐ 116 Tom Candiotti	.15	.07
☐ 117 Ray McDavid	.15	.07
☐ 118 Vince Coleman	.15	.07
☐ 119 Pete Harnisch	.15	.07
☐ 120 David Nied	.15	.07
☐ 121 Pat Rapp	.15	.07
☐ 122 Sammy Sosa	.60	.25
☐ 123 Steve Reed	.15	.07
☐ 124 Jose Oliva	.15	.07
☐ 125 Ricky Bottalico	.30	.14
☐ 126 Jose DeLeon	.15	.07
☐ 127 Pat Hentgen	.30	.14
☐ 128 Will Clark	.40	.18
☐ 129 Mark Dewey	.15	.07
☐ 130 Greg Vaughn	.15	.07
☐ 131 Darren Dreifort	.15	.07
☐ 132 Ed Sprague	.15	.07
☐ 133 Lee Smith	.30	.14
☐ 134 Charles Nagy	.30	.14
☐ 135 Phil Plantier	.15	.07
☐ 136 Jason Jacome	.15	.07
☐ 137 Jose Lima	.15	.07
☐ 138 J.R. Phillips	.15	.07
☐ 139 J.T. Snow	.30	.14
☐ 140 Michael Huff	.15	.07
☐ 141 Billy Brewer	.15	.07
☐ 142 Jeromy Burnitz	.30	.14
☐ 143 Ricky Bones	.15	.07
☐ 144 Carlos Rodriguez	.15	.07
☐ 145 Luis Gonzalez	.15	.07
☐ 146 Mark Lemke	.15	.07
☐ 147 Al Martin	.30	.14
☐ 148 Mike Bordick	.15	.07
☐ 149 Robb Nen	.15	.07
☐ 150 Wil Cordero	.15	.07
☐ 151 Edgar Martinez	.40	.18
☐ 152 Gerald Williams	.15	.07
☐ 153 Esteban Beltre	.15	.07
☐ 154 Mike Moore	.15	.07
☐ 155 Mark Langston	.15	.07
☐ 156 Mark Clark	.15	.07
☐ 157 Bobby Ayala	.15	.07
☐ 158 Rick Wilkins	.15	.07
☐ 159 Bobby Munoz	.15	.07
☐ 160 Brett Butler CL	.30	.14
☐ 161 Scott Erickson	.15	.07
☐ 162 Paul Molitor	.60	.25
☐ 163 Jon Lieber	.15	.07
☐ 164 Jason Grimsley	.15	.07
☐ 165 Norberto Martin	.15	.07
☐ 166 Javier Lopez	.40	.18
☐ 167 Brian McRae	.15	.07
☐ 168 Gary Sheffield	.60	.25
☐ 169 Marcus Moore	.15	.07
☐ 170 John Hudek	.15	.07
☐ 171 Kelly Stinnett	.15	.07
☐ 172 Chris Gomez	.15	.07
☐ 173 Rey Sanchez	.15	.07
☐ 174 Juan Guzman	.15	.07
☐ 175 Chan Ho Park	.60	.25
☐ 176 Terry Shumpert	.15	.07
☐ 177 Steve Ontiveros	.15	.07
☐ 178 Brad Ausmus	.15	.07
☐ 179 Tim Davis	.15	.07
☐ 180 Billy Ashley	.15	.07
☐ 181 Vinny Castilla	.40	.18
☐ 182 Bill Spiers	.15	.07
☐ 183 Randy Knorr	.15	.07
☐ 184 Brian Hunter	.40	.18
☐ 185 Pat Meares	.15	.07
☐ 186 Steve Buechele	.15	.07
☐ 187 Kirt Manwaring	.15	.07
☐ 188 Tim Naehring	.15	.07
☐ 189 Matt Mieske	.30	.14
☐ 190 Josias Manzanillo	.15	.07
☐ 191 Greg McMichael	.15	.07
☐ 192 Chuck Carr	.15	.07
☐ 193 Midre Cummings	.15	.07
☐ 194 Darryl Strawberry	.30	.14
☐ 195 Greg Gagne	.15	.07
☐ 196 Steve Cooke	.15	.07
☐ 197 Woody Williams	.15	.07
☐ 198 Ron Karkovice	.15	.07
☐ 199 Phil Leftwich	.15	.07
☐ 200 Jim Thome	.60	.25
☐ 201 Brady Anderson	.40	.18
☐ 202 Pedro Martinez	.60	.25
☐ 203 Steve Karsay	.15	.07
☐ 204 Reggie Sanders	.15	.07
☐ 205 Bill Risley	.15	.07
☐ 206 Jay Bell	.30	.14
☐ 207 Kevin Brown	.30	.14
☐ 208 Tim Scott	.15	.07
☐ 209 Lenny Dykstra	.30	.14
☐ 210 Willie Greene	.15	.07
☐ 211 Jim Eisenreich	.30	.14
☐ 212 Cliff Floyd	.30	.14
☐ 213 Otis Nixon	.30	.14
☐ 214 Eduardo Perez	.15	.07
☐ 215 Manuel Lee	.15	.07
☐ 216 Armando Benitez	.15	.07
☐ 217 Dave McCarty	.15	.07
☐ 218 Scott Livingstone	.15	.07

☐ 219	Chad Kreuter	.15	.07
☐ 220	Don Mattingly CL	.60	.25
☐ 221	Brian Jordan	.30	.14
☐ 222	Matt Whiteside	.15	.07
☐ 223	Jim Edmonds	.60	.25
☐ 224	Tony Gwynn	1.50	.70
☐ 225	Jose Lind	.15	.07
☐ 226	Marvin Freeman	.15	.07
☐ 227	Ken Hill	.15	.07
☐ 228	David Hulse	.15	.07
☐ 229	Joe Hesketh	.15	.07
☐ 230	Roberto Petagine	.15	.07
☐ 231	Jeffrey Hammonds	.30	.14
☐ 232	John Jaha	.15	.07
☐ 233	John Burkett	.15	.07
☐ 234	Hal Morris	.15	.07
☐ 235	Tony Castillo	.15	.07
☐ 236	Ryan Bowen	.15	.07
☐ 237	Wayne Kirby	.15	.07
☐ 238	Brent Mayne	.15	.07
☐ 239	Jim Bullinger	.15	.07
☐ 240	Mike Lieberthal	.15	.07
☐ 241	Barry Larkin	.40	.18
☐ 242	David Segui	.15	.07
☐ 243	Jose Bautista	.15	.07
☐ 244	Hector Fajardo	.15	.07
☐ 245	Orel Hershiser	.30	.14
☐ 246	James Mouton	.15	.07
☐ 247	Scott Leius	.15	.07
☐ 248	Tom Glavine	.40	.18
☐ 249	Danny Bautista	.15	.07
☐ 250	Jose Mercedes	.15	.07
☐ 251	Marquis Grissom	.30	.14
☐ 252	Charlie Hayes	.15	.07
☐ 253	Ryan Klesko	.40	.18
☐ 254	Vicente Palacios	.15	.07
☐ 255	Matias Carrillo	.15	.07
☐ 256	Gary DiSarcina	.15	.07
☐ 257	Kirk Gibson	.30	.14
☐ 258	Garey Ingram	.15	.07
☐ 259	Alex Fernandez	.30	.14
☐ 260	John Mabry	.40	.18
☐ 261	Chris Howard	.15	.07
☐ 262	Miguel Jimenez	.15	.07
☐ 263	Heath Slocumb	.15	.07
☐ 264	Albert Belle	.75	.35
☐ 265	Dave Clark	.15	.07
☐ 266	Joe Orsulak	.15	.07
☐ 267	Joey Hamilton	.30	.14
☐ 268	Mark Portugal	.15	.07
☐ 269	Kevin Tapani	.15	.07
☐ 270	Sid Fernandez	.15	.07
☐ 271	Steve Dreyer	.15	.07
☐ 272	Denny Hocking	.15	.07
☐ 273	Troy O'Leary	.15	.07
☐ 274	Milt Cuyler	.15	.07
☐ 275	Frank Thomas	2.50	1.10
☐ 276	Jorge Fabregas	.15	.07
☐ 277	Mike Gallego	.15	.07
☐ 278	Mickey Morandini	.15	.07
☐ 279	Roberto Hernandez	.15	.07
☐ 280	Henry Rodriguez	.15	.07
☐ 281	Garret Anderson	.60	.25
☐ 282	Bob Wickman	.15	.07
☐ 283	Gar Finnvold	.15	.07
☐ 284	Paul O'Neill	.30	.14
☐ 285	Royce Clayton	.15	.07
☐ 286	Chuck Knoblauch	.60	.25
☐ 287	Johnny Ruffin	.15	.07
☐ 288	Dave Nilsson	.30	.14
☐ 289	David Cone	.30	.14
☐ 290	Chuck McElroy	.15	.07
☐ 291	Kevin Stocker	.15	.07
☐ 292	Jose Rijo	.15	.07
☐ 293	Sean Berry	.15	.07
☐ 294	Ozzie Guillen	.15	.07
☐ 295	Chris Hoiles	.15	.07
☐ 296	Kevin Foster	.15	.07
☐ 297	Jeff Frye	.15	.07
☐ 298	Lance Johnson	.30	.14
☐ 299	Mike Kelly	.15	.07
☐ 300	Ellis Burks	.30	.14
☐ 301	Roberto Kelly	.15	.07
☐ 302	Dante Bichette	.40	.18
☐ 303	Alvaro Ezpinoza	.15	.07
☐ 304	Alex Cole	.15	.07
☐ 305	Rickey Henderson	.40	.18
☐ 306	Dave Weathers	.15	.07
☐ 307	Shane Reynolds	.15	.07
☐ 308	Bobby Bonilla	.30	.14
☐ 309	Junior Felix	.15	.07
☐ 310	Jeff Fassero	.15	.07
☐ 311	Darren Lewis	.15	.07
☐ 312	John Doherty	.15	.07
☐ 313	Scott Servais	.15	.07
☐ 314	Rick Helling	.15	.07
☐ 315	Pedro Martinez	.60	.25
☐ 316	Wes Chamberlain	.15	.07
☐ 317	Bryan Eversgerd	.15	.07
☐ 318	Trevor Hoffman	.30	.14
☐ 319	John Patterson	.15	.07
☐ 320	Matt Walbeck	.15	.07
☐ 321	Jeff Montgomery	.30	.14
☐ 322	Mel Rojas	.15	.07
☐ 323	Eddie Taubensee	.15	.07
☐ 324	Ray Lankford	.40	.18
☐ 325	Jose Vizcaino	.15	.07
☐ 326	Carlos Baerga	.30	.14
☐ 327	Jack Voigt	.15	.07
☐ 328	Julio Franco	.30	.14
☐ 329	Brent Gates	.15	.07
☐ 330	Kirby Puckett CL	.60	.25
☐ 331	Greg Maddux	2.00	.90
☐ 332	Jason Bere	.15	.07
☐ 333	Bill Wegman	.15	.07
☐ 334	Tuffy Rhodes	.15	.07
☐ 335	Kevin Young	.15	.07
☐ 336	Andy Benes	.15	.07
☐ 337	Pedro Astacio	.15	.07
☐ 338	Reggie Jefferson	.30	.14
☐ 339	Tim Belcher	.15	.07
☐ 340	Ken Griffey Jr.	3.00	1.35
☐ 341	Mariano Duncan	.15	.07
☐ 342	Andres Galarraga	.40	.18
☐ 343	Rondell White	.40	.18
☐ 344	Cory Bailey	.15	.07
☐ 345	Bryan Harvey	.15	.07
☐ 346	John Franco	.30	.14
☐ 347	Greg Swindell	.15	.07
☐ 348	David West	.15	.07
☐ 349	Fred McGriff	.40	.18
☐ 350	Jose Canseco	.40	.18
☐ 351	Orlando Merced	.15	.07
☐ 352	Rheal Cormier	.15	.07
☐ 353	Carlos Pulido	.15	.07
☐ 354	Terry Steinbach	.30	.14
☐ 355	Wade Boggs	.60	.25
☐ 356	B.J. Surhoff	.30	.14
☐ 357	Rafael Palmeiro	.40	.18
☐ 358	Anthony Young	.15	.07
☐ 359	Tom Brunansky	.15	.07
☐ 360	Todd Stottlemyre	.15	.07
☐ 361	Chris Turner	.15	.07
☐ 362	Joe Boever	.15	.07
☐ 363	Jeff Blauser	.15	.07
☐ 364	Derek Bell	.30	.14
☐ 365	Matt Williams	.40	.18
☐ 366	Jeremy Hernandez	.15	.07
☐ 367	Joe Girardi	.15	.07
☐ 368	Mike Devereaux	.15	.07
☐ 369	Jim Abbott	.15	.07
☐ 370	Manny Ramirez	.60	.25
☐ 371	Kenny Lofton	.75	.35
☐ 372	Mark Smith	.15	.07
☐ 373	Dave Fleming	.15	.07
☐ 374	Dave Stewart	.30	.14
☐ 375	Roger Pavlik	.15	.07
☐ 376	Hipolito Pichardo	.15	.07
☐ 377	Bill Taylor	.15	.07
☐ 378	Robin Ventura	.30	.14
☐ 379	Bernard Gilkey	.30	.14
☐ 380	Kirby Puckett	1.25	.55
☐ 381	Steve Howe	.15	.07
☐ 382	Devon White	.15	.07
☐ 383	Roberto Mejia	.15	.07
☐ 384	Darrin Jackson	.15	.07
☐ 385	Mike Morgan	.15	.07
☐ 386	Rusty Meacham	.15	.07
☐ 387	Bill Swift	.15	.07
☐ 388	Lou Frazier	.15	.07
☐ 389	Andy Van Slyke	.30	.14
☐ 390	Brett Butler	.30	.14
☐ 391	Bobby Witt	.15	.07
☐ 392	Jeff Conine	.30	.14
☐ 393	Tim Hyers	.15	.07
☐ 394	Terry Pendleton	.30	.14
☐ 395	Ricky Jordan	.15	.07
☐ 396	Eric Plunk	.15	.07
☐ 397	Melido Perez	.15	.07
☐ 398	Darryl Kile	.30	.14
☐ 399	Mark McLemore	.15	.07
☐ 400	Greg W.Harris	.15	.07
☐ 401	Jim Leyritz	.15	.07
☐ 402	Doug Strange	.15	.07
☐ 403	Tim Salmon	.60	.25
☐ 404	Terry Mulholland	.15	.07
☐ 405	Robby Thompson	.15	.07
☐ 406	Ruben Sierra	.15	.07
☐ 407	Tony Phillips	.15	.07
☐ 408	Moises Alou	.30	.14
☐ 409	Felix Fermin	.15	.07
☐ 410	Pat Listach	.15	.07
☐ 411	Kevin Bass	.15	.07
☐ 412	Ben McDonald	.15	.07
☐ 413	Scott Cooper	.15	.07
☐ 414	Jody Reed	.15	.07
☐ 415	Deion Sanders	.60	.25
☐ 416	Ricky Gutierrez	.15	.07
☐ 417	Gregg Jefferies	.30	.14
☐ 418	Jack McDowell	.15	.07
☐ 419	Al Leiter	.30	.14
☐ 420	Tony Longmire	.15	.07
☐ 421	Paul Wagner	.15	.07
☐ 422	Geronimo Pena	.15	.07
☐ 423	Ivan Rodriguez	.75	.35
☐ 424	Kevin Gross	.15	.07
☐ 425	Kirk McCaskill	.15	.07
☐ 426	Greg Myers	.15	.07
☐ 427	Roger Clemens	1.25	.55
☐ 428	Chris Hammond	.15	.07
☐ 429	Randy Myers	.15	.07
☐ 430	Roger Mason	.15	.07
☐ 431	Bret Saberhagen	.15	.07
☐ 432	Jeff Reboulet	.15	.07
☐ 433	John Olerud	.30	.14
☐ 434	Bill Gullickson	.15	.07
☐ 435	Eddie Murray	.60	.25
☐ 436	Pedro Munoz	.15	.07
☐ 437	Charlie O'Brien	.15	.07
☐ 438	Jeff Nelson	.15	.07
☐ 439	Mike Macfarlane	.15	.07
☐ 440	Don Mattingly CL	.60	.25
☐ 441	Derrick May	.15	.07
☐ 442	John Roper	.15	.07
☐ 443	Darryl Hamilton	.15	.07
☐ 444	Dan Miceli	.15	.07
☐ 445	Tony Eusebio	.15	.07
☐ 446	Jerry Browne	.15	.07
☐ 447	Wally Joyner	.30	.14
☐ 448	Brian Harper	.15	.07
☐ 449	Scott Fletcher	.15	.07
☐ 450	Bip Roberts	.15	.07
☐ 451	Pete Smith	.15	.07
☐ 452	Chili Davis	.30	.14
☐ 453	Dave Hollins	.15	.07
☐ 454	Tony Pena	.15	.07
☐ 455	Butch Henry	.15	.07
☐ 456	Craig Biggio	.40	.18
☐ 457	Zane Smith	.15	.07
☐ 458	Ryan Thompson	.15	.07
☐ 459	Mike Jackson	.15	.07
☐ 460	Mark McGwire	1.25	.55
☐ 461	John Smoltz	.40	.18
☐ 462	Steve Scarsone	.15	.07
☐ 463	Greg Colbrunn	.15	.07
☐ 464	Shawn Green	.30	.14
☐ 465	David Wells	.15	.07
☐ 466	Jose Hernandez	.15	.07
☐ 467	Chip Hale	.15	.07
☐ 468	Tony Tarasco	.15	.07
☐ 469	Kevin Mitchell	.15	.07
☐ 470	Billy Hatcher	.15	.07
☐ 471	Jay Buhner	.40	.18
☐ 472	Ken Caminiti	.60	.25
☐ 473	Tom Henke	.15	.07
☐ 474	Todd Worrell	.15	.07
☐ 475	Mark Eichhorn	.15	.07
☐ 476	Bruce Ruffin	.15	.07
☐ 477	Chuck Finley	.30	.14
☐ 478	Marc Newfield	.30	.14
☐ 479	Paul Shuey	.15	.07
☐ 480	Bob Tewksbury	.15	.07
☐ 481	Ramon J.Martinez	.30	.14
☐ 482	Melvin Nieves	.30	.14
☐ 483	Todd Zeile	.15	.07
☐ 484	Benito Santiago	.15	.07
☐ 485	Stan Javier	.15	.07
☐ 486	Kirk Rueter	.15	.07
☐ 487	Andre Dawson	.40	.18
☐ 488	Eric Karros	.30	.14
☐ 489	Dave Magadan	.15	.07
☐ 490	Joe Carter CL	.30	.14
☐ 491	Randy Velarde	.15	.07
☐ 492	Larry Walker	.60	.25
☐ 493	Cris Carpenter	.15	.07
☐ 494	Tom Gordon	.15	.07
☐ 495	Dave Burba	.15	.07
☐ 496	Darren Bragg	.30	.14
☐ 497	Darren Daulton	.30	.14
☐ 498	Don Slaught	.15	.07
☐ 499	Pat Borders	.15	.07
☐ 500	Lenny Harris	.15	.07
☐ 501	Joe Ausanio	.15	.07
☐ 502	Alan Trammell	.40	.18
☐ 503	Mike Fetters	.15	.07
☐ 504	Scott Ruffcorn	.15	.07
☐ 505	Rich Rowland	.15	.07
☐ 506	Juan Samuel	.15	.07
☐ 507	Bo Jackson	.30	.14
☐ 508	Jeff Branson	.15	.07
☐ 509	Bernie Williams	.60	.25

Card	MINT	NRMT
☐ 510 Paul Sorrento	.15	.07
☐ 511 Dennis Eckersley	.40	.18
☐ 512 Pat Mahomes	.15	.07
☐ 513 Rusty Greer	.60	.25
☐ 514 Luis Polonia	.15	.07
☐ 515 Willie Banks	.15	.07
☐ 516 John Wetteland	.30	.14
☐ 517 Mike LaValliere	.15	.07
☐ 518 Tommy Greene	.15	.07
☐ 519 Mark Grace	.40	.18
☐ 520 Bob Hamelin	.15	.07
☐ 521 Scott Sanderson	.15	.07
☐ 522 Joe Carter	.40	.18
☐ 523 Jeff Brantley	.15	.07
☐ 524 Andrew Lorraine	.15	.07
☐ 525 Rico Brogna	.15	.07
☐ 526 Shane Mack	.15	.07
☐ 527 Mark Wohlers	.30	.14
☐ 528 Scott Sanders	.15	.07
☐ 529 Chris Bosio	.15	.07
☐ 530 Andujar Cedeno	.15	.07
☐ 531 Kenny Rogers	.15	.07
☐ 532 Doug Drabek	.15	.07
☐ 533 Curt Leskanic	.15	.07
☐ 534 Craig Shipley	.15	.07
☐ 535 Craig Grebeck	.15	.07
☐ 536 Cal Eldred	.15	.07
☐ 537 Mickey Tettleton	.15	.07
☐ 538 Harold Baines	.30	.14
☐ 539 Tim Wallach	.15	.07
☐ 540 Damon Buford	.15	.07
☐ 541 Lenny Webster	.15	.07
☐ 542 Kevin Appier	.30	.14
☐ 543 Raul Mondesi	.40	.18
☐ 544 Eric Young	.30	.14
☐ 545 Russ Davis	.15	.07
☐ 546 Mike Benjamin	.15	.07
☐ 547 Mike Greenwell	.15	.07
☐ 548 Scott Brosius	.15	.07
☐ 549 Brian Dorsett	.15	.07
☐ 550 Chili Davis CL	.30	.14

1995 Donruss Press Proofs

Parallel to the basic Donruss set, the Press Proofs are distinguished by the player's name, team name and Donruss logo being done in gold foil on front. The words "Press Proof are also in gold at the top. The first 2,000 cards of the production run were stamped as such and inserted at a rate of one in every 20 first and second series packs.

	MINT	NRMT
COMPLETE SET (550)	1500.00	700.00
COMPLETE SERIES 1 (330)	1000.00	450.00
COMPLETE SERIES 2 (220)	600.00	275.00
COMMON CARD (1-550)	2.50	1.10

*STARS: 12.5X TO 25X BASIC CARDS
*YOUNG STARS: 10X TO 20X BASIC CARDS

1995 Donruss All-Stars

This 18-card standard-size set was randomly inserted into retail packs. The first series has the nine 1994 American League starters while the second series honored the National League starters. The fronts feature the playerís photo against a background of his league's all-star logo. The player and his team are identified on the bottom. His team is noted in the upper left corner. All of this is on a borderless card with a gray background. The horizontal backs have a player photo, a quick blurb about his starting role in the game and his performance in the 1994 All-Star game. The cards are numbered in the upper right with either an "AL-X" or an "NL-X."

	MINT	NRMT
COMPLETE SET (18)	150.00	70.00
COMPLETE SERIES 1 (9)	100.00	45.00
COMPLETE SERIES 2 (9)	50.00	22.00
COMMON CARD (AL1-AL9)	2.00	.90
COMMON CARD (NL1-NL9)	2.00	.90

Card	MINT	NRMT
☐ AL1 Jimmy Key	2.00	.90
☐ AL2 Ivan Rodriguez	7.50	3.40
☐ AL3 Frank Thomas	25.00	11.00
☐ AL4 Roberto Alomar	5.00	2.20
☐ AL5 Wade Boggs	5.00	2.20
☐ AL6 Cal Ripken	25.00	11.00
☐ AL7 Joe Carter	4.00	1.80
☐ AL8 Ken Griffey Jr.	30.00	13.50
☐ AL9 Kirby Puckett	12.50	5.50
☐ NL1 Greg Maddux	20.00	9.00
☐ NL2 Mike Piazza	20.00	9.00
☐ NL3 Gregg Jefferies	3.00	1.35
☐ NL4 Mariano Duncan	2.00	.90
☐ NL5 Matt Williams	4.00	1.80
☐ NL6 Ozzie Smith	7.50	3.40
☐ NL7 Barry Bonds	7.50	3.40
☐ NL8 Tony Gwynn	15.00	6.75
☐ NL9 David Justice	5.00	2.20

1995 Donruss Bomb Squad

Randomly inserted one in every 24 retail packs and one in every 16 magazine packs, this set features the top six home run hitters in the National and American League. These cards were only included in first series packs. Each of the six cards shows a different slugger on the either side of the card. Both the fronts and backs are horizontal and feature the player photo with a bomber as background. There are foil bombs to the left indicating how many homers the player hit in 1994. A dog tag indicates the player's position and rank among home run leaders in his league.

	MINT	NRMT
COMPLETE SET (6)	25.00	11.00
COMMON CARD (1-6)	1.50	.70

Card	MINT	NRMT
☐ 1 Ken Griffey Matt Williams	8.00	3.60
☐ 2 Frank Thomas Jeff Bagwell	8.00	3.60
☐ 3 Albert Belle Barry Bonds	2.50	1.10
☐ 4 Jose Canseco Fred McGriff	2.00	.90
☐ 5 Cecil Fielder Andres Galarraga	1.50	.70
☐ 6 Joe Carter Kevin Mitchell	2.00	.90

1995 Donruss Diamond Kings

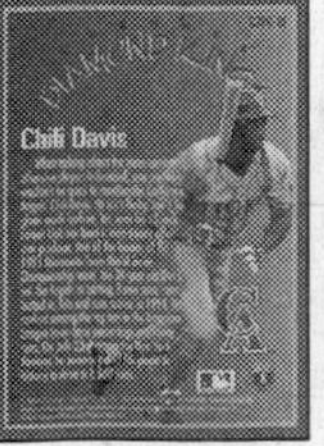

The 1995 Donruss Diamond King set consists of 29 standard-size cards that were randomly inserted in packs. The fronts feature water color player portraits by noted sports artist Dick Perez. The player's name and "Diamond Kings" are in gold foil. The backs have a dark blue border with a player photo and text. The cards are numbered on back with a DK prefix.

	MINT	NRMT
COMPLETE SET (29)	50.00	22.00
COMPLETE SERIES 1 (14)	20.00	9.00
COMPLETE SERIES 2 (15)	30.00	13.50
COMMON CARD (DK1-DK29)	1.00	.45

Card	MINT	NRMT
☐ DK1 Frank Thomas	12.00	5.50
☐ DK2 Jeff Bagwell	5.00	2.20
☐ DK3 Chili Davis	1.50	.70
☐ DK4 Dante Bichette	2.00	.90
☐ DK5 Ruben Sierra	1.00	.45
☐ DK6 Jeff Conine	1.50	.70
☐ DK7 Paul O'Neill	1.50	.70
☐ DK8 Bobby Bonilla	1.50	.70
☐ DK9 Joe Carter	2.00	.90
☐ DK10 Moises Alou	1.50	.70
☐ DK11 Kenny Lofton	3.00	1.35
☐ DK12 Matt Williams	2.00	.90
☐ DK13 Kevin Seitzer	1.00	.45
☐ DK14 Sammy Sosa	2.50	1.10
☐ DK15 Scott Cooper	1.00	.45
☐ DK16 Raul Mondesi	2.00	.90
☐ DK17 Will Clark	2.00	.90
☐ DK18 Lenny Dykstra	1.50	.70
☐ DK19 Kirby Puckett	5.00	2.20
☐ DK20 Hal Morris	1.00	.45
☐ DK21 Travis Fryman	1.50	.70
☐ DK22 Greg Maddux	8.00	3.60
☐ DK23 Rafael Palmeiro	2.00	.90
☐ DK24 Tony Gwynn	5.00	2.20
☐ DK25 David Cone	1.50	.70
☐ DK26 Al Martin	1.00	.45
☐ DK27 Ken Griffey Jr.	12.00	5.50
☐ DK28 Gregg Jefferies	1.50	.70
☐ DK29 Checklist	1.00	.45

1995 Donruss Dominators

This nine-card standard-size set was randomly inserted in second series hobby packs. Each of these cards features three of the leading players at each position. The horizontal fronts have photos of all three players and identify only their last name. The words "remove protective film" cover a significant portion of the fronts as well. The backs have small action photos of the three players along with their 1994 stats. The cards are numbered in the upper right corner as "X" of 9.

	MINT	NRMT
COMPLETE SET (9)	30.00	13.50
COMMON CARD (1-9)	1.00	.45

Card	MINT	NRMT
☐ 1 David Cone Mike Mussina Greg Maddux	5.00	2.20
☐ 2 Ivan Rodriguez Mike Piazza Darren Daulton	4.00	1.80
☐ 3 Fred McGriff Frank Thomas Jeff Bagwell	8.00	3.60
☐ 4 Roberto Alomar Carlos Baerga Craig Biggio	1.00	.45
☐ 5 Robin Ventura Travis Fryman Matt Williams	1.00	.45
☐ 6 Cal Ripken Barry Larkin Wil Cordero	6.00	2.70
☐ 7 Albert Belle Barry Bonds Moises Alou	1.50	.70
☐ 8 Ken Griffey Kenny Lofton Marquis Grissom	8.00	3.60
☐ 9 Kirby Puckett Paul O'Neill Tony Gwynn	3.00	1.35

1995 Donruss Elite

Randomly inserted one in every 210 Series 1 and 2 packs, this set consists of 12 standard-size cards that are numbered (49-60) based on where the previous year's set left off. The fronts contain an action photo surrounded by a marble border. Silver holographic foil borders the card on all four sides. Limited to 10,000, the backs are individually numbered, contain a small photo and write-up.

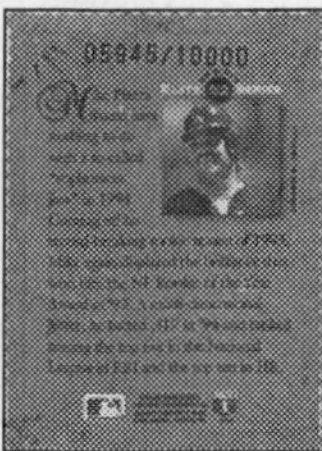

	MINT	NRMT
COMPLETE SET (12)	275.00	125.00
COMPLETE SERIES 1 (6)	150.00	70.00
COMPLETE SERIES 2 (6)	125.00	55.00
COMMON CARD (49-60)	6.00	2.70
☐ 49 Jeff Bagwell	25.00	11.00
☐ 50 Paul O'Neill	6.00	2.70
☐ 51 Greg Maddux	40.00	18.00
☐ 52 Mike Piazza	40.00	18.00
☐ 53 Matt Williams	8.00	3.60
☐ 54 Ken Griffey	60.00	27.00
☐ 55 Frank Thomas	50.00	22.00
☐ 56 Barry Bonds	15.00	6.75
☐ 57 Kirby Puckett	25.00	11.00
☐ 58 Fred McGriff	8.00	3.60
☐ 59 Jose Canseco	8.00	3.60
☐ 60 Albert Belle	15.00	6.75

1995 Donruss Long Ball Leaders

Inserted one in every 24 series one hobby packs, this set features eight top home run hitters. Metallic fronts have much ornamentation including a player photo, the length of the player's home run, the stadium and the date. Horizontal backs have a player photo and photo of the stadium with which the home run occurred. The back also includes all the particulars concerning the home run.

	MINT	NRMT
COMPLETE SET (8)	20.00	9.00
COMMON CARD (1-8)	1.00	.45
☐ 1 Frank Thomas	8.00	3.60
☐ 2 Fred McGriff	1.50	.70
☐ 3 Ken Griffey	8.00	3.60
☐ 4 Matt Williams	1.50	.70
☐ 5 Mike Piazza	5.00	2.20
☐ 6 Jose Canseco	1.00	.45
☐ 7 Barry Bonds	2.00	.90
☐ 8 Jeff Bagwell	3.00	1.35

1995 Donruss Mound Marvels

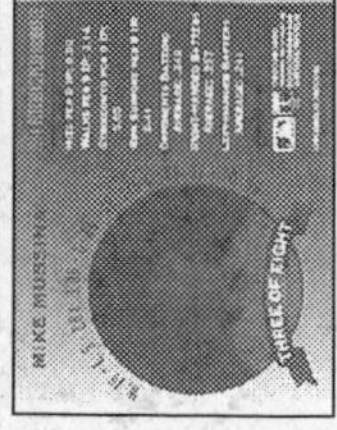

This eight-card standard-size set was randomly inserted into second series magazine jumbo and retail packs at a rate of one every 16 packs. This set features eight of the leading major league starters. The horizontal fronts feature the player's photo on the left with the words "Donruss Mound Marvels" and the player's name on the right. The back features the player's photo within a circular inset along with all his 1994 stats.

	MINT	NRMT
COMPLETE SET (8)	20.00	9.00
COMMON CARD (1-8)	1.00	.45
☐ 1 Greg Maddux	10.00	4.50
☐ 2 David Cone	1.50	.70
☐ 3 Mike Mussina	3.00	1.35
☐ 4 Bret Saberhagen	1.00	.45
☐ 5 Jimmy Key	1.00	.45
☐ 6 Doug Drabek	1.00	.45
☐ 7 Randy Johnson	3.00	1.35
☐ 8 Jason Bere	1.00	.45

1995 Donruss Top of the Order

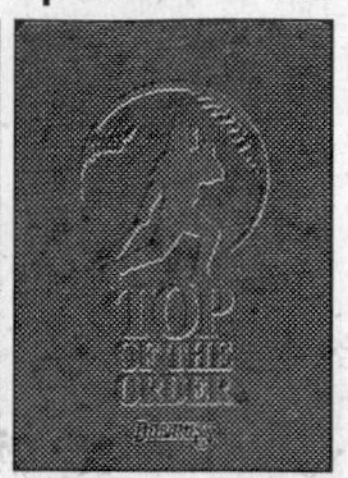

This 360-card standard-size set was distributed as a Major League Baseball Card Game. The cards were packaged in 80-card starter decks with other cards available in booster packs. The fronts carry player action photos with the player's name, team, position, and other player information needed to play the game. The green backs carry the card logo. The first 180 cards feature players in the American League with the National League represented by the second 180 cards. The cards are unnumbered and checklisted below in alphabetical order within each team. There are three levels of scarcity for these cards; common, uncommon and rare. All cards have been given either a designation of C (for common), U (for uncommon) or R (for rare).

	MINT	NRMT
COMPLETE SET (360)	600.00	275.00
COMMON CARD (1-360)	.10	.05
UNCOMMON CARD (1-360)	.50	.23
RARE CARD (1-360)	3.00	1.35
☐ 1 Brady Anderson C	.40	.18
☐ 2 Harold Baines U	1.00	.45
☐ 3 Bret Barberie U	.50	.23
☐ 4 Armando Benitez C	.10	.05
☐ 5 Bobby Bonilla U	1.00	.45
☐ 6 Scott Erickson C	.10	.05
☐ 7 Leo Gomez C	.10	.05
☐ 8 Curtis Goodwin R	3.00	1.35
☐ 9 Jeffrey Hammonds C	.10	.05
☐ 10 Chris Hoiles C	.10	.05
☐ 11 Doug Jones C	.10	.05
☐ 12 Ben McDonald U	.50	.23
☐ 13 Mike Mussina U	3.00	1.35
☐ 14 Rafael Palmeiro R	5.00	2.20
☐ 15 Cal Ripken Jr. R	25.00	11.00
☐ 16 Rick Aguilera C	.10	.05
☐ 17 Luis Alicea C	.10	.05
☐ 18 Jose Canseco U	2.00	.90
☐ 19 Roger Clemens C	.50	.23
☐ 20 Mike Greenwell U	.50	.23
☐ 21 Erik Hanson C	.10	.05
☐ 22 Mike Macfarlane C	.10	.05
☐ 23 Tim Naehring R	3.00	1.35
☐ 24 Troy O'Leary U	.50	.23
☐ 25 Ken Ryan C	.10	.05
☐ 26 Aaron Sele C	.10	.05
☐ 27 Lee Tinsley U	.50	.23
☐ 28 John Valentin R	4.00	1.80
☐ 29 Mo Vaughn R	7.50	3.40
☐ 30 Jim Abbott C	.10	.05
☐ 31 Mike Butcher C	.10	.05
☐ 32 Chili Davis R	4.00	1.80
☐ 33 Gary DiSarcina R	3.00	1.35
☐ 34 Damion Easley C	.10	.05
☐ 35 Jim Edmonds R	5.00	2.20
☐ 36 Chuck Finley U	1.00	.45
☐ 37 Mark Langston C	.25	.11
☐ 38 Greg Myers C	.10	.05
☐ 39 Spike Owen C	.10	.05
☐ 40 Troy Percival R	3.00	1.35
☐ 41 Tony Phillips U	1.00	.45
☐ 42 Tim Salmon R	6.00	2.70
☐ 43 Lee Smith R	4.00	1.80
☐ 44 J.T. Snow U	.50	.23
☐ 45 Jason Bere C	.10	.05
☐ 46 Mike Devereaux U	.50	.23
☐ 47 Ray Durham C	.50	.23
☐ 48 Alex Fernandez C	.25	.11
☐ 49 Ozzie Guillen R	3.00	1.35
☐ 50 Roberto Hernandez C	.10	.05
☐ 51 Lance Johnson U	.50	.23
☐ 52 Ron Karkovice C	.10	.05
☐ 53 Tim Raines U	1.00	.45
☐ 54 Frank Thomas R	30.00	13.50
☐ 55 Robin Ventura U	1.00	.45
☐ 56 Sandy Alomar R	4.00	1.80
☐ 57 Carlos Baerga R	5.00	2.20
☐ 58 Albert Belle R	15.00	6.75
☐ 59 Kenny Lofton R	8.00	3.60
☐ 60 Dennis Martinez C	.25	.11
☐ 61 Jose Mesa U	1.00	.45
☐ 62 Eddie Murray R	7.50	3.40
☐ 63 Charles Nagy C	.25	.11
☐ 64 Tony Pena C	.10	.05
☐ 65 Eric Plunk R	3.00	1.35
☐ 66 Manny Ramirez R	8.00	3.60
☐ 67 Paul Sorrento C	.10	.05
☐ 68 Jim Thome R	6.00	2.70
☐ 69 Omar Vizquel C	.25	.11
☐ 70 Danny Bautista C	.10	.05
☐ 71 Joe Boever C	.10	.05
☐ 72 Chad Curtis C	.10	.05
☐ 73 Cecil Fielder U	1.50	.70
☐ 74 John Flaherty U	.50	.23
☐ 75 Travis Fryman U	1.00	.45
☐ 76 Kirk Gibson C	.25	.11
☐ 77 Chris Gomez C	.10	.05
☐ 78 Mike Henneman R	3.00	1.35
☐ 79 Bob Higginson C	.75	.35
☐ 80 Alan Trammell U	1.50	.70
☐ 81 Lou Whitaker R	4.00	1.80
☐ 82 Kevin Appier R	4.00	1.80
☐ 83 Billy Brewer C	.10	.05
☐ 84 Vince Coleman R	3.00	1.35
☐ 85 Gary Gaetti C	.10	.05
☐ 86 Greg Gagne C	.10	.05
☐ 87 Tom Goodwin R	3.00	1.35
☐ 88 Tom Gordon C	.10	.05
☐ 89 Mark Gubicza C	.10	.05
☐ 90 Bob Hamelin C	.10	.05
☐ 91 Phil Hiatt C	.10	.05
☐ 92 Wally Joyner R	4.00	1.80
☐ 93 Brent Mayne C	.10	.05
☐ 94 Jeff Montgomery C	.10	.05
☐ 95 Ricky Bones C	.10	.05
☐ 96 Mike Fetters C	.10	.05
☐ 97 Darryl Hamilton C	.10	.05
☐ 98 Pat Listach C	.10	.05
☐ 99 Matt Mieske C	.10	.05
☐ 100 Dave Nilsson C	.10	.05
☐ 101 Joe Oliver U	.50	.23
☐ 102 Kevin Seitzer U	.50	.23
☐ 103 B.J. Surhoff U	.50	.23
☐ 104 Jose Valentin C	.10	.05
☐ 105 Greg Vaughn C	.25	.11
☐ 106 Bill Wegman C	.10	.05
☐ 107 Alex Cole U	.50	.23
☐ 108 Marty Cordova C	.50	.23
☐ 109 Chuck Knoblauch R	5.00	2.20
☐ 110 Scott Leius C	.10	.05
☐ 111 Pat Meares C	.10	.05
☐ 112 Pedro Munoz C	.10	.05
☐ 113 Kirby Puckett R	12.00	5.50
☐ 114 Scott Stahoviak C	.10	.05
☐ 115 Mike Trombley C	.10	.05
☐ 116 Matt Walbeck C	.10	.05
☐ 117 Wade Boggs R	5.00	2.20
☐ 118 David Cone U	1.00	.45
☐ 119 Tony Fernandez C	.10	.05
☐ 120 Don Mattingly R	15.00	6.75
☐ 121 Jack McDowell C	.25	.11
☐ 122 Paul O'Neill U	1.00	.45
☐ 123 Melido Perez C	.10	.05
☐ 124 Luis Polonia C	.10	.05
☐ 125 Ruben Sierra C	.25	.11
☐ 126 Mike Stanley C	.10	.05
☐ 127 Randy Velarde C	.10	.05
☐ 128 John Wetteland R	4.00	1.80
☐ 129 Bob Wickman C	.10	.05
☐ 130 Bernie Williams C	.40	.18
☐ 131 Gerald Williams C	.10	.05
☐ 132 Geronimo Berroa C	.25	.11
☐ 133 Mike Bordick U	.50	.23
☐ 134 Scott Brosius C	.10	.05
☐ 135 Dennis Eckersley C	.25	.11
☐ 136 Brent Gates C	.10	.05
☐ 137 Rickey Henderson U	2.00	.90
☐ 138 Stan Javier C	.10	.05
☐ 139 Mark McGwire R	10.00	4.50
☐ 140 Steve Ontiveros U	.50	.23
☐ 141 Terry Steinbach C	.25	.11
☐ 142 Todd Stottlemyre R	3.00	1.35
☐ 143 Danny Tartabull C	.25	.11
☐ 144 Bobby Ayala R	3.00	1.35

Card	MINT	NRMT
☐ 145 Andy Benes U	1.00	.45
☐ 146 Mike Blowers C	.10	.05
☐ 147 Jay Buhner U	2.00	.90
☐ 148 Joey Cora U	.50	.23
☐ 149 Alex Diaz C	.10	.05
☐ 150 Ken Griffey Jr. R	30.00	13.50
☐ 151 Randy Johnson R	6.00	2.70
☐ 152 Edgar Martinez R	5.00	2.20
☐ 153 Tino Martinez U	1.00	.45
☐ 154 Bill Risley R	3.00	1.35
☐ 155 Alex Rodriguez C	3.00	1.35
☐ 156 Dan Wilson C	.25	.11
☐ 157 Will Clark R	5.00	2.20
☐ 158 Jeff Frye U	.50	.23
☐ 159 Benji Gil C	.10	.05
☐ 160 Juan Gonzalez C	1.50	.70
☐ 161 Rusty Greer C	.40	.18
☐ 162 Mark McLemore R	3.00	1.35
☐ 163 Otis Nixon U	.50	.23
☐ 164 Dean Palmer R	4.00	1.80
☐ 165 Ivan Rodriguez R	7.50	3.40
☐ 166 Kenny Rogers C	.10	.05
☐ 167 Jeff Russell C	.10	.05
☐ 168 Mickey Tettleton C	.10	.05
☐ 169 Bob Tewksbury C	.10	.05
☐ 170 Bobby Witt C	.10	.05
☐ 171 Roberto Alomar R	8.00	3.60
☐ 172 Joe Carter R	5.00	2.20
☐ 173 Alex Gonzalez C	.25	.11
☐ 174 Candy Maldonado C	.10	.05
☐ 175 Paul Molitor C	.60	.25
☐ 176 John Olerud C	.10	.05
☐ 177 Lance Parrish C	.25	.11
☐ 178 Ed Sprague C	.10	.05
☐ 179 Devon White C	.25	.11
☐ 180 Woody Williams C	.10	.05
☐ 181 Steve Avery C	.25	.11
☐ 182 Jeff Blauser C	.10	.05
☐ 183 Tom Glavine U	2.00	.90
☐ 184 Marquis Grissom R	5.00	2.20
☐ 185 Chipper Jones C	2.00	.90
☐ 186 David Justice R	5.00	2.20
☐ 187 Ryan Klesko U	3.00	1.35
☐ 188 Mark Lemke C	.10	.05
☐ 189 Javy Lopez C	.40	.18
☐ 190 Greg Maddux R	20.00	9.00
☐ 191 Fred McGriff R	5.00	2.20
☐ 192 Greg McMichael U	.50	.23
☐ 193 John Smoltz R	6.00	2.70
☐ 194 Mark Wohlers R	4.00	1.80
☐ 195 Jim Bullinger U	.50	.23
☐ 196 Shawon Dunston R	3.00	1.35
☐ 197 Kevin Foster C	.10	.05
☐ 198 Luis Gonzalez C	.10	.05
☐ 199 Mark Grace R	5.00	2.20
☐ 200 Brian McRae R	4.00	1.80
☐ 201 Randy Myers R	3.00	1.35
☐ 202 Jaime Navarro U	.50	.23
☐ 203 Rey Sanchez U	.50	.23
☐ 204 Scott Servais C	.10	.05
☐ 205 Sammy Sosa R	6.00	2.70
☐ 206 Steve Trachsel U	.50	.23
☐ 207 Todd Zeile C	.10	.05
☐ 208 Bret Boone R	3.00	1.35
☐ 209 Jeff Branson U	.50	.23
☐ 210 Jeff Brantley R	3.00	1.35
☐ 211 Hector Carrasco C	.10	.05
☐ 212 Ron Gant R	4.00	1.80
☐ 213 Lenny Harris C	.10	.05
☐ 214 Barry Larkin R	5.00	2.20
☐ 215 Darren Lewis C	.10	.05
☐ 216 Hal Morris C	.10	.05
☐ 217 Mark Portugal C	.10	.05
☐ 218 Jose Rijo U	.50	.23
☐ 219 Reggie Sanders R	4.00	1.80
☐ 220 Pete Schourek U	.50	.23
☐ 221 John Smiley C	.10	.05
☐ 222 Eddie Taubensee C	.10	.05
☐ 223 David Wells C	.10	.05
☐ 224 Jason Bates C	.10	.05
☐ 225 Dante Bichette R	5.00	2.20
☐ 226 Vinny Castilla U	1.00	.45
☐ 227 Andres Galarraga R	5.00	2.20
☐ 228 Joe Girardi U	.50	.23
☐ 229 Mike Kingery C	.10	.05
☐ 230 Steve Reed R	3.00	1.35
☐ 231 Bruce Ruffin U	.50	.23
☐ 232 Bret Saberhagen U	1.00	.45
☐ 233 Bill Swift C	.10	.05
☐ 234 Larry Walker R	4.00	1.80
☐ 235 Walt Weiss C	.10	.05
☐ 236 Eric Young C	.25	.11
☐ 237 Kurt Abbott C	.10	.05
☐ 238 John Burkett C	.10	.05
☐ 239 Chuck Carr C	.10	.05
☐ 240 Greg Colbrunn C	.10	.05
☐ 241 Jeff Conine R	4.00	1.80
☐ 242 Andre Dawson C	.25	.11
☐ 243 Chris Hammond R	3.00	1.35
☐ 244 Charles Johnson C	.25	.11
☐ 245 Robb Nen C	.25	.11
☐ 246 Terry Pendleton U	1.00	.45
☐ 247 Gary Sheffield R	5.00	2.20
☐ 248 Quilvio Veras C	.10	.05
☐ 249 Jeff Bagwell U	6.00	2.70
☐ 250 Derek Bell R	4.00	1.80
☐ 251 Craig Biggio U	1.00	.45
☐ 252 Doug Drabek C	.10	.05
☐ 253 Tony Eusebio U	.50	.23
☐ 254 John Hudek C	.10	.05
☐ 255 Brian Hunter U	2.00	.90
☐ 256 Todd Jones R	3.00	1.35
☐ 257 Dave Magadan U	.50	.23
☐ 258 Orlando Miller C	.10	.05
☐ 259 James Mouton C	.10	.05
☐ 260 Shane Reynolds C	.25	.11
☐ 261 Greg Swindell C	.10	.05
☐ 262 Billy Ashley C	.10	.05
☐ 263 Tom Candiotti U	.50	.23
☐ 264 Delino DeShields C	.10	.05
☐ 265 Eric Karros R	4.00	1.80
☐ 266 Roberto Kelly C	.10	.05
☐ 267 Ramon Martinez C	.25	.11
☐ 268 Raul Mondesi R	5.00	2.20
☐ 269 Hideo Nomo R	15.00	6.75
☐ 270 Jose Offerman U	.50	.23
☐ 271 Mike Piazza R	20.00	9.00
☐ 272 Kevin Tapani C	.10	.05
☐ 273 Ismael Valdes U	1.00	.45
☐ 274 Tim Wallach C	.10	.05
☐ 275 Todd Worrell R	3.00	1.35
☐ 276 Moises Alou R	4.00	1.80
☐ 277 Sean Berry U	.50	.23
☐ 278 Wil Cordero U	.50	.23
☐ 279 Jeff Fassero C	.10	.05
☐ 280 Darrin Fletcher C	.10	.05
☐ 281 Mike Lansing C	.10	.05
☐ 282 Pedro Martinez R	4.00	1.80
☐ 283 Carlos Perez U	.50	.23
☐ 284 Mel Rojas U	.50	.23
☐ 285 Tim Scott R	3.00	1.35
☐ 286 David Segui U	.50	.23
☐ 287 Tony Tarasco U	.50	.23
☐ 288 Rondell White C	.25	.11
☐ 289 Rico Brogna C	.10	.05
☐ 290 Brett Butler C	.25	.11
☐ 291 John Franco C	.10	.05
☐ 292 Pete Harnisch C	.10	.05
☐ 293 Todd Hundley C	.25	.11
☐ 294 Bobby Jones C	.10	.05
☐ 295 Jeff Kent C	.10	.05
☐ 296 Joe Orsulak U	.50	.23
☐ 297 Ryan Thompson U	.50	.23
☐ 298 Jose Vizcaino C	.10	.05
☐ 299 Ricky Bottalico U	1.00	.45
☐ 300 Darren Daulton C	.25	.11
☐ 301 Mariano Duncan U	.50	.23
☐ 302 Lenny Dykstra U	1.00	.45
☐ 303 Jim Eisenreich U	.50	.23
☐ 304 Tyler Green U	.50	.23
☐ 305 Charlie Hayes U	.50	.23
☐ 306 Dave Hollins C	.10	.05
☐ 307 Gregg Jefferies C	.25	.11
☐ 308 Mickey Morandini U	.50	.23
☐ 309 Curt Schilling R	3.00	1.35
☐ 310 Heathcliff Slocumb U	.50	.23
☐ 311 Kevin Stocker C	.10	.05
☐ 312 Jay Bell C	.10	.05
☐ 313 Jacob Brumfield C	.10	.05
☐ 314 Dave Clark U	.50	.23
☐ 315 Carlos Garcia C	.10	.05
☐ 316 Mark Johnson C	.10	.05
☐ 317 Jeff King C	.10	.05
☐ 318 Nelson Liriano U	.50	.23
☐ 319 Al Martin U	.50	.23
☐ 320 Orlando Merced U	.50	.23
☐ 321 Dan Miceli U	.50	.23
☐ 322 Denny Neagle C	.25	.11
☐ 323 Mark Parent C	.10	.05
☐ 324 Dan Plesac R	3.00	1.35
☐ 325 Scott Cooper C	.10	.05
☐ 326 Bernard Gilkey R	4.00	1.80
☐ 327 Tom Henke R	3.00	1.35
☐ 328 Ken Hill C	.10	.05
☐ 329 Danny Jackson C	.10	.05
☐ 330 Brian Jordan R	5.00	2.20
☐ 331 Ray Lankford U	1.00	.45
☐ 332 John Mabry U	1.00	.45
☐ 333 Jose Oquendo C	.10	.05
☐ 334 Tom Pagnozzi C	.10	.05
☐ 335 Ozzie Smith U	4.00	1.80
☐ 336 Andy Ashby U	.50	.23
☐ 337 Brad Ausmus U	.50	.23
☐ 338 Ken Caminiti U	2.00	.90
☐ 339 Andujar Cedeno C	.10	.05
☐ 340 Steve Finley R	4.00	1.80
☐ 341 Tony Gwynn R	15.00	6.75
☐ 342 Joey Hamilton C	.40	.18
☐ 343 Trevor Hoffman C	.25	.11
☐ 344 Jody Reed C	.10	.05
☐ 345 Bip Roberts R	3.00	1.35
☐ 346 Eddie Williams C	.10	.05
☐ 347 Rod Beck U	.50	.23
☐ 348 Mike Benjamin U	.50	.23
☐ 349 Barry Bonds R	8.00	3.60
☐ 350 Royce Clayton C	.10	.05
☐ 351 Glenallen Hill C	.10	.05
☐ 352 Kirt Manwaring C	.10	.05
☐ 353 Terry Mulholland C	.10	.05
☐ 354 John Patterson C	.10	.05
☐ 355 J.R. Phillips C	.10	.05
☐ 356 Deion Sanders R	5.00	2.20
☐ 357 Steve Scarsone U	.50	.23
☐ 358 Robby Thompson C	.10	.05
☐ 359 William VanLandingham C	.10	.05
☐ 360 Matt Williams R	5.00	2.20

1996 Donruss Samples

This 8-card standard-size set was issued to preview the 1996 Donruss series. The fronts feature full-bleed color action photos. The player's number, position, team name and team logo are printed on a silver foil square at the bottom center. The horizontal backs carry a second color photo, biography, and career statistics. The disclaimer "PROMOTIONAL SAMPLE" is stamped diagonally across both sides of the cards.

	MINT	NRMT
COMPLETE SET (8)	12.00	5.50
COMMON CARD (1-8)	.50	.23
☐ 1 Frank Thomas	2.50	1.10
☐ 2 Barry Bonds	.50	.23
☐ 3 Hideo Nomo	2.00	.90
☐ 4 Ken Griffey Jr.	3.00	1.35
☐ 5 Cal Ripken	2.50	1.10
☐ 6 Manny Ramirez	1.50	.70
☐ 7 Mike Piazza	2.00	.90
☐ 8 Greg Maddux	2.00	.90

1996 Donruss

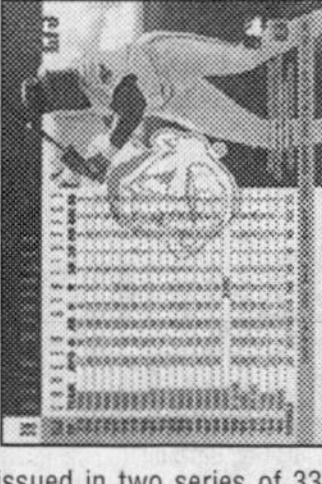

The 1996 Donruss set was issued in two series of 330 and 220 cards respectively, for a total of 550. The 12-card packs had a suggested retail price of $1.79. The full-bleed fronts feature full-color action photos. The player's name is in white ink in the upper right. The Donruss logo, team name and team logo as well as uniform number and position are located in the bottom middle set against a silver foil background. The horizontal backs feature season and career stats, text, vital stats and another photo. There are no notable Rookie Cards in this set.

	MINT	NRMT
COMPLETE SET (550)	40.00	18.00
COMPLETE SERIES 1 (330)	25.00	11.00
COMPLETE SERIES 2 (220)	15.00	6.75
COMMON CARD (1-550)	.15	.07
☐ 1 Frank Thomas	2.50	1.10
☐ 2 Jason Bates	.15	.07

☐ 3 Steve Sparks	.15	.07
☐ 4 Scott Servais	.15	.07
☐ 5 Angelo Encarnacion	.15	.07
☐ 6 Scott Sanders	.15	.07
☐ 7 Billy Ashley	.15	.07
☐ 8 Alex Rodriguez	2.50	1.10
☐ 9 Sean Bergman	.15	.07
☐ 10 Brad Radke	.15	.07
☐ 11 Andy Van Slyke	.30	.14
☐ 12 Joe Girardi	.15	.07
☐ 13 Mark Grudzielanek	.30	.14
☐ 14 Rick Aguilera	.30	.14
☐ 15 Randy Veres	.15	.07
☐ 16 Tim Bogar	.15	.07
☐ 17 Dave Veres	.15	.07
☐ 18 Kevin Stocker	.15	.07
☐ 19 Marquis Grissom	.30	.14
☐ 20 Will Clark	.40	.18
☐ 21 Jay Bell	.30	.14
☐ 22 Allen Battle	.15	.07
☐ 23 Frank Rodriguez	.30	.14
☐ 24 Terry Steinbach	.30	.14
☐ 25 Gerald Williams	.15	.07
☐ 26 Sid Roberson	.15	.07
☐ 27 Greg Zaun	.15	.07
☐ 28 Ozzie Timmons	.15	.07
☐ 29 Vaughn Eshelman	.15	.07
☐ 30 Ed Sprague	.15	.07
☐ 31 Gary DiSarcina	.15	.07
☐ 32 Joe Boever	.15	.07
☐ 33 Steve Avery	.15	.07
☐ 34 Brad Ausmus	.15	.07
☐ 35 Kirt Manwaring	.15	.07
☐ 36 Gary Sheffield	.60	.25
☐ 37 Jason Bere	.15	.07
☐ 38 Jeff Manto	.15	.07
☐ 39 David Cone	.30	.14
☐ 40 Manny Ramirez	.60	.25
☐ 41 Sandy Alomar Jr.	.30	.14
☐ 42 Curtis Goodwin	.15	.07
☐ 43 Tino Martinez	.60	.25
☐ 44 Woody Williams	.15	.07
☐ 45 Dean Palmer	.30	.14
☐ 46 Hipolito Pichardo	.15	.07
☐ 47 Jason Giambi	.30	.14
☐ 48 Lance Johnson	.15	.07
☐ 49 Bernard Gilkey	.30	.14
☐ 50 Kirby Puckett	1.25	.55
☐ 51 Tony Fernandez	.15	.07
☐ 52 Alex Gonzalez	.15	.07
☐ 53 Bret Saberhagen	.15	.07
☐ 54 Lyle Mouton	.15	.07
☐ 55 Brian McRae	.15	.07
☐ 56 Mark Gubicza	.15	.07
☐ 57 Sergio Valdez	.15	.07
☐ 58 Darrin Fletcher	.15	.07
☐ 59 Steve Parris	.15	.07
☐ 60 Johnny Damon	.30	.14
☐ 61 Rickey Henderson	.40	.18
☐ 62 Darrell Whitmore	.15	.07
☐ 63 Roberto Petagine	.15	.07
☐ 64 Trenidad Hubbard	.15	.07
☐ 65 Heathcliff Slocumb	.15	.07
☐ 66 Steve Finley	.30	.14
☐ 67 Mariano Rivera	.60	.25
☐ 68 Brian L.Hunter	.30	.14
☐ 69 Jamie Moyer	.15	.07
☐ 70 Ellis Burks	.30	.14
☐ 71 Pat Kelly	.15	.07
☐ 72 Mickey Tettleton	.15	.07
☐ 73 Garret Anderson	.30	.14
☐ 74 Andy Pettitte	.75	.35
☐ 75 Glenallen Hill	.30	.14
☐ 76 Brent Gates	.15	.07
☐ 77 Lou Whitaker	.30	.14
☐ 78 David Segui	.15	.07
☐ 79 Dan Wilson	.15	.07
☐ 80 Pat Listach	.15	.07
☐ 81 Jeff Bagwell	1.25	.55
☐ 82 Ben McDonald	.15	.07
☐ 83 John Valentin	.30	.14
☐ 84 John Jaha	.15	.07
☐ 85 Pete Schourek	.15	.07
☐ 86 Bryce Florie	.15	.07
☐ 87 Brian Jordan	.30	.14
☐ 88 Ron Karkovice	.15	.07
☐ 89 Al Leiter	.15	.07
☐ 90 Tony Longmire	.15	.07
☐ 91 Nelson Liriano	.15	.07
☐ 92 David Bell	.15	.07
☐ 93 Kevin Gross	.15	.07
☐ 94 Tom Candiotti	.15	.07
☐ 95 Dave Martinez	.15	.07
☐ 96 Greg Myers	.15	.07
☐ 97 Rheal Cormier	.15	.07
☐ 98 Chris Hammond	.15	.07
☐ 99 Randy Myers	.15	.07
☐ 100 Bill Pulsipher	.15	.07
☐ 101 Jason Isringhausen	.15	.07
☐ 102 Dave Stevens	.15	.07
☐ 103 Roberto Alomar	.60	.25
☐ 104 Bob Higginson	.40	.18
☐ 105 Eddie Murray	.60	.25
☐ 106 Matt Walbeck	.15	.07
☐ 107 Mark Wohlers	.30	.14
☐ 108 Jeff Nelson	.15	.07
☐ 109 Tom Goodwin	.15	.07
☐ 110 Cal Ripken CL	1.25	.55
☐ 111 Rey Sanchez	.15	.07
☐ 112 Hector Carrasco	.15	.07
☐ 113 B.J. Surhoff	.15	.07
☐ 114 Dan Miceli	.15	.07
☐ 115 Dean Hartgraves	.15	.07
☐ 116 John Burkett	.15	.07
☐ 117 Gary Gaetti	.30	.14
☐ 118 Ricky Bones	.15	.07
☐ 119 Mike Macfarlane	.15	.07
☐ 120 Bip Roberts	.15	.07
☐ 121 Dave Mlicki	.15	.07
☐ 122 Chili Davis	.30	.14
☐ 123 Mark Whiten	.15	.07
☐ 124 Herbert Perry	.15	.07
☐ 125 Butch Henry	.15	.07
☐ 126 Derek Bell	.30	.14
☐ 127 Al Martin	.15	.07
☐ 128 John Franco	.30	.14
☐ 129 W. VanLandingham	.15	.07
☐ 130 Mike Bordick	.15	.07
☐ 131 Mike Mordecai	.15	.07
☐ 132 Robby Thompson	.15	.07
☐ 133 Greg Colbrunn	.15	.07
☐ 134 Domingo Cedeno	.15	.07
☐ 135 Chad Curtis	.15	.07
☐ 136 Jose Hernandez	.15	.07
☐ 137 Scott Klingenbeck	.15	.07
☐ 138 Ryan Klesko	.40	.18
☐ 139 John Smiley	.15	.07
☐ 140 Charlie Hayes	.15	.07
☐ 141 Jay Buhner	.40	.18
☐ 142 Doug Drabek	.15	.07
☐ 143 Roger Pavlik	.15	.07
☐ 144 Todd Worrell	.30	.14
☐ 145 Cal Ripken	2.50	1.10
☐ 146 Steve Reed	.15	.07
☐ 147 Chuck Finley	.15	.07
☐ 148 Mike Blowers	.15	.07
☐ 149 Orel Hershiser	.30	.14
☐ 150 Allen Watson	.15	.07
☐ 151 Ramon Martinez	.30	.14
☐ 152 Melvin Nieves	.30	.14
☐ 153 Tripp Cromer	.15	.07
☐ 154 Yorkis Perez	.15	.07
☐ 155 Stan Javier	.15	.07
☐ 156 Mel Rojas	.30	.14
☐ 157 Aaron Sele	.15	.07
☐ 158 Eric Karros	.30	.14
☐ 159 Robb Nen	.15	.07
☐ 160 Raul Mondesi	.40	.18
☐ 161 John Wetteland	.30	.14
☐ 162 Tim Scott	.15	.07
☐ 163 Kenny Rogers	.15	.07
☐ 164 Melvin Bunch	.15	.07
☐ 165 Rod Beck	.30	.14
☐ 166 Andy Benes	.15	.07
☐ 167 Lenny Dykstra	.30	.14
☐ 168 Orlando Merced	.15	.07
☐ 169 Tomas Perez	.30	.14
☐ 170 Xavier Hernandez	.15	.07
☐ 171 Ruben Sierra	.15	.07
☐ 172 Alan Trammell	.40	.18
☐ 173 Mike Fetters	.15	.07
☐ 174 Wilson Alvarez	.30	.14
☐ 175 Erik Hanson	.15	.07
☐ 176 Travis Fryman	.30	.14
☐ 177 Jim Abbott	.15	.07
☐ 178 Bret Boone	.15	.07
☐ 179 Sterling Hitchcock	.15	.07
☐ 180 Pat Mahomes	.15	.07
☐ 181 Mark Acre	.15	.07
☐ 182 Charles Nagy	.30	.14
☐ 183 Rusty Greer	.60	.25
☐ 184 Mike Stanley	.15	.07
☐ 185 Jim Bullinger	.15	.07
☐ 186 Shane Andrews	.15	.07
☐ 187 Brian Keyser	.15	.07
☐ 188 Tyler Green	.15	.07
☐ 189 Mark Grace	.40	.18
☐ 190 Bob Hamelin	.15	.07
☐ 191 Luis Ortiz	.15	.07
☐ 192 Joe Carter	.30	.14
☐ 193 Eddie Taubensee	.15	.07
☐ 194 Brian Anderson	.15	.07
☐ 195 Edgardo Alfonzo	.60	.25
☐ 196 Pedro Munoz	.15	.07
☐ 197 David Justice	.40	.18
☐ 198 Trevor Hoffman	.30	.14
☐ 199 Bobby Ayala	.15	.07
☐ 200 Tony Eusebio	.15	.07
☐ 201 Jeff Russell	.15	.07
☐ 202 Mike Hampton	.15	.07
☐ 203 Walt Weiss	.15	.07
☐ 204 Joey Hamilton	.30	.14
☐ 205 Roberto Hernandez	.30	.14
☐ 206 Greg Vaughn	.15	.07
☐ 207 Felipe Lira	.15	.07
☐ 208 Harold Baines	.30	.14
☐ 209 Tim Wallach	.15	.07
☐ 210 Manny Alexander	.15	.07
☐ 211 Tim Laker	.15	.07
☐ 212 Chris Haney	.15	.07
☐ 213 Brian Maxcy	.15	.07
☐ 214 Eric Young	.30	.14
☐ 215 Darryl Strawberry	.30	.14
☐ 216 Barry Bonds	.75	.35
☐ 217 Tim Naehring	.30	.14
☐ 218 Scott Brosius	.15	.07
☐ 219 Reggie Sanders	.15	.07
☐ 220 Eddie Murray CL	.60	.25
☐ 221 Luis Alicea	.15	.07
☐ 222 Albert Belle	.75	.35
☐ 223 Benji Gil	.15	.07
☐ 224 Dante Bichette	.40	.18
☐ 225 Bobby Bonilla	.30	.14
☐ 226 Todd Stottlemyre	.15	.07
☐ 227 Jim Edmonds	.30	.14
☐ 228 Todd Jones	.15	.07
☐ 229 Shawn Green	.40	.18
☐ 230 Javier Lopez	.40	.18
☐ 231 Ariel Prieto	.15	.07
☐ 232 Tony Phillips	.15	.07
☐ 233 James Mouton	.15	.07
☐ 234 Jose Oquendo	.15	.07
☐ 235 Royce Clayton	.15	.07
☐ 236 Chuck Carr	.15	.07
☐ 237 Doug Jones	.15	.07
☐ 238 Mark McLemore	.15	.07
☐ 239 Bill Swift	.15	.07
☐ 240 Scott Leius	.15	.07
☐ 241 Russ Davis	.15	.07
☐ 242 Ray Durham	.30	.14
☐ 243 Matt Mieske	.15	.07
☐ 244 Brent Mayne	.15	.07
☐ 245 Thomas Howard	.15	.07
☐ 246 Troy O'Leary	.30	.14
☐ 247 Jacob Brumfield	.15	.07
☐ 248 Mickey Morandini	.15	.07
☐ 249 Todd Hundley	.30	.14
☐ 250 Chris Bosio	.15	.07
☐ 251 Omar Vizquel	.30	.14
☐ 252 Mike Lansing	.15	.07
☐ 253 John Mabry	.30	.14
☐ 254 Mike Perez	.15	.07
☐ 255 Delino DeShields	.15	.07
☐ 256 Wil Cordero	.15	.07
☐ 257 Mike James	.15	.07
☐ 258 Todd Van Poppel	.15	.07
☐ 259 Joey Cora	.30	.14
☐ 260 Andre Dawson	.40	.18
☐ 261 Jerry DiPoto	.15	.07
☐ 262 Rick Krivda	.15	.07
☐ 263 Glenn Dishman	.30	.14
☐ 264 Mike Mimbs	.15	.07
☐ 265 John Ericks	.15	.07
☐ 266 Jose Canseco	.40	.18
☐ 267 Jeff Branson	.15	.07
☐ 268 Curt Leskanic	.15	.07
☐ 269 Jon Nunnally	.15	.07
☐ 270 Scott Stahoviak	.15	.07
☐ 271 Jeff Montgomery	.15	.07
☐ 272 Hal Morris	.15	.07
☐ 273 Esteban Loaiza	.15	.07
☐ 274 Rico Brogna	.15	.07
☐ 275 Dave Winfield	.40	.18
☐ 276 J.R. Phillips	.15	.07
☐ 277 Todd Zeile	.15	.07
☐ 278 Tom Pagnozzi	.15	.07
☐ 279 Mark Lemke	.15	.07
☐ 280 Dave Magadan	.15	.07
☐ 281 Greg McMichael	.15	.07
☐ 282 Mike Morgan	.15	.07
☐ 283 Moises Alou	.30	.14
☐ 284 Dennis Martinez	.30	.14
☐ 285 Jeff Kent	.15	.07
☐ 286 Mark Johnson	.15	.07
☐ 287 Darren Lewis	.15	.07
☐ 288 Brad Clontz	.15	.07
☐ 289 Chad Fonville	.15	.07
☐ 290 Paul Sorrento	.15	.07
☐ 291 Lee Smith	.30	.14
☐ 292 Tom Glavine	.40	.18
☐ 293 Antonio Osuna	.15	.07

Card	MINT	NRMT
☐ 294 Kevin Foster	.15	.07
☐ 295 Sandy Martinez	.15	.07
☐ 296 Mark Leiter	.15	.07
☐ 297 Julian Tavarez	.15	.07
☐ 298 Mike Kelly	.15	.07
☐ 299 Joe Oliver	.15	.07
☐ 300 John Flaherty	.15	.07
☐ 301 Don Mattingly	1.00	.45
☐ 302 Pat Meares	.15	.07
☐ 303 John Doherty	.15	.07
☐ 304 Joe Vitiello	.15	.07
☐ 305 Vinny Castilla	.30	.14
☐ 306 Jeff Brantley	.15	.07
☐ 307 Mike Greenwell	.15	.07
☐ 308 Midre Cummings	.15	.07
☐ 309 Curt Schilling	.30	.14
☐ 310 Ken Caminiti	.60	.25
☐ 311 Scott Erickson	.15	.07
☐ 312 Carl Everett	.15	.07
☐ 313 Charles Johnson	.30	.14
☐ 314 Alex Diaz	.15	.07
☐ 315 Jose Mesa	.15	.07
☐ 316 Mark Carreon	.15	.07
☐ 317 Carlos Perez	.15	.07
☐ 318 Ismael Valdes	.30	.14
☐ 319 Frank Castillo	.15	.07
☐ 320 Tom Henke	.30	.14
☐ 321 Spike Owen	.15	.07
☐ 322 Joe Orsulak	.15	.07
☐ 323 Paul Menhart	.15	.07
☐ 324 Pedro Borbon	.15	.07
☐ 325 Paul Molitor CL	.60	.25
☐ 326 Jeff Cirillo	.30	.14
☐ 327 Edwin Hurtado	.15	.07
☐ 328 Orlando Miller	.15	.07
☐ 329 Steve Ontiveros	.15	.07
☐ 330 Kirby Puckett CL	.60	.25
☐ 331 Scott Bullett	.15	.07
☐ 332 Andres Galarraga	.60	.25
☐ 333 Cal Eldred	.15	.07
☐ 334 Sammy Sosa	.60	.25
☐ 335 Don Slaught	.15	.07
☐ 336 Jody Reed	.15	.07
☐ 337 Roger Cedeno	.15	.07
☐ 338 Ken Griffey Jr.	3.00	1.35
☐ 339 Todd Hollandsworth	.30	.14
☐ 340 Mike Trombley	.15	.07
☐ 341 Gregg Jefferies	.30	.14
☐ 342 Larry Walker	.60	.25
☐ 343 Pedro Martinez	.60	.25
☐ 344 Dwayne Hosey	.15	.07
☐ 345 Terry Pendleton	.30	.14
☐ 346 Pete Harnisch	.15	.07
☐ 347 Tony Castillo	.15	.07
☐ 348 Paul Quantrill	.15	.07
☐ 349 Fred McGriff	.40	.18
☐ 350 Ivan Rodriguez	.75	.35
☐ 351 Butch Huskey	.30	.14
☐ 352 Ozzie Smith	.75	.35
☐ 353 Marty Cordova	.15	.07
☐ 354 John Wasdin	.15	.07
☐ 355 Wade Boggs	.60	.25
☐ 356 Dave Nilsson	.30	.14
☐ 357 Rafael Palmeiro	.40	.18
☐ 358 Luis Gonzalez	.15	.07
☐ 359 Reggie Jefferson	.15	.07
☐ 360 Carlos Delgado	.30	.14
☐ 361 Orlando Palmeiro	.15	.07
☐ 362 Chris Gomez	.15	.07
☐ 363 John Smoltz	.40	.18
☐ 364 Marc Newfield	.30	.14
☐ 365 Matt Williams	.40	.18
☐ 366 Jesus Tavarez	.15	.07
☐ 367 Bruce Ruffin	.15	.07
☐ 368 Sean Berry	.15	.07
☐ 369 Randy Velarde	.15	.07
☐ 370 Tony Pena	.15	.07
☐ 371 Jim Thome	.60	.25
☐ 372 Jeffrey Hammonds	.30	.14
☐ 373 Bob Wolcott	.15	.07
☐ 374 Juan Guzman	.15	.07
☐ 375 Juan Gonzalez	1.50	.70
☐ 376 Michael Tucker	.30	.14
☐ 377 Doug Johns	.15	.07
☐ 378 Mike Cameron	1.50	.70
☐ 379 Ray Lankford	.30	.14
☐ 380 Jose Parra	.15	.07
☐ 381 Jimmy Key	.30	.14
☐ 382 John Olerud	.30	.14
☐ 383 Kevin Ritz	.15	.07
☐ 384 Tim Raines	.15	.07
☐ 385 Rich Amaral	.15	.07
☐ 386 Keith Lockhart	.15	.07
☐ 387 Steve Scarsone	.15	.07
☐ 388 Cliff Floyd	.15	.07
☐ 389 Rich Aude	.15	.07
☐ 390 Hideo Nomo	1.50	.70
☐ 391 Geronimo Berroa	.15	.07
☐ 392 Pat Rapp	.15	.07
☐ 393 Dustin Hermanson	.30	.14
☐ 394 Greg Maddux	2.00	.90
☐ 395 Darren Daulton	.30	.14
☐ 396 Kenny Lofton	.75	.35
☐ 397 Ruben Rivera	.40	.18
☐ 398 Billy Wagner	.30	.14
☐ 399 Kevin Brown	.30	.14
☐ 400 Mike Kingery	.15	.07
☐ 401 Bernie Williams	.60	.25
☐ 402 Otis Nixon	.30	.14
☐ 403 Damion Easley	.15	.07
☐ 404 Paul O'Neill	.15	.07
☐ 405 Deion Sanders	.60	.25
☐ 406 Dennis Eckersley	.40	.18
☐ 407 Tony Clark	.60	.25
☐ 408 Rondell White	.40	.18
☐ 409 Luis Sojo	.15	.07
☐ 410 David Hulse	.15	.07
☐ 411 Shane Reynolds	.15	.07
☐ 412 Chris Hoiles	.15	.07
☐ 413 Lee Tinsley	.15	.07
☐ 414 Scott Karl	.15	.07
☐ 415 Ron Gant	.30	.14
☐ 416 Brian Johnson	.15	.07
☐ 417 Jose Oliva	.15	.07
☐ 418 Jack McDowell	.15	.07
☐ 419 Paul Molitor	.60	.25
☐ 420 Ricky Bottalico	.15	.07
☐ 421 Paul Wagner	.15	.07
☐ 422 Terry Bradshaw	.15	.07
☐ 423 Bob Tewksbury	.15	.07
☐ 424 Mike Piazza	2.00	.90
☐ 425 Luis Andujar	.30	.14
☐ 426 Mark Langston	.15	.07
☐ 427 Stan Belinda	.15	.07
☐ 428 Kurt Abbott	.15	.07
☐ 429 Shawon Dunston	.15	.07
☐ 430 Bobby Jones	.15	.07
☐ 431 Jose Vizcaino	.15	.07
☐ 432 Matt Lawton	.15	.07
☐ 433 Pat Hentgen	.30	.14
☐ 434 Cecil Fielder	.30	.14
☐ 435 Carlos Baerga	.30	.14
☐ 436 Rich Becker	.30	.14
☐ 437 Chipper Jones	2.00	.90
☐ 438 Bill Risley	.15	.07
☐ 439 Kevin Appier	.30	.14
☐ 440 Wade Boggs CL	.60	.25
☐ 441 Jaime Navarro	.15	.07
☐ 442 Barry Larkin	.40	.18
☐ 443 Jose Valentin	.15	.07
☐ 444 Bryan Rekar	.15	.07
☐ 445 Rick Wilkins	.15	.07
☐ 446 Quilvio Veras	.15	.07
☐ 447 Greg Gagne	.15	.07
☐ 448 Mark Kiefer	.15	.07
☐ 449 Bobby Witt	.15	.07
☐ 450 Andy Ashby	.15	.07
☐ 451 Alex Ochoa	.15	.07
☐ 452 Jorge Fabregas	.15	.07
☐ 453 Gene Schall	.15	.07
☐ 454 Ken Hill	.15	.07
☐ 455 Tony Tarasco	.15	.07
☐ 456 Donnie Wall	.15	.07
☐ 457 Carlos Garcia	.15	.07
☐ 458 Ryan Thompson	.15	.07
☐ 459 Marvin Benard	.15	.07
☐ 460 Jose Herrera	.15	.07
☐ 461 Jeff Blauser	.15	.07
☐ 462 Chris Hook	.15	.07
☐ 463 Jeff Conine	.30	.14
☐ 464 Devon White	.15	.07
☐ 465 Danny Bautista	.15	.07
☐ 466 Steve Trachsel	.15	.07
☐ 467 C.J. Nitkowski	.15	.07
☐ 468 Mike Devereaux	.15	.07
☐ 469 David Wells	.15	.07
☐ 470 Jim Eisenreich	.30	.14
☐ 471 Edgar Martinez	.40	.18
☐ 472 Craig Biggio	.40	.18
☐ 473 Jeff Frye	.15	.07
☐ 474 Karim Garcia	.30	.14
☐ 475 Jimmy Haynes	.15	.07
☐ 476 Darren Holmes	.15	.07
☐ 477 Tim Salmon	.60	.25
☐ 478 Randy Johnson	.60	.25
☐ 479 Eric Plunk	.15	.07
☐ 480 Scott Cooper	.15	.07
☐ 481 Chan Ho Park	.60	.25
☐ 482 Ray McDavid	.15	.07
☐ 483 Mark Petkovsek	.15	.07
☐ 484 Greg Swindell	.15	.07
☐ 485 George Williams	.15	.07
☐ 486 Yamil Benitez	.30	.14
☐ 487 Tim Wakefield	.15	.07
☐ 488 Kevin Tapani	.15	.07
☐ 489 Derrick May	.15	.07
☐ 490 Ken Griffey Jr. CL	1.50	.70
☐ 491 Derek Jeter	2.00	.90
☐ 492 Jeff Fassero	.15	.07
☐ 493 Benito Santiago	.15	.07
☐ 494 Tom Gordon	.15	.07
☐ 495 Jamie Brewington	.15	.07
☐ 496 Vince Coleman	.15	.07
☐ 497 Kevin Jordan	.15	.07
☐ 498 Jeff King	.30	.14
☐ 499 Mike Simms	.15	.07
☐ 500 Jose Rijo	.15	.07
☐ 501 Denny Neagle	.30	.14
☐ 502 Jose Lima	.15	.07
☐ 503 Kevin Seitzer	.15	.07
☐ 504 Alex Fernandez	.30	.14
☐ 505 Mo Vaughn	.75	.35
☐ 506 Phil Nevin	.15	.07
☐ 507 J.T. Snow	.30	.14
☐ 508 Andujar Cedeno	.15	.07
☐ 509 Ozzie Guillen	.15	.07
☐ 510 Mark Clark	.15	.07
☐ 511 Mark McGwire	1.25	.55
☐ 512 Jeff Reboulet	.15	.07
☐ 513 Armando Benitez	.15	.07
☐ 514 LaTroy Hawkins	.15	.07
☐ 515 Brett Butler	.30	.14
☐ 516 Tavo Alvarez	.15	.07
☐ 517 Chris Snopek	.15	.07
☐ 518 Mike Mussina	.60	.25
☐ 519 Darryl Kile	.30	.14
☐ 520 Wally Joyner	.15	.07
☐ 521 Willie McGee	.15	.07
☐ 522 Kent Mercker	.15	.07
☐ 523 Mike Jackson	.15	.07
☐ 524 Troy Percival	.15	.07
☐ 525 Tony Gwynn	1.50	.70
☐ 526 Ron Coomer	.15	.07
☐ 527 Darryl Hamilton	.15	.07
☐ 528 Phil Plantier	.15	.07
☐ 529 Norm Charlton	.15	.07
☐ 530 Craig Paquette	.15	.07
☐ 531 Dave Burba	.15	.07
☐ 532 Mike Henneman	.15	.07
☐ 533 Terrell Wade	.15	.07
☐ 534 Eddie Williams	.15	.07
☐ 535 Robin Ventura	.30	.14
☐ 536 Chuck Knoblauch	.60	.25
☐ 537 Les Norman	.15	.07
☐ 538 Brady Anderson	.40	.18
☐ 539 Roger Clemens	1.25	.55
☐ 540 Mark Portugal	.15	.07
☐ 541 Mike Matheny	.15	.07
☐ 542 Jeff Parrett	.15	.07
☐ 543 Roberto Kelly	.15	.07
☐ 544 Damon Buford	.15	.07
☐ 545 Chad Ogea	.15	.07
☐ 546 Jose Offerman	.15	.07
☐ 547 Brian Barber	.15	.07
☐ 548 Danny Tartabull	.15	.07
☐ 549 Duane Singleton	.15	.07
☐ 550 Tony Gwynn CL	.60	.25

1996 Donruss Press Proofs

Randomly inserted at a rate of one in 10 first and second series packs, these cards are parallel to the regular Donruss issue. Even though they are not sequentially numbered, production on these cards were limited to 2,000 cards. Each card is noted as being a Press Proof in gold foil on the front.

	MINT	NRMT
COMPLETE SET (550)	1500.00	700.00
COMPLETE SERIES 1 (330)	900.00	400.00
COMPLETE SERIES 2 (220)	600.00	275.00
COMMON CARD (1-550)	2.00	.90

*STARS: 10X TO 20X BASIC CARDS ..
*YOUNG STARS: 7.5X TO 15X BASIC CARDS

1996 Donruss Diamond Kings

These 31 standard-size cards were randomly inserted into packs and issued in two series of 14 and 17 cards. They were inserted in first series packs at a ratio of approximately one every 60 packs. Second series cards were inserted one every 30 packs. The cards are sequentially numbered in the back lower right as "X" of 10,000. The fronts feature player portraits by noted sports artist Dick Perez. These cards are gold-foil stamped and the portraits are surrounded by gold-foil borders. The backs feature text about the player as well as a player photo. The cards are numbered on the back with a "DK" prefix.

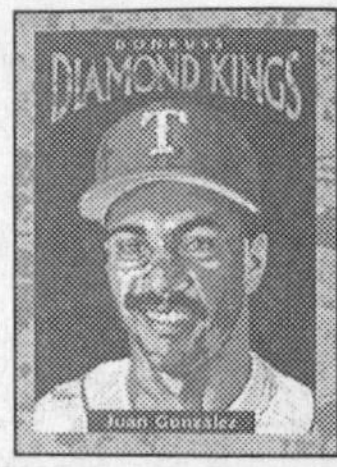

	MINT	NRMT
COMPLETE SET (31)	300.00	135.00
COMPLETE SERIES 1 (14)	150.00	70.00
COMPLETE SERIES 2 (17)	150.00	70.00
COMMON CARD (1-31)	4.00	1.80
☐ 1 Frank Thomas	40.00	18.00
☐ 2 Mo Vaughn	12.00	5.50
☐ 3 Manny Ramirez	12.00	5.50
☐ 4 Mark McGwire	20.00	9.00
☐ 5 Juan Gonzalez	25.00	11.00
☐ 6 Roberto Alomar	10.00	4.50
☐ 7 Tim Salmon	10.00	4.50
☐ 8 Barry Bonds	12.00	5.50
☐ 9 Tony Gwynn	25.00	11.00
☐ 10 Reggie Sanders	4.00	1.80
☐ 11 Larry Walker	6.00	2.70
☐ 12 Pedro Martinez	10.00	4.50
☐ 13 Jeff King	4.00	1.80
☐ 14 Mark Grace	6.00	2.70
☐ 15 Greg Maddux	25.00	11.00
☐ 16 Don Mattingly	12.00	5.50
☐ 17 Gregg Jefferies	4.00	1.80
☐ 18 Chad Curtis	4.00	1.80
☐ 19 Jason Isringhausen	4.00	1.80
☐ 20 B.J. Surhoff	4.00	1.80
☐ 21 Jeff Conine	4.00	1.80
☐ 22 Kirby Puckett	15.00	6.75
☐ 23 Derek Bell	4.00	1.80
☐ 24 Wally Joyner	4.00	1.80
☐ 25 Brian Jordan	4.00	1.80
☐ 26 Edgar Martinez	6.00	2.70
☐ 27 Hideo Nomo	20.00	9.00
☐ 28 Mike Mussina	8.00	3.60
☐ 29 Eddie Murray	10.00	4.50
☐ 30 Cal Ripken	30.00	13.50
☐ 31 Checklist	4.00	1.80

1996 Donruss Elite

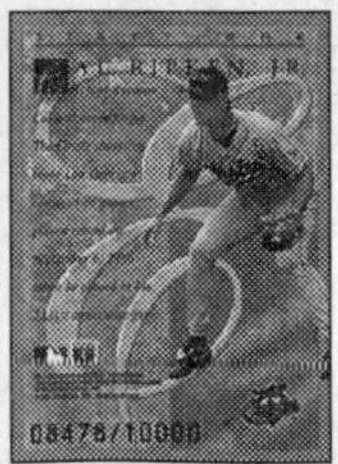

Randomly inserted one in Donruss packs, this 12-card standard-size set is continuously numbered (61-72) from the previous year. First series cards were inserted one every 40 packs. Second series cards were inserted one every 75 packs. The fronts contain an action photo surrounded by a silver border. Limited to 10,000 and sequentially numbered, the backs contain a small photo and write up.

	MINT	NRMT
COMPLETE SET (12)	270.00	120.00
COMPLETE SERIES 1 (6)	150.00	70.00
COMPLETE SERIES 2 (6)	120.00	55.00
COMMON CARD (61-72)	5.00	2.20
☐ 61 Cal Ripken	50.00	22.00
☐ 62 Hideo Nomo	40.00	18.00
☐ 63 Reggie Sanders	5.00	2.20
☐ 64 Mo Vaughn	15.00	6.75
☐ 65 Tim Salmon	8.00	3.60
☐ 66 Chipper Jones	40.00	18.00
☐ 67 Manny Ramirez	12.00	5.50
☐ 68 Greg Maddux	25.00	11.00
☐ 69 Frank Thomas	30.00	13.50
☐ 70 Ken Griffey Jr.	40.00	18.00
☐ 71 Dante Bichette	8.00	3.60
☐ 72 Tony Gwynn	20.00	9.00

1996 Donruss Freeze Frame

Randomly inserted in second series packs at a rate of one in 60, this 8-card standard-size set features the top hitters and pitchers in baseball. Just 5,000 of each card were produced and sequentially numbered. In a horizontal format with round corners, the fronts display a crosshatched color player photo that is bordered on the left and bottom by thick black borders. A second color player cutout is superposed on the photo. The backs have three small color photos, '95 season highlights, and a brief note.

	MINT	NRMT
COMPLETE SET (8)	180.00	80.00
COMMON CARD (1-8)	10.00	4.50
☐ 1 Frank Thomas	30.00	13.50
☐ 2 Ken Griffey Jr.	40.00	18.00
☐ 3 Cal Ripken	30.00	13.50
☐ 4 Hideo Nomo	20.00	9.00
☐ 5 Greg Maddux	25.00	11.00
☐ 6 Albert Belle	10.00	4.50
☐ 7 Chipper Jones	25.00	11.00
☐ 8 Mike Piazza	25.00	11.00

1996 Donruss Hit List

This 16-card standard-size set was randomly inserted in 97 Donruss and salutes the most consistent hitters in the game. The first series cards were inserted one every 105 packs while the second series cards were inserted one every 60 packs. The cards are sequentially numbered out of 10,000. The fronts feature full-color shots set against a silver-foil background that is complemented by a team color duotone and features a gold foil team logo and "Hit List" logo. The backs have a color action photo as well as having year-by-year and career hit and batting average stats.

	MINT	NRMT
COMPLETE SET (16)	100.00	45.00
COMPLETE SERIES 1 (8)	60.00	27.00
COMPLETE SERIES 2 (8)	40.00	18.00
COMMON CARD (1-16)	2.50	1.10
☐ 1 Tony Gwynn	15.00	6.75
☐ 2 Ken Griffey Jr.	30.00	13.50
☐ 3 Will Clark	3.00	1.35
☐ 4 Mike Piazza	20.00	9.00
☐ 5 Carlos Baerga	2.50	1.10
☐ 6 Mo Vaughn	8.00	3.60
☐ 7 Mark Grace	3.00	1.35
☐ 8 Kirby Puckett	12.00	5.50
☐ 9 Frank Thomas	20.00	9.00
☐ 10 Barry Bonds	6.00	2.70
☐ 11 Jeff Bagwell	10.00	4.50
☐ 12 Edgar Martinez	3.00	1.35
☐ 13 Tim Salmon	5.00	2.20
☐ 14 Wade Boggs	5.00	2.20
☐ 15 Don Mattingly	8.00	3.60
☐ 16 Eddie Murray	8.00	3.60

1996 Donruss Long Ball Leaders

This eight-card standard-size set was randomly inserted into series one retail packs. They were inserted at a rate of

approximately one in every 96 packs. The cards are sequentially numbered out of 5,000. The set highlights eight top sluggers and their farthest home run distance of 1995. The fronts feature a player photo set against a silver-foil background. The words "Long Ball Leaders" are on the top of the card while the stadium, date and distance of the blast are in the middle. The player's name is at the bottom. The back has a player photo and information about the game in which the mighty clout occurred.

	MINT	NRMT
COMPLETE SET (8)	200.00	90.00
COMMON CARD (1-8)	8.00	3.60
☐ 1 Barry Bonds	20.00	9.00
☐ 2 Ryan Klesko	12.00	5.50
☐ 3 Mark McGwire	30.00	13.50
☐ 4 Raul Mondesi	12.00	5.50
☐ 5 Cecil Fielder	8.00	3.60
☐ 6 Ken Griffey Jr.	80.00	36.00
☐ 7 Larry Walker	15.00	6.75
☐ 8 Frank Thomas	60.00	27.00

1996 Donruss Power Alley

This ten-card standard-size set was randomly inserted into series one hobby packs. They were inserted at a rate of approximately one in every 92 packs. These cards are all sequentially numbered out of 5,000. These cards feature a player photo set against a diamond design and team holographic background. The horizontal backs feature a player photo, some text and the player's 1995 power statistics.

	MINT	NRMT
COMPLETE SET (10)	150.00	70.00
COMMON CARD (1-10)	4.00	1.80
COMP.DIE CUT SET (10)	800.00	350.00
DIE CUTS: 2X TO 4X BASIC CARDS		
☐ 1 Frank Thomas	40.00	18.00
☐ 2 Barry Bonds	12.00	5.50
☐ 3 Reggie Sanders	4.00	1.80
☐ 4 Albert Belle	12.00	5.50
☐ 5 Tim Salmon	6.00	2.70
☐ 6 Dante Bichette	6.00	2.70
☐ 7 Mo Vaughn	12.00	5.50
☐ 8 Jim Edmonds	10.00	4.50
☐ 9 Manny Ramirez	12.00	5.50
☐ 10 Ken Griffey Jr.	50.00	22.00

1996 Donruss Pure Power

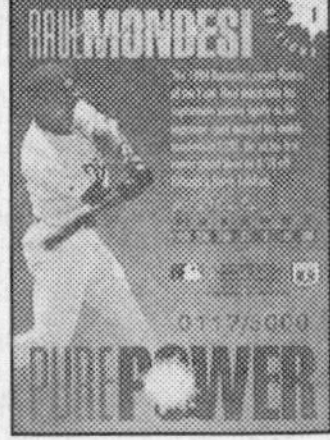

Randomly inserted in retail and magazine packs only at a rate of one in eight, this eight-card set features color ction player photos of eight of the most powerful players Major League baseball.

	MINT	NRMT
OMPLETE SET (8)	175.00	80.00
OMMON CARD (1-8)	8.00	3.60
1 Raul Mondesi	8.00	3.60
2 Barry Bonds	15.00	6.75
3 Albert Belle	15.00	6.75
4 Frank Thomas	40.00	18.00
5 Mike Piazza	40.00	18.00
6 Dante Bichette	10.00	4.50
7 Manny Ramirez	15.00	6.75
8 Mo Vaughn	15.00	6.75

1996 Donruss Round Trippers

Randomly inserted in second series hobby packs at a rate f one in 55, this 10-card standard-size set honors ten of aseball's top homerun hitters. Just 5,000 of each card were produced and consecutively numbered. On a sepia-one background with a home plate icon carrying the 1995 eason home run total, the fronts superpose a color layer cutout. The player's name and "Round Trippers" are ronze foil stamped at the bottom. The backs have a imilar design and present 1995 and career home run tatistics by a bar graph.

	MINT	NRMT
OMPLETE SET (10)	150.00	70.00
OMMON CARD (1-10)	5.00	2.20
1 Albert Belle	10.00	4.50
2 Barry Bonds	10.00	4.50
3 Jeff Bagwell	15.00	6.75
4 Tim Salmon	8.00	3.60
5 Mo Vaughn	10.00	4.50
6 Ken Griffey Jr.	40.00	18.00
7 Mike Piazza	25.00	11.00
8 Cal Ripken	30.00	13.50
9 Frank Thomas	30.00	13.50
10 Dante Bichette	5.00	2.20

1996 Donruss Showdown

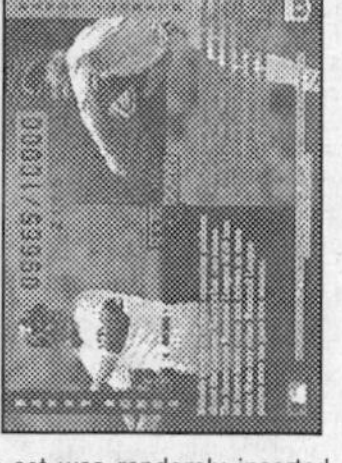

This eight-card standard-size set was randomly inserted n series one packs at a rate of one every 105 packs. These cards feature one top hitter and one top pitcher rom each league. The cards are sequentially numbered out of 10,000. The horizontal fronts feature gold foil stamping and have the words "Show Down" in the middle. The backs feature color player photos as well as some text about their accomplishments.

	MINT	NRMT
OMPLETE SET (8)	120.00	55.00
OMMON CARD (1-8)	4.00	1.80
1 Frank Thomas Hideo Nomo	30.00	13.50
2 Barry Bonds Randy Johnson	10.00	4.50
3 Greg Maddux Ken Griffey Jr.	40.00	18.00
4 Roger Clemens Tony Gwynn	20.00	9.00
5 Mike Piazza Mike Mussina	20.00	9.00
6 Cal Ripken Pedro J.Martinez	25.00	11.00
7 Tim Wakefield Matt Williams	4.00	1.80
8 Manny Ramirez Carlos Perez	5.00	2.20

1997 Donruss

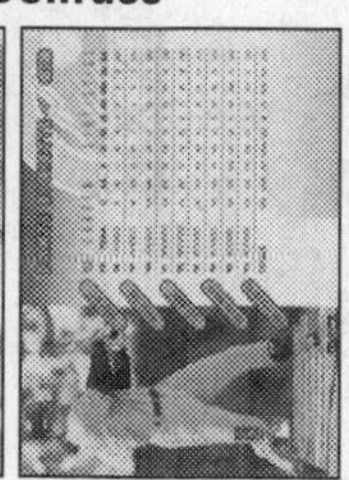

The 1997 Donruss set was issued in two separate series of 270 and 180 cards respectively. Both first series and Update cards were distributed in 10-card packs carrying a suggested retail price of $1.99 each. Card fronts feature color action player photos while the backs carry another color player photo with player information and career statistics. The following subsets are included within the set: Checklists (267-270/448-450), Rookies (353-397), Hit List (398-422), King of the Hill (423-437) and Interleague Showdown (438-447). The only key RC's in this set are Jose Cruz Jr. and Hideki Irabu.

	MINT	NRMT
COMPLETE SET (450)	45.00	20.00
COMPLETE SERIES 1 (270)	25.00	11.00
COMPLETE UPDATE (180)	20.00	9.00
COMMON CARD (1-450)	.15	.07
1 Juan Gonzalez	1.50	.70
2 Jim Edmonds	.60	.25
3 Tony Gwynn	1.50	.70
4 Andres Galarraga	.60	.25
5 Joe Carter	.30	.14
6 Raul Mondesi	.40	.18
7 Greg Maddux	2.00	.90
8 Travis Fryman	.30	.14
9 Brian Jordan	.30	.14
10 Henry Rodriguez	.15	.07
11 Manny Ramirez	.60	.25
12 Mark McGwire	1.25	.55
13 Marc Newfield	.15	.07
14 Craig Biggio	.40	.18
15 Sammy Sosa	.60	.25
16 Brady Anderson	.40	.18
17 Wade Boggs	.60	.25
18 Charles Johnson	.30	.14
19 Matt Williams	.40	.18
20 Denny Neagle	.30	.14
21 Ken Griffey Jr.	3.00	1.35
22 Robin Ventura	.30	.14
23 Barry Larkin	.40	.18
24 Todd Zeile	.15	.07
25 Chuck Knoblauch	.60	.25
26 Todd Hundley	.30	.14
27 Roger Clemens	1.25	.55
28 Michael Tucker	.30	.14
29 Rondell White	.30	.14
30 Osvaldo Fernandez	.15	.07
31 Ivan Rodriguez	.75	.35
32 Alex Fernandez	.30	.14
33 Jason Isringhausen	.15	.07
34 Chipper Jones	2.00	.90
35 Paul O'Neill	.30	.14
36 Hideo Nomo	1.50	.70
37 Roberto Alomar	.60	.25
38 Derek Bell	.30	.14
39 Paul Molitor	.60	.25
40 Andy Benes	.15	.07
41 Steve Trachsel	.15	.07
42 J.T. Snow	.30	.14
43 Jason Kendall	.30	.14
44 Alex Rodriguez	2.50	1.10
45 Joey Hamilton	.30	.14
46 Carlos Delgado	.30	.14
47 Jason Giambi	.30	.14
48 Larry Walker	.60	.25
49 Derek Jeter	2.00	.90
50 Kenny Lofton	.75	.35
51 Devon White	.15	.07
52 Matt Mieske	.15	.07
53 Melvin Nieves	.15	.07
54 Jose Canseco	.40	.18
55 Tino Martinez	.60	.25
56 Rafael Palmeiro	.40	.18
57 Edgardo Alfonzo	.30	.14
58 Jay Buhner	.40	.18
59 Shane Reynolds	.15	.07
60 Steve Finley	.30	.14
61 Bobby Higginson	.30	.14
62 Dean Palmer	.15	.07
63 Terry Pendleton	.15	.07
64 Marquis Grissom	.30	.14
65 Mike Stanley	.15	.07
66 Moises Alou	.30	.14
67 Ray Lankford	.30	.14
68 Marty Cordova	.15	.07
69 John Olerud	.15	.07
70 David Cone	.30	.14
71 Benito Santiago	.15	.07
72 Ryne Sandberg	.75	.35
73 Rickey Henderson	.40	.18
74 Roger Cedeno	.15	.07
75 Wilson Alvarez	.30	.14
76 Tim Salmon	.60	.25
77 Orlando Merced	.15	.07
78 Vinny Castilla	.30	.14
79 Ismael Valdes	.30	.14
80 Dante Bichette	.30	.14
81 Kevin Brown	.30	.14
82 Andy Pettitte	.60	.25
83 Scott Stahoviak	.15	.07
84 Mickey Tettleton	.15	.07
85 Jack McDowell	.15	.07
86 Tom Glavine	.30	.14
87 Gregg Jefferies	.15	.07
88 Chili Davis	.15	.07
89 Randy Johnson	.60	.25
90 John Mabry	.15	.07
91 Billy Wagner	.30	.14
92 Jeff Cirillo	.30	.14
93 Trevor Hoffman	.30	.14
94 Juan Guzman	.15	.07
95 Geronimo Berroa	.15	.07
96 Bernard Gilkey	.15	.07
97 Danny Tartabull	.15	.07
98 Johnny Damon	.15	.07
99 Charlie Hayes	.15	.07
100 Reggie Sanders	.15	.07
101 Robby Thompson	.15	.07
102 Bobby Bonilla	.30	.14
103 Reggie Jefferson	.30	.14
104 John Smoltz	.60	.25
105 Jim Thome	.15	.07
106 Ruben Rivera	.30	.14
107 Darren Oliver	.15	.07
108 Mo Vaughn	.75	.35
109 Roger Pavlik	.15	.07
110 Terry Steinbach	.15	.07
111 Jermaine Dye	.15	.07
112 Mark Grudzielanek	.15	.07
113 Rick Aguilera	.15	.07
114 Jamey Wright	.30	.14
115 Eddie Murray	.60	.25
116 Brian L. Hunter	.15	.07
117 Hal Morris	.15	.07
118 Tom Pagnozzi	.15	.07
119 Mike Mussina	.60	.25
120 Mark Grace	.40	.18
121 Cal Ripken	2.50	1.10
122 Tom Goodwin	.15	.07
123 Paul Sorrento	.15	.07
124 Jay Bell	.15	.07
125 Todd Hollandsworth	.15	.07
126 Edgar Martinez	.40	.18
127 George Arias	.15	.07
128 Greg Vaughn	.15	.07
129 Roberto Hernandez	.30	.14
130 Delino DeShields	.15	.07
131 Bill Pulsipher	.15	.07
132 Joey Cora	.30	.14
133 Mariano Rivera	.30	.14
134 Mike Piazza	2.00	.90
135 Carlos Baerga	.30	.14
136 Jose Mesa	.30	.14
137 Will Clark	.40	.18
138 Frank Thomas	2.50	1.10
139 John Wetteland	.30	.14
140 Shawn Estes	.30	.14
141 Garret Anderson	.30	.14
142 Andre Dawson	.40	.18
143 Eddie Taubensee	.15	.07
144 Ryan Klesko	.40	.18
145 Rocky Coppinger	.30	.14
146 Jeff Bagwell	1.25	.55
147 Donovan Osborne	.15	.07
148 Greg Myers	.15	.07
149 Brant Brown	.15	.07
150 Kevin Elster	.15	.07
151 Bob Wells	.15	.07
152 Wally Joyner	.15	.07
153 Rico Brogna	.15	.07
154 Dwight Gooden	.30	.14

☐ 155 Jermaine Allensworth	.15	.07
☐ 156 Ray Durham	.15	.07
☐ 157 Cecil Fielder	.30	.14
☐ 158 John Burkett	.15	.07
☐ 159 Gary Sheffield	.60	.25
☐ 160 Albert Belle	.75	.35
☐ 161 Tomas Perez	.15	.07
☐ 162 David Doster	.15	.07
☐ 163 John Valentin	.15	.07
☐ 164 Danny Graves	.15	.07
☐ 165 Jose Paniagua	.15	.07
☐ 166 Brian Giles	.15	.07
☐ 167 Barry Bonds	.75	.35
☐ 168 Sterling Hitchcock	.15	.07
☐ 169 Bernie Williams	.60	.25
☐ 170 Fred McGriff	.40	.18
☐ 171 George Williams	.15	.07
☐ 172 Amaury Telemaco	.15	.07
☐ 173 Ken Caminiti	.60	.25
☐ 174 Ron Gant	.30	.14
☐ 175 Dave Justice	.60	.25
☐ 176 James Baldwin	.15	.07
☐ 177 Pat Hentgen	.30	.14
☐ 178 Ben McDonald	.15	.07
☐ 179 Tim Naehring	.15	.07
☐ 180 Jim Eisenreich	.30	.14
☐ 181 Ken Hill	.15	.07
☐ 182 Paul Wilson	.30	.14
☐ 183 Marvin Benard	.15	.07
☐ 184 Alan Benes	.30	.14
☐ 185 Ellis Burks	.30	.14
☐ 186 Scott Servais	.15	.07
☐ 187 David Segui	.15	.07
☐ 188 Scott Brosius	.15	.07
☐ 189 Jose Offerman	.15	.07
☐ 190 Eric Davis	.15	.07
☐ 191 Brett Butler	.30	.14
☐ 192 Curtis Pride	.15	.07
☐ 193 Yamil Benitez	.15	.07
☐ 194 Chan Ho Park	.60	.25
☐ 195 Bret Boone	.15	.07
☐ 196 Omar Vizquel	.30	.14
☐ 197 Orlando Miller	.15	.07
☐ 198 Ramon Martinez	.30	.14
☐ 199 Harold Baines	.15	.07
☐ 200 Eric Young	.30	.14
☐ 201 Fernando Vina	.15	.07
☐ 202 Alex Gonzalez	.15	.07
☐ 203 Fernando Valenzuela	.30	.14
☐ 204 Steve Avery	.15	.07
☐ 205 Ernie Young	.15	.07
☐ 206 Kevin Appier	.30	.14
☐ 207 Randy Myers	.15	.07
☐ 208 Jeff Suppan	.30	.14
☐ 209 James Mouton	.15	.07
☐ 210 Russ Davis	.15	.07
☐ 211 Al Martin	.15	.07
☐ 212 Troy Percival	.15	.07
☐ 213 Al Leiter	.15	.07
☐ 214 Dennis Eckersley	.40	.18
☐ 215 Mark Johnson	.15	.07
☐ 216 Eric Karros	.30	.14
☐ 217 Royce Clayton	.15	.07
☐ 218 Tony Phillips	.15	.07
☐ 219 Tim Wakefield	.15	.07
☐ 220 Alan Trammell	.40	.18
☐ 221 Eduardo Perez	.15	.07
☐ 222 Butch Huskey	.15	.07
☐ 223 Tim Belcher	.15	.07
☐ 224 Jamie Moyer	.15	.07
☐ 225 F.P. Santangelo	.15	.07
☐ 226 Rusty Greer	.30	.14
☐ 227 Jeff Brantley	.15	.07
☐ 228 Mark Langston	.15	.07
☐ 229 Ray Montgomery	.15	.07
☐ 230 Rich Becker	.15	.07
☐ 231 Ozzie Smith	.75	.35
☐ 232 Rey Ordonez	.15	.07
☐ 233 Ricky Otero	.15	.07
☐ 234 Mike Cameron	.30	.14
☐ 235 Mike Sweeney	.15	.07
☐ 236 Mark Lewis	.15	.07
☐ 237 Luis Gonzalez	.15	.07
☐ 238 Marcus Jensen	.15	.07
☐ 239 Ed Sprague	.15	.07
☐ 240 Jose Valentin	.15	.07
☐ 241 Jeff Frye	.15	.07
☐ 242 Charles Nagy	.30	.14
☐ 243 Carlos Garcia	.15	.07
☐ 244 Mike Hampton	.15	.07
☐ 245 B.J. Surhoff	.30	.14
☐ 246 Wilton Guerrero	.15	.07
☐ 247 Frank Rodriguez	.15	.07
☐ 248 Gary Gaetti	.30	.14
☐ 249 Lance Johnson	.15	.07
☐ 250 Darren Bragg	.15	.07
☐ 251 Darryl Hamilton	.15	.07
☐ 252 John Jaha	.15	.07
☐ 253 Craig Paquette	.15	.07
☐ 254 Jaime Navarro	.15	.07
☐ 255 Shawon Dunston	.15	.07
☐ 256 Mark Loretta	.15	.07
☐ 257 Tim Belk	.15	.07
☐ 258 Jeff Darwin	.15	.07
☐ 259 Ruben Sierra	.15	.07
☐ 260 Chuck Finley	.15	.07
☐ 261 Darryl Strawberry	.30	.14
☐ 262 Shannon Stewart	.15	.07
☐ 263 Pedro Martinez	.60	.25
☐ 264 Neifi Perez	.30	.14
☐ 265 Jeff Conine	.30	.14
☐ 266 Orel Hershiser	.30	.14
☐ 267 Eddie Murray CL	.60	.25
☐ 268 Paul Molitor CL	.60	.25
☐ 269 Barry Bonds CL	.60	.25
☐ 270 Mark McGwire CL	.60	.25
☐ 271 Matt Williams	.40	.18
☐ 272 Todd Zeile	.15	.07
☐ 273 Roger Clemens	1.25	.55
☐ 274 Michael Tucker	.30	.14
☐ 275 J.T. Snow	.30	.14
☐ 276 Kenny Lofton	.75	.35
☐ 277 Jose Canseco	.40	.18
☐ 278 Marquis Grissom	.30	.14
☐ 279 Moises Alou	.30	.14
☐ 280 Benito Santiago	.15	.07
☐ 281 Willie McGee	.15	.07
☐ 282 Chili Davis	.30	.14
☐ 283 Ron Coomer	.15	.07
☐ 284 Orlando Merced	.15	.07
☐ 285 Delino DeShields	.15	.07
☐ 286 John Wetteland	.30	.14
☐ 287 Darren Daulton	.30	.14
☐ 288 Lee Stevens	.15	.07
☐ 289 Albert Belle	.75	.35
☐ 290 Sterling Hitchcock	.15	.07
☐ 291 David Justice	.60	.25
☐ 292 Eric Davis	.15	.07
☐ 293 Brian Hunter	.30	.14
☐ 294 Darryl Hamilton	.15	.07
☐ 295 Steve Avery	.15	.07
☐ 296 Joe Vitiello	.15	.07
☐ 297 Jaime Navarro	.15	.07
☐ 298 Eddie Murray	.60	.25
☐ 299 Randy Myers	.15	.07
☐ 300 Francisco Cordova	.15	.07
☐ 301 Javier Lopez	.15	.07
☐ 302 Geronimo Berroa	.15	.07
☐ 303 Jeffrey Hammonds	.15	.07
☐ 304 Deion Sanders	.60	.25
☐ 305 Jeff Fassero	.15	.07
☐ 306 Curt Schilling	.30	.14
☐ 307 Robb Nen	.15	.07
☐ 308 Mark McLemore	.15	.07
☐ 309 Jimmy Key	.15	.07
☐ 310 Quilvio Veras	.15	.07
☐ 311 Bip Roberts	.15	.07
☐ 312 Esteban Loaiza	.15	.07
☐ 313 Andy Ashby	.15	.07
☐ 314 Sandy Alomar Jr.	.30	.14
☐ 315 Shawn Green	.15	.07
☐ 316 Luis Castillo	.15	.07
☐ 317 Benji Gil	.15	.07
☐ 318 Otis Nixon	.15	.07
☐ 319 Aaron Sele	.15	.07
☐ 320 Brad Ausmus	.15	.07
☐ 321 Troy O'Leary	.15	.07
☐ 322 Terrell Wade	.15	.07
☐ 323 Jeff King	.15	.07
☐ 324 Kevin Seitzer	.15	.07
☐ 325 Mark Wohlers	.15	.07
☐ 326 Edgar Renteria	.30	.14
☐ 327 Dan Wilson	.15	.07
☐ 328 Brian McRae	.15	.07
☐ 329 Rod Beck	.15	.07
☐ 330 Julio Franco	.30	.14
☐ 331 Dave Nilsson	.15	.07
☐ 332 Glenallen Hill	.15	.07
☐ 333 Kevin Elster	.15	.07
☐ 334 Joe Girardi	.15	.07
☐ 335 David Wells	.15	.07
☐ 336 Jeff Blauser	.15	.07
☐ 337 Darryl Kile	.30	.14
☐ 338 Jeff Kent	.15	.07
☐ 339 Jim Leyritz	.15	.07
☐ 340 Todd Stottlemyre	.15	.07
☐ 341 Tony Clark	.60	.25
☐ 342 Chris Hoiles	.15	.07
☐ 343 Mike Lieberthal	.15	.07
☐ 344 Matt Lawton	.15	.07
☐ 345 Alex Ochoa	.15	.07
☐ 346 Chris Snopek	.15	.07
☐ 347 Rudy Pemberton	.15	.07
☐ 348 Eric Owens	.15	.07
☐ 349 Joe Randa	.15	.07
☐ 350 John Olerud	.30	.14
☐ 351 Steve Karsay	.15	.07
☐ 352 Mark Whiten	.15	.07
☐ 353 Bob Abreu	.60	.25
☐ 354 Bartolo Colon	.30	.14
☐ 355 Vladimir Guerrero	1.25	.55
☐ 356 Darin Erstad	1.00	.45
☐ 357 Scott Rolen	1.50	.70
☐ 358 Andruw Jones	1.50	.70
☐ 359 Scott Spiezio	.30	.14
☐ 360 Karim Garcia	.15	.07
☐ 361 Hideki Irabu	.75	.35
☐ 362 Nomar Garciaparra	2.00	.90
☐ 363 Dmitri Young	.30	.14
☐ 364 Bubba Trammell	.60	.25
☐ 365 Kevin Orie	.30	.14
☐ 366 Jose Rosado	.15	.07
☐ 367 Jose Guillen	.75	.35
☐ 368 Brooks Kieschnick	.30	.14
☐ 369 Pokey Reese	.15	.07
☐ 370 Glendon Rusch	.15	.07
☐ 371 Jason Dickson	.15	.07
☐ 372 Todd Walker	.15	.07
☐ 373 Justin Thompson	.30	.14
☐ 374 Todd Greene	.30	.14
☐ 375 Jeff Suppan	.30	.14
☐ 376 Trey Beamon	.15	.07
☐ 377 Damon Mashore	.15	.07
☐ 378 Wendell Magee	.15	.07
☐ 379 Shigetoshi Hasegawa	.40	.18
☐ 380 Bill Mueller	.30	.14
☐ 381 Chris Widger	.15	.07
☐ 382 Tony Graffanino	.15	.07
☐ 383 Derrek Lee	.30	.14
☐ 384 Brian Moehler	.15	.07
☐ 385 Quinton McCracken	.15	.07
☐ 386 Matt Morris	.30	.14
☐ 387 Marvin Benard	.15	.07
☐ 388 Deivi Cruz	.40	.18
☐ 389 Javier Valentin	.15	.07
☐ 390 Todd Dunwoody	.60	.25
☐ 391 Derrick Gibson	.60	.25
☐ 392 Raul Casanova	.15	.07
☐ 393 George Arias	.15	.07
☐ 394 Tony Womack	.50	.23
☐ 395 Antone Williamson	.15	.07
☐ 396 Jose Cruz Jr.	5.00	2.20
☐ 397 Desi Relaford	.15	.07
☐ 398 Frank Thomas HIT	1.25	.55
☐ 399 Ken Griffey Jr. HIT	1.50	.70
☐ 400 Cal Ripken HIT	1.25	.55
☐ 401 Chipper Jones HIT	1.00	.45
☐ 402 Mike Piazza HIT	1.00	.45
☐ 403 Gary Sheffield HIT	.60	.25
☐ 404 Alex Rodriguez HIT	1.25	.55
☐ 405 Wade Boggs HIT	.60	.25
☐ 406 Juan Gonzalez HIT	1.00	.45
☐ 407 Tony Gwynn HIT	.75	.35
☐ 408 Edgar Martinez HIT	.40	.18
☐ 409 Jeff Bagwell HIT	.60	.25
☐ 410 Larry Walker HIT	.60	.25
☐ 411 Kenny Lofton HIT	.60	.25
☐ 412 Manny Ramirez HIT	.60	.25
☐ 413 Mark McGwire HIT	.60	.25
☐ 414 Roberto Alomar HIT	.60	.25
☐ 415 Derek Jeter HIT	1.00	.45
☐ 416 Brady Anderson HIT	.40	.18
☐ 417 Paul Molitor HIT	.60	.25
☐ 418 Dante Bichette HIT	.30	.14
☐ 419 Jim Edmonds HIT	.60	.25
☐ 420 Mo Vaughn HIT	.60	.25
☐ 421 Barry Bonds HIT	.40	.18
☐ 422 Rusty Greer HIT	.30	.14
☐ 423 Greg Maddux KING	1.00	.45
☐ 424 Andy Pettitte KING	.60	.25
☐ 425 John Smoltz KING	.30	.14
☐ 426 Randy Johnson KING	.60	.25
☐ 427 Hideo Nomo KING	.75	.35
☐ 428 Roger Clemens KING	.60	.25
☐ 429 Tom Glavine KING	.30	.14
☐ 430 Pat Hentgen KING	.30	.14
☐ 431 Kevin Brown KING	.30	.14
☐ 432 Mike Mussina KING	.60	.25
☐ 433 Alex Fernandez KING	.15	.07
☐ 434 Kevin Appier KING	.15	.07
☐ 435 David Cone KING	.60	.25
☐ 436 Jeff Fassero KING	.15	.07
☐ 437 John Wetteland KING	.15	.07
☐ 438 Barry Bonds IS Ivan Rodriguez	.60	.25
☐ 439 Ken Griffey Jr. IS Andres Galarraga	1.00	.45
☐ 440 Fred McGriff IS Rafael Palmeiro	.40	.18
☐ 441 Barry Larkin IS Jim Thome	.40	.18

	MINT	NRMT
442 Sammy Sosa IS Albert Belle	.60	.25
443 Bernie Williams IS Todd Hundley	.30	.14
444 Chuck Knoblauch IS Brian Jordan	.15	.07
445 Mo Vaughn IS Jeff Conine	.15	.07
446 Ken Caminiti IS Jason Giambi	.15	.07
447 Raul Mondesi IS Tim Salmon	.40	.18
448 Cal Ripken CL	1.25	.55
449 Greg Maddux CL	1.00	.45
450 Ken Griffey Jr. CL	1.50	.70

1997 Donruss Gold Press Proofs

andomly inserted in first series at a rate of 1:32 and odate packs at an approximate rate of 1:64, cards from is 450-card set are a die-cut parallel rendition of the ore common silver Press Proof cards. Gold foil amping further distinguishes them from the silver Press oofs. Only 500 gold sets were printed.

	MINT	NRMT
OMPLETE SET (450)	3200.00	1450.00
OMPLETE SERIES 1 (270)	2000.00	900.00
OMPLETE UPDATE (180)	1200.00	550.00
OMMON CARD (1-450)	6.00	2.70
STARS: 15X TO 40X BASIC CARDS		
YOUNG STARS: 12.5X TO 30X BASIC CARDS		
ROOKIES: 8X TO 20X BASIC CARDS		

1997 Donruss Silver Press Proofs

andomly inserted in first series packs at a rate of 1:8 and pdate packs at an approximate rate of 1:16, cards from is 450-card silver foil set parallel the regular 1997 onruss set. The silver foil stamped words, "Press Proof" own the front right-hand side of the card distinguish em from their regular issue counterparts. Only 2,000 of ch card were produced.

	MINT	NRMT
OMPLETE SET (450)	1200.00	550.00
OMPLETE SERIES 1 (270)	700.00	325.00
OMPLETE UPDATE (180)	500.00	220.00
OMMON CARD (1-450)	2.00	.90
STARS: 6X TO 12X BASIC CARDS		
YOUNG STARS: 5X TO 10X BASIC CARDS		
ROOKIES: 3X TO 6X BASIC CARDS		

1997 Donruss Armed and Dangerous

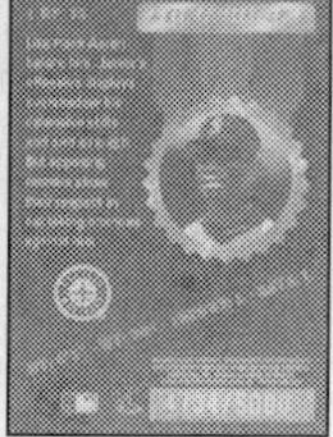

andomly inserted in hobby packs at a rate of one in 58 acks, this 15-card set features the League's hottest arms the game. The fronts carry color action player photos ith foil printing. The backs display player information nd a color player head portrait at the end of a ribbon presenting a medal. Only 5,000 of this set were oduced and are sequentially numbered.

	MINT	NRMT
OMPLETE SET (15)	150.00	70.00
OMMON CARD (1-15)	4.00	1.80
1 Ken Griffey Jr.	30.00	13.50
2 Raul Mondesi	4.00	1.80
3 Chipper Jones	20.00	9.00
4 Ivan Rodriguez	8.00	3.60
5 Randy Johnson	5.00	2.20
6 Alex Rodriguez	20.00	9.00
7 Larry Walker	5.00	2.20
8 Cal Ripken	25.00	11.00
9 Kenny Lofton	8.00	3.60
10 Barry Bonds	8.00	3.60
11 Derek Jeter	15.00	6.75
12 Charles Johnson	4.00	1.80
13 Greg Maddux	20.00	9.00
14 Roberto Alomar	6.00	2.70
15 Barry Larkin	4.00	1.80

1997 Donruss Diamond Kings

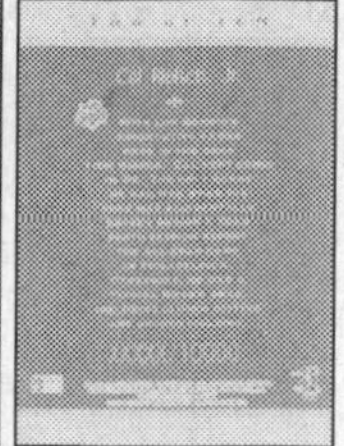

Randomly inserted in all first series packs at a rate of one in 45, this 10-card set commemorates the 15th anniversary of the annual art cards in Donruss baseball sets. Only 10,000 sets were produced each of which is sequentially numbered. Ten cards were printed with the number 1,982 representing the year the insert began and could be redeemed for an original piece of artwork by Diamond Kings artist Dan Gardiner. This was the first year Gardiner painted the Diamond King series.

	MINT	NRMT
COMPLETE SET (10)	180.00	80.00
COMMON CARD (1-10)	4.00	1.80
COMP.CANVAS SET (10)	750.00	350.00
*CANVAS: 2X TO 4X BASIC DK'S		
1 Ken Griffey Jr.	40.00	18.00
2 Cal Ripken	30.00	13.50
3 Mo Vaughn	10.00	4.50
4 Chuck Knoblauch	6.00	2.70
5 Jeff Bagwell	15.00	6.75
6 Henry Rodriguez	4.00	1.80
7 Mike Piazza	25.00	11.00
8 Ivan Rodriguez	10.00	4.50
9 Frank Thomas	30.00	13.50
10 Chipper Jones	25.00	11.00

1997 Donruss Dominators

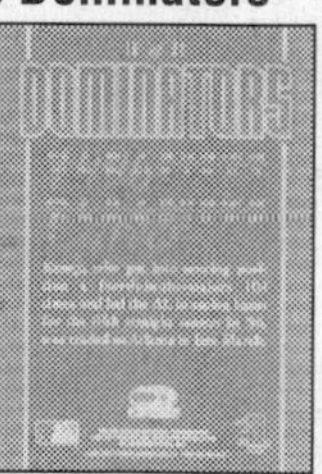

Randomly inserted in Update packs, cards from this 20-card set feature top stars with either incredible speed, awesome power, or unbelievable pitching ability. Card fronts feature red borders and silver foil stamping.

	MINT	NRMT
COMPLETE SET (20)	90.00	40.00
COMMON CARD (1-20)	1.50	.70
1 Frank Thomas	12.00	5.50
2 Ken Griffey Jr.	15.00	6.75
3 Greg Maddux	10.00	4.50
4 Cal Ripken	12.00	5.50
5 Alex Rodriguez	10.00	4.50
6 Albert Belle	4.00	1.80
7 Mark McGwire	6.00	2.70
8 Juan Gonzalez	8.00	3.60
9 Chipper Jones	10.00	4.50
10 Hideo Nomo	8.00	3.60
11 Roger Clemens	6.00	2.70
12 John Smoltz	1.50	.70
13 Mike Piazza	10.00	4.50
14 Sammy Sosa	3.00	1.35
15 Matt Williams	2.50	1.10
16 Kenny Lofton	4.00	1.80
17 Barry Larkin	2.50	1.10
18 Rafael Palmeiro	2.50	1.10
19 Ken Caminiti	3.00	1.35
20 Gary Sheffield	3.00	1.35

1997 Donruss Elite Inserts

Randomly inserted in all first series packs, this 12-card

fronts feature Micro-etched color action player photos, while the backs carry player information. Only 2,500 of this set were produced and are sequentially numbered.

	MINT	NRMT
COMPLETE SET (12)	500.00	220.00
COMMON CARD (1-12)	12.00	5.50
1 Frank Thomas	60.00	27.00
2 Paul Molitor	15.00	6.75
3 Sammy Sosa	12.00	5.50
4 Barry Bonds	20.00	9.00
5 Chipper Jones	50.00	22.00
6 Alex Rodriguez	50.00	22.00
7 Ken Griffey Jr.	80.00	36.00
8 Jeff Bagwell	30.00	13.50
9 Cal Ripken	60.00	27.00
10 Mo Vaughn	20.00	9.00
11 Mike Piazza	50.00	22.00
12 Juan Gonzalez UER name mispelled as Gonzales	40.00	18.00

1997 Donruss Franchise Features

Randomly inserted in Update hobby packs only at an approximate rate of 1:48, cards from this 15-card set feature color player photos on a unique "movie-poster" style, double-front card design. Each card highlights a superstar veteran on one side displaying a "Now Playing" banner, while the other side features a rookie prospect with a "Coming Attraction" banner. Each card is printed on an all foil card stock and serial numbered to 3,000.

	MINT	NRMT
COMPLETE SET (15)	250.00	110.00
COMMON CARD (1-15)	6.00	2.70
1 Ken Griffey Jr. Andruw Jones	40.00	18.00
2 Frank Thomas Darin Erstad	30.00	13.50
3 Alex Rodriguez Nomar Garciaparra	30.00	13.50
4 Chuck Knoblauch Wilton Guerrero	6.00	2.70
5 Juan Gonzalez BubbaTrammell	20.00	9.00
6 Chipper Jones Todd Walker	25.00	11.00
7 Barry Bonds Vladimir Guerrero	12.00	5.50
8 Mark McGwire Dmitri Young	15.00	6.75
9 Mike Piazza Mike Sweeney	25.00	11.00
10 Mo Vaughn Tony Clark	10.00	4.50
11 Gary Sheffield Jose Guillen		
12 Kenny Lofton Shannon Stewart	10.00	4.50
13 Cal Ripken Scott Rolen	30.00	13.50
14 Derek Jeter Pokey Reese	20.00	9.00
15 Tony Gwynn Bob Abreu	20.00	9.00

1997 Donruss Longball Leaders

Randomly inserted in first series retail packs only, this 15-card set honors the league's most fearsome long-ball hitters. The fronts feature color action player photos and foil stamping. The backs carry player information.

	MINT	NRMT
COMPLETE SET (15)	120.00	55.00
COMMON CARD (1-15)	2.50	1.10
☐ 1 Frank Thomas	25.00	11.00
☐ 2 Albert Belle	8.00	3.60
☐ 3 Mo Vaughn	8.00	3.60
☐ 4 Brady Anderson	4.00	1.80
☐ 5 Greg Vaughn	2.50	1.10
☐ 6 Ken Griffey Jr.	30.00	13.50
☐ 7 Jay Buhner	4.00	1.80
☐ 8 Juan Gonzalez	15.00	6.75
☐ 9 Mike Piazza	20.00	9.00
☐ 10 Jeff Bagwell	12.00	5.50
☐ 11 Sammy Sosa	5.00	2.20
☐ 12 Mark McGwire	12.00	5.50
☐ 13 Cecil Fielder	3.00	1.35
☐ 14 Ryan Klesko	4.00	1.80
☐ 15 Jose Canseco	4.00	1.80

1997 Donruss Power Alley

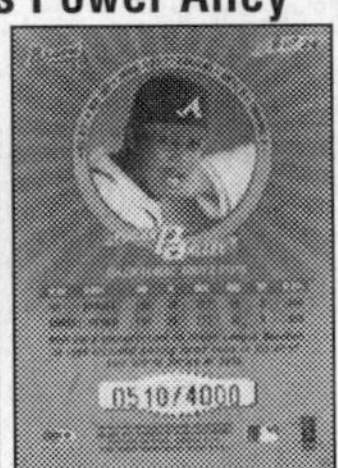

This 24-card set features color images of some of the league's top hitters printed on a micro-etched, all-foil card stock with holographic foil stamping. Using a "fractured" printing structure, 12 players utilize a green finish and are numbered to 4,000. Eight players are printed on all blue finish and number to 2,000, with the last four players utilizing a gold finish and are numbered to 1,000.

	MINT	NRMT
COMPLETE SET (24)	600.00	275.00
COMMON CARD (1-24)	5.00	2.20
*GREEN DIE CUT: 3X TO 6X BASIC GREEN		
*BLUE DIE CUT: 2X TO 4X BASIC BLUE		
*GOLD DIE CUT: 1.25X TO 2.5X BASIC GOLD		
☐ 1 Frank Thomas G	80.00	36.00
☐ 2 Ken Griffey Jr. G	100.00	45.00
☐ 3 Cal Ripken G	80.00	36.00
☐ 4 Jeff Bagwell B	25.00	11.00
☐ 5 Mike Piazza B	40.00	18.00
☐ 6 Andruw Jones GR	15.00	6.75
☐ 7 Alex Rodriguez G	60.00	27.00
☐ 8 Albert Belle GR	10.00	4.50
☐ 9 Mo Vaughn GR	10.00	4.50
☐ 10 Chipper Jones B	40.00	18.00
☐ 11 Juan Gonzalez B	30.00	13.50
☐ 12 Ken Caminiti GR	8.00	3.60
☐ 13 Manny Ramirez GR	8.00	3.60
☐ 14 Mark McGwire GR	15.00	6.75
☐ 15 Kenny Lofton B	15.00	6.75
☐ 16 Barry Bonds GR	10.00	4.50
☐ 17 Gary Sheffield GR	8.00	3.60
☐ 18 Tony Gwynn GR	20.00	9.00
☐ 19 Vladimir Guerrero B	20.00	9.00
☐ 20 Ivan Rodriguez B	15.00	6.75
☐ 21 Paul Molitor B	12.00	5.50
☐ 22 Sammy Sosa GR	8.00	3.60
☐ 23 Matt Williams GR	5.00	2.20
☐ 24 Derek Jeter GR	20.00	9.00

1997 Donruss Rated Rookies

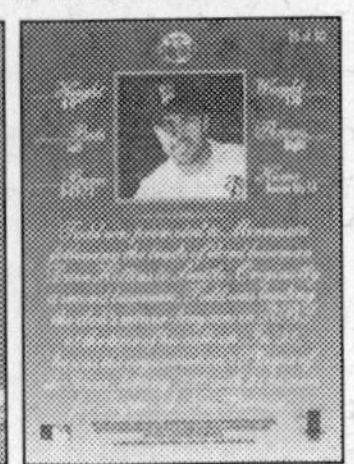

Randomly inserted in all first series packs, this 30-card set honors the top rookie prospects as chosen by Donruss to be the most likely to succeed. The fronts feature color action player photos and silver foil printing. The backs carry a player portrait and player information.

	MINT	NRMT
COMPLETE SET (30)	50.00	22.00
COMMON CARD (1-30)	1.00	.45
☐ 1 Jason Thompson	1.50	.70
☐ 2 LaTroy Hawkins	1.00	.45
☐ 3 Scott Rolen	10.00	4.50
☐ 4 Trey Beamon	1.00	.45
☐ 5 Kimera Bartee	1.00	.45
☐ 6 Nerio Rodriguez	1.00	.45
☐ 7 Jeff D'Amico	1.50	.70
☐ 8 Quinton McCracken	1.00	.45
☐ 9 John Wasdin	1.00	.45
☐ 10 Robin Jennings	1.00	.45
☐ 11 Steve Gibralter	1.00	.45
☐ 12 Tyler Houston	1.00	.45
☐ 13 Tony Clark	4.00	1.80
☐ 14 Ugueth Urbina	1.50	.70
☐ 15 Karim Garcia	1.50	.70
☐ 16 Raul Casanova	1.00	.45
☐ 17 Brooks Kieschnick	1.50	.70
☐ 18 Luis Castillo	1.00	.45
☐ 19 Edgar Renteria	1.50	.70
☐ 20 Andruw Jones	10.00	4.50
☐ 21 Chad Mottola	1.00	.45
☐ 22 Mac Suzuki	1.50	.70
☐ 23 Justin Thompson	1.50	.70
☐ 24 Darin Erstad	6.00	2.70
☐ 25 Todd Walker	1.00	.45
☐ 26 Todd Greene	1.50	.70
☐ 27 Vladimir Guerrero	8.00	3.60
☐ 28 Darren Dreifort	1.00	.45
☐ 29 John Burke	1.00	.45
☐ 30 Damon Mashore	1.00	.45

1997 Donruss Ripken The Only Way I Know

This special autobiographical tribute to Cal Ripken Jr. delivers a one-of-a-kind inside look at the modern day "Iron Man." Cards from this ten card set are printed on all foil card stock with foil stamping, utilizing exclusive photography and excerpts from his book. The first nine cards in the set were randomly seeded into packs of Donruss Update at an approximate rate of 1:24. Card #10 was available exclusively in his book, "The Only Way I Know." Ripken autographed 2,131 of these #10 cards and they were randomly inserted into the books. Because of it's separate distribution, card #10 is not commonly included in complete sets, thus the mainstream set is considered complete with cards 1-9. Only 5,000 of each 1-9 card were produced, each of which are sequentially numbered on back.

	MINT	NRMT
COMPLETE SET (9)	100.00	45.00
COMMON CARD (1-9)	12.00	5.50
☐ 1 Cal Ripken	12.00	5.50
☐ 2 Cal Ripken	12.00	5.50
☐ 3 Cal Ripken	12.00	5.50
☐ 4 Cal Ripken	12.00	5.50
☐ 5 Cal Ripken	12.00	5.50
☐ 6 Cal Ripken	12.00	5.50
☐ 7 Cal Ripken	12.00	5.50
☐ 8 Cal Ripken	12.00	5.50
☐ 9 Cal Ripken	12.00	5.50
☐ 10 Cal Ripken	6.00	2.70
distributed exclusively with book		
☐ 10A Cal Ripken BOOK AU/2131	200.00	90.00

1997 Donruss Rocket Launchers

Randomly inserted in first series magazine packs only this 15-card set honers baseball's top power hitters. The fronts feature color player photos, while the backs carry player information. Only 5,000 of this set were produced and are sequentially numbered.

	MINT	NRMT
COMPLETE SET (15)	120.00	55.00
COMMON CARD (1-15)	3.00	1.35
☐ 1 Frank Thomas	25.00	11.00
☐ 2 Albert Belle	8.00	3.60
☐ 3 Chipper Jones	20.00	9.00
☐ 4 Mike Piazza	20.00	9.00
☐ 5 Mo Vaughn	8.00	3.60
☐ 6 Juan Gonzalez	15.00	6.75
☐ 7 Fred McGriff	4.00	1.80
☐ 8 Jeff Bagwell	12.00	5.50
☐ 9 Matt Williams	4.00	1.80
☐ 10 Gary Sheffield	6.00	2.70
☐ 11 Barry Bonds	8.00	3.60
☐ 12 Manny Ramirez	10.00	4.50
☐ 13 Henry Rodriguez	3.00	1.35
☐ 14 Jason Giambi	3.50	1.55
☐ 15 Cal Ripken	25.00	11.00

1997 Donruss Rookie Diamond Kings

Randomly inserted in Update packs at an approximate rate of 1:24, cards from this 10-card set feature color portraits of some of the season's hottest rookie prospects in gold borders. Only 9,500 of each card were printed and are sequentially numbered. Please note that the numbering of each card runs to 10,000, but the first 500 of each card were Canvas parallels.

	MINT	NRMT
COMPLETE SET (10)	110.00	50.00
COMMON CARD (1-10)	4.00	1.80
*CANVAS: 2X TO 4X BASIC CARDS....		
☐ 1 Andruw Jones	20.00	9.00
☐ 2 Vladimir Guerrero	15.00	6.75
☐ 3 Scott Rolen	20.00	9.00
☐ 4 Todd Walker	4.00	1.80
☐ 5 Bartolo Colon	4.50	2.00
☐ 6 Jose Guillen	10.00	4.50
☐ 7 Nomar Garciaparra	25.00	11.00
☐ 8 Darin Erstad	12.00	5.50
☐ 9 Dmitri Young	4.50	2.00
☐ 10 Wilton Guerrero	4.00	1.80

1998 Donruss

he 1998 Donruss set was issued in one series totalling 70 cards and was distributed in 10-card packs with a uggested retail price of $1.99. The fronts feature color layer photos with player information on the backs. The et contains the topical subset: Fan Club (156-165). Each an Club card carried instructions on how the fan could ote for their favorite players to be included in the 1998 onruss Update set.

	MINT	NRMT
OMPLETE SET (170)	20.00	9.00
OMMON CARD (1-170)	.10	.05

	MINT	NRMT
☐ 1 Paul Molitor	.50	.23
☐ 2 Juan Gonzalez	1.25	.55
☐ 3 Darryl Kile	.25	.11
☐ 4 Randy Johnson	.50	.23
☐ 5 Tom Glavine	.25	.11
☐ 6 Pat Hentgen	.50	.23
☐ 7 David Justice	.50	.23
☐ 8 Kevin Brown	.25	.11
☐ 9 Mike Mussina	.50	.23
☐ 10 Ken Caminiti	.50	.23
☐ 11 Todd Hundley	.25	.11
☐ 12 Frank Thomas	2.00	.90
☐ 13 Ray Lankford	.25	.11
☐ 14 Justin Thompson	.25	.11
☐ 15 Jason Dickson	.25	.11
☐ 16 Kenny Lofton	.60	.25
☐ 17 Ivan Rodriguez	.60	.25
☐ 18 Pedro Martinez	.50	.23
☐ 19 Brady Anderson	.35	.16
☐ 20 Barry Larkin	.35	.16
☐ 21 Chipper Jones	1.50	.70
☐ 22 Tony Gwynn	1.25	.55
☐ 23 Roger Clemens	1.00	.45
☐ 24 Sandy Alomar Jr.	.25	.11
☐ 25 Tino Martinez	.50	.23
☐ 26 Jeff Bagwell	1.00	.45
☐ 27 Shawn Estes	.25	.11
☐ 28 Ken Griffey Jr.	2.50	1.10
☐ 29 Javier Lopez	.25	.11
☐ 30 Denny Neagle	.25	.11
☐ 31 Mike Piazza	1.50	.70
☐ 32 Andres Galarraga	.50	.23
☐ 33 Larry Walker	.50	.23
☐ 34 Alex Rodriguez	1.50	.70
☐ 35 Greg Maddux	1.50	.70
☐ 36 Albert Belle	.60	.25
☐ 37 Barry Bonds	.60	.25
☐ 38 Mo Vaughn	.60	.25
☐ 39 Kevin Appier	.25	.11
☐ 40 Wade Boggs	.50	.23
☐ 41 Garret Anderson	.25	.11
☐ 42 Jeffrey Hammonds	.25	.11
☐ 43 Marquis Grissom	.25	.11
☐ 44 Jim Edmonds	.50	.23
☐ 45 Brian Jordan	.25	.11
☐ 46 Raul Mondesi	.50	.23
☐ 47 John Valentin	.25	.11
☐ 48 Brad Radke	.25	.11
☐ 49 Ismael Valdes	.25	.11
☐ 50 Matt Stairs	.10	.05
☐ 51 Matt Williams	.35	.16
☐ 52 Reggie Jefferson	.25	.11
☐ 53 Alan Benes	.10	.05
☐ 54 Charles Johnson	.25	.11
☐ 55 Chuck Knoblauch	.50	.23
☐ 56 Edgar Martinez	.35	.16
☐ 57 Nomar Garciaparra	1.50	.70
☐ 58 Craig Biggio	.35	.16
☐ 59 Bernie Williams	.50	.23
☐ 60 David Cone	.25	.11
☐ 61 Cal Ripken	2.00	.90
☐ 62 Mark McGwire	1.25	.55
☐ 63 Roberto Alomar	.50	.23
☐ 64 Fred McGriff	.35	.16
☐ 65 Eric Karros	.25	.11
☐ 66 Robin Ventura	.25	.11
☐ 67 Darin Erstad	.60	.25
☐ 68 Michael Tucker	.25	.11
☐ 69 Jim Thome	.50	.23
☐ 70 Mark Grace	.35	.16
☐ 71 Lou Collier	.10	.05
☐ 72 Karim Garcia	.25	.11
☐ 73 Alex Fernandez	.10	.05
☐ 74 J.T. Snow	.25	.11
☐ 75 Reggie Sanders	.10	.05
☐ 76 John Smoltz	.25	.11
☐ 77 Tim Salmon	.50	.23
☐ 78 Paul O'Neill	.25	.11
☐ 79 Vinny Castilla	.25	.11
☐ 80 Rafael Palmeiro	.35	.16
☐ 81 Jaret Wright	1.25	.55
☐ 82 Jay Buhner	.35	.16
☐ 83 Brett Butler	.25	.11
☐ 84 Todd Greene	.10	.05
☐ 85 Scott Rolen	1.25	.55
☐ 86 Sammy Sosa	.50	.23
☐ 87 Jason Giambi	.10	.05
☐ 88 Carlos Delgado	.25	.11
☐ 89 Deion Sanders	.50	.23
☐ 90 Wilton Guerrero	.10	.05
☐ 91 Andy Pettitte	.50	.23
☐ 92 Brian Giles	.25	.11
☐ 93 Dmitri Young	.25	.11
☐ 94 Ron Coomer	.10	.05
☐ 95 Mike Cameron	.25	.11
☐ 96 Edgardo Alfonzo	.25	.11
☐ 97 Jimmy Key	.25	.11
☐ 98 Ryan Klesko	.35	.16
☐ 99 Andy Benes	.10	.05
☐ 100 Derek Jeter	1.25	.55
☐ 101 Jeff Fassero	.10	.05
☐ 102 Neifi Perez	.10	.05
☐ 103 Hideo Nomo	1.25	.55
☐ 104 Andruw Jones	1.00	.45
☐ 105 Todd Helton	.60	.25
☐ 106 Livan Hernandez	.25	.11
☐ 107 Brett Tomko	.25	.11
☐ 108 Shannon Stewart	.25	.11
☐ 109 Bartolo Colon	.25	.11
☐ 110 Matt Morris	.25	.11
☐ 111 Miguel Tejada	.60	.25
☐ 112 Pokey Reese	.10	.05
☐ 113 Fernando Tatis	.25	.11
☐ 114 Todd Dunwoody	.25	.11
☐ 115 Jose Cruz Jr.	2.00	.90
☐ 116 Chan Ho Park	.50	.23
☐ 117 Kevin Young	.10	.05
☐ 118 Rickey Henderson	.50	.23
☐ 119 Hideki Irabu	.35	.16
☐ 120 Francisco Cordova	.10	.05
☐ 121 Al Martin	.10	.05
☐ 122 Tony Clark	.50	.23
☐ 123 Curt Schilling	.25	.11
☐ 124 Rusty Greer	.25	.11
☐ 125 Jose Canseco	.35	.16
☐ 126 Edgar Renteria	.10	.05
☐ 127 Todd Walker	.10	.05
☐ 128 Wally Joyner	.25	.11
☐ 129 Bill Mueller	.10	.05
☐ 130 Jose Guillen	.35	.16
☐ 131 Manny Ramirez	.50	.23
☐ 132 Bobby Higginson	.25	.11
☐ 133 Kevin Orie	.10	.05
☐ 134 Will Clark	.35	.16
☐ 135 Dave Nilsson	.10	.05
☐ 136 Jason Kendall	.25	.11
☐ 137 Ivan Cruz	.10	.05
☐ 138 Gary Sheffield	.50	.23
☐ 139 Bubba Trammell	.25	.11
☐ 140 Vladimir Guerrero	.75	.35
☐ 141 Dennis Reyes	.10	.05
☐ 142 Bobby Bonilla	.25	.11
☐ 143 Ruben Rivera	.25	.11
☐ 144 Ben Grieve	1.00	.45
☐ 145 Moises Alou	.25	.11
☐ 146 Tony Womack	.10	.05
☐ 147 Eric Young	.10	.05
☐ 148 Paul Konerko	.75	.35
☐ 149 Dante Bichette	.25	.11
☐ 150 Joe Carter	.25	.11
☐ 151 Rondell White	.25	.11
☐ 152 Chris Holt	.10	.05
☐ 153 Shawn Green	.25	.11
☐ 154 Mark Grudzielanek UER back rudzielanek	.10	.05
☐ 155 Jermaine Dye	.10	.05
☐ 156 Ken Griffey Jr. FC	1.25	.55
☐ 157 Frank Thomas FC	1.00	.45
☐ 158 Chipper Jones FC	.75	.35
☐ 159 Mike Piazza FC	.75	.35
☐ 160 Cal Ripken FC	1.00	.45
☐ 161 Greg Maddux FC	.75	.35
☐ 162 Juan Gonzalez FC	.60	.25
☐ 163 Alex Rodriguez FC	.75	.35
☐ 164 Mark McGwire FC	.60	.25
☐ 165 Derek Jeter FC	.60	.25
☐ 166 Larry Walker CL (1-55)	.50	.23
☐ 167 Tony Gwynn CL (56-110)	.60	.25
☐ 168 Tino Martinez CL (111-170)	.50	.23
☐ 169 Scott Rolen CL (inserts)	.60	.25
☐ 170 Nomar Garciaparra CL (inserts)	.75	.35

1998 Donruss Gold Press Proofs

This 170-card set is a limited production, die-cut parallel version of the regular base set. Each card is numbered as "1 of 500."

	MINT	NRMT
COMPLETE SET (170)	2000.00	900.00
COMMON CARD (1-170)	5.00	2.20

*STARS: 20X TO 40X BASIC CARDS ..
*YOUNG STARS: 15X TO 30X BASIC CARDS

1998 Donruss Silver Press Proofs

Randomly inserted in packs, this 170-card set is a limited parallel version of the base set printed on foil board. Each card is designated as "1 of 1500" produced.

	MINT	NRMT
COMPLETE SET (170)	800.00	350.00
COMMON CARD (1-170)	2.00	.90

*STARS: 6X TO 15X BASIC CARDS ....
*YOUNG STARS: 5X TO 12X BASIC CARDS

1998 Donruss Crusade Green

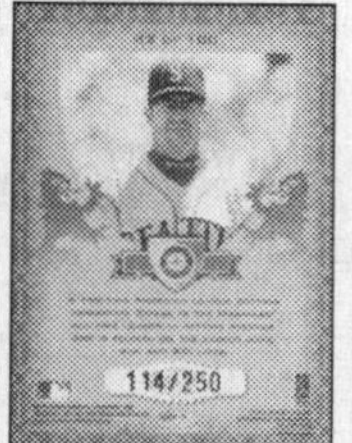

This 40-card set is skip numbered and was combined with cards from two other sets to make a complete set consisting of a total of 100 cards. The spread over the three programs were as follows: 40 players from 1998 Donruss, 30 from 1998 Leaf, and 30 from 1998 Donruss Update. The fronts feature color player photos printed with Limited "refractive" technology. The backs carry player information. Only 250 of each of these Green cards were produced and sequentially numbered.

	MINT	NRMT
COMMON CARD	12.00	5.50

*PURPLE STARS: .75X TO 1.5X GREEN
*RED STARS: 3X TO 6X GREEN

	MINT	NRMT
☐ 5 Jason Dickson	12.00	5.50
☐ 6 Todd Greene	12.00	5.50
☐ 7 Roberto Alomar	50.00	22.00
☐ 8 Cal Ripken	200.00	90.00
☐ 12 Mo Vaughn	60.00	27.00
☐ 13 Nomar Garciaparra	120.00	55.00
☐ 16 Mike Cameron	25.00	11.00
☐ 20 Sandy Alomar Jr.	25.00	11.00
☐ 21 David Justice	40.00	18.00
☐ 25 Justin Thompson	25.00	11.00
☐ 27 Kevin Appier	12.00	5.50
☐ 33 Tino Martinez	40.00	18.00
☐ 36 Hideki Irabu	25.00	11.00
☐ 37 Jose Canseco	30.00	13.50
☐ 39 Ken Griffey Jr.	250.00	110.00
☐ 42 Edgar Martinez	30.00	13.50
☐ 45 Will Clark	30.00	13.50
☐ 47 Rusty Greer	15.00	6.75
☐ 50 Shawn Green	12.00	5.50
☐ 51 Jose Cruz Jr.	150.00	70.00
☐ 52 Kenny Lofton	60.00	27.00
☐ 53 Chipper Jones	120.00	55.00
☐ 62 Kevin Orie	15.00	6.75
☐ 65 Deion Sanders	25.00	11.00
☐ 67 Larry Walker	50.00	22.00
☐ 68 Dante Bichette	15.00	6.75
☐ 71 Todd Helton	50.00	22.00
☐ 74 Bobby Bonilla	15.00	6.75
☐ 75 Kevin Brown	15.00	6.75
☐ 78 Craig Biggio	30.00	13.50
☐ 82 Wilton Guerrero	12.00	5.50
☐ 85 Pedro Martinez	40.00	18.00
☐ 86 Edgardo Alfonzo	15.00	6.75
☐ 88 Scott Rolen	100.00	45.00

	MINT	NRMT
☐ 89 Francisco Cordova	12.00	5.50
☐ 90 Jose Guillen	40.00	18.00
☐ 92 Ray Lankford	15.00	6.75
☐ 93 Mark McGwire	100.00	45.00
☐ 94 Matt Morris	12.00	5.50
☐ 100 Shawn Estes	15.00	6.75

1998 Donruss Diamond Kings

Randomly inserted in packs, this 20-card set features color player portraits of some of the greatest names in Baseball. Only 9,500 sets were produced and are sequentially numbered. The first 500 of each card were printed on actual canvas card stock. In addition, a Frank Thomas sample card was created as a promo for the 1998 Donruss 1 product. The card was sent to all wholesale accounts along with the order forms for the product. The large "SAMPLE" stamp across the back of the card makes it easy to differentiate from Thomas' standard 1998 Diamond King insert card.

	MINT	NRMT
COMPLETE SET (20)	250.00	110.00
COMMON CARD (1-20)	5.00	2.20
COMP.CANVAS SET (20)	1200.00	550.00
*CANVAS: 2X TO 4X BASIC DIAMOND KINGS		
☐ 1 Cal Ripken	30.00	13.50
☐ 2 Greg Maddux	25.00	11.00
☐ 3 Ivan Rodriguez	10.00	4.50
☐ 4 Tony Gwynn	20.00	9.00
☐ 5 Paul Molitor	8.00	3.60
☐ 6 Kenny Lofton	10.00	4.50
☐ 7 Andy Pettitte	8.00	3.60
☐ 8 Darin Erstad	8.00	3.60
☐ 9 Randy Johnson	8.00	3.60
☐ 10 Derek Jeter	20.00	9.00
☐ 11 Hideo Nomo	20.00	9.00
☐ 12 David Justice	8.00	3.60
☐ 13 Bernie Williams	8.00	3.60
☐ 14 Roger Clemens	15.00	6.75
☐ 15 Barry Larkin	5.00	2.20
☐ 16 Andruw Jones	12.00	5.50
☐ 17 Mike Piazza	25.00	11.00
☐ 18 Frank Thomas	30.00	13.50
☐ 19 Alex Rodriguez	25.00	11.00
☐ 20 Ken Griffey Jr.	40.00	18.00
☐ S20 Frank Thomas Sample	5.00	2.20

1998 Donruss Longball Leaders

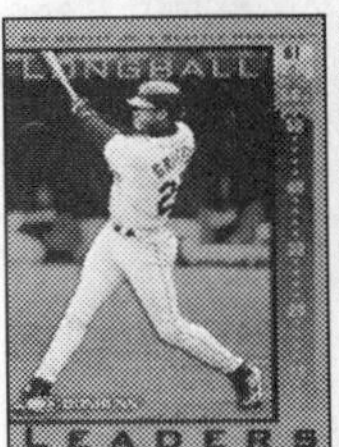
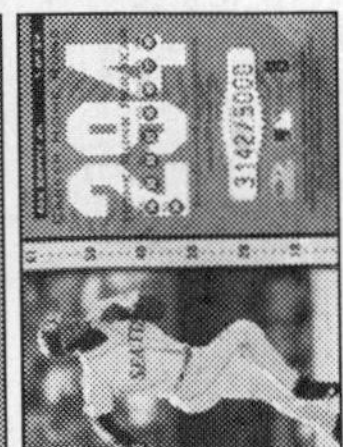

Randomly inserted in packs, this 24-card set features color photos of the top sluggers in baseball printed on micro-etched cards. Only 5000 of each card were produced and are sequentially numbered.

	MINT	NRMT
COMPLETE SET (24)	200.00	90.00
COMMON CARD (1-24)	4.00	1.80
☐ 1 Ken Griffey Jr.	30.00	13.50
☐ 2 Mark McGwire	12.00	5.50
☐ 3 Tino Martinez	6.00	2.70
☐ 4 Barry Bonds	8.00	3.60
☐ 5 Frank Thomas	25.00	11.00
☐ 6 Albert Belle	8.00	3.60
☐ 7 Mike Piazza	20.00	9.00
☐ 8 Chipper Jones	15.00	6.75
☐ 9 Vladimir Guerrero	8.00	3.60
☐ 10 Matt Williams	4.00	1.80
☐ 11 Sammy Sosa	6.00	2.70
☐ 12 Tim Salmon	6.00	2.70
☐ 13 Raul Mondesi	4.00	1.80
☐ 14 Jeff Bagwell	12.00	5.50
☐ 15 Mo Vaughn	8.00	3.60
☐ 16 Manny Ramirez	6.00	2.70
☐ 17 Jim Thome	6.00	2.70
☐ 18 Jim Edmonds	6.00	2.70
☐ 19 Tony Clark	6.00	2.70
☐ 20 Nomar Garciaparra	15.00	6.75
☐ 21 Juan Gonzalez	15.00	6.75
☐ 22 Scott Rolen	12.00	5.50
☐ 23 Larry Walker	6.00	2.70
☐ 24 Andres Galarraga	6.00	2.70

1998 Donruss Production Line Power Index

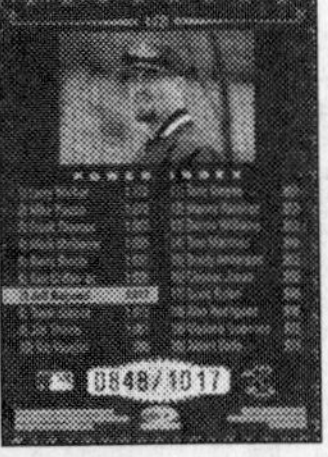

Randomly inserted in hobby packs only, this 20-card set features color player images printed on holographic board with blue highlights. Each card is sequentially numbered according to the player's power index.

	MINT	NRMT
COMPLETE SET (20)	600.00	275.00
COMMON CARD (1-20)	12.00	5.50
☐ 1 Frank Thomas/1067	80.00	36.00
☐ 2 Mark McGwire/1039	40.00	18.00
☐ 3 Barry Bonds/1031	25.00	11.00
☐ 4 Jeff Bagwell/1017	40.00	18.00
☐ 5 Ken Griffey Jr./1028	100.00	45.00
☐ 6 Alex Rodriguez/846	60.00	27.00
☐ 7 Chipper Jones/850	50.00	22.00
☐ 8 Mike Piazza/1070	60.00	27.00
☐ 9 Mo Vaughn/980	25.00	11.00
☐ 10 Brady Anderson/863	12.00	5.50
☐ 11 Manny Ramirez/953	20.00	9.00
☐ 12 Albert Belle/823	25.00	11.00
☐ 13 Jim Thome/1001	20.00	9.00
☐ 14 Bernie Williams/952	20.00	9.00
☐ 15 Scott Rolen/846	40.00	18.00
☐ 16 Vladimir Guerrero/833	25.00	11.00
☐ 17 Larry Walker/1172	20.00	9.00
☐ 18 David Justice/1013	20.00	9.00
☐ 19 Tino Martinez/948	20.00	9.00
☐ 20 Tony Gwynn/957	50.00	22.00

1998 Donruss Rated Rookies

Randomly inserted in packs, this 30-card set features color action photos of some of the top rookie prospects as chosen by Donruss to be the most likely to succeed. The backs carry player information.

	MINT	NRMT
COMPLETE SET (30)	60.00	27.00
COMMON CARD (1-30)	1.00	.45
☐ 1 Mark Kotsay	4.00	1.80
☐ 2 Neifi Perez	1.50	.70
☐ 3 Paul Konerko	6.00	2.70
☐ 4 Jose Cruz Jr.	15.00	6.75
☐ 5 Hideki Irabu	3.00	1.35
☐ 6 Mike Cameron	1.50	.70
☐ 7 Jeff Suppan	1.00	.45
☐ 8 Kevin Orie	1.50	.70
☐ 9 Pokey Reese	1.00	.45
☐ 10 Todd Dunwoody	1.50	.70
☐ 11 Miguel Tejada	5.00	2.20
☐ 12 Jose Guillen	4.00	1.80
☐ 13 Bartolo Colon	1.50	.70
☐ 14 Derrek Lee	1.50	.70
☐ 15 Antone Williamson	1.00	.45
☐ 16 Wilton Guerrero	1.00	.45
☐ 17 Jaret Wright	10.00	4.50
☐ 18 Todd Helton	5.00	2.20
☐ 19 Shannon Stewart	1.50	.70
☐ 20 Nomar Garciaparra	12.00	5.50
☐ 21 Brett Tomko	1.50	.70
☐ 22 Fernando Tatis	4.00	1.80
☐ 23 Raul Ibanez	1.00	.45
☐ 24 Dennis Reyes	1.00	.45
☐ 25 Bobby Estalella	1.50	.70
☐ 26 Lou Collier	1.00	.45
☐ 27 Bubba Trammell	1.50	.70
☐ 28 Ben Grieve	8.00	3.60
☐ 29 Ivan Cruz	1.00	.45
☐ 30 Karim Garcia	2.00	.90

1997 Donruss Elite

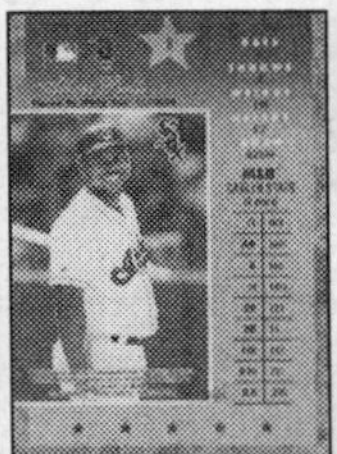

The 1997 Donruss Elite set was issued in one series totalling 150 cards. The product was distributed exclusively to hobby dealers. Each foil-wrapped pack contained eight cards and carried a suggested retail price of $3.49. Player selection was limited to the top stars (plus three player checklist cards) and card design is very similar to the Donruss Elite hockey set that was released one year earlier. Basic card fronts feature a color player photo encased by a thick silver and marble border. Backs contain another color photo and player information. Strangely enough, the backs only provide career statistics neglecting statistics from the previous season. The cards were released around February, 1997.

	MINT	NRMT
COMPLETE SET (150)	40.00	18.00
COMMON CARD (1-150)	.20	.09
☐ 1 Juan Gonzalez	2.00	.90
☐ 2 Alex Rodriguez	3.00	1.35
☐ 3 Frank Thomas	3.00	1.35
☐ 4 Greg Maddux	2.50	1.10
☐ 5 Ken Griffey Jr.	4.00	1.80
☐ 6 Cal Ripken	3.00	1.35
☐ 7 Mike Piazza	2.50	1.10
☐ 8 Chipper Jones	2.50	1.10
☐ 9 Albert Belle	1.00	.45
☐ 10 Andruw Jones	2.00	.90
☐ 11 Vladimir Guerrero	1.50	.70
☐ 12 Mo Vaughn UER front Gonzales	1.00	.45
☐ 13 Ivan Rodriguez	1.00	.45
☐ 14 Andy Pettitte	.75	.35
☐ 15 Tony Gwynn	2.00	.90
☐ 16 Barry Bonds	1.00	.45
☐ 17 Jeff Bagwell	1.50	.70
☐ 18 Manny Ramirez	.75	.35
☐ 19 Kenny Lofton	1.00	.45
☐ 20 Roberto Alomar	.75	.35
☐ 21 Mark McGwire	1.50	.70
☐ 22 Ryan Klesko	.60	.25
☐ 23 Tim Salmon	.75	.35
☐ 24 Derek Jeter	2.50	1.10
☐ 25 Eddie Murray	.75	.35
☐ 26 Jermaine Dye	.20	.09
☐ 27 Ruben Rivera	.40	.18
☐ 28 Jim Edmonds	.75	.35
☐ 29 Mike Mussina	.75	.35
☐ 30 Randy Johnson	.75	.35
☐ 31 Sammy Sosa	.75	.35
☐ 32 Hideo Nomo	2.00	.90
☐ 33 Chuck Knoblauch	.75	.35
☐ 34 Paul Molitor	.75	.35
☐ 35 Rafael Palmeiro	.60	.25

Card	MINT	NRMT
☐ 36 Brady Anderson	.60	.25
☐ 37 Will Clark	.60	.25
☐ 38 Craig Biggio	.60	.25
☐ 39 Jason Giambi	.40	.18
☐ 40 Roger Clemens	1.50	.70
☐ 41 Jay Buhner	.60	.25
☐ 42 Edgar Martinez	.60	.25
☐ 43 Gary Sheffield	.75	.35
☐ 44 Fred McGriff	.60	.25
☐ 45 Bobby Bonilla	.40	.18
☐ 46 Tom Glavine	.60	.25
☐ 47 Wade Boggs	.75	.35
☐ 48 Jeff Conine	.40	.18
☐ 49 John Smoltz	.75	.35
☐ 50 Jim Thome	.75	.35
☐ 51 Billy Wagner	.40	.18
☐ 52 Jose Canseco	.60	.25
☐ 53 Javy Lopez	.40	.18
☐ 54 Cecil Fielder	.40	.18
☐ 55 Garret Anderson	.40	.18
☐ 56 Alex Ochoa	.20	.09
☐ 57 Scott Rolen	2.00	.90
☐ 58 Darin Erstad	1.25	.55
☐ 59 Rey Ordonez	.20	.09
☐ 60 Dante Bichette	.40	.18
☐ 61 Joe Carter	.40	.18
☐ 62 Moises Alou	.40	.18
☐ 63 Jason Isringhausen	.20	.09
☐ 64 Karim Garcia	.40	.18
☐ 65 Brian Jordan	.40	.18
☐ 66 Ruben Sierra	.20	.09
☐ 67 Todd Hollandsworth	.20	.09
☐ 68 Paul Wilson	.20	.09
☐ 69 Ernie Young	.20	.09
☐ 70 Ryne Sandberg	1.00	.45
☐ 71 Raul Mondesi	.60	.25
☐ 72 George Arias	.20	.09
☐ 73 Ray Durham	.20	.09
☐ 74 Dean Palmer	.40	.18
☐ 75 Shawn Green	.20	.09
☐ 76 Eric Young	.40	.18
☐ 77 Jason Kendall	.40	.18
☐ 78 Greg Vaughn	.20	.09
☐ 79 Terrell Wade	.20	.09
☐ 80 Bill Pulsipher	.20	.09
☐ 81 Bobby Higginson	.40	.18
☐ 82 Mark Grudzielanek	.20	.09
☐ 83 Ken Caminiti	.75	.35
☐ 84 Todd Greene	.40	.18
☐ 85 Carlos Delgado	.40	.18
☐ 86 Mark Grace	.60	.25
☐ 87 Rondell White	.40	.18
☐ 88 Barry Larkin	.60	.25
☐ 89 J.T. Snow	.40	.18
☐ 90 Alex Gonzalez	.20	.09
☐ 91 Raul Casanova	.20	.09
☐ 92 Marc Newfield	.20	.09
☐ 93 Jermaine Allensworth	.20	.09
☐ 94 John Mabry	.40	.18
☐ 95 Kirby Puckett	1.50	.70
☐ 96 Travis Fryman	.40	.18
☐ 97 Kevin Brown	.40	.18
☐ 98 Andres Galarraga	.75	.35
☐ 99 Marty Cordova	.40	.18
☐ 100 Henry Rodriguez	.20	.09
☐ 101 Sterling Hitchcock	.20	.09
☐ 102 Trey Beamon	.20	.09
☐ 103 Brett Butler	.40	.18
☐ 104 Rickey Henderson	.60	.25
☐ 105 Tino Martinez	.75	.35
☐ 106 Kevin Appier	.40	.18
☐ 107 Brian Hunter	.40	.18
☐ 108 Eric Karros	.40	.18
☐ 109 Andre Dawson	.60	.25
☐ 110 Darryl Strawberry	.40	.18
☐ 111 James Baldwin	.20	.09
☐ 112 Chad Mottola	.20	.09
☐ 113 Dave Nilsson	.20	.09
☐ 114 Carlos Baerga	.40	.18
☐ 115 Chan Ho Park	.75	.35
☐ 116 John Jaha	.20	.09
☐ 117 Alan Benes	.40	.18
☐ 118 Mariano Rivera	.40	.18
☐ 119 Ellis Burks	.40	.18
☐ 120 Tony Clark	.75	.35
☐ 121 Todd Walker	.20	.09
☐ 122 Dwight Gooden	.40	.18
☐ 123 Ugueth Urbina	.40	.18
☐ 124 David Cone	.40	.18
☐ 125 Ozzie Smith	1.00	.45
☐ 126 Kimera Bartee	.20	.09
☐ 127 Rusty Greer	.40	.18
☐ 128 Pat Hentgen	.40	.18
☐ 129 Charles Johnson	.20	.09
☐ 130 Quinton McCracken	.20	.09
☐ 131 Troy Percival	.20	.09
☐ 132 Shane Reynolds	.20	.09
☐ 133 Charles Nagy	.40	.18
☐ 134 Tom Goodwin	.20	.09
☐ 135 Ron Gant	.40	.18
☐ 136 Dan Wilson	.20	.09
☐ 137 Matt Williams	.60	.25
☐ 138 LaTroy Hawkins	.20	.09
☐ 139 Kevin Seitzer	.20	.09
☐ 140 Michael Tucker	.20	.09
☐ 141 Todd Hundley	.40	.18
☐ 142 Alex Fernandez	.40	.18
☐ 143 Marquis Grissom	.40	.18
☐ 144 Steve Finley	.40	.18
☐ 145 Curtis Pride	.20	.09
☐ 146 Derek Bell	.20	.09
☐ 147 Butch Huskey	.40	.18
☐ 148 Dwight Gooden CL	.40	.18
☐ 149 Al Leiter CL	.20	.09
☐ 150 Hideo Nomo CL	1.00	.45

1997 Donruss Elite Gold Stars

Randomly seeded into one in every nine packs, cards from this set parallel the 150-card base issue. The distinctive gold foil fronts easily differentiate them from their silver-foiled base-issue brethren. The following cards were erroneously printed with a silver (rather than gold) logo on front: 6, 15, 25, 32, 42, 47, 57, 60, 69 and 70. Corrected gold logo versions of these cards do exist, but are in far shorter supply and exact values are not known at this time. The set is considered complete with the erroneous silver logo cards.

	MINT	NRMT
COMPLETE SET (150)	1000.00	450.00
COMMON CARD (1-150)	2.00	.90

*STARS: 6X TO 15X BASIC CARDS
*YOUNG STARS: 5X TO 12X BASIC CARDS

1997 Donruss Elite Leather and Lumber

This ten-card insert set features color action veteran player photos printed on two unique materials. The fronts display a player image on real wood card stock with the end of a baseball bat as background. The backs carry another player photo printed on genuine leather card stock with a baseball and glove as background. Only 500 of each card was produced and are sequentially numbered.

	MINT	NRMT
COMPLETE SET (10)	1000.00	450.00
COMMON CARD (1-10)	30.00	13.50
☐ 1 Ken Griffey Jr.	200.00	90.00
☐ 2 Alex Rodriguez	120.00	55.00
☐ 3 Frank Thomas	150.00	70.00
☐ 4 Chipper Jones	100.00	45.00
☐ 5 Ivan Rodriguez	50.00	22.00
☐ 6 Cal Ripken	150.00	70.00
☐ 7 Barry Bonds	50.00	22.00
☐ 8 Chuck Knoblauch	30.00	13.50
☐ 9 Manny Ramirez	40.00	18.00
☐ 10 Mark McGwire	80.00	36.00

1997 Donruss Elite Passing the Torch

This 12-card insert set features eight players on four double-sided cards. A color portrait of a superstar veteran is displayed on one side with a gold foil background, and a portrait of a rising young star is printed on the flipside. Each of the eight players also has his own card to round out the 12-card set. Only 1500 of this set were produced and are sequentially numbered. However, only 1,350 of each card are available without autographs.

	MINT	NRMT
COMPLETE SET (12)	500.00	220.00
COMMON CARD (1-12)	8.00	3.60

	MINT	NRMT
☐ 1 Cal Ripken	60.00	27.00
☐ 2 Alex Rodriguez	50.00	22.00
☐ 3 Cal Ripken Alex Rodriguez	100.00	45.00
☐ 4 Kirby Puckett	30.00	13.50
☐ 5 Andruw Jones	30.00	13.50
☐ 6 Kirby Puckett Andruw Jones	30.00	13.50
☐ 7 Cecil Fielder	8.00	3.60
☐ 8 Frank Thomas	60.00	27.00
☐ 9 Cecil Fielder Frank Thomas	60.00	27.00
☐ 10 Ozzie Smith	20.00	9.00
☐ 11 Derek Jeter	40.00	18.00
☐ 12 Ozzie Smith Derek Jeter	40.00	18.00

1997 Donruss Elite Passing the Torch Autographs

This 12-card set consists of the first 150 sets of the regular "Passing the Torch" set with each card displaying an authentic player autograph. The set features a double front design which captures eight of the league's top superstars, alternating one of four different megastars on the flipside. An individual card for each of the eight players rounds out the set. Each set is sequentially numbered to 150.

	MINT	NRMT
COMPLETE SET (12)	5000.00	2200.00
COMMON CARD (1-12)	100.00	45.00
☐ 1 Cal Ripken	600.00	275.00
☐ 2 Alex Rodriguez	500.00	220.00
☐ 3 Cal Ripken Alex Rodriguez	1200.00	550.00
☐ 4 Kirby Puckett	400.00	180.00
☐ 5 Andruw Jones	250.00	110.00
☐ 6 Kirby Puckett Andruw Jones	500.00	220.00
☐ 7 Cecil Fielder	100.00	45.00
☐ 8 Frank Thomas	500.00	220.00
☐ 9 Cecil Fielder Frank Thomas	500.00	220.00
☐ 10 Ozzie Smith	300.00	135.00
☐ 11 Derek Jeter	300.00	135.00
☐ 12 Ozzie Smith Derek Jeter	500.00	220.00

1997 Donruss Elite Turn of the Century

This 20-card set showcases the stars of the next millennium and features a color player image on a silver-and-black background. The backs display another player photo with a short paragraph about the player. Only 3,500 of this set were produced and are sequentially numbered.

	MINT	NRMT
COMPLETE SET (20)	150.00	70.00
COMMON CARD (1-20)	4.00	1.80
COMP.DIE CUT SET (20)	400.00	180.00

*DIE CUTS: 1.25X TO 3X BASIC JUAN

	MINT	NRMT
☐ 1 Alex Rodriguez	25.00	11.00
☐ 2 Andruw Jones	20.00	9.00
☐ 3 Chipper Jones	25.00	11.00
☐ 4 Todd Walker	4.00	1.80

Card	MINT	NRMT
5 Scott Rolen	20.00	9.00
6 Trey Beamon	4.00	1.80
7 Derek Jeter	25.00	11.00
8 Darin Erstad	12.00	5.50
9 Tony Clark	8.00	3.60
10 Todd Greene	4.00	1.80
11 Jason Giambi	5.00	2.20
12 Justin Thompson	5.00	2.20
13 Ernie Young	4.00	1.80
14 Jason Kendall	5.00	2.20
15 Alex Ochoa	4.00	1.80
16 Brooks Kieschnick	5.00	2.20
17 Bobby Higginson	5.00	2.20
18 Ruben Rivera	5.00	2.20
19 Chan Ho Park	8.00	3.60
20 Chad Mottola	4.00	1.80
P5 Scott Rolen Promo	4.00	1.80
P7 Derek Jeter Promo	6.00	2.70

1997 Donruss Limited

The 1997 Donruss Limited set was issued in one series totalling 200 cards and distributed in five-card packs with a suggested retail price of $4.99. The set is divided into four unique subsets: Counterparts, Double Team, Star Factor and Unlimited Potential/Talent. The Counterparts subset features 100 double-sided cards with full-bleed photos of two star players who play the same position. The Double Team subset displays color action photos of two star teammates back-to-back on 40 double-sided cards. The Star Factor subset highlights 40 superstars with a different photo of the same player on each side of the card plus unique player statistics. The Unlimited Potential/Talent subset features double-front cards with color photo matchups of a veteran and a rookie. Less than 1100 of each Unlimited Potential/Talent card was produced. Judging from case breakdowns provided to us from dealers in the field, the odds appear to be as follows: Double Team 1:6, Star Factor 1:24 and Unlimited Potential/Talent 1:36.

	MINT	NRMT
COMPLETE SET (200)	1900.00	850.00
COMP.COUNTER SET (100)	40.00	18.00
COMMON COUNTERPART	.25	.11
COUNTERPART UNLISTED	1.00	.45
COMP.DOUBLE SET (40)	120.00	55.00
COMMON DOUBLE TEAM	1.50	.70
COMP.STAR FACT.SET (40)	1000.00	450.00
COMMON STAR FACTOR	5.00	2.20
COMP.UNLIMITED SET (20)	800.00	350.00
COMMON UNLIMITED	4.00	1.80

Card	MINT	NRMT
1 Ken Griffey Jr. C	5.00	2.20
Rondell White		
2 Greg Maddux C	3.00	1.35
David Cone		
3 Gary Sheffield D	3.00	1.35
Moises Alou		
4 Frank Thomas S	80.00	36.00
5 Cal Ripken C	4.00	1.80
Kevin Orie		
6 Vladimir Guerrero U	25.00	11.00
Barry Bonds		
7 Eddie Murray C	.50	.23
Reggie Jefferson		
8 Manny Ramirez D	3.00	1.35
Marquis Grissom		
9 Mike Piazza S	60.00	27.00
10 Barry Larkin C	.25	.11
Rey Ordonez		
11 Jeff Bagwell C	2.00	.90
Eric Karros		
12 Chuck Knoblauch C	.25	.11
Ray Durham		
13 Alex Rodriguez C	4.00	1.80
Edgar Renteria		
14 Matt Williams C	.50	.23
Vinny Castilla		
15 Todd Hollandsworth C	.25	.11
Bob Abreu		
16 John Smoltz C	.50	.23
Pedro Martinez		
17 Jose Canseco C	.50	.23
Chili Davis		
18 Jose Cruz Jr. U	120.00	55.00
Ken Griffey Jr.		
19 Ken Griffey Jr. S	100.00	45.00
20 Paul Molitor C	.50	.23
John Olerud		
21 Roberto Alomar C	.25	.11
Luis Castillo		
22 Derek Jeter C	3.00	1.35
Lou Collier		
23 Chipper Jones C	3.00	1.35
Robin Ventura		
24 Gary Sheffield C	.50	.23
Ron Gant		
25 Ramon Martinez C	.25	.11
Bobby Jones		
26 Mike Piazza D	20.00	9.00
Raul Mondesi		
27 Darin Erstad U	40.00	18.00
Jeff Bagwell		
28 Ivan Rodriguez S	25.00	11.00
29 J.T.Snow C	.25	.11
Kevin Young		
30 Ryne Sandberg C	1.25	.55
Julio Franco		
31 Travis Fryman C	.25	.11
Chris Snopek		
32 Wade Boggs C	.25	.11
Russ Davis		
33 Brooks Kieschnick C	.25	.11
Marty Cordova		
34 Andy Pettitte C	.50	.23
Denny Neagle		
35 Paul Molitor D	1.50	.70
Matt Lawton		
36 Scott Rolen U	80.00	36.00
Cal Ripken		
37 Cal Ripken S	80.00	36.00
38 Jim Thome C	.25	.11
Dave Nilsson		
39 Tony Womack C	1.25	.55
Carlos Baerga		
40 Nomar Garciaparra C	3.00	1.35
Mark Grudzielanek		
41 Todd Greene C	.25	.11
Chris Widger		
42 Deion Sanders C	.25	.11
Bernard Gilkey		
43 Hideo Nomo C	2.50	1.10
Charles Nagy		
44 Ivan Rodriguez D	8.00	3.60
Rusty Greer		
45 Todd Walker U	50.00	22.00
Chipper Jones		
46 Greg Maddux S	60.00	27.00
47 Mo Vaughn C	1.25	.55
Cecil Fielder		
48 Craig Biggio C	.25	.11
Scott Spiezio		
49 Pokey Reese C	.25	.11
Jeff Blauser		
50 Ken Caminiti C	.25	.11
Joe Randa		
51 Albert Belle C	1.25	.55
Shawn Green		
52 Randy Johnson C	.25	.11
Jason Dickson		
53 Hideo Nomo D	15.00	6.75
Chan Ho Park		
54 Scott Spiezio U	8.00	3.60
Chuck Knoblauch		
55 Chipper Jones S	60.00	27.00
56 Tino Martinez C	.25	.11
Ryan McGuire		
57 Eric Young C	.25	.11
Wilton Guerrero		
58 Ron Coomer C	.25	.11
Dave Hollins		
59 Sammy Sosa C	.25	.11
Angel Echevarria		
60 Dennis Reyes C	1.00	.45
Jimmy Key		
61 Barry Larkin D	4.00	1.80
Deion Sanders		
62 Wilton Guerrero U	4.00	1.80
Roberto Alomar		
63 Albert Belle S	25.00	11.00
64 Mark McGwire C	2.00	.90
Andre Galarraga		
65 Edgar Martinez C	.25	.11
Todd Walker		
66 Steve Finley C	.25	.11
Rich Becker		
67 Tom Glavine C	.25	.11
Andy Ashby		
68 Sammy Sosa D	8.00	3.60
Ryne Sandberg		
69 Nomar Garciaparra U	80.00	36.00
Alex Rodriguez		
70 Jeff Bagwell S	40.00	18.00
71 Darin Erstad C	1.50	.70
Mark Grace		
72 Scott Rolen C	2.50	1.10
Edgardo Alfonzo		
73 Kenny Lofton C	1.25	.55
Lance Johnson		
74 Joey Hamilton C	.25	.11
Brett Tomko		
75 Eddie Murray D	6.00	2.70
Tim Salmon		
76 Dmitri Young U	20.00	9.00
Mo Vaughn		
77 Juan Gonzalez S	50.00	22.00
78 Frank Thomas C	5.00	2.20
Tony Clark		
79 Shannon Stewart C	.25	.11
Bip Roberts		
80 Shawn Estes C	.25	.11
Alex Fernandez		
81 John Smoltz D	3.00	1.35
Javier Lopez		
82 Todd Greene U	50.00	22.00
Mike Piazza		
83 Derek Jeter S	50.00	22.00
84 Dmitri Young C	.50	.23
Antone Williamson		
85 Rickey Henderson C	.25	.11
Darryl Hamilton		
86 Billy Wagner C	.50	.23
Dennis Eckersley		
87 Larry Walker D	1.50	.70
Eric Young		
88 Mark Kotsay U	50.00	22.00
Juan Gonzalez		
89 Barry Bonds S	25.00	11.00
90 Will Clark C	.25	.11
Jeff Conine		
91 Tony Gwynn C	2.50	1.10
Brett Butler		
92 John Wetteland C	.25	.11
Rod Beck		
93 Bernie Williams D	1.50	.70
Tony Martinez		
94 Andruw Jones U	30.00	13.50
Kenny Lofton		
95 Mo Vaughn S	25.00	11.00
96 Joe Carter C	.50	.23
Derrek Lee		
97 John Mabry C	.25	.11
F.P. Santangelo		
98 Esteban Loaiza C	.25	.11
Wilson Alvarez		
99 Matt Williams D	4.00	1.80
David Justice		
100 Derrek Lee U	60.00	27.00
Frank Thomas		
101 Mark McGwire S	40.00	18.00
102 Fred McGriff C	.25	.11
Paul Sorrento		
103 Jermaine Allensworth C	.25	.11
Bernie Williams		
104 Ismael Valdes C	.25	.11
Chris Holt		
105 Fred McGriff D	4.00	1.80
Ryan Klesko		
106 Tony Clark U	30.00	13.50
Mark McGwire		
107 Tony Gwynn S	50.00	22.00
108 Jeffrey Hammonds C	.25	.11
Ellis Burks		
109 Shane Reynolds C	.25	.11
Andy Benes		
110 Roger Clemens D	12.00	5.50
Carlos Delgado		
111 Karim Garcia U	25.00	11.00
Albert Belle		
112 Paul Molitor S	20.00	9.00
113 Trey Beamon C	.25	.11
Eric Owens		

☐ 114 Curt Schilling C .50 .23
Darryl Kile
☐ 115 Tom Glavine D 3.00 1.35
Michael Tucker
☐ 116 Pokey Reese U 40.00 18.00
Derek Jeter
☐ 117 Manny Ramirez S 20.00 9.00
☐ 118 Juan Gonzalez C 2.50 1.10
Brant Brown
☐ 119 Juan Guzman C .25 .11
Francisco Cordova
☐ 120 Randy Johnson D 4.00 1.80
Edgar Martinez
☐ 121 Hideki Irabu U 50.00 22.00
Greg Maddux
☐ 122 Alex Rodriguez S 60.00 27.00
☐ 123 Barry Bonds C 1.25 .55
Quinton McCracken
☐ 124 Roger Clemens C 2.00 .90
Andy Benes
☐ 125 Wade Boggs D 3.00 1.35
Paul O'Neill
☐ 126 Mike Cameron U 8.00 3.60
Larry Walker
☐ 127 Gary Sheffield S 15.00 6.75
☐ 128 Andruw Jones C 2.50 1.10
Raul Mondesi
☐ 129 Brady Anderson C .25 .11
Terrell Wade
☐ 130 Brady Anderson D 4.00 1.80
Rafael Palmeiro
☐ 131 Neifi Perez U 8.00 3.60
Barry Larkin
☐ 132 Ken Caminiti S 12.00 5.50
☐ 133 Larry Walker C 1.00 .45
Rusty Greer
☐ 134 Mariano Rivera C .50 .23
Mark Wohlers
☐ 135 Hideki Irabu D 6.00 2.70
Andy Pettitte
☐ 136 Jose Guillen U 40.00 18.00
Tony Gwynn
☐ 137 Hideo Nomo S 50.00 22.00
☐ 138 Vladimir Guerrero C 2.00 .90
Jim Edmonds
☐ 139 Justin Thompson C .50 .23
Dwight Gooden
☐ 140 Andres Galarraga D 3.00 1.35
Dante Bichette
☐ 141 Kenny Lofton S 25.00 11.00
☐ 142 Tim Salmon C 1.00 .45
Manny Ramirez
☐ 143 Kevin Brown C .25 .11
Matt Morris
☐ 144 Craig Biggio D 4.00 1.80
Bob Abreu
☐ 145 Roberto Alomar S 20.00 9.00
☐ 146 Jose Guillen C 1.25 .55
Brian Jordan
☐ 147 Bartolo Colon C .25 .11
Kevin Appier
☐ 148 Ray Lankford D .25 .11
Brian Jordan
☐ 149 Chuck Knoblauch S 15.00 6.75
☐ 150 Henry Rodriguez C .25 .11
Ray Lankford
☐ 151 Jaret Wright C 6.00 2.70
Ben McDonald
☐ 152 Bobby Bonilla D .25 .11
Kevin Brown
☐ 153 Barry Larkin S 12.00 5.50
☐ 154 David Justice C .25 .11
Reggie Sanders
☐ 155 Mike Mussina C .25 .11
Ken Hill
☐ 156 Mark Grace D 1.50 .70
Brooks Kieschnick
☐ 157 Jim Thome S 20.00 9.00
☐ 158 Michael Tucker C .25 .11
Curtis Goodwin
☐ 159 Jeff Suppan C .25 .11
Jeff Fassero
☐ 160 Mike Mussina D 3.00 1.35
Jeffrey Hammonds
☐ 161 John Smoltz S 10.00 4.50
☐ 162 Moises Alou C .50 .23
Eric Davis
☐ 163 Sandy Alomar Jr. C .50 .23
Dan Wilson
☐ 164 Reggie White D 1.50 .70
Henry Rodriguez
☐ 165 Roger Clemens S 40.00 18.00
☐ 166 Brady Anderson C .25 .11
Al Martin
☐ 167 Jason Kendall C .25 .11
Charles Johnson
☐ 168 Jason Giambi D 3.00 1.35
Jose Canseco
☐ 169 Larry Walker S 20.00 9.00
☐ 170 Jay Buhner C .25 .11
Geronimo Berroa
☐ 171 Ivan Rodriguez C 1.25 .55
Mike Sweeney
☐ 172 Kevin Appier D 1.50 .70
Jose Rosado
☐ 173 Bernie Williams S 15.00 6.75
☐ 174 Todd Dunwoody C .25 .11
Brian Giles
☐ 175 Javier Lopez C .25 .11
Scott Hatteberg
☐ 176 John Jaha D .25 .11
Jeff Cirillo
☐ 177 Andy Pettitte S 20.00 9.00
☐ 178 Dante Bichette C .50 .23
Butch Huskey
☐ 179 Raul Casanova C .25 .11
Todd Hundley
☐ 180 Jim Edmonds D 3.00 1.35
Garrett Anderson
☐ 181 Deion Sanders S 10.00 4.50
☐ 182 Ryan Klesko C .50 .23
Paul O'Neill
☐ 183 Joe Carter D 3.00 1.35
Pat Hentgen
☐ 184 Brady Anderson S 12.00 5.50
☐ 185 Carlos Delgado C .25 .11
Wally Joyner
☐ 186 Jermaine Dye D 1.50 .70
Johnny Damon
☐ 187 Randy Johnson S 20.00 9.00
☐ 188 Todd Hundley D 3.00 1.35
Carlos Baerga
☐ 189 Tom Glavine S 10.00 4.50
☐ 190 Damon Mashore D .25 .11
Jason McDonald
☐ 191 Wade Boggs S 20.00 9.00
☐ 192 Al Martin D 1.50 .70
Jason Kendall
☐ 193 Matt Williams S 20.00 9.00
☐ 194 Will Clark D 1.50 .70
Dean Palmer
☐ 195 Sammy Sosa S 15.00 6.75
☐ 196 Jose Cruz Jr. D 30.00 13.50
Jay Buhner
☐ 197 Eddie Murray S 20.00 9.00
☐ 198 Darin Erstad D 10.00 4.50
Jason Dickson
☐ 199 Fred McGriff S 10.00 4.50
☐ 200 Bubba Trammell D 5.00 2.20
Bobby Higginson

1997 Donruss Limited Exposure

Randomly inserted in packs, this 200-card set is parallel to the base set and was printed using Holographic Poly-Chromium technology on both sides. The set is designated by an exclusive"Limited Exposure" stamp. Less than 40 of the Star Factor subsets exist.

	MINT	NRMT
COMPLETE SET (200)	15000.00	6800.00
COMP.COUNTER SET (100)	1000.00	450.00
COMMON COUNTERPART	4.00	1.80
COUNTERPART MINORS	6.00	2.70
COUNTER.SEMIS	10.00	4.50
COUNTERPART UNLISTED	15.00	6.75
*COUNTER.STARS: 7.5X TO 15X BASIC CARDS		
*COUNTER.YOUNG STARS: 6X TO 12X BASIC CARDS		
*COUNTER.ROOKIES: 4X TO 8X BASIC CARDS		
COMP.DOUBLE SET (40)	1000.00	450.00
COMMON DOUBLE TEAM	12.00	5.50
DOUBLE TEAM MINORS	20.00	9.00
DOUBLE SEMIS	30.00	13.50
DOUBLE TEAM UNLISTED	50.00	22.00
*DOUBLE TEAM: 6X TO 12X BASIC CARDS		
COMP.STAR FACT.SET (40)	8000.00	3600.00
COMMON STAR FACTOR	40.00	18.00
STAR FACTOR MINORS	60.00	27.00
STAR FACTOR SEMIS	100.00	45.00
STAR FACTOR UNLISTED	150.00	70.00
COMP.UNLIMITED SET (20)	5000.00	2200.00
COMMON UNLIMITED	25.00	11.00
UNLIMITED MINORS	40.00	18.00
UNLIMITED SEMIS	60.00	27.00
UNLIMITED UNLISTED	100.00	45.00
*UNLIMITED: 5X TO 10X BASIC CARDS		
COMPLETE NON-GLOSS SET(100)	250.00	110.00
COMMON GLOSS	1.00	.45
*NON-GLOSS: .1X TO .25X BASIC EXPOSURE		

☐ 1 Ken Griffey Jr. C 80.00 36.00
Rondell White
☐ 2 Greg Maddux C 50.00 22.00
David Cone
☐ 4 Frank Thomas S 800.00 350.00
☐ 5 Cal Ripken C 60.00 27.00
Kevin Orie
☐ 6 Vladimir Guerrero U 150.00 70.00
Barry Bonds
☐ 9 Mike Piazza S 500.00 220.00
☐ 11 Jeff Bagwell C 30.00 13.50
Eric Karros
☐ 13 Alex Rodriguez C 60.00 27.00
Edgar Renteria
☐ 18 Jose Cruz Jr. U 800.00 350.00
Ken Griffey Jr.
☐ 19 Ken Griffey Jr. S 1000.00 450.00
☐ 22 Derek Jeter C 40.00 18.00
Lou Collier
☐ 23 Chipper Jones C 50.00 22.00
Robin Ventura
☐ 26 Mike Piazza D 150.00 70.00
Raul Mondesi
☐ 27 Darin Erstad U 250.00 110.00
Jeff Bagwell
☐ 28 Ivan Rodriguez S 200.00 90.00
☐ 30 Ryne Sandberg C 20.00 9.00
Julio Franco
☐ 36 Scott Rolen U 500.00 220.00
Cal Ripken
☐ 37 Cal Ripken S 600.00 275.00
☐ 40 Nomar Garciaparra C 50.00 22.00
Mark Grudzielanek
☐ 43 Hideo Nomo C 40.00 18.00
Charles Nagy
☐ 44 Ivan Rodriguez D 60.00 27.00
Rusty Greer
☐ 45 Todd Walker U 250.00 110.00
Chipper Jones
☐ 46 Greg Maddux S 500.00 220.00
☐ 47 Mo Vaughn C 20.00 9.00
Cecil Fielder
☐ 51 Albert Belle C 20.00 9.00
Shawn Green
☐ 53 Hideo Nomo D 120.00 55.00
Chan Ho Park
☐ 55 Chipper Jones S 400.00 180.00
☐ 63 Albert Belle S 200.00 90.00
☐ 64 Mark McGwire C 30.00 13.50
Andre Galarraga
☐ 68 Sammy Sosa D 60.00 27.00
Ryne Sandberg
☐ 69 Nomar Garciaparra U 500.00 220.00
Alex Rodriguez
☐ 70 Jeff Bagwell S 300.00 135.00
☐ 71 Darin Erstad C 25.00 11.00
Mark Grace
☐ 72 Scott Rolen C 40.00 18.00
Edgardo Alfonzo
☐ 73 Kenny Lofton C 20.00 9.00
Lance Johnson
☐ 76 Dmitri Young U 120.00 55.00
Mo Vaughn
☐ 77 Juan Gonzalez S 400.00 180.00
☐ 78 Frank Thomas C 60.00 27.00
Tony Clark
☐ 82 Todd Greene U 300.00 135.00
Mike Piazza
☐ 83 Derek Jeter S 400.00 180.00
☐ 88 Mark Kotsay U 300.00 135.00
Juan Gonzalez
☐ 89 Barry Bonds S 200.00 90.00
☐ 91 Tony Gwynn C 40.00 18.00
Brett Butler
☐ 94 Andruw Jones U 200.00 90.00
Kenny Lofton
☐ 95 Mo Vaughn S 200.00 90.00
☐ 100 Derrek Lee U 500.00 220.00
Frank Thomas
☐ 101 Mark McGwire S 300.00 135.00
☐ 106 Tony Clark U 200.00 90.00
Mark McGwire
☐ 107 Tony Gwynn S 400.00 180.00
☐ 110 Roger Clemens D 100.00 45.00
Carlos Delgado
☐ 111 Karim Garcia U 150.00 70.00

Albert Belle		
☐ 116 Pokey Reese U	250.00	110.00
Derek Jeter		
☐ 118 Juan Gonzalez C	40.00	18.00
Brant Brown		
☐ 121 Hideki Irabu U	300.00	135.00
Greg Maddux		
☐ 122 Alex Rodriguez S	500.00	220.00
☐ 123 Barry Bonds C	20.00	9.00
Quinton McCracken		
☐ 124 Roger Clemens C	30.00	13.50
Andy Benes		
☐ 128 Andruw Jones C	40.00	18.00
Raul Mondesi		
☐ 135 Hideki Irabu D	40.00	18.00
Andy Pettitte		
☐ 136 Jose Guillen U	250.00	110.00
Tony Gwynn		
☐ 137 Hideo Nomo S	600.00	275.00
☐ 138 Vladimir Guerrero C	30.00	13.50
Jim Edmonds		
☐ 141 Kenny Lofton S	200.00	90.00
☐ 151 Jaret Wright C	30.00	13.50
Ben McDonald		
☐ 165 Roger Clemens S	300.00	135.00
☐ 171 Ivan Rodriguez C	20.00	9.00
Mike Sweeney		
☐ 196 Jose Cruz Jr. D	150.00	70.00
Jay Buhner		
☐ 198 Darin Erstad D	60.00	27.00
Jason Dickson		

1997 Donruss Limited Fabric of the Game

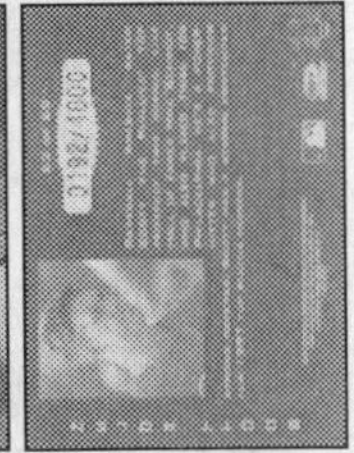

Randomly inserted in packs at a rate of 1:20, cards from this 69-card multi-fractured chase set highlights color player photos using three different technologies, each of which represents a different statistical category: Canvas (Stolen Bases), Leather (Doubles), and Wood (Homeruns). Five more levels cross the sections and are sequentially numbered: Legendary Material (numbered to 100), Hall of Fame Material (numbered to 250), Superstar Material (numbered to 500), Star Material (numbered to 750), and Major League Material (numbered to 1000)

	MINT	NRMT
COMPLETE SET (69)	2000.00	900.00
COMMON MAJOR LG MAT.	3.00	1.35
COMMON STAR MAT.	5.00	2.20
COMMON SUPERSTAR MAT.	12.00	5.50
COMMON HOF MAT.	20.00	9.00
COMMON LEGEND	50.00	22.00

☐ 1 Cal Ripken HF	150.00	70.00
☐ 2 Tony Gwynn SS	60.00	27.00
☐ 3 Ivan Rodriguez S	25.00	11.00
☐ 4 Rickey Henderson L	60.00	27.00
☐ 5 Ken Griffey Jr. SS	120.00	55.00
☐ 6 Chipper Jones ML	40.00	18.00
☐ 7 Sammy Sosa S	15.00	6.75
☐ 8 Wade Boggs HF	30.00	13.50
☐ 9 Manny Ramirez ML	12.00	5.50
☐ 10 Barry Bonds HF	50.00	22.00
☐ 11 Mike Piazza S	60.00	27.00
☐ 12 Rondell White ML	3.00	1.35
☐ 13 Albert Belle S	25.00	11.00
☐ 14 Tony Clark ML	12.00	5.50
☐ 15 Edgar Martinez SS	15.00	6.75
☐ 16 Deion Sanders S	12.00	5.50
☐ 17 Juan Gonzalez SS	60.00	27.00
☐ 18 Nomar Garciaparra ML	40.00	18.00
☐ 19 Rafael Palmeiro SS	15.00	6.75
☐ 20 Dave Justice S	20.00	9.00
☐ 21 Bob Abreu ML	12.00	5.50
☐ 22 Paul Molitor L	80.00	36.00
☐ 23 Vladimir Guerrero ML	25.00	11.00
☐ 24 Chuck Knoblauch SS	20.00	9.00
☐ 25 Tony Gwynn HF	100.00	45.00
☐ 26 Darin Erstad ML	20.00	9.00
☐ 27 Mark McGwire HF	80.00	36.00
☐ 28 Larry Walker S	20.00	9.00
☐ 29 Gary Sheffield S	15.00	6.75
☐ 30 Jose Cruz Jr. ML	60.00	27.00
☐ 31 Kenny Lofton HF	50.00	22.00
☐ 32 Andres Galarraga SS	25.00	11.00
☐ 33 Raul Mondesi ML	8.00	3.60
☐ 34 Eddie Murray L	80.00	36.00
☐ 35 Tino Martinez ML	10.00	4.50
☐ 36 Todd Walker ML	10.00	4.50
☐ 37 Frank Thomas SS	100.00	45.00
☐ 38 Ken Caminiti S	15.00	6.75
☐ 39 Pokey Reese ML	3.00	1.35
☐ 40 Barry Bonds HF	50.00	22.00
☐ 41 Barry Larkin SS	15.00	6.75
☐ 42 Bernie Williams S	15.00	6.75
☐ 43 Cal Ripken HF	150.00	70.00
☐ 44 Bobby Bonilla SS	15.00	6.75
☐ 45 Ken Griffey Jr. S	100.00	45.00
☐ 46 Tim Salmon S	15.00	6.75
☐ 47 Ryne Sandberg HF	50.00	22.00
☐ 48 Rusty Greer ML	5.00	2.20
☐ 49 Matt Williams SS	15.00	6.75
☐ 50 Eric Young S	3.00	1.35
☐ 51 Andruw Jones ML	30.00	13.50
☐ 52 Jeff Bagwell S	40.00	18.00
☐ 53 Wilton Guerrero ML	3.00	1.35
☐ 54 Fred McGriff HF	30.00	13.50
☐ 55 Jose Guillen ML	15.00	6.75
☐ 56 Brady Anderson SS	15.00	6.75
☐ 57 Mo Vaughn S	25.00	11.00
☐ 58 Craig Biggio SS	15.00	6.75
☐ 59 Dmitri Young ML	3.00	1.35
☐ 60 Frank Thomas S	80.00	36.00
☐ 61 Derek Jeter ML	40.00	18.00
☐ 62 Albert Belle SS	30.00	13.50
☐ 63 Scott Rolen ML	30.00	13.50
☐ 64 Roberto Alomar HF	40.00	18.00
☐ 65 Jeff Bagwell S	40.00	18.00
☐ 66 Mark Grace SS	15.00	6.75
☐ 67 Gary Sheffield S	15.00	6.75
☐ 68 Joe Carter HF	25.00	11.00
☐ 69 Jim Thome ML	12.00	5.50

1997 Donruss Preferred

The 1997 Donruss Preferred set was issued in one series totalling 200 cards and distributed in five-card packs with a suggested retail of $4.99. The set features color player photos on an all-foil, micro-etched card stock. The set is divided into 100 bronze (5:1 insert odds), 60 silver (1:3), 30 gold (1:12), and 10 platinum (1:48) cards.

	MINT	NRMT
COMPLETE SET (200)	950.00	425.00
COMP.BRONZE SET (100)	30.00	13.50
COMMON BRONZE	.25	.11
COMP.SILVER SET (60)	150.00	70.00
COMMON SILVER	2.00	.90
COMP.GOLD SET (30)	300.00	135.00
COMMON GOLD	6.00	2.70
COMP.PLAT.SET (10)	500.00	220.00
COMMON PLATINUM	40.00	18.00

☐ 1 Frank Thomas P	60.00	27.00
☐ 2 Ken Griffey Jr. P	80.00	36.00
☐ 3 Cecil Fielder B	.35	.16
☐ 4 Chuck Knoblauch G	10.00	4.50
☐ 5 Garret Anderson B	.35	.16
☐ 6 Greg Maddux P	50.00	22.00
☐ 7 Matt Williams S	3.00	1.35
☐ 8 Marquis Grissom S	2.50	1.10
☐ 9 Jason Isringhausen B	.25	.11
☐ 10 Larry Walker S	6.00	2.70
☐ 11 Charles Nagy B	.35	.16
☐ 12 Dan Wilson B	.25	.11
☐ 13 Albert Belle G	15.00	6.75
☐ 14 Javier Lopez B	.35	.16
☐ 15 David Cone B	.35	.16
☐ 16 Bernard Gilkey B	.25	.11
☐ 17 Andres Galarraga S	5.00	2.20
☐ 18 Bill Pulsipher B	.25	.11
☐ 19 Alex Fernandez B	.25	.11
☐ 20 Andy Pettitte S	6.00	2.70
☐ 21 Mark Grudzielanek B	.25	.11
☐ 22 Juan Gonzalez P	40.00	18.00
☐ 23 Reggie Sanders B	.25	.11
☐ 24 Kenny Lofton G	15.00	6.75
☐ 25 Andy Ashby B	.25	.11
☐ 26 John Wetteland B	.35	.16
☐ 27 Bobby Bonilla B	.35	.16
☐ 28 Hideo Nomo G	30.00	13.50
☐ 29 Joe Carter B	.35	.16
☐ 30 Jose Canseco B	.50	.23
☐ 31 Ellis Burks B	.35	.16
☐ 32 Edgar Martinez S	3.00	1.35
☐ 33 Chan Ho Park B	.75	.35
☐ 34 Dave Justice B	.75	.35
☐ 35 Carlos Delgado B	.35	.16
☐ 36 Jeff Cirillo S	2.00	.90
☐ 37 Charles Johnson B	.35	.16
☐ 38 Manny Ramirez G	12.00	5.50
☐ 39 Greg Vaughn B	.25	.11
☐ 40 Henry Rodriguez B	.25	.11
☐ 41 Darryl Strawberry B	.35	.16
☐ 42 Jim Thome G	12.00	5.50
☐ 43 Ryan Klesko S	3.00	1.35
☐ 44 Ruben Sierra B	.25	.11
☐ 45 Brian Jordan G	6.00	2.70
☐ 46 Tony Gwynn P	40.00	18.00
☐ 47 Rafael Palmeiro G	8.00	3.60
☐ 48 Dante Bichette S	2.50	1.10
☐ 49 Ivan Rodriguez G	15.00	6.75
☐ 50 Mark McGwire G	25.00	11.00
☐ 51 Tim Salmon S	5.00	2.20
☐ 52 Roger Clemens B	1.50	.70
☐ 53 Matt Lawton B	.25	.11
☐ 54 Wade Boggs S	5.00	2.20
☐ 55 Travis Fryman B	.35	.16
☐ 56 Bobby Higginson S	2.50	1.10
☐ 57 John Jaha S	2.00	.90
☐ 58 Rondell White S	2.50	1.10
☐ 59 Tom Glavine S	2.50	1.10
☐ 60 Eddie Murray S	6.00	2.70
☐ 61 Vinny Castilla B	.35	.16
☐ 62 Todd Hundley B	.35	.16
☐ 63 Jay Buhner S	3.00	1.35
☐ 64 Paul O'Neill B	.35	.16
☐ 65 Steve Finley B	.35	.16
☐ 66 Kevin Appier B	.35	.16
☐ 67 Ray Durham B	.25	.11
☐ 68 Dave Nilsson B	.25	.11
☐ 69 Jeff Bagwell G	25.00	11.00
☐ 70 Al Martin S	2.00	.90
☐ 71 Paul Molitor G	12.00	5.50
☐ 72 Kevin Brown S	2.50	1.10
☐ 73 Ron Gant B	.35	.16
☐ 74 Dwight Gooden B	.35	.16
☐ 75 Quinton McCracken B	.25	.11
☐ 76 Rusty Greer S	2.50	1.10
☐ 77 Juan Guzman B	.25	.11
☐ 78 Fred McGriff S	5.00	2.20
☐ 79 Tino Martinez B	.75	.35
☐ 80 Ray Lankford B	.35	.16
☐ 81 Ken Caminiti G	10.00	4.50
☐ 82 James Baldwin B	.25	.11
☐ 83 Jermaine Dye G	6.00	2.70
☐ 84 Mark Grace S	3.00	1.35
☐ 85 Pat Hentgen S	2.50	1.10
☐ 86 Jason Giambi S	2.50	1.10
☐ 87 Brian Hunter B	.35	.16
☐ 88 Andy Benes B	.35	.16
☐ 89 Jose Rosado B	.25	.11
☐ 90 Shawn Green B	.35	.16
☐ 91 Jason Kendall B	.35	.16
☐ 92 Alex Rodriguez P	50.00	22.00
☐ 93 Chipper Jones P	50.00	22.00
☐ 94 Barry Bonds G	15.00	6.75
☐ 95 Brady Anderson G	8.00	3.60
☐ 96 Ryne Sandberg S	8.00	3.60
☐ 97 Lance Johnson B	.25	.11
☐ 98 Cal Ripken P	60.00	27.00
☐ 99 Craig Biggio S	8.00	3.60
☐ 100 Dean Palmer B	.35	.16
☐ 101 Gary Sheffield G	10.00	4.50
☐ 102 Johnny Damon B	.25	.11
☐ 103 Mo Vaughn G	15.00	6.75
☐ 104 Randy Johnson S	6.00	2.70
☐ 105 Raul Mondesi S	3.00	1.35
☐ 106 Roberto Alomar G	12.00	5.50
☐ 107 Mike Piazza P	50.00	22.00
☐ 108 Rey Ordonez B	.25	.11
☐ 109 Barry Larkin G	8.00	3.60
☐ 110 Tony Clark S	5.00	2.20
☐ 111 Bernie Williams S	5.00	2.20
☐ 112 John Smoltz G	7.00	3.10
☐ 113 Moises Alou B	.35	.16
☐ 114 Will Clark B	.35	.16
☐ 115 Sammy Sosa G	10.00	4.50
☐ 116 Jim Edmonds S	5.00	2.20
☐ 117 Jeff Conine B	.35	.16
☐ 118 Joey Hamilton B	.25	.11

] 119 Todd Hollandsworth B	.25	.11
] 120 Troy Percival B	.25	.11
] 121 Paul Wilson B	.25	.11
] 122 Ken Hill B	.25	.11
] 123 Mariano Rivera S	2.50	1.10
] 124 Eric Karros B	.25	.11
] 125 Derek Jeter G	30.00	13.50
] 126 Eric Young S	.25	.11
] 127 John Mabry B	.25	.11
] 128 Gregg Jefferies B	.25	.11
] 129 Ismael Valdes S	.25	.11
] 130 Marty Cordova B	.25	.11
] 131 Omar Vizquel B	.35	.16
] 132 Mike Mussina S	6.00	2.70
] 133 Darin Erstad B	1.25	.55
] 134 Edgar Renteria S	2.50	1.10
] 135 Billy Wagner B	.35	.16
] 136 Alex Ochoa B	.25	.11
] 137 Luis Castillo B	.25	.11
] 138 Rocky Coppinger B	.25	.11
] 139 Mike Sweeney B	.25	.11
] 140 Michael Tucker B	.35	.16
] 141 Chris Snopek B	.25	.11
] 142 Dmitri Young S	2.00	.90
] 143 Andruw Jones P	30.00	13.50
] 144 Mike Cameron S	2.50	1.10
] 145 Brant Brown B	.25	.11
] 146 Todd Walker G	6.00	2.70
] 147 Nomar Garciaparra G	30.00	13.50
] 148 Glendon Rusch B	.25	.11
] 149 Karim Garcia S	2.00	.90
] 150 Bubba Trammell S	5.00	2.20
] 151 Todd Greene B	.25	.11
] 152 Wilton Guerrero G	6.00	2.70
] 153 Scott Spiezio B	.25	.11
] 154 Brooks Kieschnick B	.25	.11
] 155 Vladimir Guerrero G	20.00	9.00
] 156 Brian Giles S	2.00	.90
] 157 Pokey Reese B	.25	.11
] 158 Jason Dickson G	.25	.11
] 159 Kevin Orie S	7.00	3.10
] 160 Scott Rolen G	25.00	11.00
] 161 Bartolo Colon S	2.50	1.10
] 162 Shannon Stewart G	7.00	3.10
] 163 Wendell Magee B	.25	.11
] 164 Jose Guillen S	6.00	2.70
] 165 Bob Abreu S	5.00	2.20
] 166 Deivi Cruz B	.75	.35
] 167 Alex Rodriguez NT B	3.00	1.35
] 168 Frank Thomas NT B	3.00	1.35
] 169 Cal Ripken NT B	3.00	1.35
] 170 Chipper Jones NT B	2.50	1.10
] 171 Mike Piazza NT B	2.50	1.10
] 172 Tony Gwynn NT S	15.00	6.75
] 173 Juan Gonzalez NT B	2.00	.90
] 174 Kenny Lofton NT S	8.00	3.60
] 175 Ken Griffey Jr. NT B	4.00	1.80
] 176 Mark McGwire NT B	1.50	.70
] 177 Jeff Bagwell NT B	1.50	.70
] 178 Paul Molitor NT S	6.00	2.70
] 179 Andruw Jones NT B	2.00	.90
] 180 Manny Ramirez NT S	6.00	2.70
] 181 Ken Caminiti NT S	5.00	2.20
] 182 Barry Bonds NT B	1.00	.45
] 183 Mo Vaughn NT B	1.00	.45
] 184 Derek Jeter NT B	2.50	1.10
] 185 Barry Larkin NT S	3.00	1.35
] 186 Ivan Rodriguez NT B	1.00	.45
] 187 Albert Belle NT S	8.00	3.60
] 188 John Smoltz NT S	2.50	1.10
] 189 Chuck Knoblauch NT S	5.00	2.20
] 190 Brian Jordan NT S	2.00	.90
] 191 Gary Sheffield NT S	5.00	2.20
] 192 Jim Thome NT S	6.00	2.70
] 193 Brady Anderson NT S	2.50	1.10
] 194 Hideo Nomo NT S	15.00	6.75
] 195 Sammy Sosa NT S	5.00	2.20
] 196 Greg Maddux NT B	2.50	1.10
] 197 Vladimir Guerrero CL B	1.25	.55
] 198 Scott Rolen CL B	1.50	.70
] 199 Todd Walker CL B	.25	.11
200 Nomar Garciaparra CL B	2.00	.90

1997 Donruss Preferred Cut to the Chase

ese die cut cards parallel their more common non-die t siblings. The set is broken into four different oupings by color and scarcity. Pack odds for the ferent colored subsets become more difficult in this y: Bronze is the easiest, then Silver, Gold and Platinum ing the hardest to pull.

	MINT	NRMT
MP.BRONZE SET (100)	400.00	180.00
MMON BRONZE	2.00	.90

*BRONZE STARS: 5X TO 10X BASIC CARDS		
*BRONZE YNG.STARS: 4X TO 8X BASIC CARDS		
COMP.SILVER SET (60)	600.00	275.00
COMMON SILVER	8.00	3.60
*SILVER STARS: 2X TO 4X BASIC CARDS		
*SILVER YNG.STARS: 1.5X TO 3X BASIC CARDS		
COMP.GOLD SET (30)	800.00	350.00
COMMON GOLD	15.00	6.75
*GOLD STARS: 1.25X TO 2.5X BASIC CARDS		
*GOLD YOUNG STARS: 1X TO 2X BASIC CARDS		
COMP.PLAT.SET (10)	1500.00	700.00
COMMON PLATINUM	120.00	55.00
*PLAT.STARS: 1.5X TO 3X BASIC CARDS		
*PLAT.YNG.STARS: 1.25X TO 2.5X BASIC CARDS		

1997 Donruss Preferred Precious Metals

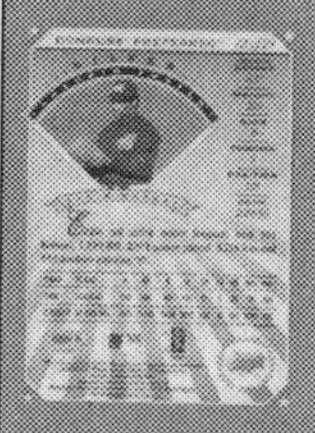

Randomly inserted in packs, this 25-card set is a partial parallel version of the regular set printed on actual silver, gold, or platinum. No more than 100 of each card was produced.

	MINT	NRMT
COMPLETE SET (25)	6000.00	2700.00
COMMON CARD (1-25)	80.00	36.00
☐ 1 Frank Thomas P	500.00	220.00
☐ 2 Ken Griffey Jr. P	600.00	275.00
☐ 3 Greg Maddux P	400.00	180.00
☐ 4 Albert Belle G	150.00	70.00
☐ 5 Juan Gonzalez P	300.00	135.00
☐ 6 Kenny Lofton G	150.00	70.00
☐ 7 Tony Gwynn P	300.00	135.00
☐ 8 Ivan Rodriguez G	150.00	70.00
☐ 9 Mark McGwire G	250.00	110.00
☐ 10 Matt Williams S	80.00	36.00
☐ 11 Wade Boggs S	100.00	45.00
☐ 12 Eddie Murray S	120.00	55.00
☐ 13 Jeff Bagwell G	250.00	110.00
☐ 14 Ken Caminiti G	80.00	36.00
☐ 15 Alex Rodriguez P	400.00	180.00
☐ 16 Chipper Jones P	300.00	135.00
☐ 17 Barry Bonds G	150.00	70.00
☐ 18 Cal Ripken P	500.00	220.00
☐ 19 Mo Vaughn G	150.00	70.00
☐ 20 Mike Piazza P	400.00	180.00
☐ 21 Derek Jeter G	300.00	135.00
☐ 22 Bernie Williams S	100.00	45.00
☐ 23 Andruw Jones P	250.00	110.00
☐ 24 Vladimir Guerrero G	200.00	90.00
☐ 25 Jose Guillen S	100.00	45.00

1997 Donruss Preferred Staremasters

Randomly inserted in packs, this 20-card set features up-close face photos of superstar players printed on all-foil card stock and accented with holographic foil stamping. Each card is sequentially numbered out of 1,500.

	MINT	NRMT
COMPLETE SET (20)	600.00	275.00
COMMON CARD (1-20)	12.00	5.50
☐ 1 Alex Rodriguez	50.00	22.00
☐ 2 Frank Thomas	60.00	27.00
☐ 3 Chipper Jones	50.00	22.00
☐ 4 Cal Ripken	60.00	27.00
☐ 5 Mike Piazza	50.00	22.00
☐ 6 Juan Gonzalez	40.00	18.00
☐ 7 Derek Jeter	40.00	18.00
☐ 8 Jeff Bagwell	30.00	13.50
☐ 9 Ken Griffey Jr.	80.00	36.00
☐ 10 Tony Gwynn	40.00	18.00
☐ 11 Barry Bonds	20.00	9.00
☐ 12 Albert Belle	20.00	9.00
☐ 13 Greg Maddux	50.00	22.00
☐ 14 Mark McGwire	30.00	13.50
☐ 15 Ken Caminiti	12.00	5.50
☐ 16 Hideo Nomo	40.00	18.00
☐ 17 Gary Sheffield	12.00	5.50
☐ 18 Andruw Jones	30.00	13.50
☐ 19 Mo Vaughn	20.00	9.00
☐ 20 Ivan Rodriguez	20.00	9.00

1997 Donruss Preferred Staremasters Samples

Promotional samples of Staremasters inserts were distributed within wholesale dealer order forms prior to the products release (one card per order). The Samples parallel the regular Staremasters inserts except for the bold "SAMPLE" text running diagonally across both front and back of the card. In addition, Sample cards are numbered as "PROMO/1500" on back rather than the typical serial numbering of the true insert cards. Please see the multiplier provided below for values on the singles.

	MINT	NRMT
COMPLETE SET (20)	60.00	27.00
COMMON CARD (1-20)	1.25	.55
*SINGLES: .1X BASIC STAREMASTERS		

1997 Donruss Preferred Tin Boxes

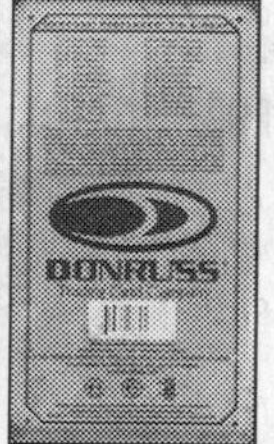

Each box of Donruss Preferred features one of 25 different players on the lid. These lids parallel the far more common blue tin packs and are each serial numbered of 1200.

	MINT	NRMT
COMPLETE SET (25)	150.00	70.00
COMMON LID (1-25)	2.00	.90
*BOX LIDS: 4X TO 8X BLUE TIN PACKS		

1997 Donruss Preferred Tin Boxes Gold

Following the successful release of the 1997 Donruss Preferred brand, Donruss/Leaf decided to re-issue an additional supply of the product a few months later, entitling Donruss Preferred Baseball Hobby Gold Edition. All of this new product was allocated to direct hobby accounts. The cards in the packs were identical to the first print run, but the large tin boxes were printed in gold with the box lids sequentially numbered to 299 (rather than the blue boxes numbered to 1200 in the first print run). This was the only way for collectors to obtain the new gold tin boxes.

	MINT	NRMT
COMPLETE SET (25)	500.00	220.00
COMMON BOX (1-25)	5.00	2.20
*GOLD BOXES: 10X TO 20X BLUE TIN PACKS		

1997 Donruss Preferred Tin Packs

Each pack of Donruss Preferred Baseball cards comes in one of 25 different player tins. These 25 tins come packed in hobby only, sequentally numbered display tins. Less than 1,200 of each Hobby-Only Display Master Tins were

produced with each featuring one of 25 star players. The tins are unnumbered and checklisted below alphabetically.

	MINT	NRMT
COMPLETE SET (25)	20.00	9.00
COMMON PACK (1-25)	.25	.11
☐ 1 Jeff Bagwell	1.00	.45
☐ 2 Albert Belle	.60	.25
☐ 3 Barry Bonds	.60	.25
☐ 4 Roger Clemens	1.00	.45
☐ 5 Juan Gonzalez	1.25	.55
☐ 6 Ken Griffey Jr.	2.50	1.10
☐ 7 Tony Gwynn	1.25	.55
☐ 8 Derek Jeter	1.50	.70
☐ 9 Andruw Jones	1.25	.55
☐ 10 Chipper Jones	1.50	.70
☐ 11 Kenny Lofton	.60	.25
☐ 12 Greg Maddux	1.50	.70
☐ 13 Mark McGwire	1.00	.45
☐ 14 Hideo Nomo	1.25	.55
☐ 15 Mike Piazza	1.50	.70
☐ 16 Manny Ramirez	.50	.23
☐ 17 Cal Ripken	2.00	.90
☐ 18 Alex Rodriguez	2.00	.90
☐ 19 Ivan Rodriguez	.60	.25
☐ 20 Ryne Sandberg	.60	.25
☐ 21 Gary Sheffield	.25	.11
☐ 22 John Smoltz	.25	.11
☐ 23 Sammy Sosa	.25	.11
☐ 24 Frank Thomas	2.00	.90
☐ 25 Mo Vaughn	.60	.25

1997 Donruss Preferred Tin Packs Gold

Each sealed box of Donruss Preferred contained one gold tin pack. These gold tins parallel the far more common blue tins and are each serial numbered of 1200. The tins are unnumbered and checklisted below alphabetically.

	MINT	NRMT
COMPLETE SET (25)	250.00	110.00
COMMON TIN (1-25)	2.50	1.10

*GOLD PACKS: 5X TO 10X BLUE TIN PACKS

1997 Donruss Preferred X-Ponential Power

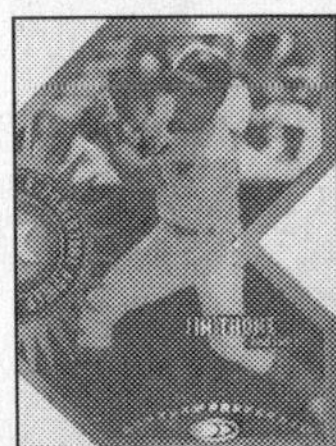

Randomly inserted in packs, this 20-card set features color player action photos of two of the best hitters from 10 of the hottest teams in the league printed on die-cut thick plastic card stock with gold holographic foil treatment. When the cards of both superstar teammates are placed side-by-side, their cards form a complete "X." Only 3,000 of each card was produced and sequentially numbered.

	MINT	NRMT
COMPLETE SET (10)	300.00	135.00
COMMON CARD (1A-10B)	5.00	2.20
☐ 1A Manny Ramirez	10.00	4.50
☐ 1B Jim Thome	10.00	4.50
☐ 2A Paul Molitor	10.00	4.50
☐ 2B Chuck Knoblauch	10.00	4.50
☐ 3A Ivan Rodriguez	12.00	5.50
☐ 3B Juan Gonzalez	25.00	11.00
☐ 4A Albert Belle	12.00	5.50
☐ 4B Frank Thomas	40.00	18.00
☐ 5A Roberto Alomar	10.00	4.50
☐ 5B Cal Ripken	40.00	18.00
☐ 6A Tim Salmon	10.00	4.50
☐ 6B Jim Edmonds	10.00	4.50
☐ 7A Ken Griffey Jr.	50.00	22.00
☐ 7B Alex Rodriguez	30.00	13.50
☐ 8A Chipper Jones	30.00	13.50
☐ 8B Andruw Jones	20.00	9.00
☐ 9A Mike Piazza	30.00	13.50
☐ 9B Raul Mondesi	5.00	2.20
☐ 10A Tony Gwynn	25.00	11.00
☐ 10B Ken Caminiti	10.00	4.50

1997 Donruss Signature

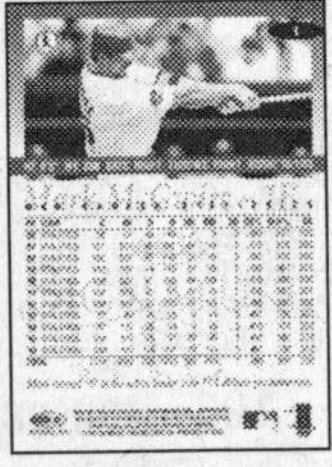

Distributed in five-card packs with one authentic autographed card per pack, this 100-card set was issued in either series packs. The fronts feature color player photos with player information on the backs. These packs carried a suggested retail price of $14.99. The only Rookie Cards of note in this set are Jose Cruz Jr. and Mark Kotsay.

	MINT	NRMT
COMPLETE SET (100)	50.00	22.00
COMMON CARD (1-100)	.25	.11
☐ 1 Mark McGwire	2.50	1.10
☐ 2 Kenny Lofton	1.25	.55
☐ 3 Tony Gwynn	2.50	1.10
☐ 4 Tony Clark	1.00	.45
☐ 5 Tim Salmon	1.00	.45
☐ 6 Ken Griffey Jr.	5.00	2.20
☐ 7 Mike Piazza	3.00	1.35
☐ 8 Greg Maddux	3.00	1.35
☐ 9 Roberto Alomar	1.00	.45
☐ 10 Andres Galarraga	1.00	.45
☐ 11 Roger Clemens	2.00	.90
☐ 12 Bernie Williams	1.00	.45
☐ 13 Rondell White	.50	.23
☐ 14 Kevin Appier	.25	.11
☐ 15 Ray Lankford	.50	.23
☐ 16 Frank Thomas	4.00	1.80
☐ 17 Will Clark	.75	.35
☐ 18 Chipper Jones	3.00	1.35
☐ 19 Jeff Bagwell	2.00	.90
☐ 20 Manny Ramirez	1.00	.45
☐ 21 Ryne Sandberg	1.25	.55
☐ 22 Paul Molitor	1.00	.45
☐ 23 Gary Sheffield	1.00	.45
☐ 24 Jim Edmonds	1.00	.45
☐ 25 Barry Larkin	.75	.35
☐ 26 Rafael Palmeiro	.75	.35
☐ 27 Alan Benes	.25	.11
☐ 28 Dave Justice	1.00	.45
☐ 29 Randy Johnson	1.00	.45
☐ 30 Barry Bonds	1.25	.55
☐ 31 Mo Vaughn	1.25	.55
☐ 32 Michael Tucker	.50	.23
☐ 33 Larry Walker	1.00	.45
☐ 34 Tino Martinez	1.00	.45
☐ 35 Jose Guillen	1.00	.45
☐ 36 Carlos Delgado	.50	.23
☐ 37 Jason Dickson	.50	.23
☐ 38 Tom Glavine	.50	.23
☐ 39 Raul Mondesi	.75	.35
☐ 40 Jose Cruz Jr.	10.00	4.50
☐ 41 Johnny Damon	.50	.23
☐ 42 Mark Grace	.75	.35
☐ 43 Juan Gonzalez	2.50	1.10
☐ 44 Vladimir Guerrero	2.00	.90
☐ 45 Kevin Brown	.50	.23
☐ 46 Justin Thompson	.50	.23
☐ 47 Eric Young	.25	.11
☐ 48 Ron Coomer	.25	.11
☐ 49 Mark Kotsay	2.50	1.10
☐ 50 Scott Rolen	2.50	1.10
☐ 51 Derek Jeter	3.00	1.35
☐ 52 Jim Thome	1.00	.45
☐ 53 Fred McGriff	.75	.35
☐ 54 Albert Belle	1.25	.55
☐ 55 Garret Anderson	.50	.23
☐ 56 Wilton Guerrero	.25	.11
☐ 57 Jose Canseco	.75	.35
☐ 58 Cal Ripken	4.00	1.80
☐ 59 Sammy Sosa	1.00	.45
☐ 60 Dmitri Young	.50	.23
☐ 61 Alex Rodriguez	4.00	1.80
☐ 62 Javier Lopez	.50	.23
☐ 63 Sandy Alomar Jr.	.50	.23
☐ 64 Joe Carter	.50	.23
☐ 65 Dante Bichette	.50	.23
☐ 66 Al Martin	.25	.11
☐ 67 Darin Erstad	1.50	.70
☐ 68 Pokey Reese	.25	.11
☐ 69 Brady Anderson	.75	.35
☐ 70 Andruw Jones	2.50	1.10
☐ 71 Ivan Rodriguez	1.25	.55
☐ 72 Nomar Garciaparra	3.00	1.35
☐ 73 Moises Alou	.50	.23
☐ 74 Andy Pettitte	1.00	.45
☐ 75 Jay Buhner	.75	.35
☐ 76 Craig Biggio	.75	.35
☐ 77 Wade Boggs	1.00	.45
☐ 78 Shawn Estes	.50	.23
☐ 79 Neifi Perez	.25	.11
☐ 80 Rusty Greer	.50	.23
☐ 81 Pedro Martinez	.50	.23
☐ 82 Mike Mussina	1.00	.45
☐ 83 Jason Giambi	.50	.23
☐ 84 Hideo Nomo	2.50	1.10
☐ 85 Todd Hundley	.50	.23
☐ 86 Deion Sanders	.75	.35
☐ 87 Mike Cameron	.50	.23
☐ 88 Bobby Bonilla	.50	.23
☐ 89 Todd Greene	.50	.23
☐ 90 Kevin Orie	.50	.23
☐ 91 Ken Caminiti	1.00	.45
☐ 92 Chuck Knoblauch	1.00	.45
☐ 93 Matt Morris	.50	.23
☐ 94 Matt Williams	.75	.35
☐ 95 Pat Hentgen	1.00	.45
☐ 96 John Smoltz	.50	.23
☐ 97 Edgar Martinez	.75	.35
☐ 98 Jason Kendall	.50	.23
☐ 99 Ken Griffey Jr. CL	2.50	1.10
☐ 100 Frank Thomas CL	2.00	.90

1997 Donruss Signature Platinum Press Proofs

Randomly inserted in packs, this set is a holo foil paralle version of the base set. Only 150 of this set wer produced. Each card is numbered "1 of 150" on the back.

	MINT	NRMT
COMPLETE SET (100)	3000.00	1350.0
COMMON CARD (1-100)	10.00	4.5

*STARS: 20X TO 40X BASIC CARDS ..
*YOUNG STARS: 15X TO 30X BASIC CARDS
*ROOKIES: 7.5X TO 15X BASIC CARDS

1997 Donruss Signature Autographs

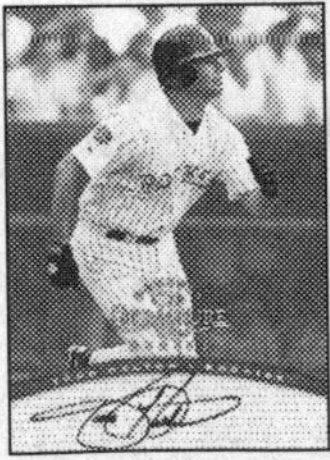

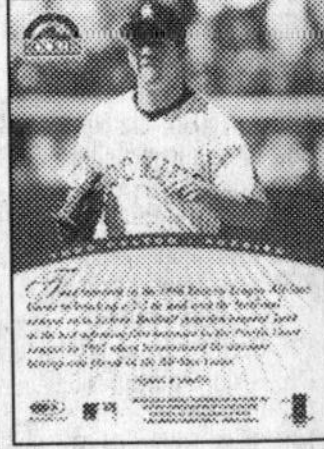

Inserted one per pack, this 117-card set features colo player autographed photos. The first 100 cards eac player signed were blue, sequentially numbered to 10 and designated as "Century Marks." The next 100 card signed were green, sequentially numbered 101-1,100, an designated as "Millenium Marks." Player autograph surpassing 1100 were red and were not numbered. Som autographed signature cards were not available at firs and were designated by blank-backed redemption card which could be redeemed by mail for the player' autograph card. The cards are checklisted below i alphabetical order. Asterisk cards were found in bot Series A and B. Print runs for how many cards each playe signed is noted below next to the players name.

	MINT	NRM
COMMON CARD	6.00	2.7

Card	MINT	NRMT
☐ 1 Jeff Abbott/3900	6.00	2.70
☐ 2 Bob Abreu/3900	8.00	3.60
☐ 3 Edgardo Alfonzo/3900	10.00	4.50
☐ 4 Roberto Alomar/150 *	100.00	45.00
☐ 5 Sandy Alomar Jr./1400	20.00	9.00
☐ 6 Moises Alou/900	20.00	9.00
☐ 7 Garret Anderson/3900	10.00	4.50
☐ 8 Andy Ashby/3900	6.00	2.70
☐ 9 Trey Beamon/3900	6.00	2.70
☐ 10 Alan Benes/3900	10.00	4.50
☐ 11 Geronimo Berroa/3900	6.00	2.70
☐ 12 Wade Boggs/150 *	100.00	45.00
☐ 13 Kevin Brown C/3900	6.00	2.70
☐ 14 Brett Butler/1400	20.00	9.00
☐ 15 Mike Cameron/3900	15.00	6.75
☐ 16 Giovanni Carrara/2900	8.00	3.60
☐ 17 Luis Castillo/3900	6.00	2.70
☐ 18 Tony Clark/3900	15.00	6.75
☐ 19 Will Clark/1400	30.00	13.50
☐ 20 Lou Collier/3900	6.00	2.70
☐ 21 Bartolo Colon/3900	8.00	3.60
☐ 22 Ron Coomer/3900	6.00	2.70
☐ 23 Marty Cordova/3900	8.00	3.60
☐ 24 Jacob Cruz/3900 *	10.00	4.50
☐ 25 Jose Cruz Jr./900 *	150.00	70.00
☐ 26 Russ Davis/3900	8.00	3.60
☐ 27 Jason Dickson/3900	10.00	4.50
☐ 28 Todd Dunwoody/3900	15.00	6.75
☐ 29 Jermaine Dye/3900	8.00	3.60
☐ 30 Jim Edmonds/3900	15.00	6.75
☐ 31 Darin Erstad/900 *	50.00	22.00
☐ 32 Bobby Estalella/3900	10.00	4.50
☐ 33 Shawn Estes/3900	10.00	4.50
☐ 34 Jeff Fassero/3900	6.00	2.70
☐ 35 Andres Galarraga/900	40.00	18.00
☐ 36 Karim Garcia/3900	12.00	5.50
☐ 37 Derrick Gibson/3900	15.00	6.75
☐ 38 Brian Giles/3900	6.00	2.70
☐ 39 Tom Glavine/150	50.00	22.00
☐ 40 Rick Gorecki/900	10.00	4.50
☐ 41 Shawn Green/1900	12.00	5.50
☐ 42 Todd Greene/3900	12.00	5.50
☐ 43 Rusty Greer/3900	10.00	4.50
☐ 44 Ben Grieve/3900	30.00	13.50
☐ 45 Mark Grudzielanek/3900	8.00	3.60
☐ 46 Vladimir Guerrero/1900 *	40.00	18.00
☐ 47 Wilton Guerrero/2150	10.00	4.50
☐ 48 Jose Guillen/2900	20.00	9.00
☐ 49 Jeffrey Hammonds/2150	10.00	4.50
☐ 50 Todd Helton/1400	30.00	13.50
☐ 51 Todd Hollandsworth/2900	10.00	4.50
☐ 52 Trenidad Hubbard/900	10.00	4.50
☐ 53 Todd Hundley/1400	15.00	6.75
☐ 54 Bobby Jones/3900	6.00	2.70
☐ 55 Brian Jordan/1400	12.00	5.50
☐ 56 David Justice/900	40.00	18.00
☐ 57 Eric Karros/650	25.00	11.00
☐ 58 Jason Kendall/3900	10.00	4.50
☐ 59 Jimmy Key/3900	10.00	4.50
☐ 60 Brooks Kieschnick/3900	8.00	3.60
☐ 61 Ryan Klesko/225	50.00	22.00
☐ 62 Paul Konerko/3900	30.00	13.50
☐ 63 Mark Kotsay/2400	30.00	13.50
☐ 64 Ray Lankford/3900	10.00	4.50
☐ 65 Barry Larkin/150 *	60.00	27.00
☐ 66 Derrek Lee/3900	15.00	6.75
☐ 67 Esteban Loaiza/3900	6.00	2.70
☐ 68 Javier Lopez/1400	20.00	9.00
☐ 69 Edgar Martinez/150 *	60.00	27.00
☐ 70 Pedro Martinez/900	40.00	18.00
☐ 71 Rafael Medina/3900	8.00	3.60
☐ 72 Raul Mondesi EXCH/650	40.00	18.00
☐ 73 Matt Morris/3900	10.00	4.50
☐ 74 Paul O'Neill/900	25.00	11.00
☐ 75 Kevin Orie/3900	12.00	5.50
☐ 76 David Ortiz/3900	10.00	4.50
☐ 77 Rafael Palmeiro/900	25.00	11.00
☐ 78 Jay Payton/3900	8.00	3.60
☐ 79 Neifi Perez/3900	8.00	3.60
☐ 80 Manny Ramirez/900	40.00	18.00
☐ 81 Joe Randa/3900	6.00	2.70
☐ 82 Calvin Reese/3900	6.00	2.70
☐ 83 Edgar Renteria EXCH/3900	10.00	4.50
☐ 84 Dennis Reyes/3900	8.00	3.60
☐ 85 Henry Rodriguez/3900	8.00	3.60
☐ 86 Scott Rolen/1900 *	50.00	22.00
☐ 87 Kirk Rueter/2900	8.00	3.60
☐ 88 Ryne Sandberg/400	120.00	55.00
☐ 89 Dwight Smith/2900	8.00	3.60
☐ 90 J.T. Snow/900	15.00	6.75
☐ 91 Scott Spiezio/3900	8.00	3.60
☐ 92 Shannon Stewart/2900	10.00	4.50
☐ 93 Jeff Suppan/1900	12.00	5.50
☐ 94 Mike Sweeney/3900	8.00	3.60
☐ 95 Miguel Tejada/3900	30.00	13.50
☐ 96 Justin Thompson/2400	15.00	6.75
☐ 97 Brett Tomko/3900	10.00	4.50
☐ 98 Bubba Trammell/3900	12.00	5.50
☐ 99 Michael Tucker/3900	8.00	3.60
☐ 100 Javier Valentin/3900	10.00	4.50
☐ 101 Mo Vaughn/150 *	100.00	45.00
☐ 102 Robin Ventura/1400	20.00	9.00
☐ 103 Terrell Wade/3900	6.00	2.70
☐ 104 Billy Wagner/3900	10.00	4.50
☐ 105 Larry Walker/900	50.00	22.00
☐ 106 Todd Walker/2400	15.00	6.75
☐ 107 Rondell White/3900	8.00	3.60
☐ 108 Kevin Wickander/900	10.00	4.50
☐ 109 Chris Widger/3900	6.00	2.70
☐ 110 Matt Williams/150 *	60.00	27.00
☐ 111 Antone Williamson/3900	6.00	2.70
☐ 112 Dan Wilson/3900	8.00	3.60
☐ 113 Tony Womack/3900	8.00	3.60
☐ 114 Jaret Wright/3900	40.00	18.00
☐ 115 Dmitri Young/3900	8.00	3.60
☐ 116 Eric Young/3900	6.00	2.70
☐ 117 Kevin Young/3900	6.00	2.70

1997 Donruss Signature Autographs Century

Randomly inserted in packs, this set, designated as blue, features the first 100 cards signed by each player. The cards are sequentially numbered. Raul Mondesi, Eddie Murray, Edgar Renteria and Jim Thome are exchange cards. The cards are checklisted below in alphabetical order. It's believed a number of Nomar Garciaparra Century marks were lost or destroyed during packaging and as few as 62 of these cards may have been inserted into packs.

	MINT	NRMT
COMMON CARD	40.00	18.00
MINOR STARS	80.00	36.00
☐ 4 Roberto Alomar *	150.00	70.00
☐ 9 Jeff Bagwell	250.00	110.00
☐ 11 Albert Belle	200.00	90.00
☐ 14 Wade Boggs *	150.00	70.00
☐ 15 Barry Bonds	200.00	90.00
☐ 19 Jay Buhner	100.00	45.00
☐ 24 Tony Clark	100.00	45.00
☐ 25 Will Clark	100.00	45.00
☐ 26 Roger Clemens *	400.00	180.00
☐ 32 Jose Cruz Jr. *	400.00	180.00
☐ 37 Jim Edmonds	100.00	45.00
☐ 38 Darin Erstad *	120.00	55.00
☐ 42 Andres Galarraga	120.00	55.00
☐ 44 Nomar Garciaparra *	300.00	135.00
☐ 48 Juan Gonzalez	400.00	180.00
☐ 53 Ben Grieve	150.00	70.00
☐ 55 Vladimir Guerrero *	150.00	70.00
☐ 57 Jose Guillen	100.00	45.00
☐ 58 Tony Gwynn *	400.00	180.00
☐ 60 Todd Helton	120.00	55.00
☐ 64 Derek Jeter *	300.00	135.00
☐ 65 Andruw Jones *	200.00	90.00
☐ 67 Chipper Jones *	400.00	180.00
☐ 69 David Justice	120.00	55.00
☐ 74 Ryan Klesko	100.00	45.00
☐ 75 Chuck Knoblauch *	100.00	45.00
☐ 76 Paul Konerko	150.00	70.00
☐ 77 Mark Kotsay	120.00	55.00
☐ 79 Barry Larkin *	100.00	45.00
☐ 83 Greg Maddux *	500.00	220.00
☐ 84 Edgar Martinez *	100.00	45.00
☐ 85 Pedro Martinez	120.00	55.00
☐ 86 Tino Martinez *	100.00	45.00
☐ 88 Raul Mondesi EXCH	100.00	45.00
☐ 90 Eddie Murray EXCH*	150.00	70.00
☐ 91 Mike Mussina	150.00	70.00
☐ 98 Andy Pettitte *	150.00	70.00
☐ 99 Manny Ramirez	120.00	55.00
☐ 104 Cal Ripken	600.00	275.00
☐ 105 Alex Rodriguez	500.00	220.00
☐ 107 Ivan Rodriguez	200.00	90.00
☐ 108 Scott Rolen *	200.00	90.00
☐ 110 Ryne Sandberg	250.00	110.00
☐ 111 Gary Sheffield *	120.00	55.00
☐ 118 Miguel Tejada	150.00	70.00
☐ 119 Frank Thomas	500.00	220.00
☐ 120 Jim Thome EXCH	150.00	70.00
☐ 126 Mo Vaughn *	150.00	70.00
☐ 130 Larry Walker	150.00	70.00
☐ 135 Bernie Williams	120.00	55.00
☐ 136 Matt Williams *	100.00	45.00
☐ 140 Jaret Wright	200.00	90.00

1997 Donruss Signature Autographs Millenium

Randomly inserted in packs, this set, designated as green, features the second 100 cards signed by each player. The cards are sequentially numbered 101-1,100 and are checklisted below in alphabetical order. It has been noted that there are some cards in existence not serially numbered.

	MINT	NRMT
COMMON CARD	15.00	6.75
☐ 1 Jeff Abbott	15.00	6.75
☐ 2 Bob Abreu	15.00	6.75
☐ 3 Edgardo Alfonzo	30.00	13.50
☐ 4 Roberto Alomar *	60.00	27.00
☐ 5 Sandy Alomar Jr.	30.00	13.50
☐ 6 Moises Alou	30.00	13.50
☐ 7 Garret Anderson	30.00	13.50
☐ 8 Andy Ashby	15.00	6.75
☐ 9 Jeff Bagwell/400	150.00	70.00
☐ 10 Trey Beamon	15.00	6.75
☐ 11 Albert Belle/400	120.00	55.00
☐ 12 Alan Benes	15.00	6.75
☐ 13 Geronimo Berroa	15.00	6.75
☐ 14 Wade Boggs *	60.00	27.00
☐ 15 Barry Bonds/400	150.00	70.00
☐ 16 Bobby Bonilla/900 *	40.00	18.00
☐ 17 Kevin Brown/900	40.00	18.00
☐ 18 Kevin Brown C	15.00	6.75
☐ 19 Jay Buhner/900	50.00	22.00
☐ 20 Brett Butler	30.00	13.50
☐ 21 Mike Cameron	30.00	13.50
☐ 22 Giovanni Carrara	15.00	6.75
☐ 23 Luis Castillo	15.00	6.75
☐ 24 Tony Clark	40.00	18.00
☐ 25 Will Clark	40.00	18.00
☐ 26 Roger Clemens/400 *	250.00	110.00
☐ 27 Lou Collier	15.00	6.75
☐ 28 Bartolo Colon	15.00	6.75
☐ 29 Ron Coomer	15.00	6.75
☐ 30 Marty Cordova	15.00	6.75
☐ 31 Jacob Cruz	15.00	6.75
☐ 32 Jose Cruz Jr. *	150.00	70.00
☐ 33 Russ Davis	15.00	6.75
☐ 34 Jason Dickson	15.00	6.75
☐ 35 Todd Dunwoody	30.00	13.50
☐ 36 Jermaine Dye	15.00	6.75
☐ 37 Jim Edmonds	30.00	13.50
☐ 38 Darin Erstad *	50.00	22.00
☐ 39 Bobby Estalella	15.00	6.75
☐ 40 Shawn Estes	15.00	6.75
☐ 41 Jeff Fassero	15.00	6.75
☐ 42 Andres Galarraga	50.00	22.00
☐ 43 Karim Garcia	15.00	6.75
☐ 44 Nomar Garciaparra/650 *	200.00	90.00
☐ 45 Derrick Gibson	30.00	13.50
☐ 46 Brian Giles	15.00	6.75
☐ 47 Tom Glavine	30.00	13.50
☐ 48 Juan Gonzalez/900	150.00	70.00
☐ 49 Rick Gorecki	15.00	6.75
☐ 50 Shawn Green	15.00	6.75
☐ 51 Todd Greene	15.00	6.75
☐ 52 Rusty Greer	30.00	13.50
☐ 53 Ben Grieve	60.00	27.00
☐ 54 Mark Grudzielanek	15.00	6.75
☐ 55 Vladimir Guerrero *	80.00	36.00
☐ 56 Wilton Guerrero	15.00	6.75
☐ 57 Jose Guillen	30.00	13.50
☐ 58 Tony Gwynn/900 *	150.00	70.00
☐ 59 Jeffrey Hammonds	15.00	6.75
☐ 60 Todd Helton	40.00	18.00
☐ 61 Todd Hundley	30.00	13.50
☐ 62 Todd Hollandsworth	15.00	6.75
☐ 63 Trenidad Hubbard	15.00	6.75
☐ 64 Derek Jeter/400 *	200.00	90.00
☐ 65 Andruw Jones/900 *	100.00	45.00
☐ 66 Bobby Jones	15.00	6.75
☐ 67 Chipper Jones/900 *	150.00	70.00
☐ 68 Brian Jordan	15.00	6.75
☐ 69 David Justice	50.00	22.00
☐ 70 Eric Karros	30.00	13.50
☐ 71 Jason Kendall	30.00	13.50
☐ 72 Jimmy Key	30.00	13.50
☐ 73 Brooks Kieschnick	15.00	6.75
☐ 74 Ryan Klesko	40.00	18.00
☐ 75 Chuck Knoblauch/900 *	50.00	22.00
☐ 76 Paul Konerko	60.00	27.00
☐ 77 Mark Kotsay	40.00	18.00
☐ 78 Ray Lankford	30.00	13.50
☐ 79 Barry Larkin *	40.00	18.00
☐ 80 Derrek Lee	30.00	13.50
☐ 81 Esteban Loaiza	15.00	6.75
☐ 82 Javier Lopez	30.00	13.50
☐ 83 Greg Maddux/400 *	350.00	160.00
☐ 84 Edgar Martinez *	40.00	18.00
☐ 85 Pedro Martinez	50.00	22.00
☐ 86 Tino Martinez/900 *	50.00	22.00
☐ 87 Rafael Medina	15.00	6.75
☐ 88 Raul Mondesi EXCH	40.00	18.00
☐ 89 Matt Morris	15.00	6.75
☐ 90 Eddie Murray/900 *	60.00	27.00

☐ 91 Mike Mussina/900	60.00	27.00
☐ 92 Paul O'Neill	30.00	13.50
☐ 93 Kevin Orie	15.00	6.75
☐ 94 David Ortiz	15.00	6.75
☐ 95 Rafael Palmeiro	30.00	13.50
☐ 96 Jay Payton	15.00	6.75
☐ 97 Neifi Perez	15.00	6.75
☐ 98 Andy Pettitte/900 *	60.00	27.00
☐ 99 Manny Ramirez	50.00	22.00
☐ 100 Joe Randa	15.00	6.75
☐ 101 Calvin Reese	15.00	6.75
☐ 102 Edgar Renteria	15.00	6.75
☐ 103 Dennis Reyes	15.00	6.75
☐ 104 Cal Ripken/400	400.00	180.00
☐ 105 Alex Rodriguez/400	300.00	135.00
☐ 106 Henry Rodriguez	15.00	6.75
☐ 107 Ivan Rodriguez/900	80.00	36.00
☐ 108 Scott Rolen *	100.00	45.00
☐ 109 Kirk Rueter	15.00	6.75
☐ 110 Ryne Sandberg	100.00	45.00
☐ 111 Gary Sheffield/400 *	80.00	36.00
☐ 112 Dwight Smith	15.00	6.75
☐ 113 J.T. Snow	30.00	13.50
☐ 114 Scott Spiezio	15.00	6.75
☐ 115 Shannon Stewart	15.00	6.75
☐ 116 Jeff Suppan	15.00	6.75
☐ 117 Mike Sweeney	15.00	6.75
☐ 118 Miguel Tejada	60.00	27.00
☐ 119 Frank Thomas/400	300.00	135.00
☐ 120 Jim Thome EXCH/900	60.00	27.00
☐ 121 Justin Thompson	30.00	13.50
☐ 122 Brett Tomko	15.00	6.75
☐ 123 Bubba Trammell	30.00	13.50
☐ 124 Michael Tucker	30.00	13.50
☐ 125 Javier Valentin	15.00	6.75
☐ 126 Mo Vaughn *	60.00	27.00
☐ 127 Robin Ventura	30.00	13.50
☐ 128 Terrell Wade	15.00	6.75
☐ 129 Billy Wagner	30.00	13.50
☐ 130 Larry Walker	60.00	27.00
☐ 131 Todd Walker	30.00	13.50
☐ 132 Rondell White	30.00	13.50
☐ 133 Kevin Wickander	15.00	6.75
☐ 134 Chris Widger	15.00	6.75
☐ 135 Bernie Williams/400	80.00	36.00
☐ 136 Matt Williams *	40.00	18.00
☐ 137 Antone Williamson	15.00	6.75
☐ 138 Dan Wilson	15.00	6.75
☐ 139 Tony Womack	15.00	6.75
☐ 140 Jaret Wright	80.00	36.00
☐ 141 Dmitri Young	15.00	6.75
☐ 142 Eric Young	15.00	6.75
☐ 143 Kevin Young	15.00	6.75

1997 Donruss Signature Notable Nicknames

Randomly inserted in packs, this 10-card set features photos of players with notable nicknames. Only 200 of this serial numbered set were produced. The cards are unnumbered and checklisted below in alphabetical order.

	MINT	NRMT
COMPLETE SET (10)	1800.00	800.00
COMMON CARD	60.00	27.00
☐ 1 Ernie Banks Mr. Cub	200.00	90.00
☐ 2 Tony Clark The Tiger	120.00	55.00
☐ 3 Roger Clemens The Rocket	300.00	135.00
☐ 4 Reggie Jackson Mr. October	250.00	110.00
☐ 5 Randy Johnson The Big Unit	150.00	70.00
☐ 6 Stan Musial The Man	300.00	135.00
☐ 7 Ivan Rodriguez Pudge	150.00	70.00
☐ 8 Frank Thomas The Big Hurt	400.00	180.00
☐ 9 Mo Vaughn The Hit Dog	120.00	55.00
☐ 10 Billy Wagner The Kid	60.00	27.00

1997 Donruss Signature Significant Signatures

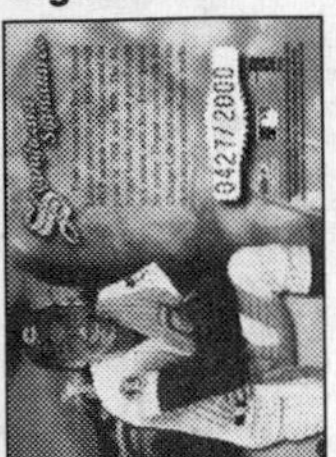

Randomly inserted in packs, this 22-card set features photos with autographs of legendary Hall of Fame players. Only 2000 of each card was produced and serially numbered. The cards are checklisted below in alphabetical order.

	MINT	NRMT
COMPLETE SET (22)	1000.00	450.00
COMMON CARD	30.00	13.50
☐ 1 Ernie Banks	50.00	22.00
☐ 2 Johnny Bench	60.00	27.00
☐ 3 Yogi Berra	60.00	27.00
☐ 4 George Brett	60.00	27.00
☐ 5 Lou Brock	40.00	18.00
☐ 6 Rod Carew	40.00	18.00
☐ 7 Steve Carlton	40.00	18.00
☐ 8 Larry Doby	30.00	13.50
☐ 9 Carlton Fisk	40.00	18.00
☐ 10 Bob Gibson	40.00	18.00
☐ 11 Reggie Jackson	60.00	27.00
☐ 12 Al Kaline	50.00	22.00
☐ 13 Harmon Killebrew	40.00	18.00
☐ 14 Don Mattingly	80.00	36.00
☐ 15 Stan Musial	80.00	36.00
☐ 16 Jim Palmer	40.00	18.00
☐ 17 Brooks Robinson	40.00	18.00
☐ 18 Frank Robinson	50.00	22.00
☐ 19 Mike Schmidt	60.00	27.00
☐ 20 Tom Seaver	60.00	27.00
☐ 21 Duke Snider	60.00	27.00
☐ 22 Carl Yastrzemski	60.00	27.00

1997 Donruss Team Sets

This 165-card set features color action player photos from eleven Major League teams printed on specially treated card stock with team color matching foil stamping. The set was distributed in five-card packs with a suggested retail price of $1.99. The Indians and Angels packs were sold exclusively at the respective ballparks during their home games. Due to manufacturing problems, Russ Davis (supposed to be #144) and Bernie Williams (supposed to be #131) were never printed, thus the set is complete at 163 cards.

	MINT	NRMT
COMP.ANGELS (1-15)	5.00	2.20
COMP.BRAVES (16-30)	6.00	2.70
COMP.ORIOLES (31-45)	4.00	1.80
COMP.RED SOX (46-60)	3.00	1.35
COMP.WHITE SOX (61-75)	4.00	1.80
COMP.INDIANS (76-90)	5.00	2.20
COMP.ROCKIES (91-105)	2.50	1.10
COMP.DODGERS (106-120)	4.00	1.80
COMP.YANKEES (121-135)	6.00	2.70
COMP.MARINERS (136-150)	10.00	4.50
COMP.CARDS (151-165)	2.00	.90
COMMON CARD (16-165)	.15	.07

☐ 1 Jim Edmonds	.60	.25
☐ 2 Tim Salmon	.60	.25
☐ 3 Tony Phillips	.15	.07
☐ 4 Garret Anderson	.30	.14
☐ 5 Troy Percival	.15	.07
☐ 6 Mark Langston	.15	.07
☐ 7 Chuck Finley	.30	.14
☐ 8 Eddie Murray	.60	.25
☐ 9 Jim Leyritz	.15	.07
☐ 10 Darin Erstad	1.00	.45
☐ 11 Jason Dickson	.40	.18
☐ 12 Allen Watson	.15	.07
☐ 13 Shigetoshi Hasegawa	.60	.25
☐ 14 Dave Hollins	.15	.07
☐ 15 Gary DiSarcina	.15	.07
☐ 16 Greg Maddux	2.00	.90
☐ 17 Denny Neagle	.30	.14
☐ 18 Chipper Jones	2.00	.90
☐ 19 Tom Glavine	.30	.14
☐ 20 John Smoltz	.30	.14
☐ 21 Ryan Klesko	.40	.18
☐ 22 Fred McGriff	.40	.18
☐ 23 Michael Tucker	.30	.14
☐ 24 Kenny Lofton	.75	.35
☐ 25 Javier Lopez	.30	.14
☐ 26 Mark Wohlers	.30	.14
☐ 27 Jeff Blauser	.15	.07
☐ 28 Andruw Jones	1.50	.70
☐ 29 Tony Graffanino	.15	.07
☐ 30 Terrell Wade	.15	.07
☐ 31 Brady Anderson	.40	.18
☐ 32 Roberto Alomar	.60	.25
☐ 33 Rafael Palmeiro	.40	.18
☐ 34 Mike Mussina	.60	.25
☐ 35 Cal Ripken	2.50	1.10
☐ 36 Rocky Coppinger	.15	.07
☐ 37 Randy Myers	.30	.14
☐ 38 B.J. Surhoff	.30	.14
☐ 39 Eric Davis	.30	.14
☐ 40 Armando Benitez	.15	.07
☐ 41 Jeffrey Hammonds	.30	.14
☐ 42 Jimmy Key	.30	.14
☐ 43 Chris Hoiles	.15	.07
☐ 44 Mike Bordick	.15	.07
☐ 45 Pete Incaviglia	.15	.07
☐ 46 Mike Stanley	.15	.07
☐ 47 Reggie Jefferson	.30	.14
☐ 48 Mo Vaughn	.75	.35
☐ 49 John Valentin	.15	.07
☐ 50 Tim Naehring	.15	.07
☐ 51 Jeff Suppan	.15	.07
☐ 52 Tim Wakefield	.15	.07
☐ 53 Jeff Frye	.15	.07
☐ 54 Darren Bragg	.15	.07
☐ 55 Steve Avery	.15	.07
☐ 56 Shane Mack	.15	.07
☐ 57 Aaron Sele	.15	.07
☐ 58 Troy O'Leary	.15	.07
☐ 59 Rudy Pemberton	.15	.07
☐ 60 Nomar Garciaparra	2.00	.90
☐ 61 Robin Ventura	.30	.14
☐ 62 Wilson Alvarez	.15	.07
☐ 63 Roberto Hernandez	.30	.14
☐ 64 Frank Thomas	3.00	1.35
☐ 65 Ray Durham	.15	.07
☐ 66 James Baldwin	.15	.07
☐ 67 Harold Baines	.30	.14
☐ 68 Doug Drabek	.15	.07
☐ 69 Mike Cameron	.15	.07
☐ 70 Albert Belle	1.00	.45
☐ 71 Jaime Navarro	.15	.07
☐ 72 Chris Snopek	.15	.07
☐ 73 Lyle Mouton	.15	.07
☐ 74 Dave Martinez	.15	.07
☐ 75 Ozzie Guillen	.15	.07
☐ 76 Manny Ramirez	.60	.25
☐ 77 Jack McDowell	.15	.07
☐ 78 Jim Thome	.60	.25
☐ 79 Jose Mesa	.30	.14
☐ 80 Brian Giles	.15	.07
☐ 81 Omar Vizquel	.15	.07
☐ 82 Charles Nagy	.15	.07
☐ 83 Orel Hershiser	.30	.14
☐ 84 Matt Williams	.40	.18
☐ 85 Marquis Grissom	.30	.14
☐ 86 David Justice	.60	.25
☐ 87 Sandy Alomar	.30	.14
☐ 88 Kevin Seitzer	.15	.07
☐ 89 Julio Franco	.30	.14
☐ 90 Bartolo Colon	.15	.07
☐ 91 Andres Galarraga	.60	.25
☐ 92 Larry Walker	.60	.25
☐ 93 Vinny Castilla	.30	.14
☐ 94 Dante Bichette	.30	.14
☐ 95 Jamey Wright	.15	.07
☐ 96 Ellis Burks	.30	.14
☐ 97 Eric Young	.30	.14

☐ 98 Neifi Perez	.15	.07
☐ 99 Quinton McCracken	.15	.07
☐ 100 Bruce Ruffin	.15	.07
☐ 101 Walt Weiss	.15	.07
☐ 102 Roger Bailey	.15	.07
☐ 103 Jeff Reed	.15	.07
☐ 104 Bill Swift	.15	.07
☐ 105 Kirt Manwaring	.15	.07
☐ 106 Raul Mondesi	.60	.25
☐ 107 Hideo Nomo	1.50	.70
☐ 108 Roger Cedeno	.15	.07
☐ 109 Ismael Valdes	.30	.14
☐ 110 Todd Hollandsworth	.15	.07
☐ 111 Mike Piazza	2.00	.90
☐ 112 Brett Butler	.30	.14
☐ 113 Chan Ho Park	.60	.25
☐ 114 Ramon Martinez	.30	.14
☐ 115 Eric Karros	.30	.14
☐ 116 Wilton Guerrero	.15	.07
☐ 117 Todd Zeile	.15	.07
☐ 118 Karim Garcia	.15	.07
☐ 119 Greg Gagne	.15	.07
☐ 120 Darren Dreifort	.15	.07
☐ 121 Wade Boggs	.60	.25
☐ 122 Paul O'Neill	.30	.14
☐ 123 Derek Jeter	2.00	.90
☐ 124 Tino Martinez	.60	.25
☐ 125 David Cone	.30	.14
☐ 126 Andy Pettitte	.30	.14
☐ 127 Charlie Hayes	.15	.07
☐ 128 Mariano Rivera	.40	.18
☐ 129 Dwight Gooden	.30	.14
☐ 130 Cecil Fielder	.30	.14
☐ 132 Darryl Strawberry	.30	.14
☐ 133 Joe Girardi	.15	.07
☐ 134 David Wells	.15	.07
☐ 135 Hideki Irabu	1.00	.45
☐ 136 Ken Griffey Jr.	3.00	1.35
☐ 137 Alex Rodriguez	2.50	1.10
☐ 138 Jay Buhner	.40	.18
☐ 139 Randy Johnson	.60	.25
☐ 140 Paul Sorrento	.15	.07
☐ 141 Edgar Martinez	.40	.18
☐ 142 Joey Cora	.30	.14
☐ 143 Bob Wells	.15	.07
☐ 145 Jamie Moyer	.15	.07
☐ 146 Jeff Fassero	.15	.07
☐ 147 Dan Wilson	.15	.07
☐ 148 Jose Cruz Jr.	5.00	2.20
☐ 149 Scott Sanders	.15	.07
☐ 150 Rich Amaral	.15	.07
☐ 151 Brian Jordan	.15	.07
☐ 152 Andy Benes	.15	.07
☐ 153 Ray Lankford	.30	.14
☐ 154 John Mabry	.15	.07
☐ 155 Tom Pagnozzi	.15	.07
☐ 156 Ron Gant	.15	.07
☐ 157 Alan Benes	.15	.07
☐ 158 Dennis Eckersley	.40	.18
☐ 159 Royce Clayton	.15	.07
☐ 160 Todd Stottlemyre	.15	.07
☐ 161 Gary Gaetti	.30	.14
☐ 162 Willie McGee	.30	.14
☐ 163 Delino DeShields	.15	.07
☐ 164 Dmitri Young	.15	.07
☐ 165 Matt Morris	.40	.18

1997 Donruss Team Sets Pennant Edition

Randomly inserted at an approximate rate of one in every six packs, cards from this 163-card set parallel the Donruss Team Sets base set and displays red and gold foil treatment.

	MINT	NRMT
COMPLETE SET (165)	750.00	350.00
COMMON CARD (1-165)	2.00	.90

*STARS: 8X TO 20X BASIC CARDS
*YOUNG STARS: 6X TO 15X BASIC CARDS
*ROOKIES: 4X TO 10X BASIC CARDS

1997 Donruss Team Sets MVP's

Randomly inserted in packs at an approximate rate of 1:36, this 18-card set features color action player photos printed on microetched foil with foil stamping. Only 1,000 sets were produced and all of the cards are sequentially numbered on back.

	MINT	NRMT
COMPLETE SET (18)	600.00	275.00
COMMON CARD (1-18)	4.00	1.80

☐ 1 Ivan Rodriguez	20.00	9.00
☐ 2 Mike Piazza	50.00	22.00
☐ 3 Frank Thomas	60.00	27.00
☐ 4 Jeff Bagwell	30.00	13.50
☐ 5 Chuck Knoblauch	15.00	6.75
☐ 6 Eric Young	4.00	1.80
☐ 7 Alex Rodriguez	60.00	27.00
☐ 8 Barry Larkin	10.00	4.50
☐ 9 Cal Ripken	60.00	27.00
☐ 10 Chipper Jones	50.00	22.00
☐ 11 Albert Belle	25.00	11.00
☐ 12 Barry Bonds	20.00	9.00
☐ 13 Ken Griffey Jr.	80.00	36.00
☐ 14 Kenny Lofton	20.00	9.00
☐ 15 Juan Gonzalez	40.00	18.00
☐ 16 Larry Walker	15.00	6.75
☐ 17 Roger Clemens	30.00	13.50
☐ 18 Greg Maddux	50.00	22.00

1997 Donruss VxP 1.0

The 1997 Donruss VxP 1.0 set was issued in one series totalling 50 cards. The cards were distributed 10 to a pack with one CD trading card and feature a small player action photo with a head shot. When tilted slightly, the card changes to another photo of the same player beside a disc photo.

	MINT	NRMT
COMPLETE SET (50)	50.00	22.00
COMMON CARD (1-50)	.30	.14

☐ 1 Darin Erstad	1.00	.45
☐ 2 Jim Thome	.60	.25
☐ 3 Alex Rodriguez	2.50	1.10
☐ 4 Greg Maddux	2.00	.90
☐ 5 Scott Rolen	1.50	.70
☐ 6 Roberto Alomar	.60	.25
☐ 7 Tony Clark	.50	.23
☐ 8 Randy Johnson	.60	.25
☐ 9 Sammy Sosa	.50	.23
☐ 10 Jose Guillen	.75	.35
☐ 11 Cal Ripken	2.50	1.10
☐ 12 Paul Molitor	.60	.25
☐ 13 Jose Cruz Jr.	5.00	2.20
☐ 14 Barry Larkin	.40	.18
☐ 15 Ken Caminiti	.40	.18
☐ 16 Rafael Palmeiro	.30	.14
☐ 17 Chuck Knoblauch	.60	.25
☐ 18 Juan Gonzalez	1.50	.70
☐ 19 Larry Walker	.60	.25
☐ 20 Tony Gwynn	1.50	.70
☐ 21 Brady Anderson	.40	.18
☐ 22 Derek Jeter	1.50	.70
☐ 23 Rusty Greer	.30	.14
☐ 24 Gary Sheffield	.50	.23
☐ 25 Barry Bonds	.75	.35
☐ 26 Mo Vaughn	.75	.35
☐ 27 Tino Martinez	.50	.23
☐ 28 Ivan Rodriguez	.75	.35
☐ 29 Jeff Bagwell	1.25	.55
☐ 30 Tim Salmon	.50	.23
☐ 31 Nomar Garciaparra	2.00	.90
☐ 32 Bernie Williams	.50	.23
☐ 33 Kenny Lofton	.75	.35
☐ 34 Mike Piazza	2.00	.90
☐ 35 Jim Edmonds	.50	.23
☐ 36 Frank Thomas	2.50	1.10
☐ 37 Andy Pettitte	.60	.25
☐ 38 Andruw Jones	1.50	.70
☐ 39 Raul Mondesi	.40	.18
☐ 40 John Smoltz	.30	.14
☐ 41 Albert Belle	.75	.35
☐ 42 Mark McGwire	1.25	.55
☐ 43 Chipper Jones	2.00	.90
☐ 44 Hideo Nomo	1.50	.70
☐ 45 David Justice	.50	.23
☐ 46 Manny Ramirez	.60	.25
☐ 47 Ken Griffey Jr.	3.00	1.35
☐ 48 Roger Clemens	1.25	.55
☐ 49 Vladimir Guerrero	1.25	.55
☐ 50 Ryne Sandberg	1.00	.45

1997 Donruss VxP 1.0 CD Roms

This set features six collectible CD-ROM trading cards shaped and styled like an actual trading card. Each CD was distributed in a pack with ten regular VxP 1.0 cards and features personal and career player information, batting and fielding strategies, video highlights, and an interactive baseball trivia game. When all six were collected and added to a hard drive, a special screen saver with an interactive desktop game was unlocked. The cards are listed below alphabetical.

	MINT	NRMT
COMPLETE SET (6)	120.00	55.00
COMMON CARD (1-6)	15.00	6.75

☐ 1 Ken Griffey Jr.	15.00	6.75
☐ 2 Greg Maddux	15.00	6.75
☐ 3 Mike Piazza	15.00	6.75
☐ 4 Cal Ripken	15.00	6.75
☐ 5 Alex Rodriguez	15.00	6.75
☐ 6 Frank Thomas	15.00	6.75

1986 Dorman's Cheese

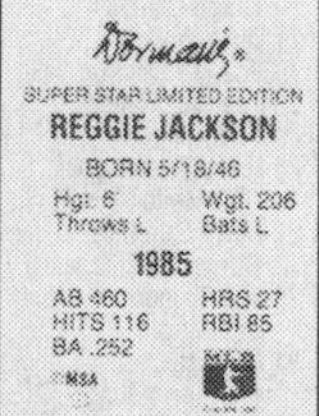

This 20-card set was issued in panels of two cards. The individual cards measure approximately 1 1/2" by 2" whereas the panels measure 3" by 2". Team logos have been removed from the photos as these cards were not licensed by Major League Baseball (team owners). The backs contain a minimum of information.

	MINT	NRMT
COMPLETE PANEL SET	18.00	8.00
COMPLETE SET	15.00	6.75
COMMON PAIR	.25	.11

☐ 1 George Brett	2.50	1.10
☐ 2 Jack Morris	.50	.23
☐ 3 Gary Carter	.75	.35
☐ 4 Cal Ripken	5.00	2.20
☐ 5 Dwight Gooden	.75	.35
☐ 6 Kent Hrbek	.25	.11
☐ 7 Rickey Henderson	1.25	.55
☐ 8 Mike Schmidt	1.50	.70
☐ 9 Keith Hernandez	.50	.23
☐ 10 Dale Murphy	1.00	.45
☐ 11 Reggie Jackson	1.50	.70
☐ 12 Eddie Murray	1.50	.70
☐ 13 Don Mattingly	3.00	1.35
☐ 14 Ryne Sandberg	2.50	1.10
☐ 15 Willie McGee	.50	.23

☐ 16 Robin Yount	.75	.35
☐ 17 Rick Sutcliffe	.25	.11
☐ 18 Wade Boggs	1.25	.55
☐ 19 Dave Winfield	1.00	.45
☐ 20 Jim Rice	.50	.23

1941 Double Play R330

The cards in this 75-card set measure approximately 2 1/2" by 3 1/8" was a blank-backed issue distributed by Gum Products. It consists of 75 numbered cards (two consecutive numbers per card), each depicting two players in sepia tone photographs. Cards 81-100 contain action poses, and the last 50 numbers of the set are slightly harder to find. Cards that have been cut in half to form "singles" have a greatly reduced value. These cards have a value from five to ten percent of the uncut strips and are very difficult to sell. The player on the left has an odd number and the other player has an even number. We are using only the odd numbers to identify these panels.

	EX-MT	VG-E
COMPLETE SET (150)	5000.00	2200.00
COMMON PAIRS (1-100)	25.00	11.00
COMMON PAIRS (101-150)	30.00	13.50
WRAPPER (1-CENT)	500.00	220.00

	EX-MT	VG-E
☐ 1 Larry French	60.00	27.00
Vance Page		
☐ 3 Billy Herman	45.00	20.00
Stan Hack		
☐ 5 Lonny Frey	35.00	16.00
Johnny VanderMeer		
☐ 7 Paul Derringer	35.00	16.00
Bucky Walters		
☐ 9 Frank McCormick	25.00	11.00
Billy Werber		
☐ 11 Johnny Ripple	45.00	20.00
Ernie Lombardi		
☐ 13 Alex Kampouris	25.00	11.00
Whitlow Wyatt		
☐ 15 Mickey Owen	45.00	20.00
Paul Waner		
☐ 17 Cookie Lavagetto	30.00	13.50
Pete Reiser		
☐ 19 James Wasdell	30.00	13.50
Dolph Camilli		
☐ 21 Dixie Walker	45.00	20.00
Joe Medwick		
☐ 23 Pee Wee Reese	200.00	90.00
Kirby Higbe		
☐ 25 Harry Danning	25.00	11.00
Cliff Melton		
☐ 27 Harry Gumbert	25.00	11.00
Burgess Whitehead		
☐ 29 Joe Orengo	25.00	11.00
Joe Moore		
☐ 31 Mel Ott	100.00	45.00
Norman Young		
☐ 33 Lee Handley	45.00	20.00
Arky Vaughan		
☐ 35 Bob Klinger	25.00	11.00
Stanley Brown		
☐ 37 Terry Moore	30.00	13.50
Gus Mancuso		
☐ 39 Johnny Mize	150.00	70.00
Enos Slaughter		
☐ 41 Johnny Cooney	25.00	11.00
Sibby Sisti		
☐ 43 Max West	25.00	11.00
Carvel Rowell		
☐ 45 Danny Litwhiler	25.00	11.00
Merrill May		
☐ 47 Frank Hayes	25.00	11.00
Al Brancato		
☐ 49 Bob Johnson	30.00	13.50
Bill Nagel		
☐ 51 Bobo Newsom	100.00	45.00
Hank Greenberg		
☐ 53 Barney McCosky	75.00	34.00
Charlie Gehringer		
☐ 55 Mike Higgins	30.00	13.50
Dick Bartell		
☐ 57 Ted Williams	500.00	220.00
Jim Tabor		
☐ 59 Joe Cronin	200.00	90.00
Jimmy Foxx		
☐ 61 Lefty Gomez	250.00	110.00
Phil Rizzuto		
☐ 63 Joe DiMaggio	750.00	350.00
Charlie Keller		
☐ 65 Red Rolfe	100.00	45.00
Bill Dickey		
☐ 67 Joe Gordon	100.00	45.00
Red Ruffing		
☐ 69 Mike Tresh	60.00	27.00
Luke Appling		
☐ 71 Moose Solters	25.00	11.00
Johnny Rigney		
☐ 73 Buddy Myer	30.00	13.50
Ben Chapman		
☐ 75 Cecil Travis	30.00	13.50
George Case		
☐ 77 Joe Krakauskas	125.00	55.00
Bob Feller		
☐ 79 Ken Keltner	30.00	13.50
Hal Trosky		
☐ 81 Ted Williams	600.00	275.00
Joe Cronin		
☐ 83 Joe Gordon	40.00	18.00
Charlie Keller		
☐ 85 Hank Greenberg	200.00	90.00
Red Ruffing		
☐ 87 Hal Trosky	30.00	13.50
George Case		
☐ 89 Mel Ott	100.00	45.00
Burgess Whitehead		
☐ 91 Harry Danning	25.00	11.00
Harry Gumbert		
☐ 93 Norman Young	25.00	11.00
Cliff Melton		
☐ 95 Jimmy Ripple	30.00	13.50
Bucky Walters		
☐ 97 Stan Hack	30.00	13.50
Bob Klinger		
☐ 99 Johnny Mize	75.00	34.00
Dan Litwhiler		
☐ 101 Dom Dallesandro	30.00	13.50
Augie Galan		
☐ 103 Bill Lee	40.00	18.00
Phil Cavarretta		
☐ 105 Lefty Grove	150.00	70.00
Bobby Doerr		
☐ 107 Frank Pytlak	60.00	27.00
Dom DiMaggio		
☐ 109 Jerry Priddy	35.00	16.00
Johnny Murphy		
☐ 111 Tommy Henrich	50.00	22.00
Marius Russo		
☐ 113 Frank Crosetti	50.00	22.00
Johnny Sturm		
☐ 115 Ival Goodman	30.00	13.50
Myron McCormick		
☐ 117 Eddie Joost	30.00	13.50
Ernie Koy		
☐ 119 Lloyd Waner	50.00	22.00
Hank Majeski		
☐ 121 Buddy Hassett	30.00	13.50
Eugene Moore		
☐ 123 Nick Etten	30.00	13.50
Johnny Rizzo		
☐ 125 Sam Chapman	30.00	13.50
Wally Moses		
☐ 127 Johnny Babich	30.00	13.50
Dick Siebert		
☐ 129 Nelson Potter	30.00	13.50
Benny McCoy		
☐ 131 Clarence Campbell	75.00	34.00
Lou Boudreau		
☐ 133 Rollie Hemsley	40.00	18.00
Mel Harder		
☐ 135 Gerald Walker	30.00	13.50
Joe Heving		
☐ 137 Johnny Rucker	30.00	13.50
Ace Adams		
☐ 139 Morris Arnovich	90.00	40.00
Carl Hubbell		
☐ 141 Lew Riggs	75.00	34.00
Leo Durocher		
☐ 143 Fred Fitzsimmons	30.00	13.50
Joe Vosmik		
☐ 145 Frank Crespi	30.00	13.50
Jim Brown		
☐ 147 Don Heffner	30.00	13.50
Harlond Clift		
☐ 149 Debs Garms	35.00	16.00
Elbie Fletcher		

1950 Drake's

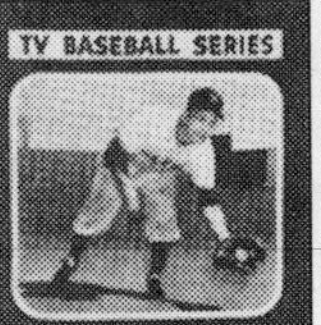

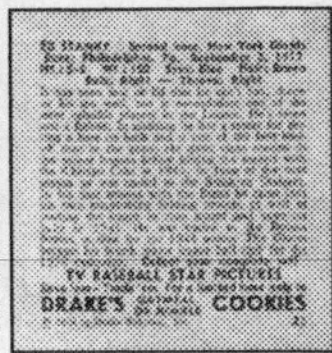

The cards in this 36-card set measure approximately 2 1/2" by 2 1/2". The 1950 Drake's Cookies set contains numbered black and white cards. The players are pictured inside a simulated television screen and the caption "TV Baseball Series" appears on the cards. The players selected for this set show a heavy representation of players from New York teams. The catalog designation for this set is D358.

	NRMT	VG-E
COMPLETE SET (36)	7000.00	3200.00
COMMON CARD (1-36)	75.00	34.00

	NRMT	VG-E
☐ 1 Preacher Roe	100.00	45.00
☐ 2 Clint Hartung	75.00	34.00
☐ 3 Earl Torgeson	75.00	34.00
☐ 4 Lou Brissie	75.00	34.00
☐ 5 Duke Snider	350.00	160.00
☐ 6 Roy Campanella	450.00	200.00
☐ 7 Sheldon Jones	75.00	34.00
☐ 8 Whitey Lockman	75.00	34.00
☐ 9 Bobby Thomson	100.00	45.00
☐ 10 Dick Sisler	75.00	34.00
☐ 11 Gil Hodges	200.00	90.00
☐ 12 Eddie Waitkus	75.00	34.00
☐ 13 Bobby Doerr	150.00	70.00
☐ 14 Warren Spahn	300.00	135.00
☐ 15 Buddy Kerr	75.00	34.00
☐ 16 Sid Gordon	75.00	34.00
☐ 17 Willard Marshall	75.00	34.00
☐ 18 Carl Furillo	100.00	45.00
☐ 19 Pee Wee Reese	300.00	135.00
☐ 20 Alvin Dark	100.00	45.00
☐ 21 Del Ennis	100.00	45.00
☐ 22 Ed Stanky	100.00	45.00
☐ 23 Tom Henrich	125.00	55.00
☐ 24 Yogi Berra	400.00	180.00
☐ 25 Phil Rizzuto	200.00	90.00
☐ 26 Jerry Coleman	100.00	45.00
☐ 27 Joe Page	100.00	45.00
☐ 28 Allie Reynolds	100.00	45.00
☐ 29 Ray Scarborough	75.00	34.00
☐ 30 Birdie Tebbetts	75.00	34.00
☐ 31 Maurice McDermott	75.00	34.00
☐ 32 Johnny Pesky	100.00	45.00
☐ 33 Dom DiMaggio	125.00	55.00
☐ 34 Vern Stephens	100.00	45.00
☐ 35 Bob Elliott	100.00	45.00
☐ 36 Enos Slaughter	175.00	80.00

1981 Drake's

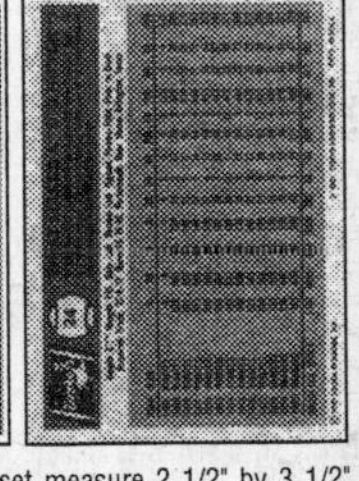

The cards in this 33-card set measure 2 1/2" by 3 1/2". The 1981 Drake's Bakeries set contains National and American League stars. Produced in conjunction with Topps and released to the public in Drake's Cakes, this set features red frames for American League players and blue frames for National League players. A Drake's Cakes logo with the words "Big Hitters" appears on the lower front of each card. The backs are quite similar to the 1981 Topps backs but contain the Drake's logo, a different card number, and a short paragraph entitled "What Makes a Big Hitter" at the top of the card.

	NRMT	VG-E
COMPLETE SET (33)	7.50	3.40
COMMON CARD (1-33)	.05	.02

	NRMT	VG-E
☐ 1 Carl Yastrzemski	.75	.35
☐ 2 Rod Carew	.75	.35
☐ 3 Pete Rose	1.25	.55
☐ 4 Dave Parker	.10	.05
☐ 5 George Brett	2.50	1.10
☐ 6 Eddie Murray	2.00	.90
☐ 7 Mike Schmidt	1.25	.55
☐ 8 Jim Rice	.20	.09

Card	NRMT	VG-E
☐ 9 Fred Lynn	.10	.05
☐ 10 Reggie Jackson	.75	.35
☐ 11 Steve Garvey	.30	.14
☐ 12 Ken Singleton	.10	.05
☐ 13 Bill Buckner	.10	.05
☐ 14 Dave Winfield	1.00	.45
☐ 15 Jack Clark	.10	.05
☐ 16 Cecil Cooper	.10	.05
☐ 17 Bob Horner	.05	.02
☐ 18 George Foster	.10	.05
☐ 19 Dave Kingman	.10	.05
☐ 20 Cesar Cedeno	.10	.05
☐ 21 Joe Charboneau	.10	.05
☐ 22 George Hendrick	.05	.02
☐ 23 Gary Carter	.40	.18
☐ 24 Al Oliver	.10	.05
☐ 25 Bruce Bochte	.05	.02
☐ 26 Jerry Mumphrey	.05	.02
☐ 27 Steve Kemp	.05	.02
☐ 28 Bob Watson	.10	.05
☐ 29 John Castino	.05	.02
☐ 30 Tony Armas	.05	.02
☐ 31 John Mayberry	.05	.02
☐ 32 Carlton Fisk	.75	.35
☐ 33 Lee Mazzilli	.05	.02

1982 Drake's

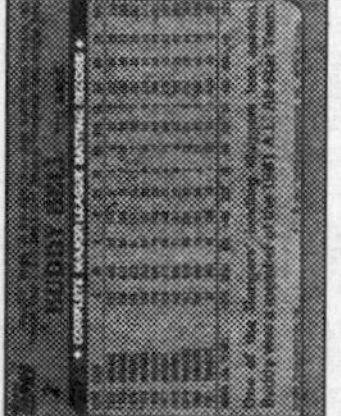

The cards in this 33-card set measure 2 1/2" by 3 1/2". The 1982 Drake's Big Hitters series cards each has the title "2nd Annual Collectors' Edition" in a ribbon design at the top of the picture area. Each color player photo has "photo mount" designs in the corners, red for the AL and green for the NL. The reverses are green and blue, the same as the regular 1982 Topps format, and the photos are larger than those of the previous year. Of the 33 hitters featured, 19 represent the National League. There are 21 returnees from the 1981 set and only one photo, that of Kennedy, is the same as that appearing in the regular Topps issue. The Drake's logo appears centered in the bottom border on the obverse. This set's card numbering is essentially in alphabetical order by the player's name.

	NRMT	VG-E
COMPLETE SET (33)	7.50	3.40
COMMON CARD (1-33)	.05	.02
☐ 1 Tony Armas	.05	.02
☐ 2 Buddy Bell	.10	.05
☐ 3 Johnny Bench	.50	.23
☐ 4 George Brett	2.00	.90
☐ 5 Bill Buckner	.10	.05
☐ 6 Rod Carew	.40	.18
☐ 7 Gary Carter	.30	.14
☐ 8 Jack Clark	.10	.05
☐ 9 Cecil Cooper	.10	.05
☐ 10 Jose Cruz	.05	.02
☐ 11 Dwight Evans	.20	.09
☐ 12 Carlton Fisk	.50	.23
☐ 13 George Foster	.10	.05
☐ 14 Steve Garvey	.30	.14
☐ 15 Kirk Gibson	.30	.14
☐ 16 Mike Hargrove	.10	.05
☐ 17 George Hendrick	.05	.02
☐ 18 Bob Horner	.05	.02
☐ 19 Reggie Jackson	.50	.23
☐ 20 Terry Kennedy	.05	.02
☐ 21 Dave Kingman	.10	.05
☐ 22 Greg Luzinski	.10	.05
☐ 23 Bill Madlock	.10	.05
☐ 24 John Mayberry	.05	.02
☐ 25 Eddie Murray	1.50	.70
☐ 26 Graig Nettles	.10	.05
☐ 27 Jim Rice	.20	.09
☐ 28 Pete Rose	1.25	.55
☐ 29 Mike Schmidt	1.25	.55
☐ 30 Ken Singleton	.05	.02
☐ 31 Dave Winfield	.60	.25
☐ 32 Butch Wynegar	.05	.02
☐ 33 Richie Zisk	.05	.02

1983 Drake's

The cards in this 33-card series measure 2 1/2" by 3 1/2". For the third year in a row, Drake's Cakes, in conjunction with Topps, issued a set entitled Big Hitters. The fronts appear very similar to those of the previous two years with slight variations on the framelines and player identification sections. The backs are the same as the Topps backs of this year except for the card number and the Drake's logo. This set's card numbering is essentially in alphabetical order by the player's name.

	NRMT	VG-E
COMPLETE SET (33)	7.50	3.40
COMMON CARD (1-33)	.05	.02
☐ 1 Don Baylor	.10	.05
☐ 2 Bill Buckner	.10	.05
☐ 3 Rod Carew	.40	.18
☐ 4 Gary Carter	.30	.14
☐ 5 Jack Clark	.10	.05
☐ 6 Cecil Cooper	.10	.05
☐ 7 Dwight Evans	.20	.09
☐ 8 George Foster	.10	.05
☐ 9 Pedro Guerrero	.05	.02
☐ 10 George Hendrick	.05	.02
☐ 11 Bob Horner	.05	.02
☐ 12 Reggie Jackson	.50	.23
☐ 13 Steve Kemp	.05	.02
☐ 14 Dave Kingman	.10	.05
☐ 15 Bill Madlock	.05	.02
☐ 16 Gary Matthews	.05	.02
☐ 17 Hal McRae	.10	.05
☐ 18 Dale Murphy	.40	.18
☐ 19 Eddie Murray	1.50	.70
☐ 20 Ben Oglivie	.05	.02
☐ 21 Al Oliver	.10	.05
☐ 22 Jim Rice	.20	.09
☐ 23 Cal Ripken	4.00	1.80
☐ 24 Pete Rose	1.00	.45
☐ 25 Mike Schmidt	1.00	.45
☐ 26 Ken Singleton	.05	.02
☐ 27 Gorman Thomas	.05	.02
☐ 28 Jason Thompson	.05	.02
☐ 29 Mookie Wilson	.10	.05
☐ 30 Willie Wilson	.05	.02
☐ 31 Dave Winfield	.60	.25
☐ 32 Carl Yastrzemski	.50	.23
☐ 33 Robin Yount	.60	.25

1984 Drake's

The cards in this 33-card set measure 2 1/2" by 3 1/2". The Fourth Annual Collectors Edition of baseball cards produced by Drake's Cakes in conjunction with Topps continued this now annual set entitled Big Hitters. As in previous years, the front contains a frameline in which the title of the set, the Drake's logo, and the player's name, his team, and position appear. The cards all feature the player in a batting action pose. While the cards fronts are different from the Topps fronts of this year, the backs differ only in the card number and the use of the Drake's logo instead of the Topps logo. This set's card numbering is essentially in alphabetical order by the player's name.

	NRMT	VG-E
COMPLETE SET (33)	7.50	3.40
COMMON CARD (1-33)	.05	.02

Card	NRMT	VG-E
☐ 1 Don Baylor	.10	.05
☐ 2 Wade Boggs	.75	.35
☐ 3 George Brett	2.00	.90
☐ 4 Bill Buckner	.10	.05
☐ 5 Rod Carew	.40	.18
☐ 6 Gary Carter	.20	.09
☐ 7 Ron Cey	.10	.05
☐ 8 Cecil Cooper	.10	.05
☐ 9 Andre Dawson	.40	.18
☐ 10 Steve Garvey	.10	.05
☐ 11 Pedro Guerrero	.10	.05
☐ 12 George Hendrick	.05	.02
☐ 13 Keith Hernandez	.10	.05
☐ 14 Bob Horner	.05	.02
☐ 15 Reggie Jackson	.50	.23
☐ 16 Steve Kemp	.05	.02
☐ 17 Ron Kittle	.05	.02
☐ 18 Greg Luzinski	.10	.05
☐ 19 Fred Lynn	.10	.05
☐ 20 Bill Madlock	.10	.05
☐ 21 Gary Matthews	.05	.02
☐ 22 Dale Murphy	.40	.18
☐ 23 Eddie Murray	1.25	.55
☐ 24 Al Oliver	.10	.05
☐ 25 Jim Rice	.20	.09
☐ 26 Cal Ripken	4.00	1.80
☐ 27 Pete Rose	1.00	.45
☐ 28 Mike Schmidt	1.00	.45
☐ 29 Darryl Strawberry	.50	.23
☐ 30 Alan Trammell	.30	.14
☐ 31 Mookie Wilson	.05	.02
☐ 32 Dave Winfield	.60	.25
☐ 33 Robin Yount	.50	.23

1985 Drake's

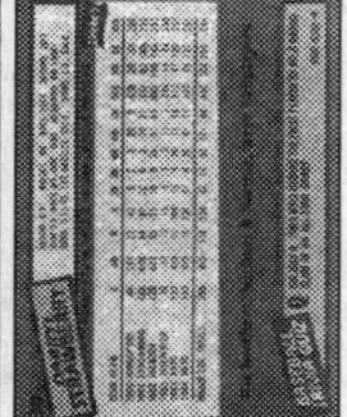

The cards in this 44-card set measure 2 1/2" by 3 1/2". The Fifth Annual Collectors Edition of baseball cards produced by Drake's Cakes in conjunction with Topps continued this apparently annual set with a new twist, for the first time, 11 pitchers were included. The "Big Hitters" are numbered 1-33 and the pitchers are numbered 34-44; each subgroup is ordered alphabetically. The cards are numbered in the upper right corner of the backs of the cards. The complete set could be obtained directly from the company by sending 2.95 with four proofs of purchase.

	NRMT	VG-E
COMPLETE FACT. SET (44)	10.00	4.50
COMPLETE SET (44)	10.00	4.50
COMMON CARD (1-33)	.05	.02
COMMON CARD (34-44)	.10	.05
☐ 1 Tony Armas	.05	.02
☐ 2 Harold Baines	.15	.07
☐ 3 Don Baylor	.10	.05
☐ 4 George Brett	1.50	.70
☐ 5 Gary Carter	.25	.11
☐ 6 Ron Cey	.15	.07
☐ 7 Jose Cruz	.05	.02
☐ 8 Alvin Davis	.05	.02
☐ 9 Chili Davis	.15	.07
☐ 10 Dwight Evans	.15	.07
☐ 11 Steve Garvey	.25	.11
☐ 12 Kirk Gibson	.35	.16
☐ 13 Pedro Guerrero	.15	.07
☐ 14 Tony Gwynn	2.00	.90
☐ 15 Keith Hernandez	.15	.07
☐ 16 Kent Hrbek	.15	.07
☐ 17 Reggie Jackson	.50	.23
☐ 18 Gary Matthews	.05	.02
☐ 19 Don Mattingly	3.00	1.35
☐ 20 Dale Murphy	.40	.18
☐ 21 Eddie Murray	1.00	.45
☐ 22 Dave Parker	.15	.07
☐ 23 Lance Parrish	.15	.07
☐ 24 Tim Raines	.15	.07
☐ 25 Jim Rice	.15	.07
☐ 26 Cal Ripken	3.00	1.35
☐ 27 Juan Samuel	.05	.02

	MINT	NRMT
☐ 28 Ryne Sandberg	1.50	.70
☐ 29 Mike Schmidt	1.00	.45
☐ 30 Darryl Strawberry	.15	.07
☐ 31 Alan Trammell	.25	.11
☐ 32 Dave Winfield	.60	.25
☐ 33 Robin Yount	.40	.18
☐ 34 Mike Boddicker	.10	.05
☐ 35 Steve Carlton	.40	.18
☐ 36 Dwight Gooden	1.50	.70
☐ 37 Willie Hernandez	.10	.05
☐ 38 Mark Langston	.25	.11
☐ 39 Dan Quisenberry	.10	.05
☐ 40 Dave Righetti	.10	.05
☐ 41 Tom Seaver	.50	.23
☐ 42 Bob Stanley	.10	.05
☐ 43 Rick Sutcliffe	.10	.05
☐ 44 Bruce Sutter	.10	.05

1986 Drake's

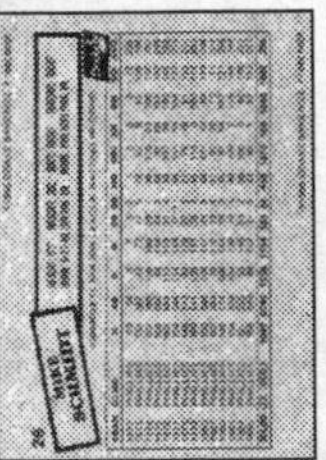

This set of 37 cards was distributed as back panels of various Drake's snack products. Each individual card measures 2 1/2" by 3 1/2". Each specially marked package features two, three, or four cards on the back. The set is easily recognized by the Drake's logo and "6th Annual Collector's Edition" at the top of the obverse. Cards are numbered on the front and the back. Cards below are coded based on the product upon which they appeared, for example, Apple Pies (AP), Cherry Pies (CP), Chocolate Donut Delites (CDD), Coffee Cake Jr. (CCJ), Creme Shortcakes (CS), Devil Dogs (DD), Fudge Brownies (FUD), Funny Bones (FB), Peanut Butter Squares (PBS), Powdered Sugar Donut Delites (PSDD), Ring Ding Jr. (RDJ), Sunny Doodles (SD), Swiss Rolls (SR), Yankee Doodles (YD), and Yodels (Y). The last nine cards are pitchers. Complete panels would be valued approximately 50 percent higher than the individual card prices listed below.

	MINT	NRMT
COMPLETE SET (37)	50.00	22.00
COMMON CARD (1-37)	.25	.11
☐ 1 Gary Carter Y	.75	.35
☐ 2 Dwight Evans Y	.50	.23
☐ 3 Reggie Jackson SR	2.00	.90
☐ 4 Dave Parker SR	.50	.23
☐ 5 Rickey Henderson FB	1.50	.70
☐ 6 Pedro Guerrero FB	.50	.23
☐ 7 Don Mattingly YD	6.00	2.70
☐ 8 Mike Marshall YD	.25	.11
☐ 9 Keith Moreland YD	.25	.11
☐ 10 Keith Hernandez CS	.50	.23
☐ 11 Cal Ripken CS	10.00	4.50
☐ 12 Dale Murphy RDJ	1.00	.45
☐ 13 Jim Rice RDJ	.50	.23
☐ 14 George Brett CCJ	5.00	2.20
☐ 15 Tim Raines CCJ	.50	.23
☐ 16 Darryl Strawberry DD	.75	.35
☐ 17 Bill Buckner DD	.50	.23
☐ 18 Dave Winfield AP	1.50	.70
☐ 19 Ryne Sandberg AP	3.00	1.35
☐ 20 Steve Balboni AP	.25	.11
☐ 21 Tommy Herr AP	.25	.11
☐ 22 Pete Rose CP	3.00	1.35
☐ 23 Willie McGee CP	.50	.23
☐ 24 Harold Baines CP	.50	.23
☐ 25 Eddie Murray CP	1.50	.70
☐ 26 Mike Schmidt SD/FUD	2.00	.90
☐ 27 Wade Boggs SD/FUD	1.50	.70
☐ 28 Kirk Gibson SD/FUD	.50	.23
☐ 29 Bret Saberhagen PBS	.50	.23
☐ 30 John Tudor PBS	.25	.11
☐ 31 Orel Hershiser PBS	.50	.23
☐ 32 Ron Guidry CDD	.50	.23
☐ 33 Nolan Ryan CDD	10.00	4.50
☐ 34 Dave Stieb CDD	.25	.11
☐ 35 Dwight Gooden SDD	.75	.35
☐ 36 Fern.Valenzuela SDD	.50	.23
☐ 37 Tom Browning SDD	.25	.11

1987 Drake's

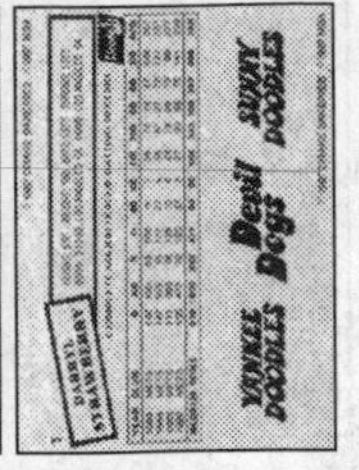

This 33-card set features 25 top hitters and eight top pitchers. Cards were printed in groups of two, three, or four on the backs of Drake's bakery products. Individual cards measure 2 1/2" by 3 1/2" and tout the 7th annual edition. Card backs feature year-by-year season statistics. The cards are numbered such that the pitchers are listed numerically last, e.g., top hitters 1-25 and pitchers 26-33). Complete panels would be valued approximately 50 percent higher than the individual card prices listed below.

	MINT	NRMT
COMPLETE SET (33)	50.00	22.00
COMMON CARD (1-33)	.25	.11
☐ 1 Darryl Strawberry	.75	.35
☐ 2 Wally Joyner	.75	.35
☐ 3 Von Hayes	.25	.11
☐ 4 Jose Canseco	3.00	1.35
☐ 5 Dave Winfield	1.50	.70
☐ 6 Cal Ripken	10.00	4.50
☐ 7 Keith Moreland	.25	.11
☐ 8 Don Mattingly	5.00	2.20
☐ 9 Willie McGee	.25	.11
☐ 10 Keith Hernandez	.50	.23
☐ 11 Tony Gwynn	4.00	1.80
☐ 12 Rickey Henderson	1.50	.70
☐ 13 Dale Murphy	1.00	.45
☐ 14 George Brett	4.00	1.80
☐ 15 Jim Rice	.50	.23
☐ 16 Wade Boggs	1.50	.70
☐ 17 Kevin Bass	.25	.11
☐ 18 Dave Parker	.50	.23
☐ 19 Kirby Puckett	4.00	1.80
☐ 20 Gary Carter	.75	.35
☐ 21 Ryne Sandberg	3.00	1.35
☐ 22 Harold Baines	.50	.23
☐ 23 Mike Schmidt	2.00	.90
☐ 24 Eddie Murray	1.50	.70
☐ 25 Steve Sax	.25	.11
☐ 26 Dwight Gooden	.75	.35
☐ 27 Jack Morris	.50	.23
☐ 28 Ron Darling	.25	.11
☐ 29 Fernando Valenzuela	.50	.23
☐ 30 John Tudor	.25	.11
☐ 31 Roger Clemens	5.00	2.20
☐ 32 Nolan Ryan	10.00	4.50
☐ 33 Mike Scott	.25	.11

1988 Drake's

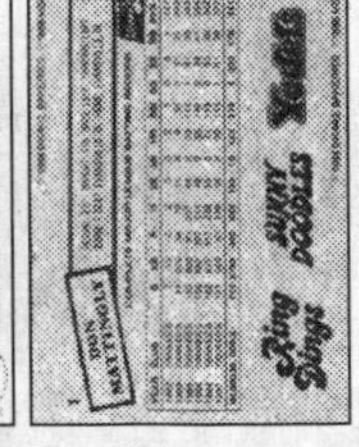

This 33-card set features 27 top hitters and six top pitchers. Cards were printed in groups of two, three, or four on the backs of Drake's bakery products. Individual cards measure approximately 2 1/2" by 3 1/2" and tout the 8th annual edition. Card backs feature year-by-year season statistics. The cards are numbered such that the pitchers are listed numerically last, e.g., top hitters 1-27 and pitchers 28-33). The product affiliations are as follows, 1-2 Ring Dings, 3-4 Devil Dogs, 5-6 Coffee Cakes, 7-9 Yankee Doodles, 10-11 Funny Bones, 12-14 Fudge Brownies, 15-18 Cherry Pies, 19-21 Sunny Doodles, 22-24 Powdered Sugar Donuts, 25-27 Chocolate Donuts, 28-29 Yodels, and 30-33 Apple Pies. Complete panels would be valued approximately 50 percent higher than the individual card prices listed below.

	MINT	NRMT
COMPLETE SET (33)	40.00	18.00
COMMON CARD (1-33)	.25	.11
☐ 1 Don Mattingly	5.00	2.20
☐ 2 Tim Raines	.50	.23
☐ 3 Darryl Strawberry	.75	.35
☐ 4 Wade Boggs	1.50	.70
☐ 5 Keith Hernandez	.50	.23
☐ 6 Mark McGwire	3.00	1.35
☐ 7 Rickey Henderson	1.50	.70
☐ 8 Mike Schmidt	2.00	.90
☐ 9 Dwight Evans	.25	.11
☐ 10 Gary Carter	.50	.23
☐ 11 Paul Molitor	2.00	.90
☐ 12 Dave Winfield	1.50	.70
☐ 13 Alan Trammell	.75	.35
☐ 14 Tony Gwynn	4.00	1.80
☐ 15 Dale Murphy	1.00	.45
☐ 16 Andre Dawson	.75	.35
☐ 17 Von Hayes	.25	.11
☐ 18 Willie Randolph	.25	.11
☐ 19 Kirby Puckett	4.00	1.80
☐ 20 Juan Samuel	.25	.11
☐ 21 Eddie Murray	1.50	.70
☐ 22 George Bell	.25	.11
☐ 23 Larry Sheets	.25	.11
☐ 24 Eric Davis	.50	.23
☐ 25 Cal Ripken	10.00	4.50
☐ 26 Pedro Guerrero	.25	.11
☐ 27 Will Clark	2.50	1.10
☐ 28 Dwight Gooden	.50	.23
☐ 29 Frank Viola	.25	.11
☐ 30 Roger Clemens	4.00	1.80
☐ 31 Rick Sutcliffe	.25	.11
☐ 32 Jack Morris	.50	.23
☐ 33 John Tudor	.25	.11

1993 Duracell Power Players I

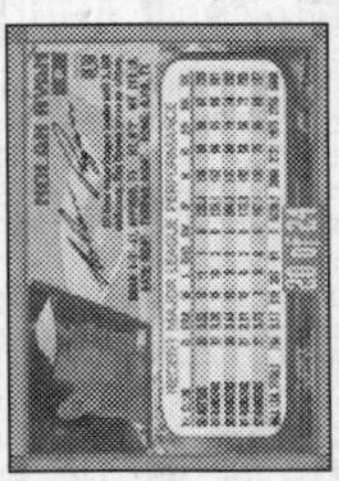

This 24-card standard-size set was divided into six packs with four cards and one Duracell Official Order Form in each pack. One pack was free with a purchase of Duracell Saver Pack or could be ordered with proof of purchase of several other Duracell products. The white-bordered color photo has a Duracell logo across the top and the player's name, team and position at the bottom edge. The horizontal back carries a close-up photo in the upper left. The player's name, autograph, biography, and recent statistics are shown superimposed over a ghosted picture of a ball park.

	MINT	NRMT
COMPLETE SET (24)	2.50	1.10
COMMON CARD (1-24)	.05	.02
☐ 1 Roger Clemens	.50	.23
☐ 2 Frank Thomas	1.00	.45
☐ 3 Andre Dawson	.15	.07
☐ 4 Orel Hershiser	.10	.05
☐ 5 Kirby Puckett	.50	.23
☐ 6 Edgar Martinez	.15	.07
☐ 7 Craig Biggio	.15	.07
☐ 8 Terry Pendleton	.05	.02
☐ 9 Mark McGwire	.50	.23
☐ 10 Dave Stewart	.05	.02
☐ 11 Ozzie Smith	.40	.18
☐ 12 Doug Drabek	.05	.02
☐ 13 Dwight Gooden	.10	.05
☐ 14 Tony Gwynn	.50	.23
☐ 15 Carlos Baerga	.10	.05
☐ 16 Robin Yount	.15	.07
☐ 17 Barry Bonds	.30	.14
☐ 18 Bip Roberts	.05	.02
☐ 19 Don Mattingly	.40	.18
☐ 20 Nolan Ryan	.75	.35
☐ 21 Tom Glavine	.10	.05
☐ 22 Will Clark	.15	.07
☐ 23 Cecil Fielder	.10	.05
☐ 24 Dave Winfield	.15	.07

1993 Duracell Power Players II

This 24-card standard-size set was divided into six packs with four cards and one Duracell Official Order Form in each pack. One pack was free with a purchase of a Duracell Saver Pack or could be ordered with proof of purchase of several other Duracell products. The white-bordered color photo has a Duracell logo across the top and the player's name, team and position at the bottom edge. The horizontal back carries a close-up photo in the upper left. The player's name, autograph, biography, and recent statistics are shown superimposed over a ghosted picture of a ballpark.

	MINT	NRMT
COMPLETE SET (24)	2.50	1.10
COMMON CARD (1-24)	.05	.02

☐ 1 Cal Ripken	1.00	.45
☐ 2 Melido Perez	.05	.02
☐ 3 John Kruk	.05	.02
☐ 4 Charlie Hayes	.05	.02
☐ 5 George Brett	.50	.23
☐ 6 Ruben Sierra	.05	.02
☐ 7 Deion Sanders	.25	.11
☐ 8 Andy Van Slyke	.05	.02
☐ 9 Fred McGriff	.15	.07
☐ 10 Benito Santiago	.05	.02
☐ 11 Charles Nagy	.10	.05
☐ 12 Greg Maddux	.75	.35
☐ 13 Ryne Sandberg	.50	.23
☐ 14 Dennis Martinez	.10	.05
☐ 15 Ken Griffey Jr.	1.25	.55
☐ 16 Jim Abbott	.10	.05
☐ 17 Barry Larkin	.15	.07
☐ 18 Gary Sheffield	.25	.11
☐ 19 Jose Canseco	.15	.07
☐ 20 Jack McDowell	.05	.02
☐ 21 Darryl Strawberry	.10	.05
☐ 22 Delino DeShields	.05	.02
☐ 23 Dennis Eckersley	.15	.07
☐ 24 Paul Molitor	.25	.11

1995 Eagle Ballpark Legends

Upper Deck produced this 9-card standard-size set as part of a promotion for Eagle Ballpark Style Peanuts. The set could be obtained by sending in a cash register receipt as evidence for the purchase of 2 cans Eagle Ballpark Style Peanuts (11 oz. or larger) and $1.00 to cover shipping and handling. The fronts freature full-bleed sepia-toned player photos. The sponsor logo appears in the upper left corner, the Upper Deck logo in the lower left, and the player's name across the bottom. The backs present player profile and career highlights. Some card sets contained randomly inserted autographed Harmon Killebrew cards. These autographed cards are valued at between 20 and 30 dollars.

	MINT	NRMT
COMPLETE SET (9)	10.00	4.50
COMMON CARD (1-9)	.75	.35

☐ 1 Nolan Ryan	5.00	2.20
☐ 2 Reggie Jackson	2.50	1.10
☐ 3 Tom Seaver	2.00	.90
☐ 4 Harmon Killebrew	.75	.35
☐ 5 Ted Williams	4.00	1.80
☐ 6 Whitey Ford	2.00	.90
☐ 7 Al Kaline	1.50	.70
☐ 8 Willie Stargell	.75	.35
☐ 9 Bob Gibson	.75	.35

1995 Emotion

This 200-card standard-size set was produced by Fleer/SkyBox. The first-year brand has double-thick card stock with borderless fronts. Card fronts and backs are either horizontal or vertical. On the front of each player card is a theme such as Class (Cal Ripken) and Confident (Barry Bonds). The backs have two player photos, '94 stats and career numbers. The checklist is arranged alphabetically by team with AL preceding NL.

	MINT	NRMT
COMPLETE SET (200)	40.00	18.00
COMMON CARD (1-200)	.25	.11

☐ 1 Brady Anderson	.75	.35
☐ 2 Kevin Brown	.50	.23
☐ 3 Curtis Goodwin	.25	.11
☐ 4 Jeffrey Hammonds	.50	.23
☐ 5 Ben McDonald	.25	.11
☐ 6 Mike Mussina	1.00	.45
☐ 7 Rafael Palmeiro	.75	.35
☐ 8 Cal Ripken Jr.	4.00	1.80
☐ 9 Jose Canseco	.75	.35
☐ 10 Roger Clemens	2.00	.90
☐ 11 Vaughn Eshelman	.25	.11
☐ 12 Mike Greenwell	.25	.11
☐ 13 Erik Hanson	.25	.11
☐ 14 Tim Naehring	.25	.11
☐ 15 Aaron Sele	.25	.11
☐ 16 John Valentin	.50	.23
☐ 17 Mo Vaughn	1.25	.55
☐ 18 Chili Davis	.50	.23
☐ 19 Gary DiSarcina	.25	.11
☐ 20 Chuck Finley	.50	.23
☐ 21 Tim Salmon	1.00	.45
☐ 22 Lee Smith	.50	.23
☐ 23 J.T. Snow	.50	.23
☐ 24 Jim Abbott	.25	.11
☐ 25 Jason Bere	.25	.11
☐ 26 Ray Durham	.50	.23
☐ 27 Ozzie Guillen	.25	.11
☐ 28 Tim Raines	.25	.11
☐ 29 Frank Thomas	4.00	1.80
☐ 30 Robin Ventura	.50	.23
☐ 31 Carlos Baerga	.50	.23
☐ 32 Albert Belle	1.25	.55
☐ 33 Orel Hershiser	.50	.23
☐ 34 Kenny Lofton	1.25	.55
☐ 35 Dennis Martinez	.50	.23
☐ 36 Eddie Murray	1.00	.45
☐ 37 Manny Ramirez	1.00	.45
☐ 38 Julian Tavarez	.25	.11
☐ 39 Jim Thome	1.00	.45
☐ 40 Dave Winfield	.75	.35
☐ 41 Chad Curtis	.25	.11
☐ 42 Cecil Fielder	.50	.23
☐ 43 Travis Fryman	.50	.23
☐ 44 Kirk Gibson	.50	.23
☐ 45 Bob Higginson	1.50	.70
☐ 46 Alan Trammell	.75	.35
☐ 47 Lou Whitaker	.50	.23
☐ 48 Kevin Appier	.50	.23
☐ 49 Gary Gaetti	.50	.23
☐ 50 Jeff Montgomery	.50	.23
☐ 51 Jon Nunnally	.50	.23
☐ 52 Ricky Bones	.25	.11
☐ 53 Cal Eldred	.25	.11
☐ 54 Joe Oliver	.25	.11
☐ 55 Kevin Seitzer	.25	.11
☐ 56 Marty Cordova	.75	.35
☐ 57 Chuck Knoblauch	1.00	.45
☐ 58 Kirby Puckett	2.00	.90
☐ 59 Wade Boggs	1.00	.45
☐ 60 Derek Jeter	3.00	1.35
☐ 61 Jimmy Key	.50	.23
☐ 62 Don Mattingly	1.50	.70
☐ 63 Jack McDowell	.25	.11
☐ 64 Paul O'Neill	.50	.23
☐ 65 Andy Pettitte	1.50	.70
☐ 66 Ruben Rivera	1.00	.45
☐ 67 Mike Stanley	.25	.11
☐ 68 John Wetteland	.50	.23
☐ 69 Geronimo Berroa	.25	.11
☐ 70 Dennis Eckersley	.75	.35
☐ 71 Rickey Henderson	.75	.35
☐ 72 Mark McGwire	2.00	.90
☐ 73 Steve Ontiveros	.25	.11
☐ 74 Ruben Sierra	.25	.11
☐ 75 Terry Steinbach	.50	.23
☐ 76 Jay Buhner	.75	.35
☐ 77 Ken Griffey Jr.	5.00	2.20
☐ 78 Randy Johnson	1.00	.45
☐ 79 Edgar Martinez	.75	.35
☐ 80 Tino Martinez	1.00	.45
☐ 81 Marc Newfield	.25	.11
☐ 82 Alex Rodriguez	4.00	1.80
☐ 83 Will Clark	.75	.35
☐ 84 Benji Gil	.25	.11
☐ 85 Juan Gonzalez	2.50	1.10
☐ 86 Rusty Greer	1.00	.45
☐ 87 Dean Palmer	.50	.23
☐ 88 Ivan Rodriguez	1.25	.55
☐ 89 Kenny Rogers	.25	.11
☐ 90 Roberto Alomar	1.00	.45
☐ 91 Joe Carter	.75	.35
☐ 92 David Cone	.50	.23
☐ 93 Alex Gonzalez	.50	.23
☐ 94 Shawn Green	.50	.23
☐ 95 Pat Hentgen	.50	.23
☐ 96 Paul Molitor	1.00	.45
☐ 97 John Olerud	.50	.23
☐ 98 Devon White	.25	.11
☐ 99 Steve Avery	.25	.11
☐ 100 Tom Glavine	.75	.35
☐ 101 Marquis Grissom	.50	.23
☐ 102 Chipper Jones	3.00	1.35
☐ 103 David Justice	1.00	.45
☐ 104 Ryan Klesko	.75	.35
☐ 105 Javier Lopez	.75	.35
☐ 106 Greg Maddux	3.00	1.35
☐ 107 Fred McGriff	.75	.35
☐ 108 John Smoltz	.75	.35
☐ 109 Shawon Dunston	.25	.11
☐ 110 Mark Grace	.75	.35
☐ 111 Brian McRae	.25	.11
☐ 112 Randy Myers	.25	.11
☐ 113 Sammy Sosa	1.00	.45
☐ 114 Steve Trachsel	.25	.11
☐ 115 Bret Boone	.25	.11
☐ 116 Ron Gant	.50	.23
☐ 117 Barry Larkin	.75	.35
☐ 118 Deion Sanders	1.00	.45
☐ 119 Reggie Sanders	.25	.11
☐ 120 Pete Schourek	.25	.11
☐ 121 John Smiley	.25	.11
☐ 122 Jason Bates	.25	.11
☐ 123 Dante Bichette	.75	.35
☐ 124 Vinny Castilla	.75	.35
☐ 125 Andres Galarraga	.75	.35
☐ 126 Larry Walker	1.00	.45
☐ 127 Greg Colbrunn	.25	.11
☐ 128 Jeff Conine	.50	.23
☐ 129 Andre Dawson	.75	.35
☐ 130 Chris Hammond	.25	.11
☐ 131 Charles Johnson	.50	.23
☐ 132 Gary Sheffield	1.00	.45
☐ 133 Quilvio Veras	.25	.11
☐ 134 Jeff Bagwell	2.00	.90
☐ 135 Derek Bell	.50	.23
☐ 136 Craig Biggio	.75	.35
☐ 137 Jim Dougherty	.25	.11
☐ 138 John Hudek	.25	.11
☐ 139 Orlando Miller	.25	.11
☐ 140 Phil Plantier	.25	.11
☐ 141 Eric Karros	.50	.23
☐ 142 Ramon Martinez	.50	.23
☐ 143 Raul Mondesi	.75	.35
☐ 144 Hideo Nomo	5.00	2.20
☐ 145 Mike Piazza	3.00	1.35
☐ 146 Ismael Valdes	.50	.23
☐ 147 Todd Worrell	.25	.11
☐ 148 Moises Alou	.50	.23
☐ 149 Yamil Benitez	.75	.35
☐ 150 Wil Cordero	.25	.11
☐ 151 Jeff Fassero	.25	.11
☐ 152 Cliff Floyd	.50	.23
☐ 153 Pedro Martinez	1.00	.45
☐ 154 Carlos Perez	.50	.23
☐ 155 Tony Tarasco	.25	.11
☐ 156 Rondell White	.75	.35
☐ 157 Edgardo Alfonzo	1.00	.45
☐ 158 Bobby Bonilla	.50	.23
☐ 159 Rico Brogna	.25	.11

	MINT	NRMT
☐ 160 Bobby Jones	.50	.23
☐ 161 Bill Pulsipher	.25	.11
☐ 162 Bret Saberhagen	.25	.11
☐ 163 Ricky Bottalico	.50	.23
☐ 164 Darren Daulton	.50	.23
☐ 165 Lenny Dykstra	.50	.23
☐ 166 Charlie Hayes	.25	.11
☐ 167 Dave Hollins	.25	.11
☐ 168 Gregg Jefferies	.50	.23
☐ 169 Michael Mimbs	.25	.11
☐ 170 Curt Schilling	.50	.23
☐ 171 Heathcliff Slocumb	.25	.11
☐ 172 Jay Bell	.50	.23
☐ 173 Micah Franklin	.25	.11
☐ 174 Mark Johnson	.25	.11
☐ 175 Jeff King	.50	.23
☐ 176 Al Martin	.50	.23
☐ 177 Dan Miceli	.25	.11
☐ 178 Denny Neagle	.50	.23
☐ 179 Bernard Gilkey	.50	.23
☐ 180 Ken Hill	.25	.11
☐ 181 Brian Jordan	.50	.23
☐ 182 Ray Lankford	.75	.35
☐ 183 Ozzie Smith	1.25	.55
☐ 184 Andy Benes	.25	.11
☐ 185 Ken Caminiti	1.00	.45
☐ 186 Steve Finley	.50	.23
☐ 187 Tony Gwynn	2.50	1.10
☐ 188 Joey Hamilton	.50	.23
☐ 189 Melvin Nieves	.50	.23
☐ 190 Scott Sanders	.25	.11
☐ 191 Rod Beck	.25	.11
☐ 192 Barry Bonds	1.25	.55
☐ 193 Royce Clayton	.25	.11
☐ 194 Glenallen Hill	.25	.11
☐ 195 Darren Lewis	.25	.11
☐ 196 Mark Portugal	.25	.11
☐ 197 Matt Williams	.75	.35
☐ 198 Checklist 1-82	.25	.11
☐ 199 Checklist 83-162	.25	.11
☐ 200 Checklist 163-200/Inserts	.25	.11
☐ P8 Cal Ripken Promo	7.50	3.40

1995 Emotion Masters

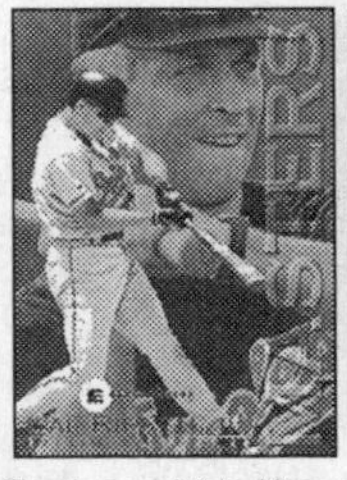

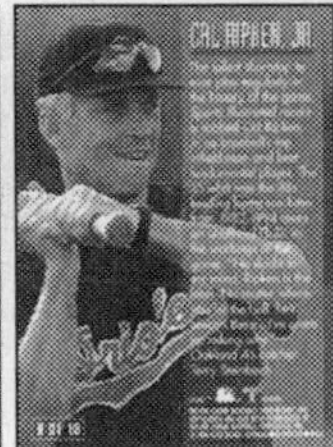

The theme of this 10-card standard-size set is the showcasing of players that come through in the clutch. Randomly inserted at a rate of one in eight packs, a player photo is superimposed over a larger photo that is ghosted in a color emblematic of that team. The player's name and the Emotion logo are at the bottom. The backs have a photo to the left and text to the right. Both sides of the card are shaded in the color scheme of the player's team.

	MINT	NRMT
COMPLETE SET (10)	60.00	27.00
COMMON CARD (1-10)	1.50	.70
☐ 1 Barry Bonds	4.00	1.80
☐ 2 Juan Gonzalez	7.50	3.40
☐ 3 Ken Griffey Jr.	15.00	6.75
☐ 4 Tony Gwynn	7.50	3.40
☐ 5 Kenny Lofton	4.00	1.80
☐ 6 Greg Maddux	10.00	4.50
☐ 7 Raul Mondesi	1.50	.70
☐ 8 Cal Ripken	12.00	5.50
☐ 9 Frank Thomas	12.00	5.50
☐ 10 Matt Williams	2.50	1.10

1995 Emotion N-Tense

Randomly inserted at a rate of one in 37 packs, this 12-card standard-size set features fronts that have a player photo surrounded by a swirling color scheme and a large holographic "N" in the background. The backs feature a like color scheme with text and player photo.

	MINT	NRMT
COMPLETE SET (12)	150.00	70.00
COMMON CARD (1-12)	5.00	2.20
☐ 1 Jeff Bagwell	15.00	6.75
☐ 2 Albert Belle	10.00	4.50

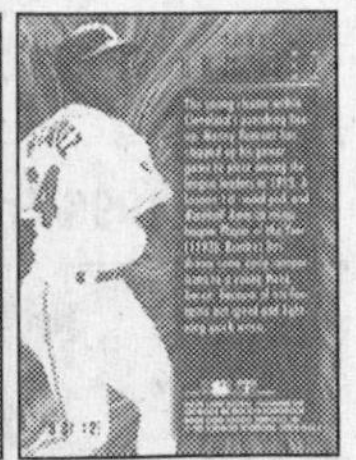

	MINT	NRMT
☐ 3 Barry Bonds	10.00	4.50
☐ 4 Cecil Fielder	5.00	2.20
☐ 5 Ron Gant	5.00	2.20
☐ 6 Ken Griffey Jr.	40.00	18.00
☐ 7 Mark McGwire	15.00	6.75
☐ 8 Mike Piazza	25.00	11.00
☐ 9 Manny Ramirez	8.00	3.60
☐ 10 Frank Thomas	30.00	13.50
☐ 11 Mo Vaughn	10.00	4.50
☐ 12 Matt Williams	7.00	3.10

1995 Emotion Ripken

This 15-card Cal Ripken standard-size set features great moments from the career of the Baltimore Orioles' great. Inserted at a rate of one in 12 packs, the moments were selected by the record-breaking shortstop. Referred to as "Timeless", an action photo of Ripken is superimposed over a silver background that includes a watch and another photo at the top. The backs elaborate on the event or events which Cal selected. This text is superimposed over a large photo. A five-card mail-in (described on wrapper) set was also made available. The expiration was 3/1/96.

	MINT	NRMT
COMPLETE SET (10)	60.00	27.00
COMMON CARD (1-10)	6.00	2.70
COMMON MAIL-IN (11-15)	6.00	2.70
☐ 1 Cal Ripken High School Pitcher	6.00	2.70
☐ 2 Cal Ripken Role Model	6.00	2.70
☐ 3 Cal Ripken Rookie of the Year	6.00	2.70
☐ 4 Cal Ripken 1st MVP Season	6.00	2.70
☐ 5 Cal Ripken 95 Consecutived Errorless Games	6.00	2.70
☐ 6 Cal Ripken All-Star MVP	6.00	2.70
☐ 7 Cal Ripken Conditioning	6.00	2.70
☐ 8 Cal Ripken Shortstop HR Record	6.00	2.70
☐ 9 Cal Ripken Literacy Work	6.00	2.70
☐ 10 Cal Ripken 2000th Consecutive Game	6.00	2.70
☐ 11 Cal Ripken 1995 All-Star Selection	6.00	2.70
☐ 12 Cal Ripken 35th Birthday	6.00	2.70
☐ 13 Cal Ripken Game 2,130	6.00	2.70
☐ 14 Cal Ripken Game 2,131	6.00	2.70
☐ 15 Cal Ripken 2,153 and Counting	6.00	2.70

1995 Emotion Rookies

This 10-card standard-size set was inserted at a rate of one in five packs. Card fronts feature an action photo superimposed over background that is in a color consistent with that of the team's. The backs have a player photo and a write-up.

	MINT	NRMT
COMPLETE SET (10)	25.00	11.00
COMMON CARD (1-10)	1.00	.45
☐ 1 Edgardo Alfonzo	4.00	1.80
☐ 2 Jason Bates	1.00	.45
☐ 3 Marty Cordova	3.00	1.35
☐ 4 Ray Durham	2.00	.90
☐ 5 Alex Gonzalez	2.00	.90
☐ 6 Shawn Green	2.00	.90
☐ 7 Charles Johnson	2.00	.90
☐ 8 Chipper Jones	8.00	3.60
☐ 9 Hideo Nomo	8.00	3.60
☐ 10 Alex Rodriguez	10.00	4.50

1996 Emotion-XL

The 1996 Emotion-XL set was issued in one series totalling 300 standard-size cards. The 7-card packs retail for $4.99 each. The fronts feature a color action player photo with either a blue, green or maroon frame and the player's name and team printed in a foil-stamped medallion. A descriptive term describing the player completes the front. The backs carry player information and statistics. The cards are grouped alphabetically by team with AL preceding NL.

	MINT	NRMT
COMPLETE SET (300)	80.00	36.00
COMMON CARD (1-300)	.40	.18
☐ 1 Roberto Alomar	.40	.18
☐ 2 Brady Anderson	1.00	.45
☐ 3 Bobby Bonilla	.75	.35
☐ 4 Jeffrey Hammonds	.40	.18
☐ 5 Chris Hoiles	.40	.18
☐ 6 Mike Mussina	1.50	.70
☐ 7 Randy Myers	.40	.18
☐ 8 Rafael Palmeiro	1.00	.45
☐ 9 Cal Ripken	6.00	2.70
☐ 10 B.J. Surhoff	.40	.18
☐ 11 Jose Canseco	1.00	.45
☐ 12 Roger Clemens	3.00	1.35
☐ 13 Wil Cordero	.40	.18
☐ 14 Mike Greenwell	.40	.18
☐ 15 Dwayne Hosey	.40	.18
☐ 16 Tim Naehring	.75	.35
☐ 17 Troy O'Leary	.40	.18
☐ 18 Mike Stanley	.40	.18
☐ 19 John Valentin	.75	.35
☐ 20 Mo Vaughn	2.00	.90
☐ 21 Jim Abbott	.75	.35
☐ 22 Garret Anderson	1.00	.45
☐ 23 George Arias	.40	.18
☐ 24 Chili Davis	.40	.18
☐ 25 Jim Edmonds	1.50	.70
☐ 26 Chuck Finley	.40	.18
☐ 27 Todd Greene	.75	.35
☐ 28 Mark Langston	.40	.18
☐ 29 Troy Percival	.75	.35
☐ 30 Tim Salmon	1.00	.45
☐ 31 Lee Smith	.75	.35
☐ 32 J.T. Snow	.75	.35
☐ 33 Harold Baines	.75	.35
☐ 34 Jason Bere	.40	.18
☐ 35 Ray Durham	.75	.35
☐ 36 Alex Fernandez	.75	.35
☐ 37 Ozzie Guillen	.40	.18
☐ 38 Darren Lewis	.40	.18

☐ 39 Lyle Mouton	.40	.18
☐ 40 Tony Phillips	.40	.18
☐ 41 Danny Tartabull	.40	.18
☐ 42 Frank Thomas	6.00	2.70
☐ 43 Robin Ventura	.75	.35
☐ 44 Sandy Alomar Jr.	.75	.35
☐ 45 Carlos Baerga	.75	.35
☐ 46 Albert Belle	2.00	.90
☐ 47 Julio Franco	.75	.35
☐ 48 Orel Hershiser	.75	.35
☐ 49 Kenny Lofton	2.00	.90
☐ 50 Dennis Martinez	.75	.35
☐ 51 Jack McDowell	.40	.18
☐ 52 Jose Mesa	.75	.35
☐ 53 Eddie Murray	1.50	.70
☐ 54 Charles Nagy	.75	.35
☐ 55 Manny Ramirez	1.50	.70
☐ 56 Jim Thome	1.50	.70
☐ 57 Omar Vizquel	.75	.35
☐ 58 Chad Curtis	.40	.18
☐ 59 Cecil Fielder	.75	.35
☐ 60 Travis Fryman	.75	.35
☐ 61 Chris Gomez	.40	.18
☐ 62 Felipe Lira	.40	.18
☐ 63 Alan Trammell	1.00	.45
☐ 64 Kevin Appier	.75	.35
☐ 65 Johnny Damon	.75	.35
☐ 66 Tom Goodwin	.40	.18
☐ 67 Mark Gubicza	.40	.18
☐ 68 Jeff Montgomery	.40	.18
☐ 69 Jon Nunnally	.40	.18
☐ 70 Bip Roberts	.40	.18
☐ 71 Ricky Bones	.40	.18
☐ 72 Chuck Carr	.40	.18
☐ 73 John Jaha	.40	.18
☐ 74 Ben McDonald	.40	.18
☐ 75 Matt Mieske	.40	.18
☐ 76 Dave Nilsson	.75	.35
☐ 77 Kevin Seitzer	.40	.18
☐ 78 Greg Vaughn	.40	.18
☐ 79 Rick Aguilera	.40	.18
☐ 80 Marty Cordova	.75	.35
☐ 81 Roberto Kelly	.40	.18
☐ 82 Chuck Knoblauch	1.50	.70
☐ 83 Pat Meares	.40	.18
☐ 84 Paul Molitor	1.50	.70
☐ 85 Kirby Puckett	3.00	1.35
☐ 86 Brad Radke	.40	.18
☐ 87 Wade Boggs	1.50	.70
☐ 88 David Cone	.75	.35
☐ 89 Dwight Gooden	.75	.35
☐ 90 Derek Jeter	5.00	2.20
☐ 91 Tino Martinez	1.50	.70
☐ 92 Paul O'Neill	.75	.35
☐ 93 Andy Pettitte	2.00	.90
☐ 94 Tim Raines	.40	.18
☐ 95 Ruben Rivera	.75	.35
☐ 96 Kenny Rogers	.40	.18
☐ 97 Ruben Sierra	.40	.18
☐ 98 John Wetteland	.75	.35
☐ 99 Bernie Williams	1.50	.70
☐ 100 Allen Battle	.40	.18
☐ 101 Geronimo Berroa	.40	.18
☐ 102 Brent Gates	.40	.18
☐ 103 Doug Johns	.40	.18
☐ 104 Mark McGwire	3.00	1.35
☐ 105 Pedro Munoz	.40	.18
☐ 106 Ariel Prieto	.40	.18
☐ 107 Terry Steinbach	.75	.35
☐ 108 Todd Van Poppel	.40	.18
☐ 109 Chris Bosio	.40	.18
☐ 110 Jay Buhner	1.00	.45
☐ 111 Joey Cora	.75	.35
☐ 112 Russ Davis	.40	.18
☐ 113 Ken Griffey Jr.	8.00	3.60
☐ 114 Sterling Hitchcock	.40	.18
☐ 115 Randy Johnson	1.50	.70
☐ 116 Edgar Martinez	1.00	.45
☐ 117 Alex Rodriguez	6.00	2.70
☐ 118 Paul Sorrento	.40	.18
☐ 119 Dan Wilson	.40	.18
☐ 120 Will Clark	1.00	.45
☐ 121 Juan Gonzalez	4.00	1.80
☐ 122 Rusty Greer	1.50	.70
☐ 123 Kevin Gross	.40	.18
☐ 124 Ken Hill	.40	.18
☐ 125 Dean Palmer	.75	.35
☐ 126 Roger Pavlik	.40	.18
☐ 127 Ivan Rodriguez	2.00	.90
☐ 128 Mickey Tettleton	.40	.18
☐ 129 Joe Carter	.75	.35
☐ 130 Carlos Delgado	.75	.35
☐ 131 Alex Gonzalez	.40	.18
☐ 132 Shawn Green	.40	.18
☐ 133 Erik Hanson	.40	.18
☐ 134 Pat Hentgen	.75	.35
☐ 135 Otis Nixon	.75	.35

☐ 136 John Olerud	.75	.35
☐ 137 Ed Sprague	.40	.18
☐ 138 Steve Avery	.40	.18
☐ 139 Jermaine Dye	.40	.18
☐ 140 Tom Glavine	1.00	.45
☐ 141 Marquis Grissom	.75	.35
☐ 142 Chipper Jones	5.00	2.20
☐ 143 David Justice	1.00	.45
☐ 144 Ryan Klesko	1.00	.45
☐ 145 Javier Lopez	.75	.35
☐ 146 Greg Maddux	5.00	2.20
☐ 147 Fred McGriff	1.00	.45
☐ 148 Jason Schmidt	.75	.35
☐ 149 John Smoltz	.75	.35
☐ 150 Mark Wohlers	.75	.35
☐ 151 Jim Bullinger	.40	.18
☐ 152 Frank Castillo	.40	.18
☐ 153 Kevin Foster	.40	.18
☐ 154 Luis Gonzalez	.40	.18
☐ 155 Mark Grace	1.00	.45
☐ 156 Brian McRae	.40	.18
☐ 157 Jaime Navarro	.40	.18
☐ 158 Rey Sanchez	.40	.18
☐ 159 Ryne Sandberg	2.00	.90
☐ 160 Sammy Sosa	1.50	.70
☐ 161 Bret Boone	.40	.18
☐ 162 Jeff Brantley	.40	.18
☐ 163 Vince Coleman	.40	.18
☐ 164 Steve Gibralter	.40	.18
☐ 165 Barry Larkin	1.00	.45
☐ 166 Hal Morris	.40	.18
☐ 167 Mark Portugal	.40	.18
☐ 168 Reggie Sanders	.40	.18
☐ 169 Pete Schourek	.40	.18
☐ 170 John Smiley	.40	.18
☐ 171 Jason Bates	.40	.18
☐ 172 Dante Bichette	1.00	.45
☐ 173 Ellis Burks	.75	.35
☐ 174 Vinny Castilla	.75	.35
☐ 175 Andres Galarraga	1.00	.45
☐ 176 Kevin Ritz	.40	.18
☐ 177 Bill Swift	.40	.18
☐ 178 Larry Walker	1.00	.45
☐ 179 Walt Weiss	.40	.18
☐ 180 Eric Young	.75	.35
☐ 181 Kurt Abbott	.40	.18
☐ 182 Kevin Brown	.75	.35
☐ 183 John Burkett	.40	.18
☐ 184 Greg Colbrunn	.40	.18
☐ 185 Jeff Conine	.75	.35
☐ 186 Chris Hammond	.40	.18
☐ 187 Charles Johnson	.75	.35
☐ 188 Terry Pendleton	.75	.35
☐ 189 Pat Rapp	.40	.18
☐ 190 Gary Sheffield	1.50	.70
☐ 191 Quilvio Veras	.40	.18
☐ 192 Devon White	.40	.18
☐ 193 Jeff Bagwell	3.00	1.35
☐ 194 Derek Bell	.75	.35
☐ 195 Sean Berry	.40	.18
☐ 196 Craig Biggio	1.00	.45
☐ 197 Doug Drabek	.40	.18
☐ 198 Tony Eusebio	.40	.18
☐ 199 Mike Hampton	.40	.18
☐ 200 Brian L.Hunter	.75	.35
☐ 201 Derrick May	.40	.18
☐ 202 Orlando Miller	.40	.18
☐ 203 Shane Reynolds	.40	.18
☐ 204 Mike Blowers	.40	.18
☐ 205 Tom Candiotti	.40	.18
☐ 206 Delino DeShields	.40	.18
☐ 207 Greg Gagne	.40	.18
☐ 208 Karim Garcia	1.50	.70
☐ 209 Todd Hollandsworth	.75	.35
☐ 210 Eric Karros	.75	.35
☐ 211 Ramon Martinez	.75	.35
☐ 212 Raul Mondesi	1.00	.45
☐ 213 Hideo Nomo	4.00	1.80
☐ 214 Chan Ho Park	1.50	.70
☐ 215 Mike Piazza	5.00	2.20
☐ 216 Ismael Valdes	.75	.35
☐ 217 Todd Worrell	.75	.35
☐ 218 Moises Alou	.75	.35
☐ 219 Yamil Benitez	.75	.35
☐ 220 Jeff Fassero	.40	.18
☐ 221 Darrin Fletcher	.40	.18
☐ 222 Cliff Floyd	.40	.18
☐ 223 Pedro Martinez	1.50	.70
☐ 224 Carlos Perez	.40	.18
☐ 225 Mel Rojas	.40	.18
☐ 226 David Segui	.40	.18
☐ 227 Rondell White	.75	.35
☐ 228 Rico Brogna	.40	.18
☐ 229 Carl Everett	.40	.18
☐ 230 John Franco	.75	.35
☐ 231 Bernard Gilkey	.40	.18
☐ 232 Todd Hundley	.75	.35

☐ 233 Jason Isringhausen	.40	.18
☐ 234 Lance Johnson	.40	.18
☐ 235 Bobby Jones	.40	.18
☐ 236 Jeff Kent	.40	.18
☐ 237 Rey Ordonez	.40	.18
☐ 238 Bill Pulsipher	.40	.18
☐ 239 Jose Vizcaino	.40	.18
☐ 240 Paul Wilson	.40	.18
☐ 241 Ricky Bottalico	.40	.18
☐ 242 Darren Daulton	.75	.35
☐ 243 Lenny Dykstra	.75	.35
☐ 244 Jim Eisenreich	.75	.35
☐ 245 Sid Fernandez	.40	.18
☐ 246 Gregg Jefferies	.40	.18
☐ 247 Mickey Morandini	.40	.18
☐ 248 Benito Santiago	.40	.18
☐ 249 Curt Schilling	.75	.35
☐ 250 Mark Whiten	.40	.18
☐ 251 Todd Zeile	.40	.18
☐ 252 Jay Bell	.75	.35
☐ 253 Carlos Garcia	.40	.18
☐ 254 Charlie Hayes	.40	.18
☐ 255 Jason Kendall	1.00	.45
☐ 256 Jeff King	.75	.35
☐ 257 Al Martin	.40	.18
☐ 258 Orlando Merced	.40	.18
☐ 259 Dan Miceli	.40	.18
☐ 260 Denny Neagle	.75	.35
☐ 261 Alan Benes	1.00	.45
☐ 262 Andy Benes	.75	.35
☐ 263 Royce Clayton	.40	.18
☐ 264 Dennis Eckersley	1.00	.45
☐ 265 Gary Gaetti	.75	.35
☐ 266 Ron Gant	.75	.35
☐ 267 Brian Jordan	.75	.35
☐ 268 Ray Lankford	1.00	.45
☐ 269 John Mabry	.75	.35
☐ 270 Tom Pagnozzi	.40	.18
☐ 271 Ozzie Smith	2.00	.90
☐ 272 Todd Stottlemyre	.40	.18
☐ 273 Andy Ashby	.40	.18
☐ 274 Brad Ausmus	.40	.18
☐ 275 Ken Caminiti	1.50	.70
☐ 276 Steve Finley	.75	.35
☐ 277 Tony Gwynn	4.00	1.80
☐ 278 Joey Hamilton	.75	.35
☐ 279 Rickey Henderson	1.50	.70
☐ 280 Trevor Hoffman	.75	.35
☐ 281 Wally Joyner	.40	.18
☐ 282 Jody Reed	.40	.18
☐ 283 Bob Tewksbury	.40	.18
☐ 284 Fernando Valenzuela	.75	.35
☐ 285 Rod Beck	.40	.18
☐ 286 Barry Bonds	2.00	.90
☐ 287 Mark Carreon	.40	.18
☐ 288 Shawon Dunston	.40	.18
☐ 289 Osvaldo Fernandez	1.00	.45
☐ 290 Glenallen Hill	.40	.18
☐ 291 Stan Javier	.40	.18
☐ 292 Mark Leiter	.40	.18
☐ 293 Kirt Manwaring	.40	.18
☐ 294 Robby Thompson	.40	.18
☐ 295 William VanLandingham	.40	.18
☐ 296 Allen Watson	.40	.18
☐ 297 Matt Williams	1.00	.45
☐ 298 Checklist	.40	.18
☐ 299 Checklist	.40	.18
☐ 300 Checklist	.40	.18
☐ P55 Manny Ramirez Promo	2.00	.90

1996 Emotion-XL D-Fense

Randomly inserted in packs at a rate of one in four, this 10-card set showcases outstanding defensive players. The fronts feature a color action player cut-out on a sepia portait background with silver foil print and border. The backs carry information about the player on another sepia portrait background.

	MINT	NRMT
COMPLETE SET (10)	30.00	13.50
COMMON CARD (1-10)	1.00	.45

	MINT	NRMT
☐ 1 Roberto Alomar	2.00	.90
☐ 2 Barry Bonds	2.50	1.10
☐ 3 Mark Grace	1.50	.70
☐ 4 Ken Griffey Jr.	10.00	4.50
☐ 5 Kenny Lofton	2.50	1.10
☐ 6 Greg Maddux	6.00	2.70
☐ 7 Raul Mondesi	1.00	.45
☐ 8 Cal Ripken	8.00	3.60
☐ 9 Ivan Rodriguez	2.50	1.10
☐ 10 Matt Williams	1.50	.70

1996 Emotion-XL Legion of Boom

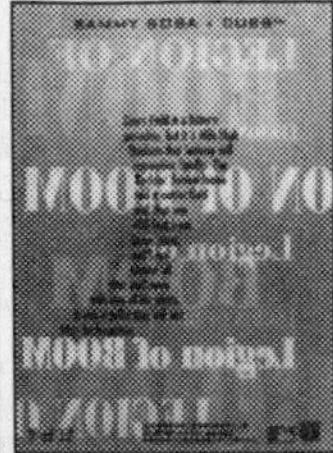

Randomly inserted in packs at a rate of one in 36, this 12-card set features the game's big hitters on cards with translucent card backs. The fronts carry a color action player cut-out with silver foil print.

	MINT	NRMT
COMPLETE SET (12)	200.00	90.00
COMMON CARD (1-12)	6.00	2.70
☐ 1 Albert Belle	12.00	5.50
☐ 2 Barry Bonds	12.00	5.50
☐ 3 Juan Gonzalez	25.00	11.00
☐ 4 Ken Griffey Jr.	50.00	22.00
☐ 5 Mark McGwire	20.00	9.00
☐ 6 Mike Piazza	30.00	13.50
☐ 7 Manny Ramirez	12.00	5.50
☐ 8 Tim Salmon	6.00	2.70
☐ 9 Sammy Sosa	8.00	3.60
☐ 10 Frank Thomas	40.00	18.00
☐ 11 Mo Vaughn	12.00	5.50
☐ 12 Matt Williams	6.00	2.70

1996 Emotion-XL N-Tense

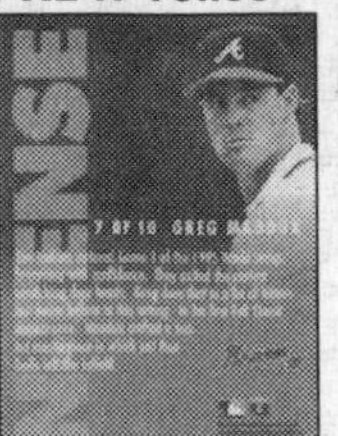

Randomly inserted in packs at a rate of one in 12, this 10-card set highlights top-clutch performers on special, front N-shaped die-cut cards. The backs carry information about the player on a player portrait background.

	MINT	NRMT
COMPLETE SET (10)	100.00	45.00
COMMON CARD (1-10)	3.00	1.35
☐ 1 Albert Belle	6.00	2.70
☐ 2 Barry Bonds	6.00	2.70
☐ 3 Jose Canseco	3.00	1.35
☐ 4 Ken Griffey Jr.	25.00	11.00
☐ 5 Tony Gwynn	10.00	4.50
☐ 6 Randy Johnson	5.00	2.20
☐ 7 Greg Maddux	15.00	6.75
☐ 8 Cal Ripken	20.00	9.00
☐ 9 Frank Thomas	20.00	9.00
☐ 10 Matt Williams	4.00	1.80

1996 Emotion-XL Rare Breed

Randomly inserted in packs at a rate of one in 100, this 10-card set showcases young stars on lenticular cards. The fronts feature color action player cut-outs on a baseball graphics background. The backs carry player information over a color player portrait.

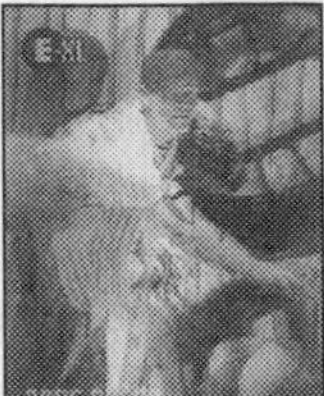

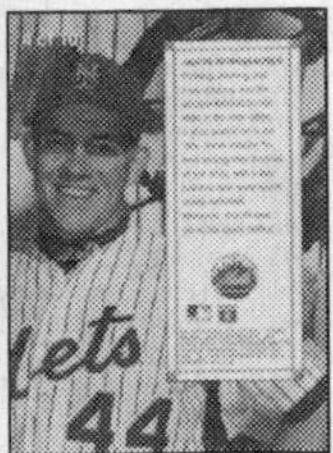

	MINT	NRMT
COMPLETE SET (10)	200.00	90.00
COMMON CARD (1-10)	6.00	2.70
☐ 1 Garret Anderson	12.00	5.50
☐ 2 Marty Cordova	6.00	2.70
☐ 3 Brian L.Hunter	8.00	3.60
☐ 4 Jason Isringhausen	6.00	2.70
☐ 5 Charles Johnson	8.00	3.60
☐ 6 Chipper Jones	80.00	36.00
☐ 7 Raul Mondesi	12.00	5.50
☐ 8 Hideo Nomo	60.00	27.00
☐ 9 Manny Ramirez	25.00	11.00
☐ 10 Rondell White	8.00	3.60

1992 Expos Donruss Durivage

Featuring the Montreal Expos, the 26-card standard-size set was produced by Donruss for Durivage (a Canadian bread company). The fronts have posed color photos of the players without hats, framed by a gray inner border and a dark green outer border. The team logo, "Durivage" set name, and player information appear at the bottom of card front. In a horizontal format, the bilingual (English and French) backs carry biography and recent major league performance statistics, on a background of gray vertical stripes that fade to white as one moves down the card. The cards are numbered on the back, "No. X de/of 20." The complete set price does include all variations and the unnumbered checklist card.

	MINT	NRMT
COMPLETE SET (26)	60.00	27.00
COMMON CARD (1-20)	1.25	.55
☐ 1 Bret Barberie	1.25	.55
☐ 2A Chris Haney	2.50	1.10
☐ 2B Brian Barnes	5.00	2.20
☐ 3A Bill Sampen	1.50	.70
☐ 3B Phil Bradley	3.00	1.35
☐ 4 Ivan Calderon	1.50	.70
☐ 5 Gary Carter	7.50	3.40
☐ 6 Delino DeShields	6.00	2.70
☐ 7 Jeff Fassero	3.00	1.35
☐ 8 Darrin Fletcher	1.50	.70
☐ 9 Mark Gardner	1.25	.55
☐ 10 Marquis Grissom	7.50	3.40
☐ 11 Ken Hill	3.00	1.35
☐ 12 Dennis Martinez	3.00	1.35
☐ 13 Chris Nabholz	1.25	.55
☐ 14 Spike Owen	1.25	.55
☐ 15A Tom Runnells MG	2.00	.90
☐ 15B Felipe Alou MG	6.00	2.70
☐ 16A John Vander Wal	2.50	1.10
☐ 16B Matt Stairs	4.00	1.80
☐ 17A Bill Landrum	1.50	.70
☐ 17B Dave Wainhouse	3.00	1.35
☐ 18 Larry Walker	10.00	4.50
☐ 19 Tim Wallach	3.00	1.35
☐ 20 John Wetteland	3.00	1.35
☐ xx0 Album	5.00	2.20
☐ NNO0 Checklist Card SP	5.00	2.20

1993 Expos Donruss McDonald's

This 33-card set was produced by Donruss for McDonald's and commemorates the Montreal Expos' 25th year in baseball. The standard-size cards have fronts displaying full-bleed action pictures with the McDonald's logo at the top left. Across the bottom, the player's name and uniform number are printed on a blue stripe, with the silver-foil 25-year Expos' logo stamped to the left. The horizontal backs carry biography, statistics, and career summaries in both French and English on a beige

background. The player's name and number appear near the top, printed in a dark blue stripe edged in red. The 25-year Expos' logo is displayed in the top left in red, white, and blue. The certified signed and numbered (out of 2,000) Felipe Alou card was reportedly inserted at a rate of one per case of 2,500 packs. The cards were distributed in four-card foil packs.

	MINT	NRMT
COMPLETE SET (33)	8.00	3.60
COMMON CARD (1-33)	.10	.05
☐ 1 Moises Alou	.25	.11
☐ 2 Andre Dawson	1.00	.45
☐ 3 Delino DeShields	.75	.35
☐ 4 Andres Galarraga	1.50	.70
☐ 5 Marquis Grissom	1.50	.70
☐ 6 Tim Raines	1.00	.45
☐ 7 Larry Walker	1.50	.70
☐ 8 Tim Wallach	.25	.11
☐ 9 Ken Hill	.25	.11
☐ 10 Dennis Martinez	.50	.23
☐ 11 Jeff Reardon	.50	.23
☐ 12 Gary Carter	1.50	.70
☐ 13 Dave Cash	.10	.05
☐ 14 Warren Cromartie	.25	.11
☐ 15 Mack Jones	.10	.05
☐ 16 Al Oliver	.50	.23
☐ 17 Larry Parrish	.25	.11
☐ 18 Rodney Scott	.10	.05
☐ 19 Ken Singleton	.25	.11
☐ 20 Rusty Staub	.50	.23
☐ 21 Ellis Valentine	.10	.05
☐ 22 Woodie Fryman	.10	.05
☐ 23 Charlie Lea	.10	.05
☐ 24 Bill Lee	.25	.11
☐ 25 Mike Marshall	.25	.11
☐ 26 Claude Raymond	.25	.11
☐ 27 Steve Renko	.10	.05
☐ 28 Steve Rogers	.25	.11
☐ 29 Bill Stoneman	.10	.05
☐ 30 Gene Mauch MG	.10	.05
☐ 31 Felipe Alou MG	.25	.11
☐ 32 Buck Rodgers MG	.10	.05
☐ 33 Checklist 1-32	.10	.05
☐ AU0 Felipe Alou AU/2000 (Certified autograph)	100.00	45.00

1994 Extra Bases

Measuring 2 1/2" by 4 3/4", this 400 card set was issued by Fleer. Each pack contained at least one insert card. Full-bleed fronts contain a large color photo with the player's name and Extra Bases logo at the bottom. The backs are also full-bleed with a large player photo and statistics. The checklist was arranged alphabetically by team and league starting with the American League. Within each team, the player listings are alphabetical. Rookie Cards include Ray Durham and Chan Ho Park.

	MINT	NRMT
COMPLETE SET (400)	35.00	16.00
COMMON CARD (1-400)	.10	.05
☐ 1 Brady Anderson	.35	.16
☐ 2 Harold Baines	.20	.09
☐ 3 Mike Devereaux	.10	.05
☐ 4 Sid Fernandez	.10	.05
☐ 5 Jeffrey Hammonds	.20	.09
☐ 6 Chris Hoiles	.10	.05
☐ 7 Ben McDonald	.10	.05

☐ 8 Mark McLemore	.10	.05
☐ 9 Mike Mussina	.50	.23
☐ 10 Mike Oquist	.10	.05
☐ 11 Rafael Palmeiro	.35	.16
☐ 12 Cal Ripken Jr.	2.50	1.10
☐ 13 Chris Sabo	.10	.05
☐ 14 Lee Smith	.20	.09
☐ 15 Wes Chamberlain	.10	.05
☐ 16 Roger Clemens	1.25	.55
☐ 17 Scott Cooper	.10	.05
☐ 18 Danny Darwin	.10	.05
☐ 19 Andre Dawson	.35	.16
☐ 20 Mike Greenwell	.10	.05
☐ 21 Tim Naehring	.10	.05
☐ 22 Otis Nixon	.10	.05
☐ 23 Jeff Russell	.10	.05
☐ 24 Ken Ryan	.10	.05
☐ 25 Aaron Sele	.10	.05
☐ 26 John Valentin	.20	.09
☐ 27 Mo Vaughn	.75	.35
☐ 28 Frank Viola	.10	.05
☐ 29 Brian Anderson	.20	.09
☐ 30 Chad Curtis	.20	.09
☐ 31 Chili Davis	.20	.09
☐ 32 Gary DiSarcina	.10	.05
☐ 33 Damion Easley	.10	.05
☐ 34 Jim Edmonds	.50	.23
☐ 35 Chuck Finley	.10	.05
☐ 36 Bo Jackson	.20	.09
☐ 37 Mark Langston	.10	.05
☐ 38 Harold Reynolds	.10	.05
☐ 39 Tim Salmon	.50	.23
☐ 40 Wilson Alvarez	.20	.09
☐ 41 James Baldwin	.20	.09
☐ 42 Jason Bere	.10	.05
☐ 43 Joey Cora	.20	.09
☐ 44 Ray Durham	.50	.23
☐ 45 Alex Fernandez	.20	.09
☐ 46 Julio Franco	.20	.09
☐ 47 Ozzie Guillen	.10	.05
☐ 48 Darrin Jackson	.10	.05
☐ 49 Lance Johnson	.20	.09
☐ 50 Ron Karkovice	.10	.05
☐ 51 Jack McDowell	.10	.05
☐ 52 Tim Raines	.20	.09
☐ 53 Frank Thomas	2.50	1.10
☐ 54 Robin Ventura	.20	.09
☐ 55 Sandy Alomar Jr.	.20	.09
☐ 56 Carlos Baerga	.20	.09
☐ 57 Albert Belle	1.00	.45
☐ 58 Mark Clark	.10	.05
☐ 59 Wayne Kirby	.10	.05
☐ 60 Kenny Lofton	.75	.35
☐ 61 Dennis Martinez	.20	.09
☐ 62 Jose Mesa	.20	.09
☐ 63 Jack Morris	.20	.09
☐ 64 Eddie Murray	.50	.23
☐ 65 Charles Nagy	.20	.09
☐ 66 Manny Ramirez	.60	.25
☐ 67 Paul Shuey	.10	.05
☐ 68 Paul Sorrento	.10	.05
☐ 69 Jim Thome	.75	.35
☐ 70 Omar Vizquel	.20	.09
☐ 71 Eric Davis	.20	.09
☐ 72 John Doherty	.10	.05
☐ 73 Cecil Fielder	.20	.09
☐ 74 Travis Fryman	.20	.09
☐ 75 Kirk Gibson	.20	.09
☐ 76 Gene Harris	.10	.05
☐ 77 Mike Henneman	.10	.05
☐ 78 Mike Moore	.10	.05
☐ 79 Tony Phillips	.10	.05
☐ 80 Mickey Tettleton	.10	.05
☐ 81 Alan Trammell	.35	.16
☐ 82 Lou Whitaker	.20	.09
☐ 83 Kevin Appier	.20	.09
☐ 84 Vince Coleman	.10	.05
☐ 85 David Cone	.20	.09
☐ 86 Gary Gaetti	.20	.09
☐ 87 Greg Gagne	.10	.05
☐ 88 Tom Gordon	.10	.05
☐ 89 Jeff Granger	.10	.05
☐ 90 Bob Hamelin	.10	.05
☐ 91 Dave Henderson	.10	.05
☐ 92 Felix Jose	.10	.05
☐ 93 Wally Joyner	.20	.09
☐ 94 Jose Lind	.10	.05
☐ 95 Mike Macfarlane	.10	.05
☐ 96 Brian McRae	.10	.05
☐ 97 Jeff Montgomery	.20	.09
☐ 98 Ricky Bones	.10	.05
☐ 99 Jeff Bronkey	.10	.05
☐ 100 Alex Diaz	.10	.05
☐ 101 Cal Eldred	.10	.05
☐ 102 Darryl Hamilton	.10	.05
☐ 103 Brian Harper	.10	.05
☐ 104 John Jaha	.10	.05
☐ 105 Pat Listach	.10	.05
☐ 106 Dave Nilsson	.20	.09
☐ 107 Jody Reed	.10	.05
☐ 108 Kevin Seitzer	.10	.05
☐ 109 Greg Vaughn	.10	.05
☐ 110 Turner Ward	.10	.05
☐ 111 Wes Weger	.10	.05
☐ 112 Bill Wegman	.10	.05
☐ 113 Rick Aguilera	.20	.09
☐ 114 Rich Becker	.10	.05
☐ 115 Alex Cole	.10	.05
☐ 116 Scott Erickson	.10	.05
☐ 117 Kent Hrbek	.20	.09
☐ 118 Chuck Knoblauch	.50	.23
☐ 119 Scott Leius	.10	.05
☐ 120 Shane Mack	.10	.05
☐ 121 Pat Mahomes	.10	.05
☐ 122 Pat Meares	.10	.05
☐ 123 Kirby Puckett	1.25	.55
☐ 124 Kevin Tapani	.10	.05
☐ 125 Matt Walbeck	.10	.05
☐ 126 Dave Winfield	.35	.16
☐ 127 Jim Abbott	.20	.09
☐ 128 Wade Boggs	.50	.23
☐ 129 Mike Gallego	.10	.05
☐ 130 Xavier Hernandez	.10	.05
☐ 131 Pat Kelly	.10	.05
☐ 132 Jimmy Key	.20	.09
☐ 133 Don Mattingly	1.25	.55
☐ 134 Terry Mulholland	.10	.05
☐ 135 Matt Nokes	.10	.05
☐ 136 Paul O'Neill	.20	.09
☐ 137 Melido Perez	.10	.05
☐ 138 Luis Polonia	.10	.05
☐ 139 Mike Stanley	.10	.05
☐ 140 Danny Tartabull	.10	.05
☐ 141 Randy Velarde	.10	.05
☐ 142 Bernie Williams	.50	.23
☐ 143 Mark Acre	.10	.05
☐ 144 Geronimo Berroa	.10	.05
☐ 145 Mike Bordick	.10	.05
☐ 146 Scott Brosius	.10	.05
☐ 147 Ron Darling	.10	.05
☐ 148 Dennis Eckersley	.35	.16
☐ 149 Brent Gates	.10	.05
☐ 150 Rickey Henderson	.35	.16
☐ 151 Stan Javier	.10	.05
☐ 152 Steve Karsay	.10	.05
☐ 153 Mark McGwire	1.00	.45
☐ 154 Troy Neel	.10	.05
☐ 155 Ruben Sierra	.10	.05
☐ 156 Terry Steinbach	.20	.09
☐ 157 Bill Taylor	.10	.05
☐ 158 Rich Amaral	.10	.05
☐ 159 Eric Anthony	.10	.05
☐ 160 Bobby Ayala	.10	.05
☐ 161 Chris Bosio	.10	.05
☐ 162 Jay Buhner	.35	.16
☐ 163 Tim Davis	.10	.05
☐ 164 Felix Fermin	.10	.05
☐ 165 Dave Fleming	.10	.05
☐ 166 Ken Griffey Jr.	3.00	1.35
☐ 167 Reggie Jefferson	.20	.09
☐ 168 Randy Johnson	.50	.23
☐ 169 Edgar Martinez	.35	.16
☐ 170 Tino Martinez	.50	.23
☐ 171 Bill Risley	.10	.05
☐ 172 Roger Salkeld	.10	.05
☐ 173 Mac Suzuki	.20	.09
☐ 174 Dan Wilson	.20	.09
☐ 175 Kevin Brown	.20	.09
☐ 176 Jose Canseco	.35	.16
☐ 177 Will Clark	.35	.16
☐ 178 Juan Gonzalez	1.50	.70
☐ 179 Rick Helling	.10	.05
☐ 180 Tom Henke	.20	.09
☐ 181 Chris James	.10	.05
☐ 182 Manuel Lee	.10	.05
☐ 183 Dean Palmer	.20	.09
☐ 184 Ivan Rodriguez	.60	.25
☐ 185 Kenny Rogers	.10	.05
☐ 186 Roberto Alomar	.50	.23
☐ 187 Pat Borders	.10	.05
☐ 188 Joe Carter	.20	.09
☐ 189 Carlos Delgado	.35	.16
☐ 190 Juan Guzman	.10	.05
☐ 191 Pat Hentgen	.50	.23
☐ 192 Paul Molitor	.50	.23
☐ 193 John Olerud	.20	.09
☐ 194 Ed Sprague	.10	.05
☐ 195 Dave Stewart	.20	.09
☐ 196 Todd Stottlemyre	.10	.05
☐ 197 Duane Ward	.10	.05
☐ 198 Devon White	.10	.05
☐ 199 Steve Avery	.10	.05
☐ 200 Jeff Blauser	.10	.05
☐ 201 Tom Glavine	.35	.16
☐ 202 David Justice	.50	.23
☐ 203 Mike Kelly	.10	.05
☐ 204 Roberto Kelly	.10	.05
☐ 205 Ryan Klesko	.35	.16
☐ 206 Mark Lemke	.10	.05
☐ 207 Javier Lopez	.20	.09
☐ 208 Greg Maddux	2.00	.90
☐ 209 Fred McGriff	.35	.16
☐ 210 Greg McMichael	.10	.05
☐ 211 Kent Mercker	.10	.05
☐ 212 Terry Pendleton	.20	.09
☐ 213 John Smoltz	.35	.16
☐ 214 Tony Tarasco	.10	.05
☐ 215 Willie Banks	.10	.05
☐ 216 Steve Buechele	.10	.05
☐ 217 Shawon Dunston	.10	.05
☐ 218 Mark Grace	.35	.16
☐ 219 Brooks Kieschnick	.20	.09
☐ 220 Derrick May	.10	.05
☐ 221 Randy Myers	.10	.05
☐ 222 Karl Rhodes	.10	.05
☐ 223 Rey Sanchez	.10	.05
☐ 224 Sammy Sosa	.50	.23
☐ 225 Steve Trachsel	.10	.05
☐ 226 Rick Wilkins	.10	.05
☐ 227 Bret Boone	.10	.05
☐ 228 Jeff Brantley	.10	.05
☐ 229 Tom Browning	.10	.05
☐ 230 Hector Carrasco	.10	.05
☐ 231 Rob Dibble	.10	.05
☐ 232 Erik Hanson	.10	.05
☐ 233 Barry Larkin	.50	.23
☐ 234 Kevin Mitchell	.20	.09
☐ 235 Hal Morris	.10	.05
☐ 236 Joe Oliver	.10	.05
☐ 237 Jose Rijo	.10	.05
☐ 238 Johnny Ruffin	.10	.05
☐ 239 Deion Sanders	.50	.23
☐ 240 Reggie Sanders	.10	.05
☐ 241 John Smiley	.10	.05
☐ 242 Dante Bichette	.35	.16
☐ 243 Ellis Burks	.20	.09
☐ 244 Andres Galarraga	.50	.23
☐ 245 Joe Girardi	.10	.05
☐ 246 Greg W.Harris	.10	.05
☐ 247 Charlie Hayes	.10	.05
☐ 248 Howard Johnson	.10	.05
☐ 249 Roberto Mejia	.10	.05
☐ 250 Marcus Moore	.10	.05
☐ 251 David Nied	.10	.05
☐ 252 Armando Reynoso	.10	.05
☐ 253 Bruce Ruffin	.10	.05
☐ 254 Mark Thompson	.20	.09
☐ 255 Walt Weiss	.10	.05
☐ 256 Kurt Abbott	.10	.05
☐ 257 Bret Barberie	.10	.05
☐ 258 Chuck Carr	.10	.05
☐ 259 Jeff Conine	.20	.09
☐ 260 Chris Hammond	.10	.05
☐ 261 Bryan Harvey	.10	.05
☐ 262 Jeremy Hernandez	.10	.05
☐ 263 Charlie Hough	.10	.05
☐ 264 Dave Magadan	.10	.05
☐ 265 Benito Santiago	.10	.05
☐ 266 Gary Sheffield	.50	.23
☐ 267 David Weathers	.10	.05
☐ 268 Jeff Bagwell	1.25	.55
☐ 269 Craig Biggio	.35	.16
☐ 270 Ken Caminiti	.50	.23
☐ 271 Andujar Cedeno	.10	.05
☐ 272 Doug Drabek	.10	.05
☐ 273 Steve Finley	.20	.09
☐ 274 Luis Gonzalez	.10	.05
☐ 275 Pete Harnisch	.10	.05
☐ 276 John Hudek	.10	.05
☐ 277 Darryl Kile	.20	.09
☐ 278 Orlando Miller	.10	.05
☐ 279 James Mouton	.10	.05
☐ 280 Shane Reynolds	.10	.05
☐ 281 Scott Servais	.10	.05
☐ 282 Greg Swindell	.10	.05
☐ 283 Pedro Astacio	.10	.05
☐ 284 Brett Butler	.20	.09
☐ 285 Tom Candiotti	.10	.05
☐ 286 Delino DeShields	.10	.05
☐ 287 Kevin Gross	.10	.05
☐ 288 Orel Hershiser	.20	.09
☐ 289 Eric Karros	.20	.09
☐ 290 Ramon Martinez	.20	.09
☐ 291 Raul Mondesi	.50	.23
☐ 292 Jose Offerman	.10	.05
☐ 293 Chan Ho Park	2.00	.90
☐ 294 Mike Piazza	2.00	.90
☐ 295 Henry Rodriguez	.10	.05
☐ 296 Cory Snyder	.10	.05
☐ 297 Tim Wallach	.10	.05
☐ 298 Todd Worrell	.10	.05

☐ 299 Moises Alou .20 .09
☐ 300 Sean Berry .10 .05
☐ 301 Wil Cordero .10 .05
☐ 302 Joey Eischen .10 .05
☐ 303 Jeff Fassero .10 .05
☐ 304 Darrin Fletcher .10 .05
☐ 305 Cliff Floyd .20 .09
☐ 306 Marquis Grissom .20 .09
☐ 307 Ken Hill .10 .05
☐ 308 Mike Lansing .20 .09
☐ 309 Pedro J.Martinez .50 .23
☐ 310 Mel Rojas .10 .05
☐ 311 Kirk Rueter .10 .05
☐ 312 Larry Walker .50 .23
☐ 313 John Wetteland .20 .09
☐ 314 Rondell White .20 .09
☐ 315 Bobby Bonilla .20 .09
☐ 316 John Franco .20 .09
☐ 317 Dwight Gooden .20 .09
☐ 318 Todd Hundley .20 .09
☐ 319 Bobby Jones .20 .09
☐ 320 Jeff Kent .10 .05
☐ 321 Kevin McReynolds .10 .05
☐ 322 Bill Pulsipher .10 .05
☐ 323 Bret Saberhagen .10 .05
☐ 324 David Segui .10 .05
☐ 325 Pete Smith .10 .05
☐ 326 Kelly Stinnett .10 .05
☐ 327 Ryan Thompson .10 .05
☐ 328 Jose Vizcaino .10 .05
☐ 329 Ricky Bottalico .35 .16
☐ 330 Darren Daulton .20 .09
☐ 331 Mariano Duncan .10 .05
☐ 332 Lenny Dykstra .20 .09
☐ 333 Tommy Greene .10 .05
☐ 334 Billy Hatcher .10 .05
☐ 335 Dave Hollins .10 .05
☐ 336 Pete Incaviglia .10 .05
☐ 337 Danny Jackson .10 .05
☐ 338 Doug Jones .10 .05
☐ 339 Ricky Jordan .10 .05
☐ 340 John Kruk .20 .09
☐ 341 Curt Schilling .20 .09
☐ 342 Kevin Stocker .10 .05
☐ 343 Jay Bell .20 .09
☐ 344 Steve Cooke .10 .05
☐ 345 Carlos Garcia .10 .05
☐ 346 Brian Hunter .10 .05
☐ 347 Jeff King .20 .09
☐ 348 Al Martin .10 .05
☐ 349 Orlando Merced .10 .05
☐ 350 Denny Neagle .20 .09
☐ 351 Don Slaught .10 .05
☐ 352 Andy Van Slyke .20 .09
☐ 353 Paul Wagner .10 .05
☐ 354 Rick White .10 .05
☐ 355 Luis Alicea .10 .05
☐ 356 Rene Arocha .10 .05
☐ 357 Rheal Cormier .10 .05
☐ 358 Bernard Gilkey .20 .09
☐ 359 Gregg Jefferies .20 .09
☐ 360 Ray Lankford .20 .09
☐ 361 Tom Pagnozzi .10 .05
☐ 362 Mike Perez .10 .05
☐ 363 Ozzie Smith .75 .35
☐ 364 Bob Tewksbury .10 .05
☐ 365 Mark Whiten .10 .05
☐ 366 Todd Zeile .10 .05
☐ 367 Andy Ashby .20 .09
☐ 368 Brad Ausmus .10 .05
☐ 369 Derek Bell .20 .09
☐ 370 Andy Benes .20 .09
☐ 371 Archi Cianfrocco .10 .05
☐ 372 Tony Gwynn 1.50 .70
☐ 373 Trevor Hoffman .20 .09
☐ 374 Tim Hyers .10 .05
☐ 375 Pedro Martinez .10 .05
☐ 376 Phil Plantier .10 .05
☐ 377 Bip Roberts .10 .05
☐ 378 Scott Sanders .10 .05
☐ 379 Dave Staton .10 .05
☐ 380 Wally Whitehurst .10 .05
☐ 381 Rod Beck .20 .09
☐ 382 Todd Benzinger .10 .05
☐ 383 Barry Bonds .75 .35
☐ 384 John Burkett .10 .05
☐ 385 Royce Clayton .20 .09
☐ 386 Bryan Hickerson .10 .05
☐ 387 Mike Jackson .10 .05
☐ 388 Darren Lewis .10 .05
☐ 389 Kirt Manwaring .10 .05
☐ 390 Willie McGee .20 .09
☐ 391 Mark Portugal .10 .05
☐ 392 Bill Swift .10 .05
☐ 393 Robby Thompson .10 .05
☐ 394 Salomon Torres .10 .05
☐ 395 Matt Williams .35 .16
☐ 396 Checklist .10 .05
☐ 397 Checklist .10 .05
☐ 398 Checklist .10 .05
☐ 399 Checklist .10 .05
☐ 400 Checklist .10 .05
☐ P1 Paul Molitor Promo 2.00 .90

1994 Extra Bases Game Breakers

Consisting of 30 cards and randomly inserted in packs at a rate of three per eight, this set features top run producers from around the major leagues. The cards measure 2 1/2" by 4 11/16" and are horizontally designed. There are two photos on the front that bleed into one another. The back has a photo and career highlights.

	MINT	NRMT
COMPLETE SET (30)	25.00	11.00
COMMON CARD (1-30)	.25	.11
☐ 1 Jeff Bagwell	2.50	1.10
☐ 2 Rod Beck	.35	.16
☐ 3 Albert Belle	2.00	.90
☐ 4 Barry Bonds	1.50	.70
☐ 5 Jose Canseco	.50	.23
☐ 6 Joe Carter	.35	.16
☐ 7 Roger Clemens	2.00	.90
☐ 8 Darren Daulton	.35	.16
☐ 9 Lenny Dykstra	.35	.16
☐ 10 Cecil Fielder	.35	.16
☐ 11 Tom Glavine	.35	.16
☐ 12 Juan Gonzalez	2.50	1.10
☐ 13 Mark Grace	.50	.23
☐ 14 Ken Griffey Jr.	5.00	2.20
☐ 15 David Justice	.75	.35
☐ 16 Greg Maddux	3.00	1.35
☐ 17 Don Mattingly	2.00	.90
☐ 18 Ben McDonald	.25	.11
☐ 19 Fred McGriff	.50	.23
☐ 20 Paul Molitor	.75	.35
☐ 21 John Olerud	.35	.16
☐ 22 Mike Piazza	3.00	1.35
☐ 23 Kirby Puckett	2.00	.90
☐ 24 Cal Ripken Jr.	4.00	1.80
☐ 25 Tim Salmon	.75	.35
☐ 26 Gary Sheffield	.75	.35
☐ 27 Frank Thomas	4.00	1.80
☐ 28 Mo Vaughn	1.00	.45
☐ 29 Matt Williams	.50	.23
☐ 30 Dave Winfield	.50	.23

1994 Extra Bases Major League Hopefuls

Randomly inserted in packs at a rate of one in eight, this 10-card set features top minor league performers. Cards measure 2 1/2" by 4 11/16". Computer generated fronts contain multiple player photos. The backs have a player photo and a write-up about the player's minor league exploits.

	MINT	NRMT
COMPLETE SET (10)	10.00	4.50
COMMON CARD (1-10)	.50	.23
☐ 1 James Baldwin	.75	.35
☐ 2 Ricky Bottalico	1.00	.45
☐ 3 Ray Durham	1.50	.70
☐ 4 Joey Eischen	.50	.23
☐ 5 Brooks Kieschnick	1.00	.45
☐ 6 Orlando Miller	.50	.23
☐ 7 Bill Pulsipher	.75	.35
☐ 8 Mac Suzuki	.75	.35
☐ 9 Mark Thompson	.50	.23
☐ 10 Wes Weger	.50	.23

1994 Extra Bases Pitchers Duel

This 10-card set measures 2 1/2" by 4 3/4". These cards were available through a wrapper offer which was good through March 31, 1995. Each card features two leading pitchers.

	MINT	NRMT
COMPLETE SET (10)	12.00	5.50
COMMON CARD (1-10)	.75	.35
☐ 1 Roger Clemens Jack McDowell	3.00	1.35
☐ 2 Ben McDonald Randy Johnson	3.00	1.35
☐ 3 David Cone Jimmy Key	1.00	.45
☐ 4 Mike Mussina Aaron Sele	2.00	.90
☐ 5 Chuck Finley Wilson Alvarez	.75	.35
☐ 6 Curt Schilling Steve Avery	.75	.35
☐ 7 Greg Maddux Jose Rijo	3.00	1.35
☐ 8 Bob Tewksbury Bret Saberhagen	.75	.35
☐ 9 Tom Glavine Bill Swift	.75	.35
☐ 10 Doug Drabek Orel Hershiser	.75	.35

1994 Extra Bases Rookie Standouts

Randomly inserted in packs at a rate of one in four, this 20-card set features those that had potential for being top rookies in 1994. The cards measure 2 1/2" by 4 11/16". Card fronts have an action photo of the player. The background is somewhat blurred and a jagged outline appears around the player as if to allow him to stand out from the rest of the card. The backs have a player photo and text on a white background.

	MINT	NRMT
COMPLETE SET (20)	18.00	8.00
COMMON CARD (1-20)	.40	.18
☐ 1 Kurt Abbott	.40	.18
☐ 2 Brian Anderson	.40	.18
☐ 3 Hector Carrasco	.40	.18
☐ 4 Tim Davis	.40	.18
☐ 5 Carlos Delgado	2.00	.90
☐ 6 Cliff Floyd	.40	.18
☐ 7 Bob Hamelin	.40	.18
☐ 8 Jeffrey Hammonds	.50	.23
☐ 9 Rick Helling	.40	.18
☐ 10 Steve Karsay	.40	.18
☐ 11 Ryan Klesko	1.50	.70
☐ 12 Javier Lopez	2.00	.90
☐ 13 Raul Mondesi	2.00	.90

☐ 14 James Mouton	.40	.18
☐ 15 Chan Ho Park	2.00	.90
☐ 16 Manny Ramirez	3.00	1.35
☐ 17 Tony Tarasco	.40	.18
☐ 18 Steve Trachsel	.40	.18
☐ 19 Rick White	.40	.18
☐ 20 Rondell White	1.50	.70

1994 Extra Bases Second Year Stars

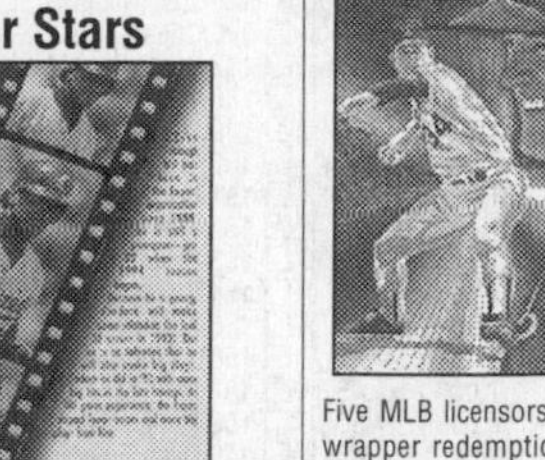

Randomly inserted in packs at a rate of one in four, Second Year Stars takes a look at 20 top second year players and reflects on their rookie campaigns of 1993. The cards measure 2 1/2" by 4 11/16". Card fronts feature multiple photos including a large full bleed photo of the player and four smaller photos that give the appearance of being captured on film. These smaller photos run the length of the card and are on the left.

	MINT	NRMT
COMPLETE SET (20)	10.00	4.50
COMMON CARD (1-20)	.50	.23
☐ 1 Bobby Ayala	.50	.23
☐ 2 Jason Bere	.50	.23
☐ 3 Chuck Carr	.50	.23
☐ 4 Jeff Conine	.75	.35
☐ 5 Steve Cooke	.50	.23
☐ 6 Wil Cordero	.50	.23
☐ 7 Carlos Garcia	.50	.23
☐ 8 Brent Gates	.50	.23
☐ 9 Trevor Hoffman	.75	.35
☐ 10 Wayne Kirby	.50	.23
☐ 11 Al Martin	.50	.23
☐ 12 Pedro Martinez	2.00	.90
☐ 13 Greg McMichael	.50	.23
☐ 14 Troy Neel	.50	.23
☐ 15 David Nied	.50	.23
☐ 16 Mike Piazza	5.00	2.20
☐ 17 Kirk Rueter	.75	.35
☐ 18 Tim Salmon	2.00	.90
☐ 19 Aaron Sele	.50	.23
☐ 20 Kevin Stocker	.50	.23

1994 FanFest Clemente

This standard-size redemption set was reportedly the brainchild of MLB's Ray Schulte, who obtained the cooperation of the five major baseball card manufacturers to each produce 15,000 special Roberto Clemente cards for the '94 All-Star FanFest in Pittsburgh, July 8-12. Each card was redeemable only at each manufacturer's booth for five wrappers of any '94 baseball product from that company. The undistributed cards were reportedly destroyed. It has been estimated that less than 10,000 of each card were distributed. All the cards are numbered on the back as "X of 5."

	MINT	NRMT
COMPLETE SET (5)	80.00	36.00
COMMON CARD (1-5)	15.00	6.75
☐ 1 Roberto Clemente Donruss Diamond King	15.00	6.75
☐ 2 Roberto Clemente 1963 Fleer Reprint	15.00	6.75
☐ 3 Roberto Clemente 1994 Pinnacle Dufex	15.00	6.75
☐ 4 Roberto Clemente 1954 Topps Archives	20.00	9.00
☐ 5 Roberto Clemente Upper Deck Electric	15.00	6.75

1995 FanFest Ryan

Five MLB licensors produced one card each as part of a wrapper redemption program featuring Nolan Ryan for All-Star FanFest in Dallas in July. Pinnacle, Ultra, and Upper Deck cards sport the design of the licensor's regular issue, while Donruss produced a special design and Topps modified Ryan's 1968 rookie card (shared with Jerry Koosman) to feature only Ryan. Again, Ray Schulte, promoter of the Pinnacle All-Star Fan Fest shows, was involved in the creation of this set. The cards are numbered on the back "X of 5."

	MINT	NRMT
COMPLETE SET (5)	40.00	18.00
COMMON CARD (1-5)	10.00	4.50
☐ 1 Nolan Ryan 1995 Upper Deck	12.00	5.50
☐ 2 Nolan Ryan 1968 Topps	10.00	4.50
☐ 3 Nolan Ryan 1995 Pinnacle	10.00	4.50
☐ 4 Nolan Ryan 1995 Ultra	12.00	5.50
☐ 5 Nolan Ryan 1995 Donruss (Special design)	10.00	4.50

1996 FanFest Carlton

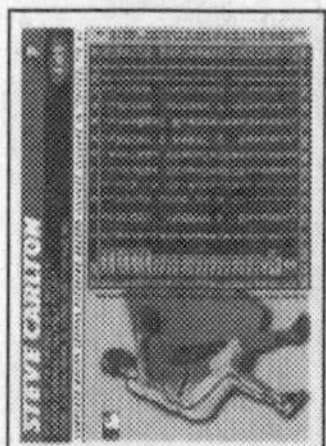

These five standard-size cards marked the third straight year that a set of one player's cards were issued in conjunction with the annual All-Star Fan Fest. MLB's Ray Schulte, who originated the idea of these cards was again instrumental in arranging for the companies to issue these cards as part of a wrapper redemption program.

	MINT	NRMT
COMPLETE SET (5)	30.00	13.50
COMMON CARD (1-5)	6.00	2.70
☐ 1 Steve Carlton Donruss	6.00	2.70
☐ 2 Steve Carlton Fleer Ultra	6.00	2.70
☐ 3 Steve Carlton Pinnacle	8.00	3.60
☐ 4 Steve Carlton 1965 Topps	8.00	3.60
☐ 5 Steve Carlton Upper Deck	6.00	2.70

1997 FanFest Jackie Robinson

These five cards marked the fourth straight year that a set of one player's cards were issued in conjunction with the annual All-Star Fan Fest. MLB's Ray Schulte, who originated the idea of these cards was again instrumental in arranging for the companies to issue these cards as part of a wrapper redemption program. Fleer/SkyBox also issued a Ultra Larry Doby card as part of the Fan Fest

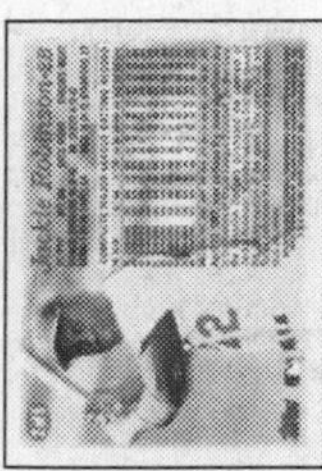

celebration. This card is priced below but not considered part of the Robinson set.

	MINT	NRMT
COMPLETE SET (5)	30.00	13.50
COMMON CARD (1-5)	6.00	2.70
☐ 1 Jackie Robinson Pinnacle	6.00	2.70
☐ 2 Jackie Robinson 1952 Topps	6.00	2.70
☐ 3 Jackie Robinson Upper Deck	6.00	2.70
☐ 4 Jackie Robinson 1949 Leaf	6.00	2.70
☐ 5 Jackie Robinson Fleer Ultra	6.00	2.70
☐ 6 Larry Doby Fleer Ultra	6.00	2.70

1913 Fatima T200

The cards in this 16-card set measure approximately 2 5/8" by 5 13/16". The 1913 Fatima Cigarettes issue contains unnumbered glossy surface team cards. Both St. Louis team cards are considered difficult to obtain. A large 13" by 21" unnumbered, heavy cardboard parallel premium issue is also known to exist and is quite scarce. These unnumbered team cards are ordered below by team alphabetical order within league.

	EX-MT	VG-E
COMPLETE SET (16)	7000.00	3200.00
COMMON TEAM (1-16)	300.00	135.00
☐ 1 Boston Red Sox	350.00	160.00
☐ 2 Chicago White Sox	400.00	180.00
☐ 3 Cleveland Indians	1000.00	450.00
☐ 4 Detroit Tigers	750.00	350.00
☐ 5 New York Yankees	800.00	350.00
☐ 6 Philadelphia Athletics	300.00	135.00
☐ 7 St. Louis Browns	600.00	275.00
☐ 8 Washington Senators	400.00	180.00
☐ 9 Boston Braves	400.00	180.00
☐ 10 Brooklyn Dodgers	300.00	135.00
☐ 11 Chicago Cubs	350.00	160.00
☐ 12 Cincinnati Reds	300.00	135.00
☐ 13 New York Giants	500.00	220.00
☐ 14 Philadelphia Phillies	300.00	135.00
☐ 15 Pittsburgh Pirates	400.00	180.00
☐ 16 St. Louis Cardinals	400.00	180.00

1993 Finest Promos

Topps gave 5,000 of these three-card promo standard-size sets to its dealer customers to promote the release of its 1993 Topps Baseball's Finest set. The standard-size cards have metallic finishes on their fronts and feature color player action photos. The words "Promotional Sample 1 of 5000" appears in red lettering superposed upon the player's biography on the back of the card. A limited amount of these cards were issued as refractors. They are valued below as well.

	MINT	NRMT
COMPLETE SET (3)	60.00	27.00
COMMON CARD	12.50	5.50
*REFRACTORS: 30X to 60X BASIC CARDS		
☐ 88 Roberto Alomar	15.00	6.75
☐ 98 Don Mattingly AS	20.00	9.00
☐ 107 Nolan Ryan	40.00	18.00

1993 Finest

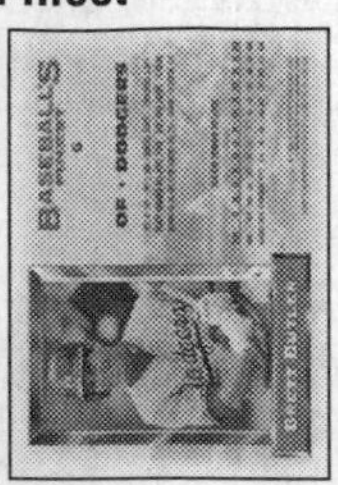

This 199-card standard-size single series set is widely recognized as one of the most important issues of the 1990's. The Finest brand was Topps first attempt at the super-premium card market. Production was announced at 4,000 cases and cards were distributed exclusively through hobby dealers in the fall of 1993. This was the first time in the history of the hobby that a major manufacturer publicly released production figures. Cards were issued in 7-card foil fin-wrapped packs that carried a suggested retail price of $3.99. The product was a smashing success upon release with pack prices immediately soaring well above suggested retail prices. The popularity of the product has continued to grow throughout the years as it's place in hobby lore is now well soldified. The cards have silver-blue metallic finishes on their fronts and feature color player action photos. The set's title appears at the top, and the player's name is shown at the bottom. J.T. Snow is the only key Rookie Card in this set.

	MINT	NRMT
COMPLETE SET (199)	250.00	110.00
COMMON CARD (1-199)	1.00	.45
☐ 1 David Justice	5.00	2.20
☐ 2 Lou Whitaker	1.50	.70
☐ 3 Bryan Harvey	1.00	.45
☐ 4 Carlos Garcia	1.00	.45
☐ 5 Sid Fernandez	1.00	.45
☐ 6 Brett Butler	1.50	.70
☐ 7 Scott Cooper	1.00	.45
☐ 8 B.J. Surhoff	1.50	.70
☐ 9 Steve Finley	1.50	.70
☐ 10 Curt Schilling	1.50	.70
☐ 11 Jeff Bagwell	10.00	4.50
☐ 12 Alex Cole	1.00	.45
☐ 13 John Olerud	1.00	.45
☐ 14 John Smiley	1.00	.45
☐ 15 Bip Roberts	1.00	.45
☐ 16 Albert Belle	6.00	2.70
☐ 17 Duane Ward	1.00	.45
☐ 18 Alan Trammell	3.00	1.35
☐ 19 Andy Benes	1.50	.70
☐ 20 Reggie Sanders	1.50	.70
☐ 21 Todd Zeile	1.00	.45
☐ 22 Rick Aguilera	1.00	.45
☐ 23 Dave Hollins	1.00	.45
☐ 24 Jose Rijo	1.00	.45
☐ 25 Matt Williams	3.00	1.35
☐ 26 Sandy Alomar	1.50	.70
☐ 27 Alex Fernandez	1.50	.70
☐ 28 Ozzie Smith	6.00	2.70
☐ 29 Ramon Martinez	1.50	.70
☐ 30 Bernie Williams	5.00	2.20
☐ 31 Gary Sheffield	5.00	2.20
☐ 32 Eric Karros	3.00	1.35
☐ 33 Frank Viola	1.00	.45
☐ 34 Kevin Young	1.00	.45
☐ 35 Ken Hill	1.50	.70
☐ 36 Tony Fernandez	1.00	.45
☐ 37 Tim Wakefield	1.50	.70
☐ 38 John Kruk	1.50	.70
☐ 39 Chris Sabo	1.00	.45
☐ 40 Marquis Grissom	1.50	.70
☐ 41 Glenn Davis	1.00	.45
☐ 42 Jeff Montgomery	1.50	.70
☐ 43 Kenny Lofton	10.00	4.50
☐ 44 John Burkett	1.00	.45
☐ 45 Darryl Hamilton	1.00	.45
☐ 46 Jim Abbott	1.00	.45
☐ 47 Ivan Rodriguez	6.00	2.70
☐ 48 Eric Young	5.00	2.20
☐ 49 Mitch Williams	1.00	.45
☐ 50 Harold Reynolds	1.00	.45
☐ 51 Brian Harper	1.00	.45
☐ 52 Rafael Palmeiro	3.00	1.35
☐ 53 Bret Saberhagen	1.00	.45
☐ 54 Jeff Conine	1.50	.70
☐ 55 Ivan Calderon	1.00	.45
☐ 56 Juan Guzman	1.00	.45
☐ 57 Carlos Baerga	1.50	.70
☐ 58 Charles Nagy	1.50	.70
☐ 59 Wally Joyner	1.50	.70
☐ 60 Charlie Hayes	1.00	.45
☐ 61 Shane Mack	1.00	.45
☐ 62 Pete Harnisch	1.00	.45
☐ 63 George Brett	10.00	4.50
☐ 64 Lance Johnson	1.00	.45
☐ 65 Ben McDonald	1.00	.45
☐ 66 Bobby Bonilla	1.50	.70
☐ 67 Terry Steinbach	1.50	.70
☐ 68 Ron Gant	1.50	.70
☐ 69 Doug Jones	1.00	.45
☐ 70 Paul Molitor	6.00	2.70
☐ 71 Brady Anderson	3.00	1.35
☐ 72 Chuck Finley	1.00	.45
☐ 73 Mark Grace	3.00	1.35
☐ 74 Mike Devereaux	1.00	.45
☐ 75 Tony Phillips	1.00	.45
☐ 76 Chuck Knoblauch	5.00	2.20
☐ 77 Tony Gwynn	12.00	5.50
☐ 78 Kevin Appier	1.50	.70
☐ 79 Sammy Sosa	5.00	2.20
☐ 80 Mickey Tettleton	1.00	.45
☐ 81 Felix Jose	1.00	.45
☐ 82 Mark Langston	1.00	.45
☐ 83 Gregg Jefferies	1.50	.70
☐ 84 Andre Dawson AS	3.00	1.35
☐ 85 Greg Maddux AS	15.00	6.75
☐ 86 Rickey Henderson AS	3.00	1.35
☐ 87 Tom Glavine AS	3.00	1.35
☐ 88 Roberto Alomar AS	6.00	2.70
☐ 89 Darryl Strawberry AS	1.50	.70
☐ 90 Wade Boggs AS	5.00	2.20
☐ 91 Bo Jackson AS	1.50	.70
☐ 92 Mark McGwire AS	10.00	4.50
☐ 93 Robin Ventura AS	1.50	.70
☐ 94 Joe Carter AS	3.00	1.35
☐ 95 Lee Smith AS	1.50	.70
☐ 96 Cal Ripken AS	20.00	9.00
☐ 97 Larry Walker AS	3.00	1.35
☐ 98 Don Mattingly AS	8.00	3.60
☐ 99 Jose Canseco AS	3.00	1.35
☐ 100 Dennis Eckersley AS	3.00	1.35
☐ 101 Terry Pendleton AS	1.50	.70
☐ 102 Frank Thomas AS	20.00	9.00
☐ 103 Barry Bonds AS	6.00	2.70
☐ 104 Roger Clemens AS	10.00	4.50
☐ 105 Ryne Sandberg AS	6.00	2.70
☐ 106 Fred McGriff AS	3.00	1.35
☐ 107 Nolan Ryan AS	20.00	9.00
☐ 108 Will Clark AS	3.00	1.35
☐ 109 Pat Listach AS	1.00	.45
☐ 110 Ken Griffey Jr. AS	25.00	11.00
☐ 111 Cecil Fielder AS	1.50	.70
☐ 112 Kirby Puckett AS	10.00	4.50
☐ 113 Dwight Gooden AS	1.50	.70
☐ 114 Barry Larkin AS	3.00	1.35
☐ 115 David Cone AS	1.50	.70
☐ 116 Juan Gonzalez AS	12.00	5.50
☐ 117 Kent Hrbek	1.50	.70
☐ 118 Tim Wallach	1.00	.45
☐ 119 Craig Biggio	3.00	1.35
☐ 120 Roberto Kelly	1.00	.45
☐ 121 Gregg Olson	1.00	.45
☐ 122 Eddie Murray UER 122 career strikeouts should be 1224	8.00	3.60
☐ 123 Wil Cordero	1.00	.45
☐ 124 Jay Buhner	3.00	1.35
☐ 125 Carlton Fisk	5.00	2.20
☐ 126 Eric Davis	1.50	.70
☐ 127 Doug Drabek	1.00	.45
☐ 128 Ozzie Guillen	1.00	.45
☐ 129 John Wetteland	1.50	.70
☐ 130 Andres Galarraga	3.00	1.35
☐ 131 Ken Caminiti	5.00	2.20
☐ 132 Tom Candiotti	1.00	.45
☐ 133 Pat Borders	1.00	.45
☐ 134 Kevin Brown	1.50	.70
☐ 135 Travis Fryman	1.50	.70
☐ 136 Kevin Mitchell	1.50	.70
☐ 137 Greg Swindell	1.00	.45
☐ 138 Benito Santiago	1.00	.45
☐ 139 Reggie Jefferson	3.00	1.35
☐ 140 Chris Bosio	1.00	.45
☐ 141 Deion Sanders	5.00	2.20
☐ 142 Scott Erickson	1.00	.45
☐ 143 Howard Johnson	1.00	.45
☐ 144 Orestes Destrade	1.00	.45
☐ 145 Jose Guzman	1.00	.45
☐ 146 Chad Curtis	1.50	.70
☐ 147 Cal Eldred	1.00	.45
☐ 148 Willie Greene	1.50	.70
☐ 149 Tommy Greene	1.00	.45
☐ 150 Erik Hanson	1.00	.45
☐ 151 Bob Welch	1.00	.45
☐ 152 John Jaha	1.50	.70
☐ 153 Harold Baines	1.50	.70
☐ 154 Randy Johnson	5.00	2.20
☐ 155 Al Martin	1.50	.70
☐ 156 J.T. Snow	6.00	2.70
☐ 157 Mike Mussina	6.00	2.70
☐ 158 Ruben Sierra	1.00	.45
☐ 159 Dean Palmer	1.50	.70
☐ 160 Steve Avery	1.00	.45
☐ 161 Julio Franco	1.50	.70
☐ 162 Dave Winfield	3.00	1.35
☐ 163 Tim Salmon	6.00	2.70
☐ 164 Tom Henke	1.00	.45
☐ 165 Mo Vaughn	6.00	2.70
☐ 166 John Smoltz	3.00	1.35
☐ 167 Danny Tartabull	1.00	.45
☐ 168 Delino DeShields	1.00	.45
☐ 169 Charlie Hough	1.00	.45
☐ 170 Paul O'Neill	1.50	.70
☐ 171 Darren Daulton	1.50	.70
☐ 172 Jack McDowell	1.00	.45
☐ 173 Junior Felix	1.00	.45
☐ 174 Jimmy Key	1.50	.70
☐ 175 George Bell	1.00	.45
☐ 176 Mike Stanton	1.00	.45
☐ 177 Len Dykstra	1.50	.70
☐ 178 Norm Charlton	1.00	.45
☐ 179 Eric Anthony	1.00	.45
☐ 180 Rob Dibble	1.00	.45
☐ 181 Otis Nixon	1.00	.45
☐ 182 Randy Myers	1.50	.70
☐ 183 Tim Raines	1.50	.70
☐ 184 Orel Hershiser	1.50	.70
☐ 185 Andy Van Slyke	1.50	.70
☐ 186 Mike Lansing	1.50	.70
☐ 187 Ray Lankford	3.00	1.35
☐ 188 Mike Morgan	1.00	.45
☐ 189 Moises Alou	1.50	.70
☐ 190 Edgar Martinez	3.00	1.35
☐ 191 John Franco	1.00	.45
☐ 192 Robin Yount	1.50	.70
☐ 193 Bob Tewksbury	1.00	.45
☐ 194 Jay Bell	1.50	.70
☐ 195 Luis Gonzalez	1.00	.45
☐ 196 Dave Fleming	1.00	.45
☐ 197 Mike Greenwell	1.00	.45
☐ 198 David Nied	1.00	.45
☐ 199 Mike Piazza	25.00	11.00

1993 Finest Refractors

Randomly inserted in packs at a rate of one in 18, these 199 standard-size cards are identical to the regular-issue 1993 Topps Finest except that their fronts have been laminated with a plastic diffraction grating that gives the card a colorful 3-D appearance. Because of the known production numbers, these cards are believed to have a print run of 241 of each card. Several cards are believed to be in short supply and are notated with an asterisk. Topps, however, has never publicly released any verification of shortprinted singles, but some of the singles are accepted as being tough to find due to poor regional distribution and hoarding. Due to their high value, these cards are extremely condition sensitive, with much attention paid to centering and minor scratches on the card fronts.

	MINT	NRMT
COMPLETE SET (199)	40000.00	18000.00
COMMON CARD (1-199)	50.00	22.00
MINOR STARS	100.00	45.00
☐ 1 David Justice	250.00	110.00
☐ 3 Bryan Harvey*	200.00	90.00
☐ 10 Curt Schilling*	250.00	110.00
☐ 11 Jeff Bagwell	1000.00	450.00
☐ 12 Alex Cole	250.00	110.00
☐ 16 Albert Belle	700.00	325.00
☐ 25 Matt Williams	500.00	220.00
☐ 26 Sandy Alomar	150.00	70.00
☐ 27 Alex Fernandez	150.00	70.00

☐ 28 Ozzie Smith	300.00	135.00
☐ 30 Bernie Williams	400.00	180.00
☐ 31 Gary Sheffield	350.00	160.00
☐ 32 Eric Karros	150.00	70.00
☐ 38 John Kruk*	200.00	90.00
☐ 39 Chris Sabo*	200.00	90.00
☐ 40 Marquis Grissom*	350.00	160.00
☐ 41 Glenn Davis*	250.00	110.00
☐ 43 Kenny Lofton	400.00	180.00
☐ 47 Ivan Rodriguez*	800.00	350.00
☐ 52 Rafael Palmeiro	200.00	90.00
☐ 54 Jeff Conine	175.00	80.00
☐ 58 Charles Nagy	175.00	80.00
☐ 63 George Brett	700.00	325.00
☐ 70 Paul Molitor	500.00	220.00
☐ 71 Brady Anderson	250.00	110.00
☐ 73 Mark Grace	250.00	110.00
☐ 76 Chuck Knoblauch	350.00	160.00
☐ 77 Tony Gwynn	700.00	325.00
☐ 79 Sammy Sosa*	500.00	220.00
☐ 80 Mickey Tettleton	125.00	55.00
☐ 81 Felix Jose*	200.00	90.00
☐ 84 Andre Dawson AS*	200.00	90.00
☐ 85 Greg Maddux AS	1200.00	550.00
☐ 86 Rickey Henderson	250.00	110.00
☐ 87 Tom Glavine AS !	150.00	70.00
☐ 88 Roberto Alomar AS	500.00	220.00
☐ 89 Darryl Strawberry AS	125.00	55.00
☐ 90 Wade Boggs AS	250.00	110.00
☐ 92 Mark McGwire AS	700.00	325.00
☐ 93 Robin Ventura AS	150.00	70.00
☐ 94 Joe Carter AS	150.00	70.00
☐ 96 Cal Ripken AS	2000.00	900.00
☐ 97 Larry Walker AS	350.00	160.00
☐ 98 Don Mattingly AS	400.00	180.00
☐ 99 Jose Canseco AS !	250.00	110.00
☐ 102 Frank Thomas AS	1200.00	550.00
☐ 103 Barry Bonds AS	700.00	325.00
☐ 104 Roger Clemens AS	600.00	275.00
☐ 105 Ryne Sandberg AS	300.00	135.00
☐ 106 Fred McGriff AS	200.00	90.00
☐ 107 Nolan Ryan AS !	1500.00	700.00
☐ 108 Will Clark AS	250.00	110.00
☐ 110 Ken Griffey Jr. AS !	2000.00	900.00
☐ 111 Cecil Fielder AS	175.00	80.00
☐ 112 Kirby Puckett AS	400.00	180.00
☐ 113 Dwight Gooden AS	150.00	70.00
☐ 114 Barry Larkin AS	250.00	110.00
☐ 115 David Cone AS	125.00	55.00
☐ 116 Juan Gonzalez AS	1500.00	700.00
☐ 119 Craig Biggio	150.00	70.00
☐ 122 Eddie Murray UER 122 career strikeouts should be 1224	400.00	180.00
☐ 124 Jay Buhner	250.00	110.00
☐ 125 Carlton Fisk	175.00	80.00
☐ 130 Andres Galarraga	250.00	110.00
☐ 131 Ken Caminiti	250.00	110.00
☐ 134 Kevin Brown*	200.00	90.00
☐ 135 Travis Fryman	150.00	70.00
☐ 141 Deion Sanders	200.00	90.00
☐ 154 Randy Johnson	500.00	220.00
☐ 155 Al Martin *	125.00	55.00
☐ 156 J.T. Snow	150.00	70.00
☐ 157 Mike Mussina	400.00	180.00
☐ 159 Dean Palmer	150.00	70.00
☐ 162 Dave Winfield	150.00	70.00
☐ 163 Tim Salmon	400.00	180.00
☐ 165 Mo Vaughn	400.00	180.00
☐ 166 John Smoltz	200.00	90.00
☐ 173 Junior Felix*	200.00	90.00
☐ 187 Ray Lankford	150.00	70.00
☐ 189 Moises Alou*	200.00	90.00
☐ 190 Edgar Martinez	250.00	110.00
☐ 192 Robin Yount	200.00	90.00
☐ 193 Bob Tewksbury*	150.00	70.00
☐ 199 Mike Piazza	1200.00	550.00

1993 Finest Jumbos

These oversized (approximately 4" by 6") cards were inserted one per sealed box of 1993 Topps Finest packs and feature reproductions of 33 players from that set's All-Star subset (84-116). Some hobby dealers believe because of the known production numbers that slightly less than 1,500 of each of these cards were produced.

	MINT	NRMT
COMPLETE SET (33)	500.00	220.00
COMMON CARD (84-116)	5.00	2.20
☐ 84 Andre Dawson	8.00	3.60
☐ 85 Greg Maddux	40.00	18.00
☐ 86 Rickey Henderson	8.00	3.60
☐ 87 Tom Glavine	8.00	3.60
☐ 88 Roberto Alomar	12.00	5.50
☐ 89 Darryl Strawberry	8.00	3.60
☐ 90 Wade Boggs	8.00	3.60
☐ 91 Bo Jackson	8.00	3.60
☐ 92 Mark McGwire	25.00	11.00
☐ 93 Robin Ventura	8.00	3.60
☐ 94 Joe Carter	8.00	3.60
☐ 95 Lee Smith	8.00	3.60
☐ 96 Cal Ripken	50.00	22.00
☐ 97 Larry Walker	8.00	3.60
☐ 98 Don Mattingly	20.00	9.00
☐ 99 Jose Canseco	8.00	3.60
☐ 100 Dennis Eckersley	8.00	3.60
☐ 101 Terry Pendleton	8.00	3.60
☐ 102 Frank Thomas	50.00	22.00
☐ 103 Barry Bonds	15.00	6.75
☐ 104 Roger Clemens	25.00	11.00
☐ 105 Ryne Sandberg	15.00	6.75
☐ 106 Fred McGriff	8.00	3.60
☐ 107 Nolan Ryan	50.00	22.00
☐ 108 Will Clark	8.00	3.60
☐ 109 Pat Listach	5.00	2.20
☐ 110 Ken Griffey Jr.	60.00	27.00
☐ 111 Cecil Fielder	8.00	3.60
☐ 112 Kirby Puckett	25.00	11.00
☐ 113 Dwight Gooden	8.00	3.60
☐ 114 Barry Larkin	8.00	3.60
☐ 115 David Cone	8.00	3.60
☐ 116 Juan Gonzalez	30.00	13.50

1994 Finest Pre-Production

This 40-card preview standard-size set is identical in design to the basic Finest set. Cards were randomly inserted at a rate of one in 36 in second series Topps packs and three cards were issued with each Topps factory set. The card numbers on back correspond to those of the regular issue. The only way to distinguish between the preview and basic cards is "Pre-Production" in small red letters on back.

	MINT	NRMT
COMPLETE SET (40)	175.00	80.00
COMMON CARD	3.00	1.35
☐ 22P Deion Sanders	10.00	4.50
☐ 23P Jose Offerman	3.00	1.35
☐ 26P Alex Fernandez	3.00	1.35
☐ 31P Steve Finley	6.00	2.70
☐ 35P Andres Galarraga	12.00	5.50
☐ 43P Reggie Sanders	6.00	2.70
☐ 47P Dave Hollins	3.00	1.35
☐ 52P David Cone	6.00	2.70
☐ 59P Dante Bichette	12.00	5.50
☐ 61P Orlando Merced	3.00	1.35
☐ 62P Brian McRae	3.00	1.35
☐ 66P Mike Mussina	20.00	9.00
☐ 76P Mike Stanley	3.00	1.35
☐ 78P Mark McGwire	40.00	18.00
☐ 79P Pat Listach	3.00	1.35
☐ 82P Dwight Gooden	6.00	2.70
☐ 84P Phil Plantier	3.00	1.35
☐ 90P Jeff Russell	3.00	1.35
☐ 92P Gregg Jefferies	6.00	2.70
☐ 93P Jose Guzman	3.00	1.35
☐ 100P John Smoltz	12.00	5.50
☐ 102P Jim Thome	25.00	11.00
☐ 121P Moises Alou	6.00	2.70
☐ 125P Devon White	3.00	1.35
☐ 126P Ivan Rodriguez	25.00	11.00
☐ 130P Dave Magadan	3.00	1.35
☐ 136P Ozzie Smith	25.00	11.00
☐ 141P Chris Hoiles	3.00	1.35
☐ 149P Jim Abbott	6.00	2.70
☐ 151P Bill Swift	3.00	1.35
☐ 154P Edgar Martinez	12.00	5.50
☐ 157P J.T. Snow	6.00	2.70
☐ 159P Alan Trammell	12.00	5.50
☐ 163P Roberto Kelly	3.00	1.35
☐ 166P Scott Erickson	6.00	2.70
☐ 168P Scott Cooper	3.00	1.35
☐ 169P Rod Beck	6.00	2.70
☐ 177P Dean Palmer	6.00	2.70
☐ 182P Todd Van Poppel	3.00	1.35
☐ 185P Paul Sorrento	3.00	1.35

1994 Finest

The 1994 Topps Finest baseball set consists of two series of 220 cards each, for a total of 440 standard-size cards. Each series includes 40 special design Finest cards: 20 top 1993 rookies (1-20), 20 top 1994 rookies (421-440) and 40 top veterans (201-240). These glossy and metallic cards have a color photo on front with green and gold borders. A color photo on back is accompanied by statistics and a "Finest Moment" note. Some series 2 packs contained either one or two series 1 cards. The only notable Rookie Card is Chan Ho Park.

	MINT	NRMT
COMPLETE SET (440)	180.00	80.00
COMPLETE SERIES 1 (220)	90.00	40.00
COMPLETE SERIES 2 (220)	90.00	40.00
COMMON CARD (1-440)	.50	.23
☐ 1 Mike Piazza FIN	8.00	3.60
☐ 2 Kevin Stocker FIN	.50	.23
☐ 3 Greg McMichael FIN	.50	.23
☐ 4 Jeff Conine FIN	1.00	.45
☐ 5 Rene Arocha FIN	.50	.23
☐ 6 Aaron Sele FIN	1.00	.45
☐ 7 Brent Gates FIN	.50	.23
☐ 8 Chuck Carr FIN	.50	.23
☐ 9 Kirk Rueter FIN	.50	.23
☐ 10 Mike Lansing FIN	1.00	.45
☐ 11 Al Martin FIN	.50	.23
☐ 12 Jason Bere FIN	1.00	.45
☐ 13 Troy Neel FIN	.50	.23
☐ 14 Armando Reynoso FIN	.50	.23
☐ 15 Jeromy Burnitz FIN	.50	.23
☐ 16 Rich Amaral FIN	.50	.23
☐ 17 David McCarty FIN	.50	.23
☐ 18 Tim Salmon FIN	2.50	1.10
☐ 19 Steve Cooke FIN	.50	.23
☐ 20 Wil Cordero FIN	.50	.23
☐ 21 Kevin Tapani	.50	.23
☐ 22 Deion Sanders	2.50	1.10
☐ 23 Jose Offerman	.50	.23
☐ 24 Mark Langston	.50	.23
☐ 25 Ken Hill	.50	.23
☐ 26 Alex Fernandez	.50	.23
☐ 27 Jeff Blauser	.50	.23
☐ 28 Royce Clayton	.50	.23
☐ 29 Brad Ausmus	.50	.23
☐ 30 Ryan Bowen	.50	.23
☐ 31 Steve Finley	1.00	.45
☐ 32 Charlie Hayes	.50	.23
☐ 33 Jeff Kent	.50	.23
☐ 34 Mike Henneman	.50	.23
☐ 35 Andres Galarraga	1.50	.70
☐ 36 Wayne Kirby	.50	.23
☐ 37 Joe Oliver	.50	.23
☐ 38 Terry Steinbach	1.00	.45
☐ 39 Ryan Thompson	.50	.23
☐ 40 Luis Alicea	.50	.23
☐ 41 Randy Velarde	.50	.23
☐ 42 Bob Tewksbury	.50	.23
☐ 43 Reggie Sanders	1.00	.45
☐ 44 Brian Williams	.50	.23
☐ 45 Joe Orsulak	.50	.23
☐ 46 Jose Lind	.50	.23
☐ 47 Dave Hollins	.50	.23
☐ 48 Graeme Lloyd	.50	.23
☐ 49 Jim Gott	.50	.23
☐ 50 Andre Dawson	1.50	.70
☐ 51 Steve Buechele	.50	.23
☐ 52 David Cone	1.00	.45
☐ 53 Ricky Gutierrez	.50	.23
☐ 54 Lance Johnson	.50	.23
☐ 55 Tino Martinez	2.50	1.10
☐ 56 Phil Hiatt	.50	.23
☐ 57 Carlos Garcia	.50	.23
☐ 58 Danny Darwin	.50	.23
☐ 59 Dante Bichette	1.50	.70
☐ 60 Scott Kamieniecki	.50	.23
☐ 61 Orlando Merced	.50	.23
☐ 62 Brian McRae	.50	.23
☐ 63 Pat Kelly	.50	.23
☐ 64 Tom Henke	.50	.23

☐ 65 Jeff King	1.00	.45
☐ 66 Mike Mussina	2.50	1.10
☐ 67 Tim Pugh	.50	.23
☐ 68 Robby Thompson	.50	.23
☐ 69 Paul O'Neill	1.00	.45
☐ 70 Hal Morris	.50	.23
☐ 71 Ron Karkovice	.50	.23
☐ 72 Joe Girardi	.50	.23
☐ 73 Eduardo Perez	.50	.23
☐ 74 Raul Mondesi	2.50	1.10
☐ 75 Mike Gallego	.50	.23
☐ 76 Mike Stanley	.50	.23
☐ 77 Kevin Roberson	.50	.23
☐ 78 Mark McGwire	5.00	2.20
☐ 79 Pat Listach	.50	.23
☐ 80 Eric Davis	1.00	.45
☐ 81 Mike Bordick	.50	.23
☐ 82 Doc Gooden	1.00	.45
☐ 83 Mike Moore	.50	.23
☐ 84 Phil Plantier	.50	.23
☐ 85 Darren Lewis	.50	.23
☐ 86 Rick Wilkins	.50	.23
☐ 87 Darryl Strawberry	1.00	.45
☐ 88 Rob Dibble	.50	.23
☐ 89 Greg Vaughn	.50	.23
☐ 90 Jeff Russell	.50	.23
☐ 91 Mark Lewis	.50	.23
☐ 92 Gregg Jefferies	1.00	.45
☐ 93 Jose Guzman	.50	.23
☐ 94 Kenny Rogers	.50	.23
☐ 95 Mark Lemke	.50	.23
☐ 96 Mike Morgan	.50	.23
☐ 97 Andujar Cedeno	.50	.23
☐ 98 Orel Hershiser	1.00	.45
☐ 99 Greg Swindell	.50	.23
☐ 100 John Smoltz	1.50	.70
☐ 101 Pedro Martinez	2.50	1.10
☐ 102 Jim Thome	3.00	1.35
☐ 103 David Segui	.50	.23
☐ 104 Charles Nagy	1.00	.45
☐ 105 Shane Mack	.50	.23
☐ 106 John Jaha	.50	.23
☐ 107 Tom Candiotti	.50	.23
☐ 108 David Wells	.50	.23
☐ 109 Bobby Jones	1.00	.45
☐ 110 Bob Hamelin	.50	.23
☐ 111 Bernard Gilkey	1.00	.45
☐ 112 Chili Davis	1.00	.45
☐ 113 Todd Stottlemyre	.50	.23
☐ 114 Derek Bell	1.00	.45
☐ 115 Mark McLemore	.50	.23
☐ 116 Mark Whiten	.50	.23
☐ 117 Mike Devereaux	.50	.23
☐ 118 Terry Pendleton	1.00	.45
☐ 119 Pat Meares	.50	.23
☐ 120 Pete Harnisch	.50	.23
☐ 121 Moises Alou	1.00	.45
☐ 122 Jay Buhner	1.50	.70
☐ 123 Wes Chamberlain	.50	.23
☐ 124 Mike Perez	.50	.23
☐ 125 Devon White	.50	.23
☐ 126 Ivan Rodriguez	3.00	1.35
☐ 127 Don Slaught	.50	.23
☐ 128 John Valentin	1.00	.45
☐ 129 Jaime Navarro	.50	.23
☐ 130 Dave Magadan	.50	.23
☐ 131 Brady Anderson	1.50	.70
☐ 132 Juan Guzman	.50	.23
☐ 133 John Wetteland	1.00	.45
☐ 134 Dave Stewart	1.00	.45
☐ 135 Scott Servais	.50	.23
☐ 136 Ozzie Smith	3.00	1.35
☐ 137 Darrin Fletcher	.50	.23
☐ 138 Jose Mesa	1.00	.45
☐ 139 Wilson Alvarez	1.00	.45
☐ 140 Pete Incaviglia	.50	.23
☐ 141 Chris Hoiles	.50	.23
☐ 142 Darryl Hamilton	.50	.23
☐ 143 Chuck Finley	.50	.23
☐ 144 Archi Cianfrocco	.50	.23
☐ 145 Bill Wegman	.50	.23
☐ 146 Joey Cora	.50	.23
☐ 147 Darrell Whitmore	.50	.23
☐ 148 David Hulse	.50	.23
☐ 149 Jim Abbott	.50	.23
☐ 150 Curt Schilling	1.00	.45
☐ 151 Bill Swift	.50	.23
☐ 152 Tommy Greene	.50	.23
☐ 153 Roberto Mejia	.50	.23
☐ 154 Edgar Martinez	1.50	.70
☐ 155 Roger Pavlik	.50	.23
☐ 156 Randy Tomlin	.50	.23
☐ 157 J.T. Snow	1.00	.45
☐ 158 Bob Welch	.50	.23
☐ 159 Alan Trammell	1.50	.70
☐ 160 Ed Sprague	.50	.23
☐ 161 Ben McDonald	.50	.23
☐ 162 Derrick May	.50	.23
☐ 163 Roberto Kelly	.50	.23
☐ 164 Bryan Harvey	.50	.23
☐ 165 Ron Gant	.50	.23
☐ 166 Scott Erickson	.50	.23
☐ 167 Anthony Young	.50	.23
☐ 168 Scott Cooper	.50	.23
☐ 169 Rod Beck	1.00	.45
☐ 170 John Franco	.50	.23
☐ 171 Gary DiSarcina	.50	.23
☐ 172 Dave Fleming	.50	.23
☐ 173 Wade Boggs	2.50	1.10
☐ 174 Kevin Appier	1.00	.45
☐ 175 Jose Bautista	.50	.23
☐ 176 Wally Joyner	1.00	.45
☐ 177 Dean Palmer	1.00	.45
☐ 178 Tony Phillips	.50	.23
☐ 179 John Smiley	.50	.23
☐ 180 Charlie Hough	.50	.23
☐ 181 Scott Fletcher	.50	.23
☐ 182 Todd Van Poppel	.50	.23
☐ 183 Mike Blowers	.50	.23
☐ 184 Willie McGee	.50	.23
☐ 185 Paul Sorrento	.50	.23
☐ 186 Eric Young	1.00	.45
☐ 187 Bret Barberie	.50	.23
☐ 188 Manuel Lee	.50	.23
☐ 189 Jeff Branson	.50	.23
☐ 190 Jim Deshaies	.50	.23
☐ 191 Ken Caminiti	2.50	1.10
☐ 192 Tim Raines	.50	.23
☐ 193 Joe Grahe	.50	.23
☐ 194 Hipolito Pichardo	.50	.23
☐ 195 Denny Neagle	1.00	.45
☐ 196 Jeff Gardner	.50	.23
☐ 197 Mike Benjamin	.50	.23
☐ 198 Milt Thompson	.50	.23
☐ 199 Bruce Ruffin	.50	.23
☐ 200 Chris Hammond UER (Back of card has Mariners; should be Marlins)	.50	.23
☐ 201 Tony Gwynn FIN	6.00	2.70
☐ 202 Robin Ventura FIN	1.00	.45
☐ 203 Frank Thomas FIN	10.00	4.50
☐ 204 Kirby Puckett FIN	5.00	2.20
☐ 205 Roberto Alomar FIN	2.50	1.10
☐ 206 Dennis Eckersley FIN	1.50	.70
☐ 207 Joe Carter FIN	1.50	.70
☐ 208 Albert Belle FIN	3.00	1.35
☐ 209 Greg Maddux FIN	8.00	3.60
☐ 210 Ryne Sandberg FIN	3.00	1.35
☐ 211 Juan Gonzalez FIN	6.00	2.70
☐ 212 Jeff Bagwell FIN	5.00	2.20
☐ 213 Randy Johnson FIN	2.50	1.10
☐ 214 Matt Williams FIN	1.50	.70
☐ 215 Dave Winfield FIN	1.50	.70
☐ 216 Larry Walker FIN	2.50	1.10
☐ 217 Roger Clemens FIN	5.00	2.20
☐ 218 Kenny Lofton FIN	3.00	1.35
☐ 219 Cecil Fielder FIN	1.00	.45
☐ 220 Darren Daulton FIN	1.00	.45
☐ 221 John Olerud FIN	1.00	.45
☐ 222 Jose Canseco FIN	1.50	.70
☐ 223 Rickey Henderson FIN	1.50	.70
☐ 224 Fred McGriff FIN	1.50	.70
☐ 225 Gary Sheffield FIN	2.50	1.10
☐ 226 Jack McDowell FIN	.50	.23
☐ 227 Rafael Palmeiro FIN	1.50	.70
☐ 228 Travis Fryman FIN	1.00	.45
☐ 229 Marquis Grissom FIN	1.00	.45
☐ 230 Barry Bonds FIN	3.00	1.35
☐ 231 Carlos Baerga FIN	1.00	.45
☐ 232 Ken Griffey Jr. FIN	12.00	5.50
☐ 233 David Justice FIN	2.50	1.10
☐ 234 Bobby Bonilla FIN	1.00	.45
☐ 235 Cal Ripken FIN	10.00	4.50
☐ 236 Sammy Sosa FIN	2.50	1.10
☐ 237 Len Dykstra FIN	1.00	.45
☐ 238 Will Clark FIN	1.50	.70
☐ 239 Paul Molitor FIN	2.50	1.10
☐ 240 Barry Larkin FIN	1.50	.70
☐ 241 Bo Jackson	1.00	.45
☐ 242 Mitch Williams	.50	.23
☐ 243 Ron Darling	.50	.23
☐ 244 Darryl Kile	1.00	.45
☐ 245 Geronimo Berroa	1.00	.45
☐ 246 Gregg Olson	.50	.23
☐ 247 Brian Harper	.50	.23
☐ 248 Rheal Cormier	.50	.23
☐ 249 Rey Sanchez	.50	.23
☐ 250 Jeff Fassero	.50	.23
☐ 251 Sandy Alomar	1.00	.45
☐ 252 Chris Bosio	.50	.23
☐ 253 Andy Stankiewicz	.50	.23
☐ 254 Harold Baines	1.00	.45
☐ 255 Andy Ashby	.50	.23
☐ 256 Tyler Green	.50	.23
☐ 257 Kevin Brown	1.00	.45
☐ 258 Mo Vaughn	3.00	1.35
☐ 259 Mike Harkey	.50	.23
☐ 260 Dave Henderson	.50	.23
☐ 261 Kent Hrbek	1.00	.45
☐ 262 Darrin Jackson	.50	.23
☐ 263 Bob Wickman	.50	.23
☐ 264 Spike Owen	.50	.23
☐ 265 Todd Jones	.50	.23
☐ 266 Pat Borders	.50	.23
☐ 267 Tom Glavine	1.50	.70
☐ 268 Dave Nilsson	1.00	.45
☐ 269 Rich Batchelor	.50	.23
☐ 270 Delino DeShields	.50	.23
☐ 271 Felix Fermin	.50	.23
☐ 272 Orestes Destrade	.50	.23
☐ 273 Mickey Morandini	.50	.23
☐ 274 Otis Nixon	1.00	.45
☐ 275 Ellis Burks	1.00	.45
☐ 276 Greg Gagne	.50	.23
☐ 277 John Doherty	.50	.23
☐ 278 Julio Franco	1.00	.45
☐ 279 Bernie Williams	2.50	1.10
☐ 280 Rick Aguilera	.50	.23
☐ 281 Mickey Tettleton	.50	.23
☐ 282 David Nied	.50	.23
☐ 283 Johnny Ruffin	.50	.23
☐ 284 Dan Wilson	1.00	.45
☐ 285 Omar Vizquel	1.00	.45
☐ 286 Willie Banks	.50	.23
☐ 287 Erik Pappas	.50	.23
☐ 288 Cal Eldred	.50	.23
☐ 289 Bobby Witt	.50	.23
☐ 290 Luis Gonzalez	.50	.23
☐ 291 Greg Pirkl	.50	.23
☐ 292 Alex Cole	.50	.23
☐ 293 Ricky Bones	.50	.23
☐ 294 Denis Boucher	.50	.23
☐ 295 John Burkett	.50	.23
☐ 296 Steve Trachsel	1.00	.45
☐ 297 Ricky Jordan	.50	.23
☐ 298 Mark Dewey	.50	.23
☐ 299 Jimmy Key	1.00	.45
☐ 300 Mike Macfarlane	.50	.23
☐ 301 Tim Belcher	.50	.23
☐ 302 Carlos Reyes	.50	.23
☐ 303 Greg A. Harris	.50	.23
☐ 304 Brian Anderson	1.00	.45
☐ 305 Terry Mulholland	.50	.23
☐ 306 Felix Jose	.50	.23
☐ 307 Darren Holmes	.50	.23
☐ 308 Jose Rijo	.50	.23
☐ 309 Paul Wagner	.50	.23
☐ 310 Bob Scanlan	.50	.23
☐ 311 Mike Jackson	.50	.23
☐ 312 Jose Vizcaino	.50	.23
☐ 313 Rob Butler	.50	.23
☐ 314 Kevin Seitzer	.50	.23
☐ 315 Geronimo Pena	.50	.23
☐ 316 Hector Carrasco	.50	.23
☐ 317 Eddie Murray	2.50	1.10
☐ 318 Roger Salkeld	.50	.23
☐ 319 Todd Hundley	1.00	.45
☐ 320 Danny Jackson	.50	.23
☐ 321 Kevin Young	.50	.23
☐ 322 Mike Greenwell	.50	.23
☐ 323 Kevin Mitchell	.50	.23
☐ 324 Chuck Knoblauch	2.50	1.10
☐ 325 Danny Tartabull	.50	.23
☐ 326 Vince Coleman	.50	.23
☐ 327 Marvin Freeman	.50	.23
☐ 328 Andy Benes	1.00	.45
☐ 329 Mike Kelly	.50	.23
☐ 330 Karl Rhodes	.50	.23
☐ 331 Allen Watson	.50	.23
☐ 332 Damion Easley	.50	.23
☐ 333 Reggie Jefferson	1.00	.45
☐ 334 Kevin McReynolds	.50	.23
☐ 335 Arthur Rhodes	.50	.23
☐ 336 Brian R. Hunter	.50	.23
☐ 337 Tom Browning	.50	.23
☐ 338 Pedro Munoz	.50	.23
☐ 339 Billy Ripken	.50	.23
☐ 340 Gene Harris	.50	.23
☐ 341 Fernando Vina	.50	.23
☐ 342 Sean Berry	.50	.23
☐ 343 Pedro Astacio	.50	.23
☐ 344 B.J. Surhoff	.50	.23
☐ 345 Doug Drabek	.50	.23
☐ 346 Jody Reed	.50	.23
☐ 347 Ray Lankford	1.50	.70
☐ 348 Steve Farr	.50	.23
☐ 349 Eric Anthony	.50	.23
☐ 350 Pete Smith	.50	.23
☐ 351 Lee Smith	1.00	.45
☐ 352 Mariano Duncan	.50	.23
☐ 353 Doug Strange	.50	.23

	MINT	NRMT
☐ 354 Tim Bogar	.50	.23
☐ 355 Dave Weathers	.50	.23
☐ 356 Eric Karros	1.00	.45
☐ 357 Randy Myers	.50	.23
☐ 358 Chad Curtis	.50	.23
☐ 359 Steve Avery	.50	.23
☐ 360 Brian Jordan	1.00	.45
☐ 361 Tim Wallach	.50	.23
☐ 362 Pedro Martinez	2.50	1.10
☐ 363 Bip Roberts	.50	.23
☐ 364 Lou Whitaker	1.00	.45
☐ 365 Luis Polonia	.50	.23
☐ 366 Benny Santiago	.50	.23
☐ 367 Brett Butler	1.00	.45
☐ 368 Shawon Dunston	.50	.23
☐ 369 Kelly Stinnett	.50	.23
☐ 370 Chris Turner	.50	.23
☐ 371 Ruben Sierra	.50	.23
☐ 372 Greg A. Harris	.50	.23
☐ 373 Xavier Hernandez	.50	.23
☐ 374 Howard Johnson	.50	.23
☐ 375 Duane Ward	.50	.23
☐ 376 Roberto Hernandez	1.00	.45
☐ 377 Scott Leius	.50	.23
☐ 378 Dave Valle	.50	.23
☐ 379 Sid Fernandez	.50	.23
☐ 380 Doug Jones	.50	.23
☐ 381 Zane Smith	.50	.23
☐ 382 Craig Biggio	1.50	.70
☐ 383 Rick White	.50	.23
☐ 384 Tom Pagnozzi	.50	.23
☐ 385 Chris James	.50	.23
☐ 386 Bret Boone	.50	.23
☐ 387 Jeff Montgomery	1.00	.45
☐ 388 Chad Kreuter	.50	.23
☐ 389 Greg Hibbard	.50	.23
☐ 390 Mark Grace	1.50	.70
☐ 391 Phil Leftwich	.50	.23
☐ 392 Don Mattingly	4.00	1.80
☐ 393 Ozzie Guillen	.50	.23
☐ 394 Gary Gaetti	1.00	.45
☐ 395 Erik Hanson	.50	.23
☐ 396 Scott Brosius	.50	.23
☐ 397 Tom Gordon	.50	.23
☐ 398 Bill Gullickson	.50	.23
☐ 399 Matt Mieske	.50	.23
☐ 400 Pat Hentgen	1.00	.45
☐ 401 Walt Weiss	.50	.23
☐ 402 Greg Blosser	.50	.23
☐ 403 Stan Javier	.50	.23
☐ 404 Doug Henry	.50	.23
☐ 405 Ramon Martinez	1.00	.45
☐ 406 Frank Viola	.50	.23
☐ 407 Mike Hampton	1.00	.45
☐ 408 Andy Van Slyke	1.00	.45
☐ 409 Bobby Ayala	.50	.23
☐ 410 Todd Zeile	.50	.23
☐ 411 Jay Bell	1.00	.45
☐ 412 Denny Martinez	1.00	.45
☐ 413 Mark Portugal	.50	.23
☐ 414 Bobby Munoz	.50	.23
☐ 415 Kirt Manwaring	.50	.23
☐ 416 John Kruk	1.00	.45
☐ 417 Trevor Hoffman	1.00	.45
☐ 418 Chris Sabo	.50	.23
☐ 419 Bret Saberhagen	.50	.23
☐ 420 Chris Nabholz	.50	.23
☐ 421 James Mouton FIN	1.00	.45
☐ 422 Tony Tarasco FIN	.50	.23
☐ 423 Carlos Delgado FIN	1.50	.70
☐ 424 Rondell White FIN	1.00	.45
☐ 425 Javier Lopez FIN	1.50	.70
☐ 426 Chan Ho Park FIN	8.00	3.60
☐ 427 Cliff Floyd FIN	1.00	.45
☐ 428 Dave Staton FIN	.50	.23
☐ 429 J.R. Phillips FIN	.50	.23
☐ 430 Manny Ramirez FIN	3.00	1.35
☐ 431 Kurt Abbott FIN	.50	.23
☐ 432 Melvin Nieves FIN	1.00	.45
☐ 433 Alex Gonzalez FIN	1.00	.45
☐ 434 Rick Helling FIN	.50	.23
☐ 435 Danny Bautista FIN	.50	.23
☐ 436 Matt Walbeck FIN	.50	.23
☐ 437 Ryan Klesko FIN	1.50	.70
☐ 438 Steve Karsay FIN	.50	.23
☐ 439 Salomon Torres FIN	.50	.23
☐ 440 Scott Ruffcorn FIN	.50	.23

1994 Finest Refractors

The 1994 Topps Finest Refractors baseball set consists of two series of 220 cards each, for a total of 440 cards. These special cards were inserted at a rate of one in every nine packs. They are identical to the basic Finest card except for a more intense luster and 3-D appearance.

	MINT	NRMT
COMPLETE SET (440)	2800.00	1250.00
COMPLETE SERIES 1 (220)	1400.00	650.00
COMPLETE SERIES 2 (220)	1400.00	650.00
COMMON CARD (1-440)	4.00	1.80
*STARS: 5X TO 10X BASIC CARDS		
*ROOKIES: 2.5X to 5X BASIC CARDS.		

1994 Finest Jumbos

Inserted one per Finest box, this 80-card over-sized set (3 1/2" by 5") was issued in two series of 40. Each of the 80 cards is identical in design to the special "Finest" cards from the basic Finest set except for the size. The "Finest" subset was designated to showcase top rookies, prospects and veterans. The card numbering is the same as the corresponding basic issue cards. Hence, the first series comprises of cards 1-20 and 201-220. The second series is cards 221-240 and 421-440.

	MINT	NRMT
COMPLETE SET (80)	350.00	160.00
COMPLETE SERIES 1 (40)	200.00	90.00
COMPLETE SERIES 2 (40)	150.00	70.00
COMMON CARD (1-20/201-220)	1.00	.45
COMMON CARD (221-240/421-440)	1.00	.45
*STARS: 1.5X to 3X BASIC CARDS		

1995 Finest

Consisting of 330 standard-size cards, this set was issued in series of 220 and 110. A protective film, designed to keep the card from scratching and to maintain original gloss, covers the front. With the Finest logo at the top, a silver baseball diamond design surrounded by green (field) form the background to an action photo. Horizontally designed backs have a photo to the right with statistical information to the left. A Finest Moment, or career highlight, is also included. Rookie Cards in this set include Bobby Higginson and Hideo Nomo.

	MINT	NRMT
COMPLETE SET (330)	120.00	55.00
COMPLETE SERIES 1 (220)	80.00	36.00
COMPLETE SERIES 2 (110)	40.00	18.00
COMMON CARD (1-330)	.40	.18

	MINT	NRMT
☐ 1 Raul Mondesi	1.25	.55
☐ 2 Kurt Abbott	.40	.18
☐ 3 Chris Gomez	.40	.18
☐ 4 Manny Ramirez	2.00	.90
☐ 5 Rondell White	1.25	.55
☐ 6 William VanLandingham	.40	.18
☐ 7 Jon Lieber	.40	.18
☐ 8 Ryan Klesko	1.25	.55
☐ 9 John Hudek	.40	.18
☐ 10 Joey Hamilton	.75	.35
☐ 11 Bob Hamelin	.40	.18
☐ 12 Brian Anderson	.40	.18
☐ 13 Mike Lieberthal	.40	.18
☐ 14 Rico Brogna	.40	.18
☐ 15 Rusty Greer	2.00	.90
☐ 16 Carlos Delgado	.75	.35
☐ 17 Jim Edmonds	2.00	.90
☐ 18 Steve Trachsel	.40	.18
☐ 19 Matt Walbeck	.40	.18
☐ 20 Armando Benitez	.40	.18
☐ 21 Steve Karsay	.40	.18
☐ 22 Jose Oliva	.40	.18
☐ 23 Cliff Floyd	.75	.35
☐ 24 Kevin Foster	.40	.18
☐ 25 Javier Lopez	1.25	.55
☐ 26 Jose Valentin	.75	.35
☐ 27 James Mouton	.40	.18
☐ 28 Hector Carrasco	.40	.18
☐ 29 Orlando Miller	.40	.18
☐ 30 Garret Anderson	1.25	.55
☐ 31 Marvin Freeman	.40	.18
☐ 32 Brett Butler	.75	.35
☐ 33 Roberto Kelly	.40	.18
☐ 34 Rod Beck	.40	.18
☐ 35 Jose Rijo	.40	.18
☐ 36 Edgar Martinez	1.25	.55
☐ 37 Jim Thome	2.00	.90
☐ 38 Rick Wilkins	.40	.18
☐ 39 Wally Joyner	.75	.35
☐ 40 Wil Cordero	.40	.18
☐ 41 Tommy Greene	.40	.18
☐ 42 Travis Fryman	.75	.35
☐ 43 Don Slaught	.40	.18
☐ 44 Brady Anderson	1.25	.55
☐ 45 Matt Williams	1.25	.55
☐ 46 Rene Arocha	.40	.18
☐ 47 Rickey Henderson	1.25	.55
☐ 48 Mike Mussina	2.00	.90
☐ 49 Greg McMichael	.40	.18
☐ 50 Jody Reed	.40	.18
☐ 51 Tino Martinez	2.00	.90
☐ 52 Dave Clark	.40	.18
☐ 53 John Valentin	.75	.35
☐ 54 Bret Boone	.40	.18
☐ 55 Walt Weiss	.40	.18
☐ 56 Kenny Lofton	2.50	1.10
☐ 57 Scott Leius	.40	.18
☐ 58 Eric Karros	.75	.35
☐ 59 John Olerud	.75	.35
☐ 60 Chris Hoiles	.40	.18
☐ 61 Sandy Alomar Jr.	.40	.18
☐ 62 Tim Wallach	.40	.18
☐ 63 Cal Eldred	.40	.18
☐ 64 Tom Glavine	1.25	.55
☐ 65 Mark Grace	1.25	.55
☐ 66 Rey Sanchez	.40	.18
☐ 67 Bobby Ayala	.40	.18
☐ 68 Dante Bichette	1.25	.55
☐ 69 Andres Galarraga	1.25	.55
☐ 70 Chuck Carr	.40	.18
☐ 71 Bobby Witt	.40	.18
☐ 72 Steve Avery	.40	.18
☐ 73 Bobby Jones	.75	.35
☐ 74 Delino DeShields	.40	.18
☐ 75 Kevin Tapani	.40	.18
☐ 76 Randy Johnson	2.00	.90
☐ 77 David Nied	.40	.18
☐ 78 Pat Hentgen	.75	.35
☐ 79 Tim Salmon	2.00	.90
☐ 80 Todd Zeile	.40	.18
☐ 81 John Wetteland	.75	.35
☐ 82 Albert Belle	2.50	1.10
☐ 83 Ben McDonald	.40	.18
☐ 84 Bobby Munoz	.40	.18
☐ 85 Bip Roberts	.40	.18
☐ 86 Mo Vaughn	2.50	1.10
☐ 87 Chuck Finley	.75	.35
☐ 88 Chuck Knoblauch	2.00	.90
☐ 89 Frank Thomas	8.00	3.60
☐ 90 Danny Tartabull	.40	.18
☐ 91 Dean Palmer	.75	.35
☐ 92 Len Dykstra	.75	.35
☐ 93 J.R. Phillips	.40	.18
☐ 94 Tom Candiotti	.40	.18
☐ 95 Marquis Grissom	.75	.35
☐ 96 Barry Larkin	1.25	.55
☐ 97 Bryan Harvey	.40	.18
☐ 98 David Justice	2.00	.90
☐ 99 David Cone	.75	.35
☐ 100 Wade Boggs	2.00	.90
☐ 101 Jason Bere	.40	.18
☐ 102 Hal Morris	.40	.18
☐ 103 Fred McGriff	1.25	.55
☐ 104 Bobby Bonilla	.75	.35
☐ 105 Jay Buhner	1.25	.55
☐ 106 Allen Watson	.40	.18
☐ 107 Mickey Tettleton	.40	.18
☐ 108 Kevin Appier	.75	.35
☐ 109 Ivan Rodriguez	2.50	1.10
☐ 110 Carlos Garcia	.40	.18
☐ 111 Andy Benes	.40	.18
☐ 112 Eddie Murray	2.00	.90
☐ 113 Mike Piazza	6.00	2.70
☐ 114 Greg Vaughn	.40	.18
☐ 115 Paul Molitor	2.00	.90
☐ 116 Terry Steinbach	.75	.35
☐ 117 Jeff Bagwell	4.00	1.80
☐ 118 Ken Griffey Jr.	10.00	4.50
☐ 119 Gary Sheffield	2.00	.90
☐ 120 Cal Ripken	8.00	3.60
☐ 121 Jeff Kent	.40	.18
☐ 122 Jay Bell	.75	.35
☐ 123 Will Clark	1.25	.55
☐ 124 Cecil Fielder	.75	.35
☐ 125 Alex Fernandez	.75	.35
☐ 126 Don Mattingly	3.00	1.35
☐ 127 Reggie Sanders	.40	.18
☐ 128 Moises Alou	.75	.35
☐ 129 Craig Biggio	1.25	.55
☐ 130 Eddie Williams	.40	.18
☐ 131 John Franco	.40	.18
☐ 132 John Kruk	.75	.35
☐ 133 Jeff King	.75	.35

☐ 134 Royce Clayton .40 .18
☐ 135 Doug Drabek .40 .18
☐ 136 Ray Lankford .75 .35
☐ 137 Roberto Alomar 2.00 .90
☐ 138 Todd Hundley .75 .35
☐ 139 Alex Cole .40 .18
☐ 140 Shawon Dunston .40 .18
☐ 141 John Roper .40 .18
☐ 142 Mark Langston .40 .18
☐ 143 Tom Pagnozzi .40 .18
☐ 144 Wilson Alvarez .75 .35
☐ 145 Scott Cooper .40 .18
☐ 146 Kevin Mitchell .75 .35
☐ 147 Mark Whiten .40 .18
☐ 148 Jeff Conine .75 .35
☐ 149 Chili Davis .75 .35
☐ 150 Luis Gonzalez .40 .18
☐ 151 Juan Guzman .40 .18
☐ 152 Mike Greenwell .40 .18
☐ 153 Mike Henneman .40 .18
☐ 154 Rick Aguilera .40 .18
☐ 155 Dennis Eckersley 1.25 .55
☐ 156 Darrin Fletcher .40 .18
☐ 157 Darren Lewis .40 .18
☐ 158 Juan Gonzalez 5.00 2.20
☐ 159 Dave Hollins .40 .18
☐ 160 Jimmy Key .75 .35
☐ 161 Roberto Hernandez .40 .18
☐ 162 Randy Myers .40 .18
☐ 163 Joe Carter 1.25 .55
☐ 164 Darren Daulton .75 .35
☐ 165 Mike Macfarlane .40 .18
☐ 166 Bret Saberhagen .40 .18
☐ 167 Kirby Puckett 4.00 1.80
☐ 168 Lance Johnson .40 .18
☐ 169 Mark McGwire 4.00 1.80
☐ 170 Jose Canseco 1.25 .55
☐ 171 Mike Stanley .40 .18
☐ 172 Lee Smith .75 .35
☐ 173 Robin Ventura .75 .35
☐ 174 Greg Gagne .40 .18
☐ 175 Brian McRae .40 .18
☐ 176 Mike Bordick .40 .18
☐ 177 Rafael Palmeiro 1.25 .55
☐ 178 Kenny Rogers .40 .18
☐ 179 Chad Curtis .40 .18
☐ 180 Devon White .75 .35
☐ 181 Paul O'Neill .75 .35
☐ 182 Ken Caminiti 2.00 .90
☐ 183 Dave Nilsson .75 .35
☐ 184 Tim Naehring .40 .18
☐ 185 Roger Clemens 4.00 1.80
☐ 186 Otis Nixon .40 .18
☐ 187 Tim Raines .40 .18
☐ 188 Denny Martinez .75 .35
☐ 189 Pedro Martinez 2.00 .90
☐ 190 Jim Abbott .40 .18
☐ 191 Ryan Thompson .40 .18
☐ 192 Barry Bonds 2.50 1.10
☐ 193 Joe Girardi .40 .18
☐ 194 Steve Finley .75 .35
☐ 195 John Jaha .40 .18
☐ 196 Tony Gwynn 5.00 2.20
☐ 197 Sammy Sosa 2.00 .90
☐ 198 John Burkett .40 .18
☐ 199 Carlos Baerga .75 .35
☐ 200 Ramon Martinez .75 .35
☐ 201 Aaron Sele .40 .18
☐ 202 Eduardo Perez .40 .18
☐ 203 Alan Trammell 1.25 .55
☐ 204 Orlando Merced .40 .18
☐ 205 Deion Sanders 2.00 .90
☐ 206 Robb Nen .40 .18
☐ 207 Jack McDowell .40 .18
☐ 208 Ruben Sierra .40 .18
☐ 209 Bernie Williams 2.00 .90
☐ 210 Kevin Seitzer .40 .18
☐ 211 Charles Nagy .75 .35
☐ 212 Tony Phillips .40 .18
☐ 213 Greg Maddux 6.00 2.70
☐ 214 Jeff Montgomery .75 .35
☐ 215 Larry Walker 2.00 .90
☐ 216 Andy Van Slyke .75 .35
☐ 217 Ozzie Smith 2.50 1.10
☐ 218 Geronimo Pena .40 .18
☐ 219 Gregg Jefferies .75 .35
☐ 220 Lou Whitaker .75 .35
☐ 221 Chipper Jones 6.00 2.70
☐ 222 Benji Gil .40 .18
☐ 223 Tony Phillips .40 .18
☐ 224 Trevor Wilson .40 .18
☐ 225 Tony Tarasco .40 .18
☐ 226 Roberto Petagine .40 .18
☐ 227 Mike Macfarlane .40 .18
☐ 228 Hideo Nomo UER 15.00 6.75
(In 3rd line agianst)
☐ 229 Mark McLemore .40 .18
☐ 230 Ron Gant .75 .35
☐ 231 Andujar Cedeno .40 .18
☐ 232 Mike Mimbs .40 .18
☐ 233 Jim Abbott .40 .18
☐ 234 Ricky Bones .40 .18
☐ 235 Marty Cordova 1.25 .55
☐ 236 Mark Johnson .40 .18
☐ 237 Marquis Grissom .75 .35
☐ 238 Tom Henke .40 .18
☐ 239 Terry Pendleton .75 .35
☐ 240 John Wetteland .75 .35
☐ 241 Lee Smith .75 .35
☐ 242 Jaime Navarro .40 .18
☐ 243 Luis Alicea .40 .18
☐ 244 Scott Cooper .40 .18
☐ 245 Gary Gaetti .75 .35
☐ 246 Edgardo Alfonzo UER 2.00 .90
(Incomplete career BA)
☐ 247 Brad Clontz .40 .18
☐ 248 Dave Mlicki .40 .18
☐ 249 Dave Winfield 1.25 .55
☐ 250 Mark Grudzielanek 2.50 1.10
☐ 251 Alex Gonzalez .75 .35
☐ 252 Kevin Brown .75 .35
☐ 253 Esteban Loaiza .40 .18
☐ 254 Vaughn Eshelman .40 .18
☐ 255 Bill Swift .40 .18
☐ 256 Brian McRae .40 .18
☐ 257 Bobby Higginson 5.00 2.20
☐ 258 Jack McDowell .40 .18
☐ 259 Scott Stahoviak .40 .18
☐ 260 Jon Nunnally .75 .35
☐ 261 Charlie Hayes .40 .18
☐ 262 Jacob Brumfield .40 .18
☐ 263 Chad Curtis .40 .18
☐ 264 Heathcliff Slocumb .40 .18
☐ 265 Mark Whiten .40 .18
☐ 266 Mickey Tettleton .40 .18
☐ 267 Jose Mesa .40 .18
☐ 268 Doug Jones .40 .18
☐ 269 Trevor Hoffman .75 .35
☐ 270 Paul Sorrento .40 .18
☐ 271 Shane Andrews .40 .18
☐ 272 Brett Butler .75 .35
☐ 273 Curtis Goodwin .40 .18
☐ 274 Larry Walker 2.00 .90
☐ 275 Phil Plantier .40 .18
☐ 276 Ken Hill .40 .18
☐ 277 Vinny Castilla UER 1.25 .55
Rockies spelled Rockie
☐ 278 Billy Ashley .40 .18
☐ 279 Derek Jeter 6.00 2.70
☐ 280 Bob Tewksbury .40 .18
☐ 281 Jose Offerman .40 .18
☐ 282 Glenallen Hill .40 .18
☐ 283 Tony Fernandez .40 .18
☐ 284 Mike Devereaux .40 .18
☐ 285 John Burkett .40 .18
☐ 286 Geronimo Berroa .40 .18
☐ 287 Quilvio Veras .40 .18
☐ 288 Jason Bates .40 .18
☐ 289 Lee Tinsley .40 .18
☐ 290 Derek Bell .75 .35
☐ 291 Jeff Fassero .40 .18
☐ 292 Ray Durham .75 .35
☐ 293 Chad Ogea .40 .18
☐ 294 Bill Pulsipher .75 .35
☐ 295 Phil Nevin .40 .18
☐ 296 Carlos Perez .75 .35
☐ 297 Roberto Kelly .40 .18
☐ 298 Tim Wakefield .40 .18
☐ 299 Jeff Manto .40 .18
☐ 300 Brian Hunter 1.25 .55
☐ 301 C.J. Nitkowski .40 .18
☐ 302 Dustin Hermanson .40 .18
☐ 303 John Mabry 1.25 .55
☐ 304 Orel Hershiser .75 .35
☐ 305 Ron Villone .40 .18
☐ 306 Sean Bergman .40 .18
☐ 307 Tom Goodwin .40 .18
☐ 308 Al Reyes .40 .18
☐ 309 Todd Stottlemyre .40 .18
☐ 310 Rich Becker .40 .18
☐ 311 Joey Cora .75 .35
☐ 312 Ed Sprague .40 .18
☐ 313 John Smoltz UER 1.25 .55
(3rd line; from spelled as form)
☐ 314 Frank Castillo .40 .18
☐ 315 Chris Hammond .40 .18
☐ 316 Ismael Valdes .75 .35
☐ 317 Pete Harnisch .40 .18
☐ 318 Bernard Gilkey .75 .35
☐ 319 John Kruk .75 .35
☐ 320 Marc Newfield .75 .35
☐ 321 Brian Johnson .40 .18
☐ 322 Mark Portugal .40 .18
☐ 323 David Hulse .40 .18
☐ 324 Luis Ortiz UER .40 .18
(Below spelled beloe)
☐ 325 Mike Benjamin .40 .18
☐ 326 Brian Jordan .75 .35
☐ 327 Shawn Green .75 .35
☐ 328 Joe Oliver .40 .18
☐ 329 Felipe Lira .40 .18
☐ 330 Andre Dawson 1.25 .55

1995 Finest Refractors

This set is a parallel to the basic Finest set, including the use of protective coating, the difference can be found in the refractive sheen. The cards were inserted at a rate of one in 12 packs.

	MINT	NRMT
COMPLETE SET (330)	4500.00	2000.00
COMPLETE SERIES 1 (220)	3500.00	1600.00
COMPLETE SERIES 2 (110)	1000.00	450.00
COMMON CARD (1-330)	10.00	4.50

*STARS: 12.5X TO 25X BASIC CARDS
*YOUNG STARS: 6X TO 12X BASIC CARDS

1995 Finest Flame Throwers

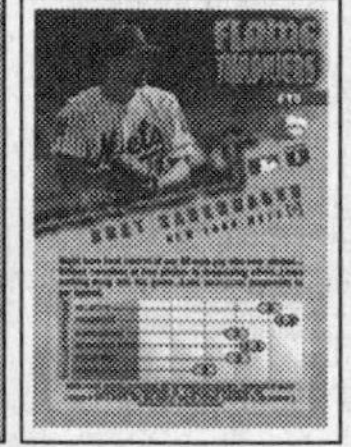

Randomly inserted in first series packs at a rate of 1:48, this nine-card set showcases strikeout leaders who bring on the heat. With a protective coating, a player photo is superimposed over a fiery orange background. The backs have a player photo with skills ratings such as velocity.

	MINT	NRMT
COMPLETE SET (9)	40.00	18.00
COMMON CARD (1-9)	3.00	1.35

☐ FT1 Jason Bere 3.00 1.35
☐ FT2 Roger Clemens 25.00 11.00
☐ FT3 Juan Guzman 3.00 1.35
☐ FT4 John Hudek 3.00 1.35
☐ FT5 Randy Johnson 12.00 5.50
☐ FT6 Pedro Martinez 8.00 3.60
☐ FT7 Jose Rijo 3.00 1.35
☐ FT8 Bret Saberhagen 3.00 1.35
☐ FT9 John Wetteland 4.00 1.80

1995 Finest Power Kings

Randomly inserted in series one packs at a rate of one in 24, Power Kings is an 18-card set highlighting top sluggers. With a protective coating, the fronts feature chromium technology that allows the player photo to be rther enhanced as if to jump out from a blue lightning olt background. The horizontal backs contain two small hotos and power production figures.

	MINT	NRMT
OMPLETE SET (18)	200.00	90.00
OMMON CARD (1-18)	4.00	1.80
☐ PK1 Bob Hamelin	4.00	1.80
☐ PK2 Raul Mondesi	6.00	2.70
☐ PK3 Ryan Klesko	6.00	2.70
☐ PK4 Carlos Delgado	6.00	2.70
☐ PK5 Manny Ramirez	10.00	4.50
☐ PK6 Mike Piazza	30.00	13.50
☐ PK7 Jeff Bagwell	20.00	9.00
☐ PK8 Mo Vaughn	12.00	5.50
☐ PK9 Frank Thomas	40.00	18.00
☐ PK10 Ken Griffey Jr.	50.00	22.00
☐ PK11 Albert Belle	12.00	5.50
☐ PK12 Sammy Sosa	10.00	4.50
☐ PK13 Dante Bichette	6.00	2.70
☐ PK14 Gary Sheffield	10.00	4.50
☐ PK15 Matt Williams	6.00	2.70
☐ PK16 Fred McGriff	6.00	2.70
☐ PK17 Barry Bonds	12.00	5.50
☐ PK18 Cecil Fielder	6.00	2.70

1995 Finest Bronze

vailable exclusively direct from Topps, this six-card set eatures 1994 league leaders. The fronts feature hromium metallized graphics, mounted on bronze and actory sealed in clear resin. The cards are numbered on he back "X of 6."

	MINT	NRMT
OMPLETE SET (6)	120.00	55.00
OMMON CARD (1-6)	5.00	2.20
☐ 1 Matt Williams	10.00	4.50
☐ 2 Tony Gwynn	20.00	9.00
☐ 3 Jeff Bagwell	20.00	9.00
☐ 4 Ken Griffey Jr.	40.00	18.00
☐ 5 Paul O'Neill	5.00	2.20
☐ 6 Frank Thomas	40.00	18.00

1996 Finest

The 1996 Finest set was issued in two series of 191 cards and 168 cards respectively, for a total of 359 cards. The six-card foil packs originally retailed for $5.00 each. A protective film, designed to keep the card from scratching and to maintain original gloss, covers the front. This product provides collectors with the opportunity to complete a number of sets within sets, each with a different degree of insertion. Each card is numbered twice to indicate the set count and the theme count. Series 1 set covers four distinct themes: Finest Phenoms, Finest Intimidators, Finest Gamers and Finest Sterling. Within the first three themes, some players will be common (bronze trim), some uncommon (silver) and some rare (gold). Finest Sterling consists of star players included within one of the other three themes, but featured with a new design and different photography. The breakdown for the player selection of common, uncommon and rare cards is completely random. There are 110 common, 55 uncommon (1:4 packs) and 25 rare cards (1:24 packs). Series 2 covers four distict themes also with common, uncommon and rare cards seeded at the same ratio. The four themes are: Finest Franchises which features 36 team leaders and bonafide superstars, Finest Additions which features 47 players who have switched teams in '96, Finest Prodigies which features 45 best up-and-coming players, and Finest Sterling with 39 top stars. In addition to the cards' special borders, each card will also have either "common," "uncommon", or "rare" written within the numbering box on the card backs to let collectors know which type of card they hold.

	MINT	NRMT
COMPLETE SET (359)	1150.00	430.00
COMPLETE SERIES 1 (191)	750.00	350.00
COMPLETE SERIES 2 (168)	400.00	180.00
COMP.BRONZE SET (220)	50.00	22.00
COMP.BRONZE SER.1 (110)	25.00	11.00
COMP.BRONZE SER.2 (110)	30.00	13.50
COMMON BRONZE	.25	.11
COMP.GOLD SET (48)	900.00	400.00
COMP.GOLD SER.1 (26)	600.00	275.00
COMP.GOLD SER.2 (22)	300.00	135.00
COMMON GOLD	8.00	3.60
COMP.SILVER SET (91)	230.00	105.00
COMP.SILVER SER.1 (55)	150.00	70.00
COMP.SILVER SER.2 (36)	80.00	36.00
COMMON SILVER	1.50	.70
☐ B5 Roberto Hernandez B	.50	.23
☐ B8 Terry Pendleton B	.50	.23
☐ B12 Ken Caminiti B	1.00	.45
☐ B15 Dan Miceli B	.25	.11
☐ B16 Chipper Jones B	3.00	1.35
☐ B17 John Wetteland B	.50	.23
☐ B19 Tim Naehring B	.25	.11
☐ B21 Eddie Murray B	1.00	.45
☐ B23 Kevin Appier B	.50	.23
☐ B24 Ken Griffey Jr. B	5.00	2.20
☐ B26 Brian McRae B	.25	.11
☐ B27 Pedro Martinez B	1.00	.45
☐ B28 Brian Jordan B	.50	.23
☐ B29 Mike Fetters B	.25	.11
☐ B30 Carlos Delgado B	.50	.23
☐ B31 Shane Reynolds B	.25	.11
☐ B32 Terry Steinbach B	.50	.23
☐ B34 Mark Leiter B	.25	.11
☐ B36 David Segui B	.25	.11
☐ B40 Fred McGriff B	.75	.35
☐ B44 Glenallen Hill B	.25	.11
☐ B45 Brady Anderson B	.75	.35
☐ B47 Jim Thome B	1.00	.45
☐ B48 Frank Thomas B	4.00	1.80
☐ B49 Chuck Knoblauch B	1.00	.45
☐ B50 Len Dykstra B	.50	.23
☐ B53 Tom Pagnozzi B	.25	.11
☐ B55 Ricky Bones B	.25	.11
☐ B56 David Justice B	.75	.35
☐ B57 Steve Avery B	.25	.11
☐ B58 Robby Thompson B	.25	.11
☐ B61 Tony Gwynn B	2.50	1.10
☐ B63 Denny Neagle B	.50	.23
☐ B67 Robin Ventura B	.50	.23
☐ B70 Kevin Seitzer B	.25	.11
☐ B71 Ramon Martinez B	.50	.23
☐ B75 Brian L.Hunter B	.50	.23
☐ B76 Alan Benes B	.50	.23
☐ B80 Ozzie Guillen B	.25	.11
☐ B82 Benji Gil B	.25	.11
☐ B85 Todd Hundley B	.50	.23
☐ B87 Pat Hentgen B	.50	.23
☐ B89 Chuck Finley B	.50	.23
☐ B92 Derek Jeter B	3.00	1.35
☐ B93 Paul O'Neill B	.50	.23
☐ B94 Darrin Fletcher B	.25	.11
☐ B96 Delino DeShields B	.25	.11
☐ B97 Tim Salmon B	1.00	.45
☐ B98 John Olerud B	.50	.23
☐ B101 Tim Wakefield B	.25	.11
☐ B103 Dave Stevens B	.25	.11
☐ B104 Orlando Merced B	.25	.11
☐ B106 Jay Bell B	.25	.11
☐ B107 John Burkett B	.25	.11
☐ B108 Chris Hoiles B	.25	.11
☐ B110 Dave Nilsson B	.25	.11
☐ B111 Rod Beck B	.25	.11
☐ B113 Mike Piazza B	3.00	1.35
☐ B114 Mark Langston B	.25	.11
☐ B116 Rico Brogna B	.25	.11
☐ B118 Tom Goodwin B	.25	.11
☐ B119 Bryan Rekar B	.25	.11
☐ B120 David Cone B	.50	.23
☐ B122 Andy Pettitte B	1.25	.55
☐ B123 Chili Davis B	.50	.23
☐ B124 John Smoltz B	.50	.23
☐ B125 Heathcliff Slocumb B	.25	.11
☐ B126 Dante Bichette B	.75	.35
☐ B128 Alex Gonzalez B	.25	.11
☐ B129 Jeff Montgomery B	.25	.11
☐ B131 Denny Martinez B	.50	.23
☐ B132 Mel Rojas B	.25	.11
☐ B133 Derek Bell B	.50	.23
☐ B134 Trevor Hoffman B	.50	.23
☐ B136 Darren Daulton B	.50	.23
☐ B137 Pete Schourek B	.25	.11
☐ B138 Phil Nevin B	.25	.11
☐ B139 Andres Galarraga B	.75	.35
☐ B140 Chad Fonville B	.25	.11
☐ B144 J.T. Snow B	.50	.23
☐ B146 Barry Bonds B	1.25	.55
☐ B147 Orel Hershiser B	.50	.23
☐ B148 Quilvio Veras B	.25	.11
☐ B149 Will Clark B	.75	.35
☐ B150 Jose Rijo B	.25	.11
☐ B152 Travis Fryman B	.50	.23
☐ B154 Alex Fernandez B	.25	.11
☐ B155 Wade Boggs B	.75	.35
☐ B156 Troy Percival B	.50	.23
☐ B157 Moises Alou B	.50	.23
☐ B158 Javy Lopez B	.50	.23
☐ B159 Jason Giambi B	.50	.23
☐ B162 Mark McGwire B	2.00	.90
☐ B163 Eric Karros B	.50	.23
☐ B166 Mickey Tettleton B	.25	.11
☐ B167 Barry Larkin B	.75	.35
☐ B169 Ruben Sierra B	.25	.11
☐ B170 Bill Swift B	.25	.11
☐ B172 Chad Curtis B	.25	.11
☐ B173 Dean Palmer B	.50	.23
☐ B175 Bobby Bonilla B	.50	.23
☐ B176 Greg Colbrunn B	.25	.11
☐ B177 Jose Mesa B	.50	.23
☐ B178 Mike Greenwell B	.25	.11
☐ B181 Doug Drabek B	.25	.11
☐ B183 Wilson Alvarez B	.50	.23
☐ B184 Marty Cordova B	.50	.23
☐ B185 Hal Morris B	.25	.11
☐ B187 Carlos Garcia B	.25	.11
☐ B190 Marquis Grissom B	.50	.23
☐ B193 Will Clark B	.75	.35
☐ B194 Paul Molitor B	1.00	.45
☐ B195 Kenny Rogers B	.25	.11
☐ B196 Reggie Sanders B	.25	.11
☐ B199 Raul Mondesi B	.75	.35
☐ B200 Lance Johnson B	.25	.11
☐ B201 Alvin Morman B	.25	.11
☐ B203 Jack McDowell B	.25	.11
☐ B204 Randy Myers B	.25	.11
☐ B205 Harold Baines B	.50	.23
☐ B206 Marty Cordova B	.50	.23
☐ B207 Rich Hunter B	.25	.11
☐ B208 Al Leiter B	.25	.11
☐ B209 Greg Gagne B	.25	.11
☐ B210 Ben McDonald B	.25	.11
☐ B212 Terry Adams B	.25	.11
☐ B213 Paul Sorrento B	.25	.11
☐ B214 Albert Belle B	1.25	.55
☐ B215 Mike Blowers B	.25	.11
☐ B216 Jim Edmonds B	1.00	.45
☐ B217 Felipe Crespo B	.25	.11
☐ B219 Shawon Dunston B	.25	.11
☐ B220 Jimmy Haynes B	.25	.11
☐ B221 Jose Canseco B	.75	.35
☐ B222 Eric Davis B	.25	.11
☐ B224 Tim Raines B	.25	.11
☐ B225 Tony Phillips B	.25	.11
☐ B226 Charlie Hayes B	.25	.11
☐ B227 Eric Owens B	.25	.11
☐ B228 Roberto Alomar B	1.00	.45
☐ B233 Kenny Lofton B	1.25	.55
☐ B236 Mark McGwire B	2.00	.90
☐ B237 Jay Buhner B	.75	.35
☐ B238 Craig Biggio B	.75	.35
☐ B240 Barry Bonds B	1.25	.55
☐ B244 Ron Gant B	.50	.23
☐ B245 Paul Wilson B	.25	.11
☐ B246 Todd Hollandsworth B	.50	.23
☐ B247 Todd Zeile B	.25	.11
☐ B248 David Justice B	.75	.35
☐ B250 Moises Alou B	.50	.23
☐ B251 Bob Wolcott B	.25	.11
☐ B252 David Wells B	.25	.11
☐ B253 Juan Gonzalez B	2.50	1.10
☐ B254 Andres Galarraga B	.75	.35
☐ B255 Dave Hollins B	.25	.11
☐ B257 Sammy Sosa B	1.00	.45
☐ B258 Ivan Rodriguez B	1.00	.45
☐ B259 Bip Roberts B	.25	.11
☐ B260 Tino Martinez B	1.00	.45
☐ B262 Mike Stanley B	.25	.11
☐ B264 Butch Huskey B	.50	.23
☐ B265 Jeff Conine B	.50	.23
☐ B267 Mark Grace B	.75	.35
☐ B268 Jason Schmidt B	.50	.23
☐ B269 Otis Nixon B	.50	.23

Card	Mint	NRMT
☐ B271 Kirby Puckett B	2.00	.90
☐ B273 Andy Benes B	.50	.23
☐ B275 Mike Piazza B	3.00	1.35
☐ B276 Rey Ordonez B	.50	.23
☐ B278 Gary Gaetti B	.50	.23
☐ B280 Robin Ventura B	.50	.23
☐ B281 Cal Ripken B	4.00	1.80
☐ B282 Carlos Baerga B	.50	.23
☐ B283 Roger Cedeno B	.25	.11
☐ B285 Terrell Wade B	.25	.11
☐ B286 Kevin Brown B	.50	.23
☐ B287 Rafael Palmeiro B	.75	.35
☐ B288 Mo Vaughn B	1.25	.55
☐ B292 Bob Tewksbury B	.25	.11
☐ B297 T.J. Mathews B	.25	.11
☐ B298 Manny Ramirez B	1.00	.45
☐ B299 Jeff Bagwell B	2.00	.90
☐ B301 Wade Boggs B	1.00	.45
☐ B303 Steve Gibralter B	.25	.11
☐ B304 B.J. Surhoff B	.25	.11
☐ B306 Royce Clayton B	.25	.11
☐ B307 Sal Fasano B	.25	.11
☐ B309 Gary Sheffield B	1.00	.45
☐ B310 Ken Hill B	.25	.11
☐ B311 Joe Girardi B	.25	.11
☐ B312 Matt Lawton B	.25	.11
☐ B314 Julio Franco B	.50	.23
☐ B315 Joe Carter B	.50	.23
☐ B316 Brooks Kieschnick B	.50	.23
☐ B318 Heathcliff Slocumb B	.25	.11
☐ B319 Barry Larkin B	.75	.35
☐ B320 Tony Gwynn B	2.50	1.10
☐ B322 Frank Thomas B	4.00	1.80
☐ B323 Edgar Martinez B	.75	.35
☐ B325 Henry Rodriguez B	.25	.11
☐ B326 Marvin Benard B	.25	.11
☐ B329 Ugueth Urbina B	.50	.23
☐ B331 Roger Salkeld B	.25	.11
☐ B332 Edgar Renteria B	.75	.35
☐ B333 Ryan Klesko B	1.00	.45
☐ B334 Ray Lankford B	.50	.23
☐ B336 Justin Thompson B	.25	.11
☐ B339 Mark Clark B	.25	.11
☐ B340 Ruben Rivera B	.50	.23
☐ B342 Matt Williams B	.75	.35
☐ B343 Francisco Cordova B	.25	.11
☐ B344 Cecil Fielder B	.50	.23
☐ B348 Mark Grudzielanek B	.25	.11
☐ B349 Ron Coomer B	.25	.11
☐ B351 Rich Aurilia B	.25	.11
☐ B352 Jose Herrera B	.25	.11
☐ B356 Tony Clark B	1.25	.55
☐ B358 Dan Naulty B	.25	.11
☐ B359 Checklist B	.25	.11
☐ G4 Marty Cordova G	8.00	3.60
☐ G6 Tony Gwynn G	40.00	18.00
☐ G9 Albert Belle G	20.00	9.00
☐ G18 Kirby Puckett G	30.00	13.50
☐ G20 Karim Garcia G	8.00	3.60
☐ G25 Cal Ripken G	60.00	27.00
☐ G33 Hideo Nomo G	40.00	18.00
☐ G39 Ryne Sandberg G	20.00	9.00
☐ G42 Jeff Bagwell G	30.00	13.50
☐ G51 Jason Isringhausen G	8.00	3.60
☐ G64 Mo Vaughn G	20.00	9.00
☐ G66 Dante Bichette G	10.00	4.50
☐ G74 Mark McGwire G	30.00	13.50
☐ G81 Kenny Lofton G	20.00	9.00
☐ G83 Jim Edmonds G	15.00	6.75
☐ G90 Mike Mussina G	15.00	6.75
☐ G100 Jeff Conine G	8.00	3.60
☐ G102 Johnny Damon G	8.00	3.60
☐ G105 Barry Bonds G	20.00	9.00
☐ G117 Jose Canseco G	10.00	4.50
☐ G135 Ken Griffey Jr. G	80.00	36.00
☐ G141 Chipper Jones G	50.00	22.00
☐ G145 Greg Maddux G	50.00	22.00
☐ G164 Jay Buhner G	10.00	4.50
☐ G186 Frank Thomas G	60.00	27.00
☐ G191 Checklist G	8.00	3.60
☐ G192 Chipper Jones G	50.00	22.00
☐ G197 Roberto Alomar G	15.00	6.75
☐ G198 Dennis Eckersley G	10.00	4.50
☐ G202 George Arias G	8.00	3.60
☐ G232 Hideo Nomo G	40.00	18.00
☐ G243 Chris Snopek G	8.00	3.60
☐ G249 Tim Salmon G	10.00	4.50
☐ G266 Matt Williams G	10.00	4.50
☐ G270 Randy Johnson G	10.00	4.50
☐ G279 Paul Molitor G	15.00	6.75
☐ G290 Cecil Fielder G	8.00	3.60
☐ G294 Livan Hernandez G	25.00	11.00
☐ G300 Marty Janzen G	8.00	3.60
☐ G308 Ron Gant G	8.00	3.60
☐ G321 Ryan Klesko G	15.00	6.75
☐ G324 Jermaine Dye G	8.00	3.60
☐ G330 Jason Giambi G	8.00	3.60
☐ G335 Edgar Martinez G	10.00	4.50
☐ G338 Rey Ordonez G	8.00	3.60
☐ G347 Sammy Sosa G	15.00	6.75
☐ G354 Juan Gonzalez G	40.00	18.00
☐ G355 Craig Biggio G	10.00	4.50
☐ S1 Greg Maddux S UER 95 stats listed as Mariners	15.00	6.75
☐ S2 Bernie Williams S	5.00	2.20
☐ S3 Ivan Rodriguez S	6.00	2.70
☐ S7 Barry Larkin S	3.00	1.35
☐ S10 Ray Lankford S	3.00	1.35
☐ S11 Mike Piazza S	15.00	6.75
☐ S13 Larry Walker S	5.00	2.20
☐ S14 Matt Williams S	3.00	1.35
☐ S22 Tim Salmon S	5.00	2.20
☐ S35 Edgar Martinez S	5.00	2.20
☐ S37 Gregg Jefferies S	2.50	1.10
☐ S38 Bill Pulsipher S	1.50	.70
☐ S41 Shawn Green S	2.50	1.10
☐ S43 Jim Abbott S	1.50	.70
☐ S46 Roger Clemens S	10.00	4.50
☐ S52 Rondell White S	3.00	1.35
☐ S54 Dennis Eckersley S	3.00	1.35
☐ S59 Hideo Nomo S	12.00	5.50
☐ S60 Gary Sheffield S	5.00	2.20
☐ S62 Will Clark S	3.00	1.35
☐ S65 Bret Boone S	1.50	.70
☐ S68 Rafael Palmeiro S	3.00	1.35
☐ S69 Carlos Baerga S	1.50	.70
☐ S72 Tom Glavine S	3.00	1.35
☐ S73 Garret Anderson S	3.00	1.35
☐ S77 Randy Johnson S	5.00	2.20
☐ S78 Jeff King S	1.50	.70
☐ S79 Kirby Puckett S	10.00	4.50
☐ S84 Cecil Fielder S	2.50	1.10
☐ S86 Reggie Sanders S	1.50	.70
☐ S88 Ryan Klesko S	3.00	1.35
☐ S91 John Valentin S	2.50	1.10
☐ S95 Manny Ramirez S	5.00	2.20
☐ S99 Vinny Castilla S	2.50	1.10
☐ S109 Carlos Perez S	1.50	.70
☐ S112 Craig Biggio S	3.00	1.35
☐ S115 Juan Gonzalez S	12.00	5.50
☐ S121 Ray Durham S	2.50	1.10
☐ S127 C.J. Nitkowski S	1.50	.70
☐ S130 Raul Mondesi S	3.00	1.35
☐ S142 Lee Smith S	2.50	1.10
☐ S143 Joe Carter S	2.50	1.10
☐ S151 Mo Vaughn S	6.00	2.70
☐ S153 Frank Rodriguez S	1.50	.70
☐ S160 Steve Finley S	2.50	1.10
☐ S161 Jeff Bagwell S	10.00	4.50
☐ S165 Cal Ripken S	20.00	9.00
☐ S168 Lyle Mouton S	1.50	.70
☐ S171 Sammy Sosa S	5.00	2.20
☐ S174 John Franco S	2.50	1.10
☐ S179 Greg Vaughn S	1.50	.70
☐ S180 Mark Wohlers S	2.50	1.10
☐ S182 Paul O'Neill S	2.50	1.10
☐ S188 Albert Belle S	6.00	2.70
☐ S189 Mark Grace S	3.00	1.35
☐ S211 Ernie Young S	1.50	.70
☐ S218 Fred McGriff S	3.00	1.35
☐ S223 Kimera Bartee S	1.50	.70
☐ S229 Rickey Henderson S	3.00	1.35
☐ S230 Sterling Hitchcock S	2.50	1.10
☐ S231 Bernard Gilkey S	2.50	1.10
☐ S234 Ryne Sandberg S	6.00	2.70
☐ S235 Greg Maddux S	15.00	6.75
☐ S239 Todd Stottlemyre S	1.50	.70
☐ S241 Jason Kendall S	3.00	1.35
☐ S242 Paul O'Neill S	2.50	1.10
☐ S256 Devon White S	1.50	.70
☐ S261 Chuck Knoblauch S	5.00	2.20
☐ S263 Wally Joyner S	2.50	1.10
☐ S272 Andy Fox S	1.50	.70
☐ S274 Sean Berry S	1.50	.70
☐ S277 Benito Santiago S	1.50	.70
☐ S284 Chad Mottola S	1.50	.70
☐ S289 Dante Bichette S	3.00	1.35
☐ S291 Doc Gooden S	2.50	1.10
☐ S293 Kevin Mitchell S	1.50	.70
☐ S295 Russ Davis S	1.50	.70
☐ S296 Chan Ho Park S	5.00	2.20
☐ S302 Larry Walker S	5.00	2.20
☐ S305 Ken Griffey Jr. S	25.00	11.00
☐ S313 Billy Wagner S	2.50	1.10
☐ S317 Mike Grace S	1.50	.70
☐ S327 Kenny Lofton S	6.00	2.70
☐ S328 Derek Bell S	1.50	.70
☐ S337 Gary Sheffield S	5.00	2.20
☐ S341 Mark Grace S	3.00	1.35
☐ S345 Andres Galarraga S	5.00	2.20
☐ S346 Brady Anderson S	3.00	1.35
☐ S350 Derek Jeter S	12.00	5.50
☐ S353 Jay Buhner S	3.00	1.35
☐ S357 Tino Martinez S	5.00	2.20

1996 Finest Refractors

This 359-card set is parallel to the basic 1996 Finest set. The first 191 cards are parallel to the regular Series 1 with the second 168 cards parallel to regular Series 2. The word "refractor" is printed above the numbers on the card backs. The rate of insertion is one in 12 for a Bronze refractor (common), one in 48 for a Silver refractor (uncommon), and one in 288 for a Gold refractor (rare).

	MINT	NRMT
COMPLETE SET (359)	6000.00	2700.00
COMPLETE SERIES 1 (191)	3800.00	1700.00
COMPLETE SERIES 2 (168)	2200.00	1000.00
COMP.BRONZE SET (220)	1100.00	500.00
COMP.BRONZE SER.1 (110)	500.00	220.00
COMP.BRONZE SER.2 (110)	600.00	275.00
COMMON BRONZE	3.00	1.35
*BRONZE STARS: 5X to 12X BASIC CARDS		
COMP.GOLD SET (48)	3500.00	1600.00
COMP.GOLD SER.1 (26)	2500.00	1100.00
COMP.GOLD SER.2 (22)	1000.00	450.00
COMMON GOLD	25.00	11.00
*GOLD STARS: 2X to 4X BASIC CARDS		
COMP.SILVER SET (91)	1400.00	650.00
COMP.SILVER SER.1 (55)	800.00	350.00
COMP.SILVER SER.2 (36)	600.00	275.00
COMMON SILVER	6.00	2.70
*SILVER STARS: 2.5X to 5X BASIC CARDS		

1996 Finest Landmark

This four-card limited edition medallion set came with a Certificate of Authenticity and was produced by Topps. Only 2,000 sets were made. The fronts feature color action player photos on a gold ball and star metallic background. The backs carry player biographical and career information including batting records.

	MINT	NRMT
COMPLETE SET (4)	120.00	55.00
COMMON CARD (1-4)	12.00	5.50
☐ 1 Greg Maddux	30.00	13.50
☐ 2 Albert Belle	25.00	11.00
☐ 3 Cal Ripken	60.00	27.00
☐ 4 Eddie Murray	12.00	5.50

1997 Finest Promos

This five-card set features one promo card for each of the five themes found in the 1997 Finest Series I set. The fronts, backs, and card numbers are identical to the regular set with the exception of the words, "Promotional Sample Not for Resale" printed in red across the back. The cards are checklisted below according to their numbers in the regular set.

	MINT	NRMT
COMPLETE SET (5)	40.00	18.00
COMMON CARD	5.00	2.20
☐ 1 Barry Bonds C	5.00	2.20
☐ 15 Derek Jeter C	12.00	5.50
☐ 30 Mark McGwire C	10.00	4.50
☐ 143 Hideo Nomo U	15.00	6.75
☐ 159 Jeff Bagwell R	10.00	4.50

1997 Finest

The 1997 Finest set was issued in two series of 175 cards each and was distributed in six-card packs with a suggested retail price of $5.00. The fronts feature a borderless action player photo while the backs carry player information with another player photo. Series 1 is divided into five distinct themes: Finest Hurlers (top pitchers), Finest Blue Chips (up-and-coming future stars), Finest Power (long-ball hitters), Finest Warriors (superstar players), and Finest Masters (hottest players). Series 2 is also divided into five distinct themes: Finest

ower (power hitters , pitchers), Finest Masters (top layers), Finest Blue Chips (top new players), Finest ompetitors (hottest players), and Finest Acquisitions atest trades and new signings). All five themes of each eries have common cards (1-100 , 176-275) designated ith bronze trim, uncommon (101-150 , 276-325) with lver trim and an insertion rate of one in four for both eries, and rare (151-175 , 326-350) with gold trim and n insertion rate of one in 24 for both series. The cards re numbered on the backs within the whole set and ithin the theme set.

	MINT	NRMT
OMPLETE SET (350)	1300.00	575.00
OMPLETE SERIES 1 (175)	650.00	300.00
OMPLETE SERIES 2 (175)	650.00	300.00
OMP.BRONZE SET (200)	60.00	27.00
OMP.BRONZE SER.1 (100)	30.00	13.50
OMP.BRONZE SER.2 (100)	30.00	13.50
OM.BRON.(1-100/176-275)	.25	.11
OMP.SILVER SET (100)	375.00	170.00
OMP.SILVER SER.1 (50)	150.00	70.00
OMP.SILVER SER.2 (50)	225.00	100.00
OM.SILV.(101-150/276-325)	1.50	.70
OMP.GOLD SET (50)	900.00	400.00
OMP.GOLD SER.1 (25)	500.00	220.00
OMP.GOLD SER.2 (25)	400.00	180.00
OM.GOLD (151-175/326-350)	8.00	3.60

Card	MINT	NRMT
☐ 1 Barry Bonds B	1.25	.55
☐ 2 Ryne Sandberg B	1.25	.55
☐ 3 Brian Jordan B	.50	.23
☐ 4 Rocky Coppinger B	.25	.11
☐ 5 Dante Bichette B UER Card is erroneously numbered 155	.75	.35
☐ 6 Al Martin B	.25	.11
☐ 7 Charles Nagy B	.50	.23
☐ 8 Otis Nixon B	.25	.11
☐ 9 Mark Johnson B	.25	.11
☐ 10 Jeff Bagwell B	2.00	.90
☐ 11 Ken Hill B	.25	.11
☐ 12 Willie Adams B	.25	.11
☐ 13 Raul Mondesi B	.75	.35
☐ 14 Reggie Sanders B	.25	.11
☐ 15 Derek Jeter B	3.00	1.35
☐ 16 Jermaine Dye B	.25	.11
☐ 17 Edgar Renteria B	.50	.23
☐ 18 Travis Fryman B	.50	.23
☐ 19 Roberto Hernandez B	.50	.23
☐ 20 Sammy Sosa B	1.00	.45
☐ 21 Garret Anderson B	.50	.23
☐ 22 Rey Ordonez B	.25	.11
☐ 23 Glenallen Hill B	.25	.11
☐ 24 Dave Nilsson B	.25	.11
☐ 25 Kevin Brown B	.50	.23
☐ 26 Brian McRae B	.25	.11
☐ 27 Joey Hamilton B	.50	.23
☐ 28 Jamey Wright B	.50	.23
☐ 29 Frank Thomas B	4.00	1.80
☐ 30 Mark McGwire B	2.00	.90
☐ 31 Ramon Martinez B	.50	.23
☐ 32 Jaime Bluma B	.25	.11
☐ 33 Frank Rodriguez B	.25	.11
☐ 34 Andy Benes B	.50	.23
☐ 35 Jay Buhner B	.75	.35
☐ 36 Justin Thompson B	.50	.23
☐ 37 Darin Erstad B	1.50	.70
☐ 38 Gregg Jefferies B	.50	.23
☐ 39 Jeff D'Amico B	.50	.23
☐ 40 Pedro Martinez B	1.00	.45
☐ 41 Nomar Garciaparra B	3.00	1.35
☐ 42 Jose Valentin B	.25	.11
☐ 43 Pat Hentgen B	.50	.23
☐ 44 Will Clark B	.75	.35
☐ 45 Bernie Williams B	1.00	.45
☐ 46 Luis Castillo B	.25	.11
☐ 47 B.J. Surhoff B	.50	.23
☐ 48 Greg Gagne B	.25	.11
☐ 49 Pete Schourek B	.25	.11
☐ 50 Mike Piazza B	3.00	1.35
☐ 51 Dwight Gooden B	.50	.23
☐ 52 Javy Lopez B	.50	.23
☐ 53 Chuck Finley B	.25	.11
☐ 54 James Baldwin B	.25	.11
☐ 55 Jack McDowell B	.25	.11
☐ 56 Royce Clayton B	.25	.11
☐ 57 Carlos Delgado B	.50	.23
☐ 58 Neifi Perez B	.50	.23
☐ 59 Eddie Taubensee B	.25	.11
☐ 60 Rafael Palmeiro B	.75	.35
☐ 61 Marty Cordova B	.25	.11
☐ 62 Wade Boggs B	1.00	.45
☐ 63 Rickey Henderson B	.75	.35
☐ 64 Mike Hampton B	.25	.11
☐ 65 Troy Percival B	.25	.11
☐ 66 Barry Larkin B	.75	.35
☐ 67 Jermaine Allensworth B	.25	.11
☐ 68 Mark Clark B	.25	.11
☐ 69 Mike Lansing B	.25	.11
☐ 70 Mark Grudzielanek B	.25	.11
☐ 71 Todd Stottlemyre B	.25	.11
☐ 72 Juan Guzman B	.25	.11
☐ 73 John Burkett B	.25	.11
☐ 74 Wilson Alvarez B	.25	.11
☐ 75 Ellis Burks B	.50	.23
☐ 76 Bobby Higginson B	.50	.23
☐ 77 Ricky Bottalico B	.25	.11
☐ 78 Omar Vizquel B	.50	.23
☐ 79 Paul Sorrento B	.25	.11
☐ 80 Denny Neagle B	.50	.23
☐ 81 Roger Pavlik B	.25	.11
☐ 82 Mike Lieberthal B	.25	.11
☐ 83 Devon White B	.25	.11
☐ 84 John Olerud B	.50	.23
☐ 85 Kevin Appier B	.50	.23
☐ 86 Joe Girardi B	.25	.11
☐ 87 Paul O'Neill B	.50	.23
☐ 88 Mike Sweeney B	.50	.23
☐ 89 John Smiley B	.25	.11
☐ 90 Ivan Rodriguez B	1.25	.55
☐ 91 Randy Myers B	.50	.23
☐ 92 Bip Roberts B	.25	.11
☐ 93 Jose Mesa B	.50	.23
☐ 94 Paul Wilson B	.25	.11
☐ 95 Mike Mussina B	1.00	.45
☐ 96 Ben McDonald B	.25	.11
☐ 97 John Mabry B	.25	.11
☐ 98 Tom Goodwin B	.25	.11
☐ 99 Edgar Martinez B	.75	.35
☐ 100 Andruw Jones B	2.50	1.10
☐ 101 Jose Canseco S	3.00	1.35
☐ 102 Billy Wagner S	2.50	1.10
☐ 103 Dante Bichette S	2.50	1.10
☐ 104 Curt Schilling S	2.50	1.10
☐ 105 Dean Palmer S	2.50	1.10
☐ 106 Larry Walker S	5.00	2.20
☐ 107 Bernie Williams S	4.00	1.80
☐ 108 Chipper Jones S	15.00	6.75
☐ 109 Gary Sheffield S	4.00	1.80
☐ 110 Randy Johnson S	5.00	2.20
☐ 111 Roberto Alomar S	5.00	2.20
☐ 112 Todd Walker S	1.50	.70
☐ 113 Sandy Alomar Jr. S	2.50	1.10
☐ 114 John Jaha S	1.50	.70
☐ 115 Ken Caminiti S UER#'d 135	4.00	1.80
☐ 116 Ryan Klesko S	3.00	1.35
☐ 117 Mariano Rivera S	2.50	1.10
☐ 118 Jason Giambi S	2.50	1.10
☐ 119 Lance Johnson S	1.50	.70
☐ 120 Robin Ventura S	2.50	1.10
☐ 121 Todd Hollandsworth S	1.50	.70
☐ 122 Johnny Damon S	2.50	1.10
☐ 123 William VanLandingham S	1.50	.70
☐ 124 Jason Kendall S	2.50	1.10
☐ 125 Vinny Castilla S	2.50	1.10
☐ 126 Harold Baines S	2.50	1.10
☐ 127 Joe Carter S	2.50	1.10
☐ 128 Craig Biggio S	3.00	1.35
☐ 129 Tony Clark S	4.00	1.80
☐ 130 Ron Gant S	2.50	1.10
☐ 131 David Segui S	1.50	.70
☐ 132 Steve Trachsel S	1.50	.70
☐ 133 Scott Rolen S	12.00	5.50
☐ 134 Mike Stanley S	1.50	.70
☐ 135 Cal Ripken S	20.00	9.00
☐ 136 John Smoltz S	2.50	1.10
☐ 137 Bobby Jones S	1.50	.70
☐ 138 Manny Ramirez S	5.00	2.20
☐ 139 Ken Griffey Jr. S	25.00	11.00
☐ 140 Chuck Knoblauch S	4.00	1.80
☐ 141 Mark Grace S	3.00	1.35
☐ 142 Chris Snopek S	1.50	.70
☐ 143 Hideo Nomo S	12.00	5.50
☐ 144 Tim Salmon S	4.00	1.80
☐ 145 David Cone S	2.50	1.10
☐ 146 Eric Young S	1.50	.70
☐ 147 Jeff Brantley S	1.50	.70
☐ 148 Jim Thome S	5.00	2.20
☐ 149 Trevor Hoffman S	1.50	.70
☐ 150 Juan Gonzalez S	12.00	5.50
☐ 151 Mike Piazza G	50.00	22.00
☐ 152 Ivan Rodriguez G	20.00	9.00
☐ 153 Mo Vaughn G	20.00	9.00
☐ 154 Brady Anderson G	10.00	4.50
☐ 155 Mark McGwire G	30.00	13.50
☐ 156 Rafael Palmeiro G	10.00	4.50
☐ 157 Barry Larkin G	10.00	4.50
☐ 158 Greg Maddux G	50.00	22.00
☐ 159 Jeff Bagwell G	30.00	13.50
☐ 160 Frank Thomas G	60.00	27.00
☐ 161 Ken Caminiti G	12.00	5.50
☐ 162 Andruw Jones G	40.00	18.00
☐ 163 Dennis Eckersley G	10.00	4.50
☐ 164 Jeff Conine G	8.00	3.60
☐ 165 Jim Edmonds G	12.00	5.50
☐ 166 Derek Jeter G	50.00	22.00
☐ 167 Vladimir Guerrero G	30.00	13.50
☐ 168 Sammy Sosa G	12.00	5.50
☐ 169 Tony Gwynn G	40.00	18.00
☐ 170 Andres Galarraga G	12.00	5.50
☐ 171 Todd Hundley G	9.00	4.00
☐ 172 Jay Buhner G UER#'d 164	10.00	4.50
☐ 173 Paul Molitor G	15.00	6.75
☐ 174 Kenny Lofton G	20.00	9.00
☐ 175 Barry Bonds G	20.00	9.00
☐ 176 Gary Sheffield B	1.00	.45
☐ 177 Dmitri Young B	.25	.11
☐ 178 Jay Bell B	.25	.11
☐ 179 David Wells B	.25	.11
☐ 180 Walt Weiss B	.25	.11
☐ 181 Paul Molitor B	1.00	.45
☐ 182 Jose Guillen B	1.25	.55
☐ 183 Al Leiter B	.25	.11
☐ 184 Mike Fetters B	.25	.11
☐ 185 Mark Langston B	.25	.11
☐ 186 Fred McGriff B	.75	.35
☐ 187 Darrin Fletcher B	.25	.11
☐ 188 Brant Brown B	.25	.11
☐ 189 Geronimo Berroa B	.25	.11
☐ 190 Jim Thome B	1.00	.45
☐ 191 Jose Vizcaino B	.25	.11
☐ 192 Andy Ashby B	.25	.11
☐ 193 Rusty Greer B	.50	.23
☐ 194 Brian Hunter B	.50	.23
☐ 195 Chris Hoiles B	.25	.11
☐ 196 Orlando Merced B	.25	.11
☐ 197 Brett Butler B	.50	.23
☐ 198 Derek Bell B	.25	.11
☐ 199 Bobby Bonilla B	.50	.23
☐ 200 Alex Ochoa B	.25	.11
☐ 201 Wally Joyner B	.25	.11
☐ 202 Mo Vaughn B	1.25	.55
☐ 203 Doug Drabek B	.25	.11
☐ 204 Tino Martinez B	1.00	.45
☐ 205 Roberto Alomar B	1.00	.45
☐ 206 Brian Giles B	.25	.11
☐ 207 Todd Worrell B	.50	.23
☐ 208 Alan Benes B	.50	.23
☐ 209 Jim Leyritz B	.25	.11
☐ 210 Darryl Hamilton B	.25	.11
☐ 211 Jimmy Key B	.50	.23
☐ 212 Juan Gonzalez B	2.50	1.10
☐ 213 Vinny Castilla B	.50	.23
☐ 214 Chuck Knoblauch B	1.00	.45
☐ 215 Tony Phillips B	.25	.11
☐ 216 Jeff Cirillo B	.50	.23
☐ 217 Carlos Garcia B	.25	.11
☐ 218 Brooks Kieschnick B	.25	.11
☐ 219 Marquis Grissom B	.50	.23
☐ 220 Dan Wilson B	.25	.11
☐ 221 Greg Vaughn B	.25	.11
☐ 222 John Wetteland B	.50	.23
☐ 223 Andres Galarraga B	.75	.35
☐ 224 Ozzie Guillen B	.25	.11
☐ 225 Kevin Elster B	.25	.11
☐ 226 Bernard Gilkey B	.25	.11
☐ 227 Mike Macfarlane B	.25	.11
☐ 228 Heathcliff Slocumb B	.25	.11
☐ 229 Wendell Magee Jr. B	.25	.11
☐ 230 Carlos Baerga B	.25	.11
☐ 231 Kevin Seitzer B	.25	.11
☐ 232 Henry Rodriguez B	.25	.11
☐ 233 Roger Clemens B	2.00	.90
☐ 234 Mark Wohlers B	.25	.11
☐ 235 Eddie Murray B	1.00	.45
☐ 236 Todd Zeile B	.25	.11
☐ 237 J.T. Snow B	.50	.23
☐ 238 Ken Griffey Jr. B	5.00	2.20
☐ 239 Sterling Hitchcock B	.25	.11
☐ 240 Albert Belle B	1.25	.55
☐ 241 Terry Steinbach B	.50	.23
☐ 242 Robb Nen B	.50	.23
☐ 243 Mark McLemore B	.25	.11
☐ 244 Jeff King B	.25	.11
☐ 245 Tony Clark B	1.00	.45
☐ 246 Tim Salmon B	1.00	.45
☐ 247 Benito Santiago B	.25	.11

Card	MINT	NRMT
☐ 248 Robin Ventura B	.50	.23
☐ 249 Bubba Trammell B	1.00	.45
☐ 250 Chili Davis B	.50	.23
☐ 251 John Valentin B	.25	.11
☐ 252 Cal Ripken B	4.00	1.80
☐ 253 Matt Williams B	.75	.35
☐ 254 Jeff Kent B	.25	.11
☐ 255 Eric Karros B	.50	.23
☐ 256 Ray Lankford B	.50	.23
☐ 257 Ed Sprague B	.25	.11
☐ 258 Shane Reynolds B	.25	.11
☐ 259 Jaime Navarro B	.25	.11
☐ 260 Eric Davis B	.25	.11
☐ 261 Orel Hershiser B	.50	.23
☐ 262 Mark Grace B	.75	.35
☐ 263 Rod Beck B	.50	.23
☐ 264 Ismael Valdes B	.50	.23
☐ 265 Manny Ramirez B	1.00	.45
☐ 266 Ken Caminiti B	1.00	.45
☐ 267 Tim Naehring B	.25	.11
☐ 268 Jose Rosado B	.25	.11
☐ 269 Greg Colbrunn B	.25	.11
☐ 270 Dean Palmer B	.25	.11
☐ 271 David Justice B	1.00	.45
☐ 272 Scott Spiezio B	.25	.11
☐ 273 Chipper Jones B	3.00	1.35
☐ 274 Mel Rojas B	.25	.11
☐ 275 Bartolo Colon B	.50	.23
☐ 276 Darin Erstad S	8.00	3.60
☐ 277 Sammy Sosa S	4.00	1.80
☐ 278 Rafael Palmeiro S	3.00	1.35
☐ 279 Frank Thomas S	20.00	9.00
☐ 280 Ruben Rivera S	1.50	.70
☐ 281 Hal Morris S	1.50	.70
☐ 282 Jay Buhner S	3.00	1.35
☐ 283 Kenny Lofton S	6.00	2.70
☐ 284 Jose Canseco S	3.00	1.35
☐ 285 Alex Fernandez S	2.50	1.10
☐ 286 Todd Helton S	8.00	3.60
☐ 287 Andy Pettitte S	5.00	2.20
☐ 288 John Franco S	2.50	1.10
☐ 289 Ivan Rodriguez S	6.00	2.70
☐ 290 Ellis Burks S	2.50	1.10
☐ 291 Julio Franco S	2.50	1.10
☐ 292 Mike Piazza S	15.00	6.75
☐ 293 Brian Jordan S	2.50	1.10
☐ 294 Greg Maddux S	15.00	6.75
☐ 295 Bob Abreu S	4.00	1.80
☐ 296 Rondell White S	2.50	1.10
☐ 297 Moises Alou S	2.50	1.10
☐ 298 Tony Gwynn S	12.00	5.50
☐ 299 Deion Sanders S	4.00	1.80
☐ 300 Jeff Montgomery S	2.50	1.10
☐ 301 Ray Durham S	2.50	1.10
☐ 302 John Wasdin S	1.50	.70
☐ 303 Ryne Sandberg S	6.00	2.70
☐ 304 Delino DeShields S	1.50	.70
☐ 305 Mark McGwire S	10.00	4.50
☐ 306 Andruw Jones S	12.00	5.50
☐ 307 Kevin Orie S	2.50	1.10
☐ 308 Matt Williams S	3.00	1.35
☐ 309 Karim Garcia S	2.50	1.10
☐ 310 Derek Jeter S	15.00	6.75
☐ 311 Mo Vaughn S	6.00	2.70
☐ 312 Brady Anderson S	3.00	1.35
☐ 313 Barry Bonds S	6.00	2.70
☐ 314 Steve Finley S	2.50	1.10
☐ 315 Vladimir Guerrero S	10.00	4.50
☐ 316 Matt Morris S	2.50	1.10
☐ 317 Tom Glavine S	2.50	1.10
☐ 318 Jeff Bagwell S	10.00	4.50
☐ 319 Albert Belle S	6.00	2.70
☐ 320 Hideki Irabu S	6.00	2.70
☐ 321 Andres Galarraga S	3.00	1.35
☐ 322 Cecil Fielder S	2.50	1.10
☐ 323 Barry Larkin S	2.50	1.10
☐ 324 Todd Hundley S	2.50	1.10
☐ 325 Fred McGriff S	3.00	1.35
☐ 326 Gary Sheffield G	12.00	5.50
☐ 327 Craig Biggio G	10.00	4.50
☐ 328 Raul Mondesi G	10.00	4.50
☐ 329 Edgar Martinez G	10.00	4.50
☐ 330 Chipper Jones G	50.00	22.00
☐ 331 Bernie Williams G	12.00	5.50
☐ 332 Juan Gonzalez G	40.00	18.00
☐ 333 Ron Gant G	8.00	3.60
☐ 334 Cal Ripken G	60.00	27.00
☐ 335 Larry Walker G	15.00	6.75
☐ 336 Matt Williams G	10.00	4.50
☐ 337 Jose Cruz Jr. G	80.00	36.00
☐ 338 Joe Carter G	9.00	4.00
☐ 339 Wilton Guerrero G	8.00	3.60
☐ 340 Cecil Fielder G	9.00	4.00
☐ 341 Todd Walker G	8.00	3.60
☐ 342 Ken Griffey Jr. G	80.00	36.00
☐ 343 Ryan Klesko G	10.00	4.50
☐ 344 Roger Clemens G	30.00	13.50
☐ 345 Hideo Nomo G	40.00	18.00
☐ 346 Dante Bichette G	10.00	4.50
☐ 347 Albert Belle G	20.00	9.00
☐ 348 Randy Johnson G	15.00	6.75
☐ 349 Manny Ramirez G	15.00	6.75
☐ 350 John Smoltz G	9.00	4.00

1997 Finest Embossed

This 150-card set is parallel to regular set numbers 101-175 of Finest Series 1 and 276-350 of Finest Series 2. There is an embossed version of cards 101-150 and 276-325 with an insertion rate of one in 16 for each series. There is an embossed die-cut version of cards 151-175 and 326-350 with an insertion rate of one in 96 packs for each series.

	MINT	NRMT
COMPLETE SET (150)	2800.00	1250.00
COMPLETE SERIES 1 (75)	1400.00	650.00
COMPLETE SERIES 2 (75)	1400.00	650.00
COMP.SILVER SER.1 (50)	400.00	180.00
COMP.SILVER SER.2 (50)	600.00	275.00
COM.SILV.(101-150/276-325)	4.00	1.80
*SILV.STARS: 1.25X TO 2.5X BASIC CARD		
*SILVER YOUNG STARS: 1X TO 2X BASIC CARD		
COMP.GOLD SER.1 (25)	1000.00	450.00
COMP.GOLD SER.2 (25)	800.00	350.00
COM.GOLD (151-175/326-350)	15.00	6.75
*GOLD STARS: 1X TO 2X BASIC CARD		
*GOLD YOUNG STARS: .75X TO 1.5X BASIC CARD		

1997 Finest Embossed Refractors

This 150-card set is a parallel version of the regular Finest Embossed set and is similar in design. The difference is found in the refractive quality of the cards.

	MINT	NRMT
COM.SILV.(101-150/276-325)	30.00	13.50
SILVER MINOR STARS	40.00	18.00
SILVER UNLISTED STARS	60.00	27.00
COM.GOLD (151-175/326-350)	125.00	55.00
GOLD MINOR STARS	150.00	70.00
GOLD UNLISTED STARS	200.00	90.00

Card	MINT	NRMT
☐ 106 Larry Walker S	80.00	36.00
☐ 108 Chipper Jones S	200.00	90.00
☐ 110 Randy Johnson S	80.00	36.00
☐ 111 Roberto Alomar S	80.00	36.00
☐ 133 Scott Rolen S	150.00	70.00
☐ 135 Cal Ripken S	300.00	135.00
☐ 138 Manny Ramirez S	80.00	36.00
☐ 139 Ken Griffey Jr. S	500.00	220.00
☐ 143 Hideo Nomo S	250.00	110.00
☐ 148 Jim Thome S	80.00	36.00
☐ 150 Juan Gonzalez S	200.00	90.00
☐ 151 Mike Piazza G	800.00	350.00
☐ 152 Ivan Rodriguez G	300.00	135.00
☐ 153 Mo Vaughn G	300.00	135.00
☐ 155 Mark McGwire G	500.00	220.00
☐ 158 Greg Maddux G	800.00	350.00
☐ 159 Jeff Bagwell G	500.00	220.00
☐ 160 Frank Thomas G	1200.00	550.00
☐ 162 Andruw Jones G	500.00	220.00
☐ 166 Derek Jeter G	600.00	275.00
☐ 167 Vladimir Guerrero G	400.00	180.00
☐ 169 Tony Gwynn G	600.00	275.00
☐ 173 Paul Molitor G	250.00	110.00
☐ 174 Kenny Lofton G	300.00	135.00
☐ 175 Barry Bonds G	300.00	135.00
☐ 276 Darin Erstad S	100.00	45.00
☐ 279 Frank Thomas S	400.00	180.00
☐ 283 Kenny Lofton S	100.00	45.00
☐ 286 Todd Helton S	100.00	45.00
☐ 287 Andy Pettitte S	80.00	36.00
☐ 289 Ivan Rodriguez S	100.00	45.00
☐ 292 Mike Piazza S	250.00	110.00
☐ 294 Greg Maddux S	250.00	110.00
☐ 298 Tony Gwynn S	200.00	90.00
☐ 303 Ryne Sandberg S	100.00	45.00
☐ 305 Mark McGwire S	150.00	70.00
☐ 306 Andruw Jones S	150.00	70.00
☐ 310 Derek Jeter S	200.00	90.00
☐ 311 Mo Vaughn S	100.00	45.00
☐ 313 Barry Bonds S	100.00	45.00
☐ 315 Vladimir Guerrero S	120.00	55.00
☐ 318 Jeff Bagwell S	150.00	70.00
☐ 319 Albert Belle S	100.00	45.00
☐ 320 Hideki Irabu S	60.00	27.00
☐ 330 Chipper Jones G	600.00	275.00
☐ 332 Juan Gonzalez G	600.00	275.00
☐ 334 Cal Ripken G	1000.00	450.00
☐ 335 Larry Walker G	250.00	110.00
☐ 337 Jose Cruz Jr. G	600.00	275.00
☐ 342 Ken Griffey Jr. G	1200.00	550.00
☐ 344 Roger Clemens G	500.00	220.00
☐ 345 Hideo Nomo G	800.00	350.00
☐ 347 Albert Belle G	300.00	135.00
☐ 348 Randy Johnson G	250.00	110.00
☐ 349 Manny Ramirez G	250.00	110.00

1997 Finest Refractors

This 350-card set is parallel and similar in design to the regular Finest set. The distinction is in the refractive quality of the card. Cards 1-100 and 176-275 have an insertion rate of one in 12 in each series packs. Cards 101-150 and 276-325 have an insertion rate of one in 48 in each series packs. Cards 151-175 and 326-350 have an insertion rate of one in 288.

	MINT	NRMT
COMPLETE SET (350)	6400.00	2900.00
COMPLETE SERIES 1 (175)	3300.00	1500.00
COMPLETE SERIES 2 (175)	3100.00	1400.00
COMP.BRONZE SER.1 (100)	500.00	220.00
COMP.BRONZE SER.2 (100)	400.00	180.00
COM.BRON.(1-100/176-275)	3.00	1.35
*BRONZE STARS: 6X TO 12X BASIC CARD		
*BRONZE YOUNG STARS: 5X TO 10X BASIC CARD		
COMP.SILVER SER.1 (50)	800.00	350.00
COMP.SILVER SER.2 (50)	1200.00	550.00
COM.SILV.(101-150/276-325)	8.00	3.60
*SILVER STARS: 2.5X TO 5X BASIC CARD		
*SILVER YOUNG STARS: 2X TO 4X BASIC CARD		
COMP.GOLD SER.1 (25)	2000.00	900.00
COMP.GOLD SER.2 (25)	1500.00	700.00
COM.GOLD (151-175/326-350)	30.00	13.50
*GOLD STARS: 2.5X TO 5X BASE CARD HI		
*GOLD YOUNG STARS: 2X TO 4X BASE HI		

1993 Flair Promos

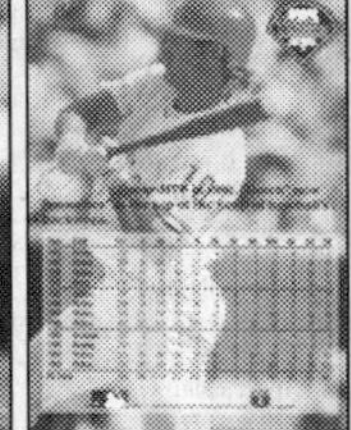

This 8-card standard-size set was issued to preview the design of the 1993 Flair series. These cards can be distinguished by triple zero on their backs; otherwise, they are identical to their regular issue counterparts. The cards are listed below in alphabetical order by player's last name. According to unverified reports, Fleer shredded a 5,000 count box of these cards to avoid potential difficulties with their licensing organizations.

	MINT	NRMT
COMPLETE SET (8)	300.00	135.00
COMMON CARD (1-8)	10.00	4.50

Card	MINT	NRMT
☐ 1 Will Clark	30.00	13.50
☐ 2 Darren Daulton	20.00	9.00
☐ 3 Andres Galarraga	40.00	18.00
☐ 4 Bryan Harvey	10.00	4.50
☐ 5 David Justice	40.00	18.00
☐ 6 Jody Reed	10.00	4.50
☐ 7 Nolan Ryan	150.00	70.00
☐ 8 Sammy Sosa	40.00	18.00

1993 Flair

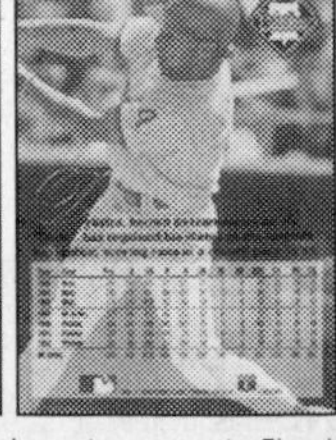

This 300-card standard-size set represents Fleer's entrance into the super-premium category of trading cards. Cards were distributed exclusively in specially encased "hardpacks". The cards are made from heavy 24 point board card stock, with an additional three points of high-gloss laminate on each side, and feature full-bleed lor fronts that sport two photos of each player, one perposed upon the other. The Flair logo appears at the p and the player's name rests at the bottom, both amped in gold foil. The cards are numbered phabetically within teams with National League eceding American league. There are no key Rookie ards in this set.

	MINT	NRMT
OMPLETE SET (300)	60.00	27.00
OMMON CARD (1-300)	.40	.18
1 Steve Avery	.40	.18
2 Jeff Blauser	.40	.18
3 Ron Gant	.60	.25
4 Tom Glavine	1.00	.45
5 David Justice	1.50	.70
6 Mark Lemke	.40	.18
7 Greg Maddux	5.00	2.20
8 Fred McGriff	1.00	.45
9 Terry Pendleton	.60	.25
10 Deion Sanders	1.50	.70
11 John Smoltz	1.00	.45
12 Mike Stanton	.40	.18
13 Steve Buechele	.40	.18
14 Mark Grace	1.00	.45
15 Greg Hibbard	.40	.18
16 Derrick May	.40	.18
17 Chuck McElroy	.40	.18
18 Mike Morgan	.40	.18
19 Randy Myers	.60	.25
20 Ryne Sandberg	2.00	.90
21 Dwight Smith	.40	.18
22 Sammy Sosa	1.50	.70
23 Jose Vizcaino	.40	.18
24 Tim Belcher	.40	.18
25 Rob Dibble	.40	.18
26 Roberto Kelly	.40	.18
27 Barry Larkin	1.00	.45
28 Kevin Mitchell	.60	.25
29 Hal Morris	.40	.18
30 Joe Oliver	.40	.18
31 Jose Rijo	.40	.18
32 Bip Roberts	.40	.18
33 Chris Sabo	.40	.18
34 Reggie Sanders	.60	.25
35 Dante Bichette	1.00	.45
36 Willie Blair	.40	.18
37 Jerald Clark	.40	.18
38 Alex Cole	.40	.18
39 Andres Galarraga	1.00	.45
40 Joe Girardi	.40	.18
41 Charlie Hayes	.40	.18
42 Chris Jones	.40	.18
43 David Nied	.40	.18
44 Eric Young	1.50	.70
45 Alex Arias	.40	.18
46 Jack Armstrong	.40	.18
47 Bret Barberie	.40	.18
48 Chuck Carr	.40	.18
49 Jeff Conine	.60	.25
50 Orestes Destrade	.40	.18
51 Chris Hammond	.40	.18
52 Bryan Harvey	.40	.18
53 Benito Santiago	.40	.18
54 Gary Sheffield	1.50	.70
55 Walt Weiss	.40	.18
56 Eric Anthony	.40	.18
57 Jeff Bagwell	3.00	1.35
58 Craig Biggio	1.00	.45
59 Ken Caminiti	1.50	.70
60 Andujar Cedeno	.40	.18
61 Doug Drabek	.40	.18
62 Steve Finley	.60	.25
63 Luis Gonzalez	.40	.18
64 Pete Harnisch	.40	.18
65 Doug Jones	.40	.18
66 Darryl Kile	.60	.25
67 Greg Swindell	.40	.18
68 Brett Butler	.60	.25
69 Jim Gott	.40	.18
70 Orel Hershiser	.60	.25
71 Eric Karros	.60	.25
72 Pedro Martinez	1.50	.70
73 Ramon Martinez	.60	.25
74 Roger McDowell	.40	.18
75 Mike Piazza	8.00	3.60
76 Jody Reed	.40	.18
77 Tim Wallach	.40	.18
78 Moises Alou	.60	.25
79 Greg Colbrunn	.40	.18
80 Wil Cordero	.60	.25
81 Delino DeShields	.40	.18
82 Jeff Fassero	.40	.18
83 Marquis Grissom	.60	.25
84 Ken Hill	.60	.25
85 Mike Lansing	.60	.25
86 Dennis Martinez	.60	.25
87 Larry Walker	1.50	.70
88 John Wetteland	.60	.25
89 Bobby Bonilla	.60	.25
90 Vince Coleman	.40	.18
91 Dwight Gooden	.60	.25
92 Todd Hundley	1.00	.45
93 Howard Johnson	.40	.18
94 Eddie Murray	1.50	.70
95 Joe Orsulak	.40	.18
96 Bret Saberhagen	.40	.18
97 Darren Daulton	.60	.25
98 Mariano Duncan	.40	.18
99 Len Dykstra	.60	.25
100 Jim Eisenreich	.60	.25
101 Tommy Greene	.40	.18
102 Dave Hollins	.40	.18
103 Pete Incaviglia	.40	.18
104 Danny Jackson	.40	.18
105 John Kruk	.60	.25
106 Terry Mulholland	.40	.18
107 Curt Schilling	.60	.25
108 Mitch Williams	.40	.18
109 Stan Belinda	.40	.18
110 Jay Bell	.60	.25
111 Steve Cooke	.40	.18
112 Carlos Garcia	.40	.18
113 Jeff King	.60	.25
114 Al Martin	.60	.25
115 Orlando Merced	.40	.18
116 Don Slaught	.40	.18
117 Andy Van Slyke	.60	.25
118 Tim Wakefield	.60	.25
119 Rene Arocha	.40	.18
120 Bernard Gilkey	.60	.25
121 Gregg Jefferies	.60	.25
122 Ray Lankford	1.00	.45
123 Donovan Osborne	.40	.18
124 Tom Pagnozzi	.40	.18
125 Erik Pappas	.40	.18
126 Geronimo Pena	.40	.18
127 Lee Smith	.60	.25
128 Ozzie Smith	2.00	.90
129 Bob Tewksbury	.40	.18
130 Mark Whiten	.40	.18
131 Derek Bell	.40	.18
132 Andy Benes	.60	.25
133 Tony Gwynn	4.00	1.80
134 Gene Harris	.40	.18
135 Trevor Hoffman	1.50	.70
136 Phil Plantier	.40	.18
137 Rod Beck	.60	.25
138 Barry Bonds	2.00	.90
139 John Burkett	.40	.18
140 Will Clark	1.00	.45
141 Royce Clayton	.60	.25
142 Mike Jackson	.40	.18
143 Darren Lewis	.40	.18
144 Kirt Manwaring	.40	.18
145 Willie McGee	.40	.18
146 Bill Swift	.40	.18
147 Robby Thompson	.40	.18
148 Matt Williams	1.00	.45
149 Brady Anderson	1.00	.45
150 Mike Devereaux	.40	.18
151 Chris Hoiles	.40	.18
152 Ben McDonald	.40	.18
153 Mark McLemore	.40	.18
154 Mike Mussina	1.50	.70
155 Gregg Olson	.40	.18
156 Harold Reynolds	.40	.18
157 Cal Ripken UER (Back refers to his games streak going into 1992; should be 1993) Also streak is spelled steak	6.00	2.70
158 Rick Sutcliffe	.40	.18
159 Fernando Valenzuela	.60	.25
160 Roger Clemens	3.00	1.35
161 Scott Cooper	.40	.18
162 Andre Dawson	1.00	.45
163 Scott Fletcher	.40	.18
164 Mike Greenwell	.40	.18
165 Greg A. Harris	.40	.18
166 Billy Hatcher	.40	.18
167 Jeff Russell	.40	.18
168 Mo Vaughn	2.00	.90
169 Frank Viola	.40	.18
170 Chad Curtis	.60	.25
171 Chili Davis	.60	.25
172 Gary DiSarcina	.40	.18
173 Damion Easley	.40	.18
174 Chuck Finley	.40	.18
175 Mark Langston	.60	.25
176 Luis Polonia	.40	.18
177 Tim Salmon	2.00	.90
178 Scott Sanderson	.40	.18
179 J.T.Snow	2.00	.90
180 Wilson Alvarez	.60	.25
181 Ellis Burks	.60	.25
182 Joey Cora	.60	.25
183 Alex Fernandez	.60	.25
184 Ozzie Guillen	.40	.18
185 Roberto Hernandez	.60	.25
186 Bo Jackson	.60	.25
187 Lance Johnson	.60	.25
188 Jack McDowell	.60	.25
189 Frank Thomas	6.00	2.70
190 Robin Ventura	.60	.25
191 Carlos Baerga	.60	.25
192 Albert Belle	2.00	.90
193 Wayne Kirby	.40	.18
194 Derek Lilliquist	.40	.18
195 Kenny Lofton	3.00	1.35
196 Carlos Martinez	.40	.18
197 Jose Mesa	.60	.25
198 Eric Plunk	.40	.18
199 Paul Sorrento	.40	.18
200 John Doherty	.40	.18
201 Cecil Fielder	.60	.25
202 Travis Fryman	.60	.25
203 Kirk Gibson	.60	.25
204 Mike Henneman	.40	.18
205 Chad Kreuter	.40	.18
206 Scott Livingstone	.40	.18
207 Tony Phillips	.40	.18
208 Mickey Tettleton	.40	.18
209 Alan Trammell	1.00	.45
210 David Wells	.40	.18
211 Lou Whitaker	.60	.25
212 Kevin Appier	.60	.25
213 George Brett	3.00	1.35
214 David Cone	.60	.25
215 Tom Gordon	.40	.18
216 Phil Hiatt	.40	.18
217 Felix Jose	.40	.18
218 Wally Joyner	.60	.25
219 Jose Lind	.40	.18
220 Mike Macfarlane	.40	.18
221 Brian McRae	.40	.18
222 Jeff Montgomery	.60	.25
223 Cal Eldred	.40	.18
224 Darryl Hamilton	.40	.18
225 John Jaha	.60	.25
226 Pat Listach	.40	.18
227 Graeme Lloyd	.40	.18
228 Kevin Reimer	.40	.18
229 Bill Spiers	.40	.18
230 B.J.Surhoff	.60	.25
231 Greg Vaughn	.40	.18
232 Robin Yount	1.00	.45
233 Rick Aguilera	.40	.18
234 Jim Deshaies	.40	.18
235 Brian Harper	.40	.18
236 Kent Hrbek	.60	.25
237 Chuck Knoblauch	1.50	.70
238 Shane Mack	.40	.18
239 David McCarty	.40	.18
240 Pedro Munoz	.40	.18
241 Mike Pagliarulo	.40	.18
242 Kirby Puckett	3.00	1.35
243 Dave Winfield	1.00	.45
244 Jim Abbott	.40	.18
245 Wade Boggs	1.50	.70
246 Pat Kelly	.40	.18
247 Jimmy Key	.60	.25
248 Jim Leyritz	.40	.18
249 Don Mattingly	2.50	1.10
250 Matt Nokes	.40	.18
251 Paul O'Neill	.60	.25
252 Mike Stanley	.40	.18
253 Danny Tartabull	.40	.18
254 Bob Wickman	.40	.18
255 Bernie Williams	1.00	.45
256 Mike Bordick	.40	.18
257 Dennis Eckersley	.60	.25
258 Brent Gates	.40	.18
259 Goose Gossage	.60	.25
260 Rickey Henderson	1.00	.45
261 Mark McGwire	3.00	1.35
262 Ruben Sierra	.40	.18
263 Terry Steinbach	.60	.25
264 Bob Welch	.40	.18
265 Bobby Witt	.40	.18
266 Rich Amaral	.40	.18
267 Chris Bosio	.40	.18
268 Jay Buhner	1.00	.45
269 Norm Charlton	.40	.18
270 Ken Griffey Jr.	8.00	3.60
271 Erik Hanson	.40	.18
272 Randy Johnson	1.50	.70
273 Edgar Martinez	1.00	.45
274 Tino Martinez	1.50	.70
275 Dave Valle	.40	.18
276 Omar Vizquel	.60	.25
277 Kevin Brown	.60	.25

Card	MINT	NRMT
☐ 278 Jose Canseco	1.00	.45
☐ 279 Julio Franco	.60	.25
☐ 280 Juan Gonzalez	4.00	1.80
☐ 281 Tom Henke	.40	.18
☐ 282 David Hulse	.40	.18
☐ 283 Rafael Palmeiro	1.00	.45
☐ 284 Dean Palmer	.60	.25
☐ 285 Ivan Rodriguez	2.00	.90
☐ 286 Nolan Ryan	6.00	2.70
☐ 287 Roberto Alomar	1.50	.70
☐ 288 Pat Borders	.40	.18
☐ 289 Joe Carter	1.00	.45
☐ 290 Juan Guzman	.40	.18
☐ 291 Pat Hentgen	1.00	.45
☐ 292 Paul Molitor	1.50	.70
☐ 293 John Olerud	.40	.18
☐ 294 Ed Sprague	.40	.18
☐ 295 Dave Stewart	.60	.25
☐ 296 Duane Ward	.40	.18
☐ 297 Devon White	.40	.18
☐ 298 Checklist 1-100	.40	.18
☐ 299 Checklist 101-200	.40	.18
☐ 300 Checklist 201-300	.40	.18

1993 Flair Wave of the Future

This 20-card standard-size limited edition insert set features a selction of top prospects. Cards were randomly seeded into1993 Flair packs. Each card is made of the same thick card stock as the regular-issue set and features full-bleed color player action photos on the fronts, with the Flair logo, player's name, and the "Wave of the Future" name and logo in gold foil, all superimposed upon an ocean breaker.

	MINT	NRMT
COMPLETE SET (20)	40.00	18.00
COMMON CARD (1-20)	1.00	.45
☐ 1 Jason Bere	1.00	.45
☐ 2 Jeromy Burnitz	1.00	.45
☐ 3 Russ Davis	1.50	.70
☐ 4 Jim Edmonds	10.00	4.50
☐ 5 Cliff Floyd	1.00	.45
☐ 6 Jeffrey Hammonds	3.00	1.35
☐ 7 Trevor Hoffman	3.00	1.35
☐ 8 Domingo Jean	1.00	.45
☐ 9 David McCarty	1.00	.45
☐ 10 Bobby Munoz	1.00	.45
☐ 11 Brad Pennington	1.00	.45
☐ 12 Mike Piazza	15.00	6.75
☐ 13 Manny Ramirez	8.00	3.60
☐ 14 John Roper	1.00	.45
☐ 15 Tim Salmon	5.00	2.20
☐ 16 Aaron Sele	1.00	.45
☐ 17 Allen Watson	1.00	.45
☐ 18 Rondell White	3.00	1.35
☐ 19 Darrell Whitmore UER (Nigel Wilson back)	1.00	.45
☐ 20 Nigel Wilson UER (Darrell Whitmore back)	1.00	.45

1994 Flair

For the second consecutive year Fleer issued a Flair brand. The set consists of 450 full bleed cards in two series of 250 and 200. The card stock is thicker than the traditional standard card. Card fronts feature two photos with the player's name and team name at the bottom in gold foil. The first letter of the player's last name appears within a gold shield to add style to this premium brand product. The backs are horizontal with a player photo and statistics. The team logo and player's name are done in gold foil. The cards are grouped alphabetically by team within each league with AL preceding NL. Notable Rookie Cards include Chan Ho Park and Alex Rodriguez.

	MINT	NRMT
COMPLETE SET (450)	60.00	27.00
COMPLETE SERIES 1 (250)	25.00	11.00
COMPLETE SERIES 2 (200)	35.00	16.00
COMMON CARD (1-450)	.25	.11
☐ 1 Harold Baines	.50	.23
☐ 2 Jeffrey Hammonds	.50	.23
☐ 3 Chris Hoiles	.25	.11
☐ 4 Ben McDonald	.25	.11
☐ 5 Mark McLemore	.25	.11
☐ 6 Jamie Moyer	.25	.11
☐ 7 Jim Poole	.25	.11
☐ 8 Cal Ripken Jr.	4.00	1.80
☐ 9 Chris Sabo	.25	.11
☐ 10 Scott Bankhead	.25	.11
☐ 11 Scott Cooper	.25	.11
☐ 12 Danny Darwin	.25	.11
☐ 13 Andre Dawson	.75	.35
☐ 14 Billy Hatcher	.25	.11
☐ 15 Aaron Sele	.50	.23
☐ 16 John Valentin	.50	.23
☐ 17 Dave Valle	.25	.11
☐ 18 Mo Vaughn	1.25	.55
☐ 19 Brian Anderson	.50	.23
☐ 20 Gary DiSarcina	.25	.11
☐ 21 Jim Edmonds	1.00	.45
☐ 22 Chuck Finley	.25	.11
☐ 23 Bo Jackson	.50	.23
☐ 24 Mark Leiter	.25	.11
☐ 25 Greg Myers	.25	.11
☐ 26 Eduardo Perez	.25	.11
☐ 27 Tim Salmon	1.00	.45
☐ 28 Wilson Alvarez	.50	.23
☐ 29 Jason Bere	.25	.11
☐ 30 Alex Fernandez	.25	.11
☐ 31 Ozzie Guillen	.25	.11
☐ 32 Joe Hall	.25	.11
☐ 33 Darrin Jackson	.25	.11
☐ 34 Kirk McCaskill	.25	.11
☐ 35 Tim Raines	.25	.11
☐ 36 Frank Thomas	4.00	1.80
☐ 37 Carlos Baerga	.50	.23
☐ 38 Albert Belle	1.25	.55
☐ 39 Mark Clark	.25	.11
☐ 40 Wayne Kirby	.25	.11
☐ 41 Dennis Martinez	.50	.23
☐ 42 Charles Nagy	.50	.23
☐ 43 Manny Ramirez	1.25	.55
☐ 44 Paul Sorrento	.25	.11
☐ 45 Jim Thome	1.25	.55
☐ 46 Eric Davis	.50	.23
☐ 47 John Doherty	.25	.11
☐ 48 Junior Felix	.25	.11
☐ 49 Cecil Fielder	.50	.23
☐ 50 Kirk Gibson	.50	.23
☐ 51 Mike Moore	.25	.11
☐ 52 Tony Phillips	.25	.11
☐ 53 Alan Trammell	.75	.35
☐ 54 Kevin Appier	.50	.23
☐ 55 Stan Belinda	.25	.11
☐ 56 Vince Coleman	.25	.11
☐ 57 Greg Gagne	.25	.11
☐ 58 Bob Hamelin	.25	.11
☐ 59 Dave Henderson	.25	.11
☐ 60 Wally Joyner	.50	.23
☐ 61 Mike Macfarlane	.25	.11
☐ 62 Jeff Montgomery	.50	.23
☐ 63 Ricky Bones	.25	.11
☐ 64 Jeff Bronkey	.25	.11
☐ 65 Alex Diaz	.25	.11
☐ 66 Cal Eldred	.25	.11
☐ 67 Darryl Hamilton	.25	.11
☐ 68 John Jaha	.25	.11
☐ 69 Mark Kiefer	.25	.11
☐ 70 Kevin Seitzer	.25	.11
☐ 71 Turner Ward	.25	.11
☐ 72 Rich Becker	.50	.23
☐ 73 Scott Erickson	.25	.11
☐ 74 Keith Garagozzo	.25	.11
☐ 75 Kent Hrbek	.50	.23
☐ 76 Scott Leius	.25	.11
☐ 77 Kirby Puckett	2.00	.90
☐ 78 Matt Walbeck	.25	.11
☐ 79 Dave Winfield	.75	.35
☐ 80 Mike Gallego	.25	.11
☐ 81 Xavier Hernandez	.25	.11
☐ 82 Jimmy Key	.50	.23
☐ 83 Jim Leyritz	.25	.11
☐ 84 Don Mattingly	1.50	.70
☐ 85 Matt Nokes	.25	.11
☐ 86 Paul O'Neill	.50	.23
☐ 87 Melido Perez	.25	.11
☐ 88 Danny Tartabull	.25	.11
☐ 89 Mike Bordick	.25	.11
☐ 90 Ron Darling	.25	.11
☐ 91 Dennis Eckersley	.50	.23
☐ 92 Stan Javier	.25	.11
☐ 93 Steve Karsay	.25	.11
☐ 94 Mark McGwire	2.00	.90
☐ 95 Troy Neel	.25	.11
☐ 96 Terry Steinbach	.50	.23
☐ 97 Bill Taylor	.25	.11
☐ 98 Eric Anthony	.25	.11
☐ 99 Chris Bosio	.25	.11
☐ 100 Tim Davis	.25	.11
☐ 101 Felix Fermin	.25	.11
☐ 102 Dave Fleming	.25	.11
☐ 103 Ken Griffey Jr.	5.00	2.20
☐ 104 Greg Hibbard	.25	.11
☐ 105 Reggie Jefferson	.75	.35
☐ 106 Tino Martinez	1.00	.45
☐ 107 Jack Armstrong	.25	.11
☐ 108 Will Clark	.75	.35
☐ 109 Juan Gonzalez	2.50	1.10
☐ 110 Rick Helling	.25	.11
☐ 111 Tom Henke	.25	.11
☐ 112 David Hulse	.25	.11
☐ 113 Manuel Lee	.25	.11
☐ 114 Doug Strange	.25	.11
☐ 115 Roberto Alomar	1.00	.45
☐ 116 Joe Carter	.75	.35
☐ 117 Carlos Delgado	.75	.35
☐ 118 Pat Hentgen	.50	.23
☐ 119 Paul Molitor	1.00	.45
☐ 120 John Olerud	.50	.23
☐ 121 Dave Stewart	.50	.23
☐ 122 Todd Stottlemyre	.25	.11
☐ 123 Mike Timlin	.25	.11
☐ 124 Jeff Blauser	.25	.11
☐ 125 Tom Glavine	.75	.35
☐ 126 David Justice	1.00	.45
☐ 127 Mike Kelly	.25	.11
☐ 128 Ryan Klesko	.75	.35
☐ 129 Javier Lopez	.75	.35
☐ 130 Greg Maddux	3.00	1.35
☐ 131 Fred McGriff	.75	.35
☐ 132 Kent Mercker	.25	.11
☐ 133 Mark Wohlers	.50	.23
☐ 134 Willie Banks	.25	.11
☐ 135 Steve Buechele	.25	.11
☐ 136 Shawon Dunston	.25	.11
☐ 137 Jose Guzman	.25	.11
☐ 138 Glenallen Hill	.25	.11
☐ 139 Randy Myers	.25	.11
☐ 140 Karl Rhodes	.25	.11
☐ 141 Ryne Sandberg	1.25	.55
☐ 142 Steve Trachsel	.50	.23
☐ 143 Bret Boone	.25	.11
☐ 144 Tom Browning	.25	.11
☐ 145 Hector Carrasco	.25	.11
☐ 146 Barry Larkin	.75	.35
☐ 147 Hal Morris	.25	.11
☐ 148 Jose Rijo	.25	.11
☐ 149 Reggie Sanders	.50	.23
☐ 150 John Smiley	.25	.11
☐ 151 Dante Bichette	.75	.35
☐ 152 Ellis Burks	.50	.23
☐ 153 Joe Girardi	.25	.11
☐ 154 Mike Harkey	.25	.11
☐ 155 Roberto Mejia	.25	.11
☐ 156 Marcus Moore	.25	.11
☐ 157 Armando Reynoso	.25	.11
☐ 158 Bruce Ruffin	.25	.11
☐ 159 Eric Young	.50	.23
☐ 160 Kurt Abbott	.25	.11
☐ 161 Jeff Conine	.50	.23
☐ 162 Orestes Destrade	.25	.11
☐ 163 Chris Hammond	.25	.11
☐ 164 Bryan Harvey	.25	.11
☐ 165 Dave Magadan	.25	.11
☐ 166 Gary Sheffield	1.00	.45
☐ 167 David Weathers	.25	.11
☐ 168 Andujar Cedeno	.25	.11
☐ 169 Tom Edens	.25	.11
☐ 170 Luis Gonzalez	.25	.11
☐ 171 Pete Harnisch	.25	.11
☐ 172 Todd Jones	.25	.11
☐ 173 Darryl Kile	.50	.23
☐ 174 James Mouton	.50	.23
☐ 175 Scott Servais	.25	.11
☐ 176 Mitch Williams	.25	.11
☐ 177 Pedro Astacio	.25	.11
☐ 178 Orel Hershiser	.50	.23
☐ 179 Raul Mondesi	.75	.35
☐ 180 Jose Offerman	.25	.11

181 Chan Ho Park	4.00	1.80
182 Mike Piazza	3.00	1.35
183 Cory Snyder	.25	.11
184 Tim Wallach	.25	.11
185 Todd Worrell	.25	.11
186 Sean Berry	.25	.11
187 Wil Cordero	.25	.11
188 Darrin Fletcher	.25	.11
189 Cliff Floyd	.75	.35
190 Marquis Grissom	.50	.23
191 Rod Henderson	.25	.11
192 Ken Hill	.25	.11
193 Pedro Martinez	1.00	.45
194 Kirk Rueter	.25	.11
195 Jeromy Burnitz	.50	.23
196 John Franco	.25	.11
197 Dwight Gooden	.50	.23
198 Todd Hundley	.50	.23
199 Bobby Jones	.50	.23
200 Jeff Kent	.25	.11
201 Mike Maddux	.25	.11
202 Ryan Thompson	.25	.11
203 Jose Vizcaino	.25	.11
204 Darren Daulton	.50	.23
205 Lenny Dykstra	.50	.23
206 Jim Eisenreich	.50	.23
207 Dave Hollins	.25	.11
208 Danny Jackson	.25	.11
209 Doug Jones	.25	.11
210 Jeff Juden	.25	.11
211 Ben Rivera	.25	.11
212 Kevin Stocker	.25	.11
213 Milt Thompson	.25	.11
214 Jay Bell	.50	.23
215 Steve Cooke	.25	.11
216 Mark Dewey	.25	.11
217 Al Martin	.25	.11
218 Orlando Merced	.25	.11
219 Don Slaught	.25	.11
220 Zane Smith	.25	.11
221 Rick White	.25	.11
222 Kevin Young	.25	.11
223 Rene Arocha	.25	.11
224 Rheal Cormier	.25	.11
225 Brian Jordan	.50	.23
226 Ray Lankford	.75	.35
227 Mike Perez	.25	.11
228 Ozzie Smith	1.25	.55
229 Mark Whiten	.25	.11
230 Todd Zeile	.25	.11
231 Derek Bell	.50	.23
232 Archi Cianfrocco	.25	.11
233 Ricky Gutierrez	.25	.11
234 Trevor Hoffman	.50	.23
235 Phil Plantier	.25	.11
236 Dave Staton	.25	.11
237 Wally Whitehurst	.25	.11
238 Todd Benzinger	.25	.11
239 Barry Bonds	1.25	.55
240 John Burkett	.25	.11
241 Royce Clayton	.25	.11
242 Bryan Hickerson	.25	.11
243 Mike Jackson	.25	.11
244 Darren Lewis	.25	.11
245 Kirt Manwaring	.25	.11
246 Mark Portugal	.25	.11
247 Salomon Torres	.25	.11
248 Checklist	.25	.11
249 Checklist	.25	.11
250 Checklist	.25	.11
251 Brady Anderson	.75	.35
252 Mike Devereaux	.25	.11
253 Sid Fernandez	.25	.11
254 Leo Gomez	.25	.11
255 Mike Mussina	1.00	.45
256 Mike Oquist	.25	.11
257 Rafael Palmeiro	.75	.35
258 Lee Smith	.50	.23
259 Damon Berryhill	.25	.11
260 Wes Chamberlain	.25	.11
261 Roger Clemens	2.00	.90
262 Gar Finnvold	.25	.11
263 Mike Greenwell	.25	.11
264 Tim Naehring	.25	.11
265 Otis Nixon	.25	.11
266 Ken Ryan	.25	.11
267 Chad Curtis	.25	.11
268 Chili Davis	.50	.23
269 Damion Easley	.25	.11
270 Jorge Fabregas	.25	.11
271 Mark Langston	.25	.11
272 Phil Leftwich	.25	.11
273 Harold Reynolds	.25	.11
274 J.T. Snow	.50	.23
275 Joey Cora	.50	.23
276 Julio Franco	.50	.23
277 Roberto Hernandez	.50	.23
☐ 278 Lance Johnson	.50	.23
☐ 279 Ron Karkovice	.25	.11
☐ 280 Jack McDowell	.25	.11
☐ 281 Robin Ventura	.50	.23
☐ 282 Sandy Alomar Jr.	.50	.23
☐ 283 Kenny Lofton	1.25	.55
☐ 284 Jose Mesa	.50	.23
☐ 285 Jack Morris	.50	.23
☐ 286 Eddie Murray	1.00	.45
☐ 287 Chad Ogea	.50	.23
☐ 288 Eric Plunk	.25	.11
☐ 289 Paul Shuey	.25	.11
☐ 290 Omar Vizquel	.50	.23
☐ 291 Danny Bautista	.25	.11
☐ 292 Travis Fryman	.50	.23
☐ 293 Greg Gohr	.25	.11
☐ 294 Chris Gomez	.25	.11
☐ 295 Mickey Tettleton	.25	.11
☐ 296 Lou Whitaker	.50	.23
☐ 297 David Cone	.50	.23
☐ 298 Gary Gaetti	.50	.23
☐ 299 Tom Gordon	.25	.11
☐ 300 Felix Jose	.25	.11
☐ 301 Jose Lind	.25	.11
☐ 302 Brian McRae	.25	.11
☐ 303 Mike Fetters	.25	.11
☐ 304 Brian Harper	.25	.11
☐ 305 Pat Listach	.25	.11
☐ 306 Matt Mieske	.25	.11
☐ 307 Dave Nilsson	.50	.23
☐ 308 Jody Reed	.25	.11
☐ 309 Greg Vaughn	.25	.11
☐ 310 Bill Wegman	.25	.11
☐ 311 Rick Aguilera	.25	.11
☐ 312 Alex Cole	.25	.11
☐ 313 Denny Hocking	.25	.11
☐ 314 Chuck Knoblauch	1.00	.45
☐ 315 Shane Mack	.25	.11
☐ 316 Pat Meares	.25	.11
☐ 317 Kevin Tapani	.25	.11
☐ 318 Jim Abbott	.25	.11
☐ 319 Wade Boggs	1.00	.45
☐ 320 Sterling Hitchcock	.50	.23
☐ 321 Pat Kelly	.25	.11
☐ 322 Terry Mulholland	.25	.11
☐ 323 Luis Polonia	.25	.11
☐ 324 Mike Stanley	.25	.11
☐ 325 Bob Wickman	.25	.11
☐ 326 Bernie Williams	1.00	.45
☐ 327 Mark Acre	.25	.11
☐ 328 Geronimo Berroa	.50	.23
☐ 329 Scott Brosius	.25	.11
☐ 330 Brent Gates	.25	.11
☐ 331 Rickey Henderson	.75	.35
☐ 332 Carlos Reyes	.25	.11
☐ 333 Ruben Sierra	.25	.11
☐ 334 Bobby Witt	.25	.11
☐ 335 Bobby Ayala	.25	.11
☐ 336 Jay Buhner	.75	.35
☐ 337 Randy Johnson	1.00	.45
☐ 338 Edgar Martinez	.75	.35
☐ 339 Bill Risley	.25	.11
☐ 340 Alex Rodriguez	20.00	9.00
☐ 341 Roger Salkeld	.25	.11
☐ 342 Dan Wilson	.50	.23
☐ 343 Kevin Brown	.50	.23
☐ 344 Jose Canseco	.75	.35
☐ 345 Dean Palmer	.50	.23
☐ 346 Ivan Rodriguez	1.25	.55
☐ 347 Kenny Rogers	.25	.11
☐ 348 Pat Borders	.25	.11
☐ 349 Juan Guzman	.25	.11
☐ 350 Ed Sprague	.25	.11
☐ 351 Devon White	.25	.11
☐ 352 Steve Avery	.25	.11
☐ 353 Roberto Kelly	.25	.11
☐ 354 Mark Lemke	.25	.11
☐ 355 Greg McMichael	.25	.11
☐ 356 Terry Pendleton	.50	.23
☐ 357 John Smoltz	.75	.35
☐ 358 Mike Stanton	.25	.11
☐ 359 Tony Tarasco	.25	.11
☐ 360 Mark Grace	.75	.35
☐ 361 Derrick May	.25	.11
☐ 362 Rey Sanchez	.25	.11
☐ 363 Sammy Sosa	1.00	.45
☐ 364 Rick Wilkins	.25	.11
☐ 365 Jeff Brantley	.25	.11
☐ 366 Tony Fernandez	.25	.11
☐ 367 Chuck McElroy	.25	.11
☐ 368 Kevin Mitchell	.25	.11
☐ 369 John Roper	.25	.11
☐ 370 Johnny Ruffin	.25	.11
☐ 371 Deion Sanders	1.00	.45
☐ 372 Marvin Freeman	.25	.11
☐ 373 Andres Galarraga	.75	.35
☐ 374 Charlie Hayes	.25	.11
☐ 375 Nelson Liriano	.25	.11
☐ 376 David Nied	.25	.11
☐ 377 Walt Weiss	.25	.11
☐ 378 Bret Barberie	.25	.11
☐ 379 Jerry Browne	.25	.11
☐ 380 Chuck Carr	.25	.11
☐ 381 Greg Colbrunn	.25	.11
☐ 382 Charlie Hough	.25	.11
☐ 383 Kurt Miller	.25	.11
☐ 384 Benito Santiago	.25	.11
☐ 385 Jeff Bagwell	2.00	.90
☐ 386 Craig Biggio	.75	.35
☐ 387 Ken Caminiti	1.00	.45
☐ 388 Doug Drabek	.25	.11
☐ 389 Steve Finley	.50	.23
☐ 390 John Hudek	.25	.11
☐ 391 Orlando Miller	.25	.11
☐ 392 Shane Reynolds	.25	.11
☐ 393 Brett Butler	.50	.23
☐ 394 Tom Candiotti	.25	.11
☐ 395 Delino DeShields	.25	.11
☐ 396 Kevin Gross	.25	.11
☐ 397 Eric Karros	.50	.23
☐ 398 Ramon Martinez	.50	.23
☐ 399 Henry Rodriguez	.25	.11
☐ 400 Moises Alou	.50	.23
☐ 401 Jeff Fassero	.25	.11
☐ 402 Mike Lansing	.50	.23
☐ 403 Mel Rojas	.25	.11
☐ 404 Larry Walker	1.00	.45
☐ 405 John Wetteland	.50	.23
☐ 406 Gabe White	.25	.11
☐ 407 Bobby Bonilla	.50	.23
☐ 408 Josias Manzanillo	.25	.11
☐ 409 Bret Saberhagen	.25	.11
☐ 410 David Segui	.25	.11
☐ 411 Mariano Duncan	.25	.11
☐ 412 Tommy Greene	.25	.11
☐ 413 Billy Hatcher	.25	.11
☐ 414 Ricky Jordan	.25	.11
☐ 415 John Kruk	.50	.23
☐ 416 Bobby Munoz	.25	.11
☐ 417 Curt Schilling	.50	.23
☐ 418 Fernando Valenzuela	.50	.23
☐ 419 David West	.25	.11
☐ 420 Carlos Garcia	.25	.11
☐ 421 Brian Hunter	.25	.11
☐ 422 Jeff King	.50	.23
☐ 423 Jon Lieber	.25	.11
☐ 424 Ravelo Manzanillo	.25	.11
☐ 425 Denny Neagle	.50	.23
☐ 426 Andy Van Slyke	.50	.23
☐ 427 Bryan Eversgerd	.25	.11
☐ 428 Bernard Gilkey	.50	.23
☐ 429 Gregg Jefferies	.50	.23
☐ 430 Tom Pagnozzi	.25	.11
☐ 431 Bob Tewksbury	.25	.11
☐ 432 Allen Watson	.25	.11
☐ 433 Andy Ashby	.25	.11
☐ 434 Andy Benes	.50	.23
☐ 435 Donnie Elliott	.25	.11
☐ 436 Tony Gwynn	2.50	1.10
☐ 437 Joey Hamilton	.50	.23
☐ 438 Tim Hyers	.25	.11
☐ 439 Luis Lopez	.25	.11
☐ 440 Bip Roberts	.25	.11
☐ 441 Scott Sanders	.25	.11
☐ 442 Rod Beck	.50	.23
☐ 443 Dave Burba	.25	.11
☐ 444 Darryl Strawberry	.50	.23
☐ 445 Bill Swift	.25	.11
☐ 446 Robby Thompson	.25	.11
☐ 447 Bill VanLandingham	.25	.11
☐ 448 Matt Williams	.75	.35
☐ 449 Checklist	.25	.11
☐ 450 Checklist	.25	.11
☐ P15 Aaron Sele Promo	1.50	.70

1994 Flair Hot Gloves

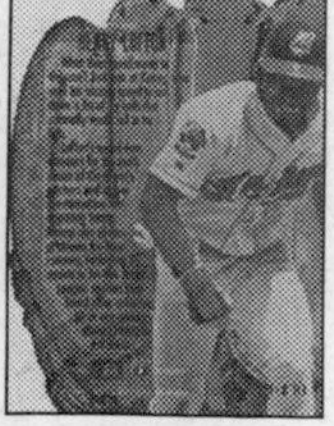

Randomly inserted in second series packs at a rate of one in 24, this set highlights 10 of the game's top players that also have outstanding defensive ability. The cards feature a special die-cut "glove" design with the player appearing within the glove. The back has a short write-up and a photo.

	MINT	NRMT
COMPLETE SET (10)	180.00	80.00
COMMON CARD (1-10)	8.00	3.60
☐ 1 Barry Bonds	15.00	6.75
☐ 2 Will Clark	10.00	4.50
☐ 3 Ken Griffey Jr.	60.00	27.00
☐ 4 Kenny Lofton	15.00	6.75
☐ 5 Greg Maddux	40.00	18.00
☐ 6 Don Mattingly	20.00	9.00
☐ 7 Kirby Puckett	25.00	11.00
☐ 8 Cal Ripken Jr.	50.00	22.00
☐ 9 Tim Salmon	12.00	5.50
☐ 10 Matt Williams	8.00	3.60

1994 Flair Hot Numbers

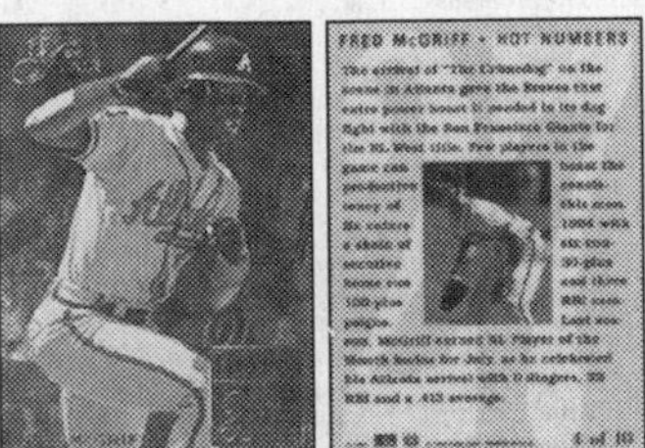

This 10-card set was randomly inserted in first series packs at a rate of one in 24. Metallic fronts feature a player photo with various numbers or statistics serving as background. The player's uniform number is part of the Hot Numbers logo at bottom left or right. The player's name is also at the bottom. The backs have a small photo centered in the middle surrounded by text highlighting achievements.

	MINT	NRMT
COMPLETE SET (10)	100.00	45.00
COMMON CARD (1-10)	1.50	.70
☐ 1 Roberto Alomar	6.00	2.70
☐ 2 Carlos Baerga	1.50	.70
☐ 3 Will Clark	4.00	1.80
☐ 4 Fred McGriff	4.00	1.80
☐ 5 Paul Molitor	6.00	2.70
☐ 6 John Olerud	1.50	.70
☐ 7 Mike Piazza	20.00	9.00
☐ 8 Cal Ripken Jr.	25.00	11.00
☐ 9 Ryne Sandberg	7.50	3.40
☐ 10 Frank Thomas	25.00	11.00

1994 Flair Infield Power

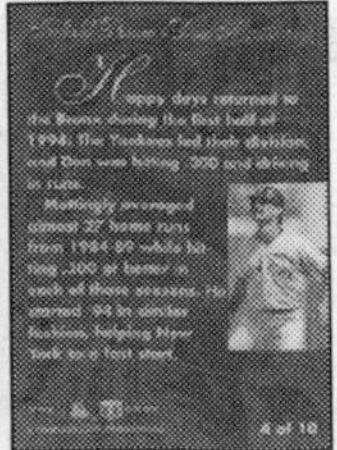

Randomly inserted in second series packs at a rate of one in five, this 10-card standard-size set spotlights major league infielders who are power hitters. Card fronts feature a horizontal format with two photos of the player. The backs contain a short write-up with emphasis on power numbers. The back also has a small photo.

	MINT	NRMT
COMPLETE SET (10)	20.00	9.00
COMMON CARD (1-10)	.50	.23
☐ 1 Jeff Bagwell	3.00	1.35
☐ 2 Will Clark	1.50	.70
☐ 3 Darren Daulton	.50	.23
☐ 4 Don Mattingly	4.00	1.80
☐ 5 Fred McGriff	1.50	.70
☐ 6 Rafael Palmeiro	1.50	.70
☐ 7 Mike Piazza	5.00	2.20
☐ 8 Cal Ripken Jr.	6.00	2.70
☐ 9 Frank Thomas	8.00	3.60
☐ 10 Matt Williams	1.50	.70

1994 Flair Outfield Power

This 10-card standard-size set was randomly inserted in both first and second series packs at a rate of one in five. Two photos on the front feature the player fielding and hitting. The player's name and Outfield Power serve as a dividing point between the photos. The back contains a small photo and text.

	MINT	NRMT
COMPLETE SET (10)	25.00	11.00
COMMON CARD (1-10)	.75	.35
☐ 1 Albert Belle	4.00	1.80
☐ 2 Barry Bonds	2.50	1.10
☐ 3 Joe Carter	1.50	.70
☐ 4 Lenny Dykstra	.75	.35
☐ 5 Juan Gonzalez	5.00	2.20
☐ 6 Ken Griffey Jr.	10.00	4.50
☐ 7 David Justice	1.50	.70
☐ 8 Kirby Puckett	4.00	1.80
☐ 9 Tim Salmon	1.50	.70
☐ 10 Dave Winfield	1.50	.70

1994 Flair Wave of the Future

This 20-card standard-size set takes a look at potential big league stars. The cards were randomly inserted in packs at a rate of one in five -- the first 10 in series 1, the second 10 in series 2. The fronts and backs have the player superimposed over a wavy colored background. The front has the Wave of the Future logo and a paragraph or two about the player along with a photo on the back.

	MINT	NRMT
COMPLETE SET (20)	55.00	25.00
COMPLETE SER.1 SET (10)	15.00	6.75
COMPLETE SER.2 SET (10)	40.00	18.00
COMMON CARD (A1-B10)	1.00	.45
☐ A1 Kurt Abbott	1.00	.45
☐ A2 Carlos Delgado	2.50	1.10
☐ A3 Steve Karsay	1.00	.45
☐ A4 Ryan Klesko	3.00	1.35
☐ A5 Javier Lopez	2.50	1.10
☐ A6 Raul Mondesi	3.00	1.35
☐ A7 James Mouton	1.00	.45
☐ A8 Chan Ho Park	8.00	3.60
☐ A9 Dave Staton	1.00	.45
☐ A10 Rick White	1.00	.45
☐ B1 Mark Acre	1.00	.45
☐ B2 Chris Gomez	1.00	.45
☐ B3 Joey Hamilton	2.50	1.10
☐ B4 John Hudek	1.00	.45
☐ B5 Jon Lieber	1.00	.45
☐ B6 Matt Mieske	1.50	.70
☐ B7 Orlando Miller	1.00	.45
☐ B8 Alex Rodriguez	30.00	13.50
☐ B9 Tony Tarasco	1.00	.45
☐ B10 William VanLandingham	1.00	.45

1995 Flair

This set was issued in two series of 216 cards for a total of 432 standard-size cards. Horizontally designed fronts have a 100 percent etched foil surface containing two player photos. The backs feature a full-bleed photo with yearly statistics superimposed. The checklist is arranged alphabetically by league with AL preceding NL.

	MINT	NRMT
COMPLETE SET (432)	80.00	36.00
COMPLETE SERIES 1 (216)	50.00	22.00
COMPLETE SERIES (216)	30.00	13.50
COMMON CARD (1-432)	.25	.11
☐ 1 Brady Anderson	.75	.35
☐ 2 Harold Baines	.50	.23
☐ 3 Leo Gomez	.25	.11
☐ 4 Alan Mills	.25	.11
☐ 5 Jamie Moyer	.25	.11
☐ 6 Mike Mussina	1.00	.45
☐ 7 Mike Oquist	.25	.11
☐ 8 Arthur Rhodes	.25	.11
☐ 9 Cal Ripken Jr.	4.00	1.80
☐ 10 Roger Clemens	2.00	.90
☐ 11 Scott Cooper	.25	.11
☐ 12 Mike Greenwell	.25	.11
☐ 13 Aaron Sele	.50	.23
☐ 14 John Valentin	.50	.23
☐ 15 Mo Vaughn	1.25	.55
☐ 16 Chad Curtis	.25	.11
☐ 17 Gary DiSarcina	.25	.11
☐ 18 Chuck Finley	.50	.23
☐ 19 Andrew Lorraine	.25	.11
☐ 20 Spike Owen	.25	.11
☐ 21 Tim Salmon	1.00	.45
☐ 22 J.T. Snow	.50	.23
☐ 23 Wilson Alvarez	.50	.23
☐ 24 Jason Bere	.25	.11
☐ 25 Ozzie Guillen	.25	.11
☐ 26 Mike LaValliere	.25	.11
☐ 27 Frank Thomas	4.00	1.80
☐ 28 Robin Ventura	.50	.23
☐ 29 Carlos Baerga	.50	.23
☐ 30 Albert Belle	1.25	.55
☐ 31 Jason Grimsley	.25	.11
☐ 32 Dennis Martinez	.50	.23
☐ 33 Eddie Murray	1.00	.45
☐ 34 Charles Nagy	.50	.23
☐ 35 Manny Ramirez	1.00	.45
☐ 36 Paul Sorrento	.25	.11
☐ 37 John Doherty	.25	.11
☐ 38 Cecil Fielder	.50	.23
☐ 39 Travis Fryman	.50	.23
☐ 40 Chris Gomez	.25	.11
☐ 41 Tony Phillips	.25	.11
☐ 42 Lou Whitaker	.50	.23
☐ 43 David Cone	.50	.23
☐ 44 Gary Gaetti	.50	.23
☐ 45 Mark Gubicza	.25	.11
☐ 46 Bob Hamelin	.25	.11
☐ 47 Wally Joyner	.50	.23
☐ 48 Rusty Meacham	.25	.11
☐ 49 Jeff Montgomery	.50	.23
☐ 50 Ricky Bones	.25	.11
☐ 51 Cal Eldred	.25	.11
☐ 52 Pat Listach	.25	.11
☐ 53 Matt Mieske	.50	.23
☐ 54 Dave Nilsson	.50	.23
☐ 55 Greg Vaughn	.25	.11
☐ 56 Bill Wegman	.25	.11
☐ 57 Chuck Knoblauch	1.00	.45
☐ 58 Scott Leius	.25	.11
☐ 59 Pat Mahomes	.25	.11
☐ 60 Pat Meares	.25	.11
☐ 61 Pedro Munoz	.25	.11
☐ 62 Kirby Puckett	2.00	.90
☐ 63 Wade Boggs	1.00	.45
☐ 64 Jimmy Key	.50	.23
☐ 65 Jim Leyritz	.25	.11
☐ 66 Don Mattingly	1.50	.70
☐ 67 Paul O'Neill	.50	.23
☐ 68 Melido Perez	.25	.11
☐ 69 Danny Tartabull	.25	.11
☐ 70 John Briscoe	.25	.11
☐ 71 Scott Brosius	.25	.11
☐ 72 Ron Darling	.25	.11
☐ 73 Brent Gates	.25	.11
☐ 74 Rickey Henderson	.75	.35
☐ 75 Stan Javier	.25	.11
☐ 76 Mark McGwire	2.00	.90
☐ 77 Todd Van Poppel	.25	.11

☐ 78 Bobby Ayala .25 .11
☐ 79 Mike Blowers .25 .11
☐ 80 Jay Buhner .75 .35
☐ 81 Ken Griffey Jr. 5.00 2.20
☐ 82 Randy Johnson 1.00 .45
☐ 83 Tino Martinez 1.00 .45
☐ 84 Jeff Nelson .25 .11
☐ 85 Alex Rodriguez 4.00 1.80
☐ 86 Will Clark .75 .35
☐ 87 Jeff Frye .25 .11
☐ 88 Juan Gonzalez 2.50 1.10
☐ 89 Rusty Greer 1.00 .45
☐ 90 Darren Oliver 1.00 .45
☐ 91 Dean Palmer .50 .23
☐ 92 Ivan Rodriguez 1.25 .55
☐ 93 Matt Whiteside .25 .11
☐ 94 Roberto Alomar 1.00 .45
☐ 95 Joe Carter .75 .35
☐ 96 Tony Castillo .25 .11
☐ 97 Juan Guzman .25 .11
☐ 98 Pat Hentgen .50 .23
☐ 99 Mike Huff .25 .11
☐ 100 John Olerud .50 .23
☐ 101 Woody Williams .25 .11
☐ 102 Roberto Kelly .25 .11
☐ 103 Ryan Klesko .75 .35
☐ 104 Javier Lopez .75 .35
☐ 105 Greg Maddux 3.00 1.35
☐ 106 Fred McGriff .75 .35
☐ 107 Jose Oliva .25 .11
☐ 108 John Smoltz .75 .35
☐ 109 Tony Tarasco .25 .11
☐ 110 Mark Wohlers .50 .23
☐ 111 Jim Bullinger .25 .11
☐ 112 Shawon Dunston .25 .11
☐ 113 Derrick May .25 .11
☐ 114 Randy Myers .25 .11
☐ 115 Karl Rhodes .25 .11
☐ 116 Rey Sanchez .25 .11
☐ 117 Steve Trachsel .25 .11
☐ 118 Eddie Zambrano .25 .11
☐ 119 Bret Boone .25 .11
☐ 120 Brian Dorsett .25 .11
☐ 121 Hal Morris .25 .11
☐ 122 Jose Rijo .25 .11
☐ 123 John Roper .25 .11
☐ 124 Reggie Sanders .25 .11
☐ 125 Pete Schourek .25 .11
☐ 126 John Smiley .25 .11
☐ 127 Ellis Burks .50 .23
☐ 128 Vinny Castilla .75 .35
☐ 129 Marvin Freeman .25 .11
☐ 130 Andres Galarraga .75 .35
☐ 131 Mike Munoz .25 .11
☐ 132 David Nied .25 .11
☐ 133 Bruce Ruffin .25 .11
☐ 134 Walt Weiss .25 .11
☐ 135 Eric Young .50 .23
☐ 136 Greg Colbrunn .25 .11
☐ 137 Jeff Conine .50 .23
☐ 138 Jeremy Hernandez .25 .11
☐ 139 Charles Johnson .50 .23
☐ 140 Robb Nen .25 .11
☐ 141 Gary Sheffield 1.00 .45
☐ 142 Dave Weathers .25 .11
☐ 143 Jeff Bagwell 2.00 .90
☐ 144 Craig Biggio .75 .35
☐ 145 Tony Eusebio .25 .11
☐ 146 Luis Gonzalez .25 .11
☐ 147 John Hudek .25 .11
☐ 148 Darryl Kile .50 .23
☐ 149 Dave Veres .25 .11
☐ 150 Billy Ashley .25 .11
☐ 151 Pedro Astacio .25 .11
☐ 152 Rafael Bournigal .25 .11
☐ 153 Delino DeShields .25 .11
☐ 154 Raul Mondesi .75 .35
☐ 155 Mike Piazza 3.00 1.35
☐ 156 Rudy Seanez .25 .11
☐ 157 Ismael Valdes .50 .23
☐ 158 Tim Wallach .25 .11
☐ 159 Todd Worrell .25 .11
☐ 160 Moises Alou .50 .23
☐ 161 Cliff Floyd .50 .23
☐ 162 Gil Heredia .25 .11
☐ 163 Mike Lansing .25 .11
☐ 164 Pedro Martinez 1.00 .45
☐ 165 Kirk Rueter .25 .11
☐ 166 Tim Scott .25 .11
☐ 167 Jeff Shaw .25 .11
☐ 168 Rondell White .75 .35
☐ 169 Bobby Bonilla .50 .23
☐ 170 Rico Brogna .25 .11
☐ 171 Todd Hundley .50 .23
☐ 172 Jeff Kent .25 .11
☐ 173 Jim Lindeman .25 .11
☐ 174 Joe Orsulak .25 .11
☐ 175 Bret Saberhagen .25 .11
☐ 176 Toby Borland .25 .11
☐ 177 Darren Daulton .50 .23
☐ 178 Lenny Dykstra .50 .23
☐ 179 Jim Eisenreich .50 .23
☐ 180 Tommy Greene .25 .11
☐ 181 Tony Longmire .25 .11
☐ 182 Bobby Munoz .25 .11
☐ 183 Kevin Stocker .25 .11
☐ 184 Jay Bell .50 .23
☐ 185 Steve Cooke .25 .11
☐ 186 Ravelo Manzanillo .25 .11
☐ 187 Al Martin .50 .23
☐ 188 Denny Neagle .50 .23
☐ 189 Don Slaught .25 .11
☐ 190 Paul Wagner .25 .11
☐ 191 Rene Arocha .25 .11
☐ 192 Bernard Gilkey .50 .23
☐ 193 Jose Oquendo .25 .11
☐ 194 Tom Pagnozzi .25 .11
☐ 195 Ozzie Smith 1.25 .55
☐ 196 Allen Watson .25 .11
☐ 197 Mark Whiten .25 .11
☐ 198 Andy Ashby .25 .11
☐ 199 Donnie Elliott .25 .11
☐ 200 Bryce Florie .25 .11
☐ 201 Tony Gwynn 2.50 1.10
☐ 202 Trevor Hoffman .50 .23
☐ 203 Brian Johnson .25 .11
☐ 204 Tim Mauser .25 .11
☐ 205 Bip Roberts .25 .11
☐ 206 Rod Beck .25 .11
☐ 207 Barry Bonds 1.25 .55
☐ 208 Royce Clayton .25 .11
☐ 209 Darren Lewis .25 .11
☐ 210 Mark Portugal .25 .11
☐ 211 Kevin Rogers .25 .11
☐ 212 Wm. VanLandingham .25 .11
☐ 213 Matt Williams .75 .35
☐ 214 Checklist .25 .11
☐ 215 Checklist .25 .11
☐ 216 Checklist .25 .11
☐ 217 Bret Barberie .25 .11
☐ 218 Armando Benitez .25 .11
☐ 219 Kevin Brown .50 .23
☐ 220 Sid Fernandez .25 .11
☐ 221 Chris Hoiles .25 .11
☐ 222 Doug Jones .25 .11
☐ 223 Ben McDonald .25 .11
☐ 224 Rafael Palmeiro .75 .35
☐ 225 Andy Van Slyke .50 .23
☐ 226 Jose Canseco .75 .35
☐ 227 Vaughn Eshelman .25 .11
☐ 228 Mike Macfarlane .25 .11
☐ 229 Tim Naehring .25 .11
☐ 230 Frank Rodriguez .50 .23
☐ 231 Lee Tinsley .25 .11
☐ 232 Mark Whiten .25 .11
☐ 233 Garret Anderson .75 .35
☐ 234 Chili Davis .50 .23
☐ 235 Jim Edmonds 1.00 .45
☐ 236 Mark Langston .25 .11
☐ 237 Troy Percival .25 .11
☐ 238 Tony Phillips .25 .11
☐ 239 Lee Smith .50 .23
☐ 240 Jim Abbott .25 .11
☐ 241 James Baldwin .50 .23
☐ 242 Mike Devereaux .25 .11
☐ 243 Ray Durham .50 .23
☐ 244 Alex Fernandez .25 .11
☐ 245 Roberto Hernandez .25 .11
☐ 246 Lance Johnson .25 .11
☐ 247 Ron Karkovice .25 .11
☐ 248 Tim Raines .25 .11
☐ 249 Sandy Alomar Jr. .25 .11
☐ 250 Orel Hershiser .50 .23
☐ 251 Julian Tavarez .25 .11
☐ 252 Jim Thome 1.00 .45
☐ 253 Omar Vizquel .50 .23
☐ 254 Dave Winfield .75 .35
☐ 255 Chad Curtis .25 .11
☐ 256 Kirk Gibson .50 .23
☐ 257 Mike Henneman .25 .11
☐ 258 Bob Higginson 1.50 .70
☐ 259 Felipe Lira .25 .11
☐ 260 Rudy Pemberton .25 .11
☐ 261 Alan Trammell .75 .35
☐ 262 Kevin Appier .50 .23
☐ 263 Pat Borders .25 .11
☐ 264 Tom Gordon .25 .11
☐ 265 Jose Lind .25 .11
☐ 266 Jon Nunnally .50 .23
☐ 267 Dilson Torres .25 .11
☐ 268 Michael Tucker .75 .35
☐ 269 Jeff Cirillo .50 .23
☐ 270 Darryl Hamilton .25 .11
☐ 271 David Hulse .25 .11
☐ 272 Mark Kiefer .25 .11
☐ 273 Graeme Lloyd .25 .11
☐ 274 Joe Oliver .25 .11
☐ 275 Al Reyes .25 .11
☐ 276 Kevin Seitzer .25 .11
☐ 277 Rick Aguilera .25 .11
☐ 278 Marty Cordova .75 .35
☐ 279 Scott Erickson .25 .11
☐ 280 LaTroy Hawkins .25 .11
☐ 281 Brad Radke 1.25 .55
☐ 282 Kevin Tapani .25 .11
☐ 283 Tony Fernandez .25 .11
☐ 284 Sterling Hitchcock .50 .23
☐ 285 Pat Kelly .25 .11
☐ 286 Jack McDowell .25 .11
☐ 287 Andy Pettitte 1.50 .70
☐ 288 Mike Stanley .25 .11
☐ 289 John Wetteland .50 .23
☐ 290 Bernie Williams 1.00 .45
☐ 291 Mark Acre .25 .11
☐ 292 Geronimo Berroa .25 .11
☐ 293 Dennis Eckersley .75 .35
☐ 294 Steve Ontiveros .25 .11
☐ 295 Ruben Sierra .25 .11
☐ 296 Terry Steinbach .50 .23
☐ 297 Dave Stewart .50 .23
☐ 298 Todd Stottlemyre .25 .11
☐ 299 Darren Bragg .50 .23
☐ 300 Joey Cora .50 .23
☐ 301 Edgar Martinez .75 .35
☐ 302 Bill Risley .25 .11
☐ 303 Ron Villone .25 .11
☐ 304 Dan Wilson .50 .23
☐ 305 Benji Gil .25 .11
☐ 306 Wilson Heredia .25 .11
☐ 307 Mark McLemore .25 .11
☐ 308 Otis Nixon .50 .23
☐ 309 Kenny Rogers .25 .11
☐ 310 Jeff Russell .25 .11
☐ 311 Mickey Tettleton .25 .11
☐ 312 Bob Tewksbury .25 .11
☐ 313 David Cone .50 .23
☐ 314 Carlos Delgado .50 .23
☐ 315 Alex Gonzalez .50 .23
☐ 316 Shawn Green .50 .23
☐ 317 Paul Molitor 1.00 .45
☐ 318 Ed Sprague .25 .11
☐ 319 Devon White .25 .11
☐ 320 Steve Avery .25 .11
☐ 321 Jeff Blauser .25 .11
☐ 322 Brad Clontz .25 .11
☐ 323 Tom Glavine .75 .35
☐ 324 Marquis Grissom .50 .23
☐ 325 Chipper Jones 3.00 1.35
☐ 326 David Justice 1.00 .45
☐ 327 Mark Lemke .25 .11
☐ 328 Kent Mercker .25 .11
☐ 329 Jason Schmidt .75 .35
☐ 330 Steve Buechele .25 .11
☐ 331 Kevin Foster .25 .11
☐ 332 Mark Grace .75 .35
☐ 333 Brian McRae .25 .11
☐ 334 Sammy Sosa 1.00 .45
☐ 335 Ozzie Timmons .25 .11
☐ 336 Rick Wilkins .25 .11
☐ 337 Hector Carrasco .25 .11
☐ 338 Ron Gant .50 .23
☐ 339 Barry Larkin .75 .35
☐ 340 Deion Sanders 1.00 .45
☐ 341 Benito Santiago .25 .11
☐ 342 Roger Bailey .25 .11
☐ 343 Jason Bates .25 .11
☐ 344 Dante Bichette .75 .35
☐ 345 Joe Girardi .25 .11
☐ 346 Bill Swift .25 .11
☐ 347 Mark Thompson .50 .23
☐ 348 Larry Walker 1.00 .45
☐ 349 Kurt Abbott .25 .11
☐ 350 John Burkett .25 .11
☐ 351 Chuck Carr .25 .11
☐ 352 Andre Dawson .75 .35
☐ 353 Chris Hammond .25 .11
☐ 354 Charles Johnson .50 .23
☐ 355 Terry Pendleton .50 .23
☐ 356 Quilvio Veras .25 .11
☐ 357 Derek Bell .50 .23
☐ 358 Jim Dougherty .25 .11
☐ 359 Doug Drabek .25 .11
☐ 360 Todd Jones .25 .11
☐ 361 Orlando Miller .25 .11
☐ 362 James Mouton .25 .11
☐ 363 Phil Plantier .25 .11
☐ 364 Shane Reynolds .25 .11
☐ 365 Todd Hollandsworth .50 .23
☐ 366 Eric Karros .50 .23
☐ 367 Ramon Martinez .50 .23
☐ 368 Hideo Nomo 5.00 2.20

	MINT	NRMT
369 Jose Offerman	.25	.11
370 Antonio Osuna	.25	.11
371 Todd Williams	.25	.11
372 Shane Andrews	.25	.11
373 Wil Cordero	.25	.11
374 Jeff Fassero	.25	.11
375 Darrin Fletcher	.25	.11
376 Mark Grudzielanek	.75	.35
377 Carlos Perez	.50	.23
378 Mel Rojas	.25	.11
379 Tony Tarasco	.25	.11
380 Edgardo Alfonzo	1.00	.45
381 Brett Butler	.50	.23
382 Carl Everett	.50	.23
383 John Franco	.50	.23
384 Pete Harnisch	.25	.11
385 Bobby Jones	.50	.23
386 Dave Mlicki	.25	.11
387 Jose Vizcaino	.25	.11
388 Ricky Bottalico	.50	.23
389 Tyler Green	.25	.11
390 Charlie Hayes	.25	.11
391 Dave Hollins	.25	.11
392 Gregg Jefferies	.50	.23
393 Michael Mimbs	.25	.11
394 Mickey Morandini	.25	.11
395 Curt Schilling	.50	.23
396 Heathcliff Slocumb	.25	.11
397 Jason Christiansen	.25	.11
398 Midre Cummings	.25	.11
399 Carlos Garcia	.25	.11
400 Mark Johnson	.25	.11
401 Jeff King	.50	.23
402 Jon Lieber	.25	.11
403 Esteban Loaiza	.25	.11
404 Orlando Merced	.25	.11
405 Gary Wilson	.25	.11
406 Scott Cooper	.25	.11
407 Tom Henke	.25	.11
408 Ken Hill	.25	.11
409 Danny Jackson	.25	.11
410 Brian Jordan	.50	.23
411 Ray Lankford	.75	.35
412 John Mabry	.75	.35
413 Todd Zeile	.25	.11
414 Andy Benes	.25	.11
415 Andres Berumen	.25	.11
416 Ken Caminiti	1.00	.45
417 Andujar Cedeno	.25	.11
418 Steve Finley	.50	.23
419 Joey Hamilton	.75	.35
420 Dustin Hermanson	.25	.11
421 Melvin Nieves	.50	.23
422 Roberto Petagine	.25	.11
423 Eddie Williams	.25	.11
424 Glenallen Hill	.25	.11
425 Kirt Manwaring	.25	.11
426 Terry Mulholland	.25	.11
427 J.R. Phillips	.25	.11
428 Joe Rosselli	.25	.11
429 Robby Thompson	.25	.11
430 Checklist	.25	.11
431 Checklist	.25	.11
432 Checklist	.25	.11

1995 Flair Hot Gloves

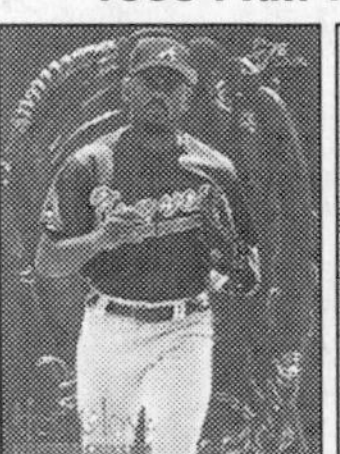

This 12-card standard-size set features players that are known for their defensive prowess. Randomly inserted in series two packs at a rate of one in 25, a player photo is superimposed over an embossed design of a bronze glove.The backs have a photo and write-up with a glove as background.

	MINT	NRMT
COMPLETE SET (12)	175.00	80.00
COMMON CARD (1-12)	5.00	2.20
1 Roberto Alomar	12.00	5.50
2 Barry Bonds	15.00	6.75
3 Ken Griffey Jr.	60.00	27.00
4 Marquis Grissom	6.00	2.70
5 Barry Larkin	8.00	3.60
6 Darren Lewis	5.00	2.20
7 Kenny Lofton	15.00	6.75
8 Don Mattingly	20.00	9.00
9 Cal Ripken	50.00	22.00
10 Ivan Rodriguez	15.00	6.75
11 Devon White	5.00	2.20
12 Matt Williams	8.00	3.60

1995 Flair Hot Numbers

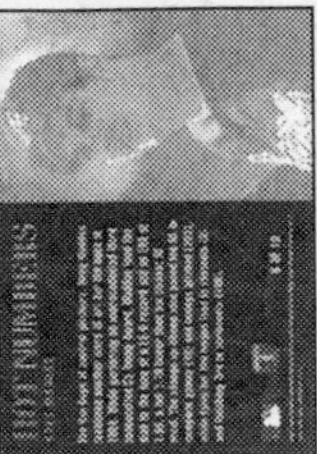

Randomly inserted in series one packs at a rate of one in nine, this 10-card standard-size set showcases top players. A player photo on front is superimposed over a gold background that contains player stats from 1994. Horizontal backs have a ghosted player photo to the right with highlights on the left.

	MINT	NRMT
COMPLETE SET (10)	60.00	27.00
COMMON CARD (1-10)	2.00	.90
1 Jeff Bagwell	6.00	2.70
2 Albert Belle	6.00	2.70
3 Barry Bonds	4.00	1.80
4 Ken Griffey Jr.	15.00	6.75
5 Kenny Lofton	4.00	1.80
6 Greg Maddux	10.00	4.50
7 Mike Piazza	10.00	4.50
8 Cal Ripken	12.00	5.50
9 Frank Thomas	15.00	6.75
10 Matt Williams	2.00	.90

1995 Flair Infield Power

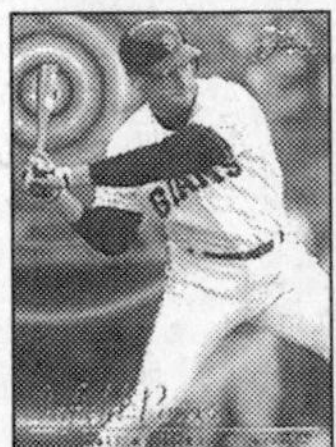

Randomly inserted in second series packs at a rate of one in six, this 10-card standard-size set features sluggers that man the infield. A player photo on front is surrounded by multiple color schemes with a horizontal back offering a player photo and highlights.

	MINT	NRMT
COMPLETE SET (10)	15.00	6.75
COMMON CARD (1-10)	.50	.23
1 Jeff Bagwell	3.00	1.35
2 Darren Daulton	.50	.23
3 Cecil Fielder	.75	.35
4 Andres Galarraga	1.00	.45
5 Fred McGriff	1.00	.45
6 Rafael Palmeiro	1.00	.45
7 Mike Piazza	5.00	2.20
8 Frank Thomas	8.00	3.60
9 Mo Vaughn	2.00	.90
10 Matt Williams	1.00	.45

1995 Flair Outfield Power

Randomly inserted in first series packs at a rate of one in six, this 10-card standard-size set features sluggers that patrol the outfield. A player photo on front is surrounded by multiple color schemes with a horizontal back offering a player photo and highlights.

	MINT	NRMT
COMPLETE SET (10)	15.00	6.75
COMMON CARD (1-10)	.50	.23
1 Albert Belle	3.00	1.35
2 Dante Bichette	1.00	.45

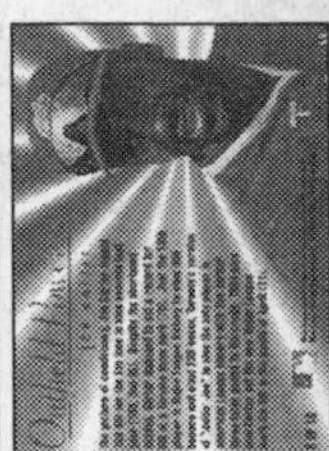

	MINT	NRMT
3 Barry Bonds	2.00	.90
4 Jose Canseco	1.00	.45
5 Joe Carter	1.00	.45
6 Juan Gonzalez	4.00	1.80
7 Ken Griffey Jr.	8.00	3.60
8 Kirby Puckett	3.00	1.35
9 Gary Sheffield	1.50	.70
10 Ruben Sierra	.50	.23

1995 Flair Ripken

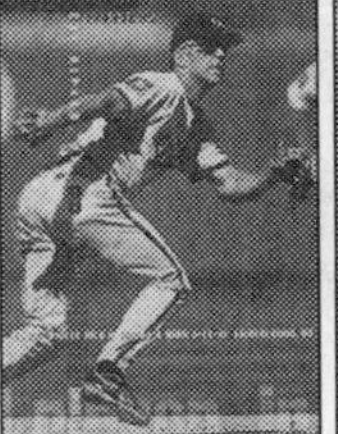

Titled "Enduring", this 10-card standard-size set is a tribute to Cal Ripken's career through the '94 season. Cards were randomly inserted in second series packs at a rate of one in 12. Full-bleed fronts have the set title in silver foil toward the bottom. The backs have a photo and a write-up on a specific achievement as selected by Cal. A five-card mail-in wrapper offer completes the set. The expiration date on this offer was March 1, 1996.

	MINT	NRMT
COMPLETE SET (10)	80.00	36.00
COMMON CARD (1-10)	10.00	4.50
COMMON MAIL-IN (11-15)	6.00	2.70
1 Cal Ripken Rookie of the Year	10.00	4.50
2 Cal Ripken 1st MVP Season	10.00	4.50
3 Cal Ripken World Series Highlight	10.00	4.50
4 Cal Ripken Family Tradition	10.00	4.50
5 Cal Ripken 8,243 Consecutive Innings	10.00	4.50
6 Cal Ripken 95 Consecutive Errorless Games	10.00	4.50
7 Cal Ripken All-Star MVP	10.00	4.50
8 Cal Ripken 1,000th RBI	10.00	4.50
9 Cal Ripken 287th Home Run	10.00	4.50
10 Cal Ripken 2,000th Consecutive Game	10.00	4.50
11 Cal Ripken Literacy	6.00	2.70
12 Cal Ripken Game 2,130	6.00	2.70
13 Cal Ripken Game 2,131	6.00	2.70
14 Cal Ripken Defensive Prowess	6.00	2.70
15 Cal Ripken 2,153 and Counting	6.00	2.70

1995 Flair Today's Spotlight

This 12-card die-cut set was randomly inserted in first series packs at a rate of one in 25 packs. The upper portion of the player photo on front has the spotlight effect as the remainder of the photo is darkened. Horizontal backs have a circular player photo to the right with text off to the left.

	MINT	NRMT
COMPLETE SET (12)	120.00	55.00
COMMON CARD (1-12)	4.00	1.80

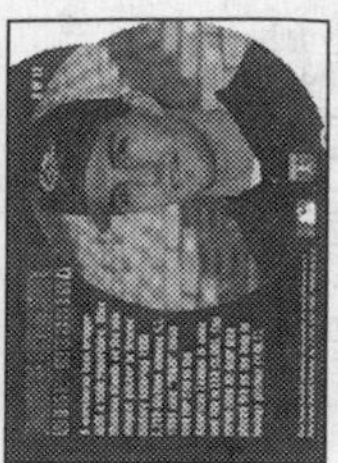

☐ 1 Jeff Bagwell	20.00	9.00
☐ 2 Jason Bere	4.00	1.80
☐ 3 Cliff Floyd	5.00	2.20
☐ 4 Chuck Knoblauch	10.00	4.50
☐ 5 Kenny Lofton	12.00	5.50
☐ 6 Javier Lopez	6.00	2.70
☐ 7 Raul Mondesi	6.00	2.70
☐ 8 Mike Mussina	10.00	4.50
☐ 9 Mike Piazza	30.00	13.50
☐ 10 Manny Ramirez	10.00	4.50
☐ 11 Tim Salmon	10.00	4.50
☐ 12 Frank Thomas	40.00	18.00

1995 Flair Wave of the Future

potlighting 10 of the game's hottest young stars, cards vere randomly inserted in second series packs at a rate of ne in nine. An action photo is superimposed over rimarily a solid background save for the player's name, eam and same name which appear several times. The acks are horizontal with a photo and write-up.

	MINT	NRMT
OMPLETE SET (10)	25.00	11.00
OMMON CARD (1-10)	1.00	.45
☐ 1 Jason Bates	1.00	.45
☐ 2 Armando Benitez	1.00	.45
☐ 3 Marty Cordova	3.00	1.35
☐ 4 Ray Durham	2.00	.90
☐ 5 Vaughn Eshelman	1.00	.45
☐ 6 Carl Everett	1.00	.45
☐ 7 Shawn Green	2.00	.90
☐ 8 Dustin Hermanson	1.00	.45
☐ 9 Chipper Jones	10.00	4.50
☐ 10 Hideo Nomo	10.00	4.50

1996 Flair

eleased in July, 1996, this 400-card set was issued in ne series and sold in seven-card packs at a suggested etail price of $4.99. Gold and Silver etched foil front ariations exist for all cards. These color variations were rinted in similar quantities and are valued equally. The onts and backs each carry a color action player cut-out n a player portrait background with player statistics on e backs. The cards are grouped alphabetically within ams and checklisted below alphabetically according to ams for each league.

	MINT	NRMT
OMPLETE SET (400)	200.00	90.00
OMMON CARD (1-400)	.50	.23
☐ 1 Roberto Alomar	2.00	.90
☐ 2 Brady Anderson	1.25	.55
☐ 3 Bobby Bonilla	.75	.35
☐ 4 Scott Erickson	.50	.23
☐ 5 Jeffrey Hammonds	.50	.23
☐ 6 Jimmy Haynes	.50	.23
☐ 7 Chris Hoiles	.50	.23
☐ 8 Kent Mercker	.50	.23
☐ 9 Mike Mussina	2.00	.90
☐ 10 Randy Myers	.50	.23
☐ 11 Rafael Palmeiro	1.25	.55
☐ 12 Cal Ripken	8.00	3.60
☐ 13 B.J. Surhoff	.50	.23
☐ 14 David Wells	.50	.23
☐ 15 Jose Canseco	1.25	.55
☐ 16 Roger Clemens	4.00	1.80
☐ 17 Wil Cordero	.50	.23
☐ 18 Tom Gordon	.50	.23
☐ 19 Mike Greenwell	.50	.23
☐ 20 Dwayne Hosey	.50	.23
☐ 21 Jose Malave	.50	.23
☐ 22 Tim Naehring	.50	.23
☐ 23 Troy O'Leary	.50	.23
☐ 24 Aaron Sele	.50	.23
☐ 25 Heathcliff Slocumb	.50	.23
☐ 26 Mike Stanley	.50	.23
☐ 27 Jeff Suppan	1.25	.55
☐ 28 John Valentin	.75	.35
☐ 29 Mo Vaughn	2.50	1.10
☐ 30 Tim Wakefield	.50	.23
☐ 31 Jim Abbott	.50	.23
☐ 32 Garret Anderson	1.25	.55
☐ 33 George Arias	.50	.23
☐ 34 Chili Davis	.50	.23
☐ 35 Gary DiSarcina	.50	.23
☐ 36 Jim Edmonds	2.00	.90
☐ 37 Chuck Finley	.50	.23
☐ 38 Todd Greene	.75	.35
☐ 39 Mark Langston	.50	.23
☐ 40 Troy Percival	.50	.23
☐ 41 Tim Salmon	1.25	.55
☐ 42 Lee Smith	.75	.35
☐ 43 J.T. Snow	.75	.35
☐ 44 Randy Velarde	.50	.23
☐ 45 Tim Wallach	.50	.23
☐ 46 Wilson Alvarez	.75	.35
☐ 47 Harold Baines	.75	.35
☐ 48 Jason Bere	.50	.23
☐ 49 Ray Durham	.75	.35
☐ 50 Alex Fernandez	.75	.35
☐ 51 Ozzie Guillen	.50	.23
☐ 52 Roberto Hernandez	.75	.35
☐ 53 Ron Karkovice	.50	.23
☐ 54 Darren Lewis	.50	.23
☐ 55 Lyle Mouton	.50	.23
☐ 56 Tony Phillips	.50	.23
☐ 57 Chris Snopek	.50	.23
☐ 58 Kevin Tapani	.50	.23
☐ 59 Danny Tartabull	.50	.23
☐ 60 Frank Thomas	8.00	3.60
☐ 61 Robin Ventura	.75	.35
☐ 62 Sandy Alomar Jr.	.75	.35
☐ 63 Carlos Baerga	.75	.35
☐ 64 Albert Belle	2.50	1.10
☐ 65 Julio Franco	.75	.35
☐ 66 Orel Hershiser	.75	.35
☐ 67 Kenny Lofton	2.50	1.10
☐ 68 Dennis Martinez	.75	.35
☐ 69 Jack McDowell	.50	.23
☐ 70 Jose Mesa	.75	.35
☐ 71 Eddie Murray	2.00	.90
☐ 72 Charles Nagy	.75	.35
☐ 73 Tony Pena	.50	.23
☐ 74 Manny Ramirez	2.00	.90
☐ 75 Julian Tavarez	.50	.23
☐ 76 Jim Thome	2.00	.90
☐ 77 Omar Vizquel	.75	.35
☐ 78 Chad Curtis	.50	.23
☐ 79 Cecil Fielder	.75	.35
☐ 80 Travis Fryman	.75	.35
☐ 81 Chris Gomez	.50	.23
☐ 82 Bob Higginson	1.25	.55
☐ 83 Mark Lewis	.50	.23
☐ 84 Felipe Lira	.50	.23
☐ 85 Alan Trammell	1.25	.55
☐ 86 Kevin Appier	.75	.35
☐ 87 Johnny Damon	.75	.35
☐ 88 Tom Goodwin	.50	.23
☐ 89 Mark Gubicza	.50	.23
☐ 90 Bob Hamelin	.50	.23
☐ 91 Keith Lockhart	.50	.23
☐ 92 Jeff Montgomery	.50	.23
☐ 93 Jon Nunnally	.50	.23
☐ 94 Bip Roberts	.50	.23
☐ 95 Michael Tucker	.75	.35
☐ 96 Joe Vitiello	.50	.23
☐ 97 Ricky Bones	.50	.23
☐ 98 Chuck Carr	.50	.23
☐ 99 Jeff Cirillo	.50	.23
☐ 100 Mike Fetters	.50	.23
☐ 101 John Jaha	.50	.23
☐ 102 Mike Matheny	.50	.23
☐ 103 Ben McDonald	.50	.23
☐ 104 Matt Mieske	.50	.23
☐ 105 Dave Nilsson	.75	.35
☐ 106 Kevin Seitzer	.50	.23
☐ 107 Steve Sparks	.50	.23
☐ 108 Jose Valentin	.50	.23
☐ 109 Greg Vaughn	.50	.23
☐ 110 Rick Aguilera	.50	.23
☐ 111 Rich Becker	.75	.35
☐ 112 Marty Cordova	.50	.23
☐ 113 LaTroy Hawkins	.50	.23
☐ 114 Dave Hollins	.50	.23
☐ 115 Roberto Kelly	.50	.23
☐ 116 Chuck Knoblauch	2.00	.90
☐ 117 Matt Lawton	.50	.23
☐ 118 Pat Meares	.50	.23
☐ 119 Paul Molitor	2.00	.90
☐ 120 Kirby Puckett	4.00	1.80
☐ 121 Brad Radke	.75	.35
☐ 122 Frank Rodriguez	.50	.23
☐ 123 Scott Stahoviak	.50	.23
☐ 124 Matt Walbeck	.50	.23
☐ 125 Wade Boggs	2.00	.90
☐ 126 David Cone	.75	.35
☐ 127 Joe Girardi	.50	.23
☐ 128 Dwight Gooden	.50	.23
☐ 129 Derek Jeter	6.00	2.70
☐ 130 Jimmy Key	.75	.35
☐ 131 Jim Leyritz	.50	.23
☐ 132 Tino Martinez	2.00	.90
☐ 133 Paul O'Neill	.75	.35
☐ 134 Andy Pettitte	2.50	1.10
☐ 135 Tim Raines	.50	.23
☐ 136 Ruben Rivera	.75	.35
☐ 137 Kenny Rogers	.50	.23
☐ 138 Ruben Sierra	.50	.23
☐ 139 John Wetteland	.75	.35
☐ 140 Bernie Williams	2.00	.90
☐ 141 Tony Batista	.50	.23
☐ 142 Allen Battle	.50	.23
☐ 143 Geronimo Berroa	.50	.23
☐ 144 Mike Bordick	.50	.23
☐ 145 Scott Brosius	.50	.23
☐ 146 Steve Cox	.50	.23
☐ 147 Brent Gates	.50	.23
☐ 148 Jason Giambi	1.25	.55
☐ 149 Doug Johns	.50	.23
☐ 150 Mark McGwire	4.00	1.80
☐ 151 Pedro Munoz	.50	.23
☐ 152 Ariel Prieto	.50	.23
☐ 153 Terry Steinbach	.75	.35
☐ 154 Todd Van Poppel	.50	.23
☐ 155 Bobby Ayala	.50	.23
☐ 156 Chris Bosio	.50	.23
☐ 157 Jay Buhner	1.25	.55
☐ 158 Joey Cora	.75	.35
☐ 159 Russ Davis	.50	.23
☐ 160 Ken Griffey Jr.	10.00	4.50
☐ 161 Sterling Hitchcock	.50	.23
☐ 162 Randy Johnson	2.00	.90
☐ 163 Edgar Martinez	1.25	.55
☐ 164 Alex Rodriguez	8.00	3.60
☐ 165 Paul Sorrento	.50	.23
☐ 166 Dan Wilson	.50	.23
☐ 167 Will Clark	1.25	.55
☐ 168 Benji Gil	.50	.23
☐ 169 Juan Gonzalez	5.00	2.20
☐ 170 Rusty Greer	2.00	.90
☐ 171 Kevin Gross	.50	.23
☐ 172 Darryl Hamilton	.50	.23
☐ 173 Mike Henneman	.50	.23
☐ 174 Ken Hill	.50	.23
☐ 175 Mark McLemore	.50	.23
☐ 176 Dean Palmer	.75	.35
☐ 177 Roger Pavlik	.50	.23
☐ 178 Ivan Rodriguez	2.50	1.10
☐ 179 Mickey Tettleton	.50	.23
☐ 180 Bobby Witt	.50	.23
☐ 181 Joe Carter	.75	.35
☐ 182 Felipe Crespo	.50	.23
☐ 183 Alex Gonzalez	.50	.23
☐ 184 Shawn Green	.50	.23
☐ 185 Juan Guzman	.50	.23
☐ 186 Erik Hanson	.50	.23
☐ 187 Pat Hentgen	.75	.35
☐ 188 Sandy Martinez	.50	.23
☐ 189 Otis Nixon	.75	.35
☐ 190 John Olerud	.75	.35
☐ 191 Paul Quantrill	.50	.23
☐ 192 Bill Risley	.50	.23
☐ 193 Ed Sprague	.50	.23
☐ 194 Steve Avery	.50	.23

☐ 195 Jeff Blauser .50 .23
☐ 196 Brad Clontz .50 .23
☐ 197 Jermaine Dye .50 .23
☐ 198 Tom Glavine 1.25 .55
☐ 199 Marquis Grissom .75 .35
☐ 200 Chipper Jones 6.00 2.70
☐ 201 David Justice 1.25 .55
☐ 202 Ryan Klesko 1.25 .55
☐ 203 Mark Lemke .50 .23
☐ 204 Javier Lopez 1.25 .55
☐ 205 Greg Maddux 6.00 2.70
☐ 206 Fred McGriff 1.25 .55
☐ 207 Greg McMichael .50 .23
☐ 208 Wonderful Monds .50 .23
☐ 209 Jason Schmidt .50 .23
☐ 210 John Smoltz .75 .35
☐ 211 Mark Wohlers .75 .35
☐ 212 Jim Bullinger .50 .23
☐ 213 Frank Castillo .50 .23
☐ 214 Kevin Foster .50 .23
☐ 215 Luis Gonzalez .50 .23
☐ 216 Mark Grace 1.25 .55
☐ 217 Robin Jennings .50 .23
☐ 218 Doug Jones .50 .23
☐ 219 Dave Magadan .50 .23
☐ 220 Brian McRae .50 .23
☐ 221 Jaime Navarro .50 .23
☐ 222 Rey Sanchez .50 .23
☐ 223 Ryne Sandberg 2.50 1.10
☐ 224 Scott Servais .50 .23
☐ 225 Sammy Sosa 2.00 .90
☐ 226 Ozzie Timmons .50 .23
☐ 227 Bret Boone .50 .23
☐ 228 Jeff Branson .50 .23
☐ 229 Jeff Brantley .50 .23
☐ 230 Dave Burba .50 .23
☐ 231 Vince Coleman .50 .23
☐ 232 Steve Gibralter .50 .23
☐ 233 Mike Kelly .50 .23
☐ 234 Barry Larkin 1.25 .55
☐ 235 Hal Morris .50 .23
☐ 236 Mark Portugal .50 .23
☐ 237 Jose Rijo .50 .23
☐ 238 Reggie Sanders .50 .23
☐ 239 Pete Schourek .50 .23
☐ 240 John Smiley .50 .23
☐ 241 Eddie Taubensee .50 .23
☐ 242 Jason Bates .50 .23
☐ 243 Dante Bichette 1.25 .55
☐ 244 Ellis Burks .75 .35
☐ 245 Vinny Castilla .75 .35
☐ 246 Andres Galarraga 2.00 .90
☐ 247 Darren Holmes .50 .23
☐ 248 Curt Leskanic .50 .23
☐ 249 Steve Reed .50 .23
☐ 250 Kevin Rtiz .50 .23
☐ 251 Bret Saberhagen .50 .23
☐ 252 Bill Swift .50 .23
☐ 253 Larry Walker 2.00 .90
☐ 254 Walt Weiss .50 .23
☐ 255 Eric Young .75 .35
☐ 256 Kurt Abbott .50 .23
☐ 257 Kevin Brown .75 .35
☐ 258 John Burkett .50 .23
☐ 259 Greg Colbrunn .50 .23
☐ 260 Jeff Conine .75 .35
☐ 261 Andre Dawson 1.25 .55
☐ 262 Chris Hammond .50 .23
☐ 263 Charles Johnson .75 .35
☐ 264 Al Leiter .50 .23
☐ 265 Robb Nen .75 .35
☐ 266 Terry Pendleton .75 .35
☐ 267 Pat Rapp .50 .23
☐ 268 Gary Sheffield 2.00 .90
☐ 269 Quilvio Veras .50 .23
☐ 270 Devon White .50 .23
☐ 271 Bob Abreu 2.00 .90
☐ 272 Jeff Bagwell 4.00 1.80
☐ 273 Derek Bell .75 .35
☐ 274 Sean Berry .50 .23
☐ 275 Craig Biggio 1.25 .55
☐ 276 Doug Drabek .50 .23
☐ 277 Tony Eusebio .50 .23
☐ 278 Richard Hidalgo 2.00 .90
☐ 279 Brian L.Hunter .75 .35
☐ 280 Todd Jones .50 .23
☐ 281 Derrick May .50 .23
☐ 282 Orlando Miller .50 .23
☐ 283 James Mouton .50 .23
☐ 284 Shane Reynolds .50 .23
☐ 285 Greg Swindell .50 .23
☐ 286 Mike Blowers .50 .23
☐ 287 Brett Butler .75 .35
☐ 288 Tom Candiotti .50 .23
☐ 289 Roger Cedeno .75 .35
☐ 290 Delino DeShields .50 .23
☐ 291 Greg Gagne .50 .23
☐ 292 Karim Garcia .75 .35
☐ 293 Todd Hollandsworth .75 .35
☐ 294 Eric Karros .75 .35
☐ 295 Ramon Martinez .75 .35
☐ 296 Raul Mondesi 1.25 .55
☐ 297 Hideo Nomo 5.00 2.20
☐ 298 Mike Piazza 6.00 2.70
☐ 299 Ismael Valdes .75 .35
☐ 300 Todd Worrell .75 .35
☐ 301 Moises Alou .75 .35
☐ 302 Shane Andrews .50 .23
☐ 303 Yamil Benitez .75 .35
☐ 304 Jeff Fassero .50 .23
☐ 305 Darrin Fletcher .50 .23
☐ 306 Cliff Floyd .50 .23
☐ 307 Mark Grudzielanek .75 .35
☐ 308 Mike Lansing .50 .23
☐ 309 Pedro Martinez 2.00 .90
☐ 310 Ryan McGuire .50 .23
☐ 311 Carlos Perez .50 .23
☐ 312 Mel Rojas .75 .35
☐ 313 David Segui .50 .23
☐ 314 Rondell White .75 .35
☐ 315 Edgardo Alfonzo 2.00 .90
☐ 316 Rico Brogna .50 .23
☐ 317 Carl Everett .50 .23
☐ 318 John Franco .75 .35
☐ 319 Bernard Gilkey .75 .35
☐ 320 Todd Hundley .75 .35
☐ 321 Jason Isringhausen .50 .23
☐ 322 Lance Johnson .50 .23
☐ 323 Bobby Jones .50 .23
☐ 324 Jeff Kent .50 .23
☐ 325 Rey Ordonez .50 .23
☐ 326 Bill Pulsipher .50 .23
☐ 327 Jose Vizcaino .50 .23
☐ 328 Paul Wilson .50 .23
☐ 329 Ricky Bottalico .75 .35
☐ 330 Darren Daulton .75 .35
☐ 331 David Doster .50 .23
☐ 332 Lenny Dykstra .75 .35
☐ 333 Jim Eisenreich .75 .35
☐ 334 Sid Fernandez .50 .23
☐ 335 Gregg Jefferies .75 .35
☐ 336 Mickey Morandini .50 .23
☐ 337 Benito Santiago .50 .23
☐ 338 Curt Schilling .75 .35
☐ 339 Kevin Stocker .50 .23
☐ 340 David West .50 .23
☐ 341 Mark Whiten .50 .23
☐ 342 Todd Zeile .50 .23
☐ 343 Jay Bell .75 .35
☐ 344 John Ericks .50 .23
☐ 345 Carlos Garcia .50 .23
☐ 346 Charlie Hayes .50 .23
☐ 347 Jason Kendall .75 .35
☐ 348 Jeff King .75 .35
☐ 349 Mike Kingery .50 .23
☐ 350 Al Martin .50 .23
☐ 351 Orlando Merced .50 .23
☐ 352 Dan Miceli .50 .23
☐ 353 Denny Neagle .75 .35
☐ 354 Alan Benes .75 .35
☐ 355 Andy Benes .50 .23
☐ 356 Royce Clayton .50 .23
☐ 357 Dennis Eckersley 1.25 .55
☐ 358 Gary Gaetti .75 .35
☐ 359 Ron Gant .75 .35
☐ 360 Brian Jordan .75 .35
☐ 361 Ray Lankford 1.25 .55
☐ 362 John Mabry .75 .35
☐ 363 T.J. Mathews .50 .23
☐ 364 Mike Morgan .50 .23
☐ 365 Donovan Osborne .50 .23
☐ 366 Tom Pagnozzi .50 .23
☐ 367 Ozzie Smith 2.50 1.10
☐ 368 Todd Stottlemyre .50 .23
☐ 369 Andy Ashby .50 .23
☐ 370 Brad Ausmus .50 .23
☐ 371 Ken Caminiti 2.00 .90
☐ 372 Andujar Cedeno .50 .23
☐ 373 Steve Finley .75 .35
☐ 374 Tony Gwynn 5.00 2.20
☐ 375 Joey Hamilton .75 .35
☐ 376 Rickey Henderson 2.00 .90
☐ 377 Trevor Hoffman .75 .35
☐ 378 Wally Joyner .50 .23
☐ 379 Marc Newfield .75 .35
☐ 380 Jody Reed .50 .23
☐ 381 Bob Tewksbury .50 .23
☐ 382 Fernando Valenzuela .75 .35
☐ 383 Rod Beck .75 .35
☐ 384 Barry Bonds 2.50 1.10
☐ 385 Mark Carreon .50 .23
☐ 386 Shawon Dunston .50 .23
☐ 387 Osvaldo Fernandez 2.00 .90
☐ 388 Glenallen Hill .50 .23
☐ 389 Stan Javier .50 .23
☐ 390 Mark Leiter .50 .23
☐ 391 Kirt Manwaring .50 .23
☐ 392 Robby Thompson .50 .23
☐ 393 William VanLandingham .50 .23
☐ 394 Allen Watson .50 .23
☐ 395 Matt Williams 1.25 .55
☐ 396 Checklist (1-92) .50 .23
☐ 397 Checklist (93-180) .50 .23
☐ 398 Checklist (181-272) .50 .23
☐ 399 Checklist (273-365) .50 .23
☐ 400 Checklist (366-400/Inserts) .50 .23

1996 Flair Diamond Cuts

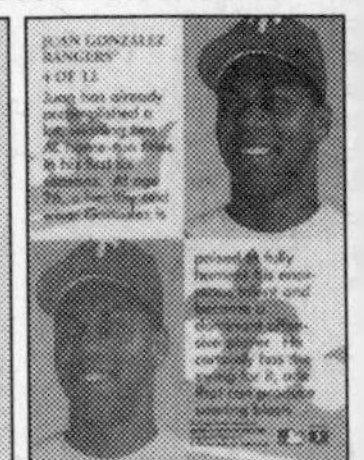

Randomly inserted in packs at a rate of one in 20, this 12-card set showcases the game's greatest stars with rainbow holofoil and glitter coating on the card.

	MINT	NRMT
COMPLETE SET (12)	150.00	70.00
COMMON CARD (1-12)	4.00	1.80
☐ 1 Jeff Bagwell	12.00	5.50
☐ 2 Albert Belle	8.00	3.60
☐ 3 Barry Bonds	8.00	3.60
☐ 4 Juan Gonzalez	15.00	6.75
☐ 5 Ken Griffey Jr.	30.00	13.50
☐ 6 Greg Maddux	20.00	9.00
☐ 7 Eddie Murray	6.00	2.70
☐ 8 Mike Piazza	20.00	9.00
☐ 9 Cal Ripken	25.00	11.00
☐ 10 Frank Thomas	25.00	11.00
☐ 11 Mo Vaughn	8.00	3.60
☐ 12 Matt Williams	4.00	1.80

1996 Flair Hot Gloves

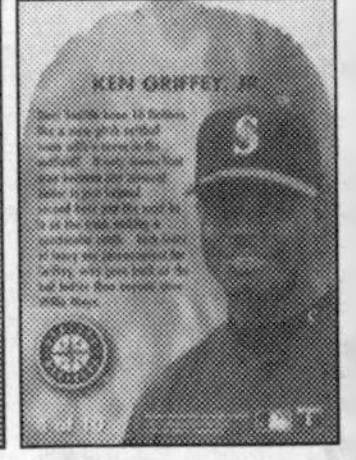

Randomly inserted in hobby packs only at a rate of one in 90, this 10-card set is printed on special, thermo-embossed die-cut cards and spotlights the best defensive players.

	MINT	NRMT
COMPLETE SET (10)	500.00	220.00
COMMON CARD (1-10)	20.00	9.00
☐ 1 Roberto Alomar	30.00	13.50
☐ 2 Barry Bonds	40.00	18.00
☐ 3 Will Clark	20.00	9.00
☐ 4 Ken Griffey Jr.	150.00	70.00
☐ 5 Kenny Lofton	40.00	18.00
☐ 6 Greg Maddux	100.00	45.00
☐ 7 Mike Piazza	100.00	45.00
☐ 8 Cal Ripken	120.00	55.00
☐ 9 Ivan Rodriguez	40.00	18.00
☐ 10 Matt Williams	20.00	9.00

1996 Flair Powerline

Randomly inserted in packs at a rate of one in 6, this 10-card set features baseball's leading power hitters. The fronts display a color action close-up player photo with a green overlay indicating his power. The backs carry a player portrait and a statement about the player's hitting power.

	MINT	NRMT
COMPLETE SET (10)	40.00	18.00
COMMON CARD (1-10)	1.00	.45

☐ 1 Albert Belle	2.50	1.10
☐ 2 Barry Bonds	2.50	1.10
☐ 3 Juan Gonzalez	5.00	2.20
☐ 4 Ken Griffey Jr.	10.00	4.50
☐ 5 Mark McGwire	4.00	1.80
☐ 6 Mike Piazza	6.00	2.70
☐ 7 Manny Ramirez	2.00	.90
☐ 8 Sammy Sosa	1.50	.70
☐ 9 Frank Thomas	8.00	3.60
☐ 10 Matt Williams	1.25	.55

1996 Flair Wave of the Future

Randomly inserted in packs at a rate of one in 72, this 20-card set highlights the top 1996 rookies and prospects on lenticular cards.

	MINT	NRMT
COMPLETE SET (20)	250.00	110.00
COMMON CARD (1-20)	10.00	4.50
☐ 1 Bob Abreu	15.00	6.75
☐ 2 George Arias	10.00	4.50
☐ 3 Tony Batista	15.00	6.75
☐ 4 Alan Benes	25.00	11.00
☐ 5 Yamil Benitez	12.50	5.50
☐ 6 Steve Cox	10.00	4.50
☐ 7 David Doster	10.00	4.50
☐ 8 Jermaine Dye	10.00	4.50
☐ 9 Osvaldo Fernandez	12.50	5.50
☐ 10 Karim Garcia	25.00	11.00
☐ 11 Steve Gibralter	10.00	4.50
☐ 12 Todd Greene	20.00	9.00
☐ 13 Richard Hidalgo	25.00	11.00
☐ 14 Robin Jennings	10.00	4.50
☐ 15 Jason Kendall	20.00	9.00
☐ 16 Jose Malave	10.00	4.50
☐ 17 Wonderful Monds	10.00	4.50
☐ 18 Rey Ordonez	15.00	6.75
☐ 19 Ruben Rivera	25.00	11.00
☐ 20 Paul Wilson	10.00	4.50

1997 Flair Showcase Row 2

The 1997 Flair Showcase set was issued in one series totalling 540 cards and was distributed in five-card packs with a suggested retail price of $4.99. This hobby exclusive set is divided into three 180-card sets (Row2/Style, Row1/Grace, and Row0/Showcase) and features holographic foil fronts with an action photo of the player silhouetted over a larger black-and-white head-shot image in the background. The thick card stock is laminated with a shiny glossy coating for a super-premium "feel." Also inserted one in every pack was a Million Dollar Moments card. Finally, 25 serial-numbered Alex Rodriguez Emerald Exchange cards were randomly seeded into packs. The card fronts were very similar in design to the regular Row 2 Rodriguez, except for green foil accents. The card back, however, consisted entirely of text explaining prize guidelines. The deadline to exchange the card was 8/1/98.

	MINT	NRMT
COMPLETE SET (180)	100.00	45.00
COMMON CARD (1-60)	.25	.11
COMMON CARD (61-120)	.40	.18
COMMON CARD (121-180)	.30	.14
☐ 1 Andruw Jones	2.50	1.10
☐ 2 Derek Jeter	3.00	1.35
☐ 3 Alex Rodriguez	4.00	1.80
☐ 4 Paul Molitor	1.00	.45
☐ 5 Jeff Bagwell	2.00	.90
☐ 6 Scott Rolen	2.50	1.10
☐ 7 Kenny Lofton	1.25	.55
☐ 8 Cal Ripken	4.00	1.80
☐ 9 Brady Anderson	.60	.25
☐ 10 Chipper Jones	3.00	1.35
☐ 11 Todd Greene	.40	.18
☐ 12 Todd Walker	.25	.11
☐ 13 Billy Wagner	.40	.18
☐ 14 Craig Biggio	.60	.25
☐ 15 Kevin Orie	.40	.18
☐ 16 Hideo Nomo	2.50	1.10
☐ 17 Kevin Appier	.40	.18
☐ 18 Bubba Trammell STY	1.00	.45
☐ 19 Juan Gonzalez	2.50	1.10
☐ 20 Randy Johnson	1.00	.45
☐ 21 Roger Clemens	2.00	.90
☐ 22 Johnny Damon	.40	.18
☐ 23 Ryne Sandberg	1.25	.55
☐ 24 Ken Griffey Jr.	5.00	2.20
☐ 25 Barry Bonds	1.25	.55
☐ 26 Nomar Garciaparra	3.00	1.35
☐ 27 Vladimir Guerrero	2.00	.90
☐ 28 Ron Gant	.40	.18
☐ 29 Joe Carter	.40	.18
☐ 30 Tim Salmon	1.00	.45
☐ 31 Mike Piazza	3.00	1.35
☐ 32 Barry Larkin	.60	.25
☐ 33 Manny Ramirez	1.00	.45
☐ 34 Sammy Sosa	1.00	.45
☐ 35 Frank Thomas	4.00	1.80
☐ 36 Melvin Nieves	.25	.11
☐ 37 Tony Gwynn	2.50	1.10
☐ 38 Gary Sheffield	1.00	.45
☐ 39 Darin Erstad	1.50	.70
☐ 40 Ken Caminiti	1.00	.45
☐ 41 Jermaine Dye	.25	.11
☐ 42 Mo Vaughn	1.25	.55
☐ 43 Raul Mondesi	.60	.25
☐ 44 Greg Maddux	3.00	1.35
☐ 45 Chuck Knoblauch	1.00	.45
☐ 46 Andy Pettitte	1.00	.45
☐ 47 Deion Sanders	1.00	.45
☐ 48 Albert Belle	1.25	.55
☐ 49 Jamey Wright	.40	.18
☐ 50 Rey Ordonez	.25	.11
☐ 51 Bernie Williams	1.00	.45
☐ 52 Mark McGwire	2.00	.90
☐ 53 Mike Mussina	1.00	.45
☐ 54 Bob Abreu	1.00	.45
☐ 55 Reggie Sanders	.25	.11
☐ 56 Brian Jordan	.40	.18
☐ 57 Ivan Rodriguez	1.25	.55
☐ 58 Roberto Alomar	1.00	.45
☐ 59 Tim Naehring	.25	.11
☐ 60 Edgar Renteria	.40	.18
☐ 61 Dean Palmer	.60	.25
☐ 62 Benito Santiago	.40	.18
☐ 63 David Cone	.60	.25
☐ 64 Carlos Delgado	.60	.25
☐ 65 Brian Giles	.40	.18
☐ 66 Alex Ochoa	.40	.18
☐ 67 Rondell White	.60	.25
☐ 68 Robin Ventura	.60	.25
☐ 69 Eric Karros	.40	.18
☐ 70 Jose Valentin	.40	.18
☐ 71 Rafael Palmeiro	1.00	.45
☐ 72 Chris Snopek	.40	.18
☐ 73 David Justice	1.25	.55
☐ 74 Tom Glavine	.60	.25
☐ 75 Rudy Pemberton	.40	.18
☐ 76 Larry Walker	1.50	.70
☐ 77 Jim Thome	1.50	.70
☐ 78 Charles Johnson	.60	.25
☐ 79 Dante Powell	.40	.18
☐ 80 Derrek Lee	1.25	.55
☐ 81 Jason Kendall	.60	.25
☐ 82 Todd Hollandsworth	.40	.18
☐ 83 Bernard Gilkey	.40	.18
☐ 84 Mel Rojas	.40	.18
☐ 85 Dmitri Young	.60	.25
☐ 86 Bret Boone	.40	.18
☐ 87 Pat Hentgen	.60	.25
☐ 88 Bobby Bonilla	.60	.25
☐ 89 John Wetteland	.60	.25
☐ 90 Todd Hundley	.60	.25
☐ 91 Wilton Guerrero	.40	.18
☐ 92 Geronimo Berroa	.40	.18
☐ 93 Al Martin	.40	.18
☐ 94 Danny Tartabull	.40	.18
☐ 95 Brian McRae	.40	.18
☐ 96 Steve Finley	.60	.25
☐ 97 Todd Stottlemyre	.40	.18
☐ 98 John Smoltz	.60	.25
☐ 99 Matt Williams	1.00	.45
☐ 100 Eddie Murray	1.50	.70
☐ 101 Henry Rodriguez	.40	.18
☐ 102 Marty Cordova	.40	.18
☐ 103 Juan Guzman	.40	.18
☐ 104 Chili Davis	.60	.25
☐ 105 Eric Young	.40	.18
☐ 106 Jeff Abbott	.40	.18
☐ 107 Shannon Stewart	.60	.25
☐ 108 Rocky Coppinger	.40	.18
☐ 109 Jose Canseco	1.00	.45
☐ 110 Dante Bichette	.40	.18
☐ 111 Dwight Gooden	.60	.25
☐ 112 Scott Brosius	.40	.18
☐ 113 Steve Avery	.40	.18
☐ 114 Andres Galarraga	1.25	.55
☐ 115 Sandy Alomar Jr.	.60	.25
☐ 116 Ray Lankford	.60	.25
☐ 117 Jorge Posada	.40	.18
☐ 118 Ryan Klesko	1.00	.45
☐ 119 Jay Buhner	1.00	.45
☐ 120 Jose Guillen	2.00	.90
☐ 121 Paul O'Neill	.50	.23
☐ 122 Jimmy Key	.50	.23
☐ 123 Hal Morris	.30	.14
☐ 124 Travis Fryman	.50	.23
☐ 125 Jim Edmonds		
☐ 126 Jeff Cirillo	.50	.23
☐ 127 Fred McGriff	.75	.35
☐ 128 Alan Benes	.30	.14
☐ 129 Derek Bell	.30	.14
☐ 130 Tony Graffanino	.30	.14
☐ 131 Shawn Green	.50	.23
☐ 132 Denny Neagle	.50	.23
☐ 133 Alex Fernandez	.30	.14
☐ 134 Mickey Morandini	.30	.14
☐ 135 Royce Clayton	.30	.14
☐ 136 Jose Mesa	.50	.23
☐ 137 Edgar Martinez	.75	.35
☐ 138 Curt Schilling	.50	.23
☐ 139 Lance Johnson	.30	.14
☐ 140 Andy Benes	.50	.23
☐ 141 Charles Nagy	.30	.14
☐ 142 Mariano Rivera	.50	.23
☐ 143 Mark Wohlers	.50	.23
☐ 144 Ken Hill	.30	.14
☐ 145 Jay Bell	.30	.14
☐ 146 Bob Higginson	.50	.23
☐ 147 Mark Grudzielanek	.50	.23
☐ 148 Ray Durham	.30	.14
☐ 149 John Olerud	.50	.23
☐ 150 Joey Hamilton	.30	.14
☐ 151 Trevor Hoffman	.50	.23
☐ 152 Dan Wilson	.30	.14
☐ 153 J.T. Snow	.50	.23
☐ 154 Marquis Grissom	.50	.23
☐ 155 Yamil Benitez	.50	.23
☐ 156 Rusty Greer	.50	.23
☐ 157 Darryl Kile	.50	.23
☐ 158 Ismael Valdes	.50	.23
☐ 159 Jeff Conine	.50	.23
☐ 160 Darren Daulton	.50	.23
☐ 161 Chan Ho Park		
☐ 162 Troy Percival	.50	.23
☐ 163 Wade Boggs		
☐ 164 Dave Nilsson	.50	.23
☐ 165 Vinny Castilla	.50	.23
☐ 166 Kevin Brown	.50	.23
☐ 167 Dennis Eckersley	.75	.35
☐ 168 Wendell Magee Jr.	.30	.14
☐ 169 John Jaha	.30	.14
☐ 170 Garret Anderson	.50	.23
☐ 171 Jason Giambi	.50	.23
☐ 172 Mark Grace	.75	.35
☐ 173 Tony Clark	1.00	.45
☐ 174 Moises Alou	.50	.23
☐ 175 Brett Butler	.50	.23
☐ 176 Cecil Fielder	.50	.23
☐ 177 Chris Widger	.30	.14
☐ 178 Doug Drabek	.30	.14
☐ 179 Ellis Burks	.50	.23

	MINT	NRMT
☐ 180 Shigetoshi Hasegawa STY	.75	.35
☐ NNO Alex Rodriguez Glove EXCH	1000.00	450.00

1997 Flair Showcase Row 1

Randomly inserted in packs at the rate of one in 25, this 180-card Grace set is parallel to the base Flair Showcase Row 2 (Style) set and features holographic foil fronts with an action photo of the player silhouetted over a larger color head-shot image in the background.

	MINT	NRMT
COMPLETE SET (180)	200.00	90.00
COMMON CARD (1-60)	.60	.25
MINOR STARS 1-60	1.00	.45
SEMISTARS 1-60	1.50	.70
UNLISTED STARS 1-60	2.50	1.10
*STARS 1-60: 1.25X TO 2.5X ROW2		
COMMON CARD (61-120)	.50	.23
MINOR STARS 61-120	.75	.35
SEMISTARS 61-120	1.25	.55
UNLISTED STARS 61-120	2.00	.90
*STARS 61-120: .6X TO 1.2X ROW 2		
COMMON CARD (121-180)	1.00	.45
MINOR STARS 121-180	1.50	.70
SEMISTARS 121-180	2.50	1.10
UNLISTED STARS 121-180	4.00	1.80
*STARS 121-180: 1.5X TO 3X ROW 2		

1997 Flair Showcase Row 0

Randomly inserted in packs at the rate of one in 24, this 180-card Showcase set is parallel to the base Flair Showcase Row 2 (Style) set and features holographic foil fronts with a head-shot image of the player silhouetted over a larger player action-shot in the background.

	MINT	NRMT
COMPLETE SET (180)	2000.00	900.00
COMMON CARD (1-60)	8.00	3.60
MINOR STARS 1-60	10.00	4.50
SEMISTARS 1-60	15.00	6.75
UNLISTED STARS 1-60	20.00	9.00
*STARS 1-60: 12.5X TO 25X STYLE		
*YOUNG STARS 1-60: 10X TO 20X STYLE		
COMMON CARD (61-120)	3.00	1.35
MINOR STARS 61-120	5.00	2.20
SEMISTARS 61-120	8.00	3.60
UNLISTED STARS 61-120		
*STARS 61-120: 4X TO 8X STYLE		
*YOUNG STARS 61-120: 3X TO 6X STYLE		
COMMON CARD (121-180)	1.25	.55
MINOR STARS 121-180	2.00	.90
SEMISTARS 121-180	3.00	1.35
UNLISTED STARS 121-180		
*STARS 121-180: 2.5X TO 5X STYLE.		
*YOUNG STARS 121-180: 2X TO 4X STYLE		
☐ 1 Andruw Jones	50.00	22.00
☐ 2 Derek Jeter	60.00	27.00
☐ 3 Alex Rodriguez	80.00	36.00
☐ 4 Paul Molitor	25.00	11.00
☐ 5 Jeff Bagwell	50.00	22.00
☐ 6 Scott Rolen	50.00	22.00
☐ 7 Kenny Lofton	30.00	13.50
☐ 8 Cal Ripken	100.00	45.00
☐ 10 Chipper Jones	80.00	36.00
☐ 16 Hideo Nomo	60.00	27.00
☐ 18 Bubba Trammell STY	20.00	9.00
☐ 19 Juan Gonzalez	60.00	27.00
☐ 20 Randy Johnson	25.00	11.00
☐ 21 Roger Clemens	50.00	22.00
☐ 23 Ryne Sandberg	30.00	13.50
☐ 24 Ken Griffey Jr.	120.00	55.00
☐ 25 Barry Bonds	30.00	13.50
☐ 26 Nomar Garciaparra	60.00	27.00
☐ 27 Vladimir Guerrero	40.00	18.00
☐ 31 Mike Piazza	80.00	36.00
☐ 33 Manny Ramirez	25.00	11.00
☐ 35 Frank Thomas	100.00	45.00
☐ 37 Tony Gwynn	60.00	27.00
☐ 39 Darin Erstad	30.00	13.50
☐ 42 Mo Vaughn	30.00	13.50
☐ 44 Greg Maddux	80.00	36.00
☐ 46 Andy Pettitte	25.00	11.00
☐ 48 Albert Belle	30.00	13.50
☐ 52 Mark McGwire	50.00	22.00
☐ 53 Mike Mussina	25.00	11.00
☐ 57 Ivan Rodriguez	30.00	13.50
☐ 58 Roberto Alomar	25.00	11.00
☐ 76 Larry Walker	12.00	5.50
☐ 77 Jim Thome	12.00	5.50
☐ 100 Eddie Murray	12.00	5.50
☐ 120 Jose Guillen	12.00	5.50
☐ 161 Chan Ho Park	4.00	1.80
☐ 163 Wade Boggs	4.00	1.80
☐ 173 Tony Clark	4.00	1.80

1997 Flair Showcase Legacy Collection

Randomly inserted in packs at a rate of one in 30, this 180-card set is parallel to the regular set. Only 100 sequentially numbered sets were produced, each featuring an "alternate" player photo printed on a matte finish/foil stamped card. Similar to the regular Showcase set, each player has three different cards. We are treating the pricing of the cards the same irregardless of the row. One of one Masterpiece cards were also made. Since there are so few produced, we are not providing pricing for them. Please refer to future issues of Beckett Baseball Card Monthly for occassional updates on key players.

	MINT	NRMT
COMMON CARD (1-180)	25.00	11.00
MINOR STARS	40.00	18.00
SEMISTARS	60.00	27.00
UNLISTED STARS	80.00	36.00
☐ 1 Andruw Jones	200.00	90.00
☐ 2 Derek Jeter	250.00	110.00
☐ 3 Alex Rodriguez	300.00	135.00
☐ 5 Jeff Bagwell	200.00	90.00
☐ 6 Scott Rolen	200.00	90.00
☐ 7 Kenny Lofton	120.00	55.00
☐ 8 Cal Ripken	400.00	180.00
☐ 10 Chipper Jones	250.00	110.00
☐ 16 Hideo Nomo	350.00	160.00
☐ 19 Juan Gonzalez	250.00	110.00
☐ 21 Roger Clemens	200.00	90.00
☐ 23 Ryne Sandberg	120.00	55.00
☐ 24 Ken Griffey Jr.	500.00	220.00
☐ 25 Barry Bonds	120.00	55.00
☐ 26 Nomar Garciaparra	250.00	110.00
☐ 27 Vladimir Guerrero	150.00	70.00
☐ 31 Mike Piazza	300.00	135.00
☐ 35 Frank Thomas	400.00	180.00
☐ 37 Tony Gwynn	250.00	110.00
☐ 39 Darin Erstad	120.00	55.00
☐ 42 Mo Vaughn	120.00	55.00
☐ 44 Greg Maddux	300.00	135.00
☐ 48 Albert Belle	120.00	55.00
☐ 52 Mark McGwire	200.00	90.00
☐ 57 Ivan Rodriguez	120.00	55.00

1997 Flair Showcase Diamond Cuts

Randomly inserted in packs at a rate of one in 20, this 20-card set features color images of baseball's brightest stars silhouetted on a holofoil-stamped die-cut diamond-design background.

	MINT	NRMT
COMPLETE SET (20)	300.00	135.00
COMMON CARD (1-20)	5.00	2.20
☐ 1 Jeff Bagwell	15.00	6.75
☐ 2 Albert Belle	10.00	4.50
☐ 3 Ken Caminiti	8.00	3.60
☐ 4 Juan Gonzalez	20.00	9.00
☐ 5 Ken Griffey Jr.	40.00	18.00
☐ 6 Tony Gwynn	20.00	9.00
☐ 7 Todd Hundley	5.00	2.20
☐ 8 Andruw Jones	15.00	6.75
☐ 9 Chipper Jones	25.00	11.00
☐ 10 Greg Maddux	25.00	11.00
☐ 11 Mark McGwire	15.00	6.75
☐ 12 Mike Piazza	25.00	11.00
☐ 13 Derek Jeter	20.00	9.00
☐ 14 Manny Ramirez	8.00	3.60
☐ 15 Cal Ripken	30.00	13.50
☐ 16 Alex Rodriguez	25.00	11.00
☐ 17 Frank Thomas	30.00	13.50
☐ 18 Mo Vaughn	10.00	4.50
☐ 19 Bernie Williams	8.00	3.60
☐ 20 Matt Williams	8.00	3.60

1997 Flair Showcase Hot Gloves

Randomly inserted in packs at a rate of one in 90, this 15-card set features color images of baseball's top glovemen silhouetted against a die-cut flame and glove background with temperature-sensitive inks.

	MINT	NRMT
COMPLETE SET (15)	700.00	325.00
COMMON CARD (1-15)	10.00	4.50
☐ 1 Roberto Alomar	20.00	9.00
☐ 2 Barry Bonds	25.00	11.00
☐ 3 Juan Gonzalez	50.00	22.00
☐ 4 Ken Griffey Jr.	100.00	45.00
☐ 5 Marquis Grissom	10.00	4.50
☐ 6 Derek Jeter	50.00	22.00
☐ 7 Chipper Jones	60.00	27.00
☐ 8 Barry Larkin	12.00	5.50
☐ 9 Kenny Lofton	25.00	11.00
☐ 10 Greg Maddux	60.00	27.00
☐ 11 Mike Piazza	60.00	27.00
☐ 12 Cal Ripken	80.00	36.00
☐ 13 Alex Rodriguez	60.00	27.00
☐ 14 Ivan Rodriguez	25.00	11.00
☐ 15 Frank Thomas	80.00	36.00

1997 Flair Showcase Wave of the Future

Randomly inserted in packs at a rate of one in four, this 27-card set features color images of top rookies silhouetted against a background of an embossed wave design with simulated sand.

	MINT	NRMT
COMPLETE SET (27)	80.00	36.00
COMMON (1-25/WF1-WF2)	1.00	.45
☐ 1 Todd Greene	1.25	.55
☐ 2 Andruw Jones	6.00	2.70
☐ 3 Randall Simon	5.00	2.20
☐ 4 Wady Almonte	1.25	.55
☐ 5 Pat Cline	1.00	.45
☐ 6 Jeff Abbott	1.00	.45
☐ 7 Justin Towle	1.00	.45
☐ 8 Richie Sexson	1.00	.45
☐ 9 Bubba Trammell	3.00	1.35
☐ 10 Bob Abreu	2.00	.90
☐ 11 David Arias-Ortiz	3.00	1.35
☐ 12 Todd Walker	1.00	.45
☐ 13 Orlando Cabrera	1.00	.45
☐ 14 Vladimir Guerrero	5.00	2.20
☐ 15 Ricky Ledee	6.00	2.70
☐ 16 Jorge Posada	1.00	.45
☐ 17 Ruben Rivera	1.25	.55
☐ 18 Scott Spiezio	1.25	.55
☐ 19 Scott Rolen	6.00	2.70
☐ 20 Emil Brown	1.00	.45
☐ 21 Jose Guillen	3.00	1.35
☐ 22 T.J. Staton	1.00	.45
☐ 23 Eli Marrero	1.25	.55
☐ 24 Fernando Tatis	8.00	3.60
☐ 25 Ryan Jones	1.00	.45
☐ WF1 Hideki Irabu	8.00	3.60
☐ WF2 Jose Cruz Jr.	30.00	13.50

1959 Fleer Ted Williams

The cards in this 80-card set measure 2 1/2" by 3 1/2". The 1959 Fleer set, with a catalog designation of R418-1, portrays the life of Ted Williams. The wording of the wrapper, "Baseball's Greatest Series," has led to speculation that Fleer contemplated similar sets honoring other baseball immortals, but chose to develop instead the format of the 1960 and 1961 issues. These packs contained either six or eight cards. Card number 68, which was withdrawn early in production, is considered scarce and has even been counterfeited; the fake has a rosy coloration and a cross-hatch pattern visible over the

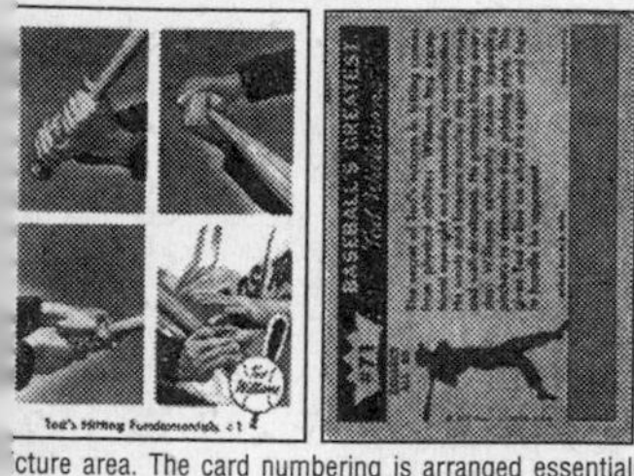

icture area. The card numbering is arranged essentially chronological order.

	NRMT	VG-E
OMPLETE SET (80)	1800.00	800.00
OMMON CARD (1-80)	12.00	5.50
VRAPPER (6-CARD)	125.00	55.00
VRAPPER (8-CARD)	150.00	70.00

☐ 1 Ted Williams 100.00 45.00
The Early Years
Choosing up sides
on the sandlots
☐ 2 Ted Williams 100.00 45.00
Babe Ruth
Meeting boyhood idol
Babe Ruth
☐ 3 Ted Williams 12.00 5.50
Practice Makes Perfect
At place practicing on the sandlots
☐ 4 Ted Williams 12.00 5.50
Learns Fine Points
Sliding at Herbert Hoover High
☐ 5 Ted Williams 12.00 5.50
Ted's Fame Spreads
At plate at Herbert Hoover High
☐ 6 Ted Williams 25.00 11.00
Ted Turns Pro
Portrait
San Diego Padres
PCL League
uniform)
☐ 7 Ted Williams 15.00 6.75
From Mound to Plate
At plate
San Diego Padres, PCL
☐ 8 Ted Williams 15.00 6.75
1937 First Full Season
Making a leaping catch
☐ 9 Ted Williams 18.00 8.00
Eddie Collins
First Step to Majors
☐ 10 Ted Williams 12.00 5.50
Gunning as Pastime
Wearing hunting gear, taking aim
☐ 11 Ted Williams 35.00 16.00
Jimmie Foxx
First Spring Training
☐ 12 Ted Williams 18.00 8.00
Burning Up Minors
Pitching for Minneapolis
American Association
☐ 13 Ted Williams 15.00 6.75
1939 Shows Will Stay
Follow-through
☐ 14 Ted Williams 15.00 6.75
Outstanding Rookie '39
Follow-through
☐ 15 Ted Williams 15.00 6.75
Licks Sophomore Jinx
Sliding into third base
for a triple
☐ 16 Ted Williams 15.00 6.75
1941 Greatest Year
Follow-through at plate
☐ 17 Ted Williams 35.00 16.00
How Ted Hit .400
Youthful Williams
as he looked in '41
☐ 18 Ted Williams 18.00 8.00
1941 All Star Hero
Crossing plate
after home run
☐ 19 Ted Williams 15.00 6.75
Wins Triple Crown
Crossing plate at Fenway Park
☐ 20 Ted Williams 12.00 5.50
On to Naval Training
In training plane
at Amherst College
☐ 21 Ted Williams 15.00 6.75
Honors for Williams
Receiving 1942 Sporting News POY
☐ 22 Ted Williams 12.00 5.50
1944 Ted Solos
In cockpit at
Pensacola, FL Navy Air Station
☐ 23 Ted Williams 15.00 6.75
Williams Wins Wings
Wearing Naval
Aviation Cadet uniform
☐ 24 Ted Williams 12.00 5.50
1945 Sharpshooter
Taking Naval eye test
☐ 25 Ted Williams 15.00 6.75
1945 Ted Discharged
In cockpit, giving
the thumbs up
☐ 26 Ted Williams 15.00 6.75
Off to Flying Start
In batters box
spring training, 1946
☐ 27 Ted Williams 15.00 6.75
7/9/46 One Man Show
Riding blooper pitch out of park
☐ 28 Ted Williams 12.00 5.50
The Williams Shift
Diagram of Cleveland Indians
position shift to defense Williams
☐ 29 Ted Williams 18.00 8.00
Ted Hits for Cycle
Close-up of follow through
☐ 30 Ted Williams 15.00 6.75
Beating Williams Shift
Crossing plate after home run
☐ 31 Ted Williams 15.00 6.75
Sox Lose Series
Sliding across plate
Sept. 14, 1946
☐ 32 Ted Williams 15.00 6.75
Joseph Cashman
Most Valuable Player
Receiving MVP Award
☐ 33 Ted Williams 12.00 5.50
Another Triple Crown
Famous Williams' Grip
☐ 34 Ted Williams 12.00 5.50
Runs Scored Record
Sliding into 2nd base
in 1947 AS Game
☐ 35 Ted Williams 12.00 5.50
Sox Miss Pennant
Checking weight on
new 36 oz. hickory bat
☐ 36 Ted Williams 15.00 6.75
Banner Year for Ted
Bunting down the
3rd base line
☐ 37 Ted Williams 15.00 6.75
1949 Sox Miss Again
Two moods: grim and determined
smiling and happy
☐ 38 Ted Williams 15.00 6.75
1949 Power Rampage
Full shot of his
batting follow through
☐ 39 Ted Williams 20.00 9.00
Joe Cronin
Eddie Collins
1950 Great Start
Signing $125,000 contract
☐ 40 Ted Williams 15.00 6.75
Ted Crashes into Wall
Making catch in
1950 All Star game
and crashing into wall
☐ 41 Ted Williams 12.00 5.50
1950 Ted Recovers
Recuperating from elbow operation
in hospital
☐ 42 Ted Williams 15.00 6.75
Tom Yawkey
Slowed by Injury
☐ 43 Ted Williams 15.00 6.75
Double Play Lead
Leaping high to
make great catch
☐ 44 Ted Williams 15.00 6.75
Back to Marines
Hanging up number 9
prior to leaving for Marines
☐ 45 Ted Williams 15.00 6.75
Farewell to Baseball
Honored at Fenway Park
prior to return to service
☐ 46 Ted Williams 12.00 5.50
Ready for Combat
Drawing jet pilot equipment
in Willow Grove
☐ 47 Ted Williams 12.00 5.50
Ted Crash Lands Jet
In flying gear
and jet he crash landed in
☐ 48 Ted Williams 18.00 8.00
Ford Frick
1953 Ted Returns
Throwing out 1st ball
at All-Star Game in Cincinnati
☐ 49 Ted Williams 12.00 5.50
Smash Return
Giving his arm
whirlpool treatment
☐ 50 Ted Williams 18.00 8.00
1954 Spring Injury
Full batting pose at plate
☐ 51 Ted Williams 12.00 5.50
Ted is Patched Up
In first workout after
fractured collar bone
☐ 52 Ted Williams 18.00 8.00
1954 Ted's Comeback
Hitting a home run
against Detroit
☐ 53 Ted Williams 15.00 6.75
Comeback is Success
Beating catcher's
tag at home plate
☐ 54 Ted Williams 15.00 6.75
Ted Hooks Big One
With prize catch
1235 lb. black marlin
☐ 55 Ted Williams 18.00 8.00
Joe Cronin
Retirement "No Go"
Returning from retirement
☐ 56 Ted Williams 15.00 6.75
2,000th Hit
8/11/55
☐ 57 Ted Williams 15.00 6.75
400th Homer
In locker room
☐ 58 Ted Williams 15.00 6.75
Williams Hits .388
Four-picture sequence
of his batting swing
☐ 59 Ted Williams 15.00 6.75
Hot September for Ted
Full shot of follow through
at plate
☐ 60 Ted Williams 15.00 6.75
More Records for Ted
Swinging and missing
☐ 61 Ted Williams 15.00 6.75
1957 Outfielder
Warming up prior
to ball game
☐ 62 Ted Williams 12.00 5.50
1958 Sixth Batting Title
Slamming pitch into stands
☐ 63 Ted Williams 75.00 34.00
Ted's All-Star Record
Portrait and facsimile autograph
☐ 64 Ted Williams 12.00 5.50
Barbara Williams
Daughter and Daddy
In uniform holding his daughter
☐ 65 Ted Williams 15.00 6.75
1958 August 30
Determination on face
connecting with ball
☐ 66 Ted Williams 12.00 5.50
1958 Powerhouse
Stance and follow through
in batters box
☐ 67 Ted Williams 40.00 18.00
Sam Snead
Two Famous Fishermen
testing fishing equipment
☐ 68 Ted Williams 1000.00 450.00
Bucky Harris
Ted Signs for 1959 SP
signing contract
☐ 69 Ted Williams 15.00 6.75
A Future Ted Williams
With eager, young newcomer
☐ 70 Ted Williams 35.00 16.00
Jim Thorpe
at Sportsmen's Show
☐ 71 Ted Williams 12.00 5.50
Hitting Fund. 1
Proper gripping of
a baseball bat
☐ 72 Ted Williams 12.00 5.50
Hitting Fund. 2
Checking his swing
☐ 73 Ted Williams 12.00 5.50
Hitting Fund. 3
Stance and follow-through
☐ 74 Ted Williams 12.00 5.50
Here's How

Demonstrating in locker room
an aspect of hitting
☐ 75 Ted Williams 50.00 22.00
Eddie Collins
Babe Ruth
Williams' Value to Sox
☐ 76 Ted Williams 12.00 5.50
On Base Record
Awaiting intentional walk
to first base
☐ 77 Ted Williams 15.00 6.75
Ted Relaxes
Displaying bonefish
which he caught
☐ 78 Ted Williams 15.00 6.75
Rep. Joe Martin
Justice Earl Warren
Honors for Williams
Clark Griffith Memorial Award
☐ 79 Ted Williams 25.00 11.00
Where Ted Stands
Wielding giant eight foot bat
when honored as modern-day Paul Bunyan
☐ 80 Ted Williams 35.00 16.00
Ted's Goals for 1959
Admiring his portrait

1960 Fleer

The cards in this 79-card set measure 2 1/2" by 3 1/2". The cards from the 1960 Fleer series of Baseball Greats are sometimes mistaken for 1930s cards by collectors not familiar with this set. The cards each contain a tinted photo of a baseball immortal, and were issued in one series. There are no known scarcities, although a number 80 card (Pepper Martin reverse with either Eddie Collins or Lefty Grove obverse) exists (this is not considered part of the set). The catalog designation for 1960 Fleer is R418-2. The cards were printed on a 96-card sheet with 17 double prints. These are noted in the checklist below by DP. On the sheet the second Eddie Collins card is typically found in the number 80 position.

	NRMT	VG-E
COMPLETE SET (79)	600.00	275.00
COMMON CARD (1-79)	4.00	1.80
WRAPPER	100.00	45.00

☐ 1 Napoleon Lajoie DP 30.00 13.50
☐ 2 Christy Mathewson 15.00 6.75
☐ 3 Babe Ruth 125.00 55.00
☐ 4 Carl Hubbell 8.00 3.60
☐ 5 Grover C. Alexander 8.00 3.60
☐ 6 Walter Johnson DP 10.00 4.50
☐ 7 Chief Bender 4.00 1.80
☐ 8 Roger Bresnahan 4.00 1.80
☐ 9 Mordecai Brown 4.00 1.80
☐ 10 Tris Speaker 8.00 3.60
☐ 11 Arky Vaughan DP 4.00 1.80
☐ 12 Zach Wheat 4.00 1.80
☐ 13 George Sisler 4.00 1.80
☐ 14 Connie Mack 8.00 3.60
☐ 15 Clark Griffith 4.00 1.80
☐ 16 Lou Boudreau DP 6.00 2.70
☐ 17 Ernie Lombardi 4.00 1.80
☐ 18 Heinie Manush 4.00 1.80
☐ 19 Marty Marion 4.00 1.80
☐ 20 Eddie Collins DP 4.00 1.80
☐ 21 Rabbit Maranville DP 4.00 1.80
☐ 22 Joe Medwick 4.00 1.80
☐ 23 Ed Barrow 4.00 1.80
☐ 24 Mickey Cochrane 6.00 2.70
☐ 25 Jimmy Collins 4.00 1.80
☐ 26 Bob Feller DP 15.00 6.75
☐ 27 Luke Appling 6.00 2.70
☐ 28 Lou Gehrig 80.00 36.00
☐ 29 Gabby Hartnett 4.00 1.80
☐ 30 Chuck Klein 4.00 1.80
☐ 31 Tony Lazzeri DP 6.00 2.70
☐ 32 Al Simmons 4.00 1.80
☐ 33 Wilbert Robinson 4.00 1.80
☐ 34 Sam Rice 4.00 1.80
☐ 35 Herb Pennock 4.00 1.80
☐ 36 Mel Ott DP 8.00 3.60
☐ 37 Lefty O'Doul 4.00 1.80
☐ 38 Johnny Mize 8.00 3.60
☐ 39 Edmund(Bing) Miller 4.00 1.80
☐ 40 Joe Tinker 4.00 1.80
☐ 41 Frank Baker DP 4.00 1.80
☐ 42 Ty Cobb 60.00 27.00
☐ 43 Paul Derringer 4.00 1.80
☐ 44 Cap Anson 4.00 1.80
☐ 45 Jim Bottomley 4.00 1.80
☐ 46 Eddie Plank DP 4.00 1.80
☐ 47 Denton(Cy) Young 10.00 4.50
☐ 48 Hack Wilson 6.00 2.70
☐ 49 Ed Walsh UER 4.00 1.80
(Photo actually
Ed Walsh Jr.)
☐ 50 Frank Chance 4.00 1.80
☐ 51 Dazzy Vance DP 4.00 1.80
☐ 52 Bill Terry 6.00 2.70
☐ 53 Jimmie Foxx 10.00 4.50
☐ 54 Lefty Gomez 8.00 3.60
☐ 55 Branch Rickey 4.00 1.80
☐ 56 Ray Schalk DP 4.00 1.80
☐ 57 Johnny Evers 4.00 1.80
☐ 58 Charley Gehringer 6.00 2.70
☐ 59 Burleigh Grimes 4.00 1.80
☐ 60 Lefty Grove 8.00 3.60
☐ 61 Rube Waddell DP 4.00 1.80
☐ 62 John(Honus) Wagner 15.00 6.75
☐ 63 Red Ruffing 4.00 1.80
☐ 64 Kenesaw M. Landis 4.00 1.80
☐ 65 Harry Heilmann 4.00 1.80
☐ 66 John McGraw DP 4.00 1.80
☐ 67 Hughie Jennings 4.00 1.80
☐ 68 Hal Newhouser 6.00 2.70
☐ 69 Waite Hoyt 4.00 1.80
☐ 70 Bobo Newsom 4.00 1.80
☐ 71 Earl Averill DP 4.00 1.80
☐ 72 Ted Williams 90.00 40.00
☐ 73 Warren Giles 4.00 1.80
☐ 74 Ford Frick 4.00 1.80
☐ 75 Kiki Cuyler 4.00 1.80
☐ 76 Paul Waner DP 4.00 1.80
☐ 77 Pie Traynor 4.00 1.80
☐ 78 Lloyd Waner 4.00 1.80
☐ 79 Ralph Kiner 10.00 4.50
☐ 80A Pepper Martin SP 2000.00 900.00
(Eddie Collins
pictured on obverse)
☐ 80B Pepper Martin SP 1500.00 700.00
(Lefty Grove
pictured on obverse)

1961 Fleer

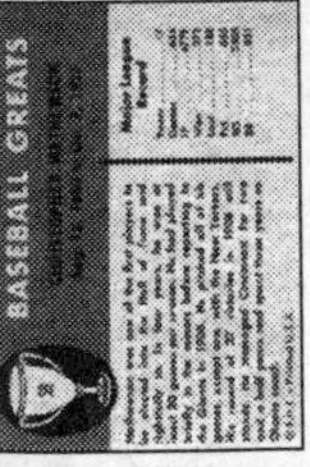

The cards in this 154-card set measure 2 1/2" by 3 1/2". In 1961, Fleer continued its Baseball Greats format by issuing this series of cards. The set was released in two distinct series, 1-88 and 89-154 (of which the latter is more difficult to obtain). The players within each series are conveniently numbered in alphabetical order. It appears that this set (the second series) continued to be issued the following year by Fleer. The catalog number for this set is F418-3. In each first series pack Fleer inserted a Major League team decal and a pennant sticker honoring past World Series winners.

	NRMT	VG-E
COMPLETE SET (154)	1200.00	550.00
COMMON CARD (1-88)	3.00	1.35
COMMON CARD (89-154)	7.00	3.10
WRAPPER (5-CENT)	100.00	45.00

☐ 1 Frank Baker CL 50.00 15.00
Ty Cobb
Zack Wheat
☐ 2 Grover C. Alexander 6.00 2.70
☐ 3 Nick Altrock 3.00 1.35
☐ 4 Cap Anson 4.00 1.80
☐ 5 Earl Averill 4.00 1.80
☐ 6 Frank Baker 4.00 1.80
☐ 7 Dave Bancroft 4.00 1.80
☐ 8 Chief Bender 4.00 1.80
☐ 9 Jim Bottomley 4.00 1.80
☐ 10 Roger Bresnahan 4.00 1.80
☐ 11 Mordecai Brown 4.00 1.80
☐ 12 Max Carey 4.00 1.80
☐ 13 Jack Chesbro 4.00 1.80
☐ 14 Ty Cobb 50.00 22.00
☐ 15 Mickey Cochrane 5.00 2.20
☐ 16 Eddie Collins 6.00 2.70
☐ 17 Earle Combs 4.00 1.80
☐ 18 Charles Comiskey 4.00 1.80
☐ 19 Kiki Cuyler 4.00 1.80
☐ 20 Paul Derringer 3.00 1.35
☐ 21 Howard Ehmke 3.00 1.35
☐ 22 Billy Evans 3.00 1.35
☐ 23 Johnny Evers 4.00 1.80
☐ 24 Urban Faber 4.00 1.80
☐ 25 Bob Feller 12.00 5.50
☐ 26 Wes Ferrell 3.00 1.35
☐ 27 Lew Fonseca 3.00 1.35
☐ 28 Jimmie Foxx 7.00 3.10
☐ 29 Ford Frick 3.00 1.35
☐ 30 Frankie Frisch 4.00 1.80
☐ 31 Lou Gehrig 75.00 34.00
☐ 32 Charley Gehringer 4.00 1.80
☐ 33 Warren Giles 3.00 1.35
☐ 34 Lefty Gomez 4.00 1.80
☐ 35 Goose Goslin 4.00 1.80
☐ 36 Clark Griffith 4.00 1.80
☐ 37 Burleigh Grimes 4.00 1.80
☐ 38 Lefty Grove 4.00 1.80
☐ 39 Chick Hafey 4.00 1.80
☐ 40 Jesse Haines 4.00 1.80
☐ 41 Gabby Hartnett 4.00 1.80
☐ 42 Harry Heilmann 4.00 1.80
☐ 43 Rogers Hornsby 7.00 3.10
☐ 44 Waite Hoyt 4.00 1.80
☐ 45 Carl Hubbell 5.00 2.20
☐ 46 Miller Huggins 4.00 1.80
☐ 47 Hughie Jennings 4.00 1.80
☐ 48 Ban Johnson 4.00 1.80
☐ 49 Walter Johnson 12.00 5.50
☐ 50 Ralph Kiner 7.00 3.10
☐ 51 Chuck Klein 4.00 1.80
☐ 52 Johnny Kling 3.00 1.35
☐ 53 Kenesaw M. Landis 4.00 1.80
☐ 54 Tony Lazzeri 4.00 1.80
☐ 55 Ernie Lombardi 4.00 1.80
☐ 56 Dolf Luque 3.00 1.35
☐ 57 Heinie Manush 4.00 1.80
☐ 58 Marty Marion 3.00 1.35
☐ 59 Christy Mathewson 12.00 5.50
☐ 60 John McGraw 4.00 1.80
☐ 61 Joe Medwick 4.00 1.80
☐ 62 Edmund(Bing) Miller 3.00 1.35
☐ 63 Johnny Mize 4.00 1.80
☐ 64 John Mostil 3.00 1.35
☐ 65 Art Nehf 3.00 1.35
☐ 66 Hal Newhouser 4.00 1.80
☐ 67 Bobo Newsom 3.00 1.35
☐ 68 Mel Ott 6.00 2.70
☐ 69 Allie Reynolds 3.00 1.35
☐ 70 Sam Rice 4.00 1.80
☐ 71 Eppa Rixey 4.00 1.80
☐ 72 Edd Roush 4.00 1.80
☐ 73 Schoolboy Rowe 3.00 1.35
☐ 74 Red Ruffing 4.00 1.80
☐ 75 Babe Ruth 125.00 55.00
☐ 76 Joe Sewell 4.00 1.80
☐ 77 Al Simmons 4.00 1.80
☐ 78 George Sisler 4.00 1.80
☐ 79 Tris Speaker 6.00 2.70
☐ 80 Fred Toney 3.00 1.35
☐ 81 Dazzy Vance 4.00 1.80
☐ 82 Hippo Vaughn 3.00 1.35
☐ 83 Ed Walsh 4.00 1.80
☐ 84 Lloyd Waner 4.00 1.80
☐ 85 Paul Waner 4.00 1.80
☐ 86 Zack Wheat 4.00 1.80
☐ 87 Hack Wilson 4.00 1.80
☐ 88 Jimmy Wilson 3.00 1.35
☐ 89 George Sisler CL 60.00 18.00
Pie Traynor
☐ 90 Babe Adams 7.00 3.10
☐ 91 Dale Alexander 7.00 3.10
☐ 92 Jim Bagby 7.00 3.10
☐ 93 Ossie Bluege 7.00 3.10
☐ 94 Lou Boudreau 10.00 4.50
☐ 95 Tommy Bridges 7.00 3.10
☐ 96 Donie Bush 7.00 3.10
☐ 97 Dolph Camilli 7.00 3.10
☐ 98 Frank Chance 10.00 4.50
☐ 99 Jimmy Collins 10.00 4.50
☐ 100 Stan Coveleskie 10.00 4.50
☐ 101 Hugh Critz 7.00 3.10
☐ 102 Alvin Crowder 7.00 3.10
☐ 103 Joe Dugan 7.00 3.10

☐ 104 Bibb Falk	7.00	3.10
☐ 105 Rick Ferrell	10.00	4.50
☐ 106 Art Fletcher	7.00	3.10
☐ 107 Dennis Galehouse	7.00	3.10
☐ 108 Chick Galloway	7.00	3.10
☐ 109 Mule Haas	7.00	3.10
☐ 110 Stan Hack	7.00	3.10
☐ 111 Bump Hadley	7.00	3.10
☐ 112 Billy Hamilton	10.00	4.50
☐ 113 Joe Hauser	7.00	3.10
☐ 114 Babe Herman	7.00	3.10
☐ 115 Travis Jackson	10.00	4.50
☐ 116 Eddie Joost	7.00	3.10
☐ 117 Addie Joss	10.00	4.50
☐ 118 Joe Judge	7.00	3.10
☐ 119 Joe Kuhel	7.00	3.10
☐ 120 Napoleon Lajoie	18.00	8.00
☐ 121 Dutch Leonard	7.00	3.10
☐ 122 Ted Lyons	10.00	4.50
☐ 123 Connie Mack	18.00	8.00
☐ 124 Rabbit Maranville	10.00	4.50
☐ 125 Fred Marberry	7.00	3.10
☐ 126 Joe McGinnity	10.00	4.50
☐ 127 Oscar Melillo	7.00	3.10
☐ 128 Ray Mueller	7.00	3.10
☐ 129 Kid Nichols	10.00	4.50
☐ 130 Lefty O'Doul	7.00	3.10
☐ 131 Bob O'Farrell	7.00	3.10
☐ 132 Roger Peckinpaugh	7.00	3.10
☐ 133 Herb Pennock	10.00	4.50
☐ 134 George Pipgras	7.00	3.10
☐ 135 Eddie Plank	12.00	5.50
☐ 136 Ray Schalk	10.00	4.50
☐ 137 Hal Schumacher	7.00	3.10
☐ 138 Luke Sewell	7.00	3.10
☐ 139 Bob Shawkey	7.00	3.10
☐ 140 Riggs Stephenson	7.00	3.10
☐ 141 Billy Sullivan	7.00	3.10
☐ 142 Bill Terry	15.00	6.75
☐ 143 Joe Tinker	10.00	4.50
☐ 144 Pie Traynor	12.00	5.50
☐ 145 Hal Trosky	7.00	3.10
☐ 146 George Uhle	7.00	3.10
☐ 147 Johnny VanderMeer	10.00	4.50
☐ 148 Arky Vaughan	10.00	4.50
☐ 149 Rube Waddell	10.00	4.50
☐ 150 Honus Wagner	50.00	22.00
☐ 151 Dixie Walker	7.00	3.10
☐ 152 Ted Williams	125.00	55.00
☐ 153 Cy Young	40.00	18.00
☐ 154 Ross Youngs	40.00	18.00

1963 Fleer

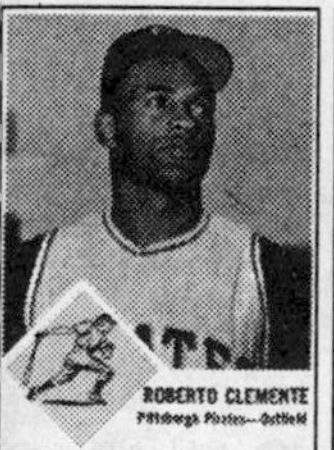

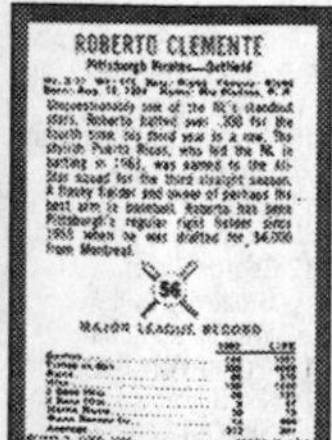

The Fleer set of current baseball players was marketed in 1963 in a gum card-style waxed wrapper package which contained a cherry cookie instead of gum. The cards were printed in sheets of 66 with the scarce card of Joe Adcock (#46) replaced by the unnumbered checklist card for the final press run. The complete set price includes the checklist card. The catalog designation for this set is R418-4. The key Rookie Card in this set is Maury Wills. The set is basically arranged numerically in alphabetical order by teams which are also in alphabetical order.

	NRMT	VG-E
COMPLETE SET (67)	2000.00	900.00
WRAPPER (5-CENT)	100.00	45.00
☐ 1 Steve Barber	30.00	9.00
☐ 2 Ron Hansen	15.00	6.75
☐ 3 Milt Pappas	20.00	9.00
☐ 4 Brooks Robinson	100.00	45.00
☐ 5 Willie Mays	200.00	90.00
☐ 6 Lou Clinton	15.00	6.75
☐ 7 Bill Monbouquette	15.00	6.75
☐ 8 Carl Yastrzemski	120.00	55.00
☐ 9 Ray Herbert	15.00	6.75
☐ 10 Jim Landis	15.00	6.75
☐ 11 Dick Donovan	15.00	6.75
☐ 12 Tito Francona	15.00	6.75
☐ 13 Jerry Kindall	15.00	6.75
☐ 14 Frank Lary	20.00	9.00
☐ 15 Dick Howser	20.00	9.00
☐ 16 Jerry Lumpe	15.00	6.75
☐ 17 Norm Siebern	15.00	6.75
☐ 18 Don Lee	15.00	6.75
☐ 19 Albie Pearson	20.00	9.00
☐ 20 Bob Rodgers	20.00	9.00
☐ 21 Leon Wagner	15.00	6.75
☐ 22 Jim Kaat	25.00	11.00
☐ 23 Vic Power	20.00	9.00
☐ 24 Rich Rollins	20.00	9.00
☐ 25 Bobby Richardson	30.00	13.50
☐ 26 Ralph Terry	20.00	9.00
☐ 27 Tom Cheney	15.00	6.75
☐ 28 Chuck Cottier	15.00	6.75
☐ 29 Jimmy Piersall	20.00	9.00
☐ 30 Dave Stenhouse	15.00	6.75
☐ 31 Glen Hobbie	15.00	6.75
☐ 32 Ron Santo	25.00	11.00
☐ 33 Gene Freese	15.00	6.75
☐ 34 Vada Pinson	20.00	9.00
☐ 35 Bob Purkey	15.00	6.75
☐ 36 Joe Amalfitano	15.00	6.75
☐ 37 Bob Aspromonte	15.00	6.75
☐ 38 Dick Farrell	15.00	6.75
☐ 39 Al Spangler	15.00	6.75
☐ 40 Tommy Davis	20.00	9.00
☐ 41 Don Drysdale	60.00	27.00
☐ 42 Sandy Koufax	200.00	90.00
☐ 43 Maury Wills	100.00	45.00
☐ 44 Frank Bolling	15.00	6.75
☐ 45 Warren Spahn	70.00	32.00
☐ 46 Joe Adcock SP	200.00	90.00
☐ 47 Roger Craig	20.00	9.00
☐ 48 Al Jackson	20.00	9.00
☐ 49 Rod Kanehl	20.00	9.00
☐ 50 Ruben Amaro	15.00	6.75
☐ 51 Johnny Callison	20.00	9.00
☐ 52 Clay Dalrymple	15.00	6.75
☐ 53 Don Demeter	15.00	6.75
☐ 54 Art Mahaffey	15.00	6.75
☐ 55 Smoky Burgess	20.00	9.00
☐ 56 Roberto Clemente	250.00	110.00
☐ 57 Roy Face	20.00	9.00
☐ 58 Vern Law	20.00	9.00
☐ 59 Bill Mazeroski	30.00	13.50
☐ 60 Ken Boyer	25.00	11.00
☐ 61 Bob Gibson	70.00	32.00
☐ 62 Gene Oliver	15.00	6.75
☐ 63 Bill White	25.00	11.00
☐ 64 Orlando Cepeda	30.00	13.50
☐ 65 Jim Davenport	15.00	6.75
☐ 66 Billy O'Dell	30.00	9.00
☐ NNO Checklist card	700.00	230.00

1970 Fleer World Series

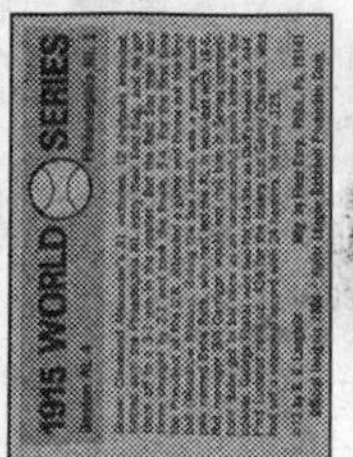

This set of 66 standard-siz cards was distributed by Fleer. The cards are in crude color on the front with light blue printing on white card stock on the back. All the years are represented except for 1904 when no World Series was played. In the list below, the winning series team is listed first. The year of the Series on the obverse is inside a white baseball. The original art for the cards in this set was drawn by sports artist R.G. Laughlin.

	NRMT	VG-E
COMPLETE SET (66)	125.00	55.00
COMMON CARD (1-66)	1.50	.70
☐ 1 1903 Red Sox/Pirates	1.50	.70
☐ 2 1905 Giants/A's (Christy Mathewson)	4.00	1.80
☐ 3 1906 White Sox/Cubs	1.50	.70
☐ 4 1907 Cubs/Tigers	1.50	.70
☐ 5 1908 Cubs/Tigers (Joe Tinker, Johnny Evers, and Frank Chance)	4.00	1.80
☐ 6 1909 Pirates/Tigers (Honus Wagner and Ty Cobb)	6.00	2.70
☐ 7 1910 A's/Cubs (Chief Bender and Jack Coombs)	2.50	1.10
☐ 8 1911 A's/Giants (John McGraw)	2.50	1.10
☐ 9 1912 Red Sox/Giants	1.50	.70
☐ 10 1913 A's/Giants	1.50	.70
☐ 11 1914 Braves/A's	1.50	.70
☐ 12 1915 Red Sox/Phillies (Babe Ruth)	6.00	2.70
☐ 13 1916 Red Sox/Dodgers (Babe Ruth)	6.00	2.70
☐ 14 1917 White Sox/Giants	1.50	.70
☐ 15 1918 Red Sox/Cubs	1.50	.70
☐ 16 1919 Reds/White Sox	6.00	2.70
☐ 17 1920 Indians/Dodgers (Stan Coveleski)	2.50	1.10
☐ 18 1921 Giants/Yankees (Commissioner Landis)	1.50	.70
☐ 19 1922 Giants/Yankees	1.50	.70
☐ 20 1923 Yankees/Giants (Babe Ruth)	6.00	2.70
☐ 21 1924 Senators/Giants (John McGraw)	2.50	1.10
☐ 22 1925 Pirates/Senators (Walter Johnson)	4.00	1.80
☐ 23 1926 Cardinals/Yankees (Grover C. Alexander and Tony Lazzeri)	2.50	1.10
☐ 24 1927 Yankees/Pirates	1.50	.70
☐ 25 1928 Yankees/Cardinals (Babe Ruth and Lou Gehrig)	6.00	2.70
☐ 26 1929 A's/Cubs	1.50	.70
☐ 27 1930 A's/Cardinals	1.50	.70
☐ 28 1931 Cardinals/A's (Pepper Martin)	1.50	.70
☐ 29 1932 Yankees/Cubs (Babe Ruth and Lou Gehrig)	6.00	2.70
☐ 30 1933 Giants/Senators (Mel Ott)	2.50	1.10
☐ 31 1934 Cardinals/Tigers	1.50	.70
☐ 32 1935 Tigers/Cubs (Charlie Gehringer and Tommy Bridges)	2.50	1.10
☐ 33 1936 Yankees/Giants	1.50	.70
☐ 34 1937 Yankees/Giants (Carl Hubbell)	2.50	1.10
☐ 35 1938 Yankees/Cubs (Lou Gehrig)	4.00	1.80
☐ 36 1939 Yankees/Reds	1.50	.70
☐ 37 1940 Reds/Tigers	1.50	.70
☐ 38 1941 Yankees/Dodgers	1.50	.70
☐ 39 1942 Cardinals/Yankees	1.50	.70
☐ 40 1943 Yankees/Cardinals	1.50	.70
☐ 41 1944 Cardinals/Browns	1.50	.70
☐ 42 1945 Tigers/Cubs (Hank Greenberg)	4.00	1.80
☐ 43 1946 Cardinals/Red Sox (Enos Slaughter)	2.50	1.10
☐ 44 1947 Yankees/Dodgers (Al Gionfriddo)	1.50	.70
☐ 45 1948 Indians/Braves	1.50	.70
☐ 46 1949 Yankees/Dodgers (Allie Reynolds and Preacher Roe)	1.50	.70
☐ 47 1950 Yankees/Phillies	1.50	.70
☐ 48 1951 Yankees/Giants	1.50	.70
☐ 49 1952 Yankees/Dodgers (Johnny Mize and Duke Snider)	4.00	1.80
☐ 50 1953 Yankees/Dodgers (Carl Erskine)	1.50	.70
☐ 51 1954 Giants/Indians (Johnny Antonelli)	1.50	.70
☐ 52 1955 Dodgers/Yankees (Johnny Podres)	1.50	.70
☐ 53 1956 Yankees/Dodgers	1.50	.70
☐ 54 1957 Braves/Yankees (Lew Burdette)	1.50	.70
☐ 55 1958 Yankees/Braves (Bob Turley)	1.50	.70
☐ 56 1959 Dodgers/White Sox (Chuck Essegian)	1.50	.70
☐ 57 1960 Pirates/Yankees	1.50	.70
☐ 58 1961 Yankees/Reds (Whitey Ford)	2.50	1.10
☐ 59 1962 Yankees/Giants	1.50	.70
☐ 60 1963 Dodgers/Yankees (Moose Skowron)	1.50	.70
☐ 61 1964 Cardinals/Yankees (Bobby Richardson)	2.50	1.10
☐ 62 1965 Dodgers/Twins	1.50	.70
☐ 63 1966 Orioles/Dodgers	1.50	.70
☐ 64 1967 Cardinals/Red Sox	1.50	.70
☐ 65 1968 Tigers/Cardinals	1.50	.70
☐ 66 1969 Mets/Orioles	2.50	1.10

1971 Fleer World Series

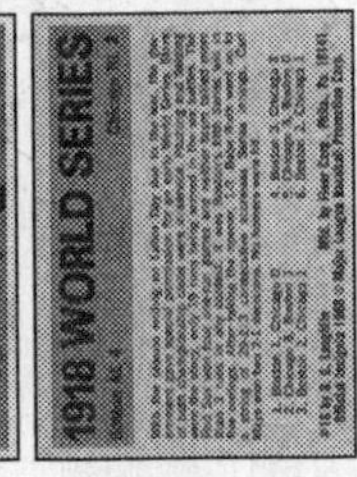

This set of 68 standard-size cards was distributed by Fleer. The cards are in crude color on the front with brown printing on white card stock on the back. All the years since 1903 are represented in this set including 1904, when no World Series was played. That year is represented by a card explaining why there was no World Series that year. In the list below, the winning series team is listed first. The year of the Series on the obverse is inside a white square over the official World Series logo.

	NRMT	VG-E
COMPLETE SET (68)	125.00	55.00
COMMON CARD (1-68)	1.50	.70
MINOR STARS	2.50	1.10
SEMISTARS	4.00	1.80
UNLISTED STARS	5.00	2.20
☐ 1 1903 Red Sox/Pirates (Cy Young)	4.00	1.80
☐ 2 1904 NO Series (John McGraw)	2.50	1.10
☐ 3 1905 Giants/A's (Christy Mathewson, Chief Bender, and Joe McGinnity)	4.00	1.80
☐ 4 1906 White Sox/Cubs	1.50	.70
☐ 5 1907 Cubs/Tigers	1.50	.70
☐ 6 1908 Cubs/Tigers (Ty Cobb)	5.00	2.20
☐ 7 1909 Pirates/Tigers	1.50	.70
☐ 8 1910 A's/Cubs (Eddie Collins)	2.50	1.10
☐ 9 1911 A's/Giants (Home Run Baker)	2.50	1.10
☐ 10 1912 Red Sox/Giants	1.50	.70
☐ 11 1913 A's/Giants (Christy Mathewson)	4.00	1.80
☐ 12 1914 Braves/A's	1.50	.70
☐ 13 1915 Red Sox/Phillies (Grover Alexander)	2.50	1.10
☐ 14 1916 Red Sox/Dodgers	1.50	.70
☐ 15 1917 White Sox/Giants (Red Faber)	2.50	1.10
☐ 16 1918 Red Sox/Cubs (Babe Ruth)	7.50	3.40
☐ 17 1919 Reds/White Sox	6.00	2.70
☐ 18 1920 Indians/Dodgers	1.50	.70
☐ 19 1921 Giants/Yankees (Waite Hoyt)	2.50	1.10
☐ 20 1922 Giants/Yankees	1.50	.70
☐ 21 1923 Yankees/Giants (Herb Pennock)	2.50	1.10
☐ 22 1924 Senators/Giants (Walter Johnson)	4.00	1.80
☐ 23 1925 Pirates/Senators (Kiki Cuyler and Walter Johnson)	2.50	1.10
☐ 24 1926 Cardinals/Yankees (Rogers Hornsby)	4.00	1.80
☐ 25 1927 Yankees/Pirates	1.50	.70
☐ 26 1928 Yankees/Cardinals (Lou Gehrig)	5.00	2.20
☐ 27 1929 A's/Cubs	1.50	.70
☐ 28 1930 A's/Cardinals (Jimmie Foxx)	4.00	1.80
☐ 29 1931 Cardinals/A's (Pepper Martin)	1.50	.70
☐ 30 1932 Yankees/Cubs (Babe Ruth)	7.50	3.40
☐ 31 1933 Giants/Senators (Carl Hubbell)	2.50	1.10
☐ 32 1934 Cardinals/Tigers	1.50	.70
☐ 33 1935 Tigers/Cubs (Mickey Cochrane)	2.50	1.10
☐ 34 1936 Yankees/Giants (Red Rolfe)	1.50	.70
☐ 35 1937 Yankees/Giants (Tony Lazzeri)	2.50	1.10
☐ 36 1938 Yankees/Cubs	1.50	.70
☐ 37 1939 Yankees/Reds	1.50	.70
☐ 38 1940 Reds/Tigers	1.50	.70
☐ 39 1941 Yankees/Dodgers	1.50	.70
☐ 40 1942 Cardinals/Yankees	1.50	.70
☐ 41 1943 Yankees/Cardinals	1.50	.70
☐ 42 1944 Cardinals/Browns	1.50	.70
☐ 43 1945 Tigers/Cubs (Hank Greenberg)	4.00	1.80
☐ 44 1946 Cardinals/Red Sox (Enos Slaughter)	2.50	1.10
☐ 45 1947 Yankees/Dodgers	1.50	.70
☐ 46 1948 Indians/Braves	1.50	.70
☐ 47 1949 Yankees/Dodgers (Preacher Roe)	1.50	.70
☐ 48 1950 Yankees/Phillies (Allie Reynolds)	1.50	.70
☐ 49 1951 Yankees/Giants (Ed Lopat)	1.50	.70
☐ 50 1952 Yankees/Dodgers (Johnny Mize)	2.50	1.10
☐ 51 1953 Yankees/Dodgers	1.50	.70
☐ 52 1954 Giants/Indians	1.50	.70
☐ 53 1955 Dodgers/Yankees (Duke Snider)	2.50	1.10
☐ 54 1956 Yankees/Dodgers	1.50	.70
☐ 55 1957 Braves/Yankees	1.50	.70
☐ 56 1958 Yankees/Braves (Hank Bauer)	1.50	.70
☐ 57 1959 Dodgers/Wh.Sox (Duke Snider)	2.50	1.10
☐ 58 1960 Pirates/Yankees	1.50	.70
☐ 59 1961 Yankees/Reds (Whitey Ford)	2.50	1.10
☐ 60 1962 Yankees/Giants	1.50	.70
☐ 61 1963 Dodgers/Yankees	1.50	.70
☐ 62 1964 Cardinals/Yankees	1.50	.70
☐ 63 1965 Dodgers/Twins	1.50	.70
☐ 64 1966 Orioles/Dodgers	1.50	.70
☐ 65 1967 Cardinals/Red Sox	1.50	.70
☐ 66 1968 Tigers/Cardinals	1.50	.70
☐ 67 1969 Mets/Orioles	1.50	.70
☐ 68 1970 Orioles/Reds	2.50	1.10

1972 Fleer Famous Feats

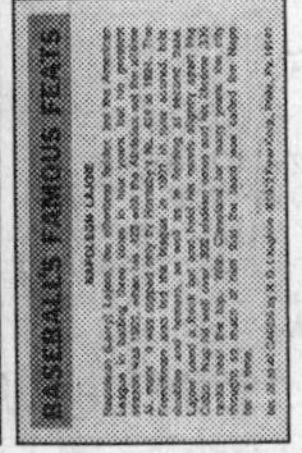

This Fleer set of 40 cards features the artwork of sports artist R.G. Laughlin. The set is titled "Baseball's Famous Feats." The cards are numbered both on the front and back. The backs are printed in light blue on white card stock. The cards measure approximately 2 1/2" by 4". This set was licensed by Major League Baseball.

	NRMT	VG-E
COMPLETE SET (40)	40.00	18.00
COMMON CARD (1-40)	.75	.35
☐ 1 Joe McGinnity	1.00	.45
☐ 2 Rogers Hornsby	2.00	.90
☐ 3 Christy Mathewson	2.00	.90
☐ 4 Dazzy Vance	1.00	.45
☐ 5 Lou Gehrig	3.00	1.35
☐ 6 Jim Bottomley	1.00	.45
☐ 7 Johnny Evers	1.00	.45
☐ 8 Walter Johnson	2.00	.90
☐ 9 Hack Wilson	1.00	.45
☐ 10 Wilbert Robinson	1.00	.45
☐ 11 Cy Young	1.50	.70
☐ 12 Rudy York	.75	.35
☐ 13 Grover C. Alexander	1.00	.45
☐ 14 Fred Toney and Hippo Vaughn	.75	.35
☐ 15 Ty Cobb	3.00	1.35
☐ 16 Jimmie Foxx	2.00	.90
☐ 17 Hub Leonard	.75	.35
☐ 18 Eddie Collins	1.00	.45
☐ 19 Joe Oeschger and Leon Cadore	.75	.35
☐ 20 Babe Ruth	4.00	1.80
☐ 21 Honus Wagner	2.00	.90
☐ 22 Red Rolfe	.75	.35
☐ 23 Ed Walsh	1.00	.45
☐ 24 Paul Waner	1.00	.45
☐ 25 Mel Ott	1.50	.70
☐ 26 Eddie Plank	1.00	.45
☐ 27 Sam Crawford	1.00	.45
☐ 28 Napoleon Lajoie	1.50	.70
☐ 29 Ed Reulbach	.75	.35
☐ 30 Pinky Higgins	.75	.35
☐ 31 Bill Klem	1.00	.45
☐ 32 Tris Speaker	1.50	.70
☐ 33 Hank Gowdy	.75	.35
☐ 34 Lefty O'Doul	.75	.35
☐ 35 Lloyd Waner	1.00	.45
☐ 36 Chuck Klein	1.00	.45
☐ 37 Deacon Phillippe	.75	.35
☐ 38 Ed Delahanty	1.00	.45
☐ 39 Jack Chesbro	1.00	.45
☐ 40 Willie Keeler	1.00	.45

1973 Fleer Wildest Days

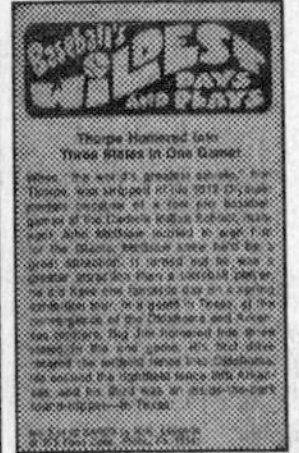

This Fleer set of 42 cards is titled "Baseball's Wildest Days and Plays" and features the artwork of sports artist R.G. Laughlin. The cards are numbered on the back. The backs are printed in dark red on white card stock. The cards measure approximately 2 1/2" by 4". This set was not licensed by Major League Baseball.

	NRMT	VG-E
COMPLETE SET (42)	30.00	13.50
COMMON CARD (1-42)	.50	.23
☐ 1 Cubs and Phillies Score 49 Runs in Game	1.00	.45
☐ 2 Frank Chance Five HBP's in One Day	.75	.35
☐ 3 Jim Thorpe Homered into 3 States	2.00	.90
☐ 4 Eddie Gaedel Midget in Majors	1.25	.55
☐ 5 Most Tied Game Ever	.50	.23
☐ 6 Seven Errors in One Inning	.50	.23
☐ 7 Four 20-Game Winners But No Pennant	.50	.23
☐ 8 Dummy Hoy Umpires Signal Strikes	1.00	.45
☐ 9 Fourteeen Hits in One Inning	.50	.23
☐ 10 Yankees Not Shut Out For Two Years	.50	.23
☐ 11 Buck Weaver 17 Straight Fouls	1.50	.70
☐ 12 George Sisler Greatest Thrill Was as a Pitcher	.75	.35
☐ 13 Wrong-Way Baserunner	.50	.23
☐ 14 Kiki Cuyler Sits Out Series	.75	.35
☐ 15 Grounder Climbed Wall	.50	.23
☐ 16 Gabby Street Washington Monument	.75	.35
☐ 17 Mel Ott Ejected Twice	1.50	.70
☐ 18 Shortest Pitching Career	.50	.23
☐ 19 Three Homers in One Inning	.50	.23
☐ 20 Bill Byron Singing Umpire	.50	.23
☐ 21 Fred Clarke Walking Steal of Home	.75	.35
☐ 22 Christy Mathewson 373rd Win Discovered	1.50	.70
☐ 23 Hitting Through the Unglaub Arc	.50	.23
☐ 24 Jim O'Rourke Catching at 52	.50	.23
☐ 25 Fired for Striking Out in Series	.50	.23
☐ 26 Eleven Run Inning on One Hit	.50	.23
☐ 27 58 Innings in 3 Days	.50	.23
☐ 28 Homer on Warm-Up Pitch	.50	.23
☐ 29 Giants Win 26 Straight But Finish Fourth	.50	.23
☐ 30 Player Who Stole	.50	.23

	NRMT	VG-E
First Base		
31 Ernie Shore Perfect Game in Relief	.75	.35
32 Greatest Comeback	.50	.23
33 All-Time Flash-In-The-Pan	.50	.23
34 Hub Pruett Fanned Ruth 19 out of 31	1.25	.55
35 Fixed Batting Race Ty Cobb Nap Lajoie	1.50	.70
36 Wild-Pitch Rebound Play	.50	.23
37 17 Straight Scoring Innings	.50	.23
38 Wildest Opening Day	.50	.23
39 Baseball's Strike One	.50	.23
40 Opening Day No Hitter That Didn't Count	.50	.23
41 Jimmie Foxx Six Straight Walks in One Game	1.50	.70
42 Entire Team Hit and Scored in Inning	1.00	.45

1974 Fleer Baseball Firsts

his Fleer set of 42 cards is titled "Baseball Firsts" and atures the artwork of sports artist R.G. Laughlin. The rds are numbered on the back. The backs are printed in ack on gray card stock. The cards measure pproximately 2 1/2" by 4". This set was not licensed by ajor League Baseball.

	NRMT	VG-E
OMPLETE SET (42)	20.00	9.00
OMMON CARD (1-42)	.30	.14
1 Slide	.60	.25
2 Spring Training	.30	.14
3 Bunt	.30	.14
4 Catcher's Mask	.30	.14
5 Lou Gehrig Four straight Homers	1.50	.70
6 Radio Broadcast	.30	.14
7 Numbered Uniforms	.30	.14
8 Shin Guards	.30	.14
9 Players Association	.30	.14
10 Knuckleball	.30	.14
11 Player With Glasses	.30	.14
12 Baseball Cards	2.00	.90
13 Standardized Rules	.30	.14
14 Grand Slam	.30	.14
15 Player Fined	.30	.14
16 Presidential Opener	.30	.14
17 Player Transaction	.30	.14
18 All-Star Game	.30	.14
19 Scoreboard	.30	.14
20 Cork Center Ball	.30	.14
21 Scorekeeping	.30	.14
22 Domed Stadium	.30	.14
23 Batting Helmet	.30	.14
24 Fatality	.30	.14
25 Unassisted Triple Play	.30	.14
26 Home Run At Night	.30	.14
27 Black Major Leaguer	.60	.25
28 Pinch Hitter	.30	.14
29 Million-Dollar World Series	.30	.14
30 Tarpaulin	.30	.14
31 Team Initials	.30	.14
32 Pennant Playoff	.30	.14
33 Glove	.30	.14
34 Curve Ball	.30	.14
35 Night Game	.30	.14
36 Admission Charge	.30	.14
37 Farm System	.30	.14
38 Telecast	.30	.14
39 Commissioner	.30	.14
40 .400 Hitter	.30	.14
41 World Series	.30	.14
42 Player Into Service	.60	.25

1975 Fleer Pioneers

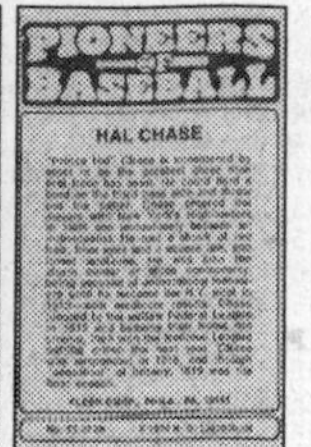

This 28-card set of brown and white sepia-toned photos of old timers is subtitled "Pioneers of Baseball. The graphics artwork was done by R.G. Laughlin. The cards measure approximately 2 1/2" X 4". The card backs are a narrative about the particular player. The cards are numbered on the back at the bottom.

	NRMT	VG-E
COMPLETE SET (28)	15.00	6.75
COMMON CARD (1-28)	.50	.23
☐ 1 Cap Anson	1.25	.55
☐ 2 Harry Wright	.75	.35
☐ 3 Buck Ewing	.75	.35
☐ 4 Al G. Spalding	.75	.35
☐ 5 Old Hoss Radbourn	.75	.35
☐ 6 Dan Brouthers	.75	.35
☐ 7 Roger Bresnahan	.75	.35
☐ 8 Mike Kelly	.75	.35
☐ 9 Ned Hanlon	.50	.23
☐ 10 Ed Delahanty	.75	.35
☐ 11 Pud Galvin	.75	.35
☐ 12 Amos Rusie	.75	.35
☐ 13 Tommy McCarthy	.75	.35
☐ 14 Ty Cobb	2.00	.90
☐ 15 John McGraw	.75	.35
☐ 16 Home Run Baker	.75	.35
☐ 17 Johnny Evers	.75	.35
☐ 18 Nap Lajoie	1.00	.45
☐ 19 Cy Young	1.25	.55
☐ 20 Eddie Collins	1.00	.45
☐ 21 John Glasscock	.50	.23
☐ 22 Hal Chase	.50	.23
☐ 23 Mordecai Brown	.75	.35
☐ 24 Jake Daubert	.50	.23
☐ 25 Mike Donlin	.50	.23
☐ 26 John Clarkson	.75	.35
☐ 27 Buck Herzog	.50	.23
☐ 28 Art Nehf	.50	.23

1981 Fleer

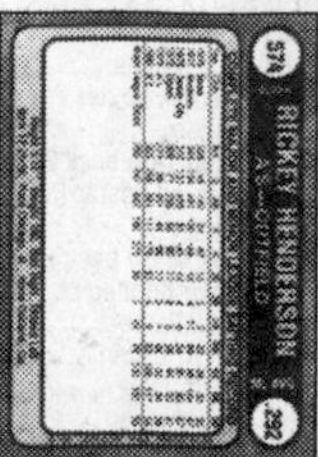

This issue of cards marks Fleer's first entry into the current player baseball card market since 1963. Cards are grouped in team order and teams are ordered based upon their standings from the 1980 season with the World Series champion Philadelphia Phillies starting off the set. Cards 638-660 feature specials and checklists. The cards of pitchers in this set erroneously show a heading (on the card backs) of "Batting Record" over their career pitching statistics. There were three distinct printings: the two following the primary run were designed to correct numerous errors. The variations caused by these multiple printings are noted in the checklist below (P1, P2, or P3). The Craig Nettles variation was corrected before the end of the first printing and thus is not included in the complete set consideration due to scarcity. Unopened packs contained 17 cards as well as a piece of gum. Unopened boxes contained 38 packs. The key Rookie Cards in this set are Danny Ainge, Harold Baines, Kirk Gibson, Jeff Reardon, and Fernando Valenzuela, whose first name was erroneously spelled Fernand on the card front.

	NRMT	VG-E
COMPLETE SET (660)	30.00	13.50
COMMON CARD (1-660)	.10	.05
☐ 1 Pete Rose UER (270 hits in '63, should be 170)	1.25	.55
☐ 2 Larry Bowa	.25	.11
☐ 3 Manny Trillo	.10	.05
☐ 4 Bob Boone	.25	.11
☐ 5 Mike Schmidt (See also 640A)	1.25	.55
☐ 6 Steve Carlton P1 Golden Arm (Back "1066 Cardinals~; Number on back 6)	1.50	.70
☐ 6B Steve Carlton P2 Pitcher of Year (Back "1066 Cardinals~)	1.50	.70
☐ 6C Steve Carlton P3 (1966 Cardinals)	2.00	.90
☐ 7 Tug McGraw (See 657A)	.25	.11
☐ 8 Larry Christenson	.10	.05
☐ 9 Bake McBride	.10	.05
☐ 10 Greg Luzinski	.25	.11
☐ 11 Ron Reed	.10	.05
☐ 12 Dickie Noles	.10	.05
☐ 13 Keith Moreland	.25	.11
☐ 14 Bob Walk	.25	.11
☐ 15 Lonnie Smith	.25	.11
☐ 16 Dick Ruthven	.10	.05
☐ 17 Sparky Lyle	.25	.11
☐ 18 Greg Gross	.10	.05
☐ 19 Garry Maddox	.10	.05
☐ 20 Nino Espinosa	.10	.05
☐ 21 George Vukovich	.10	.05
☐ 22 John Vukovich	.10	.05
☐ 23 Ramon Aviles	.10	.05
☐ 24A Kevin Saucier P1 (Name on back "Ken~)	.10	.05
☐ 24B Kevin Saucier P2 (Name on back "Ken~)	.10	.05
☐ 24C Kevin Saucier P3 (Name on back "Kevin~)	1.00	.45
☐ 25 Randy Lerch	.10	.05
☐ 26 Del Unser	.10	.05
☐ 27 Tim McCarver	.50	.23
☐ 28 George Brett (See also 655A)	2.50	1.10
☐ 29 Willie Wilson (See also 653A)	.10	.05
☐ 30 Paul Splittorff	.10	.05
☐ 31 Dan Quisenberry	.25	.11
☐ 32A Amos Otis P1 (Batting Pose; "Outfield"; 32 on back)	.25	.11
☐ 32B Amos Otis P2 Series Starter 483 on back	.25	.11
☐ 33 Steve Busby	.10	.05
☐ 34 U.L. Washington	.10	.05
☐ 35 Dave Chalk	.10	.05
☐ 36 Darrell Porter	.10	.05
☐ 37 Marty Pattin	.10	.05
☐ 38 Larry Gura	.10	.05
☐ 39 Renie Martin	.10	.05
☐ 40 Rich Gale	.10	.05
☐ 41A Hal McRae P1 ("Royals" on front in black letters)	.50	.23
☐ 41B Hal McRae P2 ("Royals" on front in blue letters)	.25	.11
☐ 42 Dennis Leonard	.10	.05
☐ 43 Willie Aikens	.10	.05
☐ 44 Frank White	.25	.11
☐ 45 Clint Hurdle	.10	.05
☐ 46 John Wathan	.10	.05
☐ 47 Pete LaCock	.10	.05
☐ 48 Rance Mulliniks	.10	.05
☐ 49 Jeff Twitty	.10	.05
☐ 50 Jamie Quirk	.10	.05
☐ 51 Art Howe	.10	.05
☐ 52 Ken Forsch	.10	.05
☐ 53 Vern Ruhle	.10	.05
☐ 54 Joe Niekro	.25	.11
☐ 55 Frank LaCorte	.10	.05
☐ 56 J.R. Richard	.25	.11
☐ 57 Nolan Ryan	5.00	2.20
☐ 58 Enos Cabell	.10	.05
☐ 59 Cesar Cedeno	.25	.11
☐ 60 Jose Cruz	.50	.23
☐ 61 Bill Virdon MG	.10	.05
☐ 62 Terry Puhl	.10	.05
☐ 63 Joaquin Andujar	.25	.11
☐ 64 Alan Ashby	.10	.05

☐ 65 Joe Sambito .10 .05
☐ 66 Denny Walling .10 .05
☐ 67 Jeff Leonard .25 .11
☐ 68 Luis Pujols .10 .05
☐ 69 Bruce Bochy .10 .05
☐ 70 Rafael Landestoy .10 .05
☐ 71 Dave Smith .25 .11
☐ 72 Danny Heep .10 .05
☐ 73 Julio Gonzalez .10 .05
☐ 74 Craig Reynolds .10 .05
☐ 75 Gary Woods .10 .05
☐ 76 Dave Bergman .10 .05
☐ 77 Randy Niemann .10 .05
☐ 78 Joe Morgan 1.00 .45
☐ 79 Reggie Jackson 1.25 .55
(See also 650A)
☐ 80 Bucky Dent .25 .11
☐ 81 Tommy John .50 .23
☐ 82 Luis Tiant .25 .11
☐ 83 Rick Cerone .10 .05
☐ 84 Dick Howser MG .25 .11
☐ 85 Lou Piniella .25 .11
☐ 86 Ron Davis .10 .05
☐ 87A Graig Nettles P1 8.00 3.60
ERR (Name on back
misspelled "Craig~)
☐ 87B Graig Nettles P2 COR .25 .11
("Graig")
☐ 88 Ron Guidry .25 .11
☐ 89 Rich Gossage .50 .23
☐ 90 Rudy May .10 .05
☐ 91 Gaylord Perry 1.00 .45
☐ 92 Eric Soderholm .10 .05
☐ 93 Bob Watson .25 .11
☐ 94 Bobby Murcer .25 .11
☐ 95 Bobby Brown .10 .05
☐ 96 Jim Spencer .10 .05
☐ 97 Tom Underwood .10 .05
☐ 98 Oscar Gamble .10 .05
☐ 99 Johnny Oates .25 .11
☐ 100 Fred Stanley .10 .05
☐ 101 Ruppert Jones .10 .05
☐ 102 Dennis Werth .10 .05
☐ 103 Joe Lefebvre .10 .05
☐ 104 Brian Doyle .10 .05
☐ 105 Aurelio Rodriguez .10 .05
☐ 106 Doug Bird .10 .05
☐ 107 Mike Griffin .10 .05
☐ 108 Tim Lollar .10 .05
☐ 109 Willie Randolph .25 .11
☐ 110 Steve Garvey .50 .23
☐ 111 Reggie Smith .25 .11
☐ 112 Don Sutton 1.00 .45
☐ 113 Burt Hooton .10 .05
☐ 114A Dave Lopes P1 .50 .23
(Small hand on back)
☐ 114B Dave Lopes P2 .25 .11
(No hand)
☐ 115 Dusty Baker .50 .23
☐ 116 Tom Lasorda MG .25 .11
☐ 117 Bill Russell .25 .11
☐ 118 Jerry Reuss UER .25 .11
("Home:" omitted)
☐ 119 Terry Forster .10 .05
☐ 120A Bob Welch P1 .25 .11
(Name on back
is "Bob~)
☐ 120B Bob Welch P2 .50 .23
(Name on back
is "Robert~)
☐ 121 Don Stanhouse .10 .05
☐ 122 Rick Monday .25 .11
☐ 123 Derrel Thomas .10 .05
☐ 124 Joe Ferguson .10 .05
☐ 125 Rick Sutcliffe .25 .11
☐ 126A Ron Cey P1 .50 .23
(Small hand on back)
☐ 126B Ron Cey P2 .25 .11
(No hand)
☐ 127 Dave Goltz .10 .05
☐ 128 Jay Johnstone .25 .11
☐ 129 Steve Yeager .10 .05
☐ 130 Gary Weiss .10 .05
☐ 131 Mike Scioscia 1.00 .45
☐ 132 Vic Davalillo .10 .05
☐ 133 Doug Rau .10 .05
☐ 134 Pepe Frias .10 .05
☐ 135 Mickey Hatcher .25 .11
☐ 136 Steve Howe .25 .11
☐ 137 Robert Castillo .10 .05
☐ 138 Gary Thomasson .10 .05
☐ 139 Rudy Law .10 .05
☐ 140 Fernando Valenzuela 2.00 .90
UER (Misspelled
Fernand on card)
☐ 141 Manny Mota .25 .11
☐ 142 Gary Carter 1.00 .45
☐ 143 Steve Rogers .10 .05
☐ 144 Warren Cromartie .10 .05
☐ 145 Andre Dawson 1.50 .70
☐ 146 Larry Parrish .10 .05
☐ 147 Rowland Office .10 .05
☐ 148 Ellis Valentine .10 .05
☐ 149 Dick Williams MG .10 .05
☐ 150 Bill Gullickson .50 .23
☐ 151 Elias Sosa .10 .05
☐ 152 John Tamargo .10 .05
☐ 153 Chris Speier .10 .05
☐ 154 Ron LeFlore .25 .11
☐ 155 Rodney Scott .10 .05
☐ 156 Stan Bahnsen .10 .05
☐ 157 Bill Lee .25 .11
☐ 158 Fred Norman .10 .05
☐ 159 Woodie Fryman .10 .05
☐ 160 David Palmer .10 .05
☐ 161 Jerry White .10 .05
☐ 162 Roberto Ramos .10 .05
☐ 163 John D'Acquisto .10 .05
☐ 164 Tommy Hutton .10 .05
☐ 165 Charlie Lea .10 .05
☐ 166 Scott Sanderson .10 .05
☐ 167 Ken Macha .10 .05
☐ 168 Tony Bernazard .10 .05
☐ 169 Jim Palmer .75 .35
☐ 170 Steve Stone .25 .11
☐ 171 Mike Flanagan .25 .11
☐ 172 Al Bumbry .25 .11
☐ 173 Doug DeCinces .25 .11
☐ 174 Scott McGregor .10 .05
☐ 175 Mark Belanger .25 .11
☐ 176 Tim Stoddard .10 .05
☐ 177A Rick Dempsey P1 .50 .23
(Small hand on front)
☐ 177B Rick Dempsey P2 .25 .11
(No hand)
☐ 178 Earl Weaver MG 1.00 .45
☐ 179 Tippy Martinez .10 .05
☐ 180 Dennis Martinez .50 .23
☐ 181 Sammy Stewart .10 .05
☐ 182 Rich Dauer .10 .05
☐ 183 Lee May .25 .11
☐ 184 Eddie Murray 2.00 .90
☐ 185 Benny Ayala .10 .05
☐ 186 John Lowenstein .10 .05
☐ 187 Gary Roenicke .10 .05
☐ 188 Ken Singleton .25 .11
☐ 189 Dan Graham .10 .05
☐ 190 Terry Crowley .10 .05
☐ 191 Kiko Garcia .10 .05
☐ 192 Dave Ford .10 .05
☐ 193 Mark Corey .10 .05
☐ 194 Lenn Sakata .10 .05
☐ 195 Doug DeCinces .25 .11
☐ 196 Johnny Bench 1.25 .55
☐ 197 Dave Concepcion .25 .11
☐ 198 Ray Knight .25 .11
☐ 199 Ken Griffey .50 .23
☐ 200 Tom Seaver 1.25 .55
☐ 201 Dave Collins .10 .05
☐ 202A George Foster P1 .50 .23
Slugger
(Number on back 216)
☐ 202B George Foster P2 .50 .23
Slugger
(Number on back 202)
☐ 203 Junior Kennedy .10 .05
☐ 204 Frank Pastore .10 .05
☐ 205 Dan Driessen .10 .05
☐ 206 Hector Cruz .10 .05
☐ 207 Paul Moskau .10 .05
☐ 208 Charlie Leibrandt .50 .23
☐ 209 Harry Spilman .10 .05
☐ 210 Joe Price .10 .05
☐ 211 Tom Hume .10 .05
☐ 212 Joe Nolan .10 .05
☐ 213 Doug Bair .10 .05
☐ 214 Mario Soto .10 .05
☐ 215A Bill Bonham P1 .50 .23
(Small hand on back)
☐ 215B Bill Bonham P2 .10 .05
(No hand)
☐ 216 George Foster .25 .11
(See 202)
☐ 217 Paul Householder .10 .05
☐ 218 Ron Oester .10 .05
☐ 219 Sam Mejias .10 .05
☐ 220 Sheldon Burnside .10 .05
☐ 221 Carl Yastrzemski 1.00 .45
☐ 222 Jim Rice .25 .11
☐ 223 Fred Lynn .25 .11
☐ 224 Carlton Fisk 1.25 .55
☐ 225 Rick Burleson .10 .05
☐ 226 Dennis Eckersley 1.00 .45
☐ 227 Butch Hobson .10 .05
☐ 228 Tom Burgmeier .10 .05
☐ 229 Garry Hancock .10 .05
☐ 230 Don Zimmer MG .10 .05
☐ 231 Steve Renko .10 .05
☐ 232 Dwight Evans .50 .23
☐ 233 Mike Torrez .10 .05
☐ 234 Bob Stanley .10 .05
☐ 235 Jim Dwyer .10 .05
☐ 236 Dave Stapleton .10 .05
☐ 237 Glenn Hoffman .10 .05
☐ 238 Jerry Remy .10 .05
☐ 239 Dick Drago .10 .05
☐ 240 Bill Campbell .10 .05
☐ 241 Tony Perez 1.00 .45
☐ 242 Phil Niekro 1.00 .45
☐ 243 Dale Murphy 1.00 .45
☐ 244 Bob Horner .25 .11
☐ 245 Jeff Burroughs .10 .05
☐ 246 Rick Camp .10 .05
☐ 247 Bobby Cox MG .25 .11
☐ 248 Bruce Benedict .10 .05
☐ 249 Gene Garber .10 .05
☐ 250 Jerry Royster .10 .05
☐ 251A Gary Matthews P1 .50 .23
(Small hand on back)
☐ 251B Gary Matthews P2 .25 .11
(No hand)
☐ 252 Chris Chambliss .25 .11
☐ 253 Luis Gomez .10 .05
☐ 254 Bill Nahorodny .10 .05
☐ 255 Doyle Alexander .10 .05
☐ 256 Brian Asselstine .10 .05
☐ 257 Biff Pocoroba .10 .05
☐ 258 Mike Lum .10 .05
☐ 259 Charlie Spikes .10 .05
☐ 260 Glenn Hubbard .10 .05
☐ 261 Tommy Boggs .10 .05
☐ 262 Al Hrabosky .10 .05
☐ 263 Rick Matula .10 .05
☐ 264 Preston Hanna .10 .05
☐ 265 Larry Bradford .10 .05
☐ 266 Rafael Ramirez .10 .05
☐ 267 Larry McWilliams .10 .05
☐ 268 Rod Carew .75 .35
☐ 269 Bobby Grich .25 .11
☐ 270 Carney Lansford .25 .11
☐ 271 Don Baylor .50 .23
☐ 272 Joe Rudi .25 .11
☐ 273 Dan Ford .10 .05
☐ 274 Jim Fregosi MG .10 .05
☐ 275 Dave Frost .10 .05
☐ 276 Frank Tanana .25 .11
☐ 277 Dickie Thon .25 .11
☐ 278 Jason Thompson .10 .05
☐ 279 Rick Miller .10 .05
☐ 280 Bert Campaneris .25 .11
☐ 281 Tom Donohue .10 .05
☐ 282 Brian Downing .25 .11
☐ 283 Fred Patek .10 .05
☐ 284 Bruce Kison .10 .05
☐ 285 Dave LaRoche .10 .05
☐ 286 Don Aase .10 .05
☐ 287 Jim Barr .10 .05
☐ 288 Alfredo Martinez .10 .05
☐ 289 Larry Harlow .10 .05
☐ 290 Andy Hassler .10 .05
☐ 291 Dave Kingman .50 .23
☐ 292 Bill Buckner .25 .11
☐ 293 Rick Reuschel .25 .11
☐ 294 Bruce Sutter .25 .11
☐ 295 Jerry Martin .10 .05
☐ 296 Scot Thompson .10 .05
☐ 297 Ivan DeJesus .10 .05
☐ 298 Steve Dillard .10 .05
☐ 299 Dick Tidrow .10 .05
☐ 300 Randy Martz .10 .05
☐ 301 Lenny Randle .10 .05
☐ 302 Lynn McGlothen .10 .05
☐ 303 Cliff Johnson .10 .05
☐ 304 Tim Blackwell .10 .05
☐ 305 Dennis Lamp .10 .05
☐ 306 Bill Caudill .10 .05
☐ 307 Carlos Lezcano .10 .05
☐ 308 Jim Tracy .10 .05
☐ 309 Doug Capilla UER .10 .05
(Cubs on front but
Braves on back)
☐ 310 Willie Hernandez .25 .11
☐ 311 Mike Vail .10 .05
☐ 312 Mike Krukow .10 .05
☐ 313 Barry Foote .10 .05
☐ 314 Larry Biittner .10 .05
☐ 315 Mike Tyson .10 .05
☐ 316 Lee Mazzilli .10 .05
☐ 317 John Stearns .10 .05
☐ 318 Alex Trevino .10 .05
☐ 319 Craig Swan .10 .05

☐ 320 Frank Taveras .10 .05
☐ 321 Steve Henderson .10 .05
☐ 322 Neil Allen .10 .05
☐ 323 Mark Bomback .10 .05
☐ 324 Mike Jorgensen .10 .05
☐ 325 Joe Torre MG .25 .11
☐ 326 Elliott Maddox .10 .05
☐ 327 Pete Falcone .10 .05
☐ 328 Ray Burris .10 .05
☐ 329 Claudell Washington .10 .05
☐ 330 Doug Flynn .10 .05
☐ 331 Joel Youngblood .10 .05
☐ 332 Bill Almon .10 .05
☐ 333 Tom Hausman .10 .05
☐ 334 Pat Zachry .10 .05
☐ 335 Jeff Reardon 1.00 .45
☐ 336 Wally Backman .25 .11
☐ 337 Dan Norman .10 .05
☐ 338 Jerry Morales .10 .05
☐ 339 Ed Farmer .10 .05
☐ 340 Bob Molinaro .10 .05
☐ 341 Todd Cruz .10 .05
☐ 342A Britt Burns P1 .50 .23
(Small hand on front)
☐ 342B Britt Burns P2 .25 .11
(No hand)
☐ 343 Kevin Bell .10 .05
☐ 344 Tony LaRussa MG .25 .11
☐ 345 Steve Trout .10 .05
☐ 346 Harold Baines 1.50 .70
☐ 347 Richard Wortham .10 .05
☐ 348 Wayne Nordhagen .10 .05
☐ 349 Mike Squires .10 .05
☐ 350 Lamar Johnson .10 .05
☐ 351 Rickey Henderson 2.00 .90
(Most Stolen Bases AL)
☐ 352 Francisco Barrios .10 .05
☐ 353 Thad Bosley .10 .05
☐ 354 Chet Lemon .10 .05
☐ 355 Bruce Kimm .10 .05
☐ 356 Richard Dotson .10 .05
☐ 357 Jim Morrison .10 .05
☐ 358 Mike Proly .10 .05
☐ 359 Greg Pryor .10 .05
☐ 360 Dave Parker .50 .23
☐ 361 Omar Moreno .10 .05
☐ 362A Kent Tekulve P1 .25 .11
(Back "1071 Waterbury~
and "1078 Pirates~)
☐ 362B Kent Tekulve P2 .25 .11
("1971 Waterbury" and
"1978 Pirates")
☐ 363 Willie Stargell .75 .35
☐ 364 Phil Garner .25 .11
☐ 365 Ed Ott .10 .05
☐ 366 Don Robinson .10 .05
☐ 367 Chuck Tanner MG .25 .11
☐ 368 Jim Rooker .10 .05
☐ 369 Dale Berra .10 .05
☐ 370 Jim Bibby .10 .05
☐ 371 Steve Nicosia .10 .05
☐ 372 Mike Easler .10 .05
☐ 373 Bill Robinson .25 .11
☐ 374 Lee Lacy .10 .05
☐ 375 John Candelaria .25 .11
☐ 376 Manny Sanguillen .25 .11
☐ 377 Rick Rhoden .10 .05
☐ 378 Grant Jackson .10 .05
☐ 379 Tim Foli .10 .05
☐ 380 Rod Scurry .10 .05
☐ 381 Bill Madlock .50 .23
☐ 382A Kurt Bevacqua .25 .11
P1 ERR
(P on cap backwards)
☐ 382B Kurt Bevacqua P2 .10 .05
COR
☐ 383 Bert Blyleven .50 .23
☐ 384 Eddie Solomon .10 .05
☐ 385 Enrique Romo .10 .05
☐ 386 John Milner .10 .05
☐ 387 Mike Hargrove .25 .11
☐ 388 Jorge Orta .10 .05
☐ 389 Toby Harrah .25 .11
☐ 390 Tom Veryzer .10 .05
☐ 391 Miguel Dilone .10 .05
☐ 392 Dan Spillner .10 .05
☐ 393 Jack Brohamer .10 .05
☐ 394 Wayne Garland .10 .05
☐ 395 Sid Monge .10 .05
☐ 396 Rick Waits .10 .05
☐ 397 Joe Charboneau 1.00 .45
☐ 398 Gary Alexander .10 .05
☐ 399 Jerry Dybzinski .10 .05
☐ 400 Mike Stanton .10 .05
☐ 401 Mike Paxton .10 .05
☐ 402 Gary Gray .10 .05
☐ 403 Rick Manning .10 .05
☐ 404 Bo Diaz .10 .05
☐ 405 Ron Hassey .10 .05
☐ 406 Ross Grimsley .10 .05
☐ 407 Victor Cruz .10 .05
☐ 408 Len Barker .10 .05
☐ 409 Bob Bailor .10 .05
☐ 410 Otto Velez .10 .05
☐ 411 Ernie Whitt .10 .05
☐ 412 Jim Clancy .10 .05
☐ 413 Barry Bonnell .10 .05
☐ 414 Dave Stieb .25 .11
☐ 415 Damaso Garcia .10 .05
☐ 416 John Mayberry .10 .05
☐ 417 Roy Howell .10 .05
☐ 418 Danny Ainge 2.00 .90
☐ 419A Jesse Jefferson P1 .10 .05
(Back says Pirates)
☐ 419B Jesse Jefferson P2 .10 .05
(Back says Pirates)
☐ 419C Jesse Jefferson P3 1.00 .45
(Back says Blue Jays)
☐ 420 Joey McLaughlin .10 .05
☐ 421 Lloyd Moseby .25 .11
☐ 422 Alvis Woods .10 .05
☐ 423 Garth Iorg .10 .05
☐ 424 Doug Ault .10 .05
☐ 425 Ken Schrom .10 .05
☐ 426 Mike Willis .10 .05
☐ 427 Steve Braun .10 .05
☐ 428 Bob Davis .10 .05
☐ 429 Jerry Garvin .10 .05
☐ 430 Alfredo Griffin .10 .05
☐ 431 Bob Mattick MG .10 .05
☐ 432 Vida Blue .25 .11
☐ 433 Jack Clark .25 .11
☐ 434 Willie McCovey .75 .35
☐ 435 Mike Ivie .10 .05
☐ 436A Darrel Evans P1 ERR .50 .23
(Name on front
"Darrel")
☐ 436B Darrell Evans P2 COR .50 .23
(Name on front
"Darrell")
☐ 437 Terry Whitfield .10 .05
☐ 438 Rennie Stennett .10 .05
☐ 439 John Montefusco .10 .05
☐ 440 Jim Wohlford .10 .05
☐ 441 Bill North .10 .05
☐ 442 Milt May .10 .05
☐ 443 Max Venable .10 .05
☐ 444 Ed Whitson .10 .05
☐ 445 Al Holland .10 .05
☐ 446 Randy Moffitt .10 .05
☐ 447 Bob Knepper .10 .05
☐ 448 Gary Lavelle .10 .05
☐ 449 Greg Minton .10 .05
☐ 450 Johnnie LeMaster .10 .05
☐ 451 Larry Herndon .10 .05
☐ 452 Rich Murray .10 .05
☐ 453 Joe Pettini .10 .05
☐ 454 Allen Ripley .10 .05
☐ 455 Dennis Littlejohn .10 .05
☐ 456 Tom Griffin .10 .05
☐ 457 Alan Hargesheimer .10 .05
☐ 458 Joe Strain .10 .05
☐ 459 Steve Kemp .10 .05
☐ 460 Sparky Anderson MG .25 .11
☐ 461 Alan Trammell 1.25 .55
☐ 462 Mark Fidrych 1.00 .45
☐ 463 Lou Whitaker 1.00 .45
☐ 464 Dave Rozema .10 .05
☐ 465 Milt Wilcox .10 .05
☐ 466 Champ Summers .10 .05
☐ 467 Lance Parrish .25 .11
☐ 468 Dan Petry .10 .05
☐ 469 Pat Underwood .10 .05
☐ 470 Rick Peters .10 .05
☐ 471 Al Cowens .10 .05
☐ 472 John Wockenfuss .10 .05
☐ 473 Tom Brookens .10 .05
☐ 474 Richie Hebner .10 .05
☐ 475 Jack Morris 1.00 .45
☐ 476 Jim Lentine .10 .05
☐ 477 Bruce Robbins .10 .05
☐ 478 Mark Wagner .10 .05
☐ 479 Tim Corcoran .10 .05
☐ 480A Stan Papi P1 .25 .11
(Front as Pitcher)
☐ 480B Stan Papi P2 .10 .05
(Front as Shortstop)
☐ 481 Kirk Gibson 2.00 .90
☐ 482 Dan Schatzeder .10 .05
☐ 483A Amos Otis P1 .25 .11
(See card 32)
☐ 483B Amos Otis P2 .25 .11
(See card 32)
☐ 484 Dave Winfield 1.50 .70
☐ 485 Rollie Fingers 1.00 .45
☐ 486 Gene Richards .10 .05
☐ 487 Randy Jones .10 .05
☐ 488 Ozzie Smith 4.00 1.80
☐ 489 Gene Tenace .25 .11
☐ 490 Bill Fahey .10 .05
☐ 491 John Curtis .10 .05
☐ 492 Dave Cash .10 .05
☐ 493A Tim Flannery P1 .25 .11
(Batting right)
☐ 493B Tim Flannery P2 .10 .05
(Batting left)
☐ 494 Jerry Mumphrey .10 .05
☐ 495 Bob Shirley .10 .05
☐ 496 Steve Mura .10 .05
☐ 497 Eric Rasmussen .10 .05
☐ 498 Broderick Perkins .10 .05
☐ 499 Barry Evans .10 .05
☐ 500 Chuck Baker .10 .05
☐ 501 Luis Salazar .10 .05
☐ 502 Gary Lucas .10 .05
☐ 503 Mike Armstrong .10 .05
☐ 504 Jerry Turner .10 .05
☐ 505 Dennis Kinney .10 .05
☐ 506 Willie Montanez UER .10 .05
(Misspelled Willy
on card front)
☐ 507 Gorman Thomas .25 .11
☐ 508 Ben Oglivie .25 .11
☐ 509 Larry Hisle .10 .05
☐ 510 Sal Bando .25 .11
☐ 511 Robin Yount 1.25 .55
☐ 512 Mike Caldwell .10 .05
☐ 513 Sixto Lezcano .10 .05
☐ 514A Bill Travers P1 ERR .25 .11
("Jerry Augustine"
with Augustine back)
☐ 514B Bill Travers P2 COR .10 .05
☐ 515 Paul Molitor 2.00 .90
☐ 516 Moose Haas .10 .05
☐ 517 Bill Castro .10 .05
☐ 518 Jim Slaton .10 .05
☐ 519 Lary Sorensen .10 .05
☐ 520 Bob McClure .10 .05
☐ 521 Charlie Moore .10 .05
☐ 522 Jim Gantner .25 .11
☐ 523 Reggie Cleveland .10 .05
☐ 524 Don Money .10 .05
☐ 525 Bill Travers .10 .05
☐ 526 Buck Martinez .10 .05
☐ 527 Dick Davis .10 .05
☐ 528 Ted Simmons .25 .11
☐ 529 Garry Templeton .10 .05
☐ 530 Ken Reitz .10 .05
☐ 531 Tony Scott .10 .05
☐ 532 Ken Oberkfell .10 .05
☐ 533 Bob Sykes .10 .05
☐ 534 Keith Smith .10 .05
☐ 535 John Littlefield .10 .05
☐ 536 Jim Kaat .25 .11
☐ 537 Bob Forsch .10 .05
☐ 538 Mike Phillips .10 .05
☐ 539 Terry Landrum .10 .05
☐ 540 Leon Durham .25 .11
☐ 541 Terry Kennedy .10 .05
☐ 542 George Hendrick .10 .05
☐ 543 Dane Iorg .10 .05
☐ 544 Mark Littell .10 .05
☐ 545 Keith Hernandez .25 .11
☐ 546 Silvio Martinez .10 .05
☐ 547A Don Hood P1 ERR .25 .11
("Pete Vuckovich"
with Vuckovich back)
☐ 547B Don Hood P2 COR .10 .05
☐ 548 Bobby Bonds .25 .11
☐ 549 Mike Ramsey .10 .05
☐ 550 Tom Herr .25 .11
☐ 551 Roy Smalley .10 .05
☐ 552 Jerry Koosman .25 .11
☐ 553 Ken Landreaux .10 .05
☐ 554 John Castino .10 .05
☐ 555 Doug Corbett .10 .05
☐ 556 Bombo Rivera .10 .05
☐ 557 Ron Jackson .10 .05
☐ 558 Butch Wynegar .10 .05
☐ 559 Hosken Powell .10 .05
☐ 560 Pete Redfern .10 .05
☐ 561 Roger Erickson .10 .05
☐ 562 Glenn Adams .10 .05
☐ 563 Rick Sofield .10 .05
☐ 564 Geoff Zahn .10 .05
☐ 565 Pete Mackanin .10 .05
☐ 566 Mike Cubbage .10 .05
☐ 567 Darrell Jackson .10 .05
☐ 568 Dave Edwards .10 .05
☐ 569 Rob Wilfong .10 .05
☐ 570 Sal Butera .10 .05

Card	NRMT	VG-E
☐ 571 Jose Morales	.10	.05
☐ 572 Rick Langford	.10	.05
☐ 573 Mike Norris	.10	.05
☐ 574 Rickey Henderson	2.50	1.10
☐ 575 Tony Armas	.25	.11
☐ 576 Dave Revering	.10	.05
☐ 577 Jeff Newman	.10	.05
☐ 578 Bob Lacey	.10	.05
☐ 579 Brian Kingman	.10	.05
☐ 580 Mitchell Page	.10	.05
☐ 581 Billy Martin MG	.50	.23
☐ 582 Rob Picciolo	.10	.05
☐ 583 Mike Heath	.10	.05
☐ 584 Mickey Klutts	.10	.05
☐ 585 Orlando Gonzalez	.10	.05
☐ 586 Mike Davis	.10	.05
☐ 587 Wayne Gross	.10	.05
☐ 588 Matt Keough	.10	.05
☐ 589 Steve McCatty	.10	.05
☐ 590 Dwayne Murphy	.10	.05
☐ 591 Mario Guerrero	.10	.05
☐ 592 Dave McKay	.10	.05
☐ 593 Jim Essian	.10	.05
☐ 594 Dave Heaverlo	.10	.05
☐ 595 Maury Wills MG	.25	.11
☐ 596 Juan Beniquez	.10	.05
☐ 597 Rodney Craig	.10	.05
☐ 598 Jim Anderson	.10	.05
☐ 599 Floyd Bannister	.10	.05
☐ 600 Bruce Bochte	.10	.05
☐ 601 Julio Cruz	.10	.05
☐ 602 Ted Cox	.10	.05
☐ 603 Dan Meyer	.10	.05
☐ 604 Larry Cox	.10	.05
☐ 605 Bill Stein	.10	.05
☐ 606 Steve Garvey	.50	.23
(Most Hits NL)		
☐ 607 Dave Roberts	.10	.05
☐ 608 Leon Roberts	.10	.05
☐ 609 Reggie Walton	.10	.05
☐ 610 Dave Edler	.10	.05
☐ 611 Larry Milbourne	.10	.05
☐ 612 Kim Allen	.10	.05
☐ 613 Mario Mendoza	.10	.05
☐ 614 Tom Paciorek	.10	.05
☐ 615 Glenn Abbott	.10	.05
☐ 616 Joe Simpson	.10	.05
☐ 617 Mickey Rivers	.25	.11
☐ 618 Jim Kern	.10	.05
☐ 619 Jim Sundberg	.25	.11
☐ 620 Richie Zisk	.10	.05
☐ 621 Jon Matlack	.10	.05
☐ 622 Ferguson Jenkins	1.00	.45
☐ 623 Pat Corrales MG	.10	.05
☐ 624 Ed Figueroa	.10	.05
☐ 625 Buddy Bell	.25	.11
☐ 626 Al Oliver	.25	.11
☐ 627 Doc Medich	.10	.05
☐ 628 Bump Wills	.10	.05
☐ 629 Rusty Staub	.25	.11
☐ 630 Pat Putnam	.10	.05
☐ 631 John Grubb	.10	.05
☐ 632 Danny Darwin	.25	.11
☐ 633 Ken Clay	.10	.05
☐ 634 Jim Norris	.10	.05
☐ 635 John Butcher	.10	.05
☐ 636 Dave Roberts	.10	.05
☐ 637 Billy Sample	.10	.05
☐ 638 Carl Yastrzemski	1.00	.45
☐ 639 Cecil Cooper	.25	.11
☐ 640 Mike Schmidt P1	1.25	.55
(Portrait;		
"Third Base";		
number on back 5)		
☐ 640B Mike Schmidt P2	2.00	.90
("1980 Home Run King";		
640 on back)		
☐ 641A CL: Phils/Royals P1	.25	.11
41 is Hal McRae		
☐ 641B CL: Phils/Royals P2	.25	.11
(41 is Hal McRae,		
Double Threat)		
☐ 642 CL: Astros/Yankees	.10	.05
☐ 643 CL: Expos/Dodgers	.10	.05
☐ 644A CL: Reds/Orioles P1	.25	.11
(202 is George Foster;		
Joe Nolan pitcher,		
should be catcher)		
☐ 644B CL: Reds/Orioles P2	.25	.11
(202 is Foster Slugger;		
Joe Nolan pitcher,		
should be catcher)		
☐ 645 Pete Rose	1.25	.55
Larry Bowa		
Mike Schmidt		
Triple Threat P1		
(No number on back)		
☐ 645B Pete Rose	2.50	1.10
Larry Bowa		
Mike Schmidt		
Triple Threat P2		
(Back numbered 645)		
☐ 646 CL: Braves/Red Sox	.10	.05
☐ 647 CL: Cubs/Angels	.10	.05
☐ 648 CL: Mets/White Sox	.10	.05
☐ 649 CL: Indians/Pirates	.10	.05
☐ 650 Reggie Jackson	1.25	.55
Mr. Baseball P1		
(Number on back 79)		
☐ 650B Reggie Jackson	1.25	.55
Mr. Baseball P2		
(Number on back 650)		
☐ 651 CL: Giants/Blue Jays	.10	.05
☐ 652A CL: Tigers/Padres P1	.25	.11
(483 is listed)		
☐ 652B CL: Tigers/Padres P2	.25	.11
(483 is deleted)		
☐ 653A Willie Wilson P1	.25	.11
Most Hits Most Runs		
(Number on back 29)		
☐ 653B Willie Wilson P2	.25	.11
Most Hits Most Runs		
(Number on back 653)		
☐ 654A CL:Brewers/Cards P1	.25	.11
(514 Jerry Augustine;		
547 Pete Vuckovich)		
☐ 654B CL:Brewers/Cards P2	.25	.11
(514 Billy Travers;		
547 Don Hood)		
☐ 655 George Brett P1	2.50	1.10
.390 Average		
(Number on back 28)		
☐ 655B George Brett P2	4.00	1.80
.390 Average		
(Number on back 655)		
☐ 656 CL: Twins/Oakland A's	.25	.11
☐ 657A Tug McGraw P1	.25	.11
Game Saver		
(Number on back 7)		
☐ 657B Tug McGraw P2	.25	.11
Game Saver		
(Number on back 657)		
☐ 658 CL: Rangers/Mariners	.10	.05
☐ 659A Checklist P1	.10	.05
of Special Cards		
(Last lines on front,		
Wilson Most Hits)		
☐ 659B Checklist P2	.10	.05
of Special Cards		
(Last lines on front,		
Otis Series Starter)		
☐ 660 Steve Carlton P1	1.50	.70
Golden Arm		
(Number on back 660;		
Back "1066 Cardinals~)		
☐ 660B Steve Carlton P2	1.50	.70
Golden Arm		
("1966 Cardinals~)		

1981 Fleer Sticker Cards

The stickers in this 128-sticker set measure 2 1/2" by 3 1/2". The 1981 Fleer Baseball Star Stickers consist of numbered cards with peelable, full-color sticker fronts and three unnumbered checklists. The backs of the numbered player cards are the same as the 1981 Fleer regular issue cards except for the numbers, while the checklist cards (cards 126-128 below) have sticker fronts of Jackson (1-42), Brett (43-83), and Schmidt (84-125).

	NRMT	VG-E
COMPLETE SET (128)	45.00	20.00
COMMON CARD (1-128)	.10	.05
☐ 1 Steve Garvey	.75	.35
☐ 2 Ron LeFlore	.10	.05
☐ 3 Ron Cey	.20	.09
☐ 4 Dave Revering	.10	.05
☐ 5 Tony Armas	.10	.05
☐ 6 Mike Norris	.10	.05
☐ 7 Steve Kemp	.10	.05
☐ 8 Bruce Bochte	.10	.05
☐ 9 Mike Schmidt	3.00	1.35
☐ 10 Scott McGregor	.10	.05
☐ 11 Buddy Bell	.20	.09
☐ 12 Carney Lansford	.20	.09
☐ 13 Carl Yastrzemski	2.00	.90
☐ 14 Ben Oglivie	.10	.05
☐ 15 Willie Stargell	1.00	.45
☐ 16 Cecil Cooper	.20	.09
☐ 17 Gene Richards	.10	.05
☐ 18 Jim Kern	.10	.05
☐ 19 Jerry Koosman	.20	.09
☐ 20 Larry Bowa	.20	.09
☐ 21 Kent Tekulve	.20	.09
☐ 22 Dan Driessen	.10	.05
☐ 23 Phil Niekro	1.00	.45
☐ 24 Dan Quisenberry	.20	.09
☐ 25 Dave Winfield	2.00	.90
☐ 26 Dave Parker	.20	.09
☐ 27 Rick Langford	.10	.05
☐ 28 Amos Otis	.20	.09
☐ 29 Bill Buckner	.20	.09
☐ 30 Al Bumbry	.10	.05
☐ 31 Bake McBride	.10	.05
☐ 32 Mickey Rivers	.20	.09
☐ 33 Rick Burleson	.10	.05
☐ 34 Dennis Eckersley	1.50	.70
☐ 35 Cesar Cedeno	.20	.09
☐ 36 Enos Cabell	.10	.05
☐ 37 Johnny Bench	2.00	.90
☐ 38 Robin Yount	2.00	.90
☐ 39 Mark Belanger	.20	.09
☐ 40 Rod Carew	1.50	.70
☐ 41 George Foster	.20	.09
☐ 42 Lee Mazzilli	.10	.05
☐ 43 Pete Rose	3.00	1.35
Larry Bowa		
Mike Schmidt		
Triple Threat		
☐ 44 J.R. Richard	.10	.05
☐ 45 Lou Piniella	.20	.09
☐ 46 Ken Landreaux	.10	.05
☐ 47 Rollie Fingers	.75	.35
☐ 48 Joaquin Andujar	.20	.09
☐ 49 Tom Seaver	2.00	.90
☐ 50 Bobby Grich	.20	.09
☐ 51 Jon Matlack	.10	.05
☐ 52 Jack Clark	.20	.09
☐ 53 Jim Rice	.20	.09
☐ 54 Rickey Henderson	5.00	2.20
☐ 55 Roy Smalley	.10	.05
☐ 56 Mike Flanagan	.10	.05
☐ 57 Steve Rogers	.10	.05
☐ 58 Carlton Fisk	2.00	.90
☐ 59 Don Sutton	1.00	.45
☐ 60 Ken Griffey	.20	.09
☐ 61 Burt Hooton	.10	.05
☐ 62 Dusty Baker	.20	.09
☐ 63 Vida Blue	.20	.09
☐ 64 Al Oliver	.20	.09
☐ 65 Jim Bibby	.10	.05
☐ 66 Tony Perez	.60	.25
☐ 67 Davey Lopes	.20	.09
☐ 68 Bill Russell	.20	.09
☐ 69 Larry Parrish	.10	.05
☐ 70 Garry Maddox	.10	.05
☐ 71 Phil Garner	.20	.09
☐ 72 Graig Nettles	.35	.16
☐ 73 Gary Carter	1.00	.45
☐ 74 Pete Rose	3.00	1.35
☐ 75 Greg Luzinski	.20	.09
☐ 76 Ron Guidry	.20	.09
☐ 77 Gorman Thomas	.10	.05
☐ 78 Jose Cruz	.20	.09
☐ 79 Bob Boone	.20	.09
☐ 80 Bruce Sutter	.20	.09
☐ 81 Chris Chambliss	.20	.09
☐ 82 Paul Molitor	3.00	1.35
☐ 83 Tug McGraw	.20	.09
☐ 84 Ferguson Jenkins	.75	.35
☐ 85 Steve Carlton	1.50	.70
☐ 86 Miguel Dilone	.10	.05
☐ 87 Reggie Smith	.20	.09
☐ 88 Rick Cerone	.10	.05
☐ 89 Alan Trammell	1.00	.45
☐ 90 Doug DeCinces	.10	.05
☐ 91 Sparky Lyle	.20	.09
☐ 92 Warren Cromartie	.10	.05
☐ 93 Rick Reuschel	.20	.09
☐ 94 Larry Hisle	.10	.05
☐ 95 Paul Splittorff	.10	.05
☐ 96 Manny Trillo	.10	.05
☐ 97 Frank White	.20	.09
☐ 98 Fred Lynn	.20	.09
☐ 99 Bob Horner	.10	.05
☐ 100 Omar Moreno	.10	.05

☐ 101 Dave Concepcion	.20	.09
☐ 102 Larry Gura	.10	.05
☐ 103 Ken Singleton	.20	.09
☐ 104 Steve Stone	.10	.05
☐ 105 Richie Zisk	.20	.09
☐ 106 Willie Wilson	.20	.09
☐ 107 Willie Randolph	.20	.09
☐ 108 Nolan Ryan	10.00	4.50
☐ 109 Joe Morgan	1.50	.70
☐ 110 Bucky Dent	.20	.09
☐ 111 Dave Kingman	.35	.16
☐ 112 John Castino	.10	.05
☐ 113 Joe Rudi	.10	.05
☐ 114 Ed Farmer	.10	.05
☐ 115 Reggie Jackson	2.00	.90
☐ 116 George Brett	5.00	2.20
☐ 117 Eddie Murray	4.00	1.80
☐ 118 Rich Gossage	.50	.23
☐ 119 Dale Murphy	1.50	.70
☐ 120 Ted Simmons	.20	.09
☐ 121 Tommy John	.50	.23
☐ 122 Don Baylor	.35	.16
☐ 123 Andre Dawson	1.50	.70
☐ 124 Jim Palmer	1.50	.70
☐ 125 Garry Templeton	.10	.05
☐ 126 Reggie Jackson CL 1 Unnumbered	1.00	.45
☐ 127 George Brett CL 2 Unnumbered	3.00	1.35
☐ 128 Mike Schmidt CL3 Unnumbered	2.00	.90

1982 Fleer

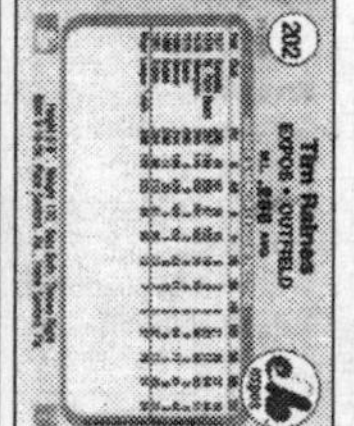

The 1982 Fleer set contains 660-card standard-size cards, of which are grouped in team order based upon standings from the previous season. Cards numbered 628 through 646 are special cards highlighting some of the stars and leaders of the 1981 season. The last 14 cards in the set (647-660) are checklist cards. The backs feature player statistics and a full-color team logo in the upper right-hand corner of each card. The complete set price below does not include any of the more valuable variation cards listed. Fleer was not allowed to insert bubble gum or other confectionary products into these packs; therefore logo stickers were included in these 15-card packs. Notable Rookie Cards in this set include Cal Ripken Jr., Lee Smith, and Dave Stewart.

	NRMT	VG-E
COMPLETE SET (660)	70.00	32.00
COMMON CARD (1-660)	.10	.05
☐ 1 Dusty Baker	.40	.18
☐ 2 Robert Castillo	.10	.05
☐ 3 Ron Cey	.20	.09
☐ 4 Terry Forster	.10	.05
☐ 5 Steve Garvey	.40	.18
☐ 6 Dave Goltz	.10	.05
☐ 7 Pedro Guerrero	.20	.09
☐ 8 Burt Hooton	.10	.05
☐ 9 Steve Howe	.10	.05
☐ 10 Jay Johnstone	.20	.09
☐ 11 Ken Landreaux	.10	.05
☐ 12 Dave Lopes	.20	.09
☐ 13 Mike A. Marshall	.20	.09
☐ 14 Bobby Mitchell	.10	.05
☐ 15 Rick Monday	.10	.05
☐ 16 Tom Niedenfuer	.10	.05
☐ 17 Ted Power	.10	.05
☐ 18 Jerry Reuss UER ("Home:" omitted)	.20	.09
☐ 19 Ron Roenicke	.10	.05
☐ 20 Bill Russell	.20	.09
☐ 21 Steve Sax	.75	.35
☐ 22 Mike Scioscia	.20	.09
☐ 23 Reggie Smith	.20	.09
☐ 24 Dave Stewart	1.00	.45
☐ 25 Rick Sutcliffe	.20	.09
☐ 26 Derrel Thomas	.10	.05
☐ 27 Fernando Valenzuela	.40	.18
☐ 28 Bob Welch	.20	.09
☐ 29 Steve Yeager	.10	.05
☐ 30 Bobby Brown	.10	.05
☐ 31 Rick Cerone	.10	.05
☐ 32 Ron Davis	.10	.05
☐ 33 Bucky Dent	.20	.09
☐ 34 Barry Foote	.10	.05
☐ 35 George Frazier	.10	.05
☐ 36 Oscar Gamble	.10	.05
☐ 37 Rich Gossage	.40	.18
☐ 38 Ron Guidry	.20	.09
☐ 39 Reggie Jackson	1.00	.45
☐ 40 Tommy John	.40	.18
☐ 41 Rudy May	.10	.05
☐ 42 Larry Milbourne	.10	.05
☐ 43 Jerry Mumphrey	.10	.05
☐ 44 Bobby Murcer	.20	.09
☐ 45 Gene Nelson	.10	.05
☐ 46 Graig Nettles	.20	.09
☐ 47 Johnny Oates	.20	.09
☐ 48 Lou Piniella	.20	.09
☐ 49 Willie Randolph	.20	.09
☐ 50 Rick Reuschel	.20	.09
☐ 51 Dave Revering	.10	.05
☐ 52 Dave Righetti	.75	.35
☐ 53 Aurelio Rodriguez	.10	.05
☐ 54 Bob Watson	.20	.09
☐ 55 Dennis Werth	.10	.05
☐ 56 Dave Winfield	1.50	.70
☐ 57 Johnny Bench	1.00	.45
☐ 58 Bruce Berenyi	.10	.05
☐ 59 Larry Biittner	.10	.05
☐ 60 Scott Brown	.10	.05
☐ 61 Dave Collins	.10	.05
☐ 62 Geoff Combe	.10	.05
☐ 63 Dave Concepcion	.20	.09
☐ 64 Dan Driessen	.10	.05
☐ 65 Joe Edelen	.10	.05
☐ 66 George Foster	.20	.09
☐ 67 Ken Griffey	.20	.09
☐ 68 Paul Householder	.10	.05
☐ 69 Tom Hume	.10	.05
☐ 70 Junior Kennedy	.10	.05
☐ 71 Ray Knight	.20	.09
☐ 72 Mike LaCoss	.10	.05
☐ 73 Rafael Landestoy	.10	.05
☐ 74 Charlie Leibrandt	.10	.05
☐ 75 Sam Mejias	.10	.05
☐ 76 Paul Moskau	.10	.05
☐ 77 Joe Nolan	.10	.05
☐ 78 Mike O'Berry	.10	.05
☐ 79 Ron Oester	.10	.05
☐ 80 Frank Pastore	.10	.05
☐ 81 Joe Price	.10	.05
☐ 82 Tom Seaver	1.00	.45
☐ 83 Mario Soto	.10	.05
☐ 84 Mike Vail	.10	.05
☐ 85 Tony Armas	.10	.05
☐ 86 Shooty Babitt	.10	.05
☐ 87 Dave Beard	.10	.05
☐ 88 Rick Bosetti	.10	.05
☐ 89 Keith Drumwright	.10	.05
☐ 90 Wayne Gross	.10	.05
☐ 91 Mike Heath	.10	.05
☐ 92 Rickey Henderson	1.50	.70
☐ 93 Cliff Johnson	.10	.05
☐ 94 Jeff Jones	.10	.05
☐ 95 Matt Keough	.10	.05
☐ 96 Brian Kingman	.10	.05
☐ 97 Mickey Klutts	.10	.05
☐ 98 Rick Langford	.10	.05
☐ 99 Steve McCatty	.10	.05
☐ 100 Dave McKay	.10	.05
☐ 101 Dwayne Murphy	.10	.05
☐ 102 Jeff Newman	.10	.05
☐ 103 Mike Norris	.10	.05
☐ 104 Bob Owchinko	.10	.05
☐ 105 Mitchell Page	.10	.05
☐ 106 Rob Picciolo	.10	.05
☐ 107 Jim Spencer	.10	.05
☐ 108 Fred Stanley	.10	.05
☐ 109 Tom Underwood	.10	.05
☐ 110 Joaquin Andujar	.20	.09
☐ 111 Steve Braun	.10	.05
☐ 112 Bob Forsch	.10	.05
☐ 113 George Hendrick	.10	.05
☐ 114 Keith Hernandez	.20	.09
☐ 115 Tom Herr	.20	.09
☐ 116 Dane Iorg	.10	.05
☐ 117 Jim Kaat	.40	.18
☐ 118 Tito Landrum	.10	.05
☐ 119 Sixto Lezcano	.10	.05
☐ 120 Mark Littell	.10	.05
☐ 121 John Martin	.10	.05
☐ 122 Silvio Martinez	.10	.05
☐ 123 Ken Oberkfell	.10	.05
☐ 124 Darrell Porter	.20	.09
☐ 125 Mike Ramsey	.10	.05
☐ 126 Orlando Sanchez	.10	.05
☐ 127 Bob Shirley	.10	.05
☐ 128 Lary Sorensen	.10	.05
☐ 129 Bruce Sutter	.20	.09
☐ 130 Bob Sykes	.10	.05
☐ 131 Garry Templeton	.10	.05
☐ 132 Gene Tenace	.20	.09
☐ 133 Jerry Augustine	.10	.05
☐ 134 Sal Bando	.20	.09
☐ 135 Mark Brouhard	.10	.05
☐ 136 Mike Caldwell	.10	.05
☐ 137 Reggie Cleveland	.10	.05
☐ 138 Cecil Cooper	.20	.09
☐ 139 Jamie Easterly	.10	.05
☐ 140 Marshall Edwards	.10	.05
☐ 141 Rollie Fingers	.75	.35
☐ 142 Jim Gantner	.20	.09
☐ 143 Moose Haas	.10	.05
☐ 144 Larry Hisle	.10	.05
☐ 145 Roy Howell	.10	.05
☐ 146 Rickey Keeton	.10	.05
☐ 147 Randy Lerch	.10	.05
☐ 148 Paul Molitor	1.25	.55
☐ 149 Don Money	.10	.05
☐ 150 Charlie Moore	.10	.05
☐ 151 Ben Oglivie	.20	.09
☐ 152 Ted Simmons	.20	.09
☐ 153 Jim Slaton	.10	.05
☐ 154 Gorman Thomas	.20	.09
☐ 155 Robin Yount	1.50	.70
☐ 156 Pete Vuckovich (Should precede Yount in the team order)	.10	.05
☐ 157 Benny Ayala	.10	.05
☐ 158 Mark Belanger	.20	.09
☐ 159 Al Bumbry	.20	.09
☐ 160 Terry Crowley	.10	.05
☐ 161 Rich Dauer	.10	.05
☐ 162 Doug DeCinces	.20	.09
☐ 163 Rick Dempsey	.20	.09
☐ 164 Jim Dwyer	.10	.05
☐ 165 Mike Flanagan	.20	.09
☐ 166 Dave Ford	.10	.05
☐ 167 Dan Graham	.10	.05
☐ 168 Wayne Krenchicki	.10	.05
☐ 169 John Lowenstein	.10	.05
☐ 170 Dennis Martinez	.20	.09
☐ 171 Tippy Martinez	.10	.05
☐ 172 Scott McGregor	.10	.05
☐ 173 Jose Morales	.10	.05
☐ 174 Eddie Murray	1.25	.55
☐ 175 Jim Palmer	.75	.35
☐ 176 Cal Ripken (Fleer Ripken cards from 1982 through 1993 erroneously have 22 games played in 1981;not 23.)	40.00	18.00
☐ 177 Gary Roenicke	.10	.05
☐ 178 Lenn Sakata	.10	.05
☐ 179 Ken Singleton	.20	.09
☐ 180 Sammy Stewart	.10	.05
☐ 181 Tim Stoddard	.10	.05
☐ 182 Steve Stone	.20	.09
☐ 183 Stan Bahnsen	.10	.05
☐ 184 Ray Burris	.10	.05
☐ 185 Gary Carter	.75	.35
☐ 186 Warren Cromartie	.10	.05
☐ 187 Andre Dawson	.75	.35
☐ 188 Terry Francona	.10	.05
☐ 189 Woodie Fryman	.10	.05
☐ 190 Bill Gullickson	.10	.05
☐ 191 Grant Jackson	.10	.05
☐ 192 Wallace Johnson	.10	.05
☐ 193 Charlie Lea	.10	.05
☐ 194 Bill Lee	.20	.09
☐ 195 Jerry Manuel	.10	.05
☐ 196 Brad Mills	.10	.05
☐ 197 John Milner	.10	.05
☐ 198 Rowland Office	.10	.05
☐ 199 David Palmer	.10	.05
☐ 200 Larry Parrish	.10	.05
☐ 201 Mike Phillips	.10	.05
☐ 202 Tim Raines	.75	.35
☐ 203 Bobby Ramos	.10	.05
☐ 204 Jeff Reardon	.20	.09
☐ 205 Steve Rogers	.10	.05
☐ 206 Scott Sanderson	.10	.05
☐ 207 Rodney Scott UER (Photo actually Tim Raines)	.40	.18
☐ 208 Elias Sosa	.10	.05
☐ 209 Chris Speier	.10	.05
☐ 210 Tim Wallach	.75	.35
☐ 211 Jerry White	.10	.05
☐ 212 Alan Ashby	.10	.05
☐ 213 Cesar Cedeno	.20	.09
☐ 214 Jose Cruz	.20	.09
☐ 215 Kiko Garcia	.10	.05

☐ 216 Phil Garner .20 .09
☐ 217 Danny Heep .10 .05
☐ 218 Art Howe .10 .05
☐ 219 Bob Knepper .10 .05
☐ 220 Frank LaCorte .10 .05
☐ 221 Joe Niekro .20 .09
☐ 222 Joe Pittman .10 .05
☐ 223 Terry Puhl .10 .05
☐ 224 Luis Pujols .10 .05
☐ 225 Craig Reynolds .10 .05
☐ 226 J.R. Richard .20 .09
☐ 227 Dave Roberts .10 .05
☐ 228 Vern Ruhle .10 .05
☐ 229 Nolan Ryan 5.00 2.20
☐ 230 Joe Sambito .10 .05
☐ 231 Tony Scott .10 .05
☐ 232 Dave Smith .10 .05
☐ 233 Harry Spilman .10 .05
☐ 234 Don Sutton .75 .35
☐ 235 Dickie Thon .10 .05
☐ 236 Denny Walling .10 .05
☐ 237 Gary Woods .10 .05
☐ 238 Luis Aguayo .10 .05
☐ 239 Ramon Aviles .10 .05
☐ 240 Bob Boone .20 .09
☐ 241 Larry Bowa .20 .09
☐ 242 Warren Brusstar .10 .05
☐ 243 Steve Carlton .75 .35
☐ 244 Larry Christenson .10 .05
☐ 245 Dick Davis .10 .05
☐ 246 Greg Gross .10 .05
☐ 247 Sparky Lyle .20 .09
☐ 248 Garry Maddox .10 .05
☐ 249 Gary Matthews .20 .09
☐ 250 Bake McBride .10 .05
☐ 251 Tug McGraw .20 .09
☐ 252 Keith Moreland .10 .05
☐ 253 Dickie Noles .10 .05
☐ 254 Mike Proly .10 .05
☐ 255 Ron Reed .10 .05
☐ 256 Pete Rose 1.00 .45
☐ 257 Dick Ruthven .10 .05
☐ 258 Mike Schmidt 1.00 .45
☐ 259 Lonnie Smith .20 .09
☐ 260 Manny Trillo .10 .05
☐ 261 Del Unser .10 .05
☐ 262 George Vukovich .10 .05
☐ 263 Tom Brookens .10 .05
☐ 264 George Cappuzzello .10 .05
☐ 265 Marty Castillo .10 .05
☐ 266 Al Cowens .10 .05
☐ 267 Kirk Gibson .75 .35
☐ 268 Richie Hebner .20 .09
☐ 269 Ron Jackson .10 .05
☐ 270 Lynn Jones .10 .05
☐ 271 Steve Kemp .10 .05
☐ 272 Rick Leach .10 .05
☐ 273 Aurelio Lopez .10 .05
☐ 274 Jack Morris .20 .09
☐ 275 Kevin Saucier .10 .05
☐ 276 Lance Parrish .40 .18
☐ 277 Rick Peters .10 .05
☐ 278 Dan Petry .10 .05
☐ 279 Dave Rozema .10 .05
☐ 280 Stan Papi .10 .05
☐ 281 Dan Schatzeder .10 .05
☐ 282 Champ Summers .10 .05
☐ 283 Alan Trammell .75 .35
☐ 284 Lou Whitaker .40 .18
☐ 285 Milt Wilcox .10 .05
☐ 286 John Wockenfuss .10 .05
☐ 287 Gary Allenson .10 .05
☐ 288 Tom Burgmeier .10 .05
☐ 289 Bill Campbell .10 .05
☐ 290 Mark Clear .10 .05
☐ 291 Steve Crawford .10 .05
☐ 292 Dennis Eckersley .75 .35
☐ 293 Dwight Evans .40 .18
☐ 294 Rich Gedman .20 .09
☐ 295 Garry Hancock .10 .05
☐ 296 Glenn Hoffman .10 .05
☐ 297 Bruce Hurst .10 .05
☐ 298 Carney Lansford .20 .09
☐ 299 Rick Miller .10 .05
☐ 300 Reid Nichols .10 .05
☐ 301 Bob Ojeda .40 .18
☐ 302 Tony Perez .75 .35
☐ 303 Chuck Rainey .10 .05
☐ 304 Jerry Remy .10 .05
☐ 305 Jim Rice .20 .09
☐ 306 Joe Rudi .10 .05
☐ 307 Bob Stanley .10 .05
☐ 308 Dave Stapleton .10 .05
☐ 309 Frank Tanana .20 .09
☐ 310 Mike Torrez .10 .05
☐ 311 John Tudor .20 .09
☐ 312 Carl Yastrzemski .75 .35
☐ 313 Buddy Bell .20 .09
☐ 314 Steve Comer .10 .05
☐ 315 Danny Darwin .10 .05
☐ 316 John Ellis .10 .05
☐ 317 John Grubb .10 .05
☐ 318 Rick Honeycutt .10 .05
☐ 319 Charlie Hough .20 .09
☐ 320 Ferguson Jenkins .75 .35
☐ 321 John Henry Johnson .10 .05
☐ 322 Jim Kern .10 .05
☐ 323 Jon Matlack .10 .05
☐ 324 Doc Medich .10 .05
☐ 325 Mario Mendoza .10 .05
☐ 326 Al Oliver .20 .09
☐ 327 Pat Putnam .10 .05
☐ 328 Mickey Rivers .10 .05
☐ 329 Leon Roberts .10 .05
☐ 330 Billy Sample .10 .05
☐ 331 Bill Stein .10 .05
☐ 332 Jim Sundberg .20 .09
☐ 333 Mark Wagner .10 .05
☐ 334 Bump Wills .10 .05
☐ 335 Bill Almon .10 .05
☐ 336 Harold Baines .75 .35
☐ 337 Ross Baumgarten .10 .05
☐ 338 Tony Bernazard .10 .05
☐ 339 Britt Burns .10 .05
☐ 340 Richard Dotson .10 .05
☐ 341 Jim Essian .10 .05
☐ 342 Ed Farmer .10 .05
☐ 343 Carlton Fisk .75 .35
☐ 344 Kevin Hickey .10 .05
☐ 345 LaMarr Hoyt .10 .05
☐ 346 Lamar Johnson .10 .05
☐ 347 Jerry Koosman .20 .09
☐ 348 Rusty Kuntz .10 .05
☐ 349 Dennis Lamp .10 .05
☐ 350 Ron LeFlore .20 .09
☐ 351 Chet Lemon .10 .05
☐ 352 Greg Luzinski .20 .09
☐ 353 Bob Molinaro .10 .05
☐ 354 Jim Morrison .10 .05
☐ 355 Wayne Nordhagen .10 .05
☐ 356 Greg Pryor .10 .05
☐ 357 Mike Squires .10 .05
☐ 358 Steve Trout .10 .05
☐ 359 Alan Bannister .10 .05
☐ 360 Len Barker .10 .05
☐ 361 Bert Blyleven .75 .35
☐ 362 Joe Charboneau .10 .05
☐ 363 John Denny .10 .05
☐ 364 Bo Diaz .10 .05
☐ 365 Miguel Dilone .10 .05
☐ 366 Jerry Dybzinski .10 .05
☐ 367 Wayne Garland .10 .05
☐ 368 Mike Hargrove .20 .09
☐ 369 Toby Harrah .20 .09
☐ 370 Ron Hassey .10 .05
☐ 371 Von Hayes .20 .09
☐ 372 Pat Kelly .10 .05
☐ 373 Duane Kuiper .10 .05
☐ 374 Rick Manning .10 .05
☐ 375 Sid Monge .10 .05
☐ 376 Jorge Orta .10 .05
☐ 377 Dave Rosello .10 .05
☐ 378 Dan Spillner .10 .05
☐ 379 Mike Stanton .10 .05
☐ 380 Andre Thornton .10 .05
☐ 381 Tom Veryzer .10 .05
☐ 382 Rick Waits .10 .05
☐ 383 Doyle Alexander .10 .05
☐ 384 Vida Blue .20 .09
☐ 385 Fred Breining .10 .05
☐ 386 Enos Cabell .10 .05
☐ 387 Jack Clark .20 .09
☐ 388 Darrell Evans .20 .09
☐ 389 Tom Griffin .10 .05
☐ 390 Larry Herndon .10 .05
☐ 391 Al Holland .10 .05
☐ 392 Gary Lavelle .10 .05
☐ 393 Johnnie LeMaster .10 .05
☐ 394 Jerry Martin .10 .05
☐ 395 Milt May .10 .05
☐ 396 Greg Minton .10 .05
☐ 397 Joe Morgan .75 .35
☐ 398 Joe Pettini .10 .05
☐ 399 Allen Ripley .10 .05
☐ 400 Billy Smith .10 .05
☐ 401 Rennie Stennett .10 .05
☐ 402 Ed Whitson .10 .05
☐ 403 Jim Wohlford .10 .05
☐ 404 Willie Aikens .10 .05
☐ 405 George Brett 1.50 .70
☐ 406 Ken Brett .10 .05
☐ 407 Dave Chalk .10 .05
☐ 408 Rich Gale .10 .05
☐ 409 Cesar Geronimo .10 .05
☐ 410 Larry Gura .10 .05
☐ 411 Clint Hurdle .10 .05
☐ 412 Mike Jones .10 .05
☐ 413 Dennis Leonard .10 .05
☐ 414 Renie Martin .10 .05
☐ 415 Lee May .20 .09
☐ 416 Hal McRae .20 .09
☐ 417 Darryl Motley .10 .05
☐ 418 Rance Mulliniks .10 .05
☐ 419 Amos Otis .20 .09
☐ 420 Ken Phelps .10 .05
☐ 421 Jamie Quirk .10 .05
☐ 422 Dan Quisenberry .20 .09
☐ 423 Paul Splittorff .10 .05
☐ 424 U.L. Washington .10 .05
☐ 425 John Wathan .10 .05
☐ 426 Frank White .20 .09
☐ 427 Willie Wilson .20 .09
☐ 428 Brian Asselstine .10 .05
☐ 429 Bruce Benedict .10 .05
☐ 430 Tommy Boggs .10 .05
☐ 431 Larry Bradford .10 .05
☐ 432 Rick Camp .10 .05
☐ 433 Chris Chambliss .20 .09
☐ 434 Gene Garber .10 .05
☐ 435 Preston Hanna .10 .05
☐ 436 Bob Horner .20 .09
☐ 437 Glenn Hubbard .10 .05
☐ 438A All Hrabosky ERR 15.00 6.75
(Height 5'1" All on reverse)
☐ 438B Al Hrabosky ERR .40 .18
(Height 5'1")
☐ 438C Al Hrabosky .20 .09
(Height 5'10")
☐ 439 Rufino Linares .10 .05
☐ 440 Rick Mahler .10 .05
☐ 441 Ed Miller .10 .05
☐ 442 John Montefusco .10 .05
☐ 443 Dale Murphy .75 .35
☐ 444 Phil Niekro .75 .35
☐ 445 Gaylord Perry .75 .35
☐ 446 Biff Pocoroba .10 .05
☐ 447 Rafael Ramirez .10 .05
☐ 448 Jerry Royster .10 .05
☐ 449 Claudell Washington .10 .05
☐ 450 Don Aase .10 .05
☐ 451 Don Baylor .40 .18
☐ 452 Juan Beniquez .10 .05
☐ 453 Rick Burleson .10 .05
☐ 454 Bert Campaneris .20 .09
☐ 455 Rod Carew .75 .35
☐ 456 Bob Clark .10 .05
☐ 457 Brian Downing .10 .05
☐ 458 Dan Ford .10 .05
☐ 459 Ken Forsch .10 .05
☐ 460A Dave Frost (5 mm space before ERA) .10 .05
☐ 460B Dave Frost .10 .05
(1 mm space)
☐ 461 Bobby Grich .20 .09
☐ 462 Larry Harlow .10 .05
☐ 463 John Harris .10 .05
☐ 464 Andy Hassler .10 .05
☐ 465 Butch Hobson .10 .05
☐ 466 Jesse Jefferson .10 .05
☐ 467 Bruce Kison .10 .05
☐ 468 Fred Lynn .20 .09
☐ 469 Angel Moreno .10 .05
☐ 470 Ed Ott .10 .05
☐ 471 Fred Patek .10 .05
☐ 472 Steve Renko .10 .05
☐ 473 Mike Witt .20 .09
☐ 474 Geoff Zahn .10 .05
☐ 475 Gary Alexander .10 .05
☐ 476 Dale Berra .10 .05
☐ 477 Kurt Bevacqua .10 .05
☐ 478 Jim Bibby .10 .05
☐ 479 John Candelaria .10 .05
☐ 480 Victor Cruz .10 .05
☐ 481 Mike Easler .10 .05
☐ 482 Tim Foli .10 .05
☐ 483 Lee Lacy .10 .05
☐ 484 Vance Law .10 .05
☐ 485 Bill Madlock .20 .09
☐ 486 Willie Montanez .10 .05
☐ 487 Omar Moreno .10 .05
☐ 488 Steve Nicosia .10 .05
☐ 489 Dave Parker .20 .09
☐ 490 Tony Pena .10 .05
☐ 491 Pascual Perez .10 .05
☐ 492 Johnny Ray .20 .09
☐ 493 Rick Rhoden .10 .05
☐ 494 Bill Robinson .10 .05
☐ 495 Don Robinson .10 .05
☐ 496 Enrique Romo .10 .05
☐ 497 Rod Scurry .10 .05

☐ 498 Eddie Solomon	.10	.05
☐ 499 Willie Stargell	.75	.35
☐ 500 Kent Tekulve	.20	.09
☐ 501 Jason Thompson	.10	.05
☐ 502 Glenn Abbott	.10	.05
☐ 503 Jim Anderson	.10	.05
☐ 504 Floyd Bannister	.10	.05
☐ 505 Bruce Bochte	.10	.05
☐ 506 Jeff Burroughs	.10	.05
☐ 507 Bryan Clark	.10	.05
☐ 508 Ken Clay	.10	.05
☐ 509 Julio Cruz	.10	.05
☐ 510 Dick Drago	.10	.05
☐ 511 Gary Gray	.10	.05
☐ 512 Dan Meyer	.10	.05
☐ 513 Jerry Narron	.10	.05
☐ 514 Tom Paciorek	.20	.09
☐ 515 Casey Parsons	.10	.05
☐ 516 Lenny Randle	.10	.05
☐ 517 Shane Rawley	.10	.05
☐ 518 Joe Simpson	.10	.05
☐ 519 Richie Zisk	.10	.05
☐ 520 Neil Allen	.10	.05
☐ 521 Bob Bailor	.10	.05
☐ 522 Hubie Brooks	.20	.09
☐ 523 Mike Cubbage	.10	.05
☐ 524 Pete Falcone	.10	.05
☐ 525 Doug Flynn	.10	.05
☐ 526 Tom Hausman	.10	.05
☐ 527 Ron Hodges	.10	.05
☐ 528 Randy Jones	.10	.05
☐ 529 Mike Jorgensen	.10	.05
☐ 530 Dave Kingman	.20	.09
☐ 531 Ed Lynch	.10	.05
☐ 532 Mike G. Marshall	.10	.05
☐ 533 Lee Mazzilli	.10	.05
☐ 534 Dyar Miller	.10	.05
☐ 535 Mike Scott	.20	.09
☐ 536 Rusty Staub	.20	.09
☐ 537 John Stearns	.10	.05
☐ 538 Craig Swan	.10	.05
☐ 539 Frank Taveras	.10	.05
☐ 540 Alex Trevino	.10	.05
☐ 541 Ellis Valentine	.10	.05
☐ 542 Mookie Wilson	.20	.09
☐ 543 Joel Youngblood	.10	.05
☐ 544 Pat Zachry	.10	.05
☐ 545 Glenn Adams	.10	.05
☐ 546 Fernando Arroyo	.10	.05
☐ 547 John Verhoeven	.10	.05
☐ 548 Sal Butera	.10	.05
☐ 549 John Castino	.10	.05
☐ 550 Don Cooper	.10	.05
☐ 551 Doug Corbett	.10	.05
☐ 552 Dave Engle	.10	.05
☐ 553 Roger Erickson	.10	.05
☐ 554 Danny Goodwin	.10	.05
☐ 555A Darrell Jackson (Black cap)	.40	.18
☐ 555B Darrell Jackson (Red cap with T)	.20	.09
☐ 555C Darrell Jackson (Red cap, no emblem)	3.00	1.35
☐ 556 Pete Mackanin	.10	.05
☐ 557 Jack O'Connor	.10	.05
☐ 558 Hosken Powell	.10	.05
☐ 559 Pete Redfern	.10	.05
☐ 560 Roy Smalley	.10	.05
☐ 561 Chuck Baker UER (Shortshop on front)	.10	.05
☐ 562 Gary Ward	.10	.05
☐ 563 Rob Wilfong	.10	.05
☐ 564 Al Williams	.10	.05
☐ 565 Butch Wynegar	.10	.05
☐ 566 Randy Bass	.10	.05
☐ 567 Juan Bonilla	.10	.05
☐ 568 Danny Boone	.10	.05
☐ 569 John Curtis	.10	.05
☐ 570 Juan Eichelberger	.10	.05
☐ 571 Barry Evans	.10	.05
☐ 572 Tim Flannery	.10	.05
☐ 573 Ruppert Jones	.10	.05
☐ 574 Terry Kennedy	.10	.05
☐ 575 Joe Lefebvre	.10	.05
☐ 576A John Littlefield ERR (Left handed; reverse negative)	200.00	90.00
☐ 576B John Littlefield COR (Right handed)	.20	.09
☐ 577 Gary Lucas	.10	.05
☐ 578 Steve Mura	.10	.05
☐ 579 Broderick Perkins	.10	.05
☐ 580 Gene Richards	.10	.05
☐ 581 Luis Salazar	.10	.05
☐ 582 Ozzie Smith	2.00	.90
☐ 583 John Urrea	.10	.05
☐ 584 Chris Welsh	.10	.05
☐ 585 Rick Wise	.10	.05
☐ 586 Doug Bird	.10	.05
☐ 587 Tim Blackwell	.10	.05
☐ 588 Bobby Bonds	.20	.09
☐ 589 Bill Buckner	.20	.09
☐ 590 Bill Caudill	.10	.05
☐ 591 Hector Cruz	.10	.05
☐ 592 Jody Davis	.10	.05
☐ 593 Ivan DeJesus	.10	.05
☐ 594 Steve Dillard	.10	.05
☐ 595 Leon Durham	.10	.05
☐ 596 Rawly Eastwick	.10	.05
☐ 597 Steve Henderson	.10	.05
☐ 598 Mike Krukow	.10	.05
☐ 599 Mike Lum	.10	.05
☐ 600 Randy Martz	.10	.05
☐ 601 Jerry Morales	.10	.05
☐ 602 Ken Reitz	.10	.05
☐ 603 Lee Smith ERR (Cubs logo reversed)	2.50	1.10
☐ 603B Lee Smith COR	6.00	2.70
☐ 604 Dick Tidrow	.10	.05
☐ 605 Jim Tracy	.10	.05
☐ 606 Mike Tyson	.10	.05
☐ 607 Ty Waller	.10	.05
☐ 608 Danny Ainge	1.00	.45
☐ 609 Jorge Bell	.75	.35
☐ 610 Mark Bomback	.10	.05
☐ 611 Barry Bonnell	.10	.05
☐ 612 Jim Clancy	.10	.05
☐ 613 Damaso Garcia	.10	.05
☐ 614 Jerry Garvin	.10	.05
☐ 615 Alfredo Griffin	.10	.05
☐ 616 Garth Iorg	.10	.05
☐ 617 Luis Leal	.10	.05
☐ 618 Ken Macha	.10	.05
☐ 619 John Mayberry	.10	.05
☐ 620 Joey McLaughlin	.10	.05
☐ 621 Lloyd Moseby	.10	.05
☐ 622 Dave Stieb	.20	.09
☐ 623 Jackson Todd	.10	.05
☐ 624 Willie Upshaw	.10	.05
☐ 625 Otto Velez	.10	.05
☐ 626 Ernie Whitt	.10	.05
☐ 627 Alvis Woods	.10	.05
☐ 628 All Star Game Cleveland, Ohio	.20	.09
☐ 629 All Star Infielders Frank White and Bucky Dent	.20	.09
☐ 630 Big Red Machine Dan Driessen Dave Concepcion George Foster	.20	.09
☐ 631 Bruce Sutter Top NL Relief Pitcher	.20	.09
☐ 632 Steve and Carlton Steve Carlton Carlton Fisk	.40	.18
☐ 633 Carl Yastrzemski 3000th Game	.75	.35
☐ 634 Dynamic Duo Johnny Bench and Tom Seaver	1.00	.45
☐ 635 West Meets East Fernando Valenzuela and Gary Carter	.20	.09
☐ 636A Fernando Valenzuela: NL SO King ("he" NL)	.75	.35
☐ 636B Fernando Valenzuela: NL SO King ("the" NL)	.75	.35
☐ 637 Mike Schmidt Home Run King	1.00	.45
☐ 638 NL All Stars Gary Carter and Dave Parker	.20	.09
☐ 639 Perfect Game UER Len Barker and Bo Diaz (Catcher actually Ron Hassey)	.20	.09
☐ 640 Pete and Re-Pete Pete Rose and Son	1.00	.45
☐ 641 Phillies Finest Lonnie Smith Mike Schmidt Steve Carlton	.75	.35
☐ 642 Red Sox Reunion Fred Lynn and Dwight Evans	.20	.09
☐ 643 Rickey Henderson Most Hits and Runs	1.00	.45
☐ 644 Rollie Fingers Most Saves AL	.20	.09
☐ 645 Tom Seaver Most 1981 Wins	.75	.35
☐ 646 Yankee Powerhouse Reggie Jackson and Dave Winfield (Comma on back after outfielder)	2.00	.90
☐ 646B Yankee Powerhouse Reggie Jackson and Dave Winfield (No comma)	2.00	.90
☐ 647 CL: Yankees/Dodgers	.10	.05
☐ 648 CL: A's/Reds	.10	.05
☐ 649 CL: Cards/Brewers	.10	.05
☐ 650 CL: Expos/Orioles	.10	.05
☐ 651 CL: Astros/Phillies	.10	.05
☐ 652 CL: Tigers/Red Sox	.10	.05
☐ 653 CL: Rangers/White Sox	.10	.05
☐ 654 CL: Giants/Indians	.10	.05
☐ 655 CL: Royals/Braves	.10	.05
☐ 656 CL: Angels/Pirates	.10	.05
☐ 657 CL: Mariners/Mets	.10	.05
☐ 658 CL: Padres/Twins	.10	.05
☐ 659 CL: Blue Jays/Cubs	.10	.05
☐ 660 Specials Checklist	.10	.05

1982 Fleer Stamps

The stamps in this 242-piece set measure 1 13/16" by 2 1/2". The 1982 Fleer stamp set consists of different individual stamps issued in strips of 10 stamps each. The stamps were issued in packages with the Fleer team logo stickers. The backs are blank and an inexpensive album is available in which to place the stamps. A checklist is provided in the back of the album which lists 25 strips of 10 stamps. The checklist below lists the individual stamps plus the strip (with prefix G) to which the stamps are supposed to belong based on the album strip checklist. Complete strips have equal value to the sum of the individual stamps on the strip. Eight stamps have been doubly printed and are noted by two different strip numbers below. The numbering is essentially in team order, e.g., Los Angeles Dodgers (1-10), Cincinnati Reds (11-20), St. Louis Cardinals (21-30), Montreal Expos (31-40), Houston Astros (41-50), Philadelphia Phillies (51-60), San Francisco Giants (61-65), Atlanta Braves (66-70), Pittsburgh Pirates (71-80), New York Mets (81-90), Chicago Cubs (91-100), San Diego Padres (101-105), Combination Stamps (106-111), New York Yankees (112-121), Oakland A's (122-131), Milwaukee Brewers (132-141), Baltimore Orioles (142-151), Detroit Tigers (152-161), Boston Red Sox (162-171), Texas Rangers (172-181), Chicago White Sox (182-191), Cleveland Indians (192-201), Kansas City Royals (202-211), California Angels (212-221), Seattle Mariners (222-226), Minnesota Twins (227-231), Toronto Blue Jays (232-236) and Combination Stamps (237-242).

	NRMT	VG-E
COMPLETE SET (242)	20.00	9.00
COMMON STAMP (1-242)	.05	.02
COMMON SHEET	.75	.35
☐ 1 Fern. Valenzuela G20	.50	.23
☐ 2 Rick Monday G16	.05	.02
☐ 3 Ron Cey G9	.10	.05
☐ 4 Dusty Baker G20	.10	.05
☐ 5 Burt Hooton G10	.05	.02
☐ 6 Pedro Guerrero G23	.10	.05
☐ 7 Jerry Reuss G12	.05	.02
☐ 8 Bill Russell G7	.05	.02
☐ 9 Steve Garvey G21	.15	.07
☐ 10 Davey Lopes G19	.10	.05
☐ 11 Tom Seaver G7	1.00	.45
☐ 12 George Foster G17	.10	.05
☐ 13 Frank Pastore G12	.05	.02
☐ 14 Dave Collins G5	.05	.02
☐ 15 Dave Concepcion G21	.10	.05
☐ 16 Ken Griffey G6	.10	.05
☐ 17 Johnny Bench G20	1.00	.45
☐ 18 Ray Knight G16	.10	.05
☐ 19 Mario Soto G9	.05	.02
☐ 20 Ron Oester G19	.05	.02
☐ 21 Ken Oberkfell G21	.05	.02

☐ 22 Bob Forsch G4 .05 .02
☐ 23 Keith Hernandez G19 .10 .05
☐ 24 Dane Iorg G9 .05 .02
☐ 25 George Hendrick G2 .05 .02
☐ 26 Gene Tenace G24 .05 .02
☐ 27 Garry Templeton G12 .05 .02
☐ 28 Bruce Sutter G18 .10 .05
☐ 29 Darrell Porter G14 .05 .02
☐ 30 Tom Herr G3 .05 .02
☐ 31 Tim Raines G11 .50 .23
☐ 32 Chris Speier G13 .05 .02
☐ 33 Warren Cromartie G22 .05 .02
☐ 34 Larry Parrish G15 .05 .02
☐ 35 Andre Dawson G10 .75 .35
☐ 36 Steve Rogers G1/G25 .05 .02
☐ 37 Jeff Reardon G23 .15 .07
☐ 38 Rodney Scott G12 .05 .02
☐ 39 Gary Carter G14 .50 .23
☐ 40 Scott Sanderson G6 .05 .02
☐ 41 Cesar Cedeno G7 .05 .02
☐ 42 Nolan Ryan G10 6.00 2.70
☐ 43 Don Sutton G24 .25 .11
☐ 44 Terry Puhl G15 .05 .02
☐ 45 Joe Niekro G13 .05 .02
☐ 46 Tony Scott G16 .05 .02
☐ 47 Joe Sambito G1 .05 .02
☐ 48 Art Howe G9 .05 .02
☐ 49 Bob Knepper G18 .05 .02
☐ 50 Jose Cruz G22 .10 .05
☐ 51 Pete Rose G16 2.00 .90
☐ 52 Dick Ruthven G12 .05 .02
☐ 53 Mike Schmidt G14 2.00 .90
☐ 54 Steve Carlton G17 1.00 .45
☐ 55 Tug McGraw G4 .10 .05
☐ 56 Larry Bowa G4 .10 .05
☐ 57 Garry Maddox G18 .05 .02
☐ 58 Gary Matthews G4 .05 .02
☐ 59 Manny Trillo G15 .05 .02
☐ 60 Lonnie Smith G20 .05 .02
☐ 61 Vida Blue G11 .10 .05
☐ 62 Milt May G12 .05 .02
☐ 63 Joe Morgan G16 .50 .23
☐ 64 Enos Cabell G8 .05 .02
☐ 65 Jack Clark G18 .10 .05
☐ 66 Claud.Washington G19 .05 .02
☐ 67 Gaylord Perry G16 .25 .11
☐ 68 Phil Niekro G22 .25 .11
☐ 69 Bob Horner G7 .05 .02
☐ 70 Chris Chambliss G11 .05 .02
☐ 71 Dave Parker G15 .10 .05
☐ 72 Tony Pena G11 .05 .02
☐ 73 Kent Tekulve G23 .05 .02
☐ 74 Mike Easler G18 .05 .02
☐ 75 Tim Foli G13 .05 .02
☐ 76 Willie Stargell G21 .50 .23
☐ 77 Bill Madlock G5 .10 .05
☐ 78 Jim Bibby G14 .05 .02
☐ 79 Omar Moreno G17 .05 .02
☐ 80 Lee Lacy G2 .05 .02
☐ 81 Hubie Brooks G24 .05 .02
☐ 82 Rusty Staub G4 .10 .05
☐ 83 Ellis Valentine G13 .05 .02
☐ 84 Neil Allen G1 .05 .02
☐ 85 Dave Kingman G9 .15 .07
☐ 86 Mookie Wilson G3 .15 .07
☐ 87 Doug Flynn G11 .05 .02
☐ 88 Pat Zachry G8 .05 .02
☐ 89 John Stearns G6 .05 .02
☐ 90 Lee Mazzilli G2 .05 .02
☐ 91 Ken Reitz G23 .05 .02
☐ 92 Mike Krukow G11 .05 .02
☐ 93 Jerry Morales G10 .05 .02
☐ 94 Leon Durham G22 .05 .02
☐ 95 Ivan DeJesus G2 .05 .02
☐ 96 Bill Buckner G17 .10 .05
☐ 97 Jim Tracy G12 .05 .02
☐ 98 Steve Henderson G14 .05 .02
☐ 99 Dick Tidrow G14 .05 .02
☐ 100 Mike Tyson G5 .05 .02
☐ 101 Ozzie Smith G12 2.50 1.10
☐ 102 Ruppert Jones G24 .05 .02
☐ 103 Brod Perkins G10 .05 .02
☐ 104 Gene Richards G15 .05 .02
☐ 105 Terry Kennedy G22 .05 .02
☐ 106 Jim Bibby and Willie Stargell G4 .15 .07
☐ 107 Pete Rose and Larry Bowa G21 .75 .35
☐ 108 Fern.Valenzuela and Warren Spahn G1/G25 .25 .11
☐ 109 Pete Rose and Dave Concepcion G8 .75 .35
☐ 110 Reggie Jackson and Dave Winfield G3 1.50 .70
☐ 111 Fernando Valenzuela and Tom Lasorda G4 .15 .07
☐ 112 Reggie Jackson G6 2.00 .90
☐ 113 Dave Winfield G3 1.50 .70
☐ 114 Lou Piniella G2 .10 .05
☐ 115 Tommy John G9 .10 .05
☐ 116 Rich Gossage G1/G25 .10 .05
☐ 117 Ron Davis G10 .05 .02
☐ 118 Rick Cerone G5 .05 .02
☐ 119 Graig Nettles G8 .10 .05
☐ 120 Ron Guidry G24 .10 .05
☐ 121 Willie Randolph G24 .10 .05
☐ 122 Dwayne Murphy G15 .05 .02
☐ 123 Rickey Henderson G16 2.00 .90
☐ 124 Wayne Gross G6 .05 .02
☐ 125 Mike Norris G8 .05 .02
☐ 126 Rick Langford G20 .05 .02
☐ 127 Jim Spencer G17 .05 .02
☐ 128 Tony Armas G12 .05 .02
☐ 129 Matt Keough G7 .05 .02
☐ 130 Jeff Jones G19 .05 .02
☐ 131 Steve McCatty G3 .05 .02
☐ 132 Rollie Fingers G7 .25 .11
☐ 133 Jim Gantner G15 .05 .02
☐ 134 Gorman Thomas G6 .05 .02
☐ 135 Robin Yount G13 1.00 .45
☐ 136 Paul Molitor G22 1.50 .70
☐ 137 Ted Simmons G10 .10 .05
☐ 138 Ben Oglivie G23 .05 .02
☐ 139 Moose Haas G21 .05 .02
☐ 140 Cecil Cooper G24 .10 .05
☐ 141 Pete Vuckovich G10 .05 .02
☐ 142 Doug DeCinces G21 .05 .02
☐ 143 Jim Palmer G9 .50 .23
☐ 144 Steve Stone G16 .05 .02
☐ 145 Mike Flanagan G19 .05 .02
☐ 146 Rick Dempsey G9 .05 .02
☐ 147 Al Bumbry G14 .05 .02
☐ 148 Mark Belanger G8 .05 .02
☐ 149 Scott McGregor G23 .05 .02
☐ 150 Ken Singleton G10 .05 .02
☐ 151 Eddie Murray G5 2.50 1.10
☐ 152 Lance Parrish G20 .15 .07
☐ 153 Dave Rozema G15 .05 .02
☐ 154 Champ Summers G13 .05 .02
☐ 155 Alan Trammell G2 .50 .23
☐ 156 Lou Whitaker G1/G25 .25 .11
☐ 157 Milt Wilcox G5 .05 .02
☐ 158 Kevin Saucier G24 .05 .02
☐ 159 Jack Morris G14 .10 .05
☐ 160 Steve Kemp G7 .05 .02
☐ 161 Kirk Gibson G3 .25 .11
☐ 162 Carl Yastrzemski G3 .75 .35
☐ 163 Jim Rice G21 .15 .07
☐ 164 Carney Lansford G15 .10 .05
☐ 165 Dennis Eckersley G6 .50 .23
☐ 166 Mike Torrez G5 .05 .02
☐ 167 Dwight Evans G19 .10 .05
☐ 168 Glenn Hoffman G18 .05 .02
☐ 169 Bob Stanley G20 .05 .02
☐ 170 Tony Perez G16 .25 .11
☐ 171 Jerry Remy G13 .05 .02
☐ 172 Buddy Bell G5 .10 .05
☐ 173 Fergie Jenkins G17 .25 .11
☐ 174 Mickey Rivers G9 .05 .02
☐ 175 Bump Wills G2 .05 .02
☐ 176 Jon Matlack G20 .05 .02
☐ 177 Steve Comer G23 .05 .02
☐ 178 Al Oliver G1/G25 .10 .05
☐ 179 Bill Stein G3 .05 .02
☐ 180 Pat Putnam G14 .05 .02
☐ 181 Jim Sundberg G4 .05 .02
☐ 182 Ron LeFlore G4 .10 .05
☐ 183 Carlton Fisk G11 1.00 .45
☐ 184 Harold Baines G18 .25 .11
☐ 185 Bill Almon G2 .05 .02
☐ 186 Richard Dotson G9 .05 .02
☐ 187 Greg Luzinski G14 .10 .05
☐ 188 Mike Squires G13 .05 .02
☐ 189 Britt Burns G19 .05 .02
☐ 190 LaMarr Hoyt G6 .05 .02
☐ 191 Chet Lemon G22 .05 .02
☐ 192 Joe Charboneau G20 .05 .02
☐ 193 Toby Harrah G16 .05 .02
☐ 194 John Denny G22 .05 .02
☐ 195 Rick Manning G8 .05 .02
☐ 196 Miguel Dilone G15 .05 .02
☐ 197 Bo Diaz G13 .05 .02
☐ 198 Mike Hargrove G17 .10 .05
☐ 199 Bert Blyleven G11 .10 .05
☐ 200 Len Barker G7 .05 .02
☐ 201 Andre Thornton G18 .05 .02
☐ 202 George Brett G24 2.00 .90
☐ 203 U.L. Washington G25 .05 .02
☐ 204 Dan Quisenberry G17 .05 .02
☐ 205 Larry Gura G17 .05 .02
☐ 206 Willie Aikens G22 .05 .02
☐ 207 Willie Wilson G21 .05 .02
☐ 208 Dennis Leonard G8 .05 .02
☐ 209 Frank White G6 .10 .05
☐ 210 Hal McRae G23 .10 .05
☐ 211 Amos Otis G18 .05 .02
☐ 212 Don Aase G23 .05 .02
☐ 213 Butch Hobson G6 .05 .02
☐ 214 Fred Lynn G18 .10 .05
☐ 215 Brian Downing G10 .05 .02
☐ 216 Dan Ford G5 .05 .02
☐ 217 Rod Carew G5 .75 .35
☐ 218 Bobby Grich G19 .10 .05
☐ 219 Rick Burleson G11 .05 .02
☐ 220 Don Baylor G3 .10 .05
☐ 221 Ken Forsch G17 .05 .02
☐ 222 Bruce Bochte .05 .02
☐ 223 Richie Zisk .05 .02
☐ 224 Tom Paciorek .05 .02
☐ 225 Julio Cruz .05 .02
☐ 226 Jeff Burroughs .05 .02
☐ 227 Doug Corbett .05 .02
☐ 228 Roy Smalley .05 .02
☐ 229 Gary Ward .05 .02
☐ 230 John Castino .05 .02
☐ 231 Rob Wilfong .05 .02
☐ 232 Dave Stieb .05 .02
☐ 233 Otto Velez .05 .02
☐ 234 Damaso Garcia .05 .02
☐ 235 John Mayberry .05 .02
☐ 236 Alfredo Griffin .05 .02
☐ 237 Ted Williams Carl Yastrzemski 2.00 .90
☐ 238 Rick Cerone Graig Nettles .10 .05
☐ 239 Buddy Bell George Brett 1.50 .70
☐ 240 Steve Carlton Jim Kaat .25 .11
☐ 241 Steve Carlton Dave Parker .25 .11
☐ 242 Ron Davis Nolan Ryan 4.00 1.80
☐ XX Stamp Album 2.00 .90

1983 Fleer

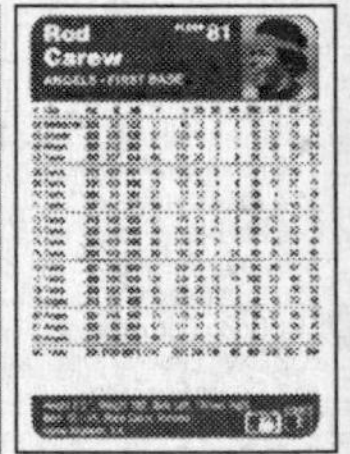

In 1983, for the third straight year, Fleer produced a baseball series of 660 standard-size cards. Of these, 1-628 are player cards, 629-646 are special cards, and 647-660 are checklist cards. The player cards are again ordered alphabetically within team and teams seeded in descending order based upon the previous season's standings. The front of each card has a colorful team logo at bottom left and the player's name and position at lower right. The reverses are done in shades of brown on white. Wax packs consisted of 15 cards plus logo stickers in a 38-pack box. Notable Rookie Cards include Wade Boggs, Tony Gwynn and Ryne Sandberg.

	NRMT	VG-E
COMPLETE SET (660)	80.00	36.00
COMMON CARD (1-660)	.10	.05

☐ 1 Joaquin Andujar .10 .05
☐ 2 Doug Bair .10 .05
☐ 3 Steve Braun .10 .05
☐ 4 Glenn Brummer .10 .05
☐ 5 Bob Forsch .10 .05
☐ 6 David Green .10 .05
☐ 7 George Hendrick .10 .05
☐ 8 Keith Hernandez .20 .09
☐ 9 Tom Herr .20 .09
☐ 10 Dane Iorg .10 .05
☐ 11 Jim Kaat .20 .09
☐ 12 Jeff Lahti .10 .05
☐ 13 Tito Landrum .10 .05
☐ 14 Dave LaPoint .10 .05
☐ 15 Willie McGee .75 .35
☐ 16 Steve Mura .10 .05
☐ 17 Ken Oberkfell .10 .05
☐ 18 Darrell Porter .10 .05
☐ 19 Mike Ramsey .10 .05
☐ 20 Gene Roof .10 .05
☐ 21 Lonnie Smith .10 .05
☐ 22 Ozzie Smith 1.50 .70

☐ 23 John Stuper .10 .05
☐ 24 Bruce Sutter .20 .09
☐ 25 Gene Tenace .20 .09
☐ 26 Jerry Augustine .10 .05
☐ 27 Dwight Bernard .10 .05
☐ 28 Mark Brouhard .10 .05
☐ 29 Mike Caldwell .10 .05
☐ 30 Cecil Cooper .20 .09
☐ 31 Jamie Easterly .10 .05
☐ 32 Marshall Edwards .10 .05
☐ 33 Rollie Fingers .75 .35
☐ 34 Jim Gantner .20 .09
☐ 35 Moose Haas .10 .05
☐ 36 Roy Howell .10 .05
☐ 37 Pete Ladd .10 .05
☐ 38 Bob McClure .10 .05
☐ 39 Doc Medich .10 .05
☐ 40 Paul Molitor 1.00 .45
☐ 41 Don Money .10 .05
☐ 42 Charlie Moore .10 .05
☐ 43 Ben Oglivie .10 .05
☐ 44 Ed Romero .10 .05
☐ 45 Ted Simmons .20 .09
☐ 46 Jim Slaton .10 .05
☐ 47 Don Sutton .40 .18
☐ 48 Gorman Thomas .10 .05
☐ 49 Pete Vuckovich .10 .05
☐ 50 Ned Yost .10 .05
☐ 51 Robin Yount 1.25 .55
☐ 52 Benny Ayala .10 .05
☐ 53 Bob Bonner .10 .05
☐ 54 Al Bumbry .20 .09
☐ 55 Terry Crowley .10 .05
☐ 56 Storm Davis .10 .05
☐ 57 Rich Dauer .10 .05
☐ 58 Rick Dempsey UER .20 .09
(Posing batting lefty)
☐ 59 Jim Dwyer .10 .05
☐ 60 Mike Flanagan .20 .09
☐ 61 Dan Ford .10 .05
☐ 62 Glenn Gulliver .10 .05
☐ 63 John Lowenstein .10 .05
☐ 64 Dennis Martinez .20 .09
☐ 65 Tippy Martinez .10 .05
☐ 66 Scott McGregor .10 .05
☐ 67 Eddie Murray 1.00 .45
☐ 68 Joe Nolan .10 .05
☐ 69 Jim Palmer .75 .35
☐ 70 Cal Ripken 10.00 4.50
☐ 71 Gary Roenicke .10 .05
☐ 72 Lenn Sakata .10 .05
☐ 73 Ken Singleton .20 .09
☐ 74 Sammy Stewart .10 .05
☐ 75 Tim Stoddard .10 .05
☐ 76 Don Aase .10 .05
☐ 77 Don Baylor .40 .18
☐ 78 Juan Beniquez .10 .05
☐ 79 Bob Boone .20 .09
☐ 80 Rick Burleson .10 .05
☐ 81 Rod Carew .60 .25
☐ 82 Bobby Clark .10 .05
☐ 83 Doug Corbett .10 .05
☐ 84 John Curtis .10 .05
☐ 85 Doug DeCinces .20 .09
☐ 86 Brian Downing .10 .05
☐ 87 Joe Ferguson .10 .05
☐ 88 Tim Foli .10 .05
☐ 89 Ken Forsch .10 .05
☐ 90 Dave Goltz .10 .05
☐ 91 Bobby Grich .20 .09
☐ 92 Andy Hassler .10 .05
☐ 93 Reggie Jackson 1.00 .45
☐ 94 Ron Jackson .10 .05
☐ 95 Tommy John .40 .18
☐ 96 Bruce Kison .10 .05
☐ 97 Fred Lynn .20 .09
☐ 98 Ed Ott .10 .05
☐ 99 Steve Renko .10 .05
☐ 100 Luis Sanchez .10 .05
☐ 101 Rob Wilfong .10 .05
☐ 102 Mike Witt .10 .05
☐ 103 Geoff Zahn .10 .05
☐ 104 Willie Aikens .10 .05
☐ 105 Mike Armstrong .10 .05
☐ 106 Vida Blue .20 .09
☐ 107 Bud Black .20 .09
☐ 108 George Brett 1.50 .70
☐ 109 Bill Castro .10 .05
☐ 110 Onix Concepcion .10 .05
☐ 111 Dave Frost .10 .05
☐ 112 Cesar Geronimo .10 .05
☐ 113 Larry Gura .10 .05
☐ 114 Steve Hammond .10 .05
☐ 115 Don Hood .10 .05
☐ 116 Dennis Leonard .10 .05
☐ 117 Jerry Martin .10 .05
☐ 118 Lee May .20 .09
☐ 119 Hal McRae .20 .09
☐ 120 Amos Otis .20 .09
☐ 121 Greg Pryor .10 .05
☐ 122 Dan Quisenberry .20 .09
☐ 123 Don Slaught .40 .18
☐ 124 Paul Splittorff .10 .05
☐ 125 U.L. Washington .10 .05
☐ 126 John Wathan .10 .05
☐ 127 Frank White .20 .09
☐ 128 Willie Wilson .20 .09
☐ 129 Steve Bedrosian UER .20 .09
(Height 6'33")
☐ 130 Bruce Benedict .10 .05
☐ 131 Tommy Boggs .10 .05
☐ 132 Brett Butler .75 .35
☐ 133 Rick Camp .10 .05
☐ 134 Chris Chambliss .20 .09
☐ 135 Ken Dayley .10 .05
☐ 136 Gene Garber .10 .05
☐ 137 Terry Harper .10 .05
☐ 138 Bob Horner .10 .05
☐ 139 Glenn Hubbard .10 .05
☐ 140 Rufino Linares .10 .05
☐ 141 Rick Mahler .10 .05
☐ 142 Dale Murphy .75 .35
☐ 143 Phil Niekro .75 .35
☐ 144 Pascual Perez .10 .05
☐ 145 Biff Pocoroba .10 .05
☐ 146 Rafael Ramirez .10 .05
☐ 147 Jerry Royster .10 .05
☐ 148 Ken Smith .10 .05
☐ 149 Bob Walk .10 .05
☐ 150 Claudell Washington .10 .05
☐ 151 Bob Watson .20 .09
☐ 152 Larry Whisenton .10 .05
☐ 153 Porfirio Altamirano .10 .05
☐ 154 Marty Bystrom .10 .05
☐ 155 Steve Carlton .75 .35
☐ 156 Larry Christenson .10 .05
☐ 157 Ivan DeJesus .10 .05
☐ 158 John Denny .10 .05
☐ 159 Bob Dernier .10 .05
☐ 160 Bo Diaz .10 .05
☐ 161 Ed Farmer .10 .05
☐ 162 Greg Gross .10 .05
☐ 163 Mike Krukow .10 .05
☐ 164 Garry Maddox .10 .05
☐ 165 Gary Matthews .20 .09
☐ 166 Tug McGraw .20 .09
☐ 167 Bob Molinaro .10 .05
☐ 168 Sid Monge .10 .05
☐ 169 Ron Reed .10 .05
☐ 170 Bill Robinson .10 .05
☐ 171 Pete Rose 1.00 .45
☐ 172 Dick Ruthven .10 .05
☐ 173 Mike Schmidt 1.00 .45
☐ 174 Manny Trillo .10 .05
☐ 175 Ozzie Virgil .10 .05
☐ 176 George Vukovich .10 .05
☐ 177 Gary Allenson .10 .05
☐ 178 Luis Aponte .10 .05
☐ 179 Wade Boggs 8.00 3.60
☐ 180 Tom Burgmeier .10 .05
☐ 181 Mark Clear .10 .05
☐ 182 Dennis Eckersley .75 .35
☐ 183 Dwight Evans .20 .09
☐ 184 Rich Gedman .10 .05
☐ 185 Glenn Hoffman .10 .05
☐ 186 Bruce Hurst .10 .05
☐ 187 Carney Lansford .20 .09
☐ 188 Rick Miller .10 .05
☐ 189 Reid Nichols .10 .05
☐ 190 Bob Ojeda .10 .05
☐ 191 Tony Perez .75 .35
☐ 192 Chuck Rainey .10 .05
☐ 193 Jerry Remy .10 .05
☐ 194 Jim Rice .20 .09
☐ 195 Bob Stanley .10 .05
☐ 196 Dave Stapleton .10 .05
☐ 197 Mike Torrez .10 .05
☐ 198 John Tudor .10 .05
☐ 199 Julio Valdez .10 .05
☐ 200 Carl Yastrzemski .75 .35
☐ 201 Dusty Baker .20 .09
☐ 202 Joe Beckwith .10 .05
☐ 203 Greg Brock .10 .05
☐ 204 Ron Cey .20 .09
☐ 205 Terry Forster .10 .05
☐ 206 Steve Garvey .40 .18
☐ 207 Pedro Guerrero .20 .09
☐ 208 Burt Hooton .10 .05
☐ 209 Steve Howe .10 .05
☐ 210 Ken Landreaux .10 .05
☐ 211 Mike Marshall .10 .05
☐ 212 Candy Maldonado .20 .09
☐ 213 Rick Monday .10 .05
☐ 214 Tom Niedenfuer .10 .05
☐ 215 Jorge Orta .10 .05
☐ 216 Jerry Reuss UER .20 .09
("Home:" omitted)
☐ 217 Ron Roenicke .10 .05
☐ 218 Vicente Romo .10 .05
☐ 219 Bill Russell .20 .09
☐ 220 Steve Sax .20 .09
☐ 221 Mike Scioscia .20 .09
☐ 222 Dave Stewart .20 .09
☐ 223 Derrel Thomas .10 .05
☐ 224 Fernando Valenzuela .40 .18
☐ 225 Bob Welch .20 .09
☐ 226 Ricky Wright .10 .05
☐ 227 Steve Yeager .10 .05
☐ 228 Bill Almon .10 .05
☐ 229 Harold Baines .40 .18
☐ 230 Salome Barojas .10 .05
☐ 231 Tony Bernazard .10 .05
☐ 232 Britt Burns .10 .05
☐ 233 Richard Dotson .10 .05
☐ 234 Ernesto Escarrega .10 .05
☐ 235 Carlton Fisk .75 .35
☐ 236 Jerry Hairston .10 .05
☐ 237 Kevin Hickey .10 .05
☐ 238 LaMarr Hoyt .20 .09
☐ 239 Steve Kemp .10 .05
☐ 240 Jim Kern .10 .05
☐ 241 Ron Kittle .40 .18
☐ 242 Jerry Koosman .20 .09
☐ 243 Dennis Lamp .10 .05
☐ 244 Rudy Law .10 .05
☐ 245 Vance Law .10 .05
☐ 246 Ron LeFlore .10 .05
☐ 247 Greg Luzinski .20 .09
☐ 248 Tom Paciorek .10 .05
☐ 249 Aurelio Rodriguez .10 .05
☐ 250 Mike Squires .10 .05
☐ 251 Steve Trout .10 .05
☐ 252 Jim Barr .10 .05
☐ 253 Dave Bergman .10 .05
☐ 254 Fred Breining .10 .05
☐ 255 Bob Brenly .10 .05
☐ 256 Jack Clark .20 .09
☐ 257 Chili Davis .75 .35
☐ 258 Darrell Evans .20 .09
☐ 259 Alan Fowlkes .10 .05
☐ 260 Rich Gale .10 .05
☐ 261 Atlee Hammaker .10 .05
☐ 262 Al Holland .10 .05
☐ 263 Duane Kuiper .10 .05
☐ 264 Bill Laskey .10 .05
☐ 265 Gary Lavelle .10 .05
☐ 266 Johnnie LeMaster .10 .05
☐ 267 Renie Martin .10 .05
☐ 268 Milt May .10 .05
☐ 269 Greg Minton .10 .05
☐ 270 Joe Morgan .75 .35
☐ 271 Tom O'Malley .10 .05
☐ 272 Reggie Smith .20 .09
☐ 273 Guy Sularz .10 .05
☐ 274 Champ Summers .10 .05
☐ 275 Max Venable .10 .05
☐ 276 Jim Wohlford .10 .05
☐ 277 Ray Burris .10 .05
☐ 278 Gary Carter .75 .35
☐ 279 Warren Cromartie .10 .05
☐ 280 Andre Dawson .75 .35
☐ 281 Terry Francona .10 .05
☐ 282 Doug Flynn .10 .05
☐ 283 Woodie Fryman .10 .05
☐ 284 Bill Gullickson .20 .09
☐ 285 Wallace Johnson .10 .05
☐ 286 Charlie Lea .10 .05
☐ 287 Randy Lerch .10 .05
☐ 288 Brad Mills .10 .05
☐ 289 Dan Norman .10 .05
☐ 290 Al Oliver .20 .09
☐ 291 David Palmer .10 .05
☐ 292 Tim Raines .75 .35
☐ 293 Jeff Reardon .20 .09
☐ 294 Steve Rogers .10 .05
☐ 295 Scott Sanderson .10 .05
☐ 296 Dan Schatzeder .10 .05
☐ 297 Bryn Smith .10 .05
☐ 298 Chris Speier .10 .05
☐ 299 Tim Wallach .20 .09
☐ 300 Jerry White .10 .05
☐ 301 Joel Youngblood .10 .05
☐ 302 Ross Baumgarten .10 .05
☐ 303 Dale Berra .10 .05
☐ 304 John Candelaria .10 .05
☐ 305 Dick Davis .10 .05
☐ 306 Mike Easler .10 .05
☐ 307 Richie Hebner .20 .09
☐ 308 Lee Lacy .10 .05
☐ 309 Bill Madlock .20 .09
☐ 310 Larry McWilliams .10 .05

- ☐ 311 John Milner .10 .05
- ☐ 312 Omar Moreno .10 .05
- ☐ 313 Jim Morrison .10 .05
- ☐ 314 Steve Nicosia .10 .05
- ☐ 315 Dave Parker .20 .09
- ☐ 316 Tony Pena .10 .05
- ☐ 317 Johnny Ray .10 .05
- ☐ 318 Rick Rhoden .10 .05
- ☐ 319 Don Robinson .10 .05
- ☐ 320 Enrique Romo .10 .05
- ☐ 321 Manny Sarmiento .10 .05
- ☐ 322 Rod Scurry .10 .05
- ☐ 323 Jimmy Smith .10 .05
- ☐ 324 Willie Stargell .75 .35
- ☐ 325 Jason Thompson .10 .05
- ☐ 326 Kent Tekulve .20 .09
- ☐ 327A Tom Brookens .10 .05 (Short .375" brown box shaded in on card back)
- ☐ 327B Tom Brookens .10 .05 (Longer 1.25" brown box shaded in on card back)
- ☐ 328 Enos Cabell .10 .05
- ☐ 329 Kirk Gibson .75 .35
- ☐ 330 Larry Herndon .10 .05
- ☐ 331 Mike Ivie .10 .05
- ☐ 332 Howard Johnson .75 .35
- ☐ 333 Lynn Jones .10 .05
- ☐ 334 Rick Leach .10 .05
- ☐ 335 Chet Lemon .10 .05
- ☐ 336 Jack Morris .40 .18
- ☐ 337 Lance Parrish .20 .09
- ☐ 338 Larry Pashnick .10 .05
- ☐ 339 Dan Petry .10 .05
- ☐ 340 Dave Rozema .10 .05
- ☐ 341 Dave Rucker .10 .05
- ☐ 342 Elias Sosa .10 .05
- ☐ 343 Dave Tobik .10 .05
- ☐ 344 Alan Trammell .75 .35
- ☐ 345 Jerry Turner .10 .05
- ☐ 346 Jerry Ujdur .10 .05
- ☐ 347 Pat Underwood .10 .05
- ☐ 348 Lou Whitaker .40 .18
- ☐ 349 Milt Wilcox .10 .05
- ☐ 350 Glenn Wilson .20 .09
- ☐ 351 John Wockenfuss .10 .05
- ☐ 352 Kurt Bevacqua .10 .05
- ☐ 353 Juan Bonilla .10 .05
- ☐ 354 Floyd Chiffer .10 .05
- ☐ 355 Luis DeLeon .10 .05
- ☐ 356 Dave Dravecky .75 .35
- ☐ 357 Dave Edwards .10 .05
- ☐ 358 Juan Eichelberger .10 .05
- ☐ 359 Tim Flannery .10 .05
- ☐ 360 Tony Gwynn 20.00 9.00
- ☐ 361 Ruppert Jones .10 .05
- ☐ 362 Terry Kennedy .10 .05
- ☐ 363 Joe Lefebvre .10 .05
- ☐ 364 Sixto Lezcano .10 .05
- ☐ 365 Tim Lollar .10 .05
- ☐ 366 Gary Lucas .10 .05
- ☐ 367 John Montefusco .10 .05
- ☐ 368 Broderick Perkins .10 .05
- ☐ 369 Joe Pittman .10 .05
- ☐ 370 Gene Richards .10 .05
- ☐ 371 Luis Salazar .10 .05
- ☐ 372 Eric Show .10 .05
- ☐ 373 Garry Templeton .10 .05
- ☐ 374 Chris Welsh .10 .05
- ☐ 375 Alan Wiggins .10 .05
- ☐ 376 Rick Cerone .10 .05
- ☐ 377 Dave Collins .10 .05
- ☐ 378 Roger Erickson .10 .05
- ☐ 379 George Frazier .10 .05
- ☐ 380 Oscar Gamble .10 .05
- ☐ 381 Rich Gossage .40 .18
- ☐ 382 Ken Griffey .20 .09
- ☐ 383 Ron Guidry .20 .09
- ☐ 384 Dave LaRoche .10 .05
- ☐ 385 Rudy May .10 .05
- ☐ 386 John Mayberry .10 .05
- ☐ 387 Lee Mazzilli .10 .05
- ☐ 388 Mike Morgan .10 .05
- ☐ 389 Jerry Mumphrey .10 .05
- ☐ 390 Bobby Murcer .20 .09
- ☐ 391 Graig Nettles .20 .09
- ☐ 392 Lou Piniella .20 .09
- ☐ 393 Willie Randolph .20 .09
- ☐ 394 Shane Rawley .10 .05
- ☐ 395 Dave Righetti .20 .09
- ☐ 396 Andre Robertson .10 .05
- ☐ 397 Roy Smalley .10 .05
- ☐ 398 Dave Winfield 1.25 .55
- ☐ 399 Butch Wynegar .10 .05
- ☐ 400 Chris Bando .10 .05
- ☐ 401 Alan Bannister .10 .05
- ☐ 402 Len Barker .10 .05
- ☐ 403 Tom Brennan .10 .05
- ☐ 404 Carmelo Castillo .10 .05
- ☐ 405 Miguel Dilone .10 .05
- ☐ 406 Jerry Dybzinski .10 .05
- ☐ 407 Mike Fischlin .10 .05
- ☐ 408 Ed Glynn UER .10 .05 (Photo actually Bud Anderson)
- ☐ 409 Mike Hargrove .20 .09
- ☐ 410 Toby Harrah .10 .05
- ☐ 411 Ron Hassey .10 .05
- ☐ 412 Von Hayes .20 .09
- ☐ 413 Rick Manning .10 .05
- ☐ 414 Bake McBride .10 .05
- ☐ 415 Larry Milbourne .10 .05
- ☐ 416 Bill Nahorodny .10 .05
- ☐ 417 Jack Perconte .10 .05
- ☐ 418 Lary Sorensen .10 .05
- ☐ 419 Dan Spillner .10 .05
- ☐ 420 Rick Sutcliffe .20 .09
- ☐ 421 Andre Thornton .10 .05
- ☐ 422 Rick Waits .10 .05
- ☐ 423 Eddie Whitson .10 .05
- ☐ 424 Jesse Barfield .20 .09
- ☐ 425 Barry Bonnell .10 .05
- ☐ 426 Jim Clancy .10 .05
- ☐ 427 Damaso Garcia .10 .05
- ☐ 428 Jerry Garvin .10 .05
- ☐ 429 Alfredo Griffin .10 .05
- ☐ 430 Garth Iorg .10 .05
- ☐ 431 Roy Lee Jackson .10 .05
- ☐ 432 Luis Leal .10 .05
- ☐ 433 Buck Martinez .10 .05
- ☐ 434 Joey McLaughlin .10 .05
- ☐ 435 Lloyd Moseby .10 .05
- ☐ 436 Rance Mulliniks .10 .05
- ☐ 437 Dale Murray .10 .05
- ☐ 438 Wayne Nordhagen .10 .05
- ☐ 439 Geno Petralli .20 .09
- ☐ 440 Hosken Powell .10 .05
- ☐ 441 Dave Stieb .20 .09
- ☐ 442 Willie Upshaw .10 .05
- ☐ 443 Ernie Whitt .10 .05
- ☐ 444 Alvis Woods .10 .05
- ☐ 445 Alan Ashby .10 .05
- ☐ 446 Jose Cruz .20 .09
- ☐ 447 Kiko Garcia .10 .05
- ☐ 448 Phil Garner .20 .09
- ☐ 449 Danny Heep .10 .05
- ☐ 450 Art Howe .10 .05
- ☐ 451 Bob Knepper .10 .05
- ☐ 452 Alan Knicely .10 .05
- ☐ 453 Ray Knight .20 .09
- ☐ 454 Frank LaCorte .10 .05
- ☐ 455 Mike LaCoss .10 .05
- ☐ 456 Randy Moffitt .10 .05
- ☐ 457 Joe Niekro .20 .09
- ☐ 458 Terry Puhl .10 .05
- ☐ 459 Luis Pujols .10 .05
- ☐ 460 Craig Reynolds .10 .05
- ☐ 461 Bert Roberge .10 .05
- ☐ 462 Vern Ruhle .10 .05
- ☐ 463 Nolan Ryan 4.00 1.80
- ☐ 464 Joe Sambito .10 .05
- ☐ 465 Tony Scott .10 .05
- ☐ 466 Dave Smith .10 .05
- ☐ 467 Harry Spilman .10 .05
- ☐ 468 Dickie Thon .10 .05
- ☐ 469 Denny Walling .10 .05
- ☐ 470 Larry Andersen .10 .05
- ☐ 471 Floyd Bannister .10 .05
- ☐ 472 Jim Beattie .10 .05
- ☐ 473 Bruce Bochte .10 .05
- ☐ 474 Manny Castillo .10 .05
- ☐ 475 Bill Caudill .10 .05
- ☐ 476 Bryan Clark .10 .05
- ☐ 477 Al Cowens .10 .05
- ☐ 478 Julio Cruz .10 .05
- ☐ 479 Todd Cruz .10 .05
- ☐ 480 Gary Gray .10 .05
- ☐ 481 Dave Henderson .10 .05
- ☐ 482 Mike Moore .20 .09
- ☐ 483 Gaylord Perry .75 .35
- ☐ 484 Dave Revering .10 .05
- ☐ 485 Joe Simpson .10 .05
- ☐ 486 Mike Stanton .10 .05
- ☐ 487 Rick Sweet .10 .05
- ☐ 488 Ed VandeBerg .10 .05
- ☐ 489 Richie Zisk .10 .05
- ☐ 490 Doug Bird .10 .05
- ☐ 491 Larry Bowa .20 .09
- ☐ 492 Bill Buckner .20 .09
- ☐ 493 Bill Campbell .10 .05
- ☐ 494 Jody Davis .10 .05
- ☐ 495 Leon Durham .10 .05
- ☐ 496 Steve Henderson .10 .05
- ☐ 497 Willie Hernandez .20 .09
- ☐ 498 Ferguson Jenkins .75 .35
- ☐ 499 Jay Johnstone .20 .09
- ☐ 500 Junior Kennedy .10 .05
- ☐ 501 Randy Martz .10 .05
- ☐ 502 Jerry Morales .10 .05
- ☐ 503 Keith Moreland .10 .05
- ☐ 504 Dickie Noles .10 .05
- ☐ 505 Mike Proly .10 .05
- ☐ 506 Allen Ripley .10 .05
- ☐ 507 Ryne Sandberg UER 12.00 5.50 (Should say High School in Spokane, Washington)
- ☐ 508 Lee Smith 2.00 .90
- ☐ 509 Pat Tabler .10 .05
- ☐ 510 Dick Tidrow .10 .05
- ☐ 511 Bump Wills .10 .05
- ☐ 512 Gary Woods .10 .05
- ☐ 513 Tony Armas .10 .05
- ☐ 514 Dave Beard .10 .05
- ☐ 515 Jeff Burroughs .10 .05
- ☐ 516 John D'Acquisto .10 .05
- ☐ 517 Wayne Gross .10 .05
- ☐ 518 Mike Heath .10 .05
- ☐ 519 Rickey Henderson UER 1.00 .45 (Brock record listed as 120 steals)
- ☐ 520 Cliff Johnson .10 .05
- ☐ 521 Matt Keough .10 .05
- ☐ 522 Brian Kingman .10 .05
- ☐ 523 Rick Langford .10 .05
- ☐ 524 Dave Lopes .20 .09
- ☐ 525 Steve McCatty .10 .05
- ☐ 526 Dave McKay .10 .05
- ☐ 527 Dan Meyer .10 .05
- ☐ 528 Dwayne Murphy .10 .05
- ☐ 529 Jeff Newman .10 .05
- ☐ 530 Mike Norris .10 .05
- ☐ 531 Bob Owchinko .10 .05
- ☐ 532 Joe Rudi .10 .05
- ☐ 533 Jimmy Sexton .10 .05
- ☐ 534 Fred Stanley .10 .05
- ☐ 535 Tom Underwood .10 .05
- ☐ 536 Neil Allen .10 .05
- ☐ 537 Wally Backman .10 .05
- ☐ 538 Bob Bailor .10 .05
- ☐ 539 Hubie Brooks .10 .05
- ☐ 540 Carlos Diaz .10 .05
- ☐ 541 Pete Falcone .10 .05
- ☐ 542 George Foster .20 .09
- ☐ 543 Ron Gardenhire .10 .05
- ☐ 544 Brian Giles .10 .05
- ☐ 545 Ron Hodges .10 .05
- ☐ 546 Randy Jones .10 .05
- ☐ 547 Mike Jorgensen .10 .05
- ☐ 548 Dave Kingman .40 .18
- ☐ 549 Ed Lynch .10 .05
- ☐ 550 Jesse Orosco .10 .05
- ☐ 551 Rick Ownbey .10 .05
- ☐ 552 Charlie Puleo .10 .05
- ☐ 553 Gary Rajsich .10 .05
- ☐ 554 Mike Scott .20 .09
- ☐ 555 Rusty Staub .20 .09
- ☐ 556 John Stearns .10 .05
- ☐ 557 Craig Swan .10 .05
- ☐ 558 Ellis Valentine .10 .05
- ☐ 559 Tom Veryzer .10 .05
- ☐ 560 Mookie Wilson .20 .09
- ☐ 561 Pat Zachry .10 .05
- ☐ 562 Buddy Bell .20 .09
- ☐ 563 John Butcher .10 .05
- ☐ 564 Steve Comer .10 .05
- ☐ 565 Danny Darwin .10 .05
- ☐ 566 Bucky Dent .20 .09
- ☐ 567 John Grubb .10 .05
- ☐ 568 Rick Honeycutt .10 .05
- ☐ 569 Dave Hostetler .10 .05
- ☐ 570 Charlie Hough .20 .09
- ☐ 571 Lamar Johnson .10 .05
- ☐ 572 Jon Matlack .10 .05
- ☐ 573 Paul Mirabella .10 .05
- ☐ 574 Larry Parrish .10 .05
- ☐ 575 Mike Richardt .10 .05
- ☐ 576 Mickey Rivers .10 .05
- ☐ 577 Billy Sample .10 .05
- ☐ 578 Dave Schmidt .10 .05
- ☐ 579 Bill Stein .10 .05
- ☐ 580 Jim Sundberg .20 .09
- ☐ 581 Frank Tanana .20 .09
- ☐ 582 Mark Wagner .10 .05
- ☐ 583 George Wright .10 .05
- ☐ 584 Johnny Bench 1.00 .45
- ☐ 585 Bruce Berenyi .10 .05
- ☐ 586 Larry Biittner .10 .05
- ☐ 587 Cesar Cedeno .20 .09
- ☐ 588 Dave Concepcion .20 .09
- ☐ 589 Dan Driessen .10 .05
- ☐ 590 Greg Harris .10 .05

□ 591 Ben Hayes .10 .05
□ 592 Paul Householder .10 .05
□ 593 Tom Hume .10 .05
□ 594 Wayne Krenchicki .10 .05
□ 595 Rafael Landestoy .10 .05
□ 596 Charlie Leibrandt .10 .05
□ 597 Eddie Milner .10 .05
□ 598 Ron Oester .10 .05
□ 599 Frank Pastore .10 .05
□ 600 Joe Price .10 .05
□ 601 Tom Seaver 1.00 .45
□ 602 Bob Shirley .10 .05
□ 603 Mario Soto .10 .05
□ 604 Alex Trevino .10 .05
□ 605 Mike Vail .10 .05
□ 606 Duane Walker .10 .05
□ 607 Tom Brunansky .20 .09
□ 608 Bobby Castillo .10 .05
□ 609 John Castino .10 .05
□ 610 Ron Davis .10 .05
□ 611 Lenny Faedo .10 .05
□ 612 Terry Felton .10 .05
□ 613 Gary Gaetti .75 .35
□ 614 Mickey Hatcher .10 .05
□ 615 Brad Havens .10 .05
□ 616 Kent Hrbek .20 .09
□ 617 Randy Johnson .10 .05
□ 618 Tim Laudner .10 .05
□ 619 Jeff Little .10 .05
□ 620 Bobby Mitchell .10 .05
□ 621 Jack O'Connor .10 .05
□ 622 John Pacella .10 .05
□ 623 Pete Redfern .10 .05
□ 624 Jesus Vega .10 .05
□ 625 Frank Viola .75 .35
□ 626 Ron Washington .10 .05
□ 627 Gary Ward .10 .05
□ 628 Al Williams .10 .05
□ 629 Red Sox All-Stars .75 .35
Carl Yastrzemski
Dennis Eckersley
Mark Clear
□ 630 300 Career Wins .20 .09
Gaylord Perry
Terry Bulling 5/6/82
□ 631 Pride of Venezuela .20 .09
Dave Concepcion and
Manny Trillo
□ 632 All-Star Infielders .75 .35
Robin Yount and
Buddy Bell
□ 633 Mr.Vet and Mr.Rookie .75 .35
Dave Winfield and
Kent Hrbek
□ 634 Fountain of Youth .75 .35
Willie Stargell and
Pete Rose
□ 635 Big Chiefs .20 .09
Toby Harrah and
Andre Thornton
□ 636 Smith Brothers .75 .35
Ozzie Smith
Lonnie Smith
□ 637 Base Stealers' Threat .20 .09
Bo Diaz and
Gary Carter
□ 638 All-Star Catchers .75 .35
Carlton Fisk and
Gary Carter
□ 639 The Silver Shoe 1.00 .45
Rickey Henderson
□ 640 Home Run Threats .75 .35
Ben Oglivie and
Reggie Jackson
□ 641 Two Teams Same Day .10 .05
Joel Youngblood
August 4, 1982
□ 642 Last Perfect Game .20 .09
Ron Hassey and
Len Barker
□ 643 Black and Blue .20 .09
Vida Blue
□ 644 Black and Blue .10 .05
Bud Black
□ 645 Speed and Power .75 .35
Reggie Jackson
□ 646 Speed and Power 1.00 .45
Rickey Henderson
□ 647 CL: Cards/Brewers .10 .05
□ 648 CL: Orioles/Angels .10 .05
□ 649 CL: Royals/Braves .10 .05
□ 650 CL: Phillies/Red Sox .10 .05
□ 651 CL: Dodgers/White Sox .10 .05
□ 652 CL: Giants/Expos .10 .05
□ 653 CL: Pirates/Tigers .10 .05
□ 654 CL: Padres/Yankees .10 .05
□ 655 CL: Indians/Blue Jays .10 .05
□ 656 CL: Astros/Mariners .10 .05
□ 657 CL: Cubs/A's .10 .05
□ 658 CL: Mets/Rangers .10 .05
□ 659 CL: Reds/Twins .10 .05
□ 660 CL: Specials/Teams .10 .05

1983 Fleer Stamps

This 288-card set features color photos of players and team logos on stamps measuring approximately 1 1/4" by 1 13/16" each. The stamps were issued on four different sheets of 72 stamps each. There are 224 player stamps and 64 team logo stamps. The team logo stamps have double and triple prints. Baseball trivia quiz questions were also included with the stamps. The stamps are unnumbered and checklisted below in alphabetical order.

	NRMT	VG-E
COMPLETE SET (288)	10.00	4.50
COMMON CARD (1-288)	.05	.02
COMMON TEAM LOGO (225-250)	.05	.02

□ 1 Willie Aikens .05 .02
□ 2 Neil Allen .05 .02
□ 3 Joaquin Andujar .05 .02
□ 4 Alan Ashby .05 .02
□ 5 Bob Bailor .05 .02
□ 6 Harold Baines .15 .07
□ 7 Dusty Baker .10 .05
□ 8 Floyd Bannister .05 .02
□ 9 Len Barker .05 .02
□ 10 Don Baylor .10 .05
□ 11 Dave Beard .05 .02
□ 12 Jim Beattie .05 .02
□ 13 Buddy Bell .10 .05
□ 14 Johnny Bench .75 .35
□ 15 Dale Berra .05 .02
□ 16 Larry Biittner .05 .02
□ 17 Vida Blue .10 .05
□ 18 Bruce Bochte .05 .02
□ 19 Wade Boggs 4.00 1.80
□ 20 Bob Boone .10 .05
□ 21 Larry Bowa .05 .02
□ 22 George Brett 2.00 .90
□ 23 Hubie Brooks .05 .02
□ 24 Tom Brunansky .05 .02
□ 25 Bill Buckner .10 .05
□ 26 Al Bumbry .05 .02
□ 27 Jeff Burroughs .05 .02
□ 28 Enos Cabell .05 .02
□ 29 Rod Carew .50 .23
□ 30 Steve Carlton .40 .18
□ 31 Gary Carter .30 .14
□ 32 Bobby Castillo .05 .02
□ 33 Bill Caudill .05 .02
□ 34 Cesar Cedeno .10 .05
□ 35 Rick Cerone .05 .02
□ 36 Ron Cey .10 .05
□ 37 Chris Chambliss .10 .05
□ 38 Larry Christenson .05 .02
□ 39 Jim Clancy .05 .02
□ 40 Jack Clark .10 .05
□ 41 Mark Clear .05 .02
□ 42 Dave Concepcion .10 .05
□ 43 Cecil Cooper .10 .05
□ 44 Warren Cromartie .05 .02
□ 45 Jose Cruz .10 .05
□ 46 Danny Darwin .10 .05
□ 47 Rich Dauer .05 .02
□ 48 Ron Davis .05 .02
□ 49 Andre Dawson .50 .23
□ 50 Doug DeCinces .05 .02
□ 51 Ivan DeJesus .05 .02
□ 52 Luis DeLeon .05 .02
□ 53 Bo Diaz .05 .02
□ 54 Brian Downing .10 .05
□ 55 Dan Driessen .05 .02
□ 56 Leon Durham .05 .02
□ 57 Mike Easler .05 .02
□ 58 Dennis Eckersley .25 .11
□ 59 Dwight Evans .15 .07
□ 60 Rollie Fingers .35 .16
□ 61 Carlton Fisk .50 .23
□ 62 Mike Flanagan .05 .02
□ 63 Bob Forsch .05 .02
□ 64 Ken Forsch .05 .02
□ 65 George Foster .10 .05
□ 66 Gene Garber .10 .05
□ 67 Damaso Garcia .05 .02
□ 68 Phil Garner .10 .05
□ 69 Steve Garvey .15 .07
□ 70 Goose Gossage .15 .07
□ 71 Ken Griffey .10 .05
□ 72 John Grubb .05 .02
□ 73 Ron Guidry .10 .05
□ 74 Atlee Hammaker .05 .02
□ 75 Mike Hargrove .10 .05
□ 76 Toby Harrah .05 .02
□ 77 Rickey Henderson 1.50 .70
□ 78 Keith Hernandez .15 .07
□ 79 Larry Herndon .05 .02
□ 80 Tom Herr .05 .02
□ 81 Al Holland .05 .02
□ 82 Burt Hooton .05 .02
□ 83 Bob Horner .05 .02
□ 84 Art Howe .10 .05
□ 85 Steve Howe .05 .02
□ 86 LaMarr Hoyt .05 .02
□ 87 Kent Hrbek .25 .11
□ 88 Tom Hume .05 .02
□ 89 Garth Iorg .05 .02
□ 90 Reggie Jackson .75 .35
□ 91 Ferguson Jenkins .30 .14
□ 92 Tommy John .15 .07
□ 93 Ruppert Jones .05 .02
□ 94 Steve Kemp .05 .02
□ 95 Bruce Kison .05 .02
□ 96 Ray Knight .10 .05
□ 97 Jerry Koosman .10 .05
□ 98 Duane Kuiper .05 .02
□ 99 Ken Landreaux .05 .02
□ 100 Carney Lansford .05 .02
□ 101 Bill Laskey .05 .02
□ 102 Gary Lavelle .05 .02
□ 103 Charlie Lea .05 .02
□ 104 Ron LeFlore .05 .02
□ 105 Dennis Leonard .05 .02
□ 106 Sixto Lezcano .05 .02
□ 107 Davey Lopes .10 .05
□ 108 John Lowenstein .05 .02
□ 109 Greg Luzinski .10 .05
□ 110 Fred Lynn .15 .07
□ 111 Garry Maddox .05 .02
□ 112 Bill Madlock .10 .05
□ 113 Rick Manning .05 .02
□ 114 Dennis Martinez .10 .05
□ 115 Tippy Martinez .05 .02
□ 116 Randy Martz .05 .02
□ 117 Jon Matlack .05 .02
□ 118 Gary Matthews .10 .05
□ 119 Milt May .05 .02
□ 120 Lee Mazzilli .05 .02
□ 121 Bob McClure .05 .02
□ 122 Tug McGraw .10 .05
□ 123 Scott McGregor .05 .02
□ 124 Hal McRae .10 .05
□ 125 Eddie Milner .05 .02
□ 126 Greg Minton .05 .02
□ 127 Paul Molitor .75 .35
□ 128 Rick Monday .05 .02
□ 129 John Montefusco .05 .02
□ 130 Keith Moreland .05 .02
□ 131 Joe Morgan .50 .23
□ 132 Jerry Mumphrey .05 .02
□ 133 Steve Mura .05 .02
□ 134 Dale Murphy .40 .18
□ 135 Dwayne Murphy .05 .02
□ 136 Eddie Murray .50 .23
□ 137 Graig Nettles .15 .07
□ 138 Joe Niekro .10 .05
□ 139 Phil Niekro .30 .14
□ 140 Ken Oberkfell .05 .02
□ 141 Ben Oglivie .05 .02
□ 142 Al Oliver .15 .07
□ 143 Amos Otis .10 .05
□ 144 Tom Paciorek .10 .05
□ 145 Jim Palmer .40 .18
□ 146 Dave Parker .10 .05
□ 147 Lance Parrish .15 .07
□ 148 Larry Parrish .10 .05
□ 149 Tony Pena .05 .02
□ 150 Gaylord Perry .30 .14
□ 151 Lou Piniella .10 .05
□ 152 Darrell Porter .05 .02
□ 153 Hosken Powell .05 .02
□ 154 Dan Quisenberry .10 .05
□ 155 Tim Raines .25 .11
□ 156 Rafael Ramirez .05 .02
□ 157 Willie Randolph .10 .05
□ 158 Johnny Ray .05 .02

☐ 159 Jeff Reardon	.10	.05
☐ 160 Ron Reed	.05	.02
☐ 161 Jerry Reuss	.05	.02
☐ 162 Rick Rhoden	.05	.02
☐ 163 Jim Rice	.10	.05
☐ 164 Mike Richardt	.05	.02
☐ 165 Cal Ripken Jr.	4.00	1.80
☐ 166 Ron Roenicke	.05	.02
☐ 167 Steve Rogers	.05	.02
☐ 168 Pete Rose	1.00	.45
☐ 169 Jerry Royster	.05	.02
☐ 170 Nolan Ryan	4.00	1.80
☐ 171 Manny Sarmiento	.05	.02
☐ 172 Steve Sax	.05	.02
☐ 173 Mike Schmidt	1.00	.45
☐ 174 Tom Seaver	.50	.23
☐ 175 Eric Show	.05	.02
☐ 176 Ted Simmons	.15	.07
☐ 177 Ken Singleton	.05	.02
☐ 178 Roy Smalley	.05	.02
☐ 179 Lonnie Smith	.05	.02
☐ 180 Ozzie Smith	2.00	.90
☐ 181 Reggie Smith	.10	.05
☐ 182 Mario Soto	.05	.02
☐ 183 Chris Speier	.05	.02
☐ 184 Dan Spillner	.05	.02
☐ 185 Bob Stanley	.05	.02
☐ 186 Willie Stargell	.30	.14
☐ 187 Rusty Staub	.15	.07
☐ 188 Dave Stieb	.05	.02
☐ 189 Jim Sundberg	.05	.02
☐ 190 Rick Sutcliffe	.05	.02
☐ 191 Bruce Sutter	.10	.05
☐ 192 Don Sutton	.30	.14
☐ 193 Craig Swan	.05	.02
☐ 194 Kent Tekulve	.05	.02
☐ 195 Gorman Thomas	.05	.02
☐ 196 Jason Thompson	.05	.02
☐ 197 Dickie Thon	.05	.02
☐ 198 Andre Thornton	.05	.02
☐ 199 Dick Tidrow	.05	.02
☐ 200 Manny Trillo	.05	.02
☐ 201 John Tudor	.05	.02
☐ 202 Tom Underwood	.05	.02
☐ 203 Willie Upshaw	.05	.02
☐ 204 Ellis Valentine	.05	.02
☐ 205 Fernando Valenzuela	.30	.14
☐ 206 Ed VandeBerg	.05	.02
☐ 207 Pete Vuckovich	.05	.02
☐ 208 Gary Ward	.05	.02
☐ 209 Claudell Washington	.05	.02
☐ 210 U.L. Washington	.05	.02
☐ 211 Bob Watson	.10	.05
☐ 212 Lou Whitaker	.25	.11
☐ 213 Frank White	.05	.02
☐ 214 Milt Wilcox	.05	.02
☐ 215 Al Williams	.05	.02
☐ 216 Bump Wills	.05	.02
☐ 217 Mookie Wilson	.10	.05
☐ 218 Willie Wilson	.05	.02
☐ 219 Dave Winfield	.75	.35
☐ 220 John Wockenfuss	.05	.02
☐ 221 Carl Yastrzemski	.50	.23
☐ 222 Robin Yount	.50	.23
☐ 223 Pat Zachry	.05	.02
☐ 224 Richie Zisk	.05	.02
☐ 225 Atlanta Braves TP	.05	.02
☐ 226 Baltimore Orioles DP	.05	.02
☐ 227 Boston Red Sox DP	.05	.02
☐ 228 California Angels TP	.05	.02
☐ 229 Chicago Cubs DP	.05	.02
☐ 230 Chicago White Sox TP	.05	.02
☐ 231 Cincinnati Reds TP	.05	.02
☐ 232 Cleveland Indians TP	.05	.02
☐ 233 Detroit Tigers DP	.05	.02
☐ 234 Houston Astros DP	.05	.02
☐ 235 Los Angeles Dodgers TP	.05	.02
☐ 236 Kansas City Royals TP	.05	.02
☐ 237 Milwaukee Brewers DP	.05	.02
☐ 238 Minnesota Twins TP	.05	.02
☐ 239 Montreal Expos TP	.05	.02
☐ 240 New York Mets DP	.05	.02
☐ 241 New York Yankees DP	.05	.02
☐ 242 Oakland A's DP	.05	.02
☐ 243 Philadelphia Phillies TP	.05	.02
☐ 244 Pittsburgh Pirates TP	.05	.02
☐ 245 St. Louis Cardinals DP	.05	.02
☐ 246 San Diego Padres DP	.05	.02
☐ 247 San Francisco Giants TP	.05	.02
☐ 248 Seattle Mariners DP	.05	.02
☐ 249 Texas Rangers DP	.05	.02
☐ 250 Toronto Blue Jays DP	.05	.02

1983 Fleer Stickers

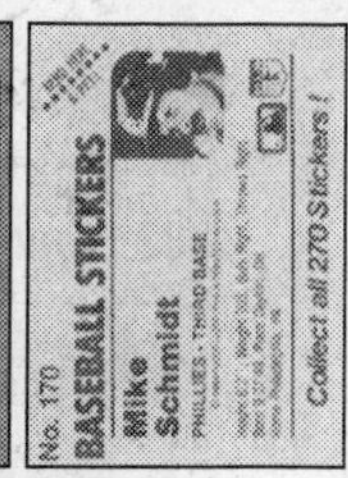

The stickers in this 270-sticker set measure approximately 1 13/16" by 2 1/2". The 1983 Fleer stickers set was issued in strips of ten stickers plus two team logos per strip. No album was issued for the stickers. The fronts contain player photos surrounded by a blue border with two red stars on the upper portion of a yellow frameline. While all of the players could be attained on 27 different strips, it was necessary to have 30 different strips to obtain all of the team logos. There are a few instances where the logo pictured on the front of the card relates to a different team checklisted on the back of the card. The backs of the logo stamps feature either a team checklist (CL) or poster offer (PO).

	NRMT	VG-E
COMPLETE SET	12.50	5.50
COMMON CARD	.05	.02
COMMON TEAM ISSUE	.05	.02
☐ 1 Bruce Sutter	.10	.05
☐ 2 Willie McGee	.30	.14
☐ 3 Darrell Porter	.05	.02
☐ 4 Lonnie Smith	.05	.02
☐ 5 Dane Iorg	.05	.02
☐ 6 Keith Hernandez	.10	.05
☐ 7 Joaquin Andujar	.05	.02
☐ 8 Ken Oberkfell	.05	.02
☐ 9 John Stuper	.05	.02
☐ 10 Ozzie Smith	1.50	.70
☐ 11 Bob Forsch	.05	.02
☐ 12 Jim Gantner	.05	.02
☐ 13 Rollie Fingers	.30	.14
☐ 14 Pete Vuckovich	.05	.02
☐ 15 Ben Oglivie	.05	.02
☐ 16 Don Sutton	.30	.14
☐ 17 Bob McClure	.05	.02
☐ 18 Robin Yount	.40	.18
☐ 19 Paul Molitor	.50	.23
☐ 20 Gorman Thomas	.05	.02
☐ 21 Mike Caldwell	.05	.02
☐ 22 Ted Simmons	.10	.05
☐ 23 Cecil Cooper	.10	.05
☐ 24 Steve Renko	.05	.02
☐ 25 Tommy John	.15	.07
☐ 26 Rod Carew	.40	.18
☐ 27 Bruce Kison	.05	.02
☐ 28 Ken Forsch	.05	.02
☐ 29 Geoff Zahn	.05	.02
☐ 30 Doug DeCinces	.05	.02
☐ 31 Fred Lynn	.10	.05
☐ 32 Reggie Jackson	.75	.35
☐ 33 Don Baylor	.10	.05
☐ 34 Bob Boone	.10	.05
☐ 35 Brian Downing	.05	.02
☐ 36 Rich Gossage	.15	.07
☐ 37 Roy Smalley	.05	.02
☐ 38 Graig Nettles	.15	.07
☐ 39 Dave Winfield	.50	.23
☐ 40 Lee Mazzilli	.05	.02
☐ 41 Jerry Mumphrey	.05	.02
☐ 42 Dave Collins	.05	.02
☐ 43 Rick Cerone	.05	.02
☐ 44 Willie Randolph	.10	.05
☐ 45 Lou Piniella	.10	.05
☐ 46 Ken Griffey	.10	.05
☐ 47 Ron Guidry	.10	.05
☐ 48 Jack Clark	.05	.02
☐ 49 Reggie Smith	.05	.02
☐ 50 Atlee Hammaker	.05	.02
☐ 51 Fred Breining	.05	.02
☐ 52 Gary Lavelle	.05	.02
☐ 53 Chili Davis	.25	.11
☐ 54 Greg Minton	.05	.02
☐ 55 Joe Morgan	.30	.14
☐ 56 Al Holland	.05	.02
☐ 57 Bill Laskey	.05	.02
☐ 58 Duane Kuiper	.05	.02
☐ 59 Tom Burgmeier	.05	.02
☐ 60 Carl Yastrzemski	.50	.23
☐ 61 Mark Clear	.05	.02
☐ 62 Mike Torrez	.05	.02
☐ 63 Dennis Eckersley	.30	.14
☐ 64 Wade Boggs	3.00	1.35
☐ 65 Bob Stanley	.05	.02
☐ 66 Jim Rice	.10	.05
☐ 67 Carney Lansford	.05	.0
☐ 68 Jerry Remy	.05	.0
☐ 69 Dwight Evans	.15	.0
☐ 70 John Candelaria	.05	.02
☐ 71 Bill Madlock	.10	.0
☐ 72 Dave Parker	.10	.0
☐ 73 Kent Tekulve	.05	.0
☐ 74 Tony Pena	.05	.02
☐ 75 Manny Sarmiento	.05	.0
☐ 76 Johnny Ray	.05	.0
☐ 77 Dale Berra	.05	.02
☐ 78 Lee Lacy	.05	.02
☐ 79 Jason Thompson	.05	.02
☐ 80 Mike Easler	.05	.02
☐ 81 Willie Stargell	.30	.14
☐ 82 Rick Camp	.05	.02
☐ 83 Bob Watson	.10	.05
☐ 84 Bob Horner	.05	.02
☐ 85 Rafael Ramirez	.05	.02
☐ 86 Chris Chambliss	.05	.02
☐ 87 Gene Garber	.05	.02
☐ 88 Claudell Washington	.05	.02
☐ 89 Steve Bedrosian	.05	.02
☐ 90 Dale Murphy	.50	.23
☐ 91 Phil Niekro	.30	.14
☐ 92 Jerry Royster	.05	.02
☐ 93 Bob Walk	.05	.02
☐ 94 Frank White	.05	.02
☐ 95 Dennis Leonard	.05	.02
☐ 96 Vida Blue	.10	.05
☐ 97 U.L. Washington	.05	.02
☐ 98 George Brett	3.00	1.35
☐ 99 Amos Otis	.05	.02
☐ 100 Dan Quisenberry	.05	.02
☐ 101 Willie Aikens	.05	.02
☐ 102 Hal McRae	.05	.02
☐ 103 Larry Gura	.05	.02
☐ 104 Willie Wilson	.05	.02
☐ 105 Damaso Garcia	.05	.02
☐ 106 Hosken Powell	.05	.02
☐ 107 Joey McLaughlin	.05	.02
☐ 108 Jim Clancy	.05	.02
☐ 109 Barry Bonnell	.05	.02
☐ 110 Garth Iorg	.05	.02
☐ 111 Dave Stieb	.05	.02
☐ 112 Fernando Valenzuela	.15	.07
☐ 113 Steve Garvey	.25	.11
☐ 114 Rick Monday	.05	.02
☐ 115 Burt Hooten	.05	.02
☐ 116 Bill Russell	.05	.02
☐ 117 Pedro Guerrero	.05	.02
☐ 118 Steve Sax	.05	.02
☐ 119 Steve Howe	.05	.02
☐ 120 Ken Landreaux	.05	.02
☐ 121 Dusty Baker	.10	.05
☐ 122 Ron Cey	.10	.05
☐ 123 Jerry Reuss	.05	.02
☐ 124 Bump Wills	.05	.02
☐ 125 Keith Moreland	.05	.02
☐ 126 Dick Tidrow	.05	.02
☐ 127 Bill Campbell	.05	.02
☐ 128 Larry Bowa	.05	.02
☐ 129 Randy Martz	.05	.02
☐ 130 Ferguson Jenkins	.30	.14
☐ 131 Leon Durham	.05	.02
☐ 132 Bill Buckner	.10	.05
☐ 133 Ron Davis	.05	.02
☐ 134 Jack O'Connor	.05	.02
☐ 135 Kent Hrbek	.10	.05
☐ 136 Gary Ward	.05	.02
☐ 137 Al Williams	.05	.02
☐ 138 Tom Brunansky	.05	.02
☐ 139 Bobby Castillo	.05	.02
☐ 140 Dusty Baker	.15	.07
Dale Murphy		
☐ 141 Nolan Ryan	2.50	1.10
Alan Ashby		
☐ 142 Omar Moreno	.05	.02
Lee Lacy		
sic, Lacey		
☐ 143 Al Oliver	.50	.23
Pete Rose		
☐ 144 Rickey Henderson	.50	.23
☐ 145 Ray Knight	.50	.23
Mike Schmidt		
Pete Rose		
☐ 146 Ben Oglivie	.05	.02
Hal McRae		
☐ 147 Ray Knight	.05	.02
Tom Hume		
☐ 148 Buddy Bell	.25	.11
Carlton Fisk		
☐ 149 Steve Kemp	.05	.02
☐ 150 Rudy Law	.05	.02
☐ 151 Ron LeFlore	.05	.02
☐ 152 Jerry Koosman	.05	.02
☐ 153 Carlton Fisk	.50	.23

- ☐ 154 Salome Barojas .05 .02
- ☐ 155 Harold Baines .10 .05
- ☐ 156 Britt Burns .05 .02
- ☐ 157 Tom Paciorek .10 .05
- ☐ 158 Greg Luzinski .05 .02
- ☐ 159 LeMarr Hoyt .05 .02
- ☐ 160 George Wright .05 .02
- ☐ 161 Danny Darwin .05 .02
- ☐ 162 Lamar Johnson .05 .02
- ☐ 163 Charlie Hough .05 .02
- ☐ 164 Buddy Bell .05 .02
- ☐ 165 Jon Matlack .05 .02
- ☐ 166 Billy Sample .05 .02
- ☐ 167 Johnny Grubb .05 .02
- ☐ 168 Larry Parrish .05 .02
- ☐ 169 Ivan DeJesus .05 .02
- ☐ 170 Mike Schmidt 1.00 .45
- ☐ 171 Tug McGraw .05 .02
- ☐ 172 Ron Reed .05 .02
- ☐ 173 Garry Maddox .05 .02
- ☐ 174 Pete Rose 1.50 .70
- ☐ 175 Manny Trillo .05 .02
- ☐ 176 Steve Carlton .75 .35
- ☐ 177 Bo Diaz .05 .02
- ☐ 178 Gary Matthews .05 .02
- ☐ 179 Bill Caudill .05 .02
- ☐ 180 Ed VandeBerg .05 .02
- ☐ 181 Gaylord Perry .30 .14
- ☐ 182 Floyd Bannister .05 .02
- ☐ 183 Richie Zisk .05 .02
- ☐ 184 Al Cowens .05 .02
- ☐ 185 Bruce Bochte .05 .02
- ☐ 186 Jeff Burroughs .05 .02
- ☐ 187 Dave Beard .05 .02
- ☐ 188 Dave Lopes .05 .02
- ☐ 189 Dwayne Murphy .05 .02
- ☐ 190 Rick Langford .05 .02
- ☐ 191 Tom Underwood .05 .02
- ☐ 192 Rickey Henderson 2.00 .90
- ☐ 193 Mike Flanagan .05 .02
- ☐ 194 Scott McGregor .05 .02
- ☐ 195 Ken Singleton .05 .02
- ☐ 196 Rich Dauer .05 .02
- ☐ 197 John Lowenstein .05 .02
- ☐ 198 Cal Ripken 5.00 2.20
- ☐ 199 Dennis Martinez .10 .05
- ☐ 200 Jim Palmer .50 .23
- ☐ 201 Tippy Martinez .05 .02
- ☐ 202 Eddie Murray 1.00 .45
- ☐ 203 Al Bumbry .05 .02
- ☐ 204 Dickie Thon .05 .02
- ☐ 205 Phil Garner .05 .02
- ☐ 206 Jose Cruz .05 .02
- ☐ 207 Nolan Ryan 5.00 2.20
- ☐ 208 Ray Knight .05 .02
- ☐ 209 Terry Puhl .05 .02
- ☐ 210 Joe Niekro .05 .02
- ☐ 211 Art Howe .10 .05
- ☐ 212 Alan Ashby .05 .02
- ☐ 213 Tom Hume .05 .02
- ☐ 214 Johnny Bench .50 .23
- ☐ 215 Larry Biittner .05 .02
- ☐ 216 Mario Soto .05 .02
- ☐ 217 Dan Driessen .05 .02
- ☐ 218 Tom Seaver .50 .23
- ☐ 219 Dave Concepcion .05 .02
- ☐ 220 Wayne Krenchicki .05 .02
- ☐ 221 Cesar Cedeno .05 .02
- ☐ 222 Randy Jones .05 .02
- ☐ 223 Terry Kennedy .05 .02
- ☐ 224 Luis DeLeon .05 .02
- ☐ 225 Eric Show .05 .02
- ☐ 226 Tim Flannery .05 .02
- ☐ 227 Garry Templeton .05 .02
- ☐ 228 Tim Lollar .05 .02
- ☐ 229 Sixto Lezcano .05 .02
- ☐ 230 Bob Bailor .05 .02
- ☐ 231 Craig Swan .05 .02
- ☐ 232 Dave Kingman .10 .05
- ☐ 233 Mookie Wilson .10 .05
- ☐ 234 John Stearns .05 .02
- ☐ 235 Ellis Valentine .05 .02
- ☐ 236 Neil Allen .05 .02
- ☐ 237 Pat Zachry .05 .02
- ☐ 238 Rusty Staub .05 .02
- ☐ 239 George Foster .05 .02
- ☐ 240 Rick Sutcliffe .05 .02
- ☐ 241 Andre Thornton .05 .02
- ☐ 242 Mike Hargrove .05 .02
- ☐ 243 Dan Spillner .05 .02
- ☐ 244 Lary Sorensen .05 .02
- ☐ 245 Len Barker .05 .02
- ☐ 246 Rick Manning .05 .02
- ☐ 247 Toby Harrah .05 .02
- ☐ 248 Milt Wilcox .05 .02
- ☐ 249 Lou Whitaker .10 .05
- ☐ 250 Tom Brookens .05 .02
- ☐ 251 Chet Lemon .05 .02
- ☐ 252 Jack Morris .10 .05
- ☐ 253 Alan Trammell .25 .11
- ☐ 254 Johnny Wockenfuss .05 .02
- ☐ 255 Lance Parrish .15 .07
- ☐ 256 Larry Herndon .05 .02
- ☐ 257 Chris Speier .05 .02
- ☐ 258 Woodie Fryman .05 .02
- ☐ 259 Scott Sanderson .05 .02
- ☐ 260 Steve Rogers .05 .02
- ☐ 261 Warren Cromartie .05 .02
- ☐ 262 Gary Carter .40 .18
- ☐ 263 Bill Gullickson .05 .02
- ☐ 264 Andre Dawson .30 .14
- ☐ 265 Tim Raines .15 .07
- ☐ 266 Charlie Lea .05 .02
- ☐ 267 Jeff Reardon .10 .05
- ☐ 268 Al Oliver .10 .05
- ☐ 269 George Hendrick .05 .02
- ☐ 270 John Montefusco .05 .02
- ☐ NNO Pittsburgh Pirates PO .05 .02
- ☐ NNO New York Mets PO .05 .02
- ☐ NNO San Diego Padres PO .05 .02
- ☐ NNO Detroit Tigers CL .05 .02
- ☐ NNO Cincinnati Reds CL .05 .02
- ☐ NNO Seattle Mariners PO .05 .02
- ☐ NNO New York Yankees CL .05 .02
- ☐ NNO Oakland A's CL .05 .02
- ☐ NNO Philadelphia Phillies CL .05 .02
- ☐ NNO Pittsburgh Pirates CL .05 .02
- ☐ NNO Cleveland Indians CL .05 .02
- ☐ NNO Chicago Cubs CL .05 .02
- ☐ NNO Los Angeles Dodgers PO .05 .02
- ☐ NNO Seattle Mariners CL .05 .02
- ☐ NNO Baltimore Orioles PO .05 .02
- ☐ NNO Cincinnati Reds PO .05 .02
- ☐ NNO San Diego Padres CL .05 .02
- ☐ NNO Texas Rangers CL .05 .02
- ☐ NNO New York Yankees PO .05 .02
- ☐ NNO Boston Red Sox CL .05 .02
- ☐ NNO St. Louis Cardinals PO .05 .02
- ☐ NNO Houston Astros PO .05 .02
- ☐ NNO Cleveland Indians PO .05 .02
- ☐ NNO Minnesota Twins CL .05 .02
- ☐ NNO St. Louis Cardinals CL .05 .02
- ☐ NNO Chicago White Sox PO .05 .02
- ☐ NNO Kansas City Royals CL .05 .02
- ☐ NNO Montreal Expos CL .05 .02
- ☐ NNO Montreal Expos PO .05 .02
- ☐ NNO Milwaukee Brewers CL .05 .02
- ☐ NNO Boston Red Sox PO .05 .02
- ☐ NNO San Francisco Giants PO .05 .02
- ☐ NNO Los Angeles Dodgers CL .05 .02
- ☐ NNO Milwaukee Brewers PO .05 .02
- ☐ NNO Baltimore Orioles CL .05 .02
- ☐ NNO California Angels PO .05 .02
- ☐ NNO Detroit Tigers PO .05 .02
- ☐ NNO California Angels CL .05 .02
- ☐ NNO Toronto Blue Jays PO .05 .02
- ☐ NNO Toronto Blue Jays CL .05 .02
- ☐ NNO New York Mets CL .05 .02
- ☐ NNO Atlanta Braves PO .05 .02
- ☐ NNO Atlanta Braves CL .05 .02
- ☐ NNO Kansas City Royals PO .05 .02
- ☐ NNO Minnesota Twins PO .05 .02
- ☐ NNO Philadelphia Phillies PO .05 .02

1984 Fleer

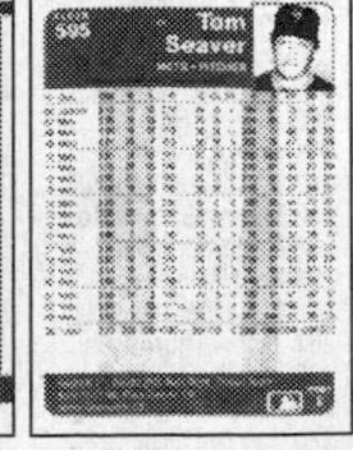

The 1984 Fleer card 660-card standard-size set featured fronts with full-color team logos along with the player's name and position and the Fleer identification. The set features many imaginative photos, several multi-player cards, and many more action shots than the 1983 card set. The backs are quite similar to the 1983 backs except that blue rather than brown ink is used. The player cards are alphabetized within team and the teams are ordered by their 1983 season finish and won-lost record. Specials (626-646) and checklist cards (647-660) make up the end of the set. Wax packs again consisted of 15 cards plus logo stickers. The key Rookie Cards in this set are Don Mattingly, Tony Phillips, Darryl Strawberry, and Andy Van Slyke.

	NRMT	VG-E
COMPLETE SET (660)	80.00	36.00
COMMON CARD (1-660)	.15	.07

- ☐ 1 Mike Boddicker .40 .18
- ☐ 2 Al Bumbry .40 .18
- ☐ 3 Todd Cruz .15 .07
- ☐ 4 Rich Dauer .15 .07
- ☐ 5 Storm Davis .15 .07
- ☐ 6 Rick Dempsey .15 .07
- ☐ 7 Jim Dwyer .15 .07
- ☐ 8 Mike Flanagan .15 .07
- ☐ 9 Dan Ford .15 .07
- ☐ 10 John Lowenstein .15 .07
- ☐ 11 Dennis Martinez .40 .18
- ☐ 12 Tippy Martinez .15 .07
- ☐ 13 Scott McGregor .15 .07
- ☐ 14 Eddie Murray 4.00 1.80
- ☐ 15 Joe Nolan .15 .07
- ☐ 16 Jim Palmer 1.25 .55
- ☐ 17 Cal Ripken 12.00 5.50
- ☐ 18 Gary Roenicke .15 .07
- ☐ 19 Lenn Sakata .15 .07
- ☐ 20 John Shelby .15 .07
- ☐ 21 Ken Singleton .15 .07
- ☐ 22 Sammy Stewart .15 .07
- ☐ 23 Tim Stoddard .15 .07
- ☐ 24 Marty Bystrom .15 .07
- ☐ 25 Steve Carlton 2.00 .90
- ☐ 26 Ivan DeJesus .15 .07
- ☐ 27 John Denny .15 .07
- ☐ 28 Bob Dernier .15 .07
- ☐ 29 Bo Diaz .15 .07
- ☐ 30 Kiko Garcia .15 .07
- ☐ 31 Greg Gross .15 .07
- ☐ 32 Kevin Gross .40 .18
- ☐ 33 Von Hayes .15 .07
- ☐ 34 Willie Hernandez .40 .18
- ☐ 35 Al Holland .15 .07
- ☐ 36 Charles Hudson .15 .07
- ☐ 37 Joe Lefebvre .15 .07
- ☐ 38 Sixto Lezcano .15 .07
- ☐ 39 Garry Maddox .15 .07
- ☐ 40 Gary Matthews .15 .07
- ☐ 41 Len Matuszek .15 .07
- ☐ 42 Tug McGraw .40 .18
- ☐ 43 Joe Morgan 1.50 .70
- ☐ 44 Tony Perez 1.50 .70
- ☐ 45 Ron Reed .15 .07
- ☐ 46 Pete Rose 2.00 .90
- ☐ 47 Juan Samuel .75 .35
- ☐ 48 Mike Schmidt 2.00 .90
- ☐ 49 Ozzie Virgil .15 .07
- ☐ 50 Juan Agosto .15 .07
- ☐ 51 Harold Baines .75 .35
- ☐ 52 Floyd Bannister .15 .07
- ☐ 53 Salome Barojas .15 .07
- ☐ 54 Britt Burns .15 .07
- ☐ 55 Julio Cruz .15 .07
- ☐ 56 Richard Dotson .15 .07
- ☐ 57 Jerry Dybzinski .15 .07
- ☐ 58 Carlton Fisk 2.00 .90
- ☐ 59 Scott Fletcher .15 .07
- ☐ 60 Jerry Hairston .15 .07
- ☐ 61 Kevin Hickey .15 .07
- ☐ 62 Marc Hill .15 .07
- ☐ 63 LaMarr Hoyt .15 .07
- ☐ 64 Ron Kittle .15 .07
- ☐ 65 Jerry Koosman .40 .18
- ☐ 66 Dennis Lamp .15 .07
- ☐ 67 Rudy Law .15 .07
- ☐ 68 Vance Law .15 .07
- ☐ 69 Greg Luzinski .40 .18
- ☐ 70 Tom Paciorek .40 .18
- ☐ 71 Mike Squires .15 .07
- ☐ 72 Dick Tidrow .15 .07
- ☐ 73 Greg Walker .40 .18
- ☐ 74 Glenn Abbott .15 .07
- ☐ 75 Howard Bailey .15 .07
- ☐ 76 Doug Bair .15 .07
- ☐ 77 Juan Berenguer .15 .07
- ☐ 78 Tom Brookens .40 .18
- ☐ 79 Enos Cabell .15 .07
- ☐ 80 Kirk Gibson 1.50 .70
- ☐ 81 John Grubb .15 .07
- ☐ 82 Larry Herndon .40 .18
- ☐ 83 Wayne Krenchicki .15 .07
- ☐ 84 Rick Leach .15 .07
- ☐ 85 Chet Lemon .40 .18
- ☐ 86 Aurelio Lopez .40 .18
- ☐ 87 Jack Morris 1.50 .70
- ☐ 88 Lance Parrish .75 .35
- ☐ 89 Dan Petry .40 .18
- ☐ 90 Dave Rozema .15 .07
- ☐ 91 Alan Trammell 1.50 .70
- ☐ 92 Lou Whitaker 1.50 .70

- ☐ 93 Milt Wilcox .15 .07
- ☐ 94 Glenn Wilson .40 .18
- ☐ 95 John Wockenfuss .15 .07
- ☐ 96 Dusty Baker .75 .35
- ☐ 97 Joe Beckwith .15 .07
- ☐ 98 Greg Brock .15 .07
- ☐ 99 Jack Fimple .15 .07
- ☐ 100 Pedro Guerrero .40 .18
- ☐ 101 Rick Honeycutt .15 .07
- ☐ 102 Burt Hooton .15 .07
- ☐ 103 Steve Howe .15 .07
- ☐ 104 Ken Landreaux .15 .07
- ☐ 105 Mike Marshall .15 .07
- ☐ 106 Rick Monday .15 .07
- ☐ 107 Jose Morales .15 .07
- ☐ 108 Tom Niedenfuer .15 .07
- ☐ 109 Alejandro Pena .40 .18
- ☐ 110 Jerry Reuss UER .15 .07
  ("Home:" omitted)
- ☐ 111 Bill Russell .40 .18
- ☐ 112 Steve Sax .40 .18
- ☐ 113 Mike Scioscia .15 .07
- ☐ 114 Derrel Thomas .15 .07
- ☐ 115 Fernando Valenzuela .40 .18
- ☐ 116 Bob Welch .15 .07
- ☐ 117 Steve Yeager .15 .07
- ☐ 118 Pat Zachry .15 .07
- ☐ 119 Don Baylor .75 .35
- ☐ 120 Bert Campaneris .40 .18
- ☐ 121 Rick Cerone .15 .07
- ☐ 122 Ray Fontenot .15 .07
- ☐ 123 George Frazier .15 .07
- ☐ 124 Oscar Gamble .15 .07
- ☐ 125 Rich Gossage .75 .35
- ☐ 126 Ken Griffey .40 .18
- ☐ 127 Ron Guidry .40 .18
- ☐ 128 Jay Howell .15 .07
- ☐ 129 Steve Kemp .15 .07
- ☐ 130 Matt Keough .15 .07
- ☐ 131 Don Mattingly 20.00 9.00
- ☐ 132 John Montefusco .15 .07
- ☐ 133 Omar Moreno .15 .07
- ☐ 134 Dale Murray .15 .07
- ☐ 135 Graig Nettles .40 .18
- ☐ 136 Lou Piniella .40 .18
- ☐ 137 Willie Randolph .40 .18
- ☐ 138 Shane Rawley .15 .07
- ☐ 139 Dave Righetti .40 .18
- ☐ 140 Andre Robertson .15 .07
- ☐ 141 Bob Shirley .15 .07
- ☐ 142 Roy Smalley .15 .07
- ☐ 143 Dave Winfield 3.00 1.35
- ☐ 144 Butch Wynegar .15 .07
- ☐ 145 Jim Acker .15 .07
- ☐ 146 Doyle Alexander .15 .07
- ☐ 147 Jesse Barfield .40 .18
- ☐ 148 Jorge Bell .40 .18
- ☐ 149 Barry Bonnell .15 .07
- ☐ 150 Jim Clancy .15 .07
- ☐ 151 Dave Collins .15 .07
- ☐ 152 Tony Fernandez 1.50 .70
- ☐ 153 Damaso Garcia .15 .07
- ☐ 154 Dave Geisel .15 .07
- ☐ 155 Jim Gott .15 .07
- ☐ 156 Alfredo Griffin .15 .07
- ☐ 157 Garth Iorg .15 .07
- ☐ 158 Roy Lee Jackson .15 .07
- ☐ 159 Cliff Johnson .15 .07
- ☐ 160 Luis Leal .15 .07
- ☐ 161 Buck Martinez .15 .07
- ☐ 162 Joey McLaughlin .15 .07
- ☐ 163 Randy Moffitt .15 .07
- ☐ 164 Lloyd Moseby .15 .07
- ☐ 165 Rance Mulliniks .15 .07
- ☐ 166 Jorge Orta .15 .07
- ☐ 167 Dave Stieb .15 .07
- ☐ 168 Willie Upshaw .15 .07
- ☐ 169 Ernie Whitt .15 .07
- ☐ 170 Len Barker .15 .07
- ☐ 171 Steve Bedrosian .15 .07
- ☐ 172 Bruce Benedict .15 .07
- ☐ 173 Brett Butler .75 .35
- ☐ 174 Rick Camp .15 .07
- ☐ 175 Chris Chambliss .15 .07
- ☐ 176 Ken Dayley .15 .07
- ☐ 177 Pete Falcone .15 .07
- ☐ 178 Terry Forster .15 .07
- ☐ 179 Gene Garber .15 .07
- ☐ 180 Terry Harper .15 .07
- ☐ 181 Bob Horner .15 .07
- ☐ 182 Glenn Hubbard .15 .07
- ☐ 183 Randy Johnson .15 .07
- ☐ 184 Craig McMurtry .15 .07
- ☐ 185 Donnie Moore .15 .07
- ☐ 186 Dale Murphy 1.50 .70
- ☐ 187 Phil Niekro 1.50 .70
- ☐ 188 Pascual Perez .15 .07
- ☐ 189 Biff Pocoroba .15 .07
- ☐ 190 Rafael Ramirez .15 .07
- ☐ 191 Jerry Royster .15 .07
- ☐ 192 Claudell Washington .15 .07
- ☐ 193 Bob Watson .40 .18
- ☐ 194 Jerry Augustine .15 .07
- ☐ 195 Mark Brouhard .15 .07
- ☐ 196 Mike Caldwell .15 .07
- ☐ 197 Tom Candiotti 1.50 .70
- ☐ 198 Cecil Cooper .40 .18
- ☐ 199 Rollie Fingers 1.50 .70
- ☐ 200 Jim Gantner .40 .18
- ☐ 201 Bob L. Gibson .15 .07
- ☐ 202 Moose Haas .15 .07
- ☐ 203 Roy Howell .15 .07
- ☐ 204 Pete Ladd .15 .07
- ☐ 205 Rick Manning .15 .07
- ☐ 206 Bob McClure .15 .07
- ☐ 207 Paul Molitor UER 3.00 1.35
  ('83 stats should say
  .270 BA and 608 AB)
- ☐ 208 Don Money .15 .07
- ☐ 209 Charlie Moore .15 .07
- ☐ 210 Ben Oglivie .15 .07
- ☐ 211 Chuck Porter .15 .07
- ☐ 212 Ed Romero .15 .07
- ☐ 213 Ted Simmons .40 .18
- ☐ 214 Jim Slaton .15 .07
- ☐ 215 Don Sutton 1.50 .70
- ☐ 216 Tom Tellmann .15 .07
- ☐ 217 Pete Vuckovich .15 .07
- ☐ 218 Ned Yost .15 .07
- ☐ 219 Robin Yount 3.00 1.35
- ☐ 220 Alan Ashby .15 .07
- ☐ 221 Kevin Bass .15 .07
- ☐ 222 Jose Cruz .40 .18
- ☐ 223 Bill Dawley .15 .07
- ☐ 224 Frank DiPino .15 .07
- ☐ 225 Bill Doran .40 .18
- ☐ 226 Phil Garner .40 .18
- ☐ 227 Art Howe .15 .07
- ☐ 228 Bob Knepper .15 .07
- ☐ 229 Ray Knight .40 .18
- ☐ 230 Frank LaCorte .15 .07
- ☐ 231 Mike LaCoss .15 .07
- ☐ 232 Mike Madden .15 .07
- ☐ 233 Jerry Mumphrey .15 .07
- ☐ 234 Joe Niekro .40 .18
- ☐ 235 Terry Puhl .15 .07
- ☐ 236 Luis Pujols .15 .07
- ☐ 237 Craig Reynolds .15 .07
- ☐ 238 Vern Ruhle .15 .07
- ☐ 239 Nolan Ryan 10.00 4.50
- ☐ 240 Mike Scott .40 .18
- ☐ 241 Tony Scott .15 .07
- ☐ 242 Dave Smith .15 .07
- ☐ 243 Dickie Thon .15 .07
- ☐ 244 Denny Walling .15 .07
- ☐ 245 Dale Berra .15 .07
- ☐ 246 Jim Bibby .15 .07
- ☐ 247 John Candelaria .15 .07
- ☐ 248 Jose DeLeon .15 .07
- ☐ 249 Mike Easler .15 .07
- ☐ 250 Cecilio Guante .15 .07
- ☐ 251 Richie Hebner .15 .07
- ☐ 252 Lee Lacy .15 .07
- ☐ 253 Bill Madlock .40 .18
- ☐ 254 Milt May .15 .07
- ☐ 255 Lee Mazzilli .15 .07
- ☐ 256 Larry McWilliams .15 .07
- ☐ 257 Jim Morrison .15 .07
- ☐ 258 Dave Parker .40 .18
- ☐ 259 Tony Pena .15 .07
- ☐ 260 Johnny Ray .15 .07
- ☐ 261 Rick Rhoden .15 .07
- ☐ 262 Don Robinson .15 .07
- ☐ 263 Manny Sarmiento .15 .07
- ☐ 264 Rod Scurry .15 .07
- ☐ 265 Kent Tekulve .40 .18
- ☐ 266 Gene Tenace .40 .18
- ☐ 267 Jason Thompson .15 .07
- ☐ 268 Lee Tunnell .15 .07
- ☐ 269 Marvell Wynne .15 .07
- ☐ 270 Ray Burris .15 .07
- ☐ 271 Gary Carter 1.50 .70
- ☐ 272 Warren Cromartie .15 .07
- ☐ 273 Andre Dawson 1.50 .70
- ☐ 274 Doug Flynn .15 .07
- ☐ 275 Terry Francona .15 .07
- ☐ 276 Bill Gullickson .15 .07
- ☐ 277 Bob James .15 .07
- ☐ 278 Charlie Lea .15 .07
- ☐ 279 Bryan Little .15 .07
- ☐ 280 Al Oliver .40 .18
- ☐ 281 Tim Raines .75 .35
- ☐ 282 Bobby Ramos .15 .07
- ☐ 283 Jeff Reardon .40 .18
- ☐ 284 Steve Rogers .15 .07
- ☐ 285 Scott Sanderson .15 .07
- ☐ 286 Dan Schatzeder .15 .07
- ☐ 287 Bryn Smith .15 .07
- ☐ 288 Chris Speier .15 .07
- ☐ 289 Manny Trillo .15 .07
- ☐ 290 Mike Vail .15 .07
- ☐ 291 Tim Wallach .40 .18
- ☐ 292 Chris Welsh .15 .07
- ☐ 293 Jim Wohlford .15 .07
- ☐ 294 Kurt Bevacqua .15 .07
- ☐ 295 Juan Bonilla .15 .07
- ☐ 296 Bobby Brown .15 .07
- ☐ 297 Luis DeLeon .15 .07
- ☐ 298 Dave Dravecky .40 .18
- ☐ 299 Tim Flannery .15 .07
- ☐ 300 Steve Garvey .75 .35
- ☐ 301 Tony Gwynn 10.00 4.50
- ☐ 302 Andy Hawkins .15 .07
- ☐ 303 Ruppert Jones .15 .07
- ☐ 304 Terry Kennedy .15 .07
- ☐ 305 Tim Lollar .15 .07
- ☐ 306 Gary Lucas .15 .07
- ☐ 307 Kevin McReynolds .75 .35
- ☐ 308 Sid Monge .15 .07
- ☐ 309 Mario Ramirez .15 .07
- ☐ 310 Gene Richards .15 .07
- ☐ 311 Luis Salazar .15 .07
- ☐ 312 Eric Show .15 .07
- ☐ 313 Elias Sosa .15 .07
- ☐ 314 Garry Templeton .15 .07
- ☐ 315 Mark Thurmond .15 .07
- ☐ 316 Ed Whitson .15 .07
- ☐ 317 Alan Wiggins .15 .07
- ☐ 318 Neil Allen .15 .07
- ☐ 319 Joaquin Andujar .15 .07
- ☐ 320 Steve Braun .15 .07
- ☐ 321 Glenn Brummer .15 .07
- ☐ 322 Bob Forsch .15 .07
- ☐ 323 David Green .15 .07
- ☐ 324 George Hendrick .15 .07
- ☐ 325 Tom Herr .40 .18
- ☐ 326 Dane Iorg .15 .07
- ☐ 327 Jeff Lahti .15 .07
- ☐ 328 Dave LaPoint .15 .07
- ☐ 329 Willie McGee .75 .35
- ☐ 330 Ken Oberkfell .15 .07
- ☐ 331 Darrell Porter .15 .07
- ☐ 332 Jamie Quirk .15 .07
- ☐ 333 Mike Ramsey .15 .07
- ☐ 334 Floyd Rayford .15 .07
- ☐ 335 Lonnie Smith .15 .07
- ☐ 336 Ozzie Smith 2.50 1.10
- ☐ 337 John Stuper .15 .07
- ☐ 338 Bruce Sutter .40 .18
- ☐ 339 Andy Van Slyke UER 1.50 .70
  (Batting and throwing
  both wrong on card back)
- ☐ 340 Dave Von Ohlen .15 .07
- ☐ 341 Willie Aikens .15 .07
- ☐ 342 Mike Armstrong .15 .07
- ☐ 343 Bud Black .15 .07
- ☐ 344 George Brett 3.00 1.35
- ☐ 345 Onix Concepcion .15 .07
- ☐ 346 Keith Creel .15 .07
- ☐ 347 Larry Gura .15 .07
- ☐ 348 Don Hood .15 .07
- ☐ 349 Dennis Leonard .15 .07
- ☐ 350 Hal McRae .40 .18
- ☐ 351 Amos Otis .40 .18
- ☐ 352 Gaylord Perry 1.50 .70
- ☐ 353 Greg Pryor .15 .07
- ☐ 354 Dan Quisenberry .15 .07
- ☐ 355 Steve Renko .15 .07
- ☐ 356 Leon Roberts .15 .07
- ☐ 357 Pat Sheridan .15 .07
- ☐ 358 Joe Simpson .15 .07
- ☐ 359 Don Slaught .40 .18
- ☐ 360 Paul Splittorff .15 .07
- ☐ 361 U.L. Washington .15 .07
- ☐ 362 John Wathan .15 .07
- ☐ 363 Frank White .40 .18
- ☐ 364 Willie Wilson .15 .07
- ☐ 365 Jim Barr .15 .07
- ☐ 366 Dave Bergman .15 .07
- ☐ 367 Fred Breining .15 .07
- ☐ 368 Bob Brenly .15 .07
- ☐ 369 Jack Clark .40 .18
- ☐ 370 Chili Davis .75 .35
- ☐ 371 Mark Davis .15 .07
- ☐ 372 Darrell Evans .40 .18
- ☐ 373 Atlee Hammaker .15 .07
- ☐ 374 Mike Krukow .15 .07
- ☐ 375 Duane Kuiper .15 .07
- ☐ 376 Bill Laskey .15 .07
- ☐ 377 Gary Lavelle .15 .07
- ☐ 378 Johnnie LeMaster .15 .07

☐ 379 Jeff Leonard .15 .07
☐ 380 Randy Lerch .15 .07
☐ 381 Renie Martin .15 .07
☐ 382 Andy McGaffigan .15 .07
☐ 383 Greg Minton .15 .07
☐ 384 Tom O'Malley .15 .07
☐ 385 Max Venable .15 .07
☐ 386 Brad Wellman .15 .07
☐ 387 Joel Youngblood .15 .07
☐ 388 Gary Allenson .15 .07
☐ 389 Luis Aponte .15 .07
☐ 390 Tony Armas .15 .07
☐ 391 Doug Bird .15 .07
☐ 392 Wade Boggs 3.00 1.35
☐ 393 Dennis Boyd .40 .18
☐ 394 Mike Brown UER P .15 .07
(shown with record
of 31-104)
☐ 395 Mark Clear .15 .07
☐ 396 Dennis Eckersley 1.50 .70
☐ 397 Dwight Evans .40 .18
☐ 398 Rich Gedman .15 .07
☐ 399 Glenn Hoffman .15 .07
☐ 400 Bruce Hurst .15 .07
☐ 401 John Henry Johnson .15 .07
☐ 402 Ed Jurak .15 .07
☐ 403 Rick Miller .15 .07
☐ 404 Jeff Newman .15 .07
☐ 405 Reid Nichols .15 .07
☐ 406 Bob Ojeda .15 .07
☐ 407 Jerry Remy .15 .07
☐ 408 Jim Rice .40 .18
☐ 409 Bob Stanley .15 .07
☐ 410 Dave Stapleton .15 .07
☐ 411 John Tudor .15 .07
☐ 412 Carl Yastrzemski 1.50 .70
☐ 413 Buddy Bell .40 .18
☐ 414 Larry Biittner .15 .07
☐ 415 John Butcher .15 .07
☐ 416 Danny Darwin .40 .18
☐ 417 Bucky Dent .40 .18
☐ 418 Dave Hostetler .15 .07
☐ 419 Charlie Hough .40 .18
☐ 420 Bobby Johnson .15 .07
☐ 421 Odell Jones .15 .07
☐ 422 Jon Matlack .15 .07
☐ 423 Pete O'Brien .40 .18
☐ 424 Larry Parrish .15 .07
☐ 425 Mickey Rivers .15 .07
☐ 426 Billy Sample .15 .07
☐ 427 Dave Schmidt .15 .07
☐ 428 Mike Smithson .15 .07
☐ 429 Bill Stein .15 .07
☐ 430 Dave Stewart .40 .18
☐ 431 Jim Sundberg .40 .18
☐ 432 Frank Tanana .40 .18
☐ 433 Dave Tobik .15 .07
☐ 434 Wayne Tolleson .15 .07
☐ 435 George Wright .15 .07
☐ 436 Bill Almon .15 .07
☐ 437 Keith Atherton .15 .07
☐ 438 Dave Beard .15 .07
☐ 439 Tom Burgmeier .15 .07
☐ 440 Jeff Burroughs .15 .07
☐ 441 Chris Codiroli .15 .07
☐ 442 Tim Conroy .15 .07
☐ 443 Mike Davis .15 .07
☐ 444 Wayne Gross .15 .07
☐ 445 Garry Hancock .15 .07
☐ 446 Mike Heath .15 .07
☐ 447 Rickey Henderson 3.00 1.35
☐ 448 Donnie Hill .15 .07
☐ 449 Bob Kearney .15 .07
☐ 450 Bill Krueger .15 .07
☐ 451 Rick Langford .15 .07
☐ 452 Carney Lansford .40 .18
☐ 453 Dave Lopes .40 .18
☐ 454 Steve McCatty .15 .07
☐ 455 Dan Meyer .15 .07
☐ 456 Dwayne Murphy .15 .07
☐ 457 Mike Norris .15 .07
☐ 458 Ricky Peters .15 .07
☐ 459 Tony Phillips 2.00 .90
☐ 460 Tom Underwood .15 .07
☐ 461 Mike Warren .15 .07
☐ 462 Johnny Bench 2.00 .90
☐ 463 Bruce Berenyi .15 .07
☐ 464 Dann Bilardello .15 .07
☐ 465 Cesar Cedeno .40 .18
☐ 466 Dave Concepcion .40 .18
☐ 467 Dan Driessen .15 .07
☐ 468 Nick Esasky .15 .07
☐ 469 Rich Gale .15 .07
☐ 470 Ben Hayes .15 .07
☐ 471 Paul Householder .15 .07
☐ 472 Tom Hume .15 .07
☐ 473 Alan Knicely .15 .07
☐ 474 Eddie Milner .15 .07
☐ 475 Ron Oester .15 .07
☐ 476 Kelly Paris .15 .07
☐ 477 Frank Pastore .15 .07
☐ 478 Ted Power .15 .07
☐ 479 Joe Price .15 .07
☐ 480 Charlie Puleo .15 .07
☐ 481 Gary Redus .15 .07
☐ 482 Bill Scherrer .15 .07
☐ 483 Mario Soto .15 .07
☐ 484 Alex Trevino .15 .07
☐ 485 Duane Walker .15 .07
☐ 486 Larry Bowa .40 .18
☐ 487 Warren Brusstar .15 .07
☐ 488 Bill Buckner .40 .18
☐ 489 Bill Campbell .15 .07
☐ 490 Ron Cey .40 .18
☐ 491 Jody Davis .15 .07
☐ 492 Leon Durham .15 .07
☐ 493 Mel Hall .40 .18
☐ 494 Ferguson Jenkins 1.50 .70
☐ 495 Jay Johnstone .40 .18
☐ 496 Craig Lefferts .15 .07
☐ 497 Carmelo Martinez .15 .07
☐ 498 Jerry Morales .15 .07
☐ 499 Keith Moreland .15 .07
☐ 500 Dickie Noles .15 .07
☐ 501 Mike Proly .15 .07
☐ 502 Chuck Rainey .15 .07
☐ 503 Dick Ruthven .15 .07
☐ 504 Ryne Sandberg 5.00 2.20
☐ 505 Lee Smith 1.50 .70
☐ 506 Steve Trout .15 .07
☐ 507 Gary Woods .15 .07
☐ 508 Juan Beniquez .15 .07
☐ 509 Bob Boone .40 .18
☐ 510 Rick Burleson .15 .07
☐ 511 Rod Carew 1.25 .55
☐ 512 Bobby Clark .15 .07
☐ 513 John Curtis .15 .07
☐ 514 Doug DeCinces .15 .07
☐ 515 Brian Downing .15 .07
☐ 516 Tim Foli .15 .07
☐ 517 Ken Forsch .15 .07
☐ 518 Bobby Grich .40 .18
☐ 519 Andy Hassler .15 .07
☐ 520 Reggie Jackson 2.00 .90
☐ 521 Ron Jackson .15 .07
☐ 522 Tommy John .75 .35
☐ 523 Bruce Kison .15 .07
☐ 524 Steve Lubratich .15 .07
☐ 525 Fred Lynn .40 .18
☐ 526 Gary Pettis .15 .07
☐ 527 Luis Sanchez .15 .07
☐ 528 Daryl Sconiers .15 .07
☐ 529 Ellis Valentine .15 .07
☐ 530 Rob Wilfong .15 .07
☐ 531 Mike Witt .15 .07
☐ 532 Geoff Zahn .15 .07
☐ 533 Bud Anderson .15 .07
☐ 534 Chris Bando .15 .07
☐ 535 Alan Bannister .15 .07
☐ 536 Bert Blyleven .40 .18
☐ 537 Tom Brennan .15 .07
☐ 538 Jamie Easterly .15 .07
☐ 539 Juan Eichelberger .15 .07
☐ 540 Jim Essian .15 .07
☐ 541 Mike Fischlin .15 .07
☐ 542 Julio Franco .75 .35
☐ 543 Mike Hargrove .40 .18
☐ 544 Toby Harrah .40 .18
☐ 545 Ron Hassey .15 .07
☐ 546 Neal Heaton .15 .07
☐ 547 Bake McBride .15 .07
☐ 548 Broderick Perkins .15 .07
☐ 549 Lary Sorensen .15 .07
☐ 550 Dan Spillner .15 .07
☐ 551 Rick Sutcliffe .40 .18
☐ 552 Pat Tabler .15 .07
☐ 553 Gorman Thomas .15 .07
☐ 554 Andre Thornton .15 .07
☐ 555 George Vukovich .15 .07
☐ 556 Darrell Brown .15 .07
☐ 557 Tom Brunansky .40 .18
☐ 558 Randy Bush .15 .07
☐ 559 Bobby Castillo .15 .07
☐ 560 John Castino .15 .07
☐ 561 Ron Davis .15 .07
☐ 562 Dave Engle .15 .07
☐ 563 Lenny Faedo .15 .07
☐ 564 Pete Filson .15 .07
☐ 565 Gary Gaetti .75 .35
☐ 566 Mickey Hatcher .15 .07
☐ 567 Kent Hrbek .40 .18
☐ 568 Rusty Kuntz .15 .07
☐ 569 Tim Laudner .15 .07
☐ 570 Rick Lysander .15 .07
☐ 571 Bobby Mitchell .15 .07
☐ 572 Ken Schrom .15 .07
☐ 573 Ray Smith .15 .07
☐ 574 Tim Teufel .15 .07
☐ 575 Frank Viola .75 .35
☐ 576 Gary Ward .15 .07
☐ 577 Ron Washington .15 .07
☐ 578 Len Whitehouse .15 .07
☐ 579 Al Williams .15 .07
☐ 580 Bob Bailor .15 .07
☐ 581 Mark Bradley .15 .07
☐ 582 Hubie Brooks .15 .07
☐ 583 Carlos Diaz .15 .07
☐ 584 George Foster .40 .18
☐ 585 Brian Giles .15 .07
☐ 586 Danny Heep .15 .07
☐ 587 Keith Hernandez .40 .18
☐ 588 Ron Hodges .15 .07
☐ 589 Scott Holman .15 .07
☐ 590 Dave Kingman .75 .35
☐ 591 Ed Lynch .15 .07
☐ 592 Jose Oquendo .40 .18
☐ 593 Jesse Orosco .15 .07
☐ 594 Junior Ortiz .15 .07
☐ 595 Tom Seaver 2.00 .90
☐ 596 Doug Sisk .15 .07
☐ 597 Rusty Staub .40 .18
☐ 598 John Stearns .15 .07
☐ 599 Darryl Strawberry 5.00 2.20
☐ 600 Craig Swan .15 .07
☐ 601 Walt Terrell .15 .07
☐ 602 Mike Torrez .15 .07
☐ 603 Mookie Wilson .40 .18
☐ 604 Jamie Allen .15 .07
☐ 605 Jim Beattie .15 .07
☐ 606 Tony Bernazard .15 .07
☐ 607 Manny Castillo .15 .07
☐ 608 Bill Caudill .15 .07
☐ 609 Bryan Clark .15 .07
☐ 610 Al Cowens .15 .07
☐ 611 Dave Henderson .40 .18
☐ 612 Steve Henderson .15 .07
☐ 613 Orlando Mercado .15 .07
☐ 614 Mike Moore .15 .07
☐ 615 Ricky Nelson UER .15 .07
(Jamie Nelson's
stats on back)
☐ 616 Spike Owen .40 .18
☐ 617 Pat Putnam .15 .07
☐ 618 Ron Roenicke .15 .07
☐ 619 Mike Stanton .15 .07
☐ 620 Bob Stoddard .15 .07
☐ 621 Rick Sweet .15 .07
☐ 622 Roy Thomas .15 .07
☐ 623 Ed VandeBerg .15 .07
☐ 624 Matt Young .15 .07
☐ 625 Richie Zisk .15 .07
☐ 626 Fred Lynn .40 .18
1982 AS Game RB
☐ 627 Manny Trillo .15 .07
1983 AS Game RB
☐ 628 Steve Garvey .75 .35
NL Iron Man
☐ 629 Rod Carew 1.50 .70
AL Batting Runner-Up
☐ 630 Wade Boggs 1.50 .70
AL Batting Champion
☐ 631 Tim Raines: Letting .40 .18
Go of the Raines
☐ 632 Al Oliver .40 .18
Double Trouble
☐ 633 Steve Sax .15 .07
AS Second Base
☐ 634 Dickie Thon .15 .07
AS Shortstop
☐ 635 Ace Firemen .15 .07
Dan Quisenberry
and Tippy Martinez
☐ 636 Reds Reunited 1.50 .70
Joe Morgan
Pete Rose
Tony Perez
☐ 637 Backstop Stars .75 .35
Lance Parrish
Bob Boone
☐ 638 George Brett and 2.00 .90
Gaylord Perry
Pine Tar 7/24/83
☐ 639 1983 No Hitters .75 .35
Dave Righetti
Mike Warren
Bob Forsch
☐ 640 Johnny Bench and 2.00 .90
Carl Yastrzemski
Retiring Superstars
☐ 641 Gaylord Perry 1.50 .70
Going Out In Style

Card	NRMT	VG-E
☐ 642 Steve Carlton 300 Club and Strikeout Record	1.50	.70
☐ 643 Joe Altobelli and Paul Owens World Series Managers	.15	.07
☐ 644 Rick Dempsey World Series MVP	.40	.18
☐ 645 Mike Boddicker WS Rookie Winner	.15	.07
☐ 646 Scott McGregor WS Clincher	.15	.07
☐ 647 CL: Orioles/Royals Joe Altobelli MG	.15	.07
☐ 648 CL: Phillies/Giants Paul Owens MG	.15	.07
☐ 649 CL: White Sox/Red Sox Tony LaRussa MG	.75	.35
☐ 650 CL: Tigers/Rangers Sparky Anderson MG	.75	.35
☐ 651 CL: Dodgers/A's Tommy Lasorda MG	.75	.35
☐ 652 CL: Yankees/Reds Billy Martin MG	.75	.35
☐ 653 CL: Blue Jays/Cubs Bobby Cox MG	.40	.18
☐ 654 CL: Braves/Angels Joe Torre MG	.75	.35
☐ 655 CL: Brewers/Indians Rene Lachemann MG	.15	.07
☐ 656 CL: Astros/Twins Bob Lillis MG	.15	.07
☐ 657 CL: Pirates/Mets Chuck Tanner MG	.15	.07
☐ 658 CL: Expos/Mariners Bill Virdon MG	.15	.07
☐ 659 CL: Padres/Specials Dick Williams MG	.40	.18
☐ 660 CL: Cardinals/Teams Whitey Herzog MG	.75	.35

1984 Fleer Update

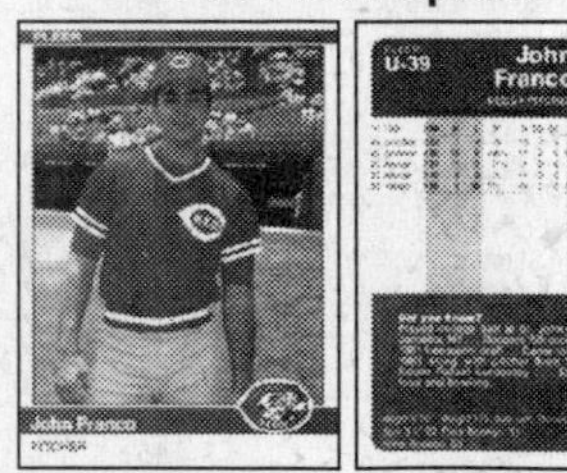

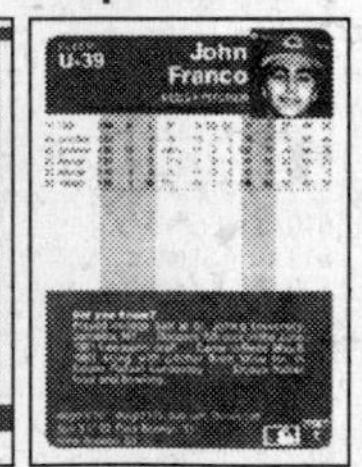

This set was Fleer's first update set and portrayed players with their proper team for the current year and to rookies who were not in their regular issue. Like the Topps Traded sets of the time, the Fleer Update sets were distributed in factory set form through hobby dealers only. The set was quite popular with collectors, and, apparently, the print run was relatively short, as the set was quickly in short supply and exhibited a rapid and dramatic price increase. The cards are numbered on the back with a U prefix and placed in alphabetical order by player name. The key (extended) Rookie Cards in this set are Roger Clemens, John Franco, Dwight Gooden, Jimmy Key, Mark Langston, Kirby Puckett, Jose Rijo, and Bret Saberhagen. Collectors are urged to be careful if purchasing single cards of Clemens, Darling, Gooden, Puckett, Rose, or Saberhagen as these specific cards have been illegally reprinted. These fakes are blurry when compared to the real cards.

	NRMT	VG-E
COMP.FACT.SET (132)	400.00	180.00
COMMON CARD (1-132)	1.00	.45

Card	NRMT	VG-E
☐ 1 Willie Aikens	1.00	.45
☐ 2 Luis Aponte	1.00	.45
☐ 3 Mark Bailey	1.00	.45
☐ 4 Bob Bailor	1.00	.45
☐ 5 Dusty Baker	4.00	1.80
☐ 6 Steve Balboni	1.00	.45
☐ 7 Alan Bannister	1.00	.45
☐ 8 Marty Barrett	4.00	1.80
☐ 9 Dave Beard	1.00	.45
☐ 10 Joe Beckwith	1.00	.45
☐ 11 Dave Bergman	1.00	.45
☐ 12 Tony Bernazard	1.00	.45
☐ 13 Bruce Bochte	1.00	.45
☐ 14 Barry Bonnell	1.00	.45
☐ 15 Phil Bradley	4.00	1.80
☐ 16 Fred Breining	1.00	.45
☐ 17 Mike C. Brown	1.00	.45
☐ 18 Bill Buckner	4.00	1.80
☐ 19 Ray Burris	1.00	.45
☐ 20 John Butcher	1.00	.45
☐ 21 Brett Butler	5.00	2.20
☐ 22 Enos Cabell	1.00	.45
☐ 23 Bill Campbell	1.00	.45
☐ 24 Bill Caudill	1.00	.45
☐ 25 Bobby Clark	1.00	.45
☐ 26 Bryan Clark	1.00	.45
☐ 27 Roger Clemens	200.00	90.00
☐ 28 Jaime Cocanower	1.00	.45
☐ 29 Ron Darling	5.00	2.20
☐ 30 Alvin Davis	4.00	1.80
☐ 31 Bob Dernier	1.00	.45
☐ 32 Carlos Diaz	1.00	.45
☐ 33 Mike Easler	1.00	.45
☐ 34 Dennis Eckersley	6.00	2.70
☐ 35 Jim Essian	1.00	.45
☐ 36 Darrell Evans	4.00	1.80
☐ 37 Mike Fitzgerald	1.00	.45
☐ 38 Tim Foli	1.00	.45
☐ 39 John Franco	8.00	3.60
☐ 40 George Frazier	1.00	.45
☐ 41 Rich Gale	1.00	.45
☐ 42 Barbaro Garbey	1.00	.45
☐ 43 Dwight Gooden	40.00	18.00
☐ 44 Rich Gossage	5.00	2.20
☐ 45 Wayne Gross	1.00	.45
☐ 46 Mark Gubicza	4.00	1.80
☐ 47 Jackie Gutierrez	1.00	.45
☐ 48 Toby Harrah	4.00	1.80
☐ 49 Ron Hassey	1.00	.45
☐ 50 Richie Hebner	1.00	.45
☐ 51 Willie Hernandez	4.00	1.80
☐ 52 Ed Hodge	1.00	.45
☐ 53 Ricky Horton	1.00	.45
☐ 54 Art Howe	1.00	.45
☐ 55 Dane Iorg	1.00	.45
☐ 56 Brook Jacoby	4.00	1.80
☐ 57 Dion James	4.00	1.80
☐ 58 Mike Jeffcoat	1.00	.45
☐ 59 Ruppert Jones	1.00	.45
☐ 60 Bob Kearney	1.00	.45
☐ 61 Jimmy Key	15.00	6.75
☐ 62 Dave Kingman	5.00	2.20
☐ 63 Brad Komminsk	1.00	.45
☐ 64 Jerry Koosman	4.00	1.80
☐ 65 Wayne Krenchicki	1.00	.45
☐ 66 Rusty Kuntz	1.00	.45
☐ 67 Frank LaCorte	1.00	.45
☐ 68 Dennis Lamp	1.00	.45
☐ 69 Tito Landrum	1.00	.45
☐ 70 Mark Langston	8.00	3.60
☐ 71 Rick Leach	1.00	.45
☐ 72 Craig Lefferts	4.00	1.80
☐ 73 Gary Lucas	1.00	.45
☐ 74 Jerry Martin	1.00	.45
☐ 75 Carmelo Martinez	1.00	.45
☐ 76 Mike Mason	1.00	.45
☐ 77 Gary Matthews	1.00	.45
☐ 78 Andy McGaffigan	1.00	.45
☐ 79 Joey McLaughlin	1.00	.45
☐ 80 Joe Morgan	8.00	3.60
☐ 81 Darryl Motley	1.00	.45
☐ 82 Graig Nettles	4.00	1.80
☐ 83 Phil Niekro	5.00	2.20
☐ 84 Ken Oberkfell	1.00	.45
☐ 85 Al Oliver	4.00	1.80
☐ 86 Jorge Orta	1.00	.45
☐ 87 Amos Otis	4.00	1.80
☐ 88 Bob Owchinko	1.00	.45
☐ 89 Dave Parker	4.00	1.80
☐ 90 Jack Perconte	1.00	.45
☐ 91 Tony Perez	6.00	2.70
☐ 92 Gerald Perry	4.00	1.80
☐ 93 Kirby Puckett	180.00	80.00
☐ 94 Shane Rawley	1.00	.45
☐ 95 Floyd Rayford	1.00	.45
☐ 96 Ron Reed	1.00	.45
☐ 97 R.J. Reynolds	1.00	.45
☐ 98 Gene Richards	1.00	.45
☐ 99 Jose Rijo	5.00	2.20
☐ 100 Jeff D. Robinson	1.00	.45
☐ 101 Ron Romanick	1.00	.45
☐ 102 Pete Rose	15.00	6.75
☐ 103 Bret Saberhagen	8.00	3.60
☐ 104 Scott Sanderson	1.00	.45
☐ 105 Dick Schofield	4.00	1.80
☐ 106 Tom Seaver	15.00	6.75
☐ 107 Jim Slaton	1.00	.45
☐ 108 Mike Smithson	1.00	.45
☐ 109 Lary Sorensen	1.00	.45
☐ 110 Tim Stoddard	1.00	.45
☐ 111 Jeff Stone	1.00	.45
☐ 112 Champ Summers	1.00	.45
☐ 113 Jim Sundberg	4.00	1.80
☐ 114 Rick Sutcliffe	4.00	1.80
☐ 115 Craig Swan	1.00	.45
☐ 116 Derrel Thomas	1.00	.45
☐ 117 Gorman Thomas	1.00	.45
☐ 118 Alex Trevino	1.00	.45
☐ 119 Manny Trillo	1.00	.45
☐ 120 John Tudor	1.00	.45
☐ 121 Tom Underwood	1.00	.45
☐ 122 Mike Vail	1.00	.45
☐ 123 Tom Waddell	1.00	.45
☐ 124 Gary Ward	1.00	.45
☐ 125 Terry Whitfield	1.00	.45
☐ 126 Curtis Wilkerson	1.00	.45
☐ 127 Frank Williams	1.00	.45
☐ 128 Glenn Wilson	1.00	.45
☐ 129 John Wockenfuss	1.00	.45
☐ 130 Ned Yost	1.00	.45
☐ 131 Mike Young	1.00	.45
☐ 132 Checklist 1-132	1.00	.45

1984 Fleer Stickers

The stickers in this 126-sticker set measure approximately 1 15/16" by 2 1/2". The 1984 Fleer sticker set is a very attractive set with a beige border. Many players are featured more than once in the set due to the fact that the album issued to house the set contains league leader categories in which to place the stickers. The checklist below is ordered by categories, e.g., Game Winning RBI's (1-5), Batting Average (6-15), Home Runs (16-23), Hits (24-31), Slugging Percentage (32-39), Pinch Hits (40-43), Designated Hitter's Hits (44-47), On Base Percentage (48-55), Won/Lost Percentage (56-64), Earned Run Average (65-66), Saves (67-77), Strikeouts (78-87), Stolen Bases (88-95), Future Hall of Famers (96-103), Rookie Stars (104-113), World Series Batting (114-122) and Playoff Managers (123-126). These stickers were originally issued in packs of six for 25 cents plus a team logo.

	NRMT	VG-E
COMPLETE SET (126)	12.00	5.50
COMMON STICKER (1-126)	.05	.02

Sticker	NRMT	VG-E
☐ 1 Dickie Thon	.05	.02
☐ 2 Ken Landreaux	.05	.02
☐ 3 Darrell Evans	.15	.07
☐ 4 Harold Baines	.15	.07
☐ 5 Dave Winfield	.50	.23
☐ 6 Bill Madlock	.05	.02
☐ 7 Lonnie Smith	.05	.02
☐ 8 Jose Cruz	.15	.07
☐ 9 George Hendrick	.05	.02
☐ 10 Ray Knight	.15	.07
☐ 11 Wade Boggs	.60	.25
☐ 12 Rod Carew	.50	.23
☐ 13 Lou Whitaker	.25	.11
☐ 14 Alan Trammell	.40	.18
☐ 15 Cal Ripken	2.00	.90
☐ 16 Mike Schmidt	.75	.35
☐ 17 Dale Murphy	.40	.18
☐ 18 Andre Dawson	.40	.18
☐ 19 Pedro Guerrero	.15	.07
☐ 20 Jim Rice	.15	.07
☐ 21 Tony Armas	.05	.02
☐ 22 Ron Kittle	.05	.02
☐ 23 Eddie Murray	.50	.23
☐ 24 Jose Cruz	.15	.07
☐ 25 Andre Dawson	.40	.18
☐ 26 Rafael Ramirez	.05	.02
☐ 27 Al Oliver	.15	.07
☐ 28 Wade Boggs	.60	.25
☐ 29 Cal Ripken	2.00	.90
☐ 30 Lou Whitaker	.15	.07
☐ 31 Cecil Cooper	.15	.07
☐ 32 Dale Murphy	.40	.18
☐ 33 Andre Dawson	.40	.18
☐ 34 Pedro Guerrero	.15	.07
☐ 35 Mike Schmidt	.60	.25
☐ 36 George Brett	1.00	.45
☐ 37 Jim Rice	.15	.07
☐ 38 Eddie Murray	.50	.23
☐ 39 Carlton Fisk	.40	.18
☐ 40 Rusty Staub	.15	.07

☐ 41 Duane Walker	.05	.02
☐ 42 Steve Braun	.05	.02
☐ 43 Kurt Bevacqua	.05	.02
☐ 44 Hal McRae	.15	.07
☐ 45 Don Baylor	.15	.07
☐ 46 Ken Singleton	.05	.02
☐ 47 Greg Luzinski	.15	.07
☐ 48 Mike Schmidt	.50	.23
☐ 49 Keith Hernandez	.15	.07
☐ 50 Dale Murphy	.40	.18
☐ 51 Tim Raines	.25	.11
☐ 52 Wade Boggs	.50	.23
☐ 53 Rickey Henderson	.50	.23
☐ 54 Rod Carew	.50	.23
☐ 55 Ken Singleton	.05	.02
☐ 56 John Denny	.05	.02
☐ 57 John Candelaria	.05	.02
☐ 58 Larry McWilliams	.05	.02
☐ 59 Pascual Perez	.05	.02
☐ 60 Jesse Orosco	.05	.02
☐ 61 Moose Haas	.05	.02
☐ 62 Richard Dotson	.05	.02
☐ 63 Mike Flanagan	.05	.02
☐ 64 Scott McGregor	.05	.02
☐ 65 Atlee Hammaker	.05	.02
☐ 66 Rick Honeycutt	.05	.02
☐ 67 Lee Smith	.40	.18
☐ 68 Al Holland	.05	.02
☐ 69 Greg Minton	.05	.02
☐ 70 Bruce Sutter	.15	.07
☐ 71 Jeff Reardon	.15	.07
☐ 72 Frank DiPino	.05	.02
☐ 73 Dan Quisenberry	.15	.07
☐ 74 Bob Stanley	.05	.02
☐ 75 Ron Davis	.05	.02
☐ 76 Bill Caudill	.05	.02
☐ 77 Peter Ladd	.05	.02
☐ 78 Steve Carlton	.50	.23
☐ 79 Mario Soto	.05	.02
☐ 80 Larry McWilliams	.05	.02
☐ 81 Fernando Valenzuela	.15	.07
☐ 82 Nolan Ryan	2.00	.90
☐ 83 Jack Morris	.25	.11
☐ 84 Floyd Bannister	.05	.02
☐ 85 Dave Stieb	.05	.02
☐ 86 Dave Righetti	.05	.02
☐ 87 Rick Sutcliffe	.15	.07
☐ 88 Tim Raines	.25	.11
☐ 89 Alan Wiggins	.05	.02
☐ 90 Steve Sax	.15	.07
☐ 91 Mookie Wilson	.25	.11
☐ 92 Rickey Henderson	.50	.23
☐ 93 Rudy Law	.05	.02
☐ 94 Willie Wilson	.15	.07
☐ 95 Julio Cruz	.05	.02
☐ 96 Johnny Bench	.50	.23
☐ 97 Carl Yastrzemski	.50	.23
☐ 98 Gaylord Perry	.40	.18
☐ 99 Pete Rose	.75	.35
☐ 100 Joe Morgan	.50	.23
☐ 101 Steve Carlton	.50	.23
☐ 102 Jim Palmer	.50	.23
☐ 103 Rod Carew	.50	.23
☐ 104 Darryl Strawberry	.60	.25
☐ 105 Craig McMurtry	.05	.02
☐ 106 Mel Hall	.05	.02
☐ 107 Lee Tunnell	.05	.02
☐ 108 Bill Dawley	.05	.02
☐ 109 Ron Kittle	.05	.02
☐ 110 Mike Boddicker	.05	.02
☐ 111 Julio Franco	.25	.11
☐ 112 Daryl Sconiers	.05	.02
☐ 113 Neal Heaton	.05	.02
☐ 114 John Shelby	.05	.02
☐ 115 Rick Dempsey	.05	.02
☐ 116 John Lowenstein	.05	.02
☐ 117 Jim Dwyer	.05	.02
☐ 118 Bo Diaz	.05	.02
☐ 119 Pete Rose	.75	.35
☐ 120 Joe Morgan	.40	.18
☐ 121 Gary Matthews	.05	.02
☐ 122 Garry Maddox	.05	.02
☐ 123 Paul Owens MG	.05	.02
☐ 124 Tom Lasorda MG	.25	.11
☐ 125 Joe Altobelli MG	.05	.02
☐ 126 Tony LaRussa MG	.15	.07

1985 Fleer

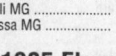

The 1985 Fleer set consists of 660 standard-size cards. Wax packs contained 15 cards plus logo stickers. Card fronts feature a full color photo, team logo along with the player's name and position. The borders enclosing the photo are color-coded to correspond to the player's team. The cards are ordered alphabetically within team. The teams are ordered based on their respective performance

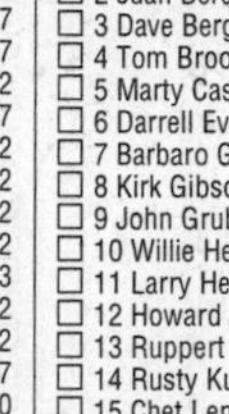

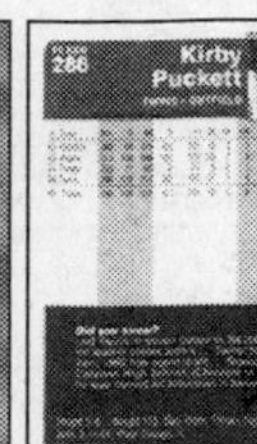

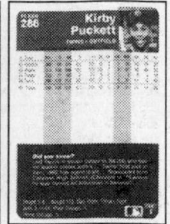

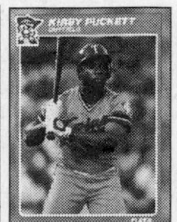

during the prior year. Subsets include Specials (626-643) and Major League Prospects (644-653). The black and white photo on the reverse is included for the third straight year. Notable Rookie Cards include Roger Clemens, Eric Davis, Shawon Dunston, John Franco, Dwight Gooden, Orel Hershiser, Jimmy Key, Mark Langston, Terry Pendleton, Kirby Puckett, Jose Rijo, Bret Saberhagen, and Danny Tartabull.

	NRMT	VG-E
COMPLETE SET (660)	100.00	45.00
COMMON CARD (1-660)	.15	.07
☐ 1 Doug Bair	.15	.07
☐ 2 Juan Berenguer	.15	.07
☐ 3 Dave Bergman	.15	.07
☐ 4 Tom Brookens	.15	.07
☐ 5 Marty Castillo	.15	.07
☐ 6 Darrell Evans	.40	.18
☐ 7 Barbaro Garbey	.15	.07
☐ 8 Kirk Gibson	.40	.18
☐ 9 John Grubb	.15	.07
☐ 10 Willie Hernandez	.15	.07
☐ 11 Larry Herndon	.15	.07
☐ 12 Howard Johnson	.40	.18
☐ 13 Ruppert Jones	.15	.07
☐ 14 Rusty Kuntz	.15	.07
☐ 15 Chet Lemon	.15	.07
☐ 16 Aurelio Lopez	.15	.07
☐ 17 Sid Monge	.15	.07
☐ 18 Jack Morris	.40	.18
☐ 19 Lance Parrish	.40	.18
☐ 20 Dan Petry	.15	.07
☐ 21 Dave Rozema	.15	.07
☐ 22 Bill Scherrer	.15	.07
☐ 23 Alan Trammell	.75	.35
☐ 24 Lou Whitaker	.40	.18
☐ 25 Milt Wilcox	.15	.07
☐ 26 Kurt Bevacqua	.15	.07
☐ 27 Greg Booker	.15	.07
☐ 28 Bobby Brown	.15	.07
☐ 29 Luis DeLeon	.15	.07
☐ 30 Dave Dravecky	.40	.18
☐ 31 Tim Flannery	.15	.07
☐ 32 Steve Garvey	.75	.35
☐ 33 Rich Gossage	.75	.35
☐ 34 Tony Gwynn	6.00	2.70
☐ 35 Greg Harris	.15	.07
☐ 36 Andy Hawkins	.15	.07
☐ 37 Terry Kennedy	.15	.07
☐ 38 Craig Lefferts	.15	.07
☐ 39 Tim Lollar	.15	.07
☐ 40 Carmelo Martinez	.15	.07
☐ 41 Kevin McReynolds	.40	.18
☐ 42 Graig Nettles	.40	.18
☐ 43 Luis Salazar	.15	.07
☐ 44 Eric Show	.15	.07
☐ 45 Garry Templeton	.15	.07
☐ 46 Mark Thurmond	.15	.07
☐ 47 Ed Whitson	.15	.07
☐ 48 Alan Wiggins	.15	.07
☐ 49 Rich Bordi	.15	.07
☐ 50 Larry Bowa	.40	.18
☐ 51 Warren Brusstar	.15	.07
☐ 52 Ron Cey	.40	.18
☐ 53 Henry Cotto	.15	.07
☐ 54 Jody Davis	.15	.07
☐ 55 Bob Dernier	.15	.07
☐ 56 Leon Durham	.15	.07
☐ 57 Dennis Eckersley	1.50	.70
☐ 58 George Frazier	.15	.07
☐ 59 Richie Hebner	.15	.07
☐ 60 Dave Lopes	.40	.18
☐ 61 Gary Matthews	.15	.07
☐ 62 Keith Moreland	.15	.07
☐ 63 Rick Reuschel	.15	.07
☐ 64 Dick Ruthven	.15	.07
☐ 65 Ryne Sandberg	3.00	1.35
☐ 66 Scott Sanderson	.15	.07
☐ 67 Lee Smith	.75	.35
☐ 68 Tim Stoddard	.15	.07
☐ 69 Rick Sutcliffe	.15	.07
☐ 70 Steve Trout	.15	.07
☐ 71 Gary Woods	.15	.07
☐ 72 Wally Backman	.15	.07
☐ 73 Bruce Berenyi	.15	.07
☐ 74 Hubie Brooks UER (Kelvin Chapman's stats on card back)	.15	.07
☐ 75 Kelvin Chapman	.15	.07
☐ 76 Ron Darling	.40	.18
☐ 77 Sid Fernandez	.40	.18
☐ 78 Mike Fitzgerald	.15	.07
☐ 79 George Foster	.40	.18
☐ 80 Brent Gaff	.15	.07
☐ 81 Ron Gardenhire	.15	.07
☐ 82 Dwight Gooden	4.00	1.80
☐ 83 Tom Gorman	.15	.07
☐ 84 Danny Heep	.15	.07
☐ 85 Keith Hernandez	.40	.18
☐ 86 Ray Knight	.40	.18
☐ 87 Ed Lynch	.15	.07
☐ 88 Jose Oquendo	.15	.07
☐ 89 Jesse Orosco	.15	.07
☐ 90 Rafael Santana	.15	.07
☐ 91 Doug Sisk	.15	.07
☐ 92 Rusty Staub	.40	.18
☐ 93 Darryl Strawberry	1.50	.70
☐ 94 Walt Terrell	.15	.07
☐ 95 Mookie Wilson	.40	.18
☐ 96 Jim Acker	.15	.07
☐ 97 Willie Aikens	.15	.07
☐ 98 Doyle Alexander	.15	.07
☐ 99 Jesse Barfield	.15	.07
☐ 100 George Bell	.40	.18
☐ 101 Jim Clancy	.15	.07
☐ 102 Dave Collins	.15	.07
☐ 103 Tony Fernandez	.40	.18
☐ 104 Damaso Garcia	.15	.07
☐ 105 Jim Gott	.15	.07
☐ 106 Alfredo Griffin	.15	.07
☐ 107 Garth Iorg	.15	.07
☐ 108 Roy Lee Jackson	.15	.07
☐ 109 Cliff Johnson	.15	.07
☐ 110 Jimmy Key	2.00	.90
☐ 111 Dennis Lamp	.15	.07
☐ 112 Rick Leach	.15	.07
☐ 113 Luis Leal	.15	.07
☐ 114 Buck Martinez	.15	.07
☐ 115 Lloyd Moseby	.15	.07
☐ 116 Rance Mulliniks	.15	.07
☐ 117 Dave Stieb	.40	.18
☐ 118 Willie Upshaw	.15	.07
☐ 119 Ernie Whitt	.15	.07
☐ 120 Mike Armstrong	.15	.07
☐ 121 Don Baylor	.75	.35
☐ 122 Marty Bystrom	.15	.07
☐ 123 Rick Cerone	.15	.07
☐ 124 Joe Cowley	.15	.07
☐ 125 Brian Dayett	.15	.07
☐ 126 Tim Foli	.15	.07
☐ 127 Ray Fontenot	.15	.07
☐ 128 Ken Griffey	.40	.18
☐ 129 Ron Guidry	.40	.18
☐ 130 Toby Harrah	.15	.07
☐ 131 Jay Howell	.15	.07
☐ 132 Steve Kemp	.15	.07
☐ 133 Don Mattingly	5.00	2.20
☐ 134 Bobby Meacham	.15	.07
☐ 135 John Montefusco	.15	.07
☐ 136 Omar Moreno	.15	.07
☐ 137 Dale Murray	.15	.07
☐ 138 Phil Niekro	.75	.35
☐ 139 Mike Pagliarulo	.15	.07
☐ 140 Willie Randolph	.40	.18
☐ 141 Dennis Rasmussen	.15	.07
☐ 142 Dave Righetti	.40	.18
☐ 143 Jose Rijo	1.50	.70
☐ 144 Andre Robertson	.15	.07
☐ 145 Bob Shirley	.15	.07
☐ 146 Dave Winfield	1.50	.70
☐ 147 Butch Wynegar	.15	.07
☐ 148 Gary Allenson	.15	.07
☐ 149 Tony Armas	.15	.07
☐ 150 Marty Barrett	.15	.07
☐ 151 Wade Boggs	2.00	.90
☐ 152 Dennis Boyd	.15	.07
☐ 153 Bill Buckner	.40	.18
☐ 154 Mark Clear	.15	.07
☐ 155 Roger Clemens	25.00	11.00
☐ 156 Steve Crawford	.15	.07
☐ 157 Mike Easler	.15	.07
☐ 158 Dwight Evans	.40	.18
☐ 159 Rich Gedman	.15	.07
☐ 160 Jackie Gutierrez (Wade Boggs shown on deck)	.40	.18
☐ 161 Bruce Hurst	.15	.07
☐ 162 John Henry Johnson	.15	.07
☐ 163 Rick Miller	.15	.07

☐ 164 Reid Nichols	.15	.07
☐ 165 Al Nipper	.15	.07
☐ 166 Bob Ojeda	.15	.07
☐ 167 Jerry Remy	.15	.07
☐ 168 Jim Rice	.40	.18
☐ 169 Bob Stanley	.15	.07
☐ 170 Mike Boddicker	.15	.07
☐ 171 Al Bumbry	.15	.07
☐ 172 Todd Cruz	.15	.07
☐ 173 Rich Dauer	.15	.07
☐ 174 Storm Davis	.15	.07
☐ 175 Rick Dempsey	.15	.07
☐ 176 Jim Dwyer	.15	.07
☐ 177 Mike Flanagan	.15	.07
☐ 178 Dan Ford	.15	.07
☐ 179 Wayne Gross	.15	.07
☐ 180 John Lowenstein	.15	.07
☐ 181 Dennis Martinez	.40	.18
☐ 182 Tippy Martinez	.15	.07
☐ 183 Scott McGregor	.15	.07
☐ 184 Eddie Murray	2.50	1.10
☐ 185 Joe Nolan	.15	.07
☐ 186 Floyd Rayford	.15	.07
☐ 187 Cal Ripken	8.00	3.60
☐ 188 Gary Roenicke	.15	.07
☐ 189 Lenn Sakata	.15	.07
☐ 190 John Shelby	.15	.07
☐ 191 Ken Singleton	.15	.07
☐ 192 Sammy Stewart	.15	.07
☐ 193 Bill Swaggerty	.15	.07
☐ 194 Tom Underwood	.15	.07
☐ 195 Mike Young	.15	.07
☐ 196 Steve Balboni	.15	.07
☐ 197 Joe Beckwith	.15	.07
☐ 198 Bud Black	.15	.07
☐ 199 George Brett	3.00	1.35
☐ 200 Onix Concepcion	.15	.07
☐ 201 Mark Gubicza	.40	.18
☐ 202 Larry Gura	.15	.07
☐ 203 Mark Huismann	.15	.07
☐ 204 Dane Iorg	.15	.07
☐ 205 Danny Jackson	.15	.07
☐ 206 Charlie Leibrandt	.15	.07
☐ 207 Hal McRae	.40	.18
☐ 208 Darryl Motley	.15	.07
☐ 209 Jorge Orta	.15	.07
☐ 210 Greg Pryor	.15	.07
☐ 211 Dan Quisenberry	.40	.18
☐ 212 Bret Saberhagen	1.50	.70
☐ 213 Pat Sheridan	.15	.07
☐ 214 Don Slaught	.15	.07
☐ 215 U.L. Washington	.15	.07
☐ 216 John Wathan	.15	.07
☐ 217 Frank White	.40	.18
☐ 218 Willie Wilson	.15	.07
☐ 219 Neil Allen	.15	.07
☐ 220 Joaquin Andujar	.15	.07
☐ 221 Steve Braun	.15	.07
☐ 222 Danny Cox	.15	.07
☐ 223 Bob Forsch	.15	.07
☐ 224 David Green	.15	.07
☐ 225 George Hendrick	.15	.07
☐ 226 Tom Herr	.40	.18
☐ 227 Ricky Horton	.15	.07
☐ 228 Art Howe	.15	.07
☐ 229 Mike Jorgensen	.15	.07
☐ 230 Kurt Kepshire	.15	.07
☐ 231 Jeff Lahti	.15	.07
☐ 232 Tito Landrum	.15	.07
☐ 233 Dave LaPoint	.15	.07
☐ 234 Willie McGee	.40	.18
☐ 235 Tom Nieto	.15	.07
☐ 236 Terry Pendleton	1.50	.70
☐ 237 Darrell Porter	.15	.07
☐ 238 Dave Rucker	.15	.07
☐ 239 Lonnie Smith	.15	.07
☐ 240 Ozzie Smith	2.00	.90
☐ 241 Bruce Sutter	.40	.18
☐ 242 Andy Van Slyke UER (Bats Right, Throws Left)	.75	.35
☐ 243 Dave Von Ohlen	.15	.07
☐ 244 Larry Andersen	.15	.07
☐ 245 Bill Campbell	.15	.07
☐ 246 Steve Carlton	.75	.35
☐ 247 Tim Corcoran	.15	.07
☐ 248 Ivan DeJesus	.15	.07
☐ 249 John Denny	.15	.07
☐ 250 Bo Diaz	.15	.07
☐ 251 Greg Gross	.15	.07
☐ 252 Kevin Gross	.15	.07
☐ 253 Von Hayes	.15	.07
☐ 254 Al Holland	.15	.07
☐ 255 Charles Hudson	.15	.07
☐ 256 Jerry Koosman	.40	.18
☐ 257 Joe Lefebvre	.15	.07
☐ 258 Sixto Lezcano	.15	.07
☐ 259 Garry Maddox	.15	.07
☐ 260 Len Matuszek	.15	.07
☐ 261 Tug McGraw	.40	.18
☐ 262 Al Oliver	.40	.18
☐ 263 Shane Rawley	.15	.07
☐ 264 Juan Samuel	.15	.07
☐ 265 Mike Schmidt	2.00	.90
☐ 266 Jeff Stone	.15	.07
☐ 267 Ozzie Virgil	.15	.07
☐ 268 Glenn Wilson	.15	.07
☐ 269 John Wockenfuss	.15	.07
☐ 270 Darrell Brown	.15	.07
☐ 271 Tom Brunansky	.40	.18
☐ 272 Randy Bush	.15	.07
☐ 273 John Butcher	.15	.07
☐ 274 Bobby Castillo	.15	.07
☐ 275 Ron Davis	.15	.07
☐ 276 Dave Engle	.15	.07
☐ 277 Pete Filson	.15	.07
☐ 278 Gary Gaetti	.40	.18
☐ 279 Mickey Hatcher	.15	.07
☐ 280 Ed Hodge	.15	.07
☐ 281 Kent Hrbek	.40	.18
☐ 282 Houston Jimenez	.15	.07
☐ 283 Tim Laudner	.15	.07
☐ 284 Rick Lysander	.15	.07
☐ 285 Dave Meier	.15	.07
☐ 286 Kirby Puckett	25.00	11.00
☐ 287 Pat Putnam	.15	.07
☐ 288 Ken Schrom	.15	.07
☐ 289 Mike Smithson	.15	.07
☐ 290 Tim Teufel	.15	.07
☐ 291 Frank Viola	.40	.18
☐ 292 Ron Washington	.15	.07
☐ 293 Don Aase	.15	.07
☐ 294 Juan Beniquez	.15	.07
☐ 295 Bob Boone	.40	.18
☐ 296 Mike C. Brown	.15	.07
☐ 297 Rod Carew	1.50	.70
☐ 298 Doug Corbett	.15	.07
☐ 299 Doug DeCinces	.15	.07
☐ 300 Brian Downing	.15	.07
☐ 301 Ken Forsch	.15	.07
☐ 302 Bobby Grich	.40	.18
☐ 303 Reggie Jackson	2.00	.90
☐ 304 Tommy John	.75	.35
☐ 305 Curt Kaufman	.15	.07
☐ 306 Bruce Kison	.15	.07
☐ 307 Fred Lynn	.40	.18
☐ 308 Gary Pettis	.15	.07
☐ 309 Ron Romanick	.15	.07
☐ 310 Luis Sanchez	.15	.07
☐ 311 Dick Schofield	.15	.07
☐ 312 Daryl Sconiers	.15	.07
☐ 313 Jim Slaton	.15	.07
☐ 314 Derrel Thomas	.15	.07
☐ 315 Rob Wilfong	.15	.07
☐ 316 Mike Witt	.15	.07
☐ 317 Geoff Zahn	.15	.07
☐ 318 Len Barker	.15	.07
☐ 319 Steve Bedrosian	.15	.07
☐ 320 Bruce Benedict	.15	.07
☐ 321 Rick Camp	.15	.07
☐ 322 Chris Chambliss	.15	.07
☐ 323 Jeff Dedmon	.15	.07
☐ 324 Terry Forster	.15	.07
☐ 325 Gene Garber	.15	.07
☐ 326 Albert Hall	.15	.07
☐ 327 Terry Harper	.15	.07
☐ 328 Bob Horner	.15	.07
☐ 329 Glenn Hubbard	.15	.07
☐ 330 Randy Johnson	.15	.07
☐ 331 Brad Komminsk	.15	.07
☐ 332 Rick Mahler	.15	.07
☐ 333 Craig McMurtry	.15	.07
☐ 334 Donnie Moore	.15	.07
☐ 335 Dale Murphy	.75	.35
☐ 336 Ken Oberkfell	.15	.07
☐ 337 Pascual Perez	.15	.07
☐ 338 Gerald Perry	.15	.07
☐ 339 Rafael Ramirez	.15	.07
☐ 340 Jerry Royster	.15	.07
☐ 341 Alex Trevino	.15	.07
☐ 342 Claudell Washington	.15	.07
☐ 343 Alan Ashby	.15	.07
☐ 344 Mark Bailey	.15	.07
☐ 345 Kevin Bass	.15	.07
☐ 346 Enos Cabell	.15	.07
☐ 347 Jose Cruz	.40	.18
☐ 348 Bill Dawley	.15	.07
☐ 349 Frank DiPino	.15	.07
☐ 350 Bill Doran	.15	.07
☐ 351 Phil Garner	.15	.07
☐ 352 Bob Knepper	.15	.07
☐ 353 Mike LaCoss	.15	.07
☐ 354 Jerry Mumphrey	.15	.07
☐ 355 Joe Niekro	.15	.07
☐ 356 Terry Puhl	.15	.07
☐ 357 Craig Reynolds	.15	.07
☐ 358 Vern Ruhle	.15	.07
☐ 359 Nolan Ryan	8.00	3.60
☐ 360 Joe Sambito	.15	.07
☐ 361 Mike Scott	.15	.07
☐ 362 Dave Smith	.15	.07
☐ 363 Julio Solano	.15	.07
☐ 364 Dickie Thon	.15	.07
☐ 365 Denny Walling	.15	.07
☐ 366 Dave Anderson	.15	.07
☐ 367 Bob Bailor	.15	.07
☐ 368 Greg Brock	.15	.07
☐ 369 Carlos Diaz	.15	.07
☐ 370 Pedro Guerrero	.40	.18
☐ 371 Orel Hershiser	2.00	.90
☐ 372 Rick Honeycutt	.15	.07
☐ 373 Burt Hooton	.15	.07
☐ 374 Ken Howell	.15	.07
☐ 375 Ken Landreaux	.15	.07
☐ 376 Candy Maldonado	.15	.07
☐ 377 Mike Marshall	.15	.07
☐ 378 Tom Niedenfuer	.15	.07
☐ 379 Alejandro Pena	.15	.07
☐ 380 Jerry Reuss UER ("Home:" omitted)	.15	.07
☐ 381 R.J. Reynolds	.15	.07
☐ 382 German Rivera	.15	.07
☐ 383 Bill Russell	.15	.07
☐ 384 Steve Sax	.15	.07
☐ 385 Mike Scioscia	.15	.07
☐ 386 Franklin Stubbs	.15	.07
☐ 387 Fernando Valenzuela	.40	.18
☐ 388 Bob Welch	.15	.07
☐ 389 Terry Whitfield	.15	.07
☐ 390 Steve Yeager	.15	.07
☐ 391 Pat Zachry	.15	.07
☐ 392 Fred Breining	.15	.07
☐ 393 Gary Carter	1.50	.70
☐ 394 Andre Dawson	1.50	.70
☐ 395 Miguel Dilone	.15	.07
☐ 396 Dan Driessen	.15	.07
☐ 397 Doug Flynn	.15	.07
☐ 398 Terry Francona	.15	.07
☐ 399 Bill Gullickson	.15	.07
☐ 400 Bob James	.15	.07
☐ 401 Charlie Lea	.15	.07
☐ 402 Bryan Little	.15	.07
☐ 403 Gary Lucas	.15	.07
☐ 404 David Palmer	.15	.07
☐ 405 Tim Raines	.40	.18
☐ 406 Mike Ramsey	.15	.07
☐ 407 Jeff Reardon	.40	.18
☐ 408 Steve Rogers	.15	.07
☐ 409 Dan Schatzeder	.15	.07
☐ 410 Bryn Smith	.15	.07
☐ 411 Mike Stenhouse	.15	.07
☐ 412 Tim Wallach	.40	.18
☐ 413 Jim Wohlford	.15	.07
☐ 414 Bill Almon	.15	.07
☐ 415 Keith Atherton	.15	.07
☐ 416 Bruce Bochte	.15	.07
☐ 417 Tom Burgmeier	.15	.07
☐ 418 Ray Burris	.15	.07
☐ 419 Bill Caudill	.15	.07
☐ 420 Chris Codiroli	.15	.07
☐ 421 Tim Conroy	.15	.07
☐ 422 Mike Davis	.15	.07
☐ 423 Jim Essian	.15	.07
☐ 424 Mike Heath	.15	.07
☐ 425 Rickey Henderson	1.50	.70
☐ 426 Donnie Hill	.15	.07
☐ 427 Dave Kingman	.40	.18
☐ 428 Bill Krueger	.15	.07
☐ 429 Carney Lansford	.40	.18
☐ 430 Steve McCatty	.15	.07
☐ 431 Joe Morgan	1.50	.70
☐ 432 Dwayne Murphy	.15	.07
☐ 433 Tony Phillips	.40	.18
☐ 434 Lary Sorensen	.15	.07
☐ 435 Mike Warren	.15	.07
☐ 436 Curt Young	.15	.07
☐ 437 Luis Aponte	.15	.07
☐ 438 Chris Bando	.15	.07
☐ 439 Tony Bernazard	.15	.07
☐ 440 Bert Blyleven	.75	.35
☐ 441 Brett Butler	.40	.18
☐ 442 Ernie Camacho	.15	.07
☐ 443 Joe Carter	5.00	2.20
☐ 444 Carmelo Castillo	.15	.07
☐ 445 Jamie Easterly	.15	.07
☐ 446 Steve Farr	.40	.18
☐ 447 Mike Fischlin	.15	.07
☐ 448 Julio Franco	.40	.18
☐ 449 Mel Hall	.15	.07
☐ 450 Mike Hargrove	.40	.18
☐ 451 Neal Heaton	.15	.07

☐ 452 Brook Jacoby .15 .07
☐ 453 Mike Jeffcoat .15 .07
☐ 454 Don Schulze .15 .07
☐ 455 Roy Smith .15 .07
☐ 456 Pat Tabler .15 .07
☐ 457 Andre Thornton .15 .07
☐ 458 George Vukovich .15 .07
☐ 459 Tom Waddell .15 .07
☐ 460 Jerry Willard .15 .07
☐ 461 Dale Berra .15 .07
☐ 462 John Candelaria .15 .07
☐ 463 Jose DeLeon .15 .07
☐ 464 Doug Frobel .15 .07
☐ 465 Cecilio Guante .15 .07
☐ 466 Brian Harper .15 .07
☐ 467 Lee Lacy .15 .07
☐ 468 Bill Madlock .40 .18
☐ 469 Lee Mazzilli .15 .07
☐ 470 Larry McWilliams .15 .07
☐ 471 Jim Morrison .15 .07
☐ 472 Tony Pena .15 .07
☐ 473 Johnny Ray .15 .07
☐ 474 Rick Rhoden .15 .07
☐ 475 Don Robinson .15 .07
☐ 476 Rod Scurry .15 .07
☐ 477 Kent Tekulve .15 .07
☐ 478 Jason Thompson .15 .07
☐ 479 John Tudor .15 .07
☐ 480 Lee Tunnell .15 .07
☐ 481 Marvell Wynne .15 .07
☐ 482 Salome Barojas .15 .07
☐ 483 Dave Beard .15 .07
☐ 484 Jim Beattie .15 .07
☐ 485 Barry Bonnell .15 .07
☐ 486 Phil Bradley .40 .18
☐ 487 Al Cowens .15 .07
☐ 488 Alvin Davis .40 .18
☐ 489 Dave Henderson .15 .07
☐ 490 Steve Henderson .15 .07
☐ 491 Bob Kearney .15 .07
☐ 492 Mark Langston 1.25 .55
☐ 493 Larry Milbourne .15 .07
☐ 494 Paul Mirabella .15 .07
☐ 495 Mike Moore .15 .07
☐ 496 Edwin Nunez .15 .07
☐ 497 Spike Owen .15 .07
☐ 498 Jack Perconte .15 .07
☐ 499 Ken Phelps .15 .07
☐ 500 Jim Presley .40 .18
☐ 501 Mike Stanton .15 .07
☐ 502 Bob Stoddard .15 .07
☐ 503 Gorman Thomas .15 .07
☐ 504 Ed VandeBerg .15 .07
☐ 505 Matt Young .15 .07
☐ 506 Juan Agosto .15 .07
☐ 507 Harold Baines .75 .35
☐ 508 Floyd Bannister .15 .07
☐ 509 Britt Burns .15 .07
☐ 510 Julio Cruz .15 .07
☐ 511 Richard Dotson .15 .07
☐ 512 Jerry Dybzinski .15 .07
☐ 513 Carlton Fisk 1.50 .70
☐ 514 Scott Fletcher .15 .07
☐ 515 Jerry Hairston .15 .07
☐ 516 Marc Hill .15 .07
☐ 517 LaMarr Hoyt .15 .07
☐ 518 Ron Kittle .15 .07
☐ 519 Rudy Law .15 .07
☐ 520 Vance Law .15 .07
☐ 521 Greg Luzinski .40 .18
☐ 522 Gene Nelson .15 .07
☐ 523 Tom Paciorek .40 .18
☐ 524 Ron Reed .15 .07
☐ 525 Bert Roberge .15 .07
☐ 526 Tom Seaver 2.00 .90
☐ 527 Roy Smalley .15 .07
☐ 528 Dan Spillner .15 .07
☐ 529 Mike Squires .15 .07
☐ 530 Greg Walker .15 .07
☐ 531 Cesar Cedeno .40 .18
☐ 532 Dave Concepcion .40 .18
☐ 533 Eric Davis 2.00 .90
☐ 534 Nick Esasky .15 .07
☐ 535 Tom Foley .15 .07
☐ 536 John Franco UER 1.00 .45
(Koufax misspelled as Kofax on back)
☐ 537 Brad Gulden .15 .07
☐ 538 Tom Hume .15 .07
☐ 539 Wayne Krenchicki .15 .07
☐ 540 Andy McGaffigan .15 .07
☐ 541 Eddie Milner .15 .07
☐ 542 Ron Oester .15 .07
☐ 543 Bob Owchinko .15 .07
☐ 544 Dave Parker .40 .18
☐ 545 Frank Pastore .15 .07
☐ 546 Tony Perez .75 .35
☐ 547 Ted Power .15 .07
☐ 548 Joe Price .15 .07
☐ 549 Gary Redus .15 .07
☐ 550 Pete Rose 2.00 .90
☐ 551 Jeff Russell .40 .18
☐ 552 Mario Soto .15 .07
☐ 553 Jay Tibbs .15 .07
☐ 554 Duane Walker .15 .07
☐ 555 Alan Bannister .15 .07
☐ 556 Buddy Bell .40 .18
☐ 557 Danny Darwin .40 .18
☐ 558 Charlie Hough .40 .18
☐ 559 Bobby Jones .15 .07
☐ 560 Odell Jones .15 .07
☐ 561 Jeff Kunkel .15 .07
☐ 562 Mike Mason .15 .07
☐ 563 Pete O'Brien .15 .07
☐ 564 Larry Parrish .15 .07
☐ 565 Mickey Rivers .15 .07
☐ 566 Billy Sample .15 .07
☐ 567 Dave Schmidt .15 .07
☐ 568 Donnie Scott .15 .07
☐ 569 Dave Stewart .40 .18
☐ 570 Frank Tanana .15 .07
☐ 571 Wayne Tolleson .15 .07
☐ 572 Gary Ward .15 .07
☐ 573 Curtis Wilkerson .15 .07
☐ 574 George Wright .15 .07
☐ 575 Ned Yost .15 .07
☐ 576 Mark Brouhard .15 .07
☐ 577 Mike Caldwell .15 .07
☐ 578 Bobby Clark .15 .07
☐ 579 Jaime Cocanower .15 .07
☐ 580 Cecil Cooper .40 .18
☐ 581 Rollie Fingers .75 .35
☐ 582 Jim Gantner .15 .07
☐ 583 Moose Haas .15 .07
☐ 584 Dion James .15 .07
☐ 585 Pete Ladd .15 .07
☐ 586 Rick Manning .15 .07
☐ 587 Bob McClure .15 .07
☐ 588 Paul Molitor 2.00 .90
☐ 589 Charlie Moore .15 .07
☐ 590 Ben Oglivie .15 .07
☐ 591 Chuck Porter .15 .07
☐ 592 Randy Ready .15 .07
☐ 593 Ed Romero .15 .07
☐ 594 Bill Schroeder .15 .07
☐ 595 Ray Searage .15 .07
☐ 596 Ted Simmons .40 .18
☐ 597 Jim Sundberg .15 .07
☐ 598 Don Sutton .75 .35
☐ 599 Tom Tellmann .15 .07
☐ 600 Rick Waits .15 .07
☐ 601 Robin Yount 2.00 .90
☐ 602 Dusty Baker .40 .18
☐ 603 Bob Brenly .15 .07
☐ 604 Jack Clark .40 .18
☐ 605 Chili Davis .40 .18
☐ 606 Mark Davis .15 .07
☐ 607 Dan Gladden .40 .18
☐ 608 Atlee Hammaker .15 .07
☐ 609 Mike Krukow .15 .07
☐ 610 Duane Kuiper .15 .07
☐ 611 Bob Lacey .15 .07
☐ 612 Bill Laskey .15 .07
☐ 613 Gary Lavelle .15 .07
☐ 614 Johnnie LeMaster .15 .07
☐ 615 Jeff Leonard .15 .07
☐ 616 Randy Lerch .15 .07
☐ 617 Greg Minton .15 .07
☐ 618 Steve Nicosia .15 .07
☐ 619 Gene Richards .15 .07
☐ 620 Jeff D. Robinson .15 .07
☐ 621 Scot Thompson .15 .07
☐ 622 Manny Trillo .15 .07
☐ 623 Brad Wellman .15 .07
☐ 624 Frank Williams .15 .07
☐ 625 Joel Youngblood .15 .07
☐ 626 Cal Ripken IA 4.00 1.80
☐ 627 Mike Schmidt IA 1.50 .70
☐ 628 Giving The Signs .40 .18
Sparky Anderson
☐ 629 AL Pitcher's Nightmare 1.50 .70
Dave Winfield
Rickey Henderson
☐ 630 NL Pitcher's Nightmare 1.50 .70
Mike Schmidt
Ryne Sandberg
☐ 631 NL All-Stars .75 .35
Darryl Strawberry
Gary Carter
Steve Garvey
Ozzie Smith
☐ 632 A-S Winning Battery .75 .35
Gary Carter
Charlie Lea
☐ 633 NL Pennant Clinchers .75 .35
Steve Garvey
Rich Gossage
☐ 634 NL Rookie Phenoms 1.50 .70
Dwight Gooden
Juan Samuel
☐ 635 Toronto's Big Guns .15 .07
Willie Upshaw
☐ 636 Toronto's Big Guns .15 .07
Lloyd Moseby
☐ 637 HOLLAND: Al Holland .15 .07
☐ 638 TUNNELL: Lee Tunnell .15 .07
☐ 639 500th Homer 1.00 .45
Reggie Jackson
☐ 640 4000th Hit 1.25 .55
Pete Rose
☐ 641 Father and Son 4.00 1.80
Cal Ripken Jr.
Cal Ripken Sr.
☐ 642 Cubs: Division Champs .40 .18
☐ 643 Two Perfect Games .40 .18
and One No-Hitter:
Mike Witt
David Palmer
Jack Morris
☐ 644 Willie Lozado and .15 .07
Vic Mata
☐ 645 Kelly Gruber and .40 .18
Randy O'Neal
☐ 646 Jose Roman and .15 .07
Joel Skinner
☐ 647 Steve Kiefer and 1.50 .70
Danny Tartabull
☐ 648 Rob Deer and .20 .09
Alejandro Sanchez
☐ 649 Billy Hatcher and 1.50 .70
Shawon Dunston
☐ 650 Ron Robinson and .15 .07
Mike Bielecki
☐ 651 Zane Smith and .40 .18
Paul Zuvella
☐ 652 Joe Hesketh and .40 .18
Glenn Davis
☐ 653 John Russell and .15 .07
Steve Jeltz
☐ 654 CL: Tigers/Padres .15 .07
and Cubs/Mets
☐ 655 CL: Blue Jays/Yankees .15 .07
and Red Sox/Orioles
☐ 656 CL: Royals/Cardinals .15 .07
and Phillies/Twins
☐ 657 CL: Angels/Braves .15 .07
and Astros/Dodgers
☐ 658 CL: Expos/A's .15 .07
and Indians/Pirates
☐ 659 CL: Mariners/White Sox .15 .07
and Reds/Rangers
☐ 660 CL: Brewers/Giants .15 .07
and Special Cards

1985 Fleer Update

This 132-card standard-size update set was issued in factory set form exclusively through hobby dealers. Design is identical to the regular-issue 1985 Fleer cards except for the U prefixed card numbers on back. Cards are ordered alphabetically by the player's name. This set features the extended Rookie Cards of Vince Coleman, Darren Daulton, Mariano Duncan, Ozzie Guillen and Mickey Tettleton.

	NRMT	VG-E
COMP.FACT.SET (132)	12.00	5.50
COMMON CARD (1-132)	.15	.07

☐ 1 Don Aase .15 .07
☐ 2 Bill Almon .15 .07
☐ 3 Dusty Baker .40 .18
☐ 4 Dale Berra .15 .07
☐ 5 Karl Best .15 .07
☐ 6 Tim Birtsas .15 .07
☐ 7 Vida Blue .40 .18
☐ 8 Rich Bordi .15 .07

☐ 9 Daryl Boston .15 .07
☐ 10 Hubie Brooks .15 .07
☐ 11 Chris Brown .15 .07
☐ 12 Tom Browning .40 .18
☐ 13 Al Bumbry .15 .07
☐ 14 Tim Burke .15 .07
☐ 15 Ray Burris .15 .07
☐ 16 Jeff Burroughs .15 .07
☐ 17 Ivan Calderon .15 .07
☐ 18 Jeff Calhoun .15 .07
☐ 19 Bill Campbell .15 .07
☐ 20 Don Carman .15 .07
☐ 21 Gary Carter
☐ 22 Bobby Castillo .15 .07
☐ 23 Bill Caudill .15 .07
☐ 24 Rick Cerone .15 .07
☐ 25 Jack Clark .40 .18
☐ 26 Pat Clements .15 .07
☐ 27 Stewart Cliburn .15 .07
☐ 28 Vince Coleman .75 .35
☐ 29 Dave Collins .15 .07
☐ 30 Fritz Connally .15 .07
☐ 31 Henry Cotto .15 .07
☐ 32 Danny Darwin .15 .07
☐ 33 Darren Daulton 8.00 3.60
☐ 34 Jerry Davis .15 .07
☐ 35 Brian Dayett .15 .07
☐ 36 Ken Dixon .15 .07
☐ 37 Tommy Dunbar .15 .07
☐ 38 Mariano Duncan .75 .35
☐ 39 Bob Fallon .15 .07
☐ 40 Brian Fisher .15 .07
☐ 41 Mike Fitzgerald .15 .07
☐ 42 Ray Fontenot .15 .07
☐ 43 Greg Gagne .15 .07
☐ 44 Oscar Gamble .15 .07
☐ 45 Jim Gott .15 .07
☐ 46 David Green .15 .07
☐ 47 Alfredo Griffin .15 .07
☐ 48 Ozzie Guillen 1.50 .70
☐ 49 Toby Harrah .15 .07
☐ 50 Ron Hassey .15 .07
☐ 51 Rickey Henderson 1.00 .45
☐ 52 Steve Henderson .15 .07
☐ 53 George Hendrick .15 .07
☐ 54 Teddy Higuera .40 .18
☐ 55 Al Holland .15 .07
☐ 56 Burt Hooton .15 .07
☐ 57 Jay Howell .15 .07
☐ 58 LaMarr Hoyt .15 .07
☐ 59 Tim Hulett .15 .07
☐ 60 Bob James .15 .07
☐ 61 Cliff Johnson .15 .07
☐ 62 Howard Johnson .40 .18
☐ 63 Ruppert Jones .15 .07
☐ 64 Steve Kemp .15 .07
☐ 65 Bruce Kison .15 .07
☐ 66 Mike LaCoss .15 .07
☐ 67 Lee Lacy .15 .07
☐ 68 Dave LaPoint .15 .07
☐ 69 Gary Lavelle .15 .07
☐ 70 Vance Law .15 .07
☐ 71 Manny Lee .15 .07
☐ 72 Sixto Lezcano .15 .07
☐ 73 Tim Lollar .15 .07
☐ 74 Urbano Lugo .15 .07
☐ 75 Fred Lynn .40 .18
☐ 76 Steve Lyons .40 .18
☐ 77 Mickey Mahler .15 .07
☐ 78 Ron Mathis .15 .07
☐ 79 Len Matuszek .15 .07
☐ 80 Oddibe McDowell UER .40 .18
(Part of bio
actually Roger's)
☐ 81 Roger McDowell UER .40 .18
(Part of bio
actually Oddibe's)
☐ 82 Donnie Moore .15 .07
☐ 83 Ron Musselman .15 .07
☐ 84 Al Oliver .40 .18
☐ 85 Joe Orsulak .40 .18
☐ 86 Dan Pasqua .40 .18
☐ 87 Chris Pittaro .15 .07
☐ 88 Rick Reuschel .15 .07
☐ 89 Earnie Riles .15 .07
☐ 90 Jerry Royster .15 .07
☐ 91 Dave Rozema .15 .07
☐ 92 Dave Rucker .15 .07
☐ 93 Vern Ruhle .15 .07
☐ 94 Mark Salas .15 .07
☐ 95 Luis Salazar .15 .07
☐ 96 Joe Sambito .15 .07
☐ 97 Billy Sample .15 .07
☐ 98 Alejandro Sanchez .15 .07
☐ 99 Calvin Schiraldi .15 .07
☐ 100 Rick Schu .15 .07
☐ 101 Larry Sheets .15 .07
☐ 102 Ron Shephard .15 .07
☐ 103 Nelson Simmons .15 .07
☐ 104 Don Slaught .15 .07
☐ 105 Roy Smalley .15 .07
☐ 106 Lonnie Smith .15 .07
☐ 107 Nate Snell .15 .07
☐ 108 Lary Sorensen .15 .07
☐ 109 Chris Speier .15 .07
☐ 110 Mike Stenhouse .15 .07
☐ 111 Tim Stoddard .15 .07
☐ 112 John Stuper .15 .07
☐ 113 Jim Sundberg .15 .07
☐ 114 Bruce Sutter .40 .18
☐ 115 Don Sutton
☐ 116 Bruce Tanner .15 .07
☐ 117 Kent Tekulve .15 .07
☐ 118 Walt Terrell .15 .07
☐ 119 Mickey Tettleton 1.50 .70
☐ 120 Rich Thompson .15 .07
☐ 121 Louis Thornton .15 .07
☐ 122 Alex Trevino .15 .07
☐ 123 John Tudor .15 .07
☐ 124 Jose Uribe .15 .07
☐ 125 Dave Valle .15 .07
☐ 126 Dave Von Ohlen .15 .07
☐ 127 Curt Wardle .15 .07
☐ 128 U.L. Washington .15 .07
☐ 129 Ed Whitson .15 .07
☐ 130 Herm Winningham .15 .07
☐ 131 Rich Yett .15 .07
☐ 132 Checklist U1-U132 .15 .07

1985 Fleer Limited Edition

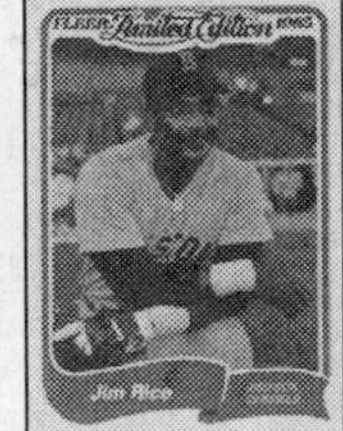

This 44-card set features standard size cards which were distributed in a colorful box as a complete set. The back of the box gives a complete checklist of the cards in the set. The cards are ordered alphabetically by the player's name. Backs of the cards are yellow and white whereas the fronts show a picture of the player inside a red banner-type border.

	NRMT	VG-E
COMPLETE SET (44)	6.00	2.70
COMMON CARD (1-44)	.05	.02

☐ 1 Buddy Bell .05 .02
☐ 2 Bert Blyleven .10 .05
☐ 3 Wade Boggs .40 .18
☐ 4 George Brett 1.25 .55
☐ 5 Rod Carew .25 .11
☐ 6 Steve Carlton .25 .11
☐ 7 Alvin Davis .05 .02
☐ 8 Andre Dawson .25 .11
☐ 9 Steve Garvey .15 .07
☐ 10 Rich Gossage .10 .05
☐ 11 Tony Gwynn 1.25 .55
☐ 12 Keith Hernandez .10 .05
☐ 13 Kent Hrbek .10 .05
☐ 14 Reggie Jackson .50 .23
☐ 15 Dave Kingman .10 .05
☐ 16 Ron Kittle .05 .02
☐ 17 Mark Langston .15 .07
☐ 18 Jeff Leonard .05 .02
☐ 19 Bill Madlock .05 .02
☐ 20 Don Mattingly 1.50 .70
☐ 21 Jack Morris .10 .05
☐ 22 Dale Murphy .25 .11
☐ 23 Eddie Murray .50 .23
☐ 24 Tony Pena .05 .02
☐ 25 Dan Quisenberry .05 .02
☐ 26 Tim Raines .10 .05
☐ 27 Jim Rice .10 .05
☐ 28 Cal Ripken 2.50 1.10
☐ 29 Pete Rose .75 .35
☐ 30 Nolan Ryan 2.50 1.10
☐ 31 Ryne Sandberg 1.00 .45
☐ 32 Steve Sax .05 .02
☐ 33 Mike Schmidt .50 .23
☐ 34 Tom Seaver .40 .18
☐ 35 Ozzie Smith 1.00 .45
☐ 36 Mario Soto .05 .02
☐ 37 Dave Stieb .05 .02
☐ 38 Darryl Strawberry .30 .14
☐ 39 Rick Sutcliffe .05 .02
☐ 40 Alan Trammell .15 .07
☐ 41 Willie Upshaw .05 .02
☐ 42 Fernando Valenzuela .10 .05
☐ 43 Dave Winfield .30 .14
☐ 44 Robin Yount .25 .11

1985 Fleer Star Stickers

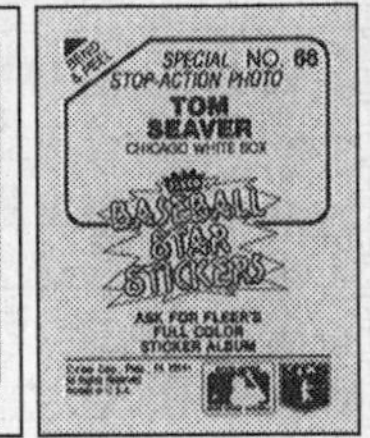

The stickers in this 126-sticker set measure approximately 1 15/16" by 2 1/2". The 1985 Fleer stickers set can be housed in a Fleer sticker album. Stickers are numbered on the fronts. A distinctive feature of the set is the inclusion of stop-action (designated SA in the checklist below) photos on cards 62 through 79. These photos are actually a series of six consecutive stickers which depict a player in action through the course of an activity; e.g., Eddie Murray's swing, Tom Seaver's wind-up and Mike Schmidt fielding. The backs of these stickers are blue and similar in design to past years.

	NRMT	VG-E
COMPLETE SET (126)	50.00	22.00
COMMON STICKER (1-126)	.10	.05

☐ 1 Pete Rose 3.00 1.35
☐ 2 Pete Rose 3.00 1.35
☐ 3 Pete Rose 3.00 1.35
☐ 4 Don Mattingly 7.50 3.40
☐ 5 Dave Winfield 1.25 .55
☐ 6 Wade Boggs 2.50 1.10
☐ 7 Buddy Bell .20 .09
☐ 8 Tony Gwynn 6.00 2.70
☐ 9 Lee Lacy .10 .05
☐ 10 Chili Davis .20 .09
☐ 11 Ryne Sandberg 4.00 1.80
☐ 12 Tony Armas .10 .05
☐ 13 Jim Rice .20 .09
☐ 14 Dave Kingman .20 .09
☐ 15 Alvin Davis .20 .09
☐ 16 Gary Carter .35 .16
☐ 17 Mike Schmidt 2.50 1.10
☐ 18 Dale Murphy .50 .23
☐ 19 Ron Cey .20 .09
☐ 20 Eddie Murray 1.50 .70
☐ 21 Harold Baines .20 .09
☐ 22 Kirk Gibson .20 .09
☐ 23 Jim Rice .20 .09
☐ 24 Gary Matthews .10 .05
☐ 25 Keith Hernandez .20 .09
☐ 26 Gary Carter .35 .16
☐ 27 George Hendrick .10 .05
☐ 28 Tony Armas .10 .05
☐ 29 Dave Kingman .20 .09
☐ 30 Dwayne Murphy .10 .05
☐ 31 Lance Parrish .20 .09
☐ 32 Andre Thornton .10 .05
☐ 33 Dale Murphy .50 .23
☐ 34 Mike Schmidt 2.50 1.10
☐ 35 Gary Carter .35 .16
☐ 36 Darryl Strawberry .60 .25
☐ 37 Don Mattingly 7.50 3.40
☐ 38 Larry Parrish .10 .05
☐ 39 George Bell .20 .09
☐ 40 Dwight Evans .20 .09
☐ 41 Cal Ripken 7.50 3.40
☐ 42 Tim Raines .20 .09
☐ 43 Johnny Ray .10 .05
☐ 44 Juan Samuel .10 .05
☐ 45 Ryne Sandberg 4.00 1.80
☐ 46 Mike Easler .10 .05
☐ 47 Andre Thornton .10 .05
☐ 48 Dave Kingman .20 .09
☐ 49 Don Baylor .20 .09
☐ 50 Rusty Staub .20 .09
☐ 51 Steve Braun .10 .05
☐ 52 Kevin Bass .10 .05
☐ 53 Greg Gross .10 .05
☐ 54 Rickey Henderson 1.25 .55
☐ 55 Dave Collins .10 .05
☐ 56 Brett Butler .20 .09

57 Gary Pettis	.10	.05
58 Tim Raines	.20	.09
59 Juan Samuel	.10	.05
60 Alan Wiggins	.10	.05
61 Lonnie Smith	.10	.05
62 Eddie Murray SA	.75	.35
63 Eddie Murray SA	.75	.35
64 Eddie Murray SA	.75	.35
65 Eddie Murray SA	.75	.35
66 Eddie Murray SA	.75	.35
67 Eddie Murray SA	.75	.35
68 Tom Seaver SA	1.00	.45
69 Tom Seaver SA	1.00	.45
70 Tom Seaver SA	1.00	.45
71 Tom Seaver SA	1.00	.45
72 Tom Seaver SA	1.00	.45
73 Tom Seaver SA	1.00	.45
74 Mike Schmidt SA	1.25	.55
75 Mike Schmidt SA	1.25	.55
76 Mike Schmidt SA	1.25	.55
77 Mike Schmidt SA	1.25	.55
78 Mike Schmidt SA	1.25	.55
79 Mike Schmidt SA	1.25	.55
80 Mike Boddicker	.10	.05
81 Bert Blyleven	.20	.09
82 Jack Morris	.20	.09
83 Dan Petry	.10	.05
84 Frank Viola	.20	.09
85 Joaquin Andujar	.10	.05
86 Mario Soto	.10	.05
87 Dwight Gooden	2.50	1.10
88 Joe Niekro	.10	.05
89 Rick Sutcliffe	.10	.05
90 Mike Boddicker	.10	.05
91 Dave Stieb	.10	.05
92 Bert Blyleven	.20	.09
93 Phil Niekro	.60	.25
94 Alejandro Pena	.10	.05
95 Dwight Gooden	2.50	1.10
96 Orel Hershiser	2.50	1.10
97 Rick Rhoden	.10	.05
98 John Candelaria	.10	.05
99 Dan Quisenberry	.10	.05
100 Bill Caudill	.10	.05
101 Willie Hernandez	.10	.05
102 Dave Righetti	.20	.09
103 Ron Davis	.10	.05
104 Bruce Sutter	.20	.09
105 Lee Smith	.35	.16
106 Jesse Orosco	.10	.05
107 Al Holland	.10	.05
108 Goose Gossage	.20	.09
109 Mark Langston	.75	.35
110 Dave Stieb	.10	.05
111 Mike Witt	.10	.05
112 Bert Blyleven	.20	.09
113 Dwight Gooden	2.50	1.10
114 Fernando Valenzuela	.20	.09
115 Nolan Ryan	7.50	3.40
116 Mario Soto	.10	.05
117 Ron Darling	.20	.09
118 Dan Gladden	.10	.05
119 Jeff Stone	.10	.05
120 John Franco	.75	.35
121 Barbaro Garbey	.10	.05
122 Kirby Puckett	10.00	4.50
123 Roger Clemens	10.00	4.50
124 Bret Saberhagen	.75	.35
125 Sparky Anderson MG	.35	.16
126 Dick Williams MG	.10	.05

1986 Fleer

ne 1986 Fleer set consists of 660-card standard-size ards. Wax packs included 15 cards plus logo stickers. ard fronts feature dark blue borders, a team logo along ith the player's name and position. The player cards are phabetized within team and the teams are ordered by eir 1985 season finish and won-lost record. Subsets clude Specials (626-643) and Major League Prospects 544-653). The Dennis and Tippy Martinez cards were pparently switched in the set numbering, as their adjacent numbers (279 and 280) were reversed on the Orioles checklist card. The set includes the Rookie Cards of Rick Aguilera, Jose Canseco, Darren Daulton, Len Dykstra, Cecil Fielder, Andres Galarraga, Paul O'Neill,and Mickey Tettleton.

	MINT	NRMT
COMPLETE SET (660)	40.00	18.00
COMP.FACT.SET (660)	50.00	22.00
COMMON CARD (1-660)	.10	.05

☐ 1 Steve Balboni	.10	.05
☐ 2 Joe Beckwith	.10	.05
☐ 3 Buddy Biancalana	.10	.05
☐ 4 Bud Black	.10	.05
☐ 5 George Brett	2.00	.90
☐ 6 Onix Concepcion	.10	.05
☐ 7 Steve Farr	.10	.05
☐ 8 Mark Gubicza	.10	.05
☐ 9 Dane Iorg	.10	.05
☐ 10 Danny Jackson	.10	.05
☐ 11 Lynn Jones	.10	.05
☐ 12 Mike Jones	.10	.05
☐ 13 Charlie Leibrandt	.10	.05
☐ 14 Hal McRae	.25	.11
☐ 15 Omar Moreno	.10	.05
☐ 16 Darryl Motley	.10	.05
☐ 17 Jorge Orta	.10	.05
☐ 18 Dan Quisenberry	.10	.05
☐ 19 Bret Saberhagen	.25	.11
☐ 20 Pat Sheridan	.10	.05
☐ 21 Lonnie Smith	.10	.05
☐ 22 Jim Sundberg	.10	.05
☐ 23 John Wathan	.10	.05
☐ 24 Frank White	.25	.11
☐ 25 Willie Wilson	.10	.05
☐ 26 Joaquin Andujar	.10	.05
☐ 27 Steve Braun	.10	.05
☐ 28 Bill Campbell	.10	.05
☐ 29 Cesar Cedeno	.25	.11
☐ 30 Jack Clark	.25	.11
☐ 31 Vince Coleman	.50	.23
☐ 32 Danny Cox	.10	.05
☐ 33 Ken Dayley	.10	.05
☐ 34 Ivan DeJesus	.10	.05
☐ 35 Bob Forsch	.10	.05
☐ 36 Brian Harper	.10	.05
☐ 37 Tom Herr	.10	.05
☐ 38 Ricky Horton	.10	.05
☐ 39 Kurt Kepshire	.10	.05
☐ 40 Jeff Lahti	.10	.05
☐ 41 Tito Landrum	.10	.05
☐ 42 Willie McGee	.25	.11
☐ 43 Tom Nieto	.10	.05
☐ 44 Terry Pendleton	.25	.11
☐ 45 Darrell Porter	.25	.11
☐ 46 Ozzie Smith	1.25	.55
☐ 47 John Tudor	.10	.05
☐ 48 Andy Van Slyke	.25	.11
☐ 49 Todd Worrell	.25	.11
☐ 50 Jim Acker	.10	.05
☐ 51 Doyle Alexander	.10	.05
☐ 52 Jesse Barfield	.10	.05
☐ 53 George Bell	.25	.11
☐ 54 Jeff Burroughs	.10	.05
☐ 55 Bill Caudill	.10	.05
☐ 56 Jim Clancy	.10	.05
☐ 57 Tony Fernandez	.10	.05
☐ 58 Tom Filer	.10	.05
☐ 59 Damaso Garcia	.10	.05
☐ 60 Tom Henke	.25	.11
☐ 61 Garth Iorg	.10	.05
☐ 62 Cliff Johnson	.10	.05
☐ 63 Jimmy Key	1.00	.45
☐ 64 Dennis Lamp	.10	.05
☐ 65 Gary Lavelle	.10	.05
☐ 66 Buck Martinez	.10	.05
☐ 67 Lloyd Moseby	.10	.05
☐ 68 Rance Mulliniks	.10	.05
☐ 69 Al Oliver	.25	.11
☐ 70 Dave Stieb	.10	.05
☐ 71 Louis Thornton	.10	.05
☐ 72 Willie Upshaw	.10	.05
☐ 73 Ernie Whitt	.10	.05
☐ 74 Rick Aguilera	1.00	.45
☐ 75 Wally Backman	.10	.05
☐ 76 Gary Carter	1.00	.45
☐ 77 Ron Darling	.10	.05
☐ 78 Len Dykstra	2.00	.90
☐ 79 Sid Fernandez	.25	.11
☐ 80 George Foster	.25	.11
☐ 81 Dwight Gooden	1.00	.45
☐ 82 Tom Gorman	.10	.05
☐ 83 Danny Heep	.10	.05
☐ 84 Keith Hernandez	.25	.11
☐ 85 Howard Johnson	.25	.11
☐ 86 Ray Knight	.25	.11
☐ 87 Terry Leach	.10	.05
☐ 88 Ed Lynch	.10	.05
☐ 89 Roger McDowell	.25	.11
☐ 90 Jesse Orosco	.10	.05
☐ 91 Tom Paciorek	.25	.11
☐ 92 Ronn Reynolds	.10	.05
☐ 93 Rafael Santana	.10	.05
☐ 94 Doug Sisk	.10	.05
☐ 95 Rusty Staub	.25	.11
☐ 96 Darryl Strawberry	1.00	.45
☐ 97 Mookie Wilson	.25	.11
☐ 98 Neil Allen	.10	.05
☐ 99 Don Baylor	.50	.23
☐ 100 Dale Berra	.10	.05
☐ 101 Rich Bordi	.10	.05
☐ 102 Marty Bystrom	.10	.05
☐ 103 Joe Cowley	.10	.05
☐ 104 Brian Fisher	.10	.05
☐ 105 Ken Griffey	.25	.11
☐ 106 Ron Guidry	.25	.11
☐ 107 Ron Hassey	.10	.05
☐ 108 Rickey Henderson UER (SB Record of 120, sic)	1.00	.45
☐ 109 Don Mattingly	1.50	.70
☐ 110 Bobby Meacham	.10	.05
☐ 111 John Montefusco	.10	.05
☐ 112 Phil Niekro	1.00	.45
☐ 113 Mike Pagliarulo	.10	.05
☐ 114 Dan Pasqua	.10	.05
☐ 115 Willie Randolph	.25	.11
☐ 116 Dave Righetti	.10	.05
☐ 117 Andre Robertson	.10	.05
☐ 118 Billy Sample	.10	.05
☐ 119 Bob Shirley	.10	.05
☐ 120 Ed Whitson	.10	.05
☐ 121 Dave Winfield	1.00	.45
☐ 122 Butch Wynegar	.10	.05
☐ 123 Dave Anderson	.10	.05
☐ 124 Bob Bailor	.10	.05
☐ 125 Greg Brock	.10	.05
☐ 126 Enos Cabell	.10	.05
☐ 127 Bobby Castillo	.10	.05
☐ 128 Carlos Diaz	.10	.05
☐ 129 Mariano Duncan	1.00	.45
☐ 130 Pedro Guerrero	.25	.11
☐ 131 Orel Hershiser	1.00	.45
☐ 132 Rick Honeycutt	.10	.05
☐ 133 Ken Howell	.10	.05
☐ 134 Ken Landreaux	.10	.05
☐ 135 Bill Madlock	.10	.05
☐ 136 Candy Maldonado	.10	.05
☐ 137 Mike Marshall	.10	.05
☐ 138 Len Matuszek	.10	.05
☐ 139 Tom Niedenfuer	.10	.05
☐ 140 Alejandro Pena	.10	.05
☐ 141 Jerry Reuss	.10	.05
☐ 142 Bill Russell	.25	.11
☐ 143 Steve Sax	.10	.05
☐ 144 Mike Scioscia	.10	.05
☐ 145 Fernando Valenzuela	.25	.11
☐ 146 Bob Welch	.10	.05
☐ 147 Terry Whitfield	.10	.05
☐ 148 Juan Beniquez	.10	.05
☐ 149 Bob Boone	.25	.11
☐ 150 John Candelaria	.10	.05
☐ 151 Rod Carew	1.00	.45
☐ 152 Stewart Cliburn	.10	.05
☐ 153 Doug DeCinces	.10	.05
☐ 154 Brian Downing	.10	.05
☐ 155 Ken Forsch	.10	.05
☐ 156 Craig Gerber	.10	.05
☐ 157 Bobby Grich	.25	.11
☐ 158 George Hendrick	.10	.05
☐ 159 Al Holland	.10	.05
☐ 160 Reggie Jackson	1.25	.55
☐ 161 Ruppert Jones	.10	.05
☐ 162 Urbano Lugo	.10	.05
☐ 163 Kirk McCaskill	.25	.11
☐ 164 Donnie Moore	.10	.05
☐ 165 Gary Pettis	.10	.05
☐ 166 Ron Romanick	.10	.05
☐ 167 Dick Schofield	.10	.05
☐ 168 Daryl Sconiers	.10	.05
☐ 169 Jim Slaton	.10	.05
☐ 170 Don Sutton	1.00	.45
☐ 171 Mike Witt	.10	.05
☐ 172 Buddy Bell	.25	.11
☐ 173 Tom Browning	.10	.05
☐ 174 Dave Concepcion	.25	.11
☐ 175 Eric Davis	.50	.23
☐ 176 Bo Diaz	.10	.05
☐ 177 Nick Esasky	.10	.05
☐ 178 John Franco	.50	.23
☐ 179 Tom Hume	.10	.05
☐ 180 Wayne Krenchicki	.10	.05
☐ 181 Andy McGaffigan	.10	.05
☐ 182 Eddie Milner	.10	.05
☐ 183 Ron Oester	.10	.05

☐ 184 Dave Parker	.25	.11
☐ 185 Frank Pastore	.10	.05
☐ 186 Tony Perez	1.00	.45
☐ 187 Ted Power	.10	.05
☐ 188 Joe Price	.10	.05
☐ 189 Gary Redus	.10	.05
☐ 190 Ron Robinson	.10	.05
☐ 191 Pete Rose	1.25	.55
☐ 192 Mario Soto	.10	.05
☐ 193 John Stuper	.10	.05
☐ 194 Jay Tibbs	.10	.05
☐ 195 Dave Van Gorder	.10	.05
☐ 196 Max Venable	.10	.05
☐ 197 Juan Agosto	.10	.05
☐ 198 Harold Baines	.50	.23
☐ 199 Floyd Bannister	.10	.05
☐ 200 Britt Burns	.10	.05
☐ 201 Julio Cruz	.10	.05
☐ 202 Joel Davis	.10	.05
☐ 203 Richard Dotson	.10	.05
☐ 204 Carlton Fisk	1.00	.45
☐ 205 Scott Fletcher	.10	.05
☐ 206 Ozzie Guillen	.50	.23
☐ 207 Jerry Hairston	.10	.05
☐ 208 Tim Hulett	.10	.05
☐ 209 Bob James	.10	.05
☐ 210 Ron Kittle	.10	.05
☐ 211 Rudy Law	.10	.05
☐ 212 Bryan Little	.10	.05
☐ 213 Gene Nelson	.10	.05
☐ 214 Reid Nichols	.10	.05
☐ 215 Luis Salazar	.10	.05
☐ 216 Tom Seaver	1.25	.55
☐ 217 Dan Spillner	.10	.05
☐ 218 Bruce Tanner	.10	.05
☐ 219 Greg Walker	.10	.05
☐ 220 Dave Wehrmeister	.10	.05
☐ 221 Juan Berenguer	.10	.05
☐ 222 Dave Bergman	.10	.05
☐ 223 Tom Brookens	.10	.05
☐ 224 Darrell Evans	.25	.11
☐ 225 Barbaro Garbey	.10	.05
☐ 226 Kirk Gibson	.25	.11
☐ 227 John Grubb	.10	.05
☐ 228 Willie Hernandez	.10	.05
☐ 229 Larry Herndon	.10	.05
☐ 230 Chet Lemon	.10	.05
☐ 231 Aurelio Lopez	.10	.05
☐ 232 Jack Morris	.25	.11
☐ 233 Randy O'Neal	.10	.05
☐ 234 Lance Parrish	.25	.11
☐ 235 Dan Petry	.10	.05
☐ 236 Alejandro Sanchez	.10	.05
☐ 237 Bill Scherrer	.10	.05
☐ 238 Nelson Simmons	.10	.05
☐ 239 Frank Tanana	.10	.05
☐ 240 Walt Terrell	.10	.05
☐ 241 Alan Trammell	.50	.23
☐ 242 Lou Whitaker	.25	.11
☐ 243 Milt Wilcox	.10	.05
☐ 244 Hubie Brooks	.10	.05
☐ 245 Tim Burke	.10	.05
☐ 246 Andre Dawson	1.00	.45
☐ 247 Mike Fitzgerald	.10	.05
☐ 248 Terry Francona	.10	.05
☐ 249 Bill Gullickson	.10	.05
☐ 250 Joe Hesketh	.10	.05
☐ 251 Bill Laskey	.10	.05
☐ 252 Vance Law	.10	.05
☐ 253 Charlie Lea	.10	.05
☐ 254 Gary Lucas	.10	.05
☐ 255 David Palmer	.10	.05
☐ 256 Tim Raines	.25	.11
☐ 257 Jeff Reardon	.25	.11
☐ 258 Bert Roberge	.10	.05
☐ 259 Dan Schatzeder	.10	.05
☐ 260 Bryn Smith	.10	.05
☐ 261 Randy St.Claire	.10	.05
☐ 262 Scot Thompson	.10	.05
☐ 263 Tim Wallach	.10	.05
☐ 264 U.L. Washington	.10	.05
☐ 265 Mitch Webster	.10	.05
☐ 266 Herm Winningham	.10	.05
☐ 267 Floyd Youmans	.10	.05
☐ 268 Don Aase	.10	.05
☐ 269 Mike Boddicker	.10	.05
☐ 270 Rich Dauer	.10	.05
☐ 271 Storm Davis	.10	.05
☐ 272 Rick Dempsey	.10	.05
☐ 273 Ken Dixon	.10	.05
☐ 274 Jim Dwyer	.10	.05
☐ 275 Mike Flanagan	.10	.05
☐ 276 Wayne Gross	.10	.05
☐ 277 Lee Lacy	.10	.05
☐ 278 Fred Lynn	.25	.11
☐ 279 Tippy Martinez	.10	.05
☐ 280 Dennis Martinez	.25	.11
☐ 281 Scott McGregor	.10	.05
☐ 282 Eddie Murray	1.25	.55
☐ 283 Floyd Rayford	.10	.05
☐ 284 Cal Ripken	4.00	1.80
☐ 285 Gary Roenicke	.10	.05
☐ 286 Larry Sheets	.10	.05
☐ 287 John Shelby	.10	.05
☐ 288 Nate Snell	.10	.05
☐ 289 Sammy Stewart	.10	.05
☐ 290 Alan Wiggins	.10	.05
☐ 291 Mike Young	.10	.05
☐ 292 Alan Ashby	.10	.05
☐ 293 Mark Bailey	.10	.05
☐ 294 Kevin Bass	.10	.05
☐ 295 Jeff Calhoun	.10	.05
☐ 296 Jose Cruz	.10	.05
☐ 297 Glenn Davis	.25	.11
☐ 298 Bill Dawley	.10	.05
☐ 299 Frank DiPino	.10	.05
☐ 300 Bill Doran	.10	.05
☐ 301 Phil Garner	.10	.05
☐ 302 Jeff Heathcock	.10	.05
☐ 303 Charlie Kerfeld	.10	.05
☐ 304 Bob Knepper	.10	.05
☐ 305 Ron Mathis	.10	.05
☐ 306 Jerry Mumphrey	.10	.05
☐ 307 Jim Pankovits	.10	.05
☐ 308 Terry Puhl	.10	.05
☐ 309 Craig Reynolds	.10	.05
☐ 310 Nolan Ryan	4.00	1.80
☐ 311 Mike Scott	.10	.05
☐ 312 Dave Smith	.10	.05
☐ 313 Dickie Thon	.10	.05
☐ 314 Denny Walling	.10	.05
☐ 315 Kurt Bevacqua	.10	.05
☐ 316 Al Bumbry	.10	.05
☐ 317 Jerry Davis	.10	.05
☐ 318 Luis DeLeon	.10	.05
☐ 319 Dave Dravecky	.25	.11
☐ 320 Tim Flannery	.10	.05
☐ 321 Steve Garvey	.50	.23
☐ 322 Rich Gossage	.50	.23
☐ 323 Tony Gwynn	2.50	1.10
☐ 324 Andy Hawkins	.10	.05
☐ 325 LaMarr Hoyt	.10	.05
☐ 326 Roy Lee Jackson	.10	.05
☐ 327 Terry Kennedy	.10	.05
☐ 328 Craig Lefferts	.10	.05
☐ 329 Carmelo Martinez	.10	.05
☐ 330 Lance McCullers	.10	.05
☐ 331 Kevin McReynolds	.10	.05
☐ 332 Graig Nettles	.25	.11
☐ 333 Jerry Royster	.10	.05
☐ 334 Eric Show	.10	.05
☐ 335 Tim Stoddard	.10	.05
☐ 336 Garry Templeton	.10	.05
☐ 337 Mark Thurmond	.10	.05
☐ 338 Ed Wojna	.10	.05
☐ 339 Tony Armas	.10	.05
☐ 340 Marty Barrett	.10	.05
☐ 341 Wade Boggs	1.00	.45
☐ 342 Dennis Boyd	.10	.05
☐ 343 Bill Buckner	.25	.11
☐ 344 Mark Clear	.10	.05
☐ 345 Roger Clemens	4.00	1.80
☐ 346 Steve Crawford	.10	.05
☐ 347 Mike Easler	.10	.05
☐ 348 Dwight Evans	.25	.11
☐ 349 Rich Gedman	.10	.05
☐ 350 Jackie Gutierrez	.10	.05
☐ 351 Glenn Hoffman	.10	.05
☐ 352 Bruce Hurst	.10	.05
☐ 353 Bruce Kison	.10	.05
☐ 354 Tim Lollar	.10	.05
☐ 355 Steve Lyons	.10	.05
☐ 356 Al Nipper	.10	.05
☐ 357 Bob Ojeda	.10	.05
☐ 358 Jim Rice	.25	.11
☐ 359 Bob Stanley	.10	.05
☐ 360 Mike Trujillo	.10	.05
☐ 361 Thad Bosley	.10	.05
☐ 362 Warren Brusstar	.10	.05
☐ 363 Ron Cey	.25	.11
☐ 364 Jody Davis	.10	.05
☐ 365 Bob Dernier	.10	.05
☐ 366 Shawon Dunston	.10	.05
☐ 367 Leon Durham	.10	.05
☐ 368 Dennis Eckersley	1.00	.45
☐ 369 Ray Fontenot	.10	.05
☐ 370 George Frazier	.10	.05
☐ 371 Billy Hatcher	.10	.05
☐ 372 Dave Lopes	.25	.11
☐ 373 Gary Matthews	.10	.05
☐ 374 Ron Meridith	.10	.05
☐ 375 Keith Moreland	.10	.05
☐ 376 Reggie Patterson	.10	.05
☐ 377 Dick Ruthven	.10	.05
☐ 378 Ryne Sandberg	1.25	.55
☐ 379 Scott Sanderson	.10	.05
☐ 380 Lee Smith	.50	.23
☐ 381 Lary Sorensen	.10	.05
☐ 382 Chris Speier	.10	.05
☐ 383 Rick Sutcliffe	.10	.05
☐ 384 Steve Trout	.10	.05
☐ 385 Gary Woods	.10	.05
☐ 386 Bert Blyleven	.50	.23
☐ 387 Tom Brunansky	.10	.05
☐ 388 Randy Bush	.10	.05
☐ 389 John Butcher	.10	.05
☐ 390 Ron Davis	.10	.05
☐ 391 Dave Engle	.10	.05
☐ 392 Frank Eufemia	.10	.05
☐ 393 Pete Filson	.10	.05
☐ 394 Gary Gaetti	.25	.11
☐ 395 Greg Gagne	.10	.05
☐ 396 Mickey Hatcher	.10	.05
☐ 397 Kent Hrbek	.25	.11
☐ 398 Tim Laudner	.10	.05
☐ 399 Rick Lysander	.10	.05
☐ 400 Dave Meier	.10	.05
☐ 401 Kirby Puckett UER (Card has him in NL, should be AL)	4.00	1.80
☐ 402 Mark Salas	.10	.05
☐ 403 Ken Schrom	.10	.05
☐ 404 Roy Smalley	.10	.05
☐ 405 Mike Smithson	.10	.05
☐ 406 Mike Stenhouse	.10	.05
☐ 407 Tim Teufel	.10	.05
☐ 408 Frank Viola	.25	.11
☐ 409 Ron Washington	.10	.05
☐ 410 Keith Atherton	.10	.05
☐ 411 Dusty Baker	.25	.11
☐ 412 Tim Birtsas	.10	.05
☐ 413 Bruce Bochte	.10	.05
☐ 414 Chris Codiroli	.10	.05
☐ 415 Dave Collins	.10	.05
☐ 416 Mike Davis	.10	.05
☐ 417 Alfredo Griffin	.10	.05
☐ 418 Mike Heath	.10	.05
☐ 419 Steve Henderson	.10	.05
☐ 420 Donnie Hill	.10	.05
☐ 421 Jay Howell	.10	.05
☐ 422 Tommy John	.50	.23
☐ 423 Dave Kingman	.25	.11
☐ 424 Bill Krueger	.10	.05
☐ 425 Rick Langford	.10	.05
☐ 426 Carney Lansford	.25	.11
☐ 427 Steve McCatty	.10	.05
☐ 428 Dwayne Murphy	.10	.05
☐ 429 Steve Ontiveros	.25	.11
☐ 430 Tony Phillips	.10	.05
☐ 431 Jose Rijo	.10	.05
☐ 432 Mickey Tettleton	2.00	.90
☐ 433 Luis Aguayo	.10	.05
☐ 434 Larry Andersen	.10	.05
☐ 435 Steve Carlton	.50	.23
☐ 436 Don Carman	.10	.05
☐ 437 Tim Corcoran	.10	.05
☐ 438 Darren Daulton	2.00	.90
☐ 439 John Denny	.10	.05
☐ 440 Tom Foley	.10	.05
☐ 441 Greg Gross	.10	.05
☐ 442 Kevin Gross	.10	.05
☐ 443 Von Hayes	.10	.05
☐ 444 Charles Hudson	.10	.05
☐ 445 Garry Maddox	.10	.05
☐ 446 Shane Rawley	.10	.05
☐ 447 Dave Rucker	.10	.05
☐ 448 John Russell	.10	.05
☐ 449 Juan Samuel	.10	.05
☐ 450 Mike Schmidt	1.25	.55
☐ 451 Rick Schu	.10	.05
☐ 452 Dave Shipanoff	.10	.05
☐ 453 Dave Stewart	.25	.11
☐ 454 Jeff Stone	.10	.05
☐ 455 Kent Tekulve	.10	.05
☐ 456 Ozzie Virgil	.10	.05
☐ 457 Glenn Wilson	.10	.05
☐ 458 Jim Beattie	.10	.05
☐ 459 Karl Best	.10	.05
☐ 460 Barry Bonnell	.10	.05
☐ 461 Phil Bradley	.10	.05
☐ 462 Ivan Calderon	.25	.11
☐ 463 Al Cowens	.10	.05
☐ 464 Alvin Davis	.10	.05
☐ 465 Dave Henderson	.10	.05
☐ 466 Bob Kearney	.10	.05
☐ 467 Mark Langston	.10	.05
☐ 468 Bob Long	.10	.05
☐ 469 Mike Moore	.10	.05
☐ 470 Edwin Nunez	.10	.05
☐ 471 Spike Owen	.10	.05
☐ 472 Jack Perconte	.10	.05

☐ 473 Jim Presley .10 .05
☐ 474 Donnie Scott .10 .05
☐ 475 Bill Swift .10 .05
☐ 476 Danny Tartabull .25 .11
☐ 477 Gorman Thomas .10 .05
☐ 478 Roy Thomas .10 .05
☐ 479 Ed VandeBerg .10 .05
☐ 480 Frank Wills .10 .05
☐ 481 Matt Young .10 .05
☐ 482 Ray Burris .10 .05
☐ 483 Jaime Cocanower .10 .05
☐ 484 Cecil Cooper .25 .11
☐ 485 Danny Darwin .10 .05
☐ 486 Rollie Fingers .50 .23
☐ 487 Jim Gantner .10 .05
☐ 488 Bob L. Gibson .10 .05
☐ 489 Moose Haas .10 .05
☐ 490 Teddy Higuera .25 .11
☐ 491 Paul Householder .10 .05
☐ 492 Pete Ladd .10 .05
☐ 493 Rick Manning .10 .05
☐ 494 Bob McClure .10 .05
☐ 495 Paul Molitor 1.00 .45
☐ 496 Charlie Moore .10 .05
☐ 497 Ben Oglivie .10 .05
☐ 498 Randy Ready .10 .05
☐ 499 Earnie Riles .10 .05
☐ 500 Ed Romero .10 .05
☐ 501 Bill Schroeder .10 .05
☐ 502 Ray Searage .10 .05
☐ 503 Ted Simmons .25 .11
☐ 504 Pete Vuckovich .10 .05
☐ 505 Rick Waits .10 .05
☐ 506 Robin Yount 1.00 .45
☐ 507 Len Barker .10 .05
☐ 508 Steve Bedrosian .10 .05
☐ 509 Bruce Benedict .10 .05
☐ 510 Rick Camp .10 .05
☐ 511 Rick Cerone .10 .05
☐ 512 Chris Chambliss .25 .11
☐ 513 Jeff Dedmon .10 .05
☐ 514 Terry Forster .10 .05
☐ 515 Gene Garber .10 .05
☐ 516 Terry Harper .10 .05
☐ 517 Bob Horner .10 .05
☐ 518 Glenn Hubbard .10 .05
☐ 519 Joe Johnson .10 .05
☐ 520 Brad Komminsk .10 .05
☐ 521 Rick Mahler .10 .05
☐ 522 Dale Murphy 1.00 .45
☐ 523 Ken Oberkfell .10 .05
☐ 524 Pascual Perez .10 .05
☐ 525 Gerald Perry .10 .05
☐ 526 Rafael Ramirez .10 .05
☐ 527 Steve Shields .10 .05
☐ 528 Zane Smith .10 .05
☐ 529 Bruce Sutter .25 .11
☐ 530 Milt Thompson .25 .11
☐ 531 Claudell Washington .10 .05
☐ 532 Paul Zuvella .10 .05
☐ 533 Vida Blue .25 .11
☐ 534 Bob Brenly .10 .05
☐ 535 Chris Brown .10 .05
☐ 536 Chili Davis .50 .23
☐ 537 Mark Davis .10 .05
☐ 538 Rob Deer .10 .05
☐ 539 Dan Driessen .10 .05
☐ 540 Scott Garrelts .10 .05
☐ 541 Dan Gladden .10 .05
☐ 542 Jim Gott .10 .05
☐ 543 David Green .10 .05
☐ 544 Atlee Hammaker .10 .05
☐ 545 Mike Jeffcoat .10 .05
☐ 546 Mike Krukow .10 .05
☐ 547 Dave LaPoint .10 .05
☐ 548 Jeff Leonard .10 .05
☐ 549 Greg Minton .10 .05
☐ 550 Alex Trevino .10 .05
☐ 551 Manny Trillo .10 .05
☐ 552 Jose Uribe .10 .05
☐ 553 Brad Wellman .10 .05
☐ 554 Frank Williams .10 .05
☐ 555 Joel Youngblood .10 .05
☐ 556 Alan Bannister .10 .05
☐ 557 Glenn Brummer .10 .05
☐ 558 Steve Buechele .25 .11
☐ 559 Jose Guzman .10 .05
☐ 560 Toby Harrah .10 .05
☐ 561 Greg Harris .10 .05
☐ 562 Dwayne Henry .10 .05
☐ 563 Burt Hooton .10 .05
☐ 564 Charlie Hough .25 .11
☐ 565 Mike Mason .10 .05
☐ 566 Oddibe McDowell .10 .05
☐ 567 Dickie Noles .10 .05
☐ 568 Pete O'Brien .10 .05
☐ 569 Larry Parrish .10 .05
☐ 570 Dave Rozema .10 .05
☐ 571 Dave Schmidt .10 .05
☐ 572 Don Slaught .10 .05
☐ 573 Wayne Tolleson .10 .05
☐ 574 Duane Walker .10 .05
☐ 575 Gary Ward .10 .05
☐ 576 Chris Welsh .10 .05
☐ 577 Curtis Wilkerson .10 .05
☐ 578 George Wright .10 .05
☐ 579 Chris Bando .10 .05
☐ 580 Tony Bernazard .10 .05
☐ 581 Brett Butler .25 .11
☐ 582 Ernie Camacho .10 .05
☐ 583 Joe Carter 2.00 .90
☐ 584 Carmen Castillo .10 .05
☐ 585 Jamie Easterly .10 .05
☐ 586 Julio Franco .50 .23
☐ 587 Mel Hall .10 .05
☐ 588 Mike Hargrove .25 .11
☐ 589 Neal Heaton .10 .05
☐ 590 Brook Jacoby .10 .05
☐ 591 Otis Nixon 1.00 .45
☐ 592 Jerry Reed .10 .05
☐ 593 Vern Ruhle .10 .05
☐ 594 Pat Tabler .10 .05
☐ 595 Rich Thompson .10 .05
☐ 596 Andre Thornton .10 .05
☐ 597 Dave Von Ohlen .10 .05
☐ 598 George Vukovich .10 .05
☐ 599 Tom Waddell .10 .05
☐ 600 Curt Wardle .10 .05
☐ 601 Jerry Willard .10 .05
☐ 602 Bill Almon .10 .05
☐ 603 Mike Bielecki .10 .05
☐ 604 Sid Bream .10 .05
☐ 605 Mike C. Brown .10 .05
☐ 606 Pat Clements .10 .05
☐ 607 Jose DeLeon .10 .05
☐ 608 Denny Gonzalez .10 .05
☐ 609 Cecilio Guante .10 .05
☐ 610 Steve Kemp .10 .05
☐ 611 Sammy Khalifa .10 .05
☐ 612 Lee Mazzilli .10 .05
☐ 613 Larry McWilliams .10 .05
☐ 614 Jim Morrison .10 .05
☐ 615 Joe Orsulak .10 .05
☐ 616 Tony Pena .10 .05
☐ 617 Johnny Ray .10 .05
☐ 618 Rick Reuschel .10 .05
☐ 619 R.J. Reynolds .10 .05
☐ 620 Rick Rhoden .10 .05
☐ 621 Don Robinson .10 .05
☐ 622 Jason Thompson .10 .05
☐ 623 Lee Tunnell .10 .05
☐ 624 Jim Winn .10 .05
☐ 625 Marvell Wynne .10 .05
☐ 626 Dwight Gooden IA 1.00 .45
☐ 627 Don Mattingly IA 1.25 .55
☐ 628 4192 (Pete Rose) .50 .23
☐ 629 3000 Career Hits 1.00 .45
Rod Carew
☐ 630 300 Career Wins 1.00 .45
Tom Seaver
Phil Niekro
☐ 631 Ouch (Don Baylor) .25 .11
☐ 632 Instant Offense .50 .23
Darryl Strawberry
Tim Raines
☐ 633 Shortstops Supreme 2.00 .90
Cal Ripken
Alan Trammell
☐ 634 Boggs and "Hero" 1.25 .55
Wade Boggs
George Brett
☐ 635 Braves Dynamic Duo .25 .11
Bob Horner
Dale Murphy
☐ 636 Cardinal Ignitors .25 .11
Willie McGee
Vince Coleman
☐ 637 Terror on Basepaths .25 .11
Vince Coleman
☐ 638 Charlie Hustle / Dr.K 1.00 .45
Pete Rose
Dwight Gooden
☐ 639 1984 and 1985 AL 1.00 .45
Batting Champs
Wade Boggs
Don Mattingly
☐ 640 NL West Sluggers .25 .11
Dale Murphy
Steve Garvey
Dave Parker
☐ 641 Staff Aces .25 .11
Fernando Valenzuela
Dwight Gooden
☐ 642 Blue Jay Stoppers 1.00 .45
Jimmy Key
Dave Stieb
☐ 643 AL All-Star Backstops .25 .11
Carlton Fisk
Rich Gedman
☐ 644 Gene Walter and 1.00 .45
Benito Santiago
☐ 645 Mike Woodard and .10 .05
Colin Ward
☐ 646 Kal Daniels and 2.00 .90
Paul O'Neill
☐ 647 Andres Galarraga and 6.00 2.70
Fred Toliver
☐ 648 Bob Kipper and .10 .05
Curt Ford
☐ 649 Jose Canseco and 8.00 3.60
Eric Plunk
☐ 650 Mark McLemore and 1.00 .45
Gus Polidor
☐ 651 Rob Woodward and .10 .05
Mickey Brantley
☐ 652 Billy Joe Robidoux and .10 .05
Mark Funderburk
☐ 653 Cecil Fielder and 3.00 1.35
Cory Snyder
☐ 654 CL: Royals/Cardinals .10 .05
Blue Jays/Mets
☐ 655 CL: Yankees/Dodgers .10 .05
Angels/Reds UER
(168 Darly Sconiers)
☐ 656 CL: White Sox/Tigers .10 .05
Expos/Orioles
(279 Dennis,
280 Tippy)
☐ 657 CL: Astros/Padres .10 .05
Red Sox/Cubs
☐ 658 CL: Twins/A's .10 .05
Phillies/Mariners
☐ 659 CL: Brewers/Braves .10 .05
Giants/Rangers
☐ 660 CL: Indians/Pirates .10 .05
Special Cards

1986 Fleer All-Stars

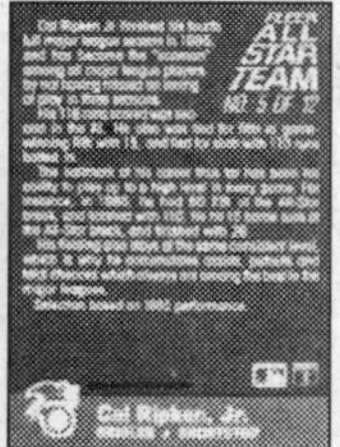

Randomly inserted in wax and cello packs, this 12-card standard-size set features top stars. The cards feature red backgrounds (American Leaguers) and blue backgrounds (National Leaguers). The 12 selections cover each position, left and right-handed starting pitchers, a reliever, and a designated hitter.

	MINT	NRMT
COMPLETE SET (12)	30.00	13.50
COMMON CARD (1-12)	.25	.11

☐ 1 Don Mattingly 6.00 2.70
☐ 2 Tom Herr .25 .11
☐ 3 George Brett 6.00 2.70
☐ 4 Gary Carter .75 .35
☐ 5 Cal Ripken 15.00 6.75
☐ 6 Dave Parker .50 .23
☐ 7 Rickey Henderson UER 2.50 1.10
(Misspelled Ricky
on card back)
☐ 8 Pedro Guerrero .50 .23
☐ 9 Dan Quisenberry .25 .11
☐ 10 Dwight Gooden .75 .35
☐ 11 Gorman Thomas .25 .11
☐ 12 John Tudor .25 .11

1986 Fleer Future Hall of Famers

These six standard-size cards were issued one per Fleer three-packs. This set features players that Fleer predicts will be "Future Hall of Famers." The card backs describe career highlights, records, and honors won by the player.

	MINT	NRMT
COMPLETE SET (6)	15.00	6.75
COMMON CARD (1-6)	2.00	.90

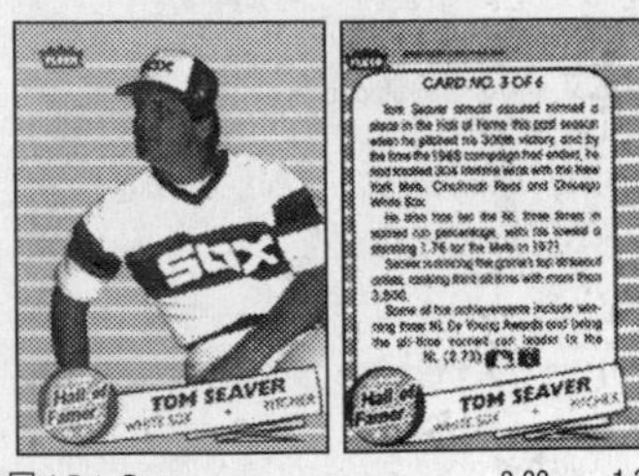

☐ 1 Pete Rose	3.00	1.35
☐ 2 Steve Carlton	2.00	.90
☐ 3 Tom Seaver	2.00	.90
☐ 4 Rod Carew	2.00	.90
☐ 5 Nolan Ryan	10.00	4.50
☐ 6 Reggie Jackson	2.50	1.10

1986 Fleer Wax Box Cards

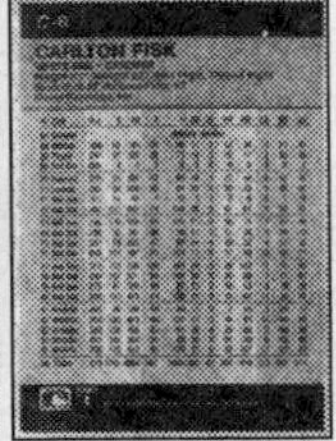

The cards in this eight-card set measure the standard size and were found on the bottom of the Fleer regular issue wax pack and cello pack boxes as four-card panel. Cards have essentially the same design as the 1986 Fleer regular issue set. These eight cards (C1 to C8) are considered a separate set in their own right and are not typically included in a complete set of the regular issue 1986 Fleer cards. The value of the panel uncut is slightly greater, perhaps by 25 percent greater, than the value of the individual cards cut up carefully.

	MINT	NRMT
COMPLETE SET (8)	5.00	2.20
COMMON CARD (C1-C8)	.25	.11
☐ C1 Royals Logo	.25	.11
☐ C2 George Brett	2.50	1.10
☐ C3 Ozzie Guillen	.50	.23
☐ C4 Dale Murphy	.75	.35
☐ C5 Cardinals Logo	.25	.11
☐ C6 Tom Browning	.25	.11
☐ C7 Gary Carter	.50	.23
☐ C8 Carlton Fisk	1.00	.45

1986 Fleer Update

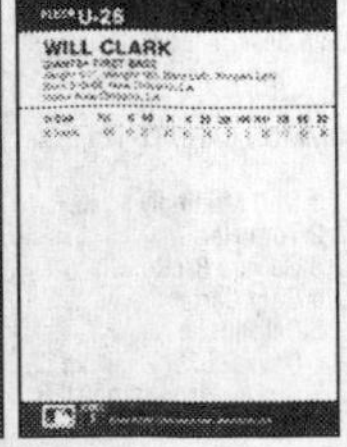

This 132-card standard-size set was distributed in factory set form through hobby dealers. In addition to the complete set of 132 cards, the box also contains 25 Team Logo Stickers.The card fronts look very similar to the 1986 Fleer regular issue. The cards are numbered (with a U prefix) alphabetically according to player's last name. The extended Rookie Cards in this set include Barry Bonds, Bobby Bonilla, Will Clark, Wally Joyner, John Kruk, Kevin Mitchell, and Ruben Sierra.

	MINT	NRMT
COMP.FACT.SET (132)	12.00	5.50
COMMON CARD (1-132)	.10	.05
☐ 1 Mike Aldrete	.10	.05
☐ 2 Andy Allanson	.10	.05
☐ 3 Neil Allen	.10	.05
☐ 4 Joaquin Andujar	.10	.05
☐ 5 Paul Assenmacher	.10	.05
☐ 6 Scott Bailes	.10	.05
☐ 7 Jay Baller	.10	.05
☐ 8 Scott Bankhead	.10	.05
☐ 9 Bill Bathe	.10	.05
☐ 10 Don Baylor	.75	.35
☐ 11 Billy Beane	.10	.05
☐ 12 Steve Bedrosian	.10	.05
☐ 13 Juan Beniquez	.10	.05
☐ 14 Barry Bonds	6.00	2.70
☐ 15 Bobby Bonilla UER (Wrong birthday)	1.50	.70
☐ 16 Rich Bordi	.10	.05
☐ 17 Bill Campbell	.10	.05
☐ 18 Tom Candiotti	.10	.05
☐ 19 John Cangelosi	.10	.05
☐ 20 Jose Canseco UER (Headings on back for a pitcher)	2.50	1.10
☐ 21 Chuck Cary	.10	.05
☐ 22 Juan Castillo	.10	.05
☐ 23 Rick Cerone	.10	.05
☐ 24 John Cerutti	.10	.05
☐ 25 Will Clark	2.50	1.10
☐ 26 Mark Clear	.10	.05
☐ 27 Darnell Coles	.10	.05
☐ 28 Dave Collins	.10	.05
☐ 29 Tim Conroy	.10	.05
☐ 30 Ed Correa	.10	.05
☐ 31 Joe Cowley	.10	.05
☐ 32 Bill Dawley	.10	.05
☐ 33 Rob Deer	.20	.09
☐ 34 John Denny	.10	.05
☐ 35 Jim Deshaies	.10	.05
☐ 36 Doug Drabek	.75	.35
☐ 37 Mike Easler	.10	.05
☐ 38 Mark Eichhorn	.10	.05
☐ 39 Dave Engle	.10	.05
☐ 40 Mike Fischlin	.10	.05
☐ 41 Scott Fletcher	.10	.05
☐ 42 Terry Forster	.10	.05
☐ 43 Terry Francona	.10	.05
☐ 44 Andres Galarraga	2.50	1.10
☐ 45 Lee Guetterman	.10	.05
☐ 46 Bill Gullickson	.10	.05
☐ 47 Jackie Gutierrez	.10	.05
☐ 48 Moose Haas	.10	.05
☐ 49 Billy Hatcher	.20	.09
☐ 50 Mike Heath	.10	.05
☐ 51 Guy Hoffman	.10	.05
☐ 52 Tom Hume	.10	.05
☐ 53 Pete Incaviglia	.75	.35
☐ 54 Dane Iorg	.10	.05
☐ 55 Chris James	.10	.05
☐ 56 Stan Javier	.20	.09
☐ 57 Tommy John	.75	.35
☐ 58 Tracy Jones	.10	.05
☐ 59 Wally Joyner	1.00	.45
☐ 60 Wayne Krenchicki	.10	.05
☐ 61 John Kruk	.75	.35
☐ 62 Mike LaCoss	.10	.05
☐ 63 Pete Ladd	.10	.05
☐ 64 Dave LaPoint	.10	.05
☐ 65 Mike LaValliere	.10	.05
☐ 66 Rudy Law	.10	.05
☐ 67 Dennis Leonard	.10	.05
☐ 68 Steve Lombardozzi	.10	.05
☐ 69 Aurelio Lopez	.10	.05
☐ 70 Mickey Mahler	.10	.05
☐ 71 Candy Maldonado	.10	.05
☐ 72 Roger Mason	.10	.05
☐ 73 Greg Mathews	.10	.05
☐ 74 Andy McGaffigan	.10	.05
☐ 75 Joel McKeon	.10	.05
☐ 76 Kevin Mitchell	.75	.35
☐ 77 Bill Mooneyham	.10	.05
☐ 78 Omar Moreno	.10	.05
☐ 79 Jerry Mumphrey	.10	.05
☐ 80 Al Newman	.20	.09
☐ 81 Phil Niekro	.75	.35
☐ 82 Randy Niemann	.10	.05
☐ 83 Juan Nieves	.10	.05
☐ 84 Bob Ojeda	.10	.05
☐ 85 Rick Ownbey	.10	.05
☐ 86 Tom Paciorek	.10	.05
☐ 87 David Palmer	.10	.05
☐ 88 Jeff Parrett	.10	.05
☐ 89 Pat Perry	.10	.05
☐ 90 Dan Plesac	.10	.05
☐ 91 Darrell Porter	.10	.05
☐ 92 Luis Quinones	.10	.05
☐ 93 Rey Quinones UER (Misspelled Quinonez)	.10	.05
☐ 94 Gary Redus	.10	.05
☐ 95 Jeff Reed	.10	.05
☐ 96 Bip Roberts	.75	.35
☐ 97 Billy Joe Robidoux	.10	.05
☐ 98 Gary Roenicke	.10	.05
☐ 99 Ron Roenicke	.10	.05
☐ 100 Angel Salazar	.10	.05
☐ 101 Joe Sambito	.10	.05
☐ 102 Billy Sample	.10	.05
☐ 103 Dave Schmidt	.10	.05
☐ 104 Ken Schrom	.10	.05
☐ 105 Ruben Sierra	1.25	.55
☐ 106 Ted Simmons	.20	.09
☐ 107 Sammy Stewart	.10	.05
☐ 108 Kurt Stillwell	.10	.05
☐ 109 Dale Sveum	.10	.05
☐ 110 Tim Teufel	.10	.05
☐ 111 Bob Tewksbury	.20	.09
☐ 112 Andres Thomas	.10	.05
☐ 113 Jason Thompson	.10	.05
☐ 114 Milt Thompson	.20	.09
☐ 115 Robby Thompson	.20	.09
☐ 116 Jay Tibbs	.10	.05
☐ 117 Fred Toliver	.10	.05
☐ 118 Wayne Tolleson	.10	.05
☐ 119 Alex Trevino	.10	.05
☐ 120 Manny Trillo	.10	.05
☐ 121 Ed VandeBerg	.10	.05
☐ 122 Ozzie Virgil	.10	.05
☐ 123 Tony Walker	.10	.05
☐ 124 Gene Walter	.10	.05
☐ 125 Duane Ward	.20	.09
☐ 126 Jerry Willard	.10	.05
☐ 127 Mitch Williams	.20	.09
☐ 128 Reggie Williams	.10	.05
☐ 129 Bobby Witt	.40	.18
☐ 130 Marvell Wynne	.10	.05
☐ 131 Steve Yeager	.10	.05
☐ 132 Checklist 1-132	.10	.05

1986 Fleer League Leaders

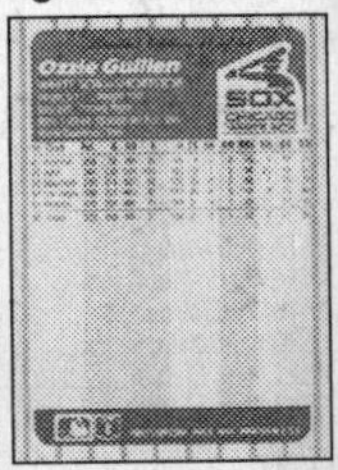

This 44-card standard-size set is also sometimes referred to as the Walgreen's set. Although the set was distributed through Walgreen's, there is no mention on the cards or box of that fact. The cards are easily recognizable by the fact that they contain the phrase "Fleer League Leaders" at the top of the obverse. Both sides of the cards are designed with a blue stripe on white pattern. The checklist for the set is given on the outside of the red, white, blue, and gold box in which the set was packaged.

	MINT	NRMT
COMPLETE SET (44)	5.00	2.20
COMMON CARD (1-44)	.05	.02
☐ 1 Wade Boggs	.50	.23
☐ 2 George Brett	1.25	.55
☐ 3 Jose Canseco	1.50	.70
☐ 4 Rod Carew	.25	.11
☐ 5 Gary Carter	.20	.09
☐ 6 Jack Clark	.10	.05
☐ 7 Vince Coleman	.10	.05
☐ 8 Jose Cruz	.10	.05
☐ 9 Alvin Davis	.05	.02
☐ 10 Mariano Duncan	.10	.05
☐ 11 Leon Durham	.05	.02
☐ 12 Carlton Fisk	.40	.18
☐ 13 Julio Franco	.10	.05
☐ 14 Scott Garrelts	.05	.02
☐ 15 Steve Garvey	.10	.05
☐ 16 Dwight Gooden	.30	.14
☐ 17 Ozzie Guillen	.10	.05
☐ 18 Willie Hernandez	.05	.02
☐ 19 Bob Horner	.05	.02
☐ 20 Kent Hrbek	.10	.05
☐ 21 Charlie Leibrandt	.05	.02
☐ 22 Don Mattingly	1.00	.45
☐ 23 Oddibe McDowell	.05	.02
☐ 24 Willie McGee	.10	.05
☐ 25 Keith Moreland	.05	.02
☐ 26 Lloyd Moseby	.05	.02
☐ 27 Dale Murphy	.30	.14
☐ 28 Phil Niekro	.40	.18
☐ 29 Joe Orsulak	.05	.02
☐ 30 Dave Parker	.10	.05
☐ 31 Lance Parrish	.10	.05
☐ 32 Kirby Puckett	1.25	.55

33 Tim Raines	.10	.05
34 Earnie Riles	.05	.02
35 Cal Ripken	2.00	.90
36 Pete Rose	.75	.35
37 Bret Saberhagen	.10	.05
38 Juan Samuel	.05	.02
39 Ryne Sandberg	.75	.35
40 Tom Seaver	.40	.18
41 Lee Smith	.20	.09
42 Ozzie Smith	1.00	.45
43 Dave Stieb	.05	.02
44 Robin Yount	.30	.14

1986 Fleer Limited Edition

e 44-card boxed standard-size set was produced by er for McCrory's. The cards have green and yellow rders. Card backs are printed in red and black on white d stock. The back of the original box gives a complete ecklist of the players in the set. The set box also ntains six logo stickers.

	MINT	NRMT
MPLETE SET (44)	5.00	2.20
MMON CARD (1-44)	.05	.02
1 Doyle Alexander	.05	.02
2 Joaquin Andujar	.05	.02
3 Harold Baines	.10	.05
4 Wade Boggs	.40	.18
5 Phil Bradley	.05	.02
6 George Brett	.75	.35
7 Hubie Brooks	.05	.02
8 Chris Brown	.05	.02
9 Tom Brunansky	.05	.02
10 Gary Carter	.20	.09
11 Vince Coleman	.10	.05
12 Cecil Cooper	.10	.05
13 Jose Cruz	.05	.02
14 Mike Davis	.05	.02
15 Carlton Fisk	.40	.18
16 Julio Franco	.10	.05
17 Damaso Garcia	.05	.02
18 Rich Gedman	.05	.02
19 Kirk Gibson	.10	.05
20 Dwight Gooden	.30	.14
21 Pedro Guerrero	.05	.02
22 Tony Gwynn	1.50	.70
23 Rickey Henderson	.40	.18
24 Orel Hershiser	.30	.14
25 LaMarr Hoyt	.05	.02
26 Reggie Jackson	.50	.23
27 Don Mattingly	1.00	.45
28 Oddibe McDowell	.05	.02
29 Willie McGee	.10	.05
30 Paul Molitor	.50	.23
31 Dale Murphy	.30	.14
32 Eddie Murray	.50	.23
33 Dave Parker	.10	.05
34 Tony Pena	.05	.02
35 Jeff Reardon	.05	.02
36 Cal Ripken	2.00	.90
37 Pete Rose	.75	.35
38 Bret Saberhagen	.10	.05
39 Juan Samuel	.05	.02
40 Ryne Sandberg	.75	.35
41 Mike Schmidt	.50	.23
42 Lee Smith	.20	.09
43 Don Sutton	.40	.18
44 Lou Whitaker	.10	.05

1986 Fleer Mini

e Fleer "Classic Miniatures" set consists of 120 small ds with all new pictures of the players as compared to 1986 Fleer regular issue. The cards are only 1 13/16" 2 9/16", making them some of the smallest (in size) duced in recent memory. Card backs provide career r-by-year statistics. The complete set was distributed red, white, and silver box along with 18 logo stickers. card numbering is done in the same team order as 1986 Fleer regular set.

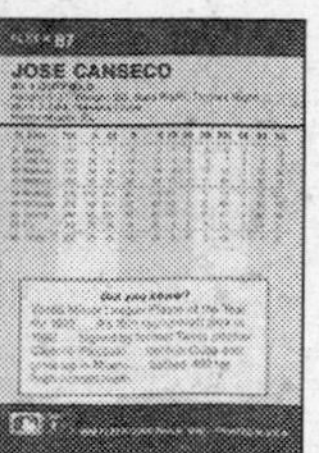

	MINT	NRMT
COMPLETE SET (120)	8.00	3.60
COMMON CARD (1-120)	.05	.02
☐ 1 George Brett	1.25	.55
☐ 2 Dan Quisenberry	.05	.02
☐ 3 Bret Saberhagen	.15	.07
☐ 4 Lonnie Smith	.05	.02
☐ 5 Willie Wilson	.10	.05
☐ 6 Jack Clark	.10	.05
☐ 7 Vince Coleman	.10	.05
☐ 8 Tom Herr	.05	.02
☐ 9 Willie McGee	.10	.05
☐ 10 Ozzie Smith	1.00	.45
☐ 11 John Tudor	.05	.02
☐ 12 Jesse Barfield	.05	.02
☐ 13 George Bell	.10	.05
☐ 14 Tony Fernandez	.05	.02
☐ 15 Damaso Garcia	.05	.02
☐ 16 Dave Stieb	.05	.02
☐ 17 Gary Carter	.15	.07
☐ 18 Ron Darling	.05	.02
☐ 19A Dwight Gooden (R on Mets logo)	.50	.23
☐ 19B Dwight Gooden (No R on Mets logo)	.50	.23
☐ 20 Keith Hernandez	.10	.05
☐ 21 Darryl Strawberry	.15	.07
☐ 22 Ron Guidry	.10	.05
☐ 23 Rickey Henderson	.50	.23
☐ 24 Don Mattingly	1.25	.55
☐ 25 Dave Righetti	.05	.02
☐ 26 Dave Winfield	.50	.23
☐ 27 Mariano Duncan	.10	.05
☐ 28 Pedro Guerrero	.10	.05
☐ 29 Bill Madlock	.10	.05
☐ 30 Mike Marshall	.05	.02
☐ 31 Fernando Valenzuela	.15	.07
☐ 32 Reggie Jackson	.50	.23
☐ 33 Gary Pettis	.05	.02
☐ 34 Ron Romanick	.05	.02
☐ 35 Don Sutton	.30	.14
☐ 36 Mike Witt	.05	.02
☐ 37 Buddy Bell	.10	.05
☐ 38 Tom Browning	.05	.02
☐ 39 Dave Parker	.10	.05
☐ 40 Pete Rose	.60	.25
☐ 41 Mario Soto	.05	.02
☐ 42 Harold Baines	.10	.05
☐ 43 Carlton Fisk	.50	.23
☐ 44 Ozzie Guillen	.10	.05
☐ 45 Ron Kittle	.05	.02
☐ 46 Tom Seaver	.50	.23
☐ 47 Kirk Gibson	.10	.05
☐ 48 Jack Morris	.15	.07
☐ 49 Lance Parrish	.10	.05
☐ 50 Alan Trammell	.15	.07
☐ 51 Lou Whitaker	.10	.05
☐ 52 Hubie Brooks	.05	.02
☐ 53 Andre Dawson	.40	.18
☐ 54 Tim Raines	.10	.05
☐ 55 Bryn Smith	.05	.02
☐ 56 Tim Wallach	.05	.02
☐ 57 Mike Boddicker	.05	.02
☐ 58 Eddie Murray	.40	.18
☐ 59 Cal Ripken	2.00	.90
☐ 60 John Shelby	.05	.02
☐ 61 Mike Young	.05	.02
☐ 62 Jose Cruz	.05	.02
☐ 63 Glenn Davis	.05	.02
☐ 64 Phil Garner	.05	.02
☐ 65 Nolan Ryan	2.00	.90
☐ 66 Mike Scott	.05	.02
☐ 67 Steve Garvey	.10	.05
☐ 68 Rich Gossage	.10	.05
☐ 69 Tony Gwynn	1.00	.45
☐ 70 Andy Hawkins	.05	.02
☐ 71 Garry Templeton	.05	.02
☐ 72 Wade Boggs	.40	.18
☐ 73 Roger Clemens	1.50	.70
☐ 74 Dwight Evans	.10	.05
☐ 75 Rich Gedman	.05	.02
☐ 76 Jim Rice	.10	.05
☐ 77 Shawon Dunston	.05	.02
☐ 78 Leon Durham	.05	.02
☐ 79 Keith Moreland	.05	.02
☐ 80 Ryne Sandberg	.60	.25
☐ 81 Rick Sutcliffe	.05	.02
☐ 82 Bert Blyleven	.10	.05
☐ 83 Tom Brunansky	.05	.02
☐ 84 Kent Hrbek	.10	.05
☐ 85 Kirby Puckett	1.50	.70
☐ 86 Bruce Bochte	.05	.02
☐ 87 Jose Canseco	.75	.35
☐ 88 Mike Davis	.05	.02
☐ 89 Jay Howell	.05	.02
☐ 90 Dwayne Murphy	.05	.02
☐ 91 Steve Carlton	.40	.18
☐ 92 Von Hayes	.05	.02
☐ 93 Juan Samuel	.05	.02
☐ 94 Mike Schmidt	.40	.18
☐ 95 Glenn Wilson	.05	.02
☐ 96 Phil Bradley	.05	.02
☐ 97 Alvin Davis	.05	.02
☐ 98 Jim Presley	.05	.02
☐ 99 Danny Tartabull	.10	.05
☐ 100 Cecil Cooper	.10	.05
☐ 101 Paul Molitor	.60	.25
☐ 102 Ernie Riles	.05	.02
☐ 103 Robin Yount	.25	.11
☐ 104 Bob Horner	.05	.02
☐ 105 Dale Murphy	.25	.11
☐ 106 Bruce Sutter	.10	.05
☐ 107 Claudell Washington	.05	.02
☐ 108 Chris Brown	.05	.02
☐ 109 Chili Davis	.10	.05
☐ 110 Scott Garrelts	.05	.02
☐ 111 Oddibe McDowell	.05	.02
☐ 112 Pete O'Brien	.05	.02
☐ 113 Gary Ward	.05	.02
☐ 114 Brett Butler	.10	.05
☐ 115 Julio Franco	.10	.05
☐ 116 Brook Jacoby	.05	.02
☐ 117 Mike C. Brown	.05	.02
☐ 118 Joe Orsulak	.05	.02
☐ 119 Tony Pena	.05	.02
☐ 120 R.J. Reynolds	.05	.02

1986 Fleer Sluggers/Pitchers

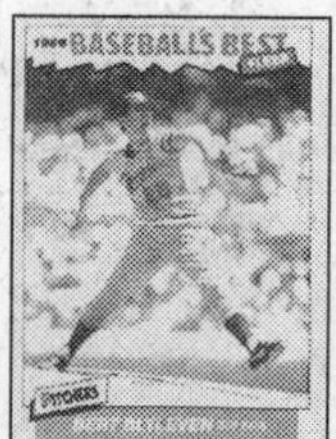

Fleer produced this 44-card boxed standard-size set although it was primarily distributed by Kress, McCrory, Newberry, T.G.Y., and other similar stores. The set features 22 sluggers and 22 pitchers and is subtitled "Baseball's Best". The set was packaged in a red, white, blue, and yellow custom box along with six logo stickers. The set checklist is given on the back of the box. The card numbering is in alphabetical order by the player's name. The Will Clark and Bobby Witt cards were the first major league cards produced of those players.

	MINT	NRMT
COMPLETE SET (44)	5.00	2.20
COMMON CARD (1-44)	.05	.02
☐ 1 Bert Blyleven	.10	.05
☐ 2 Wade Boggs	.40	.18
☐ 3 George Brett	1.00	.45
☐ 4 Tom Browning	.05	.02
☐ 5 Jose Canseco	1.00	.45
☐ 6 Will Clark	1.50	.70
☐ 7 Roger Clemens	1.00	.45
☐ 8 Alvin Davis	.05	.02
☐ 9 Julio Franco	.10	.05
☐ 10 Kirk Gibson	.10	.05
☐ 11 Dwight Gooden	.30	.14
☐ 12 Rich Gossage	.10	.05
☐ 13 Pedro Guerrero	.05	.02
☐ 14 Ron Guidry	.10	.05
☐ 15 Tony Gwynn	.75	.35
☐ 16 Orel Hershiser	.30	.14
☐ 17 Kent Hrbek	.10	.05
☐ 18 Reggie Jackson	.40	.18
☐ 19 Wally Joyner	.40	.18
☐ 20 Charlie Leibrandt	.05	.02
☐ 21 Don Mattingly	1.00	.45

☐ 22 Willie McGee .10 .05
☐ 23 Jack Morris .10 .05
☐ 24 Dale Murphy .30 .14
☐ 25 Eddie Murray .50 .23
☐ 26 Jeff Reardon .05 .02
☐ 27 Rick Reuschel .05 .02
☐ 28 Cal Ripken 2.00 .90
☐ 29 Pete Rose .50 .23
☐ 30 Nolan Ryan 1.50 .70
☐ 31 Bret Saberhagen .10 .05
☐ 32 Ryne Sandberg .60 .25
☐ 33 Mike Schmidt .50 .23
☐ 34 Tom Seaver .40 .18
☐ 35 Bryn Smith .05 .02
☐ 36 Mario Soto .05 .02
☐ 37 Dave Stieb .05 .02
☐ 38 Darryl Strawberry .20 .09
☐ 39 Rick Sutcliffe .05 .02
☐ 40 John Tudor .05 .02
☐ 41 Fernando Valenzuela .10 .05
☐ 42 Bobby Witt .10 .05
☐ 43 Mike Witt .05 .02
☐ 44 Robin Yount .30 .14

1986 Fleer Sluggers/Pitchers Box Cards

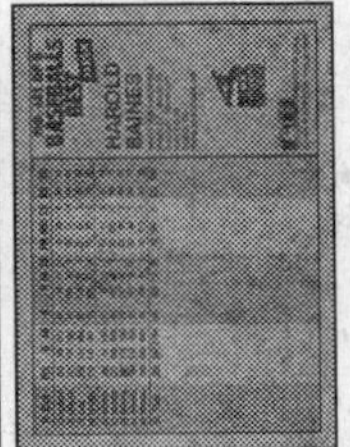

The cards in this six-card set each measure the standard size. Cards have essentially the same design as the 1986 Fleer Sluggers vs. Pitchers set of Baseball's Best. The cards were printed on the bottom of the counter display box which held 24 small boxed sets; hence theoretically these box cards are 1/24 as plentiful as the regular boxed set cards. These six cards, numbered M1 to M5 with one blank-back (unnumbered) card, are considered a separate set in their own right and are not typically included in a complete set of the 1986 Fleer Sluggers vs. Pitchers set of 44. The value of the panels uncut is slightly greater, perhaps by 25 percent greater, than the value of the individual cards cut up carefully.

	MINT	NRMT
COMPLETE SET (6)	10.00	4.50
COMMON CARD	.50	.23

☐ M1 Harold Baines .75 .35
☐ M2 Steve Carlton 1.50 .70
☐ M3 Gary Carter .75 .35
☐ M4 Vince Coleman .75 .35
☐ M5 Kirby Puckett 8.00 3.60
☐ NNO Team Logo .50 .23
(Blank back)

1986 Fleer Sticker Cards

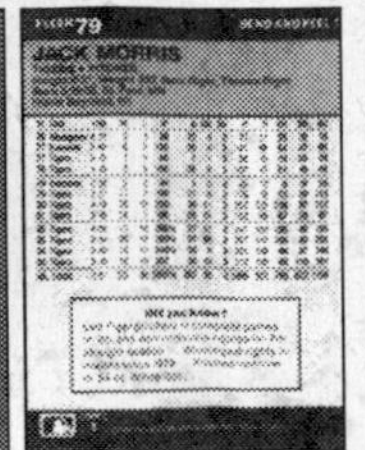

The standard-size stickers (made of card stock) 132-card set feature card photos on the front surrounded by a yellow border and a cranberry frame. The backs are printed in blue and black on white card stock. The backs contain year-by-year statistical information. They are numbered on the back in the upper left-hand corner. The card numbering is in alphabetical order by the player's name.

	MINT	NRMT
COMPLETE SET (132)	15.00	6.75
COMMON CARD (1-132)	.05	.02

☐ 1 Harold Baines .10 .05
☐ 2 Jesse Barfield .05 .02
☐ 3 Don Baylor .10 .05
☐ 4 Juan Beniquez .05 .02
☐ 5 Tim Birtsas .05 .02
☐ 6 Bert Blyleven .10 .05
☐ 7 Bruce Bochte .05 .02
☐ 8 Wade Boggs .40 .18
☐ 9 Dennis Boyd .05 .02
☐ 10 Phil Bradley .05 .02
☐ 11 George Brett 1.50 .70
☐ 12 Hubie Brooks .05 .02
☐ 13 Chris Brown .05 .02
☐ 14 Tom Browning .05 .02
☐ 15 Tom Brunansky .05 .02
☐ 16 Bill Buckner .10 .05
☐ 17 Britt Burns .05 .02
☐ 18 Brett Butler .10 .05
☐ 19 Jose Canseco 2.00 .90
☐ 20 Rod Carew .40 .18
☐ 21 Steve Carlton .40 .18
☐ 22 Don Carman .05 .02
☐ 23 Gary Carter .15 .07
☐ 24 Jack Clark .10 .05
☐ 25 Vince Coleman .15 .07
☐ 26 Cecil Cooper .10 .05
☐ 27 Jose Cruz .10 .05
☐ 28 Ron Darling .05 .02
☐ 29 Alvin Davis .05 .02
☐ 30 Jody Davis .05 .02
☐ 31 Mike Davis .05 .02
☐ 32 Andre Dawson .25 .11
☐ 33 Mariano Duncan .10 .05
☐ 34 Shawon Dunston .10 .05
☐ 35 Leon Durham .05 .02
☐ 36 Darrell Evans .10 .05
☐ 37 Tony Fernandez .05 .02
☐ 38 Carlton Fisk .40 .18
☐ 39 John Franco .25 .11
☐ 40 Julio Franco .10 .05
☐ 41 Damaso Garcia .05 .02
☐ 42 Scott Garrelts .05 .02
☐ 43 Steve Garvey .25 .11
☐ 44 Rich Gedman .05 .02
☐ 45 Kirk Gibson .10 .05
☐ 46 Dwight Gooden .30 .14
☐ 47 Pedro Guerrero .10 .05
☐ 48 Ron Guidry .10 .05
☐ 49 Ozzie Guillen .10 .05
☐ 50 Tony Gwynn 2.50 1.10
☐ 51 Andy Hawkins .05 .02
☐ 52 Von Hayes .05 .02
☐ 53 Rickey Henderson .60 .25
☐ 54 Tom Henke .05 .02
☐ 55 Keith Hernandez .10 .05
☐ 56 Willie Hernandez .05 .02
☐ 57 Tommy Herr .05 .02
☐ 58 Orel Hershiser .15 .07
☐ 59 Teddy Higuera .05 .02
☐ 60 Bob Horner .05 .02
☐ 61 Charlie Hough .10 .05
☐ 62 Jay Howell .05 .02
☐ 63 LaMarr Hoyt .05 .02
☐ 64 Kent Hrbek .10 .05
☐ 65 Reggie Jackson .60 .25
☐ 66 Bob James .05 .02
☐ 67 Dave Kingman .10 .05
☐ 68 Ron Kittle .05 .02
☐ 69 Charlie Leibrandt .05 .02
☐ 70 Fred Lynn .10 .05
☐ 71 Mike Marshall .05 .02
☐ 72 Don Mattingly 2.50 1.10
☐ 73 Oddibe McDowell .05 .02
☐ 74 Willie McGee .10 .05
☐ 75 Scott McGregor .05 .02
☐ 76 Paul Molitor .75 .35
☐ 77 Donnie Moore .05 .02
☐ 78 Keith Moreland .05 .02
☐ 79 Jack Morris .10 .05
☐ 80 Dale Murphy .25 .11
☐ 81 Eddie Murray .75 .35
☐ 82 Phil Niekro .40 .18
☐ 83 Joe Orsulak .05 .02
☐ 84 Dave Parker .10 .05
☐ 85 Lance Parrish .10 .05
☐ 86 Larry Parrish .05 .02
☐ 87 Tony Pena .05 .02
☐ 88 Gary Pettis .05 .02
☐ 89 Jim Presley .05 .02
☐ 90 Kirby Puckett 3.00 1.35
☐ 91 Dan Quisenberry .05 .02
☐ 92 Tim Raines .10 .05
☐ 93 Johnny Ray .05 .02
☐ 94 Jeff Reardon .10 .05
☐ 95 Rick Reuschel .10 .05
☐ 96 Jim Rice .10 .05
☐ 97 Dave Righetti .05 .02
☐ 98 Earnie Riles .05 .0
☐ 99 Cal Ripken 3.00 1.3
☐ 100 Ron Romanick .05 .0
☐ 101 Pete Rose 1.25 .5
☐ 102 Nolan Ryan 3.00 1.3
☐ 103 Bret Saberhagen .15 .0
☐ 104 Mark Salas .05 .0
☐ 105 Juan Samuel .05 .0
☐ 106 Ryne Sandberg 1.25 .5
☐ 107 Mike Schmidt .75 .3
☐ 108 Mike Scott .05 .0
☐ 109 Tom Seaver .40 .1
☐ 110 Bryn Smith .05 .0
☐ 111 Dave Smith .10 .0
☐ 112 Lee Smith .15 .0
☐ 113 Ozzie Smith 1.25 .5
☐ 114 Mario Soto .05 .0
☐ 115 Dave Stieb .05 .0
☐ 116 Darryl Strawberry .15 .0
☐ 117 Bruce Sutter .10 .0
☐ 118 Garry Templeton .05 .0
☐ 119 Gorman Thomas .05 .0
☐ 120 Andre Thornton .05 .0
☐ 121 Alan Trammell .15 .0
☐ 122 John Tudor .05 .0
☐ 123 Fernando Valenzuela .50 .2
☐ 124 Frank Viola .10 .0
☐ 125 Gary Ward .05 .0
☐ 126 Lou Whitaker .10 .0
☐ 127 Frank White .10 .0
☐ 128 Glenn Wilson .05 .0
☐ 129 Willie Wilson .05 .0
☐ 130 Dave Winfield .40 .1
☐ 131 Robin Yount .25 .1
☐ 132 Dwight Gooden CL .25 .1
Dale Murphy

1986 Fleer Stickers Wax Box Cards

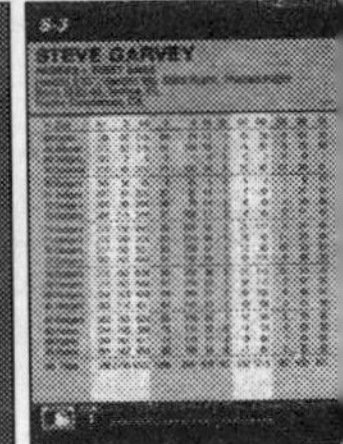

The bottoms of the Star Sticker wax boxes contained a s of four cards done in a similar format to the sticker these cards (they are not stickers but truly cards) a numbered with the prefix S and are considered a separa set. Each individual card measures 2 1/2" by 3 1/2". Th value of the panel uncut is slightly greater, perhaps by 2 percent greater, than the value of the individual cards c up carefully.

	MINT	NRM
COMPLETE SET (4)	4.00	1.8
COMMON CARD (S1-S4)	.25	.1

☐ S1 Team Logo .25 .1
(Checklist back)
☐ S2 Wade Boggs 2.00 .9
☐ S3 Steve Garvey .50 .2
☐ S4 Dave Winfield 1.50 .7

1987 Fleer

This set consists of 660 standard-size cards. Cards we primarily issued in 17-card wax packs, rack packs ar hobby and retail factory sets. Card fronts feature distinctive light blue and white blended border encasing color photo. Cards are again organized numerically t teams with team ordering based on the previous seaso ecord. The last 36 cards in the set consist of Specials 525-643), Rookie Pairs (644-653), and checklists (654-60). The key Rookie Cards in this set are Barry Bonds, obby Bonilla, Will Clark, Chuck Finley, Bo Jackson, Wally oyner, John Kruk, Barry Larkin, Kevin Mitchell, Kevin eitzer, Ruben Sierra and Devon White.

	MINT	NRMT
OMPLETE SET (660)	40.00	18.00
OMP.FACT.SET (672)	40.00	18.00
OMMON CARD (1-660)	.20	.09
1 Rick Aguilera	.40	.18
2 Richard Anderson	.20	.09
3 Wally Backman	.20	.09
4 Gary Carter	.10	.05
5 Ron Darling	.20	.09
6 Len Dykstra	.40	.18
7 Kevin Elster	.75	.35
8 Sid Fernandez	.20	.09
9 Dwight Gooden	.10	.05
10 Ed Hearn	.20	.09
11 Danny Heep	.20	.09
12 Keith Hernandez	.40	.18
13 Howard Johnson	.20	.09
14 Ray Knight	.40	.18
15 Lee Mazzilli	.20	.09
16 Roger McDowell	.20	.09
17 Kevin Mitchell	.10	.05
18 Randy Niemann	.20	.09
19 Bob Ojeda	.20	.09
20 Jesse Orosco	.20	.09
21 Rafael Santana	.20	.09
22 Doug Sisk	.20	.09
23 Darryl Strawberry	.10	.05
24 Tim Teufel	.20	.09
25 Mookie Wilson	.40	.18
26 Tony Armas	.20	.09
27 Marty Barrett	.20	.09
28 Don Baylor	.10	.05
29 Wade Boggs	.75	.35
30 Oil Can Boyd	.20	.09
31 Bill Buckner	.40	.18
32 Roger Clemens	2.00	.90
33 Steve Crawford	.20	.09
34 Dwight Evans	.40	.18
35 Rich Gedman	.20	.09
36 Dave Henderson	.20	.09
37 Bruce Hurst	.20	.09
38 Tim Lollar	.20	.09
39 Al Nipper	.20	.09
40 Spike Owen	.20	.09
41 Jim Rice	.40	.18
42 Ed Romero	.20	.09
43 Joe Sambito	.20	.09
44 Calvin Schiraldi	.20	.09
45 Tom Seaver UER	.75	.35
Lifetime saves total 0, should be 1		
46 Jeff Sellers	.20	.09
47 Bob Stanley	.20	.09
48 Sammy Stewart	.20	.09
49 Larry Andersen	.20	.09
50 Alan Ashby	.20	.09
51 Kevin Bass	.20	.09
52 Jeff Calhoun	.20	.09
53 Jose Cruz	.40	.18
54 Danny Darwin	.20	.09
55 Glenn Davis	.20	.09
56 Jim Deshaies	.20	.09
57 Bill Doran	.20	.09
58 Phil Garner	.20	.09
59 Billy Hatcher	.20	.09
60 Charlie Kerfeld	.20	.09
61 Bob Knepper	.20	.09
62 Dave Lopes	.40	.18
63 Aurelio Lopez	.20	.09
64 Jim Pankovits	.20	.09
65 Terry Puhl	.20	.09
66 Craig Reynolds	.20	.09
67 Nolan Ryan	3.00	1.35
68 Mike Scott	.20	.09
69 Dave Smith	.20	.09
70 Dickie Thon	.20	.09
71 Tony Walker	.20	.09
72 Denny Walling	.20	.09
73 Bob Boone	.40	.18
74 Rick Burleson	.20	.09
75 John Candelaria	.20	.09
76 Doug Corbett	.20	.09
77 Doug DeCinces	.20	.09
78 Brian Downing	.20	.09
79 Chuck Finley	.75	.35
80 Terry Forster	.20	.09
81 Bob Grich	.40	.18
82 George Hendrick	.20	.09
83 Jack Howell	.20	.09
84 Reggie Jackson	1.00	.45
85 Ruppert Jones	.20	.09
86 Wally Joyner	1.00	.45
87 Gary Lucas	.20	.09
88 Kirk McCaskill	.20	.09
89 Donnie Moore	.20	.09
90 Gary Pettis	.20	.09
91 Vern Ruhle	.20	.09
92 Dick Schofield	.20	.09
93 Don Sutton	.75	.35
94 Rob Wilfong	.20	.09
95 Mike Witt	.20	.09
96 Doug Drabek	.75	.35
97 Mike Easler	.20	.09
98 Mike Fischlin	.20	.09
99 Brian Fisher	.20	.09
100 Ron Guidry	.40	.18
101 Rickey Henderson	.75	.35
102 Tommy John	.40	.18
103 Ron Kittle	.20	.09
104 Don Mattingly	1.25	.55
105 Bobby Meacham	.20	.09
106 Joe Niekro	.20	.09
107 Mike Pagliarulo	.20	.09
108 Dan Pasqua	.20	.09
109 Willie Randolph	.40	.18
110 Dennis Rasmussen	.20	.09
111 Dave Righetti	.20	.09
112 Gary Roenicke	.20	.09
113 Rod Scurry	.20	.09
114 Bob Shirley	.20	.09
115 Joel Skinner	.20	.09
116 Tim Stoddard	.20	.09
117 Bob Tewksbury	.40	.18
118 Wayne Tolleson	.20	.09
119 Claudell Washington	.20	.09
120 Dave Winfield	.75	.35
121 Steve Buechele	.20	.09
122 Ed Correa	.20	.09
123 Scott Fletcher	.20	.09
124 Jose Guzman	.20	.09
125 Toby Harrah	.20	.09
126 Greg Harris	.20	.09
127 Charlie Hough	.20	.09
128 Pete Incaviglia	.40	.18
129 Mike Mason	.20	.09
130 Oddibe McDowell	.20	.09
131 Dale Mohorcic	.20	.09
132 Pete O'Brien	.20	.09
133 Tom Paciorek	.20	.09
134 Larry Parrish	.20	.09
135 Geno Petralli	.20	.09
136 Darrell Porter	.20	.09
137 Jeff Russell	.20	.09
138 Ruben Sierra	1.00	.45
139 Don Slaught	.20	.09
140 Gary Ward	.20	.09
141 Curtis Wilkerson	.20	.09
142 Mitch Williams	.40	.18
143 Bobby Witt UER	.75	.35
(Tulsa misspelled as Tusla; ERA should be 6.43, not .643)		
144 Dave Bergman	.20	.09
145 Tom Brookens	.20	.09
146 Bill Campbell	.20	.09
147 Chuck Cary	.20	.09
148 Darnell Coles	.20	.09
149 Dave Collins	.20	.09
150 Darrell Evans	.40	.18
151 Kirk Gibson	.40	.18
152 John Grubb	.20	.09
153 Willie Hernandez	.20	.09
154 Larry Herndon	.20	.09
155 Eric King	.20	.09
156 Chet Lemon	.20	.09
157 Dwight Lowry	.20	.09
158 Jack Morris	.40	.18
159 Randy O'Neal	.20	.09
160 Lance Parrish	.40	.18
161 Dan Petry	.20	.09
162 Pat Sheridan	.20	.09
163 Jim Slaton	.20	.09
164 Frank Tanana	.20	.09
165 Walt Terrell	.20	.09
166 Mark Thurmond	.20	.09
167 Alan Trammell	.10	.05
168 Lou Whitaker	.40	.18
169 Luis Aguayo	.20	.09
170 Steve Bedrosian	.20	.09
171 Don Carman	.20	.09
172 Darren Daulton	.10	.05
173 Greg Gross	.20	.09
174 Kevin Gross	.20	.09
175 Von Hayes	.20	.09
176 Charles Hudson	.20	.09
177 Tom Hume	.20	.09
178 Steve Jeltz	.20	.09
179 Mike Maddux	.20	.09
180 Shane Rawley	.20	.09
181 Gary Redus	.20	.09
182 Ron Roenicke	.20	.09
183 Bruce Ruffin	.20	.09
184 John Russell	.20	.09
185 Juan Samuel	.20	.09
186 Dan Schatzeder	.20	.09
187 Mike Schmidt	1.00	.45
188 Rick Schu	.20	.09
189 Jeff Stone	.20	.09
190 Kent Tekulve	.20	.09
191 Milt Thompson	.20	.09
192 Glenn Wilson	.20	.09
193 Buddy Bell	.40	.18
194 Tom Browning	.20	.09
195 Sal Butera	.20	.09
196 Dave Concepcion	.40	.18
197 Kal Daniels	.20	.09
198 Eric Davis	.10	.05
199 John Denny	.20	.09
200 Bo Diaz	.20	.09
201 Nick Esasky	.20	.09
202 John Franco	.40	.18
203 Bill Gullickson	.20	.09
204 Barry Larkin	5.00	2.20
205 Eddie Milner	.20	.09
206 Rob Murphy	.20	.09
207 Ron Oester	.20	.09
208 Dave Parker	.40	.18
209 Tony Perez	.75	.35
210 Ted Power	.20	.09
211 Joe Price	.20	.09
212 Ron Robinson	.20	.09
213 Pete Rose	1.00	.45
214 Mario Soto	.20	.09
215 Kurt Stillwell	.20	.09
216 Max Venable	.20	.09
217 Chris Welsh	.20	.09
218 Carl Willis	.20	.09
219 Jesse Barfield	.20	.09
220 George Bell	.20	.09
221 Bill Caudill	.20	.09
222 John Cerutti	.20	.09
223 Jim Clancy	.20	.09
224 Mark Eichhorn	.20	.09
225 Tony Fernandez	.20	.09
226 Damaso Garcia	.20	.09
227 Kelly Gruber ERR	.20	.09
(Wrong birth year)		
228 Tom Henke	.20	.09
229 Garth Iorg	.20	.09
230 Joe Johnson	.20	.09
231 Cliff Johnson	.20	.09
232 Jimmy Key	.40	.18
233 Dennis Lamp	.20	.09
234 Rick Leach	.20	.09
235 Buck Martinez	.20	.09
236 Lloyd Moseby	.20	.09
237 Rance Mulliniks	.20	.09
238 Dave Stieb	.20	.09
239 Willie Upshaw	.20	.09
240 Ernie Whitt	.20	.09
241 Andy Allanson	.20	.09
242 Scott Bailes	.20	.09
243 Chris Bando	.20	.09
244 Tony Bernazard	.20	.09
245 John Butcher	.20	.09
246 Brett Butler	.10	.05
247 Ernie Camacho	.20	.09
248 Tom Candiotti	.20	.09
249 Joe Carter	.75	.35
250 Carmen Castillo	.20	.09
251 Julio Franco	.40	.18
252 Mel Hall	.20	.09
253 Brook Jacoby	.20	.09
254 Phil Niekro	.75	.35
255 Otis Nixon	.10	.05
256 Dickie Noles	.20	.09
257 Bryan Oelkers	.20	.09
258 Ken Schrom	.20	.09
259 Don Schulze	.20	.09
260 Cory Snyder	.20	.09
261 Pat Tabler	.20	.09
262 Andre Thornton	.20	.09
263 Rich Yett	.20	.09
264 Mike Aldrete	.40	.18
265 Juan Berenguer	.20	.09
266 Vida Blue	.40	.18
267 Bob Brenly	.20	.09
268 Chris Brown	.20	.09
269 Will Clark	5.00	2.20
270 Chili Davis	.10	.05
271 Mark Davis	.20	.09
272 Kelly Downs	.20	.09
273 Scott Garrelts	.20	.09
274 Dan Gladden	.20	.09
275 Mike Krukow	.20	.09

☐ 276 Randy Kutcher .20 .09
☐ 277 Mike LaCoss .20 .09
☐ 278 Jeff Leonard .20 .09
☐ 279 Candy Maldonado .20 .09
☐ 280 Roger Mason .20 .09
☐ 281 Bob Melvin .20 .09
☐ 282 Greg Minton .20 .09
☐ 283 Jeff D. Robinson .20 .09
☐ 284 Harry Spilman .20 .09
☐ 285 Robby Thompson .40 .18
☐ 286 Jose Uribe .20 .09
☐ 287 Frank Williams .20 .09
☐ 288 Joel Youngblood .20 .09
☐ 289 Jack Clark .40 .18
☐ 290 Vince Coleman .20 .09
☐ 291 Tim Conroy .20 .09
☐ 292 Danny Cox .20 .09
☐ 293 Ken Dayley .20 .09
☐ 294 Curt Ford .20 .09
☐ 295 Bob Forsch .20 .09
☐ 296 Tom Herr .20 .09
☐ 297 Ricky Horton .20 .09
☐ 298 Clint Hurdle .20 .09
☐ 299 Jeff Lahti .20 .09
☐ 300 Steve Lake .20 .09
☐ 301 Tito Landrum .20 .09
☐ 302 Mike LaValliere .20 .09
☐ 303 Greg Mathews .20 .09
☐ 304 Willie McGee .20 .09
☐ 305 Jose Oquendo .20 .09
☐ 306 Terry Pendleton .40 .18
☐ 307 Pat Perry .20 .09
☐ 308 Ozzie Smith 1.00 .45
☐ 309 Ray Soff .20 .09
☐ 310 John Tudor .20 .09
☐ 311 Andy Van Slyke UER .40 .18
(Bats R, Throws L)
☐ 312 Todd Worrell .40 .18
☐ 313 Dann Bilardello .20 .09
☐ 314 Hubie Brooks .20 .09
☐ 315 Tim Burke .20 .09
☐ 316 Andre Dawson .75 .35
☐ 317 Mike Fitzgerald .20 .09
☐ 318 Tom Foley .20 .09
☐ 319 Andres Galarraga 1.00 .45
☐ 320 Joe Hesketh .20 .09
☐ 321 Wallace Johnson .20 .09
☐ 322 Wayne Krenchicki .20 .09
☐ 323 Vance Law .20 .09
☐ 324 Dennis Martinez .40 .18
☐ 325 Bob McClure .20 .09
☐ 326 Andy McGaffigan .20 .09
☐ 327 Al Newman .20 .09
☐ 328 Tim Raines .40 .18
☐ 329 Jeff Reardon .40 .18
☐ 330 Luis Rivera .20 .09
☐ 331 Bob Sebra .20 .09
☐ 332 Bryn Smith .20 .09
☐ 333 Jay Tibbs .20 .09
☐ 334 Tim Wallach .20 .09
☐ 335 Mitch Webster .20 .09
☐ 336 Jim Wohlford .20 .09
☐ 337 Floyd Youmans .20 .09
☐ 338 Chris Bosio .40 .18
☐ 339 Glenn Braggs .20 .09
☐ 340 Rick Cerone .20 .09
☐ 341 Mark Clear .20 .09
☐ 342 Bryan Clutterbuck .20 .09
☐ 343 Cecil Cooper .40 .18
☐ 344 Rob Deer .20 .09
☐ 345 Jim Gantner .20 .09
☐ 346 Ted Higuera .20 .09
☐ 347 John Henry Johnson .20 .09
☐ 348 Tim Leary .20 .09
☐ 349 Rick Manning .20 .09
☐ 350 Paul Molitor .75 .35
☐ 351 Charlie Moore .20 .09
☐ 352 Juan Nieves .20 .09
☐ 353 Ben Oglivie .20 .09
☐ 354 Dan Plesac .20 .09
☐ 355 Ernest Riles .20 .09
☐ 356 Billy Joe Robidoux .20 .09
☐ 357 Bill Schroeder .20 .09
☐ 358 Dale Sveum .20 .09
☐ 359 Gorman Thomas .20 .09
☐ 360 Bill Wegman .20 .09
☐ 361 Robin Yount .75 .35
☐ 362 Steve Balboni .20 .09
☐ 363 Scott Bankhead .20 .09
☐ 364 Buddy Biancalana .20 .09
☐ 365 Bud Black .20 .09
☐ 366 George Brett 1.50 .70
☐ 367 Steve Farr .20 .09
☐ 368 Mark Gubicza .20 .09
☐ 369 Bo Jackson 2.50 1.10
☐ 370 Danny Jackson .20 .09
☐ 371 Mike Kingery .40 .18
☐ 372 Rudy Law .20 .09
☐ 373 Charlie Leibrandt .20 .09
☐ 374 Dennis Leonard .20 .09
☐ 375 Hal McRae .40 .18
☐ 376 Jorge Orta .20 .09
☐ 377 Jamie Quirk .20 .09
☐ 378 Dan Quisenberry .20 .09
☐ 379 Bret Saberhagen .40 .18
☐ 380 Angel Salazar .20 .09
☐ 381 Lonnie Smith .20 .09
☐ 382 Jim Sundberg .20 .09
☐ 383 Frank White .40 .18
☐ 384 Willie Wilson .20 .09
☐ 385 Joaquin Andujar .20 .09
☐ 386 Doug Bair .20 .09
☐ 387 Dusty Baker .40 .18
☐ 388 Bruce Bochte .20 .09
☐ 389 Jose Canseco 1.50 .70
☐ 390 Chris Codiroli .20 .09
☐ 391 Mike Davis .20 .09
☐ 392 Alfredo Griffin .20 .09
☐ 393 Moose Haas .20 .09
☐ 394 Donnie Hill .20 .09
☐ 395 Jay Howell .20 .09
☐ 396 Dave Kingman .40 .18
☐ 397 Carney Lansford .40 .18
☐ 398 Dave Leiper .20 .09
☐ 399 Bill Mooneyham .20 .09
☐ 400 Dwayne Murphy .20 .09
☐ 401 Steve Ontiveros .20 .09
☐ 402 Tony Phillips .20 .09
☐ 403 Eric Plunk .20 .09
☐ 404 Jose Rijo .20 .09
☐ 405 Terry Steinbach 1.00 .45
☐ 406 Dave Stewart .40 .18
☐ 407 Mickey Tettleton .40 .18
☐ 408 Dave Von Ohlen .20 .09
☐ 409 Jerry Willard .20 .09
☐ 410 Curt Young .20 .09
☐ 411 Bruce Bochy .20 .09
☐ 412 Dave Dravecky .40 .18
☐ 413 Tim Flannery .20 .09
☐ 414 Steve Garvey .75 .35
☐ 415 Rich Gossage .40 .18
☐ 416 Tony Gwynn 2.00 .90
☐ 417 Andy Hawkins .20 .09
☐ 418 LaMarr Hoyt .20 .09
☐ 419 Terry Kennedy .20 .09
☐ 420 John Kruk 1.00 .45
☐ 421 Dave LaPoint .20 .09
☐ 422 Craig Lefferts .20 .09
☐ 423 Carmelo Martinez .20 .09
☐ 424 Lance McCullers .20 .09
☐ 425 Kevin McReynolds .20 .09
☐ 426 Graig Nettles .40 .18
☐ 427 Bip Roberts 1.00 .45
☐ 428 Jerry Royster .20 .09
☐ 429 Benito Santiago .40 .18
☐ 430 Eric Show .20 .09
☐ 431 Bob Stoddard .20 .09
☐ 432 Garry Templeton .20 .09
☐ 433 Gene Walter .20 .09
☐ 434 Ed Whitson .20 .09
☐ 435 Marvell Wynne .20 .09
☐ 436 Dave Anderson .20 .09
☐ 437 Greg Brock .20 .09
☐ 438 Enos Cabell .20 .09
☐ 439 Mariano Duncan .20 .09
☐ 440 Pedro Guerrero .40 .18
☐ 441 Orel Hershiser .40 .18
☐ 442 Rick Honeycutt .20 .09
☐ 443 Ken Howell .20 .09
☐ 444 Ken Landreaux .20 .09
☐ 445 Bill Madlock .20 .09
☐ 446 Mike Marshall .20 .09
☐ 447 Len Matuszek .20 .09
☐ 448 Tom Niedenfuer .20 .09
☐ 449 Alejandro Pena .20 .09
☐ 450 Dennis Powell .20 .09
☐ 451 Jerry Reuss .20 .09
☐ 452 Bill Russell .20 .09
☐ 453 Steve Sax .20 .09
☐ 454 Mike Scioscia .20 .09
☐ 455 Franklin Stubbs .20 .09
☐ 456 Alex Trevino .20 .09
☐ 457 Fernando Valenzuela .40 .18
☐ 458 Ed VandeBerg .20 .09
☐ 459 Bob Welch .20 .09
☐ 460 Reggie Williams .20 .09
☐ 461 Don Aase .20 .09
☐ 462 Juan Beniquez .20 .09
☐ 463 Mike Boddicker .20 .09
☐ 464 Juan Bonilla .20 .09
☐ 465 Rich Bordi .20 .09
☐ 466 Storm Davis .20 .09
☐ 467 Rick Dempsey .40 .18
☐ 468 Ken Dixon .20 .09
☐ 469 Jim Dwyer .20 .09
☐ 470 Mike Flanagan .20 .09
☐ 471 Jackie Gutierrez .20 .09
☐ 472 Brad Havens .20 .09
☐ 473 Lee Lacy .20 .09
☐ 474 Fred Lynn .40 .18
☐ 475 Scott McGregor .20 .09
☐ 476 Eddie Murray .75 .35
☐ 477 Tom O'Malley .20 .09
☐ 478 Cal Ripken Jr. 3.00 1.3
☐ 479 Larry Sheets .20 .09
☐ 480 John Shelby .20 .09
☐ 481 Nate Snell .20 .0
☐ 482 Jim Traber .20 .0
☐ 483 Mike Young .20 .0
☐ 484 Neil Allen .20 .0
☐ 485 Harold Baines .40 .1
☐ 486 Floyd Bannister .20 .09
☐ 487 Daryl Boston .20 .09
☐ 488 Ivan Calderon .20 .09
☐ 489 John Cangelosi .20 .0
☐ 490 Steve Carlton .75 .3
☐ 491 Joe Cowley .20 .09
☐ 492 Julio Cruz .20 .09
☐ 493 Bill Dawley .20 .0
☐ 494 Jose DeLeon .20 .0
☐ 495 Richard Dotson .20 .0
☐ 496 Carlton Fisk .75 .3
☐ 497 Ozzie Guillen .40 .1
☐ 498 Jerry Hairston .20 .0
☐ 499 Ron Hassey .20 .0
☐ 500 Tim Hulett .20 .0
☐ 501 Bob James .20 .0
☐ 502 Steve Lyons .20 .0
☐ 503 Joel McKeon .20 .0
☐ 504 Gene Nelson .20 .0
☐ 505 Dave Schmidt .20 .0
☐ 506 Ray Searage .20 .0
☐ 507 Bobby Thigpen .40 .1
☐ 508 Greg Walker .20 .0
☐ 509 Jim Acker .20 .0
☐ 510 Doyle Alexander .20 .0
☐ 511 Paul Assenmacher .20 .0
☐ 512 Bruce Benedict .20 .0
☐ 513 Chris Chambliss .20 .0
☐ 514 Jeff Dedmon .20 .0
☐ 515 Gene Garber .20 .0
☐ 516 Ken Griffey .40 .1
☐ 517 Terry Harper .20 .0
☐ 518 Bob Horner .20 .0
☐ 519 Glenn Hubbard .20 .0
☐ 520 Rick Mahler .20 .0
☐ 521 Omar Moreno .20 .0
☐ 522 Dale Murphy .75 .3
☐ 523 Ken Oberkfell .20 .0
☐ 524 Ed Olwine .20 .0
☐ 525 David Palmer .20 .0
☐ 526 Rafael Ramirez .20 .0
☐ 527 Billy Sample .20 .0
☐ 528 Ted Simmons .40 .1
☐ 529 Zane Smith .20 .0
☐ 530 Bruce Sutter .20 .0
☐ 531 Andres Thomas .20 .0
☐ 532 Ozzie Virgil .20 .0
☐ 533 Allan Anderson .20 .0
☐ 534 Keith Atherton .20 .0
☐ 535 Billy Beane .20 .0
☐ 536 Bert Blyleven .40 .1
☐ 537 Tom Brunansky .20 .0
☐ 538 Randy Bush .20 .0
☐ 539 George Frazier .20 .0
☐ 540 Gary Gaetti .20 .0
☐ 541 Greg Gagne .20 .0
☐ 542 Mickey Hatcher .20 .0
☐ 543 Neal Heaton .20 .0
☐ 544 Kent Hrbek .40 .1
☐ 545 Roy Lee Jackson .20 .0
☐ 546 Tim Laudner .20 .0
☐ 547 Steve Lombardozzi .20 .0
☐ 548 Mark Portugal .40 .1
☐ 549 Kirby Puckett 2.00 .9
☐ 550 Jeff Reed .20 .0
☐ 551 Mark Salas .20 .0
☐ 552 Roy Smalley .20 .0
☐ 553 Mike Smithson .20 .0
☐ 554 Frank Viola .20 .0
☐ 555 Thad Bosley .20 .0
☐ 556 Ron Cey .40 .1
☐ 557 Jody Davis .20 .0
☐ 558 Ron Davis .20 .0
☐ 559 Bob Dernier .20 .0
☐ 560 Frank DiPino .20 .0
☐ 561 Shawon Dunston UER .20 .0
(Wrong birth year listed on card back)
☐ 562 Leon Durham .20 .0
☐ 563 Dennis Eckersley .75 .3

☐ 564 Terry Francona	.20	.09
☐ 565 Dave Gumpert	.20	.09
☐ 566 Guy Hoffman	.20	.09
☐ 567 Ed Lynch	.20	.09
☐ 568 Gary Matthews	.20	.09
☐ 569 Keith Moreland	.20	.09
☐ 570 Jamie Moyer	.75	.35
☐ 571 Jerry Mumphrey	.20	.09
☐ 572 Ryne Sandberg	1.00	.45
☐ 573 Scott Sanderson	.20	.09
☐ 574 Lee Smith	.75	.35
☐ 575 Chris Speier	.20	.09
☐ 576 Rick Sutcliffe	.20	.09
☐ 577 Manny Trillo	.20	.09
☐ 578 Steve Trout	.20	.09
☐ 579 Karl Best	.20	.09
☐ 580 Scott Bradley	.20	.09
☐ 581 Phil Bradley	.20	.09
☐ 582 Mickey Brantley	.20	.09
☐ 583 Mike G. Brown P	.20	.09
☐ 584 Alvin Davis	.20	.09
☐ 585 Lee Guetterman	.20	.09
☐ 586 Mark Huismann	.20	.09
☐ 587 Bob Kearney	.20	.09
☐ 588 Pete Ladd	.20	.09
☐ 589 Mark Langston	.40	.18
☐ 590 Mike Moore	.20	.09
☐ 591 Mike Morgan	.20	.09
☐ 592 John Moses	.20	.09
☐ 593 Ken Phelps	.20	.09
☐ 594 Jim Presley	.20	.09
☐ 595 Rey Quinones UER (Quinonez on front)	.20	.09
☐ 596 Harold Reynolds	.20	.09
☐ 597 Billy Swift	.20	.09
☐ 598 Danny Tartabull	.40	.18
☐ 599 Steve Yeager	.20	.09
☐ 600 Matt Young	.20	.09
☐ 601 Bill Almon	.20	.09
☐ 602 Rafael Belliard	.20	.09
☐ 603 Mike Bielecki	.20	.09
☐ 604 Barry Bonds	20.00	9.00
☐ 605 Bobby Bonilla	2.50	1.10
☐ 606 Sid Bream	.20	.09
☐ 607 Mike C. Brown	.20	.09
☐ 608 Pat Clements	.20	.09
☐ 609 Mike Diaz	.20	.09
☐ 610 Cecilio Guante	.20	.09
☐ 611 Barry Jones	.20	.09
☐ 612 Bob Kipper	.20	.09
☐ 613 Larry McWilliams	.20	.09
☐ 614 Jim Morrison	.20	.09
☐ 615 Joe Orsulak	.20	.09
☐ 616 Junior Ortiz	.20	.09
☐ 617 Tony Pena	.20	.09
☐ 618 Johnny Ray	.20	.09
☐ 619 Rick Reuschel	.20	.09
☐ 620 R.J. Reynolds	.20	.09
☐ 621 Rick Rhoden	.20	.09
☐ 622 Don Robinson	.20	.09
☐ 623 Bob Walk	.20	.09
☐ 624 Jim Winn	.20	.09
☐ 625 Youthful Power Pete Incaviglia Jose Canseco	.75	.35
☐ 626 300 Game Winners Don Sutton Phil Niekro	.10	.05
☐ 627 AL Firemen Dave Righetti Don Aase	.20	.09
☐ 628 Rookie All-Stars Wally Joyner Jose Canseco	.75	.35
☐ 629 Magic Mets Gary Carter Sid Fernandez Dwight Gooden Keith Hernandez Darryl Strawberry	.10	.05
☐ 630 NL Best Righties Mike Scott Mike Krukow	.20	.09
☐ 631 Sensational Southpaws Fernando Valenzuela John Franco	.20	.09
☐ 632 Count'Em Bob Horner	.20	.09
☐ 633 AL Pitcher's Nightmare Jose Canseco Jim Rice Kirby Puckett	1.00	.45
☐ 634 All-Star Battery Gary Carter Roger Clemens	.40	.18
☐ 635 4000 Strikeouts Steve Carlton	.75	.35
☐ 636 Big Bats at First Glenn Davis Eddie Murray	.75	.35
☐ 637 On Base Wade Boggs Keith Hernandez	.75	.35
☐ 638 Sluggers Left Side Don Mattingly Darryl Strawberry	.75	.35
☐ 639 Former MVP's Dave Parker Ryne Sandberg	.40	.18
☐ 640 Dr. K and Super K Dwight Gooden Roger Clemens	.10	.05
☐ 641 AL West Stoppers Mike Witt Charlie Hough	.20	.09
☐ 642 Doubles and Triples Juan Samuel Tim Raines	.40	.18
☐ 643 Outfielders with Punch Harold Baines Jesse Barfield	.40	.18
☐ 644 Dave Clark and Greg Swindell	.75	.35
☐ 645 Ron Karkovice and Russ Morman	.40	.18
☐ 646 Devon White and Willie Fraser	1.00	.45
☐ 647 Mike Stanley and Jerry Browne	.75	.35
☐ 648 Dave Magadan and Phil Lombardi	.75	.35
☐ 649 Jose Gonzalez and Ralph Bryant	.20	.09
☐ 650 Jimmy Jones and Randy Asadoor	.20	.09
☐ 651 Tracy Jones and Marvin Freeman	.20	.09
☐ 652 John Stefero and Kevin Seitzer	.75	.35
☐ 653 Rob Nelson and Steve Fireovid	.20	.09
☐ 654 CL: Mets/Red Sox Astros/Angels	.20	.09
☐ 655 CL: Yankees/Rangers Tigers/Phillies	.20	.09
☐ 656 CL: Reds/Blue Jays Indians/Giants ERR (230/231 wrong)	.20	.09
☐ 657 CL: Cardinals/Expos Brewers/Royals	.20	.09
☐ 658 CL: A's/Padres Dodgers/Orioles	.20	.09
☐ 659 CL: White Sox/Braves Twins/Cubs	.20	.09
☐ 660 CL: Mariners/Pirates Special Cards ER (580/581 wrong)	.20	.09

1987 Fleer Glossy

This set parallels the regular Fleer issue. The cards were issued in a special tin which also included a glossy version of the World Series set. These 672 standard-size are differentiated only by the gloss on the front. This set was produced in fairly large quantities, although still significantly less than regular issue cards.

	MINT	NRMT
COMPLETE FACT.SET (672)	40.00	18.00
COMMON CARD (1-660)	.10	.05
COMMON WS (WS1-WS12)	.10	.05
*STARS: 1X BASIC CARDS		
*ROOKIES: 1X BASIC CARDS		

1987 Fleer All-Stars

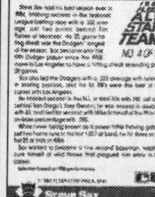

This 12-card standard-size set was distributed as an insert in packs of the Fleer regular issue. The cards are designed with a color player photo superimposed on a gray or black background with yellow stars. The player's name, team, and position are printed in orange on black or gray at the bottom of the obverse. The card backs are done predominantly in gray, red, and black and are numbered on the back in the upper right hand corner.

	MINT	NRMT
COMPLETE SET (12)	20.00	9.00
COMMON CARD (1-12)	.30	.14
☐ 1 Don Mattingly	6.00	2.70
☐ 2 Gary Carter	2.00	.90
☐ 3 Tony Fernandez	.30	.14
☐ 4 Steve Sax	.30	.14
☐ 5 Kirby Puckett	10.00	4.50
☐ 6 Mike Schmidt	2.50	1.10
☐ 7 Mike Easler	.30	.14
☐ 8 Todd Worrell	.30	.14
☐ 9 George Bell	.30	.14
☐ 10 Fernando Valenzuela	.75	.35
☐ 11 Roger Clemens	5.00	2.20
☐ 12 Tim Raines	.75	.35

1987 Fleer Headliners

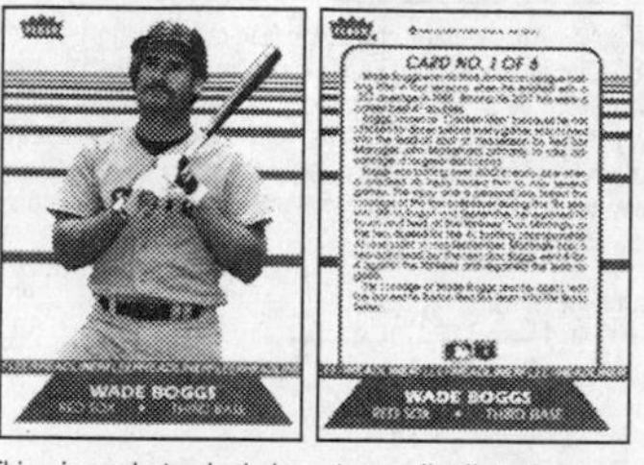

This six-card standard-size set was distributed one per rack pack as well as with three-pack wax pack rack packs. The obverse features the player photo against a beige background with irregular red stripes. The checklist below also lists each player's team affiliation. The set is sequenced in alphabetical order.

	MINT	NRMT
COMPLETE SET (6)	6.00	2.70
COMMON CARD (1-6)	.50	.23
☐ 1 Wade Boggs		
☐ 2 Jose Canseco	3.00	1.35
☐ 3 Dwight Gooden	.75	.35
☐ 4 Rickey Henderson		
☐ 5 Keith Hernandez	.50	.23
☐ 6 Jim Rice	.50	.23

1987 Fleer Wax Box Cards

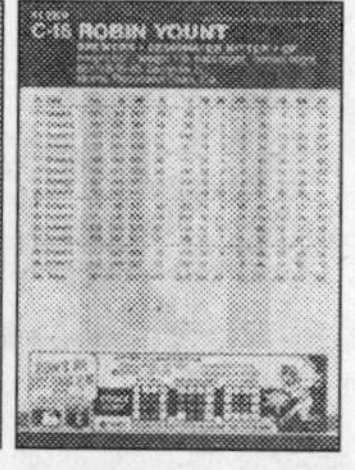

The cards in this 16-card set measure the standard, 2 1/2" by 3 1/2". Cards have essentially the same design as the 1987 Fleer regular issue set. The cards were printed on the bottoms of the regular issue wax pack boxes. These 16 cards (C1 to C16) are considered a separate set in their own right and are not typically included in a complete set of the regular issue 1987 Fleer cards. The value of the panel uncut is slightly greater, perhaps by 25 percent greater, than the value of the individual cards cut up carefully.

	MINT	NRMT
COMPLETE SET (16)	10.00	4.50
COMMON CARDS (C1-C16)	.10	.05
☐ C1 Mets Logo	.10	.05
☐ C2 Jesse Barfield	.10	.05
☐ C3 George Brett	3.00	1.35
☐ C4 Dwight Gooden	.50	.23
☐ C5 Boston Logo	.10	.05
☐ C6 Keith Hernandez	.25	.11
☐ C7 Wally Joyner	.50	.23
☐ C8 Dale Murphy	.75	.35
☐ C9 Astros Logo	.10	.05
☐ C10 Dave Parker	.25	.11

☐ C11 Kirby Puckett 2.50 1.10
☐ C12 Dave Righetti .... .10 .05
☐ C13 Angels Logo .... .10 .05
☐ C14 Ryne Sandberg .... 2.00 .90
☐ C15 Mike Schmidt .... 1.50 .70
☐ C16 Robin Yount .... .75 .35

1987 Fleer World Series

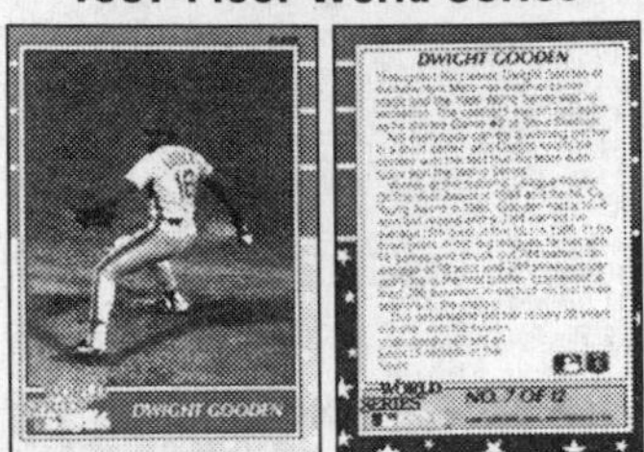

This 12-card standard-size set of features highlights of the previous year's World Series between the Mets and the Red Sox. The sets were packaged as a complete set insert with the collated sets (of the 1987 Fleer regular issue) which were sold by Fleer directly to hobby card dealers; they were not available in the general retail candy store outlets.

	MINT	NRMT
COMPLETE SET (12)	2.00	.90
COMMON CARD (1-12)	.10	.05

☐ 1 Bruce Hurst .... .10 .05
☐ 2 Keith Hernandez and .... .50 .23
Wade Boggs
☐ 3 Roger Clemens HOR .... 1.00 .45
☐ 4 Gary Carter .... .50 .23
☐ 5 Ron Darling .... .10 .05
☐ 6 Marty Barrett .... .10 .05
☐ 7 Dwight Gooden .... .50 .23
☐ 8 Strategy at Work .... .10 .05
(Mets Conference)
☐ 9 Dwight Evans .... .25 .11
Congratulated by Rich Gedman
☐ 10 Dave Henderson .... .10 .05
☐ 11 Ray Knight .... .25 .11
Darryl Strawberry
☐ 12 Ray Knight .... .10 .05

1987 Fleer Update

This 132-card standard-size set was distributed exclusively in factory set form by hobby dealers. In addition to the complete set of 132 cards, the box also contained 25 Team Logo stickers. The cards look very similar to the 1987 Fleer regular issue except for the U-prefixed numbering on back. Cards are ordered alphabetically according to player's last name. The key extended Rookie Cards in this set are Ellis Burks, Mike Greenwell, Greg Maddux, Fred McGriff, Mark McGwire and Matt Williams.

	MINT	NRMT
COMP.FACT.SET (132)	12.00	5.50
COMMON CARD (1-132)	.10	.05

☐ 1 Scott Bankhead .... .10 .05
☐ 2 Eric Bell .... .10 .05
☐ 3 Juan Beniquez .... .10 .05
☐ 4 Juan Berenguer .... .10 .05
☐ 5 Mike Birkbeck .... .10 .05
☐ 6 Randy Bockus .... .10 .05
☐ 7 Rod Booker .... .10 .05
☐ 8 Thad Bosley .... .10 .05
☐ 9 Greg Brock .... .10 .05
☐ 10 Bob Brower .... .10 .05
☐ 11 Chris Brown .... .10 .05
☐ 12 Jerry Browne .... .10 .05
☐ 13 Ralph Bryant .... .10 .05
☐ 14 DeWayne Buice .... .10 .05
☐ 15 Ellis Burks .... 1.00 .45
☐ 16 Casey Candaele .... .10 .05
☐ 17 Steve Carlton .... .50 .23
☐ 18 Juan Castillo .... .10 .05
☐ 19 Chuck Crim .... .10 .05
☐ 20 Mark Davidson .... .10 .05
☐ 21 Mark Davis .... .10 .05
☐ 22 Storm Davis .... .10 .05
☐ 23 Bill Dawley .... .10 .05
☐ 24 Andre Dawson .... .50 .23
☐ 25 Brian Dayett .... .10 .05
☐ 26 Rick Dempsey .... .25 .11
☐ 27 Ken Dowell .... .10 .05
☐ 28 Dave Dravecky .... .25 .11
☐ 29 Mike Dunne .... .10 .05
☐ 30 Dennis Eckersley .... .50 .23
☐ 31 Cecil Fielder .... .75 .35
☐ 32 Brian Fisher .... .10 .05
☐ 33 Willie Fraser .... .10 .05
☐ 34 Ken Gerhart .... .10 .05
☐ 35 Jim Gott .... .10 .05
☐ 36 Dan Gladden .... .10 .05
☐ 37 Mike Greenwell .... .10 .05
☐ 38 Cecilio Guante .... .10 .05
☐ 39 Albert Hall .... .10 .05
☐ 40 Atlee Hammaker .... .10 .05
☐ 41 Mickey Hatcher .... .10 .05
☐ 42 Mike Heath .... .10 .05
☐ 43 Neal Heaton .... .10 .05
☐ 44 Mike Henneman .... .10 .05
☐ 45 Guy Hoffman .... .10 .05
☐ 46 Charles Hudson .... .10 .05
☐ 47 Chuck Jackson .... .10 .05
☐ 48 Mike Jackson .... .50 .23
☐ 49 Reggie Jackson .... .60 .25
☐ 50 Chris James .... .10 .05
☐ 51 Dion James .... .10 .05
☐ 52 Stan Javier .... .10 .05
☐ 53 Stan Jefferson .... .10 .05
☐ 54 Jimmy Jones .... .10 .05
☐ 55 Tracy Jones .... .10 .05
☐ 56 Terry Kennedy .... .10 .05
☐ 57 Mike Kingery .... .25 .11
☐ 58 Ray Knight .... .25 .11
☐ 59 Gene Larkin .... .10 .05
☐ 60 Mike LaValliere .... .10 .05
☐ 61 Jack Lazorko .... .10 .05
☐ 62 Terry Leach .... .10 .05
☐ 63 Rick Leach .... .10 .05
☐ 64 Craig Lefferts .... .10 .05
☐ 65 Jim Lindeman .... .10 .05
☐ 66 Bill Long .... .10 .05
☐ 67 Mike Loynd .... .10 .05
☐ 68 Greg Maddux 8.00 3.60
☐ 69 Bill Madlock .... .10 .05
☐ 70 Dave Magadan .... .25 .11
☐ 71 Joe Magrane .... .10 .05
☐ 72 Fred Manrique .... .10 .05
☐ 73 Mike Mason .... .10 .05
☐ 74 Lloyd McClendon .... .10 .05
☐ 75 Fred McGriff .... .60 .25
☐ 76 Mark McGwire 2.50 1.10
☐ 77 Mark McLemore .... .10 .05
☐ 78 Kevin McReynolds .... .10 .05
☐ 79 Dave Meads .... .10 .05
☐ 80 Greg Minton .... .10 .05
☐ 81 John Mitchell .... .10 .05
☐ 82 Kevin Mitchell .... .10 .05
☐ 83 John Morris .... .10 .05
☐ 84 Jeff Musselman .... .10 .05
☐ 85 Randy Myers .... .50 .23
☐ 86 Gene Nelson .... .10 .05
☐ 87 Joe Niekro .... .10 .05
☐ 88 Tom Nieto .... .10 .05
☐ 89 Reid Nichols .... .10 .05
☐ 90 Matt Nokes .... .25 .11
☐ 91 Dickie Noles .... .10 .05
☐ 92 Edwin Nunez .... .10 .05
☐ 93 Jose Nunez .... .10 .05
☐ 94 Paul O'Neill .... .25 .11
☐ 95 Jim Paciorek .... .10 .05
☐ 96 Lance Parrish .... .25 .11
☐ 97 Bill Pecota .... .10 .05
☐ 98 Tony Pena .... .10 .05
☐ 99 Luis Polonia .... .25 .11
☐ 100 Randy Ready .... .10 .05
☐ 101 Jeff Reardon .... .25 .11
☐ 102 Gary Redus .... .10 .05
☐ 103 Rick Rhoden .... .10 .05
☐ 104 Wally Ritchie .... .10 .05
☐ 105 Jeff M. Robinson UER .... .10 .05
(Wrong Jeff's
stats on back)
☐ 106 Mark Salas .... .10 .05
☐ 107 Dave Schmidt .... .10 .05
☐ 108 Kevin Seitzer UER .... .25 .11
(Wrong birth year)
☐ 109 John Shelby .... .10 .05
☐ 110 John Smiley .... .25 .11
☐ 111 Lary Sorensen .... .10 .05
☐ 112 Chris Speier .... .10 .05
☐ 113 Randy St.Claire .... .10 .05
☐ 114 Jim Sundberg .... .10 .05
☐ 115 B.J. Surhoff .... .50 .23
☐ 116 Greg Swindell .... .10 .05
☐ 117 Danny Tartabull .... .25 .11
☐ 118 Dorn Taylor .... .10 .05
☐ 119 Lee Tunnell .... .10 .05
☐ 120 Ed VandeBerg .... .10 .05
☐ 121 Andy Van Slyke .... .25 .11
☐ 122 Gary Ward .... .10 .05
☐ 123 Devon White .... .50 .23
☐ 124 Alan Wiggins .... .10 .05
☐ 125 Bill Wilkinson .... .10 .05
☐ 126 Jim Winn .... .10 .05
☐ 127 Frank Williams .... .10 .05
☐ 128 Ken Williams .... .10 .05
☐ 129 Matt Williams 3.00 1.35
☐ 130 Herm Willingham .... .10 .05
☐ 131 Matt Young .... .10 .05
☐ 132 Checklist 1-132 .... .10 .05

1987 Fleer Update Glossy

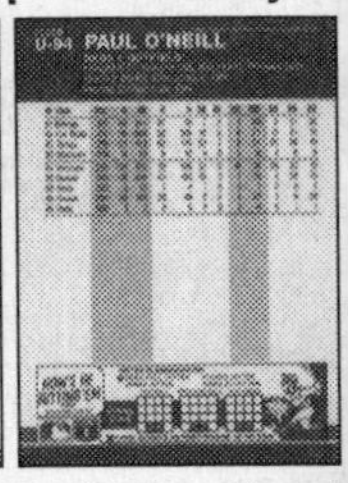

This set parallels the regular Fleer Update issue. The cards were issued in a special tin. These 132 standard-size are differentiated only by the gloss on the front. This set was produced in fairly large quantities, although still significantly less than regular issue cards.

	MINT	NRMT
COMPLETE FACT.SET (132)	12.00	5.50
COMMON CARD (1-132)	.10	.05
*STARS: 1X BASIC CARDS		
*ROOKIES: 1X BASIC CARDS		

1987 Fleer Award Winners

This small set of 44 standard-size cards was produced for 7-Eleven stores by Fleer. The cards feature full color fronts and yellow, white, and black backs. The card fronts are distinguished by their yellow frame around the player's full-color photo. The box for the cards describes the set as the "1987 Limited Edition Baseball's Award Winners." The checklist for the set is given on the back of the set box. The card numbering is in alphabetical order by player's name.

	MINT	NRMT
COMPLETE SET (44)	4.00	1.80
COMMON CARD (1-44)	.05	.02

☐ 1 Marty Barrett .... .05 .02
☐ 2 George Bell .... .05 .02
☐ 3 Bert Blyleven .... .10 .05
☐ 4 Bob Boone .... .10 .05
☐ 5 John Candelaria .... .05 .02
☐ 6 Jose Canseco .... .50 .23
☐ 7 Gary Carter .... .10 .05
☐ 8 Joe Carter .... .30 .14
☐ 9 Roger Clemens .... 1.00 .45
☐ 10 Cecil Cooper .... .10 .05
☐ 11 Eric Davis .... .05 .02
☐ 12 Tony Fernandez .... .05 .02
☐ 13 Scott Fletcher .... .05 .02

] 14 Bob Forsch	.05	.02
] 15 Dwight Gooden	.20	.09
] 16 Ron Guidry	.10	.05
] 17 Ozzie Guillen	.05	.02
] 18 Bill Gullickson	.05	.02
] 19 Tony Gwynn	1.25	.55
] 20 Bob Knepper	.05	.02
] 21 Ray Knight	.05	.02
] 22 Mark Langston	.10	.05
] 23 Candy Maldonado	.05	.02
] 24 Don Mattingly	1.00	.45
] 25 Roger McDowell	.05	.02
] 26 Dale Murphy	.30	.14
] 27 Dave Parker	.10	.05
] 28 Lance Parrish	.10	.05
] 29 Gary Pettis	.05	.02
] 30 Kirby Puckett	1.00	.45
] 31 Johnny Ray	.05	.02
] 32 Dave Righetti	.05	.02
] 33 Cal Ripken	2.00	.90
] 34 Bret Saberhagen	.10	.05
] 35 Ryne Sandberg	.75	.35
] 36 Mike Schmidt	.50	.23
] 37 Mike Scott	.05	.02
] 38 Ozzie Smith	.75	.35
] 39 Robby Thompson	.05	.02
] 40 Fernando Valenzuela	.10	.05
] 41 Mitch Webster UER (Mike on front)	.05	.02
] 42 Frank White	.10	.05
] 43 Mike Witt	.05	.02
] 44 Todd Worrell	.10	.05

1987 Fleer Baseball All-Stars

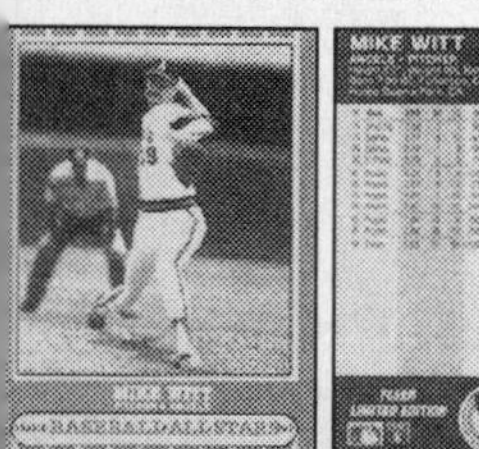
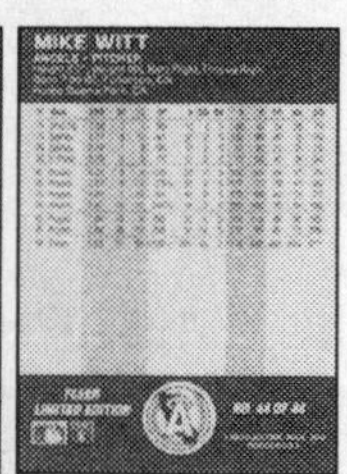

his small set of 44 standard-size cards was produced for en Franklin stores by Fleer. The cards feature full color onts and red, white, and blue backs. The card fronts are asily distinguished by their white vertical stripes over a right red background. The box for the cards proclaims imited Edition Baseball All-Stars" and is styled in the ame manner and color scheme as the cards themselves. e checklist for the set is given on the back of the set ox. The card numbering is in alphabetical order by ayer's name.

	MINT	NRMT
OMPLETE SET (44)	5.00	2.20
OMMON CARD (1-44)	.05	.02

] 1 Harold Baines	.10	.05
] 2 Jesse Barfield	.05	.02
] 3 Wade Boggs	.40	.18
] 4 Dennis Boyd	.05	.02
] 5 Scott Bradley	.05	.02
] 6 Jose Canseco	.75	.35
] 7 Gary Carter	.20	.09
] 8 Joe Carter	.30	.14
] 9 Mark Clear	.05	.02
] 10 Roger Clemens	.75	.35
] 11 Jose Cruz	.10	.05
] 12 Chili Davis	.10	.05
] 13 Jody Davis	.05	.02
] 14 Rob Deer	.05	.02
] 15 Brian Downing	.05	.02
] 16 Sid Fernandez	.05	.02
] 17 John Franco	.10	.05
] 18 Andres Galarraga	.40	.18
] 19 Dwight Gooden	.30	.14
] 20 Tony Gwynn	1.00	.45
] 21 Charlie Hough	.05	.02
] 22 Bruce Hurst	.05	.02
] 23 Wally Joyner	.20	.09
] 24 Carney Lansford	.10	.05
] 25 Fred Lynn	.10	.05
] 26 Don Mattingly	1.00	.45
] 27 Willie McGee	.10	.05
] 28 Jack Morris	.10	.05
] 29 Dale Murphy	.30	.14
] 30 Bob Ojeda	.05	.02
] 31 Tony Pena	.05	.02
] 32 Kirby Puckett	1.00	.45
☐ 33 Dan Quisenberry	.05	.02
☐ 34 Tim Raines	.10	.05
☐ 35 Willie Randolph	.10	.05
☐ 36 Cal Ripken	2.00	.90
☐ 37 Pete Rose	.75	.35
☐ 38 Nolan Ryan	2.00	.90
☐ 39 Juan Samuel	.05	.02
☐ 40 Mike Schmidt	.50	.23
☐ 41 Ozzie Smith	.75	.35
☐ 42 Andres Thomas	.05	.02
☐ 43 Fernando Valenzuela	.10	.05
☐ 44 Mike Witt	.05	.02

1987 Fleer Exciting Stars

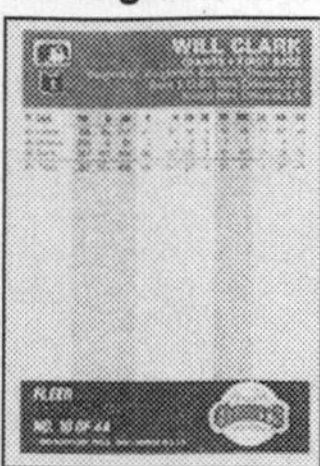

This small 44-card boxed standard-size set was produced by Fleer for distribution by the Cumberland Farm stores. The cards feature full color fronts. The set is titled "Baseball's Exciting Stars." Each individual boxed set includes the 44 cards and six logo stickers. The checklist for the set is found on the back panel of the box. The card numbering is in alphabetical order by player's name.

	MINT	NRMT
COMPLETE SET (44)	4.00	1.80
COMMON CARD (1-44)	.05	.02

☐ 1 Don Aase	.05	.02
☐ 2 Rick Aguilera	.10	.05
☐ 3 Jesse Barfield	.05	.02
☐ 4 Wade Boggs	.30	.14
☐ 5 Oil Can Boyd	.05	.02
☐ 6 Sid Bream	.05	.02
☐ 7 Jose Canseco	.75	.35
☐ 8 Steve Carlton	.30	.14
☐ 9 Gary Carter	.15	.07
☐ 10 Will Clark	.75	.35
☐ 11 Roger Clemens	.60	.25
☐ 12 Danny Cox	.05	.02
☐ 13 Alvin Davis	.05	.02
☐ 14 Eric Davis	.10	.05
☐ 15 Rob Deer	.05	.02
☐ 16 Brian Downing	.05	.02
☐ 17 Gene Garber	.10	.05
☐ 18 Steve Garvey	.25	.11
☐ 19 Dwight Gooden	.15	.07
☐ 20 Mark Gubicza	.05	.02
☐ 21 Mel Hall	.05	.02
☐ 22 Terry Harper	.05	.02
☐ 23 Von Hayes	.05	.02
☐ 24 Rickey Henderson	.25	.11
☐ 25 Tom Henke	.05	.02
☐ 26 Willie Hernandez	.05	.02
☐ 27 Ted Higuera	.05	.02
☐ 28 Rick Honeycutt	.05	.02
☐ 29 Kent Hrbek	.10	.05
☐ 30 Wally Joyner	.15	.07
☐ 31 Charlie Kerfeld	.05	.02
☐ 32 Fred Lynn	.10	.05
☐ 33 Don Mattingly	1.00	.45
☐ 34 Tim Raines	.10	.05
☐ 35 Dennis Rasmussen	.05	.02
☐ 36 Johnny Ray	.05	.02
☐ 37 Jim Rice	.10	.05
☐ 38 Pete Rose	.75	.35
☐ 39 Lee Smith	.15	.07
☐ 40 Cory Snyder	.05	.02
☐ 41 Darryl Strawberry	.15	.07
☐ 42 Kent Tekulve	.05	.02
☐ 43 Willie Wilson	.10	.05
☐ 44 Bobby Witt	.10	.05

1987 Fleer Game Winners

This small 44-card boxed standard-size set was produced by Fleer for distribution by several store chains, including Bi-Mart, Pay'n'Save, Mott's, M.E.Moses, and Winn's. The cards feature full color fronts. The set is titled "Baseball's Game Winners." Each individual boxed set includes the 44 cards and six logo stickers. The checklist for the set is found on the back panel of the box. The card numbering is in alphabetical order by player's name.

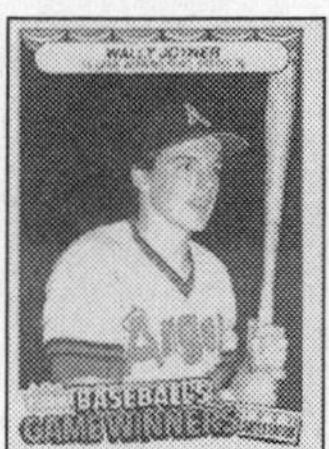

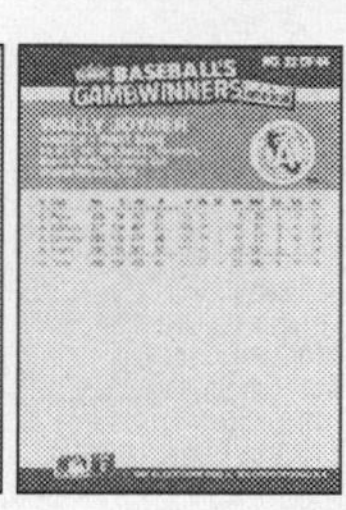

	MINT	NRMT
COMPLETE SET (44)	5.00	2.20
COMMON CARD (1-44)	.05	.02

☐ 1 Harold Baines	.10	.05
☐ 2 Don Baylor	.10	.05
☐ 3 George Bell	.05	.02
☐ 4 Tony Bernazard	.05	.02
☐ 5 Wade Boggs	.40	.18
☐ 6 George Brett	.75	.35
☐ 7 Hubie Brooks	.05	.02
☐ 8 Jose Canseco	.75	.35
☐ 9 Gary Carter	.20	.09
☐ 10 Roger Clemens	.75	.35
☐ 11 Eric Davis	.05	.02
☐ 12 Glenn Davis	.05	.02
☐ 13 Shawon Dunston	.05	.02
☐ 14 Mark Eichhorn	.05	.02
☐ 15 Gary Gaetti	.10	.05
☐ 16 Steve Garvey	.20	.09
☐ 17 Kirk Gibson	.10	.05
☐ 18 Dwight Gooden	.20	.09
☐ 19 Von Hayes	.05	.02
☐ 20 Willie Hernandez	.05	.02
☐ 21 Ted Higuera	.05	.02
☐ 22 Wally Joyner	.20	.09
☐ 23 Bob Knepper	.05	.02
☐ 24 Mike Krukow	.05	.02
☐ 25 Jeff Leonard	.05	.02
☐ 26 Don Mattingly	1.00	.45
☐ 27 Kirk McCaskill	.05	.02
☐ 28 Kevin McReynolds	.05	.02
☐ 29 Jim Morrison	.05	.02
☐ 30 Dale Murphy	.30	.14
☐ 31 Pete O'Brien	.05	.02
☐ 32 Bob Ojeda	.05	.02
☐ 33 Larry Parrish	.05	.02
☐ 34 Ken Phelps	.05	.02
☐ 35 Dennis Rasmussen	.05	.02
☐ 36 Ernest Riles	.05	.02
☐ 37 Cal Ripken	2.00	.90
☐ 38 Ron Robinson	.05	.02
☐ 39 Steve Sax	.05	.02
☐ 40 Mike Schmidt	.50	.23
☐ 41 John Tudor	.05	.02
☐ 42 Fernando Valenzuela	.10	.05
☐ 43 Mike Witt	.05	.02
☐ 44 Curt Young	.05	.02

1987 Fleer Hottest Stars

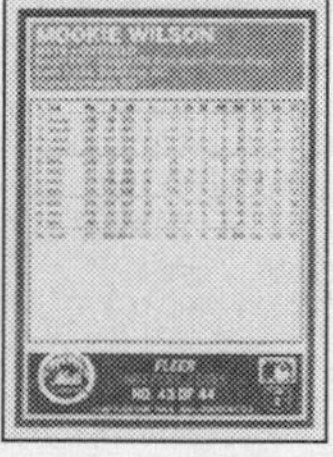

This 44-card boxed standard-size set was produced by Fleer for distribution by Revco stores all over the country. The cards feature full color fronts and red, white, and black backs. The card fronts are easily distinguished by their solid red outside borders and and white and blue inner borders framing the player's picture. The box for the cards proclaims "1987 Limited Edition Baseball's Hottest Stars" and is styled in the same manner and color scheme as the cards themselves. The checklist for the set is given on the back of the set box. The card numbering is in alphabetical order by player's name.

	MINT	NRMT
COMPLETE SET (44)	5.00	2.20
COMMON CARD (1-44)	.05	.02

☐ 1 Joaquin Andujar .05 .02
☐ 2 Harold Baines .10 .05
☐ 3 Kevin Bass .05 .02
☐ 4 Don Baylor .10 .05
☐ 5 Barry Bonds 2.00 .90
☐ 6 George Brett .75 .35
☐ 7 Tom Brunansky .05 .02
☐ 8 Brett Butler .10 .05
☐ 9 Jose Canseco .75 .35
☐ 10 Roger Clemens .75 .35
☐ 11 Ron Darling .05 .02
☐ 12 Eric Davis .05 .02
☐ 13 Andre Dawson .30 .14
☐ 14 Doug DeCinces .05 .02
☐ 15 Leon Durham .05 .02
☐ 16 Mark Eichhorn .05 .02
☐ 17 Scott Garrelts .05 .02
☐ 18 Dwight Gooden .20 .09
☐ 19 Dave Henderson .05 .02
☐ 20 Rickey Henderson .50 .23
☐ 21 Keith Hernandez .10 .05
☐ 22 Ted Higuera .05 .02
☐ 23 Bob Horner .05 .02
☐ 24 Pete Incaviglia .10 .05
☐ 25 Wally Joyner .20 .09
☐ 26 Mark Langston .05 .02
☐ 27 Don Mattingly UER 1.00 .45
(Pirates logo
on back)
☐ 28 Dale Murphy .30 .14
☐ 29 Kirk McCaskill .05 .02
☐ 30 Willie McGee .10 .05
☐ 31 Dave Righetti .05 .02
☐ 32 Pete Rose .75 .35
☐ 33 Bruce Ruffin .05 .02
☐ 34 Steve Sax .05 .02
☐ 35 Mike Schmidt .50 .23
☐ 36 Larry Sheets .05 .02
☐ 37 Eric Show .05 .02
☐ 38 Dave Smith .05 .02
☐ 39 Cory Snyder .05 .02
☐ 40 Frank Tanana .05 .02
☐ 41 Alan Trammell .30 .14
☐ 42 Reggie Williams .05 .02
☐ 43 Mookie Wilson .10 .05
☐ 44 Todd Worrell .10 .05

1987 Fleer League Leaders

This small set of 44 standard-size cards was produced for Walgreens by Fleer. The cards feature full color fronts and red, white, and blue backs. The card fronts are easily distinguished by their light blue vertical stripes over a white background. The box for the cards proclaims a "Walgreens Exclusive" and is styled in the same manner and color scheme as the cards themselves. The checklist for the set is given on the back of the set box. The card numbering is in alphabetical order by player's name.

MINT NRMT
COMPLETE SET (44) 5.00 2.20
COMMON CARD (1-44) .05 .02

☐ 1 Jesse Barfield .05 .02
☐ 2 Mike Boddicker .05 .02
☐ 3 Wade Boggs .40 .18
☐ 4 Phil Bradley .05 .02
☐ 5 George Brett .75 .35
☐ 6 Hubie Brooks .05 .02
☐ 7 Chris Brown .05 .02
☐ 8 Jose Canseco .75 .35
☐ 9 Joe Carter .30 .14
☐ 10 Roger Clemens .75 .35
☐ 11 Vince Coleman .05 .02
☐ 12 Joe Cowley .05 .02
☐ 13 Kal Daniels .05 .02
☐ 14 Glenn Davis .05 .02
☐ 15 Jody Davis .05 .02
☐ 16 Darrell Evans .10 .05
☐ 17 Dwight Evans .10 .05
☐ 18 John Franco .10 .05
☐ 19 Julio Franco .10 .05
☐ 20 Dwight Gooden .20 .09
☐ 21 Rich Gossage .10 .05
☐ 22 Tom Herr .05 .02
☐ 23 Ted Higuera .05 .02
☐ 24 Bob Horner .05 .02
☐ 25 Pete Incaviglia .10 .05
☐ 26 Wally Joyner .20 .09
☐ 27 Dave Kingman .10 .05
☐ 28 Don Mattingly 1.00 .45
☐ 29 Willie McGee .10 .05
☐ 30 Donnie Moore .05 .02
☐ 31 Keith Moreland .05 .02
☐ 32 Eddie Murray .50 .23
☐ 33 Mike Pagliarulo .05 .02
☐ 34 Larry Parrish .05 .02
☐ 35 Tony Pena .05 .02
☐ 36 Kirby Puckett 1.00 .45
☐ 37 Pete Rose .75 .35
☐ 38 Juan Samuel .05 .02
☐ 39 Ryne Sandberg .75 .35
☐ 40 Mike Schmidt .50 .23
☐ 41 Darryl Strawberry .10 .05
☐ 42 Greg Walker .05 .02
☐ 43 Bob Welch .05 .02
☐ 44 Todd Worrell .10 .05

1987 Fleer Limited Edition

This 44-card boxed standard-size set was (mass) produced by Fleer for distribution by McCrory's and is sometimes referred to as the McCrory's set. The numerical checklist on the back of the box shows that the set is numbered alphabetically.

MINT NRMT
COMPLETE SET (44) 4.00 1.80
COMMON CARD (1-44) .05 .02

☐ 1 Floyd Bannister .05 .02
☐ 2 Marty Barrett .05 .02
☐ 3 Steve Bedrosian .05 .02
☐ 4 George Bell .05 .02
☐ 5 George Brett 1.00 .45
☐ 6 Jose Canseco .60 .25
☐ 7 Joe Carter .30 .14
☐ 8 Will Clark .75 .35
☐ 9 Roger Clemens .60 .25
☐ 10 Vince Coleman .05 .02
☐ 11 Glenn Davis .05 .02
☐ 12 Mike Davis .05 .02
☐ 13 Len Dykstra .20 .09
☐ 14 John Franco .10 .05
☐ 15 Julio Franco .10 .05
☐ 16 Steve Garvey .20 .09
☐ 17 Kirk Gibson .10 .05
☐ 18 Dwight Gooden .10 .05
☐ 19 Tony Gwynn 1.00 .45
☐ 20 Keith Hernandez .10 .05
☐ 21 Teddy Higuera .05 .02
☐ 22 Kent Hrbek .10 .05
☐ 23 Wally Joyner .20 .09
☐ 24 Mike Krukow .05 .02
☐ 25 Mike Marshall .05 .02
☐ 26 Don Mattingly 1.00 .45
☐ 27 Oddibe McDowell .05 .02
☐ 28 Jack Morris .10 .05
☐ 29 Lloyd Moseby .05 .02
☐ 30 Dale Murphy .30 .14
☐ 31 Eddie Murray .60 .25
☐ 32 Tony Pena .05 .02
☐ 33 Jim Presley .05 .02
☐ 34 Jeff Reardon .05 .02
☐ 35 Jim Rice .10 .05
☐ 36 Pete Rose .75 .35
☐ 37 Mike Schmidt .50 .23
☐ 38 Mike Scott .05 .02
☐ 39 Lee Smith .20 .09
☐ 40 Lonnie Smith .05 .02
☐ 41 Gary Ward .05 .02
☐ 42 Dave Winfield .30 .14
☐ 43 Todd Worrell .05 .02
☐ 44 Robin Yount .30 .14

1987 Fleer Limited Box Cards

The cards in this six-card set each measure the standard size. Cards have essentially the same design as the 1987 Fleer Limited Edition cards which were distributed by McCrory's. The cards were printed on the bottom of the counter display box which held 24 small boxed sets hence theoretically these box cards are 1/24 as plentiful as the regular boxed set cards. These six cards, numbered C1 to C6, are considered a separate set in their own right and are not typically included in a complete set of the 1987 Fleer Limited Edition set of 44. The value of the panels uncut is slightly greater, perhaps by 25 percent greater, than the value of the individual cards cut up carefully.

MINT NRMT
COMPLETE SET (6) 2.00 .90
COMMON CARDS (C1-C6) .25 .11

☐ C1 Ron Darling .25 .11
☐ C2 Bill Buckner .50 .23
☐ C3 John Candelaria .25 .11
☐ C4 Jack Clark .50 .23
☐ C5 Bret Saberhagen 2.00 .90
☐ C6 Team Logo .25 .11
(Checklist back)

1987 Fleer Mini

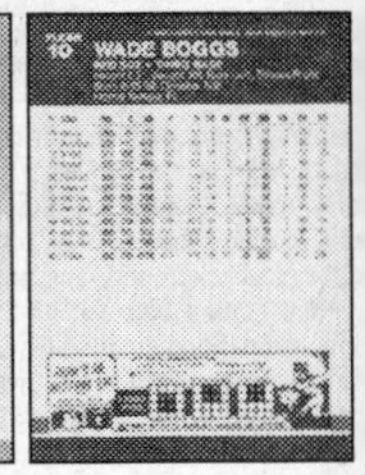

The 1987 Fleer "Classic Miniatures" set consists of 120 small cards with all new pictures of the players as compared to the 1987 Fleer regular issue. The cards are only 1 13/16" by 2 9/16", making them one of the smallest cards available. Card backs provide career year-by-year statistics. The complete set was distributed in a blue, red, white, and silver box along with 18 logo stickers. The card numbering is by alphabetical order.

MINT NRMT
COMPLETE SET (120) 6.00 2.70
COMMON CARD (1-120) .05 .02

☐ 1 Don Aase .05 .02
☐ 2 Joaquin Andujar .05 .02
☐ 3 Harold Baines .10 .05
☐ 4 Jesse Barfield .05 .02
☐ 5 Kevin Bass .05 .02
☐ 6 Don Baylor .10 .05
☐ 7 George Bell .05 .02
☐ 8 Tony Bernazard .05 .02
☐ 9 Bert Blyleven .10 .05
☐ 10 Wade Boggs .30 .14
☐ 11 Phil Bradley .05 .02
☐ 12 Sid Bream .05 .02
☐ 13 George Brett 1.00 .45
☐ 14 Hubie Brooks .05 .02
☐ 15 Chris Brown .05 .02
☐ 16 Tom Candiotti .05 .02
☐ 17 Jose Canseco .60 .25
☐ 18 Gary Carter .15 .07
☐ 19 Joe Carter .25 .11
☐ 20 Roger Clemens 1.00 .45
☐ 21 Vince Coleman .05 .02
☐ 22 Cecil Cooper .10 .05
☐ 23 Ron Darling .05 .02

☐ 24 Alvin Davis	.05	.02
☐ 25 Chili Davis	.10	.05
☐ 26 Eric Davis	.10	.05
☐ 27 Glenn Davis	.05	.02
☐ 28 Mike Davis	.05	.02
☐ 29 Doug DeCinces	.05	.02
☐ 30 Rob Deer	.05	.02
☐ 31 Jim Deshaies	.05	.02
☐ 32 Bo Diaz	.05	.02
☐ 33 Richard Dotson	.05	.02
☐ 34 Brian Downing	.05	.02
☐ 35 Shawon Dunston	.05	.02
☐ 36 Mark Eichhorn	.05	.02
☐ 37 Dwight Evans	.10	.05
☐ 38 Tony Fernandez	.05	.02
☐ 39 Julio Franco	.10	.05
☐ 40 Gary Gaetti	.10	.05
☐ 41 Andres Galarraga	.40	.18
☐ 42 Scott Garrelts	.05	.02
☐ 43 Steve Garvey	.15	.07
☐ 44 Kirk Gibson	.10	.05
☐ 45 Dwight Gooden	.15	.07
☐ 46 Ken Griffey	.10	.05
☐ 47 Mark Gubicza	.05	.02
☐ 48 Ozzie Guillen	.05	.02
☐ 49 Bill Gullickson	.05	.02
☐ 50 Tony Gwynn	1.00	.45
☐ 51 Von Hayes	.05	.02
☐ 52 Rickey Henderson	.50	.23
☐ 53 Keith Hernandez	.10	.05
☐ 54 Willie Hernandez	.05	.02
☐ 55 Ted Higuera	.05	.02
☐ 56 Charlie Hough	.05	.02
☐ 57 Kent Hrbek	.10	.05
☐ 58 Pete Incaviglia	.10	.05
☐ 59 Wally Joyner	.30	.14
☐ 60 Bob Knepper	.05	.02
☐ 61 Mike Krukow	.05	.02
☐ 62 Mark Langston	.05	.02
☐ 63 Carney Lansford	.10	.05
☐ 64 Jim Lindeman	.05	.02
☐ 65 Bill Madlock	.10	.05
☐ 66 Don Mattingly	1.00	.45
☐ 67 Kirk McCaskill	.05	.02
☐ 68 Lance McCullers	.05	.02
☐ 69 Keith Moreland	.05	.02
☐ 70 Jack Morris	.10	.05
☐ 71 Jim Morrison	.05	.02
☐ 72 Lloyd Moseby	.05	.02
☐ 73 Jerry Mumphrey	.05	.02
☐ 74 Dale Murphy	.25	.11
☐ 75 Eddie Murray	.60	.25
☐ 76 Pete O'Brien	.05	.02
☐ 77 Bob Ojeda	.05	.02
☐ 78 Jesse Orosco	.05	.02
☐ 79 Dan Pasqua	.05	.02
☐ 80 Dave Parker	.10	.05
☐ 81 Larry Parrish	.05	.02
☐ 82 Jim Presley	.05	.02
☐ 83 Kirby Puckett	1.00	.45
☐ 84 Dan Quisenberry	.05	.02
☐ 85 Tim Raines	.10	.05
☐ 86 Dennis Rasmussen	.05	.02
☐ 87 Johnny Ray	.05	.02
☐ 88 Jeff Reardon	.10	.05
☐ 89 Jim Rice	.10	.05
☐ 90 Dave Righetti	.05	.02
☐ 91 Earnest Riles	.05	.02
☐ 92 Cal Ripken	1.50	.70
☐ 93 Ron Robinson	.05	.02
☐ 94 Juan Samuel	.05	.02
☐ 95 Ryne Sandberg	.60	.25
☐ 96 Steve Sax	.05	.02
☐ 97 Mike Schmidt	.40	.18
☐ 98 Ken Schrom	.05	.02
☐ 99 Mike Scott	.05	.02
☐ 100 Ruben Sierra	.10	.05
☐ 101 Lee Smith	.15	.07
☐ 102 Ozzie Smith	.75	.35
☐ 103 Cory Snyder	.05	.02
☐ 104 Kent Tekulve	.05	.02
☐ 105 Andres Thomas	.05	.02
☐ 106 Robby Thompson	.05	.02
☐ 107 Alan Trammell	.15	.07
☐ 108 John Tudor	.05	.02
☐ 109 Fernando Valenzuela	.10	.05
☐ 110 Greg Walker	.05	.02
☐ 111 Mitch Webster	.05	.02
☐ 112 Lou Whitaker	.10	.05
☐ 113 Frank White	.10	.05
☐ 114 Reggie Williams	.05	.02
☐ 115 Glenn Wilson	.05	.02
☐ 116 Willie Wilson	.10	.05
☐ 117 Dave Winfield	.50	.23
☐ 118 Mike Witt	.05	.02
☐ 119 Todd Worrell	.10	.05
☐ 120 Floyd Youmans	.05	.02

1987 Fleer Record Setters

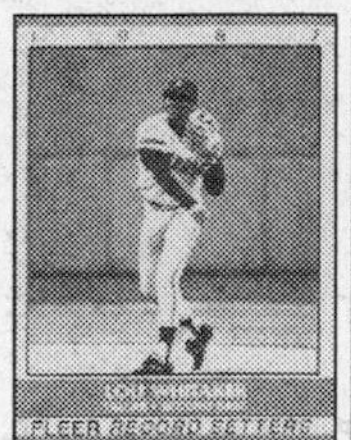

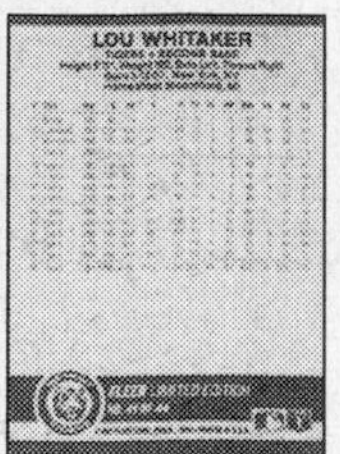

This 44-card boxed standard-size set was produced by Fleer for distribution by Eckerd's Drug Stores and is sometimes referred to as the Eckerd's set. Six team logo stickers are included in the box with the complete set. The numerical checklist on the back of the box shows that the set is numbered alphabetically.

	MINT	NRMT
COMPLETE SET (44)	4.00	1.80
COMMON CARD (1-44)	.05	.02

☐ 1 George Brett	.75	.35
☐ 2 Chris Brown	.05	.02
☐ 3 Jose Canseco UER (3 of 444 on back)	.50	.23
☐ 4 Roger Clemens	.50	.23
☐ 5 Alvin Davis UER (5 of 441 on back, upside down one)	.05	.02
☐ 6 Shawon Dunston	.05	.02
☐ 7 Tony Fernandez	.05	.02
☐ 8 Carlton Fisk UER (8 of 44' on back)	.40	.18
☐ 9 Gary Gaetti UER (9 of 444 on back)	.10	.05
☐ 10 Gene Garber	.05	.02
☐ 11 Rich Gedman	.05	.02
☐ 12 Dwight Gooden	.20	.09
☐ 13 Ozzie Guillen	.05	.02
☐ 14 Bill Gullickson	.05	.02
☐ 15 Billy Hatcher	.05	.02
☐ 16 Orel Hershiser	.10	.05
☐ 17 Wally Joyner	.40	.18
☐ 18 Ray Knight	.05	.02
☐ 19 Craig Lefferts	.05	.02
☐ 20 Don Mattingly	1.00	.45
☐ 21 Kevin Mitchell	.10	.05
☐ 22 Lloyd Moseby	.05	.02
☐ 23 Dale Murphy	.20	.09
☐ 24 Eddie Murray	.50	.23
☐ 25 Phil Niekro	.40	.18
☐ 26 Ben Oglivie	.05	.02
☐ 27 Jesse Orosco	.05	.02
☐ 28 Joe Orsulak	.05	.02
☐ 29 Larry Parrish	.05	.02
☐ 30 Tim Raines	.10	.05
☐ 31 Shane Rawley	.05	.02
☐ 32 Dave Righetti	.05	.02
☐ 33 Pete Rose	.75	.35
☐ 34 Steve Sax	.05	.02
☐ 35 Mike Schmidt	.50	.23
☐ 36 Mike Scott	.05	.02
☐ 37 Don Sutton	.40	.18
☐ 38 Alan Trammell	.20	.09
☐ 39 John Tudor	.05	.02
☐ 40 Gary Ward	.05	.02
☐ 41 Lou Whitaker	.10	.05
☐ 42 Willie Wilson	.10	.05
☐ 43 Todd Worrell	.10	.05
☐ 44 Floyd Youmans	.05	.02

1987 Fleer Sluggers/Pitchers

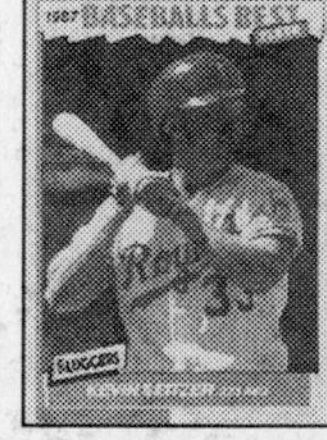

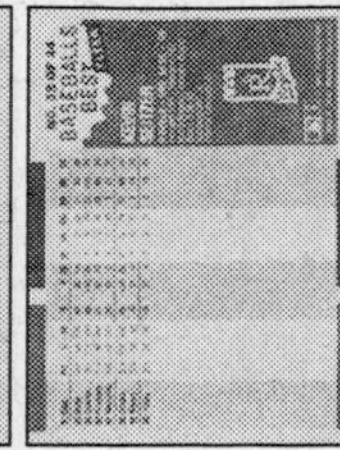

Fleer produced this 44-card boxed standard-size set although it was primarily distributed by McCrory, McLellan, Newberry, H.L.Green, T.G.Y., and other similar stores. The set features 28 sluggers and 16 pitchers and is subtitled "Baseball's Best". The set was packaged in a red, white, blue, and yellow custom box along with six logo stickers. The set checklist is given on the back of the box. The checklist on the back of the set box misspells McGwire as McGuire. The card numbering is in alphabetical order by player's name.

	MINT	NRMT
COMPLETE SET (44)	5.00	2.20
COMMON CARD (1-44)	.05	.02

☐ 1 Kevin Bass	.05	.02
☐ 2 Jesse Barfield	.05	.02
☐ 3 George Bell	.05	.02
☐ 4 Wade Boggs	.30	.14
☐ 5 Sid Bream	.05	.02
☐ 6 George Brett	1.00	.45
☐ 7 Ivan Calderon	.05	.02
☐ 8 Jose Canseco	.60	.25
☐ 9 Jack Clark	.10	.05
☐ 10 Roger Clemens	1.00	.45
☐ 11 Eric Davis	.10	.05
☐ 12 Andre Dawson	.25	.11
☐ 13 Sid Fernandez	.05	.02
☐ 14 John Franco	.10	.05
☐ 15 Dwight Gooden	.15	.07
☐ 16 Pedro Guerrero	.10	.05
☐ 17 Tony Gwynn	1.00	.45
☐ 18 Rickey Henderson	.50	.23
☐ 19 Tom Henke	.05	.02
☐ 20 Ted Higuera	.05	.02
☐ 21 Pete Incaviglia	.10	.05
☐ 22 Wally Joyner	.30	.14
☐ 23 Jeff Leonard	.05	.02
☐ 24 Joe Magrane	.05	.02
☐ 25 Don Mattingly	1.00	.45
☐ 26 Mark McGwire	2.00	.90
☐ 27 Jack Morris	.10	.05
☐ 28 Dale Murphy	.25	.11
☐ 29 Dave Parker	.10	.05
☐ 30 Ken Phelps	.05	.02
☐ 31 Kirby Puckett	1.00	.45
☐ 32 Tim Raines	.10	.05
☐ 33 Jeff Reardon	.05	.02
☐ 34 Dave Righetti	.05	.02
☐ 35 Cal Ripken	2.00	.90
☐ 36 Bret Saberhagen	.10	.05
☐ 37 Mike Schmidt	.50	.23
☐ 38 Mike Scott	.05	.02
☐ 39 Kevin Seitzer	.10	.05
☐ 40 Darryl Strawberry	.10	.05
☐ 41 Rick Sutcliffe	.05	.02
☐ 42 Pat Tabler	.05	.02
☐ 43 Fernando Valenzuela	.10	.05
☐ 44 Mike Witt	.05	.02

1987 Fleer Sluggers/Pitchers Box Cards

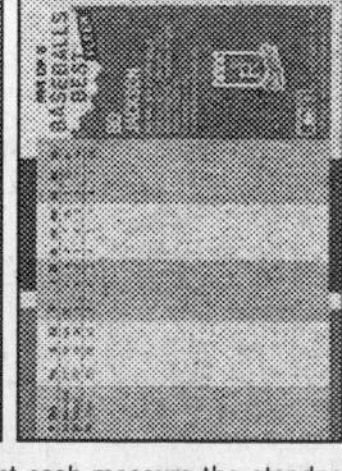

The cards in this six-card set each measure the standard size. Cards have essentially the same design as the 1987 Fleer Sluggers vs. Pitchers set of Baseball's Best. The cards were printed on the bottom of the counter display box which held 24 small boxed sets; hence theoretically these box cards are 1/24 as plentiful as the regular boxed set cards. These six cards, numbered M1 to M5 with one blank-back (unnumbered) card, are considered a separate set in their own right and are not typically included in a complete set of the 1987 Fleer Sluggers vs. Pitchers set of 44. The value of the panels uncut is slightly greater, perhaps by 25 percent greater, than the value of the individual cards cut up carefully.

	MINT	NRMT
COMPLETE SET (6)	10.00	4.50
COMMON CARD	.50	.23

☐ M1 Steve Bedrosian	.50	.23
☐ M2 Will Clark	6.00	2.70
☐ M3 Vince Coleman	.50	.23
☐ M4 Bo Jackson	3.00	1.35

Card	MINT	NRMT
☐ M5 Cory Snyder	.50	.23
☐ NNO Team Logo (Blank back)	.50	.23

1987 Fleer Sticker Cards

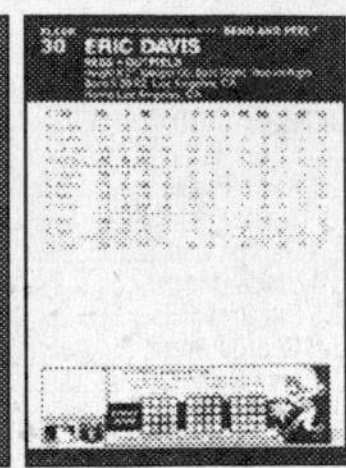

These Star Stickers were distributed as a separate issue by Fleer with five star stickers and a logo sticker in each wax pack. The 132-card (sticker) set features 2 1/2" by 3 1/2" full-color fronts and even statistics on the sticker back, which is an indication that the Fleer Company understands that these stickers are rarely used as stickers but more like traditional cards. The fronts are surrounded by a green border and the backs are printed in green and yellow on white card stock. The numbering is in alphabetical order by player's name.

	MINT	NRMT
COMPLETE SET (132)	15.00	6.75
COMMON CARD (1-132)	.05	.02
☐ 1 Don Aase	.05	.02
☐ 2 Harold Baines	.10	.05
☐ 3 Floyd Bannister	.05	.02
☐ 4 Jesse Barfield	.05	.02
☐ 5 Marty Barrett	.05	.02
☐ 6 Kevin Bass	.05	.02
☐ 7 Don Baylor	.10	.05
☐ 8 Steve Bedrosian	.05	.02
☐ 9 George Bell	.05	.02
☐ 10 Bert Blyleven	.10	.05
☐ 11 Mike Boddicker	.05	.02
☐ 12 Wade Boggs	.50	.23
☐ 13 Phil Bradley	.05	.02
☐ 14 Sid Bream	.05	.02
☐ 15 George Brett	1.50	.70
☐ 16 Hubie Brooks	.05	.02
☐ 17 Tom Brunansky	.05	.02
☐ 18 Tom Candiotti	.05	.02
☐ 19 Jose Canseco	1.00	.45
☐ 20 Gary Carter	.10	.05
☐ 21 Joe Carter	.40	.18
☐ 22 Will Clark	1.50	.70
☐ 23 Mark Clear	.05	.02
☐ 24 Roger Clemens	1.25	.55
☐ 25 Vince Coleman	.05	.02
☐ 26 Jose Cruz	.10	.05
☐ 27 Ron Darling	.05	.02
☐ 28 Alvin Davis	.05	.02
☐ 29 Chili Davis	.10	.05
☐ 30 Eric Davis	.10	.05
☐ 31 Glenn Davis	.05	.02
☐ 32 Mike Davis	.05	.02
☐ 33 Andre Dawson	.40	.18
☐ 34 Doug DeCinces	.05	.02
☐ 35 Brian Downing	.05	.02
☐ 36 Shawon Dunston	.05	.02
☐ 37 Mark Eichhorn	.05	.02
☐ 38 Dwight Evans	.10	.05
☐ 39 Tony Fernandez	.05	.02
☐ 40 Bob Forsch	.05	.02
☐ 41 John Franco	.10	.05
☐ 42 Julio Franco	.10	.05
☐ 43 Gary Gaetti	.10	.05
☐ 44 Gene Garber	.10	.05
☐ 45 Scott Garrelts	.05	.02
☐ 46 Steve Garvey	.25	.11
☐ 47 Kirk Gibson	.10	.05
☐ 48 Dwight Gooden	.10	.05
☐ 49 Ken Griffey Sr.	.10	.05
☐ 50 Ozzie Guillen	.05	.02
☐ 51 Bill Gullickson	.05	.02
☐ 52 Tony Gwynn	1.50	.70
☐ 53 Mel Hall	.05	.02
☐ 54 Greg A. Harris	.05	.02
☐ 55 Von Hayes	.05	.02
☐ 56 Rickey Henderson	.60	.25
☐ 57 Tom Henke	.05	.02
☐ 58 Keith Hernandez	.10	.05
☐ 59 Willie Hernandez	.05	.02
☐ 60 Ted Higuera	.05	.02
☐ 61 Bob Horner	.05	.02
☐ 62 Charlie Hough	.05	.02
☐ 63 Jay Howell	.05	.02
☐ 64 Kent Hrbek	.10	.05
☐ 65 Bruce Hurst	.05	.02
☐ 66 Pete Incaviglia	.10	.05
☐ 67 Bob James	.05	.02
☐ 68 Wally Joyner	.50	.23
☐ 69 Mike Krukow	.05	.02
☐ 70 Mark Langston	.05	.02
☐ 71 Carney Lansford	.10	.05
☐ 72 Fred Lynn	.10	.05
☐ 73 Bill Madlock	.10	.05
☐ 74 Don Mattingly	1.50	.70
☐ 75 Kirk McCaskill	.05	.02
☐ 76 Lance McCullers	.05	.02
☐ 77 Oddibe McDowell	.05	.02
☐ 78 Paul Molitor	.60	.25
☐ 79 Keith Moreland	.05	.02
☐ 80 Jack Morris	.10	.05
☐ 81 Jim Morrison	.05	.02
☐ 82 Jerry Mumphrey	.05	.02
☐ 83 Dale Murphy	.40	.18
☐ 84 Eddie Murray	.75	.35
☐ 85 Ben Oglivie	.05	.02
☐ 86 Bob Ojeda	.05	.02
☐ 87 Jesse Orosco	.05	.02
☐ 88 Dave Parker	.10	.05
☐ 89 Larry Parrish	.05	.02
☐ 90 Tony Pena	.05	.02
☐ 91 Jim Presley	.05	.02
☐ 92 Kirby Puckett	1.50	.70
☐ 93 Dan Quisenberry	.05	.02
☐ 94 Tim Raines	.10	.05
☐ 95 Dennis Rasmussen	.05	.02
☐ 96 Shane Rawley	.05	.02
☐ 97 Johnny Ray	.05	.02
☐ 98 Jeff Reardon	.10	.05
☐ 99 Jim Rice	.10	.05
☐ 100 Dave Righetti	.05	.02
☐ 101 Cal Ripken	3.00	1.35
☐ 102 Pete Rose	1.25	.55
☐ 103 Nolan Ryan	3.00	1.35
☐ 104 Juan Samuel	.05	.02
☐ 105 Ryne Sandberg	1.25	.55
☐ 106 Steve Sax	.05	.02
☐ 107 Mike Schmidt	.75	.35
☐ 108 Mike Scott	.05	.02
☐ 109 Dave Smith	.05	.02
☐ 110 Lee Smith	.25	.11
☐ 111 Lonnie Smith	.05	.02
☐ 112 Ozzie Smith	1.25	.55
☐ 113 Cory Snyder	.05	.02
☐ 114 Darryl Strawberry	.10	.05
☐ 115 Don Sutton	.50	.23
☐ 116 Kent Tekulve	.05	.02
☐ 117 Andres Thomas	.05	.02
☐ 118 Alan Trammell	.25	.11
☐ 119 John Tudor	.05	.02
☐ 120 Fernando Valenzuela	.10	.05
☐ 121 Bob Welch	.10	.05
☐ 122 Lou Whitaker	.10	.05
☐ 123 Frank White	.10	.05
☐ 124 Reggie Williams	.05	.02
☐ 125 Willie Wilson	.10	.05
☐ 126 Dave Winfield	.40	.18
☐ 127 Mike Witt	.05	.02
☐ 128 Todd Worrell	.10	.05
☐ 129 Curt Young	.05	.02
☐ 130 Robin Yount	.40	.18
☐ 131 Jose Canseco CL Don Mattingly	.75	.35
☐ 132 Bo Jackson CL Eric Davis	.25	.11

1987 Fleer Stickers Wax Box Cards

The bottoms of the Star Sticker wax boxes contained two different sets of four cards done in a similar format to the stickers; these cards (they are not stickers but truly cards) are numbered with the prefix S and are considered a separate set. The value of the panels uncut is slightly greater, perhaps by 25 percent greater, than the value of the individual cards cut up carefully. When cut properly, the individual cards measure standard size, 2 1/2" by 3 1/2".

	MINT	NRMT
COMPLETE SET (8)	5.00	2.20
COMMON CARD (S1-S8)	.10	.05
☐ S1 Detroit Logo	.10	.05
☐ S2 Wade Boggs	1.50	.70
☐ S3 Bert Blyleven	.25	.11
☐ S4 Jose Cruz	.10	.05
☐ S5 Glenn Davis	.10	.05
☐ S6 Phillies Logo	.10	.05
☐ S7 Bob Horner	.10	.05
☐ S8 Don Mattingly	3.00	1.35

1988 Fleer

This set consists of 660 standard-size cards. Cards were primarily issued in 15-card wax packs and hobby and retail factory sets. Each wax pack contained one of 26 different "Stadium Card" stickers. Card fronts feature a distinctive white background with red and blue diagonal stripes across the card. Cards are again organized numerically by teams and team order is based upon the previous season's record. Subsets include Specials (622-640), Rookie Pairs (641-653), and checklists (654-660). Rookie Cards in this set include Jay Bell, John Burkett, Ellis Burks, Ken Caminiti, Ron Gant, Tom Glavine, Mark Grace, Gregg Jefferies, Edgar Martinez, Jack McDowell, Jeff Montgomery, and Matt Williams.

	MINT	NRMT
COMPLETE SET (660)	20.00	9.00
COMPLETE RETAIL SET (660)	20.00	9.00
COMPLETE HOBBY SET (672)	25.00	11.00
COMMON CARD (1-660)	.10	.05
☐ 1 Keith Atherton	.10	.05
☐ 2 Don Baylor	.40	.18
☐ 3 Juan Berenguer	.10	.05
☐ 4 Bert Blyleven	.20	.09
☐ 5 Tom Brunansky	.10	.05
☐ 6 Randy Bush	.10	.05
☐ 7 Steve Carlton	.40	.18
☐ 8 Mark Davidson	.10	.05
☐ 9 George Frazier	.10	.05
☐ 10 Gary Gaetti	.10	.05
☐ 11 Greg Gagne	.10	.05
☐ 12 Dan Gladden	.10	.05
☐ 13 Kent Hrbek	.20	.09
☐ 14 Gene Larkin	.10	.05
☐ 15 Tim Laudner	.10	.05
☐ 16 Steve Lombardozzi	.10	.05
☐ 17 Al Newman	.10	.05
☐ 18 Joe Niekro	.10	.05
☐ 19 Kirby Puckett	.75	.35
☐ 20 Jeff Reardon	.20	.09
☐ 21A Dan Schatzeder ERR (Misspelled Schatzader on card front)	.20	.09
☐ 21B Dan Schatzeder COR	.10	.05
☐ 22 Roy Smalley	.10	.05
☐ 23 Mike Smithson	.10	.05
☐ 24 Les Straker	.10	.05
☐ 25 Frank Viola	.10	.05
☐ 26 Jack Clark	.20	.09
☐ 27 Vince Coleman	.10	.05
☐ 28 Danny Cox	.10	.05
☐ 29 Bill Dawley	.10	.05
☐ 30 Ken Dayley	.10	.05
☐ 31 Doug DeCinces	.10	.05
☐ 32 Curt Ford	.10	.05
☐ 33 Bob Forsch	.10	.05
☐ 34 David Green	.10	.05
☐ 35 Tom Herr	.10	.05
☐ 36 Ricky Horton	.10	.05
☐ 37 Lance Johnson	.50	.23
☐ 38 Steve Lake	.10	.05
☐ 39 Jim Lindeman	.10	.05

☐ 40 Joe Magrane .10 .05
☐ 41 Greg Mathews .10 .05
☐ 42 Willie McGee .10 .05
☐ 43 John Morris .10 .05
☐ 44 Jose Oquendo .10 .05
☐ 45 Tony Pena .10 .05
☐ 46 Terry Pendleton .20 .09
☐ 47 Ozzie Smith .50 .23
☐ 48 John Tudor .10 .05
☐ 49 Lee Tunnell .10 .05
☐ 50 Todd Worrell .10 .05
☐ 51 Doyle Alexander .10 .05
☐ 52 Dave Bergman .10 .05
☐ 53 Tom Brookens .10 .05
☐ 54 Darrell Evans .20 .09
☐ 55 Kirk Gibson .20 .09
☐ 56 Mike Heath .10 .05
☐ 57 Mike Henneman .20 .09
☐ 58 Willie Hernandez .10 .05
☐ 59 Larry Herndon .10 .05
☐ 60 Eric King .10 .05
☐ 61 Chet Lemon .10 .05
☐ 62 Scott Lusader .10 .05
☐ 63 Bill Madlock .10 .05
☐ 64 Jack Morris .40 .18
☐ 65 Jim Morrison .10 .05
☐ 66 Matt Nokes .10 .05
☐ 67 Dan Petry .10 .05
☐ 68A Jeff M. Robinson ERR .40 .18
(Stats for Jeff D. Robinson on card back, Born 12-13-60)
☐ 68B Jeff M. Robinson COR .10 .05
(Born 12-14-61)
☐ 69 Pat Sheridan .10 .05
☐ 70 Nate Snell .10 .05
☐ 71 Frank Tanana .10 .05
☐ 72 Walt Terrell .10 .05
☐ 73 Mark Thurmond .10 .05
☐ 74 Alan Trammell .10 .05
☐ 75 Lou Whitaker .20 .09
☐ 76 Mike Aldrete .10 .05
☐ 77 Bob Brenly .10 .05
☐ 78 Will Clark .50 .23
☐ 79 Chili Davis .10 .05
☐ 80 Kelly Downs .10 .05
☐ 81 Dave Dravecky .20 .09
☐ 82 Scott Garrelts .10 .05
☐ 83 Atlee Hammaker .10 .05
☐ 84 Dave Henderson .10 .05
☐ 85 Mike Krukow .10 .05
☐ 86 Mike LaCoss .10 .05
☐ 87 Craig Lefferts .10 .05
☐ 88 Jeff Leonard .10 .05
☐ 89 Candy Maldonado .10 .05
☐ 90 Eddie Milner .10 .05
☐ 91 Bob Melvin .10 .05
☐ 92 Kevin Mitchell .20 .09
☐ 93 Jon Perlman .10 .05
☐ 94 Rick Reuschel .10 .05
☐ 95 Don Robinson .10 .05
☐ 96 Chris Speier .10 .05
☐ 97 Harry Spilman .10 .05
☐ 98 Robby Thompson .10 .05
☐ 99 Jose Uribe .10 .05
☐ 100 Mark Wasinger .10 .05
☐ 101 Matt Williams 2.00 .90
☐ 102 Jesse Barfield .10 .05
☐ 103 George Bell .10 .05
☐ 104 Juan Beniquez .10 .05
☐ 105 John Cerutti .10 .05
☐ 106 Jim Clancy .10 .05
☐ 107 Rob Ducey .10 .05
☐ 108 Mark Eichhorn .10 .05
☐ 109 Tony Fernandez .10 .05
☐ 110 Cecil Fielder .10 .05
☐ 111 Kelly Gruber .10 .05
☐ 112 Tom Henke .10 .05
☐ 113A Garth Iorg ERR .40 .18
(Misspelled Iorq on card front)
☐ 113B Garth Iorg COR .10 .05
☐ 114 Jimmy Key .20 .09
☐ 115 Rick Leach .10 .05
☐ 116 Manny Lee .10 .05
☐ 117 Nelson Liriano .10 .05
☐ 118 Fred McGriff .40 .18
☐ 119 Lloyd Moseby .10 .05
☐ 120 Rance Mulliniks .10 .05
☐ 121 Jeff Musselman .10 .05
☐ 122 Jose Nunez .10 .05
☐ 123 Dave Stieb .20 .09
☐ 124 Willie Upshaw .10 .05
☐ 125 Duane Ward .10 .05
☐ 126 Ernie Whitt .10 .05
☐ 127 Rick Aguilera .10 .05
☐ 128 Wally Backman .10 .05
☐ 129 Mark Carreon .40 .18
☐ 130 Gary Carter .40 .18
☐ 131 David Cone .50 .23
☐ 132 Ron Darling .10 .05
☐ 133 Len Dykstra .20 .09
☐ 134 Sid Fernandez .10 .05
☐ 135 Dwight Gooden .10 .05
☐ 136 Keith Hernandez .20 .09
☐ 137 Gregg Jefferies .50 .23
☐ 138 Howard Johnson .10 .05
☐ 139 Terry Leach .10 .05
☐ 140 Barry Lyons .10 .05
☐ 141 Dave Magadan .10 .05
☐ 142 Roger McDowell .10 .05
☐ 143 Kevin McReynolds .10 .05
☐ 144 Keith A. Miller .10 .05
☐ 145 John Mitchell .10 .05
☐ 146 Randy Myers .40 .18
☐ 147 Bob Ojeda .10 .05
☐ 148 Jesse Orosco .10 .05
☐ 149 Rafael Santana .10 .05
☐ 150 Doug Sisk .10 .05
☐ 151 Darryl Strawberry .20 .09
☐ 152 Tim Teufel .10 .05
☐ 153 Gene Walter .10 .05
☐ 154 Mookie Wilson .20 .09
☐ 155 Jay Aldrich .10 .05
☐ 156 Chris Bosio .10 .05
☐ 157 Glenn Braggs .10 .05
☐ 158 Greg Brock .10 .05
☐ 159 Juan Castillo .10 .05
☐ 160 Mark Clear .10 .05
☐ 161 Cecil Cooper .20 .09
☐ 162 Chuck Crim .10 .05
☐ 163 Rob Deer .10 .05
☐ 164 Mike Felder .10 .05
☐ 165 Jim Gantner .10 .05
☐ 166 Ted Higuera .10 .05
☐ 167 Steve Kiefer .10 .05
☐ 168 Rick Manning .10 .05
☐ 169 Paul Molitor .40 .18
☐ 170 Juan Nieves .10 .05
☐ 171 Dan Plesac .10 .05
☐ 172 Earnest Riles .10 .05
☐ 173 Bill Schroeder .10 .05
☐ 174 Steve Stanicek .10 .05
☐ 175 B.J. Surhoff .20 .09
☐ 176 Dale Sveum .10 .05
☐ 177 Bill Wegman .10 .05
☐ 178 Robin Yount .40 .18
☐ 179 Hubie Brooks .10 .05
☐ 180 Tim Burke .10 .05
☐ 181 Casey Candaele .10 .05
☐ 182 Mike Fitzgerald .10 .05
☐ 183 Tom Foley .10 .05
☐ 184 Andres Galarraga .40 .18
☐ 185 Neal Heaton .10 .05
☐ 186 Wallace Johnson .10 .05
☐ 187 Vance Law .10 .05
☐ 188 Dennis Martinez .20 .09
☐ 189 Bob McClure .10 .05
☐ 190 Andy McGaffigan .10 .05
☐ 191 Reid Nichols .10 .05
☐ 192 Pascual Perez .10 .05
☐ 193 Tim Raines .20 .09
☐ 194 Jeff Reed .10 .05
☐ 195 Bob Sebra .10 .05
☐ 196 Bryn Smith .10 .05
☐ 197 Randy St.Claire .10 .05
☐ 198 Tim Wallach .10 .05
☐ 199 Mitch Webster .10 .05
☐ 200 Herm Winningham .10 .05
☐ 201 Floyd Youmans .10 .05
☐ 202 Brad Arnsberg .10 .05
☐ 203 Rick Cerone .10 .05
☐ 204 Pat Clements .10 .05
☐ 205 Henry Cotto .10 .05
☐ 206 Mike Easler .10 .05
☐ 207 Ron Guidry .10 .05
☐ 208 Bill Gullickson .10 .05
☐ 209 Rickey Henderson .40 .18
☐ 210 Charles Hudson .10 .05
☐ 211 Tommy John .20 .09
☐ 212 Roberto Kelly .40 .18
☐ 213 Ron Kittle .10 .05
☐ 214 Don Mattingly .60 .25
☐ 215 Bobby Meacham .10 .05
☐ 216 Mike Pagliarulo .10 .05
☐ 217 Dan Pasqua .10 .05
☐ 218 Willie Randolph .20 .09
☐ 219 Rick Rhoden .10 .05
☐ 220 Dave Righetti .20 .09
☐ 221 Jerry Royster .10 .05
☐ 222 Tim Stoddard .10 .05
☐ 223 Wayne Tolleson .10 .05
☐ 224 Gary Ward .10 .05
☐ 225 Claudell Washington .10 .05
☐ 226 Dave Winfield .40 .18
☐ 227 Buddy Bell .20 .09
☐ 228 Tom Browning .10 .05
☐ 229 Dave Concepcion .20 .09
☐ 230 Kal Daniels .10 .05
☐ 231 Eric Davis .10 .05
☐ 232 Bo Diaz .10 .05
☐ 233 Nick Esasky .10 .05
(Has a dollar sign before '87 SB totals)
☐ 234 John Franco .20 .09
☐ 235 Guy Hoffman .10 .05
☐ 236 Tom Hume .10 .05
☐ 237 Tracy Jones .10 .05
☐ 238 Bill Landrum .10 .05
☐ 239 Barry Larkin .75 .35
☐ 240 Terry McGriff .10 .05
☐ 241 Rob Murphy .10 .05
☐ 242 Ron Oester .10 .05
☐ 243 Dave Parker .20 .09
☐ 244 Pat Perry .10 .05
☐ 245 Ted Power .10 .05
☐ 246 Dennis Rasmussen .10 .05
☐ 247 Ron Robinson .10 .05
☐ 248 Kurt Stillwell .10 .05
☐ 249 Jeff Treadway .10 .05
☐ 250 Frank Williams .10 .05
☐ 251 Steve Balboni .10 .05
☐ 252 Bud Black .10 .05
☐ 253 Thad Bosley .10 .05
☐ 254 George Brett .75 .35
☐ 255 John Davis .10 .05
☐ 256 Steve Farr .10 .05
☐ 257 Gene Garber .10 .05
☐ 258 Jerry Don Gleaton .10 .05
☐ 259 Mark Gubicza .10 .05
☐ 260 Bo Jackson .40 .18
☐ 261 Danny Jackson .10 .05
☐ 262 Ross Jones .10 .05
☐ 263 Charlie Leibrandt .10 .05
☐ 264 Bill Pecota .10 .05
☐ 265 Melido Perez .20 .09
☐ 266 Jamie Quirk .10 .05
☐ 267 Dan Quisenberry .10 .05
☐ 268 Bret Saberhagen .20 .09
☐ 269 Angel Salazar .10 .05
☐ 270 Kevin Seitzer UER .20 .09
(Wrong birth year)
☐ 271 Danny Tartabull .10 .05
☐ 272 Gary Thurman .10 .05
☐ 273 Frank White .20 .09
☐ 274 Willie Wilson .10 .05
☐ 275 Tony Bernazard .10 .05
☐ 276 Jose Canseco .40 .18
☐ 277 Mike Davis .10 .05
☐ 278 Storm Davis .10 .05
☐ 279 Dennis Eckersley .20 .09
☐ 280 Alfredo Griffin .10 .05
☐ 281 Rick Honeycutt .10 .05
☐ 282 Jay Howell .10 .05
☐ 283 Reggie Jackson .50 .23
☐ 284 Dennis Lamp .10 .05
☐ 285 Carney Lansford .20 .09
☐ 286 Mark McGwire 1.50 .70
☐ 287 Dwayne Murphy .10 .05
☐ 288 Gene Nelson .10 .05
☐ 289 Steve Ontiveros .10 .05
☐ 290 Tony Phillips .10 .05
☐ 291 Eric Plunk .10 .05
☐ 292 Luis Polonia .10 .05
☐ 293 Rick Rodriguez .10 .05
☐ 294 Terry Steinbach .20 .09
☐ 295 Dave Stewart .20 .09
☐ 296 Curt Young .10 .05
☐ 297 Luis Aguayo .10 .05
☐ 298 Steve Bedrosian .10 .05
☐ 299 Jeff Calhoun .10 .05
☐ 300 Don Carman .10 .05
☐ 301 Todd Frohwirth .10 .05
☐ 302 Greg Gross .10 .05
☐ 303 Kevin Gross .10 .05
☐ 304 Von Hayes .10 .05
☐ 305 Keith Hughes .10 .05
☐ 306 Mike Jackson .40 .18
☐ 307 Chris James .10 .05
☐ 308 Steve Jeltz .10 .05
☐ 309 Mike Maddux .10 .05
☐ 310 Lance Parrish .10 .05
☐ 311 Shane Rawley .10 .05
☐ 312 Wally Ritchie .10 .05
☐ 313 Bruce Ruffin .10 .05
☐ 314 Juan Samuel .10 .05
☐ 315 Mike Schmidt .50 .23
☐ 316 Rick Schu .10 .05
☐ 317 Jeff Stone .10 .05
☐ 318 Kent Tekulve .10 .05
☐ 319 Milt Thompson .10 .05

☐ 320 Glenn Wilson	.10	.05
☐ 321 Rafael Belliard	.10	.05
☐ 322 Barry Bonds	1.00	.45
☐ 323 Bobby Bonilla UER (Wrong birth year)	.40	.18
☐ 324 Sid Bream	.10	.05
☐ 325 John Cangelosi	.10	.05
☐ 326 Mike Diaz	.10	.05
☐ 327 Doug Drabek	.20	.09
☐ 328 Mike Dunne	.10	.05
☐ 329 Brian Fisher	.10	.05
☐ 330 Brett Gideon	.10	.05
☐ 331 Terry Harper	.10	.05
☐ 332 Bob Kipper	.10	.05
☐ 333 Mike LaValliere	.10	.05
☐ 334 Jose Lind	.10	.05
☐ 335 Junior Ortiz	.10	.05
☐ 336 Vicente Palacios	.10	.05
☐ 337 Bob Patterson	.10	.05
☐ 338 Al Pedrique	.10	.05
☐ 339 R.J. Reynolds	.10	.05
☐ 340 John Smiley	.10	.05
☐ 341 Andy Van Slyke UER (Wrong batting and throwing listed)	.20	.09
☐ 342 Bob Walk	.10	.05
☐ 343 Marty Barrett	.10	.05
☐ 344 Todd Benzinger	.10	.05
☐ 345 Wade Boggs	.40	.18
☐ 346 Tom Bolton	.10	.05
☐ 347 Oil Can Boyd	.10	.05
☐ 348 Ellis Burks	1.00	.45
☐ 349 Roger Clemens	.75	.35
☐ 350 Steve Crawford	.10	.05
☐ 351 Dwight Evans	.20	.09
☐ 352 Wes Gardner	.10	.05
☐ 353 Rich Gedman	.10	.05
☐ 354 Mike Greenwell	.20	.09
☐ 355 Sam Horn	.10	.05
☐ 356 Bruce Hurst	.10	.05
☐ 357 John Marzano	.10	.05
☐ 358 Al Nipper	.10	.05
☐ 359 Spike Owen	.10	.05
☐ 360 Jody Reed	.20	.09
☐ 361 Jim Rice	.40	.18
☐ 362 Ed Romero	.10	.05
☐ 363 Kevin Romine	.10	.05
☐ 364 Joe Sambito	.10	.05
☐ 365 Calvin Schiraldi	.10	.05
☐ 366 Jeff Sellers	.10	.05
☐ 367 Bob Stanley	.10	.05
☐ 368 Scott Bankhead	.10	.05
☐ 369 Phil Bradley	.10	.05
☐ 370 Scott Bradley	.10	.05
☐ 371 Mickey Brantley	.10	.05
☐ 372 Mike Campbell	.10	.05
☐ 373 Alvin Davis	.10	.05
☐ 374 Lee Guetterman	.10	.05
☐ 375 Dave Hengel	.10	.05
☐ 376 Mike Kingery	.10	.05
☐ 377 Mark Langston	.10	.05
☐ 378 Edgar Martinez	2.00	.90
☐ 379 Mike Moore	.10	.05
☐ 380 Mike Morgan	.10	.05
☐ 381 John Moses	.10	.05
☐ 382 Donell Nixon	.10	.05
☐ 383 Edwin Nunez	.10	.05
☐ 384 Ken Phelps	.10	.05
☐ 385 Jim Presley	.10	.05
☐ 386 Rey Quinones	.10	.05
☐ 387 Jerry Reed	.10	.05
☐ 388 Harold Reynolds	.10	.05
☐ 389 Dave Valle	.10	.05
☐ 390 Bill Wilkinson	.10	.05
☐ 391 Harold Baines	.20	.09
☐ 392 Floyd Bannister	.10	.05
☐ 393 Daryl Boston	.10	.05
☐ 394 Ivan Calderon	.10	.05
☐ 395 Jose DeLeon	.10	.05
☐ 396 Richard Dotson	.10	.05
☐ 397 Carlton Fisk	.40	.18
☐ 398 Ozzie Guillen	.10	.05
☐ 399 Ron Hassey	.10	.05
☐ 400 Donnie Hill	.10	.05
☐ 401 Bob James	.10	.05
☐ 402 Dave LaPoint	.10	.05
☐ 403 Bill Lindsey	.10	.05
☐ 404 Bill Long	.10	.05
☐ 405 Steve Lyons	.10	.05
☐ 406 Fred Manrique	.10	.05
☐ 407 Jack McDowell	.40	.18
☐ 408 Gary Redus	.10	.05
☐ 409 Ray Searage	.10	.05
☐ 410 Bobby Thigpen	.10	.05
☐ 411 Greg Walker	.10	.05
☐ 412 Ken Williams	.10	.05
☐ 413 Jim Winn	.10	.05
☐ 414 Jody Davis	.10	.05
☐ 415 Andre Dawson	.40	.18
☐ 416 Brian Dayett	.10	.05
☐ 417 Bob Dernier	.10	.05
☐ 418 Frank DiPino	.10	.05
☐ 419 Shawon Dunston	.10	.05
☐ 420 Leon Durham	.10	.05
☐ 421 Les Lancaster	.10	.05
☐ 422 Ed Lynch	.10	.05
☐ 423 Greg Maddux	2.50	1.10
☐ 424 Dave Martinez	.10	.05
☐ 425A Keith Moreland ERR (Photo actually Jody Davis)	1.50	.70
☐ 425B Keith Moreland COR (Bat on shoulder)	.20	.09
☐ 426 Jamie Moyer	.10	.05
☐ 427 Jerry Mumphrey	.10	.05
☐ 428 Paul Noce	.10	.05
☐ 429 Rafael Palmeiro	.40	.18
☐ 430 Wade Rowdon	.10	.05
☐ 431 Ryne Sandberg	.50	.23
☐ 432 Scott Sanderson	.10	.05
☐ 433 Lee Smith	.10	.05
☐ 434 Jim Sundberg	.10	.05
☐ 435 Rick Sutcliffe	.10	.05
☐ 436 Manny Trillo	.10	.05
☐ 437 Juan Agosto	.10	.05
☐ 438 Larry Andersen	.10	.05
☐ 439 Alan Ashby	.10	.05
☐ 440 Kevin Bass	.10	.05
☐ 441 Ken Caminiti	2.00	.90
☐ 442 Rocky Childress	.10	.05
☐ 443 Jose Cruz	.10	.05
☐ 444 Danny Darwin	.10	.05
☐ 445 Glenn Davis	.10	.05
☐ 446 Jim Deshaies	.10	.05
☐ 447 Bill Doran	.10	.05
☐ 448 Ty Gainey	.10	.05
☐ 449 Billy Hatcher	.10	.05
☐ 450 Jeff Heathcock	.10	.05
☐ 451 Bob Knepper	.10	.05
☐ 452 Rob Mallicoat	.10	.05
☐ 453 Dave Meads	.10	.05
☐ 454 Craig Reynolds	.10	.05
☐ 455 Nolan Ryan	1.50	.70
☐ 456 Mike Scott	.10	.05
☐ 457 Dave Smith	.10	.05
☐ 458 Denny Walling	.10	.05
☐ 459 Robbie Wine	.10	.05
☐ 460 Gerald Young	.10	.05
☐ 461 Bob Brower	.10	.05
☐ 462A Jerry Browne ERR (Photo actually Bob Brower, white player)	1.50	.70
☐ 462B Jerry Browne COR (Black player)	.20	.09
☐ 463 Steve Buechele	.10	.05
☐ 464 Edwin Correa	.10	.05
☐ 465 Cecil Espy	.10	.05
☐ 466 Scott Fletcher	.10	.05
☐ 467 Jose Guzman	.10	.05
☐ 468 Greg Harris	.10	.05
☐ 469 Charlie Hough	.20	.09
☐ 470 Pete Incaviglia	.10	.05
☐ 471 Paul Kilgus	.10	.05
☐ 472 Mike Loynd	.10	.05
☐ 473 Oddibe McDowell	.10	.05
☐ 474 Dale Mohorcic	.10	.05
☐ 475 Pete O'Brien	.10	.05
☐ 476 Larry Parrish	.10	.05
☐ 477 Geno Petralli	.10	.05
☐ 478 Jeff Russell	.10	.05
☐ 479 Ruben Sierra	.10	.05
☐ 480 Mike Stanley	.20	.09
☐ 481 Curtis Wilkerson	.10	.05
☐ 482 Mitch Williams	.20	.09
☐ 483 Bobby Witt	.10	.05
☐ 484 Tony Armas	.10	.05
☐ 485 Bob Boone	.20	.09
☐ 486 Bill Buckner	.20	.09
☐ 487 DeWayne Buice	.10	.05
☐ 488 Brian Downing	.10	.05
☐ 489 Chuck Finley	.20	.09
☐ 490 Willie Fraser UER (Wrong bio stats, for George Hendrick)	.10	.05
☐ 491 Jack Howell	.10	.05
☐ 492 Ruppert Jones	.10	.05
☐ 493 Wally Joyner	.40	.18
☐ 494 Jack Lazorko	.10	.05
☐ 495 Gary Lucas	.10	.05
☐ 496 Kirk McCaskill	.10	.05
☐ 497 Mark McLemore	.10	.05
☐ 498 Darrell Miller	.10	.05
☐ 499 Greg Minton	.10	.05
☐ 500 Donnie Moore	.10	.05
☐ 501 Gus Polidor	.10	.05
☐ 502 Johnny Ray	.10	.05
☐ 503 Mark Ryal	.10	.05
☐ 504 Dick Schofield	.10	.05
☐ 505 Don Sutton	.40	.18
☐ 506 Devon White	.20	.09
☐ 507 Mike Witt	.10	.05
☐ 508 Dave Anderson	.10	.05
☐ 509 Tim Belcher	.20	.09
☐ 510 Ralph Bryant	.10	.05
☐ 511 Tim Crews	.10	.05
☐ 512 Mike Devereaux	.10	.05
☐ 513 Mariano Duncan	.10	.05
☐ 514 Pedro Guerrero	.20	.09
☐ 515 Jeff Hamilton	.10	.05
☐ 516 Mickey Hatcher	.10	.05
☐ 517 Brad Havens	.10	.05
☐ 518 Orel Hershiser	.20	.09
☐ 519 Shawn Hillegas	.10	.05
☐ 520 Ken Howell	.10	.05
☐ 521 Tim Leary	.10	.05
☐ 522 Mike Marshall	.10	.05
☐ 523 Steve Sax	.10	.05
☐ 524 Mike Scioscia	.10	.05
☐ 525 Mike Sharperson	.10	.05
☐ 526 John Shelby	.10	.05
☐ 527 Franklin Stubbs	.10	.05
☐ 528 Fernando Valenzuela	.20	.09
☐ 529 Bob Welch	.10	.05
☐ 530 Matt Young	.10	.05
☐ 531 Jim Acker	.10	.05
☐ 532 Paul Assenmacher	.10	.05
☐ 533 Jeff Blauser	.75	.35
☐ 534 Joe Boever	.10	.05
☐ 535 Martin Clary	.10	.05
☐ 536 Kevin Coffman	.10	.05
☐ 537 Jeff Dedmon	.10	.05
☐ 538 Ron Gant	.50	.23
☐ 539 Tom Glavine	1.50	.70
☐ 540 Ken Griffey	.10	.05
☐ 541 Albert Hall	.10	.05
☐ 542 Glenn Hubbard	.10	.05
☐ 543 Dion James	.10	.05
☐ 544 Dale Murphy	.40	.18
☐ 545 Ken Oberkfell	.10	.05
☐ 546 David Palmer	.10	.05
☐ 547 Gerald Perry	.10	.05
☐ 548 Charlie Puleo	.10	.05
☐ 549 Ted Simmons	.20	.09
☐ 550 Zane Smith	.10	.05
☐ 551 Andres Thomas	.10	.05
☐ 552 Ozzie Virgil	.10	.05
☐ 553 Don Aase	.10	.05
☐ 554 Jeff Ballard	.10	.05
☐ 555 Eric Bell	.10	.05
☐ 556 Mike Boddicker	.10	.05
☐ 557 Ken Dixon	.10	.05
☐ 558 Jim Dwyer	.10	.05
☐ 559 Ken Gerhart	.10	.05
☐ 560 Rene Gonzales	.10	.05
☐ 561 Mike Griffin	.10	.05
☐ 562 John Habyan UER (Misspelled Hayban on both sides of card)	.10	.05
☐ 563 Terry Kennedy	.10	.05
☐ 564 Ray Knight	.20	.09
☐ 565 Lee Lacy	.10	.05
☐ 566 Fred Lynn	.10	.05
☐ 567 Eddie Murray	.40	.18
☐ 568 Tom Niedenfuer	.10	.05
☐ 569 Bill Ripken	.20	.09
☐ 570 Cal Ripken	1.50	.70
☐ 571 Dave Schmidt	.10	.05
☐ 572 Larry Sheets	.10	.05
☐ 573 Pete Stanicek	.10	.05
☐ 574 Mark Williamson	.10	.05
☐ 575 Mike Young	.10	.05
☐ 576 Shawn Abner	.10	.05
☐ 577 Greg Booker	.10	.05
☐ 578 Chris Brown	.10	.05
☐ 579 Keith Comstock	.10	.05
☐ 580 Joey Cora	.75	.35
☐ 581 Mark Davis	.10	.05
☐ 582 Tim Flannery (With surfboard)	.40	.18
☐ 583 Goose Gossage	.10	.05
☐ 584 Mark Grant	.10	.05
☐ 585 Tony Gwynn	1.00	.45
☐ 586 Andy Hawkins	.10	.05
☐ 587 Stan Jefferson	.10	.05
☐ 588 Jimmy Jones	.10	.05
☐ 589 John Kruk	.20	.09
☐ 590 Shane Mack	.10	.05
☐ 591 Carmelo Martinez	.10	.05
☐ 592 Lance McCullers UER (6'11" tall)	.10	.05

☐ 593 Eric Nolte	.10	.05
☐ 594 Randy Ready	.10	.05
☐ 595 Luis Salazar	.10	.05
☐ 596 Benito Santiago	.10	.05
☐ 597 Eric Show	.10	.05
☐ 598 Garry Templeton	.10	.05
☐ 599 Ed Whitson	.10	.05
☐ 600 Scott Bailes	.10	.05
☐ 601 Chris Bando	.10	.05
☐ 602 Jay Bell	.75	.35
☐ 603 Brett Butler	.20	.09
☐ 604 Tom Candiotti	.10	.05
☐ 605 Joe Carter	.40	.18
☐ 606 Carmen Castillo	.10	.05
☐ 607 Brian Dorsett	.10	.05
☐ 608 John Farrell	.10	.05
☐ 609 Julio Franco	.20	.09
☐ 610 Mel Hall	.10	.05
☐ 611 Tommy Hinzo	.10	.05
☐ 612 Brook Jacoby	.10	.05
☐ 613 Doug Jones	.20	.09
☐ 614 Ken Schrom	.10	.05
☐ 615 Cory Snyder	.10	.05
☐ 616 Sammy Stewart	.10	.05
☐ 617 Greg Swindell	.10	.05
☐ 618 Pat Tabler	.10	.05
☐ 619 Ed VandeBerg	.10	.05
☐ 620 Eddie Williams	.20	.09
☐ 621 Rich Yett	.10	.05
☐ 622 Slugging Sophomores Wally Joyner Cory Snyder	.20	.09
☐ 623 Dominican Dynamite George Bell Pedro Guerrero	.10	.05
☐ 624 Oakland's Power Team Mark McGwire Jose Canseco	.75	.35
☐ 625 Classic Relief Dave Righetti Dan Plesac	.10	.05
☐ 626 All Star Righties Bret Saberhagen Mike Witt Jack Morris	.20	.09
☐ 627 Game Closers John Franco Steve Bedrosian	.10	.05
☐ 628 Masters/Double Play Ozzie Smith Ryne Sandberg	.50	.23
☐ 629 Rookie Record Setter Mark McGwire	.75	.35
☐ 630 Changing the Guard Mike Greenwell Ellis Burks Todd Benzinger	.40	.18
☐ 631 NL Batting Champs Tony Gwynn Tim Raines	.40	.18
☐ 632 Pitching Magic Mike Scott Orel Hershiser	.20	.09
☐ 633 Big Bats at First Pat Tabler Mark McGwire	.50	.23
☐ 634 Hitting King/Thief Tony Gwynn Vince Coleman	.40	.18
☐ 635 Slugging Shortstops Tony Fernandez Cal Ripken Alan Trammell	.50	.23
☐ 636 Tried/True Sluggers Mike Schmidt Gary Carter	.40	.18
☐ 637 Crunch Time Darryl Strawberry Eric Davis	.20	.09
☐ 638 AL All-Stars Matt Nokes Kirby Puckett	.10	.05
☐ 639 NL All-Stars Keith Hernandez Dale Murphy	.20	.09
☐ 640 The O's Brothers Billy Ripken Cal Ripken	.75	.35
☐ 641 Mark Grace and Darrin Jackson	2.00	.90
☐ 642 Damon Berryhill and Jeff Montgomery	.40	.18
☐ 643 Felix Fermin and Jesse Reid	.10	.05
☐ 644 Greg Myers and Greg Tabor	.10	.05
☐ 645 Joey Meyer and Jim Eppard	.10	.05
☐ 646 Adam Peterson and Randy Velarde	.20	.09
☐ 647 Pete Smith and Chris Gwynn	.20	.09
☐ 648 Tom Newell and Greg Jelks	.10	.05
☐ 649 Mario Diaz and Clay Parker	.10	.05
☐ 650 Jack Savage and Todd Simmons	.10	.05
☐ 651 John Burkett and Kirt Manwaring	.40	.18
☐ 652 Dave Otto and Walt Weiss	.20	.09
☐ 653 Jeff King and Randell Byers	.50	.23
☐ 654 CL: Twins/Cards Tigers/Giants UER (90 Bob Melvin, 91 Eddie Milner)	.10	.05
☐ 655 CL: Blue Jays/Mets Brewers/Expos UER (Mets listed before Blue Jays on card)	.10	.05
☐ 656 CL: Yankees/Reds Royals/A's	.10	.05
☐ 657 CL: Phillies/Pirates Red Sox/Mariners	.10	.05
☐ 658 CL: White Sox/Cubs Astros/Rangers	.10	.05
☐ 659 CL: Angels/Dodgers Braves/Orioles	.10	.05
☐ 660 CL: Padres/Indians Rookies/Specials	.10	.05

1988 Fleer Glossy

This 660 card set is a parallel to the regular Fleer issue. The cards are the same as the regular issue except for the glossy sheen on the front. The cards (along with the 12-card World Series insert set) were issued in a factory tin distributed exclusively through hobby dealers.

	MINT	NRMT
COMPLETE FACT.SET (672)	40.00	18.00
COMMON CARD (1-660)	.05	.02
COMMON WORLD SER. (WS1-WS12)	.05	.02
*STARS: 2X BASIC CARDS		
*ROOKIES: 2X BASIC CARDS		

1988 Fleer All-Stars

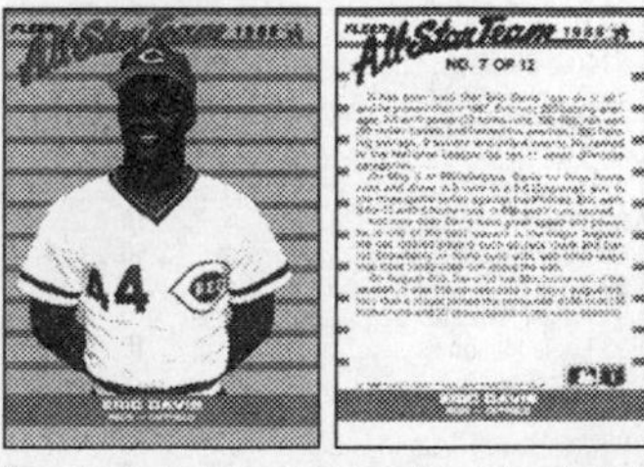

These 12 standard-size cards were inserted randomly in wax and cello packs of the 1988 Fleer set. The cards show the player silhouetted against a light green background with dark green stripes. The player's name, team, and position are printed in yellow at the bottom of the obverse. The card backs are done predominantly in green, white, and black. The players are the "best" at each position, three pitchers, eight position players, and a designated hitter.

	MINT	NRMT
COMPLETE SET (12)	6.00	2.70
COMMON CARD (1-12)	.30	.14
☐ 1 Matt Nokes	.30	.14
☐ 2 Tom Henke	.30	.14
☐ 3 Ted Higuera	.30	.14
☐ 4 Roger Clemens	2.00	.90
☐ 5 George Bell	.30	.14
☐ 6 Andre Dawson	1.00	.45
☐ 7 Eric Davis	.40	.18
☐ 8 Wade Boggs	1.00	.45
☐ 9 Alan Trammell	.40	.18
☐ 10 Juan Samuel	.30	.14
☐ 11 Jack Clark	.30	.14
☐ 12 Paul Molitor	1.50	.70

1988 Fleer Headliners

This six-card standard-size set was distributed one per rack pack. The obverse features the player photo

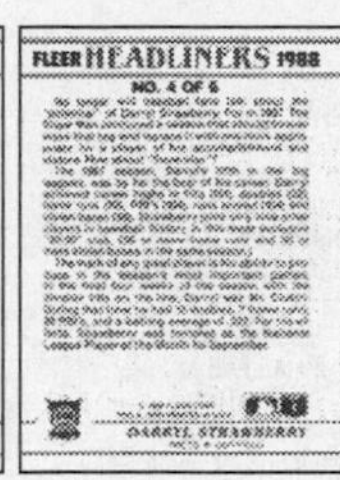

superimposed on a gray newsprint background. The cards are printed in red, black, and white on the back describing why that particular player made headlines the previous season. The set is sequenced in alphabetical order.

	MINT	NRMT
COMPLETE SET (6)	5.00	2.20
COMMON CARD (1-6)	.75	.35
☐ 1 Don Mattingly	2.50	1.10
☐ 2 Mark McGwire	2.50	1.10
☐ 3 Jack Morris	1.00	.45
☐ 4 Darryl Strawberry	1.00	.45
☐ 5 Dwight Gooden	1.00	.45
☐ 6 Tim Raines	.75	.35

1988 Fleer Wax Box Cards

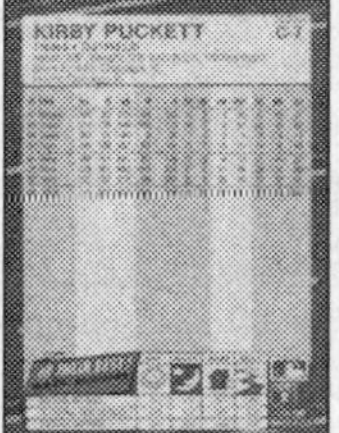

The cards in this 16-card set measure the standard size. Cards have essentially the same design as the 1988 Fleer regular issue set. The cards were printed on the bottoms of the regular issue wax pack boxes. These 16 cards (C1 to C16) are considered a separate set in their own right and are not typically included in a complete set of the regular issue 1988 Fleer cards. The value of the panel uncut is slightly greater, perhaps by 25 percent greater, than the value of the individual cards cut up carefully.

	MINT	NRMT
COMPLETE SET (16)	8.00	3.60
COMMON CARD (C1-C16)	.10	.05
☐ C1 Cardinals Logo	.10	.05
☐ C2 Dwight Evans	.25	.11
☐ C3 Andres Galarraga	1.00	.45
☐ C4 Wally Joyner	.25	.11
☐ C5 Twins Logo	.10	.05
☐ C6 Dale Murphy	.50	.23
☐ C7 Kirby Puckett	2.50	1.10
☐ C8 Shane Rawley	.10	.05
☐ C9 Giants Logo	.10	.05
☐ C10 Ryne Sandberg	2.50	1.10
☐ C11 Mike Schmidt	1.25	.55
☐ C12 Kevin Seitzer	.25	.11
☐ C13 Tigers Logo	.10	.05
☐ C14 Dave Stewart	.25	.11
☐ C15 Tim Wallach	.10	.05
☐ C16 Todd Worrell	.10	.05

1988 Fleer World Series

This 12-card standard-size set features highlights of the previous year's World Series between the Minnesota Twins and the St. Louis Cardinals. The sets were packaged as a complete set insert with the collated sets (of the 1988 Fleer regular issue) which were sold by Fleer directly to hobby card dealers; they were not available in the general retail candy store outlets. The set numbering is essentially in chronological order of the events from the immediate past World Series.

	MINT	NRMT
COMPLETE SET (12)	2.00	.90
COMMON CARD (1-12)	.10	.05
☐ 1 Dan Gladden	.10	.05
☐ 2 Randy Bush	.10	.05
☐ 3 John Tudor	.10	.05
☐ 4 Ozzie Smith	1.00	.45
☐ 5 Todd Worrell Tony Pena	.10	.05
☐ 6 Vince Coleman	.10	.05
☐ 7 Tom Herr Dan Driessen	.10	.05
☐ 8 Kirby Puckett	1.25	.55
☐ 9 Kent Hrbek	.25	.11
☐ 10 Tom Herr	.10	.05
☐ 11 Don Baylor	.25	.11
☐ 12 Frank Viola	.10	.05

1988 Fleer Update

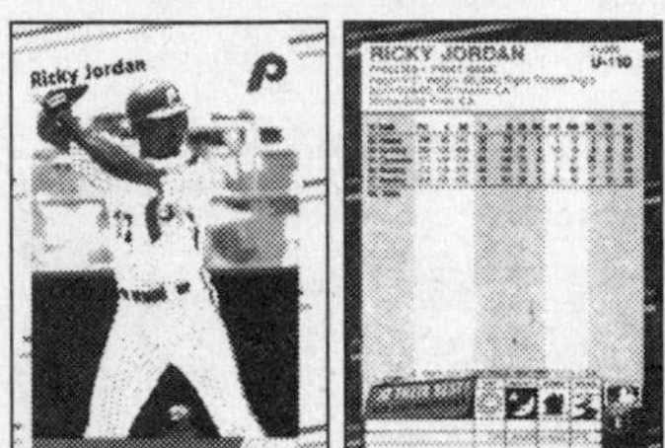

This 132-card standard-size set was distributed exclusively in factory set form in a red, white and blue, cellophane-wrapped box through hobby dealers. In addition to the complete set of 132 cards, the box also contained 25 Team Logo stickers. The cards look very similar to the 1988 Fleer regular issue except for the U-prefixed numbering on back. Cards are ordered alphabetically by player's last name. This was the first Fleer Update set to adopt the Fleer "alphabetical within team" numbering system. The key extended Rookie Cards in this set are Roberto Alomar, Craig Biggio and John Smoltz.

	MINT	NRMT
COMP.FACT.SET (132)	8.00	3.60
COMMON CARD (1-132)	.10	.05
UNLISTED STARS	.75	.35
☐ 1 Jose Bautista	.10	.05
☐ 2 Joe Orsulak	.10	.05
☐ 3 Doug Sisk	.10	.05
☐ 4 Craig Worthington	.10	.05
☐ 5 Mike Boddicker	.10	.05
☐ 6 Rick Cerone	.10	.05
☐ 7 Larry Parrish	.10	.05
☐ 8 Lee Smith	.20	.09
☐ 9 Mike Smithson	.10	.05
☐ 10 John Trautwein	.10	.05
☐ 11 Sherman Corbett	.10	.05
☐ 12 Chili Davis	.40	.18
☐ 13 Jim Eppard	.10	.05
☐ 14 Bryan Harvey	.20	.09
☐ 15 John Davis	.10	.05
☐ 16 Dave Gallagher	.10	.05
☐ 17 Ricky Horton	.10	.05
☐ 18 Dan Pasqua	.10	.05
☐ 19 Melido Perez	.20	.09
☐ 20 Jose Segura	.10	.05
☐ 21 Andy Allanson	.10	.05
☐ 22 Jon Perlman	.10	.05
☐ 23 Domingo Ramos	.10	.05
☐ 24 Rick Rodriguez	.10	.05
☐ 25 Willie Upshaw	.10	.05
☐ 26 Paul Gibson	.10	.05
☐ 27 Don Heinkel	.10	.05
☐ 28 Ray Knight	.20	.09
☐ 29 Gary Pettis	.10	.05
☐ 30 Luis Salazar	.10	.05
☐ 31 Mike Macfarlane	.20	.09
☐ 32 Jeff Montgomery	.75	.35
☐ 33 Ted Power	.10	.05
☐ 34 Israel Sanchez	.10	.05
☐ 35 Kurt Stillwell	.10	.05
☐ 36 Pat Tabler	.10	.05
☐ 37 Don August	.10	.05
☐ 38 Darryl Hamilton	.20	.09
☐ 39 Jeff Leonard	.10	.05
☐ 40 Joey Meyer	.10	.05
☐ 41 Allan Anderson	.10	.05
☐ 42 Brian Harper	.10	.05
☐ 43 Tom Herr	.10	.05
☐ 44 Charlie Lea	.10	.05
☐ 45 John Moses (Listed as Hohn on checklist card)	.10	.05
☐ 46 John Candelaria	.10	.05
☐ 47 Jack Clark	.20	.09
☐ 48 Richard Dotson	.10	.05
☐ 49 Al Leiter	.75	.35
☐ 50 Rafael Santana	.10	.05
☐ 51 Don Slaught	.10	.05
☐ 52 Todd Burns	.10	.05
☐ 53 Dave Henderson	.10	.05
☐ 54 Doug Jennings	.10	.05
☐ 55 Dave Parker	.40	.18
☐ 56 Walt Weiss	.40	.18
☐ 57 Bob Welch	.10	.05
☐ 58 Henry Cotto	.10	.05
☐ 59 Mario Diaz UER (Listed as Marion on card front)	.10	.05
☐ 60 Mike Jackson	.10	.05
☐ 61 Bill Swift	.10	.05
☐ 62 Jose Cecena	.10	.05
☐ 63 Ray Hayward	.10	.05
☐ 64 Jim Steels UER (Listed as Jim Steele on card back)	.10	.05
☐ 65 Pat Borders	.20	.09
☐ 66 Sil Campusano	.10	.05
☐ 67 Mike Flanagan	.10	.05
☐ 68 Todd Stottlemyre	.75	.35
☐ 69 David Wells	.75	.35
☐ 70 Jose Alvarez	.10	.05
☐ 71 Paul Runge	.10	.05
☐ 72 Cesar Jimenez (Card was intended for German Jiminez, it's his photo)	.10	.05
☐ 73 Pete Smith	.10	.05
☐ 74 John Smoltz	2.00	.90
☐ 75 Damon Berryhill	.10	.05
☐ 76 Goose Gossage	.40	.18
☐ 77 Mark Grace	1.50	.70
☐ 78 Darrin Jackson	.10	.05
☐ 79 Vance Law	.10	.05
☐ 80 Jeff Pico	.10	.05
☐ 81 Gary Varsho	.10	.05
☐ 82 Tim Birtsas	.10	.05
☐ 83 Rob Dibble	.20	.09
☐ 84 Danny Jackson	.10	.05
☐ 85 Paul O'Neill	.40	.18
☐ 86 Jose Rijo	.10	.05
☐ 87 Chris Sabo	.20	.09
☐ 88 John Fishel	.10	.05
☐ 89 Craig Biggio	2.50	1.10
☐ 90 Terry Puhl	.10	.05
☐ 91 Rafael Ramirez	.10	.05
☐ 92 Louie Meadows	.10	.05
☐ 93 Kirk Gibson	.20	.09
☐ 94 Alfredo Griffin	.10	.05
☐ 95 Jay Howell	.10	.05
☐ 96 Jesse Orosco	.10	.05
☐ 97 Alejandro Pena	.10	.05
☐ 98 Tracy Woodson	.10	.05
☐ 99 John Dopson	.10	.05
☐ 100 Brian Holman	.10	.05
☐ 101 Rex Hudler	.10	.05
☐ 102 Jeff Parrett	.10	.05
☐ 103 Nelson Santovenia	.10	.05
☐ 104 Kevin Elster	.20	.09
☐ 105 Jeff Innis	.10	.05
☐ 106 Mackey Sasser	.10	.05
☐ 107 Phil Bradley	.10	.05
☐ 108 Danny Clay	.10	.05
☐ 109 Greg A.Harris	.10	.05
☐ 110 Ricky Jordan	.20	.09
☐ 111 David Palmer	.10	.05
☐ 112 Jim Gott	.10	.05
☐ 113 Tommy Gregg UER (Photo actually Randy Milligan)	.10	.05
☐ 114 Barry Jones	.10	.05
☐ 115 Randy Milligan	.10	.05
☐ 116 Luis Alicea	.20	.09
☐ 117 Tom Brunansky	.10	.05
☐ 118 John Costello	.10	.05
☐ 119 Jose DeLeon	.10	.05
☐ 120 Bob Horner	.10	.05
☐ 121 Scott Terry	.10	.05
☐ 122 Roberto Alomar	4.00	1.80
☐ 123 Dave Leiper	.10	.05
☐ 124 Keith Moreland	.10	.05
☐ 125 Mark Parent	.10	.05
☐ 126 Dennis Rasmussen	.10	.05
☐ 127 Randy Bockus	.10	.05
☐ 128 Brett Butler	.20	.09
☐ 129 Donell Nixon	.10	.05
☐ 130 Earnest Riles	.10	.05
☐ 131 Roger Samuels	.10	.05
☐ 132 Checklist U1-U132	.10	.05

1988 Fleer Update Glossy

This 132 card set is a parallel to the regular Fleer Update issue. Except for a glossy sheen on the front, the cards are identical to the regular Fleer issue. The cards were issued through hobby dealers in a special tin. The cards are not as plentiful as the regular Fleer update set.

	MINT	NRMT
COMPLETE FACT.SET (132)	15.00	6.75
COMMON CARD (1-132)	.10	.05
*STARS: 2X BASIC CARDS		
*ROOKIES: 2X BASIC CARDS		

1988 Fleer Award Winners

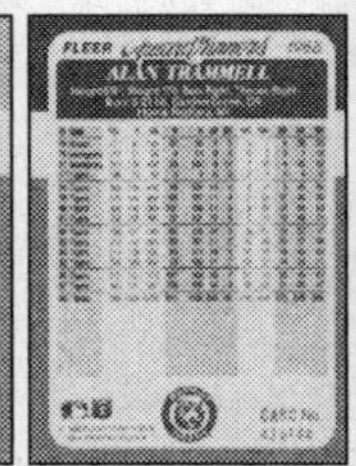

This small set of 44 standard-size cards was produced for 7-Eleven stores by Fleer. The cards feature full color fronts and red, white, and blue backs. The card fronts are distinguished by the red, white, and blue frame around the player's full-color photo. The box for the cards describes the set as the "1988 Limited Edition Baseball Award Winners." The checklist for the set is given on the back of the set box. The card numbering is in alphabetical order by player's name.

	MINT	NRMT
COMPLETE SET (44)	5.00	2.20
COMMON CARD (1-44)	.05	.02
☐ 1 Steve Bedrosian	.05	.02
☐ 2 George Bell	.05	.02
☐ 3 Wade Boggs	.40	.18
☐ 4 Jose Canseco	.60	.25
☐ 5 Will Clark	.60	.25
☐ 6 Roger Clemens	.75	.35
☐ 7 Kal Daniels	.05	.02
☐ 8 Eric Davis	.10	.05
☐ 9 Andre Dawson	.30	.14
☐ 10 Mike Dunne	.05	.02
☐ 11 Dwight Evans	.10	.05
☐ 12 Carlton Fisk	.50	.23
☐ 13 Julio Franco	.10	.05
☐ 14 Dwight Gooden	.10	.05
☐ 15 Pedro Guerrero	.05	.02
☐ 16 Tony Gwynn	1.00	.45
☐ 17 Orel Hershiser	.10	.05
☐ 18 Tom Henke	.10	.05
☐ 19 Ted Higuera	.05	.02
☐ 20 Charlie Hough	.10	.05
☐ 21 Wally Joyner	.20	.09
☐ 22 Jimmy Key	.10	.05
☐ 23 Don Mattingly	1.00	.45
☐ 24 Mark McGwire	1.25	.55
☐ 25 Paul Molitor	.50	.23
☐ 26 Jack Morris	.10	.05
☐ 27 Dale Murphy	.30	.14
☐ 28 Terry Pendleton	.10	.05
☐ 29 Kirby Puckett	1.00	.45
☐ 30 Tim Raines	.10	.05
☐ 31 Jeff Reardon	.05	.02
☐ 32 Harold Reynolds	.10	.05
☐ 33 Dave Righetti	.05	.02
☐ 34 Benito Santiago	.05	.02
☐ 35 Mike Schmidt	.50	.23
☐ 36 Mike Scott	.05	.02
☐ 37 Kevin Seitzer	.10	.05
☐ 38 Larry Sheets	.05	.02
☐ 39 Ozzie Smith	1.00	.45
☐ 40 Darryl Strawberry	.10	.05
☐ 41 Rick Sutcliffe	.05	.02
☐ 42 Danny Tartabull	.05	.02
☐ 43 Alan Trammell	.20	.09
☐ 44 Tim Wallach	.05	.02

1988 Fleer Baseball All-Stars

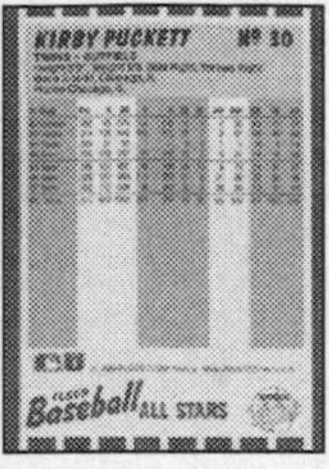

This small boxed set of 44 standard-size cards was produced exclusively for Ben Franklin Stores. The cards feature full color fronts and white and blue backs. The card fronts are distinguished by the yellow and blue striped background behind the player's full-color photo. The box for the cards describes the set as the "1988 Fleer Baseball All-Stars." The checklist for the set is given on the back of the set box. The card numbering is in alphabetical order by player's name.

	MINT	NRMT
COMPLETE SET (44)	5.00	2.20
COMMON CARD (1-44)	.05	.02
☐ 1 George Bell	.05	.02
☐ 2 Wade Boggs	.40	.18
☐ 3 Bobby Bonilla	.10	.05
☐ 4 George Brett	.75	.35
☐ 5 Jose Canseco	.60	.25
☐ 6 Jack Clark	.10	.05
☐ 7 Will Clark	.60	.25
☐ 8 Roger Clemens	1.00	.45
☐ 9 Eric Davis	.10	.05
☐ 10 Andre Dawson	.30	.14
☐ 11 Julio Franco	.10	.05
☐ 12 Dwight Gooden	.10	.05
☐ 13 Tony Gwynn	1.00	.45
☐ 14 Orel Hershiser	.10	.05
☐ 15 Teddy Higuera	.05	.02
☐ 16 Charlie Hough	.05	.02
☐ 17 Kent Hrbek	.10	.05
☐ 18 Bruce Hurst	.05	.02
☐ 19 Wally Joyner	.20	.09
☐ 20 Mark Langston	.05	.02
☐ 21 Dave LaPoint	.05	.02
☐ 22 Candy Maldonado	.05	.02
☐ 23 Don Mattingly	1.00	.45
☐ 24 Roger McDowell	.05	.02
☐ 25 Mark McGwire	1.25	.55
☐ 26 Jack Morris	.10	.05
☐ 27 Dale Murphy	.20	.09
☐ 28 Eddie Murray	.60	.25
☐ 29 Matt Nokes	.05	.02
☐ 30 Kirby Puckett	1.00	.45
☐ 31 Tim Raines	.10	.05
☐ 32 Willie Randolph	.10	.05
☐ 33 Jeff Reardon	.05	.02
☐ 34 Nolan Ryan	2.00	.90
☐ 35 Juan Samuel	.05	.02
☐ 36 Mike Schmidt	.50	.23
☐ 37 Mike Scott	.05	.02
☐ 38 Kevin Seitzer	.10	.05
☐ 39 Ozzie Smith	1.00	.45
☐ 40 Darryl Strawberry	.10	.05
☐ 41 Rick Sutcliffe	.05	.02
☐ 42 Alan Trammell	.20	.09
☐ 43 Tim Wallach	.05	.02
☐ 44 Dave Winfield	.30	.14

1988 Fleer Baseball MVP's

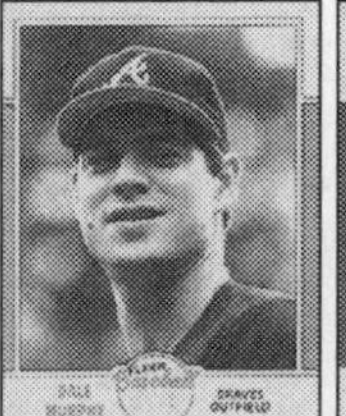
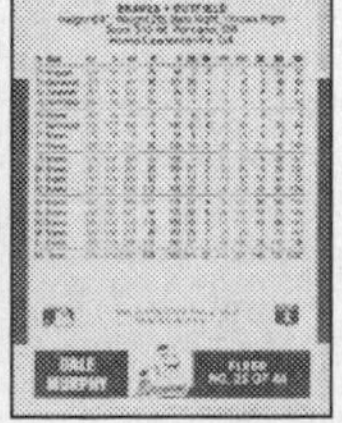

This small 44-card boxed standard-size set was produced by Fleer for distribution by the Toys'r'Us stores. The cards feature full color fronts. The set is titled "Baseball MVP." Each individual boxed set includes the 44 cards and six logo stickers. The checklist for the set is found on the back panel of the box. The card fronts have a vanilla-yellow and blue border. The box refers to Toys'r'Us but there is no mention of Toys'r'Us anywhere on the cards themselves. The card numbering is in alphabetical order by player's name.

	MINT	NRMT
COMPLETE SET (44)	5.00	2.20
COMMON CARD (1-44)	.05	.02
☐ 1 George Bell	.05	.02
☐ 2 Wade Boggs	.40	.18
☐ 3 Jose Canseco	.50	.23
☐ 4 Ivan Calderon	.05	.02
☐ 5 Will Clark	.60	.25
☐ 6 Roger Clemens	.75	.35
☐ 7 Vince Coleman	.05	.02
☐ 8 Eric Davis	.10	.05
☐ 9 Andre Dawson	.30	.14
☐ 10 Dave Dravecky	.05	.02
☐ 11 Mike Dunne	.05	.02
☐ 12 Dwight Evans	.10	.05
☐ 13 Sid Fernandez	.05	.02
☐ 14 Tony Fernandez	.05	.02
☐ 15 Julio Franco	.10	.05
☐ 16 Dwight Gooden	.10	.05
☐ 17 Tony Gwynn	1.00	.45
☐ 18 Ted Higuera	.05	.02
☐ 19 Charlie Hough	.05	.02
☐ 20 Wally Joyner	.20	.09
☐ 21 Mark Langston	.10	.05
☐ 22 Don Mattingly	1.00	.45
☐ 23 Mark McGwire	1.25	.55
☐ 24 Jack Morris	.10	.05
☐ 25 Dale Murphy	.30	.14
☐ 26 Kirby Puckett	1.00	.45
☐ 27 Tim Raines	.10	.05
☐ 28 Willie Randolph	.10	.05
☐ 29 Ryne Sandberg	.75	.35
☐ 30 Benito Santiago	.05	.02
☐ 31 Mike Schmidt	.50	.23
☐ 32 Mike Scott	.05	.02
☐ 33 Kevin Seitzer	.10	.05
☐ 34 Larry Sheets	.05	.02
☐ 35 Ozzie Smith	1.00	.45
☐ 36 Dave Stewart	.10	.05
☐ 37 Darryl Strawberry	.10	.05
☐ 38 Rick Sutcliffe	.05	.02
☐ 39 Alan Trammell	.20	.09
☐ 40 Fernando Valenzuela	.10	.05
☐ 41 Frank Viola	.05	.02
☐ 42 Tim Wallach	.05	.02
☐ 43 Dave Winfield	.50	.23
☐ 44 Robin Yount	.50	.23

1988 Fleer Exciting Stars

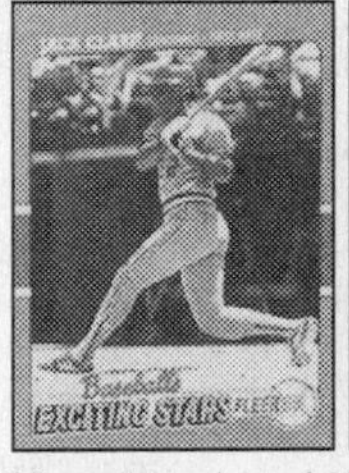

This small boxed set of 44 standard-size cards was produced exclusively for Cumberland Farm Stores. The cards feature full color fronts and red, white, and blue backs. The card fronts are distinguished by the framing of the player's full-color photo with a blue border with a red and white bar stripe across the middle. The box for the cards describes the set as the "1988 Fleer Baseball's Exciting Stars." The checklist for the set is given on the back of the set box. The card numbering is in alphabetical order by player's name.

	MINT	NRMT
COMPLETE SET (44)	5.00	2.20
COMMON CARD (1-44)	.05	.02
☐ 1 Harold Baines	.10	.05
☐ 2 Kevin Bass	.05	.02
☐ 3 George Bell	.05	.02
☐ 4 Wade Boggs	.40	.18
☐ 5 Mickey Brantley	.05	.02
☐ 6 Sid Bream	.05	.02
☐ 7 Jose Canseco	.60	.25
☐ 8 Jack Clark	.10	.05
☐ 9 Will Clark	.60	.25
☐ 10 Roger Clemens	.75	.35
☐ 11 Vince Coleman	.05	.02
☐ 12 Eric Davis	.05	.02
☐ 13 Andre Dawson	.30	.14
☐ 14 Julio Franco	.10	.05
☐ 15 Dwight Gooden	.10	.05
☐ 16 Mike Greenwell	.05	.02
☐ 17 Tony Gwynn	1.00	.45
☐ 18 Von Hayes	.05	.02
☐ 19 Tom Henke	.05	.02
☐ 20 Orel Hershiser	.10	.05
☐ 21 Teddy Higuera	.05	.02
☐ 22 Brook Jacoby	.05	.02
☐ 23 Wally Joyner	.20	.09
☐ 24 Jimmy Key	.10	.05
☐ 25 Don Mattingly	1.00	.45
☐ 26 Mark McGwire	1.00	.45
☐ 27 Jack Morris	.10	.05
☐ 28 Dale Murphy	.30	.14
☐ 29 Matt Nokes	.05	.02
☐ 30 Kirby Puckett	1.00	.45
☐ 31 Tim Raines	.10	.05
☐ 32 Ryne Sandberg	.75	.35
☐ 33 Benito Santiago	.05	.02
☐ 34 Mike Schmidt	.50	.23
☐ 35 Mike Scott	.05	.02
☐ 36 Kevin Seitzer	.10	.05
☐ 37 Larry Sheets	.05	.02
☐ 38 Ruben Sierra	.10	.05
☐ 39 Darryl Strawberry	.10	.05
☐ 40 Rick Sutcliffe	.05	.02
☐ 41 Danny Tartabull	.05	.02
☐ 42 Alan Trammell	.20	.09
☐ 43 Fernando Valenzuela	.10	.05
☐ 44 Devon White	.05	.02

1988 Fleer Hottest Stars

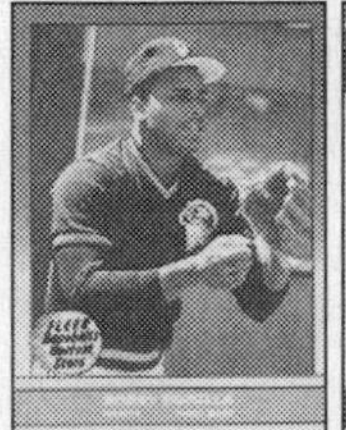
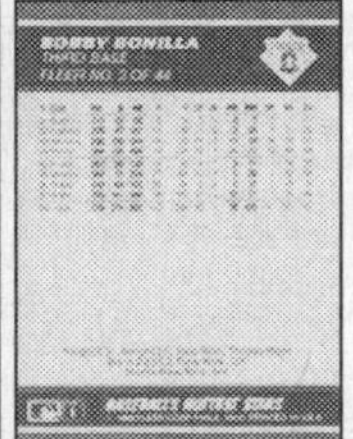

This 44-card boxed standard-size set was produced by Fleer for exclusive distribution by Revco Discount Drug stores all over the country. The cards feature full color fronts and red, white, and blue backs. The card fronts are easily distinguished by the flaming baseball in the lower right corner which says "Fleer Baseball's Hottest Stars." The player's picture is framed in red fading from orange down to yellow. The box for the cards proclaims "1988 Limited Edition Baseball's Hottest Stars" and is styled in blue, red, and yellow. The checklist for the set is given on the back of the set box. The box refers to Revco but there is no mention of Revco anywhere on the cards themselves. The card numbering is in alphabetical order by player's name.

	MINT	NRMT
COMPLETE SET (44)	5.00	2.20
COMMON CARD (1-44)	.05	.02
☐ 1 George Bell	.05	.02
☐ 2 Wade Boggs	.40	.18
☐ 3 Bobby Bonilla	.20	.09
☐ 4 George Brett	.75	.35
☐ 5 Jose Canseco	.60	.25
☐ 6 Will Clark	.60	.25
☐ 7 Roger Clemens	.75	.35
☐ 8 Eric Davis	.10	.05
☐ 9 Andre Dawson	.30	.14
☐ 10 Tony Fernandez	.05	.02
☐ 11 Julio Franco	.10	.05
☐ 12 Gary Gaetti	.10	.05
☐ 13 Dwight Gooden	.10	.05
☐ 14 Mike Greenwell	.05	.02
☐ 15 Tony Gwynn	1.00	.45
☐ 16 Rickey Henderson	.50	.23
☐ 17 Keith Hernandez	.10	.05
☐ 18 Tom Herr	.05	.02
☐ 19 Orel Hershiser	.10	.05
☐ 20 Ted Higuera	.05	.02
☐ 21 Wally Joyner	.20	.09
☐ 22 Jimmy Key	.10	.05
☐ 23 Mark Langston	.05	.02
☐ 24 Don Mattingly	1.00	.45
☐ 25 Jack McDowell	.50	.23
☐ 26 Mark McGwire	1.00	.45
☐ 27 Kevin Mitchell	.05	.02

☐ 28 Jack Morris	.10	.05
☐ 29 Dale Murphy	.30	.14
☐ 30 Kirby Puckett	1.00	.45
☐ 31 Tim Raines	.10	.05
☐ 32 Shane Rawley	.05	.02
☐ 33 Benito Santiago	.05	.02
☐ 34 Mike Schmidt	.50	.23
☐ 35 Mike Scott	.05	.02
☐ 36 Kevin Seitzer	.10	.05
☐ 37 Larry Sheets	.05	.02
☐ 38 Ruben Sierra	.10	.05
☐ 39 Dave Smith	.05	.02
☐ 40 Ozzie Smith	1.00	.45
☐ 41 Darryl Strawberry	.10	.05
☐ 42 Rick Sutcliffe	.05	.02
☐ 43 Pat Tabler	.05	.02
☐ 44 Alan Trammell	.20	.09

1988 Fleer League Leaders

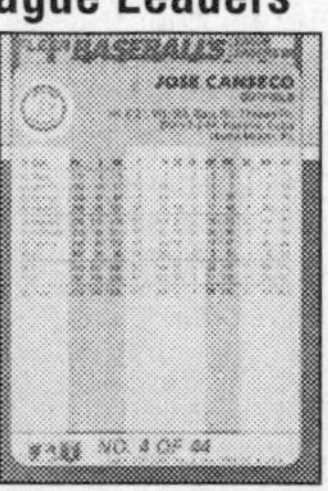

This small boxed set of 44 standard-size cards was produced exclusively for Walgreen Drug Stores. The cards feature full color fronts and pink, white, and blue backs. The card fronts are distinguished by the blue solid and striped background behind the player's full-color photo. The box for the cards describes the set as the "1988 Fleer Baseball's League Leaders." The checklist for the set is given on the back of the set box. The card numbering is in alphabetical order by player's name.

	MINT	NRMT
COMPLETE SET (44)	5.00	2.20
COMMON CARD (1-44)	.05	.02
☐ 1 George Bell	.05	.02
☐ 2 Wade Boggs	.40	.18
☐ 3 Ivan Calderon	.05	.02
☐ 4 Jose Canseco	.60	.25
☐ 5 Will Clark	.60	.25
☐ 6 Roger Clemens	.75	.35
☐ 7 Vince Coleman	.05	.02
☐ 8 Eric Davis	.05	.02
☐ 9 Andre Dawson	.30	.14
☐ 10 Bill Doran	.05	.02
☐ 11 Dwight Evans	.10	.05
☐ 12 Julio Franco	.10	.05
☐ 13 Gary Gaetti	.10	.05
☐ 14 Andres Galarraga	.30	.14
☐ 15 Dwight Gooden	.10	.05
☐ 16 Tony Gwynn	1.00	.45
☐ 17 Tom Henke	.10	.05
☐ 18 Keith Hernandez	.10	.05
☐ 19 Orel Hershiser	.10	.05
☐ 20 Ted Higuera	.05	.02
☐ 21 Kent Hrbek	.10	.05
☐ 22 Wally Joyner	.20	.09
☐ 23 Jimmy Key	.10	.05
☐ 24 Mark Langston	.05	.02
☐ 25 Don Mattingly	1.00	.45
☐ 26 Mark McGwire	1.25	.55
☐ 27 Paul Molitor	.50	.23
☐ 28 Jack Morris	.10	.05
☐ 29 Dale Murphy	.30	.14
☐ 30 Kirby Puckett	1.00	.45
☐ 31 Tim Raines	.10	.05
☐ 32 Rick Reuschel	.10	.05
☐ 33 Bret Saberhagen	.05	.02
☐ 34 Benito Santiago	.05	.02
☐ 35 Mike Schmidt	.50	.23
☐ 36 Mike Scott	.05	.02
☐ 37 Kevin Seitzer	.10	.05
☐ 38 Larry Sheets	.05	.02
☐ 39 Ruben Sierra	.10	.05
☐ 40 Darryl Strawberry	.10	.05
☐ 41 Rick Sutcliffe	.05	.02
☐ 42 Alan Trammell	.20	.09
☐ 43 Andy Van Slyke	.10	.05
☐ 44 Todd Worrell	.10	.05

1988 Fleer Mini

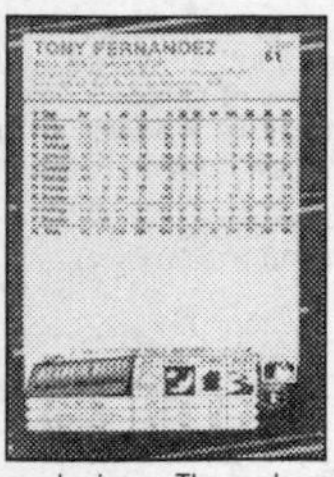

The 1988 Fleer "Classic Miniatures" set consists of 120 small cards with all new pictures of the players as compared to the 1988 Fleer regular issue. The cards are only 1 13/16" by 2 9/16", making them one of the smallest cards available. Card backs provide career year-by-year statistics. The complete set was distributed in a green, red, white, and silver box along with 18 logo stickers. The card numbering is by alphabetical team order within league and alphabetically within each team.

	MINT	NRMT
COMPLETE SET (120)	10.00	4.50
COMMON CARD (1-120)	.05	.02
☐ 1 Eddie Murray	.60	.25
☐ 2 Dave Schmidt	.05	.02
☐ 3 Larry Sheets	.05	.02
☐ 4 Wade Boggs	.30	.14
☐ 5 Roger Clemens	1.00	.45
☐ 6 Dwight Evans	.10	.05
☐ 7 Mike Greenwell	.10	.05
☐ 8 Sam Horn	.05	.02
☐ 9 Lee Smith	.15	.07
☐ 10 Brian Downing	.05	.02
☐ 11 Wally Joyner	.15	.07
☐ 12 Devon White	.10	.05
☐ 13 Mike Witt	.05	.02
☐ 14 Ivan Calderon	.05	.02
☐ 15 Ozzie Guillen	.05	.02
☐ 16 Jack McDowell	.30	.14
☐ 17 Kenny Williams	.05	.02
☐ 18 Joe Carter	.25	.11
☐ 19 Julio Franco	.10	.05
☐ 20 Pat Tabler	.05	.02
☐ 21 Doyle Alexander	.05	.02
☐ 22 Jack Morris	.10	.05
☐ 23 Matt Nokes	.05	.02
☐ 24 Walt Terrell	.05	.02
☐ 25 Alan Trammell	.15	.07
☐ 26 Bret Saberhagen	.10	.05
☐ 27 Kevin Seitzer	.10	.05
☐ 28 Danny Tartabull	.05	.02
☐ 29 Gary Thurman	.05	.02
☐ 30 Ted Higuera	.05	.02
☐ 31 Paul Molitor	.60	.25
☐ 32 Dan Plesac	.05	.02
☐ 33 Robin Yount	.25	.11
☐ 34 Gary Gaetti	.05	.02
☐ 35 Kent Hrbek	.10	.05
☐ 36 Kirby Puckett	1.00	.45
☐ 37 Jeff Reardon	.10	.05
☐ 38 Frank Viola	.05	.02
☐ 39 Jack Clark	.05	.02
☐ 40 Rickey Henderson	.50	.23
☐ 41 Don Mattingly	.75	.35
☐ 42 Willie Randolph	.10	.05
☐ 43 Dave Righetti	.05	.02
☐ 44 Dave Winfield	.50	.23
☐ 45 Jose Canseco	.60	.25
☐ 46 Mark McGwire	1.25	.55
☐ 47 Dave Parker	.10	.05
☐ 48 Dave Stewart	.10	.05
☐ 49 Walt Weiss	.15	.07
☐ 50 Bob Welch	.10	.05
☐ 51 Mickey Brantley	.05	.02
☐ 52 Mark Langston	.05	.02
☐ 53 Harold Reynolds	.10	.05
☐ 54 Scott Fletcher	.05	.02
☐ 55 Charlie Hough	.10	.05
☐ 56 Pete Incaviglia	.05	.02
☐ 57 Larry Parrish	.05	.02
☐ 58 Ruben Sierra	.10	.05
☐ 59 George Bell	.05	.02
☐ 60 Mark Eichhorn	.05	.02
☐ 61 Tony Fernandez	.05	.02
☐ 62 Tom Henke	.05	.02
☐ 63 Jimmy Key	.10	.05
☐ 64 Dion James	.05	.02
☐ 65 Dale Murphy	.25	.11
☐ 66 Zane Smith	.05	.02
☐ 67 Andre Dawson	.25	.11
☐ 68 Mark Grace	1.50	.70
☐ 69 Jerry Mumphrey	.05	.02
☐ 70 Ryne Sandberg	1.00	.45
☐ 71 Rick Sutcliffe	.05	.02
☐ 72 Kal Daniels	.05	.02
☐ 73 Eric Davis	.10	.05
☐ 74 John Franco	.10	.05
☐ 75 Ron Robinson	.05	.02
☐ 76 Jeff Treadway	.05	.02
☐ 77 Kevin Bass	.05	.02
☐ 78 Glenn Davis	.05	.02
☐ 79 Nolan Ryan	2.00	.90
☐ 80 Mike Scott	.05	.02
☐ 81 Dave Smith	.05	.02
☐ 82 Kirk Gibson	.10	.05
☐ 83 Pedro Guerrero	.05	.02
☐ 84 Orel Hershiser	.10	.05
☐ 85 Steve Sax	.05	.02
☐ 86 Fernando Valenzuela	.10	.05
☐ 87 Tim Burke	.05	.02
☐ 88 Andres Galarraga	.25	.11
☐ 89 Neal Heaton	.05	.02
☐ 90 Tim Raines	.10	.05
☐ 91 Tim Wallach	.05	.02
☐ 92 Dwight Gooden	.10	.05
☐ 93 Keith Hernandez	.10	.05
☐ 94 Gregg Jefferies	.50	.23
☐ 95 Howard Johnson	.05	.02
☐ 96 Roger McDowell	.05	.02
☐ 97 Darryl Strawberry	.10	.05
☐ 98 Steve Bedrosian	.05	.02
☐ 99 Von Hayes	.05	.02
☐ 100 Shane Rawley	.05	.02
☐ 101 Juan Samuel	.05	.02
☐ 102 Mike Schmidt	.40	.18
☐ 103 Bobby Bonilla	.10	.05
☐ 104 Mike Dunne	.05	.02
☐ 105 Andy Van Slyke	.10	.05
☐ 106 Vince Coleman	.05	.02
☐ 107 Bob Horner	.05	.02
☐ 108 Willie McGee	.10	.05
☐ 109 Ozzie Smith	1.00	.45
☐ 110 John Tudor	.05	.02
☐ 111 Todd Worrell	.05	.02
☐ 112 Tony Gwynn	.75	.35
☐ 113 John Kruk	.10	.05
☐ 114 Lance McCullers	.05	.02
☐ 115 Benito Santiago	.05	.02
☐ 116 Will Clark	.60	.25
☐ 117 Jeff Leonard	.05	.02
☐ 118 Candy Maldonado	.05	.02
☐ 119 Kirt Manwaring	.05	.02
☐ 120 Don Robinson	.05	.02

1988 Fleer Record Setters

This small boxed set of 44 standard-size cards was produced exclusively for Eckerd's Drug Stores. The cards feature full color fronts and red, white, and blue backs. The card fronts are distinguished by the red and blue frame around the player's full-color photo. The box for the cards describes the set as the "1988 Baseball Record Setters." The checklist for the set is given on the back of the set box. The card numbering is in alphabetical order by player's name.

	MINT	NRMT
COMPLETE SET (44)	5.00	2.20
COMMON CARD (1-44)	.05	.02
☐ 1 Jesse Barfield	.05	.02
☐ 2 George Bell	.05	.02
☐ 3 Wade Boggs	.40	.18
☐ 4 Jose Canseco	.60	.25
☐ 5 Jack Clark	.10	.05
☐ 6 Will Clark	.60	.25
☐ 7 Roger Clemens	.75	.35
☐ 8 Alvin Davis	.05	.02
☐ 9 Eric Davis	.05	.02
☐ 10 Andre Dawson	.30	.14
☐ 11 Mike Dunne	.05	.02
☐ 12 John Franco	.10	.05
☐ 13 Julio Franco	.10	.05
☐ 14 Dwight Gooden	.10	.05
☐ 15 Mark Gubicza (Listed as Gubiczo on box checklist)	.05	.02
☐ 16 Ozzie Guillen	.05	.02

☐ 17 Tony Gwynn	1.00	.45
☐ 18 Orel Hershiser	.10	.05
☐ 19 Teddy Higuera	.05	.02
☐ 20 Howard Johnson UER (Missing '87 stats on card back)	.05	.02
☐ 21 Wally Joyner	.20	.09
☐ 22 Jimmy Key	.10	.05
☐ 23 Jeff Leonard	.05	.02
☐ 24 Don Mattingly	1.00	.45
☐ 25 Mark McGwire	1.25	.55
☐ 26 Jack Morris	.10	.05
☐ 27 Dale Murphy	.20	.09
☐ 28 Larry Parrish	.05	.02
☐ 29 Kirby Puckett	1.00	.45
☐ 30 Tim Raines	.10	.05
☐ 31 Harold Reynolds	.10	.05
☐ 32 Dave Righetti	.10	.05
☐ 33 Cal Ripken	2.00	.90
☐ 34 Benito Santiago	.05	.02
☐ 35 Mike Schmidt	.50	.23
☐ 36 Mike Scott	.05	.02
☐ 37 Kevin Seitzer	.10	.05
☐ 38 Ozzie Smith	1.00	.45
☐ 39 Darryl Strawberry	.10	.05
☐ 40 Rick Sutcliffe	.05	.02
☐ 41 Alan Trammell	.20	.09
☐ 42 Frank Viola	.05	.02
☐ 43 Mitch Williams	.05	.02
☐ 44 Todd Worrell	.10	.05

1988 Fleer Sluggers/Pitchers

Fleer produced this 44-card boxed standard-size set although it was primarily distributed by McCrory, McLellan, J.J Newberry, H.L.Green, T.G.Y., and other similar stores. The set is subtitled "Baseball's Best". The set was packaged in a green custom box along with six logo stickers. The set checklist is given on the back of the box. The bottoms of the boxes which held the individual set boxes also contained a panel of six cards; these box bottom cards were numbered C1 through C6. The card numbering is in alphabetical order by player's name.

	MINT	NRMT
COMPLETE SET (44)	5.00	2.20
COMMON CARD (1-44)	.05	.02
☐ 1 George Bell	.05	.02
☐ 2 Wade Boggs	.40	.18
☐ 3 Bobby Bonilla	.10	.05
☐ 4 Tom Brunansky	.05	.02
☐ 5 Ellis Burks	.40	.18
☐ 6 Jose Canseco	.60	.25
☐ 7 Joe Carter	.30	.14
☐ 8 Will Clark	.60	.25
☐ 9 Roger Clemens	.75	.35
☐ 10 Eric Davis	.05	.02
☐ 11 Glenn Davis	.05	.02
☐ 12 Andre Dawson	.30	.14
☐ 13 Dennis Eckersley	.20	.09
☐ 14 Andres Galarraga	.30	.14
☐ 15 Dwight Gooden	.10	.05
☐ 16 Pedro Guerrero	.05	.02
☐ 17 Tony Gwynn	1.00	.45
☐ 18 Orel Hershiser	.10	.05
☐ 19 Ted Higuera	.05	.02
☐ 20 Pete Incaviglia	.05	.02
☐ 21 Danny Jackson	.05	.02
☐ 22 Doug Jennings	.05	.02
☐ 23 Mark Langston	.05	.02
☐ 24 Dave LaPoint	.05	.02
☐ 25 Mike LaValliere	.05	.02
☐ 26 Don Mattingly	1.00	.45
☐ 27 Mark McGwire	1.25	.55
☐ 28 Dale Murphy	.30	.14
☐ 29 Ken Phelps	.05	.02
☐ 30 Kirby Puckett	1.00	.45
☐ 31 Johnny Ray	.05	.02
☐ 32 Jeff Reardon	.05	.02
☐ 33 Dave Righetti	.10	.05
☐ 34 Cal Ripken UER (Misspelled Ripkin on card front)	2.00	.90
☐ 35 Chris Sabo	.10	.05
☐ 36 Mike Schmidt	.50	.23
☐ 37 Mike Scott	.05	.02
☐ 38 Kevin Seitzer	.10	.05
☐ 39 Dave Stewart	.10	.05
☐ 40 Darryl Strawberry	.10	.05
☐ 41 Greg Swindell	.05	.02
☐ 42 Frank Tanana	.10	.05
☐ 43 Dave Winfield	.50	.23
☐ 44 Todd Worrell	.10	.05

1988 Fleer Sluggers/Pitchers Box Cards

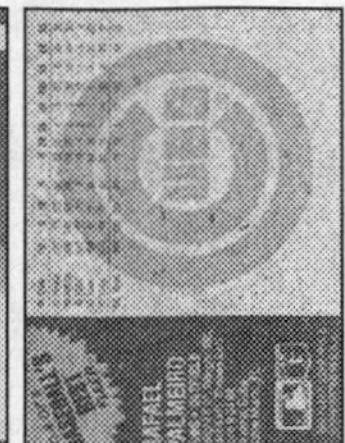

The cards in this six-card set each measure the standard size. Cards have essentially the same design as the 1988 Fleer Sluggers vs. Pitchers set of Baseball's Best. The cards were printed on the bottom of the counter display box which held 24 small boxed sets; hence theoretically these box cards are 1/24 as plentiful as the regular boxed set cards. These six cards, numbered C1 to C6 are considered a separate set in their own right and are not typically included in a complete set of the 1988 Fleer Sluggers vs. Pitchers set of 44. The value of the panels uncut is slightly greater, perhaps by 25 percent greater, than the value of the individual cards cut up carefully.

	MINT	NRMT
COMPLETE SET (6)	5.00	2.20
COMMON CARDS (C1-C6)	.25	.11
☐ C1 Ron Darling	.25	.11
☐ C2 Rickey Henderson	1.50	.70
☐ C3 Carney Lansford	.50	.23
☐ C4 Rafael Palmeiro	2.50	1.10
☐ C5 Frank Viola	.25	.11
☐ C6 Twins Logo (Checklist back)	.25	.11

1988 Fleer Sticker Cards

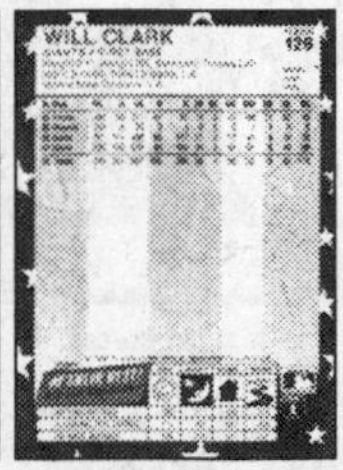

These Star Stickers were distributed as a separate issue by Fleer, with five star stickers and a logo sticker in each wax pack. The 132-card (sticker) set features 2 1/2" by 3 1/2" full-color fronts and even statistics on the sticker back, which is an indication that the Fleer Company understands that these stickers are rarely used as stickers but more like traditional cards. The fronts are surrounded by a silver-gray border and the backs are printed in red and black on white card stock. The set numbering is in alphabetical order within team and alphabetically by team within each league.

	MINT	NRMT
COMPLETE SET (132)	15.00	6.75
COMMON CARD (1-132)	.05	.02
☐ 1 Mike Boddicker	.05	.02
☐ 2 Eddie Murray	.75	.35
☐ 3 Cal Ripken	3.00	1.35
☐ 4 Larry Sheets	.05	.02
☐ 5 Wade Boggs	.50	.23
☐ 6 Ellis Burks	.50	.23
☐ 7 Roger Clemens	1.25	.55
☐ 8 Dwight Evans	.10	.05
☐ 9 Mike Greenwell	.10	.05
☐ 10 Bruce Hurst	.05	.02
☐ 11 Brian Downing	.05	.02
☐ 12 Wally Joyner	.25	.11
☐ 13 Mike Witt	.05	.02
☐ 14 Ivan Calderon	.05	.02
☐ 15 Jose DeLeon	.05	.02
☐ 16 Ozzie Guillen	.05	.02
☐ 17 Bobby Thigpen	.05	.02
☐ 18 Joe Carter	.40	.18
☐ 19 Julio Franco	.10	.05
☐ 20 Brook Jacoby	.05	.02
☐ 21 Cory Snyder	.05	.02
☐ 22 Pat Tabler	.05	.02
☐ 23 Doyle Alexander	.05	.02
☐ 24 Kirk Gibson	.10	.05
☐ 25 Mike Henneman	.10	.05
☐ 26 Jack Morris	.10	.05
☐ 27 Matt Nokes	.05	.02
☐ 28 Walt Terrell	.05	.02
☐ 29 Alan Trammell	.25	.11
☐ 30 George Brett	1.25	.55
☐ 31 Charlie Leibrandt	.05	.02
☐ 32 Bret Saberhagen	.10	.05
☐ 33 Kevin Seitzer	.10	.05
☐ 34 Danny Tartabull	.05	.02
☐ 35 Frank White	.10	.05
☐ 36 Rob Deer	.05	.02
☐ 37 Ted Higuera	.05	.02
☐ 38 Paul Molitor	.60	.25
☐ 39 Dan Plesac	.05	.02
☐ 40 Robin Yount	.40	.18
☐ 41 Bert Blyleven	.10	.05
☐ 42 Tom Brunansky	.05	.02
☐ 43 Gary Gaetti	.10	.05
☐ 44 Kent Hrbek	.10	.05
☐ 45 Kirby Puckett	1.50	.70
☐ 46 Jeff Reardon	.10	.05
☐ 47 Frank Viola	.05	.02
☐ 48 Don Mattingly	1.50	.70
☐ 49 Mike Pagliarulo	.05	.02
☐ 50 Willie Randolph	.10	.05
☐ 51 Rick Rhoden	.05	.02
☐ 52 Dave Righetti	.05	.02
☐ 53 Dave Winfield	.40	.18
☐ 54 Jose Canseco	.50	.23
☐ 55 Carney Lansford	.05	.02
☐ 56 Mark McGwire	2.00	.90
☐ 57 Dave Stewart	.05	.02
☐ 58 Curt Young	.05	.02
☐ 59 Alvin Davis	.05	.02
☐ 60 Mark Langston	.05	.02
☐ 61 Ken Phelps	.05	.02
☐ 62 Harold Reynolds	.10	.05
☐ 63 Scott Fletcher	.05	.02
☐ 64 Charlie Hough	.05	.02
☐ 65 Pete Incaviglia	.05	.02
☐ 66 Oddibe McDowell	.05	.02
☐ 67 Pete O'Brien	.05	.02
☐ 68 Larry Parrish	.05	.02
☐ 69 Ruben Sierra	.10	.05
☐ 70 Jesse Barfield	.05	.02
☐ 71 George Bell	.05	.02
☐ 72 Tony Fernandez	.05	.02
☐ 73 Tom Henke	.05	.02
☐ 74 Jimmy Key	.10	.05
☐ 75 Lloyd Moseby	.05	.02
☐ 76 Dion James	.05	.02
☐ 77 Dale Murphy	.40	.18
☐ 78 Zane Smith	.05	.02
☐ 79 Andre Dawson	.40	.18
☐ 80 Ryne Sandberg	1.25	.55
☐ 81 Rick Sutcliffe	.05	.02
☐ 82 Kal Daniels	.05	.02
☐ 83 Eric Davis	.10	.05
☐ 84 John Franco	.10	.05
☐ 85 Kevin Bass	.05	.02
☐ 86 Glenn Davis	.05	.02
☐ 87 Bill Doran	.05	.02
☐ 88 Nolan Ryan	3.00	1.35
☐ 89 Mike Scott	.05	.02
☐ 90 Dave Smith	.05	.02
☐ 91 Pedro Guerrero	.05	.02
☐ 92 Orel Hershiser	.10	.05
☐ 93 Steve Sax	.05	.02
☐ 94 Fernando Valenzuela	.10	.05
☐ 95 Tim Burke	.05	.02
☐ 96 Andres Galarraga	.40	.18
☐ 97 Tim Raines	.10	.05
☐ 98 Tim Wallach	.05	.02
☐ 99 Mitch Webster	.05	.02
☐ 100 Ron Darling	.05	.02
☐ 101 Sid Fernandez	.05	.02
☐ 102 Dwight Gooden	.10	.05
☐ 103 Keith Hernandez	.10	.05
☐ 104 Howard Johnson	.05	.02
☐ 105 Roger McDowell	.05	.02
☐ 106 Darryl Strawberry	.10	.05

☐ 107 Steve Bedrosian	.05	.02
☐ 108 Von Hayes	.05	.02
☐ 109 Shane Rawley	.05	.02
☐ 110 Juan Samuel	.05	.02
☐ 111 Mike Schmidt	.75	.35
☐ 112 Milt Thompson	.05	.02
☐ 113 Sid Bream	.05	.02
☐ 114 Bobby Bonilla	.10	.05
☐ 115 Mike Dunne	.05	.02
☐ 116 Andy Van Slyke	.10	.05
☐ 117 Vince Coleman	.05	.02
☐ 118 Willie McGee	.10	.05
☐ 119 Terry Pendleton	.10	.05
☐ 120 Ozzie Smith	1.25	.55
☐ 121 John Tudor	.05	.02
☐ 122 Todd Worrell	.05	.02
☐ 123 Tony Gwynn	1.50	.70
☐ 124 John Kruk	.10	.05
☐ 125 Benito Santiago	.05	.02
☐ 126 Will Clark	.75	.35
☐ 127 Dave Dravecky	.05	.02
☐ 128 Jeff Leonard	.05	.02
☐ 129 Candy Maldonado	.05	.02
☐ 130 Rick Reuschel	.10	.05
☐ 131 Don Robinson	.05	.02
☐ 132 Checklist Card	.05	.02

1988 Fleer Stickers Wax Box Cards

The bottoms of the Star Sticker wax boxes contained two different sets of four cards done in a similar format to the stickers; these cards (they are not stickers but truly cards) are numbered with the prefix S and are considered a separate set. The value of the panels uncut is slightly greater, perhaps by 25 percent greater, than the value of the individual cards cut up carefully.

	MINT	NRMT
COMPLETE SET (8)	4.00	1.80
COMMON CARD (S1-S8)	.25	.11
☐ S1 Don Baylor	.25	.11
☐ S2 Gary Carter	.50	.23
☐ S3 Ron Guidry	.25	.11
☐ S4 Rickey Henderson	1.25	.55
☐ S5 Kevin Mitchell	.25	.11
☐ S6 Mark McGwire and Eric Davis	2.00	.90
☐ S7 Giants Logo	.25	.11
☐ S8 Detroit Logo	.25	.11

1988 Fleer Superstars

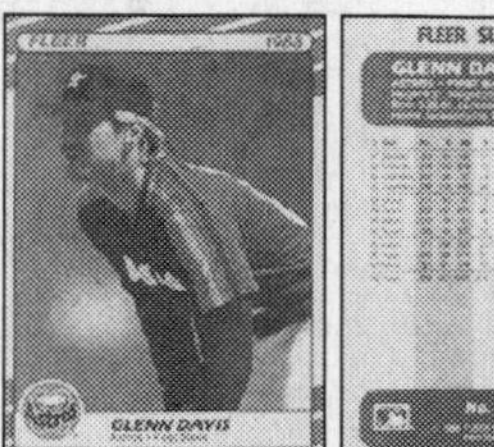

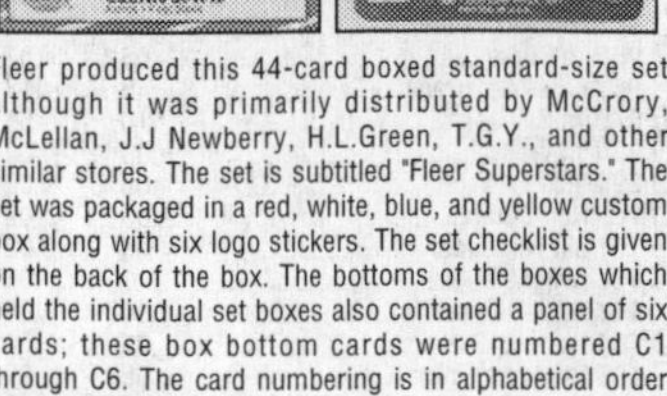

Fleer produced this 44-card boxed standard-size set although it was primarily distributed by McCrory, McLellan, J.J Newberry, H.L.Green, T.G.Y., and other similar stores. The set is subtitled "Fleer Superstars." The set was packaged in a red, white, blue, and yellow custom box along with six logo stickers. The set checklist is given on the back of the box. The bottoms of the boxes which held the individual set boxes also contained a panel of six cards; these box bottom cards were numbered C1 through C6. The card numbering is in alphabetical order by player's name.

	MINT	NRMT
COMPLETE SET (44)	5.00	2.20
COMMON CARD (1-44)	.05	.02
☐ 1 Steve Bedrosian	.05	.02
☐ 2 George Bell	.05	.02
☐ 3 Wade Boggs	.40	.18
☐ 4 Barry Bonds	1.00	.45
☐ 5 Jose Canseco	.60	.25
☐ 6 Joe Carter	.30	.14
☐ 7 Jack Clark	.10	.05
☐ 8 Will Clark	.60	.25
☐ 9 Roger Clemens	.75	.35
☐ 10 Alvin Davis	.05	.02
☐ 11 Eric Davis	.10	.05
☐ 12 Glenn Davis	.05	.02
☐ 13 Andre Dawson	.30	.14
☐ 14 Dwight Gooden	.10	.05
☐ 15 Orel Hershiser	.10	.05
☐ 16 Teddy Higuera	.05	.02
☐ 17 Kent Hrbek	.10	.05
☐ 18 Wally Joyner	.10	.05
☐ 19 Jimmy Key	.10	.05
☐ 20 John Kruk	.10	.05
☐ 21 Jeff Leonard	.05	.02
☐ 22 Don Mattingly	1.00	.45
☐ 23 Mark McGwire	1.25	.55
☐ 24 Kevin McReynolds	.05	.02
☐ 25 Dale Murphy	.30	.14
☐ 26 Matt Nokes	.05	.02
☐ 27 Terry Pendleton	.10	.05
☐ 28 Kirby Puckett	1.00	.45
☐ 29 Tim Raines	.10	.05
☐ 30 Rick Rhoden	.05	.02
☐ 31 Cal Ripken	2.00	.90
☐ 32 Benito Santiago	.05	.02
☐ 33 Mike Schmidt	.50	.23
☐ 34 Mike Scott	.05	.02
☐ 35 Kevin Seitzer	.10	.05
☐ 36 Ruben Sierra	.10	.05
☐ 37 Cory Snyder	.05	.02
☐ 38 Darryl Strawberry	.10	.05
☐ 39 Rick Sutcliffe	.05	.02
☐ 40 Danny Tartabull	.05	.02
☐ 41 Alan Trammell	.20	.09
☐ 42 Kenny Williams	.05	.02
☐ 43 Mike Witt	.05	.02
☐ 44 Robin Yount	.30	.14

1988 Fleer Superstars Box Cards

The cards in this six-card set each measure the standard size. Cards have essentially the same design as the 1988 Fleer Superstars set. The cards were printed on the bottom of the counter display box which held 24 small boxed sets; hence theoretically these box cards are 1/24 as plentiful as the regular boxed set cards. These six cards, numbered C1 to C6 are considered a separate set in their own right and are not typically included in a complete set of the 1988 Fleer Superstars set of 44. The value of the panels uncut is slightly greater, perhaps by 25 percent greater, than the value of the individual cards cut up carefully.

	MINT	NRMT
COMPLETE SET (6)	8.00	3.60
COMMON CARD (C1-C6)	.25	.11
☐ C1 Pete Incaviglia	.50	.23
☐ C2 Rickey Henderson	2.00	.90
☐ C3 Tony Fernandez	.50	.23
☐ C4 Shane Rawley	.25	.11
☐ C5 Ryne Sandberg	5.00	2.20
☐ C6 Cardinals Logo (Checklist back)	.25	.11

1988 Fleer Team Leaders

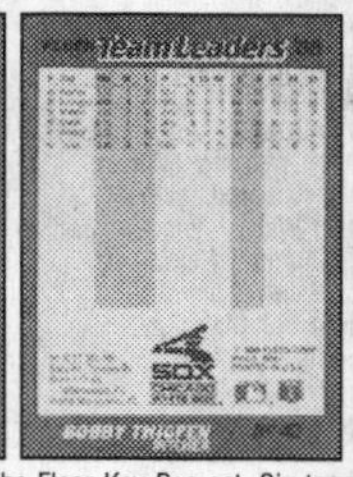

This 44-card boxed standard-size set was produced by Fleer for exclusive distribution by Kay Bee Toys and is sometimes referred to as the Fleer Kay Bee set. Six team logo stickers are included in the box with the complete set. The numerical checklist on the back of the box shows that the set is numbered alphabetically. The cards have a distinctive red border on the fronts. The Kay Bee logo is printed in the lower right corner of the obverse of each card.

	MINT	NRMT
COMPLETE SET (44)	5.00	2.20
COMMON CARD (1-44)	.05	.02
☐ 1 George Bell	.05	.02
☐ 2 Wade Boggs	.40	.18
☐ 3 Jose Canseco	.60	.25
☐ 4 Will Clark	.60	.25
☐ 5 Roger Clemens	.75	.35
☐ 6 Eric Davis	.10	.05
☐ 7 Andre Dawson	.30	.14
☐ 8 Julio Franco	.10	.05
☐ 9 Andres Galarraga	.30	.14
☐ 10 Dwight Gooden	.10	.05
☐ 11 Tony Gwynn	1.00	.45
☐ 12 Tom Henke	.05	.02
☐ 13 Orel Hershiser	.10	.05
☐ 14 Kent Hrbek	.10	.05
☐ 15 Ted Higuera	.05	.02
☐ 16 Wally Joyner	.10	.05
☐ 17 Jimmy Key	.10	.05
☐ 18 Mark Langston	.05	.02
☐ 19 Don Mattingly	1.00	.45
☐ 20 Willie McGee	.10	.05
☐ 21 Mark McGwire	1.25	.55
☐ 22 Paul Molitor	.50	.23
☐ 23 Jack Morris	.10	.05
☐ 24 Dale Murphy	.30	.14
☐ 25 Larry Parrish	.05	.02
☐ 26 Kirby Puckett	1.00	.45
☐ 27 Tim Raines	.10	.05
☐ 28 Jeff Reardon	.05	.02
☐ 29 Dave Righetti	.05	.02
☐ 30 Cal Ripken	2.00	.90
☐ 31 Don Robinson	.05	.02
☐ 32 Bret Saberhagen	.10	.05
☐ 33 Juan Samuel	.05	.02
☐ 34 Mike Schmidt	.50	.23
☐ 35 Mike Scott	.05	.02
☐ 36 Kevin Seitzer	.10	.05
☐ 37 Dave Smith	.05	.02
☐ 38 Ozzie Smith	1.00	.45
☐ 39 Zane Smith	.05	.02
☐ 40 Darryl Strawberry	.10	.05
☐ 41 Rick Sutcliffe	.05	.02
☐ 42 Bobby Thigpen	.05	.02
☐ 43 Alan Trammell	.20	.09
☐ 44 Andy Van Slyke	.10	.05

1989 Fleer

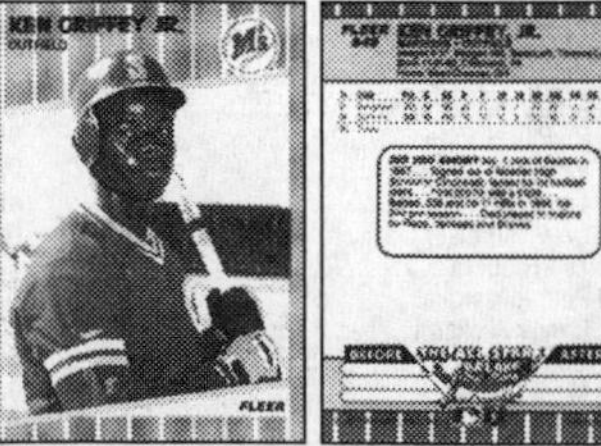

This set consists of 660 standard-size cards. Cards were primarily issued in 15-card wax packs, rack packs and hobby and retail factory sets. Card fronts feature a distinctive gray border background with white and yellow trim. Cards are again organized alphabetically within teams and teams ordered by previous season record. The last 33 cards in the set consist of Specials (628-639), Rookie Pairs (640-653), and checklists (654-660). Approximately half of the California Angels players have white rather than yellow halos. Certain Oakland A's player cards have red instead of green lines for front photo borders. Checklist cards are available either with or without positions listed for each player. Rookie Cards in this set include Sandy Alomar Jr., Brady Anderson, Dante Bichette, Craig Biggio, Ken Griffey Jr., Charlie Hayes, Ken Hill, Randy Johnson, Ramon Martinez, Hal Morris, Gary Sheffield, and John Smoltz.

	MINT	NRMT
COMPLETE SET (660)	10.00	4.50
COMP.RETAIL SET (660)	10.00	4.50
COMP.HOBBY SET (672)	12.00	5.50
COMMON CARD (1-660)	.05	.02

Card	MINT	NRMT
☐ 1 Don Baylor	.05	.02
☐ 2 Lance Blankenship	.05	.02
☐ 3 Todd Burns UER (Wrong birthdate; before/after All-Star stats missing)	.05	.02
☐ 4 Greg Cadaret UER (All-Star Break stats show 3 losses, should be 2)	.05	.02
☐ 5 Jose Canseco	.20	.09
☐ 6 Storm Davis	.05	.02
☐ 7 Dennis Eckersley	.20	.09
☐ 8 Mike Gallego	.05	.02
☐ 9 Ron Hassey	.05	.02
☐ 10 Dave Henderson	.05	.02
☐ 11 Rick Honeycutt	.05	.02
☐ 12 Glenn Hubbard	.05	.02
☐ 13 Stan Javier	.05	.02
☐ 14 Doug Jennings	.05	.02
☐ 15 Felix Jose	.05	.02
☐ 16 Carney Lansford	.10	.05
☐ 17 Mark McGwire	.40	.18
☐ 18 Gene Nelson	.05	.02
☐ 19 Dave Parker	.10	.05
☐ 20 Eric Plunk	.05	.02
☐ 21 Luis Polonia	.05	.02
☐ 22 Terry Steinbach	.10	.05
☐ 23 Dave Stewart	.10	.05
☐ 24 Walt Weiss	.05	.02
☐ 25 Bob Welch	.05	.02
☐ 26 Curt Young	.05	.02
☐ 27 Rick Aguilera	.10	.05
☐ 28 Wally Backman	.05	.02
☐ 29 Mark Carreon UER (After All-Star Break batting 7.14)	.05	.02
☐ 30 Gary Carter	.20	.09
☐ 31 David Cone	.20	.09
☐ 32 Ron Darling	.05	.02
☐ 33 Len Dykstra	.10	.05
☐ 34 Kevin Elster	.05	.02
☐ 35 Sid Fernandez	.05	.02
☐ 36 Dwight Gooden	.10	.05
☐ 37 Keith Hernandez	.10	.05
☐ 38 Gregg Jefferies	.20	.09
☐ 39 Howard Johnson	.05	.02
☐ 40 Terry Leach	.05	.02
☐ 41 Dave Magadan UER (Bio says 15 doubles, should be 13)	.05	.02
☐ 42 Bob McClure	.05	.02
☐ 43 Roger McDowell UER (Led Mets with 58, should be 62)	.05	.02
☐ 44 Kevin McReynolds	.05	.02
☐ 45 Keith A. Miller	.05	.02
☐ 46 Randy Myers	.10	.05
☐ 47 Bob Ojeda	.05	.02
☐ 48 Mackey Sasser	.05	.02
☐ 49 Darryl Strawberry	.10	.05
☐ 50 Tim Teufel	.05	.02
☐ 51 Dave West	.05	.02
☐ 52 Mookie Wilson	.10	.05
☐ 53 Dave Anderson	.05	.02
☐ 54 Tim Belcher	.05	.02
☐ 55 Mike Davis	.05	.02
☐ 56 Mike Devereaux	.05	.02
☐ 57 Kirk Gibson	.20	.09
☐ 58 Alfredo Griffin	.05	.02
☐ 59 Chris Gwynn	.05	.02
☐ 60 Jeff Hamilton	.05	.02
☐ 61A Danny Heep (Home: Lake Hills)	.20	.09
☐ 61B Danny Heep (Home: San Antonio)	.05	.02
☐ 62 Orel Hershiser	.10	.05
☐ 63 Brian Holton	.05	.02
☐ 64 Jay Howell	.05	.02
☐ 65 Tim Leary	.05	.02
☐ 66 Mike Marshall	.05	.02
☐ 67 Ramon Martinez	.25	.11
☐ 68 Jesse Orosco	.05	.02
☐ 69 Alejandro Pena	.05	.02
☐ 70 Steve Sax	.05	.02
☐ 71 Mike Scioscia	.05	.02
☐ 72 Mike Sharperson	.05	.02
☐ 73 John Shelby	.05	.02
☐ 74 Franklin Stubbs	.05	.02
☐ 75 John Tudor	.05	.02
☐ 76 Fernando Valenzuela	.10	.05
☐ 77 Tracy Woodson	.05	.02
☐ 78 Marty Barrett	.05	.02
☐ 79 Todd Benzinger	.05	.02
☐ 80 Mike Boddicker UER (Rochester in '76, should be '78)	.05	.02
☐ 81 Wade Boggs	.20	.09
☐ 82 Oil Can Boyd	.05	.02
☐ 83 Ellis Burks	.10	.05
☐ 84 Rick Cerone	.05	.02
☐ 85 Roger Clemens	.40	.18
☐ 86 Steve Curry	.05	.02
☐ 87 Dwight Evans	.10	.05
☐ 88 Wes Gardner	.05	.02
☐ 89 Rich Gedman	.05	.02
☐ 90 Mike Greenwell	.05	.02
☐ 91 Bruce Hurst	.05	.02
☐ 92 Dennis Lamp	.05	.02
☐ 93 Spike Owen	.05	.02
☐ 94 Larry Parrish UER (Before All-Star Break batting 1.90)	.05	.02
☐ 95 Carlos Quintana	.05	.02
☐ 96 Jody Reed	.05	.02
☐ 97 Jim Rice	.05	.02
☐ 98A Kevin Romine ERR (Photo actually Randy Kutcher batting)	.20	.09
☐ 98B Kevin Romine COR (Arms folded)	.05	.02
☐ 99 Lee Smith	.10	.05
☐ 100 Mike Smithson	.05	.02
☐ 101 Bob Stanley	.05	.02
☐ 102 Allan Anderson	.05	.02
☐ 103 Keith Atherton	.05	.02
☐ 104 Juan Berenguer	.05	.02
☐ 105 Bert Blyleven	.10	.05
☐ 106 Eric Bullock UER (Bats/Throws Right, should be Left)	.05	.02
☐ 107 Randy Bush	.05	.02
☐ 108 John Christensen	.05	.02
☐ 109 Mark Davidson	.05	.02
☐ 110 Gary Gaetti	.05	.02
☐ 111 Greg Gagne	.05	.02
☐ 112 Dan Gladden	.05	.02
☐ 113 German Gonzalez	.05	.02
☐ 114 Brian Harper	.05	.02
☐ 115 Tom Herr	.05	.02
☐ 116 Kent Hrbek	.10	.05
☐ 117 Gene Larkin	.05	.02
☐ 118 Tim Laudner	.05	.02
☐ 119 Charlie Lea	.05	.02
☐ 120 Steve Lombardozzi	.05	.02
☐ 121A John Moses (Home: Tempe)	.20	.09
☐ 121B John Moses (Home: Phoenix)	.05	.02
☐ 122 Al Newman	.05	.02
☐ 123 Mark Portugal	.05	.02
☐ 124 Kirby Puckett	.40	.18
☐ 125 Jeff Reardon	.10	.05
☐ 126 Fred Toliver	.05	.02
☐ 127 Frank Viola	.05	.02
☐ 128 Doyle Alexander	.05	.02
☐ 129 Dave Bergman	.05	.02
☐ 130A Tom Brookens ERR (Mike Heath back)	.75	.35
☐ 130B Tom Brookens COR	.05	.02
☐ 131 Paul Gibson	.05	.02
☐ 132A Mike Heath ERR (Tom Brookens back)	.75	.35
☐ 132B Mike Heath COR	.05	.02
☐ 133 Don Heinkel	.05	.02
☐ 134 Mike Henneman	.05	.02
☐ 135 Guillermo Hernandez	.05	.02
☐ 136 Eric King	.05	.02
☐ 137 Chet Lemon	.05	.02
☐ 138 Fred Lynn UER ('74, '75 stats missing)	.05	.02
☐ 139 Jack Morris	.10	.05
☐ 140 Matt Nokes	.05	.02
☐ 141 Gary Pettis	.05	.02
☐ 142 Ted Power	.05	.02
☐ 143 Jeff M. Robinson	.05	.02
☐ 144 Luis Salazar	.05	.02
☐ 145 Steve Searcy	.05	.02
☐ 146 Pat Sheridan	.05	.02
☐ 147 Frank Tanana	.05	.02
☐ 148 Alan Trammell	.05	.02
☐ 149 Walt Terrell	.05	.02
☐ 150 Jim Walewander	.05	.02
☐ 151 Lou Whitaker	.10	.05
☐ 152 Tim Birtsas	.05	.02
☐ 153 Tom Browning	.05	.02
☐ 154 Keith Brown	.05	.02
☐ 155 Norm Charlton	.10	.05
☐ 156 Dave Concepcion	.10	.05
☐ 157 Kal Daniels	.05	.02
☐ 158 Eric Davis	.10	.05
☐ 159 Bo Diaz	.05	.02
☐ 160 Rob Dibble	.10	.05
☐ 161 Nick Esasky	.05	.02
☐ 162 John Franco	.10	.05
☐ 163 Danny Jackson	.05	.02
☐ 164 Barry Larkin	.05	.02
☐ 165 Rob Murphy	.05	.02
☐ 166 Paul O'Neill	.10	.05
☐ 167 Jeff Reed	.05	.02
☐ 168 Jose Rijo	.05	.02
☐ 169 Ron Robinson	.05	.02
☐ 170 Chris Sabo	.05	.02
☐ 171 Candy Sierra	.05	.02
☐ 172 Van Snider	.05	.02
☐ 173A Jeff Treadway (Target registration mark above head on front in light blue)	5.00	2.20
☐ 173B Jeff Treadway (No target on front)	.05	.02
☐ 174 Frank Williams (After All-Star Break stats are jumbled)	.05	.02
☐ 175 Herm Winningham	.05	.02
☐ 176 Jim Adduci	.05	.02
☐ 177 Don August	.05	.02
☐ 178 Mike Birkbeck	.05	.02
☐ 179 Chris Bosio	.05	.02
☐ 180 Glenn Braggs	.05	.02
☐ 181 Greg Brock	.05	.02
☐ 182 Mark Clear	.05	.02
☐ 183 Chuck Crim	.05	.02
☐ 184 Rob Deer	.05	.02
☐ 185 Tom Filer	.05	.02
☐ 186 Jim Gantner	.05	.02
☐ 187 Darryl Hamilton	.10	.05
☐ 188 Ted Higuera	.05	.02
☐ 189 Odell Jones	.05	.02
☐ 190 Jeffrey Leonard	.05	.02
☐ 191 Joey Meyer	.05	.02
☐ 192 Paul Mirabella	.05	.02
☐ 193 Paul Molitor	.20	.09
☐ 194 Charlie O'Brien	.05	.02
☐ 195 Dan Plesac	.05	.02
☐ 196 Gary Sheffield	.75	.35
☐ 197 B.J. Surhoff	.10	.05
☐ 198 Dale Sveum	.05	.02
☐ 199 Bill Wegman	.05	.02
☐ 200 Robin Yount	.20	.09
☐ 201 Rafael Belliard	.05	.02
☐ 202 Barry Bonds	.40	.18
☐ 203 Bobby Bonilla	.05	.02
☐ 204 Sid Bream	.05	.02
☐ 205 Benny Distefano	.05	.02
☐ 206 Doug Drabek	.05	.02
☐ 207 Mike Dunne	.05	.02
☐ 208 Felix Fermin	.05	.02
☐ 209 Brian Fisher	.05	.02
☐ 210 Jim Gott	.05	.02
☐ 211 Bob Kipper	.05	.02
☐ 212 Dave LaPoint	.05	.02
☐ 213 Mike LaValliere	.05	.02
☐ 214 Jose Lind	.05	.02
☐ 215 Junior Ortiz	.05	.02
☐ 216 Vicente Palacios	.05	.02
☐ 217 Tom Prince	.05	.02
☐ 218 Gary Redus	.05	.02
☐ 219 R.J. Reynolds	.05	.02
☐ 220 Jeff D. Robinson	.05	.02
☐ 221 John Smiley	.05	.02
☐ 222 Andy Van Slyke	.10	.05
☐ 223 Bob Walk	.05	.02
☐ 224 Glenn Wilson	.05	.02
☐ 225 Jesse Barfield	.05	.02
☐ 226 George Bell	.05	.02
☐ 227 Pat Borders	.10	.05
☐ 228 John Cerutti	.05	.02
☐ 229 Jim Clancy	.05	.02
☐ 230 Mark Eichhorn	.05	.02
☐ 231 Tony Fernandez	.05	.02
☐ 232 Cecil Fielder	.05	.02
☐ 233 Mike Flanagan	.05	.02
☐ 234 Kelly Gruber	.05	.02
☐ 235 Tom Henke	.05	.02

☐ 236 Jimmy Key .05 .02
☐ 237 Rick Leach .05 .02
☐ 238 Manny Lee UER .05 .02
(Bio says regular shortstop, sic, Tony Fernandez)
☐ 239 Nelson Liriano .05 .02
☐ 240 Fred McGriff .20 .09
☐ 241 Lloyd Moseby .05 .02
☐ 242 Rance Mulliniks .05 .02
☐ 243 Jeff Musselman .05 .02
☐ 244 Dave Stieb .05 .02
☐ 245 Todd Stottlemyre .10 .05
☐ 246 Duane Ward .05 .02
☐ 247 David Wells .10 .05
☐ 248 Ernie Whitt UER .05 .02
(HR total 21, should be 121)
☐ 249 Luis Aguayo .05 .02
☐ 250A Neil Allen .75 .35
(Home: Sarasota, FL)
☐ 250B Neil Allen .05 .02
(Home: Syosset, NY)
☐ 251 John Candelaria .05 .02
☐ 252 Jack Clark .10 .05
☐ 253 Richard Dotson .05 .02
☐ 254 Rickey Henderson .20 .09
☐ 255 Tommy John .10 .05
☐ 256 Roberto Kelly .05 .02
☐ 257 Al Leiter .05 .02
☐ 258 Don Mattingly .30 .14
☐ 259 Dale Mohorcic .05 .02
☐ 260 Hal Morris .20 .09
☐ 261 Scott Nielsen .05 .02
☐ 262 Mike Pagliarulo UER .05 .02
(Wrong birthdate)
☐ 263 Hipolito Pena .05 .02
☐ 264 Ken Phelps .05 .02
☐ 265 Willie Randolph .10 .05
☐ 266 Rick Rhoden .05 .02
☐ 267 Dave Righetti .05 .02
☐ 268 Rafael Santana .05 .02
☐ 269 Steve Shields .05 .02
☐ 270 Joel Skinner .05 .02
☐ 271 Don Slaught .05 .02
☐ 272 Claudell Washington .05 .02
☐ 273 Gary Ward .05 .02
☐ 274 Dave Winfield .20 .09
☐ 275 Luis Aquino .05 .02
☐ 276 Floyd Bannister .05 .02
☐ 277 George Brett .40 .18
☐ 278 Bill Buckner .10 .05
☐ 279 Nick Capra .05 .02
☐ 280 Jose DeJesus .05 .02
☐ 281 Steve Farr .05 .02
☐ 282 Jerry Don Gleaton .05 .02
☐ 283 Mark Gubicza .05 .02
☐ 284 Tom Gordon UER .20 .09
(16.2 innings in '88, should be 15.2)
☐ 285 Bo Jackson .20 .09
☐ 286 Charlie Leibrandt .05 .02
☐ 287 Mike Macfarlane .05 .02
☐ 288 Jeff Montgomery .10 .05
☐ 289 Bill Pecota UER .05 .02
(Photo actually Brad Wellman)
☐ 290 Jamie Quirk .05 .02
☐ 291 Bret Saberhagen .10 .05
☐ 292 Kevin Seitzer .05 .02
☐ 293 Kurt Stillwell .05 .02
☐ 294 Pat Tabler .05 .02
☐ 295 Danny Tartabull .05 .02
☐ 296 Gary Thurman .05 .02
☐ 297 Frank White .10 .05
☐ 298 Willie Wilson .05 .02
☐ 299 Roberto Alomar .30 .14
☐ 300 Sandy Alomar Jr. UER .50 .23
(Wrong birthdate, says 6/16/66, should say 6/18/66)
☐ 301 Chris Brown .05 .02
☐ 302 Mike Brumley UER .05 .02
(133 hits in '88, should be 134)
☐ 303 Mark Davis .05 .02
☐ 304 Mark Grant .05 .02
☐ 305 Tony Gwynn .50 .23
☐ 306 Greg W. Harris .05 .02
☐ 307 Andy Hawkins .05 .02
☐ 308 Jimmy Jones .05 .02
☐ 309 John Kruk .10 .05
☐ 310 Dave Leiper .05 .02
☐ 311 Carmelo Martinez .05 .02
☐ 312 Lance McCullers .05 .02
☐ 313 Keith Moreland .05 .02
☐ 314 Dennis Rasmussen .05 .02
☐ 315 Randy Ready UER .05 .02
(1214 games in '88, should be 114)
☐ 316 Benito Santiago .05 .02
☐ 317 Eric Show .05 .02
☐ 318 Todd Simmons .05 .02
☐ 319 Garry Templeton .05 .02
☐ 320 Dickie Thon .05 .02
☐ 321 Ed Whitson .05 .02
☐ 322 Marvell Wynne .05 .02
☐ 323 Mike Aldrete .05 .02
☐ 324 Brett Butler .10 .05
☐ 325 Will Clark UER .20 .09
(Three consecutive 100 RBI seasons)
☐ 326 Kelly Downs UER .05 .02
('88 stats missing)
☐ 327 Dave Dravecky .10 .05
☐ 328 Scott Garrelts .05 .02
☐ 329 Atlee Hammaker .05 .02
☐ 330 Charlie Hayes .20 .09
☐ 331 Mike Krukow .05 .02
☐ 332 Craig Lefferts .05 .02
☐ 333 Candy Maldonado .05 .02
☐ 334 Kirt Manwaring UER .05 .02
(Bats Rights)
☐ 335 Bob Melvin .05 .02
☐ 336 Kevin Mitchell .10 .05
☐ 337 Donell Nixon .05 .02
☐ 338 Tony Perezchica .05 .02
☐ 339 Joe Price .05 .02
☐ 340 Rick Reuschel .05 .02
☐ 341 Earnest Riles .05 .02
☐ 342 Don Robinson .05 .02
☐ 343 Chris Speier .05 .02
☐ 344 Robby Thompson UER .05 .02
(West Plam Beach)
☐ 345 Jose Uribe .05 .02
☐ 346 Matt Williams .25 .11
☐ 347 Trevor Wilson .05 .02
☐ 348 Juan Agosto .05 .02
☐ 349 Larry Andersen .05 .02
☐ 350A Alan Ashby ERR 2.00 .90
(Throws Rig)
☐ 350B Alan Ashby COR .05 .02
☐ 351 Kevin Bass .05 .02
☐ 352 Buddy Bell .10 .05
☐ 353 Craig Biggio .50 .23
☐ 354 Danny Darwin .05 .02
☐ 355 Glenn Davis .05 .02
☐ 356 Jim Deshaies .05 .02
☐ 357 Bill Doran .05 .02
☐ 358 John Fishel .05 .02
☐ 359 Billy Hatcher .05 .02
☐ 360 Bob Knepper .05 .02
☐ 361 Louie Meadows UER .05 .02
(Bio says 10 EBH's and 6 SB's in '88, should be 3 and 4)
☐ 362 Dave Meads .05 .02
☐ 363 Jim Pankovits .05 .02
☐ 364 Terry Puhl .05 .02
☐ 365 Rafael Ramirez .05 .02
☐ 366 Craig Reynolds .05 .02
☐ 367 Mike Scott .05 .02
(Card number listed as 368 on Astros CL)
☐ 368 Nolan Ryan .75 .35
(Card number listed as 367 on Astros CL)
☐ 369 Dave Smith .05 .02
☐ 370 Gerald Young .05 .02
☐ 371 Hubie Brooks .05 .02
☐ 372 Tim Burke .05 .02
☐ 373 John Dopson .05 .02
☐ 374 Mike R. Fitzgerald .05 .02
☐ 375 Tom Foley .05 .02
☐ 376 Andres Galarraga UER .20 .09
(Home: Caracus)
☐ 377 Neal Heaton .05 .02
☐ 378 Joe Hesketh .05 .02
☐ 379 Brian Holman .05 .02
☐ 380 Rex Hudler .05 .02
☐ 381 Randy Johnson UER 1.00 .45
(Innings for '85 and '86 shown as 27 and 120, should be 27.1 and 119.2)
☐ 382 Wallace Johnson .05 .02
☐ 383 Tracy Jones .05 .02
☐ 384 Dave Martinez .05 .02
☐ 385 Dennis Martinez .10 .05
☐ 386 Andy McGaffigan .05 .02
☐ 387 Otis Nixon .10 .05
☐ 388 Johnny Paredes .05 .02
☐ 389 Jeff Parrett .05 .02
☐ 390 Pascual Perez .05 .02
☐ 391 Tim Raines .20 .09
☐ 392 Luis Rivera .05 .02
☐ 393 Nelson Santovenia .05 .02
☐ 394 Bryn Smith .05 .02
☐ 395 Tim Wallach .05 .02
☐ 396 Andy Allanson UER .05 .02
(1214 hits in '88, should be 114)
☐ 397 Rod Allen .05 .02
☐ 398 Scott Bailes .05 .02
☐ 399 Tom Candiotti .05 .02
☐ 400 Joe Carter .20 .09
☐ 401 Carmen Castillo UER .05 .02
(After All-Star Break batting 2.50)
☐ 402 Dave Clark UER .05 .02
(Card front shows position as Rookie; after All-Star Break batting 3.14)
☐ 403 John Farrell UER .05 .02
(Typo in runs allowed in '88)
☐ 404 Julio Franco .10 .05
☐ 405 Don Gordon .05 .02
☐ 406 Mel Hall .05 .02
☐ 407 Brad Havens .05 .02
☐ 408 Brook Jacoby .05 .02
☐ 409 Doug Jones .05 .02
☐ 410 Jeff Kaiser .05 .02
☐ 411 Luis Medina .05 .02
☐ 412 Cory Snyder .05 .02
☐ 413 Greg Swindell .05 .02
☐ 414 Ron Tingley UER .05 .02
(Hit HR in first ML at-bat, should be first AL at-bat)
☐ 415 Willie Upshaw .05 .02
☐ 416 Ron Washington .05 .02
☐ 417 Rich Yett .05 .02
☐ 418 Damon Berryhill .05 .02
☐ 419 Mike Bielecki .05 .02
☐ 420 Doug Dascenzo .05 .02
☐ 421 Jody Davis UER .05 .02
(Braves stats for '88 missing)
☐ 422 Andre Dawson .20 .09
☐ 423 Frank DiPino .05 .02
☐ 424 Shawon Dunston .05 .02
☐ 425 Rich Gossage .05 .02
☐ 426 Mark Grace UER .20 .09
(Minor League stats for '88 missing)
☐ 427 Mike Harkey .05 .02
☐ 428 Darrin Jackson .05 .02
☐ 429 Les Lancaster .05 .02
☐ 430 Vance Law .05 .02
☐ 431 Greg Maddux .75 .35
☐ 432 Jamie Moyer .05 .02
☐ 433 Al Nipper .05 .02
☐ 434 Rafael Palmeiro UER .20 .09
(170 hits in '88, should be 178)
☐ 435 Pat Perry .05 .02
☐ 436 Jeff Pico .05 .02
☐ 437 Ryne Sandberg .25 .11
☐ 438 Calvin Schiraldi .05 .02
☐ 439 Rick Sutcliffe .05 .02
☐ 440A Manny Trillo ERR 2.00 .90
(Throws Rig)
☐ 440B Manny Trillo COR .05 .02
☐ 441 Gary Varsho UER .05 .02
(Wrong birthdate; .303 should be .302; 11/28 should be 9/19)
☐ 442 Mitch Webster .05 .02
☐ 443 Luis Alicea .05 .02
☐ 444 Tom Brunansky .05 .02
☐ 445 Vince Coleman UER .05 .02
(Third straight with 83, should be fourth straight with 81)
☐ 446 John Costello UER .05 .02
(Home California, should be New York)
☐ 447 Danny Cox .05 .02
☐ 448 Ken Dayley .05 .02
☐ 449 Jose DeLeon .05 .02
☐ 450 Curt Ford .05 .02
☐ 451 Pedro Guerrero .10 .05
☐ 452 Bob Horner .05 .02
☐ 453 Tim Jones .05 .02
☐ 454 Steve Lake .05 .02
☐ 455 Joe Magrane UER .05 .02
(Des Moines, IO)
☐ 456 Greg Mathews .05 .02
☐ 457 Willie McGee .05 .02

☐ 458 Larry McWilliams	.05	.02
☐ 459 Jose Oquendo	.05	.02
☐ 460 Tony Pena	.05	.02
☐ 461 Terry Pendleton	.10	.05
☐ 462 Steve Peters UER (Lives in Harrah, not Harah)	.05	.02
☐ 463 Ozzie Smith	.25	.11
☐ 464 Scott Terry	.05	.02
☐ 465 Denny Walling	.05	.02
☐ 466 Todd Worrell	.05	.02
☐ 467 Tony Armas UER (Before All-Star Break batting 2.39)	.05	.02
☐ 468 Dante Bichette	.40	.18
☐ 469 Bob Boone	.10	.05
☐ 470 Terry Clark	.05	.02
☐ 471 Stew Cliburn	.05	.02
☐ 472 Mike Cook UER (TM near Angels logo missing from front)	.05	.02
☐ 473 Sherman Corbett	.05	.02
☐ 474 Chili Davis	.10	.05
☐ 475 Brian Downing	.05	.02
☐ 476 Jim Eppard	.05	.02
☐ 477 Chuck Finley	.10	.05
☐ 478 Willie Fraser	.05	.02
☐ 479 Bryan Harvey UER (ML record shows 0-0, should be 7-5)	.10	.05
☐ 480 Jack Howell	.05	.02
☐ 481 Wally Joyner UER (Yorba Linda, GA)	.10	.05
☐ 482 Jack Lazorko	.05	.02
☐ 483 Kirk McCaskill	.05	.02
☐ 484 Mark McLemore	.05	.02
☐ 485 Greg Minton	.05	.02
☐ 486 Dan Petry	.05	.02
☐ 487 Johnny Ray	.05	.02
☐ 488 Dick Schofield	.05	.02
☐ 489 Devon White	.05	.02
☐ 490 Mike Witt	.05	.02
☐ 491 Harold Baines	.10	.05
☐ 492 Daryl Boston	.05	.02
☐ 493 Ivan Calderon UER ('80 stats shifted)	.05	.02
☐ 494 Mike Diaz	.05	.02
☐ 495 Carlton Fisk	.20	.09
☐ 496 Dave Gallagher	.05	.02
☐ 497 Ozzie Guillen	.05	.02
☐ 498 Shawn Hillegas	.05	.02
☐ 499 Lance Johnson	.10	.05
☐ 500 Barry Jones	.05	.02
☐ 501 Bill Long	.05	.02
☐ 502 Steve Lyons	.05	.02
☐ 503 Fred Manrique	.05	.02
☐ 504 Jack McDowell	.10	.05
☐ 505 Donn Pall	.05	.02
☐ 506 Kelly Paris	.05	.02
☐ 507 Dan Pasqua	.05	.02
☐ 508 Ken Patterson	.05	.02
☐ 509 Melido Perez	.05	.02
☐ 510 Jerry Reuss	.05	.02
☐ 511 Mark Salas	.05	.02
☐ 512 Bobby Thigpen UER ('86 ERA 4.69, should be 4.68)	.05	.02
☐ 513 Mike Woodard	.05	.02
☐ 514 Bob Brower	.05	.02
☐ 515 Steve Buechele	.05	.02
☐ 516 Jose Cecena	.05	.02
☐ 517 Cecil Espy	.05	.02
☐ 518 Scott Fletcher	.05	.02
☐ 519 Cecilio Guante ('87 Yankee stats are off-centered)	.05	.02
☐ 520 Jose Guzman	.05	.02
☐ 521 Ray Hayward	.05	.02
☐ 522 Charlie Hough	.10	.05
☐ 523 Pete Incaviglia	.10	.05
☐ 524 Mike Jeffcoat	.05	.02
☐ 525 Paul Kilgus	.05	.02
☐ 526 Chad Kreuter	.05	.02
☐ 527 Jeff Kunkel	.05	.02
☐ 528 Oddibe McDowell	.05	.02
☐ 529 Pete O'Brien	.05	.02
☐ 530 Geno Petralli	.05	.02
☐ 531 Jeff Russell	.05	.02
☐ 532 Ruben Sierra	.05	.02
☐ 533 Mike Stanley	.05	.02
☐ 534A Ed VandeBerg ERR (Throws Lef)	2.00	.90
☐ 534B Ed VandeBerg COR	.05	.02
☐ 535 Curtis Wilkerson ERR (Pitcher headings at bottom)	.05	.02
☐ 536 Mitch Williams	.05	.02
☐ 537 Bobby Witt UER ('85 ERA .643, should be 6.43)	.05	.02
☐ 538 Steve Balboni	.05	.02
☐ 539 Scott Bankhead	.05	.02
☐ 540 Scott Bradley	.05	.02
☐ 541 Mickey Brantley	.05	.02
☐ 542 Jay Buhner	.25	.11
☐ 543 Mike Campbell	.05	.02
☐ 544 Darnell Coles	.05	.02
☐ 545 Henry Cotto	.05	.02
☐ 546 Alvin Davis	.05	.02
☐ 547 Mario Diaz	.05	.02
☐ 548 Ken Griffey Jr.	6.00	2.70
☐ 549 Erik Hanson	.10	.05
☐ 550 Mike Jackson UER (Lifetime ERA 3.345, should be 3.45)	.05	.02
☐ 551 Mark Langston	.05	.02
☐ 552 Edgar Martinez	.20	.09
☐ 553 Bill McGuire	.05	.02
☐ 554 Mike Moore	.05	.02
☐ 555 Jim Presley	.05	.02
☐ 556 Rey Quinones	.05	.02
☐ 557 Jerry Reed	.05	.02
☐ 558 Harold Reynolds	.05	.02
☐ 559 Mike Schooler	.05	.02
☐ 560 Bill Swift	.05	.02
☐ 561 Dave Valle	.05	.02
☐ 562 Steve Bedrosian	.05	.02
☐ 563 Phil Bradley	.05	.02
☐ 564 Don Carman	.05	.02
☐ 565 Bob Dernier	.05	.02
☐ 566 Marvin Freeman	.05	.02
☐ 567 Todd Frohwirth	.05	.02
☐ 568 Greg Gross	.05	.02
☐ 569 Kevin Gross	.05	.02
☐ 570 Greg A. Harris	.05	.02
☐ 571 Von Hayes	.05	.02
☐ 572 Chris James	.05	.02
☐ 573 Steve Jeltz	.05	.02
☐ 574 Ron Jones UER (Led IL in '88 with 85, should be 75)	.05	.02
☐ 575 Ricky Jordan	.10	.05
☐ 576 Mike Maddux	.05	.02
☐ 577 David Palmer	.05	.02
☐ 578 Lance Parrish	.05	.02
☐ 579 Shane Rawley	.05	.02
☐ 580 Bruce Ruffin	.05	.02
☐ 581 Juan Samuel	.05	.02
☐ 582 Mike Schmidt	.25	.11
☐ 583 Kent Tekulve	.05	.02
☐ 584 Milt Thompson UER (19 hits in '88, should be 109)	.05	.02
☐ 585 Jose Alvarez	.05	.02
☐ 586 Paul Assenmacher	.05	.02
☐ 587 Bruce Benedict	.05	.02
☐ 588 Jeff Blauser	.10	.05
☐ 589 Terry Blocker	.05	.02
☐ 590 Ron Gant	.10	.05
☐ 591 Tom Glavine	.25	.11
☐ 592 Tommy Gregg	.05	.02
☐ 593 Albert Hall	.05	.02
☐ 594 Dion James	.05	.02
☐ 595 Rick Mahler	.05	.02
☐ 596 Dale Murphy	.20	.09
☐ 597 Gerald Perry	.05	.02
☐ 598 Charlie Puleo	.05	.02
☐ 599 Ted Simmons	.10	.05
☐ 600 Pete Smith	.05	.02
☐ 601 Zane Smith	.05	.02
☐ 602 John Smoltz	.50	.23
☐ 603 Bruce Sutter	.05	.02
☐ 604 Andres Thomas	.05	.02
☐ 605 Ozzie Virgil	.05	.02
☐ 606 Brady Anderson	.50	.23
☐ 607 Jeff Ballard	.05	.02
☐ 608 Jose Bautista	.05	.02
☐ 609 Ken Gerhart	.05	.02
☐ 610 Terry Kennedy	.05	.02
☐ 611 Eddie Murray	.20	.09
☐ 612 Carl Nichols UER (Before All-Star Break batting 1.88)	.05	.02
☐ 613 Tom Niedenfuer	.05	.02
☐ 614 Joe Orsulak	.05	.02
☐ 615 Oswald Peraza UER (Shown as Oswaldo)	.05	.02
☐ 616A Bill Ripken ERR (Rick Face written on knob of bat)	5.00	2.20
☐ 616B Bill Ripken (Bat knob whited out)	30.00	13.50
☐ 616C Bill Ripken (Words on bat knob scribbled out)	5.00	2.20
☐ 616D Bill Ripken DP (Black box covering bat knob)	.10	.05
☐ 617 Cal Ripken	.75	.35
☐ 618 Dave Schmidt	.05	.02
☐ 619 Rick Schu	.05	.02
☐ 620 Larry Sheets	.05	.02
☐ 621 Doug Sisk	.05	.02
☐ 622 Pete Stanicek	.05	.02
☐ 623 Mickey Tettleton	.10	.05
☐ 624 Jay Tibbs	.05	.02
☐ 625 Jim Traber	.05	.02
☐ 626 Mark Williamson	.05	.02
☐ 627 Craig Worthington	.05	.02
☐ 628 Speed/Power Jose Canseco	.20	.09
☐ 629 Pitcher Perfect Tom Browning	.05	.02
☐ 630 Like Father/Like Sons Roberto Alomar Sandy Alomar Jr. (Names on card listed in wrong order) UER	.25	.11
☐ 631 NL All Stars UER Will Clark Rafael Palmeiro (Gallaraga, sic; Clark 3 consecutive 100 RBI seasons; third with 102 RBI's)	.20	.09
☐ 632 Homeruns - Coast to Coast UER Darryl Strawberry Will Clark (Homeruns should be two words)	.10	.05
☐ 633 Hot Corners - Hot Hitters UER Wade Boggs Carney Lansford (Boggs hit .366 in '86, should be '88)	.10	.05
☐ 634 Triple A's Jose Canseco Terry Steinbach Mark McGwire	.10	.05
☐ 635 Dual Heat Mark Davis Dwight Gooden	.10	.05
☐ 636 NL Pitching Power UER Danny Jackson David Cone (Hersheiser, sic)	.10	.05
☐ 637 Cannon Arms UER Chris Sabo Bobby Bonilla (Bobby Bonds, sic)	.10	.05
☐ 638 Double Trouble UER Andres Galarraga (Misspelled Gallaraga on card back) Gerald Perry	.10	.05
☐ 639 Power Center Kirby Puckett Eric Davis	.20	.09
☐ 640 Steve Wilson and Cameron Drew	.05	.02
☐ 641 Kevin Brown and Kevin Reimer	.20	.09
☐ 642 Brad Pounders and Jerald Clark	.05	.02
☐ 643 Mike Capel and Drew Hall	.05	.02
☐ 644 Joe Girardi and Rolando Roomes	.20	.09
☐ 645 Lenny Harris and Marty Brown	.10	.05
☐ 646 Luis DeLosSantos and Jim Campbell	.05	.02
☐ 647 Randy Kramer and Miguel Garcia	.05	.02
☐ 648 Torey Lovullo and Robert Palacios	.05	.02
☐ 649 Jim Corsi and Bob Milacki	.05	.02
☐ 650 Grady Hall and Mike Rochford	.05	.02
☐ 651 Terry Taylor and Vance Lovelace	.05	.02
☐ 652 Ken Hill and Dennis Cook	.40	.18
☐ 653 Scott Service and Shane Turner	.05	.02
☐ 654 CL: Oakland/Mets Dodgers/Red Sox (10 Hendersor; 68 Jess Orosco)	.05	.02

	MINT	NRMT
☐ 655A CL: Twins/Tigers ERR Reds/Brewers (179 Boslo and Twins/Tigers positions listed)	.05	.02
☐ 655B CL: Twins/Tigers COR Reds/Brewers (179 Boslo but Twins/Tigers positions not listed)	.05	.02
☐ 656 CL: Pirates/Blue Jays Yankees/Royals (225 Jess Barfield)	.05	.02
☐ 657 CL: Padres/Giants Astros/Expos (367/368 wrong)	.05	.02
☐ 658 CL: Indians/Cubs Cardinals/Angels (449 Deleon)	.05	.02
☐ 659 CL: White Sox/Rangers Mariners/Phillies	.05	.02
☐ 660 CL: Braves/Orioles Specials/Checklists (632 hyphenated differently and 650 Hali; 595 Rich Mahler; 619 Rich Schu)	.05	.02

1989 Fleer Glossy

This 660 card set turned out to be the final parallel glossy issue for Fleer. These cards are identical to the regular Fleer cards except for the glossy sheen on the front. As many dealers did not order this product, this set is considerably scarcer than the regular 1989 Fleer set. Unlike the previous two seasons, the update set was not issued in Glossy form.

	MINT	NRMT
COMPLETE FACT.SET (672)	90.00	40.00
COMMON CARD (1-660)	.10	.05
COMMON WORLD SER. (WS1-WS12)	.10	.05
*STARS: 6X BASIC CARDS		
*ROOKIES: 6X BASIC CARDS		

1989 Fleer All-Stars

This twelve-card standard-size subset was randomly inserted in Fleer wax and cello packs. The players selected are the 1989 Fleer Major League All-Star team. One player has been selected for each position along with a DH and three pitchers. The cards feature a distinctive green background on the card fronts. The set is sequenced in alphabetical order.

	MINT	NRMT
COMPLETE SET (12)	5.00	2.20
COMMON CARD (1-12)	.25	.11
☐ 1 Bobby Bonilla	.35	.16
☐ 2 Jose Canseco	1.00	.45
☐ 3 Will Clark	1.25	.55
☐ 4 Dennis Eckersley	.50	.23
☐ 5 Julio Franco	.35	.16
☐ 6 Mike Greenwell	.25	.11
☐ 7 Orel Hershiser	.40	.18
☐ 8 Paul Molitor	1.25	.55
☐ 9 Mike Scioscia	.25	.11
☐ 10 Darryl Strawberry	.35	.16
☐ 11 Alan Trammell	.40	.18
☐ 12 Frank Viola	.25	.11

1989 Fleer For The Record

This six-card standard-size insert set was distributed one per rack pack. The set is subtitled "For The Record" and commemorates record-breaking events for those players from the previous season. The card backs are printed in red, black, and gray on white card stock. The set is sequenced in alphabetical order.

	MINT	NRMT
COMPLETE SET (6)	8.00	3.60
COMMON CARD (1-6)	.30	.14
SEMISTARS	.60	.25
UNLISTED STARS	.75	.35
☐ 1 Wade Boggs	.75	.35
☐ 2 Roger Clemens	2.50	1.10
☐ 3 Andres Galarraga	1.00	.45
☐ 4 Kirk Gibson	.30	.14
☐ 5 Greg Maddux	5.00	2.20
☐ 6 Don Mattingly UER (Won batting title '83, should say '84)	2.00	.90

1989 Fleer Wax Box Cards

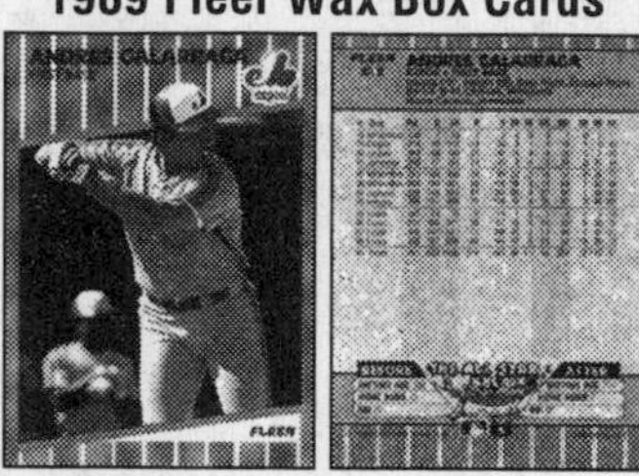

The cards in this 28-card set measure the standard 2 1/2" by 3 1/2". Cards have essentially the same design as the 1989 Fleer regular issue set. The cards were printed on the bottoms of the regular issue wax pack boxes. These 28 cards (C1 to C28) are considered a separate set in their own right and are not typically included in a complete set of the regular issue 1989 Fleer cards. The value of the panel uncut is slightly greater, perhaps by 25 percent greater, than the value of the individual cards cut up carefully. The wax box cards are further distinguished by the gray card stock used.

	MINT	NRMT
COMPLETE SET (28)	10.00	4.50
COMMON CARD (C1-C28)	.25	.11
☐ C1 Mets Logo	.25	.11
☐ C2 Wade Boggs	1.00	.45
☐ C3 George Brett	2.00	.90
☐ C4 Jose Canseco UER ('88 strikeouts 121 and career strikeouts 49, should be 128 and 491)	1.00	.45
☐ C5 A's Logo	.25	.11
☐ C6 Will Clark	1.00	.45
☐ C7 David Cone	.40	.18
☐ C8 Andres Galarraga UER (Career average .289 should be .269)	.75	.35
☐ C9 Dodgers Logo	.25	.11
☐ C10 Kirk Gibson	.40	.18
☐ C11 Mike Greenwell	.25	.11
☐ C12 Tony Gwynn	2.50	1.10
☐ C13 Tigers Logo	.25	.11
☐ C14 Orel Hershiser	.40	.18
☐ C15 Danny Jackson	.25	.11
☐ C16 Wally Joyner	.40	.18
☐ C17 Red Sox Logo	.25	.11
☐ C18 Yankees Logo	.25	.11
☐ C19 Fred McGriff UER (Career BA of .289 should be .269)	1.00	.45
☐ C20 Kirby Puckett	2.50	1.10
☐ C21 Chris Sabo	.25	.11
☐ C22 Kevin Seitzer	.25	.11
☐ C23 Pirates Logo	.25	.11
☐ C24 Astros Logo	.25	.11
☐ C25 Darryl Strawberry	.40	.18
☐ C26 Alan Trammell	.60	.25
☐ C27 Andy Van Slyke	.40	.18
☐ C28 Frank Viola	.25	.11

1989 Fleer World Series

This 12-card standard-size set features highlights of the previous year's World Series between the Dodgers and the Athletics. The sets were packaged as a complete set insert with the collated sets (of the 1989 Fleer regular issue) which were sold by Fleer directly to hobby card dealers; they were not available in the general retail candy store outlets.

	MINT	NRMT
COMPLETE SET (12)	2.00	.90
COMMON CARD (1-12)	.10	.05
☐ 1 Mickey Hatcher	.10	.05
☐ 2 Tim Belcher	.10	.05
☐ 3 Jose Canseco	.50	.23
☐ 4 Mike Scioscia	.10	.05
☐ 5 Kirk Gibson	.50	.23
☐ 6 Orel Hershiser	.25	.11
☐ 7 Mike Marshall	.10	.05
☐ 8 Mark McGwire	1.00	.45
☐ 9 Steve Sax UER actually 42 steals in '88	.10	.05
☐ 10 Walt Weiss	.10	.05
☐ 11 Orel Hershiser	.25	.11
☐ 12 Dodger Blue World Champs	.10	.05

1989 Fleer Update

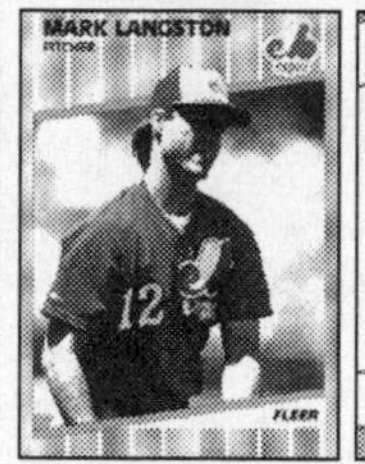

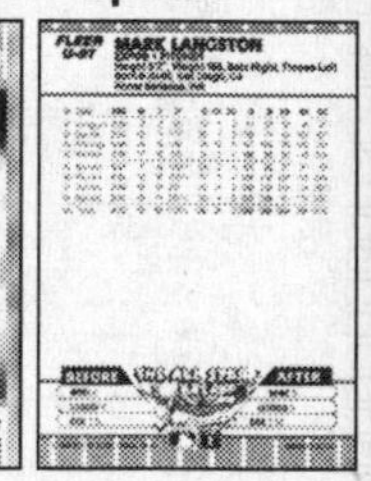

The 1989 Fleer Update set contains 132 standard-size cards. The cards were distributed exclusively in factory set form in grey and white, cellophane wrapped boxes through hobby dealers. The cards are identical in design to regular issue 1989 Fleer cards except for the U-prefixed numbering on back. The set numbering is in team order with players within teams ordered alphabetically. The set includes special cards for Nolan Ryan's 5,000th strikeout and Mike Schmidt's retirement. Rookie Cards include Kevin Appier, Joey (Albert) Belle, Deion Sanders, Greg Vaughn, Robin Ventura and Todd Zeile.

	MINT	NRMT
COMP.FACT.SET (132)	5.00	2.20
COMMON CARD (1-132)	.05	.02
☐ 1 Phil Bradley	.05	.02
☐ 2 Mike Devereaux	.05	.02
☐ 3 Steve Finley	.25	.11
☐ 4 Kevin Hickey	.05	.02
☐ 5 Brian Holton	.05	.02
☐ 6 Bob Milacki	.05	.02
☐ 7 Randy Milligan	.05	.02
☐ 8 John Dopson	.05	.02
☐ 9 Nick Esasky	.05	.02
☐ 10 Rob Murphy	.05	.02
☐ 11 Jim Abbott	.20	.09
☐ 12 Bert Blyleven	.10	.05
☐ 13 Jeff Manto	.05	.02
☐ 14 Bob McClure	.05	.02
☐ 15 Lance Parrish	.05	.02
☐ 16 Lee Stevens	.20	.09
☐ 17 Claudell Washington	.05	.02
☐ 18 Mark Davis	.05	.02
☐ 19 Eric King	.05	.02
☐ 20 Ron Kittle	.05	.02
☐ 21 Matt Merullo	.05	.02
☐ 22 Steve Rosenberg	.05	.02

Card	MINT	NRMT
☐ 23 Robin Ventura	.40	.18
☐ 24 Keith Atherton	.05	.02
☐ 25 Joey Belle	2.00	.90
☐ 26 Jerry Browne	.05	.02
☐ 27 Felix Fermin	.05	.02
☐ 28 Brad Komminsk	.05	.02
☐ 29 Pete O'Brien	.05	.02
☐ 30 Mike Brumley	.05	.02
☐ 31 Tracy Jones	.05	.02
☐ 32 Mike Schwabe	.05	.02
☐ 33 Gary Ward	.05	.02
☐ 34 Frank Williams	.05	.02
☐ 35 Kevin Appier	.25	.11
☐ 36 Bob Boone	.10	.05
☐ 37 Luis DeLosSantos	.05	.02
☐ 38 Jim Eisenreich	.20	.09
☐ 39 Jaime Navarro	.10	.05
☐ 40 Bill Spiers	.05	.02
☐ 41 Greg Vaughn	.50	.23
☐ 42 Randy Veres	.05	.02
☐ 43 Wally Backman	.05	.02
☐ 44 Shane Rawley	.05	.02
☐ 45 Steve Balboni	.05	.02
☐ 46 Jesse Barfield	.05	.02
☐ 47 Alvaro Espinoza	.05	.02
☐ 48 Bob Geren	.05	.02
☐ 49 Mel Hall	.05	.02
☐ 50 Andy Hawkins	.05	.02
☐ 51 Hensley Meulens	.05	.02
☐ 52 Steve Sax	.05	.02
☐ 53 Deion Sanders	.75	.35
☐ 54 Rickey Henderson	.20	.09
☐ 55 Mike Moore	.05	.02
☐ 56 Tony Phillips	.05	.02
☐ 57 Greg Briley	.05	.02
☐ 58 Gene Harris	.05	.02
☐ 59 Randy Johnson	1.00	.45
☐ 60 Jeffrey Leonard	.05	.02
☐ 61 Dennis Powell	.05	.02
☐ 62 Omar Vizquel	.40	.18
☐ 63 Kevin Brown	.20	.09
☐ 64 Julio Franco	.10	.05
☐ 65 Jamie Moyer	.05	.02
☐ 66 Rafael Palmeiro	.20	.09
☐ 67 Nolan Ryan	1.50	.70
☐ 68 Francisco Cabrera	.20	.09
☐ 69 Junior Felix	.05	.02
☐ 70 Al Leiter	.20	.09
☐ 71 Alex Sanchez	.05	.02
☐ 72 Geronimo Berroa	.20	.09
☐ 73 Derek Lilliquist	.05	.02
☐ 74 Lonnie Smith	.05	.02
☐ 75 Jeff Treadway	.05	.02
☐ 76 Paul Kilgus	.05	.02
☐ 77 Lloyd McClendon	.05	.02
☐ 78 Scott Sanderson	.05	.02
☐ 79 Dwight Smith	.10	.05
☐ 80 Jerome Walton	.20	.09
☐ 81 Mitch Williams	.05	.02
☐ 82 Steve Wilson	.05	.02
☐ 83 Todd Benzinger	.05	.02
☐ 84 Ken Griffey Sr.	.05	.02
☐ 85 Rick Mahler	.05	.02
☐ 86 Rolando Roomes	.05	.02
☐ 87 Scott Scudder	.05	.02
☐ 88 Jim Clancy	.05	.02
☐ 89 Rick Rhoden	.05	.02
☐ 90 Dan Schatzeder	.05	.02
☐ 91 Mike Morgan	.05	.02
☐ 92 Eddie Murray	.20	.09
☐ 93 Willie Randolph	.10	.05
☐ 94 Ray Searage	.05	.02
☐ 95 Mike Aldrete	.05	.02
☐ 96 Kevin Gross	.05	.02
☐ 97 Mark Langston	.05	.02
☐ 98 Spike Owen	.05	.02
☐ 99 Zane Smith	.05	.02
☐ 100 Don Aase	.05	.02
☐ 101 Barry Lyons	.05	.02
☐ 102 Juan Samuel	.05	.02
☐ 103 Wally Whitehurst	.05	.02
☐ 104 Dennis Cook	.05	.02
☐ 105 Len Dykstra	.10	.05
☐ 106 Charlie Hayes	.20	.09
☐ 107 Tommy Herr	.05	.02
☐ 108 Ken Howell	.05	.02
☐ 109 John Kruk	.10	.05
☐ 110 Roger McDowell	.05	.02
☐ 111 Terry Mulholland	.05	.02
☐ 112 Jeff Parrett	.05	.02
☐ 113 Neal Heaton	.05	.02
☐ 114 Jeff King	.10	.05
☐ 115 Randy Kramer	.05	.02
☐ 116 Bill Landrum	.05	.02
☐ 117 Cris Carpenter	.05	.02
☐ 118 Frank DiPino	.05	.02
☐ 119 Ken Hill	.20	.09
☐ 120 Dan Quisenberry	.05	.02
☐ 121 Milt Thompson	.05	.02
☐ 122 Todd Zeile	.20	.09
☐ 123 Jack Clark	.10	.05
☐ 124 Bruce Hurst	.05	.02
☐ 125 Mark Parent	.05	.02
☐ 126 Bip Roberts	.10	.05
☐ 127 Jeff Brantley UER (Photo actually Joe Kmak)	.10	.05
☐ 128 Terry Kennedy	.05	.02
☐ 129 Mike LaCoss	.05	.02
☐ 130 Greg Litton	.05	.02
☐ 131 Mike Schmidt	.50	.23
☐ 132 Checklist 1-132	.05	.02

1989 Fleer Baseball All-Stars

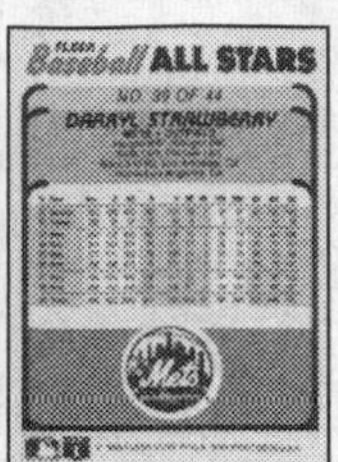

The 1989 Fleer Baseball All-Stars set contains 44 standard-size cards. The fronts are yellowish beige with salmon pinstripes; the vertically oriented backs are red, white and pink and feature career stats. The card numbering of this set is ordered alphabetically by player's name. The cards were distributed through Ben Franklin stores as a boxed set.

	MINT	NRMT
COMPLETE SET (44)	5.00	2.20
COMMON CARD (1-44)	.05	.02
☐ 1 Doyle Alexander	.05	.02
☐ 2 George Bell	.05	.02
☐ 3 Wade Boggs	.40	.18
☐ 4 Bobby Bonilla	.10	.05
☐ 5 Jose Canseco	.75	.35
☐ 6 Will Clark	.75	.35
☐ 7 Roger Clemens	1.00	.45
☐ 8 Vince Coleman	.05	.02
☐ 9 David Cone	.10	.05
☐ 10 Mark Davis	.05	.02
☐ 11 Andre Dawson	.30	.14
☐ 12 Dennis Eckersley	.20	.09
☐ 13 Andres Galarraga	.30	.14
☐ 14 Kirk Gibson	.10	.05
☐ 15 Dwight Gooden	.10	.05
☐ 16 Mike Greenwell	.05	.02
☐ 17 Mark Gubicza	.05	.02
☐ 18 Ozzie Guillen	.05	.02
☐ 19 Tony Gwynn	1.00	.45
☐ 20 Rickey Henderson	.50	.23
☐ 21 Orel Hershiser	.10	.05
☐ 22 Danny Jackson	.05	.02
☐ 23 Doug Jones	.05	.02
☐ 24 Ricky Jordan	.05	.02
☐ 25 Bob Knepper	.05	.02
☐ 26 Barry Larkin	.75	.35
☐ 27 Vance Law	.05	.02
☐ 28 Don Mattingly	1.00	.45
☐ 29 Mark McGwire	1.00	.45
☐ 30 Paul Molitor	.50	.23
☐ 31 Gerald Perry	.05	.02
☐ 32 Kirby Puckett	1.00	.45
☐ 33 Johnny Ray	.05	.02
☐ 34 Harold Reynolds	.10	.05
☐ 35 Cal Ripken	2.00	.90
☐ 36 Don Robinson	.05	.02
☐ 37 Ruben Sierra	.05	.02
☐ 38 Dave Smith	.05	.02
☐ 39 Darryl Strawberry	.10	.05
☐ 40 Dave Stieb	.05	.02
☐ 41 Alan Trammell	.20	.09
☐ 42 Andy Van Slyke	.10	.05
☐ 43 Frank Viola	.05	.02
☐ 44 Dave Winfield	.50	.23

1989 Fleer Baseball MVP's

The 1989 Fleer Baseball MVP's set contains 44 standard-size cards. The fronts and backs are green and yellow. The horizontally oriented backs feature career stats. The card numbering of this set is ordered alphabetically by player's

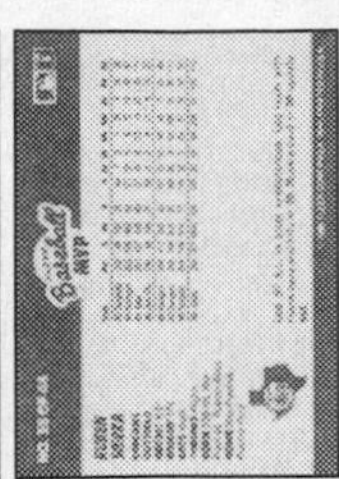

name. The cards were distributed through Toys 'R' Us stores as a boxed set.

	MINT	NRMT
COMPLETE SET (44)	6.00	2.70
COMMON CARD (1-44)	.05	.02
☐ 1 Steve Bedrosian	.05	.02
☐ 2 George Bell	.05	.02
☐ 3 Wade Boggs	.40	.18
☐ 4 George Brett	.75	.35
☐ 5 Hubie Brooks	.05	.02
☐ 6 Jose Canseco	.60	.25
☐ 7 Will Clark	.60	.25
☐ 8 Roger Clemens	.75	.35
☐ 9 Eric Davis	.10	.05
☐ 10 Glenn Davis	.05	.02
☐ 11 Andre Dawson	.30	.14
☐ 12 Andres Galarraga	.30	.14
☐ 13 Kirk Gibson	.10	.05
☐ 14 Dwight Gooden	.10	.05
☐ 15 Mark Grace	.75	.35
☐ 16 Mike Greenwell	.05	.02
☐ 17 Tony Gwynn	1.00	.45
☐ 18 Bryan Harvey	.05	.02
☐ 19 Orel Hershiser	.10	.05
☐ 20 Ted Higuera	.05	.02
☐ 21 Danny Jackson	.05	.02
☐ 22 Mike Jackson	.05	.02
☐ 23 Doug Jones	.05	.02
☐ 24 Greg Maddux	2.00	.90
☐ 25 Mike Marshall	.05	.02
☐ 26 Don Mattingly	1.00	.45
☐ 27 Fred McGriff	.60	.25
☐ 28 Mark McGwire	.75	.35
☐ 29 Kevin McReynolds	.05	.02
☐ 30 Jack Morris	.10	.05
☐ 31 Gerald Perry	.05	.02
☐ 32 Kirby Puckett	1.00	.45
☐ 33 Chris Sabo	.05	.02
☐ 34 Mike Scott	.05	.02
☐ 35 Ruben Sierra	.05	.02
☐ 36 Darryl Strawberry	.10	.05
☐ 37 Danny Tartabull	.05	.02
☐ 38 Bobby Thigpen	.05	.02
☐ 39 Alan Trammell	.20	.09
☐ 40 Andy Van Slyke	.10	.05
☐ 41 Frank Viola	.05	.02
☐ 42 Walt Weiss	.05	.02
☐ 43 Dave Winfield	.50	.23
☐ 44 Todd Worrell	.10	.05

1989 Fleer Exciting Stars

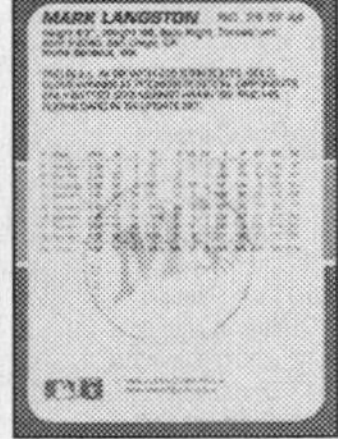

The 1989 Fleer Exciting Stars set contains 44 standard-size cards. The fronts have baby blue borders; the backs are pink and blue. The vertically oriented backs feature career stats. The card numbering of this set is ordered alphabetically by player's name. The cards were distributed as a boxed set.

	MINT	NRMT
COMPLETE SET (44)	5.00	2.20
COMMON CARD (1-44)	.05	.02
☐ 1 Harold Baines	.10	.05
☐ 2 Wade Boggs	.40	.18
☐ 3 Jose Canseco	.60	.25
☐ 4 Joe Carter	.30	.14
☐ 5 Will Clark	.60	.25

Card	MINT	NRMT
☐ 6 Roger Clemens	.75	.35
☐ 7 Vince Coleman	.05	.02
☐ 8 David Cone	.10	.05
☐ 9 Eric Davis	.10	.05
☐ 10 Glenn Davis	.05	.02
☐ 11 Andre Dawson	.30	.14
☐ 12 Dwight Evans	.10	.05
☐ 13 Andres Galarraga	.30	.14
☐ 14 Kirk Gibson	.10	.05
☐ 15 Dwight Gooden	.10	.05
☐ 16 Jim Gott	.05	.02
☐ 17 Mark Grace	.75	.35
☐ 18 Mike Greenwell	.05	.02
☐ 19 Mark Gubicza	.05	.02
☐ 20 Tony Gwynn	1.00	.45
☐ 21 Rickey Henderson	.50	.23
☐ 22 Tom Henke	.05	.02
☐ 23 Mike Henneman	.05	.02
☐ 24 Orel Hershiser	.10	.05
☐ 25 Danny Jackson	.05	.02
☐ 26 Gregg Jefferies	.10	.05
☐ 27 Ricky Jordan	.05	.02
☐ 28 Wally Joyner	.10	.05
☐ 29 Mark Langston	.05	.02
☐ 30 Tim Leary	.05	.02
☐ 31 Don Mattingly	1.00	.45
☐ 32 Mark McGwire	.75	.35
☐ 33 Dale Murphy	.30	.14
☐ 34 Kirby Puckett	1.00	.45
☐ 35 Chris Sabo	.05	.02
☐ 36 Kevin Seitzer	.05	.02
☐ 37 Ruben Sierra	.05	.02
☐ 38 Ozzie Smith	1.00	.45
☐ 39 Dave Stewart	.10	.05
☐ 40 Darryl Strawberry	.10	.05
☐ 41 Alan Trammell	.20	.09
☐ 42 Frank Viola	.05	.02
☐ 43 Dave Winfield	.40	.18
☐ 44 Robin Yount	.30	.14

1989 Fleer Heroes of Baseball

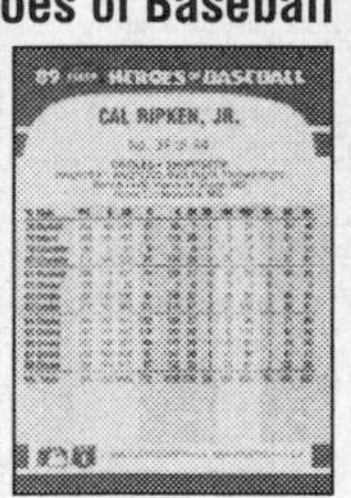

The 1989 Fleer Heroes of Baseball set contains 44 standard-size cards. The fronts and backs are red, white and blue. The vertically oriented backs feature career stats. The card numbering of this set is ordered alphabetically by player's name. The cards were distributed through Woolworth stores as a boxed set.

	MINT	NRMT
COMPLETE SET (44)	5.00	2.20
COMMON CARD (1-44)	.05	.02
☐ 1 George Bell	.05	.02
☐ 2 Wade Boggs	.40	.18
☐ 3 Barry Bonds	.75	.35
☐ 4 Tom Brunansky	.05	.02
☐ 5 Jose Canseco	.60	.25
☐ 6 Joe Carter	.30	.14
☐ 7 Will Clark	.60	.25
☐ 8 Roger Clemens	.75	.35
☐ 9 David Cone	.10	.05
☐ 10 Eric Davis	.10	.05
☐ 11 Glenn Davis	.05	.02
☐ 12 Andre Dawson	.30	.14
☐ 13 Dennis Eckersley	.20	.09
☐ 14 John Franco	.10	.05
☐ 15 Gary Gaetti	.10	.05
☐ 16 Andres Galarraga	.30	.14
☐ 17 Kirk Gibson	.10	.05
☐ 18 Dwight Gooden	.10	.05
☐ 19 Mike Greenwell	.05	.02
☐ 20 Tony Gwynn	1.00	.45
☐ 21 Bryan Harvey	.05	.02
☐ 22 Orel Hershiser	.10	.05
☐ 23 Ted Higuera	.05	.02
☐ 24 Danny Jackson	.05	.02
☐ 25 Ricky Jordan	.05	.02
☐ 26 Don Mattingly	1.00	.45
☐ 27 Fred McGriff	.60	.25
☐ 28 Mark McGwire	1.00	.45
☐ 29 Kevin McReynolds	.05	.02
☐ 30 Gerald Perry	.05	.02
☐ 31 Kirby Puckett	1.00	.45
☐ 32 Johnny Ray	.05	.02
☐ 33 Harold Reynolds	.10	.05
☐ 34 Cal Ripken	2.00	.90
☐ 35 Ryne Sandberg	.75	.35
☐ 36 Kevin Seitzer	.05	.02
☐ 37 Ruben Sierra	.05	.02
☐ 38 Darryl Strawberry	.10	.05
☐ 39 Bobby Thigpen	.05	.02
☐ 40 Alan Trammell	.20	.09
☐ 41 Andy Van Slyke	.10	.05
☐ 42 Frank Viola	.05	.02
☐ 43 Dave Winfield	.50	.23
☐ 44 Robin Yount	.30	.14

1989 Fleer League Leaders

The 1989 Fleer League Leaders set contains 44 standard-size cards. The fronts are red and yellow; the horizontally oriented backs are light blue and red, and feature career stats. The card numbering of this set is ordered alphabetically by player's name. The cards were distributed through Woolworth stores as a boxed set.

	MINT	NRMT
COMPLETE SET (44)	5.00	2.20
COMMON CARD (1-44)	.05	.02
☐ 1 Allan Anderson	.05	.02
☐ 2 Wade Boggs	.40	.18
☐ 3 Jose Canseco	.60	.25
☐ 4 Will Clark	.60	.25
☐ 5 Roger Clemens	.75	.35
☐ 6 Vince Coleman	.05	.02
☐ 7 David Cone	.10	.05
☐ 8 Kal Daniels	.05	.02
☐ 9 Chili Davis	.10	.05
☐ 10 Eric Davis	.10	.05
☐ 11 Glenn Davis	.05	.02
☐ 12 Andre Dawson	.30	.14
☐ 13 John Franco	.10	.05
☐ 14 Andres Galarraga	.30	.14
☐ 15 Kirk Gibson	.10	.05
☐ 16 Dwight Gooden	.10	.05
☐ 17 Mark Grace	.75	.35
☐ 18 Mike Greenwell	.05	.02
☐ 19 Tony Gwynn	1.00	.45
☐ 20 Orel Hershiser	.10	.05
☐ 21 Pete Incaviglia	.05	.02
☐ 22 Danny Jackson	.05	.02
☐ 23 Gregg Jefferies	.10	.05
☐ 24 Joe Magrane	.05	.02
☐ 25 Don Mattingly	1.00	.45
☐ 26 Fred McGriff	.60	.25
☐ 27 Mark McGwire	.75	.35
☐ 28 Dale Murphy	.30	.14
☐ 29 Dan Plesac	.05	.02
☐ 30 Kirby Puckett	1.00	.45
☐ 31 Harold Reynolds	.10	.05
☐ 32 Cal Ripken	2.00	.90
☐ 33 Jeff M. Robinson	.05	.02
☐ 34 Mike Scott	.05	.02
☐ 35 Ozzie Smith	1.00	.45
☐ 36 Dave Stewart	.10	.05
☐ 37 Darryl Strawberry	.10	.05
☐ 38 Greg Swindell	.05	.02
☐ 39 Bobby Thigpen	.05	.02
☐ 40 Alan Trammell	.20	.09
☐ 41 Andy Van Slyke	.10	.05
☐ 42 Frank Viola	.05	.02
☐ 43 Dave Winfield	.50	.23
☐ 44 Robin Yount	.30	.14

1989 Fleer Superstars

The 1989 Fleer Superstars set contains 44 standard-size cards. The fronts are red and beige; the horizontally oriented backs are yellow, and feature career stats. The card numbering of this set is ordered alphabetically by player's name. The cards were distributed as a boxed set. The back panel of the box contains the complete set checklist.

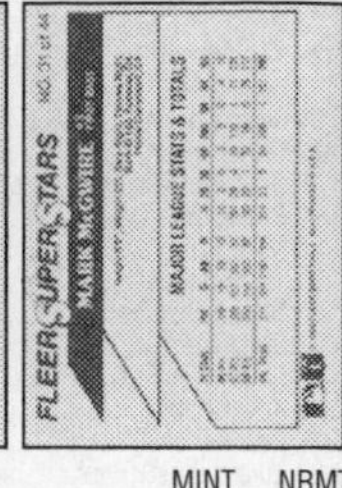

	MINT	NRMT
COMPLETE SET (44)	6.00	2.70
COMMON CARD (1-44)	.05	.02
☐ 1 Roberto Alomar	1.00	.45
☐ 2 Harold Baines	.10	.05
☐ 3 Tim Belcher	.05	.02
☐ 4 Wade Boggs	.40	.18
☐ 5 George Brett	.75	.35
☐ 6 Jose Canseco	.60	.25
☐ 7 Gary Carter	.20	.09
☐ 8 Will Clark	.60	.25
☐ 9 Roger Clemens	.75	.35
☐ 10 Kal Daniels UER (Reverse negative photo on front)	.05	.02
☐ 11 Eric Davis	.10	.05
☐ 12 Andre Dawson	.30	.14
☐ 13 Tony Fernandez	.05	.02
☐ 14 Scott Fletcher	.05	.02
☐ 15 Andres Galarraga	.30	.14
☐ 16 Kirk Gibson	.10	.05
☐ 17 Dwight Gooden	.10	.05
☐ 18 Jim Gott	.05	.02
☐ 19 Mark Grace	.75	.35
☐ 20 Mike Greenwell	.05	.02
☐ 21 Tony Gwynn	1.00	.45
☐ 22 Rickey Henderson	.50	.23
☐ 23 Orel Hershiser	.10	.05
☐ 24 Ted Higuera	.05	.02
☐ 25 Gregg Jefferies	.10	.05
☐ 26 Wally Joyner	.10	.05
☐ 27 Mark Langston	.05	.02
☐ 28 Greg Maddux	2.00	.90
☐ 29 Don Mattingly	1.00	.45
☐ 30 Fred McGriff	.60	.25
☐ 31 Mark McGwire	1.00	.45
☐ 32 Dan Plesac	.05	.02
☐ 33 Kirby Puckett	1.00	.45
☐ 34 Jeff Reardon	.05	.02
☐ 35 Chris Sabo	.05	.02
☐ 36 Mike Schmidt	.50	.23
☐ 37 Mike Scott	.05	.02
☐ 38 Cory Snyder	.05	.02
☐ 39 Darryl Strawberry	.10	.05
☐ 40 Alan Trammell	.20	.09
☐ 41 Frank Viola	.05	.02
☐ 42 Walt Weiss	.05	.02
☐ 43 Dave Winfield	.50	.23
☐ 44 Todd Worrell UER (Statistical headings on back for hitter)	.05	.02

1990 Fleer

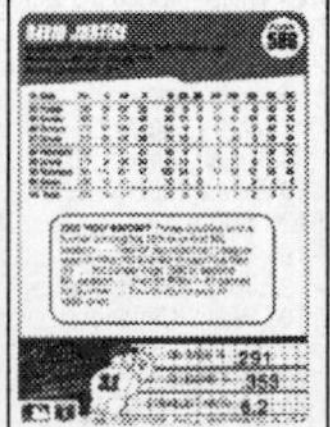

The 1990 Fleer set contains 660 standard-size cards. Cards were primarily issued in wax packs, rack packs and hobby and retail factory sets. Card fronts feature white outer borders with ribbon-like, colored inner borders. The set is again ordered numerically by teams based upon the previous season's record. Subsets include Decade Greats (621-630), Superstar Combinations (631-639), Rookie Prospects (640-653) and checklists (654-660). Rookie Cards of note include Moises Alou, Juan Gonzalez, Marquis Grissom, Dave Justice, Ben McDonald, Sammy Sosa, and Larry Walker.

	MINT	NRMT
OMPLETE SET (660)	8.00	3.60
OMP.RETAIL SET (660)	8.00	3.60
OMP.HOBBY SET (672)	10.00	4.50
OMMON CARD (1-660)	.05	.02
1 Lance Blankenship	.05	.02
2 Todd Burns	.05	.02
3 Jose Canseco	.20	.09
4 Jim Corsi	.05	.02
5 Storm Davis	.05	.02
6 Dennis Eckersley	.20	.09
7 Mike Gallego	.05	.02
8 Ron Hassey	.05	.02
9 Dave Henderson	.05	.02
10 Rickey Henderson	.20	.09
11 Rick Honeycutt	.05	.02
12 Stan Javier	.05	.02
13 Felix Jose	.05	.02
14 Carney Lansford	.10	.05
15 Mark McGwire UER (1989 runs listed as 4, should be 74)	.40	.18
16 Mike Moore	.05	.02
17 Gene Nelson	.05	.02
18 Dave Parker	.10	.05
19 Tony Phillips	.05	.02
20 Terry Steinbach	.10	.05
21 Dave Stewart	.10	.05
22 Walt Weiss	.05	.02
23 Bob Welch	.05	.02
24 Curt Young	.05	.02
25 Paul Assenmacher	.05	.02
26 Damon Berryhill	.05	.02
27 Mike Bielecki	.05	.02
28 Kevin Blankenship	.05	.02
29 Andre Dawson	.20	.09
30 Shawon Dunston	.05	.02
31 Joe Girardi	.10	.05
32 Mark Grace	.20	.09
33 Mike Harkey	.05	.02
34 Paul Kilgus	.05	.02
35 Les Lancaster	.05	.02
36 Vance Law	.05	.02
37 Greg Maddux	.60	.25
38 Lloyd McClendon	.05	.02
39 Jeff Pico	.05	.02
40 Ryne Sandberg	.25	.11
41 Scott Sanderson	.05	.02
42 Dwight Smith	.05	.02
43 Rick Sutcliffe	.05	.02
44 Jerome Walton	.05	.02
45 Mitch Webster	.05	.02
46 Curt Wilkerson	.05	.02
47 Dean Wilkins	.05	.02
48 Mitch Williams	.05	.02
49 Steve Wilson	.05	.02
50 Steve Bedrosian	.05	.02
51 Mike Benjamin	.05	.02
52 Jeff Brantley	.10	.05
53 Brett Butler	.05	.02
54 Will Clark UER (Did You Know says first in runs, should say tied for first)	.20	.09
55 Kelly Downs	.05	.02
56 Scott Garrelts	.05	.02
57 Atlee Hammaker	.05	.02
58 Terry Kennedy	.05	.02
59 Mike LaCoss	.05	.02
60 Craig Lefferts	.05	.02
61 Greg Litton	.05	.02
62 Candy Maldonado	.05	.02
63 Kirt Manwaring UER (No '88 Phoenix stats as noted in box)	.05	.02
64 Randy McCament	.05	.02
65 Kevin Mitchell	.10	.05
66 Donell Nixon	.05	.02
67 Ken Oberkfell	.05	.02
68 Rick Reuschel	.05	.02
69 Ernest Riles	.05	.02
70 Don Robinson	.05	.02
71 Pat Sheridan	.05	.02
72 Chris Speier	.05	.02
73 Robby Thompson	.05	.02
74 Jose Uribe	.05	.02
75 Matt Williams	.20	.09
76 George Bell	.05	.02
77 Pat Borders	.05	.02
78 John Cerutti	.05	.02
79 Junior Felix	.05	.02
80 Tony Fernandez	.05	.02
81 Mike Flanagan	.05	.02
82 Mauro Gozzo	.05	.02
83 Kelly Gruber	.05	.02
84 Tom Henke	.05	.02
85 Jimmy Key	.10	.05
86 Manny Lee	.05	.02
87 Nelson Liriano UER (Should say "led the IL" instead of "led the TL")	.05	.02
88 Lee Mazzilli	.05	.02
89 Fred McGriff	.20	.09
90 Lloyd Moseby	.05	.02
91 Rance Mulliniks	.05	.02
92 Alex Sanchez	.05	.02
93 Dave Stieb	.05	.02
94 Todd Stottlemyre	.10	.05
95 Duane Ward UER (Double line of '87 Syracuse stats)	.05	.02
96 David Wells	.05	.02
97 Ernie Whitt	.05	.02
98 Frank Wills	.05	.02
99 Mookie Wilson	.05	.02
100 Kevin Appier	.20	.09
101 Luis Aquino	.05	.02
102 Bob Boone	.10	.05
103 George Brett	.40	.18
104 Jose DeJesus	.05	.02
105 Luis De Los Santos	.05	.02
106 Jim Eisenreich	.10	.05
107 Steve Farr	.05	.02
108 Tom Gordon	.05	.02
109 Mark Gubicza	.05	.02
110 Bo Jackson	.20	.09
111 Terry Leach	.05	.02
112 Charlie Leibrandt	.05	.02
113 Rick Luecken	.05	.02
114 Mike Macfarlane	.05	.02
115 Jeff Montgomery	.10	.05
116 Bret Saberhagen	.10	.05
117 Kevin Seitzer	.05	.02
118 Kurt Stillwell	.05	.02
119 Pat Tabler	.05	.02
120 Danny Tartabull	.05	.02
121 Gary Thurman	.05	.02
122 Frank White	.10	.05
123 Willie Wilson	.05	.02
124 Matt Winters	.05	.02
125 Jim Abbott	.20	.09
126 Tony Armas	.05	.02
127 Dante Bichette	.20	.09
128 Bert Blyleven	.10	.05
129 Chili Davis	.10	.05
130 Brian Downing	.05	.02
131 Mike Fetters	.10	.05
132 Chuck Finley	.10	.05
133 Willie Fraser	.05	.02
134 Bryan Harvey	.05	.02
135 Jack Howell	.05	.02
136 Wally Joyner	.10	.05
137 Jeff Manto	.05	.02
138 Kirk McCaskill	.05	.02
139 Bob McClure	.05	.02
140 Greg Minton	.05	.02
141 Lance Parrish	.05	.02
142 Dan Petry	.05	.02
143 Johnny Ray	.05	.02
144 Dick Schofield	.05	.02
145 Lee Stevens	.05	.02
146 Claudell Washington	.05	.02
147 Devon White	.05	.02
148 Mike Witt	.05	.02
149 Roberto Alomar	.25	.11
150 Sandy Alomar Jr.	.20	.09
151 Andy Benes	.20	.09
152 Jack Clark	.10	.05
153 Pat Clements	.05	.02
154 Joey Cora	.20	.09
155 Mark Davis	.05	.02
156 Mark Grant	.05	.02
157 Tony Gwynn	.50	.23
158 Greg W. Harris	.05	.02
159 Bruce Hurst	.05	.02
160 Darrin Jackson	.05	.02
161 Chris James	.05	.02
162 Carmelo Martinez	.05	.02
163 Mike Pagliarulo	.05	.02
164 Mark Parent	.05	.02
165 Dennis Rasmussen	.05	.02
166 Bip Roberts	.05	.02
167 Benito Santiago	.05	.02
168 Calvin Schiraldi	.05	.02
169 Eric Show	.05	.02
170 Garry Templeton	.05	.02
171 Ed Whitson	.05	.02
172 Brady Anderson	.20	.09
173 Jeff Ballard	.05	.02
174 Phil Bradley	.05	.02
175 Mike Devereaux	.05	.02
176 Steve Finley	.20	.09
177 Pete Harnisch	.05	.02
178 Kevin Hickey	.05	.02
179 Brian Holton	.05	.02
180 Ben McDonald	.20	.09
181 Bob Melvin	.05	.02
182 Bob Milacki	.05	.02
183 Randy Milligan UER (Double line of '87 stats)	.05	.02
184 Gregg Olson	.05	.02
185 Joe Orsulak	.05	.02
186 Bill Ripken	.05	.02
187 Cal Ripken	.75	.35
188 Dave Schmidt	.05	.02
189 Larry Sheets	.05	.02
190 Mickey Tettleton	.10	.05
191 Mark Thurmond	.05	.02
192 Jay Tibbs	.05	.02
193 Jim Traber	.05	.02
194 Mark Williamson	.05	.02
195 Craig Worthington	.05	.02
196 Don Aase	.05	.02
197 Blaine Beatty	.05	.02
198 Mark Carreon	.05	.02
199 Gary Carter	.20	.09
200 David Cone	.20	.09
201 Ron Darling	.05	.02
202 Kevin Elster	.05	.02
203 Sid Fernandez	.05	.02
204 Dwight Gooden	.10	.05
205 Keith Hernandez	.10	.05
206 Jeff Innis	.05	.02
207 Gregg Jefferies	.10	.05
208 Howard Johnson	.05	.02
209 Barry Lyons UER (Double line of '87 stats)	.05	.02
210 Dave Magadan	.05	.02
211 Kevin McReynolds	.05	.02
212 Jeff Musselman	.05	.02
213 Randy Myers	.10	.05
214 Bob Ojeda	.05	.02
215 Juan Samuel	.05	.02
216 Mackey Sasser	.05	.02
217 Darryl Strawberry	.10	.05
218 Tim Teufel	.05	.02
219 Frank Viola	.05	.02
220 Juan Agosto	.05	.02
221 Larry Andersen	.05	.02
222 Eric Anthony	.10	.05
223 Kevin Bass	.05	.02
224 Craig Biggio	.20	.09
225 Ken Caminiti	.20	.09
226 Jim Clancy	.05	.02
227 Danny Darwin	.05	.02
228 Glenn Davis	.05	.02
229 Jim Deshaies	.05	.02
230 Bill Doran	.05	.02
231 Bob Forsch	.05	.02
232 Brian Meyer	.05	.02
233 Terry Puhl	.05	.02
234 Rafael Ramirez	.05	.02
235 Rick Rhoden	.05	.02
236 Dan Schatzeder	.05	.02
237 Mike Scott	.05	.02
238 Dave Smith	.05	.02
239 Alex Trevino	.05	.02
240 Glenn Wilson	.05	.02
241 Gerald Young	.05	.02
242 Tom Brunansky	.05	.02
243 Cris Carpenter	.05	.02
244 Alex Cole	.10	.05
245 Vince Coleman	.05	.02
246 John Costello	.05	.02
247 Ken Dayley	.05	.02
248 Jose DeLeon	.05	.02
249 Frank DiPino	.05	.02
250 Pedro Guerrero	.05	.02
251 Ken Hill	.20	.09
252 Joe Magrane	.05	.02
253 Willie McGee UER (No decimal point before 353)	.05	.02
254 John Morris	.05	.02
255 Jose Oquendo	.05	.02
256 Tony Pena	.05	.02
257 Terry Pendleton	.10	.05
258 Ted Power	.05	.02
259 Dan Quisenberry	.05	.02
260 Ozzie Smith	.25	.11
261 Scott Terry	.05	.02
262 Milt Thompson	.05	.02
263 Denny Walling	.05	.02
264 Todd Worrell	.05	.02
265 Todd Zeile	.10	.05
266 Marty Barrett	.05	.02
267 Mike Boddicker	.05	.02

☐ 268 Wade Boggs .20 .09
☐ 269 Ellis Burks .20 .09
☐ 270 Rick Cerone .05 .02
☐ 271 Roger Clemens .40 .18
☐ 272 John Dopson .05 .02
☐ 273 Nick Esasky .05 .02
☐ 274 Dwight Evans .10 .05
☐ 275 Wes Gardner .05 .02
☐ 276 Rich Gedman .05 .02
☐ 277 Mike Greenwell .05 .02
☐ 278 Danny Heep .05 .02
☐ 279 Eric Hetzel .05 .02
☐ 280 Dennis Lamp .05 .02
☐ 281 Rob Murphy UER .05 .02
('89 stats say Reds, should say Red Sox)
☐ 282 Joe Price .05 .02
☐ 283 Carlos Quintana .05 .02
☐ 284 Jody Reed .05 .02
☐ 285 Luis Rivera .05 .02
☐ 286 Kevin Romine .05 .02
☐ 287 Lee Smith .20 .09
☐ 288 Mike Smithson .05 .02
☐ 289 Bob Stanley .05 .02
☐ 290 Harold Baines .10 .05
☐ 291 Kevin Brown .20 .09
☐ 292 Steve Buechele .05 .02
☐ 293 Scott Coolbaugh .05 .02
☐ 294 Jack Daugherty .05 .02
☐ 295 Cecil Espy .05 .02
☐ 296 Julio Franco .10 .05
☐ 297 Juan Gonzalez 2.00 .90
☐ 298 Cecilio Guante .05 .02
☐ 299 Drew Hall .05 .02
☐ 300 Charlie Hough .05 .02
☐ 301 Pete Incaviglia .05 .02
☐ 302 Mike Jeffcoat .05 .02
☐ 303 Chad Kreuter .05 .02
☐ 304 Jeff Kunkel .05 .02
☐ 305 Rick Leach .05 .02
☐ 306 Fred Manrique .05 .02
☐ 307 Jamie Moyer .05 .02
☐ 308 Rafael Palmeiro .20 .09
☐ 309 Geno Petralli .05 .02
☐ 310 Kevin Reimer .05 .02
☐ 311 Kenny Rogers .10 .05
☐ 312 Jeff Russell .05 .02
☐ 313 Nolan Ryan .75 .35
☐ 314 Ruben Sierra .05 .02
☐ 315 Bobby Witt .05 .02
☐ 316 Chris Bosio .05 .02
☐ 317 Glenn Braggs UER .05 .02
(Stats say 111 K's, but bio says 117 K's)
☐ 318 Greg Brock .05 .02
☐ 319 Chuck Crim .05 .02
☐ 320 Rob Deer .05 .02
☐ 321 Mike Felder .05 .02
☐ 322 Tom Filer .05 .02
☐ 323 Tony Fossas .05 .02
☐ 324 Jim Gantner .05 .02
☐ 325 Darryl Hamilton .10 .05
☐ 326 Teddy Higuera .05 .02
☐ 327 Mark Knudson .05 .02
☐ 328 Bill Krueger UER .05 .02
('86 stats missing)
☐ 329 Tim McIntosh .05 .02
☐ 330 Paul Molitor .20 .09
☐ 331 Jaime Navarro .05 .02
☐ 332 Charlie O'Brien .05 .02
☐ 333 Jeff Peterek .05 .02
☐ 334 Dan Plesac .05 .02
☐ 335 Jerry Reuss .05 .02
☐ 336 Gary Sheffield UER .25 .11
(Bio says played for 3 teams in '87, but stats say in '88)
☐ 337 Bill Spiers .05 .02
☐ 338 B.J. Surhoff .10 .05
☐ 339 Greg Vaughn .10 .05
☐ 340 Robin Yount .20 .09
☐ 341 Hubie Brooks .05 .02
☐ 342 Tim Burke .05 .02
☐ 343 Mike Fitzgerald .05 .02
☐ 344 Tom Foley .05 .02
☐ 345 Andres Galarraga .20 .09
☐ 346 Damaso Garcia .05 .02
☐ 347 Marquis Grissom .40 .18
☐ 348 Kevin Gross .05 .02
☐ 349 Joe Hesketh .05 .02
☐ 350 Jeff Huson .05 .02
☐ 351 Wallace Johnson .05 .02
☐ 352 Mark Langston .05 .02
☐ 353A Dave Martinez 2.00 .90
(Yellow on front)
☐ 353B Dave Martinez .05 .02
(Red on front)
☐ 354 Dennis Martinez UER .10 .05
('87 ERA is 616, should be 6.16)
☐ 355 Andy McGaffigan .05 .02
☐ 356 Otis Nixon .05 .02
☐ 357 Spike Owen .05 .02
☐ 358 Pascual Perez .05 .02
☐ 359 Tim Raines .10 .05
☐ 360 Nelson Santovenia .05 .02
☐ 361 Bryn Smith .05 .02
☐ 362 Zane Smith .05 .02
☐ 363 Larry Walker 1.00 .45
☐ 364 Tim Wallach .05 .02
☐ 365 Rick Aguilera .10 .05
☐ 366 Allan Anderson .05 .02
☐ 367 Wally Backman .05 .02
☐ 368 Doug Baker .05 .02
☐ 369 Juan Berenguer .05 .02
☐ 370 Randy Bush .05 .02
☐ 371 Carmen Castillo .05 .02
☐ 372 Mike Dyer .05 .02
☐ 373 Gary Gaetti .10 .05
☐ 374 Greg Gagne .05 .02
☐ 375 Dan Gladden .05 .02
☐ 376 German Gonzalez UER .05 .02
(Bio says 31 saves in '88, but stats say 30)
☐ 377 Brian Harper .05 .02
☐ 378 Kent Hrbek .10 .05
☐ 379 Gene Larkin .05 .02
☐ 380 Tim Laudner UER .05 .02
(No decimal point before '85 BA of 238)
☐ 381 John Moses .05 .02
☐ 382 Al Newman .05 .02
☐ 383 Kirby Puckett .40 .18
☐ 384 Shane Rawley .05 .02
☐ 385 Jeff Reardon .10 .05
☐ 386 Roy Smith .05 .02
☐ 387 Gary Wayne .05 .02
☐ 388 Dave West .05 .02
☐ 389 Tim Belcher .05 .02
☐ 390 Tim Crews UER .05 .02
(Stats say 163 IP for '83, but bio says 136)
☐ 391 Mike Davis .05 .02
☐ 392 Rick Dempsey .05 .02
☐ 393 Kirk Gibson .10 .05
☐ 394 Jose Gonzalez .05 .02
☐ 395 Alfredo Griffin .05 .02
☐ 396 Jeff Hamilton .05 .02
☐ 397 Lenny Harris .05 .02
☐ 398 Mickey Hatcher .05 .02
☐ 399 Orel Hershiser .10 .05
☐ 400 Jay Howell .05 .02
☐ 401 Mike Marshall .05 .02
☐ 402 Ramon Martinez .10 .05
☐ 403 Mike Morgan .05 .02
☐ 404 Eddie Murray .20 .09
☐ 405 Alejandro Pena .05 .02
☐ 406 Willie Randolph .10 .05
☐ 407 Mike Scioscia .05 .02
☐ 408 Ray Searage .05 .02
☐ 409 Fernando Valenzuela .10 .05
☐ 410 Jose Vizcaino .20 .09
☐ 411 John Wetteland .20 .09
☐ 412 Jack Armstrong .05 .02
☐ 413 Todd Benzinger UER .05 .02
(Bio says .323 at Pawtucket, but stats say .321)
☐ 414 Tim Birtsas .05 .02
☐ 415 Tom Browning .05 .02
☐ 416 Norm Charlton .05 .02
☐ 417 Eric Davis .10 .05
☐ 418 Rob Dibble .05 .02
☐ 419 John Franco .05 .02
☐ 420 Ken Griffey Sr. .05 .02
☐ 421 Chris Hammond .05 .02
(No 1989 used for "Did Not Play" stat, actually did play for Nashville in 1989)
☐ 422 Danny Jackson .05 .02
☐ 423 Barry Larkin .20 .09
☐ 424 Tim Leary .05 .02
☐ 425 Rick Mahler .05 .02
☐ 426 Joe Oliver .05 .02
☐ 427 Paul O'Neill .10 .05
☐ 428 Luis Quinones UER .05 .02
('86-'88 stats are omitted from card but included in totals)
☐ 429 Jeff Reed .05 .02
☐ 430 Jose Rijo .05 .02
☐ 431 Ron Robinson .05 .02
☐ 432 Rolando Roomes .05 .02
☐ 433 Chris Sabo .05 .02
☐ 434 Scott Scudder .05 .02
☐ 435 Herm Winningham .05 .02
☐ 436 Steve Balboni .05 .02
☐ 437 Jesse Barfield .05 .02
☐ 438 Mike Blowers .20 .09
☐ 439 Tom Brookens .05 .02
☐ 440 Greg Cadaret .05 .02
☐ 441 Alvaro Espinoza UER .05 .02
(Career games say 218, should be 219)
☐ 442 Bob Geren .05 .02
☐ 443 Lee Guetterman .05 .02
☐ 444 Mel Hall .05 .02
☐ 445 Andy Hawkins .05 .02
☐ 446 Roberto Kelly .05 .02
☐ 447 Don Mattingly .30 .14
☐ 448 Lance McCullers .05 .02
☐ 449 Hensley Meulens .05 .02
☐ 450 Dale Mohorcic .05 .02
☐ 451 Clay Parker .05 .02
☐ 452 Eric Plunk .05 .02
☐ 453 Dave Righetti .05 .02
☐ 454 Deion Sanders .20 .09
☐ 455 Steve Sax .05 .02
☐ 456 Don Slaught .05 .02
☐ 457 Walt Terrell .05 .02
☐ 458 Dave Winfield .20 .09
☐ 459 Jay Bell .10 .05
☐ 460 Rafael Belliard .05 .02
☐ 461 Barry Bonds .25 .11
☐ 462 Bobby Bonilla .10 .05
☐ 463 Sid Bream .05 .02
☐ 464 Benny Distefano .05 .02
☐ 465 Doug Drabek .05 .02
☐ 466 Jim Gott .05 .02
☐ 467 Billy Hatcher UER .05 .02
(.1 hits for Cubs in 1984)
☐ 468 Neal Heaton .05 .02
☐ 469 Jeff King .10 .05
☐ 470 Bob Kipper .05 .02
☐ 471 Randy Kramer .05 .02
☐ 472 Bill Landrum .05 .02
☐ 473 Mike LaValliere .05 .02
☐ 474 Jose Lind .05 .02
☐ 475 Junior Ortiz .05 .02
☐ 476 Gary Redus .05 .02
☐ 477 Rick Reed .05 .02
☐ 478 R.J. Reynolds .05 .02
☐ 479 Jeff D. Robinson .05 .02
☐ 480 John Smiley .05 .02
☐ 481 Andy Van Slyke .10 .05
☐ 482 Bob Walk .05 .02
☐ 483 Andy Allanson .05 .02
☐ 484 Scott Bailes .05 .02
☐ 485 Joey Belle UER .50 .23
(Has Jay Bell "Did You Know")
☐ 486 Bud Black .05 .02
☐ 487 Jerry Browne .05 .02
☐ 488 Tom Candiotti .05 .02
☐ 489 Joe Carter .10 .05
☐ 490 Dave Clark .05 .02
(No '84 stats)
☐ 491 John Farrell .05 .02
☐ 492 Felix Fermin .05 .02
☐ 493 Brook Jacoby .05 .02
☐ 494 Dion James .05 .02
☐ 495 Doug Jones .05 .02
☐ 496 Brad Komminsk .05 .02
☐ 497 Rod Nichols .05 .02
☐ 498 Pete O'Brien .05 .02
☐ 499 Steve Olin .10 .05
☐ 500 Jesse Orosco .05 .02
☐ 501 Joel Skinner .05 .02
☐ 502 Cory Snyder .05 .02
☐ 503 Greg Swindell .05 .02
☐ 504 Rich Yett .05 .02
☐ 505 Scott Bankhead .05 .02
☐ 506 Scott Bradley .05 .02
☐ 507 Greg Briley UER .05 .02
(28 SB's in bio, but 27 in stats)
☐ 508 Jay Buhner .20 .09
☐ 509 Darnell Coles .05 .02
☐ 510 Keith Comstock .05 .02
☐ 511 Henry Cotto .05 .02
☐ 512 Alvin Davis .05 .02
☐ 513 Ken Griffey Jr. 1.50 .70
☐ 514 Erik Hanson .05 .02
☐ 515 Gene Harris .05 .02
☐ 516 Brian Holman .05 .02
☐ 517 Mike Jackson .05 .02
☐ 518 Randy Johnson .30 .14
☐ 519 Jeffrey Leonard .05 .02
☐ 520 Edgar Martinez .20 .09

521 Dennis Powell	.05	.02
522 Jim Presley	.05	.02
523 Jerry Reed	.05	.02
524 Harold Reynolds	.05	.02
525 Mike Schooler	.05	.02
526 Bill Swift	.05	.02
527 Dave Valle	.05	.02
528 Omar Vizquel	.20	.09
529 Ivan Calderon	.05	.02
530 Carlton Fisk UER (Bellow Falls, should be Bellows Falls)	.20	.09
531 Scott Fletcher	.05	.02
532 Dave Gallagher	.05	.02
533 Ozzie Guillen	.05	.02
534 Greg Hibbard	.05	.02
535 Shawn Hillegas	.05	.02
536 Lance Johnson	.10	.05
537 Eric King	.05	.02
538 Ron Kittle	.05	.02
539 Steve Lyons	.05	.02
540 Carlos Martinez	.05	.02
541 Tom McCarthy	.05	.02
542 Matt Merullo (Had 5 ML runs scored entering '90, not 6)	.05	.02
543 Donn Pall UER (Stats say pro career began in '85, bio says '88)	.05	.02
544 Dan Pasqua	.05	.02
545 Ken Patterson	.05	.02
546 Melido Perez	.05	.02
547 Steve Rosenberg	.05	.02
548 Sammy Sosa	.75	.35
549 Bobby Thigpen	.05	.02
550 Robin Ventura	.20	.09
551 Greg Walker	.05	.02
552 Don Carman	.05	.02
553 Pat Combs (6 walks for Phillies in '89 in stats, brief bio says 4)	.05	.02
554 Dennis Cook	.05	.02
555 Darren Daulton	.10	.05
556 Len Dykstra	.10	.05
557 Curt Ford	.05	.02
558 Charlie Hayes	.10	.05
559 Von Hayes	.05	.02
560 Tommy Herr	.05	.02
561 Ken Howell	.05	.02
562 Steve Jeltz	.05	.02
563 Ron Jones	.05	.02
564 Ricky Jordan UER (Duplicate line of statistics on back)	.05	.02
565 John Kruk	.10	.05
566 Steve Lake	.05	.02
567 Roger McDowell	.05	.02
568 Terry Mulholland UER (Did You Know refers to Dave Magadan)	.05	.02
569 Dwayne Murphy	.05	.02
570 Jeff Parrett	.05	.02
571 Randy Ready	.05	.02
572 Bruce Ruffin	.05	.02
573 Dickie Thon	.05	.02
574 Jose Alvarez UER ('78 and '79 stats are reversed)	.05	.02
575 Geronimo Berroa	.10	.05
576 Jeff Blauser	.10	.05
577 Joe Boever	.05	.02
578 Marty Clary UER (No comma between city and state)	.05	.02
579 Jody Davis	.05	.02
580 Mark Eichhorn	.05	.02
581 Darrell Evans	.10	.05
582 Ron Gant	.10	.05
583 Tom Glavine	.20	.09
584 Tommy Greene	.05	.02
585 Tommy Gregg	.05	.02
586 Dave Justice UER (Actually had 16 2B in Sumter in '86)	.75	.35
587 Mark Lemke	.10	.05
588 Derek Lilliquist	.05	.02
589 Oddibe McDowell	.05	.02
590 Kent Mercker ERA (Bio says 2.75 ERA, stats say 2.68 ERA)	.10	.05
591 Dale Murphy	.20	.09
592 Gerald Perry	.05	.02
593 Lonnie Smith	.05	.02
594 Pete Smith	.05	.02
595 John Smoltz	.20	.09

☐ 596 Mike Stanton UER (No comma between city and state)	.10	.05
☐ 597 Andres Thomas	.05	.02
☐ 598 Jeff Treadway	.05	.02
☐ 599 Doyle Alexander	.05	.02
☐ 600 Dave Bergman	.05	.02
☐ 601 Brian DuBois	.05	.02
☐ 602 Paul Gibson	.05	.02
☐ 603 Mike Heath	.05	.02
☐ 604 Mike Henneman	.05	.02
☐ 605 Guillermo Hernandez	.05	.02
☐ 606 Shawn Holman	.05	.02
☐ 607 Tracy Jones	.05	.02
☐ 608 Chet Lemon	.05	.02
☐ 609 Fred Lynn	.05	.02
☐ 610 Jack Morris	.10	.05
☐ 611 Matt Nokes	.05	.02
☐ 612 Gary Pettis	.05	.02
☐ 613 Kevin Ritz	.05	.02
☐ 614 Jeff M. Robinson ('88 stats are not in line)	.05	.02
☐ 615 Steve Searcy	.05	.02
☐ 616 Frank Tanana	.05	.02
☐ 617 Alan Trammell	.10	.05
☐ 618 Gary Ward	.05	.02
☐ 619 Lou Whitaker	.10	.05
☐ 620 Frank Williams	.05	.02
☐ 621A George Brett '80 ERR (Had 10 .390 hitting seasons)	1.50	.70
☐ 621B George Brett '80 COR	.20	.09
☐ 622 Fern.Valenzuela '81	.10	.05
☐ 623 Dale Murphy '82	.20	.09
☐ 624A Cal Ripken '83 ERR (Misspelled Ripkin on card back)	5.00	2.20
☐ 624B Cal Ripken '83 COR	.40	.18
☐ 625 Ryne Sandberg '84	.20	.09
☐ 626 Don Mattingly '85	.20	.09
☐ 627 Roger Clemens '86	.20	.09
☐ 628 George Bell '87	.05	.02
☐ 629 Jose Canseco '88 UER (Reggie won MVP in '83, should say '73)	.20	.09
☐ 630A Will Clark '89 ERR (32 total bases on card back)	1.00	.45
☐ 630B Will Clark '89 COR (321 total bases; technically still an error, listing only 24 runs)	.20	.09
☐ 631 Game Savers Mark Davis Mitch Williams	.05	.02
☐ 632 Boston Igniters Wade Boggs Mike Greenwell	.20	.09
☐ 633 Starter and Stopper Mark Gubicza Jeff Russell	.05	.02
☐ 634 League's Best Shortstops Tony Fernandez Cal Ripken	.25	.11
☐ 635 Human Dynamos Kirby Puckett Bo Jackson	.20	.09
☐ 636 300 Strikeout Club Nolan Ryan Mike Scott	.25	.11
☐ 637 The Dynamic Duo Will Clark Kevin Mitchell	.10	.05
☐ 638 AL All-Stars Don Mattingly Mark McGwire	.25	.11
☐ 639 NL East Rivals Howard Johnson Ryne Sandberg	.20	.09
☐ 640 Rudy Seanez Colin Charland	.05	.02
☐ 641 George Canale Kevin Maas UER (Canale listed as INF on front, 1B on back)	.20	.09
☐ 642 Kelly Mann and Dave Hansen	.05	.02
☐ 643 Greg Smith and Stu Tate	.05	.02
☐ 644 Tom Drees and Dann Howitt	.05	.02
☐ 645 Mike Roesler and Derrick May	.20	.09

☐ 646 Scott Hemond and Mark Gardner	.05	.02
☐ 647 John Orton and Scott Leius	.05	.02
☐ 648 Rich Monteleone and Dana Williams	.05	.02
☐ 649 Mike Huff and Steve Frey	.05	.02
☐ 650 Chuck McElroy and Moises Alou	.50	.23
☐ 651 Bobby Rose and Mike Hartley	.05	.02
☐ 652 Matt Kinzer and Wayne Edwards	.05	.02
☐ 653 Delino DeShields and Jason Grimsley	.10	.05
☐ 654 CL: A's/Cubs Giants/Blue Jays	.05	.02
☐ 655 CL: Royals/Angels Padres/Orioles	.05	.02
☐ 656 CL: Mets/Astros Cards/Red Sox	.05	.02
☐ 657 CL: Rangers/Brewers Expos/Twins	.05	.02
☐ 658 CL: Dodgers/Reds Yankees/Pirates	.05	.02
☐ 659 CL: Indians/Mariners White Sox/Phillies	.05	.02
☐ 660A CL: Braves/Tigers Specials/Checklists (Checklist-660 in smaller print on card front)	.05	.02
☐ 660B CL: Braves/Tigers Specials/Checklists (Checklist-660 in normal print on card front)	.05	.02

1990 Fleer Canadian

The 1990 Fleer Canadian set contains 660 standard-size cards. The cards were distributed in wax packs exclusively in Canada. The Canadian set differs from the U.S. version only in that it shows copyright "FLEER LTD./LTEE PTD. IN CANADA" on the card backs. Although these Canadian cards were undoubtedly produced in much lesser quantities compared to the U.S. issue, the fact that the versions are so similar has kept the demand down over the years.

	MINT	NRMT
COMPLETE SET (660)	75.00	34.00
COMMON CARD (1-660)	.15	.07
*STARS: 3X to 6X BASIC CARDS		
*YOUNG STARS: 3X to 6X BASIC CARDS		
*ROOKIES: 3X to 6X BASIC CARDS		

1990 Fleer All-Stars

The 1990 Fleer All-Star insert set includes 12 standard-size cards. The set was randomly inserted in 33-card cellos and wax packs. The set is sequenced in alphabetical order. The fronts are white with a light gray screen and bright red stripes. The player selection for the set is Fleer's opinion of the best Major Leaguer at each position.

	MINT	NRMT
COMPLETE SET (12)	3.00	1.35
COMMON CARD (1-12)	.15	.07
☐ 1 Harold Baines	.35	.16
☐ 2 Will Clark	.50	.23
☐ 3 Mark Davis	.15	.07
☐ 4 Howard Johnson UER (In middle of 5th line, the is misspelled th)	.15	.07
☐ 5 Joe Magrane	.15	.07
☐ 6 Kevin Mitchell	.15	.07
☐ 7 Kirby Puckett	1.00	.45
☐ 8 Cal Ripken	2.00	.90
☐ 9 Ryne Sandberg	.75	.35
☐ 10 Mike Scott UER Astros spelled Asatros on back	.15	.07

	MINT	NRMT
☐ 11 Ruben Sierra	.15	.07
☐ 12 Mickey Tettleton	.15	.07

1990 Fleer League Standouts

This six-card standard-size insert set was distributed one per 45-card rack pack. The set is subtitled "Standouts" and commemorates outstanding events for those players from the previous season.

	MINT	NRMT
COMPLETE SET (6)	6.00	2.70
COMMON CARD (1-6)	.50	.23
☐ 1 Barry Larkin		
☐ 2 Don Mattingly	3.00	1.35
☐ 3 Darryl Strawberry	.50	.23
☐ 4 Jose Canseco		
☐ 5 Wade Boggs	.75	.35
☐ 6 Mark Grace UER (Chris Sabo misspelled as Cris)	.75	.35

1990 Fleer Soaring Stars

The 1990 Fleer Soaring Stars set was issued exclusively in jumbo cello packs. This 12-card, standard-size set features some of the most popular young players entering the 1990 season. The set gives the visual impression of rockets exploding in the air to honor these young players.

	MINT	NRMT
COMPLETE SET (12)	25.00	11.00
COMMON CARD (1-12)	.50	.23
☐ 1 Todd Zeile	1.00	.45
☐ 2 Mike Stanton	.50	.23
☐ 3 Larry Walker	6.00	2.70
☐ 4 Robin Ventura	1.00	.45
☐ 5 Scott Coolbaugh	.50	.23
☐ 6 Ken Griffey Jr.	15.00	6.75
☐ 7 Tom Gordon	.50	.23
☐ 8 Jerome Walton	.50	.23
☐ 9 Junior Felix	.50	.23
☐ 10 Jim Abbott	1.00	.45
☐ 11 Ricky Jordan	.50	.23
☐ 12 Dwight Smith	.50	.23

1990 Fleer Wax Box Cards

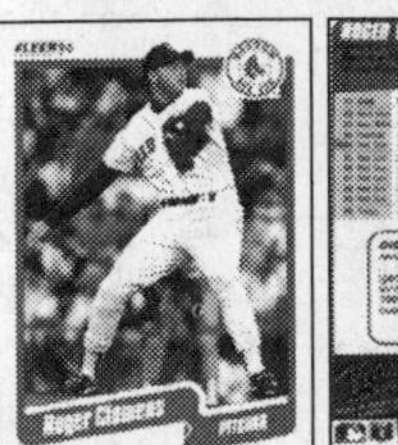
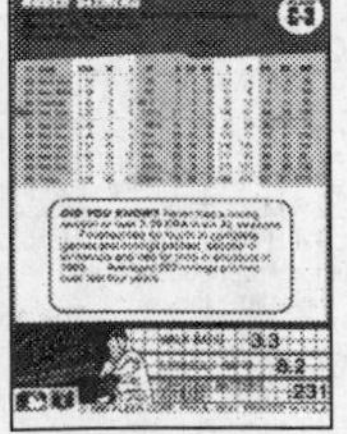

The 1990 Fleer wax box cards comprise seven different box bottoms with four cards each, for a total of 28 standard-size cards. The outer front borders are white; the inner, ribbon-like borders are different depending on the team. The vertically oriented backs are gray. The cards are numbered with a "C" prefix.

	MINT	NRMT
COMPLETE SET (28)	12.00	5.50
COMMON CARD (C1-C28)	.15	.07
☐ C1 Giants Logo	.15	.07
☐ C2 Tim Belcher	.15	.07
☐ C3 Roger Clemens	1.00	.45
☐ C4 Eric Davis	.25	.11
☐ C5 Glenn Davis	.15	.07
☐ C6 Cubs Logo	.15	.07
☐ C7 John Franco	.25	.11
☐ C8 Mike Greenwell	.15	.07
☐ C9 A's Logo	.15	.07
☐ C10 Ken Griffey Jr.	3.00	1.35
☐ C11 Pedro Guerrero	.15	.07
☐ C12 Tony Gwynn	1.50	.70
☐ C13 Blue Jays Logo	.15	.07
☐ C14 Orel Hershiser	.25	.11
☐ C15 Bo Jackson	.25	.11
☐ C16 Howard Johnson	.15	.07
☐ C17 Mets Logo	.15	.07
☐ C18 Cardinals Logo	.15	.07
☐ C19 Don Mattingly	1.25	.55
☐ C20 Mark McGwire	1.25	.55
☐ C21 Kevin Mitchell	.15	.07
☐ C22 Kirby Puckett	1.25	.55
☐ C23 Royals Logo	.15	.07
☐ C24 Orioles Logo	.15	.07
☐ C25 Ruben Sierra	.15	.07
☐ C26 Dave Stewart	.25	.11
☐ C27 Jerome Walton	.15	.07
☐ C28 Robin Yount	.75	.35

1990 Fleer World Series

This 12-card standard-size set was issued as an insert in with the Fleer factory sets, celebrating the 1989 World Series. This set marked the fourth year that Fleer issued a special World Series set in their factory (or vend) set. The design of these cards are different from the regular Fleer issue as the photo is framed by a white border with red and blue World Series cards and the player description in black.

	MINT	NRMT
COMPLETE SET (12)	1.00	.45
COMMON CARD (1-12)	.05	.02
☐ 1 Mike Moore Final piece of puzzle	.05	.02
☐ 2 Kevin Mitchell NL MVP	.05	.02
☐ 3 Terry Steinbach Game Two's Crushing Blow	.05	.02
☐ 4 Will Clark Powers Giants into Series	.25	.11
☐ 5 Jose Canseco Canseco Crushed; WS Slump	.25	.11
☐ 6 Walt Weiss Great Leather in the field	.05	.02
☐ 7 Terry Steinbach: Game 1 and A's Break Out on Top	.05	.02
☐ 8 Dave Stewart Oakland's MVP	.05	.02
☐ 9 Dave Parker Parker's Bat Produces Power	.10	.05
☐ 10 Dave Parker Jose Canseco Will Clark WS record Book Game 3	.25	.11
☐ 11 Rickey Henderson Swipes Championship Series Records	.25	.11
☐ 12 Oakland A's Celebrate Baseball's Best in 89	.10	.05

1990 Fleer Update

The 1990 Fleer Update set contains 132 standard-size cards. This set marked the seventh consecutive year Fleer issued an end of season Update set. The set was issued exclusively as a boxed set through hobby dealers. The set is checklisted alphabetically by team for each league an then alphabetically within each team. The fronts are style the same as the 1990 Fleer regular issue set. The back are numbered with the prefix "U" for Update. Rookie Card in this set include Carlos Baerga, Alex Fernandez, Trav Fryman, Todd Hundley and Frank Thomas.

	MINT	NRM
COMPLETE SET (132)	5.00	2.2
COMMON CARD (1-132)	.05	.0
☐ 1 Steve Avery	.20	.0
☐ 2 Francisco Cabrera	.05	.0
☐ 3 Nick Esasky	.05	.0
☐ 4 Jim Kremers	.05	.0
☐ 5 Greg Olson	.05	.0
☐ 6 Jim Presley	.05	.0
☐ 7 Shawn Boskie	.05	.0
☐ 8 Joe Kraemer	.05	.0
☐ 9 Luis Salazar	.05	.0
☐ 10 Hector Villanueva	.05	.0
☐ 11 Glenn Braggs	.05	.0
☐ 12 Mariano Duncan	.05	.0
☐ 13 Billy Hatcher	.05	.0
☐ 14 Tim Layana	.05	.0
☐ 15 Hal Morris	.10	.0
☐ 16 Javier Ortiz	.05	.0
☐ 17 Dave Rohde	.05	.0
☐ 18 Eric Yelding	.05	.0
☐ 19 Hubie Brooks	.05	.0
☐ 20 Kal Daniels	.05	.0
☐ 21 Dave Hansen	.05	.0
☐ 22 Mike Hartley	.05	.0
☐ 23 Stan Javier	.05	.0
☐ 24 Jose Offerman	.20	.0
☐ 25 Juan Samuel	.05	.0
☐ 26 Dennis Boyd	.05	.0
☐ 27 Delino DeShields	.10	.0
☐ 28 Steve Frey	.05	.0
☐ 29 Mark Gardner	.05	.0
☐ 30 Chris Nabholz	.05	.0
☐ 31 Bill Sampen	.05	.0
☐ 32 Dave Schmidt	.05	.0
☐ 33 Daryl Boston	.05	.0
☐ 34 Chuck Carr	.20	.0
☐ 35 John Franco	.05	.0
☐ 36 Todd Hundley	.40	.1
☐ 37 Julio Machado	.05	.0
☐ 38 Alejandro Pena	.05	.0
☐ 39 Darren Reed	.05	.0
☐ 40 Kelvin Torve	.05	.0
☐ 41 Darrel Akerfelds	.05	.0
☐ 42 Jose DeJesus	.05	.0
☐ 43 Dave Hollins UER (Misspelled Dane on card back)	.20	.0
☐ 44 Carmelo Martinez	.05	.0
☐ 45 Brad Moore	.05	.0
☐ 46 Dale Murphy	.20	.0
☐ 47 Wally Backman	.05	.0
☐ 48 Stan Belinda	.05	.0
☐ 49 Bob Patterson	.05	.0
☐ 50 Ted Power	.05	.0
☐ 51 Don Slaught	.05	.0
☐ 52 Geronimo Pena	.05	.0
☐ 53 Lee Smith	.10	.0
☐ 54 John Tudor	.05	.0
☐ 55 Joe Carter	.20	.0
☐ 56 Thomas Howard	.05	.0
☐ 57 Craig Lefferts	.05	.0
☐ 58 Rafael Valdez	.05	.0
☐ 59 Dave Anderson	.05	.0
☐ 60 Kevin Bass	.05	.0
☐ 61 John Burkett	.10	.0
☐ 62 Gary Carter	.20	.0
☐ 63 Rick Parker	.05	.0
☐ 64 Trevor Wilson	.05	.0
☐ 65 Chris Hoiles	.20	.0
☐ 66 Tim Hulett	.05	.0
☐ 67 Dave Johnson	.05	.0
☐ 68 Curt Schilling	.20	.0
☐ 69 David Segui	.20	.0
☐ 70 Tom Brunansky	.05	.0
☐ 71 Greg A. Harris	.05	.0

Card	MINT	NRMT
☐ 72 Dana Kiecker	.05	.02
☐ 73 Tim Naehring	.20	.09
☐ 74 Tony Pena	.05	.02
☐ 75 Jeff Reardon	.10	.05
☐ 76 Jerry Reed	.05	.02
☐ 77 Mark Eichhorn	.05	.02
☐ 78 Mark Langston	.05	.02
☐ 79 John Orton	.05	.02
☐ 80 Luis Polonia	.05	.02
☐ 81 Dave Winfield	.20	.09
☐ 82 Cliff Young	.05	.02
☐ 83 Wayne Edwards	.05	.02
☐ 84 Alex Fernandez	.50	.23
☐ 85 Craig Grebeck	.05	.02
☐ 86 Scott Radinsky	.05	.02
☐ 87 Frank Thomas	4.00	1.80
☐ 88 Beau Allred	.05	.02
☐ 89 Sandy Alomar Jr.	.20	.09
☐ 90 Carlos Baerga	.25	.11
☐ 91 Kevin Bearse	.05	.02
☐ 92 Chris James	.05	.02
☐ 93 Candy Maldonado	.05	.02
☐ 94 Jeff Manto	.05	.02
☐ 95 Cecil Fielder	.10	.05
☐ 96 Travis Fryman	.40	.18
☐ 97 Lloyd Moseby	.05	.02
☐ 98 Edwin Nunez	.05	.02
☐ 99 Tony Phillips	.05	.02
☐ 100 Larry Sheets	.05	.02
☐ 101 Mark Davis	.05	.02
☐ 102 Storm Davis	.05	.02
☐ 103 Gerald Perry	.05	.02
☐ 104 Terry Shumpert	.05	.02
☐ 105 Edgar Diaz	.05	.02
☐ 106 Dave Parker	.10	.05
☐ 107 Tim Drummond	.05	.02
☐ 108 Junior Ortiz	.05	.02
☐ 109 Park Pittman	.05	.02
☐ 110 Kevin Tapani	.10	.05
☐ 111 Oscar Azocar	.05	.02
☐ 112 Jim Leyritz	.20	.09
☐ 113 Kevin Maas	.10	.05
☐ 114 Alan Mills	.05	.02
☐ 115 Matt Nokes	.05	.02
☐ 116 Pascual Perez	.05	.02
☐ 117 Ozzie Canseco	.05	.02
☐ 118 Scott Sanderson	.05	.02
☐ 119 Tino Martinez	.40	.18
☐ 120 Jeff Schaefer	.05	.02
☐ 121 Matt Young	.05	.02
☐ 122 Brian Bohanon	.05	.02
☐ 123 Jeff Huson	.05	.02
☐ 124 Ramon Manon	.05	.02
☐ 125 Gary Mielke UER (Shown as Blue Jay on front)	.05	.02
☐ 126 Willie Blair	.05	.02
☐ 127 Glenallen Hill	.05	.02
☐ 128 John Olerud UER (Listed as throwing right, should be left)	.20	.09
☐ 129 Luis Sojo	.05	.02
☐ 130 Mark Whiten	.10	.05
☐ 131 Nolan Ryan	.75	.35
☐ 132 Checklist U1-U132	.05	.02

1990 Fleer Award Winners

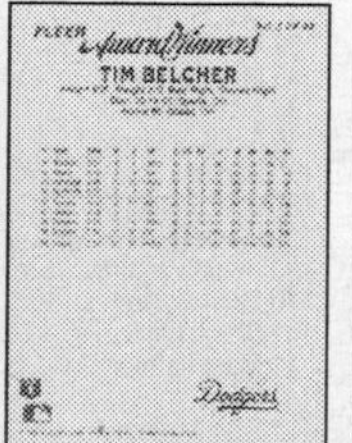

The 1990 Fleer Award Winners set was printed by Fleer for Hills stores (as well as for some 7/Eleven's) and released early in the summer of 1990. The set features a player photo within a trophy design with the player's name, team and position at the base. This 44-card standard-size set is numbered in alphabetical order, although Will Clark erroneously precedes Jack Clark. Card number 10 is listed on the box checklist as being Ron Darling, but Darling is not in the set. Consequently the numbers on the box checklist between 10 and 37 are off by one. Darryl Strawberry (38) is not listed on the box, but is included in the set. The box also includes six peel-off team logo stickers. The original suggested retail price for the set at Hills was 2.49.

	MINT	NRMT
COMPLETE SET (44)	6.00	2.70
COMMON CARD (1-44)	.05	.02
☐ 1 Jeff Ballard	.05	.02
☐ 2 Tim Belcher	.05	.02
☐ 3 Bert Blyleven	.10	.05
☐ 4 Wade Boggs	.40	.18
☐ 5 Bob Boone	.10	.05
☐ 6 Jose Canseco	.75	.35
☐ 7 Will Clark	.75	.35
☐ 8 Jack Clark	.10	.05
☐ 9 Vince Coleman	.05	.02
☐ 10 Eric Davis	.10	.05
☐ 11 Jose DeLeon	.05	.02
☐ 12 Tony Fernandez	.05	.02
☐ 13 Carlton Fisk	.50	.23
☐ 14 Scott Garrelts	.05	.02
☐ 15 Tom Gordon	.05	.02
☐ 16 Ken Griffey Jr.	4.00	1.80
☐ 17 Von Hayes	.05	.02
☐ 18 Rickey Henderson	.50	.23
☐ 19 Bo Jackson	.10	.05
☐ 20 Howard Johnson	.05	.02
☐ 21 Don Mattingly	1.50	.70
☐ 22 Fred McGriff	.60	.25
☐ 23 Kevin Mitchell	.05	.02
☐ 24 Gregg Olson	.05	.02
☐ 25 Gary Pettis	.05	.02
☐ 26 Kirby Puckett	1.50	.70
☐ 27 Harold Reynolds	.10	.05
☐ 28 Jeff Russell	.05	.02
☐ 29 Nolan Ryan	2.50	1.10
☐ 30 Bret Saberhagen	.10	.05
☐ 31 Ryne Sandberg	1.50	.70
☐ 32 Benito Santiago	.05	.02
☐ 33 Mike Scott	.05	.02
☐ 34 Ruben Sierra	.05	.02
☐ 35 Lonnie Smith	.05	.02
☐ 36 Ozzie Smith	1.50	.70
☐ 37 Dave Stewart	.10	.05
☐ 38 Darryl Strawberry	.10	.05
☐ 39 Greg Swindell	.05	.02
☐ 40 Andy Van Slyke	.10	.05
☐ 41 Tim Wallach	.05	.02
☐ 42 Jerome Walton	.05	.02
☐ 43 Mitch Williams	.05	.02
☐ 44 Robin Yount	.50	.23

1990 Fleer Baseball All-Stars

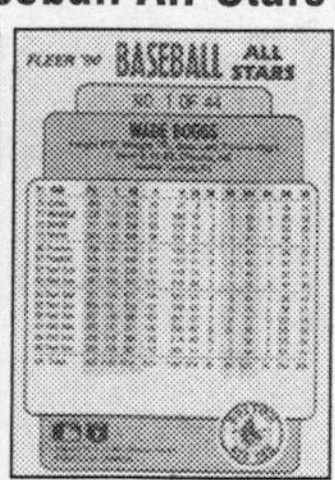

The 1990 Fleer Baseball All-Stars Set was produced by Fleer for the Ben Franklin chain and released early in the summer of 1990. This standard-size 44-card set features some of the best of today's players in alphabetical order. The design of the cards has vertical stripes on the front of the card. The set's custom box gives the set checklist on the back panel. The box also includes six peel-off team logo stickers each with a trivia quiz on back.

	MINT	NRMT
COMPLETE SET (44)	6.00	2.70
COMMON CARD (1-44)	.05	.02
☐ 1 Wade Boggs	.40	.18
☐ 2 Bobby Bonilla	.10	.05
☐ 3 Tim Burke	.05	.02
☐ 4 Jose Canseco	.60	.25
☐ 5 Will Clark	.60	.25
☐ 6 Eric Davis	.10	.05
☐ 7 Glenn Davis	.05	.02
☐ 8 Julio Franco	.10	.05
☐ 9 Tony Fernandez	.05	.02
☐ 10 Gary Gaetti	.10	.05
☐ 11 Scott Garrelts	.05	.02
☐ 12 Mark Grace	.60	.25
☐ 13 Mike Greenwell	.05	.02
☐ 14 Ken Griffey Jr.	4.00	1.80
☐ 15 Mark Gubicza	.05	.02
☐ 16 Pedro Guerrero	.05	.02
☐ 17 Von Hayes	.05	.02
☐ 18 Orel Hershiser	.10	.05
☐ 19 Bruce Hurst	.05	.02
☐ 20 Bo Jackson	.10	.05
☐ 21 Howard Johnson	.05	.02
☐ 22 Doug Jones	.05	.02
☐ 23 Barry Larkin	.60	.25
☐ 24 Don Mattingly	1.25	.55
☐ 25 Mark McGwire	1.50	.70
☐ 26 Kevin McReynolds	.05	.02
☐ 27 Kevin Mitchell	.05	.02
☐ 28 Dan Plesac	.05	.02
☐ 29 Kirby Puckett	1.50	.70
☐ 30 Cal Ripken	3.00	1.35
☐ 31 Bret Saberhagen	.10	.05
☐ 32 Ryne Sandberg	1.25	.55
☐ 33 Steve Sax	.05	.02
☐ 34 Ruben Sierra	.05	.02
☐ 35 Ozzie Smith	1.25	.55
☐ 36 John Smoltz	.40	.18
☐ 37 Darryl Strawberry	.10	.05
☐ 38 Terry Steinbach	.10	.05
☐ 39 Dave Stewart	.10	.05
☐ 40 Bobby Thigpen	.05	.02
☐ 41 Alan Trammell	.20	.09
☐ 42 Devon White	.05	.02
☐ 43 Mitch Williams	.05	.02
☐ 44 Robin Yount	.50	.23

1990 Fleer Baseball MVP's

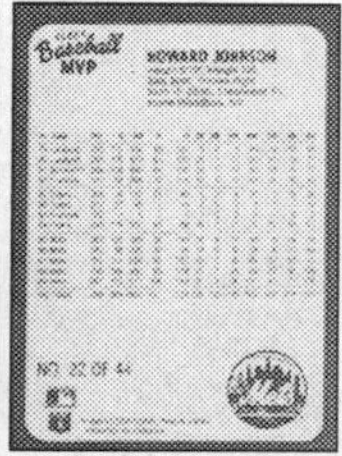

The 1990 Fleer Baseball MVP's were produced by Fleer exclusively for the Toys'R'Us chain and released early in the summer of 1990. This set has a multi-colored border, is standard size, and has 44 players arranged in alphabetical order. The set's custom box gives the set checklist on the back panel. The box also includes six peel-off team logo stickers.

	MINT	NRMT
COMPLETE SET (44)	6.00	2.70
COMMON CARD (1-44)	.05	.02
☐ 1 George Bell	.05	.02
☐ 2 Bert Blyleven	.10	.05
☐ 3 Wade Boggs	.40	.18
☐ 4 Bobby Bonilla	.10	.05
☐ 5 George Brett	1.25	.55
☐ 6 Jose Canseco	.60	.25
☐ 7 Will Clark	.60	.25
☐ 8 Roger Clemens	1.00	.45
☐ 9 Eric Davis	.10	.05
☐ 10 Glenn Davis	.05	.02
☐ 11 Tony Fernandez	.05	.02
☐ 12 Dwight Gooden	.10	.05
☐ 13 Mike Greenwell	.05	.02
☐ 14 Ken Griffey Jr.	4.00	1.80
☐ 15 Pedro Guerrero	.05	.02
☐ 16 Tony Gwynn	2.00	.90
☐ 17 Rickey Henderson	.40	.18
☐ 18 Tom Herr	.05	.02
☐ 19 Orel Hershiser	.10	.05
☐ 20 Kent Hrbek	.10	.05
☐ 21 Bo Jackson	.10	.05
☐ 22 Howard Johnson	.05	.02
☐ 23 Don Mattingly	1.50	.70
☐ 24 Fred McGriff	.60	.25
☐ 25 Mark McGwire	1.50	.70
☐ 26 Kevin Mitchell	.05	.02
☐ 27 Paul Molitor	.50	.23
☐ 28 Dale Murphy	.30	.14
☐ 29 Kirby Puckett	1.50	.70
☐ 30 Tim Raines	.10	.05
☐ 31 Cal Ripken	3.00	1.35
☐ 32 Bret Saberhagen	.10	.05
☐ 33 Ryne Sandberg	1.25	.55
☐ 34 Ruben Sierra	.05	.02
☐ 35 Dwight Smith	.05	.02
☐ 36 Ozzie Smith	1.25	.55
☐ 37 Darryl Strawberry	.10	.05
☐ 38 Dave Stewart	.10	.05
☐ 39 Greg Swindell	.05	.02
☐ 40 Bobby Thigpen	.05	.02
☐ 41 Alan Trammell	.20	.09
☐ 42 Jerome Walton	.05	.02

	MINT	NRMT
☐ 43 Mitch Williams	.05	.02
☐ 44 Robin Yount	.50	.23

1990 Fleer League Leaders

The 1990 Fleer League Leader set was issued by Fleer for Walgreen stores. This set design features solid blue borders with the players photo inset within the middle of the card. This 44-card, standard-size set is numbered in alphabetical order. The set's custom box gives the set checklist on the back panel. The box also includes six peel-off team logo stickers. The original suggested retail price for the set at Walgreen's was 2.49.

	MINT	NRMT
COMPLETE SET (44)	6.00	2.70
COMMON CARD (1-44)	.05	.02
☐ 1 Roberto Alomar	1.00	.45
☐ 2 Tim Belcher	.05	.02
☐ 3 George Bell	.05	.02
☐ 4 Wade Boggs	.40	.18
☐ 5 Jose Canseco	.60	.25
☐ 6 Will Clark	.60	.25
☐ 7 David Cone	.10	.05
☐ 8 Eric Davis	.05	.02
☐ 9 Glenn Davis	.05	.02
☐ 10 Nick Esasky	.05	.02
☐ 11 Dennis Eckersley	.20	.09
☐ 12 Mark Grace	.60	.25
☐ 13 Mike Greenwell	.05	.02
☐ 14 Ken Griffey Jr.	4.00	1.80
☐ 15 Mark Gubicza	.05	.02
☐ 16 Pedro Guerrero	.05	.02
☐ 17 Tony Gwynn	2.00	.90
☐ 18 Rickey Henderson	.50	.23
☐ 19 Bo Jackson	.10	.05
☐ 20 Doug Jones	.10	.05
☐ 21 Ricky Jordan	.05	.02
☐ 22 Barry Larkin	.60	.25
☐ 23 Don Mattingly	1.50	.70
☐ 24 Fred McGriff	.60	.25
☐ 25 Mark McGwire	1.50	.70
☐ 26 Kevin Mitchell	.05	.02
☐ 27 Jack Morris	.10	.05
☐ 28 Gregg Olson	.05	.02
☐ 29 Dan Plesac	.05	.02
☐ 30 Kirby Puckett	1.50	.70
☐ 31 Nolan Ryan	3.00	1.35
☐ 32 Bret Saberhagen	.05	.02
☐ 33 Ryne Sandberg	1.25	.55
☐ 34 Steve Sax	.05	.02
☐ 35 Mike Scott	.05	.02
☐ 36 Ruben Sierra	.05	.02
☐ 37 Lonnie Smith	.05	.02
☐ 38 Darryl Strawberry	.10	.05
☐ 39 Bobby Thigpen	.05	.02
☐ 40 Andy Van Slyke	.10	.05
☐ 41 Tim Wallach	.05	.02
☐ 42 Jerome Walton UER (Photo actually Eric Yelding)	.05	.02
☐ 43 Devon White	.05	.02
☐ 44 Robin Yount	.30	.14

1991 Fleer

The 1991 Fleer set consists of 720 standard-size cards. Cards were primarily issued in wax packs, cello packs and factory sets. This set does not have what has been a Fleer tradition in recent years, the two-player rookie cards and there are less two-player special cards than in prior years. The design features solid yellow borders with the information in black indicating name, position, and team. The set is again ordered numerically by teams, followed by combination cards, rookie prospect pairs, and checklists. Rookie Cards in this set include Jeff Conine and Brian McRae. A number of the cards in the set can be found with photos cropped (very slightly) differently as Fleer used two separate printers in their attempt to maximize production.

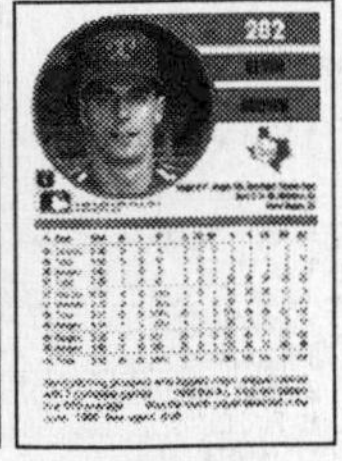

	MINT	NRMT
COMPLETE SET (720)	8.00	3.60
COMP.RETAIL SET (732)	10.00	4.50
COMP.HOBBY SET (732)	10.00	4.50
COMMON CARD (1-720)	.05	.02
☐ 1 Troy Afenir	.05	.02
☐ 2 Harold Baines	.10	.05
☐ 3 Lance Blankenship	.05	.02
☐ 4 Todd Burns	.05	.02
☐ 5 Jose Canseco	.20	.09
☐ 6 Dennis Eckersley	.20	.09
☐ 7 Mike Gallego	.05	.02
☐ 8 Ron Hassey	.05	.02
☐ 9 Dave Henderson	.05	.02
☐ 10 Rickey Henderson	.20	.09
☐ 11 Rick Honeycutt	.05	.02
☐ 12 Doug Jennings	.05	.02
☐ 13 Joe Klink	.05	.02
☐ 14 Carney Lansford	.10	.05
☐ 15 Darren Lewis	.05	.02
☐ 16 Willie McGee UER (Height 6'11")	.05	.02
☐ 17 Mark McGwire UER (183 extra base hits in 1987)	.40	.18
☐ 18 Mike Moore	.05	.02
☐ 19 Gene Nelson	.05	.02
☐ 20 Dave Otto	.05	.02
☐ 21 Jamie Quirk	.05	.02
☐ 22 Willie Randolph	.10	.05
☐ 23 Scott Sanderson	.05	.02
☐ 24 Terry Steinbach	.10	.05
☐ 25 Dave Stewart	.10	.05
☐ 26 Walt Weiss	.05	.02
☐ 27 Bob Welch	.05	.02
☐ 28 Curt Young	.05	.02
☐ 29 Wally Backman	.05	.02
☐ 30 Stan Belinda UER (Born in Huntington, should be State College)	.05	.02
☐ 31 Jay Bell	.10	.05
☐ 32 Rafael Belliard	.05	.02
☐ 33 Barry Bonds	.25	.11
☐ 34 Bobby Bonilla	.10	.05
☐ 35 Sid Bream	.05	.02
☐ 36 Doug Drabek	.05	.02
☐ 37 Carlos Garcia	.05	.02
☐ 38 Neal Heaton	.05	.02
☐ 39 Jeff King	.10	.05
☐ 40 Bob Kipper	.05	.02
☐ 41 Bill Landrum	.05	.02
☐ 42 Mike LaValliere	.05	.02
☐ 43 Jose Lind	.05	.02
☐ 44 Carmelo Martinez	.05	.02
☐ 45 Bob Patterson	.05	.02
☐ 46 Ted Power	.05	.02
☐ 47 Gary Redus	.05	.02
☐ 48 R.J. Reynolds	.05	.02
☐ 49 Don Slaught	.05	.02
☐ 50 John Smiley	.05	.02
☐ 51 Zane Smith	.05	.02
☐ 52 Randy Tomlin	.05	.02
☐ 53 Andy Van Slyke	.10	.05
☐ 54 Bob Walk	.05	.02
☐ 55 Jack Armstrong	.05	.02
☐ 56 Todd Benzinger	.05	.02
☐ 57 Glenn Braggs	.05	.02
☐ 58 Keith Brown	.05	.02
☐ 59 Tom Browning	.05	.02
☐ 60 Norm Charlton	.05	.02
☐ 61 Eric Davis	.10	.05
☐ 62 Rob Dibble	.05	.02
☐ 63 Bill Doran	.05	.02
☐ 64 Mariano Duncan	.05	.02
☐ 65 Chris Hammond	.05	.02
☐ 66 Billy Hatcher	.05	.02
☐ 67 Danny Jackson	.05	.02
☐ 68 Barry Larkin	.20	.09
☐ 69 Tim Layana (Black line over made in first text line)	.05	.02
☐ 70 Terry Lee	.05	.02
☐ 71 Rick Mahler	.05	.02
☐ 72 Hal Morris	.05	.02
☐ 73 Randy Myers	.10	.05
☐ 74 Ron Oester	.05	.02
☐ 75 Joe Oliver	.05	.02
☐ 76 Paul O'Neill	.10	.05
☐ 77 Luis Quinones	.05	.02
☐ 78 Jeff Reed	.05	.02
☐ 79 Jose Rijo	.05	.02
☐ 80 Chris Sabo	.05	.02
☐ 81 Scott Scudder	.05	.02
☐ 82 Herm Winningham	.05	.02
☐ 83 Larry Andersen	.05	.02
☐ 84 Marty Barrett	.05	.02
☐ 85 Mike Boddicker	.05	.02
☐ 86 Wade Boggs	.20	.09
☐ 87 Tom Bolton	.05	.02
☐ 88 Tom Brunansky	.05	.02
☐ 89 Ellis Burks	.10	.05
☐ 90 Roger Clemens	.40	.18
☐ 91 Scott Cooper	.05	.02
☐ 92 John Dopson	.05	.02
☐ 93 Dwight Evans	.10	.05
☐ 94 Wes Gardner	.05	.02
☐ 95 Jeff Gray	.05	.02
☐ 96 Mike Greenwell	.05	.02
☐ 97 Greg A. Harris	.05	.02
☐ 98 Daryl Irvine	.05	.02
☐ 99 Dana Kiecker	.05	.02
☐ 100 Randy Kutcher	.05	.02
☐ 101 Dennis Lamp	.05	.02
☐ 102 Mike Marshall	.05	.02
☐ 103 John Marzano	.05	.02
☐ 104 Rob Murphy	.05	.02
☐ 105 Tim Naehring	.10	.05
☐ 106 Tony Pena	.05	.02
☐ 107 Phil Plantier	.10	.05
☐ 108 Carlos Quintana	.05	.02
☐ 109 Jeff Reardon	.10	.05
☐ 110 Jerry Reed	.05	.02
☐ 111 Jody Reed	.05	.02
☐ 112 Luis Rivera UER (Born 1/3/84)	.05	.02
☐ 113 Kevin Romine	.05	.02
☐ 114 Phil Bradley	.05	.02
☐ 115 Ivan Calderon	.05	.02
☐ 116 Wayne Edwards	.05	.02
☐ 117 Alex Fernandez	.10	.05
☐ 118 Carlton Fisk	.20	.09
☐ 119 Scott Fletcher	.05	.02
☐ 120 Craig Grebeck	.05	.02
☐ 121 Ozzie Guillen	.05	.02
☐ 122 Greg Hibbard	.05	.02
☐ 123 Lance Johnson UER (Born Cincinnati, should be Lincoln Heights)	.10	.05
☐ 124 Barry Jones	.05	.02
☐ 125 Ron Karkovice	.05	.02
☐ 126 Eric King	.05	.02
☐ 127 Steve Lyons	.05	.02
☐ 128 Carlos Martinez	.05	.02
☐ 129 Jack McDowell UER (Stanford misspelled as Standford on back)	.05	.02
☐ 130 Donn Pall (No dots over any i's in text)	.05	.02
☐ 131 Dan Pasqua	.05	.02
☐ 132 Ken Patterson	.05	.02
☐ 133 Melido Perez	.05	.02
☐ 134 Adam Peterson	.05	.02
☐ 135 Scott Radinsky	.05	.02
☐ 136 Sammy Sosa	.25	.11
☐ 137 Bobby Thigpen	.05	.02
☐ 138 Frank Thomas	1.50	.70
☐ 139 Robin Ventura	.20	.09
☐ 140 Daryl Boston	.05	.02
☐ 141 Chuck Carr	.05	.02
☐ 142 Mark Carreon	.05	.02
☐ 143 David Cone	.10	.05
☐ 144 Ron Darling	.05	.02
☐ 145 Kevin Elster	.05	.02
☐ 146 Sid Fernandez	.05	.02
☐ 147 John Franco	.05	.02
☐ 148 Dwight Gooden	.10	.05
☐ 149 Tom Herr	.05	.02
☐ 150 Todd Hundley	.20	.09
☐ 151 Gregg Jefferies	.10	.05
☐ 152 Howard Johnson	.05	.02
☐ 153 Dave Magadan	.05	.02
☐ 154 Kevin McReynolds	.05	.02
☐ 155 Keith Miller UER (Text says Rochester in '87, stats say Tidewater, mixed up with other Keith Miller)	.05	.02
☐ 156 Bob Ojeda	.05	.02

☐ 157 Tom O'Malley	.05	.02
☐ 158 Alejandro Pena	.05	.02
☐ 159 Darren Reed	.05	.02
☐ 160 Mackey Sasser	.05	.02
☐ 161 Darryl Strawberry	.10	.05
☐ 162 Tim Teufel	.05	.02
☐ 163 Kelvin Torve	.05	.02
☐ 164 Julio Valera	.05	.02
☐ 165 Frank Viola	.05	.02
☐ 166 Wally Whitehurst	.05	.02
☐ 167 Jim Acker	.05	.02
☐ 168 Derek Bell	.20	.09
☐ 169 George Bell	.05	.02
☐ 170 Willie Blair	.05	.02
☐ 171 Pat Borders	.05	.02
☐ 172 John Cerutti	.05	.02
☐ 173 Junior Felix	.05	.02
☐ 174 Tony Fernandez	.05	.02
☐ 175 Kelly Gruber UER (Born in Houston, should be Bellaire)	.05	.02
☐ 176 Tom Henke	.05	.02
☐ 177 Glenallen Hill	.05	.02
☐ 178 Jimmy Key	.10	.05
☐ 179 Manny Lee	.05	.02
☐ 180 Fred McGriff	.20	.09
☐ 181 Rance Mulliniks	.05	.02
☐ 182 Greg Myers	.05	.02
☐ 183 John Olerud UER (Listed as throwing right, should be left)	.10	.05
☐ 184 Luis Sojo	.05	.02
☐ 185 Dave Stieb	.05	.02
☐ 186 Todd Stottlemyre	.05	.02
☐ 187 Duane Ward	.05	.02
☐ 188 David Wells	.05	.02
☐ 189 Mark Whiten	.05	.02
☐ 190 Ken Williams	.05	.02
☐ 191 Frank Wills	.05	.02
☐ 192 Mookie Wilson	.05	.02
☐ 193 Don Aase	.05	.02
☐ 194 Tim Belcher UER (Born Sparta, Ohio, should say Mt. Gilead)	.05	.02
☐ 195 Hubie Brooks	.05	.02
☐ 196 Dennis Cook	.05	.02
☐ 197 Tim Crews	.05	.02
☐ 198 Kal Daniels	.05	.02
☐ 199 Kirk Gibson	.10	.05
☐ 200 Jim Gott	.05	.02
☐ 201 Alfredo Griffin	.05	.02
☐ 202 Chris Gwynn	.05	.02
☐ 203 Dave Hansen	.05	.02
☐ 204 Lenny Harris	.05	.02
☐ 205 Mike Hartley	.05	.02
☐ 206 Mickey Hatcher	.05	.02
☐ 207 Carlos Hernandez	.05	.02
☐ 208 Orel Hershiser	.10	.05
☐ 209 Jay Howell UER (No 1982 Yankee stats)	.05	.02
☐ 210 Mike Huff	.05	.02
☐ 211 Stan Javier	.05	.02
☐ 212 Ramon Martinez	.10	.05
☐ 213 Mike Morgan	.05	.02
☐ 214 Eddie Murray	.20	.09
☐ 215 Jim Neidlinger	.05	.02
☐ 216 Jose Offerman	.05	.02
☐ 217 Jim Poole	.05	.02
☐ 218 Juan Samuel	.05	.02
☐ 219 Mike Scioscia	.05	.02
☐ 220 Ray Searage	.05	.02
☐ 221 Mike Sharperson	.05	.02
☐ 222 Fernando Valenzuela	.10	.05
☐ 223 Jose Vizcaino	.05	.02
☐ 224 Mike Aldrete	.05	.02
☐ 225 Scott Anderson	.05	.02
☐ 226 Dennis Boyd	.05	.02
☐ 227 Tim Burke	.05	.02
☐ 228 Delino DeShields	.05	.02
☐ 229 Mike Fitzgerald	.05	.02
☐ 230 Tom Foley	.05	.02
☐ 231 Steve Frey	.05	.02
☐ 232 Andres Galarraga	.20	.09
☐ 233 Mark Gardner	.05	.02
☐ 234 Marquis Grissom	.20	.09
☐ 235 Kevin Gross (No date given for first Expos win)	.05	.02
☐ 236 Drew Hall	.05	.02
☐ 237 Dave Martinez	.05	.02
☐ 238 Dennis Martinez	.10	.05
☐ 239 Dale Mohorcic	.05	.02
☐ 240 Chris Nabholz	.05	.02
☐ 241 Otis Nixon	.05	.02
☐ 242 Junior Noboa	.05	.02
☐ 243 Spike Owen	.05	.02
☐ 244 Tim Raines	.10	.05
☐ 245 Mel Rojas UER (Stats show 3.60 ERA, bio says 3.19 ERA)	.20	.09
☐ 246 Scott Ruskin	.05	.02
☐ 247 Bill Sampen	.05	.02
☐ 248 Nelson Santovenia	.05	.02
☐ 249 Dave Schmidt	.05	.02
☐ 250 Larry Walker	.30	.14
☐ 251 Tim Wallach	.05	.02
☐ 252 Dave Anderson	.05	.02
☐ 253 Kevin Bass	.05	.02
☐ 254 Steve Bedrosian	.05	.02
☐ 255 Jeff Brantley	.05	.02
☐ 256 John Burkett	.10	.05
☐ 257 Brett Butler	.10	.05
☐ 258 Gary Carter	.20	.09
☐ 259 Will Clark	.20	.09
☐ 260 Steve Decker	.05	.02
☐ 261 Kelly Downs	.05	.02
☐ 262 Scott Garrelts	.05	.02
☐ 263 Terry Kennedy	.05	.02
☐ 264 Mike LaCoss	.05	.02
☐ 265 Mark Leonard	.05	.02
☐ 266 Greg Litton	.05	.02
☐ 267 Kevin Mitchell	.10	.05
☐ 268 Randy O'Neal	.05	.02
☐ 269 Rick Parker	.05	.02
☐ 270 Rick Reuschel	.05	.02
☐ 271 Ernest Riles	.05	.02
☐ 272 Don Robinson	.05	.02
☐ 273 Robby Thompson	.05	.02
☐ 274 Mark Thurmond	.05	.02
☐ 275 Jose Uribe	.05	.02
☐ 276 Matt Williams	.20	.09
☐ 277 Trevor Wilson	.05	.02
☐ 278 Gerald Alexander	.05	.02
☐ 279 Brad Arnsberg	.05	.02
☐ 280 Kevin Belcher	.05	.02
☐ 281 Joe Bitker	.05	.02
☐ 282 Kevin Brown	.10	.05
☐ 283 Steve Buechele	.05	.02
☐ 284 Jack Daugherty	.05	.02
☐ 285 Julio Franco	.10	.05
☐ 286 Juan Gonzalez	.75	.35
☐ 287 Bill Haselman	.05	.02
☐ 288 Charlie Hough	.05	.02
☐ 289 Jeff Huson	.05	.02
☐ 290 Pete Incaviglia	.05	.02
☐ 291 Mike Jeffcoat	.05	.02
☐ 292 Jeff Kunkel	.05	.02
☐ 293 Gary Mielke	.05	.02
☐ 294 Jamie Moyer	.05	.02
☐ 295 Rafael Palmeiro	.20	.09
☐ 296 Geno Petralli	.05	.02
☐ 297 Gary Pettis	.05	.02
☐ 298 Kevin Reimer	.05	.02
☐ 299 Kenny Rogers	.05	.02
☐ 300 Jeff Russell	.05	.02
☐ 301 John Russell	.05	.02
☐ 302 Nolan Ryan	.75	.35
☐ 303 Ruben Sierra	.05	.02
☐ 304 Bobby Witt	.05	.02
☐ 305 Jim Abbott UER (Text on back states he won Sullivan Award (outstanding amateur athlete) in 1989;should be '88)	.10	.05
☐ 306 Kent Anderson	.05	.02
☐ 307 Dante Bichette	.20	.09
☐ 308 Bert Blyleven	.10	.05
☐ 309 Chili Davis	.10	.05
☐ 310 Brian Downing	.05	.02
☐ 311 Mark Eichhorn	.05	.02
☐ 312 Mike Fetters	.05	.02
☐ 313 Chuck Finley	.10	.05
☐ 314 Willie Fraser	.05	.02
☐ 315 Bryan Harvey	.05	.02
☐ 316 Donnie Hill	.05	.02
☐ 317 Wally Joyner	.10	.05
☐ 318 Mark Langston	.05	.02
☐ 319 Kirk McCaskill	.05	.02
☐ 320 John Orton	.05	.02
☐ 321 Lance Parrish	.05	.02
☐ 322 Luis Polonia UER (1984 Madfison, should be Madison)	.05	.02
☐ 323 Johnny Ray	.05	.02
☐ 324 Bobby Rose	.05	.02
☐ 325 Dick Schofield	.05	.02
☐ 326 Rick Schu	.05	.02
☐ 327 Lee Stevens	.05	.02
☐ 328 Devon White	.10	.05
☐ 329 Dave Winfield	.20	.09
☐ 330 Cliff Young	.05	.02
☐ 331 Dave Bergman	.05	.02
☐ 332 Phil Clark	.05	.02
☐ 333 Darnell Coles	.05	.02
☐ 334 Milt Cuyler	.05	.02
☐ 335 Cecil Fielder	.10	.05
☐ 336 Travis Fryman	.20	.09
☐ 337 Paul Gibson	.05	.02
☐ 338 Jerry Don Gleaton	.05	.02
☐ 339 Mike Heath	.05	.02
☐ 340 Mike Henneman	.05	.02
☐ 341 Chet Lemon	.05	.02
☐ 342 Lance McCullers	.05	.02
☐ 343 Jack Morris	.10	.05
☐ 344 Lloyd Moseby	.05	.02
☐ 345 Edwin Nunez	.05	.02
☐ 346 Clay Parker	.05	.02
☐ 347 Dan Petry	.05	.02
☐ 348 Tony Phillips	.05	.02
☐ 349 Jeff M. Robinson	.05	.02
☐ 350 Mark Salas	.05	.02
☐ 351 Mike Schwabe	.05	.02
☐ 352 Larry Sheets	.05	.02
☐ 353 John Shelby	.05	.02
☐ 354 Frank Tanana	.05	.02
☐ 355 Alan Trammell	.10	.05
☐ 356 Gary Ward	.05	.02
☐ 357 Lou Whitaker	.10	.05
☐ 358 Beau Allred	.05	.02
☐ 359 Sandy Alomar Jr.	.20	.09
☐ 360 Carlos Baerga	.20	.09
☐ 361 Kevin Bearse	.05	.02
☐ 362 Tom Brookens	.05	.02
☐ 363 Jerry Browne UER (No dot over i in first text line)	.05	.02
☐ 364 Tom Candiotti	.05	.02
☐ 365 Alex Cole	.05	.02
☐ 366 John Farrell UER (Born in Neptune, should be Monmouth)	.05	.02
☐ 367 Felix Fermin	.05	.02
☐ 368 Keith Hernandez	.10	.05
☐ 369 Brook Jacoby	.05	.02
☐ 370 Chris James	.05	.02
☐ 371 Dion James	.05	.02
☐ 372 Doug Jones	.05	.02
☐ 373 Candy Maldonado	.05	.02
☐ 374 Steve Olin	.05	.02
☐ 375 Jesse Orosco	.05	.02
☐ 376 Rudy Seanez	.05	.02
☐ 377 Joel Skinner	.05	.02
☐ 378 Cory Snyder	.05	.02
☐ 379 Greg Swindell	.05	.02
☐ 380 Sergio Valdez	.05	.02
☐ 381 Mike Walker	.05	.02
☐ 382 Colby Ward	.05	.02
☐ 383 Turner Ward	.05	.02
☐ 384 Mitch Webster	.05	.02
☐ 385 Kevin Wickander	.05	.02
☐ 386 Darrel Akerfelds	.05	.02
☐ 387 Joe Boever	.05	.02
☐ 388 Rod Booker	.05	.02
☐ 389 Sil Campusano	.05	.02
☐ 390 Don Carman	.05	.02
☐ 391 Wes Chamberlain	.05	.02
☐ 392 Pat Combs	.05	.02
☐ 393 Darren Daulton	.10	.05
☐ 394 Jose DeJesus	.05	.02
☐ 395A Len Dykstra Name spelled Lenny on back	.10	.05
☐ 395B Len Dykstra Name spelled Len on back	.10	.05
☐ 396 Jason Grimsley	.05	.02
☐ 397 Charlie Hayes	.05	.02
☐ 398 Von Hayes	.05	.02
☐ 399 David Hollins UER (Atl-bats, should say at-bats)	.05	.02
☐ 400 Ken Howell	.05	.02
☐ 401 Ricky Jordan	.05	.02
☐ 402 John Kruk	.10	.05
☐ 403 Steve Lake	.05	.02
☐ 404 Chuck Malone	.05	.02
☐ 405 Roger McDowell UER (Says Phillies is saves, should say in)	.05	.02
☐ 406 Chuck McElroy	.05	.02
☐ 407 Mickey Morandini	.05	.02
☐ 408 Terry Mulholland	.05	.02
☐ 409 Dale Murphy	.20	.09
☐ 410A Randy Ready ERR (No Brewers stats listed for 1983)	.05	.02
☐ 410B Randy Ready COR	.05	.02
☐ 411 Bruce Ruffin	.05	.02
☐ 412 Dickie Thon	.05	.02
☐ 413 Paul Assenmacher	.05	.02
☐ 414 Damon Berryhill	.05	.02
☐ 415 Mike Bielecki	.05	.02
☐ 416 Shawn Boskie	.05	.02
☐ 417 Dave Clark	.05	.02

☐ 418 Doug Dascenzo .05 .02
☐ 419A Andre Dawson ERR .20 .09
(No stats for 1976)
☐ 419B Andre Dawson COR .20 .09
☐ 420 Shawon Dunston .05 .02
☐ 421 Joe Girardi .10 .05
☐ 422 Mark Grace .20 .09
☐ 423 Mike Harkey .05 .02
☐ 424 Les Lancaster .05 .02
☐ 425 Bill Long .05 .02
☐ 426 Greg Maddux .60 .25
☐ 427 Derrick May .05 .02
☐ 428 Jeff Pico .05 .02
☐ 429 Domingo Ramos .05 .02
☐ 430 Luis Salazar .05 .02
☐ 431 Ryne Sandberg .25 .11
☐ 432 Dwight Smith .05 .02
☐ 433 Greg Smith .05 .02
☐ 434 Rick Sutcliffe .05 .02
☐ 435 Gary Varsho .05 .02
☐ 436 Hector Villanueva .05 .02
☐ 437 Jerome Walton .05 .02
☐ 438 Curtis Wilkerson .05 .02
☐ 439 Mitch Williams .05 .02
☐ 440 Steve Wilson .05 .02
☐ 441 Marvell Wynne .05 .02
☐ 442 Scott Bankhead .05 .02
☐ 443 Scott Bradley .05 .02
☐ 444 Greg Briley .05 .02
☐ 445 Mike Brumley UER .05 .02
(Text 40 SB's in 1988,
stats say 41)
☐ 446 Jay Buhner .20 .09
☐ 447 Dave Burba .05 .02
☐ 448 Henry Cotto .05 .02
☐ 449 Alvin Davis .05 .02
☐ 450 Ken Griffey Jr. 1.50 .70
(Bat around .300)
☐ 450A Ken Griffey Jr. 1.50 .70
(Bat .300)
☐ 451 Erik Hanson .05 .02
☐ 452 Gene Harris UER .05 .02
(63 career runs,
should be 73)
☐ 453 Brian Holman .05 .02
☐ 454 Mike Jackson .05 .02
☐ 455 Randy Johnson .25 .11
☐ 456 Jeffrey Leonard .05 .02
☐ 457 Edgar Martinez .20 .09
☐ 458 Tino Martinez .20 .09
☐ 459 Pete O'Brien UER .05 .02
(1987 BA .266,
should be .286)
☐ 460 Harold Reynolds .05 .02
☐ 461 Mike Schooler .05 .02
☐ 462 Bill Swift .05 .02
☐ 463 David Valle .05 .02
☐ 464 Omar Vizquel .20 .09
☐ 465 Matt Young .05 .02
☐ 466 Brady Anderson .20 .09
☐ 467 Jeff Ballard UER .05 .02
(Missing top of right
parenthesis after
Saberhagen in last
text line)
☐ 468 Juan Bell .05 .02
☐ 469A Mike Devereaux .10 .05
(First line of text
ends with six)
☐ 469B Mike Devereaux .10 .05
(First line of text
ends with runs)
☐ 470 Steve Finley .20 .09
☐ 471 Dave Gallagher .05 .02
☐ 472 Leo Gomez .05 .02
☐ 473 Rene Gonzales .05 .02
☐ 474 Pete Harnisch .05 .02
☐ 475 Kevin Hickey .05 .02
☐ 476 Chris Hoiles .05 .02
☐ 477 Sam Horn .05 .02
☐ 478 Tim Hulett .05 .02
(Photo shows National
Leaguer sliding into
second base)
☐ 479 Dave Johnson .05 .02
☐ 480 Ron Kittle UER .05 .02
(Edmonton misspelled
as Edmundton)
☐ 481 Ben McDonald .10 .05
☐ 482 Bob Melvin .05 .02
☐ 483 Bob Milacki .05 .02
☐ 484 Randy Milligan .05 .02
☐ 485 John Mitchell .05 .02
☐ 486 Gregg Olson .05 .02
☐ 487 Joe Orsulak .05 .02
☐ 488 Joe Price .05 .02
☐ 489 Bill Ripken .05 .02
☐ 490 Cal Ripken .75 .35
☐ 491 Curt Schilling .05 .02
☐ 492 David Segui .10 .05
☐ 493 Anthony Telford .05 .02
☐ 494 Mickey Tettleton .10 .05
☐ 495 Mark Williamson .05 .02
☐ 496 Craig Worthington .05 .02
☐ 497 Juan Agosto .05 .02
☐ 498 Eric Anthony .05 .02
☐ 499 Craig Biggio .20 .09
☐ 500 Ken Caminiti UER .20 .09
(Born 4/4, should
be 4/21)
☐ 501 Casey Candaele .05 .02
☐ 502 Andujar Cedeno .05 .02
☐ 503 Danny Darwin .05 .02
☐ 504 Mark Davidson .05 .02
☐ 505 Glenn Davis .05 .02
☐ 506 Jim Deshaies .05 .02
☐ 507 Luis Gonzalez .20 .09
☐ 508 Bill Gullickson .05 .02
☐ 509 Xavier Hernandez .05 .02
☐ 510 Brian Meyer .05 .02
☐ 511 Ken Oberkfell .05 .02
☐ 512 Mark Portugal .05 .02
☐ 513 Rafael Ramirez .05 .02
☐ 514 Karl Rhodes .05 .02
☐ 515 Mike Scott .05 .02
☐ 516 Mike Simms .05 .02
☐ 517 Dave Smith .05 .02
☐ 518 Franklin Stubbs .05 .02
☐ 519 Glenn Wilson .05 .02
☐ 520 Eric Yelding UER .05 .02
(Text has 63 steals,
stats have 64,
which is correct)
☐ 521 Gerald Young .05 .02
☐ 522 Shawn Abner .05 .02
☐ 523 Roberto Alomar .20 .09
☐ 524 Andy Benes .10 .05
☐ 525 Joe Carter .20 .09
☐ 526 Jack Clark .10 .05
☐ 527 Joey Cora .20 .09
☐ 528 Paul Faries .05 .02
☐ 529 Tony Gwynn .50 .23
☐ 530 Atlee Hammaker .05 .02
☐ 531 Greg W. Harris .05 .02
☐ 532 Thomas Howard .05 .02
☐ 533 Bruce Hurst .05 .02
☐ 534 Craig Lefferts .05 .02
☐ 535 Derek Lilliquist .05 .02
☐ 536 Fred Lynn .05 .02
☐ 537 Mike Pagliarulo .05 .02
☐ 538 Mark Parent .05 .02
☐ 539 Dennis Rasmussen .05 .02
☐ 540 Bip Roberts .05 .02
☐ 541 Richard Rodriguez .05 .02
☐ 542 Benito Santiago .05 .02
☐ 543 Calvin Schiraldi .05 .02
☐ 544 Eric Show .05 .02
☐ 545 Phil Stephenson .05 .02
☐ 546 Garry Templeton UER .05 .02
(Born 3/24/57,
should be 3/24/56)
☐ 547 Ed Whitson .05 .02
☐ 548 Eddie Williams .05 .02
☐ 549 Kevin Appier .20 .09
☐ 550 Luis Aquino .05 .02
☐ 551 Bob Boone .10 .05
☐ 552 George Brett .40 .18
☐ 553 Jeff Conine .25 .11
☐ 554 Steve Crawford .05 .02
☐ 555 Mark Davis .05 .02
☐ 556 Storm Davis .05 .02
☐ 557 Jim Eisenreich .10 .05
☐ 558 Steve Farr .05 .02
☐ 559 Tom Gordon .05 .02
☐ 560 Mark Gubicza .05 .02
☐ 561 Bo Jackson .20 .09
☐ 562 Mike Macfarlane .05 .02
☐ 563 Brian McRae .25 .11
☐ 564 Jeff Montgomery .10 .05
☐ 565 Bill Pecota .05 .02
☐ 566 Gerald Perry .05 .02
☐ 567 Bret Saberhagen .05 .02
☐ 568 Jeff Schulz .05 .02
☐ 569 Kevin Seitzer .05 .02
☐ 570 Terry Shumpert .05 .02
☐ 571 Kurt Stillwell .05 .02
☐ 572 Danny Tartabull .05 .02
☐ 573 Gary Thurman .05 .02
☐ 574 Frank White .10 .05
☐ 575 Willie Wilson .05 .02
☐ 576 Chris Bosio .05 .02
☐ 577 Greg Brock .05 .02
☐ 578 George Canale .05 .02
☐ 579 Chuck Crim .05 .02
☐ 580 Rob Deer .05 .02
☐ 581 Edgar Diaz .05 .02
☐ 582 Tom Edens .05 .02
☐ 583 Mike Felder .05 .02
☐ 584 Jim Gantner .05 .02
☐ 585 Darryl Hamilton .05 .02
☐ 586 Ted Higuera .05 .02
☐ 587 Mark Knudson .05 .02
☐ 588 Bill Krueger .05 .02
☐ 589 Tim McIntosh .05 .02
☐ 590 Paul Mirabella .05 .02
☐ 591 Paul Molitor .20 .09
☐ 592 Jaime Navarro .05 .02
☐ 593 Dave Parker .10 .05
☐ 594 Dan Plesac .05 .02
☐ 595 Ron Robinson .05 .02
☐ 596 Gary Sheffield .20 .09
☐ 597 Bill Spiers .05 .02
☐ 598 B.J. Surhoff .10 .05
☐ 599 Greg Vaughn .05 .02
☐ 600 Randy Veres .05 .02
☐ 601 Robin Yount .20 .09
☐ 602 Rick Aguilera .10 .05
☐ 603 Allan Anderson .05 .02
☐ 604 Juan Berenguer .05 .02
☐ 605 Randy Bush .05 .02
☐ 606 Carmen Castillo .05 .02
☐ 607 Tim Drummond .05 .02
☐ 608 Scott Erickson .05 .02
☐ 609 Gary Gaetti .10 .05
☐ 610 Greg Gagne .05 .02
☐ 611 Dan Gladden .05 .02
☐ 612 Mark Guthrie .05 .02
☐ 613 Brian Harper .05 .02
☐ 614 Kent Hrbek .10 .05
☐ 615 Gene Larkin .05 .02
☐ 616 Terry Leach .05 .02
☐ 617 Nelson Liriano .05 .02
☐ 618 Shane Mack .05 .02
☐ 619 John Moses .05 .02
☐ 620 Pedro Munoz .05 .02
☐ 621 Al Newman .05 .02
☐ 622 Junior Ortiz .05 .02
☐ 623 Kirby Puckett .40 .18
☐ 624 Roy Smith .05 .02
☐ 625 Kevin Tapani .05 .02
☐ 626 Gary Wayne .05 .02
☐ 627 David West .05 .02
☐ 628 Cris Carpenter .05 .02
☐ 629 Vince Coleman .05 .02
☐ 630 Ken Dayley .05 .02
☐ 631A Jose DeLeon ERR .05 .02
(missing '79 Bradenton stats)
☐ 631B Jose DeLeon COR .05 .02
(with '79 Bradenton stats)
☐ 632 Frank DiPino .05 .02
☐ 633 Bernard Gilkey .05 .02
☐ 634A Pedro Guerrero ERR .10 .05
(career SB shown as "$91")
☐ 634B Pedro Guerrero COR .10 .05
☐ 635 Ken Hill .10 .05
☐ 636 Felix Jose .05 .02
☐ 637 Ray Lankford .10 .05
☐ 638 Joe Magrane .05 .02
☐ 639 Tom Niedenfuer .05 .02
☐ 640 Jose Oquendo .05 .02
☐ 641 Tom Pagnozzi .05 .02
☐ 642 Terry Pendleton .10 .05
☐ 643 Mike Perez .05 .02
☐ 644 Bryn Smith .05 .02
☐ 645 Lee Smith .20 .09
☐ 646 Ozzie Smith .25 .11
☐ 647 Scott Terry .05 .02
☐ 648 Bob Tewksbury .05 .02
☐ 649 Milt Thompson .05 .02
☐ 650 John Tudor .05 .02
☐ 651 Denny Walling .05 .02
☐ 652 Craig Wilson .05 .02
☐ 653 Todd Worrell .05 .02
☐ 654 Todd Zeile .10 .05
☐ 655 Oscar Azocar .05 .02
☐ 656 Steve Balboni UER .05 .02
(Born 1/5/57,
should be 1/16)
☐ 657 Jesse Barfield .05 .02
☐ 658 Greg Cadaret .05 .02
☐ 659 Chuck Cary .05 .02
☐ 660 Rick Cerone .05 .02
☐ 661 Dave Eiland .05 .02
☐ 662 Alvaro Espinoza .05 .02
☐ 663 Bob Geren .05 .02
☐ 664 Lee Guetterman .05 .02
☐ 665 Mel Hall .05 .02
☐ 666 Andy Hawkins .05 .02
☐ 667 Jimmy Jones .05 .02
☐ 668 Roberto Kelly .05 .02
☐ 669 Dave LaPoint UER .05 .02

		MINT	NRMT
	(No '81 Brewers stats, totals also are wrong)		
☐ 670	Tim Leary	.05	.02
☐ 671	Jim Leyritz	.10	.05
☐ 672	Kevin Maas	.05	.02
☐ 673	Don Mattingly	.30	.14
☐ 674	Matt Nokes	.05	.02
☐ 675	Pascual Perez	.05	.02
☐ 676	Eric Plunk	.05	.02
☐ 677	Dave Righetti	.05	.02
☐ 678	Jeff D. Robinson	.05	.02
☐ 679	Steve Sax	.05	.02
☐ 680	Mike Witt	.05	.02
☐ 681	Steve Avery UER (Born in New Jersey, should say Michigan)	.10	.05
☐ 682	Mike Bell	.05	.02
☐ 683	Jeff Blauser	.05	.02
☐ 684	Francisco Cabrera UER (Born 10/16, should say 10/10)	.05	.02
☐ 685	Tony Castillo	.05	.02
☐ 686	Marty Clary UER (Shown pitching righty, but bio has left)	.05	.02
☐ 687	Nick Esasky	.05	.02
☐ 688	Ron Gant	.10	.05
☐ 689	Tom Glavine	.20	.09
☐ 690	Mark Grant	.05	.02
☐ 691	Tommy Gregg	.05	.02
☐ 692	Dwayne Henry	.05	.02
☐ 693	Dave Justice	.25	.11
☐ 694	Jimmy Kremers	.05	.02
☐ 695	Charlie Leibrandt	.05	.02
☐ 696	Mark Lemke	.05	.02
☐ 697	Oddibe McDowell	.05	.02
☐ 698	Greg Olson	.05	.02
☐ 699	Jeff Parrett	.05	.02
☐ 700	Jim Presley	.05	.02
☐ 701	Victor Rosario	.05	.02
☐ 702	Lonnie Smith	.05	.02
☐ 703	Pete Smith	.05	.02
☐ 704	John Smoltz	.20	.09
☐ 705	Mike Stanton	.05	.02
☐ 706	Andres Thomas	.05	.02
☐ 707	Jeff Treadway	.05	.02
☐ 708	Jim Vatcher	.05	.02
☐ 709	Ryne Sandberg Cecil Fielder Home Run Kings	.20	.09
☐ 710	Barry Bonds Ken Griffey Jr. 2nd Generation Stars	.50	.23
☐ 711	Bobby Bonilla Barry Larkin NLCS Team Leaders	.20	.09
☐ 712	Bobby Thigpen John Franco Top Game Savers	.05	.02
☐ 713	Chicago's 100 Club Andre Dawson Ryne Sandberg UER (Ryno misspelled Rhino)	.10	.05
☐ 714	CL:A's/Pirates Reds/Red Sox	.05	.02
☐ 715	CL:White Sox/Mets Blue Jays/Dodgers	.05	.02
☐ 716	CL:Expos/Giants Rangers/Angels	.05	.02
☐ 717	CL:Tigers/Indians Phillies/Cubs	.05	.02
☐ 718	CL:Mariners/Orioles Astros/Padres	.05	.02
☐ 719	CL:Royals/Brewers Twins/Cardinals	.05	.02
☐ 720	CL:Yankees/Braves Superstars/Specials	.05	.02

1991 Fleer All-Stars

For the sixth consecutive year Fleer issued an All-Star insert set. This year the cards were only available as random inserts in Fleer cello packs. This ten-card standard-size set is reminiscent of the 1971 Topps Greatest Moments set with two pictures on the (black-bordered) front as well as a photo on the back.

	MINT	NRMT
COMPLETE SET (10)	15.00	6.75
COMMON CARD (1-10)	.50	.23
☐ 1 Ryne Sandberg	2.00	.90
☐ 2 Barry Larkin	1.00	.45
☐ 3 Matt Williams	1.00	.45
☐ 4 Cecil Fielder	.75	.35
☐ 5 Barry Bonds	2.00	.90
☐ 6 Rickey Henderson	1.50	.70
☐ 7 Ken Griffey Jr.	10.00	4.50
☐ 8 Jose Canseco	1.00	.45
☐ 9 Benito Santiago	.50	.23
☐ 10 Roger Clemens	1.50	.70

1991 Fleer Pro-Visions

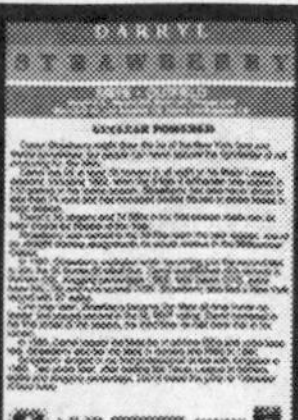

This 12-card standard-size insert set features paintings by artist Terry Smith framed by distinctive black borders on each card front. The cards were randomly inserted in wax and rack packs. An additional four-card set was issued only in 1991 Fleer factory sets. Those cards are numbered F1-F4. Unlike the 12 cards inserted in packs, these factory set cards feature white borders on front.

	MINT	NRMT
COMPLETE REG.SET (12)	4.00	1.80
COMP.FACT.SET (4)	2.00	.90
COMMON REG.CARD (R1-R12)	.20	.09
COMMON FACT.CARD (F1-F4)	.25	.11
☐ 1 Kirby Puckett UER (.326 average, should be .328)	1.25	.55
☐ 2 Will Clark UER (On tenth line, pennant misspelled pennent)	.50	.23
☐ 3 Ruben Sierra UER (No apostrophe in hasn't)	.20	.09
☐ 4 Mark McGwire UER (Fisk won ROY in '72, not '82)	1.00	.45
☐ 5 Bo Jackson (Bio says 6', others have him at 6'1~)	.30	.14
☐ 6 Jose Canseco UER (Bio 6'3~, 230, text has 6'4~, 240)	.50	.23
☐ 7 Dwight Gooden UER (2.80 ERA in Lynchburg, should be 2.50)	.30	.14
☐ 8 Mike Greenwell UER (.328 BA and 87 RBI, should be .325 and 95)	.20	.09
☐ 9 Roger Clemens	.75	.35
☐ 10 Eric Davis	.30	.14
☐ 11 Don Mattingly	1.00	.45
☐ 12 Darryl Strawberry	.30	.14
☐ F1 Barry Bonds	.75	.35
☐ F2 Rickey Henderson	.50	.23
☐ F3 Ryne Sandberg	.75	.35
☐ F4 Dave Stewart	.25	.11

1991 Fleer Wax Box Cards

These cards were issued on the bottom of 1991 Fleer wax boxes. This set celebrated the spate of no-hitters in 1990 and were printed on three different boxes. These standard size cards, come four to a box, three about the no-hitters and one team logo card on each box. The cards are blank backed and are numbered on the front in a subtle way. They are ordered below as they are numbered, which is by chronological order of their no-hitters. Only the player cards are listed below since there was a different team logo card on each box.

	MINT	NRMT
COMPLETE SET (9)	3.50	1.55
COMMON CARD (1-9)	.15	.07

	MINT	NRMT
☐ 1 Mark Langston and Mike Witt	.15	.07
☐ 2 Randy Johnson	.50	.23
☐ 3 Nolan Ryan	2.00	.90
☐ 4 Dave Stewart	.25	.11
☐ 5 Fernando Valenzuela	.25	.11
☐ 6 Andy Hawkins	.15	.07
☐ 7 Melido Perez	.15	.07
☐ 8 Terry Mulholland	.15	.07
☐ 9 Dave Stieb	.15	.07

1991 Fleer World Series

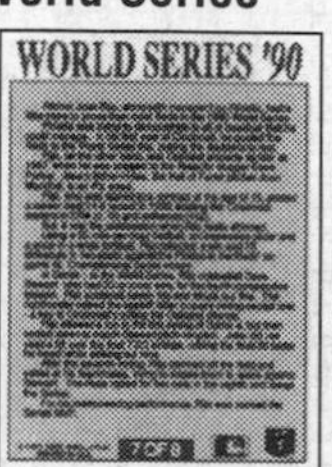

This eight-card set captures highlights from the 1990 World Series between the Cincinnati Reds and the Oakland Athletics. The set was only available as an insert with the 1991 Fleer factory sets. The standard-size cards have on the fronts color action photos, bordered in blue on a white card face. The words "World Series '90" appears in red and blue lettering above the pictures. The backs have a similar design, only with a summary of an aspect of the Series on a yellow background.

	MINT	NRMT
COMPLETE SET (8)	1.00	.45
COMMON CARD (1-8)	.10	.05
☐ 1 Eric Davis	.25	.11
☐ 2 Billy Hatcher	.10	.05
☐ 3 Jose Canseco	.50	.23
☐ 4 Rickey Henderson	.50	.23
☐ 5 Chris Sabo	.10	.05
☐ 6 Dave Stewart	.25	.11
☐ 7 Jose Rijo	.10	.05
☐ 8 Reds Celebrate	.25	.11

1991 Fleer Update

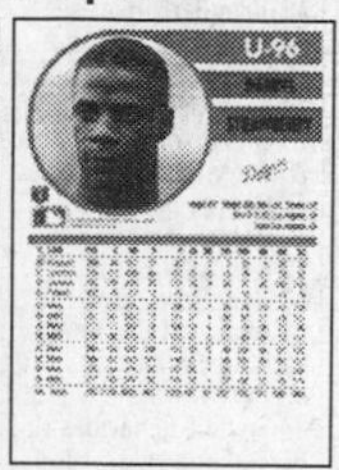

The 1991 Fleer Update set contains 132 standard-size cards. The cards were distributed exclusively in factory set form through hobby dealers. Card design is identical to regular issue 1991 Fleer cards except for the U-prefixed numbering on back. The cards are ordered alphabetically by team. The key Rookie Cards in this set are Jeff Bagwell and Ivan Rodriguez.

	MINT	NRMT
COMPLETE SET (132)	4.00	1.80
COMMON CARD (1-132)	.05	.02
☐ 1 Glenn Davis	.05	.02
☐ 2 Dwight Evans	.10	.05
☐ 3 Jose Mesa	.10	.05
☐ 4 Jack Clark	.10	.05

☐ 5 Danny Darwin	.05	.02
☐ 6 Steve Lyons	.05	.02
☐ 7 Mo Vaughn	.40	.18
☐ 8 Floyd Bannister	.05	.02
☐ 9 Gary Gaetti	.10	.05
☐ 10 Dave Parker	.10	.05
☐ 11 Joey Cora	.10	.05
☐ 12 Charlie Hough	.05	.02
☐ 13 Matt Merullo	.05	.02
☐ 14 Warren Newson	.05	.02
☐ 15 Tim Raines	.10	.05
☐ 16 Albert Belle	.30	.14
☐ 17 Glenallen Hill	.05	.02
☐ 18 Shawn Hillegas	.05	.02
☐ 19 Mark Lewis	.05	.02
☐ 20 Charles Nagy	.20	.09
☐ 21 Mark Whiten	.05	.02
☐ 22 John Cerutti	.05	.02
☐ 23 Rob Deer	.05	.02
☐ 24 Mickey Tettleton	.10	.05
☐ 25 Warren Cromartie	.05	.02
☐ 26 Kirk Gibson	.10	.05
☐ 27 David Howard	.05	.02
☐ 28 Brent Mayne	.05	.02
☐ 29 Dante Bichette	.20	.09
☐ 30 Mark Lee	.05	.02
☐ 31 Julio Machado	.05	.02
☐ 32 Edwin Nunez	.05	.02
☐ 33 Willie Randolph	.10	.05
☐ 34 Franklin Stubbs	.05	.02
☐ 35 Bill Wegman	.05	.02
☐ 36 Chili Davis	.10	.05
☐ 37 Chuck Knoblauch	.25	.11
☐ 38 Scott Leius	.05	.02
☐ 39 Jack Morris	.10	.05
☐ 40 Mike Pagliarulo	.05	.02
☐ 41 Lenny Webster	.05	.02
☐ 42 John Habyan	.05	.02
☐ 43 Steve Howe	.05	.02
☐ 44 Jeff Johnson	.05	.02
☐ 45 Scott Kamieniecki	.05	.02
☐ 46 Pat Kelly	.10	.05
☐ 47 Hensley Meulens	.05	.02
☐ 48 Wade Taylor	.05	.02
☐ 49 Bernie Williams	.25	.11
☐ 50 Kirk Dressendorfer	.05	.02
☐ 51 Ernest Riles	.05	.02
☐ 52 Rich DeLucia	.05	.02
☐ 53 Tracy Jones	.05	.02
☐ 54 Bill Krueger	.05	.02
☐ 55 Alonzo Powell	.05	.02
☐ 56 Jeff Schaefer	.05	.02
☐ 57 Russ Swan	.05	.02
☐ 58 John Barfield	.05	.02
☐ 59 Rich Gossage	.10	.05
☐ 60 Jose Guzman	.05	.02
☐ 61 Dean Palmer	.10	.05
☐ 62 Ivan Rodriguez	1.50	.70
☐ 63 Roberto Alomar	.20	.09
☐ 64 Tom Candiotti	.05	.02
☐ 65 Joe Carter	.10	.05
☐ 66 Ed Sprague	.05	.02
☐ 67 Pat Tabler	.05	.02
☐ 68 Mike Timlin	.05	.02
☐ 69 Devon White	.05	.02
☐ 70 Rafael Belliard	.05	.02
☐ 71 Juan Berenguer	.05	.02
☐ 72 Sid Bream	.05	.02
☐ 73 Marvin Freeman	.05	.02
☐ 74 Kent Mercker	.05	.02
☐ 75 Otis Nixon	.05	.02
☐ 76 Terry Pendleton	.10	.05
☐ 77 George Bell	.05	.02
☐ 78 Danny Jackson	.05	.02
☐ 79 Chuck McElroy	.05	.02
☐ 80 Gary Scott	.05	.02
☐ 81 Heathcliff Slocumb	.20	.09
☐ 82 Dave Smith	.05	.02
☐ 83 Rick Wilkins	.05	.02
☐ 84 Freddie Benavides	.05	.02
☐ 85 Ted Power	.05	.02
☐ 86 Mo Sanford	.05	.02
☐ 87 Jeff Bagwell	2.50	1.10
☐ 88 Steve Finley	.10	.05
☐ 89 Pete Harnisch	.05	.02
☐ 90 Darryl Kile	.20	.09
☐ 91 Brett Butler	.10	.05
☐ 92 John Candelaria	.05	.02
☐ 93 Gary Carter	.20	.09
☐ 94 Kevin Gross	.05	.02
☐ 95 Bob Ojeda	.05	.02
☐ 96 Darryl Strawberry	.10	.05
☐ 97 Ivan Calderon	.05	.02
☐ 98 Ron Hassey	.05	.02
☐ 99 Gilberto Reyes	.05	.02
☐ 100 Hubie Brooks	.05	.02
☐ 101 Rick Cerone	.05	.02
☐ 102 Vince Coleman	.05	.02
☐ 103 Jeff Innis	.05	.02
☐ 104 Pete Schourek	.10	.05
☐ 105 Andy Ashby	.20	.09
☐ 106 Wally Backman	.05	.02
☐ 107 Darrin Fletcher	.05	.02
☐ 108 Tommy Greene	.05	.02
☐ 109 John Morris	.05	.02
☐ 110 Mitch Williams	.05	.02
☐ 111 Lloyd McClendon	.05	.02
☐ 112 Orlando Merced	.10	.05
☐ 113 Vicente Palacios	.05	.02
☐ 114 Gary Varsho	.05	.02
☐ 115 John Wehner	.05	.02
☐ 116 Rex Hudler	.05	.02
☐ 117 Tim Jones	.05	.02
☐ 118 Geronimo Pena	.05	.02
☐ 119 Gerald Perry	.05	.02
☐ 120 Larry Andersen	.05	.02
☐ 121 Jerald Clark	.05	.02
☐ 122 Scott Coolbaugh	.05	.02
☐ 123 Tony Fernandez	.05	.02
☐ 124 Darrin Jackson	.05	.02
☐ 125 Fred McGriff	.20	.09
☐ 126 Jose Mota	.05	.02
☐ 127 Tim Teufel	.05	.02
☐ 128 Bud Black	.05	.02
☐ 129 Mike Felder	.05	.02
☐ 130 Willie McGee	.05	.02
☐ 131 Dave Righetti	.05	.02
☐ 132 Checklist U1-U132	.05	.02

1992 Fleer

The 1992 Fleer set contains 720 standard-size cards issued in one comprehensive series. The cards were distributed in plastic wrapped packs, 35-card cello packs, 42-card rack packs and factory sets. The card fronts shade from metallic pale green to white as one moves down the face. The team logo and player's name appear to the right of the picture, running the length of the card. The cards are ordered alphabetically within and according to teams for each league with AL preceding NL. Topical subsets feature Major League Prospects (652-680), Record Setters (681-687), League Leaders (688-697), Super Star Specials (698-707) and Pro Visions (708-713). The only notable Rookie Card features Vinny Castilla.

	MINT	NRMT
COMPLETE SET (720)	10.00	4.50
COMP.HOBBY SET (732)	20.00	9.00
COMP.RETAIL SET (732)	20.00	9.00
COMMON CARD (1-720)	.05	.02

	MINT	NRMT
☐ 1 Brady Anderson	.05	.02
☐ 2 Jose Bautista	.05	.02
☐ 3 Juan Bell	.05	.02
☐ 4 Glenn Davis	.05	.02
☐ 5 Mike Devereaux	.05	.02
☐ 6 Dwight Evans	.10	.05
☐ 7 Mike Flanagan	.05	.02
☐ 8 Leo Gomez	.05	.02
☐ 9 Chris Hoiles	.05	.02
☐ 10 Sam Horn	.05	.02
☐ 11 Tim Hulett	.05	.02
☐ 12 Dave Johnson	.05	.02
☐ 13 Chito Martinez	.05	.02
☐ 14 Ben McDonald	.05	.02
☐ 15 Bob Melvin	.05	.02
☐ 16 Luis Mercedes	.05	.02
☐ 17 Jose Mesa	.10	.05
☐ 18 Bob Milacki	.05	.02
☐ 19 Randy Milligan	.05	.02
☐ 20 Mike Mussina UER (Card back refers to him as Jeff)	.30	.14
☐ 21 Gregg Olson	.05	.02
☐ 22 Joe Orsulak	.05	.02
☐ 23 Jim Poole	.05	.02
☐ 24 Arthur Rhodes	.05	.02
☐ 25 Billy Ripken	.05	.02
☐ 26 Cal Ripken	.75	.35
☐ 27 David Segui	.05	.02
☐ 28 Roy Smith	.05	.02
☐ 29 Anthony Telford	.05	.02
☐ 30 Mark Williamson	.05	.02
☐ 31 Craig Worthington	.05	.02
☐ 32 Wade Boggs	.20	.09
☐ 33 Tom Bolton	.05	.02
☐ 34 Tom Brunansky	.05	.02
☐ 35 Ellis Burks	.10	.05
☐ 36 Jack Clark	.10	.05
☐ 37 Roger Clemens	.40	.18
☐ 38 Danny Darwin	.05	.02
☐ 39 Mike Greenwell	.05	.02
☐ 40 Joe Hesketh	.05	.02
☐ 41 Daryl Irvine	.05	.02
☐ 42 Dennis Lamp	.05	.02
☐ 43 Tony Pena	.05	.02
☐ 44 Phil Plantier	.05	.02
☐ 45 Carlos Quintana	.05	.02
☐ 46 Jeff Reardon	.10	.05
☐ 47 Jody Reed	.05	.02
☐ 48 Luis Rivera	.05	.02
☐ 49 Mo Vaughn	.30	.14
☐ 50 Jim Abbott	.05	.02
☐ 51 Kyle Abbott	.05	.02
☐ 52 Ruben Amaro Jr.	.05	.02
☐ 53 Scott Bailes	.05	.02
☐ 54 Chris Beasley	.05	.02
☐ 55 Mark Eichhorn	.05	.02
☐ 56 Mike Fetters	.05	.02
☐ 57 Chuck Finley	.05	.02
☐ 58 Gary Gaetti	.10	.05
☐ 59 Dave Gallagher	.05	.02
☐ 60 Donnie Hill	.05	.02
☐ 61 Bryan Harvey UER (Lee Smith led the Majors with 47 saves)	.05	.02
☐ 62 Wally Joyner	.10	.05
☐ 63 Mark Langston	.05	.02
☐ 64 Kirk McCaskill	.05	.02
☐ 65 John Orton	.05	.02
☐ 66 Lance Parrish	.05	.02
☐ 67 Luis Polonia	.05	.02
☐ 68 Bobby Rose	.05	.02
☐ 69 Dick Schofield	.05	.02
☐ 70 Luis Sojo	.05	.02
☐ 71 Lee Stevens	.05	.02
☐ 72 Dave Winfield	.05	.02
☐ 73 Cliff Young	.05	.02
☐ 74 Wilson Alvarez	.10	.05
☐ 75 Esteban Beltre	.05	.02
☐ 76 Joey Cora	.10	.05
☐ 77 Brian Drahman	.05	.02
☐ 78 Alex Fernandez	.10	.05
☐ 79 Carlton Fisk	.20	.09
☐ 80 Scott Fletcher	.05	.02
☐ 81 Craig Grebeck	.05	.02
☐ 82 Ozzie Guillen	.05	.02
☐ 83 Greg Hibbard	.05	.02
☐ 84 Charlie Hough	.05	.02
☐ 85 Mike Huff	.05	.02
☐ 86 Bo Jackson	.10	.05
☐ 87 Lance Johnson	.05	.02
☐ 88 Ron Karkovice	.05	.02
☐ 89 Jack McDowell	.05	.02
☐ 90 Matt Merullo	.05	.02
☐ 91 Warren Newson	.05	.02
☐ 92 Donn Pall UER (Called Dunn on card back)	.05	.02
☐ 93 Dan Pasqua	.05	.02
☐ 94 Ken Patterson	.05	.02
☐ 95 Melido Perez	.05	.02
☐ 96 Scott Radinsky	.05	.02
☐ 97 Tim Raines	.10	.05
☐ 98 Sammy Sosa	.20	.09
☐ 99 Bobby Thigpen	.05	.02
☐ 100 Frank Thomas	1.00	.45
☐ 101 Robin Ventura	.10	.05
☐ 102 Mike Aldrete	.05	.02
☐ 103 Sandy Alomar Jr.	.05	.02
☐ 104 Carlos Baerga	.10	.05
☐ 105 Albert Belle	.25	.11
☐ 106 Willie Blair	.05	.02
☐ 107 Jerry Browne	.05	.02
☐ 108 Alex Cole	.05	.02
☐ 109 Felix Fermin	.05	.02
☐ 110 Glenallen Hill	.05	.02
☐ 111 Shawn Hillegas	.05	.02
☐ 112 Chris James	.05	.02
☐ 113 Reggie Jefferson	.05	.02
☐ 114 Doug Jones	.05	.02
☐ 115 Eric King	.05	.02
☐ 116 Mark Lewis	.05	.02
☐ 117 Carlos Martinez	.05	.02
☐ 118 Charles Nagy UER (Throws right, but	.10	.05

card says left)		
☐ 119 Rod Nichols	.05	.02
☐ 120 Steve Olin	.05	.02
☐ 121 Jesse Orosco	.05	.02
☐ 122 Rudy Seanez	.05	.02
☐ 123 Joel Skinner	.05	.02
☐ 124 Greg Swindell	.05	.02
☐ 125 Jim Thome	.60	.25
☐ 126 Mark Whiten	.05	.02
☐ 127 Scott Aldred	.05	.02
☐ 128 Andy Allanson	.05	.02
☐ 129 John Cerutti	.05	.02
☐ 130 Milt Cuyler	.05	.02
☐ 131 Mike Dalton	.05	.02
☐ 132 Rob Deer	.05	.02
☐ 133 Cecil Fielder	.10	.05
☐ 134 Travis Fryman	.10	.05
☐ 135 Dan Gakeler	.05	.02
☐ 136 Paul Gibson	.05	.02
☐ 137 Bill Gullickson	.05	.02
☐ 138 Mike Henneman	.05	.02
☐ 139 Pete Incaviglia	.05	.02
☐ 140 Mark Leiter	.05	.02
☐ 141 Scott Livingstone	.05	.02
☐ 142 Lloyd Moseby	.05	.02
☐ 143 Tony Phillips	.05	.02
☐ 144 Mark Salas	.05	.02
☐ 145 Frank Tanana	.05	.02
☐ 146 Walt Terrell	.05	.02
☐ 147 Mickey Tettleton	.05	.02
☐ 148 Alan Trammell	.05	.02
☐ 149 Lou Whitaker	.10	.05
☐ 150 Kevin Appier	.10	.05
☐ 151 Luis Aquino	.05	.02
☐ 152 Todd Benzinger	.05	.02
☐ 153 Mike Boddicker	.05	.02
☐ 154 George Brett	.40	.18
☐ 155 Storm Davis	.05	.02
☐ 156 Jim Eisenreich	.10	.05
☐ 157 Kirk Gibson	.10	.05
☐ 158 Tom Gordon	.05	.02
☐ 159 Mark Gubicza	.05	.02
☐ 160 David Howard	.05	.02
☐ 161 Mike Macfarlane	.05	.02
☐ 162 Brent Mayne	.05	.02
☐ 163 Brian McRae	.05	.02
☐ 164 Jeff Montgomery	.10	.05
☐ 165 Bill Pecota	.05	.02
☐ 166 Harvey Pulliam	.05	.02
☐ 167 Bret Saberhagen	.05	.02
☐ 168 Kevin Seitzer	.05	.02
☐ 169 Terry Shumpert	.05	.02
☐ 170 Kurt Stillwell	.05	.02
☐ 171 Danny Tartabull	.05	.02
☐ 172 Gary Thurman	.05	.02
☐ 173 Dante Bichette	.05	.02
☐ 174 Kevin D. Brown	.05	.02
☐ 175 Chuck Crim	.05	.02
☐ 176 Jim Gantner	.05	.02
☐ 177 Darryl Hamilton	.05	.02
☐ 178 Ted Higuera	.05	.02
☐ 179 Darren Holmes	.05	.02
☐ 180 Mark Lee	.05	.02
☐ 181 Julio Machado	.05	.02
☐ 182 Paul Molitor	.20	.09
☐ 183 Jaime Navarro	.05	.02
☐ 184 Edwin Nunez	.05	.02
☐ 185 Dan Plesac	.05	.02
☐ 186 Willie Randolph	.10	.05
☐ 187 Ron Robinson	.05	.02
☐ 188 Gary Sheffield	.20	.09
☐ 189 Bill Spiers	.05	.02
☐ 190 B.J. Surhoff	.10	.05
☐ 191 Dale Sveum	.05	.02
☐ 192 Greg Vaughn	.05	.02
☐ 193 Bill Wegman	.05	.02
☐ 194 Robin Yount	.05	.02
☐ 195 Rick Aguilera	.05	.02
☐ 196 Allan Anderson	.05	.02
☐ 197 Steve Bedrosian	.05	.02
☐ 198 Randy Bush	.05	.02
☐ 199 Larry Casian	.05	.02
☐ 200 Chili Davis	.10	.05
☐ 201 Scott Erickson	.10	.05
☐ 202 Greg Gagne	.05	.02
☐ 203 Dan Gladden	.05	.02
☐ 204 Brian Harper	.05	.02
☐ 205 Kent Hrbek	.10	.05
☐ 206 Chuck Knoblauch UER (Career hit total of 59 is wrong)	.20	.09
☐ 207 Gene Larkin	.05	.02
☐ 208 Terry Leach	.05	.02
☐ 209 Scott Leius	.05	.02
☐ 210 Shane Mack	.05	.02
☐ 211 Jack Morris	.10	.05
☐ 212 Pedro Munoz	.05	.02
☐ 213 Denny Neagle	.05	.02
☐ 214 Al Newman	.05	.02
☐ 215 Junior Ortiz	.05	.02
☐ 216 Mike Pagliarulo	.05	.02
☐ 217 Kirby Puckett	.40	.18
☐ 218 Paul Sorrento	.05	.02
☐ 219 Kevin Tapani	.05	.02
☐ 220 Lenny Webster	.05	.02
☐ 221 Jesse Barfield	.05	.02
☐ 222 Greg Cadaret	.05	.02
☐ 223 Dave Eiland	.05	.02
☐ 224 Alvaro Espinoza	.05	.02
☐ 225 Steve Farr	.05	.02
☐ 226 Bob Geren	.05	.02
☐ 227 Lee Guetterman	.05	.02
☐ 228 John Habyan	.05	.02
☐ 229 Mel Hall	.05	.02
☐ 230 Steve Howe	.05	.02
☐ 231 Mike Humphreys	.05	.02
☐ 232 Scott Kamieniecki	.05	.02
☐ 233 Pat Kelly	.05	.02
☐ 234 Roberto Kelly	.05	.02
☐ 235 Tim Leary	.05	.02
☐ 236 Kevin Maas	.05	.02
☐ 237 Don Mattingly	.30	.14
☐ 238 Hensley Meulens	.05	.02
☐ 239 Matt Nokes	.05	.02
☐ 240 Pascual Perez	.05	.02
☐ 241 Eric Plunk	.05	.02
☐ 242 John Ramos	.05	.02
☐ 243 Scott Sanderson	.05	.02
☐ 244 Steve Sax	.05	.02
☐ 245 Wade Taylor	.05	.02
☐ 246 Randy Velarde	.05	.02
☐ 247 Bernie Williams	.20	.09
☐ 248 Troy Afenir	.05	.02
☐ 249 Harold Baines	.10	.05
☐ 250 Lance Blankenship	.05	.02
☐ 251 Mike Bordick	.05	.02
☐ 252 Jose Canseco	.05	.02
☐ 253 Steve Chitren	.05	.02
☐ 254 Ron Darling	.05	.02
☐ 255 Dennis Eckersley	.20	.09
☐ 256 Mike Gallego	.05	.02
☐ 257 Dave Henderson	.05	.02
☐ 258 Rickey Henderson UER (Wearing 24 on front and 22 on back)	.05	.02
☐ 259 Rick Honeycutt	.05	.02
☐ 260 Brook Jacoby	.05	.02
☐ 261 Carney Lansford	.10	.05
☐ 262 Mark McGwire	.40	.18
☐ 263 Mike Moore	.05	.02
☐ 264 Gene Nelson	.05	.02
☐ 265 Jamie Quirk	.05	.02
☐ 266 Joe Slusarski	.05	.02
☐ 267 Terry Steinbach	.10	.05
☐ 268 Dave Stewart	.10	.05
☐ 269 Todd Van Poppel	.05	.02
☐ 270 Walt Weiss	.05	.02
☐ 271 Bob Welch	.05	.02
☐ 272 Curt Young	.05	.02
☐ 273 Scott Bradley	.05	.02
☐ 274 Greg Briley	.05	.02
☐ 275 Jay Buhner	.05	.02
☐ 276 Henry Cotto	.05	.02
☐ 277 Alvin Davis	.05	.02
☐ 278 Rich DeLucia	.05	.02
☐ 279 Ken Griffey Jr.	1.25	.55
☐ 280 Erik Hanson	.05	.02
☐ 281 Brian Holman	.05	.02
☐ 282 Mike Jackson	.05	.02
☐ 283 Randy Johnson	.20	.09
☐ 284 Tracy Jones	.05	.02
☐ 285 Bill Krueger	.05	.02
☐ 286 Edgar Martinez	.05	.02
☐ 287 Tino Martinez	.20	.09
☐ 288 Rob Murphy	.05	.02
☐ 289 Pete O'Brien	.05	.02
☐ 290 Alonzo Powell	.05	.02
☐ 291 Harold Reynolds	.05	.02
☐ 292 Mike Schooler	.05	.02
☐ 293 Russ Swan	.05	.02
☐ 294 Bill Swift	.05	.02
☐ 295 Dave Valle	.05	.02
☐ 296 Omar Vizquel	.10	.05
☐ 297 Gerald Alexander	.05	.02
☐ 298 Brad Arnsberg	.05	.02
☐ 299 Kevin Brown	.10	.05
☐ 300 Jack Daugherty	.05	.02
☐ 301 Mario Diaz	.05	.02
☐ 302 Brian Downing	.05	.02
☐ 303 Julio Franco	.10	.05
☐ 304 Juan Gonzalez	.60	.25
☐ 305 Rich Gossage	.10	.05
☐ 306 Jose Guzman	.05	.02
☐ 307 Jose Hernandez	.05	.02
☐ 308 Jeff Huson	.05	.02
☐ 309 Mike Jeffcoat	.05	.02
☐ 310 Terry Mathews	.05	.02
☐ 311 Rafael Palmeiro	.20	.09
☐ 312 Dean Palmer	.10	.05
☐ 313 Geno Petralli	.05	.02
☐ 314 Gary Pettis	.05	.02
☐ 315 Kevin Reimer	.05	.02
☐ 316 Ivan Rodriguez	.40	.18
☐ 317 Kenny Rogers	.05	.02
☐ 318 Wayne Rosenthal	.05	.02
☐ 319 Jeff Russell	.05	.02
☐ 320 Nolan Ryan	.75	.35
☐ 321 Ruben Sierra	.05	.02
☐ 322 Jim Acker	.05	.02
☐ 323 Roberto Alomar	.20	.09
☐ 324 Derek Bell	.10	.05
☐ 325 Pat Borders	.05	.02
☐ 326 Tom Candiotti	.05	.02
☐ 327 Joe Carter	.10	.05
☐ 328 Rob Ducey	.05	.02
☐ 329 Kelly Gruber	.05	.02
☐ 330 Juan Guzman	.05	.02
☐ 331 Tom Henke	.05	.02
☐ 332 Jimmy Key	.10	.05
☐ 333 Manny Lee	.05	.02
☐ 334 Al Leiter	.10	.05
☐ 335 Bob MacDonald	.05	.02
☐ 336 Candy Maldonado	.05	.02
☐ 337 Rance Mulliniks	.05	.02
☐ 338 Greg Myers	.05	.02
☐ 339 John Olerud UER (1991 BA has .256, but text says .258)	.10	.05
☐ 340 Ed Sprague	.05	.02
☐ 341 Dave Stieb	.05	.02
☐ 342 Todd Stottlemyre	.05	.02
☐ 343 Mike Timlin	.05	.02
☐ 344 Duane Ward	.05	.02
☐ 345 David Wells	.05	.02
☐ 346 Devon White	.05	.02
☐ 347 Mookie Wilson	.05	.02
☐ 348 Eddie Zosky	.05	.02
☐ 349 Steve Avery	.05	.02
☐ 350 Mike Bell	.05	.02
☐ 351 Rafael Belliard	.05	.02
☐ 352 Juan Berenguer	.05	.02
☐ 353 Jeff Blauser	.05	.02
☐ 354 Sid Bream	.05	.02
☐ 355 Francisco Cabrera	.05	.02
☐ 356 Marvin Freeman	.05	.02
☐ 357 Ron Gant	.10	.05
☐ 358 Tom Glavine	.05	.02
☐ 359 Brian Hunter	.05	.02
☐ 360 Dave Justice	.20	.09
☐ 361 Charlie Leibrandt	.05	.02
☐ 362 Mark Lemke	.05	.02
☐ 363 Kent Mercker	.05	.02
☐ 364 Keith Mitchell	.05	.02
☐ 365 Greg Olson	.05	.02
☐ 366 Terry Pendleton	.10	.05
☐ 367 Armando Reynoso	.05	.02
☐ 368 Deion Sanders	.20	.09
☐ 369 Lonnie Smith	.05	.02
☐ 370 Pete Smith	.05	.02
☐ 371 John Smoltz	.05	.02
☐ 372 Mike Stanton	.05	.02
☐ 373 Jeff Treadway	.05	.02
☐ 374 Mark Wohlers	.05	.02
☐ 375 Paul Assenmacher	.05	.02
☐ 376 George Bell	.05	.02
☐ 377 Shawn Boskie	.05	.02
☐ 378 Frank Castillo	.10	.05
☐ 379 Andre Dawson	.05	.02
☐ 380 Shawon Dunston	.05	.02
☐ 381 Mark Grace	.05	.02
☐ 382 Mike Harkey	.05	.02
☐ 383 Danny Jackson	.05	.02
☐ 384 Les Lancaster	.05	.02
☐ 385 Ced Landrum	.05	.02
☐ 386 Greg Maddux	.60	.25
☐ 387 Derrick May	.05	.02
☐ 388 Chuck McElroy	.05	.02
☐ 389 Ryne Sandberg	.25	.11
☐ 390 Heathcliff Slocumb	.05	.02
☐ 391 Dave Smith	.05	.02
☐ 392 Dwight Smith	.05	.02
☐ 393 Rick Sutcliffe	.05	.02
☐ 394 Hector Villanueva	.05	.02
☐ 395 Chico Walker	.05	.02
☐ 396 Jerome Walton	.05	.02
☐ 397 Rick Wilkins	.05	.02
☐ 398 Jack Armstrong	.05	.02
☐ 399 Freddie Benavides	.05	.02
☐ 400 Glenn Braggs	.05	.02
☐ 401 Tom Browning	.05	.02
☐ 402 Norm Charlton	.05	.02
☐ 403 Eric Davis	.10	.05

☐ 404 Rob Dibble .05 .02
☐ 405 Bill Doran .05 .02
☐ 406 Mariano Duncan .05 .02
☐ 407 Kip Gross .05 .02
☐ 408 Chris Hammond .05 .02
☐ 409 Billy Hatcher .05 .02
☐ 410 Chris Jones .05 .02
☐ 411 Barry Larkin .05 .02
☐ 412 Hal Morris .05 .02
☐ 413 Randy Myers .10 .05
☐ 414 Joe Oliver .05 .02
☐ 415 Paul O'Neill .10 .05
☐ 416 Ted Power .05 .02
☐ 417 Luis Quinones .05 .02
☐ 418 Jeff Reed .05 .02
☐ 419 Jose Rijo .05 .02
☐ 420 Chris Sabo .05 .02
☐ 421 Reggie Sanders .10 .05
☐ 422 Scott Scudder .05 .02
☐ 423 Glenn Sutko .05 .02
☐ 424 Eric Anthony .05 .02
☐ 425 Jeff Bagwell .60 .25
☐ 426 Craig Biggio .05 .02
☐ 427 Ken Caminiti .20 .09
☐ 428 Casey Candaele .05 .02
☐ 429 Mike Capel .05 .02
☐ 430 Andujar Cedeno .05 .02
☐ 431 Jim Corsi .05 .02
☐ 432 Mark Davidson .05 .02
☐ 433 Steve Finley .10 .05
☐ 434 Luis Gonzalez .05 .02
☐ 435 Pete Harnisch .05 .02
☐ 436 Dwayne Henry .05 .02
☐ 437 Xavier Hernandez .05 .02
☐ 438 Jimmy Jones .05 .02
☐ 439 Darryl Kile .10 .05
☐ 440 Rob Mallicoat .05 .02
☐ 441 Andy Mota .05 .02
☐ 442 Al Osuna .05 .02
☐ 443 Mark Portugal .05 .02
☐ 444 Scott Servais .05 .02
☐ 445 Mike Simms .05 .02
☐ 446 Gerald Young .05 .02
☐ 447 Tim Belcher .05 .02
☐ 448 Brett Butler .10 .05
☐ 449 John Candelaria .05 .02
☐ 450 Gary Carter .20 .09
☐ 451 Dennis Cook .05 .02
☐ 452 Tim Crews .05 .02
☐ 453 Kal Daniels .05 .02
☐ 454 Jim Gott .05 .02
☐ 455 Alfredo Griffin .05 .02
☐ 456 Kevin Gross .05 .02
☐ 457 Chris Gwynn .05 .02
☐ 458 Lenny Harris .05 .02
☐ 459 Orel Hershiser .10 .05
☐ 460 Jay Howell .05 .02
☐ 461 Stan Javier .05 .02
☐ 462 Eric Karros .10 .05
☐ 463 Ramon Martinez UER .10 .05
(Card says bats right, should be left)
☐ 464 Roger McDowell UER .05 .02
(Wins add up to 54, totals have 51)
☐ 465 Mike Morgan .05 .02
☐ 466 Eddie Murray .20 .09
☐ 467 Jose Offerman .05 .02
☐ 468 Bob Ojeda .05 .02
☐ 469 Juan Samuel .05 .02
☐ 470 Mike Scioscia .05 .02
☐ 471 Darryl Strawberry .10 .05
☐ 472 Bret Barberie .05 .02
☐ 473 Brian Barnes .05 .02
☐ 474 Eric Bullock .05 .02
☐ 475 Ivan Calderon .05 .02
☐ 476 Delino DeShields .05 .02
☐ 477 Jeff Fassero .05 .02
☐ 478 Mike Fitzgerald .05 .02
☐ 479 Steve Frey .05 .02
☐ 480 Andres Galarraga .05 .02
☐ 481 Mark Gardner .05 .02
☐ 482 Marquis Grissom .10 .05
☐ 483 Chris Haney .05 .02
☐ 484 Barry Jones .05 .02
☐ 485 Dave Martinez .05 .02
☐ 486 Dennis Martinez .10 .05
☐ 487 Chris Nabholz .05 .02
☐ 488 Spike Owen .05 .02
☐ 489 Gilberto Reyes .05 .02
☐ 490 Mel Rojas .10 .05
☐ 491 Scott Ruskin .05 .02
☐ 492 Bill Sampen .05 .02
☐ 493 Larry Walker .20 .09
☐ 494 Tim Wallach .05 .02
☐ 495 Daryl Boston .05 .02
☐ 496 Hubie Brooks .05 .02

☐ 497 Tim Burke .05 .02
☐ 498 Mark Carreon .05 .02
☐ 499 Tony Castillo .05 .02
☐ 500 Vince Coleman .05 .02
☐ 501 David Cone .10 .05
☐ 502 Kevin Elster .05 .02
☐ 503 Sid Fernandez .05 .02
☐ 504 John Franco .05 .02
☐ 505 Dwight Gooden .10 .05
☐ 506 Todd Hundley .05 .02
☐ 507 Jeff Innis .05 .02
☐ 508 Gregg Jefferies .10 .05
☐ 509 Howard Johnson .05 .02
☐ 510 Dave Magadan .05 .02
☐ 511 Terry McDaniel .05 .02
☐ 512 Kevin McReynolds .05 .02
☐ 513 Keith Miller .05 .02
☐ 514 Charlie O'Brien .05 .02
☐ 515 Mackey Sasser .05 .02
☐ 516 Pete Schourek .05 .02
☐ 517 Julio Valera .05 .02
☐ 518 Frank Viola .05 .02
☐ 519 Wally Whitehurst .05 .02
☐ 520 Anthony Young .05 .02
☐ 521 Andy Ashby .05 .02
☐ 522 Kim Batiste .05 .02
☐ 523 Joe Boever .05 .02
☐ 524 Wes Chamberlain .05 .02
☐ 525 Pat Combs .05 .02
☐ 526 Danny Cox .05 .02
☐ 527 Darren Daulton .10 .05
☐ 528 Jose DeJesus .05 .02
☐ 529 Len Dykstra .10 .05
☐ 530 Darrin Fletcher .05 .02
☐ 531 Tommy Greene .05 .02
☐ 532 Jason Grimsley .05 .02
☐ 533 Charlie Hayes .05 .02
☐ 534 Von Hayes .05 .02
☐ 535 Dave Hollins .05 .02
☐ 536 Ricky Jordan .05 .02
☐ 537 John Kruk .10 .05
☐ 538 Jim Lindeman .05 .02
☐ 539 Mickey Morandini .05 .02
☐ 540 Terry Mulholland .05 .02
☐ 541 Dale Murphy .20 .09
☐ 542 Randy Ready .05 .02
☐ 543 Wally Ritchie UER .05 .02
(Letters in data are cut off on card)
☐ 544 Bruce Ruffin .05 .02
☐ 545 Steve Searcy .05 .02
☐ 546 Dickie Thon .05 .02
☐ 547 Mitch Williams .05 .02
☐ 548 Stan Belinda .05 .02
☐ 549 Jay Bell .10 .05
☐ 550 Barry Bonds .25 .11
☐ 551 Bobby Bonilla .05 .02
☐ 552 Steve Buechele .05 .02
☐ 553 Doug Drabek .05 .02
☐ 554 Neal Heaton .05 .02
☐ 555 Jeff King .10 .05
☐ 556 Bob Kipper .05 .02
☐ 557 Bill Landrum .05 .02
☐ 558 Mike LaValliere .05 .02
☐ 559 Jose Lind .05 .02
☐ 560 Lloyd McClendon .05 .02
☐ 561 Orlando Merced .05 .02
☐ 562 Bob Patterson .05 .02
☐ 563 Joe Redfield .05 .02
☐ 564 Gary Redus .05 .02
☐ 565 Rosario Rodriguez .05 .02
☐ 566 Don Slaught .05 .02
☐ 567 John Smiley .05 .02
☐ 568 Zane Smith .05 .02
☐ 569 Randy Tomlin .05 .02
☐ 570 Andy Van Slyke .10 .05
☐ 571 Gary Varsho .05 .02
☐ 572 Bob Walk .05 .02
☐ 573 John Wehner UER .05 .02
(Actually played for Carolina in 1991, not Cards)
☐ 574 Juan Agosto .05 .02
☐ 575 Cris Carpenter .05 .02
☐ 576 Jose DeLeon .05 .02
☐ 577 Rich Gedman .05 .02
☐ 578 Bernard Gilkey .10 .05
☐ 579 Pedro Guerrero .05 .02
☐ 580 Ken Hill .05 .02
☐ 581 Rex Hudler .05 .02
☐ 582 Felix Jose .05 .02
☐ 583 Ray Lankford .05 .02
☐ 584 Omar Olivares .05 .02
☐ 585 Jose Oquendo .05 .02
☐ 586 Tom Pagnozzi .05 .02
☐ 587 Geronimo Pena .05 .02
☐ 588 Mike Perez .05 .02

☐ 589 Gerald Perry .05 .02
☐ 590 Bryn Smith .05 .02
☐ 591 Lee Smith .10 .05
☐ 592 Ozzie Smith .25 .11
☐ 593 Scott Terry .05 .02
☐ 594 Bob Tewksbury .05 .02
☐ 595 Milt Thompson .05 .02
☐ 596 Todd Zeile .05 .02
☐ 597 Larry Andersen .05 .02
☐ 598 Oscar Azocar .05 .02
☐ 599 Andy Benes .05 .02
☐ 600 Ricky Bones .05 .02
☐ 601 Jerald Clark .05 .02
☐ 602 Pat Clements .05 .02
☐ 603 Paul Faries .05 .02
☐ 604 Tony Fernandez .05 .02
☐ 605 Tony Gwynn .50 .23
☐ 606 Greg W. Harris .05 .02
☐ 607 Thomas Howard .05 .02
☐ 608 Bruce Hurst .05 .02
☐ 609 Darrin Jackson .05 .02
☐ 610 Tom Lampkin .05 .02
☐ 611 Craig Lefferts .05 .02
☐ 612 Jim Lewis .05 .02
☐ 613 Mike Maddux .05 .02
☐ 614 Fred McGriff .05 .02
☐ 615 Jose Melendez .05 .02
☐ 616 Jose Mota .05 .02
☐ 617 Dennis Rasmussen .05 .02
☐ 618 Bip Roberts .05 .02
☐ 619 Rich Rodriguez .05 .02
☐ 620 Benito Santiago .05 .02
☐ 621 Craig Shipley .05 .02
☐ 622 Tim Teufel .05 .02
☐ 623 Kevin Ward .05 .02
☐ 624 Ed Whitson .05 .02
☐ 625 Dave Anderson .05 .02
☐ 626 Kevin Bass .05 .02
☐ 627 Rod Beck .20 .09
☐ 628 Bud Black .05 .02
☐ 629 Jeff Brantley .05 .02
☐ 630 John Burkett .05 .02
☐ 631 Will Clark .05 .02
☐ 632 Royce Clayton .10 .05
☐ 633 Steve Decker .05 .02
☐ 634 Kelly Downs .05 .02
☐ 635 Mike Felder .05 .02
☐ 636 Scott Garrelts .05 .02
☐ 637 Eric Gunderson .05 .02
☐ 638 Bryan Hickerson .05 .02
☐ 639 Darren Lewis .05 .02
☐ 640 Greg Litton .05 .02
☐ 641 Kirt Manwaring .05 .02
☐ 642 Paul McClellan .05 .02
☐ 643 Willie McGee .05 .02
☐ 644 Kevin Mitchell .05 .02
☐ 645 Francisco Oliveras .05 .02
☐ 646 Mike Remlinger .05 .02
☐ 647 Dave Righetti .05 .02
☐ 648 Robby Thompson .05 .02
☐ 649 Jose Uribe .05 .02
☐ 650 Matt Williams .05 .02
☐ 651 Trevor Wilson .05 .02
☐ 652 Tom Goodwin MLP UER .10 .05
(Timed in 3.5, should be be timed)
☐ 653 Terry Bross MLP .05 .02
☐ 654 Mike Christopher MLP .05 .02
☐ 655 Kenny Lofton MLP .75 .35
☐ 656 Chris Cron MLP .05 .02
☐ 657 Willie Banks MLP .05 .02
☐ 658 Pat Rice MLP .05 .02
☐ 659A Rob Maurer MLP ERR .75 .35
(Name misspelled as Mauer on card front)
☐ 659B Rob Maurer MLP COR .10 .05
☐ 660 Don Harris MLP .05 .02
☐ 661 Henry Rodriguez MLP .20 .09
☐ 662 Cliff Brantley MLP .05 .02
☐ 663 Mike Linskey MLP UER .05 .02
(220 pounds in data, 200 in text)
☐ 664 Gary DiSarcina MLP .05 .02
☐ 665 Gil Heredia MLP .05 .02
☐ 666 Vinny Castilla MLP .50 .23
☐ 667 Paul Abbott MLP .05 .02
☐ 668 Monty Fariss MLP UER .05 .02
(Called Paul on back)
☐ 669 Jarvis Brown MLP .05 .02
☐ 670 Wayne Kirby MLP .05 .02
☐ 671 Scott Brosius MLP .05 .02
☐ 672 Bob Hamelin MLP .05 .02
☐ 673 Joel Johnston MLP .05 .02
☐ 674 Tim Spehr MLP .05 .02
☐ 675A Jeff Gardner MLP ERR .75 .35
(P on front, should be SS)

	MINT	NRMT
☐ 675B Jeff Gardner MLP COR	.25	.11
☐ 676 Rico Rossy MLP	.05	.02
☐ 677 Roberto Hernandez MLP	.05	.02
☐ 678 Ted Wood MLP	.05	.02
☐ 679 Cal Eldred MLP	.05	.02
☐ 680 Sean Berry MLP	.05	.02
☐ 681 Rickey Henderson RS	.05	.02
☐ 682 Nolan Ryan RS	.40	.18
☐ 683 Dennis Martinez RS	.10	.05
☐ 684 Wilson Alvarez RS	.10	.05
☐ 685 Joe Carter RS	.05	.02
☐ 686 Dave Winfield RS	.20	.09
☐ 687 David Cone RS	.10	.05
☐ 688 Jose Canseco LL UER (Text on back has 42 stolen bases in '88; should be 40)	.05	.02
☐ 689 Howard Johnson LL	.05	.02
☐ 690 Julio Franco LL	.05	.02
☐ 691 Terry Pendleton LL	.05	.02
☐ 692 Cecil Fielder LL	.10	.05
☐ 693 Scott Erickson LL	.05	.02
☐ 694 Tom Glavine LL	.10	.05
☐ 695 Dennis Martinez LL	.05	.02
☐ 696 Bryan Harvey LL	.05	.02
☐ 697 Lee Smith LL	.10	.05
☐ 698 Super Siblings Roberto Alomar Sandy Alomar Jr.	.10	.05
☐ 699 The Indispensables Bobby Bonilla Will Clark	.10	.05
☐ 700 Teamwork Mark Wohlers Kent Mercker Alejandro Pena	.05	.02
☐ 701 Tiger Tandems Stacy Jones Bo Jackson Gregg Olson Frank Thomas	.50	.23
☐ 702 The Ignitors Paul Molitor Brett Butler	.20	.09
☐ 703 Indispensables II Cal Ripken Joe Carter	.40	.18
☐ 704 Power Packs Barry Larkin Kirby Puckett	.20	.09
☐ 705 Today and Tomorrow Mo Vaughn Cecil Fielder	.20	.09
☐ 706 Teenage Sensations Ramon Martinez Ozzie Guillen	.10	.05
☐ 707 Designated Hitters Harold Baines Wade Boggs	.05	.02
☐ 708 Robin Yount PV	.05	.02
☐ 709 Ken Griffey Jr. PV UER (Missing quotations on back; BA has .322, but was actually .327)	.75	.35
☐ 710 Nolan Ryan PV	.40	.18
☐ 711 Cal Ripken PV	.40	.18
☐ 712 Frank Thomas PV	.75	.35
☐ 713 Dave Justice PV	.20	.09
☐ 714 Checklist 1-101	.05	.02
☐ 715 Checklist 102-194	.05	.02
☐ 716 Checklist 195-296	.05	.02
☐ 717 Checklist 297-397	.05	.02
☐ 718 Checklist 398-494	.05	.02
☐ 719 Checklist 495-596	.05	.02
☐ 720A Checklist 597-720 ERR (659 Rob Mauer)	.05	.02
☐ 720B Checklist 597-720 COR (659 Rob Maurer)	.05	.02

1992 Fleer All-Stars

Cards from this 24-card standard-size set were randomly inserted in plastic wrap packs. Selected members of the American and National League 1991 All-Star squads comprise this set. The glossy color photos on the fronts are bordered in black and accented above and below with gold stripes and lettering. A diamond with a color head shot of the player is superimposed at the lower right corner of the picture.

	MINT	NRMT
COMPLETE SET (24)	35.00	16.00
COMMON CARD (1-24)	.50	.23
☐ 1 Felix Jose	.50	.23
☐ 2 Tony Gwynn	2.50	1.10
☐ 3 Barry Bonds	2.00	.90
☐ 4 Bobby Bonilla	.75	.35
☐ 5 Mike LaValliere	.50	.23
☐ 6 Tom Glavine	1.00	.45
☐ 7 Ramon Martinez	.75	.35
☐ 8 Lee Smith	1.00	.45
☐ 9 Mickey Tettleton	.50	.23
☐ 10 Scott Erickson	.75	.35
☐ 11 Frank Thomas	10.00	4.50
☐ 12 Danny Tartabull	.50	.23
☐ 13 Will Clark	1.00	.45
☐ 14 Ryne Sandberg	1.50	.70
☐ 15 Terry Pendleton	.50	.23
☐ 16 Barry Larkin	1.00	.45
☐ 17 Rafael Palmeiro	1.00	.45
☐ 18 Julio Franco	.50	.23
☐ 19 Robin Ventura	.75	.35
☐ 20 Cal Ripken UER (Candidte; total bases misspelled as based)	8.00	3.60
☐ 21 Joe Carter	1.00	.45
☐ 22 Kirby Puckett	2.50	1.10
☐ 23 Ken Griffey Jr.	10.00	4.50
☐ 24 Jose Canseco	1.00	.45

1992 Fleer Clemens

Roger Clemens served as a spokesperson for Fleer during 1992 and was the exclusive subject of this 15-card standard-size set. The first 12-card Clemens "Career Highlights" subseries was randomly inserted in 1992 Fleer packs. Two-thousand signed cards were randomly inserted in wax packs and could also be won by entering a drawing. However, these cards are uncertifiable as they do not have any distinguishable marks. Moreover, a three-card Clemens subset (13-15) was available through a special mail-in offer. The glossy color photos on the fronts are bordered in black and accented with gold stripes and lettering on the top of the card. On a pale yellow background with black borders, the back has player profile and career highlights.

	MINT	NRMT
COMPLETE SET (12)	10.00	4.50
COMMON CLEMENS (1-12)	1.00	.45
COMMON SEND-OFF (13-15)	1.00	.45
☐ 1 Roger Clemens Quiet Storm	1.00	.45
☐ 2 Roger Clemens Courted By Mets and Twins	1.00	.45
☐ 3 Roger Clemens The Show	1.00	.45
☐ 4 Roger Clemens Rocket Launched	1.00	.45
☐ 5 Roger Clemens Time Of Trial	1.00	.45
☐ 6 Roger Clemens Break Through	1.00	.45
☐ 7 Roger Clemens Play It Again Roger	1.00	.45
☐ 8 Roger Clemens Business As Usual	1.00	.45
☐ 9 Roger Clemens Heeee's Back	1.00	.45
☐ 10 Roger Clemens Blood, Sweat and Tears	1.00	.45
☐ 11 Roger Clemens Prime Of Life	1.00	.45
☐ 12 Roger Clemens Man For Every Season	1.00	.45
☐ 13 Roger Clemens Cooperstown Bound	1.00	.45
☐ 14 Roger Clemens The Heat of the Moment	1.00	.45
☐ 15 Roger Clemens Final Words Q and A with "The Rocket"	1.00	.45
☐ AU0 Roger Clemens AU (Uncertified signature)	80.00	36.00
☐ NNO Roger Clemens Promo with Paul Mullan	6.00	2.70

1992 Fleer Lumber Company

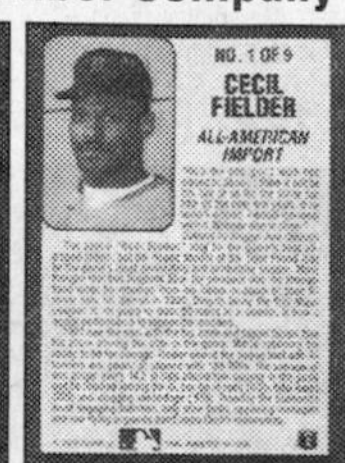

The 1992 Fleer Lumber Company standard-size set features nine outstanding hitters in Major League Baseball. This set was only available as a bonus in Fleer hobby factory sets. Inside a black glossy frame, the fronts display color action player photos, with the player's name printed in black in a gold foil bar beneath the picture. The wider right border contains the catch phrase "The Lumber Co." in the shape of a baseball bat, complete with woodgrain streaks.

	MINT	NRMT
COMPLETE SET (9)	10.00	4.50
COMMON CARD (L1-L9)	.75	.35
☐ L1 Cecil Fielder	.75	.35
☐ L2 Mickey Tettleton	.75	.35
☐ L3 Darryl Strawberry	.75	.35
☐ L4 Ryne Sandberg	1.50	.70
☐ L5 Jose Canseco	1.00	.45
☐ L6 Matt Williams UER In 17th line, cycle is spelled cyle	1.00	.45
☐ L7 Cal Ripken	8.00	3.60
☐ L8 Barry Bonds	1.50	.70
☐ L9 Ron Gant	.75	.35

1992 Fleer Rookie Sensations

Cards from the 20-card Fleer Rookie Sensations set were randomly inserted in 1992 Fleer 35-card cello packs. The cards were extremely popular upon release resulting in packs selling for levels far above suggested retail levels. The glossy color photos on the fronts have a white border on a royal blue card face. The words "Rookie Sensations" appear above the picture in gold foil lettering, while the player's name appears on a gold foil plaque beneath the picture. Through a mail-in offer for ten Fleer baseball card wrappers and 1.00 for postage and handling, Fleer offered an uncut 8 1/2" by 11" numbered promo sheet picturing ten of the 20-card set on each side in a reduced-size front-only format. The offer indicated an expiration date of July 31, 1992, or whenever the production quantity of 250,000 sheets was exhausted.

	MINT	NRMT
COMPLETE SET (20)	50.00	22.00
COMMON CARD (1-20)	1.00	.45
☐ 1 Frank Thomas	25.00	11.00
☐ 2 Todd Van Poppel	1.00	.45
☐ 3 Orlando Merced	1.00	.45
☐ 4 Jeff Bagwell	12.00	5.50
☐ 5 Jeff Fassero	2.00	.90
☐ 6 Darren Lewis	1.00	.45
☐ 7 Milt Cuyler	1.00	.45

☐ 8 Mike Timlin	1.00	.45
☐ 9 Brian McRae	1.00	.45
☐ 10 Chuck Knoblauch	4.00	1.80
☐ 11 Rich DeLucia	1.00	.45
☐ 12 Ivan Rodriguez	8.00	3.60
☐ 13 Juan Guzman	1.00	.45
☐ 14 Steve Chitren	1.00	.45
☐ 15 Mark Wohlers	2.00	.90
☐ 16 Wes Chamberlain	1.00	.45
☐ 17 Ray Lankford	3.00	1.35
☐ 18 Chito Martinez	1.00	.45
☐ 19 Phil Plantier	1.00	.45
☐ 20 Scott Leius UER (Misspelled Lieus on card front)	1.00	.45

1992 Fleer Smoke 'n Heat

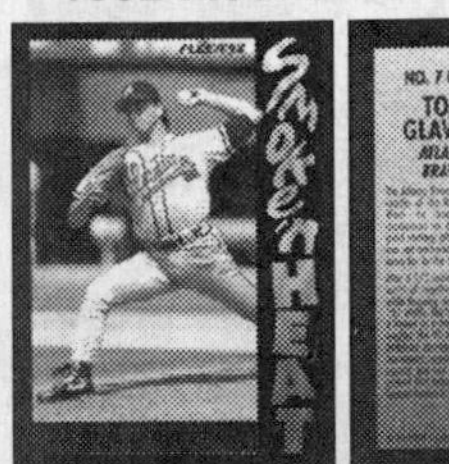

This 12-card standard-size set features outstanding major league pitchers, especially the premier fastball pitchers in both leagues. These cards were only available in Fleer's 1992 Christmas factory set. The front design features color action player photos bordered in black. The player's name appears in a gold foil bar beneath the picture, and the words "Smoke 'n Heat" are printed vertically in the wider right border.

	MINT	NRMT
COMPLETE SET (12)	10.00	4.50
COMMON CARD (S1-S12)	.50	.23
☐ S1 Lee Smith	.75	.35
☐ S2 Jack McDowell	.50	.23
☐ S3 David Cone	.75	.35
☐ S4 Roger Clemens	1.50	.70
☐ S5 Nolan Ryan	6.00	2.70
☐ S6 Scott Erickson	.50	.23
☐ S7 Tom Glavine	1.00	.45
☐ S8 Dwight Gooden	.75	.35
☐ S9 Andy Benes	.50	.23
☐ S10 Steve Avery	.50	.23
☐ S11 Randy Johnson	1.50	.70
☐ S12 Jim Abbott	.75	.35

1992 Fleer Team Leaders

Cards from the 20-card Fleer Team Leaders set were randomly inserted in 1992 Fleer 42-card rack packs. The glossy color photos on the fronts are bordered in white and green. Two gold foil stripes below the picture intersect a diamond-shaped "Team Leaders" emblem.

	MINT	NRMT
COMPLETE SET (20)	45.00	20.00
COMMON CARD (1-20)	1.00	.45
☐ 1 Don Mattingly	8.00	3.60
☐ 2 Howard Johnson	1.00	.45
☐ 3 Chris Sabo UER (Where he it, should be Where he hit)	1.00	.45
☐ 4 Carlton Fisk	3.00	1.35
☐ 5 Kirby Puckett	6.00	2.70
☐ 6 Cecil Fielder	1.50	.70
☐ 7 Tony Gwynn	6.00	2.70
☐ 8 Will Clark	2.00	.90
☐ 9 Bobby Bonilla	1.50	.70
☐ 10 Len Dykstra	1.50	.70
☐ 11 Tom Glavine	2.00	.90
☐ 12 Rafael Palmeiro	2.00	.90
☐ 13 Wade Boggs	3.00	1.35
☐ 14 Joe Carter	2.00	.90
☐ 15 Ken Griffey Jr.	20.00	9.00
☐ 16 Darryl Strawberry	1.50	.70
☐ 17 Cal Ripken	15.00	6.75
☐ 18 Danny Tartabull	1.00	.45
☐ 19 Jose Canseco	2.00	.90
☐ 20 Andre Dawson	2.00	.90

1992 Fleer Update

The 1992 Fleer Update set contains 132 standard-size cards. Cards were distributed exclusively in factory sets through hobby dealers. Factory sets included a four-card, black-bordered "92 Headliners" insert set for a total of 136 cards. Due to lackluster retail response for previous Fleer Update sets, wholesale orders for this product were low, resulting in a short print run. As word got out that the cards were in short supply, the secondary market prices soared not soon after release. The basic card design is identical to the regular issue 1992 Fleer cards except for the U-prefixed numbering on back. The cards are checklisted alphabetically within and according to teams for each league with AL preceding NL. Rookie Cards in this set include John Jaha, Mike Piazza, John Valentin and Eric Young. The Piazza card is widely recognized as one of the more desirable singles issued in the 1990's.

	MINT	NRMT
COMP.FACT.SET (136)	160.00	70.00
COMPLETE SET (132)	150.00	70.00
COMMON CARD (U1-U132)	.25	.11
☐ 1 Todd Frohwirth	.25	.11
☐ 2 Alan Mills	.25	.11
☐ 3 Rick Sutcliffe	.25	.11
☐ 4 John Valentin	2.00	.90
☐ 5 Frank Viola	.25	.11
☐ 6 Bob Zupcic	.25	.11
☐ 7 Mike Butcher	.25	.11
☐ 8 Chad Curtis	2.00	.90
☐ 9 Damion Easley	1.50	.70
☐ 10 Tim Salmon	18.00	8.00
☐ 11 Julio Valera	.25	.11
☐ 12 George Bell	.25	.11
☐ 13 Roberto Hernandez	1.50	.70
☐ 14 Shawn Jeter	.25	.11
☐ 15 Thomas Howard	.25	.11
☐ 16 Jesse Levis	.25	.11
☐ 17 Kenny Lofton	30.00	13.50
☐ 18 Paul Sorrento	.25	.11
☐ 19 Rico Brogna	.75	.35
☐ 20 John Doherty	.25	.11
☐ 21 Dan Gladden	.25	.11
☐ 22 Buddy Groom	.25	.11
☐ 23 Shawn Hare	.25	.11
☐ 24 John Kiely	.25	.11
☐ 25 Kurt Knudsen	.25	.11
☐ 26 Gregg Jefferies	.75	.35
☐ 27 Wally Joyner	.75	.35
☐ 28 Kevin Koslofski	.25	.11
☐ 29 Kevin McReynolds	.25	.11
☐ 30 Rusty Meacham	.25	.11
☐ 31 Keith Miller	.25	.11
☐ 32 Hipolito Pichardo	.25	.11
☐ 33 James Austin	.25	.11
☐ 34 Scott Fletcher	.25	.11
☐ 35 John Jaha	2.00	.90
☐ 36 Pat Listach	.25	.11
☐ 37 Dave Nilsson	2.00	.90
☐ 38 Kevin Seitzer	.25	.11
☐ 39 Tom Edens	.25	.11
☐ 40 Pat Mahomes	.25	.11
☐ 41 John Smiley	.25	.11
☐ 42 Charlie Hayes	.25	.11
☐ 43 Sam Militello	.25	.11
☐ 44 Andy Stankiewicz	.25	.11
☐ 45 Danny Tartabull	.25	.11
☐ 46 Bob Wickman	.25	.11
☐ 47 Jerry Browne	.25	.11
☐ 48 Kevin Campbell	.25	.11
☐ 49 Vince Horsman	.25	.11
☐ 50 Troy Neel	.25	.11
☐ 51 Ruben Sierra	.25	.11
☐ 52 Bruce Walton	.25	.11
☐ 53 Willie Wilson	.25	.11
☐ 54 Bret Boone	.75	.35
☐ 55 Dave Fleming	.25	.11
☐ 56 Kevin Mitchell	.75	.35
☐ 57 Jeff Nelson	.25	.11
☐ 58 Shane Turner	.25	.11
☐ 59 Jose Canseco	2.00	.90
☐ 60 Jeff Frye	.25	.11
☐ 61 Danny Leon	.25	.11
☐ 62 Roger Pavlik	1.50	.70
☐ 63 David Cone	.75	.35
☐ 64 Pat Hentgen	6.00	2.70
☐ 65 Randy Knorr	.25	.11
☐ 66 Jack Morris	.75	.35
☐ 67 Dave Winfield	1.50	.70
☐ 68 David Nied	.25	.11
☐ 69 Otis Nixon	.75	.35
☐ 70 Alejandro Pena	.25	.11
☐ 71 Jeff Reardon	.75	.35
☐ 72 Alex Arias	.25	.11
☐ 73 Jim Bullinger	.25	.11
☐ 74 Mike Morgan	.25	.11
☐ 75 Rey Sanchez	.25	.11
☐ 76 Bob Scanlan	.25	.11
☐ 77 Sammy Sosa	2.00	.90
☐ 78 Scott Bankhead	.25	.11
☐ 79 Tim Belcher	.25	.11
☐ 80 Steve Foster	.25	.11
☐ 81 Willie Greene	.75	.35
☐ 82 Bip Roberts	.25	.11
☐ 83 Scott Ruskin	.25	.11
☐ 84 Greg Swindell	.25	.11
☐ 85 Juan Guerrero	.25	.11
☐ 86 Butch Henry	.25	.11
☐ 87 Doug Jones	.25	.11
☐ 88 Brian Williams	.25	.11
☐ 89 Tom Candiotti	.25	.11
☐ 90 Eric Davis	.75	.35
☐ 91 Carlos Hernandez	.25	.11
☐ 92 Mike Piazza	100.00	45.00
☐ 93 Mike Sharperson	.25	.11
☐ 94 Eric Young	2.00	.90
☐ 95 Moises Alou	3.00	1.35
☐ 96 Greg Colbrunn	.25	.11
☐ 97 Wil Cordero	.25	.11
☐ 98 Ken Hill	.75	.35
☐ 99 John Vander Wal	.25	.11
☐ 100 John Wetteland	.75	.35
☐ 101 Bobby Bonilla	.75	.35
☐ 102 Eric Hillman	.25	.11
☐ 103 Pat Howell	.25	.11
☐ 104 Jeff Kent	2.00	.90
☐ 105 Dick Schofield	.25	.11
☐ 106 Ryan Thompson	.25	.11
☐ 107 Chico Walker	.25	.11
☐ 108 Juan Bell	.25	.11
☐ 109 Mariano Duncan	.25	.11
☐ 110 Jeff Grotewold	.25	.11
☐ 111 Ben Rivera	.25	.11
☐ 112 Curt Schilling	3.00	1.35
☐ 113 Victor Cole	.25	.11
☐ 114 Albert Martin	2.00	.90
☐ 115 Roger Mason	.25	.11
☐ 116 Blas Minor	.25	.11
☐ 117 Tim Wakefield	2.00	.90
☐ 118 Mark Clark	.75	.35
☐ 119 Rheal Cormier	.25	.11
☐ 120 Donovan Osborne	.75	.35
☐ 121 Todd Worrell	.75	.35
☐ 122 Jeremy Hernandez	.25	.11
☐ 123 Randy Myers	.75	.35
☐ 124 Frank Seminara	.25	.11
☐ 125 Gary Sheffield	2.00	.90
☐ 126 Dan Walters	.25	.11
☐ 127 Steve Hosey	.25	.11
☐ 128 Mike Jackson	.25	.11
☐ 129 Jim Pena	.25	.11
☐ 130 Cory Snyder	.25	.11
☐ 131 Bill Swift	.25	.11
☐ 132 Checklist U1-U132	.25	.11

1992 Fleer Update Headliners

Each 1992 Fleer Update factory set included a four-card set of Headliner inserts. The cards are numbered separately and have a completely different design to the base cards. Each Headliner features UV coating and black borders. The set features a selection of stars that made headlines in the 1991 season. Cards are numbered on back X of 4.

	MINT	NRMT
COMPLETE SET (4)	15.00	6.75
COMMON CARD (1-4)	.50	.23

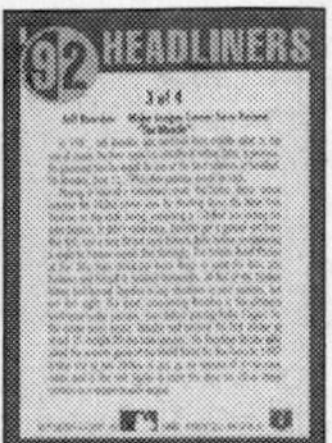

	MINT	NRMT
] 1 Ken Griffey Jr.	12.00	5.50
] 2 Robin Yount	1.50	.70
] 3 Jeff Reardon	.50	.23
] 4 Cecil Fielder	1.00	.45

1992 Fleer Citgo The Performer

his 24-card standard-size set was produced by Fleer for -Eleven. During April and May at any of the 1,600 articipating 7-Eleven stores, customers who purchased ight gallons or more of mid-grade or premium Citgo-rand gasoline received a packet of five trading cards. uring June or while supplies last, customers who vanted additional cards could receive three trading cards f their choice per eight gallon or more fill-up by sending a self-addressed envelope with 1.00 to cover postage nd handling. The front design has color action player hotos, with a metallic blue-green border that fades to vhite as one moves down the card face. The card front rominently features "The Performer". The team logo, layer's name, and his position appear in the wider right order. The top half of the backs have close-up photos, vhile the bottom half carry biography and complete career tatistics.

	MINT	NRMT
OMPLETE SET (24)	8.00	3.60
OMMON CARD (1-24)	.10	.05
] 1 Nolan Ryan	1.50	.70
] 2 Frank Thomas	1.50	.70
] 3 Ryne Sandberg	.75	.35
] 4 Ken Griffey Jr.	2.00	.90
] 5 Cal Ripken	1.50	.70
] 6 Roger Clemens	1.00	.45
] 7 Cecil Fielder	.25	.11
] 8 Dave Justice	.60	.25
] 9 Wade Boggs	.60	.25
] 10 Tony Gwynn	1.00	.45
] 11 Kirby Puckett	.75	.35
] 12 Darryl Strawberry	.25	.11
] 13 Jose Canseco	.40	.18
] 14 Barry Larkin	.40	.18
] 15 Terry Pendleton	.10	.05
] 16 Don Mattingly	.75	.35
] 17 Rickey Henderson	.40	.18
] 18 Ruben Sierra	.10	.05
] 19 Jeff Bagwell	1.00	.45
] 20 Tom Glavine	.25	.11
] 21 Ramon Martinez	.25	.11
] 22 Will Clark	.40	.18
] 23 Barry Bonds	.60	.25
] 24 Roberto Alomar	.60	.25

1992 Fleer Gwynn Casa de Amparo

his one card set was produced by the Fleer Corporation or Casa de Amparo (Spanish for house of refuge) which rovided care for over 600 children each year. Tony wynn served as a spokesperson for the house. The front eatures a color picture of Tony Gwynn hold Casa's Poster hild for 1992. The back displays information about Casa e Amparo.

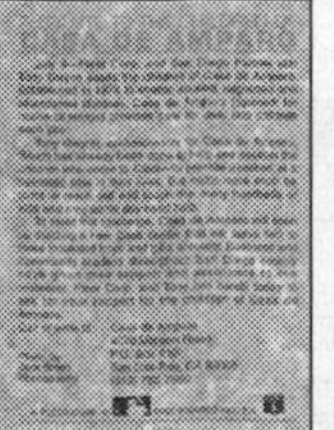

	MINT	NRMT
COMPLETE SET (1)	5.00	2.20
COMMON CARD (1)	5.00	2.20
☐ 1 Tony Gwynn	5.00	2.20

1993 Fleer

The 720-card 1993 Fleer baseball set contains two series of 360 standard-size cards. Cards were distributed in plastic wrapped packs, cello packs, jumbo packs and rack packs. For the first time in years, Fleer did not issue a factory set. In fact, Fleer discontinued issuing factory sets from 1993-on. The card fronts show glossy color action player photos bordered in silver. A team color-coded stripe edges the left side of the picture and carries the player's name and team name. The cards are checklisted below alphabetically within and according to teams for each league with NL preceding AL. Topical subsets include League Leaders (344-348/704-708), Round Trippers (349-353/709-713), and Super Star Specials (354-357/714-717). Each series concludes with checklists (358-360/718-720). There are no key Rookie Cards in this set.

	MINT	NRMT
COMPLETE SET (720)	40.00	18.00
COMPLETE SERIES 1 (360)	20.00	9.00
COMPLETE SERIES 2 (360)	20.00	9.00
COMMON CARD (1-720)	.10	.05
☐ 1 Steve Avery	.10	.05
☐ 2 Sid Bream	.10	.05
☐ 3 Ron Gant	.20	.09
☐ 4 Tom Glavine	.10	.05
☐ 5 Brian Hunter	.10	.05
☐ 6 Ryan Klesko	.50	.23
☐ 7 Charlie Leibrandt	.10	.05
☐ 8 Kent Mercker	.10	.05
☐ 9 David Nied	.10	.05
☐ 10 Otis Nixon	.10	.05
☐ 11 Greg Olson	.10	.05
☐ 12 Terry Pendleton	.20	.09
☐ 13 Deion Sanders	.40	.18
☐ 14 John Smoltz	.10	.05
☐ 15 Mike Stanton	.10	.05
☐ 16 Mark Wohlers	.20	.09
☐ 17 Paul Assenmacher	.10	.05
☐ 18 Steve Buechele	.10	.05
☐ 19 Shawon Dunston	.10	.05
☐ 20 Mark Grace	.10	.05
☐ 21 Derrick May	.10	.05
☐ 22 Chuck McElroy	.10	.05
☐ 23 Mike Morgan	.10	.05
☐ 24 Rey Sanchez	.10	.05
☐ 25 Ryne Sandberg	.50	.23
☐ 26 Bob Scanlan	.10	.05
☐ 27 Sammy Sosa	.40	.18
☐ 28 Rick Wilkins	.10	.05
☐ 29 Bobby Ayala	.10	.05
☐ 30 Tim Belcher	.10	.05
☐ 31 Jeff Branson	.10	.05
☐ 32 Norm Charlton	.10	.05
☐ 33 Steve Foster	.10	.05
☐ 34 Willie Greene	.20	.09
☐ 35 Chris Hammond	.10	.05
☐ 36 Milt Hill	.10	.05
☐ 37 Hal Morris	.10	.05
☐ 38 Joe Oliver	.10	.05
☐ 39 Paul O'Neill	.20	.09
☐ 40 Tim Pugh	.10	.05
☐ 41 Jose Rijo	.10	.05
☐ 42 Bip Roberts	.10	.05
☐ 43 Chris Sabo	.10	.05
☐ 44 Reggie Sanders	.20	.09
☐ 45 Eric Anthony	.10	.05
☐ 46 Jeff Bagwell	.75	.35
☐ 47 Craig Biggio	.10	.05
☐ 48 Joe Boever	.10	.05
☐ 49 Casey Candaele	.10	.05
☐ 50 Steve Finley	.20	.09
☐ 51 Luis Gonzalez	.10	.05
☐ 52 Pete Harnisch	.10	.05
☐ 53 Xavier Hernandez	.10	.05
☐ 54 Doug Jones	.10	.05
☐ 55 Eddie Taubensee	.10	.05
☐ 56 Brian Williams	.10	.05
☐ 57 Pedro Astacio	.10	.05
☐ 58 Todd Benzinger	.10	.05
☐ 59 Brett Butler	.20	.09
☐ 60 Tom Candiotti	.10	.05
☐ 61 Lenny Harris	.10	.05
☐ 62 Carlos Hernandez	.10	.05
☐ 63 Orel Hershiser	.20	.09
☐ 64 Eric Karros	.20	.09
☐ 65 Ramon Martinez	.20	.09
☐ 66 Jose Offerman	.10	.05
☐ 67 Mike Scioscia	.10	.05
☐ 68 Mike Sharperson	.10	.05
☐ 69 Eric Young	.40	.18
☐ 70 Moises Alou	.20	.09
☐ 71 Ivan Calderon	.10	.05
☐ 72 Archi Cianfrocco	.10	.05
☐ 73 Wil Cordero	.10	.05
☐ 74 Delino DeShields	.10	.05
☐ 75 Mark Gardner	.10	.05
☐ 76 Ken Hill	.20	.09
☐ 77 Tim Laker	.10	.05
☐ 78 Chris Nabholz	.10	.05
☐ 79 Mel Rojas	.20	.09
☐ 80 John Vander Wal UER (Misspelled Vander Wall in letters on back)	.10	.05
☐ 81 Larry Walker	.40	.18
☐ 82 Tim Wallach	.10	.05
☐ 83 John Wetteland	.20	.09
☐ 84 Bobby Bonilla	.20	.09
☐ 85 Daryl Boston	.10	.05
☐ 86 Sid Fernandez	.10	.05
☐ 87 Eric Hillman	.10	.05
☐ 88 Todd Hundley	.10	.05
☐ 89 Howard Johnson	.10	.05
☐ 90 Jeff Kent	.20	.09
☐ 91 Eddie Murray	.40	.18
☐ 92 Bill Pecota	.10	.05
☐ 93 Bret Saberhagen	.10	.05
☐ 94 Dick Schofield	.10	.05
☐ 95 Pete Schourek	.10	.05
☐ 96 Anthony Young	.10	.05
☐ 97 Ruben Amaro Jr.	.10	.05
☐ 98 Juan Bell	.10	.05
☐ 99 Wes Chamberlain	.10	.05
☐ 100 Darren Daulton	.20	.09
☐ 101 Mariano Duncan	.10	.05
☐ 102 Mike Hartley	.10	.05
☐ 103 Ricky Jordan	.10	.05
☐ 104 John Kruk	.20	.09
☐ 105 Mickey Morandini	.10	.05
☐ 106 Terry Mulholland	.10	.05
☐ 107 Ben Rivera	.10	.05
☐ 108 Curt Schilling	.10	.05
☐ 109 Keith Shepherd	.10	.05
☐ 110 Stan Belinda	.10	.05
☐ 111 Jay Bell	.20	.09
☐ 112 Barry Bonds	.50	.23
☐ 113 Jeff King	.20	.09
☐ 114 Mike LaValliere	.10	.05
☐ 115 Jose Lind	.10	.05
☐ 116 Roger Mason	.10	.05
☐ 117 Orlando Merced	.10	.05
☐ 118 Bob Patterson	.10	.05
☐ 119 Don Slaught	.10	.05
☐ 120 Zane Smith	.10	.05
☐ 121 Randy Tomlin	.10	.05
☐ 122 Andy Van Slyke	.20	.09
☐ 123 Tim Wakefield	.20	.09
☐ 124 Rheal Cormier	.10	.05
☐ 125 Bernard Gilkey	.20	.09
☐ 126 Felix Jose	.10	.05
☐ 127 Ray Lankford	.10	.05
☐ 128 Bob McClure	.10	.05
☐ 129 Donovan Osborne	.10	.05
☐ 130 Tom Pagnozzi	.10	.05
☐ 131 Geronimo Pena	.10	.05
☐ 132 Mike Perez	.10	.05

☐ 133 Lee Smith	.20	.09
☐ 134 Bob Tewksbury	.10	.05
☐ 135 Todd Worrell	.10	.05
☐ 136 Todd Zeile	.10	.05
☐ 137 Jerald Clark	.10	.05
☐ 138 Tony Gwynn	1.00	.45
☐ 139 Greg W. Harris	.10	.05
☐ 140 Jeremy Hernandez	.10	.05
☐ 141 Darrin Jackson	.10	.05
☐ 142 Mike Maddux	.10	.05
☐ 143 Fred McGriff	.10	.05
☐ 144 Jose Melendez	.10	.05
☐ 145 Rich Rodriguez	.10	.05
☐ 146 Frank Seminara	.10	.05
☐ 147 Gary Sheffield	.40	.18
☐ 148 Kurt Stillwell	.10	.05
☐ 149 Dan Walters	.10	.05
☐ 150 Rod Beck	.20	.09
☐ 151 Bud Black	.10	.05
☐ 152 Jeff Brantley	.10	.05
☐ 153 John Burkett	.10	.05
☐ 154 Will Clark	.10	.05
☐ 155 Royce Clayton	.10	.05
☐ 156 Mike Jackson	.10	.05
☐ 157 Darren Lewis	.10	.05
☐ 158 Kirt Manwaring	.10	.05
☐ 159 Willie McGee	.10	.05
☐ 160 Cory Snyder	.10	.05
☐ 161 Bill Swift	.10	.05
☐ 162 Trevor Wilson	.10	.05
☐ 163 Brady Anderson	.10	.05
☐ 164 Glenn Davis	.10	.05
☐ 165 Mike Devereaux	.10	.05
☐ 166 Todd Frohwirth	.10	.05
☐ 167 Leo Gomez	.10	.05
☐ 168 Chris Hoiles	.10	.05
☐ 169 Ben McDonald	.10	.05
☐ 170 Randy Milligan	.10	.05
☐ 171 Alan Mills	.10	.05
☐ 172 Mike Mussina	.40	.18
☐ 173 Gregg Olson	.10	.05
☐ 174 Arthur Rhodes	.10	.05
☐ 175 David Segui	.10	.05
☐ 176 Ellis Burks	.20	.09
☐ 177 Roger Clemens	.75	.35
☐ 178 Scott Cooper	.10	.05
☐ 179 Danny Darwin	.10	.05
☐ 180 Tony Fossas	.10	.05
☐ 181 Paul Quantrill	.10	.05
☐ 182 Jody Reed	.10	.05
☐ 183 John Valentin	.20	.09
☐ 184 Mo Vaughn	.50	.23
☐ 185 Frank Viola	.10	.05
☐ 186 Bob Zupcic	.10	.05
☐ 187 Jim Abbott	.10	.05
☐ 188 Gary DiSarcina	.10	.05
☐ 189 Damion Easley	.10	.05
☐ 190 Junior Felix	.10	.05
☐ 191 Chuck Finley	.10	.05
☐ 192 Joe Grahe	.10	.05
☐ 193 Bryan Harvey	.10	.05
☐ 194 Mark Langston	.10	.05
☐ 195 John Orton	.10	.05
☐ 196 Luis Polonia	.10	.05
☐ 197 Tim Salmon	.50	.23
☐ 198 Luis Sojo	.10	.05
☐ 199 Wilson Alvarez	.20	.09
☐ 200 George Bell	.10	.05
☐ 201 Alex Fernandez	.20	.09
☐ 202 Craig Grebeck	.10	.05
☐ 203 Ozzie Guillen	.10	.05
☐ 204 Lance Johnson	.10	.05
☐ 205 Ron Karkovice	.10	.05
☐ 206 Kirk McCaskill	.10	.05
☐ 207 Jack McDowell	.10	.05
☐ 208 Scott Radinsky	.10	.05
☐ 209 Tim Raines	.20	.09
☐ 210 Frank Thomas	1.50	.70
☐ 211 Robin Ventura	.20	.09
☐ 212 Sandy Alomar Jr.	.20	.09
☐ 213 Carlos Baerga	.20	.09
☐ 214 Dennis Cook	.10	.05
☐ 215 Thomas Howard	.10	.05
☐ 216 Mark Lewis	.10	.05
☐ 217 Derek Lilliquist	.10	.05
☐ 218 Kenny Lofton	.75	.35
☐ 219 Charles Nagy	.20	.09
☐ 220 Steve Olin	.10	.05
☐ 221 Paul Sorrento	.10	.05
☐ 222 Jim Thome	.75	.35
☐ 223 Mark Whiten	.10	.05
☐ 224 Milt Cuyler	.10	.05
☐ 225 Rob Deer	.10	.05
☐ 226 John Doherty	.10	.05
☐ 227 Cecil Fielder	.20	.09
☐ 228 Travis Fryman	.20	.09
☐ 229 Mike Henneman	.10	.05
☐ 230 John Kiely UER	.10	.05
(Card has batting		
stats of Pat Kelly)		
☐ 231 Kurt Knudsen	.10	.05
☐ 232 Scott Livingstone	.10	.05
☐ 233 Tony Phillips	.10	.05
☐ 234 Mickey Tettleton	.10	.05
☐ 235 Kevin Appier	.20	.09
☐ 236 George Brett	.75	.35
☐ 237 Tom Gordon	.10	.05
☐ 238 Gregg Jefferies	.20	.09
☐ 239 Wally Joyner	.20	.09
☐ 240 Kevin Koslofski	.10	.05
☐ 241 Mike Macfarlane	.10	.05
☐ 242 Brian McRae	.10	.05
☐ 243 Rusty Meacham	.10	.05
☐ 244 Keith Miller	.10	.05
☐ 245 Jeff Montgomery	.20	.09
☐ 246 Hipolito Pichardo	.10	.05
☐ 247 Ricky Bones	.10	.05
☐ 248 Cal Eldred	.10	.05
☐ 249 Mike Fetters	.10	.05
☐ 250 Darryl Hamilton	.10	.05
☐ 251 Doug Henry	.10	.05
☐ 252 John Jaha	.20	.09
☐ 253 Pat Listach	.10	.05
☐ 254 Paul Molitor	.40	.18
☐ 255 Jaime Navarro	.10	.05
☐ 256 Kevin Seitzer	.10	.05
☐ 257 B.J. Surhoff	.20	.09
☐ 258 Greg Vaughn	.10	.05
☐ 259 Bill Wegman	.10	.05
☐ 260 Robin Yount	.10	.05
☐ 261 Rick Aguilera	.10	.05
☐ 262 Chili Davis	.20	.09
☐ 263 Scott Erickson	.10	.05
☐ 264 Greg Gagne	.10	.05
☐ 265 Mark Guthrie	.10	.05
☐ 266 Brian Harper	.10	.05
☐ 267 Kent Hrbek	.20	.09
☐ 268 Terry Jorgensen	.10	.05
☐ 269 Gene Larkin	.10	.05
☐ 270 Scott Leius	.10	.05
☐ 271 Pat Mahomes	.10	.05
☐ 272 Pedro Munoz	.10	.05
☐ 273 Kirby Puckett	.75	.35
☐ 274 Kevin Tapani	.10	.05
☐ 275 Carl Willis	.10	.05
☐ 276 Steve Farr	.10	.05
☐ 277 John Habyan	.10	.05
☐ 278 Mel Hall	.10	.05
☐ 279 Charlie Hayes	.10	.05
☐ 280 Pat Kelly	.10	.05
☐ 281 Don Mattingly	.60	.25
☐ 282 Sam Militello	.10	.05
☐ 283 Matt Nokes	.10	.05
☐ 284 Melido Perez	.10	.05
☐ 285 Andy Stankiewicz	.10	.05
☐ 286 Danny Tartabull	.10	.05
☐ 287 Randy Velarde	.10	.05
☐ 288 Bob Wickman	.10	.05
☐ 289 Bernie Williams	.10	.05
☐ 290 Lance Blankenship	.10	.05
☐ 291 Mike Bordick	.10	.05
☐ 292 Jerry Browne	.10	.05
☐ 293 Dennis Eckersley	.10	.05
☐ 294 Rickey Henderson	.10	.05
☐ 295 Vince Horsman	.10	.05
☐ 296 Mark McGwire	.75	.35
☐ 297 Jeff Parrett	.10	.05
☐ 298 Ruben Sierra	.10	.05
☐ 299 Terry Steinbach	.20	.09
☐ 300 Walt Weiss	.10	.05
☐ 301 Bob Welch	.10	.05
☐ 302 Willie Wilson	.10	.05
☐ 303 Bobby Witt	.10	.05
☐ 304 Bret Boone	.10	.05
☐ 305 Jay Buhner	.10	.05
☐ 306 Dave Fleming	.10	.05
☐ 307 Ken Griffey Jr.	2.00	.90
☐ 308 Erik Hanson	.10	.05
☐ 309 Edgar Martinez	.10	.05
☐ 310 Tino Martinez	.40	.18
☐ 311 Jeff Nelson	.10	.05
☐ 312 Dennis Powell	.10	.05
☐ 313 Mike Schooler	.10	.05
☐ 314 Russ Swan	.10	.05
☐ 315 Dave Valle	.10	.05
☐ 316 Omar Vizquel	.20	.09
☐ 317 Kevin Brown	.20	.09
☐ 318 Todd Burns	.10	.05
☐ 319 Jose Canseco	.10	.05
☐ 320 Julio Franco	.20	.09
☐ 321 Jeff Frye	.10	.05
☐ 322 Juan Gonzalez	1.00	.45
☐ 323 Jose Guzman	.10	.05
☐ 324 Jeff Huson	.10	.05
☐ 325 Dean Palmer	.20	.09
☐ 326 Kevin Reimer	.10	.05
☐ 327 Ivan Rodriguez	.50	.23
☐ 328 Kenny Rogers	.10	.05
☐ 329 Dan Smith	.10	.05
☐ 330 Roberto Alomar	.40	.18
☐ 331 Derek Bell	.20	.09
☐ 332 Pat Borders	.10	.05
☐ 333 Joe Carter	.10	.05
☐ 334 Kelly Gruber	.10	.05
☐ 335 Tom Henke	.10	.05
☐ 336 Jimmy Key	.20	.09
☐ 337 Manuel Lee	.10	.05
☐ 338 Candy Maldonado	.10	.05
☐ 339 John Olerud	.10	.05
☐ 340 Todd Stottlemyre	.10	.05
☐ 341 Duane Ward	.10	.05
☐ 342 Devon White	.10	.05
☐ 343 Dave Winfield	.10	.05
☐ 344 Edgar Martinez LL	.20	.09
☐ 345 Cecil Fielder LL	.20	.09
☐ 346 Kenny Lofton LL	.40	.18
☐ 347 Jack Morris LL	.10	.05
☐ 348 Roger Clemens LL	.40	.18
☐ 349 Fred McGriff RT	.20	.09
☐ 350 Barry Bonds RT	.40	.18
☐ 351 Gary Sheffield RT	.40	.18
☐ 352 Darren Daulton RT	.20	.09
☐ 353 Dave Hollins RT	.10	.05
☐ 354 Brothers in Blue	.10	.05
Pedro Martinez		
Ramon Martinez		
☐ 355 Power Packs	.50	.23
Ivan Rodriguez		
Kirby Puckett		
☐ 356 Triple Threats	.40	.18
Ryne Sandberg		
Gary Sheffield		
☐ 357 Infield Trifecta	.40	.18
Roberto Alomar		
Chuck Knoblauch		
Carlos Baerga		
☐ 358 Checklist 1-120	.10	.05
☐ 359 Checklist 121-240	.10	.05
☐ 360 Checklist 241-360	.10	.05
☐ 361 Rafael Belliard	.10	.05
☐ 362 Damon Berryhill	.10	.05
☐ 363 Mike Bielecki	.10	.05
☐ 364 Jeff Blauser	.10	.05
☐ 365 Francisco Cabrera	.10	.05
☐ 366 Marvin Freeman	.10	.05
☐ 367 David Justice	.40	.18
☐ 368 Mark Lemke	.10	.05
☐ 369 Alejandro Pena	.10	.05
☐ 370 Jeff Reardon	.20	.09
☐ 371 Lonnie Smith	.10	.05
☐ 372 Pete Smith	.10	.05
☐ 373 Shawn Boskie	.10	.05
☐ 374 Jim Bullinger	.10	.05
☐ 375 Frank Castillo	.10	.05
☐ 376 Doug Dascenzo	.10	.05
☐ 377 Andre Dawson	.10	.05
☐ 378 Mike Harkey	.10	.05
☐ 379 Greg Hibbard	.10	.05
☐ 380 Greg Maddux	1.25	.55
☐ 381 Ken Patterson	.10	.05
☐ 382 Jeff D. Robinson	.10	.05
☐ 383 Luis Salazar	.10	.05
☐ 384 Dwight Smith	.10	.05
☐ 385 Jose Vizcaino	.10	.05
☐ 386 Scott Bankhead	.10	.05
☐ 387 Tom Browning	.10	.05
☐ 388 Darnell Coles	.10	.05
☐ 389 Rob Dibble	.10	.05
☐ 390 Bill Doran	.10	.05
☐ 391 Dwayne Henry	.10	.05
☐ 392 Cesar Hernandez	.10	.05
☐ 393 Roberto Kelly	.10	.05
☐ 394 Barry Larkin	.10	.05
☐ 395 Dave Martinez	.10	.05
☐ 396 Kevin Mitchell	.20	.09
☐ 397 Jeff Reed	.10	.05
☐ 398 Scott Ruskin	.10	.05
☐ 399 Greg Swindell	.10	.05
☐ 400 Dan Wilson	.20	.09
☐ 401 Andy Ashby	.10	.05
☐ 402 Freddie Benavides	.10	.05
☐ 403 Dante Bichette	.10	.05
☐ 404 Willie Blair	.10	.05
☐ 405 Denis Boucher	.10	.05
☐ 406 Vinny Castilla	.40	.18
☐ 407 Braulio Castillo	.10	.05
☐ 408 Alex Cole	.10	.05
☐ 409 Andres Galarraga	.10	.05
☐ 410 Joe Girardi	.10	.05
☐ 411 Butch Henry	.10	.05
☐ 412 Darren Holmes	.10	.05

☐ 413 Calvin Jones	.10	.05
☐ 414 Steve Reed	.10	.05
☐ 415 Kevin Ritz	.10	.05
☐ 416 Jim Tatum	.10	.05
☐ 417 Jack Armstrong	.10	.05
☐ 418 Bret Barberie	.10	.05
☐ 419 Ryan Bowen	.10	.05
☐ 420 Cris Carpenter	.10	.05
☐ 421 Chuck Carr	.10	.05
☐ 422 Scott Chiamparino	.10	.05
☐ 423 Jeff Conine	.20	.09
☐ 424 Jim Corsi	.10	.05
☐ 425 Steve Decker	.10	.05
☐ 426 Chris Donnels	.10	.05
☐ 427 Monty Fariss	.10	.05
☐ 428 Bob Natal	.10	.05
☐ 429 Pat Rapp	.10	.05
☐ 430 Dave Weathers	.10	.05
☐ 431 Nigel Wilson	.10	.05
☐ 432 Ken Caminiti	.40	.18
☐ 433 Andujar Cedeno	.10	.05
☐ 434 Tom Edens	.10	.05
☐ 435 Juan Guerrero	.10	.05
☐ 436 Pete Incaviglia	.10	.05
☐ 437 Jimmy Jones	.10	.05
☐ 438 Darryl Kile	.20	.09
☐ 439 Rob Murphy	.10	.05
☐ 440 Al Osuna	.10	.05
☐ 441 Mark Portugal	.10	.05
☐ 442 Scott Servais	.10	.05
☐ 443 John Candelaria	.10	.05
☐ 444 Tim Crews	.10	.05
☐ 445 Eric Davis	.20	.09
☐ 446 Tom Goodwin	.10	.05
☐ 447 Jim Gott	.10	.05
☐ 448 Kevin Gross	.10	.05
☐ 449 Dave Hansen	.10	.05
☐ 450 Jay Howell	.10	.05
☐ 451 Roger McDowell	.10	.05
☐ 452 Bob Ojeda	.10	.05
☐ 453 Henry Rodriguez	.20	.09
☐ 454 Darryl Strawberry	.20	.09
☐ 455 Mitch Webster	.10	.05
☐ 456 Steve Wilson	.10	.05
☐ 457 Brian Barnes	.10	.05
☐ 458 Sean Berry	.10	.05
☐ 459 Jeff Fassero	.10	.05
☐ 460 Darrin Fletcher	.10	.05
☐ 461 Marquis Grissom	.20	.09
☐ 462 Dennis Martinez	.20	.09
☐ 463 Spike Owen	.10	.05
☐ 464 Matt Stairs	.10	.05
☐ 465 Sergio Valdez	.10	.05
☐ 466 Kevin Bass	.10	.05
☐ 467 Vince Coleman	.10	.05
☐ 468 Mark Dewey	.10	.05
☐ 469 Kevin Elster	.10	.05
☐ 470 Tony Fernandez	.10	.05
☐ 471 John Franco	.10	.05
☐ 472 Dave Gallagher	.10	.05
☐ 473 Paul Gibson	.10	.05
☐ 474 Dwight Gooden	.20	.09
☐ 475 Lee Guetterman	.10	.05
☐ 476 Jeff Innis	.10	.05
☐ 477 Dave Magadan	.10	.05
☐ 478 Charlie O'Brien	.10	.05
☐ 479 Willie Randolph	.20	.09
☐ 480 Mackey Sasser	.10	.05
☐ 481 Ryan Thompson	.10	.05
☐ 482 Chico Walker	.10	.05
☐ 483 Kyle Abbott	.10	.05
☐ 484 Bob Ayrault	.10	.05
☐ 485 Kim Batiste	.10	.05
☐ 486 Cliff Brantley	.10	.05
☐ 487 Jose DeLeon	.10	.05
☐ 488 Len Dykstra	.15	.07
☐ 489 Tommy Greene	.10	.05
☐ 490 Jeff Grotewold	.10	.05
☐ 491 Dave Hollins	.10	.05
☐ 492 Danny Jackson	.10	.05
☐ 493 Stan Javier	.10	.05
☐ 494 Tom Marsh	.10	.05
☐ 495 Greg Mathews	.10	.05
☐ 496 Dale Murphy	.10	.05
☐ 497 Todd Pratt	.10	.05
☐ 498 Mitch Williams	.10	.05
☐ 499 Danny Cox	.10	.05
☐ 500 Doug Drabek	.10	.05
☐ 501 Carlos Garcia	.10	.05
☐ 502 Lloyd McClendon	.10	.05
☐ 503 Denny Neagle	.10	.05
☐ 504 Gary Redus	.10	.05
☐ 505 Bob Walk	.10	.05
☐ 506 John Wehner	.10	.05
☐ 507 Luis Alicea	.10	.05
☐ 508 Mark Clark	.10	.05
☐ 509 Pedro Guerrero	.10	.05
☐ 510 Rex Hudler	.10	.05
☐ 511 Brian Jordan	.20	.09
☐ 512 Omar Olivares	.10	.05
☐ 513 Jose Oquendo	.10	.05
☐ 514 Gerald Perry	.10	.05
☐ 515 Bryn Smith	.10	.05
☐ 516 Craig Wilson	.10	.05
☐ 517 Tracy Woodson	.10	.05
☐ 518 Larry Andersen	.10	.05
☐ 519 Andy Benes	.20	.09
☐ 520 Jim Deshaies	.10	.05
☐ 521 Bruce Hurst	.10	.05
☐ 522 Randy Myers	.20	.09
☐ 523 Benito Santiago	.10	.05
☐ 524 Tim Scott	.10	.05
☐ 525 Tim Teufel	.10	.05
☐ 526 Mike Benjamin	.10	.05
☐ 527 Dave Burba	.10	.05
☐ 528 Craig Colbert	.10	.05
☐ 529 Mike Felder	.10	.05
☐ 530 Bryan Hickerson	.10	.05
☐ 531 Chris James	.10	.05
☐ 532 Mark Leonard	.10	.05
☐ 533 Greg Litton	.10	.05
☐ 534 Francisco Oliveras	.10	.05
☐ 535 John Patterson	.10	.05
☐ 536 Jim Pena	.10	.05
☐ 537 Dave Righetti	.10	.05
☐ 538 Robby Thompson	.10	.05
☐ 539 Jose Uribe	.10	.05
☐ 540 Matt Williams	.10	.05
☐ 541 Storm Davis	.10	.05
☐ 542 Sam Horn	.10	.05
☐ 543 Tim Hulett	.10	.05
☐ 544 Craig Lefferts	.10	.05
☐ 545 Chito Martinez	.10	.05
☐ 546 Mark McLemore	.10	.05
☐ 547 Luis Mercedes	.10	.05
☐ 548 Bob Milacki	.10	.05
☐ 549 Joe Orsulak	.10	.05
☐ 550 Billy Ripken	.10	.05
☐ 551 Cal Ripken Jr.	1.50	.70
☐ 552 Rick Sutcliffe	.10	.05
☐ 553 Jeff Tackett	.10	.05
☐ 554 Wade Boggs	.40	.18
☐ 555 Tom Brunansky	.10	.05
☐ 556 Jack Clark	.10	.05
☐ 557 John Dopson	.10	.05
☐ 558 Mike Gardiner	.10	.05
☐ 559 Mike Greenwell	.10	.05
☐ 560 Greg A. Harris	.10	.05
☐ 561 Billy Hatcher	.10	.05
☐ 562 Joe Hesketh	.10	.05
☐ 563 Tony Pena	.10	.05
☐ 564 Phil Plantier	.10	.05
☐ 565 Luis Rivera	.10	.05
☐ 566 Herm Winningham	.10	.05
☐ 567 Matt Young	.10	.05
☐ 568 Bert Blyleven	.20	.09
☐ 569 Mike Butcher	.10	.05
☐ 570 Chuck Crim	.10	.05
☐ 571 Chad Curtis	.20	.09
☐ 572 Tim Fortugno	.10	.05
☐ 573 Steve Frey	.10	.05
☐ 574 Gary Gaetti	.20	.09
☐ 575 Scott Lewis	.10	.05
☐ 576 Lee Stevens	.10	.05
☐ 577 Ron Tingley	.10	.05
☐ 578 Julio Valera	.10	.05
☐ 579 Shawn Abner	.10	.05
☐ 580 Joey Cora	.20	.09
☐ 581 Chris Cron	.10	.05
☐ 582 Carlton Fisk	.40	.18
☐ 583 Roberto Hernandez	.20	.09
☐ 584 Charlie Hough	.10	.05
☐ 585 Terry Leach	.10	.05
☐ 586 Donn Pall	.10	.05
☐ 587 Dan Pasqua	.10	.05
☐ 588 Steve Sax	.10	.05
☐ 589 Bobby Thigpen	.10	.05
☐ 590 Albert Belle	.50	.23
☐ 591 Felix Fermin	.10	.05
☐ 592 Glenallen Hill	.10	.05
☐ 593 Brook Jacoby	.10	.05
☐ 594 Reggie Jefferson	.20	.09
☐ 595 Carlos Martinez	.10	.05
☐ 596 Jose Mesa	.20	.09
☐ 597 Rod Nichols	.10	.05
☐ 598 Junior Ortiz	.10	.05
☐ 599 Eric Plunk	.10	.05
☐ 600 Ted Power	.10	.05
☐ 601 Scott Scudder	.10	.05
☐ 602 Kevin Wickander	.10	.05
☐ 603 Skeeter Barnes	.10	.05
☐ 604 Mark Carreon	.10	.05
☐ 605 Dan Gladden	.10	.05
☐ 606 Bill Gullickson	.10	.05
☐ 607 Chad Kreuter	.10	.05
☐ 608 Mark Leiter	.10	.05
☐ 609 Mike Munoz	.10	.05
☐ 610 Rich Rowland	.10	.05
☐ 611 Frank Tanana	.10	.05
☐ 612 Walt Terrell	.10	.05
☐ 613 Alan Trammell	.10	.05
☐ 614 Lou Whitaker	.20	.09
☐ 615 Luis Aquino	.10	.05
☐ 616 Mike Boddicker	.10	.05
☐ 617 Jim Eisenreich	.20	.09
☐ 618 Mark Gubicza	.10	.05
☐ 619 David Howard	.10	.05
☐ 620 Mike Magnante	.10	.05
☐ 621 Brent Mayne	.10	.05
☐ 622 Kevin McReynolds	.10	.05
☐ 623 Ed Pierce	.10	.05
☐ 624 Bill Sampen	.10	.05
☐ 625 Steve Shifflett	.10	.05
☐ 626 Gary Thurman	.10	.05
☐ 627 Curtis Wilkerson	.10	.05
☐ 628 Chris Bosio	.10	.05
☐ 629 Scott Fletcher	.10	.05
☐ 630 Jim Gantner	.10	.05
☐ 631 Dave Nilsson	.20	.09
☐ 632 Jesse Orosco	.10	.05
☐ 633 Dan Plesac	.10	.05
☐ 634 Ron Robinson	.10	.05
☐ 635 Bill Spiers	.10	.05
☐ 636 Franklin Stubbs	.10	.05
☐ 637 Willie Banks	.10	.05
☐ 638 Randy Bush	.10	.05
☐ 639 Chuck Knoblauch	.40	.18
☐ 640 Shane Mack	.10	.05
☐ 641 Mike Pagliarulo	.10	.05
☐ 642 Jeff Reboulet	.10	.05
☐ 643 John Smiley	.10	.05
☐ 644 Mike Trombley	.10	.05
☐ 645 Gary Wayne	.10	.05
☐ 646 Lenny Webster	.10	.05
☐ 647 Tim Burke	.10	.05
☐ 648 Mike Gallego	.10	.05
☐ 649 Dion James	.10	.05
☐ 650 Jeff Johnson	.10	.05
☐ 651 Scott Kamieniecki	.10	.05
☐ 652 Kevin Maas	.10	.05
☐ 653 Rich Monteleone	.10	.05
☐ 654 Jerry Nielsen	.10	.05
☐ 655 Scott Sanderson	.10	.05
☐ 656 Mike Stanley	.10	.05
☐ 657 Gerald Williams	.10	.05
☐ 658 Curt Young	.10	.05
☐ 659 Harold Baines	.20	.09
☐ 660 Kevin Campbell	.10	.05
☐ 661 Ron Darling	.10	.05
☐ 662 Kelly Downs	.10	.05
☐ 663 Eric Fox	.10	.05
☐ 664 Dave Henderson	.10	.05
☐ 665 Rick Honeycutt	.10	.05
☐ 666 Mike Moore	.10	.05
☐ 667 Jamie Quirk	.10	.05
☐ 668 Jeff Russell	.10	.05
☐ 669 Dave Stewart	.20	.09
☐ 670 Greg Briley	.10	.05
☐ 671 Dave Cochrane	.10	.05
☐ 672 Henry Cotto	.10	.05
☐ 673 Rich DeLucia	.10	.05
☐ 674 Brian Fisher	.10	.05
☐ 675 Mark Grant	.10	.05
☐ 676 Randy Johnson	.40	.18
☐ 677 Tim Leary	.10	.05
☐ 678 Pete O'Brien	.10	.05
☐ 679 Lance Parrish	.10	.05
☐ 680 Harold Reynolds	.10	.05
☐ 681 Shane Turner	.10	.05
☐ 682 Jack Daugherty	.10	.05
☐ 683 David Hulse	.10	.05
☐ 684 Terry Mathews	.10	.05
☐ 685 Al Newman	.10	.05
☐ 686 Edwin Nunez	.10	.05
☐ 687 Rafael Palmeiro	.10	.05
☐ 688 Roger Pavlik	.10	.05
☐ 689 Geno Petralli	.10	.05
☐ 690 Nolan Ryan	1.50	.70
☐ 691 David Cone	.20	.09
☐ 692 Alfredo Griffin	.10	.05
☐ 693 Juan Guzman	.10	.05
☐ 694 Pat Hentgen	.10	.05
☐ 695 Randy Knorr	.10	.05
☐ 696 Bob MacDonald	.10	.05
☐ 697 Jack Morris	.20	.09
☐ 698 Ed Sprague	.10	.05
☐ 699 Dave Stieb	.10	.05
☐ 700 Pat Tabler	.10	.05
☐ 701 Mike Timlin	.10	.05
☐ 702 David Wells	.10	.05
☐ 703 Eddie Zosky	.10	.05

☐ 704 Gary Sheffield LL	.40	.18
☐ 705 Darren Daulton LL	.20	.09
☐ 706 Marquis Grissom LL	.20	.09
☐ 707 Greg Maddux LL	.60	.25
☐ 708 Bill Swift LL	.10	.05
☐ 709 Juan Gonzalez RT	.40	.18
☐ 710 Mark McGwire RT	.40	.18
☐ 711 Cecil Fielder RT	.20	.09
☐ 712 Albert Belle RT	.40	.18
☐ 713 Joe Carter RT	.20	.09
☐ 714 Cecil Fielder SS Frank Thomas Power Brokers	.40	.18
☐ 715 Larry Walker SS Darren Daulton Unsung Heroes	.40	.18
☐ 716 Edgar Martinez SS Robin Ventura Hot Corner Hammers	.20	.09
☐ 717 Roger Clemens SS Dennis Eckersley Start to Finish	.40	.18
☐ 718 Checklist 361-480	.10	.05
☐ 719 Checklist 481-600	.10	.05
☐ 720 Checklist 601-720	.10	.05

1993 Fleer All-Stars

This 24-card standard-size set featuring members of the American and National league All-Star squads, was randomly inserted in wax packs. 12 American League players were seeded in series 1 packs and 12 National League players in series 2. The horizontal fronts feature a color close-up photo cut out and superposed upon a black-and-white action scene framed by white borders. The player's name and the word "All-Stars" are printed in gold foil lettering across the bottom of the picture.

	MINT	NRMT
COMPLETE SET (24)	40.00	18.00
COMPLETE SER.1 (12)	25.00	11.00
COMPLETE SER.2 (12)	15.00	6.75
COMMON CARD (AL1-NL12)	.75	.35
☐ AL1 Frank Thomas	12.00	5.50
☐ AL2 Roberto Alomar	2.00	.90
☐ AL3 Edgar Martinez	1.50	.70
☐ AL4 Pat Listach	.75	.35
☐ AL5 Cecil Fielder	1.00	.45
☐ AL6 Juan Gonzalez	6.00	2.70
☐ AL7 Ken Griffey Jr.	12.00	5.50
☐ AL8 Joe Carter	1.00	.45
☐ AL9 Kirby Puckett	5.00	2.20
☐ AL10 Brian Harper	.75	.35
☐ AL11 Dave Fleming	.75	.35
☐ AL12 Jack McDowell	.75	.35
☐ NL1 Fred McGriff	1.50	.70
☐ NL2 Delino DeShields	.75	.35
☐ NL3 Gary Sheffield	2.00	.90
☐ NL4 Barry Larkin	1.50	.70
☐ NL5 Felix Jose	.75	.35
☐ NL6 Larry Walker	2.00	.90
☐ NL7 Barry Bonds	3.00	1.35
☐ NL8 Andy Van Slyke	1.00	.45
☐ NL9 Darren Daulton	1.00	.45
☐ NL10 Greg Maddux	8.00	3.60
☐ NL11 Tom Glavine	1.50	.70
☐ NL12 Lee Smith	1.00	.45

1993 Fleer Glavine

As part of the Signature Series, this 12-card standard-size set spotlights Tom Glavine. An additional three cards (13-15) were available via a mail-in offer and are generally considered to be a seperate set. The mail-in offer expired on September 30, 1993. The fronts feature glossy color action photos with white borders. The player's name and the words "Career Highlights" appear in gold foil block lettering across the bottom of the picture. The horizontal backs carry a small close-up color photo and summarize chapters of Glavine's career. The cards are numbered on

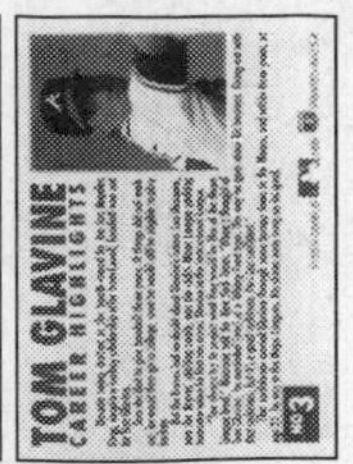

the back at the lower left corner. Reportedly, a filmmaking problem during production resulted in eight variations in this 12-card insert set. Different backs appear on eight of the 12 cards. Cards 1-4 and 7-10 in wax packs feature card-back text variations from those included in the rack and jumbo magazine packs. The text differences occur in the first few words of text on the card back. No corrections were made in Series I. The correct Glavine cards appeared in Series II wax, rack, and jumbo magazine packs.

	MINT	NRMT
COMPLETE SET (12)	4.00	1.80
COMMON GLAVINE (1-12)	.50	.23
COMMON SEND-OFF (13-15)	2.00	.90
☐ 1 Tom Glavine The Glavine family ... (Throwing to first)	.50	.23
☐ 2 Tom Glavine High School baseball ... (Pitching, with arm behind head, shot from left side)	.50	.23
☐ 3 Tom Glavine Despite being drafted ... (Pitching, close-up shot from left side)	.50	.23
☐ 4 Tom Glavine Unflappable is ... (Pitching, shot from almost directly in front)	.50	.23
☐ 5 Tom Glavine In 1989 Tom ... (Pitching, shot from right angle)	.50	.23
☐ 6 Tom Glavine Tom Glavine had ... (Pitching, with ball below waist)	.50	.23
☐ 7 Tom Glavine Tom Glavine's dream ... (Pitching, close-up shot with ball behind head)	.50	.23
☐ 8 Tom Glavine After Winning ... (Pitching, shot from directly in front)	.50	.23
☐ 9 Tom Glavine Little Leaguers ... (Pitching, just after release with left leg in air)	.50	.23
☐ 10 Tom Glavine Will success spoil ... (Pitching, ball below waist and right leg slightly raised)	.50	.23
☐ 11 Tom Glavine What makes Tom ... (Batting)	.50	.23
☐ 12 Tom Glavine It was a day ... (Pitching, close-up shot wearing dark blue top)	.50	.23
☐ 13 Tom Glavine Send-Off 1	2.00	.90
☐ 14 Tom Glavine Send-Off 2	2.00	.90
☐ 15 Tom Glavine Send-Off 3	2.00	.90
☐ AU0 Tom Glavine AU (Certified signature)	80.00	36.00

1993 Fleer Golden Moments

Cards from this six-card standard-size set, featuring memorable moments from the previous season, were randomly inserted in 1993 Fleer wax packs, three each in series 1 and 2. The fronts feature glossy color action photos framed by thin aqua and white lines and a black outer border. A gold foil baseball icon appears at each corner of the picture, and the player's name and the set

title "Golden Moments" appears in a gold foil bar toward the bottom of the picture. The cards are unnumbered and checklisted below in alphabetical order.

	MINT	NRMT
COMPLETE SET (6)	12.00	5.50
COMPLETE SER.1 (3)	4.00	1.80
COMPLETE SER.2 (3)	8.00	3.60
COMMON SERIES 1 (A1-B3)	.50	.23
☐ A1 George Brett	5.00	2.20
☐ A2 Mickey Morandini	.50	.23
☐ A3 Dave Winfield	2.00	.90
☐ B1 Dennis Eckersley	1.50	.70
☐ B2 Bip Roberts	.50	.23
☐ B3 Frank Thomas and Juan Gonzalez	8.00	3.60

1993 Fleer Major League Prospects

Cards from this 36-card standard-size set, featuring a selection of prospects, were randomly inserted in wax packs, 18 each in series 1 and 2. These cards feature black-bordered color player action photos on their fronts. The player's name appears in gold foil at the top, and the set's name and logo appear in gold foil and black at the bottom. The key card in this set is Mike Piazza.

	MINT	NRMT
COMPLETE SET (36)	30.00	13.50
COMPLETE SERIES 1 (18)	20.00	9.00
COMPLETE SERIES 2 (18)	10.00	4.50
COMMON SERIES 1 (A1-A18)	.50	.23
COMMON SERIES 2 (B1-B18)	.50	.23
☐ A1 Melvin Nieves	.75	.35
☐ A2 Sterling Hitchcock	.50	.23
☐ A3 Tim Costo	.50	.23
☐ A4 Manny Alexander	.50	.23
☐ A5 Alan Embree	.50	.23
☐ A6 Kevin Young	.50	.23
☐ A7 J.T. Snow	1.50	.70
☐ A8 Russ Springer	.50	.23
☐ A9 Billy Ashley	.50	.23
☐ A10 Kevin Rogers	.50	.23
☐ A11 Steve Hosey	.50	.23
☐ A12 Eric Wedge	.50	.23
☐ A13 Mike Piazza	15.00	6.75
☐ A14 Jesse Levis	.50	.23
☐ A15 Rico Brogna	.75	.35
☐ A16 Alex Arias	.50	.23
☐ A17 Rod Brewer	.50	.23
☐ A18 Troy Neel	.50	.23
☐ B1 Scooter Tucker	.50	.23
☐ B2 Kerry Woodson	.50	.23
☐ B3 Greg Colbrunn	.50	.23
☐ B4 Pedro Martinez	5.00	2.20
☐ B5 Dave Silvestri	.50	.23
☐ B6 Kent Bottenfield	.50	.23
☐ B7 Rafael Bournigal	.50	.23
☐ B8 J.T. Bruett	.50	.23
☐ B9 Dave Mlicki	.50	.23
☐ B10 Paul Wagner	.50	.23
☐ B11 Mike Williams	.50	.23
☐ B12 Henry Mercedes	.50	.23
☐ B13 Scott Taylor	.50	.23
☐ B14 Dennis Moeller	.50	.23
☐ B15 Javier Lopez	3.00	1.35

☐ B16 Steve Cooke	.50	.23
☐ B17 Pete Young	.50	.23
☐ B18 Ken Ryan	.50	.23

1993 Fleer Pro-Visions

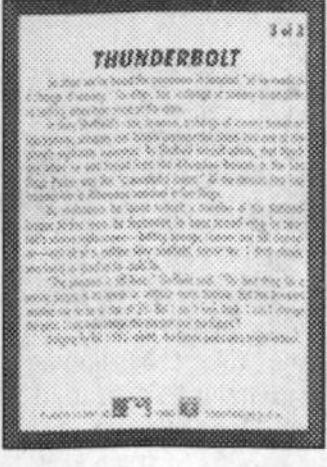

Cards from this six-card standard-size set, featuring a selection of superstars in fantasy paintings, were randomly inserted in poly packs, three each in series 1 and 2. These cards feature black-bordered fanciful color artwork of the players in action. The player's name appears in gold foil within the bottom black margin of each.

	MINT	NRMT
COMPLETE SET (6)	5.00	2.20
COMPLETE SERIES 1 (3)	3.00	1.35
COMPLETE SERIES 2 (3)	2.00	.90
COMMON SERIES 1 (A1-B3)	.75	.35
☐ A1 Roberto Alomar	2.00	.90
☐ A2 Dennis Eckersley	1.50	.70
☐ A3 Gary Sheffield	2.00	.90
☐ B1 Andy Van Slyke	.75	.35
☐ B2 Tom Glavine	1.50	.70
☐ B3 Cecil Fielder	1.00	.45

1993 Fleer Rookie Sensations

Cards from this 20-card standard-size set, featuring a selection of 1993's top rookies, were randomly inserted in cello packs, 10 each in series 1 and 2. The cards feature blue-bordered fronts with cutout color player photos, each superposed upon a silver-colored background. The set's title and the player's name appear in gold foil in an upper corner. The key card in this set is Kenny Lofton.

	MINT	NRMT
COMPLETE SET (20)	30.00	13.50
COMPLETE SERIES 1 (10)	20.00	9.00
COMPLETE SERIES 2 (10)	10.00	4.50
COMMON CARD (RSA1-RSB10)	1.00	.45
☐ RSA1 Kenny Lofton	15.00	6.75
☐ RSA2 Cal Eldred	1.00	.45
☐ RSA3 Pat Listach	1.00	.45
☐ RSA4 Roberto Hernandez	1.50	.70
☐ RSA5 Dave Fleming	1.00	.45
☐ RSA6 Eric Karros	3.00	1.35
☐ RSA7 Reggie Sanders	1.50	.70
☐ RSA8 Derrick May	1.00	.45
☐ RSA9 Mike Perez	1.00	.45
☐ RSA10 Donovan Osborne	1.00	.45
☐ RSB1 Moises Alou	1.50	.70
☐ RSB2 Pedro Astacio	1.00	.45
☐ RSB3 Jim Austin	1.00	.45
☐ RSB4 Chad Curtis	1.50	.70
☐ RSB5 Gary DiSarcina	1.00	.45
☐ RSB6 Scott Livingstone	1.00	.45
☐ RSB7 Sam Militello	1.00	.45
☐ RSB8 Arthur Rhodes	1.00	.45
☐ RSB9 Tim Wakefield	1.50	.70
☐ RSB10 Bob Zupcic	1.00	.45

1993 Fleer Team Leaders

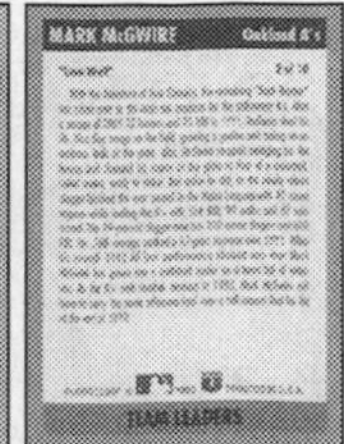

One Team Leader or Tom Glavine insert was seeded into each Fleer rack pack. Series 1 racks included 10 American League players, while series 2 racks included 10 National League players. Each of the tan-bordered standard-size cards comprising this set feature a posed color player photo on its front with a smaller cutout color action photo superposed in a lower corner. The player's name and the set's title appear vertically in gold foil along the left side within team color-coded bars.

	MINT	NRMT
COMPLETE SET (20)	70.00	32.00
COMPLETE SERIES 1 (10)	50.00	22.00
COMPLETE SERIES 2 (10)	20.00	9.00
COMMON CARD (AL1-NL10)	1.00	.45
☐ AL1 Kirby Puckett	8.00	3.60
☐ AL2 Mark McGwire	6.00	2.70
☐ AL3 Pat Listach	1.00	.45
☐ AL4 Roger Clemens	6.00	2.70
☐ AL5 Frank Thomas	20.00	9.00
☐ AL6 Carlos Baerga	1.50	.70
☐ AL7 Brady Anderson	2.50	1.10
☐ AL8 Juan Gonzalez	10.00	4.50
☐ AL9 Roberto Alomar	3.00	1.35
☐ AL10 Ken Griffey Jr.	20.00	9.00
☐ NL1 Will Clark	2.50	1.10
☐ NL2 Terry Pendleton	1.50	.70
☐ NL3 Ray Lankford	1.50	.70
☐ NL4 Eric Karros	1.50	.70
☐ NL5 Gary Sheffield	3.00	1.35
☐ NL6 Ryne Sandberg	5.00	2.20
☐ NL7 Marquis Grissom	1.50	.70
☐ NL8 John Kruk	1.50	.70
☐ NL9 Jeff Bagwell	8.00	3.60
☐ NL10 Andy Van Slyke	1.50	.70

1993 Fleer Final Edition

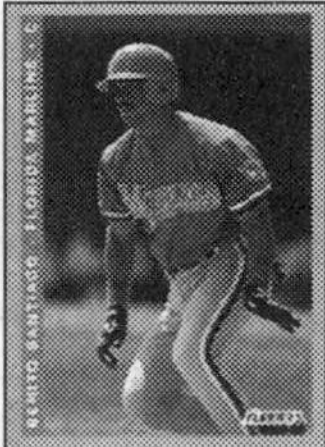
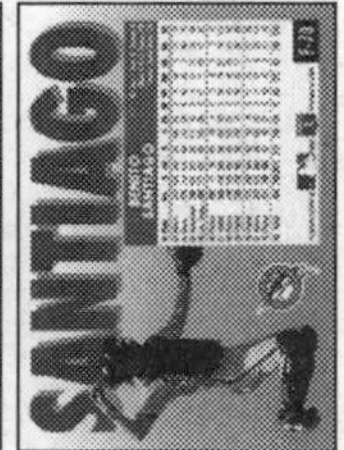

This 300-card standard-size set was issued exclusively in factory set form (along with ten Diamond Tribute inserts) to update and feature rookies not in the regular 1993 Fleer set. The cards are identical in design to regular issue 1993 Fleer cards except for the F-prefixed numbering. Cards are ordered alphabetically within teams with NL preceding AL. The set closes with checklist cards (298-300). The only key Rookie Card in this set features Jim Edmonds.

	MINT	NRMT
COMP.FACT.SET (310)	10.00	4.50
COMPLETE SET (300)	6.00	2.70
COMMON CARD (F1-F300)	.10	.05
☐ 1 Steve Bedrosian	.10	.05
☐ 2 Jay Howell	.10	.05
☐ 3 Greg Maddux	1.25	.55
☐ 4 Greg McMichael	.10	.05
☐ 5 Tony Tarasco	.10	.05
☐ 6 Jose Bautista	.10	.05
☐ 7 Jose Guzman	.10	.05
☐ 8 Greg Hibbard	.10	.05
☐ 9 Candy Maldonado	.10	.05
☐ 10 Randy Myers	.20	.09
☐ 11 Matt Walbeck	.10	.05
☐ 12 Turk Wendell	.20	.09
☐ 13 Willie Wilson	.10	.05
☐ 14 Greg Cadaret	.10	.05
☐ 15 Roberto Kelly	.10	.05
☐ 16 Randy Milligan	.10	.05
☐ 17 Kevin Mitchell	.20	.09
☐ 18 Jeff Reardon	.20	.09
☐ 19 John Roper	.10	.05
☐ 20 John Smiley	.10	.05
☐ 21 Andy Ashby	.10	.05
☐ 22 Dante Bichette	.30	.14
☐ 23 Willie Blair	.10	.05
☐ 24 Pedro Castellano	.10	.05
☐ 25 Vinny Castilla	.40	.18
☐ 26 Jerald Clark	.10	.05
☐ 27 Alex Cole	.10	.05
☐ 28 Scott Fredrickson	.10	.05
☐ 29 Jay Gainer	.10	.05
☐ 30 Andres Galarraga	.30	.14
☐ 31 Joe Girardi	.10	.05
☐ 32 Ryan Hawblitzel	.10	.05
☐ 33 Charlie Hayes	.10	.05
☐ 34 Darren Holmes	.10	.05
☐ 35 Chris Jones	.10	.05
☐ 36 David Nied	.10	.05
☐ 37 J.Owens	.10	.05
☐ 38 Lance Painter	.10	.05
☐ 39 Jeff Parrett	.10	.05
☐ 40 Steve Reed	.10	.05
☐ 41 Armando Reynoso	.10	.05
☐ 42 Bruce Ruffin	.10	.05
☐ 43 Danny Sheaffer	.10	.05
☐ 44 Keith Shepherd	.10	.05
☐ 45 Jim Tatum	.10	.05
☐ 46 Gary Wayne	.10	.05
☐ 47 Eric Young	.40	.18
☐ 48 Luis Aquino	.10	.05
☐ 49 Alex Arias	.10	.05
☐ 50 Jack Armstrong	.10	.05
☐ 51 Bret Barberie	.10	.05
☐ 52 Geronimo Berroa	.20	.09
☐ 53 Ryan Bowen	.10	.05
☐ 54 Greg Briley	.10	.05
☐ 55 Cris Carpenter	.10	.05
☐ 56 Chuck Carr	.10	.05
☐ 57 Jeff Conine	.20	.09
☐ 58 Jim Corsi	.10	.05
☐ 59 Orestes Destrade	.10	.05
☐ 60 Junior Felix	.10	.05
☐ 61 Chris Hammond	.10	.05
☐ 62 Bryan Harvey	.10	.05
☐ 63 Charlie Hough	.10	.05
☐ 64 Joe Klink	.10	.05
☐ 65 Richie Lewis UER (Refers to place of birth and residence as Illinois instead of Indiana)	.10	.05
☐ 66 Mitch Lyden	.10	.05
☐ 67 Bob Natal	.10	.05
☐ 68 Scott Pose	.10	.05
☐ 69 Rich Renteria	.10	.05
☐ 70 Benito Santiago	.10	.05
☐ 71 Gary Sheffield	.40	.18
☐ 72 Matt Turner	.10	.05
☐ 73 Walt Weiss	.10	.05
☐ 74 Darrell Whitmore	.10	.05
☐ 75 Nigel Wilson	.10	.05
☐ 76 Kevin Bass	.10	.05
☐ 77 Doug Drabek	.10	.05
☐ 78 Tom Edens	.10	.05
☐ 79 Chris James	.10	.05
☐ 80 Greg Swindell	.10	.05
☐ 81 Omar Daal	.20	.09
☐ 82 Raul Mondesi	.50	.23
☐ 83 Jody Reed	.10	.05
☐ 84 Cory Snyder	.10	.05
☐ 85 Rick Trlicek	.10	.05
☐ 86 Tim Wallach	.10	.05
☐ 87 Todd Worrell	.10	.05
☐ 88 Tavo Alvarez	.10	.05
☐ 89 Frank Bolick	.10	.05
☐ 90 Kent Bottenfield	.10	.05
☐ 91 Greg Colbrunn	.10	.05
☐ 92 Cliff Floyd	.20	.09
☐ 93 Lou Frazier	.10	.05
☐ 94 Mike Gardiner	.10	.05
☐ 95 Mike Lansing	.20	.09
☐ 96 Bill Risley	.10	.05
☐ 97 Jeff Shaw	.10	.05
☐ 98 Kevin Baez	.10	.05
☐ 99 Tim Bogar	.10	.05
☐ 100 Jeromy Burnitz	.20	.09
☐ 101 Mike Draper	.10	.05
☐ 102 Darrin Jackson	.10	.05
☐ 103 Mike Maddux	.10	.05
☐ 104 Joe Orsulak	.10	.05
☐ 105 Doug Saunders	.10	.05
☐ 106 Frank Tanana	.10	.05
☐ 107 Dave Telgheder	.10	.05
☐ 108 Larry Andersen	.10	.05
☐ 109 Jim Eisenreich	.20	.09
☐ 110 Pete Incaviglia	.10	.05
☐ 111 Danny Jackson	.10	.05
☐ 112 David West	.10	.05
☐ 113 Al Martin	.20	.09

☐ 114 Blas Minor	.10	.05
☐ 115 Dennis Moeller	.10	.05
☐ 116 William Pennyfeather	.10	.05
☐ 117 Rich Robertson	.10	.05
☐ 118 Ben Shelton	.10	.05
☐ 119 Lonnie Smith	.10	.05
☐ 120 Freddie Toliver	.10	.05
☐ 121 Paul Wagner	.10	.05
☐ 122 Kevin Young	.10	.05
☐ 123 Rene Arocha	.10	.05
☐ 124 Gregg Jefferies	.20	.09
☐ 125 Paul Kilgus	.10	.05
☐ 126 Les Lancaster	.10	.05
☐ 127 Joe Magrane	.10	.05
☐ 128 Rob Murphy	.10	.05
☐ 129 Erik Pappas	.10	.05
☐ 130 Stan Royer	.10	.05
☐ 131 Ozzie Smith	.50	.23
☐ 132 Tom Urbani	.10	.05
☐ 133 Mark Whiten	.10	.05
☐ 134 Derek Bell	.20	.09
☐ 135 Doug Brocail	.10	.05
☐ 136 Phil Clark	.10	.05
☐ 137 Mark Ettles	.10	.05
☐ 138 Jeff Gardner	.10	.05
☐ 139 Pat Gomez	.10	.05
☐ 140 Ricky Gutierrez	.10	.05
☐ 141 Gene Harris	.10	.05
☐ 142 Kevin Higgins	.10	.05
☐ 143 Trevor Hoffman	.30	.14
☐ 144 Phil Plantier	.10	.05
☐ 145 Kerry Taylor	.10	.05
☐ 146 Guillermo Velasquez	.10	.05
☐ 147 Wally Whitehurst	.10	.05
☐ 148 Tim Worrell	.10	.05
☐ 149 Todd Benzinger	.10	.05
☐ 150 Barry Bonds	.50	.23
☐ 151 Greg Brummett	.10	.05
☐ 152 Mark Carreon	.10	.05
☐ 153 Dave Martinez	.10	.05
☐ 154 Jeff Reed	.10	.05
☐ 155 Kevin Rogers	.10	.05
☐ 156 Harold Baines	.20	.09
☐ 157 Damon Buford	.10	.05
☐ 158 Paul Carey	.10	.05
☐ 159 Jeffrey Hammonds	.20	.09
☐ 160 Jamie Moyer	.10	.05
☐ 161 Sherman Obando	.10	.05
☐ 162 John O'Donoghue	.10	.05
☐ 163 Brad Pennington	.10	.05
☐ 164 Jim Poole	.10	.05
☐ 165 Harold Reynolds	.10	.05
☐ 166 Fernando Valenzuela	.20	.09
☐ 167 Jack Voigt	.10	.05
☐ 168 Mark Williamson	.10	.05
☐ 169 Scott Bankhead	.10	.05
☐ 170 Greg Blosser	.10	.05
☐ 171 Jim Byrd	.10	.05
☐ 172 Ivan Calderon	.10	.05
☐ 173 Andre Dawson	.30	.14
☐ 174 Scott Fletcher	.10	.05
☐ 175 Jose Melendez	.10	.05
☐ 176 Carlos Quintana	.10	.05
☐ 177 Jeff Russell	.10	.05
☐ 178 Aaron Sele	.20	.09
☐ 179 Rod Correia	.10	.05
☐ 180 Chili Davis	.20	.09
☐ 181 Jim Edmonds	1.00	.45
☐ 182 Rene Gonzales	.10	.05
☐ 183 Hilly Hathaway	.10	.05
☐ 184 Torey Lovullo	.10	.05
☐ 185 Greg Myers	.10	.05
☐ 186 Gene Nelson	.10	.05
☐ 187 Troy Percival	.20	.09
☐ 188 Scott Sanderson	.10	.05
☐ 189 Darryl Scott	.10	.05
☐ 190 J.T. Snow	.50	.23
☐ 191 Russ Springer	.10	.05
☐ 192 Jason Bere	.20	.09
☐ 193 Rodney Bolton	.10	.05
☐ 194 Ellis Burks	.20	.09
☐ 195 Bo Jackson	.20	.09
☐ 196 Mike LaValliere	.10	.05
☐ 197 Scott Ruffcorn	.10	.05
☐ 198 Jeff Schwartz	.10	.05
☐ 199 Jerry DiPoto	.10	.05
☐ 200 Alvaro Espinoza	.10	.05
☐ 201 Wayne Kirby	.10	.05
☐ 202 Tom Kramer	.10	.05
☐ 203 Jesse Levis	.10	.05
☐ 204 Manny Ramirez	.75	.35
☐ 205 Jeff Treadway	.10	.05
☐ 206 Bill Wertz	.10	.05
☐ 207 Cliff Young	.10	.05
☐ 208 Matt Young	.10	.05
☐ 209 Kirk Gibson	.20	.09
☐ 210 Greg Gohr	.10	.05
☐ 211 Bill Krueger	.10	.05
☐ 212 Bob MacDonald	.10	.05
☐ 213 Mike Moore	.10	.05
☐ 214 David Wells	.10	.05
☐ 215 Billy Brewer	.10	.05
☐ 216 David Cone	.20	.09
☐ 217 Greg Gagne	.10	.05
☐ 218 Mark Gardner	.10	.05
☐ 219 Chris Haney	.10	.05
☐ 220 Phil Hiatt	.10	.05
☐ 221 Jose Lind	.10	.05
☐ 222 Juan Bell	.10	.05
☐ 223 Tom Brunansky	.10	.05
☐ 224 Mike Ignasiak	.10	.05
☐ 225 Joe Kmak	.10	.05
☐ 226 Tom Lampkin	.10	.05
☐ 227 Graeme Lloyd	.10	.05
☐ 228 Carlos Maldonado	.10	.05
☐ 229 Matt Mieske	.20	.09
☐ 230 Angel Miranda	.10	.05
☐ 231 Troy O'Leary	.20	.09
☐ 232 Kevin Reimer	.10	.05
☐ 233 Larry Casian	.10	.05
☐ 234 Jim Deshaies	.10	.05
☐ 235 Eddie Guardado	.10	.05
☐ 236 Chip Hale	.10	.05
☐ 237 Mike Maksudian	.10	.05
☐ 238 David McCarty	.10	.05
☐ 239 Pat Meares	.20	.09
☐ 240 George Tsamis	.10	.05
☐ 241 Dave Winfield	.30	.14
☐ 242 Jim Abbott	.10	.05
☐ 243 Wade Boggs	.40	.18
☐ 244 Andy Cook	.10	.05
☐ 245 Russ Davis	.40	.18
☐ 246 Mike Humphreys	.10	.05
☐ 247 Jimmy Key	.20	.09
☐ 248 Jim Leyritz	.10	.05
☐ 249 Bobby Munoz	.10	.05
☐ 250 Paul O'Neill	.20	.09
☐ 251 Spike Owen	.10	.05
☐ 252 Dave Silvestri	.10	.05
☐ 253 Marcos Armas	.10	.05
☐ 254 Brent Gates	.10	.05
☐ 255 Goose Gossage	.20	.09
☐ 256 Scott Lydy	.10	.05
☐ 257 Henry Mercedes	.10	.05
☐ 258 Mike Mohler	.10	.05
☐ 259 Troy Neel	.10	.05
☐ 260 Edwin Nunez	.10	.05
☐ 261 Craig Paquette	.10	.05
☐ 262 Kevin Seitzer	.10	.05
☐ 263 Rich Amaral	.10	.05
☐ 264 Mike Blowers	.10	.05
☐ 265 Chris Bosio	.10	.05
☐ 266 Norm Charlton	.10	.05
☐ 267 Jim Converse	.10	.05
☐ 268 John Cummings	.10	.05
☐ 269 Mike Felder	.10	.05
☐ 270 Mike Hampton	.40	.18
☐ 271 Bill Haselman	.10	.05
☐ 272 Dwayne Henry	.10	.05
☐ 273 Greg Litton	.10	.05
☐ 274 Mackey Sasser	.10	.05
☐ 275 Lee Tinsley	.20	.09
☐ 276 David Wainhouse	.10	.05
☐ 277 Jeff Bronkey	.10	.05
☐ 278 Benji Gil	.10	.05
☐ 279 Tom Henke	.10	.05
☐ 280 Charlie Leibrandt	.10	.05
☐ 281 Robb Nen	.40	.18
☐ 282 Bill Ripken	.10	.05
☐ 283 Jon Shave	.10	.05
☐ 284 Doug Strange	.10	.05
☐ 285 Matt Whiteside	.10	.05
☐ 286 Scott Brow	.10	.05
☐ 287 Willie Canate	.10	.05
☐ 288 Tony Castillo	.10	.05
☐ 289 Domingo Cedeno	.10	.05
☐ 290 Darnell Coles	.10	.05
☐ 291 Danny Cox	.10	.05
☐ 292 Mark Eichhorn	.10	.05
☐ 293 Tony Fernandez	.10	.05
☐ 294 Al Leiter	.20	.09
☐ 295 Paul Molitor	.40	.18
☐ 296 Dave Stewart	.20	.09
☐ 297 Woody Williams	.10	.05
☐ 298 Checklist F1-F100	.10	.05
☐ 299 Checklist F101-F200	.10	.05
☐ 300 Checklist F201-F300	.10	.05

1993 Fleer Final Edition Diamond Tribute

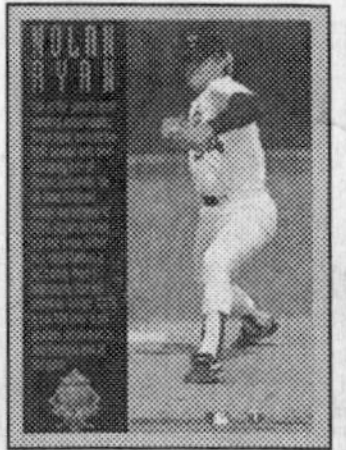

Each Fleer Final Edition factory set contained a complete 10-card set of Diamond Tribute inserts. These cards are numbered separately and feature a totally different design from the base cards. Each horizontally-designed Diamond Tribute card front features UV coating and two player images (one chest up and one full body action shot) set against the background of a blurred crowd. The set highlights a selection of top active veterans. Each card is numbered X of 10 on back.

	MINT	NRMT
COMPLETE SET (10)	4.00	1.80
COMMON CARD (1-10)	.25	.11
☐ 1 Wade Boggs	.50	.23
☐ 2 George Brett	1.25	.55
☐ 3 Andre Dawson	.35	.16
☐ 4 Carlton Fisk	.50	.23
☐ 5 Paul Molitor	.50	.23
☐ 6 Nolan Ryan	3.00	1.35
☐ 7 Lee Smith	.25	.11
☐ 8 Ozzie Smith	.75	.35
☐ 9 Dave Winfield	.35	.16
☐ 10 Robin Yount	.35	.16

1993 Fleer Atlantic

This standard-size set of 25 cards features 24 high-profile players plus a checklist and was offered free in packs of five cards with a minimum purchase of eight gallons of Atlantic gasoline. The cards were available from June 14 to July 25, 1993, at participating Atlantic retailers in New York and Pennsylvania. The action photos on the fronts are bordered in gold with the player's name, team, and position in white lettering printed on a blue stripe along the left side. The Atlantic Collector's Edition logo appears in the lower left. The horizontal back carries a color player cutout on the left side on a background that fades from white at the top to gold. The player's last name appears in bold lettering, which fades from blue to red at the top. Player statistics and biography are below. The cards are sequenced in alphabetical order. This set features one of the earliest cards picturing Barry Bonds as a member of the San Francisco Giants.

	MINT	NRMT
COMPLETE SET (25)	8.00	3.60
COMMON CARD (1-25)	.10	.05
☐ 1 Roberto Alomar	.40	.18
☐ 2 Barry Bonds	.40	.18
☐ 3 Bobby Bonilla	.20	.09
☐ 4 Will Clark	.30	.14
☐ 5 Roger Clemens	.75	.35
☐ 6 Darren Daulton	.20	.09
☐ 7 Dennis Eckersley	.30	.14
☐ 8 Cecil Fielder	.20	.09
☐ 9 Tom Glavine	.20	.09
☐ 10 Juan Gonzalez	1.25	.55
☐ 11 Ken Griffey Jr.	2.50	1.10
☐ 12 John Kruk	.15	.07
☐ 13 Greg Maddux	1.50	.70
☐ 14 Don Mattingly	1.00	.45
☐ 15 Fred McGriff	.30	.14
☐ 16 Mark McGwire	1.00	.45
☐ 17 Terry Pendleton	.10	.05
☐ 18 Kirby Puckett	.75	.35
☐ 19 Cal Ripken	2.00	.90
☐ 20 Nolan Ryan	2.00	.90
☐ 21 Ryne Sandberg	.60	.25

Card	MINT	NRMT
☐ 22 Gary Sheffield	.40	.18
☐ 23 Frank Thomas	2.00	.90
☐ 24 Andy Van Slyke	.20	.09
☐ 25 Checklist 1-25	.10	.05

1993 Fleer Fruit of the Loom

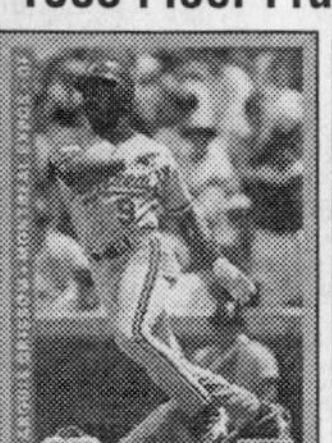

The 1993 Fleer Fruit of the Loom set consists of 66 cards measuring the standard size. Six-card packs were inserted in three-packs of Fruit of the Loom boys briefs. The cards have the same design as the regular issue 1993 Fleer. The only exception is the Fruit of the Loom logo which appears on the front. The fronts display glossy color action player photos bordered in silver. A team color-coded stripe edges the left side of the picture and carries the player's name and team. On a background that shades from white to silver, the horizontal backs have the player's last name in team color-coded block lettering, a cut-out color player photo, and a box displaying biographical and statistical information. The cards are numbered on the back ordered alphabetically by player's name.

	MINT	NRMT
COMPLETE SET (66)	80.00	36.00
COMMON CARD (1-66)	.50	.23
☐ 1 Roberto Alomar	2.00	.90
☐ 2 Brady Anderson	1.50	.70
☐ 3 Jeff Bagwell	7.50	3.40
☐ 4 Albert Belle	6.00	2.70
☐ 5 Craig Biggio	1.50	.70
☐ 6 Barry Bonds	2.50	1.10
☐ 7 George Brett	6.00	2.70
☐ 8 Brett Butler	1.00	.45
☐ 9 Jose Canseco	1.50	.70
☐ 10 Joe Carter	1.00	.45
☐ 11 Will Clark	1.50	.70
☐ 12 Roger Clemens	3.00	1.35
☐ 13 Darren Daulton	1.00	.45
☐ 14 Andre Dawson	2.00	.90
☐ 15 Delino DeShields	.50	.23
☐ 16 Rob Dibble	.50	.23
☐ 17 Doug Drabek	.50	.23
☐ 18 Dennis Eckersley	1.50	.70
☐ 19 Cecil Fielder	1.00	.45
☐ 20 Travis Fryman	1.00	.45
☐ 21 Tom Glavine	1.00	.45
☐ 22 Juan Gonzalez	7.50	3.40
☐ 23 Dwight Gooden	1.00	.45
☐ 24 Mark Grace	1.50	.70
☐ 25 Ken Griffey Jr.	15.00	6.75
☐ 26 Marquis Grissom	1.00	.45
☐ 27 Juan Guzman	.50	.23
☐ 28 Tony Gwynn	6.00	2.70
☐ 29 Rickey Henderson	1.50	.70
☐ 30 David Justice	2.00	.90
☐ 31 Eric Karros	1.50	.70
☐ 32 Chuck Knoblauch	2.50	1.10
☐ 33 John Kruk	1.00	.45
☐ 34 Ray Lankford	1.00	.45
☐ 35 Barry Larkin	1.50	.70
☐ 36 Pat Listach	.50	.23
☐ 37 Kenny Lofton	3.00	1.35
☐ 38 Shane Mack	.50	.23
☐ 39 Greg Maddux	10.00	4.50
☐ 40 Dennis Martinez	1.00	.45
☐ 41 Edgar Martinez	1.50	.70
☐ 42 Ramon Martinez	1.00	.45
☐ 43 Don Mattingly	7.50	3.40
☐ 44 Jack McDowell	.50	.23
☐ 45 Fred McGriff	1.50	.70
☐ 46 Mark McGwire	6.00	2.70
☐ 47 Jeff Montgomery	.50	.23
☐ 48 Eddie Murray	3.00	1.35
☐ 49 Charles Nagy	1.00	.45
☐ 50 Tom Pagnozzi	.50	.23
☐ 51 Terry Pendleton	.50	.23
☐ 52 Kirby Puckett	7.50	3.40
☐ 53 Jose Rijo	.50	.23
☐ 54 Cal Ripken	12.00	5.50
☐ 55 Nolan Ryan	12.00	5.50
☐ 56 Ryne Sandberg	4.00	1.80
☐ 57 Gary Sheffield	2.00	.90
☐ 58 Bill Swift	.50	.23
☐ 59 Danny Tartabull	.50	.23
☐ 60 Mickey Tettleton	.50	.23
☐ 61 Frank Thomas	12.00	5.50
☐ 62 Andy Van Slyke	1.00	.45
☐ 63 Robin Ventura	1.00	.45
☐ 64 Larry Walker	2.00	.90
☐ 65 Robin Yount	1.50	.70
☐ 66 Checklist 1-66	.50	.23

1994 Fleer

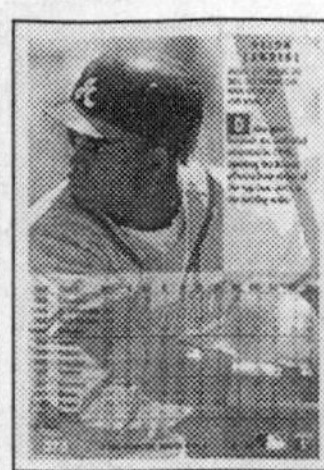

The 1994 Fleer baseball set consists of 720 standard-size cards. The white-bordered fronts feature color player action photos. In one corner, the player's name and position appear in a gold foil lettered arc; his team logo appears within. The backs are also white-bordered and feature a color player photo, some action, others posed. One side of the picture is ghosted and color-screened, and carries the player's name, biography, and career highlights. The bottom of the photo is also color-screened and ghosted, and carries the player's statistics. The cards are numbered on the back, grouped alphabetically within teams, and checklisted below alphabetically according to teams for each league with AL preceding NL. The set closes with a Superstar Specials (706-713) subset. There are no key Rookie Cards in this set.

	MINT	NRMT
COMPLETE SET (720)	50.00	22.00
COMMON CARD (1-720)	.15	.07
☐ 1 Brady Anderson	.50	.23
☐ 2 Harold Baines	.30	.14
☐ 3 Mike Devereaux	.15	.07
☐ 4 Todd Frohwirth	.15	.07
☐ 5 Jeffrey Hammonds	.30	.14
☐ 6 Chris Hoiles	.15	.07
☐ 7 Tim Hulett	.15	.07
☐ 8 Ben McDonald	.15	.07
☐ 9 Mark McLemore	.15	.07
☐ 10 Alan Mills	.15	.07
☐ 11 Jamie Moyer	.15	.07
☐ 12 Mike Mussina	.60	.25
☐ 13 Gregg Olson	.15	.07
☐ 14 Mike Pagliarulo	.15	.07
☐ 15 Brad Pennington	.15	.07
☐ 16 Jim Poole	.15	.07
☐ 17 Harold Reynolds	.15	.07
☐ 18 Arthur Rhodes	.15	.07
☐ 19 Cal Ripken Jr.	2.50	1.10
☐ 20 David Segui	.15	.07
☐ 21 Rick Sutcliffe	.15	.07
☐ 22 Fernando Valenzuela	.30	.14
☐ 23 Jack Voigt	.15	.07
☐ 24 Mark Williamson	.15	.07
☐ 25 Scott Bankhead	.15	.07
☐ 26 Roger Clemens	1.25	.55
☐ 27 Scott Cooper	.15	.07
☐ 28 Danny Darwin	.15	.07
☐ 29 Andre Dawson	.50	.23
☐ 30 Rob Deer	.15	.07
☐ 31 John Dopson	.15	.07
☐ 32 Scott Fletcher	.15	.07
☐ 33 Mike Greenwell	.15	.07
☐ 34 Greg A. Harris	.15	.07
☐ 35 Billy Hatcher	.15	.07
☐ 36 Bob Melvin	.15	.07
☐ 37 Tony Pena	.15	.07
☐ 38 Paul Quantrill	.15	.07
☐ 39 Carlos Quintana	.15	.07
☐ 40 Ernest Riles	.15	.07
☐ 41 Jeff Russell	.15	.07
☐ 42 Ken Ryan	.15	.07
☐ 43 Aaron Sele	.15	.07
☐ 44 John Valentin	.30	.14
☐ 45 Mo Vaughn	.75	.35
☐ 46 Frank Viola	.15	.07
☐ 47 Bob Zupcic	.15	.07
☐ 48 Mike Butcher	.15	.07
☐ 49 Rod Correia	.15	.07
☐ 50 Chad Curtis	.15	.07
☐ 51 Chili Davis	.30	.14
☐ 52 Gary DiSarcina	.15	.07
☐ 53 Damion Easley	.15	.07
☐ 54 Jim Edmonds	.60	.25
☐ 55 Chuck Finley	.15	.07
☐ 56 Steve Frey	.15	.07
☐ 57 Rene Gonzales	.15	.07
☐ 58 Joe Grahe	.15	.07
☐ 59 Hilly Hathaway	.15	.07
☐ 60 Stan Javier	.15	.07
☐ 61 Mark Langston	.15	.07
☐ 62 Phil Leftwich	.15	.07
☐ 63 Torey Lovullo	.15	.07
☐ 64 Joe Magrane	.15	.07
☐ 65 Greg Myers	.15	.07
☐ 66 Ken Patterson	.15	.07
☐ 67 Eduardo Perez	.15	.07
☐ 68 Luis Polonia	.15	.07
☐ 69 Tim Salmon	.60	.25
☐ 70 J.T. Snow	.50	.23
☐ 71 Ron Tingley	.15	.07
☐ 72 Julio Valera	.15	.07
☐ 73 Wilson Alvarez	.30	.14
☐ 74 Tim Belcher	.15	.07
☐ 75 George Bell	.15	.07
☐ 76 Jason Bere	.15	.07
☐ 77 Rod Bolton	.15	.07
☐ 78 Ellis Burks	.30	.14
☐ 79 Joey Cora	.30	.14
☐ 80 Alex Fernandez	.30	.14
☐ 81 Craig Grebeck	.15	.07
☐ 82 Ozzie Guillen	.15	.07
☐ 83 Roberto Hernandez	.30	.14
☐ 84 Bo Jackson	.30	.14
☐ 85 Lance Johnson	.15	.07
☐ 86 Ron Karkovice	.15	.07
☐ 87 Mike LaValliere	.15	.07
☐ 88 Kirk McCaskill	.15	.07
☐ 89 Jack McDowell	.15	.07
☐ 90 Warren Newson	.15	.07
☐ 91 Dan Pasqua	.15	.07
☐ 92 Scott Radinsky	.15	.07
☐ 93 Tim Raines	.15	.07
☐ 94 Steve Sax	.15	.07
☐ 95 Jeff Schwarz	.15	.07
☐ 96 Frank Thomas	2.50	1.10
☐ 97 Robin Ventura	.30	.14
☐ 98 Sandy Alomar Jr.	.30	.14
☐ 99 Carlos Baerga	.30	.14
☐ 100 Albert Belle	.75	.35
☐ 101 Mark Clark	.15	.07
☐ 102 Jerry DiPoto	.15	.07
☐ 103 Alvaro Espinoza	.15	.07
☐ 104 Felix Fermin	.15	.07
☐ 105 Jeremy Hernandez	.15	.07
☐ 106 Reggie Jefferson	.30	.14
☐ 107 Wayne Kirby	.15	.07
☐ 108 Tom Kramer	.15	.07
☐ 109 Mark Lewis	.15	.07
☐ 110 Derek Lilliquist	.15	.07
☐ 111 Kenny Lofton	.75	.35
☐ 112 Candy Maldonado	.15	.07
☐ 113 Jose Mesa	.30	.14
☐ 114 Jeff Mutis	.15	.07
☐ 115 Charles Nagy	.30	.14
☐ 116 Bob Ojeda	.15	.07
☐ 117 Junior Ortiz	.15	.07
☐ 118 Eric Plunk	.15	.07
☐ 119 Manny Ramirez	.75	.35
☐ 120 Paul Sorrento	.15	.07
☐ 121 Jim Thome	.75	.35
☐ 122 Jeff Treadway	.15	.07
☐ 123 Bill Wertz	.15	.07
☐ 124 Skeeter Barnes	.15	.07
☐ 125 Milt Cuyler	.15	.07
☐ 126 Eric Davis	.30	.14
☐ 127 John Doherty	.15	.07
☐ 128 Cecil Fielder	.30	.14
☐ 129 Travis Fryman	.30	.14
☐ 130 Kirk Gibson	.30	.14
☐ 131 Dan Gladden	.15	.07
☐ 132 Greg Gohr	.15	.07
☐ 133 Chris Gomez	.15	.07
☐ 134 Bill Gullickson	.15	.07
☐ 135 Mike Henneman	.15	.07
☐ 136 Kurt Knudsen	.15	.07
☐ 137 Chad Kreuter	.15	.07
☐ 138 Bill Krueger	.15	.07
☐ 139 Scott Livingstone	.15	.07
☐ 140 Bob MacDonald	.15	.07
☐ 141 Mike Moore	.15	.07
☐ 142 Tony Phillips	.15	.07
☐ 143 Mickey Tettleton	.15	.07
☐ 144 Alan Trammell	.50	.23
☐ 145 David Wells	.15	.07
☐ 146 Lou Whitaker	.30	.14

☐ 147 Kevin Appier .30 .14
☐ 148 Stan Belinda .15 .07
☐ 149 George Brett 1.25 .55
☐ 150 Billy Brewer .15 .07
☐ 151 Hubie Brooks .15 .07
☐ 152 David Cone .30 .14
☐ 153 Gary Gaetti .30 .14
☐ 154 Greg Gagne .15 .07
☐ 155 Tom Gordon .15 .07
☐ 156 Mark Gubicza .15 .07
☐ 157 Chris Gwynn .15 .07
☐ 158 John Habyan .15 .07
☐ 159 Chris Haney .15 .07
☐ 160 Phil Hiatt .15 .07
☐ 161 Felix Jose .15 .07
☐ 162 Wally Joyner .30 .14
☐ 163 Jose Lind .15 .07
☐ 164 Mike Macfarlane .15 .07
☐ 165 Mike Magnante .15 .07
☐ 166 Brent Mayne .15 .07
☐ 167 Brian McRae .15 .07
☐ 168 Kevin McReynolds .15 .07
☐ 169 Keith Miller .15 .07
☐ 170 Jeff Montgomery .30 .14
☐ 171 Hipolito Pichardo .15 .07
☐ 172 Rico Rossy .15 .07
☐ 173 Juan Bell .15 .07
☐ 174 Ricky Bones .15 .07
☐ 175 Cal Eldred .15 .07
☐ 176 Mike Fetters .15 .07
☐ 177 Darryl Hamilton .15 .07
☐ 178 Doug Henry .15 .07
☐ 179 Mike Ignasiak .15 .07
☐ 180 John Jaha .15 .07
☐ 181 Pat Listach .15 .07
☐ 182 Graeme Lloyd .15 .07
☐ 183 Matt Mieske .15 .07
☐ 184 Angel Miranda .15 .07
☐ 185 Jaime Navarro .15 .07
☐ 186 Dave Nilsson .30 .14
☐ 187 Troy O'Leary .15 .07
☐ 188 Jesse Orosco .15 .07
☐ 189 Kevin Reimer .15 .07
☐ 190 Kevin Seitzer .15 .07
☐ 191 Bill Spiers .15 .07
☐ 192 B.J. Surhoff .15 .07
☐ 193 Dickie Thon .15 .07
☐ 194 Jose Valentin .30 .14
☐ 195 Greg Vaughn .15 .07
☐ 196 Bill Wegman .15 .07
☐ 197 Robin Yount .60 .25
☐ 198 Rick Aguilera .15 .07
☐ 199 Willie Banks .15 .07
☐ 200 Bernardo Brito .15 .07
☐ 201 Larry Casian .15 .07
☐ 202 Scott Erickson .15 .07
☐ 203 Eddie Guardado .15 .07
☐ 204 Mark Guthrie .15 .07
☐ 205 Chip Hale .15 .07
☐ 206 Brian Harper .15 .07
☐ 207 Mike Hartley .15 .07
☐ 208 Kent Hrbek .30 .14
☐ 209 Terry Jorgensen .15 .07
☐ 210 Chuck Knoblauch .60 .25
☐ 211 Gene Larkin .15 .07
☐ 212 Shane Mack .15 .07
☐ 213 David McCarty .15 .07
☐ 214 Pat Meares .15 .07
☐ 215 Pedro Munoz .15 .07
☐ 216 Derek Parks .15 .07
☐ 217 Kirby Puckett 1.25 .55
☐ 218 Jeff Reboulet .15 .07
☐ 219 Kevin Tapani .15 .07
☐ 220 Mike Trombley .15 .07
☐ 221 George Tsamis .15 .07
☐ 222 Carl Willis .15 .07
☐ 223 Dave Winfield .60 .25
☐ 224 Jim Abbott .15 .07
☐ 225 Paul Assenmacher .15 .07
☐ 226 Wade Boggs .60 .25
☐ 227 Russ Davis .30 .14
☐ 228 Steve Farr .15 .07
☐ 229 Mike Gallego .15 .07
☐ 230 Paul Gibson .15 .07
☐ 231 Steve Howe .15 .07
☐ 232 Dion James .15 .07
☐ 233 Domingo Jean .15 .07
☐ 234 Scott Kamieniecki .15 .07
☐ 235 Pat Kelly .15 .07
☐ 236 Jimmy Key .30 .14
☐ 237 Jim Leyritz .15 .07
☐ 238 Kevin Maas .15 .07
☐ 239 Don Mattingly 1.00 .45
☐ 240 Rich Monteleone .15 .07
☐ 241 Bobby Munoz .15 .07
☐ 242 Matt Nokes .15 .07
☐ 243 Paul O'Neill .30 .14
☐ 244 Spike Owen .15 .07
☐ 245 Melido Perez .15 .07
☐ 246 Lee Smith .30 .14
☐ 247 Mike Stanley .15 .07
☐ 248 Danny Tartabull .15 .07
☐ 249 Randy Velarde .15 .07
☐ 250 Bob Wickman .15 .07
☐ 251 Bernie Williams .60 .25
☐ 252 Mike Aldrete .15 .07
☐ 253 Marcos Armas .15 .07
☐ 254 Lance Blankenship .15 .07
☐ 255 Mike Bordick .15 .07
☐ 256 Scott Brosius .15 .07
☐ 257 Jerry Browne .15 .07
☐ 258 Ron Darling .15 .07
☐ 259 Kelly Downs .15 .07
☐ 260 Dennis Eckersley .50 .23
☐ 261 Brent Gates .15 .07
☐ 262 Goose Gossage .30 .14
☐ 263 Scott Hemond .15 .07
☐ 264 Dave Henderson .15 .07
☐ 265 Rick Honeycutt .15 .07
☐ 266 Vince Horsman .15 .07
☐ 267 Scott Lydy .15 .07
☐ 268 Mark McGwire 1.25 .55
☐ 269 Mike Mohler .15 .07
☐ 270 Troy Neel .15 .07
☐ 271 Edwin Nunez .15 .07
☐ 272 Craig Paquette .15 .07
☐ 273 Ruben Sierra .15 .07
☐ 274 Terry Steinbach .30 .14
☐ 275 Todd Van Poppel .15 .07
☐ 276 Bob Welch .15 .07
☐ 277 Bobby Witt .15 .07
☐ 278 Rich Amaral .15 .07
☐ 279 Mike Blowers .15 .07
☐ 280 Bret Boone UER .15 .07
(Name spelled Brett on front)
☐ 281 Chris Bosio .15 .07
☐ 282 Jay Buhner .50 .23
☐ 283 Norm Charlton .15 .07
☐ 284 Mike Felder .15 .07
☐ 285 Dave Fleming .15 .07
☐ 286 Ken Griffey Jr. 3.00 1.35
☐ 287 Erik Hanson .15 .07
☐ 288 Bill Haselman .15 .07
☐ 289 Brad Holman .15 .07
☐ 290 Randy Johnson .50 .23
☐ 291 Tim Leary .15 .07
☐ 292 Greg Litton .15 .07
☐ 293 Dave Magadan .15 .07
☐ 294 Edgar Martinez .50 .23
☐ 295 Tino Martinez .60 .25
☐ 296 Jeff Nelson .15 .07
☐ 297 Erik Plantenberg .15 .07
☐ 298 Mackey Sasser .15 .07
☐ 299 Brian Turang .15 .07
☐ 300 Dave Valle .15 .07
☐ 301 Omar Vizquel .30 .14
☐ 302 Brian Bohanon .15 .07
☐ 303 Kevin Brown .30 .14
☐ 304 Jose Canseco UER .50 .23
(Back mentions 1991 as his 40/40 MVP season; should be '88)
☐ 305 Mario Diaz .15 .07
☐ 306 Julio Franco .30 .14
☐ 307 Juan Gonzalez 1.50 .70
☐ 308 Tom Henke .15 .07
☐ 309 David Hulse .15 .07
☐ 310 Manuel Lee .15 .07
☐ 311 Craig Lefferts .15 .07
☐ 312 Charlie Leibrandt .15 .07
☐ 313 Rafael Palmeiro .50 .23
☐ 314 Dean Palmer .30 .14
☐ 315 Roger Pavlik .15 .07
☐ 316 Dan Peltier .15 .07
☐ 317 Gene Petralli .15 .07
☐ 318 Gary Redus .15 .07
☐ 319 Ivan Rodriguez .75 .35
☐ 320 Kenny Rogers .15 .07
☐ 321 Nolan Ryan 2.50 1.10
☐ 322 Doug Strange .15 .07
☐ 323 Matt Whiteside .15 .07
☐ 324 Roberto Alomar .60 .25
☐ 325 Pat Borders .15 .07
☐ 326 Joe Carter .50 .23
☐ 327 Tony Castillo .15 .07
☐ 328 Darnell Coles .15 .07
☐ 329 Danny Cox .15 .07
☐ 330 Mark Eichhorn .15 .07
☐ 331 Tony Fernandez .15 .07
☐ 332 Alfredo Griffin .15 .07
☐ 333 Juan Guzman .15 .07
☐ 334 Rickey Henderson .50 .23
☐ 335 Pat Hentgen .30 .14
☐ 336 Randy Knorr .15 .07
☐ 337 Al Leiter .15 .07
☐ 338 Paul Molitor .60 .25
☐ 339 Jack Morris .30 .14
☐ 340 John Olerud .30 .14
☐ 341 Dick Schofield .15 .07
☐ 342 Ed Sprague .15 .07
☐ 343 Dave Stewart .30 .14
☐ 344 Todd Stottlemyre .15 .07
☐ 345 Mike Timlin .15 .07
☐ 346 Duane Ward .15 .07
☐ 347 Turner Ward .15 .07
☐ 348 Devon White .15 .07
☐ 349 Woody Williams .15 .07
☐ 350 Steve Avery .15 .07
☐ 351 Steve Bedrosian .15 .07
☐ 352 Rafael Belliard .15 .07
☐ 353 Damon Berryhill .15 .07
☐ 354 Jeff Blauser .15 .07
☐ 355 Sid Bream .15 .07
☐ 356 Francisco Cabrera .15 .07
☐ 357 Marvin Freeman .15 .07
☐ 358 Ron Gant .30 .14
☐ 359 Tom Glavine .50 .23
☐ 360 Jay Howell .15 .07
☐ 361 David Justice .60 .25
☐ 362 Ryan Klesko .60 .25
☐ 363 Mark Lemke .15 .07
☐ 364 Javier Lopez .50 .23
☐ 365 Greg Maddux 2.00 .90
☐ 366 Fred McGriff .50 .23
☐ 367 Greg McMichael .15 .07
☐ 368 Kent Mercker .15 .07
☐ 369 Otis Nixon .15 .07
☐ 370 Greg Olson .15 .07
☐ 371 Bill Pecota .15 .07
☐ 372 Terry Pendleton .30 .14
☐ 373 Deion Sanders .50 .23
☐ 374 Pete Smith .15 .07
☐ 375 John Smoltz .50 .23
☐ 376 Mike Stanton .15 .07
☐ 377 Tony Tarasco .15 .07
☐ 378 Mark Wohlers .30 .14
☐ 379 Jose Bautista .15 .07
☐ 380 Shawn Boskie .15 .07
☐ 381 Steve Buechele .15 .07
☐ 382 Frank Castillo .15 .07
☐ 383 Mark Grace .50 .23
☐ 384 Jose Guzman .15 .07
☐ 385 Mike Harkey .15 .07
☐ 386 Greg Hibbard .15 .07
☐ 387 Glenallen Hill .15 .07
☐ 388 Steve Lake .15 .07
☐ 389 Derrick May .15 .07
☐ 390 Chuck McElroy .15 .07
☐ 391 Mike Morgan .15 .07
☐ 392 Randy Myers .15 .07
☐ 393 Dan Plesac .15 .07
☐ 394 Kevin Roberson .15 .07
☐ 395 Rey Sanchez .15 .07
☐ 396 Ryne Sandberg .75 .35
☐ 397 Bob Scanlan .15 .07
☐ 398 Dwight Smith .15 .07
☐ 399 Sammy Sosa .60 .25
☐ 400 Jose Vizcaino .15 .07
☐ 401 Rick Wilkins .15 .07
☐ 402 Willie Wilson .15 .07
☐ 403 Eric Yelding .15 .07
☐ 404 Bobby Ayala .15 .07
☐ 405 Jeff Branson .15 .07
☐ 406 Tom Browning .15 .07
☐ 407 Jacob Brumfield .15 .07
☐ 408 Tim Costo .15 .07
☐ 409 Rob Dibble .15 .07
☐ 410 Willie Greene .30 .14
☐ 411 Thomas Howard .15 .07
☐ 412 Roberto Kelly .15 .07
☐ 413 Bill Landrum .15 .07
☐ 414 Barry Larkin .50 .23
☐ 415 Larry Luebbers .15 .07
☐ 416 Kevin Mitchell .15 .07
☐ 417 Hal Morris .15 .07
☐ 418 Joe Oliver .15 .07
☐ 419 Tim Pugh .15 .07
☐ 420 Jeff Reardon .30 .14
☐ 421 Jose Rijo .15 .07
☐ 422 Bip Roberts .15 .07
☐ 423 John Roper .15 .07
☐ 424 Johnny Ruffin .15 .07
☐ 425 Chris Sabo .15 .07
☐ 426 Juan Samuel .15 .07
☐ 427 Reggie Sanders .15 .07
☐ 428 Scott Service .15 .07
☐ 429 John Smiley .15 .07
☐ 430 Jerry Spradlin .15 .07
☐ 431 Kevin Wickander .15 .07
☐ 432 Freddie Benavides .15 .07
☐ 433 Dante Bichette .60 .25
☐ 434 Willie Blair .15 .07

☐ 435 Daryl Boston	.15	.07
☐ 436 Kent Bottenfield	.15	.07
☐ 437 Vinny Castilla	.50	.23
☐ 438 Jerald Clark	.15	.07
☐ 439 Alex Cole	.15	.07
☐ 440 Andres Galarraga	.50	.23
☐ 441 Joe Girardi	.15	.07
☐ 442 Greg W. Harris	.15	.07
☐ 443 Charlie Hayes	.15	.07
☐ 444 Darren Holmes	.15	.07
☐ 445 Chris Jones	.15	.07
☐ 446 Roberto Mejia	.15	.07
☐ 447 David Nied	.15	.07
☐ 448 J. Owens	.15	.07
☐ 449 Jeff Parrett	.15	.07
☐ 450 Steve Reed	.15	.07
☐ 451 Armando Reynoso	.15	.07
☐ 452 Bruce Ruffin	.15	.07
☐ 453 Mo Sanford	.15	.07
☐ 454 Danny Sheaffer	.15	.07
☐ 455 Jim Tatum	.15	.07
☐ 456 Gary Wayne	.15	.07
☐ 457 Eric Young	.30	.14
☐ 458 Luis Aquino	.15	.07
☐ 459 Alex Arias	.15	.07
☐ 460 Jack Armstrong	.15	.07
☐ 461 Bret Barberie	.15	.07
☐ 462 Ryan Bowen	.15	.07
☐ 463 Chuck Carr	.15	.07
☐ 464 Jeff Conine	.30	.14
☐ 465 Henry Cotto	.15	.07
☐ 466 Orestes Destrade	.15	.07
☐ 467 Chris Hammond	.15	.07
☐ 468 Bryan Harvey	.15	.07
☐ 469 Charlie Hough	.15	.07
☐ 470 Joe Klink	.15	.07
☐ 471 Richie Lewis	.15	.07
☐ 472 Bob Natal	.15	.07
☐ 473 Pat Rapp	.15	.07
☐ 474 Rich Renteria	.15	.07
☐ 475 Rich Rodriguez	.15	.07
☐ 476 Benito Santiago	.15	.07
☐ 477 Gary Sheffield	.60	.25
☐ 478 Matt Turner	.15	.07
☐ 479 David Weathers	.15	.07
☐ 480 Walt Weiss	.15	.07
☐ 481 Darrell Whitmore	.15	.07
☐ 482 Eric Anthony	.15	.07
☐ 483 Jeff Bagwell	1.25	.55
☐ 484 Kevin Bass	.15	.07
☐ 485 Craig Biggio	.50	.23
☐ 486 Ken Caminiti	.60	.25
☐ 487 Andujar Cedeno	.15	.07
☐ 488 Chris Donnels	.15	.07
☐ 489 Doug Drabek	.15	.07
☐ 490 Steve Finley	.30	.14
☐ 491 Luis Gonzalez	.15	.07
☐ 492 Pete Harnisch	.15	.07
☐ 493 Xavier Hernandez	.15	.07
☐ 494 Doug Jones	.15	.07
☐ 495 Todd Jones	.15	.07
☐ 496 Darryl Kile	.30	.14
☐ 497 Al Osuna	.15	.07
☐ 498 Mark Portugal	.15	.07
☐ 499 Scott Servais	.15	.07
☐ 500 Greg Swindell	.15	.07
☐ 501 Eddie Taubensee	.15	.07
☐ 502 Jose Uribe	.15	.07
☐ 503 Brian Williams	.15	.07
☐ 504 Billy Ashley	.15	.07
☐ 505 Pedro Astacio	.15	.07
☐ 506 Brett Butler	.30	.14
☐ 507 Tom Candiotti	.15	.07
☐ 508 Omar Daal	.15	.07
☐ 509 Jim Gott	.15	.07
☐ 510 Kevin Gross	.15	.07
☐ 511 Dave Hansen	.15	.07
☐ 512 Carlos Hernandez	.15	.07
☐ 513 Orel Hershiser	.30	.14
☐ 514 Eric Karros	.30	.14
☐ 515 Pedro Martinez	.60	.25
☐ 516 Ramon Martinez	.30	.14
☐ 517 Roger McDowell	.15	.07
☐ 518 Raul Mondesi	.60	.25
☐ 519 Jose Offerman	.15	.07
☐ 520 Mike Piazza	2.00	.90
☐ 521 Jody Reed	.15	.07
☐ 522 Henry Rodriguez	.15	.07
☐ 523 Mike Sharperson	.15	.07
☐ 524 Cory Snyder	.15	.07
☐ 525 Darryl Strawberry	.30	.14
☐ 526 Rick Trlicek	.15	.07
☐ 527 Tim Wallach	.15	.07
☐ 528 Mitch Webster	.15	.07
☐ 529 Steve Wilson	.15	.07
☐ 530 Todd Worrell	.15	.07
☐ 531 Moises Alou	.30	.14
☐ 532 Brian Barnes	.15	.07
☐ 533 Sean Berry	.15	.07
☐ 534 Greg Colbrunn	.15	.07
☐ 535 Delino DeShields	.15	.07
☐ 536 Jeff Fassero	.15	.07
☐ 537 Darrin Fletcher	.15	.07
☐ 538 Cliff Floyd	.50	.23
☐ 539 Lou Frazier	.15	.07
☐ 540 Marquis Grissom	.30	.14
☐ 541 Butch Henry	.15	.07
☐ 542 Ken Hill	.15	.07
☐ 543 Mike Lansing	.30	.14
☐ 544 Brian Looney	.15	.07
☐ 545 Dennis Martinez	.30	.14
☐ 546 Chris Nabholz	.15	.07
☐ 547 Randy Ready	.15	.07
☐ 548 Mel Rojas	.15	.07
☐ 549 Kirk Rueter	.15	.07
☐ 550 Tim Scott	.15	.07
☐ 551 Jeff Shaw	.15	.07
☐ 552 Tim Spehr	.15	.07
☐ 553 John VanderWal	.15	.07
☐ 554 Larry Walker	.60	.25
☐ 555 John Wetteland	.30	.14
☐ 556 Rondell White	.50	.23
☐ 557 Tim Bogar	.15	.07
☐ 558 Bobby Bonilla	.30	.14
☐ 559 Jeromy Burnitz	.30	.14
☐ 560 Sid Fernandez	.15	.07
☐ 561 John Franco	.30	.14
☐ 562 Dave Gallagher	.15	.07
☐ 563 Dwight Gooden	.30	.14
☐ 564 Eric Hillman	.15	.07
☐ 565 Todd Hundley	.50	.23
☐ 566 Jeff Innis	.15	.07
☐ 567 Darrin Jackson	.15	.07
☐ 568 Howard Johnson	.15	.07
☐ 569 Bobby Jones	.30	.14
☐ 570 Jeff Kent	.15	.07
☐ 571 Mike Maddux	.15	.07
☐ 572 Jeff McKnight	.15	.07
☐ 573 Eddie Murray	.60	.25
☐ 574 Charlie O'Brien	.15	.07
☐ 575 Joe Orsulak	.15	.07
☐ 576 Bret Saberhagen	.15	.07
☐ 577 Pete Schourek	.15	.07
☐ 578 Dave Telgheder	.15	.07
☐ 579 Ryan Thompson	.15	.07
☐ 580 Anthony Young	.15	.07
☐ 581 Ruben Amaro	.15	.07
☐ 582 Larry Andersen	.15	.07
☐ 583 Kim Batiste	.15	.07
☐ 584 Wes Chamberlain	.15	.07
☐ 585 Darren Daulton	.30	.14
☐ 586 Mariano Duncan	.15	.07
☐ 587 Lenny Dykstra	.30	.14
☐ 588 Jim Eisenreich	.30	.14
☐ 589 Tommy Greene	.15	.07
☐ 590 Dave Hollins	.15	.07
☐ 591 Pete Incaviglia	.15	.07
☐ 592 Danny Jackson	.15	.07
☐ 593 Ricky Jordan	.15	.07
☐ 594 John Kruk	.30	.14
☐ 595 Roger Mason	.15	.07
☐ 596 Mickey Morandini	.15	.07
☐ 597 Terry Mulholland	.15	.07
☐ 598 Todd Pratt	.15	.07
☐ 599 Ben Rivera	.15	.07
☐ 600 Curt Schilling	.30	.14
☐ 601 Kevin Stocker	.15	.07
☐ 602 Milt Thompson	.15	.07
☐ 603 David West	.15	.07
☐ 604 Mitch Williams	.15	.07
☐ 605 Jay Bell	.30	.14
☐ 606 Dave Clark	.15	.07
☐ 607 Steve Cooke	.15	.07
☐ 608 Tom Foley	.15	.07
☐ 609 Carlos Garcia	.15	.07
☐ 610 Joel Johnston	.15	.07
☐ 611 Jeff King	.30	.14
☐ 612 Al Martin	.15	.07
☐ 613 Lloyd McClendon	.15	.07
☐ 614 Orlando Merced	.15	.07
☐ 615 Blas Minor	.15	.07
☐ 616 Denny Neagle	.30	.14
☐ 617 Mark Petkovsek	.15	.07
☐ 618 Tom Prince	.15	.07
☐ 619 Don Slaught	.15	.07
☐ 620 Zane Smith	.15	.07
☐ 621 Randy Tomlin	.15	.07
☐ 622 Andy Van Slyke	.30	.14
☐ 623 Paul Wagner	.15	.07
☐ 624 Tim Wakefield	.15	.07
☐ 625 Bob Walk	.15	.07
☐ 626 Kevin Young	.15	.07
☐ 627 Luis Alicea	.15	.07
☐ 628 Rene Arocha	.15	.07
☐ 629 Rod Brewer	.15	.07
☐ 630 Rheal Cormier	.15	.07
☐ 631 Bernard Gilkey	.15	.07
☐ 632 Lee Guetterman	.15	.07
☐ 633 Gregg Jefferies	.30	.14
☐ 634 Brian Jordan	.15	.07
☐ 635 Les Lancaster	.15	.07
☐ 636 Ray Lankford	.50	.23
☐ 637 Rob Murphy	.15	.07
☐ 638 Omar Olivares	.15	.07
☐ 639 Jose Oquendo	.15	.07
☐ 640 Donovan Osborne	.15	.07
☐ 641 Tom Pagnozzi	.15	.07
☐ 642 Erik Pappas	.15	.07
☐ 643 Geronimo Pena	.15	.07
☐ 644 Mike Perez	.15	.07
☐ 645 Gerald Perry	.15	.07
☐ 646 Ozzie Smith	.75	.35
☐ 647 Bob Tewksbury	.15	.07
☐ 648 Allen Watson	.15	.07
☐ 649 Mark Whiten	.15	.07
☐ 650 Tracy Woodson	.15	.07
☐ 651 Todd Zeile	.15	.07
☐ 652 Andy Ashby	.15	.07
☐ 653 Brad Ausmus	.15	.07
☐ 654 Billy Bean	.15	.07
☐ 655 Derek Bell	.30	.14
☐ 656 Andy Benes	.30	.14
☐ 657 Doug Brocail	.15	.07
☐ 658 Jarvis Brown	.15	.07
☐ 659 Archi Cianfrocco	.15	.07
☐ 660 Phil Clark	.15	.07
☐ 661 Mark Davis	.15	.07
☐ 662 Jeff Gardner	.15	.07
☐ 663 Pat Gomez	.15	.07
☐ 664 Ricky Gutierrez	.15	.07
☐ 665 Tony Gwynn	1.50	.70
☐ 666 Gene Harris	.15	.07
☐ 667 Kevin Higgins	.15	.07
☐ 668 Trevor Hoffman	.30	.14
☐ 669 Pedro Martinez	.15	.07
☐ 670 Tim Mauser	.15	.07
☐ 671 Melvin Nieves	.15	.07
☐ 672 Phil Plantier	.15	.07
☐ 673 Frank Seminara	.15	.07
☐ 674 Craig Shipley	.15	.07
☐ 675 Kerry Taylor	.15	.07
☐ 676 Tim Teufel	.15	.07
☐ 677 Guillermo Velasquez	.15	.07
☐ 678 Wally Whitehurst	.15	.07
☐ 679 Tim Worrell	.15	.07
☐ 680 Rod Beck	.30	.14
☐ 681 Mike Benjamin	.15	.07
☐ 682 Todd Benzinger	.15	.07
☐ 683 Bud Black	.15	.07
☐ 684 Barry Bonds	.75	.35
☐ 685 Jeff Brantley	.15	.07
☐ 686 Dave Burba	.15	.07
☐ 687 John Burkett	.15	.07
☐ 688 Mark Carreon	.15	.07
☐ 689 Will Clark	.50	.23
☐ 690 Royce Clayton	.30	.14
☐ 691 Bryan Hickerson	.15	.07
☐ 692 Mike Jackson	.15	.07
☐ 693 Darren Lewis	.15	.07
☐ 694 Kirt Manwaring	.15	.07
☐ 695 Dave Martinez	.15	.07
☐ 696 Willie McGee	.15	.07
☐ 697 John Patterson	.15	.07
☐ 698 Jeff Reed	.15	.07
☐ 699 Kevin Rogers	.15	.07
☐ 700 Scott Sanderson	.15	.07
☐ 701 Steve Scarsone	.15	.07
☐ 702 Billy Swift	.15	.07
☐ 703 Robby Thompson	.15	.07
☐ 704 Matt Williams	.50	.23
☐ 705 Trevor Wilson	.15	.07
☐ 706 Brave New World	.60	.25
Fred McGriff		
Ron Gant		
David Justice		
☐ 707 1-2 Punch	.30	.14
John Olerud		
Paul Molitor		
☐ 708 American Heat	.30	.14
Mike Mussina		
Jack McDowell		
☐ 709 Together Again	.50	.23
Lou Whitaker		
Alan Trammell		
☐ 710 Lone Star Lumber	.50	.23
Rafael Palmeiro		
Juan Gonzalez		
☐ 711 Batmen	.50	.23
Brett Butler		
Tony Gwynn		
☐ 712 Twin Peaks	.60	.25

Kirby Puckett		
Chuck Knoblauch		
☐ 713 Back to Back	.75	.35
Mike Piazza		
Eric Karros		
☐ 714 Checklist 1	.15	.07
☐ 715 Checklist 2	.15	.07
☐ 716 Checklist 3	.15	.07
☐ 717 Checklist 4	.15	.07
☐ 718 Checklist 5	.15	.07
☐ 719 Checklist 6	.15	.07
☐ 720 Checklist 7	.15	.07
☐ P69 Tim Salmon Promo	1.00	.45

1994 Fleer All-Rookies

Collectors could redeem an All-Rookie Team Exchange card by mail for this nine-card set of top 1994 rookies at each position as chosen by Fleer. The expiration date to remeem this set was September 30, 1994. None of these players were in the basic 1994 Fleer set. The exchange card was randomly inserted into all pack types.

	MINT	NRMT
COMPLETE SET (9)	8.00	3.60
COMMON CARD (M1-M9)	.50	.23
☐ M1 Kurt Abbott	.75	.35
☐ M2 Rich Becker	.75	.35
☐ M3 Carlos Delgado	4.00	1.80
☐ M4 Jorge Fabregas	.50	.23
☐ M5 Bob Hamelin	.75	.35
☐ M6 John Hudek	.50	.23
☐ M7 Tim Hyers	.50	.23
☐ M8 Luis S.Lopez	.50	.23
☐ M9 James Mouton	.50	.23
☐ NNO Expired All-Rookie Exch.	1.50	.70

1994 Fleer All-Stars

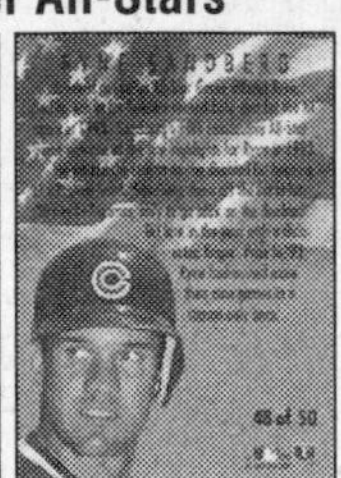

Fleer issued this 50-card standard-size set in 1994, to commemorate the All-Stars of the 1993 season. The cards were exclusively available in the Fleer wax packs at a rate of one in two. The set features 25 American League (1-25) and 25 National League (26-50) All-Stars. The full-bleed fronts feature color action player cut-out photos with an American flag background. The player's name is stamped in gold foil along the bottom edge adjacent to a 1993 All-Stars Game logo. The borderless backs carry a similar flag background with a player head shot near the bottom. The player's name and career highlights round out the back. Each league's all-stars are sequenced in alphabetical order.

	MINT	NRMT
COMPLETE SET (50)	25.00	11.00
COMMON CARD (1-50)	.25	.11
☐ 1 Roberto Alomar	.75	.35
☐ 2 Carlos Baerga	.25	.11
☐ 3 Albert Belle	1.50	.70
☐ 4 Wade Boggs	.75	.35
☐ 5 Joe Carter	.50	.23
☐ 6 Scott Cooper	.25	.11
☐ 7 Cecil Fielder	.35	.16
☐ 8 Travis Fryman	.35	.16
☐ 9 Juan Gonzalez	2.00	.90
☐ 10 Ken Griffey Jr.	4.00	1.80
☐ 11 Pat Hentgen	.35	.16
☐ 12 Randy Johnson	.75	.35
☐ 13 Jimmy Key	.35	.16
☐ 14 Mark Langston	.25	.11
☐ 15 Jack McDowell	.25	.11
☐ 16 Paul Molitor	.75	.35
☐ 17 Jeff Montgomery	.25	.11
☐ 18 Mike Mussina	.75	.35
☐ 19 John Olerud	.35	.16
☐ 20 Kirby Puckett	1.50	.70
☐ 21 Cal Ripken	3.00	1.35
☐ 22 Ivan Rodriguez	1.00	.45
☐ 23 Frank Thomas	4.00	1.80
☐ 24 Greg Vaughn	.25	.11
☐ 25 Duane Ward	.25	.11
☐ 26 Steve Avery	.25	.11
☐ 27 Rod Beck	.25	.11
☐ 28 Jay Bell	.25	.11
☐ 29 Andy Benes	.35	.16
☐ 30 Jeff Blauser	.25	.11
☐ 31 Barry Bonds	1.00	.45
☐ 32 Bobby Bonilla	.35	.16
☐ 33 John Burkett	.25	.11
☐ 34 Darren Daulton	.35	.16
☐ 35 Andres Galarraga	.50	.23
☐ 36 Tom Glavine	.50	.23
☐ 37 Mark Grace	.50	.23
☐ 38 Marquis Grissom	.35	.16
☐ 39 Tony Gwynn	1.50	.70
☐ 40 Bryan Harvey	.25	.11
☐ 41 Dave Hollins	.25	.11
☐ 42 David Justice	.75	.35
☐ 43 Darryl Kile	.35	.16
☐ 44 John Kruk	.35	.16
☐ 45 Barry Larkin	.50	.23
☐ 46 Terry Mulholland	.25	.11
☐ 47 Mike Piazza	2.50	1.10
☐ 48 Ryne Sandberg	1.00	.45
☐ 49 Gary Sheffield	.75	.35
☐ 50 John Smoltz	.50	.23

1994 Fleer Award Winners

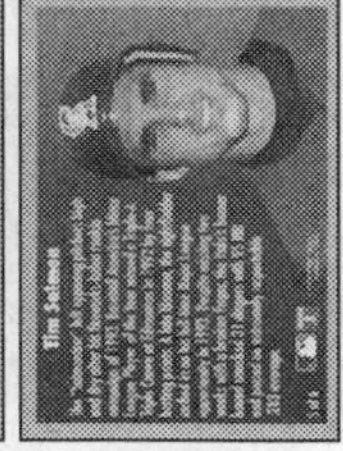

Randomly inserted in foil packs at a rate of one in 37, this six-card standard-size set spotlights six outstanding players who received awards. Inside beige borders, the horizontal fronts feature three views of the same color player photo. The words "Fleer Award Winners" and the player's name are printed in gold foil toward the bottom. The backs have a similar design to the fronts, only with one color player cutout and a season summary.

	MINT	NRMT
COMPLETE SET (6)	12.00	5.50
COMMON CARD (1-6)	.50	.23
☐ 1 Frank Thomas	4.00	1.80
☐ 2 Barry Bonds	1.25	.55
☐ 3 Jack McDowell	.50	.23
☐ 4 Greg Maddux	3.00	1.35
☐ 5 Tim Salmon	1.00	.45
☐ 6 Mike Piazza	3.00	1.35

1994 Fleer Golden Moments

These standard-size cards were issued one per blue retail jumbo pack. The fronts feature borderless color player action photos. A shrink-wrapped package containing a jumbo set was issued one per Fleer hobby case. Jumbos were later issued for retail purposes. The production number out of a total of 10,000 appears near the bottom of the jumbos. The standard-size cards are not individually numbered.

	MINT	NRMT
COMPLETE SET (10)	40.00	18.00
COMMON CARD (1-10)	.75	.35
*JUMBOS: 1.5X TO 4X BASIC CARDS		
☐ 1 Mark Whiten	.75	.35
☐ 2 Carlos Baerga	.75	.35
☐ 3 Dave Winfield	2.50	1.10
☐ 4 Ken Griffey Jr.	12.00	5.50
☐ 5 Bo Jackson	1.00	.45
☐ 6 George Brett	5.00	2.20
☐ 7 Nolan Ryan	10.00	4.50
☐ 8 Fred McGriff	1.50	.70
☐ 9 Frank Thomas	40.00	18.00
☐ 10 Chris Bosio	.75	.35
Jim Abbott		
Darryl Kile		

1994 Fleer League Leaders

Randomly inserted in all pack types at arate of one in 17, this 28-card set features six statistical leaders each for the American (1-6) and the National (7-12) Leagues. Inside a beige border, the fronts feature a color action player cutout superimposed on a black-and-white player photo. The player's name and the set title are gold foil stamped in the bottom border, while the player's achievement is printed vertically along the right edge of the picture. The horizontal backs have a color close-up shot on the left portion and a player summary on the right.

	MINT	NRMT
COMPLETE SET (12)	6.00	2.70
COMMON CARD (1-12)	.25	.11
☐ 1 John Olerud	.35	.16
☐ 2 Albert Belle	2.00	.90
☐ 3 Rafael Palmeiro	.50	.23
☐ 4 Kenny Lofton	1.50	.70
☐ 5 Jack McDowell	.25	.11
☐ 6 Kevin Appier	.35	.16
☐ 7 Andres Galarraga	.50	.23
☐ 8 Barry Bonds	1.25	.55
☐ 9 Lenny Dykstra	.35	.16
☐ 10 Chuck Carr	.25	.11
☐ 11 Tom Glavine UER	.50	.23
No number on back of card		
☐ 12 Greg Maddux	3.00	1.35

1994 Fleer Lumber Company

Randomly inserted in jumbo packs at a rate of one in five, this ten-card standard-size set features the best hitters in the game. The full-bleed fronts have a color action player cutout on a wood background. The player's name, team name, and the set title "Lumber Company" appear in an oval-shaped seal burned in the wood, just as one would find on a bat. On a background consisting of wooden bats laying on infield sand, the backs present a color headshot and a player profile on a ghosted panel. The cards are numbered alphabetically.

	MINT	NRMT
COMPLETE SET (10)	12.00	5.50
COMMON CARD (1-10)	.40	.18

	MINT	NRMT
☐ 1 Albert Belle	2.00	.90
☐ 2 Barry Bonds	1.25	.55
☐ 3 Ron Gant	.40	.18
☐ 4 Juan Gonzalez	2.50	1.10
☐ 5 Ken Griffey Jr.	5.00	2.20
☐ 6 David Justice	1.00	.45
☐ 7 Fred McGriff	.75	.35
☐ 8 Rafael Palmeiro	.75	.35
☐ 9 Frank Thomas	4.00	1.80
☐ 10 Matt Williams	.75	.35

1994 Fleer Major League Prospects

Randomly inserted in all pack types at a rate of one in six, this 35-card standard-size set showcases some of the outstanding young players in Major League Baseball. Inside beige borders, the fronts display color action photos superimposed over ghosted versions of the team logos. The set title and the player's name are gold foil stamped across the bottom of the card. On a beige background with thin blue pinstripes, the backs show a color player cutout and, on a powder blue panel, a player profile. The cards are numbered on the back "X of 35" and are sequenced in alphabetical order.

	MINT	NRMT
COMPLETE SET (35)	15.00	6.75
COMMON CARD (1-35)	.25	.11
☐ 1 Kurt Abbott	.25	.11
☐ 2 Brian Anderson	.50	.23
☐ 3 Rich Aude	.25	.11
☐ 4 Cory Bailey	.25	.11
☐ 5 Danny Bautista	.25	.11
☐ 6 Marty Cordova	1.50	.70
☐ 7 Tripp Cromer	.25	.11
☐ 8 Midre Cummings	.25	.11
☐ 9 Carlos Delgado	2.00	.90
☐ 10 Steve Dreyer	.25	.11
☐ 11 Steve Dunn	.25	.11
☐ 12 Jeff Granger	.25	.11
☐ 13 Tyrone Hill	.25	.11
☐ 14 Denny Hocking	.25	.11
☐ 15 John Hope	.25	.11
☐ 16 Butch Huskey	.50	.23
☐ 17 Miguel Jimenez	.25	.11
☐ 18 Chipper Jones	6.00	2.70
☐ 19 Steve Karsay	.25	.11
☐ 20 Mike Kelly	.25	.11
☐ 21 Mike Lieberthal	.50	.23
☐ 22 Albie Lopez	.25	.11
☐ 23 Jeff McNeely	.25	.11
☐ 24 Dan Miceli	.25	.11
☐ 25 Nate Minchey	.25	.11
☐ 26 Marc Newfield	.25	.11
☐ 27 Darren Oliver	1.00	.45
☐ 28 Luis Ortiz	.25	.11
☐ 29 Curtis Pride	.25	.11
☐ 30 Roger Salkeld	.25	.11
☐ 31 Scott Sanders	.25	.11
☐ 32 Dave Staton	.25	.11
☐ 33 Salomon Torres	.25	.11
☐ 34 Steve Trachsel	.25	.11
☐ 35 Chris Turner	.25	.11

1994 Fleer Pro-Visions

Randomly inserted in all pack types at a rate of one in 12, this nine-card standard-size set features on its fronts colorful artistic player caricatures with surrealistic backgrounds drawn by illustrator Wayne Still. The player's name is gold foil stamped at the lower right corner. When all nine cards are placed in order in a collector sheet, the backgrounds fit together to form a composite. The backs shade from one bright color to another and present career summaries. The cards are numbered on the back "X of 9."

	MINT	NRMT
COMPLETE SET (9)	4.00	1.80
COMMON CARD (1-9)	.25	.11

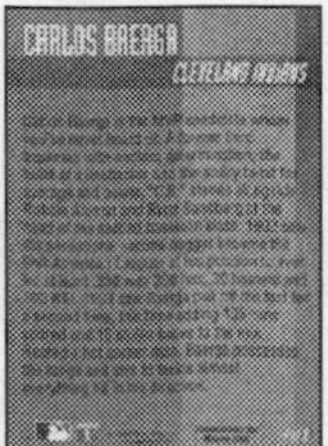

	MINT	NRMT
☐ 1 Darren Daulton	.35	.16
☐ 2 John Olerud	.35	.16
☐ 3 Matt Williams	.50	.23
☐ 4 Carlos Baerga	.25	.11
☐ 5 Ozzie Smith	1.00	.45
☐ 6 Juan Gonzalez	2.00	.90
☐ 7 Jack McDowell	.25	.11
☐ 8 Mike Piazza	2.50	1.10
☐ 9 Tony Gwynn	1.50	.70

1994 Fleer Rookie Sensations

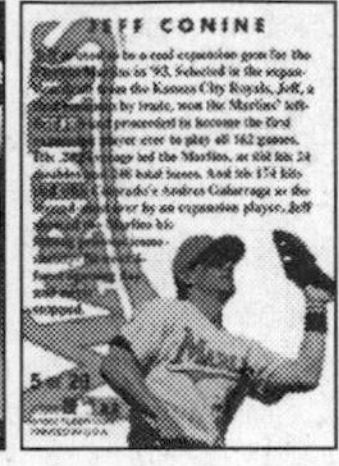

Randomly inserted in jumbo packs at a rate of one in four, this 20-card standard-size set features outstanding rookies. The fronts are "double exposed," with a player action cutout superimposed over a second photo. The team logo also appears in the team color-coded background. The set title is gold foil stamped toward the top, and the player's name is gold foil stamped on a team color-coded ribbon toward the bottom. On a white background featuring a ghosted version of the team logo, the backs have a player cutout photo and a season summary. The cards are numbered on the back "X of 20" and are sequenced in alphabetical order.

	MINT	NRMT
COMPLETE SET (20)	18.00	8.00
COMMON CARD (1-20)	.75	.35
☐ 1 Rene Arocha	.75	.35
☐ 2 Jason Bere	.75	.35
☐ 3 Jeromy Burnitz	1.50	.70
☐ 4 Chuck Carr	.75	.35
☐ 5 Jeff Conine	1.50	.70
☐ 6 Steve Cooke	.75	.35
☐ 7 Cliff Floyd	2.00	.90
☐ 8 Jeffrey Hammonds	1.50	.70
☐ 9 Wayne Kirby	.75	.35
☐ 10 Mike Lansing	1.50	.70
☐ 11 Al Martin	1.50	.70
☐ 12 Greg McMichael	.75	.35
☐ 13 Troy Neel	.75	.35
☐ 14 Mike Piazza	12.00	5.50
☐ 15 Armando Reynoso	.75	.35
☐ 16 Kirk Rueter	.75	.35
☐ 17 Tim Salmon	3.00	1.35
☐ 18 Aaron Sele	.75	.35
☐ 19 J.T. Snow	2.00	.90
☐ 20 Kevin Stocker	.75	.35

1994 Fleer Salmon

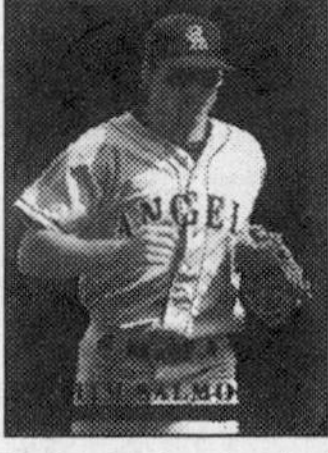

Spotlighting American League Rookie of the Year Tim Salmon, this 15-card standard size set was issued in two forms. Cards 1-12 were randomly inserted in packs (one in eight) and 13-15 were available through a mail-in offer. Ten wrappers and 1.50 were necessary to acquire the mail-ins. The mail-in expiration date was September 30, 1994. Salmon autographed more than 2,000 of his cards. The cards feature a borderless all-foil, spectra-etched design and UV coating on both sides. The fronts feature cutout color action shots of Salmon that are superposed upon the silvery foil-and-etched design. His name appears in gold lettering near the bottom, along with the words "A.L. Rookie of the Year" in silver lettering within a gold bar. The back carries a color photo of Salmon on the right side. His name appears in ocher lettering in the upper left, followed below by career highlights in black lettering.

	MINT	NRMT
COMPLETE SET (12)	25.00	11.00
COMMON SALMON (1-12)	2.50	1.10
COMMON MAIL-IN (13-15)	2.50	1.10
☐ 1 Tim Salmon Watching flight of ball after hit	2.50	1.10
☐ 2 Tim Salmon Trotting in to catch ball	2.50	1.10
☐ 3 Tim Salmon Follow through weight on front leg	2.50	1.10
☐ 4 Tim Salmon Middle of swing horizontal pose	2.50	1.10
☐ 5 Tim Salmon Sliding into base	2.50	1.10
☐ 6 Tim Salmon Pose swing end of bat in camera angle	2.50	1.10
☐ 7 Tim Salmon Running with shades on	2.50	1.10
☐ 8 Tim Salmon Bat cocked awaiting pitch	2.50	1.10
☐ 9 Tim Salmon Adjusting batting gloves bat under arm	2.50	1.10
☐ 10 Tim Salmon Running to base	2.50	1.10
☐ 11 Tim Salmon Awaiting pitch shot from left side with catcher in view	2.50	1.10
☐ 12 Tim Salmon Ready to play	2.50	1.10
☐ 13 Tim Salmon Awaiting a pitch	2.50	1.10
☐ 14 Tim Salmon Fielding	2.50	1.10
☐ 15 Tim Salmon Running the bases	2.50	1.10
☐ AU0 Tim Salmon AU (Certified autograph)	80.00	36.00

1994 Fleer Smoke 'n Heat

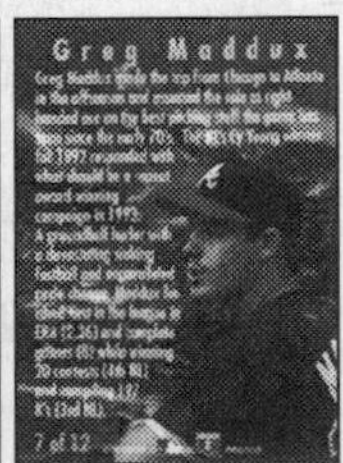

Randomly inserted in wax packs at a rate of one in 36, this 12-card standard-size set showcases the best pitchers in the game. On the fronts, color action player cutouts are superimposed on a red-and-gold fiery background that has a metallic sheen to it. The set title "Smoke 'n Heat" is printed in large block lettering. On a reddish marbleized background, the backs have another player cutout and season summary. The cards are numbered on the back "X of 12." and are sequenced in alphabetical order.

	MINT	NRMT
COMPLETE SET (12)	70.00	32.00
COMMON CARD (1-12)	2.00	.90
☐ 1 Roger Clemens	6.00	2.70
☐ 2 David Cone	3.00	1.35
☐ 3 Juan Guzman	2.00	.90
☐ 4 Pete Harnisch	2.00	.90
☐ 5 Randy Johnson	6.00	2.70

	MINT	NRMT
☐ 6 Mark Langston	2.00	.90
☐ 7 Greg Maddux	20.00	9.00
☐ 8 Mike Mussina	6.00	2.70
☐ 9 Jose Rijo	2.00	.90
☐ 10 Nolan Ryan	30.00	13.50
☐ 11 Curt Schilling	3.00	1.35
☐ 12 John Smoltz	3.00	1.35

1994 Fleer Team Leaders

Randomly inserted in all pack types, this 28-card standard-size set features Fleer's selected top player from each of the 28 major league teams. The fronts feature an action player cutout superposed on a larger close-up photo with a team color-coded background, all inside beige borders. The set title, player's name, team name, and position are printed in gold foil across the bottom. On a white background with a ghosted version of the team logo, the horizontal backs carry a second color player cutout and a summary of the player's performance. The card numbering is arranged alphabetically by city according to the American (1-14) and the National (15-28) Leagues.

	MINT	NRMT
COMPLETE SET (28)	25.00	11.00
COMMON CARD (1-28)	.25	.11
☐ 1 Cal Ripken	4.00	1.80
☐ 2 Mo Vaughn	1.25	.55
☐ 3 Tim Salmon	1.00	.45
☐ 4 Frank Thomas	5.00	2.20
☐ 5 Carlos Baerga	.35	.16
☐ 6 Cecil Fielder	.35	.16
☐ 7 Brian McRae	.25	.11
☐ 8 Greg Vaughn	.25	.11
☐ 9 Kirby Puckett	2.00	.90
☐ 10 Don Mattingly	2.50	1.10
☐ 11 Mark McGwire	1.50	.70
☐ 12 Ken Griffey Jr.	5.00	2.20
☐ 13 Juan Gonzalez	2.50	1.10
☐ 14 Paul Molitor	1.00	.45
☐ 15 David Justice	1.00	.45
☐ 16 Ryne Sandberg	1.25	.55
☐ 17 Barry Larkin	.75	.35
☐ 18 Andres Galarraga	.75	.35
☐ 19 Gary Sheffield	1.00	.45
☐ 20 Jeff Bagwell	2.00	.90
☐ 21 Mike Piazza	3.00	1.35
☐ 22 Marquis Grissom	.35	.16
☐ 23 Bobby Bonilla	.35	.16
☐ 24 Lenny Dykstra	.35	.16
☐ 25 Jay Bell	.25	.11
☐ 26 Gregg Jefferies	.35	.16
☐ 27 Tony Gwynn	2.00	.90
☐ 28 Will Clark	.75	.35

1994 Fleer Update

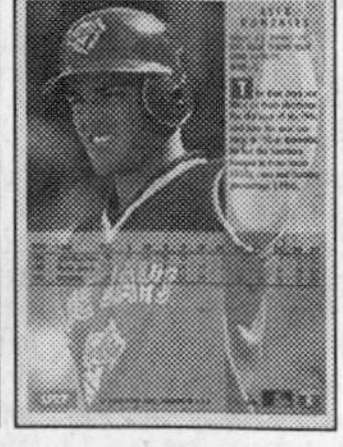

This 200-card standard-size set highlights traded players in their new uniforms and promising young rookies. The Update set was exclusively distributed in factory set form through hobby dealers. A ten card Diamond Tribute set was included in each factory set for a total of 210 cards. The cards are numbered on the back, grouped alphabetically by team by league with AL preceding NL. Key Rookie Cards include Chan Ho Park and Alex Rodriguez.

	MINT	NRMT
COMP.FACT.SET (210)	18.00	8.00
COMPLETE SET (200)	15.00	6.75
COMMON CARD (U1-U200)	.15	.07
☐ 1 Mark Eichhorn	.15	.07
☐ 2 Sid Fernandez	.15	.07
☐ 3 Leo Gomez	.15	.07
☐ 4 Mike Oquist	.15	.07
☐ 5 Rafael Palmeiro	.50	.23
☐ 6 Chris Sabo	.15	.07
☐ 7 Dwight Smith	.15	.07
☐ 8 Lee Smith	.25	.11
☐ 9 Damon Berryhill	.15	.07
☐ 10 Wes Chamberlain	.15	.07
☐ 11 Gar Finnvold	.15	.07
☐ 12 Chris Howard	.15	.07
☐ 13 Tim Naehring	.15	.07
☐ 14 Otis Nixon	.25	.11
☐ 15 Brian Anderson	.50	.23
☐ 16 Jorge Fabregas	.15	.07
☐ 17 Rex Hudler	.15	.07
☐ 18 Bo Jackson	.25	.11
☐ 19 Mark Leiter	.15	.07
☐ 20 Spike Owen	.15	.07
☐ 21 Harold Reynolds	.15	.07
☐ 22 Chris Turner	.15	.07
☐ 23 Dennis Cook	.15	.07
☐ 24 Jose DeLeon	.15	.07
☐ 25 Julio Franco	.25	.11
☐ 26 Joe Hall	.15	.07
☐ 27 Darrin Jackson	.15	.07
☐ 28 Dane Johnson	.15	.07
☐ 29 Norberto Martin	.15	.07
☐ 30 Scott Sanderson	.15	.07
☐ 31 Jason Grimsley	.15	.07
☐ 32 Dennis Martinez	.25	.11
☐ 33 Jack Morris	.25	.11
☐ 34 Eddie Murray	1.00	.45
☐ 35 Chad Ogea	.15	.07
☐ 36 Tony Pena	.15	.07
☐ 37 Paul Shuey	.15	.07
☐ 38 Omar Vizquel	.25	.11
☐ 39 Danny Bautista	.15	.07
☐ 40 Tim Belcher	.15	.07
☐ 41 Joe Boever	.15	.07
☐ 42 Storm Davis	.15	.07
☐ 43 Junior Felix	.15	.07
☐ 44 Mike Gardiner	.15	.07
☐ 45 Buddy Groom	.15	.07
☐ 46 Juan Samuel	.15	.07
☐ 47 Vince Coleman	.15	.07
☐ 48 Bob Hamelin	.15	.07
☐ 49 Dave Henderson	.15	.07
☐ 50 Rusty Meacham	.15	.07
☐ 51 Terry Shumpert	.15	.07
☐ 52 Jeff Bronkey	.15	.07
☐ 53 Alex Diaz	.15	.07
☐ 54 Brian Harper	.15	.07
☐ 55 Jose Mercedes	.15	.07
☐ 56 Jody Reed	.15	.07
☐ 57 Bob Scanlan	.15	.07
☐ 58 Turner Ward	.15	.07
☐ 59 Rich Becker	.25	.11
☐ 60 Alex Cole	.15	.07
☐ 61 Denny Hocking	.15	.07
☐ 62 Scott Leius	.15	.07
☐ 63 Pat Mahomes	.15	.07
☐ 64 Carlos Pulido	.15	.07
☐ 65 Dave Stevens	.15	.07
☐ 66 Matt Walbeck	.15	.07
☐ 67 Xavier Hernandez	.15	.07
☐ 68 Sterling Hitchcock	.25	.11
☐ 69 Terry Mulholland	.15	.07
☐ 70 Luis Polonia	.15	.07
☐ 71 Gerald Williams	.25	.11
☐ 72 Mark Acre	.15	.07
☐ 73 Geronimo Berroa	.25	.11
☐ 74 Rickey Henderson	.50	.23
☐ 75 Stan Javier	.15	.07
☐ 76 Steve Karsay	.15	.07
☐ 77 Carlos Reyes	.15	.07
☐ 78 Bill Taylor	.15	.07
☐ 79 Eric Anthony	.15	.07
☐ 80 Bobby Ayala	.15	.07
☐ 81 Tim Davis	.15	.07
☐ 82 Felix Fermin	.15	.07
☐ 83 Reggie Jefferson	.25	.11
☐ 84 Keith Mitchell	.15	.07
☐ 85 Bill Risley	.15	.07
☐ 86 Alex Rodriguez	10.00	4.50
☐ 87 Roger Salkeld	.15	.07
☐ 88 Dan Wilson	.25	.11
☐ 89 Cris Carpenter	.15	.07
☐ 90 Will Clark	.50	.23
☐ 91 Jeff Frye	.15	.07
☐ 92 Rick Helling	.15	.07
☐ 93 Chris James	.15	.07
☐ 94 Oddibe McDowell	.15	.07
☐ 95 Billy Ripken	.15	.07
☐ 96 Carlos Delgado	1.00	.45
☐ 97 Alex Gonzalez	.15	.07
☐ 98 Shawn Green	.25	.11
☐ 99 Darren Hall	.15	.07
☐ 100 Mike Huff	.15	.07
☐ 101 Mike Kelly	.15	.07
☐ 102 Roberto Kelly	.15	.07
☐ 103 Charlie O'Brien	.15	.07
☐ 104 Jose Oliva	.15	.07
☐ 105 Gregg Olson	.15	.07
☐ 106 Willie Banks	.15	.07
☐ 107 Jim Bullinger	.15	.07
☐ 108 Chuck Crim	.15	.07
☐ 109 Shawon Dunston	.15	.07
☐ 110 Karl Rhodes	.15	.07
☐ 111 Steve Trachsel	.15	.07
☐ 112 Anthony Young	.15	.07
☐ 113 Eddie Zambrano	.15	.07
☐ 114 Bret Boone	.15	.07
☐ 115 Jeff Brantley	.15	.07
☐ 116 Hector Carrasco	.15	.07
☐ 117 Tony Fernandez	.15	.07
☐ 118 Tim Fortugno	.15	.07
☐ 119 Erik Hanson	.15	.07
☐ 120 Chuck McElroy	.15	.07
☐ 121 Deion Sanders	1.00	.45
☐ 122 Ellis Burks	.25	.11
☐ 123 Marvin Freeman	.15	.07
☐ 124 Mike Harkey	.15	.07
☐ 125 Howard Johnson	.15	.07
☐ 126 Mike Kingery	.15	.07
☐ 127 Nelson Liriano	.15	.07
☐ 128 Marcus Moore	.15	.07
☐ 129 Mike Munoz	.15	.07
☐ 130 Kevin Ritz	.15	.07
☐ 131 Walt Weiss	.15	.07
☐ 132 Kurt Abbott	.15	.07
☐ 133 Jerry Browne	.15	.07
☐ 134 Greg Colbrunn	.15	.07
☐ 135 Jeremy Hernandez	.15	.07
☐ 136 Dave Magadan	.15	.07
☐ 137 Kurt Miller	.15	.07
☐ 138 Robb Nen	.25	.11
☐ 139 Jesus Tavarez	.15	.07
☐ 140 Sid Bream	.15	.07
☐ 141 Tom Edens	.15	.07
☐ 142 Tony Eusebio	.15	.07
☐ 143 John Hudek	.15	.07
☐ 144 Brian L. Hunter	1.00	.45
☐ 145 Orlando Miller	.15	.07
☐ 146 James Mouton	.25	.11
☐ 147 Shane Reynolds	.15	.07
☐ 148 Rafael Bournigal	.15	.07
☐ 149 Delino DeShields	.15	.07
☐ 150 Garey Ingram	.15	.07
☐ 151 Chan Ho Park	2.50	1.10
☐ 152 Wil Cordero	.25	.11
☐ 153 Pedro Martinez	1.00	.45
☐ 154 Randy Milligan	.15	.07
☐ 155 Lenny Webster	.15	.07
☐ 156 Rico Brogna	.15	.07
☐ 157 Josias Manzanillo	.15	.07
☐ 158 Kevin McReynolds	.15	.07
☐ 159 Mike Remlinger	.15	.07
☐ 160 David Segui	.15	.07
☐ 161 Pete Smith	.15	.07
☐ 162 Kelly Stinnett	.15	.07
☐ 163 Jose Vizcaino	.15	.07
☐ 164 Billy Hatcher	.15	.07
☐ 165 Doug Jones	.15	.07
☐ 166 Mike Lieberthal	.15	.07
☐ 167 Tony Longmire	.15	.07
☐ 168 Bobby Munoz	.15	.07
☐ 169 Paul Quantrill	.15	.07
☐ 170 Heathcliff Slocumb	.25	.11
☐ 171 Fernando Valenzuela	.25	.11
☐ 172 Mark Dewey	.15	.07
☐ 173 Brian R. Hunter	.15	.07
☐ 174 Jon Lieber	.15	.07
☐ 175 Ravelo Manzanillo	.15	.07
☐ 176 Dan Miceli	.15	.07
☐ 177 Rick White	.15	.07
☐ 178 Bryan Eversgerd	.15	.07
☐ 179 John Habyan	.15	.07
☐ 180 Terry McGriff	.15	.07
☐ 181 Vicente Palacios	.15	.07
☐ 182 Rich Rodriguez	.15	.07
☐ 183 Rick Sutcliffe	.15	.07
☐ 184 Donnie Elliott	.15	.07
☐ 185 Joey Hamilton	1.00	.45
☐ 186 Tim Hyers	.15	.07
☐ 187 Luis Lopez	.15	.07
☐ 188 Ray McDavid	.15	.07
☐ 189 Bip Roberts	.15	.07
☐ 190 Scott Sanders	.15	.07

☐ 191 Eddie Williams	.15	.07
☐ 192 Steve Frey	.15	.07
☐ 193 Pat Gomez	.15	.07
☐ 194 Rich Monteleone	.15	.07
☐ 195 Mark Portugal	.15	.07
☐ 196 Darryl Strawberry	.25	.11
☐ 197 Salomon Torres	.15	.07
☐ 198 W.VanLandingham	.15	.07
☐ 199 Checklist	.15	.07
☐ 200 Checklist	.15	.07

1994 Fleer Update Diamond Tribute

Each 1994 Fleer Update factory set contained a complete 10-card set of Diamond Tribute inserts. This was the third and final year that Fleer included an insert set in their factory boxed update sets. The 1994 Diamond Tribute inserts feature a player action shot cut out against a backdrop of clouds and baseballs. The selection once again focuses on the game's top veterans. Cards are numbered X of 10 on the back.

	MINT	NRMT
COMPLETE SET (10)	3.00	1.35
COMMON CARD (1-10)	.25	.11
☐ 1 Barry Bonds	.50	.23
☐ 2 Joe Carter	.25	.11
☐ 3 Will Clark	.35	.16
☐ 4 Roger Clemens	.40	.18
☐ 5 Tony Gwynn	.75	.35
☐ 6 Don Mattingly	1.00	.45
☐ 7 Fred McGriff	.25	.11
☐ 8 Eddie Murray	.50	.23
☐ 9 Kirby Puckett	.75	.35
☐ 10 Cal Ripken	2.00	.90

1994 Fleer Sunoco

These 25 standard-size cards feature white-bordered color player action shots on their fronts. The player's name and position appear in a white-lettered arc around his team's logo in one corner of the photo. The white-bordered back carries a posed color player photo that is ghosted, except for the rectangular area around the player's head. Upon the ghosted areas appear the player's name, biography, career highlights, and statistics. The cards are numbered on the back as "X of 25."

	MINT	NRMT
COMPLETE SET (25)	6.00	2.70
COMMON CARD (1-25)	.10	.05
☐ 1 Roberto Alomar	.40	.18
☐ 2 Carlos Baerga	.20	.09
☐ 3 Jeff Bagwell	.75	.35
☐ 4 Jay Bell	.10	.05
☐ 5 Barry Bonds	.50	.23
☐ 6 Joe Carter	.20	.09
☐ 7 Roger Clemens	.60	.25
☐ 8 Darren Daulton	.20	.09
☐ 9 Len Dykstra	.20	.09
☐ 10 Cecil Fielder	.20	.09
☐ 11 Tom Glavine	.20	.09
☐ 12 Juan Gonzalez	.75	.35
☐ 13 Ken Griffey Jr.	2.00	.90
☐ 14 David Justice	.40	.18
☐ 15 John Kruk	.10	.05
☐ 16 Greg Maddux	1.25	.55
☐ 17 Don Mattingly	.75	.35
☐ 18 Jack McDowell	.10	.05
☐ 19 John Olerud	.20	.09
☐ 20 Mike Piazza	1.25	.55
☐ 21 Kirby Puckett	.75	.35
☐ 22 Tim Salmon	.40	.18
☐ 23 Frank Thomas	1.50	.70
☐ 24 Andy Van Slyke	.10	.05
☐ 25 Checklist	.10	.05

1995 Fleer

The 1995 Fleer set consists of 600 standard-size cards issued as one series. Each pack contained at least one insert card with some 'Hot Packs" containing nothing but insert cards. Full-bleed fronts have two player photos and, atypical of baseball cards fronts, biographical information such as height, weight, etc. The backgrounds are multi-colored. The backs are horizontal and contain year-by-year statistics along with a photo. There was a different design for each of baseball's six divisions. The checklist is arranged alphabetically by teams within each league with AL preceding NL. Eight card promo sets were issued to hobby dealers. These cards are extremely difficult to tell apart from the regular cards and have the same value as the regular cards. The players in this set are Marquis Grissom, David Cone, Ozzie Smith, Roger Clemens, Tim Salmon, Paul O'Neill, Juan Gonzalez and Dante Bichette.

	MINT	NRMT
COMPLETE SET (600)	50.00	22.00
COMMON CARD (1-600)	.15	.07
☐ 1 Brady Anderson	.40	.18
☐ 2 Harold Baines	.30	.14
☐ 3 Damon Buford	.15	.07
☐ 4 Mike Devereaux	.15	.07
☐ 5 Mark Eichhorn	.15	.07
☐ 6 Sid Fernandez	.15	.07
☐ 7 Leo Gomez	.15	.07
☐ 8 Jeffrey Hammonds	.30	.14
☐ 9 Chris Hoiles	.15	.07
☐ 10 Rick Krivda	.15	.07
☐ 11 Ben McDonald	.15	.07
☐ 12 Mark McLemore	.15	.07
☐ 13 Alan Mills	.15	.07
☐ 14 Jamie Moyer	.15	.07
☐ 15 Mike Mussina	.60	.25
☐ 16 Mike Oquist	.15	.07
☐ 17 Rafael Palmeiro	.40	.18
☐ 18 Arthur Rhodes	.15	.07
☐ 19 Cal Ripken Jr.	2.50	1.10
☐ 20 Chris Sabo	.15	.07
☐ 21 Lee Smith	.30	.14
☐ 22 Jack Voigt	.15	.07
☐ 23 Damon Berryhill	.15	.07
☐ 24 Tom Brunansky	.15	.07
☐ 25 Wes Chamberlain	.15	.07
☐ 26 Roger Clemens	1.25	.55
☐ 27 Scott Cooper	.15	.07
☐ 28 Andre Dawson	.40	.18
☐ 29 Gar Finnvold	.15	.07
☐ 30 Tony Fossas	.15	.07
☐ 31 Mike Greenwell	.15	.07
☐ 32 Joe Hesketh	.15	.07
☐ 33 Chris Howard	.15	.07
☐ 34 Chris Nabholz	.15	.07
☐ 35 Tim Naehring	.15	.07
☐ 36 Otis Nixon	.15	.07
☐ 37 Carlos Rodriguez	.15	.07
☐ 38 Rich Rowland	.15	.07
☐ 39 Ken Ryan	.15	.07
☐ 40 Aaron Sele	.15	.07
☐ 41 John Valentin	.30	.14
☐ 42 Mo Vaughn	.75	.35
☐ 43 Frank Viola	.15	.07
☐ 44 Danny Bautista	.15	.07
☐ 45 Joe Boever	.15	.07
☐ 46 Milt Cuyler	.15	.07
☐ 47 Storm Davis	.15	.07
☐ 48 John Doherty	.15	.07
☐ 49 Junior Felix	.15	.07
☐ 50 Cecil Fielder	.30	.14
☐ 51 Travis Fryman	.30	.14
☐ 52 Mike Gardiner	.15	.07
☐ 53 Kirk Gibson	.30	.14
☐ 54 Chris Gomez	.15	.07
☐ 55 Buddy Groom	.15	.07
☐ 56 Mike Henneman	.15	.07
☐ 57 Chad Kreuter	.15	.07
☐ 58 Mike Moore	.15	.07
☐ 59 Tony Phillips	.15	.07
☐ 60 Juan Samuel	.15	.07
☐ 61 Mickey Tettleton	.15	.07
☐ 62 Alan Trammell	.40	.18
☐ 63 David Wells	.15	.07
☐ 64 Lou Whitaker	.30	.14
☐ 65 Jim Abbott	.15	.07
☐ 66 Joe Ausanio	.15	.07
☐ 67 Wade Boggs	.60	.25
☐ 68 Mike Gallego	.15	.07
☐ 69 Xavier Hernandez	.15	.07
☐ 70 Sterling Hitchcock	.30	.14
☐ 71 Steve Howe	.15	.07
☐ 72 Scott Kamieniecki	.15	.07
☐ 73 Pat Kelly	.15	.07
☐ 74 Jimmy Key	.30	.14
☐ 75 Jim Leyritz	.15	.07
☐ 76 Don Mattingly UER	1.00	.45
Photo is a reversed negative		
☐ 77 Terry Mulholland	.15	.07
☐ 78 Paul O'Neill	.30	.14
☐ 79 Melido Perez	.15	.07
☐ 80 Luis Polonia	.15	.07
☐ 81 Mike Stanley	.15	.07
☐ 82 Danny Tartabull	.15	.07
☐ 83 Randy Velarde	.15	.07
☐ 84 Bob Wickman	.15	.07
☐ 85 Bernie Williams	.60	.25
☐ 86 Gerald Williams	.15	.07
☐ 87 Roberto Alomar	.60	.25
☐ 88 Pat Borders	.15	.07
☐ 89 Joe Carter	.40	.18
☐ 90 Tony Castillo	.15	.07
☐ 91 Brad Cornett	.15	.07
☐ 92 Carlos Delgado	.30	.14
☐ 93 Alex Gonzalez	.30	.14
☐ 94 Shawn Green	.30	.14
☐ 95 Juan Guzman	.15	.07
☐ 96 Darren Hall	.15	.07
☐ 97 Pat Hentgen	.30	.14
☐ 98 Mike Huff	.15	.07
☐ 99 Randy Knorr	.15	.07
☐ 100 Al Leiter	.15	.07
☐ 101 Paul Molitor	.60	.25
☐ 102 John Olerud	.30	.14
☐ 103 Dick Schofield	.15	.07
☐ 104 Ed Sprague	.15	.07
☐ 105 Dave Stewart	.30	.14
☐ 106 Todd Stottlemyre	.15	.07
☐ 107 Devon White	.15	.07
☐ 108 Woody Williams	.15	.07
☐ 109 Wilson Alvarez	.30	.14
☐ 110 Paul Assenmacher	.15	.07
☐ 111 Jason Bere	.15	.07
☐ 112 Dennis Cook	.15	.07
☐ 113 Joey Cora	.15	.07
☐ 114 Jose DeLeon	.15	.07
☐ 115 Alex Fernandez	.30	.14
☐ 116 Julio Franco	.30	.14
☐ 117 Craig Grebeck	.15	.07
☐ 118 Ozzie Guillen	.15	.07
☐ 119 Roberto Hernandez	.15	.07
☐ 120 Darrin Jackson	.15	.07
☐ 121 Lance Johnson	.30	.14
☐ 122 Ron Karkovice	.15	.07
☐ 123 Mike LaValliere	.15	.07
☐ 124 Norberto Martin	.15	.07
☐ 125 Kirk McCaskill	.15	.07
☐ 126 Jack McDowell	.15	.07
☐ 127 Tim Raines	.15	.07
☐ 128 Frank Thomas	2.50	1.10
☐ 129 Robin Ventura	.30	.14
☐ 130 Sandy Alomar Jr.	.15	.07
☐ 131 Carlos Baerga	.30	.14
☐ 132 Albert Belle	.75	.35
☐ 133 Mark Clark	.15	.07
☐ 134 Alvaro Espinoza	.15	.07
☐ 135 Jason Grimsley	.15	.07
☐ 136 Wayne Kirby	.15	.07
☐ 137 Kenny Lofton	.75	.35
☐ 138 Albie Lopez	.15	.07
☐ 139 Dennis Martinez	.30	.14
☐ 140 Jose Mesa	.30	.14
☐ 141 Eddie Murray	.60	.25
☐ 142 Charles Nagy	.30	.14
☐ 143 Tony Pena	.15	.07

☐ 144 Eric Plunk .15 .07
☐ 145 Manny Ramirez .60 .25
☐ 146 Jeff Russell .15 .07
☐ 147 Paul Shuey .15 .07
☐ 148 Paul Sorrento .15 .07
☐ 149 Jim Thome .60 .25
☐ 150 Omar Vizquel .30 .14
☐ 151 Dave Winfield .40 .18
☐ 152 Kevin Appier .30 .14
☐ 153 Billy Brewer .15 .07
☐ 154 Vince Coleman .15 .07
☐ 155 David Cone .30 .14
☐ 156 Gary Gaetti .30 .14
☐ 157 Greg Gagne .15 .07
☐ 158 Tom Gordon .15 .07
☐ 159 Mark Gubicza .15 .07
☐ 160 Bob Hamelin .15 .07
☐ 161 Dave Henderson .15 .07
☐ 162 Felix Jose .15 .07
☐ 163 Wally Joyner .30 .14
☐ 164 Jose Lind .15 .07
☐ 165 Mike Macfarlane .15 .07
☐ 166 Mike Magnante .15 .07
☐ 167 Brent Mayne .15 .07
☐ 168 Brian McRae .15 .07
☐ 169 Rusty Meacham .15 .07
☐ 170 Jeff Montgomery .30 .14
☐ 171 Hipolito Pichardo .15 .07
☐ 172 Terry Shumpert .15 .07
☐ 173 Michael Tucker .40 .18
☐ 174 Ricky Bones .15 .07
☐ 175 Jeff Cirillo .30 .14
☐ 176 Alex Diaz .15 .07
☐ 177 Cal Eldred .15 .07
☐ 178 Mike Fetters .15 .07
☐ 179 Darryl Hamilton .15 .07
☐ 180 Brian Harper .15 .07
☐ 181 John Jaha .15 .07
☐ 182 Pat Listach .15 .07
☐ 183 Graeme Lloyd .15 .07
☐ 184 Jose Mercedes .15 .07
☐ 185 Matt Mieske .30 .14
☐ 186 Dave Nilsson .30 .14
☐ 187 Jody Reed .15 .07
☐ 188 Bob Scanlan .15 .07
☐ 189 Kevin Seitzer .15 .07
☐ 190 Bill Spiers .15 .07
☐ 191 B.J. Surhoff .30 .14
☐ 192 Jose Valentin .30 .14
☐ 193 Greg Vaughn .15 .07
☐ 194 Turner Ward .15 .07
☐ 195 Bill Wegman .15 .07
☐ 196 Rick Aguilera .15 .07
☐ 197 Rich Becker .15 .07
☐ 198 Alex Cole .15 .07
☐ 199 Marty Cordova .40 .18
☐ 200 Steve Dunn .15 .07
☐ 201 Scott Erickson .15 .07
☐ 202 Mark Guthrie .15 .07
☐ 203 Chip Hale .15 .07
☐ 204 LaTroy Hawkins .15 .07
☐ 205 Denny Hocking .15 .07
☐ 206 Chuck Knoblauch .60 .25
☐ 207 Scott Leius .15 .07
☐ 208 Shane Mack .15 .07
☐ 209 Pat Mahomes .15 .07
☐ 210 Pat Meares .15 .07
☐ 211 Pedro Munoz .15 .07
☐ 212 Kirby Puckett 1.25 .55
☐ 213 Jeff Reboulet .15 .07
☐ 214 Dave Stevens .15 .07
☐ 215 Kevin Tapani .15 .07
☐ 216 Matt Walbeck .15 .07
☐ 217 Carl Willis .15 .07
☐ 218 Brian Anderson .15 .07
☐ 219 Chad Curtis .15 .07
☐ 220 Chili Davis .30 .14
☐ 221 Gary DiSarcina .15 .07
☐ 222 Damion Easley .15 .07
☐ 223 Jim Edmonds .60 .25
☐ 224 Chuck Finley .30 .14
☐ 225 Joe Grahe .15 .07
☐ 226 Rex Hudler .15 .07
☐ 227 Bo Jackson .30 .14
☐ 228 Mark Langston .15 .07
☐ 229 Phil Leftwich .15 .07
☐ 230 Mark Leiter .15 .07
☐ 231 Spike Owen .15 .07
☐ 232 Bob Patterson .15 .07
☐ 233 Troy Percival .15 .07
☐ 234 Eduardo Perez .15 .07
☐ 235 Tim Salmon .60 .25
☐ 236 J.T. Snow .30 .14
☐ 237 Chris Turner .15 .07
☐ 238 Mark Acre .15 .07
☐ 239 Geronimo Berroa .15 .07
☐ 240 Mike Bordick .15 .07
☐ 241 John Briscoe .15 .07
☐ 242 Scott Brosius .15 .07
☐ 243 Ron Darling .15 .07
☐ 244 Dennis Eckersley .30 .14
☐ 245 Brent Gates .15 .07
☐ 246 Rickey Henderson .40 .18
☐ 247 Stan Javier .15 .07
☐ 248 Steve Karsay .15 .07
☐ 249 Mark McGwire 1.25 .55
☐ 250 Troy Neel .15 .07
☐ 251 Steve Ontiveros .15 .07
☐ 252 Carlos Reyes .15 .07
☐ 253 Ruben Sierra .15 .07
☐ 254 Terry Steinbach .30 .14
☐ 255 Bill Taylor .15 .07
☐ 256 Todd Van Poppel .15 .07
☐ 257 Bobby Witt .15 .07
☐ 258 Rich Amaral .15 .07
☐ 259 Eric Anthony .15 .07
☐ 260 Bobby Ayala .15 .07
☐ 261 Mike Blowers .15 .07
☐ 262 Chris Bosio .15 .07
☐ 263 Jay Buhner .40 .18
☐ 264 John Cummings .15 .07
☐ 265 Tim Davis .15 .07
☐ 266 Felix Fermin .15 .07
☐ 267 Dave Fleming .15 .07
☐ 268 Goose Gossage .30 .14
☐ 269 Ken Griffey Jr. 3.00 1.35
☐ 270 Reggie Jefferson .30 .14
☐ 271 Randy Johnson .60 .25
☐ 272 Edgar Martinez .40 .18
☐ 273 Tino Martinez .60 .25
☐ 274 Greg Pirkl .15 .07
☐ 275 Bill Risley .15 .07
☐ 276 Roger Salkeld .15 .07
☐ 277 Luis Sojo .15 .07
☐ 278 Mac Suzuki .30 .14
☐ 279 Dan Wilson .30 .14
☐ 280 Kevin Brown .30 .14
☐ 281 Jose Canseco .40 .18
☐ 282 Cris Carpenter .15 .07
☐ 283 Will Clark .40 .18
☐ 284 Jeff Frye .15 .07
☐ 285 Juan Gonzalez 1.50 .70
☐ 286 Rick Helling .15 .07
☐ 287 Tom Henke .15 .07
☐ 288 David Hulse .15 .07
☐ 289 Chris James .15 .07
☐ 290 Manuel Lee .15 .07
☐ 291 Oddibe McDowell .15 .07
☐ 292 Dean Palmer .30 .14
☐ 293 Roger Pavlik .15 .07
☐ 294 Bill Ripken .15 .07
☐ 295 Ivan Rodriguez .75 .35
☐ 296 Kenny Rogers .15 .07
☐ 297 Doug Strange .15 .07
☐ 298 Matt Whiteside .15 .07
☐ 299 Steve Avery .15 .07
☐ 300 Steve Bedrosian .15 .07
☐ 301 Rafael Belliard .15 .07
☐ 302 Jeff Blauser .15 .07
☐ 303 Dave Gallagher .15 .07
☐ 304 Tom Glavine .40 .18
☐ 305 David Justice .40 .18
☐ 306 Mike Kelly .15 .07
☐ 307 Roberto Kelly .15 .07
☐ 308 Ryan Klesko .40 .18
☐ 309 Mark Lemke .15 .07
☐ 310 Javier Lopez .40 .18
☐ 311 Greg Maddux 2.00 .90
☐ 312 Fred McGriff .40 .18
☐ 313 Greg McMichael .15 .07
☐ 314 Kent Mercker .15 .07
☐ 315 Charlie O'Brien .15 .07
☐ 316 Jose Oliva .15 .07
☐ 317 Terry Pendleton .30 .14
☐ 318 John Smoltz .40 .18
☐ 319 Mike Stanton .15 .07
☐ 320 Tony Tarasco .15 .07
☐ 321 Terrell Wade .15 .07
☐ 322 Mark Wohlers .30 .14
☐ 323 Kurt Abbott .15 .07
☐ 324 Luis Aquino .15 .07
☐ 325 Bret Barberie .15 .07
☐ 326 Ryan Bowen .15 .07
☐ 327 Jerry Browne .15 .07
☐ 328 Chuck Carr .15 .07
☐ 329 Matias Carrillo .15 .07
☐ 330 Greg Colbrunn .15 .07
☐ 331 Jeff Conine .30 .14
☐ 332 Mark Gardner .15 .07
☐ 333 Chris Hammond .15 .07
☐ 334 Bryan Harvey .15 .07
☐ 335 Richie Lewis .15 .07
☐ 336 Dave Magadan .15 .07
☐ 337 Terry Mathews .15 .07
☐ 338 Robb Nen .15 .07
☐ 339 Yorkis Perez .15 .07
☐ 340 Pat Rapp .15 .07
☐ 341 Benito Santiago .15 .07
☐ 342 Gary Sheffield .60 .25
☐ 343 Dave Weathers .15 .07
☐ 344 Moises Alou .30 .14
☐ 345 Sean Berry .15 .07
☐ 346 Wil Cordero .15 .07
☐ 347 Joey Eischen .15 .07
☐ 348 Jeff Fassero .15 .07
☐ 349 Darrin Fletcher .15 .07
☐ 350 Cliff Floyd .30 .14
☐ 351 Marquis Grissom .30 .14
☐ 352 Butch Henry .15 .07
☐ 353 Gil Heredia .15 .07
☐ 354 Ken Hill .15 .07
☐ 355 Mike Lansing .15 .07
☐ 356 Pedro Martinez .60 .25
☐ 357 Mel Rojas .15 .07
☐ 358 Kirk Rueter .15 .07
☐ 359 Tim Scott .15 .07
☐ 360 Jeff Shaw .15 .07
☐ 361 Larry Walker .60 .25
☐ 362 Lenny Webster .15 .07
☐ 363 John Wetteland .30 .14
☐ 364 Rondell White .40 .18
☐ 365 Bobby Bonilla .30 .14
☐ 366 Rico Brogna .15 .07
☐ 367 Jeromy Burnitz .30 .14
☐ 368 John Franco .30 .14
☐ 369 Dwight Gooden .30 .14
☐ 370 Todd Hundley .30 .14
☐ 371 Jason Jacome .15 .07
☐ 372 Bobby Jones .30 .14
☐ 373 Jeff Kent .15 .07
☐ 374 Jim Lindeman .15 .07
☐ 375 Josias Manzanillo .15 .07
☐ 376 Roger Mason .15 .07
☐ 377 Kevin McReynolds .15 .07
☐ 378 Joe Orsulak .15 .07
☐ 379 Bill Pulsipher .15 .07
☐ 380 Bret Saberhagen .15 .07
☐ 381 David Segui .15 .07
☐ 382 Pete Smith .15 .07
☐ 383 Kelly Stinnett .15 .07
☐ 384 Ryan Thompson .15 .07
☐ 385 Jose Vizcaino .15 .07
☐ 386 Toby Borland .15 .07
☐ 387 Ricky Bottalico .30 .14
☐ 388 Darren Daulton .30 .14
☐ 389 Mariano Duncan .15 .07
☐ 390 Lenny Dykstra .30 .14
☐ 391 Jim Eisenreich .30 .14
☐ 392 Tommy Greene .15 .07
☐ 393 Dave Hollins .15 .07
☐ 394 Pete Incaviglia .15 .07
☐ 395 Danny Jackson .15 .07
☐ 396 Doug Jones .15 .07
☐ 397 Ricky Jordan .15 .07
☐ 398 John Kruk .30 .14
☐ 399 Mike Lieberthal .15 .07
☐ 400 Tony Longmire .15 .07
☐ 401 Mickey Morandini .15 .07
☐ 402 Bobby Munoz .15 .07
☐ 403 Curt Schilling .30 .14
☐ 404 Heathcliff Slocumb .15 .07
☐ 405 Kevin Stocker .15 .07
☐ 406 Fernando Valenzuela .30 .14
☐ 407 David West .15 .07
☐ 408 Willie Banks .15 .07
☐ 409 Jose Bautista .15 .07
☐ 410 Steve Buechele .15 .07
☐ 411 Jim Bullinger .15 .07
☐ 412 Chuck Crim .15 .07
☐ 413 Shawon Dunston .15 .07
☐ 414 Kevin Foster .15 .07
☐ 415 Mark Grace .40 .18
☐ 416 Jose Hernandez .15 .07
☐ 417 Glenallen Hill .15 .07
☐ 418 Brooks Kieschnick .30 .14
☐ 419 Derrick May .15 .07
☐ 420 Randy Myers .15 .07
☐ 421 Dan Plesac .15 .07
☐ 422 Karl Rhodes .15 .07
☐ 423 Rey Sanchez .15 .07
☐ 424 Sammy Sosa .60 .25
☐ 425 Steve Trachsel .15 .07
☐ 426 Rick Wilkins .15 .07
☐ 427 Anthony Young .15 .07
☐ 428 Eddie Zambrano .15 .07
☐ 429 Bret Boone .30 .14
☐ 430 Jeff Branson .15 .07
☐ 431 Jeff Brantley .15 .07
☐ 432 Hector Carrasco .15 .07
☐ 433 Brian Dorsett .15 .07
☐ 434 Tony Fernandez .15 .07

☐ 435 Tim Fortugno	.15	.07
☐ 436 Erik Hanson	.15	.07
☐ 437 Thomas Howard	.15	.07
☐ 438 Kevin Jarvis	.15	.07
☐ 439 Barry Larkin	.40	.18
☐ 440 Chuck McElroy	.15	.07
☐ 441 Kevin Mitchell	.15	.07
☐ 442 Hal Morris	.15	.07
☐ 443 Jose Rijo	.15	.07
☐ 444 John Roper	.15	.07
☐ 445 Johnny Ruffin	.15	.07
☐ 446 Deion Sanders	.60	.25
☐ 447 Reggie Sanders	.15	.07
☐ 448 Pete Schourek	.15	.07
☐ 449 John Smiley	.15	.07
☐ 450 Eddie Taubensee	.15	.07
☐ 451 Jeff Bagwell	1.25	.55
☐ 452 Kevin Bass	.15	.07
☐ 453 Craig Biggio	.40	.18
☐ 454 Ken Caminiti	.60	.25
☐ 455 Andujar Cedeno	.15	.07
☐ 456 Doug Drabek	.15	.07
☐ 457 Tony Eusebio	.15	.07
☐ 458 Mike Felder	.15	.07
☐ 459 Steve Finley	.30	.14
☐ 460 Luis Gonzalez	.15	.07
☐ 461 Mike Hampton	.30	.14
☐ 462 Pete Harnisch	.15	.07
☐ 463 John Hudek	.15	.07
☐ 464 Todd Jones	.15	.07
☐ 465 Darryl Kile	.30	.14
☐ 466 James Mouton	.15	.07
☐ 467 Shane Reynolds	.15	.07
☐ 468 Scott Servais	.15	.07
☐ 469 Greg Swindell	.15	.07
☐ 470 Dave Veres	.15	.07
☐ 471 Brian Williams	.15	.07
☐ 472 Jay Bell	.30	.14
☐ 473 Jacob Brumfield	.15	.07
☐ 474 Dave Clark	.15	.07
☐ 475 Steve Cooke	.15	.07
☐ 476 Midre Cummings	.15	.07
☐ 477 Mark Dewey	.15	.07
☐ 478 Tom Foley	.15	.07
☐ 479 Carlos Garcia	.15	.07
☐ 480 Jeff King	.30	.14
☐ 481 Jon Lieber	.15	.07
☐ 482 Ravelo Manzanillo	.15	.07
☐ 483 Al Martin	.30	.14
☐ 484 Orlando Merced	.15	.07
☐ 485 Danny Miceli	.15	.07
☐ 486 Denny Neagle	.30	.14
☐ 487 Lance Parrish	.15	.07
☐ 488 Don Slaught	.15	.07
☐ 489 Zane Smith	.15	.07
☐ 490 Andy Van Slyke	.30	.14
☐ 491 Paul Wagner	.15	.07
☐ 492 Rick White	.15	.07
☐ 493 Luis Alicea	.15	.07
☐ 494 Rene Arocha	.15	.07
☐ 495 Rheal Cormier	.15	.07
☐ 496 Bryan Eversgerd	.15	.07
☐ 497 Bernard Gilkey	.30	.14
☐ 498 John Habyan	.15	.07
☐ 499 Gregg Jefferies	.30	.14
☐ 500 Brian Jordan	.30	.14
☐ 501 Ray Lankford	.40	.18
☐ 502 John Mabry	.40	.18
☐ 503 Terry McGriff	.15	.07
☐ 504 Tom Pagnozzi	.15	.07
☐ 505 Vicente Palacios	.15	.07
☐ 506 Geronimo Pena	.15	.07
☐ 507 Gerald Perry	.15	.07
☐ 508 Rich Rodriguez	.15	.07
☐ 509 Ozzie Smith	.75	.35
☐ 510 Bob Tewksbury	.15	.07
☐ 511 Allen Watson	.15	.07
☐ 512 Mark Whiten	.15	.07
☐ 513 Todd Zeile	.15	.07
☐ 514 Dante Bichette	.40	.18
☐ 515 Willie Blair	.15	.07
☐ 516 Ellis Burks	.30	.14
☐ 517 Marvin Freeman	.15	.07
☐ 518 Andres Galarraga	.40	.18
☐ 519 Joe Girardi	.15	.07
☐ 520 Greg W. Harris	.15	.07
☐ 521 Charlie Hayes	.15	.07
☐ 522 Mike Kingery	.15	.07
☐ 523 Nelson Liriano	.15	.07
☐ 524 Mike Munoz	.15	.07
☐ 525 David Nied	.15	.07
☐ 526 Steve Reed	.15	.07
☐ 527 Kevin Ritz	.15	.07
☐ 528 Bruce Ruffin	.15	.07
☐ 529 John Vander Wal	.15	.07
☐ 530 Walt Weiss	.15	.07
☐ 531 Eric Young	.30	.14
☐ 532 Billy Ashley	.15	.07
☐ 533 Pedro Astacio	.15	.07
☐ 534 Rafael Bournigal	.15	.07
☐ 535 Brett Butler	.30	.14
☐ 536 Tom Candiotti	.15	.07
☐ 537 Omar Daal	.15	.07
☐ 538 Delino DeShields	.15	.07
☐ 539 Darren Dreifort	.15	.07
☐ 540 Kevin Gross	.15	.07
☐ 541 Orel Hershiser	.30	.14
☐ 542 Garey Ingram	.15	.07
☐ 543 Eric Karros	.30	.14
☐ 544 Ramon Martinez	.30	.14
☐ 545 Raul Mondesi	.40	.18
☐ 546 Chan Ho Park	.60	.25
☐ 547 Mike Piazza	2.00	.90
☐ 548 Henry Rodriguez	.15	.07
☐ 549 Rudy Seanez	.15	.07
☐ 550 Ismael Valdes	.30	.14
☐ 551 Tim Wallach	.15	.07
☐ 552 Todd Worrell	.15	.07
☐ 553 Andy Ashby	.15	.07
☐ 554 Brad Ausmus	.15	.07
☐ 555 Derek Bell	.30	.14
☐ 556 Andy Benes	.15	.07
☐ 557 Phil Clark	.15	.07
☐ 558 Donnie Elliott	.15	.07
☐ 559 Ricky Gutierrez	.15	.07
☐ 560 Tony Gwynn	1.50	.70
☐ 561 Joey Hamilton	.30	.14
☐ 562 Trevor Hoffman	.30	.14
☐ 563 Luis Lopez	.15	.07
☐ 564 Pedro A. Martinez	.15	.07
☐ 565 Tim Mauser	.15	.07
☐ 566 Phil Plantier	.15	.07
☐ 567 Bip Roberts	.15	.07
☐ 568 Scott Sanders	.15	.07
☐ 569 Craig Shipley	.15	.07
☐ 570 Jeff Tabaka	.15	.07
☐ 571 Eddie Williams	.15	.07
☐ 572 Rod Beck	.15	.07
☐ 573 Mike Benjamin	.15	.07
☐ 574 Barry Bonds	.75	.35
☐ 575 Dave Burba	.15	.07
☐ 576 John Burkett	.15	.07
☐ 577 Mark Carreon	.15	.07
☐ 578 Royce Clayton	.15	.07
☐ 579 Steve Frey	.15	.07
☐ 580 Bryan Hickerson	.15	.07
☐ 581 Mike Jackson	.15	.07
☐ 582 Darren Lewis	.15	.07
☐ 583 Kirt Manwaring	.15	.07
☐ 584 Rich Monteleone	.15	.07
☐ 585 John Patterson	.15	.07
☐ 586 J.R. Phillips	.15	.07
☐ 587 Mark Portugal	.15	.07
☐ 588 Joe Rosselli	.15	.07
☐ 589 Darryl Strawberry	.30	.14
☐ 590 Bill Swift	.15	.07
☐ 591 Robby Thompson	.15	.07
☐ 592 William VanLandingham	.15	.07
☐ 593 Matt Williams	.40	.18
☐ 594 Checklist	.15	.07
☐ 595 Checklist	.15	.07
☐ 596 Checklist	.15	.07
☐ 597 Checklist	.15	.07
☐ 598 Checklist	.15	.07
☐ 599 Checklist	.15	.07
☐ 600 Checklist	.15	.07

1995 Fleer All-Fleer

This nine-card standard-size set was available through a 1995 Fleer wrapper offer. Nine of the leading players for each position are featured in this set. The wrapper redemption offer expired on September 30, 1995. The fronts feature the player's photo covering most of the card with a small section on the right set off for the words "All Fleer 9" along with the playerís name. The backs feature player information as to why they are among the best in the game.

	MINT	NRMT
COMPLETE SET (9)	10.00	4.50
COMMON CARD (1-9)	.50	.23
☐ 1 Mike Piazza	2.00	.90
☐ 2 Frank Thomas	2.50	1.10
☐ 3 Roberto Alomar	1.00	.45
☐ 4 Cal Ripken	2.50	1.10
☐ 5 Matt Williams	.75	.35
☐ 6 Barry Bonds	.75	.35
☐ 7 Ken Griffey Jr.	3.00	1.35
☐ 8 Tony Gwynn	1.00	.45
☐ 9 Greg Maddux	2.00	.90

1995 Fleer All-Rookies

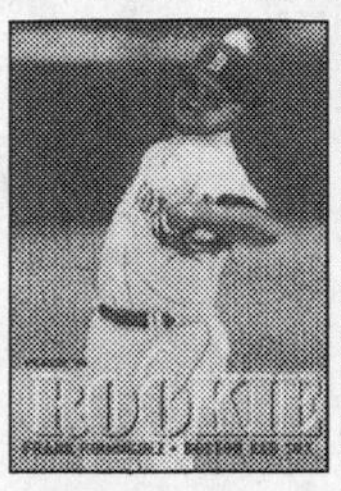

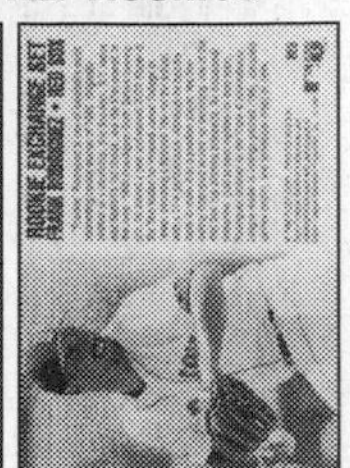

This nine-card standard-size set was available through a Rookie Exchange redemption card randomly inserted in packs. The redemption deadline was 9/30/95. This set features players who made their major league debut in 1995. The fronts have an action photo with a grainy background. The player's name and team are in gold foil at the bottom. Horizontal backs have a player photo the left and minor league highlights to the right. The set is sequenced in alphabetical order.

	MINT	NRMT
COMPLETE SET (9)	5.00	2.20
COMMON CARD (M1-M9)	.50	.23
☐ M1 Edgardo Alfonzo	2.50	1.10
☐ M2 Jason Bates	.50	.23
☐ M3 Brian Boehringer	.50	.23
☐ M4 Darren Bragg	.75	.35
☐ M5 Brad Clontz	.50	.23
☐ M6 Jim Dougherty	.50	.23
☐ M7 Todd Hollandsworth	2.50	1.10
☐ M8 Rudy Pemberton	.50	.23
☐ M9 Frank Rodriguez	.75	.35
☐ NNO Expired All-Rookie Exch.	1.50	.70

1995 Fleer All-Stars

Randomly inserted in all pack types at a rate of one in three, this 25-card standard-size set showcases those that participated in the 1994 mid-season classic held in Pittsburgh. Horizontally designed, the fronts contain photos of American League stars with the back protraying the National League player from the same position. On each side, the 1994 All-Star Game logo appears in gold foil as does either the A.L. or N.L. logo in silver foil.

	MINT	NRMT
COMPLETE SET (25)	12.00	5.50
COMMON CARD (1-25)	.25	.11
☐ 1 Ivan Rodriguez Mike Piazza	2.00	.90
☐ 2 Frank Thomas Gregg Jefferies	2.50	1.10
☐ 3 Robert Alomar Mariano Duncan	.60	.25
☐ 4 Wade Boggs Matt Williams	.35	.16
☐ 5 Cal Ripken Jr. Ozzie Smith	2.50	1.10
☐ 6 Joe Carter Barry Bonds	.75	.35
☐ 7 Ken Griffey Jr.	5.00	2.20

Tony Gwynn		
☐ 8 Kirby Puckett	1.50	.70
David Justice		
☐ 9 Jimmy Key	2.00	.90
Greg Maddux		
☐ 10 Chuck Knoblauch	.60	.25
Wil Cordero		
☐ 11 Scott Cooper	.25	.11
Ken Caminiti		
☐ 12 Will Clark	.35	.16
Carlos Garcia		
☐ 13 Paul Molitor	1.00	.45
Jeff Bagwell		
☐ 14 Travis Fryman	.50	.23
Craig Biggio		
☐ 15 Mickey Tettleton	.35	.16
Fred McGriff		
☐ 16 Kenny Lofton	.35	.16
Moises Alou		
☐ 17 Albert Belle	.75	.35
Marquis Grissom		
☐ 18 Paul O'Neill	.35	.16
Dante Bichette		
☐ 19 David Cone	.35	.16
Ken Hill		
☐ 20 Mike Mussina	.35	.16
Doug Drabek		
☐ 21 Randy Johnson	.35	.16
John Hudek		
☐ 22 Pat Hentgen	.35	.16
Danny Jackson		
☐ 23 Wilson Alvarez	.25	.11
Rod Beck		
☐ 24 Lee Smith	.35	.16
Randy Myers		
☐ 25 Jason Bere	.25	.11
Doug Jones		

1995 Fleer Award Winners

Randomly inserted in all pack types at a rate of one in 24, this six card standard-size set highlights the major award winners of 1994. Card fronts feature action photos that are full-bleed on the right border and have gold border on the left. Within the gold border are the player's name and Fleer Award Winner. The backs contain a photo with text that references 1994 accomplishments.

	MINT	NRMT
COMPLETE SET (6)	8.00	3.60
COMMON CARD (1-6)	.50	.23
☐ 1 Frank Thomas	5.00	2.20
☐ 2 Jeff Bagwell	2.00	.90
☐ 3 David Cone	.75	.35
☐ 4 Greg Maddux	3.00	1.35
☐ 5 Bob Hamelin	.50	.23
☐ 6 Raul Mondesi	1.00	.45

1995 Fleer League Leaders

Randomly inserted in all pack types at a rate of one in 12, this 10-card standard-size set features 1994 American and National League leaders in various categories. The horizontal cards have player photos on front and back. The back also has a brief write-up concerning the accomplishment.

	MINT	NRMT
COMPLETE SET (10)	8.00	3.60
COMMON CARD (1-10)	.50	.23
☐ 1 Paul O'Neill	.60	.25
☐ 2 Ken Griffey Jr.	5.00	2.20
☐ 3 Kirby Puckett	2.00	.90
☐ 4 Jimmy Key	.60	.25
☐ 5 Randy Johnson	1.00	.45
☐ 6 Tony Gwynn	2.00	.90
☐ 7 Matt Williams	.75	.35
☐ 8 Jeff Bagwell	2.00	.90
☐ 9 Greg Maddux	1.50	.70
Ken Hill		
☐ 10 Andy Benes	.50	.23

1995 Fleer Lumber Company

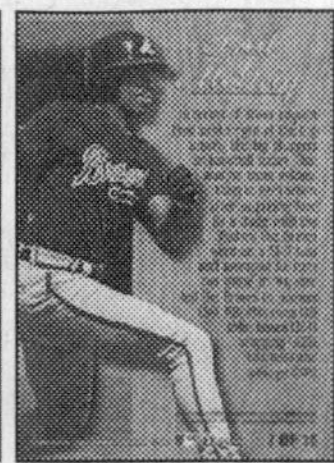

Randomly inserted in retail packs at a rate of one in 24, this standard-size set highlights 10 of the game's top sluggers. Full-bleed card fronts feature an action photo with the Lumber Company logo, which includes the player's name, toward the bottom of the photo. Card backs have a player photo and woodgrain background with a write-up that highlights individual achievements. The set is sequenced in alphabetical order.

	MINT	NRMT
COMPLETE SET (10)	40.00	18.00
COMMON CARD (1-10)	1.00	.45
☐ 1 Jeff Bagwell	6.00	2.70
☐ 2 Albert Belle	6.00	2.70
☐ 3 Barry Bonds	4.00	1.80
☐ 4 Jose Canseco	1.50	.70
☐ 5 Joe Carter	2.00	.90
☐ 6 Ken Griffey Jr.	15.00	6.75
☐ 7 Fred McGriff	2.00	.90
☐ 8 Kevin Mitchell	1.00	.45
☐ 9 Frank Thomas	15.00	6.75
☐ 10 Matt Williams	2.00	.90

1995 Fleer Major League Prospects

Randomly inserted in all pack types at a rate of one in six, this 10-card standard-size set spotlights major league hopefuls. Card fronts feature a player photo with the words "Major League Prospects" serving as part of the background. The player's name and team appear in silver foil at the bottom. The backs have a photo and a write-up on his minor league career. The cards are sequenced in alphabetical order.

	MINT	NRMT
COMPLETE SET (10)	10.00	4.50
COMMON CARD (1-10)	.50	.23
☐ 1 Garret Anderson	1.00	.45
☐ 2 James Baldwin	.75	.35
☐ 3 Alan Benes	1.00	.45
☐ 4 Armando Benitez	.50	.23
☐ 5 Ray Durham	.75	.35
☐ 6 Brian L. Hunter	1.00	.45
☐ 7 Derek Jeter	4.00	1.80
☐ 8 Charles Johnson	1.00	.45
☐ 9 Orlando Miller	.50	.23
☐ 10 Alex Rodriguez	5.00	2.20

1995 Fleer Pro-Visions

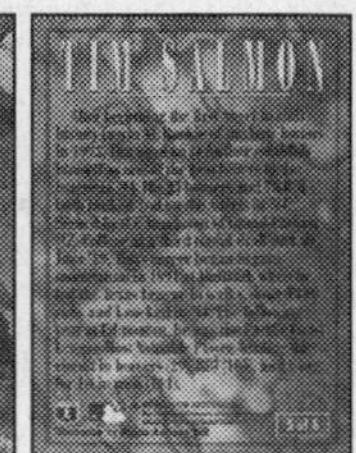

Randomly inserted in all pack types at a rate of one in nine, this six card standard-size set features top players illustrated by Wayne Anthony Still. The colorful artwork on front features the player in a surrealistic setting. The backs offer write-up on the player's previous season.

	MINT	NRMT
COMPLETE SET (6)	4.00	1.80
COMMON CARD (1-6)	.50	.23
☐ 1 Mike Mussina	1.00	.45
☐ 2 Raul Mondesi	.50	.23
☐ 3 Jeff Bagwell	1.25	.55
☐ 4 Greg Maddux	2.00	.90
☐ 5 Tim Salmon	1.00	.45
☐ 6 Manny Ramirez	1.00	.45

1995 Fleer Rookie Sensations

Randomly inserted in 18-card packs, this 20-card standard-size set features top rookies from the 1994 season. The fronts have full-bleed color photos with the team and player's name in gold foil along the right edge. The backs also have full-bleed color photos along with player information. The set is sequenced in alphabetical order.

	MINT	NRMT
COMPLETE SET (20)	50.00	22.00
COMMON CARD (1-20)	2.00	.90
☐ 1 Kurt Abbott	2.00	.90
☐ 2 Rico Brogna	3.00	1.35
☐ 3 Hector Carrasco	2.00	.90
☐ 4 Kevin Foster	2.00	.90
☐ 5 Chris Gomez	2.00	.90
☐ 6 Darren Hall	2.00	.90
☐ 7 Bob Hamelin	2.00	.90
☐ 8 Joey Hamilton	3.00	1.35
☐ 9 John Hudek	2.00	.90
☐ 10 Ryan Klesko	6.00	2.70
☐ 11 Javier Lopez	4.00	1.80
☐ 12 Matt Mieske	3.00	1.35
☐ 13 Raul Mondesi	6.00	2.70
☐ 14 Manny Ramirez	10.00	4.50
☐ 15 Shane Reynolds	3.00	1.35
☐ 16 Bill Risley	2.00	.90
☐ 17 Johnny Ruffin	2.00	.90
☐ 18 Steve Trachsel	2.00	.90
☐ 19 William VanLandingham	2.00	.90
☐ 20 Rondell White	4.00	1.80

1995 Fleer Team Leaders

Randomly inserted in 12-card hobby packs at a rate of one in 24, this 28-card standard-size set features top players from each team. Each team is represented with card the has the team's leading hitter on one side with the leading pitcher on the other side. The team logo, "Team Leaders" and the player's name are gold foil stamped on front and back.

	MINT	NRMT
COMPLETE SET (28)	225.00	100.00
COMMON CARD (1-28)	2.50	1.10
☐ 1 Cal Ripken Jr.	30.00	13.50
Mike Mussina		

☐ 2 Mo Vaughn Roger Clemens	15.00	6.75
☐ 3 Tim Salmon Chuck Finley	2.50	1.10
☐ 4 Frank Thomas Jack McDowell	30.00	13.50
☐ 5 Albert Belle Dennis Martinez	10.00	4.50
☐ 6 Cecil Fielder Mike Moore	4.00	1.80
☐ 7 Bob Hamelin David Cone	2.50	1.10
☐ 8 Greg Vaughn Ricky Bones	2.50	1.10
☐ 9 Kirby Puckett Rick Aguilera	15.00	6.75
☐ 10 Don Mattingly Jimmy Key	12.00	5.50
☐ 11 Ruben Sierra Dennis Eckersley	2.50	1.10
☐ 12 Ken Griffey Jr. Randy Johnson	40.00	18.00
☐ 13 Jose Canseco Kenny Rogers	2.50	1.10
☐ 14 Joe Carter Pat Hentgen	4.00	1.80
☐ 15 David Justice Greg Maddux	25.00	11.00
☐ 16 Sammy Sosa Steve Trachsel	4.00	1.80
☐ 17 Kevin Mitchell Jose Rijo	2.50	1.10
☐ 18 Dante Bichette Bruce Ruffin	2.50	1.10
☐ 19 Jeff Conine Robb Nen	2.50	1.10
☐ 20 Jeff Bagwell Doug Drabek	15.00	6.75
☐ 21 Mike Piazza Ramon Martinez	20.00	9.00
☐ 22 Moises Alou Ken Hill	2.50	1.10
☐ 23 Bobby Bonilla Bret Saberhagen	2.50	1.10
☐ 24 Darren Daulton Danny Jackson	4.00	1.80
☐ 25 Jay Bell Zane Smith	2.50	1.10
☐ 26 Gregg Jefferies Bob Tewksbury	2.50	1.10
☐ 27 Tony Gwynn Andy Benes	20.00	9.00
☐ 28 Matt Williams Rod Beck	2.50	1.10

1995 Fleer Update

This 200-card standard-size set features many players who were either rookies in 1995 or played for new teams. These cards were issued in either 12-card packs with a suggested retail price of $1.49 or 18-card packs that had a suggested retail price of $2.29. Each Fleer Update pack included one card from several insert sets produced with this product. Hot packs featuring only these insert cards were included one every 72 packs. The full-bleed fronts have two player photos and, atypical of baseball card fronts, biographical information such as height, weight, etc. The backgrounds are multi-colored. The backs are horizontal, have yearly statistics, a photo, and are numbered with the prefix "U". The checklist is arranged alphabetically by team within each leagueís divisions. Key Rookie Cards in this set include Bobby Higginson and Hideo Nomo.

	MINT	NRMT
COMPLETE SET (200)	15.00	6.75
COMMON CARD (1-200)	.10	.05
☐ 1 Manny Alexander	.10	.05
☐ 2 Bret Barberie	.10	.05
☐ 3 Armando Benitez	.10	.05
☐ 4 Kevin Brown	.20	.09
☐ 5 Doug Jones	.10	.05
☐ 6 Sherman Obando	.10	.05
☐ 7 Andy Van Slyke	.20	.09
☐ 8 Stan Belinda	.10	.05
☐ 9 Jose Canseco	.30	.14
☐ 10 Vaughn Eshelman	.10	.05
☐ 11 Mike Macfarlane	.10	.05
☐ 12 Troy O'Leary	.10	.05
☐ 13 Steve Rodriguez	.10	.05
☐ 14 Lee Tinsley	.10	.05
☐ 15 Tim Vanegmond	.10	.05
☐ 16 Mark Whiten	.10	.05
☐ 17 Sean Bergman	.10	.05
☐ 18 Chad Curtis	.10	.05
☐ 19 John Flaherty	.10	.05
☐ 20 Bob Higginson	.60	.25
☐ 21 Felipe Lira	.10	.05
☐ 22 Shannon Penn	.10	.05
☐ 23 Todd Steverson	.10	.05
☐ 24 Sean Whiteside	.10	.05
☐ 25 Tony Fernandez	.10	.05
☐ 26 Jack McDowell	.10	.05
☐ 27 Andy Pettitte	.60	.25
☐ 28 John Wetteland	.20	.09
☐ 29 David Cone	.20	.09
☐ 30 Mike Timlin	.10	.05
☐ 31 Duane Ward	.10	.05
☐ 32 Jim Abbott	.10	.05
☐ 33 James Baldwin	.10	.05
☐ 34 Mike Devereaux	.10	.05
☐ 35 Ray Durham	.20	.09
☐ 36 Tim Fortugno	.10	.05
☐ 37 Scott Ruffcorn	.10	.05
☐ 38 Chris Sabo	.10	.05
☐ 39 Paul Assenmacher	.10	.05
☐ 40 Bud Black	.10	.05
☐ 41 Orel Hershiser	.20	.09
☐ 42 Julian Tavarez	.10	.05
☐ 43 Dave Winfield	.30	.14
☐ 44 Pat Borders	.10	.05
☐ 45 Melvin Bunch	.10	.05
☐ 46 Tom Goodwin	.10	.05
☐ 47 Jon Nunnally	.20	.09
☐ 48 Joe Randa	.10	.05
☐ 49 Dilson Torres	.10	.05
☐ 50 Joe Vitiello	.10	.05
☐ 51 David Hulse	.10	.05
☐ 52 Scott Karl	.10	.05
☐ 53 Mark Kiefer	.10	.05
☐ 54 Derrick May	.10	.05
☐ 55 Joe Oliver	.10	.05
☐ 56 Al Reyes	.10	.05
☐ 57 Steve Sparks	.10	.05
☐ 58 Jerald Clark	.10	.05
☐ 59 Eddie Guardado	.10	.05
☐ 60 Kevin Maas	.10	.05
☐ 61 David McCarty	.10	.05
☐ 62 Brad Radke	.50	.23
☐ 63 Scott Stahoviak	.10	.05
☐ 64 Garret Anderson	.30	.14
☐ 65 Shawn Boskie	.10	.05
☐ 66 Mike James	.10	.05
☐ 67 Tony Phillips	.10	.05
☐ 68 Lee Smith	.20	.09
☐ 69 Mitch Williams	.10	.05
☐ 70 Jim Corsi	.10	.05
☐ 71 Mark Harkey	.10	.05
☐ 72 Dave Stewart	.20	.09
☐ 73 Todd Stottlemyre	.10	.05
☐ 74 Joey Cora	.10	.05
☐ 75 Chad Kreuter	.10	.05
☐ 76 Jeff Nelson	.10	.05
☐ 77 Alex Rodriguez	1.50	.70
☐ 78 Ron Villone	.10	.05
☐ 79 Bob Wells	.10	.05
☐ 80 Jose Alberro	.10	.05
☐ 81 Terry Burrows	.10	.05
☐ 82 Kevin Gross	.10	.05
☐ 83 Wilson Heredia	.10	.05
☐ 84 Mark McLemore	.10	.05
☐ 85 Otis Nixon	.20	.09
☐ 86 Jeff Russell	.10	.05
☐ 87 Mickey Tettleton	.10	.05
☐ 88 Bob Tewksbury	.10	.05
☐ 89 Pedro Borbon	.10	.05
☐ 90 Marquis Grissom	.20	.09
☐ 91 Chipper Jones	1.25	.55
☐ 92 Mike Mordecai	.10	.05
☐ 93 Jason Schmidt	.40	.18
☐ 94 John Burkett	.10	.05
☐ 95 Andre Dawson	.30	.14
☐ 96 Matt Dunbar	.10	.05
☐ 97 Charles Johnson	.20	.09
☐ 98 Terry Pendleton	.20	.09
☐ 99 Rich Scheid	.10	.05
☐ 100 Quilvio Veras	.10	.05
☐ 101 Bobby Witt	.10	.05
☐ 102 Eddie Zosky	.10	.05
☐ 103 Shane Andrews	.10	.05
☐ 104 Reid Cornelius	.10	.05
☐ 105 Chad Fonville	.10	.05
☐ 106 Mark Grudzielanek	.30	.14
☐ 107 Roberto Kelly	.10	.05
☐ 108 Carlos Perez	.20	.09
☐ 109 Tony Tarasco	.10	.05
☐ 110 Brett Butler	.20	.09
☐ 111 Carl Everett	.10	.05
☐ 112 Pete Harnisch	.10	.05
☐ 113 Doug Henry	.10	.05
☐ 114 Kevin Lomon	.10	.05
☐ 115 Blas Minor	.10	.05
☐ 116 Dave Mlicki	.10	.05
☐ 117 Ricky Otero	.10	.05
☐ 118 Norm Charlton	.10	.05
☐ 119 Tyler Green	.10	.05
☐ 120 Gene Harris	.10	.05
☐ 121 Charlie Hayes	.10	.05
☐ 122 Gregg Jefferies	.20	.09
☐ 123 Michael Mimbs	.10	.05
☐ 124 Paul Quantrill	.10	.05
☐ 125 Frank Castillo	.10	.05
☐ 126 Brian McRae	.10	.05
☐ 127 Jaime Navarro	.10	.05
☐ 128 Mike Perez	.10	.05
☐ 129 Tanyon Sturtze	.10	.05
☐ 130 Ozzie Timmons	.10	.05
☐ 131 John Courtright	.10	.05
☐ 132 Ron Gant	.20	.09
☐ 133 Xavier Hernandez	.10	.05
☐ 134 Brian Hunter	.10	.05
☐ 135 Benito Santiago	.10	.05
☐ 136 Pete Smith	.10	.05
☐ 137 Scott Sullivan	.10	.05
☐ 138 Derek Bell	.20	.09
☐ 139 Doug Brocail	.10	.05
☐ 140 Ricky Gutierrez	.10	.05
☐ 141 Pedro Martinez	.10	.05
☐ 142 Orlando Miller	.10	.05
☐ 143 Phil Plantier	.10	.05
☐ 144 Craig Shipley	.10	.05
☐ 145 Rich Aude	.10	.05
☐ 146 Jason Christiansen	.10	.05
☐ 147 Freddy Garcia	.10	.05
☐ 148 Jim Gott	.10	.05
☐ 149 Mark Johnson	.10	.05
☐ 150 Esteban Loaiza	.10	.05
☐ 151 Dan Plesac	.10	.05
☐ 152 Gary Wilson	.10	.05
☐ 153 Allen Battle	.10	.05
☐ 154 Terry Bradshaw	.10	.05
☐ 155 Scott Cooper	.10	.05
☐ 156 Tripp Cromer	.10	.05
☐ 157 John Frascatore	.10	.05
☐ 158 John Habyan	.10	.05
☐ 159 Tom Henke	.10	.05
☐ 160 Ken Hill	.10	.05
☐ 161 Danny Jackson	.10	.05
☐ 162 Donovan Osborne	.10	.05
☐ 163 Tom Urbani	.10	.05
☐ 164 Roger Bailey	.10	.05
☐ 165 Jorge Brito	.10	.05
☐ 166 Vinny Castilla	.30	.14
☐ 167 Darren Holmes	.10	.05
☐ 168 Roberto Mejia	.10	.05
☐ 169 Bill Swift	.10	.05
☐ 170 Mark Thompson	.10	.05
☐ 171 Larry Walker	.40	.18
☐ 172 Greg Hansell	.10	.05
☐ 173 Dave Hansen	.10	.05
☐ 174 Carlos Hernandez	.10	.05
☐ 175 Hideo Nomo	2.00	.90
☐ 176 Jose Offerman	.10	.05
☐ 177 Antonio Osuna	.10	.05
☐ 178 Reggie Williams	.10	.05
☐ 179 Todd Williams	.10	.05
☐ 180 Andres Berumen	.10	.05
☐ 181 Ken Caminiti	.40	.18
☐ 182 Andujar Cedeno	.10	.05
☐ 183 Steve Finley	.20	.09
☐ 184 Bryce Florie	.10	.05

Card	MINT	NRMT
☐ 185 Dustin Hermanson	.10	.05
☐ 186 Ray Holbert	.10	.05
☐ 187 Melvin Nieves	.20	.09
☐ 188 Roberto Petagine	.10	.05
☐ 189 Jody Reed	.10	.05
☐ 190 Fernando Valenzuela	.20	.09
☐ 191 Brian Williams	.10	.05
☐ 192 Mark Dewey	.10	.05
☐ 193 Glenallen Hill	.10	.05
☐ 194 Chris Hook	.10	.05
☐ 195 Terry Mulholland	.10	.05
☐ 196 Steve Scarsone	.10	.05
☐ 197 Trevor Wilson	.10	.05
☐ 198 Checklist	.10	.05
☐ 199 Checklist	.10	.05
☐ 200 Checklist	.10	.05

1995 Fleer Update Diamond Tribute

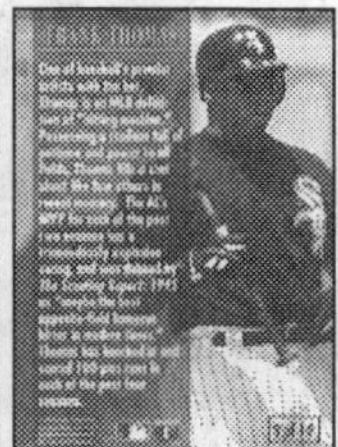

This 10-card standard-size set was inserted at a rate of one in five packs. This set features ten top players. The full-bleed fronts feature a player photo, the "Fleer 95" logo in the upper left corner, the words "Diamond Tribute" surrounding the player's team logo and the player's name on the bottom. All the words in front are in gold foil. The back is split between player information and a player photo. The cards are numbered in the lower right with an "X" of 10. The cards are sequenced in alphabetical order.

	MINT	NRMT
COMPLETE SET (10)	8.00	3.60
COMMON CARD (1-10)	.30	.14
☐ 1 Jeff Bagwell	1.25	.55
☐ 2 Albert Belle	1.25	.55
☐ 3 Barry Bonds	.75	.35
☐ 4 David Cone	.30	.14
☐ 5 Dennis Eckersley	.40	.18
☐ 6 Ken Griffey Jr.	3.00	1.35
☐ 7 Rickey Henderson	.50	.23
☐ 8 Greg Maddux	2.00	.90
☐ 9 Frank Thomas	3.00	1.35
☐ 10 Matt Williams	.50	.23

1995 Fleer Update Headliners

Inserted one every three packs, this 20-card standard-size set features various major league stars. The fronts feature the playerís photo set against a newspaper headline. The word "Headliner" as well as the playerís name is printed on the bottom on the card in gold foil. The backs have some player information as well as another player photo. The cards are numbered in the lower left as "X" of 20. The cards are sequenced in alphabetical order.

	MINT	NRMT
COMPLETE SET (20)	12.00	5.50
COMMON CARD (1-20)	.25	.11
☐ 1 Jeff Bagwell	1.25	.55
☐ 2 Albert Belle	1.25	.55
☐ 3 Barry Bonds	.75	.35
☐ 4 Jose Canseco	.50	.23
☐ 5 Joe Carter	.50	.23
☐ 6 Will Clark	.50	.23
☐ 7 Roger Clemens	.60	.25
☐ 8 Lenny Dykstra	.25	.11
☐ 9 Cecil Fielder	.35	.16
☐ 10 Juan Gonzalez	1.50	.70
☐ 11 Ken Griffey Jr.	3.00	1.35
☐ 12 Kenny Lofton	.75	.35
☐ 13 Greg Maddux	2.00	.90
☐ 14 Fred McGriff	.50	.23
☐ 15 Mike Piazza	2.00	.90
☐ 16 Kirby Puckett	1.25	.55
☐ 17 Tim Salmon	.60	.25
☐ 18 Frank Thomas	3.00	1.35
☐ 19 Mo Vaughn	.75	.35
☐ 20 Matt Williams	.50	.23

1995 Fleer Update Rookie Update

Inserted one in every four packs, this 10-card standard-size set features some of 1995's best rookies. The horizontal fronts feature the words "Rookie Update" in large letters at the top, and the "Fleer 95" logo as well as the player's name at the bottom. The rest of the card has the player's photo. To the left, the back has background information as well as a photo on the right. The cards are numbered as "X of 10". Chipper Jones and Hideo Nomo are among the players included in this set. The set is sequenced in alphabetical order.

	MINT	NRMT
COMPLETE SET (10)	15.00	6.75
COMMON CARD (1-10)	.25	.11
☐ 1 Shane Andrews	.25	.11
☐ 2 Ray Durham	.50	.23
☐ 3 Shawn Green	.50	.23
☐ 4 Charles Johnson	.75	.35
☐ 5 Chipper Jones	4.00	1.80
☐ 6 Esteban Loaiza	.25	.11
☐ 7 Hideo Nomo	4.00	1.80
☐ 8 Jon Nunnally	.25	.11
☐ 9 Alex Rodriguez	5.00	2.20
☐ 10 Julian Tavarez	.25	.11

1995 Fleer Update Smooth Leather

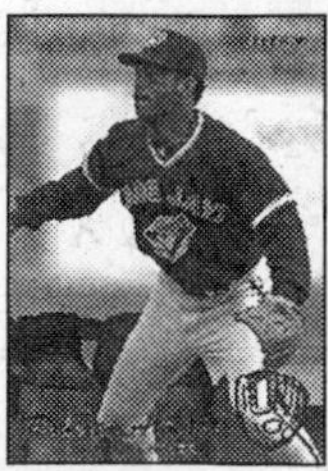
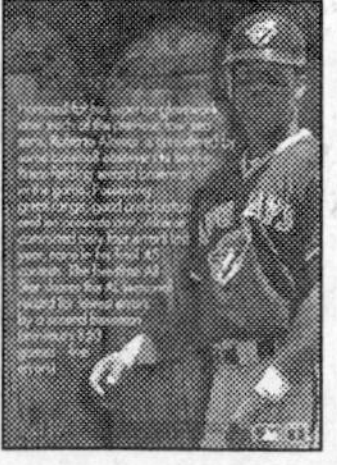

Inserted one every five jumbo packs, this 10-card standard-size set features many leading defensive wizards. The card fronts feature a player photo. Underneath the player photo, is his name along with the words "smooth leather" on the bottom. The right corner features a glove. All of this information as well as the "Fleer 95" logo is in gold print. All of this is on a card with a special leather-like coating. The back features a photo as well as fielding information. The cards are numbered in the lower left as "X of 10" and are sequenced in alphabetical order.

	MINT	NRMT
COMPLETE SET (10)	25.00	11.00
COMMON CARD (1-10)	.75	.35
☐ 1 Roberto Alomar	2.00	.90
☐ 2 Barry Bonds	2.50	1.10
☐ 3 Ken Griffey Jr.	10.00	4.50
☐ 4 Marquis Grissom	.75	.35
☐ 5 Darren Lewis	.75	.35
☐ 6 Kenny Lofton	2.50	1.10
☐ 7 Don Mattingly	5.00	2.20
☐ 8 Cal Ripken	8.00	3.60
☐ 9 Ivan Rodriguez	2.50	1.10
☐ 10 Matt Williams	1.25	.55

1995 Fleer Update Soaring Stars

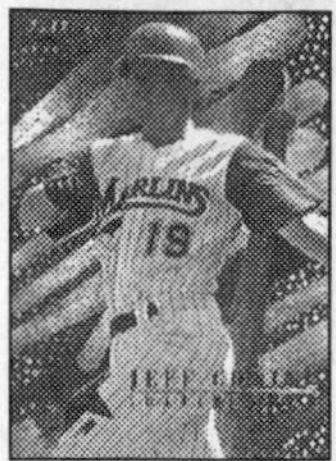

This nine-card standard-size set was inserted one every 36 packs. The fronts feature the player's photo set against a prismatic background of baseballs. The player's name, the "Soaring Stars" logo as well as a star are all printed in gold foil at the bottom. The back has a player photo, his name as well as some career information. The cards are numbered in the upper right "X of 9" and are sequenced in alphabetical order.

	MINT	NRMT
COMPLETE SET (9)	60.00	27.00
COMMON CARD (1-9)	2.50	1.10
☐ 1 Moises Alou UER (says .399 BA in 1994)	3.00	1.35
☐ 2 Jason Bere	2.50	1.10
☐ 3 Jeff Conine	3.00	1.35
☐ 4 Cliff Floyd	2.50	1.10
☐ 5 Pat Hentgen	3.00	1.35
☐ 6 Kenny Lofton	12.00	5.50
☐ 7 Raul Mondesi	5.00	2.20
☐ 8 Mike Piazza	30.00	13.50
☐ 9 Tim Salmon	8.00	3.60

1996 Fleer

The 1996 Fleer baseball set consists of 600 standard-size cards. Cards were issued in 11-card packs with a suggested retail price of $1.49. Borderless fronts are matte-finished and have full-color action shots with the player's name, team and position stamped in gold foil. Backs contain a biography and career stats on the top and a full-color head shot with a 1995 synopsis on the bottom. The matte finish on the cards was designed so collectors could have an easier surface for cards to be autographed. Fleer included in each pack a "Thanks a Million" scratch-off game card redeemable for instant-win prizes and a chance to bat for a million-dollar prize in a Major League park. Rookie Cards in this set include Matt Lawton and Mike Sweeney.

	MINT	NRMT
COMPLETE SET (600)	80.00	36.00
COMMON CARD (1-600)	.15	.07
☐ 1 Manny Alexander	.15	.07
☐ 2 Brady Anderson	.40	.18
☐ 3 Harold Baines	.30	.14
☐ 4 Armando Benitez	.15	.07
☐ 5 Bobby Bonilla	.30	.14
☐ 6 Kevin Brown	.30	.14
☐ 7 Scott Erickson	.15	.07
☐ 8 Curtis Goodwin	.15	.07
☐ 9 Jeffrey Hammonds	.15	.07
☐ 10 Jimmy Haynes	.15	.07
☐ 11 Chris Hoiles	.15	.07
☐ 12 Doug Jones	.15	.07

☐ 13 Rick Krivda .15 .07
☐ 14 Jeff Manto .15 .07
☐ 15 Ben McDonald .15 .07
☐ 16 Jamie Moyer .15 .07
☐ 17 Mike Mussina .60 .25
☐ 18 Jesse Orosco .15 .07
☐ 19 Rafael Palmeiro .40 .18
☐ 20 Cal Ripken 2.50 1.10
☐ 21 Rick Aguilera .15 .07
☐ 22 Luis Alicea .15 .07
☐ 23 Stan Belinda .15 .07
☐ 24 Jose Canseco .40 .18
☐ 25 Roger Clemens 1.25 .55
☐ 26 Vaughn Eshelman .15 .07
☐ 27 Mike Greenwell .15 .07
☐ 28 Erik Hanson .15 .07
☐ 29 Dwayne Hosey .15 .07
☐ 30 Mike Macfarlane UER .15 .07
☐ 31 Tim Naehring .15 .07
☐ 32 Troy O'Leary .15 .07
☐ 33 Aaron Sele .15 .07
☐ 34 Zane Smith .15 .07
☐ 35 Jeff Suppan .40 .18
☐ 36 Lee Tinsley .15 .07
☐ 37 John Valentin .30 .14
☐ 38 Mo Vaughn .75 .35
☐ 39 Tim Wakefield .15 .07
☐ 40 Jim Abbott .30 .14
☐ 41 Brian Anderson .15 .07
☐ 42 Garret Anderson .40 .18
☐ 43 Chili Davis .15 .07
☐ 44 Gary DiSarcina .15 .07
☐ 45 Damion Easley .15 .07
☐ 46 Jim Edmonds .60 .25
☐ 47 Chuck Finley .15 .07
☐ 48 Todd Greene .30 .14
☐ 49 Mike Harkey .15 .07
☐ 50 Mike James .15 .07
☐ 51 Mark Langston .15 .07
☐ 52 Greg Myers .15 .07
☐ 53 Orlando Palmeiro .15 .07
☐ 54 Bob Patterson .15 .07
☐ 55 Troy Percival .30 .14
☐ 56 Tony Phillips .15 .07
☐ 57 Tim Salmon .60 .25
☐ 58 Lee Smith .30 .14
☐ 59 J.T. Snow .30 .14
☐ 60 Randy Velarde .15 .07
☐ 61 Wilson Alvarez .40 .18
☐ 62 Luis Andujar .15 .07
☐ 63 Jason Bere .15 .07
☐ 64 Ray Durham .30 .14
☐ 65 Alex Fernandez .30 .14
☐ 66 Ozzie Guillen .15 .07
☐ 67 Roberto Hernandez .30 .14
☐ 68 Lance Johnson .15 .07
☐ 69 Matt Karchner .15 .07
☐ 70 Ron Karkovice .15 .07
☐ 71 Norberto Martin .15 .07
☐ 72 Dave Martinez .15 .07
☐ 73 Kirk McCaskill .15 .07
☐ 74 Lyle Mouton .15 .07
☐ 75 Tim Raines .15 .07
☐ 76 Mike Sirotka .15 .07
☐ 77 Frank Thomas 2.50 1.10
☐ 78 Larry Thomas .15 .07
☐ 79 Robin Ventura .30 .14
☐ 80 Sandy Alomar, Jr. .30 .14
☐ 81 Paul Assenmacher .15 .07
☐ 82 Carlos Baerga .30 .14
☐ 83 Albert Belle .75 .35
☐ 84 Mark Clark .15 .07
☐ 85 Alan Embree .15 .07
☐ 86 Alvaro Espinoza .15 .07
☐ 87 Orel Hershiser .30 .14
☐ 88 Ken Hill .15 .07
☐ 89 Kenny Lofton .75 .35
☐ 90 Dennis Martinez .30 .14
☐ 91 Jose Mesa .30 .14
☐ 92 Eddie Murray .60 .25
☐ 93 Charles Nagy .30 .14
☐ 94 Chad Ogea .15 .07
☐ 95 Tony Pena .15 .07
☐ 96 Herb Perry .15 .07
☐ 97 Eric Plunk .15 .07
☐ 98 Jim Poole .15 .07
☐ 99 Manny Ramirez .60 .25
☐ 100 Paul Sorrento .15 .07
☐ 101 Julian Tavarez .15 .07
☐ 102 Jim Thome .60 .25
☐ 103 Omar Vizquel .30 .14
☐ 104 Dave Winfield .40 .18
☐ 105 Danny Bautista .15 .07
☐ 106 Joe Boever .15 .07
☐ 107 Chad Curtis .15 .07
☐ 108 John Doherty .15 .07
☐ 109 Cecil Fielder .30 .14
☐ 110 John Flaherty .15 .07
☐ 111 Travis Fryman .30 .14
☐ 112 Chris Gomez .15 .07
☐ 113 Bob Higginson .40 .18
☐ 114 Mark Lewis .15 .07
☐ 115 Jose Lima .15 .07
☐ 116 Felipe Lira .15 .07
☐ 117 Brian Maxcy .15 .07
☐ 118 C.J. Nitkowski .15 .07
☐ 119 Phil Plantier .15 .07
☐ 120 Clint Sodowsky .15 .07
☐ 121 Alan Trammell .40 .18
☐ 122 Lou Whitaker .30 .14
☐ 123 Kevin Appier .30 .14
☐ 124 Johnny Damon .30 .14
☐ 125 Gary Gaetti .30 .14
☐ 126 Tom Goodwin .15 .07
☐ 127 Tom Gordon .15 .07
☐ 128 Mark Gubicza .15 .07
☐ 129 Bob Hamelin .15 .07
☐ 130 David Howard .15 .07
☐ 131 Jason Jacome .15 .07
☐ 132 Wally Joyner .15 .07
☐ 133 Keith Lockhart .15 .07
☐ 134 Brent Mayne .15 .07
☐ 135 Jeff Montgomery .15 .07
☐ 136 Jon Nunnally .15 .07
☐ 137 Juan Samuel .15 .07
☐ 138 Mike Sweeney .60 .25
☐ 139 Michael Tucker .30 .14
☐ 140 Joe Vitiello .15 .07
☐ 141 Ricky Bones .15 .07
☐ 142 Chuck Carr .15 .07
☐ 143 Jeff Cirillo .15 .07
☐ 144 Mike Fetters .15 .07
☐ 145 Darryl Hamilton .15 .07
☐ 146 David Hulse .15 .07
☐ 147 John Jaha .15 .07
☐ 148 Scott Karl .15 .07
☐ 149 Mark Kiefer .15 .07
☐ 150 Pat Listach .15 .07
☐ 151 Mark Loretta .15 .07
☐ 152 Mike Matheny .15 .07
☐ 153 Matt Mieske .15 .07
☐ 154 Dave Nilsson .30 .14
☐ 155 Joe Oliver .15 .07
☐ 156 Al Reyes .15 .07
☐ 157 Kevin Seitzer .15 .07
☐ 158 Steve Sparks .15 .07
☐ 159 B.J. Surhoff .15 .07
☐ 160 Jose Valentin .15 .07
☐ 161 Greg Vaughn .15 .07
☐ 162 Fernando Vina .15 .07
☐ 163 Rich Becker .30 .14
☐ 164 Ron Coomer .15 .07
☐ 165 Marty Cordova .30 .14
☐ 166 Chuck Knoblauch .60 .25
☐ 167 Matt Lawton .15 .07
☐ 168 Pat Meares .15 .07
☐ 169 Paul Molitor .60 .25
☐ 170 Pedro Munoz .15 .07
☐ 171 Jose Parra .15 .07
☐ 172 Kirby Puckett 1.25 .55
☐ 173 Brad Radke .30 .14
☐ 174 Jeff Reboulet .15 .07
☐ 175 Rich Robertson .15 .07
☐ 176 Frank Rodriguez .15 .07
☐ 177 Scott Stahoviak .15 .07
☐ 178 Dave Stevens .15 .07
☐ 179 Matt Walbeck .15 .07
☐ 180 Wade Boggs .60 .25
☐ 181 David Cone .30 .14
☐ 182 Tony Fernandez .15 .07
☐ 183 Joe Girardi .15 .07
☐ 184 Derek Jeter 2.00 .90
☐ 185 Scott Kamieniecki .15 .07
☐ 186 Pat Kelly .15 .07
☐ 187 Jim Leyritz .15 .07
☐ 188 Tino Martinez .60 .25
☐ 189 Don Mattingly 1.00 .45
☐ 190 Jack McDowell .15 .07
☐ 191 Jeff Nelson .15 .07
☐ 192 Paul O'Neill .15 .07
☐ 193 Melido Perez .15 .07
☐ 194 Andy Pettitte .60 .25
☐ 195 Mariano Rivera .60 .25
☐ 196 Ruben Sierra .15 .07
☐ 197 Mike Stanley .15 .07
☐ 198 Darryl Strawberry .30 .14
☐ 199 John Wetteland .30 .14
☐ 200 Bob Wickman .15 .07
☐ 201 Bernie Williams .60 .25
☐ 202 Mark Acre .15 .07
☐ 203 Geronimo Berroa .15 .07
☐ 204 Mike Bordick .15 .07
☐ 205 Scott Brosius .15 .07
☐ 206 Dennis Eckersley .40 .18
☐ 207 Brent Gates .15 .07
☐ 208 Jason Giambi .15 .07
☐ 209 Rickey Henderson .40 .18
☐ 210 Jose Herrera .15 .07
☐ 211 Stan Javier .15 .07
☐ 212 Doug Johns .15 .07
☐ 213 Mark McGwire .60 .25
☐ 214 Steve Ontiveros .15 .07
☐ 215 Craig Paquette .15 .07
☐ 216 Ariel Prieto .15 .07
☐ 217 Carlos Reyes .15 .07
☐ 218 Terry Steinbach .30 .14
☐ 219 Todd Stottlemyre .15 .07
☐ 220 Danny Tartabull .15 .07
☐ 221 Todd Van Poppel .15 .07
☐ 222 John Wasdin .15 .07
☐ 223 George Williams .15 .07
☐ 224 Steve Wojciechowski .15 .07
☐ 225 Rich Amaral .15 .07
☐ 226 Bobby Ayala .15 .07
☐ 227 Tim Belcher .15 .07
☐ 228 Andy Benes .15 .07
☐ 229 Chris Bosio .15 .07
☐ 230 Darren Bragg .15 .07
☐ 231 Jay Buhner .40 .18
☐ 232 Norm Charlton .15 .07
☐ 233 Vince Coleman .15 .07
☐ 234 Joey Cora .30 .14
☐ 235 Russ Davis .15 .07
☐ 236 Alex Diaz .15 .07
☐ 237 Felix Fermin .15 .07
☐ 238 Ken Griffey Jr. 3.00 1.35
☐ 239 Sterling Hitchcock .15 .07
☐ 240 Randy Johnson .60 .25
☐ 241 Edgar Martinez .40 .18
☐ 242 Bill Risley .15 .07
☐ 243 Alex Rodriguez 2.50 1.10
☐ 244 Luis Sojo .15 .07
☐ 245 Dan Wilson .15 .07
☐ 246 Bob Wolcott .15 .07
☐ 247 Will Clark .40 .18
☐ 248 Jeff Frye .15 .07
☐ 249 Benji Gil .15 .07
☐ 250 Juan Gonzalez 1.50 .70
☐ 251 Rusty Greer .60 .25
☐ 252 Kevin Gross .15 .07
☐ 253 Roger McDowell .15 .07
☐ 254 Mark McLemore .15 .07
☐ 255 Otis Nixon .30 .14
☐ 256 Luis Ortiz .15 .07
☐ 257 Mike Pagliarulo .15 .07
☐ 258 Dean Palmer .30 .14
☐ 259 Roger Pavlik .15 .07
☐ 260 Ivan Rodriguez .75 .35
☐ 261 Kenny Rogers .15 .07
☐ 262 Jeff Russell .15 .07
☐ 263 Mickey Tettleton .15 .07
☐ 264 Bob Tewksbury .15 .07
☐ 265 Dave Valle .15 .07
☐ 266 Matt Whiteside .15 .07
☐ 267 Roberto Alomar .60 .25
☐ 268 Joe Carter .30 .14
☐ 269 Tony Castillo .15 .07
☐ 270 Domingo Cedeno .15 .07
☐ 271 Tim Crabtree UER .15 .07
☐ 272 Carlos Delgado .30 .14
☐ 273 Alex Gonzalez .15 .07
☐ 274 Shawn Green .30 .14
☐ 275 Juan Guzman .15 .07
☐ 276 Pat Hentgen .30 .14
☐ 277 Al Leiter .15 .07
☐ 278 Sandy Martinez .15 .07
☐ 279 Paul Menhart .15 .07
☐ 280 John Olerud .30 .14
☐ 281 Paul Quantrill .15 .07
☐ 282 Ken Robinson .15 .07
☐ 283 Ed Sprague .15 .07
☐ 284 Mike Timlin .15 .07
☐ 285 Steve Avery .15 .07
☐ 286 Rafael Belliard .15 .07
☐ 287 Jeff Blauser .15 .07
☐ 288 Pedro Borbon .15 .07
☐ 289 Brad Clontz .15 .07
☐ 290 Mike Devereaux .15 .07
☐ 291 Tom Glavine .40 .18
☐ 292 Marquis Grissom .30 .14
☐ 293 Chipper Jones 2.00 .90
☐ 294 David Justice .40 .18
☐ 295 Mike Kelly .15 .07
☐ 296 Ryan Klesko .40 .18
☐ 297 Mark Lemke .15 .07
☐ 298 Javier Lopez .30 .14
☐ 299 Greg Maddux 2.00 .90
☐ 300 Fred McGriff .40 .18
☐ 301 Greg McMichael .15 .07
☐ 302 Kent Mercker .15 .07
☐ 303 Mike Mordecai .15 .07

Card	Price	Price
☐ 304 Charlie O'Brien	.15	.07
☐ 305 Eduardo Perez	.15	.07
☐ 306 Luis Polonia	.15	.07
☐ 307 Jason Schmidt	.30	.14
☐ 308 John Smoltz	.30	.14
☐ 309 Terrell Wade	.15	.07
☐ 310 Mark Wohlers	.30	.14
☐ 311 Scott Bullett	.15	.07
☐ 312 Jim Bullinger	.15	.07
☐ 313 Larry Casian	.15	.07
☐ 314 Frank Castillo	.15	.07
☐ 315 Shawon Dunston	.15	.07
☐ 316 Kevin Foster	.15	.07
☐ 317 Matt Franco	.15	.07
☐ 318 Luis Gonzalez	.15	.07
☐ 319 Mark Grace	.40	.18
☐ 320 Jose Hernandez	.15	.07
☐ 321 Mike Hubbard	.15	.07
☐ 322 Brian McRae	.15	.07
☐ 323 Randy Myers	.15	.07
☐ 324 Jaime Navarro	.15	.07
☐ 325 Mark Parent	.15	.07
☐ 326 Mike Perez	.15	.07
☐ 327 Rey Sanchez	.15	.07
☐ 328 Ryne Sandberg	.75	.35
☐ 329 Scott Servais	.15	.07
☐ 330 Sammy Sosa	.60	.25
☐ 331 Ozzie Timmons	.15	.07
☐ 332 Steve Trachsel	.15	.07
☐ 333 Todd Zeile	.30	.14
☐ 334 Bret Boone	.15	.07
☐ 335 Jeff Branson	.15	.07
☐ 336 Jeff Brantley	.15	.07
☐ 337 Dave Burba	.15	.07
☐ 338 Hector Carrasco	.15	.07
☐ 339 Mariano Duncan	.15	.07
☐ 340 Ron Gant	.30	.14
☐ 341 Lenny Harris	.15	.07
☐ 342 Xavier Hernandez	.15	.07
☐ 343 Thomas Howard	.15	.07
☐ 344 Mike Jackson	.15	.07
☐ 345 Barry Larkin	.40	.18
☐ 346 Darren Lewis	.15	.07
☐ 347 Hal Morris	.15	.07
☐ 348 Eric Owens	.15	.07
☐ 349 Mark Portugal	.15	.07
☐ 350 Jose Rijo	.15	.07
☐ 351 Reggie Sanders	.15	.07
☐ 352 Benito Santiago	.15	.07
☐ 353 Pete Schourek	.15	.07
☐ 354 John Smiley	.15	.07
☐ 355 Eddie Taubensee	.15	.07
☐ 356 Jerome Walton	.15	.07
☐ 357 David Wells	.15	.07
☐ 358 Roger Bailey	.15	.07
☐ 359 Jason Bates	.15	.07
☐ 360 Dante Bichette	.40	.18
☐ 361 Ellis Burks	.30	.14
☐ 362 Vinny Castilla	.30	.14
☐ 363 Andres Galarraga	.40	.18
☐ 364 Darren Holmes	.15	.07
☐ 365 Mike Kingery	.15	.07
☐ 366 Curt Leskanic	.15	.07
☐ 367 Quinton McCracken	.15	.07
☐ 368 Mike Munoz	.15	.07
☐ 369 David Nied	.15	.07
☐ 370 Steve Reed	.15	.07
☐ 371 Bryan Rekar	.15	.07
☐ 372 Kevin Ritz	.15	.07
☐ 373 Bruce Ruffin	.15	.07
☐ 374 Bret Saberhagen	.15	.07
☐ 375 Bill Swift	.15	.07
☐ 376 John Vander Wal	.15	.07
☐ 377 Larry Walker	.60	.25
☐ 378 Walt Weiss	.15	.07
☐ 379 Eric Young	.30	.14
☐ 380 Kurt Abbott	.15	.07
☐ 381 Alex Arias	.15	.07
☐ 382 Jerry Browne	.15	.07
☐ 383 John Burkett	.15	.07
☐ 384 Greg Colbrunn	.15	.07
☐ 385 Jeff Conine	.30	.14
☐ 386 Andre Dawson	.40	.18
☐ 387 Chris Hammond	.15	.07
☐ 388 Charles Johnson	.30	.14
☐ 389 Terry Mathews	.15	.07
☐ 390 Robb Nen	.30	.14
☐ 391 Joe Orsulak	.15	.07
☐ 392 Terry Pendleton	.30	.14
☐ 393 Pat Rapp	.15	.07
☐ 394 Gary Sheffield	.60	.25
☐ 395 Jesus Tavarez	.15	.07
☐ 396 Marc Valdes	.15	.07
☐ 397 Quilvio Veras	.15	.07
☐ 398 Randy Veres	.15	.07
☐ 399 Devon White	.15	.07
☐ 400 Jeff Bagwell	1.25	.55
☐ 401 Derek Bell	.30	.14
☐ 402 Craig Biggio	.40	.18
☐ 403 John Cangelosi	.15	.07
☐ 404 Jim Dougherty	.15	.07
☐ 405 Doug Drabek	.15	.07
☐ 406 Tony Eusebio	.15	.07
☐ 407 Ricky Gutierrez	.15	.07
☐ 408 Mike Hampton	.15	.07
☐ 409 Dean Hartgraves	.15	.07
☐ 410 John Hudek	.15	.07
☐ 411 Brian L. Hunter	.30	.14
☐ 412 Todd Jones	.15	.07
☐ 413 Darryl Kile	.30	.14
☐ 414 Dave Magadan	.15	.07
☐ 415 Derrick May	.15	.07
☐ 416 Orlando Miller	.15	.07
☐ 417 James Mouton	.15	.07
☐ 418 Shane Reynolds	.15	.07
☐ 419 Greg Swindell	.15	.07
☐ 420 Jeff Tabaka	.15	.07
☐ 421 Dave Veres	.15	.07
☐ 422 Billy Wagner	.30	.14
☐ 423 Donne Wall	.15	.07
☐ 424 Rick Wilkins	.15	.07
☐ 425 Billy Ashley	.15	.07
☐ 426 Mike Blowers	.15	.07
☐ 427 Brett Butler	.30	.14
☐ 428 Tom Candiotti	.15	.07
☐ 429 Juan Castro	.15	.07
☐ 430 John Cummings	.15	.07
☐ 431 Delino DeShields	.15	.07
☐ 432 Joey Eischen	.15	.07
☐ 433 Chad Fonville	.15	.07
☐ 434 Greg Gagne	.15	.07
☐ 435 Dave Hansen	.15	.07
☐ 436 Carlos Hernandez	.15	.07
☐ 437 Todd Hollandsworth	.30	.14
☐ 438 Eric Karros	.30	.14
☐ 439 Roberto Kelly	.15	.07
☐ 440 Ramon Martinez	.30	.14
☐ 441 Raul Mondesi	.40	.18
☐ 442 Hideo Nomo	1.50	.70
☐ 443 Antonio Osuna	.15	.07
☐ 444 Chan Ho Park	.60	.25
☐ 445 Mike Piazza	2.00	.90
☐ 446 Felix Rodriguez	.15	.07
☐ 447 Kevin Tapani	.15	.07
☐ 448 Ismael Valdes	.15	.07
☐ 449 Todd Worrell	.30	.14
☐ 450 Moises Alou	.30	.14
☐ 451 Shane Andrews	.15	.07
☐ 452 Yamil Benitez	.30	.14
☐ 453 Sean Berry	.15	.07
☐ 454 Wil Cordero	.15	.07
☐ 455 Jeff Fassero	.15	.07
☐ 456 Darrin Fletcher	.15	.07
☐ 457 Cliff Floyd	.15	.07
☐ 458 Mark Grudzielanek	.30	.14
☐ 459 Gil Heredia	.15	.07
☐ 460 Tim Laker	.15	.07
☐ 461 Mike Lansing	.15	.07
☐ 462 Pedro J.Martinez	.60	.25
☐ 463 Carlos Perez	.15	.07
☐ 464 Curtis Pride	.15	.07
☐ 465 Mel Rojas	.30	.14
☐ 466 Kirk Rueter	.15	.07
☐ 467 F.P. Santangelo	.15	.07
☐ 468 Tim Scott	.15	.07
☐ 469 David Segui	.15	.07
☐ 470 Tony Tarasco	.15	.07
☐ 471 Rondell White	.40	.18
☐ 472 Edgardo Alfonzo	.60	.25
☐ 473 Tim Bogar	.15	.07
☐ 474 Rico Brogna	.15	.07
☐ 475 Damon Buford	.15	.07
☐ 476 Paul Byrd	.15	.07
☐ 477 Carl Everett	.15	.07
☐ 478 John Franco	.30	.14
☐ 479 Todd Hundley	.30	.14
☐ 480 Butch Huskey	.30	.14
☐ 481 Jason Isringhausen	.15	.07
☐ 482 Bobby Jones	.15	.07
☐ 483 Chris Jones	.15	.07
☐ 484 Jeff Kent	.15	.07
☐ 485 Dave Mlicki	.15	.07
☐ 486 Robert Person	.15	.07
☐ 487 Bill Pulsipher	.15	.07
☐ 488 Kelly Stinnett	.15	.07
☐ 489 Ryan Thompson	.15	.07
☐ 490 Jose Vizcaino	.15	.07
☐ 491 Howard Battle	.15	.07
☐ 492 Toby Borland	.15	.07
☐ 493 Ricky Bottalico	.15	.07
☐ 494 Darren Daulton	.30	.14
☐ 495 Lenny Dykstra	.30	.14
☐ 496 Jim Eisenreich	.30	.14
☐ 497 Sid Fernandez	.15	.07
☐ 498 Tyler Green	.15	.07
☐ 499 Charlie Hayes	.15	.07
☐ 500 Gregg Jefferies	.30	.14
☐ 501 Kevin Jordan	.15	.07
☐ 502 Tony Longmire	.15	.07
☐ 503 Tom Marsh	.15	.07
☐ 504 Michael Mimbs	.15	.07
☐ 505 Mickey Morandini	.15	.07
☐ 506 Gene Schall	.15	.07
☐ 507 Curt Schilling	.30	.14
☐ 508 Heathcliff Slocumb	.15	.07
☐ 509 Kevin Stocker	.15	.07
☐ 510 Andy Van Slyke	.30	.14
☐ 511 Lenny Webster	.15	.07
☐ 512 Mark Whiten	.15	.07
☐ 513 Mike Williams	.15	.07
☐ 514 Jay Bell	.30	.14
☐ 515 Jacob Brumfield	.15	.07
☐ 516 Jason Christiansen	.15	.07
☐ 517 Dave Clark	.15	.07
☐ 518 Midre Cummings	.15	.07
☐ 519 Angelo Encarnacion	.15	.07
☐ 520 John Ericks	.15	.07
☐ 521 Carlos Garcia	.15	.07
☐ 522 Mark Johnson	.15	.07
☐ 523 Jeff King	.30	.14
☐ 524 Nelson Liriano	.15	.07
☐ 525 Esteban Loaiza	.15	.07
☐ 526 Al Martin	.15	.07
☐ 527 Orlando Merced	.15	.07
☐ 528 Dan Miceli	.15	.07
☐ 529 Ramon Morel	.15	.07
☐ 530 Denny Neagle	.30	.14
☐ 531 Steve Parris	.15	.07
☐ 532 Dan Plesac	.15	.07
☐ 533 Don Slaught	.15	.07
☐ 534 Paul Wagner	.15	.07
☐ 535 John Wehner	.15	.07
☐ 536 Kevin Young	.15	.07
☐ 537 Allen Battle	.15	.07
☐ 538 David Bell	.15	.07
☐ 539 Alan Benes	.30	.14
☐ 540 Scott Cooper	.15	.07
☐ 541 Tripp Cromer	.15	.07
☐ 542 Tony Fossas	.15	.07
☐ 543 Bernard Gilkey	.30	.14
☐ 544 Tom Henke	.30	.14
☐ 545 Brian Jordan	.30	.14
☐ 546 Ray Lankford	.30	.14
☐ 547 John Mabry	.30	.14
☐ 548 T.J. Mathews	.15	.07
☐ 549 Mike Morgan	.15	.07
☐ 550 Jose Oliva	.15	.07
☐ 551 Jose Oquendo	.15	.07
☐ 552 Donovan Osborne	.15	.07
☐ 553 Tom Pagnozzi	.15	.07
☐ 554 Mark Petkovsek	.15	.07
☐ 555 Danny Sheaffer	.15	.07
☐ 556 Ozzie Smith	.75	.35
☐ 557 Mark Sweeney	.15	.07
☐ 558 Allen Watson	.15	.07
☐ 559 Andy Ashby	.15	.07
☐ 560 Brad Ausmus	.15	.07
☐ 561 Willie Blair	.15	.07
☐ 562 Ken Caminiti	.60	.25
☐ 563 Andujar Cedeno	.15	.07
☐ 564 Glenn Dishman	.15	.07
☐ 565 Steve Finley	.30	.14
☐ 566 Bryce Florie	.15	.07
☐ 567 Tony Gwynn	1.50	.70
☐ 568 Joey Hamilton	.30	.14
☐ 569 Dustin Hermanson UER	.15	.07
☐ 570 Trevor Hoffman	.30	.14
☐ 571 Brian Johnson	.15	.07
☐ 572 Marc Kroon	.15	.07
☐ 573 Scott Livingstone	.15	.07
☐ 574 Marc Newfield	.15	.07
☐ 575 Melvin Nieves	.30	.14
☐ 576 Jody Reed	.15	.07
☐ 577 Bip Roberts	.15	.07
☐ 578 Scott Sanders	.15	.07
☐ 579 Fernando Valenzuela	.30	.14
☐ 580 Eddie Williams	.15	.07
☐ 581 Rod Beck	.30	.14
☐ 582 Marvin Benard	.15	.07
☐ 583 Barry Bonds	.75	.35
☐ 584 Jamie Brewington	.15	.07
☐ 585 Mark Carreon	.15	.07
☐ 586 Royce Clayton	.15	.07
☐ 587 Shawn Estes	.30	.14
☐ 588 Glenallen Hill	.15	.07
☐ 589 Mark Leiter	.15	.07
☐ 590 Kirt Manwaring	.15	.07
☐ 591 David McCarty	.15	.07
☐ 592 Terry Mulholland	.15	.07
☐ 593 John Patterson	.15	.07
☐ 594 J.R. Phillips	.15	.07

	MINT	NRMT
595 Deion Sanders	.60	.25
596 Steve Scarsone	.15	.07
597 Robby Thompson	.15	.07
598 Sergio Valdez	.15	.07
599 William Van Landingham	.15	.07
600 Matt Williams	.40	.18
P20 Cal Ripken Promo	2.00	.90

1996 Fleer Tiffany

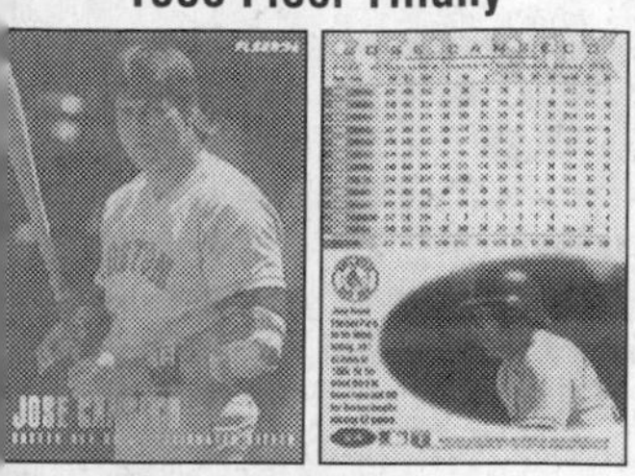

he Tiffany Collection is a 600-card parallel set that has a pecial UV coating that replaces the matte finish of the gular cards and silver holographic foil that takes the ace of gold foil for lettering. These cards were inserted regular packs at one card per pack.

	MINT	NRMT
OMPLETE SET (600)	200.00	90.00
OMMON CARD (1-600)	.25	.11
STARS: 2X to 4X BASIC CARDS		

1996 Fleer Checklists

hecklist cards were seeded one per six regular packs and ave glossy, borderless fronts with full-color shots of the lajor League's best. "Checklist" and the player's name are amped in gold foil. Backs list the entire rundown of '96 eer cards printed in black type on a white background.

	MINT	NRMT
OMPLETE SET (10)	5.00	2.20
OMMON CARD (1-10)	.25	.11
1 Barry Bonds	.50	.23
2 Ken Griffey Jr.	1.50	.70
3 Chipper Jones	1.00	.45
4 Greg Maddux	1.00	.45
5 Mike Piazza	1.00	.45
6 Manny Ramirez	.50	.23
7 Cal Ripken	1.25	.55
8 Frank Thomas	1.50	.70
9 Mo Vaughn	.50	.23
10 Matt Williams	.25	.11

1996 Fleer Golden Memories

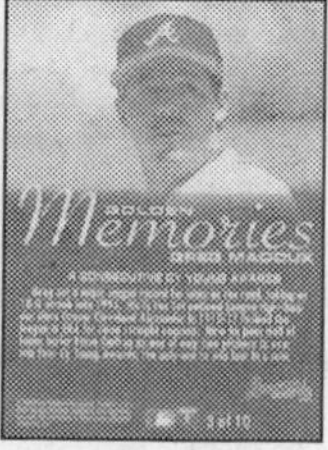

andomly inserted at a rate of one in 10 regular packs, is 10-card standard-size set features important ghlights of the 1995 season. Fronts have two action ots, one serving as a background, the other a full-color tout. "Golden Memories" and player's name are printed rtically in white type. Backs contain a biography, player ose-up and career statistics.

	MINT	NRMT
COMPLETE SET (10)	10.00	4.50
1 Albert Belle	2.00	.90
2 Barry Bonds / Sammy Sosa	1.25	.55
3 Greg Maddux	3.00	1.35
4 Edgar Martinez	.40	.18
5 Ramon Martinez	.25	.11
6 Mark McGwire	1.50	.70
7 Eddie Murray	1.25	.55
8 Cal Ripken	4.00	1.80
9 Frank Thomas	4.00	1.80
10 Alan Trammell / Lou Whitaker	.40	.18

1996 Fleer Lumber Company

This retail-exclusive 12-card set was inserted one in every nine packs and features RBI and HR power hitters. The fronts display a color action player cut-out on a wood background with embossed printing. The backs carry a player photo and information about the player.

	MINT	NRMT
COMPLETE SET (12)	30.00	13.50
COMMON CARD (1-12)	1.00	.45
1 Albert Belle	4.00	1.80
2 Dante Bichette	1.00	.45
3 Barry Bonds	2.50	1.10
4 Ken Griffey Jr.	10.00	4.50
5 Mark McGwire	3.00	1.35
6 Mike Piazza	6.00	2.70
7 Manny Ramirez	2.50	1.10
8 Tim Salmon	2.00	.90
9 Sammy Sosa	2.00	.90
10 Frank Thomas	8.00	3.60
11 Mo Vaughn	2.50	1.10
12 Matt Williams	1.50	.70

1996 Fleer Postseason Glory

Randomly inserted in regular packs at a rate of one in five, this five-card standard-size set highlights great moments of the 1996 Divisional, League Championship and World Series games. Horizontal, white-bordered fronts feature a player in three full-color action cutouts with black strips on top and bottom. "Post-Season Glory" appears on top and the player's name is printed in silver hologram foil. White-bordered backs are split between a full-color player close-up and a description of his post-season play printed in white type on a black background.

	MINT	NRMT
COMPLETE SET (5)	2.00	.90
COMMON CARD (1-5)	.10	.05
1 Tom Glavine	.20	.09
2 Ken Griffey Jr.	1.50	.70
3 Orel Hershiser	.10	.05
4 Randy Johnson	.25	.11
5 Jim Thome	.25	.11

1996 Fleer Prospects

Randomly inserted at a rate of one in six regular packs, this ten-card standard-size set focuses on players moving

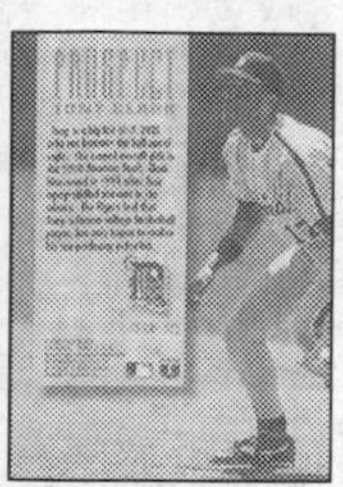

up through the farm system. Borderless fronts have full-color head shots on one-color backgrounds. "Prospect" and the player's name are stamped in silver hologram foil. Backs feature a full-color action shot with a synopsis of talent printed in a green box.

	MINT	NRMT
COMPLETE SET (10)	5.00	2.20
COMMON CARD (1-10)	.25	.11
1 Yamil Benitez	.50	.23
2 Roger Cedeno	.50	.23
3 Tony Clark	1.50	.70
4 Micah Franklin	.25	.11
5 Karim Garcia	1.50	.70
6 Todd Greene	.50	.23
7 Alex Ochoa	.25	.11
8 Ruben Rivera	1.50	.70
9 Chris Snopek	.25	.11
10 Shannon Stewart	.25	.11

1996 Fleer Road Warriors

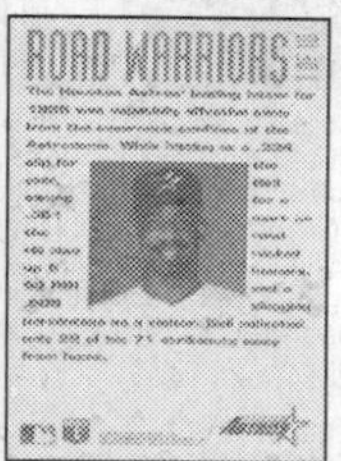

Randomly inserted in regular packs at a rate of one in 13, this 10-card standard-size set focuses on players who thrive on the road. Fronts feature a full-color player cutout set against a winding rural highway background. "Road Warriors" is printed in reverse type with a hazy white border and the player's name is printed in white type underneath. Backs include the player's road stats, biography and a close-up shot.

	MINT	NRMT
COMPLETE SET (10)	12.00	5.50
COMMON CARD (1-10)	.75	.35
1 Derek Bell	.75	.35
2 Tony Gwynn	2.00	.90
3 Greg Maddux	3.00	1.35
4 Mark McGwire	2.00	.90
5 Mike Piazza	3.00	1.35
6 Manny Ramirez	1.25	.55
7 Tim Salmon	1.25	.55
8 Frank Thomas	4.00	1.80
9 Mo Vaughn	1.25	.55
10 Matt Williams	1.00	.45

1996 Fleer Rookie Sensations

Randomly inserted at a rate of one in 11 regular packs, this 15-card standard-size set highlights 1995's best rookies. Borderless, horizontal fronts have a full-color action shot and a silver hologram strip containing the player's name and team logo. Horizontal backs have full-color head shots with a player profile all printed on a white background.

	MINT	NRMT
COMPLETE SET (15)	20.00	9.00
COMMON CARD (1-15)	1.00	.45
☐ 1 Garret Anderson	1.50	.70
☐ 2 Marty Cordova	1.50	.70
☐ 3 Johnny Damon	1.50	.70
☐ 4 Ray Durham	1.50	.70
☐ 5 Carl Everett	1.00	.45
☐ 6 Shawn Green	1.50	.70
☐ 7 Brian L.Hunter	1.50	.70
☐ 8 Jason Isringhausen	1.00	.45
☐ 9 Charles Johnson	1.50	.70
☐ 10 Chipper Jones	10.00	4.50
☐ 11 John Mabry	1.50	.70
☐ 12 Hideo Nomo	4.00	1.80
☐ 13 Troy Percival	1.50	.70
☐ 14 Andy Pettitte	5.00	2.20
☐ 15 Quilvio Veras	1.50	.70

1996 Fleer Smoke 'n Heat

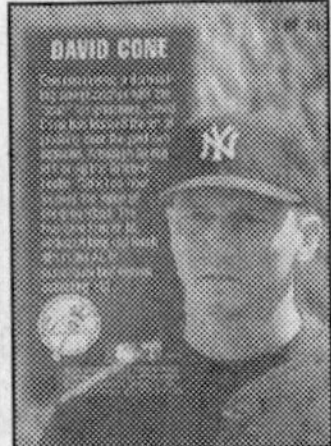

Randomly inserted at a rate of one in nine regular packs, this 10-card standard-size set celebrates the pitchers with rifle arms and a high strikeout count. Fronts feature a full-color player cutout set against a red flame background. "Smoke 'n Heat" and the player's name are printed in gold type. Backs feature the pitcher's 1995 numbers, a biography and career stats along with a full-color close-up.

	MINT	NRMT
COMPLETE SET (10)	8.00	3.60
COMMON CARD (1-10)	.25	.11
☐ 1 Kevin Appier	.35	.16
☐ 2 Roger Clemens	2.00	.90
☐ 3 David Cone	.35	.16
☐ 4 Chuck Finley	.25	.11
☐ 5 Randy Johnson	1.00	.45
☐ 6 Greg Maddux	3.00	1.35
☐ 7 Pedro Martinez	1.00	.45
☐ 8 Hideo Nomo	2.50	1.10
☐ 9 John Smoltz	.50	.23
☐ 10 Todd Stottlemyre	.25	.11

1996 Fleer Team Leaders

This hobby-exclusive 28-card set was randomly inserted one in every nine packs and features statistical and inspirational leaders. The fronts display color action player cut-out on a foil background of the team name and logo. The backs carry a player portrait and player information.

	MINT	NRMT
COMPLETE SET (28)	80.00	36.00
COMMON CARD (1-28)	1.00	.45
☐ 1 Cal Ripken	12.00	5.50
☐ 2 Mo Vaughn	4.00	1.80
☐ 3 Jim Edmonds	3.00	1.35
☐ 4 Frank Thomas	15.00	6.75
☐ 5 Kenny Lofton	4.00	1.80
☐ 6 Travis Fryman	1.50	.70
☐ 7 Gary Gaetti	1.50	.70
☐ 8 B.J. Surhoff	1.50	.70
☐ 9 Kirby Puckett	6.00	2.70
☐ 10 Don Mattingly	8.00	3.60
☐ 11 Mark McGwire	5.00	2.20
☐ 12 Ken Griffey Jr.	15.00	6.75
☐ 13 Juan Gonzalez	8.00	3.60
☐ 14 Joe Carter	1.50	.70
☐ 15 Greg Maddux	10.00	4.50
☐ 16 Sammy Sosa	3.00	1.35
☐ 17 Barry Larkin	2.00	.90
☐ 18 Dante Bichette	1.50	.70
☐ 19 Jeff Conine	1.50	.70
☐ 20 Jeff Bagwell	6.00	2.70
☐ 21 Mike Piazza	10.00	4.50
☐ 22 Rondell White	1.50	.70
☐ 23 Rico Brogna	1.00	.45
☐ 24 Darren Daulton	1.50	.70
☐ 25 Jeff King	1.00	.45
☐ 26 Ray Lankford	1.50	.70
☐ 27 Tony Gwynn	6.00	2.70
☐ 28 Barry Bonds	4.00	1.80

1996 Fleer Tomorrow's Legends

Randomly inserted in regular packs at a rate of one in 13, this 10-card set focuses on young talent with bright futures. Multicolored fronts have four panels of art that serve as a background and a full-color player cutout. "Tomorrow's Legends" and player's name are printed in white type at the bottom. Backs include the player's '95 stats, biography and a full-color close-up shot.

	MINT	NRMT
COMPLETE SET (10)	12.00	5.50
COMMON CARD (1-10)	1.00	.45
☐ 1 Garret Anderson	1.25	.55
☐ 2 Jim Edmonds	1.50	.70
☐ 3 Brian L.Hunter	1.25	.55
☐ 4 Jason Isringhausen	1.00	.45
☐ 5 Charles Johnson	1.25	.55
☐ 6 Chipper Jones	6.00	2.70
☐ 7 Ryan Klesko	1.50	.70
☐ 8 Hideo Nomo	5.00	2.20
☐ 9 Manny Ramirez	2.00	.90
☐ 10 Rondell White	1.25	.55

1996 Fleer Zone

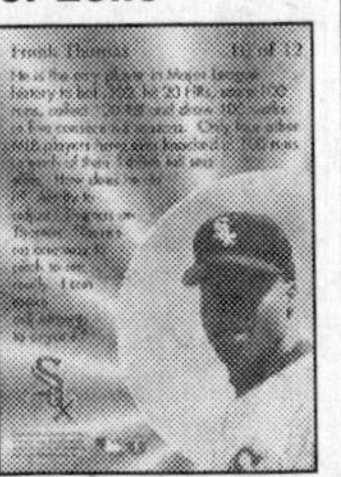

This 12-card set was randomly inserted one in every 90 packs and features "unstoppable" hitters and "unhittable" pitchers. The fronts display a color action player cut-out printed on holographic foil. The backs carry a player portrait with information as to why they were selected for this set.

	MINT	NRMT
COMPLETE SET (12)	200.00	90.00
COMMON CARD (1-12)	5.00	2.20
☐ 1 Albert Belle	10.00	4.50
☐ 2 Barry Bonds	10.00	4.50
☐ 3 Ken Griffey Jr.	40.00	18.00
☐ 4 Tony Gwynn	20.00	9.00
☐ 5 Randy Johnson	8.00	3.60
☐ 6 Kenny Lofton	10.00	4.50
☐ 7 Greg Maddux	25.00	11.00
☐ 8 Edgar Martinez	6.00	2.70
☐ 9 Mike Piazza	25.00	11.00
☐ 10 Frank Thomas	30.00	13.50
☐ 11 Mo Vaughn	10.00	4.50
☐ 12 Matt Williams	5.00	2.20

1996 Fleer Update

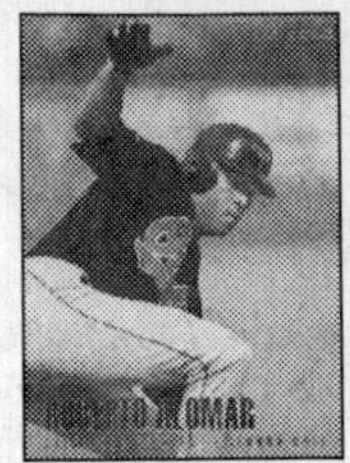

The 1996 Fleer Update set was issued in one series totalling 250 cards. The 11-card packs retail for $1.49 each. The fronts feature color action player photos. The backs carry complete player stats and a "Did you know?" fact. The cards are grouped alphabetically within teams and checklisted below alphabetically according to teams for each league with AL preceding NL. The set contains the subset: Encore (U211-U245). Notable Rookie Cards include Mike Cameron and Wilton Guerrero.

	MINT	NRMT
COMPLETE SET (250)	30.00	13.50
COMMON CARD (U1-U250)	.15	.07
☐ U1 Roberto Alomar	.60	.25
☐ U2 Mike Devereaux	.15	.07
☐ U3 Scott McClain	.15	.07
☐ U4 Roger McDowell	.15	.07
☐ U5 Kent Mercker	.15	.07
☐ U6 Jimmy Myers	.15	.07
☐ U7 Randy Myers	.30	.14
☐ U8 B.J. Surhoff	.30	.14
☐ U9 Tony Tarasco	.15	.07
☐ U10 David Wells	.15	.07
☐ U11 Wil Cordero	.15	.07
☐ U12 Tom Gordon	.15	.07
☐ U13 Reggie Jefferson	.30	.14
☐ U14 Jose Malave	.15	.07
☐ U15 Kevin Mitchell	.15	.07
☐ U16 Jamie Moyer	.15	.07
☐ U17 Heathcliff Slocumb	.15	.07
☐ U18 Mike Stanley	.15	.07
☐ U19 George Arias	.15	.07
☐ U20 Jorge Fabregas	.15	.07
☐ U21 Don Slaught	.15	.07
☐ U22 Randy Velarde	.15	.07
☐ U23 Harold Baines	.30	.14
☐ U24 Mike Cameron	1.50	.70
☐ U25 Darren Lewis	.15	.07
☐ U26 Tony Phillips	.15	.07
☐ U27 Bill Simas	.15	.07
☐ U28 Chris Snopek	.15	.07
☐ U29 Kevin Tapani	.15	.07
☐ U30 Danny Tartabull	.15	.07
☐ U31 Julio Franco	.30	.14
☐ U32 Jack McDowell	.15	.07
☐ U33 Kimera Bartee	.15	.07
☐ U34 Mark Lewis	.15	.07
☐ U35 Melvin Nieves	.15	.07
☐ U36 Mark Parent	.15	.07
☐ U37 Eddie Williams	.15	.07
☐ U38 Tim Belcher	.15	.07
☐ U39 Sal Fasano	.15	.07
☐ U40 Chris Haney	.15	.07
☐ U41 Mike Macfarlane	.15	.07
☐ U42 Jose Offerman	.15	.07
☐ U43 Joe Randa	.15	.07
☐ U44 Bip Roberts	.15	.07
☐ U45 Chuck Carr	.15	.07
☐ U46 Bobby Hughes	.15	.07
☐ U47 Graeme Lloyd	.15	.07
☐ U48 Ben McDonald	.15	.07
☐ U49 Kevin Wickander	.15	.07
☐ U50 Rick Aguilera	.30	.14
☐ U51 Mike Durant	.15	.07
☐ U52 Chip Hale	.15	.07
☐ U53 LaTroy Hawkins	.15	.07
☐ U54 Dave Hollins	.15	.07
☐ U55 Roberto Kelly	.15	.07
☐ U56 Paul Molitor	.60	.25
☐ U57 Dan Naulty	.15	.07
☐ U58 Mariano Duncan	.15	.07
☐ U59 Andy Fox	.15	.07
☐ U60 Joe Girardi	.15	.07
☐ U61 Dwight Gooden	.30	.14
☐ U62 Jimmy Key	.30	.14
☐ U63 Matt Luke	.15	.07

Card	MINT	NRMT
☐ U64 Tino Martinez	.60	.25
☐ U65 Jeff Nelson	.15	.07
☐ U66 Tim Raines	.15	.07
☐ U67 Ruben Rivera	.30	.14
☐ U68 Kenny Rogers	.15	.07
☐ U69 Gerald Williams	.15	.07
☐ U70 Tony Batista	.40	.18
☐ U71 Allen Battle	.15	.07
☐ U72 Jim Corsi	.15	.07
☐ U73 Steve Cox	.15	.07
☐ U74 Pedro Munoz	.15	.07
☐ U75 Phil Plantier	.15	.07
☐ U76 Scott Spiezio	.40	.18
☐ U77 Ernie Young	.15	.07
☐ U78 Russ Davis	.15	.07
☐ U79 Sterling Hitchcock	.15	.07
☐ U80 Edwin Hurtado	.15	.07
☐ U81 Raul Ibanez	.15	.07
☐ U82 Mike Jackson	.15	.07
☐ U83 Ricky Jordan	.15	.07
☐ U84 Paul Sorrento	.15	.07
☐ U85 Doug Strange	.15	.07
☐ U86 Mark Brandenburg	.15	.07
☐ U87 Damon Buford	.15	.07
☐ U88 Kevin Elster	.15	.07
☐ U89 Darryl Hamilton	.15	.07
☐ U90 Ken Hill	.30	.14
☐ U91 Ed Vosberg	.15	.07
☐ U92 Craig Worthington	.15	.07
☐ U93 Tilson Brito	.15	.07
☐ U94 Giovanni Carrara	.15	.07
☐ U95 Felipe Crespo	.15	.07
☐ U96 Erik Hanson	.15	.07
☐ U97 Marty Janzen	.15	.07
☐ U98 Otis Nixon	.15	.07
☐ U99 Charlie O'Brien	.15	.07
☐ U100 Robert Perez	.15	.07
☐ U101 Paul Quantrill	.15	.07
☐ U102 Bill Risley	.15	.07
☐ U103 Juan Samuel	.15	.07
☐ U104 Jermaine Dye	.15	.07
☐ U105 Wonderful Monds	.15	.07
☐ U106 Dwight Smith	.15	.07
☐ U107 Jerome Walton	.15	.07
☐ U108 Terry Adams	.15	.07
☐ U109 Leo Gomez	.15	.07
☐ U110 Robin Jennings	.15	.07
☐ U111 Doug Jones	.15	.07
☐ U112 Brooks Kieschnick	.30	.14
☐ U113 Dave Magadan	.15	.07
☐ U114 Jason Maxwell	.15	.07
☐ U115 Rodney Myers	.15	.07
☐ U116 Eric Anthony	.15	.07
☐ U117 Vince Coleman	.15	.07
☐ U118 Eric Davis	.30	.14
☐ U119 Steve Gibralter	.15	.07
☐ U120 Curtis Goodwin	.15	.07
☐ U121 Willie Greene	.30	.14
☐ U122 Mike Kelly	.15	.07
☐ U123 Marcus Moore	.15	.07
☐ U124 Chad Mottola	.15	.07
☐ U125 Chris Sabo	.15	.07
☐ U126 Roger Salkeld	.15	.07
☐ U127 Pedro Castellano	.15	.07
☐ U128 Trenidad Hubbard	.15	.07
☐ U129 Jayhawk Owens	.15	.07
☐ U130 Jeff Reed	.15	.07
☐ U131 Kevin Brown	.30	.14
☐ U132 Al Leiter	.15	.07
☐ U133 Matt Mantei	.15	.07
☐ U134 Dave Weathers	.15	.07
☐ U135 Devon White	.15	.07
☐ U136 Bob Abreu	.60	.25
☐ U137 Sean Berry	.15	.07
☐ U138 Doug Brocail	.15	.07
☐ U139 Richard Hidalgo	.60	.25
☐ U140 Alvin Morman	.15	.07
☐ U141 Mike Blowers	.15	.07
☐ U142 Roger Cedeno	.30	.14
☐ U143 Greg Gagne	.15	.07
☐ U144 Karim Garcia	.40	.18
☐ U145 Wilton Guerrero	.60	.25
☐ U146 Israel Alcantara	.15	.07
☐ U147 Omar Daal	.15	.07
☐ U148 Ryan McGuire	.15	.07
☐ U149 Sherman Obando	.15	.07
☐ U150 Jose Paniagua	.15	.07
☐ U151 Henry Rodriguez	.15	.07
☐ U152 Andy Stankiewicz	.15	.07
☐ U153 Dave Veres	.15	.07
☐ U154 Juan Acevedo	.15	.07
☐ U155 Mark Clark	.15	.07
☐ U156 Bernard Gilkey	.15	.07
☐ U157 Pete Harnisch	.15	.07
☐ U158 Lance Johnson	.15	.07
☐ U159 Brent Mayne	.15	.07
☐ U160 Rey Ordonez	.40	.18
☐ U161 Kevin Roberson	.15	.07
☐ U162 Paul Wilson	.15	.07
☐ U163 David Doster	.15	.07
☐ U164 Mike Grace	.15	.07
☐ U165 Rich Hunter	.15	.07
☐ U166 Pete Incaviglia	.15	.07
☐ U167 Mike Lieberthal	.15	.07
☐ U168 Terry Mulholland	.15	.07
☐ U169 Ken Ryan	.15	.07
☐ U170 Benito Santiago	.15	.07
☐ U171 Kevin Sefcik	.15	.07
☐ U172 Lee Tinsley	.15	.07
☐ U173 Todd Zeile	.15	.07
☐ U174 Francisco Cordova	.15	.07
☐ U175 Danny Darwin	.15	.07
☐ U176 Charlie Hayes	.15	.07
☐ U177 Jason Kendall	.40	.18
☐ U178 Mike Kingery	.15	.07
☐ U179 Jon Lieber	.15	.07
☐ U180 Zane Smith	.15	.07
☐ U181 Luis Alicea	.15	.07
☐ U182 Cory Bailey	.15	.07
☐ U183 Andy Benes	.15	.07
☐ U184 Pat Borders	.15	.07
☐ U185 Mike Busby	.15	.07
☐ U186 Royce Clayton	.15	.07
☐ U187 Dennis Eckersley	.40	.18
☐ U188 Gary Gaetti	.30	.14
☐ U189 Ron Gant	.30	.14
☐ U190 Aaron Holbert	.15	.07
☐ U191 Willie McGee	.15	.07
☐ U192 Miguel Mejia	.15	.07
☐ U193 Jeff Parrett	.15	.07
☐ U194 Todd Stottlemyre	.15	.07
☐ U195 Sean Bergman	.15	.07
☐ U196 Archi Cianfrocco	.15	.07
☐ U197 Rickey Henderson	.40	.18
☐ U198 Wally Joyner	.15	.07
☐ U199 Craig Shipley	.15	.07
☐ U200 Bob Tewksbury	.15	.07
☐ U201 Tim Worrell	.15	.07
☐ U202 Rich Aurilia	.15	.07
☐ U203 Doug Creek	.15	.07
☐ U204 Shawon Dunston	.15	.07
☐ U205 Osvaldo Fernandez	.30	.14
☐ U206 Mark Gardner	.15	.07
☐ U207 Stan Javier	.15	.07
☐ U208 Marcus Jensen	.15	.07
☐ U209 Chris Singleton	.15	.07
☐ U210 Allen Watson	.15	.07
☐ U211 Jeff Bagwell ENC	.60	.25
☐ U212 Derek Bell ENC	.15	.07
☐ U213 Albert Belle ENC	.60	.25
☐ U214 Wade Boggs ENC	.40	.18
☐ U215 Barry Bonds ENC	.60	.25
☐ U216 Jose Canseco ENC	.40	.18
☐ U217 Marty Cordova ENC	.15	.07
☐ U218 Jim Edmonds ENC	.60	.25
☐ U219 Cecil Fielder ENC	.30	.14
☐ U220 Andres Galarraga ENC	.60	.25
☐ U221 Juan Gonzalez ENC	.75	.35
☐ U222 Mark Grace ENC	.40	.18
☐ U223 Ken Griffey Jr. ENC	1.50	.70
☐ U224 Tony Gwynn ENC	.75	.35
☐ U225 Jason Isringhausen ENC	.15	.07
☐ U226 Derek Jeter ENC	1.00	.45
☐ U227 Randy Johnson ENC	.60	.25
☐ U228 Chipper Jones ENC	1.00	.45
☐ U229 Ryan Klesko ENC	.40	.18
☐ U230 Barry Larkin ENC	.40	.18
☐ U231 Kenny Lofton ENC	.60	.25
☐ U232 Greg Maddux ENC	1.00	.45
☐ U233 Raul Mondesi ENC	.60	.25
☐ U234 Hideo Nomo ENC	.75	.35
☐ U235 Mike Piazza ENC	1.00	.45
☐ U236 Manny Ramirez ENC	.60	.25
☐ U237 Cal Ripken ENC	1.25	.55
☐ U238 Tim Salmon ENC	.60	.25
☐ U239 Ryne Sandberg ENC	.60	.25
☐ U240 Reggie Sanders ENC	.15	.07
☐ U241 Gary Sheffield ENC	.60	.25
☐ U242 Sammy Sosa ENC	.60	.25
☐ U243 Frank Thomas ENC	1.25	.55
☐ U244 Mo Vaughn ENC	.50	.23
☐ U245 Matt Williams ENC	.40	.18
☐ U246 Barry Bonds CL	.40	.18
☐ U247 Ken Griffey Jr. CL	1.50	.70
☐ U248 Rey Ordonez CL	.15	.07
☐ U249 Ryne Sandberg CL	.60	.25
☐ U250 Frank Thomas CL	1.25	.55

1996 Fleer Update Tiffany

Inserted one per pack, these 250 cards parallel the basic Fleer Update cards. Unlike the basic cards, Tiffany inserts feature a layer of UV coating and a special logo on each card front.

	MINT	NRMT
COMPLETE SET (250)	100.00	45.00
COMMON CARD (U1-U250)	.25	.11
*STARS: 2X TO 4X BASIC CARDS		
*YOUNG STARS: 1.5X TO 3X BASIC CARDS		

1996 Fleer Update Diamond Tribute

Randomly inserted in packs at a rate of one in 100, this 10-card set spotlights future Hall of Famers with holographic foils in a diamond design.

	MINT	NRMT
COMPLETE SET (10)	150.00	70.00
COMMON CARD (1-10)	5.00	2.20
☐ 1 Wade Boggs	5.00	2.20
☐ 2 Barry Bonds	10.00	4.50
☐ 3 Ken Griffey Jr.	40.00	18.00
☐ 4 Tony Gwynn	15.00	6.75
☐ 5 Rickey Henderson	8.00	3.60
☐ 6 Greg Maddux	25.00	11.00
☐ 7 Eddie Murray	8.00	3.60
☐ 8 Cal Ripken	30.00	13.50
☐ 9 Ozzie Smith	10.00	4.50
☐ 10 Frank Thomas	30.00	13.50

1996 Fleer Update Headliners

Randomly inserted exclusively in retail packs at a rate of one in 20, cards from this 20-card set feature raised textured printing. The fronts carry color action player photos with the word "headliner" running continuously across the background.

	MINT	NRMT
COMPLETE SET (20)	40.00	18.00
COMMON CARD (1-20)	1.00	.45
☐ 1 Roberto Alomar	1.50	.70
☐ 2 Jeff Bagwell	3.00	1.35
☐ 3 Albert Belle	2.00	.90
☐ 4 Barry Bonds	2.00	.90
☐ 5 Cecil Fielder	1.00	.45
☐ 6 Juan Gonzalez	4.00	1.80
☐ 7 Ken Griffey Jr.	8.00	3.60
☐ 8 Tony Gwynn	4.00	1.80
☐ 9 Randy Johnson	1.50	.70
☐ 10 Chipper Jones	5.00	2.20
☐ 11 Ryan Klesko	1.25	.55
☐ 12 Kenny Lofton	1.25	.55
☐ 13 Greg Maddux	5.00	2.20
☐ 14 Hideo Nomo	4.00	1.80
☐ 15 Mike Piazza	5.00	2.20
☐ 16 Manny Ramirez	2.00	.90
☐ 17 Cal Ripken	6.00	2.70
☐ 18 Tim Salmon	1.50	.70
☐ 19 Frank Thomas	6.00	2.70
☐ 20 Matt Williams	1.25	.55

1996 Fleer Update New Horizons

Randomly inserted in hobby packs only at a rate of one in five, this 20-card set features 1996 rookies and prospects. The fronts carry player action color photos printed on foil

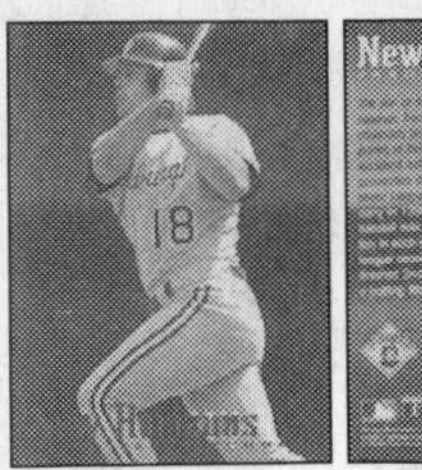

cards. The backs display a player portrait and information about the player.

	MINT	NRMT
COMPLETE SET (20)	15.00	6.75
COMMON CARD (1-20)	.25	.11
☐ 1 Bob Abreu	1.25	.55
☐ 2 George Arias	.25	.11
☐ 3 Tony Batista	1.25	.55
☐ 4 Steve Cox	.25	.11
☐ 5 Jermaine Dye	.25	.11
☐ 6 Andy Fox	.25	.11
☐ 7 Mike Grace	.25	.11
☐ 8 Todd Greene	1.50	.70
☐ 9 Wilton Guerrero	2.50	1.10
☐ 10 Richard Hidalgo	2.00	.90
☐ 11 Raul Ibanez	.25	.11
☐ 12 Robin Jennings	.25	.11
☐ 13 Marcus Jensen	.25	.11
☐ 14 Jason Kendall	1.50	.70
☐ 15 Jason Maxwell	.25	.11
☐ 16 Ryan McGuire	.25	.11
☐ 17 Miguel Mejia	.25	.11
☐ 18 Wonderful Monds	.25	.11
☐ 19 Rey Ordonez	.25	.11
☐ 20 Paul Wilson	.25	.11

1996 Fleer Update Smooth Leather

Randomly inserted in packs at a rate of one in 5, this 10-card set features ten defensive stars. The fronts display color player photos and gold foil printing. The backs carry a player portrait and information about why the player was selected for this set.

	MINT	NRMT
COMPLETE SET (10)	10.00	4.50
COMMON CARD (1-10)	.50	.23
☐ 1 Roberto Alomar	.75	.35
☐ 2 Barry Bonds	1.00	.45
☐ 3 Will Clark	.60	.25
☐ 4 Ken Griffey Jr.	4.00	1.80
☐ 5 Kenny Lofton	1.00	.45
☐ 6 Greg Maddux	2.50	1.10
☐ 7 Raul Mondesi	.60	.25
☐ 8 Rey Ordonez	.50	.23
☐ 9 Cal Ripken	3.00	1.35
☐ 10 Matt Williams	.60	.25

1996 Fleer Update Soaring Stars

Randomly inserted in packs at a rate of one in 11, this 10-card set features 10 of the hottest young players. The fronts carry color player cut-outs on a background of soaring baseballs in etched foil. The backs display another player photo on the same background with player information.

	MINT	NRMT
COMPLETE SET (10)	25.00	11.00
COMMON CARD (1-10)	1.00	.45
☐ 1 Jeff Bagwell	3.00	1.35
☐ 2 Barry Bonds	2.00	.90

	MINT	NRMT
☐ 3 Juan Gonzalez	4.00	1.80
☐ 4 Ken Griffey Jr.	8.00	3.60
☐ 5 Chipper Jones	5.00	2.20
☐ 6 Greg Maddux	5.00	2.20
☐ 7 Mike Piazza	5.00	2.20
☐ 8 Manny Ramirez	1.50	.70
☐ 9 Frank Thomas	6.00	2.70
☐ 10 Matt Williams	1.00	.45

1996 Fleer Braves

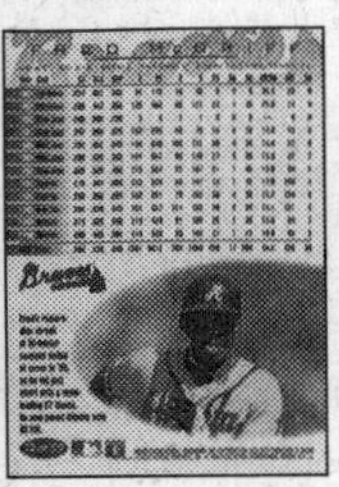

These 20 standard-size cards feature the same design as the regular Fleer issue, except they are UV coated, use silver foil and are numbered "x of 20". The team set packs were available at retail locations and hobby shops in 10-card packs for a suggested retail price of $1.99.

	MINT	NRMT
COMPLETE SET (20)	6.00	2.70
COMMON CARD (1-20)	.10	.05
☐ 1 Steve Avery	.10	.05
☐ 2 Jeff Blauser	.10	.05
☐ 3 Brad Clontz	.10	.05
☐ 4 Tom Glavine	.50	.23
☐ 5 Marquis Grissom	.20	.09
☐ 6 Chipper Jones	2.00	.90
☐ 7 David Justice	.50	.23
☐ 8 Ryan Klesko	1.00	.45
☐ 9 Mark Lemke	.10	.05
☐ 10 Javier Lopez	.40	.18
☐ 11 Greg Maddux	2.00	.90
☐ 12 Fred McGriff	.50	.23
☐ 13 Greg McMichael	.10	.05
☐ 14 Eddie Perez	.10	.05
☐ 15 Jason Schmidt	.30	.14
☐ 16 John Smoltz	.50	.23
☐ 17 Terrell Wade	.10	.05
☐ 18 Mark Wohlers	.40	.18
☐ 19 Logo card	.10	.05
☐ 20 Checklist	.10	.05

1996 Fleer Cubs

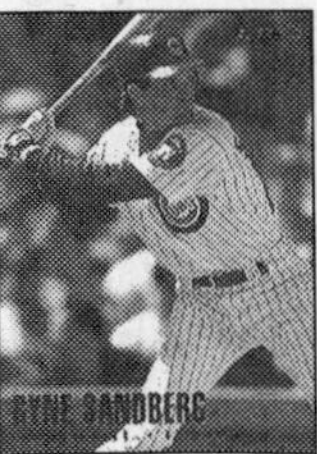

These 20 standard-size cards feature the same design as the regular Fleer issue, except they are UV coated, use silver foil and are numbered "x of 20". The team set packs were available at retail locations and hobby shops in 10-card packs for a suggested retail price of $1.99.

	MINT	NRMT
COMPLETE SET (20)	5.00	2.20
COMMON CARD (1-20)	.10	.05
☐ 1 Terry Adams	.10	.05
☐ 2 Jim Bullinger	.10	.05
☐ 3 Frank Castillo	.10	.05
☐ 4 Kevin Foster	.10	.05
☐ 5 Leo Gomez	.10	.05
☐ 6 Luis Gonzalez	.20	.09
☐ 7 Mark Grace	1.00	.45
☐ 8 Jose Hernandez	.10	.05
☐ 9 Robin Jennings	.10	.05
☐ 10 Doug Jones	.20	.09
☐ 11 Brooks Kieschnick	.20	.09
☐ 12 Brian McRae	.10	.05
☐ 13 Jaime Navarro	.10	.05
☐ 14 Rey Sanchez	.10	.05
☐ 15 Ryne Sandberg	1.50	.70
☐ 16 Scott Servais	.10	.05
☐ 17 Sammy Sosa	1.00	.45
☐ 18 Steve Trachsel	.10	.05
☐ 19 Logo card	.10	.05
☐ 20 Checklist	.10	.05

1996 Fleer Dodgers

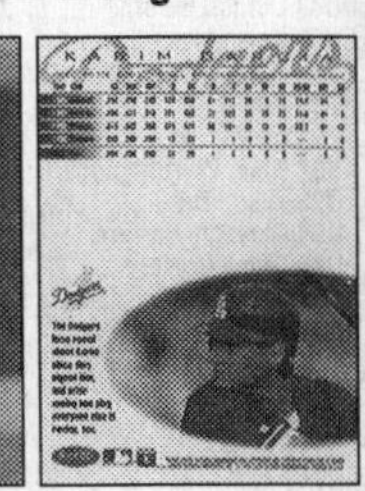

These 20 standard-size cards feature the same design as the regular Fleer issue, except they are UV coated, use silver foil and are numbered "x of 20". The team set packs were available at retail locations and hobby shops in 10-card packs for a suggested retail price of $1.99.

	MINT	NRMT
COMPLETE SET (20)	6.00	2.70
COMMON CARD (1-20)	.10	.05
☐ 1 Mike Blowers	.10	.05
☐ 2 Brett Butler	.40	.18
☐ 3 Tom Candiotti	.10	.05
☐ 4 Roger Cedeno	.30	.14
☐ 5 Delino DeShields	.10	.05
☐ 6 Chad Fonville	.10	.05
☐ 7 Greg Gagne	.10	.05
☐ 8 Karim Garcia	.40	.18
☐ 9 Todd Hollandsworth	.30	.14
☐ 10 Eric Karros	.40	.18
☐ 11 Ramon Martinez	.20	.09
☐ 12 Raul Mondesi	.75	.35
☐ 13 Hideo Nomo	3.00	1.35
☐ 14 Antonio Osuna	.10	.05
☐ 15 Chan Ho Park	1.00	.45
☐ 16 Mike Piazza	2.50	1.10
☐ 17 Ismael Valdes	.20	.09
☐ 18 Todd Worrell	.20	.09
☐ 19 Logo card	.10	.05
☐ 20 Checklist	.10	.05

1996 Fleer Indians

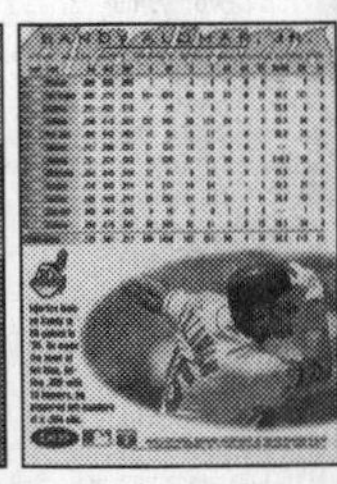

This 20-card standard-size set was issued by Fleer as a test to see how regional team issues would sell. These cards are different from the regular 1996 Fleer issues as the 10-card packs feature the Indians logo. The cards have silver-foil and are issued with UV coating and they are numbered "X" of 20. The set is sequenced in alphabetical order.

	MINT	NRMT
COMPLETE SET (20)	6.00	2.70
COMMON CARD (1-20)	.10	.05

1 Sandy Alomar Jr.	.40	.18
2 Paul Assenmacher	.10	.05
3 Carlos Baerga	.20	.09
4 Albert Belle	1.00	.45
5 Orel Hershiser	.20	.09
6 Kenny Lofton	1.25	.55
7 Dennis Martinez	.20	.09
8 Jose Mesa	.20	.09
9 Eddie Murray	.60	.25
10 Charles Nagy	.30	.14
11 Tony Pena	.10	.05
12 Herb Perry	.10	.05
13 Eric Plunk	.10	.05
14 Jim Poole	.10	.05
15 Manny Ramirez	1.00	.45
16 Julian Tavarez	.10	.05
17 Jim Thome	1.50	.70
18 Omar Vizquel	.75	.35
19 Indians Logo	.10	.05
20 Indians CL	.10	.05

1996 Fleer Orioles

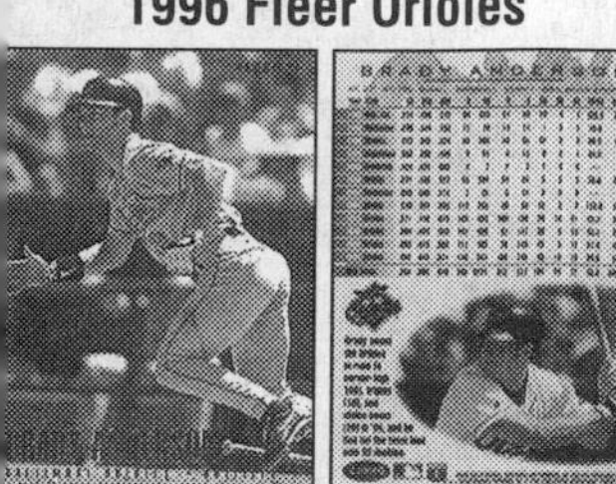

hese 20 standard-size cards feature the same design as e regular Fleer issue, except they are UV coated, use 'ver foil and are numbered "x of 20". The team set packs ere available at retail locations and hobby shops in 10-ard packs for a suggested retail price of $1.99.

	MINT	NRMT
OMPLETE SET (20)	6.00	2.70
OMMON CARD (1-20)	.10	.05
1 Roberto Alomar	1.00	.45
2 Brady Anderson	.75	.35
3 Armando Benitez	.10	.05
4 Bobby Bonilla	.30	.14
5 Scott Erickson	.20	.09
6 Jeffrey Hammonds	.20	.09
7 Jimmy Haynes	.10	.05
8 Chris Hoiles	.20	.09
9 Rick Krivda	.10	.05
10 Kent Mercker	.10	.05
11 Mike Mussina	.75	.35
12 Randy Myers	.30	.14
13 Jesse Orosco	.20	.09
14 Rafael Palmeiro	.50	.23
15 Cal Ripken	3.00	1.35
16 B.J. Surhoff	.20	.09
17 Tony Tarasco	.10	.05
18 David Wells	.10	.05
19 Logo card	.10	.05
20 Checklist	.10	.05

1996 Fleer Rangers

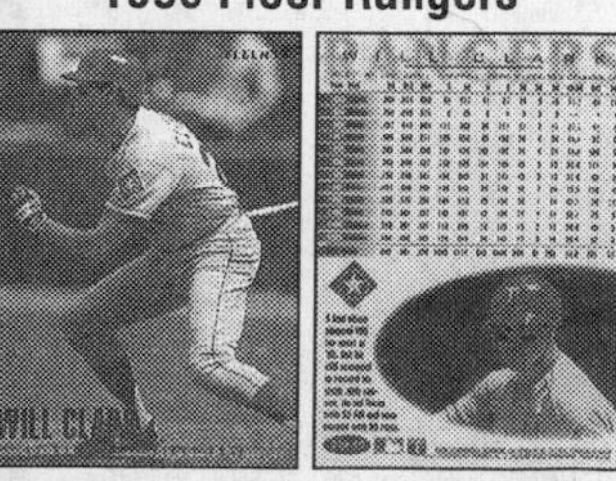

ese 20 standard-size cards have the same design as the gular Fleer issue, except they are UV coated, use silver l and are numbered "x of 20". The team set packs were ailable at retail locations and hobby shops in 10-card cks for a suggested price of $1.99.

	MINT	NRMT
MPLETE SET (20)	5.00	2.20
MMON CARD (1-20)	.10	.05
1 Mark Brandenburg	.10	.05
2 Damon Buford	.10	.05
3 Will Clark	.75	.35
4 Kevin Elster	.10	.05
5 Benji Gil	.10	.05
6 Juan Gonzalez	1.50	.70
7 Rusty Greer	.75	.35
8 Kevin Gross	.10	.05
9 Darryl Hamilton	.10	.05
10 Ken Hill	.20	.09
11 Mark McLemore	.10	.05
12 Dean Palmer	.40	.18
13 Roger Pavlik	.10	.05
14 Ivan Rodriguez	1.00	.45
15 Mickey Tettleton	.30	.14
16 Dave Valle	.10	.05
17 Ed Vosberg	.10	.05
18 Matt Whiteside	.10	.05
19 Logo card	.10	.05
20 Checklist	.10	.05

1996 Fleer Red Sox

These 20 standard-size cards feature the same design as the regular Fleer issue, except they are UV coated, use silver foil and are numbered "x of 20". The team set packs were available at retail locations and hobby shops in 10-card packs for a suggested retail price of $1.99.

	MINT	NRMT
COMPLETE SET (20)	5.00	2.20
COMMON CARD (1-20)	.10	.05
1 Stan Belinda	.10	.05
2 Jose Canseco	.50	.23
3 Roger Clemens	1.50	.70
4 Wil Cordero	.10	.05
5 Vaughn Eshelman	.10	.05
6 Tom Gordon	.10	.05
7 Mike Greenwell	.20	.09
8 Dwayne Hosey	.10	.05
9 Kevin Mitchell	.10	.05
10 Tim Naehring	.20	.09
11 Troy O'Leary	.10	.05
12 Aaron Sele	.10	.05
13 Heathcliff Slocumb	.20	.09
14 Mike Stanley	.10	.05
15 Jeff Suppan	.40	.18
16 John Valentin	.20	.09
17 Mo Vaughn	1.50	.70
18 Tim Wakefield	.10	.05
19 Logo card	.10	.05
20 Checklist	.10	.05

1996 Fleer Rockies

These 20 standard-size cards are same as the regular Fleer issue, except they are UV coated, they use silver foil and they are numbered "x of 20". The team set packs were available at retail locations and hobby shops in 10-card packs for a suggested price of $1.99.

	MINT	NRMT
COMPLETE SET (20)	6.00	2.70
COMMON CARD (1-20)	.10	.05
1 Jason Bates	.10	.05
2 Dante Bichette	.75	.35
3 Ellis Burks	.60	.25
4 Vinny Castilla	.60	.25
5 Andres Galarraga	1.00	.45
6 Darren Holmes	.10	.05
7 Curt Leskanic	.10	.05
8 Quinton McCracken	.10	.05
9 Mike Munoz	.10	.05
10 Jayhawk Owens	.10	.05
11 Steve Reed	.10	.05
12 Kevin Ritz	.10	.05
13 Bret Saberhagen	.10	.05
14 Bill Swift	.10	.05
15 John Vander Wal	.10	.05
16 Larry Walker	1.25	.55
17 Walt Weiss	.20	.09
18 Eric Young	.20	.09
19 Logo card	.10	.05
20 Checklist	.10	.05

1996 Fleer White Sox

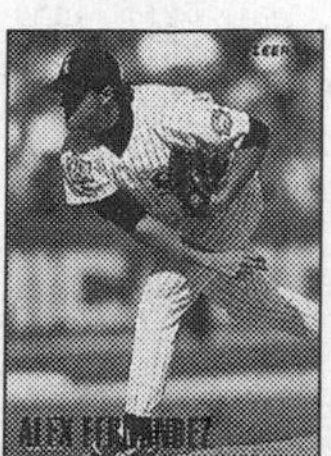

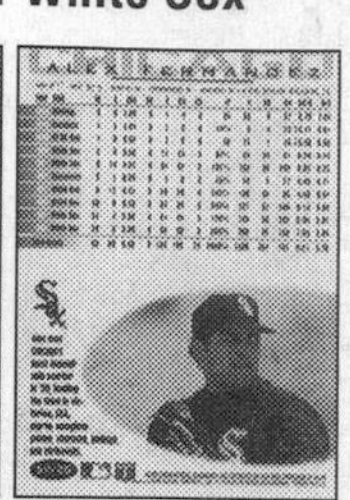

These 20 standard-size cards have the same design as the regular Fleer issue, except they are UV coated, they use silver foil and they are numbered "x of 20". The team set packs were available at retail locations and hobby shops in 10-card packs for a suggested price of $1.99.

	MINT	NRMT
COMPLETE SET (20)	6.00	2.70
COMMON CARD (1-20)	.10	.05
1 Wilson Alvarez	.20	.09
2 Harold Baines	.20	.09
3 Jason Bere	.10	.05
4 Ray Durham	.30	.14
5 Alex Fernandez	.20	.09
6 Ozzie Guillen	.10	.05
7 Roberto Hernandez	.20	.09
8 Matt Karchner	.10	.05
9 Ron Karkovice	.10	.05
10 Darren Lewis	.10	.05
11 Dave Martinez	.10	.05
12 Lyle Mouton	.10	.05
13 Tony Phillips	.10	.05
14 Chris Snopek	.10	.05
15 Kevin Tapani	.10	.05
16 Danny Tartabull	.10	.05
17 Frank Thomas	3.00	1.35
18 Robin Ventura	.50	.23
19 Logo card	.10	.05
20 Checklist	.10	.05

1997 Fleer

The 1997 Fleer Set was issued in two series totaling 761 cards and distributed in 10-card packs with a suggested retail price of $1.49. The fronts feature color action player photos with a matte finish and gold foil printing. The backs carry another player photo with player information and career statistics. Cards 491-500 are a Checklist subset of Series 1 and feature black-and-white or sepia tone photos of big-name players. Series 2 contains the following subsets: Encore (696-720) which are redesigned cards of the big-name players from Series 1, and Checklists (721-748). Cards 749 and 750 are expansion team logo cards with the insert checklists on the backs. Some delers believe that cards numbered 751-761 were short printed. Also, an Andrew Jones autographed Circa card numbered to 200 was inserted into packs.

	MINT	NRMT
COMPLETE SET (761)	80.00	36.00
COMPLETE SERIES 1 (500)	50.00	22.00

COMPLETE SERIES 2 (261)	30.00	13.50
COMMON CARD (1-761)	.15	.07
☐ 1 Roberto Alomar	.60	.25
☐ 2 Brady Anderson	.40	.18
☐ 3 Bobby Bonilla	.30	.14
☐ 4 Rocky Coppinger	.30	.14
☐ 5 Cesar Devarez	.15	.07
☐ 6 Scott Erickson	.15	.07
☐ 7 Jeffrey Hammonds	.30	.14
☐ 8 Chris Hoiles	.30	.14
☐ 9 Eddie Murray	.60	.25
☐ 10 Mike Mussina	.60	.25
☐ 11 Randy Myers	.30	.14
☐ 12 Rafael Palmeiro	.40	.18
☐ 13 Cal Ripken	2.50	1.10
☐ 14 B.J. Surhoff	.30	.14
☐ 15 David Wells	.15	.07
☐ 16 Todd Zeile	.15	.07
☐ 17 Darren Bragg	.15	.07
☐ 18 Jose Canseco	.40	.18
☐ 19 Roger Clemens	1.25	.55
☐ 20 Wil Cordero	.15	.07
☐ 21 Jeff Frye	.15	.07
☐ 22 Nomar Garciaparra	2.00	.90
☐ 23 Tom Gordon	.15	.07
☐ 24 Mike Greenwell	.15	.07
☐ 25 Reggie Jefferson	.30	.14
☐ 26 Jose Malave	.15	.07
☐ 27 Tim Naehring	.15	.07
☐ 28 Troy O'Leary	.15	.07
☐ 29 Heathcliff Slocumb	.15	.07
☐ 30 Mike Stanley	.15	.07
☐ 31 John Valentin	.15	.07
☐ 32 Mo Vaughn	.75	.35
☐ 33 Tim Wakefield	.15	.07
☐ 34 Garret Anderson	.30	.14
☐ 35 George Arias	.15	.07
☐ 36 Shawn Boskie	.15	.07
☐ 37 Chili Davis	.15	.07
☐ 38 Jason Dickson	.30	.14
☐ 39 Gary DiSarcina	.15	.07
☐ 40 Jim Edmonds	.60	.25
☐ 41 Darin Erstad	1.00	.45
☐ 42 Jorge Fabregas	.15	.07
☐ 43 Chuck Finley	.15	.07
☐ 44 Todd Greene	.30	.14
☐ 45 Mike Holtz	.15	.07
☐ 46 Rex Hudler	.15	.07
☐ 47 Mike James	.15	.07
☐ 48 Mark Langston	.15	.07
☐ 49 Troy Percival	.15	.07
☐ 50 Tim Salmon	.60	.25
☐ 51 Jeff Schmidt	.15	.07
☐ 52 J.T. Snow	.30	.14
☐ 53 Randy Velarde	.15	.07
☐ 54 Wilson Alvarez	.15	.07
☐ 55 Harold Baines	.30	.14
☐ 56 James Baldwin	.15	.07
☐ 57 Jason Bere	.15	.07
☐ 58 Mike Cameron	.60	.25
☐ 59 Ray Durham	.15	.07
☐ 60 Alex Fernandez	.30	.14
☐ 61 Ozzie Guillen	.15	.07
☐ 62 Roberto Hernandez	.30	.14
☐ 63 Ron Karkovice	.15	.07
☐ 64 Darren Lewis	.15	.07
☐ 65 Dave Martinez	.15	.07
☐ 66 Lyle Mouton	.15	.07
☐ 67 Greg Norton	.15	.07
☐ 68 Tony Phillips	.15	.07
☐ 69 Chris Snopek	.15	.07
☐ 70 Kevin Tapani	.15	.07
☐ 71 Danny Tartabull	.15	.07
☐ 72 Frank Thomas	2.50	1.10
☐ 73 Robin Ventura	.30	.14
☐ 74 Sandy Alomar Jr.	.15	.07
☐ 75 Albert Belle	.75	.35
☐ 76 Mark Carreon	.15	.07
☐ 77 Julio Franco	.15	.07
☐ 78 Brian Giles	.15	.07
☐ 79 Orel Hershiser	.30	.14
☐ 80 Kenny Lofton	.75	.35
☐ 81 Dennis Martinez	.30	.14
☐ 82 Jack McDowell	.15	.07
☐ 83 Jose Mesa	.30	.14
☐ 84 Charles Nagy	.30	.14
☐ 85 Chad Ogea	.15	.07
☐ 86 Eric Plunk	.15	.07
☐ 87 Manny Ramirez	.60	.25
☐ 88 Kevin Seitzer	.15	.07
☐ 89 Julian Tavarez	.15	.07
☐ 90 Jim Thome	.60	.25
☐ 91 Jose Vizcaino	.15	.07
☐ 92 Omar Vizquel	.30	.14
☐ 93 Brad Ausmus	.15	.07
☐ 94 Kimera Bartee	.15	.07
☐ 95 Raul Casanova	.15	.07
☐ 96 Tony Clark	.60	.25
☐ 97 John Cummings	.15	.07
☐ 98 Travis Fryman	.30	.14
☐ 99 Bob Higginson	.30	.14
☐ 100 Mark Lewis	.15	.07
☐ 101 Felipe Lira	.15	.07
☐ 102 Phil Nevin	.15	.07
☐ 103 Melvin Nieves	.15	.07
☐ 104 Curtis Pride	.15	.07
☐ 105 A.J. Sager	.15	.07
☐ 106 Ruben Sierra	.15	.07
☐ 107 Justin Thompson	.30	.14
☐ 108 Alan Trammell	.40	.18
☐ 109 Kevin Appier	.30	.14
☐ 110 Tim Belcher	.15	.07
☐ 111 Jaime Bluma	.15	.07
☐ 112 Johnny Damon	.15	.07
☐ 113 Tom Goodwin	.15	.07
☐ 114 Chris Haney	.15	.07
☐ 115 Keith Lockhart	.15	.07
☐ 116 Mike Macfarlane	.15	.07
☐ 117 Jeff Montgomery	.15	.07
☐ 118 Jose Offerman	.15	.07
☐ 119 Craig Paquette	.15	.07
☐ 120 Joe Randa	.15	.07
☐ 121 Bip Roberts	.15	.07
☐ 122 Jose Rosado	.40	.18
☐ 123 Mike Sweeney	.30	.14
☐ 124 Michael Tucker	.15	.07
☐ 125 Jeromy Burnitz	.30	.14
☐ 126 Jeff Cirillo	.30	.14
☐ 127 Jeff D'Amico	.30	.14
☐ 128 Mike Fetters	.15	.07
☐ 129 John Jaha	.30	.14
☐ 130 Scott Karl	.15	.07
☐ 131 Jesse Levis	.15	.07
☐ 132 Mark Loretta	.15	.07
☐ 133 Mike Matheny	.15	.07
☐ 134 Ben McDonald	.15	.07
☐ 135 Matt Mieske	.15	.07
☐ 136 Marc Newfield	.15	.07
☐ 137 Dave Nilsson	.15	.07
☐ 138 Jose Valentin	.15	.07
☐ 139 Fernando Vina	.15	.07
☐ 140 Bob Wickman	.15	.07
☐ 141 Gerald Williams	.15	.07
☐ 142 Rick Aguilera	.30	.14
☐ 143 Rich Becker	.15	.07
☐ 144 Ron Coomer	.15	.07
☐ 145 Marty Cordova	.30	.14
☐ 146 Roberto Kelly	.15	.07
☐ 147 Chuck Knoblauch	.60	.25
☐ 148 Matt Lawton	.15	.07
☐ 149 Pat Meares	.15	.07
☐ 150 Travis Miller	.15	.07
☐ 151 Paul Molitor	.60	.25
☐ 152 Greg Myers	.15	.07
☐ 153 Dan Naulty	.15	.07
☐ 154 Kirby Puckett	1.25	.55
☐ 155 Brad Radke	.30	.14
☐ 156 Frank Rodriguez	.15	.07
☐ 157 Scott Stahoviak	.15	.07
☐ 158 Dave Stevens	.15	.07
☐ 159 Matt Walbeck	.15	.07
☐ 160 Todd Walker	.15	.07
☐ 161 Wade Boggs	.60	.25
☐ 162 David Cone	.30	.14
☐ 163 Mariano Duncan	.15	.07
☐ 164 Cecil Fielder	.30	.14
☐ 165 Joe Girardi	.15	.07
☐ 166 Dwight Gooden	.30	.14
☐ 167 Charlie Hayes	.15	.07
☐ 168 Derek Jeter	2.00	.90
☐ 169 Jimmy Key	.15	.07
☐ 170 Jim Leyritz	.15	.07
☐ 171 Tino Martinez	.60	.25
☐ 172 Ramiro Mendoza	.40	.18
☐ 173 Jeff Nelson	.15	.07
☐ 174 Paul O'Neill	.15	.07
☐ 175 Andy Pettitte	.60	.25
☐ 176 Mariano Rivera	.30	.14
☐ 177 Ruben Rivera	.30	.14
☐ 178 Kenny Rogers	.15	.07
☐ 179 Darryl Strawberry	.30	.14
☐ 180 John Wetteland	.30	.14
☐ 181 Bernie Williams	.15	.07
☐ 182 Willie Adams	.15	.07
☐ 183 Tony Batista	.30	.14
☐ 184 Geronimo Berroa	.15	.07
☐ 185 Mike Bordick	.15	.07
☐ 186 Scott Brosius	.15	.07
☐ 187 Bobby Chouinard	.15	.07
☐ 188 Jim Corsi	.15	.07
☐ 189 Brent Gates	.15	.07
☐ 190 Jason Giambi	.30	.14
☐ 191 Jose Herrera	.15	.07
☐ 192 Damon Mashore	.15	.07
☐ 193 Mark McGwire	1.25	.55
☐ 194 Mike Mohler	.15	.07
☐ 195 Scott Spiezio	.30	.14
☐ 196 Terry Steinbach	.15	.07
☐ 197 Bill Taylor	.15	.07
☐ 198 John Wasdin	.15	.07
☐ 199 Steve Wojciechowski	.15	.07
☐ 200 Ernie Young	.15	.07
☐ 201 Rich Amaral	.15	.07
☐ 202 Jay Buhner	.40	.18
☐ 203 Norm Charlton	.15	.07
☐ 204 Joey Cora	.30	.14
☐ 205 Russ Davis	.15	.07
☐ 206 Ken Griffey Jr.	3.00	1.35
☐ 207 Sterling Hitchcock	.15	.07
☐ 208 Brian Hunter	.15	.07
☐ 209 Raul Ibanez	.15	.07
☐ 210 Randy Johnson	.60	.25
☐ 211 Edgar Martinez	.40	.18
☐ 212 Jamie Moyer	.15	.07
☐ 213 Alex Rodriguez	2.50	1.10
☐ 214 Paul Sorrento	.15	.07
☐ 215 Matt Wagner	.15	.07
☐ 216 Bob Wells	.15	.07
☐ 217 Dan Wilson	.15	.07
☐ 218 Damon Buford	.15	.07
☐ 219 Will Clark	.40	.18
☐ 220 Kevin Elster	.15	.07
☐ 221 Juan Gonzalez	1.50	.70
☐ 222 Rusty Greer	.30	.14
☐ 223 Kevin Gross	.15	.07
☐ 224 Darryl Hamilton	.15	.07
☐ 225 Mike Henneman	.15	.07
☐ 226 Ken Hill	.15	.07
☐ 227 Mark McLemore	.15	.07
☐ 228 Darren Oliver	.15	.07
☐ 229 Dean Palmer	.30	.14
☐ 230 Roger Pavlik	.15	.07
☐ 231 Ivan Rodriguez	.75	.35
☐ 232 Mickey Tettleton	.15	.07
☐ 233 Bobby Witt	.15	.07
☐ 234 Jacob Brumfield	.15	.07
☐ 235 Joe Carter	.30	.14
☐ 236 Tim Crabtree	.15	.07
☐ 237 Carlos Delgado	.30	.14
☐ 238 Huck Flener	.15	.07
☐ 239 Alex Gonzalez	.15	.07
☐ 240 Shawn Green	.15	.07
☐ 241 Juan Guzman	.15	.07
☐ 242 Pat Hentgen	.30	.14
☐ 243 Marty Janzen	.15	.07
☐ 244 Sandy Martinez	.15	.07
☐ 245 Otis Nixon	.15	.07
☐ 246 Charlie O'Brien	.15	.07
☐ 247 John Olerud	.30	.14
☐ 248 Robert Perez	.15	.07
☐ 249 Ed Sprague	.15	.07
☐ 250 Mike Timlin	.15	.07
☐ 251 Steve Avery	.15	.07
☐ 252 Jeff Blauser	.15	.07
☐ 253 Brad Clontz	.15	.07
☐ 254 Jermaine Dye	.15	.07
☐ 255 Tom Glavine	.30	.14
☐ 256 Marquis Grissom	.30	.14
☐ 257 Andruw Jones	1.50	.70
☐ 258 Chipper Jones	2.00	.90
☐ 259 David Justice	.60	.25
☐ 260 Ryan Klesko	.40	.18
☐ 261 Mark Lemke	.15	.07
☐ 262 Javier Lopez	.30	.14
☐ 263 Greg Maddux	2.00	.90
☐ 264 Fred McGriff	.40	.18
☐ 265 Greg McMichael	.15	.07
☐ 266 Denny Neagle	.15	.07
☐ 267 Terry Pendleton	.15	.07
☐ 268 Eddie Perez	.15	.07
☐ 269 John Smoltz	.30	.14
☐ 270 Terrell Wade	.15	.07
☐ 271 Mark Wohlers	.30	.14
☐ 272 Terry Adams	.15	.07
☐ 273 Brant Brown	.15	.07
☐ 274 Leo Gomez	.15	.07
☐ 275 Luis Gonzalez	.15	.07
☐ 276 Mark Grace	.40	.18
☐ 277 Tyler Houston	.15	.07
☐ 278 Robin Jennings	.15	.07
☐ 279 Brooks Kieschnick	.30	.14
☐ 280 Brian McRae	.15	.07
☐ 281 Jaime Navarro	.15	.07
☐ 282 Ryne Sandberg	.75	.35
☐ 283 Scott Servais	.15	.07
☐ 284 Sammy Sosa	.60	.25
☐ 285 Dave Swartzbaugh	.15	.07
☐ 286 Amaury Telemaco	.15	.07
☐ 287 Steve Trachsel	.15	.07
☐ 288 Pedro Valdes	.15	.07

☐ 289 Turk Wendell .15 .07
☐ 290 Bret Boone .15 .07
☐ 291 Jeff Branson .15 .07
☐ 292 Jeff Brantley .15 .07
☐ 293 Eric Davis .30 .14
☐ 294 Willie Greene .15 .07
☐ 295 Thomas Howard .15 .07
☐ 296 Barry Larkin .40 .18
☐ 297 Kevin Mitchell .15 .07
☐ 298 Hal Morris .15 .07
☐ 299 Chad Mottola .15 .07
☐ 300 Joe Oliver .15 .07
☐ 301 Mark Portugal .15 .07
☐ 302 Roger Salkeld .15 .07
☐ 303 Reggie Sanders .15 .07
☐ 304 Pete Schourek .15 .07
☐ 305 John Smiley .15 .07
☐ 306 Eddie Taubensee .15 .07
☐ 307 Dante Bichette .30 .14
☐ 308 Ellis Burks .30 .14
☐ 309 Vinny Castilla .30 .14
☐ 310 Andres Galarraga .40 .18
☐ 311 Curt Leskanic .15 .07
☐ 312 Quinton McCracken .15 .07
☐ 313 Neifi Perez .30 .14
☐ 314 Jeff Reed .15 .07
☐ 315 Steve Reed .15 .07
☐ 316 Armando Reynoso .15 .07
☐ 317 Kevin Ritz .15 .07
☐ 318 Bruce Ruffin .15 .07
☐ 319 Larry Walker .60 .25
☐ 320 Walt Weiss .15 .07
☐ 321 Jamey Wright .30 .14
☐ 322 Eric Young .30 .14
☐ 323 Kurt Abbott .15 .07
☐ 324 Alex Arias .15 .07
☐ 325 Kevin Brown .30 .14
☐ 326 Luis Castillo .30 .14
☐ 327 Greg Colbrunn .15 .07
☐ 328 Jeff Conine .30 .14
☐ 329 Andre Dawson .40 .18
☐ 330 Charles Johnson .15 .07
☐ 331 Al Leiter .15 .07
☐ 332 Ralph Milliard .15 .07
☐ 333 Robb Nen .15 .07
☐ 334 Pat Rapp .15 .07
☐ 335 Edgar Renteria .30 .14
☐ 336 Gary Sheffield .60 .25
☐ 337 Devon White .15 .07
☐ 338 Bob Abreu .60 .25
☐ 339 Jeff Bagwell 1.25 .55
☐ 340 Derek Bell .15 .07
☐ 341 Sean Berry .15 .07
☐ 342 Craig Biggio .40 .18
☐ 343 Doug Drabek .15 .07
☐ 344 Tony Eusebio .15 .07
☐ 345 Ricky Gutierrez .15 .07
☐ 346 Mike Hampton .15 .07
☐ 347 Brian Hunter .30 .14
☐ 348 Todd Jones .15 .07
☐ 349 Darryl Kile .30 .14
☐ 350 Derrick May .15 .07
☐ 351 Orlando Miller .15 .07
☐ 352 James Mouton .15 .07
☐ 353 Shane Reynolds .15 .07
☐ 354 Billy Wagner .30 .14
☐ 355 Donne Wall .15 .07
☐ 356 Mike Blowers .15 .07
☐ 357 Brett Butler .30 .14
☐ 358 Roger Cedeno .15 .07
☐ 359 Chad Curtis .15 .07
☐ 360 Delino DeShields .15 .07
☐ 361 Greg Gagne .15 .07
☐ 362 Karim Garcia .30 .14
☐ 363 Wilton Guerrero .15 .07
☐ 364 Todd Hollandsworth .30 .14
☐ 365 Eric Karros .30 .14
☐ 366 Ramon Martinez .30 .14
☐ 367 Raul Mondesi .40 .18
☐ 368 Hideo Nomo 1.50 .70
☐ 369 Antonio Osuna .15 .07
☐ 370 Chan Ho Park .60 .25
☐ 371 Mike Piazza 2.00 .90
☐ 372 Ismael Valdes .30 .14
☐ 373 Todd Worrell .30 .14
☐ 374 Moises Alou .30 .14
☐ 375 Shane Andrews .15 .07
☐ 376 Yamil Benitez .15 .07
☐ 377 Jeff Fassero .15 .07
☐ 378 Darrin Fletcher .15 .07
☐ 379 Cliff Floyd .15 .07
☐ 380 Mark Grudzielanek .15 .07
☐ 381 Mike Lansing .15 .07
☐ 382 Barry Manuel .15 .07
☐ 383 Pedro Martinez .60 .25
☐ 384 Henry Rodriguez .15 .07
☐ 385 Mel Rojas .15 .07
☐ 386 F.P. Santangelo .15 .07
☐ 387 David Segui .15 .07
☐ 388 Ugueth Urbina .30 .14
☐ 389 Rondell White .30 .14
☐ 390 Edgardo Alfonzo .30 .14
☐ 391 Carlos Baerga .30 .14
☐ 392 Mark Clark .15 .07
☐ 393 Alvaro Espinoza .15 .07
☐ 394 John Franco .15 .07
☐ 395 Bernard Gilkey .15 .07
☐ 396 Pete Harnisch .15 .07
☐ 397 Todd Hundley .30 .14
☐ 398 Butch Huskey .15 .07
☐ 399 Jason Isringhausen .15 .07
☐ 400 Lance Johnson .15 .07
☐ 401 Bobby Jones .15 .07
☐ 402 Alex Ochoa .15 .07
☐ 403 Rey Ordonez .15 .07
☐ 404 Robert Person .15 .07
☐ 405 Paul Wilson .15 .07
☐ 406 Matt Beech .15 .07
☐ 407 Ron Blazier .15 .07
☐ 408 Ricky Bottalico .15 .07
☐ 409 Lenny Dykstra .30 .14
☐ 410 Jim Eisenreich .30 .14
☐ 411 Bobby Estalella .30 .14
☐ 412 Mike Grace .15 .07
☐ 413 Gregg Jefferies .15 .07
☐ 414 Mike Lieberthal .15 .07
☐ 415 Wendell Magee .15 .07
☐ 416 Mickey Morandini .15 .07
☐ 417 Ricky Otero .15 .07
☐ 418 Scott Rolen 1.50 .70
☐ 419 Ken Ryan .15 .07
☐ 420 Benito Santiago .15 .07
☐ 421 Curt Schilling .30 .14
☐ 422 Kevin Sefcik .15 .07
☐ 423 Jermaine Allensworth .30 .14
☐ 424 Trey Beamon .15 .07
☐ 425 Jay Bell .15 .07
☐ 426 Francisco Cordova .15 .07
☐ 427 Carlos Garcia .15 .07
☐ 428 Mark Johnson .15 .07
☐ 429 Jason Kendall .30 .14
☐ 430 Jeff King .15 .07
☐ 431 Jon Lieber .15 .07
☐ 432 Al Martin .15 .07
☐ 433 Orlando Merced .15 .07
☐ 434 Ramon Morel .15 .07
☐ 435 Matt Ruebel .15 .07
☐ 436 Jason Schmidt .30 .14
☐ 437 Marc Wilkins .15 .07
☐ 438 Alan Benes .30 .14
☐ 439 Andy Benes .15 .07
☐ 440 Royce Clayton .15 .07
☐ 441 Dennis Eckersley .30 .14
☐ 442 Gary Gaetti .30 .14
☐ 443 Ron Gant .30 .14
☐ 444 Aaron Holbert .15 .07
☐ 445 Brian Jordan .30 .14
☐ 446 Ray Lankford .30 .14
☐ 447 John Mabry .30 .14
☐ 448 T.J. Mathews .15 .07
☐ 449 Willie McGee .15 .07
☐ 450 Donovan Osborne .15 .07
☐ 451 Tom Pagnozzi .15 .07
☐ 452 Ozzie Smith .75 .35
☐ 453 Todd Stottlemyre .15 .07
☐ 454 Mark Sweeney .15 .07
☐ 455 Dmitri Young .30 .14
☐ 456 Andy Ashby .15 .07
☐ 457 Ken Caminiti .60 .25
☐ 458 Archi Cianfrocco .15 .07
☐ 459 Steve Finley .30 .14
☐ 460 John Flaherty .15 .07
☐ 461 Chris Gomez .15 .07
☐ 462 Tony Gwynn 1.50 .70
☐ 463 Joey Hamilton .30 .14
☐ 464 Rickey Henderson .40 .18
☐ 465 Trevor Hoffman .15 .07
☐ 466 Brian Johnson .15 .07
☐ 467 Wally Joyner .15 .07
☐ 468 Jody Reed .15 .07
☐ 469 Scott Sanders .15 .07
☐ 470 Bob Tewksbury .15 .07
☐ 471 Fernando Valenzuela .30 .14
☐ 472 Greg Vaughn .15 .07
☐ 473 Tim Worrell .15 .07
☐ 474 Rich Aurilia .15 .07
☐ 475 Rod Beck .15 .07
☐ 476 Marvin Benard .15 .07
☐ 477 Barry Bonds .75 .35
☐ 478 Jay Canizaro .15 .07
☐ 479 Shawon Dunston .15 .07
☐ 480 Shawn Estes .15 .07
☐ 481 Mark Gardner .15 .07
☐ 482 Glenallen Hill .15 .07
☐ 483 Stan Javier .15 .07
☐ 484 Marcus Jensen .15 .07
☐ 485 Bill Mueller .15 .07
☐ 486 Wm. VanLandingham .15 .07
☐ 487 Allen Watson .15 .07
☐ 488 Rick Wilkins .15 .07
☐ 489 Matt Williams .40 .18
☐ 490 Desi Wilson .15 .07
☐ 491 Albert Belle CL .60 .25
☐ 492 Ken Griffey Jr. CL 1.50 .70
☐ 493 Andruw Jones CL 1.50 .70
☐ 494 Chipper Jones CL 1.00 .45
☐ 495 Mark McGwire CL .60 .25
☐ 496 Paul Molitor CL .60 .25
☐ 497 Mike Piazza CL 1.00 .45
☐ 498 Cal Ripken CL 1.25 .55
☐ 499 Alex Rodriguez CL 1.50 .70
☐ 500 Frank Thomas CL 1.50 .70
☐ 501 Kenny Lofton .75 .35
☐ 502 Carlos Perez .15 .07
☐ 503 Tim Raines .15 .07
☐ 504 Danny Patterson .15 .07
☐ 505 Derrick May .15 .07
☐ 506 Dave Hollins .15 .07
☐ 507 Felipe Crespo .15 .07
☐ 508 Brian Banks .15 .07
☐ 509 Jeff Kent .15 .07
☐ 510 Bubba Trammell .60 .25
☐ 511 Robert Person .15 .07
☐ 512 David Arias-Ortiz .75 .35
☐ 513 Ryan Jones .15 .07
☐ 514 David Justice .60 .25
☐ 515 Will Cunnane .15 .07
☐ 516 Russ Johnson .15 .07
☐ 517 John Burkett .15 .07
☐ 518 Robinson Checo .15 .07
☐ 519 Ricardo Rincon .15 .07
☐ 520 Woody Williams .15 .07
☐ 521 Rick Helling .15 .07
☐ 522 Jorge Posada .15 .07
☐ 523 Kevin Orie .15 .07
☐ 524 Fernando Tatis 1.50 .70
☐ 525 Jermaine Dye .15 .07
☐ 526 Brian Hunter .15 .07
☐ 527 Greg McMichael .15 .07
☐ 528 Matt Wagner .15 .07
☐ 529 Richie Sexson .15 .07
☐ 530 Scott Ruffcorn .15 .07
☐ 531 Luis Gonzalez .15 .07
☐ 532 Mike Johnson .40 .18
☐ 533 Mark Petkovsek .15 .07
☐ 534 Doug Drabek .15 .07
☐ 535 Jose Canseco .40 .18
☐ 536 Bobby Bonilla .30 .14
☐ 537 J.T. Snow .15 .07
☐ 538 Shawon Dunston .15 .07
☐ 539 John Ericks .15 .07
☐ 540 Terry Steinbach .15 .07
☐ 541 Jay Bell .15 .07
☐ 542 Joe Borowski .15 .07
☐ 543 David Wells .15 .07
☐ 544 Justin Towle .50 .23
☐ 545 Mike Blowers .15 .07
☐ 546 Shannon Stewart .15 .07
☐ 547 Rudy Pemberton .15 .07
☐ 548 Bill Swift .15 .07
☐ 549 Osvaldo Fernandez .15 .07
☐ 550 Eddie Murray .60 .25
☐ 551 Don Wengert .15 .07
☐ 552 Brad Ausmus .15 .07
☐ 553 Carlos Garcia .15 .07
☐ 554 Jose Guillen .60 .25
☐ 555 Rheal Cormier .15 .07
☐ 556 Doug Brocail .15 .07
☐ 557 Rex Hudler .15 .07
☐ 558 Armando Benitez .15 .07
☐ 559 Eli Marrero .30 .14
☐ 560 Ricky Ledee 1.25 .55
☐ 561 Bartolo Colon .15 .07
☐ 562 Quilvio Veras .15 .07
☐ 563 Alex Fernandez .15 .07
☐ 564 Darren Dreifort .15 .07
☐ 565 Benji Gil .15 .07
☐ 566 Kent Mercker .15 .07
☐ 567 Glendon Rusch .15 .07
☐ 568 Ramon Tatis .15 .07
☐ 569 Roger Clemens 1.25 .55
☐ 570 Mark Lewis .15 .07
☐ 571 Emil Brown .40 .18
☐ 572 Jaime Navarro .15 .07
☐ 573 Sherman Obando .15 .07
☐ 574 John Wasdin .15 .07
☐ 575 Calvin Maduro .15 .07
☐ 576 Todd Jones .15 .07
☐ 577 Orlando Merced .15 .07
☐ 578 Cal Eldred .15 .07
☐ 579 Mark Gubicza .15 .07

☐ 580 Michael Tucker .15 .07
☐ 581 Tony Saunders .50 .23
☐ 582 Garvin Alston .15 .07
☐ 583 Joe Roa .15 .07
☐ 584 Brady Raggio .15 .07
☐ 585 Jimmy Key .30 .14
☐ 586 Marc Sagmoen .15 .07
☐ 587 Jim Bullinger .15 .07
☐ 588 Yorkis Perez .15 .07
☐ 589 Jose Cruz Jr. 6.00 2.70
☐ 590 Mike Stanton .15 .07
☐ 591 Deivi Cruz .40 .18
☐ 592 Steve Karsay .15 .07
☐ 593 Mike Trombley .15 .07
☐ 594 Doug Glanville .15 .07
☐ 595 Scott Sanders .15 .07
☐ 596 Thomas Howard .15 .07
☐ 597 T.J. Staton .40 .18
☐ 598 Garrett Stephenson .15 .07
☐ 599 Rico Brogna .15 .07
☐ 600 Albert Belle .75 .35
☐ 601 Jose Vizcaino .15 .07
☐ 602 Chili Davis .30 .14
☐ 603 Shane Mack .15 .07
☐ 604 Jim Eisenreich .30 .14
☐ 605 Todd Zeile .15 .07
☐ 606 Brian Boehringer .15 .07
☐ 607 Paul Shuey .15 .07
☐ 608 Kevin Tapani .15 .07
☐ 609 John Wetteland .15 .07
☐ 610 Jim Leyritz .15 .07
☐ 611 Ray Montgomery .15 .07
☐ 612 Doug Bochtler .15 .07
☐ 613 Wady Almonte .50 .23
☐ 614 Danny Tartabull .15 .07
☐ 615 Orlando Miller .15 .07
☐ 616 Bobby Ayala .15 .07
☐ 617 Tony Graffanino .15 .07
☐ 618 Marc Valdes .15 .07
☐ 619 Ron Villone .15 .07
☐ 620 Derrek Lee .30 .14
☐ 621 Greg Colbrunn .15 .07
☐ 622 Felix Heredia .15 .07
☐ 623 Carl Everett .15 .07
☐ 624 Mark Thompson .15 .07
☐ 625 Jeff Granger .15 .07
☐ 626 Damian Jackson .15 .07
☐ 627 Mark Leiter .15 .07
☐ 628 Chris Holt .15 .07
☐ 629 Dario Veras .40 .18
☐ 630 Dave Burba .15 .07
☐ 631 Darryl Hamilton .15 .07
☐ 632 Mark Acre .15 .07
☐ 633 Fernando Hernandez .15 .07
☐ 634 Terry Mulholland .15 .07
☐ 635 Dustin Hermanson .15 .07
☐ 636 Delino DeShields .15 .07
☐ 637 Steve Avery .15 .07
☐ 638 Tony Womack .50 .23
☐ 639 Mark Whiten .15 .07
☐ 640 Marquis Grissom .15 .07
☐ 641 Xavier Hernandez .15 .07
☐ 642 Eric Davis .30 .14
☐ 643 Bob Tewksbury .15 .07
☐ 644 Dante Powell .15 .07
☐ 645 Carlos Castillo .40 .18
☐ 646 Chris Widger .15 .07
☐ 647 Moises Alou .30 .14
☐ 648 Pat Listach .15 .07
☐ 649 Edgar Ramos .40 .18
☐ 650 Deion Sanders .60 .25
☐ 651 John Olerud .30 .14
☐ 652 Todd Dunwoody .60 .25
☐ 653 Randall Simon 1.25 .55
☐ 654 Dan Carlson .15 .07
☐ 655 Matt Williams .40 .18
☐ 656 Jeff King .15 .07
☐ 657 Luis Alicea .15 .07
☐ 658 Brian Moehler .15 .07
☐ 659 Ariel Prieto .15 .07
☐ 660 Kevin Elster .15 .07
☐ 661 Mark Hutton .15 .07
☐ 662 Aaron Sele .15 .07
☐ 663 Graeme Lloyd .15 .07
☐ 664 John Burke .15 .07
☐ 665 Mel Rojas .15 .07
☐ 666 Sid Fernandez .15 .07
☐ 667 Pedro Astacio .15 .07
☐ 668 Jeff Abbott .15 .07
☐ 669 Darren Daulton .30 .14
☐ 670 Mike Bordick .15 .07
☐ 671 Sterling Hitchcock .15 .07
☐ 672 Damion Easley .15 .07
☐ 673 Armando Reynoso .15 .07
☐ 674 Pat Cline .15 .07
☐ 675 Orlando Cabrera .15 .07
☐ 676 Alan Embree .15 .07
☐ 677 Brian Bevil .15 .07
☐ 678 David Weathers .15 .07
☐ 679 Cliff Floyd .15 .07
☐ 680 Joe Randa .15 .07
☐ 681 Bill Haselman .15 .07
☐ 682 Jeff Fassero .15 .07
☐ 683 Matt Morris .15 .07
☐ 684 Mark Portugal .15 .07
☐ 685 Lee Smith .15 .07
☐ 686 Pokey Reese .15 .07
☐ 687 Benito Santiago .15 .07
☐ 688 Brian Johnson .15 .07
☐ 689 Brent Brede .15 .07
☐ 690 Shigetoshi Hasegawa .40 .18
☐ 691 Julio Santana .15 .07
☐ 692 Steve Kline .15 .07
☐ 693 Julian Tavarez .15 .07
☐ 694 John Hudek .15 .07
☐ 695 Manny Alexander .15 .07
☐ 696 Roberto Alomar ENC .60 .25
☐ 697 Jeff Bagwell ENC .60 .25
☐ 698 Barry Bonds ENC .60 .25
☐ 699 Ken Caminiti ENC .60 .25
☐ 700 Juan Gonzalez ENC .75 .35
☐ 701 Ken Griffey Jr. ENC 1.50 .70
☐ 702 Tony Gwynn ENC .75 .35
☐ 703 Derek Jeter ENC 1.00 .45
☐ 704 Andruw Jones ENC 1.00 .45
☐ 705 Chipper Jones ENC 1.00 .45
☐ 706 Barry Larkin ENC .40 .18
☐ 707 Greg Maddux ENC 1.00 .45
☐ 708 Mark McGwire ENC .60 .25
☐ 709 Paul Molitor ENC .60 .25
☐ 710 Hideo Nomo ENC .75 .35
☐ 711 Andy Pettitte ENC .60 .25
☐ 712 Mike Piazza ENC 1.00 .45
☐ 713 Manny Ramirez ENC .60 .25
☐ 714 Cal Ripken ENC 1.25 .55
☐ 715 Alex Rodriguez ENC 1.25 .55
☐ 716 Ryne Sandberg ENC .60 .25
☐ 717 John Smoltz ENC .30 .14
☐ 718 Frank Thomas ENC 1.25 .55
☐ 719 Mo Vaughn ENC .60 .25
☐ 720 Bernie Williams ENC .60 .25
☐ 721 Tim Salmon CL .60 .25
☐ 722 Greg Maddux CL 1.00 .45
☐ 723 Cal Ripken CL 1.25 .55
☐ 724 Mo Vaughn CL .60 .25
☐ 725 Ryne Sandberg CL .60 .25
☐ 726 Frank Thomas CL 1.25 .55
☐ 727 Barry Larkin CL .40 .18
☐ 728 Manny Ramirez CL .60 .25
☐ 729 Andres Galarraga CL .60 .25
☐ 730 Tony Clark CL .60 .25
☐ 731 Gary Sheffield CL .60 .25
☐ 732 Jeff Bagwell CL .60 .25
☐ 733 Kevin Appier CL .15 .07
☐ 734 Mike Piazza CL 1.00 .45
☐ 735 Jeff Cirillo CL .15 .07
☐ 736 Paul Molitor CL .60 .25
☐ 737 Henry Rodriguez CL .15 .07
☐ 738 Todd Hundley CL .15 .07
☐ 739 Derek Jeter CL 1.00 .45
☐ 740 Mark McGwire CL .60 .25
☐ 741 Curt Schilling CL .15 .07
☐ 742 Jason Kendall CL .15 .07
☐ 743 Tony Gwynn CL .75 .35
☐ 744 Barry Bonds CL .60 .25
☐ 745 Ken Griffey Jr. CL 1.50 .70
☐ 746 Brian Jordan CL .15 .07
☐ 747 Juan Gonzalez CL .75 .35
☐ 748 Joe Carter CL .15 .07
☐ 749 Arizona Diamondbacks CL .30 .14
☐ 750 Tampa Bay Devil Rays CL .30 .14
☐ 751 Hideki Irabu .75 .35
☐ 752 Jeremi Gonzalez .50 .23
☐ 753 Mario Valdez .30 .14
☐ 754 Aaron Boone .30 .14
☐ 755 Brett Tomko .15 .07
☐ 756 Jaret Wright 5.00 2.20
☐ 757 Ryan McGuire .15 .07
☐ 758 Jason McDonald .15 .07
☐ 759 Adrian Brown .15 .07
☐ 760 Keith Foulke .15 .07
☐ 761 Bonus Checklist (751-761) .15 .07
☐ P489 Matt Williams Promo 2.00 .90
☐ NNO Andruw Jones Circa AU200 100.00 45.00

1997 Fleer Tiffany

Randomly inserted in series one and two packs at a rate of one in 20, this 751-card set is a parallel version of the regular set featuring a glossy holographic design, foil stamping, and UV coating.

	MINT	NRMT
COMPLETE SET (761)	5500.00	2500.00
COMPLETE SERIES 1 (500)	4000.00	1800.00
COMPLETE SERIES 2 (261)	1500.00	700.00
COMMON CARD (1-761)	4.00	1.80

*STARS: 20X TO 40X BASIC CARDS
*YOUNG STARS: 15X TO 30X BASIC CARDS
*ROOKIES: 7.5X TO 15X BASIC CARDS

1997 Fleer Bleacher Blasters

Randomly inserted in Fleer 2 retail packs only at a rate of one in 36, this 10-card set features color action photos of power hitters who reach the bleachers with great frequency.

	MINT	NRMT
COMPLETE SET (10)	100.00	45.00
COMMON CARD (1-10)	3.00	1.35

☐ 1 Albert Belle 6.00 2.70
☐ 2 Barry Bonds 6.00 2.70
☐ 3 Juan Gonzalez 12.00 5.50
☐ 4 Ken Griffey Jr. 25.00 11.00
☐ 5 Mark McGwire 10.00 4.50
☐ 6 Mike Piazza 15.00 6.75
☐ 7 Alex Rodriguez 15.00 6.75
☐ 8 Frank Thomas 20.00 9.00
☐ 9 Mo Vaughn 6.00 2.70
☐ 10 Matt Williams 3.00 1.35

1997 Fleer Decade of Excellence

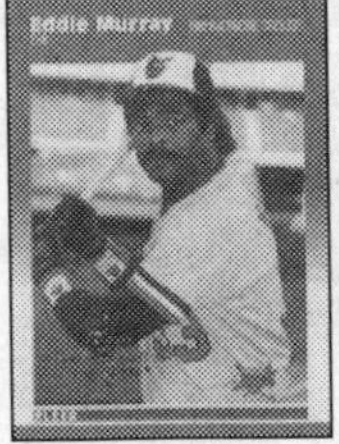

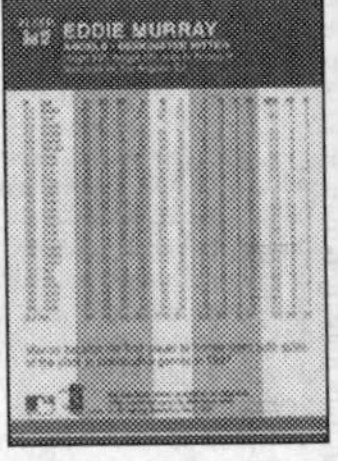

Randomly inserted in Fleer Series 2 hobby packs only at a rate of one in 36, this 12-card set spotlights players who started their major league careers no later than 1987. The set features photos of these players from the 1987 season in the 1987 Fleer Baseball card design.

	MINT	NRMT
COMPLETE SET (12)	60.00	27.00
COMMON CARD (1-12)	2.50	1.10
COMP.RARE.TRAD.SET (10)	350.00	160.00
COMMON RARE.TRAD. (1-10)	12.50	5.50

*RARE TRADITION: 2.5X TO 5X BASIC DECADE

☐ 1 Wade Boggs 4.00 1.80
☐ 2 Barry Bonds 5.00 2.20
☐ 3 Roger Clemens 8.00 3.60
☐ 4 Tony Gwynn 10.00 4.50
☐ 5 Rickey Henderson 3.50 1.55
☐ 6 Greg Maddux 12.00 5.50
☐ 7 Mark McGwire 8.00 3.60
☐ 8 Paul Molitor 4.00 1.80
☐ 9 Eddie Murray 4.00 1.80
☐ 10 Cal Ripken 15.00 6.75
☐ 11 Ryne Sandberg 5.00 2.20
☐ 12 Matt Williams 2.50 1.10

1997 Fleer Diamond Tribute

Randomly inserted in Fleer Series 2 packs at a rate of one in 288, this 12-card set features color action images of Baseball's top players on a dazzling foil background.

	MINT	NRMT
COMPLETE SET (12)	600.00	275.00
COMMON CARD (1-12)	20.00	9.00

☐ 1 Albert Belle 25.00 11.00
☐ 2 Barry Bonds 25.00 11.00

☐ 3 Juan Gonzalez	50.00	22.00
☐ 4 Ken Griffey Jr.	100.00	45.00
☐ 5 Tony Gwynn	50.00	22.00
☐ 6 Greg Maddux	60.00	27.00
☐ 7 Mark McGwire	40.00	18.00
☐ 8 Eddie Murray	20.00	9.00
☐ 9 Mike Piazza	60.00	27.00
☐ 10 Cal Ripken	80.00	36.00
☐ 11 Alex Rodriguez	60.00	27.00
☐ 12 Frank Thomas	80.00	36.00

1997 Fleer Golden Memories

Randomly inserted in first series packs at a rate of one in 16, this ten-card set commemorates major achievements by individual players from the 1996 season. The fronts feature color player images on a background of the top portion of the sun and its rays. The backs carry player information.

	MINT	NRMT
COMPLETE SET (10)	10.00	4.50
COMMON CARD (1-10)	.75	.35
☐ 1 Barry Bonds	1.50	.70
☐ 2 Dwight Gooden	.60	.25
☐ 3 Todd Hundley	.75	.35
☐ 4 Mark McGwire	2.00	.90
☐ 5 Paul Molitor	1.00	.45
☐ 6 Eddie Murray	1.00	.45
☐ 7 Hideo Nomo	1.50	.70
☐ 8 Mike Piazza	4.00	1.80
☐ 9 Cal Ripken	5.00	2.20
☐ 10 Ozzie Smith	2.00	.90

1997 Fleer Goudey Greats

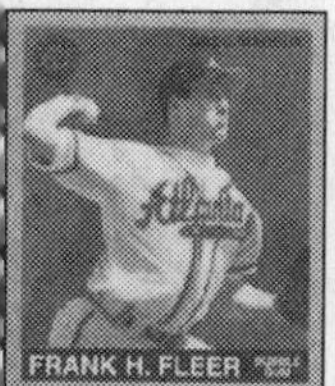

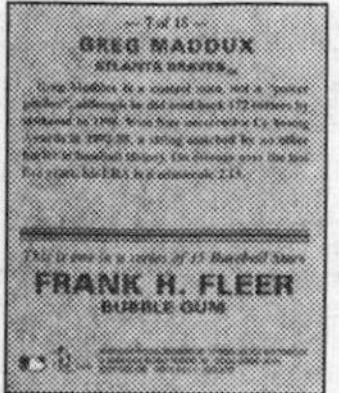

Randomly inserted in Fleer Series 2 packs at a rate of one in eight, this 15-card set features color player photos of today's stars on cards styled and sized to resemble the 1933 Goudey Baseball card set.

	MINT	NRMT
COMPLETE SET (15)	30.00	13.50
COMMON CARD (1-15)	1.00	.45
COMP.FOIL SET (15)	1500.00	700.00
COMMON FOIL (1-15)	50.00	22.00

*FOIL CARDS: 25X TO 50X BASIC GOUDEY GREATS

☐ 1 Barry Bonds	1.25	.55
☐ 2 Ken Griffey Jr.	5.00	2.20
☐ 3 Tony Gwynn	2.50	1.10
☐ 4 Derek Jeter	3.00	1.35
☐ 5 Chipper Jones	3.00	1.35
☐ 6 Kenny Lofton	1.25	.55
☐ 7 Greg Maddux	3.00	1.35
☐ 8 Mark McGwire	2.00	.90
☐ 9 Eddie Murray	1.00	.45
☐ 10 Mike Piazza	3.00	1.35
☐ 11 Cal Ripken	4.00	1.80
☐ 12 Alex Rodriguez	4.00	1.80
☐ 13 Ryne Sandberg	1.25	.55
☐ 14 Frank Thomas	4.00	1.80
☐ 15 Mo Vaughn	1.25	.55

1997 Fleer Headliners

Randomly inserted in Fleer Series 2 packs at a rate of one in two, this 20-card set features color action photos of top players who make headlines for their teams. The backs carry player information.

	MINT	NRMT
COMPLETE SET (20)	12.00	5.50
COMMON CARD (1-20)	.25	.11
☐ 1 Jeff Bagwell	.75	.35
☐ 2 Albert Belle	.50	.23
☐ 3 Barry Bonds	.50	.23
☐ 4 Ken Caminiti	.40	.18
☐ 5 Juan Gonzalez	1.00	.45
☐ 6 Ken Griffey Jr.	2.00	.90
☐ 7 Tony Gwynn	1.00	.45
☐ 8 Derek Jeter	1.25	.55
☐ 9 Andruw Jones	1.25	.55
☐ 10 Chipper Jones	1.25	.55
☐ 11 Greg Maddux	1.25	.55
☐ 12 Mark McGwire	.75	.35
☐ 13 Paul Molitor	.40	.18
☐ 14 Eddie Murray	.40	.18
☐ 15 Mike Piazza	1.25	.55
☐ 16 Cal Ripken	1.50	.70
☐ 17 Alex Rodriguez	1.50	.70
☐ 18 Ryne Sandberg	.50	.23
☐ 19 John Smoltz	.25	.11
☐ 20 Frank Thomas	1.50	.70

1997 Fleer Lumber Company

Randomly inserted exclusively in Fleer Series 1 retail packs, this 18-card set features a selection of the game's top sluggers. The innovative design displays pure die-cut circular borders, simulating the effect of a cut tree.

	MINT	NRMT
COMPLETE SET (18)	180.00	80.00
COMMON CARD (1-18)	3.00	1.35
☐ 1 Brady Anderson	4.00	1.80
☐ 2 Jeff Bagwell	12.00	5.50
☐ 3 Albert Belle	8.00	3.60
☐ 4 Barry Bonds	8.00	3.60
☐ 5 Jay Buhner	4.00	1.80
☐ 6 Ellis Burks	3.00	1.35
☐ 7 Andres Galarraga	5.00	2.20
☐ 8 Juan Gonzalez	15.00	6.75
☐ 9 Ken Griffey Jr.	30.00	13.50
☐ 10 Todd Hundley	3.00	1.35
☐ 11 Ryan Klesko	4.00	1.80
☐ 12 Mark McGwire	12.00	5.50
☐ 13 Mike Piazza	20.00	9.00
☐ 14 Alex Rodriguez	20.00	9.00
☐ 15 Gary Sheffield	5.00	2.20
☐ 16 Sammy Sosa	5.00	2.20
☐ 17 Frank Thomas	25.00	11.00
☐ 18 Mo Vaughn	8.00	3.60

1997-98 Fleer Million Dollar Moments

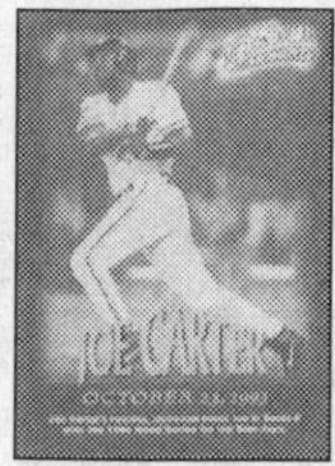

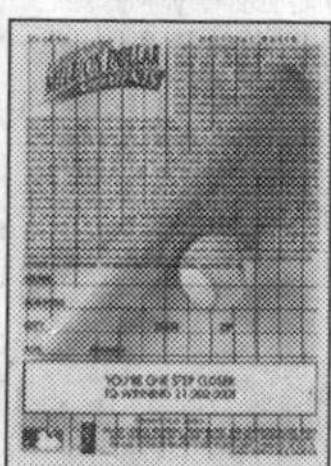

Inserted one per pack into 1997 Fleer 2, 1997 Flair Showcase, 1998 Fleer 1 and 1998 Ultra 1; these 50 cards mix a selection of retired legends with today's stars, highlighting key moments in baseball history. The first 45 cards in the set are common to find. Cards 46-50 are extremely shortprinted with each card being tougher to find than the next as you work your way up to card #50. Prior to the July 31st, 1998 deadline, collectors could mail in their 45-card sets (plus $5.99 for postage and handling) and receive a complete 50-card exchange set. The lucky collectors that managed to obtain one or more of the shortprinted cards could receive a shopping spree at card shops nationwide selected by Fleer. Each shortprinted card had to be mailed in along with a complete 45-card set to receive the following shopping allowances: #46/$100, #47/$250, #48/$500, #49/$1000. A grand prize of $1,000,000 cash (payable in increments of $50,000 annually over 20 years) was available for one collector that could obtain and redeem all five shortprint cards (#'s 46-50). This set was actually a part of a multi-sport promotion (baseball, basketball and football) for Fleer with each sport offering a separate $1,000,000 grand prize. In addition, 10,000 instant winner cards per sport (good for an assortment of material including shopping sprees, video games and various Fleer sets) were randomly seeded into packs. We are listing cards #46-50, however no prices are assigned for these cards.

	MINT	NRMT
COMPLETE SET (45)	8.00	3.60
COMMON CARD (1-45)	.10	.05
☐ 1 Checklist	.10	.05
☐ 2 Derek Jeter	.60	.25
☐ 3 Babe Ruth	1.50	.70
☐ 4 Barry Bonds	.40	.18
☐ 5 Brooks Robinson	.30	.14
☐ 6 Todd Hundley	.15	.07
☐ 7 Johnny Vander Meer	.10	.05
☐ 8 Cal Ripken	.75	.35
☐ 9 Bill Mazeroski	.15	.07
☐ 10 Chipper Jones	.60	.25
☐ 11 Frank Robinson	.30	.14
☐ 12 Roger Clemens	.40	.18
☐ 13 Bob Feller	.25	.11
☐ 14 Mike Piazza	.60	.25
☐ 15 Joe Nuxhall	.10	.05
☐ 16 Hideo Nomo	.50	.23
☐ 17 Jackie Robinson	1.00	.45
☐ 18 Orel Hershiser	.15	.07
☐ 19 Bobby Thomson	.15	.07
☐ 20 Joe Carter	.15	.07
☐ 21 Al Kaline	.30	.14
☐ 22 Bernie Williams	.25	.11
☐ 23 Don Larsen	.15	.07
☐ 24 Rickey Henderson	.15	.07
☐ 25 Maury Wills	.15	.07
☐ 26 Andruw Jones	.50	.23
☐ 27 Bobby Richardson	.15	.07
☐ 28 Alex Rodriguez	.75	.35
☐ 29 Jim Bunning	.25	.11
☐ 30 Ken Caminiti	.25	.11
☐ 31 Bob Gibson	.30	.14
☐ 32 Frank Thomas	.75	.35
☐ 33 Mickey Lolich	.15	.07
☐ 34 John Smoltz	.15	.07
☐ 35 Ron Swoboda	.10	.05
☐ 36 Albert Belle	.40	.18
☐ 37 Chris Chambliss	.15	.07
☐ 38 Juan Gonzalez	.50	.23
☐ 39 Ron Blomberg	.10	.05
☐ 40 John Wetteland	.15	.07
☐ 41 Carlton Fisk	.25	.11
☐ 42 Mo Vaughn	.25	.11

	MINT	NRMT
☐ 43 Bucky Dent	.15	.07
☐ 44 Greg Maddux	.60	.25
☐ 45 Willie Stargell	.25	.11
☐ 46 Tony Gwynn SP		
☐ 47 Joel Youngblood SP		
☐ 48 Andy Pettitte SP		
☐ 49 Mookie Wilson SP		
☐ 50 Jeff Bagwell SP		

1997 Fleer New Horizons

Randomly inserted in Fleer Series 2 packs at a rate of one in four, this 15-card set features borderless color action photos of Rookies and prospects. The backs carry player information.

	MINT	NRMT
COMPLETE SET (15)	15.00	6.75
COMMON CARD (1-15)	.25	.11
☐ 1 Bob Abreu		
☐ 2 Jose Cruz Jr.	5.00	2.20
☐ 3 Darin Erstad	1.25	.55
☐ 4 Nomar Garciaparra	2.50	1.10
☐ 5 Vladimir Guerrero	1.50	.70
☐ 6 Wilton Guerrero	.25	.11
☐ 7 Jose Guillen	1.00	.45
☐ 8 Hideki Irabu		
☐ 9 Andruw Jones	2.00	.90
☐ 10 Kevin Orie	.35	.16
☐ 11 Scott Rolen	2.00	.90
☐ 12 Scott Spiezio	.35	.16
☐ 13 Bubba Trammell	.35	.16
☐ 14 Todd Walker	.25	.11
☐ 15 Dmitri Young	.35	.16

1997 Fleer Night and Day

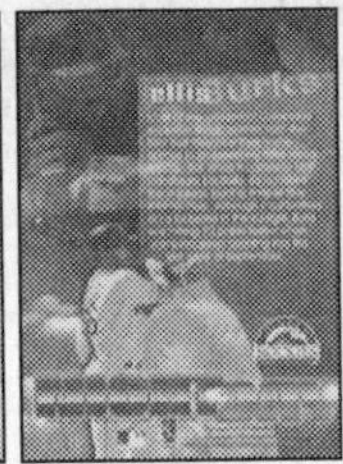

Randomly inserted in Fleer Series 1 packs at a rate of one in 240, this ten-card set features color action player photos of superstars who excel in day games, night games, or both and are printed on lenticular 3D cards. The backs carry player information.

	MINT	NRMT
COMPLETE SET (10)	350.00	160.00
COMMON CARD (1-10)	10.00	4.50
☐ 1 Barry Bonds	20.00	9.00
☐ 2 Ellis Burks	10.00	4.50
☐ 3 Juan Gonzalez	40.00	18.00
☐ 4 Ken Griffey Jr.	80.00	36.00
☐ 5 Mark McGwire	30.00	13.50
☐ 6 Mike Piazza	50.00	22.00
☐ 7 Manny Ramirez	20.00	9.00
☐ 8 Alex Rodriguez	50.00	22.00
☐ 9 John Smoltz	10.00	4.50
☐ 10 Frank Thomas	60.00	27.00

1997 Fleer Rookie Sensations

Randomly inserted in Fleer Series 1 packs at a rate of one in six, this 20-card set honors the top rookies from the 1996 season and the 1997 season rookies/prospects. The fronts freature color action player images on a multi-color swirling background. The backs carry a paragraph with information about the player.

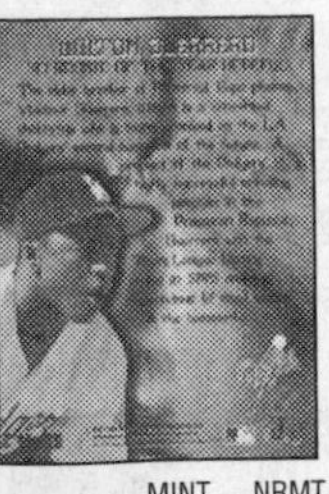

	MINT	NRMT
COMPLETE SET (20)	25.00	11.00
COMMON CARD (1-20)	.50	.23
☐ 1 Jermaine Allensworth	.50	.23
☐ 2 James Baldwin	.50	.23
☐ 3 Alan Benes	.75	.35
☐ 4 Jermaine Dye	.50	.23
☐ 5 Darin Erstad	4.00	1.80
☐ 6 Todd Hollandsworth	.75	.35
☐ 7 Derek Jeter	5.00	2.20
☐ 8 Jason Kendall	.75	.35
☐ 9 Alex Ochoa	.50	.23
☐ 10 Rey Ordonez	.50	.23
☐ 11 Edgar Renteria	.75	.35
☐ 12 Bob Abreu	1.25	.55
☐ 13 Nomar Garciaparra	3.00	1.35
☐ 14 Wilton Guerrero	.50	.23
☐ 15 Andruw Jones	8.00	3.60
☐ 16 Wendell Magee	.50	.23
☐ 17 Neifi Perez	.75	.35
☐ 18 Scott Rolen	3.00	1.35
☐ 19 Scott Spiezio	.75	.35
☐ 20 Todd Walker	.50	.23

1997 Fleer Soaring Stars

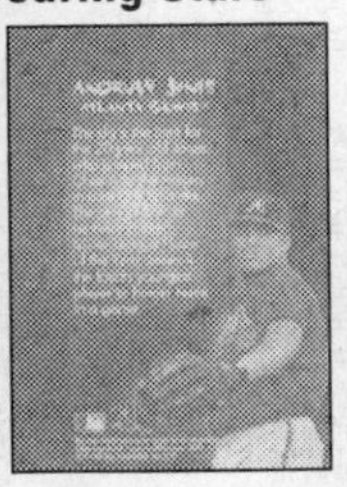

Randomly inserted in Fleer Series 2 packs at a rate of one in 12, this 12-card set features color action photos of players who enjoyed a meteoric rise to stardom and have all the skills to stay there. The player's image is set on a background of twinkling stars.

	MINT	NRMT
COMPLETE SET (12)	40.00	18.00
COMMON CARD (1-12)	1.50	.70
COMP.GLOWING SET (12)	800.00	350.00
COMMON GLOWING (1-12)	30.00	13.50
*GLOWING: 10X TO 20X BASIC CARDS		
☐ 1 Albert Belle	1.50	.70
☐ 2 Barry Bonds	1.50	.70
☐ 3 Juan Gonzalez	3.00	1.35
☐ 4 Ken Griffey Jr.	6.00	2.70
☐ 5 Derek Jeter	4.00	1.80
☐ 6 Andruw Jones	4.00	1.80
☐ 7 Chipper Jones	4.00	1.80
☐ 8 Greg Maddux	4.00	1.80
☐ 9 Mark McGwire	2.50	1.10
☐ 10 Mike Piazza	4.00	1.80
☐ 11 Alex Rodriguez	5.00	2.20
☐ 12 Frank Thomas	5.00	2.20

1997 Fleer Team Leaders

Randomly inserted in Fleer Series 1 packs at a rate of one in 20, this 28-card set honors statistical or inspirational leaders from each team on a die-cut card. The fronts feature color action player images with the player's face in the background. The backs carry a paragraph with information about the player.

	MINT	NRMT
COMPLETE SET (28)	110.00	50.00
COMMON CARD (1-28)	1.50	.70
☐ 1 Cal Ripken	15.00	6.75
☐ 2 Mo Vaughn	5.00	2.20
☐ 3 Jim Edmonds	4.00	1.80
☐ 4 Frank Thomas	15.00	6.75
☐ 5 Albert Belle	5.00	2.20
☐ 6 Bob Higginson	2.00	.90
☐ 7 Kevin Appier	2.00	.90
☐ 8 John Jaha	1.50	.70
☐ 9 Paul Molitor	4.00	1.80
☐ 10 Andy Pettitte	4.00	1.80
☐ 11 Mark McGwire	8.00	3.60
☐ 12 Ken Griffey Jr.	20.00	9.00
☐ 13 Juan Gonzalez	10.00	4.50
☐ 14 Pat Hentgen	2.00	.90
☐ 15 Chipper Jones	12.00	5.50
☐ 16 Mark Grace	3.00	1.35
☐ 17 Barry Larkin	3.00	1.35
☐ 18 Ellis Burks	2.00	.90
☐ 19 Gary Sheffield	4.00	1.80
☐ 20 Jeff Bagwell	8.00	3.60
☐ 21 Mike Piazza	12.00	5.50
☐ 22 Henry Rodriguez	1.50	.70
☐ 23 Todd Hundley	2.00	.90
☐ 24 Curt Schilling	2.00	.90
☐ 25 Jeff King	1.50	.70
☐ 26 Brian Jordan	1.50	.70
☐ 27 Tony Gwynn	10.00	4.50
☐ 28 Barry Bonds	5.00	2.20

1997 Fleer Zone

Randomly inserted in Fleer Series 1 hobby packs only at a rate of one in 80, this 20-card set features color player images of some of the 1996 season's unstoppable hitters and unhittable pitchers on a holographic card. The backs carry another color photo with a paragraph about the player.

	MINT	NRMT
COMPLETE SET (20)	250.00	110.00
COMMON CARD (1-20)	4.00	1.80
☐ 1 Jeff Bagwell	15.00	6.75
☐ 2 Albert Belle	10.00	4.50
☐ 3 Barry Bonds	10.00	4.50
☐ 4 Ken Caminiti	8.00	3.60
☐ 5 Andres Galarraga	8.00	3.60
☐ 6 Juan Gonzalez	20.00	9.00
☐ 7 Ken Griffey Jr.	40.00	18.00
☐ 8 Tony Gwynn	20.00	9.00
☐ 9 Chipper Jones	25.00	11.00
☐ 10 Greg Maddux	25.00	11.00
☐ 11 Mark McGwire	15.00	6.75
☐ 12 Dean Palmer	4.00	1.80
☐ 13 Andy Pettitte	10.00	4.50
☐ 14 Mike Piazza	25.00	11.00
☐ 15 Alex Rodriguez	25.00	11.00
☐ 16 Gary Sheffield	8.00	3.60
☐ 17 John Smoltz	4.50	2.00
☐ 18 Frank Thomas	30.00	13.50
☐ 19 Jim Thome	8.00	3.60
☐ 20 Matt Williams	5.00	2.20

1998 Fleer Diamond Ink

Randomly inserted one per Series 1 Fleer and Ultra packs, these point cards feature a selection of top stars. Collectors that saved up 500 points of a specific player could redeem the cards for a baseball signed by that player. Point cards came in 1, 5 and 10 point increments. Judging from supplies on the secondary market at the

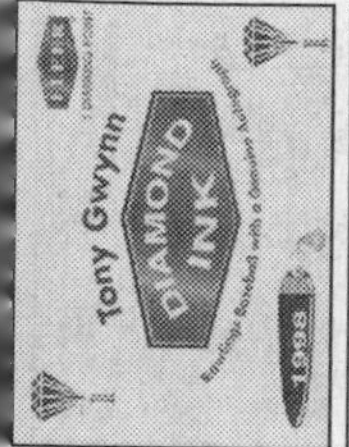

time of the promotion it appears that a few players were in much shorter supply than other - most notably Roger Clemens, Tony Gwynn, Greg Maddux and Alex Rodriguez. Finally, Greg Maddux was a late additon to the promotion, thus his point cards were made available only in Fleer 1 packs (which happened to be released about four to six weeks after Ultra 1).

	MINT	NRMT
J.BUHNER POINT	.10	.05
R.CLEMENS POINT	.25	.11
J.CRUZ JR. POINT	.25	.11
N.GARCIAPARRA POINT	.20	.09
T.GWYNN POINT	.20	.09
R.HERNANDEZ POINT	.05	.02
A.RODRIGUEZ POINT	.25	.11
S.ROLEN POINT	.15	.07
T.WOMACK POINT	.05	.02

1992 French's

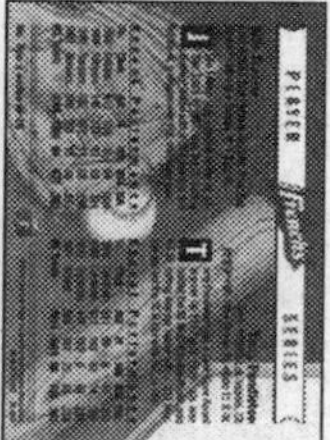

The 1992 French's Special Edition Combo Series consists of 18 two-player cards and a title/checklist card. The cards measure the standard size. Each card features one player from the American League and one player from the National League. The cards were licensed by the MLBPA and produced by MSA (Michael Schechter Associates). Collectors could obtain the title/checklist card and three free player cards through an on-pack promotion by purchasing a 16 oz. size of French's Classic Yellow Mustard (the cards were enclosed in a plastic hangtag). Alternatively, collectors could collect all 18 player cards in the series by sending in 3.00 plus 75 cents for postage and handling along with one quality seal from the 16 oz. size of French's Classic Yellow Mustard. The released production figures were 43,000 18-card sets and 1,800,000 three-card hangtags. Both sides of the card are vertically oriented; the two color action player photos on the front are bordered in green. A white stripe with the words "Player Series" cuts across the top and intersects the French's trademark logo. Two baseball bats and a ball edge the pictures at the bottom. On a green background that features a glove, ball, bat, and home plate, the backs carry biography, player profile, and recent performance statistics for each player.

	MINT	NRMT
COMPLETE SET (19)	8.00	3.60
COMMON PAIR (1-18)	.25	.11
☐ 1 Chuck Knoblauch and Jeff Bagwell	.75	.35
☐ 2 Roger Clemens and Tom Glavine	.75	.35
☐ 3 Julio Franco and Terry Pendleton	.25	.11
☐ 4 Jose Canseco and Howard Johnson	.50	.23
☐ 5 Scott Erickson and John Smiley	.25	.11
☐ 6 Bryan Harvey and Lee Smith	.25	.11
☐ 7 Kirby Puckett and Barry Bonds	1.00	.45
☐ 8 Robin Ventura and Matt Williams	.50	.23
☐ 9 Tony Pena and Tom Pagnozzi	.25	.11
☐ 10 Sandy Alomar Jr. and Benito Santiago	.40	.18
☐ 11 Don Mattingly and Will Clark	1.00	.45
☐ 12 Roberto Alomar and Ryne Sandberg	1.00	.45
☐ 13 Cal Ripken and Ozzie Smith	2.50	1.10
☐ 14 Wade Boggs and Chris Sabo	.50	.23
☐ 15 Ken Griffey Jr. and Dave Justice	2.00	.90
☐ 16 Joe Carter and Tony Gwynn	1.00	.45
☐ 17 Rickey Henderson and Darryl Strawberry	.50	.23
☐ 18 Jack Morris and Steve Avery	.25	.11
☐ NNO Title/Checklist Card	.25	.11

1993 Fun Pack

This 225-card standard-size single series set was issued by Upper Deck and targeted primarily at youngsters. Cards were distributed exclusively in hobby and retail foil fin-wrapped packs. Each card has a front that display action player photos on a bright multicolored background. The team name is printed in yellow at the top right and the player's name appears below the photo within the irregular green border. Topical subsets featured are Stars of Tomorrow (1-9), Hot Shots (10-21), Kid Stars (22-27), Upper Deck Heroes (28-36), All-Star Advice (210-215), All-Star Fold Outs (216-220), and Checklists (221-225) and randomly numbered Glow Stars. Card numbers 37-209 are arranged alphabetically according to team names, with each team subset beginning with a Glow Star card. There are no key Rookie Cards in this set.The Hot Shot subset cards were only available in retail packs or through a as a mail-in redemption promotion available in hobby packs.

	MINT	NRMT
COMPLETE SET (225)	40.00	18.00
COMMON CARD (1-225)	.05	.02
☐ 1 Wil Cordero SOT	.05	.02
☐ 2 Brent Gates SOT	.05	.02
☐ 3 Benji Gil SOT	.05	.02
☐ 4 Phil Hiatt SOT	.05	.02
☐ 5 David McCarty SOT	.05	.02
☐ 6 Mike Piazza SOT	2.00	.90
☐ 7 Tim Salmon SOT	.50	.23
☐ 8 J.T. Snow SOT	.30	.14
☐ 9 Kevin Young SOT	.05	.02
☐ 10 Roberto Alomar HS	.75	.35
☐ 11 Barry Bonds HS	1.00	.45
☐ 12 Jose Canseco HS	.20	.09
☐ 13 Will Clark HS	.20	.09
☐ 14 Roger Clemens HS	.75	.35
☐ 15 Juan Gonzalez HS	2.00	.90
☐ 16 Ken Griffey Jr. HS	4.00	1.80
☐ 17 Mark McGwire HS	1.25	.55
☐ 18 Nolan Ryan HS	4.00	1.80
☐ 19 Ryne Sandberg HS	1.00	.45
☐ 20 Gary Sheffield HS	.15	.07
☐ 21 Frank Thomas HS	4.00	1.80
☐ 22 Roberto Alomar KS	.15	.07
☐ 23 Roger Clemens KS	.15	.07
☐ 24 Ken Griffey Jr. KS	1.00	.45
☐ 25 Gary Sheffield KS	.15	.07
☐ 26 Nolan Ryan KS	.75	.35
☐ 27 Frank Thomas KS	1.00	.45
☐ 28 Reggie Jackson HERO	.15	.07
☐ 29 Roger Clemens HERO	.15	.07
☐ 30 Ken Griffey Jr. HERO	1.00	.45
☐ 31 Bo Jackson HERO	.15	.07
☐ 32 Cal Ripken Jr. HERO	.75	.35
☐ 33 Nolan Ryan HERO	.75	.35
☐ 34 Deion Sanders HERO	.15	.07
☐ 35 Ozzie Smith HERO	.15	.07
☐ 36 Frank Thomas HERO	1.00	.45
☐ 37 Tim Salmon GS	.25	.11
☐ 38 Chili Davis	.15	.07
☐ 39 Chuck Finley	.05	.02
☐ 40 Mark Langston	.05	.02
☐ 41 Luis Polonia	.05	.02
☐ 42 Jeff Bagwell GS	.15	.07
☐ 43 Jeff Bagwell	.75	.35
☐ 44 Craig Biggio	.25	.11
☐ 45 Ken Caminiti	.15	.07
☐ 46 Doug Drabek	.05	.02
☐ 47 Steve Finley	.15	.07
☐ 48 Mark McGwire GS	.15	.07
☐ 49 Dennis Eckersley	.25	.11
☐ 50 Rickey Henderson	.25	.11
☐ 51 Mark McGwire	.60	.25
☐ 52 Ruben Sierra	.05	.02
☐ 53 Terry Steinbach	.15	.07
☐ 54 Roberto Alomar GS	.25	.11
☐ 55 Roberto Alomar	.15	.07
☐ 56 Joe Carter	.25	.11
☐ 57 Juan Guzman	.05	.02
☐ 58 Paul Molitor	.15	.07
☐ 59 Jack Morris	.15	.07
☐ 60 John Olerud	.05	.02
☐ 61 Tom Glavine GS	.25	.11
☐ 62 Steve Avery	.05	.02
☐ 63 Tom Glavine	.25	.11
☐ 64 David Justice	.25	.11
☐ 65 Greg Maddux	1.25	.55
☐ 66 Terry Pendleton	.05	.02
☐ 67 Deion Sanders	.15	.07
☐ 68 John Smoltz	.25	.11
☐ 69 Robin Yount GS	.25	.11
☐ 70 Cal Eldred	.05	.02
☐ 71 Pat Listach	.05	.02
☐ 72 Greg Vaughn	.05	.02
☐ 73 Robin Yount	.25	.11
☐ 74 Ozzie Smith GS	.15	.07
☐ 75 Gregg Jefferies	.15	.07
☐ 76 Ray Lankford	.25	.11
☐ 77 Lee Smith	.15	.07
☐ 78 Ozzie Smith	.50	.23
☐ 79 Bob Tewksbury	.05	.02
☐ 80 Ryne Sandberg GS	.15	.07
☐ 81 Mark Grace	.25	.11
☐ 82 Mike Morgan	.05	.02
☐ 83 Randy Myers	.15	.07
☐ 84 Ryne Sandberg	.50	.23
☐ 85 Sammy Sosa	.15	.07
☐ 86 Eric Karros GS	.15	.07
☐ 87 Brett Butler	.15	.07
☐ 88 Orel Hershiser	.15	.07
☐ 89 Eric Karros	.15	.07
☐ 90 Ramon Martinez	.15	.07
☐ 91 Jose Offerman	.05	.02
☐ 92 Darryl Strawberry	.15	.07
☐ 93 Marquis Grissom GS	.15	.07
☐ 94 Delino DeShields	.05	.02
☐ 95 Marquis Grissom	.15	.07
☐ 96 Ken Hill	.15	.07
☐ 97 Dennis Martinez	.15	.07
☐ 98 Larry Walker	.15	.07
☐ 99 Barry Bonds GS	.15	.07
☐ 100 Barry Bonds	.50	.23
☐ 101 Will Clark	.25	.11
☐ 102 Bill Swift	.05	.02
☐ 103 Robby Thompson	.05	.02
☐ 104 Matt Williams	.25	.11
☐ 105 Carlos Baerga GS	.05	.02
☐ 106 Sandy Alomar Jr.	.15	.07
☐ 107 Carlos Baerga	.15	.07
☐ 108 Albert Belle	.75	.35
☐ 109 Kenny Lofton	.75	.35
☐ 110 Charles Nagy	.15	.07
☐ 111 Ken Griffey Jr. GS	1.00	.45
☐ 112 Jay Buhner	.25	.11
☐ 113 Dave Fleming	.05	.02
☐ 114 Ken Griffey Jr.	2.00	.90
☐ 115 Randy Johnson	.15	.07
☐ 116 Edgar Martinez	.25	.11
☐ 117 Benito Santiago GS	.05	.02
☐ 118 Bret Barberie	.05	.02
☐ 119 Jeff Conine	.15	.07
☐ 120 Brian Harvey	.05	.02
☐ 121 Benito Santiago	.05	.02
☐ 122 Walt Weiss	.05	.02
☐ 123 Dwight Gooden GS	.05	.02
☐ 124 Bobby Bonilla	.15	.07
☐ 125 Tony Fernandez	.05	.02
☐ 126 Dwight Gooden	.15	.07
☐ 127 Howard Johnson	.05	.02
☐ 128 Eddie Murray	.15	.07
☐ 129 Bret Saberhagen	.05	.02
☐ 130 Cal Ripken Jr. GS	.75	.35
☐ 131 Brady Anderson	.25	.11
☐ 132 Mike Devereaux	.05	.02
☐ 133 Ben McDonald	.05	.02
☐ 134 Mike Mussina	.15	.07

Card	MINT	NRMT
☐ 135 Cal Ripken Jr.	1.50	.70
☐ 136 Fred McGriff GS	.15	.07
☐ 137 Andy Benes	.15	.07
☐ 138 Tony Gwynn	.75	.35
☐ 139 Fred McGriff	.25	.11
☐ 140 Phil Plantier	.05	.02
☐ 141 Gary Sheffield	.15	.07
☐ 142 Darren Daulton GS	.15	.07
☐ 143 Darren Daulton	.15	.07
☐ 144 Len Dykstra	.15	.07
☐ 145 Dave Hollins	.05	.02
☐ 146 John Kruk	.15	.07
☐ 147 Mitch Williams	.05	.02
☐ 148 Andy Van Slyke GS	.05	.02
☐ 149 Jay Bell	.15	.07
☐ 150 Zane Smith	.05	.02
☐ 151 Andy Van Slyke	.15	.07
☐ 152 Tim Wakefield	.05	.02
☐ 153 Juan Gonzalez GS	.15	.07
☐ 154 Kevin Brown	.15	.07
☐ 155 Jose Canseco	.25	.11
☐ 156 Juan Gonzalez	1.00	.45
☐ 157 Rafael Palmeiro	.25	.11
☐ 158 Dean Palmer	.15	.07
☐ 159 Ivan Rodriguez	.50	.23
☐ 160 Nolan Ryan	1.50	.70
☐ 161 Roger Clemens GS	.15	.07
☐ 162 Roger Clemens	.40	.18
☐ 163 Andre Dawson	.25	.11
☐ 164 Mike Greenwell	.05	.02
☐ 165 Tony Pena	.05	.02
☐ 166 Frank Viola	.05	.02
☐ 167 Barry Larkin GS	.15	.07
☐ 168 Rob Dibble	.05	.02
☐ 169 Roberto Kelly	.05	.02
☐ 170 Barry Larkin	.25	.11
☐ 171 Kevin Mitchell	.15	.07
☐ 172 Bip Roberts	.05	.02
☐ 173 Andres Galarraga GS	.25	.11
☐ 174 Dante Bichette	.25	.11
☐ 175 Jerald Clark	.05	.02
☐ 176 Andres Galarraga	.25	.11
☐ 177 Charlie Hayes	.05	.02
☐ 178 David Nied	.05	.02
☐ 179 David Cone GS	.15	.07
☐ 180 Kevin Appier	.15	.07
☐ 181 George Brett	.75	.35
☐ 182 David Cone	.15	.07
☐ 183 Felix Jose	.05	.02
☐ 184 Wally Joyner	.15	.07
☐ 185 Cecil Fielder GS	.15	.07
☐ 186 Cecil Fielder	.15	.07
☐ 187 Travis Fryman	.15	.07
☐ 188 Tony Phillips	.05	.02
☐ 189 Mickey Tettleton	.05	.02
☐ 190 Lou Whitaker	.15	.07
☐ 191 Kirby Puckett GS	.15	.07
☐ 192 Scott Erickson	.05	.02
☐ 193 Chuck Knoblauch	.15	.07
☐ 194 Shane Mack	.05	.02
☐ 195 Kirby Puckett	.75	.35
☐ 196 Dave Winfield	.25	.11
☐ 197 Frank Thomas GS	1.00	.45
☐ 198 George Bell	.05	.02
☐ 199 Bo Jackson	.15	.07
☐ 200 Jack McDowell	.05	.02
☐ 201 Tim Raines	.15	.07
☐ 202 Frank Thomas	2.00	.90
☐ 203 Robin Ventura	.15	.07
☐ 204 Jim Abbott GS	.05	.02
☐ 205 Jim Abbott	.05	.02
☐ 206 Wade Boggs	.15	.07
☐ 207 Jimmy Key	.15	.07
☐ 208 Don Mattingly	1.00	.45
☐ 209 Danny Tartabull	.05	.02
☐ 210 Brett Butler ASA	.05	.02
☐ 211 Tony Gwynn ASA	.40	.18
☐ 212 Rickey Henderson ASA	.15	.07
☐ 213 Ramon Martinez ASA	.05	.02
☐ 214 Nolan Ryan ASA	.75	.35
☐ 215 Ozzie Smith ASA	.15	.07
☐ 216 Marquis Grissom FOLD	.15	.07
☐ 217 Dean Palmer FOLD	.15	.07
☐ 218 Cal Ripken Jr. FOLD	.75	.35
☐ 219 Deion Sanders FOLD	.15	.07
☐ 220 Darryl Strawberry FOLD	.15	.07
☐ 221 David McCarty CL	.05	.02
☐ 222 Barry Bonds CL	.15	.07
☐ 223 Juan Gonzalez CL	.15	.07
☐ 224 Ken Griffey Jr. CL	1.00	.45
☐ 225 Frank Thomas CL	1.00	.45
☐ NNO Hot Shots Card Expired	.15	.07
☐ NNO Hot Shots Card Punched	.15	.07

1993 Fun Pack All-Stars

Randomly inserted in 1993 Upper Deck Fun Packs, these nine foldouts feature combinations by position for American and National leaue All-Stars. The cards measure the standard size when closed and 2 1/2" by 7" when opened. The front of each features side-by-side color action photos of an American League and a National League player. The set's title appears above the photos within a blue stripe. The players' names appear within an irregular white stripe near the bottom. The blue-and-white back carries the rules for playing the scratch-off game and a section to keep score. The actual scratch-off lineups appear when the card is opened. The American League players and their scratch-off circles are displayed within the reddish left side of the foldout, and their National League counterparts appear within the bluish right side.

	MINT	NRMT
COMPLETE SET (9)	15.00	6.75
COMMON PAIR (AS1-AS9)	.50	.23

Card	MINT	NRMT
☐ AS1 Frank Thomas Fred McGriff	4.00	1.80
☐ AS2 Ivan Rodriguez Darren Daulton	1.00	.45
☐ AS3 Mark McGwire Will Clark	1.00	.45
☐ AS4 Roberto Alomar Ryne Sandberg	2.00	.90
☐ AS5 Robin Ventura Terry Pendleton	.50	.23
☐ AS6 Cal Ripken Ozzie Smith	4.00	1.80
☐ AS7 Juan Gonzalez Barry Bonds	2.00	.90
☐ AS8 Ken Griffey Jr. Marquis Grissom	5.00	2.20
☐ AS9 Kirby Puckett Tony Gwynn	4.00	1.80

1993 Fun Pack Mascots

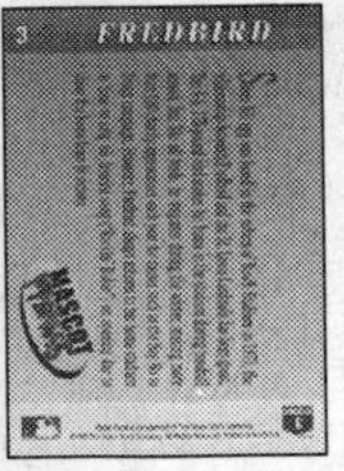

Randomly inserted in 1993 Upper Deck Fun Packs, these five standard-size horizontal cards feature two mascot photos on their fronts. On the left is a color photo, on the right is the hologram. These photos appear over a background that shades from yellow to orange, from right to left. The mascot's name appears vertically in white lettering within pink and purple stripes on the left edge. The words "Mascot Madness" appear in multicolored lettering within a yellow oval near the bottom. The back is similarly designed, except the photos are replaced by the mascot's career highlights and a white stripe up the right edge carries the Major League Baseball and the MLBPA logos.

	MINT	NRMT
COMPLETE SET (5)	4.00	1.80
COMMON CARD (1-5)	.75	.35

Card	MINT	NRMT
☐ 1 Phillie Phanatic	1.50	.70
☐ 2 Pirate Parrot	.75	.35
☐ 3 Fredbird	.75	.35
☐ 4 BJ Birdie	.75	.35
☐ 5 Youppi	.75	.35

1994 Fun Pack

Issued by Upper Deck for the second straight year, the Fun Pack set consists of 240 cards. Bright yellow and green borders surround a color player photo on the front.

The backs, with much the same color scheme, are horizontal and contain a cartoon relating to the player and statistics. The following subsets are included in this set: Stars of Tomorrow (1-9), Standouts (175-192), Pro-Files (193-198), Headline Stars (199-207), What's the Call (208-216), Foldouts (217-225) and Fun Cards (226-234). Michael Jordan's baseball Rookie Card is in this set.

	MINT	NRMT
COMPLETE SET (240)	65.00	29.00
COMMON CARD (1-240)	.10	.05

Card	MINT	NRMT
☐ 1 Manny Ramirez	1.00	.45
☐ 2 Cliff Floyd	.20	.09
☐ 3 Rondell White	.35	.16
☐ 4 Carlos Delgado	.50	.23
☐ 5 Chipper Jones	2.50	1.10
☐ 6 Javier Lopez	.35	.16
☐ 7 Ryan Klesko	.50	.23
☐ 8 Steve Karsay	.10	.05
☐ 9 Rich Becker	.20	.09
☐ 10 Gary Sheffield	.50	.23
☐ 11 Jeffrey Hammonds	.35	.16
☐ 12 Roberto Alomar	.50	.23
☐ 13 Brent Gates	.10	.05
☐ 14 Andres Galarraga	.35	.16
☐ 15 Tim Salmon	.50	.23
☐ 16 Dwight Gooden	.20	.09
☐ 17 Mark Grace	.35	.16
☐ 18 Andy Van Slyke	.20	.09
☐ 19 Juan Gonzalez	1.50	.70
☐ 20 Mickey Tettleton	.10	.05
☐ 21 Roger Clemens	.60	.25
☐ 22 Will Clark	.35	.16
☐ 23 David Justice	.50	.23
☐ 24 Ken Griffey Jr.	3.00	1.35
☐ 25 Barry Bonds	.75	.35
☐ 26 Bill Swift	.10	.05
☐ 27 Fred McGriff	.35	.16
☐ 28 Randy Myers	.10	.05
☐ 29 Joe Carter	.20	.09
☐ 30 Nigel Wilson	.10	.05
☐ 31 Mike Piazza	2.00	.90
☐ 32 Dave Winfield	.35	.16
☐ 33 Steve Avery	.10	.05
☐ 34 Kirby Puckett	1.25	.55
☐ 35 Frank Thomas	3.00	1.35
☐ 36 Aaron Sele	.10	.05
☐ 37 Ricky Gutierrez	.10	.05
☐ 38 Curt Schilling	.20	.09
☐ 39 Mike Greenwell	.10	.05
☐ 40 Andy Benes	.20	.09
☐ 41 Kevin Brown	.20	.09
☐ 42 Mo Vaughn	.75	.35
☐ 43 Dennis Eckersley	.35	.16
☐ 44 Ken Hill	.10	.05
☐ 45 Cecil Fielder	.20	.09
☐ 46 Bobby Jones	.20	.09
☐ 47 Tom Glavine	.35	.16
☐ 48 Wally Joyner	.20	.09
☐ 49 Ellis Burks	.20	.09
☐ 50 Jason Bere	.10	.05
☐ 51 Randy Johnson	.50	.23
☐ 52 Darryl Kile	.20	.09
☐ 53 Jeff Montgomery	.10	.05
☐ 54 Alex Fernandez	.10	.05
☐ 55 Kevin Appier	.20	.09
☐ 56 Brian McRae	.10	.05
☐ 57 John Wetteland	.20	.09
☐ 58 Bob Tewksbury	.10	.05
☐ 59 Todd Van Poppel	.10	.05
☐ 60 Ryne Sandberg	.75	.35
☐ 61 Bret Barberie	.10	.05
☐ 62 Phil Plantier	.10	.05
☐ 63 Chris Hoiles	.10	.05
☐ 64 Tony Phillips	.10	.05
☐ 65 Salomon Torres	.10	.05
☐ 66 Juan Guzman	.10	.05
☐ 67 Paul O'Neill	.20	.09
☐ 68 Dante Bichette	.35	.16
☐ 69 Lenny Dykstra	.20	.09
☐ 70 Ivan Rodriguez	.75	.35
☐ 71 Dean Palmer	.20	.09
☐ 72 Brett Butler	.20	.09

Card	NRMT-MT	EXC
☐ 73 Rick Aguilera	.10	.05
☐ 74 Robby Thompson	.10	.05
☐ 75 Jim Abbott	.10	.05
☐ 76 Al Martin	.10	.05
☐ 77 Roberto Hernandez	.20	.09
☐ 78 Jay Buhner	.35	.16
☐ 79 Devon White	.10	.05
☐ 80 Travis Fryman	.20	.09
☐ 81 Jeromy Burnitz	.20	.09
☐ 82 John Burkett	.10	.05
☐ 83 Orlando Merced	.10	.05
☐ 84 Jose Rijo	.10	.05
☐ 85 Eddie Murray	.50	.23
☐ 86 Howard Johnson	.10	.05
☐ 87 Chuck Carr	.10	.05
☐ 88 Pedro J. Martinez	.50	.23
☐ 89 Charlie Hayes	.10	.05
☐ 90 Matt Williams	.35	.16
☐ 91 Steve Finley	.20	.09
☐ 92 Pat Listach	.10	.05
☐ 93 Sandy Alomar Jr.	.20	.09
☐ 94 Delino DeShields	.10	.05
☐ 95 Rod Beck	.20	.09
☐ 96 Todd Zeile UER (Card misnumbered 97)	.10	.05
☐ 97 Duane Ward UER (Card misnumbered 98)	.10	.05
☐ 98 Darryl Hamilton	.10	.05
☐ 99 John Olerud	.20	.09
☐ 100 Andre Dawson	.35	.16
☐ 101 Ozzie Smith	.75	.35
☐ 102 Rick Wilkins	.10	.05
☐ 103 Alan Trammell	.35	.16
☐ 104 Jeff Blauser	.10	.05
☐ 105 Bret Boone	.10	.05
☐ 106 J.T. Snow	.20	.09
☐ 107 Kenny Lofton	1.00	.45
☐ 108 Cal Ripken Jr.	2.50	1.10
☐ 109 Carlos Baerga	.20	.09
☐ 110 Bip Roberts	.10	.05
☐ 111 Barry Larkin	.35	.16
☐ 112 Mark Langston	.10	.05
☐ 113 Ozzie Guillen	.10	.05
☐ 114 Chad Curtis	.10	.05
☐ 115 Dave Hollins	.10	.05
☐ 116 Reggie Sanders	.10	.05
☐ 117 Jeff Conine	.20	.09
☐ 118 Mark Whiten	.10	.05
☐ 119 Tony Gwynn	1.25	.55
☐ 120 John Kruk	.20	.09
☐ 121 Eduardo Perez	.10	.05
☐ 122 Walt Weiss	.10	.05
☐ 123 Don Mattingly	1.50	.70
☐ 124 Rickey Henderson	.35	.16
☐ 125 Mark McGwire	1.00	.45
☐ 126 Wade Boggs	.50	.23
☐ 127 Bobby Bonilla	.20	.09
☐ 128 Jeff King	.20	.09
☐ 129 Jack McDowell	.10	.05
☐ 130 Albert Belle	1.25	.55
☐ 131 Greg Maddux	2.00	.90
☐ 132 Dennis Martinez	.20	.09
☐ 133 Jose Canseco	.35	.16
☐ 134 Bryan Harvey	.10	.05
☐ 135 Dave Fleming	.10	.05
☐ 136 Larry Walker	.50	.23
☐ 137 Ken Caminiti	.50	.23
☐ 138 Doug Drabek	.10	.05
☐ 139 Alex Gonzalez	.10	.05
☐ 140 Darren Daulton	.20	.09
☐ 141 Ruben Sierra	.10	.05
☐ 142 Kirk Rueter	.10	.05
☐ 143 Raul Mondesi	.50	.23
☐ 144 Greg Vaughn	.10	.05
☐ 145 Danny Tartabull	.10	.05
☐ 146 Eric Karros	.20	.09
☐ 147 Chuck Knoblauch	.50	.23
☐ 148 Mike Mussina	.50	.23
☐ 149 Brady Anderson	.35	.16
☐ 150 Paul Molitor	.50	.23
☐ 151 Bo Jackson	.20	.09
☐ 152 Jeff Bagwell	1.25	.55
☐ 153 Gregg Jefferies UER Name spelled Greg on front	.20	.09
☐ 154 Rafael Palmeiro	.35	.16
☐ 155 Orel Hershiser	.20	.09
☐ 156 Derek Bell	.20	.09
☐ 157 Jeff Kent	.10	.05
☐ 158 Craig Biggio	.35	.16
☐ 159 Marquis Grissom	.20	.09
☐ 160 Matt Mieske	.10	.05
☐ 161 Jay Bell	.20	.09
☐ 162 Sammy Sosa	.50	.23
☐ 163 Robin Ventura	.20	.09
☐ 164 Deion Sanders	.50	.23
☐ 165 Jimmy Key	.20	.09
☐ 166 Cal Eldred	.10	.05
☐ 167 David McCarty	.10	.05
☐ 168 Carlos Garcia	.10	.05
☐ 169 Willie Greene	.20	.09
☐ 170 Michael Jordan	10.00	4.50
☐ 171 Roberto Mejia	.10	.05
☐ 172 Phil Hiatt UER (Card misnumbered 72)	.10	.05
☐ 173 Marc Newfield	.20	.09
☐ 174 Kevin Stocker	.10	.05
☐ 175 Randy Johnson STA	.50	.23
☐ 176 Ivan Rodriguez STA	.50	.23
☐ 177 Frank Thomas STA	1.50	.70
☐ 178 Roberto Alomar STA	.50	.23
☐ 179 Travis Fryman STA	.20	.09
☐ 180 Cal Ripken Jr. STA	1.25	.55
☐ 181 Juan Gonzalez STA	.75	.35
☐ 182 Ken Griffey Jr. STA	1.50	.70
☐ 183 Albert Belle STA	.50	.23
☐ 184 Greg Maddux STA	1.00	.45
☐ 185 Mike Piazza STA	1.00	.45
☐ 186 Fred McGriff STA	.35	.16
☐ 187 Robby Thompson STA	.10	.05
☐ 188 Matt Williams STA	.35	.16
☐ 189 Jeff Blauser STA	.10	.05
☐ 190 Barry Bonds STA	.50	.23
☐ 191 Lenny Dykstra STA	.10	.05
☐ 192 David Justice STA	.50	.23
☐ 193 Ken Griffey Jr. PF	1.50	.70
☐ 194 Barry Bonds PF	.50	.23
☐ 195 Frank Thomas PF	1.50	.70
☐ 196 Juan Gonzalez PF	.50	.23
☐ 197 Randy Johnson PF	.50	.23
☐ 198 Chuck Carr PF	.10	.05
☐ 199 Barry Bonds HES Juan Gonzalez	1.25	.55
☐ 200 Ken Griffey Jr. HES Don Mattingly	2.50	1.10
☐ 201 Roberto Alomar HES Carlos Baerga	.20	.09
☐ 202 Dave Winfield HES Robin Yount	.35	.16
☐ 203 Mike Piazza HES Tim Salmon	.75	.35
☐ 204 Albert Belle HES Frank Thomas	2.00	.90
☐ 205 Cliff Floyd HES Rondell White	.20	.09
☐ 206 Kirby Puckett HES Tony Gwynn	1.25	.55
☐ 207 Roger Clemens HES Greg Maddux	1.25	.55
☐ 208 Mike Piazza WC	1.00	.45
☐ 209 Jose Canseco WC	.35	.16
☐ 210 Frank Thomas WC	1.50	.70
☐ 211 Roberto Alomar WC	.50	.23
☐ 212 Barry Bonds WC	.50	.23
☐ 213 Rickey Henderson WC	.50	.23
☐ 214 John Kruk WC	.10	.05
☐ 215 Juan Gonzalez WC	.50	.23
☐ 216 Ken Griffey Jr. WC	1.50	.70
☐ 217 Roberto Alomar FOLD SP	.50	.23
☐ 218 Craig Biggio FOLD	.35	.16
☐ 219 Cal Ripken Jr. FOLD	1.25	.55
☐ 220 Mike Piazza FOLD	1.00	.45
☐ 221 Brent Gates FOLD	.10	.05
☐ 222 Walt Weiss FOLD	.10	.05
☐ 223 Bobby Bonilla FOLD	.20	.09
☐ 224 Ken Griffey Jr. FOLD	1.50	.70
☐ 225 Barry Bonds FOLD	.50	.23
☐ 226 Barry Bonds FUN	.50	.23
☐ 227 Joe Carter FUN	.20	.09
☐ 228 Mike Greenwell FUN	.10	.05
☐ 229 Ken Griffey Jr. FUN	1.50	.70
☐ 230 John Kruk FUN	.10	.05
☐ 231 Mike Piazza FUN	1.00	.45
☐ 232 Kirby Puckett FUN	.50	.23
☐ 233 John Smoltz FUN	.50	.23
☐ 234 Rick Wilkins FUN	.10	.05
☐ 235 Ken Griffey Jr. CL	1.50	.70
☐ 236 Frank Thomas CL	1.50	.70
☐ 237 Barry Bonds CL	.50	.23
☐ 238 Mike Piazza CL	1.00	.45
☐ 239 Tim Salmon CL	.50	.23
☐ 240 Juan Gonzalez CL	.50	.23
☐ P172 Ken Griffey Jr. Promo	3.00	1.35

1983 Giants Mother's

The cards in this 20-card set measure the standard size. For the first time in 30 years, Mother's Cookies issued a baseball card set. The full color set, produced by hobbyist Barry Colla, features San Francisco Giants players only. Fifteen cards were issued at the Houston Astros vs. San Francisco Giants game of August 7, 1983. Five of the cards were redeemable by sending in a coupon. The five additional cards received from redemption of the coupon

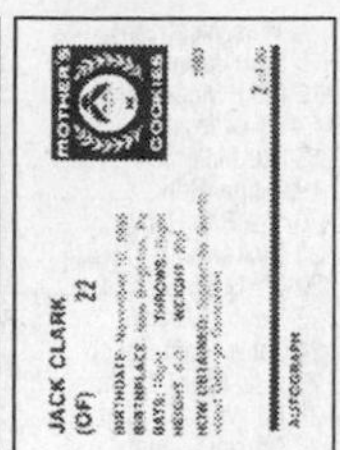

were not guaranteed to be the five needed to complete the set. The fronts feature the player's photo, his name, and the Giants' logo, while the backs feature player biographies and the Mother's Cookies logo. The backs also contain a space in which to obtain the player's autograph.

	NRMT-MT	EXC
COMPLETE SET (20)	12.00	5.50
COMMON CARD (1-20)	.50	.23
☐ 1 Frank Robinson MG	2.50	1.10
☐ 2 Jack Clark	1.00	.45
☐ 3 Chili Davis	1.50	.70
☐ 4 Johnnie LeMaster	.50	.23
☐ 5 Greg Minton	.50	.23
☐ 6 Bob Brenly	.50	.23
☐ 7 Fred Breining	.50	.23
☐ 8 Jeff Leonard	.50	.23
☐ 9 Darrell Evans	1.50	.70
☐ 10 Tom O'Malley	.50	.23
☐ 11 Duane Kuiper	.50	.23
☐ 12 Mike Krukow	.50	.23
☐ 13 Atlee Hammaker	.50	.23
☐ 14 Gary Lavelle	.50	.23
☐ 15 Bill Laskey	.50	.23
☐ 16 Max Venable	.50	.23
☐ 17 Joel Youngblood	.50	.23
☐ 18 Dave Bergman	.50	.23
☐ 19 Mike Vail	.50	.23
☐ 20 Andy McGaffigan	.50	.23

1984 Giants Mother's

The cards in this 28-card set measure the standard-size. In 1984, the Los Angeles based Mother's Cookies Co. issued five sets of cards featuring players from major league teams. The San Francisco Giants set features previous Giant All-Star selections depicted by drawings. Similar to their 1952 and 1953 issues, the cards have rounded corners. The backs of the cards contain the Mother's Cookies logo. The cards were distributed in partial sets to fans at the respective stadiums of the teams involved. Whereas 20 cards were given to each patron, a redemption card, redeemable for eight more cards was included. Unfortunately, the eight cards received by redeeming the coupon were not necessarily the eight needed to complete a set. Hobbyist Barry Colla was involved in the production of these sets.

	NRMT-MT	EXC
COMPLETE SET (28)	15.00	6.75
COMMON CARD (1-28)	.25	.11
☐ 1 Willie Mays	5.00	2.20
☐ 2 Willie McCovey	2.50	1.10
☐ 3 Juan Marichal	2.00	.90
☐ 4 Gaylord Perry	1.50	.70
☐ 5 Tom Haller	.25	.11
☐ 6 Jim Davenport	.25	.11
☐ 7 Jack Clark	.75	.35
☐ 8 Greg Minton	.25	.11
☐ 9 Atlee Hammaker	.25	.11
☐ 10 Gary Lavelle	.25	.11
☐ 11 Orlando Cepeda	1.25	.55
☐ 12 Bobby Bonds	.75	.35
☐ 13 John Antonelli	.25	.11
☐ 14 Bob Schmidt UER (Photo actually	.25	.11

Wes Westrum)
☐ 15 Sam Jones .25 .11
☐ 16 Mike McCormick .25 .11
☐ 17 Ed Bailey .25 .11
☐ 18 Stu Miller .50 .23
☐ 19 Felipe Alou 1.00 .45
☐ 20 Jim Ray Hart .25 .11
☐ 21 Dick Dietz .25 .11
☐ 22 Chris Speier .25 .11
☐ 23 Bobby Murcer 1.00 .45
☐ 24 John Montefusco .25 .11
☐ 25 Vida Blue .75 .35
☐ 26 Ed Whitson .25 .11
☐ 27 Darrell Evans 1.00 .45
☐ 28 Giants Checklist Card .50 .23
All-Star Game Logo

1985 Giants Mother's

SCOTT GARRELTS
GIANTS
MOTHER'S COOKIES
1985
GIANTS
23 of 28
SCOTT GARRELTS
(RHP)
50
AUTOGRAPH

The cards in this 28-card set measure the standard size. In 1985, the Los Angeles based Mother's Cookies Co. again issued five sets of cards featuring players from major league teams. The San Francisco Giants set features current players depicted by photos on cards with rounded corners. The backs of the cards contain the Mother's Cookies logo. Cards were passed out at the stadium on June 30.

	NRMT-MT	EXC
COMPLETE SET (28)	7.50	3.40
COMMON CARD (1-28)	.25	.11

☐ 1 Jim Davenport MG .25 .11
☐ 2 Chili Davis 1.00 .45
☐ 3 Dan Gladden .50 .23
☐ 4 Jeff Leonard .25 .11
☐ 5 Manny Trillo .25 .11
☐ 6 Atlee Hammaker .25 .11
☐ 7 Bob Brenly .25 .11
☐ 8 Greg Minton .25 .11
☐ 9 Bill Laskey .25 .11
☐ 10 Vida Blue .75 .35
☐ 11 Mike Krukow .25 .11
☐ 12 Frank Williams .25 .11
☐ 13 Jose Uribe .25 .11
☐ 14 Johnnie LeMaster .25 .11
☐ 15 Scot Thompson .25 .11
☐ 16 Dave LaPoint .25 .11
☐ 17 David Green .25 .11
☐ 18 Chris Brown .25 .11
☐ 19 Joel Youngblood .25 .11
☐ 20 Mark Davis .50 .23
☐ 21 Jim Gott .25 .11
☐ 22 Doug Gwosdz .25 .11
☐ 23 Scott Garrelts .25 .11
☐ 24 Gary Rajsich .25 .11
☐ 25 Rob Deer .50 .23
☐ 26 Brad Wellman .25 .11
☐ 27 Giants' Coaches .25 .11
Rocky Bridges
Chuck Hiller
Tom McCraw
Bob Miller
Jack Mull
☐ 28 Giants' Checklist .25 .11
Candlestick Park

1986 Giants Mother's

This set consists of 28 full-color, rounded-corner cards each measuring the standard size. Starter sets (only 20 cards but also including a certificate for eight more cards) were given out at the ballpark and collectors were encouraged to trade to fill in the rest of their set. Cards were originally given out at Candlestick Park on July 13th.

	MINT	NRMT
COMPLETE SET (28)	17.50	8.00
COMMON CARD (1-28)	.25	.11

☐ 1 Roger Craig MG .50 .23
☐ 2 Chili Davis 1.00 .45
☐ 3 Dan Gladden .25 .11
☐ 4 Jeff Leonard .25 .11

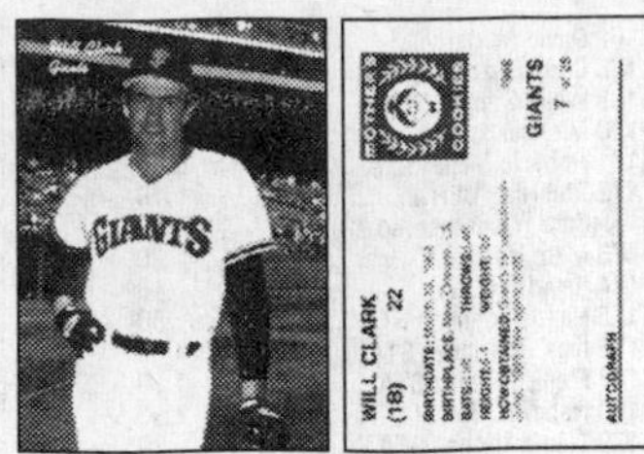

☐ 5 Bob Brenly .25 .11
☐ 6 Atlee Hammaker .25 .11
☐ 7 Will Clark 10.00 4.50
☐ 8 Greg Minton .25 .11
☐ 9 Candy Maldonado .25 .11
☐ 10 Vida Blue .75 .35
☐ 11 Mike Krukow .25 .11
☐ 12 Bob Melvin .25 .11
☐ 13 Jose Uribe .25 .11
☐ 14 Dan Driessen .25 .11
☐ 15 Jeff D. Robinson .25 .11
☐ 16 Robby Thompson .75 .35
☐ 17 Mike LaCoss .25 .11
☐ 18 Chris Brown .25 .11
☐ 19 Scott Garrelts .25 .11
☐ 20 Mark Davis .50 .23
☐ 21 Jim Gott .25 .11
☐ 22 Brad Wellman .25 .11
☐ 23 Roger Mason .25 .11
☐ 24 Bill Laskey .25 .11
☐ 25 Brad Gulden .25 .11
☐ 26 Joel Youngblood .25 .11
☐ 27 Juan Berenguer .25 .11
☐ 28 Checklist Card .25 .11
Bob Lillis CO
Gordy MacKenzie CO
Bill Fahey CO
Norm Sherry CO
Jose Morales CO

1987 Giants Mother's

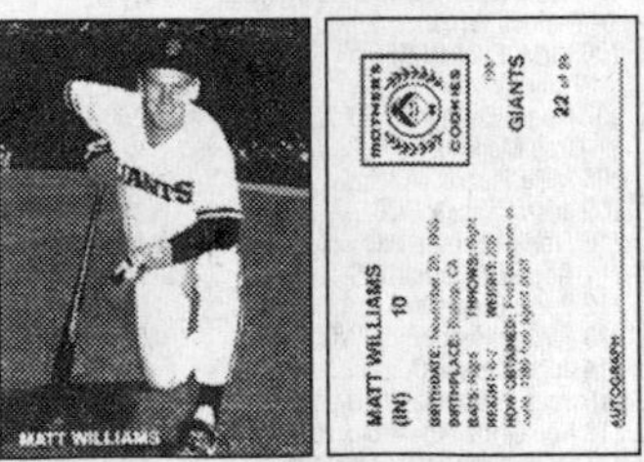

GIANTS
MATT WILLIAMS
MOTHER'S COOKIES
1987
GIANTS
22 of 28
MATT WILLIAMS
(INF)
10
AUTOGRAPH

This set consists of 28 full-color, rounded-corner cards each measuring the standard size. Starter sets (only 20 cards but also including a certificate for eight more cards) were given out at the ballpark and collectors were encouraged to trade to fill in the rest of their set. Cards were originally given out at Candlestick Park on June 27th during a game against the Astros. Photos were taken by Dennis Desprois. The sets were reportedly given out free to the first 25,000 paid admissions at the game. There is an early Matt Williams card in this set.

	MINT	NRMT
COMPLETE SET (28)	15.00	6.75
COMMON CARD (1-28)	.25	.11

☐ 1 Roger Craig MG .50 .23
☐ 2 Will Clark 6.00 2.70
☐ 3 Chili Davis 1.00 .45
☐ 4 Bob Brenly .25 .11
☐ 5 Chris Brown .25 .11
☐ 6 Mike Krukow .25 .11
☐ 7 Candy Maldonado .25 .11
☐ 8 Jeffrey Leonard .25 .11
☐ 9 Greg Minton .25 .11
☐ 10 Robby Thompson .50 .23
☐ 11 Scott Garrelts .25 .11
☐ 12 Bob Melvin .25 .11
☐ 13 Jose Uribe .25 .11
☐ 14 Mark Davis .50 .23
☐ 15 Eddie Milner .25 .11
☐ 16 Harry Spilman .25 .11
☐ 17 Kelly Downs .25 .11
☐ 18 Chris Speier .25 .11
☐ 19 Jim Gott .25 .11
☐ 20 Joel Youngblood .25 .11
☐ 21 Mike LaCoss .25 .11
☐ 22 Matt Williams 7.50 3.40
☐ 23 Roger Mason .25 .11
☐ 24 Mike Aldrete .25 .11
☐ 25 Jeff D. Robinson .25 .11
☐ 26 Mark Grant .25 .11
☐ 27 Giants' Coaches .25 .11
Don Zimmer
Bob Lillis
Jose Morales
Norm Sherry
Bill Fahey
Gordon MacKenzie
☐ 28 Checklist Card .25 .11
Candlestick Park

1988 Giants Mother's

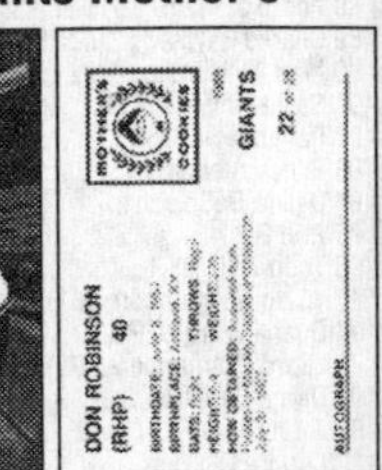

This set consists of 28 full-color, rounded-corner cards each measuring the standard size. Starter sets (only 20 cards but also including a certificate for eight more cards) were given out at the ballpark and collectors were encouraged to trade to fill in the rest of their set. Cards were originally given out at Candlestick Park on July 30th during a game. Photos were taken by Dennis Desprois. The sets were reportedly given out free to the first 35,000 paid admissions at the game.

	MINT	NRMT
COMPLETE SET (28)	10.00	4.50
COMMON CARD (1-28)	.25	.11

☐ 1 Roger Craig MG .50 .23
☐ 2 Will Clark 3.00 1.35
☐ 3 Kevin Mitchell .75 .35
☐ 4 Bob Brenly .25 .11
☐ 5 Mike Aldrete .25 .11
☐ 6 Mike Krukow .25 .11
☐ 7 Candy Maldonado .25 .11
☐ 8 Jeffrey Leonard .25 .11
☐ 9 Dave Dravecky .75 .35
☐ 10 Robby Thompson .25 .11
☐ 11 Scott Garrelts .25 .11
☐ 12 Bob Melvin .25 .11
☐ 13 Jose Uribe .25 .11
☐ 14 Brett Butler 1.00 .45
☐ 15 Rick Reuschel .50 .23
☐ 16 Harry Spilman .25 .11
☐ 17 Kelly Downs .25 .11
☐ 18 Chris Speier .25 .11
☐ 19 Atlee Hammaker .25 .11
☐ 20 Joel Youngblood .25 .11
☐ 21 Mike LaCoss .25 .11
☐ 22 Don Robinson .25 .11
☐ 23 Mark Wasinger .25 .11
☐ 24 Craig Lefferts .25 .11
☐ 25 Phil Garner .50 .23
☐ 26 Joe Price .25 .11
☐ 27 Giants' Coaches .50 .23
Dusty Baker
Bill Fahey
Bob Lillis
Jose Morales
Gordie MacKenzie
Norm Sherry
☐ 28 Checklist Card .25 .11
Giants NL Champs Logo

1989 Giants Mother's

The 1989 Mother's Cookies San Francisco Giants set contains 28 standard-size cards with rounded corners. The fronts have borderless color photos, and the horizontally oriented backs have biographical information. Starter sets containing 20 of these cards were given away at a Giants home game during the 1989 season.

	MINT	NRMT
COMPLETE SET (28)	12.00	5.50
COMMON CARD (1-28)	.25	.11

☐ 1 Roger Craig MG .50 .23
☐ 2 Will Clark 2.50 1.10
☐ 3 Kevin Mitchell .75 .35
☐ 4 Kelly Downs .25 .11
☐ 5 Brett Butler 1.00 .45

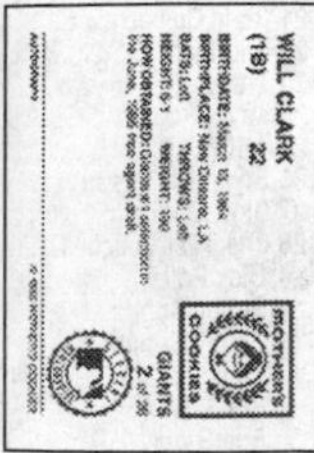

☐ 6 Mike Krukow	.25	.11
☐ 7 Candy Maldonado	.25	.11
☐ 8 Terry Kennedy	.25	.11
☐ 9 Dave Dravecky	.75	.35
☐ 10 Robby Thompson	.25	.11
☐ 11 Scott Garrelts	.25	.11
☐ 12 Matt Williams	4.00	1.80
☐ 13 Jose Uribe	.25	.11
☐ 14 Tracy Jones	.25	.11
☐ 15 Rick Reuschel	.50	.23
☐ 16 Ernest Riles	.25	.11
☐ 17 Jeff Brantley	.50	.23
☐ 18 Chris Speier	.25	.11
☐ 19 Atlee Hammaker	.25	.11
☐ 20 Ed Jurak	.25	.11
☐ 21 Mike LaCoss	.25	.11
☐ 22 Don Robinson	.25	.11
☐ 23 Kirt Manwaring	.25	.11
☐ 24 Craig Lefferts	.25	.11
☐ 25 Donell Nixon	.25	.11
☐ 26 Joe Price	.25	.11
☐ 27 Rich Gossage	.75	.35
☐ 28 Checklist Card	.50	.23
Bill Fahey CO		
Dusty Baker CO		
Bob Lillis CO		
Wendell Kim CO		
Norm Sherry CO		

1990 Giants Mother's

The 1990 Mother's Cookies San Francisco Giants set features cards with rounded corners measuring the standard size. The cards have full-color fronts and biographical information with no stats on the back. The Giants cards were given away at the July 29th game to the first 25,000 children 14 and under. They were distributed in 20-card random packets at the game and eight more at the redemption booths. However, both groups of cards were random and there was no guarantee of getting a complete set in the cards. The promotional idea was that the only way one could finish the set was to trade for them. The redemption certificates were to be used at the Labor Day San Francisco card show. In addition to this the Mother's A's cards were also redeemable at that show.

	MINT	NRMT
COMPLETE SET (28)	12.00	5.50
COMMON CARD (1-28)	.25	.11

☐ 1 Roger Craig MG	.50	.23
☐ 2 Will Clark	2.50	1.10
☐ 3 Gary Carter	1.00	.45
☐ 4 Kelly Downs	.25	.11
☐ 5 Kevin Mitchell	.75	.35
☐ 6 Steve Bedrosian	.50	.23
☐ 7 Brett Butler	1.00	.45
☐ 8 Rick Reuschel	.50	.23
☐ 9 Matt Williams	3.00	1.35
☐ 10 Robby Thompson	.25	.11
☐ 11 Mike LaCoss	.25	.11
☐ 12 Terry Kennedy	.25	.11
☐ 13 Atlee Hammaker	.25	.11
☐ 14 Rick Leach	.25	.11
☐ 15 Ernest Riles	.25	.11
☐ 16 Scott Garrelts	.25	.11
☐ 17 Jose Uribe	.25	.11
☐ 18 Greg Litton	.25	.11
☐ 19 Dave Anderson	.25	.11
☐ 20 Don Robinson	.25	.11
☐ 21 Giants Coaches	.50	.23
Dusty Baker		
Bob Lillis		
Bill Fahey		
Norm Sherry		
Wendell Kim		
☐ 22 Bill Bathe	.25	.11
☐ 23 Randy O'Neal	.25	.11
☐ 24 Kevin Bass	.25	.11
☐ 25 Jeff Brantley	.50	.23
☐ 26 John Burkett	.75	.35
☐ 27 Ernie Camacho	.25	.11
☐ 28 Checklist Card	.25	.11

1991 Giants Mother's

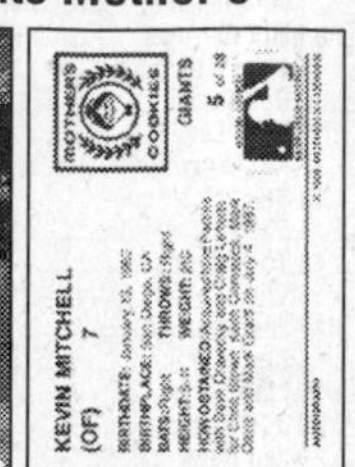

The 1991 Mother's Cookies San Francisco Giants set contains 28 cards with rounded corners measuring the standard size. The set includes an additional card advertising a trading card collectors album. The front design has borderless glossy color player photos from the waist up. The horizontally oriented backs are printed in red and purple, present biographical information, and have blank slots for player autographs.

	MINT	NRMT
COMPLETE SET (28)	10.00	4.50
COMMON CARD (1-28)	.25	.11

☐ 1 Roger Craig MG	.50	.23
☐ 2 Will Clark	2.00	.90
☐ 3 Steve Decker	.25	.11
☐ 4 Kelly Downs	.25	.11
☐ 5 Kevin Mitchell	.75	.35
☐ 6 Willie McGee	.75	.35
☐ 7 Bud Black	.25	.11
☐ 8 Dave Righetti	.50	.23
☐ 9 Matt Williams	2.50	1.10
☐ 10 Robby Thompson	.25	.11
☐ 11 Mike LaCoss	.25	.11
☐ 12 Terry Kennedy	.25	.11
☐ 13 Mark Leonard	.25	.11
☐ 14 Rick Reuschel	.50	.23
☐ 15 Mike Felder	.25	.11
☐ 16 Scott Garrelts	.25	.11
☐ 17 Jose Uribe	.25	.11
☐ 18 Greg Litton	.25	.11
☐ 19 Dave Anderson	.25	.11
☐ 20 Don Robinson	.25	.11
☐ 21 Mike Kingery	.25	.11
☐ 22 Trevor Wilson	.25	.11
☐ 23 Kirt Manwaring	.25	.11
☐ 24 Kevin Bass	.25	.11
☐ 25 Jeff Brantley	.50	.23
☐ 26 John Burkett	.75	.35
☐ 27 Giant's Coaches	.50	.23
Dusty Baker		
Bill Fahey		
Wendell Kim		
Bob Lillis		
Norm Sherry		
☐ 28 Checklist Card	.25	.11
Mark Letendre TR		
Greg Lynn TR		

1992 Giants Mother's

The set was sponsored by Mother's Cookies and features full-bleed color player photos of the San Francisco Giants. The 28 cards in this set have rounded corners and measure the standard size. The backs, printed in purple and red, have biographical information. The set included two coupons: one featured a mail-in offer to obtain a trading card collectors album for 3.95, while the second featured a mail-in offer to obtain an additional eight trading cards.

	MINT	NRMT
COMPLETE SET (28)	10.00	4.50
COMMON CARD (1-28)	.25	.11

☐ 1 Roger Craig MG	.50	.23
☐ 2 Will Clark	2.00	.90
☐ 3 Bill Swift	.25	.11
☐ 4 Royce Clayton	1.00	.45
☐ 5 John Burkett	.75	.35
☐ 6 Willie McGee	.75	.35
☐ 7 Bud Black	.25	.11
☐ 8 Dave Righetti	.50	.23
☐ 9 Matt Williams	2.50	1.10
☐ 10 Robby Thompson	.25	.11
☐ 11 Darren Lewis	.25	.11
☐ 12 Mike Jackson	.25	.11
☐ 13 Mark Leonard	.25	.11
☐ 14 Rod Beck	1.50	.70
☐ 15 Mike Felder	.25	.11
☐ 16 Bryan Hickerson	.25	.11
☐ 17 Jose Uribe	.25	.11
☐ 18 Greg Litton	.25	.11
☐ 19 Cory Snyder	.25	.11
☐ 20 Jim McNamara	.25	.11
☐ 21 Kelly Downs	.25	.11
☐ 22 Trevor Wilson	.25	.11
☐ 23 Kirt Manwaring	.25	.11
☐ 24 Kevin Bass	.25	.11
☐ 25 Jeff Brantley	.50	.23
☐ 26 Dave Burba	.25	.11
☐ 27 Chris James	.25	.11
☐ 28 Checklist Card	.50	.23
Carlos Alfonso CO		
Dusty Baker CO		
Wendell Kim CO		
Bob Brenly CO		
Bob Lillis CO		

1993 Giants Mother's

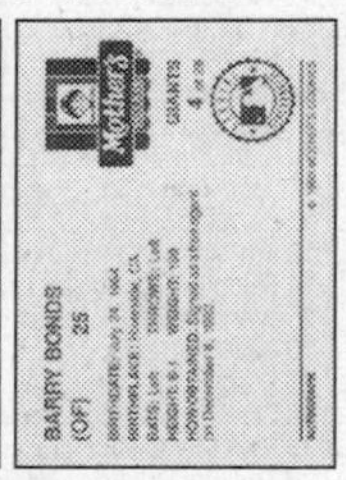

The 1993 Mother's Cookies Giants set consists of 28 standard-size cards with rounded corners. The fronts display full-bleed color player portraits shot from the waist up. The player's name and team name appear in one of the corners. On a white background in red and purple print, the horizontal backs carry biographical information and the sponsor's logo. A blank slot for the player's autograph rounds out the back.

	MINT	NRMT
COMPLETE SET (28)	12.50	5.50
COMMON CARD (1-28)	.25	.11

☐ 1 Dusty Baker MG	.50	.23
☐ 2 Will Clark	2.00	.90
☐ 3 Matt Williams	2.50	1.10
☐ 4 Barry Bonds	3.00	1.35
☐ 5 Bill Swift	.25	.11
☐ 6 Royce Clayton	.75	.35
☐ 7 John Burkett	.75	.35
☐ 8 Willie McGee	.75	.35
☐ 9 Kirt Manwaring	.25	.11
☐ 10 Dave Righetti	.50	.23
☐ 11 Todd Benzinger	.25	.11
☐ 12 Rod Beck	1.00	.45
☐ 13 Darren Lewis	.25	.11
☐ 14 Robby Thompson	.25	.11
☐ 15 Mark Carreon	.25	.11
☐ 16 Dave Martinez	.25	.11
☐ 17 Jeff Brantley	.75	.35
☐ 18 Dave Burba	.25	.11
☐ 19 Mike Benjamin	.25	.11
☐ 20 Mike Jackson	.25	.11

☐ 21 Craig Colbert	.25	.11
☐ 22 Bud Black	.25	.11
☐ 23 Trevor Wilson	.25	.11
☐ 24 Kevin Rogers	.25	.11
☐ 25 Jeff Reed	.25	.11
☐ 26 Bryan Hickerson	.25	.11
☐ 27 Gino Minutelli	.25	.11
☐ 28 Checklist/Coaches	.50	.23

Dick Pole
Bobby Bonds
Denny Sommers
Wendell Kim
Bob Lillis
Bob Brenly

1994 Giants Mother's

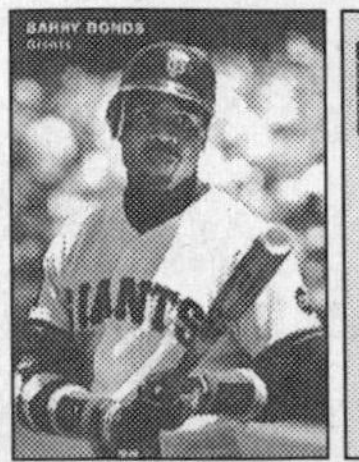

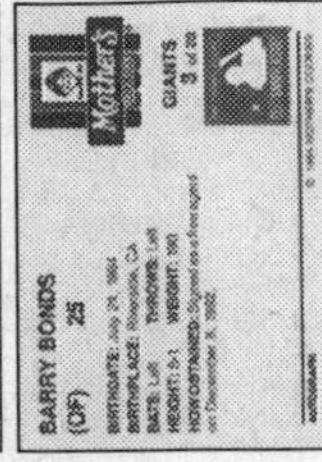

The 1994 Mother's Cookies Giants set consists of 28 standard-size cards with rounded corners. The fronts display full-bleed color player portraits shot from the waist up against a stadium background. The player's name and team name appear in one of the corners. On a white background in red and purple print, the horizontal backs carry biographical information and the sponsor's logo. A blank slot for the player's autograph rounds out the back.

	MINT	NRMT
COMPLETE SET (28)	10.00	4.50
COMMON CARD (1-28)	.25	.11
☐ 1 Dusty Baker MG	.50	.23
☐ 2 Robby Thompson	.25	.11
☐ 3 Barry Bonds	2.50	1.10
☐ 4 Royce Clayton	.75	.35
☐ 5 John Burkett	.75	.35
☐ 6 Bill Swift	.25	.11
☐ 7 Matt Williams	2.00	.90
☐ 8 Rod Beck	1.00	.45
☐ 9 Steve Scarsone	.25	.11
☐ 10 Mark Portugal	.25	.11
☐ 11 John Patterson	.25	.11
☐ 12 Darren Lewis	.25	.11
☐ 13 Kirt Manwaring	.25	.11
☐ 14 Salomon Torres	.25	.11
☐ 15 Willie McGee	.75	.35
☐ 16 Dave Martinez	.25	.11
☐ 17 Darryl Strawberry	.50	.23
☐ 18 Steve Frey	.25	.11
☐ 19 Rich Monteleone	.25	.11
☐ 20 Todd Benzinger	.25	.11
☐ 21 Jeff Reed	.25	.11
☐ 22 Mike Benjamin	.25	.11
☐ 23 Mike Jackson	.25	.11
☐ 24 Pat Gomez	.25	.11
☐ 25 Dave Burba	.25	.11
☐ 26 Bryan Hickerson	.25	.11
☐ 27 Mark Carreon	.25	.11
☐ 28 Checklist/Coaches	.50	.23

Bobby Bonds
Bob Lillis
Wendell Kim
Bob Brenly
Dick Pole
Denny Sommers

1995 Giants Mother's

This 1995 Mother's Cookies San Francisco Giants set consists of 28 standard-size cards with rounded corners. The fronts display posed color player portraits. The player's name and team name appear in one of the top corners. The horizontal backs carry biographical information and the sponsor's logo on a white background in red and purple print. A blank slot at the bottom for the player's autograph rounds out the back.

	MINT	NRMT
COMPLETE SET (28)	10.00	4.50
COMMON CARD (1-28)	.25	.11
☐ 1 Dusty Baker MG	.50	.23
☐ 2 Robby Thompson	.25	.11

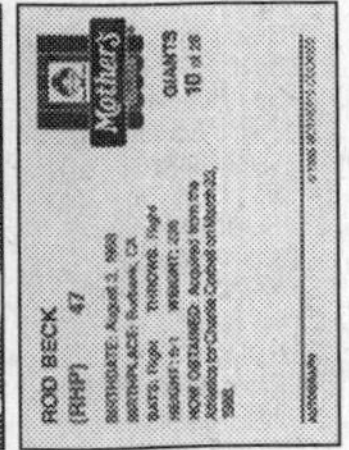

☐ 3 Barry Bonds	2.50	1.10
☐ 4 Royce Clayton	.75	.35
☐ 5 Glenallen Hill	.50	.23
☐ 6 Terry Mulholland	.25	.11
☐ 7 Matt Williams	2.00	.90
☐ 8 Mark Portugal	.25	.11
☐ 9 John Patterson	.25	.11
☐ 10 Rod Beck	1.00	.45
☐ 11 Mark Leiter	.25	.11
☐ 12 Kirt Manwaring	.25	.11
☐ 13 Steve Scarsone	.25	.11
☐ 14 Darren Lewis	.25	.11
☐ 15 Tom Lampkin	.25	.11
☐ 16 William VanLandingham	.25	.11
☐ 17 Joe Rosselli	.25	.11
☐ 18 Chris Hook	.25	.11
☐ 19 Mark Dewey	.25	.11
☐ 20 J.R. Phillips	.25	.11
☐ 21 Jeff Reed	.25	.11
☐ 22 Pat Gomez	.25	.11
☐ 23 Mike Benjamin	.25	.11
☐ 24 Trevor Wilson	.25	.11
☐ 25 Dave Burba	.25	.11
☐ 26 Jose Bautista	.25	.11
☐ 27 Mark Carreon	.25	.11
☐ 28 Coaches/Checklist	.50	.23

Dick Pole
Bobby Bonds
Wendell Kim
Bob Brenly
Bob Lillis

1996 Giants Mother's

This 28-card set consists of borderless posed color player portraits in stadium settings. The player's and team's names appear in one of the top rounded corners. The backs carry biographical information and the sponsor's logo on a white background in red and purple print. A blank slot for the player's autograph rounds out the back.

	MINT	NRMT
COMPLETE SET (28)	8.00	3.60
COMMON CARD (1-28)	.25	.11
☐ 1 Dusty Baker MG	.50	.23
☐ 2 Barry Bonds	2.50	1.10
☐ 3 Rod Beck	.50	.23
☐ 4 Matt Williams	2.00	.90
☐ 5 Robby Thompson	.25	.11
☐ 6 Glenallen Hill	.25	.11
☐ 7 Kirt Manwaring	.25	.11
☐ 8 Mark Carreon	.25	.11
☐ 9 Osvaldo Fernandez	1.00	.45
☐ 10 J.R. Phillips	.25	.11
☐ 11 Shawon Dunston	.25	.11
☐ 12 Mark Leiter	.25	.11
☐ 13 William VanLandingham	.25	.11
☐ 14 Stan Javier	.25	.11
☐ 15 Allen Watson	.25	.11
☐ 16 Mel Hall	.25	.11
☐ 17 Doug Creek	.25	.11
☐ 18 Steve Scarsone	.25	.11
☐ 19 Mark Dewey	.25	.11
☐ 20 Mark Gardner	.25	.11
☐ 21 David McCarty	.25	.11
☐ 22 Tom Lampkin	.25	.11
☐ 23 Jeff Juden	.25	.11
☐ 24 Steve Decker	.25	.11
☐ 25 Rich DeLucia	.25	.11
☐ 26 Kim Batiste	.25	.11
☐ 27 Steve Bourgeois	.25	.11
☐ 28 Coaches Card CL	.25	.11

Bob Lillis
Dick Pole
Bobby Bonds
Jim Davenport
Mike Sadek
Juan Lopez
Wendell Kim
Carlos Alfonso

1961 Golden Press

The cards in this 33-card set measure 2 1/2" by 3 1/2". The 1961 Golden Press set of full color cards features members of Baseball's Hall of Fame. The cards came in a booklet with perforations for punching the cards out of the book. The catalog designation for this set is W524. The price for the full book intact is double the complete set price listed.

	NRMT	VG-E
COMPLETE SET (33)	125.00	55.00
COMMON CARD (1-33)	1.00	.45
MINOR STARS	2.00	.90
SEMISTARS	3.00	1.35
UNLISTED STARS	4.00	1.80
☐ 1 Mel Ott	4.00	1.80
☐ 2 Grover C. Alexander	3.00	1.35
☐ 3 Babe Ruth	40.00	18.00
☐ 4 Hank Greenberg	3.00	1.35
☐ 5 Bill Terry	2.00	.90
☐ 6 Carl Hubbell	2.00	.90
☐ 7 Rogers Hornsby	5.00	2.20
☐ 8 Dizzy Dean	7.50	3.40
☐ 9 Joe DiMaggio	35.00	16.00
☐ 10 Charlie Gehringer	1.00	.45
☐ 11 Gabby Hartnett	1.00	.45
☐ 12 Mickey Cochrane	2.00	.90
☐ 13 George Sisler	1.00	.45
☐ 14 Joe Cronin	1.00	.45
☐ 15 Pie Traynor	1.00	.45
☐ 16 Lou Gehrig	35.00	16.00
☐ 17 Lefty Grove	3.00	1.35
☐ 18 Chief Bender	1.00	.45
☐ 19 Frankie Frisch	1.00	.45
☐ 20 Al Simmons	1.00	.45
☐ 21 Home Run Baker	1.00	.45
☐ 22 Jimmy Foxx	5.00	2.20
☐ 23 John McGraw	1.00	.45
☐ 24 Christy Mathewson	7.50	3.40
☐ 25 Ty Cobb	35.00	16.00
☐ 26 Dazzy Vance	1.00	.45
☐ 27 Bill Dickey	2.00	.90
☐ 28 Eddie Collins	2.00	.90
☐ 29 Walter Johnson	7.50	3.40
☐ 30 Tris Speaker	3.00	1.35
☐ 31 Nap Lajoie	3.00	1.35
☐ 32 Honus Wagner	7.50	3.40
☐ 33 Cy Young	5.00	2.20

1933 Goudey R319

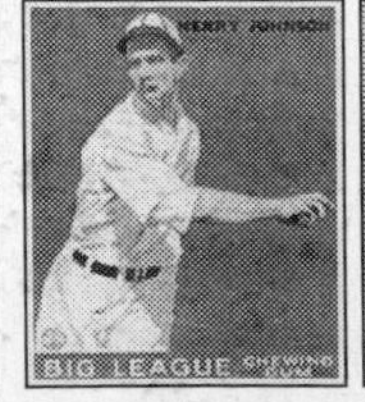

The cards in this 240-card set measure approximately 2 3/8" by 2 7/8". The 1933 Goudey set, was that company's first baseball issue. The four Babe Ruth and two Lou

Gehrig cards in the set are extremely popular with collectors. Card number 106, Napoleon Lajoie, was not printed in 1933, and was circulated to a limited number of collectors in 1934 upon request (it was printed along with the 1934 Goudey cards). An album was offered to house the 1933 set. Several minor leaguers are depicted. Card number 1 (Bengough) is very rarely found in mint condition; in fact, as a general rule all the first series cards are more difficult to find in Mint condition. Players with more than one card are also sometimes differentiated below by their pose: BAT (Batting), FIELD (Fielding), PIT (Pitching), THROW (Throwing). One of the Babe Ruth cards was double printed (DP) apparently in place of the Lajoie and hence is easier to obtain than the others. Due to the scarcity of the Lajoie card, the set is considered complete at 239 cards and is priced as such below.

	EX-MT	VG-E
COMPLETE SET (239)	40000.00	18000.00
COMMON CARD (1-52)	60.00	27.00
COMMON CARD (53-240)	50.00	22.00
WRAPPER (1-CENT, BATTER)	100.00	45.00
WRAPPER (1-CENT, AD FRONT)	175.00	80.00
☐ 1 Benny Bengough	1250.00	550.00
☐ 2 Dazzy Vance	200.00	90.00
☐ 3 Hugh Critz	60.00	27.00
☐ 4 Heinie Schuble	60.00	27.00
☐ 5 Babe Herman	75.00	34.00
☐ 6 Jimmy Dykes	75.00	34.00
☐ 7 Ted Lyons	150.00	70.00
☐ 8 Roy Johnson	60.00	27.00
☐ 9 Dave Harris	60.00	27.00
☐ 10 Glenn Myatt	60.00	27.00
☐ 11 Billy Rogell	60.00	27.00
☐ 12 George Pipgras	60.00	27.00
☐ 13 Lafayette Thompson	60.00	27.00
☐ 14 Henry Johnson	60.00	27.00
☐ 15 Victor Sorrell	60.00	27.00
☐ 16 George Blaeholder	60.00	27.00
☐ 17 Watson Clark	60.00	27.00
☐ 18 Muddy Ruel	60.00	27.00
☐ 19 Bill Dickey	350.00	160.00
☐ 20 Bill Terry THROW	250.00	110.00
☐ 21 Phil Collins	60.00	27.00
☐ 22 Pie Traynor	200.00	90.00
☐ 23 Kiki Cuyler	150.00	70.00
☐ 24 Horace Ford	60.00	27.00
☐ 25 Paul Waner	150.00	70.00
☐ 26 Chalmer Cissell	60.00	27.00
☐ 27 George Connally	60.00	27.00
☐ 28 Dick Bartell	75.00	34.00
☐ 29 Jimmie Foxx	450.00	200.00
☐ 30 Frank Hogan	60.00	27.00
☐ 31 Tony Lazzeri	375.00	170.00
☐ 32 Bud Clancy	60.00	27.00
☐ 33 Ralph Kress	60.00	27.00
☐ 34 Bob O'Farrell	60.00	27.00
☐ 35 Al Simmons	350.00	160.00
☐ 36 Tommy Thevenow	60.00	27.00
☐ 37 Jimmy Wilson	60.00	27.00
☐ 38 Fred Brickell	60.00	27.00
☐ 39 Mark Koenig	75.00	34.00
☐ 40 Taylor Douthit	60.00	27.00
☐ 41 Gus Mancuso	40.00	18.00
☐ 42 Eddie Collins	125.00	55.00
☐ 43 Lew Fonseca	40.00	18.00
☐ 44 Jim Bottomley	125.00	55.00
☐ 45 Larry Benton	60.00	27.00
☐ 46 Ethan Allen	75.00	34.00
☐ 47 Heinie Manush BAT	150.00	70.00
☐ 48 Marty McManus	60.00	27.00
☐ 49 Frankie Frisch	250.00	110.00
☐ 50 Ed Brandt	60.00	27.00
☐ 51 Charlie Grimm	75.00	34.00
☐ 52 Andy Cohen	60.00	27.00
☐ 53 Babe Ruth	4000.00	1800.00
☐ 54 Ray Kremer	50.00	22.00
☐ 55 Pat Malone	50.00	22.00
☐ 56 Red Ruffing	100.00	45.00
☐ 57 Earl Clark	50.00	22.00
☐ 58 Lefty O'Doul	75.00	34.00
☐ 59 Bing Miller	50.00	22.00
☐ 60 Waite Hoyt	100.00	45.00
☐ 61 Max Bishop	50.00	22.00
☐ 62 Pepper Martin	75.00	34.00
☐ 63 Joe Cronin BAT	125.00	55.00
☐ 64 Burleigh Grimes	100.00	45.00
☐ 65 Milt Gaston	50.00	22.00
☐ 66 George Grantham	50.00	22.00
☐ 67 Guy Bush	50.00	22.00
☐ 68 Horace Lisenbee	50.00	22.00
☐ 69 Randy Moore	50.00	22.00
☐ 70 Floyd(Pete) Scott	50.00	22.00
☐ 71 Robert J. Burke	50.00	22.00
☐ 72 Owen Carroll	50.00	22.00
☐ 73 Jesse Haines	100.00	45.00
☐ 74 Eppa Rixey	100.00	45.00
☐ 75 Willie Kamm	50.00	22.00
☐ 76 Mickey Cochrane	175.00	80.00
☐ 77 Adam Comorosky	50.00	22.00
☐ 78 Jack Quinn	50.00	22.00
☐ 79 Red Faber	100.00	45.00
☐ 80 Clyde Manion	50.00	22.00
☐ 81 Sam Jones	55.00	25.00
☐ 82 Dibrell Williams	50.00	22.00
☐ 83 Pete Jablonowski	50.00	22.00
☐ 84 Glenn Spencer	50.00	22.00
☐ 85 Heinie Sand	50.00	22.00
☐ 86 Phil Todt	50.00	22.00
☐ 87 Frank O'Rourke	50.00	22.00
☐ 88 Russell Rollings	50.00	22.00
☐ 89 Tris Speaker RET	250.00	110.00
☐ 90 Jess Petty	50.00	22.00
☐ 91 Tom Zachary	55.00	25.00
☐ 92 Lou Gehrig	2500.00	1100.00
☐ 93 John Welch	50.00	22.00
☐ 94 Bill Walker	50.00	22.00
☐ 95 Alvin Crowder	50.00	22.00
☐ 96 Willis Hudlin	50.00	22.00
☐ 97 Joe Morrissey	50.00	22.00
☐ 98 Wally Berger	75.00	34.00
☐ 99 Tony Cuccinello	55.00	25.00
☐ 100 George Uhle	50.00	22.00
☐ 101 Richard Coffman	50.00	22.00
☐ 102 Travis Jackson	100.00	45.00
☐ 103 Earle Combs	100.00	45.00
☐ 104 Fred Marberry	50.00	22.00
☐ 105 Bernie Friberg	50.00	22.00
☐ 106 Napoleon Lajoie SP (Not issued until 1934)	30000.00	13500.00
☐ 107 Heinie Manush	100.00	45.00
☐ 108 Joe Kuhel	50.00	22.00
☐ 109 Joe Cronin	125.00	55.00
☐ 110 Goose Goslin	100.00	45.00
☐ 111 Monte Weaver	50.00	22.00
☐ 112 Fred Schulte	50.00	22.00
☐ 113 Oswald Bluege	55.00	25.00
☐ 114 Luke Sewell	65.00	29.00
☐ 115 Cliff Heathcote	50.00	22.00
☐ 116 Eddie Morgan	50.00	22.00
☐ 117 Rabbit Maranville	100.00	45.00
☐ 118 Val Picinich	50.00	22.00
☐ 119 Rogers Hornsby FIELD	350.00	160.00
☐ 120 Carl Reynolds	50.00	22.00
☐ 121 Walter Stewart	50.00	22.00
☐ 122 Alvin Crowder	50.00	22.00
☐ 123 Jack Russell	50.00	22.00
☐ 124 Earl Whitehill	50.00	22.00
☐ 125 Bill Terry	250.00	110.00
☐ 126 Joe Moore	55.00	25.00
☐ 127 Mel Ott	300.00	135.00
☐ 128 Chuck Klein	150.00	70.00
☐ 129 Hal Schumacher PIT	55.00	25.00
☐ 130 Fred Fitzsimmons	55.00	25.00
☐ 131 Fred Frankhouse	50.00	22.00
☐ 132 Jim Elliott	50.00	22.00
☐ 133 Fred Lindstrom	100.00	45.00
☐ 134 Sam Rice	100.00	45.00
☐ 135 Woody English	50.00	22.00
☐ 136 Flint Rhem	50.00	22.00
☐ 137 Fred(Red) Lucas	50.00	22.00
☐ 138 Herb Pennock	100.00	45.00
☐ 139 Ben Cantwell	50.00	22.00
☐ 140 Bump Hadley	50.00	22.00
☐ 141 Ray Benge	50.00	22.00
☐ 142 Paul Richards	65.00	29.00
☐ 143 Glenn Wright	55.00	25.00
☐ 144 Babe Ruth BAT DP	3000.00	1350.00
☐ 145 Rube Walberg	50.00	22.00
☐ 146 Walter Stewart PIT	50.00	22.00
☐ 147 Leo Durocher	175.00	80.00
☐ 148 Eddie Farrell	50.00	22.00
☐ 149 Babe Ruth	4000.00	1800.00
☐ 150 Ray Kolp	50.00	22.00
☐ 151 Jake Flowers	50.00	22.00
☐ 152 Zack Taylor	50.00	22.00
☐ 153 Buddy Myer	55.00	25.00
☐ 154 Jimmie Foxx	350.00	160.00
☐ 155 Joe Judge	50.00	22.00
☐ 156 Danny MacFayden	50.00	22.00
☐ 157 Sam Byrd	50.00	22.00
☐ 158 Moe Berg	350.00	160.00
☐ 159 Oswald Bluege	55.00	25.00
☐ 160 Lou Gehrig	2500.00	1100.00
☐ 161 Al Spohrer	50.00	22.00
☐ 162 Leo Mangum	50.00	22.00
☐ 163 Luke Sewell	65.00	29.00
☐ 164 Lloyd Waner	100.00	45.00
☐ 165 Joe Sewell	100.00	45.00
☐ 166 Sam West	50.00	22.00
☐ 167 Jack Russell	50.00	22.00
☐ 168 Goose Goslin	100.00	45.00
☐ 169 Al Thomas	50.00	22.00
☐ 170 Harry McCurdy	50.00	22.00
☐ 171 Charlie Jamieson	50.00	22.00
☐ 172 Billy Hargrave	50.00	22.00
☐ 173 Roscoe Holm	50.00	22.00
☐ 174 Warren(Curly) Ogden	50.00	22.00
☐ 175 Dan Howley MG	50.00	22.00
☐ 176 John Ogden	50.00	22.00
☐ 177 Walter French	50.00	22.00
☐ 178 Jackie Warner	50.00	22.00
☐ 179 Fred Leach	50.00	22.00
☐ 180 Eddie Moore	50.00	22.00
☐ 181 Babe Ruth	4000.00	1800.00
☐ 182 Andy High	50.00	22.00
☐ 183 Rube Walberg	50.00	22.00
☐ 184 Charley Berry	55.00	25.00
☐ 185 Bob Smith	50.00	22.00
☐ 186 John Schulte	50.00	22.00
☐ 187 Heinie Manush	100.00	45.00
☐ 188 Rogers Hornsby	350.00	160.00
☐ 189 Joe Cronin	125.00	55.00
☐ 190 Fred Schulte	50.00	22.00
☐ 191 Ben Chapman	65.00	29.00
☐ 192 Walter Brown	50.00	22.00
☐ 193 Lynford Lary	50.00	22.00
☐ 194 Earl Averill	125.00	55.00
☐ 195 Evar Swanson	50.00	22.00
☐ 196 Leroy Mahaffey	50.00	22.00
☐ 197 Rick Ferrell	100.00	45.00
☐ 198 Jack Burns	50.00	22.00
☐ 199 Tom Bridges	55.00	25.00
☐ 200 Bill Hallahan	50.00	22.00
☐ 201 Ernie Orsatti	50.00	22.00
☐ 202 Gabby Hartnett	125.00	55.00
☐ 203 Lon Warneke	55.00	25.00
☐ 204 Riggs Stephenson	55.00	25.00
☐ 205 Heinie Meine	50.00	22.00
☐ 206 Gus Suhr	50.00	22.00
☐ 207 Mel Ott BAT	350.00	160.00
☐ 208 Bernie James	50.00	22.00
☐ 209 Adolfo Luque	75.00	34.00
☐ 210 Virgil Davis	50.00	22.00
☐ 211 Hack Wilson	300.00	135.00
☐ 212 Billy Urbanski	50.00	22.00
☐ 213 Earl Adams	50.00	22.00
☐ 214 John Kerr	50.00	22.00
☐ 215 Russ Van Atta	50.00	22.00
☐ 216 Lefty Gomez	300.00	135.00
☐ 217 Frank Crosetti	125.00	55.00
☐ 218 Wes Ferrell	55.00	25.00
☐ 219 Mule Haas UER (Name spelled Hass on front)	50.00	22.00
☐ 220 Lefty Grove	400.00	180.00
☐ 221 Dale Alexander	55.00	25.00
☐ 222 Charley Gehringer	250.00	110.00
☐ 223 Dizzy Dean	600.00	275.00
☐ 224 Frank Demaree	50.00	22.00
☐ 225 Bill Jurges	55.00	25.00
☐ 226 Charley Root	55.00	25.00
☐ 227 Billy Herman	125.00	55.00
☐ 228 Tony Piet	50.00	22.00
☐ 229 Arky Vaughan	125.00	55.00
☐ 230 Carl Hubbell PIT	200.00	90.00
☐ 231 Joe Moore FIELD	50.00	22.00
☐ 232 Lefty O'Doul	75.00	34.00
☐ 233 Johnny Vergez	50.00	22.00
☐ 234 Carl Hubbell	200.00	90.00
☐ 235 Fred Fitzsimmons	55.00	25.00
☐ 236 George Davis	50.00	22.00
☐ 237 Gus Mancuso	50.00	22.00
☐ 238 Hugh Critz	50.00	22.00
☐ 239 Leroy Parmelee	50.00	22.00
☐ 240 Hal Schumacher	125.00	55.00

1933 Goudey Canadian V353

The cards in this 94-card set measure approximately 2 3/8" by 2 7/8". World Wide Gum, the Canadian subsidiary of Goudey issued this set of numbered color cards in 1933. Cards 1 to 52 contain obverses identical to the American issue, but cards 53 to 94 have a slightly different order. The fronts feature white-bordered color player drawings. The words "Big League Chewing Gum"

are printed in white lettering within a red stripe near the bottom. The green ink backs are found printed in English only, or in French and English (the latter are slightly harder to find and are valued at a 25 percent premium over the prices listed below). The catalog designation for this set is V353.

	EX-MT	VG-E
COMPLETE SET (94)	20000.00	9000.00
COMMON CARD (1-94)	60.00	27.00

	EX-MT	VG-E
☐ 1 Benny Bengough	600.00	275.00
☐ 2 Dazzy Vance	125.00	55.00
☐ 3 Hugh Critz	60.00	27.00
☐ 4 Heinie Schulbe	60.00	27.00
☐ 5 Babe Herman	90.00	40.00
☐ 6 Jimmy Dykes	75.00	34.00
☐ 7 Ted Lyons	125.00	55.00
☐ 8 Roy Johnson	60.00	27.00
☐ 9 Dave Harris	60.00	27.00
☐ 10 Glenn Myatt	60.00	27.00
☐ 11 Billy Rogell	60.00	27.00
☐ 12 George Pipgras	75.00	34.00
☐ 13 Lafayette Thompson	60.00	27.00
☐ 14 Henry Johnson	60.00	27.00
☐ 15 Victor Sorrell	60.00	27.00
☐ 16 George Blaeholder	60.00	27.00
☐ 17 Watson Clark	60.00	27.00
☐ 18 Muddy Ruel	60.00	27.00
☐ 19 Bill Dickey	350.00	160.00
☐ 20 Bill Terry	175.00	80.00
☐ 21 Phil Collins	60.00	27.00
☐ 22 Pie Traynor	150.00	70.00
☐ 23 Kiki Cuyler	125.00	55.00
☐ 24 Horace Ford	60.00	27.00
☐ 25 Paul Waner	150.00	70.00
☐ 26 Chalmer Cissell	60.00	27.00
☐ 27 George Connally	60.00	27.00
☐ 28 Dick Bartell	75.00	34.00
☐ 29 Jimmy Foxx	450.00	200.00
☐ 30 Frank Hogan	60.00	27.00
☐ 31 Tony Lazzeri	175.00	80.00
☐ 32 Bud Clancy	60.00	27.00
☐ 33 Ralph Kress	60.00	27.00
☐ 34 Bob O'Farrell	75.00	34.00
☐ 35 Al Simmons	175.00	80.00
☐ 36 Tommy Thevenow	60.00	27.00
☐ 37 Jimmy Wilson	75.00	34.00
☐ 38 Fred Bickell	60.00	27.00
☐ 39 Mark Koenig	75.00	34.00
☐ 40 Taylor Douthit	60.00	27.00
☐ 41 Gus Mancuso	60.00	27.00
☐ 42 Eddie Collins	150.00	70.00
☐ 43 Lew Fonseca	75.00	34.00
☐ 44 Jim Bottomley	125.00	55.00
☐ 45 Larry Benton	60.00	27.00
☐ 46 Ethan Allen	75.00	34.00
☐ 47 Heinie Manush	125.00	55.00
☐ 48 Marty McManus	60.00	27.00
☐ 49 Frank Frisch	150.00	70.00
☐ 50 Ed Brandt	60.00	27.00
☐ 51 Charlie Grimm	75.00	34.00
☐ 52 Andy Cohen	60.00	27.00
☐ 53 Jack Quinn	75.00	34.00
☐ 54 Urban Faber	125.00	55.00
☐ 55 Lou Gehrig	3500.00	1600.00
☐ 56 John Welch	60.00	27.00
☐ 57 Bill Walker	60.00	27.00
☐ 58 Lefty O'Doul	90.00	40.00
☐ 59 Bing Miller	75.00	34.00
☐ 60 Waite Hoyt	125.00	55.00
☐ 61 Max Bishop	75.00	34.00
☐ 62 Pepper Martin	90.00	40.00
☐ 63 Joe Cronin	150.00	70.00
☐ 64 Burleigh Grimes	125.00	55.00
☐ 65 Milt Gaston	60.00	27.00
☐ 66 George Grantham	60.00	27.00
☐ 67 Guy Bush	60.00	27.00
☐ 68 Willie Kamm	60.00	27.00
☐ 69 Mickey Cochrane	200.00	90.00
☐ 70 Adam Comorosky	60.00	27.00
☐ 71 Alvin Crowder	60.00	27.00
☐ 72 Willis Hudlin	60.00	27.00
☐ 73 Eddie Farrell	60.00	27.00
☐ 74 Leo Durocher	175.00	80.00
☐ 75 Walter Stewart	60.00	27.00
☐ 76 George Walberg	60.00	27.00
☐ 77 Glenn Wright	75.00	34.00
☐ 78 Charles(Buddy) Myer	75.00	34.00
☐ 79 James(Zack) Taylor	60.00	27.00
☐ 80 George H.(Babe)Ruth	5000.00	2200.00
☐ 81 D'Arcy(Jake) Flowers	60.00	27.00
☐ 82 Ray Kolp	60.00	27.00
☐ 83 Oswald Bluege	60.00	27.00
☐ 84 Morris (Moe) Berg	250.00	110.00
☐ 85 Jimmy Foxx	450.00	200.00
☐ 86 Sam Byrd	60.00	27.00
☐ 87 Danny MacFayden	60.00	27.00
☐ 88 Joe Judge	75.00	34.00
☐ 89 Joe Sewell	125.00	55.00
☐ 90 Lloyd Waner	125.00	55.00
☐ 91 Luke Sewell	75.00	34.00
☐ 92 Leo Mangum	60.00	27.00
☐ 93 George H.(Babe)Ruth	5000.00	2200.00
☐ 94 Al Spohrer	75.00	34.00

1934 Goudey R320

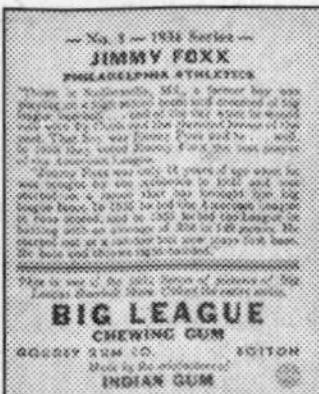

JIMMY FOXX
BIG LEAGUE
CHEWING GUM
INDIAN GUM

The cards in this 96-card color set measure approximately 2 3/8" by 2 7/8". Cards 1-48 are considered to be the easiest to find (although card number 1, Foxx, is very scarce in mint condition) while 73-96 are much more difficult to find. Cards of this 1934 Goudey series are slightly less abundant than cards of the 1933 Goudey set. Of the 96 cards, 84 contain a "Lou Gehrig Says" line on the front in a blue design, while 12 of the high series (80-91) contain a "Chuck Klein Says" line in a red design. These Chuck Klein cards are indicated in the checklist below by CK and are in fact the 12 National Leaguers in the high series.

	EX-MT	VG-E
COMPLETE SET (96)	17000.00	7600.00
COMMON CARD (1-48)	50.00	22.00
COMMON CARD (49-72)	75.00	34.00
COMMON CARD (73-96)	175.00	80.00
WRAPPER (1-CENT, WHITE)	100.00	45.00
WRAPPER (1-CENT, CLEAR)	100.00	45.00

	EX-MT	VG-E
☐ 1 Jimmie Foxx	750.00	350.00
☐ 2 Mickey Cochrane	175.00	80.00
☐ 3 Charlie Grimm	60.00	27.00
☐ 4 Woody English	50.00	22.00
☐ 5 Ed Brandt	50.00	22.00
☐ 6 Dizzy Dean	600.00	275.00
☐ 7 Leo Durocher	150.00	70.00
☐ 8 Tony Piet	50.00	22.00
☐ 9 Ben Chapman	60.00	27.00
☐ 10 Chuck Klein	150.00	70.00
☐ 11 Paul Waner	125.00	55.00
☐ 12 Carl Hubbell	165.00	75.00
☐ 13 Frankie Frisch	150.00	70.00
☐ 14 Willie Kamm	50.00	22.00
☐ 15 Alvin Crowder	50.00	22.00
☐ 16 Joe Kuhel	50.00	22.00
☐ 17 Hugh Critz	50.00	22.00
☐ 18 Heinie Manush	100.00	45.00
☐ 19 Lefty Grove	300.00	135.00
☐ 20 Frank Hogan	50.00	22.00
☐ 21 Bill Terry	200.00	90.00
☐ 22 Arky Vaughan	125.00	55.00
☐ 23 Charley Gehringer	200.00	90.00
☐ 24 Ray Benge	50.00	22.00
☐ 25 Roger Cramer	60.00	27.00
☐ 26 Gerald Walker	50.00	22.00
☐ 27 Luke Appling	150.00	70.00
☐ 28 Ed Coleman	50.00	22.00
☐ 29 Larry French	50.00	22.00
☐ 30 Julius Solters	50.00	22.00
☐ 31 Buck Jordan	50.00	22.00
☐ 32 Blondy Ryan	50.00	22.00
☐ 33 Frank Hurst	50.00	22.00
☐ 34 Chick Hafey	100.00	45.00
☐ 35 Ernie Lombardi	125.00	55.00
☐ 36 Walter Betts	50.00	22.00
☐ 37 Lou Gehrig	2700.00	1200.00
☐ 38 Oral Hildebrand	50.00	22.00
☐ 39 Fred Walker	50.00	22.00
☐ 40 John Stone	50.00	22.00
☐ 41 George Earnshaw	50.00	22.00
☐ 42 John Allen	50.00	22.00
☐ 43 Dick Porter	50.00	22.00
☐ 44 Tom Bridges	60.00	27.00
☐ 45 Oscar Melillo	50.00	22.00
☐ 46 Joe Stripp	50.00	22.00
☐ 47 John Frederick	50.00	22.00
☐ 48 Tex Carleton	50.00	22.00
☐ 49 Sam Leslie	75.00	34.00
☐ 50 Walter Beck	75.00	34.00
☐ 51 Rip Collins	75.00	34.00
☐ 52 Herman Bell	75.00	34.00
☐ 53 George Watkins	75.00	34.00
☐ 54 Wesley Schulmerich	75.00	34.00
☐ 55 Ed Holley	75.00	34.00
☐ 56 Mark Koenig	100.00	45.00
☐ 57 Bill Swift	75.00	34.00
☐ 58 Earl Grace	75.00	34.00
☐ 59 Joe Mowry	75.00	34.00
☐ 60 Lynn Nelson	75.00	34.00
☐ 61 Lou Gehrig	2700.00	1200.00
☐ 62 Hank Greenberg	375.00	170.00
☐ 63 Minter Hayes	75.00	34.00
☐ 64 Frank Grube	75.00	34.00
☐ 65 Cliff Bolton	75.00	34.00
☐ 66 Mel Harder	100.00	45.00
☐ 67 Bob Weiland	75.00	34.00
☐ 68 Bob Johnson	100.00	45.00
☐ 69 John Marcum	75.00	34.00
☐ 70 Pete Fox	75.00	34.00
☐ 71 Lyle Tinning	75.00	34.00
☐ 72 Arndt Jorgens	75.00	34.00
☐ 73 Ed Wells	175.00	80.00
☐ 74 Bob Boken	175.00	80.00
☐ 75 Bill Werber	175.00	80.00
☐ 76 Hal Trosky	200.00	90.00
☐ 77 Joe Vosmik	175.00	80.00
☐ 78 Pinky Higgins	200.00	90.00
☐ 79 Ed Durham	175.00	80.00
☐ 80 Marty McManus CK	175.00	80.00
☐ 81 Bob Brown CK	175.00	80.00
☐ 82 Bill Hallahan CK	175.00	80.00
☐ 83 Jim Mooney CK	175.00	80.00
☐ 84 Paul Derringer CK	225.00	100.00
☐ 85 Adam Comorosky CK	175.00	80.00
☐ 86 Lloyd Johnson CK	175.00	80.00
☐ 87 George Darrow CK	175.00	80.00
☐ 88 Homer Peel CK	175.00	80.00
☐ 89 Linus Frey CK	175.00	80.00
☐ 90 KiKi Cuyler CK	350.00	160.00
☐ 91 Dolph Camilli CK	200.00	90.00
☐ 92 Steve Larkin	175.00	80.00
☐ 93 Fred Ostermueller	175.00	80.00
☐ 94 Red Rolfe	200.00	90.00
☐ 95 Myril Hoag	175.00	80.00
☐ 96 James DeShong	300.00	135.00

1934 Goudey Canadian V354

The cards in this 96-card set measure approximately 2 3/8" by 2 7/8". The 1934 Canadian Goudey set was issued by World Wide Gum Company. Cards 1 to 48 have the same format as the 1933 American Goudey issue while cards 49 to 96 have the same format as the 1934 American Goudey issue. Cards numbers 49 to 96 all have the "Lou Gehrig Says" endorsement on the front of the cards. No Chuck Klein endorsement exists as it does in the 1934 American issue. The fronts feature white-bordered color player drawings. The words "Big League Chewing Gum" are printed in white lettering within a red stripe near the bottom. The green ink backs are found printed in English only, or in French and English (the latter are slightly harder to find and are valued at a 25 percent premium over the prices listed below). The catalog designation for this set is V354.

	EX-MT	VG-E
COMPLETE SET (96)	13000.00	5800.00
COMMON CARD (1-96)	60.00	27.00

	EX-MT	VG-E
☐ 1 Rogers Hornsby	600.00	275.00
☐ 2 Eddie Morgan	60.00	27.00
☐ 3 Val Picinich	60.00	27.00
☐ 4 Rabbit Maranville	125.00	55.00
☐ 5 Flint Rhem	60.00	27.00
☐ 6 Jim Elliott	60.00	27.00
☐ 7 Fred(Red) Lucas	60.00	27.00
☐ 8 Fred Marberry	60.00	27.00
☐ 9 Clifton Heathcote	60.00	27.00
☐ 10 Bernie Friberg	60.00	27.00
☐ 11 Woody English	60.00	27.00
☐ 12 Carl Reynolds	60.00	27.00
☐ 13 Ray Benge	60.00	27.00
☐ 14 Ben Cantwell	60.00	27.00
☐ 15 Bump Hadley	60.00	27.00

☐ 16 Herb Pennock	125.00	55.00
☐ 17 Fred Lindstrom	125.00	55.00
☐ 18 Edgar(Sam) Rice	125.00	55.00
☐ 19 Fred Frankhouse	60.00	27.00
☐ 20 Fred Fitzsimmons	75.00	34.00
☐ 21 Earle Combs	125.00	55.00
☐ 22 George Uhle	60.00	27.00
☐ 23 Richard Coffman	60.00	27.00
☐ 24 Travis Jackson	125.00	55.00
☐ 25 Robert J. Burke	60.00	27.00
☐ 26 Randy Moore	60.00	27.00
☐ 27 Heinie Sand	60.00	27.00
☐ 28 George (Babe) Ruth	5000.00	2200.00
☐ 29 Tris Speaker	300.00	135.00
☐ 30 Perce(Pat) Malone	60.00	27.00
☐ 31 Sam Jones	75.00	34.00
☐ 32 Eppa Rixey	125.00	55.00
☐ 33 Floyd (Pete) Scott	60.00	27.00
☐ 34 Pete Jablonowski	60.00	27.00
☐ 35 Clyde Manion	60.00	27.00
☐ 36 Dib Williams	60.00	27.00
☐ 37 Glenn Spencer	60.00	27.00
☐ 38 Ray Kremer	60.00	27.00
☐ 39 Phil Todt	60.00	27.00
☐ 40 Russell Rollings	60.00	27.00
☐ 41 Earl Clark	60.00	27.00
☐ 42 Jess Petty	60.00	27.00
☐ 43 Frank O'Rourke	60.00	27.00
☐ 44 Jesse Haines	125.00	55.00
☐ 45 Horace Lisenbee	60.00	27.00
☐ 46 Owen Carroll	60.00	27.00
☐ 47 Tom Zachary	75.00	34.00
☐ 48 Charlie(Red) Ruffing	150.00	70.00
☐ 49 Ray Benge	60.00	27.00
☐ 50 Woody English	60.00	27.00
☐ 51 Ben Chapman	75.00	34.00
☐ 52 Joe Kuhel	60.00	27.00
☐ 53 Bill Terry	200.00	90.00
☐ 54 Robert(Lefty) Grove	300.00	135.00
☐ 55 Jerome(Dizzy) Dean	750.00	350.00
☐ 56 Chuck Klein	150.00	70.00
☐ 57 Charley Gehringer	200.00	90.00
☐ 58 Jimmie Foxx	400.00	180.00
☐ 59 Mickey Cochrane	200.00	90.00
☐ 60 Willie Kamm	60.00	27.00
☐ 61 Charlie Grimm	75.00	34.00
☐ 62 Ed Brandt	60.00	27.00
☐ 63 Tony Piet	60.00	27.00
☐ 64 Frank Frisch	150.00	70.00
☐ 65 Alvin Crowder	60.00	27.00
☐ 66 Frank Hogan	60.00	27.00
☐ 67 Paul Waner	150.00	70.00
☐ 68 Heinie Manush	125.00	55.00
☐ 69 Leo Durocher	150.00	70.00
☐ 70 Arky Vaughan	125.00	55.00
☐ 71 Carl Hubbell	200.00	90.00
☐ 72 Hugh Critz	60.00	27.00
☐ 73 John(Blondy) Ryan	60.00	27.00
☐ 74 Doc Cramer	75.00	34.00
☐ 75 Baxter Jordan	60.00	27.00
☐ 76 Ed Coleman	60.00	27.00
☐ 77 Julius(Moose) Solters	60.00	27.00
☐ 78 Chick Hafey	125.00	55.00
☐ 79 Larry French	60.00	27.00
☐ 80 Frank(Don) Hurst	60.00	27.00
☐ 81 Gerald Walker	60.00	27.00
☐ 82 Ernie Lombardi	150.00	70.00
☐ 83 Walter(Huck) Betts	60.00	27.00
☐ 84 Luke Appling	150.00	70.00
☐ 85 John Frederick	60.00	27.00
☐ 86 Fred(Dixie) Walker	75.00	34.00
☐ 87 Tom Bridges	75.00	34.00
☐ 88 Dick Porter	60.00	27.00
☐ 89 John Stone	60.00	27.00
☐ 90 James(Tex) Carleton	60.00	27.00
☐ 91 Joe Stripp	60.00	27.00
☐ 92 Lou Gehrig	3500.00	1600.00
☐ 93 George Earnshaw	75.00	34.00
☐ 94 Oscar Melillo	60.00	27.00
☐ 95 Oral Hildebrand	60.00	27.00
☐ 96 John Allen	75.00	34.00

1935 Goudey Puzzle R321

The cards in this 36-card set (the number of different front pictures) measure approximately 2 3/8" by 2 7/8". The 1935 Goudey set is sometimes called the Goudey Puzzle Set, or the Goudey 4-in-1's. There are 36 different card fronts but 114 different front/back combinations. The card number in the checklist refers to the back puzzle number, as the backs can be arranged to form a puzzle picturing a player or team. To avoid the confusion caused by two different fronts having the same back number, the rarer cards have been arbitrarily given a "1" prefix. The scarcer puzzle cards are hence all listed at the numerical end of the list below, i.e. rare puzzle 1 is listed as number

11, rare puzzle 2 is listed as 12, etc. The BLUE in the checklist refers to a card with a blue border, as most cards have a red border. The set price below includes all the cards listed. The following is the list of the puzzle back pictures: 1) Detroit Tigers; 2) Chuck Klein; 3) Frankie Frisch; 4) Mickey Cochrane; 5) Joe Cronin; 6) Jimmy Foxx; 7) Al Simmons; 8) Cleveland Indians; and 9) Washington Senators.

	EX-MT	VG-E
COMPLETE SET (114)	13500.00	6100.00
COMMON CARDS (1-9)	50.00	22.00
COMMON CARDS (11-17)	75.00	34.00
WRAPPER (1-CENT, WHITE)	200.00	90.00

☐ 1A Frank Frisch	150.00	70.00
Dizzy Dean		
Ernie Orsatti		
Tex Carleton		
☐ 1B Roy Mahaffey	125.00	55.00
Jimmie Foxx		
Dib Williams		
Pinky Higgins		
☐ 1C Heinie Manush	60.00	27.00
Lyn Lary		
Monte Weaver		
Bump Hadley		
☐ 1D Mickey Cochrane	125.00	55.00
Charlie Gehringer		
Tommy Bridges		
Billy Rogell		
☐ 1E Paul Waner	100.00	45.00
Guy Bush		
Waite Hoyt		
Lloyd Waner		
☐ 1F Burleigh Grimes	100.00	45.00
Chuck Klein		
Kiki Cuyler		
Woody English		
☐ 1G Sam Leslie	50.00	22.00
Lonnie Frey		
Joe Stripp		
Watson Clark		
☐ 1H Tony Piet	60.00	27.00
Adam Comorosky		
Jim Bottomley		
Sparky Adams		
☐ 1I George Earnshaw	60.00	27.00
Jimmie Dykes		
Luke Sewell		
Luke Appling		
☐ 1J Babe Ruth	1000.00	450.00
Marty McManus		
Eddie Brandt		
Rabbit Maranville		
☐ 1K Bill Terry	100.00	45.00
Hal Schumacher		
Gus Mancuso		
Travis Jackson		
☐ 1L Willie Kamm	60.00	27.00
Oral Hildebrand		
Earl Averill		
Hal Trosky		
☐ 2A Frank Frisch	150.00	70.00
Dizzy Dean		
Ernie Orsatti		
Tex Carleton		
☐ 2B Roy Mahaffey	125.00	55.00
Jimmie Foxx		
Dib Williams		
Pinky Higgins		
☐ 2C Heinie Manush	60.00	27.00
Lyn Lary		
Monte Weaver		
Bump Hadley		
☐ 2D Mickey Cochrane	125.00	55.00
Charlie Gehringer		
Tommy Bridges		
Billy Rogell		
☐ 2E Willie Kamm	60.00	27.00
Oral Hildebrand		
Earl Averill		
Hal Trosky		
☐ 2F George Earnshaw	60.00	27.00
Jimmie Dykes		
Luke Sewell		
Luke Appling		
☐ 3A Babe Ruth	1000.00	450.00
Marty McManus		
Eddie Brandt		
Rabbit Maranville		
☐ 3B Bill Terry	100.00	45.00
Hal Schumacher		
Gus Mancuso		
Travis Jackson		
☐ 3C Paul Waner	100.00	45.00
Guy Bush		
Waite Hoyt		
Lloyd Waner		
☐ 3D Burleigh Grimes	100.00	45.00
Chuck Klein		
Kiki Cuyler		
Woody English		
☐ 3E Sam Leslie	50.00	22.00
Lonnie Frey		
Joe Stripp		
Watson Clark		
☐ 3F Tony Piet	60.00	27.00
Adam Comorosky		
Jim Bottomley		
Sparky Adams		
☐ 4A Hugh Critz BLUE	100.00	45.00
Dick Bartell		
Mel Ott		
Gus Mancuso		
☐ 4B Pie Traynor BLUE	60.00	27.00
Red Lucas		
Tom Thevenow		
Glenn Wright		
☐ 4C Charlie Berry BLUE	60.00	27.00
Bobby Burke		
Red Kress		
Dazzy Vance		
☐ 4D Red Ruffing BLUE	150.00	70.00
Pat Malone		
Tony Lazzeri		
Bill Dickey		
☐ 4E Randy Moore BLUE	50.00	22.00
Shanty Hogan		
Fred Frankhouse		
Eddie Brandt		
☐ 4F Pepper Martin BLUE	50.00	22.00
Bob O'Farrell		
Sam Byrd		
Danny MacFayden		
☐ 5A Muddy Ruel	100.00	45.00
Al Simmons		
Willie Kamm		
Mickey Cochrane		
☐ 5B Willis Hudlin	60.00	27.00
George Myatt		
Adam Comorosky		
Jim Bottomley		
☐ 5C Paul Waner	100.00	45.00
Guy Bush		
Waite Hoyt		
Lloyd Waner		
☐ 5D Sam West	50.00	22.00
Oscar Melillo		
George Blaeholder		
Dick Coffman		
☐ 5E Sam Leslie	50.00	22.00
Lonnie Frey		
Joe Stripp		
Watson Clark		
☐ 5F Heine Schuble	60.00	27.00
Fred Marberry		
Goose Goslin		
General Crowder		
☐ 6A Muddy Ruel	100.00	45.00
Al Simmons		
Willie Kamm		
Mickey Cochrane		
☐ 6B Willis Hudlin	60.00	27.00
George Myatt		
Adam Comorosky		
Jim Bottomley		
☐ 6C Jimmy Wilson	50.00	22.00
Ethan Allen		
Bubba Jonnard		
Fred Brickell		
☐ 6D Sam West	50.00	22.00
Oscar Melillo		
George Blaeholder		
Dick Coffman		
☐ 6E Joe Cronin	60.00	27.00
Carl Reynolds		
Max Bishop		
Chalmer Cissell		
☐ 6F Heine Schuble	60.00	27.00
Fred Marberry		
Goose Goslin		

General Crowder
☐ 7A Hugh Critz BLUE 100.00 45.00
Dick Bartell
Mel Ott
Gus Mancuso
☐ 7B Pie Traynor BLUE 60.00 27.00
Red Lucas
Tom Thevenow
Glenn Wright
☐ 7C Charlie Berry BLUE 60.00 27.00
Bobby Burke
Red Kress
Dazzy Vance
☐ 7D Red Ruffing BLUE 150.00 70.00
Pat Malone
Tom Lazzeri
Bill Dickey
☐ 7E Randy Moore BLUE 50.00 22.00
Shanty Hogan
Fred Frankhouse
Eddie Brandt
☐ 7F Pepper Martin BLUE 50.00 22.00
Bob O'Farrell
Sam Byrd
Danny MacFayden
☐ 8A Mark Koenig 50.00 22.00
Fred Fitzsimmons
Ray Benge
Tom Zachary
☐ 8B Minter Hayes 60.00 27.00
Ted Lyons
Mule Haas
Zeke Bonura
☐ 8C Jack Burns 50.00 22.00
Rollie Hemsley
Frank Grube
Bob Weiland
☐ 8D F.Campbell 50.00 22.00
Billy Meyers
Ival Goodman
Alex Kampouris
☐ 8E Jimmy DeShong 50.00 22.00
Johnny Allen
Red Rolfe
Dixie Walker
☐ 8F Pete Fox 100.00 45.00
Hank Greenberg
Gee Walker
Schoolboy Rowe
☐ 8G Billy Werber 60.00 27.00
Rick Ferrell
Wes Ferrell
Fritz Ostermueller
☐ 8H Joe Kuhel 50.00 22.00
Earl Whitehill
Buddy Myer
John Stone
☐ 8I Joe Vosmik 50.00 22.00
Bill Knickerbocker
Mel Harder
Lefty Stewart
☐ 8J Bob Johnson 50.00 22.00
Ed Coleman
Johnny Marcum
Doc Cramer
☐ 8K Babe Herman 60.00 27.00
Gus Suhr
Tom Padden
Cy Blanton
☐ 8L Al Spohrer 50.00 22.00
Flint Rhem
Ben Cantwell
Larry Benton
☐ 8M Mark Koenig 50.00 22.00
Fred Fitzsimmons
Ray Benge
Tom Zachary
☐ 9B Minter Hayes 60.00 27.00
Ted Lyons
Mule Haas
Zeke Bonura
☐ 9C Jack Burns 50.00 22.00
Rollie Hemsley
Frank Grube
Bob Weiland
☐ 9D Bruce Campbell 50.00 22.00
Billy Meyers
Ival Goodman
Alex Kampouris
☐ 9E Jimmy DeShong 50.00 22.00
Johnny Allen
Red Rolfe
Fred Walker
☐ 9F Pete Fox 100.00 45.00
Hank Greenberg
Gee Walker
Schoolboy Rowe
☐ 9G Billy Werber 60.00 27.00
Rick Ferrell
Wes Ferrell
F.Ostermueller
☐ 9H Joe Kuhel 50.00 22.00
Earl Whitehill
Buddy Myer
John Stone
☐ 9I Joe Vosmik 50.00 22.00
Bill Knickerbocker
Mel Harder
Lefty Stewart
☐ 9J Bob Johnson 50.00 22.00
Ed Coleman
Johnny Marcum
Doc Cramer
☐ 9K Babe Herman 60.00 27.00
Gus Suhr
Tom Padden
Cy Blanton
☐ 9L Al Spohrer 50.00 22.00
Flint Rhem
Ben Cantwell
Larry Benton
☐ 11E Jimmy Wilson 75.00 34.00
Johnny Allen
Bubba Jonnard
Fred Brickell
☐ 11F Sam West 75.00 34.00
Oscar Melillo
George Blaeholder
Dick Coffman
☐ 11G Joe Cronin 90.00 40.00
Carl Reynolds
Max Bishop
Chalmer Cissell
☐ 11H Heine Schuble 90.00 40.00
Fred Marberry
Goose Goslin
General Crowder
☐ 11J Muddy Ruel 150.00 70.00
Al Simmons
Willie Kamm
Mickey Cochrane
☐ 11K Willis Hudlin 90.00 40.00
George Myatt
Adam Comorosky
Jim Bottomley
☐ 12A Hugh Critz BLUE 150.00 70.00
Dick Bartell
Mel Ott
Gus Mancuso
☐ 12B Pie Traynor BLUE 90.00 40.00
Red Lucas
Tommy Thevenow
Glenn Wright
☐ 12C Charlie Berry BLUE 90.00 40.00
Bobby Burke
Red Kress
Dazzy Vance
☐ 12D Red Ruffing BLUE 225.00 100.00
Pat Malone
Tony Lazzeri
Bill Dickey
☐ 12E Randy Moore BLUE 75.00 34.00
Shanty Hogan
Fred Frankhouse
Eddie Brandt
☐ 12F Pepper Martin BLUE 75.00 34.00
Bob O'Farrell
Sam Byrd
Danny MacFayden
☐ 13A Muddy Ruel 150.00 70.00
Al Simmons
Willie Kamm
Mickey Cochrane
☐ 13B Willis Hudlin 90.00 40.00
George Myatt
Adam Comorosky
Jim Bottomley
☐ 13C Jimmy Wilson 75.00 34.00
Johnny Allen
Bubba Jonnard
Fred Brickell
☐ 13D Sam West 75.00 34.00
Oscar Melillo
George Blaeholder
Dick Coffman
☐ 13E Joe Cronin 90.00 40.00
Carl Reynolds
Max Bishop
Chalmer Cissell
☐ 13F Heine Schuble 90.00 40.00
Fred Marberry
Goose Goslin
General Crowder
☐ 14A Babe Ruth 1500.00 700.00
Marty McManus
Eddie Brandt
Rabbit Maranville
☐ 14B Bill Terry 150.00 70.00
Hal Schumacher
Gus Mancuso
Travis Jackson
☐ 14C Paul Waner 150.00 70.00
Guy Bush
Waite Hoyt
Lloyd Waner
☐ 14D Burleigh Grimes 150.00 70.00
Chuck Klein
Kiki Cuyler
Woody English
☐ 14E Sam Leslie 75.00 34.00
Lonnie Frey
Joe Stripp
Watson Clark
☐ 14F Tony Piet 90.00 40.00
Adam Comorosky
Jim Bottomley
Sparky Adams
☐ 15A Babe Ruth 1500.00 700.00
Marty McManus
Eddie Brandt
Rabbit Maranville
☐ 15B Bill Terry 150.00 70.00
Hal Schumacher
Gus Mancuso
Travis Jackson
☐ 15C Jimmy Wilson 75.00 34.00
Johnny Allen
Bubba Jonnard
Fred Brickell
☐ 15D Burleigh Grimes 150.00 70.00
Chuck Klein
Kiki Cuyler
Woody English
☐ 15E Joe Cronin 90.00 40.00
Carl Reynolds
Max Bishop
Chalmer Cissell
☐ 15F Tony Piet 90.00 40.00
Adam Comorosky
Jim Bottomley
Sparky Adams
☐ 16A Frank Frisch 225.00 100.00
Dizzy Dean
Ernie Orsatti
Tex Carleton
☐ 16B Roy Mahaffey 175.00 80.00
Jimmie Foxx
Dib Williams
Pinky Higgins
☐ 16C Heinie Manush 90.00 40.00
Lyn Lary
Monte Weaver
Bump Hadley
☐ 16D Mickey Cochrane 175.00 80.00
Charlie Gehringer
Tom Bridges
Billy Rogell
☐ 16E Willie Kamm 90.00 40.00
Oral Hildebrand
Earl Averill
Hal Trosky
☐ 16F George Earnshaw 90.00 40.00
Jimmie Dykes
Luke Sewell
Luke Appling
☐ 17A Frank Frisch 225.00 100.00
Dizzy Dean
Ernie Orsatti
Tex Carleton
☐ 17B Roy Mahaffey 175.00 80.00
Jimmie Foxx
Dib Williams
Pinky Higgins
☐ 17C Heinie Manush 90.00 40.00
Lyn Lary
Monte Weaver
Bump Hadley
☐ 17D Mickey Cochrane 175.00 80.00
Charlie Gehringer
Tom Bridges
Billy Rogell
☐ 17E Willie Kamm 90.00 40.00
Oral Hildebrand
Earl Averill
Hal Trosky
☐ 17F George Earnshaw 90.00 40.00
Jimmie Dykes
Luke Sewell
Luke Appling

1936 Goudey B/W R322

The cards in this 25-card black and white set measure approximately 2 3/8" by 2 7/8". In contrast to the color

THREE BAGGER

What a smash down 1st base line!--Too fast for the 1st sacker to even get near it.

OUT

artwork of its previous sets, the 1936 Goudey set contained a simple black and white player photograph. A facsimile autograph appeared within the picture area. Each card was issued with a number of different "game situation" backs, and there may be as many as 200 different front/back combinations. This unnumbered set is checklisted and numbered below in alphabetical order for convenience.

	EX-MT	VG-E
COMPLETE SET (25)	2000.00	900.00
COMMON CARD (1-25)	45.00	20.00
WRAPPER (1-CENT)	200.00	90.00
☐ 1 Wally Berger	60.00	27.00
☐ 2 Zeke Bonura	45.00	20.00
☐ 3 Frenchy Bordagaray	45.00	20.00
☐ 4 Bill Brubaker	45.00	20.00
☐ 5 Dolph Camilli	50.00	22.00
☐ 6 Clyde Castleman	45.00	20.00
☐ 7 Mickey Cochrane	200.00	90.00
☐ 8 Joe Coscarart	45.00	20.00
☐ 9 Frank Crosetti	75.00	34.00
☐ 10 Kiki Cuyler	90.00	40.00
☐ 11 Paul Derringer	50.00	22.00
☐ 12 Jimmy Dykes	50.00	22.00
☐ 13 Rick Ferrell	90.00	40.00
☐ 14 Lefty Gomez	200.00	90.00
☐ 15 Hank Greenberg	250.00	110.00
☐ 16 Bucky Harris	90.00	40.00
☐ 17 Rollie Hemsley	45.00	20.00
☐ 18 Pinky Higgins	50.00	22.00
☐ 19 Oral Hildebrand	45.00	20.00
☐ 20 Chuck Klein	125.00	55.00
☐ 21 Pepper Martin	75.00	34.00
☐ 22 Bobo Newsom	50.00	22.00
☐ 23 Joe Vosmik	45.00	20.00
☐ 24 Paul Waner	125.00	55.00
☐ 25 Bill Werber	45.00	20.00

1938 Goudey Heads Up R323

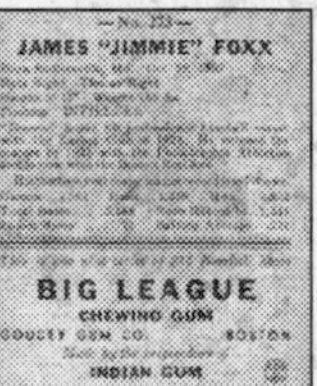

The cards in this 48-card set measure approximately 2 3/8" by 2 7/8". The 1938 Goudey set is commonly referred to as the Heads-Up set. These very popular but difficult to obtain cards came in two series of the same 24 players. The first series, numbers 241-264, is distinguished from the second series, numbers 265-288, in that the second contains etched cartoons and comments surrounding the player picture. Although the set starts with number 241, it is not a continuation of the 1933 Goudey set, but a separate set in its own right.

	EX-MT	VG-E
COMPLETE SET (48)	18000.00	8100.00
COMMON CARD (241-264)	100.00	45.00
COMMON CARD (265-288)	110.00	50.00
WRAPPER (1-CENT, 6-FIGURE)	500.00	220.00
☐ 241 Charley Gehringer	325.00	145.00
☐ 242 Pete Fox	100.00	45.00
☐ 243 Joe Kuhel	100.00	45.00
☐ 244 Frank Demaree	100.00	45.00
☐ 245 Frank Pytlak	100.00	45.00
☐ 246 Ernie Lombardi	175.00	80.00
☐ 247 Joe Vosmik	100.00	45.00
☐ 248 Dick Bartell	100.00	45.00
☐ 249 Jimmie Foxx	400.00	180.00
☐ 250 Joe DiMaggio	4500.00	2000.00
☐ 251 Bump Hadley	100.00	45.00
☐ 252 Zeke Bonura	100.00	45.00
☐ 253 Hank Greenberg	400.00	180.00
☐ 254 Van Lingle Mungo	110.00	50.00
☐ 255 Moose Solters	100.00	45.00
☐ 256 Vernon Kennedy	100.00	45.00
☐ 257 Al Lopez	175.00	80.00
☐ 258 Bobby Doerr	325.00	145.00
☐ 259 Billy Werber	100.00	45.00
☐ 260 Rudy York	110.00	50.00
☐ 261 Rip Radcliff	100.00	45.00
☐ 262 Joe Medwick	300.00	135.00
☐ 263 Marvin Owen	100.00	45.00
☐ 264 Bob Feller	700.00	325.00
☐ 265 Charley Gehringer	350.00	160.00
☐ 266 Pete Fox	110.00	50.00
☐ 267 Joe Kuhel	110.00	50.00
☐ 268 Frank Demaree	110.00	50.00
☐ 269 Frank Pytlak	110.00	50.00
☐ 270 Ernie Lombardi	200.00	90.00
☐ 271 Joe Vosmik	110.00	50.00
☐ 272 Dick Bartell	110.00	50.00
☐ 273 Jimmie Foxx	450.00	200.00
☐ 274 Joe DiMaggio	4500.00	2000.00
☐ 275 Bump Hadley	110.00	50.00
☐ 276 Zeke Bonura	110.00	50.00
☐ 277 Hank Greenberg	450.00	200.00
☐ 278 Van Lingle Mungo	125.00	55.00
☐ 279 Moose Solters	110.00	50.00
☐ 280 Vernon Kennedy	110.00	50.00
☐ 281 Al Lopez	200.00	90.00
☐ 282 Bobby Doerr	350.00	160.00
☐ 283 Billy Werber	110.00	50.00
☐ 284 Rudy York	125.00	55.00
☐ 285 Rip Radcliff	110.00	50.00
☐ 286 Joe Medwick	325.00	145.00
☐ 287 Marvin Owen	110.00	50.00
☐ 288 Bob Feller	750.00	350.00

1941 Goudey R324

The cards in this 33-card set measure 2 3/8" by 2 7/8". The 1941 Series of blank backed baseball cards was the last baseball issue marketed by Goudey before the war closed the door on that company for good. Each black and white player photo comes with four color backgrounds (blue, green, red, or yellow). Cards without numbers are probably miscut. Cards 21-25 are especially scarce in relation to the rest of the set. In fact the eight hardest to find cards in the set are, in order, 22, 24, 23, 25, 21, 27, 29 and 32.

	EX-MT	VG-E
COMPLETE SET (33)	2000.00	900.00
COMMON CARD (1-33)	30.00	13.50
WRAPPER (1-CENT)	200.00	90.00
☐ 1 Hugh Mulcahy	30.00	13.50
☐ 2 Harland Clift	30.00	13.50
☐ 3 Louis Chiozza	30.00	13.50
☐ 4 Warren Rosar	30.00	13.50
☐ 5 George McQuinn	30.00	13.50
☐ 6 George Dickman	30.00	13.50
☐ 7 Wayne Ambler	30.00	13.50
☐ 8 Bob Muncrief	30.00	13.50
☐ 9 Bill Dietrich	30.00	13.50
☐ 10 Taft Wright	30.00	13.50
☐ 11 Don Heffner	30.00	13.50
☐ 12 Fritz Ostermueller	30.00	13.50
☐ 13 Frank Hayes	30.00	13.50
☐ 14 John Kramer	30.00	13.50
☐ 15 Dario Lodigiani	30.00	13.50
☐ 16 George Case	30.00	13.50
☐ 17 Vito Tamulis	30.00	13.50
☐ 18 Whitlow Wyatt	30.00	13.50
☐ 19 Bill Posedel	30.00	13.50
☐ 20 Carl Hubbell	75.00	34.00
☐ 21 Harold Warstler SP	125.00	55.00
☐ 22 Joe Sullivan SP	300.00	135.00
☐ 23 Norman Young SP	200.00	90.00
☐ 24 Stanley Andrews SP	250.00	110.00
☐ 25 Morris Arnovich SP	125.00	55.00
☐ 26 Elbert Fletcher	30.00	13.50
☐ 27 Bill Crough	60.00	27.00
☐ 28 Al Todd	30.00	13.50
☐ 29 Debs Garms	50.00	22.00
☐ 30 Jim Tobin	30.00	13.50
☐ 31 Chester Ross	30.00	13.50
☐ 32 George Coffman	40.00	18.00
☐ 33 Mel Ott	125.00	55.00

1997-98 Highland Mint Elite Series Coins

These coins are about 1.5 inches in diameter and come in a velvet display box which converts to a display stand.The announced mintages were 5000 for bronze, 2,500 for silver, and 1000 for two-tone gold (polished silver with 24K Gold plating). The first 375 of each type are also packaged in Proof Sets of all 3 coins, each with the same serial number in a special 3 coin display box.

☐ 1 Ken Griffey Jr. G/1000	80.00	36.00
☐ 2 Ken Griffey Jr. S/2500	40.00	18.00
☐ 3 Ken Griffey Jr. B/5000	20.00	9.00
☐ 10 Chipper Jones G/1000	80.00	36.00
☐ 11 Chipper Jones S/2500	40.00	18.00
☐ 12 Chipper Jones B/5000	20.00	9.00
☐ 20 Mickey Mantle G/1000	80.00	36.00
☐ 21 Mickey Mantle S/2500	40.00	18.00
☐ 22 Mickey Mantle B/5000	20.00	9.00
☐ 30 Cal Ripken G/1000	80.00	36.00
☐ 31 Cal Ripken S/2500	40.00	18.00
☐ 32 Cal Ripken B/5000	20.00	9.00
☐ 40 Alex Rodriguez G/1000	80.00	36.00
☐ 41 Alex Rodriguez S/2500	40.00	18.00
☐ 42 Alex Rodriguez B/5000	20.00	9.00
☐ 50 Frank Thomas G/1000	80.00	36.00
☐ 51 Frank Thomas S/2500	40.00	18.00
☐ 52 Frank Thomas B/5000	20.00	9.00

1994-98 Highland Mint Magnum Series Medallions

Measuring 2 1/2" in diameter and encased in a 6" by 5" velvet box, these larger medallions feature star major leaguers. The relief on these medallions are 10 times greater than the regular medallions.

	MINT	NRMT
☐ 1 Ken Griffey Jr. G/375	250.00	110.00
☐ 2 Ken Griffey Jr. S/750	150.00	70.00
☐ 3 Ken Griffey Jr. B/3000	50.00	22.00
☐ 5 Mickey Mantle G/375	250.00	110.00
☐ 6 Mickey Mantle S/750	150.00	70.00
☐ 7 Mickey Mantle B/3000	50.00	22.00
☐ 10 Cal Ripken G/375	300.00	135.00
☐ 11 Cal Ripken S/750	150.00	70.00
☐ 12 Cal Ripken B/3000	50.00	22.00
☐ 15 Alex Rodriguez S/750	150.00	70.00
☐ 16 Alex Rodriguez B/3000	50.00	22.00
☐ 19 Babe Ruth G/375	250.00	110.00
☐ 20 Babe Ruth S/750	150.00	70.00
☐ 21 Babe Ruth B/3000	50.00	22.00
☐ 25 Nolan Ryan S/750	150.00	70.00
☐ 26 Nolan Ryan B/3000	50.00	22.00
☐ 30 Frank Thomas S/750	150.00	70.00
☐ 31 Frank Thomas B/3000	50.00	22.00

1996-98 Highland Mint Mini Mint-Cards

These mini Mint-Cards are not replicas but feature Highland Mint's own design. They are one-quarter scale of regular Mint-Cards. The high relief on the fronts is four times greater than that used on regular Mint-Cards. The backs display text and statistics. Each card is individually-numbered, includes a certificate of authenticity, and is packaged in a leather display box. Mini Mint-Cards were issued as a matching set with the cards displayed side by side. Both cards carry the same serial number. The mintage is given below with reference to gold-plated on silver, silver, and bronze quantities. The suggested retail price was $300.00 for the gold, $150.00 for the silver, and $65.00 for the bronze.

	MINT	NRMT
☐ 1 K.Griffey Jr./F.Thomas G/500	300.00	135.00
☐ 2 K.Griffey Jr./F.Thomas S/1000	180.00	80.00
☐ 3 K.Griffey Jr./F.Thomas B/5000	75.00	34.00
☐ 4 R.Johnson/N.Ryan G/375	300.00	135.00
☐ 5 R.Johnson/N.Ryan S/500	150.00	70.00
☐ 7 R.Johnson/N.Ryan B/2500	65.00	29.00
☐ 9 G.Maddux/C.Young G/375	300.00	135.00
☐ 11 G.Maddux/C.Young S/500	150.00	70.00
☐ 13 G.Maddux/C.Young B/2500	65.00	29.00
☐ 15 M.Piazza/R.Campanella S/500	150.00	70.00
☐ 17 M.Piazza/R.Campanella B/2500	65.00	29.00
☐ 19 C.Ripken/L.Gehrig G/375	400.00	180.00
☐ 21 C.Ripken/L.Gehrig S/500	225.00	100.00
☐ 23 C.Ripken/L.Gehrig B/2500	100.00	45.00

1994-98 Highland Mint Mint-Cards Pinnacle/UD

These Highland Mint cards are metal replicas of already issued Pinnacle and Upper Deck cards. All these standard size replicas contain approximately 4.25 ounces of metal. Suggested retail are 50.00 for bronze and 235.00 for silver. Each card includes a certificate of authenticity, and is packaged in a numbered album and a three-piece Lucite display. The cards are checklisted below alphabetically; the final mintage figures for each card are also listed.

	MINT	NRMT
☐ 1 Jeff Bagwell 92/S/750	200.00	90.00
☐ 2 Jeff Bagwell 92/B/2500	50.00	22.00
☐ 3 Michael Jordan 94/G/500	650.00	300.00
☐ 4 Michael Jordan 94/S/1000	300.00	135.00
☐ 5 Michael Jordan 94/B/5000	70.00	32.00
☐ 6 Greg Maddux 92/S/750	250.00	110.00
☐ 7 Greg Maddux 92/B/2500	60.00	27.00
☐ 8 Mickey Mantle 92/G/500	750.00	350.00
☐ 9 Mickey Mantle 92/S/1000	300.00	135.00
☐ 10 Mickey Mantle 92/B/5000	75.00	34.00
☐ 11 Nolan Ryan 92/G/500	650.00	300.00
☐ 12 Nolan Ryan 92/S/1000	275.00	125.00
☐ 13 Nolan Ryan 92/B/5000	60.00	27.00

1992-94 Highland Mint Mint-Cards Topps

These cards, from the Highland Mint, measure the standard size and are exact reproductions of Topps baseball cards. Each mint-card bears a serial number on its bottom edge. These cards were originally available only in hobby stores, and were packaged in a lucite display holder within an album. Each card comes with a sequentially numbered Certificate of Authenticity. When the Highland Mint/Topps relationship was ended in 1994, the remaining unsold stock was destroyed; the final available mintage according to Highland Mint is listed below. The cards are checklisted below alphabetically.

	MINT	NRMT
☐ 1 Roberto Alomar 88/S/214	225.00	100.00
☐ 2 Roberto Alomar 88/B/928	40.00	18.00
☐ 3 Ernie Banks 54/S/437	200.00	90.00
☐ 4 Ernie Banks 54/B/920	40.00	18.00
☐ 5 Johnny Bench 69/S/500	200.00	90.00
☐ 6 Johnny Bench 69/B/1384	40.00	18.00
☐ 7 Barry Bonds 86/S/596	200.00	90.00
☐ 8 Barry Bonds 86/B/2677	40.00	18.00
☐ 9 George Brett 75/S/999	200.00	90.00
☐ 10 George Brett 75/B/3560	50.00	22.00
☐ 11 Will Clark 86/S/150	350.00	160.00
☐ 12 Will Clark 86/B/1044	40.00	18.00
☐ 13 Roger Clemens 85/S/432	250.00	110.00
☐ 14 Roger Clemens 85/B/1789	40.00	18.00
☐ 15 Juan Gonzalez 90/S/365	225.00	100.00
☐ 16 Juan Gonzalez 90/B/1899	40.00	18.00
☐ 17 Ken Griffey Jr. 92/G/500	500.00	220.00
☐ 18 Ken Griffey Jr. 92/S/1000	300.00	135.00
☐ 19 Ken Griffey Jr. 92/B/5000	70.00	32.00
☐ 20 David Justice 90/S/265	200.00	90.00
☐ 21 David Justice 90/B/1396	40.00	18.00
☐ 22 Don Mattingly 84/S/414	250.00	110.00
☐ 23 Don Mattingly 84/B/1550	60.00	27.00
☐ 24 Paul Molitor 79/S/260	225.00	100.00
☐ 25 Paul Molitor 79/B/639	50.00	22.00
☐ 26 Mike Piazza 93/G/374	500.00	220.00
☐ 27 Mike Piazza 93/S/750	225.00	100.00
☐ 28 Mike Piazza 93/B/2500	50.00	22.00
☐ 29 Kirby Puckett 85/S/359	250.00	110.00
☐ 30 Kirby Puckett 85/B/1723	50.00	22.00
☐ 31 Cal Ripken 92/S/1000	350.00	160.00
☐ 32 Cal Ripken 92/B/4065	125.00	55.00
☐ 33 Brooks Robinson 57/S/796	200.00	90.00
☐ 34 Brooks Robinson 57/B/2043	40.00	18.00
☐ 35 Nolan Ryan 92/S/999	550.00	250.00
☐ 36 Nolan Ryan 92/B/5000	175.00	80.00
☐ 37 Tim Salmon 93/S/264	200.00	90.00
☐ 38 Tim Salmon 93/B/768	40.00	18.00
☐ 39 Ryne Sandberg 92/S/430	225.00	100.00
☐ 40 Ryne Sandberg 92/B/1932	60.00	27.00
☐ 41 Deion Sanders 89/S/187	200.00	90.00
☐ 42 Deion Sanders 89/B/668	40.00	18.00
☐ 43 Mike Schmidt 74/S/500	200.00	90.00
☐ 44 Mike Schmidt 74/B/1641	50.00	22.00
☐ 45 Ozzie Smith 79/S/211	300.00	135.00
☐ 46 Ozzie Smith 79/B/1088	60.00	27.00
☐ 47 Frank Thomas 92/G/500	500.00	220.00
☐ 48 Frank Thomas 92/S/1000	300.00	135.00
☐ 49 Frank Thomas 92/B/5000	70.00	32.00
☐ 50 Dave Winfield 74/S/266	300.00	135.00
☐ 51 Dave Winfield 74/B/1216	40.00	18.00
☐ 52 Carl Yastrzemski 60/S/500	200.00	90.00
☐ 53 Carl Yastrzemski 60/B/1072	50.00	22.00
☐ 54 Robin Yount 75/S/349	225.00	100.00
☐ 55 Robin Yount 75/B/1564	50.00	22.00

1992-98 Highland Mint Mint-Coins

Each of these one-troy ounce medallions is individualy numbered and accompanied by a certificate of authenticity. The fronts feature players' likenesses, names, uniform numbers and signatures; the backs show the MLBPA logo and statistics. The suggested retail prices range from $19.95 to $24.95 for silver. Nine of the silver coins (Belle, Boggs, Canseco, Clark, Gwynn, Jones, Nomo, Puckett, and Smith) were also issued as a set, protected in a cherry box and accompanied by a special certificate of authenticity featuring copies of player autographs. Just 500 of these sets were produced and all the medallions in each set carry the same serial number. These medallions represent the first 500 serial numbers from the original minting. The suggested retail price for the special set was $280. The quantities issued are listed separately for each type of metal.

	MINT	NRMT
☐ 0 Roberto Alomar S/5000	20.00	9.00
☐ 1 Jeff Bagwell S/5000	20.00	9.00
☐ 2 Jeff Bagwell B/25000	10.00	4.50
☐ 5 Albert Belle S/5000	20.00	9.00
☐ 10 Wade Boggs S/5000	20.00	9.00
☐ 15 Barry Bonds Gold Sig./1500	50.00	22.00
☐ 16 Barry Bonds S/5000	20.00	9.00
☐ 20 Jose Canseco S/5000	20.00	9.00
☐ 25 Will Clark S/5000	20.00	9.00
☐ 30 Roger Clemens Gold Sig./1500.	50.00	22.00
☐ 31 Roger Clemens S/5000	20.00	9.00
☐ 32 Roberto Clemente S/2500	25.00	11.00
☐ 33 Jose Cruz Jr. S/5000	20.00	9.00
☐ 35 Cecil Fielder S/5000	20.00	9.00
☐ 40 Ken Griffey Jr. Gold Sig./1500	75.00	34.00
☐ 41 Ken Griffey Jr. S/5000	40.00	18.00
☐ 42 Ken Griffey Jr. B/25000	12.00	5.50
☐ 45 Tony Gwynn S/5000	20.00	9.00
☐ 48 Hideki Irabu S/5000	20.00	9.00
☐ 50 Derek Jeter Gold Sig./1500	50.00	22.00
☐ 51 Derek Jeter S/5000	25.00	11.00
☐ 52 Derek Jeter B/25000	10.00	4.50
☐ 55 Andruw Jones S/5000	20.00	9.00
☐ 60 Chipper Jones Gold Sig./1500	50.00	22.00
☐ 61 Chipper Jones S/5000	20.00	9.00
☐ 62 Chipper Jones B/25000	12.00	5.50
☐ 65 Greg Maddux Gold Sig./1500	50.00	22.00
☐ 66 Greg Maddux S/5000	25.00	11.00
☐ 67 Greg Maddux B/25000	12.00	5.50
☐ 69 Mickey Mantle B/25000	12.00	5.50
☐ 70 Don Mattingly S/5000	20.00	9.00
☐ 71 Don Mattingly B/25000	10.00	4.50
☐ 72 Mark McGwire S/5000	20.00	9.00
☐ 75 Raul Mondesi S/5000	20.00	9.00
☐ 80 Eddie Murray S/5000	20.00	9.00
☐ 85 Hideo Nomo Gold Sig./1500	50.00	22.00
☐ 86 Hideo Nomo S/5000	20.00	9.00
☐ 90 Mike Piazza Gold Sig./1500	60.00	27.00
☐ 91 Mike Piazza S/5000	20.00	9.00
☐ 92 Mike Piazza B/25000	10.00	4.50
☐ 95 Kirby Puckett Gold Sig./1500	50.00	22.00
☐ 96 Kirby Puckett S/5000	20.00	9.00
☐ 100 Cal Ripken Gold Sig./1500	80.00	36.00
☐ 101 Cal Ripken S/5000	40.00	18.00
☐ 102 Cal Ripken B/15000	12.00	5.50
☐ 103 Cal Ripken B/25000	12.00	5.50
☐ 105 Alex Rodriguez Gold Sig./1500	50.00	22.00
☐ 106 Alex Rodriguez S/5000	20.00	9.00
☐ 107 Alex Rodriguez B/25000	12.00	5.50
☐ 109 Ryne Sandberg S/5000	20.00	9.00
☐ 110 Ozzie Smith S/5000	20.00	9.00
☐ 115 Frank Thomas Gold Sig./1500	70.00	32.00
☐ 116 Frank Thomas S/5000	40.00	18.00
☐ 117 Frank Thomas B/25000	12.00	5.50
☐ 120 Mo Vaughn S/5000	20.00	9.00

1958 Hires

The cards in this 66-card set measure approximately 2 5/16" by 3 1/2" or 2 5/16" by 7" with tabs. The 1958 Hires Root Beer set of numbered, colored cards was issued with detachable coupons as inserts with Hires Root Beer cartons. Cards with the coupon still intact are worth 2.5 times the prices listed below. The card front picture is surrounded by a wood grain effect which makes it look like the player is seen through a knot hole. The numbering of this set is rather strange in that it begins with 10 and skips 69.

	NRMT	VG-E
COMPLETE SET (66)	1350.00	600.00
COMMON CARD (10-76)	12.00	5.50
☐ 10 Richie Ashburn	75.00	34.00
☐ 11 Chico Carrasquel	12.00	5.50
☐ 12 Dave Philley	12.00	5.50
☐ 13 Don Newcombe	15.00	6.75
☐ 14 Wally Post	12.00	5.50
☐ 15 Rip Repulski	12.00	5.50
☐ 16 Chico Fernandez	12.00	5.50
☐ 17 Larry Doby	20.00	9.00
☐ 18 Hector Brown	12.00	5.50
☐ 19 Danny O'Connell	12.00	5.50
☐ 20 Granny Hamner	12.00	5.50
☐ 21 Dick Groat	15.00	6.75
☐ 22 Ray Narleski	12.00	5.50
☐ 23 Pee Wee Reese	75.00	34.00
☐ 24 Bob Friend	12.00	5.50
☐ 25 Willie Mays	250.00	110.00
☐ 26 Bob Nieman	12.00	5.50
☐ 27 Frank Thomas	15.00	6.75
☐ 28 Curt Simmons	15.00	6.75
☐ 29 Stan Lopata	12.00	5.50
☐ 30 Bob Skinner	12.00	5.50
☐ 31 Ron Kline	12.00	5.50
☐ 32 Willie Miranda	12.00	5.50
☐ 33 Bobby Avila	12.00	5.50
☐ 34 Clem Labine	15.00	6.75
☐ 35 Ray Jablonski	12.00	5.50
☐ 36 Bill Mazeroski	25.00	11.00
☐ 37 Billy Gardner	12.00	5.50
☐ 38 Pete Runnels	12.00	5.50
☐ 39 Jack Sanford	12.00	5.50
☐ 40 Dave Sisler	12.00	5.50
☐ 41 Don Zimmer	15.00	6.75
☐ 42 Johnny Podres	15.00	6.75
☐ 43 Dick Farrell	12.00	5.50
☐ 44 Hank Aaron	225.00	100.00
☐ 45 Bill Virdon	12.00	5.50
☐ 46 Bobby Thomson	15.00	6.75
☐ 47 Willard Nixon	12.00	5.50
☐ 48 Billy Loes	12.00	5.50
☐ 49 Hank Sauer	15.00	6.75
☐ 50 Johnny Antonelli	15.00	6.75
☐ 51 Daryl Spencer	12.00	5.50
☐ 52 Ken Lehman	12.00	5.50
☐ 53 Sammy White	12.00	5.50
☐ 54 Charley Neal	12.00	5.50
☐ 55 Don Drysdale	60.00	27.00
☐ 56 Jackie Jensen	25.00	11.00
☐ 57 Ray Katt	12.00	5.50
☐ 58 Frank Sullivan	12.00	5.50
☐ 59 Roy Face	15.00	6.75
☐ 60 Willie Jones	12.00	5.50
☐ 61 Duke Snider	75.00	34.00
☐ 62 Whitey Lockman	12.00	5.50
☐ 63 Gino Cimoli	12.00	5.50
☐ 64 Marv Grissom	12.00	5.50
☐ 65 Gene Baker	12.00	5.50
☐ 66 George Zuverink	12.00	5.50
☐ 67 Ted Kluszewski	25.00	11.00
☐ 68 Jim Busby	12.00	5.50
☐ 69 Not Issued		
☐ 70 Curt Barclay	12.00	5.50
☐ 71 Hank Foiles	12.00	5.50
☐ 72 Gene Stephens	12.00	5.50
☐ 73 Al Worthington	12.00	5.50
☐ 74 Al Walker	12.00	5.50
☐ 75 Bob Boyd	12.00	5.50
☐ 76 Al Pilarcik	12.00	5.50

1959 Home Run Derby

This 20-card set was produced in 1959 by American Motors to publicize a TV program. The cards are black and white and blank backed. The cards measure approximately 3 1/8" by 5 1/4". The cards are unnumbered and are ordered alphabetically below for convenience. During 1988, the 19 player cards in this set were publicly reprinted.

	NRMT	VG-E
COMPLETE SET (20)	3000.00	1350.00
COMMON CARD (1-20)	60.00	27.00
☐ 1 Hank Aaron	450.00	200.00
☐ 2 Bob Allison	60.00	27.00

☐ 3 Ernie Banks	175.00	80.00
☐ 4 Ken Boyer	75.00	34.00
☐ 5 Bob Cerv	60.00	27.00
☐ 6 Rocky Colavito	125.00	55.00
☐ 7 Gil Hodges	125.00	55.00
☐ 8 Jackie Jensen	75.00	34.00
☐ 9 Al Kaline	175.00	80.00
☐ 10 Harmon Killebrew	175.00	80.00
☐ 11 Jim Lemon	60.00	27.00
☐ 12 Mickey Mantle	1350.00	600.00
☐ 13 Eddie Mathews	175.00	80.00
☐ 14 Willie Mays	450.00	200.00
☐ 15 Wally Post	60.00	27.00
☐ 16 Frank Robinson	175.00	80.00
☐ 17 Mark Scott ANN	60.00	27.00
☐ 18 Duke Snider	200.00	90.00
☐ 19 Dick Stuart	60.00	27.00
☐ 20 Gus Triandos	60.00	27.00

1975 Hostess

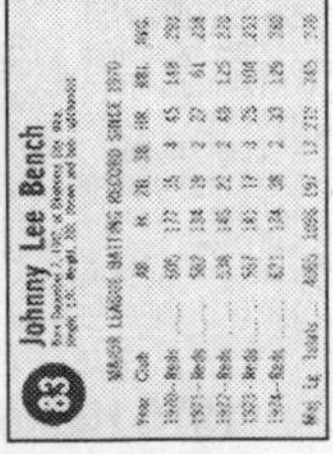

The cards in this 150-card set measure approximately 2 1/4" by 3 1/4" individually or 3 1/4" by 7 1/4" as panels of three. The 1975 Hostess set was issued in panels of three cards each on the backs of family-size packages of Hostess cakes. Card number 125, Bill Madlock, was listed correctly as an infielder and incorrectly as a pitcher. Number 11, Burt Hooton, and number 89, Doug Rader, are spelled two different ways. Some panels are more difficult to find than others as they were issued only on the backs of less popular Hostess products. These scarcer cards are shown with SP in the checklist. Although complete panel prices are not explicitly listed, they would generally have a value of 20-30 percent greater than the sum of the values of the individual players on that panel. One of the more interesting cards in the set is that of Robin Yount; Hostess issued one of the few Yount cards available in 1975, his rookie year for cards. An album to hold these cards was issued. The albums were originally intended to be given out in grocery stores. However, most seemingly were distributed through Hostess stores.

	NRMT	VG-E
COMPLETE INDIV.SET (150)	250.00	110.00
COMMON CARD (1-150)	.50	.23

☐ 1 Bob Tolan	.50	.23
☐ 2 Cookie Rojas	.50	.23
☐ 3 Darrell Evans	.75	.35
☐ 4 Sal Bando	.75	.35
☐ 5 Joe Morgan	4.00	1.80
☐ 6 Mickey Lolich	.75	.35
☐ 7 Don Sutton	3.00	1.35
☐ 8 Bill Melton	.50	.23
☐ 9 Tim Foli	.50	.23
☐ 10 Joe Lahoud	.50	.23
☐ 11A Burt Hooton ERR	1.00	.45
(Misspelled Bert		
Hooten on card		
☐ 11B Burt Hooton COR	1.00	.45
☐ 12 Paul Blair	.50	.23
☐ 13 Jim Barr	.50	.23
☐ 14 Toby Harrah	.75	.35
☐ 15 John Milner	.50	.23
☐ 16 Ken Holtzman	.50	.23
☐ 17 Cesar Cedeno	.50	.23
☐ 18 Dwight Evans	1.50	.70
☐ 19 Willie McCovey	3.00	1.35
☐ 20 Tony Oliva	1.50	.70
☐ 21 Manny Sanguillen	.50	.23
☐ 22 Mickey Rivers	.50	.23
☐ 23 Lou Brock	3.00	1.35
☐ 24 Graig Nettles UER	1.50	.70
(Craig on front)		
☐ 25 Jim Wynn	.50	.23
☐ 26 George Scott	.50	.23
☐ 27 Greg Luzinski	1.00	.45
☐ 28 Bert Campaneris	.75	.35
☐ 29 Pete Rose	12.00	5.50
☐ 30 Buddy Bell	1.00	.45
☐ 31 Gary Matthews	.75	.35
☐ 32 Freddie Patek	.50	.23
☐ 33 Mike Lum	.50	.23
☐ 34 Ellie Rodriguez	.50	.23
☐ 35 Milt May UER	.50	.23
(Photo actually		
Lee May)		
☐ 36 Willie Horton	.75	.35
☐ 37 Dave Winfield	20.00	9.00
☐ 38 Tom Grieve	.50	.23
☐ 39 Barry Foote	.50	.23
☐ 40 Joe Rudi	.50	.23
☐ 41 Bake McBride	.50	.23
☐ 42 Mike Cuellar	.50	.23
☐ 43 Garry Maddox	.50	.23
☐ 44 Carlos May	.50	.23
☐ 45 Bud Harrelson	.50	.23
☐ 46 Dave Chalk	.50	.23
☐ 47 Dave Concepcion	1.50	.70
☐ 48 Carl Yastrzemski	5.00	2.20
☐ 49 Steve Garvey	2.50	1.10
☐ 50 Amos Otis	.50	.23
☐ 51 Rick Reuschel	.50	.23
☐ 52 Rollie Fingers	3.00	1.35
☐ 53 Bob Watson	1.00	.45
☐ 54 John Ellis	.50	.23
☐ 55 Bob Bailey	.50	.23
☐ 56 Rod Carew	5.00	2.20
☐ 57 Rich Hebner	.50	.23
☐ 58 Nolan Ryan	40.00	18.00
☐ 59 Reggie Smith	.75	.35
☐ 60 Joe Coleman	.50	.23
☐ 61 Ron Cey	.75	.35
☐ 62 Darrell Porter	.75	.35
☐ 63 Steve Carlton	5.00	2.20
☐ 64 Gene Tenace	.50	.23
☐ 65 Jose Cardenal	.50	.23
☐ 66 Bill Lee	.50	.23
☐ 67 Dave Lopes	.75	.35
☐ 68 Wilbur Wood	.50	.23
☐ 69 Steve Renko	.50	.23
☐ 70 Joe Torre	1.50	.70
☐ 71 Ted Sizemore	.50	.23
☐ 72 Bobby Grich	.75	.35
☐ 73 Chris Speier	.50	.23
☐ 74 Bert Blyleven	1.00	.45
☐ 75 Tom Seaver	10.00	4.50
☐ 76 Nate Colbert	.50	.23
☐ 77 Don Kessinger	.50	.23
☐ 78 George Medich	.50	.23
☐ 79 Andy Messersmith SP	.75	.35
☐ 80 Robin Yount SP	30.00	13.50
☐ 81 Al Oliver SP	1.00	.45
☐ 82 Bill Singer SP	.75	.35
☐ 83 Johnny Bench SP	12.00	5.50
☐ 84 Gaylord Perry SP	4.00	1.80
☐ 85 Dave Kingman SP	1.00	.45
☐ 86 Ed Herrmann SP	.75	.35
☐ 87 Ralph Garr SP	.75	.35
☐ 88 Reggie Jackson SP	12.00	5.50
☐ 89A Doug Rader ERR SP	1.50	.70
(Misspelled Radar)		
☐ 89B Doug Rader COR SP	6.00	2.70
☐ 90 Elliott Maddox SP	.75	.35
☐ 91 Bill Russell SP	1.50	.70
☐ 92 John Mayberry SP	.75	.35
☐ 93 Dave Cash SP	.75	.35
☐ 94 Jeff Burroughs SP	1.00	.45
☐ 95 Ted Simmons SP	1.50	.70
☐ 96 Joe Decker SP	.75	.35
☐ 97 Bill Buckner SP	1.00	.45
☐ 98 Bobby Darwin SP	.75	.35
☐ 99 Phil Niekro SP	4.00	1.80
☐ 100 Jim Sundberg	.50	.23
☐ 101 Greg Gross	.50	.23
☐ 102 Luis Tiant	1.00	.45
☐ 103 Glenn Beckert	.50	.23
☐ 104 Hal McRae	1.00	.45
☐ 105 Mike Jorgensen	.50	.23
☐ 106 Mike Hargrove	1.00	.45
☐ 107 Don Gullett	.75	.35
☐ 108 Tito Fuentes	.50	.23
☐ 109 John Grubb	.50	.23
☐ 110 Jim Kaat	1.00	.45
☐ 111 Felix Millan	.50	.23
☐ 112 Don Money	.50	.23
☐ 113 Rick Monday	.50	.23
☐ 114 Dick Bosman	.50	.23
☐ 115 Roger Metzger	.50	.23
☐ 116 Fergie Jenkins	3.00	1.35
☐ 117 Dusty Baker	1.00	.45
☐ 118 Billy Champion SP	.75	.35
☐ 119 Bob Gibson SP	5.00	2.20
☐ 120 Bill Freehan SP	1.00	.45
☐ 121 Cesar Geronimo	.50	.23
☐ 122 Jorge Orta	.50	.23
☐ 123 Cleon Jones	.50	.23
☐ 124 Steve Busby	.50	.23
☐ 125A Bill Madlock ERR	1.50	.70
(Pitcher)		
☐ 125B Bill Madlock COR	1.50	.70
(Infielder)		
☐ 126 Jim Palmer	4.00	1.80
☐ 127 Tony Perez	2.50	1.10
☐ 128 Larry Hisle	.50	.23
☐ 129 Rusty Staub	1.00	.45
☐ 130 Hank Aaron SP	20.00	9.00
☐ 131 Rennie Stennett SP	.75	.35
☐ 132 Rico Petrocelli SP	.75	.35
☐ 133 Mike Schmidt	15.00	6.75
☐ 134 Sparky Lyle	1.00	.45
☐ 135 Willie Stargell	3.00	1.35
☐ 136 Ken Henderson	.50	.23
☐ 137 Willie Montanez	.50	.23
☐ 138 Thurman Munson	4.00	1.80
☐ 139 Richie Zisk	.50	.23
☐ 140 George Hendrick	.50	.23
☐ 141 Bobby Murcer	1.00	.45
☐ 142 Lee May	.50	.23
☐ 143 Carlton Fisk	7.50	3.40
☐ 144 Brooks Robinson	5.00	2.20
☐ 145 Bobby Bonds	1.50	.70
☐ 146 Gary Sutherland	.50	.23
☐ 147 Oscar Gamble	.50	.23
☐ 148 Jim Hunter	4.00	1.80
☐ 149 Tug McGraw	1.00	.45
☐ 150 Dave McNally	.75	.35
☐ XX Album	8.00	3.60

1975 Hostess Twinkie

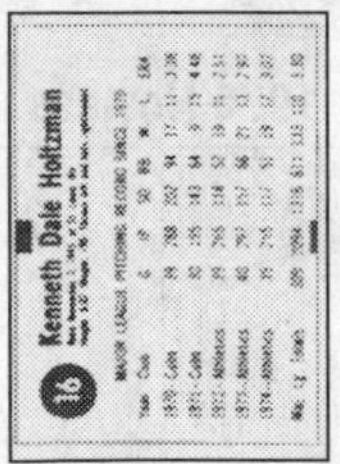

The cards in this 60-card set measure approximately 2 1/4" by 3 1/4". The 1975 Hostess Twinkie set was issued on a limited basis in the far western part of the country. The set contains the same numbers as the regular set to number 36; however, the set is skip numbered after number 36. The cards were issued as the backs for 25-cent Twinkies packs. The fronts are indistinguishable from the regular Hostess cards; however the card backs are different in that the Twinkie cards have a thick black bar in the middle of the reverse. The cards are frequently found with product stains. One of the more interesting cards in the set is that of Robin Yount; Hostess issued one of the few Yount cards available in 1975, his rookie year for cards.

	NRMT	VG-E
COMPLETE SET (60)	125.00	55.00
COMMON CARD	1.00	.45

☐ 1 Bob Tolan	1.00	.45
☐ 2 Cookie Rojas	1.00	.45
☐ 3 Darrell Evans	1.25	.55
☐ 4 Sal Bando	1.25	.55
☐ 5 Joe Morgan	6.00	2.70
☐ 6 Mickey Lolich	1.50	.70
☐ 7 Don Sutton	5.00	2.20
☐ 8 Bill Melton	1.00	.45
☐ 9 Tim Foli	1.00	.45
☐ 10 Joe Lahoud	1.00	.45
☐ 11 Burt Hooton UER	1.00	.45
(Misspelled Bert		
Hooten on card)		
☐ 12 Paul Blair	1.00	.45
☐ 13 Jim Barr	1.00	.45
☐ 14 Toby Harrah	1.00	.45

Card	NRMT	VG-E
☐ 15 John Milner	1.00	.45
☐ 16 Ken Holtzman	1.00	.45
☐ 17 Cesar Cedeno	1.25	.55
☐ 18 Dwight Evans	2.00	.90
☐ 19 Willie McCovey	5.00	2.20
☐ 20 Tony Oliva	1.50	.70
☐ 21 Manny Sanguillen	1.00	.45
☐ 22 Mickey Rivers	1.00	.45
☐ 23 Lou Brock	6.00	2.70
☐ 24 Graig Nettles UER (Craig on front)	2.00	.90
☐ 25 Jim Wynn	1.25	.55
☐ 26 George Scott	1.00	.45
☐ 27 Greg Luzinski	1.25	.55
☐ 28 Bert Campaneris	1.25	.55
☐ 29 Pete Rose	15.00	6.75
☐ 30 Buddy Bell	1.50	.70
☐ 31 Gary Matthews	1.25	.55
☐ 32 Freddie Patek	1.00	.45
☐ 33 Mike Lum	1.00	.45
☐ 34 Ellie Rodriguez	1.00	.45
☐ 35 Milt May UER (Lee May picture)	1.00	.45
☐ 36 Willie Horton	1.25	.55
☐ 40 Joe Rudi	1.25	.55
☐ 43 Garry Maddox	1.00	.45
☐ 46 Dave Chalk	1.00	.45
☐ 49 Steve Garvey	4.00	1.80
☐ 52 Rollie Fingers	5.00	2.20
☐ 58 Nolan Ryan	50.00	22.00
☐ 61 Ron Cey	1.50	.70
☐ 64 Gene Tenace	1.00	.45
☐ 65 Jose Cardenal	1.00	.45
☐ 67 Dave Lopes	1.50	.70
☐ 68 Wilbur Wood	1.00	.45
☐ 73 Chris Speier	1.00	.45
☐ 77 Don Kessinger	1.00	.45
☐ 79 Andy Messersmith	1.00	.45
☐ 80 Robin Yount	35.00	16.00
☐ 82 Bill Singer	1.00	.45
☐ 103 Glenn Beckert	1.00	.45
☐ 110 Jim Kaat	1.50	.70
☐ 112 Don Money	1.25	.55
☐ 113 Rick Monday	1.25	.55
☐ 122 Jorge Orta	1.00	.45
☐ 125 Bill Madlock	1.50	.70
☐ 130 Hank Aaron	20.00	9.00
☐ 136 Ken Henderson	1.00	.45

1976 Hostess

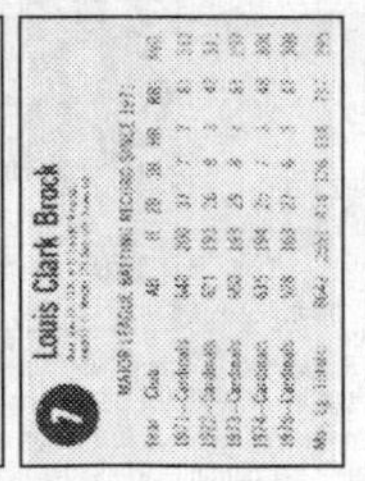

The cards in this 150-card set measure approximately 2 1/4" by 3 1/4" individually or 3 1/4" by 7 1/4" as panels of three. The 1976 Hostess set contains full-color, numbered cards issued in panels of three cards each on family-size packages of Hostess cakes. Scarcer panels (those only found on less popular Hostess products) are listed in the checklist below with SP. Complete panels of three have a value 20-30 percent more than the sum of the individual cards on the panel. Nine additional numbers (151-159) were apparently planned but never actually issued. These exist as proof cards and are quite scarce, e.g., 151 Ferguson Jenkins (even though he already appears in the set as card number 138), 152 Mike Cuellar, 153 Tom Murphy, 154 Al Cowens, 155 Barry Foote, 156 Steve Carlton, 157 Richie Zisk, 158 Ken Holtzman, and 159 Cliff Johnson. One of the more interesting cards in the set is that of Dennis Eckersley; Hostess issued one of the few Eckersley cards available in 1976, his rookie year for cards. An album to hold these cards were issued.

	NRMT	VG-E
COMPLETE INDIV.SET (150)	250.00	110.00
COMMON CARD (1-150)	.50	.23

Card	NRMT	VG-E
☐ 1 Fred Lynn	1.00	.45
☐ 2 Joe Morgan	4.00	1.80
☐ 3 Phil Niekro	4.00	1.80
☐ 4 Gaylord Perry	4.00	1.80
☐ 5 Bob Watson	.75	.35
☐ 6 Bill Freehan	.75	.35
☐ 7 Lou Brock	4.00	1.80
☐ 8 Al Fitzmorris	.50	.23
☐ 9 Rennie Stennett	.50	.23
☐ 10 Tony Oliva	1.50	.70
☐ 11 Robin Yount	20.00	9.00
☐ 12 Rick Manning	.50	.23
☐ 13 Bobby Grich	.75	.35
☐ 14 Terry Forster	.50	.23
☐ 15 Dave Kingman	.75	.35
☐ 16 Thurman Munson	4.00	1.80
☐ 17 Rick Reuschel	.50	.23
☐ 18 Bobby Bonds	1.50	.70
☐ 19 Steve Garvey	3.00	1.35
☐ 20 Vida Blue	.75	.35
☐ 21 Dave Rader	.50	.23
☐ 22 Johnny Bench	7.50	3.40
☐ 23 Luis Tiant	.75	.35
☐ 24 Darrell Evans	.75	.35
☐ 25 Larry Dierker	.75	.35
☐ 26 Willie Horton	.75	.35
☐ 27 John Ellis	.50	.23
☐ 28 Al Cowens	.50	.23
☐ 29 Jerry Reuss	.50	.23
☐ 30 Reggie Smith	.75	.35
☐ 31 Bobby Darwin SP	.75	.35
☐ 32 Fritz Peterson SP	.75	.35
☐ 33 Rod Carew SP	10.00	4.50
☐ 34 Carlos May SP	.75	.35
☐ 35 Tom Seaver SP	15.00	6.75
☐ 36 Brooks Robinson SP	10.00	4.50
☐ 37 Jose Cardenal	.50	.23
☐ 38 Ron Blomberg	.50	.23
☐ 39 Leroy Stanton	.50	.23
☐ 40 Dave Cash	.50	.23
☐ 41 John Montefusco	.50	.23
☐ 42 Bob Tolan	.50	.23
☐ 43 Carl Morton	.50	.23
☐ 44 Rick Burleson	.50	.23
☐ 45 Don Gullett	.50	.23
☐ 46 Vern Ruhle	.50	.23
☐ 47 Cesar Cedeno	.75	.35
☐ 48 Toby Harrah	.50	.23
☐ 49 Willie Stargell	4.00	1.80
☐ 50 Al Hrabosky	.50	.23
☐ 51 Amos Otis	.50	.23
☐ 52 Bud Harrelson	.50	.23
☐ 53 Jim Hughes	.50	.23
☐ 54 George Scott	.50	.23
☐ 55 Mike Vail SP	.75	.35
☐ 56 Jim Palmer SP	6.00	2.70
☐ 57 Jorge Orta SP	.75	.35
☐ 58 Chris Chambliss SP	1.00	.45
☐ 59 Dave Chalk SP	.75	.35
☐ 60 Ray Burris SP	.75	.35
☐ 61 Bert Campaneris SP	1.00	.45
☐ 62 Gary Carter SP	12.00	5.50
☐ 63 Ron Cey SP	1.00	.45
☐ 64 Carlton Fisk SP	7.50	3.40
☐ 65 Marty Perez SP	.75	.35
☐ 66 Pete Rose SP	20.00	9.00
☐ 67 Roger Metzger SP	.75	.35
☐ 68 Jim Sundberg SP	.75	.35
☐ 69 Ron LeFlore SP	.75	.35
☐ 70 Ted Sizemore SP	.75	.35
☐ 71 Steve Busby SP	.75	.35
☐ 72 Manny Sanguillen SP	.75	.35
☐ 73 Larry Hisle SP	.75	.35
☐ 74 Pete Broberg SP	.75	.35
☐ 75 Boog Powell SP	1.50	.70
☐ 76 Ken Singleton SP	.75	.35
☐ 77 Rich Gossage SP	2.00	.90
☐ 78 Jerry Grote SP	.75	.35
☐ 79 Nolan Ryan SP	50.00	22.00
☐ 80 Rick Monday SP	1.00	.45
☐ 81 Graig Nettles SP	1.50	.70
☐ 82 Chris Speier	.50	.23
☐ 83 Dave Winfield	12.00	5.50
☐ 84 Mike Schmidt	15.00	6.75
☐ 85 Buzz Capra	.50	.23
☐ 86 Tony Perez	2.50	1.10
☐ 87 Dwight Evans	1.50	.70
☐ 88 Mike Hargrove	.75	.35
☐ 89 Joe Coleman	.50	.23
☐ 90 Greg Gross	.50	.23
☐ 91 John Mayberry	.50	.23
☐ 92 John Candelaria	.75	.35
☐ 93 Bake McBride	.50	.23
☐ 94 Hank Aaron	15.00	6.75
☐ 95 Buddy Bell	.75	.35
☐ 96 Steve Braun	.50	.23
☐ 97 Jon Matlack	.50	.23
☐ 98 Lee May	.50	.23
☐ 99 Wilbur Wood	.50	.23
☐ 100 Bill Madlock	.75	.35
☐ 101 Frank Tanana	.75	.35
☐ 102 Mickey Rivers	.50	.23
☐ 103 Mike Ivie	.50	.23
☐ 104 Rollie Fingers	3.00	1.35
☐ 105 Dave Lopes	.75	.35
☐ 106 George Foster	1.00	.45
☐ 107 Denny Doyle	.50	.23
☐ 108 Earl Williams	.50	.23
☐ 109 Tom Veryzer	.50	.23
☐ 110 J.R. Richard	.75	.35
☐ 111 Jeff Burroughs	.50	.23
☐ 112 Al Oliver	.75	.35
☐ 113 Ted Simmons	1.00	.45
☐ 114 George Brett	45.00	20.00
☐ 115 Frank Duffy	.50	.23
☐ 116 Bert Blyleven	1.00	.45
☐ 117 Darrell Porter	.50	.23
☐ 118 Don Baylor	1.00	.45
☐ 119 Bucky Dent	.75	.35
☐ 120 Felix Millan	.50	.23
☐ 121 Mike Cuellar	.50	.23
☐ 122 Gene Tenace	.50	.23
☐ 123 Bobby Murcer	.75	.35
☐ 124 Willie McCovey	4.00	1.80
☐ 125 Greg Luzinski	.75	.35
☐ 126 Larry Parrish	.50	.23
☐ 127 Jim Rice	2.00	.90
☐ 128 Dave Concepcion	1.00	.45
☐ 129 Jim Wynn	.50	.23
☐ 130 Tom Grieve	.50	.23
☐ 131 Mike Cosgrove	.50	.23
☐ 132 Dan Meyer	.50	.23
☐ 133 Dave Parker	2.00	.90
☐ 134 Don Kessinger	.50	.23
☐ 135 Hal McRae	.75	.35
☐ 136 Don Money	.50	.23
☐ 137 Dennis Eckersley	20.00	9.00
☐ 138 Fergie Jenkins	3.00	1.35
☐ 139 Mike Torrez	.50	.23
☐ 140 Jerry Morales	.50	.23
☐ 141 Jim Hunter	3.00	1.35
☐ 142 Gary Matthews	.50	.23
☐ 143 Randy Jones	.50	.23
☐ 144 Mike Jorgensen	.50	.23
☐ 145 Larry Bowa	.75	.35
☐ 146 Reggie Jackson	12.00	5.50
☐ 147 Steve Yeager	.50	.23
☐ 148 Dave May	.50	.23
☐ 149 Carl Yastrzemski	6.00	2.70
☐ 150 Cesar Geronimo	.50	.23
☐ XX Album	8.00	3.60

1976 Hostess Twinkie

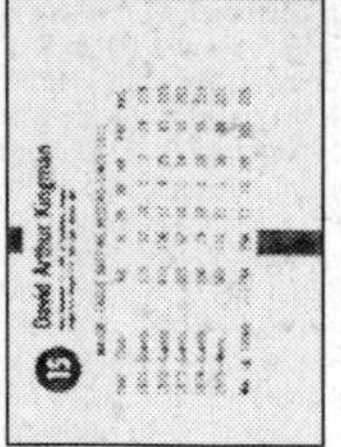

The cards in this 60-card set measure approximately 2 1/4" by 3 1/4". The 1976 Hostess Twinkies set contains the first 60 cards of the 1976 Hostess set. These cards were issued as backs on 25-cent Twinkie packages as in the 1975 Twinkies set. The fronts are indistinguishable from the regular Hostess cards; however the card backs are different in that the Twinkie cards have a thick black bar in the middle of the reverse. The cards are frequently found with product stains.

	NRMT	VG-E
COMPLETE SET (60)	125.00	55.00
COMMON CARD (1-60)	1.00	.45

Card	NRMT	VG-E
☐ 1 Fred Lynn	2.00	.90
☐ 2 Joe Morgan	6.00	2.70
☐ 3 Phil Niekro	5.00	2.20
☐ 4 Gaylord Perry	5.00	2.20
☐ 5 Bob Watson	1.25	.55
☐ 6 Bill Freehan	1.25	.55
☐ 7 Lou Brock	5.00	2.20
☐ 8 Al Fitzmorris	1.00	.45
☐ 9 Rennie Stennett	1.00	.45
☐ 10 Tony Oliva	2.00	.90
☐ 11 Robin Yount	15.00	6.75
☐ 12 Rick Manning	1.00	.45
☐ 13 Bobby Grich	1.25	.55
☐ 14 Terry Forster	1.00	.45
☐ 15 Dave Kingman	2.00	.90
☐ 16 Thurman Munson	6.00	2.70
☐ 17 Rick Reuschel	1.25	.55
☐ 18 Bobby Bonds	2.00	.90
☐ 19 Steve Garvey	6.00	2.70

Card	NRMT	VG-E
☐ 20 Vida Blue	1.50	.70
☐ 21 Dave Rader	1.00	.45
☐ 22 Johnny Bench	10.00	4.50
☐ 23 Luis Tiant	1.25	.55
☐ 24 Darrell Evans	1.25	.55
☐ 25 Larry Dierker	1.25	.55
☐ 26 Willie Horton	1.25	.55
☐ 27 John Ellis	1.00	.45
☐ 28 Al Cowens	1.00	.45
☐ 29 Jerry Reuss	1.25	.55
☐ 30 Reggie Smith	1.25	.55
☐ 31 Bobby Darwin	1.00	.45
☐ 32 Fritz Peterson	1.00	.45
☐ 33 Rod Carew	6.00	2.70
☐ 34 Carlos May	1.00	.45
☐ 35 Tom Seaver	10.00	4.50
☐ 36 Brooks Robinson	6.00	2.70
☐ 37 Jose Cardenal	1.00	.45
☐ 38 Ron Blomberg	1.00	.45
☐ 39 Leroy Stanton	1.00	.45
☐ 40 Dave Cash	1.00	.45
☐ 41 John Montefusco	1.00	.45
☐ 42 Bob Tolan	1.00	.45
☐ 43 Carl Morton	1.00	.45
☐ 44 Rick Burleson	1.25	.55
☐ 45 Don Gullett	1.25	.55
☐ 46 Vern Ruhle	1.00	.45
☐ 47 Cesar Cedeno	1.25	.55
☐ 48 Toby Harrah	1.25	.55
☐ 49 Willie Stargell	5.00	2.20
☐ 50 Al Hrabosky	1.25	.55
☐ 51 Amos Otis	1.25	.55
☐ 52 Bud Harrelson	1.25	.55
☐ 53 Jim Hughes	1.25	.55
☐ 54 George Scott	1.25	.55
☐ 55 Mike Vail	1.25	.55
☐ 56 Jim Palmer	5.00	2.20
☐ 57 Jorge Orta	1.00	.45
☐ 58 Chris Chambliss	1.50	.70
☐ 59 Dave Chalk	1.00	.45
☐ 60 Ray Burris	1.00	.45

1977 Hostess

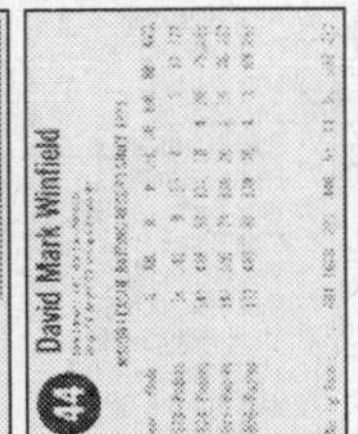

The cards in this 150-card set measure approximately 2 1/4" by 3 1/4" individually or 3 1/4" by 7 1/4" as panels of three. The 1977 Hostess set contains full-color, numbered cards issued in panels of three cards each with Hostess family-size cake products. Scarcer cards are listed in the checklist below with SP. Although complete panel prices are not explicitly listed below, they would generally have a value 20-30 percent greater than the sum of the individual players on the panel. There were ten additional cards proofed, but not produced or distributed; they are 151 Ed Kranepool, 152 Ross Grimsley, 153 Ken Brett, 154 Rowland Office, 155 Rick Wise, 156 Paul Splittorff, 157 Gerald Augustine, 158 Ken Forsch, 159 Jerry Reuss (Reuss is also number 119 in the set), and 160 Nelson Briles. There is also a complete variation set that was available one card per Twinkie package. Common cards in this Twinkie set are worth double the prices listed below, although the stars are only worth about 25 percent more. The Twinkie cards are distinguished by the thick printing bar or band printed on the card backs just below the statistics. An album to hold these cards were issued.

	NRMT	VG-E
COMPLETE INDIV.SET (150)	250.00	110.00
COMMON CARD (1-150)	.50	.23

Card	NRMT	VG-E
☐ 1 Jim Palmer	4.00	1.80
☐ 2 Joe Morgan	4.00	1.80
☐ 3 Reggie Jackson	10.00	4.50
☐ 4 Carl Yastrzemski	6.00	2.70
☐ 5 Thurman Munson	3.00	1.35
☐ 6 Johnny Bench	8.00	3.60
☐ 7 Tom Seaver	8.00	3.60
☐ 8 Pete Rose	10.00	4.50
☐ 9 Rod Carew	4.00	1.80
☐ 10 Luis Tiant	.75	.35
☐ 11 Phil Garner	.75	.35
☐ 12 Sixto Lezcano	.50	.23
☐ 13 Mike Torrez	.50	.23
☐ 14 Dave Lopes	.75	.35
☐ 15 Doug DeCinces	.50	.23
☐ 16 Jim Spencer	.50	.23
☐ 17 Hal McRae	.75	.35
☐ 18 Mike Hargrove	.75	.35
☐ 19 Willie Montanez SP	.75	.35
☐ 20 Roger Metzger SP	.75	.35
☐ 21 Dwight Evans SP	1.50	.70
☐ 22 Steve Rogers SP	.75	.35
☐ 23 Jim Rice SP	1.00	.45
☐ 24 Pete Falcone SP	.75	.35
☐ 25 Greg Luzinski SP	1.50	.70
☐ 26 Randy Jones SP	.75	.35
☐ 27 Willie Stargell SP	5.00	2.20
☐ 28 John Hiller SP	.75	.35
☐ 29 Bobby Murcer SP	1.00	.45
☐ 30 Rick Monday SP	.75	.35
☐ 31 John Montefusco SP	.75	.35
☐ 32 Lou Brock SP	5.00	2.20
☐ 33 Bill North SP	.75	.35
☐ 34 Robin Yount SP	20.00	9.00
☐ 35 Steve Garvey SP	6.00	2.70
☐ 36 George Brett SP	35.00	16.00
☐ 37 Toby Harrah SP	.75	.35
☐ 38 Jerry Royster SP	.75	.35
☐ 39 Bob Watson SP	1.00	.45
☐ 40 George Foster	.75	.35
☐ 41 Gary Carter	4.00	1.80
☐ 42 John Denny	.50	.23
☐ 43 Mike Schmidt	10.00	4.50
☐ 44 Dave Winfield	10.00	4.50
☐ 45 Al Oliver	.75	.35
☐ 46 Mark Fidrych	2.50	1.10
☐ 47 Larry Herndon	.50	.23
☐ 48 Dave Goltz	.50	.23
☐ 49 Jerry Morales	.50	.23
☐ 50 Ron LeFlore	.50	.23
☐ 51 Fred Lynn	1.00	.45
☐ 52 Vida Blue	.75	.35
☐ 53 Rick Manning	.50	.23
☐ 54 Bill Buckner	.75	.35
☐ 55 Lee May	.50	.23
☐ 56 John Mayberry	.50	.23
☐ 57 Darrel Chaney	.50	.23
☐ 58 Cesar Cedeno	.50	.23
☐ 59 Ken Griffey	1.00	.45
☐ 60 Dave Kingman	1.00	.45
☐ 61 Ted Simmons	1.00	.45
☐ 62 Larry Bowa	.75	.35
☐ 63 Frank Tanana	.75	.35
☐ 64 Jason Thompson	.50	.23
☐ 65 Ken Brett	.50	.23
☐ 66 Roy Smalley	.50	.23
☐ 67 Ray Burris	.50	.23
☐ 68 Rick Burleson	.50	.23
☐ 69 Buddy Bell	.75	.35
☐ 70 Don Sutton	4.00	1.80
☐ 71 Mark Belanger	.50	.23
☐ 72 Dennis Leonard	.50	.23
☐ 73 Gaylord Perry	4.00	1.80
☐ 74 Dick Ruthven	.50	.23
☐ 75 Jose Cruz	.50	.23
☐ 76 Cesar Geronimo	.50	.23
☐ 77 Jerry Koosman	.75	.35
☐ 78 Garry Templeton	.50	.23
☐ 79 Jim Hunter	4.00	1.80
☐ 80 John Candelaria	.50	.23
☐ 81 Nolan Ryan	40.00	18.00
☐ 82 Rusty Staub	.75	.35
☐ 83 Jim Barr	.50	.23
☐ 84 Butch Wynegar	.50	.23
☐ 85 Jose Cardenal	.50	.23
☐ 86 Claudell Washington	.50	.23
☐ 87 Bill Travers	.50	.23
☐ 88 Rick Waits	.50	.23
☐ 89 Ron Cey	.75	.35
☐ 90 Al Bumbry	.50	.23
☐ 91 Bucky Dent	.75	.35
☐ 92 Amos Otis	.50	.23
☐ 93 Tom Grieve	.50	.23
☐ 94 Enos Cabell	.50	.23
☐ 95 Dave Concepcion	1.00	.45
☐ 96 Felix Millan	.50	.23
☐ 97 Bake McBride	.50	.23
☐ 98 Chris Chambliss	.75	.35
☐ 99 Butch Metzger	.50	.23
☐ 100 Rennie Stennett	.50	.23
☐ 101 Dave Roberts	.50	.23
☐ 102 Lyman Bostock	.75	.35
☐ 103 Rick Reuschel	.50	.23
☐ 104 Carlton Fisk	7.50	3.40
☐ 105 Jim Slaton	.50	.23
☐ 106 Dennis Eckersley	6.00	2.70
☐ 107 Ken Singleton	.50	.23
☐ 108 Ralph Garr	.50	.23
☐ 109 Freddie Patek SP	.75	.35
☐ 110 Jim Sundberg SP	.75	.35
☐ 111 Phil Niekro SP	5.00	2.20
☐ 112 J.R. Richard SP	.75	.35
☐ 113 Gary Nolan SP	.75	.35
☐ 114 Jon Matlack SP	.75	.35
☐ 115 Keith Hernandez SP	.75	.35
☐ 116 Graig Nettles SP	1.50	.70
☐ 117 Steve Carlton SP	7.50	3.40
☐ 118 Bill Madlock SP	1.00	.45
☐ 119 Jerry Reuss SP	.75	.35
☐ 120 Aurelio Rodriguez SP	.75	.35
☐ 121 Dan Ford SP	.75	.35
☐ 122 Ray Fosse SP	.75	.35
☐ 123 George Hendrick SP	.75	.35
☐ 124 Alan Ashby	.50	.23
☐ 125 Joe Lis	.50	.23
☐ 126 Sal Bando	.50	.23
☐ 127 Richie Zisk	.50	.23
☐ 128 Rich Gossage	1.00	.45
☐ 129 Don Baylor	.75	.35
☐ 130 Dave McKay	.50	.23
☐ 131 Bob Grich	.75	.35
☐ 132 Dave Pagan	.50	.23
☐ 133 Dave Cash	.50	.23
☐ 134 Steve Braun	.50	.23
☐ 135 Dan Meyer	.50	.23
☐ 136 Bill Stein	.50	.23
☐ 137 Rollie Fingers	3.00	1.35
☐ 138 Brian Downing	.50	.23
☐ 139 Bill Singer	.50	.23
☐ 140 Doyle Alexander	.50	.23
☐ 141 Gene Tenace	.50	.23
☐ 142 Gary Matthews	.50	.23
☐ 143 Don Gullett	.50	.23
☐ 144 Wayne Garland	.50	.23
☐ 145 Pete Broberg	.50	.23
☐ 146 Joe Rudi	.50	.23
☐ 147 Glenn Abbott	.50	.23
☐ 148 George Scott	.50	.23
☐ 149 Bert Campaneris	.50	.23
☐ 150 Andy Messersmith	.50	.23
☐ XX Album	8.00	3.60

1978 Hostess

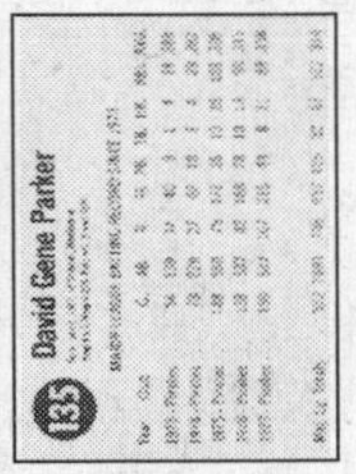

The cards in this 150-card set measure approximately 2 1/4" by 3 1/4" individually or 3 1/4" by 7 1/4" as panels of three. The 1978 Hostess set contains full-color, numbered cards issued in panels of three cards each on family packages of Hostess cake products. Scarcer cards are listed in the checklist with SP. The 1978 Hostess panels are considered by some collectors to be somewhat more difficult to obtain than Hostess panels of other years. Although complete panel prices are not explicitly listed below, they would generally have a value 20-25 percent greater than the sum of the individual players on the panel. There is additional interest in Eddie Murray number 31, since this card corresponds to his rookie year in cards. An album to hold all these cards were issued. There was an album issued for these cards. It was priced below.

	NRMT	VG-E
COMPLETE INDIV.SET (150)	250.00	110.00
COMMON CARD (1-150)	.50	.23

Card	NRMT	VG-E
☐ 1 Butch Hobson	.50	.23
☐ 2 George Foster	.75	.35
☐ 3 Bob Forsch	.50	.23
☐ 4 Tony Perez	1.50	.70
☐ 5 Bruce Sutter	1.00	.45
☐ 6 Hal McRae	.75	.35
☐ 7 Tommy John	1.50	.70
☐ 8 Greg Luzinski	.75	.35
☐ 9 Enos Cabell	.50	.23
☐ 10 Doug DeCinces	.50	.23
☐ 11 Willie Stargell	3.00	1.35
☐ 12 Ed Halicki	.50	.23
☐ 13 Larry Hisle	.50	.23
☐ 14 Jim Slaton	.50	.23
☐ 15 Buddy Bell	.75	.35
☐ 16 Earl Williams	.50	.23
☐ 17 Glenn Abbott	.50	.23

Card	NRMT	VG-E
☐ 18 Dan Ford	.50	.23
☐ 19 Gary Matthews	.50	.23
☐ 20 Eric Soderholm	.50	.23
☐ 21 Bump Wills	.50	.23
☐ 22 Keith Hernandez	1.50	.70
☐ 23 Dave Cash	.50	.23
☐ 24 George Scott	.50	.23
☐ 25 Ron Guidry	1.00	.45
☐ 26 Dave Kingman	1.00	.45
☐ 27 George Brett	30.00	13.50
☐ 28 Bob Watson SP	1.00	.45
☐ 29 Bob Boone SP	1.50	.70
☐ 30 Reggie Smith SP	.75	.35
☐ 31 Eddie Murray SP	50.00	22.00
☐ 32 Gary Lavelle SP	.75	.35
☐ 33 Rennie Stennett SP	.75	.35
☐ 34 Duane Kuiper SP	.75	.35
☐ 35 Sixto Lezcano SP	.75	.35
☐ 36 Dave Rozema SP	.75	.35
☐ 37 Butch Wynegar SP	.75	.35
☐ 38 Mitchell Page SP	.75	.35
☐ 39 Bill Stein SP	.75	.35
☐ 40 Elliott Maddox	.50	.23
☐ 41 Mike Hargrove	.75	.35
☐ 42 Bobby Bonds	1.50	.70
☐ 43 Garry Templeton	.50	.23
☐ 44 Johnny Bench	8.00	3.60
☐ 45 Jim Rice	2.00	.90
☐ 46 Bill Buckner	.75	.35
☐ 47 Reggie Jackson	8.00	3.60
☐ 48 Freddie Patek	.50	.23
☐ 49 Steve Carlton	4.00	1.80
☐ 50 Cesar Cedeno	.50	.23
☐ 51 Steve Yeager	.50	.23
☐ 52 Phil Garner	.75	.35
☐ 53 Lee May	.50	.23
☐ 54 Darrell Evans	.75	.35
☐ 55 Steve Kemp	.50	.23
☐ 56 Dusty Baker	.75	.35
☐ 57 Ray Fosse	.50	.23
☐ 58 Manny Sanguillen	.50	.23
☐ 59 Tom Johnson	.50	.23
☐ 60 Lee Stanton	.50	.23
☐ 61 Jeff Burroughs	.50	.23
☐ 62 Bobby Grich	.75	.35
☐ 63 Dave Winfield	8.00	3.60
☐ 64 Dan Driessen	.50	.23
☐ 65 Ted Simmons	1.00	.45
☐ 66 Jerry Remy	.50	.23
☐ 67 Al Cowens	.50	.23
☐ 68 Sparky Lyle	.75	.35
☐ 69 Manny Trillo	.50	.23
☐ 70 Don Sutton	3.00	1.35
☐ 71 Larry Bowa	.75	.35
☐ 72 Jose Cruz	.50	.23
☐ 73 Willie McCovey	3.00	1.35
☐ 74 Bert Blyleven	1.00	.45
☐ 75 Ken Singleton	.50	.23
☐ 76 Bill North	.50	.23
☐ 77 Jason Thompson	.50	.23
☐ 78 Dennis Eckersley	4.00	1.80
☐ 79 Jim Sundberg	.50	.23
☐ 80 Jerry Koosman	.75	.35
☐ 81 Bruce Bochte	.50	.23
☐ 82 George Hendrick	.50	.23
☐ 83 Nolan Ryan	40.00	18.00
☐ 84 Roy Howell	.50	.23
☐ 85 Roger Metzger	.50	.23
☐ 86 Doc Medich	.50	.23
☐ 87 Joe Morgan	4.00	1.80
☐ 88 Dennis Leonard	.50	.23
☐ 89 Willie Randolph	1.00	.45
☐ 90 Bobby Murcer	.75	.35
☐ 91 Rick Manning	.50	.23
☐ 92 J.R. Richard	.50	.23
☐ 93 Ron Cey	.75	.35
☐ 94 Sal Bando	.50	.23
☐ 95 Ron LeFlore	.50	.23
☐ 96 Dave Goltz	.50	.23
☐ 97 Dan Meyer	.50	.23
☐ 98 Chris Chambliss	.50	.23
☐ 99 Biff Pocoroba	.50	.23
☐ 100 Oscar Gamble	.50	.23
☐ 101 Frank Tanana	.50	.23
☐ 102 Len Randle	.50	.23
☐ 103 Tommy Hutton	.50	.23
☐ 104 John Candelaria	.50	.23
☐ 105 Jorge Orta	.50	.23
☐ 106 Ken Reitz	.50	.23
☐ 107 Bill Campbell	.50	.23
☐ 108 Dave Concepcion	1.00	.45
☐ 109 Joe Ferguson	.50	.23
☐ 110 Mickey Rivers	.50	.23
☐ 111 Paul Splittorff	.50	.23
☐ 112 Dave Lopes	.50	.23
☐ 113 Mike Schmidt	10.00	4.50
☐ 114 Joe Rudi	.50	.23
☐ 115 Milt May	.50	.23
☐ 116 Jim Palmer	4.00	1.80
☐ 117 Bill Madlock	.75	.35
☐ 118 Roy Smalley	.50	.23
☐ 119 Cecil Cooper	1.00	.45
☐ 120 Rick Langford	.50	.23
☐ 121 Ruppert Jones	.50	.23
☐ 122 Phil Niekro	3.00	1.35
☐ 123 Toby Harrah	.50	.23
☐ 124 Chet Lemon	.50	.23
☐ 125 Gene Tenace	.50	.23
☐ 126 Steve Henderson	.50	.23
☐ 127 Mike Torrez	.50	.23
☐ 128 Pete Rose	10.00	4.50
☐ 129 John Denny	.50	.23
☐ 130 Darrell Porter	.50	.23
☐ 131 Rick Reuschel	.50	.23
☐ 132 Graig Nettles	.75	.35
☐ 133 Garry Maddox	.50	.23
☐ 134 Mike Flanagan	.50	.23
☐ 135 Dave Parker	1.00	.45
☐ 136 Terry Whitfield	.50	.23
☐ 137 Wayne Garland	.50	.23
☐ 138 Robin Yount	10.00	4.50
☐ 139 Gaylord Perry	3.00	1.35
☐ 140 Rod Carew	4.00	1.80
☐ 141 Wayne Gross	.50	.23
☐ 142 Barry Bonnell	.50	.23
☐ 143 Willie Montanez	.50	.23
☐ 144 Rollie Fingers	3.00	1.35
☐ 145 Lyman Bostock	.75	.35
☐ 146 Gary Carter	3.00	1.35
☐ 147 Ron Blomberg	.50	.23
☐ 148 Bob Bailor	.50	.23
☐ 149 Tom Seaver	6.00	2.70
☐ 150 Thurman Munson	4.00	1.80
☐ XX Album	8.00	3.60

1979 Hostess

The cards in this 150-card set measure approximately 2 1/4" by 3 1/4" individually or 3 1/4" by 7 1/4" as panels of three. The 1979 Hostess set contains full color, numbered cards issued in panels of three cards each on the backs of family sized Hostess cake products. Scarcer cards are listed in the checklist below with SP. Although complete panel prices are not explicitly listed below they would generally have a value 20-25 percent greater than the sum of the individual players on the panel. The collectors who don't consider 1978 to be the most difficult Hostess to acquire, believe that 1979's are the toughest to get. The shelf life on the 1979's seemed to be slightly shorter than other years.There is additional interest in Ozzie Smith (102) since this card corresponds to his rookie year in cards. An album to hold these cards were issued.

	NRMT	VG-E
COMPLETE INDIV.SET (150)	250.00	110.00
COMMON CARD (1-150)	.50	.23
☐ 1 John Denny	.50	.23
☐ 2 Jim Rice	1.50	.70
☐ 3 Doug Bair	.50	.23
☐ 4 Darrell Porter	.50	.23
☐ 5 Ross Grimsley	.50	.23
☐ 6 Bobby Murcer	.75	.35
☐ 7 Lee Mazzilli	.50	.23
☐ 8 Steve Garvey	2.00	.90
☐ 9 Mike Schmidt	10.00	4.50
☐ 10 Terry Whitfield	.50	.23
☐ 11 Jim Palmer	4.00	1.80
☐ 12 Omar Moreno	.50	.23
☐ 13 Duane Kuiper	.50	.23
☐ 14 Mike Caldwell	.50	.23
☐ 15 Steve Kemp	.50	.23
☐ 16 Dave Goltz	.50	.23
☐ 17 Mitchell Page	.50	.23
☐ 18 Bill Stein	.50	.23
☐ 19 Gene Tenace	.50	.23
☐ 20 Jeff Burroughs	.50	.23
☐ 21 Francisco Barrios	.50	.23
☐ 22 Mike Torrez	.50	.23
☐ 23 Ken Reitz	.50	.23
☐ 24 Gary Carter	3.00	1.35
☐ 25 Al Hrabosky	.50	.23
☐ 26 Thurman Munson	4.00	1.80
☐ 27 Bill Buckner	.75	.35
☐ 28 Ron Cey SP	1.00	.45
☐ 29 J.R. Richard SP	.75	.35
☐ 30 Greg Luzinski SP	1.00	.45
☐ 31 Ed Ott SP	.75	.35
☐ 32 Dennis Martinez SP	3.00	1.35
☐ 33 Darrell Evans SP	1.00	.45
☐ 34 Ron LeFlore	.50	.23
☐ 35 Rick Waits	.50	.23
☐ 36 Cecil Cooper	.75	.35
☐ 37 Leon Roberts	.50	.23
☐ 38 Rod Carew	4.00	1.80
☐ 39 John Henry Johnson	.50	.23
☐ 40 Chet Lemon	.50	.23
☐ 41 Craig Swan	.50	.23
☐ 42 Gary Matthews	.50	.23
☐ 43 Lamar Johnson	.50	.23
☐ 44 Ted Simmons	.75	.35
☐ 45 Ken Griffey	.75	.35
☐ 46 Fred Patek	.50	.23
☐ 47 Frank Tanana	.75	.35
☐ 48 Goose Gossage	1.00	.45
☐ 49 Burt Hooton	.50	.23
☐ 50 Ellis Valentine	.50	.23
☐ 51 Ken Forsch	.50	.23
☐ 52 Bob Knepper	.50	.23
☐ 53 Dave Parker	2.00	.90
☐ 54 Doug DeCinces	.50	.23
☐ 55 Robin Yount	10.00	4.50
☐ 56 Rusty Staub	.75	.35
☐ 57 Gary Alexander	.50	.23
☐ 58 Julio Cruz	.50	.23
☐ 59 Matt Keough	.50	.23
☐ 60 Roy Smalley	.50	.23
☐ 61 Joe Morgan	4.00	1.80
☐ 62 Phil Niekro	3.00	1.35
☐ 63 Don Baylor	.75	.35
☐ 64 Dwight Evans	.75	.35
☐ 65 Tom Seaver	6.00	2.70
☐ 66 George Hendrick	.50	.23
☐ 67 Rick Reuschel	.50	.23
☐ 68 George Brett	20.00	9.00
☐ 69 Lou Piniella	.75	.35
☐ 70 Enos Cabell	.50	.23
☐ 71 Steve Carlton	4.00	1.80
☐ 72 Reggie Smith	.75	.35
☐ 73 Rick Dempsey SP	.75	.35
☐ 74 Vida Blue SP	1.00	.45
☐ 75 Phil Garner SP	1.00	.45
☐ 76 Rick Manning SP	.75	.35
☐ 77 Mark Fidrych SP	1.00	.45
☐ 78 Mario Guerrero SP	.75	.35
☐ 79 Bob Stinson SP	.75	.35
☐ 80 Al Oliver SP	1.00	.45
☐ 81 Doug Flynn SP	.75	.35
☐ 82 John Mayberry	.50	.23
☐ 83 Gaylord Perry	3.00	1.35
☐ 84 Joe Rudi	.50	.23
☐ 85 Dave Concepcion	1.00	.45
☐ 86 John Candelaria	.50	.23
☐ 87 Pete Vuckovich	.50	.23
☐ 88 Ivan DeJesus	.50	.23
☐ 89 Ron Guidry	1.50	.70
☐ 90 Hal McRae	.75	.35
☐ 91 Cesar Cedeno	.50	.23
☐ 92 Don Sutton	3.00	1.35
☐ 93 Andre Thornton	.50	.23
☐ 94 Roger Erickson	.50	.23
☐ 95 Larry Hisle	.50	.23
☐ 96 Jason Thompson	.50	.23
☐ 97 Jim Sundberg	.50	.23
☐ 98 Bob Horner	.75	.35
☐ 99 Ruppert Jones	.50	.23
☐ 100 Willie Montanez	.50	.23
☐ 101 Nolan Ryan	40.00	18.00
☐ 102 Ozzie Smith	40.00	18.00
☐ 103 Eric Soderholm	.50	.23
☐ 104 Willie Stargell	4.00	1.80
☐ 105A Bob Bailor ERR (Reverse negative)	.75	.35
☐ 105B Bob Bailor COR	1.50	.70
☐ 106 Carlton Fisk	5.00	2.20
☐ 107 George Foster	.75	.35
☐ 108 Keith Hernandez	1.50	.70
☐ 109 Dennis Leonard	.50	.23
☐ 110 Graig Nettles	1.00	.45
☐ 111 Jose Cruz	.75	.35
☐ 112 Bobby Grich	.75	.35
☐ 113 Bob Boone	.75	.35
☐ 114 Dave Lopes	.50	.23
☐ 115 Eddie Murray	20.00	9.00
☐ 116 Jack Clark	1.50	.70
☐ 117 Lou Whitaker	4.00	1.80

☐ 118 Miguel Dilone	.50	.23
☐ 119 Sal Bando	.50	.23
☐ 120 Reggie Jackson	8.00	3.60
☐ 121 Dale Murphy	8.00	3.60
☐ 122 Jon Matlack	.50	.23
☐ 123 Bruce Bochte	.50	.23
☐ 124 John Stearns	.50	.23
☐ 125 Dave Winfield	8.00	3.60
☐ 126 Jorge Orta	.50	.23
☐ 127 Garry Templeton	.50	.23
☐ 128 Johnny Bench	6.00	2.70
☐ 129 Butch Hobson	.50	.23
☐ 130 Bruce Sutter	.75	.35
☐ 131 Bucky Dent	.75	.35
☐ 132 Amos Otis	.50	.23
☐ 133 Bert Blyleven	1.00	.45
☐ 134 Larry Bowa	.75	.35
☐ 135 Ken Singleton	.50	.23
☐ 136 Sixto Lezcano	.50	.23
☐ 137 Roy Howell	.50	.23
☐ 138 Bill Madlock	.75	.35
☐ 139 Dave Revering	.50	.23
☐ 140 Richie Zisk	.50	.23
☐ 141 Butch Wynegar	.50	.23
☐ 142 Alan Ashby	.50	.23
☐ 143 Sparky Lyle	.75	.35
☐ 144 Pete Rose	10.00	4.50
☐ 145 Dennis Eckersley	2.50	1.10
☐ 146 Dave Kingman	1.00	.45
☐ 147 Buddy Bell	.75	.35
☐ 148 Mike Hargrove	.75	.35
☐ 149 Jerry Koosman	.75	.35
☐ 150 Toby Harrah	.50	.23
☐ XX Album	8.00	3.60

1987 Hostess Stickers

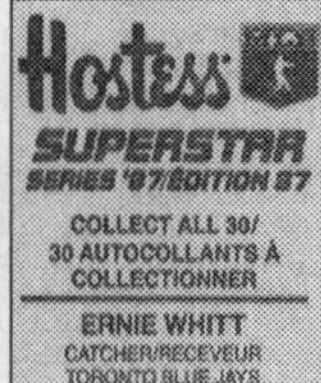

This set of 30 small, full-color stickers was produced in Canada by Hostess Potato Chips and distributed in bags of potato chips. Each sticker was loosely wrapped in cellophane (to protect against potato chip stains) and measures approximately 1 3/8" by 1 3/4" with rounded corners. The backs of the stickers contain the player's name, team and position in English as well as in French. They are numbered on the front in the lower left corner. The first six cards are Blue Jays and Expos; the rest of the set consists of one player per American team.

	MINT	NRMT
COMPLETE SET (30)	40.00	18.00
COMMON STICKER (1-30)	.50	.23
☐ 1 Jesse Barfield	.50	.23
☐ 2 Ernie Whitt	.50	.23
☐ 3 George Bell	.50	.23
☐ 4 Hubie Brooks	.50	.23
☐ 5 Tim Wallach	.50	.23
☐ 6 Floyd Youmans	.50	.23
☐ 7 Dale Murphy	1.50	.70
☐ 8 Ryne Sandberg	5.00	2.20
☐ 9 Eric Davis	.75	.35
☐ 10 Mike Scott	.50	.23
☐ 11 Fernando Valenzuela	.75	.35
☐ 12 Gary Carter	1.00	.45
☐ 13 Mike Schmidt	4.00	1.80
☐ 14 Tony Pena	.50	.23
☐ 15 Ozzie Smith	5.00	2.20
☐ 16 Tony Gwynn	6.00	2.70
☐ 17 Mike Krukow	.50	.23
☐ 18 Eddie Murray	3.00	1.35
☐ 19 Wade Boggs	2.00	.90
☐ 20 Wally Joyner	1.50	.70
☐ 21 Harold Baines	.75	.35
☐ 22 Brook Jacoby	.50	.23
☐ 23 Lou Whitaker	.75	.35
☐ 24 George Brett	5.00	2.20
☐ 25 Robin Yount	1.50	.70
☐ 26 Kirby Puckett	6.00	2.70
☐ 27 Don Mattingly	6.00	2.70
☐ 28 Jose Canseco	4.00	1.80
☐ 29 Phil Bradley	.50	.23
☐ 30 Pete O'Brien	.50	.23

1993 Hostess

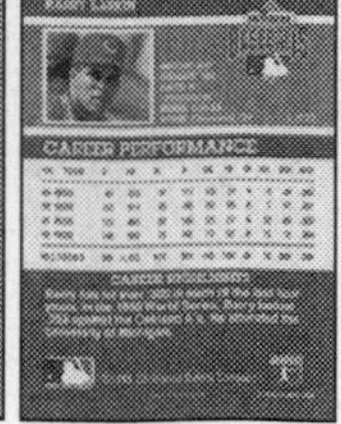

These standard-size cards were free with the purchase of packages of Hostess Baseballs, a new snack food. The frosted yellow cakes have creamy filling and were decorated with red icing to resemble the stitching of a baseball. Each two-cake snack pack contained one three-card pack and cost 85 cents, while each eight-cake family pack contained two packs and cost 2.99. The cards were issued in two series (1-16 and 17-32), the first being available nationally beginning on April 12 and the second series beginning mid-season. A checklist was included on the back of each family pack. The cards feature color action player photos inside a white inner border and an outer border consisting of blue and white diagonal pinstripes. The player's name and the team logo are on a red banner toward the bottom of the card. On blue, red, and white panels, the backs display a color head shot, biography, career performance statistics, and career highlights.

	MINT	NRMT
COMPLETE SET (32)	7.50	3.40
COMMON CARD (1-32)	.10	.05
☐ 1 Andy Van Slyke	.10	.05
☐ 2 Ryne Sandberg	.50	.23
☐ 3 Bobby Bonilla	.20	.09
☐ 4 John Kruk	.20	.09
☐ 5 Ray Lankford	.30	.14
☐ 6 Gary Sheffield	.40	.18
☐ 7 Darryl Strawberry	.20	.09
☐ 8 Barry Larkin	.30	.14
☐ 9 Terry Pendleton	.10	.05
☐ 10 Jose Canseco	.40	.18
☐ 11 Dennis Eckersley	.30	.14
☐ 12 Brian McRae	.10	.05
☐ 13 Frank Thomas	1.25	.55
☐ 14 Roberto Alomar	.40	.18
☐ 15 Carlos Baerga	.20	.09
☐ 16 Cecil Fielder	.20	.09
☐ 17 Will Clark	.30	.14
☐ 18 Andres Galarraga	.40	.18
☐ 19 Jeff Bagwell	.75	.35
☐ 20 Brett Butler	.20	.09
☐ 21 Benito Santiago	.10	.05
☐ 22 Tom Glavine	.20	.09
☐ 23 Rickey Henderson	.40	.18
☐ 24 Wally Joyner	.10	.05
☐ 25 Ken Griffey Jr.	1.50	.70
☐ 26 Cal Ripken	1.25	.55
☐ 27 Roger Clemens	.75	.35
☐ 28 Don Mattingly	.75	.35
☐ 29 Kirby Puckett	.75	.35
☐ 30 Larry Walker	.40	.18
☐ 31 Jack McDowell	.10	.05
☐ 32 Pat Listach	.10	.05

1962 Jello

The cards in this 200-card (only 197 were ever issued) set measure 2 1/2" by 3 3/8". The 1962 Jello set has the same checklist as the Post Cereal set of the same year, but is considered by some to be a test issue. The cards are grouped numerically by team. For example: New York Yankees (1-13), Detroit (14-26), Baltimore (27-36), Cleveland (37-45), Chicago White Sox (46-55), Boston (56-64), Washington (65-73), Los Angeles Angels (74-82), Minnesota (83-91), Kansas City (92-100), Los Angeles Dodgers (101-115), Cincinnati (116-130), San Francisco (131-144), Milwaukee (145-157), St. Louis (158-168), Pittsburgh (169-181), Chicago Cubs (182-191), and Philadelphia (192-200). Although the players and numbers are identical in both sets, the Jello series has its own list of scarce and difficult cards. Numbers 29, 82 and 176 were never issued. A Jello card is easily distinguished from its counterpart in Post by the absence of the Post logo. The catalog designation for this set is F229-1.

	NRMT	VG-E
COMPLETE SET (197)	5000.00	2200.00
COMMON CARD (1-200)	6.00	2.70
☐ 1 Bill Skowron	25.00	11.00
☐ 2 Bobby Richardson	25.00	11.00
☐ 3 Cletis Boyer	12.50	5.50
☐ 4 Tony Kubek	20.00	9.00
☐ 5 Mickey Mantle	1000.00	450.00
☐ 6 Roger Maris	175.00	80.00
☐ 7 Yogi Berra	125.00	55.00
☐ 8 Elston Howard	12.50	5.50
☐ 9 Whitey Ford	75.00	34.00
☐ 10 Ralph Terry	10.00	4.50
☐ 11 John Blanchard	10.00	4.50
☐ 12 Luis Arroyo	10.00	4.50
☐ 13 Bill Stafford	15.00	6.75
☐ 14 Norm Cash	12.50	5.50
☐ 15 Jake Wood	6.00	2.70
☐ 16 Steve Boros	6.00	2.70
☐ 17 Chico Fernandez	6.00	2.70
☐ 18 Bill Bruton	6.00	2.70
☐ 19 Ken Aspromonte	6.00	2.70
☐ 20 Al Kaline	60.00	27.00
☐ 21 Dick Brown	6.00	2.70
☐ 22 Frank Lary	6.00	2.70
☐ 23 Don Mossi	10.00	4.50
☐ 24 Phil Regan	6.00	2.70
☐ 25 Charley Maxwell	6.00	2.70
☐ 26 Jim Bunning	30.00	13.50
☐ 27 Jim Gentile	10.00	4.50
☐ 28 Marv Breeding	6.00	2.70
☐ 29 Not issued		
☐ 30 Ron Hansen	6.00	2.70
☐ 31 Jackie Brandt	25.00	11.00
☐ 32 Dick Williams	12.50	5.50
☐ 33 Gus Triandos	6.00	2.70
☐ 34 Milt Pappas	6.00	2.70
☐ 35 Hoyt Wilhelm	50.00	22.00
☐ 36 Chuck Estrada	6.00	2.70
☐ 37 Vic Power	6.00	2.70
☐ 38 Johnny Temple	6.00	2.70
☐ 39 Bubba Phillips	25.00	11.00
☐ 40 Tito Francona	6.00	2.70
☐ 41 Willie Kirkland	6.00	2.70
☐ 42 John Romano	6.00	2.70
☐ 43 Jim Perry	10.00	4.50
☐ 44 Woodie Held	6.00	2.70
☐ 45 Chuck Essegian	6.00	2.70
☐ 46 Roy Sievers	6.00	2.70
☐ 47 Nellie Fox	35.00	16.00
☐ 48 Al Smith	6.00	2.70
☐ 49 Luis Aparicio	40.00	18.00
☐ 50 Jim Landis	6.00	2.70
☐ 51 Minnie Minoso	25.00	11.00
☐ 52 Andy Carey	25.00	11.00
☐ 53 Sherman Lollar	6.00	2.70
☐ 54 Billy Pierce	10.00	4.50
☐ 55 Early Wynn	30.00	13.50
☐ 56 Chuck Schilling	25.00	11.00
☐ 57 Pete Runnels	10.00	4.50
☐ 58 Frank Malzone	10.00	4.50
☐ 59 Don Buddin	10.00	4.50
☐ 60 Gary Geiger	25.00	11.00
☐ 61 Carl Yastrzemski	300.00	135.00
☐ 62 Jackie Jensen	30.00	13.50
☐ 63 Jim Pagliaroni	25.00	11.00
☐ 64 Don Schwall	10.00	4.50
☐ 65 Dale Long	10.00	4.50
☐ 66 Chuck Cottier	10.00	4.50
☐ 67 Billy Klaus	25.00	11.00
☐ 68 Coot Veal	10.00	4.50
☐ 69 Marty Keough	35.00	16.00
☐ 70 Willie Tasby	35.00	16.00
☐ 71 Gene Woodling	10.00	4.50
☐ 72 Gene Green	35.00	16.00
☐ 73 Dick Donovan	10.00	4.50
☐ 74 Steve Bilko	10.00	4.50
☐ 75 Rocky Bridges	25.00	11.00
☐ 76 Eddie Yost	15.00	6.75
☐ 77 Leon Wagner	12.50	5.50
☐ 78 Albie Pearson	10.00	4.50
☐ 79 Ken Hunt	15.00	6.75
☐ 80 Earl Averill	35.00	16.00
☐ 81 Ryne Duren	12.50	5.50

Card	NRMT	VG-E
☐ 82 Not issued		
☐ 83 Bob Allison	10.00	4.50
☐ 84 Billy Martin	30.00	13.50
☐ 85 Harmon Killebrew	50.00	22.00
☐ 86 Zoilo Versalles	10.00	4.50
☐ 87 Lenny Green	30.00	13.50
☐ 88 Bill Tuttle	6.00	2.70
☐ 89 Jim Lemon	6.00	2.70
☐ 90 Earl Battey	25.00	11.00
☐ 91 Camilo Pascual	6.00	2.70
☐ 92 Norm Siebern	10.00	4.50
☐ 93 Jerry Lumpe	10.00	4.50
☐ 94 Dick Howser	12.50	5.50
☐ 95 Gene Stephens	35.00	16.00
☐ 96 Leo Posada	12.50	5.50
☐ 97 Joe Pignatano	10.00	4.50
☐ 98 Jim Archer	10.00	4.50
☐ 99 Haywood Sullivan	25.00	11.00
☐ 100 Art Ditmar	10.00	4.50
☐ 101 Gil Hodges	50.00	22.00
☐ 102 Charlie Neal	10.00	4.50
☐ 103 Daryl Spencer	10.00	4.50
☐ 104 Maury Wills	30.00	13.50
☐ 105 Tommy Davis	15.00	6.75
☐ 106 Willie Davis	15.00	6.75
☐ 107 Johnny Roseboro	35.00	16.00
☐ 108 John Podres	15.00	6.75
☐ 109 Sandy Koufax	125.00	55.00
☐ 110 Don Drysdale	60.00	27.00
☐ 111 Larry Sherry	25.00	11.00
☐ 112 Jim Gilliam	30.00	13.50
☐ 113 Norm Larker	40.00	18.00
☐ 114 Duke Snider	75.00	34.00
☐ 115 Stan Williams	25.00	11.00
☐ 116 Gordy Coleman	75.00	34.00
☐ 117 Don Blasingame	25.00	11.00
☐ 118 Gene Freese	40.00	18.00
☐ 119 Ed Kasko	40.00	18.00
☐ 120 Gus Bell	30.00	13.50
☐ 121 Vada Pinson	15.00	6.75
☐ 122 Frank Robinson	40.00	18.00
☐ 123 Bob Purkey	10.00	4.50
☐ 124 Joey Jay	10.00	4.50
☐ 125 Jim Brosnan	10.00	4.50
☐ 126 Jim O'Toole	10.00	4.50
☐ 127 Jerry Lynch	10.00	4.50
☐ 128 Wally Post	10.00	4.50
☐ 129 Ken Hunt	10.00	4.50
☐ 130 Jerry Zimmerman	10.00	4.50
☐ 131 Willie McCovey	60.00	27.00
☐ 132 Jose Pagan	30.00	13.50
☐ 133 Felipe Alou	15.00	6.75
☐ 134 Jim Davenport	12.50	5.50
☐ 135 Harvey Kuenn	15.00	6.75
☐ 136 Orlando Cepeda	30.00	13.50
☐ 137 Ed Bailey	10.00	4.50
☐ 138 Sam Jones	10.00	4.50
☐ 139 Mike McCormick	10.00	4.50
☐ 140 Juan Marichal	75.00	34.00
☐ 141 Jack Sanford	10.00	4.50
☐ 142 Willie Mays	225.00	100.00
☐ 143 Stu Miller	60.00	27.00
☐ 144 Joe Amalfitano	10.00	4.50
☐ 145 Joe Adcock	10.00	4.50
☐ 146 Frank Bolling	6.00	2.70
☐ 147 Eddie Mathews	50.00	22.00
☐ 148 Roy McMillan	6.00	2.70
☐ 149 Hank Aaron	200.00	90.00
☐ 150 Gino Cimoli	25.00	11.00
☐ 151 Frank Thomas	10.00	4.50
☐ 152 Joe Torre	20.00	9.00
☐ 153 Lew Burdette	12.50	5.50
☐ 154 Bob Buhl	6.00	2.70
☐ 155 Carlton Willey	6.00	2.70
☐ 156 Lee Maye	25.00	11.00
☐ 157 Al Spangler	35.00	16.00
☐ 158 Bill White	60.00	27.00
☐ 159 Ken Boyer	25.00	11.00
☐ 160 Joe Cunningham	10.00	4.50
☐ 161 Carl Warwick	10.00	4.50
☐ 162 Carl Sawatski	6.00	2.70
☐ 163 Lindy McDaniel	6.00	2.70
☐ 164 Ernie Broglio	10.00	4.50
☐ 165 Larry Jackson	6.00	2.70
☐ 166 Curt Flood	30.00	13.50
☐ 167 Curt Simmons	30.00	13.50
☐ 168 Alex Grammas	25.00	11.00
☐ 169 Dick Stuart	6.00	2.70
☐ 170 Bill Mazeroski	30.00	13.50
☐ 171 Don Hoak	10.00	4.50
☐ 172 Dick Groat	12.50	5.50
☐ 173 Roberto Clemente	300.00	135.00
☐ 174 Bob Skinner	25.00	11.00
☐ 175 Bill Virdon	30.00	13.50
☐ 176 Not issued		
☐ 177 Roy Face	12.50	5.50
☐ 178 Bob Friend	6.00	2.70
☐ 179 Vern Law	30.00	13.50
☐ 180 Harvey Haddix	35.00	16.00
☐ 181 Hal Smith	25.00	11.00
☐ 182 Ed Bouchee	25.00	11.00
☐ 183 Don Zimmer	12.50	5.50
☐ 184 Ron Santo	20.00	9.00
☐ 185 Andre Rodgers	6.00	2.70
☐ 186 Richie Ashburn	35.00	16.00
☐ 187 George Altman	6.00	2.70
☐ 188 Ernie Banks	35.00	16.00
☐ 189 Sam Taylor	6.00	2.70
☐ 190 Don Elston	6.00	2.70
☐ 191 Jerry Kindall	20.00	9.00
☐ 192 Pancho Herrera	6.00	2.70
☐ 193 Tony Taylor	10.00	4.50
☐ 194 Ruben Amaro	20.00	9.00
☐ 195 Don Demeter	6.00	2.70
☐ 196 Bobby Gene Smith	6.00	2.70
☐ 197 Clay Dalrymple	6.00	2.70
☐ 198 Robin Roberts	30.00	13.50
☐ 199 Art Mahaffey	6.00	2.70
☐ 200 John Buzhardt	6.00	2.70

1963 Jello

The cards in this 200-card set measure 2 1/2" by 3 3/8". The 1963 Jello set contains the same players and numbers as the Post Cereal set of the same year. The players are grouped by team with American Leaguers comprising 1-100 and National Leaguers 101-200. The ordering of teams is as follows: Minnesota (1-11), New York Yankees, Los Angeles Angels (24-34), Chicago White Sox (35-45), Detroit (46-56), Baltimore (57-66), Cleveland (67-76), Boston (77-84), Kansas City (85-92), Washington (93-100), San Francisco (101-112), Los Angeles Dodgers (113-124), Cincinnati (125-136), Pittsburgh (137-147), Milwaukee (148-157), St. Louis (158-168), Chicago Cubs (169-176), Philadelphia (177-184), Houston (185-192) and New York Mets (193-200). As in 1962, the Jello series has its own list of scarcities (many resulting from an unpopular package size). Since the Post Cereal logo was removed from the 1963 cereal set, Jello cards are primarily distinguishable by (1) smaller card size and (2) smaller print. The catalog designation is F229-2.

	NRMT	VG-E
COMPLETE SET (200)	3250.00	1450.00
COMMON CARD (1-200)	4.00	1.80

Card	NRMT	VG-E
☐ 1 Vic Power	4.00	1.80
☐ 2 Bernie Allen	20.00	9.00
☐ 3 Zoilo Versalles	25.00	11.00
☐ 4 Rich Rollins	4.00	1.80
☐ 5 Harmon Killebrew	20.00	9.00
☐ 6 Lenny Green	25.00	11.00
☐ 7 Bob Allison	4.00	1.80
☐ 8 Earl Battey	15.00	6.75
☐ 9 Camilo Pascual	6.00	2.70
☐ 10 Jim Kaat	60.00	27.00
☐ 11 Jack Kralick	4.00	1.80
☐ 12 Bill Skowron	25.00	11.00
☐ 13 Bobby Richardson	7.50	3.40
☐ 14 Cletis Boyer	6.00	2.70
☐ 15 Mickey Mantle	275.00	125.00
☐ 16 Roger Maris	100.00	45.00
☐ 17 Yogi Berra	30.00	13.50
☐ 18 Elston Howard	40.00	18.00
☐ 19 Whitey Ford	20.00	9.00
☐ 20 Ralph Terry	4.00	1.80
☐ 21 John Blanchard	15.00	6.75
☐ 22 Bill Stafford	25.00	11.00
☐ 23 Tom Tresh	7.50	3.40
☐ 24 Steve Bilko	4.00	1.80
☐ 25 Bill Moran	4.00	1.80
☐ 26 Joe Koppe	4.00	1.80
☐ 27 Felix Torres	4.00	1.80
☐ 28 Leon Wagner	4.00	1.80
☐ 29 Albie Pearson	4.00	1.80
☐ 30 Lee Thomas	4.00	1.80
☐ 31 Bob Rodgers	25.00	11.00
☐ 32 Dean Chance	6.00	2.70
☐ 33 Ken McBride	25.00	11.00
☐ 34 George Thomas	25.00	11.00
☐ 35 Joe Cunningham	25.00	11.00
☐ 36 Nellie Fox	10.00	4.50
☐ 37 Luis Aparicio	10.00	4.50
☐ 38 Al Smith	4.00	1.80
☐ 39 Floyd Robinson	4.00	1.80
☐ 40 Jim Landis	4.00	1.80
☐ 41 Charlie Maxwell	4.00	1.80
☐ 42 Sherman Lollar	6.00	2.70
☐ 43 Early Wynn	10.00	4.50
☐ 44 Juan Pizarro	20.00	9.00
☐ 45 Ray Herbert	25.00	11.00
☐ 46 Norm Cash	7.50	3.40
☐ 47 Steve Boros	30.00	13.50
☐ 48 Dick McAuliffe	6.00	2.70
☐ 49 Bill Bruton	20.00	9.00
☐ 50 Rocky Colavito	7.50	3.40
☐ 51 Al Kaline	20.00	9.00
☐ 52 Dick Brown	25.00	11.00
☐ 53 Jim Bunning	10.00	4.50
☐ 54 Hank Aguirre	4.00	1.80
☐ 55 Frank Lary	25.00	11.00
☐ 56 Don Mossi	25.00	11.00
☐ 57 Jim Gentile	6.00	2.70
☐ 58 Jackie Brandt	4.00	1.80
☐ 59 Brooks Robinson	20.00	9.00
☐ 60 Ron Hansen	4.00	1.80
☐ 61 Jerry Adair	50.00	22.00
☐ 62 Boog Powell	7.50	3.40
☐ 63 Russ Snyder	25.00	11.00
☐ 64 Steve Barber	4.00	1.80
☐ 65 Milt Pappas	25.00	11.00
☐ 66 Robin Roberts	10.00	4.50
☐ 67 Tito Francona	4.00	1.80
☐ 68 Jerry Kindall	25.00	11.00
☐ 69 Woody Held	4.00	1.80
☐ 70 Bubba Phillips	4.00	1.80
☐ 71 Chuck Essegian	4.00	1.80
☐ 72 Willie Kirkland	25.00	11.00
☐ 73 Al Luplow	4.00	1.80
☐ 74 Ty Cline	50.00	22.00
☐ 75 Dick Donovan	4.00	1.80
☐ 76 John Romano	4.00	1.80
☐ 77 Pete Runnels	6.00	2.70
☐ 78 Ed Bressoud	20.00	9.00
☐ 79 Frank Malzone	6.00	2.70
☐ 80 Carl Yastrzemski	75.00	34.00
☐ 81 Gary Geiger	4.00	1.80
☐ 82 Lou Clinton	20.00	9.00
☐ 83 Earl Wilson	4.00	1.80
☐ 84 Bill Monbouquette	4.00	1.80
☐ 85 Norm Siebern	4.00	1.80
☐ 86 Jerry Lumpe	4.00	1.80
☐ 87 Manny Jimenez	4.00	1.80
☐ 88 Gino Cimoli	4.00	1.80
☐ 89 Ed Charles	50.00	22.00
☐ 90 Ed Rakow	4.00	1.80
☐ 91 Bobby Del Greco	50.00	22.00
☐ 92 Haywood Sullivan	25.00	11.00
☐ 93 Chuck Hinton	4.00	1.80
☐ 94 Ken Retzer	25.00	11.00
☐ 95 Harry Bright	25.00	11.00
☐ 96 Bob Johnson	4.00	1.80
☐ 97 Dave Stenhouse	20.00	9.00
☐ 98 Chuck Cottier	4.00	1.80
☐ 99 Tom Cheney	4.00	1.80
☐ 100 Claude Osteen	30.00	13.50
☐ 101 Orlando Cepeda	10.00	4.50
☐ 102 Chuck Hiller	20.00	9.00
☐ 103 Jose Pagan	20.00	9.00
☐ 104 Jim Davenport	4.00	1.80
☐ 105 Harvey Kuenn	6.00	2.70
☐ 106 Willie Mays	110.00	50.00
☐ 107 Felipe Alou	7.50	3.40
☐ 108 Tom Haller	4.00	1.80
☐ 109 Juan Marichal	10.00	4.50
☐ 110 Jack Sanford	4.00	1.80
☐ 111 Bill O'Dell	4.00	1.80
☐ 112 Willie McCovey	150.00	70.00
☐ 113 Lee Walls	20.00	9.00
☐ 114 Jim Gilliam	30.00	13.50
☐ 115 Maury Wills	7.50	3.40
☐ 116 Ron Fairly	6.00	2.70
☐ 117 Tommy Davis	6.00	2.70
☐ 118 Duke Snider	15.00	6.75
☐ 119 Willie Davis	6.00	2.70
☐ 120 John Roseboro	4.00	1.80
☐ 121 Sandy Koufax	35.00	16.00
☐ 122 Stan Williams	4.00	1.80
☐ 123 Don Drysdale	10.00	4.50
☐ 124 Daryl Spencer	4.00	1.80
☐ 125 Gordy Coleman	4.00	1.80
☐ 126 Don Blasingame	25.00	11.00
☐ 127 Leo Cardenas	4.00	1.80
☐ 128 Eddie Kasko	20.00	9.00
☐ 129 Jerry Lynch	4.00	1.80
☐ 130 Vada Pinson	7.50	3.40
☐ 131 Frank Robinson	12.50	5.50
☐ 132 Johnny Edwards	25.00	11.00
☐ 133 Joey Jay	4.00	1.80
☐ 134 Bob Purkey	4.00	1.80

	MINT	NRMT
☐ 135 Marty Keough	50.00	22.00
☐ 136 Jim O'Toole	25.00	11.00
☐ 137 Dick Stuart	4.00	1.80
☐ 138 Bill Mazeroski	7.50	3.40
☐ 139 Dick Groat	6.00	2.70
☐ 140 Don Hoak	4.00	1.80
☐ 141 Bob Skinner	4.00	1.80
☐ 142 Bill Virdon	6.00	2.70
☐ 143 Roberto Clemente	150.00	70.00
☐ 144 Smoky Burgess	6.00	2.70
☐ 145 Bob Friend	4.00	1.80
☐ 146 Al McBean	25.00	11.00
☐ 147 Roy Face	6.00	2.70
☐ 148 Joe Adcock	6.00	2.70
☐ 149 Frank Bolling	4.00	1.80
☐ 150 Roy McMillan	4.00	1.80
☐ 151 Eddie Mathews	20.00	9.00
☐ 152 Hank Aaron	100.00	45.00
☐ 153 Del Crandall	25.00	11.00
☐ 154 Bob Shaw	4.00	1.80
☐ 155 Lew Burdette	6.00	2.70
☐ 156 Joe Torre	50.00	22.00
☐ 157 Tony Cloninger	30.00	13.50
☐ 158 Bill White	7.50	3.40
☐ 159 Julian Javier	25.00	11.00
☐ 160 Ken Boyer	7.50	3.40
☐ 161 Julio Gotay	25.00	11.00
☐ 162 Curt Flood	6.00	2.70
☐ 163 Charlie James	50.00	22.00
☐ 164 Gene Oliver	25.00	11.00
☐ 165 Ernie Broglio	4.00	1.80
☐ 166 Bob Gibson	100.00	45.00
☐ 167 Lindy McDaniel	20.00	9.00
☐ 168 Ray Washburn	4.00	1.80
☐ 169 Ernie Banks	20.00	9.00
☐ 170 Ron Santo	7.50	3.40
☐ 171 George Altman	4.00	1.80
☐ 172 Billy Williams	75.00	34.00
☐ 173 Andre Rodgers	25.00	11.00
☐ 174 Ken Hubbs	7.50	3.40
☐ 175 Don Landrum	25.00	11.00
☐ 176 Dick Bertell	25.00	11.00
☐ 177 Roy Sievers	6.00	2.70
☐ 178 Tony Taylor	30.00	13.50
☐ 179 Johnny Callison	6.00	2.70
☐ 180 Don Demeter	4.00	1.80
☐ 181 Tony Gonzalez	25.00	11.00
☐ 182 Wes Covington	25.00	11.00
☐ 183 Art Mahaffey	4.00	1.80
☐ 184 Clay Dalrymple	4.00	1.80
☐ 185 Al Spangler	4.00	1.80
☐ 186 Roman Mejias	4.00	1.80
☐ 187 Bob Aspromonte	30.00	13.50
☐ 188 Norm Larker	4.00	1.80
☐ 189 Johnny Temple	4.00	1.80
☐ 190 Carl Warwick	25.00	11.00
☐ 191 Bob Lillis	20.00	9.00
☐ 192 Dick Farrell	35.00	16.00
☐ 193 Gil Hodges	15.00	6.75
☐ 194 Marv Throneberry	6.00	2.70
☐ 195 Charlie Neal	25.00	11.00
☐ 196 Frank Thomas	6.00	2.70
☐ 197 Richie Ashburn	10.00	4.50
☐ 198 Felix Mantilla	20.00	9.00
☐ 199 Rod Kanehl	20.00	9.00
☐ 200 Roger Craig	35.00	16.00

1991 Jimmy Dean

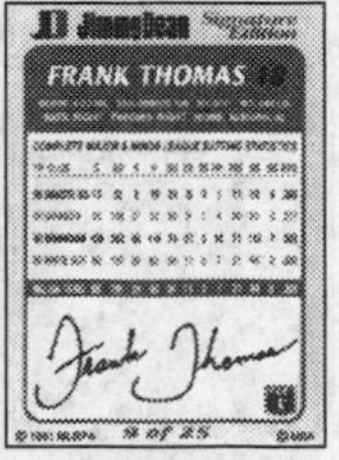

Michael Schechter Associates (MSA) produced this 25-card standard-size set on behalf of Jimmy Dean Sausage. These cards feature an obverse with a color player photo, enframed by yellow and red borders. Since these player photos were not expressly licensed by Major League Baseball, the team logos have been airbrushed out. In a red and white panel with yellow borders, the back has biographical information, complete major (and minor where appropriate) league statistics, and the player's facsimile autograph. The cards are numbered on the back. During the promotion, uncut sheets were offered by the company through a mail-in offer involving Jimmy Dean proofs of purchase.

	MINT	NRMT
COMPLETE SET (25)	12.00	5.50
COMMON CARD (1-25)	.25	.11
☐ 1 Will Clark	.60	.25
☐ 2 Ken Griffey Jr.	3.00	1.35
☐ 3 Dale Murphy	.60	.25
☐ 4 Barry Bonds	1.00	.45
☐ 5 Darryl Strawberry	.40	.18
☐ 6 Ryne Sandberg	1.25	.55
☐ 7 Gary Sheffield	.75	.35
☐ 8 Sandy Alomar Jr.	.40	.18
☐ 9 Frank Thomas	2.50	1.10
☐ 10 Barry Larkin	.75	.35
☐ 11 Kirby Puckett	1.50	.70
☐ 12 George Brett	1.25	.55
☐ 13 Kevin Mitchell	.25	.11
☐ 14 Dave Justice	.75	.35
☐ 15 Cal Ripken	2.50	1.10
☐ 16 Craig Biggio	.60	.25
☐ 17 Rickey Henderson	.60	.25
☐ 18 Roger Clemens	1.25	.55
☐ 19 Jose Canseco	.60	.25
☐ 20 Ozzie Smith	1.50	.70
☐ 21 Cecil Fielder	.40	.18
☐ 22 Dave Winfield	.60	.25
☐ 23 Kevin Maas	.25	.11
☐ 24 Nolan Ryan	2.50	1.10
☐ 25 Dwight Gooden	.40	.18

1992 Jimmy Dean

Michael Schechter Associates (MSA) produced this 18-card standard-size set for Jimmy Dean. In a cello pack, three free cards were included in any Jimmy Dean Sandwich, Flapsticks, or Links/Patties Breakfast Sausage. The fronts feature glossy color player photos with team logos airbrushed out. These pictures are bordered on the left by a black bar that includes player information printed vertically. Another bar juts out from the right at the bottom of the picture and has the company logo with the words "Jimmy Dean '92." Inside a blue border, the backs are red, white, and blue and present biography, statistics, and brief career summary.

	MINT	NRMT
COMPLETE SET (18)	8.00	3.60
COMMON CARD (1-18)	.10	.05
☐ 1 Jim Abbott	.10	.05
☐ 2 Barry Bonds	.60	.25
☐ 3 Jeff Bagwell	1.25	.55
☐ 4 Frank Thomas	1.50	.70
☐ 5 Steve Avery	.10	.05
☐ 6 Chris Sabo	.10	.05
☐ 7 Will Clark	.35	.16
☐ 8 Don Mattingly	1.00	.45
☐ 9 Darryl Strawberry	.20	.09
☐ 10 Roger Clemens	.75	.35
☐ 11 Ken Griffey Jr.	2.00	.90
☐ 12 Chuck Knoblauch	.50	.23
☐ 13 Tony Gwynn	1.00	.45
☐ 14 Juan Gonzalez	1.00	.45
☐ 15 Cecil Fielder	.20	.09
☐ 16 Bobby Bonilla	.20	.09
☐ 17 Wes Chamberlain	.10	.05
☐ 18 Ryne Sandberg	.75	.35

1992 Jimmy Dean Living Legends

This six-card standard-size set was produced by MSA (Michael Schechter Associates) and features future candidates for the Hall of Fame. Collectors could obtain the complete set through a mail-in offer detailed on packages of Jimmy Dean Breakfast Sausage or Smoked Sausage. While supplies lasted, the sets could be obtained by sending in three UPC proofs of purchase from Jimmy Dean Sausage plus 1.00 for shipping and handling. The cards feature on the fronts glossy color player photos with team logos airbrushed out. These pictures are

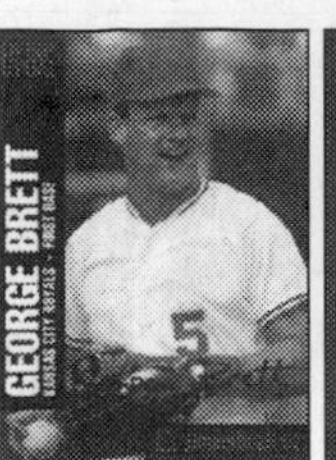

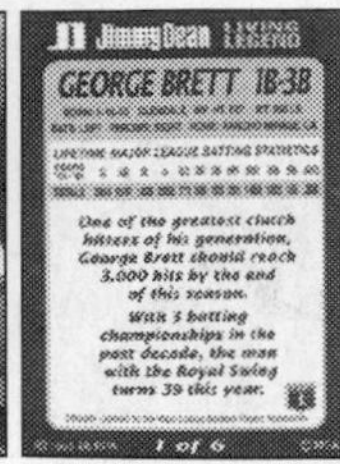

bordered on the left by a black bar that includes player information and the words "Living Legend" in gold-foil stamping. Another black bar juts out from the right at the bottom of the picture and has "Jimmy Dean '92" also in gold foil. Finally, inscribed across each photo is the player's signature in gold foil. The backs are black, yellow, and white and carry biography, statistics, and a brief career summary. Reportedly 105,000 sets were printed.

	MINT	NRMT
COMPLETE SET (6)	15.00	6.75
COMMON CARD (1-6)	1.00	.45
☐ 1 George Brett	2.50	1.10
☐ 2 Carlton Fisk	1.50	.70
☐ 3 Ozzie Smith	2.00	.90
☐ 4 Robin Yount	1.00	.45
☐ 5 Cal Ripken	5.00	2.20
☐ 6 Nolan Ryan	5.00	2.20

1992 Jimmy Dean Rookie Stars

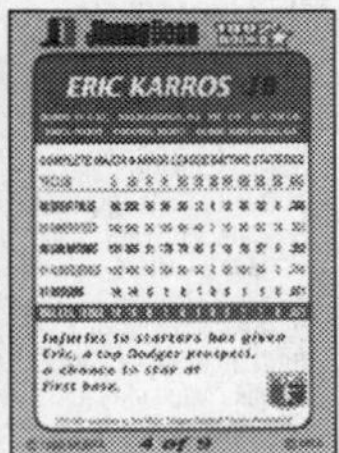

The players in this nine-card standard-size set were chosen based on actual 1992 first-half performance. Three free cards were included in specially marked packages of Jimmy Dean Sausage, Chicken Biscuits, Steak Biscuits, and MiniBurgers. The cards feature on the fronts glossy color player photos with team logos airbrushed out. These pictures are bordered on the left by a black bar that includes the player's name printed vertically in either red or blue lettering. Another bar juts out from the right at the bottom of the picture and has "Jimmy Dean '92" in black lettering. Inside light blue borders, a red and white panel displays biography, statistics, and a brief career summary. Oversized 7" by 9 3/4" versions of the cards, featuring a Rookie Star front on one side and a Living Legend front on the other, were placed at point of purchase for promotional purchases.

	MINT	NRMT
COMPLETE SET (9)	4.00	1.80
COMMON CARD (1-9)	.15	.07
☐ 1 Andy Stankiewicz	.15	.07
☐ 2 Pat Listach	.15	.07
☐ 3 Brian Jordan	1.00	.45
☐ 4 Eric Karros	.75	.35
☐ 5 Reggie Sanders	.25	.11
☐ 6 Dave Fleming	.15	.07
☐ 7 Donovan Osborne	.25	.11
☐ 8 Kenny Lofton	2.00	.90
☐ 9 Moises Alou	.75	.35

1993 Jimmy Dean

Produced by MSA (Michael Schechter Associates) for Jimmy Dean, these 28 cards measure the standard size. Eighteen cards were distributed in packs of three inside certain packages of Jimmy Dean products. The remaining ten cards were a special issue subset that could only be obtained through redemption of UPC symbols from Jimmy Dean Roll Sausage. The fronts feature full-bleed glossy color players photos with team logos airbrushed out. In one of the card's corners, two bars (a white one and a team color-coded one) carry the Jimmy Dean logo

and the player's name, respectively. On a white background with red, blue, and black print, the backs have a close-up drawing of the player as well as biographical and statistical information.

	MINT	NRMT
COMPLETE SET (28)	10.00	4.50
COMMON CARD (1-28)	.25	.11
☐ 1 Frank Thomas	3.00	1.35
☐ 2 Barry Larkin	.60	.25
☐ 3 Cal Ripken	2.50	1.10
☐ 4 Andy Van Slyke	.25	.11
☐ 5 Darren Daulton	.40	.18
☐ 6 Don Mattingly	1.25	.55
☐ 7 Roger Clemens	1.25	.55
☐ 8 Juan Gonzalez	1.50	.70
☐ 9 Mark Langston	.25	.11
☐ 10 Barry Bonds	1.00	.45
☐ 11 Ken Griffey Jr.	3.00	1.35
☐ 12 Cecil Fielder	.40	.18
☐ 13 Kirby Puckett	1.50	.70
☐ 14 Tom Glavine	.60	.25
☐ 15 George Brett	1.00	.45
☐ 16 Nolan Ryan	2.50	1.10
☐ 17 Eddie Murray	.75	.35
☐ 18 Gary Sheffield	.75	.35
☐ 19 Doug Drabek	.25	.11
☐ 20 Ray Lankford	.40	.18
☐ 21 Benito Santiago	.25	.11
☐ 22 Mark McGwire	1.25	.55
☐ 23 Kenny Lofton	1.25	.55
☐ 24 Eric Karros	.60	.25
☐ 25 Ryne Sandberg	1.00	.45
☐ 26 Charlie Hayes	.25	.11
☐ 27 Mike Mussina	.75	.35
☐ 28 Pat Listach	.25	.11

1993 Jimmy Dean Rookies

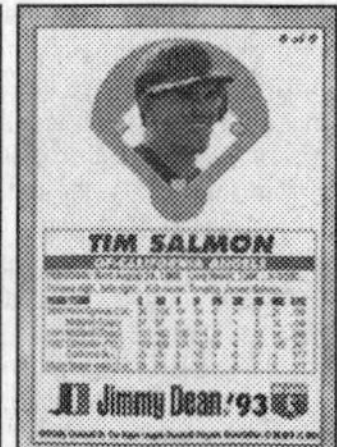

This nine-card standard-size set displays a cutout photo of the player superimposed on a gray studio background. The borderless cards carry the player's name and team on a dark gray marbleized block on the bottom. The Jimmy Dean logo and 1993 Rookies are displayed at the top left. The back carries a head shot bordered by a baseball diamond. The lower half lists the player's name, position, team, biography, and statistics. The backs are bordered in studio gray with a thin red inner border. The cards are numbered on the back following alphabetical order of the players' names.

	MINT	NRMT
COMPLETE SET (9)	6.00	2.70
COMMON CARD (1-9)	.25	.11
☐ 1 Rich Amaral	.25	.11
☐ 2 Vinny Castilla	1.00	.45
☐ 3 Jeff Conine	.50	.23
☐ 4 Brent Gates	.25	.11
☐ 5 Wayne Kirby	.25	.11
☐ 6 Mike Lansing	.50	.23
☐ 7 David Nied	.25	.11
☐ 8 Mike Piazza	3.00	1.35
☐ 9 Tim Salmon	1.50	.70

1995 Jimmy Dean All-Time Greats

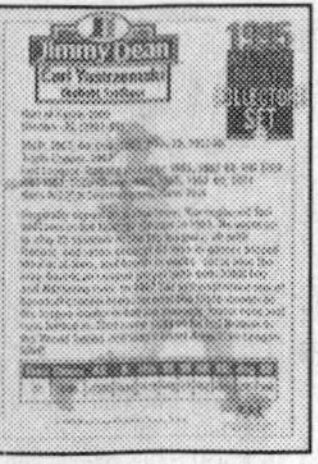

This 6-card standard-size set was cosponsored by Jimmy Dean Foods and the Major League Baseball Players Alumni Association. The cards were individually cello wrapped and inserted inside packages, and an accompanying paper insert featured coupons and a mail-in offer. (The mail-in offer was also found on boxes of Jimmy Dean Breakfast foods.) For two proofs-of-purchase plus $7.00, the collector received one autographed card featuring Billy Williams, Al Kaline, or Jim "Catfish" Hunter. Expiring December 31, 1995, the offer was limited to 12 baseball cards per original order form. The cards are checklisted below in alphabetical order.

	MINT	NRMT
COMPLETE SET (6)	5.00	2.20
COMMON CARD (1-6)	1.00	.45
☐ 1 Rod Carew	1.00	.45
☐ 2 Jim(Catfish) Hunter	1.00	.45
☐ 3 Al Kaline	1.00	.45
☐ 4 Mike Schmidt	2.00	.90
☐ 5 Billy Williams	1.00	.45
☐ 6 Carl Yastrzemski	1.50	.70
☐ NNO Billy Williams AU	20.00	9.00
☐ NNO Jim(Catfish) Hunter AU	20.00	9.00
☐ NNO Al Kaline AU	20.00	9.00

1997 Jimmy Dean

This two-card set was distributed through Jimmy Dean Products and could be obtained by sending in $12.95 and two UPCs from these products. All cards in this limited edition are autographed. The fronts feature black-and-white action player photos in a gold margin with a thin white inside border and green diamonds at the corners. The backs carry player information and career statistics. The cards are unnumbered and checklisted below in alphabetical order.

	MINT	NRMT
COMPLETE SET (2)	30.00	13.50
COMMON CARD (1-2)	15.00	6.75
☐ 1 Yogi Berra	15.00	6.75
☐ 2 Brooks Robinson	15.00	6.75

1982 K-Mart

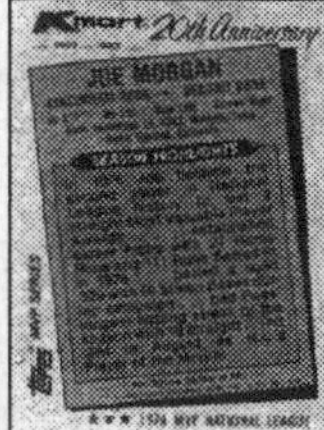

The cards in this 44-card set measure the standard size. This set was mass produced by Topps for K-Mart's 20th Anniversary Celebration and distributed in a custom box. The set features Topps cards of National and American League MVP's from 1962 through 1981. The backs highlight individual MVP winning performances. The dual National League MVP winners of 1979 and special cards commemorating the accomplishments of Drysdale (scoreless consecutive innings pitched streak), Aaron (home run record), and Rose (National League most hits lifetime record) round out the set. The 1975 Fred Lynn card is an original construction from the multi-player "Rookie Outfielders" card of Lynn of 1975. The Maury Wills card number 2, similarly, was created after the fact as Maury was not originally included in the 1962 Topps set. Topps had solved the same problem in essentially the same way in their 1975 set on card number 200.

	MINT	NRMT
COMPLETE SET (44)	2.00	.90
COMMON CARD (1-44)	.05	.02
☐ 1 Mickey Mantle: 62AL	.75	.35
☐ 2 Maury Wills: 62NL	.10	.05
☐ 3 Elston Howard: 63AL	.05	.02
☐ 4 Sandy Koufax: 63NL	.25	.11
☐ 5 Brooks Robinson: 64AL	.10	.05
☐ 6 Ken Boyer: 64NL	.05	.02
☐ 7 Zoilo Versalles: 65AL	.05	.02
☐ 8 Willie Mays: 65NL	.50	.23
☐ 9 Frank Robinson: 66AL	.10	.05
☐ 10 Bob Clemente: 66NL	.50	.23
☐ 11 Carl Yastrzemski: 67AL	.10	.05
☐ 12 Orlando Cepeda: 67NL	.05	.02
☐ 13 Denny McLain: 68AL	.05	.02
☐ 14 Bob Gibson: 68NL	.10	.05
☐ 15 Harmon Killebrew: 69AL	.10	.05
☐ 16 Willie McCovey: 69NL	.10	.05
☐ 17 Boog Powell: 70AL	.05	.02
☐ 18 Johnny Bench: 70NL	.10	.05
☐ 19 Vida Blue: 71AL	.05	.02
☐ 20 Joe Torre: 71NL	.05	.02
☐ 21 Rich Allen: 72AL	.05	.02
☐ 22 Johnny Bench: 72NL	.10	.05
☐ 23 Reggie Jackson: 73AL	.15	.07
☐ 24 Pete Rose: 73NL	.25	.11
☐ 25 Jeff Burroughs: 74AL	.05	.02
☐ 26 Steve Garvey: 74NL	.05	.02
☐ 27 Fred Lynn: 75AL	.10	.05
☐ 28 Joe Morgan: 75NL	.10	.05
☐ 29 Thurman Munson: 76AL	.05	.02
☐ 30 Joe Morgan: 76NL	.10	.05
☐ 31 Rod Carew: 77AL	.10	.05
☐ 32 George Foster: 77NL	.05	.02
☐ 33 Jim Rice: 78AL	.10	.05
☐ 34 Dave Parker: 78NL	.10	.05
☐ 35 Don Baylor: 79AL	.05	.02
☐ 36 Keith Hernandez: 79NL	.05	.02
☐ 37 Willie Stargell: 79NL	.10	.05
☐ 38 George Brett: 80AL	.40	.18
☐ 39 Mike Schmidt: 80NL	.15	.07
☐ 40 Rollie Fingers: 81AL	.10	.05
☐ 41 Mike Schmidt: 81NL	.15	.07
☐ 42 Don Drysdale '68 HL (Scoreless innings)	.10	.05
☐ 43 Hank Aaron '74 HL (Home run record)	.50	.23
☐ 44 Pete Rose '81 HL (NL most hits)	.15	.07

1987 K-Mart

Topps produced this 33-card boxed standard-size set for K-Mart. The set celebrates K-Mart's 25th anniversary and is subtitled, "Stars of the Decades." Card fronts feature a color photo of the player oriented diagonally. Card backs provide statistics for the player's best decade. The set numbering is arranged alphabetically within decade groups: 1960s (1-11), 1970s (12-22), and 1980s (23-33).

	MINT	NRMT
COMPLETE SET (33)	4.00	1.80
COMMON CARD (1-33)	.05	.02

☐ 1 Hank Aaron	.75	.35
☐ 2 Roberto Clemente	1.00	.45
☐ 3 Bob Gibson	.15	.07
☐ 4 Harmon Killebrew	.15	.07
☐ 5 Mickey Mantle	1.50	.70
☐ 6 Juan Marichal	.15	.07
☐ 7 Roger Maris	.25	.11
☐ 8 Willie Mays	.75	.35
☐ 9 Brooks Robinson	.15	.07
☐ 10 Frank Robinson	.15	.07
☐ 11 Carl Yastrzemski	.15	.07
☐ 12 Johnny Bench	.25	.11
☐ 13 Lou Brock	.25	.11
☐ 14 Rod Carew	.25	.11
☐ 15 Steve Carlton	.25	.11
☐ 16 Reggie Jackson	.40	.18
☐ 17 Jim Palmer	.25	.11
☐ 18 Jim Rice	.10	.05
☐ 19 Pete Rose	.50	.23
☐ 20 Nolan Ryan	1.50	.70
☐ 21 Tom Seaver	.40	.18
☐ 22 Willie Stargell	.25	.11
☐ 23 Wade Boggs	.40	.18
☐ 24 George Brett	.75	.35
☐ 25 Gary Carter	.10	.05
☐ 26 Dwight Gooden	.15	.07
☐ 27 Rickey Henderson	.35	.16
☐ 28 Don Mattingly	.75	.35
☐ 29 Dale Murphy	.25	.11
☐ 30 Eddie Murray	.35	.16
☐ 31 Mike Schmidt	.50	.23
☐ 32 Darryl Strawberry	.15	.07
☐ 33 Fernando Valenzuela	.10	.05

1988 K-Mart

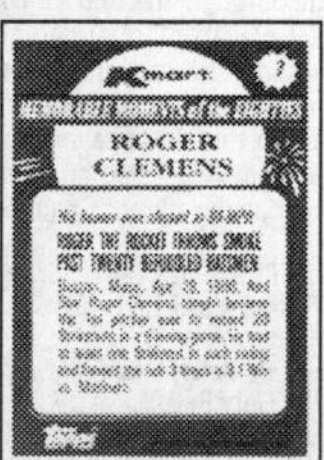

Topps produced this 33-card standard-sized boxed set exclusively for K-Mart. The set is subtitled, "Memorable Moments." Card fronts feature a color photo of the player with the K-Mart logo in lower right corner. Card backs provide details for that player's "memorable moment." The set is packaged in a bright yellow and green box with a checklist on the back panel of the box. The cards in the set were numbered by K-Mart essentially in alphabetical order.

	MINT	NRMT
COMPLETE SET (33)	4.00	1.80
COMMON CARD (1-33)	.05	.02
☐ 1 George Bell	.05	.02
☐ 2 Wade Boggs	.40	.18
☐ 3 George Brett	.75	.35
☐ 4 Jose Canseco	.40	.18
☐ 5 Jack Clark	.05	.02
☐ 6 Will Clark	.50	.23
☐ 7 Roger Clemens	.75	.35
☐ 8 Vince Coleman	.05	.02
☐ 9 Andre Dawson	.20	.09
☐ 10 Dwight Gooden	.10	.05
☐ 11 Pedro Guerrero	.05	.02
☐ 12 Tony Gwynn	1.25	.55
☐ 13 Rickey Henderson	.40	.18
☐ 14 Keith Hernandez	.05	.02
☐ 15 Don Mattingly	1.25	.55
☐ 16 Mark McGwire	1.25	.55
☐ 17 Paul Molitor	.40	.18
☐ 18 Dale Murphy	.30	.14
☐ 19 Tim Raines	.10	.05
☐ 20 Dave Righetti	.05	.02
☐ 21 Cal Ripken	2.00	.90
☐ 22 Pete Rose	.75	.35
☐ 23 Nolan Ryan	2.00	.90
☐ 24 Benito Santiago	.05	.02
☐ 25 Mike Schmidt	.50	.23
☐ 26 Mike Scott	.05	.02
☐ 27 Kevin Seitzer	.05	.02
☐ 28 Ozzie Smith	1.00	.45
☐ 29 Darryl Strawberry	.10	.05
☐ 30 Rick Sutcliffe	.05	.02
☐ 31 Fernando Valenzuela	.10	.05
☐ 32 Todd Worrell	.10	.05
☐ 33 Robin Yount	.30	.14

1989 K-Mart

The 1989 K-Mart Dream Team set contains 33 standard-size glossy cards. The fronts are blue. The cards were distributed as a boxed set through K-Mart stores. The set features 11 major league rookies of 1988 plus 11 "American League Rookies of the '80s" and 11 "National League Rookies of the '80s". The complete subject list for the set is provided on the back panel of the custom box.

	MINT	NRMT
COMPLETE SET (33)	3.00	1.35
COMMON CARD (1-33)	.05	.02
☐ 1 Mark Grace	.60	.25
☐ 2 Ron Gant	.25	.11
☐ 3 Chris Sabo	.05	.02
☐ 4 Walt Weiss	.05	.02
☐ 5 Jay Buhner	.50	.23
☐ 6 Cecil Espy	.05	.02
☐ 7 Dave Gallagher	.05	.02
☐ 8 Damon Berryhill	.05	.02
☐ 9 Tim Belcher	.05	.02
☐ 10 Paul Gibson	.05	.02
☐ 11 Gregg Jefferies	.10	.05
☐ 12 Don Mattingly	1.00	.45
☐ 13 Harold Reynolds	.10	.05
☐ 14 Wade Boggs	.50	.23
☐ 15 Cal Ripken	2.00	.90
☐ 16 Kirby Puckett	1.00	.45
☐ 17 George Bell	.05	.02
☐ 18 Jose Canseco	.50	.23
☐ 19 Terry Steinbach	.10	.05
☐ 20 Roger Clemens	.75	.35
☐ 21 Mark Langston	.05	.02
☐ 22 Harold Baines	.10	.05
☐ 23 Will Clark	.50	.23
☐ 24 Ryne Sandberg	.75	.35
☐ 25 Tim Wallach	.05	.02
☐ 26 Shawon Dunston	.05	.02
☐ 27 Tim Raines	.10	.05
☐ 28 Darryl Strawberry	.10	.05
☐ 29 Tony Gwynn	1.25	.55
☐ 30 Tony Pena	.05	.02
☐ 31 Dwight Gooden	.10	.05
☐ 32 Fernando Valenzuela	.10	.05
☐ 33 Pedro Guerrero	.05	.02

1990 K-Mart

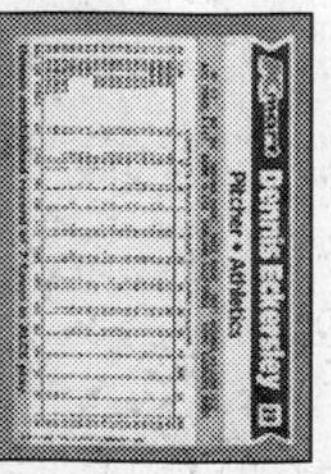

The 1990 K-Mart Superstars set is a 33-card, standard-size set issued for the K-Mart chain by the Topps Company. This set was issued with a piece of gum in the custom set box.

	MINT	NRMT
COMPLETE SET (33)	4.00	1.80
COMMON CARD (1-33)	.05	.02
☐ 1 Will Clark	.40	.18
☐ 2 Ryne Sandberg	.75	.35
☐ 3 Howard Johnson	.05	.02
☐ 4 Ozzie Smith	.75	.35
☐ 5 Tony Gwynn	1.25	.55
☐ 6 Kevin Mitchell	.05	.02
☐ 7 Jerome Walton	.05	.02
☐ 8 Craig Biggio	.40	.18
☐ 9 Mike Scott	.05	.02
☐ 10 Dwight Gooden	.10	.05
☐ 11 Sid Fernandez	.05	.02
☐ 12 Joe Magrane	.05	.02
☐ 13 Jay Howell	.05	.02
☐ 14 Mark Davis	.05	.02
☐ 15 Pedro Guerrero	.05	.02
☐ 16 Glenn Davis	.05	.02
☐ 17 Don Mattingly	1.25	.55
☐ 18 Julio Franco	.10	.05
☐ 19 Wade Boggs	.40	.18
☐ 20 Cal Ripken	2.00	.90
☐ 21 Jose Canseco	.40	.18
☐ 22 Kirby Puckett	1.25	.55
☐ 23 Rickey Henderson	.40	.18
☐ 24 Mickey Tettleton	.05	.02
☐ 25 Nolan Ryan	2.00	.90
☐ 26 Bret Saberhagen	.05	.02
☐ 27 Jeff Ballard	.05	.02
☐ 28 Chuck Finley	.05	.02
☐ 29 Dennis Eckersley	.20	.09
☐ 30 Dan Plesac	.05	.02
☐ 31 Fred McGriff	.30	.14
☐ 32 Mark McGwire	1.25	.55
☐ 33 Tony LaRussa MG and Roger Craig MG	.05	.02

1955 Kahn's

The cards in this six-card set measure 3 1/4" X 4". The 1955 Kahn's Wieners set received very limited distribution. The cards were supposedly given away at an amusement park. The set portrays the players in street clothes rather than in uniform and hence are sometimes referred to as "street clothes" Kahn's. All Kahn's sets from 1955 through 1963 are black and white and contain a 1/2" tab. Cards with the tab still intact are worth approximately 50 percent more than cards without the tab. Cards feature a facsimile autograph of the player on the front. Cards are blank-backed. Only Cincinnati Redlegs players are featured.

	NRMT	VG-E
COMPLETE SET (6)	3000.00	1350.00
COMMON CARD (1-6)	450.00	200.00
☐ 1 Gus Bell	600.00	275.00
☐ 2 Ted Kluszewski	750.00	350.00
☐ 3 Roy McMillan	450.00	200.00
☐ 4 Joe Nuxhall	500.00	220.00
☐ 5 Wally Post	450.00	200.00
☐ 6 Johnny Temple	450.00	200.00

1956 Kahn's

The cards in this 15-card set measure 3 1/4" X 4". The 1956 Kahn's set was the first set to be issued with Kahn's meat products. The cards are blank backed. The set is distinguished by the old style, short sleeve shirts on the players and the existence of backgounds (Kahn's cards of later years utilize a blank backgound). Cards which have the tab still intact are worth approximately 50 percent more than cards without the tab. Only Cincinnati Redlegs players are featured. The cards are listed and numbered below in alphabetical order by the subject's name. This set contains a very early Frank Robinson card.

	NRMT	VG-E
COMPLETE SET (15)	1700.00	750.00
COMMON CARD (1-15)	80.00	36.00

☐ 1 Ed Bailey	80.00	36.00
☐ 2 Gus Bell	90.00	40.00
☐ 3 Joe Black	100.00	45.00
☐ 4 Smoky Burgess	90.00	40.00
☐ 5 Art Fowler	80.00	36.00
☐ 6 Herschel Freeman	80.00	36.00
☐ 7 Ray Jablonski	80.00	36.00
☐ 8 John Klippstein	80.00	36.00
☐ 9 Ted Kluszewski	200.00	90.00
☐ 10 Brooks Lawrence	90.00	40.00
☐ 11 Roy McMillan	90.00	40.00
☐ 12 Joe Nuxhall	90.00	40.00
☐ 13 Wally Post	90.00	40.00
☐ 14 Frank Robinson	500.00	220.00
☐ 15 Johnny Temple	90.00	40.00

1957 Kahn's

The cards in this 29-card set measure 3 1/4" by 4". The 1957 Kahn's Wieners set contains black and white, blank backed, unnumbered cards. The set features only the Cincinnati Redlegs and Pittsburgh Pirates. The cards feature a light background. Each card features a facsimile autograph of the player on the front. The Groat card exists with a "Richard Groat" autograph and also exists with the printed name "Dick Groat" on the card. The set price inlcudes both Groats. The catalog designation is F155-3. The cards are listed and numbered below in alphabetical order by the subject's name. A Bill Mazeroski card was printed during this, his Rookie Card season.

	NRMT	VG-E
COMPLETE SET (29)	2800.00	1250.00
COMMON CARD (1-29)	60.00	27.00
☐ 1 Tom Acker	60.00	27.00
☐ 2 Ed Bailey	60.00	27.00
☐ 3 Gus Bell	75.00	34.00
☐ 4 Smoky Burgess	75.00	34.00
☐ 5 Roberto Clemente	1000.00	450.00
☐ 6 George Crowe	60.00	27.00
☐ 7 Elroy Face	90.00	40.00
☐ 8 Herschel Freeman	60.00	27.00
☐ 9 Bob Friend	75.00	34.00
☐ 10 Dick Groat	90.00	40.00
☐ 11 Richard Groat	175.00	80.00
☐ 12 Don Gross	60.00	27.00
☐ 13 Warren Hacker	60.00	27.00
☐ 14 Don Hoak	75.00	34.00
☐ 15 Hal Jeffcoat	60.00	27.00
☐ 16 Ron Kline	60.00	27.00
☐ 17 John Klippstein	60.00	27.00
☐ 18 Ted Kluszewski	175.00	80.00
☐ 19 Brooks Lawrence	75.00	34.00
☐ 20 Dale Long	60.00	27.00
☐ 21 Bill Mazeroski	200.00	90.00
☐ 22 Roy McMillan	75.00	34.00
☐ 23 Joe Nuxhall	60.00	27.00
☐ 24 Wally Post	75.00	34.00
☐ 25 Frank Robinson	400.00	180.00
☐ 26 John Temple	75.00	34.00
☐ 27 Frank Thomas	60.00	27.00
☐ 28 Bob Thurman	60.00	27.00
☐ 29 Lee Walls	60.00	27.00

1958 Kahn's

The cards in this 29-card set measure approximately 3 1/4" X 4". The 1958 Kahn's Wieners set of unnumbered, black and white cards features Cincinnati Redlegs, Philadelphia Phillies and Pittsburgh Pirates. The backs present a story for each player entitled "My Greatest Thrill in Baseball". A method of distinguishing 1958 Kahn's from 1959 Kahn's is that the word Wieners is found on the front of the 1958 but not on the front of the 1959 cards. Cards of Wally Post, Charlie Rabe and Frank Thomas are somewhat more difficult to find and are designated SP in the checklist below. The cards are listed and numbered below in alphabetical order by the subject's name.

	NRMT	VG-E
COMPLETE SET (29)	3200.00	1450.00
COMMON CARD (1-29)	50.00	22.00
☐ 1 Ed Bailey	50.00	22.00
☐ 2 Gene Baker	50.00	22.00
☐ 3 Gus Bell	60.00	27.00
☐ 4 Smoky Burgess	60.00	27.00
☐ 5 Roberto Clemente	750.00	350.00
☐ 6 George Crowe	60.00	27.00
☐ 7 Elroy Face	75.00	34.00
☐ 8 Hank Foiles	50.00	22.00
☐ 9 Dee Fondy	50.00	22.00
☐ 10 Bob Friend	60.00	27.00
☐ 11 Dick Groat	75.00	34.00
☐ 12 Harvey Haddix	60.00	27.00
☐ 13 Don Hoak	50.00	22.00
☐ 14 Hal Jeffcoat	50.00	22.00
☐ 15 Ron Kline	50.00	22.00
☐ 16 Ted Kluszewski	125.00	55.00
☐ 17 Vernon Law	60.00	27.00
☐ 18 Brooks Lawrence	60.00	27.00
☐ 19 Bill Mazeroski	100.00	45.00
☐ 20 Roy McMillan	60.00	27.00
☐ 21 Joe Nuxhall	60.00	27.00
☐ 22 Wally Post SP	350.00	160.00
☐ 23 John Powers	50.00	22.00
☐ 24 Bob Purkey	50.00	22.00
☐ 25 Charlie Rabe SP	350.00	160.00
☐ 26 Frank Robinson	250.00	110.00
☐ 27 Bob Skinner	50.00	22.00
☐ 28 Johnny Temple	60.00	27.00
☐ 29 Frank Thomas SP	350.00	160.00

1959 Kahn's

The cards in this 38-card set measure approximately 3 1/4" X 4". The 1959 Kahn's set features members of the Cincinnati Reds, Cleveland Indians and Pittsburgh Pirates. Backs feature stories entitled "The Toughest Play I have to Make," or "The Toughest Batter I Have To Face." The Brodowski card is very scarce while Haddix, Held and McLish are considered quite difficult to obtain; these scarcities are designated SP in the checklist below. The cards are listed and numbered below in alphabetical order by the subject's name.

	NRMT	VG-E
COMPLETE SET (38)	4500.00	2000.00
COMMON CARD (1-38)	50.00	22.00
☐ 1 Ed Bailey	50.00	22.00
☐ 2 Gary Bell	50.00	22.00
☐ 3 Gus Bell	60.00	27.00
☐ 4 Dick Brodowski SP	600.00	275.00
☐ 5 Smoky Burgess	60.00	27.00
☐ 6 Roberto Clemente	600.00	275.00
☐ 7 Rocky Colavito	125.00	55.00
☐ 8 Elroy Face	75.00	34.00
☐ 9 Bob Friend	60.00	27.00
☐ 10 Joe Gordon MG	60.00	27.00
☐ 11 Jim Grant	60.00	27.00
☐ 12 Dick Groat	75.00	34.00
☐ 13 Harvey Haddix SP (Blank back)	400.00	180.00
☐ 14 Woodie Held SP	400.00	180.00
☐ 15 Don Hoak	50.00	22.00
☐ 16 Ron Kline	50.00	22.00
☐ 17 Ted Kluszewski	125.00	55.00
☐ 18 Vernon Law	60.00	27.00
☐ 19 Jerry Lynch	50.00	22.00
☐ 20 Billy Martin	125.00	55.00
☐ 21 Bill Mazeroski	100.00	45.00
☐ 22 Cal McLish SP	400.00	180.00
☐ 23 Roy McMillan	50.00	22.00

☐ 24 Minnie Minoso	100.00	45.00
☐ 25 Russ Nixon	50.00	22.00
☐ 26 Joe Nuxhall	60.00	27.00
☐ 27 Jim Perry	75.00	34.00
☐ 28 Vada Pinson	100.00	45.00
☐ 29 Vic Power	50.00	22.00
☐ 30 Bob Purkey	50.00	22.00
☐ 31 Frank Robinson	200.00	90.00
☐ 32 Herb Score	75.00	34.00
☐ 33 Bob Skinner	50.00	22.00
☐ 34 George Strickland	50.00	22.00
☐ 35 Dick Stuart	60.00	27.00
☐ 36 Johnny Temple	50.00	22.00
☐ 37 Frank Thomas	60.00	27.00
☐ 38 George Witt	50.00	22.00

1960 Kahn's

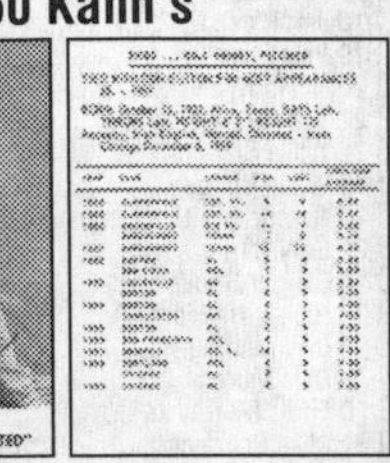

The cards in this 42-card set measure 3 1/4" X 4". The 1960 Kahn's set features players of the Chicago Cubs, Chicago White Sox, Cincinnati Redlegs, Cleveland Indians, Pittsburgh Pirates and St. Louis Cardinals. The backs give vital player information and records through the 1959 season. Kline appears with either St. Louis or Pittsburgh. The set price includes both Kline's. The Harvey Kuenn card in this set appears with a blank back and is scarce. The cards are listed and numbered below in alphabetical order by the subject's name.

	NRMT	VG-E
COMPLETE SET (43)	2000.00	900.00
COMMON CARD (1-42)	25.00	11.00
☐ 1 Ed Bailey	25.00	11.00
☐ 2 Gary Bell	25.00	11.00
☐ 3 Gus Bell	30.00	13.50
☐ 4 Smoky Burgess	30.00	13.50
☐ 5 Gino Cimoli	25.00	11.00
☐ 6 Roberto Clemente	400.00	180.00
☐ 7 Roy Face	30.00	13.50
☐ 8 Tito Francona	25.00	11.00
☐ 9 Bob Friend	30.00	13.50
☐ 10 Jim Grant	30.00	13.50
☐ 11 Dick Groat	40.00	18.00
☐ 12 Harvey Haddix	30.00	13.50
☐ 13 Woodie Held	25.00	11.00
☐ 14 Bill Henry	25.00	11.00
☐ 15 Don Hoak	25.00	11.00
☐ 16 Jay Hook	25.00	11.00
☐ 17 Eddie Kasko	25.00	11.00
☐ 18A Ron Kline (Pittsburgh)	50.00	22.00
☐ 18B Ron Kline (St. Louis)	50.00	22.00
☐ 19 Ted Kluszewski	60.00	27.00
☐ 20 Harvey Kuenn SP (Blank back)	350.00	160.00
☐ 21 Vernon Law	30.00	13.50
☐ 22 Brooks Lawrence	30.00	13.50
☐ 23 Jerry Lynch	25.00	11.00
☐ 24 Billy Martin	60.00	27.00
☐ 25 Bill Mazeroski	50.00	22.00
☐ 26 Cal McLish	25.00	11.00
☐ 27 Roy McMillan	25.00	11.00
☐ 28 Don Newcombe	40.00	18.00
☐ 29 Russ Nixon	25.00	11.00
☐ 30 Joe Nuxhall	30.00	13.50
☐ 31 Jim O'Toole	25.00	11.00
☐ 32 Jim Perry	30.00	13.50
☐ 33 Vada Pinson	50.00	22.00
☐ 34 Vic Power	25.00	11.00
☐ 35 Bob Purkey	25.00	11.00
☐ 36 Frank Robinson	150.00	70.00
☐ 37 Herb Score	30.00	13.50
☐ 38 Bob Skinner	25.00	11.00
☐ 39 Dick Stuart	30.00	13.50
☐ 40 Johnny Temple	30.00	13.50
☐ 41 Frank Thomas	30.00	13.50
☐ 42 Lee Walls	25.00	11.00

1961 Kahn's

The cards in this 43-card set measure approximately 3 1/4" X 4". The 1961 Kahn's Wieners set of black and white,

nnumbered cards features members of the Cincinnati Reds, Cleveland Indians and Pittsburgh Pirates. This year vas the first year Kahn's made complete sets available to he public; hence they are more available, especially in the better condition grades than the Kahn's of the previous ears. The backs give vital player information and year by ear career statistics through 1960. The catalog designation is F155-7. The cards are listed and numbered below in alphabetical order by the subject's name.

	NRMT	VG-E
COMPLETE SET (43)	850.00	375.00
COMMON CARD (1-43)	12.50	5.50
☐ 1 John Antonelli	12.50	5.50
☐ 2 Ed Bailey	12.50	5.50
☐ 3 Gary Bell	12.50	5.50
☐ 4 Gus Bell	15.00	6.75
☐ 5 Jim Brosnan	15.00	6.75
☐ 6 Smoky Burgess	15.00	6.75
☐ 7 Gino Cimoli	12.50	5.50
☐ 8 Roberto Clemente	300.00	135.00
☐ 9 Gordie Coleman	12.50	5.50
☐ 10 Jimmy Dykes MG	15.00	6.75
☐ 11 Roy Face	15.00	6.75
☐ 12 Tito Francona	12.50	5.50
☐ 13 Gene Freese	12.50	5.50
☐ 14 Bob Friend	15.00	6.75
☐ 15 Jim Grant	15.00	6.75
☐ 16 Dick Groat	15.00	6.75
☐ 17 Harvey Haddix	15.00	6.75
☐ 18 Woodie Held	12.50	5.50
☐ 19 Don Hoak	12.50	5.50
☐ 20 Jay Hook	12.50	5.50
☐ 21 Joey Jay	12.50	5.50
☐ 22 Eddie Kasko	12.50	5.50
☐ 23 Willie Kirkland	12.50	5.50
☐ 24 Vernon Law	15.00	6.75
☐ 25 Jerry Lynch	12.50	5.50
☐ 26 Jim Maloney	20.00	9.00
☐ 27 Bill Mazeroski	30.00	13.50
☐ 28 Wilmer Mizell	15.00	6.75
☐ 29 Rocky Nelson	12.50	5.50
☐ 30 Jim O'Toole	12.50	5.50
☐ 31 Jim Perry	15.00	6.75
☐ 32 Bubba Phillips	12.50	5.50
☐ 33 Vada Pinson	30.00	13.50
☐ 34 Wally Post	12.50	5.50
☐ 35 Vic Power	12.50	5.50
☐ 36 Bob Purkey	12.50	5.50
☐ 37 Frank Robinson	100.00	45.00
☐ 38 John Romano	12.50	5.50
☐ 39 Dick Schofield	12.50	5.50
☐ 40 Bob Skinner	12.50	5.50
☐ 41 Hal Smith	12.50	5.50
☐ 42 Dick Stuart	15.00	6.75
☐ 43 Johnny Temple	12.50	5.50

1962 Kahn's

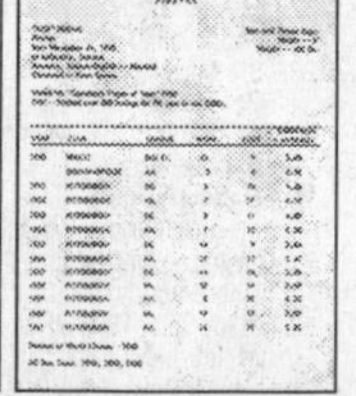

he cards in this 38-card set measure approximately 3 /4" X 4". The 1962 Kahn's Wieners set of black and white, nnumbered cards features Cincinnati, Cleveland, Minnesota and Pittsburgh players. Card numbers 1 Bell, 3 Power and 34 Purkey exist in two different forms; hese variations are listed in the checklist below. The acks of the cards contain career information. The catalog esignation is F155-8. The set price below includes the et with all variation cards. The cards are listed and numbered below in alphabetical order by the subject's name.

	NRMT	VG-E
COMPLETE SET (41)	1100.00	500.00
COMMON CARD (1-38)	10.00	4.50
☐ 1A Gary Bell (With fat man)	100.00	45.00
☐ 1B Gary Bell (No fat man)	40.00	18.00
☐ 2 Jim Brosnan	12.50	5.50
☐ 3 Smoky Burgess	12.50	5.50
☐ 4 Chico Cardenas	12.50	5.50
☐ 5 Roberto Clemente	250.00	110.00
☐ 6 Ty Cline	10.00	4.50
☐ 7 Gordon Coleman	12.50	5.50
☐ 8 Dick Donovan	10.00	4.50
☐ 9 John Edwards	10.00	4.50
☐ 10 Tito Francona	10.00	4.50
☐ 11 Gene Freese	10.00	4.50
☐ 12 Bob Friend	12.50	5.50
☐ 13 Joe Gibbon	100.00	45.00
☐ 14 Jim Grant	12.50	5.50
☐ 15 Dick Groat	15.00	6.75
☐ 16 Harvey Haddix	12.50	5.50
☐ 17 Woodie Held	10.00	4.50
☐ 18 Bill Henry	10.00	4.50
☐ 19 Don Hoak	10.00	4.50
☐ 20 Ken Hunt	10.00	4.50
☐ 21 Joey Jay	10.00	4.50
☐ 22 Eddie Kasko	10.00	4.50
☐ 23 Willie Kirkland	10.00	4.50
☐ 24 Barry Latman	10.00	4.50
☐ 25 Jerry Lynch	10.00	4.50
☐ 26 Jim Maloney	15.00	6.75
☐ 27 Bill Mazeroski	25.00	11.00
☐ 28 Jim O'Toole	10.00	4.50
☐ 29 Jim Perry	12.50	5.50
☐ 30 Bubba Phillips	10.00	4.50
☐ 31 Vada Pinson	15.00	6.75
☐ 32 Wally Post	10.00	4.50
☐ 33A Vic Power (Indians)	40.00	18.00
☐ 33B Vic Power (Twins)	100.00	45.00
☐ 34A Bob Purkey (With autograph)	40.00	18.00
☐ 34B Bob Purkey (No autograph)	100.00	45.00
☐ 35 Frank Robinson	100.00	45.00
☐ 36 John Romano	10.00	4.50
☐ 37 Dick Stuart	12.50	5.50
☐ 38 Bill Virdon	15.00	6.75

1963 Kahn's

The cards in this 30-card set measure approximately 3 1/4" X 4". The 1963 Kahn's Wieners set of black and white, unnumbered cards features players from Cincinnati, Cleveland, St. Louis, Pittsburgh and the New York Yankees. The cards feature a white border around the picture of the players. The backs contain career information. The catalog designation for this set is F155-10. The cards are listed and numbered below in alphabetical order by the subject's name.

	NRMT	VG-E
COMPLETE SET (30)	600.00	275.00
COMMON CARD (1-30)	10.00	4.50
☐ 1 Bob Bailey	10.00	4.50
☐ 2 Don Blasingame	10.00	4.50
☐ 3 Clete Boyer	15.00	6.75
☐ 4 Smoky Burgess	12.50	5.50
☐ 5 Chico Cardenas	12.50	5.50
☐ 6 Roberto Clemente	250.00	110.00
☐ 7 Donn Clendenon	12.50	5.50
☐ 8 Gordon Coleman	12.50	5.50
☐ 9 John Edwards	10.00	4.50
☐ 10 Gene Freese	10.00	4.50
☐ 11 Bob Friend	12.50	5.50
☐ 12 Joe Gibbon	10.00	4.50
☐ 13 Dick Groat	15.00	6.75
☐ 14 Harvey Haddix	12.50	5.50
☐ 15 Elston Howard	20.00	9.00
☐ 16 Joey Jay	10.00	4.50
☐ 17 Eddie Kasko	10.00	4.50
☐ 18 Tony Kubek	30.00	13.50
☐ 19 Jerry Lynch	10.00	4.50
☐ 20 Jim Maloney	15.00	6.75
☐ 21 Bill Mazeroski	25.00	11.00
☐ 22 Joe Nuxhall	12.50	5.50
☐ 23 Jim O'Toole	10.00	4.50
☐ 24 Vada Pinson	20.00	9.00
☐ 25 Bob Purkey	10.00	4.50
☐ 26 Bobby Richardson	30.00	13.50
☐ 27 Frank Robinson	100.00	45.00
☐ 28 Bill Stafford	10.00	4.50
☐ 29 Ralph Terry	12.50	5.50
☐ 30 Bill Virdon	12.50	5.50

1964 Kahn's

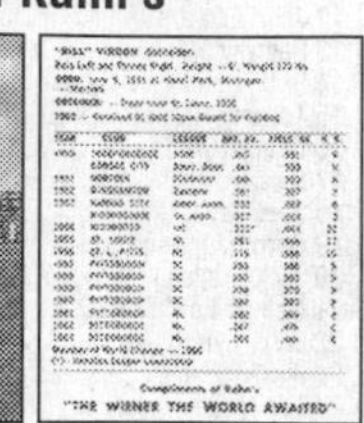

The cards in this 31-card set measure 3" X 3 1/2". The 1964 Kahn's set marks the beginning of the full color cards and the elimination of the tabs which existed on previous Kahn's cards. The set of unnumbered cards contains player information through the 1963 season on the backs. The set features Cincinnati, Cleveland and Pittsburgh players. The cards are listed and numbered below in alphabetical order by the subject's name. An early card of Pete Rose highlights this set.

	NRMT	VG-E
COMPLETE SET (31)	900.00	400.00
COMMON CARD (1-31)	10.00	4.50
☐ 1 Max Alvis	10.00	4.50
☐ 2 Bob Bailey	10.00	4.50
☐ 3 Chico Cardenas	12.50	5.50
☐ 4 Roberto Clemente	250.00	110.00
☐ 5 Donn Clendenon	12.50	5.50
☐ 6 Vic Davalillo	10.00	4.50
☐ 7 Dick Donovan	10.00	4.50
☐ 8 John Edwards	10.00	4.50
☐ 9 Bob Friend	12.50	5.50
☐ 10 Jim Grant	12.50	5.50
☐ 11 Tommy Harper	12.50	5.50
☐ 12 Woodie Held	12.50	5.50
☐ 13 Joey Jay	10.00	4.50
☐ 14 Jack Kralick	10.00	4.50
☐ 15 Jerry Lynch	10.00	4.50
☐ 16 Jim Maloney	12.50	5.50
☐ 17 Bill Mazeroski	25.00	11.00
☐ 18 Alvin McBean	10.00	4.50
☐ 19 Joe Nuxhall	12.50	5.50
☐ 20 Jim Pagliaroni	10.00	4.50
☐ 21 Vada Pinson	20.00	9.00
☐ 22 Bob Purkey	10.00	4.50
☐ 23 Pedro Ramos	10.00	4.50
☐ 24 Frank Robinson	100.00	45.00
☐ 25 John Romano	10.00	4.50
☐ 26 Pete Rose	350.00	160.00
☐ 27 John Tsitouris	10.00	4.50
☐ 28 Bob Veale	12.50	5.50
☐ 29 Bill Virdon	12.50	5.50
☐ 30 Leon Wagner	10.00	4.50
☐ 31 Fred Whitfield	10.00	4.50

1965 Kahn's

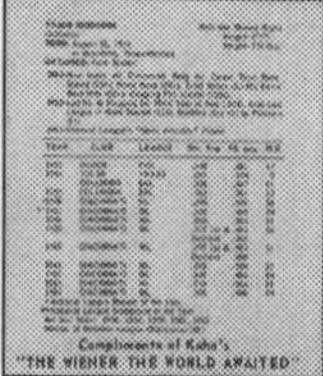

The cards in this 45-card set measure 3" X 3 1/2". The 1965 Kahn's set contains full-color, unnumbered cards. The set features Cincinnati, Cleveland, Pittsburgh and Milwaukee players. Backs contain statistical information through the 1964 season. The cards are listed and numbered below in alphabetical order by the subject's name.

	NRMT	VG-E
COMPLETE SET (45)	1000.00	450.00
COMMON CARD (1-45)	10.00	4.50
☐ 1 Henry Aaron	150.00	70.00
☐ 2 Max Alvis	12.50	5.50
☐ 3 Joe Azcue	10.00	4.50
☐ 4 Bob Bailey	10.00	4.50
☐ 5 Frank Bolling	10.00	4.50
☐ 6 Chico Cardenas	12.50	5.50
☐ 7 Rico Carty	15.00	6.75
☐ 8 Donn Clendenon	12.50	5.50
☐ 9 Tony Cloninger	12.50	5.50
☐ 10 Gordon Coleman	10.00	4.50
☐ 11 Vic Davalillo	10.00	4.50
☐ 12 John Edwards	10.00	4.50
☐ 13 Sammy Ellis	10.00	4.50
☐ 14 Bob Friend	12.50	5.50
☐ 15 Tommy Harper	12.50	5.50
☐ 16 Chuck Hinton	10.00	4.50
☐ 17 Dick Howser	12.50	5.50
☐ 18 Joey Jay	10.00	4.50
☐ 19 Deron Johnson	12.50	5.50
☐ 20 Jack Kralick	10.00	4.50
☐ 21 Denver LeMaster	10.00	4.50
☐ 22 Jerry Lynch	10.00	4.50
☐ 23 Jim Maloney	15.00	6.75
☐ 24 Lee Maye	10.00	4.50
☐ 25 Bill Mazeroski	25.00	11.00
☐ 26 Alvin McBean	10.00	4.50
☐ 27 Bill McCool	10.00	4.50
☐ 28 Sam McDowell	15.00	6.75
☐ 29 Don McMahon	10.00	4.50
☐ 30 Denis Menke	10.00	4.50
☐ 31 Joe Nuxhall	12.50	5.50
☐ 32 Gene Oliver	10.00	4.50
☐ 33 Jim O'Toole	10.00	4.50
☐ 34 Jim Pagliaroni	10.00	4.50
☐ 35 Vada Pinson	20.00	9.00
☐ 36 Frank Robinson	100.00	45.00
☐ 37 Pete Rose	200.00	90.00
☐ 38 Willie Stargell	100.00	45.00
☐ 39 Ralph Terry	12.50	5.50
☐ 40 Luis Tiant	20.00	9.00
☐ 41 Joe Torre	25.00	11.00
☐ 42 John Tsitouris	10.00	4.50
☐ 43 Bob Veale	12.50	5.50
☐ 44 Bill Virdon	12.50	5.50
☐ 45 Leon Wagner	10.00	4.50

1966 Kahn's

The cards in this 32-card set measure 2 13/16" X 4". 1966 Kahn's full-color, unnumbered set features players from Atlanta, Cincinnati, Cleveland and Pittsburgh. The set is identified by yellow and white vertical stripes and the name Kahn's written in red across a red rose at the top. The cards contain a 1 5/16" ad in the form of a tab. Cards with the ad (tab) are worth twice as much as cards without the ad. (double the prices below) The cards are listed and numbered below in alphabetical order by the subject's name.

	NRMT	VG-E
COMPLETE SET (32)	600.00	275.00
COMMON CARD (1-32)	8.00	3.60
☐ 1 Henry Aaron Portrait, no windbreaker under jersey	100.00	45.00
☐ 2 Felipe Alou: Braves Full pose batting screen in background	15.00	6.75
☐ 3 Max Alvis: Indians Kneeling full pose with bat no patch on jersey)	8.00	3.60
☐ 4 Bob Bailey	8.00	3.60
☐ 5 Wade Blasingame	8.00	3.60
☐ 6 Frank Bolling	8.00	3.60
☐ 7 Chico Cardenas: Reds Fielding feet at base	10.00	4.50
☐ 8 Roberto Clemente	125.00	55.00
☐ 9 Tony Cloninger: Braves Pitching foulpole in background	10.00	4.50
☐ 10 Vic Davalillo	8.00	3.60
☐ 11 John Edwards: Reds Catching	8.00	3.60
☐ 12 Sam Ellis: Reds White hat	8.00	3.60
☐ 13 Pedro Gonzalez	8.00	3.60
☐ 14 Tommy Harper: Reds Arm cocked	10.00	4.50
☐ 15 Deron Johnson: Reds Batting with batting cage in background	10.00	4.50
☐ 16 Mack Jones	8.00	3.60
☐ 17 Denver Lemaster	8.00	3.60
☐ 18 Jim Maloney: Reds Pitching white hat	10.00	4.50
☐ 19 Bill Mazeroski: Pirates Throwing	15.00	6.75
☐ 20 Bill McCool: Reds White hat	8.00	3.60
☐ 21 Sam McDowell: Indians Kneeling	10.00	4.50
☐ 22 Denis Menke: Braves White windbreaker under jersey	8.00	3.60
☐ 23 Joe Nuxhall	10.00	4.50
☐ 24 Jim Pagliaroni: Pirates Catching	8.00	3.60
☐ 25 Milt Pappas	10.00	4.50
☐ 26 Vada Pinson: Reds (Fielding ball on ground	15.00	6.75
☐ 27 Pete Rose: Reds With glove	125.00	55.00
☐ 28 Sonny Siebert: Indians Pitching signature at feet	10.00	4.50
☐ 29 Willie Stargell: Pirates Batting clouds in sky	40.00	18.00
☐ 30 Joe Torre: Braves Catching with hand on mask	20.00	9.00
☐ 31 Bob Veale: Pirates Hands at knee with glasses	10.00	4.50
☐ 32 Fred Whitfield	8.00	3.60

1967 Kahn's

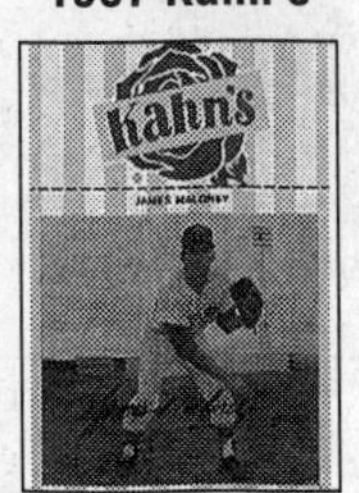

The cards in this 41-player set measure 2 13/16" X 4". The 1967 Kahn's set of full-color, unnumbered cards is almost identical in style to the 1966 issue. Different meat products had different background colors (yellow and white stripes, red and white stripes, etc.). The set features players from Atlanta, Cincinnati, Cleveland, New York Mets and Pittsburgh. Cards with the ads (see 1966 set) are worth twice as much as cards without the ad, i.e., double the prices below. The complete set price below includes all variations. The cards are listed and numbered below in alphabetical order by the subject's name.

	NRMT	VG-E
COMPLETE SET (51)	800.00	350.00
COMMON CARD (1-41)	8.00	3.60
☐ 1A Henry Aaron: Braves (Swinging pose, batting glove, ball, and hat on ground)	100.00	45.00
☐ 1B Henry Aaron: Braves (Swinging pose, batting glove, ball, and hat on ground; Cut Along Dotted Lines printed on lower tab)	125.00	55.00
☐ 2 Gene Alley: Pirates (Portrait)	10.00	4.50
☐ 3 Felipe Alou: Braves (Full pose, bat on shoulder)	15.00	6.75
☐ 4A Matty Alou: Pirates (Portrait with bat, Matio Rojas Alou"; yellow stripes)	10.00	4.50
☐ 4B Matty Alou: Pirates (Portrait with bat Matio Rojas Alou"; red stripes)	12.50	5.50
☐ 5 Max Alvis: Indians (Fielding, hands on knees)	8.00	3.60
☐ 6A Ken Boyer (Batting righthanded; autograph at waist)	12.50	5.50
☐ 6B Ken Boyer (Batting righthanded; autograph at shoulders; Cut Along Dotted Lines printed on lower tab)	15.00	6.75
☐ 7 Chico Cardenas: Reds (Fielding hand on knee)	10.00	4.50
☐ 8 Rico Carty	10.00	4.50
☐ 9 Tony Cloninger: Braves (Pitching, no foul-pole in background)	10.00	4.50
☐ 10 Tommy Davis	10.00	4.50
☐ 11 John Edwards: Reds (Kneeling with bat)	8.00	3.60
☐ 12A Sam Ellis: Reds (All red hat)	8.00	3.60
☐ 12B Sam Ellis: Reds (All red hat; Cut Along Dotted Lines printed on lower tab)	10.00	4.50
☐ 13 Jack Fisher	8.00	3.60
☐ 14 Steve Hargan: Indians (Pitching, no clouds blue sky)	8.00	3.60
☐ 15 Tommy Harper: Reds (Fielding, glove on ground)	10.00	4.50
☐ 16A Tommy Helms (Batting righthanded; top of bat visible)	10.00	4.50
☐ 16B Tommy Helms (Batting righthanded; bat chopped above hat; Cut Along Dotted Lines printed on lower tab)	12.50	5.50
☐ 17 Deron Johnson: Reds (Batting, blue sky)	10.00	4.50
☐ 18 Ken Johnson	8.00	3.60
☐ 19 Cleon Jones	10.00	4.50
☐ 20A Ed Kranepool (Ready for throw; yellow stripes)	10.00	4.50
☐ 20B Ed Kranepool (Ready for throw; red stripes)	10.00	4.50
☐ 21A Jim Maloney: Reds (Pitching, red hat, follow thru delivery; yellow stripes)	10.00	4.50
☐ 21B Jim Maloney: Reds (Pitching, red hat, follow thru delivery; red stripes)	12.50	5.50
☐ 22 Lee May: Reds (Hands on knee)	10.00	4.50
☐ 23A Bill Mazeroski: Pirates (Portrait; autograph below waist)	20.00	9.00
☐ 23B Bill Mazeroski: Pirates (Portrait; autograph above waist; Cut Along Dotted Lines printed on lower tab)	25.00	11.00
☐ 24 Bill McCool: Reds (Red hat, left hand out)	8.00	3.60
☐ 25 Sam McDowell: Indians (Pitching, left hand under glove)	12.50	5.50
☐ 26 Denis Menke: Braves (Blue sleeves)	8.00	3.60
☐ 27 Jim Pagliaroni: Pirates (Catching no chest protector)	8.00	3.60
☐ 28 Don Pavletich	8.00	3.60
☐ 29 Tony Perez: Reds (Throwing)	40.00	18.00
☐ 30 Vada Pinson: Reds	15.00	6.75

Card	NRMT	VG-E
(Ready to throw)		
☐ 31 Dennis Ribant	8.00	3.60
☐ 32 Pete Rose: Reds	125.00	55.00
(Batting)		
☐ 33 Art Shamsky: Reds	8.00	3.60
☐ 34 Bob Shaw	8.00	3.60
☐ 35 Sonny Siebert:	8.00	3.60
Indians (Pitching		
signature at knees)		
☐ 36 Willie Stargell:	40.00	18.00
Pirates (Batting		
no clouds)		
☐ 37A Joe Torre: Braves	15.00	6.75
(Catching, mask		
on ground)		
☐ 37B Joe Torre: Braves	25.00	11.00
(Catching, mask		
on ground;		
Cut Along Dotted Lines		
printed on lower tab)		
☐ 38 Bob Veale: Pirates	8.00	3.60
(Portrait, hands		
not shown)		
☐ 39 Leon Wagner: Indians	8.00	3.60
(Fielding)		
☐ 40A Fred Whitfield	8.00	3.60
(Batting lefthanded)		
☐ 40B Fred Whitfield	8.00	3.60
(Batting lefthanded;		
Cut Along Dotted Lines		
printed on lower tab)		
☐ 41 Woody Woodward	8.00	3.60

1968 Kahn's

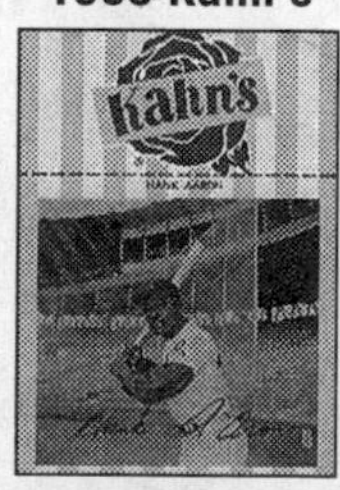

'he cards in this 50-piece set contain two different sizes. 'he smaller of the two sizes, which contains 12 cards, is 2 3/16" X 3 1/4" with the ad tab and 2 13/16" X 1 7/8" without the ad tab. The larger size, which contains 38 ards, measures 2 13/16" X 3 7/8" with the ad tab and 2 3/16" X 2 11/16" without the ad tab. The 1968 Kahn's set f full-color, blank backed, unnumbered cards features layers from Atlanta, Chicago Cubs, Chicago White Sox, incinnati, Cleveland, Detroit, New York Mets and 'ittsburgh. In the set of 12, listed with the letter A in the hecklist, Maloney exists with either yellow or yellow and reen stripes at the top of the card. The large set of 38, sted with a letter B in the checklist, contains five cards which exist in two variations. The variations in this large et have either yellow or red stripes at the top of the ards, with Maloney being an exception. Maloney has ither a yellow stripe or a Blue Mountain ad at the top. ards with the ad tabs (see other Kahn's sets) are worth wice as much as cards without the ad, i.e., double the rices below. The cards are listed and numbered below in lphabetical order (within each subset) by the subject's ame. The set features a card of Johnny Bench in his ookie Card year.

	NRMT	VG-E
OMPLETE SET (50)	1050.00	475.00
OMMON CARD	8.00	3.60
☐ A1 Hank Aaron	100.00	45.00
☐ A2 Gene Alley	10.00	4.50
☐ A3 Max Alvis	8.00	3.60
☐ A4 Clete Boyer	12.50	5.50
☐ A5 Chico Cardenas	10.00	4.50
☐ A6 Bill Freehan	12.50	5.50
☐ A7 Jim Maloney (2)	12.50	5.50
☐ A8 Lee May	12.50	5.50
☐ A9 Bill Mazeroski	20.00	9.00
☐ A10 Vada Pinson	15.00	6.75
☐ A11 Joe Torre	20.00	9.00
☐ A12 Bob Veale	10.00	4.50
☐ B1 Hank Aaron: Braves	100.00	45.00
Full pose		
batting		
bat cocked		
☐ B2 Tommy Agee	10.00	4.50
☐ B3 Gene Alley: Pirates	8.00	3.60
Fielding, full pose		
☐ B4 Felipe Alou	15.00	6.75
Full pose		
batting, swinging		
player in background		
☐ B5 Matty Alou: Pirates	10.00	4.50
Portrait with bat		
Matio Alou (2)		
☐ B6 Max Alvis	8.00	3.60
Fielding		
glove on ground		
☐ B7 Gerry Arrigo: Reds	8.00	3.60
Pitching		
followthru delivery		
☐ B8 John Bench	350.00	160.00
☐ B9 Clete Boyer	12.50	5.50
☐ B10 Larry Brown	8.00	3.60
☐ B11 Leo Cardenas: Reds	10.00	4.50
Leaping in the air		
☐ B12 Bill Freehan	12.50	5.50
☐ B13 Steve Hargan:	8.00	3.60
Indians		
Pitching		
clouds in background		
☐ B14 Joel Horlen	8.00	3.60
White Sox		
Portrait		
☐ B15 Tony Horton: Indians	8.00	3.60
Portrait		
signed Anthony		
☐ B16 Willie Horton	12.50	5.50
☐ B17 Ferguson Jenkins	40.00	18.00
☐ B18 Deron Johnson:	10.00	4.50
Braves		
☐ B19 Mack Jones: Reds	8.00	3.60
☐ B20 Bob Lee	8.00	3.60
☐ B21 Jim Maloney: Reds	12.50	5.50
Red hat		
pitching hands up (2)		
☐ B22 Lee May: Reds	10.00	4.50
Batting		
☐ B23 Bill Mazeroski:	20.00	9.00
Pirates		
Fielding		
hands in front		
of body		
☐ B24 Dick McAuliffe	8.00	3.60
☐ B25 Bill McCool	8.00	3.60
Red hat		
left hand down		
☐ B26 Sam McDowell:	12.50	5.50
Indians		
Pitching		
left hand over glove (2)		
☐ B27 Tony Perez	30.00	13.50
Fielding ball in glove (2)		
☐ B28 Gary Peters	8.00	3.60
White Sox		
Portrait		
☐ B29 Vada Pinson: Reds	10.00	4.50
Batting		
☐ B30 Chico Ruiz	8.00	3.60
☐ B31 Ron Santo: Cubs	25.00	11.00
Batting		
follow thru (2)		
☐ B32 Art Shamsky: Mets	8.00	3.60
☐ B33 Luis Tiant: Indians	15.00	6.75
Hands over head		
☐ B34 Joe Torre: Braves	20.00	9.00
Batting		
☐ B35 Bob Veale: Pirates	8.00	3.60
Hands chest high		
☐ B36 Leon Wagner: Indians	8.00	3.60
Batting		
☐ B37 Billy Williams: Cubs	40.00	18.00
Bat behind back		
☐ B38 Earl Wilson	8.00	3.60

1969 Kahn's

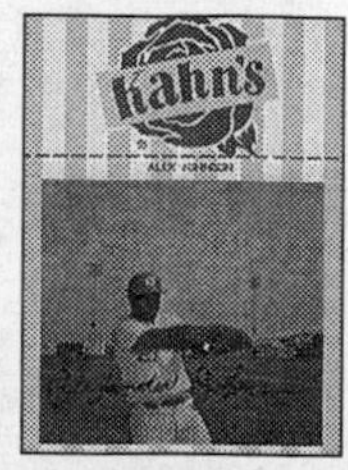

The cards in this 25-piece set contain two different sizes. The three small cards (see 1968 description) measure 2 13/16" X 3 1/4" and the 22 large cards (see 1968 description) measure 2 13/16" X 3 15/16". The 1969 Kahn's Wieners set of full-color, unnumbered cards features players from Atlanta, Chicago Cubs, Chicago White Sox, Cincinnati, Cleveland, Pittsburgh and St. Louis. The small cards have the letter A in the checklist while the large cards have the letter B in the checklist. Four of the larger cards exist in two variations (red or yellow color stripes at the top of the card). These variations are identified in the checklist below. Cards with the ad tabs (see other Kahn's sets) are worth twice as much as cards without the ad, i.e., double the prices below. The cards are listed and numbered below in alphabetical order (within each subset) by the subject's name.

	NRMT	VG-E
COMPLETE SET (25)	450.00	200.00
COMMON CARD	8.00	3.60
☐ A1 Hank Aaron	100.00	45.00
Portrait		
☐ A2 Jim Maloney	10.00	4.50
Pitching		
hands at side		
☐ A3 Tony Perez	25.00	11.00
Glove on		
☐ B1 Hank Aaron	100.00	45.00
☐ B2 Matty Alou	10.00	4.50
Batting		
☐ B3 Max Alvis	8.00	3.60
69 patch		
☐ B4 Gerry Arrigo	8.00	3.60
Leg up		
☐ B5 Steve Blass	10.00	4.50
☐ B6 Clay Carroll	8.00	3.60
☐ B7 Tony Cloninger: Reds	8.00	3.60
☐ B8 George Culver	8.00	3.60
☐ B9 Joel Horlen	10.00	4.50
Pitching		
☐ B10 Tony Horton	10.00	4.50
Batting		
☐ B11 Alex Johnson	10.00	4.50
☐ B12 Jim Maloney	10.00	4.50
☐ B13 Lee May	10.00	4.50
Foot on bag (2)		
☐ B14 Bill Mazeroski	20.00	9.00
Hands on knees (2)		
☐ B15 Sam McDowell	10.00	4.50
Leg up (2)		
☐ B16 Tony Perez	30.00	13.50
☐ B17 Gary Peters	8.00	3.60
Pitching		
☐ B18 Ron Santo	20.00	9.00
Emblem (2)		
☐ B19 Luis Tiant	15.00	6.75
Glove at knee		
☐ B20 Joe Torre: Cardinals	20.00	9.00
☐ B21 Bob Veale	10.00	4.50
Hands at knees		
no glasses		
☐ B22 Billy Williams	35.00	16.00
Bat behind head		

1989 Kahn's Cooperstown

The 1989 Kahn's Cooperstown set contains 11 standard-size cards. This set is sometimes referenced as Hillshire Farms or Kahn's Cooperstown Collection. All players included in the set are members (for the most part they are recent inductees) of the Hall of Fame. The pictures are actually paintings and are surrounded by gold borders. The fronts resemble plaques and also have facsimile autographs. The cards were available from the company via a send-in offer. A set of cards was available in return for three proofs of purchase (and $1 postage and handling) from Hillshire Farms. The last card in the set is actually a coupon card for Kahn's products; this card is not even considered part of the set by some collectors. A related promotion offered two coin cards (coins laminated on cards) featuring Johnny Bench and Carl Yastrzemski. Coin cards are 5 1/2" X 3 3/4" and are blank backed.

	MINT	NRMT
COMPLETE SET (12)	5.00	2.20
COMMON CARD (1-11)	.50	.23
☐ 1 Cool Papa Bell	.50	.23
☐ 2 Johnny Bench	1.00	.45
☐ 3 Lou Brock	.75	.35
☐ 4 Whitey Ford	.75	.35
☐ 5 Bob Gibson	.75	.35
☐ 6 Billy Herman	.50	.23
☐ 7 Harmon Killebrew	.75	.35
☐ 8 Eddie Mathews	.75	.35
☐ 9 Brooks Robinson	1.00	.45
☐ 10 Willie Stargell	1.00	.45
☐ 11 Carl Yastrzemski	1.00	.45
☐ 12 Coupon Card	.25	.11

1986 Kay-Bee

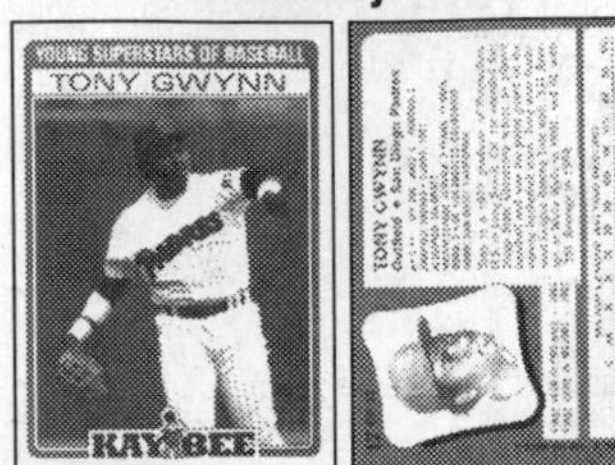

This 33-card, standard-sized set was produced by Topps but manufactured in Northern Ireland. This boxed set retailed in Kay-Bee stores for $1.99; the checklist was listed on the back of the box. The set is subtitled "Young Superstars of Baseball" and does indeed feature many young players. The cards are numbered on the back; the set card numbering is in alphabetical order by player's name.

	MINT	NRMT
COMPLETE SET (33)	4.00	1.80
COMMON CARD (1-33)	.05	.02
☐ 1 Rick Aguilera	.15	.07
☐ 2 Chris Brown	.05	.02
☐ 3 Tom Browning	.05	.02
☐ 4 Tom Brunansky	.05	.02
☐ 5 Vince Coleman	.15	.07
☐ 6 Ron Darling	.05	.02
☐ 7 Alvin Davis	.05	.02
☐ 8 Mariano Duncan	.25	.11
☐ 9 Shawon Dunston	.15	.07
☐ 10 Sid Fernandez	.05	.02
☐ 11 Tony Fernandez	.05	.02
☐ 12 Brian Fisher	.05	.02
☐ 13 John Franco	.25	.11
☐ 14 Julio Franco	.25	.11
☐ 15 Dwight Gooden	.25	.11
☐ 16 Ozzie Guillen	.25	.11
☐ 17 Tony Gwynn	1.00	.45
☐ 18 Jimmy Key	.25	.11
☐ 19 Don Mattingly	1.00	.45
☐ 20 Oddibe McDowell	.05	.02
☐ 21 Roger McDowell	.10	.05
☐ 22 Dan Pasqua	.05	.02
☐ 23 Terry Pendleton	.25	.11
☐ 24 Jim Presley	.05	.02
☐ 25 Kirby Puckett	1.00	.45
☐ 26 Earnie Riles	.05	.02
☐ 27 Bret Saberhagen	.25	.11
☐ 28 Mark Salas	.05	.02
☐ 29 Juan Samuel	.05	.02
☐ 30 Jeff Stone	.05	.02
☐ 31 Darryl Strawberry	.25	.11
☐ 32 Andy Van Slyke	.15	.07
☐ 33 Frank Viola	.15	.07

1987 Kay-Bee

This small 33-card boxed standard-size set was produced by Topps for Kay-Bee Toy Stores. The set is subtitled "Super Stars of Baseball" and has full-color fronts. The card backs are printed in blue and black on white card stock. The checklist for the set is printed on the back panel of the yellow box. The set card numbering is alphabetical by player's name.

	MINT	NRMT
COMPLETE SET (33)	4.00	1.80
COMMON CARD (1-33)	.05	.02
☐ 1 Harold Baines	.10	.05
☐ 2 Jesse Barfield	.05	.02
☐ 3 Don Baylor	.10	.05
☐ 4 Wade Boggs	.50	.23
☐ 5 George Brett	.75	.35
☐ 6 Hubie Brooks	.05	.02
☐ 7 Jose Canseco	.60	.25
☐ 8 Gary Carter	.15	.07
☐ 9 Joe Carter	.25	.11
☐ 10 Roger Clemens	.75	.35
☐ 11 Vince Coleman	.05	.02
☐ 12 Glenn Davis	.05	.02
☐ 13 Dwight Gooden	.15	.07
☐ 14 Pedro Guerrero	.05	.02
☐ 15 Tony Gwynn	1.00	.45
☐ 16 Rickey Henderson	.40	.18
☐ 17 Keith Hernandez	.15	.07
☐ 18 Wally Joyner	.10	.05
☐ 19 Don Mattingly	1.00	.45
☐ 20 Jack Morris	.15	.07
☐ 21 Dale Murphy	.25	.11
☐ 22 Eddie Murray	.40	.18
☐ 23 Dave Parker	.15	.07
☐ 24 Kirby Puckett	1.00	.45
☐ 25 Tim Raines	.15	.07
☐ 26 Jim Rice	.10	.05
☐ 27 Dave Righetti	.05	.02
☐ 28 Ryne Sandberg	.75	.35
☐ 29 Mike Schmidt	.60	.25
☐ 30 Mike Scott	.05	.02
☐ 31 Darryl Strawberry	.15	.07
☐ 32 Fernando Valenzuela	.10	.05
☐ 33 Dave Winfield	.40	.18

1988 Kay-Bee

This small 33-card boxed standard-size set was produced by Topps for Kay-Bee Toy Stores. The set is subtitled "Superstars of Baseball" and have full-color fronts. The card backs are printed in blue and green on white card stock. The checklist for the set is printed on the back panel of the box. The set card numbering is alphabetical by player's name.

	MINT	NRMT
COMPLETE SET (33)	4.00	1.80
COMMON CARD (1-33)	.05	.02
☐ 1 George Bell	.05	.02
☐ 2 Wade Boggs	.40	.18
☐ 3 Jose Canseco	.40	.18
☐ 4 Joe Carter	.25	.11
☐ 5 Jack Clark	.05	.02
☐ 6 Alvin Davis	.05	.02
☐ 7 Eric Davis	.15	.07
☐ 8 Andre Dawson	.30	.14
☐ 9 Darrell Evans	.05	.02
☐ 10 Dwight Evans	.15	.07
☐ 11 Gary Gaetti	.15	.07
☐ 12 Pedro Guerrero	.10	.05
☐ 13 Tony Gwynn	1.00	.45
☐ 14 Howard Johnson	.05	.02
☐ 15 Wally Joyner	.15	.07
☐ 16 Don Mattingly	1.00	.45
☐ 17 Willie McGee	.05	.02
☐ 18 Mark McGwire	1.25	.55
☐ 19 Paul Molitor	.40	.18
☐ 20 Dale Murphy	.25	.11
☐ 21 Dave Parker	.10	.05
☐ 22 Lance Parrish	.05	.02
☐ 23 Kirby Puckett	1.00	.45
☐ 24 Tim Raines	.10	.05
☐ 25 Cal Ripken	1.50	.70
☐ 26 Juan Samuel	.05	.02
☐ 27 Mike Schmidt	.50	.23
☐ 28 Ruben Sierra	.10	.05
☐ 29 Darryl Strawberry	.15	.07
☐ 30 Danny Tartabull	.05	.02
☐ 31 Alan Trammell	.15	.07
☐ 32 Tim Wallach	.05	.02
☐ 33 Dave Winfield	.40	.18

1989 Kay-Bee

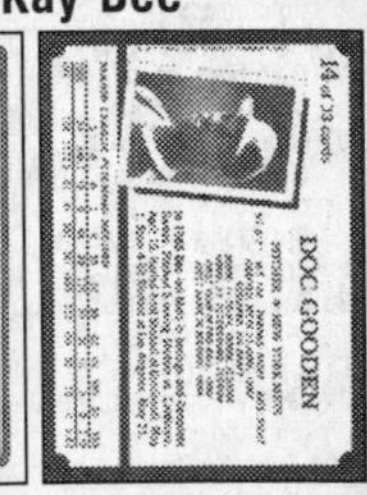

The 1989 Kay-Bee set contains 33 standard-size glossy cards. The fronts have magenta and yellow borders. The horizontally oriented backs are brown and yellow. The cards were distributed as boxed sets through Kay-Bee toy stores. The set card numbering is alphabetical by player's name.

	MINT	NRMT
COMPLETE SET (33)	4.00	1.80
COMMON CARD (1-33)	.05	.02
☐ 1 Wade Boggs	.30	.14
☐ 2 George Brett	.75	.35
☐ 3 Jose Canseco	.30	.14
☐ 4 Gary Carter	.15	.07
☐ 5 Jack Clark	.05	.02
☐ 6 Will Clark	.40	.18
☐ 7 Roger Clemens	.75	.35
☐ 8 Eric Davis	.10	.05
☐ 9 Andre Dawson	.30	.14
☐ 10 Dwight Evans	.05	.02
☐ 11 Carlton Fisk	.40	.18
☐ 12 Andres Galarraga	.30	.14
☐ 13 Kirk Gibson	.15	.07
☐ 14 Dwight Gooden	.10	.05
☐ 15 Mike Greenwell	.05	.02
☐ 16 Pedro Guerrero	.05	.02
☐ 17 Tony Gwynn	1.00	.45
☐ 18 Rickey Henderson	.30	.14
☐ 19 Orel Hershiser	.10	.05
☐ 20 Don Mattingly	.75	.35
☐ 21 Mark McGwire	1.25	.55
☐ 22 Dale Murphy	.25	.11
☐ 23 Eddie Murray	.30	.14
☐ 24 Kirby Puckett	.75	.35
☐ 25 Tim Raines	.10	.05
☐ 26 Ryne Sandberg	.60	.25
☐ 27 Mike Schmidt	.40	.18
☐ 28 Ozzie Smith	.75	.35
☐ 29 Darryl Strawberry	.10	.05
☐ 30 Alan Trammell	.15	.07
☐ 31 Frank Viola	.05	.02
☐ 32 Dave Winfield	.30	.14
☐ 33 Robin Yount	.25	.11

1990 Kay-Bee

The 1990 Kay-Bee Kings of Baseball set is a standard-size 33-card set sequenced alphabetically that Topps produced for the Kay-Bee toy store chain. A solid red border inside a purple white striped box is the major design feature of this set. The set card numbering is alphabetical by player's name.

	MINT	NRMT
COMPLETE SET (33)	4.00	1.80
COMMON CARD (1-33)	.05	.02

☐ 1 Doyle Alexander	.05	.02
☐ 2 Bert Blyleven	.05	.02
☐ 3 Wade Boggs	.30	.14
☐ 4 George Brett	.75	.35
☐ 5 John Candelaria	.05	.02
☐ 6 Gary Carter	.15	.07
☐ 7 Vince Coleman	.05	.02
☐ 8 Andre Dawson	.25	.11
☐ 9 Dennis Eckersley	.15	.07
☐ 10 Darrell Evans	.05	.02
☐ 11 Dwight Evans	.10	.05
☐ 12 Carlton Fisk	.30	.14
☐ 13 Ken Griffey Sr.	.05	.02
☐ 14 Tony Gwynn	.75	.35
☐ 15 Rickey Henderson	.30	.14
☐ 16 Keith Hernandez	.05	.02
☐ 17 Charlie Hough	.05	.02
☐ 18 Don Mattingly	.75	.35
☐ 19 Jack Morris	.10	.05
☐ 20 Dale Murphy	.25	.11
☐ 21 Eddie Murray	.40	.18
☐ 22 Dave Parker	.10	.05
☐ 23 Kirby Puckett	.75	.35
☐ 24 Tim Raines	.10	.05
☐ 25 Rick Reuschel	.05	.02
☐ 26 Jerry Reuss	.05	.02
☐ 27 Jim Rice	.10	.05
☐ 28 Nolan Ryan	1.50	.70
☐ 29 Ozzie Smith	.75	.35
☐ 30 Frank Tanana	.05	.02
☐ 31 Willie Wilson	.05	.02
☐ 32 Dave Winfield	.30	.14
☐ 33 Robin Yount	.25	.11

1970 Kellogg's

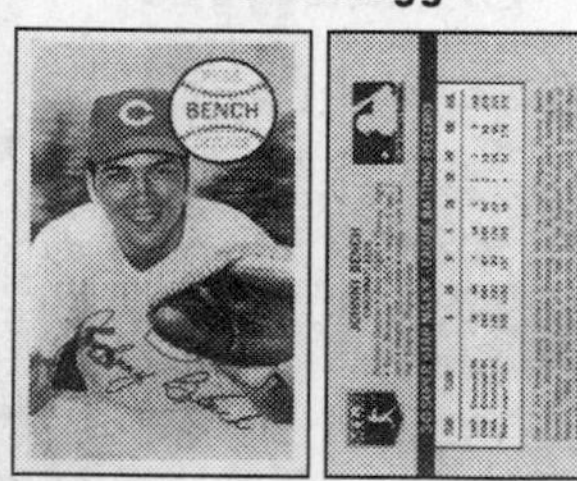

he cards in this 75-card set measure approximately 2 /4" by 3 1/2". The 1970 Kellogg's set was Kellogg's first enture into the baseball card producing field. The design ncorporates a brilliant color photo of the player set gainst an indistinct background, which is then covered vith a layer of plastic to simulate a 3-D look. Some eteran card dealers consider cards 16-30 to be in shorter upply than the other cards in the set. The cards were ndividually inserted one per specially marked boxes of ellogg's cereal. Cards still found with the wrapper intact re valued 50 percent greater than the values listed below.

	NRMT	VG-E
OMPLETE SET (75)	225.00	100.00
OMMON CARD (1-75)	1.00	.45
☐ 1 Ed Kranepool	1.50	.70
☐ 2 Pete Rose	20.00	9.00
☐ 3 Cleon Jones	1.00	.45
☐ 4 Willie McCovey	6.00	2.70
☐ 5 Mel Stottlemyre	1.50	.70
☐ 6 Frank Howard	1.50	.70
☐ 7 Tom Seaver	15.00	6.75
☐ 8 Don Sutton	3.00	1.35
☐ 9 Jim Wynn	1.00	.45
☐ 10 Jim Maloney	1.00	.45
☐ 11 Tommie Agee	1.00	.45
☐ 12 Willie Mays	20.00	9.00
☐ 13 Juan Marichal	4.00	1.80
☐ 14 Dave McNally	1.50	.70
☐ 15 Frank Robinson	8.00	3.60
☐ 16 Carlos May	1.00	.45
☐ 17 Bill Singer	1.00	.45
☐ 18 Rick Reichardt	1.00	.45
☐ 19 Boog Powell	2.00	.90
☐ 20 Gaylord Perry	6.00	2.70
☐ 21 Brooks Robinson	12.00	5.50
☐ 22 Luis Aparicio	6.00	2.70
☐ 23 Joel Horlen	1.00	.45
☐ 24 Mike Epstein	1.00	.45
☐ 25 Tom Haller	1.00	.45
☐ 26 Willie Crawford	1.00	.45
☐ 27 Roberto Clemente	30.00	13.50
☐ 28 Matty Alou	1.00	.45
☐ 29 Willie Stargell	8.00	3.60
☐ 30 Tim Cullen	1.00	.45
☐ 31 Randy Hundley	1.00	.45
☐ 32 Reggie Jackson	20.00	9.00
☐ 33 Rich Allen	2.00	.90
☐ 34 Tim McCarver	2.00	.90
☐ 35 Ray Culp	1.00	.45
☐ 36 Jim Fregosi	1.00	.45
☐ 37 Billy Williams	4.00	1.80
☐ 38 Johnny Odom	1.00	.45
☐ 39 Bert Campaneris	1.50	.70
☐ 40 Ernie Banks	10.00	4.50
☐ 41 Chris Short	1.00	.45
☐ 42 Ron Santo	2.00	.90
☐ 43 Glenn Beckert	1.00	.45
☐ 44 Lou Brock	6.00	2.70
☐ 45 Larry Hisle	1.00	.45
☐ 46 Reggie Smith	1.50	.70
☐ 47 Rod Carew	8.00	3.60
☐ 48 Curt Flood	1.50	.70
☐ 49 Jim Lonborg	1.00	.45
☐ 50 Sam McDowell	1.00	.45
☐ 51 Sal Bando	1.50	.70
☐ 52 Al Kaline	10.00	4.50
☐ 53 Gary Nolan	1.00	.45
☐ 54 Rico Petrocelli	1.50	.70
☐ 55 Ollie Brown	1.00	.45
☐ 56 Luis Tiant	1.50	.70
☐ 57 Bill Freehan	1.50	.70
☐ 58 Johnny Bench	20.00	9.00
☐ 59 Joe Pepitone	1.50	.70
☐ 60 Bobby Murcer	1.50	.70
☐ 61 Harmon Killebrew	8.00	3.60
☐ 62 Don Wilson	1.00	.45
☐ 63 Tony Oliva	2.00	.90
☐ 64 Jim Perry	1.00	.45
☐ 65 Mickey Lolich	1.50	.70
☐ 66 Jose Laboy	1.00	.45
☐ 67 Dean Chance	1.00	.45
☐ 68 Ken Harrelson	1.50	.70
☐ 69 Willie Horton	1.50	.70
☐ 70 Wally Bunker	1.00	.45
☐ 71A Bob Gibson ERR (1959 innings pitched is blank)	6.00	2.70
☐ 71B Bob Gibson COR (1959 innings is 76)	6.00	2.70
☐ 72 Joe Morgan	5.00	2.20
☐ 73 Denny McLain	1.50	.70
☐ 74 Tommy Harper	1.00	.45
☐ 75 Don Mincher	1.00	.45

1971 Kellogg's

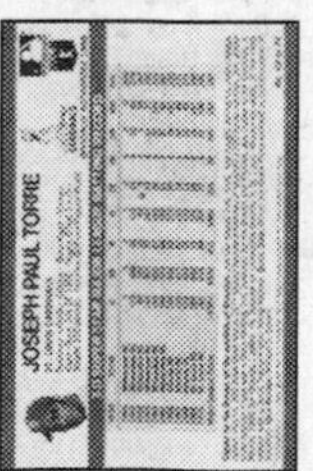

The cards in this 75-card set measure approximately 2 1/4" by 3 1/2". The 1971 set of 3-D cards marketed by the Kellogg Company is the scarcest of all that company's issues. It was distributed as single cards, one in each package of cereal, without the usual complete set mail-in offer. In addition, card dealers were unable to obtain this set in quantity, as they have in other years. All the cards are available with and without the year 1970 before XOGRAPH on the back in the lower left corner; the version without carries a slight premium for most numbers. Prices listed below are for the more common variety with the year 1970. Cards still found with the wrapper intact are valued 50 percent greater than the values listed below.

	NRMT	VG-E
COMPLETE SET (75)	900.00	400.00
COMMON CARD (1-75)	7.00	3.10
☐ 1 Wayne Simpson	7.00	3.10
☐ 2 Tom Seaver	30.00	13.50
☐ 3 Jim Perry	8.00	3.60
☐ 4 Bob Robertson	7.00	3.10
☐ 5 Roberto Clemente	60.00	27.00
☐ 6 Gaylord Perry	15.00	6.75
☐ 7 Felipe Alou	8.00	3.60
☐ 8 Denis Menke	7.00	3.10
☐ 9A Don Kessinger No 1970 date	8.00	3.60
☐ 9B Don Kessinger ERR Dated 1970 hits 167; avg. .265	8.00	3.60
☐ 9C Don Kessinger COR Dated1970 hits 168; avg. .266	8.00	3.60
☐ 10 Willie Mays	50.00	22.00
☐ 11 Jim Hickman	7.00	3.10
☐ 12 Tony Oliva	10.00	4.50
☐ 13 Manny Sanguillen	8.00	3.60
☐ 14 Frank Howard	8.00	3.60
☐ 15 Frank Robinson	25.00	11.00
☐ 16 Willie Davis	8.00	3.60
☐ 17 Lou Brock	25.00	11.00
☐ 18 Cesar Tovar	7.00	3.10
☐ 19 Luis Aparicio	15.00	6.75
☐ 20 Boog Powell	10.00	4.50
☐ 21 Dick Selma	7.00	3.10
☐ 22 Danny Walton	7.00	3.10
☐ 23 Carl Morton	7.00	3.10
☐ 24 Sonny Siebert	7.00	3.10
☐ 25 Jim Merritt	7.00	3.10
☐ 26 Jose Cardenal	7.00	3.10
☐ 27 Don Mincher	7.00	3.10
☐ 28A Clyde Wright No 1970 date team logo is Angels crest	10.00	4.50
☐ 28B Clyde Wright (No 1970 date team logo is California outline with Angels written inside	10.00	4.50
☐ 28C Clyde Wright Dated 1970 team logo is California state outline	8.00	3.60
☐ 29 Les Cain	7.00	3.10
☐ 30 Danny Cater	7.00	3.10
☐ 31 Don Sutton	15.00	6.75
☐ 32 Chuck Dobson	7.00	3.10
☐ 33 Willie McCovey	25.00	11.00
☐ 34 Mike Epstein	7.00	3.10
☐ 35 Paul Blair	7.00	3.10
☐ 36A Gary Nolan No 1970 date	8.00	3.60
☐ 36B Gary Nolan Dated 1970 1970; BB 95, SO 177	8.00	3.60
☐ 36C Gary Nolan Dated 1970 1970; BB 96, SO 181	8.00	3.60
☐ 37 Sam McDowell	8.00	3.60
☐ 38 Amos Otis	8.00	3.60
☐ 39 Ray Fosse	7.00	3.10
☐ 40 Mel Stottlemyre	8.00	3.60
☐ 41 Clarence Gaston	8.00	3.60
☐ 42 Dick Dietz	7.00	3.10
☐ 43 Roy White	7.00	3.10
☐ 44 Al Kaline	30.00	13.50
☐ 45 Carlos May	7.00	3.10
☐ 46 Tommie Agee	7.00	3.10
☐ 47 Tommy Harper	7.00	3.10
☐ 48 Larry Dierker	8.00	3.60
☐ 49 Mike Cuellar	8.00	3.60
☐ 50 Ernie Banks	30.00	13.50
☐ 51 Bob Gibson	25.00	11.00
☐ 52 Reggie Smith	8.00	3.60
☐ 53 Matty Alou	8.00	3.60
☐ 54A Alex Johnson No 1970 date team logo is Angels crest	10.00	4.50
☐ 54B Alex Johnson No 1970 date team logo is California state outline	10.00	4.50
☐ 54C Alex Johnson Dated 1970 team logo is California state outline	8.00	3.60
☐ 55 Harmon Killebrew	25.00	11.00
☐ 56 Bill Grabarkewitz	7.00	3.10
☐ 57 Richie Allen	10.00	4.50
☐ 58 Tony Perez	15.00	6.75
☐ 59 Dave McNally	8.00	3.60
☐ 60 Jim Palmer	25.00	11.00
☐ 61 Billy Williams	20.00	9.00
☐ 62 Joe Torre	12.00	5.50
☐ 63 Jim Northrup	8.00	3.60
☐ 64A Jim Fregosi No 1970 date team logo is Angels crest	10.00	4.50
☐ 64B Jim Fregosi No 1970 date team logo is California state outline	10.00	4.50
☐ 64C Jim Fregosi Dated1970 1970; Hits 166, avg. .276	8.00	3.60
☐ 64D Jim Fregosi Dated1970 1970; Hits 167, avg. .278	8.00	3.60

Card	NRMT	VG-E
☐ 65 Pete Rose	50.00	22.00
☐ 66A Bud Harrelson	8.00	3.60
No 1970 date		
☐ 66B Bud Harrelson ERR	8.00	3.60
Dated 1970		
1970 RBI 43		
☐ 66C Bud Harrelson COR	8.00	3.60
Dated 1970		
1970 RBI 42		
☐ 67 Tony Taylor	8.00	3.60
☐ 68 Willie Stargell	20.00	9.00
☐ 69 Tony Horton	8.00	3.60
☐ 70A Claude Osteen ERR	10.00	4.50
No 1970 date		
card number missing		
☐ 70B Claude Osteen COR	10.00	4.50
No 1970 date		
card number present		
☐ 70C Claude Osteen COR	8.00	3.60
Dated 1970		
☐ 71 Glenn Beckert	7.00	3.10
☐ 72 Nate Colbert	7.00	3.10
☐ 73A Rick Monday	8.00	3.60
No 1970 date		
☐ 73B Rick Monday ERR	8.00	3.60
Dated 1970		
1970; AB 377, avg. .289		
☐ 73C Rick Monday COR	8.00	3.60
Dated 1970		
1970; AB 376, avg. .290		
☐ 74 Tommy John	10.00	4.50
☐ 75 Chris Short	7.00	3.10

1972 Kellogg's

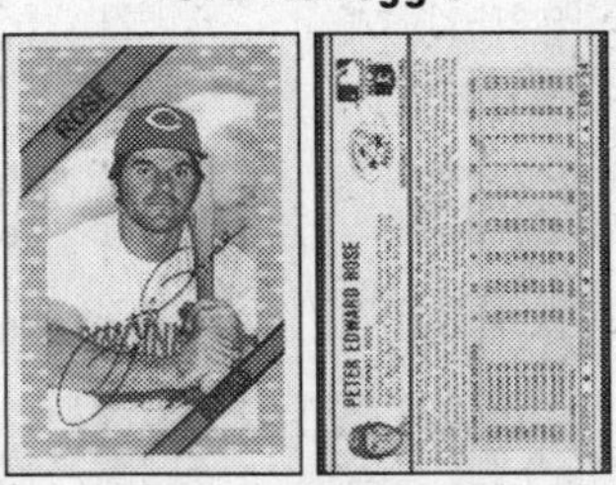

The cards in this 54-card set measure approximately 2 1/8" by 3 1/4". The dimensions of the cards in the 1972 Kellogg's set were reduced in comparison to those of the 1971 series. In addition, the length of the set was set at 54 cards rather than the 75 of the previous year. The cards of this Kellogg's set are characterized by the diagonal bands found on the obverse. Cards still found with the wrapper intact are valued 50 percent greater than the values listed below.

	NRMT	VG-E
COMPLETE SET (54)	75.00	34.00
COMMON CARD (1-54)	.75	.35
☐ 1A Tom Seaver ERR	10.00	4.50
1970 ERA 2.85		
☐ 1B Tom Seaver COR	20.00	9.00
1970 ERA 2.81		
☐ 2 Amos Otis	.75	.35
☐ 3A Willie Davis ERR	1.50	.70
Lifetime runs 842		
☐ 3B Willie Davis COR	.75	.35
Lifetime runs 841		
☐ 4 Wilbur Wood	.75	.35
☐ 5 Bill Parsons	.75	.35
☐ 6 Pete Rose	15.00	6.75
☐ 7A Willie McCovey ERR	4.00	1.80
Lifetime HR 360		
☐ 7B Willie McCovey COR	8.00	3.60
Lifetime HR 370		
☐ 8 Ferguson Jenkins	3.00	1.35
☐ 9A Vida Blue ERR	1.50	.70
Lifetime ERA 2.35		
☐ 9B Vida Blue COR	.75	.35
Lifetime ERA 2.31		
☐ 10 Joe Torre	1.50	.70
☐ 11 Merv Rettenmund	.75	.35
☐ 12 Bill Melton	.75	.35
☐ 13A Jim Palmer ERR	5.00	2.20
Lifetime games 170		
☐ 13B Jim Palmer COR	10.00	4.50
Lifetime games 168		
☐ 14 Doug Rader	.75	.35
☐ 15A Dave Roberts ERR	.75	.35
NL missing in bio		
☐ 15B Dave Roberts COR	1.50	.70
NL in bio, line 2		
☐ 16 Bobby Murcer	1.00	.45
☐ 17 Wes Parker	.75	.35
☐ 18A Joe Coleman ERR	1.50	.70
Lifetime BB 294		
☐ 18B Joe Coleman COR	.75	.35
Lifetime BB 393		
☐ 19 Manny Sanguillen	.75	.35
☐ 20 Reggie Jackson	10.00	4.50
☐ 21 Ralph Garr	.75	.35
☐ 22 Jim Hunter	3.00	1.35
☐ 23 Rick Wise	.75	.35
☐ 24 Glenn Beckert	.75	.35
☐ 25 Tony Oliva	1.50	.70
☐ 26A Bob Gibson ERR	8.00	3.60
Lifetime SO 2577		
☐ 26B Bob Gibson COR	4.00	1.80
Lifetime SO 2578		
☐ 27A Mike Cuellar ERR	1.50	.70
1971 ERA 3.80		
☐ 27B Mike Cuellar COR	.75	.35
1971 ERA 3.08		
☐ 28 Chris Speier	.75	.35
☐ 29A Dave McNally ERR	1.50	.70
Lifetime ERA 3.18		
☐ 29B Dave McNally COR	.75	.35
Lifetime ERA 3.15		
☐ 30 Leo Cardenas	.75	.35
☐ 31A Bill Freehan ERR	.75	.35
Lifetime runs 497		
☐ 31B Bill Freehan COR	1.50	.70
Lifetime runs 500		
☐ 32A Bud Harrelson ERR	1.50	.70
Lifetime hits 634		
☐ 32B Bud Harrelson COR	.75	.35
Lifetime hits 624		
☐ 33A Sam McDowell ERR	.75	.35
Bio line 3 has less than 200		
☐ 33B Sam McDowell COR	1.50	.70
Bio line 3 has less than 225		
☐ 34A Claude Osteen ERR	.75	.35
1971 ERA 3.25		
☐ 34B Claude Osteen COR	1.50	.70
1971 ERA 3.51		
☐ 35 Reggie Smith	1.00	.45
☐ 36 Sonny Siebert	.75	.35
☐ 37 Lee May	1.00	.45
☐ 38 Mickey Lolich	1.00	.45
☐ 39A Cookie Rojas ERR	1.50	.70
Lifetime 2B 149		
☐ 39B Cookie Rojas COR	.75	.35
Lifetime 2B 150		
☐ 40A Dick Drago ERR	1.50	.70
Bio line 3 has Poyals		
☐ 40B Dick Drago COR	.75	.35
Bio line 3 has Royals		
☐ 41 Nate Colbert	.75	.35
☐ 42 Andy Messersmith	.75	.35
☐ 43A Dave Johnson ERR	1.50	.70
Lifetime AB 3110, avg. .262		
☐ 43B Dave Johnson COR	1.00	.45
Lifetime AB 3113, avg. .264		
☐ 44 Steve Blass	.75	.35
☐ 45 Bob Robertson	.75	.35
☐ 46A Billy Williams ERR	4.00	1.80
Bio has "missed only one game"		
☐ 46B Billy Williams COR	7.00	3.10
Bio has that line eliminated		
☐ 47 Juan Marichal	4.00	1.80
☐ 48 Lou Brock	4.00	1.80
☐ 49 Roberto Clemente	20.00	9.00
☐ 50 Mel Stottlemyre	.75	.35
☐ 51 Don Wilson	.75	.35
☐ 52A Sal Bando ERR	.75	.35
Lifetime RBI 355		
☐ 52B Sal Bando COR	1.50	.70
Lifetime RBI 356		
☐ 53A Willie Stargell ERR	8.00	3.60
Lifetime 2B 197		
☐ 53B Willie Stargell COR	4.00	1.80
Lifetime 2B 196		
☐ 54A Willie Mays ERR	25.00	11.00
Lifetime RBI 1855		
☐ 54B Willie Mays COR	12.50	5.50
Lifetime RBI 1856		

1972 Kellogg's ATG

The cards in this 15-card set measure 2 1/4" by 3 1/2". The 1972 All-Time Greats 3-D set was issued with Kellogg's Danish Go Rounds. The set contains two different cards of Babe Ruth. The set is a reissue of a 1970 set issued by Rold Gold Pretzels to commemorate baseball's first 100 years. The Rold Gold cards are copyrighted 1970 on the reverse and are valued at approximately double the prices listed below.

	NRMT	VG-E
COMPLETE SET (15)	25.00	11.00
COMMON CARD (1-15)	1.00	.45
☐ 1 Walter Johnson	2.00	.90
☐ 2 Rogers Hornsby	1.25	.55
☐ 3 John McGraw	1.25	.55
☐ 4 Mickey Cochrane	1.25	.55
☐ 5 George Sisler	1.25	.55
☐ 6 Babe Ruth	8.00	3.60
☐ 7 Lefty Grove	1.25	.55
☐ 8 Pie Traynor	1.00	.45
☐ 9 Honus Wagner	2.00	.90
☐ 10 Eddie Collins	1.00	.45
☐ 11 Tris Speaker	1.25	.55
☐ 12 Cy Young	2.00	.90
☐ 13 Lou Gehrig	6.00	2.70
☐ 14 Babe Ruth	8.00	3.60
☐ 15 Ty Cobb	6.00	2.70

1973 Kellogg's 2D

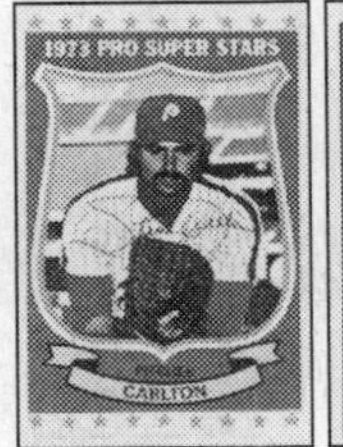

The cards in this 54-card set measure approximately 2 1/4" by 3 1/2". The 1973 Kellogg's set is the only non-3D set produced by the Kellogg Company. Apparently Kellogg's decided to have the cards produced through Visual Panographics rather than by Xograph, as in the other years. The complete set could be obtained from the company through a box-top redemption procedure. The card size is slightly larger than the previous year.

	NRMT	VG-E
COMPLETE SET (54)	75.00	34.00
COMMON CARD (1-54)	.50	.23
☐ 1 Amos Otis	.75	.35
☐ 2 Ellie Rodriguez	.50	.23
☐ 3 Mickey Lolich	1.00	.45
☐ 4 Tony Oliva	1.50	.70
☐ 5 Don Sutton	2.00	.90
☐ 6 Pete Rose	15.00	6.75
☐ 7 Steve Carlton	6.00	2.70
☐ 8 Bobby Bonds	1.00	.45
☐ 9 Wilbur Wood	.50	.23
☐ 10 Billy Williams	4.00	1.80
☐ 11 Steve Blass	.50	.23
☐ 12 Jon Matlack	.50	.23
☐ 13 Cesar Cedeno	.75	.35
☐ 14 Bob Gibson	4.00	1.80
☐ 15 Sparky Lyle	1.00	.45
☐ 16 Nolan Ryan	30.00	13.50
☐ 17 Jim Palmer	5.00	2.20
☐ 18 Ray Fosse	.50	.23
☐ 19 Bobby Murcer	.75	.35
☐ 20 Jim Hunter	3.00	1.35
☐ 21 Tom McCraw	.50	.23
☐ 22 Reggie Jackson	8.00	3.60
☐ 23 Bill Stoneman	.50	.23
☐ 24 Lou Piniella	1.00	.45
☐ 25 Willie Stargell	4.00	1.80
☐ 26 Dick Allen	1.00	.45
☐ 27 Carlton Fisk	12.00	5.50
☐ 28 Ferguson Jenkins	3.00	1.35
☐ 29 Phil Niekro	3.00	1.35
☐ 30 Gary Nolan	.50	.23
☐ 31 Joe Torre	1.00	.45
☐ 32 Bobby Tolan	.50	.23
☐ 33 Nate Colbert	.50	.23

☐ 34 Joe Morgan	4.00	1.80
☐ 35 Bert Blyleven	1.00	.45
☐ 36 Joe Rudi	.75	.35
☐ 37 Ralph Garr	.50	.23
☐ 38 Gaylord Perry	3.00	1.35
☐ 39 Bobby Grich	.75	.35
☐ 40 Lou Brock	4.00	1.80
☐ 41 Pete Broberg	.50	.23
☐ 42 Manny Sanguillen	.50	.23
☐ 43 Willie Davis	.75	.35
☐ 44 Dave Kingman	.75	.35
☐ 45 Carlos May	.50	.23
☐ 46 Tom Seaver	8.00	3.60
☐ 47 Mike Cuellar	.50	.23
☐ 48 Joe Coleman	.50	.23
☐ 49 Claude Osteen	.50	.23
☐ 50 Steve Kline	.50	.23
☐ 51 Rod Carew	5.00	2.20
☐ 52 Al Kaline	6.00	2.70
☐ 53 Larry Dierker	.75	.35
☐ 54 Ron Santo	1.00	.45

1974 Kellogg's

The cards in this 54-card set measure 2 1/8" by 3 1/4". In 1974 the Kellogg's set returned to its 3-D format; it also returned to the smaller-size card. Complete sets could be obtained from the company through a box-top offer. The cards are numbered on the back. Cards still found with the wrapper intact are valued 25 percent greater than the values listed below.

	NRMT	VG-E
COMPLETE SET (54)	60.00	27.00
COMMON CARD (1-54)	.50	.23
☐ 1 Bob Gibson	3.00	1.35
☐ 2 Rick Monday	.50	.23
☐ 3 Joe Coleman	.50	.23
☐ 4 Bert Campaneris	.75	.35
☐ 5 Carlton Fisk	5.00	2.20
☐ 6 Jim Palmer	3.00	1.35
☐ 7A Ron Santo ERR Chicago Cubs	6.00	2.70
☐ 7B Ron Santo COR Chicago White Sox	.75	.35
☐ 8 Nolan Ryan	25.00	11.00
☐ 9 Greg Luzinski	.75	.35
☐ 10 Buddy Bell	.75	.35
☐ 11 Bob Watson	.75	.35
☐ 12 Bill Singer	.50	.23
☐ 13 Dave May	.50	.23
☐ 14 Jim Brewer	.50	.23
☐ 15 Manny Sanguillen	.75	.35
☐ 16 Jeff Burroughs	.75	.35
☐ 17 Amos Otis	.75	.35
☐ 18 Ed Goodson	.50	.23
☐ 19 Nate Colbert	.50	.23
☐ 20 Reggie Jackson	8.00	3.60
☐ 21 Ted Simmons	1.00	.45
☐ 22 Bobby Murcer	1.00	.45
☐ 23 Willie Horton	.75	.35
☐ 24 Orlando Cepeda	1.50	.70
☐ 25 Ron Hunt	.50	.23
☐ 26 Wayne Twitchell	.50	.23
☐ 27 Ron Fairly	.50	.23
☐ 28 Johnny Bench	6.00	2.70
☐ 29 John Mayberry	.50	.23
☐ 30 Rod Carew	3.00	1.35
☐ 31 Ken Holtzman	.50	.23
☐ 32 Billy Williams	3.00	1.35
☐ 33 Dick Allen	1.50	.70
☐ 34A Wilbur Wood ERR (1973 K 198)	3.00	1.35
☐ 34B Wilbur Wood COR (1973 K 199)	.50	.23
☐ 35 Danny Thompson	.50	.23
☐ 36 Joe Morgan	3.00	1.35
☐ 37 Willie Stargell	3.00	1.35
☐ 38 Pete Rose	12.00	5.50
☐ 39 Bobby Bonds	1.50	.70
☐ 40 Chris Speier	.50	.23
☐ 41 Sparky Lyle	.75	.35
☐ 42 Cookie Rojas	.50	.23
☐ 43 Tommy Davis	.50	.23
☐ 44 Jim Hunter	3.00	1.35
☐ 45 Willie Davis	.50	.23
☐ 46 Bert Blyleven	.75	.35
☐ 47 Pat Kelly	.50	.23
☐ 48 Ken Singleton	.50	.23
☐ 49 Manny Mota	.75	.35
☐ 50 Dave Johnson	1.00	.45
☐ 51 Sal Bando	.75	.35
☐ 52 Tom Seaver	8.00	3.60
☐ 53 Felix Millan	.50	.23
☐ 54 Ron Blomberg	.50	.23

1975 Kellogg's

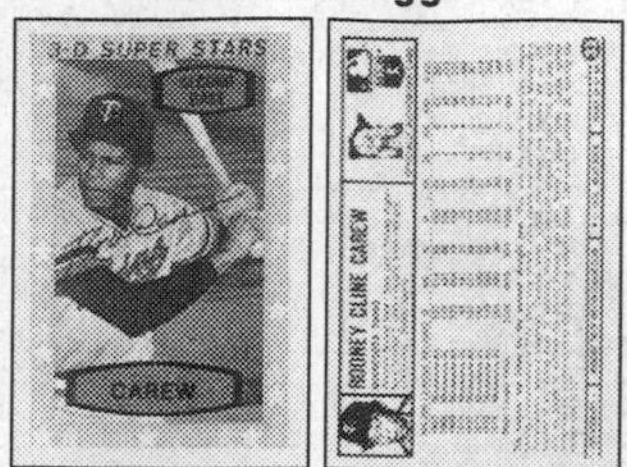

The cards in this 57-card set measure approximately 2 1/8" by 3 1/4". The 1975 Kellogg's 3-D set could be obtained card by card in cereal boxes or as a set from a box-top offer from the company. Card number 44, Jim Hunter, exists with the A's emblem or the Yankees emblem on the back of the card. Cards still found with the wrapper intact are valued 25 percent greater than the values listed below.

	NRMT	VG-E
COMPLETE SET (57)	150.00	70.00
COMMON CARD (1-57)	1.00	.45
☐ 1 Roy White	1.50	.70
☐ 2 Ross Grimsley	1.00	.45
☐ 3 Reggie Smith	1.50	.70
☐ 4A Bob Grich ERR (Bio last line begins 1973 work)	1.50	.70
☐ 4B Bob Grich COR (Bio last line begins because his fielding)	3.00	1.35
☐ 5 Greg Gross	1.00	.45
☐ 6 Bob Watson	1.50	.70
☐ 7 Johnny Bench	10.00	4.50
☐ 8 Jeff Burroughs	1.00	.45
☐ 9 Elliott Maddox	1.00	.45
☐ 10 Jon Matlack	1.00	.45
☐ 11 Pete Rose	20.00	9.00
☐ 12 Lee Stanton	1.00	.45
☐ 13 Bake McBride	1.00	.45
☐ 14 Jorge Orta	1.00	.45
☐ 15 Al Oliver	1.50	.70
☐ 16 John Briggs	1.00	.45
☐ 17 Steve Garvey	5.00	2.20
☐ 18 Brooks Robinson	7.50	3.40
☐ 19 John Hiller	1.00	.45
☐ 20 Lynn McGlothen	1.00	.45
☐ 21 Cleon Jones	1.00	.45
☐ 22 Fergie Jenkins	4.00	1.80
☐ 23 Bill North	1.00	.45
☐ 24 Steve Busby	1.00	.45
☐ 25 Richie Zisk	1.00	.45
☐ 26 Nolan Ryan	40.00	18.00
☐ 27 Joe Morgan	5.00	2.20
☐ 28 Joe Rudi	1.50	.70
☐ 29 Jose Cardenal	1.00	.45
☐ 30 Andy Messersmith	1.00	.45
☐ 31 Willie Montanez	1.00	.45
☐ 32 Bill Buckner	1.50	.70
☐ 33 Rod Carew	7.50	3.40
☐ 34 Lou Piniella	1.50	.70
☐ 35 Ralph Garr	1.00	.45
☐ 36 Mike Marshall	1.50	.70
☐ 37 Garry Maddox	1.00	.45
☐ 38 Dwight Evans	2.00	.90
☐ 39 Lou Brock	7.50	3.40
☐ 40 Ken Singleton	1.50	.70
☐ 41 Steve Braun	1.00	.45
☐ 42 Rich Allen	2.50	1.10
☐ 43 John Grubb	1.00	.45
☐ 44A Jim Hunter (Oakland A's team logo on back)	5.00	2.20
☐ 44B Jim Hunter (New York Yankees team logo on back)	15.00	6.75
☐ 45 Gaylord Perry	4.00	1.80
☐ 46 George Hendrick	1.00	.45
☐ 47 Sparky Lyle	1.50	.70
☐ 48 Dave Cash	1.00	.45
☐ 49 Luis Tiant	1.50	.70
☐ 50 Cesar Geronimo	1.00	.45
☐ 51 Carl Yastrzemski	10.00	4.50
☐ 52 Ken Brett	1.00	.45
☐ 53 Hal McRae	1.50	.70
☐ 54 Reggie Jackson	15.00	6.75
☐ 55 Rollie Fingers	5.00	2.20
☐ 56 Mike Schmidt	25.00	11.00
☐ 57 Richie Hebner	1.00	.45

1976 Kellogg's

The cards in this 57-card set measure approximately 2 1/8" by 3 1/4". The 1976 Kellogg's 3-D set could be obtained card by card in cereal boxes or as a set from the company for box-tops. Card numbers 1-3 (marked in the checklist below with SP) were apparently printed apart from the other 54 and are in shorter supply. Cards still found with the wrapper intact are valued 25 percent greater than the values listed below.

	NRMT	VG-E
COMPLETE SET (57)	75.00	34.00
COMMON CARD (1-3) SP	10.00	4.50
COMMON CARD (4-57)	.50	.23
☐ 1 Steve Hargan SP	10.00	4.50
☐ 2 Claudell Washington SP	10.00	4.50
☐ 3 Don Gullett SP	10.00	4.50
☐ 4 Randy Jones	.50	.23
☐ 5 Jim Hunter	3.00	1.35
☐ 6A Clay Carroll Team logo Cincinnati Reds on back	3.00	1.35
☐ 6B Clay Carroll Team logo Chicago White Sox on back	1.00	.45
☐ 7 Joe Rudi	.50	.23
☐ 8 Reggie Jackson	6.00	2.70
☐ 9 Felix Millan	.50	.23
☐ 10 Jim Rice	3.00	1.35
☐ 11 Bert Blyleven	.75	.35
☐ 12 Ken Singleton	.50	.23
☐ 13 Don Sutton	2.50	1.10
☐ 14 Joe Morgan	3.00	1.35
☐ 15 Dave Parker	2.00	.90
☐ 16 Dave Cash	.50	.23
☐ 17 Ron LeFlore	.50	.23
☐ 18 Greg Luzinski	.75	.35
☐ 19 Dennis Eckersley	12.00	5.50
☐ 20 Bill Madlock	.75	.35
☐ 21 George Scott	.50	.23
☐ 22 Willie Stargell	3.00	1.35
☐ 23 Al Hrabosky	.50	.23
☐ 24 Carl Yastrzemski	6.00	2.70
☐ 25A Jim Kaat Team logo Chicago White Sox on back	3.00	1.35
☐ 25B Jim Kaat Team logo Philadelphia Phillies on back	1.50	.70
☐ 26 Marty Perez	.50	.23
☐ 27 Bob Watson	.75	.35
☐ 28 Eric Soderholm	.50	.23
☐ 29 Bill Lee	.50	.23
☐ 30A Frank Tanana ERR 1975 ERA 2.63	1.00	.45
☐ 30B Frank Tanana COR 1975 ERA 2.62	.75	.35
☐ 31 Fred Lynn		
☐ 32A Tom Seaver ERR 1967 Pct. 552 with no decimal point)	7.50	3.40
☐ 32B Tom Seaver COR 1967 Pct. .552	7.50	3.40
☐ 33 Steve Busby	.50	.23
☐ 34 Gary Carter	4.00	1.80
☐ 35 Rick Wise	.50	.23
☐ 36 Johnny Bench	6.00	2.70

☐ 37 Jim Palmer	3.00	1.35
☐ 38 Bobby Murcer	.75	.35
☐ 39 Von Joshua	.50	.23
☐ 40 Lou Brock	4.00	1.80
☐ 41A Mickey Rivers	2.00	.90
No line in bio about Yankees		
☐ 41B Mickey Rivers	.75	.35
Bio has "Yankees obtained ..."		
☐ 42 Manny Sanguillen	.50	.23
☐ 43 Jerry Reuss	.50	.23
☐ 44 Ken Griffey	1.00	.45
☐ 45A Jorge Orta ERR	.75	.35
Lifetime AB 1615		
☐ 45B Jorge Orta COR	.75	.35
Lifetime AB 1616		
☐ 46 John Mayberry	.50	.23
☐ 47A Vida Blue	.75	.35
Bio "struck out more batters"		
☐ 47B Vida Blue	.75	.35
Bio "pitched more innings"		
☐ 48 Rod Carew	4.00	1.80
☐ 49A Jon Matlack ERR	.75	.35
1975 ER 87		
☐ 49B Jon Matlack COR	.75	.35
1975 ER 86		
☐ 50 Boog Powell	1.00	.45
☐ 51A Mike Hargrove ERR	1.00	.45
Lifetime AB 935		
☐ 51B Mike Hargrove COR	1.00	.45
Lifetime AB 934		
☐ 52A Paul Lindblad ERR	.75	.35
1975 ERA 2.43		
☐ 52B Paul Lindblad COR	.75	.35
1975 ERA 2.72		
☐ 53 Thurman Munson	4.00	1.80
☐ 54 Steve Garvey	2.50	1.10
☐ 55 Pete Rose	12.00	5.50
☐ 56A Greg Gross ERR	.75	.35
Lifetime games 334		
☐ 56B Greg Gross COR	.75	.35
Lifetime games 302		
☐ 57 Ted Simmons	1.00	.45

1977 Kellogg's

The cards in this 57-card set measure approximately 2 1/8" by 3 1/4". The 1977 Kellogg's series of 3-D baseball player cards could be obtained card by card from cereal boxes or by sending in box-tops and money. Each player's picture appears in miniature form on the reverse, an idea begun in 1971 and replaced in subsequent years by the use of a picture of the Kellogg's mascot. Cards still found with the wrapper intact are valued 25 percent greater than the values listed below.

	NRMT	VG-E
COMPLETE SET (57)	50.00	22.00
COMMON CARD (1-57)	.50	.23
☐ 1 George Foster	.75	.35
☐ 2 Bert Campaneris	.50	.23
☐ 3 Fergie Jenkins	2.50	1.10
☐ 4 Dock Ellis	.50	.23
☐ 5 John Montefusco	.50	.23
☐ 6 George Brett	20.00	9.00
☐ 7 John Candelaria	.50	.23
☐ 8 Fred Norman	.50	.23
☐ 9 Bill Travers	.50	.23
☐ 10 Hal McRae	.75	.35
☐ 11 Doug Rau	.50	.23
☐ 12 Greg Luzinski	.75	.35
☐ 13 Ralph Garr	.50	.23
☐ 14 Steve Garvey	2.50	1.10
☐ 15 Rick Manning	.50	.23
☐ 16A Lyman Bostock ERR	3.00	1.35
(Dock Ellis photo on back)		
☐ 16B Lyman Bostock COR	.75	.35
☐ 17 Randy Jones	.50	.23
☐ 18 Ron Cey	.75	.35
☐ 19 Dave Parker	1.50	.70
☐ 20 Pete Rose	8.00	3.60
☐ 21A Wayne Garland	.50	.23
(No trade to Cleveland is mentioned)		
☐ 21B Wayne Garland	1.50	.70
(Trade mentioned bio ends "now flip for Cleveland)		
☐ 22 Bill North	.50	.23
☐ 23 Thurman Munson	2.50	1.10
☐ 24 Tom Poquette	.50	.23
☐ 25 Ron LeFlore	.50	.23
☐ 26 Mark Fidrych	2.50	1.10
☐ 27 Sixto Lezcano	.50	.23
☐ 28 Dave Winfield	7.50	3.40
☐ 29 Jerry Koosman	.75	.35
☐ 30 Mike Hargrove	.75	.35
☐ 31 Willie Montanez	.50	.23
☐ 32 Don Stanhouse	.50	.23
☐ 33 Jay Johnstone	.50	.23
☐ 34 Bake McBride	.50	.23
☐ 35 Dave Kingman	.75	.35
☐ 36 Fred Patek	.50	.23
☐ 37 Garry Maddox	.50	.23
☐ 38A Ken Reitz	.50	.23
(No trade mentioned)		
☐ 38B Ken Reitz	1.50	.70
(Trade mentioned)		
☐ 39 Bobby Grich	.75	.35
☐ 40 Cesar Geronimo	.50	.23
☐ 41 Jim Lonborg	.50	.23
☐ 42 Ed Figueroa	.50	.23
☐ 43 Bill Madlock	.75	.35
☐ 44 Jerry Remy	.50	.23
☐ 45 Frank Tanana	.75	.35
☐ 46 Al Oliver	.75	.35
☐ 47 Charlie Hough	.75	.35
☐ 48 Lou Piniella	.75	.35
☐ 49 Ken Griffey	1.50	.70
☐ 50 Jose Cruz	.75	.35
☐ 51 Rollie Fingers	2.50	1.10
☐ 52 Chris Chambliss	.75	.35
☐ 53 Rod Carew	5.00	2.20
☐ 54 Andy Messersmith	.50	.23
☐ 55 Mickey Rivers	.75	.35
☐ 56 Butch Wynegar	.50	.23
☐ 57 Steve Carlton	5.00	2.20

1978 Kellogg's

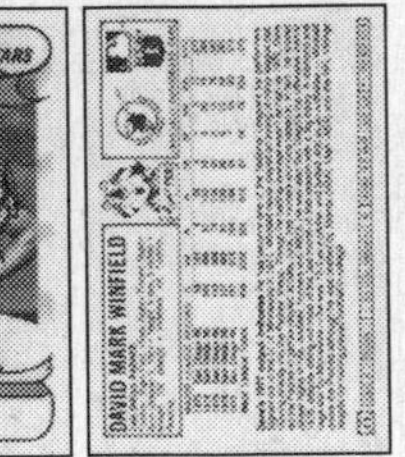

The cards in this 57-card set measure 2 1/8" by 3 1/4". This 1978 3-D Kellogg's series marks the first year in which Tony the Tiger appears on the reverse of each card next to the team and MLB logos. Once again the set could be obtained as individually wrapped cards in cereal boxes or as a set via a mail-in offer. The key card in the set is Eddie Murray, as it was one of Murray's few card issues in 1978, the year of his Topps Rookie Card. Cards still found with the wrapper intact are valued 25 percent greater than the values listed below.

	NRMT	VG-E
COMPLETE SET (57)	50.00	22.00
COMMON CARD (1-57)	.50	.23
☐ 1 Steve Carlton	4.00	1.80
☐ 2 Bucky Dent	.75	.35
☐ 3 Mike Schmidt	8.00	3.60
☐ 4 Ken Griffey	1.00	.45
☐ 5 Al Cowens	.50	.23
☐ 6 George Brett	15.00	6.75
☐ 7 Lou Brock	3.00	1.35
☐ 8 Rich Gossage	.75	.35
☐ 9 Tom Johnson	.50	.23
☐ 10 George Foster	.75	.35
☐ 11 Dave Winfield	4.00	1.80
☐ 12 Dan Meyer	.50	.23
☐ 13 Chris Chambliss	.75	.35
☐ 14 Paul Dade	.50	.23
☐ 15 Jeff Burroughs	.50	.23
☐ 16 Jose Cruz	.75	.35
☐ 17 Mickey Rivers	.75	.35
☐ 18 John Candelaria	.50	.23
☐ 19 Ellis Valentine	.50	.23
☐ 20 Hal McRae	.75	.35
☐ 21 Dave Rozema	.50	.23
☐ 22 Lenny Randle	.50	.23
☐ 23 Willie McCovey	3.00	1.35
☐ 24 Ron Cey	.75	.35
☐ 25 Eddie Murray	25.00	11.00
☐ 26 Larry Bowa	.75	.35
☐ 27 Tom Seaver	6.00	2.70
☐ 28 Garry Maddox	.50	.23
☐ 29 Rod Carew	4.00	1.80
☐ 30 Thurman Munson	2.00	.90
☐ 31 Garry Templeton	.75	.35
☐ 32 Eric Soderholm	.50	.23
☐ 33 Greg Luzinski	.75	.35
☐ 34 Reggie Smith	.75	.35
☐ 35 Dave Goltz	.50	.23
☐ 36 Tommy John	.75	.35
☐ 37 Ralph Garr	.50	.23
☐ 38 Alan Bannister	.50	.23
☐ 39 Bob Bailor	.50	.23
☐ 40 Reggie Jackson	4.00	1.80
☐ 41 Cecil Cooper	.75	.35
☐ 42 Burt Hooton	.50	.23
☐ 43 Sparky Lyle	.75	.35
☐ 44 Steve Ontiveros	.50	.23
☐ 45 Rick Reuschel	.50	.23
☐ 46 Lyman Bostock	.75	.35
☐ 47 Mitchell Page	.50	.23
☐ 48 Bruce Sutter	1.00	.45
☐ 49 Jim Rice	1.50	.70
☐ 50 Ken Forsch	.50	.23
☐ 51 Nolan Ryan	20.00	9.00
☐ 52 Dave Parker	1.00	.45
☐ 53 Bert Blyleven	.75	.35
☐ 54 Frank Tanana	.75	.35
☐ 55 Ken Singleton	.50	.23
☐ 56 Mike Hargrove	.75	.35
☐ 57 Don Sutton	2.00	.90

1979 Kellogg's

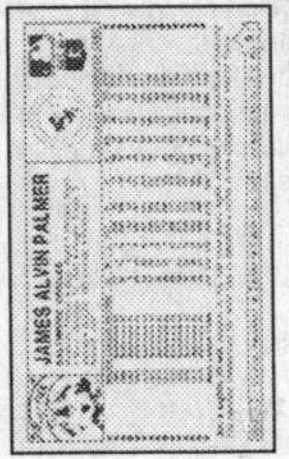

The cards in this 60-card set measure approximately 1 15/16" by 3 1/4". The 1979 edition of Kellogg's 3-D baseball cards have a 3/16" reduced width from the previous year; a nicely designed curved panel above the picture gives this set a distinctive appearance. The set contains the largest number of cards issued in a Kellogg's set since the 1971 series. Three different press runs produced numerous variations in this set. The first two printings were included in cereal boxes, while the third printing was for the complete set mail-in offer. Forty seven cards have three variations, while thirteen cards (4, 6, 9, 15, 19, 20, 30, 33, 41, 43, 45, 51, and 54) are unchanged from the second and third printings. The three printings may be distinguished by the placement of the registered symbol by Tony the Tiger and by team logos. In the third printing, four cards (16, 18, 22, 44) show the "P team logo (no registered symbol), and card numbers 56 and 57 omit the registered symbol by Tony. Cards still found with the wrapper intact are valued 25 percent greater than the values listed below.

	NRMT	VG-E
COMPLETE SET (60)	30.00	13.50
COMMON CARD (1-60)	.25	.11
☐ 1 Bruce Sutter	.50	.23
☐ 2 Ted Simmons	.50	.23
☐ 3 Ross Grimsley	.25	.11
☐ 4 Wayne Nordhagen	.25	.11
☐ 5 Jim Palmer	3.00	1.35
☐ 6 John Henry Johnson	.25	.11
☐ 7 Jason Thompson	.25	.11
☐ 8 Pat Zachry	.25	.11
☐ 9 Dennis Eckersley	3.00	1.35
☐ 10 Paul Splittorff	.25	.11
☐ 11 Ron Guidry	.75	.35
☐ 12 Jeff Burroughs	.25	.11
☐ 13 Rod Carew	3.00	1.35
☐ 14A Buddy Bell	1.50	.7
(No trade mentioned)		
☐ 14B Buddy Bell	.50	.23
(Traded to Rangers)		

☐ 15 Jim Rice	1.25	.55
☐ 16 Garry Maddox	.25	.11
☐ 17 Willie McCovey	2.00	.90
☐ 18 Steve Carlton	3.00	1.35
☐ 19 J.R. Richard	.25	.11
☐ 20 Paul Molitor	8.00	3.60
☐ 21 Dave Parker	.75	.35
☐ 22 Pete Rose	6.00	2.70
☐ 23 Vida Blue	.50	.23
☐ 24 Richie Zisk	.25	.11
☐ 25 Darrell Porter	.25	.11
☐ 26 Dan Driessen	.25	.11
☐ 27 Geoff Zahn	.25	.11
☐ 28 Phil Niekro	2.00	.90
☐ 29 Tom Seaver	4.00	1.80
☐ 30 Fred Lynn	.50	.23
☐ 31 Bill Bonham	.25	.11
☐ 32 George Foster	.50	.23
☐ 33 Terry Puhl	.25	.11
☐ 34 John Candelaria	.25	.11
☐ 35 Bob Knepper	.25	.11
☐ 36 Fred Patek	.25	.11
☐ 37 Chris Chambliss	.25	.11
☐ 38 Bob Forsch	.25	.11
☐ 39 Ken Griffey	.50	.23
☐ 40 Jack Clark	.50	.23
☐ 41 Dwight Evans	.50	.23
☐ 42 Lee Mazzilli	.25	.11
☐ 43 Mario Guerrero	.25	.11
☐ 44 Larry Bowa	.50	.23
☐ 45 Carl Yastrzemski	4.00	1.80
☐ 46 Reggie Jackson	4.00	1.80
☐ 47 Rick Reuschel	.25	.11
☐ 48 Mike Flanagan	.25	.11
☐ 49 Gaylord Perry	2.00	.90
☐ 50 George Brett	10.00	4.50
☐ 51 Craig Reynolds	.25	.11
☐ 52 Dave Lopes	.50	.23
☐ 53 Bill Almon	.25	.11
☐ 54 Roy Howell	.25	.11
☐ 55 Frank Tanana	.25	.11
☐ 56 Doug Rau	.25	.11
☐ 57 Rick Monday	.25	.11
☐ 58 Jon Matlack	.25	.11
☐ 59 Ron Jackson	.25	.11
☐ 60 Jim Sundberg	.25	.11

1980 Kellogg's

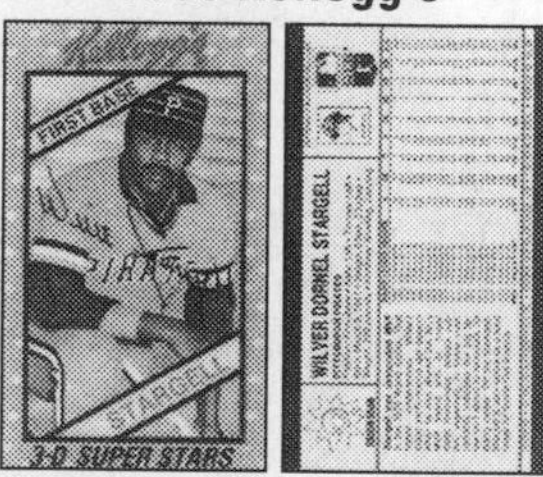

he cards in this 60-card set measure approximately 1 /8" by 3 1/4". The 1980 Kellogg's 3-D set is quite similar o, but smaller (narrower) than, the other recent Kellogg's ssues. Sets could be obtained card by card from cereal oxes or as a set from a box-top offer from the company. ards still found with the wrapper intact are valued 25 ercent greater than the values listed below.

	NRMT	VG-E
OMPLETE SET (60)	25.00	11.00
OMMON CARD (1-60)	.25	.11
☐ 1 Ross Grimsley	.25	.11
☐ 2 Mike Schmidt	5.00	2.20
☐ 3 Mike Flanagan	.25	.11
☐ 4 Ron Guidry	.50	.23
☐ 5 Bert Blyleven	.50	.23
☐ 6 Dave Kingman	.50	.23
☐ 7 Jeff Newman	.25	.11
☐ 8 Steve Rogers	.25	.11
☐ 9 George Brett	10.00	4.50
☐ 10 Bruce Sutter	.50	.23
☐ 11 Gorman Thomas	.25	.11
☐ 12 Darrell Porter	.25	.11
☐ 13 Roy Smalley	.25	.11
☐ 14 Steve Carlton	3.00	1.35
☐ 15 Jim Palmer	3.00	1.35
☐ 16 Bob Bailor	.25	.11
☐ 17 Jason Thompson	.25	.11
☐ 18 Graig Nettles	.50	.23
☐ 19 Ron Cey	.50	.23
☐ 20 Nolan Ryan	10.00	4.50
☐ 21 Ellis Valentine	.25	.11
☐ 22 Larry Hisle	.25	.11
☐ 23 Dave Parker	.75	.35
☐ 24 Eddie Murray	6.00	2.70
☐ 25 Willie Stargell	2.00	.90
☐ 26 Reggie Jackson	4.00	1.80
☐ 27 Carl Yastrzemski	3.00	1.35
☐ 28 Andre Thornton	.25	.11
☐ 29 Dave Lopes	.50	.23
☐ 30 Ken Singleton	.25	.11
☐ 31 Steve Garvey	1.50	.70
☐ 32 Dave Winfield	2.00	.90
☐ 33 Steve Kemp	.25	.11
☐ 34 Claudell Washington	.25	.11
☐ 35 Pete Rose	5.00	2.20
☐ 36 Cesar Cedeno	.25	.11
☐ 37 John Stearns	.25	.11
☐ 38 Lee Mazzilli	.50	.23
☐ 39 Larry Bowa	.50	.23
☐ 40 Fred Lynn	.50	.23
☐ 41 Carlton Fisk	3.00	1.35
☐ 42 Vida Blue	.50	.23
☐ 43 Keith Hernandez	.50	.23
☐ 44 Jim Rice	1.25	.55
☐ 45 Ted Simmons	.50	.23
☐ 46 Chet Lemon	.25	.11
☐ 47 Ferguson Jenkins	2.00	.90
☐ 48 Gary Matthews	.50	.23
☐ 49 Tom Seaver	4.00	1.80
☐ 50 George Foster	.50	.23
☐ 51 Phil Niekro	2.00	.90
☐ 52 Johnny Bench	3.00	1.35
☐ 53 Buddy Bell	.50	.23
☐ 54 Lance Parrish	.50	.23
☐ 55 Joaquin Andujar	.25	.11
☐ 56 Don Baylor	.75	.35
☐ 57 Jack Clark	.50	.23
☐ 58 J.R. Richard	.50	.23
☐ 59 Bruce Bochte	.25	.11
☐ 60 Rod Carew	3.00	1.35

1981 Kellogg's

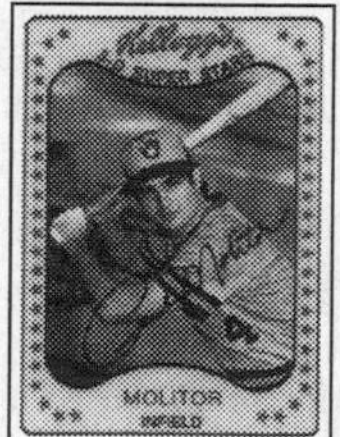

The cards in this 66-card set measure 2 1/2" by 3 1/2". The 1981 Kellogg's set witnessed an increase in both the size of the card and the size of the set. For the first time, cards were not packed in cereal packages but available only by mail-in procedure. The offer for the card set was advertised on boxes of Kellogg's Corn Flakes. The cards were printed on a different stock than in previous years, presumably to prevent the cracking problem which has plagued all Kellogg's 3-D issues. At the end of the promotion, the remainder of the sets not distributed (to cereal-eaters), were "sold" into the organized hobby, thus creating a situation where the set is relatively plentiful compared to other years of Kellogg's. Cards from this set may be found without the laminated finish that creates the 3D effect.

	NRMT	VG-E
COMPLETE SET (66)	12.00	5.50
COMMON CARD (1-66)	.10	.05
☐ 1 George Foster	.20	.09
☐ 2 Jim Palmer	1.00	.45
☐ 3 Reggie Jackson	1.50	.70
☐ 4 Al Oliver	.20	.09
☐ 5 Mike Schmidt	2.00	.90
☐ 6 Nolan Ryan	4.00	1.80
☐ 7 Bucky Dent	.20	.09
☐ 8 George Brett	3.00	1.35
☐ 9 Jim Rice	.20	.09
☐ 10 Steve Garvey	.50	.23
☐ 11 Willie Stargell	.75	.35
☐ 12 Phil Niekro	.75	.35
☐ 13 Dave Parker	.20	.09
☐ 14 Cesar Cedeno	.10	.05
☐ 15 Don Baylor	.20	.09
☐ 16 J.R. Richard	.10	.05
☐ 17 Tony Perez	.50	.23
☐ 18 Eddie Murray	1.50	.70
☐ 19 Chet Lemon	.10	.05
☐ 20 Ben Oglivie	.10	.05
☐ 21 Dave Winfield	1.50	.70
☐ 22 Joe Morgan	.75	.35
☐ 23 Vida Blue	.20	.09
☐ 24 Willie Wilson	.10	.05
☐ 25 Steve Henderson	.10	.05
☐ 26 Rod Carew	1.00	.45
☐ 27 Garry Templeton	.10	.05
☐ 28 Dave Concepcion	.20	.09
☐ 29 Dave Lopes	.20	.09
☐ 30 Ken Landreaux	.10	.05
☐ 31 Keith Hernandez	.35	.16
☐ 32 Cecil Cooper	.20	.09
☐ 33 Rickey Henderson	2.00	.90
☐ 34 Frank White	.20	.09
☐ 35 George Hendrick	.10	.05
☐ 36 Reggie Smith	.20	.09
☐ 37 Tug McGraw	.20	.09
☐ 38 Tom Seaver	1.50	.70
☐ 39 Ken Singleton	.20	.09
☐ 40 Fred Lynn	.20	.09
☐ 41 Rich Gossage	.35	.16
☐ 42 Terry Puhl	.10	.05
☐ 43 Larry Bowa	.20	.09
☐ 44 Phil Garner	.20	.09
☐ 45 Ron Guidry	.20	.09
☐ 46 Lee Mazzilli	.10	.05
☐ 47 Dave Kingman	.35	.16
☐ 48 Carl Yastrzemski	1.00	.45
☐ 49 Rick Burleson	.10	.05
☐ 50 Steve Carlton	1.00	.45
☐ 51 Alan Trammell	.75	.35
☐ 52 Tommy John	.35	.16
☐ 53 Paul Molitor	2.00	.90
☐ 54 Joe Charboneau	.35	.16
☐ 55 Rick Langford	.10	.05
☐ 56 Bruce Sutter	.20	.09
☐ 57 Robin Yount	1.25	.55
☐ 58 Steve Stone	.10	.05
☐ 59 Larry Gura	.10	.05
☐ 60 Mike Flanagan	.10	.05
☐ 61 Bob Horner	.10	.05
☐ 62 Bruce Bochte	.10	.05
☐ 63 Pete Rose	1.50	.70
☐ 64 Buddy Bell	.20	.09
☐ 65 Johnny Bench	1.50	.70
☐ 66 Mike Hargrove	.20	.09

1982 Kellogg's

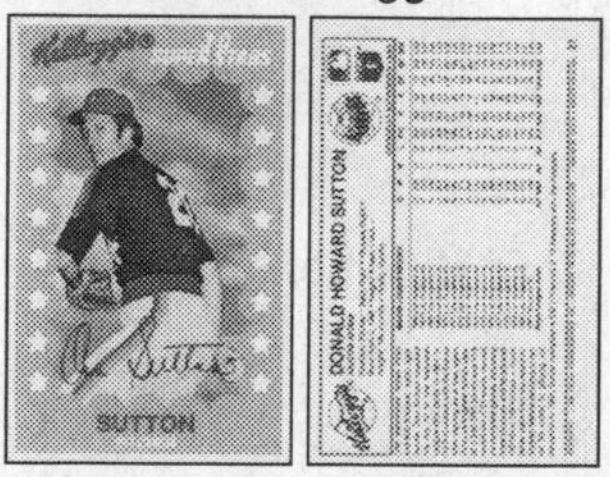

The cards in this 64-card set measure 2 1/8" by 3 1/4". The 1982 version of 3-D cards prepared for the Kellogg Company by Visual Panographics, Inc., is not only smaller in physical dimensions from the 1981 series (which was standard card size at 2 1/2" by 3 1/2") but is also two cards shorter in length (64 in '82 and 66 in '81). In addition, while retaining the policy of not inserting single cards into cereal packages and offering the sets through box-top mail-ins only, the Kellogg Company accepted box tops from four types of cereals, as opposed to only one type the previous year. Each card features a color 3-D ballplayer picture with a vertical line of white stars on each side set upon a blue background. The player's name and the word Kellogg's are printed in red on the obverse, and the card number is found on the bottom right of the reverse. Every card in the set has a statistical procedural error that was never corrected. All seasonal averages were added up and then divided by the number of seasons played.

	NRMT	VG-E
COMPLETE SET (64)	15.00	6.75
COMMON CARD (1-64)	.10	.05
☐ 1 Richie Zisk	.10	.05
☐ 2 Bill Buckner	.20	.09
☐ 3 George Brett	4.00	1.80
☐ 4 Rickey Henderson	2.00	.90
☐ 5 Jack Morris	.35	.16
☐ 6 Ozzie Smith	2.50	1.10
☐ 7 Rollie Fingers	.50	.23
☐ 8 Tom Seaver	1.50	.70
☐ 9 Fernando Valuenzuela	.50	.23
☐ 10 Hubie Brooks	.10	.05

☐ 11 Nolan Ryan	4.00	1.80
☐ 12 Dave Winfield	1.25	.55
☐ 13 Bob Horner	.20	.09
☐ 14 Reggie Jackson	1.50	.70
☐ 15 Burt Hooton	.10	.05
☐ 16 Mike Schmidt	2.00	.90
☐ 17 Bruce Sutter	.20	.09
☐ 18 Pete Rose	2.00	.90
☐ 19 Dave Kingman	.20	.09
☐ 20 Neil Allen	.10	.05
☐ 21 Don Sutton	.60	.25
☐ 22 Dave Concepcion	.20	.09
☐ 23 Keith Hernandez	.35	.16
☐ 24 Gary Carter	.50	.23
☐ 25 Carlton Fisk	1.50	.70
☐ 26 Ron Guidry	.20	.09
☐ 27 Steve Carlton	1.00	.45
☐ 28 Robin Yount	1.50	.70
☐ 29 John Castino	.10	.05
☐ 30 Johnny Bench	1.00	.45
☐ 31 Bob Knepper	.10	.05
☐ 32 Rich Gossage	.20	.09
☐ 33 Buddy Bell	.20	.09
☐ 34 Art Howe	.20	.09
☐ 35 Tony Armas	.10	.05
☐ 36 Phil Niekro	.60	.25
☐ 37 Len Barker	.10	.05
☐ 38 Bob Grich	.20	.09
☐ 39 Steve Kemp	.10	.05
☐ 40 Kirk Gibson	.50	.23
☐ 41 Carney Lansford	.10	.05
☐ 42 Jim Palmer	1.00	.45
☐ 43 Carl Yastrzemski	.75	.35
☐ 44 Rick Burleson	.10	.05
☐ 45 Dwight Evans	.20	.09
☐ 46 Ron Cey	.20	.09
☐ 47 Steve Garvey	.50	.23
☐ 48 Dave Parker	.35	.16
☐ 49 Mike Easler	.10	.05
☐ 50 Dusty Baker	.20	.09
☐ 51 Rod Carew	.75	.35
☐ 52 Chris Chambliss	.20	.09
☐ 53 Tim Raines	.50	.23
☐ 54 Chet Lemon	.10	.05
☐ 55 Bill Madlock	.20	.09
☐ 56 George Foster	.20	.09
☐ 57 Dwayne Murphy	.10	.05
☐ 58 Ken Singleton	.10	.05
☐ 59 Mike Norris	.10	.05
☐ 60 Cecil Cooper	.20	.09
☐ 61 Al Oliver	.35	.16
☐ 62 Willie Wilson	.10	.05
☐ 63 Vida Blue	.20	.09
☐ 64 Eddie Murray	1.50	.70

1983 Kellogg's

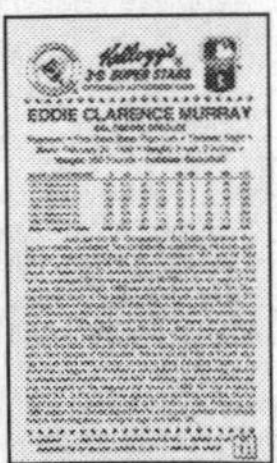

The cards in this 60-card set measure approximately 1 7/8" by 3 1/4". For the 14th year in a row, the Kellogg Company issued a card set of Major League players. The set of 3-D cards contains the photo, player's autograph, Kellogg's logo, and name and position of the player on the front of the card. The backs feature the player's team logo, career statistics, player biography, and a narrative on the player's career. Every card in the set has a statistical procedural error that was never corrected. All seasonal averages were added up and then divided by the number of seasons played.

	NRMT	VG-E
COMPLETE SET (60)	15.00	6.75
COMMON CARD (1-60)	.10	.05

☐ 1 Rod Carew	1.00	.45
☐ 2 Rollie Fingers	.50	.23
☐ 3 Reggie Jackson	1.50	.70
☐ 4 George Brett	3.00	1.35
☐ 5 Hal McRae	.20	.09
☐ 6 Pete Rose	1.50	.70
☐ 7 Fernando Valenzuela	.35	.16
☐ 8 Rickey Henderson	1.50	.70
☐ 9 Carl Yastrzemski	1.00	.45
☐ 10 Rich Gossage	.20	.09
☐ 11 Eddie Murray	1.25	.55
☐ 12 Buddy Bell	.20	.09
☐ 13 Jim Rice	.35	.16
☐ 14 Robin Yount	1.50	.70
☐ 15 Dave Winfield	1.00	.45
☐ 16 Harold Baines	.35	.16
☐ 17 Garry Templeton	.10	.05
☐ 18 Bill Madlock	.20	.09
☐ 19 Pete Vuckovich	.10	.05
☐ 20 Pedro Guerrero	.20	.09
☐ 21 Ozzie Smith	2.00	.90
☐ 22 George Foster	.20	.09
☐ 23 Willie Wilson	.10	.05
☐ 24 Johnny Ray	.10	.05
☐ 25 George Hendrick	.10	.05
☐ 26 Andre Thornton	.10	.05
☐ 27 Leon Durham	.10	.05
☐ 28 Cecil Cooper	.20	.09
☐ 29 Don Baylor	.20	.09
☐ 30 Lonnie Smith	.10	.05
☐ 31 Nolan Ryan	4.00	1.80
☐ 32 Dan Quisenberry UER Name spelled Quiesenberry on front	.20	.09
☐ 33 Len Barker	.10	.05
☐ 34 Neil Allen	.10	.05
☐ 35 Jack Morris	.20	.09
☐ 36 Dave Stieb	.10	.05
☐ 37 Bruce Sutter	.20	.09
☐ 38 Jim Sundberg	.10	.05
☐ 39 Jim Palmer	1.00	.45
☐ 40 Lance Parrish	.20	.09
☐ 41 Floyd Bannister	.10	.05
☐ 42 Larry Gura	.10	.05
☐ 43 Britt Burns	.10	.05
☐ 44 Toby Harrah	.10	.05
☐ 45 Steve Carlton	1.00	.45
☐ 46 Greg Minton	.10	.05
☐ 47 Gorman Thomas	.10	.05
☐ 48 Jack Clark	.20	.09
☐ 49 Keith Hernandez	.20	.09
☐ 50 Greg Luzinski	.20	.09
☐ 51 Fred Lynn	.20	.09
☐ 52 Dale Murphy	.50	.23
☐ 53 Kent Hrbek	.20	.09
☐ 54 Bob Horner	.10	.05
☐ 55 Gary Carter	.60	.25
☐ 56 Carlton Fisk	1.00	.45
☐ 57 Dave Concepcion	.20	.09
☐ 58 Mike Schmidt	2.00	.90
☐ 59 Bill Buckner	.20	.09
☐ 60 Bob Grich	.20	.09

1991 Kellogg's 3D

Sportflics/Optigraphics produced this 15-card set for Kellogg's, and the cards measure approximately 2 1/2" by 3 5/16". The fronts have a three-dimensional image that alternates between a posed or action color shot and a head and shoulders close-up. The card face is aqua blue, with white stripes (that turn pink) and white borders. In red and dark blue print, the horizontally oriented backs have a facial drawing of the player on the left half, and career summary on the right half. The cards are numbered on the back. The cards were inserted in specially marked boxes (18 oz. and 24 oz. only) of Kellogg's Corn Flakes. In addition, the complete set and a blue display rack were available through a mail-in offer for 4.95 and two UPC symbols.

	MINT	NRMT
COMPLETE SET (15)	8.00	3.60
COMMON CARD (1-15)	.50	.23

☐ 1 Gaylord Perry	.75	.35
☐ 2 Hank Aaron	1.50	.70
☐ 3 Willie Mays	1.50	.70
☐ 4 Ernie Banks	1.25	.55
☐ 5 Bob Gibson	.75	.35
☐ 6 Harmon Killebrew	.75	.35
☐ 7 Rollie Fingers	.75	.35
☐ 8 Steve Carlton	1.00	.45
☐ 9 Billy Williams	.75	.35
☐ 10 Lou Brock	1.00	.45
☐ 11 Yogi Berra	1.25	.55
☐ 12 Warren Spahn	1.00	.45
☐ 13 Boog Powell	.50	.23
☐ 14 Don Baylor	.50	.23
☐ 15 Ralph Kiner	.75	.35

1992 Kellogg's All-Stars

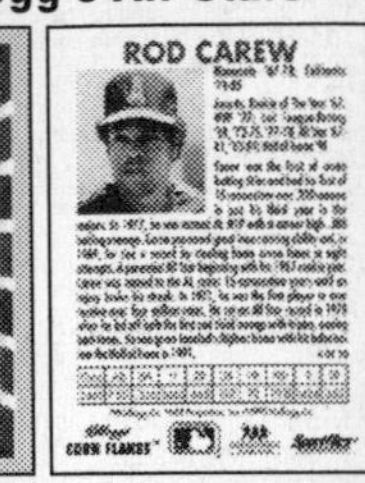

This ten-card standard-size set was produced by Optigraphics Corp. (Grand Prairie, TX) for Kellogg's and features retired baseball stars. One card was protected by a cello pack and inserted into Kellogg's cereal boxes. In the U.S., the cards were inserted in boxes of Corn Flakes, while in Canada they were inserted in Frosted Flakes and some other cereals. The complete set and a baseball display board to hold the collection were available through a mail-in offer for 4.75 and two UPC symbols from the side panel of Corn Flakes boxes (in Canada, for 7.99 and three tokens; one token was found on the side panel of each cereal box). The front of the "Double Action" cards have a three-dimensional image that alternates between two action shots and gives the impression of a batter or pitcher in motion. The pictures are bordered in red, white, and blue. The backs carry a black and white close-up photo, summary of the player's career (teams and years he played for them), awards, and career highlights. The Canadian Frosted Flakes cards are valued at two times the values listed below. The box back pictures both images of the Seaver card. While these pictures resemble the actual card, they are not standard-size or even rectangulary shaped.

	MINT	NRMT
COMPLETE SET (10)	5.00	2.20
COMMON CARD (1-10)	.25	.11

☐ 1 Willie Stargell	.75	.35
☐ 2 Tony Perez	.50	.23
☐ 3 Jim Palmer	1.00	.45
☐ 4 Rod Carew	1.00	.45
☐ 5 Tom Seaver	1.50	.70
☐ 6 Phil Niekro	.75	.35
☐ 7 Bill Madlock	.25	.11
☐ 8 Jim Rice	.50	.23
☐ 9 Dan Quisenberry	.25	.11
☐ 10 Mike Schmidt	2.00	.90

1988 King-B Discs

In 1988 King-B Quality Meat Products (Beef Jerky) introduced a set of 24 discs produced in conjunction with the Major League Baseball Players Association and Mike Schechter Associates. A single disc was inserted inside each specially marked package. The discs are numbered on the back and have a medium blue border on the front. Discs are approximately 2 3/8" in diameter. The disc backs contain very sparse personal or statistical information about the player and are printed in blue on white stock.

	MINT	NRMT
COMPLETE SET (24)	50.00	22.00
COMMON DISC (1-24)	1.00	.45

☐ 1 Mike Schmidt	3.00	1.35
☐ 2 Dale Murphy	2.00	.90
☐ 3 Kirby Puckett	10.00	4.50
☐ 4 Ozzie Smith	5.00	2.20
☐ 5 Tony Gwynn	8.00	3.60

☐ 6 Mark McGwire	10.00	4.50
☐ 7 George Brett	8.00	3.60
☐ 8 Darryl Strawberry	1.50	.70
☐ 9 Wally Joyner	2.00	.90
☐ 10 Cory Snyder	1.00	.45
☐ 11 Barry Bonds	10.00	4.50
☐ 12 Darrell Evans	1.00	.45
☐ 13 Mike Scott	1.00	.45
☐ 14 Andre Dawson	2.50	1.10
☐ 15 Don Mattingly	10.00	4.50
☐ 16 Candy Maldonado	1.00	.45
☐ 17 Alvin Davis	1.00	.45
☐ 18 Carlton Fisk	3.00	1.35
☐ 19 Fernando Valenzuela	1.50	.70
☐ 20 Roger Clemens	6.00	2.70
☐ 21 Larry Parrish	1.00	.45
☐ 22 Eric Davis	1.50	.70
☐ 23 Paul Molitor	4.00	1.80
☐ 24 Cal Ripken	12.00	5.50

1989 King-B Discs

he 1989 King-B Disc set contains 24 discs, each neasuring approximately 2 3/4" in diameter. The set was repared by MSA; there are no team logos featured on the isc. The year and lifetime statistics are featured for each layer on the back of the disc. The discs were issued one er small cannister of Beef Jerky. It has been estimated hat five million discs were produced for this set.

	MINT	NRMT
OMPLETE SET (24)	16.00	7.25
OMMON DISC (1-24)	.25	.11
☐ 1 Kirk Gibson	.75	.35
☐ 2 Eddie Murray	2.00	.90
☐ 3 Wade Boggs	1.25	.55
☐ 4 Mark McGwire	5.00	2.20
☐ 5 Ryne Sandberg	2.50	1.10
☐ 6 Ozzie Guillen	.25	.11
☐ 7 Chris Sabo	.25	.11
☐ 8 Joe Carter	.75	.35
☐ 9 Alan Trammell	.75	.35
☐ 10 Nolan Ryan	6.00	2.70
☐ 11 Bo Jackson	.50	.23
☐ 12 Orel Hershiser	.50	.23
☐ 13 Robin Yount	1.00	.45
☐ 14 Frank Viola	.25	.11
☐ 15 Darryl Strawberry	.50	.23
☐ 16 Dave Winfield	1.25	.55
☐ 17 Jose Canseco	1.50	.70
☐ 18 Von Hayes	.25	.11
☐ 19 Andy Van Slyke	.50	.23
☐ 20 Pedro Guerrero	.25	.11
☐ 21 Tony Gwynn	4.00	1.80
☐ 22 Will Clark	1.50	.70
☐ 23 Danny Jackson	.25	.11
☐ 24 Pete Incaviglia	.25	.11

1990 King-B Discs

he 1990 King-B Disc set contains 24 discs, each neasuring approximately 2 3/4" inches in diameter. The et was prepared by MSA; there are no team logos eatured on the disc. The year and lifetime statistics are eatured for each player on the back of the disc. The discs were issued one per small cannister of Beef Jerky. The ont design features a color head and shoulders player hoto, encircled by a white-and-red inner border and a lue outer border. A banner with the words "1990 King-B" superimposed at the bottom of the picture. In green rint on blue, the back presents biography and statistics.

	MINT	NRMT
OMPLETE SET (24)	20.00	9.00
OMMON DISC (1-24)	.25	.11
☐ 1 Mike Scott	.25	.11
☐ 2 Kevin Mitchell	.25	.11
☐ 3 Tony Gwynn	5.00	2.20
☐ 4 Ozzie Smith	3.00	1.35
☐ 5 Kirk Gibson	.50	.23
☐ 6 Tim Raines	.25	.11
☐ 7 Von Hayes	.25	.11
☐ 8 Bobby Bonilla	.50	.23
☐ 9 Wade Boggs	1.50	.70
☐ 10 Chris Sabo	.25	.11
☐ 11 Dale Murphy	.75	.35
☐ 12 Cory Snyder	.25	.11
☐ 13 Fred McGriff	1.50	.70
☐ 14 Don Mattingly	4.00	1.80
☐ 15 Jerome Walton	.25	.11
☐ 16 Ken Griffey Jr.	10.00	4.50
☐ 17 Bo Jackson	.50	.23
☐ 18 Robin Yount	1.00	.45
☐ 19 Rickey Henderson	1.50	.70
☐ 20 Jim Abbott	.25	.11
☐ 21 Kirby Puckett	4.00	1.80
☐ 22 Nolan Ryan	8.00	3.60
☐ 23 Gregg Olson	.25	.11
☐ 24 Lou Whitaker	.50	.23

1991 King-B Discs

This was the fourth season that MSA issued discs as inserts in King-B meat products. These discs, which measure approximately 2 3/4" in diameter, feature leading major leaguers.

	MINT	NRMT
COMPLETE SET (24)	20.00	9.00
COMMON DISC (1-24)	.25	.11
☐ 1 Willie McGee	.50	.23
☐ 2 Kevin Seitzer	.25	.11
☐ 3 Kevin Maas	.25	.11
☐ 4 Ben McDonald	.25	.11
☐ 5 Rickey Henderson	1.50	.70
☐ 6 Ken Griffey Jr.	10.00	4.50
☐ 7 John Olerud	.50	.23
☐ 8 Dwight Gooden	.50	.23
☐ 9 Ruben Sierra	.25	.11
☐ 10 Luis Polonia	.25	.11
☐ 11 Wade Boggs	1.50	.70
☐ 12 Ramon Martinez	.75	.35
☐ 13 Craig Biggio	1.25	.55
☐ 14 Cecil Fielder	.50	.23
☐ 15 Will Clark	1.50	.70
☐ 16 Matt Williams	1.00	.45
☐ 17 Sandy Alomar Jr.	.50	.23
☐ 18 Dave Justice	1.25	.55
☐ 19 Ryne Sandberg	3.00	1.35
☐ 20 Benito Santiago	.25	.11
☐ 21 Barry Bonds	2.00	.90
☐ 22 Carlton Fisk	1.50	.70
☐ 23 Kirby Puckett	4.00	1.80
☐ 24 Jose Rijo	.25	.11

1992 King-B Discs

These discs, which measure approximately 2 3/4" in diameter, feature top major league stars. These discs, inserted in beef jerky containers, were issued in conjunction with Michael Schecter Associates.

	MINT	NRMT
COMPLETE SET (24)	12.00	5.50
COMMON DISC (1-24)	.15	.07
☐ 1 Terry Pendleton	.25	.11
☐ 2 Chris Sabo	.15	.07
☐ 3 Frank Thomas	3.00	1.35
☐ 4 Todd Zeile	.15	.07
☐ 5 Bobby Bonilla	.25	.11
☐ 6 Howard Johnson	.15	.07
☐ 7 Nolan Ryan	3.00	1.35
☐ 8 Ken Griffey Jr.	4.00	1.80
☐ 9 Roger Clemens	1.50	.70
☐ 10 Tony Gwynn	3.00	1.35
☐ 11 Steve Avery	.15	.07
☐ 12 Cal Ripken	3.00	1.35
☐ 13 Danny Tartabull	.15	.07
☐ 14 Paul Molitor	.75	.35
☐ 15 Willie McGee	.25	.11
☐ 16 Wade Boggs	.75	.35
☐ 17 Cecil Fielder	.25	.11
☐ 18 Jack Morris	.25	.11
☐ 19 Ryne Sandberg	1.25	.55
☐ 20 Kirby Puckett	1.50	.70
☐ 21 Craig Biggio	.50	.23
☐ 22 Harold Baines	.25	.11
☐ 23 Scott Erickson	.15	.07
☐ 24 Joe Carter	.25	.11

1993 King-B Discs

These discs marked the sixth consecutive season that Michael Schecter Associates in conjunction with King-B meat products produced a 24 disc set. This set measure approximately 2 3/4" in diameter and features major league stars.

	MINT	NRMT
COMPLETE SET (24)	5.00	2.20
COMMON DISC (1-24)	.10	.05
☐ 1 Barry Bonds	.60	.25
☐ 2 Ken Griffey Jr.	2.50	1.10
☐ 3 Cal Ripken	2.00	.90
☐ 4 Frank Thomas	2.00	.90
☐ 5 Steve Avery	.10	.05
☐ 6 Benito Santiago	.10	.05
☐ 7 Luis Polonia	.10	.05
☐ 8 Jose Rijo	.10	.05
☐ 9 George Brett	1.00	.45
☐ 10 Darren Daulton	.20	.09
☐ 11 Cecil Fielder	.20	.09
☐ 12 Ozzie Smith	.75	.35
☐ 13 Joe Carter	.20	.09
☐ 14 Dwight Gooden	.20	.09
☐ 15 Tom Henke	.10	.05
☐ 16 Brett Butler	.20	.09
☐ 17 Nolan Ryan	1.50	.70
☐ 18 Sandy Alomar	.20	.09
☐ 19 Tom Glavine	.20	.09
☐ 20 Rafael Palmeiro	.35	.16
☐ 21 Roger Clemens	.75	.35
☐ 22 Ryne Sandberg	.75	.35
☐ 23 Doug Drabek	.10	.05
☐ 24 Chuck Knoblauch	.50	.23

1994 King-B Discs

The 1994 King-B set contains 24 round cards each measuring approximately 2 7/8" in diameter. On a white background, the fronts feature a color player portrait inside a dark purple circle that has the appearance of a disc. The player's name is printed in yellow and his team in white. All appear above the photo, while the year 1994 and the words "King B", printed on a pitcher's glove, appear under the photo. The backs present biography and statistics in purple print on white. The discs are numbered on the back.

	MINT	NRMT
COMPLETE SET (24)	5.00	2.20
COMMON DISC (1-24)	.10	.05

	MINT	NRMT
☐ 1 Fred McGriff	.35	.16
☐ 2 Paul Molitor	.50	.23
☐ 3 Jack McDowell	.10	.05
☐ 4 Darren Daulton	.20	.09
☐ 5 Wade Boggs	.50	.23
☐ 6 Ken Griffey Jr.	1.25	.55
☐ 7 Tim Salmon	.50	.23
☐ 8 Dennis Eckersley	.35	.16
☐ 9 Albert Belle	.50	.23
☐ 10 Travis Fryman	.20	.09
☐ 11 Chris Hoiles	.10	.05
☐ 12 Kirby Puckett	.60	.25
☐ 13 John Olerud	.20	.09
☐ 14 Frank Thomas	1.00	.45
☐ 15 Lenny Dykstra	.20	.09
☐ 16 Andres Galarraga	.50	.23
☐ 17 Barry Larkin	.35	.16
☐ 18 Greg Maddux	.75	.35
☐ 19 Mike Piazza	.75	.35
☐ 20 Roberto Alomar	.50	.23
☐ 21 Robin Ventura	.20	.09
☐ 22 Ryne Sandberg	.60	.25
☐ 23 Andy Van Slyke	.10	.05
☐ 24 Barry Bonds	.60	.25

1995 King-B Discs

This was the eighth year that King-B, in conjunction with MSA enterprises, issued discs. The players featured are among the best in baseball. The backs have season and career stats as well as vital statistics.

	MINT	NRMT
COMPLETE SET (24)	20.00	9.00
COMMON DISC (1-24)	.15	.07
☐ 1 Roberto Alomar	.60	.25
☐ 2 Jeff Bagwell	1.50	.70
☐ 3 Wade Boggs	.60	.25
☐ 4 Barry Bonds	.75	.35
☐ 5 Joe Carter	.25	.11
☐ 6 Mariano Duncan	.15	.07
☐ 7 Len Dykstra	.25	.11
☐ 8 Andres Galarraga	.60	.25
☐ 9 Matt Williams	.40	.18
☐ 10 Raul Mondesi	.60	.25
☐ 11 Ken Griffey Jr.	5.00	2.20
☐ 12 Gregg Jefferies	.15	.07
☐ 13 Fred McGriff	.40	.18
☐ 14 Paul Molitor	.60	.25
☐ 15 Dave Justice	.60	.25
☐ 16 Mike Piazza	3.00	1.35
☐ 17 Kirby Puckett	2.00	.90
☐ 18 Cal Ripken	4.00	1.80
☐ 19 Ivan Rodriguez	1.25	.55
☐ 20 Ozzie Smith	1.00	.45
☐ 21 Gary Sheffield	.60	.25
☐ 22 Frank Thomas	4.00	1.80
☐ 23 Greg Maddux	3.00	1.35
☐ 24 Jimmy Key	.15	.07

1996 King-B Discs

The 1996 King-B set consists of 24 round cards measuring approximately 2 7/8" in diameter. The fronts feature a color player photo with airbrushed uniforms. The year 1996 is on the left side, while the player's name and 9th annual Collectors edition appears on the bottom. The back has vital statistics, season and career statistics.

	MINT	NRMT
COMPLETE SET (24)	20.00	9.00
COMMON DISC (1-24)	.15	.07
☐ 1 Roger Clemens	1.50	.70
☐ 2 Mo Vaughn	.75	.35
☐ 3 Dante Bichette	.40	.18
☐ 4 Jeff Bagwell	2.00	.90
☐ 5 Randy Johnson	.75	.35
☐ 6 Ken Griffey Jr.	5.00	2.20
☐ 7 Kirby Puckett	1.50	.70
☐ 8 Orel Hershiser	.25	.11
☐ 9 Albert Belle	1.25	.55
☐ 10 Tony Gwynn	1.50	.70
☐ 11 Tom Glavine	.40	.18
☐ 12 Jim Abbott	.15	.07
☐ 13 Andres Galarraga	.60	.25
☐ 14 Frank Thomas	4.00	1.80
☐ 15 Barry Larkin	.40	.18
☐ 16 Mike Piazza	3.00	1.35
☐ 17 Matt Williams	.40	.18
☐ 18 Greg Maddux	3.00	1.35
☐ 19 Hideo Nomo	2.50	1.10
☐ 20 Roberto Alomar	.60	.25
☐ 21 Ivan Rodriguez	1.25	.55
☐ 22 Cal Ripken	4.00	1.80
☐ 23 Barry Bonds	.75	.35
☐ 24 Mark McGwire	2.00	.90

1997 King-B Discs

This 28-card set of rounded cards measures approximately 2 5/16" in diameter. The fronts feature color action player images on a black-and-gold marblized background. The backs carry player information and career statistics on a black-and-white player photo background. This set marks the 10th Anniversary of the King-B Discs.

	MINT	NRMT
COMPLETE SET (28)	25.00	11.00
COMMON CARD (1-28)	.25	.11
☐ 1 Brady Anderson	.75	.35
☐ 2 Barry Bonds	1.50	.70
☐ 3 Travis Fryman	.50	.23
☐ 4 Rey Ordonez	.25	.11
☐ 5 Kenny Lofton	1.25	.55
☐ 6 Mark McGwire	2.50	1.10
☐ 7 Jeff Bagwell	2.50	1.10
☐ 8 Roger Clemens	2.50	1.10
☐ 9 Juan Gonzalez	3.00	1.35
☐ 10 Mike Piazza	4.00	1.80
☐ 11 Tim Salmon	1.00	.45
☐ 12 Jeff Montgomery	.50	.23
☐ 13 Joe Carter	.50	.23
☐ 14 David Cone	.50	.23
☐ 15 Frank Thomas	5.00	2.20
☐ 16 Mickey Morandini	.25	.11
☐ 17 Ray Lankford	.50	.23
☐ 18 Pedro Martinez	1.00	.45
☐ 19 Tom Glavine	.50	.23
☐ 20 Chuck Knoblauch	1.00	.45
☐ 21 Dan Wilson	.25	.11
☐ 22 Gary Sheffield	1.00	.45
☐ 23 Dante Bichette	.50	.23
☐ 24 Al Martin	.25	.11
☐ 25 Barry Larkin	.75	.35
☐ 26 Ryne Sandberg	1.00	.45
☐ 27 Steve Finley	.50	.23
☐ 28 Matt Mieske	.25	.11

1987 Kraft Foods

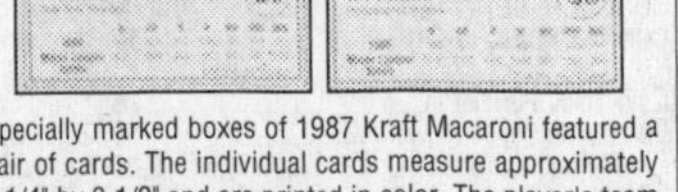

Specially marked boxes of 1987 Kraft Macaroni featured a pair of cards. The individual cards measure approximately 2 1/4" by 3 1/2" and are printed in color. The player's team insignia are airbrushed out as the set was only licensed by the Major League Baseball Players Association. The cards are blank backed and are numbered in the lower right corner of the card. The set is subtitled "Home Plate Heroes." The cards on the box provide a dotted blue line as a guide for accurately cutting the cards from the box. There were many different two-card panels. Panel prices are based on the sum of the individual player's values making up that particular panel.

	MINT	NRMT
COMPLETE SET (48)	30.00	13.50
COMMON CARD (1-48)	.15	.07
☐ 1 Eddie Murray	1.50	.70
☐ 2 Dale Murphy	1.00	.45
☐ 3 Cal Ripken	4.00	1.80
☐ 4 Mike Scott	.15	.07
☐ 5 Jim Rice	.25	.11
☐ 6 Jody Davis	.15	.07
☐ 7 Wade Boggs	1.25	.55
☐ 8 Ryne Sandberg	2.00	.90
☐ 9 Wally Joyner	.75	.35
☐ 10 Eric Davis	.50	.23
☐ 11 Ozzie Guillen	.15	.07
☐ 12 Tony Pena	.15	.07
☐ 13 Harold Baines	.25	.11
☐ 14 Johnny Ray	.15	.07
☐ 15 Joe Carter	.75	.35
☐ 16 Ozzie Smith	2.00	.90
☐ 17 Cory Snyder	.15	.07
☐ 18 Vince Coleman	.15	.07
☐ 19 Kirk Gibson	.25	.11
☐ 20 Steve Garvey	.50	.23
☐ 21 George Brett	3.00	1.35
☐ 22 John Tudor	.15	.07
☐ 23 Robin Yount	1.00	.45
☐ 24 Von Hayes	.15	.07
☐ 25 Kent Hrbek	.15	.07
☐ 26 Darryl Strawberry	.50	.23
☐ 27 Kirby Puckett	2.50	1.10
☐ 28 Ron Darling	.15	.07
☐ 29 Don Mattingly	2.50	1.10
☐ 30 Mike Schmidt	1.00	.45
☐ 31 Rickey Henderson	1.25	.55
☐ 32 Fernando Valenzuela	.25	.11
☐ 33 Dave Winfield	1.00	.45
☐ 34 Pete Rose	1.00	.45
☐ 35 Jose Canseco	1.25	.55
☐ 36 Glenn Davis	.15	.07
☐ 37 Alvin Davis	.15	.07
☐ 38 Steve Sax	.15	.07
☐ 39 Pete Incaviglia	.15	.07
☐ 40 Jeff Reardon	.15	.07
☐ 41 Jesse Barfield	.15	.07
☐ 42 Hubie Brooks	.15	.07
☐ 43 George Bell	.15	.07
☐ 44 Tony Gwynn	2.50	1.10
☐ 45 Roger Clemens	2.50	1.10
☐ 46 Chili Davis	.25	.11
☐ 47 Mike Witt	.15	.07
☐ 48 Nolan Ryan	4.00	1.80

1993 Kraft

The Kraft Singles Superstars '93 Collector's series consists of 30 pop-up cards. One card was inserted in each specially marked 12-oz., 16-oz., and 3-lb. Kraft Singles package until June. Boxed sets of all the cards could be purchased through a mail-in form enclosed with each card for 1.75 plus proof-of-purchase points from Kraft Singles packages. Also a collector's album could be purchased for 4.75 plus 36 proof-of-purchase points. The standard-size cards feature a color action photo of the player in a batting stance, and these pictures are bordered by either blue (1-15) on American League cards or green (16-30) on National League cards. The backs display a color photo of the player in a fielding stance, with the player's name written in black script running along the left edge. When the pop-up tab at the top is pulled, the front photo becomes three-dimensional and pastel yellow panels are revealed, presenting tips for playing baseball at the player's position as well as the player's career highlights and statistics. The cards are numbered on the front at the lower left corner following alphabetical order by league.

	MINT	NRMT
COMPLETE SET (30)	20.00	9.00
COMMON CARD (1-30)	.25	.11
☐ 1 Jim Abbott	.25	.11
☐ 2 Roberto Alomar	1.00	.45
☐ 3 Sandy Alomar	.50	.23
☐ 4 George Brett	2.00	.90
☐ 5 Roger Clemens	2.00	.90
☐ 6 Dennis Eckersley	.75	.35
☐ 7 Cecil Fielder	.50	.23
☐ 8 Ken Griffey Jr.	6.00	2.70
☐ 9 Don Mattingly	2.50	1.10
☐ 10 Mark McGwire	3.00	1.35
☐ 11 Kirby Puckett	2.50	1.10
☐ 12 Cal Ripken	5.00	2.20
☐ 13 Nolan Ryan	5.00	2.20
☐ 14 Robin Ventura	.50	.23
☐ 15 Robin Yount	.75	.35
☐ 16 Bobby Bonilla	.50	.23
☐ 17 Ken Caminiti	1.00	.45
☐ 18 Will Clark	1.00	.45
☐ 19 Darren Daulton	.50	.23
☐ 20 Doug Drabek	.25	.11
☐ 21 Delino DeShields	.25	.11
☐ 22 Tom Glavine	.50	.23
☐ 23 Tony Gwynn	3.00	1.35
☐ 24 Orel Hershiser	.50	.23
☐ 25 Barry Larkin	.75	.35
☐ 26 Terry Pendleton	.25	.11
☐ 27 Ryne Sandberg	2.00	.90
☐ 28 Gary Sheffield	1.00	.45
☐ 29 Lee Smith	.50	.23
☐ 30 Andy Van Slyke	.25	.11

1994 Kraft

The 1994 Kraft Singles Superstars set consists of 30 pop-up cards measuring approximately 2 1/2" by 3 3/8" and features "The Single Best Day" of 15 players from the American (1-15) and National (16-30) Leagues. One card was inserted in each specially marked 16-oz. and 3-lb. Kraft Singles package available in April and May. On-pack and in-store point-of-purchase mail-in offers enabled consumers to order a boxed American and/or National League 15-card set for $1.95 plus proof-of-purchase for each set. The fronts feature color action player shots bordered in blue on the AL cards and yellow on the NL cards. The player's name, position, and team appear in white lettering at one corner of the photo. The back displays another color player action shot that is perforated and cut out in such a way so that when the tab at the top is pulled, the photo becomes three-dimensional. White panels are also revealed, presenting a description of the player's "Single Best Day," career highlights, and statistics. The cards are numbered on the back at the upper right, following alphabetical order by league.

	MINT	NRMT
COMPLETE SET (30)	25.00	11.00
COMMON CARD (1-30)	.25	.11
☐ 1 Carlos Baerga	.50	.23
☐ 2 Dennis Eckersley	.75	.35
☐ 3 Cecil Fielder	.50	.23
☐ 4 Juan Gonzalez	3.00	1.35
☐ 5 Ken Griffey Jr.	6.00	2.70
☐ 6 Mark Langston	.25	.11
☐ 7 Brian McRae	.25	.11
☐ 8 Paul Molitor	1.00	.45
☐ 9 Kirby Puckett	2.50	1.10
☐ 10 Cal Ripken	5.00	2.20
☐ 11 Danny Tartabull	.25	.11
☐ 12 Frank Thomas	5.00	2.20
☐ 13 Greg Vaughn	.25	.11
☐ 14 Mo Vaughn	1.50	.70
☐ 15 Dave Winfield	.75	.35
☐ 16 Jeff Bagwell	2.50	1.10
☐ 17 Barry Bonds	1.50	.70
☐ 18 Bobby Bonilla	.50	.23
☐ 19 Delino DeShields	.25	.11
☐ 20 Lenny Dykstra	.25	.11
☐ 21 Andres Galarraga	1.00	.45
☐ 22 Tom Glavine	.50	.23
☐ 23 Mark Grace	.75	.35
☐ 24 Tony Gwynn	3.00	1.35
☐ 25 David Justice	1.00	.45
☐ 26 Barry Larkin	.75	.35
☐ 27 Mike Piazza	3.00	1.35
☐ 28 Gary Sheffield	1.00	.45
☐ 29 Ozzie Smith	2.00	.90
☐ 30 Andy Van Slyke	.25	.11

1995 Kraft

Consisting of 30 standard-size cards, the 1995 Kraft Singles Superstars Pop-up Action cards were included in specially-marked 12-ounce and 16-ounce packages of Kraft singles. One card was inserted in each package. The set could also be obtained through the mail by filling out the mail-in order form and sending in 36 Kraft Singles purchase points and $1.95 for each 15-card League set. The fronts feature full-bleed color action photos, with the player's name on a diagonal stripe cutting across the card. Against the background of a baseball, the back carries two panels, one displaying pitching (or hitting) record and the other presenting career highlights. The cards are arranged in alphabetical order within American (1-15) and National (16-30) Leagues.

	MINT	NRMT
COMPLETE SET (30)	25.00	11.00
COMMON CARD (1-30)	.25	.11
☐ 1 Roberto Alomar	1.00	.45
☐ 2 Joe Carter	.50	.23
☐ 3 Cecil Fielder	.50	.23
☐ 4 Juan Gonzalez	3.00	1.35
☐ 5 Ken Griffey Jr.	6.00	2.70
☐ 6 Jimmy Key	.25	.11
☐ 7 Chuck Knoblauch	1.00	.45
☐ 8 Kenny Lofton	1.50	.70
☐ 9 Mike Mussina	1.00	.45
☐ 10 Paul O'Neill	.50	.23
☐ 11 Kirby Puckett	2.50	1.10
☐ 12 Cal Ripken	5.00	2.20
☐ 13 Ivan Rodriguez	1.50	.70
☐ 14 Frank Thomas	5.00	2.20
☐ 15 Mo Vaughn	1.25	.55
☐ 16 Moises Alou	.50	.23
☐ 17 Jeff Bagwell	2.50	1.10
☐ 18 Barry Bonds	1.25	.55
☐ 19 Jeff Conine	.25	.11
☐ 20 Len Dykstra	.50	.23
☐ 21 Andres Galarraga	1.00	.45
☐ 22 Tony Gwynn	3.00	1.35
☐ 23 Gregg Jefferies	.25	.11
☐ 24 Barry Larkin	.75	.35
☐ 25 Greg Maddux	4.00	1.80
☐ 26 Mike Piazza	4.00	1.80
☐ 27 Bret Saberhagen	.25	.11
☐ 28 Ozzie Smith	2.00	.90
☐ 29 Sammy Sosa	1.00	.45
☐ 30 Matt Williams	.75	.35

1949 Leaf

The cards in this 98-card set measure 2 3/8" by 2 7/8". The 1949 Leaf set was the first post-war baseball series issued in color. In hobby circles, it has been speculated that the set was issued in the spring of 1949. This effort was not entirely successful due to a lack of refinement which resulted in many color variations and cards out of register. In addition, the set was skip numbered from 1-168, with 49 of the 98 cards printed in limited quantities (marked with SP in the checklist). Cards 102 and 136 have variations, and cards are sometimes found with overprinted, incorrect or blank backs. The notable Rookie

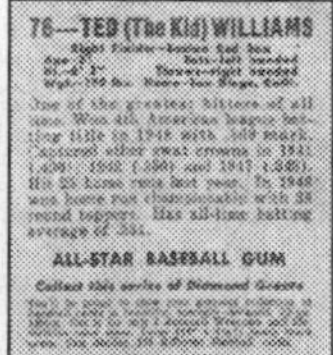

Cards in this set include Stan Musial, Satchel Paige, and Jackie Robinson.

	NRMT	VG-E
COMPLETE SET (98)	25000.00	11200.00
COMMON CARD (1-168)	25.00	11.00
COMMON SP	275.00	125.00
WRAPPER (1-CENT)	160.00	70.00
☐ 1 Joe DiMaggio	2100.00	850.00
☐ 3 Babe Ruth	2500.00	1100.00
☐ 4 Stan Musial	850.00	375.00
☐ 5 Virgil Trucks SP	350.00	160.00
☐ 8 Satchel Paige SP	2200.00	1000.00
☐ 10 Dizzy Trout	35.00	16.00
☐ 11 Phil Rizzuto	250.00	110.00
☐ 13 Cass Michaels SP	275.00	125.00
☐ 14 Billy Johnson	40.00	18.00
☐ 17 Frank Overmire	25.00	11.00
☐ 19 Johnny Wyrostek SP	275.00	125.00
☐ 20 Hank Sauer SP	350.00	160.00
☐ 22 Al Evans	25.00	11.00
☐ 26 Sam Chapman	35.00	16.00
☐ 27 Mickey Harris	25.00	11.00
☐ 28 Jim Hegan	35.00	16.00
☐ 29 Elmer Valo	35.00	16.00
☐ 30 Billy Goodman SP	300.00	135.00
☐ 31 Lou Brissie	25.00	11.00
☐ 32 Warren Spahn	275.00	125.00
☐ 33 Peanuts Lowrey SP	275.00	125.00
☐ 36 Al Zarilla SP	275.00	125.00
☐ 38 Ted Kluszewski	150.00	70.00
☐ 39 Ewell Blackwell	55.00	25.00
☐ 42 Kent Peterson	25.00	11.00
☐ 43 Ed Stevens SP	275.00	125.00
☐ 45 Ken Keltner SP	275.00	125.00
☐ 46 Johnny Mize	100.00	45.00
☐ 47 George Vico	25.00	11.00
☐ 48 Johnny Schmitz SP	275.00	125.00
☐ 49 Del Ennis	55.00	25.00
☐ 50 Dick Wakefield	25.00	11.00
☐ 51 Al Dark SP	450.00	200.00
☐ 53 Johnny VanderMeer	100.00	45.00
☐ 54 Bobby Adams SP	275.00	125.00
☐ 55 Tommy Henrich SP	450.00	200.00
☐ 56 Larry Jansen UER (Misspelled Jensen)	35.00	16.00
☐ 57 Bob McCall	25.00	11.00
☐ 59 Luke Appling	100.00	45.00
☐ 61 Jake Early	25.00	11.00
☐ 62 Eddie Joost SP	275.00	125.00
☐ 63 Barney McCosky SP	275.00	125.00
☐ 65 Robert Elliott UER (Misspelled Elliot on card front)	100.00	45.00
☐ 66 Orval Grove SP	275.00	125.00
☐ 68 Eddie Miller SP	275.00	125.00
☐ 70 Honus Wagner CO	275.00	125.00
☐ 72 Hank Edwards	25.00	11.00
☐ 73 Pat Seerey	25.00	11.00
☐ 75 Dom DiMaggio SP	550.00	250.00
☐ 76 Ted Williams	800.00	350.00
☐ 77 Roy Smalley	25.00	11.00
☐ 78 Hoot Evers SP	275.00	125.00
☐ 79 Jackie Robinson	1000.00	450.00
☐ 81 Whitey Kurowski SP	275.00	125.00
☐ 82 Johnny Lindell	35.00	16.00
☐ 83 Bobby Doerr	100.00	45.00
☐ 84 Sid Hudson	25.00	11.00
☐ 85 Dave Philley SP	300.00	135.00
☐ 86 Ralph Weigel	25.00	11.00
☐ 88 Frank Gustine SP	275.00	125.00
☐ 91 Ralph Kiner	200.00	90.00
☐ 93 Bob Feller SP	1250.00	550.00
☐ 95 George Stirnweiss	35.00	16.00
☐ 97 Marty Marion	55.00	25.00
☐ 98 Hal Newhouser SP	550.00	250.00
☐ 102A Gene Hermansk ERR	250.00	110.00
☐ 102B Gene Hermanski COR	40.00	18.00
☐ 104 Eddie Stewart SP	275.00	125.00
☐ 106 Lou Boudreau	100.00	45.00
☐ 108 Matt Batts SP	275.00	125.00
☐ 111 Jerry Priddy	25.00	11.00
☐ 113 Dutch Leonard SP	275.00	125.00
☐ 117 Joe Gordon	35.00	16.00
☐ 120 George Kell SP	550.00	250.00

☐ 121 Johnny Pesky SP	350.00	160.00
☐ 123 Cliff Fannin SP	275.00	125.00
☐ 125 Andy Pafko	25.00	11.00
☐ 127 Enos Slaughter SP	650.00	300.00
☐ 128 Buddy Rosar	25.00	11.00
☐ 129 Kirby Higbe SP	375.00	170.00
☐ 131 Sid Gordon SP	375.00	170.00
☐ 133 Tommy Holmes SP	450.00	200.00
☐ 136A Cliff Aberson (Full sleeve)	25.00	11.00
☐ 136B Cliff Aberson (Short sleeve)	250.00	110.00
☐ 137 Harry Walker SP	275.00	125.00
☐ 138 Larry Doby SP	550.00	250.00
☐ 139 Johnny Hopp	25.00	11.00
☐ 142 Danny Murtaugh SP	350.00	160.00
☐ 143 Dick Sisler SP	275.00	125.00
☐ 144 Bob Dillinger SP	375.00	170.00
☐ 146 Pete Reiser SP	450.00	200.00
☐ 149 Hank Majeski SP	275.00	125.00
☐ 153 Floyd Baker SP	275.00	125.00
☐ 158 Harry Brecheen SP	350.00	160.00
☐ 159 Mizell Platt	25.00	11.00
☐ 160 Bob Scheffing SP	275.00	125.00
☐ 161 Vern Stephens SP	350.00	160.00
☐ 163 Fred Hutchinson SP	350.00	160.00
☐ 165 Dale Mitchell SP	350.00	160.00
☐ 168 Phil Cavarretta SP UER Name spelled Cavaretta	450.00	180.00

1949 Leaf Premiums

This set of eight large, blank-backed premiums is rather scarce. They were issued as premiums with the 1949 Leaf Gum set. The catalog designation is R401-4. The set is subtitled "Baseball's Immortals" and there is no reference anywhere on the premium to Leaf, the issuing company. These large photos measure approximately 5 1/2" x 7 3/16" and are printed on thin paper.

	NRMT	VG-E
COMPLETE SET (8)	2250.00	1000.00
COMMON CARD (1-8)	150.00	70.00
☐ 1 Grover C. Alexander	200.00	90.00
☐ 2 Mickey Cochrane	200.00	90.00
☐ 3 Lou Gehrig	500.00	220.00
☐ 4 Walter Johnson	300.00	135.00
☐ 5 Christy Mathewson	300.00	135.00
☐ 6 John McGraw	200.00	90.00
☐ 7 Babe Ruth	750.00	350.00
☐ 8 Ed Walsh	150.00	70.00

1960 Leaf

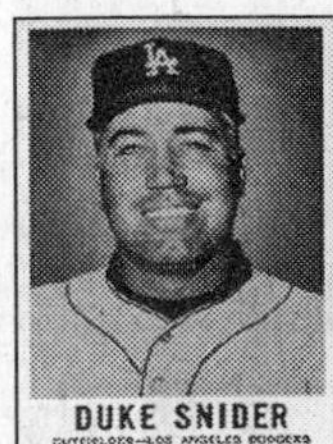

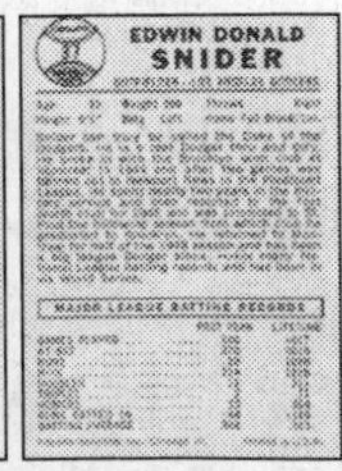

The cards in this 144-card set measure the standard size. The 1960 Leaf set was issued in a regular gum package style but with a marble instead of gum. The series was a joint production by Sports Novelties, Inc., and Leaf, two Chicago-based companies. Cards 73-144 are more difficult to find than the lower numbers. Photo variations exist (probably proof cards) for the seven cards listed with an asterisk and there is a well-known error card, number 25 showing Brooks Lawrence (in a Reds uniform) with Jim Grant's name on front, and Grant's biography and record on back. The corrected version with Grant's photo is the more difficult variety. The only notable Rookie Card in this set is Dallas Green. The complete set price below includes both versions of Jim Grant.

	NRMT	VG-E
COMPLETE SET (144)	1750.00	800.00
COMMON CARD (1-72)	3.00	1.35
COMMON CARD (73-144)	30.00	13.50
WRAPPER	50.00	22.00
☐ 1 Luis Aparicio *	25.00	6.25
☐ 2 Woody Held	3.00	1.35
☐ 3 Frank Lary	5.00	2.20
☐ 4 Camilo Pascual	5.00	2.20
☐ 5 Pancho Herrera	3.00	1.35
☐ 6 Felipe Alou	5.00	2.20
☐ 7 Benjamin Daniels	3.00	1.35
☐ 8 Roger Craig	5.00	2.20
☐ 9 Eddie Kasko	3.00	1.35
☐ 10 Bob Grim	5.00	2.20
☐ 11 Jim Busby	3.00	1.35
☐ 12 Ken Boyer	5.00	2.20
☐ 13 Bob Boyd	3.00	1.35
☐ 14 Sam Jones	5.00	2.20
☐ 15 Larry Jackson	5.00	2.20
☐ 16 Elroy Face	3.00	1.35
☐ 17 Walt Moryn *	3.00	1.35
☐ 18 Jim Gilliam	5.00	2.20
☐ 19 Don Newcombe	5.00	2.20
☐ 20 Glen Hobbie	3.00	1.35
☐ 21 Pedro Ramos	3.00	1.35
☐ 22 Ryne Duren	3.00	1.35
☐ 23 Joey Jay *	5.00	2.20
☐ 24 Lou Berberet	3.00	1.35
☐ 25A Jim Grant ERR (Photo actually Brooks Lawrence)	15.00	6.75
☐ 25B Jim Grant COR	25.00	11.00
☐ 26 Tom Borland	3.00	1.35
☐ 27 Brooks Robinson	40.00	18.00
☐ 28 Jerry Adair	3.00	1.35
☐ 29 Ron Jackson	3.00	1.35
☐ 30 George Strickland	3.00	1.35
☐ 31 Rocky Bridges	3.00	1.35
☐ 32 Bill Tuttle	3.00	1.35
☐ 33 Ken Hunt	3.00	1.35
☐ 34 Hal Griggs	3.00	1.35
☐ 35 Jim Coates *	3.00	1.35
☐ 36 Brooks Lawrence	3.00	1.35
☐ 37 Duke Snider	40.00	18.00
☐ 38 Al Spangler	3.00	1.35
☐ 39 Jim Owens	3.00	1.35
☐ 40 Bill Virdon	3.00	1.35
☐ 41 Ernie Broglio	5.00	2.20
☐ 42 Andre Rodgers	3.00	1.35
☐ 43 Julio Becquer	3.00	1.35
☐ 44 Tony Taylor	5.00	2.20
☐ 45 Jerry Lynch	5.00	2.20
☐ 46 Cletis Boyer	3.00	1.35
☐ 47 Jerry Lumpe	3.00	1.35
☐ 48 Charlie Maxwell	5.00	2.20
☐ 49 Jim Perry	5.00	2.20
☐ 50 Danny McDevitt	3.00	1.35
☐ 51 Juan Pizarro	3.00	1.35
☐ 52 Dallas Green	10.00	4.50
☐ 53 Bob Friend	5.00	2.20
☐ 54 Jack Sanford	5.00	2.20
☐ 55 Jim Rivera	3.00	1.35
☐ 56 Ted Wills	3.00	1.35
☐ 57 Milt Pappas	5.00	2.20
☐ 58 Hal Smith *	3.00	1.35
☐ 59 Bobby Avila	3.00	1.35
☐ 60 Clem Labine	5.00	2.20
☐ 61 Norman Rehm *	3.00	1.35
☐ 62 John Gabler	3.00	1.35
☐ 63 John Tsitouris	3.00	1.35
☐ 64 Dave Sisler	3.00	1.35
☐ 65 Vic Power	5.00	2.20
☐ 66 Earl Battey	3.00	1.35
☐ 67 Bob Purkey	3.00	1.35
☐ 68 Moe Drabowsky	5.00	2.20
☐ 69 Hoyt Wilhelm	15.00	6.75
☐ 70 Humberto Robinson	3.00	1.35
☐ 71 Whitey Herzog	5.00	2.20
☐ 72 Dick Donovan *	3.00	1.35
☐ 73 Gordon Jones	30.00	13.50
☐ 74 Joe Hicks	30.00	13.50
☐ 75 Ray Culp	40.00	18.00
☐ 76 Dick Drott	30.00	13.50
☐ 77 Bob Duliba	30.00	13.50
☐ 78 Art Ditmar	30.00	13.50
☐ 79 Steve Korcheck	30.00	13.50
☐ 80 Henry Mason	30.00	13.50
☐ 81 Harry Simpson	30.00	13.50
☐ 82 Gene Green	30.00	13.50
☐ 83 Bob Shaw	30.00	13.50
☐ 84 Howard Reed	30.00	13.50
☐ 85 Dick Stigman	30.00	13.50
☐ 86 Rip Repulski	30.00	13.50
☐ 87 Seth Morehead	30.00	13.50
☐ 88 Camilo Carreon	30.00	13.50
☐ 89 John Blanchard	40.00	18.00
☐ 90 Billy Hoeft	30.00	13.50
☐ 91 Fred Hopke	30.00	13.50
☐ 92 Joe Martin	30.00	13.50
☐ 93 Wally Shannon	30.00	13.50
☐ 94 Two Hal Smith's Hal R. Smith Hal W. Smith	40.00	18.00
☐ 95 Al Schroll	30.00	13.50
☐ 96 John Kucks	30.00	13.50
☐ 97 Tom Morgan	30.00	13.50
☐ 98 Willie Jones	30.00	13.50
☐ 99 Marshall Renfroe	30.00	13.50
☐ 100 Willie Tasby	30.00	13.50
☐ 101 Irv Noren	30.00	13.50
☐ 102 Russ Snyder	30.00	13.50
☐ 103 Bob Turley	40.00	18.00
☐ 104 Jim Woods	30.00	13.50
☐ 105 Ronnie Kline	30.00	13.50
☐ 106 Steve Bilko	30.00	13.50
☐ 107 Elmer Valo	30.00	13.50
☐ 108 Tom McAvoy	30.00	13.50
☐ 109 Stan Williams	30.00	13.50
☐ 110 Earl Averill Jr.	30.00	13.50
☐ 111 Lee Walls	30.00	13.50
☐ 112 Paul Richards MG	40.00	18.00
☐ 113 Ed Sadowski	30.00	13.50
☐ 114 Stover McIlwain	30.00	13.50
☐ 115 Chuck Tanner UER (Photo actually Ken Kuhn)	40.00	18.00
☐ 116 Lou Klimchock	30.00	13.50
☐ 117 Neil Chrisley	30.00	13.50
☐ 118 John Callison	40.00	18.00
☐ 119 Hal Smith	30.00	13.50
☐ 120 Carl Sawatski	30.00	13.50
☐ 121 Frank Leja	30.00	13.50
☐ 122 Earl Torgeson	30.00	13.50
☐ 123 Art Schult	30.00	13.50
☐ 124 Jim Brosnan	30.00	13.50
☐ 125 Sparky Anderson	60.00	27.00
☐ 126 Joe Pignatano	30.00	13.50
☐ 127 Rocky Nelson	30.00	13.50
☐ 128 Orlando Cepeda	60.00	27.00
☐ 129 Daryl Spencer	30.00	13.50
☐ 130 Ralph Lumenti	30.00	13.50
☐ 131 Sam Taylor	30.00	13.50
☐ 132 Harry Brecheen CO	40.00	18.00
☐ 133 Johnny Groth	30.00	13.50
☐ 134 Wayne Terwilliger	30.00	13.50
☐ 135 Kent Hadley	30.00	13.50
☐ 136 Faye Throneberry	30.00	13.50
☐ 137 Jack Meyer	30.00	13.50
☐ 138 Chuck Cottier	30.00	13.50
☐ 139 Joe DeMaestri	30.00	13.50
☐ 140 Gene Freese	30.00	13.50
☐ 141 Curt Flood	40.00	18.00
☐ 142 Gino Cimoli	30.00	13.50
☐ 143 Clay Dalrymple	30.00	13.50
☐ 144 Jim Bunning	70.00	17.50

1985 Leaf/Donruss

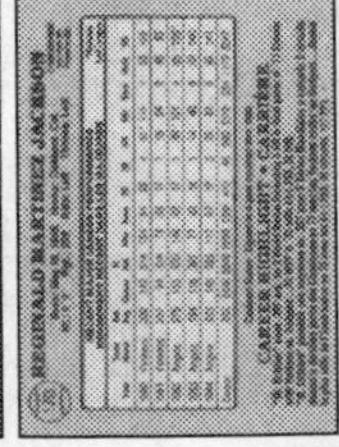

The cards in this 264-card set measure the standard size. In an effort to establish a Canadian baseball card market much as Topps' affiliate O-Pee-Chee had done, the Donruss Company in conjunction with its new parent Leaf Company issued this set to the Canadian market. The set was later released in the United States through hobby dealer channels. The cards were issued in wax packs. A piece of a large Lou Gehrig puzzle was inserted in each pack. Aside from card number differences the cards are essentially the same as the Donruss U.S. regular issue of the cards of the same players; however the backs are in both French and English. Two cards, Dick Perez artwork of Tim Raines (252) and Dave Stieb (251), are called Canadian Greats (CG) and are not contained in the Donruss U.S. set. As in most Canadian sets, the players featured are heavily biased towards Canadian teams and those American teams closest to the Canadian border. Diamond Kings (numbers 1-26 denoted DK) and Rated Rookies (number 27 denoted RR) are included just as in the American set. Those players selected for and included as Diamond Kings do not have a regular card in the set. The player cards are numbered on the back. The checklist cards (listed at the end of the list below) are numbered one, two and three (but are not given a traditional card number); the Diamond Kings checklist card is unnumbered; and the Lou Gehrig puzzle card is mistakenly numbered 635. Key cards in this set include Roger Clemens and Dwight Gooden in their Rookie Card year.

	NRMT	VG-E
COMPLETE SET (264)	75.00	34.00
COMMON CARD (1-263)	.05	.02
☐ 1 Ryne Sandberg DK	2.50	1.10
☐ 2 Doug DeCinces DK	.05	.02
☐ 3 Richard Dotson DK	.05	.02
☐ 4 Bert Blyleven DK	.10	.05
☐ 5 Lou Whitaker DK	.25	.11
☐ 6 Dan Quisenberry DK	.05	.02
☐ 7 Don Mattingly DK	4.00	1.80
☐ 8 Carney Lansford DK	.05	.02
☐ 9 Frank Tanana DK	.05	.02
☐ 10 Willie Upshaw DK	.05	.02
☐ 11 Claudell Washington DK	.05	.02
☐ 12 Mike Marshall DK	.05	.02
☐ 13 Joaquin Andujar DK	.05	.02
☐ 14 Cal Ripken DK	5.00	2.20
☐ 15 Jim Rice DK	.10	.05
☐ 16 Don Sutton DK	.50	.23
☐ 17 Frank Viola DK	.10	.05
☐ 18 Alvin Davis DK	.05	.02
☐ 19 Mario Soto DK	.05	.02
☐ 20 Jose Cruz DK	.05	.02
☐ 21 Charlie Lea DK	.05	.02
☐ 22 Jesse Orosco DK	.05	.02
☐ 23 Juan Samuel DK	.05	.02
☐ 24 Tony Pena DK	.05	.02
☐ 25 Tony Gwynn DK	4.00	1.80
☐ 26 Bob Brenly DK	.05	.02
☐ 27 Steve Kiefer RR	.05	.02
☐ 28 Joe Morgan	.50	.23
☐ 29 Luis Leal	.05	.02
☐ 30 Dan Gladden	.10	.05
☐ 31 Shane Rawley	.05	.02
☐ 32 Mark Clear	.05	.02
☐ 33 Terry Kennedy	.05	.02
☐ 34 Hal McRae	.10	.05
☐ 35 Mickey Rivers	.05	.02
☐ 36 Tom Brunansky	.05	.02
☐ 37 LaMarr Hoyt	.05	.02
☐ 38 Orel Hershiser	2.00	.90
☐ 39 Chris Bando	.05	.02
☐ 40 Lee Lacy	.05	.02
☐ 41 Lance Parrish	.10	.05
☐ 42 George Foster	.10	.05
☐ 43 Kevin McReynolds	.05	.02
☐ 44 Robin Yount	.75	.35
☐ 45 Craig McMurtry	.05	.02
☐ 46 Mike Witt	.05	.02
☐ 47 Gary Redus	.05	.02
☐ 48 Dennis Rasmussen	.05	.02
☐ 49 Gary Woods	.05	.02
☐ 50 Phil Bradley	.10	.05
☐ 51 Steve Bedrosian	.05	.02
☐ 52 Duane Walker	.05	.02
☐ 53 Geoff Zahn	.05	.02
☐ 54 Dave Stieb	.05	.02
☐ 55 Pascual Perez	.05	.02
☐ 56 Mark Langston	.50	.23
☐ 57 Bob Dernier	.05	.02
☐ 58 Joe Cowley	.05	.02
☐ 59 Dan Schatzeder	.05	.02
☐ 60 Ozzie Smith	2.00	.90
☐ 61 Bob Knepper	.05	.02
☐ 62 Keith Hernandez	.10	.05
☐ 63 Rick Rhoden	.05	.02
☐ 64 Alejandro Pena	.05	.02
☐ 65 Damaso Garcia	.05	.02
☐ 66 Chili Davis	.10	.05
☐ 67 Al Oliver	.10	.05
☐ 68 Alan Wiggins	.05	.02
☐ 69 Darryl Motley	.05	.02
☐ 70 Gary Ward	.05	.02
☐ 71 John Butcher	.05	.02
☐ 72 Scott McGregor	.05	.02
☐ 73 Bruce Hurst	.05	.02
☐ 74 Dwayne Murphy	.05	.02
☐ 75 Greg Luzinski	.10	.05
☐ 76 Pat Tabler	.05	.02
☐ 77 Chet Lemon	.05	.02
☐ 78 Jim Sundberg	.05	.02
☐ 79 Wally Backman	.05	.02
☐ 80 Terry Puhl	.05	.02
☐ 81 Storm Davis	.05	.02
☐ 82 Jim Wohlford	.05	.02
☐ 83 Willie Randolph	.10	.05
☐ 84 Ron Cey	.10	.05
☐ 85 Jim Beattie	.05	.02
☐ 86 Rafael Ramirez	.05	.02
☐ 87 Cesar Cedeno	.10	.05
☐ 88 Bobby Grich	.10	.05
☐ 89 Jason Thompson	.05	.02
☐ 90 Steve Sax	.05	.02
☐ 91 Tony Fernandez	.05	.02
☐ 92 Jeff Leonard	.05	.02
☐ 93 Von Hayes	.05	.02
☐ 94 Steve Garvey	.40	.18
☐ 95 Steve Balboni	.05	.02
☐ 96 Larry Parrish	.05	.02
☐ 97 Tim Teufel	.05	.02
☐ 98 Sammy Stewart	.05	.02
☐ 99 Roger Clemens	20.00	9.00
☐ 100 Steve Kemp	.05	.02
☐ 101 Tom Seaver	.75	.35
☐ 102 Andre Thornton	.05	.02
☐ 103 Kirk Gibson	.25	.11
☐ 104 Ted Simmons	.10	.05
☐ 105 David Palmer	.05	.02
☐ 106 Roy Lee Jackson	.05	.02
☐ 107 Kirby Puckett	15.00	6.75
☐ 108 Charlie Hough	.10	.05
☐ 109 Mike Boddicker	.05	.02
☐ 110 Willie Wilson	.10	.05
☐ 111 Tim Lollar	.05	.02
☐ 112 Tony Armas	.05	.02
☐ 113 Steve Carlton	.75	.35
☐ 114 Gary Lavelle	.05	.02
☐ 115 Cliff Johnson	.05	.02
☐ 116 Ray Burris	.05	.02
☐ 117 Rudy Law	.05	.02
☐ 118 Mike Scioscia	.05	.02
☐ 119 Kent Tekulve UER (Telukve on back)	.05	.02
☐ 120 George Vukovich	.05	.02
☐ 121 Barbaro Garbey	.05	.02
☐ 122 Mookie Wilson	.10	.05
☐ 123 Ben Oglivie	.05	.02
☐ 124 Jerry Mumphrey	.05	.02
☐ 125 Willie McGee	.10	.05
☐ 126 Jeff Reardon	.10	.05
☐ 127 Dave Winfield	1.00	.45
☐ 128 Lee Smith	.25	.11
☐ 129 Ken Phelps	.05	.02
☐ 130 Rick Camp	.05	.02
☐ 131 Dave Concepcion	.10	.05
☐ 132 Rod Carew	.75	.35
☐ 133 Andre Dawson	.50	.23
☐ 134 Doyle Alexander	.05	.02
☐ 135 Miguel Dilone	.05	.02
☐ 136 Jim Gott	.05	.02
☐ 137 Eric Show	.05	.02
☐ 138 Phil Niekro	.50	.23
☐ 139 Rick Sutcliffe	.05	.02
☐ 140 Dave Winfield Don Mattingly Two for the Title	2.00	.90
☐ 141 Ken Oberkfell	.05	.02
☐ 142 Jack Morris	.10	.05
☐ 143 Lloyd Moseby	.05	.02
☐ 144 Pete Rose	1.50	.70
☐ 145 Gary Gaetti	.10	.05
☐ 146 Don Baylor	.10	.05
☐ 147 Bobby Meacham	.05	.02
☐ 148 Frank White	.10	.05
☐ 149 Mark Thurmond	.05	.02
☐ 150 Dwight Evans	.10	.05
☐ 151 Al Holland	.05	.02
☐ 152 Joel Youngblood	.05	.02
☐ 153 Rance Mulliniks	.05	.02
☐ 154 Bill Caudill	.05	.02
☐ 155 Carlton Fisk	1.00	.45
☐ 156 Rick Honeycutt	.05	.02
☐ 157 John Candelaria	.05	.02
☐ 158 Alan Trammell	.25	.11
☐ 159 Darryl Strawberry	.50	.23
☐ 160 Aurelio Lopez	.05	.02
☐ 161 Enos Cabell	.05	.02
☐ 162 Dion James	.05	.02
☐ 163 Bruce Sutter	.10	.05
☐ 164 Razor Shines	.05	.02
☐ 165 Butch Wynegar	.05	.02
☐ 166 Rich Bordi	.05	.02
☐ 167 Spike Owen	.05	.02
☐ 168 Chris Chambliss	.05	.02
☐ 169 Dave Parker	.10	.05
☐ 170 Reggie Jackson	1.00	.45
☐ 171 Bryn Smith	.05	.02
☐ 172 Dave Collins	.05	.02
☐ 173 Dave Engle	.05	.02
☐ 174 Buddy Bell	.05	.02
☐ 175 Mike Flanagan	.05	.02
☐ 176 George Brett	3.00	1.35
☐ 177 Graig Nettles	.10	.05
☐ 178 Jerry Koosman	.05	.02
☐ 179 Wade Boggs	2.00	.90
☐ 180 Jody Davis	.05	.02
☐ 181 Ernie Whitt	.05	.02
☐ 182 Dave Kingman	.10	.05
☐ 183 Vance Law	.05	.02
☐ 184 Fernando Valenzuela	.10	.05
☐ 185 Bill Madlock	.05	.02
☐ 186 Brett Butler	.10	.05
☐ 187 Doug Sisk	.05	.02
☐ 188 Dan Petry	.05	.02
☐ 189 Joe Niekro	.05	.02
☐ 190 Rollie Fingers	.50	.23
☐ 191 David Green	.05	.02
☐ 192 Steve Rogers	.05	.02
☐ 193 Ken Griffey	.10	.05
☐ 194 Scott Sanderson	.05	.02
☐ 195 Barry Bonnell	.05	.02
☐ 196 Bruce Benedict	.05	.02
☐ 197 Keith Moreland	.05	.02
☐ 198 Fred Lynn	.10	.05
☐ 199 Tim Wallach	.05	.02
☐ 200 Kent Hrbek	.10	.05
☐ 201 Pete O'Brien	.05	.02
☐ 202 Bud Black	.05	.02
☐ 203 Eddie Murray	2.00	.90
☐ 204 Goose Gossage	.10	.05
☐ 205 Mike Schmidt	1.50	.70
☐ 206 Mike Easler	.05	.02
☐ 207 Jack Clark	.10	.05
☐ 208 Rickey Henderson	1.00	.45
☐ 209 Jesse Barfield	.05	.02
☐ 210 Ron Kittle	.05	.02
☐ 211 Pedro Guerrero	.05	.02
☐ 212 Johnny Ray	.05	.02
☐ 213 Julio Franco	.10	.05
☐ 214 Hubie Brooks	.05	.02
☐ 215 Darrell Evans	.10	.05
☐ 216 Nolan Ryan	6.00	2.70
☐ 217 Jim Gantner	.05	.02
☐ 218 Tim Raines	.10	.05
☐ 219 Dave Righetti	.05	.02
☐ 220 Gary Matthews	.05	.02
☐ 221 Jack Perconte	.05	.02
☐ 222 Dale Murphy	.50	.23
☐ 223 Brian Downing	.05	.02
☐ 224 Mickey Hatcher	.05	.02
☐ 225 Lonnie Smith	.05	.02
☐ 226 Jorge Orta	.05	.02
☐ 227 Milt Wilcox	.05	.02
☐ 228 John Denny	.05	.02
☐ 229 Marty Barrett	.05	.02
☐ 230 Alfredo Griffin	.05	.02
☐ 231 Harold Baines	.10	.05
☐ 232 Bill Russell	.10	.05
☐ 233 Marvell Wynne	.05	.02
☐ 234 Dwight Gooden	3.00	1.35
☐ 235 Willie Hernandez	.05	.02
☐ 236 Bill Gullickson	.05	.02
☐ 237 Ron Guidry	.10	.05
☐ 238 Leon Durham	.05	.02
☐ 239 Al Cowens	.05	.02
☐ 240 Bob Horner	.05	.02
☐ 241 Gary Carter	.40	.18
☐ 242 Glenn Hubbard	.05	.02
☐ 243 Steve Trout	.05	.02
☐ 244 Jay Howell	.05	.02
☐ 245 Terry Francona	.05	.02
☐ 246 Cecil Cooper	.10	.05
☐ 247 Larry McWilliams	.05	.02
☐ 248 George Bell	.05	.02
☐ 249 Larry Herndon	.05	.02
☐ 250 Ozzie Virgil	.05	.02
☐ 251 Dave Stieb CG	.05	.02
☐ 252 Tim Raines CG	.25	.11
☐ 253 Ricky Horton	.05	.02
☐ 254 Bill Buckner	.10	.05
☐ 255 Dan Driessen	.05	.02
☐ 256 Ron Darling	.05	.02
☐ 257 Doug Flynn	.05	.02
☐ 258 Darrell Porter	.05	.02
☐ 259 George Hendrick	.05	.02
☐ 260 Checklist DK 1-26 (Unnumbered)	.05	.02
☐ 261 Checklist 27-106 (Unnumbered)	.05	.02
☐ 262 Checklist 107-178 (Unnumbered)	.05	.02
☐ 263 Checklist 179-259 (Unnumbered)	.05	.02
☐ 635 Lou Gehrig Puzzle Card UER (Misnumbered)	.50	.23

1986 Leaf/Donruss

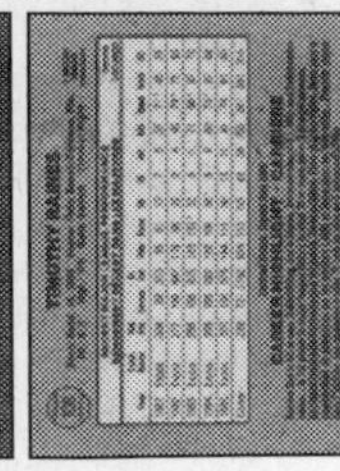

This 264-card standard-size set was issued with a puzzle of Hank Aaron. Except for the numbering, the company logo and the bilingual backs, the cards are essentially the same as the Donruss U.S. regular issue cards of the same players. On a blue and black striped background, fronts feature slightly tilted color player photos. The player's name and position appear under the photo. On a light blue background, the horizontal backs carry player biography, statistics and career hightlights in French and English. Two cards, Dick Perez artwork of Jesse Barfield (254) and Jeff Reardon (214), are called Canadian Greats (CG) and are not contained in the Donruss U.S. set. Diamond Kings (numbers 1-26, denoted DK) and Rated Rookies (numbers 27-29, denoted RR) are included just as in the American set. The cards are numbered on the back. As in most Canadian sets, the players featured are heavily biased toward Canadian teams and those American teams closest to the Canadian border. Those players selected for and included as Diamond Kings do not have a regular card in the set. The checklist cards (listed at the end of the list below) are numbered one, two and three (but are not given a traditional card number); the Diamond Kings checklist card is also unnumbered. Two key cards in this set are Andres Galarraga and Fred McGriff, who are Rookie Cards in the 1986 Donruss set.

	MINT	NRMT
COMPLETE SET (264)	25.00	11.00
COMMON CARD (1-264)	.05	.02
☐ 1 Kirk Gibson DK	.15	.07
☐ 2 Goose Gossage DK	.15	.07
☐ 3 Willie McGee DK	.10	.05
☐ 4 George Bell DK	.05	.02
☐ 5 Tony Armas DK	.05	.02
☐ 6 Chili Davis DK	.10	.05
☐ 7 Cecil Cooper DK	.10	.05
☐ 8 Mike Boddicker DK	.05	.02
☐ 9 Davey Lopes DK	.05	.02
☐ 10 Bill Doran DK	.05	.02
☐ 11 Bret Saberhagen DK	.10	.05
☐ 12 Brett Butler DK	.10	.05
☐ 13 Harold Baines DK	.10	.05
☐ 14 Mike Davis DK	.05	.02
☐ 15 Tony Perez DK	.25	.11
☐ 16 Willie Randolph DK	.10	.05
☐ 17 Bob Boone DK	.10	.05
☐ 18 Orel Hershiser DK	.15	.07
☐ 19 Johnny Ray DK	.05	.02
☐ 20 Gary Ward DK	.05	.02
☐ 21 Rick Mahler DK	.05	.02
☐ 22 Phil Bradley DK	.05	.02
☐ 23 Jerry Koosman DK	.10	.05
☐ 24 Tom Brunansky DK	.05	.02
☐ 25 Andre Dawson DK	.25	.11
☐ 26 Dwight Gooden DK	.50	.23
☐ 27 Andres Galarraga RR	4.00	1.80
☐ 28 Fred McGriff RR	6.00	2.70
☐ 29 Dave Shipanoff RR	.05	.02
☐ 30 Danny Jackson	.05	.02
☐ 31 Robin Yount	.40	.18
☐ 32 Mike Fitzgerald	.05	.02
☐ 33 Lou Whitaker	.10	.05
☐ 34 Alfredo Griffin	.05	.02
☐ 35 Oil Can Boyd	.05	.02
☐ 36 Ron Guidry	.10	.05
☐ 37 Rickey Henderson	.50	.23
☐ 38 Jack Morris	.10	.05
☐ 39 Brian Downing	.05	.02
☐ 40 Mike Marshall	.05	.02
☐ 41 Tony Gwynn	2.00	.90
☐ 42 George Brett	1.50	.70
☐ 43 Jim Gantner	.05	.02
☐ 44 Hubie Brooks	.05	.02
☐ 45 Tony Fernandez	.05	.02
☐ 46 Oddibe McDowell	.05	.02
☐ 47 Ozzie Smith	1.00	.45
☐ 48 Ken Griffey	.10	.05
☐ 49 Jose Cruz	.10	.05
☐ 50 Mariano Duncan	.25	.11
☐ 51 Mike Schmidt	.75	.35
☐ 52 Pat Tabler	.05	.02
☐ 53 Pete Rose	.75	.35
☐ 54 Frank White	.10	.05
☐ 55 Carney Lansford	.05	.02
☐ 56 Steve Garvey	.25	.11
☐ 57 Vance Law	.05	.02
☐ 58 Tony Pena	.05	.02
☐ 59 Wayne Tolleson	.05	.02
☐ 60 Dale Murphy	.30	.14
☐ 61 LaMarr Hoyt	.05	.02
☐ 62 Ryne Sandberg	1.25	.55
☐ 63 Gary Carter	.25	.11
☐ 64 Lee Smith	.15	.07
☐ 65 Alvin Davis	.05	.02
☐ 66 Edwin Nunez	.05	.02
☐ 67 Kent Hrbek	.10	.05
☐ 68 Dave Stieb	.05	.02
☐ 69 Kirby Puckett	3.00	1.35
☐ 70 Paul Molitor	.75	.35
☐ 71 Glenn Hubbard	.05	.02
☐ 72 Lloyd Moseby	.05	.02
☐ 73 Mike Smithson	.05	.02
☐ 74 Jeff Leonard	.05	.02
☐ 75 Danny Darwin	.05	.02
☐ 76 Kevin McReynolds	.05	.02
☐ 77 Bill Buckner	.10	.05
☐ 78 Ron Oester	.05	.02
☐ 79 Tommy Herr	.05	.02
☐ 80 Mike Pagliarulo	.05	.02
☐ 81 Ron Romanick	.05	.02
☐ 82 Brook Jacoby	.05	.02
☐ 83 Eddie Murray	1.00	.45
☐ 84 Gary Pettis	.05	.02
☐ 85 Chet Lemon	.05	.02
☐ 86 Toby Harrah	.05	.02
☐ 87 Mike Scioscia	.05	.02
☐ 88 Bert Blyleven	.10	.05
☐ 89 Dave Righetti	.05	.02
☐ 90 Bob Knepper	.05	.02
☐ 91 Fernando Valenzuela	.10	.05
☐ 92 Dave Dravecky	.10	.05
☐ 93 Julio Franco	.10	.05
☐ 94 Keith Moreland	.05	.02
☐ 95 Darryl Motley	.05	.02
☐ 96 Jack Clark	.10	.05
☐ 97 Tim Wallach	.05	.02
☐ 98 Steve Balboni	.05	.02
☐ 99 Storm Davis	.05	.02
☐ 100 Jay Howell	.05	.02
☐ 101 Alan Trammell	.25	.11
☐ 102 Willie Hernandez	.05	.02
☐ 103 Don Mattingly	2.00	.90
☐ 104 Lee Lacy	.05	.02
☐ 105 Pedro Guerrero	.05	.02
☐ 106 Willie Wilson	.05	.02
☐ 107 Craig Reynolds	.05	.02
☐ 108 Tim Raines	.10	.05
☐ 109 Shane Rawley	.05	.02
☐ 110 Larry Parrish	.05	.02
☐ 111 Eric Show	.05	.02
☐ 112 Mike Witt	.05	.02
☐ 113 Dennis Eckersley	.15	.07
☐ 114 Mike Moore	.05	.02
☐ 115 Vince Coleman	.10	.05
☐ 116 Damaso Garcia	.05	.02
☐ 117 Steve Carlton	.40	.18
☐ 118 Floyd Bannister	.05	.02
☐ 119 Mario Soto	.05	.02
☐ 120 Fred Lynn	.10	.05
☐ 121 Bob Horner	.05	.02
☐ 122 Rick Sutcliffe	.05	.02
☐ 123 Walt Terrell	.05	.02
☐ 124 Keith Hernandez	.10	.05
☐ 125 Dave Winfield	.50	.23
☐ 126 Frank Viola	.10	.05
☐ 127 Dwight Evans	.10	.05
☐ 128 Willie Upshaw	.05	.02
☐ 129 Andre Thornton	.05	.02
☐ 130 Donnie Moore	.05	.02
☐ 131 Darryl Strawberry	.15	.07
☐ 132 Nolan Ryan	3.00	1.35
☐ 133 Garry Templeton	.05	.02
☐ 134 John Tudor	.05	.02
☐ 135 Dave Parker	.10	.05
☐ 136 Larry McWilliams	.05	.02
☐ 137 Terry Pendleton	.15	.07
☐ 138 Terry Puhl	.05	.02
☐ 139 Bob Dernier	.05	.02
☐ 140 Ozzie Guillen	.15	.07
☐ 141 Jim Clancy	.05	.02
☐ 142 Cal Ripken	3.00	1.35
☐ 143 Mickey Hatcher	.05	.02
☐ 144 Dan Petry	.05	.02
☐ 145 Rich Gedman	.05	.02
☐ 146 Jim Rice	.10	.05
☐ 147 Butch Wynegar	.05	.02
☐ 148 Donnie Hill	.05	.02
☐ 149 Jim Sundberg	.05	.02
☐ 150 Joe Hesketh	.05	.02
☐ 151 Chris Codiroli	.05	.02
☐ 152 Charlie Hough	.10	.05
☐ 153 Herm Winningham	.05	.02
☐ 154 Dave Rozema	.05	.02
☐ 155 Don Slaught	.05	.02
☐ 156 Juan Beniquez	.05	.02
☐ 157 Ted Higuera	.05	.02
☐ 158 Andy Hawkins	.05	.02
☐ 159 Don Robinson	.05	.02
☐ 160 Glenn Wilson	.05	.02
☐ 161 Earnest Riles	.05	.02
☐ 162 Nick Esasky	.05	.02
☐ 163 Carlton Fisk	.40	.18
☐ 164 Claudell Washington	.05	.02
☐ 165 Scott McGregor	.05	.02
☐ 166 Nate Snell	.05	.02
☐ 167 Ted Simmons	.10	.05
☐ 168 Wade Boggs	.60	.25
☐ 169 Marty Barrett	.05	.02
☐ 170 Bud Black	.05	.02
☐ 171 Charlie Leibrandt	.05	.02
☐ 172 Charlie Lea	.05	.02
☐ 173 Reggie Jackson	.50	.23
☐ 174 Bryn Smith	.05	.02
☐ 175 Glenn Davis	.05	.02
☐ 176 Von Hayes	.05	.02
☐ 177 Danny Cox	.05	.02
☐ 178 Sammy Khalifa	.05	.02
☐ 179 Tom Browning	.05	.02
☐ 180 Scott Garrelts	.05	.02
☐ 181 Shawon Dunston	.10	.05
☐ 182 Doyle Alexander	.05	.02
☐ 183 Jim Presley	.05	.02
☐ 184 Al Cowens	.05	.02
☐ 185 Mark Salas	.05	.02
☐ 186 Tom Niedenfuer	.05	.02
☐ 187 Dave Henderson	.05	.02
☐ 188 Lonnie Smith	.05	.02
☐ 189 Bruce Bochte	.05	.02
☐ 190 Leon Durham	.05	.02
☐ 191 Terry Francona	.10	.05
☐ 192 Bruce Sutter	.10	.05
☐ 193 Steve Crawford	.05	.02
☐ 194 Bob Brenly	.05	.02
☐ 195 Dan Pasqua	.05	.02
☐ 196 Juan Samuel	.05	.02
☐ 197 Floyd Rayford	.05	.02
☐ 198 Tim Burke	.05	.02
☐ 199 Ben Oglivie	.05	.02
☐ 200 Don Carman	.05	.02
☐ 201 Lance Parrish	.10	.05
☐ 202 Terry Forster	.05	.02
☐ 203 Neal Heaton	.05	.02
☐ 204 Ivan Calderon	.05	.02
☐ 205 Jorge Orta	.05	.02
☐ 206 Tom Henke	.05	.02
☐ 207 Rick Reuschel	.10	.05
☐ 208 Dan Quisenberry	.10	.05
☐ 209 Pete Rose HL Ty-Breaking	1.50	.70
☐ 210 Floyd Youmans	.05	.02
☐ 211 Tom Filer	.05	.02
☐ 212 R.J. Reynolds	.05	.02
☐ 213 Gorman Thomas	.05	.02
☐ 214 Jeff Reardon CG	.10	.05
☐ 215 Chris Brown	.05	.02
☐ 216 Rick Aguilera	.25	.11
☐ 217 Ernie Whitt	.05	.02
☐ 218 Joe Orsulak	.05	.02
☐ 219 Jimmy Key	.25	.11
☐ 220 Atlee Hammaker	.05	.02
☐ 221 Ron Darling	.05	.02
☐ 222 Zane Smith	.05	.02
☐ 223 Bob Welch	.05	.02
☐ 224 Reid Nichols	.05	.02
☐ 225 Vince Coleman Willie McGee Fleet Feet	.15	.07
☐ 226 Mark Gubicza	.05	.02
☐ 227 Tim Birtsas	.05	.02
☐ 228 Mike Hargrove	.10	.05
☐ 229 Randy St. Claire	.05	.02
☐ 230 Larry Herndon	.05	.02
☐ 231 Dusty Baker	.10	.05
☐ 232 Mookie Wilson	.10	.05
☐ 233 Jeff Lahti	.05	.02
☐ 234 Tom Seaver	.40	.18
☐ 235 Mike Scott	.05	.02
☐ 236 Don Sutton	.30	.14
☐ 237 Roy Smalley	.05	.02
☐ 238 Bill Madlock	.05	.02
☐ 239 Charlie Hudson Charles on both sides	.05	.02
☐ 240 John Franco	.25	.11

Card	MINT	NRMT
241 Frank Tanana	.10	.05
242 Sid Fernandez	.05	.02
243 Phil Niekro	.25	.11
Joe Niekro		
Knuckle Brothers		
244 Dennis Lamp	.05	.02
245 Gene Nelson	.05	.02
246 Terry Harper	.05	.02
247 Vida Blue	.10	.05
248 Roger McDowell	.25	.11
249 Tony Bernazard	.05	.02
250 Cliff Johnson	.05	.02
251 Hal McRae	.10	.05
252 Garth Iorg	.05	.02
253 Mitch Webster	.05	.02
254 Jesse Barfield CG	.10	.05
255 Dan Driessen	.05	.02
256 Mike Brown	.05	.02
Pirates OF		
257 Ron Kittle	.05	.02
258 Bo Diaz	.05	.02
259 Hank Aaron Puzzle Card	.25	.11
260 Pete Rose	1.50	.70
King Of Kings		
261 Checklist DK 1-26	.05	.02
Unnumbered		
262 Checklist 27-106	.05	.02
Unnumbered		
263 Checklist 107-186	.05	.02
Unnumbered		
264 Checklist 187-260	.05	.02
Unnumbered		

1987 Leaf/Donruss

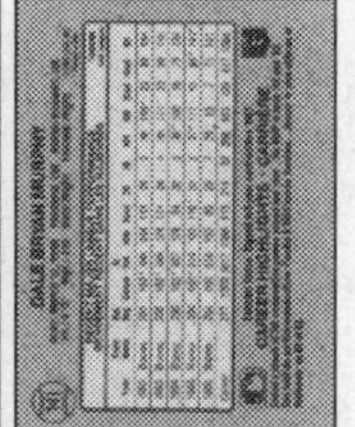

This 264-card standard-size set was issued with a puzzle of Roberto Clemente. Except for the numbering, the company logo and the bilingual backs, the cards are essentially the same as the Donruss U.S. regular issue cards of the same players. On a black background, the fronts feature color player photos with rounded corners and a thin white border. The player's name and position, and the team and manufacturer logos also appear on the front. On a golden background, the horizontal backs carry player biography, statistics and career hightlights in French and English. Two cards, Dick Perez artwork of Floyd Youmans (65) and Mark Eichhorn (173), are called Canadian Greats (CG) and are not contained in the Donruss U.S. set. Diamond Kings (numbers 1-26, denoted DK) and Rated Rookies (numbers 28-47, denoted RR) are included just as in the American set. The cards are numbered on the back. The players featured in this set are heavily biased toward Canadian teams and those American teams closest to the Canadian border. Players appearing in their Rookie Card year include Will Clark, Wally Joyner, Greg Maddux and Ruben Sierra.

	MINT	NRMT
COMPLETE SET (264)	25.00	11.00
COMMON CARD (1-264)	.05	.02
1 Wally Joyner DK	.25	.11
2 Roger Clemens DK	.75	.35
3 Dale Murphy DK	.25	.11
4 Darryl Strawberry DK	.15	.07
5 Ozzie Smith DK	.75	.35
6 Jose Canseco DK	.75	.35
7 Charlie Hough DK	.10	.05
8 Brook Jacoby DK	.05	.02
9 Fred Lynn DK	.10	.05
10 Rick Rhoden DK	.05	.02
11 Chris Brown DK	.05	.02
12 Von Hayes DK	.05	.02
13 Jack Morris DK	.10	.05
14 Kevin McReynolds DK	.05	.02
15 George Brett DK	.75	.35
16 Ted Higuera DK	.05	.02
17 Hubie Brooks DK	.05	.02
18 Mike Scott DK	.05	.02
19 Kirby Puckett DK	.75	.35
20 Dave Winfield DK	.40	.18
21 Lloyd Moseby DK	.05	.02
22 Eric Davis DK	.10	.05
23 Jim Presley DK	.05	.02
24 Keith Moreland DK	.05	.02
25 Greg Walker DK	.05	.02
26 Steve Sax DK	.05	.02
27 DK Checklist 1-26	.05	.02
28 B.J. Surhoff RR	.40	.18
29 Randy Myers RR	.50	.23
30 Ken Gerhart RR	.05	.02
31 Benito Santiago RR	.10	.05
32 Greg Swindell RR	.10	.05
33 Mike Birkbeck RR	.05	.02
34 Terry Steinbach RR	.30	.14
35 Bo Jackson RR	.40	.18
36 Greg Maddux RR	10.00	4.50
37 Jim Lindeman RR	.05	.02
38 Devon White RR	.40	.18
39 Eric Bell RR	.05	.02
40 Will Fraser RR	.05	.02
41 Jerry Browne RR	.05	.02
42 Chris James RR	.05	.02
43 Rafael Palmeiro RR	2.00	.90
44 Pat Dodson RR	.05	.02
45 Duane Ward RR	.05	.02
46 Mark McGwire RR	6.00	2.70
47 Bruce Fields RR	.05	.02
48 Jody Davis	.05	.02
49 Roger McDowell	.05	.02
50 Jose Guzman	.05	.02
51 Oddibe McDowell	.05	.02
52 Harold Baines	.10	.05
53 Dave Righetti	.05	.02
54 Moose Haas	.05	.02
55 Mark Langston	.05	.02
56 Kirby Puckett	1.50	.70
57 Dwight Evans	.10	.05
58 Willie Randolph	.10	.05
59 Wally Backman	.05	.02
60 Bryn Smith	.05	.02
61 Tim Wallach	.05	.02
62 Joe Hesketh	.05	.02
63 Garry Templeton	.05	.02
64 Robby Thompson	.05	.02
65 Floyd Youmans CG	.10	.05
66 Ernest Riles	.05	.02
67 Robin Yount	.40	.18
68 Darryl Strawberry	.15	.07
69 Ernie Whitt	.05	.02
70 Dave Winfield	.40	.18
71 Paul Molitor	.50	.23
72 Dave Stieb	.05	.02
73 Tom Henke	.05	.02
74 Frank Viola	.10	.05
75 Scott Garrelts	.05	.02
76 Mike Boddicker	.05	.02
77 Keith Moreland	.05	.02
78 Lou Whitaker	.10	.05
79 Dave Parker	.10	.05
80 Lee Smith	.15	.07
81 Tom Candiotti	.05	.02
82 Greg A. Harris	.05	.02
83 Fred Lynn	.10	.05
84 Dwight Gooden	.15	.07
85 Ron Darling	.05	.02
86 Mike Krukow	.05	.02
87 Spike Owen	.05	.02
88 Len Dykstra	.15	.07
89 Rick Aguilera	.10	.05
90 Jim Clancy	.05	.02
91 Joe Johnson	.05	.02
92 Damaso Garcia	.05	.02
93 Sid Fernandez	.05	.02
94 Bob Ojeda	.05	.02
95 Ted Higuera	.05	.02
96 George Brett	1.25	.55
97 Willie Wilson	.05	.02
98 Cal Ripken	3.00	1.35
99 Kent Hrbek	.10	.05
100 Bert Blyleven	.10	.05
101 Ron Guidry	.10	.05
102 Andy Allanson	.05	.02
103 Dave Henderson	.05	.02
104 Kirk Gibson	.10	.05
105 Lloyd Moseby	.05	.02
106 Tony Fernandez	.05	.02
107 Lance Parrish	.10	.05
108 Ozzie Smith	.75	.35
109 Gary Carter	.25	.11
110 Eddie Murray	.60	.25
111 Mike Witt	.05	.02
112 Bobby Witt	.25	.11
113 Willie McGee	.10	.05
114 Steve Garvey	.25	.11
115 Glenn Davis	.05	.02
116 Jose Cruz	.10	.05
117 Ozzie Guillen	.05	.02
118 Alvin Davis	.05	.02
119 Jose Rijo	.05	.02
120 Bill Madlock	.10	.05
121 Tommy Herr	.05	.02
122 Mike Schmidt	.75	.35
123 Mike Scioscia	.05	.02
124 Terry Pendleton	.10	.05
125 Leon Durham	.05	.02
126 Alan Trammell	.25	.11
127 Jesse Barfield	.05	.02
128 Shawon Dunston	.05	.02
129 Pete Rose	.75	.35
130 Von Hayes	.05	.02
131 Julio Franco	.10	.05
132 Juan Samuel	.05	.02
133 Joe Carter	.30	.14
134 Brook Jacoby	.05	.02
135 Jack Morris	.10	.05
136 Bob Horner	.05	.02
137 Calvin Schiraldi	.05	.02
138 Tom Browning	.05	.02
139 Shane Rawley	.05	.02
140 Mario Soto	.05	.02
141 Dale Murphy	.25	.11
142 Hubie Brooks	.05	.02
143 Jeff Reardon	.10	.05
144 Will Clark	2.00	.90
145 Ed Correa	.05	.02
146 Glenn Wilson	.05	.02
147 Johnny Ray	.05	.02
148 Fernando Valenzuela	.10	.05
149 Tim Raines	.10	.05
150 Don Mattingly	1.50	.70
151 Jose Canseco	1.00	.45
152 Gary Pettis	.05	.02
153 Don Sutton	.40	.18
154 Jim Presley	.05	.02
155 Checklist 28-105	.05	.02
156 Dale Sveum	.05	.02
157 Cory Snyder	.05	.02
158 Jeff Sellers	.05	.02
159 Denny Walling	.05	.02
160 Danny Cox	.05	.02
161 Bob Forsch	.05	.02
162 Joaquin Andujar	.05	.02
163 Roberto Clemente	.30	.14
Puzzle Card		
164 Paul Assenmacher	.10	.05
165 Marty Barrett	.05	.02
166 Ray Knight	.10	.05
167 Rafael Santana	.05	.02
168 Bruce Ruffin	.05	.02
169 Buddy Bell	.10	.05
170 Kevin Mitchell	.30	.14
171 Ken Oberkfell	.05	.02
172 Gene Garber	.10	.05
173 Mark Eichhorn CG	.10	.05
174 Don Carman	.05	.02
175 Jesse Orosco	.05	.02
176 Mookie Wilson	.10	.05
177 Gary Ward	.05	.02
178 John Franco	.10	.05
179 Eric Davis	.15	.07
180 Walt Terrell	.05	.02
181 Phil Niekro	.40	.18
182 Pat Tabler	.05	.02
183 Brett Butler	.10	.05
184 George Bell	.05	.02
185 Pete Incaviglia	.25	.11
186 Pete O'Brien	.05	.02
187 Jimmy Key	.10	.05
188 Frank White	.10	.05
189 Mike Pagliarulo	.05	.02
190 Roger Clemens	1.25	.55
191 Rickey Henderson	.40	.18
192 Mike Easler	.05	.02
193 Wade Boggs	.40	.18
194 Vince Coleman	.05	.02
195 Charlie Kerfeld	.05	.02
196 Dickie Thon	.05	.02
197 Bill Doran	.05	.02
198 Alfredo Griffin	.05	.02
199 Carlton Fisk	.40	.18
200 Phil Bradley	.05	.02
201 Reggie Jackson	.50	.23
202 Bob Boone	.10	.05
203 Steve Sax	.05	.02
204 Tom Niedenfuer	.05	.02
205 Tim Burke	.05	.02
206 Floyd Youmans	.05	.02
207 Jay Tibbs	.05	.02
208 Chili Davis	.10	.05
209 Larry Parrish	.05	.02
210 John Cerutti	.05	.02
211 Kevin Bass	.05	.02
212 Andre Dawson	.30	.14
213 Bob Sebra	.05	.02
214 Kevin McReynolds	.05	.02

Card	MINT	NRMT
☐ 215 Jim Morrison	.05	.02
☐ 216 Candy Maldonado	.05	.02
☐ 217 John Kruk	.30	.14
☐ 218 Todd Worrell	.10	.05
☐ 219 Barry Bonds	3.00	1.35
☐ 220 Andy McGaffigan	.05	.02
☐ 221 Andres Galarraga	.40	.18
☐ 222 Mike Fitzgerald	.05	.02
☐ 223 Kirk McCaskill	.05	.02
☐ 224 Dave Smith	.05	.02
☐ 225 Ruben Sierra	.30	.14
☐ 226 Scott Fletcher	.05	.02
☐ 227 Chet Lemon	.05	.02
☐ 228 Dan Petry	.05	.02
☐ 229 Mark Eichhorn	.05	.02
☐ 230 Cecil Cooper	.10	.05
☐ 231 Willie Upshaw	.05	.02
☐ 232 Don Baylor	.10	.05
☐ 233 Keith Hernandez	.10	.05
☐ 234 Ryne Sandberg	1.00	.45
☐ 235 Tony Gwynn	1.50	.70
☐ 236 Chris Brown	.05	.02
☐ 237 Pedro Guerrero	.05	.02
☐ 238 Mark Gubicza	.05	.02
☐ 239 Sid Bream	.05	.02
☐ 240 Joe Cowley	.05	.02
☐ 241 Bill Buckner	.10	.05
☐ 242 John Candelaria	.05	.02
☐ 243 Scott McGregor	.05	.02
☐ 244 Tom Brunansky	.05	.02
☐ 245 Gary Gaetti	.10	.05
☐ 246 Orel Hershiser	.10	.05
☐ 247 Jim Rice	.10	.05
☐ 248 Oil Can Boyd	.05	.02
☐ 249 Bob Knepper	.05	.02
☐ 250 Danny Tartabull	.05	.02
☐ 251 John Cangelosi	.05	.02
☐ 252 Wally Joyner	.50	.23
☐ 253 Bruce Hurst	.05	.02
☐ 254 Rich Gedman	.05	.02
☐ 255 Jim Deshaies	.05	.02
☐ 256 Tony Pena	.05	.02
☐ 257 Nolan Ryan	3.00	1.35
☐ 258 Mike Scott	.05	.02
☐ 259 Checklist 106-183	.05	.02
☐ 260 Dennis Rasmussen	.05	.02
☐ 261 Bret Saberhagen	.05	.02
☐ 262 Steve Balboni	.05	.02
☐ 263 Tom Seaver	.40	.18
☐ 264 Checklist 184-264	.05	.02

1987 Leaf Special Olympics *

This set is also known as the Candy City team as that is the logo which appears on the front of the card. This set was issued for the proceeds of the set to go to the Special Olympics. The set was in the style of the 1983 Donruss Hall of Fame Heroes set and the only additions were generic cards about various sports. The cards are standard size.

	MINT	NRMT
COMPLETE SET (18)	6.00	2.70
COMMON CARD (H1-H12)	.40	.18
COMMON CARD (S1-S6)	.10	.05
☐ H1 Mickey Mantle	3.00	1.35
☐ H2 Yogi Berra	.75	.35
☐ H3 Roy Campanella	.75	.35
☐ H4 Stan Musial	1.00	.45
☐ H5 Ted Williams	2.00	.90
☐ H6 Duke Snider	.75	.35
☐ H7 Hank Aaron	2.00	.90
☐ H8 Pee Wee Reese	.75	.35
☐ H9 Brooks Robinson	.50	.23
☐ H10 Al Kaline	.50	.23
☐ H11 Willie McCovey	.40	.18
☐ H12 Cool Papa Bell	.40	.18
☐ S1 Basketball	.30	.14
☐ S2 Softball	.10	.05
☐ S3 Track And Field	.10	.05
☐ S4 Soccer	.20	.09
☐ S5 Gymnastics	.10	.05
☐ S6 VII International Summer Games	.10	.05

1988 Leaf/Donruss

This 264-card standard-size set was issued with a puzzle of Stan Musial. Except for the numbering, the company logo and the bilingual backs, the cards are essentially the same as the Donruss U.S. regular issue cards of the same players. On a black, blue and red background, fronts feature color player photos with thin white borders. The player's name and position, and the team and manufacturer logos also appear on the front. On a light blue background, the horizontal backs carry player biography, statistics, and career hightlights in French and English. Two cards, Dick Perez artwork of George Bell (213) and Tim Wallach (255), are called Canadian Greats (CG) and are not contained in the Donruss U.S. set. Diamond Kings (numbers 1-26, denoted DK) and Rated Rookies (numbers 28-47, denoted RR) are included just as in the American set. There are also bonus cards of the the two Canadian teams' MVP's, George Bell and Tim Raines, as in the Donruss American set. The players featured are heavily biased toward Canadian teams and those American teams closest to the Canadian border. Players appearing in their Rookie Card year include Roberto Alomar, Mark Grace and Gregg Jefferies.

	MINT	NRMT
COMPLETE SET (264)	20.00	9.00
COMMON CARD (1-264)	.05	.02
☐ 1 Mark McGwire DK	1.25	.55
☐ 2 Tim Raines DK	.10	.05
☐ 3 Benito Santiago DK	.05	.02
☐ 4 Alan Trammell DK	.15	.07
☐ 5 Danny Tartabull DK	.05	.02
☐ 6 Ron Darling DK	.05	.02
☐ 7 Paul Molitor DK	.50	.23
☐ 8 Devon White DK	.10	.05
☐ 9 Andre Dawson DK	.25	.11
☐ 10 Julio Franco DK	.10	.05
☐ 11 Scott Fletcher DK	.05	.02
☐ 12 Tony Fernandez DK	.05	.02
☐ 13 Shane Rawley DK	.05	.02
☐ 14 Kal Daniels DK	.05	.02
☐ 15 Jack Clark DK	.05	.02
☐ 16 Dwight Evans DK	.10	.05
☐ 17 Tommy John DK	.10	.05
☐ 18 Andy Van Slyke DK	.10	.05
☐ 19 Gary Gaetti DK	.10	.05
☐ 20 Mark Langston DK	.05	.02
☐ 21 Will Clark DK	.50	.23
☐ 22 Glenn Hubbard DK	.05	.02
☐ 23 Billy Hatcher DK	.05	.02
☐ 24 Bob Welch DK	.05	.02
☐ 25 Ivan Calderon DK	.05	.02
☐ 26 Cal Ripken DK	2.00	.90
☐ 27 DK Checklist 1-26	.05	.02
☐ 28 Mackey Sasser RR	.05	.02
☐ 29 Jeff Treadway RR	.05	.02
☐ 30 Mike Campbell RR	.05	.02
☐ 31 Lance Johnson RR	.30	.14
☐ 32 Nelson Liriano RR	.05	.02
☐ 33 Shawn Abner RR	.05	.02
☐ 34 Roberto Alomar RR	1.50	.70
☐ 35 Shawn Hillegas RR	.05	.02
☐ 36 Joey Meyer RR	.05	.02
☐ 37 Kevin Elster RR	.25	.11
☐ 38 Jose Lind RR	.05	.02
☐ 39 Kirt Manwaring RR	.05	.02
☐ 40 Mark Grace RR	1.25	.55
☐ 41 Jody Reed RR	.10	.05
☐ 42 John Farrell RR	.05	.02
☐ 43 Al Leiter RR	.40	.18
☐ 44 Gary Thurman RR	.05	.02
☐ 45 Vicente Palacios RR	.05	.02
☐ 46 Eddie Williams RR	.05	.02
☐ 47 Jack McDowell RR	.40	.18
☐ 48 Dwight Gooden	.10	.05
☐ 49 Mike Witt	.05	.02
☐ 50 Wally Joyner	.15	.07
☐ 51 Brook Jacoby	.05	.02
☐ 52 Bert Blyleven	.10	.05
☐ 53 Ted Higuera	.05	.02
☐ 54 Mike Scott	.05	.02
☐ 55 Jose Guzman	.05	.02
☐ 56 Roger Clemens	.75	.35
☐ 57 Dave Righetti	.05	.02
☐ 58 Benito Santiago	.05	.02
☐ 59 Ozzie Guillen	.05	.02
☐ 60 Matt Nokes	.05	.02
☐ 61 Fernando Valenzuela	.10	.05
☐ 62 Orel Hershiser	.10	.05
☐ 63 Sid Fernandez	.05	.02
☐ 64 Ozzie Virgil	.05	.02
☐ 65 Wade Boggs	.40	.18
☐ 66 Floyd Youmans	.05	.02
☐ 67 Jimmy Key	.10	.05
☐ 68 Bret Saberhagen	.05	.02
☐ 69 Jody Davis	.05	.02
☐ 70 Shawon Dunston	.05	.02
☐ 71 Julio Franco	.10	.05
☐ 72 Danny Cox	.05	.02
☐ 73 Jim Clancy	.05	.02
☐ 74 Mark Eichhorn	.05	.02
☐ 75 Scott Bradley	.05	.02
☐ 76 Charlie Leibrandt	.05	.02
☐ 77 Nolan Ryan	2.00	.90
☐ 78 Ron Darling	.05	.02
☐ 79 John Franco	.10	.05
☐ 80 Dave Stieb	.05	.02
☐ 81 Mike Fitzgerald	.05	.02
☐ 82 Steve Bedrosian	.05	.02
☐ 83 Dale Murphy	.25	.11
☐ 84 Tim Burke	.05	.02
☐ 85 Jack Morris	.10	.05
☐ 86 Greg Walker	.05	.02
☐ 87 Kevin Mitchell	.05	.02
☐ 88 Doug Drabek	.05	.02
☐ 89 Charlie Hough	.10	.05
☐ 90 Tony Gwynn	1.00	.45
☐ 91 Rick Sutcliffe	.05	.02
☐ 92 Shane Rawley	.05	.02
☐ 93 George Brett	.75	.35
☐ 94 Frank Viola	.10	.05
☐ 95 Tony Pena	.05	.02
☐ 96 Jim Deshaies	.05	.02
☐ 97 Mike Scioscia	.05	.02
☐ 98 Rick Rhoden	.05	.02
☐ 99 Terry Kennedy	.05	.02
☐ 100 Cal Ripken	2.00	.90
☐ 101 Pedro Guerrero	.05	.02
☐ 102 Andy Van Slyke	.10	.05
☐ 103 Willie McGee	.10	.05
☐ 104 Mike Kingery	.05	.02
☐ 105 Kevin Seitzer	.10	.05
☐ 106 Robin Yount	.40	.18
☐ 107 Tracy Jones	.05	.02
☐ 108 Dave Magadan	.05	.02
☐ 109 Mel Hall	.05	.02
☐ 110 Billy Hatcher	.05	.02
☐ 111 Todd Benzinger	.05	.02
☐ 112 Mike LaValliere	.05	.02
☐ 113 Barry Bonds	.75	.35
☐ 114 Tim Raines	.10	.05
☐ 115 Ozzie Smith	.60	.25
☐ 116 Dave Winfield	.40	.18
☐ 117 Keith Hernandez	.10	.05
☐ 118 Jeffrey Leonard	.05	.02
☐ 119 Larry Parrish	.05	.02
☐ 120 Robby Thompson	.05	.02
☐ 121 Andres Galarraga	.30	.14
☐ 122 Mickey Hatcher	.05	.02
☐ 123 Mark Langston	.05	.02
☐ 124 Mike Schmidt	.75	.35
☐ 125 Cory Snyder	.05	.02
☐ 126 Andre Dawson	.30	.14
☐ 127 Devon White	.10	.05
☐ 128 Vince Coleman	.05	.02
☐ 129 Bryn Smith	.05	.02
☐ 130 Lance Parrish	.10	.05
☐ 131 Willie Upshaw	.05	.02
☐ 132 Pete O'Brien	.05	.02
☐ 133 Tony Fernandez	.05	.02
☐ 134 Billy Ripken	.05	.02
☐ 135 Len Dykstra	.10	.05
☐ 136 Kirk Gibson	.10	.05
☐ 137 Kevin Bass	.05	.02
☐ 138 Jose Canseco	.75	.35
☐ 139 Kent Hrbek	.10	.05
☐ 140 Lloyd Moseby	.05	.02
☐ 141 Marty Barrett	.05	.02
☐ 142 Carmelo Martinez	.05	.02
☐ 143 Tom Foley	.05	.02
☐ 144 Kirby Puckett	1.00	.45
☐ 145 Rickey Henderson	.40	.18
☐ 146 Juan Samuel	.05	.02
☐ 147 Pete Incaviglia	.05	.02

Card	MINT	NRMT
☐ 148 Greg Brock	.05	.02
☐ 149 Eric Davis	.10	.05
☐ 150 Kal Daniels	.05	.02
☐ 151 Bob Boone	.10	.05
☐ 152 John Cerutti	.05	.02
☐ 153 Mike Greenwell	.05	.02
☐ 154 Oddibe McDowell	.05	.02
☐ 155 Scott Fletcher	.05	.02
☐ 156 Gary Carter	.25	.11
☐ 157 Harold Baines	.10	.05
☐ 158 Greg Swindell	.05	.02
☐ 159 Mark McLemore	.05	.02
☐ 160 Keith Moreland	.05	.02
☐ 161 Jim Gantner	.05	.02
☐ 162 Willie Randolph	.10	.05
☐ 163 Fred Lynn	.10	.05
☐ 164 B.J. Surhoff	.10	.05
☐ 165 Ken Griffey	.10	.05
☐ 166 Chet Lemon	.05	.02
☐ 167 Alan Trammell	.10	.05
☐ 168 Paul Molitor	.50	.23
☐ 169 Lou Whitaker	.10	.05
☐ 170 Will Clark	.50	.23
☐ 171 Dwight Evans	.10	.05
☐ 172 Eddie Murray	.50	.23
☐ 173 Darrell Evans	.10	.05
☐ 174 Ellis Burks	.40	.18
☐ 175 Ivan Calderon	.05	.02
☐ 176 John Kruk	.15	.07
☐ 177 Don Mattingly	1.00	.45
☐ 178 Dick Schofield	.05	.02
☐ 179 Bruce Hurst	.05	.02
☐ 180 Ron Guidry	.10	.05
☐ 181 Jack Clark	.05	.02
☐ 182 Franklin Stubbs	.05	.02
☐ 183 Bill Doran	.05	.02
☐ 184 Joe Carter	.25	.11
☐ 185 Steve Sax	.05	.02
☐ 186 Glenn Davis	.05	.02
☐ 187 Bo Jackson	.25	.11
☐ 188 Bobby Bonilla	.15	.07
☐ 189 Willie Wilson	.05	.02
☐ 190 Danny Tartabull	.05	.02
☐ 191 Bo Diaz	.05	.02
☐ 192 Buddy Bell	.10	.05
☐ 193 Tim Wallach	.05	.02
☐ 194 Mark McGwire	2.00	.90
☐ 195 Carney Lansford	.05	.02
☐ 196 Alvin Davis	.05	.02
☐ 197 Von Hayes	.05	.02
☐ 198 Mitch Webster	.05	.02
☐ 199 Casey Candaele	.05	.02
☐ 200 Gary Gaetti	.10	.05
☐ 201 Tommy Herr	.05	.02
☐ 202 Wally Backman	.05	.02
☐ 203 Brian Downing	.05	.02
☐ 204 Rance Mulliniks	.05	.02
☐ 205 Craig Reynolds	.05	.02
☐ 206 Ruben Sierra	.10	.05
☐ 207 Ryne Sandberg	.75	.35
☐ 208 Carlton Fisk	.40	.18
☐ 209 Checklist 28-107	.05	.02
☐ 210 Gerald Young	.05	.02
☐ 211 Tim Raines MVP (Bonus card pose)	.15	.07
☐ 212 John Tudor	.05	.02
☐ 213 George Bell CG	.10	.05
☐ 214 George Bell MVP (Bonus card pose)	.10	.05
☐ 215 Jim Rice	.10	.05
☐ 216 Gerald Perry	.05	.02
☐ 217 Dave Stewart	.10	.05
☐ 218 Jose Uribe	.05	.02
☐ 219 Rick Reuschel	.10	.05
☐ 220 Darryl Strawberry	.10	.05
☐ 221 Chris Brown	.05	.02
☐ 222 Ted Simmons	.10	.05
☐ 223 Lee Mazzilli	.05	.02
☐ 224 Denny Walling	.05	.02
☐ 225 Jesse Barfield	.05	.02
☐ 226 Barry Larkin	.60	.25
☐ 227 Harold Reynolds	.10	.05
☐ 228 Kevin McReynolds	.05	.02
☐ 229 Todd Worrell	.10	.05
☐ 230 Tommy John	.10	.05
☐ 231 Rick Aguilera	.10	.05
☐ 232 Bill Madlock	.10	.05
☐ 233 Roy Smalley	.05	.02
☐ 234 Jeff Musselman	.05	.02
☐ 235 Mike Dunne	.05	.02
☐ 236 Jerry Browne	.05	.02
☐ 237 Sam Horn	.05	.02
☐ 238 Howard Johnson	.05	.02
☐ 239 Candy Maldonado	.05	.02
☐ 240 Nick Esasky	.05	.02
☐ 241 Geno Petralli	.05	.02
☐ 242 Herm Winningham	.05	.02
☐ 243 Roger McDowell	.05	.02
☐ 244 Brian Fisher	.05	.02
☐ 245 John Marzano	.05	.02
☐ 246 Terry Pendleton	.10	.05
☐ 247 Rick Leach	.05	.02
☐ 248 Pascual Perez	.05	.02
☐ 249 Mookie Wilson	.10	.05
☐ 250 Ernie Whitt	.05	.02
☐ 251 Ron Kittle	.05	.02
☐ 252 Oil Can Boyd	.05	.02
☐ 253 Jim Gott	.05	.02
☐ 254 George Bell	.05	.02
☐ 255 Tim Wallach CG	.10	.05
☐ 256 Luis Polonia	.05	.02
☐ 257 Hubie Brooks	.05	.02
☐ 258 Mickey Brantley	.05	.02
☐ 259 Gregg Jefferies	.50	.23
☐ 260 Johnny Ray	.05	.02
☐ 261 Checklist 108-187	.05	.02
☐ 262 Dennis Martinez	.10	.05
☐ 263 Stan Musial Puzzle Card	.25	.11
☐ 264 Checklist 188-264	.05	.02

1990 Leaf Previews

The 1990 Leaf Previews set contains standard-size cards which were mailed to dealers to announce the 1990 version of Donruss' second major set of the year marketed as an upscale alternative under their Leaf name. This 12-card set was presented in the same style as the other Leaf cards were done in except that "Special Preview" was imprinted in white on the back. The cards were released in two series of 264 and the first series was not released until mid-season.

	MINT	NRMT
COMPLETE SET (12)	450.00	200.00
COMMON CARD (1-12)	15.00	6.75
☐ 1 Steve Sax	15.00	6.75
☐ 2 Joe Carter	40.00	18.00
☐ 3 Dennis Eckersley	25.00	11.00
☐ 4 Ken Griffey Jr.	200.00	90.00
☐ 5 Barry Larkin	40.00	18.00
☐ 6 Mark Langston	15.00	6.75
☐ 7 Eric Anthony	15.00	6.75
☐ 8 Robin Ventura	40.00	18.00
☐ 9 Greg Vaughn	20.00	9.00
☐ 10 Bobby Bonilla	20.00	9.00
☐ 11 Gary Gaetti	20.00	9.00
☐ 12 Ozzie Smith	75.00	34.00

1990 Leaf

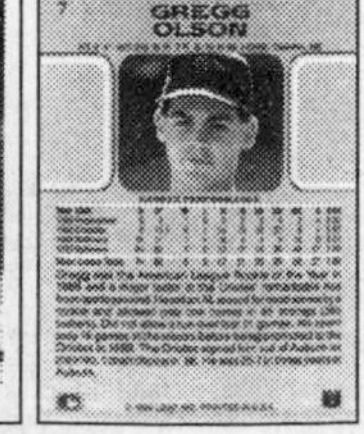

The 1990 Leaf set was the first premium set introduced by Donruss.The cards were issued in 15-card foil wrapped packs and were not available in factory sets. Each pack also contained one three-piece puzzle panel of a 63-piece Yogi Berra "Donruss Hall of Fame Diamond King" puzzle. This set, which was produced on high quality paper stock, was issued in two separate series of 264 standard-size cards each. The second series was issued approximately six weeks after the release of the first series. The cards feature full-color photos on both the front and back. Rookie Cards in the set include Carlos Baerga, Bernard Gilkey, Marquis Grissom, David Justice, Ben McDonald, Sammy Sosa, Frank Thomas and Larry Walker.

	MINT	NRMT
COMPLETE SET (528)	200.00	90.00
COMPLETE SERIES 1 (264)	80.00	36.00
COMPLETE SERIES 2 (264)	120.00	55.00
COMMON CARD (1-528)	.25	.11
☐ 1 Introductory Card	.25	.11
☐ 2 Mike Henneman	.25	.11
☐ 3 Steve Bedrosian	.25	.11
☐ 4 Mike Scott	.25	.11
☐ 5 Allan Anderson	.25	.11
☐ 6 Rick Sutcliffe	.25	.11
☐ 7 Gregg Olson	.25	.11
☐ 8 Kevin Elster	.25	.11
☐ 9 Pete O'Brien	.25	.11
☐ 10 Carlton Fisk	1.50	.70
☐ 11 Joe Magrane	.25	.11
☐ 12 Roger Clemens	3.00	1.35
☐ 13 Tom Glavine	2.00	.90
☐ 14 Tom Gordon	.50	.23
☐ 15 Todd Benzinger	.25	.11
☐ 16 Hubie Brooks	.25	.11
☐ 17 Roberto Kelly	.25	.11
☐ 18 Barry Larkin	1.50	.70
☐ 19 Mike Boddicker	.25	.11
☐ 20 Roger McDowell	.25	.11
☐ 21 Nolan Ryan	6.00	2.70
☐ 22 John Farrell	.25	.11
☐ 23 Bruce Hurst	.25	.11
☐ 24 Wally Joyner	.50	.23
☐ 25 Greg Maddux	15.00	6.75
☐ 26 Chris Bosio	.25	.11
☐ 27 John Cerutti	.25	.11
☐ 28 Tim Burke	.25	.11
☐ 29 Dennis Eckersley	1.50	.70
☐ 30 Glenn Davis	.25	.11
☐ 31 Jim Abbott	.50	.23
☐ 32 Mike LaValliere	.25	.11
☐ 33 Andres Thomas	.25	.11
☐ 34 Lou Whitaker	.50	.23
☐ 35 Alvin Davis	.25	.11
☐ 36 Melido Perez	.25	.11
☐ 37 Craig Biggio	1.50	.70
☐ 38 Rick Aguilera	.50	.23
☐ 39 Pete Harnisch	.25	.11
☐ 40 David Cone	1.50	.70
☐ 41 Scott Garrelts	.25	.11
☐ 42 Jay Howell	.25	.11
☐ 43 Eric King	.25	.11
☐ 44 Pedro Guerrero	.25	.11
☐ 45 Mike Bielecki	.25	.11
☐ 46 Bob Boone	.50	.23
☐ 47 Kevin Brown	1.50	.70
☐ 48 Jerry Browne	.25	.11
☐ 49 Mike Scioscia	.25	.11
☐ 50 Chuck Cary	.25	.11
☐ 51 Wade Boggs	1.50	.70
☐ 52 Von Hayes	.25	.11
☐ 53 Tony Fernandez	.25	.11
☐ 54 Dennis Martinez	.50	.23
☐ 55 Tom Candiotti	.25	.11
☐ 56 Andy Benes	1.00	.45
☐ 57 Rob Dibble	.25	.11
☐ 58 Chuck Crim	.25	.11
☐ 59 John Smoltz	2.50	1.10
☐ 60 Mike Heath	.25	.11
☐ 61 Kevin Gross	.25	.11
☐ 62 Mark McGwire	3.00	1.35
☐ 63 Bert Blyleven	.50	.23
☐ 64 Bob Walk	.25	.11
☐ 65 Mickey Tettleton	.50	.23
☐ 66 Sid Fernandez	.25	.11
☐ 67 Terry Kennedy	.25	.11
☐ 68 Fernando Valenzuela	.50	.23
☐ 69 Don Mattingly	2.50	1.10
☐ 70 Paul O'Neill	.50	.23
☐ 71 Robin Yount	1.50	.70
☐ 72 Bret Saberhagen	.50	.23
☐ 73 Geno Petralli	.25	.11
☐ 74 Brook Jacoby	.25	.11
☐ 75 Roberto Alomar	2.00	.90
☐ 76 Devon White	.25	.11
☐ 77 Jose Lind	.25	.11
☐ 78 Pat Combs	.25	.11
☐ 79 Dave Stieb	.25	.11
☐ 80 Tim Wallach	.25	.11
☐ 81 Dave Stewart	.50	.23
☐ 82 Eric Anthony	.50	.23
☐ 83 Randy Bush	.25	.11
☐ 84 Rickey Henderson CL	.50	.23
☐ 85 Jaime Navarro	.25	.11
☐ 86 Tommy Gregg	.25	.11
☐ 87 Frank Tanana	.25	.11
☐ 88 Omar Vizquel	2.00	.90
☐ 89 Ivan Calderon	.25	.11

☐ 90 Vince Coleman .25 .11
☐ 91 Barry Bonds 2.00 .90
☐ 92 Randy Milligan .25 .11
☐ 93 Frank Viola .25 .11
☐ 94 Matt Williams 2.00 .90
☐ 95 Alfredo Griffin .25 .11
☐ 96 Steve Sax .25 .11
☐ 97 Gary Gaetti .50 .23
☐ 98 Ryne Sandberg 2.00 .90
☐ 99 Danny Tartabull .25 .11
☐ 100 Rafael Palmeiro 1.50 .70
☐ 101 Jesse Orosco .25 .11
☐ 102 Garry Templeton .25 .11
☐ 103 Frank DiPino .25 .11
☐ 104 Tony Pena .25 .11
☐ 105 Dickie Thon .25 .11
☐ 106 Kelly Gruber .25 .11
☐ 107 Marquis Grissom 4.00 1.80
☐ 108 Jose Canseco 1.50 .70
☐ 109 Mike Blowers 1.50 .70
☐ 110 Tom Browning .25 .11
☐ 111 Greg Vaughn .50 .23
☐ 112 Oddibe McDowell .25 .11
☐ 113 Gary Ward .25 .11
☐ 114 Jay Buhner 1.50 .70
☐ 115 Eric Show .25 .11
☐ 116 Bryan Harvey .25 .11
☐ 117 Andy Van Slyke .50 .23
☐ 118 Jeff Ballard .25 .11
☐ 119 Barry Lyons .25 .11
☐ 120 Kevin Mitchell .50 .23
☐ 121 Mike Gallego .25 .11
☐ 122 Dave Smith .25 .11
☐ 123 Kirby Puckett 3.00 1.35
☐ 124 Jerome Walton .25 .11
☐ 125 Bo Jackson 1.50 .70
☐ 126 Harold Baines .50 .23
☐ 127 Scott Bankhead .25 .11
☐ 128 Ozzie Guillen .25 .11
☐ 129 Jose Oquendo UER .25 .11
(League misspelled
as Legue)
☐ 130 John Dopson .25 .11
☐ 131 Charlie Hayes .50 .23
☐ 132 Fred McGriff 1.50 .70
☐ 133 Chet Lemon .25 .11
☐ 134 Gary Carter 1.50 .70
☐ 135 Rafael Ramirez .25 .11
☐ 136 Shane Mack .25 .11
☐ 137 Mark Grace UER 1.50 .70
(Card back has OB:L,
should be B:L)
☐ 138 Phil Bradley .25 .11
☐ 139 Dwight Gooden .50 .23
☐ 140 Harold Reynolds .25 .11
☐ 141 Scott Fletcher .25 .11
☐ 142 Ozzie Smith 2.00 .90
☐ 143 Mike Greenwell .25 .11
☐ 144 Pete Smith .25 .11
☐ 145 Mark Gubicza .25 .11
☐ 146 Chris Sabo .25 .11
☐ 147 Ramon Martinez 1.00 .45
☐ 148 Tim Leary .25 .11
☐ 149 Randy Myers .50 .23
☐ 150 Jody Reed .25 .11
☐ 151 Bruce Ruffin .25 .11
☐ 152 Jeff Russell .25 .11
☐ 153 Doug Jones .25 .11
☐ 154 Tony Gwynn 4.00 1.80
☐ 155 Mark Langston .25 .11
☐ 156 Mitch Williams .25 .11
☐ 157 Gary Sheffield 4.00 1.80
☐ 158 Tom Henke .25 .11
☐ 159 Oil Can Boyd .25 .11
☐ 160 Rickey Henderson 1.50 .70
☐ 161 Bill Doran .25 .11
☐ 162 Chuck Finley .50 .23
☐ 163 Jeff King .50 .23
☐ 164 Nick Esasky .25 .11
☐ 165 Cecil Fielder 1.00 .45
☐ 166 Dave Valle .25 .11
☐ 167 Robin Ventura 2.00 .90
☐ 168 Jim Deshaies .25 .11
☐ 169 Juan Berenguer .25 .11
☐ 170 Craig Worthington .25 .11
☐ 171 Gregg Jefferies .50 .23
☐ 172 Will Clark 1.50 .70
☐ 173 Kirk Gibson .50 .23
☐ 174 Carlton Fisk CL 1.00 .45
☐ 175 Bobby Thigpen .25 .11
☐ 176 John Tudor .25 .11
☐ 177 Andre Dawson 1.50 .70
☐ 178 George Brett 3.00 1.35
☐ 179 Steve Buechele .25 .11
☐ 180 Joey Belle 10.00 4.50
☐ 181 Eddie Murray 1.50 .70
☐ 182 Bob Geren .25 .11
☐ 183 Rob Murphy .25 .11
☐ 184 Tom Herr .25 .11
☐ 185 George Bell .25 .11
☐ 186 Spike Owen .25 .11
☐ 187 Cory Snyder .25 .11
☐ 188 Fred Lynn .25 .11
☐ 189 Eric Davis 1.00 .45
☐ 190 Dave Parker .50 .23
☐ 191 Jeff Blauser .50 .23
☐ 192 Matt Nokes .25 .11
☐ 193 Delino DeShields 1.50 .70
☐ 194 Scott Sanderson .25 .11
☐ 195 Lance Parrish .25 .11
☐ 196 Bobby Bonilla .50 .23
☐ 197 Cal Ripken UER 6.00 2.70
(Reistertown, should
be Reisterstown)
☐ 198 Kevin McReynolds .25 .11
☐ 199 Robby Thompson .25 .11
☐ 200 Tim Belcher .25 .11
☐ 201 Jesse Barfield .25 .11
☐ 202 Mariano Duncan .25 .11
☐ 203 Bill Spiers .25 .11
☐ 204 Frank White .50 .23
☐ 205 Julio Franco .50 .23
☐ 206 Greg Swindell .25 .11
☐ 207 Benito Santiago .25 .11
☐ 208 Johnny Ray .25 .11
☐ 209 Gary Redus .25 .11
☐ 210 Jeff Parrett .25 .11
☐ 211 Jimmy Key 1.00 .45
☐ 212 Tim Raines .50 .23
☐ 213 Carney Lansford .50 .23
☐ 214 Gerald Young .25 .11
☐ 215 Gene Larkin .25 .11
☐ 216 Dan Plesac .25 .11
☐ 217 Lonnie Smith .25 .11
☐ 218 Alan Trammell 1.00 .45
☐ 219 Jeffrey Leonard .25 .11
☐ 220 Sammy Sosa 8.00 3.60
☐ 221 Todd Zeile .50 .23
☐ 222 Bill Landrum .25 .11
☐ 223 Mike Devereaux .25 .11
☐ 224 Mike Marshall .25 .11
☐ 225 Jose Uribe .25 .11
☐ 226 Juan Samuel .25 .11
☐ 227 Mel Hall .25 .11
☐ 228 Kent Hrbek .50 .23
☐ 229 Shawon Dunston .25 .11
☐ 230 Kevin Seitzer .25 .11
☐ 231 Pete Incaviglia .25 .11
☐ 232 Sandy Alomar Jr. 2.00 .90
☐ 233 Bip Roberts .25 .11
☐ 234 Scott Terry .25 .11
☐ 235 Dwight Evans .50 .23
☐ 236 Ricky Jordan .25 .11
☐ 237 John Olerud 2.00 .90
☐ 238 Zane Smith .25 .11
☐ 239 Walt Weiss .25 .11
☐ 240 Alvaro Espinoza .25 .11
☐ 241 Billy Hatcher .25 .11
☐ 242 Paul Molitor 1.50 .70
☐ 243 Dale Murphy 1.50 .70
☐ 244 Dave Bergman .25 .11
☐ 245 Ken Griffey Jr. 25.00 11.00
☐ 246 Ed Whitson .25 .11
☐ 247 Kirk McCaskill .25 .11
☐ 248 Jay Bell .50 .23
☐ 249 Ben McDonald 1.50 .70
☐ 250 Darryl Strawberry .50 .23
☐ 251 Brett Butler 1.00 .45
☐ 252 Terry Steinbach .50 .23
☐ 253 Ken Caminiti 2.50 1.10
☐ 254 Dan Gladden .25 .11
☐ 255 Dwight Smith .25 .11
☐ 256 Kurt Stillwell .25 .11
☐ 257 Ruben Sierra .25 .11
☐ 258 Mike Schooler .25 .11
☐ 259 Lance Johnson .50 .23
☐ 260 Terry Pendleton .50 .23
☐ 261 Ellis Burks .50 .23
☐ 262 Len Dykstra .50 .23
☐ 263 Mookie Wilson .25 .11
☐ 264 Nolan Ryan CL UER 1.50 .70
No TM after Ranger logo
☐ 265 Nolan Ryan 3.00 1.35
No Hit King
☐ 266 Brian DuBois .25 .11
☐ 267 Don Robinson .25 .11
☐ 268 Glenn Wilson .25 .11
☐ 269 Kevin Tapani .50 .23
☐ 270 Marvell Wynne .25 .11
☐ 271 Billy Ripken .25 .11
☐ 272 Howard Johnson .25 .11
☐ 273 Brian Holman .25 .11
☐ 274 Dan Pasqua .25 .11
☐ 275 Ken Dayley .25 .11
☐ 276 Jeff Reardon .50 .23
☐ 277 Jim Presley .25 .11
☐ 278 Jim Eisenreich .25 .11
☐ 279 Danny Jackson .25 .11
☐ 280 Orel Hershiser .50 .23
☐ 281 Andy Hawkins .25 .11
☐ 282 Jose Rijo .25 .11
☐ 283 Luis Rivera .25 .11
☐ 284 John Kruk .50 .23
☐ 285 Jeff Huson .25 .11
☐ 286 Joel Skinner .25 .11
☐ 287 Jack Clark .50 .23
☐ 288 Chili Davis 1.00 .45
☐ 289 Joe Girardi .50 .23
☐ 290 B.J. Surhoff .50 .23
☐ 291 Luis Sojo .25 .11
☐ 292 Tom Foley .25 .11
☐ 293 Mike Moore .25 .11
☐ 294 Ken Oberkfell .25 .11
☐ 295 Luis Polonia .25 .11
☐ 296 Doug Drabek .25 .11
☐ 297 Dave Justice 8.00 3.60
☐ 298 Paul Gibson .25 .11
☐ 299 Edgar Martinez 2.00 .90
☐ 300 Frank Thomas UER 85.00 38.00
(No B in front
of birthdate)
☐ 301 Eric Yelding .25 .11
☐ 302 Greg Gagne .25 .11
☐ 303 Brad Komminsk .25 .11
☐ 304 Ron Darling .25 .11
☐ 305 Kevin Bass .25 .11
☐ 306 Jeff Hamilton .25 .11
☐ 307 Ron Karkovice .25 .11
☐ 308 Milt Thompson UER 1.50 .70
(Ray Lankford pictured
on card back)
☐ 309 Mike Harkey .25 .11
☐ 310 Mel Stottlemyre Jr. .25 .11
☐ 311 Kenny Rogers .50 .23
☐ 312 Mitch Webster .25 .11
☐ 313 Kal Daniels .25 .11
☐ 314 Matt Nokes .25 .11
☐ 315 Dennis Lamp .25 .11
☐ 316 Ken Howell .25 .11
☐ 317 Glenallen Hill .50 .23
☐ 318 Dave Martinez .25 .11
☐ 319 Chris James .25 .11
☐ 320 Mike Pagliarulo .25 .11
☐ 321 Hal Morris .50 .23
☐ 322 Rob Deer .25 .11
☐ 323 Greg Olson .25 .11
☐ 324 Tony Phillips .25 .11
☐ 325 Larry Walker 12.00 5.50
☐ 326 Ron Hassey .25 .11
☐ 327 Jack Howell .25 .11
☐ 328 John Smiley .25 .11
☐ 329 Steve Finley 1.50 .70
☐ 330 Dave Magadan .25 .11
☐ 331 Greg Litton .25 .11
☐ 332 Mickey Hatcher .25 .11
☐ 333 Lee Guetterman .25 .11
☐ 334 Norm Charlton .25 .11
☐ 335 Edgar Diaz .25 .11
☐ 336 Willie Wilson .25 .11
☐ 337 Bobby Witt .25 .11
☐ 338 Candy Maldonado .25 .11
☐ 339 Craig Lefferts .25 .11
☐ 340 Dante Bichette 2.00 .90
☐ 341 Wally Backman .25 .11
☐ 342 Dennis Cook .25 .11
☐ 343 Pat Borders .25 .11
☐ 344 Wallace Johnson .25 .11
☐ 345 Willie Randolph .50 .23
☐ 346 Danny Darwin .25 .11
☐ 347 Al Newman .25 .11
☐ 348 Mark Knudson .25 .11
☐ 349 Joe Boever .25 .11
☐ 350 Larry Sheets .25 .11
☐ 351 Mike Jackson .25 .11
☐ 352 Wayne Edwards .25 .11
☐ 353 Bernard Gilkey 2.50 1.10
☐ 354 Don Slaught .25 .11
☐ 355 Joe Orsulak .25 .11
☐ 356 John Franco .25 .11
☐ 357 Jeff Brantley .25 .11
☐ 358 Mike Morgan .25 .11
☐ 359 Deion Sanders 3.00 1.35
☐ 360 Terry Leach .25 .11
☐ 361 Les Lancaster .25 .11
☐ 362 Storm Davis .25 .11
☐ 363 Scott Coolbaugh .25 .11
☐ 364 Ozzie Smith CL 1.00 .45
☐ 365 Cecilio Guante .25 .11
☐ 366 Joey Cora 1.50 .70
☐ 367 Willie McGee .50 .23
☐ 368 Jerry Reed .25 .11

☐ 369 Darren Daulton	.50	.23
☐ 370 Manny Lee	.25	.11
☐ 371 Mark Gardner	.25	.11
☐ 372 Rick Honeycutt	.25	.11
☐ 373 Steve Balboni	.25	.11
☐ 374 Jack Armstrong	.25	.11
☐ 375 Charlie O'Brien	.25	.11
☐ 376 Ron Gant	1.00	.45
☐ 377 Lloyd Moseby	.25	.11
☐ 378 Gene Harris	.25	.11
☐ 379 Joe Carter	1.50	.70
☐ 380 Scott Bailes	.25	.11
☐ 381 R.J. Reynolds	.25	.11
☐ 382 Bob Melvin	.25	.11
☐ 383 Tim Teufel	.25	.11
☐ 384 John Burkett	.50	.23
☐ 385 Felix Jose	.25	.11
☐ 386 Larry Andersen	.25	.11
☐ 387 David West	.25	.11
☐ 388 Luis Salazar	.25	.11
☐ 389 Mike Macfarlane	.25	.11
☐ 390 Charlie Hough	.25	.11
☐ 391 Greg Briley	.25	.11
☐ 392 Donn Pall	.25	.11
☐ 393 Bryn Smith	.25	.11
☐ 394 Carlos Quintana	.25	.11
☐ 395 Steve Lake	.25	.11
☐ 396 Mark Whiten	.50	.23
☐ 397 Edwin Nunez	.25	.11
☐ 398 Rick Parker	.25	.11
☐ 399 Mark Portugal	.25	.11
☐ 400 Roy Smith	.25	.11
☐ 401 Hector Villanueva	.25	.11
☐ 402 Bob Milacki	.25	.11
☐ 403 Alejandro Pena	.25	.11
☐ 404 Scott Bradley	.25	.11
☐ 405 Ron Kittle	.25	.11
☐ 406 Bob Tewksbury	.25	.11
☐ 407 Wes Gardner	.25	.11
☐ 408 Ernie Whitt	.25	.11
☐ 409 Terry Shumpert	.25	.11
☐ 410 Tim Layana	.25	.11
☐ 411 Chris Gwynn	.25	.11
☐ 412 Jeff D. Robinson	.25	.11
☐ 413 Scott Scudder	.25	.11
☐ 414 Kevin Romine	.25	.11
☐ 415 Jose DeJesus	.25	.11
☐ 416 Mike Jeffcoat	.25	.11
☐ 417 Rudy Seanez	.25	.11
☐ 418 Mike Dunne	.25	.11
☐ 419 Dick Schofield	.25	.11
☐ 420 Steve Wilson	.25	.11
☐ 421 Bill Krueger	.25	.11
☐ 422 Junior Felix	.25	.11
☐ 423 Drew Hall	.25	.11
☐ 424 Curt Young	.25	.11
☐ 425 Franklin Stubbs	.25	.11
☐ 426 Dave Winfield	1.50	.70
☐ 427 Rick Reed	.25	.11
☐ 428 Charlie Leibrandt	.25	.11
☐ 429 Jeff M. Robinson	.25	.11
☐ 430 Erik Hanson	.25	.11
☐ 431 Barry Jones	.25	.11
☐ 432 Alex Trevino	.25	.11
☐ 433 John Moses	.25	.11
☐ 434 Dave Johnson	.25	.11
☐ 435 Mackey Sasser	.25	.11
☐ 436 Rick Leach	.25	.11
☐ 437 Lenny Harris	.25	.11
☐ 438 Carlos Martinez	.25	.11
☐ 439 Rex Hudler	.25	.11
☐ 440 Domingo Ramos	.25	.11
☐ 441 Gerald Perry	.25	.11
☐ 442 Jeff Russell	.25	.11
☐ 443 Carlos Baerga	2.50	1.10
☐ 444 Will Clark CL	1.00	.45
☐ 445 Stan Javier	.25	.11
☐ 446 Kevin Maas	1.00	.45
☐ 447 Tom Brunansky	.25	.11
☐ 448 Carmelo Martinez	.25	.11
☐ 449 Willie Blair	1.50	.70
☐ 450 Andres Galarraga	1.50	.70
☐ 451 Bud Black	.25	.11
☐ 452 Greg W. Harris	.25	.11
☐ 453 Joe Oliver	.25	.11
☐ 454 Greg Brock	.25	.11
☐ 455 Jeff Treadway	.25	.11
☐ 456 Lance McCullers	.25	.11
☐ 457 Dave Schmidt	.25	.11
☐ 458 Todd Burns	.25	.11
☐ 459 Max Venable	.25	.11
☐ 460 Neal Heaton	.25	.11
☐ 461 Mark Williamson	.25	.11
☐ 462 Keith Miller	.25	.11
☐ 463 Mike LaCoss	.25	.11
☐ 464 Jose Offerman	1.50	.70
☐ 465 Jim Leyritz	1.50	.70
☐ 466 Glenn Braggs	.25	.11
☐ 467 Ron Robinson	.25	.11
☐ 468 Mark Davis	.25	.11
☐ 469 Gary Pettis	.25	.11
☐ 470 Keith Hernandez	.50	.23
☐ 471 Dennis Rasmussen	.25	.11
☐ 472 Mark Eichhorn	.25	.11
☐ 473 Ted Power	.25	.11
☐ 474 Terry Mulholland	.25	.11
☐ 475 Todd Stottlemyre	.50	.23
☐ 476 Jerry Goff	.25	.11
☐ 477 Gene Nelson	.25	.11
☐ 478 Rich Gedman	.25	.11
☐ 479 Brian Harper	.25	.11
☐ 480 Mike Felder	.25	.11
☐ 481 Steve Avery	.50	.23
☐ 482 Jack Morris	.50	.23
☐ 483 Randy Johnson	5.00	2.20
☐ 484 Scott Radinsky	.25	.11
☐ 485 Jose DeLeon	.25	.11
☐ 486 Stan Belinda	.25	.11
☐ 487 Brian Holton	.25	.11
☐ 488 Mark Carreon	.25	.11
☐ 489 Trevor Wilson	.25	.11
☐ 490 Mike Sharperson	.25	.11
☐ 491 Alan Mills	.25	.11
☐ 492 John Candelaria	.25	.11
☐ 493 Paul Assenmacher	.25	.11
☐ 494 Steve Crawford	.25	.11
☐ 495 Brad Arnsberg	.25	.11
☐ 496 Sergio Valdez	.25	.11
☐ 497 Mark Parent	.25	.11
☐ 498 Tom Pagnozzi	.25	.11
☐ 499 Greg A. Harris	.25	.11
☐ 500 Randy Ready	.25	.11
☐ 501 Duane Ward	.25	.11
☐ 502 Nelson Santovenia	.25	.11
☐ 503 Joe Klink	.25	.11
☐ 504 Eric Plunk	.25	.11
☐ 505 Jeff Reed	.25	.11
☐ 506 Ted Higuera	.25	.11
☐ 507 Joe Hesketh	.25	.11
☐ 508 Dan Petry	.25	.11
☐ 509 Matt Young	.25	.11
☐ 510 Jerald Clark	.25	.11
☐ 511 John Orton	.25	.11
☐ 512 Scott Ruskin	.25	.11
☐ 513 Chris Hoiles	1.50	.70
☐ 514 Daryl Boston	.25	.11
☐ 515 Francisco Oliveras	.25	.11
☐ 516 Ozzie Canseco	.25	.11
☐ 517 Xavier Hernandez	.25	.11
☐ 518 Fred Manrique	.25	.11
☐ 519 Shawn Boskie	.25	.11
☐ 520 Jeff Montgomery	.50	.23
☐ 521 Jack Daugherty	.25	.11
☐ 522 Keith Comstock	.25	.11
☐ 523 Greg Hibbard	.25	.11
☐ 524 Lee Smith	.50	.23
☐ 525 Dana Kiecker	.25	.11
☐ 526 Darrel Akerfelds	.25	.11
☐ 527 Greg Myers	.25	.11
☐ 528 Ryne Sandberg CL	.75	.35

1991 Leaf Previews

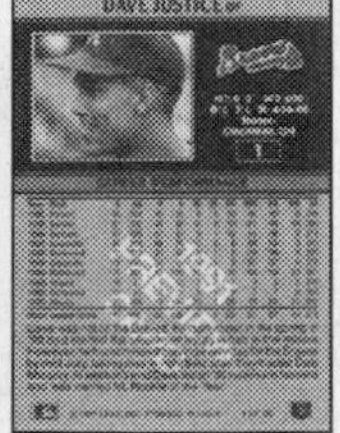

The 1991 Leaf Previews set consists of 26 standard-size cards. Cards from this set were issued as inserts (four at a time) inside specially marked 1991 Donruss hobby factory sets. The front design has color action player photos, with white and silver borders.

	MINT	NRMT
COMPLETE SET (26)	35.00	16.00
COMMON CARD (1-26)	1.00	.45
☐ 1 Dave Justice	3.00	1.35
☐ 2 Ryne Sandberg	5.00	2.20
☐ 3 Barry Larkin	2.50	1.10
☐ 4 Craig Biggio	3.00	1.35
☐ 5 Ramon Martinez	2.00	.90
☐ 6 Tim Wallach	1.00	.45
☐ 7 Dwight Gooden	2.00	.90
☐ 8 Len Dykstra	2.00	.90
☐ 9 Barry Bonds	5.00	2.20
☐ 10 Ray Lankford	2.50	1.10
☐ 11 Tony Gwynn	6.00	2.70
☐ 12 Will Clark	3.00	1.35
☐ 13 Leo Gomez	1.00	.45
☐ 14 Wade Boggs	3.00	1.35
☐ 15 Chuck Finley UER (Position on card back is First Base)	1.00	.45
☐ 16 Carlton Fisk	3.00	1.35
☐ 17 Sandy Alomar Jr.	2.00	.90
☐ 18 Cecil Fielder	2.00	.90
☐ 19 Bo Jackson	2.00	.90
☐ 20 Paul Molitor	3.00	1.35
☐ 21 Kirby Puckett	6.00	2.70
☐ 22 Don Mattingly	8.00	3.60
☐ 23 Rickey Henderson	3.00	1.35
☐ 24 Tino Martinez	3.00	1.35
☐ 25 Nolan Ryan	15.00	6.75
☐ 26 Dave Stieb	1.00	.45

1991 Leaf

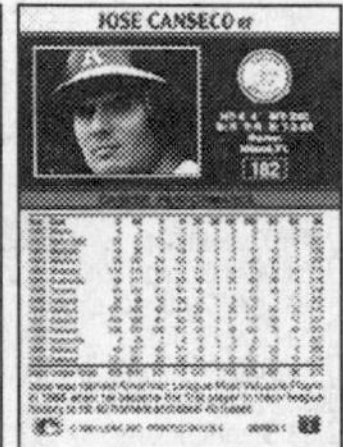

This 528-card standard size set was issued by Donruss in two separate series of 264 cards. Cards were exclusively issued in foil packs. The front design has color action player photos, with white and silver borders. A thicker stock was used for these (then) premium level cards. Rookie Cards in the set include Brian McRae and Denny Neagle.

	MINT	NRMT
COMPLETE SET (528)	15.00	6.75
COMPLETE SERIES 1 (264)	5.00	2.20
COMPLETE SERIES 2 (264)	10.00	4.50
COMMON CARD (1-528)	.10	.05
☐ 1 The Leaf Card	.10	.05
☐ 2 Kurt Stillwell	.10	.05
☐ 3 Bobby Witt	.10	.05
☐ 4 Tony Phillips	.10	.05
☐ 5 Scott Garrelts	.10	.05
☐ 6 Greg Swindell	.10	.05
☐ 7 Billy Ripken	.10	.05
☐ 8 Dave Martinez	.10	.05
☐ 9 Kelly Gruber	.10	.05
☐ 10 Juan Samuel	.10	.05
☐ 11 Brian Holman	.10	.05
☐ 12 Craig Biggio	.40	.18
☐ 13 Lonnie Smith	.10	.05
☐ 14 Ron Robinson	.10	.05
☐ 15 Mike LaValliere	.10	.05
☐ 16 Mark Davis	.10	.05
☐ 17 Jack Daugherty	.10	.05
☐ 18 Mike Henneman	.10	.05
☐ 19 Mike Greenwell	.10	.05
☐ 20 Dave Magadan	.10	.05
☐ 21 Mark Williamson	.10	.05
☐ 22 Marquis Grissom	.40	.18
☐ 23 Pat Borders	.10	.05
☐ 24 Mike Scioscia	.10	.05
☐ 25 Shawon Dunston	.10	.05
☐ 26 Randy Bush	.10	.05
☐ 27 John Smoltz	.40	.18
☐ 28 Chuck Crim	.10	.05
☐ 29 Don Slaught	.10	.05
☐ 30 Mike Macfarlane	.10	.05
☐ 31 Wally Joyner	.10	.05
☐ 32 Pat Combs	.10	.05
☐ 33 Tony Pena	.10	.05
☐ 34 Howard Johnson	.10	.05
☐ 35 Leo Gomez	.10	.05
☐ 36 Spike Owen	.10	.05
☐ 37 Eric Davis	.10	.05
☐ 38 Roberto Kelly	.10	.05
☐ 39 Jerome Walton	.10	.05
☐ 40 Shane Mack	.10	.05
☐ 41 Kent Mercker	.10	.05
☐ 42 B.J. Surhoff	.10	.05
☐ 43 Jerry Browne	.10	.05
☐ 44 Lee Smith	.10	.05
☐ 45 Chuck Finley	.10	.05

☐ 46 Terry Mulholland .10 .05
☐ 47 Tom Bolton .10 .05
☐ 48 Tom Herr .10 .05
☐ 49 Jim Deshaies .10 .05
☐ 50 Walt Weiss .10 .05
☐ 51 Hal Morris .10 .05
☐ 52 Lee Guetterman .10 .05
☐ 53 Paul Assenmacher .10 .05
☐ 54 Brian Harper .10 .05
☐ 55 Paul Gibson .10 .05
☐ 56 John Burkett .10 .05
☐ 57 Doug Jones .10 .05
☐ 58 Jose Oquendo .10 .05
☐ 59 Dick Schofield .10 .05
☐ 60 Dickie Thon .10 .05
☐ 61 Ramon Martinez .10 .05
☐ 62 Jay Buhner .40 .18
☐ 63 Mark Portugal .10 .05
☐ 64 Bob Welch .10 .05
☐ 65 Chris Sabo .10 .05
☐ 66 Chuck Cary .10 .05
☐ 67 Mark Langston .10 .05
☐ 68 Joe Boever .10 .05
☐ 69 Jody Reed .10 .05
☐ 70 Alejandro Pena .10 .05
☐ 71 Jeff King .10 .05
☐ 72 Tom Pagnozzi .10 .05
☐ 73 Joe Oliver .10 .05
☐ 74 Mike Witt .10 .05
☐ 75 Hector Villanueva .10 .05
☐ 76 Dan Gladden .10 .05
☐ 77 Dave Justice .50 .23
☐ 78 Mike Gallego .10 .05
☐ 79 Tom Candiotti .10 .05
☐ 80 Ozzie Smith .50 .23
☐ 81 Luis Polonia .10 .05
☐ 82 Randy Ready .10 .05
☐ 83 Greg A. Harris .10 .05
☐ 84 David Justice CL .20 .09
☐ 85 Kevin Mitchell .10 .05
☐ 86 Mark McLemore .10 .05
☐ 87 Terry Steinbach .10 .05
☐ 88 Tom Browning .10 .05
☐ 89 Matt Nokes .10 .05
☐ 90 Mike Harkey .10 .05
☐ 91 Omar Vizquel .40 .18
☐ 92 Dave Bergman .10 .05
☐ 93 Matt Williams .40 .18
☐ 94 Steve Olin .10 .05
☐ 95 Craig Wilson .10 .05
☐ 96 Dave Stieb .10 .05
☐ 97 Ruben Sierra .10 .05
☐ 98 Jay Howell .10 .05
☐ 99 Scott Bradley .10 .05
☐ 100 Eric Yelding .10 .05
☐ 101 Rickey Henderson .40 .18
☐ 102 Jeff Reed .10 .05
☐ 103 Jimmy Key .10 .05
☐ 104 Terry Shumpert .10 .05
☐ 105 Kenny Rogers .10 .05
☐ 106 Cecil Fielder .10 .05
☐ 107 Robby Thompson .10 .05
☐ 108 Alex Cole .10 .05
☐ 109 Randy Milligan .10 .05
☐ 110 Andres Galarraga .40 .18
☐ 111 Bill Spiers .10 .05
☐ 112 Kal Daniels .10 .05
☐ 113 Henry Cotto .10 .05
☐ 114 Casey Candaele .10 .05
☐ 115 Jeff Blauser .10 .05
☐ 116 Robin Yount .40 .18
☐ 117 Ben McDonald .10 .05
☐ 118 Bret Saberhagen .10 .05
☐ 119 Juan Gonzalez 1.50 .70
☐ 120 Lou Whitaker .10 .05
☐ 121 Ellis Burks .20 .09
☐ 122 Charlie O'Brien .10 .05
☐ 123 John Smiley .10 .05
☐ 124 Tim Burke .10 .05
☐ 125 John Olerud .10 .05
☐ 126 Eddie Murray .40 .18
☐ 127 Greg Maddux 1.25 .55
☐ 128 Kevin Tapani .10 .05
☐ 129 Ron Gant .10 .05
☐ 130 Jay Bell .10 .05
☐ 131 Chris Hoiles .10 .05
☐ 132 Tom Gordon .10 .05
☐ 133 Kevin Seitzer .10 .05
☐ 134 Jeff Huson .10 .05
☐ 135 Jerry Don Gleaton .10 .05
☐ 136 Jeff Brantley UER .10 .05
(Photo actually Rick Leach on back)
☐ 137 Felix Fermin .10 .05
☐ 138 Mike Devereaux .10 .05
☐ 139 Delino DeShields .40 .05
☐ 140 David Wells .10 .05
☐ 141 Tim Crews .10 .05
☐ 142 Erik Hanson .10 .05
☐ 143 Mark Davidson .10 .05
☐ 144 Tommy Gregg .10 .05
☐ 145 Jim Gantner .10 .05
☐ 146 Jose Lind .10 .05
☐ 147 Danny Tartabull .10 .05
☐ 148 Geno Petralli .10 .05
☐ 149 Travis Fryman .40 .18
☐ 150 Tim Naehring .10 .05
☐ 151 Kevin McReynolds .10 .05
☐ 152 Joe Orsulak .10 .05
☐ 153 Steve Frey .10 .05
☐ 154 Duane Ward .10 .05
☐ 155 Stan Javier .10 .05
☐ 156 Damon Berryhill .10 .05
☐ 157 Gene Larkin .10 .05
☐ 158 Greg Olson .10 .05
☐ 159 Mark Knudson .10 .05
☐ 160 Carmelo Martinez .10 .05
☐ 161 Storm Davis .10 .05
☐ 162 Jim Abbott .10 .05
☐ 163 Len Dykstra .10 .05
☐ 164 Tom Brunansky .10 .05
☐ 165 Dwight Gooden .10 .05
☐ 166 Jose Mesa .10 .05
☐ 167 Oil Can Boyd .10 .05
☐ 168 Barry Larkin .40 .18
☐ 169 Scott Sanderson .10 .05
☐ 170 Mark Grace .40 .18
☐ 171 Mark Guthrie .10 .05
☐ 172 Tom Glavine .40 .18
☐ 173 Gary Sheffield .40 .18
☐ 174 Roger Clemens CL .40 .18
☐ 175 Chris James .10 .05
☐ 176 Milt Thompson .10 .05
☐ 177 Donnie Hill .10 .05
☐ 178 Wes Chamberlain .10 .05
☐ 179 John Marzano .10 .05
☐ 180 Frank Viola .10 .05
☐ 181 Eric Anthony .10 .05
☐ 182 Jose Canseco .40 .18
☐ 183 Scott Scudder .10 .05
☐ 184 Dave Eiland .10 .05
☐ 185 Luis Salazar .10 .05
☐ 186 Pedro Munoz .10 .05
☐ 187 Steve Searcy .10 .05
☐ 188 Don Robinson .10 .05
☐ 189 Sandy Alomar Jr. .20 .09
☐ 190 Jose DeLeon .10 .05
☐ 191 John Orton .10 .05
☐ 192 Darren Daulton .10 .05
☐ 193 Mike Morgan .10 .05
☐ 194 Greg Briley .10 .05
☐ 195 Karl Rhodes .10 .05
☐ 196 Harold Baines .20 .09
☐ 197 Bill Doran .10 .05
☐ 198 Alvaro Espinoza .10 .05
☐ 199 Kirk McCaskill .10 .05
☐ 200 Jose DeJesus .10 .05
☐ 201 Jack Clark .10 .05
☐ 202 Daryl Boston .10 .05
☐ 203 Randy Tomlin .10 .05
☐ 204 Pedro Guerrero .10 .05
☐ 205 Billy Hatcher .10 .05
☐ 206 Tim Leary .10 .05
☐ 207 Ryne Sandberg .50 .23
☐ 208 Kirby Puckett .75 .35
☐ 209 Charlie Leibrandt .10 .05
☐ 210 Rick Honeycutt .10 .05
☐ 211 Joel Skinner .10 .05
☐ 212 Rex Hudler .10 .05
☐ 213 Bryan Harvey .10 .05
☐ 214 Charlie Hayes .10 .05
☐ 215 Matt Young .10 .05
☐ 216 Terry Kennedy .10 .05
☐ 217 Carl Nichols .10 .05
☐ 218 Mike Moore .10 .05
☐ 219 Paul O'Neill .10 .05
☐ 220 Steve Sax .10 .05
☐ 221 Shawn Boskie .10 .05
☐ 222 Rich DeLucia .10 .05
☐ 223 Lloyd Moseby .10 .05
☐ 224 Mike Kingery .10 .05
☐ 225 Carlos Baerga .10 .05
☐ 226 Bryn Smith .10 .05
☐ 227 Todd Stottlemyre .10 .05
☐ 228 Julio Franco .10 .05
☐ 229 Jim Gott .10 .05
☐ 230 Mike Schooler .10 .05
☐ 231 Steve Finley .40 .18
☐ 232 Dave Henderson .10 .05
☐ 233 Luis Quinones .10 .05
☐ 234 Mark Whiten .10 .05
☐ 235 Brian McRae .40 .18
☐ 236 Rich Gossage .10 .05
☐ 237 Rob Deer .10 .05
☐ 238 Will Clark .40 .18
☐ 239 Albert Belle .60 .25
☐ 240 Bob Melvin .10 .05
☐ 241 Larry Walker .60 .25
☐ 242 Dante Bichette .40 .18
☐ 243 Orel Hershiser .10 .05
☐ 244 Pete O'Brien .10 .05
☐ 245 Pete Harnisch .10 .05
☐ 246 Jeff Treadway .10 .05
☐ 247 Julio Machado .10 .05
☐ 248 Dave Johnson .10 .05
☐ 249 Kirk Gibson .10 .05
☐ 250 Kevin Brown .20 .09
☐ 251 Milt Cuyler .10 .05
☐ 252 Jeff Reardon .10 .05
☐ 253 David Cone .10 .05
☐ 254 Gary Redus .10 .05
☐ 255 Junior Noboa .10 .05
☐ 256 Greg Myers .10 .05
☐ 257 Dennis Cook .10 .05
☐ 258 Joe Girardi .10 .05
☐ 259 Allan Anderson .10 .05
☐ 260 Paul Marak .10 .05
☐ 261 Barry Bonds .50 .23
☐ 262 Juan Bell .10 .05
☐ 263 Russ Morman .10 .05
☐ 264 George Brett CL .30 .14
☐ 265 Jerald Clark .10 .05
☐ 266 Dwight Evans .10 .05
☐ 267 Roberto Alomar .40 .18
☐ 268 Danny Jackson .10 .05
☐ 269 Brian Downing .10 .05
☐ 270 John Cerutti .10 .05
☐ 271 Robin Ventura .40 .18
☐ 272 Gerald Perry .10 .05
☐ 273 Wade Boggs .40 .18
☐ 274 Dennis Martinez .10 .05
☐ 275 Andy Benes .20 .09
☐ 276 Tony Fossas .10 .05
☐ 277 Franklin Stubbs .10 .05
☐ 278 John Kruk .10 .05
☐ 279 Kevin Gross .10 .05
☐ 280 Von Hayes .10 .05
☐ 281 Frank Thomas 3.00 1.35
☐ 282 Rob Dibble .10 .05
☐ 283 Mel Hall .10 .05
☐ 284 Rick Mahler .10 .05
☐ 285 Dennis Eckersley .40 .18
☐ 286 Bernard Gilkey .10 .05
☐ 287 Dan Plesac .10 .05
☐ 288 Jason Grimsley .10 .05
☐ 289 Mark Lewis .10 .05
☐ 290 Tony Gwynn 1.00 .45
☐ 291 Jeff Russell .10 .05
☐ 292 Curt Schilling .40 .18
☐ 293 Pascual Perez .10 .05
☐ 294 Jack Morris .10 .05
☐ 295 Hubie Brooks .10 .05
☐ 296 Alex Fernandez .20 .09
☐ 297 Harold Reynolds .10 .05
☐ 298 Craig Worthington .10 .05
☐ 299 Willie Wilson .10 .05
☐ 300 Mike Maddux .10 .05
☐ 301 Dave Righetti .10 .05
☐ 302 Paul Molitor .40 .18
☐ 303 Gary Gaetti .10 .05
☐ 304 Terry Pendleton .10 .05
☐ 305 Kevin Elster .10 .05
☐ 306 Scott Fletcher .10 .05
☐ 307 Jeff Robinson .10 .05
☐ 308 Jesse Barfield .10 .05
☐ 309 Mike LaCoss .10 .05
☐ 310 Andy Van Slyke .10 .05
☐ 311 Glenallen Hill .10 .05
☐ 312 Bud Black .10 .05
☐ 313 Kent Hrbek .10 .05
☐ 314 Tim Teufel .10 .05
☐ 315 Tony Fernandez .10 .05
☐ 316 Beau Allred .10 .05
☐ 317 Curtis Wilkerson .10 .05
☐ 318 Bill Sampen .10 .05
☐ 319 Randy Johnson .50 .23
☐ 320 Mike Heath .10 .05
☐ 321 Sammy Sosa .50 .23
☐ 322 Mickey Tettleton .10 .05
☐ 323 Jose Vizcaino .10 .05
☐ 324 John Candelaria .10 .05
☐ 325 Dave Howard .10 .05
☐ 326 Jose Rijo .10 .05
☐ 327 Todd Zeile .10 .05
☐ 328 Gene Nelson .10 .05
☐ 329 Dwayne Henry .10 .05
☐ 330 Mike Boddicker .10 .05
☐ 331 Ozzie Guillen .10 .05
☐ 332 Sam Horn .10 .05
☐ 333 Wally Whitehurst .10 .05
☐ 334 Dave Parker .10 .05

Card	MINT	NRMT
☐ 335 George Brett	.75	.35
☐ 336 Bobby Thigpen	.10	.05
☐ 337 Ed Whitson	.10	.05
☐ 338 Ivan Calderon	.10	.05
☐ 339 Mike Pagliarulo	.10	.05
☐ 340 Jack McDowell	.10	.05
☐ 341 Dana Kiecker	.10	.05
☐ 342 Fred McGriff	.40	.18
☐ 343 Mark Lee	.10	.05
☐ 344 Alfredo Griffin	.10	.05
☐ 345 Scott Bankhead	.10	.05
☐ 346 Darrin Jackson	.10	.05
☐ 347 Rafael Palmeiro	.40	.18
☐ 348 Steve Farr	.10	.05
☐ 349 Hensley Meulens	.10	.05
☐ 350 Danny Cox	.10	.05
☐ 351 Alan Trammell	.20	.09
☐ 352 Edwin Nunez	.10	.05
☐ 353 Joe Carter	.40	.18
☐ 354 Eric Show	.10	.05
☐ 355 Vance Law	.10	.05
☐ 356 Jeff Gray	.10	.05
☐ 357 Bobby Bonilla	.20	.09
☐ 358 Ernest Riles	.10	.05
☐ 359 Ron Hassey	.10	.05
☐ 360 Willie McGee	.10	.05
☐ 361 Mackey Sasser	.10	.05
☐ 362 Glenn Braggs	.10	.05
☐ 363 Mario Diaz	.10	.05
☐ 364 Barry Bonds CL	.40	.18
☐ 365 Kevin Bass	.10	.05
☐ 366 Pete Incaviglia	.10	.05
☐ 367 Luis Sojo UER (1989 stats interspersed with 1990's)	.10	.05
☐ 368 Lance Parrish	.10	.05
☐ 369 Mark Leonard	.10	.05
☐ 370 Heathcliff Slocumb	.40	.18
☐ 371 Jimmy Jones	.10	.05
☐ 372 Ken Griffey Jr.	3.00	1.35
☐ 373 Chris Hammond	.10	.05
☐ 374 Chili Davis	.10	.05
☐ 375 Joey Cora	.20	.09
☐ 376 Ken Hill	.10	.05
☐ 377 Darryl Strawberry	.10	.05
☐ 378 Ron Darling	.10	.05
☐ 379 Sid Bream	.10	.05
☐ 380 Bill Swift	.10	.05
☐ 381 Shawn Abner	.10	.05
☐ 382 Eric King	.10	.05
☐ 383 Mickey Morandini	.10	.05
☐ 384 Carlton Fisk	.40	.18
☐ 385 Steve Lake	.10	.05
☐ 386 Mike Jeffcoat	.10	.05
☐ 387 Darren Holmes	.10	.05
☐ 388 Tim Wallach	.10	.05
☐ 389 George Bell	.10	.05
☐ 390 Craig Lefferts	.10	.05
☐ 391 Ernie Whitt	.10	.05
☐ 392 Felix Jose	.10	.05
☐ 393 Kevin Maas	.10	.05
☐ 394 Devon White	.10	.05
☐ 395 Otis Nixon	.10	.05
☐ 396 Chuck Knoblauch	.50	.23
☐ 397 Scott Coolbaugh	.10	.05
☐ 398 Glenn Davis	.10	.05
☐ 399 Manny Lee	.10	.05
☐ 400 Andre Dawson	.40	.18
☐ 401 Scott Chiamparino	.10	.05
☐ 402 Bill Gullickson	.10	.05
☐ 403 Lance Johnson	.10	.05
☐ 404 Juan Agosto	.10	.05
☐ 405 Danny Darwin	.10	.05
☐ 406 Barry Jones	.10	.05
☐ 407 Larry Andersen	.10	.05
☐ 408 Luis Rivera	.10	.05
☐ 409 Jaime Navarro	.10	.05
☐ 410 Roger McDowell	.10	.05
☐ 411 Brett Butler	.10	.05
☐ 412 Dale Murphy	.40	.18
☐ 413 Tim Raines UER (Listed as hitting .500 in 1980, should be .050)	.40	.18
☐ 414 Norm Charlton	.10	.05
☐ 415 Greg Cadaret	.10	.05
☐ 416 Chris Nabholz	.10	.05
☐ 417 Dave Stewart	.10	.05
☐ 418 Rich Gedman	.10	.05
☐ 419 Willie Randolph	.10	.05
☐ 420 Mitch Williams	.10	.05
☐ 421 Brook Jacoby	.10	.05
☐ 422 Greg W. Harris	.10	.05
☐ 423 Nolan Ryan	1.50	.70
☐ 424 Dave Rohde	.10	.05
☐ 425 Don Mattingly	.60	.25
☐ 426 Greg Gagne	.10	.05
☐ 427 Vince Coleman	.10	.05
☐ 428 Dan Pasqua	.10	.05
☐ 429 Alvin Davis	.10	.05
☐ 430 Cal Ripken	1.50	.70
☐ 431 Jamie Quirk	.10	.05
☐ 432 Benito Santiago	.10	.05
☐ 433 Jose Uribe	.10	.05
☐ 434 Candy Maldonado	.10	.05
☐ 435 Junior Felix	.10	.05
☐ 436 Deion Sanders	.40	.18
☐ 437 John Franco	.10	.05
☐ 438 Greg Hibbard	.10	.05
☐ 439 Floyd Bannister	.10	.05
☐ 440 Steve Howe	.10	.05
☐ 441 Steve Decker	.10	.05
☐ 442 Vicente Palacios	.10	.05
☐ 443 Pat Tabler	.10	.05
☐ 444 Darryl Strawberry CL	.10	.05
☐ 445 Mike Felder	.10	.05
☐ 446 Al Newman	.10	.05
☐ 447 Chris Donnels	.10	.05
☐ 448 Rich Rodriguez	.10	.05
☐ 449 Turner Ward	.10	.05
☐ 450 Bob Walk	.10	.05
☐ 451 Gilberto Reyes	.10	.05
☐ 452 Mike Jackson	.10	.05
☐ 453 Rafael Belliard	.10	.05
☐ 454 Wayne Edwards	.10	.05
☐ 455 Andy Allanson	.10	.05
☐ 456 Dave Smith	.10	.05
☐ 457 Gary Carter	.40	.18
☐ 458 Warren Cromartie	.10	.05
☐ 459 Jack Armstrong	.10	.05
☐ 460 Bob Tewksbury	.10	.05
☐ 461 Joe Klink	.10	.05
☐ 462 Xavier Hernandez	.10	.05
☐ 463 Scott Radinsky	.10	.05
☐ 464 Jeff Robinson	.10	.05
☐ 465 Gregg Jefferies	.10	.05
☐ 466 Denny Neagle	1.25	.55
☐ 467 Carmelo Martinez	.10	.05
☐ 468 Donn Pall	.10	.05
☐ 469 Bruce Hurst	.10	.05
☐ 470 Eric Bullock	.10	.05
☐ 471 Rick Aguilera	.10	.05
☐ 472 Charlie Hough	.10	.05
☐ 473 Carlos Quintana	.10	.05
☐ 474 Marty Barrett	.10	.05
☐ 475 Kevin D. Brown	.10	.05
☐ 476 Bobby Ojeda	.10	.05
☐ 477 Edgar Martinez	.40	.18
☐ 478 Bip Roberts	.10	.05
☐ 479 Mike Flanagan	.10	.05
☐ 480 John Habyan	.10	.05
☐ 481 Larry Casian	.10	.05
☐ 482 Wally Backman	.10	.05
☐ 483 Doug Dascenzo	.10	.05
☐ 484 Rick Dempsey	.10	.05
☐ 485 Ed Sprague	.10	.05
☐ 486 Steve Chitren	.10	.05
☐ 487 Mark McGwire	.75	.35
☐ 488 Roger Clemens	.75	.35
☐ 489 Orlando Merced	.10	.05
☐ 490 Rene Gonzales	.10	.05
☐ 491 Mike Stanton	.10	.05
☐ 492 Al Osuna	.10	.05
☐ 493 Rick Cerone	.10	.05
☐ 494 Mariano Duncan	.10	.05
☐ 495 Zane Smith	.10	.05
☐ 496 John Morris	.10	.05
☐ 497 Frank Tanana	.10	.05
☐ 498 Junior Ortiz	.10	.05
☐ 499 Dave Winfield	.40	.18
☐ 500 Gary Varsho	.10	.05
☐ 501 Chico Walker	.10	.05
☐ 502 Ken Caminiti	.40	.18
☐ 503 Ken Griffey Sr.	.10	.05
☐ 504 Randy Myers	.10	.05
☐ 505 Steve Bedrosian	.10	.05
☐ 506 Cory Snyder	.10	.05
☐ 507 Cris Carpenter	.10	.05
☐ 508 Tim Belcher	.10	.05
☐ 509 Jeff Hamilton	.10	.05
☐ 510 Steve Avery	.10	.05
☐ 511 Dave Valle	.10	.05
☐ 512 Tom Lampkin	.10	.05
☐ 513 Shawn Hillegas	.10	.05
☐ 514 Reggie Jefferson	.40	.18
☐ 515 Ron Karkovice	.10	.05
☐ 516 Doug Drabek	.10	.05
☐ 517 Tom Henke	.10	.05
☐ 518 Chris Bosio	.10	.05
☐ 519 Gregg Olson	.10	.05
☐ 520 Bob Scanlan	.10	.05
☐ 521 Alonzo Powell	.10	.05
☐ 522 Jeff Ballard	.10	.05
☐ 523 Ray Lankford	.40	.18
☐ 524 Tommy Greene	.10	.05
☐ 525 Mike Timlin	.10	.05
☐ 526 Juan Berenguer	.10	.05
☐ 527 Scott Erickson	.10	.05
☐ 528 Sandy Alomar Jr. CL	.10	.05

1991 Leaf Gold Rookies

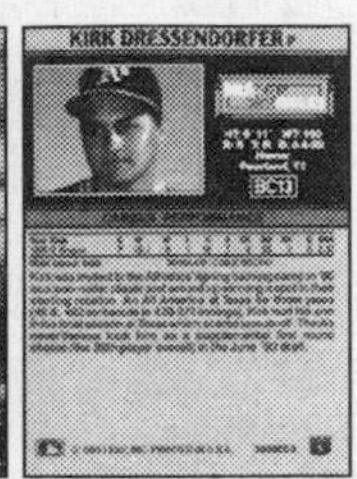

This 26-card standard size set was issued by Leaf as an insert to their 1991 Leaf regular issue.The first twelve cards were issued as random inserts in with the first series of 1991 Leaf foil packs. The rest were issued as random inserts in with the second series. The set features a selection of rookie prospects. The earliest Leaf Gold Rookie cards issued with the first series can sometimes be found with erroneous regular numbered backs 265 through 276 instead of the correct BC1 through BC12. These numbered variations are very tough to find and are valued at ten times the values listed below.

	MINT	NRMT
COMPLETE SET (26)	20.00	9.00
COMMON CARD (BC1-BC26)	.50	.23
☐ BC1 Scott Leius	.50	.23
☐ BC2 Luis Gonzalez	.75	.35
☐ BC3 Wil Cordero	.50	.23
☐ BC4 Gary Scott	.50	.23
☐ BC5 Willie Banks	.50	.23
☐ BC6 Arthur Rhodes	.75	.35
☐ BC7 Mo Vaughn	5.00	2.20
☐ BC8 Henry Rodriguez	1.50	.70
☐ BC9 Todd Van Poppel	.50	.23
☐ BC10 Reggie Sanders	1.00	.45
☐ BC11 Rico Brogna	1.00	.45
☐ BC12 Mike Mussina	3.00	1.35
☐ BC13 Kirk Dressendorfer	.50	.23
☐ BC14 Jeff Bagwell	6.00	2.70
☐ BC15 Pete Schourek	.75	.35
☐ BC16 Wade Taylor	.50	.23
☐ BC17 Pat Kelly	.50	.23
☐ BC18 Tim Costo	.50	.23
☐ BC19 Roger Salkeld	.50	.23
☐ BC20 Andujar Cedeno	.50	.23
☐ BC21 Ryan Klesko UER (1990 Sumter BA .289; should be .368)	3.00	1.35
☐ BC22 Mike Huff	.50	.23
☐ BC23 Anthony Young	.50	.23
☐ BC24 Eddie Zosky	.50	.23
☐ BC25 Nolan Ryan DP UER No Hitter 7 (Word other repeated in 7th line)	1.50	.70
☐ BC26 Rickey Henderson DP Record Steal	1.00	.45

1992 Leaf Previews

Four Leaf Preview standard-size cards were included in each 1992 Donruss hobby factory set. The cards were intended to show collectors and dealers the style of the 1992 Leaf set. The fronts carry glossy color player photos framed by silver borders.

	MINT	NRMT
COMPLETE SET (26)	50.00	22.00
COMMON CARD (1-26)	1.00	.45

	MINT	NRMT
☐ 1 Steve Avery	1.00	.45
☐ 2 Ryne Sandberg	4.00	1.80
☐ 3 Chris Sabo	1.00	.45
☐ 4 Jeff Bagwell	8.00	3.60
☐ 5 Darryl Strawberry	1.25	.55
☐ 6 Bret Barberie	1.00	.45
☐ 7 Howard Johnson	1.00	.45
☐ 8 John Kruk	1.25	.55
☐ 9 Andy Van Slyke	1.25	.55
☐ 10 Felix Jose	1.00	.45
☐ 11 Fred McGriff	1.50	.70
☐ 12 Will Clark	1.50	.70
☐ 13 Cal Ripken	10.00	4.50
☐ 14 Phil Plantier	1.00	.45
☐ 15 Lee Stevens	1.00	.45
☐ 16 Frank Thomas	18.00	8.00
☐ 17 Mark Whiten	1.00	.45
☐ 18 Cecil Fielder	1.25	.55
☐ 19 George Brett	5.00	2.20
☐ 20 Robin Yount	1.50	.70
☐ 21 Scott Erickson	1.00	.45
☐ 22 Don Mattingly	6.00	2.70
☐ 23 Jose Canseco	1.50	.70
☐ 24 Ken Griffey Jr.	18.00	8.00
☐ 25 Nolan Ryan	10.00	4.50
☐ 26 Joe Carter	1.50	.70

1992 Leaf Gold Previews

These Leaf Gold Preview cards were sent to members of the Donruss/Leaf Dealer Network who ordered 1992 Donruss Factory sets. For each set ordered, dealers received one two-card pack. These cards showed the style of the new 1992 Leaf Gold cards which would be included one per pack in the forthcoming set. The cards measure the standard size. The fronts feature color action player photos inside a gold foil picture frame and a black outer border.

	MINT	NRMT
COMPLETE SET (33)	100.00	45.00
COMMON CARD (1-33)	1.00	.45

	MINT	NRMT
☐ 1 Steve Avery	1.00	.45
☐ 2 Ryne Sandberg	8.00	3.60
☐ 3 Chris Sabo	1.00	.45
☐ 4 Jeff Bagwell	10.00	4.50
☐ 5 Darryl Strawberry	1.50	.70
☐ 6 Bret Barberie	1.00	.45
☐ 7 Howard Johnson	1.00	.45
☐ 8 John Kruk	1.00	.45
☐ 9 Andy Van Slyke	1.00	.45
☐ 10 Felix Jose	1.00	.45
☐ 11 Fred McGriff	4.00	1.80
☐ 12 Will Clark	4.00	1.80
☐ 13 Cal Ripken	15.00	6.75
☐ 14 Phil Plantier	1.00	.45
☐ 15 Lee Stevens	1.00	.45
☐ 16 Frank Thomas	20.00	9.00
☐ 17 Mark Whiten	1.00	.45
☐ 18 Cecil Fielder	1.50	.70
☐ 19 George Brett	10.00	4.50
☐ 20 Robin Yount	3.00	1.35
☐ 21 Scott Erickson	1.00	.45
☐ 22 Don Mattingly	10.00	4.50
☐ 23 Jose Canseco	4.00	1.80
☐ 24 Ken Griffey Jr.	25.00	11.00
☐ 25 Nolan Ryan	20.00	9.00
☐ 26 Joe Carter	2.50	1.10
☐ 27 Deion Sanders	4.00	1.80
☐ 28 Dean Palmer	1.50	.70
☐ 29 Andy Benes	1.50	.70
☐ 30 Gary DiSarcina	1.00	.45
☐ 31 Chris Hoiles	1.00	.45
☐ 32 Mark McGwire	10.00	4.50
☐ 33 Reggie Sanders	1.50	.70

1992 Leaf

The 1992 Leaf set consists of 528 cards, issued in two separate 264-card series. Cards were distributed in first and second series 15-card foil packs. Each pack contained

a selection of basic cards and one black gold parallel card. The basic card fronts feature color action player photos on a silver card face. The player's name appears in a black bar edged at the bottom by a thin red stripe. The team logo overlaps the bar at the right corner. There are no significant Rookie Cards in this set.

	MINT	NRMT
COMPLETE SET (528)	15.00	6.75
COMPLETE SERIES 1 (264)	5.00	2.20
COMPLETE SERIES 2 (264)	10.00	4.50
COMMON CARD (1-528)	.05	.02

	MINT	NRMT
☐ 1 Jim Abbott	.15	.07
☐ 2 Cal Eldred	.05	.02
☐ 3 Bud Black	.05	.02
☐ 4 Dave Howard	.05	.02
☐ 5 Luis Sojo	.05	.02
☐ 6 Gary Scott	.05	.02
☐ 7 Joe Oliver	.05	.02
☐ 8 Chris Gardner	.05	.02
☐ 9 Sandy Alomar Jr.	.15	.07
☐ 10 Greg W. Harris	.05	.02
☐ 11 Doug Drabek	.05	.02
☐ 12 Darryl Hamilton	.05	.02
☐ 13 Mike Mussina	.50	.23
☐ 14 Kevin Tapani	.05	.02
☐ 15 Ron Gant	.15	.07
☐ 16 Mark McGwire	.60	.25
☐ 17 Robin Ventura	.15	.07
☐ 18 Pedro Guerrero	.05	.02
☐ 19 Roger Clemens	.60	.25
☐ 20 Steve Farr	.05	.02
☐ 21 Frank Tanana	.05	.02
☐ 22 Joe Hesketh	.05	.02
☐ 23 Erik Hanson	.05	.02
☐ 24 Greg Cadaret	.05	.02
☐ 25 Rex Hudler	.05	.02
☐ 26 Mark Grace	.10	.05
☐ 27 Kelly Gruber	.05	.02
☐ 28 Jeff Bagwell	1.00	.45
☐ 29 Darryl Strawberry	.15	.07
☐ 30 Dave Smith	.05	.02
☐ 31 Kevin Appier	.15	.07
☐ 32 Steve Chitren	.05	.02
☐ 33 Kevin Gross	.05	.02
☐ 34 Rick Aguilera	.05	.02
☐ 35 Juan Guzman	.05	.02
☐ 36 Joe Orsulak	.05	.02
☐ 37 Tim Raines	.15	.07
☐ 38 Harold Reynolds	.05	.02
☐ 39 Charlie Hough	.05	.02
☐ 40 Tony Phillips	.05	.02
☐ 41 Nolan Ryan	1.25	.55
☐ 42 Vince Coleman	.05	.02
☐ 43 Andy Van Slyke	.15	.07
☐ 44 Tim Burke	.05	.02
☐ 45 Luis Polonia	.05	.02
☐ 46 Tom Browning	.05	.02
☐ 47 Willie McGee	.05	.02
☐ 48 Gary DiSarcina	.05	.02
☐ 49 Mark Lewis	.05	.02
☐ 50 Phil Plantier	.05	.02
☐ 51 Doug Dascenzo	.05	.02
☐ 52 Cal Ripken	1.25	.55
☐ 53 Pedro Munoz	.05	.02
☐ 54 Carlos Hernandez	.05	.02
☐ 55 Jerald Clark	.05	.02
☐ 56 Jeff Brantley	.05	.02
☐ 57 Don Mattingly	.50	.23
☐ 58 Roger McDowell	.05	.02
☐ 59 Steve Avery	.05	.02
☐ 60 John Olerud	.15	.07
☐ 61 Bill Gullickson	.05	.02
☐ 62 Juan Gonzalez	1.00	.45
☐ 63 Felix Jose	.05	.02
☐ 64 Robin Yount	.10	.05
☐ 65 Greg Briley	.05	.02
☐ 66 Steve Finley	.15	.07
☐ 67 Frank Thomas CL	.30	.14
☐ 68 Tom Gordon	.05	.02
☐ 69 Rob Dibble	.05	.02
☐ 70 Glenallen Hill	.05	.02
☐ 71 Calvin Jones	.05	.02
☐ 72 Joe Girardi	.05	.02
☐ 73 Barry Larkin	.10	.05
☐ 74 Andy Benes	.05	.02
☐ 75 Milt Cuyler	.05	.02
☐ 76 Kevin Bass	.05	.02
☐ 77 Pete Harnisch	.05	.02
☐ 78 Wilson Alvarez	.15	.07
☐ 79 Mike Devereaux	.05	.02
☐ 80 Doug Henry	.05	.02
☐ 81 Orel Hershiser	.15	.07
☐ 82 Shane Mack	.05	.02
☐ 83 Mike Macfarlane	.05	.02
☐ 84 Thomas Howard	.05	.02
☐ 85 Alex Fernandez	.15	.07
☐ 86 Reggie Jefferson	.10	.05
☐ 87 Leo Gomez	.05	.02
☐ 88 Mel Hall	.05	.02
☐ 89 Mike Greenwell	.05	.02
☐ 90 Jeff Russell	.05	.02
☐ 91 Steve Buechele	.05	.02
☐ 92 David Cone	.15	.07
☐ 93 Kevin Reimer	.05	.02
☐ 94 Mark Lemke	.05	.02
☐ 95 Bob Tewksbury	.05	.02
☐ 96 Zane Smith	.05	.02
☐ 97 Mark Eichhorn	.05	.02
☐ 98 Kirby Puckett	.60	.25
☐ 99 Paul O'Neill	.15	.07
☐ 100 Dennis Eckersley	.30	.14
☐ 101 Duane Ward	.05	.02
☐ 102 Matt Nokes	.05	.02
☐ 103 Mo Vaughn	.50	.23
☐ 104 Pat Kelly	.05	.02
☐ 105 Ron Karkovice	.05	.02
☐ 106 Bill Spiers	.05	.02
☐ 107 Gary Gaetti	.15	.07
☐ 108 Mackey Sasser	.05	.02
☐ 109 Robby Thompson	.05	.02
☐ 110 Marvin Freeman	.05	.02
☐ 111 Jimmy Key	.15	.07
☐ 112 Dwight Gooden	.15	.07
☐ 113 Charlie Leibrandt	.05	.02
☐ 114 Devon White	.05	.02
☐ 115 Charles Nagy	.15	.07
☐ 116 Rickey Henderson	.30	.14
☐ 117 Paul Assenmacher	.05	.02
☐ 118 Junior Felix	.05	.02
☐ 119 Julio Franco	.15	.07
☐ 120 Norm Charlton	.05	.02
☐ 121 Scott Servais	.05	.02
☐ 122 Gerald Perry	.05	.02
☐ 123 Brian McRae	.05	.02
☐ 124 Don Slaught	.05	.02
☐ 125 Juan Samuel	.05	.02
☐ 126 Harold Baines	.15	.07
☐ 127 Scott Livingstone	.05	.02
☐ 128 Jay Buhner	.10	.05
☐ 129 Darrin Jackson	.05	.02
☐ 130 Luis Mercedes	.05	.02
☐ 131 Brian Harper	.05	.02
☐ 132 Howard Johnson	.05	.02
☐ 133 Nolan Ryan CL	.30	.14
☐ 134 Dante Bichette	.10	.05
☐ 135 Dave Righetti	.05	.02
☐ 136 Jeff Montgomery	.15	.07
☐ 137 Joe Grahe	.05	.02
☐ 138 Delino DeShields	.05	.02
☐ 139 Jose Rijo	.05	.02
☐ 140 Ken Caminiti	.30	.14
☐ 141 Steve Olin	.05	.02
☐ 142 Kurt Stillwell	.05	.02
☐ 143 Jay Bell	.15	.07
☐ 144 Jaime Navarro	.05	.02
☐ 145 Ben McDonald	.05	.02
☐ 146 Greg Gagne	.05	.02
☐ 147 Jeff Blauser	.05	.02
☐ 148 Carney Lansford	.15	.07
☐ 149 Ozzie Guillen	.05	.02
☐ 150 Milt Thompson	.05	.02
☐ 151 Jeff Reardon	.15	.07
☐ 152 Scott Sanderson	.05	.02
☐ 153 Cecil Fielder	.15	.07
☐ 154 Greg A. Harris	.05	.02
☐ 155 Rich DeLucia	.05	.02
☐ 156 Roberto Kelly	.05	.02
☐ 157 Bryn Smith	.05	.02
☐ 158 Chuck McElroy	.05	.02
☐ 159 Tom Henke	.05	.02
☐ 160 Luis Gonzalez	.05	.02
☐ 161 Steve Wilson	.05	.02
☐ 162 Shawn Boskie	.05	.02
☐ 163 Mark Davis	.05	.02
☐ 164 Mike Moore	.05	.02
☐ 165 Mike Scioscia	.05	.02
☐ 166 Scott Erickson	.15	.07
☐ 167 Todd Stottlemyre	.05	.02

☐ 168 Alvin Davis	.05	.02
☐ 169 Greg Hibbard	.05	.02
☐ 170 David Valle	.05	.02
☐ 171 Dave Winfield	.10	.05
☐ 172 Alan Trammell	.10	.05
☐ 173 Kenny Rogers	.05	.02
☐ 174 John Franco	.05	.02
☐ 175 Jose Lind	.05	.02
☐ 176 Pete Schourek	.05	.02
☐ 177 Von Hayes	.05	.02
☐ 178 Chris Hammond	.05	.02
☐ 179 John Burkett	.05	.02
☐ 180 Dickie Thon	.05	.02
☐ 181 Joel Skinner	.05	.02
☐ 182 Scott Cooper	.05	.02
☐ 183 Andre Dawson	.10	.05
☐ 184 Billy Ripken	.05	.02
☐ 185 Kevin Mitchell	.05	.02
☐ 186 Brett Butler	.15	.07
☐ 187 Tony Fernandez	.05	.02
☐ 188 Cory Snyder	.05	.02
☐ 189 John Habyan	.05	.02
☐ 190 Dennis Martinez	.15	.07
☐ 191 John Smoltz	.10	.05
☐ 192 Greg Myers	.05	.02
☐ 193 Rob Deer	.05	.02
☐ 194 Ivan Rodriguez	.60	.25
☐ 195 Ray Lankford	.10	.05
☐ 196 Bill Wegman	.05	.02
☐ 197 Edgar Martinez	.10	.05
☐ 198 Darryl Kile	.05	.02
☐ 199 Cal Ripken CL	.30	.14
☐ 200 Brent Mayne	.05	.02
☐ 201 Larry Walker	.30	.14
☐ 202 Carlos Baerga	.15	.07
☐ 203 Russ Swan	.05	.02
☐ 204 Mike Morgan	.05	.02
☐ 205 Hal Morris	.05	.02
☐ 206 Tony Gwynn	.75	.35
☐ 207 Mark Leiter	.05	.02
☐ 208 Kirt Manwaring	.05	.02
☐ 209 Al Osuna	.05	.02
☐ 210 Bobby Thigpen	.05	.02
☐ 211 Chris Hoiles	.05	.02
☐ 212 B.J. Surhoff	.15	.07
☐ 213 Lenny Harris	.05	.02
☐ 214 Scott Leius	.05	.02
☐ 215 Gregg Jefferies	.05	.02
☐ 216 Bruce Hurst	.05	.02
☐ 217 Steve Sax	.05	.02
☐ 218 Dave Otto	.05	.02
☐ 219 Sam Horn	.05	.02
☐ 220 Charlie Hayes	.05	.02
☐ 221 Frank Viola	.05	.02
☐ 222 Jose Guzman	.05	.02
☐ 223 Gary Redus	.05	.02
☐ 224 Dave Gallagher	.05	.02
☐ 225 Dean Palmer	.15	.07
☐ 226 Greg Olson	.05	.02
☐ 227 Jose DeLeon	.05	.02
☐ 228 Mike LaValliere	.05	.02
☐ 229 Mark Langston	.05	.02
☐ 230 Chuck Knoblauch	.30	.14
☐ 231 Bill Doran	.05	.02
☐ 232 Dave Henderson	.05	.02
☐ 233 Roberto Alomar	.30	.14
☐ 234 Scott Fletcher	.05	.02
☐ 235 Tim Naehring	.15	.07
☐ 236 Mike Gallego	.05	.02
☐ 237 Lance Johnson	.05	.02
☐ 238 Paul Molitor	.30	.14
☐ 239 Dan Gladden	.05	.02
☐ 240 Willie Randolph	.15	.07
☐ 241 Will Clark	.10	.05
☐ 242 Sid Bream	.05	.02
☐ 243 Derek Bell	.15	.07
☐ 244 Bill Pecota	.05	.02
☐ 245 Terry Pendleton	.15	.07
☐ 246 Randy Ready	.05	.02
☐ 247 Jack Armstrong	.05	.02
☐ 248 Todd Van Poppel	.05	.02
☐ 249 Shawon Dunston	.05	.02
☐ 250 Bobby Rose	.05	.02
☐ 251 Jeff Huson	.05	.02
☐ 252 Bip Roberts	.05	.02
☐ 253 Doug Jones	.05	.02
☐ 254 Lee Smith	.15	.07
☐ 255 George Brett	.60	.25
☐ 256 Randy Tomlin	.05	.02
☐ 257 Todd Benzinger	.05	.02
☐ 258 Dave Stewart	.15	.07
☐ 259 Mark Carreon	.05	.02
☐ 260 Pete O'Brien	.05	.02
☐ 261 Tim Teufel	.05	.02
☐ 262 Bob Milacki	.05	.02
☐ 263 Mark Guthrie	.05	.02
☐ 264 Darrin Fletcher	.05	.02
☐ 265 Omar Vizquel	.15	.07
☐ 266 Chris Bosio	.05	.02
☐ 267 Jose Canseco	.10	.05
☐ 268 Mike Boddicker	.05	.02
☐ 269 Lance Parrish	.05	.02
☐ 270 Jose Vizcaino	.05	.02
☐ 271 Chris Sabo	.05	.02
☐ 272 Royce Clayton	.05	.02
☐ 273 Marquis Grissom	.15	.07
☐ 274 Fred McGriff	.10	.05
☐ 275 Barry Bonds	.40	.18
☐ 276 Greg Vaughn	.05	.02
☐ 277 Gregg Olson	.05	.02
☐ 278 Dave Hollins	.05	.02
☐ 279 Tom Glavine	.10	.05
☐ 280 Bryan Hickerson UER Name spelled Brian on front	.05	.02
☐ 281 Scott Radinsky	.05	.02
☐ 282 Omar Olivares	.05	.02
☐ 283 Ivan Calderon	.05	.02
☐ 284 Kevin Maas	.05	.02
☐ 285 Mickey Tettleton	.05	.02
☐ 286 Wade Boggs	.30	.14
☐ 287 Stan Belinda	.05	.02
☐ 288 Bret Barberie	.05	.02
☐ 289 Jose Oquendo	.05	.02
☐ 290 Frank Castillo	.15	.07
☐ 291 Dave Stieb	.05	.02
☐ 292 Tommy Greene	.05	.02
☐ 293 Eric Karros	.15	.07
☐ 294 Greg Maddux	1.00	.45
☐ 295 Jim Eisenreich	.15	.07
☐ 296 Rafael Palmeiro	.10	.05
☐ 297 Ramon Martinez	.15	.07
☐ 298 Tim Wallach	.05	.02
☐ 299 Jim Thome	1.00	.45
☐ 300 Chito Martinez	.05	.02
☐ 301 Mitch Williams	.05	.02
☐ 302 Randy Johnson	.30	.14
☐ 303 Carlton Fisk	.30	.14
☐ 304 Travis Fryman	.15	.07
☐ 305 Bobby Witt	.05	.02
☐ 306 Dave Magadan	.05	.02
☐ 307 Alex Cole	.05	.02
☐ 308 Bobby Bonilla	.15	.07
☐ 309 Bryan Harvey	.05	.02
☐ 310 Rafael Belliard	.05	.02
☐ 311 Mariano Duncan	.05	.02
☐ 312 Chuck Crim	.05	.02
☐ 313 John Kruk	.15	.07
☐ 314 Ellis Burks	.15	.07
☐ 315 Craig Biggio	.10	.05
☐ 316 Glenn Davis	.05	.02
☐ 317 Ryne Sandberg	.40	.18
☐ 318 Mike Sharperson	.05	.02
☐ 319 Rich Rodriguez	.05	.02
☐ 320 Lee Guetterman	.05	.02
☐ 321 Benito Santiago	.05	.02
☐ 322 Jose Offerman	.05	.02
☐ 323 Tony Pena	.05	.02
☐ 324 Pat Borders	.05	.02
☐ 325 Mike Henneman	.05	.02
☐ 326 Kevin Brown	.15	.07
☐ 327 Chris Nabholz	.05	.02
☐ 328 Franklin Stubbs	.05	.02
☐ 329 Tino Martinez	.30	.14
☐ 330 Mickey Morandini	.05	.02
☐ 331 Ryne Sandberg CL	.30	.14
☐ 332 Mark Gubicza	.05	.02
☐ 333 Bill Landrum	.05	.02
☐ 334 Mark Whiten	.05	.02
☐ 335 Darren Daulton	.15	.07
☐ 336 Rick Wilkins	.05	.02
☐ 337 Brian Jordan	.40	.18
☐ 338 Kevin Ward	.05	.02
☐ 339 Ruben Amaro	.05	.02
☐ 340 Trevor Wilson	.05	.02
☐ 341 Andujar Cedeno	.05	.02
☐ 342 Michael Huff	.05	.02
☐ 343 Brady Anderson	.10	.05
☐ 344 Craig Grebeck	.05	.02
☐ 345 Bobby Ojeda	.05	.02
☐ 346 Mike Pagliarulo	.05	.02
☐ 347 Terry Shumpert	.05	.02
☐ 348 Dann Bilardello	.05	.02
☐ 349 Frank Thomas	1.50	.70
☐ 350 Albert Belle	.40	.18
☐ 351 Jose Mesa	.15	.07
☐ 352 Rich Monteleone	.05	.02
☐ 353 Bob Walk	.05	.02
☐ 354 Monty Fariss	.05	.02
☐ 355 Luis Rivera	.05	.02
☐ 356 Anthony Young	.05	.02
☐ 357 Geno Petralli	.05	.02
☐ 358 Otis Nixon	.15	.07
☐ 359 Tom Pagnozzi	.05	.02
☐ 360 Reggie Sanders	.15	.07
☐ 361 Lee Stevens	.05	.02
☐ 362 Kent Hrbek	.15	.07
☐ 363 Orlando Merced	.05	.02
☐ 364 Mike Bordick	.05	.02
☐ 365 Dion James UER (Blue Jays logo on card back)	.05	.02
☐ 366 Jack Clark	.15	.07
☐ 367 Mike Stanley	.05	.02
☐ 368 Randy Velarde	.05	.02
☐ 369 Dan Pasqua	.05	.02
☐ 370 Pat Listach	.05	.02
☐ 371 Mike Fitzgerald	.05	.02
☐ 372 Tom Foley	.05	.02
☐ 373 Matt Williams	.10	.05
☐ 374 Brian Hunter	.05	.02
☐ 375 Joe Carter	.10	.05
☐ 376 Bret Saberhagen	.05	.02
☐ 377 Mike Stanton	.05	.02
☐ 378 Hubie Brooks	.05	.02
☐ 379 Eric Bell	.05	.02
☐ 380 Walt Weiss	.05	.02
☐ 381 Danny Jackson	.05	.02
☐ 382 Manuel Lee	.05	.02
☐ 383 Ruben Sierra	.05	.02
☐ 384 Greg Swindell	.05	.02
☐ 385 Ryan Bowen	.05	.02
☐ 386 Kevin Ritz	.05	.02
☐ 387 Curtis Wilkerson	.05	.02
☐ 388 Gary Varsho	.05	.02
☐ 389 Dave Hansen	.05	.02
☐ 390 Bob Welch	.05	.02
☐ 391 Lou Whitaker	.15	.07
☐ 392 Ken Griffey Jr.	2.00	.90
☐ 393 Mike Maddux	.05	.02
☐ 394 Arthur Rhodes	.05	.02
☐ 395 Chili Davis	.15	.07
☐ 396 Eddie Murray	.30	.14
☐ 397 Robin Yount CL	.10	.05
☐ 398 Dave Cochrane	.05	.02
☐ 399 Kevin Seitzer	.05	.02
☐ 400 Ozzie Smith	.40	.18
☐ 401 Paul Sorrento	.05	.02
☐ 402 Les Lancaster	.05	.02
☐ 403 Junior Noboa	.05	.02
☐ 404 David Justice	.30	.14
☐ 405 Andy Ashby	.05	.02
☐ 406 Danny Tartabull	.05	.02
☐ 407 Bill Swift	.05	.02
☐ 408 Craig Lefferts	.05	.02
☐ 409 Tom Candiotti	.05	.02
☐ 410 Lance Blankenship	.05	.02
☐ 411 Jeff Tackett	.05	.02
☐ 412 Sammy Sosa	.30	.14
☐ 413 Jody Reed	.05	.02
☐ 414 Bruce Ruffin	.05	.02
☐ 415 Gene Larkin	.05	.02
☐ 416 John Vander Wal	.05	.02
☐ 417 Tim Belcher	.05	.02
☐ 418 Steve Frey	.05	.02
☐ 419 Dick Schofield	.05	.02
☐ 420 Jeff King	.15	.07
☐ 421 Kim Batiste	.05	.02
☐ 422 Jack McDowell	.05	.02
☐ 423 Damon Berryhill	.05	.02
☐ 424 Gary Wayne	.05	.02
☐ 425 Jack Morris	.15	.07
☐ 426 Moises Alou	.10	.05
☐ 427 Mark McLemore	.05	.02
☐ 428 Juan Guerrero	.05	.02
☐ 429 Scott Scudder	.05	.02
☐ 430 Eric Davis	.15	.07
☐ 431 Joe Slusarski	.05	.02
☐ 432 Todd Zeile	.05	.02
☐ 433 Dwayne Henry	.05	.02
☐ 434 Cliff Brantley	.05	.02
☐ 435 Butch Henry	.05	.02
☐ 436 Todd Worrell	.05	.02
☐ 437 Bob Scanlan	.05	.02
☐ 438 Wally Joyner	.15	.07
☐ 439 John Flaherty	.05	.02
☐ 440 Brian Downing	.05	.02
☐ 441 Darren Lewis	.05	.02
☐ 442 Gary Carter	.30	.14
☐ 443 Wally Ritchie	.05	.02
☐ 444 Chris Jones	.05	.02
☐ 445 Jeff Kent	.30	.14
☐ 446 Gary Sheffield	.30	.14
☐ 447 Ron Darling	.05	.02
☐ 448 Deion Sanders	.30	.14
☐ 449 Andres Galarraga	.10	.05
☐ 450 Chuck Finley	.05	.02
☐ 451 Derek Lilliquist	.05	.02
☐ 452 Carl Willis	.05	.02
☐ 453 Wes Chamberlain	.05	.02
☐ 454 Roger Mason	.05	.02
☐ 455 Spike Owen	.05	.02

☐ 456 Thomas Howard	.05	.02
☐ 457 Dave Martinez	.05	.02
☐ 458 Pete Incaviglia	.05	.02
☐ 459 Keith A. Miller	.05	.02
☐ 460 Mike Fetters	.05	.02
☐ 461 Paul Gibson	.05	.02
☐ 462 George Bell	.05	.02
☐ 463 Bobby Bonilla CL	.15	.07
☐ 464 Terry Mulholland	.05	.02
☐ 465 Storm Davis	.05	.02
☐ 466 Gary Pettis	.05	.02
☐ 467 Randy Bush	.05	.02
☐ 468 Ken Hill	.15	.07
☐ 469 Rheal Cormier	.05	.02
☐ 470 Andy Stankiewicz	.05	.02
☐ 471 Dave Burba	.05	.02
☐ 472 Henry Cotto	.05	.02
☐ 473 Dale Sveum	.05	.02
☐ 474 Rich Gossage	.15	.07
☐ 475 William Suero	.05	.02
☐ 476 Doug Strange	.05	.02
☐ 477 Bill Krueger	.05	.02
☐ 478 John Wetteland	.15	.07
☐ 479 Melido Perez	.05	.02
☐ 480 Lonnie Smith	.05	.02
☐ 481 Mike Jackson	.05	.02
☐ 482 Mike Gardiner	.05	.02
☐ 483 David Wells	.05	.02
☐ 484 Barry Jones	.05	.02
☐ 485 Scott Bankhead	.05	.02
☐ 486 Terry Leach	.05	.02
☐ 487 Vince Horsman	.05	.02
☐ 488 Dave Eiland	.05	.02
☐ 489 Alejandro Pena	.05	.02
☐ 490 Julio Valera	.05	.02
☐ 491 Joe Boever	.05	.02
☐ 492 Paul Miller	.05	.02
☐ 493 Archi Cianfrocco	.05	.02
☐ 494 Dave Fleming	.05	.02
☐ 495 Kyle Abbott	.05	.02
☐ 496 Chad Kreuter	.05	.02
☐ 497 Chris James	.05	.02
☐ 498 Donnie Hill	.05	.02
☐ 499 Jacob Brumfield	.05	.02
☐ 500 Ricky Bones	.05	.02
☐ 501 Terry Steinbach	.15	.07
☐ 502 Bernard Gilkey	.15	.07
☐ 503 Dennis Cook	.05	.02
☐ 504 Len Dykstra	.15	.07
☐ 505 Mike Bielecki	.05	.02
☐ 506 Bob Kipper	.05	.02
☐ 507 Jose Melendez	.05	.02
☐ 508 Rick Sutcliffe	.05	.02
☐ 509 Ken Patterson	.05	.02
☐ 510 Andy Allanson	.05	.02
☐ 511 Al Newman	.05	.02
☐ 512 Mark Gardner	.05	.02
☐ 513 Jeff Schaefer	.05	.02
☐ 514 Jim McNamara	.05	.02
☐ 515 Peter Hoy	.05	.02
☐ 516 Curt Schilling	.15	.07
☐ 517 Kirk McCaskill	.05	.02
☐ 518 Chris Gwynn	.05	.02
☐ 519 Sid Fernandez	.05	.02
☐ 520 Jeff Parrett	.05	.02
☐ 521 Scott Ruskin	.05	.02
☐ 522 Kevin McReynolds	.05	.02
☐ 523 Rick Cerone	.05	.02
☐ 524 Jesse Orosco	.05	.02
☐ 525 Troy Afenir	.05	.02
☐ 526 John Smiley	.05	.02
☐ 527 Dale Murphy	.30	.14
☐ 528 Leaf Set Card	.05	.02

1992 Leaf Black Gold

This 528-card standard-size set was issued in two 264-card series. These Black Gold cards were inserted one per foil pack. The cards are similar to the regular issue Leaf cards, except that the card face is black rather than silver and accented by a gold foil inner border. Likewise, the horizontal backs have a gold rather than a silver background. The set is noteworthy as one of the earliest parallel issues in the hobby.

	MINT	NRMT
COMPLETE SET (528)	80.00	36.00
COMPLETE SERIES 1 (264)	30.00	13.50
COMPLETE SERIES 2 (264)	50.00	22.00
COMMON CARD (1-528)	.15	.07

*B.GOLD STARS: 2.5X TO 5X BASIC CARDS
*B.GOLD RC'S: 1.5X TO 3X BASIC CARDS

1992 Leaf Gold Rookies

This 24-card standard-size set honors 1992's most promising newcomers. The first 12 cards were randomly

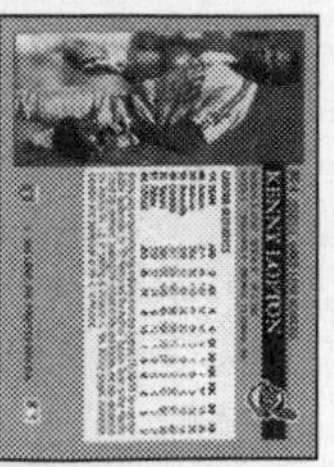

inserted in Leaf series I foil packs, while the second 12 cards were featured only in series II packs. The fronts display full-bleed color action photos highlighted by gold foil border stripes. A gold foil diamond appears at the corners of the picture frame, and the player's name appears in a black bar that extends between the bottom two diamonds. The key cards in this set are Kenny Lofton and Raul Mondesi.

	MINT	NRMT
COMPLETE SET (24)	16.00	7.25
COMPLETE SERIES 1 (12)	6.00	2.70
COMPLETE SERIES 2 (12)	10.00	4.50
COMMON CARD (BC1-BC24)	.50	.23

Card		
☐ BC1 Chad Curtis	1.00	.45
☐ BC2 Brent Gates	.50	.23
☐ BC3 Pedro Martinez	4.00	1.80
☐ BC4 Kenny Lofton	6.00	2.70
☐ BC5 Turk Wendell	.50	.23
☐ BC6 Mark Hutton	.50	.23
☐ BC7 Todd Hundley	1.50	.70
☐ BC8 Matt Stairs	.50	.23
☐ BC9 Eddie Taubensee	1.00	.45
☐ BC10 David Nied	.50	.23
☐ BC11 Salomon Torres	.50	.23
☐ BC12 Bret Boone	1.00	.45
☐ BC13 Johnny Ruffin	.50	.23
☐ BC14 Ed Martel	.50	.23
☐ BC15 Rick Trlicek	.50	.23
☐ BC16 Raul Mondesi	4.00	1.80
☐ BC17 Pat Mahomes	.50	.23
☐ BC18 Dan Wilson	1.25	.55
☐ BC19 Donovan Osborne	.50	.23
☐ BC20 Dave Silvestri	.50	.23
☐ BC21 Gary DiSarcina	.50	.23
☐ BC22 Denny Neagle	1.50	.70
☐ BC23 Steve Hosey	.50	.23
☐ BC24 John Doherty	.50	.23

1993 Leaf

The 1993 Leaf baseball set consists of three series of 220, 220, and 110 standard-size cards, respectively. Cards were distributed in 14-card foil packs, jumbo packs and magazine packs. The card fronts feature color action photos that are full-bleed except at the bottom where a diagonal black stripe (gold-foil stamped with the player's name) separates the picture from a team color-coded slate triangle. The Leaf seal embossed with gold foil is superimposed at the lower right corner. J.T. Snow is the only key Rookie Card in this set.

	MINT	NRMT
COMPLETE SET (550)	35.00	16.00
COMPLETE SERIES 1 (220)	15.00	6.75
COMPLETE SERIES 2 (220)	15.00	6.75
COMPLETE UPDATE (110)	5.00	2.20
COMMON CARD (1-550)	.15	.07

Card		
☐ 1 Ben McDonald	.15	.07
☐ 2 Sid Fernandez	.15	.07
☐ 3 Juan Guzman	.15	.07
☐ 4 Curt Schilling	.20	.09
☐ 5 Ivan Rodriguez	.75	.35
☐ 6 Don Slaught	.15	.07
☐ 7 Terry Steinbach	.30	.14
☐ 8 Todd Zeile	.15	.07
☐ 9 Andy Stankiewicz	.15	.07
☐ 10 Tim Teufel	.15	.07
☐ 11 Marvin Freeman	.15	.07
☐ 12 Jim Austin	.15	.07
☐ 13 Bob Scanlan	.15	.07
☐ 14 Rusty Meacham	.15	.07
☐ 15 Casey Candaele	.15	.07
☐ 16 Travis Fryman	.30	.14
☐ 17 Jose Offerman	.15	.07
☐ 18 Albert Belle	.75	.35
☐ 19 John Vander Wal	.15	.07
☐ 20 Dan Pasqua	.15	.07
☐ 21 Frank Viola	.15	.07
☐ 22 Terry Mulholland	.15	.07
☐ 23 Gregg Olson	.15	.07
☐ 24 Randy Tomlin	.15	.07
☐ 25 Todd Stottlemyre	.15	.07
☐ 26 Jose Oquendo	.15	.07
☐ 27 Julio Franco	.30	.14
☐ 28 Tony Gwynn	1.50	.70
☐ 29 Ruben Sierra	.15	.07
☐ 30 Robby Thompson	.15	.07
☐ 31 Jim Bullinger	.15	.07
☐ 32 Rick Aguilera	.15	.07
☐ 33 Scott Servais	.15	.07
☐ 34 Cal Eldred	.15	.07
☐ 35 Mike Piazza	3.00	1.35
☐ 36 Brent Mayne	.15	.07
☐ 37 Wil Cordero	.15	.07
☐ 38 Milt Cuyler	.15	.07
☐ 39 Howard Johnson	.15	.07
☐ 40 Kenny Lofton	1.25	.55
☐ 41 Alex Fernandez	.30	.14
☐ 42 Denny Neagle	.30	.14
☐ 43 Tony Pena	.15	.07
☐ 44 Bob Tewksbury	.15	.07
☐ 45 Glenn Davis	.15	.07
☐ 46 Fred McGriff	.20	.09
☐ 47 John Olerud	.15	.07
☐ 48 Steve Hosey	.15	.07
☐ 49 Rafael Palmeiro	.20	.09
☐ 50 David Justice	.60	.25
☐ 51 Pete Harnisch	.15	.07
☐ 52 Sam Militello	.15	.07
☐ 53 Orel Hershiser	.30	.14
☐ 54 Pat Mahomes	.15	.07
☐ 55 Greg Colbrunn	.15	.07
☐ 56 Greg Vaughn	.15	.07
☐ 57 Vince Coleman	.15	.07
☐ 58 Brian McRae	.15	.07
☐ 59 Len Dykstra	.30	.14
☐ 60 Dan Gladden	.15	.07
☐ 61 Ted Power	.15	.07
☐ 62 Donovan Osborne	.15	.07
☐ 63 Ron Karkovice	.15	.07
☐ 64 Frank Seminara	.15	.07
☐ 65 Bob Zupcic	.15	.07
☐ 66 Kirt Manwaring	.15	.07
☐ 67 Mike Devereaux	.15	.07
☐ 68 Mark Lemke	.15	.07
☐ 69 Devon White	.15	.07
☐ 70 Sammy Sosa	.60	.25
☐ 71 Pedro Astacio	.15	.07
☐ 72 Dennis Eckersley	.30	.14
☐ 73 Chris Nabholz	.15	.07
☐ 74 Melido Perez	.15	.07
☐ 75 Todd Hundley	.20	.09
☐ 76 Kent Hrbek	.30	.14
☐ 77 Mickey Morandini	.15	.07
☐ 78 Tim McIntosh	.15	.07
☐ 79 Andy Van Slyke	.30	.14
☐ 80 Kevin McReynolds	.15	.07
☐ 81 Mike Henneman	.15	.07
☐ 82 Greg W. Harris	.15	.07
☐ 83 Sandy Alomar Jr.	.30	.14
☐ 84 Mike Jackson	.15	.07
☐ 85 Ozzie Guillen	.15	.07
☐ 86 Jeff Blauser	.15	.07
☐ 87 John Valentin	.30	.14
☐ 88 Rey Sanchez	.15	.07
☐ 89 Rick Sutcliffe	.15	.07
☐ 90 Luis Gonzalez	.15	.07
☐ 91 Jeff Fassero	.15	.07
☐ 92 Kenny Rogers	.15	.07
☐ 93 Bret Saberhagen	.15	.07
☐ 94 Bob Welch	.15	.07
☐ 95 Darren Daulton	.30	.14
☐ 96 Mike Gallego	.15	.07
☐ 97 Orlando Merced	.15	.07
☐ 98 Chuck Knoblauch	.60	.25
☐ 99 Bernard Gilkey	.30	.14
☐ 100 Billy Ashley	.15	.07
☐ 101 Kevin Appier	.30	.14
☐ 102 Jeff Brantley	.15	.07
☐ 103 Bill Gullickson	.15	.07
☐ 104 John Smoltz	.20	.09
☐ 105 Paul Sorrento	.15	.07
☐ 106 Steve Buechele	.15	.07

☐ 107 Steve Sax	.15	.07
☐ 108 Andujar Cedeno	.15	.07
☐ 109 Billy Hatcher	.15	.07
☐ 110 Checklist	.15	.07
☐ 111 Alan Mills	.15	.07
☐ 112 John Franco	.15	.07
☐ 113 Jack Morris	.30	.14
☐ 114 Mitch Williams	.15	.07
☐ 115 Nolan Ryan	2.50	1.10
☐ 116 Jay Bell	.30	.14
☐ 117 Mike Bordick	.15	.07
☐ 118 Geronimo Pena	.15	.07
☐ 119 Danny Tartabull	.15	.07
☐ 120 Checklist	.15	.07
☐ 121 Steve Avery	.15	.07
☐ 122 Ricky Bones	.15	.07
☐ 123 Mike Morgan	.15	.07
☐ 124 Jeff Montgomery	.30	.14
☐ 125 Jeff Bagwell	1.25	.55
☐ 126 Tony Phillips	.15	.07
☐ 127 Lenny Harris	.15	.07
☐ 128 Glenallen Hill	.15	.07
☐ 129 Marquis Grissom	.30	.14
☐ 130 Gerald Williams UER (Bernie Williams picture and stats)	.15	.07
☐ 131 Greg A. Harris	.15	.07
☐ 132 Tommy Greene	.15	.07
☐ 133 Chris Hoiles	.15	.07
☐ 134 Bob Walk	.15	.07
☐ 135 Duane Ward	.15	.07
☐ 136 Tom Pagnozzi	.15	.07
☐ 137 Jeff Huson	.15	.07
☐ 138 Kurt Stillwell	.15	.07
☐ 139 Dave Henderson	.15	.07
☐ 140 Darrin Jackson	.15	.07
☐ 141 Frank Castillo	.15	.07
☐ 142 Scott Erickson	.15	.07
☐ 143 Darryl Kile	.30	.14
☐ 144 Bill Wegman	.15	.07
☐ 145 Steve Wilson	.15	.07
☐ 146 George Brett	1.25	.55
☐ 147 Moises Alou	.30	.14
☐ 148 Lou Whitaker	.30	.14
☐ 149 Chico Walker	.15	.07
☐ 150 Jerry Browne	.15	.07
☐ 151 Kirk McCaskill	.15	.07
☐ 152 Zane Smith	.15	.07
☐ 153 Matt Young	.15	.07
☐ 154 Lee Smith	.30	.14
☐ 155 Leo Gomez	.15	.07
☐ 156 Dan Walters	.15	.07
☐ 157 Pat Borders	.15	.07
☐ 158 Matt Williams	.20	.09
☐ 159 Dean Palmer	.30	.14
☐ 160 John Patterson	.15	.07
☐ 161 Doug Jones	.15	.07
☐ 162 John Habyan	.15	.07
☐ 163 Pedro Martinez	.60	.25
☐ 164 Carl Willis	.15	.07
☐ 165 Darrin Fletcher	.15	.07
☐ 166 B.J. Surhoff	.30	.14
☐ 167 Eddie Murray	.60	.25
☐ 168 Keith Miller	.15	.07
☐ 169 Ricky Jordan	.15	.07
☐ 170 Juan Gonzalez	1.50	.70
☐ 171 Charles Nagy	.30	.14
☐ 172 Mark Clark	.15	.07
☐ 173 Bobby Thigpen	.15	.07
☐ 174 Tim Scott	.15	.07
☐ 175 Scott Cooper	.15	.07
☐ 176 Royce Clayton	.30	.14
☐ 177 Brady Anderson	.20	.09
☐ 178 Sid Bream	.15	.07
☐ 179 Derek Bell	.30	.14
☐ 180 Otis Nixon	.30	.14
☐ 181 Kevin Gross	.15	.07
☐ 182 Ron Darling	.15	.07
☐ 183 John Wetteland	.30	.14
☐ 184 Mike Stanley	.15	.07
☐ 185 Jeff Kent	.30	.14
☐ 186 Brian Harper	.15	.07
☐ 187 Mariano Duncan	.15	.07
☐ 188 Robin Yount	.20	.09
☐ 189 Al Martin	.30	.14
☐ 190 Eddie Zosky	.15	.07
☐ 191 Mike Munoz	.15	.07
☐ 192 Andy Benes	.30	.14
☐ 193 Dennis Cook	.15	.07
☐ 194 Bill Swift	.15	.07
☐ 195 Frank Thomas	2.50	1.10
☐ 196 Damon Berryhill	.15	.07
☐ 197 Mike Greenwell	.15	.07
☐ 198 Mark Grace	.20	.09
☐ 199 Darryl Hamilton	.15	.07
☐ 200 Derrick May	.15	.07
☐ 201 Ken Hill	.30	.14
☐ 202 Kevin Brown	.30	.14
☐ 203 Dwight Gooden	.30	.14
☐ 204 Bobby Witt	.15	.07
☐ 205 Juan Bell	.15	.07
☐ 206 Kevin Maas	.15	.07
☐ 207 Jeff King	.30	.14
☐ 208 Scott Leius	.15	.07
☐ 209 Rheal Cormier	.15	.07
☐ 210 Darryl Strawberry	.30	.14
☐ 211 Tom Gordon	.15	.07
☐ 212 Bud Black	.15	.07
☐ 213 Mickey Tettleton	.15	.07
☐ 214 Pete Smith	.15	.07
☐ 215 Felix Fermin	.15	.07
☐ 216 Rick Wilkins	.15	.07
☐ 217 George Bell	.15	.07
☐ 218 Eric Anthony	.15	.07
☐ 219 Pedro Munoz	.15	.07
☐ 220 Checklist	.15	.07
☐ 221 Lance Blankenship	.15	.07
☐ 222 Deion Sanders	.60	.25
☐ 223 Craig Biggio	.20	.09
☐ 224 Ryne Sandberg	.75	.35
☐ 225 Ron Gant	.30	.14
☐ 226 Tom Brunansky	.15	.07
☐ 227 Chad Curtis	.30	.14
☐ 228 Joe Carter	.20	.09
☐ 229 Brian Jordan	.30	.14
☐ 230 Brett Butler	.30	.14
☐ 231 Frank Bolick	.15	.07
☐ 232 Rod Beck	.30	.14
☐ 233 Carlos Baerga	.30	.14
☐ 234 Eric Karros	.30	.14
☐ 235 Jack Armstrong	.15	.07
☐ 236 Bobby Bonilla	.30	.14
☐ 237 Don Mattingly	1.00	.45
☐ 238 Jeff Gardner	.15	.07
☐ 239 Dave Hollins	.15	.07
☐ 240 Steve Cooke	.15	.07
☐ 241 Jose Canseco	.20	.09
☐ 242 Ivan Calderon	.15	.07
☐ 243 Tim Belcher	.15	.07
☐ 244 Freddie Benavides	.15	.07
☐ 245 Roberto Alomar	.60	.25
☐ 246 Rob Deer	.15	.07
☐ 247 Will Clark	.20	.09
☐ 248 Mike Felder	.15	.07
☐ 249 Harold Baines	.30	.14
☐ 250 David Cone	.30	.14
☐ 251 Mark Guthrie	.15	.07
☐ 252 Ellis Burks	.30	.14
☐ 253 Jim Abbott	.15	.07
☐ 254 Chili Davis	.30	.14
☐ 255 Chris Bosio	.15	.07
☐ 256 Bret Barberie	.15	.07
☐ 257 Hal Morris	.15	.07
☐ 258 Dante Bichette	.20	.09
☐ 259 Storm Davis	.15	.07
☐ 260 Gary DiSarcina	.15	.07
☐ 261 Ken Caminiti	.60	.25
☐ 262 Paul Molitor	.60	.25
☐ 263 Joe Oliver	.15	.07
☐ 264 Pat Listach	.15	.07
☐ 265 Gregg Jefferies	.30	.14
☐ 266 Jose Guzman	.15	.07
☐ 267 Eric Davis	.30	.14
☐ 268 Delino DeShields	.15	.07
☐ 269 Barry Bonds	.75	.35
☐ 270 Mike Bielecki	.15	.07
☐ 271 Jay Buhner	.20	.09
☐ 272 Scott Pose	.15	.07
☐ 273 Tony Fernandez	.15	.07
☐ 274 Chito Martinez	.15	.07
☐ 275 Phil Plantier	.15	.07
☐ 276 Pete Incaviglia	.15	.07
☐ 277 Carlos Garcia	.15	.07
☐ 278 Tom Henke	.15	.07
☐ 279 Roger Clemens	1.25	.55
☐ 280 Rob Dibble	.15	.07
☐ 281 Daryl Boston	.15	.07
☐ 282 Greg Gagne	.15	.07
☐ 283 Cecil Fielder	.30	.14
☐ 284 Carlton Fisk	.20	.09
☐ 285 Wade Boggs	.60	.25
☐ 286 Damion Easley	.15	.07
☐ 287 Norm Charlton	.15	.07
☐ 288 Jeff Conine	.30	.14
☐ 289 Roberto Kelly	.15	.07
☐ 290 Jerald Clark	.15	.07
☐ 291 Rickey Henderson	.20	.09
☐ 292 Chuck Finley	.15	.07
☐ 293 Doug Drabek	.15	.07
☐ 294 Dave Stewart	.30	.14
☐ 295 Tom Glavine	.20	.09
☐ 296 Jaime Navarro	.15	.07
☐ 297 Ray Lankford	.20	.09
☐ 298 Greg Hibbard	.15	.07
☐ 299 Jody Reed	.15	.07
☐ 300 Dennis Martinez	.30	.14
☐ 301 Dave Martinez	.15	.07
☐ 302 Reggie Jefferson	.30	.14
☐ 303 John Cummings	.15	.07
☐ 304 Orestes Destrade	.15	.07
☐ 305 Mike Maddux	.15	.07
☐ 306 David Segui	.15	.07
☐ 307 Gary Sheffield	.60	.25
☐ 308 Danny Jackson	.15	.07
☐ 309 Craig Lefferts	.15	.07
☐ 310 Andre Dawson	.20	.09
☐ 311 Barry Larkin	.20	.09
☐ 312 Alex Cole	.15	.07
☐ 313 Mark Gardner	.15	.07
☐ 314 Kirk Gibson	.30	.14
☐ 315 Shane Mack	.15	.07
☐ 316 Bo Jackson	.30	.14
☐ 317 Jimmy Key	.30	.14
☐ 318 Greg Myers	.15	.07
☐ 319 Ken Griffey Jr.	3.00	1.35
☐ 320 Monty Fariss	.15	.07
☐ 321 Kevin Mitchell	.30	.14
☐ 322 Andres Galarraga	.20	.09
☐ 323 Mark McGwire	1.25	.55
☐ 324 Mark Langston	.15	.07
☐ 325 Steve Finley	.30	.14
☐ 326 Greg Maddux	2.00	.90
☐ 327 Dave Nilsson	.30	.14
☐ 328 Ozzie Smith	.75	.35
☐ 329 Candy Maldonado	.15	.07
☐ 330 Checklist	.15	.07
☐ 331 Tim Pugh	.15	.07
☐ 332 Joe Girardi	.15	.07
☐ 333 Junior Felix	.15	.07
☐ 334 Greg Swindell	.15	.07
☐ 335 Ramon Martinez	.30	.14
☐ 336 Sean Berry	.15	.07
☐ 337 Joe Orsulak	.15	.07
☐ 338 Wes Chamberlain	.15	.07
☐ 339 Stan Belinda	.15	.07
☐ 340 Checklist UER (306 Luis Mercedes)	.15	.07
☐ 341 Bruce Hurst	.15	.07
☐ 342 John Burkett	.15	.07
☐ 343 Mike Mussina	.60	.25
☐ 344 Scott Fletcher	.15	.07
☐ 345 Rene Gonzales	.15	.07
☐ 346 Roberto Hernandez	.30	.14
☐ 347 Carlos Martinez	.15	.07
☐ 348 Bill Krueger	.15	.07
☐ 349 Felix Jose	.15	.07
☐ 350 John Jaha	.30	.14
☐ 351 Willie Banks	.15	.07
☐ 352 Matt Nokes	.15	.07
☐ 353 Kevin Seitzer	.15	.07
☐ 354 Erik Hanson	.15	.07
☐ 355 David Hulse	.15	.07
☐ 356 Domingo Martinez	.15	.07
☐ 357 Greg Olson	.15	.07
☐ 358 Randy Myers	.30	.14
☐ 359 Tom Browning	.15	.07
☐ 360 Charlie Hayes	.15	.07
☐ 361 Bryan Harvey	.15	.07
☐ 362 Eddie Taubensee	.15	.07
☐ 363 Tim Wallach	.15	.07
☐ 364 Mel Rojas	.30	.14
☐ 365 Frank Tanana	.15	.07
☐ 366 John Kruk	.30	.14
☐ 367 Tim Laker	.15	.07
☐ 368 Rich Rodriguez	.15	.07
☐ 369 Darren Lewis	.15	.07
☐ 370 Harold Reynolds	.15	.07
☐ 371 Jose Melendez	.15	.07
☐ 372 Joe Grahe	.15	.07
☐ 373 Lance Johnson	.15	.07
☐ 374 Jose Mesa	.30	.14
☐ 375 Scott Livingstone	.15	.07
☐ 376 Wally Joyner	.30	.14
☐ 377 Kevin Reimer	.15	.07
☐ 378 Kirby Puckett	1.25	.55
☐ 379 Paul O'Neill	.30	.14
☐ 380 Randy Johnson	.60	.25
☐ 381 Manuel Lee	.15	.07
☐ 382 Dick Schofield	.15	.07
☐ 383 Darren Holmes	.15	.07
☐ 384 Charlie Hough	.15	.07
☐ 385 John Orton	.15	.07
☐ 386 Edgar Martinez	.20	.09
☐ 387 Terry Pendleton	.30	.14
☐ 388 Dan Plesac	.15	.07
☐ 389 Jeff Reardon	.30	.14
☐ 390 David Nied	.15	.07
☐ 391 Dave Magadan	.15	.07
☐ 392 Larry Walker	.60	.25
☐ 393 Ben Rivera	.15	.07
☐ 394 Lonnie Smith	.15	.07

☐ 395 Craig Shipley	.15	.07
☐ 396 Willie McGee	.15	.07
☐ 397 Arthur Rhodes	.15	.07
☐ 398 Mike Stanton	.15	.07
☐ 399 Luis Polonia	.15	.07
☐ 400 Jack McDowell	.15	.07
☐ 401 Mike Moore	.15	.07
☐ 402 Jose Lind	.15	.07
☐ 403 Bill Spiers	.15	.07
☐ 404 Kevin Tapani	.15	.07
☐ 405 Spike Owen	.15	.07
☐ 406 Tino Martinez	.60	.25
☐ 407 Charlie Leibrandt	.15	.07
☐ 408 Ed Sprague	.15	.07
☐ 409 Bryn Smith	.15	.07
☐ 410 Benito Santiago	.15	.07
☐ 411 Jose Rijo	.15	.07
☐ 412 Pete O'Brien	.15	.07
☐ 413 Willie Wilson	.15	.07
☐ 414 Bip Roberts	.15	.07
☐ 415 Eric Young	.60	.25
☐ 416 Walt Weiss	.15	.07
☐ 417 Milt Thompson	.15	.07
☐ 418 Chris Sabo	.15	.07
☐ 419 Scott Sanderson	.15	.07
☐ 420 Tim Raines	.30	.14
☐ 421 Alan Trammell	.20	.09
☐ 422 Mike Macfarlane	.15	.07
☐ 423 Dave Winfield	.20	.09
☐ 424 Bob Wickman	.15	.07
☐ 425 David Valle	.15	.07
☐ 426 Gary Redus	.15	.07
☐ 427 Turner Ward	.15	.07
☐ 428 Reggie Sanders	.30	.14
☐ 429 Todd Worrell	.15	.07
☐ 430 Julio Valera	.15	.07
☐ 431 Cal Ripken Jr.	2.50	1.10
☐ 432 Mo Vaughn	.75	.35
☐ 433 John Smiley	.15	.07
☐ 434 Omar Vizquel	.30	.14
☐ 435 Billy Ripken	.15	.07
☐ 436 Cory Snyder	.15	.07
☐ 437 Carlos Quintana	.15	.07
☐ 438 Omar Olivares	.15	.07
☐ 439 Robin Ventura	.30	.14
☐ 440 Checklist	.15	.07
☐ 441 Kevin Higgins	.15	.07
☐ 442 Carlos Hernandez	.15	.07
☐ 443 Dan Peltier	.15	.07
☐ 444 Derek Lilliquist	.15	.07
☐ 445 Tim Salmon	.75	.35
☐ 446 Sherman Obando	.15	.07
☐ 447 Pat Kelly	.15	.07
☐ 448 Todd Van Poppel	.15	.07
☐ 449 Mark Whiten	.15	.07
☐ 450 Checklist	.15	.07
☐ 451 Pat Meares	.30	.14
☐ 452 Tony Tarasco	.15	.07
☐ 453 Chris Gwynn	.15	.07
☐ 454 Armando Reynoso	.15	.07
☐ 455 Danny Darwin	.15	.07
☐ 456 Willie Greene	.30	.14
☐ 457 Mike Blowers	.15	.07
☐ 458 Kevin Roberson	.15	.07
☐ 459 Graeme Lloyd	.15	.07
☐ 460 David West	.15	.07
☐ 461 Joey Cora	.30	.14
☐ 462 Alex Arias	.15	.07
☐ 463 Chad Kreuter	.15	.07
☐ 464 Mike Lansing	.30	.14
☐ 465 Mike Timlin	.15	.07
☐ 466 Paul Wagner	.15	.07
☐ 467 Mark Portugal	.15	.07
☐ 468 Jim Leyritz	.15	.07
☐ 469 Ryan Klesko	.75	.35
☐ 470 Mario Diaz	.15	.07
☐ 471 Guillermo Velasquez	.15	.07
☐ 472 Fernando Valenzuela	.30	.14
☐ 473 Raul Mondesi	.75	.35
☐ 474 Mike Pagliarulo	.15	.07
☐ 475 Chris Hammond	.15	.07
☐ 476 Torey Lovullo	.15	.07
☐ 477 Trevor Wilson	.15	.07
☐ 478 Marcos Armas	.15	.07
☐ 479 Dave Gallagher	.15	.07
☐ 480 Jeff Treadway	.15	.07
☐ 481 Jeff Branson	.15	.07
☐ 482 Dickie Thon	.15	.07
☐ 483 Eduardo Perez	.15	.07
☐ 484 David Wells	.15	.07
☐ 485 Brian Williams	.15	.07
☐ 486 Domingo Cedeno	.15	.07
☐ 487 Tom Candiotti	.15	.07
☐ 488 Steve Frey	.15	.07
☐ 489 Greg McMichael	.15	.07
☐ 490 Marc Newfield	.30	.14
☐ 491 Larry Andersen	.15	.07
☐ 492 Damon Buford	.15	.07
☐ 493 Ricky Gutierrez	.15	.07
☐ 494 Jeff Russell	.15	.07
☐ 495 Vinny Castilla	.60	.25
☐ 496 Wilson Alvarez	.30	.14
☐ 497 Scott Bullett	.15	.07
☐ 498 Larry Casian	.15	.07
☐ 499 Jose Vizcaino	.15	.07
☐ 500 J.T. Snow	.75	.35
☐ 501 Bryan Hickerson	.15	.07
☐ 502 Jeremy Hernandez	.15	.07
☐ 503 Jeromy Burnitz	.30	.14
☐ 504 Steve Farr	.15	.07
☐ 505 J. Owens	.15	.07
☐ 506 Craig Paquette	.15	.07
☐ 507 Jim Eisenreich	.30	.14
☐ 508 Matt Whiteside	.15	.07
☐ 509 Luis Aquino	.15	.07
☐ 510 Mike LaValliere	.15	.07
☐ 511 Jim Gott	.15	.07
☐ 512 Mark McLemore	.15	.07
☐ 513 Randy Milligan	.15	.07
☐ 514 Gary Gaetti	.30	.14
☐ 515 Lou Frazier	.15	.07
☐ 516 Rich Amaral	.15	.07
☐ 517 Gene Harris	.15	.07
☐ 518 Aaron Sele	.30	.14
☐ 519 Mark Wohlers	.30	.14
☐ 520 Scott Kamieniecki	.15	.07
☐ 521 Kent Mercker	.15	.07
☐ 522 Jim Deshaies	.15	.07
☐ 523 Kevin Stocker	.15	.07
☐ 524 Jason Bere	.30	.14
☐ 525 Tim Bogar	.15	.07
☐ 526 Brad Pennington	.15	.07
☐ 527 Curt Leskanic	.15	.07
☐ 528 Wayne Kirby	.15	.07
☐ 529 Tim Costo	.15	.07
☐ 530 Doug Henry	.15	.07
☐ 531 Trevor Hoffman	.20	.09
☐ 532 Kelly Gruber	.15	.07
☐ 533 Mike Harkey	.15	.07
☐ 534 John Doherty	.15	.07
☐ 535 Erik Pappas	.15	.07
☐ 536 Brent Gates	.15	.07
☐ 537 Roger McDowell	.15	.07
☐ 538 Chris Haney	.15	.07
☐ 539 Blas Minor	.15	.07
☐ 540 Pat Hentgen	.20	.09
☐ 541 Chuck Carr	.15	.07
☐ 542 Doug Strange	.15	.07
☐ 543 Xavier Hernandez	.15	.07
☐ 544 Paul Quantrill	.15	.07
☐ 545 Anthony Young	.15	.07
☐ 546 Bret Boone	.15	.07
☐ 547 Dwight Smith	.15	.07
☐ 548 Bobby Munoz	.15	.07
☐ 549 Russ Springer	.15	.07
☐ 550 Roger Pavlik	.15	.07
☐ DW Dave Winfield 3000 Hits	1.00	.45
☐ FT Frank Thomas AU/3500 (Certified autograph)	200.00	90.00

1993 Leaf Fasttrack

These 20 standard-size cards, featuring a selection of talented young stars, were randomly inserted into 1993 Leaf retail packs; the first ten were series I inserts, the second ten were series II inserts. The fronts feature borderless color player action photos, except in the lower right corner, where an oblique white stripe carries the motion-streaked set title.

	MINT	NRMT
COMPLETE SET (20)	100.00	45.00
COMPLETE SERIES 1 (10)	60.00	27.00
COMPLETE SERIES 2 (10)	40.00	18.00
COMMON CARD (1-20)	2.00	.90
☐ 1 Frank Thomas	35.00	16.00
☐ 2 Tim Wakefield	2.00	.90
☐ 3 Kenny Lofton	15.00	6.75
☐ 4 Mike Mussina	8.00	3.60
☐ 5 Juan Gonzalez	20.00	9.00
☐ 6 Chuck Knoblauch	6.00	2.70
☐ 7 Eric Karros	3.00	1.35
☐ 8 Ray Lankford	5.00	2.20
☐ 9 Juan Guzman	2.00	.90
☐ 10 Pat Listach	2.00	.90
☐ 11 Carlos Baerga	3.00	1.35
☐ 12 Felix Jose	2.00	.90
☐ 13 Steve Avery	2.00	.90
☐ 14 Robin Ventura	3.00	1.35
☐ 15 Ivan Rodriguez	10.00	4.50
☐ 16 Cal Eldred	2.00	.90
☐ 17 Jeff Bagwell	15.00	6.75
☐ 18 David Justice	6.00	2.70
☐ 19 Travis Fryman	3.00	1.35
☐ 20 Marquis Grissom	3.00	1.35

1993 Leaf Gold All-Stars

These 30 standard-size dual-sided cards feature members of the American and National league All-Star squads. The first 20 were inserted one per 1993 Leaf jumbo packs; the first ten were series I inserts, the second ten were series II inserts. The final ten cards were randomly inserted in 1993 Leaf Update packs. The card design features full color action photos with a diagonal stripe at the base.

	MINT	NRMT
COMPLETE REG.SET (20)	40.00	18.00
COMPLETE UPDATE SET (10)	12.00	5.50
COMMON REG.CARD (R1-R20)	.50	.23
☐ R1 Ivan Rodriguez Darren Daulton	1.00	.45
☐ R2 Don Mattingly Fred McGriff	1.50	.70
☐ R3 Cecil Fielder Jeff Bagwell	2.00	.90
☐ R4 Carlos Baerga Ryne Sandberg	1.50	.70
☐ R5 Chuck Knoblauch Delino DeShields	1.00	.45
☐ R6 Robin Ventura Terry Pendleton	.50	.23
☐ R7 Ken Griffey Jr. Andy Van Slyke	5.00	2.20
☐ R8 Joe Carter Dave Justice	1.00	.45
☐ R9 Jose Canseco Tony Gwynn	2.50	1.10
☐ R10 Dennis Eckersley Rob Dibble	.50	.23
☐ R11 Mark McGwire Will Clark	2.00	.90
☐ R12 Frank Thomas Mark Grace	4.00	1.80
☐ R13 Roberto Alomar Craig Biggio	1.25	.55
☐ R14 Cal Ripken Barry Larkin	4.00	1.80
☐ R15 Edgar Martinez Gary Sheffield	1.00	.45
☐ R16 Juan Gonzalez Barry Bonds	2.50	1.10
☐ R17 Kirby Puckett Marquis Grissom	2.00	.90
☐ R18 Jim Abbott Tom Glavine	.75	.35
☐ R19 Nolan Ryan Greg Maddux	10.00	4.50
☐ R20 Roger Clemens Doug Drabek	1.00	.45
☐ U1 Mark Langston Terry Mulholland	.50	.23
☐ U2 Ivan Rodriguez Darren Daulton	.75	.35
☐ U3 John Olerud John Kruk	.50	.23
☐ U4 Roberto Alomar Ryne Sandberg	1.50	.70
☐ U5 Wade Boggs Gary Sheffield	1.25	.55

☐ U6 Cal Ripken / Barry Larkin	4.00	1.80
☐ U7 Kirby Puckett / Barry Bonds	2.50	1.10
☐ U8 Ken Griffey Jr. / Marquis Grissom	5.00	2.20
☐ U9 Joe Carter / David Justice	1.00	.45
☐ U10 Paul Molitor / Mark Grace	1.00	.45

1993 Leaf Gold Rookies

These cards of promising newcomers were randomly inserted into 1993 Leaf packs; the first ten in series I, the last ten in series II, and five in the Update product. The front of each standard-size card features a borderless color player action shot. The player's name appears in white cursive lettering within a wide gray lithic stripe near the bottom, which is set off by gold-foil lines and carries the set's title in simulated bas-relief. Leaf produced jumbo (3 1/2 by 5 inch) versions for retail repacks; they are valued at approximately double the prices below.

	MINT	NRMT
COMPLETE REG.SET (20)	40.00	18.00
COMPLETE UPDATE SET (5)	20.00	9.00
COMMON REG.CARD (R1-R20)	1.00	.45
☐ R1 Kevin Young	1.25	.55
☐ R2 Wil Cordero	1.00	.45
☐ R3 Mark Kiefer	1.00	.45
☐ R4 Gerald Williams	1.00	.45
☐ R5 Brandon Wilson	1.00	.45
☐ R6 Greg Gohr	1.00	.45
☐ R7 Ryan Thompson	1.00	.45
☐ R8 Tim Wakefield	1.25	.55
☐ R9 Troy Neel	1.00	.45
☐ R10 Tim Salmon	8.00	3.60
☐ R11 Kevin Rogers	1.00	.45
☐ R12 Rod Bolton	1.00	.45
☐ R13 Ken Ryan	1.00	.45
☐ R14 Phil Hiatt	1.00	.45
☐ R15 Rene Arocha	1.00	.45
☐ R16 Nigel Wilson	1.00	.45
☐ R17 J.T. Snow	3.00	1.35
☐ R18 Benji Gil	1.00	.45
☐ R19 Chipper Jones	20.00	9.00
☐ R20 Darrell Sherman	1.00	.45
☐ U1 Allen Watson	1.00	.45
☐ U2 Jeffrey Hammonds	1.50	.70
☐ U3 Dave McCarty	1.00	.45
☐ U4 Mike Piazza	15.00	6.75
☐ U5 Roberto Mejia	1.00	.45

1993 Leaf Heading for the Hall

Randomly inserted into 1993 Leaf series 1 and 2 packs, this ten-card standard-size set features potential Hall of Famers. Cards 1-5 were series I inserts and cards 6-10 were series II inserts. The fronts feature borderless color player action shots, with the player's name appearing within a lithic banner near the bottom, below the set's logo.

	MINT	NRMT
COMPLETE SET (10)	30.00	13.50
COMPLETE SERIES 1 (5)	20.00	9.00
COMPLETE SERIES 2 (5)	10.00	4.50
COMMON CARD (1-10)	1.50	.70
☐ 1 Nolan Ryan	12.00	5.50
☐ 2 Tony Gwynn	5.00	2.20
☐ 3 Robin Yount	1.50	.70
☐ 4 Eddie Murray	3.00	1.35
☐ 5 Cal Ripken	12.00	5.50
☐ 6 Roger Clemens	2.50	1.10
☐ 7 George Brett	5.00	2.20
☐ 8 Ryne Sandberg	3.00	1.35
☐ 9 Kirby Puckett	5.00	2.20
☐ 10 Ozzie Smith	3.00	1.35

1993 Leaf Thomas

This ten-card standard-size set spotlights Chicago White Sox slugger and Donruss/Leaf spokesperson Frank Thomas and were randomly inserted into all forms of Leaf packs. Five cards were inserted in each of the two series. The full-bleed fronts carry color action shots with "Frank" stamped in large prismatic foil letters across the bottom of the picture. Jumbo (5" by 7") versions of these cards were issued one per box of Leaf Update. The jumbos are individually numbered out of 7,500.

	MINT	NRMT
COMPLETE SET (10)	40.00	18.00
COMMON THOMAS (1-10)	5.00	2.20
COMPLETE JUMBO SET (10)	60.00	27.00
*JUMBOS: 1.5X VALUE		
☐ 1 Frank Thomas / Aggressive	5.00	2.20
☐ 2 Frank Thomas / Serious	5.00	2.20
☐ 3 Frank Thomas / Intense	5.00	2.20
☐ 4 Frank Thomas / Confident	5.00	2.20
☐ 5 Frank Thomas / Assertive	5.00	2.20
☐ 6 Frank Thomas / Power	5.00	2.20
☐ 7 Frank Thomas / Control	5.00	2.20
☐ 8 Frank Thomas / Strength	5.00	2.20
☐ 9 Frank Thomas / Concentration	5.00	2.20
☐ 10 Frank Thomas / Preparation	5.00	2.20

1994 Leaf Promos

Issued to herald the release of the 1994 Leaf set, these nine promo cards measure the standard size and parallel the corresponding regular issue 1994 Leaf cards. The "Promotional Sample" disclaimer appears diagonally on the front and back. The cards are numbered on the back as "X of 9."

	MINT	NRMT
COMPLETE SET (9)	20.00	9.00
COMMON CARD (1-9)	.50	.23
☐ 1 Roberto Alomar	1.25	.55
☐ 2 Darren Daulton	.50	.23
☐ 3 Ken Griffey Jr.	5.00	2.20
☐ 4 David Justice	1.00	.45
☐ 5 Don Mattingly	2.50	1.10
☐ 6 Mike Piazza	3.00	1.35
☐ 7 Cal Ripken	4.00	1.80
☐ 8 Ryne Sandberg	2.00	.90
☐ 9 Frank Thomas	5.00	2.20

1994 Leaf

The 1994 Leaf baseball set consists of two series of 220 standard-size cards for a total of 440. Certain "Super Packs" contained complete insert sets. The fronts feature color action player photos, with team color-coded designs on the bottom. The player's name and the Leaf logo are foil stamped, the team name appears under the player's name. The backs carry a photo of the player's home stadium in the background with a silhouetted photo of the player in the foreground. Additionally, a headshot appears in a ticket stub-like design with biographical information, while player statistics appear on the bottom. Cards featuring players from the Texas Rangers, Cleveland Indians, Milwaukee Brewers and Houston Astros were held out of the first series in order to have up-to-date photography in each team's new uniforms. A limited number of players from the San Francisco Giants are featured in the first series because of minor modifications to the team's uniforms. Randomly inserted in hobby packs at a rate of one in 36 was a stamped version of Frank Thomas' 1990 Leaf rookie card.

	MINT	NRMT
COMPLETE SET (440)	24.00	11.00
COMPLETE SERIES 1 (220)	12.00	5.50
COMPLETE SERIES 2 (220)	12.00	5.50
COMMON CARD (1-440)	.15	.07
☐ 1 Cal Ripken Jr.	2.50	1.10
☐ 2 Tony Tarasco	.15	.07
☐ 3 Joe Girardi	.15	.07
☐ 4 Bernie Williams	.60	.25
☐ 5 Chad Kreuter	.15	.07
☐ 6 Troy Neel	.15	.07
☐ 7 Tom Pagnozzi	.15	.07
☐ 8 Kirk Rueter	.15	.07
☐ 9 Chris Bosio	.15	.07
☐ 10 Dwight Gooden	.30	.14
☐ 11 Mariano Duncan	.15	.07
☐ 12 Jay Bell	.30	.14
☐ 13 Lance Johnson	.30	.14
☐ 14 Richie Lewis	.15	.07
☐ 15 Dave Martinez	.15	.07
☐ 16 Orel Hershiser	.30	.14
☐ 17 Rob Butler	.15	.07
☐ 18 Glenallen Hill	.15	.07
☐ 19 Chad Curtis	.15	.07
☐ 20 Mike Stanton	.15	.07
☐ 21 Tim Wallach	.15	.07
☐ 22 Milt Thompson	.15	.07
☐ 23 Kevin Young	.15	.07
☐ 24 John Smiley	.15	.07
☐ 25 Jeff Montgomery	.30	.14
☐ 26 Robin Ventura	.30	.14
☐ 27 Scott Lydy	.15	.07
☐ 28 Todd Stottlemyre	.15	.07
☐ 29 Mark Whiten	.15	.07
☐ 30 Robby Thompson	.15	.07
☐ 31 Bobby Bonilla	.30	.14
☐ 32 Andy Ashby	.15	.07
☐ 33 Greg Myers	.15	.07
☐ 34 Billy Hatcher	.15	.07
☐ 35 Brad Holman	.15	.07
☐ 36 Mark McLemore	.15	.07
☐ 37 Scott Sanders	.15	.07
☐ 38 Jim Abbott	.15	.07
☐ 39 David Wells	.15	.07
☐ 40 Roberto Kelly	.15	.07
☐ 41 Jeff Conine	.30	.14
☐ 42 Sean Berry	.15	.07
☐ 43 Mark Grace	.50	.23
☐ 44 Eric Young	.30	.14
☐ 45 Rick Aguilera	.15	.07
☐ 46 Chipper Jones	2.00	.90

☐ 47 Mel Rojas .15 .07
☐ 48 Ryan Thompson .15 .07
☐ 49 Al Martin .15 .07
☐ 50 Cecil Fielder .30 .14
☐ 51 Pat Kelly .15 .07
☐ 52 Kevin Tapani .15 .07
☐ 53 Tim Costo .15 .07
☐ 54 Dave Hollins .15 .07
☐ 55 Kirt Manwaring .15 .07
☐ 56 Gregg Jefferies .30 .14
☐ 57 Ron Darling .15 .07
☐ 58 Bill Haselman .15 .07
☐ 59 Phil Plantier .15 .07
☐ 60 Frank Viola .15 .07
☐ 61 Todd Zeile .15 .07
☐ 62 Bret Barberie .15 .07
☐ 63 Roberto Mejia .15 .07
☐ 64 Chuck Knoblauch .60 .25
☐ 65 Jose Lind .15 .07
☐ 66 Brady Anderson .50 .23
☐ 67 Ruben Sierra .15 .07
☐ 68 Jose Vizcaino .15 .07
☐ 69 Joe Grahe .15 .07
☐ 70 Kevin Appier .30 .14
☐ 71 Wilson Alvarez .30 .14
☐ 72 Tom Candiotti .15 .07
☐ 73 John Burkett .15 .07
☐ 74 Anthony Young .15 .07
☐ 75 Scott Cooper .15 .07
☐ 76 Nigel Wilson .15 .07
☐ 77 John Valentin .30 .14
☐ 78 Dave McCarty .15 .07
☐ 79 Archi Cianfrocco .15 .07
☐ 80 Lou Whitaker .30 .14
☐ 81 Dante Bichette .50 .23
☐ 82 Mark Dewey .15 .07
☐ 83 Danny Jackson .15 .07
☐ 84 Harold Baines .30 .14
☐ 85 Todd Benzinger .15 .07
☐ 86 Damion Easley .15 .07
☐ 87 Danny Cox .15 .07
☐ 88 Jose Bautista .15 .07
☐ 89 Mike Lansing .30 .14
☐ 90 Phil Hiatt .15 .07
☐ 91 Tim Pugh .15 .07
☐ 92 Tino Martinez .60 .25
☐ 93 Raul Mondesi .60 .25
☐ 94 Greg Maddux 2.00 .90
☐ 95 Al Leiter .15 .07
☐ 96 Benito Santiago .15 .07
☐ 97 Lenny Dykstra .30 .14
☐ 98 Sammy Sosa .60 .25
☐ 99 Tim Bogar .15 .07
☐ 100 Checklist .15 .07
☐ 101 Deion Sanders .60 .25
☐ 102 Bobby Witt .15 .07
☐ 103 Wil Cordero .30 .14
☐ 104 Rich Amaral .15 .07
☐ 105 Mike Mussina .60 .25
☐ 106 Reggie Sanders .15 .07
☐ 107 Ozzie Guillen .15 .07
☐ 108 Paul O'Neill .30 .14
☐ 109 Tim Salmon .60 .25
☐ 110 Rheal Cormier .15 .07
☐ 111 Billy Ashley .15 .07
☐ 112 Jeff Kent .15 .07
☐ 113 Derek Bell .30 .14
☐ 114 Danny Darwin .15 .07
☐ 115 Chip Hale .15 .07
☐ 116 Tim Raines .15 .07
☐ 117 Ed Sprague .15 .07
☐ 118 Darrin Fletcher .15 .07
☐ 119 Darren Holmes .15 .07
☐ 120 Alan Trammell .50 .23
☐ 121 Don Mattingly 1.00 .45
☐ 122 Greg Gagne .15 .07
☐ 123 Jose Offerman .15 .07
☐ 124 Joe Orsulak .15 .07
☐ 125 Jack McDowell .15 .07
☐ 126 Barry Larkin .50 .23
☐ 127 Ben McDonald .15 .07
☐ 128 Mike Bordick .15 .07
☐ 129 Devon White .15 .07
☐ 130 Mike Perez .15 .07
☐ 131 Jay Buhner .50 .23
☐ 132 Phil Leftwich .15 .07
☐ 133 Tommy Greene .15 .07
☐ 134 Charlie Hayes .15 .07
☐ 135 Don Slaught .15 .07
☐ 136 Mike Gallego .15 .07
☐ 137 Dave Winfield .50 .23
☐ 138 Steve Avery .15 .07
☐ 139 Derrick May .15 .07
☐ 140 Bryan Harvey .15 .07
☐ 141 Wally Joyner .30 .14
☐ 142 Andre Dawson .50 .23
☐ 143 Andy Benes .30 .14
☐ 144 John Franco .15 .07
☐ 145 Jeff King .30 .14
☐ 146 Joe Oliver .15 .07
☐ 147 Bill Gullickson .15 .07
☐ 148 Armando Reynoso .15 .07
☐ 149 Dave Fleming .15 .07
☐ 150 Checklist .15 .07
☐ 151 Todd Van Poppel .15 .07
☐ 152 Bernard Gilkey .15 .07
☐ 153 Kevin Gross .15 .07
☐ 154 Mike Devereaux .15 .07
☐ 155 Tim Wakefield .15 .07
☐ 156 Andres Galarraga .50 .23
☐ 157 Pat Meares .15 .07
☐ 158 Jim Leyritz .15 .07
☐ 159 Mike Macfarlane .15 .07
☐ 160 Tony Phillips .15 .07
☐ 161 Brent Gates .15 .07
☐ 162 Mark Langston .15 .07
☐ 163 Allen Watson .15 .07
☐ 164 Randy Johnson .60 .25
☐ 165 Doug Brocail .15 .07
☐ 166 Rob Dibble .15 .07
☐ 167 Roberto Hernandez .30 .14
☐ 168 Felix Jose .15 .07
☐ 169 Steve Cooke .15 .07
☐ 170 Darren Daulton .30 .14
☐ 171 Eric Karros .30 .14
☐ 172 Geronimo Pena .15 .07
☐ 173 Gary DiSarcina .15 .07
☐ 174 Marquis Grissom .30 .14
☐ 175 Joey Cora .30 .14
☐ 176 Jim Eisenreich .30 .14
☐ 177 Brad Pennington .15 .07
☐ 178 Terry Steinbach .30 .14
☐ 179 Pat Borders .15 .07
☐ 180 Steve Buechele .15 .07
☐ 181 Jeff Fassero .15 .07
☐ 182 Mike Greenwell .15 .07
☐ 183 Mike Henneman .15 .07
☐ 184 Ron Karkovice .15 .07
☐ 185 Pat Hentgen .30 .14
☐ 186 Jose Guzman .15 .07
☐ 187 Brett Butler .30 .14
☐ 188 Charlie Hough .15 .07
☐ 189 Terry Pendleton .30 .14
☐ 190 Melido Perez .15 .07
☐ 191 Orestes Destrade .15 .07
☐ 192 Mike Morgan .15 .07
☐ 193 Joe Carter .50 .23
☐ 194 Jeff Blauser .15 .07
☐ 195 Chris Hoiles .15 .07
☐ 196 Ricky Gutierrez .15 .07
☐ 197 Mike Moore .15 .07
☐ 198 Carl Willis .15 .07
☐ 199 Aaron Sele .15 .07
☐ 200 Checklist .15 .07
☐ 201 Tim Naehring .15 .07
☐ 202 Scott Livingstone .15 .07
☐ 203 Luis Alicea .15 .07
☐ 204 Torey Lovullo .15 .07
☐ 205 Jim Gott .15 .07
☐ 206 Bob Wickman .15 .07
☐ 207 Greg McMichael .15 .07
☐ 208 Scott Brosius .15 .07
☐ 209 Chris Gwynn .15 .07
☐ 210 Steve Sax .15 .07
☐ 211 Dick Schofield .15 .07
☐ 212 Robb Nen .30 .14
☐ 213 Ben Rivera .15 .07
☐ 214 Vinny Castilla .50 .23
☐ 215 Jamie Moyer .15 .07
☐ 216 Wally Whitehurst .15 .07
☐ 217 Frank Castillo .15 .07
☐ 218 Mike Blowers .15 .07
☐ 219 Tim Scott .15 .07
☐ 220 Paul Wagner .15 .07
☐ 221 Jeff Bagwell 1.25 .55
☐ 222 Ricky Bones .15 .07
☐ 223 Sandy Alomar Jr. .30 .14
☐ 224 Rod Beck .30 .14
☐ 225 Roberto Alomar .60 .25
☐ 226 Jack Armstrong .15 .07
☐ 227 Scott Erickson .15 .07
☐ 228 Rene Arocha .15 .07
☐ 229 Eric Anthony .15 .07
☐ 230 Jeromy Burnitz .30 .14
☐ 231 Kevin Brown .30 .14
☐ 232 Tim Belcher .15 .07
☐ 233 Bret Boone .30 .14
☐ 234 Dennis Eckersley .50 .23
☐ 235 Tom Glavine .50 .23
☐ 236 Craig Biggio .50 .23
☐ 237 Pedro Astacio .15 .07
☐ 238 Ryan Bowen .15 .07
☐ 239 Brad Ausmus .15 .07
☐ 240 Vince Coleman .15 .07
☐ 241 Jason Bere .15 .07
☐ 242 Ellis Burks .30 .14
☐ 243 Wes Chamberlain .15 .07
☐ 244 Ken Caminiti .60 .25
☐ 245 Willie Banks .15 .07
☐ 246 Sid Fernandez .15 .07
☐ 247 Carlos Baerga .30 .14
☐ 248 Carlos Garcia .15 .07
☐ 249 Jose Canseco .50 .23
☐ 250 Alex Diaz .15 .07
☐ 251 Albert Belle .75 .35
☐ 252 Moises Alou .30 .14
☐ 253 Bobby Ayala .15 .07
☐ 254 Tony Gwynn 1.50 .70
☐ 255 Roger Clemens 1.25 .55
☐ 256 Eric Davis .30 .14
☐ 257 Wade Boggs .60 .25
☐ 258 Chili Davis .30 .14
☐ 259 Rickey Henderson .50 .23
☐ 260 Andujar Cedeno .15 .07
☐ 261 Cris Carpenter .15 .07
☐ 262 Juan Guzman .15 .07
☐ 263 David Justice .60 .25
☐ 264 Barry Bonds .75 .35
☐ 265 Pete Incaviglia .15 .07
☐ 266 Tony Fernandez .15 .07
☐ 267 Cal Eldred .15 .07
☐ 268 Alex Fernandez .30 .14
☐ 269 Kent Hrbek .30 .14
☐ 270 Steve Farr .15 .07
☐ 271 Doug Drabek .15 .07
☐ 272 Brian Jordan .30 .14
☐ 273 Xavier Hernandez .15 .07
☐ 274 David Cone .30 .14
☐ 275 Brian Hunter .15 .07
☐ 276 Mike Harkey .15 .07
☐ 277 Delino DeShields .15 .07
☐ 278 David Hulse .15 .07
☐ 279 Mickey Tettleton .15 .07
☐ 280 Kevin McReynolds .15 .07
☐ 281 Darryl Hamilton .15 .07
☐ 282 Ken Hill .15 .07
☐ 283 Wayne Kirby .15 .07
☐ 284 Chris Hammond .15 .07
☐ 285 Mo Vaughn .75 .35
☐ 286 Ryan Klesko .60 .25
☐ 287 Rick Wilkins .15 .07
☐ 288 Bill Swift .15 .07
☐ 289 Rafael Palmeiro .60 .25
☐ 290 Brian Harper .15 .07
☐ 291 Chris Turner .15 .07
☐ 292 Luis Gonzalez .15 .07
☐ 293 Kenny Rogers .15 .07
☐ 294 Kirby Puckett 1.25 .55
☐ 295 Mike Stanley .15 .07
☐ 296 Carlos Reyes .15 .07
☐ 297 Charles Nagy .30 .14
☐ 298 Reggie Jefferson .30 .14
☐ 299 Bip Roberts .15 .07
☐ 300 Darrin Jackson .15 .07
☐ 301 Mike Jackson .15 .07
☐ 302 Dave Nilsson .30 .14
☐ 303 Ramon Martinez .30 .14
☐ 304 Bobby Jones .30 .14
☐ 305 Johnny Ruffin .15 .07
☐ 306 Brian McRae .15 .07
☐ 307 Bo Jackson .30 .14
☐ 308 Dave Stewart .30 .14
☐ 309 John Smoltz .50 .23
☐ 310 Dennis Martinez .30 .14
☐ 311 Dean Palmer .30 .14
☐ 312 David Nied .15 .07
☐ 313 Eddie Murray .60 .25
☐ 314 Darryl Kile .30 .14
☐ 315 Rick Sutcliffe .15 .07
☐ 316 Shawon Dunston .15 .07
☐ 317 John Jaha .15 .07
☐ 318 Salomon Torres .15 .07
☐ 319 Gary Sheffield .60 .25
☐ 320 Curt Schilling .30 .14
☐ 321 Greg Vaughn .15 .07
☐ 322 Jay Howell .15 .07
☐ 323 Todd Hundley .30 .14
☐ 324 Chris Sabo .15 .07
☐ 325 Stan Javier .15 .07
☐ 326 Willie Greene .30 .14
☐ 327 Hipolito Pichardo .15 .07
☐ 328 Doug Strange .15 .07
☐ 329 Dan Wilson .30 .14
☐ 330 Checklist .15 .07
☐ 331 Omar Vizquel .30 .14
☐ 332 Scott Servais .15 .07
☐ 333 Bob Tewksbury .15 .07
☐ 334 Matt Williams .50 .23
☐ 335 Tom Foley .15 .07
☐ 336 Jeff Russell .15 .07
☐ 337 Scott Leius .15 .07

☐ 338 Ivan Rodriguez	.75	.35
☐ 339 Kevin Seitzer	.15	.07
☐ 340 Jose Rijo	.15	.07
☐ 341 Eduardo Perez	.15	.07
☐ 342 Kirk Gibson	.30	.14
☐ 343 Randy Milligan	.15	.07
☐ 344 Edgar Martinez	.50	.23
☐ 345 Fred McGriff	.50	.23
☐ 346 Kurt Abbott	.15	.07
☐ 347 John Kruk	.30	.14
☐ 348 Mike Felder	.15	.07
☐ 349 Dave Staton	.15	.07
☐ 350 Kenny Lofton	.75	.35
☐ 351 Graeme Lloyd	.15	.07
☐ 352 David Segui	.15	.07
☐ 353 Danny Tartabull	.15	.07
☐ 354 Bob Welch	.15	.07
☐ 355 Duane Ward	.15	.07
☐ 356 Karl Rhodes	.15	.07
☐ 357 Lee Smith	.30	.14
☐ 358 Chris James	.15	.07
☐ 359 Walt Weiss	.15	.07
☐ 360 Pedro Munoz	.15	.07
☐ 361 Paul Sorrento	.15	.07
☐ 362 Todd Worrell	.15	.07
☐ 363 Bob Hamelin	.15	.07
☐ 364 Julio Franco	.30	.14
☐ 365 Roberto Petagine	.15	.07
☐ 366 Willie McGee	.15	.07
☐ 367 Pedro Martinez	.60	.25
☐ 368 Ken Griffey Jr.	3.00	1.35
☐ 369 B.J. Surhoff	.15	.07
☐ 370 Kevin Mitchell	.15	.07
☐ 371 John Doherty	.15	.07
☐ 372 Manuel Lee	.15	.07
☐ 373 Terry Mulholland	.15	.07
☐ 374 Zane Smith	.15	.07
☐ 375 Otis Nixon	.15	.07
☐ 376 Jody Reed	.15	.07
☐ 377 Doug Jones	.15	.07
☐ 378 John Olerud	.15	.07
☐ 379 Greg Swindell	.15	.07
☐ 380 Checklist	.15	.07
☐ 381 Royce Clayton	.30	.14
☐ 382 Jim Thome	.75	.35
☐ 383 Steve Finley	.30	.14
☐ 384 Ray Lankford	.50	.23
☐ 385 Henry Rodriguez	.15	.07
☐ 386 Dave Magadan	.15	.07
☐ 387 Gary Redus	.15	.07
☐ 388 Orlando Merced	.15	.07
☐ 389 Tom Gordon	.15	.07
☐ 390 Luis Polonia	.15	.07
☐ 391 Mark McGwire	1.25	.55
☐ 392 Mark Lemke	.15	.07
☐ 393 Doug Henry	.15	.07
☐ 394 Chuck Finley	.15	.07
☐ 395 Paul Molitor	.60	.25
☐ 396 Randy Myers	.15	.07
☐ 397 Larry Walker	.60	.25
☐ 398 Pete Harnisch	.15	.07
☐ 399 Darren Lewis	.15	.07
☐ 400 Frank Thomas	2.50	1.10
☐ 401 Jack Morris	.30	.14
☐ 402 Greg Hibbard	.15	.07
☐ 403 Jeffrey Hammonds	.30	.14
☐ 404 Will Clark	.50	.23
☐ 405 Travis Fryman	.30	.14
☐ 406 Scott Sanderson	.15	.07
☐ 407 Gene Harris	.15	.07
☐ 408 Chuck Carr	.15	.07
☐ 409 Ozzie Smith	.75	.35
☐ 410 Kent Mercker	.15	.07
☐ 411 Andy Van Slyke	.30	.14
☐ 412 Jimmy Key	.30	.14
☐ 413 Pat Mahomes	.15	.07
☐ 414 John Wetteland	.30	.14
☐ 415 Todd Jones	.15	.07
☐ 416 Greg Harris	.15	.07
☐ 417 Kevin Stocker	.15	.07
☐ 418 Juan Gonzalez	1.50	.70
☐ 419 Pete Smith	.15	.07
☐ 420 Pat Listach	.15	.07
☐ 421 Trevor Hoffman	.30	.14
☐ 422 Scott Fletcher	.15	.07
☐ 423 Mark Lewis	.15	.07
☐ 424 Mickey Morandini	.15	.07
☐ 425 Ryne Sandberg	.75	.35
☐ 426 Erik Hanson	.15	.07
☐ 427 Gary Gaetti	.30	.14
☐ 428 Harold Reynolds	.15	.07
☐ 429 Mark Portugal	.15	.07
☐ 430 David Valle	.15	.07
☐ 431 Mitch Williams	.15	.07
☐ 432 Howard Johnson	.15	.07
☐ 433 Hal Morris	.15	.07
☐ 434 Tom Henke	.15	.07
☐ 435 Shane Mack	.15	.07
☐ 436 Mike Piazza	2.00	.90
☐ 437 Bret Saberhagen	.15	.07
☐ 438 Jose Mesa	.30	.14
☐ 439 Jaime Navarro	.15	.07
☐ 440 Checklist	.15	.07
☐ A300 Frank Thomas Leaf 5th Anniversary	2.50	1.10

1994 Leaf Clean-Up Crew

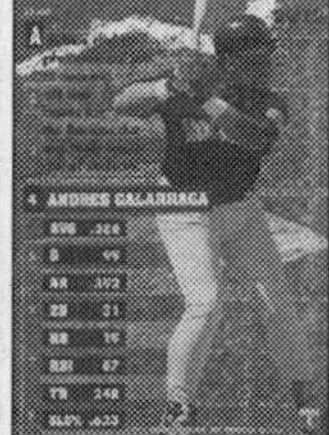

Inserted in magazine jumbo packs at a rate of one in 12, this 12-card set was issued in two series of six. Full-bleed fronts contain an action photo with the Clean-Up Crew logo at bottom right and the player's name in a colored band toward bottom left. The backs contain a photo and 1993 statistics when batting fourth. The home plate area serves as background.

	MINT	NRMT
COMPLETE SET (12)	60.00	27.00
COMPLETE SERIES 1 (6)	10.00	4.50
COMPLETE SERIES 2 (6)	50.00	22.00
COMMON CARD (1-12)	3.00	1.35
☐ 1 Larry Walker	10.00	4.50
☐ 2 Andres Galarraga	6.00	2.70
☐ 3 Dave Hollins	3.00	1.35
☐ 4 Bobby Bonilla	4.00	1.80
☐ 5 Cecil Fielder	4.00	1.80
☐ 6 Danny Tartabull	3.00	1.35
☐ 7 Juan Gonzalez	25.00	11.00
☐ 8 Joe Carter	6.00	2.70
☐ 9 Fred McGriff	6.00	2.70
☐ 10 Matt Williams	6.00	2.70
☐ 11 Albert Belle	12.00	5.50
☐ 12 Harold Baines	4.00	1.80

1994 Leaf Gamers

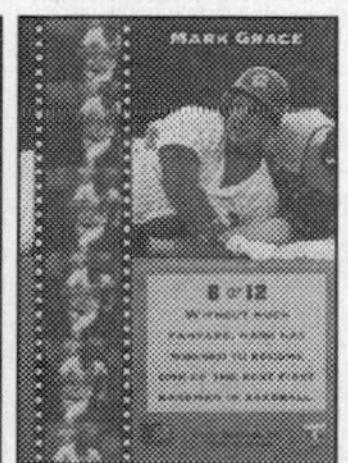

A close-up photo of the player highlights this 12-card standard-size set that was issued in two series of six. They were randomly inserted in jumbo packs at a rate of one in eight. The player's name appears at the top of the photo with the Leaf Gamers hologram logo at the bottom. The backs feature a variety of color photos including a frame by frame series resembling a film strip. There is also a small write-up.

	MINT	NRMT
COMPLETE SET (12)	150.00	70.00
COMPLETE SERIES 1 (6)	70.00	32.00
COMPLETE SERIES 2 (6)	80.00	36.00
COMMON CARD (1-12)	2.50	1.10
☐ 1 Ken Griffey Jr.	40.00	18.00
☐ 2 Lenny Dykstra	2.50	1.10
☐ 3 Juan Gonzalez	20.00	9.00
☐ 4 Don Mattingly	12.00	5.50
☐ 5 David Justice	8.00	3.60
☐ 6 Mark Grace	5.00	2.20
☐ 7 Frank Thomas	30.00	13.50
☐ 8 Barry Bonds	10.00	4.50
☐ 9 Kirby Puckett	15.00	6.75
☐ 10 Will Clark	5.00	2.20
☐ 11 John Kruk	2.50	1.10
☐ 12 Mike Piazza	25.00	11.00

1994 Leaf Gold Rookies

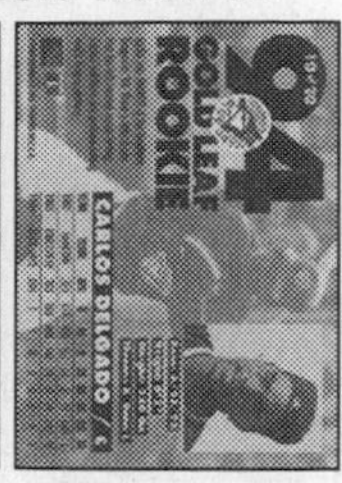

This set, which was randomly inserted in first series packs at a rate of one in 18 and second series packs at a rate of one in twelve, features 20 of the hottest young stars in the majors. A color player cutout is layed over a dark brownish background that contains "94 Gold Leaf Rookie". The player's name and team appear at the bottom in silver. Horizontal backs include career highlights and two photos.

	MINT	NRMT
COMPLETE SET (20)	16.00	7.25
COMPLETE SERIES 1 (10)	12.00	5.50
COMPLETE SERIES 2 (10)	4.00	1.80
COMMON CARD (1-20)	.50	.23
☐ 1 Javier Lopez	1.25	.55
☐ 2 Rondell White	1.25	.55
☐ 3 Butch Huskey	1.00	.45
☐ 4 Midre Cummings	.50	.23
☐ 5 Scott Ruffcorn	.50	.23
☐ 6 Manny Ramirez	4.00	1.80
☐ 7 Danny Bautista	.50	.23
☐ 8 Russ Davis	.50	.23
☐ 9 Steve Karsay	.50	.23
☐ 10 Carlos Delgado	2.00	.90
☐ 11 Bob Hamelin	.50	.23
☐ 12 Marcus Moore	.50	.23
☐ 13 Miguel Jimenez	.50	.23
☐ 14 Matt Walbeck	.50	.23
☐ 15 James Mouton	.50	.23
☐ 16 Rich Becker	1.00	.45
☐ 17 Brian Anderson	.50	.23
☐ 18 Cliff Floyd	1.00	.45
☐ 19 Steve Trachsel	.50	.23
☐ 20 Hector Carrasco	.50	.23

1994 Leaf Gold Stars

Randomly inserted in all packs at a rate of one in 90, the 15 standard-size cards in this set are individually numbered and limited to 10,000 per player. The cards were issued in two series with eight cards in series one and seven in series two. The fronts are bordered by gold and have a green marble appearance with the player appearing within a diamond (outlined in gold) in the card's upper half. The player's name, gold facsimile autograph and team name appear below the photo. The backs are similar to the fronts except for 1993 highlights and the individual numbering. They are numbered "X/10,000".

	MINT	NRMT
COMPLETE SET (15)	200.00	90.00
COMPLETE SERIES 1 (8)	125.00	55.00
COMPLETE SERIES 2 (7)	75.00	34.00
COMMON CARD (1-15)	5.00	2.20
☐ 1 Roberto Alomar	10.00	4.50
☐ 2 Barry Bonds	12.00	5.50
☐ 3 David Justice	10.00	4.50
☐ 4 Ken Griffey Jr.	50.00	22.00
☐ 5 Lenny Dykstra	6.00	2.70
☐ 6 Don Mattingly	15.00	6.75
☐ 7 Andres Galarraga	7.50	3.40
☐ 8 Greg Maddux	30.00	13.50
☐ 9 Carlos Baerga	5.00	2.20

☐ 10 Paul Molitor	10.00	4.50
☐ 11 Frank Thomas	40.00	18.00
☐ 12 John Olerud	5.00	2.20
☐ 13 Juan Gonzalez	25.00	11.00
☐ 14 Fred McGriff	7.50	3.40
☐ 15 Jack McDowell	5.00	2.20

1994 Leaf MVP Contenders

This 30-card standard-size set contains 15 players from each league who were projected to be 1994 MVP hopefuls. These unnumbered cards were randomly inserted in all second series packs at a rate of one in 36. If the player appearing on the card was named his league's MVP (Frank Thomas American League and Jeff Bagwell National League), the card could be redeemed for a 5" x 7" Frank Thomas card individually numbered out of 20,000. The backs contain all the rules and read "1 of 10,000". The expiration for redeeming Thomas and Bagwell cards was Jan. 19, 1995.

	MINT	NRMT
COMPLETE SET (30)	150.00	70.00
COMMON CARD	2.00	.90
COMP.GOLD SET (30)	150.00	70.00
*GOLD: SAME PRICE AS BASIC MVPS		

☐ A1 Carlos Baerga	3.00	1.35
☐ A2 Albert Belle	12.00	5.50
☐ A3 Jose Canseco	4.00	1.80
☐ A4 Joe Carter	4.00	1.80
☐ A5 Will Clark	4.00	1.80
☐ A6 Cecil Fielder	3.00	1.35
☐ A7 Juan Gonzalez	15.00	6.75
☐ A8 Ken Griffey Jr.	30.00	13.50
☐ A9 Paul Molitor	6.00	2.70
☐ A10 Rafael Palmeiro	4.00	1.80
☐ A11 Kirby Puckett	12.00	5.50
☐ A12 Cal Ripken Jr.	25.00	11.00
☐ A13 Frank Thomas W	25.00	11.00
☐ A14 Mo Vaughn	8.00	3.60
☐ A15 AL Bonus Card	2.00	.90
☐ N1 Jeff Bagwell W	12.00	5.50
☐ N2 Dante Bichette	4.00	1.80
☐ N3 Barry Bonds	8.00	3.60
☐ N4 Darren Daulton	3.00	1.35
☐ N5 Andres Galarraga	4.00	1.80
☐ N6 Gregg Jefferies	3.00	1.35
☐ N7 David Justice	6.00	2.70
☐ N8 Ray Lankford	4.00	1.80
☐ N9 Barry Larkin	4.00	1.80
☐ N10 Fred McGriff	4.00	1.80
☐ N11 Mike Piazza	20.00	9.00
☐ N12 Deion Sanders	6.00	2.70
☐ N13 Gary Sheffield	6.00	2.70
☐ N14 Matt Williams	6.00	2.70
☐ N15 NL Bonus Card	2.00	.90
☐ J400 Frank Thomas Jumbo	12.00	5.50

1994 Leaf Power Brokers

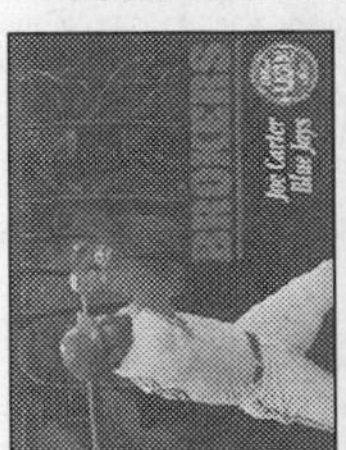

Inserted in second series retail and hobby foil packs at a rate of one in 12, this 10-card standard-size set spotlights top sluggers. Both fronts and backs are horizontal. The fronts have a small player cutout with a black background and "Power Brokers" dominating the card. Fireworks appear within "Power". The backs contain various pie charts that document the player's home run tendencies as far as home vs. away etc. There is also a small photo.

	MINT	NRMT
COMPLETE SET (10)	20.00	9.00
COMMON CARD (1-10)	.50	.23

☐ 1 Frank Thomas	8.00	3.60
☐ 2 David Justice	1.50	.70
☐ 3 Barry Bonds	2.00	.90
☐ 4 Juan Gonzalez	4.00	1.80
☐ 5 Ken Griffey Jr.	8.00	3.60
☐ 6 Mike Piazza	5.00	2.20
☐ 7 Cecil Fielder	.50	.23
☐ 8 Fred McGriff	1.00	.45
☐ 9 Joe Carter	1.00	.45
☐ 10 Albert Belle	3.00	1.35

1994 Leaf Slideshow

Randomly inserted in first and second series packs at a rate of one in 54, these ten standard-size cards simulate mounted photographic slides, but the images of the players are actually printed on acetate. The color transparencies can be seen best when they are held up to the light. The front of each transparency is framed by a simulated white slide holder, which at its bottom bears the player's name and the game from which the photo was shot. The insert sets's title is shown in blue and merges with the blue-edged bottom. The remaining edges are black. The back, in addition to the appearance of the slide's reverse image, carries comments about the player from Frank Thomas.

	MINT	NRMT
COMPLETE SET (10)	60.00	27.00
COMPLETE SERIES 1 (5)	30.00	13.50
COMPLETE SERIES 2 (5)	30.00	13.50
COMMON CARD (1-10)	1.50	.70

☐ 1 Frank Thomas	15.00	6.75
☐ 2 Mike Piazza	12.00	5.50
☐ 3 Darren Daulton	1.50	.70
☐ 4 Ryne Sandberg	5.00	2.20
☐ 5 Roberto Alomar	4.00	1.80
☐ 6 Barry Bonds	5.00	2.20
☐ 7 Juan Gonzalez	10.00	4.50
☐ 8 Tim Salmon	4.00	1.80
☐ 9 Ken Griffey Jr.	20.00	9.00
☐ 10 David Justice	4.00	1.80

1994 Leaf Statistical Standouts

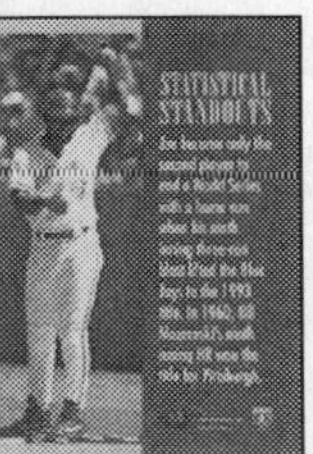

Inserted in retail and hobby foil packs at a rate of one in 12, this 10-card standard-size set features players that had significant statistical achievements in 1993. For example: Cal Ripken's home run record for a shortstop. Card fronts contain a player photo that stands out from a background that is the colors of that player's team. The back contains a photo and statistical information.

	MINT	NRMT
COMPLETE SET (10)	20.00	9.00
COMMON CARD (1-10)	.50	.23

☐ 1 Frank Thomas	4.00	1.80
☐ 2 Barry Bonds	1.25	.55
☐ 3 Juan Gonzalez	2.50	1.10
☐ 4 Mike Piazza	3.00	1.35
☐ 5 Greg Maddux	3.00	1.35
☐ 6 Ken Griffey Jr.	5.00	2.20
☐ 7 Joe Carter	.50	.23
☐ 8 Dave Winfield	.75	.35
☐ 9 Tony Gwynn	2.00	.90
☐ 10 Cal Ripken	4.00	1.80

1995 Leaf

The 1995 Leaf set was issued in two series of 200 standard-size cards for a total of 400. Full-bleed fronts contain diamond-shaped player hologram in the upper left. The team name is done in silver foil up the left side. Peculiar backs contain two photos, the card number within a stamp or seal like emblem in the upper right and '94 and career stats graph toward bottom left. Hideo Nomo is the only key Rookie Cards in this set.

	MINT	NRMT
COMPLETE SET (400)	40.00	18.00
COMPLETE SERIES 1 (200)	15.00	6.75
COMPLETE SERIES 2 (200)	25.00	11.00
COMMON CARD (1-400)	.15	.07

☐ 1 Frank Thomas	2.50	1.10
☐ 2 Carlos Garcia	.15	.07
☐ 3 Todd Hundley	.30	.14
☐ 4 Damion Easley	.15	.07
☐ 5 Roberto Mejia	.15	.07
☐ 6 John Mabry	.40	.18
☐ 7 Aaron Sele	.15	.07
☐ 8 Kenny Lofton	.75	.35
☐ 9 John Doherty	.15	.07
☐ 10 Joe Carter	.40	.18
☐ 11 Mike Lansing	.15	.07
☐ 12 John Valentin	.30	.14
☐ 13 Ismael Valdes	.30	.14
☐ 14 Dave McCarty	.15	.07
☐ 15 Melvin Nieves	.30	.14
☐ 16 Bobby Jones	.30	.14
☐ 17 Trevor Hoffman	.30	.14
☐ 18 John Smoltz	.40	.18
☐ 19 Leo Gomez	.15	.07
☐ 20 Roger Pavlik	.15	.07
☐ 21 Dean Palmer	.30	.14
☐ 22 Rickey Henderson	.40	.18
☐ 23 Eddie Taubensee	.15	.07
☐ 24 Damon Buford	.15	.07
☐ 25 Mark Wohlers	.30	.14
☐ 26 Jim Edmonds	.60	.25
☐ 27 Wilson Alvarez	.30	.14
☐ 28 Matt Williams	.40	.18
☐ 29 Jeff Montgomery	.30	.14
☐ 30 Shawon Dunston	.15	.07
☐ 31 Tom Pagnozzi	.15	.07
☐ 32 Jose Lind	.15	.07
☐ 33 Royce Clayton	.15	.07
☐ 34 Cal Eldred	.15	.07
☐ 35 Chris Gomez	.15	.07
☐ 36 Henry Rodriguez	.15	.07
☐ 37 Dave Fleming	.15	.07
☐ 38 Jon Lieber	.15	.07
☐ 39 Scott Servais	.15	.07
☐ 40 Wade Boggs	.60	.25
☐ 41 John Olerud	.30	.14
☐ 42 Eddie Williams	.15	.07
☐ 43 Paul Sorrento	.15	.07
☐ 44 Ron Karkovice	.15	.07
☐ 45 Kevin Foster	.15	.07
☐ 46 Miguel Jimenez	.15	.07
☐ 47 Reggie Sanders	.15	.07
☐ 48 Rondell White	.40	.18
☐ 49 Scott Leius	.15	.07
☐ 50 Jose Valentin	.30	.14
☐ 51 Wm. VanLandingham	.15	.07
☐ 52 Denny Hocking	.15	.07
☐ 53 Jeff Fassero	.15	.07
☐ 54 Chris Hoiles	.15	.07
☐ 55 Walt Weiss	.15	.07
☐ 56 Geronimo Berroa	.15	.07
☐ 57 Rich Rowland	.15	.07

☐ 58 Dave Weathers	.15	.07
☐ 59 Sterling Hitchcock	.30	.14
☐ 60 Raul Mondesi	.40	.18
☐ 61 Rusty Greer	.60	.25
☐ 62 David Justice	.60	.25
☐ 63 Cecil Fielder	.30	.14
☐ 64 Brian Jordan	.30	.14
☐ 65 Mike Lieberthal	.15	.07
☐ 66 Rick Aguilera	.15	.07
☐ 67 Chuck Finley	.30	.14
☐ 68 Andy Ashby	.15	.07
☐ 69 Alex Fernandez	.30	.14
☐ 70 Ed Sprague	.15	.07
☐ 71 Steve Buechele	.15	.07
☐ 72 Willie Greene	.15	.07
☐ 73 Dave Nilsson	.30	.14
☐ 74 Bret Saberhagen	.15	.07
☐ 75 Jimmy Key	.30	.14
☐ 76 Darren Lewis	.15	.07
☐ 77 Steve Cooke	.15	.07
☐ 78 Kirk Gibson	.30	.14
☐ 79 Ray Lankford	.40	.18
☐ 80 Paul O'Neill	.30	.14
☐ 81 Mike Bordick	.15	.07
☐ 82 Wes Chamberlain	.15	.07
☐ 83 Rico Brogna	.15	.07
☐ 84 Kevin Appier	.30	.14
☐ 85 Juan Guzman	.15	.07
☐ 86 Kevin Seitzer	.15	.07
☐ 87 Mickey Morandini	.15	.07
☐ 88 Pedro Martinez	.60	.25
☐ 89 Matt Mieske	.30	.14
☐ 90 Tino Martinez	.60	.25
☐ 91 Paul Shuey	.15	.07
☐ 92 Bip Roberts	.15	.07
☐ 93 Chili Davis	.30	.14
☐ 94 Deion Sanders	.60	.25
☐ 95 Darrell Whitmore	.15	.07
☐ 96 Joe Orsulak	.15	.07
☐ 97 Bret Boone	.15	.07
☐ 98 Kent Mercker	.15	.07
☐ 99 Scott Livingstone	.15	.07
☐ 100 Brady Anderson	.40	.18
☐ 101 James Mouton	.15	.07
☐ 102 Jose Rijo	.15	.07
☐ 103 Bobby Munoz	.15	.07
☐ 104 Ramon Martinez	.30	.14
☐ 105 Bernie Williams	.60	.25
☐ 106 Troy Neel	.15	.07
☐ 107 Ivan Rodriguez	.75	.35
☐ 108 Salomon Torres	.15	.07
☐ 109 Johnny Ruffin	.15	.07
☐ 110 Darryl Kile	.15	.07
☐ 111 Bobby Ayala	.15	.07
☐ 112 Ron Darling	.15	.07
☐ 113 Jose Lima	.15	.07
☐ 114 Joey Hamilton	.30	.14
☐ 115 Greg Maddux	2.00	.90
☐ 116 Greg Colbrunn	.15	.07
☐ 117 Ozzie Guillen	.15	.07
☐ 118 Brian Anderson	.15	.07
☐ 119 Jeff Bagwell	1.25	.55
☐ 120 Pat Listach	.15	.07
☐ 121 Sandy Alomar Jr.	.15	.07
☐ 122 Jose Vizcaino	.15	.07
☐ 123 Rick Helling	.15	.07
☐ 124 Allen Watson	.15	.07
☐ 125 Pedro Munoz	.15	.07
☐ 126 Craig Biggio	.40	.18
☐ 127 Kevin Stocker	.15	.07
☐ 128 Wil Cordero	.15	.07
☐ 129 Rafael Palmeiro	.40	.18
☐ 130 Gar Finnvold	.15	.07
☐ 131 Darren Hall	.15	.07
☐ 132 Heath Slocumb	.15	.07
☐ 133 Darrin Fletcher	.15	.07
☐ 134 Cal Ripken	2.50	1.10
☐ 135 Dante Bichette	.40	.18
☐ 136 Don Slaught	.15	.07
☐ 137 Pedro Astacio	.15	.07
☐ 138 Ryan Thompson	.15	.07
☐ 139 Greg Gohr	.15	.07
☐ 140 Javier Lopez	.40	.18
☐ 141 Lenny Dykstra	.30	.14
☐ 142 Pat Rapp	.15	.07
☐ 143 Mark Kiefer	.15	.07
☐ 144 Greg Gagne	.15	.07
☐ 145 Eduardo Perez	.15	.07
☐ 146 Felix Fermin	.15	.07
☐ 147 Jeff Frye	.15	.07
☐ 148 Terry Steinbach	.30	.14
☐ 149 Jim Eisenreich	.30	.14
☐ 150 Brad Ausmus	.15	.07
☐ 151 Randy Myers	.15	.07
☐ 152 Rick White	.15	.07
☐ 153 Mark Portugal	.15	.07
☐ 154 Delino DeShields	.15	.07
☐ 155 Scott Cooper	.15	.07
☐ 156 Pat Hentgen	.30	.14
☐ 157 Mark Gubicza	.15	.07
☐ 158 Carlos Baerga	.30	.14
☐ 159 Joe Girardi	.15	.07
☐ 160 Rey Sanchez	.15	.07
☐ 161 Todd Jones	.15	.07
☐ 162 Luis Polonia	.15	.07
☐ 163 Steve Trachsel	.15	.07
☐ 164 Roberto Hernandez	.15	.07
☐ 165 John Patterson	.15	.07
☐ 166 Rene Arocha	.15	.07
☐ 167 Will Clark	.40	.18
☐ 168 Jim Leyritz	.15	.07
☐ 169 Todd Van Poppel	.15	.07
☐ 170 Robb Nen	.15	.07
☐ 171 Midre Cummings	.15	.07
☐ 172 Jay Buhner	.40	.18
☐ 173 Kevin Tapani	.15	.07
☐ 174 Mark Lemke	.15	.07
☐ 175 Marcus Moore	.15	.07
☐ 176 Wayne Kirby	.15	.07
☐ 177 Rich Amaral	.15	.07
☐ 178 Lou Whitaker	.30	.14
☐ 179 Jay Bell	.30	.14
☐ 180 Rick Wilkins	.15	.07
☐ 181 Paul Molitor	.60	.25
☐ 182 Gary Sheffield	.60	.25
☐ 183 Kirby Puckett	1.25	.55
☐ 184 Cliff Floyd	.30	.14
☐ 185 Darren Oliver	.60	.25
☐ 186 Tim Naehring	.15	.07
☐ 187 John Hudek	.15	.07
☐ 188 Eric Young	.30	.14
☐ 189 Roger Salkeld	.15	.07
☐ 190 Kirt Manwaring	.15	.07
☐ 191 Kurt Abbott	.15	.07
☐ 192 David Nied	.15	.07
☐ 193 Todd Zeile	.15	.07
☐ 194 Wally Joyner	.30	.14
☐ 195 Dennis Martinez	.30	.14
☐ 196 Billy Ashley	.15	.07
☐ 197 Ben McDonald	.15	.07
☐ 198 Bob Hamelin	.15	.07
☐ 199 Chris Turner	.15	.07
☐ 200 Lance Johnson	.15	.07
☐ 201 Willie Banks	.15	.07
☐ 202 Juan Gonzalez	1.50	.70
☐ 203 Scott Sanders	.15	.07
☐ 204 Scott Brosius	.15	.07
☐ 205 Curt Schilling	.30	.14
☐ 206 Alex Gonzalez	.15	.07
☐ 207 Travis Fryman	.30	.14
☐ 208 Tim Raines	.15	.07
☐ 209 Steve Avery	.15	.07
☐ 210 Hal Morris	.15	.07
☐ 211 Ken Griffey Jr.	3.00	1.35
☐ 212 Ozzie Smith	.75	.35
☐ 213 Chuck Carr	.15	.07
☐ 214 Ryan Klesko	.40	.18
☐ 215 Robin Ventura	.30	.14
☐ 216 Luis Gonzalez	.15	.07
☐ 217 Ken Ryan	.15	.07
☐ 218 Mike Piazza	2.00	.90
☐ 219 Matt Walbeck	.15	.07
☐ 220 Jeff Kent	.15	.07
☐ 221 Orlando Miller	.15	.07
☐ 222 Kenny Rogers	.15	.07
☐ 223 J.T. Snow	.30	.14
☐ 224 Alan Trammell	.40	.18
☐ 225 John Franco	.15	.07
☐ 226 Gerald Williams	.15	.07
☐ 227 Andy Benes	.15	.07
☐ 228 Dan Wilson	.30	.14
☐ 229 Dave Hollins	.15	.07
☐ 230 Vinny Castilla	.40	.18
☐ 231 Devon White	.15	.07
☐ 232 Fred McGriff	.40	.18
☐ 233 Quilvio Veras	.15	.07
☐ 234 Tom Candiotti	.15	.07
☐ 235 Jason Bere	.15	.07
☐ 236 Mark Langston	.15	.07
☐ 237 Mel Rojas	.15	.07
☐ 238 Chuck Knoblauch	.60	.25
☐ 239 Bernard Gilkey	.30	.14
☐ 240 Mark McGwire	1.25	.55
☐ 241 Kirk Rueter	.15	.07
☐ 242 Pat Kelly	.15	.07
☐ 243 Ruben Sierra	.15	.07
☐ 244 Randy Johnson	.60	.25
☐ 245 Shane Reynolds	.15	.07
☐ 246 Danny Tartabull	.15	.07
☐ 247 Darryl Hamilton	.15	.07
☐ 248 Danny Bautista	.15	.07
☐ 249 Tom Gordon	.15	.07
☐ 250 Tom Glavine	.40	.18
☐ 251 Orlando Merced	.15	.07
☐ 252 Eric Karros	.30	.14
☐ 253 Benji Gil	.15	.07
☐ 254 Sean Bergman	.15	.07
☐ 255 Roger Clemens	1.25	.55
☐ 256 Roberto Alomar	.60	.25
☐ 257 Benito Santiago	.15	.07
☐ 258 Robby Thompson	.15	.07
☐ 259 Marvin Freeman	.15	.07
☐ 260 Jose Offerman	.15	.07
☐ 261 Greg Vaughn	.15	.07
☐ 262 David Segui	.15	.07
☐ 263 Geronimo Pena	.15	.07
☐ 264 Tim Salmon	.60	.25
☐ 265 Eddie Murray	.60	.25
☐ 266 Mariano Duncan	.15	.07
☐ 267 Hideo Nomo	3.00	1.35
☐ 268 Derek Bell	.30	.14
☐ 269 Mo Vaughn	.75	.35
☐ 270 Jeff King	.30	.14
☐ 271 Edgar Martinez	.40	.18
☐ 272 Sammy Sosa	.60	.25
☐ 273 Scott Ruffcorn	.15	.07
☐ 274 Darren Daulton	.30	.14
☐ 275 John Jaha	.15	.07
☐ 276 Andres Galarraga	.40	.18
☐ 277 Mark Grace	.40	.18
☐ 278 Mike Moore	.15	.07
☐ 279 Barry Bonds	.75	.35
☐ 280 Manny Ramirez	.60	.25
☐ 281 Ellis Burks	.30	.14
☐ 282 Greg Swindell	.15	.07
☐ 283 Barry Larkin	.40	.18
☐ 284 Albert Belle	.75	.35
☐ 285 Shawn Green	.30	.14
☐ 286 John Roper	.15	.07
☐ 287 Scott Erickson	.15	.07
☐ 288 Moises Alou	.30	.14
☐ 289 Mike Blowers	.15	.07
☐ 290 Brent Gates	.15	.07
☐ 291 Sean Berry	.15	.07
☐ 292 Mike Stanley	.15	.07
☐ 293 Jeff Conine	.30	.14
☐ 294 Tim Wallach	.15	.07
☐ 295 Bobby Bonilla	.30	.14
☐ 296 Bruce Ruffin	.15	.07
☐ 297 Chad Curtis	.15	.07
☐ 298 Mike Greenwell	.15	.07
☐ 299 Tony Gwynn	1.50	.70
☐ 300 Russ Davis	.15	.07
☐ 301 Danny Jackson	.15	.07
☐ 302 Pete Harnisch	.15	.07
☐ 303 Don Mattingly	1.00	.45
☐ 304 Rheal Cormier	.15	.07
☐ 305 Larry Walker	.60	.25
☐ 306 Hector Carrasco	.15	.07
☐ 307 Jason Jacome	.15	.07
☐ 308 Phil Plantier	.15	.07
☐ 309 Harold Baines	.30	.14
☐ 310 Mitch Williams	.15	.07
☐ 311 Charles Nagy	.30	.14
☐ 312 Ken Caminiti	.60	.25
☐ 313 Alex Rodriguez	2.50	1.10
☐ 314 Chris Sabo	.15	.07
☐ 315 Gary Gaetti	.30	.14
☐ 316 Andre Dawson	.40	.18
☐ 317 Mark Clark	.15	.07
☐ 318 Vince Coleman	.15	.07
☐ 319 Brad Clontz	.15	.07
☐ 320 Steve Finley	.30	.14
☐ 321 Doug Drabek	.15	.07
☐ 322 Mark McLemore	.15	.07
☐ 323 Stan Javier	.15	.07
☐ 324 Ron Gant	.30	.14
☐ 325 Charlie Hayes	.15	.07
☐ 326 Carlos Delgado	.30	.14
☐ 327 Ricky Bottalico	.30	.14
☐ 328 Rod Beck	.15	.07
☐ 329 Mark Acre	.15	.07
☐ 330 Chris Bosio	.15	.07
☐ 331 Tony Phillips	.15	.07
☐ 332 Garret Anderson	.40	.18
☐ 333 Pat Meares	.15	.07
☐ 334 Todd Worrell	.15	.07
☐ 335 Marquis Grissom	.30	.14
☐ 336 Brent Mayne	.15	.07
☐ 337 Lee Tinsley	.15	.07
☐ 338 Terry Pendleton	.30	.14
☐ 339 David Cone	.30	.14
☐ 340 Tony Fernandez	.15	.07
☐ 341 Jim Bullinger	.15	.07
☐ 342 Armando Benitez	.15	.07
☐ 343 John Smiley	.15	.07
☐ 344 Dan Miceli	.15	.07
☐ 345 Charles Johnson	.40	.18
☐ 346 Lee Smith	.30	.14
☐ 347 Brian McRae	.15	.07
☐ 348 Jim Thome	.60	.25

☐ 349 Jose Oliva	.15	.07
☐ 350 Terry Mulholland	.15	.07
☐ 351 Tom Henke	.15	.07
☐ 352 Dennis Eckersley	.40	.18
☐ 353 Sid Fernandez	.15	.07
☐ 354 Paul Wagner	.15	.07
☐ 355 John Dettmer	.15	.07
☐ 356 John Wetteland	.30	.14
☐ 357 John Burkett	.15	.07
☐ 358 Marty Cordova	.40	.18
☐ 359 Norm Charlton	.15	.07
☐ 360 Mike Devereaux	.15	.07
☐ 361 Alex Cole	.15	.07
☐ 362 Brett Butler	.30	.14
☐ 363 Mickey Tettleton	.15	.07
☐ 364 Al Martin	.30	.14
☐ 365 Tony Tarasco	.15	.07
☐ 366 Pat Mahomes	.15	.07
☐ 367 Gary DiSarcina	.15	.07
☐ 368 Bill Swift	.15	.07
☐ 369 Chipper Jones	2.00	.90
☐ 370 Orel Hershiser	.30	.14
☐ 371 Kevin Gross	.15	.07
☐ 372 Dave Winfield	.40	.18
☐ 373 Andujar Cedeno	.15	.07
☐ 374 Jim Abbott	.15	.07
☐ 375 Glenallen Hill	.15	.07
☐ 376 Otis Nixon	.30	.14
☐ 377 Roberto Kelly	.15	.07
☐ 378 Chris Hammond	.15	.07
☐ 379 Mike Macfarlane	.15	.07
☐ 380 J.R. Phillips	.15	.07
☐ 381 Luis Alicea	.15	.07
☐ 382 Bret Barberie	.15	.07
☐ 383 Tom Goodwin	.15	.07
☐ 384 Mark Whiten	.15	.07
☐ 385 Jeffrey Hammonds	.30	.14
☐ 386 Omar Vizquel	.30	.14
☐ 387 Mike Mussina	.60	.25
☐ 388 Ricky Bones	.15	.07
☐ 389 Steve Ontiveros	.15	.07
☐ 390 Jeff Blauser	.15	.07
☐ 391 Jose Canseco	.40	.18
☐ 392 Bob Tewksbury	.15	.07
☐ 393 Jacob Brumfield	.15	.07
☐ 394 Doug Jones	.15	.07
☐ 395 Ken Hill	.15	.07
☐ 396 Pat Borders	.15	.07
☐ 397 Carl Everett	.15	.07
☐ 398 Gregg Jefferies	.30	.14
☐ 399 Jack McDowell	.15	.07
☐ 400 Denny Neagle	.30	.14

1995 Leaf Checklists

Four checklist cards were randomly inserted in either series for a total of eight standard-size cards. Horizontal fronts feature a player photo from left to center with the start of the checklist to the right which continues on the back.

	MINT	NRMT
COMPLETE SET (8)	8.00	3.60
COMPLETE SERIES 1 (4)	4.00	1.80
COMPLETE SERIES 2 (4)	4.00	1.80
COMMON CARD (1-8)	.50	.23
☐ 1 Bob Hamelin UER (Name spelled Hamlin)	.50	.23
☐ 2 David Cone	.75	.35
☐ 3 Frank Thomas	3.00	1.35
☐ 4 Paul O'Neill	.75	.35
☐ 5 Raul Mondesi	1.00	.45
☐ 6 Greg Maddux	2.00	.90
☐ 7 Tony Gwynn	1.25	.55
☐ 8 Jeff Bagwell	1.25	.55

1995 Leaf Cornerstones

Cards from this six-card standard-size set were randomly inserted in first series packs. Horizontally designed, leading first and thrid basemen from the same team are

featured. The fronts have silver foil borders and team names with the team logo serving as background to the photos.The backs have a photo of either player with offensive and defensive stats.

	MINT	NRMT
COMPLETE SET (6)	10.00	4.50
COMMON CARD (1-6)	1.00	.45
☐ 1 Frank Thomas / Robin Ventura	5.00	2.20
☐ 2 Cecil Fielder / Travis Fryman	1.25	.55
☐ 3 Don Mattingly / Wade Boggs	2.00	.90
☐ 4 Jeff Bagwell / Ken Caminiti	2.50	1.10
☐ 5 Will Clark / Dean Palmer	1.25	.55
☐ 6 J.R. Phillips / Matt Williams	1.00	.45

1995 Leaf Gold Rookies

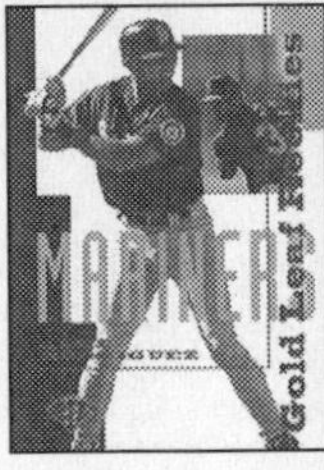

Inserted in every other first series pack, this 16-card standard-size set showcases those that were expected to have an impact in 1995. Card fronts offer two photos with various gold foil ornamentation. The backs have a large black and white photo with a smaller color photo inset at top left. The backs also contain career minor league stats.

	MINT	NRMT
COMPLETE SET (16)	6.00	2.70
COMMON CARD (1-16)	.25	.11
☐ 1 Alex Rodriguez	5.00	2.20
☐ 2 Garret Anderson	.50	.23
☐ 3 Shawn Green	.50	.23
☐ 4 Armando Benitez	.25	.11
☐ 5 Darren Dreifort	.25	.11
☐ 6 Orlando Miller	.25	.11
☐ 7 Jose Oliva	.25	.11
☐ 8 Ricky Bottalico	.50	.23
☐ 9 Charles Johnson	.50	.23
☐ 10 Brian L.Hunter	.50	.23
☐ 11 Ray McDavid	.25	.11
☐ 12 Chan Ho Park	1.50	.70
☐ 13 Mike Kelly	.25	.11
☐ 14 Cory Bailey	.25	.11
☐ 15 Alex Gonzalez	.50	.23
☐ 16 Andrew Lorraine	.25	.11

1995 Leaf Gold Stars

Randomly inserted in first and second series packs at a rate of one in 110, this 14-card standard-size set (eight first series, six second series) showcases some of the game's superstars.Individually numbered on back out of 10,000, the cards feature fronts that have a player photo superimposed metallic, refractive background. A die-cut star is in the lower left corner. The backs have a small player photo and brief write-up in addition to the numbering.

	MINT	NRMT
COMPLETE SET (14)	300.00	135.00
COMPLETE SERIES 1 (8)	150.00	70.00
COMPLETE SERIES 2 (6)	150.00	70.00
COMMON CARD (1-14)	8.00	3.60

☐ 1 Jeff Bagwell	20.00	9.00
☐ 2 Albert Belle	12.00	5.50
☐ 3 Tony Gwynn	25.00	11.00
☐ 4 Ken Griffey Jr.	50.00	22.00
☐ 5 Barry Bonds	12.00	5.50
☐ 6 Don Mattingly	15.00	6.75
☐ 7 Raul Mondesi	10.00	4.50
☐ 8 Joe Carter	10.00	4.50
☐ 9 Greg Maddux	30.00	13.50
☐ 10 Frank Thomas	40.00	18.00
☐ 11 Mike Piazza	30.00	13.50
☐ 12 Jose Canseco	8.00	3.60
☐ 13 Kirby Puckett	20.00	9.00
☐ 14 Matt Williams	10.00	4.50

1995 Leaf Great Gloves

This 16-card standard-size set was randomly inserted in series two packs at a rate of one every two packs. The players featured are leading defensive players. Action photos are set against a background that includes part of a glove. The player's name and team are stamped in gold foil. The horizontal backs feature a photo set against a glove, information about the player and their 1994 defensive statistics. The cards are numbered "X" of 16 in the upper right.

	MINT	NRMT
COMPLETE SET (16)	8.00	3.60
COMMON CARD (1-16)	.25	.11
☐ 1 Jeff Bagwell	1.25	.55
☐ 2 Roberto Alomar	.60	.25
☐ 3 Barry Bonds	.75	.35
☐ 4 Wade Boggs	.60	.25
☐ 5 Andres Galarraga	.40	.18
☐ 6 Ken Griffey Jr.	3.00	1.35
☐ 7 Marquis Grissom	.25	.11
☐ 8 Kenny Lofton	.75	.35
☐ 9 Barry Larkin	.40	.18
☐ 10 Don Mattingly	1.50	.70
☐ 11 Greg Maddux	2.00	.90
☐ 12 Kirby Puckett	1.25	.55
☐ 13 Ozzie Smith	.75	.35
☐ 14 Cal Ripken Jr.	2.50	1.10
☐ 15 Matt Williams	.40	.18
☐ 16 Ivan Rodriguez	.75	.35

1995 Leaf Heading for the Hall

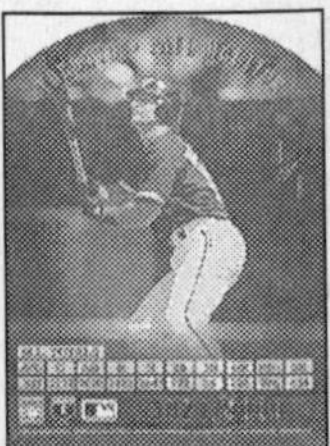

This eight-card standard-size set was randomly inserted into series two hobby packs. The cards are cut in the shape of a Hall of Fame plaque and are designed as if this ᴡere the actual information on the playerís plaque in Cooperstown. The backs feature a black and white photo along with career statistics. The cards are individually numbered out of 5,000 as well.

	MINT	NRMT
COMPLETE SET (8)	250.00	110.00
COMMON CARD (1-8)	12.00	5.50
☐ 1 Frank Thomas	50.00	22.00
☐ 2 Ken Griffey Jr.	60.00	27.00
☐ 3 Jeff Bagwell	25.00	11.00
☐ 4 Barry Bonds	15.00	6.75
☐ 5 Kirby Puckett	25.00	11.00
☐ 6 Cal Ripken	50.00	22.00
☐ 7 Tony Gwynn	30.00	13.50
☐ 8 Paul Molitor	12.00	5.50

1995 Leaf Opening Day

This eight-card standard-size set was available through a wrapper mail-in offer. Upon receipt of eight 1995 Leaf, Studio or Donruss wrappers, a collector received this set. Besides the wrappers, the set cost $2 in shipping and handling and the final deadline was Aug. 31, 1995. The fronts have the words "1995 Opening Day" on the left with the playerís picture and name on the right. The "Leaf 95" logo is in the upper right corner. All photos were taken on opening day including shots of Larry Walker as a Colorado Rockie and Jose Canseco in his Boston Red Sox debut. The horizontal backs contain the words "Opening Day" on the left with the rest of the card dedicated to the player's photo against a background of exploding fireworks. A brief inset of the playerís opening day performance is included as well. The cards are numbered "X" of 8 in the upper right corner.

	MINT	NRMT
COMPLETE SET (8)	12.00	5.50
COMMON CARD (1-8)	.40	.18
MINOR STARS	.60	.25
SEMISTARS	.75	.35
UNLISTED STARS	1.00	.45
☐ 1 Frank Thomas	2.50	1.10
☐ 2 Jeff Bagwell	1.25	.55
☐ 3 Barry Bonds	1.00	.45
☐ 4 Ken Griffey Jr.	3.00	1.35
☐ 5 Mike Piazza	2.00	.90
☐ 6 Cal Ripken	2.50	1.10
☐ 7 Jose Canseco	.40	.18
☐ 8 Larry Walker	1.00	.45

1995 Leaf Slideshow

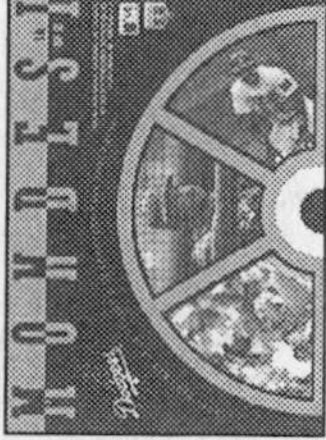

This 16-card standard-size set was issued eight per series and randomly inserted at a rate of per box. The eight cards in the first series are numbered 1A-8A and repeated with different photos in the second series as 1B-8B. Both version carry the same value. The left side of the card front is semi-circular featuring three player translucent slides".

	MINT	NRMT
COMPLETE SET (16)	80.00	36.00
COMPLETE SERIES 1 (8)	40.00	18.00
COMPLETE SERIES 2 (8)	40.00	18.00
COMMON CARD (1-8)	2.00	.90
☐ 1A Raul Mondesi	4.00	1.80
☐ 1B Raul Mondesi	4.00	1.80
☐ 2A Frank Thomas	15.00	6.75
☐ 2B Frank Thomas	12.00	5.50
☐ 3A Fred McGriff	4.00	1.80
☐ 3B Fred McGriff	4.00	1.80
☐ 4A Cal Ripken	12.00	5.50
☐ 4B Cal Ripken	12.00	5.50
☐ 5A Jeff Bagwell	6.00	2.70
☐ 5B Jeff Bagwell	6.00	2.70
☐ 6A Will Clark	2.00	.90
☐ 6B Will Clark	2.00	.90
☐ 7A Matt Williams	4.00	1.80
☐ 7B Matt Williams	4.00	1.80
☐ 8A Ken Griffey Jr.	15.00	6.75
☐ 8B Ken Griffey Jr.	15.00	6.75

1995 Leaf Statistical Standouts

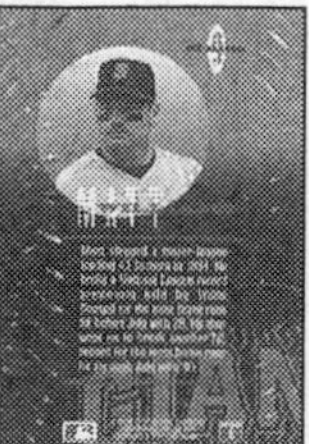

Randomly inserted in first series hobby packs at a rate of one in 70, this set features nine players who stood out from the rest statistically. The fronts contain a player photo between embossed seams or stitches of a baseball. The backs have a small circular player photo with 1994 highlights.

	MINT	NRMT
COMPLETE SET (9)	450.00	200.00
COMMON CARD (1-9)	15.00	6.75
☐ 1 Joe Carter	15.00	6.75
☐ 2 Ken Griffey Jr.	125.00	55.00
☐ 3 Don Mattingly	40.00	18.00
☐ 4 Fred McGriff	20.00	9.00
☐ 5 Paul Molitor	25.00	11.00
☐ 6 Kirby Puckett	50.00	22.00
☐ 7 Cal Ripken	100.00	45.00
☐ 8 Frank Thomas	100.00	45.00
☐ 9 Matt Williams	20.00	9.00

1995 Leaf Thomas

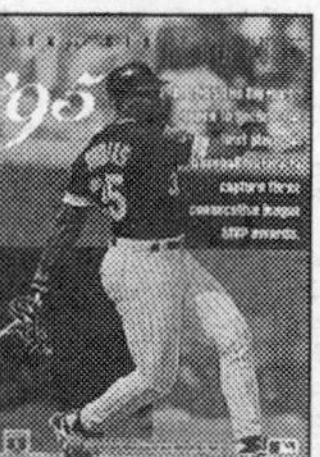

This six-card standard-size set was randomly inserted into series two packs at a rate of one in eighteen. The fronts feature an action photo and have Season "X" on the bottom. The backs have a player photo, information about a specific season in Thomas' career as well as those seasonal stats.

	MINT	NRMT
COMPLETE SET (6)	25.00	11.00
COMMON CARD (1-6)	5.00	2.20
☐ 1 Frank Thomas The Rookie	5.00	2.20
☐ 2 Frank Thomas Sophomore Stardom	5.00	2.20
☐ 3 Frank Thomas Superstar	5.00	2.20
☐ 4 Frank Thomas AL MVP	5.00	2.20
☐ 5 Frank Thomas Back-To-Back	5.00	2.20
☐ 6 Frank Thomas The Big Hurt	5.00	2.20

1995 Leaf 300 Club

Randomly inserted in first and second series mini and retail packs at a rate of one every 12 packs, this set depicts all 18 players who had a career average of .300 or better entering the 1995 campaign. A large ghosted 300 serves as background to a player photo. Gold foil is at the bottom in either corner including career average in the right corner. Full-bleed backs list the 18 players and their averages to that point.

	MINT	NRMT
COMPLETE SET (18)	120.00	55.00
COMPLETE SERIES 1 (9)	50.00	22.00
COMPLETE SERIES 2 (9)	70.00	32.00
COMMON CARD (1-18)	1.50	.70
☐ 1 Frank Thomas	20.00	9.00
☐ 2 Paul Molitor	5.00	2.20
☐ 3 Mike Piazza	15.00	6.75
☐ 4 Moises Alou	3.00	1.35
☐ 5 Mike Greenwell	1.50	.70
☐ 6 Will Clark	4.00	1.80
☐ 7 Hal Morris	1.50	.70
☐ 8 Edgar Martinez	4.00	1.80
☐ 9 Carlos Baerga	1.50	.70
☐ 10 Ken Griffey Jr.	25.00	11.00
☐ 11 Wade Boggs	5.00	2.20
☐ 12 Jeff Bagwell	10.00	4.50
☐ 13 Tony Gwynn	12.00	5.50
☐ 14 John Kruk	3.00	1.35
☐ 15 Don Mattingly	8.00	3.60
☐ 16 Mark Grace	4.00	1.80
☐ 17 Kirby Puckett	10.00	4.50
☐ 18 Kenny Lofton	6.00	2.70

1996 Leaf

The 1996 Leaf set was issued in one series totalling 220 cards. The fronts feature color action player photos with silver foil printing and lines forming a border on the left and bottom. The backs display another player photo with 1995 season and career statistics. Card number 210 is a checklist for the insert sets and cards number 211-220 feature rookies. The fronts of these 10 cards are different in design from the first 200 with a color action player cut-out over a green-shadow background of the same picture and gold lettering. The horizontal backs carry another player cut-out on a purple-and-black background with 1995 season statistics and personal information.

	MINT	NRMT
COMPLETE SET (220)	20.00	9.00
COMMON CARD (1-220)	.15	.07
☐ 1 John Smoltz	.30	.14
☐ 2 Dennis Eckersley	.40	.18
☐ 3 Delino DeShields	.15	.07
☐ 4 Cliff Floyd	.15	.07
☐ 5 Chuck Finley	.15	.07
☐ 6 Cecil Fielder	.30	.14
☐ 7 Tim Naehring	.15	.07
☐ 8 Carlos Perez	.15	.07
☐ 9 Brad Ausmus	.15	.07
☐ 10 Matt Lawton	.15	.07
☐ 11 Alan Trammell	.40	.18
☐ 12 Steve Finley	.30	.14
☐ 13 Paul O'Neill	.15	.07

Card	MINT	NRMT
☐ 14 Gary Sheffield	.60	.25
☐ 15 Mark McGwire	1.25	.55
☐ 16 Bernie Williams	.60	.25
☐ 17 Jeff Montgomery	.15	.07
☐ 18 Chan Ho Park	.60	.25
☐ 19 Greg Vaughn	.15	.07
☐ 20 Jeff Kent	.15	.07
☐ 21 Cal Ripken	2.50	1.10
☐ 22 Charles Johnson	.30	.14
☐ 23 Eric Karros	.30	.14
☐ 24 Alex Rodriguez	2.50	1.10
☐ 25 Chris Snopek	.15	.07
☐ 26 Jason Isringhausen	.15	.07
☐ 27 Chili Davis	.15	.07
☐ 28 Chipper Jones	2.00	.90
☐ 29 Bret Saberhagen	.15	.07
☐ 30 Tony Clark	.60	.25
☐ 31 Marty Cordova	.15	.07
☐ 32 Dwayne Hosey	.15	.07
☐ 33 Fred McGriff	.40	.18
☐ 34 Deion Sanders	.60	.25
☐ 35 Orlando Merced	.15	.07
☐ 36 Brady Anderson	.40	.18
☐ 37 Ray Lankford	.30	.14
☐ 38 Manny Ramirez	.60	.25
☐ 39 Alex Fernandez	.30	.14
☐ 40 Greg Colbrunn	.15	.07
☐ 41 Ken Griffey, Jr.	3.00	1.35
☐ 42 Mickey Moradini	.15	.07
☐ 43 Chuck Knoblauch	.60	.25
☐ 44 Quinton McCracken	.15	.07
☐ 45 Tim Salmon	.60	.25
☐ 46 Jose Mesa	.30	.14
☐ 47 Marquis Grissom	.30	.14
☐ 48 Checklist	.15	.07
☐ 49 Raul Mondesi	.40	.18
☐ 50 Mark Grudzielanek	.30	.14
☐ 51 Ray Durham	.40	.18
☐ 52 Matt Williams	.40	.18
☐ 53 Bob Hamelin	.15	.07
☐ 54 Lenny Dykstra	.30	.14
☐ 55 Jeff King	.15	.07
☐ 56 LaTroy Hawkins	.15	.07
☐ 57 Terry Pendleton	.15	.07
☐ 58 Kevin Stocker	.15	.07
☐ 59 Ozzie Timmons	.15	.07
☐ 60 David Justice	.60	.25
☐ 61 Ricky Bottalico	.15	.07
☐ 62 Andy Ashby	.15	.07
☐ 63 Larry Walker	.60	.25
☐ 64 Jose Canseco	.40	.18
☐ 65 Bret Boone	.15	.07
☐ 66 Shawn Green	.15	.07
☐ 67 Chad Curtis	.15	.07
☐ 68 Travis Fryman	.30	.14
☐ 69 Roger Clemens	1.25	.55
☐ 70 David Bell	.15	.07
☐ 71 Rusty Greer	.40	.18
☐ 72 Bob Higginson	.40	.18
☐ 73 Joey Hamilton	.15	.07
☐ 74 Kevin Seitzer	.15	.07
☐ 75 Julian Tavarez	.15	.07
☐ 76 Troy Percival	.15	.07
☐ 77 Kirby Puckett	1.25	.55
☐ 78 Barry Bonds	.75	.35
☐ 79 Michael Tucker	.30	.14
☐ 80 Paul Molitor	.60	.25
☐ 81 Carlos Garcia	.15	.07
☐ 82 Johnny Damon	.30	.14
☐ 83 Mike Hampton	.15	.07
☐ 84 Ariel Prieto	.15	.07
☐ 85 Tony Tarasco	.15	.07
☐ 86 Pete Schourek	.15	.07
☐ 87 Tom Glavine	.30	.14
☐ 88 Rondell White	.30	.14
☐ 89 Jim Edmonds	.60	.25
☐ 90 Robby Thompson	.15	.07
☐ 91 Wade Boggs	.60	.25
☐ 92 Pedro Martinez	.60	.25
☐ 93 Gregg Jefferies	.30	.14
☐ 94 Albert Belle	.75	.35
☐ 95 Benji Gil	.15	.07
☐ 96 Denny Neagle	.30	.14
☐ 97 Mark Langston	.15	.07
☐ 98 Sandy Alomar, Jr.	.15	.07
☐ 99 Tony Gwynn	1.50	.70
☐ 100 Todd Hundley	.30	.14
☐ 101 Dante Bichette	.40	.18
☐ 102 Eddie Murray	.60	.25
☐ 103 Lyle Mouton	.15	.07
☐ 104 John Jaha	.15	.07
☐ 105 Checklist	.15	.07
☐ 106 Jon Nunnally	.15	.07
☐ 107 Juan Gonzalez	1.50	.70
☐ 108 Kevin Appier	.15	.07
☐ 109 Brian McRae	.15	.07
☐ 110 Lee Smith	.30	.14
☐ 111 Tim Wakefield	.15	.07
☐ 112 Sammy Sosa	.60	.25
☐ 113 Jay Buhner	.60	.25
☐ 114 Garret Anderson	.30	.14
☐ 115 Edgar Martinez	.40	.18
☐ 116 Edgardo Alfonzo	.60	.25
☐ 117 Billy Ashley	.15	.07
☐ 118 Joe Carter	.30	.14
☐ 119 Javy Lopez	.30	.14
☐ 120 Bobby Bonilla	.30	.14
☐ 121 Ken Caminiti	.60	.25
☐ 122 Barry Larkin	.40	.18
☐ 123 Shannon Stewart	.15	.07
☐ 124 Orel Hershiser	.30	.14
☐ 125 Jeff Conine	.30	.14
☐ 126 Mark Grace	.40	.18
☐ 127 Kenny Lofton	.75	.35
☐ 128 Luis Gonzalez	.15	.07
☐ 129 Rico Brogna	.15	.07
☐ 130 Mo Vaughn	.75	.35
☐ 131 Brad Radke	.15	.07
☐ 132 Jose Herrera	.15	.07
☐ 133 Rick Aguilera	.15	.07
☐ 134 Gary DiSarcina	.15	.07
☐ 135 Andres Galarraga	.60	.25
☐ 136 Carl Everett	.15	.07
☐ 137 Steve Avery	.15	.07
☐ 138 Vinny Castilla	.30	.14
☐ 139 Dennis Martinez	.30	.14
☐ 140 John Wetteland	.30	.14
☐ 141 Alex Gonzalez	.15	.07
☐ 142 Brian Jordan	.30	.14
☐ 143 Todd Hollandsworth	.30	.14
☐ 144 Terrell Wade	.15	.07
☐ 145 Wilson Alvarez	.30	.14
☐ 146 Reggie Sanders	.15	.07
☐ 147 Will Clark	.40	.18
☐ 148 Hideo Nomo	1.50	.70
☐ 149 J.T.Snow	.15	.07
☐ 150 Frank Thomas	2.50	1.10
☐ 151 Ivan Rodriguez	.75	.35
☐ 152 Jay Bell	.30	.14
☐ 153 Checklist	.15	.07
☐ 154 David Cone	.30	.14
☐ 155 Roberto Alomar	.60	.25
☐ 156 Carlos Delgado	.30	.14
☐ 157 Carlos Baerga	.30	.14
☐ 158 Geronimo Berroa	.15	.07
☐ 159 Joe Vitiello	.15	.07
☐ 160 Terry Steinbach	.30	.14
☐ 161 Doug Drabek	.15	.07
☐ 162 David Segui	.15	.07
☐ 163 Ozzie Smith	.75	.35
☐ 164 Kurt Abbott	.15	.07
☐ 165 Randy Johnson	.60	.25
☐ 166 John Valentin	.30	.14
☐ 167 Mickey Tettleton	.15	.07
☐ 168 Ruben Sierra	.15	.07
☐ 169 Jim Thome	.60	.25
☐ 170 Mike Greenwell	.15	.07
☐ 171 Quilvio Veras	.15	.07
☐ 172 Robin Ventura	.30	.14
☐ 173 Bill Pulsipher	.15	.07
☐ 174 Rafael Palmeiro	.40	.18
☐ 175 Hal Morris	.15	.07
☐ 176 Ryan Klesko	.40	.18
☐ 177 Eric Young	.30	.14
☐ 178 Shane Andrews	.15	.07
☐ 179 Brian L.Hunter	.30	.14
☐ 180 Brett Butler	.30	.14
☐ 181 John Olerud	.30	.14
☐ 182 Moises Alou	.30	.14
☐ 183 Glenallen Hill	.15	.07
☐ 184 Ismael Valdes	.30	.14
☐ 185 Andy Pettitte	.75	.35
☐ 186 Yamil Benitez	.40	.18
☐ 187 Jason Bere	.15	.07
☐ 188 Dean Palmer	.30	.14
☐ 189 Jimmy Haynes	.15	.07
☐ 190 Trevor Hoffman	.30	.14
☐ 191 Mike Mussina	.60	.25
☐ 192 Greg Maddux	2.00	.90
☐ 193 Ozzie Guillen	.15	.07
☐ 194 Pat Listach	.15	.07
☐ 195 Derek Bell	.15	.07
☐ 196 Darren Daulton	.30	.14
☐ 197 John Mabry	.30	.14
☐ 198 Ramon Martinez	.30	.14
☐ 199 Jeff Bagwell	1.25	.55
☐ 200 Mike Piazza	2.00	.90
☐ 201 Al Martin	.15	.07
☐ 202 Aaron Sele	.15	.07
☐ 203 Ed Sprague	.15	.07
☐ 204 Rod Beck	.30	.14
☐ 205 Checklist	.15	.07
☐ 206 Mike Lansing	.15	.07
☐ 207 Craig Biggio	.40	.18
☐ 208 Jeffrey Hammonds	.15	.07
☐ 209 Dave Nilsson	.30	.14
☐ 210 Checklist	.15	.07
☐ 211 Derek Jeter	2.00	.90
☐ 212 Alan Benes	.30	.14
☐ 213 Jason Schmidt	.30	.14
☐ 214 Alex Ochoa	.15	.07
☐ 215 Ruben Rivera	.30	.14
☐ 216 Roger Cedeno	.30	.14
☐ 217 Jeff Suppan	.60	.25
☐ 218 Billy Wagner	.40	.18
☐ 219 Mark Loretta	.15	.07
☐ 220 Karim Garcia	.40	.18

1996 Leaf Press Proofs Bronze

This 220-card Bronze set is parallel to the regular Leaf set and between the three types of press proofs were inserted at a rate of one in 10 packs. Similar in design to the regular set, 2,000 Bronze sets were produced and feature a special holographic foil.

	MINT	NRMT
COMPLETE SET (220)	600.00	275.00
COMMON CARD (1-220)	1.00	.45

*STARS: 5X TO 12X BASIC CARDS ...
*YOUNG STARS: 4X TO 10X BASIC CARDS

1996 Leaf Press Proofs Gold

This 220-card Gold set is parallel to the regular Leaf set. Only five hundred sets were produced and they were randomly inserted into packs.

	MINT	NRMT
COMPLETE SET (220)	2500.00	1100.00
COMMON CARD (1-220)	5.00	2.20

*STARS: 20X to 50X BASIC CARDS ...
*YOUNG STARS: 15X to 40X BASIC CARDS

1996 Leaf Press Proofs Silver

This 220-card Silver set is also a parallel to the regular Leaf issue. One thousand sets were produced and the cards were randomly inserted into packs.

	MINT	NRMT
COMPLETE SET (220)	1200.00	550.00
COMMON CARD (1-220)	2.00	.90

*STARS: 10X to 25X BASIC CARDS ...
*YOUNG STARS: 8X to 20X BASIC CARDS

1996 Leaf All-Star Game MVP Contenders

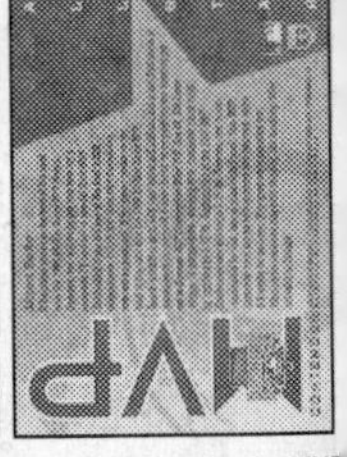

This 20 card set features possible contenders for the MVP at the 1996 All-Star Game held in Philadelphia. The cards were randomly inserted into packs. If the player on the front of the card won the MVP Award (which turned out to be Mike Piazza), the holder could send it in for a special Gold MVP Contenders set of which only 5,000 were produced. The fronts display a color action player photo. The backs carry the instructions on how to redeem the card. The expiration date for the redemption was August 15th, 1996. The Piazza card when returned with the redemption set had a hole in it to indicate the set had been redeemed.

	MINT	NRMT
COMPLETE SET (20	40.00	18.00
COMMON CARD (1-20)	.75	.35
COMP.GOLD SET (20)	40.00	18.00

*GOLD CARDS: SAME PRICE AS BASIC MVPS

Card	MINT	NRMT
☐ 1 Frank Thomas	5.00	2.20
☐ 2 Mike Piazza	6.00	2.70
☐ 3 Sammy Sosa	1.25	.55
☐ 4 Cal Ripken	5.00	2.20
☐ 5 Jeff Bagwell	2.50	1.10
☐ 6 Reggie Sanders	.75	.35
☐ 7 Mo Vaughn	1.50	.70
☐ 8 Tony Gwynn	2.50	1.10
☐ 9 Dante Bichette	1.00	.45

	MINT	NRMT
☐ 10 Tim Salmon	1.25	.55
☐ 11 Chipper Jones	4.00	1.80
☐ 12 Kenny Lofton	1.50	.70
☐ 13 Manny Ramirez	1.25	.55
☐ 14 Barry Bonds	1.50	.70
☐ 15 Raul Mondesi	1.25	.55
☐ 16 Kirby Puckett	2.50	1.10
☐ 17 Albert Belle	1.50	.70
☐ 18 Ken Griffey Jr.	6.00	2.70
☐ 19 Greg Maddux	4.00	1.80
☐ 20 Bonus Card	.75	.35

1996 Leaf Gold Stars

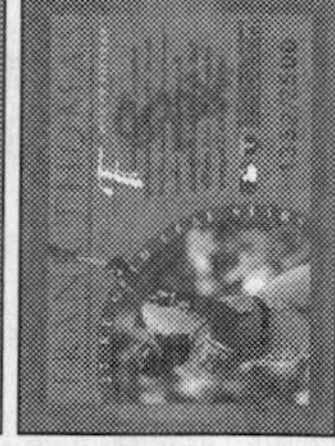

Randomly inserted in hobby and retail packs at a rate of one in 190, this 15-card set honors some of the games great players on 22 karat gold trim cards. Only 2,500 cards of each player were printed and are individually numbered.

	MINT	NRMT
COMPLETE SET (15)	500.00	220.00
COMMON CARD (1-15)	10.00	4.50
☐ 1 Frank Thomas	60.00	27.00
☐ 2 Dante Bichette	10.00	4.50
☐ 3 Sammy Sosa	15.00	6.75
☐ 4 Ken Griffey Jr.	80.00	36.00
☐ 5 Mike Piazza	50.00	22.00
☐ 6 Tim Salmon	15.00	6.75
☐ 7 Hideo Nomo	40.00	18.00
☐ 8 Cal Ripken	60.00	27.00
☐ 9 Chipper Jones	50.00	22.00
☐ 10 Albert Belle	20.00	9.00
☐ 11 Tony Gwynn	40.00	18.00
☐ 12 Mo Vaughn	20.00	9.00
☐ 13 Barry Larkin	12.50	5.50
☐ 14 Manny Ramirez	15.00	6.75
☐ 15 Greg Maddux	50.00	22.00

1996 Leaf Hats Off

Randomly inserted in retail packs only at a rate of one in 72, this 8-card set was printed and embossed on a wool-like material with the feel of a Major League ball cap. Only 5,000 of each player was produced and is individually numbered.

	MINT	NRMT
COMPLETE SET (8)	200.00	90.00
COMMON CARD (1-8)	5.00	2.20
☐ 1 Cal Ripken	30.00	13.50
☐ 2 Barry Larkin	5.00	2.20
☐ 3 Frank Thomas	30.00	13.50
☐ 4 Mo Vaughn	10.00	4.50
☐ 5 Ken Griffey Jr.	40.00	18.00
☐ 6 Hideo Nomo	20.00	9.00
☐ 7 Albert Belle	10.00	4.50
☐ 8 Greg Maddux	25.00	11.00

1996 Leaf Picture Perfect

Randomly inserted in hobby (1-6) and retail (7-12) packs at a rate of one in 140, this 12-card set is printed on real wood with gold foil trim. The fronts feature a color player action framed photo. The backs carry another player photo with player information. Only 5,000 of each card were printed and are individually numbered.

	MINT	NRMT
COMPLETE SET (12)	250.00	110.00
COMMON CARD (1-12)	8.00	3.60
☐ 1 Frank Thomas	30.00	13.50
☐ 2 Cal Ripken	30.00	13.50
☐ 3 Greg Maddux	25.00	11.00
☐ 4 Manny Ramirez	8.00	3.60
☐ 5 Chipper Jones	25.00	11.00
☐ 6 Tony Gwynn	20.00	9.00
☐ 7 Ken Griffey Jr.	40.00	18.00
☐ 8 Albert Belle	10.00	4.50
☐ 9 Jeff Bagwell	15.00	6.75
☐ 10 Mike Piazza	25.00	11.00
☐ 11 Mo Vaughn	10.00	4.50
☐ 12 Barry Bonds	10.00	4.50
☐ P10 Mike Piazza Promo	3.00	1.35

1996 Leaf Statistical Standouts

Randomly inserted in hobby packs only at a rate of one in 210, this 8-card set features eight players who stood out from the rest statistically. The cards were printed on a material with the feel of the leather that's between the seams or stitches of a baseball. Only 2,500 of each card was printed and is numbered individually.

	MINT	NRMT
COMPLETE SET (8)	450.00	200.00
COMMON CARD (1-8)	25.00	11.00
☐ 1 Cal Ripken	80.00	36.00
☐ 2 Tony Gwynn	50.00	22.00
☐ 3 Frank Thomas	80.00	36.00
☐ 4 Ken Griffey Jr.	100.00	45.00
☐ 5 Hideo Nomo	50.00	22.00
☐ 6 Greg Maddux	60.00	27.00
☐ 7 Albert Belle	25.00	11.00
☐ 8 Chipper Jones	60.00	27.00

1996 Leaf Thomas Greatest Hits

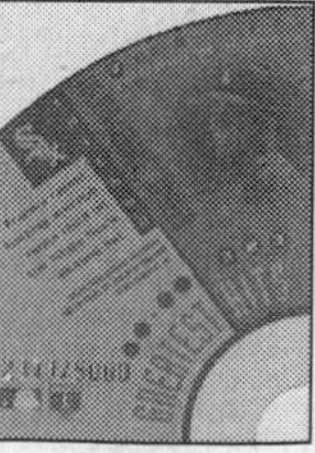

Randomly inserted in hobby (1-4) and retail (5-7) packs at a rate of one in 210, this 8-card set was printed on die-cut plastic to simulate a compact disc. The cards feature the statistical highlights of Frank Thomas. The wrapper displays the details for the special mail-in offer to obtain card number 8.

	MINT	NRMT
COMPLETE SET (8)	150.00	70.00
COMMON CARD (1-7)	25.00	11.00
COMMON EXCHANGE (8)	30.00	13.50
☐ 1 Frank Thomas 1990	25.00	11.00
☐ 2 Frank Thomas 1991	25.00	11.00
☐ 3 Frank Thomas 1992	25.00	11.00
☐ 4 Frank Thomas 1993	25.00	11.00
☐ 5 Frank Thomas 1994	25.00	11.00
☐ 6 Frank Thomas 1995	25.00	11.00
☐ 7 Frank Thomas Career	25.00	11.00
☐ 8 Frank Thomas MVP	30.00	13.50

1996 Leaf Total Bases

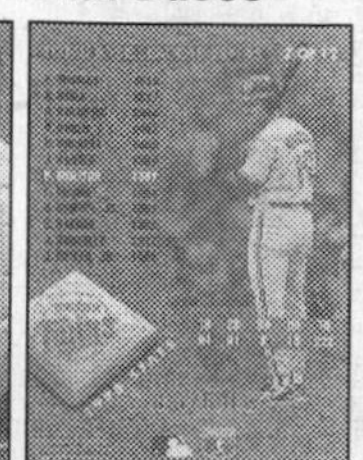

Randomly inserted in hobby packs only at a rate of one in 72, this 12-card set is printed on canvas and features the top offensive stars. Only 5,000 of each card was printed and are individually numbered. The fronts carry a color action player cut-out over a base background. The backs display another player photo and 1995 stats.

	MINT	NRMT
COMPLETE SET (12)	150.00	70.00
COMMON CARD (1-12)	3.00	1.35
☐ 1 Frank Thomas	25.00	11.00
☐ 2 Albert Belle	8.00	3.60
☐ 3 Rafael Palmeiro	5.00	2.20
☐ 4 Barry Bonds	8.00	3.60
☐ 5 Kirby Puckett	12.00	5.50
☐ 6 Joe Carter	4.00	1.80
☐ 7 Paul Molitor	6.00	2.70
☐ 8 Fred McGriff	5.00	2.20
☐ 9 Ken Griffey Jr.	30.00	13.50
☐ 10 Carlos Baerga	3.00	1.35
☐ 11 Juan Gonzalez	15.00	6.75
☐ 12 Cal Ripken	25.00	11.00

1997 Leaf

The 400-card Leaf set was issued in two separate 200-card series. 10-card packs carried a suggested retail of $2.99. Each card features color action player photos with foil enhancement. The backs carry another player photo and season and career statistics. The set contains the following subsets: Legacy (188-197/348-367), Checklists (198-200/398-400) and Gamers (368-397). The only key Rookie Cards in the set are Jose Cruz Jr. and Hideki Irabu. In a tie in with the 50th anniversary of Jackie Robinson's major league debut, Donruss/Leaf also issued some collectible items. They made 42 all-leather jackets (issued to match Robinson's uniform number). There were also 311 leather jackets produced (to match Robinson's career batting average). 1,500 lithographs were also produced of which Rachel Robinson signed 500 of them.

	MINT	NRMT
COMPLETE SET (400)	40.00	18.00
COMPLETE SERIES 1 (200)	20.00	9.00
COMPLETE SERIES 2 (200)	20.00	9.00
COMMON CARD (1-400)	.15	.07
☐ 1 Wade Boggs	.60	.25
☐ 2 Brian McRae	.15	.07
☐ 3 Jeff D'Amico	.30	.14
☐ 4 George Arias	.15	.07

☐ 5 Billy Wagner .30 .14
☐ 6 Ray Lankford .30 .14
☐ 7 Will Clark .40 .18
☐ 8 Edgar Renteria .30 .14
☐ 9 Alex Ochoa .15 .07
☐ 10 Roberto Hernandez .30 .14
☐ 11 Joe Carter .30 .14
☐ 12 Gregg Jefferies .30 .14
☐ 13 Mark Grace .40 .18
☐ 14 Roberto Alomar .60 .25
☐ 15 Joe Randa .15 .07
☐ 16 Alex Rodriguez 2.50 1.10
☐ 17 Tony Gwynn 1.50 .70
☐ 18 Steve Gibralter .15 .07
☐ 19 Scott Stahoviak .15 .07
☐ 20 Matt Williams .40 .18
☐ 21 Quinton McCracken .15 .07
☐ 22 Ugueth Urbina .30 .14
☐ 23 Jermaine Allensworth .15 .07
☐ 24 Paul Molitor .60 .25
☐ 25 Carlos Delgado .30 .14
☐ 26 Bob Abreu .60 .25
☐ 27 John Jaha .15 .07
☐ 28 Rusty Greer .30 .14
☐ 29 Kimera Bartee .15 .07
☐ 30 Ruben Rivera .30 .14
☐ 31 Jason Kendall .30 .14
☐ 32 Lance Johnson .15 .07
☐ 33 Robin Ventura .30 .14
☐ 34 Kevin Appier .30 .14
☐ 35 John Mabry .15 .07
☐ 36 Ricky Otero .15 .07
☐ 37 Mike Lansing .15 .07
☐ 38 Mark McGwire 1.25 .55
☐ 39 Tim Naehring .15 .07
☐ 40 Tom Glavine .30 .14
☐ 41 Rey Ordonez .15 .07
☐ 42 Tony Clark .60 .25
☐ 43 Rafael Palmeiro .40 .18
☐ 44 Pedro Martinez .60 .25
☐ 45 Keith Lockhart .15 .07
☐ 46 Dan Wilson .15 .07
☐ 47 John Wetteland .30 .14
☐ 48 Chan Ho Park .60 .25
☐ 49 Gary Sheffield .60 .25
☐ 50 Shawn Estes .30 .14
☐ 51 Royce Clayton .15 .07
☐ 52 Jaime Navarro .15 .07
☐ 53 Raul Casanova .15 .07
☐ 54 Jeff Bagwell 1.25 .55
☐ 55 Barry Larkin .40 .18
☐ 56 Charles Nagy .30 .14
☐ 57 Ken Caminiti .60 .25
☐ 58 Todd Hollandsworth .30 .14
☐ 59 Pat Hentgen .30 .14
☐ 60 Jose Valentin .15 .07
☐ 61 Frank Rodriguez .15 .07
☐ 62 Mickey Tettleton .15 .07
☐ 63 Marty Cordova .30 .14
☐ 64 Cecil Fielder .30 .14
☐ 65 Barry Bonds .75 .35
☐ 66 Scott Servais .15 .07
☐ 67 Ernie Young .15 .07
☐ 68 Wilson Alvarez .15 .07
☐ 69 Mike Grace .15 .07
☐ 70 Shane Reynolds .15 .07
☐ 71 Henry Rodriguez .15 .07
☐ 72 Eric Karros .30 .14
☐ 73 Mark Langston .15 .07
☐ 74 Scott Karl .15 .07
☐ 75 Trevor Hoffman .15 .07
☐ 76 Orel Hershiser .30 .14
☐ 77 John Smoltz .60 .25
☐ 78 Raul Mondesi .40 .18
☐ 79 Jeff Brantley .15 .07
☐ 80 Donne Wall .15 .07
☐ 81 Joey Cora .30 .14
☐ 82 Mel Rojas .15 .07
☐ 83 Chad Mottola .15 .07
☐ 84 Omar Vizquel .30 .14
☐ 85 Greg Maddux 2.00 .90
☐ 86 Jamey Wright .30 .14
☐ 87 Chuck Finley .15 .07
☐ 88 Brady Anderson .30 .14
☐ 89 Alex Gonzalez .15 .07
☐ 90 Andy Benes .15 .07
☐ 91 Reggie Jefferson .30 .14
☐ 92 Paul O'Neill .30 .14
☐ 93 Javier Lopez .30 .14
☐ 94 Mark Grudzielanek .15 .07
☐ 95 Marc Newfield .15 .07
☐ 96 Kevin Ritz .15 .07
☐ 97 Fred McGriff .40 .18
☐ 98 Dwight Gooden .30 .14
☐ 99 Hideo Nomo 1.50 .70
☐ 100 Steve Finley .30 .14
☐ 101 Juan Gonzalez 1.50 .70
☐ 102 Jay Buhner .40 .18
☐ 103 Paul Wilson .15 .07
☐ 104 Alan Benes .30 .14
☐ 105 Manny Ramirez .60 .25
☐ 106 Kevin Elster .15 .07
☐ 107 Frank Thomas 2.50 1.10
☐ 108 Orlando Miller .15 .07
☐ 109 Ramon Martinez .30 .14
☐ 110 Kenny Lofton .75 .35
☐ 111 Bernie Williams .60 .25
☐ 112 Robby Thompson .15 .07
☐ 113 Bernard Gilkey .15 .07
☐ 114 Ray Durham .15 .07
☐ 115 Jeff Cirillo .30 .14
☐ 116 Brian Jordan .30 .14
☐ 117 Rich Becker .15 .07
☐ 118 Al Leiter .15 .07
☐ 119 Mark Johnson .15 .07
☐ 120 Ellis Burks .30 .14
☐ 121 Sammy Sosa .60 .25
☐ 122 Willie Greene .30 .14
☐ 123 Michael Tucker .30 .14
☐ 124 Eddie Murray .60 .25
☐ 125 Joey Hamilton .30 .14
☐ 126 Antonio Osuna .15 .07
☐ 127 Bobby Higginson .30 .14
☐ 128 Tomas Perez .15 .07
☐ 129 Tim Salmon .60 .25
☐ 130 Mark Wohlers .30 .14
☐ 131 Charles Johnson .30 .14
☐ 132 Randy Johnson .60 .25
☐ 133 Brooks Kieschnick .30 .14
☐ 134 Al Martin .15 .07
☐ 135 Dante Bichette .40 .18
☐ 136 Andy Pettitte .60 .25
☐ 137 Jason Giambi .30 .14
☐ 138 James Baldwin .15 .07
☐ 139 Ben McDonald .15 .07
☐ 140 Shawn Green .15 .07
☐ 141 Geronimo Berroa .15 .07
☐ 142 Jose Offerman .15 .07
☐ 143 Curtis Pride .15 .07
☐ 144 Terrell Wade .15 .07
☐ 145 Ismael Valdes .30 .14
☐ 146 Mike Mussina .60 .25
☐ 147 Mariano Rivera .30 .14
☐ 148 Ken Hill .15 .07
☐ 149 Darin Erstad 1.00 .45
☐ 150 Jay Bell .15 .07
☐ 151 Mo Vaughn .75 .35
☐ 152 Ozzie Smith .75 .35
☐ 153 Jose Mesa .30 .14
☐ 154 Osvaldo Fernandez .15 .07
☐ 155 Vinny Castilla .30 .14
☐ 156 Jason Isringhausen .15 .07
☐ 157 B.J. Surhoff .15 .07
☐ 158 Robert Perez .15 .07
☐ 159 Ron Coomer .15 .07
☐ 160 Darren Oliver .15 .07
☐ 161 Mike Mohler .15 .07
☐ 162 Russ Davis .15 .07
☐ 163 Bret Boone .15 .07
☐ 164 Ricky Bottalico .15 .07
☐ 165 Derek Jeter 2.00 .90
☐ 166 Orlando Merced .15 .07
☐ 167 John Valentin .15 .07
☐ 168 Andruw Jones 1.50 .70
☐ 169 Angel Echevarria .15 .07
☐ 170 Todd Walker .15 .07
☐ 171 Desi Relaford .15 .07
☐ 172 Trey Beamon .15 .07
☐ 173 Brian Giles .15 .07
☐ 174 Scott Rolen 1.50 .70
☐ 175 Shannon Stewart .15 .07
☐ 176 Dmitri Young .30 .14
☐ 177 Justin Thompson .30 .14
☐ 178 Trot Nixon .15 .07
☐ 179 Josh Booty .30 .14
☐ 180 Robin Jennings .15 .07
☐ 181 Marvin Benard .15 .07
☐ 182 Luis Castillo .30 .14
☐ 183 Wendell Magee .15 .07
☐ 184 Vladimir Guerrero 1.25 .55
☐ 185 Nomar Garciaparra 2.00 .90
☐ 186 Ryan Hancock .15 .07
☐ 187 Mike Cameron .60 .25
☐ 188 Cal Ripken LG 1.25 .55
☐ 189 Chipper Jones LG 1.00 .45
☐ 190 Albert Belle LG .60 .25
☐ 191 Mike Piazza LG 1.00 .45
☐ 192 Chuck Knoblauch LG .60 .25
☐ 193 Ken Griffey Jr. LG 1.50 .70
☐ 194 Ivan Rodriguez LG .60 .25
☐ 195 Jose Canseco LG .40 .18
☐ 196 Ryne Sandberg LG .60 .25
☐ 197 Jim Thome LG .60 .25
☐ 198 Andy Pettitte CL .60 .25
☐ 199 Andruw Jones CL .75 .35
☐ 200 Derek Jeter CL 1.00 .45
☐ 201 Chipper Jones 2.00 .90
☐ 202 Albert Belle .75 .35
☐ 203 Mike Piazza 2.00 .90
☐ 204 Ken Griffey Jr. 3.00 1.35
☐ 205 Ryne Sandberg .75 .35
☐ 206 Jose Canseco .40 .18
☐ 207 Chili Davis .30 .14
☐ 208 Roger Clemens 1.25 .55
☐ 209 Deion Sanders .60 .25
☐ 210 Darryl Hamilton .15 .07
☐ 211 Jermaine Dye .15 .07
☐ 212 Matt Williams .40 .18
☐ 213 Kevin Elster .15 .07
☐ 214 John Wetteland .30 .14
☐ 215 Garret Anderson .30 .14
☐ 216 Kevin Brown .15 .07
☐ 217 Matt Lawton .15 .07
☐ 218 Cal Ripken 2.50 1.10
☐ 219 Moises Alou .30 .14
☐ 220 Chuck Knoblauch .60 .25
☐ 221 Ivan Rodriguez .75 .35
☐ 222 Travis Fryman .30 .14
☐ 223 Jim Thome .60 .25
☐ 224 Eddie Murray .60 .25
☐ 225 Eric Young .15 .07
☐ 226 Ron Gant .30 .14
☐ 227 Tony Phillips .15 .07
☐ 228 Reggie Sanders .15 .07
☐ 229 Johnny Damon .15 .07
☐ 230 Bill Pulsipher .15 .07
☐ 231 Jim Edmonds .60 .25
☐ 232 Melvin Nieves .15 .07
☐ 233 Ryan Klesko .40 .18
☐ 234 David Cone .30 .14
☐ 235 Derek Bell .15 .07
☐ 236 Julio Franco .30 .14
☐ 237 Juan Guzman .15 .07
☐ 238 Larry Walker .60 .25
☐ 239 Delino DeShields .15 .07
☐ 240 Troy Percival .15 .07
☐ 241 Andres Galarraga .60 .25
☐ 242 Rondell White .15 .07
☐ 243 John Burkett .15 .07
☐ 244 J.T. Snow .30 .14
☐ 245 Alex Fernandez .15 .07
☐ 246 Edgar Martinez .40 .18
☐ 247 Craig Biggio .40 .18
☐ 248 Todd Hundley .30 .14
☐ 249 Jimmy Key .30 .14
☐ 250 Cliff Floyd .15 .07
☐ 251 Jeff Conine .15 .07
☐ 252 Curt Schilling .30 .14
☐ 253 Jeff King .15 .07
☐ 254 Tino Martinez .60 .25
☐ 255 Carlos Baerga .30 .14
☐ 256 Jeff Fassero .15 .07
☐ 257 Dean Palmer .15 .07
☐ 258 Robb Nen .15 .07
☐ 259 Sandy Alomar Jr. .30 .14
☐ 260 Carlos Perez .15 .07
☐ 261 Rickey Henderson .40 .18
☐ 262 Bobby Bonilla .30 .14
☐ 263 Darren Daulton .30 .14
☐ 264 Jim Leyritz .15 .07
☐ 265 Dennis Martinez .30 .14
☐ 266 Butch Huskey .15 .07
☐ 267 Joe Vitiello .15 .07
☐ 268 Steve Trachsel .15 .07
☐ 269 Glenallen Hill .15 .07
☐ 270 Terry Steinbach .15 .07
☐ 271 Mark McLemore .15 .07
☐ 272 Devon White .15 .07
☐ 273 Jeff Kent .15 .07
☐ 274 Tim Raines .15 .07
☐ 275 Carlos Garcia .15 .07
☐ 276 Hal Morris .15 .07
☐ 277 Gary Gaetti .30 .14
☐ 278 John Olerud .30 .14
☐ 279 Wally Joyner .15 .07
☐ 280 Brian Hunter .30 .14
☐ 281 Steve Karsay .15 .07
☐ 282 Denny Neagle .15 .07
☐ 283 Jose Herrera .15 .07
☐ 284 Todd Stottlemyre .15 .07
☐ 285 Bip Roberts .15 .07
☐ 286 Kevin Seitzer .15 .07
☐ 287 Benji Gil .15 .07
☐ 288 Dennis Eckersley .40 .18
☐ 289 Brad Ausmus .15 .07
☐ 290 Otis Nixon .15 .07
☐ 291 Darryl Strawberry .30 .14
☐ 292 Marquis Grissom .30 .14
☐ 293 Darryl Kile .30 .14
☐ 294 Quilvio Veras .15 .07
☐ 295 Tom Goodwin .15 .07

□ 296 Benito Santiago	.15	.07
□ 297 Mike Bordick	.15	.07
□ 298 Roberto Kelly	.15	.07
□ 299 David Justice	.60	.25
□ 300 Carl Everett	.15	.07
□ 301 Mark Whiten	.15	.07
□ 302 Aaron Sele	.15	.07
□ 303 Darren Dreifort	.15	.07
□ 304 Bobby Jones	.15	.07
□ 305 Fernando Vina	.15	.07
□ 306 Ed Sprague	.15	.07
□ 307 Andy Ashby	.15	.07
□ 308 Tony Fernandez	.15	.07
□ 309 Roger Pavlik	.15	.07
□ 310 Mark Clark	.15	.07
□ 311 Mariano Duncan	.15	.07
□ 312 Tyler Houston	.15	.07
□ 313 Eric Davis	.30	.14
□ 314 Greg Vaughn	.15	.07
□ 315 David Segui	.15	.07
□ 316 Dave Nilsson	.15	.07
□ 317 F.P. Santangelo	.15	.07
□ 318 Wilton Guerrero	.15	.07
□ 319 Jose Guillen	.75	.35
□ 320 Kevin Orie	.15	.07
□ 321 Derrek Lee	.15	.07
□ 322 Bubba Trammell	.60	.25
□ 323 Pokey Reese	.15	.07
□ 324 Hideki Irabu	.75	.35
□ 325 Scott Spiezio	.30	.14
□ 326 Bartolo Colon	.15	.07
□ 327 Damon Mashore	.15	.07
□ 329 Chris Carpenter	.15	.07
□ 330 Jose Cruz Jr.	5.00	2.20
□ 331 Todd Greene	.30	.14
□ 332 Brian Moehler	.15	.07
□ 333 Mike Sweeney	.15	.07
□ 334 Neifi Perez	.15	.07
□ 335 Matt Morris	.30	.14
□ 336 Marvin Benard	.15	.07
□ 337 Karim Garcia	.15	.07
□ 338 Jason Dickson	.15	.07
□ 339 Brant Brown	.15	.07
□ 340 Jeff Suppan	.30	.14
□ 341 Deivi Cruz	.40	.18
□ 342 Antone Williamson	.15	.07
□ 343 Curtis Goodwin	.15	.07
□ 344 Brooks Kieschnick	.15	.07
□ 345 Tony Womack	.50	.23
□ 346 Rudy Pemberton	.15	.07
□ 347 Todd Dunwoody	.40	.18
□ 348 Frank Thomas LG	1.25	.55
□ 349 Andruw Jones LG	1.00	.45
□ 350 Alex Rodriguez LG	1.25	.55
□ 351 Greg Maddux LG	1.00	.45
□ 352 Jeff Bagwell LG	.60	.25
□ 353 Juan Gonzalez LG	.75	.35
□ 354 Barry Bonds LG	.60	.25
□ 355 Mark McGwire LG	.60	.25
□ 356 Tony Gwynn LG	.75	.35
□ 357 Gary Sheffield LG	.60	.25
□ 358 Derek Jeter LG	1.00	.45
□ 359 Manny Ramirez LG	.60	.25
□ 360 Hideo Nomo LG	1.00	.45
□ 361 Sammy Sosa LG	.60	.25
□ 362 Paul Molitor LG	.60	.25
□ 363 Kenny Lofton LG	.60	.25
□ 364 Eddie Murray LG	.60	.25
□ 365 Barry Larkin LG	.40	.18
□ 366 Roger Clemens LG	.60	.25
□ 367 John Smoltz LG	.15	.07
□ 368 Alex Rodriguez GM	1.25	.55
□ 369 Frank Thomas GM	1.25	.55
□ 370 Cal Ripken GM	1.25	.55
□ 371 Ken Griffey Jr. GM	1.50	.70
□ 372 Greg Maddux GM	1.00	.45
□ 373 Mike Piazza GM	1.00	.45
□ 374 Chipper Jones GM	1.00	.45
□ 375 Albert Belle GM	.60	.25
□ 376 Chuck Knoblauch GM	.60	.25
□ 377 Brady Anderson GM	.40	.18
□ 378 David Justice GM	.60	.25
□ 379 Randy Johnson GM	.60	.25
□ 380 Wade Boggs GM	.60	.25
□ 381 Kevin Brown GM	.15	.07
□ 382 Tom Glavine GM	.30	.14
□ 383 Raul Mondesi GM	.40	.18
□ 384 Ivan Rodriguez GM	.60	.25
□ 385 Larry Walker GM	.60	.25
□ 386 Bernie Williams GM	.60	.25
□ 387 Rusty Greer GM	.30	.14
□ 388 Rafael Palmeiro GM	.40	.18
□ 389 Matt Williams GM	.40	.18
□ 390 Eric Young GM	.15	.07
□ 391 Fred McGriff GM	.40	.18
□ 392 Ken Caminiti GM	.60	.25
□ 393 Roberto Alomar GM	.60	.25
□ 394 Brian Jordan GM	.15	.07
□ 395 Mark Grace GM	.40	.18
□ 396 Jim Edmonds GM	.60	.25
□ 397 Deion Sanders GM	.60	.25
□ 398 Vladimir Guerrero CL	.75	.35
□ 399 Darin Erstad CL	.60	.25
□ 400 Nomar Garciaparra CL	1.00	.45
□ NNO J.Robinson Reprint	50.00	22.00

1997 Leaf Fractal Matrix

This 400-card set is parallel to the regular Leaf issue and features color player photos with either a bronze, silver or gold finish. Only 200 cards are bronze, 120 cards are silver, and 80 cards are gold. No card is available in more than one of the colors.

	MINT	NRMT
COMPLETE SET(400)	5000.00	2200.00
COMPLETE SERIES 1 (200)	2500.00	1100.00
COMPLETE SERIES 2 (200)	2500.00	1100.00
COMMON BRONZE	1.50	.70
COMMON SILVER	5.00	2.20
COMMON GOLD	8.00	3.60
□ 1 Wade Boggs GY	40.00	18.00
□ 2 Brian McRae BY	1.50	.70
□ 3 Jeff D'Amico BY	2.50	1.10
□ 4 George Arias SY	5.00	2.20
□ 5 Billy Wagner SY	8.00	3.60
□ 6 Ray Lankford BZ	2.50	1.10
□ 7 Will Clark SY	12.00	5.50
□ 8 Edgar Renteria SY	8.00	3.60
□ 9 Alex Ochoa SY	5.00	2.20
□ 10 Roberto Hernandez BX	1.50	.70
□ 11 Joe Carter SY	8.00	3.60
□ 12 Gregg Jefferies BY	1.50	.70
□ 13 Mark Grace SY	12.00	5.50
□ 14 Roberto Alomar GY	40.00	18.00
□ 15 Joe Randa BX	1.50	.70
□ 16 Alex Rodriguez GZ	100.00	45.00
□ 17 Tony Gwynn GZ	80.00	36.00
□ 18 Steve Gibralter BY	1.50	.70
□ 19 Scott Stahoviak BX	1.50	.70
□ 20 Matt Williams SZ	12.00	5.50
□ 21 Quinton McCracken BY	1.50	.70
□ 22 Ugueth Urbina BX	1.50	.70
□ 23 Jermaine Allensworth SX	5.00	2.20
□ 24 Paul Molitor GX	60.00	27.00
□ 25 Carlos Delgado SY	8.00	3.60
□ 26 Bob Abreu SY	8.00	3.60
□ 27 John Jaha SY	8.00	3.60
□ 28 Rusty Greer SZ	8.00	3.60
□ 29 Kimera Bartee BX	1.50	.70
□ 30 Ruben Rivera SY	8.00	3.60
□ 31 Jason Kendall SY	8.00	3.60
□ 32 Lance Johnson BX	1.50	.70
□ 33 Robin Ventura BY	2.50	1.10
□ 34 Kevin Appier SX	8.00	3.60
□ 35 John Mabry SY	5.00	2.20
□ 36 Ricky Otero BX	1.50	.70
□ 37 Mike Lansing BX	1.50	.70
□ 38 Mark McGwire GZ	60.00	27.00
□ 39 Tim Naehring BX	1.50	.70
□ 40 Tom Glavine SZ	8.00	3.60
□ 41 Rey Ordonez SY	8.00	3.60
□ 42 Tony Clark SY	20.00	9.00
□ 43 Rafael Palmeiro SZ	12.00	5.50
□ 44 Pedro Martinez BX	6.00	2.70
□ 45 Keith Lockhart BX	1.50	.70
□ 46 Dan Wilson BY	1.50	.70
□ 47 John Wetteland BY	2.50	1.10
□ 48 Chan Ho Park BX	6.00	2.70
□ 49 Gary Sheffield GZ	30.00	13.50
□ 50 Shawn Estes BX	2.50	1.10
□ 51 Royce Clayton BX	1.50	.70
□ 52 Jaime Navarro BX	1.50	.70
□ 53 Raul Casanova BX	1.50	.70
□ 54 Jeff Bagwell GZ	60.00	27.00
□ 55 Barry Larkin GX	40.00	18.00
□ 56 Charles Nagy BY	2.50	1.10
□ 57 Ken Caminiti GY	20.00	9.00
□ 58 Todd Hollandsworth SZ	5.00	2.20
□ 59 Pat Hentgen SX	8.00	3.60
□ 60 Jose Valentin BX	1.50	.70
□ 61 Frank Rodriguez BX	1.50	.70
□ 62 Mickey Tettleton BX	1.50	.70
□ 63 Marty Cordova GX	12.00	5.50
□ 64 Cecil Fielder SX	8.00	3.60
□ 65 Barry Bonds GZ	40.00	18.00
□ 66 Scott Servais BX	1.50	.70
□ 67 Ernie Young BX	1.50	.70
□ 68 Wilson Alvarez BX	1.50	.70
□ 69 Mike Grace BX	1.50	.70
□ 70 Shane Reynolds SX	5.00	2.20
□ 71 Henry Rodriguez SY	8.00	3.60
□ 72 Eric Karros BX	2.50	1.10
□ 73 Mark Langston BX	1.50	.70
□ 74 Scott Karl BX	1.50	.70
□ 75 Trevor Hoffman BX	2.50	1.10
□ 76 Orel Hershiser SX	8.00	3.60
□ 77 John Smoltz GY	12.00	5.50
□ 78 Raul Mondesi GZ	20.00	9.00
□ 79 Jeff Brantley BX	1.50	.70
□ 80 Donne Wall BX	1.50	.70
□ 81 Joey Cora BX	2.50	1.10
□ 82 Mel Rojas BX	1.50	.70
□ 83 Chad Mottola BX	1.50	.70
□ 84 Omar Vizquel BX	2.50	1.10
□ 85 Greg Maddux GZ	100.00	45.00
□ 86 Jamey Wright SY	5.00	2.20
□ 87 Chuck Finley BX	1.50	.70
□ 88 Brady Anderson GY	20.00	9.00
□ 89 Alex Gonzalez SX	5.00	2.20
□ 90 Andy Benes BX	2.50	1.10
□ 91 Reggie Jefferson BX	1.50	.70
□ 92 Paul O'Neill BY	2.50	1.10
□ 93 Javier Lopez SX	8.00	3.60
□ 94 Mark Grudzielanek SX	8.00	3.60
□ 95 Marc Newfield BX	1.50	.70
□ 96 Kevin Ritz BX	1.50	.70
□ 97 Fred McGriff GY	20.00	9.00
□ 98 Dwight Gooden SX	8.00	3.60
□ 99 Hideo Nomo SY	50.00	22.00
□ 100 Steve Finley BX	2.50	1.10
□ 101 Juan Gonzalez GZ	80.00	36.00
□ 102 Jay Buhner SZ	12.00	5.50
□ 103 Paul Wilson SY	5.00	2.20
□ 104 Alan Benes BY	2.50	1.10
□ 105 Manny Ramirez GZ	30.00	13.50
□ 106 Kevin Elster BX	1.50	.70
□ 107 Frank Thomas GZ	120.00	55.00
□ 108 Orlando Miller BX	1.50	.70
□ 109 Ramon Martinez BX	2.50	1.10
□ 110 Kenny Lofton GZ	40.00	18.00
□ 111 Bernie Williams GY	30.00	13.50
□ 112 Robby Thompson BX	1.50	.70
□ 113 Bernard Gilkey BZ	2.50	1.10
□ 114 Ray Durham BX	2.50	1.10
□ 115 Jeff Cirillo SZ	8.00	3.60
□ 116 Brian Jordan GZ	12.00	5.50
□ 117 Rich Becker SY	5.00	2.20
□ 118 Al Leiter BX	1.50	.70
□ 119 Mark Johnson BX	1.50	.70
□ 120 Ellis Burks BY	2.50	1.10
□ 121 Sammy Sosa GZ	30.00	13.50
□ 122 Willie Greene BX	2.50	1.10
□ 123 Michael Tucker BX	2.50	1.10
□ 124 Eddie Murray GY	40.00	18.00
□ 125 Joey Hamilton SY	8.00	3.60
□ 126 Antonio Osuna BX	1.50	.70
□ 127 Bobby Higginson SY	8.00	3.60
□ 128 Tomas Perez BX	1.50	.70
□ 129 Tim Salmon GZ	30.00	13.50
□ 130 Mark Wohlers BX	1.50	.70
□ 131 Charles Johnson SX	8.00	3.60
□ 132 Randy Johnson SY	20.00	9.00
□ 133 Brooks Kieschnick SX	5.00	2.20
□ 134 Al Martin SY	8.00	3.60
□ 135 Dante Bichette BX	2.50	1.10
□ 136 Andy Pettitte GZ	30.00	13.50
□ 137 Jason Giambi GY	12.00	5.50
□ 138 James Baldwin SX	5.00	2.20
□ 139 Ben McDonald BX	1.50	.70
□ 140 Shawn Green SX	8.00	3.60
□ 141 Geronimo Berroa BY	1.50	.70
□ 142 Jose Offerman BX	1.50	.70
□ 143 Curtis Pride BX	1.50	.70
□ 144 Terrell Wade BX	1.50	.70
□ 145 Ismael Valdes SX	8.00	3.60
□ 146 Mike Mussina SY	20.00	9.00
□ 147 Mariano Rivera SX	8.00	3.60
□ 148 Ken Hill BY	1.50	.70
□ 149 Darin Erstad GZ	40.00	18.00
□ 150 Jay Bell BX	2.50	1.10
□ 151 Mo Vaughn GZ	40.00	18.00
□ 152 Ozzie Smith GY	50.00	22.00
□ 153 Jose Mesa BX	2.50	1.10
□ 154 Osvaldo Fernandez BX	1.50	.70
□ 155 Vinny Castilla BY	2.50	1.10
□ 156 Jason Isringhausen SY	5.00	2.20
□ 157 B.J. Surhoff BX	1.50	.70
□ 158 Robert Perez BX	1.50	.70
□ 159 Ron Coomer BX	1.50	.70
□ 160 Darren Oliver BX	1.50	.70
□ 161 Mike Mohler BX	1.50	.70
□ 162 Russ Davis BX	1.50	.70
□ 163 Bret Boone BX	1.50	.70
□ 164 Ricky Bottalico BX	2.50	1.10
□ 165 Derek Jeter GZ	80.00	36.00
□ 166 Orlando Merced BX	1.50	.70
□ 167 John Valentin BX	2.50	1.10
□ 168 Andruw Jones GZ	60.00	27.00
□ 169 Angel Echevarria BX	1.50	.70

☐ 170 Todd Walker GZ 12.00 5.50
☐ 171 Desi Relaford BY 1.50 .70
☐ 172 Trey Beamon SX 5.00 2.20
☐ 173 Brian Giles SY 5.00 2.20
☐ 174 Scott Rolen GZ 60.00 27.00
☐ 175 Shannon Stewart SZ 8.00 3.60
☐ 176 Dmitri Young GZ 12.00 5.50
☐ 177 Justin Thompson BX 4.00 1.80
☐ 178 Trot Nixon SY 5.00 2.20
☐ 179 Josh Booty SY 12.00 5.50
☐ 180 Robin Jennings BX 1.50 .70
☐ 181 Marvin Benard BX 1.50 .70
☐ 182 Luis Castillo BY 2.50 1.10
☐ 183 Wendell Magee BX 1.50 .70
☐ 184 Vladimir Guerrero GX 80.00 36.00
☐ 185 Nomar Garciaparra GX 150.00 70.00
☐ 186 Ryan Hancock BX 1.50 .70
☐ 187 Mike Cameron SX 12.00 5.50
☐ 188 Cal Ripken LG BZ 25.00 11.00
☐ 189 Chipper Jones LG SZ 50.00 22.00
☐ 190 Albert Belle LG SZ 20.00 9.00
☐ 191 Mike Piazza LG BZ 20.00 9.00
☐ 192 Chuck Knoblauch LG SY 20.00 9.00
☐ 193 Ken Griffey Jr. LG BZ 30.00 13.50
☐ 194 Ivan Rodriguez LG GZ 40.00 18.00
☐ 195 Jose Canseco LG SX 12.00 5.50
☐ 196 Ryne Sandberg LG SX 30.00 13.50
☐ 197 Jim Thome LG GY 40.00 18.00
☐ 198 Andy Pettitte CL BY 6.00 2.70
☐ 199 Andruw Jones CL BY 12.00 5.50
☐ 200 Derek Jeter CL SY 50.00 22.00
☐ 201 Chipper Jones GX 250.00 110.00
☐ 202 Albert Belle GY 50.00 22.00
☐ 203 Mike Piazza GY 120.00 55.00
☐ 204 Ken Griffey Jr. GX 500.00 220.00
☐ 205 Ryne Sandberg GZ 40.00 18.00
☐ 206 Jose Canseco SY 12.00 5.50
☐ 207 Chili Davis BX 2.50 1.10
☐ 208 Roger Clemens GZ 60.00 27.00
☐ 209 Deion Sanders GZ 12.00 5.50
☐ 210 Darryl Hamilton BX 1.50 .70
☐ 211 Jermaine Dye SX 8.00 3.60
☐ 212 Matt Williams GY 20.00 9.00
☐ 213 Kevin Elster BX 1.50 .70
☐ 214 John Wetteland SX 8.00 3.60
☐ 215 Garret Anderson GZ 12.00 5.50
☐ 216 Kevin Brown GY 12.00 5.50
☐ 217 Matt Lawton SY 5.00 2.20
☐ 218 Cal Ripken GX 400.00 180.00
☐ 219 Moises Alou GY 12.00 5.50
☐ 220 Chuck Knoblauch GZ 30.00 13.50
☐ 221 Ivan Rodriguez GY 50.00 22.00
☐ 222 Travis Fryman BY 2.50 1.10
☐ 223 Jim Thome GZ 30.00 13.50
☐ 224 Eddie Murray SZ 15.00 6.75
☐ 225 Eric Young GZ 12.00 5.50
☐ 226 Ron Gant SX 8.00 3.60
☐ 227 Tony Phillips BX 1.50 .70
☐ 228 Reggie Sanders BY 2.50 1.10
☐ 229 Johnny Damon SZ 8.00 3.60
☐ 230 Bill Pulsipher BX 1.50 .70
☐ 231 Jim Edmonds GZ 20.00 9.00
☐ 232 Melvin Nieves BX 1.50 .70
☐ 233 Ryan Klesko GZ 20.00 9.00
☐ 234 David Cone SX 8.00 3.60
☐ 235 Derek Bell BY 2.50 1.10
☐ 236 Julio Franco SX 5.00 2.20
☐ 237 Juan Guzman BX 1.50 .70
☐ 238 Larry Walker GZ 30.00 13.50
☐ 239 Delino DeShields BX 1.50 .70
☐ 240 Troy Percival BY 1.50 .70
☐ 241 Andres Galarraga GZ 30.00 13.50
☐ 242 Rondell White GZ 12.00 5.50
☐ 243 John Burkett BX 1.50 .70
☐ 244 J.T. Snow BY 2.50 1.10
☐ 245 Alex Fernandez SY 8.00 3.60
☐ 246 Edgar Martinez GZ 20.00 9.00
☐ 247 Craig Biggio GZ 20.00 9.00
☐ 248 Todd Hundley GY 12.00 5.50
☐ 249 Jimmy Key SX 8.00 3.60
☐ 250 Cliff Floyd BY 1.50 .70
☐ 251 Jeff Conine BY 2.50 1.10
☐ 252 Curt Schilling BX 2.50 1.10
☐ 253 Jeff King BX 2.50 1.10
☐ 254 Tino Martinez GZ 30.00 13.50
☐ 255 Carlos Baerga SY 8.00 3.60
☐ 256 Jeff Fassero BY 1.50 .70
☐ 257 Dean Palmer SY 8.00 3.60
☐ 258 Robb Nen BX 2.50 1.10
☐ 259 Sandy Alomar Jr. SY 8.00 3.60
☐ 260 Carlos Perez BX 1.50 .70
☐ 261 Rickey Henderson SY 12.00 5.50
☐ 262 Bobby Bonilla SY 8.00 3.60
☐ 263 Darren Daulton BX 2.50 1.10
☐ 264 Jim Leyritz BX 1.50 .70
☐ 265 Dennis Martinez BX 1.50 .70
☐ 266 Butch Huskey BX 2.50 1.10
☐ 267 Joe Vitiello SY 5.00 2.20
☐ 268 Steve Trachsel BX 1.50 .70
☐ 269 Glenallen Hill BX 1.50 .70
☐ 270 Terry Steinbach BX 2.50 1.10
☐ 271 Mark McLemore BX 1.50 .70
☐ 272 Devon White BX 1.50 .70
☐ 273 Jeff Kent BX 2.50 1.10
☐ 274 Tim Raines BX 2.50 1.10
☐ 275 Carlos Garcia BX 1.50 .70
☐ 276 Hal Morris BX 1.50 .70
☐ 277 Gary Gaetti BX 1.50 .70
☐ 278 John Olerud SY 8.00 3.60
☐ 279 Wally Joyner BX 2.50 1.10
☐ 280 Brian Hunter SX 8.00 3.60
☐ 281 Steve Karsay BX 1.50 .70
☐ 282 Denny Neagle SX 8.00 3.60
☐ 283 Jose Herrera BX 1.50 .70
☐ 284 Todd Stottlemyre BX 1.50 .70
☐ 285 Bip Roberts SX 5.00 2.20
☐ 286 Kevin Seitzer BX 1.50 .70
☐ 287 Benji Gil BX 1.50 .70
☐ 288 Dennis Eckersley SX 8.00 3.60
☐ 289 Brad Ausmus BX 1.50 .70
☐ 290 Otis Nixon BX 1.50 .70
☐ 291 Darryl Strawberry BX 2.50 1.10
☐ 292 Marquis Grissom SY 8.00 3.60
☐ 293 Darryl Kile BX 2.50 1.10
☐ 294 Quilvio Veras BX 1.50 .70
☐ 295 Tom Goodwin BX 1.50 .70
☐ 296 Benito Santiago BX 1.50 .70
☐ 297 Mike Bordick BX 1.50 .70
☐ 298 Roberto Kelly BX 1.50 .70
☐ 299 David Justice GZ 30.00 13.50
☐ 300 Carl Everett BX 1.50 .70
☐ 301 Mark Whiten BX 1.50 .70
☐ 302 Aaron Sele BX 1.50 .70
☐ 303 Darren Dreifort BX 1.50 .70
☐ 304 Bobby Jones BX 1.50 .70
☐ 305 Fernando Vina BX 1.50 .70
☐ 306 Ed Sprague BX 1.50 .70
☐ 307 Andy Ashby SX 5.00 2.20
☐ 308 Tony Fernandez BX 1.50 .70
☐ 309 Roger Pavlik BX 1.50 .70
☐ 310 Mark Clark BX 1.50 .70
☐ 311 Mariano Duncan BX 1.50 .70
☐ 312 Tyler Houston BX 1.50 .70
☐ 313 Eric Davis SY 8.00 3.60
☐ 314 Greg Vaughn BY 1.50 .70
☐ 315 David Segui SY 5.00 2.20
☐ 316 Dave Nilsson SX 8.00 3.60
☐ 317 F.P. Santangelo SX 5.00 2.20
☐ 318 Wilton Guerrero GZ 8.00 3.60
☐ 319 Jose Guillen GZ 30.00 13.50
☐ 320 Kevin Orie SY 8.00 3.60
☐ 321 Derrek Lee GZ 20.00 9.00
☐ 322 Bubba Trammell SY 20.00 9.00
☐ 323 Pokey Reese GZ 8.00 3.60
☐ 324 Hideki Irabu GX 40.00 18.00
☐ 325 Scott Spiezio SZ 8.00 3.60
☐ 326 Bartolo Colon GZ 12.00 5.50
☐ 327 Damon Mashore SY 5.00 2.20
☐ 328 Ryan McGuire SY 5.00 2.20
☐ 329 Chris Carpenter BX 2.50 1.10
☐ 330 Jose Cruz Jr. GX 300.00 135.00
☐ 331 Todd Greene SZ 8.00 3.60
☐ 332 Brian Moehler BX 1.50 .70
☐ 333 Mike Sweeney BY 2.50 1.10
☐ 334 Neifi Perez GZ 12.00 5.50
☐ 335 Matt Morris SY 8.00 3.60
☐ 336 Marvin Benard BY 1.50 .70
☐ 337 Karim Garcia SZ 8.00 3.60
☐ 338 Jason Dickson SY 8.00 3.60
☐ 339 Brant Brown SY 5.00 2.20
☐ 340 Jeff Suppan SZ 8.00 3.60
☐ 341 Deivi Cruz BX 6.00 2.70
☐ 342 Antone Williamson GZ 8.00 3.60
☐ 343 Curtis Goodwin BX 1.50 .70
☐ 344 Brooks Kieschnick SY 5.00 2.20
☐ 345 Tony Womack BX 6.00 2.70
☐ 346 Rudy Pemberton BX 1.50 .70
☐ 347 Todd Dunwoody BX 6.00 2.70
☐ 348 Frank Thomas LG SY 80.00 36.00
☐ 349 Andruw Jones LG SX 50.00 22.00
☐ 350 Alex Rodriguez LG BY 20.00 9.00
☐ 351 Greg Maddux LG SY 60.00 27.00
☐ 352 Jeff Bagwell LG BX 12.00 5.50
☐ 353 Juan Gonzalez LG SY 50.00 22.00
☐ 354 Barry Bonds LG BY 8.00 3.60
☐ 355 Mark McGwire LG BY 12.00 5.50
☐ 356 Tony Gwynn LG BY 15.00 6.75
☐ 357 Gary Sheffield LG BX 6.00 2.70
☐ 358 Derek Jeter LG SX 60.00 27.00
☐ 359 Manny Ramirez LG SY 20.00 9.00
☐ 360 Hideo Nomo LG GZ 80.00 36.00
☐ 361 Sammy Sosa LG BX 6.00 2.70
☐ 362 Paul Molitor LG SZ 20.00 9.00
☐ 363 Kenny Lofton LG BY 8.00 3.60
☐ 364 Eddie Murray LG BX 8.00 3.60
☐ 365 Barry Larkin LG SZ 12.00 5.50
☐ 366 Roger Clemens LG SY 40.00 18.00
☐ 367 John Smoltz LG BZ 2.50 1.10
☐ 368 Alex Rodriguez GM SX 80.00 36.00
☐ 369 Frank Thomas GM BX 30.00 13.50
☐ 370 Cal Ripken GM SY 80.00 36.00
☐ 371 Ken Griffey Jr. GM SY 100.00 45.00
☐ 372 Greg Maddux GM BX 25.00 11.00
☐ 373 Mike Piazza GM SX 80.00 36.00
☐ 374 Chipper Jones GM BY 20.00 9.00
☐ 375 Albert Belle GM BX 10.00 4.50
☐ 376 Chuck Knoblauch GM BX 6.00 2.70
☐ 377 Brady Anderson GM BZ 2.50 1.10
☐ 378 David Justice GM SX 20.00 9.00
☐ 379 Randy Johnson GM BZ 6.00 2.70
☐ 380 Wade Boggs GM BX 6.00 2.70
☐ 381 Kevin Brown GM BX 2.50 1.10
☐ 382 Tom Glavine GM GY 12.00 5.50
☐ 383 Raul Mondesi GM SX 12.00 5.50
☐ 384 Ivan Rodriguez GM SX 30.00 13.50
☐ 385 Larry Walker GM BY 6.00 2.70
☐ 386 Bernie Williams GM BZ 6.00 2.70
☐ 387 Rusty Greer GM GY 12.00 5.50
☐ 388 Rafael Palmeiro GM GY 12.00 5.50
☐ 389 Matt Williams GM BX 4.00 1.80
☐ 390 Eric Young GM BX 2.50 1.10
☐ 391 Fred McGriff GM BX 4.00 1.80
☐ 392 Ken Caminiti GM BX 4.00 1.80
☐ 393 Roberto Alomar GM BZ 6.00 2.70
☐ 394 Brian Jordan GM BX 2.50 1.10
☐ 395 Mark Grace GM GZ 4.00 1.80
☐ 396 Jim Edmonds GM BY 4.00 1.80
☐ 397 Deion Sanders GM SY 8.00 3.60
☐ 398 Vladimir Guerrero CL SZ 25.00 11.00
☐ 399 Darin Erstad CL SY 25.00 11.00
☐ 400 Nomar Garciaparra CL SZ 40.00 18.00

1997 Leaf Fractal Matrix Die Cuts

This 200-card series 1 set is parallel to the regular set and features three different die-cut versions in three different finishes. Only 100 of the 200-card set are produced in the X-Axis cut with 75 of those bronze, 20 of those silver, and 5 of those gold. Only 60 of the 200-card set are available in type Y-Axis cut with 20 of those bronze, 30 silver, and 10 gold. Only 40 of the 200-card set are produced in the Z-Axis cut with 5 of those bronze, 10 of those silver and 25 of those gold. No card was available in more than one color nor in more than one die-cut version.

	MINT	NRMT
COMPLETE SET (400)	10000.00	4500.00
COMPLETE SERIES 1 (200)	5000.00	2200.00
COMPLETE SERIES 2 (200)	5000.00	2200.00
COMMON X-AXIS	6.00	2.70
COMMON Y-AXIS	10.00	4.50
COMMON Z-AXIS	15.00	6.75

☐ 1 Wade Boggs GY 60.00 27.00
☐ 2 Brian McRae BY 6.00 2.70
☐ 3 Jeff D'Amico BY 10.00 4.50
☐ 4 George Arias SY 10.00 4.50
☐ 5 Billy Wagner SY 15.00 6.75
☐ 6 Ray Lankford BZ 10.00 4.50
☐ 7 Will Clark SY 25.00 11.00
☐ 8 Edgar Renteria SY 15.00 6.75
☐ 9 Alex Ochoa SY 10.00 4.50
☐ 10 Roberto Hernandez BX 6.00 2.70
☐ 11 Joe Carter SY 15.00 6.75
☐ 12 Gregg Jefferies BY 6.00 2.70
☐ 13 Mark Grace SY 25.00 11.00
☐ 14 Roberto Alomar GY 60.00 27.00
☐ 15 Joe Randa BX 6.00 2.70
☐ 16 Alex Rodriguez GZ 200.00 90.00
☐ 17 Tony Gwynn GZ 150.00 70.00
☐ 18 Steve Gibralter BY 6.00 2.70
☐ 19 Scott Stahoviak BX 6.00 2.70
☐ 20 Matt Williams SZ 25.00 11.00
☐ 21 Quinton McCracken BY 6.00 2.70
☐ 22 Ugueth Urbina BX 6.00 2.70
☐ 23 Jermaine Allensworth SX 10.00 4.50
☐ 24 Paul Molitor GX 60.00 27.00
☐ 25 Carlos Delgado SY 15.00 6.75
☐ 26 Bob Abreu SY 15.00 6.75
☐ 27 John Jaha SY 15.00 6.75
☐ 28 Rusty Greer SZ 15.00 6.75
☐ 29 Kimera Bartee BX 6.00 2.70
☐ 30 Ruben Rivera SY 15.00 6.75
☐ 31 Jason Kendall SY 15.00 6.75
☐ 32 Lance Johnson BX 6.00 2.70
☐ 33 Robin Ventura BY 10.00 4.50
☐ 34 Kevin Appier SX 15.00 6.75
☐ 35 John Mabry SY 10.00 4.50
☐ 36 Ricky Otero BX 6.00 2.70
☐ 37 Mike Lansing BX 6.00 2.70

☐ 38 Mark McGwire GZ	120.00	55.00
☐ 39 Tim Naehring BX	6.00	2.70
☐ 40 Tom Glavine SZ	15.00	6.75
☐ 41 Rey Ordonez SY	15.00	6.75
☐ 42 Tony Clark SY	40.00	18.00
☐ 43 Rafael Palmeiro SZ	25.00	11.00
☐ 44 Pedro Martinez BX	25.00	11.00
☐ 45 Keith Lockhart BX	6.00	2.70
☐ 46 Dan Wilson BY	6.00	2.70
☐ 47 John Wetteland BY	10.00	4.50
☐ 48 Chan Ho Park BX	25.00	11.00
☐ 49 Gary Sheffield GZ	60.00	27.00
☐ 50 Shawn Estes BX	10.00	4.50
☐ 51 Royce Clayton BX	6.00	2.70
☐ 52 Jaime Navarro BX	6.00	2.70
☐ 53 Raul Casanova BX	6.00	2.70
☐ 54 Jeff Bagwell GZ	120.00	55.00
☐ 55 Barry Larkin GX	40.00	18.00
☐ 56 Charles Nagy BY	10.00	4.50
☐ 57 Ken Caminiti GY	40.00	18.00
☐ 58 Todd Hollandsworth SZ	10.00	4.50
☐ 59 Pat Hentgen SX	15.00	6.75
☐ 60 Jose Valentin BX	6.00	2.70
☐ 61 Frank Rodriguez BX	6.00	2.70
☐ 62 Mickey Tettleton BX	6.00	2.70
☐ 63 Marty Cordova GX	25.00	11.00
☐ 64 Cecil Fielder SX	15.00	6.75
☐ 65 Barry Bonds GZ	80.00	36.00
☐ 66 Scott Servais BX	6.00	2.70
☐ 67 Ernie Young BX	6.00	2.70
☐ 68 Wilson Alvarez BX	6.00	2.70
☐ 69 Mike Grace BX	6.00	2.70
☐ 70 Shane Reynolds SX	10.00	4.50
☐ 71 Henry Rodriguez SY	15.00	6.75
☐ 72 Eric Karros BX	10.00	4.50
☐ 73 Mark Langston BX	6.00	2.70
☐ 74 Scott Karl BX	6.00	2.70
☐ 75 Trevor Hoffman BX	10.00	4.50
☐ 76 Orel Hershiser SX	15.00	6.75
☐ 77 John Smoltz GY	25.00	11.00
☐ 78 Raul Mondesi GZ	25.00	11.00
☐ 79 Jeff Brantley BX	6.00	2.70
☐ 80 Donne Wall BX	6.00	2.70
☐ 81 Joey Cora BX	10.00	4.50
☐ 82 Mel Rojas BX	6.00	2.70
☐ 83 Chad Mottola BX	6.00	2.70
☐ 84 Omar Vizquel BX	10.00	4.50
☐ 85 Greg Maddux GZ	200.00	90.00
☐ 86 Jamey Wright SY	10.00	4.50
☐ 87 Chuck Finley BX	6.00	2.70
☐ 88 Brady Anderson GY	40.00	18.00
☐ 89 Alex Gonzalez SX	10.00	4.50
☐ 90 Andy Benes BX	10.00	4.50
☐ 91 Reggie Jefferson BX	6.00	2.70
☐ 92 Paul O'Neill BY	10.00	4.50
☐ 93 Javier Lopez SX	15.00	6.75
☐ 94 Mark Grudzielanek SX	15.00	6.75
☐ 95 Marc Newfield BX	6.00	2.70
☐ 96 Kevin Ritz BX	6.00	2.70
☐ 97 Fred McGriff GY	40.00	18.00
☐ 98 Dwight Gooden SX	15.00	6.75
☐ 99 Hideo Nomo SY	100.00	45.00
☐ 100 Steve Finley BX	10.00	4.50
☐ 101 Juan Gonzalez GZ	150.00	70.00
☐ 102 Jay Buhner SZ	25.00	11.00
☐ 103 Paul Wilson SY	10.00	4.50
☐ 104 Alan Benes BY	10.00	4.50
☐ 105 Manny Ramirez GZ	60.00	27.00
☐ 106 Kevin Elster BX	6.00	2.70
☐ 107 Frank Thomas GZ	250.00	110.00
☐ 108 Orlando Miller BX	6.00	2.70
☐ 109 Ramon Martinez BX	10.00	4.50
☐ 110 Kenny Lofton GZ	80.00	36.00
☐ 111 Bernie Williams GY	60.00	27.00
☐ 112 Robby Thompson BX	6.00	2.70
☐ 113 Bernard Gilkey BZ	10.00	4.50
☐ 114 Ray Durham BX	10.00	4.50
☐ 115 Jeff Cirillo SZ	15.00	6.75
☐ 116 Brian Jordan GZ	25.00	11.00
☐ 117 Rich Becker SY	10.00	4.50
☐ 118 Al Leiter BX	6.00	2.70
☐ 119 Mark Johnson BX	6.00	2.70
☐ 120 Ellis Burks BY	10.00	4.50
☐ 121 Sammy Sosa GZ	60.00	27.00
☐ 122 Willie Greene BX	10.00	4.50
☐ 123 Michael Tucker BX	10.00	4.50
☐ 124 Eddie Murray GY	60.00	27.00
☐ 125 Joey Hamilton SY	15.00	6.75
☐ 126 Antonio Osuna BX	6.00	2.70
☐ 127 Bobby Higginson SY	15.00	6.75
☐ 128 Tomas Perez BX	6.00	2.70
☐ 129 Tim Salmon GZ	60.00	27.00
☐ 130 Mark Wohlers BX	6.00	2.70
☐ 131 Charles Johnson SX	15.00	6.75
☐ 132 Randy Johnson SY	40.00	18.00
☐ 133 Brooks Kieschnick SX	10.00	4.50
☐ 134 Al Martin SY	15.00	6.75
☐ 135 Dante Bichette BX	10.00	4.50
☐ 136 Andy Pettitte GZ	60.00	27.00
☐ 137 Jason Giambi GY	25.00	11.00
☐ 138 James Baldwin SX	10.00	4.50
☐ 139 Ben McDonald BX	6.00	2.70
☐ 140 Shawn Green SX	15.00	6.75
☐ 141 Geronimo Berroa BY	6.00	2.70
☐ 142 Jose Offerman BX	6.00	2.70
☐ 143 Curtis Pride BX	6.00	2.70
☐ 144 Terrell Wade BX	6.00	2.70
☐ 145 Ismael Valdes SX	15.00	6.75
☐ 146 Mike Mussina SY	40.00	18.00
☐ 147 Mariano Rivera SX	15.00	6.75
☐ 148 Ken Hill BY	6.00	2.70
☐ 149 Darin Erstad GZ	80.00	36.00
☐ 150 Jay Bell BX	10.00	4.50
☐ 151 Mo Vaughn GZ	80.00	36.00
☐ 152 Ozzie Smith GY	50.00	22.00
☐ 153 Jose Mesa BX	10.00	4.50
☐ 154 Osvaldo Fernandez BX	6.00	2.70
☐ 155 Vinny Castilla BY	10.00	4.50
☐ 156 Jason Isringhausen SY	10.00	4.50
☐ 157 B.J. Surhoff BX	6.00	2.70
☐ 158 Robert Perez BX	6.00	2.70
☐ 159 Ron Coomer BX	6.00	2.70
☐ 160 Darren Oliver BX	6.00	2.70
☐ 161 Mike Mohler BX	6.00	2.70
☐ 162 Russ Davis BX	6.00	2.70
☐ 163 Bret Boone BX	6.00	2.70
☐ 164 Ricky Bottalico BX	10.00	4.50
☐ 165 Derek Jeter GZ	150.00	70.00
☐ 166 Orlando Merced BX	6.00	2.70
☐ 167 John Valentin BX	10.00	4.50
☐ 168 Andruw Jones GZ	120.00	55.00
☐ 169 Angel Echevarria BX	6.00	2.70
☐ 170 Todd Walker GZ	25.00	11.00
☐ 171 Desi Relaford BY	6.00	2.70
☐ 172 Trey Beamon SX	10.00	4.50
☐ 173 Brian Giles SY	10.00	4.50
☐ 174 Scott Rolen GZ	120.00	55.00
☐ 175 Shannon Stewart SZ	15.00	6.75
☐ 176 Dmitri Young GZ	25.00	11.00
☐ 177 Justin Thompson BX	15.00	6.75
☐ 178 Trot Nixon SY	10.00	4.50
☐ 179 Josh Booty SY	25.00	11.00
☐ 180 Robin Jennings BX	6.00	2.70
☐ 181 Marvin Benard BX	6.00	2.70
☐ 182 Luis Castillo BY	10.00	4.50
☐ 183 Wendell Magee BX	6.00	2.70
☐ 184 Vladimir Guerrero GX	40.00	18.00
☐ 185 Nomar Garciaparra GX	60.00	27.00
☐ 186 Ryan Hancock BX	6.00	2.70
☐ 187 Mike Cameron SX	25.00	11.00
☐ 188 Cal Ripken LGD BZ	250.00	110.00
☐ 189 Chipper Jones LGD SZ	150.00	70.00
☐ 190 Albert Belle LGD SZ	80.00	36.00
☐ 191 Mike Piazza LGD BZ	200.00	90.00
☐ 192 Chuck Knoblauch LGD SY	40.00	18.00
☐ 193 Ken Griffey Jr. LGD BZ	300.00	135.00
☐ 194 Ivan Rodriguez LGD GZ	80.00	36.00
☐ 195 Jose Canseco LGD SX	25.00	11.00
☐ 196 Ryne Sandberg LGD SX	30.00	13.50
☐ 197 Jim Thome LGD GY	60.00	27.00
☐ 198 Andy Pettitte CL BY	25.00	11.00
☐ 199 Andruw Jones CL BY	80.00	36.00
☐ 200 Derek Jeter CL SY	100.00	45.00
☐ 201 Chipper Jones GX	80.00	36.00
☐ 202 Albert Belle GY	50.00	22.00
☐ 203 Mike Piazza GY	120.00	55.00
☐ 204 Ken Griffey Jr. GX	120.00	55.00
☐ 205 Ryne Sandberg GZ	80.00	36.00
☐ 206 Jose Canseco SY	25.00	11.00
☐ 207 Chili Davis BX	10.00	4.50
☐ 208 Roger Clemens GZ	120.00	55.00
☐ 209 Deion Sanders GZ	25.00	11.00
☐ 210 Darryl Hamilton BX	6.00	2.70
☐ 211 Jermaine Dye SX	15.00	6.75
☐ 212 Matt Williams GY	40.00	18.00
☐ 213 Kevin Elster BX	6.00	2.70
☐ 214 John Wetteland SX	15.00	6.75
☐ 215 Garret Anderson GZ	25.00	11.00
☐ 216 Kevin Brown GY	25.00	11.00
☐ 217 Matt Lawton SY	10.00	4.50
☐ 218 Cal Ripken GX	100.00	45.00
☐ 219 Moises Alou GY	25.00	11.00
☐ 220 Chuck Knoblauch GZ	60.00	27.00
☐ 221 Ivan Rodriguez GY	50.00	22.00
☐ 222 Travis Fryman BY	10.00	4.50
☐ 223 Jim Thome GZ	60.00	27.00
☐ 224 Eddie Murray SZ	40.00	18.00
☐ 225 Eric Young GZ	25.00	11.00
☐ 226 Ron Gant SX	15.00	6.75
☐ 227 Tony Phillips BX	6.00	2.70
☐ 228 Reggie Sanders BY	10.00	4.50
☐ 229 Johnny Damon SZ	15.00	6.75
☐ 230 Bill Pulsipher BX	6.00	2.70
☐ 231 Jim Edmonds GZ	40.00	18.00
☐ 232 Melvin Nieves BX	6.00	2.70
☐ 233 Ryan Klesko GZ	40.00	18.00
☐ 234 David Cone SX	15.00	6.75
☐ 235 Derek Bell BY	10.00	4.50
☐ 236 Julio Franco SX	10.00	4.50
☐ 237 Juan Guzman BX	6.00	2.70
☐ 238 Larry Walker GZ	60.00	27.00
☐ 239 Delino DeShields BX	6.00	2.70
☐ 240 Troy Percival BY	6.00	2.70
☐ 241 Andres Galarraga GZ	60.00	27.00
☐ 242 Rondell White GZ	25.00	11.00
☐ 243 John Burkett BX	6.00	2.70
☐ 244 J.T. Snow BY	10.00	4.50
☐ 245 Alex Fernandez SY	15.00	6.75
☐ 246 Edgar Martinez GZ	40.00	18.00
☐ 247 Craig Biggio GZ	40.00	18.00
☐ 248 Todd Hundley GY	25.00	11.00
☐ 249 Jimmy Key SX	15.00	6.75
☐ 250 Cliff Floyd BY	6.00	2.70
☐ 251 Jeff Conine BY	10.00	4.50
☐ 252 Curt Schilling BX	10.00	4.50
☐ 253 Jeff King BX	10.00	4.50
☐ 254 Tino Martinez GZ	60.00	27.00
☐ 255 Carlos Baerga SY	15.00	6.75
☐ 256 Jeff Fassero BY	6.00	2.70
☐ 257 Dean Palmer SY	15.00	6.75
☐ 258 Robb Nen BX	10.00	4.50
☐ 259 Sandy Alomar Jr. SY	15.00	6.75
☐ 260 Carlos Perez BX	6.00	2.70
☐ 261 Rickey Henderson SY	25.00	11.00
☐ 262 Bobby Bonilla SY	15.00	6.75
☐ 263 Darren Daulton BX	10.00	4.50
☐ 264 Jim Leyritz BX	6.00	2.70
☐ 265 Dennis Martinez BX	6.00	2.70
☐ 266 Butch Huskey BX	10.00	4.50
☐ 267 Joe Vitiello SY	10.00	4.50
☐ 268 Steve Trachsel BX	6.00	2.70
☐ 269 Glenallen Hill BX	6.00	2.70
☐ 270 Terry Steinbach BX	10.00	4.50
☐ 271 Mark McLemore BX	6.00	2.70
☐ 272 Devon White BX	6.00	2.70
☐ 273 Jeff Kent BX	10.00	4.50
☐ 274 Tim Raines BX	10.00	4.50
☐ 275 Carlos Garcia BX	6.00	2.70
☐ 276 Hal Morris BX	6.00	2.70
☐ 277 Gary Gaetti BX	6.00	2.70
☐ 278 John Olerud SY	15.00	6.75
☐ 279 Wally Joyner BX	10.00	4.50
☐ 280 Brian Hunter SX	15.00	6.75
☐ 281 Steve Karsay BX	6.00	2.70
☐ 282 Denny Neagle SX	15.00	6.75
☐ 283 Jose Herrera BX	6.00	2.70
☐ 284 Todd Stottlemyre BX	6.00	2.70
☐ 285 Bip Roberts SX	10.00	4.50
☐ 286 Kevin Seitzer BX	6.00	2.70
☐ 287 Benji Gil BX	6.00	2.70
☐ 288 Dennis Eckersley SX	15.00	6.75
☐ 289 Brad Ausmus BX	6.00	2.70
☐ 290 Otis Nixon BX	6.00	2.70
☐ 291 Darryl Strawberry BX	10.00	4.50
☐ 292 Marquis Grissom SY	15.00	6.75
☐ 293 Darryl Kile BX	10.00	4.50
☐ 294 Quilvio Veras BX	6.00	2.70
☐ 295 Tom Goodwin BX	6.00	2.70
☐ 296 Benito Santiago BX	6.00	2.70
☐ 297 Mike Bordick BX	6.00	2.70
☐ 298 Roberto Kelly BX	6.00	2.70
☐ 299 David Justice GZ	60.00	27.00
☐ 300 Carl Everett BX	6.00	2.70
☐ 301 Mark Whiten BX	6.00	2.70
☐ 302 Aaron Sele BX	6.00	2.70
☐ 303 Darren Dreifort BX	6.00	2.70
☐ 304 Bobby Jones BX	6.00	2.70
☐ 305 Fernando Vina BX	6.00	2.70
☐ 306 Ed Sprague BX	6.00	2.70
☐ 307 Andy Ashby SX	10.00	4.50
☐ 308 Tony Fernandez BX	6.00	2.70
☐ 309 Roger Pavlik BX	6.00	2.70
☐ 310 Mark Clark BX	6.00	2.70
☐ 311 Mariano Duncan BX	6.00	2.70
☐ 312 Tyler Houston BX	6.00	2.70
☐ 313 Eric Davis SY	15.00	6.75
☐ 314 Greg Vaughn BY	6.00	2.70
☐ 315 David Segui SY	10.00	4.50
☐ 316 Dave Nilsson SX	15.00	6.75
☐ 317 F.P. Santangelo SX	10.00	4.50
☐ 318 Wilton Guerrero GZ	15.00	6.75
☐ 319 Jose Guillen GZ	60.00	27.00
☐ 320 Kevin Orie SY	15.00	6.75
☐ 321 Derrek Lee GZ	40.00	18.00
☐ 322 Bubba Trammell SY	40.00	18.00
☐ 323 Pokey Reese GZ	15.00	6.75
☐ 324 Hideki Irabu GX	15.00	6.75
☐ 325 Scott Spiezio SZ	15.00	6.75
☐ 326 Bartolo Colon GZ	25.00	11.00
☐ 327 Damon Mashore SY	10.00	4.50
☐ 328 Ryan McGuire SY	10.00	4.50

☐ 329 Chris Carpenter BX	10.00	4.50
☐ 330 Jose Cruz Jr. GX	100.00	45.00
☐ 331 Todd Greene SZ	15.00	6.75
☐ 332 Brian Moehler BX	6.00	2.70
☐ 333 Mike Sweeney BY	10.00	4.50
☐ 334 Neifi Perez GZ	25.00	11.00
☐ 335 Matt Morris SY	15.00	6.75
☐ 336 Marvin Benard BY	6.00	2.70
☐ 337 Karim Garcia SZ	15.00	6.75
☐ 338 Jason Dickson SY	15.00	6.75
☐ 339 Brant Brown SY	10.00	4.50
☐ 340 Jeff Suppan SZ	15.00	6.75
☐ 341 Deivi Cruz BX	25.00	11.00
☐ 342 Antone Williamson GZ	15.00	6.75
☐ 343 Curtis Goodwin BX	6.00	2.70
☐ 344 Brooks Kieschnick SY	10.00	4.50
☐ 345 Tony Womack BX	25.00	11.00
☐ 346 Rudy Pemberton BX	6.00	2.70
☐ 347 Todd Dunwoody BX	25.00	11.00
☐ 348 Frank Thomas LG SY	150.00	70.00
☐ 349 Andruw Jones LG SX	50.00	22.00
☐ 350 Alex Rodriguez LG BY	120.00	55.00
☐ 351 Greg Maddux LG SY	120.00	55.00
☐ 352 Jeff Bagwell LG BY	80.00	36.00
☐ 353 Juan Gonzalez LG SY	100.00	45.00
☐ 354 Barry Bonds LG BY	50.00	22.00
☐ 355 Mark McGwire LG BY	80.00	36.00
☐ 356 Tony Gwynn LG BY	100.00	45.00
☐ 357 Gary Sheffield LG BX	25.00	11.00
☐ 358 Derek Jeter LG SX	60.00	27.00
☐ 359 Manny Ramirez LG SY	40.00	18.00
☐ 360 Hideo Nomo LG GZ	200.00	90.00
☐ 361 Sammy Sosa LG BX	25.00	11.00
☐ 362 Paul Molitor LG SZ	40.00	18.00
☐ 363 Kenny Lofton LG BY	50.00	22.00
☐ 364 Eddie Murray LG BX	25.00	11.00
☐ 365 Barry Larkin LG SZ	25.00	11.00
☐ 366 Roger Clemens LG SY	80.00	36.00
☐ 367 John Smoltz LG BZ	10.00	4.50
☐ 368 Alex Rodriguez GM SX	80.00	36.00
☐ 369 Frank Thomas GM BX	100.00	45.00
☐ 370 Cal Ripken GM SY	150.00	70.00
☐ 371 Ken Griffey Jr. GM SY	200.00	90.00
☐ 372 Greg Maddux GM BX	80.00	36.00
☐ 373 Mike Piazza GM SX	80.00	36.00
☐ 374 Chipper Jones GM BY	100.00	45.00
☐ 375 Albert Belle GM BX	30.00	13.50
☐ 376 Chuck Knoblauch GM BX	25.00	11.00
☐ 377 Brady Anderson GM BZ	10.00	4.50
☐ 378 David Justice GM SX	40.00	18.00
☐ 379 Randy Johnson GM BZ	25.00	11.00
☐ 380 Wade Boggs GM BX	25.00	11.00
☐ 381 Kevin Brown GM BX	10.00	4.50
☐ 382 Tom Glavine GM GY	25.00	11.00
☐ 383 Raul Mondesi GM SX	25.00	11.00
☐ 384 Ivan Rodriguez GM SX	30.00	13.50
☐ 385 Larry Walker GM BY	25.00	11.00
☐ 386 Bernie Williams GM BZ	25.00	11.00
☐ 387 Rusty Greer GM GY	25.00	11.00
☐ 388 Rafael Palmeiro GM GY	25.00	11.00
☐ 389 Matt Williams GM BX	15.00	6.75
☐ 390 Eric Young GM BX	10.00	4.50
☐ 391 Fred McGriff GM BX	15.00	6.75
☐ 392 Ken Caminiti GM BX	15.00	6.75
☐ 393 Roberto Alomar GM BZ	25.00	11.00
☐ 394 Brian Jordan GM BX	10.00	4.50
☐ 395 Mark Grace GM GZ	15.00	6.75
☐ 396 Jim Edmonds GM BY	15.00	6.75
☐ 397 Deion Sanders GM SY	15.00	6.75
☐ 398 Vladimir Guerrero CL SZ	100.00	45.00
☐ 399 Darin Erstad CL SY	50.00	22.00
☐ 400 Nomar Garciaparra CL SZ	150.00	70.00

1997 Leaf Banner Season

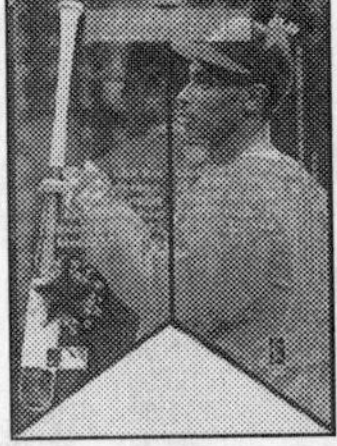

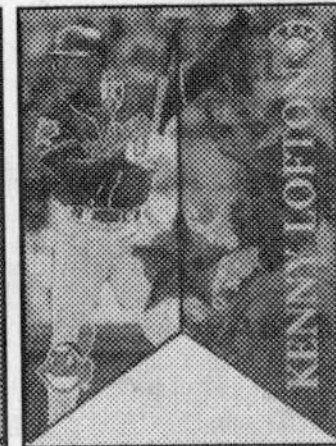

Randomly inserted in series one magazine packs, this 15-card set features color action player photos on die-cut cards and is printed on canvas card stock. Only 2500 of each card was produced and are sequentially numbered.

	MINT	NRMT
COMPLETE SET (15)	250.00	110.00
COMMON CARD (1-15)	4.00	1.80
☐ 1 Jeff Bagwell	20.00	9.00
☐ 2 Ken Griffey Jr.	60.00	27.00
☐ 3 Juan Gonzalez	25.00	11.00
☐ 4 Frank Thomas	50.00	22.00
☐ 5 Alex Rodriguez	30.00	13.50
☐ 6 Kenny Lofton	12.00	5.50
☐ 7 Chuck Knoblauch	8.00	3.60
☐ 8 Mo Vaughn	12.00	5.50
☐ 9 Chipper Jones	30.00	13.50
☐ 10 Ken Caminiti	8.00	3.60
☐ 11 Craig Biggio	6.00	2.70
☐ 12 John Smoltz	5.00	2.20
☐ 13 Pat Hentgen	5.00	2.20
☐ 14 Derek Jeter	25.00	11.00
☐ 15 Todd Hollandsworth	4.00	1.80

1997 Leaf Dress for Success

Randomly inserted in series one retail packs, this 18-card retail only set features color player photos prined on a jersey-simulated, nylon card stock and is accented with flocking on the team logo and gold-foil stamping. Only 3,500 of each card were produced and are sequentially numbered.

	MINT	NRMT
COMPLETE SET (18)	300.00	135.00
COMMON CARD (1-18)	4.00	1.80
☐ 1 Greg Maddux	25.00	11.00
☐ 2 Cal Ripken	30.00	13.50
☐ 3 Albert Belle	10.00	4.50
☐ 4 Frank Thomas	30.00	13.50
☐ 5 Dante Bichette	5.00	2.20
☐ 6 Gary Sheffield	6.00	2.70
☐ 7 Jeff Bagwell	15.00	6.75
☐ 8 Mike Piazza	25.00	11.00
☐ 9 Mark McGwire	15.00	6.75
☐ 10 Ken Caminiti	6.00	2.70
☐ 11 Alex Rodriguez	25.00	11.00
☐ 12 Ken Griffey Jr.	40.00	18.00
☐ 13 Juan Gonzalez	20.00	9.00
☐ 14 Brian Jordan	4.00	1.80
☐ 15 Mo Vaughn	10.00	4.50
☐ 16 Ivan Rodriguez	10.00	4.50
☐ 17 Andruw Jones	15.00	6.75
☐ 18 Chipper Jones	25.00	11.00

1997 Leaf Get-A-Grip

Randomly inserted in series one hobby packs, this 16-card double player insert set features color player photos of some of the current top pitchers matched against some of the league's current power hitters. The set is printed on full-silver, ploy-laminated card stock with gold-foil stamping. Only 3,500 of each card was produced and are sequentially numbered.

	MINT	NRMT
COMPLETE SET (16)	250.00	110.00
COMMON CARD (1-16)	6.00	2.70
☐ 1 Ken Griffey Jr. / Greg Maddux	40.00	18.00
☐ 2 John Smoltz / Frank Thomas	25.00	11.00
☐ 3 Mike Piazza / Andy Pettitte	25.00	11.00
☐ 4 Randy Johnson / Chipper Jones	25.00	11.00
☐ 5 Tom Glavine / Alex Rodriguez	30.00	13.50
☐ 6 Pat Hentgen / Jeff Bagwell	12.00	5.50
☐ 7 Kevin Brown / Juan Gonzalez	15.00	6.75
☐ 8 Barry Bonds / Mike Mussina	10.00	4.50
☐ 9 Hideo Nomo / Albert Belle	15.00	6.75
☐ 10 Troy Percival / Andruw Jones	15.00	6.75
☐ 11 Roger Clemens / Brian Jordan	10.00	4.50

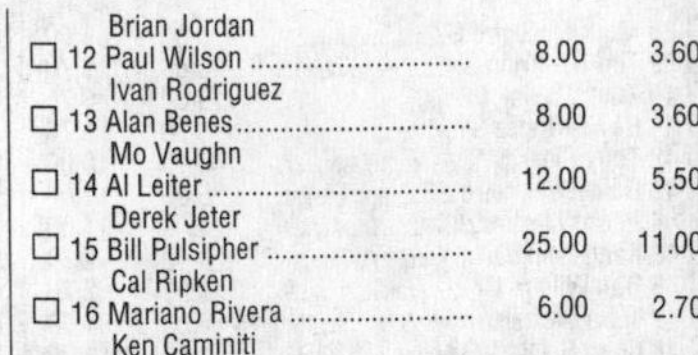

☐ 12 Paul Wilson / Ivan Rodriguez	8.00	3.60
☐ 13 Alan Benes / Mo Vaughn	8.00	3.60
☐ 14 Al Leiter / Derek Jeter	12.00	5.50
☐ 15 Bill Pulsipher / Cal Ripken	25.00	11.00
☐ 16 Mariano Rivera / Ken Caminiti	6.00	2.70

1997 Leaf Gold Stars

Randomly inserted in series two packs, this 36-card set features color action images of some of Baseball's hottest names with actual 24kt. gold foil stamping. Only 2,500 of each card were produced and are sequentially numbered.

	MINT	NRMT
COMPLETE SET (36)	600.00	275.00
COMMON CARD (1-36)	8.00	3.60
☐ 1 Frank Thomas	50.00	22.00
☐ 2 Alex Rodriguez	40.00	18.00
☐ 3 Ken Griffey Jr.	60.00	27.00
☐ 4 Andruw Jones	25.00	11.00
☐ 5 Chipper Jones	40.00	18.00
☐ 6 Jeff Bagwell	25.00	11.00
☐ 7 Derek Jeter	30.00	13.50
☐ 8 Deion Sanders	10.00	4.50
☐ 9 Ivan Rodriguez	15.00	6.75
☐ 10 Juan Gonzalez	30.00	13.50
☐ 11 Greg Maddux	40.00	18.00
☐ 12 Andy Pettitte	12.00	5.50
☐ 13 Roger Clemens	25.00	11.00
☐ 14 Hideo Nomo	30.00	13.50
☐ 15 Tony Gwynn	30.00	13.50
☐ 16 Barry Bonds	15.00	6.75
☐ 17 Kenny Lofton	15.00	6.75
☐ 18 Paul Molitor	12.00	5.50
☐ 19 Jim Thome	12.00	5.50
☐ 20 Albert Belle	15.00	6.75
☐ 21 Cal Ripken	50.00	22.00
☐ 22 Mark McGwire	25.00	11.00
☐ 23 Barry Larkin	10.00	4.50
☐ 24 Mike Piazza	40.00	18.00
☐ 25 Darin Erstad	15.00	6.75
☐ 26 Chuck Knoblauch	12.00	5.50
☐ 27 Vladimir Guerrero	20.00	9.00
☐ 28 Tony Clark	12.00	5.50
☐ 29 Scott Rolen	25.00	11.00
☐ 30 Nomar Garciaparra	20.00	9.00
☐ 31 Eric Young	8.00	3.60
☐ 32 Ryne Sandberg	15.00	6.75
☐ 33 Roberto Alomar	12.00	5.50
☐ 34 Eddie Murray	12.00	5.50
☐ 35 Rafael Palmeiro	10.00	4.50
☐ 36 Jose Guillen	12.00	5.50

1997 Leaf Knot-Hole Gang

This 12-card insert set features color action player photos printed on wooden card stock. The die-cut card resembles a wooden fence with the player being seen in action through a knot hole. Only 5,000 of this set was produced and is sequentially numbered. In addition, a promo card featuring Ryan Klesko was distributed to dealers with ordering forms for the product.

	MINT	NRMT
OMPLETE SET (12)	150.00	70.00
OMMON CARD (1-12)	3.00	1.35
☐ 1 Chuck Knoblauch	6.00	2.70
☐ 2 Ken Griffey Jr.	30.00	13.50
☐ 3 Frank Thomas	25.00	11.00
☐ 4 Tony Gwynn	15.00	6.75
☐ 5 Mike Piazza	20.00	9.00
☐ 6 Jeff Bagwell	12.00	5.50
☐ 7 Rusty Greer	3.00	1.35
☐ 8 Cal Ripken	25.00	11.00
☐ 9 Chipper Jones	20.00	9.00
☐ 10 Ryan Klesko	5.00	2.20
☐ 11 Barry Larkin	5.00	2.20
☐ 12 Paul Molitor	6.00	2.70
☐ P10 Ryan Klesko Promo	2.00	.90

1997 Leaf Leagues of the Nation

Randomly inserted in series two packs, this 15-card set celebrates the first season of interleague play with double-sided, die-cut cards that highlight some of the best interleague match-ups. Using flocking technology, the cards display color action player photos with the place and date of the game where the match-up between the pictured players took place. Only 2,500 of each card were produced and are sequentially numbered.

	MINT	NRMT
OMPLETE SET (15)	350.00	160.00
OMMON CARD (1-15)	10.00	4.50
☐ 1 Juan Gonzalez Barry Bonds	25.00	11.00
☐ 2 Cal Ripken Chipper Jones	40.00	18.00
☐ 3 Mark McGwire Ken Caminiti	20.00	9.00
☐ 4 Derek Jeter Kenny Lofton	25.00	11.00
☐ 5 Ivan Rodriguez Mike Piazza	30.00	13.50
☐ 6 Ken Griffey Jr. Larry Walker	60.00	27.00
☐ 7 Frank Thomas Sammy Sosa	40.00	18.00
☐ 8 Paul Molitor Barry Larkin	10.00	4.50
☐ 9 Albert Belle Deion Sanders	12.00	5.50
☐ 10 Matt Williams Jeff Bagwell	20.00	9.00
☐ 11 Mo Vaughn Gary Sheffield	12.00	5.50
☐ 12 Alex Rodriguez Tony Gwynn	40.00	18.00
☐ 13 Tino Martinez Scott Rolen	20.00	9.00
☐ 14 Darin Erstad Wilton Guerrero	12.00	5.50
☐ 15 Tony Clark Vladimir Guerrero	20.00	9.00

1997 Leaf Statistical Standouts

his 15-card insert set showcases some of the league's tatistical leaders and is printed on full-leather, die-cut, oil-stamped card stock. The player's statistics are isplayed beside a color player photo. Only 1,000 of this et were produced and are sequentially numbered.

	MINT	NRMT
OMPLETE SET (15)	1000.00	450.00
OMMON CARD (1-15)	15.00	6.75
☐ 1 Albert Belle	40.00	18.00
☐ 2 Juan Gonzalez	80.00	36.00
☐ 3 Ken Griffey Jr.	150.00	70.00
☐ 4 Alex Rodriguez	100.00	45.00

	MINT	NRMT
☐ 5 Frank Thomas	120.00	55.00
☐ 6 Chipper Jones	80.00	36.00
☐ 7 Greg Maddux	100.00	45.00
☐ 8 Mike Piazza	100.00	45.00
☐ 9 Cal Ripken	120.00	55.00
☐ 10 Mark McGwire	60.00	27.00
☐ 11 Barry Bonds	40.00	18.00
☐ 12 Derek Jeter	80.00	36.00
☐ 13 Ken Caminiti	25.00	11.00
☐ 14 John Smoltz	15.00	6.75
☐ 15 Paul Molitor	30.00	13.50

1997 Leaf Thomas Collection

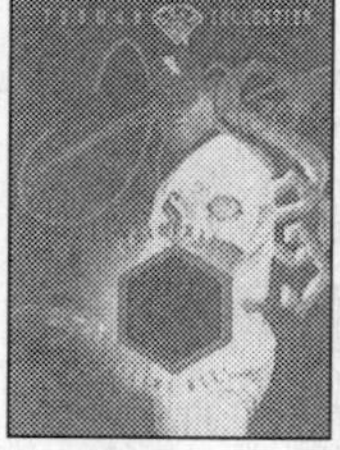

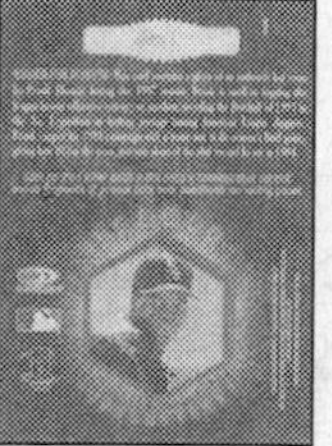

Randomly inserted in series two packs, this six-card set commemorates the multi-faceted talents of first baseman Frank Thomas with actual pieces of his game-used hats, jerseys (home and away), sweatbands, batting gloves or bats embedded in the cards. Only 100 of each card were produced and are sequentially numbered.

	MINT	NRMT
COMPLETE SET (6)	2500.00	1100.00
COMMON CARD (1-6)	400.00	180.00
☐ 1 Frank Thomas Game Hat/Blue Text	400.00	180.00
☐ 2 Frank Thomas Home Jersey/Orange Text	500.00	220.00
☐ 3 Frank Thomas Batting Glove/Yellow Text	400.00	180.00
☐ 4 Frank Thomas Bat/Green Text	400.00	180.00
☐ 5 Frank Thomas Sweatband/Purple Text	400.00	180.00
☐ 6 Frank Thomas Away Jersey/Red Text	500.00	220.00

1997 Leaf Warning Track

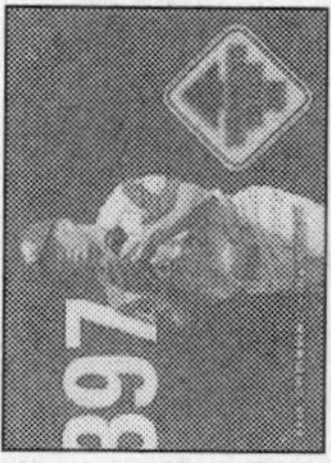

Randomly inserted in series two packs, this 18-card set features color action photos of outstanding outfielders printed on embossed canvas card stock. Only 3,500 of each card were produced and are sequentially numbered.

	MINT	NRMT
COMPLETE SET (18)	120.00	55.00
COMMON CARD (1-18)	3.00	1.35
☐ 1 Ken Griffey Jr.	30.00	13.50
☐ 2 Albert Belle	8.00	3.60
☐ 3 Barry Bonds	8.00	3.60
☐ 4 Andruw Jones	12.00	5.50
☐ 5 Kenny Lofton	8.00	3.60
☐ 6 Tony Gwynn	15.00	6.75
☐ 7 Manny Ramirez	6.00	2.70
☐ 8 Rusty Greer	4.00	1.80
☐ 9 Bernie Williams	6.00	2.70
☐ 10 Gary Sheffield	6.00	2.70
☐ 11 Juan Gonzalez	15.00	6.75
☐ 12 Raul Mondesi	6.00	2.70
☐ 13 Brady Anderson	5.00	2.20
☐ 14 Rondell White	3.00	1.35
☐ 15 Sammy Sosa	6.00	2.70
☐ 16 Deion Sanders	6.00	2.70
☐ 17 Dave Justice	6.00	2.70
☐ 18 Jim Edmonds	6.00	2.70

1997 Leaf Thomas Info

This card was put into the front of every 12 card Leaf Blister pack. The front has an action photo of Thomas while the back explains more about the 97 Leaf Product. The card is a stand alone and not inserted in the unopened part of the pack. The blister pack retailed for $2.99,

	MINT	NRMT
COMPLETE SET (1)	1.00	.45
COMMON CARD (1)	1.00	.45
☐ 1 Frank Thomas	1.00	.45

1997 Leaf Thomas Leukemia

This four-card set was produced by Donruss for the Frank Thomas Charitable Foundation. The cards feature borderless color photos of Frank Thomas, who lost a sister to Leukemia, with other people who have some connection to the illness. The back of card #1 displays a portrait of a Leukemia victim. All proceeds from the sale of the set went to the Foundation. The cards could be ordered by mail from Big Heart Charity Card for $20 each. Only 2500 of each card was produced and are sequentially numbered.

	MINT	NRMT
COMPLETE SET (4)	100.00	45.00
COMMON CARD (1-4)	25.00	11.00
☐ 1 Frank Thomas Rod Carew Michelle Carew(on back)	30.00	13.50
☐ 2 Frank Thomas Portrait Photo	25.00	11.00
☐ 3 Frank Thomas Facing Right	25.00	11.00
☐ 4 Frank Thomas Facing Front	25.00	11.00

1994 Leaf Limited

This 160-card standard-size set was issued exclusively to hobby dealers. The fronts display silver holographic Spectra Tech foiling and a silhouetted player action photo over full silver foil. The backs contain silver holographic Spectra Tech foil, two photos, and a quote about the player by well-known baseball personalities. The set is organized alphabetically within teams with AL preceding NL.

	MINT	NRMT
COMPLETE SET (160)	100.00	45.00
COMMON CARD (1-160)	.50	.23

□ 1 Jeffrey Hammonds .75 .35
□ 2 Ben McDonald .50 .23
□ 3 Mike Mussina 2.00 .90
□ 4 Rafael Palmeiro 1.25 .55
□ 5 Cal Ripken Jr. 8.00 3.60
□ 6 Lee Smith .75 .35
□ 7 Roger Clemens 4.00 1.80
□ 8 Scott Cooper .50 .23
□ 9 Andre Dawson 1.25 .55
□ 10 Mike Greenwell .50 .23
□ 11 Aaron Sele .50 .23
□ 12 Mo Vaughn 2.50 1.10
□ 13 Brian Anderson 1.25 .55
□ 14 Chad Curtis .50 .23
□ 15 Chili Davis .75 .35
□ 16 Gary DiSarcina .50 .23
□ 17 Mark Langston .50 .23
□ 18 Tim Salmon 2.00 .90
□ 19 Wilson Alvarez .75 .35
□ 20 Jason Bere .50 .23
□ 21 Julio Franco .75 .35
□ 22 Jack McDowell .50 .23
□ 23 Tim Raines .50 .23
□ 24 Frank Thomas 8.00 3.60
□ 25 Robin Ventura .75 .35
□ 26 Carlos Baerga .75 .35
□ 27 Albert Belle 2.50 1.10
□ 28 Kenny Lofton 2.50 1.10
□ 29 Eddie Murray 2.00 .90
□ 30 Manny Ramirez 2.50 1.10
□ 31 Cecil Fielder .75 .35
□ 32 Travis Fryman .75 .35
□ 33 Mickey Tettleton .50 .23
□ 34 Alan Trammell 1.25 .55
□ 35 Lou Whitaker .75 .35
□ 36 David Cone .75 .35
□ 37 Gary Gaetti .75 .35
□ 38 Greg Gagne .50 .23
□ 39 Bob Hamelin .50 .23
□ 40 Wally Joyner .75 .35
□ 41 Brian McRae .50 .23
□ 42 Ricky Bones .50 .23
□ 43 Brian Harper .50 .23
□ 44 John Jaha .50 .23
□ 45 Pat Listach .50 .23
□ 46 Dave Nilsson .75 .35
□ 47 Greg Vaughn .50 .23
□ 48 Kent Hrbek .75 .35
□ 49 Chuck Knoblauch 2.00 .90
□ 50 Shane Mack .50 .23
□ 51 Kirby Puckett 4.00 1.80
□ 52 Dave Winfield 1.25 .55
□ 53 Jim Abbott .50 .23
□ 54 Wade Boggs 2.00 .90
□ 55 Jimmy Key .75 .35
□ 56 Don Mattingly 3.00 1.35
□ 57 Paul O'Neill .75 .35
□ 58 Danny Tartabull .50 .23
□ 59 Dennis Eckersley 1.25 .55
□ 60 Rickey Henderson 1.25 .55
□ 61 Mark McGwire 4.00 1.80
□ 62 Troy Neel .50 .23
□ 63 Ruben Sierra .50 .23
□ 64 Eric Anthony .50 .23
□ 65 Jay Buhner 1.25 .55
□ 66 Ken Griffey Jr. 10.00 4.50
□ 67 Randy Johnson 2.00 .90
□ 68 Edgar Martinez 1.25 .55
□ 69 Tino Martinez 2.00 .90
□ 70 Jose Canseco 1.25 .55
□ 71 Will Clark 1.25 .55
□ 72 Juan Gonzalez 5.00 2.20
□ 73 Dean Palmer .75 .35
□ 74 Ivan Rodriguez 2.50 1.10
□ 75 Roberto Alomar 2.00 .90
□ 76 Joe Carter 1.25 .55
□ 77 Carlos Delgado 2.00 .90
□ 78 Paul Molitor 2.00 .90
□ 79 John Olerud .50 .23
□ 80 Devon White .50 .23
□ 81 Steve Avery .50 .23
□ 82 Tom Glavine 1.25 .55
□ 83 David Justice 2.00 .90
□ 84 Roberto Kelly .50 .23
□ 85 Ryan Klesko 1.25 .55
□ 86 Javier Lopez 1.25 .55
□ 87 Greg Maddux 6.00 2.70
□ 88 Fred McGriff 1.25 .55
□ 89 Shawon Dunston .50 .23
□ 90 Mark Grace 1.25 .55
□ 91 Derrick May .50 .23
□ 92 Sammy Sosa 2.00 .90
□ 93 Rick Wilkins .50 .23
□ 94 Bret Boone .50 .23
□ 95 Barry Larkin 1.25 .55
□ 96 Kevin Mitchell .50 .23
□ 97 Hal Morris .50 .23
□ 98 Deion Sanders 2.00 .90
□ 99 Reggie Sanders .50 .23
□ 100 Dante Bichette 1.25 .55
□ 101 Ellis Burks .75 .35
□ 102 Andres Galarraga 1.25 .55
□ 103 Joe Girardi .50 .23
□ 104 Charlie Hayes .50 .23
□ 105 Chuck Carr .50 .23
□ 106 Jeff Conine .75 .35
□ 107 Bryan Harvey .50 .23
□ 108 Benito Santiago .50 .23
□ 109 Gary Sheffield 2.00 .90
□ 110 Jeff Bagwell 4.00 1.80
□ 111 Craig Biggio 1.25 .55
□ 112 Ken Caminiti 2.00 .90
□ 113 Andujar Cedeno .50 .23
□ 114 Doug Drabek .50 .23
□ 115 Luis Gonzalez .50 .23
□ 116 Brett Butler .75 .35
□ 117 Delino DeShields .50 .23
□ 118 Eric Karros .75 .35
□ 119 Raul Mondesi 2.00 .90
□ 120 Mike Piazza 6.00 2.70
□ 121 Henry Rodriguez .50 .23
□ 122 Tim Wallach .50 .23
□ 123 Moises Alou .75 .35
□ 124 Cliff Floyd .75 .35
□ 125 Marquis Grissom .75 .35
□ 126 Ken Hill .50 .23
□ 127 Larry Walker 2.00 .90
□ 128 John Wetteland .75 .35
□ 129 Bobby Bonilla .75 .35
□ 130 John Franco .75 .35
□ 131 Jeff Kent .50 .23
□ 132 Bret Saberhagen .50 .23
□ 133 Ryan Thompson .50 .23
□ 134 Darren Daulton .75 .35
□ 135 Mariano Duncan .50 .23
□ 136 Lenny Dykstra .75 .35
□ 137 Danny Jackson .50 .23
□ 138 John Kruk .75 .35
□ 139 Jay Bell .75 .35
□ 140 Jeff King .75 .35
□ 141 Al Martin .50 .23
□ 142 Orlando Merced .50 .23
□ 143 Andy Van Slyke .75 .35
□ 144 Bernard Gilkey .50 .23
□ 145 Gregg Jefferies .75 .35
□ 146 Ray Lankford 1.25 .55
□ 147 Ozzie Smith 2.50 1.10
□ 148 Mark Whiten .50 .23
□ 149 Todd Zeile .50 .23
□ 150 Derek Bell .75 .35
□ 151 Andy Benes .75 .35
□ 152 Tony Gwynn 5.00 2.20
□ 153 Phil Plantier .50 .23
□ 154 Bip Roberts .50 .23
□ 155 Rod Beck .75 .35
□ 156 Barry Bonds 2.50 1.10
□ 157 John Burkett .50 .23
□ 158 Royce Clayton .75 .35
□ 159 Bill Swift .50 .23
□ 160 Matt Williams 1.25 .55

1994 Leaf Limited Gold All-Stars

Randomly inserted in packs at a rate of one in seven, this 18-card standard-size set features the starting players at each position in both the National and American leagues for the 1994 All-Star Game. They are identical in design to the basic Limited product except for being gold and individually numbered out of 10,000.

	MINT	NRMT
COMPLETE SET (18)	175.00	80.00
COMMON CARD (1-18)	3.00	1.35

□ 1 Frank Thomas 40.00 18.00
□ 2 Gregg Jefferies 4.00 1.80
□ 3 Roberto Alomar 8.00 3.60
□ 4 Mariano Duncan 3.00 1.35

□ 5 Wade Boggs 6.00 2.70
□ 6 Matt Williams 6.00 2.70
□ 7 Cal Ripken Jr. 30.00 13.50
□ 8 Ozzie Smith 10.00 4.50
□ 9 Kirby Puckett 15.00 6.75
□ 10 Barry Bonds 10.00 4.50
□ 11 Ken Griffey Jr. 40.00 18.00
□ 12 Tony Gwynn 15.00 6.75
□ 13 Joe Carter 6.00 2.70
□ 14 David Justice 8.00 3.60
□ 15 Ivan Rodriguez 10.00 4.50
□ 16 Mike Piazza 25.00 11.00
□ 17 Jimmy Key 4.00 1.80
□ 18 Greg Maddux 25.00 11.00

1994 Leaf Limited Rookies

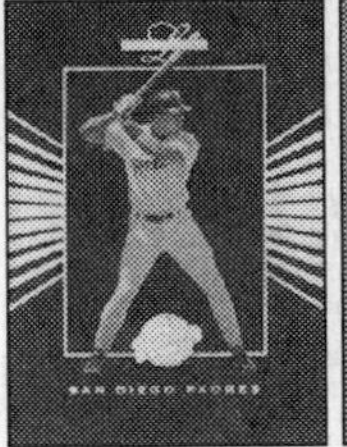

This 80-card standard-size set was issued exclusively to hobby dealers. The set showcases top rookies and prospects of 1994. The fronts display silver holographic Spectra Tech foiling and a silhouetted player action photo over full silver foil. The word "Rookies" appears in black letters above the Leaf Limited logo at top. The backs contain silver holographic Spectra Tech foil, two photos and a quote about the player by well-known baseball personalities. Rookie Cards in this set include Kurt Ho Park, Rusty Greer, Bill VanLandingham and Ismael Valdes

	MINT	NRMT
COMPLETE SET (80)	25.00	11.00
COMMON CARD (1-80)	.40	.18

□ 1 Charles Johnson 1.50 .70
□ 2 Rico Brogna .40 .18
□ 3 Melvin Nieves .40 .18
□ 4 Rich Becker .75 .35
□ 5 Russ Davis 1.00 .45
□ 6 Matt Mieske .40 .18
□ 7 Paul Shuey .40 .18
□ 8 Hector Carrasco .40 .18
□ 9 J.R. Phillips .40 .18
□ 10 Scott Ruffcorn .40 .18
□ 11 Kurt Abbott .40 .18
□ 12 Danny Bautista .40 .18
□ 13 Rick White .40 .18
□ 14 Steve Dunn .40 .18
□ 15 Joe Ausanio .40 .18
□ 16 Salomon Torres .40 .18
□ 17 Ricky Bottalico 1.00 .45
□ 18 Johnny Ruffin .40 .18
□ 19 Kevin Foster .40 .18
□ 20 W.VanLandingham .40 .18
□ 21 Troy O'Leary .40 .18
□ 22 Mark Acre .40 .18
□ 23 Norberto Martin .40 .18
□ 24 Jason Jacome .40 .18
□ 25 Steve Trachsel .40 .18
□ 26 Denny Hocking .40 .18
□ 27 Mike Lieberthal .40 .18
□ 28 Gerald Williams .40 .18
□ 29 John Mabry 1.00 .45
□ 30 Greg Blosser .40 .18
□ 31 Carl Everett .40 .18
□ 32 Steve Karsay .40 .18
□ 33 Jose Valentin .75 .35
□ 34 Jon Lieber .40 .18
□ 35 Chris Gomez .40 .18
□ 36 Jesus Tavarez .40 .18

☐ 37 Tony Longmire	.40	.18
☐ 38 Luis Lopez	.40	.18
☐ 39 Matt Walbeck	.40	.18
☐ 40 Rikkert Faneyte	.40	.18
☐ 41 Shane Reynolds	.75	.35
☐ 42 Joey Hamilton	1.50	.70
☐ 43 Ismael Valdes	2.00	.90
☐ 44 Danny Miceli	.40	.18
☐ 45 Darren Bragg	.75	.35
☐ 46 Alex Gonzalez	.75	.35
☐ 47 Rick Helling	.40	.18
☐ 48 Jose Oliva	.40	.18
☐ 49 Jim Edmonds	1.50	.70
☐ 50 Miguel Jimenez	.40	.18
☐ 51 Tony Eusebio	.40	.18
☐ 52 Shawn Green	.75	.35
☐ 53 Billy Ashley	.40	.18
☐ 54 Rondell White	1.00	.45
☐ 55 Cory Bailey	.40	.18
☐ 56 Tim Davis	.40	.18
☐ 57 John Hudek	.40	.18
☐ 58 Darren Hall	.40	.18
☐ 59 Darren Dreifort	.40	.18
☐ 60 Mike Kelly	.40	.18
☐ 61 Marcus Moore	.40	.18
☐ 62 Garret Anderson	1.50	.70
☐ 63 Brian L.Hunter	1.50	.70
☐ 64 Mark Smith	.40	.18
☐ 65 Garey Ingram	.40	.18
☐ 66 Rusty Greer	6.00	2.70
☐ 67 Marc Newfield	.75	.35
☐ 68 Gar Finnvold	.40	.18
☐ 69 Paul Spoljaric	.40	.18
☐ 70 Ray McDavid	.40	.18
☐ 71 Orlando Miller	.40	.18
☐ 72 Jorge Fabregas	.40	.18
☐ 73 Ray Holbert	.40	.18
☐ 74 Armando Benitez	.40	.18
☐ 75 Ernie Young	.40	.18
☐ 76 James Mouton	.75	.35
☐ 77 Robert Perez	.40	.18
☐ 78 Chan Ho Park	6.00	2.70
☐ 79 Roger Salkeld	.40	.18
☐ 80 Tony Tarasco	.40	.18

1994 Leaf Limited Rookies Phenoms

This 10-card standard-size set was randomly inserted in Leaf Limited Rookies packs at a rate of approximately of one in twelve. Limited to 5,000, the set showcases top 1994 rookies. The fronts are designed much like the Limited Rookies except the card is comprised of gold foil instead of silver. Gold backs are also virtually identical to the Limited Rookies in terms of content and layout. The cards are individually numbered on back out of 5,000.

	MINT	NRMT
COMPLETE SET (10)	150.00	70.00
COMMON CARD (1-10)	8.00	3.60
☐ 1 Raul Mondesi	15.00	6.75
☐ 2 Bob Hamelin	8.00	3.60
☐ 3 Midre Cummings	8.00	3.60
☐ 4 Carlos Delgado	12.00	5.50
☐ 5 Cliff Floyd	10.00	4.50
☐ 6 Jeffrey Hammonds	10.00	4.50
☐ 7 Ryan Klesko	15.00	6.75
☐ 8 Javier Lopez	12.00	5.50
☐ 9 Manny Ramirez	25.00	11.00
☐ 10 Alex Rodriguez	80.00	36.00

1995 Leaf Limited

This 192 standard-size card set was issued in two series. Each series contained 96 cards. These cards were issued in six-box cases with 20 packs per box and five cards per pack. Forty-five thousand boxes of each series was produced. The fronts feature a player photo shot against a silver holographic foil background. The player is identified on the top with his team name on the right. The "Leaf

Limited" logo is on the bottom of the card. The horizontal backs contain two player photos along with career stats broken down on a monthly basis. The cards are numbered in the upper right corner. Rookie Cards in this set include Bob Higginson and Hideo Nomo.

	MINT	NRMT
COMPLETE SET (192)	60.00	27.00
COMPLETE SERIES 1 (96)	30.00	13.50
COMPLETE SERIES 2 (96)	30.00	13.50
COMMON CARD (1-192)	.25	.11
☐ 1 Frank Thomas	6.00	2.70
☐ 2 Geronimo Berroa	.25	.11
☐ 3 Tony Phillips	.25	.11
☐ 4 Roberto Alomar	1.50	.70
☐ 5 Steve Avery	.25	.11
☐ 6 Darryl Hamilton	.25	.11
☐ 7 Scott Cooper	.25	.11
☐ 8 Mark Grace	1.00	.45
☐ 9 Billy Ashley	.25	.11
☐ 10 Wil Cordero	.25	.11
☐ 11 Barry Bonds	2.00	.90
☐ 12 Kenny Lofton	2.00	.90
☐ 13 Jay Buhner	1.00	.45
☐ 14 Alex Rodriguez	6.00	2.70
☐ 15 Bobby Bonilla	.50	.23
☐ 16 Brady Anderson	1.00	.45
☐ 17 Ken Caminiti	1.00	.45
☐ 18 Charlie Hayes	.25	.11
☐ 19 Jay Bell	.25	.11
☐ 20 Will Clark	1.00	.45
☐ 21 Jose Canseco	1.00	.45
☐ 22 Bret Boone	.25	.11
☐ 23 Dante Bichette	1.00	.45
☐ 24 Kevin Appier	.25	.11
☐ 25 Chad Curtis	.25	.11
☐ 26 Marty Cordova	1.00	.45
☐ 27 Jason Bere	.25	.11
☐ 28 Jimmy Key	.50	.23
☐ 29 Rickey Henderson	1.00	.45
☐ 30 Tim Salmon	1.50	.70
☐ 31 Joe Carter	1.00	.45
☐ 32 Tom Glavine	1.00	.45
☐ 33 Pat Listach	.25	.11
☐ 34 Brian Jordan	.50	.23
☐ 35 Brian McRae	.25	.11
☐ 36 Eric Karros	.50	.23
☐ 37 Pedro Martinez	1.00	.45
☐ 38 Royce Clayton	.25	.11
☐ 39 Eddie Murray	1.50	.70
☐ 40 Randy Johnson	1.50	.70
☐ 41 Jeff Conine	.50	.23
☐ 42 Brett Butler	.50	.23
☐ 43 Jeffrey Hammonds	.50	.23
☐ 44 Andujar Cedeno	.25	.11
☐ 45 Dave Hollins	.25	.11
☐ 46 Jeff King	.50	.23
☐ 47 Benji Gil	.25	.11
☐ 48 Roger Clemens	3.00	1.35
☐ 49 Barry Larkin	1.00	.45
☐ 50 Joe Girardi	.25	.11
☐ 51 Bob Hamelin	.25	.11
☐ 52 Travis Fryman	.50	.23
☐ 53 Chuck Knoblauch	1.50	.70
☐ 54 Ray Durham	.50	.23
☐ 55 Don Mattingly	2.50	1.10
☐ 56 Ruben Sierra	.25	.11
☐ 57 J.T. Snow	.50	.23
☐ 58 Derek Bell	.50	.23
☐ 59 David Cone	.50	.23
☐ 60 Marquis Grissom	.50	.23
☐ 61 Kevin Seitzer	.25	.11
☐ 62 Ozzie Smith	2.00	.90
☐ 63 Rick Wilkins	.25	.11
☐ 64 Hideo Nomo	8.00	3.60
☐ 65 Tony Tarasco	.25	.11
☐ 66 Manny Ramirez	1.50	.70
☐ 67 Charles Johnson	1.00	.45
☐ 68 Craig Biggio	1.00	.45
☐ 69 Bobby Jones	.50	.23
☐ 70 Mike Mussina	1.50	.70
☐ 71 Alex Gonzalez	.50	.23
☐ 72 Gregg Jefferies	.50	.23
☐ 73 Rusty Greer	1.50	.70
☐ 74 Mike Greenwell	.25	.11
☐ 75 Hal Morris	.25	.11
☐ 76 Paul O'Neill	.50	.23
☐ 77 Luis Gonzalez	.25	.11
☐ 78 Chipper Jones	5.00	2.20
☐ 79 Mike Piazza	5.00	2.20
☐ 80 Rondell White	.50	.23
☐ 81 Glenallen Hill	.25	.11
☐ 82 Shawn Green	.50	.23
☐ 83 Bernie Williams	1.50	.70
☐ 84 Jim Thome	1.50	.70
☐ 85 Terry Pendleton	.50	.23
☐ 86 Rafael Palmeiro	1.00	.45
☐ 87 Tony Gwynn	4.00	1.80
☐ 88 Mickey Tettleton	.25	.11
☐ 89 John Valentin	.50	.23
☐ 90 Deion Sanders	1.50	.70
☐ 91 Larry Walker	1.50	.70
☐ 92 Michael Tucker	1.00	.45
☐ 93 Alan Trammell	1.00	.45
☐ 94 Tim Raines	.25	.11
☐ 95 David Justice	1.50	.70
☐ 96 Tino Martinez	1.50	.70
☐ 97 Cal Ripken, Jr.	6.00	2.70
☐ 98 Deion Sanders	1.50	.70
☐ 99 Darren Daulton	.50	.23
☐ 100 Paul Molitor	1.50	.70
☐ 101 Randy Myers	.25	.11
☐ 102 Wally Joyner	.50	.23
☐ 103 Carlos Perez	.50	.23
☐ 104 Brian Hunter	1.00	.45
☐ 105 Wade Boggs	1.50	.70
☐ 106 Bob Higginson	2.50	1.10
☐ 107 Jeff Kent	.25	.11
☐ 108 Jose Offerman	.25	.11
☐ 109 Dennis Eckersley	1.00	.45
☐ 110 Dave Nilsson	.50	.23
☐ 111 Chuck Finley	.50	.23
☐ 112 Devon White	.25	.11
☐ 113 Bip Roberts	.25	.11
☐ 114 Ramon Martinez	.50	.23
☐ 115 Greg Maddux	5.00	2.20
☐ 116 Curtis Goodwin	.25	.11
☐ 117 John Jaha	.25	.11
☐ 118 Ken Griffey Jr.	8.00	3.60
☐ 119 Geronimo Pena	.25	.11
☐ 120 Shawon Dunston	.25	.11
☐ 121 Ariel Prieto	.50	.23
☐ 122 Kirby Puckett	3.00	1.35
☐ 123 Carlos Baerga	.50	.23
☐ 124 Todd Hundley	.50	.23
☐ 125 Tim Naehring	.25	.11
☐ 126 Gary Sheffield	1.50	.70
☐ 127 Dean Palmer	.50	.23
☐ 128 Rondell White	1.00	.45
☐ 129 Greg Gagne	.25	.11
☐ 130 Jose Rijo	.25	.11
☐ 131 Ivan Rodriguez	2.00	.90
☐ 132 Jeff Bagwell	3.00	1.35
☐ 133 Greg Vaughn	.25	.11
☐ 134 Chili Davis	.50	.23
☐ 135 Al Martin	.50	.23
☐ 136 Kenny Rogers	.25	.11
☐ 137 Aaron Sele	.25	.11
☐ 138 Raul Mondesi	1.00	.45
☐ 139 Cecil Fielder	.50	.23
☐ 140 Tim Wallach	.25	.11
☐ 141 Andres Galarraga	1.00	.45
☐ 142 Lou Whitaker	.50	.23
☐ 143 Jack McDowell	.25	.11
☐ 144 Matt Williams	1.00	.45
☐ 145 Ryan Klesko	1.00	.45
☐ 146 Carlos Garcia	.25	.11
☐ 147 Albert Belle	2.00	.90
☐ 148 Ryan Thompson	.25	.11
☐ 149 Roberto Kelly	.25	.11
☐ 150 Edgar Martinez	1.00	.45
☐ 151 Robby Thompson	.25	.11
☐ 152 Mo Vaughn	2.00	.90
☐ 153 Todd Zeile	.25	.11
☐ 154 Harold Baines	.50	.23
☐ 155 Phil Plantier	.25	.11
☐ 156 Mike Stanley	.25	.11
☐ 157 Ed Sprague	.25	.11
☐ 158 Moises Alou	.50	.23
☐ 159 Quilvio Veras	.25	.11
☐ 160 Reggie Sanders	.50	.23
☐ 161 Delino DeShields	.25	.11
☐ 162 Rico Brogna	.25	.11
☐ 163 Greg Colbrunn	.25	.11
☐ 164 Steve Finley	.50	.23
☐ 165 Orlando Merced	.25	.11
☐ 166 Mark McGwire	3.00	1.35
☐ 167 Garret Anderson	.50	.23
☐ 168 Paul Sorrento	.25	.11
☐ 169 Mark Langston	.25	.11

☐ 170 Danny Tartabull	.25	.11
☐ 171 Vinny Castilla	1.00	.45
☐ 172 Javier Lopez	1.00	.45
☐ 173 Bret Saberhagen	.25	.11
☐ 174 Eddie Williams	.25	.11
☐ 175 Scott Leius	.25	.11
☐ 176 Juan Gonzalez	4.00	1.80
☐ 177 Gary Gaetti	.50	.23
☐ 178 Jim Edmonds	1.50	.70
☐ 179 John Olerud	.25	.11
☐ 180 Lenny Dykstra	.50	.23
☐ 181 Ray Lankford	1.00	.45
☐ 182 Ron Gant	.50	.23
☐ 183 Doug Drabek	.25	.11
☐ 184 Fred McGriff	1.00	.45
☐ 185 Andy Benes	.25	.11
☐ 186 Kurt Abbott	.25	.11
☐ 187 Bernard Gilkey	.50	.23
☐ 188 Sammy Sosa	1.50	.70
☐ 189 Lee Smith	.50	.23
☐ 190 Dennis Martinez	.50	.23
☐ 191 Ozzie Guillen	.25	.11
☐ 192 Robin Ventura	.50	.23

1995 Leaf Limited Gold

These 24 standard-size quasi-parallel cards were inserted one per series one pack. Players from both series were included in this set. While using the same design as the regular issue, they are distinguished by different photos, different numbers and gold holographic foil.

	MINT	NRMT
COMPLETE SET (24)	50.00	22.00
COMMON CARD (1-24)	.50	.23
☐ 1 Frank Thomas	6.00	2.70
☐ 2 Jeff Bagwell	3.00	1.35
☐ 3 Raul Mondesi	1.00	.45
☐ 4 Barry Bonds	1.50	.70
☐ 5 Albert Belle	3.00	1.35
☐ 6 Ken Griffey Jr.	8.00	3.60
☐ 7 Cal Ripken UER Name spelled Ripkin on card	6.00	2.70
☐ 8 Will Clark	1.00	.45
☐ 9 Jose Canseco	1.00	.45
☐ 10 Larry Walker	1.25	.55
☐ 11 Kirby Puckett	3.00	1.35
☐ 12 Don Mattingly	4.00	1.80
☐ 13 Tim Salmon	1.25	.55
☐ 14 Roberto Alomar	1.25	.55
☐ 15 Greg Maddux	5.00	2.20
☐ 16 Mike Piazza	5.00	2.20
☐ 17 Matt Williams	1.00	.45
☐ 18 Kenny Lofton	1.50	.70
☐ 19 Alex Rodriguez UER Name spelled Rodriquez on card	8.00	3.60
☐ 20 Tony Gwynn	4.00	1.80
☐ 21 Mo Vaughn	2.00	.90
☐ 22 Chipper Jones	5.00	2.20
☐ 23 Manny Ramirez	1.50	.70
☐ 24 Deion Sanders	.50	.23

1995 Leaf Limited Bat Patrol

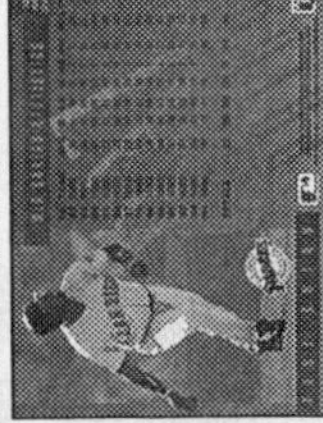

These 24 standard-size cards were inserted one per series two pack. The fronts feature a full-bleed player photo with the player being identified on the top and the words "Bat Patrol" covering most of the middle. The horizontal backs feature another player photo as well as a year by year breakdown. The cards are numbered in the upper right corner as "X" of 24.

	MINT	NRMT
COMPLETE SET (24)	25.00	11.00
COMMON CARD (1-24)	.75	.35
☐ 1 Frank Thomas	8.00	3.60
☐ 2 Tony Gwynn	3.00	1.35
☐ 3 Wade Boggs	1.50	.70
☐ 4 Larry Walker	1.50	.70
☐ 5 Ken Griffey, Jr.	8.00	3.60
☐ 6 Jeff Bagwell	3.00	1.35
☐ 7 Manny Ramirez	1.50	.70
☐ 8 Mark Grace	1.25	.55
☐ 9 Kenny Lofton	2.00	.90
☐ 10 Mike Piazza	5.00	2.20
☐ 11 Will Clark	1.25	.55
☐ 12 Mo Vaughn	2.00	.90
☐ 13 Carlos Baerga	.75	.35
☐ 14 Rafael Palmeiro	1.25	.55
☐ 15 Barry Bonds	2.00	.90
☐ 16 Kirby Puckett	3.00	1.35
☐ 17 Roberto Alomar	1.50	.70
☐ 18 Barry Larkin	1.25	.55
☐ 19 Eddie Murray	1.50	.70
☐ 20 Tim Salmon	1.50	.70
☐ 21 Don Mattingly	4.00	1.80
☐ 22 Fred McGriff	1.25	.55
☐ 23 Albert Belle	3.00	1.35
☐ 24 Dante Bichette	1.25	.55

1995 Leaf Limited Lumberjacks

These eight standard-size cards were randomly inserted into second series packs. The cards are individually numbered out of 5,000. The fronts feature a player photo surrounded by his name, the word "Lumberjacks" and "Handcrafted" in an semi-circular pattern. The team logo is in the background. The UV-coated horizontal backs feature a player photo against a forest background on the right along with some information on the left side. The player's career statistics are directly above the individual numbering (out of 5,000) of the card. The cards are numbered in the upper right corner.

	MINT	NRMT
COMPLETE SET (16)	600.00	275.00
COMPLETE SERIES 1 (8)	275.00	125.00
COMPLETE SERIES 2 (8)	325.00	145.00
COMMON CARD (1-16)	8.00	3.60
☐ 1 Albert Belle	20.00	9.00
☐ 2 Barry Bonds	20.00	9.00
☐ 3 Juan Gonzalez	40.00	18.00
☐ 4 Ken Griffey Jr.	80.00	36.00
☐ 5 Fred McGriff	12.00	5.50
☐ 6 Mike Piazza	40.00	18.00
☐ 7 Kirby Puckett	30.00	13.50
☐ 8 Mo Vaughn	20.00	9.00
☐ 9 Frank Thomas	60.00	27.00
☐ 10 Jeff Bagwell	30.00	13.50
☐ 11 Matt Williams	12.00	5.50
☐ 12 Jose Canseco	10.00	4.50
☐ 13 Raul Mondesi	12.00	5.50
☐ 14 Manny Ramirez	15.00	6.75
☐ 15 Cecil Fielder	8.00	3.60
☐ 16 Cal Ripken, Jr.	60.00	27.00

1996 Leaf Limited

The 1996 Leaf Limited set was issued exclusively to hobby outlets with a maximum production run of 45,000 boxes. Each box contained two smaller mini-boxes, enabling the dealer to use his imagination in the marketing of this product. The five-card packs carried a suggested retail price of $3.24. Each Master Box was sequentially- numbered via a box topper. If this number matched the 1996 year-ending stats, the collector and the

dealer both had a chance to win prizes such as a Frank Thomas game-used bat, autographed batting glove, or a "Two Biggest Weapons" poster. The collector would return the winning box number to the hobby shop, and the dealer would mail it to Donruss with both receiving the same prize. The card fronts displayed color player photos with another photo and player information on the backs.

	MINT	NRMT
COMPLETE SET (90)	50.00	22.00
COMMON CARD (1-90)	.40	.18
☐ 1 Ivan Rodriguez	2.00	.90
☐ 2 Roger Clemens	3.00	1.35
☐ 3 Gary Sheffield	1.50	.70
☐ 4 Tino Martinez	1.50	.70
☐ 5 Sammy Sosa	1.50	.70
☐ 6 Reggie Sanders	.40	.18
☐ 7 Ray Lankford	.75	.35
☐ 8 Manny Ramirez	1.50	.70
☐ 9 Jeff Bagwell	3.00	1.35
☐ 10 Greg Maddux	5.00	2.20
☐ 11 Ken Griffey Jr.	8.00	3.60
☐ 12 Rondell White	.75	.35
☐ 13 Mike Piazza	5.00	2.20
☐ 14 Marc Newfield	.40	.18
☐ 15 Cal Ripken	6.00	2.70
☐ 16 Carlos Delgado	.75	.35
☐ 17 Tim Salmon	1.50	.70
☐ 18 Andres Galarraga	1.50	.70
☐ 19 Chuck Knoblauch	1.50	.70
☐ 20 Matt Williams	1.00	.45
☐ 21 Mark McGwire	3.00	1.35
☐ 22 Ben McDonald	.40	.18
☐ 23 Frank Thomas	6.00	2.70
☐ 24 Johnny Damon	.75	.35
☐ 25 Gregg Jefferies	.75	.35
☐ 26 Travis Fryman	.75	.35
☐ 27 Chipper Jones	5.00	2.20
☐ 28 David Cone	.75	.35
☐ 29 Kenny Lofton	2.00	.90
☐ 30 Mike Mussina	1.50	.70
☐ 31 Alex Rodriguez	6.00	2.70
☐ 32 Carlos Baerga	.40	.18
☐ 33 Brian Hunter	.75	.35
☐ 34 Juan Gonzalez	4.00	1.80
☐ 35 Bernie Williams	1.50	.70
☐ 36 Wally Joyner	.40	.18
☐ 37 Fred McGriff	1.00	.45
☐ 38 Randy Johnson	1.50	.70
☐ 39 Marty Cordova	.75	.35
☐ 40 Garret Anderson	.75	.35
☐ 41 Albert Belle	2.00	.90
☐ 42 Edgar Martinez	1.00	.45
☐ 43 Barry Larkin	1.00	.45
☐ 44 Paul O'Neill	.40	.18
☐ 45 Cecil Fielder	.75	.35
☐ 46 Rusty Greer	1.00	.45
☐ 47 Mo Vaughn	2.00	.90
☐ 48 Dante Bichette	1.00	.45
☐ 49 Ryan Klesko	1.00	.45
☐ 50 Roberto Alomar	1.50	.70
☐ 51 Raul Mondesi	1.00	.45
☐ 52 Robin Ventura	.75	.35
☐ 53 Tony Gwynn	4.00	1.80
☐ 54 Mark Grace	1.00	.45
☐ 55 Jim Thome	1.50	.70
☐ 56 Jason Giambi	.75	.35
☐ 57 Tom Glavine	1.00	.45
☐ 58 Jim Edmonds	1.50	.70
☐ 59 Pedro Martinez	1.50	.70
☐ 60 Charles Johnson	.75	.35
☐ 61 Wade Boggs	1.50	.70
☐ 62 Orlando Merced	.40	.18
☐ 63 Craig Biggio	1.00	.45
☐ 64 Brady Anderson	1.00	.45
☐ 65 Hideo Nomo	4.00	1.80
☐ 66 Ozzie Smith	2.00	.90
☐ 67 Eddie Murray	1.50	.70
☐ 68 Will Clark	1.00	.45
☐ 69 Jay Buhner	1.00	.45
☐ 70 Kirby Puckett	3.00	1.35
☐ 71 Barry Bonds	2.00	.90

	MINT	NRMT
☐ 72 Ray Durham	.75	.35
☐ 73 Sterling Hitchcock	.40	.18
☐ 74 John Smoltz	1.00	.45
☐ 75 Andre Dawson	1.00	.45
☐ 76 Joe Carter	.75	.35
☐ 77 Ryne Sandberg	2.00	.90
☐ 78 Rickey Henderson	1.00	.45
☐ 79 Brian Jordan	.75	.35
☐ 80 Greg Vaughn	.40	.18
☐ 81 Andy Pettitte	2.00	.90
☐ 82 Dean Palmer	.75	.35
☐ 83 Paul Molitor	1.50	.70
☐ 84 Rafael Palmeiro	1.00	.45
☐ 85 Henry Rodriguez	.40	.18
☐ 86 Larry Walker	1.50	.70
☐ 87 Ismael Valdes	.75	.35
☐ 88 Derek Bell	.40	.18
☐ 89 J.T. Snow	.75	.35
☐ 90 Jack McDowell	.40	.18

1996 Leaf Limited Gold

Randomly inserted into one in every 11 packs, cards from this 90-card insert set parallel the regular Leaf Limited issue. Similar in design, it differs from the regular set with its gold holographic foil treatment.

	MINT	NRMT
COMPLETE SET (90)	500.00	220.00
COMMON CARD (1-90)	2.50	1.10
*STARS: 4X to 10X BASIC CARDS		

1996 Leaf Limited Lumberjacks

Printed with maple stock that puts wood grains on both sides, this 10-card insert set features the league's top sluggers. The fronts carry color player photos with player information and statistics on the backs. Only 5,000 sets were produced and each card is individually numbered.

	MINT	NRMT
COMPLETE SET (10)	250.00	110.00
COMMON CARD (1-10)	8.00	3.60
*BLACK: 1.5X TO 4X BASIC CARDS		
☐ 1 Ken Griffey Jr.	50.00	22.00
☐ 2 Sammy Sosa	8.00	3.60
☐ 3 Cal Ripken	40.00	18.00
☐ 4 Frank Thomas	40.00	18.00
☐ 5 Alex Rodriguez	30.00	13.50
☐ 6 Mo Vaughn	12.00	5.50
☐ 7 Chipper Jones	30.00	13.50
☐ 8 Mike Piazza	30.00	13.50
☐ 9 Jeff Bagwell	20.00	9.00
☐ 10 Mark McGwire	20.00	9.00
☐ P8 Mike Piazza Promo	5.00	2.20

1996 Leaf Limited Pennant Craze

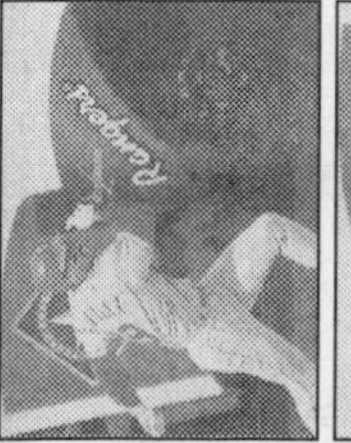

This 10-card insert set features 10 superstars who have a thirst for the pennant. A special flocking technique puts the felt feel of a pennant on a die cut card. Only 2,500 sets were produced and are individually numbered.

	MINT	NRMT
COMPLETE SET (10)	500.00	220.00
COMMON CARD (1-10)	15.00	6.75
☐ 1 Juan Gonzalez	40.00	18.00
☐ 2 Cal Ripken	60.00	27.00
☐ 3 Frank Thomas	60.00	27.00
☐ 4 Ken Griffey Jr.	80.00	36.00
☐ 5 Albert Belle	20.00	9.00
☐ 6 Greg Maddux	50.00	22.00
☐ 7 Paul Molitor	15.00	6.75
☐ 8 Alex Rodriguez	50.00	22.00
☐ 9 Barry Bonds	20.00	9.00
☐ 10 Chipper Jones	50.00	22.00

1996 Leaf Limited Rookies

Randomly inserted in packs at a rate of one in seven, this 10-card set printed in silver holographic foil features some of the hottest rookies of the year.

	MINT	NRMT
COMPLETE SET (10)	70.00	32.00
COMMON CARD (1-10)	2.50	1.10
COMP.GOLD SET (10)	180.00	80.00
*GOLD: 1X TO 2.5X BASIC CARDS		
☐ 1 Alex Ochoa	2.50	1.10
☐ 2 Darin Erstad	15.00	6.75
☐ 3 Ruben Rivera	3.00	1.35
☐ 4 Derek Jeter	15.00	6.75
☐ 5 Jermaine Dye	2.50	1.10
☐ 6 Jason Kendall	5.00	2.20
☐ 7 Mike Grace	2.50	1.10
☐ 8 Andruw Jones	15.00	6.75
☐ 9 Rey Ordonez	2.50	1.10
☐ 10 George Arias	2.50	1.10

1996 Leaf Preferred

The 1996 Leaf Preferred set was issued in one series totalling 150 cards. The 6-card packs retail for $3.49 each. Each card was printed on 20-point card stock for extra thickness and durability. The fronts feature a color action player photo and silver foil printing. The backs carry another player photo, player information and statistics. One in every ten packs contains an insert card.

	MINT	NRMT
COMPLETE SET (150)	25.00	11.00
COMMON CARD (1-150)	.15	.07
☐ 1 Ken Griffey Jr.	3.00	1.35
☐ 2 Rico Brogna	.15	.07
☐ 3 Gregg Jefferies	.30	.14
☐ 4 Reggie Sanders	.15	.07
☐ 5 Manny Ramirez	.75	.35
☐ 6 Shawn Green	.30	.14
☐ 7 Tino Martinez	.60	.25
☐ 8 Jeff Bagwell	1.25	.55
☐ 9 Marc Newfield	.30	.14
☐ 10 Ray Lankford	.30	.14
☐ 11 Jay Bell	.15	.07
☐ 12 Greg Maddux	2.00	.90
☐ 13 Frank Thomas	2.50	1.10
☐ 14 Travis Fryman	.30	.14
☐ 15 Mark McGwire	1.25	.55
☐ 16 Chuck Knoblauch	.60	.25
☐ 17 Sammy Sosa	.60	.25
☐ 18 Matt Williams	.40	.18
☐ 19 Roger Clemens	1.25	.55
☐ 20 Rondell White	.30	.14
☐ 21 Ivan Rodriguez	.75	.35
☐ 22 Cal Ripken	2.50	1.10
☐ 23 Ben McDonald	.15	.07
☐ 24 Kenny Lofton	.75	.35
☐ 25 Mike Piazza	2.00	.90
☐ 26 David Cone	.30	.14
☐ 27 Gary Sheffield	.60	.25
☐ 28 Tim Salmon	.60	.25
☐ 29 Andres Galarraga	.40	.18
☐ 30 Johnny Damon	.30	.14
☐ 31 Ozzie Smith	.75	.35
☐ 32 Carlos Baerga	.30	.14
☐ 33 Raul Mondesi	.40	.18
☐ 34 Moises Alou	.30	.14
☐ 35 Alex Rodriguez	2.50	1.10
☐ 36 Mike Mussina	.60	.25
☐ 37 Jason Isringhausen	.15	.07
☐ 38 Barry Larkin	.40	.18
☐ 39 Bernie Williams	.60	.25
☐ 40 Chipper Jones	2.00	.90
☐ 41 Joey Hamilton	.30	.14
☐ 42 Charles Johnson	.30	.14
☐ 43 Juan Gonzalez	1.50	.70
☐ 44 Greg Vaughn	.15	.07
☐ 45 Robin Ventura	.30	.14
☐ 46 Albert Belle	.75	.35
☐ 47 Rafael Palmeiro	.40	.18
☐ 48 Brian L.Hunter	.30	.14
☐ 49 Mo Vaughn	.75	.35
☐ 50 Paul O'Neill	.15	.07
☐ 51 Mark Grace	.40	.18
☐ 52 Randy Johnson	.60	.25
☐ 53 Pedro Martinez	.60	.25
☐ 54 Marty Cordova	.15	.07
☐ 55 Garret Anderson	.30	.14
☐ 56 Joe Carter	.30	.14
☐ 57 Jim Thome	.60	.25
☐ 58 Edgardo Alfonzo	.15	.07
☐ 59 Dante Bichette	.40	.18
☐ 60 Darryl Hamilton	.15	.07
☐ 61 Roberto Alomar	.60	.25
☐ 62 Fred McGriff	.30	.14
☐ 63 Kirby Puckett	1.25	.55
☐ 64 Hideo Nomo	1.50	.70
☐ 65 Alex Fernandez	.15	.07
☐ 66 Ryan Klesko	.30	.14
☐ 67 Wade Boggs	.60	.25
☐ 68 Eddie Murray	.60	.25
☐ 69 Eric Karros	.15	.07
☐ 70 Jim Edmonds	.60	.25
☐ 71 Edgar Martinez	.40	.18
☐ 72 Andy Pettitte	.75	.35
☐ 73 Mark Grudzielanek	.30	.14
☐ 74 Tom Glavine	.30	.14
☐ 75 Ken Caminiti	.60	.25
☐ 76 Will Clark	.40	.18
☐ 77 Craig Biggio	.40	.18
☐ 78 Brady Anderson	.40	.18
☐ 79 Tony Gwynn	1.50	.70
☐ 80 Larry Walker	.60	.25
☐ 81 Brian Jordan	.30	.14
☐ 82 Lenny Dykstra	.30	.14
☐ 83 Butch Huskey	.30	.14
☐ 84 Jack McDowell	.15	.07
☐ 85 Cecil Fielder	.30	.14
☐ 86 Jose Canseco	.40	.18
☐ 87 Jason Giambi	.30	.14
☐ 88 Rickey Henderson	.40	.18
☐ 89 Kevin Seitzer	.15	.07
☐ 90 Carlos Delgado	.30	.14
☐ 91 Ryne Sandberg	.75	.35
☐ 92 Dwight Gooden	.30	.14
☐ 93 Michael Tucker	.30	.14
☐ 94 Barry Bonds	.75	.35
☐ 95 Eric Young	.30	.14
☐ 96 Dean Palmer	.30	.14
☐ 97 Henry Rodriguez	.15	.07
☐ 98 John Mabry	.30	.14
☐ 99 J.T. Snow	.30	.14
☐ 100 Andre Dawson	.40	.18
☐ 101 Ismael Valdes	.30	.14
☐ 102 Charles Nagy	.30	.14
☐ 103 Jay Buhner	.40	.18
☐ 104 Derek Bell	.15	.07
☐ 105 Paul Molitor	.60	.25
☐ 106 Hal Morris	.15	.07
☐ 107 Ray Durham	.30	.14
☐ 108 Bernard Gilkey	.30	.14
☐ 109 John Valentin	.30	.14
☐ 110 Melvin Nieves	.30	.14
☐ 111 John Smoltz	.40	.18
☐ 112 Terrell Wade	.15	.07
☐ 113 Chad Mottola	.15	.07
☐ 114 Tony Clark	.60	.25

	MINT	NRMT
☐ 115 John Wasdin	.15	.07
☐ 116 Derek Jeter	2.00	.90
☐ 117 Rey Ordonez	.30	.14
☐ 118 Jason Thompson	.15	.07
☐ 119 Robin Jennings	.15	.07
☐ 120 Rocky Coppinger	.30	.14
☐ 121 Billy Wagner	.40	.18
☐ 122 Steve Gibralter	.15	.07
☐ 123 Jermaine Dye	.15	.07
☐ 124 Jason Kendall	.60	.25
☐ 125 Mike Grace	.15	.07
☐ 126 Jason Schmidt	.30	.14
☐ 127 Paul Wilson	.15	.07
☐ 128 Alan Benes	.30	.14
☐ 129 Justin Thompson	.40	.18
☐ 130 Brooks Kieschnick	.30	.14
☐ 131 George Arias	.15	.07
☐ 132 Osvaldo Fernandez	.30	.14
☐ 133 Todd Hollandsworth	.30	.14
☐ 134 Eric Owens	.15	.07
☐ 135 Chan Ho Park	.60	.25
☐ 136 Mark Loretta	.15	.07
☐ 137 Ruben Rivera	.30	.14
☐ 138 Jeff Suppan	.40	.18
☐ 139 Ugueth Urbina	.30	.14
☐ 140 LaTroy Hawkins	.15	.07
☐ 141 Chris Snopek	.15	.07
☐ 142 Edgar Renteria	.40	.18
☐ 143 Raul Casanova	.15	.07
☐ 144 Jose Herrera	.15	.07
☐ 145 Matt Lawton	.15	.07
☐ 146 Ralph Milliard	.15	.07
☐ 147 Frank Thomas CL	1.50	.70
☐ 148 Jeff Bagwell CL	.60	.25
☐ 149 Ken Griffey Jr. CL	1.50	.70
☐ 150 Mike Piazza CL	1.00	.45

1996 Leaf Preferred Press Proofs

Parallel to the regular set except for gold foil printing on front, these 150 cards are each individually numbered to 500. The cards were seeded at an approximate rate of one in every 48 packs.

	MINT	NRMT
COMPLETE SET (150)	2000.00	900.00
COMMON CARD (1-150)	4.00	1.80

*STARS: 20X TO 40X BASIC CARDS..
*YOUNG STARS: 15X TO 30X BASIC CARDS

1996 Leaf Preferred Staremaster

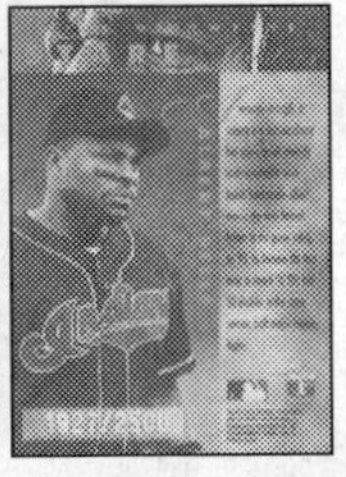

Randomly inserted at an approximate rate of one in every 144 packs, these twelve cards feature mug shots of the games most intense stares. Each card is printed on silver holographic card stock. Only 2,500 of each card was produced and are individually numbered.

	MINT	NRMT
COMPLETE SET (12)	500.00	220.00
COMMON CARD (1-12)	20.00	9.00

	MINT	NRMT
☐ 1 Chipper Jones	50.00	22.00
☐ 2 Alex Rodriguez	50.00	22.00
☐ 3 Derek Jeter	40.00	18.00
☐ 4 Tony Gwynn	40.00	18.00
☐ 5 Frank Thomas	60.00	27.00
☐ 6 Ken Griffey Jr.	80.00	36.00
☐ 7 Cal Ripken	60.00	27.00
☐ 8 Greg Maddux	50.00	22.00
☐ 9 Albert Belle	20.00	9.00
☐ 10 Barry Bonds	20.00	9.00
☐ 11 Jeff Bagwell	30.00	13.50
☐ 12 Mike Piazza	50.00	22.00

1996 Leaf Preferred Steel

Seeded one per pack, this all-steel, metalized set features silver framed color action player photos of the leagues most dominant players on a silver tinted background with a scriptive letter "S". The backs carry another player photo with the card logo as background and player statistics.

	MINT	NRMT
COMPLETE SET (77)	120.00	55.00
COMMON CARD (1-77)	1.00	.45
COMP.GOLD SET (77)	1200.00	550.00

*GOLD STARS: 4X TO 10X BASIC CARDS

	MINT	NRMT
☐ 1 Frank Thomas	10.00	4.50
☐ 2 Paul Molitor	2.00	.90
☐ 3 Kenny Lofton	2.50	1.10
☐ 4 Travis Fryman	1.25	.55
☐ 5 Jeff Conine	1.25	.55
☐ 6 Barry Bonds	2.50	1.10
☐ 7 Gregg Jefferies	1.25	.55
☐ 8 Alex Rodriguez	10.00	4.50
☐ 9 Wade Boggs	2.00	.90
☐ 10 David Justice	2.00	.90
☐ 11 Hideo Nomo	2.50	1.10
☐ 12 Roberto Alomar	2.00	.90
☐ 13 Todd Hollandsworth	1.25	.55
☐ 14 Mark McGwire	3.00	1.35
☐ 15 Rafael Palmeiro	1.50	.70
☐ 16 Will Clark	1.50	.70
☐ 17 Cal Ripken	8.00	3.60
☐ 18 Derek Bell	1.00	.45
☐ 19 Gary Sheffield	2.00	.90
☐ 20 Juan Gonzalez	5.00	2.20
☐ 21 Garret Anderson	1.25	.55
☐ 22 Mo Vaughn	2.50	1.10
☐ 23 Robin Ventura	1.25	.55
☐ 24 Carlos Baerga	1.25	.55
☐ 25 Tim Salmon	2.00	.90
☐ 26 Matt Williams	1.50	.70
☐ 27 Fred McGriff	1.50	.70
☐ 28 Rondell White	1.25	.55
☐ 29 Ray Lankford	1.25	.55
☐ 30 Lenny Dykstra	1.25	.55
☐ 31 J.T. Snow	1.25	.55
☐ 32 Sammy Sosa	2.00	.90
☐ 33 Chipper Jones	6.00	2.70
☐ 34 Bobby Bonilla	1.25	.55
☐ 35 Paul Wilson	1.00	.45
☐ 36 Darren Daulton	1.25	.55
☐ 37 Larry Walker	2.00	.90
☐ 38 Raul Mondesi	1.50	.70
☐ 39 Jeff Bagwell	4.00	1.80
☐ 40 Derek Jeter	6.00	2.70
☐ 41 Kirby Puckett	4.00	1.80
☐ 42 Jason Isringhausen	1.00	.45
☐ 43 Vinny Castilla	1.25	.55
☐ 44 Jim Edmonds	2.00	.90
☐ 45 Ron Gant	1.25	.55
☐ 46 Carlos Delgado	1.25	.55
☐ 47 Jose Canseco	1.50	.70
☐ 48 Tony Gwynn	4.00	1.80
☐ 49 Mike Mussina	2.00	.90
☐ 50 Charles Johnson	1.25	.55
☐ 51 Mike Piazza	6.00	2.70
☐ 52 Ken Griffey Jr.	10.00	4.50
☐ 53 Greg Maddux	6.00	2.70
☐ 54 Mark Grace	1.50	.70
☐ 55 Ryan Klesko	1.50	.70
☐ 56 Dennis Eckersley	1.50	.70
☐ 57 Rickey Henderson	1.50	.70
☐ 58 Michael Tucker	1.25	.55
☐ 59 Joe Carter	1.25	.55
☐ 60 Randy Johnson	2.00	.90
☐ 61 Brian Jordan	1.25	.55
☐ 62 Shawn Green	1.00	.45
☐ 63 Roger Clemens	2.00	.90
☐ 64 Andres Galarraga	2.00	.90
☐ 65 Johnny Damon	1.25	.55
☐ 66 Ryne Sandberg	2.50	1.10
☐ 67 Alan Benes	1.25	.55
☐ 68 Albert Belle	4.00	1.80
☐ 69 Barry Larkin	1.50	.70
☐ 70 Marty Cordova	1.00	.45
☐ 71 Dante Bichette	1.25	.55
☐ 72 Craig Biggio	1.50	.70
☐ 73 Reggie Sanders	1.00	.45
☐ 74 Moises Alou	1.25	.55
☐ 75 Chuck Knoblauch	2.00	.90
☐ 76 Cecil Fielder	1.25	.55
☐ 77 Manny Ramirez	2.00	.90

1996 Leaf Preferred Steel Power

This eight-card set combines a micro-etched foil card with corner interior lightening-symbol diecutting and honors eight of the top power hitters. The fronts carry a color player photo while the backs display a statement explaining why the player is included in the set along with his 1995 season hitting statistics. Only 5,000 sets were produced, and each card carries a serial number.

	MINT	NRMT
COMPLETE SET (8)	200.00	90.00
COMMON CARD (1-8)	12.00	5.50

	MINT	NRMT
☐ 1 Albert Belle	12.00	5.50
☐ 2 Mo Vaughn	12.00	5.50
☐ 3 Ken Griffey Jr.	50.00	22.00
☐ 4 Cal Ripken	40.00	18.00
☐ 5 Mike Piazza	30.00	13.50
☐ 6 Barry Bonds	12.00	5.50
☐ 7 Jeff Bagwell	20.00	9.00
☐ 8 Frank Thomas	40.00	18.00

1996 Leaf Signature

The 1996 Leaf Signature Set was issued in two series totalling 150 cards. The four-card packs have a suggested retail price of $9.99 each. It's interesting to note that the Extended Series was the last of the 1996 releases. In fact, it was released in January, 1997 - so late in the year that it's categorization as a 1996 issue is a bit of a stretch. Production for the Extended Series was only 40% that of the regular issue. Extended series packs actually contained a mix of both series 1 and 2 cards, thus the Extended series cards are somewhat scarcer. Card fronts feature borderless color action player photos with the card name printed in a silver foil emblem. The backs carry player information. The only notable Rookie Card is of Darin Erstad.

	MINT	NRMT
COMPLETE SET (150)	90.00	40.00
COMPLETE SERIES 1 (100)	50.00	22.00
COMPLETE SERIES 2 (50)	40.00	18.00
COMMON CARD (1-100)	.25	.11
COMMON CARD (101-150)	.50	.23

	MINT	NRMT
☐ 1 Mike Piazza	3.00	1.35
☐ 2 Juan Gonzalez	2.50	1.10
☐ 3 Greg Maddux	3.00	1.35
☐ 4 Marc Newfield	.25	.11
☐ 5 Wade Boggs	1.00	.45
☐ 6 Ray Lankford	.50	.23
☐ 7 Frank Thomas	4.00	1.80
☐ 8 Rico Brogna	.25	.11
☐ 9 Tim Salmon	1.00	.45
☐ 10 Ken Griffey Jr.	5.00	2.20
☐ 11 Manny Ramirez	1.00	.45
☐ 12 Cecil Fielder	.50	.23
☐ 13 Gregg Jefferies	.50	.23
☐ 14 Rondell White	.50	.23
☐ 15 Cal Ripken	4.00	1.80

☐ 16 Alex Rodriguez	4.00	1.80
☐ 17 Bernie Williams	1.00	.45
☐ 18 Andres Galarraga	1.00	.45
☐ 19 Mike Mussina	1.00	.45
☐ 20 Chuck Knoblauch	1.00	.45
☐ 21 Joe Carter	.50	.23
☐ 22 Jeff Bagwell	2.00	.90
☐ 23 Mark McGwire	2.00	.90
☐ 24 Sammy Sosa	1.00	.45
☐ 25 Reggie Sanders	.25	.11
☐ 26 Chipper Jones	3.00	1.35
☐ 27 Jeff Cirillo	.50	.23
☐ 28 Roger Clemens	2.00	.90
☐ 29 Craig Biggio	.75	.35
☐ 30 Gary Sheffield	1.00	.45
☐ 31 Paul O'Neill	.50	.23
☐ 32 Johnny Damon	.50	.23
☐ 33 Jason Isringhausen	.25	.11
☐ 34 Jay Bell	.25	.11
☐ 35 Henry Rodriguez	.25	.11
☐ 36 Matt Williams	.75	.35
☐ 37 Randy Johnson	1.00	.45
☐ 38 Fred McGriff	.75	.35
☐ 39 Jason Giambi	.50	.23
☐ 40 Ivan Rodriguez	1.25	.55
☐ 41 Raul Mondesi	.75	.35
☐ 42 Barry Larkin	.75	.35
☐ 43 Ryan Klesko	.75	.35
☐ 44 Joey Hamilton	.50	.23
☐ 45 Todd Hundley	.50	.23
☐ 46 Jim Edmonds	1.00	.45
☐ 47 Dante Bichette	.50	.23
☐ 48 Roberto Alomar	1.00	.45
☐ 49 Mark Grace	.75	.35
☐ 50 Brady Anderson	.75	.35
☐ 51 Hideo Nomo	2.50	1.10
☐ 52 Ozzie Smith	1.25	.55
☐ 53 Robin Ventura	.50	.23
☐ 54 Andy Pettitte	1.25	.55
☐ 55 Kenny Lofton	1.25	.55
☐ 56 John Mabry	.50	.23
☐ 57 Paul Molitor	1.00	.45
☐ 58 Rey Ordonez	.25	.11
☐ 59 Albert Belle	1.25	.55
☐ 60 Charles Johnson	.50	.23
☐ 61 Edgar Martinez	.75	.35
☐ 62 Derek Bell	.50	.23
☐ 63 Carlos Delgado	.50	.23
☐ 64 Raul Casanova	.25	.11
☐ 65 Ismael Valdes	.50	.23
☐ 66 J.T. Snow	1.00	.45
☐ 67 Derek Jeter	3.00	1.35
☐ 68 Jason Kendall	1.00	.45
☐ 69 John Smoltz	.50	.23
☐ 70 Chad Mottola	.25	.11
☐ 71 Jim Thome	1.00	.45
☐ 72 Will Clark	.75	.35
☐ 73 Mo Vaughn	1.25	.55
☐ 74 John Wasdin	.25	.11
☐ 75 Rafael Palmeiro	.75	.35
☐ 76 Mark Grudzielanek	.50	.23
☐ 77 Larry Walker	1.00	.45
☐ 78 Alan Benes	.25	.11
☐ 79 Michael Tucker	.50	.23
☐ 80 Billy Wagner	.50	.23
☐ 81 Paul Wilson	.50	.23
☐ 82 Greg Vaughn	.25	.11
☐ 83 Dean Palmer	.50	.23
☐ 84 Ryne Sandberg	1.25	.55
☐ 85 Eric Young	.50	.23
☐ 86 Jay Buhner	1.00	.45
☐ 87 Tony Clark	1.00	.45
☐ 88 Jermaine Dye	.25	.11
☐ 89 Barry Bonds	1.25	.55
☐ 90 Ugueth Urbina	.50	.23
☐ 91 Charles Nagy	.50	.23
☐ 92 Ruben Rivera	.50	.23
☐ 93 Todd Hollandsworth	.50	.23
☐ 94 Darin Erstad	5.00	2.20
☐ 95 Brooks Kieschnick	.50	.23
☐ 96 Edgar Renteria	.75	.35
☐ 97 Lenny Dykstra	.50	.23
☐ 98 Tony Gwynn	2.50	1.10
☐ 99 Kirby Puckett	2.00	.90
☐ 100 Checklist	.25	.11
☐ 101 Andruw Jones	5.00	2.20
☐ 102 Alex Ochoa	.50	.23
☐ 103 David Cone	1.50	.70
☐ 104 Rusty Greer	1.50	.70
☐ 105 Jose Canseco	1.50	.70
☐ 106 Ken Caminiti	2.00	.90
☐ 107 Mariano Rivera	2.00	.90
☐ 108 Ron Gant	1.50	.70
☐ 109 Darryl Strawberry	1.50	.70
☐ 110 Vladimir Guerrero	4.00	1.80
☐ 111 George Arias	.50	.23
☐ 112 Jeff Conine	1.50	.70
☐ 113 Bobby Higginson	1.50	.70
☐ 114 Eric Karros	1.50	.70
☐ 115 Brian Hunter	.50	.23
☐ 116 Eddie Murray	2.00	.90
☐ 117 Todd Walker	3.00	1.35
☐ 118 Chan Ho Park	2.00	.90
☐ 119 John Jaha	.50	.23
☐ 120 Dave Justice	2.00	.90
☐ 121 Makoto Suzuki	1.00	.45
☐ 122 Scott Rolen	5.00	2.20
☐ 123 Tino Martinez	2.00	.90
☐ 124 Kimera Bartee	.50	.23
☐ 125 Garret Anderson	1.50	.70
☐ 126 Brian Jordan	1.50	.70
☐ 127 Andre Dawson	2.00	.90
☐ 128 Javier Lopez	.50	.23
☐ 129 Bill Pulsipher	.50	.23
☐ 130 Dwight Gooden	1.50	.70
☐ 131 Al Martin	.50	.23
☐ 132 Terrell Wade	.50	.23
☐ 133 Steve Gibralter	.50	.23
☐ 134 Tom Glavine	2.00	.90
☐ 135 Kevin Appier	1.50	.70
☐ 136 Tim Raines	.50	.23
☐ 137 Curtis Pride	.50	.23
☐ 138 Todd Greene	1.00	.45
☐ 139 Bobby Bonilla	1.50	.70
☐ 140 Trey Beamon	1.50	.70
☐ 141 Marty Cordova	1.50	.70
☐ 142 Rickey Henderson	1.50	.70
☐ 143 Ellis Burks	1.50	.70
☐ 144 Dennis Eckersley	1.50	.70
☐ 145 Kevin Brown	1.50	.70
☐ 146 Carlos Baerga	.50	.23
☐ 147 Brett Butler	1.00	.45
☐ 148 Marquis Grissom	1.50	.70
☐ 149 Karim Garcia	1.50	.70
☐ 150 Frank Thomas CL	4.00	1.80

1996 Leaf Signature Press Proofs Gold

Randomly inserted in first series packs at an approximate rate of one in 12 and second series packs at an approximate rate of one in 8, this 150-card set is parallel to the regular version. Card numbers 1-100 were seeded into first series packs and 101-150 in Extended series packs. The design is similar to the regular card with the exception of the card name being printed in a gold foil emblem and the words "Press Proof" printed in gold foil vertically down the side.

	MINT	NRMT
COMPLETE SET (150)	1200.00	550.00
COMPLETE SERIES 1 (100)	800.00	350.00
COMPLETE SERIES 2 (50)	400.00	180.00
COMMON CARD (1-150)	3.00	1.35

*SER.1 STARS: 6X TO 15X BASIC CARDS
*SER.1 YOUNG STARS: 5X TO 12X BASIC CARDS
*SER.2 STARS: 3X TO 8X BASIC CARDS
*SER.2 YOUNG STARS: 2.5X TO 6X BASIC CARDS

1996 Leaf Signature Press Proofs Platinum

Randomly inserted exclusively into Extended Series packs at the rate of one in 24, this 150-card set is parallel to the regular Leaf Signature Set. Only 150 sets were produced. Unlike the multi-series base set and Gold Press Proofs, these scarce Platinum cards were issued in one comprehensive series. The cards are similar in design to the regular set with the exception of holographic platinum foil stamping. A set price has not been provided due to scarcity.

	MINT	NRMT
COMPLETE SET (150)	4000.00	1800.00
COMMON CARD (1-150)	8.00	3.60

*SER.1 STARS: 20X TO 40X BASIC CARDS
*SER.1 YOUNG STARS: 15X TO 30X BASIC CARDS
*SER.2 STARS: 10X TO 20X BASIC CARDS
*SER.2 YOUNG STARS: 7.5X TO 15X BASIC CARDS

1996 Leaf Signature Autographs

Inserted into 1996 Leaf Signature Series first series packs, these unnumbered cards were one of the first major autograph issues featured in an MLB-licensed trading card set. First series packs contained at least one autograph, with the chance of getting more. Donruss/Leaf reports that all but 10 players in the Leaf Signature Series signed close to 5,000 total autographs (3,500 bronze, 1,000 silver, 500 gold). The 10 players who signed 1,000 (700 bronze, 200 silver, 100 gold) are: Roberto Alomar, Wade Boggs, Derek Jeter, Kenny Lofton, Paul Molitor, Raul Mondesi, Manny Ramirez, Alex Rodriguez, Frank Thomas and Mo Vaughn. It's also important to note that six additional players did not submit their cards in time to be included in first series packs. Thus, their cards were thrown into Extended series packs. Those six players are as follows: Brian L.Hunter, Carlos Delgado, Phil Plantier, Jim Thome, Terrell Wade and Ernie Young. Thome signed only silver and gold foil cards, thus the Bronze set is considered complete at 251 cards. Prices below refer exclusively to Bronze versions. Blue and black ink variations have been found for Carlos Delgado, Alex Rodriguez and Michael Tucker. No consistent premiums for these variations has been tracked. Finally, an autographed jumbo silver foil version of the Frank Thomas card was distributed to dealers in March, 1997. Dealers received either this first series or the Extended Series jumbo Thomas for every Extended Series case ordered. Each Thomas jumbo is individually serial numbered to 1,500.

	MINT	NRMT
COMPLETE SET (251)	2200.00	1000.00
COMMON CARD (1-251)	4.00	1.80

☐ 1 Kurt Abbott	4.00	1.80
☐ 2 Juan Acevedo	4.00	1.80
☐ 3 Terry Adams	4.00	1.80
☐ 4 Manny Alexander	4.00	1.80
☐ 5 Roberto Alomar SP	120.00	55.00
☐ 6 Moises Alou	8.00	3.60
☐ 7 Wilson Alvarez	8.00	3.60
☐ 8 Garret Anderson	8.00	3.60
☐ 9 Shane Andrews	4.00	1.80
☐ 10 Andy Ashby	4.00	1.80
☐ 11 Pedro Astacio	8.00	3.60
☐ 12 Brad Ausmus	4.00	1.80
☐ 13 Bobby Ayala	4.00	1.80
☐ 14 Carlos Baerga	8.00	3.60
☐ 15 Harold Baines	8.00	3.60
☐ 16 Jason Bates	4.00	1.80
☐ 17 Allen Battle	4.00	1.80
☐ 18 Rich Becker	4.00	1.80
☐ 19 David Bell	4.00	1.80
☐ 20 Rafael Belliard	4.00	1.80
☐ 21 Andy Benes	8.00	3.60
☐ 22 Armando Benitez	4.00	1.80
☐ 23 Jason Bere	4.00	1.80
☐ 24 Geronimo Berroa	4.00	1.80
☐ 25 Willie Blair	4.00	1.80
☐ 26 Mike Blowers	4.00	1.80
☐ 27 Wade Boggs SP	200.00	90.00
☐ 28 Ricky Bones	4.00	1.80
☐ 29 Mike Bordick	4.00	1.80
☐ 30 Toby Borland	4.00	1.80
☐ 31 Ricky Bottalico	4.00	1.80
☐ 32 Darren Bragg	4.00	1.80
☐ 33 Jeff Branson	4.00	1.80
☐ 34 Tilson Brito	4.00	1.80
☐ 35 Rico Brogna	4.00	1.80
☐ 36 Scott Brosius	4.00	1.80
☐ 37 Damon Buford	4.00	1.80
☐ 38 Mike Busby	4.00	1.80
☐ 39 Tom Candiotti	4.00	1.80
☐ 40 Frank Castillo	4.00	1.80

Card	Mint	Nrmt
☐ 41 Andujar Cedeno	4.00	1.80
☐ 42 Domingo Cedeno	4.00	1.80
☐ 43 Roger Cedeno	8.00	3.60
☐ 44 Norm Charlton	4.00	1.80
☐ 45 Jeff Cirillo	8.00	3.60
☐ 46 Will Clark	15.00	6.75
☐ 47 Jeff Conine	8.00	3.60
☐ 48 Steve Cooke	4.00	1.80
☐ 49 Joey Cora	8.00	3.60
☐ 50 Marty Cordova	8.00	3.60
☐ 51 Rheal Cormier	4.00	1.80
☐ 52 Felipe Crespo	4.00	1.80
☐ 53 Chad Curtis	4.00	1.80
☐ 54 Johnny Damon	8.00	3.60
☐ 55 Russ Davis	8.00	3.60
☐ 56 Andre Dawson	12.00	5.50
☐ 57 Carlos Delgado	8.00	3.60
☐ 58 Doug Drabek	4.00	1.80
☐ 59 Darren Dreifort	4.00	1.80
☐ 60 Shawon Dunston	4.00	1.80
☐ 61 Ray Durham	8.00	3.60
☐ 62 Jim Edmonds	15.00	6.75
☐ 63 Joey Eischen	4.00	1.80
☐ 64 Jim Eisenreich	4.00	1.80
☐ 65 Sal Fasano	4.00	1.80
☐ 66 Jeff Fassero	8.00	3.60
☐ 67 Alex Fernandez	8.00	3.60
☐ 68 Darrin Fletcher	4.00	1.80
☐ 69 Chad Fonville	4.00	1.80
☐ 70 Kevin Foster	4.00	1.80
☐ 71 John Franco	8.00	3.60
☐ 72 Julio Franco	8.00	3.60
☐ 73 Marvin Freeman	4.00	1.80
☐ 74 Travis Fryman	8.00	3.60
☐ 75 Gary Gaetti	8.00	3.60
☐ 76 Carlos Garcia	4.00	1.80
☐ 77 Jason Giambi	8.00	3.60
☐ 78 Benji Gil	4.00	1.80
☐ 79 Greg Gohr	4.00	1.80
☐ 80 Chris Gomez	4.00	1.80
☐ 81 Leo Gomez	4.00	1.80
☐ 82 Tom Goodwin	4.00	1.80
☐ 83 Mike Grace	4.00	1.80
☐ 84 Mike Greenwell	4.00	1.80
☐ 85 Rusty Greer	12.00	5.50
☐ 86 Mark Grudzielanek	8.00	3.60
☐ 87 Mark Gubicza	4.00	1.80
☐ 88 Juan Guzman	4.00	1.80
☐ 89 Darryl Hamilton	4.00	1.80
☐ 90 Joey Hamilton	8.00	3.60
☐ 91 Chris Hammond	4.00	1.80
☐ 92 Mike Hampton	4.00	1.80
☐ 93 Chris Haney	4.00	1.80
☐ 94 Todd Haney	4.00	1.80
☐ 95 Erik Hanson	4.00	1.80
☐ 96 Pete Harnisch	4.00	1.80
☐ 97 LaTroy Hawkins	4.00	1.80
☐ 98 Charlie Hayes	4.00	1.80
☐ 99 Jimmy Haynes	4.00	1.80
☐ 100 Roberto Hernandez	8.00	3.60
☐ 101 Bobby Higginson	8.00	3.60
☐ 102 Glenallen Hill	4.00	1.80
☐ 103 Ken Hill	8.00	3.60
☐ 104 Sterling Hitchcock	4.00	1.80
☐ 105 Trevor Hoffman	8.00	3.60
☐ 106 Dave Hollins	4.00	1.80
☐ 107 Dwayne Hosey	4.00	1.80
☐ 108 Thomas Howard	4.00	1.80
☐ 109 Steve Howe	4.00	1.80
☐ 110 John Hudek	4.00	1.80
☐ 111 Rex Hudler	4.00	1.80
☐ 112 Brian L. Hunter	8.00	3.60
☐ 113 Butch Huskey	8.00	3.60
☐ 114 Mark Hutton	4.00	1.80
☐ 115 Jason Jacome	4.00	1.80
☐ 116 John Jaha	8.00	3.60
☐ 117 Reggie Jefferson	8.00	3.60
☐ 118 Derek Jeter SP	175.00	80.00
☐ 119 Bobby Jones	4.00	1.80
☐ 120 Todd Jones	4.00	1.80
☐ 121 Brian Jordan	8.00	3.60
☐ 122 Kevin Jordan	4.00	1.80
☐ 123 Jeff Juden	4.00	1.80
☐ 124 Ron Karkovice	4.00	1.80
☐ 125 Roberto Kelly	4.00	1.80
☐ 126 Mark Kiefer	4.00	1.80
☐ 127 Brooks Kieschnick	8.00	3.60
☐ 128 Jeff King	8.00	3.60
☐ 129 Mike Lansing	8.00	3.60
☐ 130 Matt Lawton	8.00	3.60
☐ 131 Al Leiter	4.00	1.80
☐ 132 Mark Leiter	4.00	1.80
☐ 133 Curtis Leskanic	4.00	1.80
☐ 134 Darren Lewis	4.00	1.80
☐ 135 Mark Lewis	4.00	1.80
☐ 136 Felipe Lira	4.00	1.80
☐ 137 Pat Listach	4.00	1.80
☐ 138 Keith Lockhart	4.00	1.80
☐ 139 Kenny Lofton SP	120.00	55.00
☐ 140 John Mabry	8.00	3.60
☐ 141 Mike Macfarlane	4.00	1.80
☐ 142 Kirt Manwaring	4.00	1.80
☐ 143 Al Martin	4.00	1.80
☐ 144 Norberto Martin	4.00	1.80
☐ 145 Dennis Martinez	8.00	3.60
☐ 146 Pedro Martinez	18.00	8.00
☐ 147 Sandy Martinez	4.00	1.80
☐ 148 Mike Matheny	4.00	1.80
☐ 149 T.J. Mathews	4.00	1.80
☐ 150 David McCarty	4.00	1.80
☐ 151 Ben McDonald	4.00	1.80
☐ 152 Pat Meares	4.00	1.80
☐ 153 Orlando Merced	4.00	1.80
☐ 154 Jose Mesa	8.00	3.60
☐ 155 Matt Mieske	4.00	1.80
☐ 156 Orlando Miller	4.00	1.80
☐ 157 Mike Mimbs	4.00	1.80
☐ 158 Paul Molitor SP	100.00	45.00
☐ 159 Raul Mondesi SP	60.00	27.00
☐ 160 Jeff Montgomery	4.00	1.80
☐ 161 Mickey Morandini	4.00	1.80
☐ 162 Lyle Mouton	4.00	1.80
☐ 163 James Mouton	4.00	1.80
☐ 164 Jamie Moyer	4.00	1.80
☐ 165 Rodney Myers	4.00	1.80
☐ 166 Denny Neagle	12.00	5.50
☐ 167 Robb Nen	8.00	3.60
☐ 168 Marc Newfield	4.00	1.80
☐ 169 Dave Nilsson	8.00	3.60
☐ 170 Jon Nunnally	4.00	1.80
☐ 171 Chad Ogea	4.00	1.80
☐ 172 Troy O'Leary	4.00	1.80
☐ 173 Rey Ordonez	8.00	3.60
☐ 174 Jayhawk Owens	4.00	1.80
☐ 175 Tom Pagnozzi	4.00	1.80
☐ 176 Dean Palmer	8.00	3.60
☐ 177 Roger Pavlik	4.00	1.80
☐ 178 Troy Percival	8.00	3.60
☐ 179 Carlos Perez	4.00	1.80
☐ 180 Robert Perez	4.00	1.80
☐ 181 Andy Pettitte	30.00	13.50
☐ 182 Phil Plantier	4.00	1.80
☐ 183 Mike Potts	4.00	1.80
☐ 184 Curtis Pride	4.00	1.80
☐ 185 Ariel Prieto	4.00	1.80
☐ 186 Bill Pulsipher	4.00	1.80
☐ 187 Brad Radke	8.00	3.60
☐ 188 Manny Ramirez SP	40.00	18.00
☐ 189 Joe Randa	4.00	1.80
☐ 190 Pat Rapp	4.00	1.80
☐ 191 Bryan Rekar	4.00	1.80
☐ 192 Shane Reynolds	4.00	1.80
☐ 193 Arthur Rhodes	4.00	1.80
☐ 194 Mariano Rivera	12.00	5.50
☐ 195 Alex Rodriguez SP	250.00	110.00
☐ 196 Frank Rodriguez	4.00	1.80
☐ 197 Mel Rojas	4.00	1.80
☐ 198 Ken Ryan	4.00	1.80
☐ 199 Bret Saberhagen	8.00	3.60
☐ 200 Tim Salmon	20.00	9.00
☐ 201 Rey Sanchez	4.00	1.80
☐ 202 Scott Sanders	4.00	1.80
☐ 203 Steve Scarsone	4.00	1.80
☐ 204 Curt Schilling	8.00	3.60
☐ 205 Jason Schmidt	8.00	3.60
☐ 206 David Segui	4.00	1.80
☐ 207 Kevin Seitzer	4.00	1.80
☐ 208 Scott Servais	4.00	1.80
☐ 209 Don Slaught	4.00	1.80
☐ 210 Zane Smith	4.00	1.80
☐ 211 Paul Sorrento	4.00	1.80
☐ 212 Scott Stahoviak	4.00	1.80
☐ 213 Mike Stanley	4.00	1.80
☐ 214 Terry Steinbach	8.00	3.60
☐ 215 Kevin Stocker	4.00	1.80
☐ 216 Jeff Suppan	10.00	4.50
☐ 217 Bill Swift	4.00	1.80
☐ 218 Greg Swindell	4.00	1.80
☐ 219 Kevin Tapani	4.00	1.80
☐ 220 Danny Tartabull	4.00	1.80
☐ 221 Julian Tavarez	4.00	1.80
☐ 222 Frank Thomas SP	250.00	110.00
☐ 223 Ozzie Timmons	4.00	1.80
☐ 224 Michael Tucker	8.00	3.60
☐ 225 Ismael Valdes	8.00	3.60
☐ 226 Jose Valentin	4.00	1.80
☐ 227 Todd Van Poppel	4.00	1.80
☐ 228 Mo Vaughn SP	100.00	45.00
☐ 229 Quilvio Veras	8.00	3.60
☐ 230 Fernando Vina	4.00	1.80
☐ 231 Joe Vitiello	4.00	1.80
☐ 232 Jose Vizcaino	4.00	1.80
☐ 233 Omar Vizquel	8.00	3.60
☐ 234 Terrell Wade	4.00	1.80
☐ 235 Paul Wagner	4.00	1.80
☐ 236 Matt Walbeck	4.00	1.80
☐ 237 Jerome Walton	4.00	1.80
☐ 238 Turner Ward	4.00	1.80
☐ 239 Allen Watson	4.00	1.80
☐ 240 David Weathers	4.00	1.80
☐ 241 Walt Weiss	4.00	1.80
☐ 242 Turk Wendell	4.00	1.80
☐ 243 Rondell White	8.00	3.60
☐ 244 Brian Williams	4.00	1.80
☐ 245 George Williams	4.00	1.80
☐ 246 Paul Wilson	4.00	1.80
☐ 247 Bobby Witt	4.00	1.80
☐ 248 Bob Wolcott	4.00	1.80
☐ 249 Eric Young	8.00	3.60
☐ 250 Ernie Young	4.00	1.80
☐ 251 Greg Zaun	4.00	1.80
☐ NNO F.Thomas Jumbo AU	80.00	36.00

1996 Leaf Signature Autographs Gold

Randomly inserted primarily in first series packs, this 252-card set is parallel to the regular set and is similar in design with the exception of the gold foil printing on each card front. Each player signed 500 cards, except for the SP's of which only 100 of each are signed. Jim Thome erroneously signed 514 Gold cards.

	MINT	NRMT
COMPLETE SET (252)	4000.00	1800.00
COMMON CARD (1-252)	10.00	4.50
*GOLD: 1.25X to 2X BRONZE CARDS.		
☐ 223 Jim Thome SP514	80.00	36.00

1996 Leaf Signature Autographs Silver

Randomly inserted primarily in first series packs, this 252-card set is parallel to the regular set and is similar in design with the exception of the silver foil printing on each card front. Each player signed 1000 silver cards, except for the SP's of which only 200 are signed. Jim Thome erroneously signed 410 Silver cards.

	MINT	NRMT
COMPLETE SET (252)	3000.00	1350.00
COMMON CARD (1-252)	6.00	2.70
*SILVER: .75X to 1.5X BRONZE CARDS		
☐ 223 Jim Thome SP410	80.00	36.00

1996 Leaf Signature Extended Autographs

At least two autographed cards from this 217-card set were inserted in every Extended Series pack. Super Packs with four autographed cards were seeded one in every 12 packs. Most players signed 5000 cards, but short prints (500-2500 of each) do exist. On average, one in every nine packs contains a short print. All short print cards are individually noted below. By mistake, Andruw Jones, Ryan Klesko, Andy Pettitte, Kirby Puckett and Frank Thomas signed a few hundred of each of their cards in blue ink instead of black. No difference in price has been noted. Also, the Juan Gonzalez, Andruw Jones and Alex Rodriguez cards available in packs were not signed. All three cards had information on the back on how to mail them into Donruss/Leaf for an actual signed version. The deadline to exchange these cards was December 31st, 1998. In addition, middle relievers Doug Creek and Steve Parris failed to sign all 5000 of their cards. Creek submitted 1,950 cards and Parris submitted 1,800. Finally, an autographed jumbo version of the Extended Series Frank Thomas card was distributed to dealers in March, 1997. Dealers received either this card or the first series jumbo Thomas for every Extended Series case ordered. Each Extended Thomas jumbo is individually serial numbered to 1,500.

	MINT	NRMT
COMPLETE SET (217)	3000.00	1350.00
COMMON CARD (1-217)	4.00	1.80

	MINT	NRMT
☐ 1 Scott Aldred	4.00	1.80
☐ 2 Mike Aldrete	4.00	1.80
☐ 3 Rich Amaral	4.00	1.80
☐ 4 Alex Arias	4.00	1.80
☐ 5 Paul Assenmacher	4.00	1.80
☐ 6 Roger Bailey	4.00	1.80
☐ 7 Erik Bennett	4.00	1.80
☐ 8 Sean Bergman	4.00	1.80
☐ 9 Doug Bochtler	4.00	1.80
☐ 10 Tim Bogar	4.00	1.80
☐ 11 Pat Borders	4.00	1.80
☐ 12 Pedro Borbon	4.00	1.80
☐ 13 Shawn Boskie	4.00	1.80
☐ 14 Rafael Bournigal	4.00	1.80
☐ 15 Mark Brandenburg	4.00	1.80
☐ 16 John Briscoe	4.00	1.80
☐ 17 Jorge Brito	4.00	1.80
☐ 18 Doug Brocail	4.00	1.80
☐ 19 Jay Buhner SP1000	50.00	22.00
☐ 20 Scott Bullett	4.00	1.80
☐ 21 Dave Burba	4.00	1.80
☐ 22 Ken Caminiti SP1000	50.00	22.00
☐ 23 John Cangelosi	4.00	1.80
☐ 24 Cris Carpenter	4.00	1.80
☐ 25 Chuck Carr	4.00	1.80
☐ 26 Larry Casian	4.00	1.80
☐ 27 Tony Castillo	4.00	1.80
☐ 28 Jason Christiansen	4.00	1.80
☐ 29 Archi Cianfrocco	4.00	1.80
☐ 30 Mark Clark	4.00	1.80
☐ 31 Terry Clark	4.00	1.80
☐ 32 Roger Clemens SP1000	150.00	70.00
☐ 33 Jim Converse	4.00	1.80
☐ 34 Dennis Cook	4.00	1.80
☐ 35 Francisco Cordova	4.00	1.80
☐ 36 Jim Corsi	4.00	1.80
☐ 37 Tim Crabtree	4.00	1.80
☐ 38 Doug Creek SP1950	12.00	5.50
☐ 39 John Cummings	4.00	1.80
☐ 40 Omar Daal	4.00	1.80
☐ 41 Rich DeLucia	4.00	1.80
☐ 42 Mark Dewey	4.00	1.80
☐ 43 Alex Diaz	4.00	1.80
☐ 44 Jermaine Dye SP2500	15.00	6.75
☐ 45 Ken Edenfield	4.00	1.80
☐ 46 Mark Eichhorn	4.00	1.80
☐ 47 John Ericks	4.00	1.80
☐ 48 Darin Erstad	40.00	18.00
☐ 49 Alvaro Espinoza	4.00	1.80
☐ 50 Jorge Fabregas	4.00	1.80
☐ 51 Mike Fetters	4.00	1.80
☐ 52 John Flaherty	4.00	1.80
☐ 53 Bryce Florie	4.00	1.80
☐ 54 Tony Fossas	4.00	1.80
☐ 55 Lou Frazier	4.00	1.80
☐ 56 Mike Gallego	4.00	1.80
☐ 57 Karim Garcia SP2500	25.00	11.00
☐ 58 Jason Giambi	6.00	2.70
☐ 59 Ed Giovanola	4.00	1.80
☐ 60 Tom Glavine SP1250	40.00	18.00
☐ 61 Juan Gonzalez SP1000	150.00	70.00
☐ 62 Craig Grebeck	4.00	1.80
☐ 63 Buddy Groom	4.00	1.80
☐ 64 Kevin Gross	4.00	1.80
☐ 65 Eddie Guardado	4.00	1.80
☐ 66 Mark Guthrie	4.00	1.80
☐ 67 Tony Gwynn SP1000	150.00	70.00
☐ 68 Chip Hale	4.00	1.80
☐ 69 Darren Hall	4.00	1.80
☐ 70 Lee Hancock	4.00	1.80
☐ 71 Dave Hansen	4.00	1.80
☐ 72 Bryan Harvey	4.00	1.80
☐ 73 Bill Haselman	4.00	1.80
☐ 74 Mike Henneman	4.00	1.80
☐ 75 Doug Henry	4.00	1.80
☐ 76 Gil Heredia	4.00	1.80
☐ 77 Carlos Hernandez	4.00	1.80
☐ 78 Jose Hernandez	4.00	1.80
☐ 79 Darren Holmes	4.00	1.80
☐ 80 Mark Holzemer	4.00	1.80
☐ 81 Rick Honeycutt	4.00	1.80
☐ 82 Chris Hook	4.00	1.80
☐ 83 Chris Howard	4.00	1.80
☐ 84 Jack Howell	4.00	1.80
☐ 85 David Hulse	4.00	1.80
☐ 86 Edwin Hurtado	4.00	1.80
☐ 87 Jeff Huson	4.00	1.80
☐ 88 Mike James	4.00	1.80
☐ 89 Derek Jeter SP1000	150.00	70.00
☐ 90 Brian Johnson	4.00	1.80
☐ 91 Randy Johnson SP1000	80.00	36.00
☐ 92 Mark Johnson	4.00	1.80
☐ 93 Andruw Jones SP2000	80.00	36.00
☐ 94 Chris Jones	4.00	1.80
☐ 95 Ricky Jordan	4.00	1.80
☐ 96 Matt Karchner	4.00	1.80
☐ 97 Scott Karl	4.00	1.80
☐ 98 Jason Kendall SP2500	20.00	9.00
☐ 99 Brian Keyser	4.00	1.80
☐ 100 Mike Kingery	4.00	1.80
☐ 101 Wayne Kirby	4.00	1.80
☐ 102 Ryan Klesko SP1000	50.00	22.00
☐ 103 Chuck Knoblauch SP1000	60.00	27.00
☐ 104 Chad Kreuter	4.00	1.80
☐ 105 Tom Lampkin	4.00	1.80
☐ 106 Scott Leius	4.00	1.80
☐ 107 Jon Lieber	4.00	1.80
☐ 108 Nelson Liriano	4.00	1.80
☐ 109 Scott Livingstone	4.00	1.80
☐ 110 Graeme Lloyd	4.00	1.80
☐ 111 Kenny Lofton SP1000	80.00	36.00
☐ 112 Luis Lopez	4.00	1.80
☐ 113 Torey Lovullo	4.00	1.80
☐ 114 Greg Maddux SP500	400.00	180.00
☐ 115 Mike Maddux	4.00	1.80
☐ 116 Dave Magadan	4.00	1.80
☐ 117 Mike Magnante	4.00	1.80
☐ 118 Joe Magrane	4.00	1.80
☐ 119 Pat Mahomes	4.00	1.80
☐ 120 Matt Mantei	4.00	1.80
☐ 121 John Marzano	4.00	1.80
☐ 122 Terry Mathews	4.00	1.80
☐ 123 Chuck McElroy	4.00	1.80
☐ 124 Fred McGriff SP1000	40.00	18.00
☐ 125 Mark McLemore	4.00	1.80
☐ 126 Greg McMichael	4.00	1.80
☐ 127 Blas Minor	4.00	1.80
☐ 128 Dave Mlicki	4.00	1.80
☐ 129 Mike Mohler	4.00	1.80
☐ 130 Paul Molitor SP1000	80.00	36.00
☐ 131 Steve Montgomery	4.00	1.80
☐ 132 Mike Mordecai	4.00	1.80
☐ 133 Mike Morgan	4.00	1.80
☐ 134 Mike Munoz	4.00	1.80
☐ 135 Greg Myers	4.00	1.80
☐ 136 Jimmy Myers	4.00	1.80
☐ 137 Mike Myers	4.00	1.80
☐ 138 Bob Natal	4.00	1.80
☐ 139 Dan Naulty	4.00	1.80
☐ 140 Jeff Nelson	4.00	1.80
☐ 141 Warren Newson	4.00	1.80
☐ 142 Chris Nichting	4.00	1.80
☐ 143 Melvin Nieves	4.00	1.80
☐ 144 Charlie O'Brien	4.00	1.80
☐ 145 Alex Ochoa	4.00	1.80
☐ 146 Omar Olivares	4.00	1.80
☐ 147 Joe Oliver	4.00	1.80
☐ 148 Lance Painter	4.00	1.80
☐ 149 Rafael Palmeiro SP2000	25.00	11.00
☐ 150 Mark Parent	4.00	1.80
☐ 151 Steve Parris SP1800	20.00	9.00
☐ 152 Bob Patterson	4.00	1.80
☐ 153 Tony Pena	4.00	1.80
☐ 154 Eddie Perez	4.00	1.80
☐ 155 Yorkis Perez	4.00	1.80
☐ 156 Robert Person	4.00	1.80
☐ 157 Mark Petkovsek	4.00	1.80
☐ 158 Andy Pettitte SP1000	60.00	27.00
☐ 159 J.R. Phillips	4.00	1.80
☐ 160 Hipolito Pichardo	4.00	1.80
☐ 161 Eric Plunk	4.00	1.80
☐ 162 Jimmy Poole	4.00	1.80
☐ 163 Kirby Puckett SP1000	150.00	70.00
☐ 164 Paul Quantrill	4.00	1.80
☐ 165 Tom Quinlan	4.00	1.80
☐ 166 Jeff Reboulet	4.00	1.80
☐ 167 Jeff Reed	4.00	1.80
☐ 168 Steve Reed	4.00	1.80
☐ 169 Carlos Reyes	4.00	1.80
☐ 170 Bill Risley	4.00	1.80
☐ 171 Kevin Ritz	4.00	1.80
☐ 172 Kevin Roberson	4.00	1.80
☐ 173 Rich Robertson	4.00	1.80
☐ 174 Alex Rodriguez SP500	300.00	135.00
☐ 175 Ivan Rodriguez SP1250	80.00	36.00
☐ 176 Bruce Ruffin	4.00	1.80
☐ 177 Juan Samuel	4.00	1.80
☐ 178 Tim Scott	4.00	1.80
☐ 179 Kevin Sefcik	4.00	1.80
☐ 180 Jeff Shaw	4.00	1.80
☐ 181 Danny Sheaffer	4.00	1.80
☐ 182 Craig Shipley	4.00	1.80
☐ 183 Dave Silvestri	4.00	1.80
☐ 184 Aaron Small	4.00	1.80
☐ 185 John Smoltz SP1000	40.00	18.00
☐ 186 Luis Sojo	4.00	1.80
☐ 187 Sammy Sosa SP1000	60.00	27.00
☐ 188 Steve Sparks	4.00	1.80
☐ 189 Tim Spehr	4.00	1.80
☐ 190 Russ Springer	4.00	1.80
☐ 191 Matt Stairs	4.00	1.80
☐ 192 Andy Stankiewicz	4.00	1.80
☐ 193 Mike Stanton	4.00	1.80
☐ 194 Kelly Stinnett	4.00	1.80
☐ 195 Doug Strange	4.00	1.80
☐ 196 Mark Sweeney	4.00	1.80
☐ 197 Jeff Tabaka	4.00	1.80
☐ 198 Jesus Tavarez	4.00	1.80
☐ 199 Frank Thomas SP1000	200.00	90.00
☐ 200 Larry Thomas	4.00	1.80
☐ 201 Mark Thompson	4.00	1.80
☐ 202 Mike Timlin	4.00	1.80
☐ 203 Steve Trachsel	4.00	1.80
☐ 204 Tom Urbani	4.00	1.80
☐ 205 Julio Valera	4.00	1.80
☐ 206 Dave Valle	4.00	1.80
☐ 207 William VanLandingham	4.00	1.80
☐ 208 Mo Vaughn SP1000	80.00	36.00
☐ 209 Dave Veres	4.00	1.80
☐ 210 Ed Vosberg	4.00	1.80
☐ 211 Don Wengert	4.00	1.80
☐ 212 Matt Whiteside	4.00	1.80
☐ 213 Bob Wickman	4.00	1.80
☐ 214 Matt Williams SP1250	50.00	22.00
☐ 215 Mike Williams	4.00	1.80
☐ 216 Woody Williams	4.00	1.80
☐ 217 Craig Worthington	4.00	1.80
☐ NNO F.Thomas Jumbo AU	80.00	36.00

1996 Leaf Signature Extended Autographs Century Marks

Randomly inserted exclusively into Extended Series packs, cards from this 31-card parallel set feature a selection of star and rising young prospect players taken from the more comprehensive 217-card Extended Autograph set. The cards differ by a special blue holographic foil treatment. Only 100 of each card exists. In addition, Juan Gonzalez, Derek Jeter, Andrew Jones, Rafael Palmeiro and Alex Rodriguez did not sign the cards distributed in packs. All of these players cards had information on the back on how to mail them into Leaf/Donruss to receive a signed version.

	MINT	NRMT
COMPLETE SET (31)	6000.00	2700.00
COMMON CARD (1-31)	60.00	27.00

	MINT	NRMT
☐ 1 Jay Buhner	125.00	55.00
☐ 2 Ken Caminiti	125.00	55.00
☐ 3 Roger Clemens	400.00	180.00
☐ 4 Jermaine Dye	60.00	27.00
☐ 5 Darin Erstad	200.00	90.00
☐ 6 Karim Garcia	100.00	45.00
☐ 7 Jason Giambi	80.00	36.00
☐ 8 Tom Glavine	100.00	45.00
☐ 9 Juan Gonzalez	400.00	180.00
☐ 10 Tony Gwynn	400.00	180.00
☐ 11 Derek Jeter	325.00	145.00
☐ 12 Randy Johnson	200.00	90.00
☐ 13 Andruw Jones	300.00	135.00
☐ 14 Jason Kendall	80.00	36.00
☐ 15 Ryan Klesko	100.00	45.00
☐ 16 Chuck Knoblauch	125.00	55.00
☐ 17 Kenny Lofton	200.00	90.00
☐ 18 Greg Maddux	600.00	275.00
☐ 19 Fred McGriff	100.00	45.00
☐ 20 Paul Molitor	150.00	70.00
☐ 21 Alex Ochoa	60.00	27.00
☐ 22 Rafael Palmeiro	100.00	45.00
☐ 23 Andy Pettitte	150.00	70.00
☐ 24 Kirby Puckett	400.00	180.00
☐ 25 Alex Rodriguez	500.00	220.00
☐ 26 Ivan Rodriguez	200.00	90.00
☐ 27 John Smoltz	100.00	45.00
☐ 28 Sammy Sosa	125.00	55.00
☐ 29 Frank Thomas	500.00	220.00
☐ 30 Mo Vaughn	200.00	90.00
☐ 31 Matt Williams	125.00	55.00

1984 Mariners Mother's

The cards in this 28-card set measure the standard size. In 1984, The Los Angeles-based Mother's Cookies Co. issued five sets of cards featuring players from major league teams. The Seattle Mariners set features current players depicted by photos. Similar to their 1952 and 1953 issues, the cards have rounded corners. The backs of the cards contain the Mother's Cookies logo. The cards were distributed in partial sets to fans at the respective stadiums of the teams involved. Whereas 20 cards were given to each patron, a redemption card, redeemable for eight more cards was included. Unfortunately, the eight cards received by redeeming the coupon were not

necessarily the eight needed to complete a set. Hobbyist Barry Colla was involved in the production of these sets. The key card in the set is Mark Langston, one of his earliest cards issued.

	NRMT	VG-E
COMPLETE SET (28)	12.50	5.50
COMMON CARD (1-28)	.25	.11

	NRMT	VG-E
☐ 1 Del Crandall MG	.25	.11
☐ 2 Barry Bonnell	.25	.11
☐ 3 Dave Henderson	.50	.23
☐ 4 Bob Kearney	.25	.11
☐ 5 Mike Moore	.50	.23
☐ 6 Spike Owen	.50	.23
☐ 7 Gorman Thomas	.50	.23
☐ 8 Ed VandeBerg	.25	.11
☐ 9 Matt Young	.25	.11
☐ 10 Larry Milbourne	.25	.11
☐ 11 Dave Beard	.25	.11
☐ 12 Jim Beattie	.25	.11
☐ 13 Mark Langston	4.00	1.80
☐ 14 Orlando Mercado	.25	.11
☐ 15 Jack Perconte	.25	.11
☐ 16 Pat Putnam	.25	.11
☐ 17 Paul Mirabella	.25	.11
☐ 18 Domingo Ramos	.25	.11
☐ 19 Al Cowens	.25	.11
☐ 20 Mike Stanton	.25	.11
☐ 21 Steve Henderson	.25	.11
☐ 22 Bob Stoddard	.25	.11
☐ 23 Alvin Davis	1.00	.45
☐ 24 Phil Bradley	.75	.35
☐ 25 Roy Thomas	.25	.11
☐ 26 Darnell Coles	.50	.23
☐ 27 Mariners' Coaches Rick Sweet Frank Funk Ben Hines Chuck Cottier Phil Roof	.25	.11
☐ 28 Mariners' Checklist Seattle Kingdome	.25	.11

1985 Mariners Mother's

The cards in this 28-card set measure the standard size. In 1985, the Los Angeles based Mother's Cookies Co. again issued five sets of cards featuring players from major league teams. The Seattle Mariners set features current players depicted by photos on cards with rounded corners. The backs of the cards contain the Mother's Cookies logo. Cards were passed out at the stadium on August 10.

	NRMT	VG-E
COMPLETE SET (28)	7.50	3.40
COMMON CARD (1-28)	.25	.11

	NRMT	VG-E
☐ 1 Chuck Cottier MG	.25	.11
☐ 2 Alvin Davis	.75	.35
☐ 3 Mark Langston	1.50	.70
☐ 4 Dave Henderson	.50	.23
☐ 5 Ed VandeBerg	.25	.11
☐ 6 Al Cowens	.25	.11
☐ 7 Spike Owen	.25	.11
☐ 8 Mike Moore	.25	.11
☐ 9 Gorman Thomas	.50	.23
☐ 10 Barry Bonnell	.25	.11
☐ 11 Jack Perconte	.25	.11
☐ 12 Domingo Ramos	.25	.11
☐ 13 Bob Kearney	.25	.11
☐ 14 Matt Young	.25	.11
☐ 15 Jim Beattie	.25	.11
☐ 16 Mike Stanton	.25	.11
☐ 17 David Valle	.25	.11
☐ 18 Ken Phelps	.25	.11
☐ 19 Salome Barojas	.25	.11
☐ 20 Jim Presley	.50	.23
☐ 21 Phil Bradley	.50	.23
☐ 22 Dave Geisel	.25	.11
☐ 23 Harold Reynolds	1.50	.70
☐ 24 Ed Nunez	.25	.11
☐ 25 Mike Morgan	.25	.11
☐ 26 Ivan Calderon	.50	.23
☐ 27 Mariners' Coaches Marty Martinez Jim Mahoney Phil Roof Phil Regan Deron Johnson	.25	.11
☐ 28 Checklist Card Seattle Kingdome	.25	.11

1986 Mariners Mother's

This set consists of 28 full-color, rounded-corner cards each measuring the standard size. Starter sets (only 20 cards but also including a certificate for eight more cards) were given out at the ballpark and collectors were encouraged to trade to fill in the rest of their set. Cards were originally given out on July 27th at the Seattle Kingdome.

	MINT	NRMT
COMPLETE SET (28)	8.00	3.60
COMMON CARD (1-28)	.25	.11

	MINT	NRMT
☐ 1 Dick Williams MG	.50	.23
☐ 2 Alvin Davis	.50	.23
☐ 3 Mark Langston	1.00	.45
☐ 4 Dave Henderson	.50	.23
☐ 5 Steve Yeager	.25	.11
☐ 6 Al Cowens	.25	.11
☐ 7 Jim Presley	.25	.11
☐ 8 Phil Bradley	.25	.11
☐ 9 Gorman Thomas	.25	.11
☐ 10 Barry Bonnell	.25	.11
☐ 11 Milt Wilcox	.25	.11
☐ 12 Domingo Ramos	.25	.11
☐ 13 Paul Mirabella	.25	.11
☐ 14 Matt Young	.25	.11
☐ 15 Ivan Calderon	.50	.23
☐ 16 Bill Swift	.50	.23
☐ 17 Pete Ladd	.25	.11
☐ 18 Ken Phelps	.25	.11
☐ 19 Karl Best	.25	.11
☐ 20 Spike Owen	.25	.11
☐ 21 Mike Moore	.25	.11
☐ 22 Danny Tartabull	1.00	.45
☐ 23 Bob Kearney	.25	.11
☐ 24 Edwin Nunez	.25	.11
☐ 25 Mike Morgan	.25	.11
☐ 26 Roy Thomas	.25	.11
☐ 27 Jim Beattie	.25	.11
☐ 28 Checklist Card Deron Johnson CO Marty Martinez CO Phil Roof CO Phil Regan CO Ozzie Virgil CO	.25	.11

1987 Mariners Mother's

This set consists of 28 full-color, rounded-corner cards each measuring the standard size. Starter sets (only 20 cards but also including a certificate for eight more cards) were given out at the ballpark and collectors were encouraged to trade to fill in the rest of their set. Cards were originally given out on August 9th at the Seattle Kingdome. Photos were taken by Barry Colla. The sets

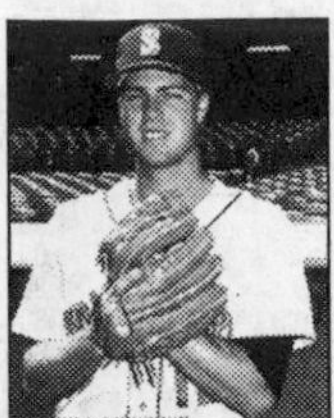

were reportedly given out free to the first 20,000 paid admissions at the game.

	MINT	NRMT
COMPLETE SET (28)	7.50	3.40
COMMON CARD (1-28)	.25	.11

	MINT	NRMT
☐ 1 Dick Williams MG	.50	.23
☐ 2 Alvin Davis	.50	.23
☐ 3 Mike Moore	.25	.11
☐ 4 Jim Presley	.25	.11
☐ 5 Mark Langston	1.00	.45
☐ 6 Phil Bradley	.25	.11
☐ 7 Ken Phelps	.25	.11
☐ 8 Mike Morgan	.25	.11
☐ 9 David Valle	.25	.11
☐ 10 Harold Reynolds	.50	.23
☐ 11 Edwin Nunez	.25	.11
☐ 12 Bob Kearney	.25	.11
☐ 13 Scott Bankhead	.25	.11
☐ 14 Scott Bradley	.25	.11
☐ 15 Mickey Brantley	.25	.11
☐ 16 Mark Huismann	.25	.11
☐ 17 Mike Kingery	.50	.23
☐ 18 John Moses	.25	.11
☐ 19 Donell Nixon	.25	.11
☐ 20 Rey Quinones	.25	.11
☐ 21 Domingo Ramos	.25	.11
☐ 22 Jerry Reed	.25	.11
☐ 23 Rich Renteria	.25	.11
☐ 24 Rich Monteleone	.25	.11
☐ 25 Mike Trujillo	.25	.11
☐ 26 Bill Wilkinson	.25	.11
☐ 27 John Christensen	.25	.11
☐ 28 Checklist Card Billy Connors CO Frank Howard CO Bobby Tolan CO Ozzie Virgil CO Phil Roof CO	.50	.23

1988 Mariners Mother's

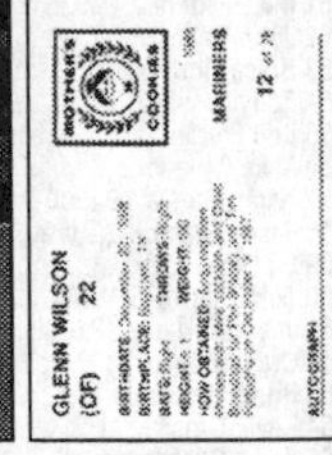

This set consists of 28 full-color, rounded-corner cards each measuring the standard size. Starter sets (only 20 cards but also including a certificate for eight more cards) were given out at the ballpark and collectors were encouraged to trade to fill in the rest of their set. Cards were originally given out on August 14th at the Seattle Kingdome. Photos were taken by Barry Colla. The sets were reportedly given out free to the first 20,000 paid admissions at the game.

	MINT	NRMT
COMPLETE SET (28)	7.50	3.40
COMMON CARD (1-28)	.25	.11

	MINT	NRMT
☐ 1 Dick Williams MG	.50	.23
☐ 2 Alvin Davis	.50	.23
☐ 3 Mike Moore	.25	.11
☐ 4 Jim Presley	.25	.11
☐ 5 Mark Langston	1.00	.45
☐ 6 Henry Cotto	.25	.11
☐ 7 Ken Phelps	.25	.11
☐ 8 Steve Trout	.25	.11
☐ 9 David Valle	.25	.11
☐ 10 Harold Reynolds	.50	.23
☐ 11 Edwin Nunez	.25	.11
☐ 12 Glenn Wilson	.25	.11
☐ 13 Scott Bankhead	.25	.11

	MINT	NRMT
☐ 14 Scott Bradley	.25	.11
☐ 15 Mickey Brantley	.25	.11
☐ 16 Bruce Fields	.25	.11
☐ 17 Mike Kingery	.25	.11
☐ 18 Mike Campbell	.25	.11
☐ 19 Mike Jackson	.75	.35
☐ 20 Rey Quinones	.25	.11
☐ 21 Mario Diaz	.25	.11
☐ 22 Jerry Reed	.25	.11
☐ 23 Rich Renteria	.25	.11
☐ 24 Julio Solano	.25	.11
☐ 25 Bill Swift	.25	.11
☐ 26 Bill Wilkinson	.25	.11
☐ 27 Mariners Coaches	.25	.11
☐ 28 Checklist Card Henry Genzale EQMG Rick Griffin TR	.25	.11

1989 Mariners Mother's

The 1989 Mother's Cookies Seattle Mariners set contains 28 standard-size cards with rounded corners. The fronts have borderless color photos, and the horizontally oriented backs have biographical information. Starter sets containing 20 of these cards were given away at a Mariners home game during the 1989 season. Ken Griffey Jr. has a card in his Rookie Card season in this set.

	MINT	NRMT
COMPLETE SET (28)	20.00	9.00
COMMON CARD (1-28)	.25	.11
☐ 1 Jim Lefebvre MG	.50	.23
☐ 2 Alvin Davis	.50	.23
☐ 3 Ken Griffey Jr.	10.00	4.50
☐ 4 Jim Presley	.25	.11
☐ 5 Mark Langston	.50	.23
☐ 6 Henry Cotto	.25	.11
☐ 7 Mickey Brantley	.25	.11
☐ 8 Jeffrey Leonard	.25	.11
☐ 9 Dave Valle	.25	.11
☐ 10 Harold Reynolds	.50	.23
☐ 11 Edgar Martinez	3.00	1.35
☐ 12 Tom Niedenfuer	.25	.11
☐ 13 Scott Bankhead	.25	.11
☐ 14 Scott Bradley	.25	.11
☐ 15 Omar Vizquel	2.00	.90
☐ 16 Erik Hanson	.50	.23
☐ 17 Bill Swift	.25	.11
☐ 18 Mike Campbell	.25	.11
☐ 19 Mike Jackson	.50	.23
☐ 20 Rich Renteria	.25	.11
☐ 21 Mario Diaz	.25	.11
☐ 22 Jerry Reed	.25	.11
☐ 23 Darnell Coles	.25	.11
☐ 24 Steve Trout	.25	.11
☐ 25 Mike Schooler	.25	.11
☐ 26 Julio Solano	.25	.11
☐ 27 Mariners Coaches Mike Paul Gene Clines Bill Plummer Bob Didier Rusty Kuntz	.25	.11
☐ 28 Checklist Card Henry Genzale EQMG Rick Griffin TR	.25	.11

1990 Mariners Mother's

1990 Mother's Cookies Seattle Mariners set contains 28 standard-size cards with the traditional Mother's Cookies rounded corners. The cards have full-color fronts and biographical information with no stats on the back. These Mariners cards were released for the August 5th game and given to the first 25,000 people who passed through the gates. They were distributed in 20-card random packets at the game and eight more at the redemption booths. However, both groups of cards were random and there was no guarantee of getting a complete set in the cards. The promotional idea was that the only way one could finish the set was to trade for them. The redemption

for eight more cards were available at the Kingdome Card Show on August 12, 1990.

	MINT	NRMT
COMPLETE SET (28)	15.00	6.75
COMMON CARD (1-28)	.25	.11
☐ 1 Jim Lefebvre MG	.25	.11
☐ 2 Alvin Davis	.50	.23
☐ 3 Ken Griffey Jr.	7.50	3.40
☐ 4 Jeffrey Leonard	.25	.11
☐ 5 David Valle	.25	.11
☐ 6 Harold Reynolds	.50	.23
☐ 7 Jay Buhner	2.50	1.10
☐ 8 Erik Hanson	.50	.23
☐ 9 Henry Cotto	.25	.11
☐ 10 Edgar Martinez	2.50	1.10
☐ 11 Bill Swift	.25	.11
☐ 12 Omar Vizquel	1.00	.45
☐ 13 Randy Johnson	2.50	1.10
☐ 14 Greg Briley	.25	.11
☐ 15 Gene Harris	.25	.11
☐ 16 Matt Young	.25	.11
☐ 17 Pete O'Brien	.25	.11
☐ 18 Brent Knackert	.25	.11
☐ 19 Mike Jackson	.50	.23
☐ 20 Brian Holman	.25	.11
☐ 21 Mike Schooler	.25	.11
☐ 22 Darnell Coles	.25	.11
☐ 23 Keith Comstock	.25	.11
☐ 24 Scott Bankhead	.25	.11
☐ 25 Scott Bradley	.25	.11
☐ 26 Mike Brumley	.25	.11
☐ 27 Mariners Coaches Rusty Kuntz Gene Clines Bill Plummer Mike Paul Bob Didier	.25	.11
☐ 28 Checklist Card Mariners Personnel Henry Genzale EQ.MG Tom Newberg ATR Rick Griffin TR	.25	.11

1992 Mariners Mother's

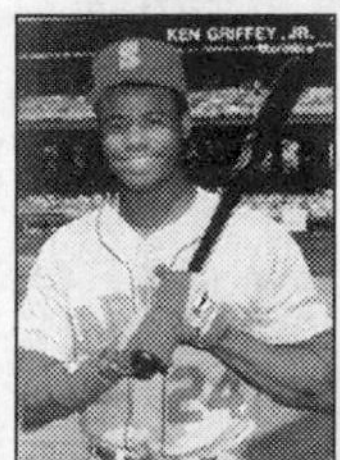

The 1992 Mother's Cookies Mariners set contains 28 cards with rounded corners measuring the standard size. The front design has borderless glossy color player photos. The player's name and team name appear in one of the upper corners. The horizontal backs are printed in red and purple, and present biography and a "how obtained" remark where appropriate. A blank slot for the player's autograph rounds out the back.

	MINT	NRMT
COMPLETE SET (28)	12.00	5.50
COMMON CARD (1-28)	.25	.11
☐ 1 Bill Plummer MG	.25	.11
☐ 2 Ken Griffey Jr.	6.00	2.70
☐ 3 Harold Reynolds	.50	.23
☐ 4 Kevin Mitchell	.50	.23
☐ 5 David Valle	.25	.11
☐ 6 Jay Buhner	1.50	.70
☐ 7 Erik Hanson	.50	.23
☐ 8 Pete O'Brien	.25	.11
☐ 9 Henry Cotto	.25	.11
☐ 10 Mike Schooler	.25	.11
☐ 11 Tino Martinez	2.50	1.10
☐ 12 Dennis Powell	.25	.11
☐ 13 Randy Johnson	2.00	.90
☐ 14 Dave Cochrane	.25	.11
☐ 15 Greg Briley	.25	.11
☐ 16 Omar Vizquel	.75	.35
☐ 17 Dave Fleming	.25	.11
☐ 18 Matt Sinatro	.25	.11
☐ 19 Jeff Nelson	.25	.11
☐ 20 Edgar Martinez	1.50	.70
☐ 21 Calvin Jones	.25	.11
☐ 22 Russ Swan	.25	.11
☐ 23 Jim Acker	.25	.11
☐ 24 Jeff Schaefer	.25	.11
☐ 25 Clay Parker	.25	.11
☐ 26 Brian Holman	.25	.11
☐ 27 Coaches Dan Warthen Russ Nixon Rusty Kuntz Marty Martinez Gene Clines Roger Hansen	.25	.11
☐ 28 Checklist	.25	.11

1993 Mariners Mother's

The 1993 Mother's Cookies Mariners set consists of 28 standard-size cards with rounded corners. The fronts display full-bleed color player portraits shot from the waist up in stadium settings. The player's name and team name appear in one of the corners. On a white background in red and purple print, the horizontal backs carry biographical information and the sponsor's logo. A blank slot for the player's autograph rounds out the back.

	MINT	NRMT
COMPLETE SET (28)	12.00	5.50
COMMON CARD (1-28)	.25	.11
☐ 1 Lou Piniella MG	.75	.35
☐ 2 Dave Fleming	.25	.11
☐ 3 Pete O'Brien	.25	.11
☐ 4 Ken Griffey Jr.	6.00	2.70
☐ 5 Henry Cotto	.25	.11
☐ 6 Jay Buhner	1.50	.70
☐ 7 David Valle	.25	.11
☐ 8 Dwayne Henry	.25	.11
☐ 9 Mike Felder	.25	.11
☐ 10 Norm Charlton	.50	.23
☐ 11 Edgar Martinez	1.50	.70
☐ 12 Erik Hanson	.50	.23
☐ 13 Mike Blowers	.25	.11
☐ 14 Omar Vizquel	.75	.35
☐ 15 Randy Johnson	2.00	.90
☐ 16 Russ Swan	.25	.11
☐ 17 Tino Martinez	2.00	.90
☐ 18 Rich DeLucia	.25	.11
☐ 19 Jeff Nelson	.25	.11
☐ 20 Chris Bosio	.25	.11
☐ 21 Tim Leary	.25	.11
☐ 22 Mackey Sasser	.25	.11
☐ 23 Dennis Powell	.25	.11
☐ 24 Mike Hampton	.75	.35
☐ 25 Fernando Vina	1.00	.45
☐ 26 John Cummings	.25	.11
☐ 27 Rich Amaral	.25	.11
☐ 28 Checklist/Coaches Sam Perlozzo Sam Mejias Lee Elia Sammy Ellis John McLaren Ken Griffey Sr.	.50	.23

1994 Mariners Mother's

The 1994 Mariners Mother's Cookies set consists of 28 standard-size cards with rounded corners. The fronts display posed full-bleed color player portraits shot from the waist up in stadium settings. The player's name and team name appear in one of the upper corners. On a white

background in red and purple print, the horizontal backs carry biographical information and the sponsor's logo. A blank slot for the player's autograph rounds out the back. The set includes a coupon with a mail-in offer to obtain a trading card collectors album for 3.95. The set had limited distribution since the original Mother's promotion night was cancelled due to the Kingdome closure and then the baseball strike.

	MINT	NRMT
COMPLETE SET (28)	17.50	8.00
COMMON CARD (1-28)	.25	.11

	MINT	NRMT
☐ 1 Lou Piniella MG	.75	.35
☐ 2 Randy Johnson	2.00	.90
☐ 3 Eric Anthony	.25	.11
☐ 4 Ken Griffey Jr.	6.00	2.70
☐ 5 Felix Fermin	.25	.11
☐ 6 Jay Buhner	1.50	.70
☐ 7 Chris Bosio	.25	.11
☐ 8 Reggie Jefferson	1.00	.45
☐ 9 Greg Hibbard	.25	.11
☐ 10 Dave Fleming	.25	.11
☐ 11 Rich Amaral	.25	.11
☐ 12 Rich Gossage	1.00	.45
☐ 13 Edgar Martinez	1.50	.70
☐ 14 Bobby Ayala	.25	.11
☐ 15 Darren Bragg	.50	.23
☐ 16 Tino Martinez	2.00	.90
☐ 17 Mike Blowers	.25	.11
☐ 18 John Cummings	.25	.11
☐ 19 Keith Mitchell	.25	.11
☐ 20 Bill Haselman	.25	.11
☐ 21 Greg Pirkl	.25	.11
☐ 22 Mackey Sasser	.25	.11
☐ 23 Tim Davis	.25	.11
☐ 24 Dan Wilson	1.25	.55
☐ 25 Jeff Nelson	.25	.11
☐ 26 Kevin King	.25	.11
☐ 27 Torey Lovullo	.25	.11
☐ 28 Checklist/Coaches Sam Perlozzo Lee Elia Sammy Ellis John McLaren Sam Mejias	.25	.11

1995 Mariners Mother's

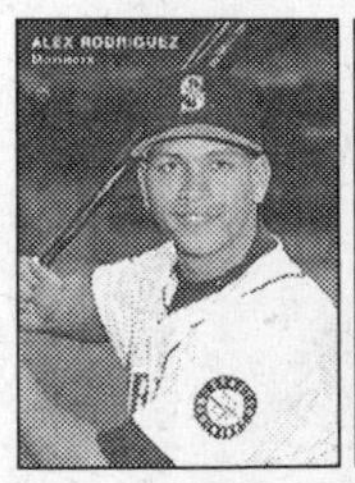

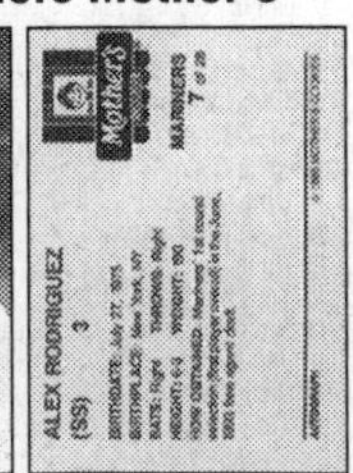

This 1995 Mother's Cookies Seattle Mariners set consists of 28 standard-size cards with rounded corners. The fronts display posed color player portraits. The player's name and team name appear in one of the top corners. The horizontal backs carry biographical information and the sponsor's logo on a white background in red and purple print. A blank slot at the bottom for the player's autograph rounds out the back.

	MINT	NRMT
COMPLETE SET (28)	17.50	8.00
COMMON CARD (1-28)	.25	.11

	MINT	NRMT
☐ 1 Lou Piniella MG	.75	.35
☐ 2 Randy Johnson	1.50	.70
☐ 3 Dave Fleming	.25	.11
☐ 4 Ken Griffey Jr.	5.00	2.20
☐ 5 Edgar Martinez	1.25	.55
☐ 6 Jay Buhner	1.25	.55
☐ 7 Alex Rodriguez	7.50	3.40
☐ 8 Joey Cora	1.00	.45
☐ 9 Tim Davis	.25	.11
☐ 10 Mike Blowers	.25	.11
☐ 11 Chris Bosio	.25	.11
☐ 12 Dan Wilson	.75	.35
☐ 13 Rich Amaral	.25	.11
☐ 14 Bobby Ayala	.25	.11
☐ 15 Darren Bragg	.50	.23
☐ 16 Bob Wells	.25	.11
☐ 17 Doug Strange	.25	.11
☐ 18 Chad Kreuter	.25	.11
☐ 19 Rafael Carmona	.25	.11
☐ 20 Luis Sojo	.25	.11
☐ 21 Tim Belcher	.25	.11
☐ 22 Steve Frey	.25	.11
☐ 23 Tino Martinez	1.50	.70
☐ 24 Felix Fermin	.25	.11
☐ 25 Jeff Nelson	.25	.11
☐ 26 Alex Diaz	.25	.11
☐ 27 Bill Risley	.25	.11
☐ 28 Coaches/Checklist Sam Perlozzo Matt Sinatro Lee Elia Sam Mejias John McLaren Bobby Cuellar	.25	.11

1995 Mariners Pacific

Produced by Pacific, this 50-card boxed standard-size set highlights the events leading up to the Seattle Mariners clinching the American League Western Division Pennant and their playoff run during the Division Series and the American League Championship Series. The set divides into game action shots (1-17) and player (and manager) cards (18-50). The fronts of all cards feature glossy, full-bleed color photos, with the caption or player's name stamped in silver foil across the bottom. The backs of the game action cards are beige and have the format of a newspaper headline and story wrapped around a small color inset photo. The backs of the player cards display a color closeup photo, 1995 stats, and a 1995 season summary.

	MINT	NRMT
COMPLETE SET (50)	15.00	6.75
COMMON CARD (1-50)	.10	.05

	MINT	NRMT
☐ 1 Ken Griffey Jr. IA	1.50	.70
☐ 2 Vince Coleman IA	.10	.05
☐ 3 Luis Sojo IA	.10	.05
☐ 4 Mariners win the West	.40	.18
☐ 5 Randy Johnson IA	.60	.25
☐ 6 Ken Griffey Jr. IA	1.50	.70
☐ 7 Tino Martinez HL Edgar Martinez	.60	.25
☐ 8 Edgar Martinez IA	.40	.18
☐ 9 Ken Griffey Jr. IA	1.50	.70
☐ 10 Thunder in the Kingdome	.25	.11
☐ 11 Win ends years of futility	.25	.11
☐ 12 Bob Wolcott IA	.10	.05
☐ 13 Jay Buhner IA	.40	.18
☐ 14 Randy Johnson IA	.60	.25
☐ 15 Lou Piniella IA	.25	.11
☐ 16 Joey Cora IA	.25	.11
☐ 17 Dave Niehaus ANN	.25	.11
☐ 18 Rich Amaral	.10	.05
☐ 19 Bobby Ayala	.10	.05
☐ 20 Tim Belcher	.10	.05
☐ 21 Andy Benes	.25	.11
☐ 22 Mike Blowers	.10	.05
☐ 23 Chris Bosio	.10	.05
☐ 24 Darren Bragg	.25	.11
☐ 25 Jay Buhner	.75	.35
☐ 26 Rafael Carmona	.10	.05
☐ 27 Norm Charlton	.25	.11
☐ 28 Vince Coleman	.10	.05
☐ 29 Joey Cora	.60	.25
☐ 30 Alex Diaz	.10	.05
☐ 31 Felix Fermin	.10	.05
☐ 32 Ken Griffey Jr.	3.00	1.35
☐ 33 Lee Guetterman	.10	.05
☐ 34 Randy Johnson	.75	.35
☐ 35 Edgar Martinez	.60	.25
☐ 36 Tino Martinez	.75	.35
☐ 37 Jeff Nelson	.10	.05
☐ 38 Warren Newson	.10	.05
☐ 39 Greg Pirkl	.10	.05
☐ 40 Arquimedez Pozo	.25	.11
☐ 41 Bill Risley	.10	.05
☐ 42 Alex Rodriguez	2.50	1.10
☐ 43 Luis Sojo	.10	.05
☐ 44 Doug Strange	.10	.05
☐ 45 Salomon Torres	.10	.05
☐ 46 Bob Wells	.10	.05
☐ 47 Chris Widger	.10	.05
☐ 48 Dan Wilson	.60	.25
☐ 49 Bob Wolcott	.25	.11
☐ 50 Lou Piniella MG	.25	.11

1996 Mariners Mother's

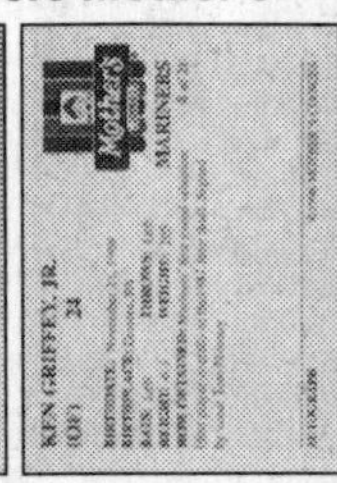

This 28-card set consists of borderless posed color player portraits. The player's and team's names appear in one of the top rounded corners. The backs carry biographical information and the sponsor's logo on a white background in red and purple print. A blank slot for the player's autograph rounds out the back.

	MINT	NRMT
COMPLETE SET (28)	12.00	5.50
COMMON CARD (1-28)	.25	.11

	MINT	NRMT
☐ 1 Lou Piniella MG	.75	.35
☐ 2 Randy Johnson	1.50	.70
☐ 3 Jay Buhner	1.25	.55
☐ 4 Ken Griffey Jr.	4.00	1.80
☐ 5 Ricky Jordan	.25	.11
☐ 6 Rich Amaral	.25	.11
☐ 7 Edgar Martinez	1.25	.55
☐ 8 Joey Cora	1.00	.45
☐ 9 Alex Rodriguez	3.00	1.35
☐ 10 Sterling Hitchcock	.50	.23
☐ 11 Chris Bosio	.25	.11
☐ 12 John Marzano	.25	.11
☐ 13 Bob Wells	.25	.11
☐ 14 Rafael Carmona	.25	.11
☐ 15 Dan Wilson	.75	.35
☐ 16 Norm Charlton	.50	.23
☐ 17 Paul Sorrento	.75	.35
☐ 18 Mike Jackson	.25	.11
☐ 19 Luis Sojo	.25	.11
☐ 20 Bobby Ayala	.25	.11
☐ 21 Alex Diaz	.25	.11
☐ 22 Doug Strange	.25	.11
☐ 23 Bob Wolcott	.50	.23
☐ 24 Darren Bragg	.50	.23
☐ 25 Paul Menhart	.25	.11
☐ 26 Edwin Hurtado	.25	.11
☐ 27 Russ Davis	.50	.23
☐ 28 Coaches Card CL Lee Elia John McLarren Steve Smith Matt Sinatro Sam Mejias Bobby Cuellar	.25	.11

1997 Marlins Pacific

This 33-card set was produced by Pacific for the Florida Marlins and sponsored by NationsBank. The cards were distributed to 16,000 kids twelve years old and under at the Marlins Kids Opening Day game on June 27, 1996. The fronts feature borderless color action player photos. The backs carry a small player portrait, player information and statistics printed in both Spanish and English.

	MINT	NRMT
COMPLETE SET (33)	8.00	3.60
COMMON CARD (1-32)	.25	.11

	MINT	NRMT
☐ 1 Kurt Abbott	.25	.11
☐ 2 Moises Alou	.50	.22

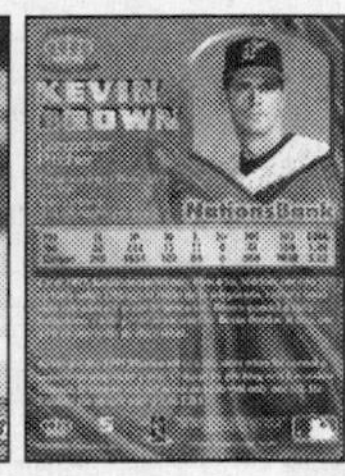

☐ 3 Alex Arias	.25	.11
☐ 4 Bobby Bonilla	.50	.22
☐ 5 Kevin Brown	.50	.22
☐ 6 John Cangelosi	.25	.11
☐ 7 Luis Castillo	.25	.11
☐ 8 Jeff Conine	.25	.11
☐ 9 Jim Eisenreich	.25	.11
☐ 10 Alex Fernandez	.50	.22
☐ 11 Cliff Floyd	.25	.11
☐ 12 Rick Helling	.25	.11
☐ 13 Felix Heredia	.25	.11
☐ 14 Mark Hutton	.25	.11
☐ 15 Charles Johnson	.50	.22
☐ 16 Al Leiter	.25	.11
☐ 17 Robb Nen	.50	.22
☐ 18 Jay Powell	.25	.11
☐ 19 Pat Rapp	.25	.11
☐ 20 Edgar Renteria	.50	.22
☐ 21 Tony Saunders	.50	.22
☐ 22 Gary Sheffield	1.00	.45
☐ 23 Devon White	.25	.11
☐ 24 Gregg Zaun	.25	.11
☐ 25 Jim Leyland MG	.25	.11
☐ 26 Rich Donnelly CO	.25	.11
☐ 27 Bruce Kimm CO	.25	.11
☐ 28 Jerry Manuel CO	.25	.11
☐ 29 Milt May CO	.25	.11
☐ 30 Larry Rothschild CO	.25	.11
☐ 31 Tommy Sandt CO	.25	.11
☐ 32 Billy the Marlin(Mascot)	.25	.11
☐ NNO Title Card CL	.25	.11

1895 Mayo N300

The Mayo Tobacco Works of Richmond, Va., issued this set of 48 ballplayers about 1895. Some recent speculation has been made that this set was issued beginning in 1894. The cards contain sepia portraits although some pictures appear to be black and white. There are 40 different individuals known in the set; cards 1 to 28 appear in uniform, while the last twelve (29-40) appear in street clothes. Eight of the former also appear with variations in uniform. The player's name appears within the picture area and a "Mayo's Cut Plug" ad is printed in a panel at the base of the card. Similar to the football set issued around the same time, the cards have black blank backs.

	EX-MT	VG-E
COMPLETE SET (48)	25000.00	11200.00
COMMON CARD (1-40)	375.00	170.00
☐ 1 Cap Anson: Chicago	2250.00	1000.00
☐ 2 Jimmy Bannon RF: Boston	375.00	170.00
☐ 3A Dan Brouthers 1B: Baltimore	750.00	350.00
☐ 3B Dan Brouthers 1B: Louisville	1000.00	450.00
☐ 4 John Clarkson P: St. Louis	750.00	350.00
☐ 5 Tommy W. Corcoran SS Brooklyn	375.00	170.00
☐ 6 Lave Cross 2B: Philadelphia	375.00	170.00
☐ 7 Hugh Duffy CF: Boston	750.00	350.00
☐ 8A Buck Ewing RF: Cincinnati	1000.00	450.00
☐ 8B Buck Ewing RF: Cleveland	1000.00	450.00
☐ 9 Dave Foutz 1B: Brooklyn	375.00	170.00
☐ 10 Charlie Ganzel C: Boston	375.00	170.00
☐ 11A Jack Glasscock SS: Pittsburgh	425.00	190.00
☐ 11B Jack Glasscock SS: Louisville	425.00	190.00
☐ 12 Mike Griffin CF: Brooklyn	375.00	170.00
☐ 13A George Haddock P: Philadelphia	375.00	170.00
☐ 13B George Haddock P: no team	375.00	170.00
☐ 14 Bill Joyce CF: Brooklyn	375.00	170.00
☐ 15 Wm.(Brickyard) Kennedy P: Brooklyn	375.00	170.00
☐ 16A Tom F. Kinslow C: Pitts.	375.00	170.00
☐ 16B Tom F. Kinslow C: no team	375.00	170.00
☐ 17 Arlie Latham 3B: Cincinnati	425.00	190.00
☐ 18 Herman Long SS: Boston	425.00	190.00
☐ 19 Tom Lovett P: Boston	375.00	170.00
☐ 20 Link Lowe 2B: Boston	425.00	190.00
☐ 21 Tommy McCarthy LF: Boston	750.00	350.00
☐ 22 Yale Murphy SS: New York	375.00	170.00
☐ 23 Billy Nash 3B: Boston	375.00	170.00
☐ 24 Kid Nicols P: Boston	750.00	350.00
☐ 25A Fred Pfeffer 2B: Louisville	375.00	170.00
☐ 25B Fred Pfeffer (Retired)	375.00	170.00
☐ 26A Amos Rusie P: New York	1200.00	550.00
☐ 26B Amos Russie (Sic) P: New York	1000.00	450.00
☐ 27 Tommy Tucker 1B: Boston	375.00	170.00
☐ 28A John Ward 2B: New York	750.00	350.00
☐ 28B John Ward (Retired)	1000.00	450.00
☐ 29 Charlie S. Abbey CF: Washington	375.00	170.00
☐ 30 Ed W. Cartwright FB: Washington	375.00	170.00
☐ 31 William F. Dahlen SS: Chicago	425.00	190.00
☐ 32 Tom P. Daly 2B: Brooklyn	375.00	170.00
☐ 33 Ed J. Delehanty LF: Phila.	1200.00	550.00
☐ 34 Bill W. Hallman 2B: Phila.	375.00	170.00
☐ 35 Billy Hamilton CF: Phila.	750.00	350.00
☐ 36 Wilbert Robinson C: Baltimore	750.00	350.00
☐ 37 James Ryan RF: Chicago	425.00	190.00
☐ 38 Billy Shindle 3B: Brooklyn	375.00	170.00
☐ 39 George J. Smith SS: Cinc.	375.00	170.00
☐ 40 Otis H. Stockdale P: Washington	375.00	170.00

1911 Mecca Double Folders T201

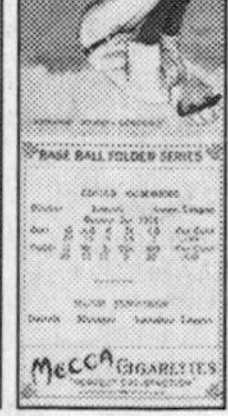

The cards in this 50-card set measure approximately 2 1/4" by 4 11/16". The 1911 Mecca Double Folder issue contains unnumbered cards. This issue was one of the first to list statistics of players portrayed on the cards. Each card portrays two players, one when the card is folded, another when the card is unfolded. The card of Dougherty and Lord is considered scarce.

	EX-MT	VG-E
COMPLETE SET (50)	5000.00	2200.00
COMMON PAIR (1-50)	45.00	20.00
☐ 1 Frank Baker / Eddie Collins	200.00	90.00
☐ 2 Jack Barry / Jack Lapp	45.00	20.00
☐ 3 Bill Bergen / Zach Wheat	120.00	55.00
☐ 4 Walter Blair / Roy Hartzell	45.00	20.00
☐ 5 Roger Bresnahan / Miller Huggins	175.00	80.00
☐ 6 Al Bridwell / Christy Matthewson UER Mathewson	350.00	160.00
☐ 7 Johnny Butler / Bill Abstein	45.00	20.00
☐ 8 Bobby Byrne / Fred Clarke	90.00	40.00
☐ 9 Frank Chance / Johnny Evers	300.00	135.00
☐ 10 Tommy Clarke / Harry Gaspar	45.00	20.00
☐ 11 Ty Cobb / Sam Crawford	1200.00	550.00
☐ 12 Leonard Cole / Johnny Kling	45.00	20.00
☐ 13 Jack Coombs / Ira Thomas	45.00	20.00
☐ 14 Jake Daubert / Nap Rucker	45.00	20.00
☐ 15 Patsy Dougherty / Harry Lord	300.00	135.00
☐ 16 Red Dooin / John Titus	45.00	20.00
☐ 17 Tom Downey / H Baker	45.00	20.00
☐ 18 Jimmy Dygert / Cy Seymour	45.00	20.00
☐ 19 Kid Elberfeld / George McBride UER	45.00	20.00
☐ 20 Cy Falkenberg / Nap Lajoie	200.00	90.00
☐ 21 E.Fitzpatrick / Ed Killian	45.00	20.00
☐ 22 Larry Gardner / Tris Speaker	175.00	80.00
☐ 23 George Gibson / Tommy Leach	45.00	20.00
☐ 24 Peaches Graham / Al Mattern	45.00	20.00
☐ 25 Arnold Hauser / Johnny Lush	45.00	20.00
☐ 26 Buck Herzog / Dots Miller	45.00	20.00
☐ 27 Harry Hinchman / Charles Hickman	45.00	20.00
☐ 28 Solly Hofman / Mordecai Brown	125.00	55.00
☐ 29 Hugh Jennings / Ed Summers	90.00	40.00
☐ 30 Otis Johnson / Russ Ford	45.00	20.00
☐ 31 Tom McCarty / Joe McGinnity	100.00	45.00
☐ 32 Ulysses McGlyn / Jimmy Barrett	45.00	20.00
☐ 33 Larry McLean / Eddie Grant	45.00	20.00
☐ 34 Fred Merkle / Hooks Wiltse	45.00	20.00
☐ 35 Chief Meyers / Larry Doyle	45.00	20.00
☐ 36 Earl Moore / Hans Lobert	45.00	20.00
☐ 37 Fred Odwell / Red Downs	45.00	20.00
☐ 38 Rube Oldring / Chief Bender	100.00	45.00
☐ 39 Fred Payne / Ed Walsh	90.00	40.00
☐ 40 Michael Simon / Lefty Leifield	45.00	20.00
☐ 41 Charles Starr / James McCabe	45.00	20.00
☐ 42 James Stephens / Frank LaPorte	45.00	20.00
☐ 43 George Stovall / Terry Turner	45.00	20.00
☐ 44 Gabby Street / Walter Johnson	500.00	220.00
☐ 45 Ralph Stroud	45.00	20.00

Bill Donovan		
☐ 46 Ed Sweeney	45.00	20.00
Hal Chase		
☐ 47 Johny Thoney	90.00	40.00
Eddie Cicotte		
☐ 48 Bobby Wallace	90.00	40.00
Joe Lake		
☐ 49 Joseph Ward	45.00	20.00
Edward Foster		
☐ 50 O.Williams	45.00	20.00
Sam Woodruff		

1996 Metal Universe Promo Sheet

This set consists of one sheet picturing samples of nine cards. The front features color action player photos of nine different players each on a different metallic background. The back carries color portraits of the same players with biographical and statistical information. The words, "Promotional Sample," are stamped diagonally on both the front and back of each player's card. The cards are numbered below according to their numbers in the regular set.

	MINT	NRMT
COMPLETE SET (9)	5.00	2.20
COMMON CARD	.25	.11
☐ 28 Todd Greene	.50	.23
☐ 67 Jon Nunnally	.25	.11
☐ 81 Brad Radke	.50	.23
☐ 90 Don Mattingly	1.00	.45
☐ 110 Alex Rodriguez	2.00	.90
☐ 116 Ivan Rodriguez	.75	.35
☐ 129 Chipper Jones	1.50	.70
☐ 183 Eric Karros	.50	.23
☐ 216 Jeff King	.25	.11

1996 Metal Universe

The Fleer Metal Universe set was issued in one series totalling 250 standard-size cards. The cards were issued in foil-wrapped packs. The theme for the set was based on intermingling fantasy comic book elements with baseball, thus each card features a player set against a wide variety of bizarre backgrounds. The cards are grouped alphabetically within teams below.

	MINT	NRMT
COMPLETE SET (250)	40.00	18.00
COMMON CARD (1-250)	.15	.07
☐ 1 Roberto Alomar	.60	.25
☐ 2 Brady Anderson	.40	.18
☐ 3 Bobby Bonilla	.30	.14
☐ 4 Chris Hoiles	.15	.07
☐ 5 Ben McDonald	.15	.07
☐ 6 Mike Mussina	.60	.25
☐ 7 Randy Myers	.15	.07
☐ 8 Rafael Palmeiro	.40	.18
☐ 9 Cal Ripken	2.50	1.10
☐ 10 B.J. Surhoff	.15	.07
☐ 11 Luis Alicea	.15	.07
☐ 12 Jose Canseco	.40	.18
☐ 13 Roger Clemens	1.25	.55
☐ 14 Will Cordero	.15	.07
☐ 15 Tom Gordon	.15	.07
☐ 16 Mike Greenwall	.15	.07
☐ 17 Tim Naehring	.15	.07
☐ 18 Troy O'Leary	.15	.07
☐ 19 Mike Stanley	.15	.07
☐ 20 John Valentin	.30	.14
☐ 21 Mo Vaughn	.75	.35
☐ 22 Tim Wakefield	.15	.07
☐ 23 Garret Anderson	.30	.14
☐ 24 Chili Davis	.15	.07
☐ 25 Gary DiSarcina	.15	.07
☐ 26 Jim Edmonds	.60	.25
☐ 27 Chuck Finley	.15	.07
☐ 28 Todd Greene	.15	.07
☐ 29 Mark Langston	.15	.07
☐ 30 Troy Percival	.15	.07
☐ 31 Tony Phillips	.15	.07
☐ 32 Tim Salmon	.60	.25
☐ 33 Lee Smith	.30	.14
☐ 34 J.T. Snow	.30	.14
☐ 35 Ray Durham	.30	.14
☐ 36 Alex Fernandez	.30	.14
☐ 37 Ozzie Guillen	.15	.07
☐ 38 Roberto Hernandez	.30	.14
☐ 39 Lyle Mouton	.15	.07
☐ 40 Frank Thomas	2.50	1.10
☐ 41 Robin Ventura	.30	.14
☐ 42 Sandy Alomar, Jr.	.15	.07
☐ 43 Carlos Baerga	.15	.07
☐ 44 Albert Belle	.75	.35
☐ 45 Orel Hershiser	.30	.14
☐ 46 Kenny Lofton	.75	.35
☐ 47 Dennis Martinez	.30	.14
☐ 48 Jack McDowell	.15	.07
☐ 49 Jose Mesa	.30	.14
☐ 50 Eddie Murray	.60	.25
☐ 51 Charles Nagy	.30	.14
☐ 52 Manny Ramirez	.60	.25
☐ 53 Julian Tavarez	.15	.07
☐ 54 Jim Thome	.60	.25
☐ 55 Omar Vizquel	.30	.14
☐ 56 Chad Curtis	.15	.07
☐ 57 Cecil Fielder	.30	.14
☐ 58 John Flaherty	.15	.07
☐ 59 Travis Fryman	.30	.14
☐ 60 Chris Gomez	.15	.07
☐ 61 Felipe Lira	.15	.07
☐ 62 Kevin Appier	.30	.14
☐ 63 Johnny Damon	.30	.14
☐ 64 Tom Goodwin	.15	.07
☐ 65 Mark Gubicza	.15	.07
☐ 66 Jeff Montgomery	.15	.07
☐ 67 Jon Nunnally	.15	.07
☐ 68 Ricky Bones	.15	.07
☐ 69 Jeff Cirillo	.30	.14
☐ 70 John Jaha	.15	.07
☐ 71 Dave Nilsson	.30	.14
☐ 72 Joe Oliver	.15	.07
☐ 73 Kevin Seitzer	.15	.07
☐ 74 Greg Vaughn	.15	.07
☐ 75 Marty Cordova	.30	.14
☐ 76 Chuck Knoblauch	.60	.25
☐ 77 Pat Meares	.15	.07
☐ 78 Paul Molitor	.60	.25
☐ 79 Pedro Munoz	.15	.07
☐ 80 Kirby Puckett	1.25	.55
☐ 81 Brad Radke	.15	.07
☐ 82 Scott Stahoviak	.15	.07
☐ 83 Matt Walbeck	.15	.07
☐ 84 Wade Boggs	.60	.25
☐ 85 David Cone	.30	.14
☐ 86 Joe Girardi	.15	.07
☐ 87 Derek Jeter	2.00	.90
☐ 88 Jim Leyritz	.15	.07
☐ 89 Tino Martinez	.60	.25
☐ 90 Don Mattingly	1.00	.45
☐ 91 Paul O'Neill	.30	.14
☐ 92 Andy Pettitte	.75	.35
☐ 93 Tim Raines	.15	.07
☐ 94 Kenny Rogers	.15	.07
☐ 95 Ruben Sierra	.15	.07
☐ 96 John Wetteland	.30	.14
☐ 97 Bernie Williams	.60	.25
☐ 98 Geronimo Berroa	.15	.07
☐ 99 Dennis Eckersley	.40	.18
☐ 100 Brent Gates	.15	.07
☐ 101 Mark McGwire	1.25	.55
☐ 102 Steve Ontiveros	.15	.07
☐ 103 Terry Steinbach	.30	.14
☐ 104 Jay Buhner	.40	.18
☐ 105 Vince Coleman	.15	.07
☐ 106 Joey Cora	.15	.07
☐ 107 Ken Griffey, Jr.	3.00	1.35
☐ 108 Randy Johnson	.60	.25
☐ 109 Edgar Martinez	.40	.18
☐ 110 Alex Rodriguez	2.50	1.10
☐ 111 Paul Sorrento	.15	.07
☐ 112 Will Clark	.40	.18
☐ 113 Juan Gonzalez	1.50	.70
☐ 114 Rusty Greer	.60	.25
☐ 115 Dean Palmer	.30	.14
☐ 116 Ivan Rodriguez	.75	.35
☐ 117 Mickey Tettleton	.15	.07
☐ 118 Joe Carter	.30	.14
☐ 119 Alex Gonzalez	.15	.07
☐ 120 Shawn Green	.15	.07
☐ 121 Erik Hanson	.15	.07
☐ 122 Pat Hentgen	.30	.14
☐ 123 Sandy Martinez	.15	.07
☐ 124 Otis Nixon	.15	.07
☐ 125 John Olerud	.30	.14
☐ 126 Steve Avery	.15	.07
☐ 127 Tom Glavine	.30	.14
☐ 128 Marquis Grissom	.30	.14
☐ 129 Chipper Jones	2.00	.90
☐ 130 David Justice	.60	.25
☐ 131 Ryan Klesko	.40	.18
☐ 132 Mark Lemke	.15	.07
☐ 133 Javier Lopez	.30	.14
☐ 134 Greg Maddux	2.00	.90
☐ 135 Fred McGriff	.40	.18
☐ 136 John Smoltz	.30	.14
☐ 137 Mark Wohlers	.30	.14
☐ 138 Frank Castillo	.15	.07
☐ 139 Shawon Dunston	.15	.07
☐ 140 Luis Gonzalez	.15	.07
☐ 141 Mark Grace	.40	.18
☐ 142 Brian McRae	.15	.07
☐ 143 Jaime Navarro	.15	.07
☐ 144 Rey Sanchez	.15	.07
☐ 145 Ryne Sandberg	.75	.35
☐ 146 Sammy Sosa	.60	.25
☐ 147 Bret Boone	.15	.07
☐ 148 Curtis Goodwin	.15	.07
☐ 149 Barry Larkin	.40	.18
☐ 150 Hal Morris	.15	.07
☐ 151 Reggie Sanders	.15	.07
☐ 152 Pete Schourek	.15	.07
☐ 153 John Smiley	.15	.07
☐ 154 Dante Bichette	.40	.18
☐ 155 Vinny Castilla	.30	.14
☐ 156 Andres Galarraga	.40	.18
☐ 157 Bret Saberhagen	.15	.07
☐ 158 Bill Swift	.15	.07
☐ 159 Larry Walker	.60	.25
☐ 160 Walt Weiss	.15	.07
☐ 161 Kurt Abbott	.15	.07
☐ 162 John Burkett	.15	.07
☐ 163 Greg Colbrunn	.15	.07
☐ 164 Jeff Conine	.30	.14
☐ 165 Chris Hammond	.15	.07
☐ 166 Charles Johnson	.30	.14
☐ 167 Al Leiter	.15	.07
☐ 168 Pat Rapp	.15	.07
☐ 169 Gary Sheffield	.60	.25
☐ 170 Quilvio Veras	.15	.07
☐ 171 Devon White	.15	.07
☐ 172 Jeff Bagwell	1.25	.55
☐ 173 Derek Bell	.15	.07
☐ 174 Sean Berry	.15	.07
☐ 175 Craig Biggio	.40	.18
☐ 176 Doug Drabek	.15	.07
☐ 177 Tony Eusebio	.15	.07
☐ 178 Brian L.Hunter	.30	.14
☐ 179 Orlando Miller	.15	.07
☐ 180 Shane Reynolds	.15	.07
☐ 181 Mike Blowers	.15	.07
☐ 182 Roger Cedeno	.15	.07
☐ 183 Eric Karros	.30	.14
☐ 184 Ramon Martinez	.30	.14
☐ 185 Raul Mondesi	.40	.18
☐ 186 Hideo Nomo	1.50	.70
☐ 187 Mike Piazza	2.00	.90
☐ 188 Moises Alou	.30	.14
☐ 189 Yamil Benitez	.30	.14
☐ 190 Darrin Fletcher	.15	.07
☐ 191 Cliff Floyd	.15	.07
☐ 192 Pedro Martinez	.60	.25
☐ 193 Carlos Perez	.15	.07
☐ 194 David Segui	.15	.07
☐ 195 Tony Tarasco	.15	.07
☐ 196 Rondell White	.30	.14
☐ 197 Edgardo Alfonzo	.40	.18
☐ 198 Rico Brogna	.30	.14
☐ 199 Carl Everett	.15	.07
☐ 200 Todd Hundley	.30	.14
☐ 201 Jason Isringhausen	.15	.07
☐ 202 Lance Johnson	.30	.14
☐ 203 Bobby Jones	.15	.07
☐ 204 Jeff Kent	.15	.07
☐ 205 Bill Pulsipher	.15	.07
☐ 206 Jose Vizcaino	.15	.07
☐ 207 Ricky Bottalico	.15	.07
☐ 208 Darren Daulton	.30	.14
☐ 209 Lenny Dykstra	.30	.14
☐ 210 Jim Eisenreich	.30	.14
☐ 211 Gregg Jefferies	.30	.14
☐ 212 Mickey Morandini	.15	.07
☐ 213 Heathcliff Slocumb	.15	.07
☐ 214 Jay Bell	.30	.14
☐ 215 Carlos Garcia	.15	.07
☐ 216 Jeff King	.30	.14
☐ 217 Al Martin	.15	.07
☐ 218 Orlando Merced	.15	.07
☐ 219 Dan Miceli	.15	.07
☐ 220 Denny Neagle	.30	.14
☐ 221 Andy Benes	.30	.14
☐ 222 Royce Clayton	.15	.07
☐ 223 Gary Gaetti	.30	.14

		MINT	NRMT
☐ 224 Ron Gant		.30	.14
☐ 225 Bernard Gilkey		.30	.14
☐ 226 Brian Jordan		.30	.14
☐ 227 Ray Lankford		.30	.14
☐ 228 John Mabry		.30	.14
☐ 229 Ozzie Smith		.75	.35
☐ 230 Todd Stottlemyre		.15	.07
☐ 231 Andy Ashby		.15	.07
☐ 232 Brad Ausmus		.15	.07
☐ 233 Ken Caminiti		.60	.25
☐ 234 Steve Finley		.30	.14
☐ 235 Tony Gwynn		1.50	.70
☐ 236 Joey Hamilton		.15	.07
☐ 237 Rickey Henderson		.40	.18
☐ 238 Trevor Hoffman		.30	.14
☐ 239 Wally Joyner		.15	.07
☐ 240 Rod Beck		.30	.14
☐ 241 Barry Bonds		.75	.35
☐ 242 Glenallen Hill		.15	.07
☐ 243 Stan Javier		.15	.07
☐ 244 Mark Leiter		.15	.07
☐ 245 Deion Sanders		.60	.25
☐ 246 William Van Landingham		.15	.07
☐ 247 Matt Williams		.40	.18
☐ 248 Checklist		.15	.07
☐ 249 Checklist		.15	.07
☐ 250 Checklist		.15	.07

1996 Metal Universe Platinum

The 1996 Fleer Metal Universe Platinum is a 250-card parallel version of the regular series and were inserted one per pack. The silver foil backgrounds differentiate these from the regular cards.

	MINT	NRMT
COMPLETE SET (250)	150.00	70.00
COMMON CARD (1-250)	.25	.11

*STARS: 2X TO 4X BASIC CARDS
*YOUNG STARS: 1.5X TO 3X BASIC CARDS

1996 Metal Universe Heavy Metal

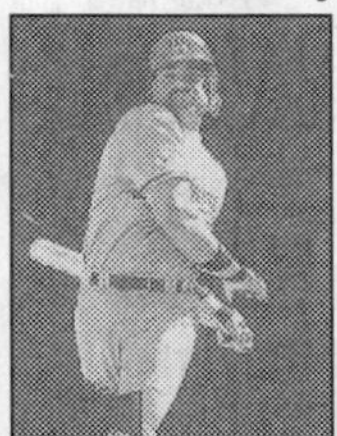

Randomly inserted in packs at a rate of one in 8 this 10-card set features the Power Hitters of Baseball. The fronts feature a color action player cut-out over a silver foil background. The backs carry a player portrait and information about the player.

	MINT	NRMT
COMPLETE SET (10)	25.00	11.00
COMMON CARD (1-10)	1.50	.70
☐ 1 Albert Belle	2.50	1.10
☐ 2 Barry Bonds	2.50	1.10
☐ 3 Juan Gonzalez	5.00	2.20
☐ 4 Ken Griffey Jr.	10.00	4.50
☐ 5 Mark McGwire	4.00	1.80
☐ 6 Mike Piazza	6.00	2.70
☐ 7 Sammy Sosa	1.50	.70
☐ 8 Frank Thomas	8.00	3.60
☐ 9 Mo Vaughn	2.50	1.10
☐ 10 Matt Williams	2.00	.90

1996 Metal Universe Mining For Gold

Randomly inserted in retail packs only at a rate of one in 12, this 12-card set highlights major prospects and rookies.

	MINT	NRMT
COMPLETE SET (12)	60.00	27.00
COMMON CARD (1-12)	1.50	.70
☐ 1 Yamil Benitez	4.00	1.80
☐ 2 Marty Cordova	2.50	1.10
☐ 3 Shawn Green	1.50	.70
☐ 4 Todd Greene	6.00	2.70
☐ 5 Brian Hunter	2.50	1.10
☐ 6 Derek Jeter	15.00	6.75
☐ 7 Charles Johnson	2.50	1.10
☐ 8 Chipper Jones	20.00	9.00
☐ 9 Hideo Nomo	15.00	6.75
☐ 10 Alex Ochoa	1.50	.70
☐ 11 Andy Pettitte	8.00	3.60
☐ 12 Quilvio Veras	1.50	.70

1996 Metal Universe Mother Lode

Randomly inserted in hobby packs only at a rate of one in 12, this 12-card set features multi-tool players. The fronts carry a color action player cut-out over a silver-foil, scroll-design background. The backs display another player photo and information about the player.

	MINT	NRMT
COMPLETE SET (12)	60.00	27.00
COMMON CARD (1-12)	2.00	.90
☐ 1 Barry Bonds	4.00	1.80
☐ 2 Jim Edmonds	3.00	1.35
☐ 3 Ken Griffey Jr.	15.00	6.75
☐ 4 Kenny Lofton	4.00	1.80
☐ 5 Raul Mondesi	2.50	1.10
☐ 6 Rafael Palmeiro	2.50	1.10
☐ 7 Manny Ramirez	3.00	1.35
☐ 8 Cal Ripken	12.00	5.50
☐ 9 Tim Salmon	3.00	1.35
☐ 10 Ryne Sandberg	4.00	1.80
☐ 11 Frank Thomas	15.00	6.75
☐ 12 Matt Williams	2.00	.90

1996 Metal Universe Platinum Portraits

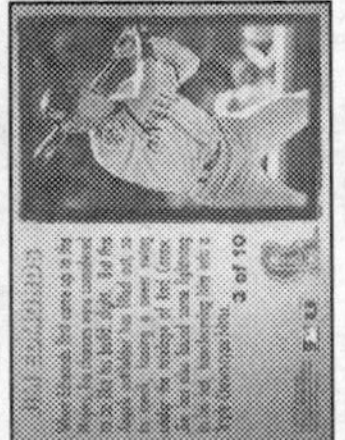

Randomly inserted in packs at a rate of one in four, this 10-card set features ten of the hottest young stars. The fronts display a player portrait on a platinum foil background. The backs carry a color action player photo and why the player is hot.

	MINT	NRMT
COMPLETE SET (10)	12.00	5.50
COMMON CARD (1-10)	.50	.23
☐ 1 Garret Anderson	.75	.35
☐ 2 Marty Cordova	.50	.23
☐ 3 Jim Edmonds	1.50	.70
☐ 4 Jason Isringhausen	.50	.23
☐ 5 Chipper Jones	5.00	2.20
☐ 6 Ryan Klesko	1.00	.45
☐ 7 Hideo Nomo	4.00	1.80
☐ 8 Carlos Perez	.50	.23
☐ 9 Manny Ramirez	1.50	.70
☐ 10 Rondell White	.75	.35

1996 Metal Universe Titanium

Randomly inserted in packs at a rate of one in 24, this 10-card set features ten of the fans' favorite players. The fronts feature an action color player cut-out on a foil baseball background. The backs display a player portrait and why the player is liked by the fans.

	MINT	NRMT
COMPLETE SET (10)	125.00	55.00
COMMON CARD (1-10)	3.00	1.35

	MINT	NRMT
☐ 1 Albert Belle	10.00	4.50
☐ 2 Barry Bonds	6.00	2.70
☐ 3 Ken Griffey Jr.	25.00	11.00
☐ 4 Tony Gwynn	10.00	4.50
☐ 5 Greg Maddux	15.00	6.75
☐ 6 Mike Piazza	15.00	6.75
☐ 7 Cal Ripken	20.00	9.00
☐ 8 Frank Thomas	25.00	11.00
☐ 9 Mo Vaughn	6.00	2.70
☐ 10 Matt Williams	3.00	1.35

1997 Metal Universe

The 1997 Metal Universe set was issued in one series totalling 250 cards and distributed in eight-card foil packs with a suggested retail price of $2.49. Printed in 100% etched foil with UV-coating, the fronts features color photos of star players on full-bleed backgrounds of comic book art with the player's name, team, position and card logo printed near the bottom of the card. The backs carry another player photo and statistics.

	MINT	NRMT
COMPLETE SET (250)	40.00	18.00
COMMON CARD (1-250)	.15	.07
☐ 1 Roberto Alomar	.60	.25
☐ 2 Brady Anderson	.40	.18
☐ 3 Rocky Coppinger	.30	.14
☐ 4 Chris Hoiles	.15	.07
☐ 5 Eddie Murray	.60	.25
☐ 6 Mike Mussina	.60	.25
☐ 7 Rafael Palmeiro	.40	.18
☐ 8 Cal Ripken	2.50	1.10
☐ 9 B.J. Surhoff	.30	.14
☐ 10 Brant Brown	.15	.07
☐ 11 Mark Grace	.40	.18
☐ 12 Brian McRae	.15	.07
☐ 13 Jaime Navarro	.15	.07
☐ 14 Ryne Sandberg	.75	.35
☐ 15 Sammy Sosa	.60	.25
☐ 16 Amaury Telemaco	.15	.07
☐ 17 Steve Trachsel	.15	.07
☐ 18 Darren Bragg	.15	.07
☐ 19 Jose Canseco	.40	.18
☐ 20 Roger Clemens	1.25	.55
☐ 21 Nomar Garciaparra	2.00	.90
☐ 22 Tom Gordon	.15	.07
☐ 23 Tim Naehring	.15	.07
☐ 24 Mike Stanley	.15	.07
☐ 25 John Valentin	.15	.07
☐ 26 Mo Vaughn	.75	.35
☐ 27 Jermaine Dye	.15	.07
☐ 28 Tom Glavine	.30	.14
☐ 29 Marquis Grissom	.30	.14
☐ 30 Andruw Jones	1.50	.70
☐ 31 Chipper Jones	2.00	.90
☐ 32 Ryan Klesko	.60	.25
☐ 33 Greg Maddux	2.00	.90
☐ 34 Fred McGriff	.40	.18
☐ 35 John Smoltz	.30	.14
☐ 36 Garret Anderson	.30	.14
☐ 37 George Arias	.15	.07
☐ 38 Gary DiSarcina	.15	.07
☐ 39 Jim Edmonds	.60	.25
☐ 40 Darin Erstad	1.00	.45
☐ 41 Chuck Finley	.15	.07
☐ 42 Troy Percival	.15	.07

Card	Mint	NRMT
☐ 43 Tim Salmon	.60	.25
☐ 44 Bret Boone	.15	.07
☐ 45 Jeff Brantley	.15	.07
☐ 46 Eric Davis	.15	.07
☐ 47 Barry Larkin	.40	.18
☐ 48 Hal Morris	.15	.07
☐ 49 Mark Portugal	.15	.07
☐ 50 Reggie Sanders	.15	.07
☐ 51 John Smiley	.15	.07
☐ 52 Wilson Alvarez	.15	.07
☐ 53 Harold Baines	.30	.14
☐ 54 James Baldwin	.15	.07
☐ 55 Albert Belle	1.00	.45
☐ 56 Mike Cameron	.30	.14
☐ 57 Ray Durham	.15	.07
☐ 58 Alex Fernandez	.30	.14
☐ 59 Roberto Hernandez	.30	.14
☐ 60 Tony Phillips	.15	.07
☐ 61 Frank Thomas	2.50	1.10
☐ 62 Robin Ventura	.30	.14
☐ 63 Jeff Cirillo	.30	.14
☐ 64 Jeff D'Amico	.30	.14
☐ 65 John Jaha	.15	.07
☐ 66 Scott Karl	.15	.07
☐ 67 Ben McDonald	.15	.07
☐ 68 Marc Newfield	.15	.07
☐ 69 Dave Nilsson	.15	.07
☐ 70 Jose Valentin	.15	.07
☐ 71 Dante Bichette	.30	.14
☐ 72 Ellis Burks	.30	.14
☐ 73 Vinny Castilla	.30	.14
☐ 74 Andres Galarraga	.60	.25
☐ 75 Kevin Ritz	.15	.07
☐ 76 Larry Walker	.60	.25
☐ 77 Walt Weiss	.15	.07
☐ 78 Jamey Wright	.30	.14
☐ 79 Eric Young	.30	.14
☐ 80 Julio Franco	.30	.14
☐ 81 Orel Hershiser	.30	.14
☐ 82 Kenny Lofton	.75	.35
☐ 83 Jack McDowell	.15	.07
☐ 84 Jose Mesa	.30	.14
☐ 85 Charles Nagy	.30	.14
☐ 86 Manny Ramirez	.60	.25
☐ 87 Jim Thome	.60	.25
☐ 88 Omar Vizquel	.30	.14
☐ 89 Matt Williams	.40	.18
☐ 90 Kevin Appier	.30	.14
☐ 91 Johnny Damon	.15	.07
☐ 92 Chili Davis	.30	.14
☐ 93 Tom Goodwin	.15	.07
☐ 94 Keith Lockhart	.15	.07
☐ 95 Jeff Montgomery	.15	.07
☐ 96 Craig Paquette	.15	.07
☐ 97 Jose Rosado	.30	.14
☐ 98 Michael Tucker	.30	.14
☐ 99 Wilton Guerrero	.15	.07
☐ 100 Todd Hollandsworth	.30	.14
☐ 101 Eric Karros	.30	.14
☐ 102 Ramon Martinez	.30	.14
☐ 103 Raul Mondesi	.40	.18
☐ 104 Hideo Nomo	1.25	.55
☐ 105 Mike Piazza	2.00	.90
☐ 106 Ismael Valdes	.30	.14
☐ 107 Todd Worrell	.30	.14
☐ 108 Tony Clark	.60	.25
☐ 109 Travis Fryman	.30	.14
☐ 110 Bob Higginson	.30	.14
☐ 111 Mark Lewis	.15	.07
☐ 112 Melvin Nieves	.15	.07
☐ 113 Justin Thompson	.30	.14
☐ 114 Wade Boggs	.60	.25
☐ 115 David Cone	.30	.14
☐ 116 Cecil Fielder	.30	.14
☐ 117 Dwight Gooden	.30	.14
☐ 118 Derek Jeter	2.00	.90
☐ 119 Tino Martinez	.60	.25
☐ 120 Paul O'Neill	.30	.14
☐ 121 Andy Pettitte	.60	.25
☐ 122 Mariano Rivera	.30	.14
☐ 123 Darryl Strawberry	.30	.14
☐ 124 John Wetteland	.30	.14
☐ 125 Bernie Williams	.60	.25
☐ 126 Tony Batista	.30	.14
☐ 127 Geronimo Berroa	.15	.07
☐ 128 Scott Brosius	.15	.07
☐ 129 Jason Giambi	.30	.14
☐ 130 Jose Herrera	.15	.07
☐ 131 Mark McGwire	1.25	.55
☐ 132 John Wasdin	.15	.07
☐ 133 Bob Abreu	.60	.25
☐ 134 Jeff Bagwell	1.25	.55
☐ 135 Derek Bell	.15	.07
☐ 136 Craig Biggio	.40	.18
☐ 137 Brian Hunter	.30	.14
☐ 138 Darryl Kile	.30	.14
☐ 139 Orlando Miller	.15	.07
☐ 140 Shane Reynolds	.15	.07
☐ 141 Billy Wagner	.30	.14
☐ 142 Donne Wall	.15	.07
☐ 143 Jay Buhner	.40	.18
☐ 144 Jeff Fassero	.15	.07
☐ 145 Ken Griffey Jr.	3.00	1.35
☐ 146 Sterling Hitchcock	.15	.07
☐ 147 Randy Johnson	.60	.25
☐ 148 Edgar Martinez	.40	.18
☐ 149 Alex Rodriguez	2.50	1.10
☐ 150 Paul Sorrento	.30	.14
☐ 151 Dan Wilson	.15	.07
☐ 152 Moises Alou	.30	.14
☐ 153 Darrin Fletcher	.15	.07
☐ 154 Cliff Floyd	.15	.07
☐ 155 Mark Grudzielanek	.15	.07
☐ 156 Vladimir Guerrero	1.25	.55
☐ 157 Mike Lansing	.15	.07
☐ 158 Pedro Martinez	.60	.25
☐ 159 Henry Rodriguez	.15	.07
☐ 160 Rondell White	.15	.07
☐ 161 Will Clark	.40	.18
☐ 162 Juan Gonzalez	1.50	.70
☐ 163 Rusty Greer	.30	.14
☐ 164 Ken Hill	.15	.07
☐ 165 Mark McLemore	.15	.07
☐ 166 Dean Palmer	.15	.07
☐ 167 Roger Pavlik	.15	.07
☐ 168 Ivan Rodriguez	.75	.35
☐ 169 Mickey Tettleton	.15	.07
☐ 170 Bobby Bonilla	.30	.14
☐ 171 Kevin Brown	.30	.14
☐ 172 Greg Colbrunn	.15	.07
☐ 173 Jeff Conine	.30	.14
☐ 174 Jim Eisenreich	.30	.14
☐ 175 Charles Johnson	.30	.14
☐ 176 Al Leiter	.15	.07
☐ 177 Robb Nen	.15	.07
☐ 178 Edgar Renteria	.30	.14
☐ 179 Gary Sheffield	.60	.25
☐ 180 Devon White	.15	.07
☐ 181 Joe Carter	.30	.14
☐ 182 Carlos Delgado	.30	.14
☐ 183 Alex Gonzalez	.15	.07
☐ 184 Shawn Green	.30	.14
☐ 185 Juan Guzman	.15	.07
☐ 186 Pat Hentgen	.30	.14
☐ 187 Orlando Merced	.15	.07
☐ 188 John Olerud	.30	.14
☐ 189 Robert Perez	.15	.07
☐ 190 Ed Sprague	.15	.07
☐ 191 Mark Clark	.15	.07
☐ 192 John Franco	.30	.14
☐ 193 Bernard Gilkey	.15	.07
☐ 194 Todd Hundley	.30	.14
☐ 195 Lance Johnson	.15	.07
☐ 196 Bobby Jones	.15	.07
☐ 197 Alex Ochoa	.15	.07
☐ 198 Rey Ordonez	.15	.07
☐ 199 Paul Wilson	.15	.07
☐ 200 Ricky Bottalico	.30	.14
☐ 201 Gregg Jefferies	.30	.14
☐ 202 Wendell Magee	.15	.07
☐ 203 Mickey Morandini	.15	.07
☐ 204 Ricky Otero	.15	.07
☐ 205 Scott Rolen	1.50	.70
☐ 206 Benito Santiago	.15	.07
☐ 207 Curt Schilling	.30	.14
☐ 208 Rich Becker	.15	.07
☐ 209 Marty Cordova	.30	.14
☐ 210 Chuck Knoblauch	.60	.25
☐ 211 Pat Meares	.15	.07
☐ 212 Paul Molitor	.60	.25
☐ 213 Frank Rodriguez	.15	.07
☐ 214 Terry Steinbach	.15	.07
☐ 215 Todd Walker	.15	.07
☐ 216 Andy Ashby	.15	.07
☐ 217 Ken Caminiti	.60	.25
☐ 218 Steve Finley	.30	.14
☐ 219 Tony Gwynn	1.50	.70
☐ 220 Joey Hamilton	.30	.14
☐ 221 Rickey Henderson	.40	.18
☐ 222 Trevor Hoffman	.15	.07
☐ 223 Wally Joyner	.15	.07
☐ 224 Scott Sanders	.15	.07
☐ 225 Fernando Valenzuela	.30	.14
☐ 226 Greg Vaughn	.15	.07
☐ 227 Alan Benes	.30	.14
☐ 228 Andy Benes	.15	.07
☐ 229 Dennis Eckersley	.40	.18
☐ 230 Ron Gant	.30	.14
☐ 231 Brian Jordan	.30	.14
☐ 232 Ray Lankford	.30	.14
☐ 233 John Mabry	.30	.14
☐ 234 Tom Pagnozzi	.15	.07
☐ 235 Todd Stottlemyre	.15	.07
☐ 236 Jermaine Allensworth	.15	.07
☐ 237 Francisco Cordova	.15	.07
☐ 238 Jason Kendall	.30	.14
☐ 239 Jeff King	.30	.14
☐ 240 Al Martin	.15	.07
☐ 241 Rod Beck	.30	.14
☐ 242 Barry Bonds	.75	.35
☐ 243 Shawn Estes	.30	.14
☐ 244 Mark Gardner	.15	.07
☐ 245 Glenallen Hill	.15	.07
☐ 246 Bill Mueller	.15	.07
☐ 247 J.T. Snow	.15	.07
☐ 248 Checklist (1-107)	.15	.07
☐ 249 Checklist (108-207)	.15	.07
☐ 250 Checklist (208-250/inserts)	.15	.07
☐ P149 Alex Rodriguez Promo	2.00	.90

1997 Metal Universe Blast Furnace

Randomly inserted in hobby packs only at a rate of one in 48, this 12-card set features color photos of some of baseball's biggest sluggers.

	MINT	NRMT
COMPLETE SET (12)	200.00	90.00
COMMON CARD (1-12)	4.00	1.80
☐ 1 Jeff Bagwell	15.00	6.75
☐ 2 Albert Belle	10.00	4.50
☐ 3 Barry Bonds	10.00	4.50
☐ 4 Andres Galarraga	6.00	2.70
☐ 5 Juan Gonzalez	20.00	9.00
☐ 6 Ken Griffey Jr.	40.00	18.00
☐ 7 Todd Hundley	4.00	1.80
☐ 8 Mark McGwire	15.00	6.75
☐ 9 Mike Piazza	25.00	11.00
☐ 10 Alex Rodriguez	25.00	11.00
☐ 11 Frank Thomas	30.00	13.50
☐ 12 Mo Vaughn	10.00	4.50

1997 Metal Universe Emerald Autographs

One of six different exchange cards were randomly inserted in hobby boxes as chiptoppers (sealed inside the box, but laying on top of the packs) at a rate of one in 20 hobby boxes The exchange cards parallel the corresponding basic cards except for emerald foil on front. In addition, the area used for the card number on back of the regular issue card is replaced by a logo stating "certified emerald autograph". The exchange cards are unnumbered and have been assigned numbers based upon alphabetical order of each player's last name for cataloguing purposes. The deadline to exchange these cards was February 1st, 1998.

	MINT	NRMT
COMPLETE SET (6)	300.00	135.00
COMMON CARD	12.00	5.50
*EXCH.CARDS: .1X TO .2X BASIC CARDS		
☐ AU1 Darin Erstad	60.00	27.00
☐ AU2 Todd Hollandsworth	15.00	6.75
☐ AU3 Alex Ochoa	12.00	5.50
☐ AU4 Alex Rodriguez	150.00	70.00
☐ AU5 Scott Rolen	80.00	36.00
☐ AU6 Todd Walker	20.00	9.00

1997 Metal Universe Magnetic Field

Randomly inserted in packs at a rate of one in 12, this ten-card set honors "Gold Glovers" who appear to have a special attraction to the ball. The fronts feature color player photos on refractive foil backgrounds.

	MINT	NRMT
COMPLETE SET (10)	40.00	18.00
COMMON CARD (1-10)	1.00	.45
☐ 1 Roberto Alomar	2.00	.90
☐ 2 Jeff Bagwell	5.00	2.20
☐ 3 Barry Bonds	3.00	1.35
☐ 4 Ken Griffey Jr.	12.00	5.50
☐ 5 Derek Jeter	8.00	3.60
☐ 6 Kenny Lofton	3.00	1.35
☐ 7 Edgar Renteria	1.00	.45
☐ 8 Cal Ripken	10.00	4.50
☐ 9 Alex Rodriguez	12.00	5.50
☐ 10 Matt Williams	2.00	.90

1997 Metal Universe Mining for Gold

Randomly inserted in packs at a rate of one in nine, this 10-card set features some of baseball's brightest young stars on die-cut "ingot" cards with pearlized gold coating.

	MINT	NRMT
COMPLETE SET (10)	20.00	9.00
COMMON CARD (1-10)	1.00	.45
☐ 1 Bob Abreu	2.00	.90
☐ 2 Kevin L.Brown C	1.00	.45
☐ 3 Nomar Garciaparra	4.00	1.80
☐ 4 Vladimir Guerrero	6.00	2.70
☐ 5 Wilton Guerrero	1.00	.45
☐ 6 Andruw Jones	10.00	4.50
☐ 7 Curt Lyons	1.00	.45
☐ 8 Neifi Perez	1.25	.55
☐ 9 Scott Rolen	4.00	1.80
☐ 10 Todd Walker	1.00	.45

1997 Metal Universe Mother Lode

Randomly inserted in packs at a rate of one in 288, this 12-card set features color player photos on die-cut cards in 100% etched foil.

	MINT	NRMT
COMPLETE SET (12)	800.00	350.00
COMMON CARD (1-12)	20.00	9.00
☐ 1 Roberto Alomar	25.00	11.00
☐ 2 Jeff Bagwell	50.00	22.00
☐ 3 Barry Bonds	30.00	13.50
☐ 4 Ken Griffey Jr.	120.00	55.00
☐ 5 Andruw Jones	50.00	22.00
☐ 6 Chipper Jones	80.00	36.00
☐ 7 Kenny Lofton	30.00	13.50
☐ 8 Mike Piazza	80.00	36.00
☐ 9 Cal Ripken	100.00	45.00
☐ 10 Alex Rodriguez	80.00	36.00
☐ 11 Frank Thomas	100.00	45.00
☐ 12 Matt Williams	20.00	9.00

1997 Metal Universe Platinum Portraits

Randomly inserted in packs at a rate of one in 36, this 10-card set features color photos of some of Baseball's rising stars with backgrounds of platinum-colored etched foil.

	MINT	NRMT
COMPLETE SET (10)	80.00	36.00
COMMON CARD (1-10)	2.50	1.10
☐ 1 James Baldwin	2.50	1.10
☐ 2 Jermaine Dye	2.50	1.10
☐ 3 Todd Hollandsworth	3.00	1.35
☐ 4 Derek Jeter	15.00	6.75
☐ 5 Chipper Jones	20.00	9.00
☐ 6 Jason Kendall	3.00	1.35
☐ 7 Rey Ordonez	2.50	1.10
☐ 8 Andy Pettitte	8.00	3.60
☐ 9 Edgar Renteria	3.00	1.35
☐ 10 Alex Rodriguez	20.00	9.00

1997 Metal Universe Titanium

Randomly inserted in packs at a rate of one in 24, this 10-card set honors some of baseball's favorite superstars. The fronts feature color player photos printed on die-cut embossed cards and sculpted on 100% etched foil.

	MINT	NRMT
COMPLETE SET (10)	100.00	45.00
COMMON CARD (1-10)	5.00	2.20
☐ 1 Jeff Bagwell	8.00	3.60
☐ 2 Albert Belle	5.00	2.20
☐ 3 Ken Griffey Jr.	20.00	9.00
☐ 4 Chipper Jones	12.00	5.50
☐ 5 Greg Maddux	12.00	5.50
☐ 6 Mark McGwire	8.00	3.60
☐ 7 Mike Piazza	12.00	5.50
☐ 8 Cal Ripken	15.00	6.75
☐ 9 Alex Rodriguez	12.00	5.50
☐ 10 Frank Thomas	15.00	6.75

1984 Mets Fan Club

The cards in this eight-player set measure 2 1/2" by 3 1/2". The sheets were produced by Topps for the New York Mets and feature only Mets players. The full sheet measures 7 1/2" by 10 1/2". Cards are together on the sheet but are perforated for those collectors who want to separate the

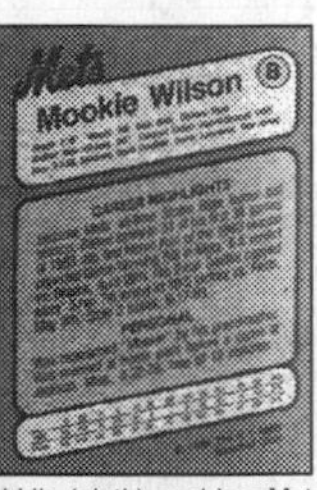

individual player cards. The middle (ninth) card is a Mets Fan club membership card which details various promotional days at Shea Stadium on the back. The cards are numbered on the back and printed in orange and blue.

	NRMT	VG-E
COMPLETE SET (8)	7.50	3.40
COMMON CARD (1-8)	.50	.23
☐ 1 Dave Johnson MG	.75	.35
☐ 2 Ron Darling	1.00	.45
☐ 3 George Foster	1.00	.45
☐ 4 Keith Hernandez	.75	.35
☐ 5 Jesse Orosco	.50	.23
☐ 6 Rusty Staub	1.25	.55
☐ 7 Darryl Strawberry	2.00	.90
☐ 8 Mookie Wilson	.75	.35
☐ NNO Membership Card	.50	.23

1985 Mets Fan Club

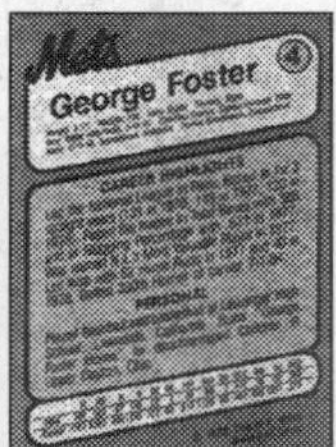

The cards in this eight-player set measure 2 1/2" by 3 1/2". The sheets were produced by Topps for the New York Mets and feature only Mets players. The full sheet measures approximately 7 1/2" by 10 1/2". Cards are together on the sheet but are perforated for those collectors who want to separate the individual player cards. The middle (ninth) card is a Mets Fan club membership card. The set was available as a membership premium for joining the Junior Mets Fan Club for 4.00. The cards are listed below in alphabetical order for convenience.

	NRMT	VG-E
COMPLETE SET (8)	8.00	3.60
COMMON CARD (1-8)	.50	.23
☐ 1 Wally Backman	.50	.23
☐ 2 Bruce Berenyi	.50	.23
☐ 3 Gary Carter	1.25	.55
☐ 4 George Foster	1.00	.45
☐ 5 Dwight Gooden	2.50	1.10
☐ 6 Keith Hernandez	1.00	.45
☐ 7 Doug Sisk	.50	.23
☐ 8 Darryl Strawberry	1.50	.70
☐ NNO Membership Card	.50	.23

1986 Mets Fan Club

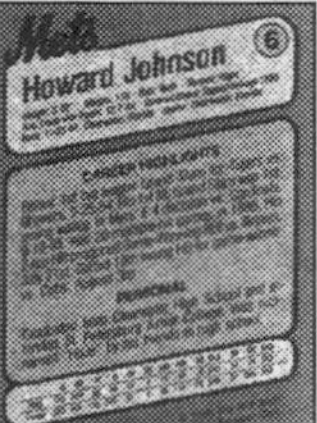

The cards in this eight-player set measure 2 1/2" by 3 1/2". The sheets were produced by Topps for the New York Mets and feature only Mets. The full sheet measures approximately 7 1/2" by 10 1/2". Cards are together on the sheet but are perforated for those collectors who want to separate the individual player cards. The middle (ninth) card is a Mets Fan club membership card. The set was available as a membership premium for joining the Junior Mets Fan Club for 5.00. The cards are listed below in alphabetical order for convenience.

	MINT	NRMT
COMPLETE SET (8)	8.00	3.60
COMMON CARD (1-8)	.50	.23
☐ 1 Wally Backman	.50	.23
☐ 2 Gary Carter	1.25	.55
☐ 3 Ron Darling	.75	.35
☐ 4 Dwight Gooden	1.25	.55
☐ 5 Keith Hernandez	1.00	.45
☐ 6 Howard Johnson	.75	.35
☐ 7 Roger McDowell	.75	.35
☐ 8 Darryl Strawberry	1.00	.45
☐ NNO Membership Card	.50	.23

1988 Mets Kahn's

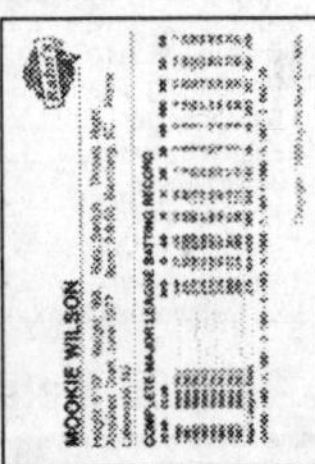

These 32-card standard-size sets were issued to the first 48,000 fans at the June 30th game between the New York Mets and the Houston Astros at Shea Stadium. The set includes 30 players, a team card, and a discount coupon card (to be redeemed at the grocery store). The cards are unnumbered except for uniform number and feature full-color photos bordered in blue and orange on the front. The Kahn's logo is printed in red in the corner of the reverse.

	MINT	NRMT
COMPLETE SET (32)	12.50	5.50
COMMON CARD	.25	.11
☐ 1 Mookie Wilson	.50	.23
☐ 2 Mackey Sasser	.25	.11
☐ 3 Bud Harrelson CO	.50	.23
☐ 4 Len Dykstra	.75	.35
☐ 5 Davey Johnson MG	.50	.23
☐ 6 Wally Backman	.25	.11
☐ 8 Gary Carter	1.50	.70
☐ 11 Tim Teufel	.25	.11
☐ 12 Ron Darling	.50	.23
☐ 13 Lee Mazzilli	.50	.23
☐ 15 Rick Aguilera	.75	.35
☐ 16 Dwight Gooden	1.50	.70
☐ 17 Keith Hernandez	1.25	.55
☐ 18 Darryl Strawberry	1.25	.55
☐ 19 Bob Ojeda	.50	.23
☐ 20 Howard Johnson	.75	.35
☐ 21 Kevin Elster	1.25	.55
☐ 22 Kevin McReynolds	.50	.23
☐ 26 Terry Leach	.25	.11
☐ 28 Bill Robinson CO	.25	.11
☐ 29 Dave Magadan	.50	.23
☐ 30 Mel Stottlemyre CO	.50	.23
☐ 31 Gene Walter	.25	.11
☐ 33 Barry Lyons	.25	.11
☐ 34 Sam Perlozzo CO	.25	.11
☐ 42 Roger McDowell	.50	.23
☐ 44 David Cone	2.00	.90
☐ 48 Randy Myers	1.00	.45
☐ 50 Sid Fernandez	.75	.35
☐ 52 Greg Pavlick CO	.25	.11
☐ NNO Team Photo Card	.50	.23
☐ NNO Discount Coupon	.25	.11

1989 Mets Fan Club

This set was produced by Topps for the Mets Fan Club as a sheet of nine cards each featuring a member of the New York Mets. The individual cards are standard size; however the set is typically traded as a sheet rather than as individual cards.

	MINT	NRMT
COMPLETE SET (9)	6.00	2.70
COMMON CARD	.50	.23
☐ 8 Gary Carter	1.25	.55
☐ 9 Gregg Jefferies	1.50	.70
☐ 16 Dwight Gooden	1.25	.55

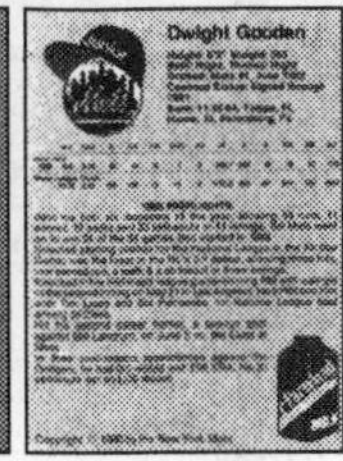

	MINT	NRMT
☐ 18 Darryl Strawberry	.75	.35
☐ 22 Kevin McReynolds	1.00	.45
☐ 25 Keith Miller	.50	.23
☐ 42 Roger McDowell	.50	.23
☐ 44 David Cone	1.50	.70
☐ NNO Mets Team Card (Eastern Div. Champs)	.50	.23

1989 Mets Kahn's

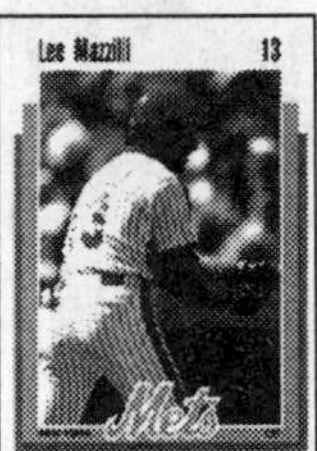

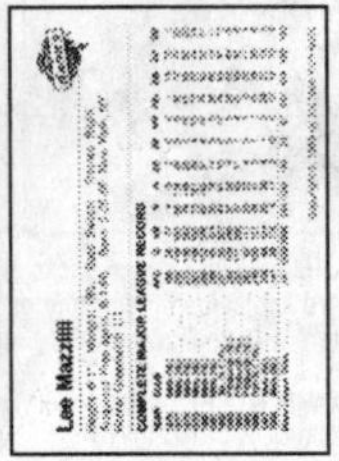

The 1989 Kahn's Mets set contains 36 (32 original and four update) standard-size cards. The fronts have color photos with Mets' colored borders (blue, orange and white). The horizontally oriented backs have career stats. The cards were available from Kahn's by sending three UPC symbols from Kahn's products and a coupon appearing in certain local newspapers. There was also a small late-season update set of Kahn's Mets showing new players who joined the Mets during the season, Jeff Innis, Keith Miller, Jeff Musselman, and Frank Viola. This "Update" subset was distributed at a different Mets Baseball Card Night game than the main set. The main set is referenced alphabetically by subject's name. The update cards are given the prefix "U" in the checklist below.

	MINT	NRMT
COMPLETE SET (36)	8.00	3.60
COMMON CARD (1-32)	.10	.05
☐ 1 Don Aase	.10	.05
☐ 2 Rick Aguilera	.60	.25
☐ 3 Mark Carreon	.10	.05
☐ 4 Gary Carter	1.00	.45
☐ 5 David Cone	1.00	.45
☐ 6 Ron Darling	.25	.11
☐ 7 Kevin Elster	.25	.11
☐ 8 Sid Fernandez	.40	.18
☐ 9 Dwight Gooden	1.00	.45
☐ 10 Bud Harrelson CO	.60	.25
☐ 11 Keith Hernandez	.60	.25
☐ 12 Gregg Jefferies	.75	.35
☐ 13 Davey Johnson MG	.25	.11
☐ 14 Howard Johnson	.40	.18
☐ 15 Barry Lyons	.10	.05
☐ 16 Dave Magadan	.10	.05
☐ 17 Lee Mazzilli	.25	.11
☐ 18 Kevin McReynolds	.25	.11
☐ 19 Randy Myers	.60	.25
☐ 20 Bob Ojeda	.25	.11
☐ 21 Greg Pavlick CO	.10	.05
☐ 22 Sam Perlozzo CO	.10	.05
☐ 23 Bill Robinson CO	.10	.05
☐ 24 Juan Samuel	.10	.05
☐ 25 Mackey Sasser	.10	.05
☐ 26 Mel Stottlemyre CO	.25	.11
☐ 27 Darryl Strawberry	.60	.25
☐ 28 Tim Teufel	.10	.05
☐ 29 Dave West	.10	.05
☐ 30 Mookie Wilson	.25	.11
☐ 31 Mets Team Photo	.25	.11
☐ 32 Sponsors Card	.10	.05
☐ U1 Jeff Innis	.60	.25
☐ U2 Keith Miller	.60	.25
☐ U3 Jeff Musselman	.60	.25
☐ U4 Frank Viola	1.00	.45

1990 Mets Kahn's

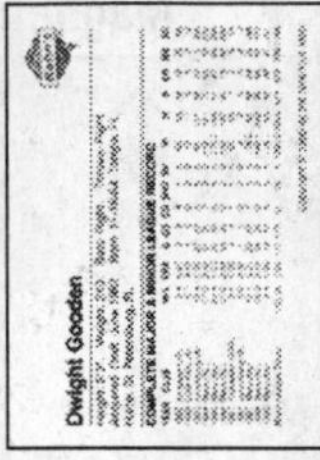

The 1990 Kahn's Mets set was given away as a New York Mets stadium promotion. This standard-size set is skip-numbered by uniform number within the set and features 34 cards and two Kahn's coupon cards. Three players, Thornton, Magadan, and Mercado are wearing different uniform numbers than listed on the front of their cards. In addition to the Shea Stadium promotion, the complete set was also available in specially marked three-packs of Kahn's Wieners.

	MINT	NRMT
COMPLETE SET (34)	7.50	3.40
COMMON CARD	.25	.11
☐ 1 Lou Thornton	.25	.11
☐ 2 Mackey Sasser	.25	.11
☐ 3 Bud Harrelson CO	.40	.18
☐ 4 Mike Cubbage CO	.25	.11
☐ 5 Davey Johnson MG	.40	.18
☐ 6 Mike Marshall	.25	.11
☐ 9 Gregg Jefferies	.40	.18
☐ 10 Dave Magadan	.25	.11
☐ 11 Tim Teufel	.25	.11
☐ 13 Jeff Musselman	.25	.11
☐ 15 Ron Darling	.40	.18
☐ 16 Dwight Gooden	1.00	.45
☐ 18 Darryl Strawberry	.75	.35
☐ 19 Bob Ojeda	.40	.18
☐ 20 Howard Johnson	.60	.25
☐ 21 Kevin Elster	.40	.18
☐ 22 Kevin McReynolds	.25	.11
☐ 25 Keith Miller	.25	.11
☐ 26 Alejandro Pena	.25	.11
☐ 27 Tom O'Malley	.25	.11
☐ 29 Frank Viola	.40	.18
☐ 30 Mel Stottlemyre CO	.40	.18
☐ 31 John Franco	.75	.35
☐ 32 Doc Edwards CO	.25	.11
☐ 33 Barry Lyons	.25	.11
☐ 35 Orlando Mercado	.25	.11
☐ 40 Jeff Innis	.25	.11
☐ 44 David Cone	1.00	.45
☐ 45 Mark Carreon	.25	.11
☐ 47 Wally Whitehurst	.25	.11
☐ 48 Julio Machado	.25	.11
☐ 50 Sid Fernandez	.60	.25
☐ 52 Greg Pavlick CO	.25	.11
☐ NNO Team Photo	.40	.18

1991 Mets Kahn's

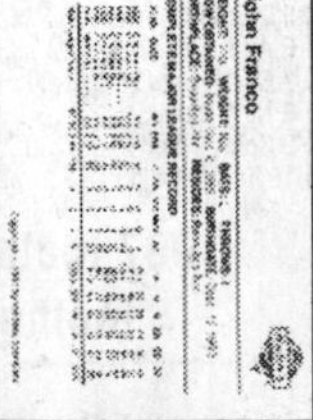

The 1991 Kahn's Mets set contains 33 cards measuring the standard size. The set is skip-numbered on the card fronts by uniform number and includes two Kahn's coupon cards. The front features color action player photos, on a white and blue pinstripe pattern. The player's name is given in an orange stripe below the picture. In a horizontal format the back presents biographical information, major league statistics, and minor league statistics where appropriate. A complete set was given away to each fan attending the New York Mets game at Shea Stadium on June 17, 1991.

	MINT	NRMT
COMPLETE SET (33)	7.50	3.40
COMMON CARD	.25	.11

☐ 1 Vince Coleman	.40	.18
☐ 2 Mackey Sasser	.25	.11
☐ 3 Bud Harrelson MG	.40	.18
☐ 4 Mike Cubbage CO	.25	.11
☐ 5 Charlie O'Brien	.25	.11
☐ 7 Hubie Brooks	.40	.18
☐ 8 Daryl Boston	.25	.11
☐ 9 Gregg Jefferies	.60	.25
☐ 10 Dave Magadan	.25	.11
☐ 11 Tim Teufel	.25	.11
☐ 13 Rick Cerone	.25	.11
☐ 15 Ron Darling	.40	.18
☐ 16 Dwight Gooden	1.00	.45
☐ 17 David Cone	1.00	.45
☐ 20 Howard Johnson	.60	.25
☐ 21 Kevin Elster	.40	.18
☐ 22 Kevin McReynolds	.25	.11
☐ 25 Keith Miller	.25	.11
☐ 26 Alejandro Pena	.25	.11
☐ 28 Tom Herr	.25	.11
☐ 29 Frank Viola	.40	.18
☐ 30 Mel Stottlemyre CO	.40	.18
☐ 31 John Franco	.75	.35
☐ 32 Doc Edwards CO	.25	.11
☐ 40 Jeff Innis	.25	.11
☐ 43 Doug Simons	.25	.11
☐ 45 Mark Carreon	.25	.11
☐ 47 Wally Whitehurst	.25	.11
☐ 48 Pete Schourek	.60	.25
☐ 50 Sid Fernandez	.40	.18
☐ 51 Tom Spencer CO	.25	.11
☐ 52 Greg Pavlick CO	.25	.11
☐ NNO 1991 New York Mets Team photo	.40	.18

1992 Mets Kahn's

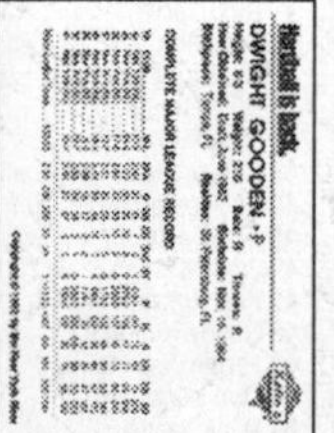

The 1992 Kahn's New York Mets set consists of 35 standard-size cards. The set included two manufacturer's coupons (one for 50 cents off Kahn's Beef Franks and another for the same amount off Kahn's Corn Dogs). The fronts feature color action player photos with a white inner border on a royal blue card face. The upper left corner of the picture is cut off to create space for the team name. An orange stripe bearing the player's name appears beneath the picture and intersects at the lower right corner a baseball with the player's uniform number. In a horizontal format, the backs carry the motto "Hardball is back," biography, and complete major league statistics. The Kahn's logo in red rounds out the back. The cards are skip-numbered by uniform number on the front and checklisted below accordingly.

	MINT	NRMT
COMPLETE SET (35)	7.50	3.40
COMMON CARD	.25	.11
☐ 1 Vince Coleman	.40	.18
☐ 2 Mackey Sasser	.25	.11
☐ 3 Junior Noboa	.25	.11
☐ 4 Mike Cubbage CO	.25	.11
☐ 6 Daryl Boston	.25	.11
☐ 8 Dave Gallagher	.25	.11
☐ 9 Todd Hundley	1.25	.55
☐ 10 Jeff Torborg MG	.25	.11
☐ 11 Dick Schofield	.25	.11
☐ 12 Willie Randolph	.60	.25
☐ 15 Kevin Elster	.40	.18
☐ 16 Dwight Gooden	.75	.35
☐ 17 David Cone	.75	.35
☐ 18 Bret Saberhagen	.40	.18
☐ 19 Anthony Young	.25	.11
☐ 20 Howard Johnson	.60	.25
☐ 22 Charlie O'Brien	.25	.11
☐ 25 Bobby Bonilla	.75	.35
☐ 26 Barry Foote CO	.25	.11
☐ 27 Tom McCraw CO	.25	.11
☐ 28 Dave LaRoche CO	.25	.11
☐ 29 Dave Magadan	.25	.11
☐ 30 Mel Stottlemyre CO	.40	.18
☐ 31 John Franco	.75	.35
☐ 32 Bill Pecota	.25	.11
☐ 33 Eddie Murray	1.25	.55
☐ 40 Jeff Innis	.25	.11
☐ 44 Tim Burke	.25	.11
☐ 45 Paul Gibson	.25	.11
☐ 47 Wally Whitehurst	.25	.11
☐ 50 Sid Fernandez	.40	.18
☐ 51 John Stephenson CO	.25	.11
☐ NNO Team Photo	.40	.18
☐ NNO Manufacturer's Coupon Kahn's Beef Franks	.25	.11
☐ NNO Manufacturer's Coupon Kahn's Corn Dogs	.25	.11

1993 Mets Kahn's

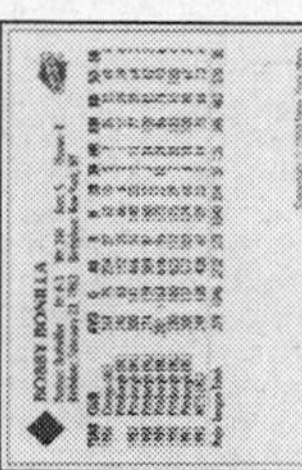

This 29-card set measures the standard size and features white-bordered color player photos on their fronts. The player's name appears in blue lettering in the upper white margin, along with his uniform number and position within orange diamonds on either side. The horizontal white backs are framed by a thin red line and carry the player's statistics. The cards are skip-numbered by uniform number on the front and checklisted below accordingly.

	MINT	NRMT
COMPLETE SET (29)	7.50	3.40
COMMON CARD	.25	.11
☐ 1 Tony Fernandez	.40	.18
☐ 6 Joe Orsulak	.25	.11
☐ 7 Jeff McKnight	.25	.11
☐ 8 Dave Gallagher	.25	.11
☐ 9 Todd Hundley	1.00	.45
☐ 11 Vince Coleman	.40	.18
☐ 12 Jeff Kent	1.50	.70
☐ 16 Dwight Gooden	.75	.35
☐ 18 Bret Saberhagen	.40	.18
☐ 19 Anthony Young	.25	.11
☐ 20 Howard Johnson	.60	.25
☐ 21 Darren Reed	.25	.11
☐ 22 Charlie O'Brien	.25	.11
☐ 23 Tim Bogar	.25	.11
☐ 25 Bobby Bonilla	.75	.35
☐ 29 Frank Tanana	.40	.18
☐ 31 John Franco	.75	.35
☐ 33 Eddie Murray	1.25	.55
☐ 34 Chico Walker	.25	.11
☐ 40 Jeff Innis	.25	.11
☐ 44 Ryan Thompson	.25	.11
☐ 47 Mike Draper	.25	.11
☐ 48 Pete Schourek	.40	.18
☐ 50 Sid Fernandez	.40	.18
☐ 51 Mike Maddux	.25	.11
☐ NNO Team Photo	.40	.18
☐ NNO Title Card	.25	.11
☐ NNO Manufacturer's Coupon Kahn's Corn Dogs	.25	.11
☐ NNO Manufacturer's Coupon Kahn's Hot Dogs	.25	.11

1995 Mets Kahn's

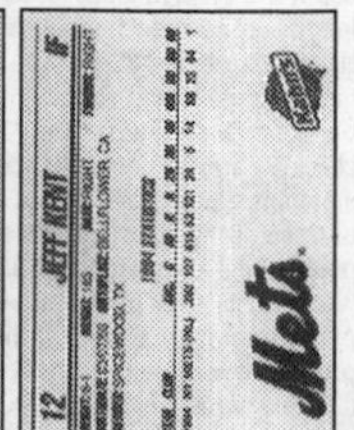

This 34-card set was sponsored by Kahn's and was issued with two manufacturer's coupons. The fronts display color player photos inside an orange picture frame. The surrounding border is gray with thin navy blue pinstripes. The player's name, number, and position are printed in team color-coded lettering in the wider bottom border. In black and red print on white, the backs present biography and 1994 statistics, as well as team and sponsor logos. The cards are unnumbered and checklisted below in alphabetical order.

	MINT	NRMT
COMPLETE SET (34)	6.00	2.70
COMMON CARD (1-34)	.10	.05
☐ 1 Edgardo Alfonzo	.75	.35
☐ 2 Jeff Barry	.10	.05
☐ 3 Tim Bogar	.10	.05
☐ 4 Bobby Bonilla	.50	.23
☐ 5 Rico Brogna	.50	.23
☐ 6 Brett Butler	.50	.23
☐ 7 Mike Cubbage CO	.10	.05
☐ 8 Jerry DiPoto	.10	.05
☐ 9 John Franco	.50	.23
☐ 10 Dallas Green MG	.20	.09
☐ 11 Eric Gunderson	.10	.05
☐ 12 Pete Harnisch	.10	.05
☐ 13 Doug Henry	.10	.05
☐ 14 Frank Howard CO	.35	.16
☐ 15 Todd Hundley	.60	.25
☐ 16 Jason Isringhausen	.20	.09
☐ 17 Bobby Jones	.35	.16
☐ 18 Chris Jones	.10	.05
☐ 19 Jeff Kent	.50	.23
☐ 20 Aaron Ledesma	.10	.05
☐ 21 Tom McCraw CO	.10	.05
☐ 22 Dave Mlicki	.10	.05
☐ 23 Blas Minor	.10	.05
☐ 24 Joe Orsulak	.10	.05
☐ 25 Ricky Otero	.10	.05
☐ 26 Greg Pavlick CO	.10	.05
☐ 27 Bill Pulsipher	.20	.09
☐ 28 Bret Saberhagen	.20	.09
☐ 29 Bill Spiers	.10	.05
☐ 30 Kelly Stinnett	.10	.05
☐ 31 Steve Swisher CO	.10	.05
☐ 32 Ryan Thompson	.10	.05
☐ 33 Jose Vizcaino	.20	.09
☐ 34 Bobby Wine CO	.10	.05

1996 Mets Kahn's

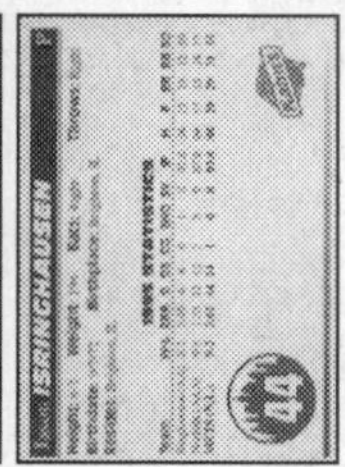

This 34-card set was sponsored by Kahn's and issued with two manufacturer's coupons. The fronts display color player photos set on a black background with the team logo at the bottom and red and gray bars across the top. The backs carry player information and career statistics. The cards are unnumbered and checklisted below in alphabetical order.

	MINT	NRMT
COMPLETE SET (34)	12.00	5.50
COMMON CARD (1- 34)	.25	.11
☐ 1 Edgardo Alfonzo	1.00	.45
☐ 2 Tim Bogar	.25	.11
☐ 3 Rico Brogna	1.00	.45
☐ 4 Paul Byrd	.25	.11
☐ 5 Mark Clark	.25	.11
☐ 6 Mike Cubbage CO	.25	.11
☐ 7 Jerry DiPoto	.25	.11
☐ 8 Carl Everett	.50	.23
☐ 9 John Franco	1.00	.45
☐ 10 Bernard Gilkey	.75	.35
☐ 11 Dallas Green MG	.25	.11
☐ 12 Pete Harnisch	.25	.11
☐ 13 Doug Henry	.25	.11
☐ 14 Frank Howard CO	.50	.23
☐ 15 Todd Hundley	1.00	.45
☐ 16 Butch Huskey	.25	.11
☐ 17 Jason Isringhausen	.50	.23
☐ 18 Lance Johnson	.75	.35
☐ 19 Bobby Jones	.50	.23
☐ 20 Chris Jones	.25	.11
☐ 21 Brent Mayne	.25	.11
☐ 22 Tom McCraw CO	.25	.11
☐ 23 Dave Mlicki	.25	.11
☐ 24 Alex Ochoa	.50	.23

☐ 25 Rey Ordonez	.50	.23
☐ 26 Greg Pavlick CO	.25	.11
☐ 27 Robert Person	.25	.11
☐ 28 Bill Pulsipher	.50	.23
☐ 29 Steve Swisher	.25	.11
☐ 30 Andy Tomberlin	.25	.11
☐ 31 Paul Wilson	.50	.23
☐ 32 Bobby Wine CO	.25	.11
☐ NNO Manufacturer's Coupon Kahn's Corn Dogs	.25	.11
☐ NNO Manufacturer's Coupon Kahn's Hot Dogs	.25	.11

1993 Metz Baking

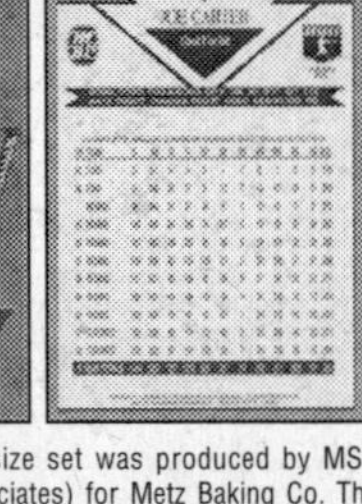

This 40-card standard-size set was produced by MSA (Michael Schechter Associates) for Metz Baking Co. The cards were issued in two series and feature on their fronts oval color drawings of the players with team names or logos airbrushed from their caps and uniforms. These drawings are bordered in red, white, and black and are displayed between two baseball bat icons. In a black banner beneath the drawing, the player's name and team appear in yellow and red, respectively. The player's position is shown within a baseball icon near the bottom of the card. In the first series, the blue fronts are edged in tan and have vertical yellow pinstripes. The second series has yellow fronts edged in red with blue pinstripes. The gray-bordered white backs all carry the same design regardless of the series. The player's name and position appear at the top. His biography appears below within a black banner, and beneath that, a stat table. The Metz and MLBPA logos in the upper corners round out the back. One card was inserted into packages of Metz products distributed in the Midwest. The cards are unnumbered and checklisted below in alphabetical order within each 20-card series.

	MINT	NRMT
COMPLETE SET (40)	5.00	2.20
COMMON CARD (1-40)	.05	.02
☐ 1 Wade Boggs	.30	.14
☐ 2 Barry Bonds	.40	.18
☐ 3 Bobby Bonilla	.10	.05
☐ 4 Joe Carter	.10	.05
☐ 5 Roger Clemens	.60	.25
☐ 6 Doug Drabek	.05	.02
☐ 7 Cecil Fielder	.10	.05
☐ 8 Dwight Gooden	.10	.05
☐ 9 Ken Griffey Jr.	1.00	.45
☐ 10 Tony Gwynn	.50	.23
☐ 11 Howard Johnson	.05	.02
☐ 12 Wally Joyner	.10	.05
☐ 13 Dave Justice	.30	.14
☐ 14 Don Mattingly	.50	.23
☐ 15 Jack McDowell	.05	.02
☐ 16 Kirby Puckett	.50	.23
☐ 17 Cal Ripken	.75	.35
☐ 18 Ryne Sandberg	.40	.18
☐ 19 Darryl Strawberry	.10	.05
☐ 20 Danny Tartabull	.05	.02
☐ 21 Dante Bichette	.20	.09
☐ 22 Jose Canseco	.20	.09
☐ 23 Will Clark	.20	.09
☐ 24 Shawon Dunston	.05	.02
☐ 25 Dennis Eckersley	.20	.09
☐ 26 Carlton Fisk	.30	.14
☐ 27 Andres Galarraga	.30	.14
☐ 28 Kirk Gibson	.10	.05
☐ 29 Mark Grace	.20	.09
☐ 30 Rickey Henderson	.20	.09
☐ 31 Kent Hrbek	.05	.02
☐ 32 Barry Larkin	.20	.09
☐ 33 Paul Molitor	.30	.14
☐ 34 Terry Pendleton	.05	.02
☐ 35 Nolan Ryan	.75	.35
☐ 36 Ozzie Smith	.40	.18
☐ 37 Mickey Tettleton	.05	.02
☐ 38 Alan Trammell	.20	.09
☐ 39 Andy Van Slyke	.05	.02
☐ 40 Dave Winfield	.30	.14

1993 Milk Bone Super Stars

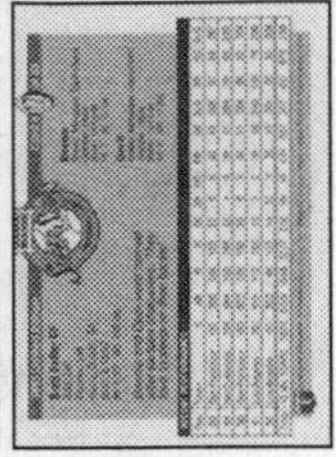

This 20-card standard-size set was featured in specially marked packages of Milk Bone Flavor Snacks and Dog Treats. Two cards were inserted in each package. Also the complete set could be obtained by sending in a mail-in form along with three Super Star Seals plus 2.50. The fronts feature a color picture of the player at home with his dog(s). At the lower left corner appears a small photo of the player in game action. The player's name and the dog's name are printed on an orange box at the lower right corner. On a pastel green panel, the horizontal backs carry player information (biography and recent performance statistics) as well as information and a player quote about the dog.

	MINT	NRMT
COMPLETE SET (20)	12.00	5.50
COMMON CARD (1-20)	.25	.11
☐ 1 Paul Molitor	1.00	.45
☐ 2 Tom Glavine	.50	.23
☐ 3 Barry Larkin	.75	.35
☐ 4 Mark McGwire	4.00	1.80
☐ 5 Bill Swift	.25	.11
☐ 6 Ken Caminiti	1.00	.45
☐ 7 Will Clark	1.00	.45
☐ 8 Rafael Palmeiro	.75	.35
☐ 9 Matt Young	.25	.11
☐ 10 Todd Zeile	.25	.11
☐ 11 Wally Joyner	.25	.11
☐ 12 Cal Ripken	6.00	2.70
☐ 13 Tom Foley	.25	.11
☐ 14 Ben McDonald	.25	.11
☐ 15 Larry Walker	1.50	.70
☐ 16 Rob Dibble	.25	.11
☐ 17 Brett Butler	.50	.23
☐ 18 Joe Girardi	.25	.11
☐ 19 Brady Anderson	.75	.35
☐ 20 Craig Biggio	.75	.35

1971 Milk Duds

The cards in this 69-card set measure 1 13/16" by 2 5/8". The 1971 Milk Duds set contains 32 American League cards and 37 National League cards. The cards are actually numbered, but the very small number appears only on the flap of the box; nevertheless the numbers below are ordered alphabetically by player's name within league. American Leaguers are numbered 1-32 and National Leaguers 33-69. The cards are sepia toned on a tan background and were issued on the backs of five-cent boxes of Milk Duds candy. The prices listed in the checklist are for complete boxes. Cards cut from boxes are approximately one-half of the listed price. The names of three of the players in the set were misspelled and are noted in the checklist below as errors. Three of the boxes were double printed, i.e., twice as many were produced or printed compared to the other players. These double-printed players are indicated below by DP in the checklist after the player's name.

	NRMT	VG-E
COMPLETE SET (69)	1200.00	550.00
COMMON CARD (1-69)	8.00	3.60
☐ 1 Luis Aparicio	20.00	9.00
☐ 2 Stan Bahnsen	8.00	3.60
☐ 3 Danny Cater	8.00	3.60
☐ 4 Ray Culp	8.00	3.60
☐ 5 Ray Fosse	8.00	3.60
☐ 6 Bill Freehan	12.50	5.50
☐ 7 Jim Fregosi	10.00	4.50
☐ 8 Tommy Harper	8.00	3.60
☐ 9 Frank Howard	12.50	5.50
☐ 10 Jim Hunter	25.00	11.00
☐ 11 Tommy John	12.50	5.50
☐ 12 Alex Johnson	8.00	3.60
☐ 13 Dave Johnson	10.00	4.50
☐ 14 Harmon Killebrew DP	15.00	6.75
☐ 15 Sam McDowell	10.00	4.50
☐ 16 Dave McNally	8.00	3.60
☐ 17 Bill Melton	8.00	3.60
☐ 18 Andy Messersmith	8.00	3.60
☐ 19 Thurman Munson	20.00	9.00
☐ 20 Tony Oliva	15.00	6.75
☐ 21 Jim Palmer	20.00	9.00
☐ 22 Jim Perry	10.00	4.50
☐ 23 Fritz Peterson	8.00	3.60
☐ 24 Rico Petrocelli	8.00	3.60
☐ 25 Boog Powell	12.50	5.50
☐ 26 Brooks Robinson DP	15.00	6.75
☐ 27 Frank Robinson	25.00	11.00
☐ 28 George Scott	8.00	3.60
☐ 29 Reggie Smith	10.00	4.50
☐ 30 Mel Stottlemyer ERR (sic, Stottlemyre)	10.00	4.50
☐ 31 Cesar Tovar	8.00	3.60
☐ 32 Roy White	8.00	3.60
☐ 33 Hank Aaron	50.00	22.00
☐ 34 Ernie Banks	40.00	18.00
☐ 35 Glen Beckert ERR (sic, Glenn)	8.00	3.60
☐ 36 Johnny Bench	40.00	18.00
☐ 37 Lou Brock	30.00	13.50
☐ 38 Rico Carty	10.00	4.50
☐ 39 Orlando Cepeda	15.00	6.75
☐ 40 Roberto Clemente	100.00	45.00
☐ 41 Willie Davis	8.00	3.60
☐ 42 Dick Dietz	8.00	3.60
☐ 43 Bob Gibson	20.00	9.00
☐ 44 Bill Grabarkewitz	8.00	3.60
☐ 45 Bud Harrelson	8.00	3.60
☐ 46 Jim Hickman	8.00	3.60
☐ 47 Ken Holtzman	8.00	3.60
☐ 48 Randy Hundley	10.00	4.50
☐ 49 Fergie Jenkins	20.00	9.00
☐ 50 Don Kessinger	10.00	4.50
☐ 51 Willie Mays	60.00	27.00
☐ 52 Willie McCovey	20.00	9.00
☐ 53 Dennis Menke	8.00	3.60
☐ 54 Jim Merritt	8.00	3.60
☐ 55 Felix Millan	8.00	3.60
☐ 56 Claud Osteen ERR (sic, Claude)	8.00	3.60
☐ 57 Milt Pappas (pictured in Oriole uniform)	10.00	4.50
☐ 58 Tony Perez	15.00	6.75
☐ 59 Gaylord Perry	20.00	9.00
☐ 60 Pete Rose DP	40.00	18.00
☐ 61 Manny Sanguillen	10.00	4.50
☐ 62 Ron Santo	15.00	6.75
☐ 63 Tom Seaver	25.00	11.00
☐ 64 Wayne Simpson	8.00	3.60
☐ 65 Rusty Staub	12.50	5.50
☐ 66 Bobby Tolan	8.00	3.60
☐ 67 Joe Torre	15.00	6.75
☐ 68 Luke Walker	8.00	3.60
☐ 69 Billy Williams	20.00	9.00

1969 Milton Bradley

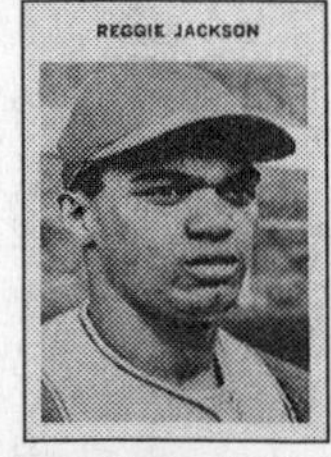

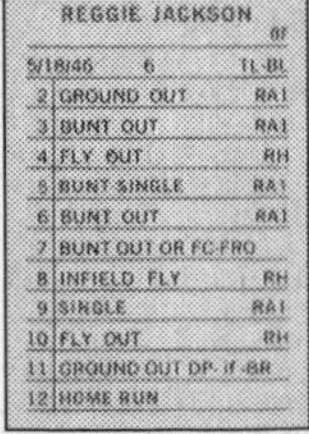

These cards were distributed as part of a baseball game produced by Milton Bradley in 1969. The cards each measure approximately 2" by 3" and have square corners. The card fronts show a black and white photo of the player with his name above the photo in a white border. The game outcomes are printed on the card backs. The game was played by rolling two dice. The outcomes (two through twelve) on the back of the player's card related to the sum of the two dice. The card backs are printed in red and black on white card stock; the player's name on back and successful outcomes for the batter such as hits are printed in red. Team logos have been airbrushed from the photos in this set. The cards are typically found with perforation notches visible. Since the cards are unnumbered, they are listed below in alphabetical order. One way to tell the 1969 and 1972 Milton Bradley sets apart is that the 1969 cards all the red digits do not have a base while the 1972 red digit cards all have a base.

	NRMT	VG-E
COMPLETE SET (296)	225.00	100.00
COMMON CARD (1-296)	.25	.11
☐ 1 Hank Aaron	15.00	6.75
☐ 2 Ted Abernathy	.25	.11
☐ 3 Jerry Adair	.25	.11
☐ 4 Tommy Agee	.25	.11
☐ 5 Bernie Allen	.25	.11
☐ 6 Hank Allen	.25	.11
☐ 7 Richie Allen	1.50	.70
☐ 8 Gene Alley	.25	.11
☐ 9 Bob Allison	.50	.23
☐ 10 Felipe Alou	1.00	.45
☐ 11 Jesus Alou	.25	.11
☐ 12 Matty Alou	.75	.35
☐ 13 Max Alvis	.25	.11
☐ 14 Mike Andrews	.25	.11
☐ 15 Luis Aparicio	3.00	1.35
☐ 16 Jose Arcia	.25	.11
☐ 17 Bob Aspromonte	.25	.11
☐ 18 Joe Azcue	.25	.11
☐ 19 Ernie Banks	7.50	3.40
☐ 20 Steve Barber	.25	.11
☐ 21 John Bateman	.25	.11
☐ 22 Glenn Beckert	.25	.11
☐ 23 Gary Bell	.25	.11
☐ 24 Johnny Bench	12.00	5.50
☐ 25 Ken Berry	.25	.11
☐ 26 Frank Bertaina	.25	.11
☐ 27 Paul Blair	.25	.11
☐ 28 Wade Blasingame	.25	.11
☐ 29 Curt Blefary	.25	.11
☐ 30 John Boccabella	.25	.11
☐ 31 Bobby Bonds	3.00	1.35
☐ 32 Sam Bowens	.25	.11
☐ 33 Ken Boyer	1.00	.45
☐ 34 Charles Bradford	.25	.11
☐ 35 Darrell Brandon	.25	.11
☐ 36 Jim Brewer	.25	.11
☐ 37 John Briggs	.25	.11
☐ 38 Nelson Briles	.25	.11
☐ 39 Ed Brinkman	.25	.11
☐ 40 Lou Brock	6.00	2.70
☐ 41 Gates Brown	.25	.11
☐ 42 Larry Brown	.25	.11
☐ 43 George Brunet	.25	.11
☐ 44 Jerry Buchek	.25	.11
☐ 45 Don Buford	.25	.11
☐ 46 Jim Bunning	3.00	1.35
☐ 47 Johnny Callison	.75	.35
☐ 48 Bert Campaneris	.75	.35
☐ 49 Jose Cardenal	.50	.23
☐ 50 Leo Cardenas	.25	.11
☐ 51 Don Cardwell	.25	.11
☐ 52 Rod Carew	7.50	3.40
☐ 53 Paul Casanova	.25	.11
☐ 54 Norm Cash	1.50	.70
☐ 55 Danny Cater	.25	.11
☐ 56 Orlando Cepeda	2.50	1.10
☐ 57 Dean Chance	.50	.23
☐ 58 Ed Charles	.25	.11
☐ 59 Horace Clarke	.25	.11
☐ 60 Roberto Clemente	20.00	9.00
☐ 61 Donn Clendenon	.25	.11
☐ 62 Ty Cline	.25	.11
☐ 63 Nate Colbert	.25	.11
☐ 64 Joe Coleman	.25	.11
☐ 65 Bob Cox	2.00	.90
☐ 66 Mike Cuellar	1.00	.45
☐ 67 Ray Culp	.25	.11
☐ 68 Clay Dalrymple	.25	.11
☐ 69 Jim Davenport	.25	.11
☐ 70 Vic Davalillo	.25	.11
☐ 71 Ron Davis	.25	.11
☐ 72 Tommy Davis	.75	.35
☐ 73 Willie Davis	.50	.23
☐ 74 Chuck Dobson	.25	.11
☐ 75 John Donaldson	.25	.11
☐ 76 Al Downing	.25	.11
☐ 77 Moe Drabowsky	.25	.11
☐ 78 Dick Ellsworth	.25	.11
☐ 79 Mike Epstein	.25	.11
☐ 80 Andy Etchebarren	.25	.11
☐ 81 Ron Fairly	.50	.23
☐ 82 Dick Farrell	.25	.11
☐ 83 Curt Flood	1.00	.45
☐ 84 Joe Foy	.25	.11
☐ 85 Tito Francona	.25	.11
☐ 86 Bill Freehan	1.00	.45
☐ 87 Jim Fregosi	.75	.35
☐ 88 Woodie Fryman	.25	.11
☐ 89 Len Gabrielson	.25	.11
☐ 90 Clarence Gaston	1.25	.55
☐ 91 Jake Gibbs	.25	.11
☐ 92 Russ Gibson	.25	.11
☐ 93 Dave Giusti	.25	.11
☐ 94 Tony Gonzalez	.25	.11
☐ 95 Jim Gosger	.25	.11
☐ 96 Julio Gotay	.25	.11
☐ 97 Dick Green	.25	.11
☐ 98 Jerry Grote	.50	.23
☐ 99 Jimmie Hall	.25	.11
☐ 100 Tom Haller	.25	.11
☐ 101 Steve Hamilton	.25	.11
☐ 102 Ron Hansen	.25	.11
☐ 103 Jim Hardin	.25	.11
☐ 104 Tommy Harper	.50	.23
☐ 105 Bud Harrelson	.50	.23
☐ 106 Ken Harrelson	1.00	.45
☐ 107 Jim Ray Hart	.25	.11
☐ 108 Woodie Held	.25	.11
☐ 109 Tommy Helms	.25	.11
☐ 110 Elrod Hendricks	.25	.11
☐ 111 Mike Hershberger	.25	.11
☐ 112 Jack Hiatt	.25	.11
☐ 113 Jim Hickman	.25	.11
☐ 114 John Hiller	.25	.11
☐ 115 Chuck Hinton	.25	.11
☐ 116 Ken Holtzman	.50	.23
☐ 117 Joel Horlen	.25	.11
☐ 118 Tony Horton	.50	.23
☐ 119 Willie Horton	.75	.35
☐ 120 Frank Howard	1.00	.45
☐ 121 Dick Howser	.50	.23
☐ 122 Randy Hundley	.50	.23
☐ 123 Ron Hunt	.25	.11
☐ 124 Jim Hunter	4.00	1.80
☐ 125 Al Jackson	.25	.11
☐ 126 Larry Jackson	.50	.23
☐ 127 Reggie Jackson	20.00	9.00
☐ 128 Sonny Jackson	.25	.11
☐ 129 Pat Jarvis	.25	.11
☐ 130 Julian Javier	.25	.11
☐ 131 Ferguson Jenkins	4.00	1.80
☐ 132 Manny Jimenez	.25	.11
☐ 133 Tommy John	2.00	.90
☐ 134 Bob Johnson	.25	.11
☐ 135 Dave Johnson	1.00	.45
☐ 136 Deron Johnson	.25	.11
☐ 137 Lou Johnson	.25	.11
☐ 138 Jay Johnstone	1.00	.45
☐ 139 Cleon Jones	.50	.23
☐ 140 Dalton Jones	.25	.11
☐ 141 Duane Josephson	.25	.11
☐ 142 Jim Kaat	2.00	.90
☐ 143 Al Kaline	7.50	3.40
☐ 144 Don Kessinger	.50	.23
☐ 145 Harmon Killebrew	5.00	2.20
☐ 146 Hal King	.25	.11
☐ 147 Ed Kirkpatrick	.25	.11
☐ 148 Fred Klages	.25	.11
☐ 149 Ron Kline	.25	.11
☐ 150 Bobby Knoop	.25	.11
☐ 151 Gary Kolb	.25	.11
☐ 152 Andy Kosco	.25	.11
☐ 153 Ed Kranepool	.50	.23
☐ 154 Lew Krausse	.25	.11
☐ 155 Hal Lanier	.25	.11
☐ 156 Jim LeFebvre	.25	.11
☐ 157 Denny Lemaster	.25	.11
☐ 158 Dave Leonhard	.25	.11
☐ 159 Don Lock	.25	.11
☐ 160 Mickey Lolich	1.00	.45
☐ 161 Jim Lonborg	1.00	.45
☐ 162 Mike Lum	.25	.11
☐ 163 Sparky Lyle	2.00	.90
☐ 164 Jim Maloney	.50	.23
☐ 165 Juan Marichal	4.00	1.80
☐ 166 J.C. Martin	.25	.11
☐ 167 Marty Martinez	.25	.11
☐ 168 Tom Matchick	.25	.11
☐ 169 Ed Mathews	6.00	2.70
☐ 170 Jerry May	.25	.11
☐ 171 Lee May	.50	.23
☐ 172 Lee Maye	.25	.11
☐ 173 Willie Mays	15.00	6.75
☐ 174 Dal Maxvill	.25	.11
☐ 175 Bill Mazeroski	2.00	.90
☐ 176 Dick McAuliffe	.25	.11
☐ 177 Al McBean	.25	.11
☐ 178 Tim McCarver	1.50	.70
☐ 179 Bill McCool	.25	.11
☐ 180 Mike McCormick	.50	.23
☐ 181 Willie McCovey	6.00	2.70
☐ 182 Tom McCraw	.25	.11
☐ 183 Lindy McDaniel	.25	.11
☐ 184 Sam McDowell	.75	.35
☐ 185 Orlando McFarlane	.25	.11
☐ 186 Jim McGlothlin	.25	.11
☐ 187 Denny McLain	1.50	.70
☐ 188 Ken McMullen	.25	.11
☐ 189 Dave McNally	1.00	.45
☐ 190 Gerry McNertney	.25	.11
☐ 191 Denis Menke	.25	.11
☐ 192 Felix Millan	.25	.11
☐ 193 Don Mincher	.25	.11
☐ 194 Rick Monday	.50	.23
☐ 195 Joe Morgan	5.00	2.20
☐ 196 Bubba Morton	.25	.11
☐ 197 Manny Mota	.50	.23
☐ 198 Jim Nash	.25	.11
☐ 199 Dave Nelson	.25	.11
☐ 200 Dick Nen	.25	.11
☐ 201 Phil Niekro	4.00	1.80
☐ 202 Jim Northrup	.50	.23
☐ 203 Rich Nye	.25	.11
☐ 204 Johnny Odom	.25	.11
☐ 205 Tony Oliva	2.00	.90
☐ 206 Gene Oliver	.25	.11
☐ 207 Phil Ortega	.25	.11
☐ 208 Claude Osteen	.50	.23
☐ 209 Ray Oyler	.25	.11
☐ 210 Jose Pagan	.25	.11
☐ 211 Jim Pagliaroni	.25	.11
☐ 212 Milt Pappas	.50	.23
☐ 213 Wes Parker	.25	.11
☐ 214 Camilo Pascual	.25	.11
☐ 215 Don Pavletich	.25	.11
☐ 216 Joe Pepitone	.75	.35
☐ 217 Tony Perez	2.50	1.10
☐ 218 Gaylord Perry	4.00	1.80
☐ 219 Jim Perry	1.00	.45
☐ 220 Gary Peters	.25	.11
☐ 221 Rico Petrocelli	.50	.23
☐ 222 Adolpho Phillips	.25	.11
☐ 223 Tom Phoebus	.25	.11
☐ 224 Vada Pinson	1.50	.70
☐ 225 Boog Powell	2.00	.90
☐ 226 Frank Quilici	.25	.11
☐ 227 Doug Rader	.25	.11
☐ 228 Rich Reese	.25	.11
☐ 229 Phil Regan	.25	.11
☐ 230 Rick Reichardt	.25	.11
☐ 231 Rick Renick	.25	.11
☐ 232 Roger Repoz	.25	.11
☐ 233 Dave Ricketts	.25	.11
☐ 234 Bill Robinson	.25	.11
☐ 235 Brooks Robinson	7.50	3.40
☐ 236 Frank Robinson	7.50	3.40
☐ 237 Bob Rodgers	.25	.11
☐ 238 Cookie Rojas	.25	.11
☐ 239 Rich Rollins	.25	.11
☐ 240 Phil Roof	.25	.11
☐ 241 Pete Rose	15.00	6.75
☐ 242 John Roseboro	.50	.23
☐ 243 Chico Ruiz	.25	.11
☐ 244 Ray Sadecki	.25	.11
☐ 245 Chico Salmon	.25	.11
☐ 246 Jose Santiago	.25	.11
☐ 247 Ron Santo	1.50	.70
☐ 248 Tom Satriano	.25	.11
☐ 249 Paul Schaal	.25	.11
☐ 250 Tom Seaver	12.00	5.50
☐ 251 Art Shamsky	.25	.11
☐ 252 Mike Shannon	.75	.35
☐ 253 Chris Short	.25	.11
☐ 254 Dick Simpson	.25	.11
☐ 255 Duke Sims	.25	.11
☐ 256 Reggie Smith	1.00	.45
☐ 257 Willie Smith	.25	.11
☐ 258 Russ Snyder	.25	.11
☐ 259 Al Spangler	.25	.11
☐ 260 Larry Stahl	.25	.11
☐ 261 Lee Stange	.25	.11
☐ 262 Mickey Stanley	.25	.11
☐ 263 Willie Stargell	6.00	2.70
☐ 264 Rusty Staub	1.50	.70
☐ 265 Mel Stottlemyre	1.00	.45
☐ 266 Ed Stroud	.25	.11
☐ 267 Don Sutton	4.00	1.80
☐ 268 Ron Swoboda	.50	.23
☐ 269 Jose Tartabull	.25	.11
☐ 270 Tony Taylor	.50	.23
☐ 271 Luis Tiant	1.50	.70
☐ 272 Bill Tillman	.25	.11
☐ 273 Bobby Tolan	.25	.11
☐ 274 Jeff Torborg	.25	.11
☐ 275 Joe Torre	2.50	1.10
☐ 276 Cesar Tovar	.25	.11

☐ 277 Dick Tracewski .25 .11
☐ 278 Tom Tresh 1.00 .45
☐ 279 Ted Uhlaender .25 .11
☐ 280 Del Unser .25 .11
☐ 281 Sandy Valdespino .25 .11
☐ 282 Fred Valentine .25 .11
☐ 283 Bob Veale .25 .11
☐ 284 Zoilo Versalles .50 .23
☐ 285 Pete Ward .25 .11
☐ 286 Al Weis .25 .11
☐ 287 Don Wert .25 .11
☐ 288 Bill White 1.00 .45
☐ 289 Roy White .50 .23
☐ 290 Fred Whitfield .25 .11
☐ 291 Hoyt Wilhelm 3.00 1.35
☐ 292 Billy Williams 5.00 2.20
☐ 293 Maury Wills 2.00 .90
☐ 294 Earl Wilson .25 .11
☐ 295 Wilbur Wood .25 .11
☐ 296 Jerry Zimmerman .25 .11

1970 Milton Bradley

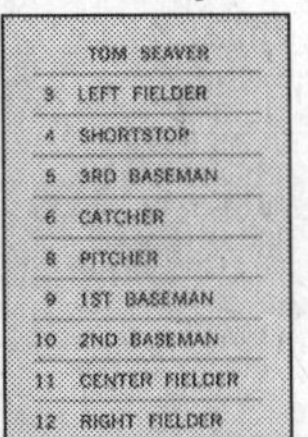

TOM SEAVER
3 LEFT FIELDER
4 SHORTSTOP
5 3RD BASEMAN
6 CATCHER
8 PITCHER
9 1ST BASEMAN
10 2ND BASEMAN
11 CENTER FIELDER
12 RIGHT FIELDER

These cards were distributed as part of a baseball game produced by Milton Bradley in 1970. The cards each measure approximately 2 3/16" by 3 1/2" and have rounded corners. The card fronts show a black and white photo of the player with his name and vital statistics below the photo in a white border. The game outcomes are printed on the card backs. The card backs are printed in red and black on white card stock; the player's name is printed in red at the top of the card. Team logos have been airbrushed from the photos in this set. Since the cards are unnumbered, they are listed below in alphabetical order.

	NRMT	VG-E
COMPLETE SET (28)	150.00	70.00
COMMON CARD (1-28)	.50	.23

☐ 1 Hank Aaron 20.00 9.00
☐ 2 Lou Brock 7.50 3.40
☐ 3 Ernie Banks 7.50 3.40
☐ 4 Rod Carew 7.50 3.40
☐ 5 Roberto Clemente 25.00 11.00
☐ 6 Tommy Davis .75 .35
☐ 7 Bill Freehan .75 .35
☐ 8 Jim Fregosi .75 .35
☐ 9 Tom Haller .50 .23
☐ 10 Frank Howard 1.00 .45
☐ 11 Reggie Jackson 15.00 6.75
☐ 12 Harmon Killebrew 6.00 2.70
☐ 13 Mickey Lolich 1.00 .45
☐ 14 Juan Marichal 6.00 2.70
☐ 15 Willie Mays 20.00 9.00
☐ 16 Willie McCovey 7.50 3.40
☐ 17 Sam McDowell .75 .35
☐ 18 Denis Menke .50 .23
☐ 19 Don Mincher .50 .23
☐ 20 Phil Niekro 6.00 2.70
☐ 21 Rico Petrocelli .75 .35
☐ 22 Boog Powell 1.50 .70
☐ 23 Frank Robinson 7.50 3.40
☐ 24 Pete Rose 20.00 9.00
☐ 25 Ron Santo 1.50 .70
☐ 26 Tom Seaver 15.00 6.75
☐ 27 Mel Stottlemyre .75 .35
☐ 28 Tony Taylor .50 .23

1972 Milton Bradley

These cards were distributed as part of a baseball game produced by Milton Bradley in 1972. The cards each measure approximately 2" by 3" and have square corners. The card fronts show a black and white photo of the player with his name above the photo in a white border. The game outcomes are printed on the card backs. The game was played by rolling two dice. The outcomes (two through twelve) on the back of the player's card related to the sum of the two dice. The card backs are printed in red and black on white card stock; successful outcomes for the batter such as hits are printed in red. Team logos have been airbrushed from the photos in this set. The cards are typically found with perforation notches visible. Since the cards are unnumbered, they are listed below in alphabetical order.

	NRMT	VG-E
COMPLETE SET (372)	250.00	110.00
COMMON CARD (1-372)	.25	.11

☐ 1 Hank Aaron 20.00 9.00
☐ 2 Tommie Aaron .25 .11
☐ 3 Ted Abernathy .25 .11
☐ 4 Jerry Adair .25 .11
☐ 5 Tommy Agee .25 .11
☐ 6 Bernie Allen .25 .11
☐ 7 Hank Allen .25 .11
☐ 8 Richie Allen 2.00 .90
☐ 9 Gene Alley .25 .11
☐ 10 Bob Allison .50 .23
☐ 11 Sandy Alomar .25 .11
☐ 12 Felipe Alou 1.00 .45
☐ 13 Jesus Alou .25 .11
☐ 14 Matty Alou .75 .35
☐ 15 Max Alvis .25 .11
☐ 16 Brant Alyea .25 .11
☐ 17 Mike Andrews .25 .11
☐ 18 Luis Aparicio 4.00 1.80
☐ 19 Jose Arcia .25 .11
☐ 20 Jerry Arrigo .25 .11
☐ 21 Bob Aspromonte .25 .11
☐ 22 Joe Azcue .25 .11
☐ 23 Bob Bailey .25 .11
☐ 24 Sal Bando 1.00 .45
☐ 25 Ernie Banks 10.00 4.50
☐ 26 Steve Barber .25 .11
☐ 27 Bob Barton .25 .11
☐ 28 John Bateman .25 .11
☐ 29 Glenn Beckert .25 .11
☐ 30 Johnny Bench 15.00 6.75
☐ 31 Ken Berry .25 .11
☐ 32 Frank Bertaina .25 .11
☐ 33 Paul Blair .25 .11
☐ 34 Steve Blass .25 .11
☐ 35 Curt Blefary .25 .11
☐ 36 Bobby Bolin .25 .11
☐ 37 Bobby Bonds 2.00 .90
☐ 38 Don Bosch .25 .11
☐ 39 Dick Bosman .25 .11
☐ 40 Dave Boswell .25 .11
☐ 41 Ken Boswell .25 .11
☐ 42 Cletis Boyer .75 .35
☐ 43 Charles Bradford .25 .11
☐ 44 Ron Brand .25 .11
☐ 45 Ken Brett .25 .11
☐ 46 Jim Brewer .25 .11
☐ 47 John Briggs .25 .11
☐ 48 Nelson Briles .25 .11
☐ 49 Ed Brinkman .25 .11
☐ 50 Jim Britton .25 .11
☐ 51 Lou Brock 8.00 3.60
☐ 52 Gates Brown .25 .11
☐ 53 Larry Brown .25 .11
☐ 54 Ollie Brown .25 .11
☐ 55 George Brunet .25 .11
☐ 56 Don Buford .25 .11
☐ 57 Wally Bunker .25 .11
☐ 58 Jim Bunning 3.00 1.35
☐ 59 Bill Butler .25 .11
☐ 60 Johnny Callison .75 .35
☐ 61 Bert Campaneris .75 .35
☐ 62 Jose Cardenal .50 .23
☐ 63 Leo Cardenas .25 .11
☐ 64 Don Cardwell .25 .11
☐ 65 Rod Carew 8.00 3.60
☐ 66 Cisco Carlos .25 .11
☐ 67 Steve Carlton 10.00 4.50
☐ 68 Clay Carroll .25 .11
☐ 69 Paul Casanova .25 .11
☐ 70 Norm Cash 2.00 .90
☐ 71 Danny Cater .25 .11
☐ 72 Orlando Cepeda 2.50 1.10
☐ 73 Dean Chance .50 .23
☐ 74 Horace Clarke .25 .11
☐ 75 Roberto Clemente 30.00 13.50
☐ 76 Donn Clendenon .25 .11
☐ 77 Ty Cline .25 .11
☐ 78 Nate Colbert .25 .11
☐ 79 Joe Coleman .25 .11
☐ 80 Billy Conigliaro .25 .11
☐ 81 Casey Cox .25 .11
☐ 82 Mike Cuellar .75 .35
☐ 83 Ray Culp .25 .11
☐ 84 George Culver .25 .11
☐ 85 Jim Davenport .25 .11
☐ 86 Vic Davalillo .25 .11
☐ 87 Tommy Davis .75 .35
☐ 88 Willie Davis .50 .23
☐ 89 Larry Dierker 1.00 .45
☐ 90 Dick Dietz .25 .11
☐ 91 Chuck Dobson .25 .11
☐ 92 Pat Dobson .25 .11
☐ 93 John Donaldson .25 .11
☐ 94 Al Downing .25 .11
☐ 95 Moe Drabowsky .25 .11
☐ 96 John Edwards .25 .11
☐ 97 Thomas Egan .25 .11
☐ 98 Dick Ellsworth .25 .11
☐ 99 Mike Epstein .25 .11
☐ 100 Andy Etchebarren .25 .11
☐ 101 Ron Fairly .75 .35
☐ 102 Frank Fernandez .25 .11
☐ 103 Al Ferrara .25 .11
☐ 104 Mike Fiore .25 .11
☐ 105 Curt Flood 1.00 .45
☐ 106 Joe Foy .25 .11
☐ 107 Tito Francona .25 .11
☐ 108 Bill Freehan 1.00 .45
☐ 109 Jim Fregosi .75 .35
☐ 110 Woodie Fryman .25 .11
☐ 111 Vern Fuller .25 .11
☐ 112 Phil Gagliano .25 .11
☐ 113 Clarence Gaston .75 .35
☐ 114 Jake Gibbs .25 .11
☐ 115 Russ Gibson .25 .11
☐ 116 Dave Giusti .25 .11
☐ 117 Fred Gladding .25 .11
☐ 118 Tony Gonzalez .25 .11
☐ 119 Jim Gosger .25 .11
☐ 120 Jim Grant .25 .11
☐ 121 Dick Green .25 .11
☐ 122 Tom Griffin .25 .11
☐ 123 Jerry Grote .25 .11
☐ 124 Tom Hall .25 .11
☐ 125 Tom Haller .25 .11
☐ 126 Steve Hamilton .25 .11
☐ 127 Bill Hands .25 .11
☐ 128 Jim Hannan .25 .11
☐ 129 Ron Hansen .25 .11
☐ 130 Jim Hardin .25 .11
☐ 131 Steve Hargan .25 .11
☐ 132 Tommy Harper .50 .23
☐ 133 Bud Harrelson .50 .23
☐ 134 Ken Harrelson 1.00 .45
☐ 135 Jim Ray Hart .25 .11
☐ 136 Richie Hebner .50 .23
☐ 137 Mike Hedlund .25 .11
☐ 138 Tommy Helms .25 .11
☐ 139 Elrod Hendricks .25 .11
☐ 140 Ron Herbel .25 .11
☐ 141 Jackie Hernandez .25 .11
☐ 142 Mike Hershberger .25 .11
☐ 143 Jack Hiatt .25 .11
☐ 144 Dennis Higgins .25 .11
☐ 146 John Hiller .25 .11
☐ 147 Chuck Hinton .25 .11
☐ 148 Larry Hisle .50 .23
☐ 149 Ken Holtzman .50 .23
☐ 150 Joel Horlen .25 .11
☐ 151 Tony Horton .25 .11
☐ 152 Willie Horton .75 .35
☐ 153 Frank Howard 1.00 .45
☐ 154 Bob Humphreys .25 .11
☐ 155 Randy Hundley .50 .23
☐ 156 Ron Hunt .25 .11
☐ 157 Jim Hunter 5.00 2.20
☐ 158 Grant Jackson .25 .11
☐ 159 Reggie Jackson 15.00 6.75
☐ 160 Sonny Jackson .25 .11
☐ 161 Pat Jarvis .25 .11
☐ 162 Larry Jaster .25 .11
☐ 163 Julian Javier .25 .11
☐ 164 Ferguson Jenkins 5.00 2.20
☐ 165 Tommy John 2.00 .90
☐ 166 Alex Johnson .25 .11
☐ 167 Bob Johnson .25 .11
☐ 168 Dave Johnson 1.00 .45
☐ 169 Deron Johnson .25 .11
☐ 170 Jay Johnstone 1.00 .45
☐ 171 Cleon Jones .25 .11
☐ 172 Dalton Jones .25 .11
☐ 173 Mack Jones .25 .11
☐ 174 Rick Joseph .25 .11
☐ 175 Duane Josephson .25 .11
☐ 176 Jim Kaat 2.00 .90
☐ 177 Al Kaline 10.00 4.50
☐ 178 Dick Kelley .25 .11
☐ 179 Pat Kelly .25 .11
☐ 180 Jerry Kenney .25 .11
☐ 181 Don Kessinger .25 .11
☐ 182 Harmon Killebrew 6.00 2.70
☐ 183 Ed Kirkpatrick .25 .11
☐ 184 Bobby Knoop .25 .11
☐ 185 Cal Koonce .25 .11
☐ 186 Jerry Koosman 1.50 .70

☐ 187 Andy Kosco .25 .11
☐ 188 Ed Kranepool .50 .23
☐ 189 Ted Kubiak .25 .11
☐ 190 Jose Laboy .25 .11
☐ 191 Joe Lahoud .25 .11
☐ 192 Bill Landis .25 .11
☐ 193 Hal Lanier .25 .11
☐ 194 Fred Lasher .25 .11
☐ 195 John Lazar .25 .11
☐ 196 Jim LeFebvre .25 .11
☐ 197 Denny Lemaster .25 .11
☐ 198 Dave Leonhard .25 .11
☐ 199 Frank Linzy .25 .11
☐ 200 Mickey Lolich 1.00 .45
☐ 201 Jim Lonborg .75 .35
☐ 202 Sparky Lyle 1.00 .45
☐ 203 Jim Maloney .50 .23
☐ 204 Juan Marichal 5.00 2.20
☐ 205 David Marshall .25 .11
☐ 206 J.C. Martin .25 .11
☐ 207 Marty Martinez .25 .11
☐ 208 Tom Matchick .25 .11
☐ 209 Carlos May .25 .11
☐ 210 Jerry May .25 .11
☐ 211 Lee May .50 .23
☐ 212 Lee Maye .25 .11
☐ 213 Willie Mays 20.00 9.00
☐ 214 Dal Maxvill .25 .11
☐ 215 Bill Mazeroski 1.50 .70
☐ 216 Dick McAuliffe .25 .11
☐ 217 Al McBean .25 .11
☐ 218 Tim McCarver 1.50 .70
☐ 219 Bill McCool .25 .11
☐ 220 Mike McCormick .50 .23
☐ 221 Willie McCovey 8.00 3.60
☐ 222 Tom McCraw .25 .11
☐ 223 Lindy McDaniel .25 .11
☐ 224 Sam McDowell .75 .35
☐ 225 Leon McFadden .25 .11
☐ 226 Dan McGinn .25 .11
☐ 227 Jim McGlothlin .25 .11
☐ 228 Tug McGraw 1.50 .70
☐ 229 Denny McLain 1.50 .70
☐ 230 Ken McMullen .25 .11
☐ 231 Dave McNally 1.00 .45
☐ 232 Gerry McNertney .25 .11
☐ 233 Bill Melton .25 .11
☐ 234 Denis Menke .25 .11
☐ 235 Andy Messersmith .50 .23
☐ 236 Felix Millan .25 .11
☐ 237 Norm Miller .25 .11
☐ 238 Don Mincher .25 .11
☐ 239 Rick Monday .50 .23
☐ 240 Don Money .25 .11
☐ 241 Barry Moore .25 .11
☐ 242 Bob Moose .25 .11
☐ 243 Dave Morehead .25 .11
☐ 244 Joe Morgan 6.00 2.70
☐ 245 Manny Mota .50 .23
☐ 246 Curt Motton .25 .11
☐ 247 Bob Murcer 1.50 .70
☐ 248 Tom Murphy .25 .11
☐ 249 Ivan Murrell .25 .11
☐ 250 Jim Nash .25 .11
☐ 251 Joe Niekro 1.00 .45
☐ 252 Phil Niekro 5.00 2.20
☐ 253 Gary Nolan .25 .11
☐ 254 Jim Northrup .50 .23
☐ 255 Rich Nye .25 .11
☐ 256 Johnny Odom .25 .11
☐ 257 John O'Donoghue .25 .11
☐ 258 Tony Oliva 1.50 .70
☐ 259 Bob Oliver .25 .11
☐ 260 Claude Osteen .50 .23
☐ 261 Ray Oyler .25 .11
☐ 262 Jose Pagan .25 .11
☐ 263 Jim Palmer 5.00 2.20
☐ 264 Milt Pappas .50 .23
☐ 265 Wes Parker .25 .11
☐ 266 Freddie Patek .50 .23
☐ 267 Mike Paul .25 .11
☐ 268 Joe Pepitone .75 .35
☐ 269 Tony Perez 2.00 .90
☐ 270 Gaylord Perry 5.00 2.20
☐ 271 Jim Perry 1.00 .45
☐ 272 Gary Peters .25 .11
☐ 273 Rico Petrocelli .50 .23
☐ 274 Tom Phoebus .25 .11
☐ 275 Lou Piniella 1.50 .70
☐ 276 Vada Pinson 1.25 .55
☐ 277 Boog Powell 1.50 .70
☐ 278 Jimmie Price .25 .11
☐ 279 Frank Quilici .25 .11
☐ 280 Doug Rader .25 .11
☐ 281 Ron Reed .25 .11
☐ 282 Rich Reese .25 .11
☐ 283 Phil Regan .25 .11
☐ 284 Rick Reichardt .25 .11
☐ 285 Rick Renick .25 .11
☐ 286 Roger Repoz .25 .11
☐ 287 Merv Rettenmund .25 .11
☐ 288 Dave Ricketts .25 .11
☐ 289 Juan Rios .25 .11
☐ 290 Bill Robinson .25 .11
☐ 291 Brooks Robinson 10.00 4.50
☐ 292 Frank Robinson 10.00 4.50
☐ 293 Aurelio Rodriguez .25 .11
☐ 294 Ellie Rodriguez .25 .11
☐ 295 Cookie Rojas .25 .11
☐ 296 Rich Rollins .25 .11
☐ 297 Vincente Romo .25 .11
☐ 298 Phil Roof .25 .11
☐ 299 Pete Rose 20.00 9.00
☐ 300 John Roseboro .50 .23
☐ 301 Chico Ruiz .25 .11
☐ 302 Mike Ryan .25 .11
☐ 303 Ray Sadecki .25 .11
☐ 304 Chico Salmon .25 .11
☐ 305 Manny Sanguillen .75 .35
☐ 306 Ron Santo 1.50 .70
☐ 307 Tom Satriano .25 .11
☐ 308 Ted Savage .25 .11
☐ 309 Paul Schaal .25 .11
☐ 310 Dick Schofield .25 .11
☐ 311 George Scott .50 .23
☐ 312 Tom Seaver 15.00 6.75
☐ 313 Art Shamsky .25 .11
☐ 314 Mike Shannon .75 .35
☐ 315 Chris Short .25 .11
☐ 316 Duke Sims .25 .11
☐ 317 Bill Singer .25 .11
☐ 318 Reggie Smith 1.00 .45
☐ 319 Willie Smith .25 .11
☐ 320 Russ Snyder .25 .11
☐ 321 Al Spangler .25 .11
☐ 322 Jim Spencer .25 .11
☐ 323 Ed Spiezio .25 .11
☐ 324 Larry Stahl .25 .11
☐ 325 Lee Stange .25 .11
☐ 326 Mickey Stanley .25 .11
☐ 327 Willie Stargell 8.00 3.60
☐ 328 Rusty Staub 1.50 .70
☐ 329 Jim Stewart .25 .11
☐ 330 George Stone .25 .11
☐ 331 Bill Stoneman .25 .11
☐ 332 Mel Stottlemyre 1.00 .45
☐ 333 Ed Stroud .25 .11
☐ 334 Ken Suarez .25 .11
☐ 335 Gary Sutherland .25 .11
☐ 336 Don Sutton 4.00 1.80
☐ 337 Ron Swoboda .50 .23
☐ 338 Fred Talbot .25 .11
☐ 339 Jose Tartabull .25 .11
☐ 340 Ken Tatum .25 .11
☐ 341 Tony Taylor .50 .23
☐ 342 Luis Tiant 1.50 .70
☐ 343 Bob Tillman .25 .11
☐ 344 Bobby Tolan .25 .11
☐ 345 Jeff Torborg .25 .11
☐ 346 Joe Torre 1.50 .70
☐ 347 Cesar Tovar .25 .11
☐ 348 Tom Tresh 1.00 .45
☐ 349 Ted Uhlaender .25 .11
☐ 350 Del Unser .25 .11
☐ 351 Bob Veale .25 .11
☐ 352 Zoilo Versalles .50 .23
☐ 353 Luke Walker .25 .11
☐ 354 Pete Ward .25 .11
☐ 355 Eddie Watt .25 .11
☐ 356 Ramon Webster .25 .11
☐ 357 Al Weis .25 .11
☐ 358 Don Wert .25 .11
☐ 359 Bill White 1.00 .45
☐ 360 Roy White .50 .23
☐ 361 Hoyt Wilhelm 3.00 1.35
☐ 362 Billy Williams 6.00 2.70
☐ 363 Walt Williams .25 .11
☐ 364 Maury Wills 1.50 .70
☐ 365 Don Wilson .25 .11
☐ 366 Earl Wilson .25 .11
☐ 367 Bobby Wine .25 .11
☐ 368 Rick Wise .50 .23
☐ 369 Wilbur Wood .25 .11
☐ 370 Woody Woodward .25 .11
☐ 371 Clyde Wright .25 .11
☐ 372 Jim Wynn 1.00 .45

1984 Milton Bradley

The cards in this 30-card set measure the standard size. This set of full color cards was produced by Topps for the Milton Bradley Co. The set was included in a board game entitled Championship Baseball. The fronts feature

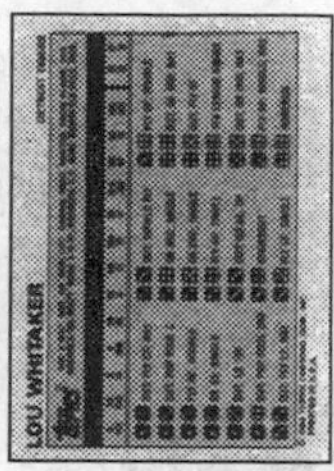

portraits of the players and the name, Championship Baseball, by Milton Bradley. The backs feature the Topps logo, statistics for the past year (pitchers' cards have career statistics), and dice rolls which are part of the board game. Pitcher cards have no dice roll charts. There are 15 players from each league. These unnumbered cards are listed below in alphabetical order. The cap logos and uniforms have been air-brushed to remove all team references.

	MINT	NRMT
COMPLETE SET (30)	12.50	5.50
COMMON CARD (1-30)	.10	.05

☐ 1 Wade Boggs 1.25 .55
☐ 2 George Brett 3.00 1.35
☐ 3 Rod Carew .75 .35
☐ 4 Steve Carlton .75 .35
☐ 5 Gary Carter .60 .25
☐ 6 Dave Concepcion .25 .11
☐ 7 Cecil Cooper .25 .11
☐ 8 Andre Dawson .75 .35
☐ 9 Carlton Fisk 1.00 .45
☐ 10 Steve Garvey .25 .11
☐ 11 Pedro Guerrero .10 .05
☐ 12 Ron Guidry .25 .11
☐ 13 Rickey Henderson 1.25 .55
☐ 14 Reggie Jackson 1.00 .45
☐ 15 Ron Kittle .10 .05
☐ 16 Bill Madlock .10 .05
☐ 17 Dale Murphy .75 .35
☐ 18 Al Oliver .10 .05
☐ 19 Darrell Porter .10 .05
☐ 20 Cal Ripken 6.00 2.70
☐ 21 Pete Rose 1.50 .70
☐ 22 Steve Sax .10 .05
☐ 23 Mike Schmidt 1.50 .70
☐ 24 Ted Simmons .25 .11
☐ 25 Ozzie Smith 2.00 .90
☐ 26 Dave Stieb .10 .05
☐ 27 Fernando Valenzuela .25 .11
☐ 28 Lou Whitaker .60 .25
☐ 29 Dave Winfield 1.00 .45
☐ 30 Robin Yount .75 .35

1987 M and M's Star Lineup

The Mars Candy Company is the sponsor of this 24-card set of cards. The cards were printed in perforated pairs. The pairs measure approximately 5" by 3 1/2" whereas the individual cards measure the standard 2 1/2" by 3 1/2". The players are shown without team logos. The cards were designed and produced by MSA, Mike Schechter Associates. The cards are numbered on the front and back. The backs show statistics for every year since 1980 even if the player was not even playing during those earlier years. The values below are for individual players; panels intact would be valued at 25 percent more than the sum of the two individual players.

	MINT	NRMT
COMPLETE PANEL SET	10.00	4.50
COMPLETE IND. SET (24)	6.00	2.70
COMMON CARD (1-24)	.10	.05

☐ 1 Wally Joyner .60 .25
☐ 2 Tony Pena .10 .05
☐ 3 Mike Schmidt .75 .35
☐ 4 Ryne Sandberg 1.25 .55

☐ 5 Wade Boggs .60 .25
☐ 6 Jack Morris .35 .16
☐ 7 Roger Clemens 1.00 .45
☐ 8 Harold Baines .10 .05
☐ 9 Dale Murphy .30 .14
☐ 10 Jose Canseco .75 .35
☐ 11 Don Mattingly 1.25 .55
☐ 12 Gary Carter .35 .16
☐ 13 Cal Ripken 2.50 1.10
☐ 14 George Brett 1.25 .55
☐ 15 Kirby Puckett 1.50 .70
☐ 16 Joe Carter .50 .23
☐ 17 Mike Witt .10 .05
☐ 18 Mike Scott .10 .05
☐ 19 Fernando Valenzuela .20 .09
☐ 20 Steve Garvey .35 .16
☐ 21 Steve Sax .10 .05
☐ 22 Nolan Ryan 2.50 1.10
☐ 23 Tony Gwynn 1.50 .70
☐ 24 Ozzie Smith 1.25 .55

1991 MooTown Snackers

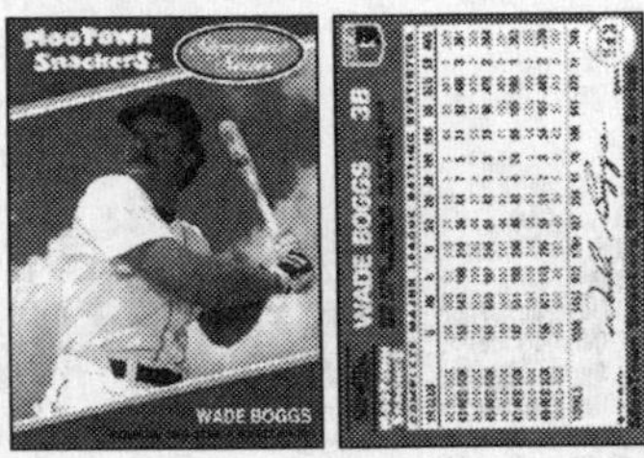

This 24-card standard-size set was sponsored by MooTown Snackers. One player card and an attached mail-in certificate (with checklist on back) were included in five-ounce packages of MooTown Snackers cheese snacks. The complete set could be purchased through the mail by sending in the mail-in certificate, three MooTown Snackers UPC codes, and 5.95. The mail-in sets did not come with the attached mail-in tab; cards with tabs are valued approximately twice the prices listed in the checklist below. The card front features a high gloss color action player photo, which is mounted diagonally on the card face. White and yellow stripes border the picture above and below. At the card top appears the company logo on a red triangle, while the words "Signature Series" appears in an aqua blue oval in the upper right corner. The player's name appears in the red triangle below the picture. The backs present statistical information in red, white, and black. On the bottom of the card a facsimile autograph and a card number round out the back.

	MINT	NRMT
COMPLETE SET (24)	25.00	11.00
COMMON CARD (1-24)	.25	.11

☐ 1 Jose Canseco 1.00 .45
☐ 2 Kirby Puckett 3.00 1.35
☐ 3 Barry Bonds 1.50 .70
☐ 4 Ken Griffey Jr. 6.00 2.70
☐ 5 Ryne Sandberg 2.50 1.10
☐ 6 Tony Gwynn 3.00 1.35
☐ 7 Kal Daniels .25 .11
☐ 8 Ozzie Smith 2.50 1.10
☐ 9 Dave Justice 1.00 .45
☐ 10 Sandy Alomar Jr. .50 .23
☐ 11 Wade Boggs .75 .35
☐ 12 Ozzie Guillen .25 .11
☐ 13 Dave Magadan .25 .11
☐ 14 Cal Ripken 5.00 2.20
☐ 15 Don Mattingly 3.00 1.35
☐ 16 Ruben Sierra .25 .11
☐ 17 Robin Yount .75 .35
☐ 18 Len Dykstra .50 .23
☐ 19 George Brett 3.00 1.35
☐ 20 Lance Parrish .25 .11
☐ 21 Chris Sabo .25 .11
☐ 22 Craig Biggio 1.00 .45
☐ 23 Kevin Mitchell .25 .11
☐ 24 Cecil Fielder .50 .23

1992 MooTown Snackers

This 24-card standard-size set was produced by MSA (Michael Schechter Associates) for MooTown Snackers. The cards were inserted inside 5 ounce and 10 ounce cheese snack packages. It is reported that more than two million cards were produced. Collectors could also obtain the complete set through a mail-in offer. The cards obtained via mail did not come with the mali-in offer tabs.

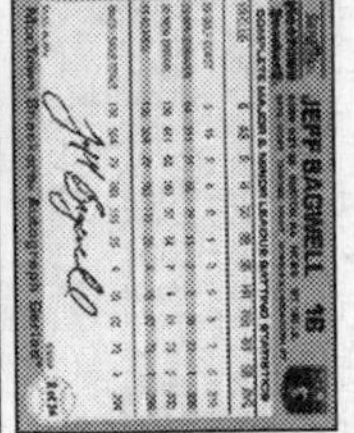

Cards with tabs have twice the value of the prices below. The color player photos on the fronts are bordered above and below by diagonal white and red stripes that edge a yellow border. Team logos were airbrushed out of the photos. In black print on a yellow and white background, the backs present biography, complete batting or pitching statistics, and facsimile autograph.

	MINT	NRMT
COMPLETE SET (24)	25.00	11.00
COMMON CARD (1-24)	.25	.11

☐ 1 Albert Belle 1.50 .70
☐ 2 Jeff Bagwell 2.50 1.10
☐ 3 Jose Rijo .25 .11
☐ 4 Roger Clemens 2.00 .90
☐ 5 Kevin Maas .25 .11
☐ 6 Kirby Puckett 2.50 1.10
☐ 7 Ken Griffey Jr. 5.00 2.20
☐ 8 Will Clark 1.00 .45
☐ 9 Felix Jose .25 .11
☐ 10 Cecil Fielder .50 .23
☐ 11 Darryl Strawberry .50 .23
☐ 12 John Smiley .25 .11
☐ 13 Roberto Alomar 1.00 .45
☐ 14 Paul Molitor 1.00 .45
☐ 15 Andre Dawson .75 .35
☐ 16 Terry Mulholland .25 .11
☐ 17 Fred McGriff .75 .35
☐ 18 Dwight Gooden .50 .23
☐ 19 Rickey Henderson 1.00 .45
☐ 20 Nolan Ryan 4.00 1.80
☐ 21 George Brett 2.50 1.10
☐ 22 Tom Glavine .75 .35
☐ 23 Cal Ripken 4.00 1.80
☐ 24 Frank Thomas 4.00 1.80

1992 Mr. Turkey Superstars

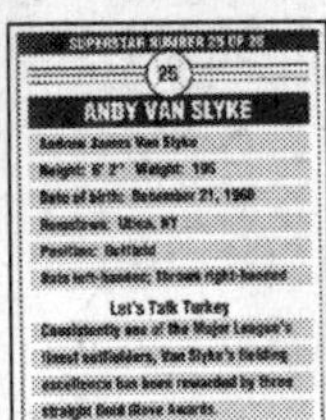

This 26-card set was sponsored by Mr. Turkey. One card was found on the back panel of Mr. Turkey products, such as Hardwood Smoked Turkey Pastrami. The standard-size player card is not perforated. On a pinstripe background whose color is team color-coded, the front design has a color action player photo cut out to fit a circular format. The extreme right portion of the circle extends off the right edge of the card. Team logos have been airbrushed out of the photos. The player's name and team name appear in a colored banner above the player photo. At the lower left corner appears the Mr. Turkey 1992 Superstar emblem, which is designed like a baseball diamond. The backs are printed in blue and carry biography and a "Let's Talk Turkey" trivia fact about the player. The cards are numbered on the back; the card numbering is actually alphabetical by player's name.

	MINT	NRMT
COMPLETE SET (26)	20.00	9.00
COMMON CARD (1-26)	.25	.11

☐ 1 Jim Abbott .25 .11
☐ 2 Roberto Alomar 1.00 .45
☐ 3 Sandy Alomar Jr. .50 .23
☐ 4 Craig Biggio .75 .35
☐ 5 George Brett 2.00 .90
☐ 6 Will Clark 1.00 .45
☐ 7 Roger Clemens 2.00 .90
☐ 8 Cecil Fielder .50 .23
☐ 9 Carlton Fisk .75 .35
☐ 10 Andres Galarraga 1.00 .45
☐ 11 Dwight Gooden .50 .23
☐ 12 Ken Griffey Jr. 5.00 2.20
☐ 13 Tony Gwynn 2.50 1.10
☐ 14 Rickey Henderson .75 .35
☐ 15 Dave Justice 1.00 .45
☐ 16 Don Mattingly 2.50 1.10
☐ 17 Dale Murphy .75 .35
☐ 18 Kirby Puckett 2.50 1.10
☐ 19 Cal Ripken 4.00 1.80
☐ 20 Nolan Ryan 4.00 1.80
☐ 21 Chris Sabo .25 .11
☐ 22 Ryne Sandberg 2.00 .90
☐ 23 Ozzie Smith 2.00 .90
☐ 24 Darryl Strawberry .50 .23
☐ 25 Andy Van Slyke .25 .11
☐ 26 Robin Yount .75 .35

1995 Mr. Turkey Baseball Greats

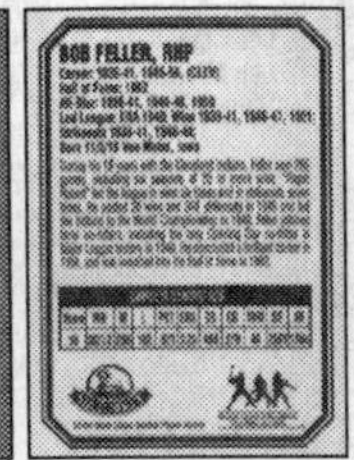

These five standard-size cards were sponsored by Mr. Turkey. On a brown background, the fronts feature sepia-toned and color action player photos. The player's name appears in a red banner on top, while the set's logo is printed in the lower right corner. All team logos have been airbrushed out of the photos. The backs carry player biography, profile and career statistics. The cards are unnumbered and checklisted below in alphabetical order.

	MINT	NRMT
COMPLETE SET (5)	8.00	3.60
COMMON CARD (1-5)	1.00	.45

☐ 1 Bob Feller 2.50 1.10
☐ 2 Al Kaline 2.50 1.10
☐ 3 Tug McGraw 1.00 .45
☐ 4 Boog Powell 1.50 .70
☐ 5 Warren Spahn 2.50 1.10

1969 Nabisco Team Flakes

The cards in this 24-card set measure either 1 15/16" by 3" or 1 3/4" by 2 15/16" depending on the amount of yellow border area provided between the "cut lines." The 1969 Nabisco Team Flakes set of full color, blank-backed and unnumbered cards was issued on the backs of Team Flakes cereal boxes. The cards are numbered in the checklist below in alphabetical order. There were three different panels or box backs containing eight cards each. The cards have yellow borders and are devoid of team insignias. The catalog designation is F275-34.

	NRMT	VG-E
COMPLETE SET (24)	600.00	275.00
COMMON CARD (1-24)	6.00	2.70

☐ 1 Hank Aaron 60.00 27.00
☐ 2 Richie Allen 15.00 6.75
☐ 3 Lou Brock 35.00 16.00
☐ 4 Paul Casanova 6.00 2.70
☐ 5 Roberto Clemente 100.00 45.00
☐ 6 Al Ferrara 6.00 2.70
☐ 7 Bill Freehan 10.00 4.50
☐ 8 Jim Fregosi 10.00 4.50
☐ 9 Bob Gibson 35.00 16.00

	MINT	NRMT
☐ 10 Tony Horton	6.00	2.70
☐ 11 Tommy John	15.00	6.75
☐ 12 Al Kaline	40.00	18.00
☐ 13 Jim Lonborg	6.00	2.70
☐ 14 Juan Marichal	35.00	16.00
☐ 15 Willie Mays	75.00	34.00
☐ 16 Rick Monday	6.00	2.70
☐ 17 Tony Oliva	15.00	6.75
☐ 18 Brooks Robinson	40.00	18.00
☐ 19 Frank Robinson	40.00	18.00
☐ 20 Pete Rose	60.00	27.00
☐ 21 Ron Santo	20.00	9.00
☐ 22 Tom Seaver	50.00	22.00
☐ 23 Rusty Staub	10.00	4.50
☐ 24 Mel Stottlemyre	6.00	2.70

1993 Nabisco All-Star Autographs

Available by sending two proofs of purchase from specially marked Nabisco packages and 5.00, each card features an autographed color action photo of a former star on its front and comes in a special card holder along with a certificate of authenticity. Each photo is trimmed with a blue line and bordered in white. The set logo appears in the upper left and a star rests in each remaining corner. The player's name appears in white within a blue and white trimmed red rectangle at the bottom. The back has a star in each corner and is trimmed by a fine blue line. The player's name and position appear in red at the top and is followed below by the player's biography, childhood photo, and stats. Don Drysdale tragically passed away between his signing the cards and the beginning of the promotion. Nabisco honored all requests until they ran out of cards on Drysdale. The Nabisco and MLBPA logos at the bottom round out the back. The cards are unnumbered and checklisted below in alphabetical order.

	MINT	NRMT
COMPLETE SET (6)	100.00	45.00
COMMON CARD (1-6)	10.00	4.50
☐ 1 Ernie Banks	15.00	6.75
☐ 2 Don Drysdale	75.00	34.00
☐ 3 Catfish Hunter	10.00	4.50
☐ 4 Phil Niekro	10.00	4.50
☐ 5 Brooks Robinson	15.00	6.75
☐ 6 Willie Stargell	10.00	4.50

1994 Nabisco All-Star Autographs

The Nabisco Biscuit Company and the Major League Baseball Players Alumni Assocation cosponsored the Nabisco All-Star Legends" program, which featured these four autographed baseball cards as well as All-Star appearances nationwide and free tickets to minor league baseball games. Measuring the standard size, one card could be obtained by mailing 5.00 and two proofs of purchase from Oreo, Oreo Double Stuff, Chips Ahoy, Ritz, Wheat Thins, Better Cheddars, Nabisco Grahams, and Honey Maid Grahams crackers. Each autographed card was accompanied by an MLBPAA certificate of authenticity. The fronts feature full-bleed color action photos that are accented by a thin gold picture frame. The player's autograph is inscribed in blue ink. The backs have a photo from the player's youth, career highlights, statistics, and an "All-Star Attitude" quote. The cards are unnumbered and checklisted below in alphabetical order.

	MINT	NRMT
COMPLETE SET (4)	60.00	27.00
COMMON CARD (1-4)	15.00	6.75
☐ 1 Bob Gibson AU	20.00	9.00
☐ 2 Jim Palmer AU	15.00	6.75
☐ 3 Frank Robinson AU	20.00	9.00
☐ 4 Duke Snider AU	20.00	9.00

1995 National Packtime

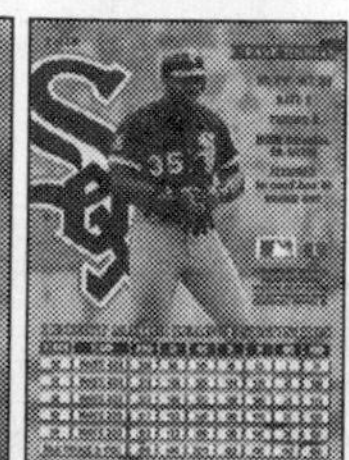

This 18-card standard-size set was sponsored by MLB, MLBPA, and the six leading card companies (Donruss, Fleer, Pacific, Pinnacle, Topps, and Upper Deck). Each of the six companies produced three cards for the set, which was available only through a mail-in offer for 28 wrappers from any of the six companies listed above plus $2.00 for shipping and handling. All orders had to be postmarked by June 30, 1995; any card sets not purchased by that date were destroyed. Except for the Topps card (which has a ragged white border), all the fronts display full-bleed color action photos. The backs carry a second color photo as well as biography and statistics. The cards are numbered on the back "X of 18." An unnumbered offer card, with a checklist on its back, was found in various 1995 baseball products.

	MINT	NRMT
COMPLETE SET (18)	8.00	3.60
COMMON CARD (1-18)	.25	.11
☐ 1 Frank Thomas	2.50	1.10
☐ 2 Matt Williams	.60	.25
☐ 3 Juan Gonzalez	1.25	.55
☐ 4 Bob Hamelin	.25	.11
☐ 5 Mike Piazza	1.50	.70
☐ 6 Ken Griffey Jr.	3.00	1.35
☐ 7 Barry Bonds	1.00	.45
☐ 8 Tim Salmon	.75	.35
☐ 9 Jose Canseco	.60	.25
☐ 10 Cal Ripken	2.50	1.10
☐ 11 Raul Mondesi	.75	.35
☐ 12 Alex Rodriguez	2.50	1.10
☐ 13 Will Clark	.60	.25
☐ 14 Fred McGriff	.60	.25
☐ 15 Tony Gwynn	1.50	.70
☐ 16 Kenny Lofton	.75	.35
☐ 17 Deion Sanders	.75	.35
☐ 18 Jeff Bagwell	1.50	.70

1995 National Packtime 2

This six-card set was sponsored by MLB, MLBPA and the six leading card companies (Donruss, Fleer, Pacific, Pinnacle, Topps, and Upper Deck) who each produced one card for the set. The fronts feature borderless color action player photos, while the backs carry player information. The cards are checklisted below in alphabetical order.

	MINT	NRMT
COMPLETE SET (6)	6.00	2.70
COMMON CARD (1-6)	.25	.11
☐ 1 Albert Belle	1.00	.45
☐ 2 Darren Daulton	.25	.11
☐ 3 Randy Johnson	.50	.23
☐ 4 Greg Maddux	1.50	.70
☐ 5 Don Mattingly	1.00	.45
☐ 6 Hideo Nomo	2.00	.90

1984 Nestle 792

The cards in this 792-card standard-size set are extremely similar to the 1984 Topps regular issue (except for the Nestle logo instead of Topps logo on the front). In conjunction with Topps, the Nestle Company issued this set as six sheets available as a premium. The set was (as detailed on the back of the checklist card for the Nestle Dream Team cards) originally available from the Nestle Company in full sheets of 132 cards, 24" by 48", for 4.95 plus five Nestle candy wrappers per sheet. The backs are virtually identical to the Topps cards of this year, i.e., same player-number correspondence. These sheets have been cut up into individual cards and are available from a few dealers around the country. This is one of the few instances in this hobby where the complete uncut sheet is worth considerably less than the sum of the individual cards due to the expense required in having the sheet cut professionally (and precisely) into individual cards. Supposedly less than 5000 sets were printed. Since the checklist is exactly the same as that of the 1984 Topps, these Nestle cards are generally priced as a multiple of the corresponding Topps card. Individual Nestle cards are priced at up to eight times the corresponding 1984 Topps price. Please see multiplication tables below. Beware also on this set to look for fakes and forgeries. Cards billed as Nestle proofs in black and white are fakes; there are even a few counterfeits in color.

	NRMT	VG-E
COMPLETE CUT SET (792)	425.00	190.00
COMMON CARD (1-792)	.25	.11
*STARS:6X to 12X BASIC CARDS		
*ROOKIES: 4X to 8X BASIC CARDS		

1984 Nestle Dream Team

The cards in this 22-card set measure the standard size. In conjunction with Topps, the Nestle Company issued this set entitled the Dream Team. The fronts have the Nestle trademark in the upper frameline, and the backs are identical to the Topps cards of this year except for the number and the Nestle's logo. Cards 1-11 feature stars of the American League while cards 12-22 show National League stars. Each league's "Dream Team" consists of eight position players and three pitchers. The cards were included with the Nestle chocolate bars as a pack of four (three player cards and a checklist header card. This set should not be confused with the Nestle 792-card (same player-number correspondence as 1984 Topps 792) set.

	NRMT	VG-E
COMPLETE SET (22)	25.00	11.00
COMMON CARD (1-22)	.25	.11

Card	MINT	NRMT
☐ 1 Eddie Murray	2.00	.90
☐ 2 Lou Whitaker	1.00	.45
☐ 3 George Brett	4.00	1.80
☐ 4 Cal Ripken	8.00	3.60
☐ 5 Jim Rice	.75	.35
☐ 6 Dave Winfield	1.25	.55
☐ 7 Lloyd Moseby	.25	.11
☐ 8 Lance Parrish	.75	.35
☐ 9 LaMarr Hoyt	.25	.11
☐ 10 Ron Guidry	.50	.23
☐ 11 Dan Quisenberry	.25	.11
☐ 12 Steve Garvey	1.00	.45
☐ 13 Johnny Ray	.25	.11
☐ 14 Mike Schmidt	3.00	1.35
☐ 15 Ozzie Smith	3.00	1.35
☐ 16 Andre Dawson	1.25	.55
☐ 17 Tim Raines	.75	.35
☐ 18 Dale Murphy	1.00	.45
☐ 19 Tony Pena	.25	.11
☐ 20 John Denny	.25	.11
☐ 21 Steve Carlton	1.25	.55
☐ 22 Al Holland	.25	.11
☐ NNO Checklist	.25	.11

1987 Nestle Dream Team

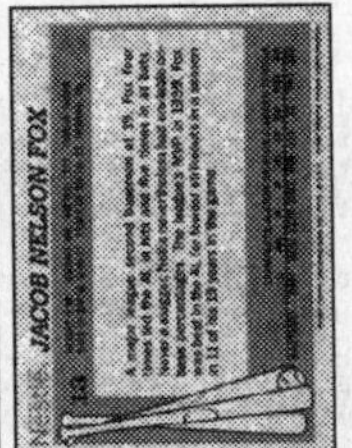

This 33-card standard-size set is, in a sense, three sets: Golden Era (1-11 gold), AL Modern Era (12-22 red), and NL Modern Era (23-33 blue). Cards have color coded borders by era. The first 11 card photos are in black and white. The Nestle set was apparently not licensed by Major League Baseball and hence the team logos are not shown in the photos. Six-packs of certain Nestle candy bars contained three cards; cards were also available through a send-in offer.

	MINT	NRMT
COMPLETE SET (33)	15.00	6.75
COMMON CARD (1-33)	.15	.07
☐ 1 Lou Gehrig	1.50	.70
☐ 2 Rogers Hornsby	.25	.11
☐ 3 Pie Traynor	.25	.11
☐ 4 Honus Wagner	1.00	.45
☐ 5 Babe Ruth	2.00	.90
☐ 6 Tris Speaker	.25	.11
☐ 7 Ty Cobb	2.00	.90
☐ 8 Mickey Cochrane	.25	.11
☐ 9 Walter Johnson	1.00	.45
☐ 10 Carl Hubbell	.25	.11
☐ 11 Jimmy Foxx	.60	.25
☐ 12 Rod Carew	.40	.18
☐ 13 Nellie Fox	.25	.11
☐ 14 Brooks Robinson	.40	.18
☐ 15 Luis Aparicio	.25	.11
☐ 16 Frank Robinson	.25	.11
☐ 17 Mickey Mantle	2.50	1.10
☐ 18 Ted Williams	2.00	.90
☐ 19 Yogi Berra	1.00	.45
☐ 20 Bob Feller	.40	.18
☐ 21 Whitey Ford	.40	.18
☐ 22 Harmon Killebrew	.25	.11
☐ 23 Stan Musial	1.50	.70
☐ 24 Jackie Robinson	2.00	.90
☐ 25 Eddie Mathews	.25	.11
☐ 26 Ernie Banks	.40	.18
☐ 27 Roberto Clemente	2.00	.90
☐ 28 Willie Mays	2.00	.90
☐ 29 Hank Aaron	2.00	.90
☐ 30 Johnny Bench	.40	.18
☐ 31 Bob Gibson	.40	.18
☐ 32 Warren Spahn	.25	.11
☐ 33 Duke Snider	1.00	.45
☐ NNO Checklist	.15	.07

1988 Nestle

This 44-card standard-size set has yellow borders. This set was produced for Nestle by Mike Schechter Associates and was printed in Canada. The Nestle set was apparently not licensed by Major League Baseball and hence the team logos are not shown in the photos. The backs are printed in red and blue on white card stock.

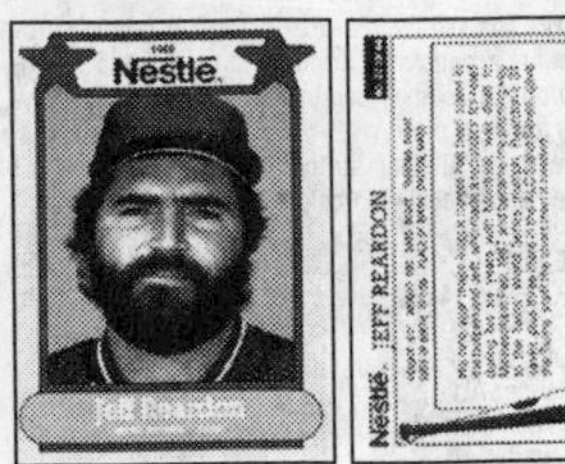

	MINT	NRMT
COMPLETE SET (44)	25.00	11.00
COMMON CARD (1-44)	.25	.11
☐ 1 Roger Clemens	2.50	1.10
☐ 2 Dale Murphy	1.00	.45
☐ 3 Eric Davis	.50	.23
☐ 4 Gary Gaetti	.50	.23
☐ 5 Ozzie Smith	2.50	1.10
☐ 6 Mike Schmidt	2.00	.90
☐ 7 Ozzie Guillen	.25	.11
☐ 8 John Franco	.50	.23
☐ 9 Andre Dawson	1.25	.55
☐ 10 Mark McGwire	5.00	2.20
☐ 11 Bret Saberhagen	.50	.23
☐ 12 Benito Santiago	.25	.11
☐ 13 Jose Uribe	.25	.11
☐ 14 Will Clark	1.25	.55
☐ 15 Don Mattingly	3.00	1.35
☐ 16 Juan Samuel	.25	.11
☐ 17 Jack Clark	.25	.11
☐ 18 Darryl Strawberry	.50	.23
☐ 19 Bill Doran	.25	.11
☐ 20 Pete Incaviglia	.25	.11
☐ 21 Dwight Gooden	.50	.23
☐ 22 Willie Randolph	.25	.11
☐ 23 Tim Wallach	.25	.11
☐ 24 Pedro Guerrero	.25	.11
☐ 25 Steve Bedrosian	.25	.11
☐ 26 Gary Carter	1.00	.45
☐ 27 Jeff Reardon	.25	.11
☐ 28 Dave Righetti	.25	.11
☐ 29 Frank White	.50	.23
☐ 30 Buddy Bell	.25	.11
☐ 31 Tim Raines	.75	.35
☐ 32 Wade Boggs	1.25	.55
☐ 33 Dave Winfield	1.25	.55
☐ 34 George Bell	.25	.11
☐ 35 Alan Trammell	.75	.35
☐ 36 Joe Carter	1.00	.45
☐ 37 Jose Canseco	1.00	.45
☐ 38 Carlton Fisk	1.25	.55
☐ 39 Kirby Puckett	3.00	1.35
☐ 40 Tony Gwynn	3.00	1.35
☐ 41 Matt Nokes	.25	.11
☐ 42 Keith Hernandez	.50	.23
☐ 43 Nolan Ryan	5.00	2.20
☐ 44 Wally Joyner	.75	.35

1997 New Pinnacle

The 1997 New Pinnacle set was issued in one series totalling 200 cards and distributed in 10-card packs with a suggested retail price of $2.99. The fronts feature borderless color action player photos with gold printing. The backs carry another smaller player photo and biographical and statistical information.

	MINT	NRMT
COMPLETE SET (200)	25.00	11.00
COMMON CARD (1-200)	.15	.07
☐ 1 Ken Griffey Jr.	3.00	1.35
☐ 2 Sammy Sosa	.60	.25
☐ 3 Greg Maddux	2.00	.90
☐ 4 Matt Williams	.40	.18
☐ 5 Jason Isringhausen	.15	.07
☐ 6 Gregg Jefferies	.30	.14
☐ 7 Chili Davis	.30	.14
☐ 8 Paul O'Neill	.30	.14
☐ 9 Larry Walker	.60	.25
☐ 10 Ellis Burks	.30	.14
☐ 11 Cliff Floyd	.15	.07
☐ 12 Albert Belle	.75	.35
☐ 13 Javier Lopez	.30	.14
☐ 14 David Cone	.30	.14
☐ 15 Jose Canseco	.40	.18
☐ 16 Todd Zeile	.15	.07
☐ 17 Bernard Gilkey	.15	.07
☐ 18 Andres Galarraga	.60	.25
☐ 19 Chris Snopek	.15	.07
☐ 20 Tim Salmon	.60	.25
☐ 21 Roger Clemens	1.25	.55
☐ 22 Reggie Sanders	.15	.07
☐ 23 John Jaha	.15	.07
☐ 24 Andy Pettitte	.60	.25
☐ 25 Kenny Lofton	.75	.35
☐ 26 Robb Nen	.15	.07
☐ 27 John Wetteland	.30	.14
☐ 28 Bobby Bonilla	.30	.14
☐ 29 Hideo Nomo	1.50	.70
☐ 30 Cecil Fielder	.30	.14
☐ 31 Garret Anderson	.30	.14
☐ 32 Pat Hentgen	.30	.14
☐ 33 Dave Justice	.60	.25
☐ 34 Billy Wagner	.30	.14
☐ 35 Al Leiter	.15	.07
☐ 36 Mark Wohlers	.30	.14
☐ 37 Rondell White	.30	.14
☐ 38 Charles Johnson	.15	.07
☐ 39 Mark Grace	.40	.18
☐ 40 Pedro Martinez	.60	.25
☐ 41 Tom Goodwin	.15	.07
☐ 42 Manny Ramirez	.60	.25
☐ 43 Greg Vaughn	.15	.07
☐ 44 Brian Jordan	.15	.07
☐ 45 Mike Piazza	2.00	.90
☐ 46 Roberto Hernandez	.15	.07
☐ 47 Wade Boggs	.60	.25
☐ 48 Scott Sanders	.15	.07
☐ 49 Alex Gonzalez	.15	.07
☐ 50 Kevin Brown	.30	.14
☐ 51 Bob Higginson	.30	.14
☐ 52 Ken Caminiti	.60	.25
☐ 53 Derek Jeter	2.00	.90
☐ 54 Carlos Baerga	.15	.07
☐ 55 Jay Buhner	.40	.18
☐ 56 Tim Naehring	.15	.07
☐ 57 Jeff Bagwell	1.25	.55
☐ 58 Steve Finley	.30	.14
☐ 59 Kevin Appier	.15	.07
☐ 60 Jay Bell	.15	.07
☐ 61 Ivan Rodriguez	.75	.35
☐ 62 Terrell Wade	.15	.07
☐ 63 Rusty Greer	.30	.14
☐ 64 Juan Guzman	.15	.07
☐ 65 Fred McGriff	.40	.18
☐ 66 Tino Martinez	.60	.25
☐ 67 Ray Lankford	.30	.14
☐ 68 Juan Gonzalez	1.50	.70
☐ 69 Ron Gant	.15	.07
☐ 70 Jack McDowell	.15	.07
☐ 71 Tony Gwynn	1.50	.70
☐ 72 Joe Carter	.30	.14
☐ 73 Wilson Alvarez	.30	.14
☐ 74 Jason Giambi	.30	.14
☐ 75 Brian Hunter	.30	.14
☐ 76 Michael Tucker	.30	.14
☐ 77 Andy Benes	.15	.07
☐ 78 Brady Anderson	.40	.18
☐ 79 Ramon Martinez	.30	.14
☐ 80 Troy Percival	.30	.14
☐ 81 Alex Rodriguez	2.50	1.10
☐ 82 Jim Thome	.60	.25
☐ 83 Denny Neagle	.30	.14
☐ 84 Rafael Palmeiro	.40	.18
☐ 85 Jose Valentin	.15	.07
☐ 86 Marc Newfield	.15	.07
☐ 87 Mariano Rivera	.30	.14
☐ 88 Alan Benes	.15	.07
☐ 89 Jimmy Key	.30	.14
☐ 90 Joe Randa	.15	.07
☐ 91 Cal Ripken	2.50	1.10
☐ 92 Craig Biggio	.40	.18
☐ 93 Dean Palmer	.15	.07
☐ 94 Gary Sheffield	.60	.25
☐ 95 Ismael Valdes	.30	.14
☐ 96 John Valentin	.15	.07
☐ 97 Johnny Damon	.15	.07
☐ 98 Mo Vaughn	.75	.35
☐ 99 Paul Sorrento	.15	.07
☐ 100 Randy Johnson	.60	.25
☐ 101 Raul Mondesi	.40	.18
☐ 102 Roberto Alomar	.60	.25
☐ 103 Royce Clayton	.15	.07

☐ 104 Mark Grudzielanek .15 .07
☐ 105 Wally Joyner .15 .07
☐ 106 Wil Cordero .15 .07
☐ 107 Will Clark .40 .18
☐ 108 Chuck Knoblauch .60 .25
☐ 109 Derek Bell .15 .07
☐ 110 Henry Rodriguez .15 .07
☐ 111 Edgar Renteria .30 .14
☐ 112 Travis Fryman .15 .07
☐ 113 Eric Young .15 .07
☐ 114 Sandy Alomar Jr. .30 .14
☐ 115 Darin Erstad 1.00 .45
☐ 116 Barry Larkin .30 .14
☐ 117 Barry Bonds .75 .35
☐ 118 Frank Thomas 2.50 1.10
☐ 119 Carlos Delgado .30 .14
☐ 120 Jason Kendall .30 .14
☐ 121 Todd Hollandsworth .15 .07
☐ 122 Jim Edmonds .60 .25
☐ 123 Chipper Jones 2.00 .90
☐ 124 Jeff Fassero .15 .07
☐ 125 Deion Sanders .60 .25
☐ 126 Matt Lawton .15 .07
☐ 127 Ryan Klesko .40 .18
☐ 128 Mike Mussina .60 .25
☐ 129 Paul Molitor .60 .25
☐ 130 Dante Bichette .30 .14
☐ 131 Bill Pulsipher .15 .07
☐ 132 Todd Hundley .30 .14
☐ 133 J.T. Snow .30 .14
☐ 134 Chuck Finley .15 .07
☐ 135 Shawn Green .30 .14
☐ 136 Charles Nagy .15 .07
☐ 137 Willie Greene .30 .14
☐ 138 Marty Cordova .15 .07
☐ 139 Eddie Murray .60 .25
☐ 140 Ryne Sandberg .75 .35
☐ 141 Alex Fernandez .15 .07
☐ 142 Mark McGwire 1.25 .55
☐ 143 Eric Davis .30 .14
☐ 144 Jermaine Dye .15 .07
☐ 145 Ruben Sierra .15 .07
☐ 146 Damon Buford .15 .07
☐ 147 John Smoltz .30 .14
☐ 148 Alex Ochoa .15 .07
☐ 149 Moises Alou .30 .14
☐ 150 Rico Brogna .15 .07
☐ 151 Terry Steinbach .15 .07
☐ 152 Jeff King .15 .07
☐ 153 Carlos Garcia .15 .07
☐ 154 Tom Glavine .30 .14
☐ 155 Edgar Martinez .40 .18
☐ 156 Kevin Elster .15 .07
☐ 157 Darryl Hamilton .15 .07
☐ 158 Jason Dickson .15 .07
☐ 159 Kevin Orie .15 .07
☐ 160 Bubba Trammell .60 .25
☐ 161 Jose Guillen .75 .35
☐ 162 Brant Brown .15 .07
☐ 163 Wendell Magee .15 .07
☐ 164 Scott Spiezio .15 .07
☐ 165 Todd Walker .15 .07
☐ 166 Rod Myers .15 .07
☐ 167 Damon Mashore .15 .07
☐ 168 Wilton Guerrero .15 .07
☐ 169 Vladimir Guerrero 1.25 .55
☐ 170 Nomar Garciaparra 2.00 .90
☐ 171 Shannon Stewart .30 .14
☐ 172 Scott Rolen 1.50 .70
☐ 173 Bob Abreu .60 .25
☐ 174 Danny Patterson .15 .07
☐ 175 Andruw Jones 1.50 .70
☐ 176 Brian Giles .15 .07
☐ 177 Dmitri Young .15 .07
☐ 178 Cal Ripken EMW 1.25 .55
☐ 179 Chuck Knoblauch EMW .60 .25
☐ 180 Alex Rodriguez EMW 1.25 .55
☐ 181 Andres Galarraga EMW .60 .25
☐ 182 Pedro Martinez EMW .60 .25
☐ 183 Brady Anderson EMW .40 .18
☐ 184 Barry Bonds EMW .60 .25
☐ 185 Ivan Rodriguez EMW .60 .25
☐ 186 Gary Sheffield EMW .60 .25
☐ 187 Denny Neagle EMW .15 .07
☐ 188 Mark McGwire AURA .60 .25
☐ 189 Ellis Burks AURA .15 .07
☐ 190 Alex Rodriguez AURA 1.25 .55
☐ 191 Mike Piazza AURA .60 .25
☐ 192 Barry Bonds AURA .60 .25
☐ 193 Albert Belle AURA .60 .25
☐ 194 Chipper Jones AURA .60 .25
☐ 195 Juan Gonzalez AURA .60 .25
☐ 196 Brady Anderson AURA .40 .18
☐ 197 Frank Thomas AURA 1.25 .55
☐ 198 Vladimir Guerrero CL .60 .25
☐ 199 Todd Walker CL .15 .07
☐ 200 Scott Rolen CL .60 .25

1997 New Pinnacle Artist's Proof

Randomly inserted in packs at a rate of one in 39, this 200-card set is a fractured parallel version of the regular set and features exclusive Dufex all-foil print technology in varying levels of scarcity utilizing finishes of Red, Blue and Green foil. The 125 Reds are scarce, 50 Blues are scarcer, and the 25 Greens represent the top stars with the scarcest printing. Each card is stamped with the "Artist's Proof" seal.

	MINT	NRMT
COMPLETE SET (200)	4300.00	1900.00
COMP.RED SET (125)	600.00	275.00
COMMON RED	5.00	2.20
COMP.BLUE SET (50)	1200.00	550.00
COMMON BLUE	20.00	9.00
COMP.GREEN SET (25)	2500.00	1100.00
COMMON GREEN	30.00	13.50

☐ 1 Ken Griffey Jr. G 250.00 110.00
☐ 2 Sammy Sosa B 40.00 18.00
☐ 3 Greg Maddux G 150.00 70.00
☐ 4 Matt Williams B 25.00 11.00
☐ 5 Jason Isringhausen R 5.00 2.20
☐ 6 Gregg Jefferies R 5.00 2.20
☐ 7 Chili Davis R 8.00 3.60
☐ 8 Paul O'Neill R 8.00 3.60
☐ 9 Larry Walker R 15.00 6.75
☐ 10 Ellis Burks B 20.00 9.00
☐ 11 Cliff Floyd R 5.00 2.20
☐ 12 Albert Belle G 60.00 27.00
☐ 13 Javier Lopez R 8.00 3.60
☐ 14 David Cone R 8.00 3.60
☐ 15 Jose Canseco B 25.00 11.00
☐ 16 Todd Zeile R 8.00 3.60
☐ 17 Bernard Gilkey B 20.00 9.00
☐ 18 Andres Galarraga B 40.00 18.00
☐ 19 Chris Snopek R 5.00 2.20
☐ 20 Tim Salmon B 40.00 18.00
☐ 21 Roger Clemens B 80.00 36.00
☐ 22 Reggie Sanders R 8.00 3.60
☐ 23 John Jaha R 8.00 3.60
☐ 24 Andy Pettitte B 40.00 18.00
☐ 25 Kenny Lofton G 60.00 27.00
☐ 26 Robb Nen R 8.00 3.60
☐ 27 John Wetteland B 20.00 9.00
☐ 28 Bobby Bonilla R 8.00 3.60
☐ 29 Hideo Nomo G 150.00 70.00
☐ 30 Cecil Fielder R 8.00 3.60
☐ 31 Garret Anderson R 8.00 3.60
☐ 32 Pat Hentgen R 8.00 3.60
☐ 33 Dave Justice R 15.00 6.75
☐ 34 Billy Wagner R 8.00 3.60
☐ 35 Al Leiter R 5.00 2.20
☐ 36 Mark Wohlers R 5.00 2.20
☐ 37 Rondell White R 8.00 3.60
☐ 38 Charles Johnson R 8.00 3.60
☐ 39 Mark Grace R 10.00 4.50
☐ 40 Pedro Martinez R 15.00 6.75
☐ 41 Tom Goodwin R 5.00 2.20
☐ 42 Manny Ramirez B 40.00 18.00
☐ 43 Greg Vaughn R 5.00 2.20
☐ 44 Brian Jordan B 20.00 9.00
☐ 45 Mike Piazza G 150.00 70.00
☐ 46 Roberto Hernandez R 5.00 2.20
☐ 47 Wade Boggs B 40.00 18.00
☐ 48 Scott Sanders R 5.00 2.20
☐ 49 Alex Gonzalez R 5.00 2.20
☐ 50 Kevin Brown R 8.00 3.60
☐ 51 Bob Higginson B 20.00 9.00
☐ 52 Ken Caminiti B 25.00 11.00
☐ 53 Derek Jeter G 120.00 55.00
☐ 54 Carlos Baerga R 8.00 3.60
☐ 55 Jay Buhner B 25.00 11.00
☐ 56 Tim Naehring R 5.00 2.20
☐ 57 Jeff Bagwell G 100.00 45.00
☐ 58 Steve Finley R 8.00 3.60
☐ 59 Kevin Appier R 8.00 3.60
☐ 60 Jay Bell R 8.00 3.60
☐ 61 Ivan Rodriguez B 50.00 22.00
☐ 62 Terrell Wade R 5.00 2.20
☐ 63 Rusty Greer R 8.00 3.60
☐ 64 Juan Guzman R 5.00 2.20
☐ 65 Fred McGriff R 10.00 4.50
☐ 66 Tino Martinez R 15.00 6.75
☐ 67 Ray Lankford R 8.00 3.60
☐ 68 Juan Gonzalez G 120.00 55.00
☐ 69 Ron Gant R 8.00 3.60
☐ 70 Jack McDowell R 5.00 2.20
☐ 71 Tony Gwynn B 100.00 45.00
☐ 72 Joe Carter B 20.00 9.00
☐ 73 Wilson Alvarez R 5.00 2.20
☐ 74 Jason Giambi R 8.00 3.60
☐ 75 Brian Hunter R 8.00 3.60
☐ 76 Michael Tucker R 8.00 3.60
☐ 77 Andy Benes R 8.00 3.60
☐ 78 Brady Anderson B 25.00 11.00
☐ 79 Ramon Martinez R 8.00 3.60
☐ 80 Troy Percival B 20.00 9.00
☐ 81 Alex Rodriguez G 150.00 70.00
☐ 82 Jim Thome B 40.00 18.00
☐ 83 Denny Neagle R 8.00 3.60
☐ 84 Rafael Palmeiro B 25.00 11.00
☐ 85 Jose Valentin R 5.00 2.20
☐ 86 Marc Newfield R 5.00 2.20
☐ 87 Mariano Rivera B 20.00 9.00
☐ 88 Alan Benes R 8.00 3.60
☐ 89 Jimmy Key R 8.00 3.60
☐ 90 Joe Randa R 5.00 2.20
☐ 91 Cal Ripken G 200.00 90.00
☐ 92 Craig Biggio R 10.00 4.50
☐ 93 Dean Palmer R 8.00 3.60
☐ 94 Gary Sheffield B 40.00 18.00
☐ 95 Ismael Valdes R 8.00 3.60
☐ 96 John Valentin R 8.00 3.60
☐ 97 Johnny Damon R 8.00 3.60
☐ 98 Mo Vaughn G 60.00 27.00
☐ 99 Paul Sorrento R 5.00 2.20
☐ 100 Randy Johnson B 40.00 18.00
☐ 101 Raul Mondesi B 25.00 11.00
☐ 102 Roberto Alomar B 40.00 18.00
☐ 103 Royce Clayton R 5.00 2.20
☐ 104 Mark Grudzielanek R 8.00 3.60
☐ 105 Wally Joyner R 8.00 3.60
☐ 106 Wil Cordero R 5.00 2.20
☐ 107 Will Clark B 25.00 11.00
☐ 108 Chuck Knoblauch B 40.00 18.00
☐ 109 Derek Bell R 8.00 3.60
☐ 110 Henry Rodriguez R 8.00 3.60
☐ 111 Edgar Renteria R 8.00 3.60
☐ 112 Travis Fryman R 8.00 3.60
☐ 113 Eric Young R 8.00 3.60
☐ 114 Sandy Alomar Jr. R 8.00 3.60
☐ 115 Darin Erstad B 50.00 22.00
☐ 116 Barry Larkin B 25.00 11.00
☐ 117 Barry Bonds B 50.00 22.00
☐ 118 Frank Thomas G 200.00 90.00
☐ 119 Carlos Delgado R 8.00 3.60
☐ 120 Jason Kendall R 8.00 3.60
☐ 121 Todd Hollandsworth R 5.00 2.20
☐ 122 Jim Edmonds R 10.00 4.50
☐ 123 Chipper Jones G 120.00 55.00
☐ 124 Jeff Fassero R 5.00 2.20
☐ 125 Deion Sanders B 20.00 9.00
☐ 126 Matt Lawton R 5.00 2.20
☐ 127 Ryan Klesko R 10.00 4.50
☐ 128 Mike Mussina R 15.00 6.75
☐ 129 Paul Molitor B 40.00 18.00
☐ 130 Dante Bichette R 8.00 3.60
☐ 131 Bill Pulsipher R 5.00 2.20
☐ 132 Todd Hundley B 20.00 9.00
☐ 133 J.T. Snow R 8.00 3.60
☐ 134 Chuck Finley R 5.00 2.20
☐ 135 Shawn Green R 8.00 3.60
☐ 136 Charles Nagy R 8.00 3.60
☐ 137 Willie Greene R 8.00 3.60
☐ 138 Marty Cordova R 8.00 3.60
☐ 139 Eddie Murray R 15.00 6.75
☐ 140 Ryne Sandberg R 20.00 9.00
☐ 141 Alex Fernandez R 8.00 3.60
☐ 142 Mark McGwire G 100.00 45.00
☐ 143 Eric Davis R 8.00 3.60
☐ 144 Jermaine Dye R 8.00 3.60
☐ 145 Ruben Sierra R 5.00 2.20
☐ 146 Damon Buford R 5.00 2.20
☐ 147 John Smoltz B 20.00 9.00
☐ 148 Alex Ochoa R 5.00 2.20
☐ 149 Moises Alou R 8.00 3.60
☐ 150 Rico Brogna R 5.00 2.20
☐ 151 Terry Steinbach R 8.00 3.60
☐ 152 Jeff King R 8.00 3.60
☐ 153 Carlos Garcia R 5.00 2.20
☐ 154 Tom Glavine R 8.00 3.60
☐ 155 Edgar Martinez B 25.00 11.00
☐ 156 Kevin Elster R 5.00 2.20
☐ 157 Darryl Hamilton R 5.00 2.20
☐ 158 Jason Dickson R 8.00 3.60
☐ 159 Kevin Orie R 8.00 3.60
☐ 160 Bubba Trammell R 15.00 6.75
☐ 161 Jose Guillen B 40.00 18.00
☐ 162 Brant Brown R 5.00 2.20
☐ 163 Wendell Magee R 5.00 2.20
☐ 164 Scott Spiezio R 8.00 3.60
☐ 165 Todd Walker B 20.00 9.00
☐ 166 Rod Myers R 8.00 3.60
☐ 167 Damon Mashore R 5.00 2.20
☐ 168 Wilton Guerrero B 20.00 9.00
☐ 169 Vladimir Guerrero G 80.00 36.00
☐ 170 Nomar Garciaparra B 100.00 45.00
☐ 171 Shannon Stewart R 8.00 3.60
☐ 172 Scott Rolen R 30.00 13.50
☐ 173 Bob Abreu R 8.00 3.60

☐ 174 Danny Patterson R	5.00	2.20
☐ 175 Andruw Jones G	100.00	45.00
☐ 176 Brian Giles R	5.00	2.20
☐ 177 Dmitri Young R	8.00	3.60
☐ 178 Cal Ripken EMW G	100.00	45.00
☐ 179 Chuck Knoblauch EMW B	40.00	18.00
☐ 180 Alex Rodriguez EMW G	80.00	36.00
☐ 181 Andres Galarraga EMW R	15.00	6.75
☐ 182 Pedro Martinez EMW R	15.00	6.75
☐ 183 Brady Anderson EMW R	10.00	4.50
☐ 184 Barry Bonds EMW B	40.00	18.00
☐ 185 Ivan Rodriguez EMW B	40.00	18.00
☐ 186 Gary Sheffield EMW B	40.00	18.00
☐ 187 Denny Neagle EMW B	20.00	9.00
☐ 188 Mark McGwire AURA B	40.00	18.00
☐ 189 Ellis Burks AURA R	8.00	3.60
☐ 190 Alex Rodriguez AURA G	80.00	36.00
☐ 191 Mike Piazza AURA G	80.00	36.00
☐ 192 Barry Bonds AURA B	40.00	18.00
☐ 193 Albert Belle AURA G	30.00	13.50
☐ 194 Chipper Jones AURA G	80.00	36.00
☐ 195 Juan Gonzalez AURA G	60.00	27.00
☐ 196 Brady Anderson AURA B	25.00	11.00
☐ 197 Frank Thomas AURA G	100.00	45.00
☐ 198 Vladimir Guerrero CL R	15.00	6.75
☐ 199 Todd Walker CL R	8.00	3.60
☐ 200 Scott Rolen CL R	15.00	6.75

1997 New Pinnacle Museum Collection

Randomly inserted in packs at a rate of one in nine, this 200-card set is a dufex parallel version of the regular set printed on full gold foil.

	MINT	NRMT
COMPLETE SET (200)	600.00	275.00
COMMON CARD (1-200)	1.50	.70

*STARS: 7.5X TO 15X BASIC CARDS.
*YOUNG STARS: 6X TO 12X BASIC CARDS

1997 New Pinnacle Press Plates

Randomly inserted in packs at the rate of one in 1,250, this all-aluminum set consists of the Authentic Press Plate that transfers the ink to the cardboard for each individual card back and front. Each plate displays an authentication seal on the back along with the personal signature of Pinnacle Chairman and CEO, Jerry Meyer. Each card has eight press plates for each of the four colors used in printing the front and the back. A collector who put together any combination of the four press plates from the same card front or back could return the plates to Pinnacle by August 22, 1997 for a bounty of $35,000. A sliding reward scale was imposed with a $30,000 bounty for plates received by August 29, 1997, $25,000 for those received by September 5, 1997, and $20,000 for those received after September 5 but before December 31, 1997. Since supply is so limited, only common card pricing is provided. However, please refer to future issues of BBCM (Beckett Baseball Card Monthly) for updates on key cards

	MINT	NRMT
COMMON FRONT	100.00	45.00
COMMON BACK	60.00	27.00

1997 New Pinnacle Interleague Encounter

Randomly inserted in packs at a rate of one in 240, this 10-card set features a double-front card design printed on mirror blue mylar foil with red foil treatments. A top AL star player is carried on one side with a top NL mega-star on the filpside and the date of the first match-up of the two teams.

	MINT	NRMT
COMPLETE SET (10)	600.00	275.00
COMMON CARD (1-10)	30.00	13.50
☐ 1 Albert Belle Brian Jordan	30.00	13.50
☐ 2 Andruw Jones Brady Anderson	50.00	22.00
☐ 3 Ken Griffey Jr. Tony Gwynn	120.00	55.00
☐ 4 Cal Ripken Chipper Jones	100.00	45.00
☐ 5 Mike Piazza Ivan Rodriguez	80.00	36.00
☐ 6 Derek Jeter Vladimir Guerrero	80.00	36.00
☐ 7 Greg Maddux Mo Vaughn	80.00	36.00
☐ 8 Alex Rodriguez Hideo Nomo	100.00	45.00
☐ 9 Juan Gonzalez Barry Bonds	60.00	27.00
☐ 10 Frank Thomas Jeff Bagwell	100.00	45.00

1997 New Pinnacle Keeping the Pace

Randomly inserted in packs at a rate of one in 89, this 18-card set features dot matrix holograms of the 18 hitters most likely to keep a 61-home run pace.

	MINT	NRMT
COMPLETE SET (18)	600.00	275.00
COMMON CARD (1-18)	6.00	2.70
☐ 1 Juan Gonzalez	40.00	18.00
☐ 2 Greg Maddux	50.00	22.00
☐ 3 Ivan Rodriguez	20.00	9.00
☐ 4 Ken Griffey Jr.	80.00	36.00
☐ 5 Alex Rodriguez	50.00	22.00
☐ 6 Barry Bonds	20.00	9.00
☐ 7 Frank Thomas	60.00	27.00
☐ 8 Chuck Knoblauch	15.00	6.75
☐ 9 Derek Jeter	40.00	18.00
☐ 10 Roger Clemens	30.00	13.50
☐ 11 Kenny Lofton	20.00	9.00
☐ 12 Tony Gwynn	40.00	18.00
☐ 13 Troy Percival	6.00	2.70
☐ 14 Cal Ripken	60.00	27.00
☐ 15 Andy Pettitte	20.00	9.00
☐ 16 Hideo Nomo	40.00	18.00
☐ 17 Randy Johnson	20.00	9.00
☐ 18 Mike Piazza	50.00	22.00

1997 New Pinnacle Spellbound

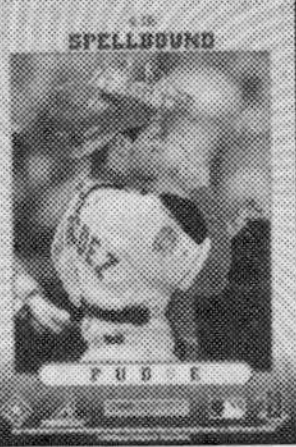

Randomly inserted in both hobby and retail packs at a rate of one in 19, this 50-card set features color action player photos superimposed over one of the letters of the player's name and printed on a full-foil, micro-etched card. The completed set for each star player spells both the player's name and the word "Spellbound."

	MINT	NRMT
COMMON A.BELLE CARD	6.00	2.70
COMMON A.JONES CARD	12.00	5.50
COMMON A.RODRIGUEZ CARD	20.00	9.00
COMMON C.JONES CARD	15.00	6.75
COMMON C.RIPKEN CARD	20.00	9.00
COMMON F.THOMAS CARD	20.00	9.00
COMMON I.RODRIGUEZ CARD	6.00	2.70
COMMON K.GRIFFEY JR. CARD	25.00	11.00
COMMON M.PIAZZA CARD	15.00	6.75

1989 Nissen

The 1989 J.J. Nissen set contains 20 standard-size cards. The fronts have airbrushed facial photos with white and yellow borders and orange trim. The backs are white and feature career stats. The complete set price below does not include the error version of Mark Grace.

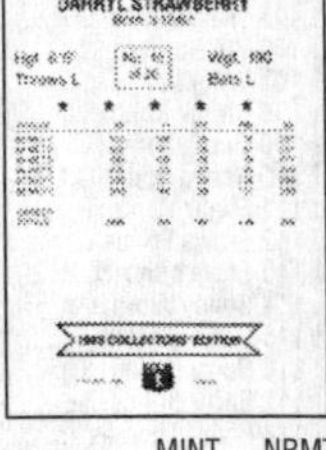

	MINT	NRMT
COMPLETE SET (20)	6.00	2.70
COMMON CARD (1-20)	.10	.05
☐ 1 Wally Joyner	.25	.11
☐ 2 Wade Boggs	.75	.35
☐ 3 Ellis Burks	.60	.25
☐ 4 Don Mattingly	1.50	.70
☐ 5 Jose Canseco	.40	.18
☐ 6 Mike Greenwell	.10	.05
☐ 7 Eric Davis	.25	.11
☐ 8 Kirby Puckett	2.00	.90
☐ 9 Kevin Seitzer	.10	.05
☐ 10 Darryl Strawberry	.25	.11
☐ 11 Gregg Jefferies	.40	.18
☐ 12A Mark Grace ERR (Photo actually Vance Law)	5.00	2.20
☐ 12B Mark Grace COR	1.00	.45
☐ 13 Matt Nokes	.10	.05
☐ 14 Mark McGwire	2.50	1.10
☐ 15 Bobby Bonilla	.40	.18
☐ 16 Roger Clemens	2.50	1.10
☐ 17 Frank Viola	.10	.05
☐ 18 Orel Hershiser	.25	.11
☐ 19 David Cone	.40	.18
☐ 20 Ted Williams	2.50	1.10

1960 Nu-Card Hi-Lites

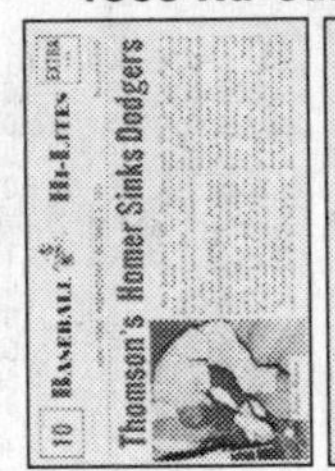

The cards in this 72-card set measure approximately 3 1/4" by 5 3/8". In 1960, the Nu-Card Company introduced its Baseball Hi-Lites set of newspaper style cards. Each card singled out an individual baseball achievement with a picture and story. The reverses contain a baseball quiz. Cards 1-18 are more valuable if found printed totally in black on the front; these are copy-righted CVC as opposed to the NCI designation found on the red and black printed fronts.

	NRMT	VG-E
COMPLETE SET (72)	450.00	200.00
COMMON CARD (1-72)	3.00	1.35
☐ 1 Babe Ruth Hits 3 Homers In A Series Game	40.00	18.00
☐ 2 Johnny Podres Pitching Wins Series	3.00	1.35
☐ 3 Bill Bevans Pitches No-Hitter, Almost	3.00	1.35
☐ 4 Box Score Devised By Reporter	3.00	1.35
☐ 5 Johnny VanderMeer Pitches Two No Hitters	3.00	1.35
☐ 6 Indians Take Bums	3.00	1.35
☐ 7 Joe DiMaggio Comes Thru	40.00	18.00
☐ 8 Christy Mathewson Pitches Three WS Shutouts	8.00	3.60
☐ 9 Harvey Haddix Pitches 12 Perfect Innings	3.00	1.35
☐ 10 Bobby Thomson Homer Sinks Dodgers	12.00	5.50
☐ 11 Carl Hubbell Strikes Out 5 A.L. Stars	8.00	3.60
☐ 12 Pickoff Ends Series	3.00	1.35
☐ 13 Cards Take Series From Yanks	3.00	1.35

☐ 14 Dizzy Dean	8.00	3.60
Daffy Dean		
Win Series		
☐ 15 Mickey Owen	3.00	1.35
Drops Third Strike		
☐ 16 Babe Ruth	40.00	18.00
Calls Shot		
☐ 17 Fred Merkle	5.00	2.20
Pulls Boner		
☐ 18 Don Larsen	8.00	3.60
Hurls Perfect W.S. Game		
☐ 19 Mickey Cochrane	5.00	2.20
Bean Ball Ends Career		
☐ 20 Ernie Banks	15.00	6.75
Belts 47 Homers		
Earns MVP		
☐ 21 Stan Musial	20.00	9.00
Hits 5 Homers in One Day		
☐ 22 Mickey Mantle	50.00	22.00
Hits Longest Homer		
☐ 23 Roy Sievers	3.00	1.35
Captures Home Run Title		
☐ 24 Lou Gehrig	50.00	22.00
2130 Consecutive Game		
Record Ends		
☐ 25 Red Schoendienst	5.00	2.20
Key Player		
Braves Pennant		
☐ 26 Eddie Gaedel	5.00	2.20
Midget Pinch-Hits		
For St. Louis		
☐ 27 Willie Mays	25.00	11.00
Makes Greatest Catch		
☐ 28 Yogi Berra	15.00	6.75
Homer Puts Yanks In 1st		
☐ 29 Roy Campanella	15.00	6.75
NL MVP		
☐ 30 Bob Turley	3.00	1.35
Hurls Yankees To		
WS Champions		
☐ 31 Dodgers Take Series	3.00	1.35
From Sox in Six		
☐ 32 Carl Furillo	3.00	1.35
Hero as Dodgers		
Beat Chicago		
in 3rd WS Game		
☐ 33 Joe Adcock	3.00	1.35
Gets 4 Homers		
And A Double		
☐ 34 Bill Dickey	5.00	2.20
Chosen All-Star Catcher		
☐ 35 Lew Burdette	3.00	1.35
Beats Yanks In		
Three World Series Games		
☐ 36 Umpires Clear	3.00	1.35
White Sox Bench		
☐ 37 Pee Wee Reese	12.00	5.50
Honored As Greatest Dodger SS		
☐ 38 Joe DiMaggio	40.00	18.00
Hits In 56 Straight		
☐ 39 Ted Williams	35.00	16.00
Hits .406 For Season		
☐ 40 Walter Johnson	10.00	4.50
Pitches 56 Straight		
☐ 41 Gil Hodges	5.00	2.20
Hits 4 Home Runs		
In Nite Game		
☐ 42 Hank Greenberg	8.00	3.60
Returns to Tigers From Army		
☐ 43 Ty Cobb	25.00	11.00
Named Best Player Of All Time		
☐ 44 Robin Roberts	5.00	2.20
Wins 28 Games		
☐ 45 Phil Rizzuto	10.00	4.50
Two Runs Save 1st Place		
☐ 46 Tigers Beat Out	3.00	1.35
Senators For Pennant		
☐ 47 Babe Ruth	40.00	18.00
Hits 60th Home Run		
☐ 48 Cy Young	5.00	2.20
Honored		
☐ 49 Harmon Killebrew	12.00	5.50
Starts Spring Training		
☐ 50 Mickey Mantle	50.00	22.00
Hits Longest Homer		
at Stadium		
☐ 51 Braves Take Pennant	3.00	1.35
☐ 52 Ted Williams	35.00	16.00
Hero Of All-Star Game		
☐ 53 Jackie Robinson	35.00	16.00
Saves Dodgers For		
Play-off Series		
☐ 54 Fred Snodgrass	3.00	1.35
Muffs Fly		
☐ 55 Duke Snider	15.00	6.75
Belts 2 Homers, Ties Record		
☐ 56 Giants Win 26 Straight	3.00	1.35
☐ 57 Ted Kluszewski	5.00	2.20
Stars In 1st Series Win		
☐ 58 Mel Ott	5.00	2.20
Walks 5 Times In Single Game		
☐ 59 Harvey Kuenn	3.00	1.35
Takes A.L. Batting Title		
☐ 60 Bob Feller	10.00	4.50
Hurls 3rd No-Hitter of Career		
☐ 61 Yankees Champs Again	3.00	1.35
☐ 62 Hank Aaron	20.00	9.00
Bat Beats Yankees		
In Series		
☐ 63 Warren Spahn	10.00	4.50
Beats Yanks in W.S.		
☐ 64 Ump's Wrong Call Helps	3.00	1.35
Dodgers Beat Yanks		
☐ 65 Al Kaline	12.00	5.50
Hits 3 Homers		
Two In Same Inning		
☐ 66 Bob Allison	3.00	1.35
Named AL ROY		
☐ 67 Willie McCovey	10.00	4.50
Blasts Way Into Giant Lineup		
☐ 68 Rocky Colavito	15.00	6.75
Hits 4 Homers in One Game		
☐ 69 Carl Erskine	3.00	1.35
Sets Strike Out Record		
in World Series		
☐ 70 Sal Maglie	3.00	1.35
Pitches No-Hit Game		
☐ 71 Early Wynn	5.00	2.20
Victory Crushes Yanks		
☐ 72 Nellie Fox	15.00	6.75
AL MVP		

1961 Nu-Card Scoops

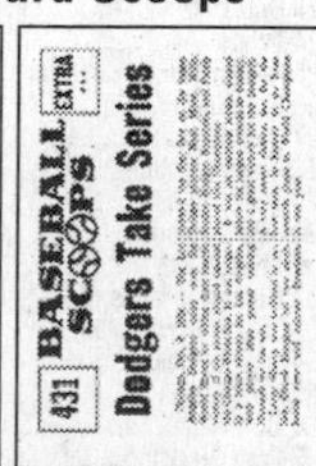

The cards in this 80-card set measure 2 1/2" by 3 1/2". This series depicts great moments in the history of individual ballplayers. Each card is designed as a miniature newspaper front-page, complete with data and picture. Both the number (401-480) and title are printed in red on the obverse, and the story is found on the back. An album was issued to hold the set. The set has been illegally reprinted, which has served to suppress the demand for the originals as well as the reprints.

	NRMT	VG-E
COMPLETE SET (80)	250.00	110.00
COMMON CARD (401-480)	.75	.35
☐ 401 Jim Gentile	1.00	.45
☐ 402 Warren Spahn	3.00	1.35
(No-hitter)		
☐ 403 Bill Mazeroski	1.50	.70
☐ 404 Willie Mays:	12.50	5.50
(Three triples)		
☐ 405 Woodie Held	.75	.35
☐ 406 Vern Law	1.00	.45
☐ 407 Pete Runnels	.75	.35
☐ 408 Lew Burdette	1.00	.45
(No-hitter)		
☐ 409 Dick Stuart	.75	.35
☐ 410 Don Cardwell	.75	.35
☐ 411 Camilo Pascual	.75	.35
☐ 412 Eddie Mathews	3.00	1.35
☐ 413 Dick Groat	1.00	.45
☐ 414 Gene Autry OWN	5.00	2.20
☐ 415 Bobby Richardson	2.00	.90
☐ 416 Roger Maris	7.50	3.40
☐ 417 Fred Merkle	.75	.35
☐ 418 Don Larsen	1.00	.45
☐ 419 Mickey Cochrane	1.50	.70
☐ 420 Ernie Banks	4.00	1.80
☐ 421 Stan Musial	10.00	4.50
☐ 422 Mickey Mantle	30.00	13.50
(Longest homer)		
☐ 423 Roy Sievers	.75	.35
☐ 424 Lou Gehrig	15.00	6.75
☐ 425 Red Schoendienst	2.00	.90
☐ 426 Eddie Gaedel	3.00	1.35
☐ 427 Willie Mays	15.00	6.75
(Greatest catch)		
☐ 428 Jackie Robinson	15.00	6.75
☐ 429 Roy Campanella	7.50	3.40
☐ 430 Bob Turley	.75	.35
☐ 431 Larry Sherry	.75	.35
☐ 432 Carl Furillo	1.00	.45
☐ 433 Joe Adcock	.75	.35
☐ 434 Bill Dickey	1.50	.70
☐ 435 Lew Burdette 3 wins	.75	.35
☐ 436 Umpire Clears Bench	.75	.35
☐ 437 Pee Wee Reese	3.00	1.35
☐ 438 Joe DiMaggio	15.00	6.75
(56 Game Hit Streak)		
☐ 439 Ted Williams	15.00	6.75
(Hits .406)		
☐ 440 Walter Johnson	3.00	1.35
☐ 441 Gil Hodges	2.00	.90
☐ 442 Hank Greenberg	3.00	1.35
☐ 443 Ty Cobb	12.50	5.50
☐ 444 Robin Roberts	3.00	1.35
☐ 445 Phil Rizzuto	3.00	1.35
☐ 446 Hal Newhouser	3.00	1.35
☐ 447 Babe Ruth 60th Homer	30.00	13.50
☐ 448 Cy Young	3.00	1.35
☐ 449 Harmon Killebrew	3.00	1.35
☐ 450 Mickey Mantle	30.00	13.50
(Longest homer)		
☐ 451 Braves Take Pennant	.75	.35
☐ 452 Ted Williams	15.00	6.75
(All-Star Hero)		
☐ 453 Yogi Berra	7.50	3.40
☐ 454 Fred Snodgrass	.75	.35
☐ 455 Babe Ruth 3 Homers	25.00	11.00
☐ 456 Giants 26 Game Streak	.75	.35
☐ 457 Ted Kluszewski	1.50	.70
☐ 458 Mel Ott	2.00	.90
☐ 459 Harvey Kuenn	1.00	.45
☐ 460 Bob Feller	4.00	1.80
☐ 461 Casey Stengel	3.00	1.35
☐ 462 Hank Aaron	12.50	5.50
☐ 463 Spahn Beats Yanks	2.50	1.10
☐ 464 Ump's Wrong Call	.75	.35
☐ 465 Al Kaline	4.00	1.80
☐ 466 Bob Allison	.75	.35
☐ 467 Joe DiMaggio	15.00	6.75
(Four Homers)		
☐ 468 Rocky Colavito	3.00	1.35
☐ 469 Carl Erskine	1.00	.45
☐ 470 Sal Maglie	1.00	.45
☐ 471 Early Wynn	2.00	.90
☐ 472 Nellie Fox	2.50	1.10
☐ 473 Marty Marion	1.00	.45
☐ 474 Johnny Podres	1.00	.45
☐ 475 Mickey Owen	.75	.35
☐ 476 Dean Brothers	2.50	1.10
(Dizzy and Daffy)		
☐ 477 Christy Mathewson	3.00	1.35
☐ 478 Harvey Haddix	.75	.35
☐ 479 Carl Hubbell	1.50	.70
☐ 480 Bobby Thomson	1.50	.70

1937 O-Pee-Chee Batter Ups V300

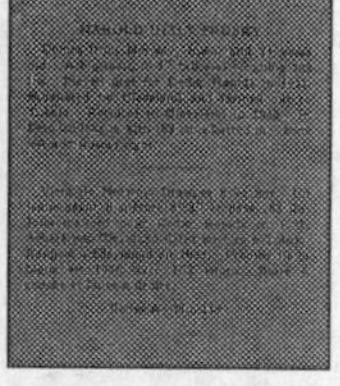

The cards in this 40-card set measure approximately 2 3/8" by 2 7/8". The fronts feature black-and-white die-cut player photos against a ballpark background with small players. The backs carry a short biography and career summary in English and French. The set is peculiar in that card numbering begins with 101. Cards without tops have greatly reduced value. The small ballplayer designs on the obverses are similar to those used on the 1934 American Goudey cards.

	EX-MT	VG-E
COMPLETE SET (40)	8500.00	3800.00
COMMON CARD (101-140)	60.00	27.00
☐ 101 John Lewis	60.00	27.00
☐ 102 Jack Hayes	60.00	27.00
☐ 103 Earl Averill	125.00	55.00
☐ 104 Harland Clift	60.00	27.00
☐ 105 Beau Bell	60.00	27.00
☐ 106 Jimmie Foxx	350.00	160.00

☐ 107 Hank Greenberg	275.00	125.00
☐ 108 George Selkirk	75.00	34.00
☐ 109 Wally Moses	75.00	34.00
☐ 110 Gerry Walker	60.00	27.00
☐ 111 Goose Goslin	125.00	55.00
☐ 112 Charlie Gehringer	225.00	100.00
☐ 113 Hal Trosky	60.00	27.00
☐ 114 Buddy Myer	60.00	27.00
☐ 115 Luke Appling	125.00	55.00
☐ 116 Zeke Bonura	60.00	27.00
☐ 117 Tony Lazzeri	125.00	55.00
☐ 118 Joe DiMaggio	4500.00	2000.00
☐ 119 Bill Dickey	275.00	125.00
☐ 120 Bob Feller	600.00	275.00
☐ 121 Harry Kelley	60.00	27.00
☐ 122 Johnny Allen	75.00	34.00
☐ 123 Bob Johnson	75.00	34.00
☐ 124 Joe Cronin	150.00	70.00
☐ 125 Rip Radcliff	60.00	27.00
☐ 126 Cecil Travis	75.00	34.00
☐ 127 Joe Kuhel	60.00	27.00
☐ 128 Odell Hale	60.00	27.00
☐ 129 Sam West	60.00	27.00
☐ 130 Ben Chapman	75.00	34.00
☐ 131 Monte Pearson	60.00	27.00
☐ 132 Rick Ferrell	125.00	55.00
☐ 133 Tommy Bridges	75.00	34.00
☐ 134 Schoolboy Rowe	75.00	34.00
☐ 135 Vernon Kennedy	60.00	27.00
☐ 136 Red Ruffing	150.00	70.00
☐ 137 Lefty Grove	275.00	125.00
☐ 138 Wes Ferrell	75.00	34.00
☐ 139 Buck Newsom	75.00	34.00
☐ 140 Rogers Hornsby	400.00	180.00

1965 O-Pee-Chee

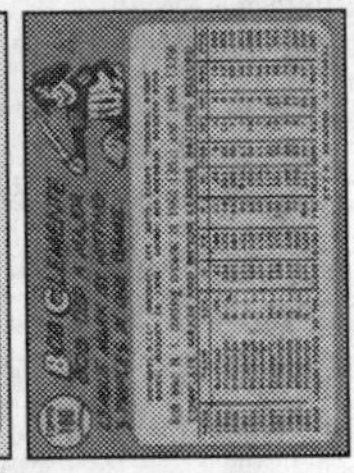

The cards in this 283-card set measure the standard size. This set is essentially the same as the regular 1965 Topps set, except that the words "Printed in Canada" appear on the bottom of the back. On a white border, the fronts feature color player photos with rounded corners. The team name appears within a pennant design below the photo. The player's name and position are also printed on the front. On a blue background, the horizontal backs carry player biography and statistics on a gray card stock. Remember the prices below apply only to the O-Pee- Chee cards -- NOT to the 1965 Topps cards which are much more plentiful.

	NRMT	VG-E
COMPLETE SET (283)	2500.00	1100.00
COMMON CARD (1-198)	4.00	1.80
COMMON CARD (199-283)	6.00	2.70

Card	NRMT	VG-E
☐ 1 AL Batting Leaders	25.00	11.00
Tony Oliva		
Elston Howard		
Brooks Robinson		
☐ 2 NL Batting Leaders	30.00	13.50
Bob Clemente		
Hank Aaron		
Rico Carty		
☐ 3 AL Home Run Leaders	50.00	22.00
Harmon Killebrew		
Mickey Mantle		
Boog Powell		
☐ 4 NL Home Run Leaders	20.00	9.00
Willie Mays		
Billy Williams		
Jim Ray Hart		
Orlando Cepeda		
Johnny Callison		
☐ 5 AL RBI Leaders	50.00	22.00
Brooks Robinson		
Harmon Killebrew		
Mickey Mantle		
Dick Stuart		
☐ 6 NL RBI Leaders	15.00	6.75
Ken Boyer		
Willie Mays		
Ron Santo		
☐ 7 AL ERA Leaders	7.50	3.40
Dean Chance		
Joel Horlen		
☐ 8 NL ERA Leaders	25.00	11.00
Sandy Koufax		
Don Drysdale		
☐ 9 AL Pitching Leaders	7.50	3.40
Dean Chance		
Gary Peters		
Dave Wickersham		
Juan Pizarro		
Wally Bunker		
☐ 10 NL Pitching Leaders	7.50	3.40
Larry Jackson		
Ray Sadecki		
Juan Marichal		
☐ 11 AL Strikeout Leaders	7.50	3.40
Al Downing		
Dean Chance		
Camilo Pascual		
☐ 12 NL Strikeout Leaders	7.50	3.40
Bob Veale		
Don Drysdale		
Bob Gibson		
☐ 13 Pedro Ramos	4.00	1.80
☐ 14 Len Gabrielson	4.00	1.80
☐ 15 Robin Roberts	12.50	5.50
☐ 16 Houston Rookies:	75.00	34.00
Joe Morgan		
Sonny Jackson		
☐ 17 John Romano	4.00	1.80
☐ 18 Bill McCool	4.00	1.80
☐ 19 Gates Brown	4.00	1.80
☐ 20 Jim Bunning	12.50	5.50
☐ 21 Don Blasingame	4.00	1.80
☐ 22 Charlie Smith	4.00	1.80
☐ 23 Bob Tiefenauer	4.00	1.80
☐ 24 Twins Team	7.50	3.40
☐ 25 Al McBean	4.00	1.80
☐ 26 Bob Knoop	4.00	1.80
☐ 27 Dick Bertell	4.00	1.80
☐ 28 Barney Schultz	4.00	1.80
☐ 29 Felix Mantilla	4.00	1.80
☐ 30 Jim Bouton	7.50	3.40
☐ 31 Mike White	4.00	1.80
☐ 32 Herman Franks MG	4.00	1.80
☐ 33 Jackie Brandt	4.00	1.80
☐ 34 Cal Koonce	4.00	1.80
☐ 35 Ed Charles	4.00	1.80
☐ 36 Bob Wine	4.00	1.80
☐ 37 Fred Gladding	4.00	1.80
☐ 38 Jim King	4.00	1.80
☐ 39 Gerry Arrigo	4.00	1.80
☐ 40 Frank Howard	6.00	2.70
☐ 41 White Sox Rookies	4.00	1.80
Bruce Howard		
Marv Staehle		
☐ 42 Earl Wilson	4.00	1.80
☐ 43 Mike Shannon	5.00	2.20
☐ 44 Wade Blasingame	4.00	1.80
☐ 45 Roy McMillan	5.00	2.20
☐ 46 Bob Lee	4.00	1.80
☐ 47 Tommy Harper	5.00	2.20
☐ 48 Claude Raymond	5.00	2.20
☐ 49 Orioles Rookies	6.00	2.70
Curt Blefary		
John Miller		
☐ 50 Juan Marichal	12.50	5.50
☐ 51 Bill Bryan	4.00	1.80
☐ 52 Ed Roebuck	4.00	1.80
☐ 53 Dick McAuliffe	5.00	2.20
☐ 54 Joe Gibbon	4.00	1.80
☐ 55 Tony Conigliaro	20.00	9.00
☐ 56 Ron Kline	4.00	1.80
☐ 57 Cardinals Team	7.50	3.40
☐ 58 Fred Talbot	4.00	1.80
☐ 59 Nate Oliver	4.00	1.80
☐ 60 Jim O'Toole	4.00	1.80
☐ 61 Chris Cannizzaro	4.00	1.80
☐ 62 Jim Kaat UER	7.50	3.40
(Misspelled Katt)		
☐ 63 Ty Cline	4.00	1.80
☐ 64 Lou Burdette	5.00	2.20
☐ 65 Tony Kubek	6.00	2.70
☐ 66 Bill Rigney MG	4.00	1.80
☐ 67 Harvey Haddix	5.00	2.20
☐ 68 Del Crandall	5.00	2.20
☐ 69 Bill Virdon	5.00	2.20
☐ 70 Bill Skowron	5.00	2.20
☐ 71 John O'Donoghue	4.00	1.80
☐ 72 Tony Gonzalez	4.00	1.80
☐ 73 Dennis Ribant	4.00	1.80
☐ 74 Red Sox Rookies	15.00	6.75
Rico Petrocelli		
Jerry Stephenson		
☐ 75 Deron Johnson	5.00	2.20
☐ 76 Sam McDowell	6.00	2.70
☐ 77 Doug Camilli	4.00	1.80
☐ 78 Dal Maxvill	5.00	2.20
☐ 79 Checklist 1-88	10.00	4.50
☐ 80 Turk Farrell	4.00	1.80
☐ 81 Don Buford	5.00	2.20
☐ 82 Braves Rookies:	7.50	3.40
Santos Alomar		
John Braun		
☐ 83 George Thomas	4.00	1.80
☐ 84 Ron Herbel	4.00	1.80
☐ 85 Willie Smith	4.00	1.80
☐ 86 Les Narum	4.00	1.80
☐ 87 Nelson Mathews	4.00	1.80
☐ 88 Jack Lamabe	4.00	1.80
☐ 89 Mike Hershberger	4.00	1.80
☐ 90 Rich Rollins	4.00	1.80
☐ 91 Cubs Team	7.50	3.40
☐ 92 Dick Howser	5.00	2.20
☐ 93 Jack Fisher	4.00	1.80
☐ 94 Charlie Lau	4.00	1.80
☐ 95 Bill Mazeroski	7.50	3.40
☐ 96 Sonny Siebert	5.00	2.20
☐ 97 Pedro Gonzalez	4.00	1.80
☐ 98 Bob Miller	4.00	1.80
☐ 99 Gil Hodges MG	10.00	4.50
☐ 100 Ken Boyer	6.00	2.70
☐ 101 Fred Newman	4.00	1.80
☐ 102 Steve Boros	4.00	1.80
☐ 103 Harvey Kuenn	5.00	2.20
☐ 104 Checklist 89-176	10.00	4.50
☐ 105 Chico Salmon	4.00	1.80
☐ 106 Gene Oliver	4.00	1.80
☐ 107 Phillies Rookies:	5.00	2.20
Pat Corrales		
Costen Shockley		
☐ 108 Don Mincher	4.00	1.80
☐ 109 Walt Bond	4.00	1.80
☐ 110 Ron Santo	7.50	3.40
☐ 111 Lee Thomas	4.00	1.80
☐ 112 Derrell Griffith	4.00	1.80
☐ 113 Steve Barber	4.00	1.80
☐ 114 Jim Hickman	4.00	1.80
☐ 115 Bobby Richardson	7.50	3.40
☐ 116 Cardinals Rookies:	5.00	2.20
Dave Dowling		
Bob Tolan		
☐ 117 Wes Stock	4.00	1.80
☐ 118 Hal Lanier	4.00	1.80
☐ 119 John Kennedy	4.00	1.80
☐ 120 Frank Robinson	40.00	18.00
☐ 121 Gene Alley	5.00	2.20
☐ 122 Bill Pleis	4.00	1.80
☐ 123 Frank Thomas	5.00	2.20
☐ 124 Tom Satriano	4.00	1.80
☐ 125 Juan Pizarro	4.00	1.80
☐ 126 Dodgers Team	7.50	3.40
☐ 127 Frank Lary	4.00	1.80
☐ 128 Vic Davalillo	4.00	1.80
☐ 129 Bennie Daniels	4.00	1.80
☐ 130 Al Kaline	40.00	18.00
☐ 131 Johnny Keane MG	4.00	1.80
☐ 132 Mike Shannon WS	7.50	3.40
☐ 133 Mel Stottlemyre WS	7.50	3.40
☐ 134 Mickey Mantle WS	100.00	45.00
☐ 135 Ken Boyer WS	7.50	3.40
☐ 136 Tim McCarver WS	7.50	3.40
☐ 137 Jim Bouton WS	7.50	3.40
☐ 138 Bob Gibson WS	15.00	6.75
☐ 139 World Series Summary	7.50	3.40
Cards celebrate		
☐ 140 Dean Chance	5.00	2.20
☐ 141 Charlie James	4.00	1.80
☐ 142 Bill Monbouquette	4.00	1.80
☐ 143 Pirates Rookies	4.00	1.80
John Gelnar		
Jerry May		
☐ 144 Ed Kranepool	5.00	2.20
☐ 145 Luis Tiant	25.00	11.00
☐ 146 Ron Hansen	4.00	1.80
☐ 147 Dennis Bennett	4.00	1.80
☐ 148 Willie Kirkland	4.00	1.80
☐ 149 Wayne Schurr	4.00	1.80
☐ 150 Brooks Robinson	40.00	18.00
☐ 151 Athletics Team	7.50	3.40
☐ 152 Phil Ortega	4.00	1.80
☐ 153 Norm Cash	7.50	3.40
☐ 154 Bob Humphreys	4.00	1.80
☐ 155 Roger Maris	50.00	22.00
☐ 156 Bob Sadowski	4.00	1.80
☐ 157 Zoilo Versalles	5.00	2.20
☐ 158 Dick Sisler MG	4.00	1.80
☐ 159 Jim Duffalo	4.00	1.80
☐ 160 Roberto Clemente !	175.00	80.00
☐ 161 Frank Baumann	4.00	1.80
☐ 162 Russ Nixon	4.00	1.80
☐ 163 John Briggs	4.00	1.80
☐ 164 Al Spangler	4.00	1.80

Card	NRMT	VG-E
☐ 165 Dick Ellsworth	4.00	1.80
☐ 166 Indians Rookies	6.00	2.70
George Culver		
Tommie Agee		
☐ 167 Bill Wakefield	4.00	1.80
☐ 168 Dick Green	5.00	2.20
☐ 169 Dave Vineyard	4.00	1.80
☐ 170 Hank Aaron	125.00	55.00
☐ 171 Jim Roland	4.00	1.80
☐ 172 Jim Piersall	6.00	2.70
☐ 173 Tigers Team	7.50	3.40
☐ 174 Joe Jay	4.00	1.80
☐ 175 Bob Aspromonte	4.00	1.80
☐ 176 Willie McCovey	25.00	11.00
☐ 177 Pete Mikkelsen	4.00	1.80
☐ 178 Dalton Jones	4.00	1.80
☐ 179 Hal Woodeschick	4.00	1.80
☐ 180 Bob Allison	4.00	1.80
☐ 181 Senators Rookies	4.00	1.80
Don Loun		
Joe McCabe		
☐ 182 Mike de la Hoz	4.00	1.80
☐ 183 Dave Nicholson	4.00	1.80
☐ 184 John Boozer	4.00	1.80
☐ 185 Max Alvis	4.00	1.80
☐ 186 Bill Cowan	4.00	1.80
☐ 187 Casey Stengel MG	20.00	9.00
☐ 188 Sam Bowens	4.00	1.80
☐ 189 Checklist 177-264	10.00	4.50
☐ 190 Bill White	6.00	2.70
☐ 191 Phil Regan	5.00	2.20
☐ 192 Jim Coker	4.00	1.80
☐ 193 Gaylord Perry	20.00	9.00
☐ 194 Rookie Stars	5.00	2.20
Bill Kelso		
Rick Reichardt		
☐ 195 Bob Veale	5.00	2.20
☐ 196 Ron Fairly	5.00	2.20
☐ 197 Diego Segui	4.00	1.80
☐ 198 Smoky Burgess	5.00	2.20
☐ 199 Bob Heffner	6.00	2.70
☐ 200 Joe Torre	10.00	4.50
☐ 201 Twins Rookies	6.00	2.70
Sandy Valdespino		
Cesar Tovar		
☐ 202 Leo Burke	6.00	2.70
☐ 203 Dallas Green	6.00	2.70
☐ 204 Russ Snyder	6.00	2.70
☐ 205 Warren Spahn	35.00	16.00
☐ 206 Willie Horton	10.00	4.50
☐ 207 Pete Rose	175.00	80.00
☐ 208 Tommy John	10.00	4.50
☐ 209 Pirates Team	10.00	4.50
☐ 210 Jim Fregosi	7.50	3.40
☐ 211 Steve Ridzik	6.00	2.70
☐ 212 Ron Brand	6.00	2.70
☐ 213 Jim Davenport	6.00	2.70
☐ 214 Bob Purkey	6.00	2.70
☐ 215 Pete Ward	6.00	2.70
☐ 216 Al Worthington	6.00	2.70
☐ 217 Walt Alston MG	10.00	4.50
☐ 218 Dick Schofield	6.00	2.70
☐ 219 Bob Meyer	6.00	2.70
☐ 220 Billy Williams	12.50	5.50
☐ 221 John Tsitouris	6.00	2.70
☐ 222 Bob Tillman	6.00	2.70
☐ 223 Dan Osinski	6.00	2.70
☐ 224 Bob Chance	6.00	2.70
☐ 225 Bo Belinsky	7.50	3.40
☐ 226 Yankees Rookies	6.00	2.70
Elvio Jimenez		
Jake Gibbs		
☐ 227 Bobby Klaus	6.00	2.70
☐ 228 Jack Sanford	6.00	2.70
☐ 229 Lou Clinton	6.00	2.70
☐ 230 Ray Sadecki	6.00	2.70
☐ 231 Jerry Adair	6.00	2.70
☐ 232 Steve Blass	6.00	2.70
☐ 233 Don Zimmer	7.50	3.40
☐ 234 White Sox Team	10.00	4.50
☐ 235 Chuck Hinton	6.00	2.70
☐ 236 Dennis McLain	40.00	18.00
☐ 237 Bernie Allen	6.00	2.70
☐ 238 Joe Moeller	6.00	2.70
☐ 239 Doc Edwards	6.00	2.70
☐ 240 Bob Bruce	6.00	2.70
☐ 241 Mack Jones	6.00	2.70
☐ 242 George Brunet	6.00	2.70
☐ 243 Reds Rookies	7.50	3.40
Ted Davidson		
Tommy Helms		
☐ 244 Lindy McDaniel	7.50	3.40
☐ 245 Joe Pepitone	7.50	3.40
☐ 246 Tom Butters	6.00	2.70
☐ 247 Wally Moon	7.50	3.40
☐ 248 Gus Triandos	6.00	2.70
☐ 249 Dave McNally	7.50	3.40
☐ 250 Willie Mays	125.00	55.00
☐ 251 Billy Herman MG	7.50	3.40
☐ 252 Pete Richert	6.00	2.70
☐ 253 Danny Cater	6.00	2.70
☐ 254 Roland Sheldon	6.00	2.70
☐ 255 Camilo Pascual	7.50	3.40
☐ 256 Tito Francona	6.00	2.70
☐ 257 Jim Wynn	7.50	3.40
☐ 258 Larry Bearnarth	6.00	2.70
☐ 259 Tigers Rookies	10.00	4.50
Jim Northrup		
Ray Oyler		
☐ 260 Don Drysdale	25.00	11.00
☐ 261 Duke Carmel	6.00	2.70
☐ 262 Bud Daley	6.00	2.70
☐ 263 Marty Keough	6.00	2.70
☐ 264 Bob Buhl	6.00	2.70
☐ 265 Jim Pagliaroni	6.00	2.70
☐ 266 Bert Campaneris	10.00	4.50
☐ 267 Senators Team	10.00	4.50
☐ 268 Ken McBride	6.00	2.70
☐ 269 Frank Bolling	6.00	2.70
☐ 270 Milt Pappas	6.00	2.70
☐ 271 Don Wert	6.00	2.70
☐ 272 Chuck Schilling	6.00	2.70
☐ 273 4th Series Checklist	12.50	5.50
☐ 274 Lum Harris MG	6.00	2.70
☐ 275 Dick Groat	7.50	3.40
☐ 276 Hoyt Wilhelm	12.50	5.50
☐ 277 Johnny Lewis	6.00	2.70
☐ 278 Ken Retzer	6.00	2.70
☐ 279 Dick Tracewski	6.00	2.70
☐ 280 Dick Stuart	7.50	3.40
☐ 281 Bill Stafford	6.00	2.70
☐ 282 Giants Rookies	50.00	22.00
Dick Estelle		
Masanori Murakami		
☐ 283 Fred Whitfield	7.50	3.40

1966 O-Pee-Chee

The cards in this 196-card set measure 2 1/2" by 3 1/2". This set is essentially the same as the regular 1966 Topps set, except that the words "Printed in Canada" appear on the bottom of the back, and the background colors are slightly different. On a white border, the fronts feature color player photos. The team name appears within a tilted bar in the top right corner, while the player's name and position are printed inside a bar under the photo. The horizontal backs carry player biography and statistics. Remember the prices below apply only to the O-Pee- Chee cards -- NOT to the 1966 Topps cards which are much more plentiful.

	NRMT	VG-E
COMPLETE SET (196)	1500.00	700.00
COMMON CARD (1-196)	3.00	1.35
☐ 1 Willie Mays	200.00	90.00
☐ 2 Ted Abernathy	3.00	1.35
☐ 3 Sam Mele MG	3.00	1.35
☐ 4 Ray Culp	3.00	1.35
☐ 5 Jim Fregosi	4.00	1.80
☐ 6 Chuck Schilling	3.00	1.35
☐ 7 Tracy Stallard	3.00	1.35
☐ 8 Floyd Robinson	3.00	1.35
☐ 9 Clete Boyer	4.00	1.80
☐ 10 Tony Cloninger	3.00	1.35
☐ 11 Senators Rookies	3.00	1.35
Brant Alyea		
Pete Craig		
☐ 12 John Tsitouris	3.00	1.35
☐ 13 Lou Johnson	3.00	1.35
☐ 14 Norm Siebern	3.00	1.35
☐ 15 Vern Law	4.00	1.80
☐ 16 Larry Brown	3.00	1.35
☐ 17 John Stephenson	3.00	1.35
☐ 18 Roland Sheldon	3.00	1.35
☐ 19 Giants Team	6.00	2.70
☐ 20 Willie Horton	4.00	1.80
☐ 21 Don Nottebart	3.00	1.35
☐ 22 Joe Nossek	3.00	1.35
☐ 23 Jack Sanford	3.00	1.35
☐ 24 Don Kessinger	6.00	2.70
☐ 25 Pete Ward	3.00	1.35
☐ 26 Ray Sadecki	3.00	1.35
☐ 27 Orioles Rookies	3.00	1.35
Darold Knowles		
Andy Etchebarren		
☐ 28 Phil Niekro	25.00	11.00
☐ 29 Mike Brumley	3.00	1.35
☐ 30 Pete Rose	50.00	22.00
☐ 31 Jack Cullen	3.00	1.35
☐ 32 Adolfo Phillips	3.00	1.35
☐ 33 Jim Pagliaroni	3.00	1.35
☐ 34 Checklist 1-88	8.00	2.00
☐ 35 Ron Swoboda	6.00	2.70
☐ 36 Jim Hunter	25.00	11.00
☐ 37 Billy Herman MG	4.00	1.80
☐ 38 Ron Nischwitz	3.00	1.35
☐ 39 Ken Henderson	3.00	1.35
☐ 40 Jim Grant	3.00	1.35
☐ 41 Don LeJohn	3.00	1.35
☐ 42 Aubrey Gatewood	3.00	1.35
☐ 43 Don Landrum	3.00	1.35
☐ 44 Indians Rookies	3.00	1.35
Bill Davis		
Tom Kelley		
☐ 45 Jim Gentile	4.00	1.80
☐ 46 Howie Koplitz	3.00	1.35
☐ 47 J.C. Martin	3.00	1.35
☐ 48 Paul Blair	4.00	1.80
☐ 49 Woody Woodward	3.00	1.35
☐ 50 Mickey Mantle	300.00	135.00
☐ 51 Gordon Richardson	3.00	1.35
☐ 52 Power Plus	6.00	2.70
Wes Covington		
Johnny Callison		
☐ 53 Bob Duliba	3.00	1.35
☐ 54 Jose Pagan	3.00	1.35
☐ 55 Ken Harrelson	4.00	1.80
☐ 56 Sandy Valdespino	3.00	1.35
☐ 57 Jim Lefebvre	4.00	1.80
☐ 58 Dave Wickersham	3.00	1.35
☐ 59 Reds Team	6.00	2.70
☐ 60 Curt Flood	6.00	2.70
☐ 61 Bob Bolin	3.00	1.35
☐ 62 Merritt Ranew (with sold line)	3.00	1.35
☐ 63 Jim Stewart	3.00	1.35
☐ 64 Bob Bruce	3.00	1.35
☐ 65 Leon Wagner	3.00	1.35
☐ 66 Al Weis	3.00	1.35
☐ 67 Mets Rookies	4.00	1.80
Cleon Jones		
Dick Selma		
☐ 68 Hal Reniff	3.00	1.35
☐ 69 Ken Hamlin	3.00	1.35
☐ 70 Carl Yastrzemski	35.00	16.00
☐ 71 Frank Carpin	3.00	1.35
☐ 72 Tony Perez	35.00	16.00
☐ 73 Jerry Zimmerman	3.00	1.35
☐ 74 Don Mossi	4.00	1.80
☐ 75 Tommy Davis	4.00	1.80
☐ 76 Red Schoendienst MG	6.00	2.70
☐ 77 Johnny Orsino	3.00	1.35
☐ 78 Frank Linzy	3.00	1.35
☐ 79 Joe Pepitone	4.00	1.80
☐ 80 Richie Allen	8.00	3.60
☐ 81 Ray Oyler	3.00	1.35
☐ 82 Bob Hendley	3.00	1.35
☐ 83 Albie Pearson	4.00	1.80
☐ 84 Braves Rookies	3.00	1.35
Jim Beauchamp		
Dick Kelley		
☐ 85 Eddie Fisher	3.00	1.35
☐ 86 John Bateman	3.00	1.35
☐ 87 Dan Napoleon	3.00	1.35
☐ 88 Fred Whitfield	3.00	1.35
☐ 89 Ted Davidson	3.00	1.35
☐ 90 Luis Aparicio	10.00	4.50
☐ 91 Bob Uecker (with traded line)	25.00	11.00
☐ 92 Yankees Team	15.00	6.75
☐ 93 Jim Lonborg	6.00	2.70
☐ 94 Matty Alou	4.00	1.80
☐ 95 Pete Richert	3.00	1.35
☐ 96 Felipe Alou	6.00	2.70
☐ 97 Jim Merritt	3.00	1.35
☐ 98 Don Demeter	3.00	1.35
☐ 99 Buc Belters	10.00	4.50
Willie Stargell		
Donn Clendenon		
☐ 100 Sandy Koufax	125.00	55.00
☐ 101 Checklist 89-176	8.00	2.00
☐ 102 Ed Kirkpatrick	3.00	1.35
☐ 103 Dick Groat (with traded line)	4.00	1.80
☐ 104 Alex Johnson	3.00	1.35

(with traded line)
☐ 105 Milt Pappas 4.00 1.80
☐ 106 Rusty Staub 6.00 2.70
☐ 107 A's Rookies 3.00 1.35
Larry Stahl
Ron Tompkins
☐ 108 Bobby Klaus 3.00 1.35
☐ 109 Ralph Terry 4.00 1.80
☐ 110 Ernie Banks 35.00 16.00
☐ 111 Gary Peters 3.00 1.35
☐ 112 Manny Mota 4.00 1.80
☐ 113 Hank Aguirre 3.00 1.35
☐ 114 Jim Gosger 3.00 1.35
☐ 115 Bill Henry 3.00 1.35
☐ 116 Walt Alston MG 6.00 2.70
☐ 117 Jake Gibbs 3.00 1.35
☐ 118 Mike McCormick 4.00 1.80
☐ 119 Art Shamsky 3.00 1.35
☐ 120 Harmon Killebrew 25.00 11.00
☐ 121 Ray Herbert 3.00 1.35
☐ 122 Joe Gaines 3.00 1.35
☐ 123 Pirates Rookies 3.00 1.35
Frank Bork
Jerry May
☐ 124 Tug McGraw 6.00 2.70
☐ 125 Lou Brock 25.00 11.00
☐ 126 Jim Palmer 150.00 70.00
☐ 127 Ken Berry 3.00 1.35
☐ 128 Jim Landis 3.00 1.35
☐ 129 Jack Kralick 3.00 1.35
☐ 130 Joe Torre 8.00 3.60
☐ 131 Angels Team 8.00 3.60
☐ 132 Orlando Cepeda 8.00 3.60
☐ 133 Don McMahon 3.00 1.35
☐ 134 Wes Parker 4.00 1.80
☐ 135 Dave Morehead 3.00 1.35
☐ 136 Woody Held 3.00 1.35
☐ 137 Pat Corrales 3.00 1.35
☐ 138 Roger Repoz 3.00 1.35
☐ 139 Cubs Rookies 3.00 1.35
Byron Browne
Don Young
☐ 140 Jim Maloney 4.00 1.80
☐ 141 Tom McCraw 3.00 1.35
☐ 142 Don Dennis 3.00 1.35
☐ 143 Jose Tartabull 3.00 1.35
☐ 144 Don Schwall 3.00 1.35
☐ 145 Bill Freehan 4.00 1.80
☐ 146 George Altman 3.00 1.35
☐ 147 Lum Harris MG 3.00 1.35
☐ 148 Bob Johnson 3.00 1.35
☐ 149 Dick Nen 3.00 1.35
☐ 150 Rocky Colavito 15.00 6.75
☐ 151 Gary Wagner 3.00 1.35
☐ 152 Frank Malzone 4.00 1.80
☐ 153 Rico Carty 4.00 1.80
☐ 154 Chuck Hiller 4.00 1.80
☐ 155 Marcelino Lopez 3.00 1.35
☐ 156 Double Play Combo 4.00 1.80
Dick Schofield
Hal Lanier
☐ 157 Rene Lachemann 4.00 1.80
☐ 158 Jim Brewer 3.00 1.35
☐ 159 Chico Ruiz 3.00 1.35
☐ 160 Whitey Ford 35.00 16.00
☐ 161 Jerry Lumpe 3.00 1.35
☐ 162 Lee Maye 3.00 1.35
☐ 163 Tito Francona 3.00 1.35
☐ 164 White Sox Rookies 4.00 1.80
Tommie Agee
Marv Staehle
☐ 165 Don Lock 3.00 1.35
☐ 166 Chris Krug 3.00 1.35
☐ 167 Boog Powell 10.00 4.50
☐ 168 Dan Osinski 3.00 1.35
☐ 169 Duke Sims 3.00 1.35
☐ 170 Cookie Rojas 4.00 1.80
☐ 171 Nick Willhite 3.00 1.35
☐ 172 Mets Team 8.00 3.60
☐ 173 Al Spangler 3.00 1.35
☐ 174 Ron Taylor 3.00 1.35
☐ 175 Bert Campaneris 6.00 2.70
☐ 176 Jim Davenport 3.00 1.35
☐ 177 Hector Lopez 3.00 1.35
☐ 178 Bob Tillman 3.00 1.35
☐ 179 Cards Rookies 3.00 1.35
Dennis Aust
Bob Tolan
☐ 180 Vada Pinson 6.00 2.70
☐ 181 Al Worthington 3.00 1.35
☐ 182 Jerry Lynch 3.00 1.35
☐ 183 Checklist 177-264 8.00 2.00
☐ 184 Denis Menke 3.00 1.35
☐ 185 Bob Buhl 4.00 1.80
☐ 186 Ruben Amaro 3.00 1.35
☐ 187 Chuck Dressen MG 4.00 1.80
☐ 188 Al Luplow 3.00 1.35
☐ 189 John Roseboro 4.00 1.80
☐ 190 Jimmie Hall 3.00 1.35
☐ 191 Darrell Sutherland 3.00 1.35
☐ 192 Vic Power 4.00 1.80
☐ 193 Dave McNally 4.00 1.80
☐ 194 Senators Team 8.00 3.60
☐ 195 Joe Morgan 20.00 9.00
☐ 196 Don Pavletich 4.00 1.80

1967 O-Pee-Chee

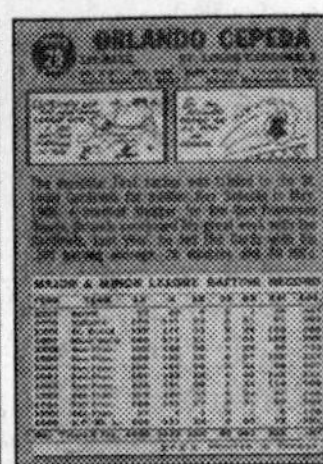

The cards in this 196-card set measure 2 1/2" by 3 1/2". This set is essentially the same as the regular 1967 Topps set, except that the words "Printed in Canada" appear on the bottom right corner of the back. On a white border, fronts feature color player photos with a thin black border. The player's name and position appear in the top part, while the team name is printed in big letters in the bottom part of the photo. On a green background, the backs carry player biography and statistics and two cartoon-like facts. Each checklist card features a small circular picture of a popular player included in that series. Remember the prices below apply only to the O-Pee-Chee cards -- NOT to the 1967 Topps cards which are much more plentiful.

	NRMT	VG-E
COMPLETE SET (196)	1250.00	550.00
COMMON CARD (1-196)	3.00	1.35

☐ 1 The Champs 25.00 11.00
Frank Robinson
Hank Bauer
Brooks Robinson
☐ 2 Jack Hamilton 3.00 1.35
☐ 3 Duke Sims 3.00 1.35
☐ 4 Hal Lanier 3.00 1.35
☐ 5 Whitey Ford 25.00 11.00
☐ 6 Dick Simpson 3.00 1.35
☐ 7 Don McMahon 3.00 1.35
☐ 8 Chuck Harrison 3.00 1.35
☐ 9 Ron Hansen 3.00 1.35
☐ 10 Matty Alou 4.00 1.80
☐ 11 Barry Moore 3.00 1.35
☐ 12 Dodgers Rookies 4.00 1.80
Jim Campanis
Bill Singer
☐ 13 Joe Sparma 4.00 1.80
☐ 14 Phil Linz 4.00 1.80
☐ 15 Earl Battey 3.00 1.35
☐ 16 Bill Hands 3.00 1.35
☐ 17 Jim Gosger 3.00 1.35
☐ 18 Gene Oliver 3.00 1.35
☐ 19 Jim McGlothlin 3.00 1.35
☐ 20 Orlando Cepeda 8.00 3.60
☐ 21 Dave Bristol MG 3.00 1.35
☐ 22 Gene Brabender 3.00 1.35
☐ 23 Larry Elliot 3.00 1.35
☐ 24 Bob Allen 3.00 1.35
☐ 25 Elston Howard 6.00 2.70
☐ 26 Bob Priddy 3.00 1.35
(with traded line)
☐ 27 Bob Saverine 3.00 1.35
☐ 28 Barry Latman 3.00 1.35
☐ 29 Tommy McCraw 3.00 1.35
☐ 30 Al Kaline 20.00 9.00
☐ 31 Jim Brewer 3.00 1.35
☐ 32 Bob Bailey 4.00 1.80
☐ 33 Athletics Rookies 6.00 2.70
Sal Bando
Randy Schwartz
☐ 34 Pete Cimino 3.00 1.35
☐ 35 Rico Carty 4.00 1.80
☐ 36 Bob Tillman 3.00 1.35
☐ 37 Rick Wise 4.00 1.80
☐ 38 Bob Johnson 3.00 1.35
☐ 39 Curt Simmons 4.00 1.80
☐ 40 Rick Reichardt 3.00 1.35
☐ 41 Joe Hoerner 3.00 1.35
☐ 42 Mets Team 10.00 4.50
☐ 43 Chico Salmon 3.00 1.35
☐ 44 Joe Nuxhall 4.00 1.80
☐ 45 Roger Maris 45.00 20.00
☐ 46 Lindy McDaniel 4.00 1.80
☐ 47 Ken McMullen 3.00 1.35
☐ 48 Bill Freehan 4.00 1.80
☐ 49 Roy Face 4.00 1.80
☐ 50 Tony Oliva 8.00 3.60
☐ 51 Astros Rookies 3.00 1.35
Dave Adlesh
Wes Bales
☐ 52 Dennis Higgins 3.00 1.35
☐ 53 Clay Dalrymple 3.00 1.35
☐ 54 Dick Green 3.00 1.35
☐ 55 Don Drysdale 20.00 9.00
☐ 56 Jose Tartabull 3.00 1.35
☐ 57 Pat Jarvis 3.00 1.35
☐ 58 Paul Schaal 3.00 1.35
☐ 59 Ralph Terry 4.00 1.80
☐ 60 Luis Aparicio 10.00 4.50
☐ 61 Gordy Coleman 3.00 1.35
☐ 62 Frank Robinson CL 8.00 2.00
☐ 63 Cards' Clubbers 10.00 4.50
Lou Brock
Curt Flood
☐ 64 Fred Valentine 3.00 1.35
☐ 65 Tom Haller 4.00 1.80
☐ 66 Manny Mota 4.00 1.80
☐ 67 Ken Berry 3.00 1.35
☐ 68 Bob Buhl 4.00 1.80
☐ 69 Vic Davalillo 3.00 1.35
☐ 70 Ron Santo 8.00 3.60
☐ 71 Camilo Pascual 4.00 1.80
☐ 72 Tigers Rookies 3.00 1.35
George Korince
(photo actually
John Brown)
John (Tom) Matchick
☐ 73 Rusty Staub 6.00 2.70
☐ 74 Wes Stock 3.00 1.35
☐ 75 George Scott 4.00 1.80
☐ 76 Jim Barbieri 3.00 1.35
☐ 77 Dooley Womack 3.00 1.35
☐ 78 Pat Corrales 4.00 1.80
☐ 79 Bubba Morton 3.00 1.35
☐ 80 Jim Maloney 4.00 1.80
☐ 81 Eddie Stanky MG 4.00 1.80
☐ 82 Steve Barber 3.00 1.35
☐ 83 Ollie Brown 3.00 1.35
☐ 84 Tommie Sisk 3.00 1.35
☐ 85 Johnny Callison 4.00 1.80
☐ 86 Mike McCormick 4.00 1.80
(with traded line)
☐ 87 George Altman 3.00 1.35
☐ 88 Mickey Lolich 6.00 2.70
☐ 89 Felix Millan 4.00 1.80
☐ 90 Jim Nash 3.00 1.35
☐ 91 Johnny Lewis 3.00 1.35
☐ 92 Ray Washburn 3.00 1.35
☐ 93 Yankees Rookies 6.00 2.70
Stan Bahnsen
Bobby Murcer
☐ 94 Ron Fairly 4.00 1.80
☐ 95 Sonny Siebert 3.00 1.35
☐ 96 Art Shamsky 3.00 1.35
☐ 97 Mike Cuellar 6.00 2.70
☐ 98 Rich Rollins 3.00 1.35
☐ 99 Lee Stange 3.00 1.35
☐ 100 Frank Robinson 18.00 8.00
☐ 101 Ken Johnson 3.00 1.35
☐ 102 Phillies Team 6.00 2.70
☐ 103 Mickey Mantle CL 25.00 11.00
☐ 104 Minnie Rojas 3.00 1.35
☐ 105 Ken Boyer 4.00 1.80
☐ 106 Randy Hundley 4.00 1.80
☐ 107 Joel Horlen 3.00 1.35
☐ 108 Alex Johnson 4.00 1.80
☐ 109 Tribe Thumpers 6.00 2.70
Rocky Colavito
Leon Wagner
☐ 110 Jack Aker 3.00 1.35
☐ 111 John Kennedy 3.00 1.35
☐ 112 Dave Wickersham 3.00 1.35
☐ 113 Dave Nicholson 3.00 1.35
☐ 114 Jack Baldschun 3.00 1.35
☐ 115 Paul Casanova 3.00 1.35
☐ 116 Herman Franks MG 3.00 1.35
☐ 117 Darrell Brandon 3.00 1.35
☐ 118 Bernie Allen 3.00 1.35
☐ 119 Wade Blasingame 3.00 1.35
☐ 120 Floyd Robinson 3.00 1.35
☐ 121 Ed Bressoud 3.00 1.35
☐ 122 George Brunet 3.00 1.35
☐ 123 Pirates Rookies 3.00 1.35
Jim Price
Luke Walker
☐ 124 Jim Stewart 3.00 1.35
☐ 125 Moe Drabowsky 4.00 1.80
☐ 126 Tony Taylor 4.00 1.80
☐ 127 John O'Donoghue 3.00 1.35
☐ 128 Ed Spiezio 3.00 1.35

☐ 129 Phil Roof 3.00 1.35
☐ 130 Phil Regan 4.00 1.80
☐ 131 Yankees Team 10.00 4.50
☐ 132 Ozzie Virgil 3.00 1.35
☐ 133 Ron Kline 3.00 1.35
☐ 134 Gates Brown 4.00 1.80
☐ 135 Deron Johnson 4.00 1.80
☐ 136 Carroll Sembera 3.00 1.35
☐ 137 Twins Rookies 3.00 1.35
Ron Clark
Jim Ollom
☐ 138 Dick Kelley 3.00 1.35
☐ 139 Dalton Jones 3.00 1.35
☐ 140 Willie Stargell 25.00 11.00
☐ 141 John Miller 3.00 1.35
☐ 142 Jackie Brandt 3.00 1.35
☐ 143 Sox Sockers 6.00 2.70
Pete Ward
Don Buford
☐ 144 Bill Hepler 3.00 1.35
☐ 145 Larry Brown 3.00 1.35
☐ 146 Steve Carlton 100.00 45.00
☐ 147 Tom Egan 3.00 1.35
☐ 148 Adolfo Phillips 3.00 1.35
☐ 149 Joe Moeller 3.00 1.35
☐ 150 Mickey Mantle 350.00 160.00
☐ 151 Moe Drabowsky WS 6.00 2.70
☐ 152 Jim Palmer WS 10.00 4.50
☐ 153 Paul Blair WS 6.00 2.70
☐ 154 Brooks Robinson WS 6.00 2.70
Dave McNally
☐ 155 World Series Summary 6.00 2.70
Winners celebrate
☐ 156 Ron Herbel 3.00 1.35
☐ 157 Danny Cater 3.00 1.35
☐ 158 Jimmie Coker 3.00 1.35
☐ 159 Bruce Howard 3.00 1.35
☐ 160 Willie Davis 4.00 1.80
☐ 161 Dick Williams MG 4.00 1.80
☐ 162 Billy O'Dell 3.00 1.35
☐ 163 Vic Roznovsky 3.00 1.35
☐ 164 Dwight Siebler 3.00 1.35
☐ 165 Cleon Jones 4.00 1.80
☐ 166 Eddie Mathews 20.00 9.00
☐ 167 Senators Rookies 3.00 1.35
Joe Coleman
Tim Cullen
☐ 168 Ray Culp 3.00 1.35
☐ 169 Horace Clarke 3.00 1.35
☐ 170 Dick McAuliffe 4.00 1.80
☐ 171 Calvin Koonce 3.00 1.35
☐ 172 Bill Heath 3.00 1.35
☐ 173 Cardinals Team 6.00 2.70
☐ 174 Dick Radatz 3.00 1.35
☐ 175 Bobby Knoop 3.00 1.35
☐ 176 Sammy Ellis 3.00 1.35
☐ 177 Tito Fuentes 3.00 1.35
☐ 178 John Buzhardt 3.00 1.35
☐ 179 Braves Rookies 3.00 1.35
Charles Vaughan
Cecil Upshaw
☐ 180 Curt Blefary 3.00 1.35
☐ 181 Terry Fox 3.00 1.35
☐ 182 Ed Charles 3.00 1.35
☐ 183 Jim Pagliaroni 3.00 1.35
☐ 184 George Thomas 3.00 1.35
☐ 185 Ken Holtzman 6.00 2.70
☐ 186 Mets Maulers 6.00 2.70
Ed Kranepool
Ron Swoboda
☐ 187 Pedro Ramos 3.00 1.35
☐ 188 Ken Harrelson 4.00 1.80
☐ 189 Chuck Hinton 3.00 1.35
☐ 190 Turk Farrell 3.00 1.35
☐ 191 Willie Mays CL 15.00 6.75
☐ 192 Fred Gladding 3.00 1.35
☐ 193 Jose Cardenal 4.00 1.80
☐ 194 Bob Allison 4.00 1.80
☐ 195 Al Jackson 3.00 1.35
☐ 196 Johnny Romano 4.00 1.80

1967 O-Pee-Chee Paper Inserts

'hese posters measure approximately 5" by 7" and are ery similar to the American Topps poster (paper insert) ssue, except that they say "Ptd. in Canada" on the bottom. 'he fronts feature color player photos with thin borders. 'he player's name and position, team name, and the card umber appear inside a circle in the lower right. A acsimile player autograph rounds out the front. The acks are blank. This Canadian version is much more ifficult to find than the American version. These umbered "All-Star" inserts have fold lines which are enerally not very noticeable when stored carefully. There

is some confusion as to whether these posters were issued in 1967 or 1968.

	NRMT	VG-E
COMPLETE SET (32)	250.00	110.00
COMMON CARD (1-32)	2.00	.90

☐ 1 Boog Powell 5.00 2.20
☐ 2 Bert Campaneris 3.00 1.35
☐ 3 Brooks Robinson 12.50 5.50
☐ 4 Tommie Agee .... 2.00 .90
☐ 5 Carl Yastrzemski 20.00 9.00
☐ 6 Mickey Mantle 100.00 45.00
☐ 7 Frank Howard 4.00 1.80
☐ 8 Sam McDowell 3.00 1.35
☐ 9 Orlando Cepeda 7.50 3.40
☐ 10 Chico Cardenas .... 2.00 .90
☐ 11 Bob Clemente 50.00 22.00
☐ 12 Willie Mays 35.00 16.00
☐ 13 Cleon Jones .... 2.00 .90
☐ 14 John Callison .... 2.00 .90
☐ 15 Hank Aaron 35.00 16.00
☐ 16 Don Drysdale 12.50 5.50
☐ 17 Bobby Knoop .... 2.00 .90
☐ 18 Tony Oliva 5.00 2.20
☐ 19 Frank Robinson 12.50 5.50
☐ 20 Denny McLain 5.00 2.20
☐ 21 Al Kaline 12.50 5.50
☐ 22 Joe Pepitone 3.00 1.35
☐ 23 Harmon Killebrew 12.50 5.50
☐ 24 Leon Wagner .... 2.00 .90
☐ 25 Joe Morgan 12.50 5.50
☐ 26 Ron Santo 5.00 2.20
☐ 27 Joe Torre 5.00 2.20
☐ 28 Juan Marichal 12.50 5.50
☐ 29 Matty Alou 3.00 1.35
☐ 30 Felipe Alou 4.00 1.80
☐ 31 Ron Hunt .... 2.00 .90
☐ 32 Willie McCovey 12.50 5.50

1968 O-Pee-Chee

The cards in this 196-card set measure 2 1/2" by 3 1/2". This set is essentially the same as the regular 1968 Topps set, except that the words "Printed in Canada" appear on the bottom of the back and the backgrounds have a different color. The fronts feature color player photos with rounded corners. The player's name is printed under the photo, while his position and team name appear in a circle in the lower right. On a light brown background, the backs carry player biography and statistics and a cartoon-like trivia question. Each checklist card features a small circular picture of a popular player included in that series. Remember the prices below apply only to the O-Pee-Chee cards -- NOT to the 1968 Topps cards which are much more plentiful. The key card in the set is Nolan Ryan in his Rookie Card year. The first OPC cards of Hall of Famers Rod Carew and Tom Seaver also appear in this set.

	NRMT	VG-E
COMPLETE SET (196)	2500.00	1100.00
COMMON CARD (1-196)	3.00	1.35

☐ 1 NL Batting Leaders 35.00 16.00
Bob Clemente
Tony Gonzalez
Matty Alou
☐ 2 AL Batting Leaders 18.00 8.00
Carl Yastrzemski
Frank Robinson
Al Kaline
☐ 3 NL RBI Leaders 25.00 11.00
Orlando Cepeda
Bob Clemente
Hank Aaron
☐ 4 AL RBI Leaders 15.00 6.75
Carl Yastrzemski
Harmon Killebrew
Frank Robinson
☐ 5 NL Home Run Leaders 10.00 4.50
Hank Aaron
Jim Wynn
Ron Santo
Willie McCovey
☐ 6 AL Home Run Leaders 10.00 4.50
Carl Yastrzemski
Harmon Killebrew
Frank Howard
☐ 7 NL ERA Leaders 6.00 2.70
Phil Niekro
Jim Bunning
Chris Short
☐ 8 AL ERA Leaders 6.00 2.70
Joel Horlen
Gary Peters
Sonny Siebert
☐ 9 NL Pitching Leaders 6.00 2.70
Mike McCormick
Ferguson Jenkins
Jim Bunning
Claude Osteen
☐ 10 AL Pitching Leaders 6.00 2.70
Jim Lonborg
Earl Wilson
Dean Chance
☐ 11 NL Strikeout Leaders 6.00 2.70
Jim Bunning
Ferguson Jenkins
Gaylord Perry
☐ 12 AL Strikeout Leaders 6.00 2.70
Jim Lonborg
Sam McDowell
Dean Chance
☐ 13 Chuck Hartenstein 3.00 1.35
☐ 14 Jerry McNertney 3.00 1.35
☐ 15 Ron Hunt 3.00 1.35
☐ 16 Indians Rookies 6.00 2.70
Lou Piniella
Richie Scheinblum
☐ 17 Dick Hall 3.00 1.35
☐ 18 Mike Hershberger 3.00 1.35
☐ 19 Juan Pizarro 3.00 1.35
☐ 20 Brooks Robinson 30.00 13.50
☐ 21 Ron Davis 3.00 1.35
☐ 22 Pat Dobson 4.00 1.80
☐ 23 Chico Cardenas 4.00 1.80
☐ 24 Bobby Locke 3.00 1.35
☐ 25 Julian Javier 4.00 1.80
☐ 26 Darrell Brandon 3.00 1.35
☐ 27 Gil Hodges MG 10.00 4.50
☐ 28 Ted Uhlaender 3.00 1.35
☐ 29 Joe Verbanic 3.00 1.35
☐ 30 Joe Torre 6.00 2.70
☐ 31 Ed Stroud 3.00 1.35
☐ 32 Joe Gibbon 3.00 1.35
☐ 33 Pete Ward 3.00 1.35
☐ 34 Al Ferrara 3.00 1.35
☐ 35 Steve Hargan 3.00 1.35
☐ 36 Pirates Rookies 4.00 1.80
Bob Moose
Bob Robertson
☐ 37 Billy Williams 10.00 4.50
☐ 38 Tony Pierce 3.00 1.35
☐ 39 Cookie Rojas 3.00 1.35
☐ 40 Denny McLain 15.00 6.75
☐ 41 Julio Gotay 3.00 1.35
☐ 42 Larry Haney 3.00 1.35
☐ 43 Gary Bell 3.00 1.35
☐ 44 Frank Kostro 3.00 1.35
☐ 45 Tom Seaver 75.00 34.00
☐ 46 Dave Ricketts 3.00 1.35
☐ 47 Ralph Houk MG 4.00 1.80
☐ 48 Ted Davidson 3.00 1.35
☐ 49 Ed Brinkman 3.00 1.35
☐ 50 Willie Mays 75.00 34.00
☐ 51 Bob Locker 3.00 1.35
☐ 52 Hawk Taylor 3.00 1.35
☐ 53 Gene Alley 4.00 1.80
☐ 54 Stan Williams 3.00 1.35
☐ 55 Felipe Alou 6.00 2.70
☐ 56 Orioles Rookies 3.00 1.35
Dave Leonhard
Dave May
☐ 57 Dan Schneider 3.00 1.35
☐ 58 Ed Mathews 20.00 9.00
☐ 59 Don Lock 3.00 1.35
☐ 60 Ken Holtzman 4.00 1.80

Card	NRMT	VG-E
☐ 61 Reggie Smith	6.00	2.70
☐ 62 Chuck Dobson	3.00	1.35
☐ 63 Dick Kenworthy	3.00	1.35
☐ 64 Jim Merritt	3.00	1.35
☐ 65 John Roseboro	4.00	1.80
☐ 66 Casey Cox	3.00	1.35
☐ 67 Jim Kaat CL	8.00	2.00
☐ 68 Ron Willis	3.00	1.35
☐ 69 Tom Tresh	4.00	1.80
☐ 70 Bob Veale	4.00	1.80
☐ 71 Vern Fuller	3.00	1.35
☐ 72 Tommy John	6.00	2.70
☐ 73 Jim Ray Hart	4.00	1.80
☐ 74 Milt Pappas	4.00	1.80
☐ 75 Don Mincher	3.00	1.35
☐ 76 Braves Rookies	4.00	1.80
Jim Britton		
Ron Reed		
☐ 77 Don Wilson	4.00	1.80
☐ 78 Jim Northrup	4.00	1.80
☐ 79 Ted Kubiak	3.00	1.35
☐ 80 Rod Carew	65.00	29.00
☐ 81 Larry Jackson	4.00	1.80
☐ 82 Sam Bowens	3.00	1.35
☐ 83 John Stephenson	3.00	1.35
☐ 84 Bob Tolan	3.00	1.35
☐ 85 Gaylord Perry	10.00	4.50
☐ 86 Willie Stargell	10.00	4.50
☐ 87 Dick Williams MG	4.00	1.80
☐ 88 Phil Regan	4.00	1.80
☐ 89 Jake Gibbs	3.00	1.35
☐ 90 Vada Pinson	6.00	2.70
☐ 91 Jim Ollom	3.00	1.35
☐ 92 Ed Kranepool	4.00	1.80
☐ 93 Tony Cloninger	3.00	1.35
☐ 94 Lee Maye	3.00	1.35
☐ 95 Bob Aspromonte	3.00	1.35
☐ 96 Senators Rookies	3.00	1.35
Frank Coggins		
Dick Nold		
☐ 97 Tom Phoebus	3.00	1.35
☐ 98 Gary Sutherland	3.00	1.35
☐ 99 Rocky Colavito	8.00	3.60
☐ 100 Bob Gibson	30.00	13.50
☐ 101 Glenn Beckert	4.00	1.80
☐ 102 Jose Cardenal	4.00	1.80
☐ 103 Don Sutton	10.00	4.50
☐ 104 Dick Dietz	3.00	1.35
☐ 105 Al Downing	4.00	1.80
☐ 106 Dalton Jones	3.00	1.35
☐ 107 Juan Marichal CL	8.00	2.00
☐ 108 Don Pavletich	3.00	1.35
☐ 109 Bert Campaneris	4.00	1.80
☐ 110 Hank Aaron	75.00	34.00
☐ 111 Rich Reese	3.00	1.35
☐ 112 Woody Fryman	3.00	1.35
☐ 113 Tigers Rookies	4.00	1.80
Tom Matchick		
Daryl Patterson		
☐ 114 Ron Swoboda	4.00	1.80
☐ 115 Sam McDowell	4.00	1.80
☐ 116 Ken McMullen	3.00	1.35
☐ 117 Larry Jaster	3.00	1.35
☐ 118 Mark Belanger	4.00	1.80
☐ 119 Ted Savage	3.00	1.35
☐ 120 Mel Stottlemyre	6.00	2.70
☐ 121 Jimmie Hall	3.00	1.35
☐ 122 Gene Mauch MG	4.00	1.80
☐ 123 Jose Santiago	3.00	1.35
☐ 124 Nate Oliver	3.00	1.35
☐ 125 Joel Horlen	3.00	1.35
☐ 126 Bobby Etheridge	3.00	1.35
☐ 127 Paul Lindblad	3.00	1.35
☐ 128 Astros Rookies	3.00	1.35
Tom Dukes		
Alonzo Harris		
☐ 129 Mickey Stanley	6.00	2.70
☐ 130 Tony Perez	10.00	4.50
☐ 131 Frank Bertaina	3.00	1.35
☐ 132 Bud Harrelson	4.00	1.80
☐ 133 Fred Whitfield	3.00	1.35
☐ 134 Pat Jarvis	3.00	1.35
☐ 135 Paul Blair	4.00	1.80
☐ 136 Randy Hundley	4.00	1.80
☐ 137 Twins Team	6.00	2.70
☐ 138 Ruben Amaro	3.00	1.35
☐ 139 Chris Short	3.00	1.35
☐ 140 Tony Conigliaro	10.00	4.50
☐ 141 Dal Maxvill	3.00	1.35
☐ 142 White Sox Rookies	3.00	1.35
Buddy Bradford		
Bill Voss		
☐ 143 Pete Cimino	3.00	1.35
☐ 144 Joe Morgan	15.00	6.75
☐ 145 Don Drysdale	15.00	6.75
☐ 146 Sal Bando	4.00	1.80
☐ 147 Frank Linzy	3.00	1.35
☐ 148 Dave Bristol MG	3.00	1.35
☐ 149 Bob Saverine	3.00	1.35
☐ 150 Bob Clemente	100.00	45.00
☐ 151 Lou Brock WS	12.50	5.50
☐ 152 Carl Yastrzemski WS	12.50	5.50
☐ 153 Nellie Briles WS	6.00	2.70
☐ 154 Bob Gibson WS	12.50	5.50
☐ 155 Jim Lonborg WS	6.00	2.70
☐ 156 Rico Petrocelli WS	6.00	2.70
☐ 157 World Series Game 7	6.00	2.70
St. Louis wins it		
☐ 158 World Series Summary	6.00	2.70
Cardinals celebrate		
☐ 159 Don Kessinger	4.00	1.80
☐ 160 Earl Wilson	4.00	1.80
☐ 161 Norm Miller	3.00	1.35
☐ 162 Cards Rookies	4.00	1.80
Hal Gilson		
Mike Torrez		
☐ 163 Gene Brabender	3.00	1.35
☐ 164 Ramon Webster	3.00	1.35
☐ 165 Tony Oliva	8.00	3.60
☐ 166 Claude Raymond	4.00	1.80
☐ 167 Elston Howard	6.00	2.70
☐ 168 Dodgers Team	6.00	2.70
☐ 169 Bob Bolin	3.00	1.35
☐ 170 Jim Fregosi	4.00	1.80
☐ 171 Don Nottebart	3.00	1.35
☐ 172 Walt Williams	3.00	1.35
☐ 173 John Boozer	3.00	1.35
☐ 174 Bob Tillman	3.00	1.35
☐ 175 Maury Wills	8.00	3.60
☐ 176 Bob Allen	3.00	1.35
☐ 177 Mets Rookies	1000.00	450.00
Jerry Koosman		
Nolan Ryan		
☐ 178 Don Wert	4.00	1.80
☐ 179 Bill Stoneman	3.00	1.35
☐ 180 Curt Flood	4.00	1.80
☐ 181 Jerry Zimmerman	3.00	1.35
☐ 182 Dave Giusti	3.00	1.35
☐ 183 Bob Kennedy MG	4.00	1.80
☐ 184 Lou Johnson	3.00	1.35
☐ 185 Tom Haller	3.00	1.35
☐ 186 Eddie Watt	3.00	1.35
☐ 187 Sonny Jackson	3.00	1.35
☐ 188 Cap Peterson	3.00	1.35
☐ 189 Bill Landis	3.00	1.35
☐ 190 Bill White	4.00	1.80
☐ 191 Dan Frisella	3.00	1.35
☐ 192 Carl Yastrzemski CL	10.00	4.50
☐ 193 Jack Hamilton	3.00	1.35
☐ 194 Don Buford	3.00	1.35
☐ 195 Joe Pepitone	4.00	1.80
☐ 196 Gary Nolan	4.00	1.80

1969 O-Pee-Chee

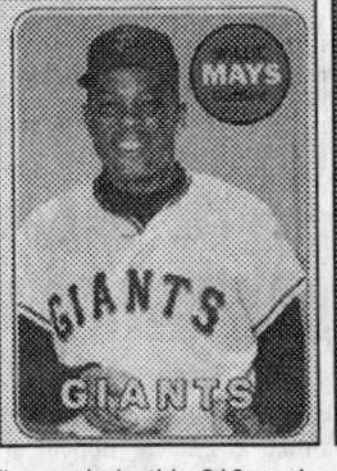

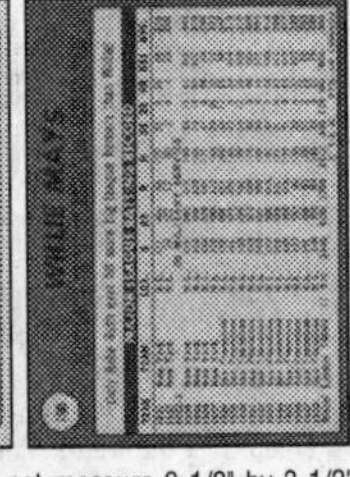

The cards in this 218-card set measure 2 1/2" by 3 1/2". This set is essentially the same as the regular 1969 Topps set, except that the words "Printed in Canada" appear on the bottom of the back and the backgrounds have a purple color. The fronts feature color player photos with rounded corners and thin black borders. The player's name and position are printed inside a circle in the top right corner, while the team name appears in the lower part of the photo. On a magenta background, the backs carry player biography and statistics. Each checklist card features a small circular picture of a popular player included in that series. Remember the prices below apply only to the O-Pee-Chee cards -- NOT to the 1969 Topps cards which are much more plentiful.

	NRMT	VG-E
COMPLETE SET (218)	1000.00	450.00
COMMON CARD (1-218)	2.50	1.10
☐ 1 AL Batting Leaders	18.00	8.00
Carl Yastrzemski		
Danny Cater		
Tony Oliva		
☐ 2 NL Batting Leaders	8.00	3.60
Pete Rose		
Matty Alou		
Felipe Alou		
☐ 3 AL RBI Leaders	6.00	2.70
Ken Harrelson		
Frank Howard		
Jim Northrup		
☐ 4 NL RBI Leaders	8.00	3.60
Willie McCovey		
Ron Santo		
Billy Williams		
☐ 5 AL Home Run Leaders	6.00	2.70
Frank Howard		
Willie Horton		
Ken Harrelson		
☐ 6 NL Home Run Leaders	8.00	3.60
Willie McCovey		
Richie Allen		
Ernie Banks		
☐ 7 AL ERA Leaders	6.00	2.70
Luis Tiant		
Sam McDowell		
Dave McNally		
☐ 8 NL ERA Leaders	8.00	3.60
Bob Gibson		
Bobby Bolin		
Bob Veale		
☐ 9 AL Pitching Leaders	6.00	2.70
Denny McLain		
Dave McNally		
Luis Tiant		
Mel Stottlemyre		
☐ 10 NL Pitching Leaders	8.00	3.60
Juan Marichal		
Bob Gibson		
Fergie Jenkins		
☐ 11 AL Strikeout Leaders	8.00	3.60
Sam McDowell		
Denny McLain		
Luis Tiant		
☐ 12 NL Strikeout Leaders	8.00	3.60
Bob Gibson		
Fergie Jenkins		
Bill Singer		
☐ 13 Mickey Stanley	4.00	1.80
☐ 14 Al McBean	2.50	1.10
☐ 15 Boog Powell	8.00	3.60
☐ 16 Giants Rookies	2.50	1.10
Cesar Gutierrez		
Rich Robertson		
☐ 17 Mike Marshall	4.00	1.80
☐ 18 Dick Schofield	2.50	1.10
☐ 19 Ken Suarez	2.50	1.10
☐ 20 Ernie Banks	25.00	11.00
☐ 21 Jose Santiago	2.50	1.10
☐ 22 Jesus Alou	4.00	1.80
☐ 23 Lew Krausse	2.50	1.10
☐ 24 Walt Alston MG	6.00	2.70
☐ 25 Roy White	4.00	1.80
☐ 26 Clay Carroll	4.00	1.80
☐ 27 Bernie Allen	2.50	1.10
☐ 28 Mike Ryan	2.50	1.10
☐ 29 Dave Morehead	2.50	1.10
☐ 30 Bob Allison	4.00	1.80
☐ 31 Mets Rookies	6.00	2.70
Gary Gentry		
Amos Otis		
☐ 32 Sammy Ellis	2.50	1.10
☐ 33 Wayne Causey	2.50	1.10
☐ 34 Gary Peters	2.50	1.10
☐ 35 Joe Morgan	10.00	4.50
☐ 36 Luke Walker	2.50	1.10
☐ 37 Curt Motton	2.50	1.10
☐ 38 Zoilo Versalles	4.00	1.80
☐ 39 Dick Hughes	2.50	1.10
☐ 40 Mayo Smith MG	2.50	1.10
☐ 41 Bob Barton	2.50	1.10
☐ 42 Tommy Harper	4.00	1.80
☐ 43 Joe Niekro	4.00	1.80
☐ 44 Danny Cater	2.50	1.10
☐ 45 Maury Wills	8.00	3.60
☐ 46 Fritz Peterson	2.50	1.10
☐ 47 Paul Popovich	2.50	1.10
☐ 48 Brant Alyea	2.50	1.10
☐ 49 Royals Rookies	2.50	1.10
Steve Jones		
Ellie Rodriguez		
☐ 50 Roberto Clemente	75.00	34.00
(Bob on card)		
☐ 51 Woody Fryman	4.00	1.80
☐ 52 Mike Andrews	2.50	1.10
☐ 53 Sonny Jackson	2.50	1.10
☐ 54 Cisco Carlos	2.50	1.10
☐ 55 Jerry Grote	4.00	1.80
☐ 56 Rich Reese	2.50	1.10
☐ 57 Checklist 1-109	8.00	3.60
Denny McLain		
☐ 58 Fred Gladding	2.50	1.10

Card	NRMT	VG-E
☐ 59 Jay Johnstone	4.00	1.80
☐ 60 Nelson Briles	4.00	1.80
☐ 61 Jimmie Hall	2.50	1.10
☐ 62 Chico Salmon	2.50	1.10
☐ 63 Jim Hickman	2.50	1.10
☐ 64 Bill Monbouquette	2.50	1.10
☐ 65 Willie Davis	4.00	1.80
☐ 66 Orioles Rookies	2.50	1.10
Mike Adamson		
Merv Rettenmund		
☐ 67 Bill Stoneman	4.00	1.80
☐ 68 Dave Duncan	4.00	1.80
☐ 69 Steve Hamilton	2.50	1.10
☐ 70 Tommy Helms	4.00	1.80
☐ 71 Steve Whitaker	2.50	1.10
☐ 72 Ron Taylor	4.00	1.80
☐ 73 Johnny Briggs	2.50	1.10
☐ 74 Preston Gomez MG	2.50	1.10
☐ 75 Luis Aparicio	10.00	4.50
☐ 76 Norm Miller	2.50	1.10
☐ 77 Ron Perranoski	4.00	1.80
☐ 78 Tom Satriano	2.50	1.10
☐ 79 Milt Pappas	4.00	1.80
☐ 80 Norm Cash	6.00	2.70
☐ 81 Mel Queen	2.50	1.10
☐ 82 Pirates Rookies	10.00	4.50
Rich Hebner		
Al Oliver		
☐ 83 Mike Ferraro	4.00	1.80
☐ 84 Bob Humphreys	2.50	1.10
☐ 85 Lou Brock	20.00	9.00
☐ 86 Pete Richert	2.50	1.10
☐ 87 Horace Clarke	2.50	1.10
☐ 88 Rich Nye	2.50	1.10
☐ 89 Russ Gibson	2.50	1.10
☐ 90 Jerry Koosman	8.00	3.60
☐ 91 Al Dark MG	4.00	1.80
☐ 92 Jack Billingham	4.00	1.80
☐ 93 Joe Foy	2.50	1.10
☐ 94 Hank Aguirre	2.50	1.10
☐ 95 Johnny Bench	60.00	27.00
☐ 96 Denver LeMaster	2.50	1.10
☐ 97 Buddy Bradford	2.50	1.10
☐ 98 Dave Giusti	2.50	1.10
☐ 99 Twins Rookies	20.00	9.00
Danny Morris		
Graig Nettles		
☐ 100 Hank Aaron	60.00	27.00
☐ 101 Daryl Patterson	2.50	1.10
☐ 102 Jim Davenport	2.50	1.10
☐ 103 Roger Repoz	2.50	1.10
☐ 104 Steve Blass	2.50	1.10
☐ 105 Rick Monday	4.00	1.80
☐ 106 Jim Hannan	2.50	1.10
☐ 107 Bob Gibson CL	8.00	3.60
☐ 108 Tony Taylor	4.00	1.80
☐ 109 Jim Lonborg	4.00	1.80
☐ 110 Mike Shannon	4.00	1.80
☐ 111 Johnny Morris	2.50	1.10
☐ 112 J.C. Martin	2.50	1.10
☐ 113 Dave May	2.50	1.10
☐ 114 Yankees Rookies	2.50	1.10
Alan Closter		
John Cumberland		
☐ 115 Bill Hands	2.50	1.10
☐ 116 Chuck Harrison	2.50	1.10
☐ 117 Jim Fairey	4.00	1.80
☐ 118 Stan Williams	2.50	1.10
☐ 119 Doug Rader	4.00	1.80
☐ 120 Pete Rose	30.00	13.50
☐ 121 Joe Grzenda	2.50	1.10
☐ 122 Ron Fairly	4.00	1.80
☐ 123 Wilbur Wood	4.00	1.80
☐ 124 Hank Bauer MG	4.00	1.80
☐ 125 Ray Sadecki	2.50	1.10
☐ 126 Dick Tracewski	2.50	1.10
☐ 127 Kevin Collins	2.50	1.10
☐ 128 Tommie Aaron	4.00	1.80
☐ 129 Bill McCool	2.50	1.10
☐ 130 Carl Yastrzemski	25.00	11.00
☐ 131 Chris Cannizzaro	2.50	1.10
☐ 132 Dave Baldwin	2.50	1.10
☐ 133 Johnny Callison	4.00	1.80
☐ 134 Jim Weaver	2.50	1.10
☐ 135 Tommy Davis	4.00	1.80
☐ 136 Cards Rookies	2.50	1.10
Steve Huntz		
Mike Torrez		
☐ 137 Wally Bunker	2.50	1.10
☐ 138 John Bateman	2.50	1.10
☐ 139 Andy Kosco	2.50	1.10
☐ 140 Jim Lefebvre	4.00	1.80
☐ 141 Bill Dillman	2.50	1.10
☐ 142 Woody Woodward	4.00	1.80
☐ 143 Joe Nossek	2.50	1.10
☐ 144 Bob Hendley	2.50	1.10
☐ 145 Max Alvis	2.50	1.10
☐ 146 Jim Perry	4.00	1.80
☐ 147 Leo Durocher MG	8.00	3.60
☐ 148 Lee Stange	2.50	1.10
☐ 149 Ollie Brown	2.50	1.10
☐ 150 Denny McLain	8.00	3.60
☐ 151 Clay Dalrymple	4.00	1.80
(Catching, Phillies)		
☐ 152 Tommie Sisk	2.50	1.10
☐ 153 Ed Brinkman	2.50	1.10
☐ 154 Jim Britton	2.50	1.10
☐ 155 Pete Ward	4.00	1.80
☐ 156 Houston Rookies	2.50	1.10
Hal Gilson		
Leon McFadden		
☐ 157 Bob Rodgers	4.00	1.80
☐ 158 Joe Gibbon	2.50	1.10
☐ 159 Jerry Adair	2.50	1.10
☐ 160 Vada Pinson	8.00	3.60
☐ 161 John Purdin	2.50	1.10
☐ 162 Bob Gibson WS	10.00	4.50
fans 17		
☐ 163 Willie Horton WS	8.00	3.60
☐ 164 Tim McCarver WS	10.00	4.50
with Roger Maris		
☐ 165 Lou Brock WS	10.00	4.50
☐ 166 Al Kaline WS	10.00	4.50
☐ 167 Jim Northrup WS	8.00	3.60
☐ 168 Mickey Lolich WS	10.00	4.50
Bob Gibson		
☐ 169 Tigers celebrate	8.00	3.60
Dick McAuliffe		
Denny McLain		
Willie Horton		
☐ 170 Frank Howard	6.00	2.70
☐ 171 Glenn Beckert	4.00	1.80
☐ 172 Jerry Stephenson	2.50	1.10
☐ 173 White Sox Rookies	2.50	1.10
Bob Christian		
Gerry Nyman		
☐ 174 Grant Jackson	2.50	1.10
☐ 175 Jim Bunning	10.00	4.50
☐ 176 Joe Azcue	2.50	1.10
☐ 177 Ron Reed	2.50	1.10
☐ 178 Ray Oyler	4.00	1.80
☐ 179 Don Pavletich	2.50	1.10
☐ 180 Willie Horton	4.00	1.80
☐ 181 Mel Nelson	2.50	1.10
☐ 182 Bill Rigney MG	2.50	1.10
☐ 183 Don Shaw	4.00	1.80
☐ 184 Roberto Pena	2.50	1.10
☐ 185 Tom Phoebus	2.50	1.10
☐ 186 John Edwards	2.50	1.10
☐ 187 Leon Wagner	2.50	1.10
☐ 188 Rick Wise	4.00	1.80
☐ 189 Red Sox Rookies	2.50	1.10
Joe Lahoud		
John Thibodeau		
☐ 190 Willie Mays	60.00	27.00
☐ 191 Lindy McDaniel	4.00	1.80
☐ 192 Jose Pagan	2.50	1.10
☐ 193 Don Cardwell	2.50	1.10
☐ 194 Ted Uhlaender	2.50	1.10
☐ 195 John Odom	4.00	1.80
☐ 196 Lum Harris MG	2.50	1.10
☐ 197 Dick Selma	2.50	1.10
☐ 198 Willie Smith	2.50	1.10
☐ 199 Jim French	2.50	1.10
☐ 200 Bob Gibson	15.00	6.75
☐ 201 Russ Snyder	2.50	1.10
☐ 202 Don Wilson	4.00	1.80
☐ 203 Dave Johnson	6.00	2.70
☐ 204 Jack Hiatt	2.50	1.10
☐ 205 Rick Reichardt	2.50	1.10
☐ 206 Phillies Rookies	4.00	1.80
Larry Hisle		
Barry Lersch		
☐ 207 Roy Face	4.00	1.80
☐ 208 Donn Clendenon	4.00	1.80
(Montreal Expos)		
☐ 209 Larry Haney UER	2.50	1.10
(Reversed negative)		
☐ 210 Felix Millan	2.50	1.10
☐ 211 Galen Cisco	2.50	1.10
☐ 212 Tom Tresh	4.00	1.80
☐ 213 Gerry Arrigo	2.50	1.10
☐ 214 Checklist 3	8.00	3.60
With 69T deckle CL		
on back (no player)		
☐ 215 Rico Petrocelli	4.00	1.80
☐ 216 Don Sutton	10.00	4.50
☐ 217 John Donaldson	2.50	1.10
☐ 218 John Roseboro	4.00	1.80

1969 O-Pee-Chee Deckle

This set is very similar to the U.S. deckle version produced by Topps. The cards measure approximately 2 1/8" by 3 1/8" (slightly smaller than the American issue) and are cut with deckle edges. The fronts feature black-and-white player photos with white borders and facsimile autographs in black ink (instead of blue ink like the Topps issue). The backs are blank. The cards are unnumbered and checklisted below in alphabetical order. Remember the prices below apply only to the O-Pee-Chee Deckle cards -- NOT to the 1969 Topps Deckle cards which are much more plentiful.

	NRMT	VG-E
COMPLETE SET (24)	200.00	90.00
COMMON CARD (1-24)	3.00	1.35
☐ 1 Richie Allen	7.50	3.40
☐ 2 Luis Aparicio	10.00	4.50
☐ 3 Rod Carew	15.00	6.75
☐ 4 Roberto Clemente	40.00	18.00
☐ 5 Curt Flood	5.00	2.20
☐ 6 Bill Freehan	5.00	2.20
☐ 7 Bob Gibson	15.00	6.75
☐ 8 Ken Harrelson	5.00	2.20
☐ 9 Tommy Helms	3.00	1.35
☐ 10 Tom Haller	3.00	1.35
☐ 11 Willie Horton	5.00	2.20
☐ 12 Frank Howard	7.50	3.40
☐ 13 Willie McCovey	15.00	6.75
☐ 14 Denny McLain	7.50	3.40
☐ 15 Juan Marichal	10.00	4.50
☐ 16 Willie Mays	30.00	13.50
☐ 17 Boog Powell	7.50	3.40
☐ 18 Brooks Robinson	15.00	6.75
☐ 19 Ron Santo	7.50	3.40
☐ 20 Rusty Staub	5.00	2.20
☐ 21 Mel Stottlemyre	3.00	1.35
☐ 22 Luis Tiant	3.00	1.35
☐ 23 Maury Wills	5.00	2.20
☐ 24 Carl Yastrzemski	15.00	6.75

1970 O-Pee-Chee

The cards in this 546-card set measure 2 1/2" by 3 1/2". This set is essentially the same as the regular 1970 Topps set, except that the words "Printed in Canada" appear on the backs and the backs are bilingual. On a gray border, the fronts feature color player photos with thin white borders. The player's name and position are printed under the photo, while the team name appears in the upper part of the picture. The horizontal backs carry player biography and statistics in French and English. The card stock is a deeper shade of yellow on the reverse for the O-Pee-Chee cards. Remember the prices below apply only to the O-Pee-Chee cards -- NOT to the 1970 Topps cards which are much more plentiful.

	NRMT	VG-E
COMPLETE SET (546)	1500.00	700.00
COMMON CARD (1-459)	1.50	.70
COMMON CARD (460-546)	2.00	.90
☐ 1 New York Mets	20.00	9.00
Team Card		
☐ 2 Diego Segui	2.00	.90
☐ 3 Darrel Chaney	1.50	.70
☐ 4 Tom Egan	1.50	.70
☐ 5 Wes Parker	2.00	.90
☐ 6 Grant Jackson	1.50	.70
☐ 7 Indians Rookies	1.50	.70
Gary Boyd		

Russ Nagelson
☐ 8 Jose Martinez 1.50 .70
☐ 9 Checklist 1-132 15.00 6.75
☐ 10 Carl Yastrzemski 18.00 8.00
☐ 11 Nate Colbert 1.50 .70
☐ 12 John Hiller 2.00 .90
☐ 13 Jack Hiatt 1.50 .70
☐ 14 Hank Allen 1.50 .70
☐ 15 Larry Dierker 1.50 .70
☐ 16 Charlie Metro MG 1.50 .70
☐ 17 Hoyt Wilhelm 6.00 2.70
☐ 18 Carlos May 2.00 .90
☐ 19 John Boccabella 1.50 .70
☐ 20 Dave McNally 2.00 .90
☐ 21 A's Rookies 6.00 2.70
Vida Blue
Gene Tenace
☐ 22 Ray Washburn 1.50 .70
☐ 23 Bill Robinson 2.00 .90
☐ 24 Dick Selma 1.50 .70
☐ 25 Cesar Tovar 1.50 .70
☐ 26 Tug McGraw 3.00 1.35
☐ 27 Chuck Hinton 1.50 .70
☐ 28 Billy Wilson 1.50 .70
☐ 29 Sandy Alomar 2.00 .90
☐ 30 Matty Alou 2.00 .90
☐ 31 Marty Pattin 2.00 .90
☐ 32 Harry Walker MG 1.50 .70
☐ 33 Don Wert 1.50 .70
☐ 34 Willie Crawford 1.50 .70
☐ 35 Joel Horlen 1.50 .70
☐ 36 Red Rookies 2.00 .90
Danny Breeden
Bernie Carbo
☐ 37 Dick Drago 1.50 .70
☐ 38 Mack Jones 1.50 .70
☐ 39 Mike Nagy 1.50 .70
☐ 40 Rich Allen 3.00 1.35
☐ 41 George Lauzerique 1.50 .70
☐ 42 Tito Fuentes 1.50 .70
☐ 43 Jack Aker 1.50 .70
☐ 44 Roberto Pena 1.50 .70
☐ 45 Dave Johnson 2.50 1.10
☐ 46 Ken Rudolph 1.50 .70
☐ 47 Bob Miller 1.50 .70
☐ 48 Gil Garrido 1.50 .70
☐ 49 Tim Cullen 1.50 .70
☐ 50 Tommie Agee 2.00 .90
☐ 51 Bob Christian 1.50 .70
☐ 52 Bruce Dal Canton 1.50 .70
☐ 53 John Kennedy 1.50 .70
☐ 54 Jeff Torborg 2.00 .90
☐ 55 John Odom 2.00 .90
☐ 56 Phillies Rookies 1.50 .70
Joe Lis
Scott Reid
☐ 57 Pat Kelly 1.50 .70
☐ 58 Dave Marshall 1.50 .70
☐ 59 Dick Ellsworth 1.50 .70
☐ 60 Jim Wynn 2.00 .90
☐ 61 NL Batting Leaders 15.00 6.75
Pete Rose
Bob Clemente
Cleon Jones
☐ 62 AL Batting Leaders 4.00 1.80
Rod Carew
Reggie Smith
Tony Oliva
☐ 63 NL RBI Leaders 4.00 1.80
Willie McCovey
Ron Santo
Tony Perez
☐ 64 AL RBI Leaders 6.00 2.70
Harmon Killebrew
Boog Powell
Reggie Jackson
☐ 65 NL Home Run Leaders 6.00 2.70
Willie McCovey
Hank Aaron
Lee May
☐ 66 AL Home Run Leaders 6.00 2.70
Harmon Killebrew
Frank Howard
Reggie Jackson
☐ 67 NL ERA Leaders 7.00 3.10
Juan Marichal
Steve Carlton
Bob Gibson
☐ 68 AL ERA Leaders 4.00 1.80
Dick Bosman
Jim Palmer
Mike Cuellar
☐ 69 NL Pitching Leaders 7.00 3.10
Tom Seaver
Phil Niekro
Fergie Jenkins
Juan Marichal
☐ 70 AL Pitching Leaders 4.00 1.80
Dennis McLain
Mike Cuellar
Dave Boswell
Dave McNally
Jim Perry
Mel Stottlemyre
☐ 71 NL Strikeout Leaders 4.00 1.80
Fergie Jenkins
Bob Gibson
Bill Singer
☐ 72 AL Strikeout Leaders 4.00 1.80
Sam McDowell
Mickey Lolich
Andy Messersmith
☐ 73 Wayne Granger 1.50 .70
☐ 74 Angels Rookies 1.50 .70
Greg Washburn
Wally Wolf
☐ 75 Jim Kaat 4.00 1.80
☐ 76 Carl Taylor 1.50 .70
☐ 77 Frank Linzy 1.50 .70
☐ 78 Joe Lahoud 1.50 .70
☐ 79 Clay Kirby 1.50 .70
☐ 80 Don Kessinger 2.00 .90
☐ 81 Dave May 1.50 .70
☐ 82 Frank Fernandez 1.50 .70
☐ 83 Don Cardwell 1.50 .70
☐ 84 Paul Casanova 1.50 .70
☐ 85 Max Alvis 1.50 .70
☐ 86 Lum Harris MG 1.50 .70
☐ 87 Steve Renko 2.00 .90
☐ 88 Pilots Rookies 2.00 .90
Miguel Fuentes
Dick Baney
☐ 89 Juan Rios 1.50 .70
☐ 90 Tim McCarver 4.00 1.80
☐ 91 Rich Morales 1.50 .70
☐ 92 George Culver 1.50 .70
☐ 93 Rick Renick 1.50 .70
☐ 94 Fred Patek 2.00 .90
☐ 95 Earl Wilson 2.00 .90
☐ 96 Cardinals Rookies 5.00 2.20
Leron Lee
Jerry Reuss
☐ 97 Joe Moeller 1.50 .70
☐ 98 Gates Brown 2.00 .90
☐ 99 Bobby Pfeil 1.50 .70
☐ 100 Mel Stottlemyre 2.00 .90
☐ 101 Bobby Floyd 1.50 .70
☐ 102 Joe Rudi 2.00 .90
☐ 103 Frank Reberger 1.50 .70
☐ 104 Gerry Moses 1.50 .70
☐ 105 Tony Gonzalez 1.50 .70
☐ 106 Darold Knowles 1.50 .70
☐ 107 Bobby Etheridge 1.50 .70
☐ 108 Tom Burgmeier 1.50 .70
☐ 109 Expos Rookies 2.00 .90
Garry Jestadt
Carl Morton
☐ 110 Bob Moose 1.50 .70
☐ 111 Mike Hegan 2.00 .90
☐ 112 Dave Nelson 1.50 .70
☐ 113 Jim Ray 1.50 .70
☐ 114 Gene Michael 2.00 .90
☐ 115 Alex Johnson 2.00 .90
☐ 116 Sparky Lyle 3.00 1.35
☐ 117 Don Young 1.50 .70
☐ 118 George Mitterwald 1.50 .70
☐ 119 Chuck Taylor 1.50 .70
☐ 120 Sal Bando 2.00 .90
☐ 121 Orioles Rookies 1.50 .70
Fred Beene
Terry Crowley
☐ 122 George Stone 1.50 .70
☐ 123 Don Gutteridge MG 1.50 .70
☐ 124 Larry Jaster 1.50 .70
☐ 125 Deron Johnson 2.00 .90
☐ 126 Marty Martinez 1.50 .70
☐ 127 Joe Coleman 1.50 .70
☐ 128 Checklist 133-263 6.00 2.70
☐ 129 Jimmie Price 1.50 .70
☐ 130 Ollie Brown 1.50 .70
☐ 131 Dodgers Rookies 2.00 .90
Ray Lamb
Bob Stinson
☐ 132 Jim McGlothlin 1.50 .70
☐ 133 Clay Carroll 1.50 .70
☐ 134 Danny Walton 1.50 .70
☐ 135 Dick Dietz 1.50 .70
☐ 136 Steve Hargan 1.50 .70
☐ 137 Art Shamsky 1.50 .70
☐ 138 Joe Foy 1.50 .70
☐ 139 Rich Nye 1.50 .70
☐ 140 Reggie Jackson 60.00 27.00
☐ 141 Pirates Rookies 2.00 .90
Dave Cash
Johnny Jeter
☐ 142 Fritz Peterson 1.50 .70
☐ 143 Phil Gagliano 1.50 .70
☐ 144 Ray Culp 1.50 .70
☐ 145 Rico Carty 2.00 .90
☐ 146 Danny Murphy 1.50 .70
☐ 147 Angel Hermoso 1.50 .70
☐ 148 Earl Weaver MG 6.00 2.70
☐ 149 Billy Champion 1.50 .70
☐ 150 Harmon Killebrew 10.00 4.50
☐ 151 Dave Roberts 1.50 .70
☐ 152 Ike Brown 1.50 .70
☐ 153 Gary Gentry 1.50 .70
☐ 154 Senators Rookies 1.50 .70
Jim Miles
Jan Dukes
☐ 155 Denis Menke 1.50 .70
☐ 156 Eddie Fisher 1.50 .70
☐ 157 Manny Mota 2.50 1.10
☐ 158 Jerry McNertney 2.00 .90
☐ 159 Tommy Helms 2.00 .90
☐ 160 Phil Niekro 5.00 2.20
☐ 161 Richie Scheinblum 1.50 .70
☐ 162 Jerry Johnson 1.50 .70
☐ 163 Syd O'Brien 1.50 .70
☐ 164 Ty Cline 1.50 .70
☐ 165 Ed Kirkpatrick 1.50 .70
☐ 166 Al Oliver 4.00 1.80
☐ 167 Bill Burbach 1.50 .70
☐ 168 Dave Watkins 1.50 .70
☐ 169 Tom Hall 1.50 .70
☐ 170 Billy Williams 7.50 3.40
☐ 171 Jim Nash 1.50 .70
☐ 172 Braves Rookies 3.00 1.35
Garry Hill
Ralph Garr
☐ 173 Jim Hicks 1.50 .70
☐ 174 Ted Sizemore 2.00 .90
☐ 175 Dick Bosman 1.50 .70
☐ 176 Jim Ray Hart 2.00 .90
☐ 177 Jim Northrup 2.00 .90
☐ 178 Denny LeMaster 1.50 .70
☐ 179 Ivan Murrell 1.50 .70
☐ 180 Tommy John 4.00 1.80
☐ 181 Sparky Anderson MG 6.00 2.70
☐ 182 Dick Hall 1.50 .70
☐ 183 Jerry Grote 2.00 .90
☐ 184 Ray Fosse 2.00 .90
☐ 185 Don Mincher 2.00 .90
☐ 186 Rick Joseph 1.50 .70
☐ 187 Mike Hedlund 1.50 .70
☐ 188 Manny Sanguillen 2.00 .90
☐ 189 Yankees Rookies 60.00 27.00
Thurman Munson
Dave McDonald
☐ 190 Joe Torre 3.00 1.35
☐ 191 Vicente Romo 1.50 .70
☐ 192 Jim Qualls 1.50 .70
☐ 193 Mike Wegener 1.50 .70
☐ 194 Chuck Manuel 1.50 .70
☐ 195 Tom Seaver NLCS 20.00 9.00
☐ 196 Ken Boswell NLCS 3.00 1.35
☐ 197 Nolan Ryan NLCS 40.00 18.00
☐ 198 Mets Celebrate 20.00 9.00
Includes Nolan Ryan
Tommie Agee
Wayne Garrett
☐ 199 Mike Cuellar ALCS 3.00 1.35
☐ 200 Boog Powell ALCS 4.00 1.80
☐ 201 Boog Powell ALCS 3.00 1.35
Andy Etchebarren
☐ 202 AL Playoff Summary 3.00 1.35
Orioles celebrate
☐ 203 Rudy May 1.50 .70
☐ 204 Len Gabrielson 1.50 .70
☐ 205 Bert Campaneris 2.50 1.10
☐ 206 Clete Boyer 2.00 .90
☐ 207 Tigers Rookies 1.50 .70
Norman McRae
Bob Reed
☐ 208 Fred Gladding 1.50 .70
☐ 209 Ken Suarez 1.50 .70
☐ 210 Juan Marichal 7.50 3.40
☐ 211 Ted Williams MG 15.00 6.75
☐ 212 Al Santorini 1.50 .70
☐ 213 Andy Etchebarren 1.50 .70
☐ 214 Ken Boswell 1.50 .70
☐ 215 Reggie Smith 3.00 1.35
☐ 216 Chuck Hartenstein 1.50 .70
☐ 217 Ron Hansen 1.50 .70
☐ 218 Ron Stone 1.50 .70
☐ 219 Jerry Kenney 1.50 .70
☐ 220 Steve Carlton 18.00 8.00
☐ 221 Ron Brand 1.50 .70
☐ 222 Jim Rooker 1.50 .70
☐ 223 Nate Oliver 1.50 .70
☐ 224 Steve Barber 2.00 .90
☐ 225 Lee May 2.50 1.10
☐ 226 Ron Perranoski 2.00 .90

☐ 227 Astros Rookies 2.50 1.10
John Mayberry
Bob Watkins
☐ 228 Aurelio Rodriguez 2.00 .90
☐ 229 Rich Robertson 1.50 .70
☐ 230 Brooks Robinson 18.00 8.00
☐ 231 Luis Tiant 3.00 1.35
☐ 232 Bob Didier 1.50 .70
☐ 233 Lew Krausse 1.50 .70
☐ 234 Tommy Dean 1.50 .70
☐ 235 Mike Epstein 1.50 .70
☐ 236 Bob Veale 1.50 .70
☐ 237 Russ Gibson 1.50 .70
☐ 238 Jose Laboy 1.50 .70
☐ 239 Ken Berry 1.50 .70
☐ 240 Fergie Jenkins 7.50 3.40
☐ 241 Royals Rookies 1.50 .70
Al Fitzmorris
Scott Northey
☐ 242 Walter Alston MG 3.00 1.35
☐ 243 Joe Sparma 2.00 .90
☐ 244 Checklist 264-372 6.00 2.70
☐ 245 Leo Cardenas 1.50 .70
☐ 246 Jim McAndrew 1.50 .70
☐ 247 Lou Klimchock 1.50 .70
☐ 248 Jesus Alou 1.50 .70
☐ 249 Bob Locker 1.50 .70
☐ 250 Willie McCovey 12.50 5.50
☐ 251 Dick Schofield 1.50 .70
☐ 252 Lowell Palmer 1.50 .70
☐ 253 Ron Woods 1.50 .70
☐ 254 Camilo Pascual 2.00 .90
☐ 255 Jim Spencer 1.50 .70
☐ 256 Vic Davalillo 1.50 .70
☐ 257 Dennis Higgins 1.50 .70
☐ 258 Paul Popovich 1.50 .70
☐ 259 Tommie Reynolds 1.50 .70
☐ 260 Claude Osteen 2.00 .90
☐ 261 Curt Motton 1.50 .70
☐ 262 Twins Rookies 1.50 .70
Jerry Morales
Jim Williams
☐ 263 Duane Josephson 2.00 .90
☐ 264 Rich Hebner 2.00 .90
☐ 265 Randy Hundley 1.50 .70
☐ 266 Wally Bunker 1.50 .70
☐ 267 Twins Rookies 1.50 .70
Herman Hill
Paul Ratliff
☐ 268 Claude Raymond 1.50 .70
☐ 269 Cesar Gutierrez 1.50 .70
☐ 270 Chris Short 1.50 .70
☐ 271 Greg Goossen 2.00 .90
☐ 272 Hector Torres 1.50 .70
☐ 273 Ralph Houk MG 2.00 .90
☐ 274 Gerry Arrigo 1.50 .70
☐ 275 Duke Sims 1.50 .70
☐ 276 Ron Hunt 1.50 .70
☐ 277 Paul Doyle 1.50 .70
☐ 278 Tommie Aaron 2.00 .90
☐ 279 Bill Lee 3.00 1.35
☐ 280 Donn Clendenon 2.00 .90
☐ 281 Casey Cox 1.50 .70
☐ 282 Steve Huntz 1.50 .70
☐ 283 Angel Bravo 1.50 .70
☐ 284 Jack Baldschun 1.50 .70
☐ 285 Paul Blair 2.00 .90
☐ 286 Dodgers Rookies 6.00 2.70
Jack Jenkins
Bill Buckner
☐ 287 Fred Talbot 1.50 .70
☐ 288 Larry Hisle 2.00 .90
☐ 289 Gene Brabender 1.50 .70
☐ 290 Rod Carew 20.00 9.00
☐ 291 Leo Durocher MG 4.00 1.80
☐ 292 Eddie Leon 1.50 .70
☐ 293 Bob Bailey 2.00 .90
☐ 294 Jose Azcue 1.50 .70
☐ 295 Cecil Upshaw 1.50 .70
☐ 296 Woody Woodward 1.50 .70
☐ 297 Curt Blefary 1.50 .70
☐ 298 Ken Henderson 1.50 .70
☐ 299 Buddy Bradford 1.50 .70
☐ 300 Tom Seaver 50.00 22.00
☐ 301 Chico Salmon 1.50 .70
☐ 302 Jeff James 1.50 .70
☐ 303 Brant Alyea 1.50 .70
☐ 304 Bill Russell 6.00 2.70
☐ 305 Don Buford WS 3.00 1.35
☐ 306 Donn Clendenon WS 3.00 1.35
☐ 307 Tommie Agee WS 3.00 1.35
☐ 308 J.C. Martin WS 3.00 1.35
☐ 309 Jerry Koosman WS 4.00 1.80
☐ 310 World Series Celebration 5.00 2.20
Includes Ed Kranepool
Tug McGraw
Ed Charles

☐ 311 Dick Green 1.50 .70
☐ 312 Mike Torrez 2.00 .90
☐ 313 Mayo Smith MG 1.50 .70
☐ 314 Bill McCool 1.50 .70
☐ 315 Luis Aparicio 5.00 2.20
☐ 316 Skip Guinn 1.50 .70
☐ 317 Red Sox Rookies 2.00 .90
Billy Conigliaro
Luis Alvarado
☐ 318 Willie Smith 1.50 .70
☐ 319 Clay Dalrymple 1.50 .70
☐ 320 Jim Maloney 2.00 .90
☐ 321 Lou Piniella 3.00 1.35
☐ 322 Luke Walker 1.50 .70
☐ 323 Wayne Comer 1.50 .70
☐ 324 Tony Taylor 2.00 .90
☐ 325 Dave Boswell 1.50 .70
☐ 326 Bill Voss 1.50 .70
☐ 327 Hal King 1.50 .70
☐ 328 George Brunet 1.50 .70
☐ 329 Chris Cannizzaro 1.50 .70
☐ 330 Lou Brock 12.00 5.50
☐ 331 Chuck Dobson 1.50 .70
☐ 332 Bobby Wine 2.00 .90
☐ 333 Bobby Murcer 3.00 1.35
☐ 334 Phil Regan 1.50 .70
☐ 335 Bill Freehan 2.00 .90
☐ 336 Del Unser 2.00 .90
☐ 337 Mike McCormick 2.00 .90
☐ 338 Paul Schaal 1.50 .70
☐ 339 Johnny Edwards 1.50 .70
☐ 340 Tony Conigliaro 4.00 1.80
☐ 341 Bill Sudakis 1.50 .70
☐ 342 Wilbur Wood 2.00 .90
☐ 343 Checklist 373-459 6.00 2.70
☐ 344 Marcelino Lopez 1.50 .70
☐ 345 Al Ferrara 1.50 .70
☐ 346 Red Schoendienst MG 3.00 1.35
☐ 347 Russ Snyder 1.50 .70
☐ 348 Mets Rookies 2.00 .90
Mike Jorgensen
Jesse Hudson
☐ 349 Steve Hamilton 1.50 .70
☐ 350 Roberto Clemente 90.00 40.00
☐ 351 Tom Murphy 1.50 .70
☐ 352 Bob Barton 1.50 .70
☐ 353 Stan Williams 1.50 .70
☐ 354 Amos Otis 2.50 1.10
☐ 355 Doug Rader 2.00 .90
☐ 356 Fred Lasher 1.50 .70
☐ 357 Bob Burda 1.50 .70
☐ 358 Pedro Borbon 2.50 1.10
☐ 359 Phil Roof 1.50 .70
☐ 360 Curt Flood 3.00 1.35
☐ 361 Ray Jarvis 1.50 .70
☐ 362 Joe Hague 1.50 .70
☐ 363 Tom Shopay 1.50 .70
☐ 364 Dan McGinn 1.50 .70
☐ 365 Zoilo Versalles 2.00 .90
☐ 366 Barry Moore 1.50 .70
☐ 367 Mike Lum 1.50 .70
☐ 368 Ed Herrmann 1.50 .70
☐ 369 Alan Foster 1.50 .70
☐ 370 Tommy Harper 2.00 .90
☐ 371 Rod Gaspar 1.50 .70
☐ 372 Dave Giusti 1.50 .70
☐ 373 Roy White 2.00 .90
☐ 374 Tommie Sisk 1.50 .70
☐ 375 Johnny Callison 2.50 1.10
☐ 376 Lefty Phillips MG 1.50 .70
☐ 377 Bill Butler 1.50 .70
☐ 378 Jim Davenport 1.50 .70
☐ 379 Tom Tischinski 1.50 .70
☐ 380 Tony Perez 7.50 3.40
☐ 381 Athletics Rookies 1.50 .70
Bobby Brooks
Mike Olivo
☐ 382 Jack DiLauro 1.50 .70
☐ 383 Mickey Stanley 2.00 .90
☐ 384 Gary Neibauer 1.50 .70
☐ 385 George Scott 2.00 .90
☐ 386 Bill Dillman 1.50 .70
☐ 387 Orioles Team 4.00 1.80
☐ 388 Byron Browne 1.50 .70
☐ 389 Jim Shellenback 1.50 .70
☐ 390 Willie Davis 2.50 1.10
☐ 391 Larry Brown 1.50 .70
☐ 392 Walt Hriniak 2.00 .90
☐ 393 John Gelnar 1.50 .70
☐ 394 Gil Hodges MG 5.00 2.20
☐ 395 Walt Williams 1.50 .70
☐ 396 Steve Blass 2.00 .90
☐ 397 Roger Repoz 1.50 .70
☐ 398 Bill Stoneman 1.50 .70
☐ 399 Yankees Team 4.00 1.80
☐ 400 Denny McLain 3.00 1.35
☐ 401 Giants Rookies 1.50 .70

John Harrell
Bernie Williams
☐ 402 Ellie Rodriguez 1.50 .70
☐ 403 Jim Bunning 4.00 1.80
☐ 404 Rich Reese 1.50 .70
☐ 405 Bill Hands 1.50 .70
☐ 406 Mike Andrews 1.50 .70
☐ 407 Bob Watson 2.50 1.10
☐ 408 Paul Lindblad 1.50 .70
☐ 409 Bob Tolan 1.50 .70
☐ 410 Boog Powell 4.00 1.80
☐ 411 Dodgers Team 4.00 1.80
☐ 412 Larry Burchart 1.50 .70
☐ 413 Sonny Jackson 1.50 .70
☐ 414 Paul Edmondson 1.50 .70
☐ 415 Julian Javier 2.00 .90
☐ 416 Joe Verbanic 1.50 .70
☐ 417 John Bateman 1.50 .70
☐ 418 John Donaldson 1.50 .70
☐ 419 Ron Taylor 2.00 .90
☐ 420 Ken McMullen 2.00 .90
☐ 421 Pat Dobson 2.00 .90
☐ 422 Royals Team 3.00 1.35
☐ 423 Jerry May 1.50 .70
☐ 424 Mike Kilkenny 1.50 .70
☐ 425 Bobby Bonds 6.00 2.70
☐ 426 Bill Rigney MG 1.50 .70
☐ 427 Fred Norman 1.50 .70
☐ 428 Don Buford 1.50 .70
☐ 429 Cubs Rookies 1.50 .70
Randy Bobb
Jim Cosman
☐ 430 Andy Messersmith 2.00 .90
☐ 431 Ron Swoboda 1.50 .70
☐ 432 Checklist 460-546 6.00 2.70
☐ 433 Ron Bryant 1.50 .70
☐ 434 Felipe Alou 2.50 1.10
☐ 435 Nelson Briles 2.00 .90
☐ 436 Phillies Team 3.00 1.35
☐ 437 Danny Cater 1.50 .70
☐ 438 Pat Jarvis 1.50 .70
☐ 439 Lee Maye 1.50 .70
☐ 440 Bill Mazeroski 3.00 1.35
☐ 441 John O'Donoghue 1.50 .70
☐ 442 Gene Mauch MG 2.00 .90
☐ 443 Al Jackson 1.50 .70
☐ 444 White Sox Rookies 1.50 .70
Billy Farmer
John Matias
☐ 445 Vada Pinson 3.00 1.35
☐ 446 Billy Grabarkewitz 1.50 .70
☐ 447 Lee Stange 1.50 .70
☐ 448 Astros Team 3.00 1.35
☐ 449 Jim Palmer 15.00 6.75
☐ 450 Willie McCovey AS 7.50 3.40
☐ 451 Boog Powell AS 4.00 1.80
☐ 452 Felix Millan AS 3.00 1.35
☐ 453 Rod Carew AS 7.50 3.40
☐ 454 Ron Santo AS 4.00 1.80
☐ 455 Brooks Robinson AS 7.50 3.40
☐ 456 Don Kessinger AS 3.50 1.55
☐ 457 Rico Petrocelli AS 3.50 1.55
☐ 458 Pete Rose AS 18.00 8.00
☐ 459 Reggie Jackson AS 18.00 8.00
☐ 460 Matty Alou AS 4.00 1.80
☐ 461 Carl Yastrzemski AS 12.50 5.50
☐ 462 Hank Aaron AS 18.00 8.00
☐ 463 Frank Robinson AS 8.00 3.60
☐ 464 Johnny Bench AS 18.00 8.00
☐ 465 Bill Freehan AS 5.00 2.20
☐ 466 Juan Marichal AS 6.00 2.70
☐ 467 Denny McLain AS 5.00 2.20
☐ 468 Jerry Koosman AS 5.00 2.20
☐ 469 Sam McDowell AS 5.00 2.20
☐ 470 Willie Stargell 12.00 5.50
☐ 471 Chris Zachary 2.00 .90
☐ 472 Braves Team 4.00 1.80
☐ 473 Don Bryant 2.00 .90
☐ 474 Dick Kelley 2.00 .90
☐ 475 Dick McAuliffe 3.00 1.35
☐ 476 Don Shaw 2.00 .90
☐ 477 Orioles Rookies 2.00 .90
Al Severinsen
Roger Freed
☐ 478 Bob Heise 2.00 .90
☐ 479 Dick Woodson 2.00 .90
☐ 480 Glenn Beckert 2.00 .90
☐ 481 Jose Tartabull 2.00 .90
☐ 482 Tom Hilgendorf 2.00 .90
☐ 483 Gail Hopkins 2.00 .90
☐ 484 Gary Nolan 3.00 1.35
☐ 485 Jay Johnstone 3.00 1.35
☐ 486 Terry Harmon 2.00 .90
☐ 487 Cisco Carlos 2.00 .90
☐ 488 J.C. Martin 2.00 .90
☐ 489 Eddie Kasko MG 2.00 .90
☐ 490 Bill Singer 2.50 1.10
☐ 491 Graig Nettles 7.50 3.40

Card	NRMT	VG-E
☐ 492 Astros Rookies	2.00	.90
Keith Lampard		
Scipio Spinks		
☐ 493 Lindy McDaniel	2.50	1.10
☐ 494 Larry Stahl	2.00	.90
☐ 495 Dave Morehead	2.00	.90
☐ 496 Steve Whitaker	2.00	.90
☐ 497 Eddie Watt	2.00	.90
☐ 498 Al Weis	2.00	.90
☐ 499 Skip Lockwood	2.00	.90
☐ 500 Hank Aaron	70.00	32.00
☐ 501 White Sox Team	4.00	1.80
☐ 502 Rollie Fingers	12.50	5.50
☐ 503 Dal Maxvill	2.00	.90
☐ 504 Don Pavletich	2.00	.90
☐ 505 Ken Holtzman	3.00	1.35
☐ 506 Ed Stroud	2.00	.90
☐ 507 Pat Corrales	2.00	.90
☐ 508 Joe Niekro	2.50	1.10
☐ 509 Expos Team	4.00	1.80
☐ 510 Tony Oliva	5.00	2.20
☐ 511 Joe Hoerner	2.00	.90
☐ 512 Billy Harris	2.00	.90
☐ 513 Preston Gomez MG	2.00	.90
☐ 514 Steve Hovley	2.00	.90
☐ 515 Don Wilson	2.00	.90
☐ 516 Yankees Rookies	2.00	.90
John Ellis		
Jim Lyttle		
☐ 517 Joe Gibbon	2.00	.90
☐ 518 Bill Melton	2.00	.90
☐ 519 Don McMahon	2.00	.90
☐ 520 Willie Horton	3.00	1.35
☐ 521 Cal Koonce	2.00	.90
☐ 522 Angels Team	4.00	1.80
☐ 523 Jose Pena	2.00	.90
☐ 524 Alvin Dark MG	3.00	1.35
☐ 525 Jerry Adair	2.00	.90
☐ 526 Ron Herbel	2.00	.90
☐ 527 Don Bosch	2.00	.90
☐ 528 Elrod Hendricks	3.00	1.35
☐ 529 Bob Aspromonte	2.00	.90
☐ 530 Bob Gibson	18.00	8.00
☐ 531 Ron Clark	2.00	.90
☐ 532 Danny Murtaugh MG	3.00	1.35
☐ 533 Buzz Stephen	2.00	.90
☐ 534 Twins Team	4.00	1.80
☐ 535 Andy Kosco	2.00	.90
☐ 536 Mike Kekich	2.00	.90
☐ 537 Joe Morgan	12.50	5.50
☐ 538 Bob Humphreys	2.00	.90
☐ 539 Phillies Rookies	6.00	2.70
Denny Doyle		
Larry Bowa		
☐ 540 Gary Peters	2.00	.90
☐ 541 Bill Heath	2.00	.90
☐ 542 Checklist 547-633	6.00	2.70
☐ 543 Clyde Wright	2.00	.90
☐ 544 Reds Team	5.00	2.20
☐ 545 Ken Harrelson	3.00	1.35
☐ 546 Ron Reed	3.00	1.35

1971 O-Pee-Chee

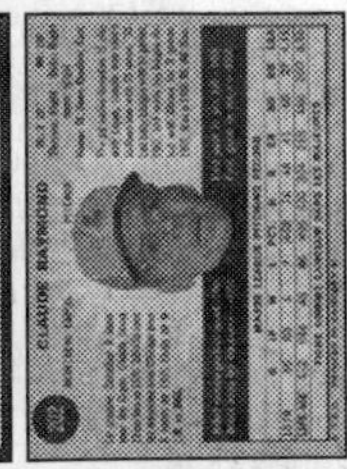

The cards in this 752-card set measure 2 1/2" by 3 1/2". The 1971 O-Pee-Chee set is a challenge to complete in "Mint" condition because the black borders are easily scratched and damaged. The O-Pee-Chee cards seem to have been cut (into individual cards) not as sharply as the Topps cards; the borders frequently appear slightly frayed. The players are also pictured in black and white on the back of the card. The next-to-last series (524-643) and the last series (644-752) are somewhat scarce. The O-Pee-Chee cards can be distinguished from Topps cards by the "Printed in Canada" on the bottom of the reverse. The reverse color is yellow instead of the green found on the backs of the 1971 Topps cards. The card backs are written in both French and English, except for cards 524-752 which were printed in English only. There are several cards which are different from the corresponding Topps card with a different pose or different team noted in bold type, i.e. "Recently Traded to ..." These changed cards are numbers 31, 32, 73, 144, 151, 161, 172, 182, 191, 202, 207, 248, 289 and 578. Remember, the prices below apply only to the 1971 O-Pee-Chee cards -- NOT Topps cards which are much more plentiful.

	NRMT	VG-E
COMPLETE SET (752)	2750.00	1250.00
COMMON CARD (1-393)	2.00	.90
COMMON CARD (394-523)	2.50	1.10
COMMON CARD (524-643)	5.00	2.20
COMMON CARD (644-752)	10.00	4.50

Card	NRMT	VG-E
☐ 1 Orioles Team	18.00	8.00
☐ 2 Dock Ellis	2.50	1.10
☐ 3 Dick McAuliffe	2.50	1.10
☐ 4 Vic Davalillo	2.00	.90
☐ 5 Thurman Munson	20.00	9.00
☐ 6 Ed Spiezio	2.00	.90
☐ 7 Jim Holt	2.00	.90
☐ 8 Mike McQueen	2.00	.90
☐ 9 George Scott	2.50	1.10
☐ 10 Claude Osteen	2.50	1.10
☐ 11 Elliott Maddox	2.50	1.10
☐ 12 Johnny Callison	2.50	1.10
☐ 13 White Sox Rookies	2.00	.90
Charlie Brinkman		
Dick Moloney		
☐ 14 Dave Concepcion	20.00	9.00
☐ 15 Andy Messersmith	2.50	1.10
☐ 16 Ken Singleton	4.00	1.80
☐ 17 Billy Sorrell	2.00	.90
☐ 18 Norm Miller	2.00	.90
☐ 19 Skip Pitlock	2.00	.90
☐ 20 Reggie Jackson	30.00	13.50
☐ 21 Dan McGinn	2.00	.90
☐ 22 Phil Roof	2.00	.90
☐ 23 Oscar Gamble	2.50	1.10
☐ 24 Rich Hand	2.00	.90
☐ 25 Clarence Gaston	3.00	1.35
☐ 26 Bert Blyleven	10.00	4.50
☐ 27 Pirates Rookies	2.00	.90
Fred Cambria		
Gene Clines		
☐ 28 Ron Klimkowski	2.00	.90
☐ 29 Don Buford	2.00	.90
☐ 30 Phil Niekro	5.00	2.20
☐ 31 John Bateman	2.50	1.10
(different pose)		
☐ 32 Jerry DeVanon	2.50	1.10
Recently Traded To Orioles		
☐ 33 Del Unser	2.00	.90
☐ 34 Sandy Vance	2.00	.90
☐ 35 Lou Piniella	3.00	1.35
☐ 36 Dean Chance	2.50	1.10
☐ 37 Rich McKinney	2.00	.90
☐ 38 Jim Colborn	2.00	.90
☐ 39 Tiger Rookies	2.00	.90
Lerrin LaGrow		
Gene Lamont		
☐ 40 Lee May	2.50	1.10
☐ 41 Rick Austin	2.00	.90
☐ 42 Boots Day	2.50	1.10
☐ 43 Steve Kealey	2.00	.90
☐ 44 Johnny Edwards	2.00	.90
☐ 45 Jim Hunter	7.00	3.10
☐ 46 Dave Campbell	2.50	1.10
☐ 47 Johnny Jeter	2.00	.90
☐ 48 Dave Baldwin	2.00	.90
☐ 49 Don Money	2.50	1.10
☐ 50 Willie McCovey	10.00	4.50
☐ 51 Steve Kline	2.00	.90
☐ 52 Braves Rookies	2.00	.90
Oscar Brown		
Earl Williams		
☐ 53 Paul Blair	2.50	1.10
☐ 54 Checklist 1-132	6.00	2.70
☐ 55 Steve Carlton	18.00	8.00
☐ 56 Duane Josephson	2.00	.90
☐ 57 Von Joshua	2.00	.90
☐ 58 Bill Lee	2.50	1.10
☐ 59 Gene Mauch MG	2.50	1.10
☐ 60 Dick Bosman	2.00	.90
☐ 61 AL Batting Leaders	4.00	1.80
Alex Johnson		
Carl Yastrzemski		
Tony Oliva		
☐ 62 NL Batting Leaders	3.00	1.35
Rico Carty		
Joe Torre		
Manny Sanguillen		
☐ 63 AL RBI Leaders	4.00	1.80
Frank Robinson		
Tony Conigliaro		
Boog Powell		
☐ 64 NL RBI Leaders	6.00	2.70
Johnny Bench		
Tony Perez		
Billy Williams		
☐ 65 AL HR Leaders	4.00	1.80
Frank Howard		
Harmon Killebrew		
Carl Yastrzemski		
☐ 66 NL HR Leaders	6.00	2.70
Johnny Bench		
Billy Williams		
Tony Perez		
☐ 67 AL ERA Leaders	4.00	1.80
Diego Segui		
Jim Palmer		
Clyde Wright		
☐ 68 NL ERA Leaders	4.00	1.80
Tom Seaver		
Wayne Simpson		
Luke Walker		
☐ 69 AL Pitching Leaders	3.00	1.35
Mike Cuellar		
Dave McNally		
Jim Perry		
☐ 70 NL Pitching Leaders	6.00	2.70
Bob Gibson		
Gaylord Perry		
Fergie Jenkins		
☐ 71 AL Strikeout Leaders	3.00	1.35
Sam McDowell		
Mickey Lolich		
Bob Johnson		
☐ 72 NL Strikeout Leaders	7.00	3.10
Tom Seaver		
Bob Gibson		
Fergie Jenkins		
☐ 73 George Brunet	2.00	.90
(St. Louis Cardinals)		
☐ 74 Twins Rookies	2.00	.90
Pete Hamm		
Jim Nettles		
☐ 75 Gary Nolan	2.50	1.10
☐ 76 Ted Savage	2.00	.90
☐ 77 Mike Compton	2.00	.90
☐ 78 Jim Spencer	2.00	.90
☐ 79 Wade Blasingame	2.00	.90
☐ 80 Bill Melton	2.00	.90
☐ 81 Felix Millan	2.00	.90
☐ 82 Casey Cox	2.00	.90
☐ 83 Met Rookies	2.50	1.10
Tim Foli		
Randy Bobb		
☐ 84 Marcel Lachemann	2.50	1.10
☐ 85 Bill Grabarkewitz	2.00	.90
☐ 86 Mike Kilkenny	2.00	.90
☐ 87 Jack Heidemann	2.00	.90
☐ 88 Hal King	2.00	.90
☐ 89 Ken Brett	2.50	1.10
☐ 90 Joe Pepitone	2.50	1.10
☐ 91 Bob Lemon MG	3.00	1.35
☐ 92 Fred Wenz	2.00	.90
☐ 93 Senators Rookies	2.00	.90
Norm McRae		
Denny Riddleberger		
☐ 94 Don Hahn	2.00	.90
☐ 95 Luis Tiant	2.50	1.10
☐ 96 Joe Hague	2.00	.90
☐ 97 Floyd Wicker	2.00	.90
☐ 98 Joe Decker	2.00	.90
☐ 99 Mark Belanger	2.50	1.10
☐ 100 Pete Rose	30.00	13.50
☐ 101 Les Cain	2.00	.90
☐ 102 Astros Rookies	2.50	1.10
Ken Forsch		
Larry Howard		
☐ 103 Rich Severson	2.00	.90
☐ 104 Dan Frisella	2.00	.90
☐ 105 Tony Conigliaro	3.00	1.35
☐ 106 Tom Dukes	2.00	.90
☐ 107 Roy Foster	2.00	.90
☐ 108 John Cumberland	2.00	.90
☐ 109 Steve Hovley	2.00	.90
☐ 110 Bill Mazeroski	3.00	1.35
☐ 111 Yankee Rookies	2.50	1.10
Loyd Colson		
Bobby Mitchell		
☐ 112 Manny Mota	2.50	1.10
☐ 113 Jerry Crider	2.00	.90
☐ 114 Billy Conigliaro	2.00	.90
☐ 115 Donn Clendenon	2.50	1.10
☐ 116 Ken Sanders	2.00	.90
☐ 117 Ted Simmons	15.00	6.75
☐ 118 Cookie Rojas	2.50	1.10
☐ 119 Frank Lucchesi MG	2.00	.90
☐ 120 Willie Horton	2.50	1.10
☐ 121 Cubs Rookies	2.00	.90
Jim Dunegan		
Roe Skidmore		
☐ 122 Eddie Watt	2.00	.90
☐ 123 Checklist 133-263	6.00	2.70
☐ 124 Don Gullett	3.00	1.35

☐ 125 Ray Fosse	2.50	1.10
☐ 126 Danny Coombs	2.00	.90
☐ 127 Danny Thompson	2.00	.90
☐ 128 Frank Johnson	2.00	.90
☐ 129 Aurelio Monteagudo	2.00	.90
☐ 130 Denis Menke	2.00	.90
☐ 131 Curt Blefary	2.00	.90
☐ 132 Jose Laboy	2.00	.90
☐ 133 Mickey Lolich	2.50	1.10
☐ 134 Jose Arcia	2.00	.90
☐ 135 Rick Monday	2.50	1.10
☐ 136 Duffy Dyer	2.00	.90
☐ 137 Marcelino Lopez	2.00	.90
☐ 138 Phillies Rookies	2.50	1.10
Joe Lis		
Willie Montanez		
☐ 139 Paul Casanova	2.00	.90
☐ 140 Gaylord Perry	8.00	3.60
☐ 141 Frank Quilici MG	2.00	.90
☐ 142 Mack Jones	2.00	.90
☐ 143 Steve Blass	2.50	1.10
☐ 144 Jackie Hernandez	2.50	1.10
(Pittsburgh Pirates)		
☐ 145 Bill Singer	2.50	1.10
☐ 146 Ralph Houk MG	2.50	1.10
☐ 147 Bob Priddy	2.00	.90
☐ 148 John Mayberry	2.50	1.10
☐ 149 Mike Hershberger	2.00	.90
☐ 150 Sam McDowell	2.50	1.10
☐ 151 Tommy Davis	3.00	1.35
(Oakland A's)		
☐ 152 Angels Rookies	2.00	.90
Lloyd Allen		
Winston Llenas		
☐ 153 Gary Ross	2.00	.90
☐ 154 Cesar Gutierrez	2.00	.90
☐ 155 Ken Henderson	2.00	.90
☐ 156 Bart Johnson	2.00	.90
☐ 157 Bob Bailey	2.50	1.10
☐ 158 Jerry Reuss	2.50	1.10
☐ 159 Jarvis Tatum	2.00	.90
☐ 160 Tom Seaver	25.00	11.00
☐ 161 Ron Hunt	4.00	1.80
(different pose)		
☐ 162 Jack Billingham	2.50	1.10
☐ 163 Buck Martinez	2.00	.90
☐ 164 Reds Rookies	2.50	1.10
Frank Duffy		
Milt Wilcox		
☐ 165 Cesar Tovar	2.00	.90
☐ 166 Joe Hoerner	2.00	.90
☐ 167 Tom Grieve	2.50	1.10
☐ 168 Bruce Dal Canton	2.00	.90
☐ 169 Ed Herrmann	2.00	.90
☐ 170 Mike Cuellar	2.50	1.10
☐ 171 Bobby Wine	2.00	.90
☐ 172 Duke Sims	2.50	1.10
(Los Angeles Dodgers)		
☐ 173 Gil Garrido	2.00	.90
☐ 174 Dave LaRoche	2.00	.90
☐ 175 Jim Hickman	2.00	.90
☐ 176 Red Sox Rookies	2.50	1.10
Bob Montgomery		
Doug Griffin		
☐ 177 Hal McRae	3.00	1.35
☐ 178 Dave Duncan	2.00	.90
☐ 179 Mike Corkins	2.00	.90
☐ 180 Al Kaline	20.00	9.00
☐ 181 Hal Lanier	2.50	1.10
☐ 182 Al Downing	2.50	1.10
(Los Angeles Dodgers)		
☐ 183 Gil Hodges MG	5.00	2.20
☐ 184 Stan Bahnsen	2.00	.90
☐ 185 Julian Javier	2.00	.90
☐ 186 Bob Spence	2.00	.90
☐ 187 Ted Abernathy	2.00	.90
☐ 188 Dodgers Rookies	4.00	1.80
Bob Valentine		
Mike Strahler		
☐ 189 George Mitterwald	2.00	.90
☐ 190 Bob Tolan	2.50	1.10
☐ 191 Mike Andrews	2.50	1.10
(Chicago White Sox)		
☐ 192 Billy Wilson	2.00	.90
☐ 193 Bob Grich	4.00	1.80
☐ 194 Mike Lum	2.50	1.10
☐ 195 Boog Powell ALCS	4.00	1.80
☐ 196 Dave McNally ALCS	4.00	1.80
☐ 197 Jim Palmer ALCS	5.00	2.20
☐ 198 AL Playoff Summary	4.00	1.80
Orioles Celebrate		
☐ 199 Ty Cline NLCS	4.00	1.80
☐ 200 Bobby Tolan NLCS	4.00	1.80
☐ 201 Ty Cline NLCS	4.00	1.80
☐ 202 Claude Raymond	2.50	1.10
(different pose)		
☐ 203 Larry Gura	2.50	1.10
☐ 204 Brewers Rookies	2.00	.90
Bernie Smith		
George Kopacz		
☐ 205 Gerry Moses	2.00	.90
☐ 206 Checklist 264-393	6.00	2.70
☐ 207 Alan Foster	2.50	1.10
(Cleveland Indians)		
☐ 208 Billy Martin MG	4.00	1.80
☐ 209 Steve Renko	2.50	1.10
☐ 210 Rod Carew	20.00	9.00
☐ 211 Phil Hennigan	2.00	.90
☐ 212 Rich Hebner	2.50	1.10
☐ 213 Frank Baker	2.00	.90
☐ 214 Al Ferrara	2.00	.90
☐ 215 Diego Segui	2.00	.90
☐ 216 Cardinals Rookies	2.00	.90
Reggie Cleveland		
Luis Melendez		
☐ 217 Ed Stroud	2.00	.90
☐ 218 Tony Cloninger	2.00	.90
☐ 219 Elrod Hendricks	2.00	.90
☐ 220 Ron Santo	3.00	1.35
☐ 221 Dave Morehead	2.00	.90
☐ 222 Bob Watson	2.50	1.10
☐ 223 Cecil Upshaw	2.00	.90
☐ 224 Alan Gallagher	2.00	.90
☐ 225 Gary Peters	2.00	.90
☐ 226 Bill Russell	2.50	1.10
☐ 227 Floyd Weaver	2.00	.90
☐ 228 Wayne Garrett	2.00	.90
☐ 229 Jim Hannan	2.00	.90
☐ 230 Willie Stargell	10.00	4.50
☐ 231 Indians Rookies	2.50	1.10
Vince Colbert		
John Lowenstein		
☐ 232 John Strohmayer	2.00	.90
☐ 233 Larry Bowa	3.00	1.35
☐ 234 Jim Lyttle	2.00	.90
☐ 235 Nate Colbert	2.50	1.10
☐ 236 Bob Humphreys	2.00	.90
☐ 237 Cesar Cedeno	3.00	1.35
☐ 238 Chuck Dobson	2.00	.90
☐ 239 Red Schoendienst MG	3.00	1.35
☐ 240 Clyde Wright	2.00	.90
☐ 241 Dave Nelson	2.00	.90
☐ 242 Jim Ray	2.00	.90
☐ 243 Carlos May	2.00	.90
☐ 244 Bob Tillman	2.00	.90
☐ 245 Jim Kaat	3.00	1.35
☐ 246 Tony Taylor	2.00	.90
☐ 247 Royals Rookies	2.50	1.10
Jerry Cram		
Paul Splittorff		
☐ 248 Hoyt Wilhelm	6.00	2.70
(Atlanta Braves)		
☐ 249 Chico Salmon	2.00	.90
☐ 250 Johnny Bench	20.00	9.00
☐ 251 Frank Reberger	2.00	.90
☐ 252 Eddie Leon	2.00	.90
☐ 253 Bill Sudakis	2.00	.90
☐ 254 Cal Koonce	2.00	.90
☐ 255 Bob Robertson	2.50	1.10
☐ 256 Tony Gonzalez	2.00	.90
☐ 257 Nelson Briles	2.00	.90
☐ 258 Dick Green	2.00	.90
☐ 259 Dave Marshall	2.00	.90
☐ 260 Tommy Harper	2.50	1.10
☐ 261 Darold Knowles	2.00	.90
☐ 262 Padres Rookies	2.00	.90
Jim Williams		
Dave Robinson		
☐ 263 John Ellis	2.00	.90
☐ 264 Joe Morgan	10.00	4.50
☐ 265 Jim Northrup	2.50	1.10
☐ 266 Bill Stoneman	2.50	1.10
☐ 267 Rich Morales	2.00	.90
☐ 268 Phillies Team	4.00	1.80
☐ 269 Gail Hopkins	2.00	.90
☐ 270 Rico Carty	2.50	1.10
☐ 271 Bill Zepp	2.00	.90
☐ 272 Tommy Helms	2.50	1.10
☐ 273 Pete Richert	2.00	.90
☐ 274 Ron Slocum	2.00	.90
☐ 275 Vada Pinson	2.50	1.10
☐ 276 Giants Rookies	10.00	4.50
Mike Davison		
George Foster		
☐ 277 Gary Waslewski	2.00	.90
☐ 278 Jerry Grote	2.50	1.10
☐ 279 Lefty Phillips MG	2.00	.90
☐ 280 Fergie Jenkins	7.00	3.10
☐ 281 Danny Walton	2.00	.90
☐ 282 Jose Pagan	2.00	.90
☐ 283 Dick Such	2.00	.90
☐ 284 Jim Gosger	2.00	.90
☐ 285 Sal Bando	2.50	1.10
☐ 286 Jerry McNertney	2.00	.90
☐ 287 Mike Fiore	2.00	.90
☐ 288 Joe Moeller	2.00	.90
☐ 289 Rusty Staub	7.50	3.40
(Different pose)		
☐ 290 Tony Oliva	3.00	1.35
☐ 291 George Culver	2.00	.90
☐ 292 Jay Johnstone	2.50	1.10
☐ 293 Pat Corrales	2.50	1.10
☐ 294 Steve Dunning	2.00	.90
☐ 295 Bobby Bonds	5.00	2.20
☐ 296 Tom Timmermann	2.00	.90
☐ 297 Johnny Briggs	2.00	.90
☐ 298 Jim Nelson	2.00	.90
☐ 299 Ed Kirkpatrick	2.00	.90
☐ 300 Brooks Robinson	20.00	9.00
☐ 301 Earl Wilson	2.00	.90
☐ 302 Phil Gagliano	2.00	.90
☐ 303 Lindy McDaniel	2.50	1.10
☐ 304 Ron Brand	2.00	.90
☐ 305 Reggie Smith	2.50	1.10
☐ 306 Jim Nash	2.00	.90
☐ 307 Don Wert	2.00	.90
☐ 308 Cardinals Team	4.00	1.80
☐ 309 Dick Ellsworth	2.00	.90
☐ 310 Tommie Agee	2.50	1.10
☐ 311 Lee Stange	2.00	.90
☐ 312 Harry Walker MG	2.00	.90
☐ 313 Tom Hall	2.00	.90
☐ 314 Jeff Torborg	2.50	1.10
☐ 315 Ron Fairly	2.50	1.10
☐ 316 Fred Scherman	2.00	.90
☐ 317 Athletic Rookies	2.00	.90
Jim Driscoll		
Angel Mangual		
☐ 318 Rudy May	2.50	1.10
☐ 319 Ty Cline	2.00	.90
☐ 320 Dave McNally	2.50	1.10
☐ 321 Tom Matchick	2.00	.90
☐ 322 Jim Beauchamp	2.00	.90
☐ 323 Billy Champion	2.00	.90
☐ 324 Graig Nettles	3.00	1.35
☐ 325 Juan Marichal	7.00	3.10
☐ 326 Richie Scheinblum	2.00	.90
☐ 327 Boog Powell WS	5.00	2.20
☐ 328 Don Buford WS	4.00	1.80
☐ 329 Frank Robinson WS	6.00	2.70
☐ 330 World Series Game 4	4.00	1.80
Reds stay alive		
☐ 331 Brooks Robinson WS	7.50	3.40
☐ 332 World Series Summary	4.00	1.80
Orioles Celebrate		
☐ 333 Clay Kirby	2.00	.90
☐ 334 Roberto Pena	2.00	.90
☐ 335 Jerry Koosman	3.00	1.35
☐ 336 Tigers Team	4.00	1.80
☐ 337 Jesus Alou	2.00	.90
☐ 338 Gene Tenace	2.50	1.10
☐ 339 Wayne Simpson	2.00	.90
☐ 340 Rico Petrocelli	2.50	1.10
☐ 341 Steve Garvey	30.00	13.50
☐ 342 Frank Tepedino	2.00	.90
☐ 343 Pirates Rookies	2.50	1.10
Ed Acosta		
Milt May		
☐ 344 Ellie Rodriguez	2.00	.90
☐ 345 Joel Horlen	2.00	.90
☐ 346 Lum Harris MG	2.00	.90
☐ 347 Ted Uhlaender	2.00	.90
☐ 348 Fred Norman	2.00	.90
☐ 349 Rich Reese	2.00	.90
☐ 350 Billy Williams	8.00	3.60
☐ 351 Jim Shellenback	2.00	.90
☐ 352 Denny Doyle	2.00	.90
☐ 353 Carl Taylor	2.00	.90
☐ 354 Don McMahon	2.00	.90
☐ 355 Bud Harrelson	3.50	1.55
☐ 356 Bob Locker	2.00	.90
☐ 357 Reds Team	4.00	1.80
☐ 358 Danny Cater	2.00	.90
☐ 359 Ron Reed	2.00	.90
☐ 360 Jim Fregosi	2.50	1.10
☐ 361 Don Sutton	7.00	3.10
☐ 362 Orioles Rookies	2.00	.90
Mike Adamson		
Roger Freed		
☐ 363 Mike Nagy	2.00	.90
☐ 364 Tommy Dean	2.00	.90
☐ 365 Bob Johnson	2.00	.90
☐ 366 Ron Stone	2.00	.90
☐ 367 Dalton Jones	2.00	.90
☐ 368 Bob Veale	2.50	1.10
☐ 369 Checklist 394-523	6.00	2.70
☐ 370 Joe Torre	3.00	1.35
☐ 371 Jack Hiatt	2.00	.90
☐ 372 Lew Krausse	2.00	.90
☐ 373 Tom McCraw	2.00	.90
☐ 374 Clete Boyer	2.50	1.10

☐ 375 Steve Hargan 2.00 .90
☐ 376 Expos Rookies 2.00 .90
Clyde Mashore
Ernie McAnally
☐ 377 Greg Garrett 2.00 .90
☐ 378 Tito Fuentes 2.50 1.10
☐ 379 Wayne Granger 2.00 .90
☐ 380 Ted Williams MG 12.00 5.50
☐ 381 Fred Gladding 2.00 .90
☐ 382 Jake Gibbs 2.00 .90
☐ 383 Rod Gaspar 2.00 .90
☐ 384 Rollie Fingers 6.00 2.70
☐ 385 Maury Wills 3.00 1.35
☐ 386 Red Sox Team 4.00 1.80
☐ 387 Ron Herbel 2.00 .90
☐ 388 Al Oliver 3.00 1.35
☐ 389 Ed Brinkman 2.00 .90
☐ 390 Glenn Beckert 2.50 1.10
☐ 391 Twins Rookies 2.50 1.10
Steve Brye
Cotton Nash
☐ 392 Grant Jackson 2.00 .90
☐ 393 Merv Rettenmund 2.50 1.10
☐ 394 Clay Carroll 2.50 1.10
☐ 395 Roy White 3.50 1.55
☐ 396 Dick Schofield 2.50 1.10
☐ 397 Alvin Dark MG 3.50 1.55
☐ 398 Howie Reed 2.50 1.10
☐ 399 Jim French 2.50 1.10
☐ 400 Hank Aaron 75.00 34.00
☐ 401 Tom Murphy 2.50 1.10
☐ 402 Dodgers Team 5.00 2.20
☐ 403 Joe Coleman 2.50 1.10
☐ 404 Astros Rookies 2.50 1.10
Buddy Harris
Roger Metzger
☐ 405 Leo Cardenas 3.50 1.55
☐ 406 Ray Sadecki 2.50 1.10
☐ 407 Joe Rudi 3.50 1.55
☐ 408 Rafael Robles 2.50 1.10
☐ 409 Don Pavletich 2.50 1.10
☐ 410 Ken Holtzman 3.50 1.55
☐ 411 George Spriggs 2.50 1.10
☐ 412 Jerry Johnson 2.50 1.10
☐ 413 Pat Kelly 2.50 1.10
☐ 414 Woodie Fryman 2.50 1.10
☐ 415 Mike Hegan 2.50 1.10
☐ 416 Gene Alley 2.50 1.10
☐ 417 Dick Hall 2.50 1.10
☐ 418 Adolfo Phillips 2.50 1.10
☐ 419 Ron Hansen 2.50 1.10
☐ 420 Jim Merritt 2.50 1.10
☐ 421 John Stephenson 2.50 1.10
☐ 422 Frank Bertaina 2.50 1.10
☐ 423 Tigers Rookies 2.50 1.10
Dennis Saunders
Tim Marting
☐ 424 Roberto Rodriquez 2.50 1.10
☐ 425 Doug Rader 3.50 1.55
☐ 426 Chris Cannizzaro 2.50 1.10
☐ 427 Bernie Allen 2.50 1.10
☐ 428 Jim McAndrew 2.50 1.10
☐ 429 Chuck Hinton 2.50 1.10
☐ 430 Wes Parker 2.50 1.10
☐ 431 Tom Burgmeier 2.50 1.10
☐ 432 Bob Didier 2.50 1.10
☐ 433 Skip Lockwood 2.50 1.10
☐ 434 Gary Sutherland 2.50 1.10
☐ 435 Jose Cardenal 3.50 1.55
☐ 436 Wilbur Wood 3.50 1.55
☐ 437 Danny Murtaugh MG 3.50 1.55
☐ 438 Mike McCormick 3.50 1.55
☐ 439 Phillies Rookies 8.00 3.60
Greg Luzinski
Scott Reid
☐ 440 Bert Campaneris 3.50 1.55
☐ 441 Milt Pappas 3.50 1.55
☐ 442 Angels Team 5.00 2.20
☐ 443 Rich Robertson 2.50 1.10
☐ 444 Jimmie Price 2.50 1.10
☐ 445 Art Shamsky 2.50 1.10
☐ 446 Bobby Bolin 2.50 1.10
☐ 447 Cesar Geronimo 3.50 1.55
☐ 448 Dave Roberts 2.50 1.10
☐ 449 Brant Alyea 2.50 1.10
☐ 450 Bob Gibson 20.00 9.00
☐ 451 Joe Keough 2.50 1.10
☐ 452 John Boccabella 2.50 1.10
☐ 453 Terry Crowley 2.50 1.10
☐ 454 Mike Paul 2.50 1.10
☐ 455 Don Kessinger 3.50 1.55
☐ 456 Bob Meyer 2.50 1.10
☐ 457 Willie Smith 2.50 1.10
☐ 458 White Sox Rookies 2.50 1.10
Ron Lolich
Dave Lemonds
☐ 459 Jim Lefebvre 2.50 1.10
☐ 460 Fritz Peterson 2.50 1.10
☐ 461 Jim Ray Hart 2.50 1.10
☐ 462 Senators Team 5.00 2.20
☐ 463 Tom Kelley 2.50 1.10
☐ 464 Aurelio Rodriguez 2.50 1.10
☐ 465 Tim McCarver 4.00 1.80
☐ 466 Ken Berry 2.50 1.10
☐ 467 Al Santorini 2.50 1.10
☐ 468 Frank Fernandez 2.50 1.10
☐ 469 Bob Aspromonte 2.50 1.10
☐ 470 Bob Oliver 2.50 1.10
☐ 471 Tom Griffin 2.50 1.10
☐ 472 Ken Rudolph 2.50 1.10
☐ 473 Gary Wagner 2.50 1.10
☐ 474 Jim Fairey 2.50 1.10
☐ 475 Ron Perranoski 3.50 1.55
☐ 476 Dal Maxvill 2.50 1.10
☐ 477 Earl Weaver MG 5.00 2.20
☐ 478 Bernie Carbo 2.50 1.10
☐ 479 Dennis Higgins 2.50 1.10
☐ 480 Manny Sanguillen 3.50 1.55
☐ 481 Daryl Patterson 2.50 1.10
☐ 482 Padres Team 5.00 2.20
☐ 483 Gene Michael 2.50 1.10
☐ 484 Don Wilson 2.50 1.10
☐ 485 Ken McMullen 2.50 1.10
☐ 486 Steve Huntz 2.50 1.10
☐ 487 Paul Schaal 2.50 1.10
☐ 488 Jerry Stephenson 2.50 1.10
☐ 489 Luis Alvarado 2.50 1.10
☐ 490 Deron Johnson 2.50 1.10
☐ 491 Jim Hardin 2.50 1.10
☐ 492 Ken Boswell 2.50 1.10
☐ 493 Dave May 2.50 1.10
☐ 494 Braves Rookies 3.50 1.55
Ralph Garr
Rick Kester
☐ 495 Felipe Alou 3.50 1.55
☐ 496 Woody Woodward 2.50 1.10
☐ 497 Horacio Pina 2.50 1.10
☐ 498 John Kennedy 2.50 1.10
☐ 499 Checklist 524-643 6.00 2.70
☐ 500 Jim Perry 3.50 1.55
☐ 501 Andy Etchebarren 2.50 1.10
☐ 502 Cubs Team 5.00 2.20
☐ 503 Gates Brown 3.50 1.55
☐ 504 Ken Wright 2.50 1.10
☐ 505 Ollie Brown 2.50 1.10
☐ 506 Bobby Knoop 2.50 1.10
☐ 507 George Stone 2.50 1.10
☐ 508 Roger Repoz 2.50 1.10
☐ 509 Jim Grant 2.50 1.10
☐ 510 Ken Harrelson 3.50 1.55
☐ 511 Chris Short 4.00 1.80
☐ 512 Red Sox Rookies 2.50 1.10
Dick Mills
Mike Garman
☐ 513 Nolan Ryan 300.00 135.00
☐ 514 Ron Woods 2.50 1.10
☐ 515 Carl Morton 2.50 1.10
☐ 516 Ted Kubiak 2.50 1.10
☐ 517 Charlie Fox MG 2.50 1.10
☐ 518 Joe Grzenda 2.50 1.10
☐ 519 Willie Crawford 2.50 1.10
☐ 520 Tommy John 5.00 2.20
☐ 521 Leron Lee 2.50 1.10
☐ 522 Twins Team 5.00 2.20
☐ 523 John Odom 3.50 1.55
☐ 524 Mickey Stanley 6.00 2.70
☐ 525 Ernie Banks 60.00 27.00
☐ 526 Ray Jarvis 5.00 2.20
☐ 527 Cleon Jones 6.00 2.70
☐ 528 Wally Bunker 5.00 2.20
☐ 529 NL Rookie Infielders 6.00 2.70
Enzo Hernandez
Bill Buckner
Marty Perez
☐ 530 Carl Yastrzemski 50.00 22.00
☐ 531 Mike Torrez 6.00 2.70
☐ 532 Bill Rigney MG 5.00 2.20
☐ 533 Mike Ryan 5.00 2.20
☐ 534 Luke Walker 5.00 2.20
☐ 535 Curt Flood 7.50 3.40
☐ 536 Claude Raymond 5.00 2.20
☐ 537 Tom Egan 5.00 2.20
☐ 538 Angel Bravo 5.00 2.20
☐ 539 Larry Brown 5.00 2.20
☐ 540 Larry Dierker 7.50 3.40
☐ 541 Bob Burda 5.00 2.20
☐ 542 Bob Miller 5.00 2.20
☐ 543 Yankees Team 10.00 4.50
☐ 544 Vida Blue 10.00 4.50
☐ 545 Dick Dietz 5.00 2.20
☐ 546 John Matias 5.00 2.20
☐ 547 Pat Dobson 5.00 2.20
☐ 548 Don Mason 5.00 2.20
☐ 549 Jim Brewer 5.00 2.20
☐ 550 Harmon Killebrew 30.00 13.50
☐ 551 Frank Linzy 5.00 2.20
☐ 552 Buddy Bradford 5.00 2.20
☐ 553 Kevin Collins 5.00 2.20
☐ 554 Lowell Palmer 5.00 2.20
☐ 555 Walt Williams 5.00 2.20
☐ 556 Jim McGlothlin 5.00 2.20
☐ 557 Tom Satriano 5.00 2.20
☐ 558 Hector Torres 5.00 2.20
☐ 559 AL Rookie Pitchers 5.00 2.20
Terry Cox
Bill Gogolewski
Gary Jones
☐ 560 Rusty Staub 7.50 3.40
☐ 561 Syd O'Brien 5.00 2.20
☐ 562 Dave Giusti 5.00 2.20
☐ 563 Giants Team 10.00 4.50
☐ 564 Al Fitzmorris 5.00 2.20
☐ 565 Jim Wynn 7.50 3.40
☐ 566 Tim Cullen 5.00 2.20
☐ 567 Walt Alston MG 10.00 4.50
☐ 568 Sal Campisi 5.00 2.20
☐ 569 Ivan Murrell 5.00 2.20
☐ 570 Jim Palmer 35.00 16.00
☐ 571 Ted Sizemore 5.00 2.20
☐ 572 Jerry Kenney 5.00 2.20
☐ 573 Ed Kranepool 7.50 3.40
☐ 574 Jim Bunning 10.00 4.50
☐ 575 Bill Freehan 7.50 3.40
☐ 576 Cubs Rookies 5.00 2.20
Adrian Garrett
Brock Davis
Garry Jestadt
☐ 577 Jim Lonborg 7.50 3.40
☐ 578 Eddie Kasko 7.50 3.40
(Topps 578 is
Ron Hunt)
☐ 579 Marty Pattin 5.00 2.20
☐ 580 Tony Perez 20.00 9.00
☐ 581 Roger Nelson 5.00 2.20
☐ 582 Dave Cash 7.50 3.40
☐ 583 Ron Cook 5.00 2.20
☐ 584 Indians Team 10.00 4.50
☐ 585 Willie Davis 7.50 3.40
☐ 586 Dick Woodson 5.00 2.20
☐ 587 Sonny Jackson 5.00 2.20
☐ 588 Tom Bradley 5.00 2.20
☐ 589 Bob Barton 5.00 2.20
☐ 590 Alex Johnson 6.00 2.70
☐ 591 Jackie Brown 5.00 2.20
☐ 592 Randy Hundley 5.00 2.20
☐ 593 Jack Aker 5.00 2.20
☐ 594 Cards Rookies 7.50 3.40
Bob Chlupsa
Bob Stinson
Al Hrabosky
☐ 595 Dave Johnson 7.50 3.40
☐ 596 Mike Jorgensen 7.50 3.40
☐ 597 Ken Suarez 5.00 2.20
☐ 598 Rick Wise 5.00 2.20
☐ 599 Norm Cash 7.50 3.40
☐ 600 Willie Mays 100.00 45.00
☐ 601 Ken Tatum 5.00 2.20
☐ 602 Marty Martinez 5.00 2.20
☐ 603 Pirates Team 10.00 4.50
☐ 604 John Gelnar 5.00 2.20
☐ 605 Orlando Cepeda 10.00 4.50
☐ 606 Chuck Taylor 5.00 2.20
☐ 607 Paul Ratliff 5.00 2.20
☐ 608 Mike Wegener 5.00 2.20
☐ 609 Leo Durocher MG 10.00 4.50
☐ 610 Amos Otis 7.50 3.40
☐ 611 Tom Phoebus 5.00 2.20
☐ 612 Indians Rookies 5.00 2.20
Lou Camilli
Ted Ford
Steve Mingori
☐ 613 Pedro Borbon 5.00 2.20
☐ 614 Billy Cowan 5.00 2.20
☐ 615 Mel Stottlemyre 7.50 3.40
☐ 616 Larry Hisle 7.50 3.40
☐ 617 Clay Dalrymple 5.00 2.20
☐ 618 Tug McGraw 7.50 3.40
☐ 619 Checklist 644-752 10.00 4.50
☐ 620 Frank Howard 7.50 3.40
☐ 621 Ron Bryant 5.00 2.20
☐ 622 Joe Lahoud 5.00 2.20
☐ 623 Pat Jarvis 5.00 2.20
☐ 624 Athletics Team 10.00 4.50
☐ 625 Lou Brock 35.00 16.00
☐ 626 Freddie Patek 7.50 3.40
☐ 627 Steve Hamilton 5.00 2.20
☐ 628 John Bateman 5.00 2.20
☐ 629 John Hiller 7.50 3.40
☐ 630 Roberto Clemente 125.00 55.00
☐ 631 Eddie Fisher 5.00 2.20
☐ 632 Darrel Chaney 5.00 2.20

□ 633 AL Rookie Outfielders 5.00 2.20
Bobby Brooks
Pete Koegel
Scott Northey
□ 634 Phil Regan 5.00 2.20
□ 635 Bobby Murcer 7.50 3.40
□ 636 Denny LeMaster 5.00 2.20
□ 637 Dave Bristol MG 5.00 2.20
□ 638 Stan Williams 5.00 2.20
□ 639 Tom Haller 5.00 2.20
□ 640 Frank Robinson 50.00 22.00
□ 641 Mets Team 20.00 9.00
□ 642 Jim Roland 5.00 2.20
□ 643 Rick Reichardt 5.00 2.20
□ 644 Jim Stewart 10.00 4.50
□ 645 Jim Maloney 12.50 5.50
□ 646 Bobby Floyd 10.00 4.50
□ 647 Juan Pizarro 10.00 4.50
□ 648 Mets Rookies 20.00 9.00
Rich Folkers
Ted Martinez
Jon Matlack
□ 649 Sparky Lyle 16.00 7.25
□ 650 Rich Allen 40.00 18.00
□ 651 Jerry Robertson 10.00 4.50
□ 652 Braves Team 20.00 9.00
□ 653 Russ Snyder 10.00 4.50
□ 654 Don Shaw 10.00 4.50
□ 655 Mike Epstein 10.00 4.50
□ 656 Gerry Nyman 10.00 4.50
□ 657 Jose Azcue 10.00 4.50
□ 658 Paul Lindblad 10.00 4.50
□ 659 Byron Browne 10.00 4.50
□ 660 Ray Culp 10.00 4.50
□ 661 Chuck Tanner MG 15.00 6.75
□ 662 Mike Hedlund 10.00 4.50
□ 663 Marv Staehle 10.00 4.50
□ 664 Rookie Pitchers 15.00 6.75
Archie Reynolds
Bob Reynolds
Ken Reynolds
□ 665 Ron Swoboda 16.00 7.25
□ 666 Gene Brabender 10.00 4.50
□ 667 Pete Ward 10.00 4.50
□ 668 Gary Neibauer 10.00 4.50
□ 669 Ike Brown 10.00 4.50
□ 670 Bill Hands 10.00 4.50
□ 671 Bill Voss 10.00 4.50
□ 672 Ed Crosby 10.00 4.50
□ 673 Gerry Janeski 10.00 4.50
□ 674 Expos Team 20.00 9.00
□ 675 Dave Boswell 10.00 4.50
□ 676 Tommie Reynolds 10.00 4.50
□ 677 Jack DiLauro 10.00 4.50
□ 678 George Thomas 10.00 4.50
□ 679 Don O'Riley 10.00 4.50
□ 680 Don Mincher 10.00 4.50
□ 681 Bill Butler 10.00 4.50
□ 682 Terry Harmon 10.00 4.50
□ 683 Bill Burbach 10.00 4.50
□ 684 Curt Motton 10.00 4.50
□ 685 Moe Drabowsky 10.00 4.50
□ 686 Chico Ruiz 10.00 4.50
□ 687 Ron Taylor 10.00 4.50
□ 688 Sparky Anderson MG 40.00 18.00
□ 689 Frank Baker 10.00 4.50
□ 690 Bob Moose 10.00 4.50
□ 691 Bob Heise 10.00 4.50
□ 692 AL Rookie Pitchers 10.00 4.50
Hal Haydel
Rogelio Moret
Wayne Twitchell
□ 693 Jose Pena 10.00 4.50
□ 694 Rick Renick 10.00 4.50
□ 695 Joe Niekro 15.00 6.75
□ 696 Jerry Morales 10.00 4.50
□ 697 Rickey Clark 10.00 4.50
□ 698 Brewers Team 20.00 9.00
□ 699 Jim Britton 10.00 4.50
□ 700 Boog Powell 25.00 11.00
□ 701 Bob Garibaldi 10.00 4.50
□ 702 Milt Ramirez 10.00 4.50
□ 703 Mike Kekich 10.00 4.50
□ 704 J.C. Martin 10.00 4.50
□ 705 Dick Selma 10.00 4.50
□ 706 Joe Foy 10.00 4.50
□ 707 Fred Lasher 10.00 4.50
□ 708 Russ Nagelson 10.00 4.50
□ 709 Rookie Outfielders 90.00 40.00
Dusty Baker
Don Baylor
Tom Paciorek
□ 710 Sonny Siebert 10.00 4.50
□ 711 Larry Stahl 10.00 4.50
□ 712 Jose Martinez 10.00 4.50
□ 713 Mike Marshall 15.00 6.75
□ 714 Dick Williams MG 15.00 6.75
□ 715 Horace Clarke 10.00 4.50
□ 716 Dave Leonhard 10.00 4.50
□ 717 Tommie Aaron 15.00 6.75
□ 718 Billy Wynne 10.00 4.50
□ 719 Jerry May 10.00 4.50
□ 720 Matty Alou 15.00 6.75
□ 721 John Morris 10.00 4.50
□ 722 Astros Team 20.00 9.00
□ 723 Vicente Romo 10.00 4.50
□ 724 Tom Tischinski 10.00 4.50
□ 725 Gary Gentry 10.00 4.50
□ 726 Paul Popovich 10.00 4.50
□ 727 Ray Lamb 10.00 4.50
□ 728 NL Rookie Outfielders 10.00 4.50
Wayne Redmond
Keith Lampard
Bernie Williams
□ 729 Dick Billings 10.00 4.50
□ 730 Jim Rooker 10.00 4.50
□ 731 Jim Qualls 10.00 4.50
□ 732 Bob Reed 10.00 4.50
□ 733 Lee Maye 10.00 4.50
□ 734 Rob Gardner 10.00 4.50
□ 735 Mike Shannon 12.50 5.50
□ 736 Mel Queen 10.00 4.50
□ 737 Preston Gomez MG 10.00 4.50
□ 738 Russ Gibson 10.00 4.50
□ 739 Barry Lersch 10.00 4.50
□ 740 Luis Aparicio 25.00 11.00
□ 741 Skip Guinn 10.00 4.50
□ 742 Royals Team 20.00 9.00
□ 743 John O'Donoghue 10.00 4.50
□ 744 Chuck Manuel 10.00 4.50
□ 745 Sandy Alomar 15.00 6.75
□ 746 Andy Kosco 10.00 4.50
□ 747 NL Rookie Pitchers 10.00 4.50
Al Severinsen
Scipio Spinks
Balor Moore
□ 748 John Purdin 10.00 4.50
□ 749 Ken Szotkiewicz 10.00 4.50
□ 750 Denny McLain 20.00 9.00
□ 751 Al Weis 14.00 6.25
□ 752 Dick Drago 12.00 5.50

1972 O-Pee-Chee

The cards in this 525-card set measure 2 1/2" by 3 1/2". The 1972 O-Pee-Chee set is very similar to the 1972 Topps set. On a white background, the fronts feature color player photos with multicolored frames, rounded bottom corners and the top part of the photo also rounded. The player's name and team name appear on the front. The horizontal backs carry player biography and statistics in French and English and have a different color than the 1972 Topps cards. Features appearing for the first time were "Boyhood Photos" (KP: 341-348 and 491-498) and "In Action" cards. The O-Pee-Chee cards can be distinguished from Topps cards by the "Printed in Canada" on the bottom of the back. This was the first year the cards denoted O.P.C. in the copyright line rather than T.C.G. There is one card in the set which is notably different from the corresponding Topps number on the back, No. 465 Gil Hodges, which notes his death in April of 1972. Remember, the prices below apply only to the O-Pee-Chee cards -- NOT Topps cards which are much more plentiful.

	NRMT	VG-E
COMPLETE SET (525)	1500.00	700.00
COMMON CARD (1-263)	1.00	.45
COMMON CARD (264-394)	2.00	.90
COMMON CARD (395-525)	2.50	1.10

□ 1 Pirates Team 8.00 3.60
□ 2 Ray Culp 1.00 .45
□ 3 Bob Tolan 1.00 .45
□ 4 Checklist 1-132 4.00 1.80
□ 5 John Bateman 1.00 .45
□ 6 Fred Scherman 1.00 .45
□ 7 Enzo Hernandez 1.00 .45
□ 8 Ron Swoboda 1.50 .70
□ 9 Stan Williams 1.00 .45
□ 10 Amos Otis 1.50 .70
□ 11 Bobby Valentine 1.50 .70
□ 12 Jose Cardenal 1.00 .45
□ 13 Joe Grzenda 1.00 .45
□ 14 Phillies Rookies 1.00 .45
Pete Koegel
Mike Anderson
Wayne Twitchell
□ 15 Walt Williams 1.00 .45
□ 16 Mike Jorgensen 1.50 .70
□ 17 Dave Duncan 1.00 .45
□ 18 Juan Pizarro 1.00 .45
□ 19 Billy Cowan 1.00 .45
□ 20 Don Wilson 1.00 .45
□ 21 Braves Team 2.00 .90
□ 22 Rob Gardner 1.00 .45
□ 23 Ted Kubiak 1.00 .45
□ 24 Ted Ford 1.00 .45
□ 25 Bill Singer 1.00 .45
□ 26 Andy Etchebarren 1.00 .45
□ 27 Bob Johnson 1.00 .45
□ 28 Twins Rookies 1.00 .45
Bob Gebhard
Steve Brye
Hal Haydel
□ 29 Bill Bonham 1.00 .45
□ 30 Rico Petrocelli 1.50 .70
□ 31 Cleon Jones 1.50 .70
□ 32 Cleon Jones IA 1.00 .45
□ 33 Billy Martin MG 4.00 1.80
□ 34 Billy Martin IA 2.00 .90
□ 35 Jerry Johnson 1.00 .45
□ 36 Jerry Johnson IA 1.00 .45
□ 37 Carl Yastrzemski 12.00 5.50
□ 38 Carl Yastrzemski IA 6.00 2.70
□ 39 Bob Barton 1.00 .45
□ 40 Bob Barton IA 1.00 .45
□ 41 Tommy Davis 1.50 .70
□ 42 Tommy Davis IA 1.00 .45
□ 43 Rick Wise 1.50 .70
□ 44 Rick Wise IA 1.00 .45
□ 45 Glenn Beckert 1.00 .45
□ 46 Glenn Beckert IA 1.00 .45
□ 47 John Ellis 1.00 .45
□ 48 John Ellis IA 1.00 .45
□ 49 Willie Mays 30.00 13.50
□ 50 Willie Mays IA 15.00 6.75
□ 51 Harmon Killebrew 8.00 3.60
□ 52 Harmon Killebrew IA 4.00 1.80
□ 53 Bud Harrelson 1.50 .70
□ 54 Bud Harrelson IA 1.00 .45
□ 55 Clyde Wright 1.00 .45
□ 56 Rich Chiles 1.00 .45
□ 57 Bob Oliver 1.00 .45
□ 58 Ernie McAnally 1.00 .45
□ 59 Fred Stanley 1.00 .45
□ 60 Manny Sanguillen 1.50 .70
□ 61 Cubs Rookies 1.50 .70
Burt Hooton
Gene Hiser
Earl Stephenson
□ 62 Angel Mangual 1.00 .45
□ 63 Duke Sims 1.00 .45
□ 64 Pete Broberg 1.00 .45
□ 65 Cesar Cedeno 1.50 .70
□ 66 Ray Corbin 1.00 .45
□ 67 Red Schoendienst MG 2.00 .90
□ 68 Jim York 1.00 .45
□ 69 Roger Freed 1.00 .45
□ 70 Mike Cuellar 1.50 .70
□ 71 Angels Team 2.00 .90
□ 72 Bruce Kison 1.50 .70
□ 73 Steve Huntz 1.00 .45
□ 74 Cecil Upshaw 1.00 .45
□ 75 Bert Campaneris 1.50 .70
□ 76 Don Carrithers 1.00 .45
□ 77 Ron Theobald 1.00 .45
□ 78 Steve Arlin 1.00 .45
□ 79 Red Sox Rookies 75.00 34.00
Mike Garman
Cecil Cooper
Carlton Fisk
□ 80 Tony Perez 4.00 1.80
□ 81 Mike Hedlund 1.00 .45
□ 82 Ron Woods 1.00 .45
□ 83 Dalton Jones 1.00 .45
□ 84 Vince Colbert 1.00 .45
□ 85 NL Batting Leaders 3.00 1.35
Joe Torre
Ralph Garr
Glenn Beckert
□ 86 AL Batting Leaders 3.00 1.35
Tony Oliva
Bobby Murcer
Merv Rettenmund
□ 87 NL RBI Leaders 5.00 2.20

Joe Torre		
Willie Stargell		
Hank Aaron		
☐ 88 AL RBI Leaders	4.00	1.80
Harmon Killebrew		
Frank Robinson		
Reggie Smith		
☐ 89 NL Home Run Leaders	5.00	2.20
Willie Stargell		
Hank Aaron		
Lee May		
☐ 90 AL Home Run Leaders	4.00	1.80
Bill Melton		
Norm Cash		
Reggie Jackson		
☐ 91 NL ERA Leaders	4.00	1.80
Tom Seaver		
Dave Roberts		
(photo actually		
Danny Coombs)		
Don Wilson		
☐ 92 AL ERA Leaders	4.00	1.80
Vida Blue		
Wilbur Wood		
Jim Palmer		
☐ 93 NL Pitching Leaders	5.00	2.20
Fergie Jenkins		
Steve Carlton		
Al Downing		
Tom Seaver		
☐ 94 AL Pitching Leaders	3.00	1.35
Mickey Lolich		
Vida Blue		
Wilbur Wood		
☐ 95 NL Strikeout Leaders	4.00	1.80
Tom Seaver		
Fergie Jenkins		
Bill Stoneman		
☐ 96 AL Strikeout Leaders	3.00	1.35
Mickey Lolich		
Vida Blue		
Joe Coleman		
☐ 97 Tom Kelley	1.00	.45
☐ 98 Chuck Tanner MG	1.50	.70
☐ 99 Ross Grimsley	1.00	.45
☐ 100 Frank Robinson	10.00	4.50
☐ 101 Astros Rookies	3.00	1.35
Bill Greif		
J.R. Richard		
Ray Busse		
☐ 102 Lloyd Allen	1.00	.45
☐ 103 Checklist 133-263	4.00	1.80
☐ 104 Toby Harrah	2.50	1.10
☐ 105 Gary Gentry	1.00	.45
☐ 106 Brewers Team	2.00	.90
☐ 107 Jose Cruz	3.00	1.35
☐ 108 Gary Waslewski	1.00	.45
☐ 109 Jerry May	1.00	.45
☐ 110 Ron Hunt	1.00	.45
☐ 111 Jim Grant	1.00	.45
☐ 112 Greg Luzinski	3.00	1.35
☐ 113 Rogelio Moret	1.00	.45
☐ 114 Bill Buckner	2.00	.90
☐ 115 Jim Fregosi	1.50	.70
☐ 116 Ed Farmer	1.00	.45
☐ 117 Cleo James	1.00	.45
☐ 118 Skip Lockwood	1.00	.45
☐ 119 Marty Perez	1.00	.45
☐ 120 Bill Freehan	1.50	.70
☐ 121 Ed Sprague	1.00	.45
☐ 122 Larry Biittner	1.00	.45
☐ 123 Ed Acosta	1.00	.45
☐ 124 Yankees Rookies	1.00	.45
Alan Closter		
Rusty Torres		
Roger Hambright		
☐ 125 Dave Cash	1.50	.70
☐ 126 Bart Johnson	1.00	.45
☐ 127 Duffy Dyer	1.00	.45
☐ 128 Eddie Watt	1.00	.45
☐ 129 Charlie Fox MG	1.00	.45
☐ 130 Bob Gibson	10.00	4.50
☐ 131 Jim Nettles	1.00	.45
☐ 132 Joe Morgan	7.50	3.40
☐ 133 Joe Keough	1.00	.45
☐ 134 Carl Morton	1.00	.45
☐ 135 Vada Pinson	1.50	.70
☐ 136 Darrel Chaney	1.00	.45
☐ 137 Dick Williams MG	1.50	.70
☐ 138 Mike Kekich	1.00	.45
☐ 139 Tim McCarver	1.50	.70
☐ 140 Pat Dobson	1.00	.45
☐ 141 Mets Rookies	1.50	.70
Buzz Capra		
Leroy Stanton		
Jon Matlack		
☐ 142 Chris Chambliss	5.00	2.20
☐ 143 Garry Jestadt	1.00	.45
☐ 144 Marty Pattin	1.00	.45
☐ 145 Don Kessinger	1.50	.70
☐ 146 Steve Kealey	1.00	.45
☐ 147 Dave Kingman	5.00	2.20
☐ 148 Dick Billings	1.00	.45
☐ 149 Gary Neibauer	1.00	.45
☐ 150 Norm Cash	1.50	.70
☐ 151 Jim Brewer	1.00	.45
☐ 152 Gene Clines	1.00	.45
☐ 153 Rick Auerbach	1.00	.45
☐ 154 Ted Simmons	3.00	1.35
☐ 155 Larry Dierker	1.00	.45
☐ 156 Twins Team	2.00	.90
☐ 157 Don Gullett	1.50	.70
☐ 158 Jerry Kenney	1.00	.45
☐ 159 John Boccabella	1.00	.45
☐ 160 Andy Messersmith	1.50	.70
☐ 161 Brock Davis	1.00	.45
☐ 162 Brewers Rookies UER	2.00	.90
Jerry Bell		
Darrell Porter		
Bob Reynolds		
(Porter and Bell		
photos switched)		
☐ 163 Tug McGraw	1.50	.70
☐ 164 Tug McGraw IA	1.50	.70
☐ 165 Chris Speier	1.50	.70
☐ 166 Chris Speier IA	1.50	.70
☐ 167 Deron Johnson	1.00	.45
☐ 168 Deron Johnson IA	1.00	.45
☐ 169 Vida Blue	2.00	.90
☐ 170 Vida Blue IA	1.50	.70
☐ 171 Darrell Evans	2.00	.90
☐ 172 Darrell Evans IA	1.50	.70
☐ 173 Clay Kirby	1.00	.45
☐ 174 Clay Kirby IA	1.00	.45
☐ 175 Tom Haller	1.00	.45
☐ 176 Tom Haller IA	1.00	.45
☐ 177 Paul Schaal	1.00	.45
☐ 178 Paul Schaal IA	1.00	.45
☐ 179 Dock Ellis	1.00	.45
☐ 180 Dock Ellis IA	1.00	.45
☐ 181 Ed Kranepool	1.00	.45
☐ 182 Ed Kranepool IA	1.00	.45
☐ 183 Bill Melton	1.00	.45
☐ 184 Bill Melton IA	1.00	.45
☐ 185 Ron Bryant	1.00	.45
☐ 186 Ron Bryant IA	1.00	.45
☐ 187 Gates Brown	1.00	.45
☐ 188 Frank Lucchesi MG	1.00	.45
☐ 189 Gene Tenace	1.50	.70
☐ 190 Dave Giusti	1.00	.45
☐ 191 Jeff Burroughs	2.00	.90
☐ 192 Cubs Team	2.00	.90
☐ 193 Kurt Bevacqua	1.00	.45
☐ 194 Fred Norman	1.00	.45
☐ 195 Orlando Cepeda	3.00	1.35
☐ 196 Mel Queen	1.00	.45
☐ 197 Johnny Briggs	1.00	.45
☐ 198 Dodgers Rookies	6.00	2.70
Charlie Hough		
Bob O'Brien		
Mike Strahler		
☐ 199 Mike Fiore	1.00	.45
☐ 200 Lou Brock	10.00	4.50
☐ 201 Phil Roof	1.00	.45
☐ 202 Scipio Spinks	1.00	.45
☐ 203 Ron Blomberg	1.00	.45
☐ 204 Tommy Helms	1.00	.45
☐ 205 Dick Drago	1.00	.45
☐ 206 Dal Maxvill	1.00	.45
☐ 207 Tom Egan	1.00	.45
☐ 208 Milt Pappas	1.50	.70
☐ 209 Joe Rudi	1.50	.70
☐ 210 Denny McLain	1.50	.70
☐ 211 Gary Sutherland	1.00	.45
☐ 212 Grant Jackson	1.00	.45
☐ 213 Angels Rookies	1.00	.45
Billy Parker		
Art Kusnyer		
Tom Silverio		
☐ 214 Mike McQueen	1.00	.45
☐ 215 Alex Johnson	1.00	.45
☐ 216 Joe Niekro	1.50	.70
☐ 217 Roger Metzger	1.00	.45
☐ 218 Eddie Kasko MG	1.00	.45
☐ 219 Rennie Stennett	1.50	.70
☐ 220 Jim Perry	1.50	.70
☐ 221 NL Playoffs	2.00	.90
Bucs champs		
☐ 222 Brooks Robinson ALCS	4.00	1.80
☐ 223 Dave McNally WS	3.00	1.35
☐ 224 Dave Johnson WS	3.00	1.35
Mark Belanger		
☐ 225 Manny Sanguillen WS	3.00	1.35
☐ 226 Roberto Clemente WS	10.00	4.50
☐ 227 Nellie Briles WS	3.00	1.35
☐ 228 Frank Robinson WS	4.00	1.80
Manny Sanguillen		
☐ 229 Steve Blass WS	3.00	1.35
☐ 230 World Series Summary	3.00	1.35
Pirates celebrate		
☐ 231 Casey Cox	1.00	.45
☐ 232 Giants Rookies	1.00	.45
Chris Arnold		
Jim Barr		
Dave Rader		
☐ 233 Jay Johnstone	1.50	.70
☐ 234 Ron Taylor	1.00	.45
☐ 235 Merv Rettenmund	1.00	.45
☐ 236 Jim McGlothlin	1.00	.45
☐ 237 Yankees Team	2.00	.90
☐ 238 Leron Lee	1.00	.45
☐ 239 Tom Timmermann	1.00	.45
☐ 240 Rich Allen	3.00	1.35
☐ 241 Rollie Fingers	6.00	2.70
☐ 242 Don Mincher	1.00	.45
☐ 243 Frank Linzy	1.00	.45
☐ 244 Steve Braun	1.00	.45
☐ 245 Tommie Agee	1.50	.70
☐ 246 Tom Burgmeier	1.00	.45
☐ 247 Milt May	1.00	.45
☐ 248 Tom Bradley	1.00	.45
☐ 249 Harry Walker MG	1.00	.45
☐ 250 Boog Powell	3.00	1.35
☐ 251 Checklist 264-394	5.00	2.20
☐ 252 Ken Reynolds	1.00	.45
☐ 253 Sandy Alomar	1.50	.70
☐ 254 Boots Day	1.00	.45
☐ 255 Jim Lonborg	1.50	.70
☐ 256 George Foster	3.00	1.35
☐ 257 Tigers Rookies	1.00	.45
Jim Foor		
Tim Hosley		
Paul Jata		
☐ 258 Randy Hundley	1.00	.45
☐ 259 Sparky Lyle	1.50	.70
☐ 260 Ralph Garr	1.50	.70
☐ 261 Steve Mingori	1.00	.45
☐ 262 Padres Team	2.00	.90
☐ 263 Felipe Alou	1.50	.70
☐ 264 Tommy John	4.00	1.80
☐ 265 Wes Parker	3.00	1.35
☐ 266 Bobby Bolin	2.00	.90
☐ 267 Dave Concepcion	4.00	1.80
☐ 268 A's Rookies	2.00	.90
Dwain Anderson		
Chris Floethe		
☐ 269 Don Hahn	2.00	.90
☐ 270 Jim Palmer	10.00	4.50
☐ 271 Ken Rudolph	2.00	.90
☐ 272 Mickey Rivers	4.00	1.80
☐ 273 Bobby Floyd	2.00	.90
☐ 274 Al Severinsen	2.00	.90
☐ 275 Cesar Tovar	3.00	1.35
☐ 276 Gene Mauch MG	2.00	.90
☐ 277 Elliott Maddox	2.00	.90
☐ 278 Dennis Higgins	2.00	.90
☐ 279 Larry Brown	2.00	.90
☐ 280 Willie McCovey	10.00	4.50
☐ 281 Bill Parsons	2.00	.90
☐ 282 Astros Team	4.00	1.80
☐ 283 Darrell Brandon	2.00	.90
☐ 284 Ike Brown	2.00	.90
☐ 285 Gaylord Perry	7.50	3.40
☐ 286 Gene Alley	2.00	.90
☐ 287 Jim Hardin	2.00	.90
☐ 288 Johnny Jeter	2.00	.90
☐ 289 Syd O'Brien	2.00	.90
☐ 290 Sonny Siebert	2.00	.90
☐ 291 Hal McRae	4.00	1.80
☐ 292 Hal McRae IA	3.00	1.35
☐ 293 Danny Frisella	2.00	.90
☐ 294 Danny Frisella IA	2.00	.90
☐ 295 Dick Dietz	2.00	.90
☐ 296 Dick Dietz IA	2.00	.90
☐ 297 Claude Osteen	3.00	1.35
☐ 298 Claude Osteen IA	2.00	.90
☐ 299 Hank Aaron	50.00	22.00
☐ 300 Hank Aaron IA	25.00	11.00
☐ 301 George Mitterwald	2.00	.90
☐ 302 George Mitterwald IA	2.00	.90
☐ 303 Joe Pepitone	3.00	1.35
☐ 304 Joe Pepitone IA	2.00	.90
☐ 305 Ken Boswell	2.00	.90
☐ 306 Ken Boswell IA	2.00	.90
☐ 307 Steve Renko	2.00	.90
☐ 308 Steve Renko IA	2.00	.90
☐ 309 Roberto Clemente	60.00	27.00
☐ 310 Roberto Clemente IA	30.00	13.50
☐ 311 Clay Carroll	2.00	.90
☐ 312 Clay Carroll IA	2.00	.90
☐ 313 Luis Aparicio	6.00	2.70
☐ 314 Luis Aparicio IA	3.00	1.35

Card	NRMT	VG-E
☐ 315 Paul Splittorff	2.00	.90
☐ 316 Cardinals Rookies	3.00	1.35
Jim Bibby		
Jorge Roque		
Santiago Guzman		
☐ 317 Rich Hand	2.00	.90
☐ 318 Sonny Jackson	2.00	.90
☐ 319 Aurelio Rodriguez	2.00	.90
☐ 320 Steve Blass	3.00	1.35
☐ 321 Joe Lahoud	2.00	.90
☐ 322 Jose Pena	2.00	.90
☐ 323 Earl Weaver MG	5.00	2.20
☐ 324 Mike Ryan	2.00	.90
☐ 325 Mel Stottlemyre	3.00	1.35
☐ 326 Pat Kelly	2.00	.90
☐ 327 Steve Stone	3.00	1.35
☐ 328 Red Sox Team	4.00	1.80
☐ 329 Roy Foster	2.00	.90
☐ 330 Jim Hunter	6.00	2.70
☐ 331 Stan Swanson	2.00	.90
☐ 332 Buck Martinez	2.00	.90
☐ 333 Steve Barber	2.00	.90
☐ 334 Rangers Rookies	2.00	.90
Bill Fahey		
Jim Mason		
Tom Ragland		
☐ 335 Bill Hands	2.00	.90
☐ 336 Marty Martinez	2.00	.90
☐ 337 Mike Kilkenny	2.00	.90
☐ 338 Bob Grich	4.00	1.80
☐ 339 Ron Cook	2.00	.90
☐ 340 Roy White	3.00	1.35
☐ 341 Joe Torre KP	4.00	1.80
☐ 342 Wilbur Wood KP	3.00	1.35
☐ 343 Willie Stargell KP	5.00	2.20
☐ 344 Dave McNally KP	3.00	1.35
☐ 345 Rick Wise KP	3.00	1.35
☐ 346 Jim Fregosi KP	3.00	1.35
☐ 347 Tom Seaver KP	7.50	3.40
☐ 348 Sal Bando KP	3.00	1.35
☐ 349 Al Fitzmorris	2.00	.90
☐ 350 Frank Howard	3.00	1.35
☐ 351 Braves Rookies	2.00	.90
Tom House		
Rick Kester		
Jimmy Britton		
☐ 352 Dave LaRoche	2.00	.90
☐ 353 Art Shamsky	2.00	.90
☐ 354 Tom Murphy	2.00	.90
☐ 355 Bob Watson	3.00	1.35
☐ 356 Gerry Moses	2.00	.90
☐ 357 Woodie Fryman	2.00	.90
☐ 358 Sparky Anderson MG	4.00	1.80
☐ 359 Don Pavletich	2.00	.90
☐ 360 Dave Roberts	2.00	.90
☐ 361 Mike Andrews	2.00	.90
☐ 362 Mets Team	4.00	1.80
☐ 363 Ron Klimkowski	2.00	.90
☐ 364 Johnny Callison	3.00	1.35
☐ 365 Dick Bosman	3.00	1.35
☐ 366 Jimmy Rosario	2.00	.90
☐ 367 Ron Perranoski	3.00	1.35
☐ 368 Danny Thompson	2.00	.90
☐ 369 Jim LeFebvre	3.00	1.35
☐ 370 Don Buford	2.00	.90
☐ 371 Denny LeMaster	2.00	.90
☐ 372 Royals Rookies	2.00	.90
Lance Clemons		
Monty Montgomery		
☐ 373 John Mayberry	3.00	1.35
☐ 374 Jack Heidemann	2.00	.90
☐ 375 Reggie Cleveland	2.00	.90
☐ 376 Andy Kosco	2.00	.90
☐ 377 Terry Harmon	2.00	.90
☐ 378 Checklist 395-525	5.00	2.20
☐ 379 Ken Berry	2.00	.90
☐ 380 Earl Williams	2.00	.90
☐ 381 White Sox Team	4.00	1.80
☐ 382 Joe Gibbon	2.00	.90
☐ 383 Brant Alyea	2.00	.90
☐ 384 Dave Campbell	3.00	1.35
☐ 385 Mickey Stanley	3.00	1.35
☐ 386 Jim Colborn	2.00	.90
☐ 387 Horace Clarke	2.00	.90
☐ 388 Charlie Williams	2.00	.90
☐ 389 Bill Rigney MG	2.00	.90
☐ 390 Willie Davis	3.00	1.35
☐ 391 Ken Sanders	2.00	.90
☐ 392 Pirates Rookies	3.00	1.35
Fred Cambria		
Richie Zisk		
☐ 393 Curt Motton	2.00	.90
☐ 394 Ken Forsch	3.00	1.35
☐ 395 Matty Alou	3.00	1.35
☐ 396 Paul Lindblad	2.50	1.10
☐ 397 Phillies Team	5.00	2.20
☐ 398 Larry Hisle	3.00	1.35
☐ 399 Milt Wilcox	2.50	1.10
☐ 400 Tony Oliva	5.00	2.20
☐ 401 Jim Nash	2.50	1.10
☐ 402 Bobby Heise	2.50	1.10
☐ 403 John Cumberland	2.50	1.10
☐ 404 Jeff Torborg	3.00	1.35
☐ 405 Ron Fairly	3.00	1.35
☐ 406 George Hendrick	5.00	2.20
☐ 407 Chuck Taylor	2.50	1.10
☐ 408 Jim Northrup	2.50	1.10
☐ 409 Frank Baker	2.50	1.10
☐ 410 Fergie Jenkins	7.50	3.40
☐ 411 Bob Montgomery	2.50	1.10
☐ 412 Dick Kelley	2.50	1.10
☐ 413 White Sox Rookies	2.50	1.10
Don Eddy		
Dave Lemonds		
☐ 414 Bob Miller	2.50	1.10
☐ 415 Cookie Rojas	3.00	1.35
☐ 416 Johnny Edwards	2.50	1.10
☐ 417 Tom Hall	2.50	1.10
☐ 418 Tom Shopay	2.50	1.10
☐ 419 Jim Spencer	2.50	1.10
☐ 420 Steve Carlton	20.00	9.00
☐ 421 Ellie Rodriguez	2.50	1.10
☐ 422 Ray Lamb	2.50	1.10
☐ 423 Oscar Gamble	3.00	1.35
☐ 424 Bill Gogolewski	2.50	1.10
☐ 425 Ken Singleton	3.00	1.35
☐ 426 Ken Singleton IA	2.50	1.10
☐ 427 Tito Fuentes	2.50	1.10
☐ 428 Tito Fuentes IA	2.50	1.10
☐ 429 Bob Robertson	2.50	1.10
☐ 430 Bob Robertson IA	2.50	1.10
☐ 431 Clarence Gaston	5.00	2.20
☐ 432 Clarence Gaston IA	3.00	1.35
☐ 433 Johnny Bench	30.00	13.50
☐ 434 Johnny Bench IA	15.00	6.75
☐ 435 Reggie Jackson	30.00	13.50
☐ 436 Reggie Jackson IA	15.00	6.75
☐ 437 Maury Wills	5.00	2.20
☐ 438 Maury Wills IA	3.00	1.35
☐ 439 Billy Williams	6.00	2.70
☐ 440 Billy Williams IA	3.00	1.35
☐ 441 Thurman Munson	20.00	9.00
☐ 442 Thurman Munson IA	10.00	4.50
☐ 443 Ken Henderson	2.50	1.10
☐ 444 Ken Henderson IA	2.50	1.10
☐ 445 Tom Seaver	40.00	18.00
☐ 446 Tom Seaver IA	20.00	9.00
☐ 447 Willie Stargell	10.00	4.50
☐ 448 Willie Stargell IA	5.00	2.20
☐ 449 Bob Lemon MG	4.00	1.80
☐ 450 Mickey Lolich	4.00	1.80
☐ 451 Tony LaRussa	5.00	2.20
☐ 452 Ed Herrmann	2.50	1.10
☐ 453 Barry Lersch	2.50	1.10
☐ 454 A's Team	5.00	2.20
☐ 455 Tommy Harper	3.00	1.35
☐ 456 Mark Belanger	3.00	1.35
☐ 457 Padres Rookies	2.50	1.10
Darcy Fast		
Derrel Thomas		
Mike Ivie		
☐ 458 Aurelio Monteagudo	2.50	1.10
☐ 459 Rick Renick	2.50	1.10
☐ 460 Al Downing	2.50	1.10
☐ 461 Tim Cullen	2.50	1.10
☐ 462 Rickey Clark	2.50	1.10
☐ 463 Bernie Carbo	2.50	1.10
☐ 464 Jim Roland	2.50	1.10
☐ 465 Gil Hodges MG	25.00	11.00
(Mentions his		
death on 4/2/72)		
☐ 466 Norm Miller	2.50	1.10
☐ 467 Steve Kline	2.50	1.10
☐ 468 Richie Scheinblum	2.50	1.10
☐ 469 Ron Herbel	2.50	1.10
☐ 470 Ray Fosse	2.50	1.10
☐ 471 Luke Walker	2.50	1.10
☐ 472 Phil Gagliano	2.50	1.10
☐ 473 Dan McGinn	2.50	1.10
☐ 474 Orioles Rookies	20.00	9.00
Don Baylor		
Roric Harrison		
Johnny Oates		
☐ 475 Gary Nolan	2.50	1.10
☐ 476 Lee Richard	2.50	1.10
☐ 477 Tom Phoebus	2.50	1.10
☐ 478 Checklist 5th Series	6.00	2.70
☐ 479 Don Shaw	2.50	1.10
☐ 480 Lee May	3.00	1.35
☐ 481 Billy Conigliaro	2.50	1.10
☐ 482 Joe Hoerner	2.50	1.10
☐ 483 Ken Suarez	2.50	1.10
☐ 484 Lum Harris MG	2.50	1.10
☐ 485 Phil Regan	2.50	1.10
☐ 486 John Lowenstein	2.50	1.10
☐ 487 Tigers Team	5.00	2.20
☐ 488 Mike Nagy	2.50	1.10
☐ 489 Expos Rookies	2.50	1.10
Terry Humphrey		
Keith Lampard		
☐ 490 Dave McNally	3.00	1.35
☐ 491 Lou Piniella KP	5.00	2.20
☐ 492 Mel Stottlemyre KP	4.00	1.80
☐ 493 Bob Bailey KP	4.00	1.80
☐ 494 Willie Horton KP	4.00	1.80
☐ 495 Bill Melton KP	3.00	1.35
☐ 496 Bud Harrelson KP	4.00	1.80
☐ 497 Jim Perry KP	4.00	1.80
☐ 498 Brooks Robinson KP	6.00	2.70
☐ 499 Vicente Romo	2.50	1.10
☐ 500 Joe Torre	4.00	1.80
☐ 501 Pete Hamm	2.50	1.10
☐ 502 Jackie Hernandez	2.50	1.10
☐ 503 Gary Peters	2.50	1.10
☐ 504 Ed Spiezio	2.50	1.10
☐ 505 Mike Marshall	3.00	1.35
☐ 506 Indians Rookies	3.00	1.35
Terry Ley		
Jim Moyer		
Dick Tidrow		
☐ 507 Fred Gladding	2.50	1.10
☐ 508 Ellie Hendricks	2.50	1.10
☐ 509 Don McMahon	2.50	1.10
☐ 510 Ted Williams MG	15.00	6.75
☐ 511 Tony Taylor	2.50	1.10
☐ 512 Paul Popovich	2.50	1.10
☐ 513 Lindy McDaniel	3.00	1.35
☐ 514 Ted Sizemore	2.50	1.10
☐ 515 Bert Blyleven	5.00	2.20
☐ 516 Oscar Brown	2.50	1.10
☐ 517 Ken Brett	3.00	1.35
☐ 518 Wayne Garrett	2.50	1.10
☐ 519 Ted Abernathy	2.50	1.10
☐ 520 Larry Bowa	5.00	2.20
☐ 521 Alan Foster	2.50	1.10
☐ 522 Dodgers Team	5.00	2.20
☐ 523 Chuck Dobson	2.50	1.10
☐ 524 Reds Rookies	2.50	1.10
Ed Armbrister		
Mel Behney		
☐ 525 Carlos May	3.00	1.35

1973 O-Pee-Chee

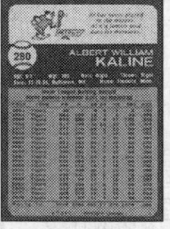

The cards in this 660-card set measure 2 1/2" by 3 1/2". This set is essentially the same as the regular 1973 Topps set, except that the words "Printed in Canada" appear on the backs and the backs are bilingual. On a white border, the fronts feature color player photos with rounded corners and thin black borders. The player's name and position and the team name are also printed on the front. An "All-Time Leaders" series (471-478) appears in this set. Kid pictures appeared again for the second year in a row (341-346). The backs carry player biography and statistics in French and English. The cards are numbered on the back. The backs appear to be more "yellow" than the Topps backs. Remember, the prices below apply only to the O-Pee-Chee cards -- NOT Topps cards which are more plentiful. Unlike the 1973 Topps set, all cards in this set were issued equally and at the same time, i.e., there were no scarce series with the O-Pee-Chee cards. Although there are no scarce series, cards 529-660 attract a slight premium. Because of the premium that high series Topps cards attract, there is a perception that O-Pee-Chee cards of the same number sequence are less available. The key card in this set is Mike Schmidt.

	NRMT	VG-E
COMPLETE SET (660)	900.00	400.00
COMMON CARD (1-528)	.75	.35
COMMON CARD (529-660)	1.75	.80
☐ 1 All-Time HR Leaders:	50.00	22.00
714 Babe Ruth		
673 Hank Aaron		
654 Willie Mays		

☐ 2 Rich Hebner	1.00	.45
☐ 3 Jim Lonborg	1.00	.45
☐ 4 John Milner	.75	.35
☐ 5 Ed Brinkman	.75	.35
☐ 6 Mac Scarce	.75	.35
☐ 7 Texas Rangers Team	1.50	.70
☐ 8 Tom Hall	.75	.35
☐ 9 Johnny Oates	1.00	.45
☐ 10 Don Sutton	2.00	.90
☐ 11 Chris Chambliss	1.25	.55
☐ 12 Padres Leaders	1.00	.45
Don Zimmer MG		
Dave Garcia CO		
Johnny Podres CO		
Bob Skinner CO		
Whitey Wietelmann CO		
☐ 13 George Hendrick	1.00	.45
☐ 14 Sonny Siebert	.75	.35
☐ 15 Ralph Garr	1.00	.45
☐ 16 Steve Braun	.75	.35
☐ 17 Fred Gladding	.75	.35
☐ 18 Leroy Stanton	.75	.35
☐ 19 Tim Foli	.75	.35
☐ 20 Stan Bahnsen	.75	.35
☐ 21 Randy Hundley	.75	.35
☐ 22 Ted Abernathy	.75	.35
☐ 23 Dave Kingman	1.25	.55
☐ 24 Al Santorini	.75	.35
☐ 25 Roy White	1.00	.45
☐ 26 Pirates Team	1.50	.70
☐ 27 Bill Gogolewski	.75	.35
☐ 28 Hal McRae	1.25	.55
☐ 29 Tony Taylor	1.00	.45
☐ 30 Tug McGraw	1.00	.45
☐ 31 Buddy Bell	3.00	1.35
☐ 32 Fred Norman	.75	.35
☐ 33 Jim Breazeale	.75	.35
☐ 34 Pat Dobson	.75	.35
☐ 35 Willie Davis	1.00	.45
☐ 36 Steve Barber	.75	.35
☐ 37 Bill Robinson	1.00	.45
☐ 38 Mike Epstein	.75	.35
☐ 39 Dave Roberts	.75	.35
☐ 40 Reggie Smith	1.00	.45
☐ 41 Tom Walker	.75	.35
☐ 42 Mike Andrews	.75	.35
☐ 43 Randy Moffitt	.75	.35
☐ 44 Rick Monday	1.00	.45
☐ 45 Ellie Rodriguez	.75	.35
(photo actually		
John Felske)		
☐ 46 Lindy McDaniel	1.00	.45
☐ 47 Luis Melendez	.75	.35
☐ 48 Paul Splittorff	.75	.35
☐ 49 Twins Leaders	1.00	.45
Frank Quilici MG		
Vern Morgan CO		
Bob Rodgers CO		
Ralph Rowe CO		
Al Worthington CO		
☐ 50 Roberto Clemente	75.00	34.00
☐ 51 Chuck Seelbach	.75	.35
☐ 52 Denis Menke	.75	.35
☐ 53 Steve Dunning	.75	.35
☐ 54 Checklist 1-132	3.00	1.35
☐ 55 Jon Matlack	1.00	.45
☐ 56 Merv Rettenmund	.75	.35
☐ 57 Derrel Thomas	.75	.35
☐ 58 Mike Paul	.75	.35
☐ 59 Steve Yeager	2.00	.90
☐ 60 Ken Holtzman	1.00	.45
☐ 61 Batting Leaders	3.00	1.35
Billy Williams		
Rod Carew		
☐ 62 Home Run Leaders	2.50	1.10
Johnny Bench		
Dick Allen		
☐ 63 RBI Leaders	2.50	1.10
Johnny Bench		
Dick Allen		
☐ 64 Stolen Base Leaders	2.00	.90
Lou Brock		
Bert Campaneris		
☐ 65 ERA Leaders	2.00	.90
Steve Carlton		
Luis Tiant		
☐ 66 Victory Leaders	2.00	.90
Steve Carlton		
Gaylord Perry		
Wilbur Wood		
☐ 67 Strikeout Leaders	35.00	16.00
Steve Carlton		
Nolan Ryan		
☐ 68 Leading Firemen	1.50	.70
Clay Carroll		
Sparky Lyle		
☐ 69 Phil Gagliano	.75	.35
☐ 70 Milt Pappas	1.00	.45
☐ 71 Johnny Briggs	.75	.35
☐ 72 Ron Reed	.75	.35
☐ 73 Ed Herrmann	.75	.35
☐ 74 Billy Champion	.75	.35
☐ 75 Vada Pinson	1.00	.45
☐ 76 Doug Rader	.75	.35
☐ 77 Mike Torrez	1.00	.45
☐ 78 Richie Scheinblum	.75	.35
☐ 79 Jim Willoughby	.75	.35
☐ 80 Tony Oliva	1.50	.70
☐ 81 Chicago Cubs Leaders	2.00	.90
Whitey Lockman MG		
Hank Aguirre CO		
Ernie Banks CO		
Larry Jansen CO		
Pete Reiser CO		
☐ 82 Fritz Peterson	.75	.35
☐ 83 Leron Lee	.75	.35
☐ 84 Rollie Fingers	5.00	2.20
☐ 85 Ted Simmons	2.00	.90
☐ 86 Tom McCraw	.75	.35
☐ 87 Ken Boswell	.75	.35
☐ 88 Mickey Stanley	1.00	.45
☐ 89 Jack Billingham	.75	.35
☐ 90 Brooks Robinson	8.00	3.60
☐ 91 Dodgers Team	1.50	.70
☐ 92 Jerry Bell	.75	.35
☐ 93 Jesus Alou	.75	.35
☐ 94 Dick Billings	.75	.35
☐ 95 Steve Blass	1.00	.45
☐ 96 Doug Griffin	.75	.35
☐ 97 Willie Montanez	.75	.35
☐ 98 Dick Woodson	.75	.35
☐ 99 Carl Taylor	.75	.35
☐ 100 Hank Aaron	35.00	16.00
☐ 101 Ken Henderson	.75	.35
☐ 102 Rudy May	.75	.35
☐ 103 Celerino Sanchez	.75	.35
☐ 104 Reggie Cleveland	.75	.35
☐ 105 Carlos May	.75	.35
☐ 106 Terry Humphrey	.75	.35
☐ 107 Phil Hennigan	.75	.35
☐ 108 Bill Russell	1.00	.45
☐ 109 Doyle Alexander	1.00	.45
☐ 110 Bob Watson	1.00	.45
☐ 111 Dave Nelson	.75	.35
☐ 112 Gary Ross	.75	.35
☐ 113 Jerry Grote	1.00	.45
☐ 114 Lynn McGlothen	.75	.35
☐ 115 Ron Santo	1.50	.70
☐ 116 Yankees Leaders	1.00	.45
Ralph Houk MG		
Jim Hegan CO		
Elston Howard CO		
Dick Howser CO		
Jim Turner CO		
☐ 117 Ramon Hernandez	.75	.35
☐ 118 John Mayberry	1.00	.45
☐ 119 Larry Bowa	1.00	.45
☐ 120 Joe Coleman	.75	.35
☐ 121 Dave Rader	.75	.35
☐ 122 Jim Strickland	.75	.35
☐ 123 Sandy Alomar	1.00	.45
☐ 124 Jim Hardin	.75	.35
☐ 125 Ron Fairly	1.00	.45
☐ 126 Jim Brewer	.75	.35
☐ 127 Brewers Team	1.50	.70
☐ 128 Ted Sizemore	.75	.35
☐ 129 Terry Forster	1.00	.45
☐ 130 Pete Rose	18.00	8.00
☐ 131 Red Sox Leaders	1.00	.45
Eddie Kasko MG		
Doug Camilli CO		
Don Lenhardt CO		
Eddie Popowski CO		
Lee Stange CO		
☐ 132 Matty Alou	1.00	.45
☐ 133 Dave Roberts	.75	.35
☐ 134 Milt Wilcox	.75	.35
☐ 135 Lee May	1.00	.45
☐ 136 Orioles Leaders	3.00	1.35
Earl Weaver MG		
George Bamberger CO		
Jim Frey CO		
Billy Hunter CO		
George Staller CO		
☐ 137 Jim Beauchamp	.75	.35
☐ 138 Horacio Pina	.75	.35
☐ 139 Carmen Fanzone	.75	.35
☐ 140 Lou Piniella	1.25	.55
☐ 141 Bruce Kison	.75	.35
☐ 142 Thurman Munson	7.50	3.40
☐ 143 John Curtis	.75	.35
☐ 144 Marty Perez	.75	.35
☐ 145 Bobby Bonds	2.00	.90
☐ 146 Woodie Fryman	.75	.35
☐ 147 Mike Anderson	.75	.35
☐ 148 Dave Goltz	.75	.35
☐ 149 Ron Hunt	.75	.35
☐ 150 Wilbur Wood	1.00	.45
☐ 151 Wes Parker	1.00	.45
☐ 152 Dave May	.75	.35
☐ 153 Al Hrabosky	1.00	.45
☐ 154 Jeff Torborg	1.00	.45
☐ 155 Sal Bando	1.00	.45
☐ 156 Cesar Geronimo	.75	.35
☐ 157 Denny Riddleberger	.75	.35
☐ 158 Astros Team	1.50	.70
☐ 159 Clarence Gaston	1.25	.55
☐ 160 Jim Palmer	10.00	4.50
☐ 161 Ted Martinez	.75	.35
☐ 162 Pete Broberg	.75	.35
☐ 163 Vic Davalillo	.75	.35
☐ 164 Monty Montgomery	.75	.35
☐ 165 Luis Aparicio	3.00	1.35
☐ 166 Terry Harmon	.75	.35
☐ 167 Steve Stone	1.00	.45
☐ 168 Jim Northrup	1.00	.45
☐ 169 Ron Schueler	.75	.35
☐ 170 Harmon Killebrew	6.00	2.70
☐ 171 Bernie Carbo	.75	.35
☐ 172 Steve Kline	.75	.35
☐ 173 Hal Breeden	1.00	.45
☐ 174 Rich Gossage	8.00	3.60
☐ 175 Frank Robinson	10.00	4.50
☐ 176 Chuck Taylor	.75	.35
☐ 177 Bill Plummer	.75	.35
☐ 178 Don Rose	.75	.35
☐ 179 Oakland A's Leaders	1.00	.45
Dick Williams MG		
Jerry Adair CO		
Vern Hoscheit CO		
Irv Noren CO		
Wes Stock CO		
☐ 180 Fergie Jenkins	5.00	2.20
☐ 181 Jack Brohamer	.75	.35
☐ 182 Mike Caldwell	1.00	.45
☐ 183 Don Buford	.75	.35
☐ 184 Jerry Koosman	1.00	.45
☐ 185 Jim Wynn	1.00	.45
☐ 186 Bill Fahey	.75	.35
☐ 187 Luke Walker	.75	.35
☐ 188 Cookie Rojas	1.00	.45
☐ 189 Greg Luzinski	1.50	.70
☐ 190 Bob Gibson	10.00	4.50
☐ 191 Tigers Team	1.50	.70
☐ 192 Pat Jarvis	.75	.35
☐ 193 Carlton Fisk	12.50	5.50
☐ 194 Jorge Orta	.75	.35
☐ 195 Clay Carroll	.75	.35
☐ 196 Ken McMullen	.75	.35
☐ 197 Ed Goodson	.75	.35
☐ 198 Horace Clarke	.75	.35
☐ 199 Bert Blyleven	2.00	.90
☐ 200 Billy Williams	5.00	2.20
☐ 201 George Hendrick ALCS	1.50	.70
☐ 202 George Foster NLCS	1.50	.70
☐ 203 Gene Tenace WS	1.50	.70
☐ 204 World Series Game 2	1.50	.70
A's two straight		
☐ 205 Tony Perez WS	1.50	.70
☐ 206 Gene Tenace WS	1.50	.70
☐ 207 Blue Moon Odom WS	1.50	.70
☐ 208 Johnny Bench WS	6.00	2.70
☐ 209 Bert Campaneris WS	1.50	.70
☐ 210 World Series Summary	1.50	.70
World champions:		
A's Win		
☐ 211 Balor Moore	.75	.35
☐ 212 Joe Lahoud	.75	.35
☐ 213 Steve Garvey	6.00	2.70
☐ 214 Steve Hamilton	.75	.35
☐ 215 Dusty Baker	2.00	.90
☐ 216 Toby Harrah	1.00	.45
☐ 217 Don Wilson	.75	.35
☐ 218 Aurelio Rodriguez	.75	.35
☐ 219 Cardinals Team	1.50	.70
☐ 220 Nolan Ryan	125.00	55.00
☐ 221 Fred Kendall	.75	.35
☐ 222 Rob Gardner	.75	.35
☐ 223 Bud Harrelson	1.00	.45
☐ 224 Bill Lee	1.00	.45
☐ 225 Al Oliver	1.50	.70
☐ 226 Ray Fosse	.75	.35
☐ 227 Wayne Twitchell	.75	.35
☐ 228 Bobby Darwin	.75	.35
☐ 229 Roric Harrison	.75	.35
☐ 230 Joe Morgan	7.50	3.40
☐ 231 Bill Parsons	.75	.35
☐ 232 Ken Singleton	1.00	.45
☐ 233 Ed Kirkpatrick	.75	.35
☐ 234 Bill North	.75	.35
☐ 235 Jim Hunter	4.00	1.80

☐ 236 Tito Fuentes	.75	.35
☐ 237 Braves Leaders	2.50	1.10
Eddie Mathews MG		
Lew Burdette CO		
Jim Busby CO		
Roy Hartsfield CO		
Ken Silvestri CO		
☐ 238 Tony Muser	.75	.35
☐ 239 Pete Richert	.75	.35
☐ 240 Bobby Murcer	1.00	.45
☐ 241 Dwain Anderson	.75	.35
☐ 242 George Culver	.75	.35
☐ 243 Angels Team	1.50	.70
☐ 244 Ed Acosta	.75	.35
☐ 245 Carl Yastrzemski	10.00	4.50
☐ 246 Ken Sanders	.75	.35
☐ 247 Del Unser	.75	.35
☐ 248 Jerry Johnson	.75	.35
☐ 249 Larry Biittner	.75	.35
☐ 250 Manny Sanguillen	1.00	.45
☐ 251 Roger Nelson	.75	.35
☐ 252 Giants Leaders	1.00	.45
Charlie Fox MG		
Joe Amalfitano CO		
Andy Gilbert CO		
Don McMahon CO		
John McNamara CO		
☐ 253 Mark Belanger	1.00	.45
☐ 254 Bill Stoneman	.75	.35
☐ 255 Reggie Jackson	20.00	9.00
☐ 256 Chris Zachary	.75	.35
☐ 257 N.Y. Mets Leaders	6.00	2.70
Yogi Berra MG		
Roy McMillan CO		
Joe Pignatano CO		
Rube Walker CO		
Eddie Yost CO		
☐ 258 Tommy John	1.50	.70
☐ 259 Jim Holt	.75	.35
☐ 260 Gary Nolan	1.00	.45
☐ 261 Pat Kelly	.75	.35
☐ 262 Jack Aker	.75	.35
☐ 263 George Scott	1.00	.45
☐ 264 Checklist 133-264	3.00	1.35
☐ 265 Gene Michael	.75	.35
☐ 266 Mike Lum	.75	.35
☐ 267 Lloyd Allen	.75	.35
☐ 268 Jerry Morales	.75	.35
☐ 269 Tim McCarver	1.50	.70
☐ 270 Luis Tiant	1.00	.45
☐ 271 Tom Hutton	.75	.35
☐ 272 Ed Farmer	.75	.35
☐ 273 Chris Speier	.75	.35
☐ 274 Darold Knowles	.75	.35
☐ 275 Tony Perez	4.00	1.80
☐ 276 Joe Lovitto	.75	.35
☐ 277 Bob Miller	.75	.35
☐ 278 Orioles Team	1.50	.70
☐ 279 Mike Strahler	.75	.35
☐ 280 Al Kaline	10.00	4.50
☐ 281 Mike Jorgensen	.75	.35
☐ 282 Steve Hovley	.75	.35
☐ 283 Ray Sadecki	.75	.35
☐ 284 Glenn Borgmann	.75	.35
☐ 285 Don Kessinger	1.00	.45
☐ 286 Frank Linzy	.75	.35
☐ 287 Eddie Leon	.75	.35
☐ 288 Gary Gentry	.75	.35
☐ 289 Bob Oliver	.75	.35
☐ 290 Cesar Cedeno	1.00	.45
☐ 291 Rogelio Moret	.75	.35
☐ 292 Jose Cruz	1.00	.45
☐ 293 Bernie Allen	.75	.35
☐ 294 Steve Arlin	.75	.35
☐ 295 Bert Campaneris	1.00	.45
☐ 296 Reds Leaders	2.50	1.10
Sparky Anderson MG		
Alex Grammas CO		
Ted Kluszewski CO		
George Scherger CO		
Larry Shepard CO		
☐ 297 Walt Williams	.75	.35
☐ 298 Ron Bryant	.75	.35
☐ 299 Ted Ford	.75	.35
☐ 300 Steve Carlton	12.50	5.50
☐ 301 Billy Grabarkewitz	.75	.35
☐ 302 Terry Crowley	.75	.35
☐ 303 Nelson Briles	.75	.35
☐ 304 Duke Sims	.75	.35
☐ 305 Willie Mays	40.00	18.00
☐ 306 Tom Burgmeier	.75	.35
☐ 307 Boots Day	.75	.35
☐ 308 Skip Lockwood	.75	.35
☐ 309 Paul Popovich	.75	.35
☐ 310 Dick Allen	1.50	.70
☐ 311 Joe Decker	.75	.35
☐ 312 Oscar Brown	.75	.35
☐ 313 Jim Ray	.75	.35
☐ 314 Ron Swoboda	.75	.35
☐ 315 John Odom	.75	.35
☐ 316 Padres Team	1.50	.70
☐ 317 Danny Cater	.75	.35
☐ 318 Jim McGlothlin	.75	.35
☐ 319 Jim Spencer	.75	.35
☐ 320 Lou Brock	7.50	3.40
☐ 321 Rich Hinton	.75	.35
☐ 322 Garry Maddox	3.00	1.35
☐ 323 Tigers Leaders	2.00	.90
Billy Martin MG		
Art Fowler CO		
Charlie Silvera CO		
Dick Tracewski CO		
☐ 324 Al Downing	.75	.35
☐ 325 Boog Powell	1.50	.70
☐ 326 Darrell Brandon	.75	.35
☐ 327 John Lowenstein	.75	.35
☐ 328 Bill Bonham	.75	.35
☐ 329 Ed Kranepool	.75	.35
☐ 330 Rod Carew	10.00	4.50
☐ 331 Carl Morton	.75	.35
☐ 332 John Felske	.75	.35
☐ 333 Gene Clines	.75	.35
☐ 334 Freddie Patek	1.00	.45
☐ 335 Bob Tolan	.75	.35
☐ 336 Tom Bradley	.75	.35
☐ 337 Dave Duncan	.75	.35
☐ 338 Checklist 265-396	3.00	1.35
☐ 339 Dick Tidrow	.75	.35
☐ 340 Nate Colbert	.75	.35
☐ 341 Jim Palmer KP	1.50	.70
☐ 342 Sam McDowell KP	1.00	.45
☐ 343 Bobby Murcer KP	1.00	.45
☐ 344 Jim Hunter KP	1.50	.70
☐ 345 Chris Speier KP	1.00	.45
☐ 346 Gaylord Perry KP	1.50	.70
☐ 347 Royals Team	1.50	.70
☐ 348 Rennie Stennett	.75	.35
☐ 349 Dick McAuliffe	.75	.35
☐ 350 Tom Seaver	15.00	6.75
☐ 351 Jimmy Stewart	.75	.35
☐ 352 Don Stanhouse	.75	.35
☐ 353 Steve Brye	.75	.35
☐ 354 Billy Parker	.75	.35
☐ 355 Mike Marshall	1.00	.45
☐ 356 White Sox Leaders	1.00	.45
Chuck Tanner MG		
Joe Lonnett CO		
Jim Mahoney CO		
Al Monchak CO		
Johnny Sain CO		
☐ 357 Ross Grimsley	.75	.35
☐ 358 Jim Nettles	.75	.35
☐ 359 Cecil Upshaw	.75	.35
☐ 360 Joe Rudi	1.00	.45
(photo actually		
Gene Tenace)		
☐ 361 Fran Healy	.75	.35
☐ 362 Eddie Watt	.75	.35
☐ 363 Jackie Hernandez	.75	.35
☐ 364 Rick Wise	.75	.35
☐ 365 Rico Petrocelli	1.00	.45
☐ 366 Brock Davis	.75	.35
☐ 367 Burt Hooton	1.00	.45
☐ 368 Bill Buckner	1.00	.45
☐ 369 Lerrin LaGrow	.75	.35
☐ 370 Willie Stargell	7.50	3.40
☐ 371 Mike Kekich	.75	.35
☐ 372 Oscar Gamble	1.00	.45
☐ 373 Clyde Wright	.75	.35
☐ 374 Darrell Evans	1.00	.45
☐ 375 Larry Dierker	.75	.35
☐ 376 Frank Duffy	.75	.35
☐ 377 Expos Leaders	.75	.35
Gene Mauch MG		
Dave Bristol CO		
Larry Doby CO		
Cal McLish CO		
Jerry Zimmerman CO		
☐ 378 Lenny Randle	.75	.35
☐ 379 Cy Acosta	.75	.35
☐ 380 Johnny Bench	15.00	6.75
☐ 381 Vicente Romo	.75	.35
☐ 382 Mike Hegan	.75	.35
☐ 383 Diego Segui	.75	.35
☐ 384 Don Baylor	4.00	1.80
☐ 385 Jim Perry	1.00	.45
☐ 386 Don Money	1.00	.45
☐ 387 Jim Barr	.75	.35
☐ 388 Ben Oglivie	1.00	.45
☐ 389 Mets Team	3.00	1.35
☐ 390 Mickey Lolich	1.00	.45
☐ 391 Lee Lacy	1.00	.45
☐ 392 Dick Drago	.75	.35
☐ 393 Jose Cardenal	.75	.35
☐ 394 Sparky Lyle	1.00	.45
☐ 395 Roger Metzger	.75	.35
☐ 396 Grant Jackson	.75	.35
☐ 397 Dave Cash	1.00	.45
☐ 398 Rich Hand	.75	.35
☐ 399 George Foster	2.00	.90
☐ 400 Gaylord Perry	5.00	2.20
☐ 401 Clyde Mashore	.75	.35
☐ 402 Jack Hiatt	.75	.35
☐ 403 Sonny Jackson	.75	.35
☐ 404 Chuck Brinkman	.75	.35
☐ 405 Cesar Tovar	.75	.35
☐ 406 Paul Lindblad	.75	.35
☐ 407 Felix Millan	.75	.35
☐ 408 Jim Colborn	.75	.35
☐ 409 Ivan Murrell	.75	.35
☐ 410 Willie McCovey	7.50	3.40
☐ 411 Ray Corbin	.75	.35
☐ 412 Manny Mota	1.00	.45
☐ 413 Tom Timmerman	.75	.35
☐ 414 Ken Rudolph	.75	.35
☐ 415 Marty Pattin	.75	.35
☐ 416 Paul Schaal	.75	.35
☐ 417 Scipio Spinks	.75	.35
☐ 418 Bobby Grich	1.00	.45
☐ 419 Casey Cox	.75	.35
☐ 420 Tommie Agee	.75	.35
☐ 421 Angels Leaders	.75	.35
Bobby Winkles MG		
Tom Morgan CO		
Salty Parker CO		
Jimmie Reese CO		
John Roseboro CO		
☐ 422 Bob Robertson	.75	.35
☐ 423 Johnny Jeter	.75	.35
☐ 424 Denny Doyle	.75	.35
☐ 425 Alex Johnson	.75	.35
☐ 426 Dave LaRoche	.75	.35
☐ 427 Rick Auerbach	.75	.35
☐ 428 Wayne Simpson	.75	.35
☐ 429 Jim Fairey	.75	.35
☐ 430 Vida Blue	1.50	.70
☐ 431 Gerry Moses	.75	.35
☐ 432 Dan Frisella	.75	.35
☐ 433 Willie Horton	1.00	.45
☐ 434 Giants Team	1.50	.70
☐ 435 Rico Carty	1.00	.45
☐ 436 Jim McAndrew	.75	.35
☐ 437 John Kennedy	.75	.35
☐ 438 Enzo Hernandez	.75	.35
☐ 439 Eddie Fisher	.75	.35
☐ 440 Glenn Beckert	.75	.35
☐ 441 Gail Hopkins	.75	.35
☐ 442 Dick Dietz	.75	.35
☐ 443 Danny Thompson	.75	.35
☐ 444 Ken Brett	.75	.35
☐ 445 Ken Berry	.75	.35
☐ 446 Jerry Reuss	1.00	.45
☐ 447 Joe Hague	.75	.35
☐ 448 John Hiller	1.00	.45
☐ 449 Indians Leaders	4.00	1.80
Ken Aspromonte MG		
Rocky Colavito CO		
Joe Lutz CO		
Warren Spahn CO		
☐ 450 Joe Torre	1.50	.70
☐ 451 John Vuckovich	.75	.35
☐ 452 Paul Casanova	.75	.35
☐ 453 Checklist 397-528	3.00	1.35
☐ 454 Tom Haller	.75	.35
☐ 455 Bill Melton	.75	.35
☐ 456 Dick Green	.75	.35
☐ 457 John Strohmayer	.75	.35
☐ 458 Jim Mason	.75	.35
☐ 459 Jimmy Howarth	.75	.35
☐ 460 Bill Freehan	1.00	.45
☐ 461 Mike Corkins	.75	.35
☐ 462 Ron Blomberg	.75	.35
☐ 463 Ken Tatum	.75	.35
☐ 464 Chicago Cubs Team	1.50	.70
☐ 465 Dave Giusti	.75	.35
☐ 466 Jose Arcia	.75	.35
☐ 467 Mike Ryan	.75	.35
☐ 468 Tom Griffin	.75	.35
☐ 469 Dan Monzon	.75	.35
☐ 470 Mike Cuellar	1.00	.45
☐ 471 Ty Cobb ATL	10.00	4.50
4191 Hits		
☐ 472 Lou Gehrig ATL	18.00	8.00
23 Grand Slams		
☐ 473 Hank Aaron ATL	12.50	5.50
6172 Total Bases		
☐ 474 Babe Ruth ATL	20.00	9.00
2209 RBI's		
☐ 475 Ty Cobb ATL	10.00	4.50
.367 Batting Average		
☐ 476 Walter Johnson ATL	4.00	1.80

113 Shutouts
☐ 477 Cy Young ATL 4.00 1.80
511 Wins
☐ 478 Walter Johnson ATL 4.00 1.80
3508 Strikeouts
☐ 479 Hal Lanier .75 .35
☐ 480 Juan Marichal 5.00 2.20
☐ 481 White Sox Team Card 1.50 .70
☐ 482 Rick Reuschel 3.00 1.35
☐ 483 Dal Maxvill .75 .35
☐ 484 Ernie McAnally .75 .35
☐ 485 Norm Cash 1.00 .45
☐ 486 Phillies Leaders 2.00 .90
Danny Ozark MG
Carroll Beringer CO
Billy DeMars CO
Ray Rippelmeyer CO
Bobby Wine CO
☐ 487 Bruce Dal Canton .75 .35
☐ 488 Dave Campbell .75 .35
☐ 489 Jeff Burroughs 1.00 .45
☐ 490 Claude Osteen 1.00 .45
☐ 491 Bob Montgomery .75 .35
☐ 492 Pedro Borbon .75 .35
☐ 493 Duffy Dyer .75 .35
☐ 494 Rich Morales .75 .35
☐ 495 Tommy Helms .75 .35
☐ 496 Ray Lamb .75 .35
☐ 497 Cardinals Leaders 3.00 1.35
Red Schoendienst MG
Vern Benson CO
George Kissell CO
Barney Schultz CO
☐ 498 Graig Nettles 2.50 1.10
☐ 499 Bob Moose .75 .35
☐ 500 Oakland A's Team 1.50 .70
☐ 501 Larry Gura .75 .35
☐ 502 Bobby Valentine .75 .35
☐ 503 Phil Niekro 5.00 2.20
☐ 504 Earl Williams .75 .35
☐ 505 Bob Bailey .75 .35
☐ 506 Bart Johnson .75 .35
☐ 507 Darrel Chaney .75 .35
☐ 508 Gates Brown .75 .35
☐ 509 Jim Nash .75 .35
☐ 510 Amos Otis 1.00 .45
☐ 511 Sam McDowell 1.00 .45
☐ 512 Dalton Jones .75 .35
☐ 513 Dave Marshall .75 .35
☐ 514 Jerry Kenney .75 .35
☐ 515 Andy Messersmith 1.00 .45
☐ 516 Danny Walton .75 .35
☐ 517 Pirates Leaders 2.00 .90
Bill Virdon MG
Don Leppert CO
Bill Mazeroski CO
Dave Ricketts CO
Mel Wright CO
☐ 518 Bob Veale .75 .35
☐ 519 John Edwards .75 .35
☐ 520 Mel Stottlemyre 1.00 .45
☐ 521 Atlanta Braves Team 1.50 .70
☐ 522 Leo Cardenas .75 .35
☐ 523 Wayne Granger .75 .35
☐ 524 Gene Tenace 1.00 .45
☐ 525 Jim Fregosi 1.00 .45
☐ 526 Ollie Brown .75 .35
☐ 527 Dan McGinn .75 .35
☐ 528 Paul Blair 1.00 .45
☐ 529 Milt May 1.75 .80
☐ 530 Jim Kaat 5.00 2.20
☐ 531 Ron Woods 1.75 .80
☐ 532 Steve Mingori 1.75 .80
☐ 533 Larry Stahl 1.75 .80
☐ 534 Dave Lemonds 1.75 .80
☐ 535 John Callison 2.50 1.10
☐ 536 Phillies Team 5.00 2.20
☐ 537 Bill Slayback 1.75 .80
☐ 538 Jim Ray Hart 1.75 .80
☐ 539 Tom Murphy 1.75 .80
☐ 540 Cleon Jones 1.75 .80
☐ 541 Bob Bolin 1.75 .80
☐ 542 Pat Corrales 2.50 1.10
☐ 543 Alan Foster 1.75 .80
☐ 544 Von Joshua 1.75 .80
☐ 545 Orlando Cepeda 5.00 2.20
☐ 546 Jim York 1.75 .80
☐ 547 Bobby Heise 1.75 .80
☐ 548 Don Durham 1.75 .80
☐ 549 Rangers Leaders 5.00 2.20
Whitey Herzog MG
Chuck Estrada CO
Chuck Hiller CO
Jackie Moore CO
☐ 550 Dave Johnson 2.50 1.10
☐ 551 Mike Kilkenny 1.75 .80
☐ 552 J.C. Martin 1.75 .80
☐ 553 Mickey Scott 1.75 .80
☐ 554 Dave Concepcion 5.00 2.20
☐ 555 Bill Hands 1.75 .80
☐ 556 Yankees Team 8.00 3.60
☐ 557 Bernie Williams 1.75 .80
☐ 558 Jerry May 1.75 .80
☐ 559 Barry Lersch 1.75 .80
☐ 560 Frank Howard 3.50 1.55
☐ 561 Jim Geddes 1.75 .80
☐ 562 Wayne Garrett 1.75 .80
☐ 563 Larry Haney 1.75 .80
☐ 564 Mike Thompson 1.75 .80
☐ 565 Jim Hickman 1.75 .80
☐ 566 Lew Krausse 1.75 .80
☐ 567 Bob Fenwick 1.75 .80
☐ 568 Ray Newman 1.75 .80
☐ 569 Dodgers Leaders 5.00 2.20
Walt Alston MG
Red Adams CO
Monty Basgall CO
Jim Gilliam CO
Tom Lasorda CO
☐ 570 Bill Singer 1.75 .80
☐ 571 Rusty Torres 1.75 .80
☐ 572 Gary Sutherland 1.75 .80
☐ 573 Fred Beene 1.75 .80
☐ 574 Bob Didier 1.75 .80
☐ 575 Dock Ellis 2.50 1.10
☐ 576 Expos Team 5.00 2.20
☐ 577 Eric Soderholm 1.75 .80
☐ 578 Ken Wright 1.75 .80
☐ 579 Tom Grieve 2.50 1.10
☐ 580 Joe Pepitone 2.50 1.10
☐ 581 Steve Kealey 1.75 .80
☐ 582 Darrell Porter 2.50 1.10
☐ 583 Bill Greif 1.75 .80
☐ 584 Chris Arnold 1.75 .80
☐ 585 Joe Niekro 2.50 1.10
☐ 586 Bill Sudakis 1.75 .80
☐ 587 Rich McKinney 1.75 .80
☐ 588 Checklist 529-660 15.00 6.75
☐ 589 Ken Forsch 1.75 .80
☐ 590 Deron Johnson 1.75 .80
☐ 591 Mike Hedlund 1.75 .80
☐ 592 John Boccabella 1.75 .80
☐ 593 Royals Leaders 1.75 .80
Jack McKeon MG
Galen Cisco CO
Harry Dunlop CO
Charlie Lau CO
☐ 594 Vic Harris 1.75 .80
☐ 595 Don Gullett 2.50 1.10
☐ 596 Red Sox Team 5.00 2.20
☐ 597 Mickey Rivers 2.50 1.10
☐ 598 Phil Roof 1.75 .80
☐ 599 Ed Crosby 1.75 .80
☐ 600 Dave McNally 2.50 1.10
☐ 601 Rookie Catchers 1.50 .70
Sergio Robles
George Pena
Rick Stelmaszek
☐ 602 Rookie Pitchers 1.50 .70
Mel Behney
Ralph Garcia
Doug Rau
☐ 603 Rookie 3rd Basemen 1.50 .70
Terry Hughes
Bill McNulty
Ken Reitz
☐ 604 Rookie Pitchers 1.50 .70
Jesse Jefferson
Dennis O'Toole
Bob Strampe
☐ 605 Rookie 1st Basemen 5.00 2.20
Enos Cabell
Pat Bourque
Gonzalo Marquez
☐ 606 Rookie Outfielders 5.00 2.20
Gary Matthews
Tom Paciorek
Jorge Roque
☐ 607 Rookie Shortstops 1.50 .70
Pepe Frias
Ray Busse
Mario Guerrero
☐ 608 Rookie Pitchers 5.00 2.20
Steve Busby
Dick Colpaert
George Medich
☐ 609 Rookie 2nd Basemen 6.00 2.70
Larvell Blanks
Pedro Garcia
Dave Lopes
☐ 610 Rookie Pitchers 5.00 2.20
Jimmy Freeman
Charlie Hough
Hank Webb
☐ 611 Rookie Outfielders 1.50 .70
Rich Coggins
Jim Wohlford
Richie Zisk
☐ 612 Rookie Pitchers 1.50 .70
Steve Lawson
Bob Reynolds
Brent Strom
☐ 613 Rookie Catchers 20.00 9.00
Bob Boone
Skip Jutze
Mike Ivie
☐ 614 Rookie Outfielders 20.00 9.00
Al Bumbry
Dwight Evans
Charlie Spikes
☐ 615 Rookie 3rd Basemen 300.00 135.00
Ron Cey
John Hilton
Mike Schmidt
☐ 616 Rookie Pitchers 1.50 .70
Norm Angelini
Steve Blateric
Mike Garman
☐ 617 Rich Chiles 1.75 .80
☐ 618 Andy Etchebarren 1.75 .80
☐ 619 Billy Wilson 1.75 .80
☐ 620 Tommy Harper 2.50 1.10
☐ 621 Joe Ferguson 2.50 1.10
☐ 622 Larry Hisle 2.50 1.10
☐ 623 Steve Renko 1.75 .80
☐ 624 Astros Leaders 6.00 2.70
Leo Durocher MG
Preston Gomez CO
Grady Hatton CO
Hub Kittle CO
Jim Owens CO
☐ 625 Angel Mangual 1.75 .80
☐ 626 Bob Barton 1.75 .80
☐ 627 Luis Alvarado 1.75 .80
☐ 628 Jim Slaton 1.75 .80
☐ 629 Indians Team 5.00 2.20
☐ 630 Denny McLain 5.00 2.20
☐ 631 Tom Matchick 1.75 .80
☐ 632 Dick Selma 1.75 .80
☐ 633 Ike Brown 1.75 .80
☐ 634 Alan Closter 1.75 .80
☐ 635 Gene Alley 2.50 1.10
☐ 636 Rickey Clark 1.75 .80
☐ 637 Norm Miller 1.75 .80
☐ 638 Ken Reynolds 1.75 .80
☐ 639 Willie Crawford 1.75 .80
☐ 640 Dick Bosman 1.75 .80
☐ 641 Reds Team 5.00 2.20
☐ 642 Jose Laboy 1.75 .80
☐ 643 Al Fitzmorris 1.75 .80
☐ 644 Jack Heidemann 1.75 .80
☐ 645 Bob Locker 1.75 .80
☐ 646 Brewers Leaders 2.50 1.10
Del Crandall MG
Harvey Kuenn CO
Joe Nossek CO
Bob Shaw CO
Jim Walton CO
☐ 647 George Stone 1.75 .80
☐ 648 Tom Egan 1.75 .80
☐ 649 Rich Folkers 1.75 .80
☐ 650 Felipe Alou 3.50 1.55
☐ 651 Don Carrithers 1.75 .80
☐ 652 Ted Kubiak 1.75 .80
☐ 653 Joe Hoerner 1.75 .80
☐ 654 Twins Team 5.00 2.20
☐ 655 Clay Kirby 1.75 .80
☐ 656 John Ellis 1.75 .80
☐ 657 Bob Johnson 1.75 .80
☐ 658 Elliott Maddox 1.75 .80
☐ 659 Jose Pagan 1.75 .80
☐ 660 Fred Scherman 4.00 1.80

1973 O-Pee-Chee Blue Team Checklists

This 24-card standard-size set is somewhat difficult to find. These blue-bordered team checklist cards are very similar in design to the mass produced red trim team checklist cards issued by O-Pee-Chee the next year and obviously very similar to the Topps issue. The primary difference compared to the Topps issue is the existence of a little French language on the reverse of the O-Pee-Chee. The fronts feature facsimile autographs on a white background. On an orange background, the backs carry the team checklists. The words "Team Checklist" are printed in French and English. The cards are unnumbered and checklisted below in alphabetical order.

	NRMT	VG-E
COMPLETE SET (24)	125.00	55.00
COMMON TEAM (1-24)	6.00	2.70

☐ 1 Atlanta Braves	6.00	2.70
☐ 2 Baltimore Orioles	6.00	2.70
☐ 3 Boston Red Sox	6.00	2.70
☐ 4 California Angels	6.00	2.70
☐ 5 Chicago Cubs	6.00	2.70
☐ 6 Chicago White Sox	6.00	2.70
☐ 7 Cincinnati Reds	6.00	2.70
☐ 8 Cleveland Indians	6.00	2.70
☐ 9 Detroit Tigers	6.00	2.70
☐ 10 Houston Astros	6.00	2.70
☐ 11 Kansas City Royals	6.00	2.70
☐ 12 Los Angeles Dodgers	6.00	2.70
☐ 13 Milwaukee Brewers	6.00	2.70
☐ 14 Minnesota Twins	6.00	2.70
☐ 15 Montreal Expos	6.00	2.70
☐ 16 New York Mets	6.00	2.70
☐ 17 New York Yankees	6.00	2.70
☐ 18 Oakland A's	6.00	2.70
☐ 19 Philadelphia Phillies	6.00	2.70
☐ 20 Pittsburgh Pirates	6.00	2.70
☐ 21 San Diego Padres	6.00	2.70
☐ 22 San Francisco Giants	6.00	2.70
☐ 23 St. Louis Cardinals	6.00	2.70
☐ 24 Texas Rangers	6.00	2.70

1974 O-Pee-Chee

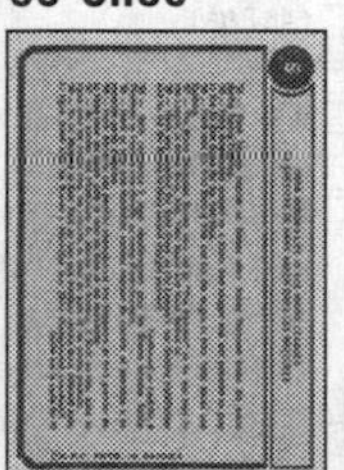

The cards in this 660-card set measure 2 1/2" by 3 1/2". The 1974 O-Pee-Chee cards are very similar to the 1974 Topps cards. Since the O-Pee-Chee cards were printed substantially later than the Topps cards, there was no "San Diego rumored moving to Washington" problem in the O-Pee-Chee set. On a white background, the fronts feature color player photos with rounded corners and blue borders. The player's name and position and the team name also appear on the front. The horizontal backs are golden yellow instead of green like the 1974 Topps and carry player biography and statistics in French and English. There are a number of obverse differences between the two sets as well; they are numbers 3, 4, 5, 6, 7, 8, 9, 99, 166 and 196. The Aaron Specials generally feature two past cards per card instead of four as in the Topps. Remember, the prices below apply only to O-Pee-Chee cards -- they are NOT prices for Topps cards as the Topps cards are generally much more available.

	NRMT	VG-E
COMPLETE SET (660)	1000.00	450.00
COMMON CARD (1-660)	.50	.23
☐ 1 Hank Aaron Complete ML record	50.00	22.00
☐ 2 Hank Aaron Special 54-57 Records on back	8.00	3.60
☐ 3 Hank Aaron Special 58-59	12.00	5.50
☐ 4 Hank Aaron Special 60-61	12.00	5.50
☐ 5 Hank Aaron Special 62-63	12.00	5.50
☐ 6 Hank Aaron Special 64-65	12.00	5.50
☐ 7 Hank Aaron Special 66-67	12.00	5.50
☐ 8 Hank Aaron Special 68-69	12.00	5.50
☐ 9 Hank Aaron Special 70-73 Milestone homers	12.00	5.50
☐ 10 Johnny Bench	15.00	6.75
☐ 11 Jim Bibby	.50	.23
☐ 12 Dave May	.50	.23
☐ 13 Tom Hilgendorf	.50	.23
☐ 14 Paul Popovich	.50	.23
☐ 15 Joe Torre	1.00	.45
☐ 16 Orioles Team	1.00	.45
☐ 17 Doug Bird	.50	.23
☐ 18 Gary Thomasson	.50	.23
☐ 19 Gerry Moses	.50	.23
☐ 20 Nolan Ryan	75.00	34.00
☐ 21 Bob Gallagher	.50	.23
☐ 22 Cy Acosta	.50	.23
☐ 23 Craig Robinson	.50	.23
☐ 24 John Hiller	.75	.35
☐ 25 Ken Singleton	.75	.35
☐ 26 Bill Campbell	.75	.35
☐ 27 George Scott	.75	.35
☐ 28 Manny Sanguillen	.75	.35
☐ 29 Phil Niekro	3.00	1.35
☐ 30 Bobby Bonds	2.00	.90
☐ 31 Astros Leaders Preston Gomez MG Roger Craig CO Hub Kittle CO Grady Hatton CO Bob Lillis CO	.50	.23
☐ 32 Johnny Grubb	.50	.23
☐ 33 Don Newhauser	.50	.23
☐ 34 Andy Kosco	.50	.23
☐ 35 Gaylord Perry	3.00	1.35
☐ 36 Cardinals Team	1.00	.45
☐ 37 Dave Sells	.50	.23
☐ 38 Don Kessinger	.75	.35
☐ 39 Ken Suarez	.50	.23
☐ 40 Jim Palmer	6.00	2.70
☐ 41 Bobby Floyd	.50	.23
☐ 42 Claude Osteen	.75	.35
☐ 43 Jim Wynn	.75	.35
☐ 44 Mel Stottlemyre	.75	.35
☐ 45 Dave Johnson	.75	.35
☐ 46 Pat Kelly	.50	.23
☐ 47 Dick Ruthven	.50	.23
☐ 48 Dick Sharon	.50	.23
☐ 49 Steve Renko	.75	.35
☐ 50 Rod Carew	6.00	2.70
☐ 51 Bob Heise	.50	.23
☐ 52 Al Oliver	1.00	.45
☐ 53 Fred Kendall	.50	.23
☐ 54 Elias Sosa	.50	.23
☐ 55 Frank Robinson	7.50	3.40
☐ 56 New York Mets Team	1.00	.45
☐ 57 Darold Knowles	.50	.23
☐ 58 Charlie Spikes	.50	.23
☐ 59 Ross Grimsley	.50	.23
☐ 60 Lou Brock	6.00	2.70
☐ 61 Luis Aparicio	3.00	1.35
☐ 62 Bob Locker	.50	.23
☐ 63 Bill Sudakis	.50	.23
☐ 64 Doug Rau	.50	.23
☐ 65 Amos Otis	.75	.35
☐ 66 Sparky Lyle	.75	.35
☐ 67 Tommy Helms	.50	.23
☐ 68 Grant Jackson	.50	.23
☐ 69 Del Unser	.50	.23
☐ 70 Dick Allen	1.00	.45
☐ 71 Dan Frisella	.50	.23
☐ 72 Aurelio Rodriguez	.50	.23
☐ 73 Mike Marshall	.75	.35
☐ 74 Twins Team	1.00	.45
☐ 75 Jim Colborn	.50	.23
☐ 76 Mickey Rivers	.75	.35
☐ 77 Rich Troedson	.50	.23
☐ 78 Giants Leaders Charlie Fox MG John McNamara CO Joe Amalfitano CO Andy Gilbert CO Don McMahon CO	.50	.23
☐ 79 Gene Tenace	.75	.35
☐ 80 Tom Seaver	14.00	6.25
☐ 81 Frank Duffy	.50	.23
☐ 82 Dave Giusti	.50	.23
☐ 83 Orlando Cepeda	1.50	.70
☐ 84 Rick Wise	.50	.23
☐ 85 Joe Morgan	6.00	2.70
☐ 86 Joe Ferguson	.50	.23
☐ 87 Fergie Jenkins	3.00	1.35
☐ 88 Fred Patek	.75	.35
☐ 89 Jackie Brown	.50	.23
☐ 90 Bobby Murcer	1.00	.45
☐ 91 Ken Forsch	.50	.23
☐ 92 Paul Blair	.75	.35
☐ 93 Rod Gilbreath	.50	.23
☐ 94 Tigers Team	1.00	.45
☐ 95 Steve Carlton	7.50	3.40
☐ 96 Jerry Hairston	.50	.23
☐ 97 Bob Bailey	.75	.35
☐ 98 Bert Blyleven	1.00	.45
☐ 99 George Theodore (Topps 99 is Brewers Leaders)	1.00	.45
☐ 100 Willie Stargell	5.00	2.20
☐ 101 Bobby Valentine	.75	.35
☐ 102 Bill Greif	.50	.23
☐ 103 Sal Bando	.75	.35
☐ 104 Ron Bryant	.50	.23
☐ 105 Carlton Fisk	14.00	6.25
☐ 106 Harry Parker	.50	.23
☐ 107 Alex Johnson	.50	.23
☐ 108 Al Hrabosky	.75	.35
☐ 109 Bobby Grich	.75	.35
☐ 110 Billy Williams	4.00	1.80
☐ 111 Clay Carroll	.50	.23
☐ 112 Dave Lopes	1.00	.45
☐ 113 Dick Drago	.50	.23
☐ 114 Angels Team	1.00	.45
☐ 115 Willie Horton	.75	.35
☐ 116 Jerry Reuss	.75	.35
☐ 117 Ron Blomberg	.50	.23
☐ 118 Bill Lee	.75	.35
☐ 119 Phillies Leaders Danny Ozark MG Ray Rippelmeyer CO Bobby Wine CO Carroll Beringer CO Billy DeMars CO	.50	.23
☐ 120 Wilbur Wood	.50	.23
☐ 121 Larry Lintz	.50	.23
☐ 122 Jim Holt	.50	.23
☐ 123 Nellie Briles	.50	.23
☐ 124 Bobby Coluccio	.50	.23
☐ 125 Nate Colbert	.50	.23
☐ 126 Checklist 1-132	2.50	1.10
☐ 127 Tom Paciorek	.75	.35
☐ 128 John Ellis	.50	.23
☐ 129 Chris Speier	.50	.23
☐ 130 Reggie Jackson	18.00	8.00
☐ 131 Bob Boone	2.00	.90
☐ 132 Felix Millan	.50	.23
☐ 133 David Clyde	.50	.23
☐ 134 Denis Menke	.50	.23
☐ 135 Roy White	.75	.35
☐ 136 Rick Reuschel	1.00	.45
☐ 137 Al Bumbry	.50	.23
☐ 138 Eddie Brinkman	.50	.23
☐ 139 Aurelio Monteagudo	.50	.23
☐ 140 Darrell Evans	1.00	.45
☐ 141 Pat Bourque	.50	.23
☐ 142 Pedro Garcia	.50	.23
☐ 143 Dick Woodson	.50	.23
☐ 144 Dodgers Leaders Walter Alston MG Tom Lasorda CO Jim Gilliam CO Red Adams CO Monty Basgall CO	1.50	.70
☐ 145 Dock Ellis	.50	.23
☐ 146 Ron Fairly	.75	.35
☐ 147 Bart Johnson	.50	.23
☐ 148 Dave Hilton	.50	.23
☐ 149 Mac Scarce	.50	.23
☐ 150 John Mayberry	.75	.35
☐ 151 Diego Segui	.50	.23
☐ 152 Oscar Gamble	.75	.35
☐ 153 Jon Matlack	.75	.35
☐ 154 Astros Team	1.00	.45
☐ 155 Bert Campaneris	.75	.35
☐ 156 Randy Moffitt	.50	.23
☐ 157 Vic Harris	.50	.23
☐ 158 Jack Billingham	.50	.23
☐ 159 Jim Ray Hart	.50	.23
☐ 160 Brooks Robinson	7.50	3.40
☐ 161 Ray Burris	.75	.35
☐ 162 Bill Freehan	.75	.35
☐ 163 Ken Berry	.50	.23
☐ 164 Tom House	.50	.23
☐ 165 Willie Davis	.75	.35
☐ 166 Mickey Lolich (Topps 166 is Royals Leaders)	1.50	.70
☐ 167 Luis Tiant	.75	.35
☐ 168 Danny Thompson	.50	.23
☐ 169 Steve Rogers	.75	.35
☐ 170 Bill Melton	.50	.23
☐ 171 Eduardo Rodriguez	.50	.23
☐ 172 Gene Clines	.50	.23
☐ 173 Randy Jones	1.00	.45
☐ 174 Bill Robinson	.75	.35
☐ 175 Reggie Cleveland	.50	.23
☐ 176 John Lowenstein	.50	.23
☐ 177 Dave Roberts	.50	.23
☐ 178 Garry Maddox	.75	.35

☐ 179 N.Y. Mets Leaders 2.00 .90
Yogi Berra MG
Rube Walker CO
Eddie Yost CO
Roy McMillan CO
Joe Pignatano CO
☐ 180 Ken Holtzman .75 .35
☐ 181 Cesar Geronimo .50 .23
☐ 182 Lindy McDaniel .75 .35
☐ 183 Johnny Oates .75 .35
☐ 184 Rangers Team 1.00 .45
☐ 185 Jose Cardenal .50 .23
☐ 186 Fred Scherman .50 .23
☐ 187 Don Baylor 3.00 1.35
☐ 188 Rudy Meoli .50 .23
☐ 189 Jim Brewer .50 .23
☐ 190 Tony Oliva 1.00 .45
☐ 191 Al Fitzmorris .50 .23
☐ 192 Mario Guerrero .50 .23
☐ 193 Tom Walker .50 .23
☐ 194 Darrell Porter .75 .35
☐ 195 Carlos May .50 .23
☐ 196 Jim Hunter 6.00 2.70
(Topps 196 is
Jim Fregosi)
☐ 197 Vicente Romo .50 .23
☐ 198 Dave Cash .50 .23
☐ 199 Mike Kekich .50 .23
☐ 200 Cesar Cedeno .75 .35
☐ 201 Batting Leaders 6.00 2.70
Rod Carew
Pete Rose
☐ 202 Home Run Leaders 6.00 2.70
Reggie Jackson
Willie Stargell
☐ 203 RBI Leaders 6.00 2.70
Reggie Jackson
Willie Stargell
☐ 204 Stolen Base Leaders 1.50 .70
Tommy Harper
Lou Brock
☐ 205 Victory Leaders 1.00 .45
Wilbur Wood
Ron Bryant
☐ 206 ERA Leaders 6.00 2.70
Jim Palmer
Tom Seaver
☐ 207 Strikeout Leaders 25.00 11.00
Nolan Ryan
Tom Seaver
☐ 208 Leading Firemen 1.00 .45
John Hiller
Mike Marshall
☐ 209 Ted Sizemore .50 .23
☐ 210 Bill Singer .50 .23
☐ 211 Chicago Cubs Team 1.00 .45
☐ 212 Rollie Fingers 3.00 1.35
☐ 213 Dave Rader .50 .23
☐ 214 Bill Grabarkewitz .50 .23
☐ 215 Al Kaline 6.00 2.70
☐ 216 Ray Sadecki .50 .23
☐ 217 Tim Foli .50 .23
☐ 218 John Briggs .50 .23
☐ 219 Doug Griffin .50 .23
☐ 220 Don Sutton 2.50 1.10
☐ 221 White Sox Leaders .75 .35
Chuck Tanner MG
Jim Mahoney CO
Alex Monchak CO
Johnny Sain CO
Joe Lonnett CO
☐ 222 Ramon Hernandez .50 .23
☐ 223 Jeff Burroughs 1.00 .45
☐ 224 Roger Metzger .50 .23
☐ 225 Paul Splittorff .50 .23
☐ 226 Padres Team Card 1.00 .45
☐ 227 Mike Lum .50 .23
☐ 228 Ted Kubiak .50 .23
☐ 229 Fritz Peterson .50 .23
☐ 230 Tony Perez 3.00 1.35
☐ 231 Dick Tidrow .50 .23
☐ 232 Steve Brye .50 .23
☐ 233 Jim Barr .50 .23
☐ 234 John Milner .50 .23
☐ 235 Dave McNally .75 .35
☐ 236 Cardinals Leaders 1.00 .45
Red Schoendienst MG
Barney Schultz CO
George Kissell CO
Johnny Lewis CO
Vern Benson CO
☐ 237 Ken Brett .50 .23
☐ 238 Fran Healy .75 .35
☐ 239 Bill Russell .75 .35
☐ 240 Joe Coleman .50 .23
☐ 241 Glenn Beckert .50 .23
☐ 242 Bill Gogolewski .50 .23
☐ 243 Bob Oliver .50 .23
☐ 244 Carl Morton .50 .23
☐ 245 Cleon Jones .50 .23
☐ 246 Athletics Team 1.00 .45
☐ 247 Rick Miller .50 .23
☐ 248 Tom Hall .50 .23
☐ 249 George Mitterwald .50 .23
☐ 250 Willie McCovey 6.00 2.70
☐ 251 Graig Nettles 2.00 .90
☐ 252 Dave Parker 12.50 5.50
☐ 253 John Boccabella .50 .23
☐ 254 Stan Bahnsen .50 .23
☐ 255 Larry Bowa .75 .35
☐ 256 Tom Griffin .50 .23
☐ 257 Buddy Bell 1.00 .45
☐ 258 Jerry Morales .50 .23
☐ 259 Bob Reynolds .50 .23
☐ 260 Ted Simmons 1.50 .70
☐ 261 Jerry Bell .50 .23
☐ 262 Ed Kirkpatrick .50 .23
☐ 263 Checklist 133-264 2.50 1.10
☐ 264 Joe Rudi .75 .35
☐ 265 Tug McGraw 1.00 .45
☐ 266 Jim Northrup .75 .35
☐ 267 Andy Messersmith .75 .35
☐ 268 Tom Grieve .75 .35
☐ 269 Bob Johnson .50 .23
☐ 270 Ron Santo 1.00 .45
☐ 271 Bill Hands .50 .23
☐ 272 Paul Casanova .50 .23
☐ 273 Checklist 265-396 2.50 1.10
☐ 274 Fred Beene .50 .23
☐ 275 Ron Hunt .50 .23
☐ 276 Angels Leaders .75 .35
Bobby Winkles MG
John Roseboro CO
Tom Morgan CO
Jimmie Reese CO
Salty Parker CO
☐ 277 Gary Nolan .75 .35
☐ 278 Cookie Rojas .75 .35
☐ 279 Jim Crawford .50 .23
☐ 280 Carl Yastrzemski 7.50 3.40
☐ 281 Giants Team 1.00 .45
☐ 282 Doyle Alexander .75 .35
☐ 283 Mike Schmidt 60.00 27.00
☐ 284 Dave Duncan .50 .23
☐ 285 Reggie Smith 1.00 .45
☐ 286 Tony Muser .50 .23
☐ 287 Clay Kirby .50 .23
☐ 288 Gorman Thomas 1.00 .45
☐ 289 Rick Auerbach .50 .23
☐ 290 Vida Blue 1.00 .45
☐ 291 Don Hahn .50 .23
☐ 292 Chuck Seelbach .50 .23
☐ 293 Milt May .50 .23
☐ 294 Steve Foucault .50 .23
☐ 295 Rick Monday .75 .35
☐ 296 Ray Corbin .50 .23
☐ 297 Hal Breeden .50 .23
☐ 298 Roric Harrison .50 .23
☐ 299 Gene Michael .50 .23
☐ 300 Pete Rose 18.00 8.00
☐ 301 Bob Montgomery .50 .23
☐ 302 Rudy May .50 .23
☐ 303 George Hendrick .75 .35
☐ 304 Don Wilson .50 .23
☐ 305 Tito Fuentes .50 .23
☐ 306 Orioles Leaders 2.00 .90
Earl Weaver MG
Jim Frey CO
George Bamberger CO
Billy Hunter CO
George Staller CO
☐ 307 Luis Melendez .50 .23
☐ 308 Bruce Dal Canton .50 .23
☐ 309 Dave Roberts .50 .23
☐ 310 Terry Forster .75 .35
☐ 311 Jerry Grote .75 .35
☐ 312 Deron Johnson .50 .23
☐ 313 Barry Lersch .50 .23
☐ 314 Brewers Team 1.00 .45
☐ 315 Ron Cey 1.00 .45
☐ 316 Jim Perry 1.00 .45
☐ 317 Richie Zisk .75 .35
☐ 318 Jim Merritt .50 .23
☐ 319 Randy Hundley .50 .23
☐ 320 Dusty Baker 2.00 .90
☐ 321 Steve Braun .50 .23
☐ 322 Ernie McAnally .50 .23
☐ 323 Richie Scheinblum .50 .23
☐ 324 Steve Kline .50 .23
☐ 325 Tommy Harper .75 .35
☐ 326 Reds Leaders 2.50 1.10
Sparky Anderson MG
Larry Shepard CO
George Scherger CO
Alex Grammas CO
Ted Kluszewski CO
☐ 327 Tom Timmermann .50 .23
☐ 328 Skip Jutze .50 .23
☐ 329 Mark Belanger .75 .35
☐ 330 Juan Marichal 3.00 1.35
☐ 331 All-Star Catchers: 6.00 2.70
Carlton Fisk
Johnny Bench
☐ 332 All-Star 1B: 6.00 2.70
Dick Allen
Hank Aaron
☐ 333 All-Star 2B: 2.50 1.10
Rod Carew
Joe Morgan
☐ 334 All-Star 3B: 2.50 1.10
Brooks Robinson
Ron Santo
☐ 335 All-Star SS 1.00 .45
Bert Campaneris
Chris Speier
☐ 336 All-Star LF: 3.00 1.35
Bobby Murcer
Pete Rose
☐ 337 All-Star CF 1.00 .45
Amos Otis
Cesar Cedeno
☐ 338 All-Star RF: 6.00 2.70
Reggie Jackson
Billy Williams
☐ 339 All-Star Pitchers: 1.50 .70
Jim Hunter
Rick Wise
☐ 340 Thurman Munson 7.50 3.40
☐ 341 Dan Driessen 1.00 .45
☐ 342 Jim Lonborg .75 .35
☐ 343 Royals Team 1.00 .45
☐ 344 Mike Caldwell .50 .23
☐ 345 Bill North .50 .23
☐ 346 Ron Reed .50 .23
☐ 347 Sandy Alomar .50 .23
☐ 348 Pete Richert .50 .23
☐ 349 John Vukovich .50 .23
☐ 350 Bob Gibson 6.00 2.70
☐ 351 Dwight Evans 3.00 1.35
☐ 352 Bill Stoneman .50 .23
☐ 353 Rich Coggins .50 .23
☐ 354 Chicago Cubs Leaders .75 .35
Whitey Lockman MG
J.C. Martin CO
Hank Aguirre CO
Al Spangler CO
Jim Marshall CO
☐ 355 Dave Nelson .50 .23
☐ 356 Jerry Koosman 1.00 .45
☐ 357 Buddy Bradford .50 .23
☐ 358 Dal Maxvill .50 .23
☐ 359 Brent Strom .50 .23
☐ 360 Greg Luzinski 1.00 .45
☐ 361 Don Carrithers .50 .23
☐ 362 Hal King .50 .23
☐ 363 Yankees Team 1.00 .45
☐ 364 Cito Gaston .75 .35
☐ 365 Steve Busby .75 .35
☐ 366 Larry Hisle .75 .35
☐ 367 Norm Cash 1.00 .45
☐ 368 Manny Mota .75 .35
☐ 369 Paul Lindblad .50 .23
☐ 370 Bob Watson .75 .35
☐ 371 Jim Slaton .50 .23
☐ 372 Ken Reitz .50 .23
☐ 373 John Curtis .50 .23
☐ 374 Marty Perez .50 .23
☐ 375 Earl Williams .50 .23
☐ 376 Jorge Orta .50 .23
☐ 377 Ron Woods .50 .23
☐ 378 Burt Hooton .75 .35
☐ 379 Rangers Leaders 1.00 .45
Billy Martin MG
Frank Lucchesi CO
Art Fowler CO
Charlie Silvera CO
Jackie Moore CO
☐ 380 Bud Harrelson .75 .35
☐ 381 Charlie Sands .50 .23
☐ 382 Bob Moose .50 .23
☐ 383 Phillies Team 1.00 .45
☐ 384 Chris Chambliss .75 .35
☐ 385 Don Gullett .75 .35
☐ 386 Gary Matthews .75 .35
☐ 387 Rich Morales .50 .23
☐ 388 Phil Roof .50 .23
☐ 389 Gates Brown .50 .23
☐ 390 Lou Piniella 1.50 .70
☐ 391 Billy Champion .50 .23
☐ 392 Dick Green .50 .23
☐ 393 Orlando Pena .50 .23
☐ 394 Ken Henderson .50 .23

☐ 395 Doug Rader	.50	.23
☐ 396 Tommy Davis	.75	.35
☐ 397 George Stone	.50	.23
☐ 398 Duke Sims	.50	.23
☐ 399 Mike Paul	.50	.23
☐ 400 Harmon Killebrew	6.00	2.70
☐ 401 Elliott Maddox	.50	.23
☐ 402 Jim Rooker	.50	.23
☐ 403 Red Sox Leaders	.75	.35
Darrell Johnson MG		
Eddie Popowski CO		
Lee Stange CO		
Don Zimmer CO		
Don Bryant CO		
☐ 404 Jim Howarth	.50	.23
☐ 405 Ellie Rodriguez	.50	.23
☐ 406 Steve Arlin	.50	.23
☐ 407 Jim Wohlford	.50	.23
☐ 408 Charlie Hough	1.00	.45
☐ 409 Ike Brown	.50	.23
☐ 410 Pedro Borbon	.50	.23
☐ 411 Frank Baker	.50	.23
☐ 412 Chuck Taylor	.50	.23
☐ 413 Don Money	.50	.23
☐ 414 Checklist 397-528	2.50	1.10
☐ 415 Gary Gentry	.50	.23
☐ 416 White Sox Team	1.00	.45
☐ 417 Rich Folkers	.50	.23
☐ 418 Walt Williams	.50	.23
☐ 419 Wayne Twitchell	.50	.23
☐ 420 Ray Fosse	.50	.23
☐ 421 Dan Fife	.50	.23
☐ 422 Gonzalo Marquez	.50	.23
☐ 423 Fred Stanley	.50	.23
☐ 424 Jim Beauchamp	.50	.23
☐ 425 Pete Broberg	.50	.23
☐ 426 Rennie Stennett	.50	.23
☐ 427 Bobby Bolin	.50	.23
☐ 428 Gary Sutherland	.50	.23
☐ 429 Dick Lange	.50	.23
☐ 430 Matty Alou	.75	.35
☐ 431 Gene Garber	1.00	.45
☐ 432 Chris Arnold	.50	.23
☐ 433 Lerrin LaGrow	.50	.23
☐ 434 Ken McMullen	.50	.23
☐ 435 Dave Concepcion	2.50	1.10
☐ 436 Don Hood	.50	.23
☐ 437 Jim Lyttle	.50	.23
☐ 438 Ed Herrmann	.50	.23
☐ 439 Norm Miller	.50	.23
☐ 440 Jim Kaat	1.50	.70
☐ 441 Tom Ragland	.50	.23
☐ 442 Alan Foster	.50	.23
☐ 443 Tom Hutton	.50	.23
☐ 444 Vic Davalillo	.50	.23
☐ 445 George Medich	.50	.23
☐ 446 Len Randle	.50	.23
☐ 447 Twins Leaders	.75	.35
Frank Quilici MG		
Ralph Rowe CO		
Bob Rodgers CO		
Vern Morgan CO		
☐ 448 Ron Hodges	.50	.23
☐ 449 Tom McCraw	.50	.23
☐ 450 Rich Hebner	.75	.35
☐ 451 Tommy John	1.50	.70
☐ 452 Gene Hiser	.50	.23
☐ 453 Balor Moore	.50	.23
☐ 454 Kurt Bevacqua	.50	.23
☐ 455 Tom Bradley	.50	.23
☐ 456 Dave Winfield	125.00	55.00
☐ 457 Chuck Goggin	.50	.23
☐ 458 Jim Ray	.50	.23
☐ 459 Reds Team	1.00	.45
☐ 460 Boog Powell	1.00	.45
☐ 461 John Odom	.50	.23
☐ 462 Luis Alvarado	.50	.23
☐ 463 Pat Dobson	.50	.23
☐ 464 Jose Cruz	.75	.35
☐ 465 Dick Bosman	.50	.23
☐ 466 Dick Billings	.50	.23
☐ 467 Winston Llenas	.50	.23
☐ 468 Pepe Frias	.50	.23
☐ 469 Joe Decker	.50	.23
☐ 470 Reggie Jackson ALCS	6.00	2.70
☐ 471 Jon Matlack NLCS	1.00	.45
☐ 472 Darold Knowles WS	.50	.23
☐ 473 Willie Mays WS	10.00	4.50
☐ 474 Bert Campaneris WS	1.00	.45
☐ 475 Rusty Staub WS	1.00	.45
☐ 476 Cleon Jones WS	1.00	.45
☐ 477 Reggie Jackson WS	7.50	3.40
☐ 478 Bert Campaneris WS	1.00	.45
☐ 479 World Series Summary	1.00	.45
A's Celebrate; Win		
2nd cons. championship		
☐ 480 Willie Crawford	.50	.23
☐ 481 Jerry Terrell	.50	.23
☐ 482 Bob Didier	.50	.23
☐ 483 Braves Team	1.00	.45
☐ 484 Carmen Fanzone	.50	.23
☐ 485 Felipe Alou	1.00	.45
☐ 486 Steve Stone	.75	.35
☐ 487 Ted Martinez	.50	.23
☐ 488 Andy Etchebarren	.50	.23
☐ 489 Pirates Leaders	1.00	.45
Danny Murtaugh MG		
Don Osborn CO		
Don Leppert CO		
Bill Mazeroski CO		
Bob Skinner CO		
☐ 490 Vada Pinson	1.00	.45
☐ 491 Roger Nelson	.50	.23
☐ 492 Mike Rogodzinski	.50	.23
☐ 493 Joe Hoerner	.50	.23
☐ 494 Ed Goodson	.50	.23
☐ 495 Dick McAuliffe	.75	.35
☐ 496 Tom Murphy	.50	.23
☐ 497 Bobby Mitchell	.50	.23
☐ 498 Pat Corrales	.50	.23
☐ 499 Rusty Torres	.50	.23
☐ 500 Lee May	.75	.35
☐ 501 Eddie Leon	.50	.23
☐ 502 Dave LaRoche	.50	.23
☐ 503 Eric Soderholm	.50	.23
☐ 504 Joe Niekro	.75	.35
☐ 505 Bill Buckner	1.00	.45
☐ 506 Ed Farmer	.50	.23
☐ 507 Larry Stahl	.50	.23
☐ 508 Expos Team	1.00	.45
☐ 509 Jesse Jefferson	.50	.23
☐ 510 Wayne Garrett	.50	.23
☐ 511 Toby Harrah	.75	.35
☐ 512 Joe Lahoud	.50	.23
☐ 513 Jim Campanis	.50	.23
☐ 514 Paul Schaal	.50	.23
☐ 515 Willie Montanez	.50	.23
☐ 516 Horacio Pina	.50	.23
☐ 517 Mike Hegan	.50	.23
☐ 518 Derrel Thomas	.50	.23
☐ 519 Bill Sharp	.50	.23
☐ 520 Tim McCarver	1.00	.45
☐ 521 Indians Leaders	.50	.23
Ken Aspromonte MG		
Clay Bryant CO		
Tony Pacheco CO		
☐ 522 J.R. Richard	.75	.35
☐ 523 Cecil Cooper	1.00	.45
☐ 524 Bill Plummer	.50	.23
☐ 525 Clyde Wright	.50	.23
☐ 526 Frank Tepedino	.50	.23
☐ 527 Bobby Darwin	.50	.23
☐ 528 Bill Bonham	.50	.23
☐ 529 Horace Clarke	.50	.23
☐ 530 Mickey Stanley	.75	.35
☐ 531 Expos Leaders	.75	.35
Gene Mauch MG		
Dave Bristol CO		
Cal McLish CO		
Larry Doby CO		
Jerry Zimmerman CO		
☐ 532 Skip Lockwood	.50	.23
☐ 533 Mike Phillips	.50	.23
☐ 534 Eddie Watt	.50	.23
☐ 535 Bob Tolan	.50	.23
☐ 536 Duffy Dyer	.50	.23
☐ 537 Steve Mingori	.50	.23
☐ 538 Cesar Tovar	.50	.23
☐ 539 Lloyd Allen	.50	.23
☐ 540 Bob Robertson	.50	.23
☐ 541 Indians Team	1.00	.45
☐ 542 Rich Gossage	3.00	1.35
☐ 543 Danny Cater	.50	.23
☐ 544 Ron Schueler	.50	.23
☐ 545 Billy Conigliaro	.75	.35
☐ 546 Mike Corkins	.50	.23
☐ 547 Glenn Borgmann	.50	.23
☐ 548 Sonny Siebert	.50	.23
☐ 549 Mike Jorgensen	.50	.23
☐ 550 Sam McDowell	.75	.35
☐ 551 Von Joshua	.50	.23
☐ 552 Denny Doyle	.50	.23
☐ 553 Jim Willoughby	.50	.23
☐ 554 Tim Johnson	.50	.23
☐ 555 Woody Fryman	.50	.23
☐ 556 Dave Campbell	.75	.35
☐ 557 Jim McGlothlin	.50	.23
☐ 558 Bill Fahey	.50	.23
☐ 559 Darrell Chaney	.50	.23
☐ 560 Mike Cuellar	.75	.35
☐ 561 Ed Kranepool	.50	.23
☐ 562 Jack Aker	.50	.23
☐ 563 Hal McRae	1.00	.45
☐ 564 Mike Ryan	.50	.23
☐ 565 Milt Wilcox	.50	.23
☐ 566 Jackie Hernandez	.50	.23
☐ 567 Red Sox Team	1.00	.45
☐ 568 Mike Torrez	.75	.35
☐ 569 Rick Dempsey	.75	.35
☐ 570 Ralph Garr	.75	.35
☐ 571 Rich Hand	.50	.23
☐ 572 Enzo Hernandez	.50	.23
☐ 573 Mike Adams	.50	.23
☐ 574 Bill Parsons	.50	.23
☐ 575 Steve Garvey	4.00	1.80
☐ 576 Scipio Spinks	.50	.23
☐ 577 Mike Sadek	.50	.23
☐ 578 Ralph Houk MG	.75	.35
☐ 579 Cecil Upshaw	.50	.23
☐ 580 Jim Spencer	.50	.23
☐ 581 Fred Norman	.50	.23
☐ 582 Bucky Dent	5.00	2.20
☐ 583 Marty Pattin	.50	.23
☐ 584 Ken Rudolph	.50	.23
☐ 585 Merv Rettenmund	.50	.23
☐ 586 Jack Brohamer	.50	.23
☐ 587 Larry Christenson	.50	.23
☐ 588 Hal Lanier	.50	.23
☐ 589 Boots Day	.75	.35
☐ 590 Rogelio Moret	.50	.23
☐ 591 Sonny Jackson	.50	.23
☐ 592 Ed Bane	.50	.23
☐ 593 Steve Yeager	.50	.23
☐ 594 Leroy Stanton	.50	.23
☐ 595 Steve Blass	.75	.35
☐ 596 Rookie Pitchers	.75	.35
Wayne Garland		
Fred Holdsworth		
Mark Littell		
Dick Pole		
☐ 597 Rookie Shortstops	1.50	.70
Dave Chalk		
John Gamble		
Pete MacKanin		
Manny Trillo		
☐ 598 Rookie Outfielders:	18.00	8.00
Dave Augustine		
Ken Griffey		
Steve Ontiveros		
Jim Tyrone		
☐ 599 Rookie Pitchers	1.00	.45
Ron Diorio		
Dave Freisleben		
Frank Riccelli		
Greg Shanahan		
☐ 600 Rookie Infielders:	6.00	2.70
Ron Cash		
Jim Cox		
Bill Madlock		
Reggie Sanders		
☐ 601 Rookie Outfielders:	3.00	1.35
Ed Armbrister		
Rich Bladt		
Brian Downing		
Bake McBride		
☐ 602 Rookie Pitchers	.75	.35
Glenn Abbott		
Rick Henninger		
Craig Swan		
Dan Vossler		
☐ 603 Rookie Catchers	.75	.35
Barry Foote		
Tom Lundstedt		
Charlie Moore		
Sergio Robles		
☐ 604 Rookie Infielders:	6.00	2.70
Terry Hughes		
John Knox		
Andy Thornton		
Frank White		
☐ 605 Rookie Pitchers:	5.00	2.20
Vic Albury		
Ken Frailing		
Kevin Kobel		
Frank Tanana		
☐ 606 Rookie Outfielders	.75	.35
Jim Fuller		
Wilbur Howard		
Tommy Smith		
Otto Velez		
☐ 607 Rookie Shortstops	.75	.35
Leo Foster		
Tom Heintzelman		
Dave Rosello		
Frank Taveras		
☐ 608 Rookie Pitchers UER	1.00	.45
Bob Apodaca		
Dick Baney		
John D'Acquisto		
Mike Wallace		
Apodaca is spellled Apodaco		

	NRMT	VG-E
☐ 609 Rico Petrocelli	.75	.35
☐ 610 Dave Kingman	1.00	.45
☐ 611 Rich Stelmaszek	.50	.23
☐ 612 Luke Walker	.50	.23
☐ 613 Dan Monzon	.50	.23
☐ 614 Adrian Devine	.50	.23
☐ 615 John Jeter	.50	.23
☐ 616 Larry Gura	.50	.23
☐ 617 Ted Ford	.50	.23
☐ 618 Jim Mason	.50	.23
☐ 619 Mike Anderson	.50	.23
☐ 620 Al Downing	.50	.23
☐ 621 Bernie Carbo	.50	.23
☐ 622 Phil Gagliano	.50	.23
☐ 623 Celerino Sanchez	.50	.23
☐ 624 Bob Miller	.50	.23
☐ 625 Ollie Brown	.50	.23
☐ 626 Pirates Team	1.00	.45
☐ 627 Carl Taylor	.50	.23
☐ 628 Ivan Murrell	.50	.23
☐ 629 Rusty Staub	1.00	.45
☐ 630 Tommy Agee	.75	.35
☐ 631 Steve Barber	.50	.23
☐ 632 George Culver	.50	.23
☐ 633 Dave Hamilton	.50	.23
☐ 634 Braves Leaders Eddie Mathews MG Herm Starrette CO Connie Ryan CO Jim Busby CO Ken Silvestri CO	1.00	.45
☐ 635 John Edwards	.50	.23
☐ 636 Dave Goltz	.50	.23
☐ 637 Checklist 529-660	2.50	1.10
☐ 638 Ken Sanders	.50	.23
☐ 639 Joe Lovitto	.50	.23
☐ 640 Milt Pappas	.75	.35
☐ 641 Chuck Brinkman	.50	.23
☐ 642 Terry Harmon	.50	.23
☐ 643 Dodgers Team	1.00	.45
☐ 644 Wayne Granger	.50	.23
☐ 645 Ken Boswell	.50	.23
☐ 646 George Foster	1.50	.70
☐ 647 Juan Beniquez	.50	.23
☐ 648 Terry Crowley	.50	.23
☐ 649 Fernando Gonzalez	.50	.23
☐ 650 Mike Epstein	.50	.23
☐ 651 Leron Lee	.50	.23
☐ 652 Gail Hopkins	.50	.23
☐ 653 Bob Stinson	.75	.35
☐ 654 Jesus Alou	.75	.35
☐ 655 Mike Tyson	.50	.23
☐ 656 Adrian Garrett	.50	.23
☐ 657 Jim Shellenback	.50	.23
☐ 658 Lee Lacy	.50	.23
☐ 659 Joe Lis	.50	.23
☐ 660 Larry Dierker	1.50	.70

1974 O-Pee-Chee Team Checklists

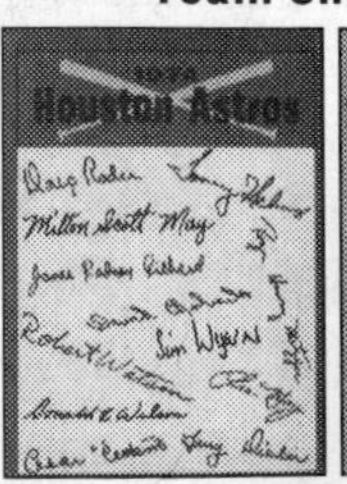

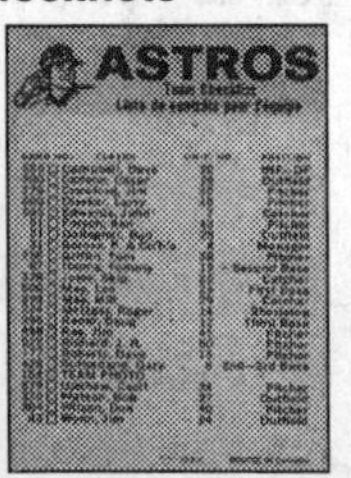

The cards in this 24-card set measure 2 1/2" by 3 1/2". The fronts have red borders and feature the year and team name in a green panel decorated by a crossed bats design, below which is a white area containing facsimile autographs of various players. On a light yellow background, the backs list team members alphabetically, along with their card number, uniform number and position. The words "Team Checklist" appear in French and English. The cards are unnumbered and checklisted below in alphabetical order.

	NRMT	VG-E
COMPLETE SET (24)	50.00	22.00
COMMON TEAM (1-24)	2.50	1.10
☐ 1 Atlanta Braves	2.50	1.10
☐ 2 Baltimore Orioles	2.50	1.10
☐ 3 Boston Red Sox	2.50	1.10
☐ 4 California Angels	2.50	1.10
☐ 5 Chicago Cubs	2.50	1.10
☐ 6 Chicago White Sox	2.50	1.10
☐ 7 Cincinnati Reds	2.50	1.10
☐ 8 Cleveland Indians	2.50	1.10
☐ 9 Detroit Tigers	2.50	1.10
☐ 10 Houston Astros	2.50	1.10
☐ 11 Kansas City Royals	2.50	1.10
☐ 12 Los Angeles Dodgers	2.50	1.10
☐ 13 Milwaukee Brewers	2.50	1.10
☐ 14 Minnesota Twins	2.50	1.10
☐ 15 Montreal Expos	2.50	1.10
☐ 16 New York Mets	2.50	1.10
☐ 17 New York Yankees	2.50	1.10
☐ 18 Oakland A's	2.50	1.10
☐ 19 Philadelphia Phillies	2.50	1.10
☐ 20 Pittsburgh Pirates	2.50	1.10
☐ 21 San Diego Padres	2.50	1.10
☐ 22 San Francisco Giants	2.50	1.10
☐ 23 St. Louis Cardinals	2.50	1.10
☐ 24 Texas Rangers	2.50	1.10

1975 O-Pee-Chee

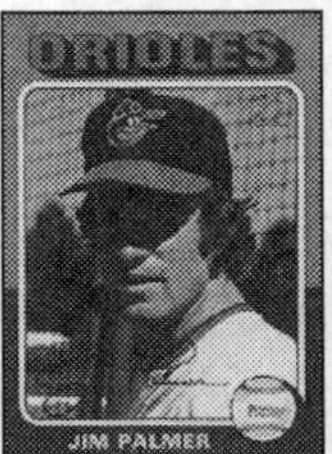

The cards in this 660-card set measure 2 1/2" by 3 1/2". The 1975 O-Pee-Chee cards are very similar to the 1975 Topps cards, yet rather different from previous years' issues. The most prominent change for the fronts is the use of a two-color fram colors surrounding the picture area rather than a single, subdued color. The fronts feature color player photos with rounded corners. The player's name and position, the team name and a facsimile autograph round out the front. The backs are printed in red and green on a yellow-vanilla card stock and carry player biography and statistics in French and English. Cards 189-212 depict the MVPs of both leagues from 1951 through 1974. The first six cards (1-6) feature players breaking records or achieving milestones during the previous season. Cards 306-313 picture league leaders in various statistical categories. Cards 459-466 depict the results of post-season action. Team cards feature a checklist back for players on that team. Remember, the prices below apply only to O-Pee-Chee cards -- they are NOT prices for Topps cards as the Topps cards are generally much more available.

	NRMT	VG-E
COMPLETE SET (660)	1000.00	450.00
COMMON CARD (1-660)	.50	.23
☐ 1 Hank Aaron RB Sets Homer Mark	35.00	16.00
☐ 2 Lou Brock RB 118 Stolen Bases	4.00	1.80
☐ 3 Bob Gibson RB 3000th Strikeout	4.00	1.80
☐ 4 Al Kaline RB 3000 Hit Club	5.00	2.20
☐ 5 Nolan Ryan RB Fans 300 for 3rd Year in a Row	35.00	16.00
☐ 6 Mike Marshall RB Hurls 106 Games	1.00	.45
☐ 7 No Hit Pitchers: Steve Busby Dick Bosman Nolan Ryan	15.00	6.75
☐ 8 Rogelio Moret	.50	.23
☐ 9 Frank Tepedino	.50	.23
☐ 10 Willie Davis	.75	.35
☐ 11 Bill Melton	.50	.23
☐ 12 David Clyde	.50	.23
☐ 13 Gene Locklear	.75	.35
☐ 14 Milt Wilcox	.50	.23
☐ 15 Jose Cardenal	.50	.23
☐ 16 Frank Tanana	2.00	.90
☐ 17 Dave Concepcion	2.00	.90
☐ 18 Tigers: Team/MG Ralph Houk	2.00	.90
☐ 19 Jerry Koosman	1.00	.45
☐ 20 Thurman Munson	7.50	3.40
☐ 21 Rollie Fingers	3.00	1.35
☐ 22 Dave Cash	.75	.35
☐ 23 Bill Russell	.75	.35
☐ 24 Al Fitzmorris	.50	.23
☐ 25 Lee May	.75	.35
☐ 26 Dave McNally	.75	.35
☐ 27 Ken Reitz	.50	.23
☐ 28 Tom Murphy	.50	.23
☐ 29 Dave Parker	5.00	2.20
☐ 30 Bert Blyleven	1.00	.45
☐ 31 Dave Rader	.50	.23
☐ 32 Reggie Cleveland	.50	.23
☐ 33 Dusty Baker	2.00	.90
☐ 34 Steve Renko	.50	.23
☐ 35 Ron Santo	1.00	.45
☐ 36 Joe Lovitto	.50	.23
☐ 37 Dave Freisleben	.50	.23
☐ 38 Buddy Bell	1.00	.45
☐ 39 Andre Thornton	.75	.35
☐ 40 Bill Singer	.50	.23
☐ 41 Cesar Geronimo	.50	.23
☐ 42 Joe Coleman	.50	.23
☐ 43 Cleon Jones	.75	.35
☐ 44 Pat Dobson	.50	.23
☐ 45 Joe Rudi	.75	.35
☐ 46 Phillies: Team/MG Danny Ozark	2.00	.90
☐ 47 Tommy John	1.50	.70
☐ 48 Freddie Patek	.50	.23
☐ 49 Larry Dierker	.50	.23
☐ 50 Brooks Robinson	7.50	3.40
☐ 51 Bob Forsch	1.00	.45
☐ 52 Darrell Porter	.75	.35
☐ 53 Dave Giusti	.50	.23
☐ 54 Eric Soderholm	.50	.23
☐ 55 Bobby Bonds	2.00	.90
☐ 56 Rick Wise	.75	.35
☐ 57 Dave Johnson	.75	.35
☐ 58 Chuck Taylor	.50	.23
☐ 59 Ken Henderson	.50	.23
☐ 60 Fergie Jenkins	3.00	1.35
☐ 61 Dave Winfield	60.00	27.00
☐ 62 Fritz Peterson	.50	.23
☐ 63 Steve Swisher	.50	.23
☐ 64 Dave Chalk	.50	.23
☐ 65 Don Gullett	1.00	.45
☐ 66 Willie Horton	.75	.35
☐ 67 Tug McGraw	1.00	.45
☐ 68 Ron Blomberg	.50	.23
☐ 69 John Odom	.50	.23
☐ 70 Mike Schmidt	60.00	27.00
☐ 71 Charlie Hough	1.00	.45
☐ 72 Royals: Team/MG Jack McKeon	2.00	.90
☐ 73 J.R. Richard	.75	.35
☐ 74 Mark Belanger	.75	.35
☐ 75 Ted Simmons	1.00	.45
☐ 76 Ed Sprague	.50	.23
☐ 77 Richie Zisk	.75	.35
☐ 78 Ray Corbin	.50	.23
☐ 79 Gary Matthews	.75	.35
☐ 80 Carlton Fisk	15.00	6.75
☐ 81 Ron Reed	.50	.23
☐ 82 Pat Kelly	.50	.23
☐ 83 Jim Merritt	.50	.23
☐ 84 Enzo Hernandez	.50	.23
☐ 85 Bill Bonham	.50	.23
☐ 86 Joe Lis	.50	.23
☐ 87 George Foster	1.50	.70
☐ 88 Tom Egan	.50	.23
☐ 89 Jim Ray	.50	.23
☐ 90 Rusty Staub	1.00	.45
☐ 91 Dick Green	.50	.23
☐ 92 Cecil Upshaw	.50	.23
☐ 93 Dave Lopes	1.00	.45
☐ 94 Jim Lonborg	.75	.35
☐ 95 John Mayberry	.75	.35
☐ 96 Mike Cosgrove	.50	.23
☐ 97 Earl Williams	.50	.23
☐ 98 Rich Folkers	.50	.23
☐ 99 Mike Hegan	.50	.23
☐ 100 Willie Stargell	5.00	2.20
☐ 101 Expos: Team/MG Gene Mauch	2.00	.90
☐ 102 Joe Decker	.50	.23
☐ 103 Rick Miller	.50	.23
☐ 104 Bill Madlock	1.00	.45
☐ 105 Buzz Capra	.50	.23
☐ 106 Mike Hargrove	3.00	1.35
☐ 107 Jim Barr	.50	.23
☐ 108 Tom Hall	.50	.23
☐ 109 George Hendrick	.75	.35
☐ 110 Wilbur Wood	.50	.23
☐ 111 Wayne Garrett	.50	.23
☐ 112 Larry Hardy	.50	.23
☐ 113 Elliott Maddox	.50	.23
☐ 114 Dick Lange	.50	.23
☐ 115 Joe Ferguson	.50	.23
☐ 116 Lerrin LaGrow	.50	.23
☐ 117 Orioles: Team/MG Earl Weaver	2.00	.90

☐ 118 Mike Anderson .50 .23
☐ 119 Tommy Helms .50 .23
☐ 120 Steve Busby .75 .35
(photo actually
Fran Healy)
☐ 121 Bill North .50 .23
☐ 122 Al Hrabosky .75 .35
☐ 123 Johnny Briggs .50 .23
☐ 124 Jerry Reuss 1.00 .45
☐ 125 Ken Singleton .75 .35
☐ 126 Checklist 1-132 2.00 .90
☐ 127 Glenn Borgmann .50 .23
☐ 128 Bill Lee .75 .35
☐ 129 Rick Monday .75 .35
☐ 130 Phil Niekro 3.00 1.35
☐ 131 Toby Harrah .75 .35
☐ 132 Randy Moffitt .50 .23
☐ 133 Dan Driessen .75 .35
☐ 134 Ron Hodges .50 .23
☐ 135 Charlie Spikes .50 .23
☐ 136 Jim Mason .50 .23
☐ 137 Terry Forster .50 .23
☐ 138 Del Unser .50 .23
☐ 139 Horacio Pina .50 .23
☐ 140 Steve Garvey 5.00 2.20
☐ 141 Mickey Stanley .75 .35
☐ 142 Bob Reynolds .50 .23
☐ 143 Cliff Johnson .75 .35
☐ 144 Jim Wohlford .50 .23
☐ 145 Ken Holtzman .75 .35
☐ 146 Padres: Team/MG 2.00 .90
John McNamara
☐ 147 Pedro Garcia .50 .23
☐ 148 Jim Rooker .50 .23
☐ 149 Tim Foli .50 .23
☐ 150 Bob Gibson 6.00 2.70
☐ 151 Steve Brye .50 .23
☐ 152 Mario Guerrero .50 .23
☐ 153 Rick Reuschel .75 .35
☐ 154 Mike Lum .50 .23
☐ 155 Jim Bibby .50 .23
☐ 156 Dave Kingman 1.00 .45
☐ 157 Pedro Borbon .50 .23
☐ 158 Jerry Grote .50 .23
☐ 159 Steve Arlin .50 .23
☐ 160 Graig Nettles 2.00 .90
☐ 161 Stan Bahnsen .50 .23
☐ 162 Willie Montanez .50 .23
☐ 163 Jim Brewer .50 .23
☐ 164 Mickey Rivers .75 .35
☐ 165 Doug Rader .75 .35
☐ 166 Woodie Fryman .50 .23
☐ 167 Rich Coggins .50 .23
☐ 168 Bill Greif .50 .23
☐ 169 Cookie Rojas .75 .35
☐ 170 Bert Campaneris .75 .35
☐ 171 Ed Kirkpatrick .50 .23
☐ 172 Red Sox: Team/MG 2.00 .90
Darrell Johnson
☐ 173 Steve Rogers .75 .35
☐ 174 Bake McBride .75 .35
☐ 175 Don Money .75 .35
☐ 176 Burt Hooton .75 .35
☐ 177 Vic Correll .50 .23
☐ 178 Cesar Tovar .50 .23
☐ 179 Tom Bradley .50 .23
☐ 180 Joe Morgan 6.00 2.70
☐ 181 Fred Beene .50 .23
☐ 182 Don Hahn .50 .23
☐ 183 Mel Stottlemyre .75 .35
☐ 184 Jorge Orta .50 .23
☐ 185 Steve Carlton 7.50 3.40
☐ 186 Willie Crawford .50 .23
☐ 187 Denny Doyle .50 .23
☐ 188 Tom Griffin .50 .23
☐ 189 1951 MVP's: 3.50 1.55
Larry (Yogi) Berra
Roy Campanella
(Campy never issued)
☐ 190 1952 MVP's 1.00 .45
Bobby Shantz
Hank Sauer
☐ 191 1953 MVP's: 2.00 .90
Al Rosen
Roy Campanella
☐ 192 1954 MVP's: 4.00 1.80
Yogi Berra
Willie Mays
☐ 193 1955 MVP's: 4.00 1.80
Yogi Berra
Roy Campanella
(Campy never issued)
☐ 194 1956 MVP's: 18.00 8.00
Mickey Mantle
Don Newcombe
☐ 195 1957 MVP's: 30.00 13.50
Mickey Mantle
Hank Aaron
☐ 196 1958 MVP's 1.00 .45
Jackie Jensen
Ernie Banks
☐ 197 1959 MVP's: 1.50 .70
Nellie Fox
Ernie Banks
☐ 198 1960 MVP's 1.00 .45
Roger Maris
Dick Groat
☐ 199 1961 MVP's: 3.00 1.35
Roger Maris
Frank Robinson
☐ 200 1962 MVP's: 18.00 8.00
Mickey Mantle
Maury Wills
(Wills never issued)
☐ 201 1963 MVP's: 1.50 .70
Elston Howard
Sandy Koufax
☐ 202 1964 MVP's: 1.50 .70
Brooks Robinson
Ken Boyer
☐ 203 1965 MVP's: 1.50 .70
Zoilo Versalles
Willie Mays
☐ 204 1966 MVP's: 6.00 2.70
Frank Robinson
Bob Clemente
☐ 205 1967 MVP's: 1.50 .70
Carl Yastrzemski
Orlando Cepeda
☐ 206 1968 MVP's: 1.50 .70
Denny McLain
Bob Gibson
☐ 207 1969 MVP's: 1.50 .70
Harmon Killebrew
Willie McCovey
☐ 208 1970 MVP's: 1.50 .70
Boog Powell
Johnny Bench
☐ 209 1971 MVP's 1.00 .45
Vida Blue
Joe Torre
☐ 210 1972 MVP's: 1.50 .70
Rich Allen
Johnny Bench
☐ 211 1973 MVP's: 6.00 2.70
Reggie Jackson
Pete Rose
☐ 212 1974 MVP's 1.00 .45
Jeff Burroughs
Steve Garvey
☐ 213 Oscar Gamble .75 .35
☐ 214 Harry Parker .50 .23
☐ 215 Bobby Valentine .50 .23
☐ 216 Giants: Team/MG 2.00 .90
Wes Westrum
☐ 217 Lou Piniella 1.50 .70
☐ 218 Jerry Johnson .50 .23
☐ 219 Ed Herrmann .50 .23
☐ 220 Don Sutton 2.50 1.10
☐ 221 Aurelio Rodriguez .50 .23
☐ 222 Dan Spillner .50 .23
☐ 223 Robin Yount 125.00 55.00
☐ 224 Ramon Hernandez .50 .23
☐ 225 Bob Grich .75 .35
☐ 226 Bill Campbell .50 .23
☐ 227 Bob Watson .75 .35
☐ 228 George Brett 225.00 100.00
☐ 229 Barry Foote .75 .35
☐ 230 Jim Hunter 3.00 1.35
☐ 231 Mike Tyson .50 .23
☐ 232 Diego Segui .50 .23
☐ 233 Billy Grabarkewitz .50 .23
☐ 234 Tom Grieve .50 .23
☐ 235 Jack Billingham .50 .23
☐ 236 Angels: Team/MG 2.00 .90
Dick Williams
☐ 237 Carl Morton .50 .23
☐ 238 Dave Duncan .50 .23
☐ 239 George Stone .50 .23
☐ 240 Garry Maddox .75 .35
☐ 241 Dick Tidrow .50 .23
☐ 242 Jay Johnstone .75 .35
☐ 243 Jim Kaat 1.00 .45
☐ 244 Bill Buckner 1.00 .45
☐ 245 Mickey Lolich 1.00 .45
☐ 246 Cardinals: Team/MG 2.00 .90
Red Schoendienst
☐ 247 Enos Cabell .50 .23
☐ 248 Randy Jones .75 .35
☐ 249 Danny Thompson .50 .23
☐ 250 Ken Brett .50 .23
☐ 251 Fran Healy .50 .23
☐ 252 Fred Scherman .50 .23
☐ 253 Jesus Alou .50 .23
☐ 254 Mike Torrez .75 .35
☐ 255 Dwight Evans 2.00 .90
☐ 256 Billy Champion .50 .23
☐ 257 Checklist 133-264 2.00 .90
☐ 258 Dave LaRoche .50 .23
☐ 259 Len Randle .50 .23
☐ 260 Johnny Bench 15.00 6.75
☐ 261 Andy Hassler .50 .23
☐ 262 Rowland Office .50 .23
☐ 263 Jim Perry .75 .35
☐ 264 John Milner .50 .23
☐ 265 Ron Bryant .50 .23
☐ 266 Sandy Alomar .50 .23
☐ 267 Dick Ruthven .50 .23
☐ 268 Hal McRae 1.00 .45
☐ 269 Doug Rau .50 .23
☐ 270 Ron Fairly .75 .35
☐ 271 Jerry Moses .50 .23
☐ 272 Lynn McGlothen .50 .23
☐ 273 Steve Braun .50 .23
☐ 274 Vicente Romo .50 .23
☐ 275 Paul Blair .75 .35
☐ 276 White Sox Team/MG 2.00 .90
Chuck Tanner
☐ 277 Frank Taveras .50 .23
☐ 278 Paul Lindblad .50 .23
☐ 279 Milt May .50 .23
☐ 280 Carl Yastrzemski 7.50 3.40
☐ 281 Jim Slaton .50 .23
☐ 282 Jerry Morales .50 .23
☐ 283 Steve Foucault .50 .23
☐ 284 Ken Griffey 5.00 2.20
☐ 285 Ellie Rodriguez .50 .23
☐ 286 Mike Jorgensen .50 .23
☐ 287 Roric Harrison .50 .23
☐ 288 Bruce Ellingsen .50 .23
☐ 289 Ken Rudolph .50 .23
☐ 290 Jon Matlack .50 .23
☐ 291 Bill Sudakis .50 .23
☐ 292 Ron Schueler .50 .23
☐ 293 Dick Sharon .50 .23
☐ 294 Geoff Zahn .50 .23
☐ 295 Vada Pinson 1.00 .45
☐ 296 Alan Foster .50 .23
☐ 297 Craig Kusick .50 .23
☐ 298 Johnny Grubb .50 .23
☐ 299 Bucky Dent 1.00 .45
☐ 300 Reggie Jackson 20.00 9.00
☐ 301 Dave Roberts .50 .23
☐ 302 Rick Burleson 1.00 .45
☐ 303 Grant Jackson .50 .23
☐ 304 Pirates: Team/MG 2.00 .90
Danny Murtaugh
☐ 305 Jim Colborn .50 .23
☐ 306 Batting Leaders: 1.50 .70
Rod Carew
Ralph Garr
☐ 307 Home Run Leaders: 3.50 1.55
Dick Allen
Mike Schmidt
☐ 308 RBI Leaders: 1.50 .70
Jeff Burroughs
Johnny Bench
☐ 309 Stolen Base Leaders: 1.50 .70
Bill North
Lou Brock
☐ 310 Victory Leaders: 1.50 .70
Jim Hunter
Fergie Jenkins
Andy Messersmith
Phil Niekro
☐ 311 ERA Leaders: 1.50 .70
Jim Hunter
Buzz Capra
☐ 312 Strikeout Leaders: 25.00 11.00
Nolan Ryan
Steve Carlton
☐ 313 Leading Firemen 1.00 .45
Terry Forster
Mike Marshall
☐ 314 Buck Martinez .50 .23
☐ 315 Don Kessinger .75 .35
☐ 316 Jackie Brown .50 .23
☐ 317 Joe Lahoud .50 .23
☐ 318 Ernie McAnally .50 .23
☐ 319 Johnny Oates .50 .23
☐ 320 Pete Rose 20.00 9.00
☐ 321 Rudy May .50 .23
☐ 322 Ed Goodson .50 .23
☐ 323 Fred Holdsworth .50 .23
☐ 324 Ed Kranepool .50 .23
☐ 325 Tony Oliva 1.00 .45
☐ 326 Wayne Twitchell .50 .23
☐ 327 Jerry Hairston .50 .23
☐ 328 Sonny Siebert .50 .23
☐ 329 Ted Kubiak .50 .23
☐ 330 Mike Marshall .75 .35
☐ 331 Indians: Team/MG 2.00 .90

Frank Robinson
☐ 332 Fred Kendall .50 .23
☐ 333 Dick Drago .50 .23
☐ 334 Greg Gross .50 .23
☐ 335 Jim Palmer 6.00 2.70
☐ 336 Rennie Stennett .50 .23
☐ 337 Kevin Kobel .50 .23
☐ 338 Rick Stelmaszek .50 .23
☐ 339 Jim Fregosi .75 .35
☐ 340 Paul Splittorff .50 .23
☐ 341 Hal Breeden .50 .23
☐ 342 Leroy Stanton .50 .23
☐ 343 Danny Frisella .50 .23
☐ 344 Ben Oglivie .75 .35
☐ 345 Clay Carroll .50 .23
☐ 346 Bobby Darwin .50 .23
☐ 347 Mike Caldwell .50 .23
☐ 348 Tony Muser .50 .23
☐ 349 Ray Sadecki .50 .23
☐ 350 Bobby Murcer 1.00 .45
☐ 351 Bob Boone 1.50 .70
☐ 352 Darold Knowles .50 .23
☐ 353 Luis Melendez .50 .23
☐ 354 Dick Bosman .50 .23
☐ 355 Chris Cannizzaro .50 .23
☐ 356 Rico Petrocelli .75 .35
☐ 357 Ken Forsch .50 .23
☐ 358 Al Bumbry .50 .23
☐ 359 Paul Popovich .50 .23
☐ 360 George Scott .75 .35
☐ 361 Dodgers: Team/MG 2.00 .90
Walter Alston
☐ 362 Steve Hargan .50 .23
☐ 363 Carmen Fanzone .50 .23
☐ 364 Doug Bird .50 .23
☐ 365 Bob Bailey .50 .23
☐ 366 Ken Sanders .50 .23
☐ 367 Craig Robinson .50 .23
☐ 368 Vic Albury .50 .23
☐ 369 Merv Rettenmund .50 .23
☐ 370 Tom Seaver 18.00 8.00
☐ 371 Gates Brown .50 .23
☐ 372 John D'Acquisto .50 .23
☐ 373 Bill Sharp .50 .23
☐ 374 Eddie Watt .50 .23
☐ 375 Roy White .75 .35
☐ 376 Steve Yeager .50 .23
☐ 377 Tom Hilgendorf .50 .23
☐ 378 Derrel Thomas .50 .23
☐ 379 Bernie Carbo .50 .23
☐ 380 Sal Bando .75 .35
☐ 381 John Curtis .50 .23
☐ 382 Don Baylor 3.00 1.35
☐ 383 Jim York .50 .23
☐ 384 Brewers: Team/MG 2.00 .90
Del Crandall
☐ 385 Dock Ellis .50 .23
☐ 386 Checklist 265-396 2.00 .90
☐ 387 Jim Spencer .50 .23
☐ 388 Steve Stone .75 .35
☐ 389 Tony Solaita .50 .23
☐ 390 Ron Cey 1.00 .45
☐ 391 Don DeMola .50 .23
☐ 392 Bruce Bochte 1.00 .45
☐ 393 Gary Gentry .50 .23
☐ 394 Larvell Blanks .50 .23
☐ 395 Bud Harrelson .75 .35
☐ 396 Fred Norman .75 .35
☐ 397 Bill Freehan .75 .35
☐ 398 Elias Sosa .50 .23
☐ 399 Terry Harmon .50 .23
☐ 400 Dick Allen 1.00 .45
☐ 401 Mike Wallace .50 .23
☐ 402 Bob Tolan .50 .23
☐ 403 Tom Buskey .50 .23
☐ 404 Ted Sizemore .50 .23
☐ 405 John Montague .50 .23
☐ 406 Bob Gallagher .50 .23
☐ 407 Herb Washington 1.00 .45
☐ 408 Clyde Wright .50 .23
☐ 409 Bob Robertson .50 .23
☐ 410 Mike Cueller .75 .35
(sic, Cuellar)
☐ 411 George Mitterwald .50 .23
☐ 412 Bill Hands .50 .23
☐ 413 Marty Pattin .50 .23
☐ 414 Manny Mota .75 .35
☐ 415 John Hiller .75 .35
☐ 416 Larry Lintz .50 .23
☐ 417 Skip Lockwood .50 .23
☐ 418 Leo Foster .50 .23
☐ 419 Dave Goltz .50 .23
☐ 420 Larry Bowa 1.00 .45
☐ 421 Mets: Team/MG 2.00 .90
Yogi Berra
☐ 422 Brian Downing 1.00 .45
☐ 423 Clay Kirby .50 .23
☐ 424 John Lowenstein .50 .23
☐ 425 Tito Fuentes .50 .23
☐ 426 George Medich .50 .23
☐ 427 Clarence Gaston 1.00 .45
☐ 428 Dave Hamilton .50 .23
☐ 429 Jim Dwyer .50 .23
☐ 430 Luis Tiant 1.00 .45
☐ 431 Rod Gilbreath .50 .23
☐ 432 Ken Berry .50 .23
☐ 433 Larry Demery .50 .23
☐ 434 Bob Locker .50 .23
☐ 435 Dave Nelson .50 .23
☐ 436 Ken Frailing .50 .23
☐ 437 Al Cowens 1.00 .45
☐ 438 Don Carrithers .50 .23
☐ 439 Ed Brinkman .50 .23
☐ 440 Andy Messersmith .75 .35
☐ 441 Bobby Heise .50 .23
☐ 442 Maximino Leon .50 .23
☐ 443 Twins: Team/MG 2.00 .90
Frank Quilici
☐ 444 Gene Garber .75 .35
☐ 445 Felix Millan .50 .23
☐ 446 Bart Johnson .50 .23
☐ 447 Terry Crowley .50 .23
☐ 448 Frank Duffy .50 .23
☐ 449 Charlie Williams .50 .23
☐ 450 Willie McCovey 6.00 2.70
☐ 451 Rick Dempsey .75 .35
☐ 452 Angel Mangual .50 .23
☐ 453 Claude Osteen .75 .35
☐ 454 Doug Griffin .50 .23
☐ 455 Don Wilson .50 .23
☐ 456 Bob Coluccio .50 .23
☐ 457 Mario Mendoza .50 .23
☐ 458 Ross Grimsley .50 .23
☐ 459 1974 AL Champs 1.00 .45
A's over Orioles
(Second base
action pictured)
☐ 460 Frank Taveras NCLS 1.50 .70
Steve Garvey
☐ 461 Reggie Jackson WS 5.00 2.20
☐ 462 World Series Game 2 1.00 .45
(Dodger dugout)
☐ 463 Rollie Fingers WS 1.50 .70
☐ 464 World Series Game 4 1.00 .45
(A's batter)
☐ 465 Joe Rudi WS 1.00 .45
☐ 466 World Series Summary: 1.50 .70
A's do it again
Win 3rd straight
(A's group)
☐ 467 Ed Halicki .50 .23
☐ 468 Bobby Mitchell .50 .23
☐ 469 Tom Dettore .50 .23
☐ 470 Jeff Burroughs .75 .35
☐ 471 Bob Stinson .50 .23
☐ 472 Bruce Dal Canton .50 .23
☐ 473 Ken McMullen .50 .23
☐ 474 Luke Walker .50 .23
☐ 475 Darrell Evans 1.00 .45
☐ 476 Ed Figueroa .50 .23
☐ 477 Tom Hutton .50 .23
☐ 478 Tom Burgmeier .50 .23
☐ 479 Ken Boswell .50 .23
☐ 480 Carlos May .50 .23
☐ 481 Will McEnaney .75 .35
☐ 482 Tom McCraw .50 .23
☐ 483 Steve Ontiveros .50 .23
☐ 484 Glenn Beckert .50 .23
☐ 485 Sparky Lyle 1.00 .45
☐ 486 Ray Fosse .50 .23
☐ 487 Astros: Team/MG 2.00 .90
Preston Gomez
☐ 488 Bill Travers .50 .23
☐ 489 Cecil Cooper 1.00 .45
☐ 490 Reggie Smith 1.00 .45
☐ 491 Doyle Alexander .75 .35
☐ 492 Rich Hebner .75 .35
☐ 493 Don Stanhouse .50 .23
☐ 494 Pete LaCock .50 .23
☐ 495 Nelson Briles .75 .35
☐ 496 Pepe Frias .50 .23
☐ 497 Jim Nettles .50 .23
☐ 498 Al Downing .50 .23
☐ 499 Marty Perez .50 .23
☐ 500 Nolan Ryan 90.00 40.00
☐ 501 Bill Robinson .75 .35
☐ 502 Pat Bourque .50 .23
☐ 503 Fred Stanley .50 .23
☐ 504 Buddy Bradford .50 .23
☐ 505 Chris Speier .50 .23
☐ 506 Leron Lee .50 .23
☐ 507 Tom Carroll .50 .23
☐ 508 Bob Hansen .50 .23
☐ 509 Dave Hilton .50 .23
☐ 510 Vida Blue 1.00 .45
☐ 511 Rangers: Team/MG 2.00 .90
Billy Martin
☐ 512 Larry Milbourne .50 .23
☐ 513 Dick Pole .50 .23
☐ 514 Jose Cruz .75 .35
☐ 515 Manny Sanguillen .75 .35
☐ 516 Don Hood .50 .23
☐ 517 Checklist 397-528 2.00 .90
☐ 518 Leo Cardenas .50 .23
☐ 519 Jim Todd .50 .23
☐ 520 Amos Otis .75 .35
☐ 521 Dennis Blair .50 .23
☐ 522 Gary Sutherland .50 .23
☐ 523 Tom Paciorek .50 .23
☐ 524 John Doherty .50 .23
☐ 525 Tom House .50 .23
☐ 526 Larry Hisle .75 .35
☐ 527 Mac Scarce .50 .23
☐ 528 Eddie Leon .50 .23
☐ 529 Gary Thomasson .50 .23
☐ 530 Gaylord Perry 3.00 1.35
☐ 531 Reds: Team/MG 5.00 2.20
Sparky Anderson
☐ 532 Gorman Thomas .75 .35
☐ 533 Rudy Meoli .50 .23
☐ 534 Alex Johnson .50 .23
☐ 535 Gene Tenace .75 .35
☐ 536 Bob Moose .50 .23
☐ 537 Tommy Harper .75 .35
☐ 538 Duffy Dyer .50 .23
☐ 539 Jesse Jefferson .50 .23
☐ 540 Lou Brock 6.00 2.70
☐ 541 Roger Metzger .50 .23
☐ 542 Pete Broberg .50 .23
☐ 543 Larry Biittner .50 .23
☐ 544 Steve Mingori .50 .23
☐ 545 Billy Williams 3.50 1.55
☐ 546 John Knox .50 .23
☐ 547 Von Joshua .50 .23
☐ 548 Charlie Sands .50 .23
☐ 549 Bill Butler .50 .23
☐ 550 Ralph Garr 1.00 .45
☐ 551 Larry Christenson .50 .23
☐ 552 Jack Brohamer .50 .23
☐ 553 John Boccabella .50 .23
☐ 554 Rich Gossage 2.00 .90
☐ 555 Al Oliver 1.00 .45
☐ 556 Tim Johnson .50 .23
☐ 557 Larry Gura .50 .23
☐ 558 Dave Roberts .50 .23
☐ 559 Bob Montgomery .50 .23
☐ 560 Tony Perez 3.00 1.35
☐ 561 A's: Team/MG 2.00 .90
Alvin Dark
☐ 562 Gary Nolan .75 .35
☐ 563 Wilbur Howard .50 .23
☐ 564 Tommy Davis .75 .35
☐ 565 Joe Torre 1.00 .45
☐ 566 Ray Burris .50 .23
☐ 567 Jim Sundberg 1.50 .70
☐ 568 Dale Murray .50 .23
☐ 569 Frank White 1.00 .45
☐ 570 Jim Wynn .75 .35
☐ 571 Dave Lemanczyk .50 .23
☐ 572 Roger Nelson .50 .23
☐ 573 Orlando Pena .50 .23
☐ 574 Tony Taylor .75 .35
☐ 575 Gene Clines .50 .23
☐ 576 Phil Roof .50 .23
☐ 577 John Morris .50 .23
☐ 578 Dave Tomlin .50 .23
☐ 579 Skip Pitlock .50 .23
☐ 580 Frank Robinson 7.50 3.40
☐ 581 Darrel Chaney .50 .23
☐ 582 Eduardo Rodriguez .50 .23
☐ 583 Andy Etchebarren .50 .23
☐ 584 Mike Garman .50 .23
☐ 585 Chris Chambliss .75 .35
☐ 586 Tim McCarver 1.00 .45
☐ 587 Chris Ward .50 .23
☐ 588 Rick Auerbach .50 .23
☐ 589 Braves: Team/MG 2.00 .90
Clyde King
☐ 590 Cesar Cedeno .75 .35
☐ 591 Glenn Abbott .50 .23
☐ 592 Balor Moore .50 .23
☐ 593 Gene Lamont .50 .23
☐ 594 Jim Fuller .50 .23
☐ 595 Joe Niekro 1.00 .45
☐ 596 Ollie Brown .50 .23
☐ 597 Winston Llenas .50 .23
☐ 598 Bruce Kison .50 .23
☐ 599 Nate Colbert .50 .23
☐ 600 Rod Carew 6.00 2.70
☐ 601 Juan Beniquez .50 .23
☐ 602 John Vukovich .50 .23
☐ 603 Lew Krausse .50 .23

☐ 604 Oscar Zamora .50 .23
☐ 605 John Ellis .50 .23
☐ 606 Bruce Miller .50 .23
☐ 607 Jim Holt .50 .23
☐ 608 Gene Michael .50 .23
☐ 609 Elrod Hendricks .50 .23
☐ 610 Ron Hunt .50 .23
☐ 611 Yankees: Team/MG 2.00 .90
Bill Virdon
☐ 612 Terry Hughes .50 .23
☐ 613 Bill Parsons .50 .23
☐ 614 Rookie Pitchers 1.00 .45
Jack Kucek
Dyar Miller
Vern Ruhle
Paul Siebert
☐ 615 Rookie Pitchers: 1.50 .70
Pat Darcy
Dennis Leonard
Tom Underwood
Hank Webb
☐ 616 Rookie Outfielders: 15.00 6.75
Dave Augustine
Pepe Mangual
Jim Rice
John Scott
☐ 617 Rookie Infielders: 2.50 1.10
Mike Cubbage
Doug DeCinces
Reggie Sanders
Manny Trillo
☐ 618 Rookie Pitchers: 1.50 .70
Jamie Easterly
Tom Johnson
Scott McGregor
Rick Rhoden
☐ 619 Rookie Outfielders 1.00 .45
Benny Ayala
Nyls Nyman
Tommy Smith
Jerry Turner
☐ 620 Rookie Catcher/OF: 30.00 13.50
Gary Carter
Marc Hill
Danny Meyer
Leon Roberts
☐ 621 Rookie Pitchers: 1.50 .70
John Denny
Rawly Eastwick
Jim Kern
Juan Veintidos
☐ 622 Rookie Outfielders: 7.50 3.40
Ed Armbrister
Fred Lynn
Tom Poquette
Terry Whitfield
☐ 623 Rookie Infielders: 7.50 3.40
Phil Garner
Keith Hernandez
Bob Sheldon
Tom Veryzer
☐ 624 Rookie Pitchers 1.00 .45
Doug Konieczny
Gary Lavelle
Jim Otten
Eddie Solomon
☐ 625 Boog Powell 1.00 .45
☐ 626 Larry Haney .50 .23
(photo actually
Dave Duncan)
☐ 627 Tom Walker .50 .23
☐ 628 Ron LeFlore 1.00 .45
☐ 629 Joe Hoerner .50 .23
☐ 630 Greg Luzinski 1.00 .45
☐ 631 Lee Lacy .50 .23
☐ 632 Morris Nettles .50 .23
☐ 633 Paul Casanova .50 .23
☐ 634 Cy Acosta .50 .23
☐ 635 Chuck Dobson .50 .23
☐ 636 Charlie Moore .50 .23
☐ 637 Ted Martinez .50 .23
☐ 638 Cubs: Team/MG 2.00 .90
Jim Marshall
☐ 639 Steve Kline .50 .23
☐ 640 Harmon Killebrew 6.00 2.70
☐ 641 Jim Northrup .50 .23
☐ 642 Mike Phillips .50 .23
☐ 643 Brent Strom .50 .23
☐ 644 Bill Fahey .50 .23
☐ 645 Danny Cater .50 .23
☐ 646 Checklist 529-660 2.00 .90
☐ 647 Claudell Washington 1.00 .45
☐ 648 Dave Pagan .50 .23
☐ 649 Jack Heidemann .50 .23
☐ 650 Dave May .50 .23
☐ 651 John Morlan .50 .23
☐ 652 Lindy McDaniel .50 .23
☐ 653 Lee Richard .50 .23
☐ 654 Jerry Terrell .50 .23
☐ 655 Rico Carty 1.00 .45
☐ 656 Bill Plummer .50 .23
☐ 657 Bob Oliver .50 .23
☐ 658 Vic Harris .50 .23
☐ 659 Bob Apodaca .50 .23
☐ 660 Hank Aaron 40.00 18.00

1976 O-Pee-Chee

This is a 660-card standard-size set. The 1976 O-Pee-Chee cards are very similar to the 1976 Topps cards, yet rather different from previous years' issues. The most prominent change is that the backs are much brighter than their American counterparts. The cards parallel the American issue and it is a challenge to find well centered examples of these cards.

	NRMT	VG-E
COMPLETE SET (660)	500.00	220.00
COMMON CARD (1-660)	.25	.11

☐ 1 Hank Aaron RB 20.00 9.00
Most RBI's, 2262
☐ 2 Bobby Bonds RB 1.00 .45
Most leadoff
homers, 32;
Plus 3 Seasons of
30 HR's and 30 SB's
☐ 3 Mickey Lolich RB .75 .35
Lefthander, Most
Strikeouts 2679
☐ 4 Dave Lopes RB .75 .35
Most consecutive
SB attempts, 38
☐ 5 Tom Seaver RB 5.00 2.20
Most cons. seasons
with 200 SO's, 8
☐ 6 Rennie Stennett RB .50 .23
Most hits in a 9
inning game, 7
☐ 7 Jim Umbarger .25 .11
☐ 8 Tito Fuentes .25 .11
☐ 9 Paul Lindblad .25 .11
☐ 10 Lou Brock 5.00 2.20
☐ 11 Jim Hughes .25 .11
☐ 12 Richie Zisk .50 .23
☐ 13 John Wockenfuss .25 .11
☐ 14 Gene Garber .50 .23
☐ 15 George Scott .50 .23
☐ 16 Bob Apodaca .25 .11
☐ 17 New York Yankees 1.50 .70
Team Card
☐ 18 Dale Murray .25 .11
☐ 19 George Brett 75.00 34.00
☐ 20 Bob Watson .50 .23
☐ 21 Dave LaRoche .25 .11
☐ 22 Bill Russell .50 .23
☐ 23 Brian Downing .50 .23
☐ 24 Cesar Geronimo .50 .23
☐ 25 Mike Torrez .50 .23
☐ 26 Andre Thornton .50 .23
☐ 27 Ed Figueroa .25 .11
☐ 28 Dusty Baker 1.25 .55
☐ 29 Rick Burleson .25 .11
☐ 30 John Montefusco .50 .23
☐ 31 Len Randle .25 .11
☐ 32 Danny Frisella .25 .11
☐ 33 Bill North .25 .11
☐ 34 Mike Garman .25 .11
☐ 35 Tony Oliva .75 .35
☐ 36 Frank Taveras .25 .11
☐ 37 John Hiller .50 .23
☐ 38 Garry Maddox .50 .23
☐ 39 Pete Broberg .25 .11
☐ 40 Dave Kingman .75 .35
☐ 41 Tippy Martinez .75 .35
☐ 42 Barry Foote .50 .23
☐ 43 Paul Splittorff .25 .11
☐ 44 Doug Rader .25 .11
☐ 45 Boog Powell .75 .35
☐ 46 Los Angeles Dodgers 1.50 .70
Team Card
Walt Alston MG
(Checklist back)
☐ 47 Jesse Jefferson .25 .11
☐ 48 Dave Concepcion 1.25 .55
☐ 49 Dave Duncan .25 .11
☐ 50 Fred Lynn 1.50 .70
☐ 51 Ray Burris .25 .11
☐ 52 Dave Chalk .25 .11
☐ 53 Mike Beard .25 .11
☐ 54 Dave Rader .25 .11
☐ 55 Gaylord Perry 2.50 1.10
☐ 56 Bob Tolan .25 .11
☐ 57 Phil Garner .75 .35
☐ 58 Ron Reed .25 .11
☐ 59 Larry Hisle .50 .23
☐ 60 Jerry Reuss .50 .23
☐ 61 Ron LeFlore .50 .23
☐ 62 Johnny Oates .50 .23
☐ 63 Bobby Darwin .25 .11
☐ 64 Jerry Koosman .75 .35
☐ 65 Chris Chambliss .50 .23
☐ 66 Gus Bell FS .50 .23
Buddy Bell
☐ 67 Ray Boone FS .50 .23
Bob Boone
☐ 68 Joe Coleman FS .25 .11
Joe Coleman Jr.
☐ 69 Jim Hegan FS .25 .11
Mike Hegan
☐ 70 Roy Smalley FS .50 .23
Roy Smalley Jr.
☐ 71 Steve Rogers .75 .35
☐ 72 Hal McRae .75 .35
☐ 73 Baltimore Orioles 1.50 .70
Team Card
Earl Weaver MG
(Checklist back)
☐ 74 Oscar Gamble .50 .23
☐ 75 Larry Dierker .25 .11
☐ 76 Willie Crawford .25 .11
☐ 77 Pedro Borbon .50 .23
☐ 78 Cecil Cooper .75 .35
☐ 79 Jerry Morales .25 .11
☐ 80 Jim Kaat .75 .35
☐ 81 Darrell Evans .75 .35
☐ 82 Von Joshua .25 .11
☐ 83 Jim Spencer .25 .11
☐ 84 Brent Strom .25 .11
☐ 85 Mickey Rivers .50 .23
☐ 86 Mike Tyson .25 .11
☐ 87 Tom Burgmeier .25 .11
☐ 88 Duffy Dyer .25 .11
☐ 89 Vern Ruhle .25 .11
☐ 90 Sal Bando .50 .23
☐ 91 Tom Hutton .25 .11
☐ 92 Eduardo Rodriguez .25 .11
☐ 93 Mike Phillips .25 .11
☐ 94 Jim Dwyer .25 .11
☐ 95 Brooks Robinson 6.00 2.70
☐ 96 Doug Bird .25 .11
☐ 97 Wilbur Howard .25 .11
☐ 98 Dennis Eckersley 50.00 22.00
☐ 99 Lee Lacy .25 .11
☐ 100 Jim Hunter 2.50 1.10
☐ 101 Pete LaCock .25 .11
☐ 102 Jim Willoughby .25 .11
☐ 103 Biff Pocoroba .25 .11
☐ 104 Cincinnati Reds 2.00 .90
Team Card
Sparky Anderson MG
(Checklist back)
☐ 105 Gary Lavelle .25 .11
☐ 106 Tom Grieve .25 .11
☐ 107 Dave Roberts .25 .11
☐ 108 Don Kirkwood .25 .11
☐ 109 Larry Lintz .25 .11
☐ 110 Carlos May .25 .11
☐ 111 Danny Thompson .25 .11
☐ 112 Kent Tekulve 1.50 .70
☐ 113 Gary Sutherland .25 .11
☐ 114 Jay Johnstone .50 .23
☐ 115 Ken Holtzman .50 .23
☐ 116 Charlie Moore .25 .11
☐ 117 Mike Jorgensen .50 .23
☐ 118 Boston Red Sox 1.50 .70
Team Card
Darrell Johnson
(Checklist back)
☐ 119 Checklist 1-132 1.50 .70
☐ 120 Rusty Staub .50 .23
☐ 121 Tony Solaita .25 .11
☐ 122 Mike Cosgrove .25 .11
☐ 123 Walt Williams .25 .11
☐ 124 Doug Rau .25 .11
☐ 125 Don Baylor 2.00 .90
☐ 126 Tom Dettore .25 .11
☐ 127 Larvell Blanks .25 .11

☐ 128 Ken Griffey	2.50	1.10
☐ 129 Andy Etchebarren	.25	.11
☐ 130 Luis Tiant	.75	.35
☐ 131 Bill Stein	.25	.11
☐ 132 Don Hood	.25	.11
☐ 133 Gary Matthews	.50	.23
☐ 134 Mike Ivie	.25	.11
☐ 135 Bake McBride	.50	.23
☐ 136 Dave Goltz	.25	.11
☐ 137 Bill Robinson	.50	.23
☐ 138 Lerrin LaGrow	.25	.11
☐ 139 Gorman Thomas	.50	.23
☐ 140 Vida Blue	.75	.35
☐ 141 Larry Parrish	.75	.35
☐ 142 Dick Drago	.25	.11
☐ 143 Jerry Grote	.50	.23
☐ 144 Al Fitzmorris	.25	.11
☐ 145 Larry Bowa	.75	.35
☐ 146 George Medich	.25	.11
☐ 147 Houston Astros	1.50	.70
Team Card		
Bill Virdon MG		
(Checklist back)		
☐ 148 Stan Thomas	.25	.11
☐ 149 Tommy Davis	.50	.23
☐ 150 Steve Garvey	4.00	1.80
☐ 151 Bill Bonham	.25	.11
☐ 152 Leroy Stanton	.25	.11
☐ 153 Buzz Capra	.25	.11
☐ 154 Bucky Dent	.50	.23
☐ 155 Jack Billingham	.50	.23
☐ 156 Rico Carty	.50	.23
☐ 157 Mike Caldwell	.25	.11
☐ 158 Ken Reitz	.25	.11
☐ 159 Jerry Terrell	.25	.11
☐ 160 Dave Winfield	25.00	11.00
☐ 161 Bruce Kison	.25	.11
☐ 162 Jack Pierce	.25	.11
☐ 163 Jim Slaton	.25	.11
☐ 164 Pepe Mangual	.25	.11
☐ 165 Gene Tenace	.50	.23
☐ 166 Skip Lockwood	.25	.11
☐ 167 Freddie Patek	.50	.23
☐ 168 Tom Hilgendorf	.25	.11
☐ 169 Graig Nettles	.75	.35
☐ 170 Rick Wise	.25	.11
☐ 171 Greg Gross	.25	.11
☐ 172 Texas Rangers	1.50	.70
Team Card		
Frank Lucchesi MG		
(Checklist back)		
☐ 173 Steve Swisher	.25	.11
☐ 174 Charlie Hough	.75	.35
☐ 175 Ken Singleton	.50	.23
☐ 176 Dick Lange	.25	.11
☐ 177 Marty Perez	.25	.11
☐ 178 Tom Buskey	.25	.11
☐ 179 George Foster	1.00	.45
☐ 180 Rich Gossage	2.00	.90
☐ 181 Willie Montanez	.25	.11
☐ 182 Harry Rasmussen	.25	.11
☐ 183 Steve Braun	.25	.11
☐ 184 Bill Greif	.25	.11
☐ 185 Dave Parker	2.00	.90
☐ 186 Tom Walker	.25	.11
☐ 187 Pedro Garcia	.25	.11
☐ 188 Fred Scherman	.25	.11
☐ 189 Claudell Washington	.50	.23
☐ 190 Jon Matlack	.50	.23
☐ 191 NL Batting Leaders	.75	.35
Bill Madlock		
Ted Simmons		
Manny Sanguillen		
☐ 192 AL Batting Leaders:	2.00	.90
Rod Carew		
Fred Lynn		
Thurman Munson		
☐ 193 NL Home Run Leaders:	4.00	1.80
Mike Schmidt		
Dave Kingman		
Greg Luzinski		
☐ 194 AL Home Run Leaders:	2.50	1.10
Reggie Jackson		
George Scott		
John Mayberry		
☐ 195 NL RBI Leaders:	1.50	.70
Greg Luzinski		
Johnny Bench		
Tony Perez		
☐ 196 AL RBI Leaders	.75	.35
George Scott		
John Mayberry		
Fred Lynn		
☐ 197 NL Steals Leaders:	1.50	.70
Dave Lopes		
Joe Morgan		
Lou Brock		
☐ 198 AL Steals Leaders	.75	.35
Mickey Rivers		
Claudell Washington		
Amos Otis		
☐ 199 NL Victory Leaders:	1.50	.70
Tom Seaver		
Randy Jones		
Andy Messersmith		
☐ 200 AL Victory Leaders:	1.50	.70
Jim Hunter		
Jim Palmer		
Vida Blue		
☐ 201 NL ERA Leaders	1.50	.70
Randy Jones		
Andy Messersmith		
Tom Seaver		
☐ 202 AL ERA Leaders	5.00	2.20
Jim Palmer		
Jim Hunter		
Dennis Eckersley		
☐ 203 NL Strikeout Leaders	1.50	.70
Tom Seaver		
John Montefusco		
Andy Messersmith		
☐ 204 AL Strikeout Leaders	.75	.35
Frank Tanana		
Bert Blyleven		
Gaylord Perry		
☐ 205 Leading Firemen	.75	.35
Al Hrabosky		
Rich Gossage		
☐ 206 Manny Trillo	.25	.11
☐ 207 Andy Hassler	.25	.11
☐ 208 Mike Lum	.25	.11
☐ 209 Alan Ashby	.75	.35
☐ 210 Lee May	.50	.23
☐ 211 Clay Carroll	.25	.11
☐ 212 Pat Kelly	.25	.11
☐ 213 Dave Heaverlo	.25	.11
☐ 214 Eric Soderholm	.25	.11
☐ 215 Reggie Smith	.50	.23
☐ 216 Montreal Expos	1.50	.70
Team Card		
Karl Kuehl MG		
(Checklist back)		
☐ 217 Dave Freisleben	.25	.11
☐ 218 John Knox	.25	.11
☐ 219 Tom Murphy	.25	.11
☐ 220 Manny Sanguillen	.50	.23
☐ 221 Jim Todd	.25	.11
☐ 222 Wayne Garrett	.25	.11
☐ 223 Ollie Brown	.25	.11
☐ 224 Jim York	.25	.11
☐ 225 Roy White	.50	.23
☐ 226 Jim Sundberg	.50	.23
☐ 227 Oscar Zamora	.25	.11
☐ 228 John Hale	.25	.11
☐ 229 Jerry Remy	.25	.11
☐ 230 Carl Yastrzemski	6.00	2.70
☐ 231 Tom House	.25	.11
☐ 232 Frank Duffy	.25	.11
☐ 233 Grant Jackson	.25	.11
☐ 234 Mike Sadek	.25	.11
☐ 235 Bert Blyleven	.75	.35
☐ 236 Kansas City Royals	1.50	.70
Team Card		
Whitey Herzog MG		
(Checklist back)		
☐ 237 Dave Hamilton	.25	.11
☐ 238 Larry Biittner	.25	.11
☐ 239 John Curtis	.25	.11
☐ 240 Pete Rose	15.00	6.75
☐ 241 Hector Torres	.25	.11
☐ 242 Dan Meyer	.25	.11
☐ 243 Jim Rooker	.25	.11
☐ 244 Bill Sharp	.25	.11
☐ 245 Felix Millan	.25	.11
☐ 246 Cesar Tovar	.25	.11
☐ 247 Terry Harmon	.25	.11
☐ 248 Dick Tidrow	.25	.11
☐ 249 Cliff Johnson	.50	.23
☐ 250 Fergie Jenkins	2.50	1.10
☐ 251 Rick Monday	.50	.23
☐ 252 Tim Nordbrook	.25	.11
☐ 253 Bill Buckner	.75	.35
☐ 254 Rudy Meoli	.25	.11
☐ 255 Fritz Peterson	.25	.11
☐ 256 Rowland Office	.25	.11
☐ 257 Ross Grimsley	.25	.11
☐ 258 Nyls Nyman	.25	.11
☐ 259 Darrel Chaney	.25	.11
☐ 260 Steve Busby	.25	.11
☐ 261 Gary Thomasson	.25	.11
☐ 262 Checklist 133-264	1.50	.70
☐ 263 Lyman Bostock	1.00	.45
☐ 264 Steve Renko	.25	.11
☐ 265 Willie Davis	.50	.23
☐ 266 Alan Foster	.25	.11
☐ 267 Aurelio Rodriguez	.25	.11
☐ 268 Del Unser	.25	.11
☐ 269 Rick Austin	.25	.11
☐ 270 Willie Stargell	4.00	1.80
☐ 271 Jim Lonborg	.50	.23
☐ 272 Rick Dempsey	.50	.23
☐ 273 Joe Niekro	.50	.23
☐ 274 Tommy Harper	.50	.23
☐ 275 Rick Manning	.25	.11
☐ 276 Mickey Scott	.25	.11
☐ 277 Chicago Cubs	1.50	.70
Team Card		
Jim Marshall MG		
(Checklist back)		
☐ 278 Bernie Carbo	.25	.11
☐ 279 Roy Howell	.25	.11
☐ 280 Burt Hooton	.50	.23
☐ 281 Dave May	.25	.11
☐ 282 Dan Osborn	.25	.11
☐ 283 Merv Rettenmund	.25	.11
☐ 284 Steve Ontiveros	.25	.11
☐ 285 Mike Cuellar	.50	.23
☐ 286 Jim Wohlford	.25	.11
☐ 287 Pete Mackanin	.25	.11
☐ 288 Bill Campbell	.25	.11
☐ 289 Enzo Hernandez	.25	.11
☐ 290 Ted Simmons	.75	.35
☐ 291 Ken Sanders	.25	.11
☐ 292 Leon Roberts	.25	.11
☐ 293 Bill Castro	.25	.11
☐ 294 Ed Kirkpatrick	.25	.11
☐ 295 Dave Cash	.25	.11
☐ 296 Pat Dobson	.25	.11
☐ 297 Roger Metzger	.25	.11
☐ 298 Dick Bosman	.25	.11
☐ 299 Champ Summers	.25	.11
☐ 300 Johnny Bench	10.00	4.50
☐ 301 Jackie Brown	.25	.11
☐ 302 Rick Miller	.25	.11
☐ 303 Steve Foucault	.25	.11
☐ 304 California Angels	1.50	.70
Team Card		
Dick Williams MG		
(Checklist back)		
☐ 305 Andy Messersmith	.50	.23
☐ 306 Rod Gilbreath	.25	.11
☐ 307 Al Bumbry	.50	.23
☐ 308 Jim Barr	.25	.11
☐ 309 Bill Melton	.25	.11
☐ 310 Randy Jones	.50	.23
☐ 311 Cookie Rojas	.25	.11
☐ 312 Don Carrithers	.25	.11
☐ 313 Dan Ford	.25	.11
☐ 314 Ed Kranepool	.25	.11
☐ 315 Al Hrabosky	.25	.11
☐ 316 Robin Yount	35.00	16.00
☐ 317 John Candelaria	2.00	.90
☐ 318 Bob Boone	.75	.35
☐ 319 Larry Gura	.25	.11
☐ 320 Willie Horton	.75	.35
☐ 321 Jose Cruz	.50	.23
☐ 322 Glenn Abbott	.25	.11
☐ 323 Rob Sperring	.25	.11
☐ 324 Jim Bibby	.25	.11
☐ 325 Tony Perez	2.00	.90
☐ 326 Dick Pole	.25	.11
☐ 327 Dave Moates	.25	.11
☐ 328 Carl Morton	.25	.11
☐ 329 Joe Ferguson	.25	.11
☐ 330 Nolan Ryan	75.00	34.00
☐ 331 San Diego Padres	1.50	.70
Team Card		
John McNamara MG		
(Checklist back)		
☐ 332 Charlie Williams	.25	.11
☐ 333 Bob Coluccio	.25	.11
☐ 334 Dennis Leonard	.50	.23
☐ 335 Bob Grich	.50	.23
☐ 336 Vic Albury	.25	.11
☐ 337 Bud Harrelson	.50	.23
☐ 338 Bob Bailey	.25	.11
☐ 339 John Denny	.50	.23
☐ 340 Jim Rice	5.00	2.20
☐ 341 Lou Gehrig ATG	12.00	5.50
☐ 342 Rogers Hornsby ATG	4.00	1.80
☐ 343 Pie Traynor ATG	1.00	.45
☐ 344 Honus Wagner ATG	6.00	2.70
☐ 345 Babe Ruth ATG	18.00	8.00
☐ 346 Ty Cobb ATG	10.00	4.50
☐ 347 Ted Williams ATG	12.50	5.50
☐ 348 Mickey Cochrane ATG	1.00	.45
☐ 349 Walter Johnson ATG	4.00	1.80
☐ 350 Lefty Grove ATG	1.00	.45
☐ 351 Randy Hundley	.25	.11
☐ 352 Dave Giusti	.25	.11
☐ 353 Sixto Lezcano	.50	.23

☐ 354 Ron Blomberg	.25	.11
☐ 355 Steve Carlton	6.00	2.70
☐ 356 Ted Martinez	.25	.11
☐ 357 Ken Forsch	.25	.11
☐ 358 Buddy Bell	.50	.23
☐ 359 Rick Reuschel	.50	.23
☐ 360 Jeff Burroughs	.50	.23
☐ 361 Detroit Tigers	1.50	.70
Team Card		
Ralph Houk MG		
(Checklist back)		
☐ 362 Will McEnaney	.50	.23
☐ 363 Dave Collins	.50	.23
☐ 364 Elias Sosa	.25	.11
☐ 365 Carlton Fisk	8.00	3.60
☐ 366 Bobby Valentine	.25	.11
☐ 367 Bruce Miller	.25	.11
☐ 368 Wilbur Wood	.25	.11
☐ 369 Frank White	.50	.23
☐ 370 Ron Cey	.75	.35
☐ 371 Ellie Hendricks	.25	.11
☐ 372 Rick Baldwin	.25	.11
☐ 373 Johnny Briggs	.25	.11
☐ 374 Dan Warthen	.25	.11
☐ 375 Ron Fairly	.50	.23
☐ 376 Rich Hebner	.50	.23
☐ 377 Mike Hegan	.25	.11
☐ 378 Steve Stone	.50	.23
☐ 379 Ken Boswell	.25	.11
☐ 380 Bobby Bonds	1.50	.70
☐ 381 Denny Doyle	.25	.11
☐ 382 Matt Alexander	.25	.11
☐ 383 John Ellis	.25	.11
☐ 384 Philadelphia Phillies	1.50	.70
Team Card		
Danny Ozark MG		
(Checklist back)		
☐ 385 Mickey Lolich	.75	.35
☐ 386 Ed Goodson	.25	.11
☐ 387 Mike Miley	.25	.11
☐ 388 Stan Perzanowski	.25	.11
☐ 389 Glenn Adams	.25	.11
☐ 390 Don Gullett	.75	.35
☐ 391 Jerry Hairston	.25	.11
☐ 392 Checklist 265-396	1.50	.70
☐ 393 Paul Mitchell	.25	.11
☐ 394 Fran Healy	.25	.11
☐ 395 Jim Wynn	.50	.23
☐ 396 Bill Lee	.50	.23
☐ 397 Tim Foli	.25	.11
☐ 398 Dave Tomlin	.25	.11
☐ 399 Luis Melendez	.25	.11
☐ 400 Rod Carew	5.00	2.20
☐ 401 Ken Brett	.25	.11
☐ 402 Don Money	.25	.11
☐ 403 Geoff Zahn	.25	.11
☐ 404 Enos Cabell	.25	.11
☐ 405 Rollie Fingers	2.50	1.10
☐ 406 Ed Herrmann	.25	.11
☐ 407 Tom Underwood	.25	.11
☐ 408 Charlie Spikes	.25	.11
☐ 409 Dave Lemanczyk	.25	.11
☐ 410 Ralph Garr	.50	.23
☐ 411 Bill Singer	.25	.11
☐ 412 Toby Harrah	.50	.23
☐ 413 Pete Varney	.25	.11
☐ 414 Wayne Garland	.25	.11
☐ 415 Vada Pinson	.75	.35
☐ 416 Tommy John	.75	.35
☐ 417 Gene Clines	.25	.11
☐ 418 Jose Morales	.25	.11
☐ 419 Reggie Cleveland	.25	.11
☐ 420 Joe Morgan	5.00	2.20
☐ 421 Oakland A's	1.50	.70
Team Card		
(No MG on front;		
checklist back)		
☐ 422 Johnny Grubb	.25	.11
☐ 423 Ed Halicki	.25	.11
☐ 424 Phil Roof	.25	.11
☐ 425 Rennie Stennett	.25	.11
☐ 426 Bob Forsch	.25	.11
☐ 427 Kurt Bevacqua	.25	.11
☐ 428 Jim Crawford	.25	.11
☐ 429 Fred Stanley	.25	.11
☐ 430 Jose Cardenal	.50	.23
☐ 431 Dick Ruthven	.25	.11
☐ 432 Tom Veryzer	.25	.11
☐ 433 Rick Waits	.25	.11
☐ 434 Morris Nettles	.25	.11
☐ 435 Phil Niekro	2.50	1.10
☐ 436 Bill Fahey	.25	.11
☐ 437 Terry Forster	.25	.11
☐ 438 Doug DeCinces	.50	.23
☐ 439 Rick Rhoden	.50	.23
☐ 440 John Mayberry	.50	.23
☐ 441 Gary Carter	7.50	3.40
☐ 442 Hank Webb	.25	.11
☐ 443 San Francisco Giants	1.50	.70
Team Card		
(No MG on front;		
checklist back)		
☐ 444 Gary Nolan	.50	.23
☐ 445 Rico Petrocelli	.50	.23
☐ 446 Larry Haney	.25	.11
☐ 447 Gene Locklear	.50	.23
☐ 448 Tom Johnson	.25	.11
☐ 449 Bob Robertson	.25	.11
☐ 450 Jim Palmer	5.00	2.20
☐ 451 Buddy Bradford	.25	.11
☐ 452 Tom Hausman	.25	.11
☐ 453 Lou Piniella	1.00	.45
☐ 454 Tom Griffin	.25	.11
☐ 455 Dick Allen	.75	.35
☐ 456 Joe Coleman	.25	.11
☐ 457 Ed Crosby	.25	.11
☐ 458 Earl Williams	.25	.11
☐ 459 Jim Brewer	.25	.11
☐ 460 Cesar Cedeno	.50	.23
☐ 461 NL and AL Champs	.75	.35
Reds sweep Bucs;		
Bosox surprise A's		
☐ 462 World Series	.75	.35
Reds Champs		
☐ 463 Steve Hargan	.25	.11
☐ 464 Ken Henderson	.25	.11
☐ 465 Mike Marshall	.50	.23
☐ 466 Bob Stinson	.25	.11
☐ 467 Woodie Fryman	.25	.11
☐ 468 Jesus Alou	.25	.11
☐ 469 Rawly Eastwick	.25	.11
☐ 470 Bobby Murcer	.50	.23
☐ 471 Jim Burton	.25	.11
☐ 472 Bob Davis	.25	.11
☐ 473 Paul Blair	.50	.23
☐ 474 Ray Corbin	.25	.11
☐ 475 Joe Rudi	.50	.23
☐ 476 Bob Moose	.25	.11
☐ 477 Cleveland Indians	1.50	.70
Team Card		
Frank Robinson MG		
(Checklist back)		
☐ 478 Lynn McGlothen	.25	.11
☐ 479 Bobby Mitchell	.25	.11
☐ 480 Mike Schmidt	30.00	13.50
☐ 481 Rudy May	.25	.11
☐ 482 Tim Hosley	.25	.11
☐ 483 Mickey Stanley	.25	.11
☐ 484 Eric Raich	.25	.11
☐ 485 Mike Hargrove	.50	.23
☐ 486 Bruce Dal Canton	.25	.11
☐ 487 Leron Lee	.25	.11
☐ 488 Claude Osteen	.50	.23
☐ 489 Skip Jutze	.25	.11
☐ 490 Frank Tanana	.75	.35
☐ 491 Terry Crowley	.25	.11
☐ 492 Martin Pattin	.25	.11
☐ 493 Derrel Thomas	.25	.11
☐ 494 Craig Swan	.25	.11
☐ 495 Nate Colbert	.50	.23
☐ 496 Juan Beniquez	.25	.11
☐ 497 Joe McIntosh	.25	.11
☐ 498 Glenn Borgmann	.25	.11
☐ 499 Mario Guerrero	.25	.11
☐ 500 Reggie Jackson	15.00	6.75
☐ 501 Billy Champion	.25	.11
☐ 502 Tim McCarver	.75	.35
☐ 503 Elliott Maddox	.25	.11
☐ 504 Pittsburgh Pirates	1.50	.70
Team Card		
Danny Murtaugh MG		
(Checklist back)		
☐ 505 Mark Belanger	.50	.23
☐ 506 George Mitterwald	.25	.11
☐ 507 Ray Bare	.25	.11
☐ 508 Duane Kuiper	.25	.11
☐ 509 Bill Hands	.25	.11
☐ 510 Amos Otis	.50	.23
☐ 511 Jamie Easterley	.25	.11
☐ 512 Ellie Rodriguez	.25	.11
☐ 513 Bart Johnson	.25	.11
☐ 514 Dan Driessen	.50	.23
☐ 515 Steve Yeager	.50	.23
☐ 516 Wayne Granger	.25	.11
☐ 517 John Milner	.25	.11
☐ 518 Doug Flynn	.25	.11
☐ 519 Steve Brye	.25	.11
☐ 520 Willie McCovey	5.00	2.20
☐ 521 Jim Colborn	.25	.11
☐ 522 Ted Sizemore	.25	.11
☐ 523 Bob Montgomery	.25	.11
☐ 524 Pete Falcone	.25	.11
☐ 525 Billy Williams	2.50	1.10
☐ 526 Checklist 397-528	1.50	.70
☐ 527 Mike Anderson	.25	.11
☐ 528 Dock Ellis	.25	.11
☐ 529 Deron Johnson	.25	.11
☐ 530 Don Sutton	1.50	.70
☐ 531 New York Mets	1.50	.70
Team Card		
Joe Frazier MG		
(Checklist back)		
☐ 532 Milt May	.25	.11
☐ 533 Lee Richard	.25	.11
☐ 534 Stan Bahnsen	.25	.11
☐ 535 Dave Nelson	.25	.11
☐ 536 Mike Thompson	.25	.11
☐ 537 Tony Muser	.25	.11
☐ 538 Pat Darcy	.25	.11
☐ 539 John Balaz	.50	.23
☐ 540 Bill Freehan	.50	.23
☐ 541 Steve Mingori	.25	.11
☐ 542 Keith Hernandez	1.50	.70
☐ 543 Wayne Twitchell	.25	.11
☐ 544 Pepe Frias	.25	.11
☐ 545 Sparky Lyle	.50	.23
☐ 546 Dave Rosello	.25	.11
☐ 547 Roric Harrison	.25	.11
☐ 548 Manny Mota	.50	.23
☐ 549 Randy Tate	.25	.11
☐ 550 Hank Aaron	30.00	13.50
☐ 551 Jerry DaVanon	.25	.11
☐ 552 Terry Humphrey	.25	.11
☐ 553 Randy Moffitt	.25	.11
☐ 554 Ray Fosse	.25	.11
☐ 555 Dyar Miller	.25	.11
☐ 556 Minnesota Twins	1.50	.70
Team Card		
Gene Mauch MG		
(Checklist back)		
☐ 557 Dan Spillner	.25	.11
☐ 558 Clarence Gaston	.75	.35
☐ 559 Clyde Wright	.25	.11
☐ 560 Jorge Orta	.25	.11
☐ 561 Tom Carroll	.25	.11
☐ 562 Adrian Garrett	.25	.11
☐ 563 Larry Demery	.25	.11
☐ 564 Bubble Gum Champ:	.75	.35
Kurt Bevacqua		
☐ 565 Tug McGraw	.50	.23
☐ 566 Ken McMullen	.25	.11
☐ 567 George Stone	.25	.11
☐ 568 Rob Andrews	.25	.11
☐ 569 Nelson Briles	.50	.23
☐ 570 George Hendrick	.50	.23
☐ 571 Don DeMola	.25	.11
☐ 572 Rich Coggins	.25	.11
☐ 573 Bill Travers	.25	.11
☐ 574 Don Kessinger	.50	.23
☐ 575 Dwight Evans	1.50	.70
☐ 576 Maximino Leon	.25	.11
☐ 577 Marc Hill	.25	.11
☐ 578 Ted Kubiak	.25	.11
☐ 579 Clay Kirby	.25	.11
☐ 580 Bert Campaneris	.50	.23
☐ 581 St. Louis Cardinals	1.50	.70
Team Card		
Red Schoendienst MG		
(Checklist back)		
☐ 582 Mike Kekich	.25	.11
☐ 583 Tommy Helms	.25	.11
☐ 584 Stan Wall	.25	.11
☐ 585 Joe Torre	.75	.35
☐ 586 Ron Schueler	.25	.11
☐ 587 Leo Cardenas	.25	.11
☐ 588 Kevin Kobel	.25	.11
☐ 589 Rookie Pitchers:	1.50	.70
Santo Alcala		
Mike Flanagan		
Joe Pactwa		
Pablo Torrealba		
☐ 590 Rookie Outfielders:	1.00	.45
Henry Cruz		
Chet Lemon		
Ellis Valentine		
Terry Whitfield		
☐ 591 Rookie Pitchers	.50	.23
Steve Grilli		
Craig Mitchell		
Jose Sosa		
George Throop		
☐ 592 Rookie Infielders:	7.50	3.40
Willie Randolph		
Dave McKay		
Jerry Royster		
Roy Staiger		
☐ 593 Rookie Pitchers	.50	.23
Larry Anderson		
Ken Crosby		
Mark Littell		
Butch Metzger		

☐ 594 Rookie Catchers/OF .50 .23
Andy Merchant
Ed Ott
Royle Stillman
Jerry White
☐ 595 Rookie Pitchers .50 .23
Art DeFillipis
Randy Lerch
Sid Monge
Steve Barr
☐ 596 Rookie Infielders .50 .23
Craig Reynolds
Lamar Johnson
Johnnie LeMaster
Jerry Manuel
☐ 597 Rookie Pitchers .50 .23
Don Aase
Jack Kucek
Frank LaCorte
Mike Pazik
☐ 598 Rookie Outfielders .50 .23
Hector Cruz
Jamie Quirk
Jerry Turner
Joe Wallis
☐ 599 Rookie Pitchers 7.50 3.40
Rob Dressler
Ron Guidry
Bob McClure
Pat Zachry
☐ 600 Tom Seaver 10.00 4.50
☐ 601 Ken Rudolph .25 .11
☐ 602 Doug Konieczny .25 .11
☐ 603 Jim Holt .25 .11
☐ 604 Joe Lovitto .25 .11
☐ 605 Al Downing .25 .11
☐ 606 Milwaukee Brewers 1.50 .70
Team Card
Alex Grammas MG
(Checklist back)
☐ 607 Rich Hinton .25 .11
☐ 608 Vic Correll .25 .11
☐ 609 Fred Norman .25 .11
☐ 610 Greg Luzinski .75 .35
☐ 611 Rich Folkers .25 .11
☐ 612 Joe Lahoud .25 .11
☐ 613 Tim Johnson .25 .11
☐ 614 Fernando Arroyo .25 .11
☐ 615 Mike Cubbage .25 .11
☐ 616 Buck Martinez .25 .11
☐ 617 Darold Knowles .25 .11
☐ 618 Jack Brohamer .25 .11
☐ 619 Bill Butler .25 .11
☐ 620 Al Oliver .75 .35
☐ 621 Tom Hall .25 .11
☐ 622 Rick Auerbach .25 .11
☐ 623 Bob Allietta .25 .11
☐ 624 Tony Taylor .50 .23
☐ 625 J.R. Richard .50 .23
☐ 626 Bob Sheldon .25 .11
☐ 627 Bill Plummer .25 .11
☐ 628 John D'Acquisto .25 .11
☐ 629 Sandy Alomar .25 .11
☐ 630 Chris Speier .25 .11
☐ 631 Atlanta Braves 1.50 .70
Team Card
Dave Bristol MG
(Checklist back)
☐ 632 Rogelio Moret .25 .11
☐ 633 John Stearns .50 .23
☐ 634 Larry Christenson .25 .11
☐ 635 Jim Fregosi .50 .23
☐ 636 Joe Decker .25 .11
☐ 637 Bruce Bochte .25 .11
☐ 638 Doyle Alexander .50 .23
☐ 639 Fred Kendall .25 .11
☐ 640 Bill Madlock .75 .35
☐ 641 Tom Paciorek .50 .23
☐ 642 Dennis Blair .25 .11
☐ 643 Checklist 529-660 1.50 .70
☐ 644 Tom Bradley .25 .11
☐ 645 Darrell Porter .50 .23
☐ 646 John Lowenstein .25 .11
☐ 647 Ramon Hernandez .25 .11
☐ 648 Al Cowens .25 .11
☐ 649 Dave Roberts .25 .11
☐ 650 Thurman Munson 6.00 2.70
☐ 651 John Odom .25 .11
☐ 652 Ed Armbrister .25 .11
☐ 653 Mike Norris .50 .23
☐ 654 Doug Griffin .25 .11
☐ 655 Mike Vail .25 .11
☐ 656 Chicago White Sox 1.50 .70
Team Card
Chuck Tanner MG
(Checklist back)
☐ 657 Roy Smalley .50 .23
☐ 658 Jerry Johnson .25 .11
☐ 659 Ben Oglivie .50 .23
☐ 660 Dave Lopes 1.00 .45

1977 O-Pee-Chee

The 1977 O-Pee-Chee set of 264 standard-size cards is not only much smaller numerically than its American counterpart, but also contains many different poses and is loaded with players from the two Canadian teams, including many players from the inaugural year of the Blue Jays and many single cards of players who were on multiplayer rookie cards. On a white background, the fronts feature color player photos with thin black borders. The player's name and position, a facsimile autograph, and the team name also appear on the front. The horizontal backs carry player biography and statistics in French and English. The numbering of this set is different than the U.S. issue, the backs have different colors and the words "O-Pee-Chee Printed in Canada" are printed on the back.

	NRMT	VG-E
COMPLETE SET (264)	300.00	135.00
COMMON CARD (1-264)	.25	.11

☐ 1 Batting Leaders 7.50 3.40
George Brett
Bill Madlock
☐ 2 Home Run Leaders 2.00 .90
Graig Nettles
Mike Schmidt
☐ 3 RBI Leaders .50 .23
Lee May
George Foster
☐ 4 Stolen Base Leaders .50 .23
Bill North
Dave Lopes
☐ 5 Victory Leaders .75 .35
Jim Palmer
Randy Jones
☐ 6 Strikeout Leaders 15.00 6.75
Nolan Ryan
Tom Seaver
☐ 7 ERA Leaders .50 .23
Mark Fidrych
John Denny
☐ 8 Leading Firemen .50 .23
Bill Campbell
Rawly Eastwick
☐ 9 Mike Jorgensen .35 .16
☐ 10 Jim Hunter 4.00 1.80
☐ 11 Ken Griffey 2.00 .90
☐ 12 Bill Campbell .25 .11
☐ 13 Otto Velez .50 .23
☐ 14 Milt May .25 .11
☐ 15 Dennis Eckersley 6.00 2.70
☐ 16 John Mayberry .50 .23
☐ 17 Larry Bowa .50 .23
☐ 18 Don Carrithers .35 .16
☐ 19 Ken Singleton .35 .16
☐ 20 Bill Stein .25 .11
☐ 21 Ken Brett .25 .11
☐ 22 Gary Woods .50 .23
☐ 23 Steve Swisher .25 .11
☐ 24 Don Sutton 2.50 1.10
☐ 25 Willie Stargell 3.50 1.55
☐ 26 Jerry Koosman .35 .16
☐ 27 Del Unser .35 .16
☐ 28 Bob Grich .35 .16
☐ 29 Jim Slaton .25 .11
☐ 30 Thurman Munson 5.00 2.20
☐ 31 Dan Driessen .25 .11
☐ 32 Tom Bruno .50 .23
☐ 33 Larry Hisle .35 .16
☐ 34 Phil Garner .35 .16
☐ 35 Mike Hargrove .35 .16
☐ 36 Jackie Brown .35 .16
☐ 37 Carl Yastrzemski 5.00 2.20
☐ 38 Dave Roberts .25 .11
☐ 39 Ray Fosse .25 .11
☐ 40 Dave McKay .50 .23
☐ 41 Paul Splittorff .25 .11
☐ 42 Garry Maddox .25 .11
☐ 43 Phil Niekro 3.00 1.35
☐ 44 Roger Metzger .25 .11
☐ 45 Gary Carter 5.00 2.20
☐ 46 Jim Spencer .25 .11
☐ 47 Ross Grimsley .25 .11
☐ 48 Bob Bailor .50 .23
☐ 49 Chris Chambliss .35 .16
☐ 50 Will McEnaney .35 .16
☐ 51 Lou Brock 5.00 2.20
☐ 52 Rollie Fingers 3.50 1.55
☐ 53 Chris Speier .25 .11
☐ 54 Bombo Rivera .35 .16
☐ 55 Pete Broberg .25 .11
☐ 56 Bill Madlock 1.00 .45
☐ 57 Rick Rhoden .25 .11
☐ 58 Blue Jays Coaches .50 .23
Don Leppert
Bob Miller
Jackie Moore
Harry Warner
☐ 59 John Candelaria .35 .16
☐ 60 Ed Kranepool .25 .11
☐ 61 Dave LaRoche .25 .11
☐ 62 Jim Rice 5.00 2.20
☐ 63 Don Stanhouse .35 .16
☐ 64 Jason Thompson .35 .16
☐ 65 Nolan Ryan 50.00 22.00
☐ 66 Tom Poquette .25 .11
☐ 67 Leon Hooten .50 .23
☐ 68 Bob Boone .25 .11
☐ 69 Mickey Rivers .35 .16
☐ 70 Gary Nolan .25 .11
☐ 71 Sixto Lezcano .25 .11
☐ 72 Larry Parrish .50 .23
☐ 73 Dave Goltz .25 .11
☐ 74 Bert Campaneris .35 .16
☐ 75 Vida Blue .35 .16
☐ 76 Rick Cerone .50 .23
☐ 77 Ralph Garr .35 .16
☐ 78 Ken Forsch .25 .11
☐ 79 Willie Montanez .25 .11
☐ 80 Jim Palmer 5.00 2.20
☐ 81 Jerry White .50 .23
☐ 82 Gene Tenace .35 .16
☐ 83 Bobby Murcer .35 .16
☐ 84 Garry Templeton 1.25 .55
☐ 85 Bill Singer .50 .23
☐ 86 Buddy Bell .35 .16
☐ 87 Luis Tiant .50 .23
☐ 88 Rusty Staub .50 .23
☐ 89 Sparky Lyle .35 .16
☐ 90 Jose Morales .35 .16
☐ 91 Dennis Leonard .25 .11
☐ 92 Tommy Smith .25 .11
☐ 93 Steve Carlton 5.00 2.20
☐ 94 John Scott .50 .23
☐ 95 Bill Bonham .25 .11
☐ 96 Dave Lopes .35 .16
☐ 97 Jerry Reuss .35 .16
☐ 98 Dave Kingman .50 .23
☐ 99 Dan Warthen .35 .16
☐ 100 Johnny Bench 7.50 3.40
☐ 101 Bert Blyleven 2.00 .90
☐ 102 Cecil Cooper .50 .23
☐ 103 Mike Willis .50 .23
☐ 104 Dan Ford .25 .11
☐ 105 Frank Tanana .50 .23
☐ 106 Bill North .25 .11
☐ 107 Joe Ferguson .25 .11
☐ 108 Dick Williams MG .50 .23
☐ 109 John Denny .25 .11
☐ 110 Willie Randolph 3.00 1.35
☐ 111 Reggie Cleveland .35 .16
☐ 112 Doug Howard .50 .23
☐ 113 Randy Jones .25 .11
☐ 114 Rico Carty .50 .23
☐ 115 Mark Fidrych 7.50 3.40
☐ 116 Darrell Porter .35 .16
☐ 117 Wayne Garrett .35 .16
☐ 118 Greg Luzinski .50 .23
☐ 119 Jim Barr .25 .11
☐ 120 George Foster 1.00 .45
☐ 121 Phil Roof .50 .23
☐ 122 Bucky Dent .35 .16
☐ 123 Steve Braun .25 .11
☐ 124 Checklist 1-132 1.25 .55
☐ 125 Lee May .35 .16
☐ 126 Woodie Fryman .35 .16
☐ 127 Jose Cardenal .25 .11
☐ 128 Doug Rau .25 .11
☐ 129 Rennie Stennett .25 .11
☐ 130 Pete Vuckovich .50 .23
☐ 131 Cesar Cedeno .35 .16
☐ 132 Jon Matlack .25 .11
☐ 133 Don Baylor 2.00 .90

☐ 134 Darrel Chaney	.25	.11
☐ 135 Tony Perez	2.50	1.10
☐ 136 Aurelio Rodriguez	.25	.11
☐ 137 Carlton Fisk	7.50	3.40
☐ 138 Wayne Garland	.25	.11
☐ 139 Dave Hilton	.50	.23
☐ 140 Rawly Eastwick	.25	.11
☐ 141 Amos Otis	.35	.16
☐ 142 Tug McGraw	.35	.16
☐ 143 Rod Carew	7.50	3.40
☐ 144 Mike Torrez	.35	.16
☐ 145 Sal Bando	.25	.11
☐ 146 Dock Ellis	.25	.11
☐ 147 Jose Cruz	.35	.16
☐ 148 Alan Ashby	.50	.23
☐ 149 Gaylord Perry	3.00	1.35
☐ 150 Keith Hernandez	1.50	.70
☐ 151 Dave Pagan	.25	.11
☐ 152 Richie Zisk	.25	.11
☐ 153 Steve Rogers	.50	.23
☐ 154 Mark Belanger	.25	.11
☐ 155 Andy Messersmith	.35	.16
☐ 156 Dave Winfield	20.00	9.00
☐ 157 Chuck Hartenstein	.50	.23
☐ 158 Manny Trillo	.25	.11
☐ 159 Steve Yeager	.25	.11
☐ 160 Cesar Geronimo	.25	.11
☐ 161 Jim Rooker	.25	.11
☐ 162 Tim Foli	.35	.16
☐ 163 Fred Lynn	1.50	.70
☐ 164 Ed Figueroa	.25	.11
☐ 165 Johnny Grubb	.25	.11
☐ 166 Pedro Garcia	.50	.23
☐ 167 Ron LeFlore	.35	.16
☐ 168 Rich Hebner	.25	.11
☐ 169 Larry Herndon	.25	.11
☐ 170 George Brett	40.00	18.00
☐ 171 Joe Kerrigan	.35	.16
☐ 172 Bud Harrelson	.25	.11
☐ 173 Bobby Bonds	1.50	.70
☐ 174 Bill Travers	.25	.11
☐ 175 John Lowenstein	.50	.23
☐ 176 Butch Wynegar	.25	.11
☐ 177 Pete Falcone	.25	.11
☐ 178 Claudell Washington	.35	.16
☐ 179 Checklist 133-264	1.25	.55
☐ 180 Dave Cash	.35	.16
☐ 181 Fred Norman	.25	.11
☐ 182 Roy White	.25	.11
☐ 183 Marty Perez	.25	.11
☐ 184 Jesse Jefferson	.50	.23
☐ 185 Jim Sundberg	.25	.11
☐ 186 Dan Meyer	.25	.11
☐ 187 Fergie Jenkins	3.00	1.35
☐ 188 Tom Veryzer	.25	.11
☐ 189 Dennis Blair	.35	.16
☐ 190 Rick Manning	.25	.11
☐ 191 Doug Bird	.25	.11
☐ 192 Al Bumbry	.25	.11
☐ 193 Dave Roberts	.25	.11
☐ 194 Larry Christenson	.25	.11
☐ 195 Chet Lemon	.35	.16
☐ 196 Ted Simmons	1.00	.45
☐ 197 Ray Burris	.25	.11
☐ 198 Expos Coaches Jim Brewer Billy Gardner Mickey Vernon Ozzie Virgil	.50	.23
☐ 199 Ron Cey	.50	.23
☐ 200 Reggie Jackson	10.00	4.50
☐ 201 Pat Zachry	.25	.11
☐ 202 Doug Ault	.50	.23
☐ 203 Al Oliver	.50	.23
☐ 204 Robin Yount	20.00	9.00
☐ 205 Tom Seaver	10.00	4.50
☐ 206 Joe Rudi	.25	.11
☐ 207 Barry Foote	.35	.16
☐ 208 Toby Harrah	.35	.16
☐ 209 Jeff Burroughs	.25	.11
☐ 210 George Scott	.35	.16
☐ 211 Jim Mason	.50	.23
☐ 212 Vern Ruhle	.25	.11
☐ 213 Fred Kendall	.25	.11
☐ 214 Rick Reuschel	.35	.16
☐ 215 Hal McRae	.50	.23
☐ 216 Chip Lang	.35	.16
☐ 217 Graig Nettles	.25	.11
☐ 218 George Hendrick	.35	.16
☐ 219 Glenn Abbott	.25	.11
☐ 220 Joe Morgan	6.00	2.70
☐ 221 Sam Ewing	.50	.23
☐ 222 George Medich	.25	.11
☐ 223 Reggie Smith	.35	.16
☐ 224 Dave Hamilton	.25	.11
☐ 225 Pepe Frias	.35	.16
☐ 226 Jay Johnstone	.25	.11
☐ 227 J.R. Richard	.35	.16
☐ 228 Doug DeCinces	.35	.16
☐ 229 Dave Lemanczyk	.50	.23
☐ 230 Rick Monday	.25	.11
☐ 231 Manny Sanguillen	.25	.11
☐ 232 John Montefusco	.25	.11
☐ 233 Duane Kuiper	.25	.11
☐ 234 Ellis Valentine	.35	.16
☐ 235 Dick Tidrow	.25	.11
☐ 236 Ben Oglivie	.35	.16
☐ 237 Rick Burleson	.25	.11
☐ 238 Roy Hartsfield MG	.50	.23
☐ 239 Lyman Bostock	.35	.16
☐ 240 Pete Rose	15.00	6.75
☐ 241 Mike Ivie	.25	.11
☐ 242 Dave Parker	3.00	1.35
☐ 243 Bill Greif	.35	.16
☐ 244 Freddie Patek	.25	.11
☐ 245 Mike Schmidt	20.00	9.00
☐ 246 Brian Downing	.35	.16
☐ 247 Steve Hargan	.50	.23
☐ 248 Dave Collins	.25	.11
☐ 249 Felix Millan	.25	.11
☐ 250 Don Gullett	.35	.16
☐ 251 Jerry Royster	.25	.11
☐ 252 Earl Williams	.50	.23
☐ 253 Frank Duffy	.25	.11
☐ 254 Tippy Martinez	.25	.11
☐ 255 Steve Garvey	3.00	1.35
☐ 256 Alvis Woods	.50	.23
☐ 257 John Hiller	.35	.16
☐ 258 Dave Concepcion	1.50	.70
☐ 259 Dwight Evans	2.50	1.10
☐ 260 Pete MacKanin	.35	.16
☐ 261 George Brett RB Most Consec. Games Three Or More Hits	15.00	6.75
☐ 262 Minnie Minoso RB Oldest Player To Hit Safely	.50	.23
☐ 263 Jose Morales RB Most Pinch-hits, Season	.50	.23
☐ 264 Nolan Ryan RB Most Seasons 300 Or More Strikeouts	20.00	9.00

1978 O-Pee-Chee

The 242 standard-size cards comprising the 1978 O-Pee-Chee set differ from the cards of the 1978 Topps set by having a higher ratio of cards of players from the two Canadian teams, a practice begun by O-Pee-Chee in 1977 and continued to 1988. The fronts feature white-bordered color player photos, each framed by a colored line. The player's name appears in black lettering at the right of lower white margin. His team name appears in colored cursive lettering, interrupting the framing line at the bottom left of the photo; his position appears within a white baseball icon in an upper corner. The tan and brown horizontal backs carry the player's name, team and position in the brown border at the bottom. Biography, major league statistics, career highlights in both French and English and a bilingual result of an "at bat" in the "Play Ball" game also appear. The asterisked cards have an extra line on the front indicating team change. Double-printed (DP) cards are also noted below. The key card in this set is Eddie Murray.

	NRMT	VG-E
COMPLETE SET (242)	225.00	100.00
COMMON CARD (1-242)	.20	.09
COMMON CARD DP (1-242)	.10	.05
☐ 1 Batting Leaders Dave Parker Rod Carew	1.50	.70
☐ 2 Home Run Leaders DP George Foster Jim Rice	.40	.18
☐ 3 RBI Leaders George Foster Larry Hisle	.40	.18
☐ 4 Stolen Base Leaders DP Frank Taveras Freddie Patek	.30	.14
☐ 5 Victory Leaders Steve Carlton Dave Goltz Dennis Leonard Jim Palmer	2.00	.90
☐ 6 Strikeout Leaders DP Phil Niekro Nolan Ryan	5.00	2.20
☐ 7 ERA Leaders DP John Candelaria Frank Tanana	.30	.14
☐ 8 Firemen Leaders Rollie Fingers Bill Campbell	.75	.35
☐ 9 Steve Rogers DP	.20	.09
☐ 10 Graig Nettles DP	.30	.14
☐ 11 Doug Capilla	.20	.09
☐ 12 George Scott	.30	.14
☐ 13 Gary Woods	.20	.09
☐ 14 Tom Veryzer Now with Cleveland as of 12-9-77	.40	.18
☐ 15 Wayne Garland	.20	.09
☐ 16 Amos Otis	.30	.14
☐ 17 Larry Christenson	.20	.09
☐ 18 Dave Cash	.30	.14
☐ 19 Jim Barr	.20	.09
☐ 20 Ruppert Jones	.20	.09
☐ 21 Eric Soderholm	.20	.09
☐ 22 Jesse Jefferson	.20	.09
☐ 23 Jerry Morales	.20	.09
☐ 24 Doug Rau	.20	.09
☐ 25 Rennie Stennett	.20	.09
☐ 26 Lee Mazzilli	.30	.14
☐ 27 Dick Williams MG	.30	.14
☐ 28 Joe Rudi	.30	.14
☐ 29 Robin Yount	15.00	6.75
☐ 30 Don Gullett DP	.20	.09
☐ 31 Roy Howell DP	.10	.05
☐ 32 Cesar Geronimo	.20	.09
☐ 33 Rick Langford DP	.10	.05
☐ 34 Dan Ford	.20	.09
☐ 35 Gene Tenace	.30	.14
☐ 36 Santo Alcala	.30	.14
☐ 37 Rick Burleson	.20	.09
☐ 38 Dave Rozema	.20	.09
☐ 39 Duane Kuiper	.20	.09
☐ 40 Ron Fairly Now with California as of 12-8-77	.40	.18
☐ 41 Dennis Leonard	.30	.14
☐ 42 Greg Luzinski	.40	.18
☐ 43 Willie Montanez Now with N.Y. Mets as of 12-8-77	.40	.18
☐ 44 Enos Cabell	.20	.09
☐ 45 Ellis Valentine	.30	.14
☐ 46 Steve Stone	.30	.14
☐ 47 Lee May DP	.30	.14
☐ 48 Roy White	.30	.14
☐ 49 Jerry Garvin	.20	.09
☐ 50 Johnny Bench	5.00	2.20
☐ 51 Garry Templeton	.30	.14
☐ 52 Doyle Alexander	.30	.14
☐ 53 Steve Henderson	.20	.09
☐ 54 Stan Bahnsen	.20	.09
☐ 55 Dan Meyer	.20	.09
☐ 56 Rick Reuschel	.30	.14
☐ 57 Reggie Smith	.30	.14
☐ 58 Blue Jays Team DP	.40	.18
☐ 59 John Montefusco	.20	.09
☐ 60 Dave Parker	1.50	.70
☐ 61 Jim Bibby	.20	.09
☐ 62 Fred Lynn	1.00	.45
☐ 63 Jose Morales	.20	.09
☐ 64 Aurelio Rodriguez	.20	.09
☐ 65 Frank Tanana	.30	.14
☐ 66 Darrell Porter	.30	.14
☐ 67 Otto Velez	.20	.09
☐ 68 Larry Bowa	.40	.18
☐ 69 Jim Hunter	2.50	1.10
☐ 70 George Foster	1.00	.45
☐ 71 Cecil Cooper DP	.30	.14
☐ 72 Gary Alexander DP	.10	.05
☐ 73 Paul Thormodsgard	.20	.09
☐ 74 Toby Harrah	.30	.14
☐ 75 Mitchell Page	.20	.09
☐ 76 Alan Ashby	.20	.09
☐ 77 Jorge Orta	.20	.09
☐ 78 Dave Winfield	12.50	5.50
☐ 79 Andy Messersmith Now with N.Y. Yankees as of 12-8-77	.40	.18
☐ 80 Ken Singleton	.30	.14
☐ 81 Will McEnaney	.30	.14
☐ 82 Lou Piniella	.40	.18
☐ 83 Bob Forsch	.20	.09
☐ 84 Dan Driessen	.20	.09

☐ 85 Dave Lemanczyk	.20	.09
☐ 86 Paul Dade	.20	.09
☐ 87 Bill Campbell	.20	.09
☐ 88 Ron LeFlore	.30	.14
☐ 89 Bill Madlock	.40	.18
☐ 90 Tony Perez DP	1.25	.55
☐ 91 Freddie Patek	.20	.09
☐ 92 Glenn Abbott	.20	.09
☐ 93 Garry Maddox	.20	.09
☐ 94 Steve Staggs	.20	.09
☐ 95 Bobby Murcer	.30	.14
☐ 96 Don Sutton	2.00	.90
☐ 97 Al Oliver	.75	.35
Now with Texas Rangers as of 12-8-77		
☐ 98 Jon Matlack	.30	.14
Now with Texas Rangers as of 12-8-77		
☐ 99 Sam Mejias	.30	.14
☐ 100 Pete Rose DP	5.00	2.20
☐ 101 Randy Jones	.20	.09
☐ 102 Sixto Lezcano	.20	.09
☐ 103 Jim Clancy DP	.10	.05
☐ 104 Butch Wynegar	.20	.09
☐ 105 Nolan Ryan	40.00	18.00
☐ 106 Wayne Gross	.20	.09
☐ 107 Bob Watson	.30	.14
☐ 108 Joe Kerrigan	.30	.14
Now with Baltimore as of 12-8-77		
☐ 109 Keith Hernandez	1.00	.45
☐ 110 Reggie Jackson	8.00	3.60
☐ 111 Denny Doyle	.20	.09
☐ 112 Sam Ewing	.30	.14
☐ 113 Bert Blyleven	.50	.23
Now with Pittsburgh as of 12-8-77		
☐ 114 Andre Thornton	.30	.14
☐ 115 Milt May	.20	.09
☐ 116 Jim Colborn	.20	.09
☐ 117 Warren Cromartie	.40	.18
☐ 118 Ted Sizemore	.20	.09
☐ 119 Checklist 1-121	1.25	.55
☐ 120 Tom Seaver	4.00	1.80
☐ 121 Luis Gomez	.20	.09
☐ 122 Jim Spencer	.30	.14
Now with N.Y. Yankees as of 12-12-77		
☐ 123 Leroy Stanton	.20	.09
☐ 124 Luis Tiant	.40	.18
☐ 125 Mark Belanger	.30	.14
☐ 126 Jackie Brown	.20	.09
☐ 127 Bill Buckner	.40	.18
☐ 128 Bill Robinson	.30	.14
☐ 129 Rick Cerone	.30	.14
☐ 130 Ron Cey	.40	.18
☐ 131 Jose Cruz	.30	.14
☐ 132 Len Randle DP	.10	.05
☐ 133 Bob Grich	.30	.14
☐ 134 Jeff Burroughs	.30	.14
☐ 135 Gary Carter	2.50	1.10
☐ 136 Milt Wilcox	.20	.09
☐ 137 Carl Yastrzemski	3.00	1.35
☐ 138 Dennis Eckersley	4.00	1.80
☐ 139 Tim Nordbrook	.20	.09
☐ 140 Ken Griffey	1.00	.45
☐ 141 Bob Boone	.30	.14
☐ 142 Dave Goltz DP	.10	.05
☐ 143 Al Cowens	.20	.09
☐ 144 Bill Atkinson	.20	.09
☐ 145 Chris Chambliss	.30	.14
☐ 146 Jim Slaton	.30	.14
Now with Detroit Tigers as of 12-9-77		
☐ 147 Bill Stein	.20	.09
☐ 148 Bob Bailor	.20	.09
☐ 149 J.R. Richard	.30	.14
☐ 150 Ted Simmons	.30	.14
☐ 151 Rick Manning	.20	.09
☐ 152 Lerrin LaGrow	.20	.09
☐ 153 Larry Parrish	.40	.18
☐ 154 Eddie Murray	125.00	55.00
☐ 155 Phil Niekro	2.50	1.10
☐ 156 Bake McBride	.30	.14
☐ 157 Pete Vuckovich	.30	.14
☐ 158 Ivan DeJesus	.20	.09
☐ 159 Rick Rhoden	.20	.09
☐ 160 Joe Morgan	2.50	1.10
☐ 161 Ed Ott	.20	.09
☐ 162 Don Stanhouse	.30	.14
☐ 163 Jim Rice	2.00	.90
☐ 164 Bucky Dent	.30	.14
☐ 165 Jim Kern	.20	.09
☐ 166 Doug Rader	.20	.09
☐ 167 Steve Kemp	.30	.14
☐ 168 John Mayberry	.30	.14
☐ 169 Tim Foli	.30	.14
Now with N.Y. Mets as of 12-7-77		
☐ 170 Steve Carlton	3.00	1.35
☐ 171 Pepe Frias	.30	.14
☐ 172 Pat Zachry	.20	.09
☐ 173 Don Baylor	.75	.35
☐ 174 Sal Bando DP	.30	.14
☐ 175 Alvis Woods	.30	.14
☐ 176 Mike Hargrove	.40	.18
☐ 177 Vida Blue	.30	.14
☐ 178 George Hendrick	.30	.14
☐ 179 Jim Palmer	2.50	1.10
☐ 180 Andre Dawson	15.00	6.75
☐ 181 Paul Moskau	.20	.09
☐ 182 Mickey Rivers	.40	.18
☐ 183 Checklist 122-242	1.25	.55
☐ 184 Jerry Johnson	.30	.14
☐ 185 Willie McCovey	2.50	1.10
☐ 186 Enrique Romo	.20	.09
☐ 187 Butch Hobson	.20	.09
☐ 188 Rusty Staub	.40	.18
☐ 189 Wayne Twitchell	.30	.14
☐ 190 Steve Garvey	1.50	.70
☐ 191 Rick Waits	.20	.09
☐ 192 Doug DeCinces	.30	.14
☐ 193 Tom Murphy	.20	.09
☐ 194 Rich Hebner	.30	.14
☐ 195 Ralph Garr	.30	.14
☐ 196 Bruce Sutter	.40	.18
☐ 197 Tom Poquette	.20	.09
☐ 198 Wayne Garrett	.20	.09
☐ 199 Pedro Borbon	.30	.14
☐ 200 Thurman Munson	3.00	1.35
☐ 201 Rollie Fingers	2.50	1.10
☐ 202 Doug Ault	.20	.09
☐ 203 Phil Garner DP	.30	.14
☐ 204 Lou Brock	2.50	1.10
☐ 205 Ed Kranepool	.20	.09
☐ 206 Bobby Bonds	.50	.23
Now with White Sox as of 12-15-77		
☐ 207 Expos Team DP	.40	.18
☐ 208 Bump Wills	.20	.09
☐ 209 Gary Matthews	.30	.14
☐ 210 Carlton Fisk	4.00	1.80
☐ 211 Jeff Byrd	.30	.14
☐ 212 Jason Thompson	.20	.09
☐ 213 Larvell Blanks	.20	.09
☐ 214 Sparky Lyle	.30	.14
☐ 215 George Brett	25.00	11.00
☐ 216 Del Unser	.20	.09
☐ 217 Manny Trillo	.20	.09
☐ 218 Roy Hartsfield MG	.20	.09
☐ 219 Carlos Lopez	.40	.18
Now with Baltimore as of 12-7-77		
☐ 220 Dave Concepcion	.50	.23
☐ 221 John Candelaria	.30	.14
☐ 222 Dave Lopes	.30	.14
☐ 223 Tim Blackwell DP	.30	.14
Now with Chicago Cubs as of 2-1-78		
☐ 224 Chet Lemon	.30	.14
☐ 225 Mike Schmidt	12.50	5.50
☐ 226 Cesar Cedeno	.30	.14
☐ 227 Mike Willis	.20	.09
☐ 228 Willie Randolph	.50	.23
☐ 229 Doug Bair	.20	.09
☐ 230 Rod Carew	2.50	1.10
☐ 231 Mike Flanagan	.30	.14
☐ 232 Chris Speier	.20	.09
☐ 233 Don Aase	.30	.14
Now with California as of 12-8-77		
☐ 234 Buddy Bell	.30	.14
☐ 235 Mark Fidrych	1.50	.70
☐ 236 Lou Brock RB Most Steals, Lifetime	2.00	.90
☐ 237 Sparky Lyle RB Most Games Pure Relief, Lifetime	.50	.23
☐ 238 Willie McCovey RB Most Times 2 HR's in Inning, Lifetime	1.50	.70
☐ 239 Brooks Robinson RB Most Consecutive Seasons with one club	2.00	.90
☐ 240 Pete Rose RB Most Hits, Switch- hitter, Lifetime	3.50	1.55
☐ 241 Nolan Ryan RB Most games 10 or More Strikeouts, Lifetime	15.00	6.75
☐ 242 Reggie Jackson RB Most Homers, One World Series	4.00	1.80

1979 O-Pee-Chee

This set is an abridgement of the 1979 Topps set. The 374 standard-size cards comprising the 1979 O-Pee-Chee set differ from the cards of the 1979 Topps set by having a higher ratio of cards of players from the two Canadian teams, a practice begun by O-Pee-Chee in 1977 and continued to 1988. The 1979 O-Pee-Chee set was the largest (374) original baseball card set issued (up to that time) by O-Pee-Chee. The fronts feature white-bordered

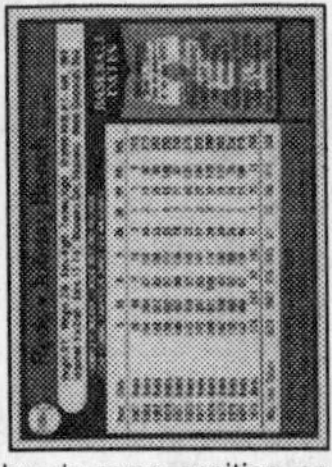

color player photos. The player's name, position, and team appear in colored lettering within the lower white margin. The green and white horizontal backs carry the player's name, team and position at the top. Biography, major league statistics, career highlights in both French and English and a bilingual trivia question and answer also appear. The asterisked cards have an extra line on the front indicating team change. Double-printed (DP) cards are also noted below. The fronts have an O-Pee-Chee logo in the lower left corner comparable to the Topps logo on the 1979 American Set. The cards are sequenced in the same order as the Topps cards; the O-Pee-Chee cards are in effect a compressed version of the Topps set. The key card in this set is Ozzie Smith.

	NRMT	VG-E
COMPLETE SET (374)	200.00	90.00
COMMON CARD (1-374)	.20	.09
COMMON CARD DP (1-374)	.10	.05

Card	NRMT	VG-E
☐ 1 Lee May	.50	.23
☐ 2 Dick Drago	.20	.09
☐ 3 Paul Dade	.20	.09
☐ 4 Ross Grimsley	.20	.09
☐ 5 Joe Morgan DP	1.00	.45
☐ 6 Kevin Kobel	.20	.09
☐ 7 Terry Forster	.20	.09
☐ 8 Paul Molitor	20.00	9.00
☐ 9 Steve Carlton	2.50	1.10
☐ 10 Dave Goltz	.20	.09
☐ 11 Dave Winfield	8.00	3.60
☐ 12 Dave Rozema	.20	.09
☐ 13 Ed Figueroa	.20	.09
☐ 14 Alan Ashby	.35	.16
Trade with Blue Jays 11-28-78		
☐ 15 Dale Murphy	5.00	2.20
☐ 16 Dennis Eckersley	2.00	.90
☐ 17 Ron Blomberg	.20	.09
☐ 18 Wayne Twitchell	.35	.16
Free Agent as of 3-1-79		
☐ 19 Al Hrabosky	.20	.09
☐ 20 Fred Norman	.20	.09
☐ 21 Steve Garvey DP	.75	.35
☐ 22 Willie Stargell	1.50	.70
☐ 23 John Hale	.20	.09
☐ 24 Mickey Rivers	.35	.16
☐ 25 Jack Brohamer	.20	.09
☐ 26 Tom Underwood	.20	.09
☐ 27 Mark Belanger	.35	.16
☐ 28 Elliott Maddox	.20	.09
☐ 29 John Candelaria	.35	.16
☐ 30 Shane Rawley	.20	.09
☐ 31 Steve Yeager	.20	.09
☐ 32 Warren Cromartie	.35	.16
☐ 33 Jason Thompson	.35	.16
☐ 34 Roger Erickson	.20	.09
☐ 35 Gary Matthews	.35	.16
☐ 36 Pete Falcone	.50	.23
Traded 12-5-78		
☐ 37 Dick Tidrow	.20	.09
☐ 38 Bob Boone	.50	.23
☐ 39 Jim Bibby	.20	.09
☐ 40 Len Barker	.35	.16
Trade with Rangers 10-3-78		
☐ 41 Robin Yount	10.00	4.50
☐ 42 Sam Mejias	.35	.16
Traded 12-14-78		
☐ 43 Ray Burris	.20	.09
☐ 44 Tom Seaver DP	2.00	.90
☐ 45 Roy Howell	.20	.09
☐ 46 Jim Todd	.35	.16
Free Agent 3-1-79		
☐ 47 Frank Duffy	.20	.09
☐ 48 Joel Youngblood	.20	.09
☐ 49 Vida Blue	.35	.16
☐ 50 Cliff Johnson	.20	.09
☐ 51 Nolan Ryan	30.00	13.50
☐ 52 Ozzie Smith	90.00	40.00
☐ 53 Jim Sundberg	.20	.09
☐ 54 Mike Paxton	.20	.09
☐ 55 Lou Whitaker	10.00	4.50
☐ 56 Dan Schatzeder	.20	.09
☐ 57 Rick Burleson	.20	.09

☐ 58 Doug Bair	.20	.09
☐ 59 Ted Martinez	.20	.09
☐ 60 Bob Watson	.35	.16
☐ 61 Jim Clancy	.20	.09
☐ 62 Rowland Office	.20	.09
☐ 63 Bobby Murcer	.35	.16
☐ 64 Don Gullett	.35	.16
☐ 65 Tom Paciorek	.35	.16
☐ 66 Rick Rhoden	.20	.09
☐ 67 Duane Kuiper	.20	.09
☐ 68 Bruce Boisclair	.20	.09
☐ 69 Manny Sarmiento	.20	.09
☐ 70 Wayne Cage	.20	.09
☐ 71 John Hiller	.35	.16
☐ 72 Rick Cerone	.20	.09
☐ 73 Dwight Evans	.50	.23
☐ 74 Buddy Solomon	.20	.09
☐ 75 Roy White	.35	.16
☐ 76 Mike Flanagan	.50	.23
☐ 77 Tom Johnson	.20	.09
☐ 78 Glenn Burke	.20	.09
☐ 79 Frank Taveras	.20	.09
☐ 80 Don Sutton	.75	.35
☐ 81 Leon Roberts	.20	.09
☐ 82 George Hendrick	.35	.16
☐ 83 Aurelio Rodriguez	.20	.09
☐ 84 Ron Reed	.20	.09
☐ 85 Alvis Woods	.20	.09
☐ 86 Jim Beattie DP	.10	.05
☐ 87 Larry Hisle	.20	.09
☐ 88 Mike Garman	.20	.09
☐ 89 Tim Johnson	.20	.09
☐ 90 Paul Splittorff	.20	.09
☐ 91 Darrel Chaney	.20	.09
☐ 92 Mike Torrez	.20	.09
☐ 93 Eric Soderholm	.20	.09
☐ 94 Ron Cey	.35	.16
☐ 95 Randy Jones	.20	.09
☐ 96 Bill Madlock	.35	.16
☐ 97 Steve Kemp DP	.10	.05
☐ 98 Bob Apodaca	.20	.09
☐ 99 Johnny Grubb	.20	.09
☐ 100 Larry Milbourne	.20	.09
☐ 101 Johnny Bench DP	2.00	.90
☐ 102 Dave Lemanczyk	.20	.09
☐ 103 Reggie Cleveland	.20	.09
☐ 104 Larry Bowa	.35	.16
☐ 105 Denny Martinez	1.50	.70
☐ 106 Bill Travers	.20	.09
☐ 107 Willie McCovey	2.00	.90
☐ 108 Wilbur Wood	.20	.09
☐ 109 Dennis Leonard	.35	.16
☐ 110 Roy Smalley	.35	.16
☐ 111 Cesar Geronimo	.20	.09
☐ 112 Jesse Jefferson	.20	.09
☐ 113 Dave Revering	.20	.09
☐ 114 Rich Gossage	.50	.23
☐ 115 Steve Stone	.50	.23
Free Agent 11-25-78		
☐ 116 Doug Flynn	.20	.09
☐ 117 Bob Forsch	.20	.09
☐ 118 Paul Mitchell	.20	.09
☐ 119 Toby Harrah	.50	.23
Traded 12-8-78		
☐ 120 Steve Rogers	.20	.09
☐ 121 Checklist 1-125 DP	.60	.25
☐ 122 Balor Moore	.20	.09
☐ 123 Rick Reuschel	.35	.16
☐ 124 Jeff Burroughs	.20	.09
☐ 125 Willie Randolph	.35	.16
☐ 126 Bob Stinson	.20	.09
☐ 127 Rick Wise	.20	.09
☐ 128 Luis Gomez	.35	.16
☐ 129 Tommy John	1.00	.45
Signed as Free Agent 11-22-78		
☐ 130 Richie Zisk	.20	.09
☐ 131 Mario Guerrero	.20	.09
☐ 132 Oscar Gamble	.35	.16
Trade with Padres 10-25-78		
☐ 133 Don Money	.20	.09
☐ 134 Joe Rudi	.35	.16
☐ 135 Woodie Fryman	.20	.09
☐ 136 Butch Hobson	.20	.09
☐ 137 Jim Colborn	.20	.09
☐ 138 Tom Grieve	.35	.16
Traded 12-5-78		
☐ 139 Andy Messersmith	.35	.16
Free Agent 2-7-79		
☐ 140 Andre Thornton	.35	.16
☐ 141 Ken Kravec	.20	.09
☐ 142 Bobby Bonds	.75	.35
Trade with Rangers 10-3-78		
☐ 143 Jose Cruz	.35	.16
☐ 144 Dave Lopes	.35	.16
☐ 145 Jerry Garvin	.20	.09
☐ 146 Pepe Frias	.20	.09
☐ 147 Mitchell Page	.20	.09
☐ 148 Ted Sizemore	.35	.16
Traded 2-23-79		
☐ 149 Rich Gale	.20	.09
☐ 150 Steve Ontiveros	.20	.09
☐ 151 Rod Carew	3.00	1.35
Traded 2-5-79		
☐ 152 Lary Sorensen DP	.10	.05
☐ 153 Willie Montanez	.20	.09
☐ 154 Floyd Bannister	.35	.16
Traded 12-8-78		
☐ 155 Bert Blyleven	.50	.23
☐ 156 Ralph Garr	.35	.16
☐ 157 Thurman Munson	2.50	1.10
☐ 158 Bob Robertson	.35	.16
Free Agent 3-1-79		
☐ 159 Jon Matlack	.20	.09
☐ 160 Carl Yastrzemski	2.50	1.10
☐ 161 Gaylord Perry	1.00	.45
☐ 162 Mike Tyson	.20	.09
☐ 163 Cecil Cooper	.35	.16
☐ 164 Pedro Borbon	.20	.09
☐ 165 Art Howe DP	.20	.09
☐ 166 Joe Coleman	.35	.16
Free Agent 3-1-79		
☐ 167 George Brett	20.00	9.00
☐ 168 Gary Alexander	.20	.09
☐ 169 Chet Lemon	.35	.16
☐ 170 Craig Swan	.20	.09
☐ 171 Chris Chambliss	.35	.16
☐ 172 John Montague	.20	.09
☐ 173 Ron Jackson	.35	.16
Traded 12-4-78		
☐ 174 Jim Palmer	2.00	.90
☐ 175 Willie Upshaw	.50	.23
☐ 176 Tug McGraw	.35	.16
☐ 177 Bill Buckner	.35	.16
☐ 178 Doug Rau	.20	.09
☐ 179 Andre Dawson	8.00	3.60
☐ 180 Jim Wright	.20	.09
☐ 181 Garry Templeton	.35	.16
☐ 182 Bill Bonham	.20	.09
☐ 183 Lee Mazzilli	.20	.09
☐ 184 Alan Trammell	12.00	5.50
☐ 185 Amos Otis	.35	.16
☐ 186 Tom Dixon	.20	.09
☐ 187 Mike Cubbage	.20	.09
☐ 188 Sparky Lyle	.50	.23
Traded 11-10-78		
☐ 189 Juan Bernhardt	.20	.09
☐ 190 Bump Wills	.50	.23
(Texas Rangers)		
☐ 191 Dave Kingman	.50	.23
☐ 192 Lamar Johnson	.20	.09
☐ 193 Lance Rautzhan	.20	.09
☐ 194 Ed Herrmann	.20	.09
☐ 195 Bill Campbell	.20	.09
☐ 196 Gorman Thomas	.20	.09
☐ 197 Paul Moskau	.20	.09
☐ 198 Dale Murray	.20	.09
☐ 199 John Mayberry	.35	.16
☐ 200 Phil Garner	.35	.16
☐ 201 Dan Ford	.35	.16
Traded 12-4-78		
☐ 202 Gary Thomasson	.35	.16
Traded 2-15-79		
☐ 203 Rollie Fingers	1.00	.45
☐ 204 Al Oliver	.50	.23
☐ 205 Doug Ault	.20	.09
☐ 206 Scott McGregor	.35	.16
☐ 207 Dave Cash	.20	.09
☐ 208 Bill Plummer	.20	.09
☐ 209 Ivan DeJesus	.20	.09
☐ 210 Jim Rice	1.50	.70
☐ 211 Ray Knight	.35	.16
☐ 212 Paul Hartzell	.35	.16
Traded 2-5-79		
☐ 213 Tim Foli	.20	.09
☐ 214 Butch Wynegar DP	.10	.05
☐ 215 Darrell Evans	.50	.23
☐ 216 Ken Griffey	.75	.35
☐ 217 Doug DeCinces	.35	.16
☐ 218 Ruppert Jones	.20	.09
☐ 219 Bob Montgomery	.20	.09
☐ 220 Rick Manning	.20	.09
☐ 221 Chris Speier	.20	.09
☐ 222 Bobby Valentine	.20	.09
☐ 223 Dave Parker	.75	.35
☐ 224 Larry Biittner	.20	.09
☐ 225 Ken Clay	.20	.09
☐ 226 Gene Tenace	.35	.16
☐ 227 Frank White	.35	.16
☐ 228 Rusty Staub	.50	.23
☐ 229 Lee Lacy	.20	.09
☐ 230 Doyle Alexander	.20	.09
☐ 231 Bruce Bochte	.20	.09
☐ 232 Steve Henderson	.20	.09
☐ 233 Jim Lonborg	.35	.16
☐ 234 Dave Concepcion	.50	.23
☐ 235 Jerry Morales	.35	.16
Traded 12-4-78		
☐ 236 Len Randle	.20	.09
☐ 237 Bill Lee DP	.35	.16
Traded 12-7-78		
☐ 238 Bruce Sutter	.35	.16
☐ 239 Jim Essian	.20	.09
☐ 240 Graig Nettles	.50	.23
☐ 241 Otto Velez	.20	.09
☐ 242 Checklist 126-250 DP	.60	.25
☐ 243 Reggie Smith	.35	.16
☐ 244 Stan Bahnsen DP	.10	.05
☐ 245 Garry Maddox DP	.20	.09
☐ 246 Joaquin Andujar	.35	.16
☐ 247 Dan Driessen	.20	.09
☐ 248 Bob Grich	.35	.16
☐ 249 Fred Lynn	.35	.16
☐ 250 Skip Lockwood	.20	.09
☐ 251 Craig Reynolds	.35	.16
Traded 12-5-78		
☐ 252 Willie Horton	.35	.16
☐ 253 Rick Waits	.20	.09
☐ 254 Bucky Dent	.35	.16
☐ 255 Bob Knepper	.20	.09
☐ 256 Miguel Dilone	.20	.09
☐ 257 Bob Owchinko	.20	.09
☐ 258 Al Cowens	.20	.09
☐ 259 Bob Bailor	.20	.09
☐ 260 Larry Christenson	.20	.09
☐ 261 Tony Perez	1.00	.45
☐ 262 Blue Jays Team	1.00	.45
Roy Hartsfield MG		
(Team checklist back)		
☐ 263 Glenn Abbott	.20	.09
☐ 264 Ron Guidry	.35	.16
☐ 265 Ed Kranepool	.20	.09
☐ 266 Charlie Hough	.35	.16
☐ 267 Ted Simmons	.50	.23
☐ 268 Jack Clark	.35	.16
☐ 269 Enos Cabell	.20	.09
☐ 270 Gary Carter	2.00	.90
☐ 271 Sam Ewing	.20	.09
☐ 272 Tom Burgmeier	.20	.09
☐ 273 Freddie Patek	.20	.09
☐ 274 Frank Tanana	.35	.16
☐ 275 Leroy Stanton	.20	.09
☐ 276 Ken Forsch	.20	.09
☐ 277 Ellis Valentine	.20	.09
☐ 278 Greg Luzinski	.35	.16
☐ 279 Rick Bosetti	.20	.09
☐ 280 John Stearns	.20	.09
☐ 281 Enrique Romo	.35	.16
Traded 12-5-78		
☐ 282 Bob Bailey	.20	.09
☐ 283 Sal Bando	.35	.16
☐ 284 Matt Keough	.20	.09
☐ 285 Biff Pocoroba	.20	.09
☐ 286 Mike Lum	.35	.16
Free Agent 3-1-79		
☐ 287 Jay Johnstone	.35	.16
☐ 288 John Montefusco	.20	.09
☐ 289 Ed Ott	.20	.09
☐ 290 Dusty Baker	.50	.23
☐ 291 Rico Carty	.50	.23
Waivers from A's 10-2-78		
☐ 292 Nino Espinosa	.20	.09
☐ 293 Rich Hebner	.20	.09
☐ 294 Cesar Cedeno	.35	.16
☐ 295 Darrell Porter	.20	.09
☐ 296 Rod Gilbreath	.20	.09
☐ 297 Jim Kern	.35	.16
Trade with Indians 10-3-78		
☐ 298 Claudell Washington	.35	.16
☐ 299 Luis Tiant	.50	.23
Signed as Free Agent 11-14-78		
☐ 300 Mike Parrott	.20	.09
☐ 301 Pete Broberg	.35	.16
Free Agent 3-1-79		
☐ 302 Greg Gross	.35	.16
Traded 2-23-79		
☐ 303 Darold Knowles	.35	.16
Free Agent 2-12-79		
☐ 304 Paul Blair	.20	.09
☐ 305 Julio Cruz	.20	.09
☐ 306 Hal McRae	.50	.23
☐ 307 Ken Reitz	.20	.09
☐ 308 Tom Murphy	.20	.09
☐ 309 Terry Whitfield	.20	.09
☐ 310 J.R. Richard	.35	.16
☐ 311 Mike Hargrove	.50	.23
Trade with Rangers 10-25-78		
☐ 312 Rick Dempsey	.35	.16
☐ 313 Phil Niekro	1.50	.70
☐ 314 Bob Stanley	.20	.09
☐ 315 Jim Spencer	.20	.09
☐ 316 George Foster	.35	.16

Card	NRMT	VG-E
☐ 317 Dave LaRoche	.20	.09
☐ 318 Rudy May	.20	.09
☐ 319 Jeff Newman	.20	.09
☐ 320 Rick Monday DP	.20	.09
☐ 321 Omar Moreno	.20	.09
☐ 322 Dave McKay	.20	.09
☐ 323 Mike Schmidt	8.00	3.60
☐ 324 Ken Singleton	.35	.16
☐ 325 Jerry Remy	.20	.09
☐ 326 Bert Campaneris	.35	.16
☐ 327 Pat Zachry	.20	.09
☐ 328 Larry Herndon	.20	.09
☐ 329 Mark Fidrych	1.00	.45
☐ 330 Del Unser	.20	.09
☐ 331 Gene Garber	.35	.16
☐ 332 Bake McBride	.35	.16
☐ 333 Jorge Orta	.20	.09
☐ 334 Don Kirkwood	.20	.09
☐ 335 Don Baylor	.75	.35
☐ 336 Bill Robinson	.35	.16
☐ 337 Manny Trillo	.35	.16
Traded 2-23-79		
☐ 338 Eddie Murray	30.00	13.50
☐ 339 Tom Hausman	.20	.09
☐ 340 George Scott DP	.20	.09
☐ 341 Rick Sweet	.20	.09
☐ 342 Lou Piniella	.35	.16
☐ 343 Pete Rose	7.50	3.40
Free Agent 12-5-79		
☐ 344 Stan Papi	.35	.16
Traded 12-7-78		
☐ 345 Jerry Koosman	.50	.23
Traded 12-8-78		
☐ 346 Hosken Powell	.20	.09
☐ 347 George Medich	.20	.09
☐ 348 Ron LeFlore DP	.20	.09
☐ 349 Montreal Expos Team	1.00	.45
Dick Williams MG		
(Team checklist back)		
☐ 350 Lou Brock	2.00	.90
☐ 351 Bill North	.20	.09
☐ 352 Jim Hunter DP	.75	.35
☐ 353 Checklist 251-374 DP	.60	.25
☐ 354 Ed Halicki	.20	.09
☐ 355 Tom Hutton	.20	.09
☐ 356 Mike Caldwell	.20	.09
☐ 357 Larry Parrish	.35	.16
☐ 358 Geoff Zahn	.20	.09
☐ 359 Derrel Thomas	.35	.16
Signed as Free Agent 11-14-78		
☐ 360 Carlton Fisk	2.50	1.10
☐ 361 John Henry Johnson	.20	.09
☐ 362 Dave Chalk	.20	.09
☐ 363 Dan Meyer DP	.10	.05
☐ 364 Sixto Lezcano	.20	.09
☐ 365 Rennie Stennett	.20	.09
☐ 366 Mike Willis	.20	.09
☐ 367 Buddy Bell DP	.50	.23
Traded 12-8-78		
☐ 368 Mickey Stanley	.20	.09
☐ 369 Dave Rader	.35	.16
Traded 2-23-79		
☐ 370 Burt Hooton	.20	.09
☐ 371 Keith Hernandez	.75	.35
☐ 372 Bill Stein	.20	.09
☐ 373 Hal Dues	.20	.09
☐ 374 Reggie Jackson DP	2.00	.90

1980 O-Pee-Chee

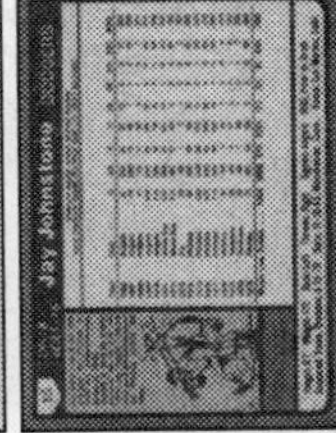

This set is an abridgement of the 1980 Topps set. The cards are printed on white stock rather than the gray stock used by Topps. The 374 standard-size cards also differ from their Topps counterparts by having a higher ratio of cards of players from the two Canadian teams, a practice begun by O-Pee-Chee in 1977 and continued to 1988. The fronts feature white-bordered color player photos framed by a colored line. The player's name appears in the white border at the top and also as a simulated autograph across the photo. The player's position appears within a colored banner at the upper left; his team name appears within a colored banner at the lower right. The blue and white horizontal backs carry the player's name, team and position at the top. Biography, major league statistics and career highlights in both French and English also appear. The cards are numbered on the back. The asterisked cards have an extra line, "Now with (new team name)" on the front indicating team change. Color changes, to correspond to the new team, are apparent on the pennant name and frame on the front. Double-printed (DP) cards are also noted below. The cards in this set were produced in lower quantities than other O-Pee-Chee sets of this era reportedly due to the company being on strike. The cards are sequenced in the same order as the Topps cards.

	NRMT	VG-E
COMPLETE SET (374)	90.00	40.00
COMMON CARD (1-374)	.15	.07
COMMON CARD DP (1-374)	.05	.02

Card	NRMT	VG-E
☐ 1 Craig Swan	.15	.07
☐ 2 Dennis Martinez	1.50	.70
☐ 3 Dave Cash	.15	.07
Now With Padres		
☐ 4 Bruce Sutter	.30	.14
☐ 5 Ron Jackson	.15	.07
☐ 6 Balor Moore	.15	.07
☐ 7 Dan Ford	.15	.07
☐ 8 Pat Putnam	.15	.07
☐ 9 Derrel Thomas	.15	.07
☐ 10 Jim Slaton	.15	.07
☐ 11 Lee Mazzilli	.30	.14
☐ 12 Del Unser	.15	.07
☐ 13 Mark Wagner	.15	.07
☐ 14 Vida Blue	.60	.25
☐ 15 Jay Johnstone	.30	.14
☐ 16 Julio Cruz DP	.05	.02
☐ 17 Tony Scott	.15	.07
☐ 18 Jeff Newman DP	.05	.02
☐ 19 Luis Tiant	.30	.14
☐ 20 Carlton Fisk	4.00	1.80
☐ 21 Dave Palmer	.15	.07
☐ 22 Bombo Rivera	.15	.07
☐ 23 Bill Fahey	.15	.07
☐ 24 Frank White	.60	.25
☐ 25 Rico Carty	.30	.14
☐ 26 Bill Bonham DP	.05	.02
☐ 27 Rick Miller	.15	.07
☐ 28 J.R. Richard	.30	.14
☐ 29 Joe Ferguson DP	.05	.02
☐ 30 Bill Madlock	.30	.14
☐ 31 Pete Vuckovich	.15	.07
☐ 32 Doug Flynn	.15	.07
☐ 33 Bucky Dent	.30	.14
☐ 34 Mike Ivie	.15	.07
☐ 35 Bob Stanley	.15	.07
☐ 36 Al Bumbry	.15	.07
☐ 37 Gary Carter	1.25	.55
☐ 38 John Milner DP	.05	.02
☐ 39 Sid Monge	.15	.07
☐ 40 Bill Russell	.30	.14
☐ 41 John Stearns	.15	.07
☐ 42 Dave Stieb	1.00	.45
☐ 43 Ruppert Jones	.15	.07
Now with Yankees		
☐ 44 Bob Owchinko	.15	.07
☐ 45 Ron LeFlore	.30	.14
Now with Expos		
☐ 46 Ted Sizemore	.15	.07
☐ 47 Ted Simmons	.30	.14
☐ 48 Pepe Frias	.15	.07
Now with Rangers		
☐ 49 Ken Landreaux	.15	.07
☐ 50 Manny Trillo	.30	.14
☐ 51 Rick Dempsey	.30	.14
☐ 52 Cecil Cooper	.30	.14
☐ 53 Bill Lee	.30	.14
☐ 54 Victor Cruz	.15	.07
☐ 55 Johnny Bench	5.00	2.20
☐ 56 Rich Dauer	.15	.07
☐ 57 Frank Tanana	.30	.14
☐ 58 Francisco Barrios	.15	.07
☐ 59 Bob Horner	.15	.07
☐ 60 Fred Lynn DP	.30	.14
☐ 61 Bob Knepper	.15	.07
☐ 62 Sparky Lyle	.30	.14
☐ 63 Larry Cox	.15	.07
☐ 64 Dock Ellis	.15	.07
Now with Pirates		
☐ 65 Phil Garner	.30	.14
☐ 66 Greg Luzinski	.30	.14
☐ 67 Checklist 1-125	.30	.14
☐ 68 Dave Lemanczyk	.15	.07
☐ 69 Tony Perez	1.00	.45
Now with Red Sox		
☐ 70 Gary Thomasson	.15	.07
☐ 71 Craig Reynolds	.15	.07
☐ 72 Amos Otis	.30	.14
☐ 73 Biff Pocoroba	.15	.07
☐ 74 Matt Keough	.15	.07
☐ 75 Bill Buckner	.30	.14
☐ 76 John Castino	.15	.07
☐ 77 Rich Gossage	1.00	.45
☐ 78 Gary Alexander	.15	.07
☐ 79 Phil Huffman	.15	.07
☐ 80 Bruce Bochte	.15	.07
☐ 81 Darrell Evans	.30	.14
☐ 82 Terry Puhl	.15	.07
☐ 83 Jason Thompson	.15	.07
☐ 84 Lary Sorensen	.15	.07
☐ 85 Jerry Remy	.15	.07
☐ 86 Tony Brizzolara	.15	.07
☐ 87 Willie Wilson DP	.30	.14
☐ 88 Eddie Murray	20.00	9.00
☐ 89 Larry Christenson	.15	.07
☐ 90 Bob Randall	.15	.07
☐ 91 Greg Pryor	.15	.07
☐ 92 Glenn Abbott	.15	.07
☐ 93 Jack Clark	.30	.14
☐ 94 Rick Waits	.15	.07
☐ 95 Luis Gomez	.15	.07
Now with Braves		
☐ 96 Burt Hooton	.30	.14
☐ 97 John Henry Johnson	.15	.07
☐ 98 Ray Knight	.30	.14
☐ 99 Rick Reuschel	.30	.14
☐ 100 Champ Summers	.15	.07
☐ 101 Ron Davis	.15	.07
☐ 102 Warren Cromartie	.15	.07
☐ 103 Ken Reitz	.15	.07
☐ 104 Hal McRae	.60	.25
☐ 105 Alan Ashby	.15	.07
☐ 106 Kevin Kobel	.15	.07
☐ 107 Buddy Bell	.30	.14
☐ 108 Dave Goltz	.15	.07
Now with Dodgers		
☐ 109 John Montefusco	.30	.14
☐ 110 Lance Parrish	.30	.14
☐ 111 Mike LaCoss	.15	.07
☐ 112 Jim Rice	.30	.14
☐ 113 Steve Carlton	4.00	1.80
☐ 114 Sixto Lezcano	.15	.07
☐ 115 Ed Halicki	.15	.07
☐ 116 Jose Morales	.15	.07
☐ 117 Dave Concepcion	.60	.25
☐ 118 Joe Cannon	.15	.07
☐ 119 Willie Montanez	.15	.07
Now with Padres		
☐ 120 Lou Piniella	.60	.25
☐ 121 Bill Stein	.15	.07
☐ 122 Dave Winfield	7.50	3.40
☐ 123 Alan Trammell	7.50	3.40
☐ 124 Andre Dawson	7.50	3.40
☐ 125 Marc Hill	.15	.07
☐ 126 Don Aase	.15	.07
☐ 127 Dave Kingman	.30	.14
☐ 128 Checklist 126-250	.30	.14
☐ 129 Dennis Lamp	.15	.07
☐ 130 Phil Niekro	1.50	.70
☐ 131 Tim Foli DP	.05	.02
☐ 132 Jim Clancy	.15	.07
☐ 133 Bill Atkinson	.15	.07
Now with White Sox		
☐ 134 Paul Dade DP	.05	.02
☐ 135 Dusty Baker	.30	.14
☐ 136 Al Oliver	.30	.14
☐ 137 Dave Chalk	.15	.07
☐ 138 Bill Robinson	.15	.07
☐ 139 Robin Yount	10.00	4.50
☐ 140 Dan Schatzeder	.15	.07
Now with Tigers		
☐ 141 Mike Schmidt DP	5.00	2.20
☐ 142 Ralph Garr	.30	.14
Now with Angels		
☐ 143 Dale Murphy	4.00	1.80
☐ 144 Jerry Koosman	.30	.14
☐ 145 Tom Veryzer	.15	.07
☐ 146 Rick Bosetti	.15	.07
☐ 147 Jim Spencer	.15	.07
☐ 148 Gaylord Perry	1.50	.70
Now with Rangers		
☐ 149 Paul Blair	.30	.14
☐ 150 Don Baylor	.60	.25
☐ 151 Dave Rozema	.15	.07
☐ 152 Steve Garvey	1.00	.45
☐ 153 Elias Sosa	.15	.07
☐ 154 Larry Gura	.15	.07
☐ 155 Tim Johnson	.15	.07
☐ 156 Steve Henderson	.15	.07
☐ 157 Ron Guidry	.30	.14
☐ 158 Mike Edwards	.15	.07
☐ 159 Butch Wynegar	.15	.07
☐ 160 Randy Jones	.15	.07
☐ 161 Denny Walling	.15	.07
☐ 162 Mike Hargrove	.30	.14
☐ 163 Dave Parker	1.00	.45

☐ 164 Roger Metzger .15 .07
☐ 165 Johnny Grubb .15 .07
☐ 166 Steve Kemp .15 .07
☐ 167 Bob Lacey .15 .07
☐ 168 Chris Speier .15 .07
☐ 169 Dennis Eckersley 2.00 .90
☐ 170 Keith Hernandez .30 .14
☐ 171 Claudell Washington .30 .14
☐ 172 Tom Underwood .15 .07
Now with Yankees
☐ 173 Dan Driessen .15 .07
☐ 174 Al Cowens .15 .07
Now with Angels
☐ 175 Rich Hebner .15 .07
Now with Tigers
☐ 176 Willie McCovey 2.00 .90
☐ 177 Carney Lansford .30 .14
☐ 178 Ken Singleton .30 .14
☐ 179 Jim Essian .15 .07
☐ 180 Mike Vail .15 .07
☐ 181 Randy Lerch .15 .07
☐ 182 Larry Parrish .30 .14
☐ 183 Checklist 251-374 .30 .14
☐ 184 George Hendrick .30 .14
☐ 185 Bob Davis .15 .07
☐ 186 Gary Matthews .30 .14
☐ 187 Lou Whitaker 6.00 2.70
☐ 188 Darrell Porter DP .05 .02
☐ 189 Wayne Gross .15 .07
☐ 190 Bobby Murcer .30 .14
☐ 191 Willie Aikens .15 .07
Now with Royals
☐ 192 Jim Kern .15 .07
☐ 193 Cesar Cedeno .30 .14
☐ 194 Joel Youngblood .15 .07
☐ 195 Ross Grimsley .15 .07
☐ 196 Jerry Mumphrey .15 .07
Now with Padres
☐ 197 Kevin Bell .15 .07
☐ 198 Garry Maddox .30 .14
☐ 199 Dave Freisleben .15 .07
☐ 200 Ed Ott .15 .07
☐ 201 Enos Cabell .15 .07
☐ 202 Pete LaCock .15 .07
☐ 203 Fergie Jenkins 1.50 .70
☐ 204 Milt Wilcox .15 .07
☐ 205 Ozzie Smith 25.00 11.00
☐ 206 Ellis Valentine .15 .07
☐ 207 Dan Meyer .15 .07
☐ 208 Barry Foote .15 .07
☐ 209 George Foster .30 .14
☐ 210 Dwight Evans .30 .14
☐ 211 Paul Molitor 15.00 6.75
☐ 212 Tony Solaita .15 .07
☐ 213 Bill North .15 .07
☐ 214 Paul Splittorff .15 .07
☐ 215 Bobby Bonds .60 .25
Now with Cardinals
☐ 216 Butch Hobson .30 .14
☐ 217 Mark Belanger .30 .14
☐ 218 Grant Jackson .15 .07
☐ 219 Tom Hutton DP .05 .02
☐ 220 Pat Zachry .15 .07
☐ 221 Duane Kuiper .15 .07
☐ 222 Larry Hisle DP .05 .02
☐ 223 Mike Krukow .15 .07
☐ 224 Johnnie LeMaster .15 .07
☐ 225 Billy Almon .15 .07
Now with Expos
☐ 226 Joe Niekro .30 .14
☐ 227 Dave Revering .15 .07
☐ 228 Don Sutton 1.00 .45
☐ 229 John Hiller .15 .07
☐ 230 Alvis Woods .15 .07
☐ 231 Mark Fidrych .30 .14
☐ 232 Duffy Dyer .15 .07
☐ 233 Nino Espinosa .15 .07
☐ 234 Doug Bair .15 .07
☐ 235 George Brett 25.00 11.00
☐ 236 Mike Torrez .15 .07
☐ 237 Frank Taveras .15 .07
☐ 238 Bert Blyleven .60 .25
☐ 239 Willie Randolph .30 .14
☐ 240 Mike Sadek DP .05 .02
☐ 241 Jerry Royster .15 .07
☐ 242 John Denny .15 .07
Now with Indians
☐ 243 Rick Monday .15 .07
☐ 244 Jesse Jefferson .15 .07
☐ 245 Aurelio Rodriguez .15 .07
Now with Padres
☐ 246 Bob Boone .60 .25
☐ 247 Cesar Geronimo .15 .07
☐ 248 Bob Shirley .15 .07
☐ 249 Expos Checklist .60 .25
☐ 250 Bob Watson .30 .14
Now with Yankees
☐ 251 Mickey Rivers .30 .14
☐ 252 Mike Tyson DP .05 .02
Now with Cubs
☐ 253 Wayne Nordhagen .15 .07
☐ 254 Roy Howell .15 .07
☐ 255 Lee May .30 .14
☐ 256 Jerry Martin .15 .07
☐ 257 Bake McBride .15 .07
☐ 258 Silvio Martinez .15 .07
☐ 259 Jim Mason .15 .07
☐ 260 Tom Seaver 5.00 2.20
☐ 261 Rich Wortham DP .05 .02
☐ 262 Mike Cubbage .15 .07
☐ 263 Gene Garber .15 .07
☐ 264 Bert Campaneris .30 .14
☐ 265 Tom Buskey .15 .07
☐ 266 Leon Roberts .15 .07
☐ 267 Ron Cey .30 .14
☐ 268 Steve Ontiveros .15 .07
☐ 269 Mike Caldwell .15 .07
☐ 270 Nelson Norman .15 .07
☐ 271 Steve Rogers .15 .07
☐ 272 Jim Morrison .15 .07
☐ 273 Clint Hurdle .15 .07
☐ 274 Dale Murray .15 .07
☐ 275 Jim Barr .15 .07
☐ 276 Jim Sundberg DP .30 .14
☐ 277 Willie Horton .30 .14
☐ 278 Andre Thornton .15 .07
☐ 279 Bob Forsch .15 .07
☐ 280 Joe Strain .15 .07
☐ 281 Rudy May .15 .07
Now with Yankees
☐ 282 Pete Rose 6.00 2.70
☐ 283 Jeff Burroughs .30 .14
☐ 284 Rick Langford .15 .07
☐ 285 Ken Griffey .30 .14
☐ 286 Bill Nahorodny .15 .07
Now with Braves
☐ 287 Art Howe .30 .14
☐ 288 Ed Figueroa .15 .07
☐ 289 Joe Rudi .30 .14
☐ 290 Alfredo Griffin .15 .07
☐ 291 Dave Lopes .30 .14
☐ 292 Rick Manning .15 .07
☐ 293 Dennis Leonard .30 .14
☐ 294 Bud Harrelson .30 .14
☐ 295 Skip Lockwood .15 .07
Now with Red Sox
☐ 296 Roy Smalley .15 .07
☐ 297 Kent Tekulve .30 .14
☐ 298 Scot Thompson .15 .07
☐ 299 Ken Kravec .15 .07
☐ 300 Blue Jays Checklist .60 .25
☐ 301 Scott Sanderson .30 .14
☐ 302 Charlie Moore .15 .07
☐ 303 Nolan Ryan 30.00 13.50
Now with Astros
☐ 304 Bob Bailor .15 .07
☐ 305 Bob Stinson .15 .07
☐ 306 Al Hrabosky .15 .07
Now with Braves
☐ 307 Mitchell Page .15 .07
☐ 308 Garry Templeton .15 .07
☐ 309 Chet Lemon .30 .14
☐ 310 Jim Palmer 2.00 .90
☐ 311 Rick Cerone .15 .07
Now with Yankees
☐ 312 Jon Matlack .15 .07
☐ 313 Don Money .15 .07
☐ 314 Reggie Jackson 5.00 2.20
☐ 315 Brian Downing .15 .07
☐ 316 Woodie Fryman .15 .07
☐ 317 Alan Bannister .15 .07
☐ 318 Ron Reed .15 .07
☐ 319 Willie Stargell 2.00 .90
☐ 320 Jerry Garvin DP .05 .02
☐ 321 Cliff Johnson .15 .07
☐ 322 Doug DeCinces .30 .14
☐ 323 Gene Richards .15 .07
☐ 324 Joaquin Andujar .30 .14
☐ 325 Richie Zisk .15 .07
☐ 326 Bob Grich .30 .14
☐ 327 Gorman Thomas .30 .14
☐ 328 Chris Chambliss .30 .14
Now with Braves
☐ 329 Blue Jays Prospects .15 .07
Butch Edge
Pat Kelly
Ted Wilborn
☐ 330 Larry Bowa .30 .14
☐ 331 Barry Bonnell .15 .07
Now with Blue Jays
☐ 332 John Candelaria .30 .14
☐ 333 Toby Harrah .30 .14
☐ 334 Larry Biittner .15 .07
☐ 335 Mike Flanagan .30 .14
☐ 336 Ed Kranepool .15 .07
☐ 337 Ken Forsch DP .05 .02
☐ 338 John Mayberry .30 .14
☐ 339 Rick Burleson .15 .07
☐ 340 Milt May .15 .07
Now with Giants
☐ 341 Roy White .15 .07
☐ 342 Joe Morgan 2.00 .90
☐ 343 Rollie Fingers 1.50 .70
☐ 344 Mario Mendoza .15 .07
☐ 345 Stan Bahnsen .15 .07
☐ 346 Tug McGraw .30 .14
☐ 347 Rusty Staub .30 .14
☐ 348 Tommy John .60 .25
☐ 349 Ivan DeJesus .15 .07
☐ 350 Reggie Smith .30 .14
☐ 351 Expos Prospects .60 .25
Tony Bernazard
Randy Miller
John Tamargo
☐ 352 Floyd Bannister .15 .07
☐ 353 Rod Carew DP 1.50 .70
☐ 354 Otto Velez .15 .07
☐ 355 Gene Tenace .30 .14
☐ 356 Freddie Patek .15 .07
Now with Angels
☐ 357 Elliott Maddox .15 .07
☐ 358 Pat Underwood .15 .07
☐ 359 Graig Nettles .30 .14
☐ 360 Rodney Scott .15 .07
☐ 361 Terry Whitfield .15 .07
☐ 362 Fred Norman .15 .07
Now with Expos
☐ 363 Sal Bando .30 .14
☐ 364 Greg Gross .15 .07
☐ 365 Carl Yastrzemski DP 2.00 .90
☐ 366 Paul Hartzell .15 .07
☐ 367 Jose Cruz .30 .14
☐ 368 Shane Rawley .15 .07
☐ 369 Jerry White .15 .07
☐ 370 Rick Wise .15 .07
Now with Padres
☐ 371 Steve Yeager .30 .14
☐ 372 Omar Moreno .15 .07
☐ 373 Bump Wills .15 .07
☐ 374 Craig Kusick .15 .07
Now with Padres

1981 O-Pee-Chee

This set is an abridgement of the 1981 Topps set. The 374 standard-size cards comprising the 1981 O-Pee-Chee set differ from the cards of the 1981 Topps set by having a higher ratio of cards of players from the two Canadian teams, a practice begun by O-Pee-Chee in 1977 and continued to 1988. The fronts feature white-bordered color player photos framed by a colored line that is wider at the bottom. The player's name appears in that wider colored area. The player's position and team appear within a colored baseball cap icon at the lower left. The red and white horizontal backs carry the player's name and position at the top. Biography, major league statistics, and career highlights in both French and English also appear. In cases where a player changed teams or was traded before press time, a small line of print on the obverse makes note of the change. Double-printed (DP) cards are also noted below. The card backs are typically found printed on white card stock. There is, however, a "variation" set printed on gray card stock; gray backs are worth 50 percent more than corresponding white backs listed below. Cards of Harold Baines, Kirk Gibson and Tim Raines are featured in their American Rookie Card year.

	NRMT	VG-E
COMPLETE SET (374)	50.00	22.00
COMMON CARD (1-374)	.10	.05
COMMON CARD DP (1-374)	.05	.02

☐ 1 Frank Pastore .10 .05
☐ 2 Phil Huffman .10 .05
☐ 3 Len Barker .10 .05
☐ 4 Robin Yount 2.00 .90

☐ 5 Dave Stieb .25 .11
☐ 6 Gary Carter .25 .11
☐ 7 Butch Hobson .10 .05
Now with Angels
☐ 8 Lance Parrish .25 .11
☐ 9 Bruce Sutter .25 .11
Now with Cardinals
☐ 10 Mike Flanagan .25 .11
☐ 11 Paul Mirabella .10 .05
☐ 12 Craig Reynolds .10 .05
☐ 13 Joe Charboneau .50 .23
☐ 14 Dan Driessen .10 .05
☐ 15 Larry Parrish .10 .05
☐ 16 Ron Davis .10 .05
☐ 17 Cliff Johnson .10 .05
Now with Athletics
☐ 18 Bruce Bochte .10 .05
☐ 19 Jim Clancy .10 .05
☐ 20 Bill Russell .25 .11
☐ 21 Ron Oester .10 .05
☐ 22 Danny Darwin .25 .11
☐ 23 Willie Aikens .10 .05
☐ 24 Don Stanhouse .10 .05
☐ 25 Sixto Lezcano .10 .05
Now with Cardinals
☐ 26 U.L. Washington .10 .05
☐ 27 Champ Summers DP .05 .02
☐ 28 Enrique Romo .10 .05
☐ 29 Gene Tenace .25 .11
☐ 30 Jack Clark .25 .11
☐ 31 Checklist 1-125 DP .05 .02
☐ 32 Ken Oberkfell .10 .05
☐ 33 Rick Honeycutt .10 .05
Now with Rangers
☐ 34 Al Bumbry .10 .05
☐ 35 John Tamargo DP .05 .02
☐ 36 Ed Farmer .10 .05
☐ 37 Gary Roenicke .10 .05
☐ 38 Tim Foli DP .05 .02
☐ 39 Eddie Murray 6.00 2.70
☐ 40 Roy Howell .10 .05
Now with Brewers
☐ 41 Bill Gullickson .50 .23
☐ 42 Jerry White DP .05 .02
☐ 43 Tim Blackwell .10 .05
☐ 44 Steve Henderson .10 .05
☐ 45 Enos Cabell .10 .05
Now with Giants
☐ 46 Rick Bosetti .10 .05
☐ 47 Bill North .10 .05
☐ 48 Rich Gossage .50 .23
☐ 49 Bob Shirley .10 .05
Now with Cardinals
☐ 50 Dave Lopes .25 .11
☐ 51 Shane Rawley .10 .05
☐ 52 Lloyd Moseby .25 .11
☐ 53 Burt Hooton .10 .05
☐ 54 Ivan DeJesus .10 .05
☐ 55 Mike Norris .10 .05
☐ 56 Del Unser .10 .05
☐ 57 Dave Revering .10 .05
☐ 58 Joel Youngblood .10 .05
☐ 59 Steve McCatty .10 .05
☐ 60 Willie Randolph .25 .11
☐ 61 Butch Wynegar .10 .05
☐ 62 Gary Lavelle .10 .05
☐ 63 Willie Montanez .10 .05
☐ 64 Terry Puhl .10 .05
☐ 65 Scott McGregor .10 .05
☐ 66 Buddy Bell .25 .11
☐ 67 Toby Harrah .25 .11
☐ 68 Jim Rice .25 .11
☐ 69 Darrell Evans .25 .11
☐ 70 Al Oliver DP .25 .11
☐ 71 Hal Dues .10 .05
☐ 72 Barry Evans DP .05 .02
☐ 73 Doug Bair .10 .05
☐ 74 Mike Hargrove .25 .11
☐ 75 Reggie Smith .25 .11
☐ 76 Mario Mendoza .10 .05
Now with Rangers
☐ 77 Mike Barlow .10 .05
☐ 78 Garth Iorg .10 .05
☐ 79 Jeff Reardon 1.50 .70
☐ 80 Roger Erickson .10 .05
☐ 81 Dave Stapleton .10 .05
☐ 82 Barry Bonnell .10 .05
☐ 83 Dave Concepcion .25 .11
☐ 84 Johnnie LeMaster .10 .05
☐ 85 Mike Caldwell .10 .05
☐ 86 Wayne Gross .10 .05
☐ 87 Rick Camp .10 .05
☐ 88 Joe Lefebvre .10 .05
☐ 89 Darrell Jackson .10 .05
☐ 90 Bake McBride .10 .05
☐ 91 Tim Stoddard DP .05 .02
☐ 92 Mike Easler .10 .05
☐ 93 Jim Bibby .10 .05
☐ 94 Kent Tekulve .25 .11
☐ 95 Jim Sundberg .25 .11
☐ 96 Tommy John .50 .23
☐ 97 Chris Speier .10 .05
☐ 98 Clint Hurdle .10 .05
☐ 99 Phil Garner .25 .11
☐ 100 Rod Carew 1.50 .70
☐ 101 Steve Stone .10 .05
☐ 102 Joe Niekro .10 .05
☐ 103 Jerry Martin .10 .05
Now with Giants
☐ 104 Ron LeFlore DP .05 .02
Now with White Sox
☐ 105 Jose Cruz .25 .11
☐ 106 Don Money .10 .05
☐ 107 Bobby Brown .10 .05
☐ 108 Larry Herndon .10 .05
☐ 109 Dennis Eckersley .75 .35
☐ 110 Carl Yastrzemski 1.50 .70
☐ 111 Greg Minton .10 .05
☐ 112 Dan Schatzeder .10 .05
☐ 113 George Brett 8.00 3.60
☐ 114 Tom Underwood .10 .05
☐ 115 Roy Smalley .10 .05
☐ 116 Carlton Fisk 2.00 .90
Now with White Sox
☐ 117 Pete Falcone .10 .05
☐ 118 Dale Murphy 1.50 .70
☐ 119 Tippy Martinez .10 .05
☐ 120 Larry Bowa .25 .11
☐ 121 Julio Cruz .10 .05
☐ 122 Jim Gantner .25 .11
☐ 123 Al Cowens .10 .05
☐ 124 Jerry Garvin .10 .05
☐ 125 Andre Dawson 2.00 .90
☐ 126 Charlie Leibrandt .50 .23
☐ 127 Willie Stargell 1.00 .45
☐ 128 Andre Thornton .25 .11
☐ 129 Art Howe .25 .11
☐ 130 Larry Gura .10 .05
☐ 131 Jerry Remy .10 .05
☐ 132 Rick Dempsey .25 .11
☐ 133 Alan Trammell DP 1.00 .45
☐ 134 Mike LaCoss .10 .05
☐ 135 Gorman Thomas .10 .05
☐ 136 Expos Future Stars 7.50 3.40
Tim Raines
Roberto Ramos
Bobby Pate
☐ 137 Bill Madlock .25 .11
☐ 138 Rich Dotson DP .05 .02
☐ 139 Oscar Gamble .10 .05
☐ 140 Bob Forsch .10 .05
☐ 141 Miguel Dilone .10 .05
☐ 142 Jackson Todd .10 .05
☐ 143 Dan Meyer .10 .05
☐ 144 Garry Templeton .10 .05
☐ 145 Mickey Rivers .25 .11
☐ 146 Alan Ashby .10 .05
☐ 147 Dale Berra .10 .05
☐ 148 Randy Jones .10 .05
Now with Mets
☐ 149 Joe Nolan .10 .05
☐ 150 Mark Fidrych .50 .23
☐ 151 Tony Armas .10 .05
☐ 152 Steve Kemp .10 .05
☐ 153 Jerry Reuss .25 .11
☐ 154 Rick Langford .10 .05
☐ 155 Chris Chambliss .25 .11
☐ 156 Bob McClure .10 .05
☐ 157 John Wathan .10 .05
☐ 158 John Curtis .10 .05
☐ 159 Steve Howe .25 .11
☐ 160 Garry Maddox .10 .05
☐ 161 Dan Graham .10 .05
☐ 162 Doug Corbett .10 .05
☐ 163 Rob Dressler .10 .05
☐ 164 Bucky Dent .25 .11
☐ 165 Alvis Woods .10 .05
☐ 166 Floyd Bannister .10 .05
☐ 167 Lee Mazzilli .10 .05
☐ 168 Don Robinson DP .05 .02
☐ 169 John Mayberry .10 .05
☐ 170 Woodie Fryman .10 .05
☐ 171 Gene Richards .10 .05
☐ 172 Rick Burleson .10 .05
Now with Angels
☐ 173 Bump Wills .10 .05
☐ 174 Glenn Abbott .10 .05
☐ 175 Dave Collins .10 .05
☐ 176 Mike Krukow .10 .05
☐ 177 Rick Monday .25 .11
☐ 178 Dave Parker .25 .11
☐ 179 Rudy May .10 .05
☐ 180 Pete Rose 3.00 1.35
☐ 181 Elias Sosa .10 .05
☐ 182 Bob Grich .25 .11
☐ 183 Fred Norman .10 .05
☐ 184 Jim Dwyer .10 .05
Now with Orioles
☐ 185 Dennis Leonard .10 .05
☐ 186 Gary Matthews .10 .05
☐ 187 Ron Hassey DP .05 .02
☐ 188 Doug DeCinces .25 .11
☐ 189 Craig Swan .10 .05
☐ 190 Cesar Cedeno .25 .11
☐ 191 Rick Sutcliffe .25 .11
☐ 192 Kiko Garcia .10 .05
☐ 193 Pete Vuckovich .10 .05
Now with Brewers
☐ 194 Tony Bernazard .10 .05
Now with White Sox
☐ 195 Keith Hernandez .25 .11
☐ 196 Jerry Mumphrey .10 .05
☐ 197 Jim Kern .10 .05
☐ 198 Jerry Dybzinski .10 .05
☐ 199 John Lowenstein .10 .05
☐ 200 George Foster .25 .11
☐ 201 Phil Niekro .50 .23
☐ 202 Bill Buckner .25 .11
☐ 203 Steve Carlton 1.50 .70
☐ 204 John D'Acquisto .10 .05
Now with Angels
☐ 205 Rick Reuschel .25 .11
☐ 206 Dan Quisenberry .25 .11
☐ 207 Mike Schmidt DP 2.00 .90
☐ 208 Bob Watson .25 .11
☐ 209 Jim Spencer .10 .05
☐ 210 Jim Palmer 1.00 .45
☐ 211 Derrel Thomas .10 .05
☐ 212 Steve Nicosia .10 .05
☐ 213 Omar Moreno .10 .05
☐ 214 Richie Zisk .10 .05
Now with Mariners
☐ 215 Larry Hisle .10 .05
☐ 216 Mike Torrez .10 .05
☐ 217 Rich Hebner .10 .05
☐ 218 Britt Burns .10 .05
☐ 219 Ken Landreaux .10 .05
☐ 220 Tom Seaver 2.00 .90
☐ 221 Bob Davis .10 .05
Now with Angels
☐ 222 Jorge Orta .10 .05
☐ 223 Bobby Bonds .25 .11
☐ 224 Pat Zachry .10 .05
☐ 225 Ruppert Jones .10 .05
☐ 226 Duane Kuiper .10 .05
☐ 227 Rodney Scott .10 .05
☐ 228 Tom Paciorek .10 .05
☐ 229 Rollie Fingers .75 .35
Now with Brewers
☐ 230 George Hendrick .10 .05
☐ 231 Tony Perez .75 .35
☐ 232 Grant Jackson .10 .05
☐ 233 Damaso Garcia .10 .05
☐ 234 Lou Whitaker 1.25 .55
☐ 235 Scott Sanderson .10 .05
☐ 236 Mike Ivie .10 .05
☐ 237 Charlie Moore .10 .05
☐ 238 Blue Jays Rookies .10 .05
Luis Leal
Brian Milner
Ken Schrom
☐ 239 Rick Miller DP .05 .02
Now with Red Sox
☐ 240 Nolan Ryan 10.00 4.50
☐ 241 Checklist 126-250 DP .05 .02
☐ 242 Chet Lemon .10 .05
☐ 243 Dave Palmer .10 .05
☐ 244 Ellis Valentine .10 .05
☐ 245 Carney Lansford .25 .11
Now with Red Sox
☐ 246 Ed Ott DP .05 .02
☐ 247 Glenn Hubbard DP .05 .02
☐ 248 Joey McLaughlin .10 .05
☐ 249 Jerry Narron .10 .05
☐ 250 Ron Guidry .25 .11
☐ 251 Steve Garvey .50 .23
☐ 252 Victor Cruz .10 .05
☐ 253 Bobby Murcer .25 .11
☐ 254 Ozzie Smith 8.00 3.60
☐ 255 John Stearns .10 .05
☐ 256 Bill Campbell .10 .05
☐ 257 Rennie Stennett .10 .05
☐ 258 Rick Waits .10 .05
☐ 259 Gary Lucas .10 .05
☐ 260 Ron Cey .25 .11
☐ 261 Rickey Henderson 8.00 3.60
☐ 262 Sammy Stewart .10 .05
☐ 263 Brian Downing .10 .05
☐ 264 Mark Bomback .10 .05
☐ 265 John Candelaria .25 .11
☐ 266 Renie Martin .10 .05

☐ 267 Stan Bahnsen .10 .05
☐ 268 Montreal Expos CL .50 .23
☐ 269 Ken Forsch .10 .05
☐ 270 Greg Luzinski .25 .11
☐ 271 Ron Jackson .10 .05
☐ 272 Wayne Garland .10 .05
☐ 273 Milt May .10 .05
☐ 274 Rick Wise .10 .05
☐ 275 Dwight Evans .50 .23
☐ 276 Sal Bando .25 .11
☐ 277 Alfredo Griffin .10 .05
☐ 278 Rick Sofield .10 .05
☐ 279 Bob Knepper .10 .05
Now with Astros
☐ 280 Ken Griffey .25 .11
☐ 281 Ken Singleton .25 .11
☐ 282 Ernie Whitt .10 .05
☐ 283 Billy Sample .10 .05
☐ 284 Jack Morris .75 .35
☐ 285 Dick Ruthven .10 .05
☐ 286 Johnny Bench 2.00 .90
☐ 287 Dave Smith .25 .11
☐ 288 Amos Otis .25 .11
☐ 289 Dave Goltz .10 .05
☐ 290 Bob Boone DP .25 .11
☐ 291 Aurelio Lopez .10 .05
☐ 292 Tom Hume .10 .05
☐ 293 Charlie Lea .10 .05
☐ 294 Bert Blyleven .50 .23
Now with Indians
☐ 295 Hal McRae .25 .11
☐ 296 Bob Stanley .10 .05
☐ 297 Bob Bailor .10 .05
Now with Mets
☐ 298 Jerry Koosman .25 .11
☐ 299 Elliott Maddox .10 .05
Now with Yankees
☐ 300 Paul Molitor 5.00 2.20
☐ 301 Matt Keough .10 .05
☐ 302 Pat Putnam .10 .05
☐ 303 Dan Ford .10 .05
☐ 304 John Castino .10 .05
☐ 305 Barry Foote .10 .05
☐ 306 Lou Piniella .25 .11
☐ 307 Gene Garber .10 .05
☐ 308 Rick Manning .10 .05
☐ 309 Don Baylor .50 .23
☐ 310 Vida Blue DP .25 .11
☐ 311 Doug Flynn .10 .05
☐ 312 Rick Rhoden .10 .05
☐ 313 Fred Lynn .25 .11
Now with Angels
☐ 314 Rich Dauer .10 .05
☐ 315 Kirk Gibson 3.00 1.35
☐ 316 Ken Reitz .10 .05
Now with Cubs
☐ 317 Lonnie Smith .25 .11
☐ 318 Steve Yeager .10 .05
☐ 319 Rowland Office .10 .05
☐ 320 Tom Burgmeier .10 .05
☐ 321 Leon Durham .25 .11
Now with Cubs
☐ 322 Neil Allen .10 .05
☐ 323 Ray Burris .10 .05
Now with Expos
☐ 324 Mike Willis .10 .05
☐ 325 Ray Knight .25 .11
☐ 326 Rafael Landestoy .10 .05
☐ 327 Moose Haas .10 .05
☐ 328 Ross Baumgarten .10 .05
☐ 329 Joaquin Andujar .25 .11
☐ 330 Frank White .25 .11
☐ 331 Toronto Blue Jays CL .10 .05
☐ 332 Dick Drago .10 .05
☐ 333 Sid Monge .10 .05
☐ 334 Joe Sambito .10 .05
☐ 335 Rick Cerone .10 .05
☐ 336 Eddie Whitson .10 .05
☐ 337 Sparky Lyle .25 .11
☐ 338 Checklist 251-374 .10 .05
☐ 339 Jon Matlack .10 .05
☐ 340 Ben Oglivie .10 .05
☐ 341 Dwayne Murphy .10 .05
☐ 342 Terry Crowley .10 .05
☐ 343 Frank Taveras .10 .05
☐ 344 Steve Rogers .10 .05
☐ 345 Warren Cromartie .10 .05
☐ 346 Bill Caudill .10 .05
☐ 347 Harold Baines 2.50 1.10
☐ 348 Frank LaCorte .10 .05
☐ 349 Glenn Hoffman .10 .05
☐ 350 J.R. Richard .10 .05
☐ 351 Otto Velez .10 .05
☐ 352 Ted Simmons .25 .11
Now with Brewers
☐ 353 Terry Kennedy .10 .05
Now with Padres
☐ 354 Al Hrabosky .10 .05
☐ 355 Bob Horner .25 .11
☐ 356 Cecil Cooper .25 .11
☐ 357 Bob Welch .25 .11
☐ 358 Paul Moskau .10 .05
☐ 359 Dave Rader .10 .05
Now with Angels
☐ 360 Willie Wilson .25 .11
☐ 361 Dave Kingman DP .25 .11
☐ 362 Joe Rudi .10 .05
Now with Red Sox
☐ 363 Rich Gale .10 .05
☐ 364 Steve Trout .10 .05
☐ 365 Graig Nettles DP .25 .11
☐ 366 Lamar Johnson .05 .02
☐ 367 Denny Martinez .75 .35
☐ 368 Manny Trillo .10 .05
☐ 369 Frank Tanana .25 .11
Now with White Sox
☐ 370 Reggie Jackson 2.00 .90
☐ 371 Bill Lee .25 .11
☐ 372 Jay Johnstone .25 .11
☐ 373 Jason Thompson .10 .05
☐ 374 Tom Hutton .10 .05

1981 O-Pee-Chee Posters

The 24 full-color posters comprising the 1981 O-Pee-Chee poster insert set were inserted one per regular wax pack and feature players of the Montreal Expos (numbered 1-12) and the Toronto Blue Jays (numbered 13-24). These posters are typically found with two folds and measure approximately 4 7/8" by 6 7/8". The posters are blank-backed and are numbered at the bottom in French and English. A distinctive red (Expos) or blue (Blue Jays) border surrounds the player photo.

	NRMT	VG-E
COMPLETE SET (24)	8.00	3.60
COMMON CARD (1-24)	.25	.11

☐ 1 Willie Montanez .25 .11
☐ 2 Rodney Scott .25 .11
☐ 3 Chris Speier .25 .11
☐ 4 Larry Parrish .50 .23
☐ 5 Warren Cromartie .50 .23
☐ 6 Andre Dawson 2.00 .90
☐ 7 Ellis Valentine .25 .11
☐ 8 Gary Carter 1.50 .70
☐ 9 Steve Rogers .25 .11
☐ 10 Woodie Fryman .25 .11
☐ 11 Jerry White .25 .11
☐ 12 Scott Sanderson .25 .11
☐ 13 John Mayberry .50 .23
☐ 14 Damaso Garcia UER .25 .11
(Misspelled Damasa)
☐ 15 Alfredo Griffin .25 .11
☐ 16 Garth Iorg .25 .11
☐ 17 Alvis Woods .25 .11
☐ 18 Rick Bosetti .25 .11
☐ 19 Barry Bonnell .25 .11
☐ 20 Ernie Whitt .25 .11
☐ 21 Jim Clancy .25 .11
☐ 22 Dave Stieb .75 .35
☐ 23 Otto Velez .25 .11
☐ 24 Lloyd Moseby .50 .23

1982 O-Pee-Chee

This set is an abridgement of the 1982 Topps set. The 396 standard-size cards comprising the 1982 O-Pee-Chee set differ from the cards of the 1982 Topps set by having a higher ratio of cards of players from the two Canadian teams, a practice begun by O-Pee-Chee in 1977 and continued to 1988. The set contains virtually the same pictures for the players also featured in the 1982 Topps issue, but the O-Pee-Chee photos appear brighter. The fronts feature white-bordered color player photos with colored lines within the wide white margin on the left. The player's name, team and bilingual position appear in colored lettering within the wide bottom margin. The player's name also appears as a simulated autograph across the photo. The blue print on green horizontal backs carry the player's name, bilingual position and biography at the top. The player's major league statistics follow below. The cards are numbered on the back. The asterisked cards have an extra line on the front inside the picture area indicating team change. In Action (IA) and All-Star (AS) cards are indicated in the checklist below; these are included in the set in addition to the player's regular card. The 396 cards in the set were the largest "original" or distinct set total printed up to that time by O-Pee-Chee; the previous high had been 374 in 1979, 1980 and 1981.

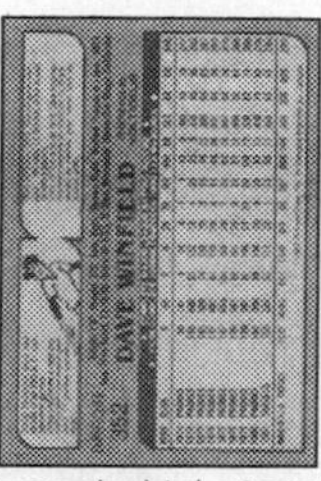

	NRMT	VG-E
COMPLETE SET (396)	45.00	20.00
COMMON CARD (1-396)	.10	.05

☐ 1 Dan Spillner .10 .05
☐ 2 Ken Singleton AS .10 .05
☐ 3 John Candelaria .10 .05
☐ 4 Frank Tanana .25 .11
Traded to Royals Jan. 15/82
☐ 5 Reggie Smith .25 .11
☐ 6 Rick Monday .10 .05
☐ 7 Scott Sanderson .10 .05
☐ 8 Rich Dauer .10 .05
☐ 9 Ron Guidry .25 .11
☐ 10 Ron Guidry IA .25 .11
☐ 11 Tom Brookens .10 .05
☐ 12 Moose Haas .10 .05
☐ 13 Chet Lemon .10 .05
Traded to Tigers Nov. 27/81
☐ 14 Steve Howe .10 .05
☐ 15 Ellis Valentine .10 .05
☐ 16 Toby Harrah .25 .11
☐ 17 Darrell Evans .25 .11
☐ 18 Johnny Bench 2.00 .90
☐ 19 Ernie Whitt .10 .05
☐ 20 Garry Maddox .10 .05
☐ 21 Graig Nettles IA .25 .11
☐ 22 Al Oliver IA .25 .11
☐ 23 Bob Boone .25 .11
Traded to Angels Dec. 9/81
☐ 24 Pete Rose IA 1.50 .70
☐ 25 Jerry Remy .10 .05
☐ 26 Jorge Orta .10 .05
Traded to Dodgers Dec 9/81
☐ 27 Bobby Bonds .25 .11
☐ 28 Jim Clancy .10 .05
☐ 29 Dwayne Murphy .10 .05
☐ 30 Tom Seaver 2.00 .90
☐ 31 Tom Seaver IA 1.00 .45
☐ 32 Claudell Washington .10 .05
☐ 33 Bob Shirley .10 .05
☐ 34 Bob Forsch .10 .05
☐ 35 Willie Aikens .10 .05
☐ 36 Rod Carew AS .75 .35
☐ 37 Willie Randolph .25 .11
☐ 38 Charlie Lea .10 .05
☐ 39 Lou Whitaker .75 .35
☐ 40 Dave Parker .25 .11
☐ 41 Dave Parker IA .25 .11
☐ 42 Mark Belanger .25 .11
Traded to Dodgers Dec. 24/81
☐ 43 Rick Langford .10 .05
☐ 44 Rollie Fingers IA .60 .25
☐ 45 Rick Cerone .10 .05
☐ 46 Johnny Wockenfuss .10 .05
☐ 47 Jack Morris AS .25 .11
☐ 48 Cesar Cedeno .10 .05
Traded to Reds Dec. 18/81
☐ 49 Alvis Woods .10 .05
☐ 50 Buddy Bell .25 .11
☐ 51 Mickey Rivers IA .10 .05
☐ 52 Steve Rogers .10 .05
☐ 53 Blue Jays Leaders .10 .05
John Mayberry
Dave Stieb
(Team checklist
on back)
☐ 54 Ron Hassey .10 .05
☐ 55 Rick Burleson .10 .05

☐ 56 Harold Baines .60 .25
☐ 57 Craig Reynolds .10 .05
☐ 58 Carlton Fisk AS .75 .35
☐ 59 Jim Kern .10 .05
Traded to Reds Feb. 10/82
☐ 60 Tony Armas .10 .05
☐ 61 Warren Cromartie .10 .05
☐ 62 Graig Nettles .25 .11
☐ 63 Jerry Koosman .25 .11
☐ 64 Pat Zachry .10 .05
☐ 65 Terry Kennedy .10 .05
☐ 66 Richie Zisk .10 .05
☐ 67 Rich Gale .10 .05
Traded to Giants Dec. 10/81
☐ 68 Steve Carlton 1.50 .70
☐ 69 Greg Luzinski IA .25 .11
☐ 70 Tim Raines 2.00 .90
☐ 71 Roy Lee Jackson .10 .05
☐ 72 Carl Yastrzemski 1.50 .70
☐ 73 John Castino .10 .05
☐ 74 Joe Niekro .25 .11
☐ 75 Tommy John .60 .25
☐ 76 Dave Winfield AS .75 .35
☐ 77 Miguel Dilone .10 .05
☐ 78 Gary Gray .10 .05
☐ 79 Tom Hume .10 .05
☐ 80 Jim Palmer 1.25 .55
☐ 81 Jim Palmer IA .60 .25
☐ 82 Vida Blue IA .25 .11
☐ 83 Garth Iorg .10 .05
☐ 84 Rennie Stennett .10 .05
☐ 85 Dave Lopes IA .25 .11
Traded to A's Feb. 8/82
☐ 86 Dave Concepcion .25 .11
☐ 87 Matt Keough .10 .05
☐ 88 Jim Spencer .10 .05
☐ 89 Steve Henderson .10 .05
☐ 90 Nolan Ryan 10.00 4.50
☐ 91 Carney Lansford .25 .11
☐ 92 Bake McBride .10 .05
☐ 93 Dave Stapleton .10 .05
☐ 94 Expos Team Leaders .10 .05
Warren Cromartie
Bill Gullickson
(Team checklist
on back)
☐ 95 Ozzie Smith 8.00 3.60
Traded to Cardinals Feb. 11/82
☐ 96 Rich Hebner .10 .05
☐ 97 Tim Foli .10 .05
Traded to Angels Dec. 11/82
☐ 98 Darrell Porter .10 .05
☐ 99 Barry Bonnell .10 .05
☐ 100 Mike Schmidt 3.00 1.35
☐ 101 Mike Schmidt IA 1.50 .70
☐ 102 Dan Briggs .10 .05
☐ 103 Al Cowens .10 .05
☐ 104 Grant Jackson .10 .05
Traded to Royals Jan. 19/82
☐ 105 Kirk Gibson .75 .35
☐ 106 Dan Schatzeder .10 .05
Traded to Giants Dec. 9/81
☐ 107 Juan Berenguer .10 .05
☐ 108 Jack Morris .25 .11
☐ 109 Dave Revering .10 .05
☐ 110 Carlton Fisk 1.50 .70
☐ 111 Carlton Fisk IA .75 .35
☐ 112 Billy Sample .10 .05
☐ 113 Steve McCatty .10 .05
☐ 114 Ken Landreaux .10 .05
☐ 115 Gaylord Perry .75 .35
☐ 116 Elias Sosa .10 .05
☐ 117 Rich Gossage IA .25 .11
☐ 118 Expos Future Stars .40 .18
Terry Francona
Brad Mills
Bryn Smith
☐ 119 Billy Almon .10 .05
☐ 120 Gary Lucas .10 .05
☐ 121 Ken Oberkfell .10 .05
☐ 122 Steve Carlton IA .75 .35
☐ 123 Jeff Reardon .60 .25
☐ 124 Bill Buckner .25 .11
☐ 125 Danny Ainge .75 .35
Voluntarily Retired Nov. 30/81
☐ 126 Paul Splittorff .10 .05
☐ 127 Lonnie Smith .10 .05
Traded to Cardinals Nov. 19/81
☐ 128 Rudy May .10 .05
☐ 129 Checklist 1-132 .10 .05
☐ 130 Julio Cruz .10 .05
☐ 131 Stan Bahnsen .10 .05
☐ 132 Pete Vuckovich .10 .05
☐ 133 Luis Salazar .10 .05
☐ 134 Dan Ford .10 .05
Traded to Orioles Jan. 28/82
☐ 135 Denny Martinez .60 .25
☐ 136 Lary Sorensen .10 .05
☐ 137 Fergie Jenkins .75 .35
Traded to Cubs Dec. 15/81
☐ 138 Rick Camp .10 .05
☐ 139 Wayne Nordhagen .10 .05
☐ 140 Ron LeFlore .25 .11
☐ 141 Rick Sutcliffe .25 .11
☐ 142 Rick Waits .10 .05
☐ 143 Mookie Wilson .75 .35
☐ 144 Greg Minton .10 .05
☐ 145 Bob Horner .25 .11
☐ 146 Joe Morgan IA .60 .25
☐ 147 Larry Gura .10 .05
☐ 148 Alfredo Griffin .10 .05
☐ 149 Pat Putnam .10 .05
☐ 150 Ted Simmons .25 .11
☐ 151 Gary Matthews .25 .11
☐ 152 Greg Luzinski .25 .11
☐ 153 Mike Flanagan .25 .11
☐ 154 Jim Morrison .10 .05
☐ 155 Otto Velez .10 .05
☐ 156 Frank White .25 .11
☐ 157 Doug Corbett .10 .05
☐ 158 Brian Downing .10 .05
☐ 159 Willie Randolph IA .25 .11
☐ 160 Luis Tiant .25 .11
☐ 161 Andre Thornton .10 .05
☐ 162 Amos Otis .25 .11
☐ 163 Paul Mirabella .10 .05
☐ 164 Bert Blyleven .60 .25
☐ 165 Rowland Office .10 .05
☐ 166 Gene Tenace .25 .11
☐ 167 Cecil Cooper .25 .11
☐ 168 Bruce Benedict .10 .05
☐ 169 Mark Clear .10 .05
☐ 170 Jim Bibby .10 .05
☐ 171 Ken Griffey IA .25 .11
Traded to Yankees Nov 4/81
☐ 172 Bill Gullickson .10 .05
☐ 173 Mike Scioscia .10 .05
☐ 174 Doug DeCinces .10 .05
Traded to Angels Jan 28/82
☐ 175 Jerry Mumphrey .10 .05
☐ 176 Rollie Fingers .75 .35
☐ 177 George Foster IA .25 .11
Traded to Mets Feb 10/82
☐ 178 Mitchell Page .10 .05
☐ 179 Steve Garvey .60 .25
☐ 180 Steve Garvey IA .40 .18
☐ 181 Woodie Fryman .10 .05
☐ 182 Larry Herndon .10 .05
Traded to Tigers Dec. 9/81
☐ 183 Frank White IA .25 .11
☐ 184 Alan Ashby .10 .05
☐ 185 Phil Niekro .75 .35
☐ 186 Leon Roberts .10 .05
☐ 187 Rod Carew 1.50 .70
☐ 188 Willie Stargell IA .60 .25
☐ 189 Joel Youngblood .10 .05
☐ 190 J.R. Richard .10 .05
☐ 191 Tim Wallach .60 .25
☐ 192 Broderick Perkins .10 .05
☐ 193 Johnny Grubb .10 .05
☐ 194 Larry Bowa .25 .11
Traded to Cubs Jan. 27/82
☐ 195 Paul Molitor 3.00 1.35
☐ 196 Willie Upshaw .10 .05
☐ 197 Roy Smalley .10 .05
☐ 198 Chris Speier .10 .05
☐ 199 Don Aase .10 .05
☐ 200 George Brett 6.00 2.70
☐ 201 George Brett IA 3.00 1.35
☐ 202 Rick Manning .10 .05
☐ 203 Blue Jays Prospects .60 .25
Jesse Barfield
Brian Milner
Boomer Wells
☐ 204 Rick Reuschel .25 .11
☐ 205 Neil Allen .10 .05
☐ 206 Leon Durham .10 .05
☐ 207 Jim Gantner .25 .11
☐ 208 Joe Morgan 1.00 .45
☐ 209 Gary Lavelle .10 .05
☐ 210 Keith Hernandez .25 .11
☐ 211 Joe Charboneau .10 .05
☐ 212 Mario Mendoza .10 .05
☐ 213 Willie Randolph AS .25 .11
☐ 214 Lance Parrish .40 .18
☐ 215 Mike Krukow .10 .05
Traded to Phillies Dec. 8/81
☐ 216 Ron Cey .25 .11
☐ 217 Ruppert Jones .10 .05
☐ 218 Dave Lopes .25 .11
Traded to A's Feb. 8/82
☐ 219 Steve Yeager .10 .05
☐ 220 Manny Trillo .10 .05
☐ 221 Dave Concepcion IA .25 .11
☐ 222 Butch Wynegar .10 .05
☐ 223 Lloyd Moseby .10 .05
☐ 224 Bruce Bochte .10 .05
☐ 225 Ed Ott .10 .05
☐ 226 Checklist 133-264 .10 .05
☐ 227 Ray Burris .10 .05
☐ 228 Reggie Smith IA .25 .11
☐ 229 Oscar Gamble .10 .05
☐ 230 Willie Wilson .10 .05
☐ 231 Brian Kingman .10 .05
☐ 232 John Stearns .10 .05
☐ 233 Duane Kuiper .10 .05
Traded to Giants Nov. 16/81
☐ 234 Don Baylor .25 .11
☐ 235 Mike Easler .10 .05
☐ 236 Lou Piniella .25 .11
☐ 237 Robin Yount 1.50 .70
☐ 238 Kevin Saucier .10 .05
☐ 239 Jon Matlack .10 .05
☐ 240 Bucky Dent .25 .11
☐ 241 Bucky Dent IA .25 .11
☐ 242 Milt May .10 .05
☐ 243 Lee Mazzilli .10 .05
☐ 244 Gary Carter .75 .35
☐ 245 Ken Reitz .10 .05
☐ 246 Scott McGregor AS .10 .05
☐ 247 Pedro Guerrero .25 .11
☐ 248 Art Howe .10 .05
☐ 249 Dick Tidrow .10 .05
☐ 250 Tug McGraw .25 .11
☐ 251 Fred Lynn .25 .11
☐ 252 Fred Lynn IA .25 .11
☐ 253 Gene Richards .10 .05
☐ 254 Jorge Bell .10 .05
☐ 255 Tony Perez .60 .25
☐ 256 Tony Perez IA .40 .18
☐ 257 Rich Dotson .10 .05
☐ 258 Bo Diaz .10 .05
Traded to Phillies Nov. 19/81
☐ 259 Rodney Scott .10 .05
☐ 260 Bruce Sutter .25 .11
☐ 261 George Brett AS 3.00 1.35
☐ 262 Rick Dempsey .25 .11
☐ 263 Mike Phillips .10 .05
☐ 264 Jerry Garvin .10 .05
☐ 265 Al Bumbry .10 .05
☐ 266 Hubie Brooks .10 .05
☐ 267 Vida Blue .25 .11
☐ 268 Rickey Henderson 4.00 1.80
☐ 269 Rick Peters .10 .05
☐ 270 Rusty Staub .25 .11
☐ 271 Sixto Lezcano .10 .05
Traded to Padres Dec. 10/81
☐ 272 Bump Wills .10 .05
☐ 273 Gary Allenson .10 .05
☐ 274 Randy Jones .10 .05
☐ 275 Bob Watson .25 .11
☐ 276 Dave Kingman .25 .11
☐ 277 Terry Puhl .10 .05
☐ 278 Jerry Reuss .25 .11
☐ 279 Sammy Stewart .10 .05
☐ 280 Ben Oglivie .10 .05
☐ 281 Kent Tekulve .25 .11
☐ 282 Ken Macha .10 .05
☐ 283 Ron Davis .10 .05
☐ 284 Bob Grich .25 .11
☐ 285 Sparky Lyle .25 .11
☐ 286 Rich Gossage AS .25 .11
☐ 287 Dennis Eckersley .60 .25
☐ 288 Garry Templeton .10 .05
Traded to Padres Dec. 10/81
☐ 289 Bob Stanley .10 .05
☐ 290 Ken Singleton .10 .05
☐ 291 Mickey Hatcher .10 .05
☐ 292 Dave Palmer .10 .05
☐ 293 Damaso Garcia .10 .05
☐ 294 Don Money .10 .05
☐ 295 George Hendrick .10 .05
☐ 296 Steve Kemp .10 .05
Traded to White Sox Nov. 27/81
☐ 297 Dave Smith .10 .05
☐ 298 Bucky Dent AS .10 .05
☐ 299 Steve Trout .10 .05
☐ 300 Reggie Jackson 3.00 1.35
Traded to Angels Jan. 26/82
☐ 301 Reggie Jackson IA 1.50 .70
Traded to Angels Jan. 26/82
☐ 302 Doug Flynn .10 .05
Traded to Rangers Dec. 14/81
☐ 303 Wayne Gross .10 .05
☐ 304 Johnny Bench IA 1.00 .45
☐ 305 Don Sutton 1.00 .45
☐ 306 Don Sutton IA .60 .25
☐ 307 Mark Bomback .10 .05
☐ 308 Charlie Moore .10 .05
☐ 309 Jeff Burroughs .10 .05
☐ 310 Mike Hargrove .25 .11

Card	NRMT	VG-E
☐ 311 Enos Cabell	.10	.05
☐ 312 Lenny Randle	.10	.05
☐ 313 Ivan DeJesus	.10	.05
Traded to Phillies Jan. 27/82		
☐ 314 Buck Martinez	.10	.05
☐ 315 Burt Hooton	.10	.05
☐ 316 Scott McGregor	.10	.05
☐ 317 Dick Ruthven	.10	.05
☐ 318 Mike Heath	.10	.05
☐ 319 Ray Knight	.25	.11
Traded to Astros Dec. 18/81		
☐ 320 Chris Chambliss	.10	.05
☐ 321 Chris Chambliss IA	.10	.05
☐ 322 Ross Baumgarten	.10	.05
☐ 323 Bill Lee	.25	.11
☐ 324 Gorman Thomas	.10	.05
☐ 325 Jose Cruz	.25	.11
☐ 326 Al Oliver	.25	.11
☐ 327 Jackson Todd	.10	.05
☐ 328 Ed Farmer	.10	.05
Traded to Phillies Jan. 28/82		
☐ 329 U.L. Washington	.10	.05
☐ 330 Ken Griffey	.25	.11
Traded to Yankees Nov. 4/81		
☐ 331 John Milner	.10	.05
☐ 332 Don Robinson	.10	.05
☐ 333 Cliff Johnson	.10	.05
☐ 334 Fernando Valenzuela	1.00	.45
☐ 335 Jim Sundberg	.25	.11
☐ 336 George Foster	.25	.11
Traded to Mets Feb. 10/82		
☐ 337 Pete Rose AS	1.50	.70
☐ 338 Dave Lopes AS	.25	.11
Traded to A's Feb. 8/82		
☐ 339 Mike Schmidt AS	1.50	.70
☐ 340 Dave Concepcion AS	.10	.05
☐ 341 Andre Dawson AS	.75	.35
☐ 342 George Foster AS	.25	.11
Traded to Mets Feb. 10/82		
☐ 343 Dave Parker AS	.25	.11
☐ 344 Gary Carter AS	.25	.11
☐ 345 Fernando Valenzuela AS	.60	.25
☐ 346 Tom Seaver AS	1.00	.45
☐ 347 Bruce Sutter AS	.25	.11
☐ 348 Darrell Porter IA	.10	.05
☐ 349 Dave Collins	.10	.05
Traded to Yankees Dec. 23/81		
☐ 350 Amos Otis IA	.10	.05
☐ 351 Frank Taveras	.10	.05
Traded to Expos Dec. 14/81		
☐ 352 Dave Winfield	1.50	.70
☐ 353 Larry Parrish	.10	.05
☐ 354 Roberto Ramos	.10	.05
☐ 355 Dwight Evans	.25	.11
☐ 356 Mickey Rivers	.10	.05
☐ 357 Butch Hobson	.10	.05
☐ 358 Carl Yastrzemski IA	.75	.35
☐ 359 Ron Jackson	.10	.05
☐ 360 Len Barker	.10	.05
☐ 361 Pete Rose	3.00	1.35
☐ 362 Kevin Hickey	.10	.05
☐ 363 Rod Carew IA	.75	.35
☐ 364 Hector Cruz	.10	.05
☐ 365 Bill Madlock	.25	.11
☐ 366 Jim Rice	.25	.11
☐ 367 Ron Cey IA	.25	.11
☐ 368 Luis Leal	.10	.05
☐ 369 Dennis Leonard	.10	.05
☐ 370 Mike Norris	.10	.05
☐ 371 Tom Paciorek	.10	.05
Traded to White Sox Dec. 11/81		
☐ 372 Willie Stargell	1.00	.45
☐ 373 Dan Driessen	.10	.05
☐ 374 Larry Bowa IA	.25	.11
Traded to Cubs Jan. 27/82		
☐ 375 Dusty Baker	.25	.11
☐ 376 Joey McLaughlin	.10	.05
☐ 377 Reggie Jackson AS	1.50	.70
Traded to Angels Jan. 26/82		
☐ 378 Mike Caldwell	.10	.05
☐ 379 Andre Dawson	1.50	.70
☐ 380 Dave Stieb	.10	.05
☐ 381 Alan Trammell	1.00	.45
☐ 382 John Mayberry	.10	.05
☐ 383 John Wathan	.10	.05
☐ 384 Hal McRae	.25	.11
☐ 385 Ken Forsch	.10	.05
☐ 386 Jerry White	.10	.05
☐ 387 Tom Veryzer	.10	.05
Traded to Mets Jan. 8/82		
☐ 388 Joe Rudi	.10	.05
Traded to A's Dec. 4/81		
☐ 389 Bob Knepper	.10	.05
☐ 390 Eddie Murray	4.00	1.80
☐ 391 Dale Murphy	1.00	.45
☐ 392 Bob Boone IA	.25	.11
Traded to Angels Dec. 6/81		
☐ 393 Al Hrabosky	.10	.05
☐ 394 Checklist 265-396	.10	.05
☐ 395 Omar Moreno	.10	.05
☐ 396 Rich Gossage	.60	.25

1982 O-Pee-Chee Posters

These 24 full-color posters comprising the 1982 O-Pee-Chee poster insert set were inserted one per regular wax pack and feature players of the Montreal Expos (numbered 13-24) and the Toronto Blue Jays (numbered 1-12). These posters are typically found with two folds and measure approximately 4 7/8" by 6 7/8". The posters are blank-backed and are numbered at the bottom in French and English. A distinctive red (Blue Jays) or blue (Expos) border surrounds the player photo.

	NRMT	VG-E
COMPLETE SET (24)	8.00	3.60
COMMON CARD (1-24)	.25	.11
☐ 1 John Mayberry	.50	.23
☐ 2 Damaso Garcia	.25	.11
☐ 3 Ernie Whitt	.25	.11
☐ 4 Lloyd Moseby	.25	.11
☐ 5 Alvis Woods	.25	.11
☐ 6 Dave Stieb	.75	.35
☐ 7 Roy Lee Jackson	.25	.11
☐ 8 Joey McLaughlin	.25	.11
☐ 9 Luis Leal	.25	.11
☐ 10 Aurelio Rodriguez	.25	.11
☐ 11 Otto Velez	.25	.11
☐ 12 Juan Berenguer UER	.25	.11
(Misspelled Berenger)		
☐ 13 Warren Cromartie	.25	.11
☐ 14 Rodney Scott	.25	.11
☐ 15 Larry Parrish	.50	.23
☐ 16 Gary Carter	1.25	.55
☐ 17 Tim Raines	1.50	.70
☐ 18 Andre Dawson	2.00	.90
☐ 19 Terry Francona	.50	.23
☐ 20 Steve Rogers	.25	.11
☐ 21 Bill Gullickson	.50	.23
☐ 22 Scott Sanderson	.25	.11
☐ 23 Jeff Reardon	1.00	.45
☐ 24 Jerry White	.25	.11

1983 O-Pee-Chee

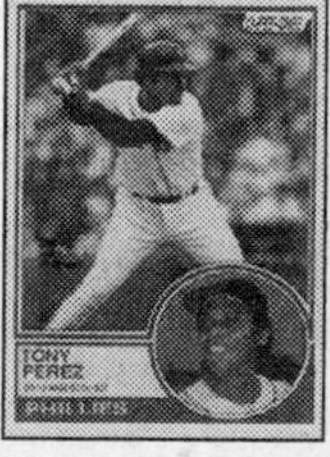

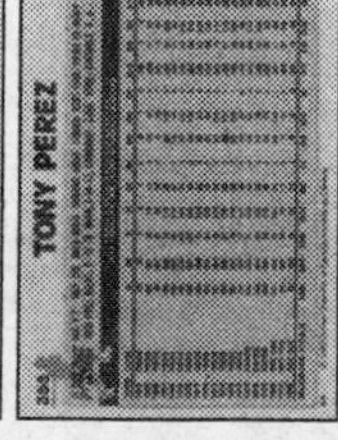

This set is an abridgement of the 1983 Topps set. The 396 standard-size cards comprising the 1983 O-Pee-Chee set differ from the cards of the 1983 Topps set by having a higher ratio of cards of players from the two Canadian teams, a practice begun by O-Pee-Chee in 1977 and continued to 1988. The set contains virtually the same pictures for the players also featured in the 1983 Topps issue. The fronts feature white-bordered color player action photos framed by a colored line. A circular color player head shot also appears on the front at the lower right. The player's name, team and bilingual position appear at the lower left. The pink and white horizontal backs carry the player's name and biography at the top. The player's major league statistics and bilingual career highlights follow below. The asterisked cards have an extra line on the front inside the picture area indicating team change. The O-Pee-Chee logo appears on the front of every card. Super Veteran (SV) and All-Star (AS) cards are indicated in the checklist below; these are included in the set in addition to the player's regular card. The set features rookie year cards of Tony Gwynn and Ryne Sandberg.

	NRMT	VG-E
COMPLETE SET (396)	60.00	27.00
COMMON CARD (1-396)	.10	.05
☐ 1 Rusty Staub	.25	.11
☐ 2 Larry Parrish	.10	.05
☐ 3 George Brett	5.00	2.20
☐ 4 Carl Yastrzemski	1.50	.70
☐ 5 Al Oliver SV	.25	.11
☐ 6 Bill Virdon MG	.10	.05
☐ 7 Gene Richards	.10	.05
☐ 8 Steve Balboni	.10	.05
☐ 9 Joey McLaughlin	.10	.05
☐ 10 Gorman Thomas	.10	.05
☐ 11 Chris Chambliss	.25	.11
☐ 12 Ray Burris	.10	.05
☐ 13 Larry Herndon	.10	.05
☐ 14 Ozzie Smith	3.00	1.35
☐ 15 Ron Cey	.25	.11
Now with Cubs		
☐ 16 Willie Wilson	.25	.11
☐ 17 Kent Tekulve	.10	.05
☐ 18 Kent Tekulve SV	.10	.05
☐ 19 Oscar Gamble	.10	.05
☐ 20 Carlton Fisk	1.25	.55
☐ 21 Dale Murphy AS	.60	.25
☐ 22 Randy Lerch	.10	.05
☐ 23 Dale Murphy	.75	.35
☐ 24 Steve Mura	.10	.05
Now with White Sox		
☐ 25 Hal McRae	.25	.11
☐ 26 Dennis Lamp	.10	.05
☐ 27 Ron Washington	.10	.05
☐ 28 Bruce Bochte	.10	.05
☐ 29 Randy Jones	.10	.05
Now with Pirates		
☐ 30 Jim Rice	.25	.11
☐ 31 Bill Gullickson	.25	.11
☐ 32 Dave Concepcion AS	.25	.11
☐ 33 Ted Simmons SV	.25	.11
☐ 34 Bobby Cox MG	.10	.05
☐ 35 Rollie Fingers	.75	.35
☐ 36 Rollie Fingers SV	.40	.18
☐ 37 Mike Hargrove	.25	.11
☐ 38 Roy Smalley	.10	.05
☐ 39 Terry Puhl	.10	.05
☐ 40 Fernando Valenzuela	.60	.25
☐ 41 Garry Maddox	.10	.05
☐ 42 Dale Murray	.40	.18
Now with Yankees		
☐ 43 Bob Dernier	.10	.05
☐ 44 Don Robinson	.10	.05
☐ 45 John Mayberry	.10	.05
☐ 46 Richard Dotson	.10	.05
☐ 47 Wayne Nordhagen	.10	.05
Now with Cubs		
☐ 48 Lary Sorensen	.10	.05
☐ 49 Willie McGee	1.00	.45
☐ 50 Bob Horner	.10	.05
☐ 51 Rusty Staub SV	.25	.11
☐ 52 Tom Seaver	3.00	1.35
Now with Mets		
☐ 53 Chet Lemon	.10	.05
☐ 54 Scott Sanderson	.10	.05
☐ 55 Mookie Wilson	.25	.11
☐ 56 Reggie Jackson	2.00	.90
☐ 57 Tim Blackwell	.10	.05
☐ 58 Keith Moreland	.10	.05
☐ 59 Alvis Woods	.10	.05
Now with Athletics		
☐ 60 Johnny Bench	2.00	.90
☐ 61 Johnny Bench SV	1.00	.45
☐ 62 Jim Gott	.10	.05
☐ 63 Rick Monday	.10	.05
☐ 64 Gary Matthews	.25	.11
☐ 65 Jack Morris	.25	.11
☐ 66 Lou Whitaker	.60	.25
☐ 67 U.L. Washington	.10	.05
☐ 68 Eric Show	.10	.05
☐ 69 Lee Lacy	.10	.05
☐ 70 Steve Carlton	1.25	.55
☐ 71 Steve Carlton SV	.75	.35
☐ 72 Tom Paciorek	.25	.11
☐ 73 Manny Trillo	.10	.05
Now with Indians		
☐ 74 Tony Perez SV	.60	.25
☐ 75 Amos Otis	.25	.11
☐ 76 Rick Mahler	.10	.05
☐ 77 Hosken Powell	.10	.05
☐ 78 Bill Caudill	.10	.05
☐ 79 Dan Petry	.10	.05
☐ 80 George Foster	.25	.11
☐ 81 Joe Morgan	1.00	.45

Now with Phillies		
☐ 82 Burt Hooton	.10	.05
☐ 83 Ryne Sandberg	15.00	6.75
☐ 84 Alan Ashby	.10	.05
☐ 85 Ken Singleton	.25	.11
☐ 86 Tom Hume	.10	.05
☐ 87 Dennis Leonard	.10	.05
☐ 88 Jim Gantner	.25	.11
☐ 89 Leon Roberts	.10	.05
Now with Royals		
☐ 90 Jerry Reuss	.25	.11
☐ 91 Ben Oglivie	.10	.05
☐ 92 Sparky Lyle SV	.25	.11
☐ 93 John Castino	.10	.05
☐ 94 Phil Niekro	.75	.35
☐ 95 Alan Trammell	.60	.25
☐ 96 Gaylord Perry	.75	.35
☐ 97 Tom Herr	.10	.05
☐ 98 Vance Law	.10	.05
☐ 99 Dickie Noles	.10	.05
☐ 100 Pete Rose	3.00	1.35
☐ 101 Pete Rose SV	1.50	.70
☐ 102 Dave Concepcion	.25	.11
☐ 103 Darrell Porter	.10	.05
☐ 104 Ron Guidry	.25	.11
☐ 105 Don Baylor	.25	.11
Now with Yankees		
☐ 106 Steve Rogers AS	.10	.05
☐ 107 Greg Minton	.10	.05
☐ 108 Glenn Hoffman	.10	.05
☐ 109 Luis Leal	.10	.05
☐ 110 Ken Griffey	.25	.11
☐ 111 Expos Leaders Al Oliver Steve Rogers (Team checklist on back)	.25	.11
☐ 112 Luis Pujols	.10	.05
☐ 113 Julio Cruz	.10	.05
☐ 114 Jim Slaton	.10	.05
☐ 115 Chili Davis	.75	.35
☐ 116 Pedro Guerrero	.25	.11
☐ 117 Mike Ivie	.10	.05
☐ 118 Chris Welsh	.10	.05
☐ 119 Frank Pastore	.10	.05
☐ 120 Len Barker	.10	.05
☐ 121 Chris Speier	.10	.05
☐ 122 Bobby Murcer	.25	.11
☐ 123 Bill Russell	.25	.11
☐ 124 Lloyd Moseby	.10	.05
☐ 125 Leon Durham	.10	.05
☐ 126 Carl Yastrzemski SV	.75	.35
☐ 127 John Candelaria	.10	.05
☐ 128 Phil Garner	.25	.11
☐ 129 Checklist 1-132	.10	.05
☐ 130 Dave Stieb	.10	.05
☐ 131 Geoff Zahn	.10	.05
☐ 132 Todd Cruz	.10	.05
☐ 133 Tony Pena	.25	.11
☐ 134 Hubie Brooks	.10	.05
☐ 135 Dwight Evans	.25	.11
☐ 136 Willie Aikens	.10	.05
☐ 137 Woodie Fryman	.10	.05
☐ 138 Rick Dempsey	.25	.11
☐ 139 Bruce Berenyi	.10	.05
☐ 140 Willie Randolph	.25	.11
☐ 141 Eddie Murray	3.00	1.35
☐ 142 Mike Caldwell	.10	.05
☐ 143 Tony Gwynn	30.00	13.50
☐ 144 Tommy John SV	.25	.11
☐ 145 Don Sutton	.75	.35
☐ 146 Don Sutton SV	.40	.18
☐ 147 Rick Manning	.10	.05
☐ 148 George Hendrick	.10	.05
☐ 149 Johnny Ray	.10	.05
☐ 150 Bruce Sutter	.25	.11
☐ 151 Bruce Sutter SV	.25	.11
☐ 152 Jay Johnstone	.25	.11
☐ 153 Jerry Koosman	.25	.11
☐ 154 Johnnie LeMaster	.10	.05
☐ 155 Dan Quisenberry	.25	.11
☐ 156 Luis Salazar	.10	.05
☐ 157 Steve Bedrosian	.25	.11
☐ 158 Jim Sundberg	.10	.05
☐ 159 Gaylord Perry SV	.40	.18
☐ 160 Dave Kingman	.25	.11
☐ 161 Dave Kingman SV	.25	.11
☐ 162 Mark Clear	.10	.05
☐ 163 Cal Ripken	15.00	6.75
☐ 164 Dave Palmer	.10	.05
☐ 165 Dan Driessen	.10	.05
☐ 166 Tug McGraw	.25	.11
☐ 167 Dennis Martinez	.25	.11
☐ 168 Juan Eichelberger	.10	.05
Now with Indians		
☐ 169 Doug Flynn	.10	.05
☐ 170 Steve Howe	.10	.05
☐ 171 Frank White	.25	.11
☐ 172 Mike Flanagan	.25	.11
☐ 173 Andre Dawson AS	.60	.25
☐ 174 Manny Trillo AS	.10	.05
Now with Indians		
☐ 175 Bo Diaz	.10	.05
☐ 176 Dave Righetti	.25	.11
☐ 177 Harold Baines	.60	.25
☐ 178 Vida Blue	.25	.11
☐ 179 Luis Tiant SV	.25	.11
☐ 180 Rickey Henderson	3.00	1.35
☐ 181 Rick Rhoden	.10	.05
☐ 182 Fred Lynn	.25	.11
☐ 183 Ed VandeBerg	.10	.05
☐ 184 Dwayne Murphy	.10	.05
☐ 185 Tim Lollar	.10	.05
☐ 186 Dave Tobik	.10	.05
☐ 187 Tug McGraw SV	.25	.11
☐ 188 Rick Miller	.10	.05
☐ 189 Dan Schatzeder	.10	.05
☐ 190 Cecil Cooper	.25	.11
☐ 191 Jim Beattie	.10	.05
☐ 192 Rich Dauer	.10	.05
☐ 193 Al Cowens	.10	.05
☐ 194 Roy Lee Jackson	.10	.05
☐ 195 Mike Gates	.10	.05
☐ 196 Tommy John	.60	.25
☐ 197 Bob Forsch	.10	.05
☐ 198 Steve Garvey	.60	.25
Now with Padres		
☐ 199 Brad Mills	.10	.05
☐ 200 Rod Carew	1.25	.55
☐ 201 Rod Carew SV	.75	.35
☐ 202 Blue Jays Leaders Dave Stieb Damaso Garcia (Team checklist back)	.10	.05
☐ 203 Floyd Bannister	.10	.05
Now with White Sox		
☐ 204 Bruce Benedict	.10	.05
☐ 205 Dave Parker	.25	.11
☐ 206 Ken Oberkfell	.10	.05
☐ 207 Graig Nettles SV	.25	.11
☐ 208 Sparky Lyle	.25	.11
☐ 209 Jason Thompson	.10	.05
☐ 210 Jack Clark	.25	.11
☐ 211 Jim Kaat	.25	.11
☐ 212 John Stearns	.10	.05
☐ 213 Tom Burgmeier	.10	.05
☐ 214 Jerry White	.10	.05
☐ 215 Mario Soto	.10	.05
☐ 216 Scott McGregor	.10	.05
☐ 217 Tim Stoddard	.10	.05
☐ 218 Bill Laskey	.10	.05
☐ 219 Reggie Jackson SV	1.00	.45
☐ 220 Dusty Baker	.25	.11
☐ 221 Joe Niekro	.25	.11
☐ 222 Damaso Garcia	.10	.05
☐ 223 John Montefusco	.10	.05
☐ 224 Mickey Rivers	.10	.05
☐ 225 Enos Cabell	.10	.05
☐ 226 LaMarr Hoyt	.10	.05
☐ 227 Tim Raines	.60	.25
☐ 228 Joaquin Andujar	.10	.05
☐ 229 Tim Wallach	.25	.11
☐ 230 Fergie Jenkins	.75	.35
☐ 231 Fergie Jenkins SV	.40	.18
☐ 232 Tom Brunansky	.25	.11
☐ 233 Ivan DeJesus	.10	.05
☐ 234 Bryn Smith	.10	.05
☐ 235 Claudell Washington	.10	.05
☐ 236 Steve Renko	.10	.05
☐ 237 Dan Norman	.10	.05
☐ 238 Cesar Cedeno	.25	.11
☐ 239 Dave Stapleton	.10	.05
☐ 240 Rich Gossage	.60	.25
☐ 241 Rich Gossage SV	.40	.18
☐ 242 Bob Stanley	.10	.05
☐ 243 Rich Gale	.10	.05
Now with Reds		
☐ 244 Sixto Lezcano	.10	.05
☐ 245 Steve Sax	.25	.11
☐ 246 Jerry Mumphrey	.10	.05
☐ 247 Dave Smith	.10	.05
☐ 248 Bake McBride	.10	.05
☐ 249 Checklist 133-264	.10	.05
☐ 250 Bill Buckner	.25	.11
☐ 251 Kent Hrbek	.75	.35
☐ 252 Gene Tenace	.10	.05
Now with Pirates		
☐ 253 Charlie Lea	.10	.05
☐ 254 Rick Cerone	.10	.05
☐ 255 Gene Garber	.10	.05
☐ 256 Gene Garber SV	.10	.05
☐ 257 Jesse Barfield	.25	.11
☐ 258 Dave Winfield	1.25	.55
☐ 259 Don Money	.10	.05
☐ 260 Steve Kemp	.10	.05
Now with Yankees		
☐ 261 Steve Yeager	.10	.05
☐ 262 Keith Hernandez	.25	.11
☐ 263 Tippy Martinez	.10	.05
☐ 264 Joe Morgan SV	.60	.25
Now with Phillies		
☐ 265 Joel Youngblood	.10	.05
Now with Giants		
☐ 266 Bruce Sutter AS	.25	.11
☐ 267 Terry Francona	.10	.05
☐ 268 Neil Allen	.10	.05
☐ 269 Ron Oester	.10	.05
☐ 270 Dennis Eckersley	.60	.25
☐ 271 Dale Berra	.10	.05
☐ 272 Al Bumbry	.10	.05
☐ 273 Lonnie Smith	.10	.05
☐ 274 Terry Kennedy	.10	.05
☐ 275 Ray Knight	.25	.11
☐ 276 Mike Norris	.10	.05
☐ 277 Rance Mulliniks	.10	.05
☐ 278 Dan Spillner	.10	.05
☐ 279 Bucky Dent	.25	.11
☐ 280 Bert Blyleven	.60	.25
☐ 281 Barry Bonnell	.10	.05
☐ 282 Reggie Smith	.25	.11
☐ 283 Reggie Smith SV	.25	.11
☐ 284 Ted Simmons	.25	.11
☐ 285 Lance Parrish	.25	.11
☐ 286 Larry Christenson	.10	.05
☐ 287 Ruppert Jones	.10	.05
☐ 288 Bob Welch	.25	.11
☐ 289 John Wathan	.10	.05
☐ 290 Jeff Reardon	.25	.11
☐ 291 Dave Revering	.10	.05
☐ 292 Craig Swan	.10	.05
☐ 293 Graig Nettles	.25	.11
☐ 294 Alfredo Griffin	.10	.05
☐ 295 Jerry Remy	.10	.05
☐ 296 Joe Sambito	.10	.05
☐ 297 Ron LeFlore	.10	.05
☐ 298 Brian Downing	.10	.05
☐ 299 Jim Palmer	1.00	.45
☐ 300 Mike Schmidt	2.50	1.10
☐ 301 Mike Schmidt SV	1.25	.55
☐ 302 Ernie Whitt	.10	.05
☐ 303 Andre Dawson	1.00	.45
☐ 304 Bobby Murcer SV	.25	.11
☐ 305 Larry Bowa	.25	.11
☐ 306 Lee Mazzilli	.10	.05
Now with Pirates		
☐ 307 Lou Piniella	.25	.11
☐ 308 Buck Martinez	.10	.05
☐ 309 Jerry Martin	.10	.05
☐ 310 Greg Luzinski	.25	.11
☐ 311 Al Oliver	.25	.11
☐ 312 Mike Torrez	.10	.05
Now with Mets		
☐ 313 Dick Ruthven	.10	.05
☐ 314 Gary Carter AS	.25	.11
☐ 315 Rick Burleson	.10	.05
☐ 316 Phil Niekro SV	.40	.18
☐ 317 Moose Haas	.10	.05
☐ 318 Carney Lansford	.25	.11
Now with Athletics		
☐ 319 Tim Foli	.10	.05
☐ 320 Steve Rogers	.10	.05
☐ 321 Kirk Gibson	.60	.25
☐ 322 Glenn Hubbard	.10	.05
☐ 323 Luis DeLeon	.10	.05
☐ 324 Mike Marshall	.10	.05
☐ 325 Von Hayes	.10	.05
Now with Phillies		
☐ 326 Garth Iorg	.10	.05
☐ 327 Jose Cruz	.25	.11
☐ 328 Jim Palmer SV	.40	.18
☐ 329 Darrell Evans	.25	.11
☐ 330 Buddy Bell	.25	.11
☐ 331 Mike Krukow	.10	.05
Now with Giants		
☐ 332 Omar Moreno	.10	.05
Now with Astros		
☐ 333 Dave LaRoche	.10	.05
☐ 334 Dave LaRoche SV	.10	.05
☐ 335 Bill Madlock	.25	.11
☐ 336 Garry Templeton	.10	.05
☐ 337 John Lowenstein	.10	.05
☐ 338 Willie Upshaw	.10	.05
☐ 339 Dave Hostetler	.10	.05
☐ 340 Larry Gura	.10	.05
☐ 341 Doug DeCinces	.25	.11
☐ 342 Mike Schmidt AS	1.25	.55
☐ 343 Charlie Hough	.25	.11
☐ 344 Andre Thornton	.10	.05
☐ 345 Jim Clancy	.10	.05
☐ 346 Ken Forsch	.10	.05
☐ 347 Sammy Stewart	.10	.05
☐ 348 Alan Bannister	.10	.05
☐ 349 Checklist 265-396	.10	.05

☐ 350 Robin Yount	1.25	.55
☐ 351 Warren Cromartie	.10	.05
☐ 352 Tim Raines AS	.60	.25
☐ 353 Tony Armas Now with Red Sox	.10	.05
☐ 354 Tom Seaver SV Now with Mets	1.50	.70
☐ 355 Tony Perez Now with Phillies	.60	.25
☐ 356 Toby Harrah	.10	.05
☐ 357 Dan Ford	.10	.05
☐ 358 Charlie Puleo Now with Reds	.10	.05
☐ 359 Dave Collins Now with Blue Jays	.10	.05
☐ 360 Nolan Ryan	10.00	4.50
☐ 361 Nolan Ryan SV	5.00	2.20
☐ 362 Bill Almon Now with Athletics	.10	.05
☐ 363 Eddie Milner	.10	.05
☐ 364 Gary Lucas	.10	.05
☐ 365 Dave Lopes	.25	.11
☐ 366 Bob Boone	.25	.11
☐ 367 Biff Pocoroba	.10	.05
☐ 368 Richie Zisk	.10	.05
☐ 369 Tony Bernazard	.10	.05
☐ 370 Gary Carter	.75	.35
☐ 371 Paul Molitor	1.50	.70
☐ 372 Art Howe	.10	.05
☐ 373 Pete Rose AS	1.50	.70
☐ 374 Glenn Adams	.10	.05
☐ 375 Pete Vuckovich	.10	.05
☐ 376 Gary Lavelle	.10	.05
☐ 377 Lee May	.25	.11
☐ 378 Lee May SV	.25	.11
☐ 379 Butch Wynegar	.10	.05
☐ 380 Ron Davis	.10	.05
☐ 381 Bob Grich	.25	.11
☐ 382 Gary Roenicke	.10	.05
☐ 383 Jim Kaat SV	.25	.11
☐ 384 Steve Carlton AS	.75	.35
☐ 385 Mike Easler	.10	.05
☐ 386 Rod Carew AS	.75	.35
☐ 387 Bob Grich AS	.25	.11
☐ 388 George Brett AS	2.50	1.10
☐ 389 Robin Yount AS	1.00	.45
☐ 390 Reggie Jackson AS	1.00	.45
☐ 391 Rickey Henderson AS	1.00	.45
☐ 392 Fred Lynn AS	.25	.11
☐ 393 Carlton Fisk AS	.60	.25
☐ 394 Pete Vuckovich AS	.10	.05
☐ 395 Larry Gura AS	.10	.05
☐ 396 Dan Quisenberry AS	.10	.05

1984 O-Pee-Chee

This set is an abridgement of the 1984 Topps set. The 396 standard-size cards comprising the 1984 O-Pee-Chee set differ from the cards of the 1984 Topps set by having a higher ratio of cards of players from the two Canadian teams, a practice begun by O-Pee-Chee in 1977 and continued to 1988. The set contains virtually the same pictures for the players also featured in the 1984 Topps issue. The fronts feature white-bordered color player action photos. A color player head shot also appears on the front at the lower left. The player's name and position appear in colored lettering within the white margin at the lower right. His team name appears in vertical colored lettering within the white margin on the left. The red, white and blue horizontal backs carry the player's name and biography at the top. The player's major league statistics and bilingual career highlights follow below. The asterisked cards have an extra line on the front inside the picture area indicating team change. The O-Pee-Chee logo appears on the front of every card. All-Star (AS) cards are indicated in the checklist below; they are included in the set in addition to the player's regular card. The set features Don Mattingly and Darryl Strawberry in their Rookie Card season.

	NRMT	VG-E
COMPLETE SET (396)	35.00	16.00
COMMON CARD (1-396)	.05	.02
☐ 1 Pascual Perez	.05	.02
☐ 2 Cal Ripken AS	3.00	1.35
☐ 3 Lloyd Moseby AS	.05	.02
☐ 4 Mel Hall	.05	.02
☐ 5 Willie Wilson	.05	.02
☐ 6 Mike Morgan	.05	.02
☐ 7 Gary Lucas Now with Expos	.05	.02
☐ 8 Don Mattingly	10.00	4.50
☐ 9 Jim Gott	.05	.02
☐ 10 Robin Yount	.75	.35
☐ 11 Joey McLaughlin	.05	.02
☐ 12 Billy Sample	.05	.02
☐ 13 Oscar Gamble	.05	.02
☐ 14 Bill Russell	.05	.02
☐ 15 Burt Hooton	.05	.02
☐ 16 Omar Moreno	.05	.02
☐ 17 Dave Lopes	.10	.05
☐ 18 Dale Berra	.05	.02
☐ 19 Rance Mulliniks	.05	.02
☐ 20 Greg Luzinski	.10	.05
☐ 21 Doug Sisk	.05	.02
☐ 22 Don Robinson	.05	.02
☐ 23 Keith Moreland	.05	.02
☐ 24 Richard Dotson	.05	.02
☐ 25 Glenn Hubbard	.05	.02
☐ 26 Rod Carew	1.00	.45
☐ 27 Alan Wiggins	.05	.02
☐ 28 Frank Viola	.40	.18
☐ 29 Phil Niekro Now with Yankees	.50	.23
☐ 30 Wade Boggs	2.50	1.10
☐ 31 Dave Parker Now with Reds	.10	.05
☐ 32 Bobby Ramos	.05	.02
☐ 33 Tom Burgmeier	.05	.02
☐ 34 Eddie Milner	.05	.02
☐ 35 Don Sutton	.50	.23
☐ 36 Glenn Wilson	.05	.02
☐ 37 Mike Krukow	.05	.02
☐ 38 Dave Collins	.05	.02
☐ 39 Garth Iorg	.05	.02
☐ 40 Dusty Baker	.10	.05
☐ 41 Tony Bernazard Now with Indians	.05	.02
☐ 42 Claudell Washington	.05	.02
☐ 43 Cecil Cooper	.10	.05
☐ 44 Dan Driessen	.05	.02
☐ 45 Jerry Mumphrey	.05	.02
☐ 46 Rick Rhoden	.05	.02
☐ 47 Rudy Law	.05	.02
☐ 48 Julio Franco	.40	.18
☐ 49 Mike Norris	.05	.02
☐ 50 Chris Chambliss	.05	.02
☐ 51 Pete Falcone	.05	.02
☐ 52 Mike Marshall	.05	.02
☐ 53 Amos Otis Now with Pirates	.05	.02
☐ 54 Jesse Orosco	.05	.02
☐ 55 Dave Concepcion	.10	.05
☐ 56 Gary Allenson	.05	.02
☐ 57 Dan Schatzeder	.05	.02
☐ 58 Jerry Remy	.05	.02
☐ 59 Carney Lansford	.10	.05
☐ 60 Paul Molitor	1.00	.45
☐ 61 Chris Codiroli	.05	.02
☐ 62 Dave Hostetler	.05	.02
☐ 63 Ed VandeBerg	.05	.02
☐ 64 Ryne Sandberg	4.00	1.80
☐ 65 Kirk Gibson	.40	.18
☐ 66 Nolan Ryan	6.00	2.70
☐ 67 Gary Ward Now with Rangers	.05	.02
☐ 68 Luis Salazar	.05	.02
☐ 69 Dan Quisenberry AS	.05	.02
☐ 70 Gary Matthews	.05	.02
☐ 71 Pete O'Brien	.10	.05
☐ 72 John Wathan	.05	.02
☐ 73 Jody Davis	.05	.02
☐ 74 Kent Tekulve	.05	.02
☐ 75 Bob Forsch	.05	.02
☐ 76 Alfredo Griffin	.05	.02
☐ 77 Bryn Smith	.05	.02
☐ 78 Mike Torrez	.05	.02
☐ 79 Mike Hargrove	.10	.05
☐ 80 Steve Rogers	.05	.02
☐ 81 Bake McBride	.05	.02
☐ 82 Doug DeCinces	.05	.02
☐ 83 Richie Zisk	.05	.02
☐ 84 Randy Bush	.05	.02
☐ 85 Atlee Hammaker	.05	.02
☐ 86 Chet Lemon	.05	.02
☐ 87 Frank Pastore	.05	.02
☐ 88 Alan Trammell	.40	.18
☐ 89 Terry Francona	.05	.02
☐ 90 Pedro Guerrero	.10	.05
☐ 91 Dan Spillner	.05	.02
☐ 92 Lloyd Moseby	.05	.02
☐ 93 Bob Knepper	.05	.02
☐ 94 Ted Simmons AS	.10	.05
☐ 95 Aurelio Lopez	.05	.02
☐ 96 Bill Buckner	.10	.05
☐ 97 LaMarr Hoyt	.05	.02
☐ 98 Tom Brunansky	.10	.05
☐ 99 Ron Oester	.05	.02
☐ 100 Reggie Jackson	1.25	.55
☐ 101 Ron Davis	.05	.02
☐ 102 Ken Oberkfell	.05	.02
☐ 103 Dwayne Murphy	.05	.02
☐ 104 Jim Slaton Now with Angels	.05	.02
☐ 105 Tony Armas	.05	.02
☐ 106 Ernie Whitt	.05	.02
☐ 107 Johnnie LeMaster	.05	.02
☐ 108 Randy Moffitt	.05	.02
☐ 109 Terry Forster	.05	.02
☐ 110 Ron Guidry	.10	.05
☐ 111 Bill Virdon MG	.05	.02
☐ 112 Doyle Alexander	.05	.02
☐ 113 Lonnie Smith	.05	.02
☐ 114 Checklist 1-132	.05	.02
☐ 115 Andre Thornton	.05	.02
☐ 116 Jeff Reardon	.10	.05
☐ 117 Tom Herr	.10	.05
☐ 118 Charlie Hough	.10	.05
☐ 119 Phil Garner	.10	.05
☐ 120 Keith Hernandez	.25	.11
☐ 121 Rich Gossage Now with Padres	.25	.11
☐ 122 Ted Simmons	.10	.05
☐ 123 Butch Wynegar	.05	.02
☐ 124 Damaso Garcia	.05	.02
☐ 125 Britt Burns	.05	.02
☐ 126 Bert Blyleven	.10	.05
☐ 127 Carlton Fisk	.75	.35
☐ 128 Rick Manning	.05	.02
☐ 129 Bill Laskey	.05	.02
☐ 130 Ozzie Smith	2.00	.90
☐ 131 Bo Diaz	.05	.02
☐ 132 Tom Paciorek	.05	.02
☐ 133 Dave Rozema	.05	.02
☐ 134 Dave Stieb	.05	.02
☐ 135 Brian Downing	.05	.02
☐ 136 Rick Camp	.05	.02
☐ 137 Willie Aikens Now with Blue Jays	.05	.02
☐ 138 Charlie Moore	.05	.02
☐ 139 George Frazier Now with Indians	.05	.02
☐ 140 Storm Davis	.05	.02
☐ 141 Glenn Hoffman	.05	.02
☐ 142 Charlie Lea	.05	.02
☐ 143 Mike Vail	.05	.02
☐ 144 Steve Sax	.10	.05
☐ 145 Gary Lavelle	.05	.02
☐ 146 Gorman Thomas Now with Mariners	.05	.02
☐ 147 Dan Petry	.05	.02
☐ 148 Mark Clear	.05	.02
☐ 149 Dave Beard Now with Mariners	.05	.02
☐ 150 Dale Murphy	.50	.23
☐ 151 Steve Trout	.05	.02
☐ 152 Tony Pena	.05	.02
☐ 153 Geoff Zahn	.05	.02
☐ 154 Dave Henderson	.10	.05
☐ 155 Frank White	.10	.05
☐ 156 Dick Ruthven	.05	.02
☐ 157 Gary Gaetti	.25	.11
☐ 158 Lance Parrish	.10	.05
☐ 159 Joe Price	.05	.02
☐ 160 Mario Soto	.05	.02
☐ 161 Tug McGraw	.10	.05
☐ 162 Bob Ojeda	.05	.02
☐ 163 George Hendrick	.05	.02
☐ 164 Scott Sanderson Now with Cubs	.05	.02
☐ 165 Ken Singleton	.05	.02
☐ 166 Terry Kennedy	.05	.02
☐ 167 Gene Garber	.05	.02
☐ 168 Juan Bonilla	.05	.02
☐ 169 Larry Parrish	.05	.02
☐ 170 Jerry Reuss	.05	.02
☐ 171 John Tudor Now with Pirates	.05	.02
☐ 172 Dave Kingman	.10	.05
☐ 173 Garry Templeton	.05	.02
☐ 174 Bob Boone	.10	.05
☐ 175 Graig Nettles	.10	.05
☐ 176 Lee Smith	.50	.23
☐ 177 LaMarr Hoyt AS	.05	.02

☐ 178 Bill Krueger	.05	.02
☐ 179 Buck Martinez	.05	.02
☐ 180 Manny Trillo	.05	.02
Now with Giants		
☐ 181 Lou Whitaker AS	.10	.05
☐ 182 Darryl Strawberry	3.00	1.35
☐ 183 Neil Allen	.05	.02
☐ 184 Jim Rice AS	.10	.05
☐ 185 Sixto Lezcano	.05	.02
☐ 186 Tom Hume	.05	.02
☐ 187 Garry Maddox	.05	.02
☐ 188 Bryan Little	.05	.02
☐ 189 Jose Cruz	.10	.05
☐ 190 Ben Oglivie	.05	.02
☐ 191 Cesar Cedeno	.10	.05
☐ 192 Nick Esasky	.05	.02
☐ 193 Ken Forsch	.05	.02
☐ 194 Jim Palmer	.60	.25
☐ 195 Jack Morris	.10	.05
☐ 196 Steve Howe	.05	.02
☐ 197 Harold Baines	.10	.05
☐ 198 Bill Doran	.10	.05
☐ 199 Willie Hernandez	.10	.05
☐ 200 Andre Dawson	.50	.23
☐ 201 Bruce Kison	.05	.02
☐ 202 Bobby Cox MG	.10	.05
☐ 203 Matt Keough	.05	.02
☐ 204 Ron Guidry AS	.10	.05
☐ 205 Greg Minton	.05	.02
☐ 206 Al Holland	.05	.02
☐ 207 Luis Leal	.05	.02
☐ 208 Jose Oquendo	.05	.02
☐ 209 Leon Durham	.05	.02
☐ 210 Joe Morgan	.60	.25
Now with Athletics		
☐ 211 Lou Whitaker	.10	.05
☐ 212 George Brett	3.00	1.35
☐ 213 Bruce Hurst	.05	.02
☐ 214 Steve Carlton	1.00	.45
☐ 215 Tippy Martinez	.05	.02
☐ 216 Ken Landreaux	.05	.02
☐ 217 Alan Ashby	.05	.02
☐ 218 Dennis Eckersley	.40	.18
☐ 219 Craig McMurtry	.05	.02
☐ 220 Fernando Valenzuela	.10	.05
☐ 221 Cliff Johnson	.05	.02
☐ 222 Rick Honeycutt	.05	.02
☐ 223 George Brett AS	1.50	.70
☐ 224 Rusty Staub	.10	.05
☐ 225 Lee Mazzilli	.05	.02
☐ 226 Pat Putnam	.05	.02
☐ 227 Bob Welch	.05	.02
☐ 228 Rick Cerone	.05	.02
☐ 229 Lee Lacy	.05	.02
☐ 230 Rickey Henderson	1.50	.70
☐ 231 Gary Redus	.05	.02
☐ 232 Tim Wallach	.10	.05
☐ 233 Checklist 133-264	.05	.02
☐ 234 Rafael Ramirez	.05	.02
☐ 235 Matt Young	.05	.02
☐ 236 Ellis Valentine	.05	.02
☐ 237 John Castino	.05	.02
☐ 238 Eric Show	.05	.02
☐ 239 Bob Horner	.05	.02
☐ 240 Eddie Murray	1.25	.55
☐ 241 Billy Almon	.05	.02
☐ 242 Greg Brock	.05	.02
☐ 243 Bruce Sutter	.10	.05
☐ 244 Dwight Evans	.10	.05
☐ 245 Rick Sutcliffe	.10	.05
☐ 246 Terry Crowley	.05	.02
☐ 247 Fred Lynn	.10	.05
☐ 248 Bill Dawley	.05	.02
☐ 249 Dave Stapleton	.05	.02
☐ 250 Bill Madlock	.05	.02
☐ 251 Jim Sundberg	.10	.05
Now with Brewers		
☐ 252 Steve Yeager	.05	.02
☐ 253 Jim Wohlford	.05	.02
☐ 254 Shane Rawley	.05	.02
☐ 255 Bruce Benedict	.05	.02
☐ 256 Dave Geisel	.05	.02
Now with Mariners		
☐ 257 Julio Cruz	.05	.02
☐ 258 Luis Sanchez	.05	.02
☐ 259 Von Hayes	.05	.02
☐ 260 Scott McGregor	.05	.02
☐ 261 Tom Seaver	1.50	.70
Now with White Sox		
☐ 262 Doug Flynn	.05	.02
☐ 263 Wayne Gross	.05	.02
Now with Orioles		
☐ 264 Larry Gura	.05	.02
☐ 265 John Montefusco	.05	.02
☐ 266 Dave Winfield AS	.40	.18
☐ 267 Tim Lollar	.05	.02
☐ 268 Ron Washington	.05	.02
☐ 269 Mickey Rivers	.05	.02
☐ 270 Mookie Wilson	.10	.05
☐ 271 Moose Haas	.05	.02
☐ 272 Rick Dempsey	.10	.05
☐ 273 Dan Quisenberry	.05	.02
☐ 274 Steve Henderson	.05	.02
☐ 275 Len Matuszek	.05	.02
☐ 276 Frank Tanana	.10	.05
☐ 277 Dave Righetti	.05	.02
☐ 278 Jorge Bell	.25	.11
☐ 279 Ivan DeJesus	.05	.02
☐ 280 Floyd Bannister	.05	.02
☐ 281 Dale Murray	.05	.02
☐ 282 Andre Robertson	.05	.02
☐ 283 Rollie Fingers	.50	.23
☐ 284 Tommy John	.25	.11
☐ 285 Darrell Porter	.05	.02
☐ 286 Lary Sorensen	.05	.02
Now with Athletics		
☐ 287 Warren Cromartie	.05	.02
Now playing in Japan		
☐ 288 Jim Beattie	.05	.02
☐ 289 Blue Jays Leaders	.05	.02
Lloyd Moseby		
Dave Stieb		
(Team checklist back)		
☐ 290 Dave Dravecky	.10	.05
☐ 291 Eddie Murray AS	.60	.25
☐ 292 Greg Bargar	.05	.02
☐ 293 Tom Underwood	.05	.02
Now with Orioles		
☐ 294 U.L. Washington	.05	.02
☐ 295 Mike Flanagan	.05	.02
☐ 296 Rich Gedman	.05	.02
☐ 297 Bruce Berenyi	.05	.02
☐ 298 Jim Gantner	.10	.05
☐ 299 Bill Caudill	.05	.02
Now with Athletics		
☐ 300 Pete Rose	2.50	1.10
Now with Expos		
☐ 301 Steve Kemp	.05	.02
☐ 302 Barry Bonnell	.05	.02
Now with Mariners		
☐ 303 Joel Youngblood	.05	.02
☐ 304 Rick Langford	.05	.02
☐ 305 Roy Smalley	.05	.02
☐ 306 Ken Griffey	.10	.05
☐ 307 Al Oliver	.10	.05
☐ 308 Ron Hassey	.05	.02
☐ 309 Len Barker	.05	.02
☐ 310 Willie McGee	.25	.11
☐ 311 Jerry Koosman	.10	.05
Now with Phillies		
☐ 312 Jorge Orta	.05	.02
Now with Royals		
☐ 313 Pete Vuckovich	.05	.02
☐ 314 George Wright	.05	.02
☐ 315 Bob Grich	.10	.05
☐ 316 Jesse Barfield	.10	.05
☐ 317 Willie Upshaw	.05	.02
☐ 318 Bill Gullickson	.05	.02
☐ 319 Ray Burris	.05	.02
Now with Athletics		
☐ 320 Bob Stanley	.05	.02
☐ 321 Ray Knight	.10	.05
☐ 322 Ken Schrom	.05	.02
☐ 323 Johnny Ray	.05	.02
☐ 324 Brian Giles	.05	.02
☐ 325 Darrell Evans	.10	.05
Now with Tigers		
☐ 326 Mike Caldwell	.05	.02
☐ 327 Ruppert Jones	.05	.02
☐ 328 Chris Speier	.05	.02
☐ 329 Bobby Castillo	.05	.02
☐ 330 John Candelaria	.05	.02
☐ 331 Bucky Dent	.10	.05
☐ 332 Expos Leaders	.10	.05
Al Oliver		
Charlie Lea		
(Team checklist back)		
☐ 333 Larry Herndon	.05	.02
☐ 334 Chuck Rainey	.05	.02
☐ 335 Don Baylor	.10	.05
☐ 336 Bob James	.05	.02
☐ 337 Jim Clancy	.05	.02
☐ 338 Duane Kuiper	.05	.02
☐ 339 Roy Lee Jackson	.05	.02
☐ 340 Hal McRae	.10	.05
☐ 341 Larry McWilliams	.05	.02
☐ 342 Tim Foli	.05	.02
Now with Yankees		
☐ 343 Fergie Jenkins	.50	.23
☐ 344 Dickie Thon	.05	.02
☐ 345 Kent Hrbek	.25	.11
☐ 346 Larry Bowa	.10	.05
☐ 347 Buddy Bell	.10	.05
☐ 348 Toby Harrah	.05	.02
Now with Yankees		
☐ 349 Dan Ford	.05	.02
☐ 350 George Foster	.10	.05
☐ 351 Lou Piniella	.10	.05
☐ 352 Dave Stewart	.40	.18
☐ 353 Mike Easler	.05	.02
Now with Red Sox		
☐ 354 Jeff Burroughs	.05	.02
☐ 355 Jason Thompson	.05	.02
☐ 356 Glenn Abbott	.05	.02
☐ 357 Ron Cey	.10	.05
☐ 358 Bob Dernier	.05	.02
☐ 359 Jim Acker	.05	.02
☐ 360 Willie Randolph	.10	.05
☐ 361 Mike Schmidt	1.50	.70
☐ 362 David Green	.05	.02
☐ 363 Cal Ripken	6.00	2.70
☐ 364 Jim Rice	.10	.05
☐ 365 Steve Bedrosian	.05	.02
☐ 366 Gary Carter	.50	.23
☐ 367 Chili Davis	.10	.05
☐ 368 Hubie Brooks	.05	.02
☐ 369 Steve McCatty	.05	.02
☐ 370 Tim Raines	.40	.18
☐ 371 Joaquin Andujar	.05	.02
☐ 372 Gary Roenicke	.05	.02
☐ 373 Ron Kittle	.05	.02
☐ 374 Rich Dauer	.05	.02
☐ 375 Dennis Leonard	.05	.02
☐ 376 Rick Burleson	.05	.02
☐ 377 Eric Rasmussen	.05	.02
☐ 378 Dave Winfield	.75	.35
☐ 379 Checklist 265-396	.05	.02
☐ 380 Steve Garvey	.25	.11
☐ 381 Jack Clark	.10	.05
☐ 382 Odell Jones	.05	.02
☐ 383 Terry Puhl	.05	.02
☐ 384 Joe Niekro	.10	.05
☐ 385 Tony Perez	.40	.18
Now with Reds		
☐ 386 George Hendrick AS	.05	.02
☐ 387 Johnny Ray AS	.05	.02
☐ 388 Mike Schmidt AS	.75	.35
☐ 389 Ozzie Smith AS	1.00	.45
☐ 390 Tim Raines AS	.25	.11
☐ 391 Dale Murphy AS	.25	.11
☐ 392 Andre Dawson AS	.25	.11
☐ 393 Gary Carter AS	.10	.05
☐ 394 Steve Rogers AS	.05	.02
☐ 395 Steve Carlton AS	.50	.23
☐ 396 Jesse Orosco AS	.05	.02

1985 O-Pee-Chee

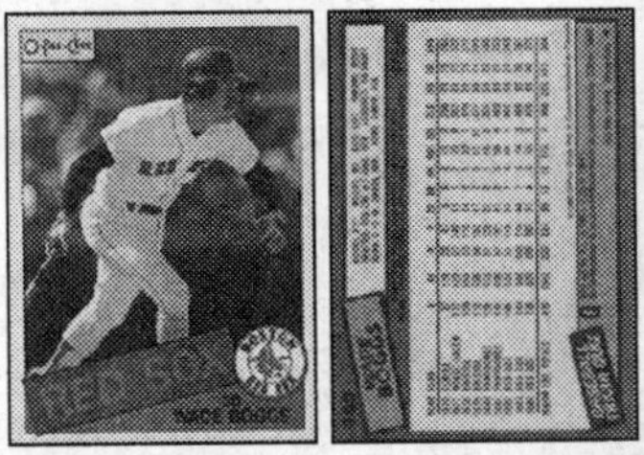

This set is an abridgement of the 1985 Topps set. The 396 standard-size cards comprising the 1985 O-Pee-Chee set differ from the cards of the 1985 Topps set by having a higher ratio of cards of players from the two Canadian teams, a practice begun by O-Pee-Chee in 1977 and continued to 1988. The set contains virtually the same pictures for the players also featured in the 1985 Topps issue. The fronts feature white-bordered color player photos. The player's name, position and team name and logo appear at the bottom of the photo. The green and white horizontal backs carry the player's name and biography at the top. The player's major league statistics and bilingual profile follow below. A bilingual trivia question and answer round out the back. The O-Pee-Chee logo appears on the front of every card. The set features Dwight Gooden and Kirby Puckett in their Rookie Card seasons.

	NRMT	VG-E
COMPLETE SET (396)	25.00	11.00
COMMON CARD (1-396)	.05	.02
☐ 1 Tom Seaver	.40	.18
☐ 2 Gary Lavelle	.05	.02
Traded to Blue Jays 1-26-85		
☐ 3 Tim Wallach	.10	.05
☐ 4 Jim Wohlford	.05	.02
☐ 5 Jeff Robinson	.05	.02

☐ 6 Willie Wilson .05 .02
☐ 7 Cliff Johnson .05 .02
Free Agent with Rangers 12-20-84
☐ 8 Willie Randolph .10 .05
☐ 9 Larry Herndon .05 .02
☐ 10 Kirby Puckett 10.00 4.50
☐ 11 Mookie Wilson .10 .05
☐ 12 Dave Lopes .10 .05
Traded to Cubs 8-81-84
☐ 13 Tim Lollar .05 .02
Traded to White Sox 12-6-84
☐ 14 Chris Bando .05 .02
☐ 15 Jerry Koosman .05 .02
☐ 16 Bobby Meacham .05 .02
☐ 17 Mike Scott .05 .02
☐ 18 Rich Gedman .05 .02
☐ 19 George Frazier .05 .02
☐ 20 Chet Lemon .05 .02
☐ 21 Dave Concepcion .10 .05
☐ 22 Jason Thompson .05 .02
☐ 23 Bret Saberhagen .40 .18
☐ 24 Jesse Barfield .05 .02
☐ 25 Steve Bedrosian .05 .02
☐ 26 Roy Smalley .05 .02
Traded to Twins 2-19-85
☐ 27 Bruce Berenyi .05 .02
☐ 28 Butch Wynegar .05 .02
☐ 29 Alan Ashby .05 .02
☐ 30 Cal Ripken 4.00 1.80
☐ 31 Luis Leal .05 .02
☐ 32 Dave Dravecky .10 .05
☐ 33 Tito Landrum .05 .02
☐ 34 Pedro Guerrero .10 .05
☐ 35 Graig Nettles .10 .05
☐ 36 Fred Breining .05 .02
☐ 37 Roy Lee Jackson .05 .02
☐ 38 Steve Henderson .05 .02
☐ 39 Gary Pettis UER .05 .02
Photo actually
Lynn Pettis
☐ 40 Phil Niekro .50 .23
☐ 41 Dwight Gooden 2.00 .90
☐ 42 Luis Sanchez .05 .02
☐ 43 Lee Smith .30 .14
☐ 44 Dickie Thon .05 .02
☐ 45 Greg Minton .05 .02
☐ 46 Mike Flanagan .05 .02
☐ 47 Bud Black .05 .02
☐ 48 Tony Fernandez .10 .05
☐ 49 Carlton Fisk .40 .18
☐ 50 John Candelaria .05 .02
☐ 51 Bob Watson .10 .05
Announced his Retirement
☐ 52 Rick Leach .05 .02
☐ 53 Rick Rhoden .05 .02
☐ 54 Cesar Cedeno .10 .05
☐ 55 Frank Tanana .05 .02
☐ 56 Larry Bowa .10 .05
☐ 57 Willie McGee .10 .05
☐ 58 Rich Dauer .05 .02
☐ 59 Jorge Bell .10 .05
☐ 60 George Hendrick .05 .02
Traded to Pirates 12-12-84
☐ 61 Donnie Moore .05 .02
Drafted by Angels 1-24-85
☐ 62 Mike Ramsey .05 .02
☐ 63 Nolan Ryan 3.00 1.35
☐ 64 Mark Bailey .05 .02
☐ 65 Bill Buckner .10 .05
☐ 66 Jerry Reuss .05 .02
☐ 67 Mike Schmidt 1.00 .45
☐ 68 Von Hayes .05 .02
☐ 69 Phil Bradley .10 .05
☐ 70 Don Baylor .10 .05
☐ 71 Julio Cruz .05 .02
☐ 72 Rick Sutcliffe .05 .02
☐ 73 Storm Davis .05 .02
☐ 74 Mike Krukow .05 .02
☐ 75 Willie Upshaw .05 .02
☐ 76 Craig Lefferts .05 .02
☐ 77 Lloyd Moseby .05 .02
☐ 78 Ron Davis .05 .02
☐ 79 Rick Mahler .05 .02
☐ 80 Keith Hernandez .10 .05
☐ 81 Vance Law .05 .02
Traded to Expos 12-7-84
☐ 82 Joe Price .05 .02
☐ 83 Dennis Lamp .05 .02
☐ 84 Gary Ward .05 .02
☐ 85 Mike Marshall .05 .02
☐ 86 Marvell Wynne .05 .02
☐ 87 David Green .05 .02
☐ 88 Bryn Smith .05 .02
☐ 89 Sixto Lezcano .05 .02
Free Agent with Pirates 1-26-85
☐ 90 Rich Gossage .10 .05
☐ 91 Jeff Burroughs .05 .02
Purchased by Blue Jays 12-22-84
☐ 92 Bobby Brown .05 .02
☐ 93 Oscar Gamble .05 .02
☐ 94 Rick Dempsey .10 .05
☐ 95 Jose Cruz .10 .05
☐ 96 Johnny Ray .05 .02
☐ 97 Joel Youngblood .05 .02
☐ 98 Eddie Whitson .05 .02
Free Agent with 12-28-84
☐ 99 Milt Wilcox .05 .02
☐ 100 George Brett 3.00 1.35
☐ 101 Jim Acker .05 .02
☐ 102 Jim Sundberg .05 .02
Traded to Royals 1-18-85
☐ 103 Ozzie Virgil .05 .02
☐ 104 Mike Fitzgerald .05 .02
Traded to Expos 12-10-84
☐ 105 Ron Kittle .05 .02
☐ 106 Pascual Perez .05 .02
☐ 107 Barry Bonnell .05 .02
☐ 108 Lou Whitaker .30 .14
☐ 109 Gary Roenicke .05 .02
☐ 110 Alejandro Pena .05 .02
☐ 111 Doug DeCinces .05 .02
☐ 112 Doug Flynn .05 .02
☐ 113 Tom Herr .10 .05
☐ 114 Bob James .05 .02
Traded to White Sox 12-7-84
☐ 115 Rickey Henderson 1.25 .55
Traded to Yankees 12-8-84
☐ 116 Pete Rose .75 .35
☐ 117 Greg Gross .05 .02
☐ 118 Eric Show .05 .02
☐ 119 Buck Martinez .05 .02
☐ 120 Steve Kemp .05 .02
Traded to Pirates 12-20-84
☐ 121 Checklist 1-132 .05 .02
☐ 122 Tom Brunansky .10 .05
☐ 123 Dave Kingman .10 .05
☐ 124 Garry Templeton .05 .02
☐ 125 Kent Tekulve .05 .02
☐ 126 Darryl Strawberry .40 .18
☐ 127 Mark Gubicza .10 .05
☐ 128 Ernie Whitt .05 .02
☐ 129 Don Robinson .05 .02
☐ 130 Al Oliver .10 .05
Traded to Dodgers 2-4-85
☐ 131 Mario Soto .05 .02
☐ 132 Jeff Leonard .05 .02
☐ 133 Andre Dawson .40 .18
☐ 134 Bruce Hurst .05 .02
☐ 135 Bobby Cox MG .10 .05
(Team checklist back)
☐ 136 Matt Young .05 .02
☐ 137 Bob Forsch .05 .02
☐ 138 Ron Darling .10 .05
☐ 139 Steve Trout .05 .02
☐ 140 Geoff Zahn .05 .02
☐ 141 Ken Forsch .05 .02
☐ 142 Jerry Willard .05 .02
☐ 143 Bill Gullickson .05 .02
☐ 144 Mike Mason .05 .02
☐ 145 Alvin Davis .10 .05
☐ 146 Gary Redus .05 .02
☐ 147 Willie Aikens .05 .02
☐ 148 Steve Yeager .05 .02
☐ 149 Dickie Noles .05 .02
☐ 150 Jim Rice .10 .05
☐ 151 Moose Haas .05 .02
☐ 152 Steve Balboni .05 .02
☐ 153 Frank LaCorte .05 .02
☐ 154 Argenis Salazar .05 .02
Drafted by Cardinals 1-24-85
☐ 155 Bob Grich .10 .05
☐ 156 Craig Reynolds .05 .02
☐ 157 Bill Madlock .05 .02
☐ 158 Pat Tabler .05 .02
☐ 159 Don Slaught .05 .02
Traded to Rangers 1-18-85
☐ 160 Lance Parrish .10 .05
☐ 161 Ken Schrom .05 .02
☐ 162 Wally Backman .05 .02
☐ 163 Dennis Eckersley .30 .14
☐ 164 Dave Collins .05 .02
Traded to A's 12-8-84
☐ 165 Dusty Baker .10 .05
☐ 166 Claudell Washington .05 .02
☐ 167 Rick Camp .05 .02
☐ 168 Garth Iorg .05 .02
☐ 169 Shane Rawley .05 .02
☐ 170 George Foster .10 .05
☐ 171 Tony Bernazard .05 .02
☐ 172 Don Sutton .40 .18
Traded to A's 12-8-84
☐ 173 Jerry Remy .05 .02
☐ 174 Rick Honeycutt .05 .02
☐ 175 Dave Parker .10 .05
☐ 176 Buddy Bell .10 .05
☐ 177 Steve Garvey .20 .09
☐ 178 Miguel Dilone .05 .02
☐ 179 Tommy John .20 .09
☐ 180 Dave Winfield .75 .35
☐ 181 Alan Trammell .30 .14
☐ 182 Rollie Fingers .50 .23
☐ 183 Larry McWilliams .05 .02
☐ 184 Carmen Castillo .05 .02
☐ 185 Al Holland .05 .02
☐ 186 Jerry Mumphrey .05 .02
☐ 187 Chris Chambliss .05 .02
☐ 188 Jim Clancy .05 .02
☐ 189 Glenn Wilson .05 .02
☐ 190 Rusty Staub .10 .05
☐ 191 Ozzie Smith 2.00 .90
☐ 192 Howard Johnson .10 .05
Traded to Mets 12-7-84
☐ 193 Jimmy Key .60 .25
☐ 194 Terry Kennedy .05 .02
☐ 195 Glenn Hubbard .05 .02
☐ 196 Pete O'Brien .05 .02
☐ 197 Keith Moreland .05 .02
☐ 198 Eddie Milner .05 .02
☐ 199 Dave Engle .05 .02
☐ 200 Reggie Jackson .60 .25
☐ 201 Burt Hooton .05 .02
Free Agent with Rangers 1-3-85
☐ 202 Gorman Thomas .05 .02
☐ 203 Larry Parrish .05 .02
☐ 204 Bob Stanley .05 .02
☐ 205 Steve Rogers .05 .02
☐ 206 Phil Garner .10 .05
☐ 207 Ed VandeBerg .05 .02
☐ 208 Jack Clark .10 .05
Traded to Cardinals 2-1-85
☐ 209 Bill Campbell .05 .02
☐ 210 Gary Matthews .05 .02
☐ 211 Dave Palmer .05 .02
☐ 212 Tony Perez .30 .14
☐ 213 Sammy Stewart .05 .02
☐ 214 John Tudor .05 .02
Traded to Cardinals 12-12-84
☐ 215 Bob Brenly .05 .02
☐ 216 Jim Gantner .05 .02
☐ 217 Bryan Clark .05 .02
☐ 218 Doyle Alexander .05 .02
☐ 219 Bo Diaz .05 .02
☐ 220 Fred Lynn .10 .05
Free Agent with Orioles 12-11-84
☐ 221 Eddie Murray .75 .35
☐ 222 Hubie Brooks .05 .02
Traded to Expos 12-10-84
☐ 223 Tom Hume .05 .02
☐ 224 Al Cowens .05 .02
☐ 225 Mike Boddicker .05 .02
☐ 226 Len Matuszek .05 .02
☐ 227 Danny Darwin .05 .02
Traded to Brewers 1-18-85
☐ 228 Scott McGregor .05 .02
☐ 229 Dave LaPoint .05 .02
Traded to Giants 2-1-85
☐ 230 Gary Carter .40 .18
Traded to Mets 12-10-84
☐ 231 Joaquin Andujar .05 .02
☐ 232 Rafael Ramirez .05 .02
☐ 233 Wayne Gross .05 .02
☐ 234 Neil Allen .05 .02
☐ 235 Garry Maddox .05 .02
☐ 236 Mark Thurmond .05 .02
☐ 237 Julio Franco .20 .09
☐ 238 Ray Burris .05 .02
Traded to Brewers 12-8-84
☐ 239 Tim Teufel .05 .02
☐ 240 Dave Stieb .05 .02
☐ 241 Brett Butler .10 .05
☐ 242 Greg Brock .05 .02
☐ 243 Barbaro Garbey .05 .02
☐ 244 Greg Walker .05 .02
☐ 245 Chili Davis .10 .05
☐ 246 Darrell Porter .05 .02
☐ 247 Tippy Martinez .05 .02
☐ 248 Terry Forster .05 .02
☐ 249 Harold Baines .10 .05
☐ 250 Jesse Orosco .05 .02
☐ 251 Brad Gulden .05 .02
☐ 252 Mike Hargrove .10 .05
☐ 253 Nick Esasky .05 .02
☐ 254 Frank Williams .05 .02
☐ 255 Lonnie Smith .05 .02
☐ 256 Daryl Sconiers .05 .02
☐ 257 Bryan Little .05 .02
Traded to White Sox 12-7-84
☐ 258 Terry Francona .05 .02
☐ 259 Mark Langston .40 .18
☐ 260 Dave Righetti .10 .05
☐ 261 Checklist 133-264 .05 .02
☐ 262 Bob Horner .05 .02

☐ 263 Mel Hall	.05	.02
☐ 264 John Shelby	.05	.02
☐ 265 Juan Samuel	.05	.02
☐ 266 Frank Viola	.10	.05
☐ 267 Jim Fanning MG	.05	.02
Now Vice President Player, Development and Scouting		
☐ 268 Dick Ruthven	.05	.02
☐ 269 Bobby Ramos	.05	.02
☐ 270 Dan Quisenberry	.05	.02
☐ 271 Dwight Evans	.10	.05
☐ 272 Andre Thornton	.05	.02
☐ 273 Orel Hershiser	1.00	.45
☐ 274 Ray Knight	.10	.05
☐ 275 Bill Caudill	.05	.02
Traded to Blue Jays 12-8-84		
☐ 276 Charlie Hough	.10	.05
☐ 277 Tim Raines	.20	.09
☐ 278 Mike Squires	.05	.02
☐ 279 Alex Trevino	.05	.02
☐ 280 Ron Romanick	.05	.02
☐ 281 Tom Niedenfuer	.05	.02
☐ 282 Mike Stenhouse	.05	.02
Traded to Twins 1-9-85		
☐ 283 Terry Puhl	.05	.02
☐ 284 Hal McRae	.10	.05
☐ 285 Dan Driessen	.05	.02
☐ 286 Rudy Law	.05	.02
☐ 287 Walt Terrell	.05	.02
Traded to Tigers 12-7-84		
☐ 288 Jeff Kunkel	.05	.02
☐ 289 Bob Knepper	.05	.02
☐ 290 Cecil Cooper	.10	.05
☐ 291 Bob Welch	.05	.02
☐ 292 Frank Pastore	.05	.02
☐ 293 Dan Schatzeder	.05	.02
☐ 294 Tom Nieto	.05	.02
☐ 295 Joe Niekro	.05	.02
☐ 296 Ryne Sandberg	2.00	.90
☐ 297 Gary Lucas	.05	.02
☐ 298 John Castino	.05	.02
☐ 299 Bill Doran	.05	.02
☐ 300 Rod Carew	.50	.23
☐ 301 John Montefusco	.05	.02
☐ 302 Johnnie LeMaster	.05	.02
☐ 303 Jim Beattie	.05	.02
☐ 304 Gary Gaetti	.10	.05
☐ 305 Dale Berra	.05	.02
Traded to Yankees 12-20-84		
☐ 306 Rick Reuschel	.05	.02
☐ 307 Ken Oberkfell	.05	.02
☐ 308 Kent Hrbek	.20	.09
☐ 309 Mike Witt	.05	.02
☐ 310 Manny Trillo	.05	.02
☐ 311 Jim Gott	.05	.02
Traded to Giants 1-26-85		
☐ 312 LaMarr Hoyt	.05	.02
Traded to Padres 12-6-84		
☐ 313 Dave Schmidt	.05	.02
☐ 314 Ron Oester	.05	.02
☐ 315 Doug Sisk	.05	.02
☐ 316 John Lowenstein	.05	.02
☐ 317 Derrel Thomas	.05	.02
Traded to Angels 9-6-84		
☐ 318 Ted Simmons	.10	.05
☐ 319 Darrell Evans	.10	.05
☐ 320 Dale Murphy	.20	.09
☐ 321 Ricky Horton	.05	.02
☐ 322 Ken Phelps	.05	.02
☐ 323 Lee Mazzilli	.05	.02
☐ 324 Don Mattingly	4.00	1.80
☐ 325 John Denny	.05	.02
☐ 326 Ken Singleton	.05	.02
☐ 327 Brook Jacoby	.05	.02
☐ 328 Greg Luzinski	.10	.05
Announced his Retirement		
☐ 329 Bob Ojeda	.05	.02
☐ 330 Leon Durham	.05	.02
☐ 331 Bill Laskey	.05	.02
☐ 332 Ben Oglivie	.05	.02
☐ 333 Willie Hernandez	.05	.02
☐ 334 Bob Dernier	.05	.02
☐ 335 Bruce Benedict	.05	.02
☐ 336 Rance Mulliniks	.05	.02
☐ 337 Rick Cerone	.05	.02
Traded to Braves 12-6-84		
☐ 338 Britt Burns	.05	.02
☐ 339 Danny Heep	.05	.02
☐ 340 Robin Yount	.75	.35
☐ 341 Andy Van Slyke	.30	.14
☐ 342 Curt Wilkerson	.05	.02
☐ 343 Bill Russell	.05	.02
☐ 344 Dave Henderson	.05	.02
☐ 345 Charlie Lea	.05	.02
☐ 346 Terry Pendleton	.60	.25
☐ 347 Carney Lansford	.05	.02
☐ 348 Bob Boone	.10	.05
☐ 349 Mike Easler	.05	.02
☐ 350 Wade Boggs	1.00	.45
☐ 351 Atlee Hammaker	.05	.02
☐ 352 Joe Morgan	.50	.23
☐ 353 Damaso Garcia	.05	.02
☐ 354 Floyd Bannister	.05	.02
☐ 355 Bert Blyleven	.10	.05
☐ 356 John Butcher	.05	.02
☐ 357 Fernando Valenzuela	.10	.05
☐ 358 Tony Pena	.05	.02
☐ 359 Mike Smithson	.05	.02
☐ 360 Steve Carlton	.40	.18
☐ 361 Alfredo Griffin	.05	.02
Traded to A's 12-8-84		
☐ 362 Craig McMurtry	.05	.02
☐ 363 Bill Dawley	.05	.02
☐ 364 Richard Dotson	.05	.02
☐ 365 Carmelo Martinez	.05	.02
☐ 366 Ron Cey	.10	.05
☐ 367 Tony Scott	.05	.02
☐ 368 Dave Bergman	.05	.02
☐ 369 Steve Sax	.05	.02
☐ 370 Bruce Sutter	.10	.05
☐ 371 Mickey Rivers	.05	.02
☐ 372 Kirk Gibson	.10	.05
☐ 373 Scott Sanderson	.05	.02
☐ 374 Brian Downing	.05	.02
☐ 375 Jeff Reardon	.10	.05
☐ 376 Frank DiPino	.05	.02
☐ 377 Checkist 265-396	.05	.02
☐ 378 Alan Wiggins	.05	.02
☐ 379 Charles Hudson	.05	.02
☐ 380 Ken Griffey	.10	.05
☐ 381 Tom Paciorek	.05	.02
☐ 382 Jack Morris	.10	.05
☐ 383 Tony Gwynn	3.00	1.35
☐ 384 Jody Davis	.05	.02
☐ 385 Jose DeLeon	.05	.02
☐ 386 Bob Kearney	.05	.02
☐ 387 George Wright	.05	.02
☐ 388 Ron Guidry	.10	.05
☐ 389 Rick Manning	.05	.02
☐ 390 Sid Fernandez	.10	.05
☐ 391 Bruce Bochte	.05	.02
☐ 392 Dan Petry	.05	.02
☐ 393 Tim Stoddard	.05	.02
Free Agent with Padres 1-2-85		
☐ 394 Tony Armas	.05	.02
☐ 395 Paul Molitor	.75	.35
☐ 396 Mike Heath	.05	.02

1985 O-Pee-Chee Posters

The 24 full-color posters in the 1985 O-Pee-Chee poster insert set were inserted one per regular wax pack and feature players of the Montreal Expos (numbered 1-12) and the Toronto Blue Jays (numbered 13-24). These posters are typically found with two folds and measure approximately 4 7/8" by 6 7/8". The posters are blank-backed and are numbered at the bottom in French and English. A distinctive blue (Blue Jays) or red (Expos) border surrounds the player photo.

	NRMT	VG-E
COMPLETE SET (24)	6.00	2.70
COMMON CARD (1-24)	.25	.11

☐ 1 Mike Fitzgerald	.25	.11
☐ 2 Dan Driessen	.25	.11
☐ 3 Dave Palmer	.25	.11
☐ 4 U.L. Washington	.25	.11
☐ 5 Hubie Brooks	.25	.11
☐ 6 Tim Wallach	.50	.23
☐ 7 Tim Raines	.75	.35
☐ 8 Herm Winningham	.25	.11
☐ 9 Andre Dawson	1.50	.70
☐ 10 Charlie Lea	.25	.11
☐ 11 Steve Rogers	.25	.11
☐ 12 Jeff Reardon	.50	.23
☐ 13 Buck Martinez	.25	.11
☐ 14 Willie Upshaw	.25	.11
☐ 15 Damaso Garcia UER (Misspelled Domaso)	.25	.11
☐ 16 Tony Fernandez	.75	.35
☐ 17 Rance Mulliniks	.25	.11
☐ 18 George Bell	.50	.23
☐ 19 Lloyd Moseby	.25	.11
☐ 20 Jesse Barfield	.50	.23
☐ 21 Doyle Alexander	.25	.11
☐ 22 Dave Stieb	.50	.23
☐ 23 Bill Caudill	.25	.11
☐ 24 Gary Lavelle	.25	.11

1986 O-Pee-Chee

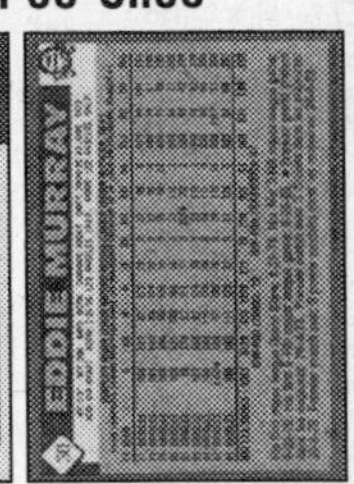

This set is an abridgement of the 1986 Topps set. The 396 standard-size cards comprising the 1986 O-Pee-Chee set differ from the cards of the 1986 Topps set by having a higher ratio of cards of players from the two Canadian teams, a practice begun by O-Pee-Chee in 1977 and continued to 1988. The fronts feature black-and white-bordered color player photos. The player's name appears within the white margin at the bottom. His team name appears within the black margin at the top and his position appears within a colored circle at the photo's lower left. The red horizontal backs carry the player's name and biography at the top. The player's major league statistics follow below. Some backs also have bilingual career highlights, some have bilingual baseball facts and still others have neither. The cards are numbered on the back. The asterisked cards have an extra line on the front inside the picture area indicating team change. The O-Pee-Chee logo appears on the front of every card.

	MINT	NRMT
COMPLETE SET (396)	12.00	5.50
COMMON CARD (1-396)	.05	.02

☐ 1 Pete Rose	1.00	.45
☐ 2 Ken Landreaux	.05	.02
☐ 3 Rob Picciolo	.05	.02
☐ 4 Steve Garvey	.15	.07
☐ 5 Andy Hawkins	.05	.02
☐ 6 Rudy Law	.05	.02
☐ 7 Lonnie Smith	.05	.02
☐ 8 Dwayne Murphy	.05	.02
☐ 9 Moose Haas	.05	.02
☐ 10 Tony Gwynn	1.25	.55
☐ 11 Bob Ojeda	.05	.02
Now with Mets		
☐ 12 Jose Uribe	.05	.02
☐ 13 Bob Kearney	.05	.02
☐ 14 Julio Cruz	.05	.02
☐ 15 Eddie Whitson	.05	.02
☐ 16 Rick Schu	.05	.02
☐ 17 Mike Stenhouse	.05	.02
Now with Red Sox		
☐ 18 Lou Thornton	.05	.02
☐ 19 Ryne Sandberg	.75	.35
☐ 20 Lou Whitaker	.10	.05
☐ 21 Mark Brouhard	.05	.02
☐ 22 Gary Lavelle	.05	.02
☐ 23 Manny Lee	.05	.02
☐ 24 Don Slaught	.05	.02
☐ 25 Willie Wilson	.05	.02
☐ 26 Mike Marshall	.05	.02
☐ 27 Ray Knight	.10	.05
☐ 28 Mario Soto	.05	.02
☐ 29 Dave Anderson	.05	.02
☐ 30 Eddie Murray	.75	.35
☐ 31 Dusty Baker	.10	.05
☐ 32 Steve Yeager	.05	.02
Now with Mariners		
☐ 33 Andy Van Slyke	.10	.05
☐ 34 Dave Righetti	.05	.02
☐ 35 Jeff Reardon	.10	.05
☐ 36 Burt Hooton	.05	.02
☐ 37 Johnny Ray	.05	.02
☐ 38 Glenn Hoffman	.05	.02
☐ 39 Rick Mahler	.05	.02
☐ 40 Ken Griffey	.10	.05
☐ 41 Brad Wellman	.05	.02
☐ 42 Joe Hesketh	.05	.02
☐ 43 Mark Salas	.05	.02
☐ 44 Jorge Orta	.05	.02

☐ 45 Damaso Garcia .05 .02
☐ 46 Jim Acker .05 .02
☐ 47 Bill Madlock .05 .02
☐ 48 Bill Almon .05 .02
☐ 49 Rick Manning .05 .02
☐ 50 Dan Quisenberry .05 .02
☐ 51 Jim Gantner .05 .02
☐ 52 Kevin Bass .05 .02
☐ 53 Len Dykstra .75 .35
☐ 54 John Franco .15 .07
☐ 55 Fred Lynn .10 .05
☐ 56 Jim Morrison .05 .02
☐ 57 Bill Doran .05 .02
☐ 58 Leon Durham .05 .02
☐ 59 Andre Thornton .05 .02
☐ 60 Dwight Evans .10 .05
☐ 61 Larry Herndon .05 .02
☐ 62 Bob Boone .10 .05
☐ 63 Kent Hrbek .15 .07
☐ 64 Floyd Bannister .05 .02
☐ 65 Harold Baines .15 .07
☐ 66 Pat Tabler .05 .02
☐ 67 Carmelo Martinez .05 .02
☐ 68 Ed Lynch .05 .02
☐ 69 George Foster .10 .05
☐ 70 Dave Winfield .40 .18
☐ 71 Ken Schrom .05 .02
Now with Indians
☐ 72 Toby Harrah .05 .02
☐ 73 Jackie Gutierrez .05 .02
Now with Orioles
☐ 74 Rance Mulliniks .05 .02
☐ 75 Jose DeLeon .05 .02
☐ 76 Ron Romanick .05 .02
☐ 77 Charlie Leibrandt .05 .02
☐ 78 Bruce Benedict .05 .02
☐ 79 Dave Schmidt .05 .02
Now with White Sox
☐ 80 Darryl Strawberry .15 .07
☐ 81 Wayne Krenchicki .05 .02
☐ 82 Tippy Martinez .05 .02
☐ 83 Phil Garner .10 .05
☐ 84 Darrell Porter .05 .02
Now with Rangers
☐ 85 Tony Perez .25 .11
Eric Davis also
shown in photo
☐ 86 Tom Waddell .05 .02
☐ 87 Tim Hulett .05 .02
☐ 88 Barbaro Garbey .05 .02
Now with A's
☐ 89 Randy St. Claire .05 .02
☐ 90 Garry Templeton .05 .02
☐ 91 Tim Teufel .05 .02
Now with Mets
☐ 92 Al Cowens .05 .02
☐ 93 Scot Thompson .05 .02
☐ 94 Tom Herr .05 .02
☐ 95 Ozzie Virgil .05 .02
Now with Braves
☐ 96 Jose Cruz .05 .02
☐ 97 Gary Gaetti .10 .05
☐ 98 Roger Clemens 2.00 .90
☐ 99 Vance Law .05 .02
☐ 100 Nolan Ryan 1.50 .70
☐ 101 Mike Smithson .05 .02
☐ 102 Rafael Santana .05 .02
☐ 103 Darrell Evans .10 .05
☐ 104 Rich Gossage .10 .05
☐ 105 Gary Ward .05 .02
☐ 106 Jim Gott .05 .02
☐ 107 Rafael Ramirez .05 .02
☐ 108 Ted Power .05 .02
☐ 109 Ron Guidry .10 .05
☐ 110 Scott McGregor .05 .02
☐ 111 Mike Scioscia .05 .02
☐ 112 Glenn Hubbard .05 .02
☐ 113 U.L. Washington .05 .02
☐ 114 Al Oliver .10 .05
☐ 115 Jay Howell .05 .02
☐ 116 Brook Jacoby .05 .02
☐ 117 Willie McGee .10 .05
☐ 118 Jerry Royster .05 .02
☐ 119 Barry Bonnell .05 .02
☐ 120 Steve Carlton .30 .14
☐ 121 Alfredo Griffin .05 .02
☐ 122 David Green .05 .02
Now with Brewers
☐ 123 Greg Walker .05 .02
☐ 124 Frank Tanana .05 .02
☐ 125 Dave Lopes .10 .05
☐ 126 Mike Krukow .05 .02
☐ 127 Jack Howell .05 .02
☐ 128 Greg Harris .05 .02
☐ 129 Herm Winningham .05 .02
☐ 130 Alan Trammell .15 .07
☐ 131 Checklist 1-132 .05 .02
☐ 132 Razor Shines .05 .02
☐ 133 Bruce Sutter .10 .05
☐ 134 Carney Lansford .05 .02
☐ 135 Joe Niekro .05 .02
☐ 136 Ernie Whitt .05 .02
☐ 137 Charlie Moore .05 .02
☐ 138 Mel Hall .05 .02
☐ 139 Roger McDowell .05 .02
☐ 140 John Candelaria .05 .02
☐ 141 Bob Rodgers MG .05 .02
Team checklist back
☐ 142 Manny Trillo .05 .02
Now with Cubs
☐ 143 Dave Palmer .10 .05
Now with Braves
☐ 144 Robin Yount .30 .14
☐ 145 Pedro Guerrero .10 .05
☐ 146 Von Hayes .05 .02
☐ 147 Lance Parrish .10 .05
☐ 148 Mike Heath .05 .02
Now with Cardinals
☐ 149 Brett Butler .10 .05
☐ 150 Joaquin Andujar .05 .02
Now with A's
☐ 151 Graig Nettles .10 .05
☐ 152 Pete Vuckovich .05 .02
☐ 153 Jason Thompson .05 .02
☐ 154 Bert Roberge .05 .02
☐ 155 Bob Grich .10 .05
☐ 156 Roy Smalley .05 .02
☐ 157 Ron Hassey .05 .02
☐ 158 Bob Stanley .05 .02
☐ 159 Orel Hershiser .40 .18
☐ 160 Chet Lemon .05 .02
☐ 161 Terry Puhl .05 .02
☐ 162 Dave LaPoint .05 .02
Now with Tigers
☐ 163 Onix Concepcion .05 .02
☐ 164 Steve Balboni .05 .02
☐ 165 Mike Davis .05 .02
☐ 166 Dickie Thon .05 .02
☐ 167 Zane Smith .05 .02
☐ 168 Jeff Burroughs .05 .02
☐ 169 Alex Trevino .05 .02
Now with Dodgers
☐ 170 Gary Carter .15 .07
☐ 171 Tito Landrum .05 .02
☐ 172 Sammy Stewart .05 .02
Now with Red Sox
☐ 173 Wayne Gross .05 .02
☐ 174 Britt Burns .05 .02
Now with Yankees
☐ 175 Steve Sax .05 .02
☐ 176 Jody Davis .05 .02
☐ 177 Joel Youngblood .05 .02
☐ 178 Fernando Valenzuela .10 .05
☐ 179 Storm Davis .05 .02
☐ 180 Don Mattingly 1.25 .55
☐ 181 Steve Bedrosian .05 .02
Now with Phillies
☐ 182 Jesse Orosco .05 .02
☐ 183 Gary Roenicke .05 .02
Now with Yankees
☐ 184 Don Baylor .10 .05
☐ 185 Rollie Fingers .30 .14
☐ 186 Ruppert Jones .05 .02
☐ 187 Scott Fletcher .05 .02
Now with Rangers
☐ 188 Bob Dernier .05 .02
☐ 189 Mike Mason .05 .02
☐ 190 George Hendrick .05 .02
☐ 191 Wally Backman .05 .02
☐ 192 Oddibe McDowell .05 .02
☐ 193 Bruce Hurst .05 .02
☐ 194 Ron Cey .10 .05
☐ 195 Dave Concepcion .10 .05
☐ 196 Doyle Alexander .05 .02
☐ 197 Dale Murray .05 .02
☐ 198 Mark Langston .15 .07
☐ 199 Dennis Eckersley .25 .11
☐ 200 Mike Schmidt .40 .18
☐ 201 Nick Esasky .05 .02
☐ 202 Ken Dayley .05 .02
☐ 203 Rick Cerone .05 .02
☐ 204 Larry McWilliams .05 .02
☐ 205 Brian Downing .05 .02
☐ 206 Danny Darwin .05 .02
☐ 207 Bill Caudill .05 .02
☐ 208 Dave Rozema .05 .02
☐ 209 Eric Show .05 .02
☐ 210 Brad Komminsk .05 .02
☐ 211 Chris Bando .05 .02
☐ 212 Chris Speier .05 .02
☐ 213 Jim Clancy .05 .02
☐ 214 Randy Bush .05 .02
☐ 215 Frank White .10 .05
☐ 216 Dan Petry .05 .02
☐ 217 Tim Wallach .05 .02
☐ 218 Mitch Webster .05 .02
☐ 219 Dennis Lamp .05 .02
☐ 220 Bob Horner .05 .02
☐ 221 Dave Henderson .05 .02
☐ 222 Dave Smith .05 .02
☐ 223 Willie Upshaw .05 .02
☐ 224 Cesar Cedeno .10 .05
☐ 225 Ron Darling .05 .02
☐ 226 Lee Lacy .05 .02
☐ 227 John Tudor .05 .02
☐ 228 Jim Presley .05 .02
☐ 229 Bill Gullickson .05 .02
Now with Reds
☐ 230 Terry Kennedy .05 .02
☐ 231 Bob Knepper .05 .02
☐ 232 Rick Rhoden .05 .02
☐ 233 Richard Dotson .05 .02
☐ 234 Jesse Barfield .05 .02
☐ 235 Butch Wynegar .05 .02
☐ 236 Jerry Reuss .10 .05
☐ 237 Juan Samuel .05 .02
☐ 238 Larry Parrish .05 .02
☐ 239 Bill Buckner .10 .05
☐ 240 Pat Sheridan .05 .02
☐ 241 Tony Fernandez .05 .02
☐ 242 Rich Thompson .05 .02
Now with Brewers
☐ 243 Rickey Henderson .40 .18
☐ 244 Craig Lefferts .05 .02
☐ 245 Jim Sundberg .05 .02
☐ 246 Phil Niekro .30 .14
☐ 247 Terry Harper .05 .02
☐ 248 Spike Owen .05 .02
☐ 249 Bret Saberhagen .25 .11
☐ 250 Dwight Gooden .25 .11
☐ 251 Rich Dauer .05 .02
☐ 252 Keith Hernandez .10 .05
☐ 253 Bo Diaz .05 .02
☐ 254 Ozzie Guillen .15 .07
☐ 255 Tony Armas .05 .02
☐ 256 Andre Dawson .25 .11
☐ 257 Doug DeCinces .05 .02
☐ 258 Tim Burke .05 .02
☐ 259 Dennis Boyd .05 .02
☐ 260 Tony Pena .05 .02
☐ 261 Sal Butera .05 .02
Now with Reds
☐ 262 Wade Boggs .60 .25
☐ 263 Checklist 133-264 .05 .02
☐ 264 Ron Oester .05 .02
☐ 265 Ron Davis .05 .02
☐ 266 Keith Moreland .05 .02
☐ 267 Paul Molitor .50 .23
☐ 268 John Denny .05 .02
Now with Reds
☐ 269 Frank Viola .10 .05
☐ 270 Jack Morris .10 .05
☐ 271 Dave Collins .05 .02
Now with Tigers
☐ 272 Bert Blyleven .10 .05
☐ 273 Jerry Willard .05 .02
☐ 274 Matt Young .05 .02
☐ 275 Charlie Hough .10 .05
☐ 276 Dave Dravecky .10 .05
☐ 277 Garth Iorg .05 .02
☐ 278 Hal McRae .10 .05
☐ 279 Curt Wilkerson .05 .02
☐ 280 Tim Raines .10 .05
☐ 281 Bill Laskey .05 .02
Now with Giants
☐ 282 Jerry Mumphrey .05 .02
Now with Cubs
☐ 283 Pat Clements .05 .02
☐ 284 Bob James .05 .02
☐ 285 Buddy Bell .10 .05
☐ 286 Tom Brookens .05 .02
☐ 287 Dave Parker .10 .05
☐ 288 Ron Kittle .05 .02
☐ 289 Johnnie LeMaster .05 .02
☐ 290 Carlton Fisk .25 .11
☐ 291 Jimmy Key .15 .07
☐ 292 Gary Matthews .05 .02
☐ 293 Marvell Wynne .05 .02
☐ 294 Danny Cox .05 .02
☐ 295 Kirk Gibson .10 .05
☐ 296 Mariano Duncan .15 .07
☐ 297 Ozzie Smith 1.00 .45
☐ 298 Craig Reynolds .05 .02
☐ 299 Bryn Smith .05 .02
☐ 300 George Brett 1.00 .45
☐ 301 Walt Terrell .05 .02
☐ 302 Greg Gross .05 .02
☐ 303 Claudell Washington .05 .02
☐ 304 Howard Johnson .10 .05
☐ 305 Phil Bradley .05 .02
☐ 306 R.J. Reynolds .05 .02

	MINT	NRMT
☐ 307 Bob Brenly	.05	.02
☐ 308 Hubie Brooks	.05	.02
☐ 309 Alvin Davis	.05	.02
☐ 310 Donnie Hill	.05	.02
☐ 311 Dick Schofield	.05	.02
☐ 312 Tom Filer	.05	.02
☐ 313 Mike Fitzgerald	.05	.02
☐ 314 Marty Barrett	.05	.02
☐ 315 Mookie Wilson	.10	.05
☐ 316 Alan Knicely	.05	.02
☐ 317 Ed Romero	.05	.02
Now with Red Sox		
☐ 318 Glenn Wilson	.05	.02
☐ 319 Bud Black	.05	.02
☐ 320 Jim Rice	.10	.05
☐ 321 Terry Pendleton	.15	.07
☐ 322 Dave Kingman	.10	.05
☐ 323 Gary Pettis	.05	.02
☐ 324 Dan Schatzeder	.05	.02
☐ 325 Juan Beniquez	.05	.02
Now with Orioles		
☐ 326 Kent Tekulve	.05	.02
☐ 327 Mike Pagliarulo	.05	.02
☐ 328 Pete O'Brien	.05	.02
☐ 329 Kirby Puckett	2.00	.90
☐ 330 Rick Sutcliffe	.05	.02
☐ 331 Alan Ashby	.05	.02
☐ 332 Willie Randolph	.10	.05
☐ 333 Tom Henke	.10	.05
☐ 334 Ken Oberkfell	.05	.02
☐ 335 Don Sutton	.30	.14
☐ 336 Dan Gladden	.05	.02
☐ 337 George Vukovich	.05	.02
☐ 338 Jorge Bell	.10	.05
☐ 339 Jim Dwyer	.05	.02
☐ 340 Cal Ripken	1.50	.70
☐ 341 Willie Hernandez	.05	.02
☐ 342 Gary Redus	.05	.02
Now with Phillies		
☐ 343 Jerry Koosman	.10	.05
☐ 344 Jim Wohlford	.05	.02
☐ 345 Donnie Moore	.05	.02
☐ 346 Floyd Youmans	.05	.02
☐ 347 Gorman Thomas	.05	.02
☐ 348 Cliff Johnson	.05	.02
☐ 349 Ken Howell	.05	.02
☐ 350 Jack Clark	.10	.05
☐ 351 Gary Lucas	.05	.02
Now with Angels		
☐ 352 Bob Clark	.05	.02
☐ 353 Dave Stieb	.05	.02
☐ 354 Tony Bernazard	.05	.02
☐ 355 Lee Smith	.25	.11
☐ 356 Mickey Hatcher	.05	.02
☐ 357 Ed VandeBerg	.05	.02
Now with Dodgers		
☐ 358 Rick Dempsey	.05	.02
☐ 359 Bobby Cox MG	.10	.05
Now General Manager of Atlanta Braves		
Team checklist back		
☐ 360 Lloyd Moseby	.05	.02
☐ 361 Shane Rawley	.05	.02
☐ 362 Garry Maddox	.05	.02
☐ 363 Buck Martinez	.05	.02
☐ 364 Ed Nunez	.05	.02
☐ 365 Luis Leal	.05	.02
☐ 366 Dale Berra	.05	.02
☐ 367 Mike Boddicker	.05	.02
☐ 368 Greg Brock	.05	.02
☐ 369 Al Holland	.05	.02
☐ 370 Vince Coleman	.15	.07
☐ 371 Rod Carew	.30	.14
☐ 372 Ben Oglivie	.05	.02
☐ 373 Lee Mazzilli	.05	.02
☐ 374 Terry Francona	.10	.05
☐ 375 Rich Gedman	.05	.02
☐ 376 Charlie Lea	.05	.02
☐ 377 Joe Carter	1.00	.45
☐ 378 Bruce Bochte	.05	.02
☐ 379 Bobby Meacham	.05	.02
☐ 380 LaMarr Hoyt	.05	.02
☐ 381 Jeff Leonard	.05	.02
☐ 382 Ivan Calderon	.10	.05
☐ 383 Chris Brown	.05	.02
☐ 384 Steve Trout	.05	.02
☐ 385 Cecil Cooper	.10	.05
☐ 386 Cecil Fielder	1.50	.70
☐ 387 Tim Flannery	.05	.02
☐ 388 Chris Codiroli	.05	.02
☐ 389 Glenn Davis	.05	.02
☐ 390 Tom Seaver	.30	.14
☐ 391 Julio Franco	.15	.07
☐ 392 Tom Brunansky	.05	.02
☐ 393 Rob Wilfong	.05	.02
☐ 394 Reggie Jackson	.30	.14
☐ 395 Scott Garrelts	.05	.02
☐ 396 Checklist 265-396	.05	.02

1986 O-Pee-Chee Box Bottoms

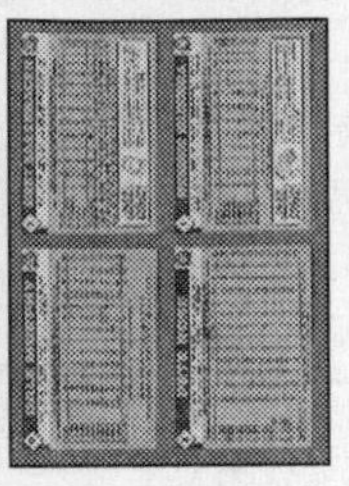

O-Pee-Chee printed four different four-card panels on the bottoms of its 1986 wax pack boxes. If cut, each card would measure approximately the standard size. These 16 cards, in alphabetical order and designated A through P, are considered a separate set from the regular issue, but are styled almost exactly the same, differing only in the player photo and colors for the team name, borders and position on the front. The backs are identical, except for the letter designations instead of numbers.

	MINT	NRMT
COMPLETE SET (16)	8.00	3.60
COMMON CARD (A-P)	.25	.11
☐ A George Bell	.25	.11
☐ B Wade Boggs	1.25	.55
☐ C George Brett	2.50	1.10
☐ D Vince Coleman	.25	.11
☐ E Carlton Fisk	1.00	.45
☐ F Dwight Gooden	.75	.35
☐ G Pedro Guerrero	.25	.11
☐ H Ron Guidry	.50	.23
☐ I Reggie Jackson	1.25	.55
☐ J Don Mattingly	2.50	1.10
☐ K Oddibe McDowell	.25	.11
☐ L Willie McGee	.50	.23
☐ M Dale Murphy	1.00	.45
☐ N Pete Rose	1.25	.55
☐ O Bret Saberhagen	.50	.23
☐ P Fernando Valenzuela	.50	.23

1987 O-Pee-Chee

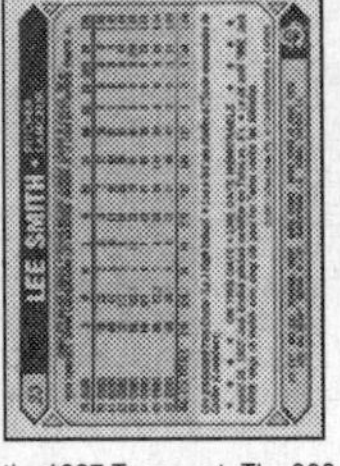

This set is an abridgement of the 1987 Topps set. The 396 standard-size cards comprising the 1987 O-Pee-Chee set differ from the cards of the 1987 Topps set by having a higher ratio of cards of players from the two Canadian teams, a practice begun by O-Pee-Chee in 1977 and continued to 1988. The fronts feature wood grain bordered color player photos. The player's name appears in the colored rectangle at the lower right. His team logo appears at the upper left. The yellow, white and blue horizontal backs carry the player's name and bilingual position at the top. The player's major league statistics follow below. Some backs also have bilingual career highlights, some have bilingual baseball facts and still others have both or neither. The cards are numbered on the back. The asterisked cards have an extra line on the front inside the picture area indicating team change. The O-Pee-Chee logo appears on the front of every card.

	MINT	NRMT
COMPLETE SET (396)	15.00	6.75
COMMON CARD (1-396)	.05	.02
☐ 1 Ken Oberkfell	.05	.02
☐ 2 Jack Howell	.05	.02
☐ 3 Hubie Brooks	.05	.02
☐ 4 Bob Grich	.10	.05
☐ 5 Rick Leach	.05	.02
☐ 6 Phil Niekro	.30	.14
☐ 7 Rickey Henderson	.30	.14
☐ 8 Terry Pendleton	.10	.05
☐ 9 Jay Tibbs	.05	.02
☐ 10 Cecil Cooper	.10	.05
☐ 11 Mario Soto	.05	.02
☐ 12 George Bell	.05	.02
☐ 13 Nick Esasky	.05	.02
☐ 14 Larry McWilliams	.05	.02
☐ 15 Dan Quisenberry	.05	.02
☐ 16 Ed Lynch	.05	.02
☐ 17 Pete O'Brien	.05	.02
☐ 18 Luis Aguayo	.05	.02
☐ 19 Matt Young	.05	.02
Now with Dodgers		
☐ 20 Gary Carter	.25	.11
☐ 21 Tom Paciorek	.05	.02
☐ 22 Doug DeCinces	.05	.02
☐ 23 Lee Smith	.15	.07
☐ 24 Jesse Barfield	.05	.02
☐ 25 Bert Blyleven	.10	.05
☐ 26 Greg Brock	.05	.02
Now with Brewers		
☐ 27 Dan Petry	.05	.02
☐ 28 Rick Dempsey	.05	.02
Now with Indians		
☐ 29 Jimmy Key	.10	.05
☐ 30 Tim Raines	.15	.07
☐ 31 Bruce Hurst	.05	.02
☐ 32 Manny Trillo	.05	.02
☐ 33 Andy Van Slyke	.10	.05
☐ 34 Ed VandeBerg	.05	.02
Now with Indians		
☐ 35 Sid Bream	.05	.02
☐ 36 Dave Winfield	.25	.11
☐ 37 Scott Garrelts	.05	.02
☐ 38 Dennis Leonard	.05	.02
☐ 39 Marty Barrett	.05	.02
☐ 40 Dave Righetti	.05	.02
☐ 41 Bo Diaz	.05	.02
☐ 42 Gary Redus	.05	.02
☐ 43 Tom Niedenfuer	.05	.02
☐ 44 Greg Harris	.05	.02
☐ 45 Jim Presley	.05	.02
☐ 46 Danny Gladden	.05	.02
☐ 47 Roy Smalley	.05	.02
☐ 48 Wally Backman	.05	.02
☐ 49 Tom Seaver	.30	.14
☐ 50 Dave Smith	.05	.02
☐ 51 Mel Hall	.05	.02
☐ 52 Tim Flannery	.05	.02
☐ 53 Julio Cruz	.05	.02
☐ 54 Dick Schofield	.05	.02
☐ 55 Tim Wallach	.05	.02
☐ 56 Glenn Davis	.05	.02
☐ 57 Darren Daulton	.15	.07
☐ 58 Chico Walker	.05	.02
☐ 59 Garth Iorg	.05	.02
☐ 60 Tony Pena	.05	.02
☐ 61 Ron Hassey	.05	.02
☐ 62 Dave Dravecky	.10	.05
☐ 63 Jorge Orta	.05	.02
☐ 64 Al Nipper	.05	.02
☐ 65 Tom Browning	.05	.02
☐ 66 Marc Sullivan	.05	.02
☐ 67 Todd Worrell	.10	.05
☐ 68 Glenn Hubbard	.05	.02
☐ 69 Carney Lansford	.05	.02
☐ 70 Charlie Hough	.05	.02
☐ 71 Lance McCullers	.05	.02
☐ 72 Walt Terrell	.05	.02
☐ 73 Bob Kearney	.05	.02
☐ 74 Dan Pasqua	.05	.02
☐ 75 Ron Darling	.05	.02
☐ 76 Robin Yount	.25	.11
☐ 77 Pat Tabler	.05	.02
☐ 78 Tom Foley	.05	.02
☐ 79 Juan Nieves	.05	.02
☐ 80 Wally Joyner	.40	.18
☐ 81 Wayne Krenchicki	.05	.02
☐ 82 Kirby Puckett	.75	.35
☐ 83 Bob Ojeda	.05	.02
☐ 84 Mookie Wilson	.10	.05
☐ 85 Kevin Bass	.05	.02
☐ 86 Kent Tekulve	.05	.02
☐ 87 Mark Salas	.05	.02
☐ 88 Brian Downing	.05	.02
☐ 89 Ozzie Guillen	.05	.02
☐ 90 Dave Stieb	.05	.02
☐ 91 Rance Mulliniks	.05	.02
☐ 92 Mike Witt	.05	.02
☐ 93 Charlie Moore	.05	.02
☐ 94 Jose Uribe	.05	.02
☐ 95 Oddibe McDowell	.05	.02
☐ 96 Ray Soff	.05	.02
☐ 97 Glenn Wilson	.05	.02
☐ 98 Brook Jacoby	.05	.02
☐ 99 Darryl Motley	.05	.02
Now with Braves		
☐ 100 Steve Garvey	.15	.07
☐ 101 Frank White	.10	.05
☐ 102 Mike Moore	.05	.02
☐ 103 Rick Aguilera	.10	.05

☐ 104 Buddy Bell	.10	.05
☐ 105 Floyd Youmans	.05	.02
☐ 106 Lou Whitaker	.10	.05
☐ 107 Ozzie Smith	.75	.35
☐ 108 Jim Gantner	.05	.02
☐ 109 R.J. Reynolds	.05	.02
☐ 110 John Tudor	.05	.02
☐ 111 Alfredo Griffin	.05	.02
☐ 112 Mike Flanagan	.05	.02
☐ 113 Neil Allen	.05	.02
☐ 114 Ken Griffey	.10	.05
☐ 115 Donnie Moore	.05	.02
☐ 116 Bob Horner	.05	.02
☐ 117 Ron Shepherd	.05	.02
☐ 118 Cliff Johnson	.05	.02
☐ 119 Vince Coleman	.05	.02
☐ 120 Eddie Murray	.30	.14
☐ 121 Dwayne Murphy	.05	.02
☐ 122 Jim Clancy	.05	.02
☐ 123 Ken Landreaux	.05	.02
☐ 124 Tom Nieto	.05	.02
Now with Twins		
☐ 125 Bob Brenly	.05	.02
☐ 126 George Brett	.75	.35
☐ 127 Vance Law	.05	.02
☐ 128 Checklist 1-132	.05	.02
☐ 129 Bob Knepper	.05	.02
☐ 130 Dwight Gooden	.15	.07
☐ 131 Juan Bonilla	.05	.02
☐ 132 Tim Burke	.05	.02
☐ 133 Bob McClure	.05	.02
☐ 134 Scott Bailes	.05	.02
☐ 135 Mike Easler	.05	.02
Now with Phillies		
☐ 136 Ron Romanick	.05	.02
Now with Yankees		
☐ 137 Rich Gedman	.05	.02
☐ 138 Bob Dernier	.05	.02
☐ 139 John Denny	.05	.02
☐ 140 Bret Saberhagen	.10	.05
☐ 141 Herm Winningham	.05	.02
☐ 142 Rick Sutcliffe	.05	.02
☐ 143 Ryne Sandberg	.40	.18
☐ 144 Mike Scioscia	.05	.02
☐ 145 Charlie Kerfeld	.05	.02
☐ 146 Jim Rice	.10	.05
☐ 147 Steve Trout	.05	.02
☐ 148 Jesse Orosco	.05	.02
☐ 149 Mike Boddicker	.05	.02
☐ 150 Wade Boggs	.30	.14
☐ 151 Dane Iorg	.05	.02
☐ 152 Rick Burleson	.05	.02
Now with Orioles		
☐ 153 Duane Ward	.10	.05
☐ 154 Rick Reuschel	.05	.02
☐ 155 Nolan Ryan	.75	.35
☐ 156 Bill Caudill	.05	.02
☐ 157 Danny Darwin	.05	.02
☐ 158 Ed Romero	.05	.02
☐ 159 Bill Almon	.05	.02
☐ 160 Julio Franco	.10	.05
☐ 161 Kent Hrbek	.10	.05
☐ 162 Chili Davis	.10	.05
☐ 163 Kevin Gross	.05	.02
☐ 164 Carlton Fisk	.25	.11
☐ 165 Jeff Reardon	.10	.05
Now with Twins		
☐ 166 Bob Boone	.10	.05
☐ 167 Rick Honeycutt	.05	.02
☐ 168 Dan Schatzeder	.05	.02
☐ 169 Jim Wohlford	.05	.02
☐ 170 Phil Bradley	.05	.02
☐ 171 Ken Schrom	.05	.02
☐ 172 Ron Oester	.05	.02
☐ 173 Juan Beniquez	.05	.02
Now with Royals		
☐ 174 Tony Armas	.05	.02
☐ 175 Bob Stanley	.05	.02
☐ 176 Steve Buechele	.05	.02
☐ 177 Keith Moreland	.05	.02
☐ 178 Cecil Fielder	.15	.07
☐ 179 Gary Gaetti	.10	.05
☐ 180 Chris Brown	.05	.02
☐ 181 Tom Herr	.05	.02
☐ 182 Lee Lacy	.05	.02
☐ 183 Ozzie Virgil	.05	.02
☐ 184 Paul Molitor	.30	.14
☐ 185 Roger McDowell	.05	.02
☐ 186 Mike Marshall	.05	.02
☐ 187 Ken Howell	.05	.02
☐ 188 Rob Deer	.05	.02
☐ 189 Joe Hesketh	.05	.02
☐ 190 Jim Sundberg	.05	.02
☐ 191 Kelly Gruber	.05	.02
☐ 192 Cory Snyder	.05	.02
☐ 193 Dave Concepcion	.10	.05
☐ 194 Kirk McCaskill	.05	.02
☐ 195 Mike Pagliarulo	.05	.02
☐ 196 Rick Manning	.05	.02
☐ 197 Brett Butler	.10	.05
☐ 198 Tony Gwynn	.75	.35
☐ 199 Mariano Duncan	.05	.02
☐ 200 Pete Rose	.30	.14
☐ 201 John Cangelosi	.05	.02
☐ 202 Danny Cox	.05	.02
☐ 203 Butch Wynegar	.05	.02
Now with Angels		
☐ 204 Chris Chambliss	.05	.02
☐ 205 Graig Nettles	.10	.05
☐ 206 Chet Lemon	.05	.02
☐ 207 Don Aase	.05	.02
☐ 208 Mike Mason	.05	.02
☐ 209 Alan Trammell	.15	.07
☐ 210 Lloyd Moseby	.05	.02
☐ 211 Richard Dotson	.05	.02
☐ 212 Mike Fitzgerald	.05	.02
☐ 213 Darrell Porter	.05	.02
☐ 214 Checklist 265-396	.05	.02
☐ 215 Mark Langston	.05	.02
☐ 216 Steve Farr	.05	.02
☐ 217 Dann Bilardello	.05	.02
☐ 218 Gary Ward	.05	.02
Now with Yankees		
☐ 219 Cecilio Guante	.05	.02
Now with Yankees		
☐ 220 Joe Carter	.25	.11
☐ 221 Ernie Whitt	.05	.02
☐ 222 Denny Walling	.05	.02
☐ 223 Charlie Leibrandt	.05	.02
☐ 224 Wayne Tolleson	.05	.02
☐ 225 Mike Smithson	.05	.02
☐ 226 Zane Smith	.05	.02
☐ 227 Terry Puhl	.05	.02
☐ 228 Eric Davis	.15	.07
☐ 229 Don Mattingly	.75	.35
☐ 230 Don Baylor	.10	.05
☐ 231 Frank Tanana	.05	.02
☐ 232 Tom Brookens	.05	.02
☐ 233 Steve Bedrosian	.05	.02
☐ 234 Wallace Johnson	.05	.02
☐ 235 Alvin Davis	.05	.02
☐ 236 Tommy John	.10	.05
☐ 237 Jim Morrison	.05	.02
☐ 238 Ricky Horton	.05	.02
☐ 239 Shane Rawley	.05	.02
☐ 240 Steve Balboni	.05	.02
☐ 241 Mike Krukow	.05	.02
☐ 242 Rick Mahler	.05	.02
☐ 243 Bill Doran	.05	.02
☐ 244 Mark Clear	.05	.02
☐ 245 Willie Upshaw	.05	.02
☐ 246 Hal McRae	.10	.05
☐ 247 Jose Canseco	.60	.25
☐ 248 George Hendrick	.05	.02
☐ 249 Doyle Alexander	.05	.02
☐ 250 Teddy Higuera	.05	.02
☐ 251 Tom Hume	.05	.02
☐ 252 Denny Martinez	.10	.05
☐ 253 Eddie Milner	.05	.02
Now with Giants		
☐ 254 Steve Sax	.05	.02
☐ 255 Juan Samuel	.05	.02
☐ 256 Dave Bergman	.05	.02
☐ 257 Bob Forsch	.05	.02
☐ 258 Steve Yeager	.05	.02
☐ 259 Don Sutton	.30	.14
☐ 260 Vida Blue	.10	.05
Now with A's		
☐ 261 Tom Brunansky	.05	.02
☐ 262 Joe Sambito	.05	.02
☐ 263 Mitch Webster	.05	.02
☐ 264 Checklist 133-264	.05	.02
☐ 265 Darrell Evans	.10	.05
☐ 266 Dave Kingman	.10	.05
☐ 267 Howard Johnson	.05	.02
☐ 268 Greg Pryor	.05	.02
☐ 269 Tippy Martinez	.05	.02
☐ 270 Jody Davis	.05	.02
☐ 271 Steve Carlton	.30	.14
☐ 272 Andres Galarraga	.50	.23
☐ 273 Fernando Valenzuela	.10	.05
☐ 274 Jeff Hearron	.05	.02
☐ 275 Ray Knight	.10	.05
Now with Orioles		
☐ 276 Bill Madlock	.10	.05
☐ 277 Tom Henke	.10	.05
☐ 278 Gary Pettis	.05	.02
☐ 279 Jimy Williams MG	.05	.02
team checklist back		
☐ 280 Jeffrey Leonard	.05	.02
☐ 281 Bryn Smith	.05	.02
☐ 282 John Cerutti	.05	.02
☐ 283 Gary Roenicke	.05	.02
Now with Braves		
☐ 284 Joaquin Andujar	.05	.02
☐ 285 Dennis Boyd	.05	.02
☐ 286 Tim Hulett	.05	.02
☐ 287 Craig Lefferts	.05	.02
☐ 288 Tito Landrum	.05	.02
☐ 289 Manny Lee	.05	.02
☐ 290 Leon Durham	.05	.02
☐ 291 Johnny Ray	.05	.02
☐ 292 Franklin Stubbs	.05	.02
☐ 293 Bob Rodgers MG	.05	.02
team checklist back		
☐ 294 Terry Francona	.10	.05
☐ 295 Len Dykstra	.15	.07
☐ 296 Tom Candiotti	.05	.02
☐ 297 Frank DiPino	.05	.02
☐ 298 Craig Reynolds	.05	.02
☐ 299 Jerry Hairston	.05	.02
☐ 300 Reggie Jackson	.30	.14
Now with A's		
☐ 301 Luis Aquino	.05	.02
☐ 302 Greg Walker	.05	.02
☐ 303 Terry Kennedy	.05	.02
Now with Orioles		
☐ 304 Phil Garner	.10	.05
☐ 305 John Franco	.10	.05
☐ 306 Bill Buckner	.10	.05
☐ 307 Kevin Mitchell	.25	.11
Now with Padres		
☐ 308 Don Slaught	.05	.02
☐ 309 Harold Baines	.10	.05
☐ 310 Frank Viola	.05	.02
☐ 311 Dave Lopes	.10	.05
☐ 312 Cal Ripken	.75	.35
☐ 313 John Candelaria	.05	.02
☐ 314 Bob Sebra	.05	.02
☐ 315 Bud Black	.05	.02
☐ 316 Brian Fisher	.05	.02
Now with Pirates		
☐ 317 Clint Hurdle	.05	.02
☐ 318 Earnest Riles	.05	.02
☐ 319 Dave LaPoint	.05	.02
Now with Cardinals		
☐ 320 Barry Bonds	1.25	.55
☐ 321 Tim Stoddard	.05	.02
☐ 322 Ron Cey	.10	.05
Now with A's		
☐ 323 Al Newman	.05	.02
☐ 324 Jerry Royster	.05	.02
Now with White Sox		
☐ 325 Garry Templeton	.05	.02
☐ 326 Mark Gubicza	.05	.02
☐ 327 Andre Thornton	.05	.02
☐ 328 Bob Welch	.10	.05
☐ 329 Tony Fernandez	.05	.02
☐ 330 Mike Scott	.05	.02
☐ 331 Jack Clark	.10	.05
☐ 332 Danny Tartabull	.05	.02
Now with Royals		
☐ 333 Greg Minton	.05	.02
☐ 334 Ed Correa	.05	.02
☐ 335 Candy Maldonado	.05	.02
☐ 336 Dennis Lamp	.05	.02
Now with Indians		
☐ 337 Sid Fernandez	.05	.02
☐ 338 Greg Gross	.05	.02
☐ 339 Willie Hernandez	.05	.02
☐ 340 Roger Clemens	.75	.35
☐ 341 Mickey Hatcher	.05	.02
☐ 342 Bob James	.05	.02
☐ 343 Jose Cruz	.10	.05
☐ 344 Bruce Sutter	.05	.02
☐ 345 Andre Dawson	.25	.11
☐ 346 Shawon Dunston	.10	.05
☐ 347 Scott McGregor	.05	.02
☐ 348 Carmelo Martinez	.05	.02
☐ 349 Storm Davis	.05	.02
Now with Padres		
☐ 350 Keith Hernandez	.10	.05
☐ 351 Andy McGaffigan	.05	.02
☐ 352 Dave Parker	.10	.05
☐ 353 Ernie Camacho	.05	.02
☐ 354 Eric Show	.05	.02
☐ 355 Don Carman	.05	.02
☐ 356 Floyd Bannister	.05	.02
☐ 357 Willie McGee	.10	.05
☐ 358 Atlee Hammaker	.05	.02
☐ 359 Dale Murphy	.15	.07
☐ 360 Pedro Guerrero	.10	.05
☐ 361 Will Clark	.60	.25
☐ 362 Bill Campbell	.05	.02
☐ 363 Alejandro Pena	.05	.02
☐ 364 Dennis Rasmussen	.05	.02
☐ 365 Rick Rhoden	.05	.02
Now with Yankees		
☐ 366 Randy St. Claire	.05	.02
☐ 367 Willie Wilson	.05	.02
☐ 368 Dwight Evans	.10	.05

	MINT	NRMT
☐ 369 Moose Haas	.05	.02
☐ 370 Fred Lynn	.10	.05
☐ 371 Mark Eichhorn	.05	.02
☐ 372 Dave Schmidt	.05	.02
Now with Orioles		
☐ 373 Jerry Reuss	.05	.02
☐ 374 Lance Parrish	.10	.05
☐ 375 Ron Guidry	.10	.05
☐ 376 Jack Morris	.10	.05
☐ 377 Willie Randolph	.10	.05
☐ 378 Joel Youngblood	.05	.02
☐ 379 Darryl Strawberry	.15	.07
☐ 380 Rich Gossage	.10	.05
☐ 381 Dennis Eckersley	.15	.07
☐ 382 Gary Lucas	.05	.02
☐ 383 Ron Davis	.05	.02
☐ 384 Pete Incaviglia	.10	.05
☐ 385 Orel Hershiser	.15	.07
☐ 386 Kirk Gibson	.10	.05
☐ 387 Don Robinson	.05	.02
☐ 388 Darnell Coles	.05	.02
☐ 389 Von Hayes	.05	.02
☐ 390 Gary Matthews	.05	.02
☐ 391 Jay Howell	.05	.02
☐ 392 Tim Laudner	.05	.02
☐ 393 Rod Scurry	.05	.02
☐ 394 Tony Bernazard	.05	.02
☐ 395 Damaso Garcia	.05	.02
Now with Braves		
☐ 396 Mike Schmidt	.40	.18

1987 O-Pee-Chee Box Bottoms

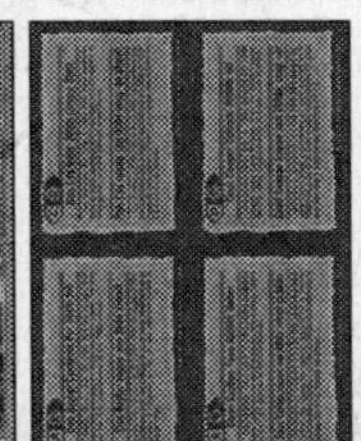

O-Pee-Chee printed two different four-card panels on the bottoms of its 1987 wax pack boxes. If cut, each card would measure approximately 2 1/8" by 3". These eight cards, in alphabetical order and designated A through H, are considered a separate set from the regular issue, but are styled almost exactly the same, differing only in the player photo and colors for the team name, borders and position on the front. On the horizontal backs, purple borders frame a yellow panel that presents bilingual text describing an outstanding achievement or milestone in the player's career.

	MINT	NRMT
COMPLETE SET (8)	4.00	1.80
COMMON CARD (A-H)	.25	.11
☐ A Don Baylor	.50	.23
☐ B Steve Carlton	1.00	.45
☐ C Ron Cey	.25	.11
☐ D Cecil Cooper	.25	.11
☐ E Rickey Henderson	1.25	.55
☐ F Jim Rice	.50	.23
☐ G Don Sutton	1.00	.45
☐ H Dave Winfield	1.00	.45

1988 O-Pee-Chee

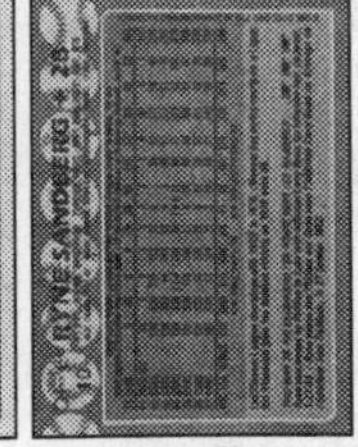

This set is an abridgement of the 1988 Topps set. The 396 standard-size cards comprising the 1988 O-Pee-Chee set differ from the cards of the 1988 Topps set by having a higher ratio of cards of players from the two Canadian teams, a practice begun by O-Pee-Chee in 1977 and continued to 1988. The fronts feature white-bordered color player photos framed by a colored line. The player's name appears in the colored diagonal stripe at the lower right. His team name appears at the top. The orange horizontal backs carry the player's name, position and biography printed across the row of baseball icons at the top. The player's major league statistics follow below. Some backs also have bilingual career highlights, some have bilingual baseball facts and still others have both or neither. The cards are numbered on the back. The asterisked cards have an extra line on the front inside the picture area indicating team change. They are styled like the 1988 Topps regular issue cards. The O-Pee-Chee logo appears on the front of every card. This set includes the first two 1987 draft picks of both the Montreal Expos and the Toronto Blue Jays.

	MINT	NRMT
COMPLETE SET (396)	12.00	5.50
COMMON CARD (1-396)	.05	.02
☐ 1 Chris James	.05	.02
☐ 2 Steve Buechele	.05	.02
☐ 3 Mike Henneman	.05	.02
☐ 4 Eddie Murray	.30	.14
☐ 5 Bret Saberhagen	.10	.05
☐ 6 Nathan Minchey	.05	.02
Expos' second draft choice		
☐ 7 Harold Reynolds	.10	.05
☐ 8 Bo Jackson	.15	.07
☐ 9 Mike Easler	.05	.02
☐ 10 Ryne Sandberg	.30	.14
☐ 11 Mike Young	.05	.02
☐ 12 Tony Phillips	.05	.02
☐ 13 Andres Thomas	.05	.02
☐ 14 Tim Burke	.05	.02
☐ 15 Chili Davis	.10	.05
Now with Angels		
☐ 16 Jim Lindeman	.05	.02
☐ 17 Ron Oester	.05	.02
☐ 18 Craig Reynolds	.05	.02
☐ 19 Juan Samuel	.05	.02
☐ 20 Kevin Gross	.05	.02
☐ 21 Cecil Fielder	.15	.07
☐ 22 Greg Swindell	.05	.02
☐ 23 Jose DeLeon	.05	.02
☐ 24 Jim Deshaies	.05	.02
☐ 25 Andres Galarraga	.25	.11
☐ 26 Mitch Williams	.05	.02
☐ 27 R.J. Reynolds	.05	.02
☐ 28 Jose Nunez	.05	.02
☐ 29 Argenis Salazar	.05	.02
☐ 30 Sid Fernandez	.05	.02
☐ 31 Keith Moreland	.05	.02
☐ 32 John Kruk	.15	.07
☐ 33 Rob Deer	.05	.02
☐ 34 Ricky Horton	.05	.02
☐ 35 Harold Baines	.10	.05
☐ 36 Jamie Moyer	.05	.02
☐ 37 Kevin McReynolds	.05	.02
☐ 38 Ron Darling	.05	.02
☐ 39 Ozzie Smith	.50	.23
☐ 40 Orel Hershiser	.10	.05
☐ 41 Bob Melvin	.05	.02
☐ 42 Alfredo Griffin	.05	.02
Now with Dodgers		
☐ 43 Dick Schofield	.05	.02
☐ 44 Terry Steinbach	.15	.07
☐ 45 Kent Hrbek	.05	.02
☐ 46 Darnell Coles	.05	.02
☐ 47 Jimmy Key	.10	.05
☐ 48 Alan Ashby	.05	.02
☐ 49 Julio Franco	.10	.05
☐ 50 Hubie Brooks	.05	.02
☐ 51 Chris Bando	.05	.02
☐ 52 Fernando Valenzuela	.10	.05
☐ 53 Kal Daniels	.05	.02
☐ 54 Jim Clancy	.05	.02
☐ 55 Phil Bradley	.05	.02
Now with Phillies		
☐ 56 Andy McGaffigan	.05	.02
☐ 57 Mike LaValliere	.05	.02
☐ 58 Dave Magadan	.05	.02
☐ 59 Danny Cox	.05	.02
☐ 60 Rickey Henderson	.25	.11
☐ 61 Jim Rice	.15	.07
☐ 62 Calvin Schiraldi	.05	.02
Now with Cubs		
☐ 63 Jerry Mumphrey	.05	.02
☐ 64 Ken Caminiti	.50	.23
☐ 65 Leon Durham	.05	.02
☐ 66 Shane Rawley	.05	.02
☐ 67 Ken Oberkfell	.05	.02
☐ 68 Keith Hernandez	.10	.05
☐ 69 Bob Brenly	.05	.02
☐ 70 Roger Clemens	.50	.23
☐ 71 Gary Pettis	.05	.02
Now with Tigers		
☐ 72 Dennis Eckersley	.15	.07
☐ 73 Dave Smith	.05	.02
☐ 74 Cal Ripken	1.50	.70
☐ 75 Joe Carter	.15	.07
☐ 76 Denny Martinez	.10	.05
☐ 77 Juan Beniquez	.05	.02
☐ 78 Tim Laudner	.05	.02
☐ 79 Ernie Whitt	.05	.02
☐ 80 Mark Langston	.05	.02
☐ 81 Dale Sveum	.05	.02
☐ 82 Dion James	.05	.02
☐ 83 Dave Valle	.05	.02
☐ 84 Bill Wegman	.05	.02
☐ 85 Howard Johnson	.05	.02
☐ 86 Benito Santiago	.05	.02
☐ 87 Casey Candaele	.05	.02
☐ 88 Delino DeShields	.75	.35
Expos' first draft choice		
☐ 89 Dave Winfield	.25	.11
☐ 90 Dale Murphy	.25	.11
☐ 91 Jay Howell	.05	.02
Now with Dodgers		
☐ 92 Ken Williams	.05	.02
☐ 93 Bob Sebra	.05	.02
☐ 94 Tim Wallach	.05	.02
☐ 95 Lance Parrish	.05	.02
☐ 96 Todd Benzinger	.05	.02
☐ 97 Scott Garrelts	.05	.02
☐ 98 Jose Guzman	.05	.02
☐ 99 Jeff Reardon	.05	.02
☐ 100 Jack Clark	.10	.05
☐ 101 Tracy Jones	.05	.02
☐ 102 Barry Larkin	.75	.35
☐ 103 Curt Young	.05	.02
☐ 104 Juan Nieves	.05	.02
☐ 105 Terry Pendleton	.05	.02
☐ 106 Rob Ducey	.05	.02
☐ 107 Scott Bailes	.05	.02
☐ 108 Eric King	.05	.02
☐ 109 Mike Pagliarulo	.05	.02
☐ 110 Teddy Higuera	.05	.02
☐ 111 Pedro Guerrero	.05	.02
☐ 112 Chris Brown	.05	.02
☐ 113 Kelly Gruber	.05	.02
☐ 114 Jack Howell	.05	.02
☐ 115 Johnny Ray	.05	.02
☐ 116 Mark Eichhorn	.05	.02
☐ 117 Tony Pena	.05	.02
☐ 118 Bob Welch	.05	.02
Now with Athletics		
☐ 119 Mike Kingery	.05	.02
☐ 120 Kirby Puckett	.75	.35
☐ 121 Charlie Hough	.10	.05
☐ 122 Tony Bernazard	.05	.02
☐ 123 Tom Candiotti	.05	.02
☐ 124 Ray Knight	.10	.05
☐ 125 Bruce Hurst	.05	.02
☐ 126 Steve Jeltz	.05	.02
☐ 127 Ron Guidry	.05	.02
☐ 128 Duane Ward	.05	.02
☐ 129 Greg Minton	.05	.02
☐ 130 Buddy Bell	.10	.05
☐ 131 Denny Walling	.05	.02
☐ 132 Donnie Hill	.05	.02
☐ 133 Wayne Tolleson	.05	.02
☐ 134 Bob Rodgers MG	.05	.02
Team checklist back		
☐ 135 Todd Worrell	.05	.02
☐ 136 Brian Dayett	.05	.02
☐ 137 Chris Bosio	.05	.02
☐ 138 Mitch Webster	.05	.02
☐ 139 Jerry Browne	.05	.02
☐ 140 Jesse Barfield	.05	.02
☐ 141 Doug DeCinces	.05	.02
Now with Cardinals		
☐ 142 Andy Van Slyke	.10	.05
☐ 143 Doug Drabek	.10	.05
☐ 144 Jeff Parrett	.05	.02
☐ 145 Bill Madlock	.10	.05
☐ 146 Larry Herndon	.05	.02
☐ 147 Bill Buckner	.10	.05
☐ 148 Carmelo Martinez	.05	.02
☐ 149 Ken Howell	.05	.02
☐ 150 Eric Davis	.05	.02
☐ 151 Randy Ready	.05	.02
☐ 152 Jeffrey Leonard	.05	.02
☐ 153 Dave Stieb	.05	.02
☐ 154 Jeff Stone	.05	.02
☐ 155 Dave Righetti	.05	.02
☐ 156 Gary Matthews	.10	.05
☐ 157 Gary Carter	.25	.11
☐ 158 Bob Boone	.10	.05
☐ 159 Glenn Davis	.05	.02
☐ 160 Willie McGee	.10	.05
☐ 161 Bryn Smith	.05	.02
☐ 162 Mark McLemore	.05	.02
☐ 163 Dale Mohorcic	.05	.02

☐ 164 Mike Flanagan .05 .02
☐ 165 Robin Yount .15 .07
☐ 166 Bill Doran .05 .02
☐ 167 Rance Mulliniks .05 .02
☐ 168 Wally Joyner .15 .07
☐ 169 Cory Snyder .05 .02
☐ 170 Rich Gossage .15 .07
☐ 171 Rick Mahler .05 .02
☐ 172 Henry Cotto .05 .02
☐ 173 George Bell .05 .02
☐ 174 B.J. Surhoff .15 .07
☐ 175 Kevin Bass .05 .02
☐ 176 Jeff Reed .05 .02
☐ 177 Frank Tanana .05 .02
☐ 178 Darryl Strawberry .10 .05
☐ 179 Lou Whitaker .10 .05
☐ 180 Terry Kennedy .05 .02
☐ 181 Mariano Duncan .05 .02
☐ 182 Ken Phelps .05 .02
☐ 183 Bob Dernier .05 .02
Now with Phillies
☐ 184 Ivan Calderon .05 .02
☐ 185 Rick Rhoden .05 .02
☐ 186 Rafael Palmeiro .60 .25
☐ 187 Kelly Downs .05 .02
☐ 188 Spike Owen .05 .02
☐ 189 Bobby Bonilla .15 .07
☐ 190 Candy Maldonado .05 .02
☐ 191 John Cerutti .05 .02
☐ 192 Devon White .10 .05
☐ 193 Brian Fisher .05 .02
☐ 194 Alex Sanchez .05 .02
Blue Jays' first
draft choice
☐ 195 Dan Quisenberry .05 .02
☐ 196 Dave Engle .05 .02
☐ 197 Lance McCullers .05 .02
☐ 198 Franklin Stubbs .05 .02
☐ 199 Scott Bradley .05 .02
☐ 200 Wade Boggs .15 .07
☐ 201 Kirk Gibson .10 .05
☐ 202 Brett Butler .10 .05
Now with Giants
☐ 203 Dave Anderson .05 .02
☐ 204 Donnie Moore .05 .02
☐ 205 Nelson Liriano .05 .02
☐ 206 Danny Gladden .05 .02
☐ 207 Dan Pasqua .05 .02
Now with White Sox
☐ 208 Robby Thompson .05 .02
☐ 209 Richard Dotson .05 .02
Now with Yankees
☐ 210 Willie Randolph .10 .05
☐ 211 Danny Tartabull .05 .02
☐ 212 Greg Brock .05 .02
☐ 213 Albert Hall .05 .02
☐ 214 Dave Schmidt .05 .02
☐ 215 Von Hayes .05 .02
☐ 216 Herm Winningham .05 .02
☐ 217 Mike Davis .05 .02
Now with Dodgers
☐ 218 Charlie Leibrandt .05 .02
☐ 219 Mike Stanley .05 .02
☐ 220 Tom Henke .05 .02
☐ 221 Dwight Evans .10 .05
☐ 222 Willie Wilson .05 .02
☐ 223 Stan Jefferson .05 .02
☐ 224 Mike Dunne .05 .02
☐ 225 Mike Scioscia .05 .02
☐ 226 Larry Parrish .05 .02
☐ 227 Mike Scott .05 .02
☐ 228 Wallace Johnson .05 .02
☐ 229 Jeff Musselman .05 .02
☐ 230 Pat Tabler .05 .02
☐ 231 Paul Molitor .25 .11
☐ 232 Bob James .05 .02
☐ 233 Joe Niekro .05 .02
☐ 234 Oddibe McDowell .05 .02
☐ 235 Gary Ward .05 .02
☐ 236 Ted Power .05 .02
Now with Royals
☐ 237 Pascual Perez .05 .02
☐ 238 Luis Polonia .10 .05
☐ 239 Mike Diaz .05 .02
☐ 240 Lee Smith .10 .05
Now with Red Sox
☐ 241 Willie Upshaw .05 .02
☐ 242 Tom Niedenfuer .05 .02
☐ 243 Tim Raines .10 .05
☐ 244 Jeff D. Robinson .05 .02
☐ 245 Rich Gedman .05 .02
☐ 246 Scott Bankhead .05 .02
☐ 247 Andre Dawson .15 .07
☐ 248 Brook Jacoby .05 .02
☐ 249 Mike Marshall .05 .02
☐ 250 Nolan Ryan 1.50 .70
☐ 251 Tom Foley .05 .02

☐ 252 Bob Brower .05 .02
☐ 253 Checklist .05 .02
☐ 254 Scott McGregor .05 .02
☐ 255 Ken Griffey .10 .05
☐ 256 Ken Schrom .05 .02
☐ 257 Gary Gaetti .10 .05
☐ 258 Ed Nunez .05 .02
☐ 259 Frank Viola .05 .02
☐ 260 Vince Coleman .05 .02
☐ 261 Reid Nichols .05 .02
☐ 262 Tim Flannery .05 .02
☐ 263 Glenn Braggs .05 .02
☐ 264 Garry Templeton .05 .02
☐ 265 Bo Diaz .05 .02
☐ 266 Matt Nokes .05 .02
☐ 267 Barry Bonds 1.00 .45
☐ 268 Bruce Ruffin .05 .02
☐ 269 Ellis Burks .50 .23
☐ 270 Mike Witt .05 .02
☐ 271 Ken Gerhart .05 .02
☐ 272 Lloyd Moseby .05 .02
☐ 273 Garth Iorg .05 .02
☐ 274 Mike Greenwell .10 .05
☐ 275 Kevin Seitzer .10 .05
☐ 276 Luis Salazar .05 .02
☐ 277 Shawon Dunston .05 .02
☐ 278 Rick Reuschel .10 .05
☐ 279 Randy St.Claire .05 .02
☐ 280 Pete Incaviglia .05 .02
☐ 281 Mike Boddicker .05 .02
☐ 282 Jay Tibbs .05 .02
☐ 283 Shane Mack .05 .02
☐ 284 Walt Terrell .05 .02
☐ 285 Jim Presley .05 .02
☐ 286 Greg Walker .05 .02
☐ 287 Dwight Gooden .15 .07
☐ 288 Jim Morrison .05 .02
☐ 289 Gene Garber .05 .02
☐ 290 Tony Fernandez .05 .02
☐ 291 Ozzie Virgil .05 .02
☐ 292 Carney Lansford .05 .02
☐ 293 Jim Acker .05 .02
☐ 294 Tommy Hinzo .05 .02
☐ 295 Bert Blyleven .10 .05
☐ 296 Ozzie Guillen .05 .02
☐ 297 Zane Smith .05 .02
☐ 298 Milt Thompson .05 .02
☐ 299 Len Dykstra .10 .05
☐ 300 Don Mattingly .75 .35
☐ 301 Bud Black .05 .02
☐ 302 Jose Uribe .05 .02
☐ 303 Manny Lee .05 .02
☐ 304 Sid Bream .05 .02
☐ 305 Steve Sax .05 .02
☐ 306 Billy Hatcher .05 .02
☐ 307 John Shelby .05 .02
☐ 308 Lee Mazzilli .05 .02
☐ 309 Bill Long .05 .02
☐ 310 Tom Herr .05 .02
☐ 311 Derek Bell .75 .35
Blue Jays' second
draft choice
☐ 312 George Brett .60 .25
☐ 313 Bob McClure .05 .02
☐ 314 Jimy Williams MG .05 .02
Team checklist back
☐ 315 Dave Parker .10 .05
Now with Athletics
☐ 316 Doyle Alexander .05 .02
☐ 317 Dan Plesac .05 .02
☐ 318 Mel Hall .05 .02
☐ 319 Ruben Sierra .10 .05
☐ 320 Alan Trammell .15 .07
☐ 321 Mike Schmidt .30 .14
☐ 322 Wally Ritchie .05 .02
☐ 323 Rick Leach .05 .02
☐ 324 Danny Jackson .05 .02
Now with Reds
☐ 325 Glenn Hubbard .05 .02
☐ 326 Frank White .10 .05
☐ 327 Larry Sheets .05 .02
☐ 328 John Cangelosi .05 .02
☐ 329 Bill Gullickson .05 .02
☐ 330 Eddie Whitson .05 .02
☐ 331 Brian Downing .10 .05
☐ 332 Gary Redus .05 .02
☐ 333 Wally Backman .05 .02
☐ 334 Dwayne Murphy .05 .02
☐ 335 Claudell Washington .05 .02
☐ 336 Dave Concepcion .10 .05
☐ 337 Jim Gantner .05 .02
☐ 338 Marty Barrett .05 .02
☐ 339 Mickey Hatcher .05 .02
☐ 340 Jack Morris .15 .07
☐ 341 John Franco .10 .05
☐ 342 Ron Robinson .05 .02
☐ 343 Greg Gagne .05 .02

☐ 344 Steve Bedrosian .05 .02
☐ 345 Scott Fletcher .05 .02
☐ 346 Vance Law .05 .02
Now with Cubs
☐ 347 Joe Johnson .05 .02
Now with Angels
☐ 348 Jim Eisenreich .15 .07
☐ 349 Alvin Davis .05 .02
☐ 350 Will Clark .50 .23
☐ 351 Mike Aldrete .05 .02
☐ 352 Billy Ripken .05 .02
☐ 353 Dave Stewart .10 .05
☐ 354 Neal Heaton .05 .02
☐ 355 Roger McDowell .05 .02
☐ 356 John Tudor .05 .02
☐ 357 Floyd Bannister .05 .02
Now with Royals
☐ 358 Rey Quinones .05 .02
☐ 359 Glenn Wilson .05 .02
Now with Mariners
☐ 360 Tony Gwynn .60 .25
☐ 361 Greg Maddux 3.00 1.35
☐ 362 Juan Castillo .05 .02
☐ 363 Willie Fraser .05 .02
☐ 364 Nick Esasky .05 .02
☐ 365 Floyd Youmans .05 .02
☐ 366 Chet Lemon .05 .02
☐ 367 Matt Young .05 .02
Now with A's
☐ 368 Gerald Young .05 .02
☐ 369 Bob Stanley .05 .02
☐ 370 Jose Canseco .25 .11
☐ 371 Joe Hesketh .05 .02
☐ 372 Rick Sutcliffe .05 .02
☐ 373 Checklist 133-264 .05 .02
☐ 374 Checklist 265-396 .05 .02
☐ 375 Tom Brunansky .05 .02
☐ 376 Jody Davis .05 .02
☐ 377 Sam Horn .05 .02
☐ 378 Mark Gubicza .05 .02
☐ 379 Rafael Ramirez .05 .02
Now with Astros
☐ 380 Joe Magrane .05 .02
☐ 381 Pete O'Brien .05 .02
☐ 382 Lee Guetterman .05 .02
☐ 383 Eric Bell .05 .02
☐ 384 Gene Larkin .05 .02
☐ 385 Carlton Fisk .15 .07
☐ 386 Mike Fitzgerald .05 .02
☐ 387 Kevin Mitchell .10 .05
☐ 388 Jim Winn .05 .02
☐ 389 Mike Smithson .05 .02
☐ 390 Darrell Evans .10 .05
☐ 391 Terry Leach .05 .02
☐ 392 Charlie Kerfeld .05 .02
☐ 393 Mike Krukow .05 .02
☐ 394 Mark McGwire 1.25 .55
☐ 395 Fred McGriff .50 .23
☐ 396 DeWayne Buice .05 .02

1988 O-Pee-Chee Box Bottoms

O-Pee-Chee printed four different four-card panels on the bottoms of its 1988 wax pack boxes. If cut, each card would measure approximately the standard size. These 16 cards, in alphabetical order and designated A through P, are considered a separate set from the regular issue but are styled almost exactly the same, differing only in the player photo and colors for the team name, borders and position on the front. The backs are identical, except for the letter designations instead of numbers.

	MINT	NRMT
COMPLETE SET (16)	8.00	3.60
COMMON CARD (A-P)	.10	.05

☐ A Don Baylor .25 .11
☐ B Steve Bedrosian .10 .05
☐ C Juan Beniquez .10 .05
☐ D Bob Boone .25 .11
☐ E Darrell Evans .25 .11
☐ F Tony Gwynn 1.50 .70
☐ G John Kruk .40 .18

☐ H Marvell Wynne	.10	.05
☐ I Joe Carter	.60	.25
☐ J Eric Davis	.25	.11
☐ K Howard Johnson	.10	.05
☐ L Darryl Strawberry	.25	.11
☐ M Rickey Henderson	.75	.35
☐ N Nolan Ryan	3.00	1.35
☐ O Mike Schmidt	1.25	.55
☐ P Kent Tekulve	.10	.05

1989 O-Pee-Chee

The 1989 O-Pee-Chee baseball set contains 396 standard-size cards that feature white bordered color player photos framed by colored lines. The player's name and team appear at the lower right. The bilingual pinkish horizontal backs are bordered in black and carry the player's biography and statistics.

	MINT	NRMT
COMPLETE SET (396)	15.00	6.75
COMPLETE FACT. SET (396)	15.00	6.75
COMMON CARD (1-396)	.05	.02

☐ 1 Brook Jacoby	.05	.02
☐ 2 Atlee Hammaker	.05	.02
☐ 3 Jack Clark	.05	.02
☐ 4 Dave Stieb	.05	.02
☐ 5 Bud Black	.05	.02
☐ 6 Damon Berryhill	.05	.02
☐ 7 Mike Scioscia	.05	.02
☐ 8 Jose Uribe	.05	.02
☐ 9 Mike Aldrete	.05	.02
☐ 10 Andre Dawson	.15	.07
☐ 11 Bruce Sutter	.05	.02
☐ 12 Dale Sveum	.05	.02
☐ 13 Dan Quisenberry	.05	.02
☐ 14 Tom Niedenfuer	.05	.02
☐ 15 Robby Thompson	.05	.02
☐ 16 Ron Robinson	.05	.02
☐ 17 Brian Downing	.05	.02
☐ 18 Rick Rhoden	.05	.02
☐ 19 Greg Gagne	.05	.02
☐ 20 Allan Anderson	.05	.02
☐ 21 Eddie Whitson	.05	.02
☐ 22 Billy Ripken	.05	.02
☐ 23 Mike Fitzgerald	.05	.02
☐ 24 Shane Rawley	.05	.02
☐ 25 Frank White	.10	.05
☐ 26 Don Mattingly	1.00	.45
☐ 27 Fred Lynn	.05	.02
☐ 28 Mike Moore	.05	.02
☐ 29 Kelly Gruber	.05	.02
☐ 30 Dwight Gooden	.10	.05
☐ 31 Dan Pasqua	.05	.02
☐ 32 Dennis Rasmussen	.05	.02
☐ 33 B.J. Surhoff	.10	.05
☐ 34 Sid Fernandez	.05	.02
☐ 35 John Tudor	.05	.02
☐ 36 Mitch Webster	.05	.02
☐ 37 Doug Drabek	.05	.02
☐ 38 Bobby Witt	.05	.02
☐ 39 Mike Maddux	.05	.02
☐ 40 Steve Sax	.05	.02
☐ 41 Orel Hershiser	.10	.05
☐ 42 Pete Incaviglia	.05	.02
☐ 43 Guillermo Hernandez	.05	.02
☐ 44 Kevin Coffman	.05	.02
☐ 45 Kal Daniels	.05	.02
☐ 46 Carlton Fisk	.25	.11
☐ 47 Carney Lansford	.05	.02
☐ 48 Tim Burke	.05	.02
☐ 49 Alan Trammell	.15	.07
☐ 50 George Bell	.05	.02
☐ 51 Tony Gwynn	1.00	.45
☐ 52 Bob Brenly	.05	.02
☐ 53 Ruben Sierra	.05	.02
☐ 54 Otis Nixon	.10	.05
☐ 55 Julio Franco	.10	.05
☐ 56 Pat Tabler	.05	.02
☐ 57 Alvin Davis	.05	.02
☐ 58 Kevin Seitzer	.05	.02
☐ 59 Mark Davis	.05	.02
☐ 60 Tom Brunansky	.05	.02
☐ 61 Jeff Treadway	.05	.02
☐ 62 Alfredo Griffin	.05	.02
☐ 63 Keith Hernandez	.10	.05
☐ 64 Alex Trevino	.05	.02
☐ 65 Rick Reuschel	.05	.02
☐ 66 Bob Walk	.05	.02
☐ 67 Dave Palmer	.05	.02
☐ 68 Pedro Guerrero	.05	.02
☐ 69 Jose Oquendo	.05	.02
☐ 70 Mark McGwire	1.00	.45
☐ 71 Mike Boddicker	.05	.02
☐ 72 Wally Backman	.05	.02
☐ 73 Pascual Perez	.05	.02
☐ 74 Joe Hesketh	.05	.02
☐ 75 Tom Henke	.05	.02
☐ 76 Nelson Liriano	.05	.02
☐ 77 Doyle Alexander	.05	.02
☐ 78 Tim Wallach	.05	.02
☐ 79 Scott Bankhead	.05	.02
☐ 80 Cory Snyder	.05	.02
☐ 81 Dave Magadan	.05	.02
☐ 82 Randy Ready	.05	.02
☐ 83 Steve Buechele	.05	.02
☐ 84 Bo Jackson	.15	.07
☐ 85 Kevin McReynolds	.05	.02
☐ 86 Jeff Reardon	.10	.05
☐ 87 Tim Raines (Named Rock on card)	.10	.05
☐ 88 Melido Perez	.05	.02
☐ 89 Dave LaPoint	.05	.02
☐ 90 Vince Coleman	.05	.02
☐ 91 Floyd Youmans	.05	.02
☐ 92 Buddy Bell	.10	.05
☐ 93 Andres Galarraga	.25	.11
☐ 94 Tony Pena	.05	.02
☐ 95 Gerald Young	.05	.02
☐ 96 Rick Cerone	.05	.02
☐ 97 Ken Oberkfell	.05	.02
☐ 98 Larry Sheets	.05	.02
☐ 99 Chuck Crim	.05	.02
☐ 100 Mike Schmidt	.30	.14
☐ 101 Ivan Calderon	.05	.02
☐ 102 Kevin Bass	.05	.02
☐ 103 Chili Davis	.10	.05
☐ 104 Randy Myers	.10	.05
☐ 105 Ron Darling	.05	.02
☐ 106 Willie Upshaw	.05	.02
☐ 107 Jose DeLeon	.05	.02
☐ 108 Fred Manrique	.05	.02
☐ 109 Johnny Ray	.05	.02
☐ 110 Paul Molitor	.30	.14
☐ 111 Rance Mulliniks	.05	.02
☐ 112 Jim Presley	.05	.02
☐ 113 Lloyd Moseby	.05	.02
☐ 114 Lance Parrish	.05	.02
☐ 115 Jody Davis	.05	.02
☐ 116 Matt Nokes	.05	.02
☐ 117 Dave Anderson	.05	.02
☐ 118 Checklist 1-132	.05	.02
☐ 119 Rafael Belliard	.05	.02
☐ 120 Frank Viola	.05	.02
☐ 121 Roger Clemens	.50	.23
☐ 122 Luis Salazar	.05	.02
☐ 123 Mike Stanley	.05	.02
☐ 124 Jim Traber	.05	.02
☐ 125 Mike Krukow	.05	.02
☐ 126 Sid Bream	.05	.02
☐ 127 Joel Skinner	.05	.02
☐ 128 Milt Thompson	.05	.02
☐ 129 Terry Clark	.05	.02
☐ 130 Gerald Perry	.05	.02
☐ 131 Bryn Smith	.05	.02
☐ 132 Kirby Puckett	1.00	.45
☐ 133 Bill Long	.05	.02
☐ 134 Jim Gantner	.05	.02
☐ 135 Jose Rijo	.05	.02
☐ 136 Joey Meyer	.05	.02
☐ 137 Geno Petralli	.05	.02
☐ 138 Wallace Johnson	.05	.02
☐ 139 Mike Flanagan	.05	.02
☐ 140 Shawon Dunston	.05	.02
☐ 141 Eric Plunk	.05	.02
☐ 142 Bobby Bonilla	.15	.07
☐ 143 Jack McDowell	.40	.18
☐ 144 Mookie Wilson	.10	.05
☐ 145 Dave Stewart	.10	.05
☐ 146 Gary Pettis	.05	.02
☐ 147 Eric Show	.05	.02
☐ 148 Eddie Murray	.40	.18
☐ 149 Lee Smith	.10	.05
☐ 150 Fernando Valenzuela	.10	.05
☐ 151 Bob Walk	.05	.02
☐ 152 Harold Baines	.10	.05
☐ 153 Albert Hall	.05	.02
☐ 154 Don Carman	.05	.02
☐ 155 Marty Barrett	.05	.02
☐ 156 Chris Sabo	.05	.02
☐ 157 Bret Saberhagen	.05	.02
☐ 158 Danny Cox	.05	.02
☐ 159 Tom Foley	.05	.02
☐ 160 Jeffrey Leonard	.05	.02
☐ 161 Brady Anderson	1.00	.45
☐ 162 Rich Gossage	.10	.05
☐ 163 Greg Brock	.05	.02
☐ 164 Joe Carter	.15	.07
☐ 165 Mike Dunne	.05	.02
☐ 166 Jeff Russell	.05	.02
☐ 167 Dan Plesac	.05	.02
☐ 168 Willie Wilson	.05	.02
☐ 169 Mike Jackson	.05	.02
☐ 170 Tony Fernandez	.05	.02
☐ 171 Jamie Moyer	.05	.02
☐ 172 Jim Gott	.05	.02
☐ 173 Mel Hall	.05	.02
☐ 174 Mark McGwire	1.00	.45
☐ 175 John Shelby	.05	.02
☐ 176 Jeff Parrett	.05	.02
☐ 177 Tim Belcher	.05	.02
☐ 178 Rich Gedman	.05	.02
☐ 179 Ozzie Virgil	.05	.02
☐ 180 Mike Scott	.05	.02
☐ 181 Dickie Thon	.05	.02
☐ 182 Rob Murphy	.05	.02
☐ 183 Oddibe McDowell	.05	.02
☐ 184 Wade Boggs	.30	.14
☐ 185 Claudell Washington	.05	.02
☐ 186 Randy Johnson	1.25	.55
☐ 187 Paul O'Neill	.10	.05
☐ 188 Todd Benzinger	.05	.02
☐ 189 Kevin Mitchell	.10	.05
☐ 190 Mike Witt	.05	.02
☐ 191 Sil Campusano	.05	.02
☐ 192 Ken Gerhart	.05	.02
☐ 193 Bob Rodgers	.05	.02
☐ 194 Floyd Bannister	.05	.02
☐ 195 Ozzie Guillen	.05	.02
☐ 196 Ron Gant	.25	.11
☐ 197 Neal Heaton	.05	.02
☐ 198 Bill Swift	.05	.02
☐ 199 Dave Parker	.15	.07
☐ 200 George Brett	.75	.35
☐ 201 Bo Diaz	.05	.02
☐ 202 Brad Moore	.05	.02
☐ 203 Rob Ducey	.05	.02
☐ 204 Bert Blyleven	.10	.05
☐ 205 Dwight Evans	.10	.05
☐ 206 Roberto Alomar	.75	.35
☐ 207 Henry Cotto	.05	.02
☐ 208 Harold Reynolds	.10	.05
☐ 209 Jose Guzman	.05	.02
☐ 210 Dale Murphy	.15	.07
☐ 211 Mike Pagliarulo	.05	.02
☐ 212 Jay Howell	.05	.02
☐ 213 Rene Gonzales	.05	.02
☐ 214 Scott Garrelts	.05	.02
☐ 215 Kevin Gross	.05	.02
☐ 216 Jack Howell	.05	.02
☐ 217 Kurt Stillwell	.05	.02
☐ 218 Mike LaValliere	.05	.02
☐ 219 Jim Clancy	.05	.02
☐ 220 Gary Gaetti	.05	.02
☐ 221 Hubie Brooks	.05	.02
☐ 222 Bruce Ruffin	.05	.02
☐ 223 Jay Buhner	.40	.18
☐ 224 Cecil Fielder	.10	.05
☐ 225 Willie McGee	.10	.05
☐ 226 Bill Doran	.05	.02
☐ 227 John Farrell	.05	.02
☐ 228 Nelson Santovenia	.05	.02
☐ 229 Jimmy Key	.10	.05
☐ 230 Ozzie Smith	.75	.35
☐ 231 Dave Schmidt	.05	.02
☐ 232 Jody Reed	.05	.02
☐ 233 Gregg Jefferies	.15	.07
☐ 234 Tom Browning	.05	.02
☐ 235 John Kruk	.10	.05
☐ 236 Charles Hudson	.05	.02
☐ 237 Todd Stottlemyre	.10	.05
☐ 238 Don Slaught	.05	.02
☐ 239 Tim Laudner	.05	.02
☐ 240 Greg Maddux	1.25	.55
☐ 241 Brett Butler	.10	.05
☐ 242 Checklist 133-264	.05	.02
☐ 243 Bob Boone	.10	.05
☐ 244 Willie Randolph	.10	.05
☐ 245 Jim Rice	.15	.07
☐ 246 Rey Quinones	.05	.02
☐ 247 Checklist 265-396	.05	.02
☐ 248 Stan Javier	.05	.02
☐ 249 Tim Leary	.05	.02
☐ 250 Cal Ripken	1.50	.70
☐ 251 John Dopson	.05	.02
☐ 252 Billy Hatcher	.05	.02

☐ 253 Robin Yount .15 .07
☐ 254 Mickey Hatcher .05 .02
☐ 255 Bob Horner .05 .02
☐ 256 Benny Santiago .05 .02
☐ 257 Luis Rivera .05 .02
☐ 258 Fred McGriff .15 .07
☐ 259 Dave Wells .05 .02
☐ 260 Dave Winfield .25 .11
☐ 261 Rafael Ramirez .05 .02
☐ 262 Nick Esasky .05 .02
☐ 263 Barry Bonds .50 .23
☐ 264 Joe Magrane .05 .02
☐ 265 Kent Hrbek .05 .02
☐ 266 Jack Morris .10 .05
☐ 267 Jeff M. Robinson .05 .02
☐ 268 Ron Kittle .05 .02
☐ 269 Candy Maldonado .05 .02
☐ 270 Wally Joyner .10 .05
☐ 271 Glenn Braggs .05 .02
☐ 272 Ron Hassey .05 .02
☐ 273 Jose Lind .05 .02
☐ 274 Mark Eichhorn .05 .02
☐ 275 Danny Tartabull .05 .02
☐ 276 Paul Kilgus .05 .02
☐ 277 Mike Davis .05 .02
☐ 278 Andy McGaffigan .05 .02
☐ 279 Scott Bradley .05 .02
☐ 280 Bob Knepper .05 .02
☐ 281 Gary Redus .05 .02
☐ 282 Rickey Henderson .25 .11
☐ 283 Andy Allanson .05 .02
☐ 284 Rick Leach .05 .02
☐ 285 John Candelaria .05 .02
☐ 286 Dick Schofield .05 .02
☐ 287 Bryan Harvey .10 .05
☐ 288 Randy Bush .05 .02
☐ 289 Ernie Whitt .05 .02
☐ 290 John Franco .10 .05
☐ 291 Todd Worrell .05 .02
☐ 292 Teddy Higuera .05 .02
☐ 293 Keith Moreland .05 .02
☐ 294 Juan Berenguer .05 .02
☐ 295 Scott Fletcher .05 .02
☐ 296 Roger McDowell .05 .02
Now with Indians 12-6-88
☐ 297 Mark Grace .75 .35
☐ 298 Chris James .05 .02
☐ 299 Frank Tanana .05 .02
☐ 300 Darryl Strawberry .10 .05
☐ 301 Charlie Leibrandt .05 .02
☐ 302 Gary Ward .05 .02
☐ 303 Brian Fisher .05 .02
☐ 304 Terry Steinbach .10 .05
☐ 305 Dave Smith .05 .02
☐ 306 Greg Minton .05 .02
☐ 307 Lance McCullers .05 .02
☐ 308 Phil Bradley .05 .02
☐ 309 Terry Kennedy .05 .02
☐ 310 Rafael Palmeiro .25 .11
☐ 311 Ellis Burks .25 .11
☐ 312 Doug Jones .05 .02
☐ 313 Denny Martinez .10 .05
☐ 314 Pete O'Brien .05 .02
☐ 315 Greg Swindell .05 .02
☐ 316 Walt Weiss .05 .02
☐ 317 Pete Stanicek .05 .02
☐ 318 Gene Nelson .05 .02
☐ 319 Danny Jackson .05 .02
☐ 320 Lou Whitaker .10 .05
☐ 321 Will Clark .30 .14
☐ 322 John Smiley .05 .02
☐ 323 Mike Marshall .05 .02
☐ 324 Gary Carter .25 .11
☐ 325 Jesse Barfield .05 .02
☐ 326 Dennis Boyd .05 .02
☐ 327 Dave Henderson .05 .02
☐ 328 Chet Lemon .05 .02
☐ 329 Bob Melvin .05 .02
☐ 330 Eric Davis .10 .05
☐ 331 Ted Power .05 .02
☐ 332 Carmelo Martinez .05 .02
☐ 333 Bob Ojeda .05 .02
☐ 334 Steve Lyons .05 .02
☐ 335 Dave Righetti .05 .02
☐ 336 Steve Balboni .05 .02
☐ 337 Calvin Schiraldi .05 .02
☐ 338 Vance Law .05 .02
☐ 339 Zane Smith .05 .02
☐ 340 Kirk Gibson .15 .07
☐ 341 Jim Deshaies .05 .02
☐ 342 Tom Brookens .05 .02
☐ 343 Pat Borders .05 .02
☐ 344 Devon White .10 .05
☐ 345 Charlie Hough .10 .05
☐ 346 Rex Hudler .05 .02
☐ 347 John Cerutti .05 .02
☐ 348 Kirk McCaskill .05 .02
☐ 349 Len Dykstra .10 .05
☐ 350 Andy Van Slyke .10 .05
☐ 351 Jeff D. Robinson .05 .02
☐ 352 Rick Schu .05 .02
☐ 353 Bruce Benedict .05 .02
☐ 354 Bill Wegman .05 .02
☐ 355 Mark Langston .05 .02
☐ 356 Steve Farr .05 .02
☐ 357 Richard Dotson .05 .02
☐ 358 Andres Thomas .05 .02
☐ 359 Alan Ashby .05 .02
☐ 360 Ryne Sandberg .75 .35
☐ 361 Kelly Downs .05 .02
☐ 362 Jeff Musselman .05 .02
☐ 363 Barry Larkin .25 .11
☐ 364 Rob Deer .05 .02
☐ 365 Mike Henneman .05 .02
☐ 366 Nolan Ryan 1.50 .70
☐ 367 Johnny Paredes .05 .02
☐ 368 Bobby Thigpen .05 .02
☐ 369 Mickey Brantley .05 .02
☐ 370 Dennis Eckersley .15 .07
☐ 371 Manny Lee .05 .02
☐ 372 Juan Samuel .05 .02
☐ 373 Tracy Jones .05 .02
☐ 374 Mike Greenwell .05 .02
☐ 375 Terry Pendleton .10 .05
☐ 376 Steve Lombardozzi .05 .02
☐ 377 Mitch Williams .05 .02
☐ 378 Glenn Davis .05 .02
☐ 379 Mark Gubicza .05 .02
☐ 380 Orel Hershiser WS .10 .05
☐ 381 Jimy Williams .05 .02
☐ 382 Kirk Gibson WS .30 .14
☐ 383 Howard Johnson .05 .02
☐ 384 David Cone .25 .11
☐ 385 Von Hayes .05 .02
☐ 386 Luis Polonia .10 .05
☐ 387 Danny Gladden .05 .02
☐ 388 Pete Smith .05 .02
☐ 389 Jose Canseco .30 .14
☐ 390 Mickey Hatcher .05 .02
☐ 391 Wil Tejada .05 .02
☐ 392 Duane Ward .05 .02
☐ 393 Rick Mahler .05 .02
☐ 394 Rick Sutcliffe .05 .02
☐ 395 Dave Martinez .05 .02
☐ 396 Ken Dayley .05 .02

1989 O-Pee-Chee Box Bottoms

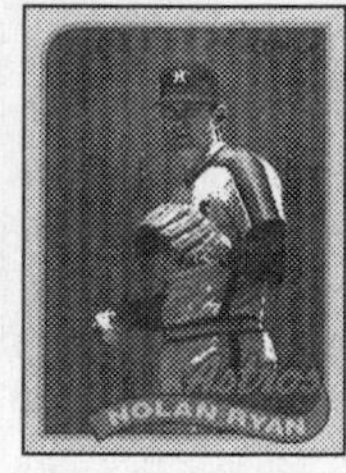

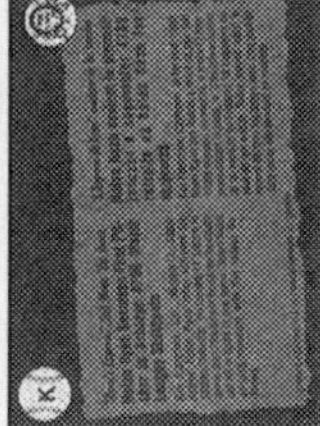

These standard-size box bottom cards feature on their fronts blue-bordered color player photos. The player's name and team appear at the bottom right. The horizontal black back carries bilingual career highlights within a purple panel. The value of the panels uncut is slightly greater, perhaps by 25 percent greater, than the value of the individual cards cut up carefully. The sixteen cards in this set honor players (and one manager) who reached career milestones during the 1988 season.The cards are lettered on the back.

	MINT	NRMT
COMPLETE SET (16)	6.00	2.70
COMMON CARD (A-K)	.10	.05

☐ A George Brett 1.00 .45
(475th Double)
☐ B Bill Buckner .25 .11
(2600th Hit)
☐ C Darrell Evans .25 .11
(400th Home Run)
☐ D Rich Gossage .40 .18
(300th Save)
☐ E Greg Gross .10 .05
(125th Pinch Hit)
☐ F Rickey Henderson .60 .25
(775th Stolen Base)
☐ G Keith Hernandez .25 .11
(125th GW-RBI)
☐ H Tom Lasorda MG .25 .11
(1000th Managerial Win)
☐ I Jim Rice .25 .11
(1400th Run Batted In)
☐ J Cal Ripken 2.00 .90
(1000th Cons. Game)
☐ K Nolan Ryan 2.00 .90
(4700th Strikeout)
☐ L Mike Schmidt .60 .25
(1000th Long Hit)
☐ M Bruce Sutter .10 .05
(300th Save)
☐ N Don Sutton .60 .25
(750th Game Started)
☐ O Kent Tekulve .10 .05
(1000th Appearance)
☐ P Dave Winfield .40 .18
(1400th RBI)

1990 O-Pee-Chee

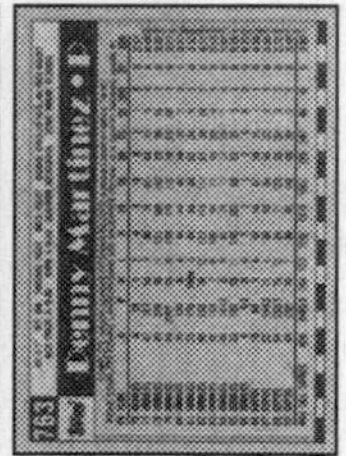

The 1990 O-Pee-Chee baseball set was a 792-card standard-size set. For the first time since 1976, O-Pee-Chee issued the exact same set as Topps. The only distinctions are the bilingual text and the O-Pee-Chee copyright on the backs. The fronts feature color player photos bordered in various colors. The player's name appears at the bottom and his team name is printed at the top. The yellow horizontal backs carry the player's name, biography and position at the top, followed below by major league statistics. Cards 385-407 feature All-Stars, while cards 661-665 are Turn Back the Clock cards. Players appearing in their Rookie Cards year include Delino DeShields (who had been on a 1988 OPC card), Juan Gonzalez, Marquis Grissom, Ben McDonald, Frank Thomas and Larry Walker.

	MINT	NRMT
COMPLETE SET (792)	25.00	11.00
COMPLETE FACT.SET (792)	25.00	11.00
COMMON CARD (1-792)	.05	.02

☐ 1 Nolan Ryan 1.50 .70
☐ 2 Nolan Ryan Salute .75 .35
New York Mets
☐ 3 Nolan Ryan Salute .75 .35
California Angels
☐ 4 Nolan Ryan Salute .75 .35
Houston Astros
☐ 5 Nolan Ryan Salute .75 .35
Texas Rangers UER
(Says Texas Stadium
rather than
Arlington Stadium)
☐ 6 Vince Coleman RB .05 .02
50 consecutive SB's
☐ 7 Rickey Henderson RB .25 .11
40 career leadoff HR's
☐ 8 Cal Ripken RB .75 .35
20 or more homers for
8 consecutive years
record for shortstops
☐ 9 Eric Plunk .05 .02
☐ 10 Barry Larkin .15 .07
☐ 11 Paul Gibson .05 .02
☐ 12 Joe Girardi .10 .05
☐ 13 Mark Williamson .05 .02
☐ 14 Mike Fetters .05 .02
☐ 15 Teddy Higuera .05 .02
☐ 16 Kent Anderson .05 .02
☐ 17 Kelly Downs .05 .02
☐ 18 Carlos Quintana .05 .02
☐ 19 Al Newman .05 .02
☐ 20 Mark Gubicza .05 .02
☐ 21 Jeff Torborg MG .05 .02
☐ 22 Bruce Ruffin .05 .02
☐ 23 Randy Velarde .05 .02
☐ 24 Joe Hesketh .05 .02
☐ 25 Willie Randolph .10 .05
☐ 26 Don Slaught .05 .02
Now with Pirates
12/4/89
☐ 27 Rick Leach .05 .02
☐ 28 Duane Ward .05 .02
☐ 29 John Cangelosi .05 .02
☐ 30 David Cone .15 .07

☐ 31 Henry Cotto .05 .02
☐ 32 John Farrell .05 .02
☐ 33 Greg Walker .05 .02
☐ 34 Tony Fossas .05 .02
☐ 35 Benito Santiago .05 .02
☐ 36 John Costello .05 .02
☐ 37 Domingo Ramos .05 .02
☐ 38 Wes Gardner .05 .02
☐ 39 Curt Ford .05 .02
☐ 40 Jay Howell .05 .02
☐ 41 Matt Williams .25 .11
☐ 42 Jeff M. Robinson .05 .02
☐ 43 Dante Bichette .30 .14
☐ 44 Roger Salkeld FDP .05 .02
☐ 45 Dave Parker UER .10 .05
Born in Jackson
not Calhoun
☐ 46 Rob Dibble .05 .02
☐ 47 Brian Harper .05 .02
☐ 48 Zane Smith .05 .02
☐ 49 Tom Lawless .05 .02
☐ 50 Glenn Davis .05 .02
☐ 51 Doug Rader MG .05 .02
☐ 52 Jack Daugherty .05 .02
☐ 53 Mike LaCoss .05 .02
☐ 54 Joel Skinner .05 .02
☐ 55 Darrell Evans UER .10 .05
HR total should be
414, not 424
☐ 56 Franklin Stubbs .05 .02
☐ 57 Greg Vaughn .10 .05
☐ 58 Keith Miller .05 .02
☐ 59 Ted Power .05 .02
Now with Pirates
11/21/89
☐ 60 George Brett .75 .35
☐ 61 Deion Sanders .30 .14
☐ 62 Ramon Martinez .15 .07
☐ 63 Mike Pagliarulo .05 .02
☐ 64 Danny Darwin .05 .02
☐ 65 Devon White .10 .05
☐ 66 Greg Litton .05 .02
☐ 67 Scott Sanderson .05 .02
Now with Athletics
12/13/89
☐ 68 Dave Henderson .05 .02
☐ 69 Todd Frohwirth .05 .02
☐ 70 Mike Greenwell .05 .02
☐ 71 Allan Anderson .05 .02
☐ 72 Jeff Huson .05 .02
☐ 73 Bob Milacki .05 .02
☐ 74 Jeff Jackson FDP .05 .02
☐ 75 Doug Jones .05 .02
☐ 76 Dave Valle .05 .02
☐ 77 Dave Bergman .05 .02
☐ 78 Mike Flanagan .05 .02
☐ 79 Ron Kittle .05 .02
☐ 80 Jeff Russell .05 .02
☐ 81 Bob Rodgers MG .05 .02
☐ 82 Scott Terry .05 .02
☐ 83 Hensley Meulens .05 .02
☐ 84 Ray Searage .05 .02
☐ 85 Juan Samuel .05 .02
Now with Dodgers
12/20/89
☐ 86 Paul Kilgus .05 .02
Now with Blue Jays
12/7/89
☐ 87 Rick Luecken .05 .02
Now with Braves
12/17/89
☐ 88 Glenn Braggs .05 .02
☐ 89 Clint Zavaras .05 .02
☐ 90 Jack Clark .10 .05
☐ 91 Steve Frey .05 .02
☐ 92 Mike Stanley .05 .02
☐ 93 Shawn Hillegas .05 .02
☐ 94 Herm Winningham .05 .02
☐ 95 Todd Worrell .05 .02
☐ 96 Jody Reed .05 .02
☐ 97 Curt Schilling .25 .11
☐ 98 Jose Gonzalez .05 .02
☐ 99 Rich Monteleone .05 .02
☐ 100 Will Clark .25 .11
☐ 101 Shane Rawley .05 .02
Now with Red Sox
1/9/90
☐ 102 Stan Javier .05 .02
☐ 103 Marvin Freeman .05 .02
☐ 104 Bob Knepper .05 .02
☐ 105 Randy Myers .10 .05
Now with Reds
12/8/89
☐ 106 Charlie O'Brien .05 .02
☐ 107 Fred Lynn .10 .05
Now with Padres
12/7/89
☐ 108 Rod Nichols .05 .02
☐ 109 Roberto Kelly .05 .02
☐ 110 Tommy Helms MG .05 .02
☐ 111 Ed Whited .05 .02
☐ 112 Glenn Wilson .05 .02
☐ 113 Manny Lee .05 .02
☐ 114 Mike Bielecki .05 .02
☐ 115 Tony Pena .05 .02
Now with Red Sox
11/28/89
☐ 116 Floyd Bannister .05 .02
☐ 117 Mike Sharperson .05 .02
☐ 118 Erik Hanson .05 .02
☐ 119 Billy Hatcher .05 .02
☐ 120 John Franco .10 .05
Now with Mets
12/8/89
☐ 121 Robin Ventura .15 .07
☐ 122 Shawn Abner .05 .02
☐ 123 Rich Gedman .05 .02
☐ 124 Dave Dravecky .10 .05
☐ 125 Kent Hrbek .10 .05
☐ 126 Randy Kramer .05 .02
☐ 127 Mike Devereaux .05 .02
☐ 128 Checklist 1 .05 .02
☐ 129 Ron Jones .05 .02
☐ 130 Bert Blyleven .10 .05
☐ 131 Matt Nokes .05 .02
☐ 132 Lance Blankenship .05 .02
☐ 133 Ricky Horton .05 .02
☐ 134 Earl Cunningham FDP .05 .02
☐ 135 Dave Magadan .05 .02
☐ 136 Kevin Brown .15 .07
☐ 137 Marty Pevey .05 .02
☐ 138 Al Leiter .10 .05
☐ 139 Greg Brock .05 .02
☐ 140 Andre Dawson .25 .11
☐ 141 John Hart MG .05 .02
☐ 142 Jeff Wetherby .05 .02
☐ 143 Rafael Belliard .05 .02
☐ 144 Bud Black .05 .02
☐ 145 Terry Steinbach .10 .05
☐ 146 Rob Richie .05 .02
☐ 147 Chuck Finley .10 .05
☐ 148 Edgar Martinez .30 .14
☐ 149 Steve Farr .05 .02
☐ 150 Kirk Gibson .10 .05
☐ 151 Rick Mahler .05 .02
☐ 152 Lonnie Smith .05 .02
☐ 153 Randy Milligan .05 .02
☐ 154 Mike Maddux .05 .02
Now with Dodgers
12/21/89
☐ 155 Ellis Burks .15 .07
☐ 156 Ken Patterson .05 .02
☐ 157 Craig Biggio .30 .14
☐ 158 Craig Lefferts .05 .02
Now with Padres
12/7/89
☐ 159 Mike Felder .05 .02
☐ 160 Dave Righetti .05 .02
☐ 161 Harold Reynolds .10 .05
☐ 162 Todd Zeile .10 .05
☐ 163 Phil Bradley .05 .02
☐ 164 Jeff Juden FDP .25 .11
☐ 165 Walt Weiss .05 .02
☐ 166 Bobby Witt .05 .02
☐ 167 Kevin Appier .15 .07
☐ 168 Jose Lind .05 .02
☐ 169 Richard Dotson .05 .02
Now with Royals
12/6/89
☐ 170 George Bell .05 .02
☐ 171 Russ Nixon MG .05 .02
☐ 172 Tom Lampkin .05 .02
☐ 173 Tim Belcher .05 .02
☐ 174 Jeff Kunkel .05 .02
☐ 175 Mike Moore .05 .02
☐ 176 Luis Quinones .05 .02
☐ 177 Mike Henneman .05 .02
☐ 178 Chris James .05 .02
Now with Indians
12/6/89
☐ 179 Brian Holton .05 .02
☐ 180 Tim Raines .10 .05
☐ 181 Juan Agosto .05 .02
☐ 182 Mookie Wilson .05 .02
☐ 183 Steve Lake .05 .02
☐ 184 Danny Cox .05 .02
☐ 185 Ruben Sierra .05 .02
☐ 186 Dave LaPoint .05 .02
☐ 187 Rick Wrona .05 .02
☐ 188 Mike Smithson .05 .02
Now with Angels
12/19/89
☐ 189 Dick Schofield .05 .02
☐ 190 Rick Reuschel .10 .05
☐ 191 Pat Borders .05 .02
☐ 192 Don August .05 .02
☐ 193 Andy Benes .15 .07
☐ 194 Glenallen Hill .10 .05
☐ 195 Tim Burke .05 .02
☐ 196 Gerald Young .05 .02
☐ 197 Doug Drabek .05 .02
☐ 198 Mike Marshall .05 .02
Now with Mets
12/20/89
☐ 199 Sergio Valdez .05 .02
☐ 200 Don Mattingly .60 .25
☐ 201 Cito Gaston MG .05 .02
☐ 202 Mike Macfarlane .05 .02
☐ 203 Mike Roesler .05 .02
☐ 204 Bob Dernier .05 .02
☐ 205 Mark Davis .05 .02
Now with Royals
12/11/89
☐ 206 Nick Esasky .05 .02
Now with Braves
11/17/89
☐ 207 Bob Ojeda .05 .02
☐ 208 Brook Jacoby .05 .02
☐ 209 Greg Mathews .05 .02
☐ 210 Ryne Sandberg .50 .23
☐ 211 John Cerutti .05 .02
☐ 212 Joe Orsulak .05 .02
☐ 213 Scott Bankhead .05 .02
☐ 214 Terry Francona .05 .02
☐ 215 Kirk McCaskill .05 .02
☐ 216 Ricky Jordan .05 .02
☐ 217 Don Robinson .05 .02
☐ 218 Wally Backman .05 .02
☐ 219 Donn Pall .05 .02
☐ 220 Barry Bonds .50 .23
☐ 221 Gary Mielke .05 .02
☐ 222 Kurt Stillwell UER .05 .02
Graduate misspelled
as gradute
☐ 223 Tommy Gregg .05 .02
☐ 224 Delino DeShields .30 .14
☐ 225 Jim Deshaies .05 .02
☐ 226 Mickey Hatcher .05 .02
☐ 227 Kevin Tapani .10 .05
☐ 228 Dave Martinez .05 .02
☐ 229 David Wells .05 .02
☐ 230 Keith Hernandez .10 .05
Now with Indians
12/7/89
☐ 231 Jack McKeon MG .05 .02
☐ 232 Darnell Coles .05 .02
☐ 233 Ken Hill .15 .07
☐ 234 Mariano Duncan .05 .02
☐ 235 Jeff Reardon .10 .05
Now with Red Sox
12/6/89
☐ 236 Hal Morris .10 .05
Now with Reds
12/12/89
☐ 237 Kevin Ritz .05 .02
☐ 238 Felix Jose .05 .02
☐ 239 Eric Show .05 .02
☐ 240 Mark Grace .30 .14
☐ 241 Mike Krukow .05 .02
☐ 242 Fred Manrique .05 .02
☐ 243 Barry Jones .05 .02
☐ 244 Bill Schroeder .05 .02
☐ 245 Roger Clemens .75 .35
☐ 246 Jim Eisenreich .10 .05
☐ 247 Jerry Reed .05 .02
☐ 248 Dave Anderson .05 .02
Now with Giants,(11/29/89
☐ 249 Mike(Texas) Smith .05 .02
☐ 250 Jose Canseco .15 .07
☐ 251 Jeff Blauser .05 .02
☐ 252 Otis Nixon .10 .05
☐ 253 Mark Portugal .05 .02
☐ 254 Francisco Cabrera .05 .02
☐ 255 Bobby Thigpen .05 .02
☐ 256 Marvell Wynne .05 .02
☐ 257 Jose DeLeon .05 .02
☐ 258 Barry Lyons .05 .02
☐ 259 Lance McCullers .05 .02
☐ 260 Eric Davis .10 .05
☐ 261 Whitey Herzog MG .10 .05
☐ 262 Checklist 2 .05 .02
☐ 263 Mel Stottlemyre Jr. .05 .02
☐ 264 Bryan Clutterbuck .05 .02
☐ 265 Pete O'Brien .05 .02
Now with Mariners
12/7/89
☐ 266 German Gonzalez .05 .02
☐ 267 Mark Davidson .05 .02
☐ 268 Rob Murphy .05 .02
☐ 269 Dickie Thon .05 .02
☐ 270 Dave Stewart .10 .05

271 Chet Lemon	.05	.02
272 Bryan Harvey	.05	.02
273 Bobby Bonilla	.10	.05
274 Mauro Gozzo	.05	.02
275 Mickey Tettleton	.10	.05
276 Gary Thurman	.05	.02
277 Lenny Harris	.05	.02
278 Pascual Perez	.05	.02
Now with Yankees		
11/27/89		
279 Steve Buechele	.05	.02
280 Lou Whitaker	.10	.05
281 Kevin Bass	.05	.02
Now with Giants		
11/20/89		
282 Derek Lilliquist	.05	.02
283 Joey Belle	1.00	.45
284 Mark Gardner	.05	.02
285 Willie McGee	.10	.05
286 Lee Guetterman	.05	.02
287 Vance Law	.05	.02
288 Greg Briley	.05	.02
289 Norm Charlton	.05	.02
290 Robin Yount	.15	.07
291 Dave Johnson MG	.10	.05
292 Jim Gott	.05	.02
Now with Dodgers		
12/7/89		
293 Mike Gallego	.05	.02
294 Craig McMurtry	.05	.02
295 Fred McGriff	.15	.07
296 Jeff Ballard	.05	.02
297 Tom Herr	.05	.02
298 Dan Gladden	.05	.02
299 Adam Peterson	.05	.02
300 Bo Jackson	.10	.05
301 Don Aase	.05	.02
302 Marcus Lawton	.05	.02
303 Rick Cerone	.05	.02
Now with Yankees		
12/19/89		
304 Marty Clary	.05	.02
305 Eddie Murray	.50	.23
306 Tom Niedenfuer	.05	.02
307 Bip Roberts	.05	.02
308 Jose Guzman	.05	.02
309 Eric Yelding	.05	.02
310 Steve Bedrosian	.05	.02
311 Dwight Smith	.05	.02
312 Dan Quisenberry	.05	.02
313 Gus Polidor	.05	.02
314 Donald Harris FDP	.05	.02
315 Bruce Hurst	.05	.02
316 Carney Lansford	.10	.05
317 Mark Guthrie	.05	.02
318 Wallace Johnson	.05	.02
319 Dion James	.05	.02
320 Dave Stieb	.10	.05
321 Joe Morgan MG	.05	.02
322 Junior Ortiz	.05	.02
323 Willie Wilson	.10	.05
324 Pete Harnisch	.05	.02
325 Robby Thompson	.05	.02
326 Tom McCarthy	.05	.02
327 Ken Williams	.05	.02
328 Curt Young	.05	.02
329 Oddibe McDowell	.05	.02
330 Ron Darling	.05	.02
331 Juan Gonzalez	3.00	1.35
332 Paul O'Neill	.10	.05
333 Bill Wegman	.05	.02
334 Johnny Ray	.05	.02
335 Andy Hawkins	.05	.02
336 Ken Griffey Jr.	3.00	1.35
337 Lloyd McClendon	.05	.02
338 Dennis Lamp	.05	.02
339 Dave Clark	.05	.02
Now with Cubs		
11/20/89		
340 Fernando Valenzuela	.10	.05
341 Tom Foley	.05	.02
342 Alex Trevino	.05	.02
343 Frank Tanana	.10	.05
344 George Canale	.05	.02
345 Harold Baines	.10	.05
346 Jim Presley	.05	.02
347 Junior Felix	.05	.02
348 Gary Wayne	.05	.02
349 Steve Finley	.25	.11
350 Bret Saberhagen	.05	.02
351 Roger Craig MG	.05	.02
352 Bryn Smith	.05	.02
Now with Cardinals		
11/29/89		
353 Sandy Alomar Jr.	.15	.07
Now with Indians		
12/6/89		
354 Stan Belinda	.05	.02
355 Marty Barrett	.05	.02
356 Randy Ready	.05	.02
357 Dave West	.05	.02
358 Andres Thomas	.05	.02
359 Jimmy Jones	.05	.02
360 Paul Molitor	.40	.18
361 Randy McCament	.05	.02
362 Damon Berryhill	.05	.02
363 Dan Petry	.05	.02
364 Rolando Roomes	.05	.02
365 Ozzie Guillen	.05	.02
366 Mike Heath	.05	.02
367 Mike Morgan	.05	.02
368 Bill Doran	.05	.02
369 Todd Burns	.05	.02
370 Tim Wallach	.05	.02
371 Jimmy Key	.10	.05
372 Terry Kennedy	.05	.02
373 Alvin Davis	.05	.02
374 Steve Cummings	.05	.02
375 Dwight Evans	.10	.05
376 Checklist 3 UER	.05	.02
Higuera misalphabet-		
ized in Brewer list		
377 Mickey Weston	.05	.02
378 Luis Salazar	.05	.02
379 Steve Rosenberg	.05	.02
380 Dave Winfield	.25	.11
381 Frank Robinson MG	.15	.07
382 Jeff Musselman	.05	.02
383 John Morris	.05	.02
384 Pat Combs	.05	.02
385 Fred McGriff AS	.15	.07
386 Julio Franco AS	.05	.02
387 Wade Boggs AS	.25	.11
388 Cal Ripken AS	.75	.35
389 Robin Yount AS	.15	.07
390 Ruben Sierra AS	.05	.02
391 Kirby Puckett AS	.40	.18
392 Carlton Fisk AS	.10	.05
393 Bret Saberhagen AS	.05	.02
394 Jeff Ballard AS	.05	.02
395 Jeff Russell AS	.05	.02
396 A.Bartlett Giamatti	.25	.11
COMM MEM		
397 Will Clark AS	.15	.07
398 Ryne Sandberg AS	.25	.11
399 Howard Johnson AS	.05	.02
400 Ozzie Smith AS	.25	.11
401 Kevin Mitchell AS	.05	.02
402 Eric Davis AS	.05	.02
403 Tony Gwynn AS	.50	.23
404 Craig Biggio AS	.15	.07
405 Mike Scott AS	.05	.02
406 Joe Magrane AS	.05	.02
407 Mark Davis AS	.05	.02
Now with Royals		
12/11/89		
408 Trevor Wilson	.05	.02
409 Tom Brunansky	.05	.02
410 Joe Boever	.05	.02
411 Ken Phelps	.05	.02
412 Jamie Moyer	.05	.02
413 Brian DuBois	.05	.02
414 Frank Thomas FDP	6.00	2.70
415 Shawon Dunston	.05	.02
416 Dave Johnson (P)	.05	.02
417 Jim Gantner	.05	.02
418 Tom Browning	.05	.02
419 Beau Allred	.05	.02
420 Carlton Fisk	.25	.11
421 Greg Minton	.05	.02
422 Pat Sheridan	.05	.02
423 Fred Toliver	.05	.02
Now with Yankees		
9/27/89		
424 Jerry Reuss	.05	.02
425 Bill Landrum	.05	.02
426 Jeff Hamilton UER	.05	.02
Stats say he fanned		
197 times in 1987		
but he only had 147 at bats		
427 Carmen Castillo	.05	.02
428 Steve Davis	.05	.02
Now with Dodgers		
12/12/89		
429 Tom Kelly MG	.05	.02
430 Pete Incaviglia	.05	.02
431 Randy Johnson	.60	.25
432 Damaso Garcia	.05	.02
Now with Yankees		
12/22/89		
433 Steve Olin	.10	.05
434 Mark Carreon	.05	.02
435 Kevin Seitzer	.05	.02
436 Mel Hall	.05	.02
437 Les Lancaster	.05	.02
438 Greg Myers	.05	.02
439 Jeff Parrett	.05	.02
440 Alan Trammell	.15	.07
441 Bob Kipper	.05	.02
442 Jerry Browne	.05	.02
443 Cris Carpenter	.05	.02
444 Kyle Abbott FDP	.05	.02
445 Danny Jackson	.05	.02
446 Dan Pasqua	.05	.02
447 Atlee Hammaker	.05	.02
448 Greg Gagne	.05	.02
449 Dennis Rasmussen	.05	.02
450 Rickey Henderson	.30	.14
451 Mark Lemke	.10	.05
452 Luis DeLosSantos	.05	.02
453 Jody Davis	.05	.02
454 Jeff King	.10	.05
455 Jeffrey Leonard	.05	.02
456 Chris Gwynn	.05	.02
457 Gregg Jefferies	.10	.05
458 Bob McClure	.05	.02
459 Jim Lefebvre MG	.05	.02
460 Mike Scott	.05	.02
461 Carlos Martinez	.05	.02
462 Denny Walling	.05	.02
463 Drew Hall	.05	.02
464 Jerome Walton	.05	.02
465 Kevin Gross	.05	.02
466 Rance Mulliniks	.05	.02
467 Juan Nieves	.05	.02
468 Bill Ripken	.05	.02
469 John Kruk	.10	.05
470 Frank Viola	.05	.02
471 Mike Brumley	.05	.02
Now with Orioles		
1/10/90		
472 Jose Uribe	.05	.02
473 Joe Price	.05	.02
474 Rich Thompson	.05	.02
475 Bob Welch	.10	.05
476 Brad Komminsk	.05	.02
477 Willie Fraser	.05	.02
478 Mike LaValliere	.05	.02
479 Frank White	.10	.05
480 Sid Fernandez	.05	.02
481 Garry Templeton	.05	.02
482 Steve Carter	.05	.02
483 Alejandro Pena	.05	.02
Now with Mets		
12/20/89		
484 Mike Fitzgerald	.05	.02
485 John Candelaria	.05	.02
486 Jeff Treadway	.05	.02
487 Steve Searcy	.05	.02
488 Ken Oberkfell	.05	.02
Now with Astros		
12/6/89		
489 Nick Leyva MG	.05	.02
490 Dan Plesac	.05	.02
491 Dave Cochrane	.05	.02
492 Ron Oester	.05	.02
493 Jason Grimsley	.05	.02
494 Terry Puhl	.05	.02
495 Lee Smith	.10	.05
496 Cecil Espy UER	.05	.02
'88 stats have 3 SB's		
should be 33		
497 Dave Schmidt	.05	.02
Now with Expos		
12/13/89		
498 Rick Schu	.05	.02
499 Bill Long	.05	.02
500 Kevin Mitchell	.05	.02
501 Matt Young	.05	.02
Now with Mariners		
12/8/89		
502 Mitch Webster	.05	.02
Now with Indians		
11/20/89		
503 Randy St.Claire	.05	.02
504 Tom O'Malley	.05	.02
505 Kelly Gruber	.05	.02
506 Tom Glavine	.25	.11
507 Gary Redus	.05	.02
508 Terry Leach	.05	.02
509 Tom Pagnozzi	.05	.02
510 Dwight Gooden	.10	.05
511 Clay Parker	.05	.02
512 Gary Pettis	.05	.02
Now with Rangers		
11/24/89		
513 Mark Eichhorn	.05	.02
Now with Angels		
12/13/89		
514 Andy Allanson	.05	.02
515 Len Dykstra	.10	.05

☐ 516 Tim Leary .05 .02
☐ 517 Roberto Alomar .50 .23
☐ 518 Bill Krueger .05 .02
☐ 519 Bucky Dent MG .05 .02
☐ 520 Mitch Williams .05 .02
☐ 521 Craig Worthington .05 .02
☐ 522 Mike Dunne .05 .02
Now with Padres
12/4/89
☐ 523 Jay Bell .10 .05
☐ 524 Daryl Boston .05 .02
☐ 525 Wally Joyner .10 .05
☐ 526 Checklist 4 .05 .02
☐ 527 Ron Hassey .05 .02
☐ 528 Kevin Wickander UER .05 .02
Monthly scoreboard
strikeout total was 2.2
that was his innings
pitched total
☐ 529 Greg A. Harris .05 .02
☐ 530 Mark Langston .05 .02
Now with Angels
12/4/89
☐ 531 Ken Caminiti .25 .11
☐ 532 Cecilio Guante .05 .02
Now with Indians
11/21/89
☐ 533 Tim Jones .05 .02
☐ 534 Louie Meadows .05 .02
☐ 535 John Smoltz .30 .14
☐ 536 Bob Geren .05 .02
☐ 537 Mark Grant .05 .02
☐ 538 Bill Spiers UER .05 .02
Photo actually George Canale
☐ 539 Neal Heaton .05 .02
☐ 540 Danny Tartabull .05 .02
☐ 541 Pat Perry .05 .02
☐ 542 Darren Daulton .10 .05
☐ 543 Nelson Liriano .05 .02
☐ 544 Dennis Boyd .05 .02
Now with Expos
12/7/89
☐ 545 Kevin McReynolds .05 .02
☐ 546 Kevin Hickey .05 .02
☐ 547 Jack Howell .05 .02
☐ 548 Pat Clements .05 .02
☐ 549 Don Zimmer MG .05 .02
☐ 550 Julio Franco .10 .05
☐ 551 Tim Crews .05 .02
☐ 552 Mike(Miss.) Smith .05 .02
☐ 553 Scott Scudder UER .05 .02
Cedar Rapids
☐ 554 Jay Buhner .25 .11
☐ 555 Jack Morris .10 .05
☐ 556 Gene Larkin .05 .02
☐ 557 Jeff Innis .05 .02
☐ 558 Rafael Ramirez .05 .02
☐ 559 Andy McGaffigan .05 .02
☐ 560 Steve Sax .05 .02
☐ 561 Ken Dayley .05 .02
☐ 562 Chad Kreuter .05 .02
☐ 563 Alex Sanchez .05 .02
☐ 564 Tyler Houston FDP .10 .05
☐ 565 Scott Fletcher .05 .02
☐ 566 Mark Knudson .05 .02
☐ 567 Ron Gant .15 .07
☐ 568 John Smiley .10 .05
☐ 569 Ivan Calderon .05 .02
☐ 570 Cal Ripken 1.50 .70
☐ 571 Brett Butler .10 .05
☐ 572 Greg W. Harris .05 .02
☐ 573 Danny Heep .05 .02
☐ 574 Bill Swift .05 .02
☐ 575 Lance Parrish .05 .02
☐ 576 Mike Dyer .05 .02
☐ 577 Charlie Hayes .05 .02
☐ 578 Joe Magrane .05 .02
☐ 579 Art Howe MG .05 .02
☐ 580 Joe Carter .15 .07
☐ 581 Ken Griffey Sr. .05 .02
☐ 582 Rick Honeycutt .05 .02
☐ 583 Bruce Benedict .05 .02
☐ 584 Phil Stephenson .05 .02
☐ 585 Kal Daniels .05 .02
☐ 586 Edwin Nunez .05 .02
☐ 587 Lance Johnson .10 .05
☐ 588 Rick Rhoden .05 .02
☐ 589 Mike Aldrete .05 .02
☐ 590 Ozzie Smith .50 .23
☐ 591 Todd Stottlemyre .05 .02
☐ 592 R.J. Reynolds .05 .02
☐ 593 Scott Bradley .05 .02
☐ 594 Luis Sojo .05 .02
☐ 595 Greg Swindell .05 .02
☐ 596 Jose DeJesus .05 .02
☐ 597 Chris Bosio .05 .02
☐ 598 Brady Anderson .15 .07
☐ 599 Frank Williams .05 .02
☐ 600 Darryl Strawberry .10 .05
☐ 601 Luis Rivera .05 .02
☐ 602 Scott Garrelts .05 .02
☐ 603 Tony Armas .05 .02
☐ 604 Ron Robinson .05 .02
☐ 605 Mike Scioscia .05 .02
☐ 606 Storm Davis .05 .02
Now with Royals
12/7/89
☐ 607 Steve Jeltz .05 .02
☐ 608 Eric Anthony .05 .02
☐ 609 Sparky Anderson MG .10 .05
☐ 610 Pedro Guerrero .05 .02
☐ 611 Walt Terrell .05 .02
Now with Pirates
11/29/89
☐ 612 Dave Gallagher .05 .02
☐ 613 Jeff Pico .05 .02
☐ 614 Nelson Santovenia .05 .02
☐ 615 Rob Deer .05 .02
☐ 616 Brian Holman .05 .02
☐ 617 Geronimo Berroa .05 .02
☐ 618 Ed Whitson .05 .02
☐ 619 Rob Ducey .05 .02
☐ 620 Tony Castillo .05 .02
☐ 621 Melido Perez .05 .02
☐ 622 Sid Bream .05 .02
☐ 623 Jim Corsi .05 .02
☐ 624 Darrin Jackson .05 .02
☐ 625 Roger McDowell .05 .02
☐ 626 Bob Melvin .05 .02
☐ 627 Jose Rijo .05 .02
☐ 628 Candy Maldonado .05 .02
Now with Indians
11/28/89
☐ 629 Eric Hetzel .05 .02
☐ 630 Gary Gaetti .10 .05
☐ 631 John Wetteland .15 .07
☐ 632 Scott Lusader .05 .02
☐ 633 Dennis Cook .05 .02
☐ 634 Luis Polonia .05 .02
☐ 635 Brian Downing .05 .02
☐ 636 Jesse Orosco .05 .02
☐ 637 Craig Reynolds .05 .02
☐ 638 Jeff Montgomery .10 .05
☐ 639 Tony LaRussa MG .10 .05
☐ 640 Rick Sutcliffe .05 .02
☐ 641 Doug Strange .05 .02
☐ 642 Jack Armstrong .05 .02
☐ 643 Alfredo Griffin .05 .02
☐ 644 Paul Assenmacher .05 .02
☐ 645 Jose Oquendo .05 .02
☐ 646 Checklist 5 .05 .02
☐ 647 Rex Hudler .05 .02
☐ 648 Jim Clancy .05 .02
☐ 649 Dan Murphy .05 .02
☐ 650 Mike Witt .05 .02
☐ 651 Rafael Santana .05 .02
Now with Indians
1/10/90
☐ 652 Mike Boddicker .05 .02
☐ 653 John Moses .05 .02
☐ 654 Paul Coleman FDP .05 .02
☐ 655 Gregg Olson .05 .02
☐ 656 Mackey Sasser .05 .02
☐ 657 Terry Mulholland .05 .02
☐ 658 Donell Nixon .05 .02
☐ 659 Greg Cadaret .05 .02
☐ 660 Vince Coleman .05 .02
☐ 661 Dick Howser TBC'85 .05 .02
UER
Seaver's 300th on 7/11/85
should be 8/4/85
☐ 662 Mike Schmidt TBC'80 .15 .07
☐ 663 Fred Lynn TBC'75 .05 .02
☐ 664 Johnny Bench TBC'70 .15 .07
☐ 665 Sandy Koufax TBC'65 .50 .23
☐ 666 Brian Fisher .05 .02
☐ 667 Curt Wilkerson .05 .02
☐ 668 Joe Oliver .05 .02
☐ 669 Tom Lasorda MG .25 .11
☐ 670 Dennis Eckersley .15 .07
☐ 671 Bob Boone .10 .05
☐ 672 Roy Smith .05 .02
☐ 673 Joey Meyer .05 .02
☐ 674 Spike Owen .05 .02
☐ 675 Jim Abbott .10 .05
☐ 676 Randy Kutcher .05 .02
☐ 677 Jay Tibbs .05 .02
☐ 678 Kirt Manwaring UER .05 .02
'88 Phoenix stats repeated
☐ 679 Gary Ward .05 .02
☐ 680 Howard Johnson .05 .02
☐ 681 Mike Schooler .05 .02
☐ 682 Dann Bilardello .05 .02
☐ 683 Kenny Rogers .10 .05
☐ 684 Julio Machado .05 .02
☐ 685 Tony Fernandez .05 .02
☐ 686 Carmelo Martinez .05 .02
Now with Phillies
12/4/89
☐ 687 Tim Birtsas .05 .02
☐ 688 Milt Thompson .05 .02
☐ 689 Rich Yett .05 .02
Now with Twins
12/26/89
☐ 690 Mark McGwire .75 .35
☐ 691 Chuck Cary .05 .02
☐ 692 Sammy Sosa 1.50 .70
☐ 693 Calvin Schiraldi .05 .02
☐ 694 Mike Stanton .10 .05
☐ 695 Tom Henke .05 .02
☐ 696 B.J. Surhoff .10 .05
☐ 697 Mike Davis .05 .02
☐ 698 Omar Vizquel .15 .07
☐ 699 Jim Leyland MG .05 .02
☐ 700 Kirby Puckett .75 .35
☐ 701 Bernie Williams 1.50 .70
☐ 702 Tony Phillips .05 .02
Now with Tigers
12/5/89
☐ 703 Jeff Brantley .10 .05
☐ 704 Chip Hale .05 .02
☐ 705 Claudell Washington .05 .02
☐ 706 Geno Petralli .05 .02
☐ 707 Luis Aquino .05 .02
☐ 708 Larry Sheets .05 .02
Now with Tigers
1/10/90
☐ 709 Juan Berenguer .05 .02
☐ 710 Von Hayes .05 .02
☐ 711 Rick Aguilera .10 .05
☐ 712 Todd Benzinger .05 .02
☐ 713 Tim Drummond .05 .02
☐ 714 Marquis Grissom .75 .35
☐ 715 Greg Maddux 1.25 .55
☐ 716 Steve Balboni .05 .02
☐ 717 Ron Karkovice .05 .02
☐ 718 Gary Sheffield .50 .23
☐ 719 Wally Whitehurst .05 .02
☐ 720 Andres Galarraga .25 .11
☐ 721 Lee Mazzilli .05 .02
☐ 722 Felix Fermin .05 .02
☐ 723 Jeff D. Robinson .05 .02
Now with Yankees
12/4/89
☐ 724 Juan Bell .05 .02
☐ 725 Terry Pendleton .10 .05
☐ 726 Gene Nelson .05 .02
☐ 727 Pat Tabler .05 .02
☐ 728 Jim Acker .05 .02
☐ 729 Bobby Valentine MG .05 .02
☐ 730 Tony Gwynn 1.00 .45
☐ 731 Don Carman .05 .02
☐ 732 Ernest Riles .05 .02
☐ 733 John Dopson .05 .02
☐ 734 Kevin Elster .05 .02
☐ 735 Charlie Hough .10 .05
☐ 736 Rick Dempsey .05 .02
☐ 737 Chris Sabo .05 .02
☐ 738 Gene Harris .05 .02
☐ 739 Dale Sveum .05 .02
☐ 740 Jesse Barfield .05 .02
☐ 741 Steve Wilson .05 .02
☐ 742 Ernie Whitt .05 .02
☐ 743 Tom Candiotti .05 .02
☐ 744 Kelly Mann .05 .02
☐ 745 Hubie Brooks .05 .02
☐ 746 Dave Smith .05 .02
☐ 747 Randy Bush .05 .02
☐ 748 Doyle Alexander .05 .02
☐ 749 Mark Parent UER .05 .02
'87 BA .80, should be .080
☐ 750 Dale Murphy .15 .07
☐ 751 Steve Lyons .05 .02
☐ 752 Tom Gordon .05 .02
☐ 753 Chris Speier .05 .02
☐ 754 Bob Walk .05 .02
☐ 755 Rafael Palmeiro .15 .07
☐ 756 Ken Howell .05 .02
☐ 757 Larry Walker 2.00 .90
☐ 758 Mark Thurmond .05 .02
☐ 759 Tom Trebelhorn MG .05 .02
☐ 760 Wade Boggs .30 .14
☐ 761 Mike Jackson .05 .02
☐ 762 Doug Dascenzo .05 .02
☐ 763 Dennis Martinez .10 .05
☐ 764 Tim Teufel .05 .02
☐ 765 Chili Davis .10 .05
☐ 766 Brian Meyer .05 .02
☐ 767 Tracy Jones .05 .02
☐ 768 Chuck Crim .05 .02
☐ 769 Greg Hibbard .05 .02

	MINT	NRMT
☐ 770 Cory Snyder	.05	.02
☐ 771 Pete Smith	.05	.02
☐ 772 Jeff Reed	.05	.02
☐ 773 Dave Leiper	.05	.02
☐ 774 Ben McDonald	.25	.11
☐ 775 Andy Van Slyke	.10	.05
☐ 776 Charlie Leibrandt	.05	.02
Now with Braves 12/17/89		
☐ 777 Tim Laudner	.05	.02
☐ 778 Mike Jeffcoat	.05	.02
☐ 779 Lloyd Moseby	.05	.02
Now with Tigers 12/7/89		
☐ 780 Orel Hershiser	.10	.05
☐ 781 Mario Diaz	.05	.02
☐ 782 Jose Alvarez	.05	.02
Now with Giants 12/4/89		
☐ 783 Checklist 6	.05	.02
☐ 784 Scott Bailes	.05	.02
Now with Angels 1/9/90		
☐ 785 Jim Rice	.10	.05
☐ 786 Eric King	.05	.02
☐ 787 Rene Gonzales	.05	.02
☐ 788 Frank DiPino	.05	.02
☐ 789 John Wathan MG	.05	.02
☐ 790 Gary Carter	.25	.11
☐ 791 Alvaro Espinoza	.05	.02
☐ 792 Gerald Perry	.05	.02

1990 O-Pee-Chee Box Bottoms

The 1990 O-Pee-Chee box bottom cards comprise four different box bottoms from the bottoms of wax pack boxes, with four cards each, for a total of 16 standard-size cards. The cards are nearly identical to the 1990 Topps Box Bottom cards. The fronts feature green-bordered color player action shots. The player's name appears at the bottom and his team name appears at the upper left. The yellow-green horizontal backs carry player career highlights in both English and French. The cards are lettered (A-P) rather than numbered on the back.

	MINT	NRMT
COMPLETE SET (16)	5.00	2.20
COMMON CARD (A-P)	.10	.05
☐ A Wade Boggs	.50	.23
☐ B George Brett	1.00	.45
☐ C Andre Dawson	.35	.16
☐ D Darrell Evans	.10	.05
☐ E Dwight Gooden	.20	.09
☐ F Rickey Henderson	.50	.23
☐ G Tom Lasorda MG	.35	.16
☐ H Fred Lynn	.10	.05
☐ I Mark McGwire	.75	.35
☐ J Dave Parker	.20	.09
☐ K Jeff Reardon	.10	.05
☐ L Rick Reuschel	.10	.05
☐ M Jim Rice	.20	.09
☐ N Cal Ripken	2.50	1.10
☐ O Nolan Ryan	2.50	1.10
☐ P Ryne Sandberg	1.00	.45

1991 O-Pee-Chee

The 1991 O-Pee-Chee baseball set contains 792 standard-size cards. For the second time since 1976, O-Pee-Chee issued the exact same set as Topps. The only distinctions are the bilingual text and the O-Pee-Chee copyright on the backs. The fronts feature white-bordered color action player photos framed by two different colored lines. The player's name and position appear at the bottom of the photo, with his team name appearing just above. The Topps 40th anniversary logo appears in the upper left corner. The traded players have their new teams and dates of trade printed on the photo. The pinkish horizontal backs present player biography, statistics and bilingual career highlights. Cards 386-407 are an All-Star subset. Five

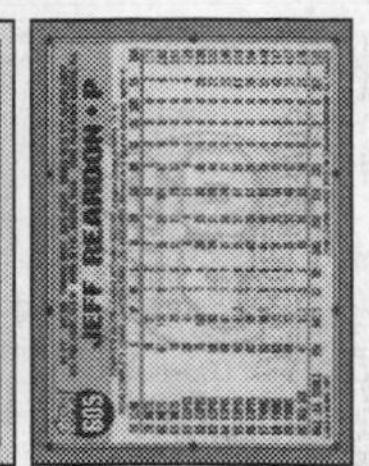

players are listed as Future Stars: 114 Lance Dickson, 211 Brian Barnes, 561 Tim McIntosh, 587 Jose Offerman, and 594 Rich Garces. Nine players are listed as First Draft Picks: 74 Shane Andrews, 103 Tim Costo, 113 Carl Everett, 278 Alex Fernandez, 471 Mike Lieberthal, 491 Kurt Miller, 529 Marc Newfield, 596 Ronnie Walden and 767 Dan Wilson.

	MINT	NRMT
COMPLETE SET (792)	25.00	11.00
COMPLETE FACT.SET (792)	25.00	11.00
COMMON CARD (1-792)	.05	.02
☐ 1 Nolan Ryan	1.50	.70
☐ 2 George Brett RB	.40	.18
☐ 3 Carlton Fisk RB	.15	.07
☐ 4 Kevin Maas RB	.05	.02
☐ 5 Cal Ripken RB	.75	.35
☐ 6 Nolan Ryan RB	.75	.35
☐ 7 Ryne Sandberg RB	.15	.07
☐ 8 Bobby Thigpen RB	.05	.02
☐ 9 Darrin Fletcher	.05	.02
☐ 10 Gregg Olson	.05	.02
☐ 11 Roberto Kelly	.05	.02
☐ 12 Paul Assenmacher	.05	.02
☐ 13 Mariano Duncan	.05	.02
☐ 14 Dennis Lamp	.05	.02
☐ 15 Von Hayes	.05	.02
☐ 16 Mike Heath	.05	.02
☐ 17 Jeff Brantley	.05	.02
☐ 18 Nelson Liriano	.05	.02
☐ 19 Jeff D. Robinson	.05	.02
☐ 20 Pedro Guerrero	.05	.02
☐ 21 Joe Morgan MG	.05	.02
☐ 22 Storm Davis	.05	.02
☐ 23 Jim Gantner	.05	.02
☐ 24 Dave Martinez	.05	.02
☐ 25 Tim Belcher	.05	.02
☐ 26 Luis Sojo UER	.05	.02
Born in Barquisimeto not Caracas		
Now with Angels 12/2/90		
☐ 27 Bobby Witt	.05	.02
☐ 28 Alvaro Espinoza	.05	.02
☐ 29 Bob Walk	.05	.02
☐ 30 Gregg Jefferies	.10	.05
☐ 31 Colby Ward	.05	.02
☐ 32 Mike Simms	.05	.02
☐ 33 Barry Jones	.05	.02
☐ 34 Atlee Hammaker	.05	.02
☐ 35 Greg Maddux	1.25	.55
☐ 36 Donnie Hill	.05	.02
☐ 37 Tom Bolton	.05	.02
☐ 38 Scott Bradley	.05	.02
☐ 39 Jim Neidlinger	.05	.02
☐ 40 Kevin Mitchell	.10	.05
☐ 41 Ken Dayley	.05	.02
Now with Blue Jays 11/26/90		
☐ 42 Chris Hoiles	.10	.05
☐ 43 Roger McDowell	.05	.02
☐ 44 Mike Felder	.05	.02
☐ 45 Chris Sabo	.05	.02
☐ 46 Tim Drummond	.05	.02
☐ 47 Brook Jacoby	.05	.02
☐ 48 Dennis Boyd	.05	.02
☐ 49 Pat Borders	.05	.02
☐ 50 Bob Welch	.05	.02
☐ 51 Art Howe MG	.05	.02
☐ 52 Francisco Oliveras	.05	.02
☐ 53 Mike Sharperson UER	.05	.02
Born in 1961, not 1960		
☐ 54 Gary Mielke	.05	.02
☐ 55 Jeffrey Leonard	.05	.02
☐ 56 Jeff Parrett	.05	.02
☐ 57 Jack Howell	.05	.02
☐ 58 Mel Stottlemyre Jr.	.05	.02
☐ 59 Eric Yelding	.05	.02
☐ 60 Frank Viola	.05	.02
☐ 61 Stan Javier	.05	.02
☐ 62 Lee Guetterman	.05	.02
☐ 63 Milt Thompson	.05	.02
☐ 64 Tom Herr	.05	.02
☐ 65 Bruce Hurst	.05	.02
☐ 66 Terry Kennedy	.05	.02
☐ 67 Rick Honeycutt	.05	.02
☐ 68 Gary Sheffield	.25	.11
☐ 69 Steve Wilson	.05	.02
☐ 70 Ellis Burks	.10	.05
☐ 71 Jim Acker	.05	.02
☐ 72 Junior Ortiz	.05	.02
☐ 73 Craig Worthington	.05	.02
☐ 74 Shane Andrews	.10	.05
☐ 75 Jack Morris	.10	.05
☐ 76 Jerry Browne	.05	.02
☐ 77 Drew Hall	.05	.02
☐ 78 Geno Petralli	.05	.02
☐ 79 Frank Thomas	3.00	1.35
☐ 80 Fernando Valenzuela	.10	.05
☐ 81 Cito Gaston MG	.05	.02
☐ 82 Tom Glavine	.15	.07
☐ 83 Daryl Boston	.05	.02
☐ 84 Bob McClure	.05	.02
☐ 85 Jesse Barfield	.05	.02
☐ 86 Les Lancaster	.05	.02
☐ 87 Tracy Jones	.05	.02
☐ 88 Bob Tewksbury	.05	.02
☐ 89 Darren Daulton	.10	.05
☐ 90 Danny Tartabull	.05	.02
☐ 91 Greg Colbrunn	.15	.07
☐ 92 Danny Jackson	.05	.02
Now with Cubs 11/21/90		
☐ 93 Ivan Calderon	.05	.02
☐ 94 John Dopson	.05	.02
☐ 95 Paul Molitor	.30	.14
☐ 96 Trevor Wilson	.05	.02
☐ 97 Brady Anderson	.15	.07
☐ 98 Sergio Valdez	.05	.02
☐ 99 Chris Gwynn	.05	.02
☐ 100 Don Mattingly	.60	.25
☐ 101 Rob Ducey	.05	.02
☐ 102 Gene Larkin	.05	.02
☐ 103 Tim Costo	.05	.02
☐ 104 Don Robinson	.05	.02
☐ 105 Kevin McReynolds	.05	.02
☐ 106 Ed Nunez	.05	.02
Now with Brewers 12/4/90		
☐ 107 Luis Polonia	.05	.02
☐ 108 Matt Young	.05	.02
Now with Red Sox 12/4/90		
☐ 109 Greg Riddoch MG	.05	.02
☐ 110 Tom Henke	.05	.02
☐ 111 Andres Thomas	.05	.02
☐ 112 Frank DiPino	.05	.02
☐ 113 Carl Everett	.30	.14
☐ 114 Lance Dickson	.05	.02
☐ 115 Hubie Brooks	.05	.02
Now with Mets 12/15/90		
☐ 116 Mark Davis	.05	.02
☐ 117 Dion James	.05	.02
☐ 118 Tom Edens	.05	.02
☐ 119 Carl Nichols	.05	.02
☐ 120 Joe Carter	.15	.07
Now with Blue Jays 12/5/90		
☐ 121 Eric King	.05	.02
Now with Indians 12/4/90		
☐ 122 Paul O'Neill	.10	.05
☐ 123 Greg A. Harris	.05	.02
☐ 124 Randy Bush	.05	.02
☐ 125 Steve Bedrosian	.05	.02
Now with Twins 12/5/90		
☐ 126 Bernard Gilkey	.10	.05
☐ 127 Joe Price	.05	.02
☐ 128 Travis Fryman	.25	.11
Front has SS, back has SS-3B		
☐ 129 Mark Eichhorn	.05	.02
☐ 130 Ozzie Smith	.50	.23
☐ 131 Checklist 1	.05	.02
☐ 132 Jamie Quirk	.05	.02
☐ 133 Greg Briley	.05	.02
☐ 134 Kevin Elster	.05	.02
☐ 135 Jerome Walton	.05	.02
☐ 136 Dave Schmidt	.05	.02
☐ 137 Randy Ready	.05	.02
☐ 138 Jamie Moyer	.05	.02
Now with Cardinals 1/10/91		
☐ 139 Jeff Treadway	.05	.02
☐ 140 Fred McGriff	.15	.07
Now with Padres 12/5/90		
☐ 141 Nick Leyva MG	.05	.02
☐ 142 Curt Wilkerson	.05	.02

Now with Pirates
1/9/91
☐ 143 John Smiley .05 .02
☐ 144 Dave Henderson .05 .02
☐ 145 Lou Whitaker .10 .05
☐ 146 Dan Plesac .05 .02
☐ 147 Carlos Baerga .15 .07
☐ 148 Rey Palacios .05 .02
☐ 149 Al Osuna UER .05 .02
Shown with glove on
right hand
bio says throws right
☐ 150 Cal Ripken 1.50 .70
☐ 151 Tom Browning .05 .02
☐ 152 Mickey Hatcher .05 .02
☐ 153 Bryan Harvey .05 .02
☐ 154 Jay Buhner .15 .07
☐ 155 Dwight Evans .10 .05
Now with Orioles
12/6/90
☐ 156 Carlos Martinez .05 .02
☐ 157 John Smoltz .15 .07
☐ 158 Jose Uribe .05 .02
☐ 159 Joe Boever .05 .02
☐ 160 Vince Coleman .05 .02
☐ 161 Tim Leary .05 .02
☐ 162 Ozzie Canseco .05 .02
☐ 163 Dave Johnson .05 .02
☐ 164 Edgar Diaz .05 .02
☐ 165 Sandy Alomar Jr. .10 .05
☐ 166 Harold Baines .10 .05
☐ 167 Randy Tomlin .05 .02
☐ 168 John Olerud .10 .05
☐ 169 Luis Aquino .05 .02
☐ 170 Carlton Fisk .25 .11
☐ 171 Tony LaRussa MG .10 .05
☐ 172 Pete Incaviglia .05 .02
☐ 173 Jason Grimsley .05 .02
☐ 174 Ken Caminiti .25 .11
☐ 175 Jack Armstrong .05 .02
☐ 176 John Orton .05 .02
☐ 177 Reggie Harris .05 .02
☐ 178 Dave Valle .05 .02
☐ 179 Pete Harnisch .05 .02
Now with Astros
1/10/91
☐ 180 Tony Gwynn 1.00 .45
☐ 181 Duane Ward .05 .02
☐ 182 Junior Noboa .05 .02
☐ 183 Clay Parker .05 .02
☐ 184 Gary Green .05 .02
☐ 185 Joe Magrane .05 .02
☐ 186 Rod Booker .05 .02
☐ 187 Greg Cadaret .05 .02
☐ 188 Damon Berryhill .05 .02
☐ 189 Daryl Irvine .05 .02
☐ 190 Matt Williams .15 .07
☐ 191 Willie Blair .05 .02
Now with Indians
11/6/90
☐ 192 Rob Deer .05 .02
Now with Tigers
11/21/90
☐ 193 Felix Fermin .05 .02
☐ 194 Xavier Hernandez .05 .02
☐ 195 Wally Joyner .10 .05
☐ 196 Jim Vatcher .05 .02
☐ 197 Chris Nabholz .05 .02
☐ 198 R.J. Reynolds .05 .02
☐ 199 Mike Hartley .05 .02
☐ 200 Darryl Strawberry .10 .05
Now with Dodgers
11/8/90
☐ 201 Tom Kelly MG .05 .02
☐ 202 Jim Leyritz .10 .05
☐ 203 Gene Harris .05 .02
☐ 204 Herm Winningham .05 .02
☐ 205 Mike Perez .05 .02
☐ 206 Carlos Quintana .05 .02
☐ 207 Gary Wayne .05 .02
☐ 208 Willie Wilson .05 .02
☐ 209 Ken Howell .05 .02
☐ 210 Lance Parrish .10 .05
☐ 211 Brian Barnes .05 .02
☐ 212 Steve Finley .15 .07
Now with Astros
1/10/91
☐ 213 Frank Wills .05 .02
☐ 214 Joe Girardi .05 .02
☐ 215 Dave Smith .05 .02
Now with Cubs
12/17/90
☐ 216 Greg Gagne .05 .02
☐ 217 Chris Bosio .05 .02
☐ 218 Rick Parker .05 .02
☐ 219 Jack McDowell .10 .05
☐ 220 Tim Wallach .05 .02
☐ 221 Don Slaught .05 .02
☐ 222 Brian McRae .30 .14
☐ 223 Allan Anderson .05 .02
☐ 224 Juan Gonzalez 1.50 .70
☐ 225 Randy Johnson .50 .23
☐ 226 Alfredo Griffin .05 .02
☐ 227 Steve Avery UER .05 .02
Pitched 13 games for
Durham in 1989, not 2
☐ 228 Rex Hudler .05 .02
☐ 229 Rance Mulliniks .05 .02
☐ 230 Sid Fernandez .05 .02
☐ 231 Doug Rader MG .05 .02
☐ 232 Jose DeJesus .05 .02
☐ 233 Al Leiter .10 .05
☐ 234 Scott Erickson .10 .05
☐ 235 Dave Parker .10 .05
☐ 236 Frank Tanana .10 .05
☐ 237 Rick Cerone .05 .02
☐ 238 Mike Dunne .05 .02
☐ 239 Darren Lewis .05 .02
Now with Giants
12/4/90
☐ 240 Mike Scott .05 .02
☐ 241 Dave Clark UER .05 .02
Career totals 19 HR and 5 3B
should be 22 and 3
☐ 242 Mike LaCoss .05 .02
☐ 243 Lance Johnson .10 .05
☐ 244 Mike Jeffcoat .05 .02
☐ 245 Kal Daniels .05 .02
☐ 246 Kevin Wickander .05 .02
☐ 247 Jody Reed .05 .02
☐ 248 Tom Gordon .05 .02
☐ 249 Bob Melvin .05 .02
☐ 250 Dennis Eckersley .15 .07
☐ 251 Mark Lemke .05 .02
☐ 252 Mel Rojas .10 .05
☐ 253 Garry Templeton .05 .02
☐ 254 Shawn Boskie .05 .02
☐ 255 Brian Downing .05 .02
☐ 256 Greg Hibbard .05 .02
☐ 257 Tom O'Malley .05 .02
☐ 258 Chris Hammond .05 .02
☐ 259 Hensley Meulens .05 .02
☐ 260 Harold Reynolds .10 .05
☐ 261 Bud Harrelson MG .05 .02
☐ 262 Tim Jones .05 .02
☐ 263 Checklist 2 .05 .02
☐ 264 Dave Hollins .05 .02
☐ 265 Mark Gubicza .05 .02
☐ 266 Carmelo Castillo .05 .02
☐ 267 Mark Knudson .05 .02
☐ 268 Tom Brookens .05 .02
☐ 269 Joe Hesketh .05 .02
☐ 270 Mark McGwire .75 .35
☐ 271 Omar Olivares .05 .02
☐ 272 Jeff King .10 .05
☐ 273 Johnny Ray .05 .02
☐ 274 Ken Williams .05 .02
☐ 275 Alan Trammell .15 .07
☐ 276 Bill Swift .05 .02
☐ 277 Scott Coolbaugh .05 .02
Now with Padres
12/12/90
☐ 278 Alex Fernandez UER .15 .07
No '90 White Sox stats
☐ 279 Jose Gonzalez .05 .02
☐ 280 Bret Saberhagen .10 .05
☐ 281 Larry Sheets .05 .02
☐ 282 Don Carman .05 .02
☐ 283 Marquis Grissom .15 .07
☐ 284 Billy Spiers .05 .02
☐ 285 Jim Abbott .10 .05
☐ 286 Ken Oberkfell .05 .02
☐ 287 Mark Grant .05 .02
☐ 288 Derrick May .05 .02
☐ 289 Tim Birtsas .05 .02
☐ 290 Steve Sax .05 .02
☐ 291 John Wathan MG .05 .02
☐ 292 Bud Black .05 .02
☐ 293 Jay Bell .10 .05
☐ 294 Mike Moore .05 .02
☐ 295 Rafael Palmeiro .15 .07
☐ 296 Mark Williamson .05 .02
☐ 297 Manny Lee .05 .02
☐ 298 Omar Vizquel .15 .07
☐ 299 Scott Radinsky .05 .02
☐ 300 Kirby Puckett .75 .35
☐ 301 Steve Farr .05 .02
Now with Yankees
11/26/90
☐ 302 Tim Teufel .05 .02
☐ 303 Mike Boddicker .05 .02
Now with Royals
11/21/90
☐ 304 Kevin Reimer .05 .02
☐ 305 Mike Scioscia .05 .02
☐ 306 Lonnie Smith .05 .02
☐ 307 Andy Benes .10 .05
☐ 308 Tom Pagnozzi .05 .02
☐ 309 Norm Charlton .05 .02
☐ 310 Gary Carter .15 .07
☐ 311 Jeff Pico .05 .02
☐ 312 Charlie Hayes .05 .02
☐ 313 Ron Robinson .05 .02
☐ 314 Gary Pettis .05 .02
☐ 315 Roberto Alomar .25 .11
☐ 316 Gene Nelson .05 .02
☐ 317 Mike Fitzgerald .05 .02
☐ 318 Rick Aguilera .10 .05
☐ 319 Jeff McKnight .05 .02
☐ 320 Tony Fernandez .05 .02
Now with Padres
12/5/90
☐ 321 Bob Rodgers MG .05 .02
☐ 322 Terry Shumpert .05 .02
☐ 323 Cory Snyder .05 .02
☐ 324 Ron Kittle .05 .02
☐ 325 Brett Butler .10 .05
Now with Dodgers
12/15/90
☐ 326 Ken Patterson .05 .02
☐ 327 Ron Hassey .05 .02
☐ 328 Walt Terrell .05 .02
☐ 329 Dave Justice UER .30 .14
Drafted third round on card
should say fourth pick
☐ 330 Dwight Gooden .10 .05
☐ 331 Eric Anthony .05 .02
☐ 332 Kenny Rogers .05 .02
Now with White Sox
12/4/90
☐ 333 Chipper Jones FDP 5.00 2.20
☐ 334 Todd Benzinger .05 .02
☐ 335 Mitch Williams .05 .02
☐ 336 Matt Nokes .05 .02
☐ 337 Keith Comstock .05 .02
☐ 338 Luis Rivera .05 .02
☐ 339 Larry Walker .60 .25
☐ 340 Ramon Martinez .10 .05
☐ 341 John Moses .05 .02
☐ 342 Mickey Morandini .05 .02
☐ 343 Jose Oquendo .05 .02
☐ 344 Jeff Russell .05 .02
☐ 345 Len Dykstra .10 .05
☐ 346 Jesse Orosco .05 .02
☐ 347 Greg Vaughn .05 .02
☐ 348 Todd Stottlemyre .10 .05
☐ 349 Dave Gallagher .05 .02
Now with Angels
12/4/90
☐ 350 Glenn Davis .05 .02
☐ 351 Joe Torre MG .10 .05
☐ 352 Frank White .10 .05
☐ 353 Tony Castillo .05 .02
☐ 354 Sid Bream .05 .02
Now with Braves
12/5/90
☐ 355 Chili Davis .10 .05
☐ 356 Mike Marshall .05 .02
☐ 357 Jack Savage .05 .02
☐ 358 Mark Parent .05 .02
Now with Rangers
12/12/90
☐ 359 Chuck Cary .05 .02
☐ 360 Tim Raines .10 .05
Now with White Sox
12/23/90
☐ 361 Scott Garrelts .05 .02
☐ 362 Hector Villanueva .05 .02
☐ 363 Rick Mahler .05 .02
☐ 364 Dan Pasqua .05 .02
☐ 365 Mike Schooler .05 .02
☐ 366 Checklist 3 .05 .02
☐ 367 Dave Walsh .05 .02
☐ 368 Felix Jose .05 .02
☐ 369 Steve Searcy .05 .02
☐ 370 Kelly Gruber .05 .02
☐ 371 Jeff Montgomery .05 .02
☐ 372 Spike Owen .05 .02
☐ 373 Darrin Jackson .05 .02
☐ 374 Larry Casian .05 .02
☐ 375 Tony Pena .05 .02
☐ 376 Mike Harkey .05 .02
☐ 377 Rene Gonzales .05 .02
☐ 378 Wilson Alvarez .15 .07
☐ 379 Randy Velarde .05 .02
☐ 380 Willie McGee .10 .05
Now with Giants
12/3/90
☐ 381 Jim Leyland MG .05 .02
☐ 382 Mackey Sasser .05 .02
☐ 383 Pete Smith .05 .02
☐ 384 Gerald Perry .05 .02

Now with Cardinals 12/13/90		
☐ 385 Mickey Tettleton	.10	.05
Now with Tigers 1/12/90		
☐ 386 Cecil Fielder AS	.10	.05
☐ 387 Julio Franco AS	.05	.02
☐ 388 Kelly Gruber AS	.05	.02
☐ 389 Alan Trammell AS	.10	.05
☐ 390 Jose Canseco AS	.15	.07
☐ 391 Rickey Henderson AS	.15	.07
☐ 392 Ken Griffey Jr. AS	1.50	.70
☐ 393 Carlton Fisk AS	.15	.07
☐ 394 Bob Welch AS	.05	.02
☐ 395 Chuck Finley AS	.05	.02
☐ 396 Bobby Thigpen AS	.05	.02
☐ 397 Eddie Murray AS	.15	.07
☐ 398 Ryne Sandberg AS	.15	.07
☐ 399 Matt Williams AS	.15	.07
☐ 400 Barry Larkin AS	.15	.07
☐ 401 Barry Bonds AS	.25	.11
☐ 402 Darryl Strawbery AS	.10	.05
☐ 403 Bobby Bonilla AS	.10	.05
☐ 404 Mike Scioscia AS	.05	.02
☐ 405 Doug Drabek AS	.05	.02
☐ 406 Frank Viola AS	.05	.02
☐ 407 John Franco AS	.05	.02
☐ 408 Earnie Riles	.05	.02
Now with Athletics 12/4/90		
☐ 409 Mike Stanley	.05	.02
☐ 410 Dave Righetti	.05	.02
Now with Giants 12/4/90		
☐ 411 Lance Blankenship	.05	.02
☐ 412 Dave Bergman	.05	.02
☐ 413 Terry Mulholland	.05	.02
☐ 414 Sammy Sosa	.50	.23
☐ 415 Rick Sutcliffe	.05	.02
☐ 416 Randy Milligan	.05	.02
☐ 417 Bill Krueger	.05	.02
☐ 418 Nick Esasky	.05	.02
☐ 419 Jeff Reed	.05	.02
☐ 420 Bobby Thigpen	.05	.02
☐ 421 Alex Cole	.05	.02
☐ 422 Rick Reuschel	.10	.05
☐ 423 Rafael Ramirez UER	.05	.02
Born 1959, not 1958		
☐ 424 Calvin Schiraldi	.05	.02
☐ 425 Andy Van Slyke	.10	.05
☐ 426 Joe Grahe	.05	.02
☐ 427 Rick Dempsey	.05	.02
☐ 428 John Barfield	.05	.02
☐ 429 Stump Merrill MG	.05	.02
☐ 430 Gary Gaetti	.10	.05
☐ 431 Paul Gibson	.05	.02
☐ 432 Delino DeShields	.05	.02
☐ 433 Pat Tabler	.05	.02
Now with Blue Jays 12/5/90		
☐ 434 Julio Machado	.05	.02
☐ 435 Kevin Maas	.05	.02
☐ 436 Scott Bankhead	.05	.02
☐ 437 Doug Dascenzo	.05	.02
☐ 438 Vicente Palacios	.05	.02
☐ 439 Dickie Thon	.05	.02
☐ 440 George Bell	.05	.02
Now with Cubs 12/6/90		
☐ 441 Zane Smith	.05	.02
☐ 442 Charlie O'Brien	.05	.02
☐ 443 Jeff Innis	.05	.02
☐ 444 Glenn Braggs	.05	.02
☐ 445 Greg Swindell	.05	.02
☐ 446 Craig Grebeck	.05	.02
☐ 447 John Burkett	.05	.02
☐ 448 Craig Lefferts	.05	.02
☐ 449 Juan Berenguer	.05	.02
☐ 450 Wade Boggs	.25	.11
☐ 451 Neal Heaton	.05	.02
☐ 452 Bill Schroeder	.05	.02
☐ 453 Lenny Harris	.05	.02
☐ 454 Kevin Appier	.15	.07
☐ 455 Walt Weiss	.05	.02
☐ 456 Charlie Leibrandt	.05	.02
☐ 457 Todd Hundley	.25	.11
☐ 458 Brian Holman	.05	.02
☐ 459 Tom Trebelhorn MG	.05	.02
☐ 460 Dave Stieb	.05	.02
☐ 461 Robin Ventura	.15	.07
☐ 462 Steve Frey	.05	.02
☐ 463 Dwight Smith	.05	.02
☐ 464 Steve Buechele	.05	.02
☐ 465 Ken Griffey Sr.	.05	.02
☐ 466 Charles Nagy	.15	.07
☐ 467 Dennis Cook	.05	.02
☐ 468 Tim Hulett	.05	.02
☐ 469 Chet Lemon	.05	.02
☐ 470 Howard Johnson	.05	.02
☐ 471 Mike Lieberthal	.30	.14
☐ 472 Kirt Manwaring	.05	.02
☐ 473 Curt Young	.05	.02
☐ 474 Phil Plantier	.10	.05
☐ 475 Teddy Higuera	.05	.02
☐ 476 Glenn Wilson	.05	.02
☐ 477 Mike Fetters	.05	.02
☐ 478 Kurt Stillwell	.05	.02
☐ 479 Bob Patterson	.05	.02
☐ 480 Dave Magadan	.05	.02
☐ 481 Eddie Whitson	.05	.02
☐ 482 Tino Martinez	.25	.11
☐ 483 Mike Aldrete	.05	.02
☐ 484 Dave LaPoint	.05	.02
☐ 485 Terry Pendleton	.10	.05
Now with Braves 12/3/90		
☐ 486 Tommy Greene	.05	.02
☐ 487 Rafael Belliard	.05	.02
Now with Braves 12/18/90		
☐ 488 Jeff Manto	.05	.02
☐ 489 Bobby Valentine MG	.05	.02
☐ 490 Kirk Gibson	.10	.05
Now with Royals 12/1/90		
☐ 491 Kurt Miller	.05	.02
☐ 492 Ernie Whitt	.05	.02
☐ 493 Jose Rijo	.05	.02
☐ 494 Chris James	.05	.02
☐ 495 Charlie Hough	.05	.02
Now with White Sox 12/20/90		
☐ 496 Marty Barrett	.05	.02
☐ 497 Ben McDonald	.10	.05
☐ 498 Mark Salas	.05	.02
☐ 499 Melido Perez	.05	.02
☐ 500 Will Clark	.15	.07
☐ 501 Mike Bielecki	.05	.02
☐ 502 Carney Lansford	.05	.02
☐ 503 Roy Smith	.05	.02
☐ 504 Julio Valera	.05	.02
☐ 505 Chuck Finley	.10	.05
☐ 506 Darnell Coles	.05	.02
☐ 507 Steve Jeltz	.05	.02
☐ 508 Mike York	.05	.02
☐ 509 Glenallen Hill	.05	.02
☐ 510 John Franco	.10	.05
☐ 511 Steve Balboni	.05	.02
☐ 512 Jose Mesa	.10	.05
☐ 513 Jerald Clark	.05	.02
☐ 514 Mike Stanton	.05	.02
☐ 515 Alvin Davis	.05	.02
☐ 516 Karl Rhodes	.05	.02
☐ 517 Joe Oliver	.05	.02
☐ 518 Cris Carpenter	.05	.02
☐ 519 Sparky Anderson MG	.10	.05
☐ 520 Mark Grace	.25	.11
☐ 521 Joe Orsulak	.05	.02
☐ 522 Stan Belinda	.05	.02
☐ 523 Rodney McCray	.05	.02
☐ 524 Darrel Akerfelds	.05	.02
☐ 525 Willie Randolph	.10	.05
☐ 526 Moises Alou	.15	.07
☐ 527 Checklist 4	.05	.02
☐ 528 Denny Martinez	.10	.05
☐ 529 Marc Newfield	.30	.14
☐ 530 Roger Clemens	.75	.35
☐ 531 Dave Rohde	.05	.02
☐ 532 Kirk McCaskill	.05	.02
☐ 533 Oddibe McDowell	.05	.02
☐ 534 Mike Jackson	.05	.02
☐ 535 Ruben Sierra	.05	.02
☐ 536 Mike Witt	.05	.02
☐ 537 Jose Lind	.05	.02
☐ 538 Bip Roberts	.05	.02
☐ 539 Scott Terry	.05	.02
☐ 540 George Brett	.75	.35
☐ 541 Domingo Ramos	.05	.02
☐ 542 Rob Murphy	.05	.02
☐ 543 Junior Felix	.05	.02
☐ 544 Alejandro Pena	.05	.02
☐ 545 Dale Murphy	.15	.07
☐ 546 Jeff Ballard	.05	.02
☐ 547 Mike Pagliarulo	.05	.02
☐ 548 Jaime Navarro	.05	.02
☐ 549 John McNamara MG	.05	.02
☐ 550 Eric Davis	.10	.05
☐ 551 Bob Kipper	.05	.02
☐ 552 Jeff Hamilton	.05	.02
☐ 553 Joe Klink	.05	.02
☐ 554 Brian Harper	.05	.02
☐ 555 Turner Ward	.05	.02
☐ 556 Gary Ward	.05	.02
☐ 557 Wally Whitehurst	.05	.02
☐ 558 Otis Nixon	.10	.05
☐ 559 Adam Peterson	.05	.02
☐ 560 Greg Smith	.05	.02
Now with Dodgers 12/14/90		
☐ 561 Tim McIntosh	.05	.02
☐ 562 Jeff Kunkel	.05	.02
☐ 563 Brent Knackert	.05	.02
☐ 564 Dante Bichette	.15	.07
☐ 565 Craig Biggio	.15	.07
☐ 566 Craig Wilson	.05	.02
☐ 567 Dwayne Henry	.05	.02
☐ 568 Ron Karkovice	.05	.02
☐ 569 Curt Schilling	.10	.05
Now with Astros 1/10/91		
☐ 570 Barry Bonds	.50	.23
☐ 571 Pat Combs	.05	.02
☐ 572 Dave Anderson	.05	.02
☐ 573 Rich Rodriguez UER	.05	.02
Stats say drafted 4th but bio says 9th round		
☐ 574 John Marzano	.05	.02
☐ 575 Robin Yount	.25	.11
☐ 576 Jeff Kaiser	.05	.02
☐ 577 Bill Doran	.05	.02
☐ 578 Dave West	.05	.02
☐ 579 Roger Craig MG	.05	.02
☐ 580 Dave Stewart	.10	.05
☐ 581 Luis Quinones	.05	.02
☐ 582 Marty Clary	.05	.02
☐ 583 Tony Phillips	.05	.02
☐ 584 Kevin Brown	.10	.05
☐ 585 Pete O'Brien	.05	.02
☐ 586 Fred Lynn	.05	.02
☐ 587 Jose Offerman UER	.05	.02
Text says signed 7/24/88 but bio says 1986		
☐ 588 Mark Whiten	.05	.02
☐ 589 Scott Ruskin	.05	.02
☐ 590 Eddie Murray	.40	.18
☐ 591 Ken Hill	.10	.05
☐ 592 B.J. Surhoff	.10	.05
☐ 593 Mike Walker	.05	.02
☐ 594 Rich Garces	.05	.02
☐ 595 Bill Landrum	.05	.02
☐ 596 Ronnie Walden	.05	.02
☐ 597 Jerry Don Gleaton	.05	.02
☐ 598 Sam Horn	.05	.02
☐ 599 Greg Myers	.05	.02
☐ 600 Bo Jackson	.10	.05
☐ 601 Bob Ojeda	.05	.02
Now with Dodgers 12/15/90		
☐ 602 Casey Candaele	.05	.02
☐ 603 Wes Chamberlain	.05	.02
☐ 604 Billy Hatcher	.05	.02
☐ 605 Jeff Reardon	.05	.02
☐ 606 Jim Gott	.05	.02
☐ 607 Edgar Martinez	.15	.07
☐ 608 Todd Burns	.05	.02
☐ 609 Jeff Torborg MG	.05	.02
☐ 610 Andres Galarraga	.25	.11
☐ 611 Dave Eiland	.05	.02
☐ 612 Steve Lyons	.05	.02
☐ 613 Eric Show	.05	.02
Now with Athletics 12/10/90		
☐ 614 Luis Salazar	.05	.02
☐ 615 Bert Blyleven	.10	.05
☐ 616 Todd Zeile	.10	.05
☐ 617 Bill Wegman	.05	.02
☐ 618 Sil Campusano	.05	.02
☐ 619 David Wells	.05	.02
☐ 620 Ozzie Guillen	.05	.02
☐ 621 Ted Power	.05	.02
Now with Reds 12/14/90		
☐ 622 Jack Daugherty	.05	.02
☐ 623 Jeff Blauser	.05	.02
☐ 624 Tom Candiotti	.05	.02
☐ 625 Terry Steinbach	.10	.05
☐ 626 Gerald Young	.05	.02
☐ 627 Tim Layana	.05	.02
☐ 628 Greg Litton	.05	.02
☐ 629 Wes Gardner	.05	.02
Now with Padres 12/15/90		
☐ 630 Dave Winfield	.15	.07
☐ 631 Mike Morgan	.05	.02
☐ 632 Lloyd Moseby	.05	.02
☐ 633 Kevin Tapani	.05	.02
☐ 634 Henry Cotto	.05	.02
☐ 635 Andy Hawkins	.05	.02
☐ 636 Geronimo Pena	.05	.02
☐ 637 Bruce Ruffin	.05	.02
☐ 638 Mike Macfarlane	.05	.02
☐ 639 Frank Robinson MG	.10	.05

☐ 640 Andre Dawson	.25	.11
☐ 641 Mike Henneman	.05	.02
☐ 642 Hal Morris	.05	.02
☐ 643 Jim Presley	.05	.02
☐ 644 Chuck Crim	.05	.02
☐ 645 Juan Samuel	.05	.02
☐ 646 Andujar Cedeno	.05	.02
☐ 647 Mark Portugal	.05	.02
☐ 648 Lee Stevens	.05	.02
☐ 649 Bill Sampen	.05	.02
☐ 650 Jack Clark	.05	.02
Now with Red Sox 12/15/90		
☐ 651 Alan Mills	.05	.02
☐ 652 Kevin Romine	.05	.02
☐ 653 Anthony Telford	.05	.02
☐ 654 Paul Sorrento	.10	.05
☐ 655 Erik Hanson	.05	.02
☐ 656 Checklist 5	.05	.02
☐ 657 Mike Kingery	.05	.02
☐ 658 Scott Aldred	.05	.02
☐ 659 Oscar Azocar	.05	.02
☐ 660 Lee Smith	.15	.07
☐ 661 Steve Lake	.05	.02
☐ 662 Rob Dibble	.05	.02
☐ 663 Greg Brock	.05	.02
☐ 664 John Farrell	.05	.02
☐ 665 Mike LaValliere	.05	.02
☐ 666 Danny Darwin	.05	.02
Now with Red Sox 12/19/90		
☐ 667 Kent Anderson	.05	.02
☐ 668 Bill Long	.05	.02
☐ 669 Lou Piniella MG	.05	.02
☐ 670 Rickey Henderson	.25	.11
☐ 671 Andy McGaffigan	.05	.02
☐ 672 Shane Mack	.05	.02
☐ 673 Greg Olson UER	.05	.02
6 RBI in '88 at Tidewater and 2 RBI in '87 should be 48 and 15		
☐ 674 Kevin Gross	.05	.02
Now with Dodgers 12/3/90		
☐ 675 Tom Brunansky	.05	.02
☐ 676 Scott Chiamparino	.05	.02
☐ 677 Billy Ripken	.05	.02
☐ 678 Mark Davidson	.05	.02
☐ 679 Bill Bathe	.05	.02
☐ 680 David Cone	.10	.05
☐ 681 Jeff Schaefer	.05	.02
☐ 682 Ray Lankford	.25	.11
☐ 683 Derek Lilliquist	.05	.02
☐ 684 Milt Cuyler	.05	.02
☐ 685 Doug Drabek	.05	.02
☐ 686 Mike Gallego	.05	.02
☐ 687 John Cerutti	.05	.02
☐ 688 Rosario Rodriguez	.05	.02
Now with Pirates 12/20/90		
☐ 689 John Kruk	.10	.05
☐ 690 Orel Hershiser	.10	.05
☐ 691 Mike Blowers	.05	.02
☐ 692 Efrain Valdez	.05	.02
☐ 693 Francisco Cabrera	.05	.02
☐ 694 Randy Veres	.05	.02
☐ 695 Kevin Seitzer	.05	.02
☐ 696 Steve Olin	.05	.02
☐ 697 Shawn Abner	.05	.02
☐ 698 Mark Guthrie	.05	.02
☐ 699 Jim Lefebvre MG	.05	.02
☐ 700 Jose Canseco	.25	.11
☐ 701 Pascual Perez	.05	.02
☐ 702 Tim Naehring	.10	.05
☐ 703 Juan Agosto	.05	.02
Now with Cardinals 12/14/90		
☐ 704 Devon White	.05	.02
Now with Blue Jays 12/2/90		
☐ 705 Robby Thompson	.05	.02
☐ 706 Brad Arnsberg	.05	.02
☐ 707 Jim Eisenreich	.10	.05
☐ 708 John Mitchell	.05	.02
☐ 709 Matt Sinatro	.05	.02
☐ 710 Kent Hrbek	.05	.02
☐ 711 Jose DeLeon	.05	.02
☐ 712 Ricky Jordan	.05	.02
☐ 713 Scott Scudder	.05	.02
☐ 714 Marvell Wynne	.05	.02
☐ 715 Tim Burke	.05	.02
☐ 716 Bob Geren	.05	.02
☐ 717 Phil Bradley	.05	.02
☐ 718 Steve Crawford	.05	.02
☐ 719 Keith Miller	.05	.02
☐ 720 Cecil Fielder	.10	.05
☐ 721 Mark Lee	.05	.02
☐ 722 Wally Backman	.05	.02
☐ 723 Candy Maldonado	.05	.02
☐ 724 David Segui	.10	.05
☐ 725 Ron Gant	.10	.05
☐ 726 Phil Stephenson	.05	.02
☐ 727 Mookie Wilson	.05	.02
☐ 728 Scott Sanderson	.05	.02
Now with Yankees 12/31/90		
☐ 729 Don Zimmer MG	.05	.02
☐ 730 Barry Larkin	.15	.07
☐ 731 Jeff Gray	.05	.02
☐ 732 Franklin Stubbs	.05	.02
Now with Brewers 12/5/90		
☐ 733 Kelly Downs	.05	.02
☐ 734 John Russell	.05	.02
☐ 735 Ron Darling	.05	.02
☐ 736 Dick Schofield	.05	.02
☐ 737 Tim Crews	.05	.02
☐ 738 Mel Hall	.05	.02
☐ 739 Russ Swan	.05	.02
☐ 740 Ryne Sandberg	.50	.23
☐ 741 Jimmy Key	.10	.05
☐ 742 Tommy Gregg	.05	.02
☐ 743 Bryn Smith	.05	.02
☐ 744 Nelson Santovenia	.05	.02
☐ 745 Doug Jones	.05	.02
☐ 746 John Shelby	.05	.02
☐ 747 Tony Fossas	.05	.02
☐ 748 Al Newman	.05	.02
☐ 749 Greg W. Harris	.05	.02
☐ 750 Bobby Bonilla	.10	.05
☐ 751 Wayne Edwards	.05	.02
☐ 752 Kevin Bass	.05	.02
☐ 753 Paul Marak UER	.05	.02
Stats say drafted in May but bio says Jan.		
☐ 754 Bill Pecota	.05	.02
☐ 755 Mark Langston	.05	.02
☐ 756 Jeff Huson	.05	.02
☐ 757 Mark Gardner	.05	.02
☐ 758 Mike Devereaux	.05	.02
☐ 759 Bobby Cox MG	.05	.02
☐ 760 Benny Santiago	.05	.02
☐ 761 Larry Andersen	.05	.02
Now with Padres 12/21/90		
☐ 762 Mitch Webster	.05	.02
☐ 763 Dana Kiecker	.05	.02
☐ 764 Mark Carreon	.05	.02
☐ 765 Shawon Dunston	.05	.02
☐ 766 Jeff M. Robinson	.05	.02
Now with Orioles 1/12/91		
☐ 767 Dan Wilson	.50	.23
☐ 768 Donn Pall	.05	.02
☐ 769 Tim Sherrill	.05	.02
☐ 770 Jay Howell	.05	.02
☐ 771 Gary Redus UER	.05	.02
Born in Tanner, should say Athens		
☐ 772 Kent Mercker UER	.05	.02
Born in Indianapolis should say Dublin, Ohio		
☐ 773 Tom Foley	.05	.02
☐ 774 Dennis Rasmussen	.05	.02
☐ 775 Julio Franco	.10	.05
☐ 776 Brent Mayne	.05	.02
☐ 777 John Candelaria	.05	.02
☐ 778 Dan Gladden	.05	.02
☐ 779 Carmelo Martinez	.05	.02
☐ 780 Randy Myers	.05	.02
☐ 781 Darryl Hamilton	.05	.02
☐ 782 Jim Deshaies	.05	.02
☐ 783 Joel Skinner	.05	.02
☐ 784 Willie Fraser	.05	.02
Now with Blue Jays 12/2/90		
☐ 785 Scott Fletcher	.05	.02
☐ 786 Eric Plunk	.05	.02
☐ 787 Checklist 6	.05	.02
☐ 788 Bob Milacki	.05	.02
☐ 789 Tom Lasorda MG	.25	.11
☐ 790 Ken Griffey Jr.	3.00	1.35
☐ 791 Mike Benjamin	.05	.02
☐ 792 Mike Greenwell	.05	.02

1991 O-Pee-Chee Box Bottoms

The 1991 O-Pee-Chee Box Bottom cards comprise four different box bottoms from the bottoms of wax pack boxes, with four cards each, for a total of 16 standard-size cards. The cards are nearly identical to the 1991 Topps Box Bottom cards. The fronts feature yellow-bordered color player action shots. The player's name and position appear at the bottom and his team name appears just

above. The traded players have their new teams and dates of trade printed on the photo. The pink and blue horizontal backs carry player career highlights in both English and French. The cards are lettered (A-P) rather than numbered on the back.

	MINT	NRMT
COMPLETE SET (16)	4.00	1.80
COMMON CARD (A-P)	.10	.05
☐ A Bert Blyleven	.25	.11
☐ B George Brett	1.25	.55
☐ C Brett Butler	.25	.11
☐ D Andre Dawson	.40	.18
☐ E Dwight Evans	.25	.11
☐ F Carlton Fisk	.40	.18
☐ G Alfredo Griffin	.10	.05
☐ H Rickey Henderson	.60	.25
☐ I Willie McGee	.25	.11
☐ J Dale Murphy	.40	.18
☐ K Eddie Murray	.60	.25
☐ L Dave Parker	.25	.11
☐ M Jeff Reardon	.10	.05
☐ N Nolan Ryan	2.50	1.10
☐ O Juan Samuel	.10	.05
☐ P Robin Yount	.60	.25

1992 O-Pee-Chee

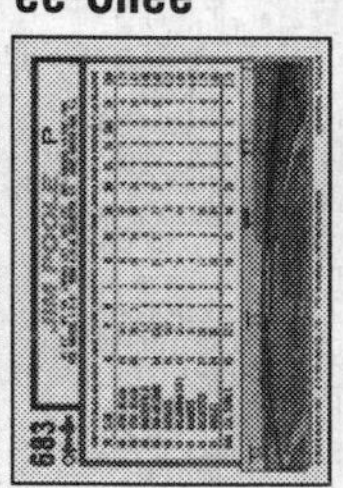

The 1992 O-Pee-Chee set contains 792 standard-size cards. These cards were sold in ten-card wax packs with a stick of bubble gum. The fronts have either posed or action color player photos on a white card face. Different color stripes frame the pictures, and the player's name and team name appear in two short color stripes respectively at the bottom. In English and French, the horizontally oriented backs have biography and complete career batting or pitching record. In addition, some of the cards have a picture of a baseball field and stadium on the back. Special subsets included are Record Breakers (2-5), Prospects (58, 126, 179, 473, 551, 591, 618, 656, 676) and a five-card tribute to Gary Carter (45, 387, 389, 399, 402). Each wax pack wrapper served as an entry blank offering each collector the chance to win one of 1,000 complete factory sets of 1992 O-Pee-Chee Premier baseball cards.

	MINT	NRMT
COMPLETE SET (792)	25.00	11.00
COMPLETE FACT.SET (792)	25.00	11.00
COMMON CARD (1-792)	.05	.02
☐ 1 Nolan Ryan	1.50	.70
☐ 2 Rickey Henderson RB	.15	.07
(Some cards have print marks that show 1.991 on the front)		
☐ 3 Jeff Reardon RB	.05	.02
☐ 4 Nolan Ryan RB	.75	.35
☐ 5 Dave Winfield RB	.15	.07
☐ 6 Brien Taylor	.05	.02
☐ 7 Jim Olander	.05	.02
☐ 8 Bryan Hickerson	.05	.02
☐ 9 Jon Farrell	.05	.02
☐ 10 Wade Boggs	.25	.11
☐ 11 Jack McDowell	.10	.05
☐ 12 Luis Gonzalez	.05	.02
☐ 13 Mike Scioscia	.05	.02
☐ 14 Wes Chamberlain	.05	.02

☐ 15 Dennis Martinez .10 .05
☐ 16 Jeff Montgomery .10 .05
☐ 17 Randy Milligan .05 .02
☐ 18 Greg Cadaret .05 .02
☐ 19 Jamie Quirk .05 .02
☐ 20 Bip Roberts .05 .02
☐ 21 Buck Rodgers MG .05 .02
☐ 22 Bill Wegman .05 .02
☐ 23 Chuck Knoblauch .25 .11
☐ 24 Randy Myers .10 .05
☐ 25 Ron Gant .10 .05
☐ 26 Mike Bielecki .05 .02
☐ 27 Juan Gonzalez 1.25 .55
☐ 28 Mike Schooler .05 .02
☐ 29 Mickey Tettleton .05 .02
☐ 30 John Kruk .10 .05
☐ 31 Bryn Smith .05 .02
☐ 32 Chris Nabholz .05 .02
☐ 33 Carlos Baerga .10 .05
☐ 34 Jeff Juden .05 .02
☐ 35 Dave Righetti .05 .02
☐ 36 Scott Ruffcorn .05 .02
☐ 37 Luis Polonia .05 .02
☐ 38 Tom Candiotti .05 .02
Now with Dodgers
12-3-91
☐ 39 Greg Olson .05 .02
☐ 40 Cal Ripken 4.00 1.80
Lou Gehrig
☐ 41 Craig Lefferts .05 .02
☐ 42 Mike Macfarlane .05 .02
☐ 43 Jose Lind .05 .02
☐ 44 Rick Aguilera .05 .02
☐ 45 Gary Carter .25 .11
☐ 46 Steve Farr .05 .02
☐ 47 Rex Hudler .05 .02
☐ 48 Scott Scudder .05 .02
☐ 49 Damon Berryhill .05 .02
☐ 50 Ken Griffey Jr. 2.50 1.10
☐ 51 Tom Runnells MG .05 .02
☐ 52 Juan Bell .05 .02
☐ 53 Tommy Gregg .05 .02
☐ 54 David Wells .05 .02
☐ 55 Rafael Palmeiro .15 .07
☐ 56 Charlie O'Brien .05 .02
☐ 57 Donn Pall .05 .02
☐ 58 1992 Prospects C .25 .11
Brad Ausmus
Jim Campanis Jr.
Dave Nilsson
Doug Robbins
☐ 59 Mo Vaughn .60 .25
☐ 60 Tony Fernandez .05 .02
☐ 61 Paul O'Neill .10 .05
☐ 62 Gene Nelson .05 .02
☐ 63 Randy Ready .05 .02
☐ 64 Bob Kipper .05 .02
Now with Twins
12-17-91
☐ 65 Willie McGee .10 .05
☐ 66 Scott Stahoviak .05 .02
☐ 67 Luis Salazar .05 .02
☐ 68 Marvin Freeman .05 .02
☐ 69 Kenny Lofton 1.50 .70
Now with Indians
12-10-91
☐ 70 Gary Gaetti .10 .05
☐ 71 Erik Hanson .05 .02
☐ 72 Eddie Zosky .05 .02
☐ 73 Brian Barnes .05 .02
☐ 74 Scott Leius .05 .02
☐ 75 Bret Saberhagen .05 .02
☐ 76 Mike Gallego .05 .02
☐ 77 Jack Armstrong .05 .02
Now with Indians
11-15-91
☐ 78 Ivan Rodriguez .75 .35
☐ 79 Jesse Orosco .05 .02
☐ 80 David Justice .25 .11
☐ 81 Ced Landrum .05 .02
☐ 82 Doug Simons .05 .02
☐ 83 Tommy Greene .05 .02
☐ 84 Leo Gomez .05 .02
☐ 85 Jose DeLeon .05 .02
☐ 86 Steve Finley .10 .05
☐ 87 Bob MacDonald .05 .02
☐ 88 Darrin Jackson .05 .02
☐ 89 Neal Heaton .05 .02
☐ 90 Robin Yount .15 .07
☐ 91 Jeff Reed .05 .02
☐ 92 Lenny Harris .05 .02
☐ 93 Reggie Jefferson .10 .05
☐ 94 Sammy Sosa .25 .11
☐ 95 Scott Bailes .05 .02
☐ 96 Tom McKinnon .05 .02
☐ 97 Luis Rivera .05 .02
☐ 98 Mike Harkey .05 .02
☐ 99 Jeff Treadway .05 .02
☐ 100 Jose Canseco .15 .07
☐ 101 Omar Vizquel .10 .05
☐ 102 Scott Kamieniecki .05 .02
☐ 103 Ricky Jordan .05 .02
☐ 104 Jeff Ballard .05 .02
☐ 105 Felix Jose .05 .02
☐ 106 Mike Boddicker .05 .02
☐ 107 Dan Pasqua .05 .02
☐ 108 Mike Timlin .05 .02
☐ 109 Roger Craig MG .05 .02
☐ 110 Ryne Sandberg .50 .23
☐ 111 Mark Carreon .05 .02
☐ 112 Oscar Azocar .05 .02
☐ 113 Mike Greenwell .05 .02
☐ 114 Mark Portugal .05 .02
☐ 115 Terry Pendleton .05 .02
☐ 116 Willie Randolph .10 .05
Now with Mets
12-20-91
☐ 117 Scott Terry .05 .02
☐ 118 Chili Davis .10 .05
☐ 119 Mark Gardner .05 .02
☐ 120 Alan Trammell .15 .07
☐ 121 Derek Bell .15 .07
☐ 122 Gary Varsho .05 .02
☐ 123 Bob Ojeda .05 .02
☐ 124 Shawn Livsey .05 .02
☐ 125 Chris Hoiles .05 .02
☐ 126 1992 Prospects 1B .75 .35
Ryan Klesko
John Jaha
Rico Brogna
Dave Staton
☐ 127 Carlos Quintana .05 .02
☐ 128 Kurt Stillwell .05 .02
☐ 129 Melido Perez .05 .02
☐ 130 Alvin Davis .05 .02
☐ 131 Checklist 1-132 .05 .02
☐ 132 Eric Show .05 .02
☐ 133 Rance Mulliniks .05 .02
☐ 134 Darryl Kile .10 .05
☐ 135 Von Hayes .05 .02
Now with Angels
12-8-91
☐ 136 Bill Doran .05 .02
☐ 137 Jeff D. Robinson .05 .02
☐ 138 Monty Fariss .05 .02
☐ 139 Jeff Innis .05 .02
☐ 140 Mark Grace UER .25 .11
(Home Calie., should
be Calif.)
☐ 141 Jim Leyland MG UER .10 .05
(No closed parenthesis
after East in 1991)
☐ 142 Todd Van Poppel .05 .02
☐ 143 Paul Gibson .05 .02
☐ 144 Bill Swift .05 .02
☐ 145 Danny Tartabull .05 .02
Now with Yankees
1-6-92
☐ 146 Al Newman .05 .02
☐ 147 Cris Carpenter .05 .02
☐ 148 Anthony Young .05 .02
☐ 149 Brian Bohanon .05 .02
☐ 150 Roger Clemens UER .75 .35
(League leading ERA in
1990 not italicized)
☐ 151 Jeff Hamilton .05 .02
☐ 152 Charlie Leibrandt .05 .02
☐ 153 Ron Karkovice .05 .02
☐ 154 Hensley Meulens .05 .02
☐ 155 Scott Bankhead .05 .02
☐ 156 Manny Ramirez 2.00 .90
☐ 157 Keith Miller .05 .02
Now with Royals
12-11-91
☐ 158 Todd Frohwirth .05 .02
☐ 159 Darrin Fletcher .05 .02
Now with Expos
12-9-91
☐ 160 Bobby Bonilla .10 .05
☐ 161 Casey Candaele .05 .02
☐ 162 Paul Faries .05 .02
☐ 163 Dana Kiecker .05 .02
☐ 164 Shane Mack .05 .02
☐ 165 Mark Langston .05 .02
☐ 166 Geronimo Pena .05 .02
☐ 167 Andy Allanson .05 .02
☐ 168 Dwight Smith .05 .02
☐ 169 Chuck Crim .05 .02
Now with Angels
12-10-91
☐ 170 Alex Cole .05 .02
☐ 171 Bill Plummer MG .05 .02
☐ 172 Juan Berenguer .05 .02
☐ 173 Brian Downing .05 .02
☐ 174 Steve Frey .05 .02
☐ 175 Orel Hershiser .10 .05
☐ 176 Ramon Garcia .05 .02
☐ 177 Dan Gladden .05 .02
Now with Tigers
12-19-91
☐ 178 Jim Acker .05 .02
☐ 179 1992 Prospects 2B .05 .02
Bobby DeJardin
Cesar Bernhardt
Armando Moreno
Andy Stankiewicz
☐ 180 Kevin Mitchell .05 .02
☐ 181 Hector Villanueva .05 .02
☐ 182 Jeff Reardon .05 .02
☐ 183 Brent Mayne .05 .02
☐ 184 Jimmy Jones .05 .02
☐ 185 Benito Santiago .05 .02
☐ 186 Cliff Floyd .15 .07
☐ 187 Ernie Riles .05 .02
☐ 188 Jose Guzman .05 .02
☐ 189 Junior Felix .05 .02
☐ 190 Glenn Davis .05 .02
☐ 191 Charlie Hough .05 .02
☐ 192 Dave Fleming .05 .02
☐ 193 Omar Olivares .05 .02
☐ 194 Eric Karros .15 .07
☐ 195 David Cone .10 .05
☐ 196 Frank Castillo .05 .02
☐ 197 Glenn Braggs .05 .02
☐ 198 Scott Aldred .05 .02
☐ 199 Jeff Blauser .05 .02
☐ 200 Len Dykstra .10 .05
☐ 201 Buck Showalter MG .25 .11
☐ 202 Rick Honeycutt .05 .02
☐ 203 Greg Myers .05 .02
☐ 204 Trevor Wilson .05 .02
☐ 205 Jay Howell .05 .02
☐ 206 Luis Sojo .05 .02
☐ 207 Jack Clark .05 .02
☐ 208 Julio Machado .05 .02
☐ 209 Lloyd McClendon .05 .02
☐ 210 Ozzie Guillen .05 .02
☐ 211 Jeremy Hernandez .05 .02
☐ 212 Randy Velarde .05 .02
☐ 213 Les Lancaster .05 .02
☐ 214 Andy Mota .05 .02
☐ 215 Rich Gossage .10 .05
☐ 216 Brent Gates .10 .05
☐ 217 Brian Harper .05 .02
☐ 218 Mike Flanagan .05 .02
☐ 219 Jerry Browne .05 .02
☐ 220 Jose Rijo .05 .02
☐ 221 Skeeter Barnes .05 .02
☐ 222 Jaime Navarro .05 .02
☐ 223 Mel Hall .05 .02
☐ 224 Bret Barberie .05 .02
☐ 225 Roberto Alomar .25 .11
☐ 226 Pete Smith .05 .02
☐ 227 Daryl Boston .05 .02
☐ 228 Eddie Whitson .05 .02
☐ 229 Shawn Boskie .05 .02
☐ 230 Dick Schofield .05 .02
☐ 231 Brian Drahman .05 .02
☐ 232 John Smiley .05 .02
☐ 233 Mitch Webster .05 .02
☐ 234 Terry Steinbach .10 .05
☐ 235 Jack Morris .10 .05
Now with Blue Jays
12-18-91
☐ 236 Bill Pecota .05 .02
Now with Mets
12-11-91
☐ 237 Jose Hernandez .05 .02
☐ 238 Greg Litton .05 .02
☐ 239 Brian Holman .05 .02
☐ 240 Andres Galarraga .25 .11
☐ 241 Gerald Young .05 .02
☐ 242 Mike Mussina .50 .23
☐ 243 Alvaro Espinoza .05 .02
☐ 244 Darren Daulton .10 .05
☐ 245 John Smoltz .15 .07
☐ 246 Jason Pruitt .05 .02
☐ 247 Chuck Finley .10 .05
☐ 248 Jim Gantner .05 .02
☐ 249 Tony Fossas .05 .02
☐ 250 Ken Griffey Sr. .10 .05
☐ 251 Kevin Elster .05 .02
☐ 252 Dennis Rasmussen .05 .02
☐ 253 Terry Kennedy .05 .02
☐ 254 Ryan Bowen .05 .02
☐ 255 Robin Ventura .10 .05
☐ 256 Mike Aldrete .05 .02
☐ 257 Jeff Russell .05 .02
☐ 258 Jim Lindeman .05 .02
☐ 259 Ron Darling .05 .02
☐ 260 Devon White .05 .02

- ☐ 261 Tom Lasorda MG .25 .11
- ☐ 262 Terry Lee .05 .02
- ☐ 263 Bob Patterson .05 .02
- ☐ 264 Checklist 133-264 .05 .02
- ☐ 265 Teddy Higuera .05 .02
- ☐ 266 Roberto Kelly .05 .02
- ☐ 267 Steve Bedrosian .05 .02
- ☐ 268 Brady Anderson .15 .07
- ☐ 269 Ruben Amaro Jr. .05 .02
- ☐ 270 Tony Gwynn 1.00 .45
- ☐ 271 Tracy Jones .05 .02
- ☐ 272 Jerry Don Gleaton .05 .02
- ☐ 273 Craig Grebeck .05 .02
- ☐ 274 Bob Scanlan .05 .02
- ☐ 275 Todd Zeile .05 .02
- ☐ 276 Shawn Green .50 .23
- ☐ 277 Scott Chiamparino .05 .02
- ☐ 278 Darryl Hamilton .05 .02
- ☐ 279 Jim Clancy .05 .02
- ☐ 280 Carlos Martinez .05 .02
- ☐ 281 Kevin Appier .10 .05
- ☐ 282 John Wehner .05 .02
- ☐ 283 Reggie Sanders .15 .07
- ☐ 284 Gene Larkin .05 .02
- ☐ 285 Bob Welch .05 .02
- ☐ 286 Gilberto Reyes .05 .02
- ☐ 287 Pete Schourek .05 .02
- ☐ 288 Andujar Cedeno .05 .02
- ☐ 289 Mike Morgan .05 .02
  Now with Cubs
  12-3-91
- ☐ 290 Bo Jackson .10 .05
- ☐ 291 Phil Garner MG .05 .02
- ☐ 292 Ray Lankford .15 .07
- ☐ 293 Mike Henneman .05 .02
- ☐ 294 Dave Valle .05 .02
- ☐ 295 Alonzo Powell .05 .02
- ☐ 296 Tom Brunansky .05 .02
- ☐ 297 Kevin Brown .10 .05
- ☐ 298 Kelly Gruber .05 .02
- ☐ 299 Charles Nagy .10 .05
- ☐ 300 Don Mattingly .60 .25
- ☐ 301 Kirk McCaskill .05 .02
  Now with White Sox
  12-28-91
- ☐ 302 Joey Cora .10 .05
- ☐ 303 Dan Plesac .05 .02
- ☐ 304 Joe Oliver .05 .02
- ☐ 305 Tom Glavine .15 .07
- ☐ 306 Al Shirley .05 .02
- ☐ 307 Bruce Ruffin .05 .02
- ☐ 308 Craig Shipley .05 .02
- ☐ 309 Dave Martinez .05 .02
  Now with Reds
  12-11-91
- ☐ 310 Jose Mesa .10 .05
- ☐ 311 Henry Cotto .05 .02
- ☐ 312 Mike LaValliere .05 .02
- ☐ 313 Kevin Tapani .05 .02
- ☐ 314 Jeff Huson .05 .02
- ☐ 315 Juan Samuel .05 .02
- ☐ 316 Curt Schilling .10 .05
- ☐ 317 Mike Bordick .05 .02
- ☐ 318 Steve Howe .05 .02
- ☐ 319 Tony Phillips .05 .02
- ☐ 320 George Bell .05 .02
- ☐ 321 Lou Piniella MG .05 .02
- ☐ 322 Tim Burke .05 .02
- ☐ 323 Milt Thompson .05 .02
- ☐ 324 Danny Darwin .05 .02
- ☐ 325 Joe Orsulak .05 .02
- ☐ 326 Eric King .05 .02
- ☐ 327 Jay Buhner .15 .07
- ☐ 328 Joel Johnston .05 .02
- ☐ 329 Franklin Stubbs .05 .02
- ☐ 330 Will Clark .15 .07
- ☐ 331 Steve Lake .05 .02
- ☐ 332 Chris Jones .05 .02
  Now with Astros
  12-19-91
- ☐ 333 Pat Tabler .05 .02
- ☐ 334 Kevin Gross .05 .02
- ☐ 335 Dave Henderson .05 .02
- ☐ 336 Greg Anthony .05 .02
- ☐ 337 Alejandro Pena .05 .02
- ☐ 338 Shawn Abner .05 .02
- ☐ 339 Tom Browning .05 .02
- ☐ 340 Otis Nixon .10 .05
- ☐ 341 Bob Geren .05 .02
  Now with Reds
  12-2-91
- ☐ 342 Tim Spehr .05 .02
- ☐ 343 John Vander Wal .05 .02
- ☐ 344 Jack Daugherty .05 .02
- ☐ 345 Zane Smith .05 .02
- ☐ 346 Rheal Cormier .05 .02
- ☐ 347 Kent Hrbek .10 .05
- ☐ 348 Rick Wilkins .05 .02
- ☐ 349 Steve Lyons .05 .02
- ☐ 350 Gregg Olson .05 .02
- ☐ 351 Greg Riddoch MG .05 .02
- ☐ 352 Ed Nunez .05 .02
- ☐ 353 Braulio Castillo .05 .02
- ☐ 354 Dave Bergman .05 .02
- ☐ 355 Warren Newson .05 .02
- ☐ 356 Luis Quinones .05 .02
  Now with Twins
  1-9-92
- ☐ 357 Mike Witt .05 .02
- ☐ 358 Ted Wood .05 .02
- ☐ 359 Mike Moore .05 .02
- ☐ 360 Lance Parrish .05 .02
- ☐ 361 Barry Jones .05 .02
- ☐ 362 Javier Ortiz .05 .02
- ☐ 363 John Candelaria .05 .02
- ☐ 364 Glenallen Hill .05 .02
- ☐ 365 Duane Ward .05 .02
- ☐ 366 Checklist 265-396 .05 .02
- ☐ 367 Rafael Belliard .05 .02
- ☐ 368 Bill Krueger .05 .02
- ☐ 369 Steve Whitaker .05 .02
- ☐ 370 Shawon Dunston .05 .02
- ☐ 371 Dante Bichette .15 .07
- ☐ 372 Kip Gross .05 .02
  Now with Dodgers
  11-27-91
- ☐ 373 Don Robinson .05 .02
- ☐ 374 Bernie Williams .40 .18
- ☐ 375 Bert Blyleven .10 .05
- ☐ 376 Chris Donnels .05 .02
- ☐ 377 Bob Zupcic .05 .02
- ☐ 378 Joel Skinner .05 .02
- ☐ 379 Steve Chitren .05 .02
- ☐ 380 Barry Bonds .50 .23
- ☐ 381 Sparky Anderson MG .10 .05
- ☐ 382 Sid Fernandez .05 .02
- ☐ 383 Dave Hollins .05 .02
- ☐ 384 Mark Lee .05 .02
- ☐ 385 Tim Wallach .05 .02
- ☐ 386 Lance Blankenship .05 .02
- ☐ 387 Gary Carter .25 .11
  Tribute
- ☐ 388 Ron Tingley .05 .02
- ☐ 389 Gary Carter .25 .11
  Tribute
- ☐ 390 Gene Harris .05 .02
- ☐ 391 Jeff Schaefer .05 .02
- ☐ 392 Mark Grant .05 .02
- ☐ 393 Carl Willis .05 .02
- ☐ 394 Al Leiter .10 .05
- ☐ 395 Ron Robinson .05 .02
- ☐ 396 Tim Hulett .05 .02
- ☐ 397 Craig Worthington .05 .02
- ☐ 398 John Orton .05 .02
- ☐ 399 Gary Carter .25 .11
  Tribute
- ☐ 400 John Dopson .05 .02
- ☐ 401 Moises Alou .25 .11
- ☐ 402 Gary Carter .25 .11
  Tribute
- ☐ 403 Matt Young .05 .02
- ☐ 404 Wayne Edwards .05 .02
- ☐ 405 Nick Esasky .05 .02
- ☐ 406 Dave Eiland .05 .02
- ☐ 407 Mike Brumley .05 .02
- ☐ 408 Bob Milacki .05 .02
- ☐ 409 Geno Petralli .05 .02
- ☐ 410 Dave Stewart .10 .05
- ☐ 411 Mike Jackson .05 .02
- ☐ 412 Luis Aquino .05 .02
- ☐ 413 Tim Teufel .05 .02
- ☐ 414 Jeff Ware .05 .02
- ☐ 415 Jim Deshaies .05 .02
- ☐ 416 Ellis Burks .10 .05
- ☐ 417 Allan Anderson .05 .02
- ☐ 418 Alfredo Griffin .05 .02
- ☐ 419 Wally Whitehurst .05 .02
- ☐ 420 Sandy Alomar Jr. .10 .05
- ☐ 421 Juan Agosto .05 .02
- ☐ 422 Sam Horn .05 .02
- ☐ 423 Jeff Fassero .10 .05
- ☐ 424 Paul McClellan .05 .02
- ☐ 425 Cecil Fielder .10 .05
- ☐ 426 Tim Raines .10 .05
- ☐ 427 Eddie Taubensee .05 .02
- ☐ 428 Dennis Boyd .05 .02
- ☐ 429 Tony LaRussa MG .10 .05
- ☐ 430 Steve Sax .05 .02
- ☐ 431 Tom Gordon .05 .02
- ☐ 432 Billy Hatcher .05 .02
- ☐ 433 Cal Eldred .05 .02
- ☐ 434 Wally Backman .05 .02
- ☐ 435 Mark Eichhorn .05 .02
- ☐ 436 Mookie Wilson .10 .05
- ☐ 437 Scott Servais .05 .02
- ☐ 438 Mike Maddux .05 .02
- ☐ 439 Chico Walker .05 .02
- ☐ 440 Doug Drabek .05 .02
- ☐ 441 Rob Deer .05 .02
- ☐ 442 Dave West .05 .02
- ☐ 443 Spike Owen .05 .02
- ☐ 444 Tyrone Hill .05 .02
- ☐ 445 Matt Williams .15 .07
- ☐ 446 Mark Lewis .05 .02
- ☐ 447 David Segui .05 .02
- ☐ 448 Tom Pagnozzi .05 .02
- ☐ 449 Jeff Johnson .05 .02
- ☐ 450 Mark McGwire .75 .35
- ☐ 451 Tom Henke .05 .02
- ☐ 452 Wilson Alvarez .15 .07
- ☐ 453 Gary Redus .05 .02
- ☐ 454 Darren Holmes .05 .02
- ☐ 455 Pete O'Brien .05 .02
- ☐ 456 Pat Combs .05 .02
- ☐ 457 Hubie Brooks .05 .02
  Now with Angels
  12-10-91
- ☐ 458 Frank Tanana .05 .02
- ☐ 459 Tom Kelly MG .05 .02
- ☐ 460 Andre Dawson .15 .07
- ☐ 461 Doug Jones .05 .02
- ☐ 462 Rich Rodriguez .05 .02
- ☐ 463 Mike Simms .05 .02
- ☐ 464 Mike Jeffcoat .05 .02
- ☐ 465 Barry Larkin .15 .07
- ☐ 466 Stan Belinda .05 .02
- ☐ 467 Lonnie Smith .05 .02
- ☐ 468 Greg A. Harris .05 .02
- ☐ 469 Jim Eisenreich .10 .05
- ☐ 470 Pedro Guerrero .05 .02
- ☐ 471 Jose DeJesus .05 .02
- ☐ 472 Rich Rowland .05 .02
- ☐ 473 1992 Prospects 3B UER .15 .07
  Frank Bolick
  Craig Paquette
  Tom Redington
  Paul Russo
  (Line around top border)
- ☐ 474 Mike Rossiter .05 .02
- ☐ 475 Robby Thompson .05 .02
- ☐ 476 Randy Bush .05 .02
- ☐ 477 Greg Hibbard .05 .02
- ☐ 478 Dale Sveum .05 .02
  Now with Phillies
  12-11-91
- ☐ 479 Chito Martinez .05 .02
- ☐ 480 Scott Sanderson .05 .02
- ☐ 481 Tino Martinez .25 .11
- ☐ 482 Jimmy Key .10 .05
- ☐ 483 Terry Shumpert .05 .02
- ☐ 484 Mike Hartley .05 .02
- ☐ 485 Chris Sabo .05 .02
- ☐ 486 Bob Walk .05 .02
- ☐ 487 John Cerutti .05 .02
- ☐ 488 Scott Cooper .05 .02
- ☐ 489 Bobby Cox MG .10 .05
- ☐ 490 Julio Franco .10 .05
- ☐ 491 Jeff Brantley .10 .05
- ☐ 492 Mike Devereaux .05 .02
- ☐ 493 Jose Offerman .05 .02
- ☐ 494 Gary Thurman .05 .02
- ☐ 495 Carney Lansford .05 .02
- ☐ 496 Joe Grahe .05 .02
- ☐ 497 Andy Ashby .10 .05
- ☐ 498 Gerald Perry .05 .02
- ☐ 499 Dave Otto .05 .02
- ☐ 500 Vince Coleman .05 .02
- ☐ 501 Rob Mallicoat .05 .02
- ☐ 502 Greg Briley .05 .02
- ☐ 503 Pascual Perez .05 .02
- ☐ 504 Aaron Sele .15 .07
- ☐ 505 Bobby Thigpen .05 .02
- ☐ 506 Todd Benzinger .05 .02
- ☐ 507 Candy Maldonado .05 .02
- ☐ 508 Bill Gullickson .05 .02
- ☐ 509 Doug Dascenzo .05 .02
- ☐ 510 Frank Viola .05 .02
- ☐ 511 Kenny Rogers .10 .05
- ☐ 512 Mike Heath .05 .02
- ☐ 513 Kevin Bass .05 .02
- ☐ 514 Kim Batiste .05 .02
- ☐ 515 Delino DeShields .10 .05
- ☐ 516 Ed Sprague .10 .05
- ☐ 517 Jim Gott .05 .02
- ☐ 518 Jose Melendez .05 .02
- ☐ 519 Hal McRae MG .05 .02
- ☐ 520 Jeff Bagwell 1.25 .55
- ☐ 521 Joe Hesketh .05 .02
- ☐ 522 Milt Cuyler .05 .02
- ☐ 523 Shawn Hillegas .05 .02
- ☐ 524 Don Slaught .05 .02

☐ 525 Randy Johnson .25 .11
☐ 526 Doug Piatt .05 .02
☐ 527 Checklist 397-528 .05 .02
☐ 528 Steve Foster .05 .02
☐ 529 Joe Girardi .05 .02
☐ 530 Jim Abbott .05 .02
☐ 531 Larry Walker .25 .11
☐ 532 Mike Huff .05 .02
☐ 533 Mackey Sasser .05 .02
☐ 534 Benji Gil .05 .02
☐ 535 Dave Stieb .05 .02
☐ 536 Willie Wilson .10 .05
☐ 537 Mark Leiter .05 .02
☐ 538 Jose Uribe .05 .02
☐ 539 Thomas Howard .05 .02
☐ 540 Ben McDonald .05 .02
☐ 541 Jose Tolentino .05 .02
☐ 542 Keith Mitchell .05 .02
☐ 543 Jerome Walton .05 .02
☐ 544 Cliff Brantley .05 .02
☐ 545 Andy Van Slyke .05 .02
☐ 546 Paul Sorrento .05 .02
☐ 547 Herm Winningham .05 .02
☐ 548 Mark Guthrie .05 .02
☐ 549 Joe Torre MG .10 .05
☐ 550 Darryl Strawberry .10 .05
☐ 551 1992 Prospects SS UER 3.00 1.35
Wilfredo Cordero
Chipper Jones
Manny Alexander
Alex Arias
(No line around
top border)
☐ 552 Dave Gallagher .05 .02
☐ 553 Edgar Martinez .15 .07
☐ 554 Donald Harris .05 .02
☐ 555 Frank Thomas 2.00 .90
☐ 556 Storm Davis .05 .02
☐ 557 Dickie Thon .05 .02
☐ 558 Scott Garrelts .05 .02
☐ 559 Steve Olin .05 .02
☐ 560 Rickey Henderson .25 .11
☐ 561 Jose Vizcaino .05 .02
☐ 562 Wade Taylor .05 .02
☐ 563 Pat Borders .05 .02
☐ 564 Jimmy Gonzalez .05 .02
☐ 565 Lee Smith .10 .05
☐ 566 Bill Sampen .05 .02
☐ 567 Dean Palmer .10 .05
☐ 568 Bryan Harvey .05 .02
☐ 569 Tony Pena .05 .02
☐ 570 Lou Whitaker .10 .05
☐ 571 Randy Tomlin .05 .02
☐ 572 Greg Vaughn .05 .02
☐ 573 Kelly Downs .05 .02
☐ 574 Steve Avery UER .05 .02
(Should be 13 games
for Durham in 1989)
☐ 575 Kirby Puckett .75 .35
☐ 576 Heathcliff Slocumb .05 .02
☐ 577 Kevin Seitzer .05 .02
☐ 578 Lee Guetterman .05 .02
☐ 579 Johnny Oates MG .05 .02
☐ 580 Greg Maddux 1.25 .55
☐ 581 Stan Javier .05 .02
☐ 582 Vicente Palacios .05 .02
☐ 583 Mel Rojas .10 .05
☐ 584 Wayne Rosenthal .05 .02
☐ 585 Lenny Webster .05 .02
☐ 586 Rod Nichols .05 .02
☐ 587 Mickey Morandini .05 .02
☐ 588 Russ Swan .05 .02
☐ 589 Mariano Duncan .05 .02
Now with Phillies
12-10-91
☐ 590 Howard Johnson .05 .02
☐ 591 1992 Prospects OF .15 .07
Jeromy Burnitz
Jacob Brumfield
Alan Cockrell
D.J. Dozier
☐ 592 Denny Neagle .15 .07
☐ 593 Steve Decker .05 .02
☐ 594 Brian Barber .05 .02
☐ 595 Bruce Hurst .05 .02
☐ 596 Kent Mercker .05 .02
☐ 597 Mike Magnante .05 .02
☐ 598 Jody Reed .05 .02
☐ 599 Steve Searcy .05 .02
☐ 600 Paul Molitor .25 .11
☐ 601 Dave Smith .05 .02
☐ 602 Mike Fetters .05 .02
☐ 603 Luis Mercedes .05 .02
☐ 604 Chris Gwynn .05 .02
Now with Royals
12-11-91
☐ 605 Scott Erickson .10 .05

☐ 606 Brook Jacoby .05 .02
☐ 607 Todd Stottlemyre .10 .05
☐ 608 Scott Bradley .05 .02
☐ 609 Mike Hargrove MG .10 .05
☐ 610 Eric Davis .10 .05
☐ 611 Brian Hunter .05 .02
☐ 612 Pat Kelly .05 .02
☐ 613 Pedro Munoz .05 .02
☐ 614 Al Osuna .05 .02
☐ 615 Matt Merullo .05 .02
☐ 616 Larry Andersen .05 .02
☐ 617 Junior Ortiz .05 .02
☐ 618 1992 Prospects OF .05 .02
Cesar Hernandez
Steve Hosey
Jeff McNeely
Dan Peltier
☐ 619 Danny Jackson .05 .02
☐ 620 George Brett .75 .35
☐ 621 Dan Gakeler .05 .02
☐ 622 Steve Buechele .05 .02
☐ 623 Bob Tewksbury .05 .02
☐ 624 Shawn Estes .75 .35
☐ 625 Kevin McReynolds .05 .02
☐ 626 Chris Haney .05 .02
☐ 627 Mike Sharperson .05 .02
☐ 628 Mark Williamson .05 .02
☐ 629 Wally Joyner .10 .05
☐ 630 Carlton Fisk .15 .07
☐ 631 Armando Reynoso .05 .02
☐ 632 Felix Fermin .05 .02
☐ 633 Mitch Williams .05 .02
☐ 634 Manuel Lee .05 .02
☐ 635 Harold Baines .10 .05
☐ 636 Greg W. Harris .05 .02
☐ 637 Orlando Merced .05 .02
☐ 638 Chris Bosio .05 .02
☐ 639 Wayne Housie .05 .02
☐ 640 Xavier Hernandez .05 .02
☐ 641 David Howard .05 .02
☐ 642 Tim Crews .05 .02
☐ 643 Rick Cerone .05 .02
☐ 644 Terry Leach .05 .02
☐ 645 Deion Sanders .15 .07
☐ 646 Craig Wilson .05 .02
☐ 647 Marquis Grissom .10 .05
☐ 648 Scott Fletcher .05 .02
☐ 649 Norm Charlton .05 .02
☐ 650 Jesse Barfield .05 .02
☐ 651 Joe Slusarski .05 .02
☐ 652 Bobby Rose .05 .02
☐ 653 Dennis Lamp .05 .02
☐ 654 Allen Watson .05 .02
☐ 655 Brett Butler .10 .05
☐ 656 1992 Prospects OF .15 .07
Rudy Pemberton
Henry Rodriguez
Lee Tinsley
Gerald Williams
☐ 657 Dave Johnson .05 .02
☐ 658 Checklist 529-660 .05 .02
☐ 659 Brian McRae .10 .05
☐ 660 Fred McGriff .15 .07
☐ 661 Bill Landrum .05 .02
☐ 662 Juan Guzman .10 .05
☐ 663 Greg Gagne .05 .02
☐ 664 Ken Hill .10 .05
Now with Expos
11-25-91
☐ 665 Dave Haas .05 .02
☐ 666 Tom Foley .05 .02
☐ 667 Roberto Hernandez .10 .05
☐ 668 Dwayne Henry .05 .02
☐ 669 Jim Fregosi MG .05 .02
☐ 670 Harold Reynolds .10 .05
☐ 671 Mark Whiten .05 .02
☐ 672 Eric Plunk .05 .02
☐ 673 Todd Hundley .10 .05
☐ 674 Mo Sanford .05 .02
☐ 675 Bobby Witt .05 .02
☐ 676 1992 Prospects P .05 .02
Sam Militello
Pat Mahomes
Turk Wendell
Roger Salkeld
☐ 677 John Marzano .05 .02
☐ 678 Joe Klink .05 .02
☐ 679 Pete Incaviglia .05 .02
☐ 680 Dale Murphy .25 .11
☐ 681 Rene Gonzales .05 .02
☐ 682 Andy Benes .10 .05
☐ 683 Jim Poole .05 .02
☐ 684 Trever Miller .05 .02
☐ 685 Scott Livingstone .05 .02
☐ 686 Rich DeLucia .05 .02
☐ 687 Harvey Pulliam .05 .02
☐ 688 Tim Belcher .05 .02

☐ 689 Mark Lemke .05 .02
☐ 690 John Franco .10 .05
☐ 691 Walt Weiss .05 .02
☐ 692 Scott Ruskin .05 .02
Now with Reds
12-11-91
☐ 693 Jeff King .05 .02
☐ 694 Mike Gardiner .05 .02
☐ 695 Gary Sheffield .25 .11
☐ 696 Joe Boever .05 .02
☐ 697 Mike Felder .05 .02
☐ 698 John Habyan .05 .02
☐ 699 Cito Gaston MG .05 .02
☐ 700 Ruben Sierra .05 .02
☐ 701 Scott Radinsky .05 .02
☐ 702 Lee Stevens .05 .02
☐ 703 Mark Wohlers .10 .05
☐ 704 Curt Young .05 .02
☐ 705 Dwight Evans .10 .05
☐ 706 Rob Murphy .05 .02
☐ 707 Gregg Jefferies .10 .05
Now with Royals
12-11-91
☐ 708 Tom Bolton .05 .02
☐ 709 Chris James .05 .02
☐ 710 Kevin Maas .05 .02
☐ 711 Ricky Bones .05 .02
☐ 712 Curt Wilkerson .05 .02
☐ 713 Roger McDowell .05 .02
☐ 714 Calvin Reese .10 .05
☐ 715 Craig Biggio .15 .07
☐ 716 Kirk Dressendorfer .05 .02
☐ 717 Ken Dayley .05 .02
☐ 718 B.J. Surhoff .10 .05
☐ 719 Terry Mulholland .05 .02
☐ 720 Kirk Gibson .10 .05
☐ 721 Mike Pagliarulo .05 .02
☐ 722 Walt Terrell .05 .02
☐ 723 Jose Oquendo .05 .02
☐ 724 Kevin Morton .05 .02
☐ 725 Dwight Gooden .10 .05
☐ 726 Kirt Manwaring .05 .02
☐ 727 Chuck McElroy .05 .02
☐ 728 Dave Burba .05 .02
☐ 729 Art Howe MG .05 .02
☐ 730 Ramon Martinez .10 .05
☐ 731 Donnie Hill .05 .02
☐ 732 Nelson Santovenia .05 .02
☐ 733 Bob Melvin .05 .02
☐ 734 Scott Hatteberg .05 .02
☐ 735 Greg Swindell .05 .02
Now with Reds
11-15-91
☐ 736 Lance Johnson .05 .02
☐ 737 Kevin Reimer .05 .02
☐ 738 Dennis Eckersley .15 .07
☐ 739 Rob Ducey .05 .02
☐ 740 Ken Caminiti .25 .11
☐ 741 Mark Gubicza .05 .02
☐ 742 Billy Spiers .05 .02
☐ 743 Darren Lewis .05 .02
☐ 744 Chris Hammond .05 .02
☐ 745 Dave Magadan .05 .02
☐ 746 Bernard Gilkey .10 .05
☐ 747 Willie Banks .05 .02
☐ 748 Matt Nokes .05 .02
☐ 749 Jerald Clark .05 .02
☐ 750 Travis Fryman .15 .07
☐ 751 Steve Wilson .05 .02
☐ 752 Billy Ripken .05 .02
☐ 753 Paul Assenmacher .05 .02
☐ 754 Charlie Hayes .05 .02
☐ 755 Alex Fernandez .10 .05
☐ 756 Gary Pettis .05 .02
☐ 757 Rob Dibble .05 .02
☐ 758 Tim Naehring .10 .05
☐ 759 Jeff Torborg MG .05 .02
☐ 760 Ozzie Smith .50 .23
☐ 761 Mike Fitzgerald .05 .02
☐ 762 John Burkett .10 .05
☐ 763 Kyle Abbott .05 .02
☐ 764 Tyler Green .05 .02
☐ 765 Pete Harnisch .05 .02
☐ 766 Mark Davis .05 .02
☐ 767 Kal Daniels .05 .02
☐ 768 Jim Thome 1.25 .55
☐ 769 Jack Howell .05 .02
☐ 770 Sid Bream .05 .02
☐ 771 Arthur Rhodes .05 .02
☐ 772 Garry Templeton .05 .02
☐ 773 Hal Morris .05 .02
☐ 774 Bud Black .05 .02
☐ 775 Ivan Calderon .05 .02
☐ 776 Doug Henry .05 .02
☐ 777 John Olerud .10 .05
☐ 778 Tim Leary .05 .02
☐ 779 Jay Bell .05 .02

☐ 780 Eddie Murray	.30	.14
Now with Mets		
11-27-91		
☐ 781 Paul Abbott	.05	.02
☐ 782 Phil Plantier	.05	.02
☐ 783 Joe Magrane	.05	.02
☐ 784 Ken Patterson	.05	.02
☐ 785 Albert Belle	.50	.23
☐ 786 Royce Clayton	.10	.05
☐ 787 Checklist 661-792	.05	.02
☐ 788 Mike Stanton	.05	.02
☐ 789 Bobby Valentine MG	.05	.02
☐ 790 Joe Carter	.10	.05
☐ 791 Danny Cox	.05	.02
☐ 792 Dave Winfield	.25	.11
Now with Blue Jays		
12-19-91		

1992 O-Pee-Chee Box Bottoms

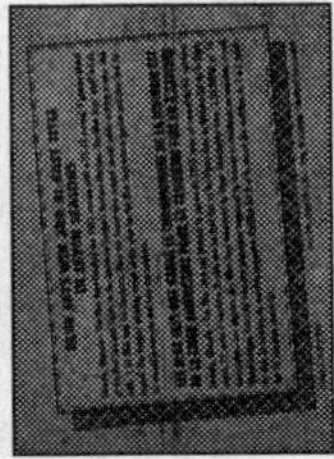

This set consists of four display box bottoms, each featuring one of four team photos of the divisional champions from the 1991 season. The oversized cards measure approximately 5" by 7" and the card's title appears within a ghosted rectangle near the bottom of the white-bordered color photo. The unnumbered horizontal plain-cardboard backs carry the team's season highlights in both English and French in blue lettering.

	MINT	NRMT
COMPLETE SET (4)	3.00	1.35
COMMON CARD (1-4)	.50	.23
☐ 1 Pirates Prevail	.50	.23
☐ 2 Braves Beat Bucs	.75	.35
☐ 3 Blue Jays Claim Crown	1.00	.45
☐ 4 Kirby Puckett	1.50	.70
Twins Tally in Tenth		

1993 O-Pee-Chee

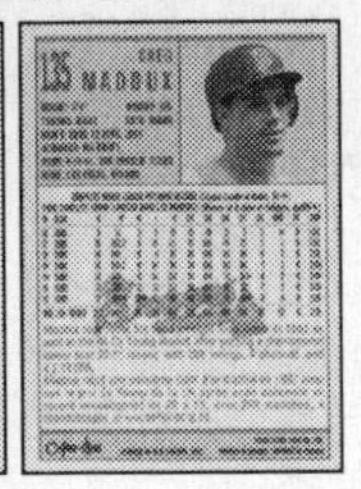

The 1993 O-Pee-Chee baseball set consists of 396 standard-size cards. This is the first year that the regular series differs from the series that Topps issued. The set was sold in wax packs with eight cards plus a random insert card from either a four-card World Series Heroes subset or an 18-card World Series Champions subset. The fronts features color action player photos with white borders. The player's name appears in a silver stripe across the bottom that overlaps the O-Pee-Chee logo. The backs display color close-ups next to a panel containing biographical data. The panel and a stripe at the bottom reflect the team colors. A white box in the center of the card contains statistics and bilingual (English and French) career highlights.

	MINT	NRMT
COMPLETE SET (396)	50.00	22.00
COMMON CARD (1-396)	.10	.05
☐ 1 Jim Abbott	.25	.11
Now with Yankees		
12/6/92		
☐ 2 Eric Anthony	.10	.05
☐ 3 Harold Baines	.25	.11
☐ 4 Roberto Alomar	.60	.25
☐ 5 Steve Avery	.10	.05
☐ 6 James Austin	.10	.05
☐ 7 Mark Wohlers	.25	.11
☐ 8 Steve Buechele	.10	.05
☐ 9 Pedro Astacio	.10	.05
☐ 10 Moises Alou	.25	.11
☐ 11 Rod Beck	.25	.11
☐ 12 Sandy Alomar	.25	.11
☐ 13 Bret Boone	.10	.05
☐ 14 Bryan Harvey	.10	.05
☐ 15 Bobby Bonilla	.25	.11
☐ 16 Brady Anderson	.40	.18
☐ 17 Andy Benes	.25	.11
☐ 18 Ruben Amaro Jr.	.10	.05
☐ 19 Jay Bell	.10	.05
☐ 20 Kevin Brown	.25	.11
☐ 21 Scott Bankhead	.10	.05
Now with Red Sox		
12/8/92		
☐ 22 Denis Boucher	.10	.05
☐ 23 Kevin Appier	.25	.11
☐ 24 Pat Kelly	.10	.05
☐ 25 Rick Aguilera	.25	.11
☐ 26 George Bell	.10	.05
☐ 27 Steve Farr	.10	.05
☐ 28 Chad Curtis	.25	.11
☐ 29 Jeff Bagwell	2.00	.90
☐ 30 Lance Blankenship	.10	.05
☐ 31 Derek Bell	.25	.11
☐ 32 Damon Berryhill	.10	.05
☐ 33 Ricky Bones	.10	.05
☐ 34 Rheal Cormier	.10	.05
☐ 35 Andre Dawson	.40	.18
Now with Red Sox		
12/2/92		
☐ 36 Brett Butler	.25	.11
☐ 37 Sean Berry	.10	.05
☐ 38 Bud Black	.10	.05
☐ 39 Carlos Baerga	.25	.11
☐ 40 Jay Buhner	.40	.18
☐ 41 Charlie Hough	.25	.11
☐ 42 Sid Fernandez	.10	.05
☐ 43 Luis Mercedes	.10	.05
☐ 44 Jerald Clark	.10	.05
Now with Rockies		
11/17/92		
☐ 45 Wes Chamberlain	.10	.05
☐ 46 Barry Bonds	1.00	.45
Now with Giants		
12/8/92		
☐ 47 Jose Canseco	.40	.18
☐ 48 Tim Belcher	.10	.05
☐ 49 David Nied	.10	.05
☐ 50 George Brett	1.50	.70
☐ 51 Cecil Fielder	.25	.11
☐ 52 Chili Davis	.25	.11
Now with Angels		
12/11/92		
☐ 53 Alex Fernandez	.25	.11
☐ 54 Charlie Hayes	.10	.05
Now with Rockies		
11/17/92		
☐ 55 Rob Ducey	.10	.05
☐ 56 Craig Biggio	.40	.18
☐ 57 Mike Bordick	.10	.05
☐ 58 Pat Borders	.10	.05
☐ 59 Jeff Blauser	.10	.05
☐ 60 Chris Bosio	.10	.05
Now with Mariners		
12/3/92		
☐ 61 Bernard Gilkey	.25	.11
☐ 62 Shawon Dunston	.10	.05
☐ 63 Tom Candiotti	.10	.05
☐ 64 Darrin Fletcher	.10	.05
☐ 65 Jeff Brantley	.10	.05
☐ 66 Albert Belle	1.00	.45
☐ 67 Dave Fleming	.10	.05
☐ 68 John Franco	.25	.11
☐ 69 Glenn Davis	.10	.05
☐ 70 Tony Fernandez	.10	.05
Now with Mets		
10/26/92		
☐ 71 Darren Daulton	.25	.11
☐ 72 Doug Drabek	.10	.05
Now with Astros		
12/1/92		
☐ 73 Julio Franco	.25	.11
☐ 74 Tom Browning	.10	.05
☐ 75 Tom Gordon	.10	.05
☐ 76 Travis Fryman	.25	.11
☐ 77 Scott Erickson	.10	.05
☐ 78 Carlton Fisk	.60	.25
☐ 79 Roberto Kelly	.10	.05
Now with Reds		
11/3/92		
☐ 80 Gary DiSarcina	.10	.05
☐ 81 Ken Caminiti	.60	.25
☐ 82 Ron Darling	.10	.05
☐ 83 Joe Carter	.25	.11
☐ 84 Sid Bream	.10	.05
☐ 85 Cal Eldred	.10	.05
☐ 86 Mark Grace	.60	.25
☐ 87 Eric Davis	.10	.05
☐ 88 Ivan Calderon	.10	.05
Now with Red Sox		
12/8/92		
☐ 89 John Burkett	.10	.05
☐ 90 Felix Fermin	.10	.05
☐ 91 Ken Griffey Jr.	4.00	1.80
☐ 92 Dwight Gooden	.25	.11
☐ 93 Mike Devereaux	.10	.05
☐ 94 Tony Gwynn	2.00	.90
☐ 95 Mariano Duncan	.10	.05
☐ 96 Jeff King	.10	.05
☐ 97 Juan Gonzalez	2.00	.90
☐ 98 Norm Charlton	.10	.05
Now with Mariners		
11/17/92		
☐ 99 Mark Gubicza	.10	.05
☐ 100 Danny Gladden	.10	.05
☐ 101 Greg Gagne	.10	.05
Now with Royals		
12/8/92		
☐ 102 Ozzie Guillen	.10	.05
☐ 103 Don Mattingly	2.00	.90
☐ 104 Damion Easley	.10	.05
☐ 105 Casey Candaele	.10	.05
☐ 106 Dennis Eckersley	.40	.18
☐ 107 David Cone	.25	.11
Now with Royals		
12/8/92		
☐ 108 Ron Gant	.25	.11
☐ 109 Mike Fetters	.10	.05
☐ 110 Mike Harkey	.10	.05
☐ 111 Kevin Gross	.10	.05
☐ 112 Archi Cianfrocco	.10	.05
☐ 113 Will Clark	.60	.25
☐ 114 Glenallen Hill	.10	.05
☐ 115 Erik Hanson	.10	.05
☐ 116 Todd Hundley	.25	.11
☐ 117 Leo Gomez	.10	.05
☐ 118 Bruce Hurst	.10	.05
☐ 119 Len Dykstra	.25	.11
☐ 120 Jose Lind	.10	.05
Now with Royals		
11/19/92		
☐ 121 Jose Guzman	.10	.05
Now with Cubs		
12/1/92		
☐ 122 Rob Dibble	.10	.05
☐ 123 Gregg Jefferies	.25	.11
☐ 124 Bill Gullickson	.10	.05
☐ 125 Brian Harper	.10	.05
☐ 126 Roberto Hernandez	.10	.05
☐ 127 Sam Militello	.10	.05
☐ 128 Junior Felix	.10	.05
Now with Marlins		
11/17/92		
☐ 129 Andujar Cedeno	.10	.05
☐ 130 Rickey Henderson	.60	.25
☐ 131 Bob MacDonald	.10	.05
☐ 132 Tom Glavine	.40	.18
☐ 133 Scott Fletcher	.10	.05
Now with Red Sox		
11/30/92		
☐ 134 Brian Jordan	.25	.11
☐ 135 Greg Maddux	3.00	1.35
Now with Braves		
12/9/92		
☐ 136 Orel Hershiser	.25	.11
☐ 137 Greg Colbrunn	.10	.05
☐ 138 Royce Clayton	.10	.05
☐ 139 Thomas Howard	.10	.05
☐ 140 Randy Johnson	.60	.25
☐ 141 Jeff Innis	.10	.05
☐ 142 Chris Hoiles	.10	.05
☐ 143 Darrin Jackson	.10	.05
☐ 144 Tommy Greene	.10	.05
☐ 145 Mike LaValliere	.10	.05
☐ 146 David Hulse	.10	.05
☐ 147 Barry Larkin	.60	.25
☐ 148 Wally Joyner	.10	.05
☐ 149 Mike Henneman	.10	.05
☐ 150 Kent Hrbek	.10	.05
☐ 151 Bo Jackson	.25	.11
☐ 152 Rich Monteleone	.10	.05
☐ 153 Chuck Finley	.25	.11
☐ 154 Steve Finley	.25	.11
☐ 155 Dave Henderson	.10	.05
☐ 156 Kelly Gruber	.10	.05
Now with Angels		
12/8/92		
☐ 157 Brian Hunter	.10	.05
☐ 158 Darryl Hamilton	.10	.05
☐ 159 Derrick May	.10	.05
☐ 160 Jay Howell	.10	.05

☐ 161 Wil Cordero .10 .05
☐ 162 Bryan Hickerson .10 .05
☐ 163 Reggie Jefferson .25 .11
☐ 164 Edgar Martinez .40 .18
☐ 165 Nigel Wilson .10 .05
☐ 166 Howard Johnson .10 .05
☐ 167 Tim Hulett .10 .05
☐ 168 Mike Maddux .10 .05
Now with Mets
12/17/92
☐ 169 Dave Hollins .10 .05
☐ 170 Zane Smith .10 .05
☐ 171 Rafael Palmeiro .60 .25
☐ 172 Dave Martinez .10 .05
Now with Giants
12/9/92
☐ 173 Rusty Meacham .10 .05
☐ 174 Mark Leiter .10 .05
☐ 175 Chuck Knoblauch .60 .25
☐ 176 Lance Johnson .25 .11
☐ 177 Matt Nokes .10 .05
☐ 178 Luis Gonzalez .10 .05
☐ 179 Jack Morris .25 .11
☐ 180 David Justice .40 .18
☐ 181 Doug Henry .10 .05
☐ 182 Felix Jose .10 .05
☐ 183 Delino DeShields .10 .05
☐ 184 Rene Gonzales .10 .05
☐ 185 Pete Harnisch .10 .05
☐ 186 Mike Moore .10 .05
Now with Tigers
12/9/92
☐ 187 Juan Guzman .10 .05
☐ 188 John Olerud .25 .11
☐ 189 Ryan Klesko .75 .35
☐ 190 John Jaha .25 .11
☐ 191 Ray Lankford .25 .11
☐ 192 Jeff Fassero .10 .05
☐ 193 Darren Lewis .10 .05
☐ 194 Mark Lewis .10 .05
☐ 195 Alan Mills .10 .05
☐ 196 Wade Boggs .60 .25
Now with Yankees
12/15/92
☐ 197 Hal Morris .10 .05
☐ 198 Ron Karkovice .10 .05
☐ 199 Joe Grahe .10 .05
☐ 200 Butch Henry .10 .05
Now with Rockies
11/17/92
☐ 201 Mark McGwire 1.50 .70
☐ 202 Tom Henke .25 .11
Now with Rangers
12/15/92
☐ 203 Ed Sprague .10 .05
☐ 204 Charlie Leibrandt .10 .05
Now with Rangers
12/9/92
☐ 205 Pat Listach .10 .05
☐ 206 Omar Olivares .10 .05
☐ 207 Mike Morgan .10 .05
☐ 208 Eric Karros .25 .11
☐ 209 Marquis Grissom .25 .11
☐ 210 Willie McGee .25 .11
☐ 211 Derek Lilliquist .10 .05
☐ 212 Tino Martinez .60 .25
☐ 213 Jeff Kent .25 .11
☐ 214 Mike Mussina 1.00 .45
☐ 215 Randy Myers .10 .05
Now with Cubs
12/9/92
☐ 216 John Kruk .25 .11
☐ 217 Tom Brunansky .10 .05
☐ 218 Paul O'Neill .25 .11
Now with Yankees
11/3/92
☐ 219 Scott Livingstone .10 .05
☐ 220 John Valentin .25 .11
☐ 221 Eddie Zosky .10 .05
☐ 222 Pete Smith .10 .05
☐ 223 Bill Wegman .10 .05
☐ 224 Todd Zeile .10 .05
☐ 225 Tim Wallach .10 .05
Now with Dodgers
12/24/92
☐ 226 Mitch Williams .10 .05
☐ 227 Tim Wakefield .10 .05
☐ 228 Frank Viola .10 .05
☐ 229 Nolan Ryan 3.00 1.35
☐ 230 Kirk McCaskill .10 .05
☐ 231 Melido Perez .10 .05
☐ 232 Mark Langston .10 .05
☐ 233 Xavier Hernandez .10 .05
☐ 234 Jerry Browne .10 .05
☐ 235 Dave Stieb .10 .05
Now with White Sox
12/8/92

☐ 236 Mark Lemke .10 .05
☐ 237 Paul Molitor .75 .35
Now with Blue Jays
12/7/92
☐ 238 Geronimo Pena .10 .05
☐ 239 Ken Hill .25 .11
☐ 240 Jack Clark .10 .05
☐ 241 Greg Myers .10 .05
☐ 242 Pete Incaviglia .10 .05
Now with Phillies
12/8/92
☐ 243 Ruben Sierra .10 .05
☐ 244 Todd Stottlemyre .10 .05
☐ 245 Pat Hentgen .40 .18
☐ 246 Melvin Nieves .25 .11
☐ 247 Jaime Navarro .10 .05
☐ 248 Donovan Osborne .10 .05
☐ 249 Brian Barnes .10 .05
☐ 250 Cory Snyder .10 .05
Now with Dodgers
12/5/92
☐ 251 Kenny Lofton .75 .35
☐ 252 Kevin Mitchell .10 .05
Now with Reds
11/17/92
☐ 253 Dave Magadan .10 .05
Now with Marlins
12/8/92
☐ 254 Ben McDonald .10 .05
☐ 255 Fred McGriff .40 .18
☐ 256 Mickey Morandini .10 .05
☐ 257 Randy Tomlin .10 .05
☐ 258 Dean Palmer .25 .11
☐ 259 Roger Clemens 1.25 .55
☐ 260 Joe Oliver .10 .05
☐ 261 Jeff Montgomery .10 .05
☐ 262 Tony Phillips .10 .05
☐ 263 Shane Mack .10 .05
☐ 264 Jack McDowell .25 .11
☐ 265 Mike Macfarlane .10 .05
☐ 266 Luis Polonia .10 .05
☐ 267 Doug Jones .10 .05
☐ 268 Terry Steinbach .10 .05
☐ 269 Jimmy Key .25 .11
Now with Yankees
12/10/92
☐ 270 Pat Tabler .10 .05
☐ 271 Otis Nixon .25 .11
☐ 272 Dave Nilsson .10 .05
☐ 273 Tom Pagnozzi .10 .05
☐ 274 Ryne Sandberg 1.50 .70
☐ 275 Ramon Martinez .25 .11
☐ 276 Tim Laker .10 .05
☐ 277 Bill Swift .10 .05
☐ 278 Charles Nagy .25 .11
☐ 279 Harold Reynolds .25 .11
Now with Orioles
12/11/92
☐ 280 Eddie Murray .75 .35
☐ 281 Gregg Olson .10 .05
☐ 282 Frank Seminara .10 .05
☐ 283 Terry Mulholland .10 .05
☐ 284 Kevin Reimer .10 .05
Now with Brewers
11/17/92
☐ 285 Mike Greenwell .10 .05
☐ 286 Jose Rijo .10 .05
☐ 287 Brian McRae .10 .05
☐ 288 Frank Tanana .10 .05
Now with Mets
12/10/92
☐ 289 Pedro Munoz .10 .05
☐ 290 Tim Raines .25 .11
☐ 291 Andy Stankiewicz .10 .05
☐ 292 Tim Salmon 1.50 .70
☐ 293 Jimmy Jones .10 .05
☐ 294 Dave Stewart .25 .11
Now with Blue Jays
12/8/92
☐ 295 Mike Timlin .10 .05
☐ 296 Greg Olson .10 .05
☐ 297 Dan Plesac .10 .05
Now with Cubs
12/8/92
☐ 298 Mike Perez .10 .05
☐ 299 Jose Offerman .10 .05
☐ 300 Denny Martinez .25 .11
☐ 301 Robby Thompson .10 .05
☐ 302 Bret Saberhagen .10 .05
☐ 303 Joe Orsulak .10 .05
Now with Mets
12/18/92
☐ 304 Tim Naehring .10 .05
☐ 305 Bip Roberts .10 .05
☐ 306 Kirby Puckett 2.00 .90
☐ 307 Steve Sax .10 .05
☐ 308 Danny Tartabull .10 .05

☐ 309 Jeff Juden .10 .05
☐ 310 Duane Ward .10 .05
☐ 311 Alejandro Pena .10 .05
Now with Pirates
12/10/92
☐ 312 Kevin Seitzer .10 .05
☐ 313 Ozzie Smith 1.00 .45
☐ 314 Mike Piazza 3.00 1.35
☐ 315 Chris Nabholz .10 .05
☐ 316 Tony Pena .10 .05
☐ 317 Gary Sheffield .60 .25
☐ 318 Mark Portugal .10 .05
☐ 319 Walt Weiss .10 .05
Now with Marlins
11/17/92
☐ 320 Manuel Lee .10 .05
Now with Rangers
12/19/92
☐ 321 David Wells .10 .05
☐ 322 Terry Pendleton .10 .05
☐ 323 Billy Spiers .10 .05
☐ 324 Lee Smith .25 .11
☐ 325 Bob Scanlan .10 .05
☐ 326 Mike Scioscia .10 .05
☐ 327 Spike Owen .10 .05
Now with Yankees
12/4/92
☐ 328 Mackey Sasser .10 .05
Now with Mariners
12/23/92
☐ 329 Arthur Rhodes .10 .05
☐ 330 Ben Rivera .10 .05
☐ 331 Ivan Rodriguez 1.00 .45
☐ 332 Phil Plantier .10 .05
Now with Padres
12/10/92
☐ 333 Chris Sabo .10 .05
☐ 334 Mickey Tettleton .10 .05
☐ 335 John Smiley .10 .05
Now with Reds
11/30/92
☐ 336 Bobby Thigpen .10 .05
☐ 337 Randy Velarde .10 .05
☐ 338 Luis Sojo .10 .05
Now with Blue Jays
12/8/92
☐ 339 Scott Servais .10 .05
☐ 340 Bob Welch .10 .05
☐ 341 Devon White .10 .05
☐ 342 Jeff Reardon .10 .05
☐ 343 B.J. Surhoff .25 .11
☐ 344 Bob Tewksbury .10 .05
☐ 345 Jose Vizcaino .10 .05
☐ 346 Mike Sharperson .10 .05
☐ 347 Mel Rojas .10 .05
☐ 348 Matt Williams .40 .18
☐ 349 Steve Olin .10 .05
☐ 350 Mike Schooler .10 .05
☐ 351 Ryan Thompson .10 .05
☐ 352 Cal Ripken 3.00 1.35
☐ 353 Benito Santiago .10 .05
Now with Marlins
12/16/92
☐ 354 Curt Schilling .25 .11
☐ 355 Andy Van Slyke .10 .05
☐ 356 Kenny Rogers .10 .05
☐ 357 Jody Reed .10 .05
Now with Dodgers
11/17/92
☐ 358 Reggie Sanders .25 .11
☐ 359 Kevin McReynolds .10 .05
☐ 360 Alan Trammell .40 .18
☐ 361 Kevin Tapani .10 .05
☐ 362 Frank Thomas 3.00 1.35
☐ 363 Bernie Williams .75 .35
☐ 364 John Smoltz .25 .11
☐ 365 Robin Yount .40 .18
☐ 366 John Wetteland .25 .11
☐ 367 Bob Zupcic .10 .05
☐ 368 Julio Valera .10 .05
☐ 369 Brian Williams .10 .05
☐ 370 Willie Wilson .10 .05
Now with Cubs
12/18/92
☐ 371 Dave Winfield .75 .35
Now with Twins
12/17/92
☐ 372 Deion Sanders .60 .25
☐ 373 Greg Vaughn .10 .05
☐ 374 Todd Worrell .25 .11
Now with Dodgers
12/9/92
☐ 375 Darryl Strawberry .25 .11
☐ 376 John Vander Wal .10 .05
☐ 377 Mike Benjamin .10 .05
☐ 378 Mark Whiten .10 .05
☐ 379 Omar Vizquel .25 .11

☐ 380 Anthony Young .10 .05
☐ 381 Rick Sutcliffe .10 .05
☐ 382 Candy Maldonado .10 .05
Now with Cubs
12/11/92
☐ 383 Francisco Cabrera .10 .05
☐ 384 Larry Walker .75 .35
☐ 385 Scott Cooper .10 .05
☐ 386 Gerald Williams .10 .05
☐ 387 Robin Ventura .25 .11
☐ 388 Carl Willis .10 .05
☐ 389 Lou Whitaker .25 .11
☐ 390 Hipolito Pichardo .10 .05
☐ 391 Rudy Seanez .10 .05
☐ 392 Greg Swindell .10 .05
Now with Astros
12/4/92
☐ 393 Mo Vaughn .75 .35
☐ 394 Checklist 1-132 .10 .05
☐ 395 Checklist 133-264 .10 .05
☐ 396 Checklist 265-396 .10 .05

1993 O-Pee-Chee World Champions

This 18-card standard-size set was randomly inserted in 1993 O-Pee-Chee wax packs and features the Toronto Blue Jays, the 1992 World Series Champions. The standard-size cards are similar to the regular issue, with glossy color action player photos with white borders on the fronts. They differ in having a gold (rather than silver) stripe across the bottom, which intersects a 1992 World Champions logo. The backs carry statistics on a burnt orange box against a light blue panel with bilingual (English and French) career highlights.

	MINT	NRMT
COMPLETE SET (18)	4.00	1.80
COMMON CARD (1-18)	.10	.05

☐ 1 Roberto Alomar 1.00 .45
☐ 2 Pat Borders .10 .05
☐ 3 Joe Carter .40 .18
☐ 4 David Cone .25 .11
☐ 5 Kelly Gruber .10 .05
☐ 6 Juan Guzman .10 .05
☐ 7 Tom Henke .25 .11
☐ 8 Jimmy Key .25 .11
☐ 9 Manuel Lee .10 .05
☐ 10 Candy Maldonado .10 .05
☐ 11 Jack Morris .25 .11
☐ 12 John Olerud .25 .11
☐ 13 Ed Sprague .10 .05
☐ 14 Todd Stottlemyre .10 .05
☐ 15 Duane Ward .10 .05
☐ 16 Devon White .10 .05
☐ 17 Dave Winfield .75 .35
☐ 18 Cito Gaston MG .10 .05

1993 O-Pee-Chee World Series Heroes

This four-card standard-size set was randomly inserted in 1993 O-Pee-Chee wax packs. These cards were more difficult to find than the 18-card World Series Champions insert set. The fronts feature color action player photos with white borders. The words "World Series Heroes" appear in a dark blue stripe above the picture, while the player's name is printed in the bottom white border. A 1992 World Series logo overlays the picture at the lower right corner. Over a ghosted version of the 1992 World Series logo, the backs summarize, in English and French, the player's outstanding performance in the 1992 World Series. The cards are numbered on the back in alphabetical order by player's name.

	MINT	NRMT
COMPLETE SET (4)	2.00	.90
COMMON CARD (1-4)	.25	.11

☐ 1 Pat Borders .25 .11
☐ 2 Jimmy Key .50 .23
☐ 3 Ed Sprague .50 .23
☐ 4 Dave Winfield 1.00 .45

1994 O-Pee-Chee

The 1994 O-Pee-Chee baseball set consists of 270 standard-size cards.Production was limited to 2,500 individually numbered cases. Each display box contained 36 packs and one 5" by 7" All-Star Jumbo card. Each foil pack contained 14 regular cards plus eiher one chase card or one redemption card.

	MINT	NRMT
COMPLETE SET (270)	15.00	6.75
COMMON CARD (1-270)	.05	.02

☐ 1 Paul Molitor .40 .18
☐ 2 Kirt Manwaring .05 .02
☐ 3 Brady Anderson .15 .07
☐ 4 Scott Cooper .05 .02
☐ 5 Kevin Stocker .05 .02
☐ 6 Alex Fernandez .10 .05
☐ 7 Jeff Montgomery .05 .02
☐ 8 Danny Tartabull .05 .02
☐ 9 Damion Easley .05 .02
☐ 10 Andujar Cedeno .05 .02
☐ 11 Steve Karsay .05 .02
☐ 12 Dave Stewart .10 .05
☐ 13 Fred McGriff .15 .07
☐ 14 Jaime Navarro .05 .02
☐ 15 Allen Watson .05 .02
☐ 16 Ryne Sandberg .60 .25
☐ 17 Arthur Rhodes .05 .02
☐ 18 Marquis Grissom .10 .05
☐ 19 John Burkett .05 .02
☐ 20 Robby Thompson .05 .02
☐ 21 Denny Martinez .10 .05
☐ 22 Ken Griffey Jr. 2.00 .90
☐ 23 Orestes Destrade .05 .02
☐ 24 Dwight Gooden .10 .05
☐ 25 Rafael Palmeiro .15 .07
☐ 26 Pedro A.Martinez .05 .02
☐ 27 Wes Chamberlain .05 .02
☐ 28 Juan Gonzalez 1.00 .45
☐ 29 Kevin Mitchell .05 .02
☐ 30 Dante Bichette .10 .05
☐ 31 Howard Johnson .05 .02
☐ 32 Mickey Tettleton .05 .02
☐ 33 Robin Ventura .10 .05
☐ 34 Terry Mulholland .05 .02
☐ 35 Bernie Williams .30 .14
☐ 36 Eduardo Perez .05 .02
☐ 37 Rickey Henderson .30 .14
☐ 38 Terry Pendleton .05 .02
☐ 39 John Smoltz .10 .05
☐ 40 Derrick May .05 .02
☐ 41 Pedro J.Martinez .25 .11
☐ 42 Mark Portugal .05 .02
☐ 43 Albert Belle .60 .25
☐ 44 Edgar Martinez .15 .07
☐ 45 Gary Sheffield .25 .11
☐ 46 Bret Saberhagen .05 .02
☐ 47 Ricky Gutierrez .05 .02
☐ 48 Orlando Merced .05 .02
☐ 49 Mike Greenwell .05 .02
☐ 50 Jose Rijo .05 .02
☐ 51 Jeff Granger .05 .02
☐ 52 Mike Henneman .05 .02
☐ 53 Dave Winfield .25 .11
☐ 54 Don Mattingly 1.00 .45
☐ 55 J.T. Snow .10 .05
☐ 56 Todd Van Poppel .05 .02
☐ 57 Chipper Jones 1.50 .70
☐ 58 Darryl Hamilton .05 .02
☐ 59 Delino DeShields .05 .02
☐ 60 Rondell White .15 .07
☐ 61 Eric Anthony .05 .02
☐ 62 Charlie Hough .10 .05
☐ 63 Sid Fernandez .05 .02
☐ 64 Derek Bell .10 .05
☐ 65 Phil Plantier .05 .02
☐ 66 Curt Schilling .10 .05
☐ 67 Roger Clemens .60 .25
☐ 68 Jose Lind .05 .02
☐ 69 Andres Galarraga .25 .11
☐ 70 Tim Belcher .05 .02
☐ 71 Ron Karkovice .05 .02
☐ 72 Alan Trammell .15 .07
☐ 73 Pete Harnisch .05 .02
☐ 74 Mark McGwire .75 .35
☐ 75 Ryan Klesko .25 .11
☐ 76 Ramon Martinez .10 .05
☐ 77 Gregg Jefferies .10 .05
☐ 78 Steve Buechele .05 .02
☐ 79 Bill Swift .05 .02
☐ 80 Matt Williams .15 .07
☐ 81 Randy Johnson .25 .11
☐ 82 Mike Mussina .40 .18
☐ 83 Andy Benes .10 .05
☐ 84 Dave Staton .05 .02
☐ 85 Steve Cooke .05 .02
☐ 86 Andy Van Slyke .05 .02
☐ 87 Ivan Rodriguez .50 .23
☐ 88 Frank Viola .05 .02
☐ 89 Aaron Sele .05 .02
☐ 90 Ellis Burks .10 .05
☐ 91 Wally Joyner .10 .05
☐ 92 Rick Aguilera .10 .05
☐ 93 Kirby Puckett 1.00 .45
☐ 94 Roberto Hernandez .05 .02
☐ 95 Mike Stanley .05 .02
☐ 96 Roberto Alomar .35 .16
☐ 97 James Mouton .05 .02
☐ 98 Chad Curtis .10 .05
☐ 99 Mitch Williams .05 .02
☐ 100 Carlos Delgado .40 .18
☐ 101 Greg Maddux 1.25 .55
☐ 102 Brian Harper .05 .02
☐ 103 Tom Pagnozzi .05 .02
☐ 104 Jose Offerman .05 .02
☐ 105 John Wetteland .10 .05
☐ 106 Carlos Baerga .10 .05
☐ 107 Dave Magadan .05 .02
☐ 108 Bobby Jones .10 .05
☐ 109 Tony Gwynn 1.00 .45
☐ 110 Jeromy Burnitz .05 .02
☐ 111 Bip Roberts .05 .02
☐ 112 Carlos Garcia .05 .02
☐ 113 Jeff Russell .05 .02
☐ 114 Armando Reynoso .05 .02
☐ 115 Ozzie Guillen .05 .02
☐ 116 Bo Jackson .10 .05
☐ 117 Terry Steinbach .05 .02
☐ 118 Deion Sanders .25 .11
☐ 119 Randy Myers .05 .02
☐ 120 Mark Whiten .05 .02
☐ 121 Manny Ramirez .40 .18
☐ 122 Ben McDonald .05 .02
☐ 123 Darren Daulton .10 .05
☐ 124 Kevin Young .05 .02
☐ 125 Barry Larkin .25 .11
☐ 126 Cecil Fielder .10 .05
☐ 127 Frank Thomas 1.50 .70
☐ 128 Luis Polonia .05 .02
☐ 129 Steve Finley .10 .05
☐ 130 John Olerud .10 .05
☐ 131 John Jaha .05 .02
☐ 132 Darren Lewis .05 .02
☐ 133 Orel Hershiser .10 .05
☐ 134 Chris Bosio .05 .02
☐ 135 Ryan Thompson .05 .02
☐ 136 Chris Sabo .05 .02
☐ 137 Tommy Greene .05 .02
☐ 138 Andre Dawson .15 .07
☐ 139 Roberto Kelly .05 .02
☐ 140 Ken Hill .05 .02
☐ 141 Greg Gagne .05 .02
☐ 142 Julio Franco .05 .02
☐ 143 Chili Davis .10 .05
☐ 144 Dennis Eckersley .15 .07
☐ 145 Joe Carter .10 .05
☐ 146 Mark Grace .25 .11
☐ 147 Mike Piazza 1.25 .55
☐ 148 J.R. Phillips .05 .02
☐ 149 Rich Amaral .05 .02

☐ 150 Benny Santiago .05 .02
☐ 151 Jeff King .05 .02
☐ 152 Dean Palmer .10 .05
☐ 153 Hal Morris .05 .02
☐ 154 Mike Macfarlane .05 .02
☐ 155 Chuck Knoblauch .25 .11
☐ 156 Pat Kelly .05 .02
☐ 157 Greg Swindell .05 .02
☐ 158 Chuck Finley .10 .05
☐ 159 Devon White .05 .02
☐ 160 Duane Ward .05 .02
☐ 161 Sammy Sosa .25 .11
☐ 162 Javy Lopez .15 .07
☐ 163 Eric Karros .10 .05
☐ 164 Royce Clayton .05 .02
☐ 165 Salomon Torres .05 .02
☐ 166 Jeff Kent .05 .02
☐ 167 Chris Hoiles .05 .02
☐ 168 Len Dykstra .10 .05
☐ 169 Jose Canseco .30 .14
☐ 170 Bret Boone .05 .02
☐ 171 Charlie Hayes .05 .02
☐ 172 Lou Whitaker .10 .05
☐ 173 Jack McDowell .10 .05
☐ 174 Jimmy Key .10 .05
☐ 175 Mark Langston .05 .02
☐ 176 Darryl Kile .10 .05
☐ 177 Juan Guzman .05 .02
☐ 178 Pat Borders .05 .02
☐ 179 Cal Eldred .05 .02
☐ 180 Jose Guzman .05 .02
☐ 181 Ozzie Smith .60 .25
☐ 182 Rod Beck .05 .02
☐ 183 Dave Fleming .05 .02
☐ 184 Eddie Murray .40 .18
☐ 185 Cal Ripken 1.50 .70
☐ 186 Dave Hollins .05 .02
☐ 187 Will Clark .30 .14
☐ 188 Otis Nixon .10 .05
☐ 189 Joe Oliver .05 .02
☐ 190 Roberto Mejia .05 .02
☐ 191 Felix Jose .05 .02
☐ 192 Tony Phillips .05 .02
☐ 193 Wade Boggs .25 .11
☐ 194 Tim Salmon .40 .18
☐ 195 Ruben Sierra .05 .02
☐ 196 Steve Avery .05 .02
☐ 197 B.J. Surhoff .05 .02
☐ 198 Todd Zeile .05 .02
☐ 199 Raul Mondesi .25 .11
☐ 200 Barry Bonds .50 .23
☐ 201 Sandy Alomar .10 .05
☐ 202 Bobby Bonilla .10 .05
☐ 203 Mike Devereaux .05 .02
☐ 204 Rickey Bottalico .25 .11
☐ 205 Kevin Brown .10 .05
☐ 206 Jason Bere .05 .02
☐ 207 Reggie Sanders .10 .05
☐ 208 David Nied .05 .02
☐ 209 Travis Fryman .10 .05
☐ 210 James Baldwin .10 .05
☐ 211 Jim Abbott .05 .02
☐ 212 Jeff Bagwell 1.00 .45
☐ 213 Bob Welch .05 .02
☐ 214 Jeff Blauser .05 .02
☐ 215 Brett Butler .10 .05
☐ 216 Pat Listach .05 .02
☐ 217 Bob Tewksbury .05 .02
☐ 218 Mike Lansing .05 .02
☐ 219 Wayne Kirby .05 .02
☐ 220 Chuck Carr .05 .02
☐ 221 Harold Baines .10 .05
☐ 222 Jay Bell .05 .02
☐ 223 Ciff Floyd .05 .02
☐ 224 Rob Dibble .05 .02
☐ 225 Kevin Appier .10 .05
☐ 226 Eric Davis .10 .05
☐ 227 Matt Walbeck .05 .02
☐ 228 Tim Raines .10 .05
☐ 229 Paul O'Neill .10 .05
☐ 230 Craig Biggio .15 .07
☐ 231 Brent Gates .05 .02
☐ 232 Rob Butler .05 .02
☐ 233 David Justice .25 .11
☐ 234 Rene Arocha .05 .02
☐ 235 Mike Morgan .05 .02
☐ 236 Denis Boucher .05 .02
☐ 237 Kenny Lofton .40 .18
☐ 238 Jeff Conine .10 .05
☐ 239 Bryan Harvey .05 .02
☐ 240 Danny Jackson .05 .02
☐ 241 Al Martin .05 .02
☐ 242 Tom Henke .10 .05
☐ 243 Erik Hanson .05 .02
☐ 244 Walt Weiss .05 .02
☐ 245 Brian McRae .05 .02
☐ 246 Kevin Tapani .05 .02
☐ 247 David McCarty .05 .02
☐ 248 Doug Drabek .05 .02
☐ 249 Troy Neel .05 .02
☐ 250 Tom Glavine .10 .05
☐ 251 Ray Lankford .10 .05
☐ 252 Wil Cordero .05 .02
☐ 253 Larry Walker .25 .11
☐ 254 Charles Nagy .10 .05
☐ 255 Kirk Rueter .05 .02
☐ 256 John Franco .10 .05
☐ 257 John Kruk .10 .05
☐ 258 Alex Gonzalez .05 .02
☐ 259 Mo Vaughn .50 .23
☐ 260 David Cone .10 .05
☐ 261 Kent Hrbek .05 .02
☐ 262 Lance Johnson .05 .02
☐ 263 Luis Gonzalez .05 .02
☐ 264 Mike Bordick .05 .02
☐ 265 Ed Sprague .05 .02
☐ 266 Moises Alou .10 .05
☐ 267 Omar Vizquel .10 .05
☐ 268 Jay Buhner .15 .07
☐ 269 Checklist .05 .02
☐ 270 Checklist .05 .02

1994 O-Pee-Chee All-Star Redemptions

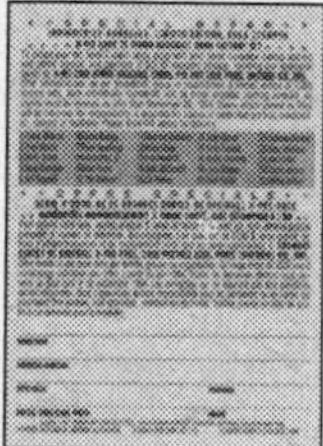

Inserted one per pack, this standard-size, 25-card redemption set features some of the game's top stars. White borders surround a color player photo on front. The backs contain redemption information. Any five cards from this set and $20 CDN could be redeemed for a foil version of the jumbo set that was issued one per wax box. The redemption deadline was September 30, 1994.

	MINT	NRMT
COMPLETE SET (25)	12.00	5.50
COMMON CARD (1-25)	.20	.09
☐ 1 Frank Thomas	3.00	1.35
☐ 2 Paul Molitor	.75	.35
☐ 3 Barry Bonds	1.00	.45
☐ 4 Juan Gonzalez	2.00	.90
☐ 5 Jeff Bagwell	2.00	.90
☐ 6 Carlos Baerga	.40	.18
☐ 7 Ryne Sandberg	1.00	.45
☐ 8 Ken Griffey Jr.	4.00	1.80
☐ 9 Mike Piazza	3.00	1.35
☐ 10 Tim Salmon	.75	.35
☐ 11 Marquis Grissom	.40	.18
☐ 12 Albert Belle	1.25	.55
☐ 13 Fred McGriff	.60	.25
☐ 14 Jack McDowell	.20	.09
☐ 15 Cal Ripken	3.00	1.35
☐ 16 John Olerud	.40	.18
☐ 17 Kirby Puckett	2.00	.90
☐ 18 Roger Clemens	1.50	.70
☐ 19 Larry Walker	.75	.35
☐ 20 Cecil Fielder	.40	.18
☐ 21 Roberto Alomar	.75	.35
☐ 22 Greg Maddux	2.50	1.10
☐ 23 Joe Carter	.40	.18
☐ 24 David Justice	.75	.35
☐ 25 Kenny Lofton	1.00	.45

1994 O-Pee-Chee Jumbo All-Stars

These 5" by 7" parallel cards were included as a bonus at the bottom of every 1994 OPC box. According to published reports, approximately 2,400 of each card was produced. A foil version exists for these cards. They are currently valued the same as the regular cards.

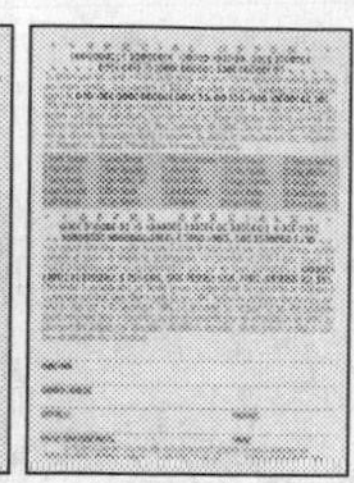

	MINT	NRMT
COMPLETE SET (25)	25.00	11.00
COMMON CARD (1-25)	.40	.18
☐ 1 Frank Thomas	8.00	3.60
☐ 2 Paul Molitor	2.00	.90
☐ 3 Barry Bonds	2.50	1.10
☐ 4 Juan Gonzalez	5.00	2.20
☐ 5 Jeff Bagwell	5.00	2.20
☐ 6 Carlos Baerga	.60	.25
☐ 7 Ryne Sandberg	2.50	1.10
☐ 8 Ken Griffey Jr.	10.00	4.50
☐ 9 Mike Piazza	6.00	2.70
☐ 10 Tim Salmon	1.00	.45
☐ 11 Marquis Grissom	.75	.35
☐ 12 Albert Belle	3.00	1.35
☐ 13 Fred McGriff	.75	.35
☐ 14 Jack McDowell	.40	.18
☐ 15 Cal Ripken	8.00	3.60
☐ 16 John Olerud	.60	.25
☐ 17 Kirby Puckett	5.00	2.20
☐ 18 Roger Clemens	2.50	1.10
☐ 19 Larry Walker	1.00	.45
☐ 20 Cecil Fielder	.60	.25
☐ 21 Roberto Alomar	1.00	.45
☐ 22 Greg Maddux	6.00	2.70
☐ 23 Joe Carter	.60	.25
☐ 24 David Justice	1.00	.45
☐ 25 Kenny Lofton	2.00	.90

1994 O-Pee-Chee Diamond Dynamos

This 18-card standard-size set was randomly inserted into 1994 OPC packs. According to the company approximately 5,000 sets were produced. The fronts feature player photos as well as red foil lettering while the backs have gold foil stamping. Between one or two cards from this set was included in each box.

	MINT	NRMT
COMPLETE SET (18)	45.00	20.00
COMMON CARD (1-18)	2.00	.90
☐ 1 Mike Piazza	20.00	9.00
☐ 2 Robert Mejia	2.00	.90
☐ 3 Wayne Kirby	2.00	.90
☐ 4 Kevin Stocker	2.00	.90
☐ 5 Chris Gomez	2.00	.90
☐ 6 Bobby Jones	3.00	1.35
☐ 7 David McCarty	2.00	.90
☐ 8 Kirk Rueter	2.00	.90
☐ 9 J.T. Snow	4.00	1.80
☐ 10 Wil Cordero	2.00	.90
☐ 11 Tim Salmon	7.50	3.40
☐ 12 Jeff Conine	3.00	1.35
☐ 13 Jason Bere	2.00	.90
☐ 14 Greg McMichael	2.00	.90
☐ 15 Brent Gates	2.00	.90
☐ 16 Allen Watson	2.00	.90
☐ 17 Aaron Sele	2.00	.90
☐ 18 Carlos Garcia	2.00	.90

1994 O-Pee-Chee Hot Prospects

This nine-card standard-size insert set features some of 1994's leading prospects. According to the manufacturer, approximately 6,666 sets were produced. The cards features gold and red foil stamping, player photos on both sides and complete minor league stats. An average of one card was included in each display box.

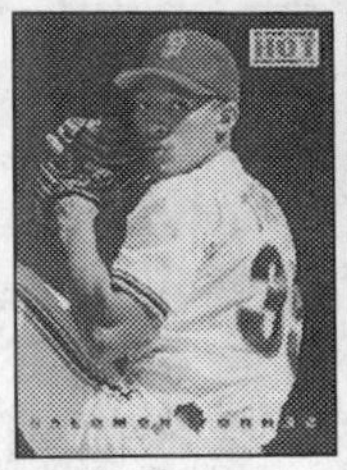

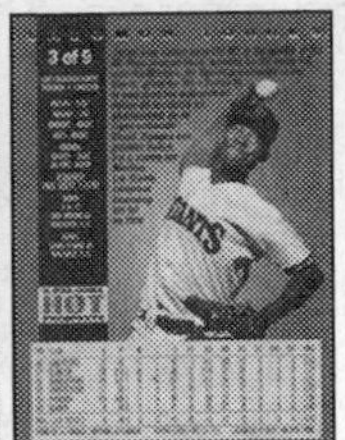

	MINT	NRMT
COMPLETE SET (9)	30.00	13.50
COMMON CARD (1-9)	1.00	.45

	MINT	NRMT
☐ 1 Cliff Floyd	1.50	.70
☐ 2 James Mouton	1.00	.45
☐ 3 Salomon Torres	1.00	.45
☐ 4 Raul Mondesi	6.00	2.70
☐ 5 Carlos Delgado	5.00	2.20
☐ 6 Manny Ramirez	10.00	4.50
☐ 7 Javy Lopez	5.00	2.20
☐ 8 Alex Gonzalez	1.00	.45
☐ 9 Ryan Klesko	6.00	2.70

1994 O-Pee-Chee World Champions

This nine card insert set features members of the 1993 World Series champion Toronto Blue Jays. Randomly inserted in packs at a rate of one in 36, the player is superimposed over a background containing the phrase, "1993 World Series Champions". The backs contain World Series statistics from 1992 and 1993 and highlights.

	MINT	NRMT
COMPLETE SET (9)	20.00	9.00
COMMON CARD (1-9)	1.00	.45

	MINT	NRMT
☐ 1 Rickey Henderson	4.00	1.80
☐ 2 Devon White	1.00	.45
☐ 3 Paul Molitor	4.00	1.80
☐ 4 Joe Carter	2.00	.90
☐ 5 John Olerud	1.50	.70
☐ 6 Roberto Alomar	4.00	1.80
☐ 7 Ed Sprague	1.00	.45
☐ 8 Pat Borders	1.00	.45
☐ 9 Tony Fernandez	1.00	.45

1991 O-Pee-Chee Premier

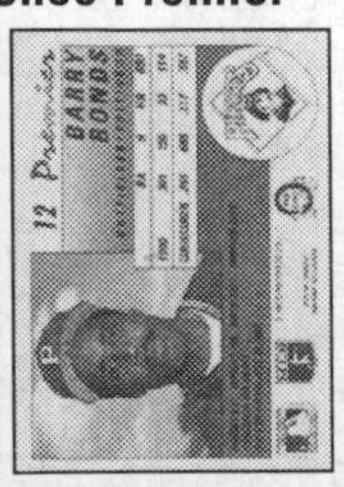

The 1991 OPC Premier set contains 132 standard-size cards. The fronts feature color action player photos on a white card face. All the pictures are bordered in gold above, while the color of the border stripes on the other three sides varies from card to card. The player's name, team name, and position (the last item in English and French) appear below the picture. In a horizontal format, the backs have a color head shot and the team logo in a circular format. Biography and statistics (1990 and career) are presented on an orange and yellow striped background. The cards are arranged in alphabetical order and numbered on the back. Small packs of these cards were given out at the Fan Fest to commemorate the 1991 All-Star Game in Canada.

	MINT	NRMT
COMPLETE SET (132)	10.00	4.50
COMPLETE FACT.SET (132)	15.00	6.75
COMMON CARD (1-132)	.05	.02

	MINT	NRMT
☐ 1 Roberto Alomar	.30	.14
☐ 2 Sandy Alomar Jr.	.10	.05
☐ 3 Moises Alou	.15	.07
☐ 4 Brian Barnes	.05	.02
☐ 5 Steve Bedrosian	.05	.02
☐ 6 George Bell	.05	.02
☐ 7 Juan Bell	.05	.02
☐ 8 Albert Belle	.75	.35
☐ 9 Bud Black	.05	.02
☐ 10 Mike Boddicker	.05	.02
☐ 11 Wade Boggs	.30	.14
☐ 12 Barry Bonds	.40	.18
☐ 13 Denis Boucher	.05	.02
☐ 14 George Brett	.75	.35
☐ 15 Hubie Brooks	.05	.02
☐ 16 Brett Butler	.10	.05
☐ 17 Ivan Calderon	.05	.02
☐ 18 Jose Canseco	.30	.14
☐ 19 Gary Carter	.25	.11
☐ 20 Joe Carter	.10	.05
☐ 21 Jack Clark	.05	.02
☐ 22 Will Clark	.25	.11
☐ 23 Roger Clemens	.50	.23
☐ 24 Alex Cole	.05	.02
☐ 25 Vince Coleman	.05	.02
☐ 26 Jeff Conine	.40	.18
☐ 27 Milt Cuyler	.05	.02
☐ 28 Danny Darwin	.05	.02
☐ 29 Eric Davis	.10	.05
☐ 30 Glenn Davis	.05	.02
☐ 31 Andre Dawson	.15	.07
☐ 32 Ken Dayley	.05	.02
☐ 33 Steve Decker	.05	.02
☐ 34 Delino DeShields	.05	.02
☐ 35 Lance Dickson	.05	.02
☐ 36 Kirk Dressendorfer	.05	.02
☐ 37 Shawon Dunston	.05	.02
☐ 38 Dennis Eckersley	.15	.07
☐ 39 Dwight Evans	.10	.05
☐ 40 Howard Farmer	.05	.02
☐ 41 Junior Felix	.05	.02
☐ 42 Alex Fernandez	.15	.07
☐ 43 Tony Fernandez	.05	.02
☐ 44 Cecil Fielder	.10	.05
☐ 45 Carlton Fisk	.25	.11
☐ 46 Willie Fraser	.05	.02
☐ 47 Gary Gaetti	.05	.02
☐ 48 Andres Galarraga	.25	.11
☐ 49 Ron Gant	.10	.05
☐ 50 Kirk Gibson	.10	.05
☐ 51 Bernard Gilkey	.10	.05
☐ 52 Leo Gomez	.05	.02
☐ 53 Rene Gonzales	.05	.02
☐ 54 Juan Gonzalez	1.00	.45
☐ 55 Dwight Gooden	.10	.05
☐ 56 Ken Griffey Jr.	2.00	.90
☐ 57 Kelly Gruber	.05	.02
☐ 58 Pedro Guerrero	.05	.02
☐ 59 Tony Gwynn	.75	.35
☐ 60 Chris Hammond	.05	.02
☐ 61 Ron Hassey	.05	.02
☐ 62 Rickey Henderson 939 Stolen Bases	.40	.18
☐ 63 Tom Henke	.10	.05
☐ 64 Orel Hershiser	.10	.05
☐ 65 Chris Hoiles	.05	.02
☐ 66 Todd Hundley	.25	.11
☐ 67 Pete Incaviglia	.05	.02
☐ 68 Danny Jackson	.05	.02
☐ 69 Barry Jones	.05	.02
☐ 70 Dave Justice	.40	.18
☐ 71 Jimmy Key	.10	.05
☐ 72 Ray Lankford	.15	.07
☐ 73 Darren Lewis	.05	.02
☐ 74 Kevin Maas	.05	.02
☐ 75 Denny Martinez	.10	.05
☐ 76 Tino Martinez	.25	.11
☐ 77 Don Mattingly	1.00	.45
☐ 78 Willie McGee	.10	.05
☐ 79 Fred McGriff	.25	.11
☐ 80 Hensley Meulens	.05	.02
☐ 81 Kevin Mitchell	.05	.02
☐ 82 Paul Molitor	.40	.18
☐ 83 Mickey Morandini	.05	.02
☐ 84 Jack Morris	.10	.05
☐ 85 Dale Murphy	.25	.11
☐ 86 Eddie Murray	.30	.14
☐ 87 Chris Nabholz	.05	.02
☐ 88 Tim Naehring	.10	.05
☐ 89 Otis Nixon	.10	.05
☐ 90 Jose Offerman	.05	.02
☐ 91 Bob Ojeda	.05	.02
☐ 92 John Olerud	.10	.05
☐ 93 Gregg Olson	.05	.02
☐ 94 Dave Parker	.10	.05
☐ 95 Terry Pendleton	.10	.05
☐ 96 Kirby Puckett	1.00	.45
☐ 97 Tim Raines	.10	.05
☐ 98 Jeff Reardon	.05	.02
☐ 99 Dave Righetti	.05	.02
☐ 100 Cal Ripken	1.50	.70
☐ 101 Mel Rojas	.15	.07
☐ 102 Nolan Ryan 7th No-Hitter	1.50	.70
☐ 103 Ryne Sandberg	.40	.18
☐ 104 Scott Sanderson	.05	.02
☐ 105 Benny Santiago	.05	.02
☐ 106 Pete Schourek	.05	.02
☐ 107 Gary Scott	.05	.02
☐ 108 Terry Shumpert	.05	.02
☐ 109 Ruben Sierra	.05	.02
☐ 110 Doug Simons	.05	.02
☐ 111 Dave Smith	.05	.02
☐ 112 Ozzie Smith	.50	.23
☐ 113 Cory Snyder	.05	.02
☐ 114 Luis Sojo	.05	.02
☐ 115 Dave Stewart	.10	.05
☐ 116 Dave Stieb	.05	.02
☐ 117 Darryl Strawberry	.10	.05
☐ 118 Pat Tabler	.05	.02
☐ 119 Wade Taylor	.05	.02
☐ 120 Bobby Thigpen	.05	.02
☐ 121 Frank Thomas	2.00	.90
☐ 122 Mike Timlin	.05	.02
☐ 123 Alan Trammell	.15	.07
☐ 124 Mo Vaughn	.50	.23
☐ 125 Tim Wallach	.05	.02
☐ 126 Devon White	.05	.02
☐ 127 Mark Whiten	.05	.02
☐ 128 Bernie Williams	.50	.23
☐ 129 Willie Wilson	.05	.02
☐ 130 Dave Winfield	.25	.11
☐ 131 Robin Yount	.15	.07
☐ 132 Checklist 1-132	.05	.02

1992 O-Pee-Chee Premier

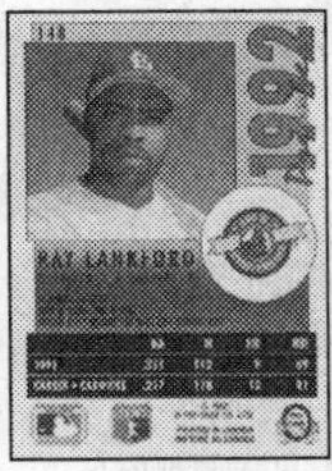

The 1992 OPC Premier baseball set consists of 198 standard-size cards. The fronts feature a mix of color action and posed player photos bordered in white. Gold stripes edge the picture on top and below, while colored stripes edge the pictures on the left and right sides. The player's name, position, and team appear in the bottom white border. In addition to a color head shot, the backs carry biography and the team logo on a panel that shades from green to blue as well as statistics on a black panel.

	MINT	NRMT
COMPLETE SET (198)	10.00	4.50
COMPLETE FACT.SET (198)	15.00	6.75
COMMON CARD (1-198)	.05	.02

	MINT	NRMT
☐ 1 Wade Boggs	.25	.11
☐ 2 John Smiley	.05	.02
☐ 3 Checklist 1-99	.05	.02
☐ 4 Ron Gant	.10	.05
☐ 5 Mike Bordick	.05	.02
☐ 6 Charlie Hayes	.05	.02
☐ 7 Kevin Morton	.05	.02
☐ 8 Checklist 100-198	.05	.02
☐ 9 Chris Gwynn	.05	.02
☐ 10 Melido Perez	.05	.02
☐ 11 Dan Gladden	.05	.02
☐ 12 Brian McRae	.10	.05
☐ 13 Dennis Martinez	.10	.05
☐ 14 Bob Scanlan	.05	.02
☐ 15 Julio Franco	.10	.05
☐ 16 Ruben Amaro Jr.	.05	.02
☐ 17 Mo Sanford	.05	.02
☐ 18 Scott Bankhead	.05	.02
☐ 19 Dickie Thon	.05	.02
☐ 20 Chris James	.05	.02
☐ 21 Mike Huff	.05	.02
☐ 22 Orlando Merced	.05	.02

☐ 23 Chris Sabo .05 .02
☐ 24 Jose Canseco .15 .07
☐ 25 Reggie Sanders .10 .05
☐ 26 Chris Nabholz .05 .02
☐ 27 Kevin Seitzer .05 .02
☐ 28 Ryan Bowen .05 .02
☐ 29 Gary Carter .15 .07
☐ 30 Wayne Rosenthal .05 .02
☐ 31 Alan Trammell .15 .07
☐ 32 Doug Drabek .05 .02
☐ 33 Craig Shipley .05 .02
☐ 34 Ryne Sandberg .30 .14
☐ 35 Chuck Knoblauch .35 .16
☐ 36 Bret Barberie .05 .02
☐ 37 Tim Naehring .10 .05
☐ 38 Omar Olivares .05 .02
☐ 39 Royce Clayton .05 .02
☐ 40 Brent Mayne .05 .02
☐ 41 Darrin Fletcher .05 .02
☐ 42 Howard Johnson .05 .02
☐ 43 Steve Sax .05 .02
☐ 44 Greg Swindell .05 .02
☐ 45 Andre Dawson .15 .07
☐ 46 Kent Hrbek .05 .02
☐ 47 Dwight Gooden .10 .05
☐ 48 Mark Leiter .05 .02
☐ 49 Tom Glavine .10 .05
☐ 50 Mo Vaughn .50 .23
☐ 51 Doug Jones .05 .02
☐ 52 Brian Barnes .05 .02
☐ 53 Rob Dibble .05 .02
☐ 54 Kevin McReynolds .05 .02
☐ 55 Ivan Rodriguez .40 .18
☐ 56 Scott Livingstone UER .05 .02
(Photo actually
Travis Fryman)
☐ 57 Mike Magnante .05 .02
☐ 58 Pete Schourek .05 .02
☐ 59 Frank Thomas 1.50 .70
☐ 60 Kirk McCaskill .05 .02
☐ 61 Wally Joyner .05 .02
☐ 62 Rick Aguilera .10 .05
☐ 63 Eric Karros .15 .07
☐ 64 Tino Martinez .25 .11
☐ 65 Bryan Hickerson .05 .02
☐ 66 Ruben Sierra .05 .02
☐ 67 Willie Randolph .10 .05
☐ 68 Bill Landrum .05 .02
☐ 69 Bip Roberts .05 .02
☐ 70 Cecil Fielder .10 .05
☐ 71 Pat Kelly .05 .02
☐ 72 Kenny Lofton .75 .35
☐ 73 John Franco .05 .02
☐ 74 Phil Plantier .05 .02
☐ 75 Dave Martinez .05 .02
☐ 76 Warren Newson .05 .02
☐ 77 Chito Martinez .05 .02
☐ 78 Brian Hunter .05 .02
☐ 79 Jack Morris .10 .05
☐ 80 Eric King .05 .02
☐ 81 Nolan Ryan 1.50 .70
☐ 82 Bret Saberhagen .10 .05
☐ 83 Roberto Kelly .05 .02
☐ 84 Ozzie Smith .50 .23
☐ 85 Chuck McElroy .05 .02
☐ 86 Carlton Fisk .25 .11
☐ 87 Mike Mussina .50 .23
☐ 88 Mark Carreon .05 .02
☐ 89 Ken Hill .10 .05
☐ 90 Rick Cerone .05 .02
☐ 91 Deion Sanders .25 .11
☐ 92 Don Mattingly .75 .35
☐ 93 Danny Tartabull .05 .02
☐ 94 Keith Miller .05 .02
☐ 95 Gregg Jefferies .10 .05
☐ 96 Barry Larkin .15 .07
☐ 97 Kevin Mitchell .05 .02
☐ 98 Rick Sutcliffe .05 .02
☐ 99 Mark McGwire .75 .35
☐ 100 Albert Belle .50 .23
☐ 101 Gregg Olson .05 .02
☐ 102 Kirby Puckett .75 .35
☐ 103 Luis Gonzalez .05 .02
☐ 104 Randy Myers .05 .02
☐ 105 Roger Clemens .50 .23
☐ 106 Tony Gwynn .75 .35
☐ 107 Jeff Bagwell 1.00 .45
☐ 108 John Wetteland .10 .05
☐ 109 Bernie Williams .35 .16
☐ 110 Scott Kamieniecki .05 .02
☐ 111 Robin Yount .25 .11
☐ 112 Dean Palmer .10 .05
☐ 113 Tim Belcher .05 .02
☐ 114 George Brett .75 .35
☐ 115 Frank Viola .05 .02
☐ 116 Kelly Gruber .05 .02
☐ 117 David Justice .25 .11
☐ 118 Scott Leius .05 .02
☐ 119 Jeff Fassero .10 .05
☐ 120 Sammy Sosa .25 .11
☐ 121 Al Osuna .05 .02
☐ 122 Wilson Alvarez .15 .07
☐ 123 Jose Offerman .05 .02
☐ 124 Mel Rojas .05 .02
☐ 125 Shawon Dunston .05 .02
☐ 126 Pete Incaviglia .05 .02
☐ 127 Von Hayes .05 .02
☐ 128 Dave Gallagher .05 .02
☐ 129 Eric Davis .10 .05
☐ 130 Roberto Alomar .25 .11
☐ 131 Mike Gallego .05 .02
☐ 132 Robin Ventura .10 .05
☐ 133 Bill Swift .05 .02
☐ 134 John Kruk .10 .05
☐ 135 Craig Biggio .15 .07
☐ 136 Eddie Taubensee .05 .02
☐ 137 Cal Ripken 1.50 .70
☐ 138 Charles Nagy .10 .05
☐ 139 Jose Melendez .05 .02
☐ 140 Jim Abbott .10 .05
☐ 141 Paul Molitor .25 .11
☐ 142 Tom Candiotti .05 .02
☐ 143 Bobby Bonilla .10 .05
☐ 144 Matt Williams .15 .07
☐ 145 Brett Butler .10 .05
☐ 146 Will Clark .15 .07
☐ 147 Rickey Henderson .25 .11
☐ 148 Ray Lankford .15 .07
☐ 149 Bill Pecota .05 .02
☐ 150 Dave Winfield .25 .11
☐ 151 Darren Lewis .05 .02
☐ 152 Bob MacDonald .05 .02
☐ 153 David Segui .05 .02
☐ 154 Benny Santiago .05 .02
☐ 155 Chuck Finley .10 .05
☐ 156 Andujar Cedeno .05 .02
☐ 157 Barry Bonds .30 .14
☐ 158 Joe Grahe .05 .02
☐ 159 Frank Castillo .05 .02
☐ 160 Dave Burba .05 .02
☐ 161 Leo Gomez .05 .02
☐ 162 Orel Hershiser .10 .05
☐ 163 Delino DeShields .05 .02
☐ 164 Sandy Alomar Jr. .10 .05
☐ 165 Denny Neagle .10 .05
☐ 166 Fred McGriff .25 .11
☐ 167 Ken Griffey Jr. 2.00 .90
☐ 168 Juan Guzman .05 .02
☐ 169 Bobby Rose .05 .02
☐ 170 Steve Avery .05 .02
☐ 171 Rich DeLucia .05 .02
☐ 172 Mike Timlin .05 .02
☐ 173 Randy Johnson .25 .11
☐ 174 Paul Gibson .05 .02
☐ 175 David Cone .10 .05
☐ 176 Marquis Grissom .10 .05
☐ 177 Kurt Stillwell .05 .02
☐ 178 Mark Whiten .05 .02
☐ 179 Darryl Strawberry .10 .05
☐ 180 Mike Morgan .05 .02
☐ 181 Scott Scudder .05 .02
☐ 182 George Bell .05 .02
☐ 183 Alvin Davis .05 .02
☐ 184 Len Dykstra .10 .05
☐ 185 Kyle Abbott .05 .02
☐ 186 Chris Haney .05 .02
☐ 187 Junior Noboa .05 .02
☐ 188 Dennis Eckersley .15 .07
☐ 189 Derek Bell .05 .02
☐ 190 Lee Smith .15 .07
☐ 191 Andres Galarraga .25 .11
☐ 192 Jack Armstrong .05 .02
☐ 193 Eddie Murray .35 .16
☐ 194 Joe Carter .10 .05
☐ 195 Terry Pendleton .10 .05
☐ 196 Darryl Kile .10 .05
☐ 197 Rod Beck .25 .11
☐ 198 Hubie Brooks .05 .02

1993 O-Pee-Chee Premier

The 1993 OPC Premier set consists of 132 standard-size cards. The foil packs contain eight regular cards and one Star Performer insert card. The white-bordered fronts feature a mix of color action and posed player photos. The player's name and position are printed in the lower left border. The backs carry a color head shot, biography, 1992 statistics, and the team logo. According to O-Pee-Chee, only 4,000 cases were produced.

	MINT	NRMT
COMPLETE SET (132)	5.00	2.20
COMMON CARD (1-132)	.05	.02

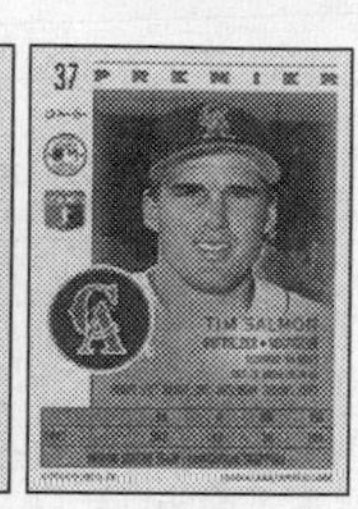

☐ 1 Barry Bonds .30 .14
☐ 2 Chad Curtis .10 .05
☐ 3 Chris Bosio .05 .02
☐ 4 Cal Eldred .05 .02
☐ 5 Dan Walters .05 .02
☐ 6 Rene Arocha .05 .02
☐ 7 Delino DeShields .05 .02
☐ 8 Spike Owen .05 .02
☐ 9 Jeff Russell .05 .02
☐ 10 Phil Plantier .05 .02
☐ 11 Mike Christopher .05 .02
☐ 12 Darren Daulton .10 .05
☐ 13 Scott Cooper .05 .02
☐ 14 Paul O'Neill .10 .05
☐ 15 Jimmy Key .10 .05
☐ 16 Dickie Thon .05 .02
☐ 17 Greg Gohr .05 .02
☐ 18 Andre Dawson .15 .07
☐ 19 Steve Cooke .05 .02
☐ 20 Tony Fernandez .05 .02
☐ 21 Mark Gardner .05 .02
☐ 22 Dave Martinez .05 .02
☐ 23 Jose Guzman .05 .02
☐ 24 Chili Davis .10 .05
☐ 25 Randy Knorr .05 .02
☐ 26 Mike Piazza 1.00 .45
☐ 27 Benji Gil .05 .02
☐ 28 Dave Winfield .25 .11
☐ 29 Wil Cordero .05 .02
☐ 30 Butch Henry .05 .02
☐ 31 Eric Young .25 .11
☐ 32 Orestes Destrade .05 .02
☐ 33 Randy Myers .10 .05
☐ 34 Tom Brunansky .05 .02
☐ 35 Dan Wilson .10 .05
☐ 36 Juan Guzman .05 .02
☐ 37 Tim Salmon .50 .23
☐ 38 Bill Krueger .05 .02
☐ 39 Larry Walker .25 .11
☐ 40 David Hulse .05 .02
☐ 41 Ken Ryan .05 .02
☐ 42 Jose Lind .05 .02
☐ 43 Benny Santiago .05 .02
☐ 44 Ray Lankford .10 .05
☐ 45 Dave Stewart .10 .05
☐ 46 Don Mattingly .75 .35
☐ 47 Fernando Valenzuela .10 .05
☐ 48 Scott Fletcher .05 .02
☐ 49 Wade Boggs .25 .11
☐ 50 Norm Charlton .05 .02
☐ 51 Carlos Baerga .10 .05
☐ 52 John Olerud .10 .05
☐ 53 Willie Wilson .10 .05
☐ 54 Dennis Moeller .05 .02
☐ 55 Joe Orsulak .05 .02
☐ 56 John Smiley .05 .02
☐ 57 Al Martin .10 .05
☐ 58 Andres Galarraga .25 .11
☐ 59 Billy Ripken .05 .02
☐ 60 Dave Stieb .05 .02
☐ 61 Dave Magadan .05 .02
☐ 62 Todd Worrell .10 .05
☐ 63 Sherman Obando .05 .02
☐ 64 Kent Bottenfield .05 .02
☐ 65 Vinny Castilla .25 .11
☐ 66 Charlie Hayes .05 .02
☐ 67 Mike Hartley .05 .02
☐ 68 Harold Baines .10 .05
☐ 69 John Cummings .05 .02
☐ 70 J.T. Snow .40 .18
☐ 71 Graeme Lloyd .05 .02
☐ 72 Frank Bolick .05 .02
☐ 73 Doug Drabek .05 .02
☐ 74 Milt Thompson .05 .02
☐ 75 Tim Pugh .05 .02
☐ 76 John Kruk .10 .05
☐ 77 Tom Henke .10 .05
☐ 78 Kevin Young .05 .02
☐ 79 Ryan Thompson .05 .02
☐ 80 Mike Hampton .15 .07
☐ 81 Jose Canseco .25 .11
☐ 82 Mike Lansing .15 .07
☐ 83 Candy Maldonado .05 .02

☐ 84 Alex Arias	.05	.02
☐ 85 Troy Neel	.05	.02
☐ 86 Greg Swindell	.05	.02
☐ 87 Tim Wallach	.05	.02
☐ 88 Andy Van Slyke	.05	.02
☐ 89 Harold Reynolds	.10	.05
☐ 90 Bryan Harvey	.05	.02
☐ 91 Jerald Clark	.05	.02
☐ 92 David Cone	.10	.05
☐ 93 Ellis Burks	.10	.05
☐ 94 Scott Bankhead	.05	.02
☐ 95 Pete Incaviglia	.05	.02
☐ 96 Cecil Fielder	.10	.05
☐ 97 Sean Berry	.05	.02
☐ 98 Gregg Jefferies	.10	.05
☐ 99 Billy Brewer	.05	.02
☐ 100 Scott Sanderson	.05	.02
☐ 101 Walt Weiss	.05	.02
☐ 102 Travis Fryman	.10	.05
☐ 103 Barry Larkin	.15	.07
☐ 104 Darren Holmes	.05	.02
☐ 105 Ivan Calderon	.05	.02
☐ 106 Terry Jorgensen	.05	.02
☐ 107 David Nied	.05	.02
☐ 108 Tim Bogar	.05	.02
☐ 109 Roberto Kelly	.05	.02
☐ 110 Mike Moore	.05	.02
☐ 111 Carlos Garcia	.05	.02
☐ 112 Mike Bielecki	.05	.02
☐ 113 Trevor Hoffman	.25	.11
☐ 114 Rich Amaral	.05	.02
☐ 115 Jody Reed	.05	.02
☐ 116 Charlie Liebrandt	.05	.02
☐ 117 Greg Gagne	.05	.02
☐ 118 Darrell Sherman	.05	.02
☐ 119 Jeff Conine	.10	.05
☐ 120 Tim Laker	.05	.02
☐ 121 Kevin Seitzer	.05	.02
☐ 122 Jeff Mutis	.05	.02
☐ 123 Rico Rossy	.05	.02
☐ 124 Paul Molitor	.25	.11
☐ 125 Cal Ripken	1.00	.45
☐ 126 Greg Maddux	.75	.35
☐ 127 Greg McMichael	.05	.02
☐ 128 Felix Jose	.05	.02
☐ 129 Dick Schofield	.05	.02
☐ 130 Jim Abbott	.10	.05
☐ 131 Kevin Reimer	.05	.02
☐ 132 Checklist 1-132	.05	.02

1993 O-Pee-Chee Premier Star Performers

The 1993 OPC Premier Star Performers 22-card standard-size set was inserted one per 1993 OPC Premier foil packs. The fronts display a gold outer border with a narrow white inner border that frames a color action player photo. The subset title is printed on a green stripe across the top of the photo and the player's name and position are printed below the photo on the lower border. The backs contain a kelly-green border surrounding a white box that carries a player head shot, biography and career summary in both French and English. A ghosted team logo appears beneath the career summary. A parallel set of Foil Star Performers was randomly inserted in foil packs. The gold foil-stamped set logo rests in a lower corner. The Foil Star Performers are valued at a multiple of the regular Star Performers cards.

	MINT	NRMT
COMPLETE SET (22)	10.00	4.50
COMMON CARD (1-22)	.10	.05
*FOIL STARS: 12.5X TO 25X BASIC CARDS		
☐ 1 Frank Thomas	1.50	.70
☐ 2 Fred McGriff	.25	.11
☐ 3 Roberto Alomar	.40	.18
☐ 4 Ryne Sandberg	.60	.25
☐ 5 Edgar Martinez	.20	.09
☐ 6 Gary Sheffield	.25	.11
☐ 7 Juan Gonzalez	1.00	.45
☐ 8 Eric Karros	.15	.07
☐ 9 Ken Griffey Jr.	2.00	.90
☐ 10 Deion Sanders	.25	.11
☐ 11 Kirby Puckett	1.00	.45
☐ 12 Will Clark	.20	.09
☐ 13 Joe Carter	.15	.07
☐ 14 Barry Bonds	.50	.23
☐ 15 Pat Listach	.10	.05
☐ 16 Mark McGwire	.75	.35
☐ 17 Kenny Lofton	.50	.23
☐ 18 Roger Clemens	.60	.25
☐ 19 Greg Maddux	1.25	.55
☐ 20 Nolan Ryan	1.50	.70
☐ 21 Tom Glavine	.15	.07
☐ 22 Dennis Eckersley	.20	.09

1993 O-Pee-Chee Premier Top Draft Picks

Randomly inserted in foil packs, this four-card standard-size set features the top two draft picks of the Toronto Blue Jays and Montreal Expos. Each borderless front carries a posed color player photo, with the player's name and team appearing vertically in gold foil within a team color-coded stripe. The set's gold foil-highlighted logo rests in a lower corner. The back carries a posed player color headshot in the upper left of a mottled, light blue panel. The player's team's logo appears alongside and his career highlights follow below.

	MINT	NRMT
COMPLETE SET (4)	8.00	3.60
COMMON CARD (1-4)	1.00	.45
☐ 1 B.J. Wallace	1.00	.45
☐ 2 Shannon Stewart	4.00	1.80
☐ 3 Rod Henderson	1.00	.45
☐ 4 Todd Steverson	2.50	1.10

1887-90 Old Judge N172

The Goodwin Company's baseball series depicts hundreds of ballplayers from more than 40 major and minor league teams as well as boxers and wrestlers. The cards (approximately 1 1/2" by 2 1/2") are actually photographs from the Hall studio in New York which were pasted onto thick cardboard. The pictures are sepia in color with either a white or pink cast, and the cards are blank backed. They are found either numbered or unnumbered, with or without a copyright date, and with hand printed or machine printed names. All known cards have the name "Goodwin Co., New York" at the base. The cards were marketed during the period 1887-1890 in packs of "Old Judge" and "Gypsy Queen" cigarettes (cards marked with the latter brand are worth double the values listed below). They have been listed alphabetically and assigned numbers in the checklist below for simplicity's sake; the various poses known for some players also have not been listed for the same reason. Some of the players are pictured in horizontal (HOR) poses. In all, more than 2300 different Goodwin cards are known to collectors, with more being discovered every year. Cards from the "Spotted Tie" sub-series are denoted in the checklist below by SPOT.

	EX-MT	VG-E
COMPLETE SET	170000.00	76500.00
COMMON CARD	150.00	70.00
COMMON CARD (DOUBLE)	200.00	90.00
COMMON BROWNS CHAMP	250.00	110.00
COMMON CARD (PCL)	2500.00	1100.00
COMMON SPOTTED TIE	450.00	200.00
☐ 1 Gus Albert: Cleveland-Milwaukee	150.00	70.00
☐ 2 Charles Alcott: St. Louis Whites-Mansfield	150.00	70.00
☐ 3 Alexander: Des Moines	150.00	70.00
☐ 4 Myron Allen: K.C.	150.00	70.00
☐ 5 Bob Allen: Pitts.-Phila. N.L.	150.00	70.00
☐ 6 Uncle Bill Alvord: Toledo-Des Moines	150.00	70.00
☐ 7 Varney Anderson: St.Paul	1500.00	700.00
☐ 8 Ed Andrews: Phila.	150.00	70.00
☐ 9 Ed Andrews and Buster Hoover: Philadelphia	200.00	90.00
☐ 10 Wally Andrews: Omaha	150.00	70.00
☐ 11 Bill Annis: Omaha-Worchester	150.00	70.00
☐ 12A Cap Anson: Chicago (In uniform)	15000.00	6800.00
☐ 12B Cap Anson: Chicago (Not in uniform)	2250.00	1000.00
☐ 13 Old Hoss Ardner: Kansas City-St. Joe	150.00	70.00
☐ 14 Tug Arundel: Indianapolis-Whites	150.00	70.00
☐ 15 Jersey Bakley: Cleve.	150.00	70.00
☐ 16 Clarence Baldwin: Cincinnati	150.00	70.00
☐ 17 Mark(Fido) Baldwin: Chicago-Columbus	150.00	70.00
☐ 18 Lady Baldwin: Detroit	150.00	70.00
☐ 19 James Banning: Wash.	150.00	70.00
☐ 20 Samuel Barkley: Pittsburgh-K.C.	150.00	70.00
☐ 22 Bald Billy Barnie: Mgr. Baltimore	175.00	80.00
☐ 23 Charles Bassett: Indianapolis-N.Y.	150.00	70.00
☐ 24 Charles Bastian: Phila.-Chicago	150.00	70.00
☐ 25 Charles Bastian and Schriver: Philadelphia	200.00	90.00
☐ 26 Ollie Beard: Cinc.	150.00	70.00
☐ 27 Ebenezer Beatin: Cleve.	150.00	70.00
☐ 28 Jake Beckley: Eagle Eye Whites-Pittsburgh	600.00	275.0
☐ 29 Stephen Behel SPOT	1250.00	550.0
☐ 30 Charles Bennett: Detroit-Boston	150.00	70.0
☐ 31 Louis Bierbauer: A's	150.00	70.0
☐ 32 Louis Bierbauer and Robert Gamble: Athletics	200.00	90.0
☐ 33 Bill Bishop: Pittsburgh-Syracuse	150.00	70.0
☐ 34 William Blair: A's-Hamiltons	150.00	70.0
☐ 35 Ned Bligh: Columbus	150.00	70.0
☐ 36 Bogart: Indianapolis	150.00	70.0
☐ 37 Boyce: Washington	150.00	70.0
☐ 38 Jake Boyd: Maroons	175.00	80.0
☐ 39 Honest John Boyle: St. Louis-Chicago	150.00	70.0
☐ 40 Handsome Henry Boyle Indianapolis-N.Y.	150.00	70.0
☐ 41 Nick Bradley: K.C.- Worchester	150.00	70.0
☐ 42 George(Grin) Bradley Sioux City	150.00	70.0
☐ 43 Stephen Brady SPOT	500.00	220.0

☐ 44 E.L. Breckinridge: Sacramento PCL	2500.00	1100.00
☐ 45 Jim Brennan: Kansas City- A's	150.00	70.00
☐ 46 Timothy Brosnan: Minn.-Sioux City	150.00	70.00
☐ 47 Cal Broughton: St. Paul	150.00	70.00
☐ 48 Big Dan Brouthers: Detroit-Boston	500.00	220.00
☐ 49 Thomas Brown: Pittsburgh-Boston	150.00	70.00
☐ 50 California Brown: New York	150.00	70.00
☐ 51 Pete Browning: Gladiator Louisville	300.00	135.00
☐ 52 Charles Brynan: Chicago-Des Moines	150.00	70.00
☐ 53 Al Buckenberger MG: Columbus	150.00	70.00
☐ 54 Dick Buckley: Indianapolis-N.Y.	150.00	70.00
☐ 55 Charles Buffington: Philadelphia	150.00	70.00
☐ 56 Ernest Burch: Brooklyn-Whites	150.00	70.00
☐ 57 Bill Burdick: Omaha-Indianapolis	150.00	70.00
☐ 58 Black Jack Burdock: Boston-Brooklyn	150.00	70.00
☐ 59 Robert Burks: Sioux City	150.00	70.00
☐ 60 George Burnham Watch Mgr. Indianapolis	175.00	80.00
☐ 61 Burns: Omaha	150.00	70.00
☐ 62 Jimmy Burns: K.C.	150.00	70.00
☐ 63 Tommy(Oyster) Burns Baltimore-Brooklyn	150.00	70.00
☐ 64 Thomas E. Burns: Chicago	150.00	70.00
☐ 65A Doc Bushong: Brook.	150.00	70.00
☐ 65B Doc Bushong: Browns Champs	250.00	110.00
☐ 66 Patsy Cahill: Ind.	150.00	70.00
☐ 67 Count Campau: Kansas City-Detroit	150.00	70.00
☐ 68 Jimmy Canavan: Omaha	150.00	70.00
☐ 69 Bart Cantz: Whites-Baltimore	150.00	70.00
☐ 70 Handsome Jack Carney Washington	150.00	70.00
☐ 71 Hick Carpenter Cincinnati	150.00	70.00
☐ 72 Cliff Carroll: Wash.	150.00	70.00
☐ 73 Scrappy Carroll: St.Paul-Chicago	150.00	70.00
☐ 74 Frederick Carroll: Pitts.	150.00	70.00
☐ 75 Jumbo Cartwright: Kansas City-St. Joe	150.00	70.00
☐ 76A Bob Caruthers: Parisian Brooklyn	175.00	80.00
☐ 76B Bob Caruthers: Parisian Browns Champs	300.00	135.00
☐ 77 Daniel Casey: Phila.	150.00	70.00
☐ 78 Icebox Chamberlain: St. Louis	150.00	70.00
☐ 79 Cupid Childs: Phila.-Syracuse	150.00	70.00
☐ 80 Bob Clark: Washington	150.00	70.00
☐ 81 Owen Clark: Washington	150.00	70.00
☐ 82 Clarke and Mickey Hughes: Brooklyn HOR	200.00	90.00
☐ 83 William(Dad) Clarke: Chicago-Omaha	150.00	70.00
☐ 84 John Clarkson: Chicago-Boston	500.00	220.00
☐ 85 Jack Clements: Philadelphia	150.00	70.00
☐ 86 Elmer Cleveland: Omaha-New York	150.00	70.00
☐ 87 Monk Cline: K.C.-Sioux City	150.00	70.00
☐ 88 Cody: Des Moines	150.00	70.00
☐ 89 John Coleman: Pittsburgh - A's	150.00	70.00
☐ 90 Bill Collins: New York-Newark	150.00	70.00
☐ 91 Hub Collins: Louisville-Brooklyn	150.00	70.00
☐ 92A Charles Comiskey: Browns Champs	900.00	400.00
☐ 92B Commy Comiskey: St. Louis-Chicago	750.00	350.00
☐ 93 Pete Connell: Des Moines	150.00	70.00
☐ 94A Roger Connor: Script	600.00	275.00
☐ 94B Roger Connor: New York	600.00	275.00
☐ 95 Richard Conway: Boston-Worchester	150.00	70.00
☐ 96 Peter Conway: Det.-Pitts.-Ind.	150.00	70.00
☐ 97 James Conway: K.C.	150.00	70.00
☐ 98 Paul Cook: Louisville	150.00	70.00
☐ 99 Jimmy Cooney: Omaha-Chicago	150.00	70.00
☐ 100 Larry Corcoran: Indianapolis-London	175.00	80.00
☐ 101 Pop Corkhill: Cincinnati-Brooklyn	150.00	70.00
☐ 102 Roscoe Coughlin: Maroons-Chicago	175.00	80.00
☐ 103 Cannon Ball Crane: New York	150.00	70.00
☐ 104 Samuel Crane: Wash.	150.00	70.00
☐ 105 Jack Crogan: Maroons	175.00	80.00
☐ 106 John Crooks: Whites-Omaha	150.00	70.00
☐ 107 Lave Cross: Louisville-A's-Phila.	150.00	70.00
☐ 108 Bill Crossley: Milw.	150.00	70.00
☐ 109A Joe Crotty SPOT	450.00	200.00
☐ 109B Joe Crotty: Sioux City	150.00	70.00
☐ 110 Billy Crowell: Cleveland-St. Joe	150.00	70.00
☐ 111 Jim Cudworth: St. Louis-Worchester	150.00	70.00
☐ 112 Bert Cunningham: Baltimore-Phila.	150.00	70.00
☐ 113 Tacks Curtis: St. Joe	150.00	70.00
☐ 114A Ed Cushman SPOT	500.00	220.00
☐ 114B Ed Cushman: Toledo	1200.00	550.00
☐ 115 Tony Cusick: Mil.	1500.00	700.00
☐ 116 Vincent Dailey: Oakland PCL	2500.00	1100.00
☐ 117 Edward Dailey: Phil.-Wash.-Columbus	150.00	70.00
☐ 118 Bill Daley: Boston	150.00	70.00
☐ 119 Con Daley: Boston-Indianapolis	150.00	70.00
☐ 120 Abner Dalrymple: Pittsburgh-Denver	150.00	70.00
☐ 121 Tom Daly: Chicago-Wash.-Cleve.	150.00	70.00
☐ 122 James Daly: Minn.	150.00	70.00
☐ 123 Law Daniels: K.C.	150.00	70.00
☐ 124 Dell Darling: Chicago	150.00	70.00
☐ 125 Wm. Darnbrough: Denver	150.00	70.00
☐ 126 D. Davin: Milwaukee	150.00	70.00
☐ 127 Jumbo Davis: K.C.	150.00	70.00
☐ 128 Pat Dealey: Wash.	150.00	70.00
☐ 129 Thomas Deasley: New York-Washington	150.00	70.00
☐ 130 Edward Decker: Phil.	150.00	70.00
☐ 131 Big Ed Delahanty: Philadelphia	1200.00	550.00
☐ 132 Jeremiah Denny: Indianapolis-New York	150.00	70.00
☐ 133 James Devlin: St.L.	150.00	70.00
☐ 134 Thomas Dolan: Whites-St. Louis-Denver	150.00	70.00
☐ 135 Jack Donahue: San Francisco PCL	2500.00	1100.00
☐ 136A James Donahue SPOT	450.00	200.00
☐ 136B James Donahue: K.C.	150.00	70.00
☐ 137 James Donnelly: Washington	150.00	70.00
☐ 138 Charles Dooley: Oakland PCL	2500.00	1100.00
☐ 139 J. Doran: Omaha	150.00	70.00
☐ 140 Michael Dorgan: N.Y.	150.00	70.00
☐ 141 Cornelius Doyle: San Fran. PCL	2500.00	1100.00
☐ 142 Homerun Duffe: St.L.	150.00	70.00
☐ 143 Hugh Duffy: Chicago	600.00	275.00
☐ 144 Dan Dugdale: Maroons-Minneapolis	175.00	80.00
☐ 145 Dugrahm: Maroons	175.00	80.00
☐ 146 Duck Duke: Minn.	150.00	70.00
☐ 147 Sure Shot Dunlap: Pittsburgh	150.00	70.00
☐ 148 J. Dunn: Maroons	175.00	80.00
☐ 149 Jesse(Cyclone)Duryea St. Paul-Cinc.	150.00	70.00
☐ 150 John Dwyer: Chicago-Maroons	175.00	80.00
☐ 151 Billy Earle: Cincinnati-St.Paul	150.00	70.00
☐ 152 Buck Ebright: Wash.	150.00	70.00
☐ 153 Red Ehret: Louisville	150.00	70.00
☐ 154 R. Emmerke: Des Moines	150.00	70.00
☐ 155 Dude Esterbrook: Louisville-Ind.-New York-All Star	150.00	70.00
☐ 156 Henry Esterday: K.C.-Columbus	150.00	70.00
☐ 157 Long John Ewing: Louisville-N.Y.	150.00	70.00
☐ 158 Buck Ewing: New York	500.00	220.00
☐ 159 Buck Ewing and Mascot: New York	500.00	220.00
☐ 160 Jay Faatz: Cleveland	150.00	70.00
☐ 161 Clinkgers Fagan: Kansas City-Denver	150.00	70.00
☐ 162 William Farmer: Pittsburgh-St. Paul	150.00	70.00
☐ 163 Sidney Farrar: Philadelphia	175.00	80.00
☐ 164 John(Moose) Farrell: Wash.-Baltimore	150.00	70.00
☐ 165 Charles(Duke)Farrell Chicago	150.00	70.00
☐ 166 Frank Fennelly: Cincinnati-A's	150.00	70.00
☐ 167 Chas. Ferguson: Phila.	150.00	70.00
☐ 168 Colonel Ferson: Washington	150.00	70.00
☐ 169 Wallace Fessenden: Umpire National	175.00	80.00
☐ 170 Jocko Fields: Pitts.	150.00	70.00
☐ 171 Fischer: Maroons	175.00	80.00
☐ 172 Thomas Flanigan: Cleve.-Sioux City	150.00	70.00
☐ 173 Silver Flint: Chicago	150.00	70.00
☐ 174 Thomas Flood: St. Joe	150.00	70.00
☐ 175 Flynn: Omaha	1200.00	550.00
☐ 176 James Fogarty: Philadelphia	150.00	70.00
☐ 177 Frank(Monkey)Foreman Baltimore-Cinc.	150.00	70.00
☐ 178 Thomas Forster: Milwaukee-Hartford	150.00	70.00
☐ 179A Elmer E. Foster SPOT	450.00	200.00
☐ 179B Elmer Foster: New York-Chicago	150.00	70.00
☐ 180 F.W. Foster SPOT T.W. Forster (Sic)	500.00	220.00
☐ 181A Scissors Foutz: Browns Champ	250.00	110.00
☐ 181B Scissors Foutz: Brooklyn	150.00	70.00
☐ 182 Julie Freeman: St.L.-Milwaukee	150.00	70.00
☐ 183 Will Fry: St. Joe	150.00	70.00
☐ 184 Fred Fudger: Oakland PCL	2500.00	1100.00
☐ 185 William Fuller: Milwaukee	150.00	70.00
☐ 186 Shorty Fuller: St.Louis	150.00	70.00
☐ 187 Christopher Fullmer: Baltimore	150.00	70.00
☐ 188 Christopher Fullmer and Tom Tucker: Baltimore HOR	200.00	90.00
☐ 189 Honest John Gaffney: Mgr. Washington	175.00	80.00
☐ 190 Pud Galvin: Pitts.	600.00	275.00
☐ 191 Robert Gamble: A's	150.00	70.00
☐ 192 Charles Ganzel: Detroit-Boston	150.00	70.00
☐ 193 Frank(Gid) Gardner: Phila.-Washington	150.00	70.00
☐ 194 Gid Gardner and Miah Murray: Washington HOR	200.00	90.00
☐ 195 Ed Gastfield: Omaha	150.00	70.00
☐ 196 Hank Gastreich: Columbus	150.00	70.00

☐ 197 Emil Geiss: Chicago 150.00 70.00
☐ 198 Frenchy Genins: Sioux City 150.00 70.00
☐ 199 William George: N.Y. 150.00 70.00
☐ 200 Move Up Joe Gerhardt All Star-Jersey City 150.00 70.00
☐ 201 Pretzels Getzein: Detroit-Ind. 150.00 70.00
☐ 202 Lee Gibson: A's 150.00 70.00
☐ 203 Robert Gilks: Cleve. 150.00 70.00
☐ 204 Pete Gillespie: N.Y. 150.00 70.00
☐ 205 Barney Gilligan Washington-Detroit 150.00 70.00
☐ 206 Frank Gilmore: Wash. 150.00 70.00
☐ 207 Pebbly Jack Glasscock Indianapolis-N.Y. 175.00 80.00
☐ 208 Kid Gleason: Phila. 175.00 80.00
☐ 209A Brother Bill Gleason A's-Louisville 150.00 70.00
☐ 209B William Bill Gleason Browns Champs 250.00 110.00
☐ 210 Mouse Glenn: Sioux City 150.00 70.00
☐ 211 Walt Goldsby: Balt. 150.00 70.00
☐ 212 Michael Goodfellow: Cleveland-Detroit 150.00 70.00
☐ 213 George Gore (Pianolegs) New York 150.00 70.00
☐ 214 Frank Graves: Minn. 150.00 70.00
☐ 215 William Greenwood: Baltimore-Columbus 150.00 70.00
☐ 216 Michael Greer: Cleveland-Brooklyn 150.00 70.00
☐ 217 Mike Griffin: Baltimore-Phila NL 150.00 70.00
☐ 218 Clark Griffith: Milwaukee 600.00 275.00
☐ 219 Henry Gruber: Cleve. 150.00 70.00
☐ 220 Addison Gumbert: Chicago-Boston 150.00 70.00
☐ 221 Thomas Gunning: Philadelphia-A's 150.00 70.00
☐ 222 Joseph Gunson: K.C. 150.00 70.00
☐ 223 George Haddock: Washington 150.00 70.00
☐ 224 William Hafner: K.C. 150.00 70.00
☐ 225 Willie Hahm: Chicago Mascot 150.00 70.00
☐ 226 William Hallman: Philadelphia 150.00 70.00
☐ 227 Charlie Hallstrom: Minn. 150.00 70.00
☐ 228 Billy Hamilton: Kansas City-Phila. 750.00 350.00
☐ 229 Willie Hamm and Ned Williamson: Chicago 200.00 90.00
☐ 230A Frank Hankinson: SPOT 450.00 200.00
☐ 230B Frank Hankinson: Kansas City 150.00 70.00
☐ 231 Ned Hanlon: Det.-Boston-Pitts. 175.00 80.00
☐ 232 William Hanrahan: Maroons-Minn. 175.00 80.00
☐ 233 A.G. Hapeman: Sacramento PCL 2500.00 1100.00
☐ 234 Pa Harkins: Brooklyn-Baltimore 150.00 70.00
☐ 235 William Hart: Cinc.-Des Moines 150.00 70.00
☐ 236 Wm. Hasamdear: K.C. 150.00 70.00
☐ 237 Colonel Hatfield: New York 150.00 70.00
☐ 238 Egyptian Healey: Wash.-Indianapolis 150.00 70.00
☐ 239 J.C. Healy: Omaha-Denver 150.00 70.00
☐ 240 Guy Hecker: Louisville 150.00 70.00
☐ 241 Tony Hellman: Sioux City 150.00 70.00
☐ 242 Hardie Henderson: Brook.-Pitts.-Balt. 150.00 70.00
☐ 243 Hardie Henderson and Michael Greer: Brooklyn 200.00 90.00
☐ 244 Moxie Hengle: Maroons-Minneapolis 175.00 80.00
☐ 245 John Henry: Phila. 150.00 70.00
☐ 246 Edward Herr: Whites-Milwaukee 150.00 70.00
☐ 247 Hunkey Hines: Whites 150.00 70.00
☐ 248 Paul Hines: Wash.-Indianapolis 150.00 70.00
☐ 249 Texas Wonder Hoffman: Denver 150.00 70.00
☐ 250 Eddie Hogan: Cleve. 150.00 70.00
☐ 251A William Holbert SPOT 450.00 200.00
☐ 251B William Holbert: Brooklyn-Mets-Jersey City 150.00 70.00
☐ 252 James(Bugs) Holliday: Des Moines-Cinc. 150.00 70.00
☐ 253 Charles Hoover: Maroons-Chi.-K.C. 175.00 80.00
☐ 254 Buster Hoover: Phila.-Toronto 150.00 70.00
☐ 255 Jack Horner: Milwaukee-New Haven 150.00 70.00
☐ 256 Jack Horner and E.H. Warner: Milwaukee 200.00 90.00
☐ 257 Michael Horning: Boston-Balt.-N.Y. 150.00 70.00
☐ 258 Pete Hotaling: Cleveland 150.00 70.00
☐ 259 William Howes: Minn.-St. Paul 150.00 70.00
☐ 260 Dummy Hoy: Washington 500.00 220.00
☐ 261A Nat Hudson: Browns Champ 250.00 110.00
☐ 261B Nat Hudson: St. Louis 150.00 70.00
☐ 262 Mickey Hughes: Brk. 150.00 70.00
☐ 263 Hungler: Sioux City 150.00 70.00
☐ 264 Wild Bill Hutchinson: Chicago 150.00 70.00
☐ 265 John Irwin: Wash.-Wilkes Barre 150.00 70.00
☐ 266 Cutrate Irwin: Phila.-Boston-Wash. 150.00 70.00
☐ 267 A.C. Jantzen: Minn. 150.00 70.00
☐ 268 Frederick Jevne: Minn.-St. Paul 150.00 70.00
☐ 269 John Johnson: K.C.-Columbus 150.00 70.00
☐ 270 Richard Johnston: Boston 150.00 70.00
☐ 271 Jordan: Minneapolis 150.00 70.00
☐ 272 Heinie Kappell: Columbus-Cincinnati 150.00 70.00
☐ 273 Keas: Milwaukee 150.00 70.00
☐ 274 Sir Timothy Keefe: New York 500.00 220.00
☐ 275 Tim Keefe and Danny Richardson: Stealing 2nd Base New York HOR 450.00 200.00
☐ 276 George Keefe: Wash. 150.00 70.00
☐ 277 James Keenan: Cinc. 150.00 70.00
☐ 278 Mike(King) Kelly 10,000 Chic-Boston 1250.00 550.00
☐ 279 Honest John Kelly: Mgr. Louisville 175.00 80.00
☐ 280 Kelly: (Umpire) Western Association 175.00 80.00
☐ 281 Charles Kelly: Philadelphia 150.00 70.00
☐ 282 Kelly and Powell: Umpire and Manager Sioux City 200.00 90.00
☐ 283A Rudolph Kemmler: Browns Champ 250.00 110.00
☐ 283B Rudolph Kemmler: St. Paul 150.00 70.00
☐ 284 Theodore Kennedy: Des Moines-Omaha 200.00 90.00
☐ 285 J.J. Kenyon: Whites-Des Moines 150.00 70.00
☐ 286 John Kerins: Louisville 150.00 70.00
☐ 287 Matthew Kilroy: Baltimore-Boston 150.00 70.00
☐ 288 Charles King: St.L.-Chi. 150.00 70.00
☐ 289 Aug. Kloff: Minn.-St.Joe 150.00 70.00
☐ 290 William Klusman: Milwaukee-Denver 150.00 70.00
☐ 291 Phillip Knell: St. Joe-Phila. 150.00 70.00
☐ 292 Fred Knouf: St. Louis 150.00 70.00
☐ 293 Charles Kremmeyer: Sacramento PCL 2500.00 1100.00
☐ 294 William Krieg: Wash.-St. Joe-Minn. 150.00 70.00
☐ 295 William Krieg and Aug. Kloff: Minneapolis 200.00 90.00
☐ 296 Gus Krock: Chicago 150.00 70.00
☐ 297 Willie Kuehne: Pittsburgh 150.00 70.00
☐ 298 Frederick Lange: Maroons 175.00 80.00
☐ 299 Ted Larkin: A's 150.00 70.00
☐ 300A Arlie Latham: Browns Champ 250.00 110.00
☐ 300B Arlie Latham: St. Louis-Chicago 175.00 80.00
☐ 301 John Lauer: Pittsburgh 150.00 70.00
☐ 302 Lawless: Columbus 150.00 70.00
☐ 303 John Leighton: Omaha 150.00 70.00
☐ 304 Rube Levy: San Fran. PCL 2500.00 1100.00
☐ 305 Tom Loftus MG: Whites-Cleveland 150.00 70.00
☐ 306 Lohbeck: Cleveland 150.00 70.00
☐ 307 Herman(Germany)Long Maroons-K.C. 200.00 90.00
☐ 308 Danny Long: Oak. PCL 2500.00 1100.00
☐ 309 Tom Lovett: Omaha-Brooklyn 150.00 70.00
☐ 310 Bobby(Link) Lowe: Milwaukee 200.00 90.00
☐ 311A Jack Lynch SPOT 500.00 220.00
☐ 311B John Lynch: All Stars 150.00 70.00
☐ 312 Dennis Lyons: A's 150.00 70.00
☐ 313 Harry Lyons: St. L. 150.00 70.00
☐ 314 Connie Mack: Wash. 1500.00 700.00
☐ 315 Joe(Reddie) Mack: Louisville 150.00 70.00
☐ 316 James(Little Mack) Macullar: Des Moines-Milwaukee 150.00 70.00
☐ 317 Kid Madden: Boston 150.00 70.00
☐ 318 Daniel Mahoney: St. Joe 150.00 70.00
☐ 319 Willard(Grasshopper) Maines: St. Paul 150.00 70.00
☐ 320 Fred Mann: St.Louis-Hartford 150.00 70.00
☐ 321 Jimmy Manning: K.C. 150.00 70.00
☐ 322 Charles(Lefty) Marr: Col.-Cinc. 150.00 70.00
☐ 323 Mascot(Willie Breslin): New York 175.00 80.00
☐ 324 Samuel Maskery: Milwaukee-Des Moines 150.00 70.00
☐ 325 Bobby Mathews: A's 150.00 70.00
☐ 326 Michael Mattimore: New York-A's 150.00 70.00
☐ 327 Albert Maul: Pitts. 150.00 70.00
☐ 328A Albert Mays SPOT 450.00 200.00
☐ 328B Albert Mays: Columbus 150.00 70.00
☐ 329 James McAleer: Cleveland 150.00 70.00
☐ 330 Thomas McCarthy: Phila.-St. Louis 500.00 220.00
☐ 331 John McCarthy: K.C. 150.00 70.00
☐ 332 James McCauley: Maroons-Phila. 175.00 80.00
☐ 333 William McClellan: Brooklyn-Denver 150.00 70.00
☐ 334 John McCormack: Whites 150.00 70.00
☐ 335 Big Jim McCormick: Chicago-Pittsburgh 150.00 70.00
☐ 336 McCreachery: Mgr. Indianapolis 175.00 80.00
☐ 337 Thomas McCullum: Minneapolis 150.00 70.00
☐ 338 James(Chippy)McGarr: St. Louis-K.C. 150.00 70.00
☐ 339 Jack McGeachy: Ind. 150.00 70.00
☐ 340 John McGlone: Cleveland-Detroit 150.00 70.00
☐ 341 James(Deacon)McGuire Phila.-Toronto 150.00 70.00
☐ 342 Bill(Gunner) McGunnigle: Mgr. Brooklyn 175.00 80.00
☐ 343 Ed McKean: Cleveland 150.00 70.00
☐ 344 Alex McKinnon: Pittsburgh 150.00 70.00
☐ 345 Thomas McLaughlin SPOT 450.00 200.00
☐ 346 John(Bid) McPhee: Cincinnati 175.00 80.00
☐ 347 James McQuaid: Denver 150.00 70.00
☐ 348 John McQuaid: Umpire Amer. Assoc. 175.00 80.00
☐ 349 Jame McTamany: 150.00 70.00

Brook.-Col.-K.C.
☐ 350 George McVey: Mil.-Denver-St. Joe 150.00 70.00
☐ 351 Peter Meegan San Fran. PCL 2500.00 1100.00
☐ 352 John Messitt: Omaha 150.00 70.00
☐ 353 George(Doggie)Miller Pittsburgh 150.00 70.00
☐ 354 Joseph Miller: Omaha-Minneapolis 150.00 70.00
☐ 355 Jocko Milligan: St. Louis-Phila. 150.00 70.00
☐ 356 E.L. Mills: Milwaukee 150.00 70.00
☐ 357 Minnehan: Minneapolis 150.00 70.00
☐ 358 Samuel Moffet: Ind. 150.00 70.00
☐ 359 Honest Morrell: Boston-Washington 150.00 70.00
☐ 360 Ed Morris (Cannonball): Pittsburgh 150.00 70.00
☐ 361 Morrisey: St. Paul 150.00 70.00
☐ 362 Tony(Count) Mullane: Cincinnati 200.00 90.00
☐ 363 Joseph Mulvey: Philadelphia 150.00 70.00
☐ 364 P.L. Murphy: St. Paul 150.00 70.00
☐ 365 Pat J. Murphy: New York 150.00 70.00
☐ 366 Miah Murray: Wash. 150.00 70.00
☐ 367 James(Truthful) Mutrie: Mgr. N.Y. 175.00 80.00
☐ 368 George Myers: Indianapolis-Phila. 150.00 70.00
☐ 369 Al(Cod) Myers: Washington 150.00 70.00
☐ 370 Thomas Nagle: Omaha-Chi. 150.00 70.00
☐ 371 Billy Nash: Boston 150.00 70.00
☐ 372 Jack(Candy) Nelson: SPOT 450.00 200.00
☐ 373 Kid Nichols: Omaha 900.00 400.00
☐ 374 Samuel Nichols: Pittsburgh 150.00 70.00
☐ 375 J.W. Nicholson Maroons-Minn. 175.00 80.00
☐ 376 Tom Nicholson (Parson) Whites-Cleveland 150.00 70.00
☐ 377A Nicholls Nicol Browns Champ 250.00 110.00
☐ 377B Hugh Nicol: Cinc. 150.00 70.00
☐ 378 Hugh Nicol and Long John Reilly: Cincinnati 200.00 90.00
☐ 379 Frederick Nyce Whites-Burlington 150.00 70.00
☐ 380 Doc Oberlander Cleveland-Syracuse 150.00 70.00
☐ 381 Jack O'Brien Brooklyn-Baltimore 150.00 70.00
☐ 382 William O'Brien: Washington 150.00 70.00
☐ 383 William O'Brien and John Irwin: Washington 200.00 90.00
☐ 384 Darby O'Brien: Brooklyn 150.00 70.00
☐ 385 John O'Brien: Cleve. 150.00 70.00
☐ 386 P.J. O'Connell: Omaha-Des Moines 150.00 70.00
☐ 387 John O'Connor: Cincinnati-Columbus 150.00 70.00
☐ 388 Hank O'Day: Washington-New York 175.00 80.00
☐ 389 O'Day Sacramento 150.00 70.00
☐ 390A James O'Neil: St. Louis-Chicago 150.00 70.00
☐ 390B James O'Neil: Browns Champs 250.00 110.00
☐ 391 Norris "Tip" O'Neill Oakland PCL 2500.00 1100.00
☐ 392 Orator O'Rourke: New York 600.00 275.00
☐ 393 Thomas O'Rourke: Boston-Jersey City 150.00 70.00
☐ 394A David Orr SPOT 450.00 200.00
☐ 394B David Orr: All Star-Brooklyn-Columbus 150.00 70.00
☐ 395 Parsons: Minneapolis 150.00 70.00
☐ 396 Owen Patton: Minn.-Des Moines 150.00 70.00
☐ 397 James Peeples: Brooklyn-Columbus 150.00 70.00
☐ 398 James Peeples and Hardie Henderson: Brooklyn 200.00 90.00
☐ 399 Hip Perrier: San Francisco PCL 2500.00 1100.00
☐ 400 Patrick Pettee: Milwaukee-London 150.00 70.00
☐ 401 Patrick Pettee and Bobby Lowe: Milwaukee 200.00 90.00
☐ 402 Bob Pettit: Chicago 150.00 70.00
☐ 403 Dandelion Pfeffer: Chi. 150.00 70.00
☐ 404 Dick Phelan: Des Moines 150.00 70.00
☐ 405 William Phillips: Brooklyn-Kansas City 150.00 70.00
☐ 406 Horace Phillips: Pittsburgh 150.00 70.00
☐ 407 John Pickett: St. Paul-K.C.-Phila. 150.00 70.00
☐ 408 George Pinkney: Brooklyn 150.00 70.00
☐ 409 Thomas Poorman: A's-Milwaukee 150.00 70.00
☐ 410 Henry Porter: Brooklyn-Kansas City 150.00 70.00
☐ 411 James Powell: Sioux City 150.00 70.00
☐ 412 Tom Powers: San Francisco PCL 2500.00 1100.00
☐ 413 Bill Purcell: (Blondie) Baltimore-A's 150.00 70.00
☐ 414 Thomas Quinn: Baltimore 150.00 70.00
☐ 415 Joseph Quinn: Des Moines-Boston 150.00 70.00
☐ 416A Old Hoss Radbourne: Boston (Portrait) 900.00 400.00
☐ 416B Old Hoss Radbourne: Boston (Non-portrait) 600.00 275.00
☐ 417 Shorty Radford: Brooklyn-Cleveland 150.00 70.00
☐ 418 Tom Ramsey: Louisville 150.00 70.00
☐ 419 Rehse: Minneapolis 150.00 70.00
☐ 420 Long John Reilly: Cincinnati 150.00 70.00
☐ 421 Charles Reilly: (Princeton) St.Paul 150.00 70.00
☐ 422 Charles Reynolds: Kansas City 150.00 70.00
☐ 423 Hardie Richardson Detroit-Boston 150.00 70.00
☐ 424 Danny Richardson: New York 150.00 70.00
☐ 425 Frank Ringo: St. Paul 150.00 70.00
☐ 426 Charles Ripslager SPOT 450.00 200.00
☐ 427 John Roach: New York 150.00 70.00
☐ 428 Wilbert Robinson Uncle Robbie: A's 750.00 350.00
☐ 429 M.C. Robinson: Minn. 150.00 70.00
☐ 430A Yank Robinson: St. Louis 150.00 70.00
☐ 430B Wm.(Yank) Robinson: Browns Champs 250.00 110.00
☐ 431 George Rooks: Maroons-Detroit 175.00 80.00
☐ 432 James(Chief) Roseman SPOT 1000.00 450.00
☐ 433 Davis Rowe: Mgr. K.C.-Denver 150.00 70.00
☐ 434 Jack Rowe: Detroit-Pittsburgh 150.00 70.00
☐ 435 Amos (Hoosier Thunderbolt) Rusie: Ind.-New York 1000.00 450.00
☐ 436 James Ryan: Chicago 175.00 80.00
☐ 437 Henry Sage: Des Moines-Toledo 150.00 70.00
☐ 438 Henry Sage and William Van Dyke: Des Moines-Toledo 200.00 90.00
☐ 439 Frank Salee Omaha-Boston 150.00 70.00
☐ 440 Sanders: Omaha 150.00 70.00
☐ 441 Al(Ben) Sanders: Philadelphia 150.00 70.00
☐ 442 Frank Scheibeck: Detroit 150.00 70.00
☐ 443 Albert Schellhase: St. Joseph 150.00 70.00
☐ 444 William Schenkle: Milwaukee 150.00 70.00
☐ 445 Bill Schildknecht: Des Moines-Milwaukee 150.00 70.00
☐ 446 Gus(Pink Whiskers) Schmelz Mgr. Cincinnati 150.00 70.00
☐ 447 R. F. Schoch: Wash. 150.00 70.00
☐ 448 Lewis Schoeneck (Jumbo): Maroons-Indianapolis 175.00 80.00
☐ 449 Pop Schriver: Phila. 150.00 70.00
☐ 450 John Seery: Ind. 150.00 70.00
☐ 451 William Serad Cincinnati-Toronto 150.00 70.00
☐ 452 Edward Seward: A's 150.00 70.00
☐ 453 George(Orator)Shafer Des Moines 150.00 70.00
☐ 454 Frank Shafer: St. Paul 150.00 70.00
☐ 455 Daniel Shannon: Omaha-L'ville-Phila. 150.00 70.00
☐ 456 William Sharsig: Mgr. Athletics 175.00 80.00
☐ 457 Samuel Shaw: Baltimore-Newark 150.00 70.00
☐ 458 John Shaw: Minneapolis 150.00 70.00
☐ 459 William Shindle: Baltimore-Phila. 150.00 70.00
☐ 460 George Shock: Wash. 150.00 70.00
☐ 461 Otto Shomberg: Ind. 150.00 70.00
☐ 462 Lev Shreve: Ind. 150.00 70.00
☐ 463 Ed(Baldy) Silch: Brooklyn-Denver 150.00 70.00
☐ 464 Michael Slattery: New York 150.00 70.00
☐ 465 Sam(Skyrocket)Smith: Louisville 150.00 70.00
☐ 466A John(Phenomenal) Smith (Portrait) 1000.00 450.00
☐ 466B John(Phenomenal) Smith: Balt.-A's (Non-portrait) 175.00 80.00
☐ 467 Elmer Smith: Cincinnati 150.00 70.00
☐ 468 Fred(Sam) Smith: Des Moines 150.00 70.00
☐ 469 George Smith (Germany) Brooklyn 150.00 70.00
☐ 470 Pop Smith: Pitt.-Bos.-Phila. 150.00 70.00
☐ 471 Nick Smith: St. Joe 150.00 70.00
☐ 472 Pop Snyder: Cleve. 150.00 70.00
☐ 473 P.T. Somers: St. Louis 150.00 70.00
☐ 474 Joe Sommer: Balt. 150.00 70.00
☐ 475 Pete Sommers: Chicago-New York 150.00 70.00
☐ 476 William Sowders: Boston-Pittsburgh 150.00 70.00
☐ 477 John Sowders: St. Paul-Kansas City 150.00 70.00
☐ 478 Charles Sprague: Maroons-Chi.-Cleve. 175.00 80.00
☐ 479 Edward Sproat: Whites 150.00 70.00
☐ 480 Harry Staley: Whites-Pittsburgh 150.00 70.00
☐ 481 Daniel Stearns: Des Moines-K.C. 150.00 70.00
☐ 482 Billy(Cannonball) Stemmyer: Boston-Cleveland 150.00 70.00
☐ 483 Stengel: Columbus 150.00 70.00
☐ 484 B.F. Stephens: Milw. 150.00 70.00
☐ 485 John C. Sterling: Minneapolis 150.00 70.00
☐ 486 Leonard Stockwell S.F. PCL 2500.00 1100.00
☐ 487 Harry Stovey: A's-Boston 300.00 135.00
☐ 488 C. Scott Stratton: Louisville 150.00 70.00
☐ 489 Joseph Straus: Omaha-Milwaukee 150.00 70.00
☐ 490 John(Cub) Stricker: Cleveland 150.00 70.00
☐ 491 J.O. Struck: Milw. 150.00 70.00
☐ 492 Marty Sullivan: Chicago-Ind. 150.00 70.00
☐ 493 Michael Sullivan: A's 150.00 70.00
☐ 494 Billy Sunday: Chicago-Pittsburgh 750.00 350.00
☐ 495 Sy Sutcliffe: Cleve. 150.00 70.00
☐ 496 Ezra Sutton: Boston-Milwaukee 150.00 70.00
☐ 497 Ed Cyrus Swartwood: Brook.-D.Moines- 150.00 70.00

Card	MINT	NRMT
Ham.		
☐ 498 Parke Swartzel: K.C.	150.00	70.00
☐ 499 Peter Sweeney: Wash.	150.00	70.00
☐ 500 Louis Sylvester#[Sacra. PCL	2500.00	1100.00
☐ 501 Ed(Dimples) Tate: Boston-Baltimore	150.00	70.00
☐ 502 Patsy Tebeau: Chi.-Cleve.-Minn.	175.00	80.00
☐ 503 John Tener: Chicago	175.00	80.00
☐ 504 Bill(Adonis) Terry: Brooklyn	150.00	70.00
☐ 505 Big Sam Thompson: Detroit- Philadelphia	500.00	220.00
☐ 506 Silent Mike Tiernan: New York	150.00	70.00
☐ 507 Ledell Titcomb: N.Y.	150.00	70.00
☐ 508 Phillip Tomney: Louisville	150.00	70.00
☐ 509 Stephen Toole: Brooklyn-K.C.- Rochester	150.00	70.00
☐ 510 George Townsend: A's	150.00	70.00
☐ 511 William Traffley: Des Moines	150.00	70.00
☐ 512 George Treadway: St. Paul-Denver	150.00	70.00
☐ 513 Samuel Trott: Baltimore-Newark	150.00	70.00
☐ 514 Sam Trott and Tommy(Oyster) Burns: Baltimore HOR	200.00	90.00
☐ 515 Tom(Foghorn) Tucker: Baltimore	150.00	70.00
☐ 516 William Tuckerman: St. Paul	150.00	70.00
☐ 517 Turner: Minneapolis	150.00	70.00
☐ 518 Lawrence Twitchell: Detroit-Cleveland	150.00	70.00
☐ 519 James Tyng: Phila	150.00	70.00
☐ 520 William Van Dyke: Des Moines-Toledo	150.00	70.00
☐ 521 George(Rip) VanHaltren Chicago	150.00	70.00
☐ 522 Harry Vaughn: (Farmer) Louisville-New York	150.00	70.00
☐ 523 Peek-a-Boo Veach: St. Paul	300.00	135.00
☐ 524 Veach: Sacra. PCL	2500.00	1100.00
☐ 525 Leon Viau: Cincinnati	150.00	70.00
☐ 526 William Vinton: Minneapolis	150.00	70.00
☐ 527 Joseph Visner: Brooklyn	150.00	70.00
☐ 528 Christian VonDer Ahe Owner Browns Champs	300.00	135.00
☐ 529 Joseph Walsh: Omaha	150.00	70.00
☐ 530 John(Monte) Ward: New York	600.00	275.00
☐ 531 E.H. Warner: Milwaukee	250.00	110.00
☐ 532 William Watkins: Mgr. Detroit- Kansas City	175.00	80.00
☐ 533 Bill Weaver: (Farmer) Louisville	150.00	70.00
☐ 534 Charles Weber: Sioux City	150.00	70.00
☐ 535 George Weidman (Stump): Detroit-New York	150.00	70.00
☐ 536 William Weidner: Columbus	150.00	70.00
☐ 537A Curtis Welch: Browns Champ	250.00	110.00
☐ 537B Curtis Welch: A's	150.00	70.00
☐ 538 Curtis Welch and Bill Gleason: Athletics	200.00	90.00
☐ 539 Smilin'Mickey Welch: All Star-New York	600.00	275.00
☐ 540 Jake Wells: K.C.	150.00	70.00
☐ 541 Frank Wells: Des Moines-Mil.	175.00	80.00
☐ 542 Joseph Werrick: Louisville-St. Paul	150.00	70.00
☐ 543 Milton(Buck) West: Minneapolis	150.00	70.00
☐ 544 Gus(Cannonball) Weyhing: A's	150.00	70.00
☐ 545 John Weyhing: Athletics-Columbus	150.00	70.00
☐ 546 Bobby Wheelock: Boston-Detroit	150.00	70.00
☐ 547 Whitacre: A's	150.00	70.00
☐ 548 Pat Whitaker: Balt.	150.00	70.00
☐ 549 Deacon White: Detroit-Pittsburgh	175.00	80.00
☐ 550 William White: Louisville	150.00	70.00
☐ 551 Jim(Grasshopper) Whitney: Wash.-Indianapolis	150.00	70.00
☐ 552 Arthur Whitney: Pittsburgh-New York	150.00	70.00
☐ 553 G. Whitney: St. Joseph	150.00	70.00
☐ 554 James Williams: Mgr. Cleveland	175.00	80.00
☐ 555 Ned Williamson: Chi.	175.00	80.00
☐ 556 Williamson and Mascot	200.00	90.00
☐ 557 C.H. Willis: Omaha	150.00	70.00
☐ 558 Walt Wilmot: Washington-Chicago	150.00	70.00
☐ 559 George Winkleman: Minneapolis- Hartford	250.00	110.00
☐ 560 Samuel Wise: Boston-Washington	150.00	70.00
☐ 561 William Wolf (Chicken) Louisville	150.00	70.00
☐ 562 George(Dandy) Wood: Philadelphia	150.00	70.00
☐ 563 Peter Wood: Phila.	150.00	70.00
☐ 564 Harry Wright: Mgr. Philadelphia	1500.00	700.00
☐ 565 Charles Zimmer (Chief) Cleveland	150.00	70.00
☐ 566 Frank Zinn: Athletics	150.00	70.00

1994 Oscar Mayer Round-Ups

The 1994 Oscar Mayer Superstar Round-Up set consists of 30 circular pop-up cards measuring about 2 1/2" in diameter and features 15 players from the American (1-15) and National (16-30) Leagues. One card was inserted in each specially marked 16-oz. package of Oscar Mayer bologna available in April and May. On-pack and in-store point-of-purchase mail-in offers enabled consumers to order a boxed American and/or National League 15-card set for 1.95 plus proof-of-purchase for each set. The black-bordered fronts feature color action player shots that are perforated and cut out in such a way so that when the tab at the top is pulled, the photo becomes three-dimensional. Also revealed is a trivia question and answer, and the player's statistics. The set's title appears at the top within the black border in blue lettering on American League cards and green lettering on National League cards. The player's name, position, and team appear below the photo. The back displays the player's name, position, team, and career highlights. A color player action cutout appears alongside. The cards are numbered on the front toward the lower right, following alphabetical order by league.

	MINT	NRMT
COMPLETE SET (30)	12.00	5.50
COMMON CARD (1-30)	.25	.11
☐ 1 Jim Abbott	.25	.11
☐ 2 Kevin Appier	.50	.23
☐ 3 Roger Clemens	1.00	.45
☐ 4 Cecil Fielder	.50	.23
☐ 5 Juan Gonzalez	2.00	.90
☐ 6 Ken Griffey Jr.	4.00	1.80
☐ 7 Kenny Lofton	1.00	.45
☐ 8 Jack McDowell	.25	.11
☐ 9 Paul Molitor	1.00	.45
☐ 10 Kirby Puckett	2.00	.90
☐ 11 Cal Ripken Jr.	3.00	1.35
☐ 12 Tim Salmon	1.00	.45
☐ 13 Ruben Sierra	.25	.11
☐ 14 Frank Thomas	3.00	1.35
☐ 15 Greg Vaughn	.25	.11
☐ 16 Jeff Bagwell	2.00	.90
☐ 17 Barry Bonds	1.00	.45
☐ 18 Bobby Bonilla	.50	.23
☐ 19 Jeff Conine	.50	.23
☐ 20 Lenny Dykstra	.50	.23
☐ 21 Andres Galarraga	1.00	.45
☐ 22 Marquis Grissom	.50	.23
☐ 23 Tony Gwynn	2.00	.90
☐ 24 Gregg Jefferies	.50	.23
☐ 25 John Kruk	.50	.23
☐ 26 Greg Maddux	2.00	.90
☐ 27 Mike Piazza	2.50	1.10
☐ 28 Jose Rijo	.25	.11
☐ 29 Ryne Sandberg	1.50	.70
☐ 30 Andy Van Slyke	.50	.23

1991 Pacific Ryan Texas Express I

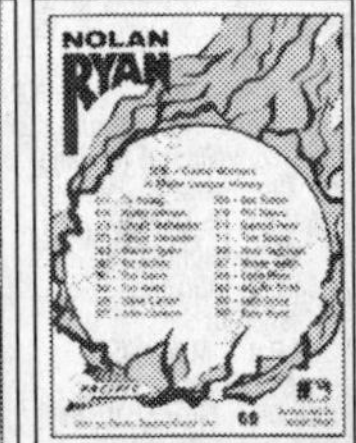

This 110-card standard-size set, Texas Express, traces the career of Nolan Ryan from the start of his career into the 1991 season as well as his personal life with his family on his ranch in Alvin, Texas. This set features glossy full-color photos on the front and either biographical information or an action shot of Ryan on the back which is framed by a fireball. The backs are printed in purple and red on a white background. Inside a flaming baseball design, one finds biography, career highlights, player quote, or an extended caption to the front picture. The cards are numbered on the back. This set was issued by Pacific Trading cards and was the first set featuring an individual baseball player to be sold in wax packs since the 1959 Fleer Ted Williams issue. The cards were available in 12-card foil packs and factory sets. Moreover, eight unnumbered bonus cards (1-6 No Hitters, 1991 25th Season, and Rookie year with the Mets) were produced in quantities of 1,000 of each card in gold foil and 10,000 of each card in silver foil; these bonus cards were randomly inserted in foil packs only. After the first and second series of Pacific Nolan Ryan Texas Express had sold out, Pacific reissued card numbers 1-220 in 1993, and the cards produced in this reissue may be distinguished by the 27th season logo, which was introduced to collectors in the 30-card 27th Season series. Currently there is no value differential between the two types.

	MINT	NRMT
COMPLETE SET (110)	12.00	5.50
COMMON CARD (1-110)	.10	.05
☐ 1 Nolan Ryan Future Hall of Famer	.35	.16
☐ 2 Nolan Ryan From Little League to the Major Leagues	.10	.05
☐ 3 Nolan Ryan A Dream Come True	.10	.05
☐ 4 Nolan Ryan Signed by the Mets	.10	.05
☐ 5 Nolan Ryan Fireball Pitcher	.10	.05
☐ 6 Nolan Ryan New York Mets Rookie Pitcher	.10	.05
☐ 7 Nolan Ryan First Major League Win	.10	.05
☐ 8 Nolan Ryan Early in 1969	.10	.05
☐ 9 Nolan Ryan Tensions of a Pennant Race	.10	.05
☐ 10 Nolan Ryan Mets Clinch NL East	.10	.05
☐ 11 Nolan Ryan Gil Hodges Keep the Ball Down	.25	.11
☐ 12 Nolan Ryan Playoff Victory	.10	.05
☐ 13 Nolan Ryan World Series Victory	.10	.05
☐ 14 Nolan Ryan The Amazin' Mets	.10	.05
☐ 15 Nolan Ryan Sets Met Record for Strikeouts	.10	.05

☐ 16 Nolan Ryan .10 .05
One of the Worst
Trades in Baseball
☐ 17 Nolan Ryan .10 .05
Slow Start with Mets
☐ 18 Nolan Ryan .10 .05
Pitcher New York Mets
☐ 19 Nolan Ryan .10 .05
Traded to the Angels
☐ 20 Nolan Ryan .10 .05
Meeting New Friends
☐ 21 Nolan Ryan .10 .05
Throwing Fast Balls
☐ 22 Nolan Ryan .10 .05
Move the Ball Around
☐ 23 Nolan Ryan .10 .05
Nolan Heat
☐ 24 Nolan Ryan .10 .05
No-Hitter Number 1
☐ 25 Nolan Ryan .10 .05
Looking Back on Number 1
☐ 26 Nolan Ryan .10 .05
No-Hitter Number 2
☐ 27 Nolan Ryan .10 .05
Single Season Strikeout Record
☐ 28 Nolan Ryan .10 .05
21 Wins in 1973
☐ 29 Nolan Ryan .15 .07
Fastest Pitch Ever Thrown
Clocked at 100.9 MPH
☐ 30 Nolan Ryan .15 .07
No-Hitter Number 3
☐ 31 Nolan Ryan .15 .07
No-Hitter Number 4
☐ 32 Nolan Ryan .15 .07
Frank Tanana
☐ 33 Nolan Ryan .10 .05
Learning Change-Up
☐ 34 Nolan Ryan .10 .05
Pitcher California Angels
☐ 35 Nolan Ryan .10 .05
Joins Astros
☐ 36 Nolan Ryan .15 .07
Starting Pitcher
☐ 37 Nolan Ryan .10 .05
Taking Batting Practice
☐ 38 Nolan Ryan .10 .05
The Game's Greatest
Power Pitcher
☐ 39 Nolan Ryan .10 .05
3,000 Career Strikeout
☐ 40 Nolan Ryan .15 .07
Home Run
☐ 41 Nolan Ryan .10 .05
The Fast Ball Grip
☐ 42 Nolan Ryan .15 .07
Record 5th No-Hitter
☐ 43 Nolan Ryan .15 .07
No-Hitter Number 5
☐ 44 Nolan Ryan .10 .05
A Dream Fulfilled
☐ 45 Nolan Ryan .25 .11
Passes Walter Johnson
☐ 46 Nolan Ryan .15 .07
Strikeout 4000
☐ 47 Nolan Ryan .10 .05
Astros win
Western Division Title
☐ 48 Nolan Ryan .10 .05
Pitcher Houston Astros
☐ 49 Nolan Ryan .10 .05
Milestone Strikeouts
☐ 50 Nolan Ryan .10 .05
Post Season Participant
☐ 51 Nolan Ryan .10 .05
Hurling for Houston
☐ 52 Nolan Ryan .10 .05
135 NL Wins
☐ 53 Nolan Ryan .10 .05
Through with Chew
☐ 54 Nolan Ryan .10 .05
Signed by Rangers 1989
☐ 55 Nolan Ryan .10 .05
Pleasant Change for Nolan
☐ 56 Nolan Ryan .10 .05
Real Special Moment
☐ 57 Nolan Ryan .10 .05
Enters 1989 All-Star Game
☐ 58 Nolan Ryan .10 .05
Pitching in
1989 All-Star Game
☐ 59 Nolan Ryan .15 .07
5,000 Strikeouts
A Standing Ovation
☐ 60 Nolan Ryan .10 .05
Great Moments in 1989
☐ 61 Nolan Ryan .15 .07
Dan Smith
☐ 62 Nolan Ryan .10 .05
Ranger Club Record
16 Strikeouts
☐ 63 Nolan Ryan .15 .07
Last Pitch No-Hitter Number 6
☐ 64 Nolan Ryan .15 .07
Sweet Number 6
☐ 65 Nolan Ryan .10 .05
Oldest To Throw No-Hitter
☐ 66 Nolan Ryan .10 .05
Another Win
☐ 67 Nolan Ryan .10 .05
20th Pitcher to Win 300
Acknowledging the Fans
☐ 68 Nolan Ryan .25 .11
Brad Arnsberg
Geno Petralli
300 Game Win Battery
☐ 69 Nolan Ryan .10 .05
A 300 Game Winner
☐ 70 Nolan Ryan .10 .05
Perfect Mechanics
☐ 71 Nolan Ryan .10 .05
22 Seasons with
100 or more Strikeouts
☐ 72 Nolan Ryan .10 .05
11th Strikeout Title
☐ 73 Nolan Ryan .10 .05
232 Strikeouts in 1990
☐ 74 Nolan Ryan .10 .05
The 1990 Season
☐ 75 Nolan Ryan .15 .07
Pitcher Texas Rangers
☐ 76 Nolan Ryan .10 .05
1991: Nolan's 25th Season
☐ 77 Nolan Ryan .25 .11
Throwing Spirals
☐ 78 Nolan Ryan .10 .05
Running the Steps
☐ 79 Nolan Ryan .10 .05
Hard Work and Conditioning
☐ 80 Nolan Ryan .10 .05
The Rigid Workout
☐ 81 Nolan Ryan .10 .05
Ryan's Routine
☐ 82 Nolan Ryan .10 .05
Ryan's Routine Between Starts
☐ 83 Nolan Ryan .10 .05
Running in Outfield
Before the Big Game
☐ 84 Nolan Ryan .10 .05
B.P. in Texas
☐ 85 Nolan Ryan .10 .05
18 Career Low-Hitters
☐ 86 Nolan Ryan .10 .05
My Job is to Give My
Team a Chance to Win
☐ 87 Nolan Ryan .10 .05
The Spring Workout
☐ 88 Nolan Ryan .10 .05
Power versus Power
☐ 89 Nolan Ryan .10 .05
Awesome Power
☐ 90 Nolan Ryan .10 .05
Blazing Speed
☐ 91 Nolan Ryan .10 .05
The Pick Off
☐ 92 Nolan Ryan 1.00 .45
A Real Gamer
Bloody lip
and blood all over jersey)
☐ 93 Nolan Ryan .25 .11
Jim Sundberg
Ranger Battery Mates
☐ 94 Nolan Ryan .10 .05
The Glare
☐ 95 Nolan Ryan .10 .05
The High Leg Kick
☐ 96 Nolan Ryan .10 .05
Day Off from Pitcher
☐ 97 Nolan Ryan .10 .05
A New Ball for Nolan
☐ 98 Nolan Ryan .10 .05
Going to Rosin Bag
☐ 99 Nolan Ryan .10 .05
Time for Relief
☐ 100 Nolan Ryan .10 .05
A Lone Star Legend
☐ 101 Nolan Ryan .10 .05
Fans' Favorite
☐ 102 Nolan Ryan .10 .05
Watching Nolan Pitch
☐ 103 Nolan Ryan .10 .05
Our Family of Five
☐ 104 Nolan Ryan .10 .05
Texas Beefmaster
☐ 105 Nolan Ryan .10 .05
Gentleman Rancher
☐ 106 Nolan Ryan .10 .05
Texas Cowboy Life
☐ 107 Nolan Ryan .15 .07
The Ryan Family
☐ 108 Nolan Ryan .10 .05
Participating in
Cutting Horse Contest
☐ 109 Nolan Ryan .10 .05
Nolan Interviews
☐ 110 Nolan Ryan .35 .16
Lynn Nolan Ryan

1991 Pacific Ryan Inserts 8

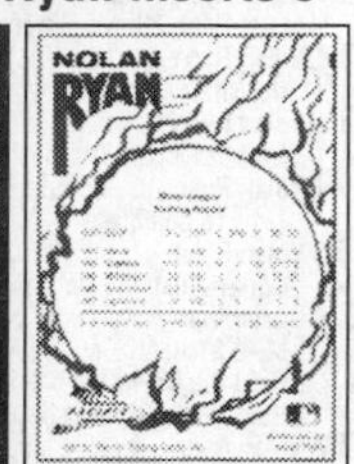

These eight standard-size cards were inserts in 1991 Pacific Nolan Ryan Texas Express foil packs. As with the regular issue, the fronts display glossy color photos that are bordered in silver foil and either purple/red or red/orange border stripes. Inside a flaming baseball design, the back presents either a player photo, statistics, or career highlights. The cards are unnumbered and checklisted below in chronological order. Besides the silver cards, they were also issued on a much more limited basis in gold. The gold versions are valued at quadruple the prices listed below.

	MINT	NRMT
COMPLETE SET (8)	100.00	45.00
COMMON CARD (1-8)	15.00	6.75

☐ 1 Nolan Ryan 15.00 6.75
New York Mets Rookie Pitcher
☐ 2 Nolan Ryan 15.00 6.75
No-Hitter 1
☐ 3 Nolan Ryan 15.00 6.75
No-Hitter 2
☐ 4 Nolan Ryan 15.00 6.75
No-Hitter 3
☐ 5 Nolan Ryan 15.00 6.75
No-Hitter 4
☐ 6 Nolan Ryan 15.00 6.75
No-Hitter 5
☐ 7 Nolan Ryan 15.00 6.75
Sweet 6
☐ 8 Nolan Ryan 15.00 6.75
1991: Nolan's 25th Season

1991 Pacific Ryan 7th No-Hitter

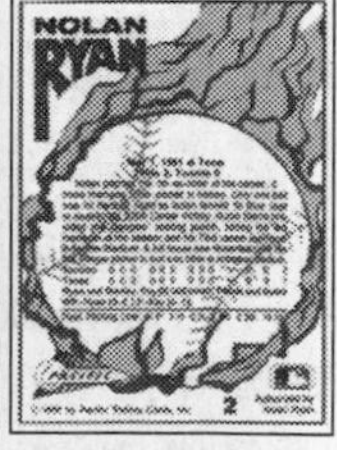

This seven-card set was produced by Pacific Trading Cards Inc. to capture various moments of Nolan Ryan's 7th no-hitter. These cards were produced in the following numbers: 1,000 of each card in gold foil and 10,000 of each card in silver foil. The cards measure the standard size and were randomly inserted in foil packs only. The fronts feature glossy color photos, with silver or gold borders on the sides and faded red borders above and below the picture. In addition, the player's name is written vertically in a multi-colored stripe on the left side of the picture. A flaming baseball in the lower left corner completes the card face. The backs are printed in purple and red on a white background. Inside a flaming baseball design, one finds an extended caption to the front picture. The cards are numbered on the back in the lower left corner. Supposedly as many as half of the cards were destroyed and never released. The prices below refer to the silver versions; the gold versions would be valued at quadruple the prices below. In addition to silver and gold, two other border versions have surfaced. One type has silver prism borders, the other has gold hologram-like borders. It is not known how these cards were distributed, but they are scarcer than the gold border cards and are valued at six times the prices below.

	MINT	NRMT
COMPLETE SET (7)	100.00	45.00
COMMON CARD (1-7)	15.00	6.75

☐ 1 Nolan Ryan 15.00 6.75
Last Pitch 7th No-Hitter
☐ 2 Nolan Ryan 15.00 6.75
No-Hitter Number 7
☐ 3 Nolan Ryan 15.00 6.75
Number 7 was The Best
☐ 4 Nolan Ryan 15.00 6.75
Time to Celebrate
☐ 5 Nolan Ryan 15.00 6.75
Congratulations from Ranger Fans
☐ 6 Nolan Ryan 15.00 6.75
Mike Stanley
Hold the No-Hitter Ball UER
Back reads Bryan, should read Ryan
☐ 7 Nolan Ryan 15.00 6.75
All in a Day's Work

1992 Pacific Ryan Magazine 6

These six standard size cards were inserted (bound) into the July 1992 Volume 2, Issue 2 of Trading Cards magazine as a pair of two-card strips. These are very similar to the hard-to-find inserts that Pacific inserted into the Ryan Texas Express second series foil packs. These "magazine cards" are only differentiable by the fact that they lack the words "Limited Edition" on the copyright line on their backs.

	MINT	NRMT
COMPLETE SET (6)	8.00	3.60
COMMON CARD (1-6)	1.50	.70

☐ 1 Nolan Ryan .... 1.50 .70
Pitching, side view
☐ 2 Nolan Ryan .... 1.50 .70
Pitching, front view
gray uniform
☐ 3 Nolan Ryan .... 1.50 .70
The Texas Express
☐ 4 Nolan Ryan .... 1.50 .70
The Seventh No-Hitter
☐ 5 Nolan Ryan .... 1.50 .70
A Texas Legacy
☐ 6 Nolan Ryan .... 1.50 .70
A Quarter of a Century

1992 Pacific Ryan Texas Express II

For the second year, Pacific issued a 110-card standard-size set titled Texas Express. A six-card insert set was randomly inserted in foil packs, with 1,000 autographed and numbered of card number 1. The fronts feature glossy posed and action photos (some color, some black-and-white) of Ryan in various stages of his life and career. The pictures are bordered at the top and bottom in varying shades of red, orange and purple. His name is printed in silver vertically down the left edge of the card on either red, orange or purple. A fiery baseball overlaps the border and photo at the bottom. The backs show the fiery baseball with either statistics, career highlights, pictures, or quotes about Nolan printed in blue on the baseball. This set is essentially an extension or second series of the 1991 Pacific Nolan Ryan set and is numbered that way. After the first and second series of Pacific Nolan Ryan Texas Express had sold out, Pacific reissued card numbers 1-220 in 1993, and the cards produced in this reissue may be distinguished by the 27th season logo, which was introduced to collectors in the 30-card 27th Season series. Currently there is no value differential between the two types.

	MINT	NRMT
COMPLETE SET (110)	10.00	4.50
COMMON CARD (111-220)	.10	.05

☐ 111 Nolan Ryan .... .25 .11
The Golden Arm
☐ 112 Nolan Ryan .... .10 .05
Little League All-Star
☐ 113 Nolan Ryan .... .10 .05
All-State Pitcher
☐ 114 Nolan Ryan .... .10 .05
Nolan Ryan Field
☐ 115 Nolan Ryan .... .10 .05
at Age 20
☐ 116 Nolan Ryan .... .10 .05
Jacksonville Suns
☐ 117 Nolan Ryan .... .10 .05
Surrounded By Friends
☐ 118 Nolan Ryan .... .15 .07
The Cowboy
☐ 119 Nolan Ryan .... .10 .05
The Simple Life
☐ 120 Nolan Ryan .... .10 .05
Loves Animals
☐ 121 Nolan Ryan .... .10 .05
Growing Up in New York
☐ 122 Nolan Ryan .... .15 .07
New York Strikeout Record
☐ 123 Nolan Ryan .... .10 .05
Traded
☐ 124 Nolan Ryan .... .25 .11
Hall of Fame Victims
☐ 125 Nolan Ryan .... .10 .05
Number 500
☐ 126 Nolan Ryan .... .10 .05
California Victory
☐ 127 Nolan Ryan .... .10 .05
20 Win Season
☐ 128 Nolan Ryan .... .10 .05
Throwing Heat
☐ 129 Nolan Ryan .... .15 .07
Strikeout Record
☐ 130 Nolan Ryan .... .15 .07
Number One
☐ 131 Nolan Ryan .... .10 .05
1,000th Strikeout
☐ 132 Nolan Ryan .... .15 .07
Number Two
☐ 133 Nolan Ryan .... .10 .05
2,000th Strikeout
☐ 134 Nolan Ryan .... .15 .07
Number Three
☐ 135 Nolan Ryan .... .25 .11
Bob Feller
Pure Speed
☐ 136 Nolan Ryan .... .10 .05
Independence Day Fireworks
☐ 137 Nolan Ryan .... .10 .05
Fast Ball Pitcher
☐ 138 Nolan Ryan .... .15 .07
Number Four
☐ 139 Nolan Ryan .... .10 .05
Free Agent
☐ 140 Nolan Ryan .... .10 .05
Houston Bound
☐ 141 Nolan Ryan .... .10 .05
Big Dollars
☐ 142 Nolan Ryan .... .15 .07
Strong Houston Staff
☐ 143 Nolan Ryan .... .15 .07
Number Five
☐ 144 Nolan Ryan .... .10 .05
Astro MVP
☐ 145 Nolan Ryan .... .10 .05
Western Division Game
☐ 146 Nolan Ryan .... .10 .05
National League All-Star
☐ 147 Nolan Ryan .... .10 .05
Major League Record
☐ 148 Nolan Ryan .... .25 .11
Breaks Walter Johnson's Record
☐ 149 Nolan Ryan .... .25 .11
Reese Ryan
☐ 150 Nolan Ryan .... .10 .05
100th National League Win
☐ 151 Nolan Ryan .... .10 .05
4,000th Strikeout
☐ 152 Nolan Ryan .... .10 .05
League Leader
☐ 153 Nolan Ryan .... .10 .05
250th Career Win
☐ 154 Nolan Ryan .... .10 .05
The Seldom of Swat
☐ 155 Nolan Ryan .... .10 .05
4,500th Strikeout
☐ 156 Nolan Ryan .... .15 .07
Like Father Like Son
☐ 157 Nolan Ryan .... .10 .05
Spoiled in the Ninth
☐ 158 Nolan Ryan .... .10 .05
Leaving Houston in Style
☐ 159 Nolan Ryan .... .10 .05
Houston Star
☐ 160 Nolan Ryan .... .10 .05
Tests Free Agency
☐ 161 Nolan Ryan .... .10 .05
Awesome Heat
☐ 162 Nolan Ryan .... .10 .05
Brotherly Love
☐ 163 Nolan Ryan .... .10 .05
Astros Return of
The Prodigious Son
☐ 164 Nolan Ryan .... .10 .05
Texas Size Decision
☐ 165 Nolan Ryan .... .10 .05
Texas Legend
☐ 166 Nolan Ryan .... .10 .05
Drawing a Crowd
☐ 167 Nolan Ryan .... .10 .05
Great Start
☐ 168 Nolan Ryan .... .10 .05
5,000th Strikeout
☐ 169 Nolan Ryan .... .10 .05
Texas All-Star
☐ 170 Nolan Ryan .... .15 .07
Number Six
☐ 171 Nolan Ryan .... .15 .07
300th Win
☐ 172 Nolan Ryan .... .10 .05
1990 League Leader
☐ 173 Nolan Ryan .... .25 .11
Man of the Year
☐ 174 Nolan Ryan .... .10 .05
Spring Training 1991
☐ 175 Nolan Ryan .... .10 .05
Fast Ball Grip
☐ 176 Nolan Ryan .... .10 .05
Strong Arm
☐ 177 Nolan Ryan .... .15 .07
Mike Stanley
Stanley's Delight
☐ 178 Nolan Ryan .... .15 .07
After Nolan's 7th No-Hitter
☐ 179 Nolan Ryan .... .10 .05
Stretching Before the Game
☐ 180 Nolan Ryan .... .10 .05
The Rangers Sign Nolan
For 1992 and 1993
☐ 181 Nolan Ryan .... .10 .05
Heading to the Bullpen
to Warmup
☐ 182 Nolan Ryan .... .10 .05
Banker
☐ 183 Nolan Ryan .... .10 .05
Time with Fans
☐ 184 Nolan Ryan .... .10 .05
Solid 1991 Season
☐ 185 Nolan Ryan .... .10 .05
Ranger Team Leader
☐ 186 Nolan Ryan .... .10 .05
Sets More Records
☐ 187 Nolan Ryan .... .15 .07
Number Seven
☐ 188 Nolan Ryan .... .15 .07
Passes Phil Niekro
☐ 189 Nolan Ryan .... .15 .07
Trails Don Sutton
☐ 190 Nolan Ryan .... .10 .05
Ranger Strikeout Mark
☐ 191 Nolan Ryan .... .10 .05
Consecutive K's
☐ 192 Nolan Ryan .... .10 .05
5,500th Strikeout
☐ 193 Nolan Ryan .... .10 .05
Twenty-Five First Timers
☐ 194 Nolan Ryan .... .10 .05

	MINT	NRMT
No-Hitters Ended in the Ninth		
☐ 195 Nolan Ryan	.10	.05
Constant Work-Outs		
☐ 196 Nolan Ryan	.10	.05
In Motion		
☐ 197 Nolan Ryan	.10	.05
Pitching in Fenway Park		
☐ 198 Nolan Ryan	.25	.11
Goose Gossage		
☐ 199 Nolan Ryan	.10	.05
Talking Over Strategy		
☐ 200 Nolan Ryan	.35	.16
Roger Clemens Don't Mess With Texas		
☐ 201 Nolan Ryan	.10	.05
314-278 Thru 1991		
☐ 202 Nolan Ryan	.10	.05
All-Time Leader		
☐ 203 Nolan Ryan	.10	.05
High Praise		
☐ 204 Nolan Ryan	.15	.07
Bobby Valentine Manager's Delight		
☐ 205 Nolan Ryan	.10	.05
733 Major League Starts		
☐ 206 Nolan Ryan	.25	.11
The Quarterback		
☐ 207 Nolan Ryan	.10	.05
Hard Work Pays Off		
☐ 208 Nolan Ryan	.15	.07
Tom House Passing Along Wisdom		
☐ 209 Nolan Ryan	.10	.05
Still Dominant		
☐ 210 Nolan Ryan	.10	.05
Fast Ball Is Just a Blur		
☐ 211 Nolan Ryan	.15	.07
Seven No-Hitters		
☐ 212 Nolan Ryan	.10	.05
Training for Perfection		
☐ 213 Nolan Ryan	.10	.05
Edge and Speed		
☐ 214 Nolan Ryan	.10	.05
This One was for Them		
☐ 215 Nolan Ryan	.10	.05
Another Day's Work		
☐ 216 Nolan Ryan	.10	.05
Pick Off at Third		
☐ 217 Nolan Ryan	.10	.05
Ready to Pitch		
☐ 218 Nolan Ryan	.10	.05
Spring Training 1992		
☐ 219 Nolan Ryan	.15	.07
Receives The Victor Award		
☐ 220 Nolan Ryan	.25	.11
1992: Nolan's 26th Season		

1992 Pacific Ryan Gold

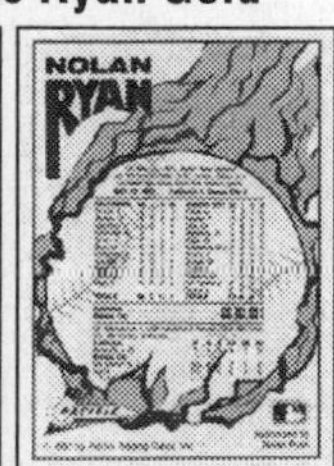

These eight standard size cards were one of two insert subsets randomly packed in 1992 Pacific Nolan Ryan Texas Express II 12-card and 24-card foil packs. Supposedly 10,000 of each card were produced. The cards feature high gloss color action photos of Ryan pitching his seven no-hitters. The pictures are bordered in gold foil and either red/orange (1-4) or purple/red border (5-8) stripes. Inside a flaming baseball design, the backs of cards 1-7 display statistics for that no-hitter while card no. 8 summarizes all seven no-hitters. The cards are unnumbered and checklisted below in chronological order of the events.

	MINT	NRMT
COMPLETE SET (8)	175.00	80.00
COMMON CARD (1-8)	25.00	11.00
☐ 1 Nolan Ryan	25.00	11.00
Number One		
☐ 2 Nolan Ryan	25.00	11.00
Number Two		
☐ 3 Nolan Ryan	25.00	11.00
Number Three		
☐ 4 Nolan Ryan	25.00	11.00
Number Four		
☐ 5 Nolan Ryan	25.00	11.00
Number Five		
☐ 6 Nolan Ryan	25.00	11.00
Number Six		
☐ 7 Nolan Ryan	25.00	11.00
Number Seven		
☐ 8 Nolan Ryan	25.00	11.00
Seven No-Hitters		

1992 Pacific Ryan Limited

These six standard size cards were one of two insert subsets randomly packed in 1992 Pacific Nolan Ryan Texas Express II 12-card and 24-card foil packs. Only 3,000 of each card were produced and, as an added bonus, 1,000 of card number 1 were autographed by Ryan. A similar-looking pair of two-card strips was inserted (bound) into all issues of the July 1992 Volume 2, Issue 2 of Trading Cards magazine. However these "magazine cards" lack the words "Limited Edition" on the copyright line on their backs. The six career highlight cards feature high gloss color action photos on their fronts edged by a graded blue stripe on the left side and framed by a white outer border. The Texas Rangers and Pacific logos overlap the picture. The horizontal backs feature a second action color photo. Nolan's name appears in a red, white, and blue bar above a red box containing either career highlights (2, 3, 6), statistics (4) or a poem (5).

	MINT	NRMT
COMPLETE SET (6)	125.00	55.00
COMMON CARD (1-6)	25.00	11.00
☐ 1 Nolan Ryan	25.00	11.00
Pitching, side view limited edition on back		
☐ 2 Nolan Ryan	25.00	11.00
(Pitching, front view gray uniform limited edition on back		
☐ 3 Nolan Ryan	25.00	11.00
The Texas Express Limited edition on back		
☐ 4 Nolan Ryan	25.00	11.00
The Seventh No-Hitter Limited edition on back		
☐ 5 Nolan Ryan	25.00	11.00
A Texas Legacy Limited edition on back		
☐ 6 Nolan Ryan	25.00	11.00
A Quarter of a Century Limited edition on back		

1992 Pacific Seaver

This 110-card standard-size set traces the career of Tom Seaver. The set was sold in 12-card foil packs or as a factory set for $12.95 through a mail-in offer. The fronts feature glossy color player photos with silver, purple, or red borders. Also white border stripes appear on the left and right sides of the pictures. At the lower left corner the nickname "Tom Terrific" in yellow lettering wraps around a white baseball icon. The back design is based on a larger version of this baseball icon, with a second color photo, career summary, or highlights inside the ball. Behind the ball appears a skyline with tall buildings. Autograph cards of Tom Seaver were randomly inserted into packs, they are valued at the bottom of the listings.

	MINT	NRMT
COMPLETE SET (110)	7.50	3.40
COMMON CARD (1-110)	.10	.05
☐ 1 Tom Seaver	.35	.16
Stand-out High School Basketball Player		
☐ 2 Tom Seaver	.10	.05
Pro Ball Player		
☐ 3 Tom Seaver	.10	.05
Destined to be a Met		
☐ 4 Tom Seaver	.10	.05
Brave or Met		
☐ 5 Tom Seaver	.10	.05
Mets Luck of the Draw		
☐ 6 Tom Seaver	.10	.05
Sent to Jacksonville		
☐ 7 Tom Seaver	.10	.05
First Major League Win		
☐ 8 Tom Seaver	.15	.07
1967 Rookie of the Year		
☐ 9 Tom Seaver	.10	.05
Humble Beginnings		
☐ 10 Tom Seaver	.10	.05
Predicting the Future		
☐ 11 Tom Seaver	.10	.05
Rookie All-Star		
☐ 12 Tom Seaver	.10	.05
16 Wins in 1968		
☐ 13 Tom Seaver	.10	.05
1968 National League All-Star		
☐ 14 Tom Seaver	.10	.05
The Amazing Mets		
☐ 15 Tom Seaver	.15	.07
1969 Cy Young Winner		
☐ 16 Tom Seaver	.15	.07
Pitcher of the Year		
☐ 17 Tom Seaver	.10	.05
Strikeout Leader		
☐ 18 Tom Seaver	.10	.05
Ties Major League Record		
☐ 19 Tom Seaver	.10	.05
Mr. Consistency		
☐ 20 Tom Seaver	.10	.05
Finishing in Style		
☐ 21 Tom Seaver	.10	.05
Twenty-Game Winner		
☐ 22 Tom Seaver	.15	.07
Second Cy Young Award		
☐ 23 Tom Seaver	.10	.05
Batting Star		
☐ 24 Tom Seaver	.10	.05
At Bat in the World Series		
☐ 25 Tom Seaver	.10	.05
Championship Series Record		
☐ 26 Tom Seaver	.10	.05
Injury Plagued Season		
☐ 27 Tom Seaver	.10	.05
Comeback		
☐ 28 Tom Seaver	.10	.05
Super September		
☐ 29 Tom Seaver	.10	.05
Sporting News All-Star		
☐ 30 Tom Seaver	.10	.05
Strikeout Record		
☐ 31 Tom Seaver	.10	.05
USC Alumni Star		
☐ 32 Tom Seaver	.10	.05
Winning Smile		
☐ 33 Tom Seaver	.10	.05
One-Hitter		
☐ 34 Tom Seaver	.10	.05
Traded to the Reds		
☐ 35 Tom Seaver	.10	.05
New York Mets Pitcher		
☐ 36 Tom Seaver	.10	.05
Winning with the Reds		
☐ 37 Tom Seaver	.10	.05
No-Hitter		
☐ 38 Tom Seaver	.10	.05
National League Leader		
☐ 39 Tom Seaver	.10	.05
Smooth Swing		
☐ 40 Tom Seaver	.10	.05
No Decision in the Championship Series		
☐ 41 Tom Seaver	.10	.05
Injury Shortened Season		
☐ 42 Tom Seaver	.10	.05
Bouncing Back		
☐ 43 Tom Seaver	.10	.05
Eighth All-Star Appearance		
☐ 44 Tom Seaver	.10	.05

Spring Training 1982		
☐ 45 Tom Seaver	.10	.05
Back to New York		
☐ 46 Tom Seaver	.10	.05
Cincinnati Reds Pitcher		
☐ 47 Tom Seaver	.10	.05
Back in the Big Apple		
☐ 48 Tom Seaver	.10	.05
Opening Day Star		
☐ 49 Tom Seaver	.10	.05
Not Much Run Support		
☐ 50 Tom Seaver	.10	.05
A Pair of Shutouts		
☐ 51 Tom Seaver	.10	.05
4,000 Inning Mark		
☐ 52 Tom Seaver	.10	.05
One Season in New York		
☐ 53 Tom Seaver	.10	.05
Chicago Bound		
☐ 54 Tom Seaver	.15	.07
Chicago White Sox Pitcher		
☐ 55 Tom Seaver	.10	.05
Win 300		
☐ 56 Tom Seaver	.10	.05
16 Wins in 1985		
☐ 57 Tom Seaver	.10	.05
Luke Appling		
Ozzie Guillen		
Blast From the Past		
☐ 58 Tom Seaver	.10	.05
Moving Up in the		
Record Book		
☐ 59 Tom Seaver	.15	.07
LaMarr Hoyt		
Cy Young Winners		
☐ 60 Tom Seaver	.25	.11
Carlton Fisk		
Two Legends of the Game		
☐ 61 Tom Seaver	.15	.07
Placido Domingo		
Singing Praise		
☐ 62 Tom Seaver	.10	.05
300th Win Tribute		
☐ 63 Tom Seaver	.15	.07
Sarah Seaver		
Anne Seaver		
Nancy Seaver		
The Seaver Family		
☐ 64 Tom Seaver	.10	.05
20th Major League Season		
☐ 65 Tom Seaver	.15	.07
Traded to the Red Sox		
☐ 66 Tom Seaver	.10	.05
Chicago White Sox		
Career Record		
☐ 67 Tom Seaver	.15	.07
Red Sox Man		
☐ 68 Tom Seaver	.15	.07
Boston Red Sox Pitcher		
☐ 69 Tom Seaver	.10	.05
One Last Try		
☐ 70 Tom Seaver	.10	.05
Major League Records		
☐ 71 Tom Seaver	.10	.05
Lowest National League		
Career ERA		
☐ 72 Tom Seaver	.10	.05
Pitching in Comiskey Park		
☐ 73 Tom Seaver	.10	.05
273 National League Wins		
☐ 74 Tom Seaver	.10	.05
300 Win Honors		
☐ 75 Tom Seaver	.10	.05
311 Major League Wins		
☐ 76 Tom Seaver	.10	.05
41 Retired		
☐ 77 Tom Seaver	.10	.05
Championship Series 2.84 ERA		
☐ 78 Tom Seaver	.10	.05
June 1976 Age 32		
☐ 79 Tom Seaver	.10	.05
8-Time National League		
All-Star Pitcher		
☐ 80 Tom Seaver	.10	.05
Broadcasting Career		
☐ 81 Tom Seaver	.10	.05
300th Game Win Celebration		
☐ 82 Tom Seaver	.35	.16
Nolan Ryan		
☐ 83 Tom Seaver	.10	.05
4th Best ERA All-Time		
☐ 84 Tom Seaver	.10	.05
15th All-Time in Victories		
☐ 85 Tom Seaver	.35	.16
Nolan Ryan		
300 Win Club		
☐ 86 Tom Seaver#[Hall of Fame	.10	.05
☐ 87 Tom Seaver	.10	.05
Pitching in Wrigley Field		
☐ 88 Tom Seaver	.10	.05
Power Pitching		
☐ 89 Tom Seaver	.10	.05
Spring Training 1980		
☐ 90 Tom Seaver	.10	.05
Pitching in		
Riverfront Stadium, 1980		
☐ 91 Tom Seaver	.15	.07
Tom Terrific		
☐ 92 Tom Seaver	.15	.07
Super Seaver		
☐ 93 Tom Seaver	.10	.05
Top 10 All-Time		
☐ 94 Tom Seaver	.10	.05
16 Opening Day		
Starting Asignments		
☐ 95 Tom Seaver	.10	.05
3,272 Major League Strikeouts		
☐ 96 Tom Seaver	.10	.05
Six Opening Day Wins		
☐ 97 Tom Seaver	.10	.05
239 Innings Pitched in 1985		
☐ 98 Tom Seaver	.10	.05
A Day Off		
☐ 99 Tom Seaver	.10	.05
Concentration		
(You Can't Let Up)		
☐ 100 Tom Seaver	.10	.05
Velocity, Movement and Location		
☐ 101 Tom Seaver	.10	.05
Strikeout King		
☐ 102 Tom Seaver	.10	.05
The Most Important Pitch		
☐ 103 Tom Seaver	.10	.05
Cincinnati Reds Number 41		
☐ 104 Tom Seaver	.15	.07
George Thomas Seaver		
☐ 105 Tom Seaver	.10	.05
Dazzling Dean of		
the Reds' Staff		
☐ 106 Tom Seaver	.15	.07
Receives the		
Judge Emil Fuchs Award		
☐ 107 Tom Seaver	.10	.05
Boston Mound Ace		
☐ 108 Tom Seaver	.10	.05
Fly Ball to Center		
☐ 109 Tom Seaver	.10	.05
August 4, 1985		
Yankee Stadium		
☐ 110 Tom Seaver	.15	.07
Breaking Walter Johnson's		
Strikeout Record		

1992 Pacific Seaver Inserts 6

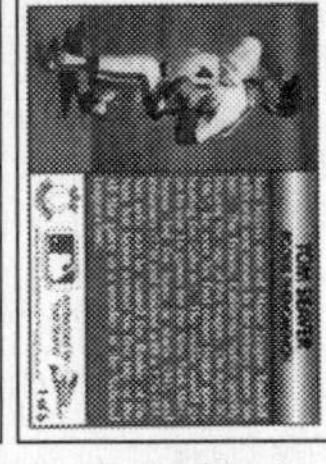

These six standard-size cards were one of two insert subsets (depicting career highlights of Tom Seaver) randomly packed in 1992 Pacific Tom Seaver 12-card foil packs. The two insert sets are numbered the same, the primary physical difference being a white border or a gold foil border on the card front. Only 3,000 of each non-gold card were produced and, as an added bonus, 1,000 of card number 1 were autographed by Seaver. According to Pacific, 10,000 of each gold card were produced. However, it seems like the numbers reported by Pacific were actually transposed when the cards were issued. There seem to be more non-gold (White) card issued than Gold cards. The six career highlight cards feature high gloss color action player photos on their fronts edged by a color stripe on the left and framed by a white (or gold) outer border. The "Tom Terrific" logo overlays the stripe at the lower left corner. The horizontal backs display a second action color photo. Seaver's name and the card subtitle appear in a graded color bar above a color-coded panel containing career highlights. The backs of the gold foil insert cards are identical to those of the regular inserts and are distinguished only by their non-glossy finish. The values for the gold and white versions are the same at this time.

	MINT	NRMT
COMPLETE SET (6)	125.00	55.00
COMMON CARD (1-6)	25.00	11.00
☐ 1 Tom Seaver	25.00	11.00
Rookie Phenomenon		
☐ 2 Tom Seaver	25.00	11.00
Miracle Mets		
☐ 3 Tom Seaver	25.00	11.00
Strikeout Record		
☐ 4 Tom Seaver	25.00	11.00
No-Hitter		
☐ 5 Tom Seaver	25.00	11.00
300th Win		
☐ 6 Tom Seaver	25.00	11.00
Hall of Fame		
☐ AU1 Tom Seaver AU	75.00	34.00

1993 Pacific Ryan 27th Season

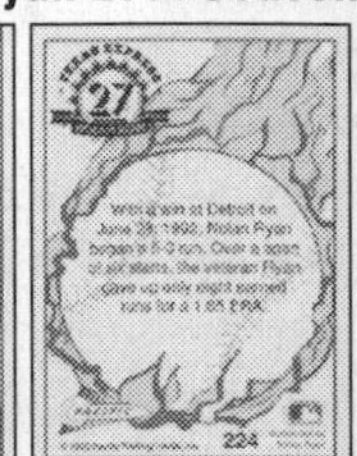

Pacific issued this 30-card set to honor Nolan Ryan being the first player in Major League Baseball history to appear in 27 seasons. The series was available in collector sets inside an attractive complete set box as well as in 25-cent five-card foil packs; the foil packs contained series I, series II, 27th Season series, and randomly inserted bonus cards. The cards measure the standard size and capture Ryan's 1992 highlights. The set features glossy color photos that are bordered in blue and red stripes. The 27th season logo appears in the lower left corner. In a flaming baseball design, the back presents career highlights. The cards are numbered on the back in continuation of the Texas Express first and second series. Beginning in mid-June, displays of Advil featuring Ryan and two-card packs appeared in stores nationwide. The two-card foil packs were available with the purchase of a bottle of 24 or more Advil Tablets or Caplets. On June 20, 1993, an offer to purchase the entire set was featured in Sunday newspapers. By mailing the Advil proof of purchase and $3.49 plus $1.50 for shipping to Pacific, the complete 30-card set could be obtained; the offer expired Dec. 31, 1993.

	MINT	NRMT
COMPLETE SET (30)	12.00	5.50
COMMON CARD (221-250)	.25	.11
☐ 221 Nolan Ryan	.25	.11
Ranger's Opening Night Pitcher		
☐ 222 Nolan Ryan	.25	.11
Slow Start in 1992		
☐ 223 Nolan Ryan	.25	.11
Still Productive		
☐ 224 Nolan Ryan	.25	.11
Getting Hot		
☐ 225 Nolan Ryan	.25	.11
Closing Strong in 1992		
☐ 226 Nolan Ryan	.25	.11
No Decision		
☐ 227 Nolan Ryan	.25	.11
No Run Support		
☐ 228 Nolan Ryan	.25	.11
Two Complete Games		
☐ 229 Nolan Ryan	.25	.11
8 2/3 Inning Shutout		
☐ 230 Nolan Ryan	.25	.11
Multiple Strikeout Games		
☐ 231 Nolan Ryan	.25	.11
Ejected		
☐ 232 Nolan Ryan	.25	.11
319 And Counting		
☐ 233 Nolan Ryan	.25	.11
Strikeout King		
☐ 234 Nolan Ryan	.25	.11
24 of 26 Seasons		
☐ 235 Nolan Ryan	.25	.11
Smile, Nolan		
☐ 236 Nolan Ryan	.25	.11
Texas Ranger Marks		
☐ 237 Nolan Ryan	.25	.11
Ranger Ace		
☐ 238 Nolan Ryan	.25	.11

Another Record		
❑ 239 Nolan Ryan	.25	.11
6th Place All-Time		
Career Innings Pitched		
❑ 240 Nolan Ryan	.25	.11
27 Games Started in 1992		
❑ 241 Nolan Ryan	.75	.35
Tom Seaver		
❑ 242 Nolan Ryan	.75	.35
Rod Carew		
Angels' Number 30 Retired		
❑ 243 Nolan Ryan	.25	.11
Angels' Nolan Ryan Night		
❑ 244 Nolan Ryan	.25	.11
Angels' Hall of Fame		
❑ 245 Nolan Ryan	.50	.23
Jimmie Reese		
Great Friends		
❑ 246 Nolan Ryan	.50	.23
Gene Autry		
Cowboys		
❑ 247 Nolan Ryan	.25	.11
Spring Training 1993		
❑ 248 Nolan Ryan	.25	.11
Smokin' Fastball		
❑ 249 Nolan Ryan	.25	.11
The Texas Express		
❑ 250 Nolan Ryan	.50	.23
Tom Seaver		
Pacific Pride		
❑ NNO Pacific Trading Cards	.15	.07
(Advertisement;		
Cover card)		

1993 Pacific Ryan Farewell McCormick

Given away to fans attending a Texas Rangers game at Arlington Stadium during Nolan Ryan Appreciation Week, this 21-card, standard-size set was produced by Pacific Trading Cards, Inc. for McCormick and Company. The fronts feature posed and action glossy photos of Ryan in various stages of his life and career. The pictures are bordered at the top and bottom in shades of coral red. His name is printed in silver vertically down the left edge of the card on a blue stripe. A logo for "1993 Nolan Ryan Farewell to a Legend" overlaps the corner of the border and the picture. The backs display Ryan's career statistics and milestones superimposed over a ghosted action shot of Ryan. The white-edged card backs have a McCormick logo in the upper left corner, a Brookshire's logo in the upper right corner, and the card number inside a flaming baseball design.

	MINT	NRMT
COMPLETE SET (21)	10.00	4.50
COMMON CARD (1-20)	.50	.23
❑ 1 Nolan Ryan	.50	.23
No-Hitter 1		
❑ 2 Nolan Ryan#[No-Hitter 2	.50	.23
❑ 3 Nolan Ryan	.50	.23
No-Hitter 3		
❑ 4 Nolan Ryan	.50	.23
No-Hitter 4		
❑ 5 Nolan Ryan	.50	.23
No-Hitter 5		
❑ 6 Nolan Ryan	.50	.23
Last Pitch No-Hitter 6		
❑ 7 Nolan Ryan	.50	.23
No-Hitter 7		
❑ 8 Nolan Ryan	.50	.23
1st Strikeout		
❑ 9 Nolan Ryan	.50	.23
1,000 Strikeout		
❑ 10 Nolan Ryan	.50	.23
2,000 Strikeout		
❑ 11 Nolan Ryan	.50	.23
3,000th Strikeout		
❑ 12 Nolan Ryan	.50	.23
Breaks Walter Johnson's Record		
❑ 13 Nolan Ryan	.50	.23
4,000 Strikeout		
❑ 14 Nolan Ryan	.50	.23
5,000 Strikeout		
❑ 15 Nolan Ryan	.50	.23
5,500 Strikeout		
❑ 16 Nolan Ryan	.50	.23
First Major League Win		
❑ 17 Nolan Ryan	.50	.23
250th Career Win		
❑ 18 Nolan Ryan	.50	.23
300th Career Win		
❑ 19 Nolan Ryan	.50	.23
Fastest Pitch Ever		
Thrown Clocked at		
100.9 MPH		
❑ 20 Nolan Ryan	.50	.23
A Lone Star Legend		
❑ NNO Title Card	.25	.11
(Manufacturer's Coupon)		

1993 Pacific Ryan Limited

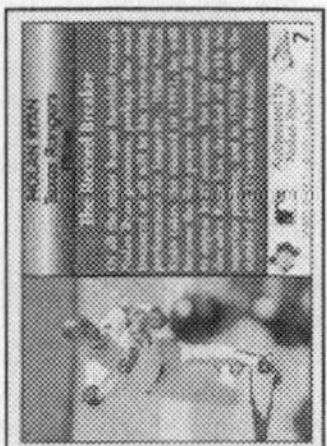

Six more cards (7-12), numbered in continuation of the 1992 set, were issued in 1993 and have a 1993 copyright notice on the card back. The card design was not significantly altered, and the backs contain the words "Limited Edition", as do the first six cards. The cards measure 2 1/2" by 3 1/2". Card numbers 7-12 were issued with gold foil borders, and the production run was 3,000 of each card. Gold foil versions of card Nos. 7-9 were given away only at the Bellevue (WA) Sports Collectors Classic IV each day of the show; card numbers 10-12 were randomly inserted in the 25-cent Changemaker packs. Although the cards are most commonly found with gold borders, white border cards have also been reported. The white border cards are valued at 20 percent of the prices below.

	MINT	NRMT
COMPLETE SET (6)	125.00	55.00
COMMON CARD (7-12)	25.00	11.00
❑ 7 Nolan Ryan	25.00	11.00
The Record Breaker		
Limited edition on back		
❑ 8 Nolan Ryan	25.00	11.00
Strikeout Leader		
Limited edition on back		
❑ 9 Nolan Ryan	25.00	11.00
Seven No-Hit Games		
Limited edition on back		
❑ 10 Nolan Ryan	25.00	11.00
Baseball Legend		
Limited edition on back		
❑ 11 Nolan Ryan	25.00	11.00
Favorite Son		
Limited edition on back		
❑ 12 Nolan Ryan	25.00	11.00
Hometown Charm		
Limited edition on back		

1993 Pacific Ryan Prism Inserts

This 20-card prism set was issued by Pacific to honor the career of Nolan Ryan. The cards were randomly inserted into 1993 Nolan Ryan 25-cent Changemaker five-card packs. The production figures were reportedly 10,000 of each card. The cards measure the standard size and feature a cut-out photo of Nolan Ryan against a prism background. His name appears at the bottom in red letters outlined in white and blue. The horizontal backs show a cut-out photo of Ryan against either a variegated blue or red panel that is bordered by a team color-coded design. Included on the panel are career highlights that correspond to the year the photo was taken. A white outer border rounds out the card back. Gold and silver versions of these sets are known as well. There is not currently enough market information to price these cards.

	MINT	NRMT
COMPLETE SET (20)	100.00	45.00
COMMON CARD (1-20)	7.50	3.40
❑ 1 Nolan Ryan	7.50	3.40
Mets - 1965		
❑ 2 Nolan Ryan	7.50	3.40
Mets - 1969		
❑ 3 Nolan Ryan	7.50	3.40
Mets - 1973		
1st No-Hitter		
❑ 4 Nolan Ryan	7.50	3.40
Angels - 1973		
1st No-Hitter		
❑ 5 Nolan Ryan	7.50	3.40
Angels - 1973		
❑ 6 Nolan Ryan	7.50	3.40
Astros - 1979		
❑ 7 Nolan Ryan	7.50	3.40
Astros - 1981		
❑ 8 Nolan Ryan	7.50	3.40
Astros - 1983		
❑ 9 Nolan Ryan	7.50	3.40
Rangers - 1988		
❑ 10 Nolan Ryan	7.50	3.40
Rangers - 1989		
5,000 Strike Outs		
❑ 11 Nolan Ryan	7.50	3.40
Rangers - 1989		
❑ 12 Nolan Ryan	7.50	3.40
Rangers - 1990		
❑ 13 Nolan Ryan	7.50	3.40
Rangers - 1990		
6th No-Hitter		
❑ 14 Nolan Ryan	7.50	3.40
Rangers - 1990		
300th Win		
❑ 15 Nolan Ryan	7.50	3.40
Rangers - 1991		
❑ 16 Nolan Ryan	7.50	3.40
Rangers - 1991		
❑ 17 Nolan Ryan	7.50	3.40
Rangers - 1991		
7th No-Hitter		
❑ 18 Nolan Ryan	7.50	3.40
Rangers - 1992		
❑ 19 Nolan Ryan	7.50	3.40
Rangers - 1992		
❑ 20 Nolan Ryan	7.50	3.40
Rangers - 1993		

1993 Pacific Spanish

Issued in two 330-card series, these 660 standard-size cards represent Pacific's first effort at a nationally distributed, MLB-licensed card set. The fronts display glossy color action photos bordered in white. Two team color-coded stripes, carrying the player's name and position, edge the pictures on the left and bottom respectively, and the team logo appears on a home plate icon at their intersection in the lower left corner. On gradated panels framed by different color edges, the horizontal backs show a color close-up photo, biography, statistics, and brief player profile. All text on both sides is in Spanish. The cards are numbered on the back, grouped alphabetically within teams, and checklisted below alphabetically according to teams in both series. Each series card numbering is alphabetical by players within teams with the teams themselves in order by team nickname. Very early in the printing, Rob Maurer (#313) was printed with, very obviously, someone else's photo on the card. This very tough card is rarely seen in the hobby and since it is so thinly traded there is no established market value. On the Third Annual Latin Night at Yankee Stadium (July 22, 1993; New York Yankees versus California Angels), four-card foil packs, featuring a title card and three player cards, were given away.

	MINT	NRMT
COMPLETE SET (660)	40.00	18.00
COMPLETE SERIES 1 (330)	25.00	11.00

COMPLETE SERIES 2 (330)	17.50	8.00
COMMON CARD (1-660)	.05	.02
☐ 1 Rafael Belliard	.05	.02
☐ 2 Sid Bream	.05	.02
☐ 3 Francisco Cabrera	.05	.02
☐ 4 Marvin Freeman	.05	.02
☐ 5 Ron Gant	.10	.05
☐ 6 Tom Glavine	.10	.05
☐ 7 Brian Hunter	.05	.02
☐ 8 David Justice	.40	.18
☐ 9 Ryan Klesko	.40	.18
☐ 10 Melvin Nieves	.10	.05
☐ 11 Deion Sanders	.40	.18
☐ 12 John Smoltz	.15	.07
☐ 13 Mark Wohlers	.10	.05
☐ 14 Brady Anderson	.15	.07
☐ 15 Glenn Davis	.05	.02
☐ 16 Mike Devereaux	.05	.02
☐ 17 Leo Gomez	.05	.02
☐ 18 Chris Hoiles	.10	.05
☐ 19 Chito Martinez	.05	.02
☐ 20 Ben McDonald	.05	.02
☐ 21 Mike Mussina	.50	.23
☐ 22 Gregg Olson	.05	.02
☐ 23 Joe Orsulak	.05	.02
☐ 24 Cal Ripken	3.00	1.35
☐ 25 David Segui	.05	.02
☐ 26 Rick Sutcliffe	.05	.02
☐ 27 Wade Boggs	.40	.18
☐ 28 Tom Brunansky	.05	.02
☐ 29 Ellis Burks	.10	.05
☐ 30 Roger Clemens	1.00	.45
☐ 31 John Dopson	.05	.02
☐ 32 John Flaherty	.05	.02
☐ 33 Mike Greenwell	.05	.02
☐ 34 Tony Pena	.05	.02
☐ 35 Carlos Quintana	.05	.02
☐ 36 Luis Rivera	.05	.02
☐ 37 Mo Vaughn	.75	.35
☐ 38 Frank Viola	.10	.05
☐ 39 Matt Young	.05	.02
☐ 40 Scott Bailes	.05	.02
☐ 41 Bert Blyleven	.10	.05
☐ 42 Chad Curtis	.05	.02
☐ 43 Gary DiSarcina	.05	.02
☐ 44 Chuck Finley	.05	.02
☐ 45 Mike Fitzgerald	.05	.02
☐ 46 Gary Gaetti	.05	.02
☐ 47 Rene Gonzales	.05	.02
☐ 48 Mark Langston	.05	.02
☐ 49 Scott Lewis	.05	.02
☐ 50 Luis Polonia	.05	.02
☐ 51 Tim Salmon	1.00	.45
☐ 52 Lee Stevens	.05	.02
☐ 53 Steve Buechele	.05	.02
☐ 54 Frank Castillo	.05	.02
☐ 55 Doug Dascenzo	.05	.02
☐ 56 Andre Dawson	.15	.07
☐ 57 Shawon Dunston	.05	.02
☐ 58 Mark Grace	.35	.16
☐ 59 Mike Morgan	.05	.02
☐ 60 Luis Salazar	.05	.02
☐ 61 Rey Sanchez	.05	.02
☐ 62 Ryne Sandberg	.75	.35
☐ 63 Dwight Smith	.05	.02
☐ 64 Jerome Walton	.05	.02
☐ 65 Rick Wilkins	.05	.02
☐ 66 Wilson Alvarez	.10	.05
☐ 67 George Bell	.05	.02
☐ 68 Joey Cora	.10	.05
☐ 69 Alex Fernandez	.10	.05
☐ 70 Carlton Fisk	.25	.11
☐ 71 Craig Grebeck	.05	.02
☐ 72 Ozzie Guillen	.05	.02
☐ 73 Jack McDowell	.05	.02
☐ 74 Scott Radinsky	.05	.02
☐ 75 Tim Raines	.10	.05
☐ 76 Bobby Thigpen	.05	.02
☐ 77 Frank Thomas	3.00	1.35
☐ 78 Robin Ventura	.10	.05
☐ 79 Tom Browning	.05	.02
☐ 80 Jacob Brumfield	.05	.02
☐ 81 Rob Dibble	.05	.02
☐ 82 Bill Doran	.05	.02
☐ 83 Billy Hatcher	.05	.02
☐ 84 Barry Larkin	.35	.16
☐ 85 Hal Morris	.10	.05
☐ 86 Joe Oliver	.05	.02
☐ 87 Jeff Reed	.05	.02
☐ 88 Jose Rijo	.05	.02
☐ 89 Bip Roberts	.05	.02
☐ 90 Chris Sabo	.05	.02
☐ 91 Sandy Alomar Jr.	.10	.05
☐ 92 Brad Arnsberg	.05	.02
☐ 93 Carlos Baerga	.10	.05
☐ 94 Albert Belle	1.00	.45
☐ 95 Felix Fermin	.05	.02
☐ 96 Mark Lewis	.05	.02
☐ 97 Kenny Lofton	1.25	.55
☐ 98 Carlos Martinez	.05	.02
☐ 99 Rod Nichols	.05	.02
☐ 100 Dave Rohde	.05	.02
☐ 101 Scott Scudder	.05	.02
☐ 102 Paul Sorrento	.05	.02
☐ 103 Mark Whiten	.05	.02
☐ 104 Mark Carreon	.05	.02
☐ 105 Milt Cuyler	.05	.02
☐ 106 Rob Deer	.05	.02
☐ 107 Cecil Fielder	.10	.05
☐ 108 Travis Fryman	.10	.05
☐ 109 Dan Gladden	.05	.02
☐ 110 Bill Gullickson	.05	.02
☐ 111 Les Lancaster	.05	.02
☐ 112 Mark Leiter	.05	.02
☐ 113 Tony Phillips	.05	.02
☐ 114 Mickey Tettleton	.05	.02
☐ 115 Alan Trammell	.15	.07
☐ 116 Lou Whitaker	.10	.05
☐ 117 Jeff Bagwell	2.00	.90
☐ 118 Craig Biggio	.15	.07
☐ 119 Joe Boever	.05	.02
☐ 120 Casey Candaele	.05	.02
☐ 121 Andujar Cedeno	.05	.02
☐ 122 Steve Finley	.10	.05
☐ 123 Luis Gonzalez	.05	.02
☐ 124 Pete Harnisch	.05	.02
☐ 125 Jimmy Jones	.05	.02
☐ 126 Mark Portugal	.05	.02
☐ 127 Rafael Ramirez	.05	.02
☐ 128 Mike Simms	.05	.02
☐ 129 Eric Yelding	.05	.02
☐ 130 Luis Aquino	.05	.02
☐ 131 Kevin Appier	.10	.05
☐ 132 Mike Boddicker	.05	.02
☐ 133 George Brett	1.50	.70
☐ 134 Tom Gordon	.05	.02
☐ 135 Mark Gubicza	.05	.02
☐ 136 David Howard	.05	.02
☐ 137 Gregg Jefferies	.10	.05
☐ 138 Wally Joyner	.10	.05
☐ 139 Brian McRae	.05	.02
☐ 140 Jeff Montgomery	.05	.02
☐ 141 Terry Shumpert	.05	.02
☐ 142 Curtis Wilkerson	.05	.02
☐ 143 Brett Butler	.10	.05
☐ 144 Eric Davis	.10	.05
☐ 145 Kevin Gross	.05	.02
☐ 146 Dave Hansen	.05	.02
☐ 147 Lenny Harris	.05	.02
☐ 148 Carlos Hernandez	.05	.02
☐ 149 Orel Hershiser	.10	.05
☐ 150 Jay Howell	.05	.02
☐ 151 Eric Karros	.10	.05
☐ 152 Ramon Martinez	.10	.05
☐ 153 Jose Offerman	.05	.02
☐ 154 Mike Sharperson	.05	.02
☐ 155 Darryl Strawberry	.10	.05
☐ 156 Jim Gantner	.05	.02
☐ 157 Darryl Hamilton	.05	.02
☐ 158 Doug Henry	.05	.02
☐ 159 John Jaha	.15	.07
☐ 160 Pat Listach	.05	.02
☐ 161 Jaime Navarro	.05	.02
☐ 162 Dave Nilsson	.10	.05
☐ 163 Jesse Orosco	.05	.02
☐ 164 Kevin Seitzer	.05	.02
☐ 165 B.J. Surhoff	.10	.05
☐ 166 Greg Vaughn	.05	.02
☐ 167 Robin Yount	.15	.07
☐ 168 Rick Aguilera	.05	.02
☐ 169 Scott Erickson	.05	.02
☐ 170 Mark Guthrie	.05	.02
☐ 171 Kent Hrbek	.10	.05
☐ 172 Chuck Knoblauch	.40	.18
☐ 173 Gene Larkin	.05	.02
☐ 174 Shane Mack	.05	.02
☐ 175 Pedro Munoz	.05	.02
☐ 176 Mike Pagliarulo	.05	.02
☐ 177 Kirby Puckett	1.50	.70
☐ 178 Kevin Tapani	.05	.02
☐ 179 Gary Wayne	.05	.02
☐ 180 Moises Alou	.10	.05
☐ 181 Brian Barnes	.05	.02
☐ 182 Archi Cianfrocco	.05	.02
☐ 183 Delino DeShields	.05	.02
☐ 184 Darrin Fletcher	.05	.02
☐ 185 Marquis Grissom	.10	.05
☐ 186 Ken Hill	.10	.05
☐ 187 Dennis Martinez	.10	.05
☐ 188 Bill Sampen	.05	.02
☐ 189 John Vander Wal	.05	.02
☐ 190 Larry Walker	.30	.14
☐ 191 Tim Wallach	.05	.02
☐ 192 Bobby Bonilla	.10	.05
☐ 193 Daryl Boston	.05	.02
☐ 194 Vince Coleman	.05	.02
☐ 195 Kevin Elster	.05	.02
☐ 196 Sid Fernandez	.05	.02
☐ 197 John Franco	.10	.05
☐ 198 Dwight Gooden	.10	.05
☐ 199 Howard Johnson	.05	.02
☐ 200 Willie Randolph	.05	.02
☐ 201 Bret Saberhagen	.10	.05
☐ 202 Dick Schofield	.05	.02
☐ 203 Pete Schourek	.05	.02
☐ 204 Greg Cadaret	.05	.02
☐ 205 John Habyan	.05	.02
☐ 206 Pat Kelly	.05	.02
☐ 207 Kevin Maas	.05	.02
☐ 208 Don Mattingly	1.50	.70
☐ 209 Matt Nokes	.05	.02
☐ 210 Melido Perez	.05	.02
☐ 211 Scott Sanderson	.05	.02
☐ 212 Andy Stankiewicz	.05	.02
☐ 213 Danny Tartabull	.05	.02
☐ 214 Randy Velarde	.05	.02
☐ 215 Bernie Williams	.60	.25
☐ 216 Harold Baines	.10	.05
☐ 217 Mike Bordick	.05	.02
☐ 218 Scott Brosius	.05	.02
☐ 219 Jerry Browne	.05	.02
☐ 220 Ron Darling	.05	.02
☐ 221 Dennis Eckersley	.15	.07
☐ 222 Rickey Henderson	.30	.14
☐ 223 Rick Honeycutt	.05	.02
☐ 224 Mark McGwire	1.50	.70
☐ 225 Ruben Sierra	.05	.02
☐ 226 Terry Steinbach	.10	.05
☐ 227 Bob Welch	.05	.02
☐ 228 Willie Wilson	.10	.05
☐ 229 Ruben Amaro	.05	.02
☐ 230 Kim Batiste	.05	.02
☐ 231 Juan Bell	.05	.02
☐ 232 Wes Chamberlain	.05	.02
☐ 233 Darren Daulton	.10	.05
☐ 234 Mariano Duncan	.05	.02
☐ 235 Lenny Dykstra	.10	.05
☐ 236 Dave Hollins	.05	.02
☐ 237 Stan Javier	.05	.02
☐ 238 John Kruk	.10	.05
☐ 239 Mickey Morandini	.05	.02
☐ 240 Terry Mulholland	.05	.02
☐ 241 Mitch Williams	.05	.02
☐ 242 Stan Belinda	.05	.02
☐ 243 Jay Bell	.10	.05
☐ 244 Carlos Garcia	.05	.02
☐ 245 Jeff King	.05	.02
☐ 246 Mike LaValliere	.05	.02
☐ 247 Lloyd McClendon	.05	.02
☐ 248 Orlando Merced	.05	.02
☐ 249 Paul Miller	.05	.02
☐ 250 Gary Redus	.05	.02
☐ 251 Don Slaught	.05	.02
☐ 252 Zane Smith	.05	.02
☐ 253 Andy Van Slyke	.05	.02
☐ 254 Tim Wakefield	.05	.02
☐ 255 Andy Benes	.10	.05
☐ 256 Dann Bilardello	.05	.02
☐ 257 Tony Gwynn	1.50	.70
☐ 258 Greg W. Harris	.05	.02
☐ 259 Darrin Jackson	.05	.02
☐ 260 Mike Maddux	.05	.02
☐ 261 Fred McGriff	.50	.23
☐ 262 Rich Rodriguez	.05	.02
☐ 263 Benito Santiago	.05	.02
☐ 264 Gary Sheffield	.25	.11
☐ 265 Kurt Stillwell	.05	.02
☐ 266 Tim Teufel	.05	.02
☐ 267 Bud Black	.05	.02
☐ 268 John Burkett	.05	.02
☐ 269 Will Clark	.40	.18
☐ 270 Royce Clayton	.10	.05
☐ 271 Bryan Hickerson	.05	.02
☐ 272 Chris James	.05	.02
☐ 273 Darren Lewis	.05	.02
☐ 274 Willie McGee	.10	.05
☐ 275 Jim McNamara	.05	.02
☐ 276 Francisco Oliveras	.05	.02
☐ 277 Robby Thompson	.05	.02
☐ 278 Matt Williams	.15	.07
☐ 279 Trevor Wilson	.05	.02
☐ 280 Bret Boone	.10	.05
☐ 281 Greg Briley	.05	.02
☐ 282 Jay Buhner	.15	.07
☐ 283 Henry Cotto	.05	.02
☐ 284 Rich DeLucia	.05	.02
☐ 285 Dave Fleming	.05	.02
☐ 286 Ken Griffey Jr.	4.00	1.80
☐ 287 Erik Hanson	.05	.02
☐ 288 Randy Johnson	.40	.18
☐ 289 Tino Martinez	.25	.11

☐ 290 Edgar Martinez	.15	.07
☐ 291 Dave Valle	.05	.02
☐ 292 Omar Vizquel	.10	.05
☐ 293 Luis Alicea	.05	.02
☐ 294 Bernard Gilkey	.10	.05
☐ 295 Felix Jose	.05	.02
☐ 296 Ray Lankford	.10	.05
☐ 297 Omar Olivares	.05	.02
☐ 298 Jose Oquendo	.05	.02
☐ 299 Tom Pagnozzi	.05	.02
☐ 300 Geronimo Pena	.05	.02
☐ 301 Gerald Perry	.05	.02
☐ 302 Ozzie Smith	.75	.35
☐ 303 Lee Smith	.10	.05
☐ 304 Bob Tewksbury	.05	.02
☐ 305 Todd Zeile	.05	.02
☐ 306 Kevin Brown	.10	.05
☐ 307 Todd Burns	.05	.02
☐ 308 Jose Canseco	.30	.14
☐ 309 Hector Fajardo	.05	.02
☐ 310 Julio Franco	.10	.05
☐ 311A Juan Gonzalez White uniform on back	2.00	.90
☐ 311B Juan Gonzalez Blue uniform on back	2.00	.90
☐ 312 Jeff Huson	.05	.02
☐ 313 Rob Maurer	.05	.02
☐ 314 Rafael Palmeiro	.15	.07
☐ 315 Dean Palmer	.10	.05
☐ 316 Ivan Rodriguez	1.25	.55
☐ 317 Nolan Ryan	3.00	1.35
☐ 318 Dickie Thon	.05	.02
☐ 319 Roberto Alomar	.50	.23
☐ 320 Derek Bell	.10	.05
☐ 321 Pat Borders	.05	.02
☐ 322 Joe Carter	.10	.05
☐ 323 Kelly Gruber	.05	.02
☐ 324 Juan Guzman	.05	.02
☐ 325 Manny Lee	.05	.02
☐ 326 Jack Morris	.10	.05
☐ 327 John Olerud	.10	.05
☐ 328 Ed Sprague	.05	.02
☐ 329 Todd Stottlemyre	.10	.05
☐ 330 Duane Ward	.05	.02
☐ 331 Steve Avery	.05	.02
☐ 332 Damon Berryhill	.05	.02
☐ 333 Jeff Blauser	.05	.02
☐ 334 Mark Lemke	.05	.02
☐ 335 Greg Maddux	2.00	.90
☐ 336 Kent Mercker	.05	.02
☐ 337 Otis Nixon	.10	.05
☐ 338 Greg Olson	.05	.02
☐ 339 Bill Pecota	.05	.02
☐ 340 Terry Pendleton	.10	.05
☐ 341 Mike Stanton	.05	.02
☐ 342 Todd Frohwirth	.05	.02
☐ 343 Tim Hulett	.05	.02
☐ 344 Mark McLemore	.05	.02
☐ 345 Luis Mercedes	.05	.02
☐ 346 Alan Mills	.05	.02
☐ 347 Sherman Obando	.05	.02
☐ 348 Jim Poole	.05	.02
☐ 349 Harold Reynolds	.10	.05
☐ 350 Arthur Rhodes	.05	.02
☐ 351 Jeff Tackett	.05	.02
☐ 352 Fernando Valenzuela	.10	.05
☐ 353 Scott Bankhead	.05	.02
☐ 354 Ivan Calderon	.05	.02
☐ 355 Scott Cooper	.05	.02
☐ 356 Danny Darwin	.05	.02
☐ 357 Scott Fletcher	.05	.02
☐ 358 Tony Fossas	.05	.02
☐ 359 Greg A. Harris	.05	.02
☐ 360 Joe Hesketh	.05	.02
☐ 361 Jose Melendez	.05	.02
☐ 362 Paul Quantrill	.05	.02
☐ 363 John Valentin	.10	.05
☐ 364 Mike Butcher	.05	.02
☐ 365 Chuck Crim	.05	.02
☐ 366 Chili Davis	.10	.05
☐ 367 Damion Easley	.05	.02
☐ 368 Steve Frey	.05	.02
☐ 369 Joe Grahe	.05	.02
☐ 370 Greg Myers	.05	.02
☐ 371 John Orton	.05	.02
☐ 372 J.T. Snow	.50	.23
☐ 373 Ron Tingley	.05	.02
☐ 374 Julio Valera	.05	.02
☐ 375 Paul Assenmacher	.05	.02
☐ 376 Jose Bautista	.05	.02
☐ 377 Jose Guzman	.05	.02
☐ 378 Greg Hibbard	.05	.02
☐ 379 Candy Maldonado	.05	.02
☐ 380 Derrick May	.05	.02
☐ 381 Dan Plesac	.05	.02
☐ 382 Tommy Shields	.05	.02
☐ 383 Sammy Sosa	.35	.16
☐ 384 Jose Vizcaino	.05	.02
☐ 385 Matt Walbeck	.05	.02
☐ 386 Ellis Burks	.10	.05
☐ 387 Roberto Hernandez	.10	.05
☐ 388 Mike Huff	.05	.02
☐ 389 Bo Jackson	.10	.05
☐ 390 Lance Johnson	.10	.05
☐ 391 Ron Karkovice	.05	.02
☐ 392 Kirk McCaskill	.05	.02
☐ 393 Donn Pall	.05	.02
☐ 394 Dan Pasqua	.05	.02
☐ 395 Steve Sax	.05	.02
☐ 396 Dave Stieb	.05	.02
☐ 397 Bobby Ayala	.05	.02
☐ 398 Tim Belcher	.05	.02
☐ 399 Jeff Branson	.05	.02
☐ 400 Cesar Hernandez	.05	.02
☐ 401 Roberto Kelly	.05	.02
☐ 402 Randy Milligan	.05	.02
☐ 403 Kevin Mitchell	.10	.05
☐ 404 Juan Samuel	.05	.02
☐ 405 Reggie Sanders	.15	.07
☐ 406 John Smiley	.05	.02
☐ 407 Dan Wilson	.25	.11
☐ 408 Mike Christopher	.05	.02
☐ 409 Dennis Cook	.05	.02
☐ 410 Alvaro Espinoza	.05	.02
☐ 411 Glenallen Hill	.05	.02
☐ 412 Reggie Jefferson	.10	.05
☐ 413 Derek Lilliquist	.05	.02
☐ 414 Jose Mesa	.05	.02
☐ 415 Charles Nagy	.10	.05
☐ 416 Junior Ortiz	.05	.02
☐ 417 Eric Plunk	.05	.02
☐ 418 Ted Power	.05	.02
☐ 419 Scott Aldred	.05	.02
☐ 420 Andy Ashby	.05	.02
☐ 421 Freddie Benavides	.05	.02
☐ 422 Dante Bichette	.15	.07
☐ 423 Willie Blair	.05	.02
☐ 424 Vinny Castilla	.25	.11
☐ 425 Jerald Clark	.05	.02
☐ 426 Alex Cole	.05	.02
☐ 427 Andres Galarraga	.25	.11
☐ 428 Joe Girardi	.05	.02
☐ 429 Charlie Hayes	.05	.02
☐ 430 Butch Henry	.05	.02
☐ 431 Darren Holmes	.05	.02
☐ 432 Dale Murphy	.25	.11
☐ 433 David Nied	.05	.02
☐ 434 Jeff Parrett	.05	.02
☐ 435 Steve Reed	.05	.02
☐ 436 Armando Reynoso	.05	.02
☐ 437 Bruce Ruffin	.05	.02
☐ 438 Bryn Smith	.05	.02
☐ 439 Jim Tatum	.05	.02
☐ 440 Eric Young	.10	.05
☐ 441 Skeeter Barnes	.05	.02
☐ 442 Tom Bolton	.05	.02
☐ 443 Kirk Gibson	.10	.05
☐ 444 Chad Kreuter	.05	.02
☐ 445 Bill Krueger	.05	.02
☐ 446 Scott Livingstone	.05	.02
☐ 447 Bob MacDonald	.05	.02
☐ 448 Mike Moore	.05	.02
☐ 449 Mike Munoz	.05	.02
☐ 450 Gary Thurman	.05	.02
☐ 451 David Wells	.05	.02
☐ 452 Alex Arias	.05	.02
☐ 453 Jack Armstrong	.05	.02
☐ 454 Bret Barberie	.05	.02
☐ 455 Ryan Bowen	.05	.02
☐ 456 Cris Carpenter	.05	.02
☐ 457 Chuck Carr	.05	.02
☐ 458 Jeff Conine	.10	.05
☐ 459 Steve Decker	.05	.02
☐ 460 Orestes Destrade	.05	.02
☐ 461 Monty Fariss	.05	.02
☐ 462 Junior Felix	.05	.02
☐ 463 Bryan Harvey	.10	.05
☐ 464 Trevor Hoffman	.25	.11
☐ 465 Charlie Hough	.05	.02
☐ 466 Dave Magadan	.05	.02
☐ 467 Bob McClure	.05	.02
☐ 468 Rob Natal	.05	.02
☐ 469 Scott Pose	.05	.02
☐ 470 Rich Renteria	.05	.02
☐ 471 Benito Santiago	.10	.05
☐ 472 Matt Turner	.05	.02
☐ 473 Walt Weiss	.05	.02
☐ 474 Eric Anthony	.05	.02
☐ 475 Chris Donnels	.05	.02
☐ 476 Doug Drabek	.10	.05
☐ 477 Xavier Hernandez	.05	.02
☐ 478 Doug Jones	.05	.02
☐ 479 Darryl Kile	.10	.05
☐ 480 Scott Servais	.05	.02
☐ 481 Greg Swindell	.05	.02
☐ 482 Eddie Taubensee	.05	.02
☐ 483 Jose Uribe	.05	.02
☐ 484 Brian Williams	.05	.02
☐ 485 Billy Brewer	.05	.02
☐ 486 David Cone	.10	.05
☐ 487 Greg Gagne	.05	.02
☐ 488 Phil Hiatt	.05	.02
☐ 489 Jose Lind	.05	.02
☐ 490 Brent Mayne	.05	.02
☐ 491 Kevin McReynolds	.05	.02
☐ 492 Keith Miller	.05	.02
☐ 493 Hipolito Pichardo	.05	.02
☐ 494 Harvey Pulliam	.05	.02
☐ 495 Rico Rossy	.05	.02
☐ 496 Pedro Astacio	.10	.05
☐ 497 Tom Candiotti	.05	.02
☐ 498 Tom Goodwin	.05	.02
☐ 499 Jim Gott	.05	.02
☐ 500 Pedro Martinez	.25	.11
☐ 501 Roger McDowell	.05	.02
☐ 502 Mike Piazza	4.00	1.80
☐ 503 Jody Reed	.05	.02
☐ 504 Rick Trlicek	.05	.02
☐ 505 Mitch Webster	.05	.02
☐ 506 Steve Wilson	.05	.02
☐ 507 James Austin	.05	.02
☐ 508 Ricky Bones	.05	.02
☐ 509 Alex Diaz	.05	.02
☐ 510 Mike Fetters	.05	.02
☐ 511 Teddy Higuera	.05	.02
☐ 512 Graeme Lloyd	.05	.02
☐ 513 Carlos Maldonado	.05	.02
☐ 514 Josias Manzanillo	.05	.02
☐ 515 Kevin Reimer	.05	.02
☐ 516 Bill Spiers	.05	.02
☐ 517 Bill Wegman	.05	.02
☐ 518 Willie Banks	.05	.02
☐ 519 J.T. Bruett	.05	.02
☐ 520 Brian Harper	.05	.02
☐ 521 Terry Jorgensen	.05	.02
☐ 522 Scott Leius	.05	.02
☐ 523 Pat Mahomes	.05	.02
☐ 524 Dave McCarty	.05	.02
☐ 525 Jeff Reboulet	.05	.02
☐ 526 Mike Trombley	.05	.02
☐ 527 Carl Willis	.05	.02
☐ 528 Dave Winfield	.30	.14
☐ 529 Sean Berry	.05	.02
☐ 530 Frank Bolick	.05	.02
☐ 531 Kent Bottenfield	.05	.02
☐ 532 Wilfredo Cordero	.05	.02
☐ 533 Jeff Fassero	.10	.05
☐ 534 Tim Laker	.05	.02
☐ 535 Mike Lansing	.15	.07
☐ 536 Chris Nabholz	.05	.02
☐ 537 Mel Rojas	.05	.02
☐ 538 John Wetteland	.10	.05
☐ 539 Ted Wood	.05	.02
☐ 540 Mike Draper	.05	.02
☐ 541 Tony Fernandez	.05	.02
☐ 542 Todd Hundley	.10	.05
☐ 543 Jeff Innis	.05	.02
☐ 544 Jeff McKnight	.05	.02
☐ 545 Eddie Murray	.75	.35
☐ 546 Charlie O'Brien	.05	.02
☐ 547 Frank Tanana	.05	.02
☐ 548 Ryan Thompson	.05	.02
☐ 549 Chico Walker	.05	.02
☐ 550 Anthony Young	.05	.02
☐ 551 Jim Abbott	.10	.05
☐ 552 Wade Boggs	.50	.23
☐ 553 Steve Farr	.05	.02
☐ 554 Neal Heaton	.05	.02
☐ 555 Steve Howe	.05	.02
☐ 556 Dion James	.05	.02
☐ 557 Scott Kamieniecki	.05	.02
☐ 558 Jimmy Key	.10	.05
☐ 559 Jim Leyritz	.05	.02
☐ 560 Paul O'Neill	.10	.05
☐ 561 Spike Owen	.05	.02
☐ 562 Lance Blankenship	.05	.02
☐ 563 Joe Boever	.05	.02
☐ 564 Storm Davis	.05	.02
☐ 565 Kelly Downs	.05	.02
☐ 566 Eric Fox	.05	.02
☐ 567 Rich Gossage	.15	.07
☐ 568 Dave Henderson	.05	.02
☐ 569 Shawn Hillegas	.05	.02
☐ 570 Mike Mohler	.05	.02
☐ 571 Troy Neel	.05	.02
☐ 572 Dale Sveum	.05	.02
☐ 573 Larry Andersen	.05	.02
☐ 574 Bob Ayrault	.05	.02
☐ 575 Jose DeLeon	.05	.02
☐ 576 Jim Eisenreich	.10	.05
☐ 577 Pete Incaviglia	.05	.02

☐ 578 Danny Jackson	.05	.02
☐ 579 Ricky Jordan	.05	.02
☐ 580 Ben Rivera	.05	.02
☐ 581 Curt Schilling	.10	.05
☐ 582 Milt Thompson	.05	.02
☐ 583 David West	.05	.02
☐ 584 John Candelaria	.05	.02
☐ 585 Steve Cooke	.05	.02
☐ 586 Tom Foley	.05	.02
☐ 587 Al Martin	.05	.02
☐ 588 Blas Minor	.05	.02
☐ 589 Dennis Moeller	.05	.02
☐ 590 Denny Neagle	.10	.05
☐ 591 Tom Prince	.05	.02
☐ 592 Randy Tomlin	.05	.02
☐ 593 Bob Walk	.05	.02
☐ 594 Kevin Young	.05	.02
☐ 595 Pat Gomez	.05	.02
☐ 596 Ricky Gutierrez	.05	.02
☐ 597 Gene Harris	.05	.02
☐ 598 Jeremy Hernandez	.05	.02
☐ 599 Phil Plantier	.05	.02
☐ 600 Tim Scott	.05	.02
☐ 601 Frank Seminara	.05	.02
☐ 602 Darrell Sherman	.05	.02
☐ 603 Craig Shipley	.05	.02
☐ 604 Guillermo Velasquez	.05	.02
☐ 605 Dan Walters	.05	.02
☐ 606 Mike Benjamin	.05	.02
☐ 607 Barry Bonds	1.00	.45
☐ 608 Jeff Brantley	.05	.02
☐ 609 Dave Burba	.05	.02
☐ 610 Craig Colbert	.05	.02
☐ 611 Mike Jackson	.05	.02
☐ 612 Kirt Manwaring	.05	.02
☐ 613 Dave Martinez	.05	.02
☐ 614 Dave Righetti	.05	.02
☐ 615 Kevin Rogers	.05	.02
☐ 616 Bill Swift	.05	.02
☐ 617 Rich Amaral	.05	.02
☐ 618 Mike Blowers	.05	.02
☐ 619 Chris Bosio	.05	.02
☐ 620 Norm Charlton	.05	.02
☐ 621 John Cummings	.05	.02
☐ 622 Mike Felder	.05	.02
☐ 623 Bill Haselman	.05	.02
☐ 624 Tim Leary	.05	.02
☐ 625 Pete O'Brien	.05	.02
☐ 626 Russ Swan	.05	.02
☐ 627 Fernando Vina	.05	.02
☐ 628 Rene Arocha	.05	.02
☐ 629 Rod Brewer	.05	.02
☐ 630 Ozzie Canseco	.05	.02
☐ 631 Rheal Cormier	.05	.02
☐ 632 Brian Jordan	.15	.07
☐ 633 Joe Magrane	.05	.02
☐ 634 Donovan Osborne	.05	.02
☐ 635 Mike Perez	.05	.02
☐ 636 Stan Royer	.05	.02
☐ 637 Hector Villanueva	.05	.02
☐ 638 Tracy Woodson	.05	.02
☐ 639 Benji Gil	.05	.02
☐ 640 Tom Henke	.10	.05
☐ 641 David Hulse	.05	.02
☐ 642 Charlie Leibrandt	.05	.02
☐ 643 Robb Nen	.05	.02
☐ 644 Dan Peltier	.05	.02
☐ 645 Billy Ripken	.05	.02
☐ 646 Kenny Rogers	.05	.02
☐ 647 John Russell	.05	.02
☐ 648 Dan Smith	.05	.02
☐ 649 Matt Whiteside	.05	.02
☐ 650 William Canate	.05	.02
☐ 651 Darnell Coles	.05	.02
☐ 652 Al Leiter	.10	.05
☐ 653 Domingo Martinez	.05	.02
☐ 654 Paul Molitor	.50	.23
☐ 655 Luis Sojo	.05	.02
☐ 656 Dave Stewart	.10	.05
☐ 657 Mike Timlin	.05	.02
☐ 658 Turner Ward	.05	.02
☐ 659 Devon White	.10	.05
☐ 660 Eddie Zosky	.05	.02

1993 Pacific Beisbol Amigos

Randomly inserted in 1993 Pacific Spanish second series foil packs, this 30-card standard-size set by Pacific features Hispanic baseball players. The portrait style photos are overlaid on a baseball motif background and edged in white. Across the bottom edge is a diamond-shaped logo for Beisbol Amigos 1993 followed by the players' names pictured on the card. With the exception of the first, all the cards in the set carry photos of two or more players. The horizontal backs are edged in white with a gray marbleized background and list players' career highlights.

	MINT	NRMT
COMPLETE SET (30)	50.00	22.00
COMMON CARD (1-30)	1.00	.45
☐ 1 Edgar Martinez	3.00	1.35
☐ 2 Luis Polonia Stan Javier	1.00	.45
☐ 3 George Bell Julio Franco	1.00	.45
☐ 4 Ozzie Guillen Ivan Rodriguez	4.00	1.80
☐ 5 Carlos Baerga Sandy Alomar Jr.	2.00	.90
☐ 6 Intercambio Extranjero Sandy Alomar Jr. Alvaro Espinoza Paul Sorrento Carlos Baerga Felix Fermin Junior Ortiz Jose Mesa Carlos Martinez	2.00	.90
☐ 7 Sandy Alomar Jr. Roberto Alomar	4.00	1.80
☐ 8 Jose Lind Felix Jose	1.00	.45
☐ 9 Ricky Bones Jaime Navarro	1.00	.45
☐ 10 Jamie Navarro Jesse Orosco	1.00	.45
☐ 11 Tino Martinez Edgar Martinez	2.50	1.10
☐ 12 Juan Gonzalez Ivan Rodriguez	10.00	4.50
☐ 13 Juan Gonzalez Julio Franco	6.00	2.70
☐ 14 Julio Franco Jose Canseco Rafael Palmeiro	6.00	2.70
☐ 15 Juan Gonzalez Jose Canseco	12.50	5.50
☐ 16 Ivan Rodriguez Benji Gil	2.50	1.10
☐ 17 Jose Guzman Frank Castillo	1.00	.45
☐ 18 Rey Sanchez Jose Vizcaino	1.00	.45
☐ 19 Derrick May Sammy Sosa	2.50	1.10
☐ 20 Sammy Sosa UER Candy Maldonado Sammy is from Dominican Republic not Puerto Rico	2.50	1.10
☐ 21 Jose Rijo Juan Samuel	1.00	.45
☐ 22 Freddie Benavides Andres Galarraga	1.50	.70
☐ 23 Guillermo Velasquez Benito Santiago	1.00	.45
☐ 24 Luis Gonzalez Andujar Cedeno	1.00	.45
☐ 25 Wilfredo Cordero Dennis Martinez	1.50	.70
☐ 26 Moises Alou Wilfredo Cordero	1.50	.70
☐ 27 Ozzie Canseco Jose Canseco	2.50	1.10
☐ 28 Jose Oquendo Luis Alicea	1.00	.45
☐ 29 Luis Alicea Rene Arocha	1.00	.45
☐ 30 Geronimo Pena Luis Alicea	1.00	.45

1993 Pacific Spanish Gold Estrellas

Randomly inserted Spanish first series foil packs, this 20-card standard-size set features the top Latin players at each position. Just 10,000 complete sets were produced for insertion. The fronts display color action player photos within gold foil borders. All the text on this set is in Spanish. The words "Estrellas De Beisbol" (Stars of Baseball) appears vertically to the left of the picture in a variegated blue, purple, and red stripe. The player's name appears at the bottom. The backs are diagonally oriented and carry career hightlights against a red, white, and blue background.

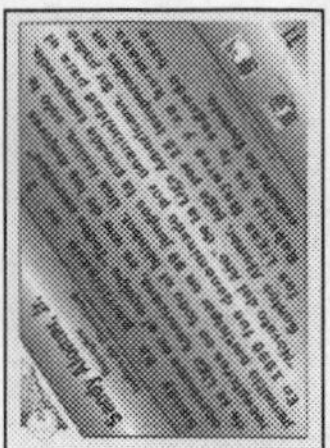

	MINT	NRMT
COMPLETE SET (20)	40.00	18.00
COMMON CARD (1-20)	1.00	.45
☐ 1 Moises Alou	1.50	.70
☐ 2 Bobby Bonilla	2.00	.90
☐ 3 Tony Fernandez	1.00	.45
☐ 4 Felix Jose	1.00	.45
☐ 5 Dennis Martinez	1.50	.70
☐ 6 Orlando Merced	1.00	.45
☐ 7 Jose Oquendo	1.00	.45
☐ 8 Geronimo Pena	1.00	.45
☐ 9 Jose Rijo	1.00	.45
☐ 10 Benito Santiago	1.00	.45
☐ 11 Sandy Alomar Jr.	1.50	.70
☐ 12 Carlos Baerga	1.50	.70
☐ 13 Jose Canseco	6.00	2.70
☐ 14 Juan Gonzalez	10.00	4.50
☐ 15 Juan Guzman	1.50	.70
☐ 16 Edgar Martinez	5.00	2.20
☐ 17 Rafael Palmeiro	7.50	3.40
☐ 18 Ruben Sierra	1.00	.45
☐ 19 Danny Tartabull	1.00	.45
☐ 20 Omar Vizquel	1.50	.70

1993 Pacific Jugadores Calientes

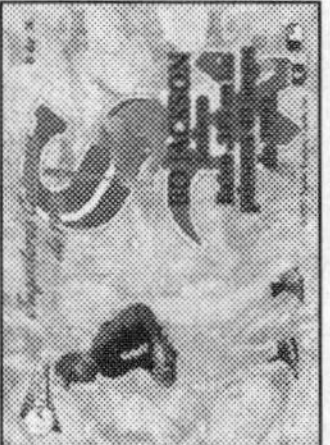

Randomly inserted in 1993 Pacific Spanish second series foil packs,This 36-card standard-size set by Pacific is titled "Jugadores Calientes" and features cut-out action photos of the players over a borderless, prismatic background. The player's name is printed on the lower edge in bold shadowed lettering. The horizontal backs with gray marbleized background carry a close-up, cut-out picture on the left. The player's name, position, and a career highlight overlay on a ghosted logo of his team with a ghosted action photo. The cards are numbered on the back and are arranged alphabetically according to the American (1-18) and National (19-36) Leagues.

	MINT	NRMT
COMPLETE SET (36)	175.00	80.00
COMMON CARD (1-36)	1.50	.70
☐ 1 Rich Amaral	1.50	.70
☐ 2 George Brett	15.00	6.75
☐ 3 Jay Buhner	4.00	1.80
☐ 4 Roger Clemens	10.00	4.50
☐ 5 Kirk Gibson	2.50	1.10
☐ 6 Juan Gonzalez	15.00	6.75
☐ 7 Ken Griffey Jr.	30.00	13.50
☐ 8 Bo Jackson	2.50	1.10
☐ 9 Kenny Lofton	10.00	4.50
☐ 10 Mark McGwire	12.50	5.50
☐ 11 Sherman Obando	1.50	.70
☐ 12 John Olerud	2.50	1.10
☐ 13 Carlos Quintana	1.50	.70
☐ 14 Ivan Rodriguez	7.50	3.40

☐ 15 Nolan Ryan	25.00	11.00
☐ 16 J.T. Snow	6.00	2.70
☐ 17 Fernando Valenzuela	2.50	1.10
☐ 18 Dave Winfield	6.00	2.70
☐ 19 Moises Alou	2.50	1.10
☐ 20 Jeff Bagwell	15.00	6.75
☐ 21 Barry Bonds	6.00	2.70
☐ 22 Bobby Bonilla	2.50	1.10
☐ 23 Vinny Castilla	4.00	1.80
☐ 24 Andujar Cedeno	1.50	.70
☐ 25 Orestes Destrade	1.50	.70
☐ 26 Andres Galarraga	6.00	2.70
☐ 27 Mark Grace	6.00	2.70
☐ 28 Tony Gwynn	12.00	5.50
☐ 29 Roberto Kelly	1.50	.70
☐ 30 John Kruk	2.50	1.10
☐ 31 Dave Magadan	1.50	.70
☐ 32 Derrick May	1.50	.70
☐ 33 Orlando Merced	1.50	.70
☐ 34 Mike Piazza	25.00	11.00
☐ 35 Armando Reynoso	1.50	.70
☐ 36 Jose Vizcaino	1.50	.70

1993 Pacific Spanish Prism Inserts

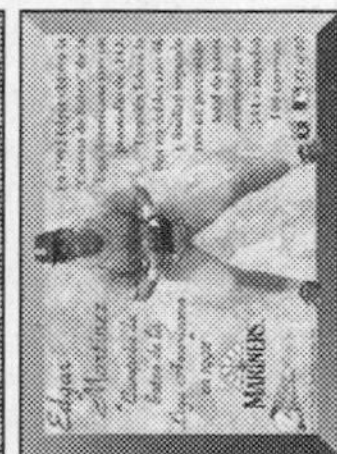

Randomly inserted into Spanish series I foil packs, this 20-card standard-size set highlights top Latin players in Major League Baseball. Ten thousand of these sets were produced for insertion. The fronts display color cut-out player photos against a prism background. The player's name appears below the picture in team color-coded block letters. The backs carry cut-out close-up photos against a marbleized background. The background and borders are team color-coded. Career highlights are featured in Spanish on either side of the picture.

	MINT	NRMT
COMPLETE SET (20)	100.00	45.00
COMMON CARD (1-20)	3.00	1.35
☐ 1 Francisco Cabrera	3.00	1.35
☐ 2 Jose Lind	3.00	1.35
☐ 3 Dennis Martinez	4.00	1.80
☐ 4 Ramon Martinez	4.00	1.80
☐ 5 Jose Rijo	3.00	1.35
☐ 6 Benito Santiago	3.00	1.35
☐ 7 Roberto Alomar	10.00	4.50
☐ 8 Sandy Alomar Jr.	5.00	2.20
☐ 9 Carlos Baerga	4.00	1.80
☐ 10 George Bell	3.00	1.35
☐ 11 Jose Canseco	8.00	3.60
☐ 12 Alex Fernandez	4.00	1.80
☐ 13 Julio Franco	4.00	1.80
☐ 14 Juan Gonzalez	15.00	6.75
☐ 15 Ozzie Guillen	4.00	1.80
☐ 16 Teddy Higuera	3.00	1.35
☐ 17 Edgar Martinez	7.50	3.40
☐ 18 Hipolito Pichardo	3.00	1.35
☐ 19 Luis Polonia	3.00	1.35
☐ 20 Ivan Rodriguez	12.50	5.50

1994 Pacific Promos

Measuring the standard size, these eight promo cards were issued to show the design of the forthcoming 1994 Pacific Crown Collection set. The cards were given away at the Super Bowl Card Show in Atlanta, to Pacific's master hobby lists of dealers and writers, and used as sales samples. The production run was reportedly approximately 10,000 sets. The fronts feature full-bleed color action player photos, except at the bottom where a gold foil stripe separates the picture from a marbleized team color-coded stripe. The disclaimer "For Promotional Use Only" is stamped diagonally in black lettering across both sides of the card. The cards are arranged alphabetically and numbered on the back with a "P" prefix.

	MINT	NRMT
COMPLETE SET (8)	10.00	4.50
COMMON CARD (P1-P8)	.25	.11
☐ P1 Carlos Baerga	.25	.11
☐ P2 Joe Carter	.50	.23
☐ P3 Juan Gonzalez	1.50	.70
☐ P4 Ken Griffey Jr.	3.00	1.35
☐ P5 Greg Maddux	1.75	.80
☐ P6 Mike Piazza	2.50	1.10
☐ P7 Tim Salmon	.75	.35
☐ P8 Frank Thomas	3.00	1.35

1994 Pacific

The 660 standard-size cards comprising this set feature color player action shots on their fronts that are borderless, except at the bottom, where a team color-coded marbleized border set off by a gold-foil line carries the team color-coded player's name. The set's gold-foil-stamped crown logo rests at the lower left. The back carries another color player action photo that is bordered only at the bottom, where the photo appears "torn away," revealing the gray marbleized area that carries the player's name, biography in both English and Spanish, statistics, and a ghosted team logo. The cards are numbered on the back, grouped alphabetically within teams. The set closes with an Award Winners subset (655-660). There are no key Rookie Cards in this set.

	MINT	NRMT
COMPLETE SET (660)	30.00	13.50
COMMON CARD (1-660)	.10	.05
COMP.CHECKLIST SET (6)	2.00	.90
COMMON CHECKLIST	.35	.16
☐ 1 Steve Avery	.10	.05
☐ 2 Steve Bedrosian	.10	.05
☐ 3 Damon Berryhill	.10	.05
☐ 4 Jeff Blauser	.10	.05
☐ 5 Sid Bream	.10	.05
☐ 6 Francisco Cabrera	.10	.05
☐ 7 Ramon Caraballo	.10	.05
☐ 8 Ron Gant	.20	.09
☐ 9 Tom Glavine	.30	.14
☐ 10 Chipper Jones	1.25	.55
☐ 11 Dave Justice	.40	.18
☐ 12 Ryan Klesko	.30	.14
☐ 13 Mark Lemke	.10	.05
☐ 14 Javier Lopez	.30	.14
☐ 15 Greg Maddux	1.25	.55
☐ 16 Fred McGriff	.30	.14
☐ 17 Greg McMichael	.10	.05
☐ 18 Kent Mercker	.10	.05
☐ 19 Otis Nixon	.20	.09
☐ 20 Terry Pendleton	.20	.09
☐ 21 Deion Sanders	.40	.18
☐ 22 John Smoltz	.30	.14
☐ 23 Tony Tarasco	.10	.05
☐ 24 Manny Alexander	.10	.05
☐ 25 Brady Anderson	.30	.14
☐ 26 Harold Baines	.20	.09
☐ 27 Damon Buford	.10	.05
☐ 28 Paul Carey	.10	.05
☐ 29 Mike Devereaux	.10	.05
☐ 30 Todd Frohwirth	.10	.05
☐ 31 Leo Gomez	.10	.05
☐ 32 Jeffrey Hammonds	.20	.09
☐ 33 Chris Hoiles	.10	.05
☐ 34 Tim Hulett	.10	.05
☐ 35 Ben McDonald	.10	.05
☐ 36 Mark McLemore	.10	.05
☐ 37 Alan Mills	.10	.05
☐ 38 Mike Mussina	.40	.18
☐ 39 Sherman Obando	.10	.05
☐ 40 Gregg Olson	.10	.05
☐ 41 Mike Pagliarulo	.10	.05
☐ 42 Jim Poole	.10	.05
☐ 43 Harold Reynolds	.10	.05
☐ 44 Cal Ripken	1.50	.70
☐ 45 David Segui	.10	.05
☐ 46 Fernando Valenzuela	.20	.09
☐ 47 Jack Voigt	.10	.05
☐ 48 Scott Bankhead	.10	.05
☐ 49 Roger Clemens	.75	.35
☐ 50 Scott Cooper	.10	.05
☐ 51 Danny Darwin	.10	.05
☐ 52 Andre Dawson	.30	.14
☐ 53 John Dopson	.10	.05
☐ 54 Scott Fletcher	.10	.05
☐ 55 Tony Fossas	.10	.05
☐ 56 Mike Greenwell	.10	.05
☐ 57 Billy Hatcher	.10	.05
☐ 58 Jeff McNeely	.10	.05
☐ 59 Jose Melendez	.10	.05
☐ 60 Tim Naehring	.10	.05
☐ 61 Tony Pena	.10	.05
☐ 62 Carlos Quintana	.10	.05
☐ 63 Paul Quantrill	.10	.05
☐ 64 Luis Rivera	.10	.05
☐ 65 Jeff Russell	.10	.05
☐ 66 Aaron Sele	.10	.05
☐ 67 John Valentin	.20	.09
☐ 68 Mo Vaughn	.50	.23
☐ 69 Frank Viola	.10	.05
☐ 70 Bob Zupcic	.10	.05
☐ 71 Mike Butcher	.10	.05
☐ 72 Rod Correia	.10	.05
☐ 73 Chad Curtis	.10	.05
☐ 74 Chili Davis	.20	.09
☐ 75 Gary DiSarcina	.10	.05
☐ 76 Damion Easley	.10	.05
☐ 77 John Farrell	.10	.05
☐ 78 Chuck Finley	.10	.05
☐ 79 Joe Grahe	.10	.05
☐ 80 Stan Javier	.10	.05
☐ 81 Mark Langston	.10	.05
☐ 82 Phil Leftwich	.10	.05
☐ 83 Torey Lovullo	.10	.05
☐ 84 Joe Magrane	.10	.05
☐ 85 Greg Myers	.10	.05
☐ 86 Eduardo Perez	.10	.05
☐ 87 Luis Polonia	.10	.05
☐ 88 Tim Salmon	.40	.18
☐ 89 J.T. Snow	.20	.09
☐ 90 Kurt Stillwell	.10	.05
☐ 91 Ron Tingley	.10	.05
☐ 92 Chris Turner	.10	.05
☐ 93 Julio Valera	.10	.05
☐ 94 Jose Bautista	.10	.05
☐ 95 Shawn Boskie	.10	.05
☐ 96 Steve Buechele	.10	.05
☐ 97 Frank Castillo	.10	.05
☐ 98 Mark Grace UER (stats have 98 home runs in 1993; should be 14)	.30	.14
☐ 99 Jose Guzman	.10	.05
☐ 100 Mike Harkey	.10	.05
☐ 101 Greg Hibbard	.10	.05
☐ 102 Doug Jennings	.10	.05
☐ 103 Derrick May	.10	.05
☐ 104 Mike Morgan	.10	.05
☐ 105 Randy Myers	.10	.05
☐ 106 Karl Rhodes	.10	.05
☐ 107 Kevin Roberson	.10	.05
☐ 108 Rey Sanchez	.10	.05
☐ 109 Ryne Sandberg	.50	.23
☐ 110 Tommy Shields	.10	.05
☐ 111 Dwight Smith	.10	.05
☐ 112 Sammy Sosa	.40	.18
☐ 113 Jose Vizcaino	.10	.05
☐ 114 Turk Wendell	.10	.05
☐ 115 Rick Wilkins	.10	.05
☐ 116 Willie Wilson	.10	.05
☐ 117 Eduardo Zambrano	.10	.05
☐ 118 Wilson Alvarez	.20	.09
☐ 119 Tim Belcher	.10	.05
☐ 120 Jason Bere	.10	.05
☐ 121 Rodney Bolton	.10	.05
☐ 122 Ellis Burks	.20	.09
☐ 123 Joey Cora	.20	.09
☐ 124 Alex Fernandez	.20	.09
☐ 125 Ozzie Guillen	.10	.05
☐ 126 Craig Grebeck	.10	.05
☐ 127 Roberto Hernandez	.20	.09
☐ 128 Bo Jackson	.20	.09
☐ 129 Lance Johnson	.10	.05
☐ 130 Ron Karkovice	.10	.05
☐ 131 Mike LaValliere	.10	.05

☐ 132 Norberto Martin .10 .05
☐ 133 Kirk McCaskill .10 .05
☐ 134 Jack McDowell .10 .05
☐ 135 Scott Radinsky .10 .05
☐ 136 Tim Raines .10 .05
☐ 137 Steve Sax .10 .05
☐ 138 Frank Thomas 1.50 .70
☐ 139 Dan Pasqua .10 .05
☐ 140 Robin Ventura .20 .09
☐ 141 Jeff Branson .10 .05
☐ 142 Tom Browning .10 .05
☐ 143 Jacob Brumfield .10 .05
☐ 144 Tim Costo .10 .05
☐ 145 Rob Dibble .10 .05
☐ 146 Brian Dorsett .10 .05
☐ 147 Steve Foster .10 .05
☐ 148 Cesar Hernandez .10 .05
☐ 149 Roberto Kelly .10 .05
☐ 150 Barry Larkin .30 .14
☐ 151 Larry Luebbers .10 .05
☐ 152 Kevin Mitchell .10 .05
☐ 153 Joe Oliver .10 .05
☐ 154 Tim Pugh .10 .05
☐ 155 Jeff Reardon .20 .09
☐ 156 Jose Rijo .10 .05
☐ 157 Bip Roberts .10 .05
☐ 158 Chris Sabo .10 .05
☐ 159 Juan Samuel .10 .05
☐ 160 Reggie Sanders .10 .05
☐ 161 John Smiley .10 .05
☐ 162 Jerry Spradlin .10 .05
☐ 163 Gary Varsho .10 .05
☐ 164 Sandy Alomar Jr. .20 .09
☐ 165 Albert Belle .50 .23
☐ 166 Carlos Baerga .20 .09
☐ 167 Mark Clark .10 .05
☐ 168 Alvaro Espinoza .10 .05
☐ 169 Felix Fermin .10 .05
☐ 170 Reggie Jefferson .20 .09
☐ 171 Wayne Kirby .10 .05
☐ 172 Tom Kramer .10 .05
☐ 173 Kenny Lofton .50 .23
☐ 174 Jesse Levis .10 .05
☐ 175 Candy Maldonado .10 .05
☐ 176 Carlos Martinez .10 .05
☐ 177 Jose Mesa .20 .09
☐ 178 Jeff Mutis .10 .05
☐ 179 Charles Nagy .20 .09
☐ 180 Bob Ojeda .10 .05
☐ 181 Junior Ortiz .10 .05
☐ 182 Eric Plunk .10 .05
☐ 183 Manny Ramirez .50 .23
☐ 184 Paul Sorrento .10 .05
☐ 185 Jeff Treadway .10 .05
☐ 186 Bill Wertz .10 .05
☐ 187 Freddie Benavides .10 .05
☐ 188 Dante Bichette .30 .14
☐ 189 Willie Blair .10 .05
☐ 190 Daryl Boston .10 .05
☐ 191 Pedro Castellano .10 .05
☐ 192 Vinny Castilla .30 .14
☐ 193 Jerald Clark .10 .05
☐ 194 Alex Cole .10 .05
☐ 195 Andres Galarraga .30 .14
☐ 196 Joe Girardi .10 .05
☐ 197 Charlie Hayes .10 .05
☐ 198 Darren Holmes .10 .05
☐ 199 Chris Jones .10 .05
☐ 200 Curt Leskanic .10 .05
☐ 201 Roberto Mejia .10 .05
☐ 202 David Nied .10 .05
☐ 203 J. Owens .10 .05
☐ 204 Steve Reed .10 .05
☐ 205 Armando Reynoso .10 .05
☐ 206 Bruce Ruffin .10 .05
☐ 207 Keith Shepherd .10 .05
☐ 208 Jim Tatum .10 .05
☐ 209 Eric Young .20 .09
☐ 210 Skeeter Barnes .10 .05
☐ 211 Danny Bautista .10 .05
☐ 212 Tom Bolton .10 .05
☐ 213 Eric Davis .20 .09
☐ 214 Storm Davis .10 .05
☐ 215 Cecil Fielder .20 .09
☐ 216 Travis Fryman .20 .09
☐ 217 Kirk Gibson .20 .09
☐ 218 Dan Gladden .10 .05
☐ 219 John Doherty .10 .05
☐ 220 Chris Gomez .10 .05
☐ 221 David Haas .10 .05
☐ 222 Bill Krueger .10 .05
☐ 223 Chad Kreuter .10 .05
☐ 224 Mark Leiter .10 .05
☐ 225 Bob MacDonald .10 .05
☐ 226 Mike Moore .10 .05
☐ 227 Tony Phillips .10 .05
☐ 228 Rich Rowland .10 .05
☐ 229 Mickey Tettleton .10 .05
☐ 230 Alan Trammell .30 .14
☐ 231 David Wells .10 .05
☐ 232 Lou Whitaker .20 .09
☐ 233 Luis Aquino .10 .05
☐ 234 Alex Arias .10 .05
☐ 235 Jack Armstrong .10 .05
☐ 236 Ryan Bowen .10 .05
☐ 237 Chuck Carr .10 .05
☐ 238 Matias Carrillo .10 .05
☐ 239 Jeff Conine .20 .09
☐ 240 Henry Cotto .10 .05
☐ 241 Orestes Destrade .10 .05
☐ 242 Chris Hammond .10 .05
☐ 243 Bryan Harvey .10 .05
☐ 244 Charlie Hough .10 .05
☐ 245 Richie Lewis .10 .05
☐ 246 Mitch Lyden .10 .05
☐ 247 Dave Magadan .10 .05
☐ 248 Bob Natal .10 .05
☐ 249 Benito Santiago .10 .05
☐ 250 Gary Sheffield .40 .18
☐ 251 Matt Turner .10 .05
☐ 252 David Weathers .10 .05
☐ 253 Walt Weiss .10 .05
☐ 254 Darrell Whitmore .10 .05
☐ 255 Nigel Wilson .10 .05
☐ 256 Eric Anthony .10 .05
☐ 257 Jeff Bagwell .75 .35
☐ 258 Kevin Bass .10 .05
☐ 259 Craig Biggio .30 .14
☐ 260 Ken Caminiti .40 .18
☐ 261 Andujar Cedeno .10 .05
☐ 262 Chris Donnels .10 .05
☐ 263 Doug Drabek .10 .05
☐ 264 Tom Edens .10 .05
☐ 265 Steve Finley .20 .09
☐ 266 Luis Gonzalez .10 .05
☐ 267 Pete Harnisch .10 .05
☐ 268 Xavier Hernandez .10 .05
☐ 269 Todd Jones .10 .05
☐ 270 Darryl Kile .20 .09
☐ 271 Al Osuna .10 .05
☐ 272 Rick Parker .10 .05
☐ 273 Mark Portugal .10 .05
☐ 274 Scott Servais .10 .05
☐ 275 Greg Swindell .10 .05
☐ 276 Eddie Taubensee .10 .05
☐ 277 Jose Uribe .10 .05
☐ 278 Brian Williams .10 .05
☐ 279 Kevin Appier .20 .09
☐ 280 Billy Brewer .10 .05
☐ 281 David Cone .20 .09
☐ 282 Greg Gagne .10 .05
☐ 283 Tom Gordon .10 .05
☐ 284 Chris Gwynn .10 .05
☐ 285 John Habyan .10 .05
☐ 286 Chris Haney .10 .05
☐ 287 Phil Hiatt .10 .05
☐ 288 David Howard .10 .05
☐ 289 Felix Jose .10 .05
☐ 290 Wally Joyner .20 .09
☐ 291 Kevin Koslofski .10 .05
☐ 292 Jose Lind .10 .05
☐ 293 Brent Mayne .10 .05
☐ 294 Mike Macfarlane .10 .05
☐ 295 Brian McRae .10 .05
☐ 296 Kevin McReynolds .10 .05
☐ 297 Keith Miller .10 .05
☐ 298 Jeff Montgomery .20 .09
☐ 299 Hipolito Pichardo .10 .05
☐ 300 Rico Rossy .10 .05
☐ 301 Curtis Wilkerson .10 .05
☐ 302 Pedro Astacio .10 .05
☐ 303 Rafael Bournigal .10 .05
☐ 304 Brett Butler .20 .09
☐ 305 Tom Candiotti .10 .05
☐ 306 Omar Daal .10 .05
☐ 307 Jim Gott .10 .05
☐ 308 Kevin Gross .10 .05
☐ 309 Dave Hansen .10 .05
☐ 310 Carlos Hernandez .10 .05
☐ 311 Orel Hershiser .20 .09
☐ 312 Eric Karros .20 .09
☐ 313 Pedro Martinez .40 .18
☐ 314 Ramon Martinez .20 .09
☐ 315 Roger McDowell .10 .05
☐ 316 Raul Mondesi .30 .14
☐ 317 Jose Offerman .10 .05
☐ 318 Mike Piazza 1.25 .55
☐ 319 Jody Reed .10 .05
☐ 320 Henry Rodriguez .10 .05
☐ 321 Cory Snyder .10 .05
☐ 322 Darryl Strawberry .20 .09
☐ 323 Tim Wallach .10 .05
☐ 324 Steve Wilson .10 .05
☐ 325 Juan Bell .10 .05
☐ 326 Ricky Bones .10 .05
☐ 327 Alex Diaz .10 .05
☐ 328 Cal Eldred .10 .05
☐ 329 Darryl Hamilton .10 .05
☐ 330 Doug Henry .10 .05
☐ 331 John Jaha .10 .05
☐ 332 Pat Listach .10 .05
☐ 333 Graeme Lloyd .10 .05
☐ 334 Carlos Maldonado .10 .05
☐ 335 Angel Miranda .10 .05
☐ 336 Jaime Navarro .10 .05
☐ 337 Dave Nilsson .20 .09
☐ 338 Rafael Novoa .10 .05
☐ 339 Troy O'Leary .10 .05
☐ 340 Jesse Orosco .10 .05
☐ 341 Kevin Seitzer .10 .05
☐ 342 Bill Spiers .10 .05
☐ 343 William Suero .10 .05
☐ 344 B.J. Surhoff .10 .05
☐ 345 Dickie Thon .10 .05
☐ 346 Jose Valentin .20 .09
☐ 347 Greg Vaughn .10 .05
☐ 348 Robin Yount .30 .14
☐ 349 Willie Banks .10 .05
☐ 350 Bernardo Brito .10 .05
☐ 351 Scott Erickson .10 .05
☐ 352 Mark Guthrie .10 .05
☐ 353 Chip Hale .10 .05
☐ 354 Brian Harper .10 .05
☐ 355 Kent Hrbek .20 .09
☐ 356 Terry Jorgensen .10 .05
☐ 357 Chuck Knoblauch .40 .18
☐ 358 Gene Larkin .10 .05
☐ 359 Scott Leius .10 .05
☐ 360 Shane Mack .10 .05
☐ 361 David McCarty .10 .05
☐ 362 Pat Meares .10 .05
☐ 363 Pedro Munoz .10 .05
☐ 364 Derek Parks .10 .05
☐ 365 Kirby Puckett .75 .35
☐ 366 Jeff Reboulet .10 .05
☐ 367 Kevin Tapani .10 .05
☐ 368 Mike Trombley .10 .05
☐ 369 George Tsamis .10 .05
☐ 370 Carl Willis .10 .05
☐ 371 Dave Winfield .30 .14
☐ 372 Moises Alou .20 .09
☐ 373 Brian Barnes .10 .05
☐ 374 Sean Berry .10 .05
☐ 375 Frank Bolick .10 .05
☐ 376 Wil Cordero .20 .09
☐ 377 Delino DeShields .10 .05
☐ 378 Jeff Fassero .10 .05
☐ 379 Darrin Fletcher .10 .05
☐ 380 Cliff Floyd .20 .09
☐ 381 Lou Frazier .10 .05
☐ 382 Marquis Grissom .20 .09
☐ 383 Gil Heredia .10 .05
☐ 384 Mike Lansing .20 .09
☐ 385 Oreste Marrero .10 .05
☐ 386 Dennis Martinez .20 .09
☐ 387 Curtis Pride .20 .09
☐ 388 Mel Rojas .10 .05
☐ 389 Kirk Rueter .10 .05
☐ 390 Joe Siddall .10 .05
☐ 391 John Vander Wal .10 .05
☐ 392 Larry Walker .40 .18
☐ 393 John Wetteland .20 .09
☐ 394 Rondell White .30 .14
☐ 395 Tim Bogar .10 .05
☐ 396 Bobby Bonilla .20 .09
☐ 397 Jeromy Burnitz .20 .09
☐ 398 Mike Draper .10 .05
☐ 399 Sid Fernandez .10 .05
☐ 400 John Franco .10 .05
☐ 401 Dave Gallagher .10 .05
☐ 402 Dwight Gooden .20 .09
☐ 403 Eric Hillman .10 .05
☐ 404 Todd Hundley .20 .09
☐ 405 Butch Huskey .20 .09
☐ 406 Jeff Innis .10 .05
☐ 407 Howard Johnson .10 .05
☐ 408 Jeff Kent .10 .05
☐ 409 Ced Landrum .10 .05
☐ 410 Mike Maddux .10 .05
☐ 411 Josias Manzanillo .10 .05
☐ 412 Jeff McKnight .10 .05
☐ 413 Eddie Murray .40 .18
☐ 414 Tito Navarro .10 .05
☐ 415 Joe Orsulak .10 .05
☐ 416 Bret Saberhagen .10 .05
☐ 417 Dave Telgheder .10 .05
☐ 418 Ryan Thompson .10 .05
☐ 419 Chico Walker .10 .05
☐ 420 Jim Abbott .10 .05
☐ 421 Wade Boggs .40 .18
☐ 422 Mike Gallego .10 .05

☐ 423 Mark Hutton .10 .05
☐ 424 Dion James .10 .05
☐ 425 Domingo Jean .10 .05
☐ 426 Pat Kelly .10 .05
☐ 427 Jimmy Key .20 .09
☐ 428 Jim Leyritz .10 .05
☐ 429 Kevin Maas .10 .05
☐ 430 Don Mattingly .60 .25
☐ 431 Bobby Munoz .10 .05
☐ 432 Matt Nokes .10 .05
☐ 433 Paul O'Neill .20 .09
☐ 434 Spike Owen .10 .05
☐ 435 Melido Perez .10 .05
☐ 436 Lee Smith .20 .09
☐ 437 Andy Stankiewicz .10 .05
☐ 438 Mike Stanley .10 .05
☐ 439 Danny Tartabull .10 .05
☐ 440 Randy Velarde .10 .05
☐ 441 Bernie Williams .40 .18
☐ 442 Gerald Williams .10 .05
☐ 443 Mike Witt .10 .05
☐ 444 Marcos Armas .10 .05
☐ 445 Lance Blankenship .10 .05
☐ 446 Mike Bordick .10 .05
☐ 447 Ron Darling UER .10 .05
Reversed negative on front
☐ 448 Dennis Eckersley .30 .14
☐ 449 Brent Gates .10 .05
☐ 450 Goose Gossage .20 .09
☐ 451 Scott Hemond .10 .05
☐ 452 Dave Henderson .10 .05
☐ 453 Shawn Hillegas .10 .05
☐ 454 Rick Honeycutt .10 .05
☐ 455 Scott Lydy .10 .05
☐ 456 Mark McGwire .75 .35
☐ 457 Henry Mercedes .10 .05
☐ 458 Mike Mohler .10 .05
☐ 459 Troy Neel .10 .05
☐ 460 Edwin Nunez .10 .05
☐ 461 Craig Paquette .10 .05
☐ 462 Ruben Sierra .10 .05
☐ 463 Terry Steinbach .20 .09
☐ 464 Todd Van Poppel .10 .05
☐ 465 Bob Welch .10 .05
☐ 466 Bobby Witt .10 .05
☐ 467 Ruben Amaro .10 .05
☐ 468 Larry Andersen .10 .05
☐ 469 Kim Batiste .10 .05
☐ 470 Wes Chamberlain .10 .05
☐ 471 Darren Daulton .20 .09
☐ 472 Mariano Duncan .10 .05
☐ 473 Len Dykstra .20 .09
☐ 474 Jim Eisenreich .20 .09
☐ 475 Tommy Greene .10 .05
☐ 476 Dave Hollins .10 .05
☐ 477 Pete Incaviglia .10 .05
☐ 478 Danny Jackson .10 .05
☐ 479 John Kruk .20 .09
☐ 480 Tony Longmire .10 .05
☐ 481 Jeff Manto .10 .05
☐ 482 Mickey Morandini .10 .05
☐ 483 Terry Mulholland .10 .05
☐ 484 Todd Pratt .10 .05
☐ 485 Ben Rivera .10 .05
☐ 486 Curt Schilling .20 .09
☐ 487 Kevin Stocker .10 .05
☐ 488 Milt Thompson .10 .05
☐ 489 David West .10 .05
☐ 490 Mitch Williams .10 .05
☐ 491 Jeff Ballard .10 .05
☐ 492 Jay Bell .20 .09
☐ 493 Scott Bullett .10 .05
☐ 494 Dave Clark .10 .05
☐ 495 Steve Cooke .10 .05
☐ 496 Midre Cummings .10 .05
☐ 497 Mark Dewey .10 .05
☐ 498 Carlos Garcia .10 .05
☐ 499 Jeff King .20 .09
☐ 500 Al Martin .10 .05
☐ 501 Lloyd McClendon .10 .05
☐ 502 Orlando Merced .10 .05
☐ 503 Blas Minor .10 .05
☐ 504 Denny Neagle .20 .09
☐ 505 Tom Prince .10 .05
☐ 506 Don Slaught .10 .05
☐ 507 Zane Smith .10 .05
☐ 508 Randy Tomlin .10 .05
☐ 509 Andy Van Slyke .20 .09
☐ 510 Paul Wagner .10 .05
☐ 511 Tim Wakefield .10 .05
☐ 512 Bob Walk .10 .05
☐ 513 John Wehner .10 .05
☐ 514 Kevin Young .10 .05
☐ 515 Billy Bean .10 .05
☐ 516 Andy Benes .20 .09
☐ 517 Derek Bell .20 .09
☐ 518 Doug Brocail .10 .05
☐ 519 Jarvis Brown .10 .05
☐ 520 Phil Clark .10 .05
☐ 521 Mark Davis .10 .05
☐ 522 Jeff Gardner .10 .05
☐ 523 Pat Gomez .10 .05
☐ 524 Ricky Gutierrez .10 .05
☐ 525 Tony Gwynn 1.00 .45
☐ 526 Gene Harris .10 .05
☐ 527 Kevin Higgins .10 .05
☐ 528 Trevor Hoffman .20 .09
☐ 529 Luis Lopez .10 .05
☐ 530 Pedro Martinez .10 .05
☐ 531 Melvin Nieves .20 .09
☐ 532 Phil Plantier .10 .05
☐ 533 Frank Seminara .10 .05
☐ 534 Craig Shipley .10 .05
☐ 535 Tim Teufel .10 .05
☐ 536 Guillermo Velasquez .10 .05
☐ 537 Wally Whitehurst .10 .05
☐ 538 Rod Beck .20 .09
☐ 539 Todd Benzinger .10 .05
☐ 540 Barry Bonds .50 .23
☐ 541 Jeff Brantley .10 .05
☐ 542 Dave Burba .10 .05
☐ 543 John Burkett .10 .05
☐ 544 Will Clark .30 .14
☐ 545 Royce Clayton .20 .09
☐ 546 Bryan Hickerson .10 .05
☐ 547 Mike Jackson .10 .05
☐ 548 Darren Lewis .10 .05
☐ 549 Kirt Manwaring .10 .05
☐ 550 Dave Martinez .10 .05
☐ 551 Willie McGee .10 .05
☐ 552 Jeff Reed .10 .05
☐ 553 Dave Righetti .10 .05
☐ 554 Kevin Rogers .10 .05
☐ 555 Steve Scarsone .10 .05
☐ 556 Bill Swift .10 .05
☐ 557 Robby Thompson .10 .05
☐ 558 Salomon Torres .10 .05
☐ 559 Matt Williams .30 .14
☐ 560 Trevor Wilson .10 .05
☐ 561 Rich Amaral .10 .05
☐ 562 Mike Blowers .10 .05
☐ 563 Chris Bosio .10 .05
☐ 564 Jay Buhner .30 .14
☐ 565 Norm Charlton .10 .05
☐ 566 Jim Converse .10 .05
☐ 567 Rich DeLucia .10 .05
☐ 568 Mike Felder .10 .05
☐ 569 Dave Fleming .10 .05
☐ 570 Ken Griffey Jr. 2.00 .90
☐ 571 Bill Haselman .10 .05
☐ 572 Dwayne Henry .10 .05
☐ 573 Brad Holman .10 .05
☐ 574 Randy Johnson .40 .18
☐ 575 Greg Litton .10 .05
☐ 576 Edgar Martinez .30 .14
☐ 577 Tino Martinez .40 .18
☐ 578 Jeff Nelson .10 .05
☐ 579 Marc Newfield .20 .09
☐ 580 Roger Salkeld .10 .05
☐ 581 Mackey Sasser .10 .05
☐ 582 Brian Turang .10 .05
☐ 583 Omar Vizquel .20 .09
☐ 584 Dave Valle .10 .05
☐ 585 Luis Alicea .10 .05
☐ 586 Rene Arocha .10 .05
☐ 587 Rheal Cormier .10 .05
☐ 588 Tripp Cromer .10 .05
☐ 589 Bernard Gilkey .20 .09
☐ 590 Lee Guetterman .10 .05
☐ 591 Gregg Jefferies .20 .09
☐ 592 Tim Jones .10 .05
☐ 593 Paul Kilgus .10 .05
☐ 594 Les Lancaster .10 .05
☐ 595 Omar Olivares .10 .05
☐ 596 Jose Oquendo .10 .05
☐ 597 Donovan Osborne .10 .05
☐ 598 Tom Pagnozzi .10 .05
☐ 599 Erik Pappas .10 .05
☐ 600 Geronimo Pena .10 .05
☐ 601 Mike Perez .10 .05
☐ 602 Gerald Perry .10 .05
☐ 603 Stan Royer .10 .05
☐ 604 Ozzie Smith .50 .23
☐ 605 Bob Tewksbury .10 .05
☐ 606 Allen Watson .10 .05
☐ 607 Mark Whiten .10 .05
☐ 608 Todd Zeile .10 .05
☐ 609 Jeff Bronkey .10 .05
☐ 610 Kevin Brown .20 .09
☐ 611 Jose Canseco .30 .14
☐ 612 Doug Dascenzo .10 .05
☐ 613 Butch Davis .10 .05
☐ 614 Mario Diaz .10 .05
☐ 615 Julio Franco .20 .09
☐ 616 Benji Gil .10 .05
☐ 617 Juan Gonzalez 1.00 .45
☐ 618 Tom Henke .10 .05
☐ 619 Jeff Huson .10 .05
☐ 620 David Hulse .10 .05
☐ 621 Craig Lefferts .10 .05
☐ 622 Rafael Palmeiro .30 .14
☐ 623 Dean Palmer .20 .09
☐ 624 Bob Patterson .10 .05
☐ 625 Roger Pavlik .10 .05
☐ 626 Gary Redus .10 .05
☐ 627 Ivan Rodriguez .50 .23
☐ 628 Kenny Rogers .10 .05
☐ 629 Jon Shave .10 .05
☐ 630 Doug Strange .10 .05
☐ 631 Matt Whiteside .10 .05
☐ 632 Roberto Alomar .40 .18
☐ 633 Pat Borders .10 .05
☐ 634 Scott Brow .10 .05
☐ 635 Rob Butler .10 .05
☐ 636 Joe Carter .30 .14
☐ 637 Tony Castillo .10 .05
☐ 638 Mark Eichhorn .10 .05
☐ 639 Tony Fernandez .10 .05
☐ 640 Huck Flener .10 .05
☐ 641 Alfredo Griffin .10 .05
☐ 642 Juan Guzman .10 .05
☐ 643 Rickey Henderson .30 .14
☐ 644 Pat Hentgen .20 .09
☐ 645 Randy Knorr .10 .05
☐ 646 Al Leiter .10 .05
☐ 647 Domingo Martinez .10 .05
☐ 648 Paul Molitor .40 .18
☐ 649 Jack Morris .20 .09
☐ 650 John Olerud .20 .09
☐ 651 Ed Sprague .10 .05
☐ 652 Dave Stewart .20 .09
☐ 653 Devon White .10 .05
☐ 654 Woody Williams .10 .05
☐ 655 Barry Bonds MVP .40 .18
☐ 656 Greg Maddux CY .60 .25
☐ 657 Jack McDowell CY .10 .05
☐ 658 Mike Piazza ROY .60 .25
☐ 659 Tim Salmon ROY .40 .18
☐ 660 Frank Thomas MVP 1.00 .45

1994 Pacific All-Latino

Randomly inserted in Pacific purple foil packs at a rate of one in 25, this 20-card standard-size set spotlights the greatest Latin players chosen by the Pacific staff. Print run was limited to 8,000 sets. The fronts feature a full-bleed color player photo with gold foil stamping. The player's name in gold foil appears on the bottom of the photo. Superimposed on the player's native country's flag, the horizontal backs show a close-up color player photo on the left, while 1993 highlights, printed in English and Spanish, appear on the right. The set subdivides into National League (1-10) and American League (11-20) players.

	MINT	NRMT
COMPLETE SET (20)	25.00	11.00
COMMON CARD (1-20)	1.00	.45

☐ 1 Benito Santiago 1.00 .45
☐ 2 Dave Magadan 1.00 .45
☐ 3 Andres Galarraga 1.50 .70
☐ 4 Luis Gonzalez 1.00 .45
☐ 5 Jose Offerman 1.00 .45
☐ 6 Bobby Bonilla 1.50 .70
☐ 7 Dennis Martinez 1.00 .45
☐ 8 Mariano Duncan 1.00 .45
☐ 9 Orlando Merced 1.00 .45
☐ 10 Jose Rijo 1.00 .45
☐ 11 Danny Tartabull 1.00 .45
☐ 12 Ruben Sierra 1.00 .45
☐ 13 Ivan Rodriguez 6.00 2.70
☐ 14 Juan Gonzalez 12.00 5.50
☐ 15 Jose Canseco 1.50 .70
☐ 16 Rafael Palmeiro 1.50 .70
☐ 17 Roberto Alomar 5.00 2.20

☐ 18 Eduardo Perez	1.00	.45
☐ 19 Alex Fernandez	1.50	.70
☐ 20 Omar Vizquel	1.50	.70

1994 Pacific Gold Prisms

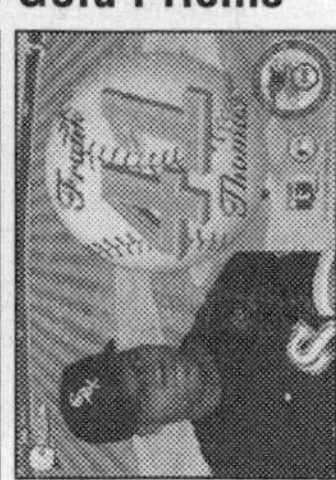

Randomly inserted in Pacific purple foil packs at a rate of one in 25, this 20-card standard-size prismatic "Home Run Leaders" set honors the top 1993 home run leaders. Print run was reportedly limited to 8,000 sets. The fronts feature a cut-out color player photo against a gold prism background. The player's name appears at the bottom, highlighted in team colors. Superimposed on a baseball field, the horizontal backs show a close-up color player photo on the left, while the number of home runs the player hit in 1993 is highlighted on a large baseball icon on the right. The set subdivides into American League (1-10) and National League (11-20) players.

	MINT	NRMT
COMPLETE SET (20)	90.00	40.00
COMMON CARD (1-20)	1.50	.70
☐ 1 Juan Gonzalez	12.00	5.50
☐ 2 Ken Griffey Jr.	25.00	11.00
☐ 3 Frank Thomas	20.00	9.00
☐ 4 Albert Belle	6.00	2.70
☐ 5 Rafael Palmeiro	3.00	1.35
☐ 6 Joe Carter	2.00	.90
☐ 7 Dean Palmer	2.00	.90
☐ 8 Mickey Tettleton	1.50	.70
☐ 9 Tim Salmon	4.00	1.80
☐ 10 Danny Tartabull	1.50	.70
☐ 11 Barry Bonds	6.00	2.70
☐ 12 Dave Justice	4.00	1.80
☐ 13 Matt Williams	3.00	1.35
☐ 14 Fred McGriff	3.00	1.35
☐ 15 Ron Gant	2.00	.90
☐ 16 Mike Piazza	15.00	6.75
☐ 17 Bobby Bonilla	2.00	.90
☐ 18 Phil Plantier	1.50	.70
☐ 19 Sammy Sosa	4.00	1.80
☐ 20 Rick Wilkins	1.50	.70

1994 Pacific Silver Prisms

Randomly inserted in Pacific foil packs, this 36-card standard-size set is also known as "Jewels of the Crown". The triangular versions were randomly inserted in purple packs and the more common circular one per black retail pack. The print run was reportedly limited to 8,000 sets. The set divides into American League (1-18) and National League (19-36) players. The cards measure the standard size. The fronts feature a cut-out color player photo against a prism background that is either circular or triangular. The player's name appears at the bottom, highlighted in team colors.

	MINT	NRMT
COMPLETE SET (36)	125.00	55.00
COMMON CARD (1-36)	1.00	.45
COMP.CIRCULAR SET (36)	60.00	27.00

*CIRCULAR STARS: 2X TO 5X BASIC CARDS

Card	MINT	NRMT
☐ 1 Robin Yount	2.50	1.10
☐ 2 Juan Gonzalez	10.00	4.50
☐ 3 Rafael Palmeiro	2.50	1.10
☐ 4 Paul Molitor	4.00	1.80
☐ 5 Roberto Alomar	4.00	1.80
☐ 6 John Olerud	1.50	.70
☐ 7 Randy Johnson	4.00	1.80
☐ 8 Ken Griffey Jr.	20.00	9.00
☐ 9 Wade Boggs	4.00	1.80
☐ 10 Don Mattingly	8.00	3.60
☐ 11 Kirby Puckett	8.00	3.60
☐ 12 Tim Salmon	4.00	1.80
☐ 13 Frank Thomas	15.00	6.75
☐ 14 Fernando Valenzuela	1.50	.70
☐ 15 Cal Ripken	15.00	6.75
☐ 16 Carlos Baerga	1.00	.45
☐ 17 Kenny Lofton	5.00	2.20
☐ 18 Cecil Fielder	1.50	.70
☐ 19 John Burkett	1.00	.45
☐ 20 Andres Galarraga	2.50	1.10
☐ 21 Charlie Hayes	1.00	.45
☐ 22 Orestes Destrade	1.00	.45
☐ 23 Jeff Conine	1.50	.70
☐ 24 Jeff Bagwell	8.00	3.60
☐ 25 Mark Grace	2.50	1.10
☐ 26 Ryne Sandberg	5.00	2.20
☐ 27 Gregg Jefferies	1.00	.45
☐ 28 Barry Bonds	5.00	2.20
☐ 29 Mike Piazza	12.00	5.50
☐ 30 Greg Maddux	12.00	5.50
☐ 31 Darren Daulton	1.50	.70
☐ 32 John Kruk	1.50	.70
☐ 33 Lenny Dykstra	1.50	.70
☐ 34 Orlando Merced	1.00	.45
☐ 35 Tony Gwynn	10.00	4.50
☐ 36 Robby Thompson	1.00	.45

1995 Pacific

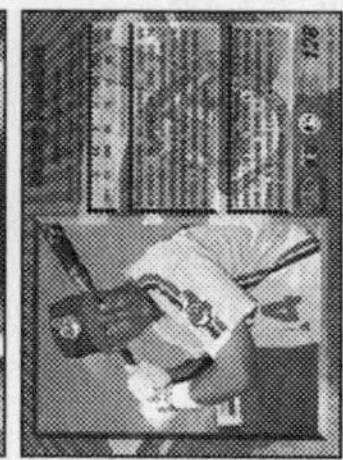

This 450-card standard-size set was issued in one series. The full-bleed fronts have action photos; the "Pacific Collection" logo is on the upper left and the player's name is at the bottom. The horizontal backs have a player photo on the left with 1994 stats and some career highlights on the right. The career highlights are in both English and Spanish. The cards are numbered in the lower right corner. The cards are grouped alphabetically within teams and checklisted below alphabetically according to teams for each league. There are no key Rookie Cards in this set.

	MINT	NRMT
COMPLETE SET (450)	30.00	13.50
COMMON CARD (1-450)	.10	.05
☐ 1 Steve Avery	.10	.05
☐ 2 Rafael Belliard	.10	.05
☐ 3 Jeff Blauser	.10	.05
☐ 4 Tom Glavine	.30	.14
☐ 5 David Justice	.40	.18
☐ 6 Mike Kelly	.10	.05
☐ 7 Roberto Kelly	.10	.05
☐ 8 Ryan Klesko	.30	.14
☐ 9 Mark Lemke	.10	.05
☐ 10 Javier Lopez	.30	.14
☐ 11 Greg Maddux	1.25	.55
☐ 12 Fred McGriff	.30	.14
☐ 13 Greg McMichael	.10	.05
☐ 14 Jose Oliva	.10	.05
☐ 15 John Smoltz	.30	.14
☐ 16 Tony Tarasco	.10	.05
☐ 17 Brady Anderson	.30	.14
☐ 18 Harold Baines	.20	.09
☐ 19 Armando Benitez	.10	.05
☐ 20 Mike Devereaux	.10	.05
☐ 21 Leo Gomez	.10	.05
☐ 22 Jeffrey Hammonds	.20	.09
☐ 23 Chris Hoiles	.10	.05
☐ 24 Ben McDonald	.10	.05
☐ 25 Mark McLemore	.10	.05
☐ 26 Jamie Moyer	.10	.05
☐ 27 Mike Mussina	.40	.18
☐ 28 Rafael Palmeiro	.30	.14
☐ 29 Jim Poole	.10	.05
☐ 30 Cal Ripken Jr.	1.50	.70
☐ 31 Lee Smith	.20	.09
☐ 32 Mark Smith	.10	.05
☐ 33 Jose Canseco	.30	.14
☐ 34 Roger Clemens	.75	.35
☐ 35 Scott Cooper	.10	.05
☐ 36 Andre Dawson	.30	.14
☐ 37 Tony Fossas	.10	.05
☐ 38 Mike Greenwell	.10	.05
☐ 39 Chris Howard	.10	.05
☐ 40 Jose Melendez	.10	.05
☐ 41 Nate Minchey	.10	.05
☐ 42 Tim Naehring	.10	.05
☐ 43 Otis Nixon	.20	.09
☐ 44 Carlos Rodriguez	.10	.05
☐ 45 Aaron Sele	.10	.05
☐ 46 Lee Tinsley	.10	.05
☐ 47 Sergio Valdez	.10	.05
☐ 48 John Valentin	.20	.09
☐ 49 Mo Vaughn	.50	.23
☐ 50 Brian Anderson	.10	.05
☐ 51 Garret Anderson	.30	.14
☐ 52 Rod Correia	.10	.05
☐ 53 Chad Curtis	.10	.05
☐ 54 Mark Dalesandro	.10	.05
☐ 55 Chili Davis	.20	.09
☐ 56 Gary DiSarcina	.10	.05
☐ 57 Damion Easley	.10	.05
☐ 58 Jim Edmonds	.30	.14
☐ 59 Jorge Fabregas	.10	.05
☐ 60 Chuck Finley	.20	.09
☐ 61 Bo Jackson	.20	.09
☐ 62 Mark Langston	.10	.05
☐ 63 Eduardo Perez	.10	.05
☐ 64 Tim Salmon	.40	.18
☐ 65 J.T. Snow	.20	.09
☐ 66 Willie Banks	.10	.05
☐ 67 Jose Bautista	.10	.05
☐ 68 Shawon Dunston	.10	.05
☐ 69 Kevin Foster	.10	.05
☐ 70 Mark Grace	.30	.14
☐ 71 Jose Guzman	.10	.05
☐ 72 Jose Hernandez	.10	.05
☐ 73 Blaise Ilsley	.10	.05
☐ 74 Derrick May	.10	.05
☐ 75 Randy Myers	.10	.05
☐ 76 Karl Rhodes	.10	.05
☐ 77 Kevin Roberson	.10	.05
☐ 78 Rey Sanchez	.10	.05
☐ 79 Sammy Sosa	.40	.18
☐ 80 Steve Trachsel	.10	.05
☐ 81 Eddie Zambrano	.10	.05
☐ 82 Wilson Alvarez	.20	.09
☐ 83 Jason Bere	.10	.05
☐ 84 Joey Cora	.20	.09
☐ 85 Jose DeLeon	.10	.05
☐ 86 Alex Fernandez	.20	.09
☐ 87 Julio Franco	.20	.09
☐ 88 Ozzie Guillen	.10	.05
☐ 89 Joe Hall	.10	.05
☐ 90 Roberto Hernandez	.10	.05
☐ 91 Darrin Jackson	.10	.05
☐ 92 Lance Johnson	.20	.09
☐ 93 Norberto Martin	.10	.05
☐ 94 Jack McDowell	.10	.05
☐ 95 Tim Raines	.10	.05
☐ 96 Olmedo Saenz	.10	.05
☐ 97 Frank Thomas	1.50	.70
☐ 98 Robin Ventura	.20	.09
☐ 99 Bret Boone	.10	.05
☐ 100 Jeff Brantley	.10	.05
☐ 101 Jacob Brumfield	.10	.05
☐ 102 Hector Carrasco	.10	.05
☐ 103 Brian Dorsett	.10	.05
☐ 104 Tony Fernandez	.10	.05
☐ 105 Willie Greene	.20	.09
☐ 106 Erik Hanson	.10	.05
☐ 107 Kevin Jarvis	.10	.05
☐ 108 Barry Larkin	.30	.14
☐ 109 Kevin Mitchell	.10	.05
☐ 110 Hal Morris	.10	.05
☐ 111 Jose Rijo	.10	.05
☐ 112 Johnny Ruffin	.10	.05
☐ 113 Deion Sanders	.30	.14
☐ 114 Reggie Sanders	.10	.05
☐ 115 Sandy Alomar Jr.	.10	.05
☐ 116 Ruben Amaro	.10	.05
☐ 117 Carlos Baerga	.20	.09
☐ 118 Albert Belle	.50	.23
☐ 119 Alvaro Espinoza	.10	.05
☐ 120 Rene Gonzales	.10	.05
☐ 121 Wayne Kirby	.10	.05
☐ 122 Kenny Lofton	.50	.23
☐ 123 Candy Maldonado	.10	.05
☐ 124 Dennis Martinez	.20	.09
☐ 125 Eddie Murray	.40	.18
☐ 126 Charles Nagy	.20	.09
☐ 127 Tony Pena	.10	.05
☐ 128 Manny Ramirez	.40	.18
☐ 129 Paul Sorrento	.10	.05

☐ 130 Jim Thome	.40	.18
☐ 131 Omar Vizquel	.20	.09
☐ 132 Dante Bichette	.30	.14
☐ 133 Ellis Burks	.20	.09
☐ 134 Vinny Castilla	.30	.14
☐ 135 Marvin Freeman	.10	.05
☐ 136 Andres Galarraga	.30	.14
☐ 137 Joe Girardi	.10	.05
☐ 138 Charlie Hayes	.10	.05
☐ 139 Mike Kingery	.10	.05
☐ 140 Nelson Liriano	.10	.05
☐ 141 Roberto Mejia	.10	.05
☐ 142 David Nied	.10	.05
☐ 143 Steve Reed	.10	.05
☐ 144 Armando Reynoso	.10	.05
☐ 145 Bruce Ruffin	.10	.05
☐ 146 John VanderWal	.10	.05
☐ 147 Walt Weiss	.10	.05
☐ 148 Skeeter Barnes	.10	.05
☐ 149 Tim Belcher	.10	.05
☐ 150 Junior Felix	.10	.05
☐ 151 Cecil Fielder	.20	.09
☐ 152 Travis Fryman	.20	.09
☐ 153 Kirk Gibson	.20	.09
☐ 154 Chris Gomez	.10	.05
☐ 155 Buddy Groom	.10	.05
☐ 156 Chad Kreuter	.10	.05
☐ 157 Mike Moore	.10	.05
☐ 158 Tony Phillips	.10	.05
☐ 159 Juan Samuel	.10	.05
☐ 160 Mickey Tettleton	.10	.05
☐ 161 Alan Trammell	.30	.14
☐ 162 David Wells	.10	.05
☐ 163 Lou Whitaker	.20	.09
☐ 164 Kurt Abbott	.10	.05
☐ 165 Luis Aquino	.10	.05
☐ 166 Alex Arias	.10	.05
☐ 167 Bret Barberie	.10	.05
☐ 168 Jerry Browne	.10	.05
☐ 169 Chuck Carr	.10	.05
☐ 170 Matias Carrillo	.10	.05
☐ 171 Greg Colbrunn	.10	.05
☐ 172 Jeff Conine	.20	.09
☐ 173 Carl Everett	.10	.05
☐ 174 Robb Nen	.10	.05
☐ 175 Yorkis Perez	.10	.05
☐ 176 Pat Rapp	.10	.05
☐ 177 Benito Santiago	.10	.05
☐ 178 Gary Sheffield	.40	.18
☐ 179 Darrell Whitmore	.10	.05
☐ 180 Jeff Bagwell	.75	.35
☐ 181 Kevin Bass	.10	.05
☐ 182 Craig Biggio	.30	.14
☐ 183 Andujar Cedeno	.10	.05
☐ 184 Doug Drabek	.10	.05
☐ 185 Tony Eusebio	.10	.05
☐ 186 Steve Finley	.20	.09
☐ 187 Luis Gonzalez	.10	.05
☐ 188 Pete Harnisch	.10	.05
☐ 189 John Hudek	.10	.05
☐ 190 Orlando Miller	.10	.05
☐ 191 James Mouton	.10	.05
☐ 192 Roberto Petagine	.10	.05
☐ 193 Shane Reynolds	.10	.05
☐ 194 Greg Swindell	.10	.05
☐ 195 Dave Veres	.10	.05
☐ 196 Kevin Appier	.20	.09
☐ 197 Stan Belinda	.10	.05
☐ 198 Vince Coleman	.10	.05
☐ 199 David Cone	.20	.09
☐ 200 Gary Gaetti	.20	.09
☐ 201 Greg Gagne	.10	.05
☐ 202 Mark Gubicza	.10	.05
☐ 203 Bob Hamelin	.10	.05
☐ 204 Dave Henderson	.10	.05
☐ 205 Felix Jose	.10	.05
☐ 206 Wally Joyner	.20	.09
☐ 207 Jose Lind	.10	.05
☐ 208 Mike Macfarlane	.10	.05
☐ 209 Brian McRae	.10	.05
☐ 210 Jeff Montgomery	.20	.09
☐ 211 Hipolito Pichardo	.10	.05
☐ 212 Pedro Astacio	.10	.05
☐ 213 Brett Butler	.20	.09
☐ 214 Omar Daal	.10	.05
☐ 215 Delino DeShields	.10	.05
☐ 216 Darren Dreifort	.10	.05
☐ 217 Carlos Hernandez	.10	.05
☐ 218 Orel Hershiser	.20	.09
☐ 219 Garey Ingram	.10	.05
☐ 220 Eric Karros	.20	.09
☐ 221 Ramon Martinez	.20	.09
☐ 222 Raul Mondesi	.30	.14
☐ 223 Jose Offerman	.10	.05
☐ 224 Mike Piazza	1.25	.55
☐ 225 Henry Rodriguez	.10	.05
☐ 226 Ismael Valdes	.20	.09
☐ 227 Tim Wallach	.10	.05
☐ 228 Jeff Cirillo	.20	.09
☐ 229 Alex Diaz	.10	.05
☐ 230 Cal Eldred	.10	.05
☐ 231 Mike Fetters	.10	.05
☐ 232 Brian Harper	.10	.05
☐ 233 Ted Higuera	.10	.05
☐ 234 John Jaha	.10	.05
☐ 235 Graeme Lloyd	.10	.05
☐ 236 Jose Mercedes	.10	.05
☐ 237 Jaime Navarro	.10	.05
☐ 238 Dave Nilsson	.20	.09
☐ 239 Jesse Orosco	.10	.05
☐ 240 Jody Reed	.10	.05
☐ 241 Jose Valentin	.20	.09
☐ 242 Greg Vaughn	.10	.05
☐ 243 Turner Ward	.10	.05
☐ 244 Rick Aguilera	.10	.05
☐ 245 Rich Becker	.10	.05
☐ 246 Jim Deshaies	.10	.05
☐ 247 Steve Dunn	.10	.05
☐ 248 Scott Erickson	.10	.05
☐ 249 Kent Hrbek	.20	.09
☐ 250 Chuck Knoblauch	.30	.14
☐ 251 Scott Leius	.10	.05
☐ 252 David McCarty	.10	.05
☐ 253 Pat Meares	.10	.05
☐ 254 Pedro Munoz	.10	.05
☐ 255 Kirby Puckett	.75	.35
☐ 256 Carlos Pulido	.10	.05
☐ 257 Kevin Tapani	.10	.05
☐ 258 Matt Walbeck	.10	.05
☐ 259 Dave Winfield	.30	.14
☐ 260 Moises Alou	.20	.09
☐ 261 Juan Bell	.10	.05
☐ 262 Freddie Benavides	.10	.05
☐ 263 Sean Berry	.10	.05
☐ 264 Wil Cordero	.10	.05
☐ 265 Jeff Fassero	.10	.05
☐ 266 Darrin Fletcher	.10	.05
☐ 267 Cliff Floyd	.10	.05
☐ 268 Marquis Grissom	.20	.09
☐ 269 Gil Heredia	.10	.05
☐ 270 Ken Hill	.10	.05
☐ 271 Pedro J. Martinez	.40	.18
☐ 272 Mel Rojas	.10	.05
☐ 273 Larry Walker	.40	.18
☐ 274 John Wetteland	.20	.09
☐ 275 Rondell White	.30	.14
☐ 276 Tim Bogar	.10	.05
☐ 277 Bobby Bonilla	.20	.09
☐ 278 Rico Brogna	.10	.05
☐ 279 Jeromy Burnitz	.20	.09
☐ 280 John Franco	.20	.09
☐ 281 Eric Hillman	.10	.05
☐ 282 Todd Hundley	.20	.09
☐ 283 Jeff Kent	.10	.05
☐ 284 Mike Maddux	.10	.05
☐ 285 Joe Orsulak	.10	.05
☐ 286 Luis Rivera	.10	.05
☐ 287 Bret Saberhagen	.10	.05
☐ 288 David Segui	.10	.05
☐ 289 Ryan Thompson	.10	.05
☐ 290 Fernando Vina	.10	.05
☐ 291 Jose Vizcaino	.10	.05
☐ 292 Jim Abbott	.10	.05
☐ 293 Wade Boggs	.40	.18
☐ 294 Russ Davis	.10	.05
☐ 295 Mike Gallego	.10	.05
☐ 296 Xavier Hernandez	.10	.05
☐ 297 Steve Howe	.10	.05
☐ 298 Jimmy Key	.20	.09
☐ 299 Don Mattingly	.60	.25
☐ 300 Terry Mulholland	.10	.05
☐ 301 Paul O'Neill	.20	.09
☐ 302 Luis Polonia	.10	.05
☐ 303 Mike Stanley	.10	.05
☐ 304 Danny Tartabull	.10	.05
☐ 305 Randy Velarde	.10	.05
☐ 306 Bob Wickman	.10	.05
☐ 307 Bernie Williams	.40	.18
☐ 308 Mark Acre	.10	.05
☐ 309 Geronimo Berroa	.10	.05
☐ 310 Mike Bordick	.10	.05
☐ 311 Dennis Eckersley	.30	.14
☐ 312 Rickey Henderson	.30	.14
☐ 313 Stan Javier	.10	.05
☐ 314 Miguel Jimenez	.10	.05
☐ 315 Francisco Matos	.10	.05
☐ 316 Mark McGwire	.75	.35
☐ 317 Troy Neel	.10	.05
☐ 318 Steve Ontiveros	.10	.05
☐ 319 Carlos Reyes	.10	.05
☐ 320 Ruben Sierra	.10	.05
☐ 321 Terry Steinbach	.20	.09
☐ 322 Bob Welch	.10	.05
☐ 323 Bobby Witt	.10	.05
☐ 324 Larry Andersen	.10	.05
☐ 325 Kim Batiste	.10	.05
☐ 326 Darren Daulton	.20	.09
☐ 327 Mariano Duncan	.10	.05
☐ 328 Lenny Dykstra	.20	.09
☐ 329 Jim Eisenreich	.20	.09
☐ 330 Danny Jackson	.10	.05
☐ 331 John Kruk	.20	.09
☐ 332 Tony Longmire	.10	.05
☐ 333 Tom Marsh	.10	.05
☐ 334 Mickey Morandini	.10	.05
☐ 335 Bobby Munoz	.10	.05
☐ 336 Todd Pratt	.10	.05
☐ 337 Tom Quinlan	.10	.05
☐ 338 Kevin Stocker	.10	.05
☐ 339 Fernando Valenzuela	.20	.09
☐ 340 Jay Bell	.20	.09
☐ 341 Dave Clark	.10	.05
☐ 342 Steve Cooke	.10	.05
☐ 343 Carlos Garcia	.10	.05
☐ 344 Jeff King	.20	.09
☐ 345 Jon Lieber	.10	.05
☐ 346 Ravelo Manzanillo	.10	.05
☐ 347 Al Martin	.20	.09
☐ 348 Orlando Merced	.10	.05
☐ 349 Denny Neagle	.20	.09
☐ 350 Alejandro Pena	.10	.05
☐ 351 Don Slaught	.10	.05
☐ 352 Zane Smith	.10	.05
☐ 353 Andy Van Slyke	.20	.09
☐ 354 Rick White	.10	.05
☐ 355 Kevin Young	.10	.05
☐ 356 Andy Ashby	.10	.05
☐ 357 Derek Bell	.20	.09
☐ 358 Andy Benes	.10	.05
☐ 359 Phil Clark	.10	.05
☐ 360 Donnie Elliott	.10	.05
☐ 361 Ricky Gutierrez	.10	.05
☐ 362 Tony Gwynn	1.00	.45
☐ 363 Trevor Hoffman	.20	.09
☐ 364 Tim Hyers	.10	.05
☐ 365 Luis Lopez	.10	.05
☐ 366 Jose Martinez	.10	.05
☐ 367 Pedro A. Martinez	.10	.05
☐ 368 Phil Plantier	.10	.05
☐ 369 Bip Roberts	.10	.05
☐ 370 A.J. Sager	.10	.05
☐ 371 Jeff Tabaka	.10	.05
☐ 372 Todd Benzinger	.10	.05
☐ 373 Barry Bonds	.50	.23
☐ 374 John Burkett	.10	.05
☐ 375 Mark Carreon	.10	.05
☐ 376 Royce Clayton	.10	.05
☐ 377 Pat Gomez	.10	.05
☐ 378 Erik Johnson	.10	.05
☐ 379 Darren Lewis	.10	.05
☐ 380 Kirt Manwaring	.10	.05
☐ 381 Dave Martinez	.10	.05
☐ 382 John Patterson	.10	.05
☐ 383 Mark Portugal	.10	.05
☐ 384 Darryl Strawberry	.20	.09
☐ 385 Salomon Torres	.10	.05
☐ 386 Wm. VanLandingham	.10	.05
☐ 387 Matt Williams	.30	.14
☐ 388 Rich Amaral	.10	.05
☐ 389 Bobby Ayala	.10	.05
☐ 390 Mike Blowers	.10	.05
☐ 391 Chris Bosio	.10	.05
☐ 392 Jay Buhner	.30	.14
☐ 393 Jim Converse	.10	.05
☐ 394 Tim Davis	.10	.05
☐ 395 Felix Fermin	.10	.05
☐ 396 Dave Fleming	.10	.05
☐ 397 Goose Gossage	.20	.09
☐ 398 Ken Griffey Jr.	2.00	.90
☐ 399 Randy Johnson	.40	.18
☐ 400 Edgar Martinez	.30	.14
☐ 401 Tino Martinez	.40	.18
☐ 402 Alex Rodriguez	1.50	.70
☐ 403 Dan Wilson	.20	.09
☐ 404 Luis Alicea	.10	.05
☐ 405 Rene Arocha	.10	.05
☐ 406 Bernard Gilkey	.20	.09
☐ 407 Gregg Jefferies	.20	.09
☐ 408 Ray Lankford	.20	.09
☐ 409 Terry McGriff	.10	.05
☐ 410 Omar Olivares	.10	.05
☐ 411 Jose Oquendo	.10	.05
☐ 412 Vicente Palacios	.10	.05
☐ 413 Geronimo Pena	.10	.05
☐ 414 Mike Perez	.10	.05
☐ 415 Gerald Perry	.10	.05
☐ 416 Ozzie Smith	.50	.23
☐ 417 Bob Tewksbury	.10	.05
☐ 418 Mark Whiten	.10	.05
☐ 419 Todd Zeile	.10	.05
☐ 420 Esteban Beltre	.10	.05

☐ 421 Kevin Brown	.20	.09
☐ 422 Cris Carpenter	.10	.05
☐ 423 Will Clark	.30	.14
☐ 424 Hector Fajardo	.10	.05
☐ 425 Jeff Frye	.10	.05
☐ 426 Juan Gonzalez	1.00	.45
☐ 427 Rusty Greer	.40	.18
☐ 428 Rick Honeycutt	.10	.05
☐ 429 David Hulse	.10	.05
☐ 430 Manny Lee	.10	.05
☐ 431 Junior Ortiz	.10	.05
☐ 432 Dean Palmer	.20	.09
☐ 433 Ivan Rodriguez	.50	.23
☐ 434 Dan Smith	.10	.05
☐ 435 Roberto Alomar	.40	.18
☐ 436 Pat Borders	.10	.05
☐ 437 Scott Brow	.10	.05
☐ 438 Rob Butler	.10	.05
☐ 439 Joe Carter	.30	.14
☐ 440 Tony Castillo	.10	.05
☐ 441 Domingo Cedeno	.10	.05
☐ 442 Brad Cornett	.10	.05
☐ 443 Carlos Delgado	.30	.14
☐ 444 Alex Gonzalez	.20	.09
☐ 445 Juan Guzman	.10	.05
☐ 446 Darren Hall	.10	.05
☐ 447 Paul Molitor	.40	.18
☐ 448 John Olerud	.20	.09
☐ 449 Robert Perez	.10	.05
☐ 450 Devon White	.10	.05

1995 Pacific Gold Crown Die Cuts

Inserted approximately one in every 18 packs, these cards are in a diecut design. The player photo goes to the full-bleed bottom borders while the top has a gold crown. The player is identified on the bottom. The back of the card features a gold crown, player information in both English and Spanish, and a player photo against a blue background. The cards are sequenced in alphabetical order according to team name.

	MINT	NRMT
COMPLETE SET (20)	250.00	110.00
COMMON CARD (1-20)	3.00	1.35
☐ 1 Greg Maddux	25.00	11.00
☐ 2 Fred McGriff	6.00	2.70
☐ 3 Rafael Palmeiro	6.00	2.70
☐ 4 Cal Ripken Jr.	30.00	13.50
☐ 5 Jose Canseco	6.00	2.70
☐ 6 Frank Thomas	30.00	13.50
☐ 7 Albert Belle	10.00	4.50
☐ 8 Manny Ramirez	8.00	3.60
☐ 9 Andres Galarraga	6.00	2.70
☐ 10 Jeff Bagwell	15.00	6.75
☐ 11 Chan Ho Park	8.00	3.60
☐ 12 Raul Mondesi	6.00	2.70
☐ 13 Mike Piazza	25.00	11.00
☐ 14 Kirby Puckett	15.00	6.75
☐ 15 Barry Bonds	10.00	4.50
☐ 16 Ken Griffey Jr.	40.00	18.00
☐ 17 Alex Rodriguez	30.00	13.50
☐ 18 Juan Gonzalez	20.00	9.00
☐ 19 Roberto Alomar	8.00	3.60
☐ 20 Carlos Delgado	3.00	1.35

1995 Pacific Gold Prisms

This 36-card standard-size set was inserted approximately one in every 12 packs. The fronts feature a player photo set against a gold metallic background. The player is identified on the bottom of the card. The horizontal backs feature a player photo set against a group of baseballs on the left side. Another photo is on the right along with the player's name, his career totals and some brief information in English and Spanish.

	MINT	NRMT
COMPLETE SET (36)	150.00	70.00
COMMON CARD (1-36)	1.50	.70

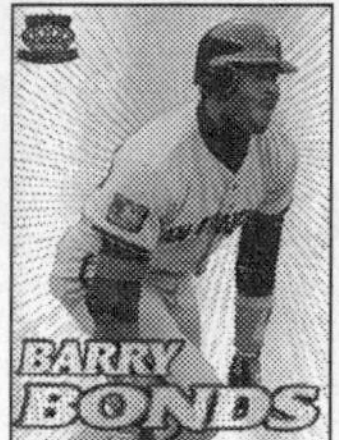

☐ 1 Jose Canseco	3.00	1.35
☐ 2 Gregg Jefferies	1.50	.70
☐ 3 Fred McGriff	3.00	1.35
☐ 4 Joe Carter	3.00	1.35
☐ 5 Tim Salmon	4.00	1.80
☐ 6 Wade Boggs	4.00	1.80
☐ 7 Dave Winfield	3.00	1.35
☐ 8 Bob Hamelin	1.50	.70
☐ 9 Cal Ripken Jr.	20.00	9.00
☐ 10 Don Mattingly	10.00	4.50
☐ 11 Juan Gonzalez	12.00	5.50
☐ 12 Carlos Delgado	2.00	.90
☐ 13 Barry Bonds	5.00	2.20
☐ 14 Albert Belle	10.00	4.50
☐ 15 Raul Mondesi	3.00	1.35
☐ 16 Jeff Bagwell	10.00	4.50
☐ 17 Mike Piazza	15.00	6.75
☐ 18 Rafael Palmeiro	3.00	1.35
☐ 19 Frank Thomas	20.00	9.00
☐ 20 Matt Williams	3.00	1.35
☐ 21 Ken Griffey Jr.	25.00	11.00
☐ 22 Will Clark	3.00	1.35
☐ 23 Bobby Bonilla	2.00	.90
☐ 24 Kenny Lofton	5.00	2.20
☐ 25 Paul Molitor	4.00	1.80
☐ 26 Kirby Puckett	10.00	4.50
☐ 27 David Justice	4.00	1.80
☐ 28 Jeff Conine	2.00	.90
☐ 29 Bret Boone	1.50	.70
☐ 30 Larry Walker	4.00	1.80
☐ 31 Cecil Fielder	2.00	.90
☐ 32 Manny Ramirez	4.00	1.80
☐ 33 Javier Lopez	3.00	1.35
☐ 34 Jimmy Key	1.50	.70
☐ 35 Andres Galarraga	3.00	1.35
☐ 36 Tony Gwynn	10.00	4.50

1995 Pacific Latinos Destacados

This 36-card standard size set was inserted approximately one in every nine packs. A literal translation for this set is Hot Hispanics and features only Spanish players. The full-bleed fronts feature color photos with the playerís name at the bottom along with a fire design. The backs have the player's name spelled vertically in the upper left with a sentence in both English and Spanish. The bottom left has the team logo while the right side had a player photo. The cards are numbered and arranged in alphabetical order.

	MINT	NRMT
COMPLETE SET (36)	50.00	22.00
COMMON CARD (1-36)	1.00	.45
☐ 1 Roberto Alomar	4.00	1.80
☐ 2 Moises Alou	1.50	.70
☐ 3 Wilson Alvarez	1.50	.70
☐ 4 Carlos Baerga	1.50	.70
☐ 5 Geronimo Berroa	1.00	.45
☐ 6 Jose Canseco	2.50	1.10
☐ 7 Hector Carrasco	1.00	.45
☐ 8 Wil Cordero	1.00	.45
☐ 9 Carlos Delgado	1.50	.70
☐ 10 Damion Easley	1.00	.45
☐ 11 Tony Eusebio	1.00	.45
☐ 12 Hector Fajardo	1.00	.45
☐ 13 Andres Galarraga	2.50	1.10
☐ 14 Carlos Garcia	1.00	.45
☐ 15 Chris Gomez	1.00	.45
☐ 16 Alex Gonzalez	1.00	.45
☐ 17 Juan Gonzalez	10.00	4.50
☐ 18 Luis Gonzalez	1.00	.45
☐ 19 Felix Jose	1.00	.45
☐ 20 Javier Lopez	2.50	1.10
☐ 21 Luis Lopez	1.00	.45
☐ 22 Dennis Martinez	1.50	.70
☐ 23 Orlando Miller	1.00	.45
☐ 24 Raul Mondesi	2.50	1.10
☐ 25 Jose Oliva	1.00	.45
☐ 26 Rafael Palmeiro	2.50	1.10
☐ 27 Yorkis Perez	1.00	.45
☐ 28 Manny Ramirez	4.00	1.80
☐ 29 Jose Rijo	1.00	.45
☐ 30 Alex Rodriguez	18.00	8.00
☐ 31 Ivan Rodriguez	5.00	2.20
☐ 32 Carlos Rodriguez	1.00	.45
☐ 33 Sammy Sosa	4.00	1.80
☐ 34 Tony Tarasco	1.00	.45
☐ 35 Ismael Valdes	1.00	.45
☐ 36 Bernie Williams	4.00	1.80

1996 Pacific

This 450-card set was issued in 12-card packs. The fronts feature borderless color action player photos with double-etched gold foil printing. The horizontal backs carry a color player portrait with player information in both English and Spanish and 1995 season player statistics.

	MINT	NRMT
COMPLETE SET (450)	30.00	13.50
COMMON CARD (1-450)	.10	.05
☐ 1 Steve Avery	.10	.05
☐ 2 Ryan Klesko	.30	.14
☐ 3 Pedro Borbon	.10	.05
☐ 4 Chipper Jones	1.25	.55
☐ 5 Kent Mercker	.10	.05
☐ 6 Greg Maddux	1.25	.55
☐ 7 Greg McMichael	.10	.05
☐ 8 Mark Wohlers	.20	.09
☐ 9 Fred McGriff	.30	.14
☐ 10 John Smoltz	.20	.09
☐ 11 Rafael Belliard	.10	.05
☐ 12 Mark Lemke	.10	.05
☐ 13 Tom Glavine	.30	.14
☐ 14 Javier Lopez	.20	.09
☐ 15 Jeff Blauser	.10	.05
☐ 16 David Justice	.40	.18
☐ 17 Marquis Grissom	.20	.09
☐ 18 Greg Maddux CY	.60	.25
☐ 19 Randy Myers	.10	.05
☐ 20 Scott Servais	.10	.05
☐ 21 Sammy Sosa	.40	.18
☐ 22 Kevin Foster	.10	.05
☐ 23 Jose Hernandez	.10	.05
☐ 24 Jim Bullinger	.10	.05
☐ 25 Mike Perez	.10	.05
☐ 26 Shawon Dunston	.10	.05
☐ 27 Rey Sanchez	.10	.05
☐ 28 Frank Castillo	.10	.05
☐ 29 Jaime Navarro	.10	.05
☐ 30 Brian McRae	.10	.05
☐ 31 Mark Grace	.30	.14
☐ 32 Roberto Rivera	.10	.05
☐ 33 Luis Gonzalez	.10	.05
☐ 34 Hector Carrasco	.10	.05
☐ 35 Bret Boone	.10	.05
☐ 36 Thomas Howard	.10	.05
☐ 37 Hal Morris	.10	.05
☐ 38 John Smiley	.10	.05
☐ 39 Jeff Brantley	.10	.05
☐ 40 Barry Larkin	.30	.14
☐ 41 Mariano Duncan	.10	.05
☐ 42 Xavier Hernandez	.10	.05
☐ 43 Pete Schourek	.10	.05
☐ 44 Reggie Sanders	.10	.05
☐ 45 Dave Burba	.10	.05
☐ 46 Jeff Branson	.10	.05
☐ 47 Mark Portugal	.10	.05

☐ 48 Ron Gant	.20	.09
☐ 49 Benito Santiago	.10	.05
☐ 50 Barry Larkin MVP	.30	.14
☐ 51 Steve Reed	.10	.05
☐ 52 Kevin Ritz	.10	.05
☐ 53 Dante Bichette	.20	.09
☐ 54 Darren Holmes	.10	.05
☐ 55 Ellis Burks	.20	.09
☐ 56 Walt Weiss	.10	.05
☐ 57 Armando Reynoso	.10	.05
☐ 58 Vinny Castilla	.20	.09
☐ 59 Jason Bates	.10	.05
☐ 60 Mike Kingery	.10	.05
☐ 61 Bryan Rekar	.10	.05
☐ 62 Curtis Leskanic	.10	.05
☐ 63 Bret Saberhagen	.10	.05
☐ 64 Andres Galarraga	.40	.18
☐ 65 Larry Walker	.40	.18
☐ 66 Joe Girardi	.10	.05
☐ 67 Quilvio Veras	.10	.05
☐ 68 Robb Nen	.10	.05
☐ 69 Mario Diaz	.10	.05
☐ 70 Chuck Carr	.10	.05
☐ 71 Alex Arias	.10	.05
☐ 72 Pat Rapp	.10	.05
☐ 73 Rich Garces	.10	.05
☐ 74 Kurt Abbott	.10	.05
☐ 75 Andre Dawson	.30	.14
☐ 76 Greg Colbrunn	.10	.05
☐ 77 John Burkett	.10	.05
☐ 78 Terry Pendleton	.20	.09
☐ 79 Jesus Tavarez	.10	.05
☐ 80 Charles Johnson	.20	.09
☐ 81 Yorkis Perez	.10	.05
☐ 82 Jeff Conine	.20	.09
☐ 83 Gary Sheffield	.40	.18
☐ 84 Brian L. Hunter	.20	.09
☐ 85 Derrick May	.10	.05
☐ 86 Greg Swindell	.10	.05
☐ 87 Derek Bell	.20	.09
☐ 88 Dave Veres	.10	.05
☐ 89 Jeff Bagwell	.75	.35
☐ 90 Todd Jones	.10	.05
☐ 91 Orlando Miller	.10	.05
☐ 92 Pedro A. Martinez	.10	.05
☐ 93 Tony Eusebio	.10	.05
☐ 94 Craig Biggio	.30	.14
☐ 95 Shane Reynolds	.10	.05
☐ 96 James Mouton	.10	.05
☐ 97 Doug Drabek	.10	.05
☐ 98 Dave Magadan	.10	.05
☐ 99 Ricky Gutierrez	.10	.05
☐ 100 Hideo Nomo	1.00	.45
☐ 101 Delino DeShields	.10	.05
☐ 102 Tom Candiotti	.10	.05
☐ 103 Mike Piazza	1.25	.55
☐ 104 Ramon Martinez	.20	.09
☐ 105 Pedro Astacio	.10	.05
☐ 106 Chad Fonville	.10	.05
☐ 107 Raul Mondesi	.30	.14
☐ 108 Ismael Valdes	.20	.09
☐ 109 Jose Offerman	.10	.05
☐ 110 Todd Worrell	.20	.09
☐ 111 Eric Karros	.20	.09
☐ 112 Brett Butler	.20	.09
☐ 113 Juan Castro	.10	.05
☐ 114 Roberto Kelly	.10	.05
☐ 115 Omar Daal	.10	.05
☐ 116 Antonio Osuna	.10	.05
☐ 117 Hideo Nomo ROY	.30	.14
☐ 118 Mike Lansing	.10	.05
☐ 119 Mel Rojas	.10	.05
☐ 120 Sean Berry	.10	.05
☐ 121 David Segui	.10	.05
☐ 122 Tavo Alvarez	.10	.05
☐ 123 Pedro J.Martinez	.40	.18
☐ 124 F.P. Santangelo	.10	.05
☐ 125 Rondell White	.20	.09
☐ 126 Cliff Floyd	.10	.05
☐ 127 Henry Rodriguez	.10	.05
☐ 128 Tony Tarasco	.10	.05
☐ 129 Yamil Benitez	.20	.09
☐ 130 Carlos Perez	.10	.05
☐ 131 Wil Cordero	.10	.05
☐ 132 Jeff Fassero	.10	.05
☐ 133 Moises Alou	.20	.09
☐ 134 John Franco	.20	.09
☐ 135 Rico Brogna	.10	.05
☐ 136 Dave Mlicki	.10	.05
☐ 137 Bill Pulsipher	.10	.05
☐ 138 Jose Vizcaino	.10	.05
☐ 139 Carl Everett	.10	.05
☐ 140 Edgardo Alfonzo	.30	.14
☐ 141 Bobby Jones	.10	.05
☐ 142 Alberto Castillo	.10	.05
☐ 143 Joe Orsulak	.10	.05
☐ 144 Jeff Kent	.10	.05
☐ 145 Ryan Thompson	.10	.05
☐ 146 Jason Isringhausen	.10	.05
☐ 147 Todd Hundley	.20	.09
☐ 148 Alex Ochoa	.10	.05
☐ 149 Charlie Hayes	.10	.05
☐ 150 Michael Mimbs	.10	.05
☐ 151 Darren Daulton	.20	.09
☐ 152 Toby Borland	.10	.05
☐ 153 Andy Van Slyke	.20	.09
☐ 154 Mickey Morandini	.10	.05
☐ 155 Sid Fernandez	.10	.05
☐ 156 Tom Marsh	.10	.05
☐ 157 Kevin Stocker	.10	.05
☐ 158 Paul Quantrill	.10	.05
☐ 159 Gregg Jefferies	.20	.09
☐ 160 Ricky Bottalico	.10	.05
☐ 161 Lenny Dykstra	.20	.09
☐ 162 Mark Whiten	.10	.05
☐ 163 Tyler Green	.10	.05
☐ 164 Jim Eisenreich	.20	.09
☐ 165 Heathcliff Slocumb	.10	.05
☐ 166 Esteban Loaiza	.10	.05
☐ 167 Rich Aude	.10	.05
☐ 168 Jason Christiansen	.10	.05
☐ 169 Ramon Morel	.10	.05
☐ 170 Orlando Merced	.10	.05
☐ 171 Paul Wagner	.10	.05
☐ 172 Jeff King	.20	.09
☐ 173 Jay Bell	.20	.09
☐ 174 Jacob Brumfield	.10	.05
☐ 175 Nelson Liriano	.10	.05
☐ 176 Dan Miceli	.10	.05
☐ 177 Carlos Garcia	.10	.05
☐ 178 Denny Neagle	.20	.09
☐ 179 Angelo Encarnacion	.10	.05
☐ 180 Al Martin	.10	.05
☐ 181 Midre Cummings	.10	.05
☐ 182 Eddie Williams	.10	.05
☐ 183 Roberto Petagine	.10	.05
☐ 184 Tony Gwynn	1.00	.45
☐ 185 Andy Ashby	.10	.05
☐ 186 Melvin Nieves	.20	.09
☐ 187 Phil Clark	.10	.05
☐ 188 Brad Ausmus	.10	.05
☐ 189 Bip Roberts	.10	.05
☐ 190 Fernando Valenzuela	.20	.09
☐ 191 Marc Newfield	.10	.05
☐ 192 Steve Finley	.20	.09
☐ 193 Trevor Hoffman	.20	.09
☐ 194 Andujar Cedeno	.10	.05
☐ 195 Jody Reed	.10	.05
☐ 196 Ken Caminiti	.40	.18
☐ 197 Joey Hamilton	.20	.09
☐ 198 Tony Gwynn BAC	.40	.18
☐ 199 Shawn Barton	.10	.05
☐ 200 Deion Sanders	.40	.18
☐ 201 Rikkert Faneyte	.10	.05
☐ 202 Barry Bonds	.50	.23
☐ 203 Matt Williams	.30	.14
☐ 204 Jose Bautista	.10	.05
☐ 205 Mark Leiter	.10	.05
☐ 206 Mark Carreon	.10	.05
☐ 207 Robby Thompson	.10	.05
☐ 208 Terry Mulholland	.10	.05
☐ 209 Rod Beck	.10	.05
☐ 210 Royce Clayton	.10	.05
☐ 211 J.R. Phillips	.10	.05
☐ 212 Kirt Manwaring	.10	.05
☐ 213 Glenallen Hill	.10	.05
☐ 214 William VanLandingham	.10	.05
☐ 215 Scott Cooper	.10	.05
☐ 216 Bernard Gilkey	.20	.09
☐ 217 Allen Watson	.10	.05
☐ 218 Donovan Osborne	.10	.05
☐ 219 Ray Lankford	.20	.09
☐ 220 Tony Fossas	.10	.05
☐ 221 Tom Pagnozzi	.10	.05
☐ 222 John Mabry	.20	.09
☐ 223 Tripp Cromer	.10	.05
☐ 224 Mark Petkovsek	.10	.05
☐ 225 Mike Morgan	.10	.05
☐ 226 Ozzie Smith	.50	.23
☐ 227 Tom Henke	.20	.09
☐ 228 Jose Oquendo	.10	.05
☐ 229 Brian Jordan	.20	.09
☐ 230 Cal Ripken	1.50	.70
☐ 231 Scott Erickson	.10	.05
☐ 232 Harold Baines	.20	.09
☐ 233 Jeff Manto	.10	.05
☐ 234 Jesse Orosco	.10	.05
☐ 235 Jeffrey Hammonds	.10	.05
☐ 236 Brady Anderson	.30	.14
☐ 237 Manny Alexander	.10	.05
☐ 238 Chris Hoiles	.10	.05
☐ 239 Rafael Palmeiro	.30	.14
☐ 240 Ben McDonald	.10	.05
☐ 241 Curtis Goodwin	.10	.05
☐ 242 Bobby Bonilla	.20	.09
☐ 243 Mike Mussina	.40	.18
☐ 244 Kevin Brown	.20	.09
☐ 245 Armando Benitez	.10	.05
☐ 246 Jose Canseco	.30	.14
☐ 247 Erik Hanson	.10	.05
☐ 248 Mo Vaughn	.50	.23
☐ 249 Tim Naehring	.10	.05
☐ 250 Vaughn Eshelman	.10	.05
☐ 251 Mike Greenwell	.10	.05
☐ 252 Troy O'Leary	.10	.05
☐ 253 Tim Wakefield	.10	.05
☐ 254 Dwayne Hosey	.10	.05
☐ 255 John Valentin	.20	.09
☐ 256 Rick Aguilera	.10	.05
☐ 257 Mike Macfarlane	.10	.05
☐ 258 Roger Clemens	.75	.35
☐ 259 Luis Alicea	.10	.05
☐ 260 Mo Vaughn MVP	.40	.18
☐ 261 Mark Langston	.10	.05
☐ 262 Jim Edmonds	.40	.18
☐ 263 Rod Correia	.10	.05
☐ 264 Tim Salmon	.40	.18
☐ 265 J.T. Snow	.20	.09
☐ 266 Orlando Palmeiro	.10	.05
☐ 267 Jorge Fabregas	.10	.05
☐ 268 Jim Abbott	.20	.09
☐ 269 Eduardo Perez	.10	.05
☐ 270 Lee Smith	.20	.09
☐ 271 Gary DiSarcina	.10	.05
☐ 272 Damion Easley	.10	.05
☐ 273 Tony Phillips	.10	.05
☐ 274 Garret Anderson	.20	.09
☐ 275 Chuck Finley	.10	.05
☐ 276 Chili Davis	.10	.05
☐ 277 Lance Johnson	.10	.05
☐ 278 Alex Fernandez	.20	.09
☐ 279 Robin Ventura	.20	.09
☐ 280 Chris Snopek	.10	.05
☐ 281 Brian Keyser	.10	.05
☐ 282 Lyle Mouton	.10	.05
☐ 283 Luis Andujar	.10	.05
☐ 284 Tim Raines	.10	.05
☐ 285 Larry Thomas	.10	.05
☐ 286 Ozzie Guillen	.10	.05
☐ 287 Frank Thomas	1.50	.70
☐ 288 Roberto Hernandez	.20	.09
☐ 289 Dave Martinez	.10	.05
☐ 290 Ray Durham	.20	.09
☐ 291 Ron Karkovice	.10	.05
☐ 292 Wilson Alvarez	.20	.09
☐ 293 Omar Vizquel	.20	.09
☐ 294 Eddie Murray	.40	.18
☐ 295 Sandy Alomar, Jr.	.10	.05
☐ 296 Orel Hershiser	.20	.09
☐ 297 Jose Mesa	.20	.09
☐ 298 Julian Tavarez	.10	.05
☐ 299 Dennis Martinez	.20	.09
☐ 300 Carlos Baerga	.20	.09
☐ 301 Manny Ramirez	.40	.18
☐ 302 Jim Thome	.40	.18
☐ 303 Kenny Lofton	.50	.23
☐ 304 Tony Pena	.10	.05
☐ 305 Alvaro Espinoza	.10	.05
☐ 306 Paul Sorrento	.10	.05
☐ 307 Albert Belle	.50	.23
☐ 308 Danny Bautista	.10	.05
☐ 309 Chris Gomez	.10	.05
☐ 310 Jose Lima	.10	.05
☐ 311 Phil Nevin	.10	.05
☐ 312 Alan Trammell	.30	.14
☐ 313 Chad Curtis	.10	.05
☐ 314 John Flaherty	.10	.05
☐ 315 Travis Fryman	.20	.09
☐ 316 Todd Steverson	.10	.05
☐ 317 Brian Bohanon	.10	.05
☐ 318 Lou Whitaker	.20	.09
☐ 319 Bobby Higginson	.20	.09
☐ 320 Steve Rodriguez	.10	.05
☐ 321 Cecil Fielder	.20	.09
☐ 322 Felipe Lira	.10	.05
☐ 323 Juan Samuel	.10	.05
☐ 324 Bob Hamelin	.10	.05
☐ 325 Tom Goodwin	.10	.05
☐ 326 Johnny Damon	.20	.09
☐ 327 Hipolito Pichardo	.10	.05
☐ 328 Dilson Torres	.10	.05
☐ 329 Kevin Appier	.20	.09
☐ 330 Mark Gubicza	.10	.05
☐ 331 Jon Nunnally	.10	.05
☐ 332 Gary Gaetti	.20	.09
☐ 333 Brent Mayne	.10	.05
☐ 334 Brent Cookson	.10	.05
☐ 335 Tom Gordon	.10	.05
☐ 336 Wally Joyner	.10	.05
☐ 337 Greg Gagne	.10	.05
☐ 338 Fernando Vina	.10	.05

☐ 339 Joe Oliver	.10	.05
☐ 340 John Jaha	.10	.05
☐ 341 Jeff Cirillo	.20	.09
☐ 342 Pat Listach	.10	.05
☐ 343 Dave Nilsson	.20	.09
☐ 344 Steve Sparks	.10	.05
☐ 345 Ricky Bones	.10	.05
☐ 346 David Hulse	.10	.05
☐ 347 Scott Karl	.10	.05
☐ 348 Darryl Hamilton	.10	.05
☐ 349 B.J. Surhoff	.20	.09
☐ 350 Angel Miranda	.10	.05
☐ 351 Sid Roberson	.10	.05
☐ 352 Matt Mieske	.10	.05
☐ 353 Jose Valentin	.10	.05
☐ 354 Matt Lawton	.10	.05
☐ 355 Eddie Guardado	.10	.05
☐ 356 Brad Radke	.20	.09
☐ 357 Pedro Munoz	.10	.05
☐ 358 Scott Stahoviak	.10	.05
☐ 359 Erik Schullstrom	.10	.05
☐ 360 Pat Meares	.10	.05
☐ 361 Marty Cordova	.10	.05
☐ 362 Scott Leius	.10	.05
☐ 363 Matt Walbeck	.10	.05
☐ 364 Rich Becker	.10	.05
☐ 365 Kirby Puckett	.75	.35
☐ 366 Oscar Munoz	.10	.05
☐ 367 Chuck Knoblauch	.40	.18
☐ 368 Marty Cordova ROY	.20	.09
☐ 369 Bernie Williams	.40	.18
☐ 370 Mike Stanley	.10	.05
☐ 371 Andy Pettitte	.50	.23
☐ 372 Jack McDowell	.10	.05
☐ 373 Sterling Hitchcock	.10	.05
☐ 374 David Cone	.20	.09
☐ 375 Randy Velarde	.10	.05
☐ 376 Don Mattingly	.60	.25
☐ 377 Melido Perez	.10	.05
☐ 378 Wade Boggs	.40	.18
☐ 379 Ruben Sierra	.10	.05
☐ 380 Tony Fernandez	.10	.05
☐ 381 John Wetteland	.20	.09
☐ 382 Mariano Rivera	.40	.18
☐ 383 Derek Jeter	1.25	.55
☐ 384 Paul O'Neill	.10	.05
☐ 385 Mark McGwire	.75	.35
☐ 386 Scott Brosius	.10	.05
☐ 387 Don Wengert	.10	.05
☐ 388 Terry Steinbach	.20	.09
☐ 389 Brent Gates	.10	.05
☐ 390 Craig Paquette	.10	.05
☐ 391 Mike Bordick	.10	.05
☐ 392 Ariel Prieto	.10	.05
☐ 393 Dennis Eckersley	.30	.14
☐ 394 Carlos Reyes	.10	.05
☐ 395 Todd Stottleymyre	.10	.05
☐ 396 Rickey Henderson	.30	.14
☐ 397 Geronimo Berroa	.10	.05
☐ 398 Steve Ontiveros	.10	.05
☐ 399 Mike Gallego	.10	.05
☐ 400 Stan Javier	.10	.05
☐ 401 Randy Johnson	.40	.18
☐ 402 Norm Charlton	.10	.05
☐ 403 Mike Blowers	.10	.05
☐ 404 Tino Martinez	.40	.18
☐ 405 Dan Wilson	.10	.05
☐ 406 Andy Benes	.10	.05
☐ 407 Alex Diaz	.10	.05
☐ 408 Edgar Martinez	.30	.14
☐ 409 Chris Bosio	.10	.05
☐ 410 Ken Griffey, Jr.	2.00	.90
☐ 411 Luis Sojo	.10	.05
☐ 412 Bob Wolcott	.10	.05
☐ 413 Vince Coleman	.10	.05
☐ 414 Rich Amaral	.10	.05
☐ 415 Jay Buhner	.30	.14
☐ 416 Alex Rodriguez	1.50	.70
☐ 417 Joey Cora	.20	.09
☐ 418 Randy Johnson CY	.40	.18
☐ 419 Edgar Martinez BAC	.20	.09
☐ 420 Ivan Rodriguez	.50	.23
☐ 421 Mark McLemore	.10	.05
☐ 422 Mickey Tettleton	.10	.05
☐ 423 Juan Gonzalez	1.00	.45
☐ 424 Will Clark	.30	.14
☐ 425 Kevin Gross	.10	.05
☐ 426 Dean Palmer	.20	.09
☐ 427 Kenny Rogers	.10	.05
☐ 428 Bob Tewksbury	.10	.05
☐ 429 Benji Gil	.10	.05
☐ 430 Jeff Russell	.10	.05
☐ 431 Rusty Greer	.30	.14
☐ 432 Roger Pavlik	.10	.05
☐ 433 Esteban Beltre	.10	.05
☐ 434 Otis Nixon	.10	.05
☐ 435 Paul Molitor	.40	.18
☐ 436 Carlos Delgado	.20	.09
☐ 437 Ed Sprague	.10	.05
☐ 438 Juan Guzman	.10	.05
☐ 439 Domingo Cedeno	.10	.05
☐ 440 Pat Hentgen	.20	.09
☐ 441 Tomas Perez	.10	.05
☐ 442 John Olerud	.10	.05
☐ 443 Shawn Green	.20	.09
☐ 444 Al Leiter	.10	.05
☐ 445 Joe Carter	.20	.09
☐ 446 Robert Perez	.10	.05
☐ 447 Devon White	.10	.05
☐ 448 Tony Castillo	.10	.05
☐ 449 Alex Gonzalez	.10	.05
☐ 450 Roberto Alomar	.40	.18

1996 Pacific Cramer's Choice

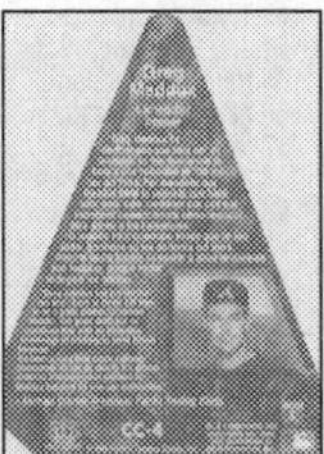

Randomly inserted in packs at a rate of one in 721, this 10-card set features the top Major League Baseball players as chosen by Pacific President and CEO, Michael Cramer. The fronts display a color player cut-out on a pyramid diecut shaped background. The backs carry information about why the player was selected for this set in both English and Spanish.

	MINT	NRMT
COMPLETE SET (10)	1200.00	550.00
COMMON CARD (CC1-CC10)	40.00	18.00
☐ CC1 Roberto Alomar	50.00	22.00
☐ CC2 Wade Boggs	40.00	18.00
☐ CC3 Cal Ripken	200.00	90.00
☐ CC4 Greg Maddux	150.00	70.00
☐ CC5 Frank Thomas	200.00	90.00
☐ CC6 Tony Gwynn	120.00	55.00
☐ CC7 Mike Piazza	150.00	70.00
☐ CC8 Ken Griffey Jr.	250.00	110.00
☐ CC9 Manny Ramirez	50.00	22.00
☐ CC10 Edgar Martinez	40.00	18.00

1996 Pacific Estrellas Latinas

Randomly inserted in packs at a rate of four in 37, this 36-card set salutes the great Latino players in the major leagues today. The fronts feature color player action cut-outs on a black and gold foil background. The horizontal backs carry a player portrait with information about the player in both English and Spanish.

	MINT	NRMT
COMPLETE SET (36)	50.00	22.00
COMMON CARD (EL1-EL36)	1.00	.45
☐ EL1 Roberto Alomar	2.50	1.10
☐ EL2 Moises Alou	1.50	.70
☐ EL3 Carlos Baerga	1.50	.70
☐ EL4 Geronimo Berroa	1.00	.45
☐ EL5 Ricky Bones	1.00	.45
☐ EL6 Bobby Bonilla	1.50	.70
☐ EL7 Jose Canseco	2.00	.90
☐ EL8 Vinny Castilla	1.50	.70
☐ EL9 Pedro Martinez	2.50	1.10
☐ EL10 John Valentin	1.00	.45
☐ EL11 Andres Galarraga	2.00	.90
☐ EL12 Juan Gonzalez	8.00	3.60
☐ EL13 Ozzie Guillen	1.00	.45
☐ EL14 Esteban Loaiza	1.00	.45
☐ EL15 Javier Lopez	1.50	.70
☐ EL16 Dennis Martinez	1.50	.70
☐ EL17 Edgar Martinez	2.00	.90
☐ EL18 Tino Martinez	2.50	1.10
☐ EL19 Orlando Merced	1.00	.45
☐ EL20 Jose Mesa	1.00	.45
☐ EL21 Raul Mondesi	2.00	.90
☐ EL22 Jaime Navarro	1.00	.45
☐ EL23 Rafael Palmeiro	2.00	.90
☐ EL24 Carlos Perez	1.00	.45
☐ EL25 Manny Ramirez	2.50	1.10
☐ EL26 Alex Rodriguez	15.00	6.75
☐ EL27 Ivan Rodriguez	4.00	1.80
☐ EL28 David Segui	1.00	.45
☐ EL29 Ruben Sierra	1.00	.45
☐ EL30 Sammy Sosa	2.50	1.10
☐ EL31 Julian Tavarez	1.00	.45
☐ EL32 Ismael Valdes	1.00	.45
☐ EL33 Fernando Valenzuela	1.50	.70
☐ EL34 Quilvio Veras	1.00	.45
☐ EL35 Omar Vizquel	1.50	.70
☐ EL36 Bernie Williams	2.50	1.10

1996 Pacific Gold Crown Die Cuts

Randomly inserted in packs at a rate of one in 37, this 36-card set features 1996 Major League Baseball Super Stars. The fronts display color action player photos with a diecut gold crown at the top and gold foil printing. The backs carry a color player portrait and information about the player in English and Spanish.

	MINT	NRMT
COMPLETE SET (36)	450.00	200.00
COMMON CARD (DC1-DC36)	4.00	1.80
☐ DC1 Roberto Alomar	10.00	4.50
☐ DC2 Will Clark	6.00	2.70
☐ DC3 Johnny Damon	5.00	2.20
☐ DC4 Don Mattingly	15.00	6.75
☐ DC5 Edgar Martinez	6.00	2.70
☐ DC6 Manny Ramirez	10.00	4.50
☐ DC7 Mike Piazza	30.00	13.50
☐ DC8 Quilvio Veras	4.00	1.80
☐ DC9 Rickey Henderson	6.00	2.70
☐ DC10 Jeff Bagwell	20.00	9.00
☐ DC11 Andres Galarraga	10.00	4.50
☐ DC12 Tim Salmon	10.00	4.50
☐ DC13 Ken Griffey Jr.	50.00	22.00
☐ DC14 Sammy Sosa	10.00	4.50
☐ DC15 Cal Ripken	40.00	18.00
☐ DC16 Raul Mondesi	6.00	2.70
☐ DC17 Jose Canseco	6.00	2.70
☐ DC18 Frank Thomas	40.00	18.00
☐ DC19 Hideo Nomo	25.00	11.00
☐ DC20 Wade Boggs	10.00	4.50
☐ DC21 Reggie Sanders	4.00	1.80
☐ DC22 Carlos Baerga	4.00	1.80
☐ DC23 Mo Vaughn	12.00	5.50
☐ DC24 Ivan Rodriguez	12.00	5.50
☐ DC25 Kirby Puckett	20.00	9.00
☐ DC26 Albert Belle	12.00	5.50
☐ DC27 Vinny Castilla	5.00	2.20
☐ DC28 Greg Maddux	30.00	13.50
☐ DC29 Dante Bichette	6.00	2.70
☐ DC30 Deion Sanders	10.00	4.50
☐ DC31 Chipper Jones	30.00	13.50
☐ DC32 Cecil Fielder	5.00	2.20
☐ DC33 Randy Johnson	10.00	4.50
☐ DC34 Mark McGwire	20.00	9.00
☐ DC35 Tony Gwynn	25.00	11.00
☐ DC36 Barry Bonds	12.00	5.50

1996 Pacific Hometowns

Randomly inserted in packs at a rate of two in 37, this 20-card set features color action player photos with a gold foil border on the left and gold foil printing. The backs carry a player portrait with the player's hometown or city and country and player information printed in both English and Spanish.

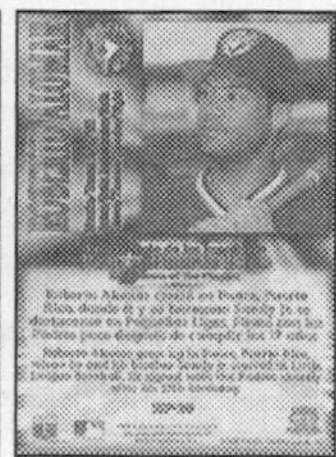

	MINT	NRMT
COMPLETE SET (20)	120.00	55.00
COMMON CARD (HP1-HP20)	1.50	.70
☐ HP1 Mike Piazza	12.00	5.50
☐ HP2 Greg Maddux	12.00	5.50
☐ HP3 Tony Gwynn	8.00	3.60
☐ HP4 Carlos Baerga	1.50	.70
☐ HP5 Don Mattingly	8.00	3.60
☐ HP6 Cal Ripken	15.00	6.75
☐ HP7 Chipper Jones	12.00	5.50
☐ HP8 Andres Galarraga	3.00	1.35
☐ HP9 Manny Ramirez	3.00	1.35
☐ HP10 Roberto Alomar	3.00	1.35
☐ HP11 Ken Griffey Jr.	20.00	9.00
☐ HP12 Jose Canseco	2.50	1.10
☐ HP13 Frank Thomas	15.00	6.75
☐ HP14 Vinny Castilla	2.00	.90
☐ HP15 Roberto Kelly	1.50	.70
☐ HP16 Dennis Martinez	2.00	.90
☐ HP17 Kirby Puckett	8.00	3.60
☐ HP18 Raul Mondesi	2.50	1.10
☐ HP19 Hideo Nomo	10.00	4.50
☐ HP20 Edgar Martinez	2.50	1.10

1996 Pacific Milestones

Randomly inserted in packs at a rate of one in 37, this 10-card set denotes the outstanding milestone and record-breaking achievements of baseball's superstars in 1995. The fronts feature a color action player cut-out on a blue foil background with embossed symbols represting the team logo, baseball, and the milestone or achievement. The backs carry a player portrait with the milestone or achievement printed in both English and Spanish.

	MINT	NRMT
COMPLETE SET (10)	75.00	34.00
COMMON CARD (M1-M10)	2.50	1.10
☐ M1 Albert Belle	5.00	2.20
☐ M2 Don Mattingly	8.00	3.60
☐ M3 Tony Gwynn	10.00	4.50
☐ M4 Jose Canseco	3.50	1.55
☐ M5 Marty Cordova	2.50	1.10
☐ M6 Wade Boggs	4.00	1.80
☐ M7 Greg Maddux	12.00	5.50
☐ M8 Eddie Murray	3.50	1.55
☐ M9 Ken Griffey Jr.	20.00	9.00
☐ M10 Cal Ripken	15.00	6.75

1996 Pacific October Moments

Randomly inserted in packs at a rate of one in 37, this 20-card set highlights 1995 postseason heroics and the players involved. The fronts feature borderless color player action photos with a bronze foil background and printing. The backs carry a player portrait with the heroic action printed in both English and Spanish.

	MINT	NRMT
COMPLETE SET (20)	150.00	70.00
COMMON CARD (OM1-OM20)	2.00	.90
☐ OM1 Carlos Baerga	2.00	.90
☐ OM2 Albert Belle	8.00	3.60
☐ OM3 Dante Bichette	3.00	1.35
☐ OM4 Jose Canseco	4.00	1.80
☐ OM5 Tom Glavine	4.00	1.80
☐ OM6 Ken Griffey Jr.	30.00	13.50
☐ OM7 Randy Johnson	6.00	2.70
☐ OM8 Chipper Jones	20.00	9.00
☐ OM9 David Justice	6.00	2.70
☐ OM10 Ryan Klesko	4.00	1.80
☐ OM11 Kenny Lofton	8.00	3.60
☐ OM12 Javier Lopez	3.00	1.35
☐ OM13 Greg Maddux	20.00	9.00
☐ OM14 Edgar Martinez	4.00	1.80
☐ OM15 Don Mattingly	10.00	4.50
☐ OM16 Hideo Nomo	15.00	6.75
☐ OM17 Mike Piazza	20.00	9.00
☐ OM18 Manny Ramirez	6.00	2.70
☐ OM19 Reggie Sanders	2.00	.90
☐ OM20 Jim Thome	6.00	2.70

1996 Pacific/Advil Nolan Ryan

This 27-card standard-size set features all-time strikeout king, Nolan Ryan. The set was available directly with a proof of purchase of Advil products. Each full-bleed card features a different highlight of Ryan's career. There was also an A , B card which were included at retail stores as part of the store display. A collector got a pack with these cards if they a big enough package. They were not available as part of the regular set.

	MINT	NRMT
COMPLETE SET (27)	15.00	6.75
COMMON CARD (1-27)	.60	.25
☐ 1 Nolan Ryan New York Mets	.60	.25
☐ 2 Nolan Ryan California Angels	.60	.25
☐ 3 Nolan Ryan Houston Astros	.60	.25
☐ 4 Nolan Ryan Texas Rangers	.60	.25
☐ 5 Nolan Ryan No-Hitter #1	.60	.25
☐ 6 Nolan Ryan No-Hitter #2	.60	.25
☐ 7 Nolan Ryan No-Hitter #3	.60	.25
☐ 8 Nolan Ryan No-Hitter #4	.60	.25
☐ 9 Nolan Ryan No-Hitter #5	.60	.25
☐ 10 Nolan Ryan No-Hitter #6	.60	.25
☐ 11 Nolan Ryan No-Hitter #7	.60	.25
☐ 12 Nolan Ryan 1st Major League Win	.60	.25
☐ 13 Nolan Ryan 250th Win	.60	.25
☐ 14 Nolan Ryan 300th Win	.60	.25
☐ 15 Nolan Ryan 324th Win	.60	.25
☐ 16 Nolan Ryan 1,000 Strikeout	.60	.25
☐ 17 Nolan Ryan 2,000 Strikeout	.60	.25
☐ 18 Nolan Ryan 3,000 Strikeout	.60	.25
☐ 19 Nolan Ryan Strikeout Record	.60	.25
☐ 20 Nolan Ryan 4,000 Strikeout	.60	.25
☐ 21 Nolan Ryan 5,000 Strikeout	.60	.25
☐ 22 Nolan Ryan World Series Victory	.60	.25
☐ 23 Nolan Ryan Fastest Pitch	.60	.25
☐ 24 Nolan Ryan Ryan Homerun	.60	.25
☐ 25 Nolan Ryan Power Pitcher	.60	.25
☐ 26 Nolan Ryan 1989 All-Star Game	.60	.25
☐ 27 Nolan Ryan Last Appearence	.60	.25
☐ A Nolan Ryan	2.50	1.10
☐ B Nolan Ryan	2.50	1.10

1996 Pacific Baerga Softball

This eight card set features major league baseball players who donated their time to participate in the Second Annual Carlos Baerga Celebrities Softball Game, played Dec. 8 in Bayamon, Puerto Rico. Two cards from the set were distributed to each attendee of the game. The fronts carry colored action player photos from the softball game. The backs display color player portraits with player information in both Spanish and English.

	MINT	NRMT
COMPLETE SET (8)	6.00	2.70
COMMON CARD (1-8)	.25	.11
☐ 1 Carlos Baerga	.25	.11
☐ 2 Mike Piazza	2.50	1.10
☐ 3 Bernie Williams	1.00	.45
☐ 4 Frank Thomas	3.00	1.35
☐ 5 Roberto Alomar	1.00	.45
☐ 6 Edgar Martinez	.75	.35
☐ 7 Kenny Lofton	1.25	.55
☐ 8 Sammy Sosa	1.00	.45

1997 Pacific

This 450-card set was issued in one series and distributed in 12-card packs. The fronts feature color action player photos foiled in gold. The backs carry player information in both English and Spanish with player statistics.

	MINT	NRMT
COMPLETE SET (450)	40.00	18.00
COMMON CARD (1-450)	.15	.07
☐ 1 Garret Anderson	.30	.14
☐ 2 George Arias	.15	.07
☐ 3 Chili Davis	.30	.14
☐ 4 Gary DiSarcina	.15	.07
☐ 5 Jim Edmonds	.60	.25
☐ 6 Darin Erstad	1.00	.45
☐ 7 Jorge Fabregas	.15	.07
☐ 8 Chuck Finley	.15	.07
☐ 9 Rex Hudler	.15	.07
☐ 10 Mark Langston	.15	.07
☐ 11 Orlando Palmeiro	.15	.07
☐ 12 Troy Percival	.15	.07
☐ 13 Tim Salmon	.60	.25
☐ 14 J.T. Snow	.30	.14
☐ 15 Randy Velarde	.15	.07

☐ 16 Manny Alexander .15 .07
☐ 17 Roberto Alomar .60 .25
☐ 18 Brady Anderson .40 .18
☐ 19 Armando Benitez .15 .07
☐ 20 Bobby Bonilla .30 .14
☐ 21 Rocky Coppinger .30 .14
☐ 22 Scott Erickson .15 .07
☐ 23 Jeffrey Hammonds .15 .07
☐ 24 Chris Hoiles .15 .07
☐ 25 Eddie Murray .60 .25
☐ 26 Mike Mussina .60 .25
☐ 27 Randy Myers .15 .07
☐ 28 Rafael Palmeiro .40 .18
☐ 29 Cal Ripken 2.50 1.10
☐ 30 B.J. Surhoff .30 .14
☐ 31 Tony Tarasco .15 .07
☐ 32 Esteban Beltre .15 .07
☐ 33 Darren Bragg .15 .07
☐ 34 Jose Canseco .40 .18
☐ 35 Roger Clemens 1.25 .55
☐ 36 Wil Cordero .15 .07
☐ 37 Alex Delgado .15 .07
☐ 38 Jeff Frye .15 .07
☐ 39 Nomar Garciaparra 2.00 .90
☐ 40 Tom Gordon .15 .07
☐ 41 Mike Greenwell .15 .07
☐ 42 Reggie Jefferson .30 .14
☐ 43 Tim Naehring .15 .07
☐ 44 Troy O'Leary .15 .07
☐ 45 Heathcliff Slocumb .30 .14
☐ 46 Lee Tinsley .15 .07
☐ 47 John Valentin .15 .07
☐ 48 Mo Vaughn .75 .35
☐ 49 Wilson Alvarez .30 .14
☐ 50 Harold Baines .15 .07
☐ 51 Ray Durham .15 .07
☐ 52 Alex Fernandez .30 .14
☐ 53 Ozzie Guillen .15 .07
☐ 54 Roberto Hernandez .30 .14
☐ 55 Ron Karkovice .15 .07
☐ 56 Darren Lewis .15 .07
☐ 57 Norberto Martin .15 .07
☐ 58 Dave Martinez .15 .07
☐ 59 Lyle Mouton .15 .07
☐ 60 Jose Munoz .15 .07
☐ 61 Tony Phillips .15 .07
☐ 62 Kevin Tapani .15 .07
☐ 63 Danny Tartabull .15 .07
☐ 64 Frank Thomas 2.50 1.10
☐ 65 Robin Ventura .30 .14
☐ 66 Sandy Alomar Jr. .30 .14
☐ 67 Albert Belle .75 .35
☐ 68 Julio Franco .30 .14
☐ 69 Brian Giles .15 .07
☐ 70 Danny Graves .15 .07
☐ 71 Orel Hershiser .30 .14
☐ 72 Jeff Kent .15 .07
☐ 73 Kenny Lofton .75 .35
☐ 74 Dennis Martinez .30 .14
☐ 75 Jack McDowell .15 .07
☐ 76 Jose Mesa .30 .14
☐ 77 Charles Nagy .30 .14
☐ 78 Manny Ramirez .60 .25
☐ 79 Julian Tavarez .15 .07
☐ 80 Jim Thome .60 .25
☐ 81 Jose Vizcaino .15 .07
☐ 82 Omar Vizquel .30 .14
☐ 83 Brad Ausmus .15 .07
☐ 84 Kimera Bartee .15 .07
☐ 85 Raul Casanova .15 .07
☐ 86 Tony Clark .60 .25
☐ 87 Travis Fryman .30 .14
☐ 88 Bobby Higginson .30 .14
☐ 89 Mark Lewis .15 .07
☐ 90 Jose Lima .15 .07
☐ 91 Felipe Lira .15 .07
☐ 92 Phil Nevin .15 .07
☐ 93 Melvin Nieves .15 .07
☐ 94 Curtis Pride .15 .07
☐ 95 Ruben Sierra .15 .07
☐ 96 Alan Trammell .30 .14
☐ 97 Kevin Appier .30 .14
☐ 98 Tim Belcher .15 .07
☐ 99 Johnny Damon .15 .07
☐ 100 Tom Goodwin .15 .07
☐ 101 Bob Hamelin .15 .07
☐ 102 David Howard .15 .07
☐ 103 Jason Jacome .15 .07
☐ 104 Keith Lockhart .15 .07
☐ 105 Mike Macfarlane .15 .07
☐ 106 Jeff Montgomery .15 .07
☐ 107 Jose Offerman .15 .07
☐ 108 Hipolito Pichardo .15 .07
☐ 109 Joe Randa .15 .07
☐ 110 Bip Roberts .15 .07
☐ 111 Chris Stynes .15 .07
☐ 112 Mike Sweeney .15 .07
☐ 113 Joe Vitiello .15 .07
☐ 114 Jeromy Burnitz .30 .14
☐ 115 Chuck Carr .15 .07
☐ 116 Jeff Cirillo .30 .14
☐ 117 Mike Fetters .15 .07
☐ 118 David Hulse .15 .07
☐ 119 John Jaha .15 .07
☐ 120 Scott Karl .15 .07
☐ 121 Jesse Levis .15 .07
☐ 122 Mark Loretta .15 .07
☐ 123 Mike Matheny .15 .07
☐ 124 Ben McDonald .15 .07
☐ 125 Matt Mieske .15 .07
☐ 126 Angel Miranda .15 .07
☐ 127 Dave Nilsson .15 .07
☐ 128 Jose Valentin .15 .07
☐ 129 Fernando Vina .15 .07
☐ 130 Ron Villone .15 .07
☐ 131 Gerald Williams .15 .07
☐ 132 Rick Aguilera .15 .07
☐ 133 Rich Becker .15 .07
☐ 134 Ron Coomer .15 .07
☐ 135 Marty Cordova .30 .14
☐ 136 Eddie Guardado .15 .07
☐ 137 Denny Hocking .15 .07
☐ 138 Roberto Kelly .15 .07
☐ 139 Chuck Knoblauch .60 .25
☐ 140 Matt Lawton .15 .07
☐ 141 Pat Meares .15 .07
☐ 142 Paul Molitor .60 .25
☐ 143 Greg Myers .15 .07
☐ 144 Jeff Reboulet .15 .07
☐ 145 Scott Stahoviak .15 .07
☐ 146 Todd Walker .15 .07
☐ 147 Wade Boggs .60 .25
☐ 148 David Cone .30 .14
☐ 149 Mariano Duncan .15 .07
☐ 150 Cecil Fielder .30 .14
☐ 151 Dwight Gooden .30 .14
☐ 152 Derek Jeter 2.00 .90
☐ 153 Jim Leyritz .15 .07
☐ 154 Tino Martinez .60 .25
☐ 155 Paul O'Neill .30 .14
☐ 156 Andy Pettitte .60 .25
☐ 157 Tim Raines .15 .07
☐ 158 Mariano Rivera .30 .14
☐ 159 Ruben Rivera .30 .14
☐ 160 Kenny Rogers .15 .07
☐ 161 Darryl Strawberry .30 .14
☐ 162 John Wetteland .30 .14
☐ 163 Bernie Williams .60 .25
☐ 164 Tony Batista .30 .14
☐ 165 Geronimo Berroa .15 .07
☐ 166 Mike Bordick .15 .07
☐ 167 Scott Brosius .15 .07
☐ 168 Brent Gates .15 .07
☐ 169 Jason Giambi .30 .14
☐ 170 Jose Herrera .15 .07
☐ 171 Brian Lesher .15 .07
☐ 172 Damon Mashore .15 .07
☐ 173 Mark McGwire 1.25 .55
☐ 174 Ariel Prieto .15 .07
☐ 175 Carlos Reyes .15 .07
☐ 176 Matt Stairs .15 .07
☐ 177 Terry Steinbach .30 .14
☐ 178 John Wasdin .15 .07
☐ 179 Ernie Young .15 .07
☐ 180 Rich Amaral .15 .07
☐ 181 Bobby Ayala .15 .07
☐ 182 Jay Buhner .40 .18
☐ 183 Rafael Carmona .15 .07
☐ 184 Norm Charlton .15 .07
☐ 185 Joey Cora .30 .14
☐ 186 Ken Griffey Jr. 3.00 1.35
☐ 187 Sterling Hitchcock .15 .07
☐ 188 Dave Hollins .15 .07
☐ 189 Randy Johnson .60 .25
☐ 190 Edgar Martinez .40 .18
☐ 191 Jamie Moyer .15 .07
☐ 192 Alex Rodriguez 2.50 1.10
☐ 193 Paul Sorrento .15 .07
☐ 194 Salomon Torres .15 .07
☐ 195 Bob Wells .15 .07
☐ 196 Dan Wilson .15 .07
☐ 197 Will Clark .40 .18
☐ 198 Kevin Elster .15 .07
☐ 199 Rene Gonzales .15 .07
☐ 200 Juan Gonzalez 1.50 .70
☐ 201 Rusty Greer .30 .14
☐ 202 Darryl Hamilton .15 .07
☐ 203 Mike Henneman .15 .07
☐ 204 Ken Hill .15 .07
☐ 205 Mark McLemore .15 .07
☐ 206 Darren Oliver .15 .07
☐ 207 Dean Palmer .15 .07
☐ 208 Roger Pavlik .15 .07
☐ 209 Ivan Rodriguez .75 .35
☐ 210 Kurt Stillwell .15 .07
☐ 211 Mickey Tettleton .15 .07
☐ 212 Bobby Witt .15 .07
☐ 213 Tilson Brito .15 .07
☐ 214 Jacob Brumfield .15 .07
☐ 215 Miguel Cairo .15 .07
☐ 216 Joe Carter .30 .14
☐ 217 Felipe Crespo .15 .07
☐ 218 Carlos Delgado .30 .14
☐ 219 Alex Gonzalez .15 .07
☐ 220 Shawn Green .15 .07
☐ 221 Juan Guzman .15 .07
☐ 222 Pat Hentgen .30 .14
☐ 223 Charlie O'Brien .15 .07
☐ 224 John Olerud .30 .14
☐ 225 Robert Perez .15 .07
☐ 226 Tomas Perez .15 .07
☐ 227 Juan Samuel .15 .07
☐ 228 Ed Sprague .15 .07
☐ 229 Mike Timlin .15 .07
☐ 230 Rafael Belliard .15 .07
☐ 231 Jermaine Dye .15 .07
☐ 232 Tom Glavine .30 .14
☐ 233 Marquis Grissom .30 .14
☐ 234 Andruw Jones 1.50 .70
☐ 235 Chipper Jones 2.00 .90
☐ 236 David Justice .60 .25
☐ 237 Ryan Klesko .40 .18
☐ 238 Mark Lemke .15 .07
☐ 239 Javier Lopez .30 .14
☐ 240 Greg Maddux 2.00 .90
☐ 241 Fred McGriff .40 .18
☐ 242 Denny Neagle .30 .14
☐ 243 Eddie Perez .15 .07
☐ 244 John Smoltz .30 .14
☐ 245 Mark Wohlers .30 .14
☐ 246 Brant Brown .15 .07
☐ 247 Scott Bullett .15 .07
☐ 248 Leo Gomez .15 .07
☐ 249 Luis Gonzalez .15 .07
☐ 250 Mark Grace .40 .18
☐ 251 Jose Hernandez .15 .07
☐ 252 Brooks Kieschnick .30 .14
☐ 253 Brian McRae .15 .07
☐ 254 Jaime Navarro .15 .07
☐ 255 Mike Perez .15 .07
☐ 256 Rey Sanchez .15 .07
☐ 257 Ryne Sandberg .75 .35
☐ 258 Scott Servais .15 .07
☐ 259 Sammy Sosa .60 .25
☐ 260 Pedro Valdes .15 .07
☐ 261 Turk Wendell .15 .07
☐ 262 Bret Boone .15 .07
☐ 263 Jeff Branson .15 .07
☐ 264 Jeff Brantley .15 .07
☐ 265 Dave Burba .15 .07
☐ 266 Hector Carrasco .15 .07
☐ 267 Eric Davis .30 .14
☐ 268 Willie Greene .30 .14
☐ 269 Lenny Harris .15 .07
☐ 270 Thomas Howard .15 .07
☐ 271 Barry Larkin .40 .18
☐ 272 Hal Morris .15 .07
☐ 273 Joe Oliver .15 .07
☐ 274 Eric Owens .15 .07
☐ 275 Jose Rijo .15 .07
☐ 276 Reggie Sanders .15 .07
☐ 277 Eddie Taubensee .15 .07
☐ 278 Jason Bates .15 .07
☐ 279 Dante Bichette .30 .14
☐ 280 Ellis Burks .30 .14
☐ 281 Vinny Castilla .30 .14
☐ 282 Andres Galarraga .60 .25
☐ 283 Quinton McCracken .15 .07
☐ 284 Jayhawk Owens .15 .07
☐ 285 Jeff Reed .15 .07
☐ 286 Bryan Rekar .15 .07
☐ 287 Armando Reynoso .15 .07
☐ 288 Kevin Ritz .15 .07
☐ 289 Bruce Ruffin .15 .07
☐ 290 John Vander Wal .15 .07
☐ 291 Larry Walker .60 .25
☐ 292 Walt Weiss .15 .07
☐ 293 Eric Young .15 .07
☐ 294 Kurt Abbott .15 .07
☐ 295 Alex Arias .15 .07
☐ 296 Miguel Batista .15 .07
☐ 297 Kevin Brown .30 .14
☐ 298 Luis Castillo .15 .07
☐ 299 Greg Colbrunn .15 .07
☐ 300 Jeff Conine .30 .14
☐ 301 Charles Johnson .30 .14
☐ 302 Al Leiter .15 .07
☐ 303 Robb Nen .30 .14
☐ 304 Joe Orsulak .15 .07
☐ 305 Yorkis Perez .15 .07
☐ 306 Edgar Renteria .30 .14

Card	MINT	NRMT
☐ 307 Gary Sheffield	.60	.25
☐ 308 Jesus Tavarez	.15	.07
☐ 309 Quilvio Veras	.15	.07
☐ 310 Devon White	.15	.07
☐ 311 Jeff Bagwell	1.25	.55
☐ 312 Derek Bell	.15	.07
☐ 313 Sean Berry	.15	.07
☐ 314 Craig Biggio	.40	.18
☐ 315 Doug Drabek	.15	.07
☐ 316 Tony Eusebio	.15	.07
☐ 317 Ricky Gutierrez	.15	.07
☐ 318 Xavier Hernandez	.15	.07
☐ 319 Brian L. Hunter	.30	.14
☐ 320 Darryl Kile	.30	.14
☐ 321 Derrick May	.15	.07
☐ 322 Orlando Miller	.15	.07
☐ 323 James Mouton	.15	.07
☐ 324 Bill Spiers	.15	.07
☐ 325 Pedro Astacio	.15	.07
☐ 326 Brett Butler	.30	.14
☐ 327 Juan Castro	.15	.07
☐ 328 Roger Cedeno	.15	.07
☐ 329 Delino DeShields	.15	.07
☐ 330 Karim Garcia	.30	.14
☐ 331 Todd Hollandsworth	.30	.14
☐ 332 Eric Karros	.30	.14
☐ 333 Oreste Marrero	.15	.07
☐ 334 Ramon Martinez	.30	.14
☐ 335 Raul Mondesi	.40	.18
☐ 336 Hideo Nomo	1.50	.70
☐ 337 Antonio Osuna	.15	.07
☐ 338 Chan Ho Park	.60	.25
☐ 339 Mike Piazza	2.00	.90
☐ 340 Ismael Valdes	.30	.14
☐ 341 Moises Alou	.30	.14
☐ 342 Omar Daal	.15	.07
☐ 343 Jeff Fassero	.15	.07
☐ 344 Cliff Floyd	.15	.07
☐ 345 Mark Grudzielanek	.15	.07
☐ 346 Mike Lansing	.15	.07
☐ 347 Pedro Martinez	.60	.25
☐ 348 Sherman Obando	.15	.07
☐ 349 Jose Paniagua	.15	.07
☐ 350 Henry Rodriguez	.15	.07
☐ 351 Mel Rojas	.15	.07
☐ 352 F.P. Santangelo	.15	.07
☐ 353 David Segui	.15	.07
☐ 354 Dave Silvestri	.15	.07
☐ 355 Ugueth Urbina	.30	.14
☐ 356 Rondell White	.30	.14
☐ 357 Edgardo Alfonzo	.30	.14
☐ 358 Carlos Baerga	.30	.14
☐ 359 Tim Bogar	.15	.07
☐ 360 Rico Brogna	.15	.07
☐ 361 Alvaro Espinoza	.15	.07
☐ 362 Carl Everett	.15	.07
☐ 363 John Franco	.30	.14
☐ 364 Bernard Gilkey	.15	.07
☐ 365 Todd Hundley	.30	.14
☐ 366 Butch Huskey	.15	.07
☐ 367 Jason Isringhausen	.15	.07
☐ 368 Bobby Jones	.15	.07
☐ 369 Lance Johnson	.15	.07
☐ 370 Brent Mayne	.15	.07
☐ 371 Alex Ochoa	.15	.07
☐ 372 Rey Ordonez	.15	.07
☐ 373 Ron Blazier	.15	.07
☐ 374 Ricky Bottalico	.15	.07
☐ 375 David Doster	.15	.07
☐ 376 Lenny Dykstra	.30	.14
☐ 377 Jim Eisenreich	.30	.14
☐ 378 Bobby Estalella	.30	.14
☐ 379 Gregg Jefferies	.15	.07
☐ 380 Kevin Jordan	.15	.07
☐ 381 Ricardo Jordan	.15	.07
☐ 382 Mickey Morandini	.15	.07
☐ 383 Ricky Otero	.15	.07
☐ 384 Benito Santiago	.15	.07
☐ 385 Gene Schall	.15	.07
☐ 386 Curt Schilling	.30	.14
☐ 387 Kevin Sefcik	.15	.07
☐ 388 Kevin Stocker	.15	.07
☐ 389 Jermaine Allensworth	.30	.14
☐ 390 Jay Bell	.15	.07
☐ 391 Jason Christiansen	.15	.07
☐ 392 Francisco Cordova	.15	.07
☐ 393 Mark Johnson	.15	.07
☐ 394 Jason Kendall	.30	.14
☐ 395 Jeff King	.15	.07
☐ 396 Jon Lieber	.15	.07
☐ 397 Nelson Liriano	.15	.07
☐ 398 Esteban Loaiza	.15	.07
☐ 399 Al Martin	.15	.07
☐ 400 Orlando Merced	.15	.07
☐ 401 Ramon Morel	.15	.07
☐ 402 Luis Alicea	.15	.07
☐ 403 Alan Benes	.30	.14
☐ 404 Andy Benes	.15	.07
☐ 405 Terry Bradshaw	.15	.07
☐ 406 Royce Clayton	.15	.07
☐ 407 Dennis Eckersley	.30	.14
☐ 408 Gary Gaetti	.30	.14
☐ 409 Mike Gallego	.15	.07
☐ 410 Ron Gant	.30	.14
☐ 411 Brian Jordan	.30	.14
☐ 412 Ray Lankford	.30	.14
☐ 413 John Mabry	.30	.14
☐ 414 Willie McGee	.15	.07
☐ 415 Tom Pagnozzi	.15	.07
☐ 416 Ozzie Smith	.75	.35
☐ 417 Todd Stottlemyre	.15	.07
☐ 418 Mark Sweeney	.15	.07
☐ 419 Andy Ashby	.15	.07
☐ 420 Ken Caminiti	.60	.25
☐ 421 Archi Cianfrocco	.15	.07
☐ 422 Steve Finley	.15	.07
☐ 423 Chris Gomez	.15	.07
☐ 424 Tony Gwynn	1.50	.70
☐ 425 Joey Hamilton	.30	.14
☐ 426 Rickey Henderson	.40	.18
☐ 427 Trevor Hoffman	.15	.07
☐ 428 Brian Johnson	.15	.07
☐ 429 Wally Joyner	.15	.07
☐ 430 Scott Livingstone	.15	.07
☐ 431 Jody Reed	.15	.07
☐ 432 Craig Shipley	.15	.07
☐ 433 Fernando Valenzuela	.30	.14
☐ 434 Greg Vaughn	.15	.07
☐ 435 Rich Aurilia	.15	.07
☐ 436 Kim Batiste	.15	.07
☐ 437 Jose Bautista	.15	.07
☐ 438 Rod Beck	.30	.14
☐ 439 Marvin Benard	.15	.07
☐ 440 Barry Bonds	.75	.35
☐ 441 Shawon Dunston	.15	.07
☐ 442 Shawn Estes	.30	.14
☐ 443 Osvaldo Fernandez	.15	.07
☐ 444 Stan Javier	.15	.07
☐ 445 David McCarty	.15	.07
☐ 446 Bill Mueller	.15	.07
☐ 447 Steve Scarsone	.15	.07
☐ 448 Robby Thompson	.15	.07
☐ 449 Rick Wilkins	.15	.07
☐ 450 Matt Williams	.40	.18

1997 Pacific Light Blue

These Light Blue parallel foil cards were found one per pack exclusively in Wal-Mart and Sam's 14-card retail packs. The cards are very similar in design to the scarce Silver parallels randomly seeded in basic packs resulting in a source of confusion for dealers and collectors alike. The Light Blue parallels are not as reflective as the Silvers. Collectors should take extreme caution when purchasing Silver or Light Blue cards.

	MINT	NRMT
COMPLETE SET (450)	300.00	135.00
COMMON CARD (1-450)	.25	.11

*STARS: 4X TO 8X BASIC CARDS
*YOUNG STARS: 3X TO 6X BASIC CARDS

1997 Pacific Silver

Randomly inserted in packs at a rate of one in 73, this 450-card set is a silver foil parallel version of the regular set and is similar in design. Only 67 of these sets were produced.

	MINT	NRMT
COMPLETE SET (450)	8000.00	3600.00
COMMON CARD (1-450)	12.00	5.50

*STARS: 60X TO 100X BASIC CARDS
*YOUNG STARS: 50X TO 80X BASIC CARDS

1997 Pacific Card-Supials

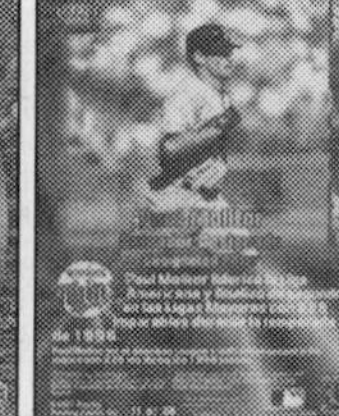

Randomly inserted in packs at a rate of one in 37, this 36-paired-card insert set features color action player photos of some of the greatest players in the Major Leagues. A smaller card was made to pair with the regular size card of the same player. The backs carry a slot for insertion of the small card.

	MINT	NRMT
COMP.LARGE SET (36)	350.00	160.00
COMMON LARGE (1-36)	3.00	1.35
COMP.MINI SET (36)	200.00	90.00
COMMON MINI (1A-36A)	2.00	.90

*MINIS: .3X TO .6X BASIC CARDS

Card	MINT	NRMT
☐ 1 Roberto Alomar	6.00	2.70
☐ 2 Brady Anderson	4.00	1.80
☐ 3 Eddie Murray	8.00	3.60
☐ 4 Cal Ripken	25.00	11.00
☐ 5 Jose Canseco	4.00	1.80
☐ 6 Mo Vaughn	8.00	3.60
☐ 7 Frank Thomas	25.00	11.00
☐ 8 Albert Belle	8.00	3.60
☐ 9 Omar Vizquel	3.50	1.55
☐ 10 Chuck Knoblauch	6.00	2.70
☐ 11 Paul Molitor	6.00	2.70
☐ 12 Wade Boggs	6.00	2.70
☐ 13 Derek Jeter	15.00	6.75
☐ 14 Andy Pettitte	8.00	3.60
☐ 15 Mark McGwire	12.00	5.50
☐ 16 Jay Buhner	4.00	1.80
☐ 17 Ken Griffey Jr.	30.00	13.50
☐ 18 Alex Rodriguez	20.00	9.00
☐ 19 Juan Gonzalez	15.00	6.75
☐ 20 Ivan Rodriguez	8.00	3.60
☐ 21 Andruw Jones	15.00	6.75
☐ 22 Chipper Jones	20.00	9.00
☐ 23 Ryan Klesko	4.00	1.80
☐ 24 Greg Maddux	20.00	9.00
☐ 25 Ryne Sandberg	8.00	3.60
☐ 26 Andres Galarraga	6.00	2.70
☐ 27 Gary Sheffield	6.00	2.70
☐ 28 Jeff Bagwell	12.00	5.50
☐ 29 Todd Hollandsworth	3.00	1.35
☐ 30 Hideo Nomo	15.00	6.75
☐ 31 Mike Piazza	20.00	9.00
☐ 32 Todd Hundley	3.50	1.55
☐ 33 Dennis Eckersley	4.00	1.80
☐ 34 Ken Caminiti	6.00	2.70
☐ 35 Tony Gwynn	15.00	6.75
☐ 36 Barry Bonds	8.00	3.60

1997 Pacific Cramer's Choice

Randomly inserted in packs at a rate of one in 721, this 10-card set features the top Major League Baseball players as chosen by Pacific President and CEO, Michael Cramer. The fronts display a color player cut-out on a pyramid die-cut shaped background. The backs carry information about why the player was selected for this set in both English and Spanish.

	MINT	NRMT
COMPLETE SET (10)	900.00	400.00
COMMON CARD (1-10)	30.00	13.50

Card	MINT	NRMT
☐ 1 Roberto Alomar	40.00	18.00
☐ 2 Frank Thomas	150.00	70.00
☐ 3 Albert Belle	50.00	22.00
☐ 4 Andy Pettitte	40.00	18.00
☐ 5 Ken Griffey Jr.	200.00	90.00
☐ 6 Alex Rodriguez	120.00	55.00
☐ 7 Chipper Jones	100.00	45.00
☐ 8 John Smoltz	30.00	13.50
☐ 9 Mike Piazza	120.00	55.00
☐ 10 Tony Gwynn	100.00	45.00

1997 Pacific Fireworks Die Cuts

Randomly inserted in packs at a rate of one in 73, this 20-card set features color action player photos on a fireworks die-cut background. The backs carry player information in both English and Spanish.

	MINT	NRMT
COMPLETE SET (20)	400.00	180.00
COMMON CARD (1-20)	5.00	2.20

Card	MINT	NRMT
☐ 1 Roberto Alomar	10.00	4.50
☐ 2 Brady Anderson	7.00	3.10
☐ 3 Eddie Murray	12.00	5.50
☐ 4 Cal Ripken	40.00	18.00
☐ 5 Frank Thomas	40.00	18.00
☐ 6 Albert Belle	12.00	5.50
☐ 7 Derek Jeter	25.00	11.00
☐ 8 Andy Pettitte	12.00	5.50
☐ 9 Bernie Williams	10.00	4.50
☐ 10 Mark McGwire	20.00	9.00
☐ 11 Ken Griffey Jr.	50.00	22.00
☐ 12 Alex Rodriguez	30.00	13.50
☐ 13 Juan Gonzalez	25.00	11.00
☐ 14 Andruw Jones	20.00	9.00
☐ 15 Chipper Jones	30.00	13.50
☐ 16 Hideo Nomo	25.00	11.00
☐ 17 Mike Piazza	30.00	13.50
☐ 18 Henry Rodriguez	5.00	2.20
☐ 19 Tony Gwynn	25.00	11.00
☐ 20 Barry Bonds	12.00	5.50

1997 Pacific Gold Crown Die Cuts

Randomly inserted in packs at a rate of one in 37, this 36-card set honors some of Major League Baseball's Super Stars of today. The fronts feature color action player photos with a die-cut gold crown at the top and gold foil printing. The backs carry player information in both English and Spanish.

	MINT	NRMT
COMPLETE SET (36)	400.00	180.00
COMMON CARD (1-36)	4.00	1.80

Card	MINT	NRMT
☐ 1 Roberto Alomar	8.00	3.60
☐ 2 Brady Anderson	5.00	2.20
☐ 3 Mike Mussina	8.00	3.60
☐ 4 Eddie Murray	10.00	4.50
☐ 5 Cal Ripken	30.00	13.50
☐ 6 Jose Canseco	5.00	2.20
☐ 7 Frank Thomas	30.00	13.50
☐ 8 Albert Belle	10.00	4.50
☐ 9 Omar Vizquel	4.50	2.00
☐ 10 Wade Boggs	8.00	3.60
☐ 11 Derek Jeter	20.00	9.00
☐ 12 Andy Pettitte	10.00	4.50
☐ 13 Mariano Rivera	4.50	2.00
☐ 14 Bernie Williams	8.00	3.60
☐ 15 Mark McGwire	15.00	6.75
☐ 16 Ken Griffey Jr.	40.00	18.00
☐ 17 Edgar Martinez	5.00	2.20
☐ 18 Alex Rodriguez	25.00	11.00
☐ 19 Juan Gonzalez	20.00	9.00
☐ 20 Ivan Rodriguez	10.00	4.50
☐ 21 Andruw Jones	15.00	6.75
☐ 22 Chipper Jones	25.00	11.00
☐ 23 Ryan Klesko	5.00	2.20
☐ 24 John Smoltz	4.50	2.00
☐ 25 Ryne Sandberg	10.00	4.50
☐ 26 Andres Galarraga	8.00	3.60
☐ 27 Edgar Renteria	4.00	1.80
☐ 28 Jeff Bagwell	15.00	6.75
☐ 29 Todd Hollandsworth	4.00	1.80
☐ 30 Hideo Nomo	20.00	9.00
☐ 31 Mike Piazza	25.00	11.00
☐ 32 Todd Hundley	4.50	2.00
☐ 33 Brian Jordan	4.00	1.80
☐ 34 Ken Caminiti	8.00	3.60
☐ 35 Tony Gwynn	20.00	9.00
☐ 36 Barry Bonds	10.00	4.50

1997 Pacific Latinos of the Major Leagues

Randomly inserted in packs at a rate of two in 37, this 36-card set salutes the great Latino players in the Major Leagues today. The fronts feature color player action images on a gold foil background of their name. The backs carry player information in both English and Spanish.

	MINT	NRMT
COMPLETE SET (36)	80.00	36.00
COMMON CARD (1-36)	1.00	.45

Card	MINT	NRMT
☐ 1 George Arias	1.00	.45
☐ 2 Roberto Alomar	4.00	1.80
☐ 3 Rafael Palmeiro	3.00	1.35
☐ 4 Bobby Bonilla	2.00	.90
☐ 5 Jose Canseco	3.00	1.35
☐ 6 Wilson Alvarez	2.00	.90
☐ 7 Dave Martinez	1.00	.45
☐ 8 Julio Franco	2.00	.90
☐ 9 Manny Ramirez	4.00	1.80
☐ 10 Omar Vizquel	2.00	.90
☐ 11 Marty Cordova	2.00	.90
☐ 12 Roberto Kelly	1.00	.45
☐ 13 Tino Martinez	4.00	1.80
☐ 14 Mariano Rivera	2.00	.90
☐ 15 Ruben Rivera	2.00	.90
☐ 16 Bernie Williams	4.00	1.80
☐ 17 Geronimo Berroa	1.00	.45
☐ 18 Joey Cora	2.00	.90
☐ 19 Edgar Martinez	3.00	1.35
☐ 20 Alex Rodriguez	12.00	5.50
☐ 21 Juan Gonzalez	10.00	4.50
☐ 22 Ivan Rodriguez	5.00	2.20
☐ 23 Andruw Jones	10.00	4.50
☐ 24 Javier Lopez	2.00	.90
☐ 25 Sammy Sosa	4.00	1.80
☐ 26 Vinny Castilla	2.00	.90
☐ 27 Andres Galarraga	4.00	1.80
☐ 28 Ramon Martinez	2.00	.90
☐ 29 Raul Mondesi	3.00	1.35
☐ 30 Ismael Valdes	2.00	.90
☐ 31 Pedro Martinez	4.00	1.80
☐ 32 Henry Rodriguez	1.00	.45
☐ 33 Carlos Baerga	2.00	.90
☐ 34 Rey Ordonez	1.00	.45
☐ 35 Fernando Valenzuela	2.00	.90
☐ 36 Osvaldo Fernandez	1.00	.45

1997 Pacific Triple Crown Die Cuts

Randomly inserted in packs at a rate of one in 145, this 20-card set features color player images over a gold foil diamond-shaped background with a die-cut gold crown at the top. The backs carry player information in both English and Spanish.

	MINT	NRMT
COMPLETE SET (20)	600.00	275.00
COMMON CARD (1-20)	8.00	3.60

Card	MINT	NRMT
☐ 1 Brady Anderson	10.00	4.50
☐ 2 Rafael Palmeiro	10.00	4.50
☐ 3 Mo Vaughn	20.00	9.00
☐ 4 Frank Thomas	60.00	27.00
☐ 5 Albert Belle	20.00	9.00
☐ 6 Jim Thome	20.00	9.00
☐ 7 Cecil Fielder	8.00	3.60
☐ 8 Mark McGwire	30.00	13.50
☐ 9 Ken Griffey Jr.	80.00	36.00
☐ 10 Alex Rodriguez	50.00	22.00
☐ 11 Juan Gonzalez	40.00	18.00
☐ 12 Andruw Jones	30.00	13.50
☐ 13 Chipper Jones	50.00	22.00
☐ 14 Dante Bichette	10.00	4.50
☐ 15 Ellis Burks	10.00	4.50
☐ 16 Andres Galarraga	15.00	6.75
☐ 17 Jeff Bagwell	30.00	13.50
☐ 18 Mike Piazza	50.00	22.00
☐ 19 Ken Caminiti	15.00	6.75
☐ 20 Barry Bonds	20.00	9.00

1997 Pacific Baerga Softball

This 10-card set features major league baseball players who donated their time to participate in the Fourth Annual Carlos Baerga Celebrities Softball Game, played December 14 in Hayto Rey, Puerto Rico, with proceeds from the game going to various Children's foundations throughout Puerto Rico. Two cards from the set were distributed in promo packs to the first 12,000 people at the game. The fronts carry color action player photos from the previous year's softball game, gold-foil stamping, and the game's official logo. The backs display color player portraits with player information in both Spanish and English.

	MINT	NRMT
COMPLETE SET (10)	10.00	4.50
COMMON CARD (1-10)	.25	.11

Card	MINT	NRMT
☐ 1 Carlos Baerga	.25	.11
☐ 2 Bernie Williams	1.50	.70
☐ 3 Ivan Rodriguez	2.50	1.10
☐ 4 Sandy Alomar Jr.	.50	.23
☐ 5 Joey Cora	.50	.23
☐ 6 Roberto Alomar	1.50	.70
☐ 7 Moises Alou	.50	.23
☐ 8 Rey Ordonez	.25	.11
☐ 9 Derek Jeter	5.00	2.20
☐ 10 David Justice	1.50	.70

1998 Pacific

The 1998 Pacific set was issued in one series totalling 450 cards and distributed in 12-card packs with a suggested retail price of $2.49. The fronts features borderless color player photos with gold foil highlights. The backs carry player information in both Spanish and English.

	MINT	NRMT
COMPLETE SET (450)	50.00	22.00
COMMON CARD (1-450)	.15	.07

Card	MINT	NRMT
☐ 1 Luis Alicea	.15	.07
☐ 2 Garret Anderson	.30	.14
☐ 3 Jason Dickson	.30	.14
☐ 4 Gary DiSarcina	.15	.07
☐ 5 Jim Edmonds	.60	.25
☐ 6 Darin Erstad	.75	.35

☐ 7 Chuck Finley	.30	.14
☐ 8 Shigetoshi Hasegawa	.30	.14
☐ 9 Rickey Henderson	.40	.18
☐ 10 Dave Hollins	.15	.07
☐ 11 Mark Langston	.15	.07
☐ 12 Orlando Palmeiro	.15	.07
☐ 13 Troy Percival	.30	.14
☐ 14 Tony Phillips	.15	.07
☐ 15 Tim Salmon	.60	.25
☐ 16 Allen Watson	.15	.07
☐ 17 Roberto Alomar	.60	.25
☐ 18 Brady Anderson	.40	.18
☐ 19 Harold Baines	.30	.14
☐ 20 Armando Benitez	.15	.07
☐ 21 Geronimo Berroa	.15	.07
☐ 22 Mike Bordick	.15	.07
☐ 23 Eric Davis	.30	.14
☐ 24 Scott Erickson	.30	.14
☐ 25 Chris Hoiles	.15	.07
☐ 26 Jimmy Key	.30	.14
☐ 27 Aaron Ledesma	.15	.07
☐ 28 Mike Mussina	.60	.25
☐ 29 Randy Myers	.30	.14
☐ 30 Jesse Orosco	.15	.07
☐ 31 Rafael Palmeiro	.40	.18
☐ 32 Jeff Reboulet	.15	.07
☐ 33 Cal Ripken	2.50	1.10
☐ 34 B.J. Surhoff	.15	.07
☐ 35 Steve Avery	.15	.07
☐ 36 Darren Bragg	.15	.07
☐ 37 Wil Cordero	.15	.07
☐ 38 Jeff Frye	.15	.07
☐ 39 Nomar Garciaparra	2.00	.90
☐ 40 Tom Gordon	.15	.07
☐ 41 Bill Haselman	.15	.07
☐ 42 Scott Hatteberg	.15	.07
☐ 43 Butch Henry	.15	.07
☐ 44 Reggie Jefferson	.30	.14
☐ 45 Tim Naehring	.15	.07
☐ 46 Troy O'Leary	.15	.07
☐ 47 Jeff Suppan	.15	.07
☐ 48 John Valentin	.15	.07
☐ 49 Mo Vaughn	.75	.35
☐ 50 Tim Wakefield	.15	.07
☐ 51 James Baldwin	.15	.07
☐ 52 Albert Belle	.75	.35
☐ 53 Tony Castillo	.15	.07
☐ 54 Doug Drabek	.15	.07
☐ 55 Ray Durham	.30	.14
☐ 56 Jorge Fabregas	.15	.07
☐ 57 Ozzie Guillen	.15	.07
☐ 58 Matt Karchner	.15	.07
☐ 59 Norberto Martin	.15	.07
☐ 60 Dave Martinez	.15	.07
☐ 61 Lyle Mouton	.15	.07
☐ 62 Jaime Navarro	.15	.07
☐ 63 Frank Thomas	2.50	1.10
☐ 64 Mario Valdez	.30	.14
☐ 65 Robin Ventura	.30	.14
☐ 66 Sandy Alomar Jr.	.30	.14
☐ 67 Paul Assenmacher	.15	.07
☐ 68 Tony Fernandez	.15	.07
☐ 69 Brian Giles	.15	.07
☐ 70 Marquis Grissom	.30	.14
☐ 71 Orel Hershiser	.30	.14
☐ 72 Mike Jackson	.15	.07
☐ 73 David Justice	.60	.25
☐ 74 Albie Lopez	.15	.07
☐ 75 Jose Mesa	.30	.14
☐ 76 Charles Nagy	.30	.14
☐ 77 Chad Ogea	.15	.07
☐ 78 Manny Ramirez	.60	.25
☐ 79 Jim Thome	.60	.25
☐ 80 Omar Vizquel	.30	.14
☐ 81 Matt Williams	.40	.18
☐ 82 Jaret Wright	1.50	.70
☐ 83 Willie Blair	.15	.07
☐ 84 Raul Casanova	.15	.07
☐ 85 Tony Clark	.60	.25
☐ 86 Deivi Cruz	.15	.07
☐ 87 Damion Easley	.15	.07
☐ 88 Travis Fryman	.30	.14
☐ 89 Bobby Higginson	.30	.14
☐ 90 Brian L. Hunter	.30	.14
☐ 91 Todd Jones	.15	.07
☐ 92 Dan Miceli	.15	.07
☐ 93 Brian Moehler	.15	.07
☐ 94 Mel Nieves	.15	.07
☐ 95 Jody Reed	.15	.07
☐ 96 Justin Thompson	.15	.07
☐ 97 Bubba Trammell	.15	.07
☐ 98 Kevin Appier	.15	.07
☐ 99 Jay Bell	.15	.07
☐ 100 Yamil Benitez	.15	.07
☐ 101 Johnny Damon	.15	.07
☐ 102 Chili Davis	.30	.14
☐ 103 Jermaine Dye	.15	.07

☐ 104 Jed Hansen	.15	.07
☐ 105 Jeff King	.15	.07
☐ 106 Mike Macfarlane	.15	.07
☐ 107 Felix Martinez	.15	.07
☐ 108 Jeff Montgomery	.15	.07
☐ 109 Jose Offerman	.15	.07
☐ 110 Dean Palmer	.30	.14
☐ 111 Hipolito Pichardo	.15	.07
☐ 112 Jose Rosado	.15	.07
☐ 113 Jeromy Burnitz	.30	.14
☐ 114 Jeff Cirillo	.15	.07
☐ 115 Cal Eldred	.15	.07
☐ 116 John Jaha	.15	.07
☐ 117 Doug Jones	.15	.07
☐ 118 Scott Karl	.15	.07
☐ 119 Jesse Levis	.15	.07
☐ 120 Mark Loretta	.15	.07
☐ 121 Ben McDonald	.15	.07
☐ 122 Jose Mercedes	.15	.07
☐ 123 Matt Mieske	.15	.07
☐ 124 Dave Nilsson	.30	.14
☐ 125 Jose Valentin	.15	.07
☐ 126 Fernando Vina	.15	.07
☐ 127 Gerald Williams	.15	.07
☐ 128 Rick Aguilera	.30	.14
☐ 129 Rich Becker	.15	.07
☐ 130 Ron Coomer	.15	.07
☐ 131 Marty Cordova	.30	.14
☐ 132 Eddie Guardado	.15	.07
☐ 133 LaTroy Hawkins	.15	.07
☐ 134 Denny Hocking	.15	.07
☐ 135 Chuck Knoblauch	.60	.25
☐ 136 Matt Lawton	.15	.07
☐ 137 Pat Meares	.15	.07
☐ 138 Paul Molitor	.60	.25
☐ 139 David Ortiz	.15	.07
☐ 140 Brad Radke	.30	.14
☐ 141 Terry Steinbach	.30	.14
☐ 142 Bob Tewksbury	.15	.07
☐ 143 Javier Valentin	.15	.07
☐ 144 Wade Boggs	.60	.25
☐ 145 David Cone	.30	.14
☐ 146 Chad Curtis	.15	.07
☐ 147 Cecil Fielder	.30	.14
☐ 148 Joe Girardi	.15	.07
☐ 149 Dwight Gooden	.30	.14
☐ 150 Hideki Irabu	.40	.18
☐ 151 Derek Jeter	1.50	.70
☐ 152 Tino Martinez	.60	.25
☐ 153 Ramiro Mendoza	.15	.07
☐ 154 Paul O'Neill	.30	.14
☐ 155 Andy Pettitte	.60	.25
☐ 156 Jorge Posada	.15	.07
☐ 157 Mariano Rivera	.30	.14
☐ 158 Rey Sanchez	.15	.07
☐ 159 Luis Sojo	.15	.07
☐ 160 David Wells	.15	.07
☐ 161 Bernie Williams	.60	.25
☐ 162 Rafael Bournigal	.15	.07
☐ 163 Scott Brosius	.15	.07
☐ 164 Jose Canseco	.40	.18
☐ 165 Jason Giambi	.15	.07
☐ 166 Ben Grieve	1.25	.55
☐ 167 Dave Magadan	.15	.07
☐ 168 Brent Mayne	.15	.07
☐ 169 Jason McDonald	.30	.14
☐ 170 Izzy Molina	.15	.07
☐ 171 Ariel Prieto	.15	.07
☐ 172 Carlos Reyes	.15	.07
☐ 173 Scott Spiezio	.30	.14
☐ 174 Matt Stairs	.15	.07
☐ 175 Bill Taylor	.15	.07
☐ 176 Dave Telgheder	.15	.07
☐ 177 Steve Wojciechowski	.15	.07
☐ 178 Rich Amaral	.15	.07
☐ 179 Bobby Ayala	.15	.07
☐ 180 Jay Buhner	.40	.18
☐ 181 Rafael Carmona	.15	.07
☐ 182 Ken Cloude	.15	.07
☐ 183 Joey Cora	.30	.14
☐ 184 Russ Davis	.15	.07
☐ 185 Jeff Fassero	.15	.07
☐ 186 Ken Griffey Jr.	3.00	1.35
☐ 187 Raul Ibanez	.15	.07
☐ 188 Randy Johnson	.60	.25
☐ 189 Roberto Kelly	.15	.07
☐ 190 Edgar Martinez	.40	.18
☐ 191 Jamie Moyer	.15	.07
☐ 192 Omar Olivares	.15	.07
☐ 193 Alex Rodriguez	2.00	.90
☐ 194 Heathcliff Slocumb	.15	.07
☐ 195 Paul Sorrento	.15	.07
☐ 196 Dan Wilson	.15	.07
☐ 197 Scott Bailes	.15	.07
☐ 198 John Burkett	.15	.07
☐ 199 Domingo Cedeno	.15	.07
☐ 200 Will Clark	.40	.18

☐ 201 Hanley Frias	.15	.07
☐ 202 Juan Gonzalez	1.50	.70
☐ 203 Tom Goodwin	.15	.07
☐ 204 Rusty Greer	.30	.14
☐ 205 Wilson Heredia	.15	.07
☐ 206 Darren Oliver	.15	.07
☐ 207 Bill Ripken	.15	.07
☐ 208 Ivan Rodriguez	.30	.14
☐ 209 Lee Stevens	.15	.07
☐ 210 Fernando Tatis	.15	.07
☐ 211 John Wetteland	.30	.14
☐ 212 Bobby Witt	.15	.07
☐ 213 Jacob Brumfield	.15	.07
☐ 214 Joe Carter	.30	.14
☐ 215 Roger Clemens	1.25	.55
☐ 216 Felipe Crespo	.15	.07
☐ 217 Jose Cruz Jr.	2.50	1.10
☐ 218 Carlos Delgado	.30	.14
☐ 219 Mariano Duncan	.15	.07
☐ 220 Carlos Garcia	.15	.07
☐ 221 Alex Gonzalez	.15	.07
☐ 222 Juan Guzman	.15	.07
☐ 223 Pat Hentgen	.60	.25
☐ 224 Orlando Merced	.15	.07
☐ 225 Tomas Perez	.15	.07
☐ 226 Paul Quantrill	.15	.07
☐ 227 Benito Santiago	.15	.07
☐ 228 Woody Williams	.15	.07
☐ 229 Rafael Belliard	.15	.07
☐ 230 Jeff Blauser	.15	.07
☐ 231 Pedro Borbon	.15	.07
☐ 232 Tom Glavine	.30	.14
☐ 233 Tony Graffanino	.15	.07
☐ 234 Andruw Jones	1.25	.55
☐ 235 Chipper Jones	2.00	.90
☐ 236 Ryan Klesko	.40	.18
☐ 237 Mark Lemke	.15	.07
☐ 238 Kenny Lofton	.75	.35
☐ 239 Javier Lopez	.30	.14
☐ 240 Fred McGriff	.40	.18
☐ 241 Greg Maddux	2.00	.90
☐ 242 Denny Neagle	.30	.14
☐ 243 John Smoltz	.30	.14
☐ 244 Michael Tucker	.30	.14
☐ 245 Mark Wohlers	.30	.14
☐ 246 Manny Alexander	.15	.07
☐ 247 Miguel Batista	.15	.07
☐ 248 Mark Clark	.15	.07
☐ 249 Doug Glanville	.15	.07
☐ 250 Jeremi Gonzalez	.30	.14
☐ 251 Mark Grace	.40	.18
☐ 252 Jose Hernandez	.15	.07
☐ 253 Lance Johnson	.15	.07
☐ 254 Brooks Kieschnick	.30	.14
☐ 255 Kevin Orie	.30	.14
☐ 256 Ryne Sandberg	.75	.35
☐ 257 Scott Servais	.15	.07
☐ 258 Sammy Sosa	.60	.25
☐ 259 Kevin Tapani	.15	.07
☐ 260 Ramon Tatis	.15	.07
☐ 261 Bret Boone	.15	.07
☐ 262 Dave Burba	.15	.07
☐ 263 Brook Fordyce	.15	.07
☐ 264 Willie Greene	.30	.14
☐ 265 Barry Larkin	.40	.18
☐ 266 Pedro A. Martinez	.15	.07
☐ 267 Hal Morris	.15	.07
☐ 268 Joe Oliver	.15	.07
☐ 269 Eduardo Perez	.15	.07
☐ 270 Pokey Reese	.15	.07
☐ 271 Felix Rodriguez	.15	.07
☐ 272 Deion Sanders	.60	.25
☐ 273 Reggie Sanders	.15	.07
☐ 274 Jeff Shaw	.15	.07
☐ 275 Scott Sullivan	.15	.07
☐ 276 Brett Tomko	.30	.14
☐ 277 Roger Bailey	.15	.07
☐ 278 Dante Bichette	.30	.14
☐ 279 Ellis Burks	.30	.14
☐ 280 Vinny Castilla	.30	.14
☐ 281 Frank Castillo	.15	.07
☐ 282 Mike DeJean	.15	.07
☐ 283 Andres Galarraga	.60	.25
☐ 284 Darren Holmes	.15	.07
☐ 285 Kirt Manwaring	.15	.07
☐ 286 Quinton McCracken	.15	.07
☐ 287 Neifi Perez	.30	.14
☐ 288 Steve Reed	.15	.07
☐ 289 John Thomson	.15	.07
☐ 290 Larry Walker	.60	.25
☐ 291 Walt Weiss	.15	.07
☐ 292 Kurt Abbott	.15	.07
☐ 293 Antonio Alfonseca	.15	.07
☐ 294 Moises Alou	.30	.14
☐ 295 Alex Arias	.15	.07
☐ 296 Bobby Bonilla	.30	.14
☐ 297 Kevin Brown	.30	.14

Card	MINT	NRMT
☐ 298 Craig Counsell	.15	.07
☐ 299 Darren Daulton	.30	.14
☐ 300 Jim Eisenreich	.30	.14
☐ 301 Alex Fernandez	.15	.07
☐ 302 Felix Heredia	.15	.07
☐ 303 Livan Hernandez	.30	.14
☐ 304 Charles Johnson	.30	.14
☐ 305 Al Leiter	.15	.07
☐ 306 Robb Nen	.30	.14
☐ 307 Edgar Renteria	.30	.14
☐ 308 Gary Sheffield	.60	.25
☐ 309 Devon White	.15	.07
☐ 310 Bob Abreu	.40	.18
☐ 311 Brad Ausmus	.15	.07
☐ 312 Jeff Bagwell	1.25	.55
☐ 313 Derek Bell	.15	.07
☐ 314 Sean Berry	.15	.07
☐ 315 Craig Biggio	.40	.18
☐ 316 Ramon Garcia	.15	.07
☐ 317 Luis Gonzalez	.15	.07
☐ 318 Ricky Gutierrez	.15	.07
☐ 319 Mike Hampton	.15	.07
☐ 320 Richard Hidalgo	.15	.07
☐ 321 Thomas Howard	.15	.07
☐ 322 Darryl Kile	.30	.14
☐ 323 Jose Lima	.15	.07
☐ 324 Shane Reynolds	.15	.07
☐ 325 Bill Spiers	.15	.07
☐ 326 Tom Candiotti	.15	.07
☐ 327 Roger Cedeno	.15	.07
☐ 328 Greg Gagne	.15	.07
☐ 329 Karim Garcia	.30	.14
☐ 330 Wilton Guerrero	.15	.07
☐ 331 Todd Hollandsworth	.30	.14
☐ 332 Eric Karros	.30	.14
☐ 333 Ramon Martinez	.30	.14
☐ 334 Raul Mondesi	.60	.25
☐ 335 Otis Nixon	.30	.14
☐ 336 Hideo Nomo	1.50	.70
☐ 337 Antonio Osuna	.15	.07
☐ 338 Chan Ho Park	.60	.25
☐ 339 Mike Piazza	2.00	.90
☐ 340 Dennis Reyes	.30	.14
☐ 341 Ismael Valdes	.30	.14
☐ 342 Todd Worrell	.30	.14
☐ 343 Todd Zeile	.30	.14
☐ 344 Darrin Fletcher	.15	.07
☐ 345 Mark Grudzielanek	.15	.07
☐ 346 Vladimir Guerrero	1.00	.45
☐ 347 Dustin Hermanson	.15	.07
☐ 348 Mike Lansing	.15	.07
☐ 349 Pedro Martinez	.60	.25
☐ 350 Ryan McGuire	.15	.07
☐ 351 Jose Paniagua	.15	.07
☐ 352 Carlos Perez	.15	.07
☐ 353 Henry Rodriguez	.15	.07
☐ 354 F.P. Santangelo	.15	.07
☐ 355 David Segui	.15	.07
☐ 356 Ugueth Urbina	.15	.07
☐ 357 Marc Valdes	.15	.07
☐ 358 Jose Vidro	.15	.07
☐ 359 Rondell White	.30	.14
☐ 360 Juan Acevedo	.15	.07
☐ 361 Edgardo Alfonzo	.30	.14
☐ 362 Carlos Baerga	.30	.14
☐ 363 Carl Everett	.15	.07
☐ 364 John Franco	.30	.14
☐ 365 Bernard Gilkey	.15	.07
☐ 366 Todd Hundley	.30	.14
☐ 367 Butch Huskey	.30	.14
☐ 368 Bobby Jones	.15	.07
☐ 369 Takashi Kashiwada	.60	.25
☐ 370 Greg McMichael	.15	.07
☐ 371 Brian McRae	.15	.07
☐ 372 Alex Ochoa	.15	.07
☐ 373 John Olerud	.30	.14
☐ 374 Rey Ordonez	.15	.07
☐ 375 Turk Wendell	.15	.07
☐ 376 Ricky Bottalico	.15	.07
☐ 377 Rico Brogna	.30	.14
☐ 378 Len Dykstra	.30	.14
☐ 379 Bobby Estalella	.30	.14
☐ 380 Wayne Gomes	.15	.07
☐ 381 Tyler Green	.15	.07
☐ 382 Gregg Jefferies	.30	.14
☐ 383 Mark Leiter	.15	.07
☐ 384 Mike Lieberthal	.15	.07
☐ 385 Mickey Morandini	.15	.07
☐ 386 Scott Rolen	1.50	.70
☐ 387 Curt Schilling	.30	.14
☐ 388 Kevin Stocker	.15	.07
☐ 389 Danny Tartabull	.15	.07
☐ 390 Jermaine Allensworth	.15	.07
☐ 391 Adrian Brown	.15	.07
☐ 392 Jason Christiansen	.15	.07
☐ 393 Steve Cooke	.15	.07
☐ 394 Francisco Cordova	.15	.07
☐ 395 Jose Guillen	.40	.18
☐ 396 Jason Kendall	.15	.07
☐ 397 Jon Lieber	.15	.07
☐ 398 Esteban Loaiza	.15	.07
☐ 399 Al Martin	.15	.07
☐ 400 Kevin Polcovich	.15	.07
☐ 401 Joe Randa	.15	.07
☐ 402 Ricardo Rincon	.15	.07
☐ 403 Tony Womack	.15	.07
☐ 404 Kevin Young	.15	.07
☐ 405 Andy Benes	.15	.07
☐ 406 Royce Clayton	.15	.07
☐ 407 Delino DeShields	.15	.07
☐ 408 Mike Difelice	.15	.07
☐ 409 Dennis Eckersley	.40	.18
☐ 410 John Frascatore	.15	.07
☐ 411 Gary Gaetti	.30	.14
☐ 412 Ron Gant	.30	.14
☐ 413 Brian Jordan	.30	.14
☐ 414 Ray Lankford	.30	.14
☐ 415 Willie McGee	.30	.14
☐ 416 Mark McGwire	1.50	.70
☐ 417 Matt Morris	.30	.14
☐ 418 Luis Ordaz	.15	.07
☐ 419 Todd Stottlemyre	.15	.07
☐ 420 Andy Ashby	.15	.07
☐ 421 Jim Bruske	.15	.07
☐ 422 Ken Caminiti	.60	.25
☐ 423 Will Cunnane	.15	.07
☐ 424 Steve Finley	.30	.14
☐ 425 John Flaherty	.15	.07
☐ 426 Chris Gomez	.15	.07
☐ 427 Tony Gwynn	1.50	.70
☐ 428 Joey Hamilton	.15	.07
☐ 429 Carlos Hernandez	.15	.07
☐ 430 Sterling Hitchcock	.15	.07
☐ 431 Trevor Hoffman	.30	.14
☐ 432 Wally Joyner	.30	.14
☐ 433 Greg Vaughn	.15	.07
☐ 434 Quilvio Veras	.15	.07
☐ 435 Wilson Alvarez	.30	.14
☐ 436 Rod Beck	.30	.14
☐ 437 Barry Bonds	.75	.35
☐ 438 Jacob Cruz	.30	.14
☐ 439 Shawn Estes	.30	.14
☐ 440 Darryl Hamilton	.15	.07
☐ 441 Roberto Hernandez	.15	.07
☐ 442 Glenallen Hill	.15	.07
☐ 443 Stan Javier	.15	.07
☐ 444 Brian Johnson	.15	.07
☐ 445 Jeff Kent	.30	.14
☐ 446 Bill Mueller	.15	.07
☐ 447 Kirk Rueter	.15	.07
☐ 448 J.T. Snow	.15	.07
☐ 449 Julian Tavarez	.15	.07
☐ 450 Jose Vizcaino	.15	.07

1998 Pacific Platinum Blue

Randomly inserted in packs at the rate of one in 73, this 450 card set is parallel to the base set and is similar in design. The difference is found in the platinum blue foil highlights. According to the manufacturer, only 67 sets were produced.

	MINT	NRMT
COMPLETE SET (450)	8000.00	3600.00
COMMON CARD (1-450)	15.00	6.75
MINOR STARS	25.00	11.00
SEMISTARS	40.00	18.00
UNLISTED STARS	60.00	27.00

*STARS 50X TO 100X BASIC CARDS
*YOUNG STARS: 40X TO 80X BASIC CARDS

Card	MINT	NRMT
☐ 33 Cal Ripken	250.00	110.00
☐ 39 Nomar Garciaparra	150.00	70.00
☐ 63 Frank Thomas	250.00	110.00
☐ 82 Jaret Wright	120.00	55.00
☐ 151 Derek Jeter	150.00	70.00
☐ 186 Ken Griffey Jr.	300.00	135.00
☐ 193 Alex Rodriguez	200.00	90.00
☐ 202 Juan Gonzalez	150.00	70.00
☐ 215 Roger Clemens	120.00	55.00
☐ 217 Jose Cruz Jr.	200.00	90.00
☐ 235 Chipper Jones	150.00	70.00
☐ 241 Greg Maddux	200.00	90.00
☐ 312 Jeff Bagwell	120.00	55.00
☐ 336 Hideo Nomo	200.00	90.00
☐ 339 Mike Piazza	200.00	90.00
☐ 386 Scott Rolen	120.00	55.00
☐ 416 Mark McGwire	120.00	55.00
☐ 427 Tony Gwynn	150.00	70.00

1998 Pacific Silver

Inserted one per pack, this 450-card set is parallel to the base set and is similar in design. The difference is found in the silver foil highlights.

	MINT	NRMT
COMPLETE SET (450)	250.00	110.00
COMMON CARD (1-450)	.25	.11

*SILVER STARS: 2.5X TO 5X BASIC CARDS
*SILVER YOUNG STARS: 2X TO 4X BASIC CARDS

1998 Pacific Cramer's Choice

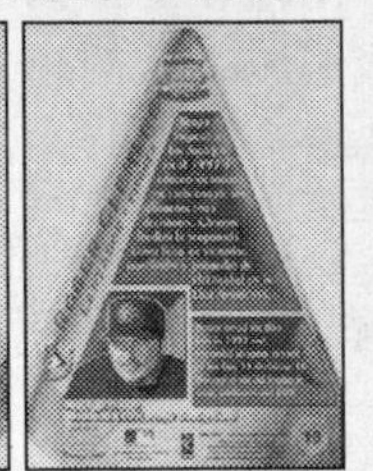

Randomly inserted in packs at the rate of one in 721, this 10-card set features top Major League players as chosen by Michael Cramer. The fronts display a color player cut-out on a pyramid die-cut shaped background. The backs carry information about why the player was selected for this set in both Spanish and English.

	MINT	NRMT
COMPLETE SET (10)	900.00	400.00
COMMON CARD (1-10)	40.00	18.00

Card	MINT	NRMT
☐ 1 Greg Maddux	120.00	55.00
☐ 2 Roberto Alomar	40.00	18.00
☐ 3 Cal Ripken	150.00	70.00
☐ 4 Nomar Garciaparra	100.00	45.00
☐ 5 Larry Walker	40.00	18.00
☐ 6 Mike Piazza	120.00	55.00
☐ 7 Mark McGwire	80.00	36.00
☐ 8 Tony Gwynn	100.00	45.00
☐ 9 Ken Griffey Jr.	200.00	90.00
☐ 10 Roger Clemens	80.00	36.00

1998 Pacific Gold Crown Die Cuts

Randomly inserted in packs at the rate of one in 37, this 36-card set features color action player photos with a die-cut crown at the top printed on a holographic silver foil background and gold etching on the trim. The backs carry player information in both Spanish and English.

	MINT	NRMT
COMPLETE SET (36)	450.00	200.00
COMMON CARD (1-36)	4.00	1.80

Card	MINT	NRMT
☐ 1 Chipper Jones	20.00	9.00
☐ 2 Greg Maddux	25.00	11.00
☐ 3 Denny Neagle	4.00	1.80
☐ 4 Roberto Alomar	8.00	3.60
☐ 5 Rafael Palmeiro	6.00	2.70
☐ 6 Cal Ripken	30.00	13.50
☐ 7 Nomar Garciaparra	20.00	9.00
☐ 8 Mo Vaughn	10.00	4.50
☐ 9 Frank Thomas	30.00	13.50
☐ 10 Sandy Alomar Jr.	5.00	2.20
☐ 11 David Justice	8.00	3.60
☐ 12 Manny Ramirez	8.00	3.60
☐ 13 Andres Galarraga	8.00	3.60
☐ 14 Larry Walker	8.00	3.60
☐ 15 Moises Alou	5.00	2.20
☐ 16 Livan Hernandez	5.00	2.20
☐ 17 Gary Sheffield	8.00	3.60
☐ 18 Jeff Bagwell	15.00	6.75
☐ 19 Raul Mondesi	4.00	1.80
☐ 20 Hideo Nomo	20.00	9.00
☐ 21 Mike Piazza	25.00	11.00
☐ 22 Derek Jeter	20.00	9.00
☐ 23 Tino Martinez	8.00	3.60
☐ 24 Bernie Williams	8.00	3.60
☐ 25 Ben Grieve	12.00	5.50
☐ 26 Mark McGwire	15.00	6.75

	MINT	NRMT
☐ 27 Tony Gwynn	20.00	9.00
☐ 28 Barry Bonds	10.00	4.50
☐ 29 Ken Griffey Jr.	40.00	18.00
☐ 30 Randy Johnson	8.00	3.60
☐ 31 Edgar Martinez	6.00	2.70
☐ 32 Alex Rodriguez	25.00	11.00
☐ 33 Juan Gonzalez	20.00	9.00
☐ 34 Ivan Rodriguez	10.00	4.50
☐ 35 Roger Clemens	15.00	6.75
☐ 36 Jose Cruz Jr.	25.00	11.00

1998 Pacific Home Run Hitters

Randomly inserted in packs at the rate of one in 73, this 20-card set features color player cut-outs of top home run hitters printed on full-foil cards with the number of home runs they hit in 1997 embossed in the background. The backs carry player information in both Spanish and English.

	MINT	NRMT
COMPLETE SET (20)	300.00	135.00
COMMON CARD (1-20)	5.00	2.20
☐ 1 Rafael Palmeiro	8.00	3.60
☐ 2 Mo Vaughn	12.00	5.50
☐ 3 Sammy Sosa	10.00	4.50
☐ 4 Albert Belle	12.00	5.50
☐ 5 Frank Thomas	40.00	18.00
☐ 6 David Justice	10.00	4.50
☐ 7 Jim Thome	10.00	4.50
☐ 8 Matt Williams	8.00	3.60
☐ 9 Vinny Castilla	5.00	2.20
☐ 10 Andres Galarraga	10.00	4.50
☐ 11 Larry Walker	10.00	4.50
☐ 12 Jeff Bagwell	20.00	9.00
☐ 13 Mike Piazza	30.00	13.50
☐ 14 Tino Martinez	10.00	4.50
☐ 15 Mark McGwire	20.00	9.00
☐ 16 Barry Bonds	12.00	5.50
☐ 17 Jay Buhner	8.00	3.60
☐ 18 Ken Griffey Jr.	50.00	22.00
☐ 19 Alex Rodriguez	30.00	13.50
☐ 20 Juan Gonzalez	25.00	11.00

1998 Pacific In The Cage

Randomly inserted in packs at the rate of one in 145, this 20-card set features color player cut-outs of the league's best hitters printed on a die-cut card with a laser-cut batting cage as the background. The backs carry player information in both Spanish and English.

	MINT	NRMT
COMPLETE SET (20)	600.00	275.00
COMMON CARD (1-20)	8.00	3.60
☐ 1 Chipper Jones	40.00	18.00
☐ 2 Roberto Alomar	15.00	6.75
☐ 3 Cal Ripken	60.00	27.00
☐ 4 Nomar Garciaparra	40.00	18.00
☐ 5 Frank Thomas	60.00	27.00
☐ 6 Sandy Alomar Jr.	10.00	4.50
☐ 7 David Justice	15.00	6.75
☐ 8 Larry Walker	15.00	6.75
☐ 9 Bobby Bonilla	8.00	3.60
☐ 10 Mike Piazza	50.00	22.00
☐ 11 Tino Martinez	15.00	6.75
☐ 12 Bernie Williams	15.00	6.75

	MINT	NRMT
☐ 13 Mark McGwire	30.00	13.50
☐ 14 Tony Gwynn	40.00	18.00
☐ 15 Barry Bonds	20.00	9.00
☐ 16 Ken Griffey Jr.	80.00	36.00
☐ 17 Edgar Martinez	12.00	5.50
☐ 18 Alex Rodriguez	50.00	22.00
☐ 19 Juan Gonzalez	40.00	18.00
☐ 20 Ivan Rodriguez	20.00	9.00

1998 Pacific Latinos of the Major Leagues

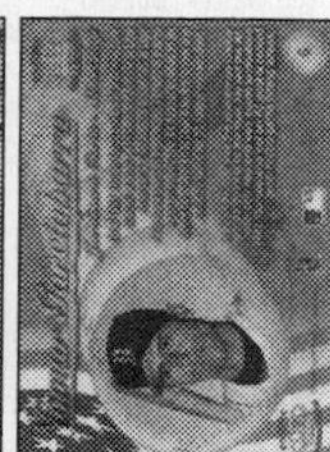

Randomly inserted in packs at the rate of two in 37, this 36-card set features color action photos of top players of Hispanic decent printed on foil cards with images of South and North America, the player's team logo, and the United States Flag in the background. The backs carry player information in both Spanish and English.

	MINT	NRMT
COMPLETE SET (36)	80.00	36.00
COMMON CARD (1-36)	1.00	.45
☐ 1 Andruw Jones	6.00	2.70
☐ 2 Javier Lopez	2.00	.90
☐ 3 Roberto Alomar	3.00	1.35
☐ 4 Geronimo Berroa	1.00	.45
☐ 5 Rafael Palmeiro	2.00	.90
☐ 6 Nomar Garciaparra	10.00	4.50
☐ 7 Sammy Sosa	3.00	1.35
☐ 8 Ozzie Guillen	1.00	.45
☐ 9 Sandy Alomar Jr.	2.00	.90
☐ 10 Manny Ramirez	3.00	1.35
☐ 11 Omar Vizquel	2.00	.90
☐ 12 Vinny Castilla	2.00	.90
☐ 13 Andres Galarraga	3.00	1.35
☐ 14 Moises Alou	2.00	.90
☐ 15 Bobby Bonilla	2.00	.90
☐ 16 Livan Hernandez	2.50	1.10
☐ 17 Edgar Renteria	2.00	.90
☐ 18 Wilton Guerrero	2.00	.90
☐ 19 Raul Mondesi	2.50	1.10
☐ 20 Ismael Valdes	2.00	.90
☐ 21 Fernando Vina	1.00	.45
☐ 22 Pedro Martinez	3.00	1.35
☐ 23 Edgardo Alfonzo	2.50	1.10
☐ 24 Carlos Baerga	1.00	.45
☐ 25 Rey Ordonez	2.00	.90
☐ 26 Tino Martinez	3.00	1.35
☐ 27 Mariano Rivera	2.00	.90
☐ 28 Bernie Williams	3.00	1.35
☐ 29 Jose Canseco	2.50	1.10
☐ 30 Joey Cora	2.00	.90
☐ 31 Roberto Kelly	1.00	.45
☐ 32 Edgar Martinez	2.50	1.10
☐ 33 Alex Rodriguez	12.00	5.50
☐ 34 Juan Gonzalez	10.00	4.50
☐ 35 Ivan Rodriguez	5.00	2.20
☐ 36 Jose Cruz Jr.	12.00	5.50

1998 Pacific Team Checklists

Randomly inserted in packs at the rate of one in 37, this 30-card set features color player photos printed on a die-cut card in the shape of the end of a baseball bat with a laser cut team logo. The two 1998 expansion teams, the Arizona Diamondbacks and the Tampa Bay Devil Rays, are included in these checklists.

	MINT	NRMT
COMPLETE SET (30)	300.00	135.00
COMMON CARD (1-30)	2.00	.90
☐ 1 Tim Salmon Jim Edmonds	6.00	2.70
☐ 2 Cal Ripken Roberto Alomar	25.00	11.00
☐ 3 Nomar Garciaparra Mo Vaughn	15.00	6.75
☐ 4 Frank Thomas Albert Belle	25.00	11.00
☐ 5 Sandy Alomar Jr. Manny Ramirez	6.00	2.70
☐ 6 Justin Thompson Tony Clark	6.00	2.70
☐ 7 Johnny Damon Jermaine Dye	3.00	1.35
☐ 8 Dave Nilsson Jeff Cirillo	2.00	.90
☐ 9 Paul Molitor Chuck Knoblauch	6.00	2.70
☐ 10 Tino Martinez Derek Jeter	15.00	6.75
☐ 11 Ben Grieve Jose Canseco	10.00	4.50
☐ 12 Ken Griffey Jr. Alex Rodriguez	40.00	18.00
☐ 13 Juan Gonzalez Ivan Rodriguez	15.00	6.75
☐ 14 Jose Cruz Jr. Roger Clemens	25.00	11.00
☐ 15 Greg Maddux Chipper Jones	25.00	11.00
☐ 16 Sammy Sosa Mark Grace	6.00	2.70
☐ 17 Barry Larkin Deion Sanders	4.00	1.80
☐ 18 Larry Walker Andres Galarraga	6.00	2.70
☐ 19 Moises Alou Bobby Bonilla	3.00	1.35
☐ 20 Jeff Bagwell Craig Biggio	12.00	5.50
☐ 21 Mike Piazza Hideo Nomo	25.00	11.00
☐ 22 Pedro Martinez Henry Rodriguez	4.00	1.80
☐ 23 Rey Ordonez Carlos Baerga	2.00	.90
☐ 24 Curt Schilling Scott Rolen	12.00	5.50
☐ 25 Al Martin Tony Womack	2.00	.90
☐ 26 Mark McGwire Dennis Eckersley	15.00	6.75
☐ 27 Tony Gwynn Wally Joyner	15.00	6.75
☐ 28 Barry Bonds J.T.Snow	8.00	3.60
☐ 29 Matt Williams Jay Bell	4.00	1.80
☐ 30 Fred McGriff Roberto Hernandez	3.00	1.35

1995 Pacific Prisms

This 144-card standard-size set was issued for the first time as a stand alone set instead as an insert set. Total production of this product was 2,999 individually numbered cases that contained 20 boxes of 36 packs. The full-bleed fronts feature a player photo against a silver prismatic background with the playerís name on the bottom. The backs have a full-color photo with some biographical information. The cards are grouped alphabetically according to teams for each league with AL and NL intermingled. There are no key Rookie Cards in this set. A checklist or team logo card was seeded into every pack.

	MINT	NRMT
COMPLETE SET (144)	150.00	70.00
COMMON CARD (1-144)	1.00	.45
COMP.TEAM LOGO SET (28)	5.00	2.20

Card	MINT	NRMT
1 David Justice	3.00	1.35
2 Ryan Klesko	2.00	.90
3 Javier Lopez	2.00	.90
4 Greg Maddux	10.00	4.50
5 Fred McGriff	2.00	.90
6 Tony Tarasco	1.00	.45
7 Jeffrey Hammonds	1.50	.70
8 Mike Mussina	3.00	1.35
9 Rafael Palmeiro	2.00	.90
10 Cal Ripken	12.00	5.50
11 Lee Smith	1.50	.70
12 Roger Clemens	6.00	2.70
13 Scott Cooper	1.00	.45
14 Mike Greenwell	1.00	.45
15 Carlos Rodriguez	1.00	.45
16 Mo Vaughn	4.00	1.80
17 Chili Davis	1.50	.70
18 Jim Edmonds	3.00	1.35
19 Jorge Fabregas	1.00	.45
20 Bo Jackson	1.50	.70
21 Tim Salmon	3.00	1.35
22 Mark Grace	2.00	.90
23 Jose Guzman	1.00	.45
24 Randy Myers	1.00	.45
25 Rey Sanchez	1.00	.45
26 Sammy Sosa	3.00	1.35
27 Wilson Alvarez	1.50	.70
28 Julio Franco	1.50	.70
29 Ozzie Guillen	1.00	.45
30 Jack McDowell	1.00	.45
31 Frank Thomas	12.00	5.50
32 Bret Boone	1.00	.45
33 Barry Larkin	2.00	.90
34 Hal Morris	1.00	.45
35 Jose Rijo	1.00	.45
36 Deion Sanders	3.00	1.35
37 Carlos Baerga	1.50	.70
38 Albert Belle	4.00	1.80
39 Kenny Lofton	4.00	1.80
40 Dennis Martinez	1.50	.70
41 Manny Ramirez	3.00	1.35
42 Omar Vizquel	1.50	.70
43 Dante Bichette	2.00	.90
44 Marvin Freeman	1.00	.45
45 Andres Galarraga	2.00	.90
46 Mike Kingery	1.00	.45
47 Danny Bautista	1.00	.45
48 Cecil Fielder	1.50	.70
49 Travis Fryman	1.50	.70
50 Tony Phillips	1.00	.45
51 Alan Trammell	2.00	.90
52 Lou Whitaker	1.50	.70
53 Alex Arias	1.00	.45
54 Bret Barberie	1.00	.45
55 Jeff Conine	1.50	.70
56 Charles Johnson	1.50	.70
57 Gary Sheffield	3.00	1.35
58 Jeff Bagwell	6.00	2.70
59 Craig Biggio	2.00	.90
60 Doug Drabek	1.00	.45
61 Tony Eusebio	1.00	.45
62 Luis Gonzalez	1.00	.45
63 David Cone	1.50	.70
64 Bob Hamelin	1.00	.45
65 Felix Jose	1.00	.45
66 Wally Joyner	1.50	.70
67 Brian McRae	1.00	.45
68 Brett Butler	1.50	.70
69 Garey Ingram	1.00	.45
70 Ramon Martinez	1.50	.70
71 Raul Mondesi	2.00	.90
72 Mike Piazza	10.00	4.50
73 Henry Rodriguez	1.00	.45
74 Ricky Bones	1.00	.45
75 Pat Listach	1.00	.45
76 Dave Nilsson	1.50	.70
77 Jose Valentin	1.50	.70
78 Rick Aguilera	1.00	.45
79 Denny Hocking	1.00	.45
80 Shane Mack	1.00	.45
81 Pedro Munoz	1.00	.45
82 Kirby Puckett	6.00	2.70
83 Dave Winfield	2.00	.90
84 Moises Alou	1.50	.70
85 Wil Cordero	1.00	.45
86 Cliff Floyd	1.50	.70
87 Marquis Grissom	1.50	.70
88 Pedro J. Martinez	3.00	1.35
89 Larry Walker	3.00	1.35
90 Bobby Bonilla	1.50	.70
91 Jeromy Burnitz	1.50	.70
92 John Franco	1.50	.70
93 Jeff Kent	1.00	.45
94 Jose Vizcaino	1.00	.45
95 Wade Boggs	3.00	1.35
96 Jimmy Key	1.50	.70
97 Don Mattingly	6.00	2.70
98 Paul O'Neill	1.50	.70
99 Luis Polonia	1.00	.45
100 Danny Tartabull	1.00	.45
101 Geronimo Berroa	1.00	.45
102 Rickey Henderson	2.00	.90
103 Ruben Sierra	1.00	.45
104 Terry Steinbach	1.50	.70
105 Darren Daulton	1.50	.70
106 Mariano Duncan	1.00	.45
107 Lenny Dykstra	1.50	.70
108 Mike Lieberthal	1.00	.45
109 Tony Longmire	1.00	.45
110 Tom Marsh	1.00	.45
111 Jay Bell	1.50	.70
112 Carlos Garcia	1.00	.45
113 Orlando Merced	1.00	.45
114 Andy Van Slyke	1.50	.70
115 Derek Bell	1.50	.70
116 Tony Gwynn	8.00	3.60
117 Luis Lopez	1.00	.45
118 Bip Roberts	1.00	.45
119 Rod Beck	1.00	.45
120 Barry Bonds	4.00	1.80
121 Darryl Strawberry	1.50	.70
122 Wm. Van Landingham	1.00	.45
123 Matt Williams	2.00	.90
124 Jay Buhner	2.00	.90
125 Felix Fermin	1.00	.45
126 Ken Griffey Jr.	15.00	6.75
127 Randy Johnson	3.00	1.35
128 Edgar Martinez	2.00	.90
129 Alex Rodriguez	12.00	5.50
130 Rene Arocha	1.00	.45
131 Gregg Jefferies	1.50	.70
132 Mike Perez	1.00	.45
133 Ozzie Smith	4.00	1.80
134 Jose Canseco	2.00	.90
135 Will Clark	2.00	.90
136 Juan Gonzalez	8.00	3.60
137 Ivan Rodriguez	4.00	1.80
138 Roberto Alomar	3.00	1.35
139 Joe Carter	2.00	.90
140 Carlos Delgado	1.50	.70
141 Alex Gonzalez	1.00	.45
142 Juan Guzman	1.00	.45
143 Paul Molitor	3.00	1.35
144 John Olerud	1.50	.70
CL1 Checklist	.25	.11
CL2 Checklist	.25	.11

1996 Pacific Prisms

This 144-card set features a color action player cut-out over a double-etched silver foil prismatic background. The backs carry a color player portrait with information about the player in both English and Spanish.

	MINT	NRMT
COMPLETE SET (144)	150.00	70.00
COMMON CARD (1-144)	.75	.35

Card	MINT	NRMT
P1 Tom Glavine	1.25	.55
P2 Chipper Jones	10.00	4.50
P3 David Justice	3.00	1.35
P4 Ryan Klesko	2.00	.90
P5 Javy Lopez	1.25	.55
P6 Greg Maddux	10.00	4.50
P7 Fred McGriff	2.00	.90
P8 Frank Castillo	.75	.35
P9 Luis Gonzalez	.75	.35
P10 Mark Grace	2.00	.90
P11 Brian McRae	.75	.35
P12 Jaime Navarro	.75	.35
P13 Sammy Sosa	3.00	1.35
P14 Bret Boone	.75	.35
P15 Ron Gant	1.25	.55
P16 Barry Larkin	2.00	.90
P17 Reggie Sanders	.75	.35
P18 Benito Santiago	.75	.35
P19 Dante Bichette	1.25	.55
P20 Vinny Castilla	1.25	.55
P21 Andres Galarraga	3.00	1.35
P22 Bryan Rekar	.75	.35
P23 Roberto Alomar	3.00	1.35
P24 Jeff Conine	1.25	.55
P25 Andre Dawson	2.00	.90
P26 Charles Johnson	1.25	.55
P27 Gary Sheffield	3.00	1.35
P28 Quilvio Veras	.75	.35
P29 Jeff Bagwell	6.00	2.70
P30 Derek Bell	1.25	.55
P31 Craig Biggio	2.00	.90
P32 Tony Eusebio	.75	.35
P33 Karim Garcia	1.25	.55
P34 Eric Karros	1.25	.55
P35 Ramon Martinez	1.25	.55
P36 Raul Mondesi	2.00	.90
P37 Hideo Nomo	8.00	3.60
P38 Mike Piazza	10.00	4.50
P39 Ismael Valdes	1.25	.55
P40 Moises Alou	1.25	.55
P41 Wil Cordero	.75	.35
P42 Pedro Martinez	3.00	1.35
P43 Mel Rojas	.75	.35
P44 David Segui	.75	.35
P45 Edfardo Alfonzo	2.00	.90
P46 Rico Brogna	.75	.35
P47 John Franco	.75	.35
P48 Jason Isringhausen	.75	.35
P49 Jose Vizcaino	.75	.35
P50 Ricky Bottalico	.75	.35
P51 Darren Daulton	1.25	.55
P52 Lenny Dykstra	1.25	.55
P53 Tyler Green	.75	.35
P54 Gregg Jefferies	1.25	.55
P55 Jay Bell	1.25	.55
P56 Jason Christiansen	.75	.35
P57 Carlos Garcia	.75	.35
P58 Esteban Loaiza	.75	.35
P59 Orlando Merced	.75	.35
P60 Andujar Cedeno	.75	.35
P61 Tony Gwynn	8.00	3.60
P62 Melvin Nieves	.75	.35
P63 Phil Plantier	.75	.35
P64 Fernando Valenzuela	1.25	.55
P65 Barry Bonds	4.00	1.80
P66 J.R. Phillips	.75	.35
P67 Deion Sanders	3.00	1.35
P68 Matt Williams	2.00	.90
P69 Bernard Gilkey	.75	.35
P70 Tom Henke	1.25	.55
P71 Brian Jordan	1.25	.55
P72 Ozzie Smith	4.00	1.80
P73 Manny Alexander	.75	.35
P74 Bobby Bonilla	1.25	.55
P75 Mike Mussina	3.00	1.35
P76 Rafael Palmeiro	2.00	.90
P77 Cal Ripken	12.00	5.50
P78 Jose Canseco	2.00	.90
P79 Roger Clemens	6.00	2.70
P80 John Valentin	1.25	.55
P81 Mo Vaughn	4.00	1.80
P82 Tim Wakefield	.75	.35
P83 Garret Anderson	1.25	.55
P84 Damion Easley	.75	.35
P85 Jim Edmonds	3.00	1.35
P86 Tim Salmon	3.00	1.35
P87 Wilson Alvarez	1.25	.55
P88 Alex Fernandez	1.25	.55
P89 Ozzie Guillen	.75	.35
P90 Roberto Hernandez	1.25	.55
P91 Frank Thomas	12.00	5.50
P92 Robin Ventura	1.25	.55
P93 Carlos Baerga	.75	.35
P94 Albert Belle	4.00	1.80
P95 Kenny Lofton	4.00	1.80
P96 Dennis Martinez	1.25	.55
P97 Eddie Murray	3.00	1.35
P98 Manny Ramirez	3.00	1.35
P99 Omar Vizquel	1.25	.55
P100 Chad Curtis	.75	.35
P101 Cecil Fielder	1.25	.55
P102 Felipe Lira	.75	.35
P103 Alan Trammell	2.00	.90
P104 Kevin Appier	1.25	.55
P105 Johnny Damon	1.25	.55
P106 Gary Gaetti	1.25	.55
P107 Wally Joyner	.75	.35
P108 Ricky Bones	.75	.35
P109 John Jaha	.75	.35
P110 B.J. Surhoff	.75	.35
P111 Jose Valentin	.75	.35
P112 Fernando Vina	.75	.35
P113 Marty Cordova	.75	.35

☐ P114 Chuck Knoblauch	3.00	1.35
☐ P115 Scott Leius	.75	.35
☐ P116 Pedro Munoz	.75	.35
☐ P117 Kirby Puckett	6.00	2.70
☐ P118 Wade Boggs	3.00	1.35
☐ P119 Don Mattingly	5.00	2.20
☐ P120 Jack McDowell	.75	.35
☐ P121 Paul O'Neill	1.25	.55
☐ P122 Ruben Rivera	1.25	.55
☐ P123 Bernie Williams	3.00	1.35
☐ P124 Geronimo Berroa	.75	.35
☐ P125 Rickey Henderson	2.00	.90
☐ P126 Mark McGwire	6.00	2.70
☐ P127 Terry Steinbach	1.25	.55
☐ P128 Danny Tartabull	.75	.35
☐ P129 Jay Buhner	2.00	.90
☐ P130 Joey Cora	1.25	.55
☐ P131 Ken Griffey, Jr.	15.00	6.75
☐ P132 Randy Johnson	3.00	1.35
☐ P133 Edgar Martinez	2.00	.90
☐ P134 Tino Martinez	3.00	1.35
☐ P135 Will Clark	2.00	.90
☐ P136 Juan Gonzalez	8.00	3.60
☐ P137 Dean Palmer	1.25	.55
☐ P138 Ivan Rodriguez	4.00	1.80
☐ P139 Mickey Tettleton	.75	.35
☐ P140 Larry Walker	3.00	1.35
☐ P141 Joe Carter	1.25	.55
☐ P142 Carlos Delgado	1.25	.55
☐ P143 Alex Gonzalez	.75	.35
☐ P144 Paul Molitor	3.00	1.35

1996 Pacific Prisms Gold

This 144-card parallel set features the same design as the Pacific Prisms set except the prismatic background on the front is printed in double-etched gold foil. The horizontal backs contain player information in both English and Spanish.

	MINT	NRMT
COMPLETE SET (144)	600.00	275.00
COMMON CARD (1-144)	3.00	1.35
*STARS: 2X to 4X BASIC CARDS		

1996 Pacific Prisms Fence Busters

Randomly inserted in packs at a rate of one in 37, this 20-card set highlights 20 of baseball's hardest hitters. The fronts feature an embossed color player action cut-out with a borderless foil baseball field as background. The backs carry a player photo with information as to why the player was selected for this set in both English and Spanish.

	MINT	NRMT
COMPLETE SET (20)	180.00	80.00
COMMON CARD (1-20)	3.00	1.35
☐ FB1 Albert Belle	10.00	4.50
☐ FB2 Dante Bichette	4.00	1.80
☐ FB3 Barry Bonds	10.00	4.50
☐ FB4 Jay Buhner	5.00	2.20
☐ FB5 Jose Canseco	5.00	2.20
☐ FB6 Ken Griffey Jr.	40.00	18.00
☐ FB7 Chipper Jones	25.00	11.00
☐ FB8 Dave Justice	8.00	3.60
☐ FB9 Eric Karros	3.00	1.35
☐ FB10 Edgar Martinez	5.00	2.20
☐ FB11 Mark McGwire	15.00	6.75
☐ FB12 Eddie Murray	8.00	3.60
☐ FB13 Mike Piazza	25.00	11.00
☐ FB14 Kirby Puckett	15.00	6.75
☐ FB15 Cal Ripken	30.00	13.50
☐ FB16 Tim Salmon	8.00	3.60
☐ FB17 Sammy Sosa	8.00	3.60
☐ FB18 Frank Thomas	30.00	13.50
☐ FB19 Mo Vaughn	10.00	4.50
☐ FB20 Larry Walker	8.00	3.60

1996 Pacific Prisms Flame Throwers

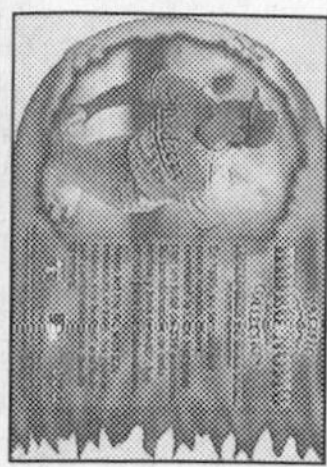

Randomly inserted in packs at a rate of one in 73, this 10-card set features 10 of Major League Baseball's hardest throwing pitchers. The fronts display a color action player photo printed on a diecut baseball-shaped card with gold foil flames indicating the force of the thrown ball. The backs carry another player photo with information of why the player was selected for this set printed in both English and Spanish.

	MINT	NRMT
COMPLETE SET (10)	150.00	70.00
COMMON CARD (1-10)	5.00	2.20
☐ FT1 Randy Johnson	20.00	9.00
☐ FT2 Mike Mussina	20.00	9.00
☐ FT3 Roger Clemens	40.00	18.00
☐ FT4 Tom Glavine	8.00	3.60
☐ FT5 Hideo Nomo	50.00	22.00
☐ FT6 Jose Rijo	5.00	2.20
☐ FT7 Greg Maddux	60.00	27.00
☐ FT8 David Cone	8.00	3.60
☐ FT9 Ramon Martinez	8.00	3.60
☐ FT10 Jose Mesa	5.00	2.20

1996 Pacific Prisms Red Hot Stars

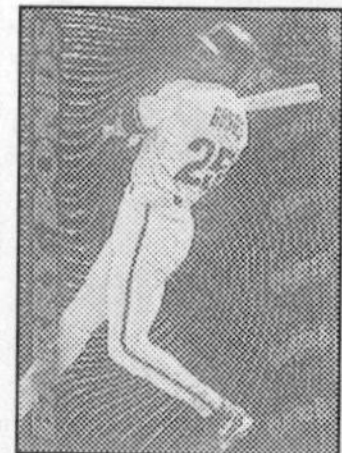

Randomly inserted in packs at a rate of one in 37, this 20-card set features 20 of Major League Baseball's hottest stars. The fronts display a color action player cut-out on a red foil background. The backs carry a color player photo with information about the player printed in both English and Spanish.

	MINT	NRMT
COMPLETE SET (20)	250.00	110.00
COMMON CARD (1-20)	3.00	1.35
☐ RH1 Roberto Alomar	8.00	3.60
☐ RH2 Jose Canseco	5.00	2.20
☐ RH3 Chipper Jones	25.00	11.00
☐ RH4 Mike Piazza	25.00	11.00
☐ RH5 Tim Salmon	8.00	3.60
☐ RH6 Jeff Bagwell	15.00	6.75
☐ RH7 Ken Griffey Jr.	40.00	18.00
☐ RH8 Greg Maddux	25.00	11.00
☐ RH9 Kirby Puckett	15.00	6.75
☐ RH10 Frank Thomas	30.00	13.50
☐ RH11 Albert Belle	10.00	4.50
☐ RH12 Tony Gwynn	20.00	9.00
☐ RH13 Edgar Martinez	3.00	1.35
☐ RH14 Manny Ramirez	8.00	3.60
☐ RH15 Barry Bonds	10.00	4.50
☐ RH16 Wade Boggs	8.00	3.60
☐ RH17 Randy Johnson	8.00	3.60
☐ RH18 Don Mattingly	12.00	5.50
☐ RH19 Cal Ripken	40.00	18.00
☐ RH20 Mo Vaughn	10.00	4.50

1997 Pacific Prisms

The 1997 Pacific Prism set was issued in one series totalling 150 cards and displays color action photos of

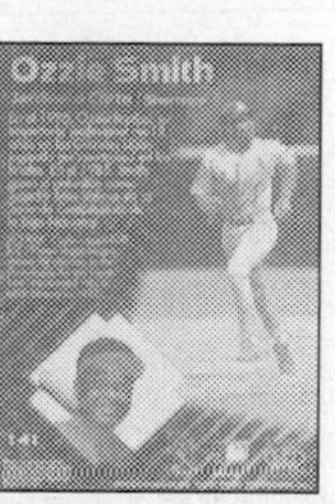

many of the top players from last season. Foiled in gold, the set features a visually stunning inlaid transparent cel on each card. The backs carry player information in both Spanish and English.

	MINT	NRMT
COMPLETE SET (150)	180.00	80.00
COMMON CARD (1-150)	1.00	.45
☐ 1 Chili Davis	1.50	.70
☐ 2 Jim Edmonds	2.50	1.10
☐ 3 Darin Erstad	5.00	2.20
☐ 4 Orlando Palmeiro	1.00	.45
☐ 5 Tim Salmon	2.50	1.10
☐ 6 J.T. Snow	1.50	.70
☐ 7 Roberto Alomar	3.00	1.35
☐ 8 Brady Anderson	2.00	.90
☐ 9 Eddie Murray	3.00	1.35
☐ 10 Mike Mussina	3.00	1.35
☐ 11 Rafael Palmeiro	2.00	.90
☐ 12 Cal Ripken	12.00	5.50
☐ 13 Jose Canseco	2.00	.90
☐ 14 Roger Clemens	6.00	2.70
☐ 15 Nomar Garciaparra	10.00	4.50
☐ 16 Reggie Jefferson	1.50	.70
☐ 17 Mo Vaughn	4.00	1.80
☐ 18 Wilson Alvarez	1.50	.70
☐ 19 Harold Baines	1.50	.70
☐ 20 Alex Fernandez	1.50	.70
☐ 21 Danny Tartabull	1.00	.45
☐ 22 Frank Thomas	12.00	5.50
☐ 23 Robin Ventura	1.50	.70
☐ 24 Sandy Alomar Jr.	1.50	.70
☐ 25 Albert Belle	4.00	1.80
☐ 26 Kenny Lofton	4.00	1.80
☐ 27 Jim Thome	3.00	1.35
☐ 28 Omar Vizquel	1.50	.70
☐ 29 Raul Casanova	1.00	.45
☐ 30 Tony Clark	2.50	1.10
☐ 31 Travis Fryman	1.50	.70
☐ 32 Bobby Higginson	1.50	.70
☐ 33 Melvin Nieves	1.00	.45
☐ 34 Justin Thompson	1.50	.70
☐ 35 Johnny Damon	1.00	.45
☐ 36 Tom Goodwin	1.00	.45
☐ 37 Jeff Montgomery	1.00	.45
☐ 38 Jose Offerman	1.00	.45
☐ 39 John Jaha	1.00	.45
☐ 40 Jeff Cirillo	1.50	.70
☐ 41 Dave Nilsson	1.00	.45
☐ 42 Jose Valentin	1.00	.45
☐ 43 Fernando Vina	1.00	.45
☐ 44 Marty Cordova	1.00	.45
☐ 45 Roberto Kelly	1.00	.45
☐ 46 Chuck Knoblauch	2.50	1.10
☐ 47 Paul Molitor	3.00	1.35
☐ 48 Todd Walker	1.00	.45
☐ 49 Wade Boggs	2.50	1.10
☐ 50 Cecil Fielder	1.50	.70
☐ 51 Derek Jeter	10.00	4.50
☐ 52 Tino Martinez	2.50	1.10
☐ 53 Andy Pettitte	3.00	1.35
☐ 54 Mariano Rivera	1.50	.70
☐ 55 Bernie Williams	2.50	1.10
☐ 56 Tony Batista	1.50	.70
☐ 57 Geronimo Berroa	1.00	.45
☐ 58 Jason Giambi	1.50	.70
☐ 59 Mark McGwire	6.00	2.70
☐ 60 Terry Steinbach	1.50	.70
☐ 61 Jay Buhner	2.00	.90
☐ 62 Joey Cora	1.50	.70
☐ 63 Ken Griffey Jr.	15.00	6.75
☐ 64 Edgar Martinez	2.00	.90
☐ 65 Alex Rodriguez	12.00	5.50
☐ 66 Paul Sorrento	1.00	.45
☐ 67 Will Clark	2.00	.90
☐ 68 Juan Gonzalez	8.00	3.60
☐ 69 Rusty Greer	1.50	.70
☐ 70 Dean Palmer	1.50	.70
☐ 71 Ivan Rodriguez	4.00	1.80
☐ 72 Joe Carter	1.50	.70
☐ 73 Carlos Delgado	1.50	.70
☐ 74 Juan Guzman	1.00	.45
☐ 75 Pat Hentgen	1.50	.70

Card	MINT	NRMT
☐ 76 Ed Sprague	1.00	.45
☐ 77 Jermaine Dye	1.00	.45
☐ 78 Andruw Jones	8.00	3.60
☐ 79 Chipper Jones	10.00	4.50
☐ 80 Ryan Klesko	2.00	.90
☐ 81 Javier Lopez	1.50	.70
☐ 82 Greg Maddux	10.00	4.50
☐ 83 John Smoltz	1.50	.70
☐ 84 Mark Grace	2.00	.90
☐ 85 Luis Gonzalez	1.00	.45
☐ 86 Brooks Kieschnick	1.50	.70
☐ 87 Jaime Navarro	1.00	.45
☐ 88 Ryne Sandberg	4.00	1.80
☐ 89 Sammy Sosa	2.50	1.10
☐ 90 Bret Boone	1.00	.45
☐ 91 Jeff Brantley	1.00	.45
☐ 92 Eric Davis	1.00	.45
☐ 93 Barry Larkin	2.00	.90
☐ 94 Reggie Sanders	1.00	.45
☐ 95 Ellis Burks	1.50	.70
☐ 96 Dante Bichette	1.50	.70
☐ 97 Vinny Castilla	1.50	.70
☐ 98 Andres Galarraga	2.50	1.10
☐ 99 Eric Young	1.00	.45
☐ 100 Kevin Brown	1.50	.70
☐ 101 Jeff Conine	1.50	.70
☐ 102 Charles Johnson	1.50	.70
☐ 103 Edgar Renteria	2.00	.90
☐ 104 Gary Sheffield	2.50	1.10
☐ 105 Jeff Bagwell	6.00	2.70
☐ 106 Derek Bell	1.00	.45
☐ 107 Sean Berry	1.00	.45
☐ 108 Craig Biggio	2.00	.90
☐ 109 Shane Reynolds	1.00	.45
☐ 110 Karim Garcia	1.50	.70
☐ 111 Todd Hollandsworth	1.50	.70
☐ 112 Ramon Martinez	1.50	.70
☐ 113 Raul Mondesi	2.00	.90
☐ 114 Hideo Nomo	8.00	3.60
☐ 115 Mike Piazza	10.00	4.50
☐ 116 Ismael Valdes	1.50	.70
☐ 117 Moises Alou	1.50	.70
☐ 118 Mark Grudzielanek	1.00	.45
☐ 119 Pedro Martinez	2.50	1.10
☐ 120 Henry Rodriguez	1.00	.45
☐ 121 F.P. Santangelo	1.00	.45
☐ 122 Carlos Baerga	1.50	.70
☐ 123 Bernard Gilkey	1.00	.45
☐ 124 Todd Hundley	1.50	.70
☐ 125 Lance Johnson	1.00	.45
☐ 126 Alex Ochoa	1.00	.45
☐ 127 Rey Ordonez	1.00	.45
☐ 128 Lenny Dykstra	1.50	.70
☐ 129 Gregg Jefferies	1.50	.70
☐ 130 Ricky Otero	1.00	.45
☐ 131 Benito Santiago	1.00	.45
☐ 132 Jermaine Allensworth	1.50	.70
☐ 133 Francisco Cordova	1.00	.45
☐ 134 Carlos Garcia	1.00	.45
☐ 135 Jason Kendall	1.50	.70
☐ 136 Al Martin	1.00	.45
☐ 137 Dennis Eckersley	2.00	.90
☐ 138 Ron Gant	1.50	.70
☐ 139 Brian Jordan	1.50	.70
☐ 140 John Mabry	1.50	.70
☐ 141 Ozzie Smith	4.00	1.80
☐ 142 Ken Caminiti	2.50	1.10
☐ 143 Steve Finley	1.50	.70
☐ 144 Tony Gwynn	8.00	3.60
☐ 145 Wally Joyner	1.00	.45
☐ 146 Fernando Valenzuela	1.50	.70
☐ 147 Barry Bonds	4.00	1.80
☐ 148 Jacob Cruz	1.00	.45
☐ 149 Osvaldo Fernandez	1.00	.45
☐ 150 Matt Williams	2.00	.90

1997 Pacific Prisms Light Blue

Distributed exclusively in retail outlets at a rate of 2:37 packs, cards from this 150-card set parallel the standard 1997 Pacific Prisms. The light blue foil fronts easily differentiate them from their bronze basic issue counterparts.

	MINT	NRMT
COMPLETE SET (150)	900.00	400.00
COMMON CARD (1-150)	6.00	2.70
*STARS: 3X to 6X BASIC CARDS		

1997 Pacific Prisms Platinum

Randomly inserted in packs at a rate of two in 37, this set is a platinum foiled parallel version of the regular set.

	MINT	NRMT
COMPLETE SET (150)	750.00	350.00
COMMON CARD (1-150)	5.00	2.20
*STARS: 2.5X TO 5X BASIC CARDS		

1997 Pacific Prisms Gate Attractions

Randomly inserted in packs at a rate of one in 73, this 32-card set features some of the league's current most popular players. The fronts display a player image on a baseball with a borderless photo of the inside of a baseball glove as background. The backs contain player information in both Spanish and English.

	MINT	NRMT
COMPLETE SET (32)	600.00	275.00
COMMON CARD (GA1-GA32)	6.00	2.70
☐ GA1 Roberto Alomar	12.00	5.50
☐ GA2 Brady Anderson	8.00	3.60
☐ GA3 Cal Ripken	50.00	22.00
☐ GA4 Frank Thomas	50.00	22.00
☐ GA5 Kenny Lofton	15.00	6.75
☐ GA6 Omar Vizquel	7.00	3.10
☐ GA7 Paul Molitor	12.00	5.50
☐ GA8 Wade Boggs	12.00	5.50
☐ GA9 Derek Jeter	30.00	13.50
☐ GA10 Andy Pettitte	15.00	6.75
☐ GA11 Bernie Williams	12.00	5.50
☐ GA12 Geronimo Berroa	6.00	2.70
☐ GA13 Mark McGwire	25.00	11.00
☐ GA14 Ken Griffey Jr.	60.00	27.00
☐ GA15 Alex Rodriguez	40.00	18.00
☐ GA16 Juan Gonzalez	30.00	13.50
☐ GA17 Andruw Jones	25.00	11.00
☐ GA18 Chipper Jones	40.00	18.00
☐ GA19 Greg Maddux	40.00	18.00
☐ GA20 Ryne Sandberg	15.00	6.75
☐ GA21 Sammy Sosa	12.00	5.50
☐ GA22 Andres Galarraga	12.00	5.50
☐ GA23 Jeff Bagwell	25.00	11.00
☐ GA24 Todd Hollandsworth	6.00	2.70
☐ GA25 Hideo Nomo	30.00	13.50
☐ GA26 Mike Piazza	40.00	18.00
☐ GA27 Todd Hundley	7.00	3.10
☐ GA28 Lance Johnson	6.00	2.70
☐ GA29 Ozzie Smith	15.00	6.75
☐ GA30 Ken Caminiti	12.00	5.50
☐ GA31 Tony Gwynn	30.00	13.50
☐ GA32 Barry Bonds	15.00	6.75

1997 Pacific Prisms Gems of the Diamond

Randomly inserted at the rate of approximately two per pack, this 220 card bonus set features color action photos with the player's name printed in the bottom gold border. A diamond replica displays the name of the player's team. The backs carry player information in both Spanish and English.

	MINT	NRMT
COMPLETE SET (220)	50.00	22.00
COMMON CARD (GD1-GD220)	.25	.11
☐ GD1 Jim Abbott	.50	.23
☐ GD2 Shawn Boskie	.25	.11
☐ GD3 Gary Disarcina	.25	.11
☐ GD4 Jim Edmonds	1.00	.45
☐ GD5 Todd Greene	.50	.23
☐ GD6 Jack Howell	.25	.11
☐ GD7 Jeff Schmidt	.25	.11
☐ GD8 Shad Williams	.25	.11
☐ GD9 Roberto Alomar	1.00	.45
☐ GD10 Cesar Devarez	.25	.11
☐ GD11 Alan Mills	.25	.11
☐ GD12 Eddie Murray	1.25	.55
☐ GD13 Jesse Orosco	.25	.11
☐ GD14 Arthur Rhodes	.25	.11
☐ GD15 Bill Ripken	.25	.11
☐ GD16 Cal Ripken	4.00	1.80
☐ GD17 Mark Smith	.25	.11
☐ GD18 Roger Clemens	2.00	.90
☐ GD19 Vaughn Eshelman	.25	.11
☐ GD20 Rich Garces	.25	.11
☐ GD21 Bill Haselman	.25	.11
☐ GD22 Dwayne Hosey	.25	.11
☐ GD23 Mike Maddux	.25	.11
☐ GD24 Jose Malave	.25	.11
☐ GD25 Aaron Sele	.25	.11
☐ GD26 James Baldwin	.25	.11
☐ GD27 Pat Borders	.25	.11
☐ GD28 Mike Cameron	.50	.23
☐ GD29 Tony Castillo	.25	.11
☐ GD30 Domingo Cedeno	.25	.11
☐ GD31 Greg Norton	.25	.11
☐ GD32 Frank Thomas	4.00	1.80
☐ GD33 Albert Belle	1.25	.55
☐ GD34 Edgar Diaz	.25	.11
☐ GD35 Alan Embree	.25	.11
☐ GD36 Albie Lopez	.25	.11
☐ GD37 Chad Ogea	.25	.11
☐ GD38 Tony Pena	.25	.11
☐ GD39 Joe Roa	.25	.11
☐ GD40 Fausto Cruz	.25	.11
☐ GD41 Joey Eischen	.25	.11
☐ GD42 Travis Fryman	.50	.23
☐ GD43 Mike Myers	.25	.11
☐ GD44 A.J. Sager	.25	.11
☐ GD45 Duane Singleton	.25	.11
☐ GD46 Justin Thompson	.50	.23
☐ GD47 Jeff Granger	.25	.11
☐ GD48 Les Norman	.25	.11
☐ GD49 Jon Nunnally	.25	.11
☐ GD50 Craig Paquette	.25	.11
☐ GD51 Michael Tucker	.50	.23
☐ GD52 Julio Valera	.25	.11
☐ GD53 Kevin Young	.25	.11
☐ GD54 Cal Eldred	.25	.11
☐ GD55 Ramon Garcia	.25	.11
☐ GD56 Marc Newfield	.25	.11
☐ GD57 Al Reyes	.25	.11
☐ GD58 Tim Unroe	.25	.11
☐ GD59 Tim Vanegmond	.25	.11
☐ GD60 Turner Ward	.25	.11
☐ GD61 Bob Wickman	.25	.11
☐ GD62 Chuck Knoblauch	1.00	.45
☐ GD63 Paul Molitor	1.00	.45
☐ GD64 Kirby Puckett	2.00	.90
☐ GD65 Tom Quinlan	.25	.11
☐ GD66 Rich Robertson	.25	.11
☐ GD67 Dave Stevens	.25	.11
☐ GD68 Matt Walbeck	.25	.11
☐ GD69 Wade Boggs	1.00	.45
☐ GD70 Tony Fernandez	.25	.11
☐ GD71 Andy Fox	.25	.11
☐ GD72 Joe Girardi	.25	.11
☐ GD73 Charlie Hayes	.25	.11
☐ GD74 Pat Kelly	.25	.11
☐ GD75 Jeff Nelson	.25	.11
☐ GD76 Melido Perez	.25	.11
☐ GD77 Mark Acre	.25	.11
☐ GD78 Allen Battle	.25	.11
☐ GD79 Rafael Bournigal	.25	.11
☐ GD80 Mark McGwire	2.00	.90
☐ GD81 Pedro Munoz	.25	.11
☐ GD82 Scott Spiezio	.50	.23
☐ GD83 Don Wengert	.25	.11
☐ GD84 Steve Wojciechowski	.25	.11
☐ GD85 Alex Diaz	.25	.11
☐ GD86 Ken Griffey Jr.	5.00	2.20
☐ GD87 Raul Ibanez	.25	.11
☐ GD88 Mike Jackson	.25	.11
☐ GD89 John Marzano	.25	.11
☐ GD90 Greg McCarthy	.25	.11
☐ GD91 Alex Rodriguez	4.00	1.80
☐ GD92 Andy Sheets	.25	.11
☐ GD93 Mac Suzuki	.50	.23
☐ GD94 Benji Gil	.25	.11
☐ GD95 Juan Gonzalez	2.50	1.10
☐ GD96 Kevin Gross	.25	.11
☐ GD97 Gil Heredia	.25	.11
☐ GD98 Luis Ortiz	.25	.11
☐ GD99 Jeff Russell	.25	.11
☐ GD100 Dave Valle	.25	.11
☐ GD101 Marty Janzen	.25	.11
☐ GD102 Sandy Martinez	.25	.11
☐ GD103 Julio Mosquera	.25	.11

☐ GD104 Otis Nixon .25 .11
☐ GD105 Paul Spoljaric .25 .11
☐ GD106 Shannon Stewart .25 .11
☐ GD107 Woody Williams .25 .11
☐ GD108 Steve Avery .25 .11
☐ GD109 Mike Bielecki .25 .11
☐ GD110 Pedro Borbon .25 .11
☐ GD111 Ed Giovanola .25 .11
☐ GD112 Chipper Jones 3.00 1.35
☐ GD113 Greg Maddux 3.00 1.35
☐ GD114 Mike Mordecai .25 .11
☐ GD115 Terrell Wade .25 .11
☐ GD116 Terry Adams .25 .11
☐ GD117 Brian Dorsett .25 .11
☐ GD118 Doug Glanville .25 .11
☐ GD119 Tyler Houston .25 .11
☐ GD120 Robin Jennings .25 .11
☐ GD121 Ryne Sandberg 1.25 .55
☐ GD122 Terry Shumpert .25 .11
☐ GD123 Amaury Telemaco .25 .11
☐ GD124 Steve Trachsel .25 .11
☐ GD125 Curtis Goodwin .25 .11
☐ GD126 Mike Kelly .25 .11
☐ GD127 Chad Mottola .25 .11
☐ GD128 Mark Portugal .25 .11
☐ GD129 Roger Salkeld .25 .11
☐ GD130 John Smiley .25 .11
☐ GD131 Lee Smith .50 .23
☐ GD132 Roger Bailey .25 .11
☐ GD133 Andres Galarraga 1.00 .45
☐ GD134 Darren Holmes .25 .11
☐ GD135 Curtis Leskanic .25 .11
☐ GD136 Mike Munoz .25 .11
☐ GD137 Jeff Reed .25 .11
☐ GD138 Mark Thompson .25 .11
☐ GD139 Jamey Wright .50 .23
☐ GD140 Andre Dawson .60 .25
☐ GD141 Craig Grebeck .25 .11
☐ GD142 Matt Mantei .25 .11
☐ GD143 Billy McMillon .25 .11
☐ GD144 Kurt Miller .25 .11
☐ GD145 Ralph Milliard .25 .11
☐ GD146 Bob Natal .25 .11
☐ GD147 Joe Siddall .25 .11
☐ GD148 Bob Abreu 1.00 .45
☐ GD149 Doug Brocail .25 .11
☐ GD150 Danny Darwin .25 .11
☐ GD151 Mike Hampton .25 .11
☐ GD152 Todd Jones .25 .11
☐ GD153 Kirt Manwaring .25 .11
☐ GD154 Alvin Morman .25 .11
☐ GD155 Billy Ashley .25 .11
☐ GD156 Tom Candiotti .25 .11
☐ GD157 Darren Dreifort .25 .11
☐ GD158 Greg Gagne .25 .11
☐ GD159 Wilton Guerrero .50 .23
☐ GD160 Hideo Nomo 2.50 1.10
☐ GD161 Mike Piazza 3.00 1.35
☐ GD162 Tom Prince .25 .11
☐ GD163 Todd Worrell .25 .11
☐ GD164 Moises Alou .50 .23
☐ GD165 Shane Andrews .25 .11
☐ GD166 Derek Aucoin .25 .11
☐ GD167 Raul Chavez .25 .11
☐ GD168 Darrin Fletcher .25 .11
☐ GD169 Mark Leiter .25 .11
☐ GD170 Henry Rodriguez .25 .11
☐ GD171 Dave Veres .25 .11
☐ GD172 Paul Byrd .25 .11
☐ GD173 Alberto Castillo .25 .11
☐ GD174 Mark Clark .25 .11
☐ GD175 Rey Ordonez .25 .11
☐ GD176 Roberto Petagine .25 .11
☐ GD177 Andy Tomberlin .25 .11
☐ GD178 Derek Wallace .25 .11
☐ GD179 Paul Wilson .25 .11
☐ GD180 Ruben Amaro Jr. .25 .11
☐ GD181 Toby Borland .25 .11
☐ GD182 Rich Hunter .25 .11
☐ GD183 Tony Longmire .25 .11
☐ GD184 Wendell Magee .25 .11
☐ GD185 Bobby Munoz .25 .11
☐ GD186 Scott Rolen 2.50 1.10
☐ GD187 Mike Williams .25 .11
☐ GD188 Trey Beamon .25 .11
☐ GD189 Jason Christiansen .25 .11
☐ GD190 Elmer Dessens .25 .11
☐ GD191 Angelo Encarnacion .25 .11
☐ GD192 Carlos Garcia .25 .11
☐ GD193 Mike Kingery .25 .11
☐ GD194 Chris Peters .25 .11
☐ GD195 Tony Womack .25 .11
☐ GD196 Brian Barber .25 .11
☐ GD197 David Bell .25 .11
☐ GD198 Tony Fossas .25 .11
☐ GD199 Rick Honeycutt .25 .11
☐ GD200 T.J. Mathews .25 .11

☐ GD201 Miguel Mejia .25 .11
☐ GD202 Donovan Osborne .25 .11
☐ GD203 Ozzie Smith 1.25 .55
☐ GD204 Andres Berumen .25 .11
☐ GD205 Ken Caminiti 1.00 .45
☐ GD206 Chris Gwynn .25 .11
☐ GD207 Tony Gwynn 2.50 1.10
☐ GD208 Rickey Henderson .60 .25
☐ GD209 Scott Sanders .25 .11
☐ GD210 Jason Thompson .25 .11
☐ GD211 Fernando Valenzuela .50 .23
☐ GD212 Tim Worrell .25 .11
☐ GD213 Barry Bonds 1.25 .55
☐ GD214 Jay Canizaro .25 .11
☐ GD215 Doug Creek .25 .11
☐ GD216 Jacob Cruz .25 .11
☐ GD217 Glenallen Hill .25 .11
☐ GD218 Tom Lampkin .25 .11
☐ GD219 Jim Poole .25 .11
☐ GD220 Desi Wilson .25 .11

1997 Pacific Prisms Sizzling Lumber

Randomly inserted in packs at a rate of one in 37, this 36-card set features color photos of three top hitters from each of twelve major league teams. The die-cut cards display red-and-gold foil flames coming from a portion of a baseball bat. The three player cards from the same team form a complete bat on fire when laid top to bottom according to the letters found after the card number. Information is printed in both Spanish and English.

	MINT	NRMT
COMPLETE SET (36)	400.00	180.00
COMMON CARD (SL1A-SL12B)	4.00	1.80

☐ SL1A Cal Ripken 30.00 13.50
☐ SL1B Rafael Palmeiro 5.00 2.20
☐ SL1C Roberto Alomar 8.00 3.60
☐ SL2A Frank Thomas 30.00 13.50
☐ SL2B Robin Ventura 4.50 2.00
☐ SL2C Harold Baines 4.50 2.00
☐ SL3A Albert Belle 10.00 4.50
☐ SL3B Manny Ramirez 10.00 4.50
☐ SL3C Kenny Lofton 10.00 4.50
☐ SL4A Derek Jeter 20.00 9.00
☐ SL4B Bernie Williams 8.00 3.60
☐ SL4C Wade Boggs 8.00 3.60
☐ SL5A Mark McGwire 15.00 6.75
☐ SL5B Jason Giambi 4.50 2.00
☐ SL5C Geronimo Berroa 4.00 1.80
☐ SL6A Ken Griffey Jr. 40.00 18.00
☐ SL6B Alex Rodriguez 25.00 11.00
☐ SL6C Jay Buhner 5.00 2.20
☐ SL7A Juan Gonzalez 20.00 9.00
☐ SL7B Dean Palmer 4.00 1.80
☐ SL7C Ivan Rodriguez 10.00 4.50
☐ SL8A Ryan Klesko 5.00 2.20
☐ SL8B Chipper Jones 25.00 11.00
☐ SL8C Andruw Jones 15.00 6.75
☐ SL9A Dante Bichette 4.50 2.00
☐ SL9B Andres Galarraga 8.00 3.60
☐ SL9C Vinny Castilla 4.50 2.00
☐ SL10A Jeff Bagwell 15.00 6.75
☐ SL10B Craig Biggio 5.00 2.20
☐ SL10C Derek Bell 4.00 1.80
☐ SL11A Mike Piazza 25.00 11.00
☐ SL11B Raul Mondesi 5.00 2.20
☐ SL11C Karim Garcia 4.00 1.80
☐ SL12A Tony Gwynn 20.00 9.00
☐ SL12B Ken Caminiti 8.00 3.60
☐ SL12C Greg Vaughn 4.00 1.80

1997 Pacific Prisms Sluggers and Hurlers

Randomly inserted in packs at a rate of one in 145, cards from this 24-card set feature top hitters and pitchers for a dozen teams printed in a two-card puzzle style matching

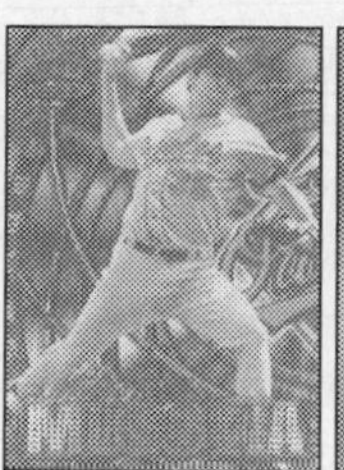

the hitter and pitcher from the same team to form a complete background picture displaying the team's name.

	MINT	NRMT
COMPLETE SET (24)	900.00	400.00
COMMON CARD (SH1A-SH12B)	5.00	2.20

☐ SH1A Cal Ripken 80.00 36.00
☐ SH1B Mike Mussina 20.00 9.00
☐ SH2A Jose Canseco 12.00 5.50
☐ SH2B Roger Clemens 40.00 18.00
☐ SH3A Frank Thomas 80.00 36.00
☐ SH3B Wilson Alvarez 8.00 3.60
☐ SH4A Kenny Lofton 25.00 11.00
☐ SH4B Orel Hershiser 8.00 3.60
☐ SH5A Derek Jeter 50.00 22.00
☐ SH5B Andy Pettitte 25.00 11.00
☐ SH6A Ken Griffey Jr. 100.00 45.00
☐ SH6B Randy Johnson 15.00 6.75
☐ SH7A Alex Rodriguez 60.00 27.00
☐ SH7B Jamie Moyer 5.00 2.20
☐ SH8A Andruw Jones 40.00 18.00
☐ SH8B Greg Maddux 60.00 27.00
☐ SH9A Chipper Jones 60.00 27.00
☐ SH9B John Smoltz 8.00 3.60
☐ SH10A Jeff Bagwell 40.00 18.00
☐ SH10B Shane Reynolds 5.00 2.20
☐ SH11A Mike Piazza 60.00 27.00
☐ SH11B Hideo Nomo 50.00 22.00
☐ SH12A Tony Gwynn 50.00 22.00
☐ SH12B Fernando Valenzuela 8.00 3.60

1984 Padres Mother's

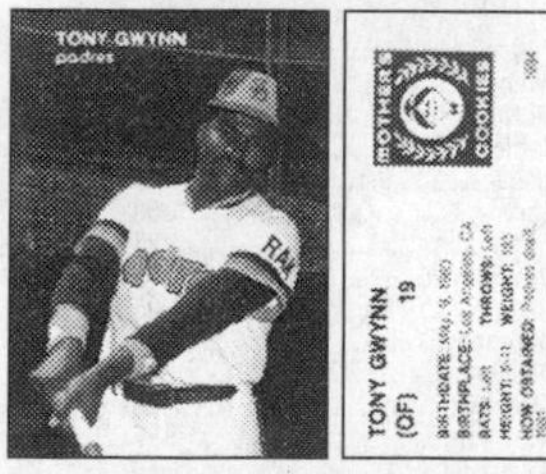

The cards in this 28-card set measure 2 1/2" by 3 1/2". In 1984, the Los Angeles based Mother's Cookies Co. issued five sets of cards featuring players from major league teams. The San Diego Padres set features current players depicted by photos. Similar to their 1952 and 1953 issues, the cards have rounded corners. The backs of the cards contain the Mother's Cookies logo. The cards were distributed in partial sets to fans at the respective stadiums of the teams involved. Whereas 20 cards were given to each patron, a redemption card, redeemable for eight more cards was included. Unfortunately, the eight cards received by redeeming the coupon were not necessarily the eight needed to complete a set. Hobbyist Barry Colla was involved in the production of these sets.

	NRMT	VG-E
COMPLETE SET (28)	20.00	9.00
COMMON CARD (1-28)	.25	.11

☐ 1 Dick Williams MG .50 .23
☐ 2 Rich Gossage 1.00 .45
☐ 3 Tim Lollar .25 .11
☐ 4 Eric Show .25 .11
☐ 5 Terry Kennedy .50 .23
☐ 6 Kurt Bevacqua .50 .23
☐ 7 Steve Garvey 2.00 .90
☐ 8 Garry Templeton .50 .23
☐ 9 Tony Gwynn 12.50 5.50
☐ 10 Alan Wiggins .25 .11
☐ 11 Dave Dravecky 1.50 .70
☐ 12 Tim Flannery .25 .11
☐ 13 Kevin McReynolds 1.00 .45
☐ 14 Bobby Brown .25 .11
☐ 15 Ed Whitson .25 .11
☐ 16 Doug Gwosdz .25 .11

☐ 17 Luis DeLeon	.25	.11
☐ 18 Andy Hawkins	.50	.23
☐ 19 Craig Lefferts	.50	.23
☐ 20 Carmelo Martinez	.25	.11
☐ 21 Sid Monge	.25	.11
☐ 22 Graig Nettles	1.00	.45
☐ 23 Mario Ramirez	.25	.11
☐ 24 Luis Salazar	.25	.11
☐ 25 Champ Summers	.25	.11
☐ 26 Mark Thurmond	.25	.11
☐ 27 Padres' Coaches Harry Dunlop Jack Krol Ozzie Virgil Norm Sherry Deacon Jones	.25	.11
☐ 28 Padres' Checklist	.25	.11

1985 Padres Mother's

The cards in this 28-card set measure 2 1/2" by 3 1/2". In 1985, the Los Angeles based Mother's Cookies Co. again issued five sets of cards featuring players from major league teams. The San Diego Padres set features current players depicted by photos on cards with rounded corners. The backs of the cards contain the Mother's Cookies logo. Cards were passed out at the stadium on August 11.

	NRMT	VG-E
COMPLETE SET (28)	10.00	4.50
COMMON CARD (1-28)	.25	.11

☐ 1 Dick Williams MG	.50	.23
☐ 2 Tony Gwynn	5.00	2.20
☐ 3 Kevin McReynolds	.50	.23
☐ 4 Graig Nettles	1.00	.45
☐ 5 Rich Gossage	1.00	.45
☐ 6 Steve Garvey	1.50	.70
☐ 7 Garry Templeton	.25	.11
☐ 8 Dave Dravecky	.75	.35
☐ 9 Eric Show	.25	.11
☐ 10 Terry Kennedy	.50	.23
☐ 11 Luis DeLeon	.25	.11
☐ 12 Bruce Bochy	.25	.11
☐ 13 Andy Hawkins	.25	.11
☐ 14 Kurt Bevacqua	.50	.23
☐ 15 Craig Lefferts	.25	.11
☐ 16 Mario Ramirez	.25	.11
☐ 17 LaMarr Hoyt	.25	.11
☐ 18 Jerry Royster	.25	.11
☐ 19 Tim Stoddard	.25	.11
☐ 20 Tim Flannery	.25	.11
☐ 21 Mark Thurmond	.25	.11
☐ 22 Greg Booker	.25	.11
☐ 23 Bobby Brown	.25	.11
☐ 24 Carmelo Martinez	.25	.11
☐ 25 Al Bumbry	.25	.11
☐ 26 Jerry Davis	.25	.11
☐ 27 Padres' Coaches Jack Krol Harry Dunlop Deacon Jones	.25	.11
☐ 28 Padres' Checklist Jack Murphy Stadium	.25	.11

1992 Padres Mother's

The 1992 Mother's Cookies Padres set contains 28 cards with rounded corners measuring the standard size. The front design has borderless glossy color player photos. The player's name and team name appear in one of the upper corners. The horizontal backs are printed in red and purple, and present biography and a "how obtained" remark where appropriate. A blank slot for the player's autograph rounds out the back.

	MINT	NRMT
COMPLETE SET (28)	12.00	5.50
COMMON CARD (1-28)	.25	.11
SEMISTARS	.75	.35

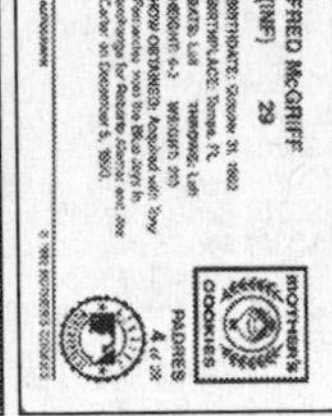

☐ 1 Greg Riddoch MG	.25	.11
☐ 2 Greg W. Harris	.25	.11
☐ 3 Gary Sheffield	1.50	.70
☐ 4 Fred McGriff	2.00	.90
☐ 5 Kurt Stillwell	.25	.11
☐ 6 Benito Santiago	.50	.23
☐ 7 Tony Gwynn	4.00	1.80
☐ 8 Tony Fernandez	.50	.23
☐ 9 Jerald Clark	.25	.11
☐ 10 Dave Eiland	.25	.11
☐ 11 Randy Myers	.75	.35
☐ 12 Oscar Azocar	.25	.11
☐ 13 Dann Bilardello	.25	.11
☐ 14 Jose Melendez	.25	.11
☐ 15 Darrin Jackson	.25	.11
☐ 16 Andy Benes	1.00	.45
☐ 17 Tim Teufel	.25	.11
☐ 18 Jeremy Hernandez	.25	.11
☐ 19 Kevin Ward	.25	.11
☐ 20 Bruce Hurst	.25	.11
☐ 21 Larry Andersen	.25	.11
☐ 22 Rich Rodriguez	.25	.11
☐ 23 Pat Clements	.25	.11
☐ 24 Craig Lefferts	.25	.11
☐ 25 Craig Shipley	.25	.11
☐ 26 Mike Maddux	.25	.11
☐ 27 Coaches Jim Snyder Mike Roarke Rob Picciolo Merv Rettenmund Bruce Kimm	.25	.11
☐ 28 Checklist	.25	.11

1993 Padres Mother's

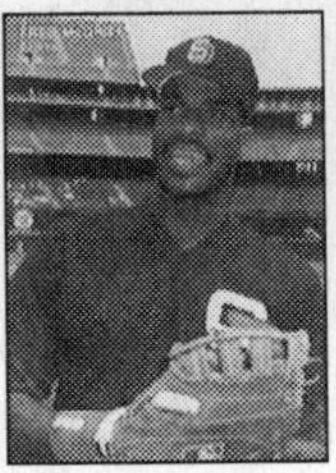
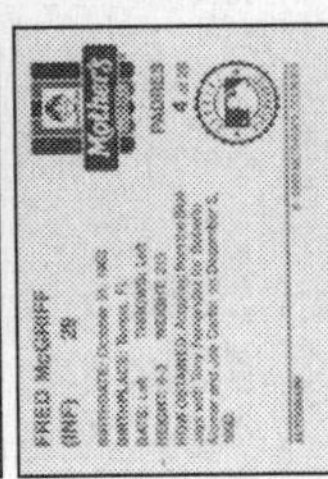

The 1993 Mother's Cookies Padres set consists of 28 standard-size cards with rounded corners. The fronts display full-bleed color player portraits shot from the waist up in stadium settings. The player's name and team name appear in one of the corners. On a white background in red and purple print, the horizontal backs carry biographical information and the sponsor's logo. A blank slot for the player's autograph rounds out the back.

	MINT	NRMT
COMPLETE SET (28)	12.00	5.50
COMMON CARD (1-28)	.25	.11

☐ 1 Jim Riggleman MG	.25	.11
☐ 2 Gary Sheffield	1.50	.70
☐ 3 Tony Gwynn	4.00	1.80
☐ 4 Fred McGriff	1.50	.70
☐ 5 Greg W. Harris	.25	.11
☐ 6 Tim Teufel	.25	.11
☐ 7 Dave Eiland	.25	.11
☐ 8 Phil Plantier	.25	.11
☐ 9 Bruce Hurst	.25	.11
☐ 10 Ricky Gutierrez	.25	.11
☐ 11 Rich Rodriguez	.25	.11
☐ 12 Derek Bell	.50	.23
☐ 13 Bob Geren	.25	.11
☐ 14 Andy Benes	.75	.35
☐ 15 Darrell Sherman	.25	.11
☐ 16 Frank Seminara	.25	.11
☐ 17 Guillermo Velasquez	.25	.11
☐ 18 Gene Harris	.25	.11
☐ 19 Dan Walters	.25	.11
☐ 20 Craig Shipley	.25	.11
☐ 21 Phil Clark	.25	.11
☐ 22 Jeff Gardner	.25	.11
☐ 23 Mike Scioscia	.25	.11
☐ 24 Wally Whitehurst	.25	.11
☐ 25 Roger Mason	.25	.11
☐ 26 Kerry Taylor	.25	.11
☐ 27 Tim Scott	.25	.11
☐ 28 Checklist/Coaches Bruce Bochy Dan Radison Mike Roarke Dave Bialas Rob Picciolo Merv Rettenmund	.25	.11

1994 Padres Mother's

The 1994 Mother's Cookies Padres set consists of 28 standard-size cards with rounded corners. The fronts display full-bleed color player portraits shot from the waist up against a stadium background. The player's name and team name appear in one of the corners. On a white background in red and purple print, the horizontal backs carry biographical information and the sponsor's logo. A blank slot for the player's autograph rounds out the back.

	MINT	NRMT
COMPLETE SET (28)	8.00	3.60
COMMON CARD (1-28)	.25	.11

☐ 1 Jim Riggleman MG	.25	.11
☐ 2 Tony Gwynn	2.50	1.10
☐ 3 Andy Benes	.75	.35
☐ 4 Bip Roberts	.50	.23
☐ 5 Phil Clark	.25	.11
☐ 6 Wally Whitehurst	.25	.11
☐ 7 Archi Cianfrocco	.25	.11
☐ 8 Derek Bell	.50	.23
☐ 9 Ricky Gutierrez	.25	.11
☐ 10 Mark Davis	.25	.11
☐ 11 Phil Plantier	.25	.11
☐ 12 Brian Johnson	.25	.11
☐ 13 Billy Bean	.25	.11
☐ 14 Craig Shipley	.25	.11
☐ 15 Tim Hyers	.25	.11
☐ 16 Gene Harris	.25	.11
☐ 17 Scott Sanders	.50	.23
☐ 18 A.J. Sager	.25	.11
☐ 19 Keith Lockhart	.25	.11
☐ 20 Tim Mauser	.25	.11
☐ 21 Andy Ashby	.50	.23
☐ 22 Brad Ausmus	.25	.11
☐ 23 Trevor Hoffman	1.00	.45
☐ 24 Luis Lopez	.25	.11
☐ 25 Doug Brocail	.25	.11
☐ 26 Dave Staton	.25	.11
☐ 27 Pedro Martinez	.25	.11
☐ 28 Checklist/Coaches Sonny Siebert Rob Picciolo Dave Bialas Dan Radison Merv Rettenmund Bruce Bochy	.25	.11

1995 Padres Mother's

The 1995 Mother's Cookies San Diego Padres set consists of 28 standard-size cards with rounded corners. The fronts display posed color player portraits in stadium settings. The player's name and team name appear in one of the top corners. The backs carry biographical information and the sponsor's logo on a white background in red and purple print. A blank slot for the player's autograph rounds out the back.

	MINT	NRMT
COMPLETE SET (28)	10.00	4.5
COMMON CARD (1-28)	.25	.1

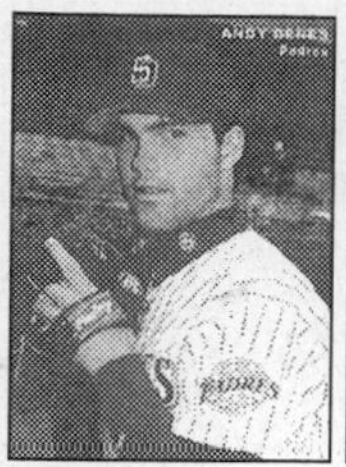

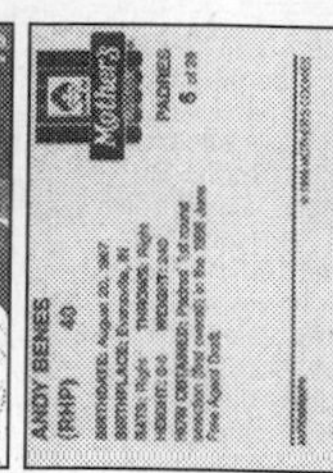

	MINT	NRMT
☐ 1 Bruce Bochy MG	.25	.11
☐ 2 Tony Gwynn	2.50	1.10
☐ 3 Ken Caminiti	1.50	.70
☐ 4 Bip Roberts	.50	.23
☐ 5 Andujar Cedeno	.25	.11
☐ 6 Andy Benes	.75	.35
☐ 7 Phil Clark	.25	.11
☐ 8 Fernando Valenzuela	.75	.35
☐ 9 Roberto Petagine	.25	.11
☐ 10 Brian Johnson	.25	.11
☐ 11 Scott Livingstone	.25	.11
☐ 12 Brian Williams	.25	.11
☐ 13 Jody Reed	.25	.11
☐ 14 Steve Finley	1.00	.45
☐ 15 Jeff Tabaka	.25	.11
☐ 16 Ray Holbert	.25	.11
☐ 17 Tim Worrell	.25	.11
☐ 18 Eddie Williams	.25	.11
☐ 19 Brad Ausmus	.25	.11
☐ 20 Willie Blair	.25	.11
☐ 21 Trevor Hoffman	.50	.23
☐ 22 Scott Sanders	.50	.23
☐ 23 Andy Ashby	.50	.23
☐ 24 Joey Hamilton	.75	.35
☐ 25 Andres Berumen	.25	.11
☐ 26 Melvin Nieves	.50	.23
☐ 27 Bryce Florie	.25	.11
☐ 28 Coaches/Checklist Merv Rettenmund Graig Nettles Davey Lopes Sonny Siebert Rob Picciolo Ty Waller	.50	.23

1996 Padres Mother's

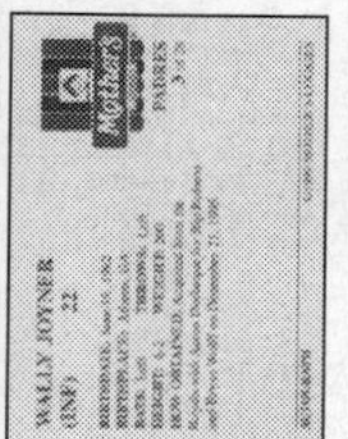

This 28-card set consists of borderless posed color player portraits in stadium settings. The player's and team's names appear in one of the top rounded corners. The backs carry biographical information and the sponsor's logo on a white background in red and purple print. A blank slot for the player's autograph rounds out the back.

	MINT	NRMT
COMPLETE SET (28)	10.00	4.50
COMMON CARD (1-28)	.25	.11

	MINT	NRMT
☐ 1 Bruce Bochy MG	.25	.11
☐ 2 Tony Gwynn	2.50	1.10
☐ 3 Wally Joyner	.50	.23
☐ 4 Rickey Henderson	1.50	.70
☐ 5 Ken Caminiti	1.50	.70
☐ 6 Scott Sanders	.50	.23
☐ 7 Steve Finley	1.00	.45
☐ 8 Fernando Valenzuela	.75	.35
☐ 9 Brian Johnson	.25	.11
☐ 10 Jody Reed	.25	.11
☐ 11 Bob Tewksbury	.25	.11
☐ 12 Andujar Cedeno	.25	.11
☐ 13 Sean Bergman	.25	.11
☐ 14 Marc Newfield	.50	.23
☐ 15 Craig Shipley	.25	.11
☐ 16 Scott Livingstone	.25	.11
☐ 17 Trevor Hoffman	.50	.23
☐ 18 Doug Bochtler	.25	.11
☐ 19 Archi Cianfrocco	.25	.11
☐ 20 Joey Hamilton	.50	.23
☐ 21 Andy Ashby	.50	.23
☐ 22 Chris Gwynn	.25	.11
☐ 23 Luis Lopez	.25	.11
☐ 24 Tim Worrell	.25	.11
☐ 25 Brad Ausmus	.25	.11
☐ 26 Willie Blair	.50	.23
☐ 27 Bryce Florie	.25	.11
☐ 28 Coaches Card CL Dan Warthen Rob Picciolo Davey Lopes Grady Little Tim Flannery Merv Rettenmund	.25	.11

1997 Padres Mother's

This 28-card set of the San Diego Padres sponsored by Mother's Cookies consists of posed color player photos with rounded corners. The backs carry biographical information and the sponsor's logo on a white background in red and purple print. A blank slot for the player's autograph rounds out the back.

	MINT	NRMT
COMPLETE SET (28)	12.00	5.50
COMMON CARD (1-28)	.25	.11

	MINT	NRMT
☐ 1 Bruce Bochy MG	.25	.11
☐ 2 Tony Gwynn	2.50	1.10
☐ 3 Ken Caminiti	1.25	.55
☐ 4 Wally Joyner	1.00	.45
☐ 5 Rickey Henderson	1.25	.55
☐ 6 Greg Vaughn	.50	.23
☐ 7 Steve Finley	1.00	.45
☐ 8 Fernando Valenzuela	.75	.35
☐ 9 John Flaherty	.25	.11
☐ 10 Sterling Hitchcock	.50	.23
☐ 11 Quilvio Veras	.50	.23
☐ 12 Don Slaught	.25	.11
☐ 13 Sean Bergman	.25	.11
☐ 14 Chris Gomez	.25	.11
☐ 15 Craig Shipley	.25	.11
☐ 16 Joey Hamilton	.50	.23
☐ 17 Scott Livingstone	.25	.11
☐ 18 Trevor Hoffman	.50	.23
☐ 19 Doug Bochtler	.25	.11
☐ 20 Chris Jones	.25	.11
☐ 21 Andy Ashby	.25	.11
☐ 22 Archi Cianfrocco	.25	.11
☐ 23 Tim Worrell	.25	.11
☐ 24 Will Cunnane	.25	.11
☐ 25 Carlos Hernandez	.25	.11
☐ 26 Tim Scott	.25	.11
☐ 27 Dario Veras	.25	.11
☐ 28 Coaches Card CL Greg Booker Tim Flannery Davey Lopes Rob Picciolo Merv Rettenmund Dan Warthen	.25	.11

1988 Panini Stickers

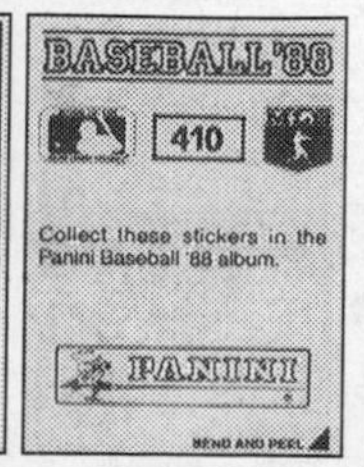

These 480 stickers measure approximately 1 15/16" by 2 11/16" (regular) and 2 1/8" by 2 11/16" (foils). The fronts of the regular stickers have white borders and feature color player head shots on a colored background. The player's name, along with his team name and logo, appear at the bottom. In addition to carrying the stickers' numbers, the white backs carry the logos for MLB, the MLBPA and Panini. There are 80 foil stickers in the set; these foils are essentially the non-player stickers. A 64-page album onto which the stickers could be affixed was available at retail stores (for 59 cents) and was also given away to Little Leaguers as part of a national promotion. The album features Don Mattingly on the front and a photo of a gold glove on the back. The album and the sticker numbering are organized alphabetically by team with AL teams preceding NL teams. The last 26 stickers in the album are actually lettered rather than numbered but are listed below as numbers 455-480. The stickers were also sold at retail outlets packed with the album as a "Complete Collectors Set." The 1988 Panini Sticker set was heavily promoted as Panini entered the baseball sticker market under its own label after producing Topps' stickers for the previous seven years.

	MINT	NRMT
COMPLETE SET (480)	40.00	18.00
COMMON STICKER (1-480)	.05	.02

	MINT	NRMT
☐ 1 1987 WS Trophy	.05	.02
☐ 2 Orioles Emblem	.05	.02
☐ 3 Orioles Uniform	.05	.02
☐ 4 Eric Bell	.05	.02
☐ 5 Mike Boddicker	.05	.02
☐ 6 Dave Schmidt	.05	.02
☐ 7 Terry Kennedy	.05	.02
☐ 8 Eddie Murray	1.00	.45
☐ 9 Bill Ripken	.05	.02
☐ 10 Orioles TL (Action photo)	.05	.02
☐ 11 Orioles W-L Breakdown Cal Ripken IA	1.50	.70
☐ 12 Ray Knight	.05	.02
☐ 13 Cal Ripken	4.00	1.80
☐ 14 Ken Gerhart	.05	.02
☐ 15 Fred Lynn	.05	.02
☐ 16 Larry Sheets	.05	.02
☐ 17 Mike Young	.05	.02
☐ 18 Red Sox Emblem	.05	.02
☐ 19 Red Sox Uniform	.05	.02
☐ 20 Oil Can Boyd	.05	.02
☐ 21 Roger Clemens	1.50	.70
☐ 22 Bruce Hurst	.05	.02
☐ 23 Bob Stanley	.05	.02
☐ 24 Rich Gedman	.05	.02
☐ 25 Dwight Evans	.15	.07
☐ 26 Red Sox TL (Action photo)	.05	.02
☐ 27 Red Sox W-L Breakdown (Action photo)	.05	.02
☐ 28 Marty Barrett	.05	.02
☐ 29 Wade Boggs	.50	.23
☐ 30 Spike Owen	.05	.02
☐ 31 Ellis Burks	.60	.25
☐ 32 Mike Greenwell	.15	.07
☐ 33 Jim Rice	.15	.07
☐ 34 Angels Emblem	.05	.02
☐ 35 Angels Uniform	.05	.02
☐ 36 Kirk McCaskill	.05	.02
☐ 37 Don Sutton	.40	.18
☐ 38 Mike Witt	.05	.02
☐ 39 Bob Boone	.15	.07
☐ 40 Wally Joyner	.25	.11
☐ 41 Mark McLemore	.15	.07
☐ 42 Angels TL (Action photo)	.05	.02
☐ 43 Angels W-L Breakdown Devon White IA	.15	.07
☐ 44 Jack Howell	.05	.02
☐ 45 Dick Schofield	.05	.02
☐ 46 Brian Downing	.05	.02
☐ 47 Ruppert Jones	.05	.02
☐ 48 Gary Pettis	.05	.02
☐ 49 Devon White	.25	.11
☐ 50 White Sox Emblem	.05	.02
☐ 51 White Sox Uniform	.05	.02
☐ 52 Floyd Bannister	.05	.02
☐ 53 Richard Dotson	.05	.02
☐ 54 Bob James	.05	.02
☐ 55 Carlton Fisk	.40	.18
☐ 56 Greg Walker	.05	.02
☐ 57 Fred Manrique	.05	.02
☐ 58 White Sox TL (Action photo)	.05	.02
☐ 59 White Sox W-L Breakdown (Action photo)	.05	.02
☐ 60 Steve Lyons	.05	.02
☐ 61 Ozzie Guillen	.15	.07
☐ 62 Harold Baines	.15	.07
☐ 63 Ivan Calderon	.05	.02
☐ 64 Gary Redus	.05	.02

☐ 65 Ken Williams	.05	.02
☐ 66 Indians Emblem	.05	.02
☐ 67 Indians Uniform	.05	.02
☐ 68 Scott Bailes	.05	.02
☐ 69 Tom Candiotti	.05	.02
☐ 70 Greg Swindell	.05	.02
☐ 71 Chris Bando	.05	.02
☐ 72 Joe Carter	.25	.11
☐ 73 Tommy Hinzo	.05	.02
☐ 74 Indians TL	.05	.02
(Action photo)		
☐ 75 Indians W-L Breakdown	.05	.02
Juan Bonilla IA		
☐ 76 Brook Jacoby	.05	.02
☐ 77 Julio Franco	.15	.07
☐ 78 Brett Butler	.15	.07
☐ 79 Mel Hall	.05	.02
☐ 80 Cory Snyder	.05	.02
☐ 81 Pat Tabler	.05	.02
☐ 82 Tigers Emblem	.05	.02
☐ 83 Tigers Uniform	.05	.02
☐ 84 Willie Hernandez	.05	.02
☐ 85 Jack Morris	.15	.07
☐ 86 Frank Tanana	.05	.02
☐ 87 Walt Terrell	.05	.02
☐ 88 Matt Nokes	.05	.02
☐ 89 Darrell Evans	.15	.07
☐ 90 Tigers TL	.15	.07
Darrell Evans IA		
☐ 91 Tigers W-L Breakdown	.25	.11
Carlton Fisk IA		
☐ 92 Lou Whitaker	.15	.07
☐ 93 Tom Brookens	.05	.02
☐ 94 Alan Trammell	.25	.11
☐ 95 Kirk Gibson	.15	.07
☐ 96 Chet Lemon	.05	.02
☐ 97 Pat Sheridan	.05	.02
☐ 98 Royals Emblem	.05	.02
☐ 99 Royals Uniform	.05	.02
☐ 100 Charlie Leibrandt	.05	.02
☐ 101 Dan Quisenberry	.05	.02
☐ 102 Bret Saberhagen	.15	.07
☐ 103 Jamie Quirk	.05	.02
☐ 104 George Brett	1.25	.55
☐ 105 Frank White	.15	.07
☐ 106 Royals TL	.15	.07
Bret Saberhagen IA		
☐ 107 Royals W-L Breakdown	.15	.07
Bret Saberhagen IA		
☐ 108 Kevin Seitzer	.15	.07
☐ 109 Angel Salazar	.05	.02
☐ 110 Bo Jackson	.25	.11
☐ 111 Lonnie Smith	.05	.02
☐ 112 Danny Tartabull	.05	.02
☐ 113 Willie Wilson	.05	.02
☐ 114 Brewers Emblem	.05	.02
☐ 115 Brewers Uniform	.05	.02
☐ 116 Ted Higuera	.05	.02
☐ 117 Juan Nieves	.05	.02
☐ 118 Dan Plesac	.05	.02
☐ 119 Bill Wegman	.05	.02
☐ 120 B.J. Surhoff	.15	.07
☐ 121 Greg Brock	.05	.02
☐ 122 Brewers TL	.15	.07
Lou Whitaker IA		
☐ 123 Brewers W-L Breakdown	.05	.02
Jim Gantner IA		
☐ 124 Jim Gantner	.05	.02
☐ 125 Paul Molitor	.60	.25
☐ 126 Dale Sveum	.05	.02
☐ 127 Glenn Braggs	.05	.02
☐ 128 Rob Deer	.05	.02
☐ 129 Robin Yount	.40	.18
☐ 130 Twins Emblem	.05	.02
☐ 131 Twins Uniform	.05	.02
☐ 132 Bert Blyleven	.15	.07
☐ 133 Jeff Reardon	.15	.07
☐ 134 Frank Viola	.05	.02
☐ 135 Tim Laudner	.05	.02
☐ 136 Kent Hrbek	.15	.07
☐ 137 Steve Lombardozzi	.05	.02
☐ 138 Twins TL	.05	.02
(Action photo)		
☐ 139 Twins W-L Breakdown	.05	.02
(Action photo)		
☐ 140 Gary Gaetti	.15	.07
☐ 141 Greg Gagne	.05	.02
☐ 142 Tom Brunansky	.05	.02
☐ 143 Dan Gladden	.05	.02
☐ 144 Kirby Puckett	2.00	.90
☐ 145 Gene Larkin	.05	.02
☐ 146 Team Emblem	.05	.02
New York Yankees		
☐ 147 Team Uniform	.05	.02
New York Yankees		
☐ 148 Tommy John	.15	.07
☐ 149 Rick Rhoden	.05	.02
☐ 150 Dave Righetti	.05	.02
☐ 151 Rick Cerone	.05	.02
☐ 152 Don Mattingly	2.00	.90
☐ 153 Willie Randolph	.15	.07
☐ 154 1987 Team Leaders	.05	.02
Scott Fletcher IA		
☐ 155 1987 W-L Breakdown	.75	.35
Don Mattingly IA		
☐ 156 Mike Pagliarulo	.05	.02
☐ 157 Wayne Tolleson	.05	.02
☐ 158 Rickey Henderson	.40	.18
☐ 159 Dan Pasqua	.05	.02
☐ 160 Gary Ward	.05	.02
☐ 161 Dave Winfield	.50	.23
☐ 162 Team Emblem	.05	.02
Oakland A's		
☐ 163 Team Uniform	.05	.02
Oakland A's		
☐ 164 Dave Stewart	.15	.07
☐ 165 Curt Young	.05	.02
☐ 166 Terry Steinbach	.25	.11
☐ 167 Mark McGwire	3.00	1.35
☐ 168 Tony Phillips	.05	.02
☐ 169 Carney Lansford	.15	.07
☐ 170 1987 Team Leaders	.05	.02
(Action photo)		
☐ 171 1987 W-L Breakdown	.05	.02
(Action photo)		
☐ 172 Alfredo Griffin	.05	.02
☐ 173 Jose Canseco	1.00	.45
☐ 174 Mike Davis	.05	.02
☐ 175 Reggie Jackson	.50	.23
☐ 176 Dwayne Murphy	.05	.02
☐ 177 Luis Polonia	.15	.07
☐ 178 Team Emblem	.05	.02
Seattle Mariners		
☐ 179 Team Uniform	.05	.02
Seattle Mariners		
☐ 180 Scott Bankhead	.05	.02
☐ 181 Mark Langston	.15	.07
☐ 182 Edwin Nunez	.05	.02
☐ 183 Scott Bradley	.05	.02
☐ 184 Dave Valle	.05	.02
☐ 185 Alvin Davis	.05	.02
☐ 186 1987 Team Leaders	.05	.02
Rey Quinones IA		
☐ 187 1987 W-L Breakdown	.05	.02
Jack Howell IA		
☐ 188 Harold Reynolds	.15	.07
☐ 189 Jim Presley	.05	.02
☐ 190 Rey Quinones	.05	.02
☐ 191 Phil Bradley	.05	.02
☐ 192 Mickey Brantley	.05	.02
☐ 193 Mike Kingery	.05	.02
☐ 194 Team Emblem	.05	.02
Texas Rangers		
☐ 195 Team Uniform	.05	.02
Texas Rangers		
☐ 196 Edwin Correa	.05	.02
☐ 197 Charlie Hough	.15	.07
☐ 198 Bobby Witt	.05	.02
☐ 199 Mike Stanley	.05	.02
☐ 200 Pete O'Brien	.05	.02
☐ 201 Jerry Browne	.05	.02
☐ 202 1987 Team Leaders	.05	.02
(Action photo)		
☐ 203 1987 W-L Breakdown	.35	.16
Steve Buechele and		
Eddie Murray IA		
☐ 204 Steve Buechele	.05	.02
☐ 205 Larry Parrish	.05	.02
☐ 206 Scott Fletcher	.05	.02
☐ 207 Pete Incaviglia	.05	.02
☐ 208 Oddibe McDowell	.05	.02
☐ 209 Ruben Sierra	.15	.07
☐ 210 Team Emblem	.05	.02
Toronto Blue Jays		
☐ 211 Team Uniform	.05	.02
Toronto Blue Jays		
☐ 212 Mark Eichhorn	.05	.02
☐ 213 Tom Henke	.05	.02
☐ 214 Jimmy Key	.15	.07
☐ 215 Dave Stieb	.05	.02
☐ 216 Ernie Whitt	.05	.02
☐ 217 Willie Upshaw	.05	.02
☐ 218 1987 Team Leaders	.05	.02
Willie Upshaw IA		
☐ 219 1987 W-L Breakdown	.05	.02
Harold Reynolds IA		
☐ 220 Garth Iorg	.05	.02
☐ 221 Kelly Gruber	.05	.02
☐ 222 Tony Fernandez	.05	.02
☐ 223 Jesse Barfield	.05	.02
☐ 224 George Bell	.05	.02
☐ 225 Lloyd Moseby	.05	.02
☐ 226A AL Logo	.05	.02
☐ 226B NL Logo	.05	.02
☐ 227 Terry Kennedy and	.75	.35
Don Mattingly		
☐ 228 Willie Randolph and	.35	.16
Wade Boggs		
☐ 229 Bret Saberhagen	.15	.07
☐ 230 Cal Ripken and	2.00	.90
George Bell		
☐ 231 Rickey Henderson and	.40	.18
Dave Winfield		
☐ 232 Gary Carter and	.15	.07
Jack Clark		
☐ 233 Mike Scott	.05	.02
☐ 234 Ryne Sandberg and	.75	.35
Mike Schmidt		
☐ 235 Ozzie Smith and	.50	.23
Eric Davis		
☐ 236 Andre Dawson and	.15	.07
Darryl Strawberry		
☐ 237 Team Emblem	.05	.02
Atlanta Braves		
☐ 238 Team Uniform	.05	.02
Atlanta Braves		
☐ 239 Rick Mahler	.05	.02
☐ 240 Zane Smith	.05	.02
☐ 241 Ozzie Virgil	.05	.02
☐ 242 Gerald Perry	.05	.02
☐ 243 Glenn Hubbard	.05	.02
☐ 244 Ken Oberkfell	.05	.02
☐ 245 1987 Team Leaders	.05	.02
(Action photo)		
☐ 246 1987 W-L Breakdown	.05	.02
Jeffrey Leonard IA		
☐ 247 Rafael Ramirez	.05	.02
☐ 248 Ken Griffey	.15	.07
☐ 249 Albert Hall	.05	.02
☐ 250 Dion James	.05	.02
☐ 251 Dale Murphy	.35	.16
☐ 252 Gary Roenicke	.05	.02
☐ 253 Team Emblem	.05	.02
Chicago Cubs		
☐ 254 Team Uniform	.05	.02
Chicago Cubs		
☐ 255 Jamie Moyer	.15	.07
☐ 256 Lee Smith	.15	.07
☐ 257 Rick Sutcliffe	.05	.02
☐ 258 Jody Davis	.05	.02
☐ 259 Leon Durham	.05	.02
☐ 260 Ryne Sandberg	1.00	.45
☐ 261 1987 Team Leaders	.05	.02
(Action photo)		
☐ 262 1987 W-L Breakdown	.05	.02
Jody Davis IA		
☐ 263 Keith Moreland	.05	.02
☐ 264 Shawon Dunston	.05	.02
☐ 265 Andre Dawson	.35	.16
☐ 266 Dave Martinez	.05	.02
☐ 267 Jerry Mumphrey	.05	.02
☐ 268 Rafael Palmeiro	.75	.35
☐ 269 Team Emblem	.05	.02
Cincinnati Reds		
☐ 270 Team Uniform	.05	.02
Cincinnati Reds		
☐ 271 John Franco	.15	.07
☐ 272 Ted Power	.05	.02
☐ 273 Bo Diaz	.05	.02
☐ 274 Nick Esasky	.05	.02
☐ 275 Dave Concepcion	.15	.07
☐ 276 Kurt Stillwell	.05	.02
☐ 277 1987 Team Leaders	.15	.07
Dave Parker IA		
☐ 278 1987 W-L Breakdown	.05	.02
(Action photo)		
☐ 279 Buddy Bell	.15	.07
☐ 280 Barry Larkin	1.00	.45
☐ 281 Kal Daniels	.05	.02
☐ 282 Eric Davis	.15	.07
☐ 283 Tracy Jones	.05	.02
☐ 284 Dave Parker	.15	.07
☐ 285 Team Emblem	.05	.02
Houston Astros		
☐ 286 Team Uniform	.05	.02
Houston Astros		
☐ 287 Jim Deshaies	.05	.02
☐ 288 Nolan Ryan	4.00	1.80
☐ 289 Mike Scott	.05	.02
☐ 290 Dave Smith	.05	.02
☐ 291 Alan Ashby	.05	.02
☐ 292 Glenn Davis	.05	.02
☐ 293 1987 Team Leaders	.05	.02
(Action photo)		
☐ 294 1987 W-L Breakdown	.05	.02
(Action photo)		
☐ 295 Bill Doran	.05	.02
☐ 296 Denny Walling	.05	.02
☐ 297 Craig Reynolds	.05	.02
☐ 298 Kevin Bass	.05	.02
☐ 299 Jose Cruz	.15	.07

☐ 300 Billy Hatcher	.05	.02
☐ 301 Team Emblem Los Angeles Dodgers	.05	.02
☐ 302 Team Uniform Los Angeles Dodgers	.05	.02
☐ 303 Orel Hershiser	.15	.07
☐ 304 Fernando Valenzuela	.15	.07
☐ 305 Bob Welch	.15	.07
☐ 306 Matt Young	.05	.02
☐ 307 Mike Scioscia	.05	.02
☐ 308 Franklin Stubbs	.05	.02
☐ 309 1987 Team Leaders (Action photo)	.05	.02
☐ 310 1987 W-L Breakdown (Action photo)	.05	.02
☐ 311 Steve Sax	.05	.02
☐ 312 Jeff Hamilton	.05	.02
☐ 313 Dave Anderson	.05	.02
☐ 314 Pedro Guerrero	.05	.02
☐ 315 Mike Marshall	.05	.02
☐ 316 John Shelby	.05	.02
☐ 317 Team Emblem Montreal Expos	.05	.02
☐ 318 Team Uniform Montreal Expos	.05	.02
☐ 319 Neal Heaton	.05	.02
☐ 320 Bryn Smith	.05	.02
☐ 321 Floyd Youmans	.05	.02
☐ 322 Mike Fitzgerald	.05	.02
☐ 323 Andres Galarraga	.50	.23
☐ 324 Vance Law	.05	.02
☐ 325 1987 Team Leaders Tim Raines IA	.15	.07
☐ 326 1987 W-L Breakdown John Kruk IA	.15	.07
☐ 327 Tim Wallach	.05	.02
☐ 328 Hubie Brooks	.05	.02
☐ 329 Casey Candaele	.05	.02
☐ 330 Tim Raines	.15	.07
☐ 331 Mitch Webster	.05	.02
☐ 332 Herm Winningham	.05	.02
☐ 333 Team Emblem New York Mets	.05	.02
☐ 334 Team Uniform New York Mets	.05	.02
☐ 335 Ron Darling	.05	.02
☐ 336 Sid Fernandez	.05	.02
☐ 337 Dwight Gooden	.15	.07
☐ 338 Gary Carter	.25	.11
☐ 339 Keith Hernandez	.15	.07
☐ 340 Wally Backman	.05	.02
☐ 341 1987 Team Leaders Junior Ortiz IA	.05	.02
☐ 342 1987 W-L Breakdown Mookie Wilson, Darryl Strawberry, and Tim Teufel IA	.15	.07
☐ 343 Howard Johnson	.05	.02
☐ 344 Rafael Santana	.05	.02
☐ 345 Lenny Dykstra	.15	.07
☐ 346 Kevin McReynolds	.05	.02
☐ 347 Darryl Strawberry	.15	.07
☐ 348 Mookie Wilson	.15	.07
☐ 349 Team Emblem Philadelphia Phillies	.05	.02
☐ 350 Team Uniform Philadelphia Phillies	.05	.02
☐ 351 Steve Bedrosian	.05	.02
☐ 352 Shane Rawley	.05	.02
☐ 353 Bruce Ruffin	.05	.02
☐ 354 Kent Tekulve	.05	.02
☐ 355 Lance Parrish	.05	.02
☐ 356 Von Hayes	.05	.02
☐ 357 1987 Team Leaders (Action photo)	.05	.02
☐ 358 1987 W-L Breakdown Glenn Wilson IA	.05	.02
☐ 359 Juan Samuel	.05	.02
☐ 360 Mike Schmidt	1.00	.45
☐ 361 Steve Jeltz	.05	.02
☐ 362 Chris James	.05	.02
☐ 363 Milt Thompson	.05	.02
☐ 364 Glenn Wilson	.05	.02
☐ 365 Team Emblem Pittsburgh Pirates	.05	.02
☐ 366 Team Uniform Pittsburgh Pirates	.05	.02
☐ 367 Mike Dunne	.05	.02
☐ 368 Brian Fisher	.05	.02
☐ 369 Mike LaValliere	.05	.02
☐ 370 Sid Bream	.05	.02
☐ 371 Jose Lind	.05	.02
☐ 372 Bobby Bonilla	.25	.11
☐ 373 1987 Team Leaders Bobby Bonilla IA	.25	.11
☐ 374 1987 W-L Breakdown (Action photo)	.05	.02
☐ 375 Al Pedrique	.05	.02
☐ 376 Barry Bonds	1.50	.70
☐ 377 John Cangelosi	.05	.02
☐ 378 Mike Diaz	.05	.02
☐ 379 R.J. Reynolds	.05	.02
☐ 380 Andy Van Slyke	.15	.07
☐ 381 Team Emblem St. Louis Cardinals	.05	.02
☐ 382 Team Uniform St. Louis Cardinals	.05	.02
☐ 383 Danny Cox	.05	.02
☐ 384 Bob Forsch	.05	.02
☐ 385 Joe Magrane	.05	.02
☐ 386 Todd Worrell	.15	.07
☐ 387 Tony Pena	.05	.02
☐ 388 Jack Clark	.05	.02
☐ 389 1987 Team Leaders Tommy Herr IA	.05	.02
☐ 390 1987 W-L Breakdown (Action photo)	.05	.02
☐ 391 Tom Herr	.05	.02
☐ 392 Terry Pendleton	.15	.07
☐ 393 Ozzie Smith	1.00	.45
☐ 394 Vince Coleman	.05	.02
☐ 395 Curt Ford	.05	.02
☐ 396 Willie McGee	.15	.07
☐ 397 Team Emblem San Diego Padres	.05	.02
☐ 398 Team Uniform San Diego Padres	.05	.02
☐ 399 Lance McCullers	.05	.02
☐ 400 Eric Show	.05	.02
☐ 401 Ed Whitson	.05	.02
☐ 402 Benito Santiago	.05	.02
☐ 403 John Kruk	.25	.11
☐ 404 Tim Flannery	.05	.02
☐ 405 1987 Team Leaders Benito Santiago IA	.05	.02
☐ 406 1987 W-L Breakdown (Action photo)	.05	.02
☐ 407 Randy Ready	.05	.02
☐ 408 Chris Brown	.05	.02
☐ 409 Garry Templeton	.05	.02
☐ 410 Tony Gwynn	1.50	.70
☐ 411 Stan Jefferson	.05	.02
☐ 412 Carmelo Martinez	.05	.02
☐ 413 Team Emblem San Francisco Giants	.05	.02
☐ 414 Team Uniform San Francisco Giants	.05	.02
☐ 415 Kelly Downs	.05	.02
☐ 416 Scott Garrelts	.05	.02
☐ 417 Mike Krukow	.05	.02
☐ 418 Mike LaCoss	.05	.02
☐ 419 Bob Brenly	.05	.02
☐ 420 Will Clark	1.00	.45
☐ 421 1987 Team Leaders Will Clark IA	.25	.11
☐ 422 1987 W-L Breakdown (Action photo)	.05	.02
☐ 423 Robby Thompson	.05	.02
☐ 424 Kevin Mitchell	.15	.07
☐ 425 Jose Uribe	.05	.02
☐ 426 Mike Aldrete	.05	.02
☐ 427 Jeffrey Leonard	.05	.02
☐ 428 Candy Maldonado	.05	.02
☐ 429 Mike Schmidt	1.00	.45
☐ 430 Don Mattingly	2.00	.90
☐ 431 Juan Nieves	.05	.02
☐ 432 Paul Molitor	.75	.35
☐ 433 Benito Santiago	.05	.02
☐ 434 Rickey Henderson	.40	.18
☐ 435 Nolan Ryan	4.00	1.80
☐ 436 Kevin Seitzer	.15	.07
☐ 437 Tony Gwynn	1.50	.70
☐ 438 Mark McGwire	3.00	1.35
☐ 439 Howard Johnson (switch-hitting)	.05	.02
☐ 440 Steve Bedrosian	.05	.02
☐ 441 Darrell Evans	.15	.07
☐ 442 Eddie Murray (switch-hitting)	1.00	.45
☐ 443 Lou Whitaker IA	.15	.07
☐ 444 Kirby Puckett and Alan Trammell IA	1.00	.45
☐ 445 Gary Gaetti	.15	.07
☐ 446 Jeffrey Leonard	.05	.02
☐ 447 Tony Pena IA	.05	.02
☐ 448 Kevin Mitchell IA	.15	.07
☐ 449 Tony Pena IA	.05	.02
☐ 450 Randy Bush IA	.05	.02
☐ 451 Minnesota Twins UL (celebrating)	.05	.02
☐ 452 Minnesota Twins UR (celebrating)	.05	.02
☐ 453 Minnesota Twins LL (celebrating)	.05	.02
☐ 454 Minnesota Twins LR (celebrating)	.05	.02
☐ 455 Baltimore Orioles A Pennant and Logo	.05	.02
☐ 456 Boston Red Sox B Pennant and Logo	.05	.02
☐ 457 California Angels C Pennant and Logo	.05	.02
☐ 458 Chicago White Sox D Pennant and Logo	.05	.02
☐ 459 Cleveland Indians E Pennant and Logo	.05	.02
☐ 460 Detroit Tigers F Pennant and Logo	.05	.02
☐ 461 Kansas City Royals G Pennant and Logo	.05	.02
☐ 462 Milwaukee Brewers H Pennant and Logo	.05	.02
☐ 463 Minnesota Twins I Pennant and Logo	.05	.02
☐ 464 New York Yankees J Pennant and Logo	.05	.02
☐ 465 Oakland A's K Pennant and Logo	.05	.02
☐ 466 Seattle Mariners L Pennant and Logo	.05	.02
☐ 467 Texas Rangers M Pennant and Logo	.05	.02
☐ 468 Toronto Blue Jays N Pennant and Logo	.05	.02
☐ 469 Atlanta Braves O Pennant and Logo	.05	.02
☐ 470 Chicago Cubs P Pennant and Logo	.05	.02
☐ 471 Cincinnati Reds Q Pennant and Logo	.05	.02
☐ 472 Houston Astros R Pennant and Logo	.05	.02
☐ 473 Los Angeles Dodgers S Pennant and Logo	.05	.02
☐ 474 Montreal Expos T Pennant and Logo	.05	.02
☐ 475 New York Mets U Pennant and Logo	.05	.02
☐ 476 Phila. Phillies W Pennant and Logo	.05	.02
☐ 477 Pittsburgh Pirates W Pennant and Logo	.05	.02
☐ 478 St. Louis Cardinals X Pennant and Logo	.05	.02
☐ 479 San Diego Padres Y Pennant and Logo	.05	.02
☐ 480 San Fran. Giants Z Pennant and Logo	.05	.02
☐ xx Sticker Album Don Mattingly on front	1.00	.45

1989 Panini Stickers

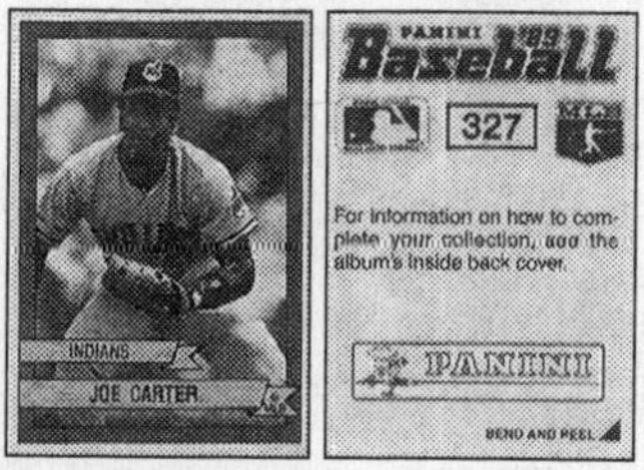

COMMON STICKER (1-480)	.05	.02
☐ 1 World Series Trophy	.05	.02
☐ 2 World Series Trophy	.05	.02
☐ 3 Mike Schmidt	.50	.23
☐ 4 Tom Browning	.05	.02
☐ 5 Doug Jones	.05	.02
☐ 6 Wrigley Field	.05	.02
☐ 7 Wade Boggs	.40	.18
☐ 8 Jose Canseco	.50	.23
☐ 9 Orel Hershiser	.10	.05
☐ 10 Oakland wins ALCS	.05	.02
☐ 11 Oakland wins ALCS	.05	.02
☐ 12 Dennis Eckersley ALCS	.10	.05
☐ 13 Orel Hershiser NLCS	.10	.05
☐ 14 Dodgers win NLCS	.05	.02
☐ 15 Dodgers win NLCS	.05	.02
☐ 16 Kirk Gibson	.20	.09
☐ 17 Kirk Gibson	.20	.09
☐ 18 Orel Hershiser	.10	.05
☐ 19 Orel Hershiser	.10	.05
☐ 20 Mark McGwire	1.50	.70
☐ 21 Tim Belcher	.05	.02
☐ 22 Jay Howell	.05	.02

□ 23 Mickey Hatcher .05 .02
□ 24 Mike Davis .05 .02
□ 25 Orel Hershiser WS MVP .10 .05
□ 26 Dodgers win AS .05 .02
□ 27 Dodgers win AS .05 .02
□ 28 Dodgers win AS .05 .02
□ 29 Dodgers win AS .05 .02
□ 30 Atlanta team logo .05 .02
□ 31 Jose Alvarez .05 .02
□ 32 Tommy Gregg .05 .02
□ 33 Paul Assenmacher .05 .02
□ 34 Tom Glavine .75 .35
□ 35 Rick Mahler .05 .02
□ 36 Pete Smith .05 .02
□ 37 Atlanta-Fulton County Stadium .05 .02
□ 38 Atlanta team lettering .05 .02
□ 39 Bruce Sutter .05 .02
□ 40 Gerald Perry .05 .02
□ 41 Jeff Blauser .10 .05
□ 42 Ron Gant .35 .16
□ 43 Andres Thomas .05 .02
□ 44 Dion James .05 .02
□ 45 Dale Murphy .30 .14
□ 46 Cubs team logo .05 .02
□ 47 Doug Dascenzo .05 .02
□ 48 Mike Harkey .05 .02
□ 49 Greg Maddux 2.00 .90
□ 50 Jeff Pico .05 .02
□ 51 Rick Sutcliffe .05 .02
□ 52 Damon Berryhill .05 .02
□ 53 Wrigley Field .05 .02
□ 54 Cubs lettering .05 .02
□ 55 Mark Grace .75 .35
□ 56 Ryne Sandberg .75 .35
□ 57 Vance Law .05 .02
□ 58 Shawon Dunston .05 .02
□ 59 Andre Dawson .30 .14
□ 60 Rafael Palmeiro .30 .14
□ 61 Mitch Webster .05 .02
□ 62 Reds team logo .05 .02
□ 63 Jack Armstrong .05 .02
□ 64 Chris Sabo .05 .02
□ 65 Tom Browning .05 .02
□ 66 John Franco .10 .05
□ 67 Danny Jackson .05 .02
□ 68 Jose Rijo .05 .02
□ 69 Riverfront Stadium .05 .02
□ 70 Reds team lettering .05 .02
□ 71 Bo Diaz .05 .02
□ 72 Nick Esasky .05 .02
□ 73 Jeff Treadway .05 .02
□ 74 Barry Larkin .50 .23
□ 75 Kal Daniels .05 .02
□ 76 Eric Davis .10 .05
□ 77 Paul O'Neill .10 .05
□ 78 Astros team logo .05 .02
□ 79 Craig Biggio 1.00 .45
□ 80 John Fishel .05 .02
□ 81 Juan Agosto .05 .02
□ 82 Bob Knepper .05 .02
□ 83 Nolan Ryan 3.00 1.35
□ 84 Mike Scott .05 .02
□ 85 The Astrodome .05 .02
□ 86 Astros team lettering .05 .02
□ 87 Dave Smith .05 .02
□ 88 Glenn Davis .05 .02
□ 89 Bill Doran .05 .02
□ 90 Rafael Ramirez .05 .02
□ 91 Kevin Bass .05 .02
□ 92 Billy Hatcher .05 .02
□ 93 Gerald Young .05 .02
□ 94 Dodgers team logo .05 .02
□ 95 Tim Belcher .05 .02
□ 96 Tim Crews .05 .02
□ 97 Orel Hershiser .10 .05
□ 98 Jay Howell .05 .02
□ 99 Tim Leary .05 .02
□ 100 John Tudor .05 .02
□ 101 Dodger Stadium .05 .02
□ 102 Dodgers team lettering .05 .02
□ 103 Fernando Valenzuela .10 .05
□ 104 Mike Scioscia .05 .02
□ 105 Mickey Hatcher .05 .02
□ 106 Steve Sax .05 .02
□ 107 Kirk Gibson .20 .09
□ 108 Mike Marshall .05 .02
□ 109 John Shelby .05 .02
□ 110 Expos team logo .05 .02
□ 111 Randy Johnson 1.50 .70
□ 112 Nelson Santovenia .05 .02
□ 113 Tim Burke .05 .02
□ 114 Dennis Martinez .10 .05
□ 115 Pascual Perez .05 .02
□ 116 Bryn Smith .05 .02
□ 117 Olympic Stadium .05 .02
□ 118 Expos team lettering .05 .02
□ 119 Andres Galarraga .30 .14
□ 120 Wallace Johnson .05 .02
□ 121 Tom Foley .05 .02
□ 122 Tim Wallach .05 .02
□ 123 Hubie Brooks .05 .02
□ 124 Tracy Jones .05 .02
□ 125 Tim Raines .10 .05
□ 126 Mets team logo .05 .02
□ 127 Kevin Elster .05 .02
□ 128 Gregg Jefferies .30 .14
□ 129 David Cone .30 .14
□ 130 Ron Darling .05 .02
□ 131 Dwight Gooden .10 .05
□ 132 Roger McDowell .05 .02
□ 133 Shea Stadium .05 .02
□ 134 Mets team lettering .05 .02
□ 135 Randy Myers .10 .05
□ 136 Gary Carter .20 .09
□ 137 Keith Hernandez .10 .05
□ 138 Lenny Dykstra .10 .05
□ 139 Kevin McReynolds .05 .02
□ 140 Darryl Strawberry .10 .05
□ 141 Mookie Wilson .05 .02
□ 142 Phillies team logo .05 .02
□ 143 Ron Jones .05 .02
□ 144 Ricky Jordan .05 .02
□ 145 Steve Bedrosian .05 .02
□ 146 Don Carman .05 .02
□ 147 Kevin Gross .05 .02
□ 148 Bruce Ruffin .05 .02
□ 149 Veterans Stadium .05 .02
□ 150 Phillies team lettering .05 .02
□ 151 Von Hayes .05 .02
□ 152 Juan Samuel .05 .02
□ 153 Mike Schmidt .75 .35
□ 154 Phil Bradley .05 .02
□ 155 Bob Dernier .05 .02
□ 156 Chris James .05 .02
□ 157 Milt Thompson .05 .02
□ 158 Pirates team logo .05 .02
□ 159 Randy Kramer .05 .02
□ 160 Scott Medvin .05 .02
□ 161 Doug Drabek .05 .02
□ 162 Mike Dunne .05 .02
□ 163 Jim Gott .05 .02
□ 164 Jeff D. Robinson .05 .02
□ 165 Three Rivers Stadium .05 .02
□ 166 Pirates team lettering .05 .02
□ 167 John Smiley .05 .02
□ 168 Mike LaValliere .05 .02
□ 169 Sid Bream .05 .02
□ 170 Jose Lind .05 .02
□ 171 Bobby Bonilla .20 .09
□ 172 Barry Bonds .75 .35
□ 173 Andy Van Slyke .10 .05
□ 174 Cardinals team logo .05 .02
□ 175 Luis Alicea .05 .02
□ 176 John Costello .05 .02
□ 177 Jose DeLeon .05 .02
□ 178 Joe Magrane .05 .02
□ 179 Todd Worrell .05 .02
□ 180 Tony Pena .05 .02
□ 181 Busch Stadium .05 .02
□ 182 Cardinals team lettering .05 .02
□ 183 Pedro Guerrero .05 .02
□ 184 Jose Oquendo .05 .02
□ 185 Terry Pendleton .10 .05
□ 186 Ozzie Smith .75 .35
□ 187 Tom Brunansky .05 .02
□ 188 Vince Coleman .05 .02
□ 189 Willie McGee .10 .05
□ 190 Padres team logo .05 .02
□ 191 Roberto Alomar 1.00 .45
□ 192 Sandy Alomar Jr. .75 .35
□ 193 Mark Davis .05 .02
□ 194 Andy Hawkins .05 .02
□ 195 Dennis Rasmussen .05 .02
□ 196 Eric Show .05 .02
□ 197 Jack Murphy Stadium .05 .02
□ 198 Padres team lettering .05 .02
□ 199 Benito Santiago .05 .02
□ 200 John Kruk .10 .05
□ 201 Randy Ready .05 .02
□ 202 Garry Templeton .05 .02
□ 203 Tony Gwynn 1.50 .70
□ 204 Carmelo Martinez .05 .02
□ 205 Marvell Wynne .05 .02
□ 206 Giants Team Logo .05 .02
□ 207 Dennis Cook .05 .02
□ 208 Kirt Manwaring .05 .02
□ 209 Kelly Downs .05 .02
□ 210 Rick Reuschel .10 .05
□ 211 Don Robinson .05 .02
□ 212 Will Clark .50 .23
□ 213 Candlestick Park .05 .02
□ 214 Giants team lettering .05 .02
□ 215 Robby Thompson .05 .02
□ 216 Kevin Mitchell .05 .02
□ 217 Jose Uribe .05 .02
□ 218 Matt Williams .75 .35
□ 219 Mike Aldrete .05 .02
□ 220 Brett Butler .10 .05
□ 221 Candy Maldonado .05 .02
□ 222 Tony Gwynn 1.50 .70
□ 223 Darryl Strawberry .10 .05
□ 224 Andres Galarraga .30 .14
□ 225 Orel Hershiser Danny Jackson .10 .05
□ 226 Nolan Ryan 3.00 1.35
□ 227 Dwight Gooden AS .10 .05
□ 228 Gary Carter AS .20 .09
□ 229 Vince Coleman AS .05 .02
□ 230 Andre Dawson AS .20 .09
□ 231 Darryl Strawberry AS .10 .05
□ 232 Will Clark AS .20 .09
□ 233 Ryne Sandberg AS .35 .16
□ 234 Bobby Bonilla AS .10 .05
□ 235 Ozzie Smith AS .35 .16
□ 236 Terry Steinbach AS .10 .05
□ 237 Frank Viola AS .05 .02
□ 238 Jose Canseco AS .20 .09
□ 239 Rickey Henderson AS .30 .14
□ 240 Dave Winfield AS .30 .14
□ 241 Cal Ripken Jr. AS 1.50 .70
□ 242 Wade Boggs AS .30 .14
□ 243 Paul Molitor AS .30 .14
□ 244 Mark McGwire AS .60 .25
□ 245 Wade Boggs AS .30 .14
□ 246 Jose Canseco .50 .23
□ 247 Kirby Puckett 1.50 .70
□ 248 Frank Viola .05 .02
□ 249 Roger Clemens .75 .35
□ 250 Orioles team logo .05 .02
□ 251 Bob Milacki .05 .02
□ 252 Craig Worthington .05 .02
□ 253 Jeff Ballard .05 .02
□ 254 Tom Niedenfuer .05 .02
□ 255 Dave Schmidt .05 .02
□ 256 Terry Kennedy .05 .02
□ 257 Memorial Stadium .05 .02
□ 258 Orioles team lettering .05 .02
□ 259 Mickey Tettleton .10 .05
□ 260 Eddie Murray .75 .35
□ 261 Bill Ripken .05 .02
□ 262 Cal Ripken Jr. 3.00 1.35
□ 263 Joe Orsulak .05 .02
□ 264 Larry Sheets .05 .02
□ 265 Pete Stanicek .05 .02
□ 266 Red Sox team logo .05 .02
□ 267 Steve Curry .05 .02
□ 268 Jody Reed .05 .02
□ 269 Oil Can Boyd .05 .02
□ 270 Roger Clemens .75 .35
□ 271 Bruce Hurst .05 .02
□ 272 Lee Smith .10 .05
□ 273 Fenway Park .05 .02
□ 274 Red Sox team lettering .05 .02
□ 275 Todd Benzinger .05 .02
□ 276 Marty Barrett .05 .02
□ 277 Wade Boggs .40 .18
□ 278 Ellis Burks .20 .09
□ 279 Dwight Evans .10 .05
□ 280 Mike Greenwell .05 .02
□ 281 Jim Rice .10 .05
□ 282 Angels team logo .05 .02
□ 283 Dante Bichette 1.50 .70
□ 284 Bryan Harvey .05 .02
□ 285 Kirk McCaskill .05 .02
□ 286 Mike Witt .05 .02
□ 287 Bob Boone .10 .05
□ 288 Brian Downing .10 .05
□ 289 Anaheim Stadium .05 .02
□ 290 Angels team lettering .05 .02
□ 291 Wally Joyner .10 .05
□ 292 Johnny Ray .05 .02
□ 293 Jack Howell .05 .02
□ 294 Dick Schofield .05 .02
□ 295 Tony Armas .05 .02
□ 296 Chili Davis .10 .05
□ 297 Devon White .10 .05
□ 298 White Sox team logo .05 .02
□ 299 Dave Gallagher .05 .02
□ 300 Melido Perez .05 .02
□ 301 Shawn Hillegas .05 .02
□ 302 Jack McDowell .10 .05
□ 303 Bobby Thigpen .05 .02
□ 304 Carlton Fisk .30 .14

☐ 305 Comiskey Park	.05	.02
☐ 306 White Sox team lettering	.05	.02
☐ 307 Greg Walker	.05	.02
☐ 308 Steve Lyons	.05	.02
☐ 309 Ozzie Guillen	.05	.02
☐ 310 Harold Baines	.10	.05
☐ 311 Daryl Boston	.05	.02
☐ 312 Lance Johnson	.10	.05
☐ 313 Dan Pasqua	.05	.02
☐ 314 Indians team logo	.05	.02
☐ 315 Luis Medina	.05	.02
☐ 316 Ron Tingley	.05	.02
☐ 317 Tom Candiotti	.05	.02
☐ 318 John Farrell	.05	.02
☐ 319 Doug Jones	.05	.02
☐ 320 Greg Swindell	.05	.02
☐ 321 Cleveland Stadium	.05	.02
☐ 322 Indians team lettering	.05	.02
☐ 323 Andy Allanson	.05	.02
☐ 324 Willie Upshaw	.05	.02
☐ 325 Julio Franco	.10	.05
☐ 326 Brook Jacoby	.05	.02
☐ 327 Joe Carter	.20	.09
☐ 328 Mel Hall	.05	.02
☐ 329 Cory Snyder	.05	.02
☐ 330 Tigers team logo	.05	.02
☐ 331 Paul Gibson	.05	.02
☐ 332 Torey Lovullo	.05	.02
☐ 333 Mike Henneman	.05	.02
☐ 334 Jack Morris	.10	.05
☐ 335 Jeff M. Robinson	.05	.02
☐ 336 Frank Tanana	.05	.02
☐ 337 Tiger Stadium	.05	.02
☐ 338 Tigers team lettering	.05	.02
☐ 339 Matt Nokes	.05	.02
☐ 340 Tom Brookens	.05	.02
☐ 341 Lou Whitaker	.10	.05
☐ 342 Luis Salazar	.05	.02
☐ 343 Alan Trammell	.20	.09
☐ 344 Chet Lemon	.05	.02
☐ 345 Gary Pettis	.05	.02
☐ 346 Royals team logo	.05	.02
☐ 347 Luis de los Santos	.05	.02
☐ 348 Gary Thurman	.05	.02
☐ 349 Steve Farr	.05	.02
☐ 350 Mark Gubicza	.05	.02
☐ 351 Charlie Leibrandt	.05	.02
☐ 352 Bret Saberhagen	.10	.05
☐ 353 Royals Stadium	.05	.02
☐ 354 Royals team lettering	.05	.02
☐ 355 George Brett	1.25	.55
☐ 356 Frank White	.10	.05
☐ 357 Kevin Seitzer	.05	.02
☐ 358 Bo Jackson	.20	.09
☐ 359 Pat Tabler	.05	.02
☐ 360 Danny Tartabull	.10	.05
☐ 361 Willie Wilson	.10	.05
☐ 362 Brewers team logo	.05	.02
☐ 363 Joey Meyer	.05	.02
☐ 364 Gary Sheffield	2.00	.90
☐ 365 Don August	.05	.02
☐ 366 Ted Higuera	.05	.02
☐ 367 Dan Plesac	.05	.02
☐ 368 B.J. Surhoff	.10	.05
☐ 369 Milwaukee County Stadium	.05	.02
☐ 370 Brewers team lettering	.05	.02
☐ 371 Greg Brock	.05	.02
☐ 372 Jim Gantner	.05	.02
☐ 373 Paul Molitor	.75	.35
☐ 374 Dale Sveum	.05	.02
☐ 375 Glenn Braggs	.05	.02
☐ 376 Rob Deer	.05	.02
☐ 377 Robin Yount	.20	.09
☐ 378 Twins team logo	.05	.02
☐ 379 German Gonzalez	.05	.02
☐ 380 Kelvin Torve	.05	.02
☐ 381 Allan Anderson	.05	.02
☐ 382 Jeff Reardon	.10	.05
☐ 383 Frank Viola	.05	.02
☐ 384 Tim Laudner	.05	.02
☐ 385 Hubert H. Humphrey Metrodome	.05	.02
☐ 386 Twins team lettering	.05	.02
☐ 387 Kent Hrbek	.10	.05
☐ 388 Gene Larkin	.05	.02
☐ 389 Gary Gaetti	.10	.05
☐ 390 Greg Gagne	.05	.02
☐ 391 Randy Bush	.05	.02
☐ 392 Dan Gladden	.05	.02
☐ 393 Kirby Puckett	1.50	.70
☐ 394 Yankees team logo	.05	.02
☐ 395 Roberto Kelly	.05	.02
☐ 396 Al Leiter	.10	.05
☐ 397 John Candelaria	.05	.02
☐ 398 Rich Dotson	.05	.02
☐ 399 Rick Rhoden	.05	.02
☐ 400 Dave Righetti	.05	.02
☐ 401 Yankee Stadium	.05	.02
☐ 402 Yankees team lettering	.05	.02
☐ 403 Don Slaught	.05	.02
☐ 404 Don Mattingly	1.50	.70
☐ 405 Willie Randolph	.10	.05
☐ 406 Mike Pagliarulo	.05	.02
☐ 407 Rafael Santana	.05	.02
☐ 408 Rickey Henderson	.30	.14
☐ 409 Dave Winfield	.30	.14
☐ 410 Athletics team logo	.05	.02
☐ 411 Todd Burns	.05	.02
☐ 412 Walt Weiss	.05	.02
☐ 413 Storm Davis	.05	.02
☐ 414 Dennis Eckersley	.20	.09
☐ 415 Dave Stewart	.10	.05
☐ 416 Bob Welch	.10	.05
☐ 417 Oakland Alameda County Coliseum	.05	.02
☐ 418 Athletics team lettering	.05	.02
☐ 419 Terry Steinbach	.10	.05
☐ 420 Mark McGwire	1.50	.70
☐ 421 Carney Lansford	.05	.02
☐ 422 Jose Canseco	.50	.23
☐ 423 Dave Henderson	.05	.02
☐ 424 Dave Parker	.10	.05
☐ 425 Luis Polonia	.10	.05
☐ 426 Mariners team logo	.05	.02
☐ 427 Mario Diaz	.05	.02
☐ 428 Edgar Martinez	.40	.18
☐ 429 Scott Bankhead	.05	.02
☐ 430 Mark Langston	.05	.02
☐ 431 Mike Moore	.05	.02
☐ 432 Scott Bradley	.05	.02
☐ 433 The Kingdome	.05	.02
☐ 434 Mariners team lettering	.05	.02
☐ 435 Alvin Davis	.05	.02
☐ 436 Harold Reynolds	.10	.05
☐ 437 Jim Presley	.05	.02
☐ 438 Rey Quinones	.05	.02
☐ 439 Mickey Brantley	.05	.02
☐ 440 Jay Buhner	.50	.23
☐ 441 Henry Cotto	.05	.02
☐ 442 Rangers team logo	.05	.02
☐ 443 Cecil Espy	.05	.02
☐ 444 Chad Kreuter	.05	.02
☐ 445 Jose Guzman	.05	.02
☐ 446 Charlie Hough	.10	.05
☐ 447 Jeff Russell	.05	.02
☐ 448 Bobby Witt	.05	.02
☐ 449 Arlington Stadium	.05	.02
☐ 450 Rangers team lettering	.05	.02
☐ 451 Geno Petralli	.05	.02
☐ 452 Pete O'Brien	.05	.02
☐ 453 Steve Buechele	.05	.02
☐ 454 Scott Fletcher	.05	.02
☐ 455 Pete Incaviglia	.05	.02
☐ 456 Oddibe McDowell	.05	.02
☐ 457 Ruben Sierra	.05	.02
☐ 458 Blue Jays team logo	.05	.02
☐ 459 Rob Ducey	.05	.02
☐ 460 Todd Stottlemyre	.10	.05
☐ 461 Tom Henke	.05	.02
☐ 462 Jimmy Key	.10	.05
☐ 463 Dave Stieb	.05	.02
☐ 464 Pat Borders	.05	.02
☐ 465 Exhibition Stadium	.05	.02
☐ 466 Blue Jays team lettering	.05	.02
☐ 467 Fred McGriff	.40	.18
☐ 468 Manny Lee	.05	.02
☐ 469 Kelly Gruber	.05	.02
☐ 470 Tony Fernandez	.05	.02
☐ 471 Jesse Barfield	.05	.02
☐ 472 George Bell	.05	.02
☐ 473 Lloyd Moseby	.05	.02
☐ 474 Orel Hershiser	.10	.05
☐ 475 Frank Viola	.05	.02
☐ 476 Chris Sabo	.05	.02
☐ 477 Jose Canseco	.50	.23
☐ 478 Walt Weiss	.05	.02
☐ 479 Kirk Gibson	.20	.09
☐ 480 Jose Canseco	.50	.23
☐ xx Sticker Album (Jose Canseco on front)	.75	.35

1990 Panini Stickers

These 388 stickers measure approximately 2 1/8" by 3" and feature on their fronts white-bordered color player

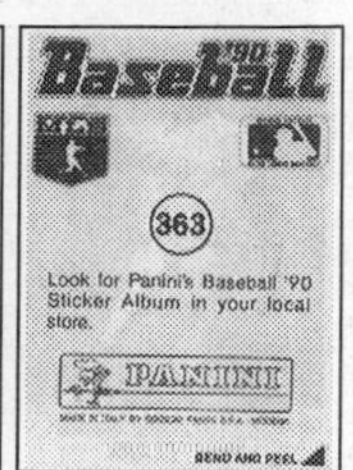

action shots. The player's name and team name, along with a baseball icon, appear within the broad white margin at the bottom. In addition to carrying the stickers' numbers, the white backs carry the logos for MLB, the MLBPA and Panini. Stickers 186-197 are foils. An album onto which the stickers could be affixed was available at retail stores. The album featured Nolan Ryan on the front and an ad for the Panini 1990 Fan Club Pop Star Sticker Collection on the back. The album also featured a four-page insert without stickers on the 1989 post-season. The album and the sticker numbering are organized by team alphabetically by city with AL teams preceding NL teams. Subsets include 1989 AL Stat Leaders (183-185), 1989 League Championship Series (Foil, 186-187), Excellence in the '80s (Foil, 188-197), 1989 All-Stars (198-213), 1989 NL Stat Leaders (214-216), Tomorrow's Headliners (373-382) and 1989 Highlights (383-388).

	MINT	NRMT
COMPLETE SET (388)	15.00	6.75
COMMON STICKER (1-388)	.05	.02
☐ 1 Randy Milligan	.05	.02
☐ 2 Gregg Olson	.05	.02
☐ 3 Bill Ripken	.05	.02
☐ 4 Phil Bradley	.05	.02
☐ 5 Joe Orsulak	.05	.02
☐ 6 Bob Milacki	.05	.02
☐ 7 Cal Ripken	2.50	1.10
☐ 8 Mickey Tettleton	.10	.05
☐ 9 Orioles Logo	.05	.02
☐ 10 Orioles Helmet	.05	.02
☐ 11 Craig Worthington	.05	.02
☐ 12 Mike Devereaux	.05	.02
☐ 13 Jeff Ballard	.05	.02
☐ 14 Lee Smith	.15	.07
☐ 15 Marty Barrett	.05	.02
☐ 16 Mike Greenwell	.05	.02
☐ 17 Dwight Evans	.10	.05
☐ 18 John Dopson	.05	.02
☐ 19 Wade Boggs	.35	.16
☐ 20 Mike Boddicker	.05	.02
☐ 21 Ellis Burks	.15	.07
☐ 22 Red Sox Logo	.05	.02
☐ 23 Red Sox Helmet	.05	.02
☐ 24 Roger Clemens	.60	.25
☐ 25 Jody Reed	.05	.02
☐ 26 Nick Esasky	.05	.02
☐ 27 Brian Downing	.10	.05
☐ 28 Bert Blyleven	.10	.05
☐ 29 Devon White	.10	.05
☐ 30 Claudell Washington	.05	.02
☐ 31 Wally Joyner	.10	.05
☐ 32 Chuck Finley	.10	.05
☐ 33 Johnny Ray	.05	.02
☐ 34 Jim Abbott	.10	.05
☐ 35 Angels Logo	.05	.02
☐ 36 Angels Helmet	.05	.02
☐ 37 Kirk McCaskill	.05	.02
☐ 38 Lance Parrish	.05	.02
☐ 39 Chili Davis	.10	.05
☐ 40 Steve Lyons	.05	.02
☐ 41 Ozzie Guillen	.05	.02
☐ 42 Melido Perez	.05	.02
☐ 43 Scott Fletcher	.05	.02
☐ 44 Carlton Fisk	.25	.11
☐ 45 Greg Walker	.05	.02
☐ 46 Dave Gallagher	.05	.02
☐ 47 Ivan Calderon	.05	.02
☐ 48 White Sox Logo	.05	.02
☐ 49 White Sox Helmet	.05	.02
☐ 50 Bobby Thigpen	.05	.02
☐ 51 Ron Kittle	.05	.02
☐ 52 Daryl Boston	.05	.02
☐ 53 John Farrell	.05	.02
☐ 54 Jerry Browne	.05	.02
☐ 55 Pete O'Brien	.05	.02
☐ 56 Cory Snyder	.05	.02
☐ 57 Tom Candiotti	.05	.02
☐ 58 Brook Jacoby	.05	.02
☐ 59 Greg Swindell	.05	.02
☐ 60 Felix Fermin	.05	.02
☐ 61 Indians Logo	.05	.02

☐ 62 Indians Helmet	.05	.02
☐ 63 Doug Jones	.05	.02
☐ 64 Dion James	.05	.02
☐ 65 Joe Carter	.10	.05
☐ 66 Mike Heath	.05	.02
☐ 67 Dave Bergman	.05	.02
☐ 68 Gary Ward	.05	.02
☐ 69 Mike Henneman	.05	.02
☐ 70 Alan Trammell	.15	.07
☐ 71 Lou Whitaker	.10	.05
☐ 72 Frank Tanana	.05	.02
☐ 73 Fred Lynn	.10	.05
☐ 74 Tigers Logo	.05	.02
☐ 75 Tigers Helmet	.05	.02
☐ 76 Jack Morris	.10	.05
☐ 77 Chet Lemon	.05	.02
☐ 78 Gary Pettis	.05	.02
☐ 79 Kurt Stillwell	.05	.02
☐ 80 Jim Eisenreich	.10	.05
☐ 81 Bret Saberhagen	.05	.02
☐ 82 Mark Gubicza	.05	.02
☐ 83 Frank White	.10	.05
☐ 84 Bo Jackson	.10	.05
☐ 85 Jeff Montgomery	.10	.05
☐ 86 Kevin Seitzer	.05	.02
☐ 87 Royals Logo	.05	.02
☐ 88 Royals Helmet	.05	.02
☐ 89 Tom Gordon	.05	.02
☐ 90 Danny Tartabull	.05	.02
☐ 91 George Brett	1.25	.55
☐ 92 Robin Yount	.25	.11
☐ 93 B.J. Surhoff	.10	.05
☐ 94 Jim Gantner	.05	.02
☐ 95 Dan Plesac	.05	.02
☐ 96 Ted Higuera	.05	.02
☐ 97 Glenn Braggs	.05	.02
☐ 98 Paul Molitor	.75	.35
☐ 99 Chris Bosio	.05	.02
☐ 100 Brewers Logo	.05	.02
☐ 101 Brewers Helmet	.05	.02
☐ 102 Rob Deer	.05	.02
☐ 103 Chuck Crim	.05	.02
☐ 104 Greg Brock	.05	.02
☐ 105 Kirby Puckett	1.50	.70
☐ 106 Gary Gaetti	.10	.05
☐ 107 Roy Smith	.05	.02
☐ 108 Jeff Reardon	.10	.05
☐ 109 Randy Bush	.05	.02
☐ 110 Al Newman	.05	.02
☐ 111 Dan Gladden	.05	.02
☐ 112 Kent Hrbek	.10	.05
☐ 113 Twins Logo	.05	.02
☐ 114 Twins Helmet	.05	.02
☐ 115 Greg Gagne	.05	.02
☐ 116 Brian Harper	.05	.02
☐ 117 Allan Anderson	.05	.02
☐ 118 Lee Guetterman	.05	.02
☐ 119 Roberto Kelly	.05	.02
☐ 120 Jesse Barfield	.05	.02
☐ 121 Alvaro Espinoza	.05	.02
☐ 122 Mel Hall	.05	.02
☐ 123 Chuck Cary	.05	.02
☐ 124 Dave Righetti	.05	.02
☐ 125 Don Mattingly	1.50	.70
☐ 126 Yankees Logo	.05	.02
☐ 127 Yankees Helmet	.05	.02
☐ 128 Bob Geren	.05	.02
☐ 129 Steve Sax	.05	.02
☐ 130 Andy Hawkins	.05	.02
☐ 131 Bob Welch	.05	.02
☐ 132 Mark McGwire	1.25	.55
☐ 133 Dave Henderson	.05	.02
☐ 134 Carney Lansford	.05	.02
☐ 135 Walt Weiss	.05	.02
☐ 136 Mike Moore	.05	.02
☐ 137 Dennis Eckersley	.15	.07
☐ 138 Rickey Henderson	.25	.11
☐ 139 Athletics Logo	.05	.02
☐ 140 Athletics Helmet	.05	.02
☐ 141 Dave Stewart	.10	.05
☐ 142 Jose Canseco	.35	.16
☐ 143 Terry Steinbach	.10	.05
☐ 144 Harold Reynolds	.10	.05
☐ 145 Darnell Coles	.05	.02
☐ 146 Brian Holman	.05	.02
☐ 147 Scott Bankhead	.05	.02
☐ 148 Greg Briley	.05	.02
☐ 149 Alvin Davis	.05	.02
☐ 150 Jeffrey Leonard	.05	.02
☐ 151 Mike Schooler	.05	.02
☐ 152 Mariners Logo	.05	.02
☐ 153 Mariners Helmet	.05	.02
☐ 154 Randy Johnson	1.00	.45
☐ 155 Ken Griffey Jr.	3.00	1.35
☐ 156 Dave Valle	.05	.02
☐ 157 Pete Incaviglia	.05	.02
☐ 158 Fred Manrique	.05	.02
☐ 159 Jeff Russell	.05	.02
☐ 160 Nolan Ryan	2.50	1.10
☐ 161 Geno Petralli	.05	.02
☐ 162 Ruben Sierra	.05	.02
☐ 163 Julio Franco	.10	.05
☐ 164 Rafael Palmeiro	.15	.07
☐ 165 Rangers Logo	.05	.02
☐ 166 Rangers Helmet	.05	.02
☐ 167 Harold Baines	.10	.05
☐ 168 Kevin Brown	.15	.07
☐ 169 Steve Buechele	.05	.02
☐ 170 Fred McGriff	.35	.16
☐ 171 Kelly Gruber	.05	.02
☐ 172 Todd Stottlemyre	.10	.05
☐ 173 Dave Stieb	.05	.02
☐ 174 Mookie Wilson	.05	.02
☐ 175 Pat Borders	.05	.02
☐ 176 Tony Fernandez	.05	.02
☐ 177 John Cerutti	.05	.02
☐ 178 Blue Jays Logo	.05	.02
☐ 179 Blue Jays Helmet	.05	.02
☐ 180 George Bell	.05	.02
☐ 181 Jimmy Key	.05	.02
☐ 182 Nelson Liriano	.05	.02
☐ 183 Kirby Puckett	1.50	.70
☐ 184 Carney Lansford	.10	.05
☐ 185 Nolan Ryan	2.50	1.10
☐ 186 AL Logo	.05	.02
☐ 187 NL Logo	.05	.02
☐ 188 World Championship Trophy	.05	.02
☐ 189 '88 World Championship LA Dodgers Ring	.05	.02
☐ 190 '87 World Championship Minnesota Twins Ring	.05	.02
☐ 191 '86 World Championship NY Mets Ring	.05	.02
☐ 192 '85 World Championship KC Royals Ring	.05	.02
☐ 193 '84 World Championship Detroit Tigers Ring	.05	.02
☐ 194 '83 World Championship Baltimore Orioles Ring	.05	.02
☐ 195 '82 World Championship St.Louis Cardinals Ring	.05	.02
☐ 196 '81 World Championship LA Dodgers Ring	.05	.02
☐ 197 '80 World Championship Philadelphia Phillies Ring	.05	.02
☐ 198 Dave Stewart Bo Jackson	.10	.05
☐ 199 Wade Boggs Kirby Puckett	.15	.07
☐ 200 Harold Baines	.10	.05
☐ 201 Julio Franco	.10	.05
☐ 202 Cal Ripken	2.50	1.10
☐ 203 Ruben Sierra	.05	.02
☐ 204 Mark McGwire	1.00	.45
☐ 205 Terry Steinbach	.10	.05
☐ 206 Rick Reuschel Ozzie Smith	.15	.07
☐ 207 Tony Gwynn Will Clark	.60	.25
☐ 208 Kevin Mitchell	.05	.02
☐ 209 Eric Davis	.10	.05
☐ 210 Howard Johnson	.05	.02
☐ 211 Pedro Guerrero	.05	.02
☐ 212 Ryne Sandberg	.75	.35
☐ 213 Benito Santiago	.05	.02
☐ 214 Kevin Mitchell	.05	.02
☐ 215 Mark Davis	.05	.02
☐ 216 Vince Coleman	.05	.02
☐ 217 Jeff Blauser	.05	.02
☐ 218 Jeff Treadway	.05	.02
☐ 219 Tom Glavine	.50	.23
☐ 220 Joe Boever	.05	.02
☐ 221 Oddibe McDowell	.05	.02
☐ 222 Dale Murphy	.15	.07
☐ 223 Derek Lilliquist	.05	.02
☐ 224 Tommy Gregg	.05	.02
☐ 225 Braves Logo	.05	.02
☐ 226 Braves Helmet	.05	.02
☐ 227 Lonnie Smith	.05	.02
☐ 228 John Smoltz	.75	.35
☐ 229 Andres Thomas	.05	.02
☐ 230 Jerome Walton	.05	.02
☐ 231 Ryne Sandberg	.75	.35
☐ 232 Mitch Williams	.05	.02
☐ 233 Rick Sutcliffe	.05	.02
☐ 234 Damon Berryhill	.05	.02
☐ 235 Dwight Smith	.05	.02
☐ 236 Shawon Dunston	.05	.02
☐ 237 Greg Maddux	2.00	.90
☐ 238 Cubs Logo	.05	.02
☐ 239 Cubs Helmet	.05	.02
☐ 240 Andre Dawson	.25	.11
☐ 241 Mark Grace	.25	.11
☐ 242 Mike Bielecki	.05	.02
☐ 243 Jose Rijo	.05	.02
☐ 244 John Franco	.10	.05
☐ 245 Paul O'Neill	.10	.05
☐ 246 Eric Davis	.10	.05
☐ 247 Tom Browning	.05	.02
☐ 248 Chris Sabo	.05	.02
☐ 249 Rob Dibble	.05	.02
☐ 250 Todd Benzinger	.05	.02
☐ 251 Reds Logo	.05	.02
☐ 252 Reds Helmet	.05	.02
☐ 253 Barry Larkin	.35	.16
☐ 254 Rolando Roomes	.05	.02
☐ 255 Danny Jackson	.05	.02
☐ 256 Terry Puhl	.05	.02
☐ 257 Dave Smith	.05	.02
☐ 258 Glenn Davis	.05	.02
☐ 259 Craig Biggio	.30	.14
☐ 260 Ken Caminiti	.40	.18
☐ 261 Kevin Bass	.05	.02
☐ 262 Mike Scott	.05	.02
☐ 263 Gerald Young	.05	.02
☐ 264 Astros Logo	.05	.02
☐ 265 Astros Helmet	.05	.02
☐ 266 Rafael Ramirez	.05	.02
☐ 267 Jim Deshaies	.05	.02
☐ 268 Bill Doran	.05	.02
☐ 269 Fernando Valenzuela	.10	.05
☐ 270 Alfredo Griffin	.05	.02
☐ 271 Kirk Gibson	.10	.05
☐ 272 Mike Marshall	.05	.02
☐ 273 Eddie Murray	.60	.25
☐ 274 Jay Howell	.05	.02
☐ 275 Orel Hershiser	.10	.05
☐ 276 Mike Scioscia	.05	.02
☐ 277 Dodgers Logo	.05	.02
☐ 278 Dodgers Helmet	.05	.02
☐ 279 Willie Randolph	.10	.05
☐ 280 Kal Daniels	.05	.02
☐ 281 Tim Belcher	.05	.02
☐ 282 Pascual Perez	.05	.02
☐ 283 Tim Raines	.10	.05
☐ 284 Andres Galarraga	.25	.11
☐ 285 Spike Owen	.05	.02
☐ 286 Tim Wallach	.05	.02
☐ 287 Mark Langston	.05	.02
☐ 288 Dennis Martinez	.10	.05
☐ 289 Nelson Santovenia	.05	.02
☐ 290 Expos Logo	.05	.02
☐ 291 Expos Helmet	.05	.02
☐ 292 Tom Foley	.05	.02
☐ 293 Dave Martinez	.05	.02
☐ 294 Tim Burke	.05	.02
☐ 295 Ron Darling	.05	.02
☐ 296 Kevin Elster	.05	.02
☐ 297 Dwight Gooden	.10	.05
☐ 298 Gregg Jefferies	.10	.05
☐ 299 Sid Fernandez	.05	.02
☐ 300 Dave Magadan	.05	.02
☐ 301 David Cone	.15	.07
☐ 302 Darryl Strawberry	.10	.05
☐ 303 Mets Logo	.05	.02
☐ 304 Mets Helmet	.05	.02
☐ 305 Kevin McReynolds	.05	.02
☐ 306 Howard Johnson	.05	.02
☐ 307 Randy Myers	.10	.05
☐ 308 Roger McDowell	.05	.02
☐ 309 Tom Herr	.05	.02
☐ 310 John Kruk	.10	.05
☐ 311 Randy Ready	.05	.02
☐ 312 Jeff Parrett	.05	.02
☐ 313 Lenny Dykstra	.10	.05
☐ 314 Ken Howell	.05	.02
☐ 315 Ricky Jordan	.05	.02
☐ 316 Phillies Logo	.05	.02
☐ 317 Phillies Helmet	.05	.02
☐ 318 Dickie Thon	.05	.02
☐ 319 Von Hayes	.05	.02
☐ 320 Dennis Cook	.05	.02
☐ 321 Jay Bell	.10	.05
☐ 322 Barry Bonds	.75	.35
☐ 323 John Smiley	.05	.02
☐ 324 Andy Van Slyke	.10	.05
☐ 325 Bobby Bonilla	.10	.05
☐ 326 Bill Landrum	.05	.02
☐ 327 Randy Kramer	.05	.02
☐ 328 Jose Lind	.05	.02
☐ 329 Pirates Logo	.05	.02
☐ 330 Pirates Helmet	.05	.02
☐ 331 Gary Redus	.05	.02
☐ 332 Doug Drabek	.05	.02
☐ 333 Mike LaValliere	.05	.02
☐ 334 Jose DeLeon	.05	.02
☐ 335 Pedro Guerrero	.05	.02
☐ 336 Vince Coleman	.05	.02
☐ 337 Terry Pendleton	.10	.05

☐ 338 Ozzie Smith	.75	.35
☐ 339 Willie McGee	.10	.05
☐ 340 Todd Worrell	.05	.02
☐ 341 Jose Oquendo	.05	.02
☐ 342 Cardinals Logo	.05	.02
☐ 343 Cardinals Helmet	.05	.02
☐ 344 Tom Brunansky	.05	.02
☐ 345 Milt Thompson	.05	.02
☐ 346 Joe Magrane	.05	.02
☐ 347 Ed Whitson	.05	.02
☐ 348 Jack Clark	.05	.02
☐ 349 Roberto Alomar	.75	.35
☐ 350 Chris James	.05	.02
☐ 351 Tony Gwynn	1.50	.70
☐ 352 Mark Davis	.05	.02
☐ 353 Greg W. Harris	.05	.02
☐ 354 Garry Templeton	.05	.02
☐ 355 Padres Logo	.05	.02
☐ 356 Padres Helmet	.05	.02
☐ 357 Bruce Hurst	.05	.02
☐ 358 Benito Santiago	.05	.02
☐ 359 Bip Roberts	.05	.02
☐ 360 Dave Dravecky	.05	.02
☐ 361 Kevin Mitchell	.05	.02
☐ 362 Craig Lefferts	.05	.02
☐ 363 Will Clark	.35	.16
☐ 364 Steve Bedrosian	.05	.02
☐ 365 Brett Butler	.10	.05
☐ 366 Matt Williams	.35	.16
☐ 367 Scott Garrelts	.05	.02
☐ 368 Giants Logo	.05	.02
☐ 369 Giants Helmet	.05	.02
☐ 370 Rick Reuschel	.05	.02
☐ 371 Robby Thompson	.05	.02
☐ 372 Jose Uribe	.05	.02
☐ 373 Ben McDonald	.25	.11
☐ 374 Carlos Martinez	.05	.02
☐ 375 Steve Olin	.10	.05
☐ 376 Bill Spiers	.05	.02
☐ 377 Junior Felix	.05	.02
☐ 378 Joe Oliver	.05	.02
☐ 379 Eric Anthony	.05	.02
☐ 380 Ramon Martinez	.15	.07
☐ 381 Todd Zeile	.10	.05
☐ 382 Andy Benes	.15	.07
☐ 383 Vince Coleman	.05	.02
☐ 384 Bo Jackson	.10	.05
☐ 385 Howard Johnson	.05	.02
☐ 386 Dave Dravecky	.05	.02
☐ 387 Nolan Ryan	2.50	1.10
☐ 388 Cal Ripken	2.50	1.10
☐ xx Sticker Album (Nolan Ryan on front)	1.50	.70

1991 Panini Stickers

The 1991 Panini baseball set contains 271 stickers measuring 1 1/2" by 2 1/2". The fronts display color action player photos bordered in white. The player's name, positon, brief biography, 1990 statistics and career totals are given beneath the picture. Included in the set are 54 foil stickers of team pennants, logos and league insignias. The stickers may be pasted in a collectible sticker album that measures 8 1/4" by 10 1/2". The stickers are numbered on the back. After a "Year of the No-Hitter 1990" (1-9) subset, the stickers are checklisted alphabetically according to teams within the NL and then the AL.

	MINT	NRMT
COMPLETE SET (271)	15.00	6.75
COMMON STICKER (1-271)	.05	.02

☐ 1 Mark Langston	.05	.02
☐ 2 Randy Johnson	.30	.14
☐ 3 Nolan Ryan	2.50	1.10
☐ 4 Dave Stewart	.10	.05
☐ 5 Fernando Valenzuela	.10	.05
☐ 6 Andy Hawkins	.05	.02
☐ 7 Melido Perez	.05	.02
☐ 8 Terry Mulholland	.05	.02
☐ 9 Dave Stieb	.05	.02
☐ 10 Craig Biggio	.30	.14
☐ 11 Jim Deshaies	.05	.02
☐ 12 Dave Smith	.05	.02
☐ 13 Eric Yelding	.05	.02
☐ 14 Astros Pennant	.05	.02
☐ 15 Astros Logo	.05	.02
☐ 16 Mike Scott	.05	.02
☐ 17 Ken Caminiti	.40	.18
☐ 18 Danny Darwin	.05	.02
☐ 19 Glenn Davis	.05	.02
☐ 20 Braves Pennant	.05	.02
☐ 21 Braves Logo	.05	.02
☐ 22 Lonnie Smith	.05	.02
☐ 23 Charlie Leibrandt	.05	.02
☐ 24 Jim Presley	.05	.02
☐ 25 Greg Olson	.05	.02
☐ 26 John Smoltz	.40	.18
☐ 27 Ron Gant	.10	.05
☐ 28 Jeff Treadway	.05	.02
☐ 29 Dave Justice	.40	.18
☐ 30 Jose Oquendo	.05	.02
☐ 31 Joe Magrane	.05	.02
☐ 32 Cardinals Pennant	.05	.02
☐ 33 Cardinals Logo	.05	.02
☐ 34 Todd Zeile	.05	.02
☐ 35 Vince Coleman	.05	.02
☐ 36 Bob Tewksbury	.05	.02
☐ 37 Pedro Guerrero	.05	.02
☐ 38 Lee Smith	.10	.05
☐ 39 Ozzie Smith	.75	.35
☐ 40 Ryne Sandberg	.75	.35
☐ 41 Andre Dawson	.25	.11
☐ 42 Cubs Pennant	.05	.02
☐ 43 Greg Maddux	2.00	.90
☐ 44 Jerome Walton	.05	.02
☐ 45 Cubs Logo	.05	.02
☐ 46 Mike Harkey	.05	.02
☐ 47 Shawon Dunston	.05	.02
☐ 48 Mark Grace	.35	.16
☐ 49 Joe Girardi	.05	.02
☐ 50 Ramon Martinez	.15	.07
☐ 51 Lenny Harris	.05	.02
☐ 52 Mike Morgan	.05	.02
☐ 53 Eddie Murray	.60	.25
☐ 54 Dodgers Pennant	.05	.02
☐ 55 Dodgers Logo	.05	.02
☐ 56 Hubie Brooks	.05	.02
☐ 57 Mike Scioscia	.05	.02
☐ 58 Kal Daniels	.05	.02
☐ 59 Fernando Valenzuela	.10	.05
☐ 60 Expos Pennant	.05	.02
☐ 61 Expos Logo	.05	.02
☐ 62 Spike Owen	.05	.02
☐ 63 Tim Raines	.10	.05
☐ 64 Tim Wallach	.05	.02
☐ 65 Larry Walker	.50	.23
☐ 66 Dave Martinez	.05	.02
☐ 67 Mark Gardner	.05	.02
☐ 68 Dennis Martinez	.10	.05
☐ 69 Delino DeShields	.05	.02
☐ 70 Jeff Brantley	.05	.02
☐ 71 Kevin Mitchell	.05	.02
☐ 72 Giants Pennant	.05	.02
☐ 73 Giants Logo	.05	.02
☐ 74 Don Robinson	.05	.02
☐ 75 Brett Butler	.10	.05
☐ 76 Matt Williams	.35	.16
☐ 77 Robby Thompson	.05	.02
☐ 78 John Burkett	.05	.02
☐ 79 Will Clark	.35	.16
☐ 80 David Cone	.10	.05
☐ 81 Dave Magadan	.05	.02
☐ 82 Mets Pennant	.05	.02
☐ 83 Gregg Jefferies	.10	.05
☐ 84 Frank Viola	.05	.02
☐ 85 Mets Logo	.05	.02
☐ 86 Howard Johnson	.05	.02
☐ 87 John Franco	.10	.05
☐ 88 Darryl Strawberry	.10	.05
☐ 89 Dwight Gooden	.10	.05
☐ 90 Joe Carter	.10	.05
☐ 91 Ed Whitson	.05	.02
☐ 92 Andy Benes	.10	.05
☐ 93 Benito Santiago	.05	.02
☐ 94 Padres Pennant	.05	.02
☐ 95 Padres Logo	.05	.02
☐ 96 Roberto Alomar	.50	.23
☐ 97 Bip Roberts	.05	.02
☐ 98 Jack Clark	.05	.02
☐ 99 Tony Gwynn	1.50	.70
☐ 100 Phillies Pennant	.05	.02
☐ 101 Phillies Logo	.05	.02
☐ 102 Charlie Hayes	.05	.02
☐ 103 Len Dykstra	.10	.05
☐ 104 Dale Murphy	.25	.11
☐ 105 Von Hayes	.05	.02
☐ 106 Dickie Thon	.05	.02
☐ 107 John Kruk	.10	.05
☐ 108 Ken Howell	.05	.02
☐ 109 Darren Daulton	.10	.05
☐ 110 Jay Bell	.05	.02
☐ 111 Bobby Bonilla	.10	.05
☐ 112 Pirates Pennant	.05	.02
☐ 113 Pirates Logo	.05	.02
☐ 114 Barry Bonds	.50	.23
☐ 115 Neal Heaton	.05	.02
☐ 116 Doug Drabek	.05	.02
☐ 117 Jose Lind	.05	.02
☐ 118 Andy Van Slyke	.05	.02
☐ 119 Sid Bream	.05	.02
☐ 120 Paul O'Neill	.10	.05
☐ 121 Randy Myers	.05	.02
☐ 122 Reds Pennant	.05	.02
☐ 123 Mariano Duncan	.05	.02
☐ 124 Eric Davis	.10	.05
☐ 125 Reds Logo	.05	.02
☐ 126 Jack Armstrong	.05	.02
☐ 127 Chris Sabo	.05	.02
☐ 128 Rob Dibble	.05	.02
☐ 129 Barry Larkin	.35	.16
☐ 130 National League Logo	.05	.02
☐ 131 American League Logo	.05	.02
☐ 132 Dave Winfield	.25	.11
☐ 133 Lance Parrish	.05	.02
☐ 134 Chili Davis	.10	.05
☐ 135 Chuck Finley	.10	.05
☐ 136 Angels Pennant	.05	.02
☐ 137 Angels Logo	.05	.02
☐ 138 Johnny Ray	.05	.02
☐ 139 Dante Bichette	.50	.23
☐ 140 Jim Abbott	.10	.05
☐ 141 Wally Joyner	.10	.05
☐ 142 Athletics Pennant	.05	.02
☐ 143 Athletics Logo	.05	.02
☐ 144 Dave Stewart	.10	.05
☐ 145 Mark McGwire	1.25	.55
☐ 146 Rickey Henderson	.35	.16
☐ 147 Walt Weiss	.05	.02
☐ 148 Dennis Eckersley	.15	.07
☐ 149 Jose Canseco	.35	.16
☐ 150 Dave Henderson	.05	.02
☐ 151 Bob Welch	.05	.02
☐ 152 Tony Fernandez	.05	.02
☐ 153 David Wells	.05	.02
☐ 154 Blue Jays Pennant	.05	.02
☐ 155 Blue Jays Logo	.05	.02
☐ 156 Pat Borders	.05	.02
☐ 157 Fred McGriff	.35	.16
☐ 158 George Bell	.05	.02
☐ 159 John Olerud	.15	.07
☐ 160 Dave Stieb	.05	.02
☐ 161 Kelly Gruber	.05	.02
☐ 162 Bill Spiers	.05	.02
☐ 163 Dan Plesac	.05	.02
☐ 164 Brewers Pennant	.05	.02
☐ 165 Mark Knudson	.05	.02
☐ 166 Robin Yount	.25	.11
☐ 167 Brewers Logo	.05	.02
☐ 168 Paul Molitor	.60	.25
☐ 169 B.J. Surhoff	.10	.05
☐ 170 Gary Sheffield	.40	.18
☐ 171 Dave Parker	.10	.05
☐ 172 Sandy Alomar Jr.	.10	.05
☐ 173 Doug Jones	.05	.02
☐ 174 Tom Candiotti	.05	.02
☐ 175 Mitch Webster	.05	.02
☐ 176 Indians Pennant	.05	.02
☐ 177 Indians Logo	.05	.02
☐ 178 Brook Jacoby	.05	.02
☐ 179 Candy Maldonado	.05	.02
☐ 180 Carlos Baerga	.25	.11
☐ 181 Chris James	.05	.02
☐ 182 Mariners Pennant	.05	.02
☐ 183 Mariners Logo	.05	.02
☐ 184 Mike Schooler	.05	.02
☐ 185 Alvin Davis	.05	.02
☐ 186 Erik Hanson	.05	.02
☐ 187 Edgar Martinez	.35	.16
☐ 188 Randy Johnson	.40	.18
☐ 189 Ken Griffey Jr.	3.00	1.35
☐ 190 Jay Buhner	.35	.16
☐ 191 Harold Reynolds	.10	.05
☐ 192 Cal Ripken	2.50	1.10
☐ 193 Gregg Olson	.05	.02
☐ 194 Orioles Pennant	.05	.02
☐ 195 Orioles Logo	.05	.02
☐ 196 Mike Devereaux	.05	.02
☐ 197 Ben McDonald	.05	.02
☐ 198 Craig Worthington	.05	.02
☐ 199 Dave Johnson	.05	.02
☐ 200 Joe Orsulak	.05	.02
☐ 201 Randy Milligan	.05	.02
☐ 202 Ruben Sierra	.05	.02
☐ 203 Bobby Witt	.05	.02

☐ 204 Rangers Pennant	.05	.02
☐ 205 Nolan Ryan	2.50	1.10
☐ 206 Jeff Huson	.05	.02
☐ 207 Rangers Logo	.05	.02
☐ 208 Kevin Brown	.10	.05
☐ 209 Steve Buechele	.05	.02
☐ 210 Julio Franco	.10	.05
☐ 211 Rafael Palmeiro	.35	.16
☐ 212 Ellis Burks	.10	.05
☐ 213 Dwight Evans	.10	.05
☐ 214 Wade Boggs	.30	.14
☐ 215 Roger Clemens	.75	.35
☐ 216 Red Sox Pennant	.05	.02
☐ 217 Red Sox Logo	.05	.02
☐ 218 Jeff Reardon	.05	.02
☐ 219 Tony Pena	.05	.02
☐ 220 Jody Reed	.05	.02
☐ 221 Carlos Quintana	.05	.02
☐ 222 Royals Pennant	.05	.02
☐ 223 Royals Logo	.05	.02
☐ 224 George Brett	1.25	.55
☐ 225 Bret Saberhagen	.05	.02
☐ 226 Bo Jackson	.10	.05
☐ 227 Kevin Seitzer	.05	.02
☐ 228 Mark Gubicza	.05	.02
☐ 229 Jim Eisenreich	.10	.05
☐ 230 Gerald Perry	.05	.02
☐ 231 Tom Gordon	.05	.02
☐ 232 Cecil Fielder	.10	.05
☐ 233 Lou Whitaker	.10	.05
☐ 234 Tigers Pennant	.05	.02
☐ 235 Tigers Logo	.05	.02
☐ 236 Mike Henneman	.05	.02
☐ 237 Mike Heath	.05	.02
☐ 238 Alan Trammell	.15	.07
☐ 239 Lloyd Moseby	.05	.02
☐ 240 Dan Petry	.05	.02
☐ 241 Dave Bergman	.05	.02
☐ 242 Brian Harper	.05	.02
☐ 243 Rick Aguilera	.10	.05
☐ 244 Twins Pennant	.05	.02
☐ 245 Greg Gagne	.05	.02
☐ 246 Gene Larkin	.05	.02
☐ 247 Twins Logo	.05	.02
☐ 248 Kirby Puckett	1.50	.70
☐ 249 Kevin Tapani	.05	.02
☐ 250 Gary Gaetti	.10	.05
☐ 251 Kent Hrbek	.10	.05
☐ 252 Bobby Thigpen	.05	.02
☐ 253 Lance Johnson	.10	.05
☐ 254 Greg Hibbard	.05	.02
☐ 255 Carlton Fisk	.25	.11
☐ 256 White Sox Pennant	.05	.02
☐ 257 White Sox Logo	.05	.02
☐ 258 Ivan Calderon	.05	.02
☐ 259 Barry Jones	.05	.02
☐ 260 Robin Ventura	.15	.07
☐ 261 Ozzie Guillen	.05	.02
☐ 262 Yankees Pennant	.05	.02
☐ 263 Yankees Logo	.05	.02
☐ 264 Kevin Maas	.05	.02
☐ 265 Bob Geren	.05	.02
☐ 266 Dave Righetti	.05	.02
☐ 267 Don Mattingly	1.50	.70
☐ 268 Roberto Kelly	.05	.02
☐ 269 Alvaro Espinoza	.05	.02
☐ 270 Oscar Azocar	.05	.02
☐ 271 Steve Sax	.05	.02

1991 Panini Canadian Top 15

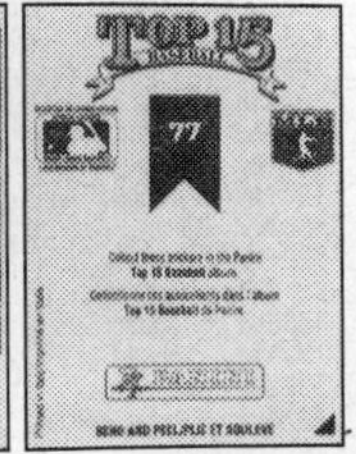

The 1991 Panini Top 15 sticker set consists of 136 stickers and features Major League's best players and teams in various statistical categories. An American and a Canadian version were issued. The stickers resemble cards insofar as they measure the standard size and are printed on a thick cardboard stock. The fronts have glossy color player photos with white borders. The player's name, team and statistical category (the last item in French and English in the Canadian version) appear below the picture. Moreover, the front also has a number (1-4) indicating the player's finish in that category, the statistic and different color emblems for the National League (blue) and the American League (red). The Gold glove winners have a gold emblem, irrespective of league. The set is subdivided according to the following statistical categories, with National League winners listed first (e.g., 1-4) and then American League winners (e.g., 5-8): batting average (1-8); home runs (9-16); runs batted in (17-24); hits (25-32); slugging average (33-40); stolen bases (41-48); runs (49-56); wins (57-64); earned run average (65-72); strikeouts (73-80); saves (81-88); shutouts (89-96); National League logo (97) and gold glove (98-106); American League logo (107) and gold glove (108-16); and team statistical leaders (117-36). The NL logo (97), AL logo (107) and all the team stickers (117-36) are foil.

	MINT	NRMT
COMPLETE SET (136)	30.00	13.50
COMMON STICKER (1-136)	.05	.02
☐ 1 Willie McGee	.10	.05
☐ 2 Eddie Murray	1.25	.55
☐ 3 Dave Magadan	.05	.02
☐ 4 Lenny Dykstra	.10	.05
☐ 5 George Brett	2.00	.90
☐ 6 Rickey Henderson	.50	.23
☐ 7 Rafael Palmeiro	.40	.18
☐ 8 Alan Trammell	.20	.09
☐ 9 Ryne Sandberg	1.25	.55
☐ 10 Darryl Strawberry	.10	.05
☐ 11 Kevin Mitchell	.05	.02
☐ 12 Barry Bonds	1.25	.55
☐ 13 Cecil Fielder	.10	.05
☐ 14 Mark McGwire	1.50	.70
☐ 15 Jose Canseco	.60	.25
☐ 16 Fred McGriff	.50	.23
☐ 17 Matt Williams	.75	.35
☐ 18 Bobby Bonilla	.10	.05
☐ 19 Joe Carter	.10	.05
☐ 20 Barry Bonds	1.25	.55
☐ 21 Cecil Fielder	.10	.05
☐ 22 Kelly Gruber	.05	.02
☐ 23 Mark McGwire	1.50	.70
☐ 24 Jose Canseco	.60	.25
☐ 25 Brett Butler	.10	.05
☐ 26 Lenny Dykstra	.10	.05
☐ 27 Ryne Sandberg	1.25	.55
☐ 28 Barry Larkin	.40	.18
☐ 29 Rafael Palmeiro	.50	.23
☐ 30 Wade Boggs	.60	.25
☐ 31 Roberto Kelly	.05	.02
☐ 32 Mike Greenwell	.05	.02
☐ 33 Barry Bonds	1.25	.55
☐ 34 Ryne Sandberg	1.25	.55
☐ 35 Kevin Mitchell	.05	.02
☐ 36 Ron Gant	.10	.05
☐ 37 Cecil Fielder	.10	.05
☐ 38 Rickey Henderson	.50	.23
☐ 39 Jose Canseco	.60	.25
☐ 40 Fred McGriff	.50	.23
☐ 41 Vince Coleman	.05	.02
☐ 42 Eric Yelding	.05	.02
☐ 43 Barry Bonds	1.25	.55
☐ 44 Brett Butler	.10	.05
☐ 45 Rickey Henderson	.50	.23
☐ 46 Steve Sax	.05	.02
☐ 47 Roberto Kelly	.05	.02
☐ 48 Alex Cole	.05	.02
☐ 49 Ryne Sandberg	1.25	.55
☐ 50 Bobby Bonilla	.10	.05
☐ 51 Brett Butler	.10	.05
☐ 52 Ron Gant	.10	.05
☐ 53 Rickey Henderson	.50	.23
☐ 54 Cecil Fielder	.10	.05
☐ 55 Harold Reynolds	.10	.05
☐ 56 Robin Yount	.40	.18
☐ 57 Doug Drabek	.05	.02
☐ 58 Ramon Martinez	.20	.09
☐ 59 Frank Viola	.05	.02
☐ 60 Dwight Gooden	.10	.05
☐ 61 Bob Welch	.05	.02
☐ 62 Dave Stewart	.10	.05
☐ 63 Roger Clemens	1.00	.45
☐ 64 Dave Stieb	.05	.02
☐ 65 Danny Darwin	.05	.02
☐ 66 Zane Smith	.05	.02
☐ 67 Ed Whitson	.05	.02
☐ 68 Frank Viola	.05	.02
☐ 69 Roger Clemens	1.00	.45
☐ 70 Chuck Finley	.10	.05
☐ 71 Dave Stewart	.10	.05
☐ 72 Kevin Appier	.20	.09
☐ 73 David Cone	.10	.05
☐ 74 Dwight Gooden	.10	.05
☐ 75 Ramon Martinez	.10	.05
☐ 76 Frank Viola	.05	.02
☐ 77 Nolan Ryan	3.00	1.35
☐ 78 Bobby Witt	.05	.02
☐ 79 Erik Hanson	.05	.02
☐ 80 Roger Clemens	1.00	.45
☐ 81 John Franco	.10	.05
☐ 82 Randy Myers	.10	.05
☐ 83 Lee Smith	.10	.05
☐ 84 Craig Lefferts	.05	.02
☐ 85 Bobby Thigpen	.05	.02
☐ 86 Dennis Eckersley	.20	.09
☐ 87 Doug Jones	.05	.02
☐ 88 Gregg Olson	.05	.02
☐ 89 Mike Morgan	.05	.02
☐ 90 Bruce Hurst	.05	.02
☐ 91 Mark Gardner	.05	.02
☐ 92 Doug Drabek	.05	.02
☐ 93 Dave Stewart	.10	.05
☐ 94 Roger Clemens	1.00	.45
☐ 95 Kevin Appier	.20	.09
☐ 96 Melido Perez	.05	.02
☐ 97 National League	.05	.02
☐ 98 Greg Maddux	3.00	1.35
☐ 99 Benito Santiago	.05	.02
☐ 100 Andres Galarraga	.50	.23
☐ 101 Ryne Sandberg	1.25	.55
☐ 102 Tim Wallach	.05	.02
☐ 103 Ozzie Smith	1.25	.55
☐ 104 Tony Gwynn	2.00	.90
☐ 105 Barry Bonds	1.25	.55
☐ 106 Andy Van Slyke	.10	.05
☐ 107 American League	.05	.02
☐ 108 Mike Boddicker	.05	.02
☐ 109 Sandy Alomar Jr.	.10	.05
☐ 110 Mark McGwire	1.50	.70
☐ 111 Harold Reynolds	.10	.05
☐ 112 Kelly Gruber	.05	.02
☐ 113 Ozzie Guillen	.05	.02
☐ 114 Ellis Burks	.10	.05
☐ 115 Gary Pettis	.05	.02
☐ 116 Ken Griffey Jr.	5.00	2.20
☐ 117 Cincinnati Reds Highest Batting Average	.05	.02
☐ 118 New York Mets Most Home Runs	.05	.02
☐ 119 New York Mets Most Runs Scored	.05	.02
☐ 120 Chicago Cubs Most Hits	.05	.02
☐ 121 Montreal Expos Most Stolen Bases	.05	.02
☐ 122 Boston Red Sox Highest Batting Average	.05	.02
☐ 123 Detroit Tigers Most Home Runs	.05	.02
☐ 124 Toronto Blue Jays Most Runs Scored	.05	.02
☐ 125 Boston Red Sox Most Hits	.05	.02
☐ 126 Milwaukee Brewers Most Stolen Bases	.05	.02
☐ 127 Philadelphia Phillies Most Double Plays	.05	.02
☐ 128 Cincinnati Reds Fewest Errors	.05	.02
☐ 129 Montreal Expos Best ERA	.05	.02
☐ 130 New York Mets Most Shutouts	.05	.02
☐ 131 Cincinnati Reds Most Saves	.05	.02
☐ 132 California Angels Most Double Plays	.05	.02
☐ 133 Toronto Blue Jays Fewest Errors	.05	.02
☐ 134 Oakland Athletics Best ERA	.05	.02
☐ 135 Oakland Athletics Most Shutouts	.05	.02
☐ 136 Chicago White Sox Most Saves	.05	.02

1991 Panini French Stickers

The French version of the 1991 Panini baseball set contains 360 stickers measuring approximately 2 1/8" by 3". The fronts display color action player photos bordered in white. The player's name and team are given beneath the picture. NL players have a blue stripe in the lower left corner, while AL players have a red stripe in the same location. Included in the set are foil stickers of team pennants, logos and league insignias. The stickers may be pasted in a collectible sticker album that measures 8 1/4" by 10 1/2". The stickers are checklisted alphabetically according to teams within the NL and then the AL, with the Canadian teams listed after each league. A special

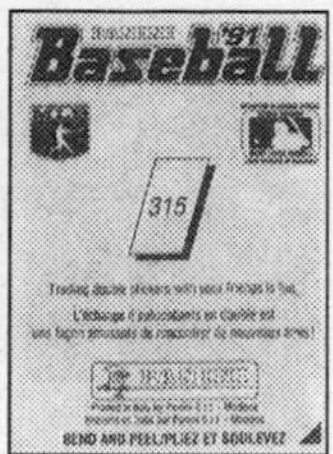

Year of the No-Hitter (352-360) subset is included at the end of the set.

	MINT	NRMT
COMPLETE SET (360)	25.00	11.00
COMMON STICKER (1-360)	.05	.02
☐ 1 MLB Logo	.05	.02
☐ 2 MLBPA Logo	.05	.02
☐ 3 Panini Baseball 1991 Logo	.05	.02
☐ 4 Astros Pennant	.05	.02
☐ 5 Astros Logo	.05	.02
☐ 6 Craig Biggio	.40	.18
☐ 7 Glenn Davis	.05	.02
☐ 8 Casey Candaele	.05	.02
☐ 9 Ken Caminiti	.40	.18
☐ 10 Rafael Ramirez	.05	.02
☐ 11 Glenn Wilson	.05	.02
☐ 12 Eric Yelding	.05	.02
☐ 13 Franklin Stubbs	.05	.02
☐ 14 Mike Scott	.05	.02
☐ 15 Danny Darwin	.05	.02
☐ 16 Braves Pennant	.05	.02
☐ 17 Braves Logo	.05	.02
☐ 18 Greg Olson	.05	.02
☐ 19 Tommy Gregg	.05	.02
☐ 20 Jeff Treadway	.05	.02
☐ 21 Jim Presley	.05	.02
☐ 22 Jeff Blauser	.05	.02
☐ 23 Ron Gant	.10	.05
☐ 24 Lonnie Smith	.05	.02
☐ 25 Dave Justice	.50	.23
☐ 26 John Smoltz	.40	.18
☐ 27 Charlie Leibrandt	.05	.02
☐ 28 Cardinals Pennant	.05	.02
☐ 29 Cardinals Logo	.05	.02
☐ 30 Tom Pagnozzi	.05	.02
☐ 31 Pedro Guerrero	.05	.02
☐ 32 Jose Oquendo	.05	.02
☐ 33 Todd Zeile	.05	.02
☐ 34 Ozzie Smith	.75	.35
☐ 35 Vince Coleman	.05	.02
☐ 36 Milt Thompson	.05	.02
☐ 37 Rex Hudler	.05	.02
☐ 38 Joe Magrane	.05	.02
☐ 39 Lee Smith	.10	.05
☐ 40 Cubs Pennant	.05	.02
☐ 41 Cubs Logo	.05	.02
☐ 42 Joe Girardi	.05	.02
☐ 43 Mark Grace	.35	.16
☐ 44 Ryne Sandberg	.75	.35
☐ 45 Luis Salazar	.05	.02
☐ 46 Shawon Dunston	.05	.02
☐ 47 Dwight Smith	.05	.02
☐ 48 Jerome Walton	.05	.02
☐ 49 Andre Dawson	.25	.11
☐ 50 Greg Maddux	2.00	.90
☐ 51 Mike Harkey	.05	.02
☐ 52 Dodgers Pennant	.05	.02
☐ 53 Dodgers Logo	.05	.02
☐ 54 Mike Scioscia	.05	.02
☐ 55 Eddie Murray	.75	.35
☐ 56 Juan Samuel	.05	.02
☐ 57 Lenny Harris	.05	.02
☐ 58 Alfredo Griffin	.05	.02
☐ 59 Hubie Brooks	.05	.02
☐ 60 Kal Daniels	.05	.02
☐ 61 Stan Javier	.05	.02
☐ 62 Ramon Martinez	.15	.07
☐ 63 Mike Morgan	.05	.02
☐ 64 Giants Pennant	.05	.02
☐ 65 Giants Logo	.05	.02
☐ 66 Terry Kennedy	.05	.02
☐ 67 Will Clark	.35	.16
☐ 68 Robby Thompson	.05	.02
☐ 69 Matt Williams	.35	.16
☐ 70 Jose Uribe	.05	.02
☐ 71 Kevin Mitchell	.05	.02
☐ 72 Brett Butler	.10	.05
☐ 73 Don Robinson	.05	.02
☐ 74 John Burkett	.05	.02
☐ 75 Jeff Brantley	.05	.02
☐ 76 Mets Pennant	.05	.02
☐ 77 Mets Logo	.05	.02
☐ 78 Mackey Sasser	.05	.02
☐ 79 Dave Magadan	.05	.02
☐ 80 Gregg Jefferies	.10	.05
☐ 81 Howard Johnson	.05	.02
☐ 82 Kevin Elster	.05	.02
☐ 83 Kevin McReynolds	.05	.02
☐ 84 Daryl Boston	.05	.02
☐ 85 Darryl Strawberry	.10	.05
☐ 86 Dwight Gooden	.10	.05
☐ 87 Frank Viola	.05	.02
☐ 88 Padres Pennant	.05	.02
☐ 89 Padres Logo	.05	.02
☐ 90 Benito Santiago	.05	.02
☐ 91 Jack Clark	.05	.02
☐ 92 Roberto Alomar	.60	.25
☐ 93 Mike Pagliarulo	.05	.02
☐ 94 Garry Templeton	.05	.02
☐ 95 Joe Carter	.10	.05
☐ 96 Bip Roberts	.05	.02
☐ 97 Tony Gwynn	1.50	.70
☐ 98 Ed Whitson	.05	.02
☐ 99 Andy Benes	.10	.05
☐ 100 Phillies Pennant	.05	.02
☐ 101 Phillies Logo	.05	.02
☐ 102 Darren Daulton	.10	.05
☐ 103 Ricky Jordan	.05	.02
☐ 104 Randy Ready	.05	.02
☐ 105 Charlie Hayes	.05	.02
☐ 106 Dickie Thon	.05	.02
☐ 107 Von Hayes	.05	.02
☐ 108 Len Dykstra	.10	.05
☐ 109 Dale Murphy	.25	.11
☐ 110 Ken Howell	.05	.02
☐ 111 Roger McDowell	.05	.02
☐ 112 Pirates Pennant	.05	.02
☐ 113 Pirates Logo	.05	.02
☐ 114 Mike LaValliere	.05	.02
☐ 115 Sid Bream	.05	.02
☐ 116 Jose Lind	.05	.02
☐ 117 Jeff King	.05	.02
☐ 118 Jay Bell	.05	.02
☐ 119 Barry Bonds	.75	.35
☐ 120 Bobby Bonilla	.10	.05
☐ 121 Andy Van Slyke	.10	.05
☐ 122 Doug Drabek	.05	.02
☐ 123 Neal Heaton	.05	.02
☐ 124 Reds Pennant	.05	.02
☐ 125 Reds Logo	.05	.02
☐ 126 Joe Oliver	.05	.02
☐ 127 Todd Benzinger	.05	.02
☐ 128 Mariano Duncan	.05	.02
☐ 129 Chris Sabo	.05	.02
☐ 130 Barry Larkin	.40	.18
☐ 131 Eric Davis	.10	.05
☐ 132 Billy Hatcher	.05	.02
☐ 133 Paul O'Neill	.10	.05
☐ 134 Jose Rijo	.05	.02
☐ 135 Randy Myers	.10	.05
☐ 136 Expos Pennant	.05	.02
☐ 137 Expos Logo	.05	.02
☐ 138 Mike Fitzgerald	.05	.02
☐ 139 Andres Galarraga	.35	.16
☐ 140 Delino DeShields	.05	.02
☐ 141 Tim Wallach	.05	.02
☐ 142 Spike Owen	.05	.02
☐ 143 Tim Raines	.10	.05
☐ 144 Dave Martinez	.05	.02
☐ 145 Larry Walker	.50	.23
☐ 146 Expos Helmet	.05	.02
☐ 147 Dennis Boyd	.05	.02
☐ 148 Tim Burke	.05	.02
☐ 149 Bill Sampen	.05	.02
☐ 150 Dennis Martinez	.10	.05
☐ 151 Marquis Grissom	.50	.23
☐ 152 Otis Nixon	.10	.05
☐ 153 Jerry Goff	.05	.02
☐ 154 Steve Frey	.05	.02
☐ 155 NL Emblem	.05	.02
☐ 156 AL Emblem	.05	.02
☐ 157 Benito Santiago	.05	.02
☐ 158 Will Clark	.35	.16
☐ 159 Ryne Sandberg	.75	.35
☐ 160 Chris Sabo	.05	.02
☐ 161 Ozzie Smith	.75	.35
☐ 162 Kevin Mitchell	.05	.02
☐ 163 Len Dykstra	.10	.05
☐ 164 Darryl Strawberry	.10	.05
☐ 165 Jack Armstrong	.05	.02
☐ 166 Sandy Alomar Jr.	.10	.05
☐ 167 Mark McGwire	1.00	.45
☐ 168 Steve Sax	.05	.02
☐ 169 Wade Boggs	.35	.16
☐ 170 Cal Ripken	2.50	1.10
☐ 171 Rickey Henderson	.40	.18
☐ 172 Ken Griffey Jr.	3.00	1.35
☐ 173 Jose Canseco	.40	.18
☐ 174 Bob Welch	.05	.02
☐ 175 Wrigley Field	.05	.02
☐ 176 World Series Trophy	.05	.02
☐ 177 Angels Pennant	.05	.02
☐ 178 Angels Logo	.05	.02
☐ 179 Lance Parrish	.05	.02
☐ 180 Wally Joyner	.10	.05
☐ 181 Johnny Ray	.05	.02
☐ 182 Jack Howell	.05	.02
☐ 183 Dick Schofield	.05	.02
☐ 184 Dave Winfield	.40	.18
☐ 185 Devon White	.05	.02
☐ 186 Dante Bichette	.40	.18
☐ 187 Chuck Finley	.10	.05
☐ 188 Jim Abbott	.10	.05
☐ 189 Athletics Pennant	.05	.02
☐ 190 Athletics Logo	.05	.02
☐ 191 Terry Steinbach	.05	.02
☐ 192 Mark McGwire	1.00	.45
☐ 193 Willie Randolph	.10	.05
☐ 194 Carney Lansford	.05	.02
☐ 195 Walt Weiss	.05	.02
☐ 196 Rickey Henderson	.35	.16
☐ 197 Dave Henderson	.05	.02
☐ 198 Jose Canseco	.40	.18
☐ 199 Dave Stewart	.10	.05
☐ 200 Dennis Eckersley	.15	.07
☐ 201 Brewers Pennant	.05	.02
☐ 202 Brewers Logo	.05	.02
☐ 203 B.J. Surhoff	.10	.05
☐ 204 Greg Brock	.05	.02
☐ 205 Paul Molitor	.75	.35
☐ 206 Gary Sheffield	.50	.23
☐ 207 Bill Spiers	.05	.02
☐ 208 Robin Yount	.40	.18
☐ 209 Rob Deer	.05	.02
☐ 210 Dave Parker	.10	.05
☐ 211 Mark Knudson	.05	.02
☐ 212 Dan Plesac	.05	.02
☐ 213 Indians Pennant	.05	.02
☐ 214 Indians Logo	.05	.02
☐ 215 Sandy Alomar Jr.	.10	.05
☐ 216 Brook Jacoby	.05	.02
☐ 217 Jerry Browne	.05	.02
☐ 218 Carlos Baerga	.40	.18
☐ 219 Felix Fermin	.05	.02
☐ 220 Candy Maldonado	.05	.02
☐ 221 Cory Snyder	.05	.02
☐ 222 Alex Cole	.05	.02
☐ 223 Tom Candiotti	.05	.02
☐ 224 Doug Jones	.05	.02
☐ 225 Mariners Pennant	.05	.02
☐ 226 Mariners Logo	.05	.02
☐ 227 Dave Valle	.05	.02
☐ 228 Pete O'Brien	.05	.02
☐ 229 Harold Reynolds	.10	.05
☐ 230 Edgar Martinez	.35	.16
☐ 231 Omar Vizquel	.25	.11
☐ 232 Henry Cotto	.05	.02
☐ 233 Ken Griffey Jr.	3.00	1.35
☐ 234 Jay Buhner	.35	.16
☐ 235 Erik Hanson	.05	.02
☐ 236 Mike Schooler	.05	.02
☐ 237 Orioles Pennant	.05	.02
☐ 238 Orioles Logo	.05	.02
☐ 239 Mickey Tettleton	.05	.02
☐ 240 Randy Milligan	.05	.02
☐ 241 Bill Ripken	.05	.02
☐ 242 Craig Worthington	.05	.02
☐ 243 Cal Ripken	2.50	1.10
☐ 244 Steve Finley	.10	.05
☐ 245 Mike Devereaux	.05	.02
☐ 246 Joe Orsulak	.05	.02
☐ 247 Ben McDonald	.05	.02
☐ 248 Gregg Olson	.05	.02
☐ 249 Rangers Pennant	.05	.02
☐ 250 Rangers Logo	.05	.02
☐ 251 Geno Petralli	.05	.02
☐ 252 Rafael Palmeiro	.35	.16
☐ 253 Julio Franco	.10	.05
☐ 254 Steve Buechele	.05	.02
☐ 255 Jeff Huson	.05	.02
☐ 256 Gary Pettis	.05	.02
☐ 257 Ruben Sierra	.05	.02
☐ 258 Pete Incaviglia	.05	.02
☐ 259 Nolan Ryan	2.50	1.10
☐ 260 Bobby Witt	.05	.02
☐ 261 Red Sox Pennant	.05	.02
☐ 262 Red Sox Logo	.05	.02
☐ 263 Tony Pena	.05	.02
☐ 264 Carlos Quintana	.05	.02
☐ 265 Jody Reed	.05	.02
☐ 266 Wade Boggs	.35	.16
☐ 267 Luis Rivera	.05	.02
☐ 268 Mike Greenwell	.05	.02
☐ 269 Ellis Burks	.10	.05
☐ 270 Tom Brunansky	.05	.02

☐ 271 Roger Clemens	.75	.35
☐ 272 Jeff Reardon	.05	.02
☐ 273 Royals Pennant	.05	.02
☐ 274 Royals Logo	.05	.02
☐ 275 Mike Macfarlane	.05	.02
☐ 276 George Brett	1.25	.55
☐ 277 Bill Pecota	.05	.02
☐ 278 Kevin Seitzer	.05	.02
☐ 279 Kurt Stillwell	.05	.02
☐ 280 Jim Eisenreich	.10	.05
☐ 281 Bo Jackson	.10	.05
☐ 282 Danny Tartabull	.05	.02
☐ 283 Bret Saberhagen	.10	.05
☐ 284 Tom Gordon	.05	.02
☐ 285 Tigers Pennant	.05	.02
☐ 286 Tigers Logo	.05	.02
☐ 287 Mike Heath	.05	.02
☐ 288 Cecil Fielder	.10	.05
☐ 289 Lou Whitaker	.10	.05
☐ 290 Tony Phillips	.05	.02
☐ 291 Alan Trammell	.15	.07
☐ 292 Chet Lemon	.05	.02
☐ 293 Lloyd Moseby	.05	.02
☐ 294 Gary Ward	.05	.02
☐ 295 Dan Petry	.05	.02
☐ 296 Jack Morris	.10	.05
☐ 297 Twins Pennant	.05	.02
☐ 298 Twins Logo	.05	.02
☐ 299 Brian Harper	.05	.02
☐ 300 Kent Hrbek	.10	.05
☐ 301 Al Newman	.05	.02
☐ 302 Gary Gaetti	.05	.02
☐ 303 Greg Gagne	.05	.02
☐ 304 Dan Gladden	.05	.02
☐ 305 Kirby Puckett	1.50	.70
☐ 306 Gene Larkin	.05	.02
☐ 307 Kevin Tapani	.05	.02
☐ 308 Rick Aguilera	.10	.05
☐ 309 White Sox Pennant	.05	.02
☐ 310 White Sox Logo	.05	.02
☐ 311 Carlton Fisk	.40	.18
☐ 312 Carlos Martinez	.05	.02
☐ 313 Scott Fletcher	.05	.02
☐ 314 Robin Ventura	.10	.05
☐ 315 Ozzie Guillen	.05	.02
☐ 316 Sammy Sosa	.60	.25
☐ 317 Lance Johnson	.10	.05
☐ 318 Ivan Calderon	.05	.02
☐ 319 Greg Hibbard	.05	.02
☐ 320 Bobby Thigpen	.05	.02
☐ 321 Yankees Pennant	.05	.02
☐ 322 Yankees Logo	.05	.02
☐ 323 Bob Geren	.05	.02
☐ 324 Don Mattingly	1.50	.70
☐ 325 Steve Sax	.05	.02
☐ 326 Jim Leyritz	.05	.02
☐ 327 Alvaro Espinoza	.05	.02
☐ 328 Roberto Kelly	.05	.02
☐ 329 Oscar Azocar	.05	.02
☐ 330 Jesse Barfield	.05	.02
☐ 331 Chuck Cary	.05	.02
☐ 332 Dave Righetti	.05	.02
☐ 333 Blue Jays Pennant	.05	.02
☐ 334 Blue Jays Logo	.05	.02
☐ 335 Pat Borders	.05	.02
☐ 336 Fred McGriff	.35	.16
☐ 337 Manny Lee	.05	.02
☐ 338 Kelly Gruber	.05	.02
☐ 339 Tony Fernandez	.05	.02
☐ 340 George Bell	.05	.02
☐ 341 Mookie Wilson	.05	.02
☐ 342 Junior Felix	.05	.02
☐ 343 Blue Jays Helmet	.05	.02
☐ 344 Dave Stieb	.05	.02
☐ 345 Tom Henke	.10	.05
☐ 346 Greg Myers	.05	.02
☐ 347 Glenallen Hill	.05	.02
☐ 348 John Olerud	.10	.05
☐ 349 Todd Stottlemyre	.10	.05
☐ 350 David Wells	.05	.02
☐ 351 Jimmy Key	.10	.05
☐ 352 Mark Langston	.05	.02
☐ 353 Randy Johnson	.50	.23
☐ 354 Nolan Ryan	2.50	1.10
☐ 355 Dave Stewart	.10	.05
☐ 356 Fernando Valenzuela	.10	.05
☐ 357 Andy Hawkins	.05	.02
☐ 358 Melido Perez	.05	.02
☐ 359 Terry Mulholland	.05	.02
☐ 360 Dave Stieb	.05	.02

1992 Panini Stickers

These 288 stickers measure approximately 2 1/8" by 3" and feature on their fronts white-bordered color player action shots that are serrated on their left sides and are

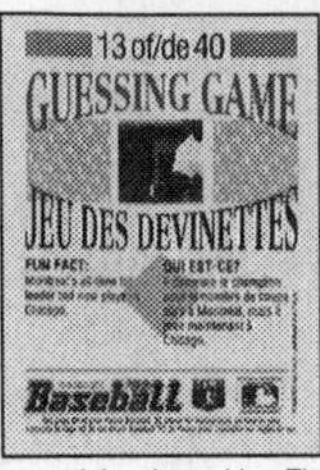

framed by a colored line on the remaining three sides. The stickers and album used to store them are organized by team. The Best of the Best AL (144-146), The Best of the Best NL (147-149) and 1991 All-Stars (270-288) are the subsets included within the set.

	MINT	NRMT
COMPLETE SET (288)	15.00	6.75
COMMON STICKER (1-288)	.05	.02

☐ 1 Panini Baseball 1992 Logo	.05	.02
☐ 2 MLB Logo	.05	.02
☐ 3 MLBPA Logo	.05	.02
☐ 4 Lance Parrish	.05	.02
☐ 5 Wally Joyner	.10	.05
☐ 6 Luis Sojo	.05	.02
☐ 7 Gary Gaetti	.05	.02
☐ 8 Dick Schofield	.05	.02
☐ 9 Junior Felix	.05	.02
☐ 10 Luis Polonia	.05	.02
☐ 11 Mark Langston	.05	.02
☐ 12 Jim Abbott	.10	.05
☐ 13 Angels Team Logo	.05	.02
☐ 14 Terry Steinbach	.05	.02
☐ 15 Mark McGwire	1.00	.45
☐ 16 Mike Gallego	.05	.02
☐ 17 Carney Lansford	.05	.02
☐ 18 Walt Weiss	.05	.02
☐ 19 Jose Canseco	.40	.18
☐ 20 Dave Henderson	.05	.02
☐ 21 Rickey Henderson	.30	.14
☐ 22 Dennis Eckersley	.15	.07
☐ 23 Athletics Team Logo	.05	.02
☐ 24 Pat Borders	.05	.02
☐ 25 John Olerud	.10	.05
☐ 26 Roberto Alomar	.40	.18
☐ 27 Kelly Gruber	.05	.02
☐ 28 Manuel Lee	.05	.02
☐ 29 Joe Carter	.10	.05
☐ 30 Devon White	.05	.02
☐ 31 Candy Maldonado	.05	.02
☐ 32 Dave Stieb	.05	.02
☐ 33 Blue Jays Team Logo	.05	.02
☐ 34 B.J. Surhoff	.10	.05
☐ 35 Franklin Stubbs	.05	.02
☐ 36 Willie Randolph	.10	.05
☐ 37 Jim Gantner	.05	.02
☐ 38 Bill Spiers	.05	.02
☐ 39 Dante Bichette	.15	.07
☐ 40 Robin Yount	.25	.11
☐ 41 Greg Vaughn	.05	.02
☐ 42 Chris Bosio	.05	.02
☐ 43 Brewers Team Logo	.05	.02
☐ 44 Sandy Alomar Jr.	.10	.05
☐ 45 Mike Aldrete	.05	.02
☐ 46 Mark Lewis	.05	.02
☐ 47 Carlos Baerga	.10	.05
☐ 48 Felix Fermin	.05	.02
☐ 49 Mark Whiten	.05	.02
☐ 50 Alex Cole	.05	.02
☐ 51 Albert Belle	.75	.35
☐ 52 Greg Swindell	.05	.02
☐ 53 Indians Team Logo	.05	.02
☐ 54 Dave Valle	.05	.02
☐ 55 Pete O'Brien	.05	.02
☐ 56 Harold Reynolds	.10	.05
☐ 57 Edgar Martinez	.30	.14
☐ 58 Omar Vizquel	.10	.05
☐ 59 Jay Buhner	.30	.14
☐ 60 Ken Griffey Jr.	2.50	1.10
☐ 61 Greg Briley	.05	.02
☐ 62 Randy Johnson	.40	.18
☐ 63 Mariners Team Logo	.05	.02
☐ 64 Chris Hoiles	.05	.02
☐ 65 Randy Milligan	.05	.02
☐ 66 Bill Ripken	.05	.02
☐ 67 Leo Gomez	.05	.02
☐ 68 Cal Ripken	2.00	.90
☐ 69 Dwight Evans	.10	.05
☐ 70 Mike Devereaux	.05	.02
☐ 71 Joe Orsulak	.05	.02
☐ 72 Gregg Olson	.05	.02
☐ 73 Orioles Team Logo	.05	.02
☐ 74 Ivan Rodriguez	1.00	.45
☐ 75 Rafael Palmeiro	.30	.14
☐ 76 Julio Franco	.10	.05
☐ 77 Dean Palmer	.10	.05
☐ 78 Jeff Huson	.05	.02
☐ 79 Ruben Sierra	.05	.02
☐ 80 Gary Pettis	.05	.02
☐ 81 Juan Gonzalez	1.25	.55
☐ 82 Nolan Ryan	2.00	.90
☐ 83 Rangers Team Logo	.05	.02
☐ 84 Tony Pena	.05	.02
☐ 85 Carlos Quintana	.05	.02
☐ 86 Jody Reed	.05	.02
☐ 87 Wade Boggs	.30	.14
☐ 88 Luis Rivera	.05	.02
☐ 89 Tom Brunansky	.05	.02
☐ 90 Ellis Burks	.10	.05
☐ 91 Mike Greenwell	.05	.02
☐ 92 Roger Clemens	.50	.23
☐ 93 Red Sox Team Logo	.05	.02
☐ 94 Todd Benzinger	.05	.02
☐ 95 Terry Shumpert	.05	.02
☐ 96 Bill Pecota	.05	.02
☐ 97 Kurt Stillwell	.05	.02
☐ 98 Danny Tartabull	.05	.02
☐ 99 Brian McRae	.05	.02
☐ 100 Kirk Gibson	.10	.05
☐ 101 Bret Saberhagen	.10	.05
☐ 102 George Brett	1.00	.45
☐ 103 Royals Team Logo	.05	.02
☐ 104 Mickey Tettleton	.05	.02
☐ 105 Cecil Fielder	.10	.05
☐ 106 Lou Whitaker	.10	.05
☐ 107 Travis Fryman	.15	.07
☐ 108 Alan Trammell	.15	.07
☐ 109 Rob Deer	.05	.02
☐ 110 Milt Cuyler	.05	.02
☐ 111 Lloyd Moseby	.05	.02
☐ 112 Bill Gullickson	.05	.02
☐ 113 Tigers Team Logo	.05	.02
☐ 114 Brian Harper	.05	.02
☐ 115 Kent Hrbek	.10	.05
☐ 116 Chuck Knoblauch	.50	.23
☐ 117 Mike Pagliarulo	.05	.02
☐ 118 Greg Gagne	.05	.02
☐ 119 Shane Mack	.05	.02
☐ 120 Kirby Puckett	1.25	.55
☐ 121 Dan Gladden	.05	.02
☐ 122 Jack Morris	.10	.05
☐ 123 Twins Team Logo	.05	.02
☐ 124 Carlton Fisk	.25	.11
☐ 125 Frank Thomas	2.50	1.10
☐ 126 Joey Cora	.10	.05
☐ 127 Robin Ventura	.10	.05
☐ 128 Ozzie Guillen	.05	.02
☐ 129 Sammy Sosa	.30	.14
☐ 130 Lance Johnson	.10	.05
☐ 131 Tim Raines	.10	.05
☐ 132 Bobby Thigpen	.05	.02
☐ 133 White Sox Team Logo	.05	.02
☐ 134 Matt Nokes	.05	.02
☐ 135 Don Mattingly	1.25	.55
☐ 136 Steve Sax	.05	.02
☐ 137 Pat Kelly	.05	.02
☐ 138 Alvaro Espinoza	.05	.02
☐ 139 Jesse Barfield	.05	.02
☐ 140 Roberto Kelly	.05	.02
☐ 141 Mel Hall	.05	.02
☐ 142 Scott Sanderson	.05	.02
☐ 143 Yankees Team Logo	.05	.02
☐ 144 Cecil Fielder Jose Canseco	.15	.07
☐ 145 Julio Franco	.10	.05
☐ 146 Roger Clemens	.50	.23
☐ 147 Howard Johnson	.05	.02
☐ 148 Terry Pendleton	.05	.02
☐ 149 Dennis Martinez	.10	.05
☐ 150 Astros Team Logo	.05	.02
☐ 151 Craig Biggio	.15	.07
☐ 152 Jeff Bagwell	1.25	.55
☐ 153 Casey Candaele	.05	.02
☐ 154 Ken Caminiti	.30	.14
☐ 155 Andujar Cedeno	.05	.02
☐ 156 Mike Simms	.05	.02
☐ 157 Steve Finley	.10	.05
☐ 158 Luis Gonzalez	.05	.02
☐ 159 Pete Harnisch	.05	.02
☐ 160 Braves Team Logo	.05	.02
☐ 161 Greg Olson	.05	.02
☐ 162 Sid Bream	.05	.02
☐ 163 Mark Lemke	.05	.02
☐ 164 Terry Pendleton	.05	.02
☐ 165 Rafael Belliard	.05	.02
☐ 166 Dave Justice	.25	.11
☐ 167 Ron Gant	.10	.05
☐ 168 Lonnie Smith	.05	.02
☐ 169 Steve Avery	.05	.02

☐ 170 Cardinals Team Logo .05 .02
☐ 171 Tom Pagnozzi .05 .02
☐ 172 Pedro Guerrero .05 .02
☐ 173 Jose Oquendo .05 .02
☐ 174 Todd Zeile .05 .02
☐ 175 Ozzie Smith .60 .25
☐ 176 Felix Jose .05 .02
☐ 177 Ray Lankford .15 .07
☐ 178 Jose DeLeon .05 .02
☐ 179 Lee Smith .10 .05
☐ 180 Cubs Team Logo .05 .02
☐ 181 Hector Villanueva .05 .02
☐ 182 Mark Grace .15 .07
☐ 183 Ryne Sandberg .60 .25
☐ 184 Luis Salazar .05 .02
☐ 185 Shawon Dunston .05 .02
☐ 186 Andre Dawson .25 .11
☐ 187 Jerome Walton .05 .02
☐ 188 George Bell .05 .02
☐ 189 Greg Maddux 1.50 .70
☐ 190 Dodgers Team Logo .05 .02
☐ 191 Mike Scioscia .05 .02
☐ 192 Eddie Murray .60 .25
☐ 193 Juan Samuel .05 .02
☐ 194 Lenny Harris .05 .02
☐ 195 Alfredo Griffin .05 .02
☐ 196 Darryl Strawberry .10 .05
☐ 197 Brett Butler .10 .05
☐ 198 Kal Daniels .05 .02
☐ 199 Orel Hershiser .10 .05
☐ 200 Expos Team Logo .05 .02
☐ 201 Gilberto Reyes .05 .02
☐ 202 Andres Galarraga .30 .14
☐ 203 Delino DeShields .05 .02
☐ 204 Tim Wallach .05 .02
☐ 205 Spike Owen .05 .02
☐ 206 Larry Walker .40 .18
☐ 207 Marquis Grissom .40 .18
☐ 208 Ivan Calderon .05 .02
☐ 209 Dennis Martinez .10 .05
☐ 210 Giants Team Logo .05 .02
☐ 211 Steve Decker .05 .02
☐ 212 Will Clark .30 .14
☐ 213 Robby Thompson .05 .02
☐ 214 Matt Williams .40 .18
☐ 215 Jose Uribe .05 .02
☐ 216 Kevin Bass .05 .02
☐ 217 Willie McGee .10 .05
☐ 218 Kevin Mitchell .05 .02
☐ 219 Dave Righetti .05 .02
☐ 220 Mets Team Logo .05 .02
☐ 221 Rick Cerone .05 .02
☐ 222 Dave Magadan .05 .02
☐ 223 Gregg Jefferies .10 .05
☐ 224 Howard Johnson .05 .02
☐ 225 Kevin Elster .05 .02
☐ 226 Hubie Brooks .05 .02
☐ 227 Vince Coleman .05 .02
☐ 228 Kevin McReynolds .05 .02
☐ 229 Frank Viola .05 .02
☐ 230 Padres Team Logo .05 .02
☐ 231 Benito Santiago .05 .02
☐ 232 Fred McGriff .30 .14
☐ 233 Bip Roberts .05 .02
☐ 234 Jack Howell .05 .02
☐ 235 Tony Fernandez .05 .02
☐ 236 Tony Gwynn 1.25 .55
☐ 237 Darrin Jackson .05 .02
☐ 238 Bruce Hurst .05 .02
☐ 239 Craig Lefferts .05 .02
☐ 240 Phillies Team Logo .05 .02
☐ 241 Darren Daulton .10 .05
☐ 242 John Kruk .10 .05
☐ 243 Mickey Morandini .05 .02
☐ 244 Charlie Hayes .05 .02
☐ 245 Dickie Thon .05 .02
☐ 246 Dale Murphy .25 .11
☐ 247 Lenny Dykstra .10 .05
☐ 248 Von Hayes .05 .02
☐ 249 Terry Mulholland .05 .02
☐ 250 Pirates Team Logo .05 .02
☐ 251 Mike LaValliere .05 .02
☐ 252 Orlando Merced .05 .02
☐ 253 Jose Lind .05 .02
☐ 254 Steve Buechele .05 .02
☐ 255 Jay Bell .05 .02
☐ 256 Bobby Bonilla .10 .05
☐ 257 Andy Van Slyke .05 .02
☐ 258 Barry Bonds .60 .25
☐ 259 Doug Drabek .05 .02
☐ 260 Reds Team Logo .05 .02
☐ 261 Joe Oliver .05 .02
☐ 262 Hal Morris .05 .02
☐ 263 Bill Doran .05 .02
☐ 264 Chris Sabo .05 .02
☐ 265 Barry Larkin .25 .11
☐ 266 Paul O'Neill .10 .05
☐ 267 Eric Davis .10 .05
☐ 268 Glenn Braggs .05 .02
☐ 269 Jose Rijo .05 .02
☐ 270 Toronto Skydome .05 .02
☐ 271 Sandy Alomar Jr. AS .10 .05
☐ 272 Cecil Fielder AS .10 .05
☐ 273 Roberto Alomar AS .25 .11
☐ 274 Wade Boggs AS .25 .11
☐ 275 Cal Ripken AS 1.00 .45
☐ 276 Dave Henderson AS .05 .02
☐ 277 Ken Griffey Jr. AS 1.25 .55
☐ 278 Rickey Henderson AS .25 .11
☐ 279 Jack Morris AS .10 .05
☐ 280 Benito Santiago AS .05 .02
☐ 281 Will Clark AS .15 .07
☐ 282 Ryne Sandberg AS .30 .14
☐ 283 Chris Sabo AS .05 .02
☐ 284 Ozzie Smith AS .30 .14
☐ 285 Andre Dawson AS .15 .07
☐ 286 Tony Gwynn AS .50 .23
☐ 287 Ivan Calderon AS .05 .02
☐ 288 Tom Glavine AS .10 .05

1993 Panini Stickers

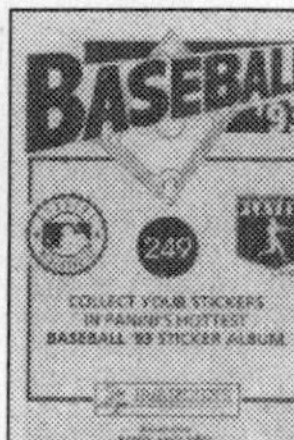

The 300 stickers in this set measure approximately 2 3/8" by 3 3/8" and were to be pasted in a 9" by 11" album. Six stickers were distributed in each 49-cent foil pack. The fronts feature color action player photos with white borders. The player's team name appears on a team color-coded angled bar at the top and the player's name is printed on a second team color-coded bar at the bottom. The team logo is located in the lower left corner. The backs are white and carry the set name, sticker number and manufacturer logo. Ten players from each of the American and National League teams are featured, including one glitter sticker of Panini's Future Stars. One card for each team displays the team's logo on the front. The stickers are numbered on the back and checklisted below according to special subsets and teams.

	MINT	NRMT
COMPLETE SET (300)	15.00	6.75
COMMON STICKER (1-300)	.05	.02

☐ 1 Angels Logo .05 .02
☐ 2 Mark Langston .05 .02
☐ 3 Ron Tingley .05 .02
☐ 4 Gary Gaetti .10 .05
☐ 5 Kelly Gruber .05 .02
☐ 6 Gary DiSarcina .05 .02
☐ 7 Damion Easley .05 .02
☐ 8 Luis Polonia .05 .02
☐ 9 Lee Stevens .05 .02
☐ 10 Chad Curtis .10 .05
☐ 11 Rene Gonzales .05 .02
☐ 12 Athletics Logo .05 .02
☐ 13 Dennis Eckersley .15 .07
☐ 14 Terry Steinbach .05 .02
☐ 15 Mark McGwire 1.00 .45
☐ 16 Mike Bordick .05 .02
☐ 17 Carney Lansford .05 .02
☐ 18 Jerry Browne .05 .02
☐ 19 Rickey Henderson .30 .14
☐ 20 Dave Henderson .05 .02
☐ 21 Ruben Sierra .05 .02
☐ 22 Ron Darling .05 .02
☐ 23 Blue Jays Logo .05 .02
☐ 24 Jack Morris .10 .05
☐ 25 Pat Borders .05 .02
☐ 26 John Olerud .10 .05
☐ 27 Roberto Alomar .40 .18
☐ 28 Luis Sojo .05 .02
☐ 29 Dave Stewart .10 .05
☐ 30 Devon White .05 .02
☐ 31 Joe Carter .10 .05
☐ 32 Derek Bell .10 .05
☐ 33 Juan Guzman .05 .02
☐ 34 Brewers Logo .05 .02
☐ 35 Jaime Navarro .05 .02
☐ 36 B.J. Surhoff .10 .05
☐ 37 Franklin Stubbs .05 .02
☐ 38 Bill Spiers .05 .02
☐ 39 Pat Listach .05 .02
☐ 40 Kevin Seitzer .05 .02
☐ 41 Darryl Hamilton .05 .02
☐ 42 Robin Yount .25 .11
☐ 43 Kevin Reimer .05 .02
☐ 44 Greg Vaughn .05 .02
☐ 45 Indians Logo .05 .02
☐ 46 Charles Nagy .10 .05
☐ 47 Sandy Alomar Jr. .10 .05
☐ 48 Reggie Jefferson .10 .05
☐ 49 Mark Lewis .05 .02
☐ 50 Felix Fermin .05 .02
☐ 51 Carlos Baerga .10 .05
☐ 52 Albert Belle 1.00 .45
☐ 53 Kenny Lofton .75 .35
☐ 54 Mark Whiten .05 .02
☐ 55 Paul Sorrento .05 .02
☐ 56 Mariners Logo .05 .02
☐ 57 Dave Fleming .05 .02
☐ 58 Dave Valle .05 .02
☐ 59 Pete O'Brien .05 .02
☐ 60 Randy Johnson .30 .14
☐ 61 Omar Vizquel .10 .05
☐ 62 Edgar Martinez .25 .11
☐ 63 Ken Griffey Jr. 2.50 1.10
☐ 64 Henry Cotto .05 .02
☐ 65 Jay Buhner .25 .11
☐ 66 Tino Martinez .25 .11
☐ 67 Orioles Logo .05 .02
☐ 68 Ben McDonald .05 .02
☐ 69 Mike Mussina .50 .23
☐ 70 Chris Hoiles .05 .02
☐ 71 Randy Milligan .05 .02
☐ 72 Billy Ripken .05 .02
☐ 73 Cal Ripken 2.00 .90
☐ 74 Leo Gomez .05 .02
☐ 75 Mike Devereaux .05 .02
☐ 76 Brady Anderson .15 .07
☐ 77 Joe Orsulak .05 .02
☐ 78 Rangers Logo .05 .02
☐ 79 Kevin Brown .10 .05
☐ 80 Ivan Rodriguez .60 .25
☐ 81 Rafael Palmeiro .30 .14
☐ 82 Julio Franco .10 .05
☐ 83 Jeff Huson .05 .02
☐ 84 Dean Palmer .10 .05
☐ 85 Jose Canseco .30 .14
☐ 86 Juan Gonzalez 1.25 .55
☐ 87 Nolan Ryan 2.00 .90
☐ 88 Brian Downing .05 .02
☐ 89 Red Sox Logo .05 .02
☐ 90 Roger Clemens .75 .35
☐ 91 Tony Pena .05 .02
☐ 92 Mo Vaughn .60 .25
☐ 93 Scott Cooper .05 .02
☐ 94 Luis Rivera .05 .02
☐ 95 Ellis Burks .10 .05
☐ 96 Mike Greenwell .05 .02
☐ 97 Andre Dawson .25 .11
☐ 98 Ivan Calderon .05 .02
☐ 99 Phil Plantier .05 .02
☐ 100 Royals Logo .05 .02
☐ 101 Kevin Appier .10 .05
☐ 102 Mike Macfarlane .05 .02
☐ 103 Wally Joyner .10 .05
☐ 104 Jim Eisenreich .10 .05
☐ 105 Greg Gagne .05 .02
☐ 106 Gregg Jefferies .10 .05
☐ 107 Kevin McReynolds .05 .02
☐ 108 Brian McRae .05 .02
☐ 109 Keith Miller .05 .02
☐ 110 George Brett 1.00 .45
☐ 111 Tigers Logo .05 .02
☐ 112 Bill Gullickson .05 .02
☐ 113 Mickey Tettleton .05 .02
☐ 114 Cecil Fielder .10 .05
☐ 115 Tony Phillips .05 .02
☐ 116 Scott Livingstone .05 .02
☐ 117 Travis Fryman .10 .05
☐ 118 Dan Gladden .05 .02
☐ 119 Rob Deer .05 .02
☐ 120 Frank Tanana .05 .02
☐ 121 Skeeter Barnes .05 .02
☐ 122 Twins Logo .05 .02
☐ 123 Scott Erickson .05 .02
☐ 124 Brian Harper .05 .02
☐ 125 Kent Hrbek .05 .02
☐ 126 Chuck Knoblauch .40 .18
☐ 127 Willie Banks .05 .02
☐ 128 Scott Leius .05 .02
☐ 129 Shane Mack .05 .02
☐ 130 Kirby Puckett 1.25 .55
☐ 131 Chili Davis .10 .05
☐ 132 Pedro Munoz .05 .02
☐ 133 White Sox Logo .05 .02
☐ 134 Jack McDowell .10 .05

☐ 135 Carlton Fisk .15 .07
☐ 136 Frank Thomas 2.50 1.10
☐ 137 Steve Sax .05 .02
☐ 138 Ozzie Guillen .05 .02
☐ 139 Robin Ventura .10 .05
☐ 140 Tim Raines .10 .05
☐ 141 Lance Johnson .10 .05
☐ 142 Ron Karkovice .05 .02
☐ 143 George Bell .05 .02
☐ 144 Yankees Logo .05 .02
☐ 145 Scott Sanderson .05 .02
☐ 146 Matt Nokes .05 .02
☐ 147 Kevin Maas .05 .02
☐ 148 Randy Velarde .05 .02
☐ 149 Andy Stankiewicz .05 .02
☐ 150 Pat Kelly .05 .02
☐ 151 Paul O'Neill .10 .05
☐ 152 Wade Boggs .30 .14
☐ 153 Danny Tartabull .05 .02
☐ 154 Don Mattingly 1.25 .55
☐ 155 Edgar Martinez LL .15 .07
☐ 156 Kevin Brown LL .10 .05
☐ 157 Dennis Eckersley LL .15 .07
☐ 158 Gary Sheffield LL .25 .11
☐ 159 Tom Glavine LL .60 .25
Greg Maddux
☐ 160 Lee Smith LL .10 .05
☐ 161 Dennis Eckersley CY .15 .07
☐ 162 Dennis Eckersley MVP .15 .07
☐ 163 Pat Listach ROY .05 .02
☐ 164 Greg Maddux CY .75 .35
☐ 165 Barry Bonds MVP .25 .11
☐ 166 Eric Karros ROY .15 .07
☐ 167 Astros Logo .05 .02
☐ 168 Pete Harnisch .05 .02
☐ 169 Eddie Taubensee .05 .02
☐ 170 Jeff Bagwell 1.25 .55
☐ 171 Craig Biggio .15 .07
☐ 172 Andujar Cedeno .05 .02
☐ 173 Ken Caminiti .40 .18
☐ 174 Steve Finley .10 .05
☐ 175 Luis Gonzalez .05 .02
☐ 176 Eric Anthony .05 .02
☐ 177 Casey Candaele .05 .02
☐ 178 Braves Logo .05 .02
☐ 179 Tom Glavine .30 .14
☐ 180 Greg Olson .05 .02
☐ 181 Sid Bream .05 .02
☐ 182 Mark Lemke .05 .02
☐ 183 Jeff Blauser .05 .02
☐ 184 Terry Pendleton .05 .02
☐ 185 Ron Gant .10 .05
☐ 186 Otis Nixon .10 .05
☐ 187 Dave Justice .25 .11
☐ 188 Deion Sanders .40 .18
☐ 189 Cardinals Logo .05 .02
☐ 190 Bob Tewksbury .05 .02
☐ 191 Tom Pagnozzi .05 .02
☐ 192 Lee Smith .10 .05
☐ 193 Geronimo Pena .05 .02
☐ 194 Ozzie Smith .60 .25
☐ 195 Todd Zeile .05 .02
☐ 196 Ray Lankford .10 .05
☐ 197 Bernard Gilkey .10 .05
☐ 198 Felix Jose .05 .02
☐ 199 Donovan Osborne .05 .02
☐ 200 Cubs Logo .05 .02
☐ 201 Mike Morgan .05 .02
☐ 202 Rick Wilkins .05 .02
☐ 203 Mark Grace .40 .18
☐ 204 Ryne Sandberg .60 .25
☐ 205 Shawon Dunston .05 .02
☐ 206 Steve Buechele .05 .02
☐ 207 Kal Daniels .05 .02
☐ 208 Sammy Sosa .40 .18
☐ 209 Derrick May .05 .02
☐ 210 Doug Dascenzo .05 .02
☐ 211 Dodgers Logo .05 .02
☐ 212 Ramon Martinez .10 .05
☐ 213 Mike Scioscia .05 .02
☐ 214 Eric Karros .15 .07
☐ 215 Tim Wallach .05 .02
☐ 216 Jose Offerman .05 .02
☐ 217 Mike Sharperson .05 .02
☐ 218 Brett Butler .10 .05
☐ 219 Darryl Strawberry .10 .05
☐ 220 Lenny Harris .05 .02
☐ 221 Eric Davis .10 .05
☐ 222 Expos Logo .05 .02
☐ 223 Ken Hill .10 .05
☐ 224 Darrin Fletcher .05 .02
☐ 225 Greg Colbrunn .05 .02
☐ 226 Delino DeShields .05 .02
☐ 227 Wil Cordero .05 .02
☐ 228 Dennis Martinez .10 .05
☐ 229 John Vander Wal .05 .02
☐ 230 Marquis Grissom .10 .05
☐ 231 Larry Walker .25 .11
☐ 232 Moises Alou .10 .05
☐ 233 Giants Logo .05 .02
☐ 234 Bill Swift .05 .02
☐ 235 Kirt Manwaring .05 .02
☐ 236 Will Clark .40 .18
☐ 237 Robby Thompson .05 .02
☐ 238 Royce Clayton .05 .02
☐ 239 Matt Williams .40 .18
☐ 240 Willie McGee .05 .02
☐ 241 Mark Leonard .05 .02
☐ 242 Cory Snyder .05 .02
☐ 243 Barry Bonds .50 .23
☐ 244 Mets Logo .05 .02
☐ 245 Dwight Gooden .10 .05
☐ 246 Todd Hundley .10 .05
☐ 247 Eddie Murray .40 .18
☐ 248 Sid Fernandez .05 .02
☐ 249 Tony Fernandez .05 .02
☐ 250 Dave Magadan .05 .02
☐ 251 Howard Johnson .05 .02
☐ 252 Vince Coleman .05 .02
☐ 253 Bobby Bonilla .10 .05
☐ 254 Daryl Boston .05 .02
☐ 255 Padres Logo .05 .02
☐ 256 Bruce Hurst .05 .02
☐ 257 Dan Walters .05 .02
☐ 258 Fred McGriff .40 .18
☐ 259 Kurt Stillwell .05 .02
☐ 260 Craig Shipley .05 .02
☐ 261 Gary Sheffield .25 .11
☐ 262 Tony Gwynn 1.25 .55
☐ 263 Oscar Azocar .05 .02
☐ 264 Darrin Jackson .05 .02
☐ 265 Andy Benes .10 .05
☐ 266 Phillies Logo .05 .02
☐ 267 Terry Mulholland .05 .02
☐ 268 Curt Schilling .10 .05
☐ 269 Darren Daulton .10 .05
☐ 270 John Kruk .10 .05
☐ 271 Mickey Morandini .05 .02
☐ 272 Mariano Duncan .05 .02
☐ 273 Dave Hollins .05 .02
☐ 274 Lenny Dykstra .10 .05
☐ 275 Wes Chamberlain .05 .02
☐ 276 Stan Javier .05 .02
☐ 277 Pirates Logo .05 .02
☐ 278 Zane Smith .05 .02
☐ 279 Tim Wakefield .05 .02
☐ 280 Mike LaValliere .05 .02
☐ 281 Orlando Merced .05 .02
☐ 282 Stan Belinda .05 .02
☐ 283 Jay Bell .05 .02
☐ 284 Jeff King .05 .02
☐ 285 Andy Van Slyke .10 .05
☐ 286 Bob Walk .05 .02
☐ 287 Gary Varsho .05 .02
☐ 288 Reds Logo .05 .02
☐ 289 Jose Rijo .05 .02
☐ 290 Joe Oliver .05 .02
☐ 291 Hal Morris .05 .02
☐ 292 Bip Roberts .05 .02
☐ 293 Barry Larkin .25 .11
☐ 294 Chris Sabo .05 .02
☐ 295 Roberto Kelly .05 .02
☐ 296 Kevin Mitchell .05 .02
☐ 297 Rob Dibble .05 .02
☐ 298 Reggie Sanders .15 .07
☐ 299 Marlins Logo .05 .02
☐ 300 Rockies Logo .10 .05

1994 Panini Stickers

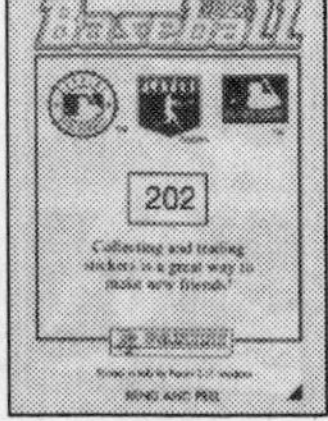

This set of 1994 Panini Baseball consists of 268 stickers measuring approximately 2 3/8" by 3 3/8". The stickers were sold in Panini packets of six, with 50 packets (suggested retail price of 49 cents each) per box. The collectible sticker album measures 9 1/8" by 10 5/8" (suggested retail price of 99 cents) and features eight baseball players on the bright yellow, UV coated cover. The album's inside front cover carries 1993 Team Statistics for the American and National Leagues and also lists the 1993 League Standings. The back inside cover provides information on how to order missing stickers and take advantage of the mail in offer of 30 stickers for $4.00, plus ten '94 Panini wrappers. The sticker fronts feature kelly-green bordered action player shots. A white baseball pennant icon across the bottom carries the player's name and team logo. After presenting the American (5-10) and National League Leaders (11-16), the set is arranged grouped alphabetically within teams and checklisted below alphabetically according to teams for each league.

	MINT	NRMT
COMPLETE SET (268)	15.00	6.75
COMMON STICKER (1-268)	.05	.02

☐ 1 WS Opening Ceremony .05 .02
(Upper left)
☐ 2 WS Opening Ceremony .05 .02
(Upper right)
☐ 3 WS Opening Ceremony .05 .02
(Lower left)
☐ 4 WS Opening Ceremony .05 .02
(Lower right)
☐ 5 John Olerud .10 .05
Highest Batting Average
☐ 6 Juan Gonzalez .50 .23
Most Home Runs
☐ 7 Albert Belle .50 .23
Most Runs Batted In
☐ 8 Jack McDowell .05 .02
Most Wins
☐ 9 Randy Johnson .25 .11
Most Strikeouts
☐ 10 Jeff Montgomery .05 .02
Duane Ward
Most Saves (tie)
☐ 11 Andres Galarraga .25 .11
Highest Batting Average
☐ 12 Barry Bonds .30 .14
Most Home Runs
☐ 13 Barry Bonds .30 .14
Most Runs Batted In
☐ 14 Tom Glavine .10 .05
John Burkett
Most Wins (tie)
☐ 15 Jose Rijo .05 .02
Most Strikeouts
☐ 16 Randy Myers .05 .02
Most Saves
☐ 17 Brady Anderson .15 .07
☐ 18 Harold Baines .10 .05
☐ 19 Mike Devereaux .05 .02
☐ 20 Chris Hoiles .05 .02
☐ 21 Mike Mussina .40 .18
☐ 22 Harold Reynolds .10 .05
☐ 23 Cal Ripken Jr. 1.50 .70
☐ 24 David Segui .05 .02
☐ 25 Fernando Valenzuela .10 .05
☐ 26 Roger Clemens .30 .14
☐ 27 Scott Cooper .05 .02
☐ 28 Andre Dawson .15 .07
☐ 29 Scott Fletcher .05 .02
☐ 30 Mike Greenwell .05 .02
☐ 31 Billy Hatcher .05 .02
☐ 32 Tony Pena .05 .02
☐ 33 John Valentin .10 .05
☐ 34 Mo Vaughn .50 .23
☐ 35 Chad Curtis .05 .02
☐ 36 Gary DiSarcina .05 .02
☐ 37 Damion Easley .05 .02
☐ 38 Mark Langston .05 .02
☐ 39 Torey Lovullo .05 .02
☐ 40 Greg Myers .05 .02
☐ 41 Luis Polonia .05 .02
☐ 42 Tim Salmon .40 .18
☐ 43 J.T. Snow .10 .05
☐ 44 George Bell .05 .02
☐ 45 Ellis Burks .10 .05
☐ 46 Joey Cora .10 .05
☐ 47 Ozzie Guillen .05 .02
☐ 48 Roberto Hernandez .05 .02
☐ 49 Bo Jackson .10 .05
☐ 50 Jack McDowell .05 .02
☐ 51 Frank Thomas 2.00 .90
☐ 52 Robin Ventura .10 .05
☐ 53 Sandy Alomar Jr. .10 .05
☐ 54 Carlos Baerga .10 .05
☐ 55 Albert Belle .75 .35
☐ 56 Felix Fermin .05 .02
☐ 57 Wayne Kirby .05 .02
☐ 58 Kenny Lofton .60 .25
☐ 59 Charles Nagy .10 .05
☐ 60 Paul Sorrento .05 .02
☐ 61 Jeff Treadway .05 .02
☐ 62 Eric Davis .10 .05
☐ 63 Cecil Fielder .10 .05
☐ 64 Travis Fryman .10 .05

☐ 65 Bill Gullickson .05 .02
☐ 66 Mike Moore .05 .02
☐ 67 Tony Phillips .05 .02
☐ 68 Mickey Tettleton .10 .05
☐ 69 Alan Trammell .15 .07
☐ 70 Lou Whitaker .10 .05
☐ 71 Kevin Appier .10 .05
☐ 72 Greg Gagne .05 .02
☐ 73 Tom Gordon .05 .02
☐ 74 Felix Jose .05 .02
☐ 75 Wally Joyner .10 .05
☐ 76 Jose Lind .05 .02
☐ 77 Mike Macfarlane .05 .02
☐ 78 Brian McRae .05 .02
☐ 79 Kevin McReynolds .05 .02
☐ 80 Darryl Hamilton .05 .02
☐ 81 Teddy Higuera .05 .02
☐ 82 John Jaha .05 .02
☐ 83 Pat Listach .05 .02
☐ 84 Dave Nilsson .05 .02
☐ 85 Kevin Reimer .05 .02
☐ 86 Kevin Seitzer .05 .02
☐ 87 B.J. Surhoff .10 .05
☐ 88 Greg Vaughn .05 .02
☐ 89 Willie Banks .05 .02
☐ 90 Brian Harper .05 .02
☐ 91 Kent Hrbek .05 .02
☐ 92 Chuck Knoblauch .40 .18
☐ 93 Shane Mack .05 .02
☐ 94 Pat Meares .05 .02
☐ 95 Pedro Munoz .05 .02
☐ 96 Kirby Puckett 1.00 .45
☐ 97 Dave Winfield .25 .11
☐ 98 Jim Abbott .10 .05
☐ 99 Wade Boggs .25 .11
☐ 100 Mike Gallego .05 .02
☐ 101 Pat Kelly .05 .02
☐ 102 Don Mattingly 1.00 .45
☐ 103 Paul O'Neill .10 .05
☐ 104 Mike Stanley .05 .02
☐ 105 Danny Tartabull .05 .02
☐ 106 Bernie Williams .50 .23
☐ 107 Mike Bordick .05 .02
☐ 108 Dennis Eckersley .15 .07
☐ 109 Dave Henderson .05 .02
☐ 110 Mark McGwire .75 .35
☐ 111 Troy Neel .05 .02
☐ 112 Ruben Sierra .05 .02
☐ 113 Terry Steinbach .05 .02
☐ 114 Todd Van Poppel .05 .02
☐ 115 Bob Welch .05 .02
☐ 116 Bret Boone .05 .02
☐ 117 Jay Buhner .15 .07
☐ 118 Ken Griffey Jr. 2.00 .90
☐ 119 Randy Johnson .30 .14
☐ 120 Rich Amaral .05 .02
☐ 121 Edgar Martinez .15 .07
☐ 122 Tino Martinez .25 .11
☐ 123 Dave Valle .05 .02
☐ 124 Omar Vizquel .10 .05
☐ 125 Jose Canseco .25 .11
☐ 126 Julio Franco .10 .05
☐ 127 Juan Gonzalez 1.00 .45
☐ 128 Tom Henke .10 .05
☐ 129 Manuel Lee .05 .02
☐ 130 Rafael Palmeiro .25 .11
☐ 131 Dean Palmer .10 .05
☐ 132 Ivan Rodriguez .50 .23
☐ 133 Doug Strange .05 .02
☐ 134 Roberto Alomar .40 .18
☐ 135 Pat Borders .05 .02
☐ 136 Joe Carter .10 .05
☐ 137 Tony Fernandez .05 .02
☐ 138 Juan Guzman .05 .02
☐ 139 Rickey Henderson .25 .11
☐ 140 Paul Molitor .40 .18
☐ 141 John Olerud .10 .05
☐ 142 Devon White .05 .02
☐ 143 Jeff Blauser .05 .02
☐ 144 Ron Gant .10 .05
☐ 145 Tom Glavine .10 .05
☐ 146 Dave Justice .25 .11
☐ 147 Greg Maddux 1.25 .55
☐ 148 Fred McGriff .15 .07
☐ 149 Terry Pendleton .05 .02
☐ 150 Deion Sanders .25 .11
☐ 151 John Smoltz .15 .07
☐ 152 Shawon Dunston .05 .02
☐ 153 Mark Grace .30 .14
☐ 154 Derrick May .05 .02
☐ 155 Randy Myers .05 .02
☐ 156 Ryne Sandberg .50 .23
☐ 157 Dwight Smith .05 .02
☐ 158 Sammy Sosa .25 .11
☐ 159 Jose Vizcaino .05 .02
☐ 160 Rick Wilkins .05 .02
☐ 161 Tom Browning .05 .02
☐ 162 Roberto Kelly .05 .02
☐ 163 Barry Larkin .15 .07
☐ 164 Kevin Mitchell .05 .02
☐ 165 Hal Morris .05 .02
☐ 166 Joe Oliver .05 .02
☐ 167 Jose Rijo .05 .02
☐ 168 Chris Sabo .05 .02
☐ 169 Reggie Sanders .10 .05
☐ 170 Freddie Benavides .05 .02
☐ 171 Dante Bichette .15 .07
☐ 172 Vinny Castilla .15 .07
☐ 173 Jerald Clark .05 .02
☐ 174 Andres Galarraga .25 .11
☐ 175 Charlie Hayes .05 .02
☐ 176 Chris Jones .05 .02
☐ 177 Roberto Mejia .05 .02
☐ 178 Eric Young .10 .05
☐ 179 Bret Barberie .05 .02
☐ 180 Chuck Carr .05 .02
☐ 181 Jeff Conine .10 .05
☐ 182 Orestes Destrade .05 .02
☐ 183 Bryan Harvey .05 .02
☐ 184 Rich Renteria .05 .02
☐ 185 Benito Santiago .05 .02
☐ 186 Gary Sheffield .25 .11
☐ 187 Walt Weiss .05 .02
☐ 188 Eric Anthony .05 .02
☐ 189 Jeff Bagwell 1.00 .45
☐ 190 Craig Biggio .15 .07
☐ 191 Ken Caminiti .25 .11
☐ 192 Andujar Cedeno .05 .02
☐ 193 Doug Drabek .05 .02
☐ 194 Steve Finley .15 .07
☐ 195 Doug Jones .05 .02
☐ 196 Darryl Kile .10 .05
☐ 197 Brett Butler .10 .05
☐ 198 Tom Candiotti .05 .02
☐ 199 Dave Hansen .05 .02
☐ 200 Orel Hershiser .10 .05
☐ 201 Eric Karros .10 .05
☐ 202 Jose Offerman .05 .02
☐ 203 Mike Piazza 1.25 .55
☐ 204 Cory Snyder .05 .02
☐ 205 Darryl Strawberry .10 .05
☐ 206 Moises Alou .10 .05
☐ 207 Sean Berry .05 .02
☐ 208 Wil Cordero .05 .02
☐ 209 Delino DeShields .05 .02
☐ 210 Marquis Grissom .10 .05
☐ 211 Ken Hill .05 .02
☐ 212 Mike Lansing .05 .02
☐ 213 Larry Walker .25 .11
☐ 214 John Wetteland .10 .05
☐ 215 Bobby Bonilla .10 .05
☐ 216 Jeromy Burnitz .10 .05
☐ 217 Dwight Gooden .10 .05
☐ 218 Todd Hundley .10 .05
☐ 219 Howard Johnson .05 .02
☐ 220 Jeff Kent .10 .05
☐ 221 Eddie Murray .40 .18
☐ 222 Bret Saberhagen .10 .05
☐ 223 Ryan Thompson .05 .02
☐ 224 Darren Daulton .10 .05
☐ 225 Mariano Duncan .05 .02
☐ 226 Lenny Dykstra .10 .05
☐ 227 Jim Eisenreich .10 .05
☐ 228 Dave Hollins .05 .02
☐ 229 John Kruk .10 .05
☐ 230 Curt Schilling .10 .05
☐ 231 Kevin Stocker .05 .02
☐ 232 Mitch Williams .05 .02
☐ 233 Jay Bell .05 .02
☐ 234 Steve Cooke .05 .02
☐ 235 Carlos Garcia .05 .02
☐ 236 Jeff King .05 .02
☐ 237 Orlando Merced .05 .02
☐ 238 Don Slaught .05 .02
☐ 239 Zane Smith .05 .02
☐ 240 Andy Van Slyke .05 .02
☐ 241 Kevin Young .05 .02
☐ 242 Bernard Gilkey .10 .05
☐ 243 Gregg Jefferies .10 .05
☐ 244 Brian Jordan .10 .05
☐ 245 Ray Lankford .10 .05
☐ 246 Tom Pagnozzi .05 .02
☐ 247 Geronimo Perez .05 .02
☐ 248 Ozzie Smith .50 .23
☐ 249 Bob Tewksbury .05 .02
☐ 250 Mark Whiten .05 .02
☐ 251 Brad Ausmus .05 .02
☐ 252 Derek Bell .10 .05
☐ 253 Andy Benes .10 .05
☐ 254 Phil Clark .05 .02
☐ 255 Jeff Gardner .05 .02
☐ 256 Tony Gwynn .75 .35
☐ 257 Trevor Hoffman .10 .05
☐ 258 Phil Plantier .05 .02
☐ 259 Craig Shipley .05 .02
☐ 260 Rod Beck .05 .02
☐ 261 Barry Bonds .60 .25
☐ 262 John Burkett .05 .02
☐ 263 Will Clark .25 .11
☐ 264 Royce Clayton .05 .02
☐ 265 Willie McGee .10 .05
☐ 266 Bill Swift .05 .02
☐ 267 Robby Thompson .05 .02
☐ 268 Matt Williams .25 .11

1995 Panini Stickers

This 156-sticker set measures approximately 1 15/16" by 3" and was distributed by Fleer. The fronts feature color action player photos framed in different colors on a white background. The player's name and team logo appear in a bar at the bottom. The backs carry the sponsor logos. The set closes with team logos (129-156).

	MINT	NRMT
COMPLETE SET (156)	20.00	9.00
COMMON STICKER (1-156)	.05	.02

☐ 1 Tom Glavine .10 .05
☐ 2 Doug Drabek .05 .02
☐ 3 Rod Beck .05 .02
☐ 4 Pedro Martinez .25 .11
☐ 5 Danny Jackson .05 .02
☐ 6 Greg Maddux 2.00 .90
☐ 7 Bret Saberhagen .10 .05
☐ 8 Ken Hill .05 .02
☐ 9 Marvin Freeman .05 .02
☐ 10 Andy Benes .10 .05
☐ 11 Wilson Alvarez .10 .05
☐ 12 Jimmy Key .05 .02
☐ 13 Mike Mussina .40 .18
☐ 14 Roger Clemens .75 .35
☐ 15 Pat Hentgen .25 .11
☐ 16 Randy Johnson .30 .14
☐ 17 Lee Smith .10 .05
☐ 18 David Cone .10 .05
☐ 19 Jason Bere .05 .02
☐ 20 Dennis Martinez .10 .05
☐ 21 Darren Daulton .10 .05
☐ 22 Darrin Fletcher .05 .02
☐ 23 Tom Pagnozzi .05 .02
☐ 24 Mike Piazza 1.50 .70
☐ 25 Benito Santiago .05 .02
☐ 26 Sandy Alomar Jr. .05 .02
☐ 27 Chris Hoiles .05 .02
☐ 28 Ivan Rodriguez .75 .35
☐ 29 Mike Stanley .05 .02
☐ 30 Dave Nilsson .05 .02
☐ 31 Jeff Bagwell 1.50 .70
☐ 32 Mark Grace .40 .18
☐ 33 Gregg Jefferies .10 .05
☐ 34 Andres Galarraga .40 .18
☐ 35 Fred McGriff .40 .18
☐ 36 Will Clark .40 .18
☐ 37 Mo Vaughn .75 .35
☐ 38 Don Mattingly 1.50 .70
☐ 39 Frank Thomas 2.50 1.10
☐ 40 Cecil Fielder .10 .05
☐ 41 Robby Thompson .05 .02
☐ 42 Delino DeShields .05 .02
☐ 43 Carlos Garcia .05 .02
☐ 44 Bret Boone .05 .02
☐ 45 Craig Biggio .15 .07
☐ 46 Roberto Alomar .40 .18
☐ 47 Chuck Knoblauch .60 .25
☐ 48 Jose Lind .05 .02
☐ 49 Carlos Baerga .10 .05
☐ 50 Lou Whitaker .10 .05
☐ 51 Bobby Bonilla .10 .05
☐ 52 Tim Wallach .05 .02
☐ 53 Todd Zeile .05 .02
☐ 54 Matt Williams .40 .18
☐ 55 Ken Caminiti .40 .18
☐ 56 Robin Ventura .10 .05
☐ 57 Wade Boggs .30 .14
☐ 58 Scott Cooper .05 .02
☐ 59 Travis Fryman .10 .05

☐ 60 Dean Palmer .10 .05
☐ 61 Jay Bell .05 .02
☐ 62 Barry Larkin .25 .11
☐ 63 Ozzie Smith .75 .35
☐ 64 Wil Cordero .05 .02
☐ 65 Royce Clayton .05 .02
☐ 66 Chris Gomez .05 .02
☐ 67 Ozzie Guillen .05 .02
☐ 68 Cal Ripken Jr. 2.50 1.10
☐ 69 Omar Vizquel .10 .05
☐ 70 Gary DiSarcina .05 .02
☐ 71 Dante Bichette .10 .05
☐ 72 Lenny Dykstra .10 .05
☐ 73 Barry Bonds .60 .25
☐ 74 Gary Sheffield .25 .11
☐ 75 Larry Walker .25 .11
☐ 76 Raul Mondesi .25 .11
☐ 77 Dave Justice .25 .11
☐ 78 Moises Alou .10 .05
☐ 79 Tony Gwynn 1.25 .55
☐ 80 Deion Sanders .25 .11
☐ 81 Kenny Lofton .75 .35
☐ 82 Kirby Puckett 1.50 .70
☐ 83 Juan Gonzalez 1.50 .70
☐ 84 Jay Buhner .15 .07
☐ 85 Joe Carter .10 .05
☐ 86 Ken Griffey Jr. 3.00 1.35
☐ 87 Ruben Sierra .05 .02
☐ 88 Tim Salmon .50 .23
☐ 89 Paul O'Neill .10 .05
☐ 90 Albert Belle 1.00 .45
☐ 91 Danny Tartabull .05 .02
☐ 92 Jose Canseco .15 .07
☐ 93 Harold Baines .10 .05
☐ 94 Kirk Gibson .10 .05
☐ 95 Chili Davis .10 .05
☐ 96 Eddie Murray .75 .35
☐ 97 Bob Hamelin .05 .02
☐ 98 Paul Molitor .75 .35
☐ 99 Raul Mondesi .60 .25
☐ 100 Ryan Klesko .50 .23
☐ 101 Cliff Floyd .05 .02
☐ 102 William VanLandingham .05 .02
☐ 103 Joey Hamilton .15 .07
☐ 104 John Hudek .05 .02
☐ 105 Manny Ramirez .75 .35
☐ 106 Bob Hamelin .05 .02
☐ 107 Rusty Greer 1.00 .45
☐ 108 Chris Gomez .05 .02
☐ 109 Greg Maddux 2.00 .90
☐ 110 Jeff Bagwell 1.50 .70
☐ 111 Raul Mondesi .60 .25
☐ 112 David Cone .10 .05
☐ 113 Frank Thomas 2.00 .90
☐ 114 Bob Hamelin .05 .02
☐ 115 Tony Gwynn 1.25 .55
☐ 116 Matt Williams .40 .18
☐ 117 Jeff Bagwell 1.50 .70
☐ 118 Craig Biggio .15 .07
☐ 119 Andy Benes .10 .05
☐ 120 Greg Maddux 2.00 .90
☐ 121 John Franco .10 .05
☐ 122 Paul O'Neill .10 .05
☐ 123 Ken Griffey Jr. 3.00 1.35
☐ 124 Kirby Puckett 1.50 .70
☐ 125 Kenny Lofton .75 .35
☐ 126 Randy Johnson .30 .14
☐ 127 Jimmy Key .05 .02
☐ 128 Lee Smith .10 .05
☐ 129 San Francisco Giants .05 .02
☐ 130 Montreal Expos .05 .02
☐ 131 Cincinnati Reds .05 .02
☐ 132 Los Angeles Dodgers .05 .02
☐ 133 New York Mets .05 .02
☐ 134 San Diego Padres .05 .02
☐ 135 Colorado Rockies .05 .02
☐ 136 Pittsburgh Pirates .05 .02
☐ 137 Florida Marlins .05 .02
☐ 138 Philadelphia Phillies .05 .02
☐ 139 Atlanta Braves .05 .02
☐ 140 Houston Astros .05 .02
☐ 141 St. Louis Cardinals .05 .02
☐ 142 Chicago Cubs .05 .02
☐ 143 Cleveland Indians .05 .02
☐ 144 New York Yankees .05 .02
☐ 145 Kansas City Royals .05 .02
☐ 146 Chicago White Sox .05 .02
☐ 147 Baltimore Orioles .05 .02
☐ 148 Seattle Mariners .05 .02
☐ 149 Boston Red Sox .05 .02
☐ 150 California Angels .05 .02
☐ 151 Toronto Blue Jays .05 .02
☐ 152 Detroit Tigers .05 .02
☐ 153 Texas Rangers .05 .02
☐ 154 Oakland Athletics .05 .02
☐ 155 Milwaukee Brewers .05 .02
☐ 156 Minnesota Twins .05 .02

1996 Panini Stickers

This 246-sticker set was distributed as a complete set in a cellophane wrapper with a suggested retail price of $8. A 60-page album to hold the stickers was included with the set. The stickers feature color action player photos with the same lighter image in the background inside a green border. Player information and statistics are found in the album below each sticker. Stickers to finish ones set were available from the Panini Missing Sticker Club at a cost of $4 for 20 different stickers or $4 for 30 stickers as long as 10 wrappers were sent as well.

	MINT	NRMT
COMPLETE SET (246)	12.00	5.50
COMMON CARD (1-246)	.05	.02

☐ 1 David Justice .25 .11
☐ 2 Tom Glavine .15 .07
☐ 3 Javier Lopez .05 .02
☐ 4 Greg Maddux .60 .25
☐ 5 Marquis Grissom .10 .05
☐ 6 Atlanta Braves Team Logo .05 .02
☐ 7 Ryan Klesko .25 .11
☐ 8 Chipper Jones .60 .25
☐ 9 Quilvio Veras .05 .02
☐ 10 Chris Hammond .05 .02
☐ 11 Charles Johnson .10 .05
☐ 12 John Burkett .05 .02
☐ 13 Florida Marlins Team Logo .05 .02
☐ 14 Jeff Conine .10 .05
☐ 15 Gary Sheffield .25 .11
☐ 16 Greg Colbrunn .05 .02
☐ 17 Moises Alou .10 .05
☐ 18 Pedro Martinez .25 .11
☐ 19 Rondell White .10 .05
☐ 20 Tony Tarasco .05 .02
☐ 21 Montreal Expos Team Logo .05 .02
☐ 22 Carlos Perez .05 .02
☐ 23 David Segui .05 .02
☐ 24 Wil Cordero .05 .02
☐ 25 Jason Isringhausen .05 .02
☐ 26 Rico Brogna .10 .05
☐ 27 Edgardo Alfonzo .25 .11
☐ 28 Todd Hundley .10 .05
☐ 29 New York Mets Team Logo .05 .02
☐ 30 Bill Pulsipher .05 .02
☐ 31 Carl Everett .05 .02
☐ 32 Jose Vizcaino .05 .02
☐ 33 Lenny Dykstra .10 .05
☐ 34 Charlie Hayes .05 .02
☐ 35 Heathcliff Slocumb .05 .02
☐ 36 Darren Daulton .10 .05
☐ 37 Philadelphia Phillies Team Logo .05 .02
☐ 38 Mickey Morandini .05 .02
☐ 39 Gregg Jefferies .10 .05
☐ 40 Jim Eisenreich .10 .05
☐ 41 Brian McRae .05 .02
☐ 42 Luis Gonzalez .05 .02
☐ 43 Randy Myers .10 .05
☐ 44 Shawon Dunston .05 .02
☐ 45 Chicago Cubs Team Logo .05 .02
☐ 46 Jaime Navarro .05 .02
☐ 47 Mark Grace .25 .11
☐ 48 Sammy Sosa .25 .11
☐ 49 Barry Larkin .15 .07
☐ 50 Pete Schourek .05 .02
☐ 51 John Smiley .05 .02
☐ 52 Reggie Sanders .10 .05
☐ 53 Cincinnati Reds Team Logo .05 .02
☐ 54 Hal Morris .05 .02
☐ 55 Ron Gant .10 .05
☐ 56 Bret Boone .05 .02
☐ 57 Craig Biggio .15 .07
☐ 58 Brian Hunter .05 .02
☐ 59 Jeff Bagwell .50 .23
☐ 60 Shane Reynolds .05 .02
☐ 61 Houston Astros Team Logo .05 .02
☐ 62 Derek Bell .10 .05
☐ 63 Doug Drabek .05 .02
☐ 64 Orlando Miller .05 .02
☐ 65 Jay Bell .05 .02
☐ 66 Dan Miceli .05 .02
☐ 67 Orlando Merced .05 .02
☐ 68 Jeff King .05 .02
☐ 69 Carlos Garcia .05 .02
☐ 70 Pittsburgh Pirates Team Logo .05 .02
☐ 71 Al Martin .05 .02
☐ 72 Denny Neagle .05 .02
☐ 73 Ray Lankford .10 .05
☐ 74 Ozzie Smith .30 .14
☐ 75 Bernard Gilkey .05 .02
☐ 76 John Mabry .10 .05
☐ 77 St. Louis Cardinals Team Logo .05 .02
☐ 78 Brian Jordan .10 .05
☐ 79 Scott Cooper .05 .02
☐ 80 Allen Watson .05 .02
☐ 81 Dante Bichette .15 .07
☐ 82 Bret Saberhagen .05 .02
☐ 83 Walt Weiss .05 .02
☐ 84 Andres Galarraga .25 .11
☐ 85 Colorado Rockies Team Logo .05 .02
☐ 86 Larry Walker .25 .11
☐ 87 Bill Swift .05 .02
☐ 88 Vinny Castilla .10 .05
☐ 89 Raul Mondesi .25 .11
☐ 90 Roger Cedeno .05 .02
☐ 91 Chad Fonville .05 .02
☐ 92 Hideo Nomo .60 .25
☐ 93 Los Angeles Dodgers Team Logo .05 .02
☐ 94 Ramon Martinez .10 .05
☐ 95 Mike Piazza .60 .25
☐ 96 Eric Karros .10 .05
☐ 97 Tony Gwynn .40 .18
☐ 98 Brad Ausmus .05 .02
☐ 99 Trevor Hoffman .05 .02
☐ 100 Ken Caminiti .25 .11
☐ 101 San Diego Padres Team Logo .05 .02
☐ 102 Andy Ashby .05 .02
☐ 103 Steve Finley .15 .07
☐ 104 Joey Hamilton .10 .05
☐ 105 Matt Williams .15 .07
☐ 106 Rod Beck .10 .05
☐ 107 Barry Bonds .30 .14
☐ 108 William VanLandingham .05 .02
☐ 109 San Francisco Giants Team Logo .05 .02
☐ 110 Deion Sanders .25 .11
☐ 111 Royce Clayton .05 .02
☐ 112 Glenallen Hill .05 .02
☐ 113 Tony Gwynn .40 .18
☐ 114 Dante Bichette .15 .07
☐ 115 Dante Bichette .15 .07
☐ 116 Quilvio Veras .05 .02
☐ 117 Hideo Nomo .60 .25
☐ 118 Greg Maddux .60 .25
☐ 119 Randy Myers .10 .05
☐ 120 Edgar Martinez .15 .07
☐ 121 Albert Belle .50 .23
☐ 122 Mo Vaughn .30 .14
☐ 123 Kenny Lofton .30 .14
☐ 124 Randy Johnson .25 .11
☐ 125 Mike Mussina .25 .11
☐ 126 Jose Mesa .05 .02
☐ 127 Mike Mussina .25 .11
☐ 128 Cal Ripken Jr. .75 .35
☐ 129 Rafael Palmeiro .15 .07
☐ 130 Ben McDonald .05 .02
☐ 131 Baltimore Orioles Team Logo .05 .02
☐ 132 Chris Hoiles .05 .02
☐ 133 Bobby Bonilla .10 .05
☐ 134 Brady Anderson .15 .07
☐ 135 Jose Canseco .15 .07
☐ 136 Roger Clemens .40 .18
☐ 137 Mo Vaughn .25 .11
☐ 138 Mike Greenwell .05 .02
☐ 139 Boston Red Sox Team Logo .05 .02
☐ 140 Tim Wakefield .05 .02
☐ 141 John Valentin .05 .02
☐ 142 Tim Naehring .05 .02
☐ 143 Travis Fryman .10 .05
☐ 144 Chad Curtis .10 .05
☐ 145 Felipe Lira .05 .02
☐ 146 Cecil Fielder .10 .05
☐ 147 Detroit Tigers Team Logo .05 .02
☐ 148 John Flaherty .05 .02
☐ 149 Chris Gomez .05 .02
☐ 150 Sean Bergman .05 .02
☐ 151 Don Mattingly .50 .23
☐ 152 Andy Pettitte .40 .18
☐ 153 Wade Boggs .25 .11
☐ 154 Paul O'Neill .10 .05
☐ 155 New York Yankees Team Logo .05 .02
☐ 156 Bernie Williams .25 .11
☐ 157 Jack McDowell .05 .02
☐ 158 David Cone .10 .05
☐ 159 Roberto Alomar .25 .11
☐ 160 Paul Molitor .25 .11
☐ 161 Shawn Green .05 .02
☐ 162 Joe Carter .10 .05
☐ 163 Toronto Blue Jays Team Logo .05 .02

☐ 164 Alex Gonzalez	.05	.02
☐ 165 Al Leiter	.05	.02
☐ 166 John Olerud	.10	.05
☐ 167 Alex Fernandez	.10	.05
☐ 168 Ray Durham	.10	.05
☐ 169 Lance Johnson	.05	.02
☐ 170 Ozzie Guillen	.05	.02
☐ 171 Chicago White Sox Team Logo	.05	.02
☐ 172 Robin Ventura	.10	.05
☐ 173 Frank Thomas	1.00	.45
☐ 174 Tim Raines	.10	.05
☐ 175 Albert Belle	.50	.23
☐ 176 Manny Ramirez	.25	.11
☐ 177 Eddie Murray	.25	.11
☐ 178 Orel Hershiser	.10	.05
☐ 179 Cleveland Indians Team Logo	.05	.02
☐ 180 Kenny Lofton	.25	.11
☐ 181 Carlos Baerga	.10	.05
☐ 182 Jose Mesa	.10	.05
☐ 183 Gary Gaetti	.10	.05
☐ 184 Tom Goodwin	.05	.02
☐ 185 Kevin Appier	.10	.05
☐ 186 Jon Nunnally	.05	.02
☐ 187 Kansas City Royals Team Logo	.05	.02
☐ 188 Wally Joyner	.05	.02
☐ 189 Jeff Montgomery	.05	.02
☐ 190 Johnny Damon	.10	.05
☐ 191 B.J. Surhoff	.10	.05
☐ 192 Ricky Bones	.05	.02
☐ 193 John Jaha	.05	.02
☐ 194 Dave Nilsson	.05	.02
☐ 195 Milwaukee Brewers Team Logo	.05	.02
☐ 196 Greg Vaughn	.05	.02
☐ 197 Kevin Seitzer	.05	.02
☐ 198 Joe Oliver	.05	.02
☐ 199 Chuck Knoblauch	.25	.11
☐ 200 Kirby Puckett	.50	.23
☐ 201 Marty Cordova	.10	.05
☐ 202 Pat Meares	.05	.02
☐ 203 Minnesota Twins Team Logo	.05	.02
☐ 204 Scott Stahoviak	.05	.02
☐ 205 Matt Walbeck	.05	.02
☐ 206 Pedro Munoz	.05	.02
☐ 207 Garret Anderson	.10	.05
☐ 208 Chili Davis	.10	.05
☐ 209 Tim Salmon	.25	.11
☐ 210 J.T. Snow	.10	.05
☐ 211 California Angels Team Logo	.05	.02
☐ 212 Jim Edmonds	.25	.11
☐ 213 Chuck Finley	.05	.02
☐ 214 Mark Langston	.05	.02
☐ 215 Dennis Eckersley	.15	.07
☐ 216 Todd Stottlemyre	.05	.02
☐ 217 Geronimo Berroa	.05	.02
☐ 218 Mark McGwire	.40	.18
☐ 219 Oakland A's Team Logo	.05	.02
☐ 220 Brent Gates	.05	.02
☐ 221 Terry Steinbach	.10	.05
☐ 222 Rickey Henderson	.25	.11
☐ 223 Ken Griffey Jr.	1.25	.55
☐ 224 Alex Rodriguez	1.00	.45
☐ 225 Tino Martinez	.25	.11
☐ 226 Randy Johnson	.25	.11
☐ 227 Seattle Mariners Team Logo	.05	.02
☐ 228 Jay Buhner	.15	.07
☐ 229 Vince Coleman	.05	.02
☐ 230 Edgar Martinez	.15	.07
☐ 231 Will Clark	.15	.07
☐ 232 Juan Gonzalez	.50	.23
☐ 233 Kenny Rogers	.05	.02
☐ 234 Ivan Rodriguez	.30	.14
☐ 235 Texas Rangers Team Logo	.05	.02
☐ 236 Mickey Tettleton	.05	.02
☐ 237 Dean Palmer	.10	.05
☐ 238 Otis Nixon	.10	.05
☐ 239 Hideo Nomo	.60	.25
☐ 240 Quilvio Veras	.05	.02
☐ 241 Jason Isringhausen	.05	.02
☐ 242 Andy Pettitte	.40	.18
☐ 243 Chipper Jones	.60	.25
☐ 244 Garret Anderson	.10	.05
☐ 245 Charles Johnson	.10	.05
☐ 246 Marty Cordova	.10	.05

1978 Pepsi

Sponsored by Pepsi-Cola and produced by MSA, this set of 40 collector cards measures approximately 2 1/8" by 9 1/2" and features members of the Cincinnati Reds and 15 national players. On a red background and inside a star cut-out, the fronts have a sepia toned player portrait in the top part. The player's name appears under the photo, along with short biography. A checklist for the Cincinnati Reds (1-25) and for the 15 National players (26-40) is printed below. The bottom part of the front has information on how to get a deck of Superstar playing

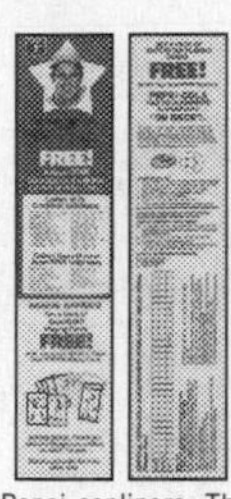

cards free for 250 Pepsi capliners. The backs carry an order form and more detailed information. The cards are unnumbered and checklisted below in alphabetical order by grouping.

	NRMT	VG-E
COMPLETE SET (40)	75.00	34.00
COMMON CARD (1-40)	1.00	.45
☐ 1 Sparky Anderson MG	2.50	1.10
☐ 2 Rick Auerbach	1.00	.45
☐ 3 Doug Bair	1.00	.45
☐ 4 Johnny Bench	7.50	3.40
☐ 5 Bill Bonham	1.00	.45
☐ 6 Pedro Borbon	1.00	.45
☐ 7 Dave Collins	1.00	.45
☐ 8 Dave Concepcion	2.50	1.10
☐ 9 Dan Driessen	1.50	.70
☐ 10 George Foster	2.00	.90
☐ 11 Cesar Geronimo	1.00	.45
☐ 12 Ken Griffey	2.50	1.10
☐ 13 Ken Henderson	1.00	.45
☐ 14 Tom Hume	1.00	.45
☐ 15 Junior Kennedy	1.00	.45
☐ 16 Ray Knight	2.00	.90
☐ 17 Mike Lum	1.00	.45
☐ 18 Joe Morgan	5.00	2.20
☐ 19 Paul Moskau	1.00	.45
☐ 20 Fred Norman	1.00	.45
☐ 21 Pete Rose	7.50	3.40
☐ 22 Manny Sarmiento	1.00	.45
☐ 23 Tom Seaver	7.50	3.40
☐ 24 Dave Tomlin	1.00	.45
☐ 25 Don Werner	1.00	.45
☐ 26 Buddy Bell	2.00	.90
☐ 27 Larry Bowa	1.50	.70
☐ 28 George Brett	15.00	6.75
☐ 29 Jeff Burroughs	1.00	.45
☐ 30 Rod Carew	5.00	2.20
☐ 31 Steve Garvey	3.00	1.35
☐ 32 Reggie Jackson	7.50	3.40
☐ 33 Dave Kingman	2.00	.90
☐ 34 Jerry Koosman	1.50	.70
☐ 35 Bill Madlock	1.50	.70
☐ 36 Jim Palmer	5.00	2.20
☐ 37 Nolan Ryan	15.00	6.75
☐ 38 Ted Simmons	2.00	.90
☐ 39 Carl Yastrzemski	5.00	2.20
☐ 40 Richie Zisk	1.00	.45

1991 Pepsi Superstar

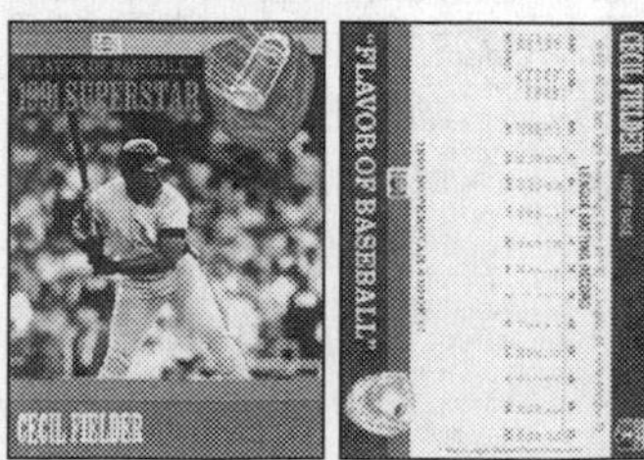

This 17-card set was sponsored by Pepsi-Cola of Florida as part of the "Flavor of Baseball" promotion. The promotion featured a chance to win one of 104 rare, older cards, including one 1952 Mickey Mantle card. The Superstar cards were glued inside specially marked 12 packs of Pepsi-Cola products in Orlando, Tampa, and Miami. It is difficult to remove the cards without creasing them; reportedly area supervisors for Pepsi each received a few sets. The cards measure slightly wider than standard size (2 5/8" by 3 1/2"). The fronts have color action player photos, with a baseball glove "catching" a can of Pepsi superimposed at the upper right corner of the picture. The player photo has two top (purple and red/blue) and two bottom (red and purple) color stripes serving as borders but none on its sides. In a horizontal format, the backs have blue and red stripes, and present Major League statistics as well as biography.

	MINT	NRMT
COMPLETE SET (17)	50.00	22.00
COMMON CARD (1-17)	1.00	.45
☐ 1 Dwight Gooden	3.00	1.35
☐ 2 Andre Dawson	3.00	1.35
☐ 3 Ryne Sandberg	10.00	4.50
☐ 4 Dave Stieb	1.00	.45
☐ 5 Jose Rijo	1.00	.45
☐ 6 Roger Clemens	6.00	2.70
☐ 7 Barry Bonds	5.00	2.20
☐ 8 Cal Ripken	20.00	9.00
☐ 9 Dave Justice	3.00	1.35
☐ 10 Cecil Fielder	1.50	.70
☐ 11 Don Mattingly	12.50	5.50
☐ 12 Ozzie Smith	10.00	4.50
☐ 13 Kirby Puckett	12.50	5.50
☐ 14 Rafael Palmeiro	2.50	1.10
☐ 15 Bobby Bonilla	1.50	.70
☐ 16 Len Dykstra	1.50	.70
☐ 17 Jose Canseco	5.00	2.20

1980-96 Perez-Steele Hall of Fame Postcards

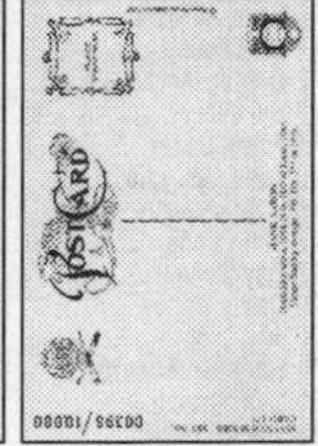

President Ronald Reagan was given the first numbered set issued on May 27th, 1981 at the White House.The sets were also issued with continuation rights. These rights have been transferable over the years. These 3 1/2" by 5 1/2" cards feature noted sports artist Dick Perez drawings. The cards are distributed through Perez Steele galleries. According to the producer, many of these cards are sold to art or postcard collectors. Just 10,000 of these sets were produced.

	NRMT	VG-E
COMPLETE SET	1000.00	450.00
COMMON CARD	1.00	.45
☐ 1 Ty Cobb	35.00	16.00
☐ 2 Walter Johnson	10.00	4.50
☐ 3 Christy Mathewson	10.00	4.50
☐ 4 Babe Ruth	60.00	27.00
☐ 5 Honus Wagner	10.00	4.50
☐ 6 Morgan Bulkeley	1.00	.45
☐ 7 Ban Johnson	1.00	.45
☐ 8 Nap Lajoie	5.00	2.20
☐ 9 Connie Mack	5.00	2.20
☐ 10 John McGraw	5.00	2.20
☐ 11 Tris Speaker	5.00	2.20
☐ 12 George Wright	1.00	.45
☐ 13 Cy Young	5.00	2.20
☐ 14 Grover Alexander	5.00	2.20
☐ 15 Alex. Cartwright	1.00	.45
☐ 16 Henry Chadwick	1.00	.45
☐ 17 Cap Anson	2.50	1.10
☐ 18 Eddie Collins	5.00	2.20
☐ 19 Candy Cummings	1.50	.70
☐ 20 Charles Comiskey	1.00	.45
☐ 21 Buck Ewing	1.50	.70
☐ 22 Lou Gehrig	35.00	16.00
☐ 23 Willie Keeler	1.50	.70
☐ 24 Hoss Radbourne	1.50	.70
☐ 25 George Sisler	15.00	6.75
☐ 26 A.G. Spalding	1.50	.70
☐ 27 Rogers Hornsby	5.00	2.20
☐ 28 Kenesaw Landis	1.00	.45
☐ 29 Roger Bresnahan	1.50	.70
☐ 30 Dan Brouthers	1.50	.70
☐ 31 Fred Clarke	1.50	.70
☐ 32 Jimmy Collins	1.50	.70
☐ 33 Ed Delahanty	1.50	.70
☐ 34 Hugh Duffy	1.50	.70
☐ 35 Hughie Jennings	1.50	.70
☐ 36 King Kelly	2.50	1.10
☐ 37 Jim O'Rourke	1.50	.70
☐ 38 Wilbert Robinson	1.50	.70
☐ 39 Jesse Burkett	1.50	.70
☐ 40 Frank Chance	5.00	2.20
☐ 41 Jack Chesbro	1.50	.70

☐ 42 Johnny Evers 5.00 2.20
☐ 43 Clark Griffith 1.50 .70
☐ 44 Thomas McCarthy 1.50 .70
☐ 45 Joe McGinnity 1.50 .70
☐ 46 Eddie Plank 1.50 .70
☐ 47 Joe Tinker 5.00 2.20
☐ 48 Rube Waddell 1.50 .70
☐ 49 Ed Walsh 1.50 .70
☐ 50 Mickey Cochrane 5.00 2.20
☐ 51 Frankie Frisch 5.00 2.20
☐ 52 Lefty Grove 5.00 2.20
☐ 53 Carl Hubbell 10.00 4.50
☐ 54 Herb Pennock 1.50 .70
☐ 55 Pie Traynor 2.50 1.10
☐ 56 Mordecai Brown 1.50 .70
☐ 57 Charlie Gehringer 2.50 1.10
☐ 58 Kid Nichols 1.50 .70
☐ 59 Jimmy Foxx 15.00 6.75
☐ 60 Mel Ott 10.00 4.50
☐ 61 Harry Heilmann 1.50 .70
☐ 62 Paul Waner 5.00 2.20
☐ 63 Edward Barrow 1.00 .45
☐ 64 Chief Bender 5.00 2.20
☐ 65 Tom Connolly 1.00 .45
☐ 66 Dizzy Dean 15.00 6.75
☐ 67 Bill Klem 1.00 .45
☐ 68 Al Simmons 5.00 2.20
☐ 69 Bobby Wallace 1.50 .70
☐ 70 Harry Wright 1.50 .70
☐ 71 Bill Dickey 5.00 2.20
☐ 72 Rabbit Maranville 1.50 .70
☐ 73 Bill Terry 7.50 3.40
☐ 74 Frank Baker 1.50 .70
☐ 75 Joe DiMaggio 60.00 27.00
☐ 76 Gabby Hartnett 1.50 .70
☐ 77 Ted Lyons 1.50 .70
☐ 78 Ray Schalk 1.50 .70
☐ 79 Dazzy Vance 1.50 .70
☐ 80 Joe Cronin 2.50 1.10
☐ 81 Hank Greenberg 20.00 9.00
☐ 82 Sam Crawford 5.00 2.20
☐ 83 Joe McCarthy 1.00 .45
☐ 84 Zack Wheat 1.50 .70
☐ 85 Max Carey 1.50 .70
☐ 86 Billy Hamilton 1.50 .70
☐ 87 Bob Feller 20.00 9.00
☐ 88 Bill McKechnie 1.00 .45
☐ 89 Jackie Robinson 25.00 11.00
☐ 90 Edd Roush 2.50 1.10
☐ 91 John Clarkson 1.50 .70
☐ 92 Elmer Flick 1.50 .70
☐ 93 Sam Rice 5.00 2.20
☐ 94 Eppa Rixey 1.50 .70
☐ 95 Luke Appling 2.50 1.10
☐ 96 Red Faber 1.50 .70
☐ 97 Burleigh Grimes 1.50 .70
☐ 98 Miller Huggins 1.50 .70
☐ 99 Tim Keefe 1.50 .70
☐ 100 Heinie Manush 1.50 .70
☐ 101 John Ward 1.50 .70
☐ 102 Pud Galvin 1.50 .70
☐ 103 Casey Stengel 10.00 4.50
☐ 104 Ted Williams 60.00 27.00
☐ 105 Branch Rickey 1.50 .70
☐ 106 Red Ruffing 1.50 .70
☐ 107 Lloyd Waner 1.50 .70
☐ 108 Kiki Cuyler 1.50 .70
☐ 109 Goose Goslin 5.00 2.20
☐ 110 Joe Medwick 1.50 .70
☐ 111 Roy Campanella 10.00 4.50
☐ 112 Stan Coveleski 1.50 .70
☐ 113 Waite Hoyt 1.50 .70
☐ 114 Stan Musial 35.00 16.00
☐ 115 Lou Boudreau 12.00 5.50
☐ 116 Earl Combs 1.50 .70
☐ 117 Ford Frick 1.00 .45
☐ 118 Jesse Haines 1.50 .70
☐ 119 David Bancroft 1.50 .70
☐ 120 Jake Beckley 1.50 .70
☐ 121 Chick Hafey 1.00 .45
☐ 122 Harry Hooper 1.50 .70
☐ 123 Joe Kelley 1.50 .70
☐ 124 Rube Marquard 5.00 2.20
☐ 125 Satchel Paige 25.00 11.00
☐ 126 George Weiss 1.00 .45
☐ 127 Yogi Berra 15.00 6.75
☐ 128 Josh Gibson 5.00 2.20
☐ 129 Lefty Gomez 2.50 1.10
☐ 130 William Harridge 1.00 .45
☐ 131 Sandy Koufax 20.00 9.00
☐ 132 Buck Leonard 15.00 6.75
☐ 133 Early Wynn 7.50 3.40
☐ 134 Ross Youngs 1.50 .70
☐ 135 Roberto Clemente 50.00 22.00
☐ 136 Billy Evans 1.00 .45
☐ 137 Monte Irvin 8.00 3.60
☐ 138 George Kelly 1.50 .70
☐ 139 Warren Spahn 10.00 4.50
☐ 140 Mickey Welch 1.50 .70
☐ 141 Cool Papa Bell 8.00 3.60
☐ 142 Jim Bottomley 1.50 .70
☐ 143 Jocko Conlan 1.00 .45
☐ 144 Whitey Ford 20.00 9.00
☐ 145 Mickey Mantle 60.00 27.00
☐ 146 Sam Thompson 1.50 .70
☐ 147 Earl Averill 2.50 1.10
☐ 148 Bucky Harris 1.50 .70
☐ 149 Billy Herman 2.50 1.10
☐ 150 Judy Johnson 10.00 4.50
☐ 151 Ralph Kiner 10.00 4.50
☐ 152 Oscar Charleston 2.50 1.10
☐ 153 Roger Connor 1.50 .70
☐ 154 Cal Hubbard 1.00 .45
☐ 155 Bob Lemon 8.00 3.60
☐ 156 Fred Lindstrom 1.50 .70
☐ 157 Robin Roberts 10.00 4.50
☐ 158 Ernie Banks 15.00 6.75
☐ 159 Martin Dihigo 5.00 2.20
☐ 160 John Lloyd 5.00 2.20
☐ 161 Al Lopez 12.00 5.50
☐ 162 Amos Rusie 1.50 .70
☐ 163 Joe Sewell 1.50 .70
☐ 164 Addie Joss 1.50 .70
☐ 165 Larry MacPhail 1.00 .45
☐ 166 Eddie Mathews 10.00 4.50
☐ 167 Warren Giles 1.00 .45
☐ 168 Willie Mays 35.00 16.00
☐ 169 Hack Wilson 1.50 .70
☐ 170 Al Kaline 20.00 9.00
☐ 171 Chuck Klein 1.50 .70
☐ 172 Duke Snider 20.00 9.00
☐ 173 Tom Yawkey 1.00 .45
☐ 174 Rube Foster 1.00 .45
☐ 175 Bob Gibson 10.00 4.50
☐ 176 Johnny Mize 2.50 1.10
☐ 177 Hank Aaron 20.00 9.00
☐ 178 Happy Chandler 1.00 .45
☐ 179 Travis Jackson 1.50 .70
☐ 180 Frank Robinson 20.00 9.00
☐ 181 Walter Alston 8.00 3.60
☐ 182 George Kell 8.00 3.60
☐ 183 Juan Marichal 6.00 2.70
☐ 184 Brooks Robinson 20.00 9.00
☐ 185 Luis Aparicio 10.00 4.50
☐ 186 Don Drysdale 5.00 2.20
☐ 187 Rick Ferrell 1.50 .70
☐ 188 Harmon Killebrew 10.00 4.50
☐ 189 Pee Wee Reese 20.00 9.00
☐ 190 Lou Brock 15.00 6.75
☐ 191 Enos Slaughter 8.00 3.60
☐ 192 Arky Vaughan 1.50 .70
☐ 193 Hoyt Wilhelm 8.00 3.60
☐ 194 Bobby Doerr 8.00 3.60
☐ 195 Ernie Lombardi 1.50 .70
☐ 196 Willie McCovey 6.00 2.70
☐ 197 Ray Dandridge 5.00 2.20
☐ 198 Catfish Hunter 8.00 3.60
☐ 199 Billy Williams 8.00 3.60
☐ 200 Willie Stargell 6.00 2.70
☐ 201 Al Barlick 2.50 1.10
☐ 202 Johnny Bench 6.00 2.70
☐ 203 Red Schoendienst 8.00 3.60
☐ 204 Carl Yastrzemski 20.00 9.00
☐ 205 Joe Morgan 20.00 9.00
☐ 206 Jim Palmer 6.00 2.70
☐ 207 Rod Carew 15.00 6.75
☐ 208 Ferguson Jenkins 10.00 4.50
☐ 209 Tony Lazzeri 1.50 .70
☐ 210 Gaylord Perry 8.00 3.60
☐ 211 Bill Veeck 1.00 .45
☐ 212 Rollie Fingers 8.00 3.60
☐ 213 Bill McGowan 1.00 .45
☐ 214 Hal Newhouser 15.00 6.75
☐ 215 Tom Seaver 20.00 9.00
☐ 216 Reggie Jackson 20.00 9.00
☐ 217 Steve Carlton 15.00 6.75
☐ 218 Leo Durocher 5.00 2.20
☐ 219 Phil Rizzuto 20.00 9.00
☐ 220 Richie Ashburn 10.00 4.50
☐ 221 Leon Day 2.50 1.10
☐ 222 William Hulbert 1.00 .45
☐ 223 Mike Schmidt 20.00 9.00
☐ 224 Vic Willis 5.00 2.20
☐ 225 Jim Bunning 10.00 4.50
☐ 226 Bill Foster 5.00 2.20
☐ 227 Ned Hanlon 5.00 2.20
☐ 228 Earl Weaver 10.00 4.50
☐ A Abner Doubleday 5.00 2.20
☐ B Stephen C. Clark 1.00 .45
☐ C Paul S. Kerr 1.00 .45
☐ D Edward W. Stack 1.00 .45
☐ E Perez-Steele Galleries 1.00 .45
☐ F George W. Bush 2.50 1.10
Edward W. Stack

1989 Perez-Steele Celebration Postcards

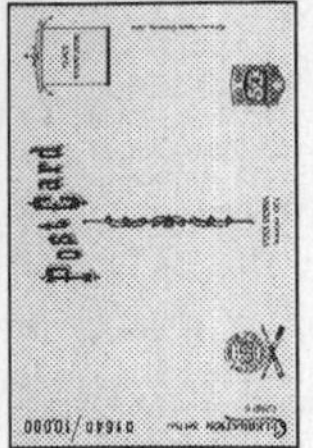

This 44-card set celebrates the 50th Anniversary of the National Baseball Hall of Fame and Museum. The cards measure approximately 3 1/2" by 5 1/2" and feature art work by artist Dick Perez. The backs carry a postcard format.

	MINT	NRMT
COMPLETE SET (44)	125.00	55.00
COMMON CARD (1-44)	2.00	.90

☐ 1 Hank Aaron 6.00 2.70
☐ 2 Luis Aparicio 4.00 1.80
☐ 3 Ernie Banks 6.00 2.70
☐ 4 Cool Papa Bell 3.00 1.35
☐ 5 Johnny Bench 4.00 1.80
☐ 6 Yogi Berra 6.00 2.70
☐ 7 Lou Boudreau 4.00 1.80
☐ 8 Roy Campanella 5.00 2.20
☐ 9 Happy Chandler 2.00 .90
☐ 10 Jocko Conlan 2.00 .90
☐ 11 Ray Dandridge 3.00 1.35
☐ 12 Bill Dickey 4.00 1.80
☐ 13 Bobby Doerr 4.00 1.80
☐ 14 Rick Ferrell 3.00 1.35
☐ 15 Charlie Gehringer 4.00 1.80
☐ 16 Lefty Gomez 4.00 1.80
☐ 17 Billy Herman 2.50 1.10
☐ 18 Carfish Hunter 4.00 1.80
☐ 19 Monte Irvin 4.00 1.80
☐ 20 Judy Johnson 4.00 1.80
☐ 21 Al Kaline 6.00 2.70
☐ 22 George Kell 4.00 1.80
☐ 23 Harmon Killebrew 5.00 2.20
☐ 24 Ralph Kiner 4.00 1.80
☐ 25 Bob Lemon 3.00 1.35
☐ 26 Buck Leonard 4.00 1.80
☐ 27 Al Lopez 2.50 1.10
☐ 28 Mickey Mantle 10.00 4.50
☐ 29 Juan Marichal 4.00 1.80
☐ 30 Eddie Mathews 4.00 1.80
☐ 31 Willie McCovey 4.00 1.80
☐ 32 Johnny Mize 4.00 1.80
☐ 33 Stan Musial 6.00 2.70
☐ 34 Pee Wee Reese 4.00 1.80
☐ 35 Brooks Robinson 5.00 2.20
☐ 36 Joe Sewell 3.00 1.35
☐ 37 Enos Slaughter 4.00 1.80
☐ 38 Duke Snider 4.00 1.80
☐ 39 Warren Spahn 5.00 2.20
☐ 40 Willie Stargell 4.00 1.80
☐ 41 Bill Terry 4.00 1.80
☐ 42 Billy Williams 3.00 1.35
☐ 43 Ted Williams 10.00 4.50
☐ 44 Carl Yastrzemski 4.00 1.80

1990-92 Perez-Steele Master Works

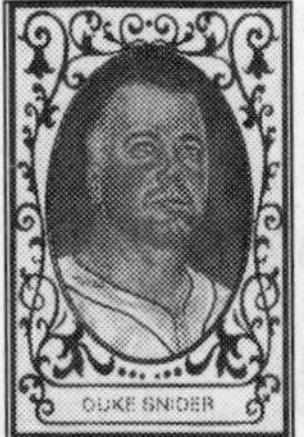

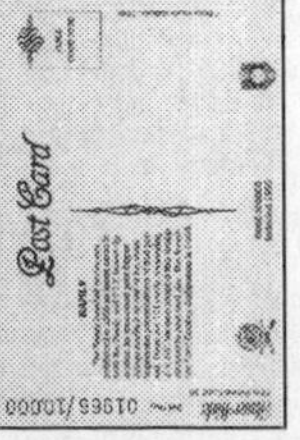

This 50-card set measures 3 1/2" by 5 1/2" and again features the fine artwork of Dick Perez. The set honors living Hall-of-Famers at the time of issue and depicts them as if they might have appeared on several vintage card sets. The sets imitated are the Goodwin Champions of

1888, Rose Postcards of 1908, the T205 Gold Borders, 1909 Ramlys and one original design. The sets are numbered and are limited to 10,000 sets. The original issue price for each series was $135.

	MINT	NRMT
COMPLETE SET (50)	225.00	100.00
COMMON CARD (1-50)	2.00	.90
☐ 1 Charlie Gehringer	2.00	.90
Ramly		
☐ 2 Charlie Gehringer	2.00	.90
Goodwin		
☐ 3 Charlie Gehringer	2.00	.90
Rose		
☐ 4 Charlie Gehringer	2.00	.90
T205		
☐ 5 Charlie Gehringer	2.00	.90
Original Drawing		
☐ 6 Mickey Mantle	15.00	6.75
Ramly		
☐ 7 Mickey Mantle	15.00	6.75
Goodwin		
☐ 8 Mickey Mantle	15.00	6.75
Rose		
☐ 9 Mickey Mantle	15.00	6.75
T205		
☐ 10 Mickey Mantle	15.00	6.75
Original Drawing		
☐ 11 Willie Mays	12.50	5.50
Ramly		
☐ 12 Willie Mays	12.50	5.50
Goodwin		
☐ 13 Willie Mays	12.50	5.50
Rose		
☐ 14 Willie Mays	12.50	5.50
T205		
☐ 15 Willie Mays	12.50	5.50
Original Drawing		
☐ 16 Duke Snider	7.50	3.40
Ramly		
☐ 17 Duke Snider	7.50	3.40
Goodwin		
☐ 18 Duke Snider	7.50	3.40
Rose		
☐ 19 Duke Snider	7.50	3.40
T205		
☐ 20 Duke Snider	7.50	3.40
Original Drawing		
☐ 21 Warren Spahn	3.00	1.35
Ramly		
☐ 22 Warren Spahn	3.00	1.35
Goodwin		
☐ 23 Warren Sphan	3.00	1.35
Rose		
☐ 24 Warren Spahn	3.00	1.35
T205		
☐ 25 Warren Spahn	3.00	1.35
Original Drawing		
☐ 26 Yogi Berra	5.00	2.20
Ramly		
☐ 27 Yogi Berra	5.00	2.20
Goodwin		
☐ 28 Yogi Berra	5.00	2.20
Rose		
☐ 29 Yogi Berra	5.00	2.20
T205		
☐ 30 Yogi Berra	5.00	2.20
Original Drawing		
☐ 31 Johnny Mize	2.00	.90
Ramly		
☐ 32 Johnny Mize	2.00	.90
Goodwin		
☐ 33 Johnny Mize	2.00	.90
Rose		
☐ 34 Johnny Mize	2.00	.90
T205		
☐ 35 Johnny Mize	2.00	.90
Original Drawing		
☐ 36 Willie Stargell	3.00	1.35
Ramly		
☐ 37 Willie Stargell	3.00	1.35
Goodwin		
☐ 38 Willie Stargell	3.00	1.35
Rose		
☐ 39 Willie Stargell	3.00	1.35
T205		
☐ 40 Willie Stargell	3.00	1.35
Original Drawing		
☐ 41 Ted Williams	12.50	5.50
Ramly		
☐ 42 Ted Williams	12.50	5.50
Goodwin		
☐ 43 Ted Williams	12.50	5.50
Rose		
☐ 44 Ted Williams	12.50	5.50
T205		
☐ 45 Ted Williams	12.50	5.50
Original Drawing		
☐ 46 Carl Yastrzemski	5.00	2.20
Ramly		
☐ 47 Carl Yastrzemski	5.00	2.20
Goodwin		
☐ 48 Carl Yastrzemski	5.00	2.20
Rose		
☐ 49 Carl Yastrzemski	5.00	2.20
T205		
☐ 50 Carl Yastrzemski	5.00	2.20
Original Drawing		

1990-97 Perez-Steele Great Moments

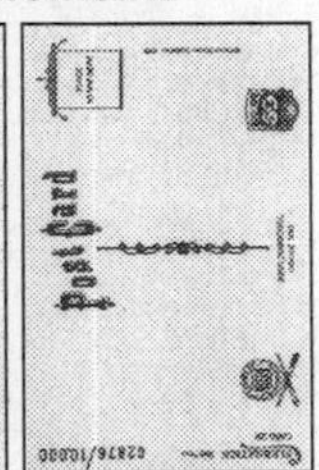

These cards were issued in series of 12 cards each. So far, nine series have been issued. The cards measure 3 1/2" by 5 1/2" and feature leading moments in Hall of Famers careers. These sets are also issued with continuation rights.

	MINT	NRMT
COMPLETE SET (108)	300.00	135.00
COMMON CARD	2.00	.90
☐ 1 Babe Ruth	20.00	9.00
☐ 2 Al Kaline	3.00	1.35
☐ 3 Jackie Robinson	15.00	6.75
☐ 4 Lou Gehrig	15.00	6.75
☐ 5 Whitey Ford	5.00	2.20
☐ 6 Christy Mathewson	7.50	3.40
☐ 7 Roy Campanella	5.00	2.20
☐ 8 Walter Johnson	7.50	3.40
☐ 9 Hank Aaron	15.00	6.75
☐ 10 Cy Young	7.50	3.40
☐ 11 Stan Musial	7.50	3.40
☐ 12 Ty Cobb	15.00	6.75
☐ 13 Ted Williams	15.00	6.75
☐ 14 Warren Spahn	3.00	1.35
☐ 15 Paul Waner	3.00	1.35
Lloyd Waner		
☐ 16 Sandy Koufax	7.50	3.40
☐ 17 Robin Roberts	3.00	1.35
☐ 18 Dizzy Dean	5.00	2.20
☐ 19 Mickey Mantle	20.00	9.00
☐ 20 Satchel Paige	10.00	4.50
☐ 21 Ernie Banks	7.50	3.40
☐ 22 Willie McCovey	3.00	1.35
☐ 23 Johnny Mize	2.00	.90
☐ 24 Honus Wagner	5.00	2.20
☐ 25 Willie Keeler	2.00	.90
☐ 26 Pee Wee Reese	5.00	2.20
☐ 27 Monte Irvin	2.00	.90
☐ 28 Eddie Mathews	5.00	2.20
☐ 29 Enos Slaughter	3.00	1.35
☐ 30 Rube Marquard	2.00	.90
☐ 31 Charlie Gehringer	3.00	1.35
☐ 32 Roberto Clemente	15.00	6.75
☐ 33 Duke Snider	7.50	3.40
☐ 34 Ray Dandridge	2.00	.90
☐ 35 Carl Hubbell	3.00	1.35
☐ 36 Bobby Doerr	3.00	1.35
☐ 37 Bill Dickey	3.00	1.35
☐ 38 Willie Stargell	3.00	1.35
☐ 39 Brooks Robinson	5.00	2.20
☐ 40 Joe Tinker	5.00	2.20
Johnny Evers		
Frank Chance		
☐ 41 Billy Herman	2.00	.90
☐ 42 Grover Alexander	5.00	2.20
☐ 43 Luis Aparicio	3.00	1.35
☐ 44 Lefty Gomez	2.00	.90
☐ 45 Eddie Collins	2.00	.90
☐ 46 Judy Johnson	3.00	1.35
☐ 47 Harry Heilmann	2.00	.90
☐ 48 Harmon Killebrew	3.00	1.35
☐ 49 Johnny Bench	7.50	3.40
☐ 50 Max Carey	2.00	.90
☐ 51 Cool Papa Bell	3.00	1.35
☐ 52 Rube Waddell	2.00	.90
☐ 53 Yogi Berra	7.50	3.40
☐ 54 Herb Pennock	2.00	.90
☐ 55 Red Schoendienst	3.00	1.35
☐ 56 Juan Marichal	5.00	2.20
☐ 57 Frankie Frisch	2.00	.90
☐ 58 Buck Leonard	3.00	1.35
☐ 59 George Kell	3.00	1.35
☐ 60 Chuck Klein	2.00	.90
☐ 61 King Kelly	2.00	.90
☐ 62 Catfish Hunter	5.00	2.20
☐ 63 Lou Boudreau	3.00	1.35
☐ 64 Al Lopez	3.00	1.35
☐ 65 Willie Mays	15.00	6.75
☐ 66 Lou Brock	5.00	2.20
☐ 67 Bob Lemon	3.00	1.35
☐ 68 Joe Sewell	2.00	.90
☐ 69 Billy Williams	3.00	1.35
☐ 70 Rick Ferrell	2.00	.90
☐ 71 Arky Vaughan	2.00	.90
☐ 72 Carl Yastrzemski	7.50	3.40
☐ 73 Tom Seaver	5.00	2.20
☐ 74 Rollie Fingers	4.00	1.80
☐ 75 Ralph Kiner	4.00	1.80
☐ 76 Frank Baker	3.00	1.35
☐ 77 Rod Carew	4.00	1.80
☐ 78 Goose Goslin	3.00	1.35
☐ 79 Gaylord Perry	4.00	1.80
☐ 80 Hack Wilson	4.00	1.80
☐ 81 Hal Newhouser	2.00	.90
☐ 82 Early Wynn	2.00	.90
☐ 83 Bob Feller	5.00	2.20
☐ 84 Branch Rickey	2.00	.90
☐ 85 Jim Palmer	4.00	1.80
☐ 86 Al Barlick	2.00	.90
☐ 87 Mickey Mantle	10.00	4.50
Willie Mays		
Duke Snider		
☐ 88 Hank Greenberg	4.00	1.80
☐ 89 Joe Morgan	4.00	1.80
☐ 90 Chief Bender	3.00	1.35
☐ 91 Pee Wee Reese	5.00	2.20
Jackie Robinson		
☐ 92 Jim Bottomley	3.00	1.35
☐ 93 Ferguson Jenkins	4.00	1.80
☐ 94 Frank Robinson	5.00	2.20
☐ 95 Hoyt Wilhelm	2.00	.90
☐ 96 Cap Anson	3.00	1.35
☐ 97 Jim Bunning	3.00	1.35
☐ 98 Richie Ashburn	4.00	1.80
☐ 99 Steve Carlton	5.00	2.20
☐ 100 Mike Schmidt	5.00	2.20
☐ 101 Nellie Fox	3.00	1.35
☐ 102 Tom Lasorda	3.00	1.35
☐ 103 Leo Durocher	2.00	.90
☐ 104 Reggie Jackson	5.00	2.20
☐ 105 Phil Rizzuto	4.00	1.80
☐ 106 Phil Niekro	3.00	1.35
☐ 107 Willie Wells	2.00	.90
☐ 108 Earl Weaver	2.00	.90

1981 Perma-Graphic All-Stars

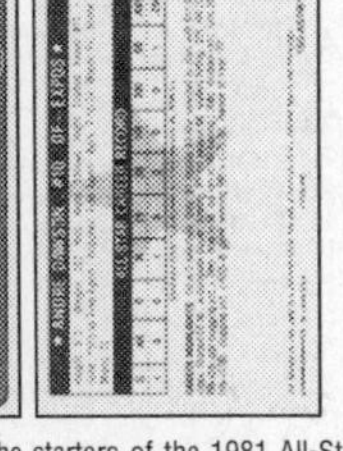

This set commemorates the starters of the 1981 All-Star game. This 18-card set measure 2 1/8" by 3 3/8" and has rounded corners. Because of the players strike of 1981 plenty of time was available to prepare the player's biography with appropriate notes. The set is framed on the front in red for the National League and blue for the American League.

	NRMT	VG-E
COMPLETE SET (18)	50.00	22.00
COMMON CARD (1-18)	1.00	.45
☐ 1 Gary Carter	6.00	2.70
☐ 2 Dave Concepcion	2.50	1.10
☐ 3 Andre Dawson	6.00	2.70
☐ 4 George Foster	1.00	.45
☐ 5 Davey Lopes	2.50	1.10
☐ 6 Dave Parker	2.50	1.10
☐ 7 Pete Rose	7.50	3.40
☐ 8 Mike Schmidt	8.00	3.60
☐ 9 Fernando Valenzuela	2.50	1.10
☐ 10 George Brett	12.50	5.50
☐ 11 Rod Carew	5.00	2.20
☐ 12 Bucky Dent	2.50	1.10

Card	NRMT	VG-E
☐ 13 Carlton Fisk	5.00	2.20
☐ 14 Reggie Jackson	6.00	2.70
☐ 15 Jack Morris	4.00	1.80
☐ 16 Willie Randolph	2.50	1.10
☐ 17 Ken Singleton	1.00	.45
☐ 18 Dave Winfield	6.00	2.70

1981 Perma-Graphic Credit Cards

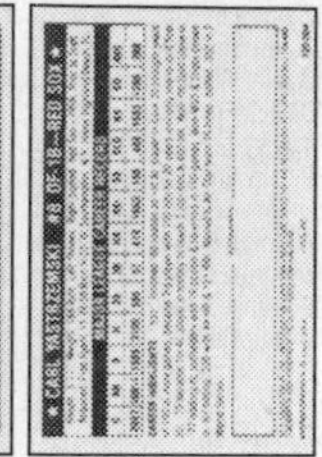

Perma-Graphic began their three-year foray into card manufacturing with this 32-card set of "credit cards" each measuring approximately 2 1/8" by 3 3/8". The set featured 32 of the leading players of 1981. This set's design is split on the front between a full-color photo of the player and an identification of said player while the back has one line of career statistics and lines of career highlights. These sets (made of plastic) were issued with the cooperation of Topps Chewing Gum. This first set of Perma-Graphic cards seems to have been produced in greater quantities than the other five Perma-Graphic sets.

	NRMT	VG-E
COMPLETE SET (32)	50.00	22.00
COMMON CARD (1-32)	1.00	.45

Card	NRMT	VG-E
☐ 1 Johnny Bench	4.00	1.80
☐ 2 Mike Schmidt	7.50	3.40
☐ 3 George Brett	10.00	4.50
☐ 4 Carl Yastrzemski	4.00	1.80
☐ 5 Pete Rose	5.00	2.20
☐ 6 Bob Horner	1.00	.45
☐ 7 Reggie Jackson	6.00	2.70
☐ 8 Keith Hernandez	2.00	.90
☐ 9 George Foster	1.00	.45
☐ 10 Garry Templeton	1.00	.45
☐ 11 Tom Seaver	4.00	1.80
☐ 12 Steve Garvey	2.00	.90
☐ 13 Dave Parker	2.00	.90
☐ 14 Willie Stargell	3.00	1.35
☐ 15 Cecil Cooper	1.00	.45
☐ 16 Steve Carlton	4.00	1.80
☐ 17 Ted Simmons	1.00	.45
☐ 18 Dave Kingman	2.00	.90
☐ 19 Rickey Henderson	10.00	4.50
☐ 20 Fred Lynn	2.00	.90
☐ 21 Dave Winfield	5.00	2.20
☐ 22 Rod Carew	4.00	1.80
☐ 23 Jim Rice	2.00	.90
☐ 24 Bruce Sutter	2.00	.90
☐ 25 Cesar Cedeno	1.00	.45
☐ 26 Nolan Ryan	12.50	5.50
☐ 27 Dusty Baker	1.00	.45
☐ 28 Jim Palmer	4.00	1.80
☐ 29 Gorman Thomas	1.00	.45
☐ 30 Ben Oglivie	1.00	.45
☐ 31 Willie Wilson	1.00	.45
☐ 32 Gary Carter	3.00	1.35

1982 Perma-Graphic All-Stars

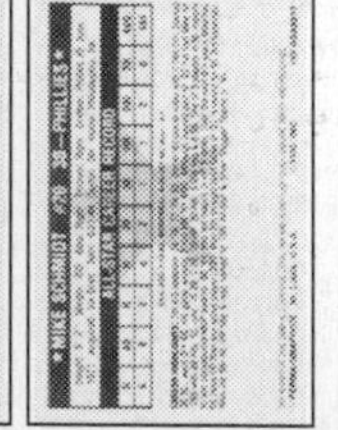

For the second time Perma-Graphic issued a special set commemorating the starters of the 1982 All-Star game. This 18-card set measures 2 1/8" by 3 3/8" and features a colorful design framing the players photo on the front The back again feature one line of complete All-Star game statistics including the 1982 game and career highlites. Perma-Graphic also issued the set in a limited (reportedly 1200 sets produced) "gold" edition, i.e., with a gold tint to the cards. The gold edition cards are valued at a multiplte of the regular set. Please refer to the multiplication table below.

	NRMT	VG-E
COMPLETE SET (18)	50.00	22.00
COMMON CARD (1-18)	1.50	.70
*GOLD CARDS:3X BASIC CARDS		

Card	NRMT	VG-E
☐ 1 Dennis Eckersley	4.00	1.80
☐ 2 Cecil Cooper	1.50	.70
☐ 3 Carlton Fisk	5.00	2.20
☐ 4 Robin Yount	5.00	2.20
☐ 5 Bobby Grich	1.50	.70
☐ 6 Rickey Henderson	6.00	2.70
☐ 7 Reggie Jackson	6.00	2.70
☐ 8 Fred Lynn	2.50	1.10
☐ 9 George Brett	10.00	4.50
☐ 10 Gary Carter	4.00	1.80
☐ 11 Dave Concepcion	1.50	.70
☐ 12 Andre Dawson	4.00	1.80
☐ 13 Tim Raines	2.50	1.10
☐ 14 Dale Murphy	4.00	1.80
☐ 15 Steve Rogers	1.50	.70
☐ 16 Pete Rose	6.00	2.70
☐ 17 Mike Schmidt	6.00	2.70
☐ 18 Manny Trillo	1.50	.70

1982 Perma-Graphic Credit Cards

For the second year Perma-Graphic, in association with Topps produced a high-quality set on plastic honoring the leading players in baseball of 1982. The players photo is on the front middle of the card and is framed by a brown border with many innovative designs. This 24-card set features plastic cards each measuring approximately 2 1/8" by 3 3/8". On the card back there is one line of career statistics along with career highlights. Perma-Graphic also issued the set in a limited (reportedly 900 sets produced) "gold" edition, i.e., with a gold tint to the cards. The gold edition cards are valued at a mulitple of the regular cards. Please see information below for the multiplication value. Again in 1982 Perma-Graphic issued these sets in conjuction and with the approval of Topps Chewing Gum.

	NRMT	VG-E
COMPLETE SET (24)	50.00	22.00
COMMON CARD (1-24)	1.00	.45
*GOLD CARDS: 3X BASIC CARDS		

Card	NRMT	VG-E
☐ 1 Johnny Bench	4.00	1.80
☐ 2 Tom Seaver	4.00	1.80
☐ 3 Mike Schmidt	6.00	2.70
☐ 4 Gary Carter	3.00	1.35
☐ 5 Willie Stargell	3.00	1.35
☐ 6 Tim Raines	2.00	.90
☐ 7 Bill Madlock	1.00	.45
☐ 8 Keith Hernandez	2.00	.90
☐ 9 Pete Rose	6.00	2.70
☐ 10 Steve Carlton	4.00	1.80
☐ 11 Steve Garvey	2.00	.90
☐ 12 Fernando Valenzuela	2.00	.90
☐ 13 Carl Yastrzemski	4.00	1.80
☐ 14 Dave Winfield	4.00	1.80
☐ 15 Carney Lansford	1.00	.45
☐ 16 Rollie Fingers	2.00	.90
☐ 17 Tony Armas	1.00	.45
☐ 18 Cecil Cooper	1.00	.45
☐ 19 George Brett	10.00	4.50
☐ 20 Reggie Jackson	6.00	2.70
☐ 21 Rod Carew	4.00	1.80
☐ 22 Eddie Murray	7.50	3.40
☐ 23 Rickey Henderson	6.00	2.70
☐ 24 Kirk Gibson	3.00	1.35

1983 Perma-Graphic All-Stars

The 1983 All-Star Set was the third set Perma-Graphic issued commemorating the starters of the All-Star game.

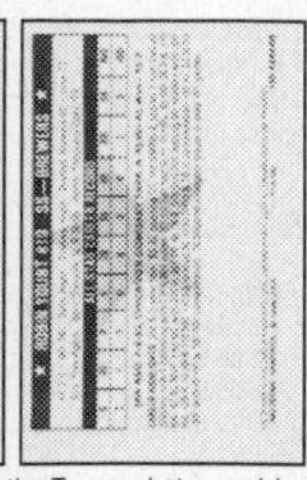

Again, Perma-Graphic used the Topps photos and issued their sets of plastic cards. This 18-card set features cards each measuring approximately 2 1/8" by 3 3/8". Perma-Graphic also issued the set in a limited "gold" edition, i.e., with a gold tint to the cards. The gold edition cards are valued at a multiple of the regular issue cards. Please see information below for values.

	NRMT	VG-E
COMPLETE SET (18)_	50.00	22.00
COMMON CARD (1-18)	1.25	.55
*GOLD CARDS:3X BASIC CARDS		

Card	NRMT	VG-E
☐ 1 George Brett	10.00	4.50
☐ 2 Rod Carew	4.00	1.80
☐ 3 Fred Lynn	2.00	.90
☐ 4 Jim Rice	2.00	.90
☐ 5 Ted Simmons	1.25	.55
☐ 6 Dave Stieb	1.25	.55
☐ 7 Dave Winfield	4.00	1.80
☐ 8 Manny Trillo	1.25	.55
☐ 9 Robin Yount	4.00	1.80
☐ 10 Gary Carter	3.00	1.35
☐ 11 Andre Dawson	3.00	1.35
☐ 12 Dale Murphy	3.00	1.35
☐ 13 Al Oliver	1.25	.55
☐ 14 Tim Raines	2.00	.90
☐ 15 Steve Sax	1.25	.55
☐ 16 Mike Schmidt	6.00	2.70
☐ 17 Ozzie Smith	7.50	3.40
☐ 18 Mario Soto	1.25	.55

1983 Perma-Graphic Credit Cards

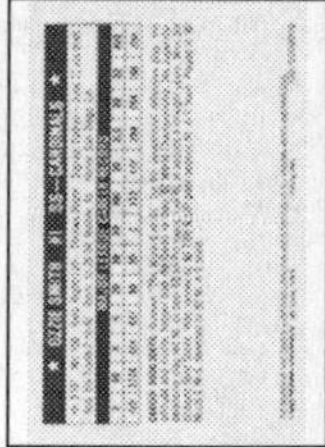

This set was the third straight year Perma-Graphic, with approval from Topps issued their high-quality plastic set. This 36-card set which measures 2 1/8" by 3 3/8" have the players photos framed by colorful backgrounds. The backs again feature one line of career statistics and several informative lines of career highlights. Perma-Graphic also issued the set in a limited (reportedly 1000 sets produced) "gold" edition, i.e., with a gold tint to the cards. The gold edition cards are valued at a multiple of the regular issue cards. Please see information below for values.

	NRMT	VG-E
COMPLETE SET (36)	50.00	22.00
COMMON CARD (1-36)	1.00	.45
*GOLD CARDS:3X BASIC CARDS		

Card	NRMT	VG-E
☐ 1 Bill Buckner	1.00	.45
☐ 2 Steve Carlton	4.00	1.80
☐ 3 Gary Carter	3.00	1.35
☐ 4 Andre Dawson	3.00	1.35
☐ 5 Pedro Guerrero	1.00	.45
☐ 6 George Hendrick	1.00	.45
☐ 7 Keith Hernandez	2.00	.90
☐ 8 Bill Madlock	1.00	.45
☐ 9 Dale Murphy	3.00	1.35
☐ 10 Al Oliver	1.00	.45
☐ 11 Dave Parker	2.00	.90
☐ 12 Darrell Porter	1.00	.45
☐ 13 Pete Rose	6.00	2.70
☐ 14 Mike Schmidt	6.00	2.70
☐ 15 Lonnie Smith	1.00	.45
☐ 16 Ozzie Smith	7.50	3.40

☐ 17 Bruce Sutter	2.00	.90
☐ 18 Fernando Valenzuela	3.00	1.35
☐ 19 George Brett	10.00	4.50
☐ 20 Rod Carew	4.00	1.80
☐ 21 Cecil Cooper	1.00	.45
☐ 22 Doug DeCinces	1.00	.45
☐ 23 Rollie Fingers	3.00	1.35
☐ 24 Damaso Garcia	1.00	.45
☐ 25 Toby Harrah	1.00	.45
☐ 26 Rickey Henderson	6.00	2.70
☐ 27 Reggie Jackson	6.00	2.70
☐ 28 Hal McRae	1.00	.45
☐ 29 Eddie Murray	6.00	2.70
☐ 30 Lance Parrish	2.00	.90
☐ 31 Jim Rice	2.00	.90
☐ 32 Gorman Thomas	1.00	.45
☐ 33 Willie Wilson	1.00	.45
☐ 34 Dave Winfield	4.00	1.80
☐ 35 Carl Yastrzemski	4.00	1.80
☐ 36 Robin Yount	3.00	1.35

1979 Phillies Burger King

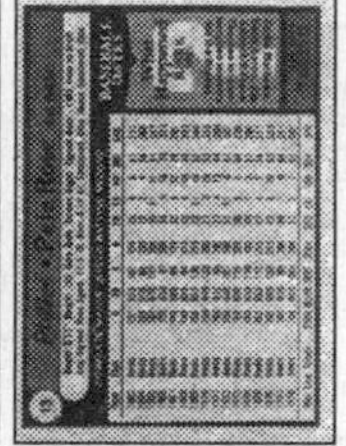

The cards in this 23-card set measure 2 1/2" by 3 1/2". The 1979 Burger King Phillies set follows the regular format of 22 player cards and one unnumbered checklist card. The asterisk indicates where the pose differs from the Topps card of that year. The set features the first card of Pete Rose as a member of the Philadelphia Phillies.

	NRMT	VG-E
COMPLETE SET (23)	10.00	4.50
COMMON CARD (1-22)	.10	.05
☐ 1 Danny Ozark MG *	.20	.09
☐ 2 Bob Boone	.50	.23
☐ 3 Tim McCarver	.50	.23
☐ 4 Steve Carlton	2.50	1.10
☐ 5 Larry Christenson	.10	.05
☐ 6 Dick Ruthven	.10	.05
☐ 7 Ron Reed	.10	.05
☐ 8 Randy Lerch	.10	.05
☐ 9 Warren Brusstar	.10	.05
☐ 10 Tug McGraw	.35	.16
☐ 11 Nino Espinosa *	.10	.05
☐ 12 Doug Bird *	.10	.05
☐ 13 Pete Rose * (Shown as Reds in 1979 Topps)	4.00	1.80
☐ 14 Manny Trillo *	.20	.09
☐ 15 Larry Bowa	.35	.16
☐ 16 Mike Schmidt	4.00	1.80
☐ 17 Pete Mackanin *	.10	.05
☐ 18 Jose Cardenal	.10	.05
☐ 19 Greg Luzinski	.35	.16
☐ 20 Garry Maddox	.20	.09
☐ 21 Bake McBride	.10	.05
☐ 22 Greg Gross *	.10	.05
☐ NNO Checklist Card TP	.05	.02

1980 Phillies Burger King

The cards in this 23-card set measure 2 1/2" by 3 1/2". The 1980 edition of Burger King Phillies follows the established pattern of 22 numbered player cards and one unnumbered checklist. Cards marked with asterisks contain poses different from those found in the regular 1980 Topps cards. This was the first Burger King set to carry the Burger King logo and hence does not generate the same confusion that the three previous years do for collectors trying to distinguish Burger King cards from the very similar Topps cards of the same years.

	NRMT	VG-E
COMPLETE SET (23)	8.00	3.60
COMMON CARD (1-22)	.10	.05
☐ 1 Dallas Green MG *	.30	.14
☐ 2 Bob Boone	.30	.14
☐ 3 Keith Moreland *	.20	.09
☐ 4 Pete Rose	4.00	1.80
☐ 5 Manny Trillo	.20	.09
☐ 6 Mike Schmidt	4.00	1.80
☐ 7 Larry Bowa	.20	.09
☐ 8 John Vukovich *	.10	.05
☐ 9 Bake McBride	.10	.05
☐ 10 Garry Maddox	.20	.09
☐ 11 Greg Luzinski	.20	.09
☐ 12 Greg Gross	.10	.05
☐ 13 Del Unser	.10	.05
☐ 14 Lonnie Smith *	.20	.09
☐ 15 Steve Carlton	2.50	1.10
☐ 16 Larry Christenson	.10	.05
☐ 17 Nino Espinosa	.10	.05
☐ 18 Randy Lerch	.10	.05
☐ 19 Dick Ruthven	.10	.05
☐ 20 Tug McGraw	.30	.14
☐ 21 Ron Reed	.10	.05
☐ 22 Kevin Saucier *	.10	.05
☐ NNO Checklist Card TP	.05	.02

1988 Phillies Topps Ashburn Sheet

This 13-card set was issued on one perforated sheet measuring approximately 10" by 14" commemorating Richie Ashburn's 40 years in baseball. Sponsored by Campbell's, the sheet features 12 smaller versions of different Topps cards printed on a sky-blue and flag background with a bigger 5" by 7" portrait card in the middle. The back of this card displayed his complete Major League batting record and accomplishments. The cards are listed below according to the year they appeared in the Topps sets.

	MINT	NRMT
COMPLETE SET (13)	10.00	4.50
COMMON CARD (1-13)	1.00	.45
☐ 1 1952 Bowman	1.00	.45
☐ 2 1952 Topps	1.00	.45
☐ 3 1954 Topps	1.00	.45
☐ 4 1956 Topps	1.00	.45
☐ 5 1957 Topps	1.00	.45
☐ 6 1958 Topps	1.00	.45
☐ 7 1959 Topps	1.00	.45
☐ 8 1959 Topps with Willie Mays	1.00	.45
☐ 9 1960 Topps	1.00	.45
☐ 10 1961 Topps	1.00	.45
☐ 11 1962 Topps	1.00	.45
☐ 12 1963 Topps	1.00	.45
☐ 13 1988 Richie Ashburn	1.00	.45

1992 Pinnacle

The 1992 Pinnacle set (issued by Score) consists of two series each with 310 standard-size cards. Cards were distributed in first and second series 16-card foil packs and 27-card cello packs. The card fronts feature glossy color player photos, on a black background accented by thin white borders. An anti-counterfeit device appears in the bottom border of each card back. A special ribbed plastic lenticular detector card was made available that allowed the user to view the anti-counterfeit device and unscramble the coding with the word "Pinnacle" appearing. Special subsets featured include '92 Rookie Prospects (52, 55, 168, 247-261, 263-280), Idols (281-286/584-591), Sidelines (287-294/592-596), Draft Picks (295-304), Shades (305-310/601-605), Grips (606-612), and Technicians (614-620). Rookie Cards in the set include Brian Jordan and Manny Ramirez.

	MINT	NRMT
COMPLETE SET (620)	40.00	18.00
COMPLETE SERIES 1 (310)	25.00	11.00
COMPLETE SERIES 2 (310)	15.00	6.75
COMMON CARD (1-620)	.10	.05
☐ 1 Frank Thomas	2.00	.90
☐ 2 Benito Santiago	.10	.05
☐ 3 Carlos Baerga	.20	.09
☐ 4 Cecil Fielder	.20	.09
☐ 5 Barry Larkin	.15	.07
☐ 6 Ozzie Smith	.50	.23
☐ 7 Willie McGee	.10	.05
☐ 8 Paul Molitor	.40	.18
☐ 9 Andy Van Slyke	.20	.09
☐ 10 Ryne Sandberg	.50	.23
☐ 11 Kevin Seitzer	.10	.05
☐ 12 Len Dykstra	.20	.09
☐ 13 Edgar Martinez	.15	.07
☐ 14 Ruben Sierra	.10	.05
☐ 15 Howard Johnson	.10	.05
☐ 16 Dave Henderson	.10	.05
☐ 17 Devon White	.10	.05
☐ 18 Terry Pendleton	.20	.09
☐ 19 Steve Finley	.20	.09
☐ 20 Kirby Puckett	.75	.35
☐ 21 Orel Hershiser	.20	.09
☐ 22 Hal Morris	.10	.05
☐ 23 Don Mattingly	.60	.25
☐ 24 Delino DeShields	.10	.05
☐ 25 Dennis Eckersley	.40	.18
☐ 26 Ellis Burks	.20	.09
☐ 27 Jay Buhner	.15	.07
☐ 28 Matt Williams	.15	.07
☐ 29 Lou Whitaker	.20	.09
☐ 30 Alex Fernandez	.20	.09
☐ 31 Albert Belle	.50	.23
☐ 32 Todd Zeile	.10	.05
☐ 33 Tony Pena	.10	.05
☐ 34 Jay Bell	.20	.09
☐ 35 Rafael Palmeiro	.15	.07
☐ 36 Wes Chamberlain	.10	.05
☐ 37 George Bell	.10	.05
☐ 38 Robin Yount	.15	.07
☐ 39 Vince Coleman	.10	.05
☐ 40 Bruce Hurst	.10	.05
☐ 41 Harold Baines	.20	.09
☐ 42 Chuck Finley	.10	.05
☐ 43 Ken Caminiti	.40	.18
☐ 44 Ben McDonald	.10	.05
☐ 45 Roberto Alomar	.40	.18
☐ 46 Chili Davis	.20	.09
☐ 47 Bill Doran	.10	.05
☐ 48 Jerald Clark	.10	.05
☐ 49 Jose Lind	.10	.05
☐ 50 Nolan Ryan	1.50	.70
☐ 51 Phil Plantier	.10	.05
☐ 52 Gary DiSarcina	.10	.05
☐ 53 Kevin Bass	.10	.05
☐ 54 Pat Kelly	.10	.05
☐ 55 Mark Wohlers	.40	.18
☐ 56 Walt Weiss	.10	.05
☐ 57 Lenny Harris	.10	.05
☐ 58 Ivan Calderon	.10	.05
☐ 59 Harold Reynolds	.10	.05
☐ 60 George Brett	.75	.35
☐ 61 Gregg Olson	.10	.05
☐ 62 Orlando Merced	.10	.05
☐ 63 Steve Decker	.10	.05
☐ 64 John Franco	.10	.05
☐ 65 Greg Maddux	1.25	.55
☐ 66 Alex Cole	.10	.05
☐ 67 Dave Hollins	.10	.05
☐ 68 Kent Hrbek	.20	.09
☐ 69 Tom Pagnozzi	.10	.05
☐ 70 Jeff Bagwell	1.25	.55
☐ 71 Jim Gantner	.10	.05
☐ 72 Matt Nokes	.10	.05
☐ 73 Brian Harper	.10	.05
☐ 74 Andy Benes	.20	.09

☐ 75 Tom Glavine .15 .07
☐ 76 Terry Steinbach .20 .09
☐ 77 Dennis Martinez .20 .09
☐ 78 John Olerud .20 .09
☐ 79 Ozzie Guillen .10 .05
☐ 80 Darryl Strawberry .20 .09
☐ 81 Gary Gaetti .20 .09
☐ 82 Dave Righetti .10 .05
☐ 83 Chris Hoiles .10 .05
☐ 84 Andujar Cedeno .10 .05
☐ 85 Jack Clark .20 .09
☐ 86 David Howard .10 .05
☐ 87 Bill Gullickson .10 .05
☐ 88 Bernard Gilkey .20 .09
☐ 89 Kevin Elster .10 .05
☐ 90 Kevin Maas .10 .05
☐ 91 Mark Lewis .10 .05
☐ 92 Greg Vaughn .10 .05
☐ 93 Bret Barberie .10 .05
☐ 94 Dave Smith .10 .05
☐ 95 Roger Clemens .75 .35
☐ 96 Doug Drabek .10 .05
☐ 97 Omar Vizquel .20 .09
☐ 98 Jose Guzman .10 .05
☐ 99 Juan Samuel .10 .05
☐ 100 Dave Justice .40 .18
☐ 101 Tom Browning .10 .05
☐ 102 Mark Gubicza .10 .05
☐ 103 Mickey Morandini .10 .05
☐ 104 Ed Whitson .10 .05
☐ 105 Lance Parrish .10 .05
☐ 106 Scott Erickson .20 .09
☐ 107 Jack McDowell .10 .05
☐ 108 Dave Stieb .10 .05
☐ 109 Mike Moore .10 .05
☐ 110 Travis Fryman .20 .09
☐ 111 Dwight Gooden .20 .09
☐ 112 Fred McGriff .15 .07
☐ 113 Alan Trammell .15 .07
☐ 114 Roberto Kelly .10 .05
☐ 115 Andre Dawson .15 .07
☐ 116 Bill Landrum .10 .05
☐ 117 Brian McRae .10 .05
☐ 118 B.J. Surhoff .20 .09
☐ 119 Chuck Knoblauch .40 .18
☐ 120 Steve Olin .10 .05
☐ 121 Robin Ventura .20 .09
☐ 122 Will Clark .15 .07
☐ 123 Tino Martinez .40 .18
☐ 124 Dale Murphy .40 .18
☐ 125 Pete O'Brien .10 .05
☐ 126 Ray Lankford .40 .18
☐ 127 Juan Gonzalez 1.25 .55
☐ 128 Ron Gant .20 .09
☐ 129 Marquis Grissom .20 .09
☐ 130 Jose Canseco .15 .07
☐ 131 Mike Greenwell .10 .05
☐ 132 Mark Langston .10 .05
☐ 133 Brett Butler .20 .09
☐ 134 Kelly Gruber .10 .05
☐ 135 Chris Sabo .10 .05
☐ 136 Mark Grace .15 .07
☐ 137 Tony Fernandez .10 .05
☐ 138 Glenn Davis .10 .05
☐ 139 Pedro Munoz .10 .05
☐ 140 Craig Biggio .15 .07
☐ 141 Pete Schourek .10 .05
☐ 142 Mike Boddicker .10 .05
☐ 143 Robby Thompson .10 .05
☐ 144 Mel Hall .10 .05
☐ 145 Bryan Harvey .10 .05
☐ 146 Mike LaValliere .10 .05
☐ 147 John Kruk .20 .09
☐ 148 Joe Carter .15 .07
☐ 149 Greg Olson .10 .05
☐ 150 Julio Franco .20 .09
☐ 151 Darryl Hamilton .10 .05
☐ 152 Felix Fermin .10 .05
☐ 153 Jose Offerman .10 .05
☐ 154 Paul O'Neill .20 .09
☐ 155 Tommy Greene .10 .05
☐ 156 Ivan Rodriguez .75 .35
☐ 157 Dave Stewart .20 .09
☐ 158 Jeff Reardon .20 .09
☐ 159 Felix Jose .10 .05
☐ 160 Doug Dascenzo .10 .05
☐ 161 Tim Wallach .10 .05
☐ 162 Dan Plesac .10 .05
☐ 163 Luis Gonzalez .10 .05
☐ 164 Mike Henneman .10 .05
☐ 165 Mike Devereaux .10 .05
☐ 166 Luis Polonia .10 .05
☐ 167 Mike Sharperson .10 .05
☐ 168 Chris Donnels .10 .05
☐ 169 Greg W. Harris .10 .05
☐ 170 Deion Sanders .40 .18
☐ 171 Mike Schooler .10 .05
☐ 172 Jose DeJesus .10 .05
☐ 173 Jeff Montgomery .20 .09
☐ 174 Milt Cuyler .10 .05
☐ 175 Wade Boggs .40 .18
☐ 176 Kevin Tapani .10 .05
☐ 177 Bill Spiers .10 .05
☐ 178 Tim Raines .20 .09
☐ 179 Randy Milligan .10 .05
☐ 180 Rob Dibble .10 .05
☐ 181 Kirt Manwaring .10 .05
☐ 182 Pascual Perez .10 .05
☐ 183 Juan Guzman .10 .05
☐ 184 John Smiley .10 .05
☐ 185 David Segui .10 .05
☐ 186 Omar Olivares .10 .05
☐ 187 Joe Slusarski .10 .05
☐ 188 Erik Hanson .10 .05
☐ 189 Mark Portugal .10 .05
☐ 190 Walt Terrell .10 .05
☐ 191 John Smoltz .15 .07
☐ 192 Wilson Alvarez .20 .09
☐ 193 Jimmy Key .20 .09
☐ 194 Larry Walker .40 .18
☐ 195 Lee Smith .20 .09
☐ 196 Pete Harnisch .10 .05
☐ 197 Mike Harkey .10 .05
☐ 198 Frank Tanana .10 .05
☐ 199 Terry Mulholland .10 .05
☐ 200 Cal Ripken 1.50 .70
☐ 201 Dave Magadan .10 .05
☐ 202 Bud Black .10 .05
☐ 203 Terry Shumpert .10 .05
☐ 204 Mike Mussina .60 .25
☐ 205 Mo Vaughn .60 .25
☐ 206 Steve Farr .10 .05
☐ 207 Darrin Jackson .10 .05
☐ 208 Jerry Browne .10 .05
☐ 209 Jeff Russell .10 .05
☐ 210 Mike Scioscia .10 .05
☐ 211 Rick Aguilera .10 .05
☐ 212 Jaime Navarro .10 .05
☐ 213 Randy Tomlin .10 .05
☐ 214 Bobby Thigpen .10 .05
☐ 215 Mark Gardner .10 .05
☐ 216 Norm Charlton .10 .05
☐ 217 Mark McGwire .75 .35
☐ 218 Skeeter Barnes .10 .05
☐ 219 Bob Tewksbury .10 .05
☐ 220 Junior Felix .10 .05
☐ 221 Sam Horn .10 .05
☐ 222 Jody Reed .10 .05
☐ 223 Luis Sojo .10 .05
☐ 224 Jerome Walton .10 .05
☐ 225 Darryl Kile .20 .09
☐ 226 Mickey Tettleton .10 .05
☐ 227 Dan Pasqua .10 .05
☐ 228 Jim Gott .10 .05
☐ 229 Bernie Williams .40 .18
☐ 230 Shane Mack .10 .05
☐ 231 Steve Avery .10 .05
☐ 232 Dave Valle .10 .05
☐ 233 Mark Leonard .10 .05
☐ 234 Spike Owen .10 .05
☐ 235 Gary Sheffield .40 .18
☐ 236 Steve Chitren .10 .05
☐ 237 Zane Smith .10 .05
☐ 238 Tom Gordon .10 .05
☐ 239 Jose Oquendo .10 .05
☐ 240 Todd Stottlemyre .10 .05
☐ 241 Darren Daulton .20 .09
☐ 242 Tim Naehring .20 .09
☐ 243 Tony Phillips .10 .05
☐ 244 Shawon Dunston .10 .05
☐ 245 Manuel Lee .10 .05
☐ 246 Mike Pagliarulo .10 .05
☐ 247 Jim Thome 1.25 .55
☐ 248 Luis Mercedes .10 .05
☐ 249 Cal Eldred .10 .05
☐ 250 Derek Bell .20 .09
☐ 251 Arthur Rhodes .10 .05
☐ 252 Scott Cooper .10 .05
☐ 253 Roberto Hernandez .20 .09
☐ 254 Mo Sanford .10 .05
☐ 255 Scott Servais .10 .05
☐ 256 Eric Karros .20 .09
☐ 257 Andy Mota .10 .05
☐ 258 Keith Mitchell .10 .05
☐ 259 Joel Johnston .10 .05
☐ 260 John Wehner .10 .05
☐ 261 Gino Minutelli .10 .05
☐ 262 Greg Gagne .10 .05
☐ 263 Stan Royer .10 .05
☐ 264 Carlos Garcia .10 .05
☐ 265 Andy Ashby .10 .05
☐ 266 Kim Batiste .10 .05
☐ 267 Julio Valera .10 .05
☐ 268 Royce Clayton .20 .09
☐ 269 Gary Scott .10 .05
☐ 270 Kirk Dressendorfer .10 .05
☐ 271 Sean Berry .10 .05
☐ 272 Lance Dickson .10 .05
☐ 273 Rob Maurer .10 .05
☐ 274 Scott Brosius .10 .05
☐ 275 Dave Fleming .10 .05
☐ 276 Lenny Webster .10 .05
☐ 277 Mike Humphreys .10 .05
☐ 278 Freddie Benavides .10 .05
☐ 279 Harvey Pulliam .10 .05
☐ 280 Jeff Carter .10 .05
☐ 281 Jim Abbott I .40 .18
Nolan Ryan
☐ 282 Wade Boggs I .40 .18
George Brett
☐ 283 Ken Griffey Jr. I .75 .35
Rickey Henderson
☐ 284 Wally Joyner I .20 .09
Dale Murphy
☐ 285 Chuck Knoblauch I .40 .18
Ozzie Smith
☐ 286 Robin Ventura I .50 .23
Lou Gehrig
☐ 287 Robin Yount SIDE .15 .07
☐ 288 Bob Tewksbury SIDE .10 .05
☐ 289 Kirby Puckett SIDE .40 .18
☐ 290 Kenny Lofton SIDE 1.25 .55
☐ 291 Jack McDowell SIDE .10 .05
☐ 292 John Burkett SIDE .10 .05
☐ 293 Dwight Smith SIDE .10 .05
☐ 294 Nolan Ryan SIDE .75 .35
☐ 295 Manny Ramirez DP 2.50 1.10
☐ 296 Cliff Floyd DP UER .40 .18
(Throws right, not left as indicated on back)
☐ 297 Al Shirley DP .20 .09
☐ 298 Brian Barber DP .20 .09
☐ 299 Jon Farrell DP .10 .05
☐ 300 Scott Ruffcorn DP .10 .05
☐ 301 Tyrone Hill DP .10 .05
☐ 302 Benji Gil DP .20 .09
☐ 303 Tyler Green DP .20 .09
☐ 304 Allen Watson DP .20 .09
☐ 305 Jay Buhner SH .15 .07
☐ 306 Roberto Alomar SH .40 .18
☐ 307 Chuck Knoblauch SH .40 .18
☐ 308 Darryl Strawberry SH .20 .09
☐ 309 Danny Tartabull SH .10 .05
☐ 310 Bobby Bonilla SH .20 .09
☐ 311 Mike Felder .10 .05
☐ 312 Storm Davis .10 .05
☐ 313 Tim Teufel .10 .05
☐ 314 Tom Brunansky .10 .05
☐ 315 Rex Hudler .10 .05
☐ 316 Dave Otto .10 .05
☐ 317 Jeff King .20 .09
☐ 318 Dan Gladden .10 .05
☐ 319 Bill Pecota .10 .05
☐ 320 Franklin Stubbs .10 .05
☐ 321 Gary Carter .40 .18
☐ 322 Melido Perez .10 .05
☐ 323 Eric Davis .20 .09
☐ 324 Greg Myers .10 .05
☐ 325 Pete Incaviglia .10 .05
☐ 326 Von Hayes .10 .05
☐ 327 Greg Swindell .10 .05
☐ 328 Steve Sax .10 .05
☐ 329 Chuck McElroy .10 .05
☐ 330 Gregg Jefferies .20 .09
☐ 331 Joe Oliver .10 .05
☐ 332 Paul Faries .10 .05
☐ 333 David West .10 .05
☐ 334 Craig Grebeck .10 .05
☐ 335 Chris Hammond .10 .05
☐ 336 Billy Ripken .10 .05
☐ 337 Scott Sanderson .10 .05
☐ 338 Dick Schofield .10 .05
☐ 339 Bob Milacki .10 .05
☐ 340 Kevin Reimer .10 .05
☐ 341 Jose DeLeon .10 .05
☐ 342 Henry Cotto .10 .05
☐ 343 Daryl Boston .10 .05
☐ 344 Kevin Gross .10 .05
☐ 345 Milt Thompson .10 .05
☐ 346 Luis Rivera .10 .05
☐ 347 Al Osuna .10 .05
☐ 348 Rob Deer .10 .05
☐ 349 Tim Leary .10 .05
☐ 350 Mike Stanton .10 .05
☐ 351 Dean Palmer .20 .09
☐ 352 Trevor Wilson .10 .05
☐ 353 Mark Eichhorn .10 .05
☐ 354 Scott Aldred .10 .05
☐ 355 Mark Whiten .10 .05
☐ 356 Leo Gomez .10 .05
☐ 357 Rafael Belliard .10 .05

☐ 358 Carlos Quintana .10 .05
☐ 359 Mark Davis .10 .05
☐ 360 Chris Nabholz .10 .05
☐ 361 Carlton Fisk .40 .18
☐ 362 Joe Orsulak .10 .05
☐ 363 Eric Anthony .10 .05
☐ 364 Greg Hibbard .10 .05
☐ 365 Scott Leius .10 .05
☐ 366 Hensley Meulens .10 .05
☐ 367 Chris Bosio .10 .05
☐ 368 Brian Downing .10 .05
☐ 369 Sammy Sosa .40 .18
☐ 370 Stan Belinda .10 .05
☐ 371 Joe Grahe .10 .05
☐ 372 Luis Salazar .10 .05
☐ 373 Lance Johnson .10 .05
☐ 374 Kal Daniels .10 .05
☐ 375 Dave Winfield .15 .07
☐ 376 Brook Jacoby .10 .05
☐ 377 Mariano Duncan .10 .05
☐ 378 Ron Darling .10 .05
☐ 379 Randy Johnson .40 .18
☐ 380 Chito Martinez .10 .05
☐ 381 Andres Galarraga .15 .07
☐ 382 Willie Randolph .20 .09
☐ 383 Charles Nagy .20 .09
☐ 384 Tim Belcher .10 .05
☐ 385 Duane Ward .10 .05
☐ 386 Vicente Palacios .10 .05
☐ 387 Mike Gallego .10 .05
☐ 388 Rich DeLucia .10 .05
☐ 389 Scott Radinsky .10 .05
☐ 390 Damon Berryhill .10 .05
☐ 391 Kirk McCaskill .10 .05
☐ 392 Pedro Guerrero .10 .05
☐ 393 Kevin Mitchell .20 .09
☐ 394 Dickie Thon .10 .05
☐ 395 Bobby Bonilla .20 .09
☐ 396 Bill Wegman .10 .05
☐ 397 Dave Martinez .10 .05
☐ 398 Rick Sutcliffe .10 .05
☐ 399 Larry Andersen .10 .05
☐ 400 Tony Gwynn 1.00 .45
☐ 401 Rickey Henderson .15 .07
☐ 402 Greg Cadaret .10 .05
☐ 403 Keith Miller .10 .05
☐ 404 Bip Roberts .10 .05
☐ 405 Kevin Brown .20 .09
☐ 406 Mitch Williams .10 .05
☐ 407 Frank Viola .10 .05
☐ 408 Darren Lewis .10 .05
☐ 409 Bob Welch .10 .05
☐ 410 Bob Walk .10 .05
☐ 411 Todd Frohwirth .10 .05
☐ 412 Brian Hunter .10 .05
☐ 413 Ron Karkovice .10 .05
☐ 414 Mike Morgan .10 .05
☐ 415 Joe Hesketh .10 .05
☐ 416 Don Slaught .10 .05
☐ 417 Tom Henke .10 .05
☐ 418 Kurt Stillwell .10 .05
☐ 419 Hector Villaneuva .10 .05
☐ 420 Glenallen Hill .10 .05
☐ 421 Pat Borders .10 .05
☐ 422 Charlie Hough .10 .05
☐ 423 Charlie Leibrandt .10 .05
☐ 424 Eddie Murray .40 .18
☐ 425 Jesse Barfield .10 .05
☐ 426 Mark Lemke .10 .05
☐ 427 Kevin McReynolds .10 .05
☐ 428 Gilberto Reyes .10 .05
☐ 429 Ramon Martinez .20 .09
☐ 430 Steve Buechele .10 .05
☐ 431 David Wells .10 .05
☐ 432 Kyle Abbott .10 .05
☐ 433 John Habyan .10 .05
☐ 434 Kevin Appier .20 .09
☐ 435 Gene Larkin .10 .05
☐ 436 Sandy Alomar Jr. .20 .09
☐ 437 Mike Jackson .10 .05
☐ 438 Todd Benzinger .10 .05
☐ 439 Teddy Higuera .10 .05
☐ 440 Reggie Sanders .20 .09
☐ 441 Mark Carreon .10 .05
☐ 442 Bret Saberhagen .10 .05
☐ 443 Gene Nelson .10 .05
☐ 444 Jay Howell .10 .05
☐ 445 Roger McDowell .10 .05
☐ 446 Sid Bream .10 .05
☐ 447 Mackey Sasser .10 .05
☐ 448 Bill Swift .10 .05
☐ 449 Hubie Brooks .10 .05
☐ 450 David Cone .20 .09
☐ 451 Bobby Witt .10 .05
☐ 452 Brady Anderson .15 .07
☐ 453 Lee Stevens .10 .05
☐ 454 Luis Aquino .10 .05
☐ 455 Carney Lansford .20 .09
☐ 456 Carlos Hernandez .10 .05
☐ 457 Danny Jackson .10 .05
☐ 458 Gerald Young .10 .05
☐ 459 Tom Candiotti .10 .05
☐ 460 Billy Hatcher .10 .05
☐ 461 John Wetteland .20 .09
☐ 462 Mike Bordick .10 .05
☐ 463 Don Robinson .10 .05
☐ 464 Jeff Johnson .10 .05
☐ 465 Lonnie Smith .10 .05
☐ 466 Paul Assenmacher .10 .05
☐ 467 Alvin Davis .10 .05
☐ 468 Jim Eisenreich .20 .09
☐ 469 Brent Mayne .10 .05
☐ 470 Jeff Brantley .10 .05
☐ 471 Tim Burke .10 .05
☐ 472 Pat Mahomes .10 .05
☐ 473 Ryan Bowen .10 .05
☐ 474 Bryn Smith .10 .05
☐ 475 Mike Flanagan .10 .05
☐ 476 Reggie Jefferson .20 .09
☐ 477 Jeff Blauser .10 .05
☐ 478 Craig Lefferts .10 .05
☐ 479 Todd Worrell .10 .05
☐ 480 Scott Scudder .10 .05
☐ 481 Kirk Gibson .20 .09
☐ 482 Kenny Rogers .10 .05
☐ 483 Jack Morris .20 .09
☐ 484 Russ Swan .10 .05
☐ 485 Mike Huff .10 .05
☐ 486 Ken Hill .20 .09
☐ 487 Geronimo Pena .10 .05
☐ 488 Charlie O'Brien .10 .05
☐ 489 Mike Maddux .10 .05
☐ 490 Scott Livingstone .10 .05
☐ 491 Carl Willis .10 .05
☐ 492 Kelly Downs .10 .05
☐ 493 Dennis Cook .10 .05
☐ 494 Joe Magrane .10 .05
☐ 495 Bob Kipper .10 .05
☐ 496 Jose Mesa .20 .09
☐ 497 Charlie Hayes .10 .05
☐ 498 Joe Girardi .10 .05
☐ 499 Doug Jones .10 .05
☐ 500 Barry Bonds .50 .23
☐ 501 Bill Krueger .10 .05
☐ 502 Glenn Braggs .10 .05
☐ 503 Eric King .10 .05
☐ 504 Frank Castillo .20 .09
☐ 505 Mike Gardiner .10 .05
☐ 506 Cory Snyder .10 .05
☐ 507 Steve Howe .10 .05
☐ 508 Jose Rijo .10 .05
☐ 509 Sid Fernandez .10 .05
☐ 510 Archi Cianfrocco .10 .05
☐ 511 Mark Guthrie .10 .05
☐ 512 Bob Ojeda .10 .05
☐ 513 John Doherty .10 .05
☐ 514 Dante Bichette .15 .07
☐ 515 Juan Berenguer .10 .05
☐ 516 Jeff M. Robinson .10 .05
☐ 517 Mike Macfarlane .10 .05
☐ 518 Matt Young .10 .05
☐ 519 Otis Nixon .20 .09
☐ 520 Brian Holman .10 .05
☐ 521 Chris Haney .10 .05
☐ 522 Jeff Kent .40 .18
☐ 523 Chad Curtis .40 .18
☐ 524 Vince Horsman .10 .05
☐ 525 Rod Nichols .10 .05
☐ 526 Peter Hoy .10 .05
☐ 527 Shawn Boskie .10 .05
☐ 528 Alejandro Pena .10 .05
☐ 529 Dave Burba .10 .05
☐ 530 Ricky Jordan .10 .05
☐ 531 Dave Silvestri .10 .05
☐ 532 John Patterson UER .10 .05
(Listed as being born in 1960; should be 1967)
☐ 533 Jeff Branson .10 .05
☐ 534 Derrick May .10 .05
☐ 535 Esteban Beltre .10 .05
☐ 536 Jose Melendez .10 .05
☐ 537 Wally Joyner .20 .09
☐ 538 Eddie Taubensee .10 .05
☐ 539 Jim Abbott .10 .05
☐ 540 Brian Williams .10 .05
☐ 541 Donovan Osborne .20 .09
☐ 542 Patrick Lennon .10 .05
☐ 543 Mike Groppuso .10 .05
☐ 544 Jarvis Brown .10 .05
☐ 545 Shawn Livsey .10 .05
☐ 546 Jeff Ware .10 .05
☐ 547 Danny Tartabull .10 .05
☐ 548 Bobby Jones .40 .18
☐ 549 Ken Griffey Jr. 2.50 1.10
☐ 550 Rey Sanchez .10 .05
☐ 551 Pedro Astacio .20 .09
☐ 552 Juan Guerrero .10 .05
☐ 553 Jacob Brumfield .10 .05
☐ 554 Ben Rivera .10 .05
☐ 555 Brian Jordan .50 .23
☐ 556 Denny Neagle .40 .18
☐ 557 Cliff Brantley .10 .05
☐ 558 Anthony Young .10 .05
☐ 559 John Vander Wal .10 .05
☐ 560 Monty Fariss .10 .05
☐ 561 Russ Springer .10 .05
☐ 562 Pat Listach .10 .05
☐ 563 Pat Hentgen .40 .18
☐ 564 Andy Stankiewicz .10 .05
☐ 565 Mike Perez .10 .05
☐ 566 Mike Bielecki .10 .05
☐ 567 Butch Henry .10 .05
☐ 568 Dave Nilsson .20 .09
☐ 569 Scott Hatteberg .10 .05
☐ 570 Ruben Amaro Jr. .10 .05
☐ 571 Todd Hundley .15 .07
☐ 572 Moises Alou .15 .07
☐ 573 Hector Fajardo .10 .05
☐ 574 Todd Van Poppel .10 .05
☐ 575 Willie Banks .10 .05
☐ 576 Bob Zupcic .10 .05
☐ 577 J.J. Johnson .20 .09
☐ 578 John Burkett .10 .05
☐ 579 Trever Miller .10 .05
☐ 580 Scott Bankhead .10 .05
☐ 581 Rich Amaral .10 .05
☐ 582 Kenny Lofton 1.50 .70
☐ 583 Matt Stairs .10 .05
☐ 584 Don Mattingly .40 .18
Rod Carew IDOLS
☐ 585 Steve Avery .20 .09
Jack Morris IDOLS
☐ 586 Roberto Alomar .15 .07
Sandy Alomar SR. IDOLS
☐ 587 Scott Sanderson .20 .09
Catfish Hunter IDOLS
☐ 588 Dave Justice .40 .18
Willie Stargell IDOLS
☐ 589 Rex Hudler .40 .18
Roger Staubach IDOLS
☐ 590 David Cone .20 .09
Jackie Gleason IDOLS
☐ 591 Tony Gwynn .40 .18
Willie Davis IDOLS
☐ 592 Orel Hershiser SIDE .20 .09
☐ 593 John Wetteland SIDE .20 .09
☐ 594 Tom Glavine SIDE .20 .09
☐ 595 Randy Johnson SIDE .40 .18
☐ 596 Jim Gott SIDE .10 .05
☐ 597 Donald Harris .10 .05
☐ 598 Shawn Hare .10 .05
☐ 599 Chris Gardner .10 .05
☐ 600 Rusty Meacham .10 .05
☐ 601 Benito Santiago .10 .05
☐ 602 Eric Davis SHADE .10 .05
☐ 603 Jose Lind SHADE .10 .05
☐ 604 Dave Justice SHADE .20 .09
☐ 605 Tim Raines SHADE .20 .09
☐ 606 Randy Tomlin GRIP .10 .05
☐ 607 Jack McDowell GRIP .10 .05
☐ 608 Greg Maddux GRIP .60 .25
☐ 609 Charles Nagy GRIP .10 .05
☐ 610 Tom Candiotti GRIP .10 .05
☐ 611 David Cone GRIP .20 .09
☐ 612 Steve Avery GRIP .10 .05
☐ 613 Rod Beck GRIP .40 .18
☐ 614 Rickey Henderson TECH .15 .07
☐ 615 Benito Santiago TECH .10 .05
☐ 616 Ruben Sierra TECH .10 .05
☐ 617 Ryne Sandberg TECH .40 .18
☐ 618 Nolan Ryan TECH .75 .35
☐ 619 Brett Butler TECH .20 .09
☐ 620 Dave Justice TECH .40 .18

1992 Pinnacle Rookie Idols

This 18-card insert set is a spin-off on the Idols subset featured in the regular series. The cards were randomly inserted in Series II wax packs. The set features full-bleed color photos of 18 rookies along with their pick of sports figures or other individuals who had the greatest impact on their careers. Both sides of the cards are horizontally oriented. The fronts carry a close-up photo of the rookie superimposed on an action game shot of his idol.

	MINT	NRMT
COMPLETE SET (18)	120.00	55.00
COMMON PAIR (1-18)	3.00	1.35

☐ 1 Reggie Sanders 3.50 1.55
and Eric Davis

☐ 2 Hector Fajardo and Jim Abbott	3.00	1.35
☐ 3 Gary Cooper and George Brett	12.00	5.50
☐ 4 Mark Wohlers and Roger Clemens	15.00	6.75
☐ 5 Luis Mercedes and Julio Franco	3.00	1.35
☐ 6 Willie Banks and Doc Gooden	3.00	1.35
☐ 7 Kenny Lofton and Rickey Henderson	25.00	11.00
☐ 8 Keith Mitchell and Dave Henderson	3.00	1.35
☐ 9 Kim Batiste and Barry Larkin		
☐ 10 Todd Hundley and Thurman Munson	8.00	3.60
☐ 11 Eddie Zosky and Cal Ripken	25.00	11.00
☐ 12 Todd Van Poppel and Nolan Ryan	25.00	11.00
☐ 13 Jim Thome and Ryne Sandberg	25.00	11.00
☐ 14 Dave Fleming and Bobby Murcer	3.00	1.35
☐ 15 Royce Clayton and Ozzie Smith	8.00	3.60
☐ 16 Donald Harris and Darryl Strawberry	3.00	1.35
☐ 17 Chad Curtis and Alan Trammell		
☐ 18 Derek Bell and Dave Winfield	6.00	2.70

1992 Pinnacle Slugfest

This 15-card set highlights the games top sluggers.The cards were issued exclusively as an one per pack insert in specially marked cello packs. The horizontally oriented fronts feature glossy photos of players at bat. The player's name is printed in gold and the word "Slugfest" is printed in red in a black border across the bottom of the picture.

	MINT	NRMT
COMPLETE SET (15)	40.00	18.00
COMMON CARD (1-15)	.75	.35
☐ 1 Cecil Fielder	1.00	.45
☐ 2 Mark McGwire	3.00	1.35
☐ 3 Jose Canseco	1.25	.55
☐ 4 Barry Bonds	2.00	.90
☐ 5 David Justice	1.50	.70
☐ 6 Bobby Bonilla	1.00	.45
☐ 7 Ken Griffey Jr.	10.00	4.50
☐ 8 Ron Gant	1.00	.45
☐ 9 Ryne Sandberg	2.00	.90
☐ 10 Ruben Sierra	.75	.35
☐ 11 Frank Thomas	8.00	3.60
☐ 12 Will Clark	1.25	.55
☐ 13 Kirby Puckett	4.00	1.80
☐ 14 Cal Ripken	8.00	3.60
☐ 15 Jeff Bagwell	5.00	2.20

1992 Pinnacle Team 2000

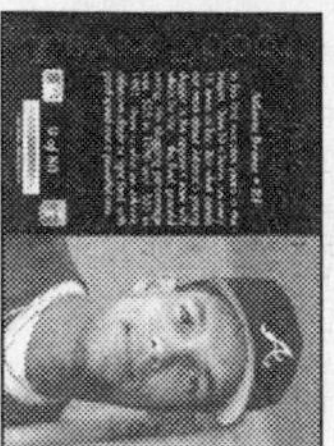

This 80-card standard-size set focuses on young players who were projected to be stars in the year 2000. Cards 1-40 were inserted in Series 1 jumbo packs while cards 41-80 were featured in Series 2 jumbo packs. The insertion rate was three per jumbo pack in either series. The fronts features action color player photos. The cards are bordered by a 1/2" black stripe that runs along the left edge and bottom forming a right angle. The two ends of the black stripe are sloped. The words "Team 2000" and the player's name appear in gold foil in the stripe. The team logo is displayed in the lower left corner.

	MINT	NRMT
COMPLETE SET (80)	30.00	13.50
COMPLETE SERIES 1 (40)	20.00	9.00
COMPLETE SERIES 2 (40)	10.00	4.50
COMMON CARD (1-80)	.15	.07
☐ 1 Mike Mussina	1.00	.45
☐ 2 Phil Plantier	.15	.07
☐ 3 Frank Thomas	5.00	2.20
☐ 4 Travis Fryman	.25	.11
☐ 5 Kevin Appier	.25	.11
☐ 6 Chuck Knoblauch	.60	.25
☐ 7 Pat Kelly	.15	.07
☐ 8 Ivan Rodriguez	1.25	.55
☐ 9 Dave Justice	.60	.25
☐ 10 Jeff Bagwell	2.00	.90
☐ 11 Marquis Grissom	.25	.11
☐ 12 Andy Benes	.15	.07
☐ 13 Gregg Olson	.15	.07
☐ 14 Kevin Morton	.15	.07
☐ 15 Tim Naehring	.25	.11
☐ 16 Dave Hollins	.15	.07
☐ 17 Sandy Alomar Jr.	.25	.11
☐ 18 Albert Belle	1.50	.70
☐ 19 Charles Nagy	.25	.11
☐ 20 Brian McRae	.15	.07
☐ 21 Larry Walker	.60	.25
☐ 22 Delino DeShields	.25	.11
☐ 23 Jeff Johnson	.15	.07
☐ 24 Bernie Williams	.60	.25
☐ 25 Jose Offerman	.15	.07
☐ 26 Juan Gonzalez	3.00	1.35
☐ 27A Juan Guzman (Pinnacle logo at top)	.25	.11
☐ 27B Juan Guzman (Pinnacle logo at bottom)	.25	.11
☐ 28 Eric Anthony	.15	.07
☐ 29 Brian Hunter	.15	.07
☐ 30 John Smoltz	.40	.18
☐ 31 Deion Sanders	.60	.25
☐ 32 Greg Maddux	3.00	1.35
☐ 33 Andujar Cedeno	.15	.07
☐ 34 Royce Clayton	.25	.11
☐ 35 Kenny Lofton	2.50	1.10
☐ 36 Cal Eldred	.15	.07
☐ 37 Jim Thome	3.00	1.35
☐ 38 Gary DiSarcina	.15	.07
☐ 39 Brian Jordan	.60	.25
☐ 40 Chad Curtis	.25	.11
☐ 41 Ben McDonald	.15	.07
☐ 42 Jim Abbott	.15	.07
☐ 43 Robin Ventura	.25	.11
☐ 44 Milt Cuyler	.15	.07
☐ 45 Gregg Jefferies	.15	.07
☐ 46 Scott Radinsky	.15	.07
☐ 47 Ken Griffey Jr.	5.00	2.20
☐ 48 Roberto Alomar	.40	.18
☐ 49 Ramon Martinez	.25	.11
☐ 50 Bret Barberie	.15	.07
☐ 51 Ray Lankford	.40	.18
☐ 52 Leo Gomez	.15	.07
☐ 53 Tommy Greene	.15	.07
☐ 54 Mo Vaughn	1.50	.70
☐ 55 Sammy Sosa	.60	.25
☐ 56 Carlos Baerga	.15	.07
☐ 57 Mark Lewis	.15	.07
☐ 58 Tom Gordon	.15	.07
☐ 59 Gary Sheffield	.60	.25
☐ 60 Scott Erickson	.25	.11
☐ 61 Pedro Munoz	.15	.07
☐ 62 Tino Martinez	.60	.25
☐ 63 Darren Lewis	.15	.07
☐ 64 Dean Palmer	.25	.11
☐ 65 John Olerud	.25	.11
☐ 66 Steve Avery	.15	.07
☐ 67 Pete Harnisch	.15	.07
☐ 68 Luis Gonzalez	.15	.07
☐ 69 Kim Batiste	.15	.07
☐ 70 Reggie Sanders	.25	.11
☐ 71 Luis Mercedes	.15	.07
☐ 72 Todd Van Poppel	.15	.07
☐ 73 Gary Scott	.15	.07
☐ 74 Monty Fariss	.15	.07
☐ 75 Kyle Abbott	.15	.07
☐ 76 Eric Karros	.40	.18
☐ 77 Mo Sanford	.15	.07
☐ 78 Todd Hundley	.60	.25
☐ 79 Reggie Jefferson	.15	.07
☐ 80 Pat Mahomes	.15	.07

1992 Pinnacle Team Pinnacle

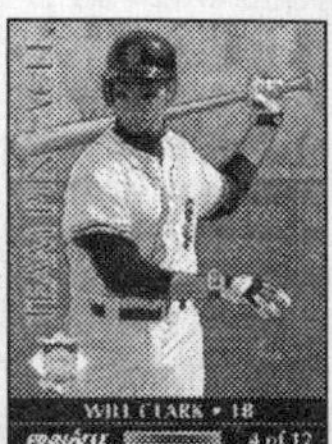

This 12-card, double-sided insert set features the National League and American League All-Star team as selected by Pinnacle. The standard-size cards were randomly inserted in Series I wax packs. The cards feature illustrations by sports artist Chris Greco with the National League All-Star on one side and the corresponding American League All-Star by position on the other. The words "Team Pinnacle" are printed vertically down the left side of the card in red for American League on one side and blue for National League on the other.

	MINT	NRMT
COMPLETE SET (12)	80.00	36.00
COMMON PAIR (1-12)	3.00	1.35
☐ 1 Roger Clemens and Ramon Martinez	8.00	3.60
☐ 2 Jim Abbott and Steve Avery	3.00	1.35
☐ 3 Ivan Rodriguez and Benito Santiago	8.00	3.60
☐ 4 Frank Thomas and Will Clark	20.00	9.00
☐ 5 Roberto Alomar and Ryne Sandberg	8.00	3.60
☐ 6 Robin Ventura and Matt Williams	4.00	1.80
☐ 7 Cal Ripken and Barry Larkin	20.00	9.00
☐ 8 Danny Tartabull and Barry Bonds	5.00	2.20
☐ 9 Ken Griffey Jr. and Brett Butler	25.00	11.00
☐ 10 Ruben Sierra and Dave Justice	3.00	1.35
☐ 11 Dennis Eckersley and Rob Dibble	3.00	1.35
☐ 12 Scott Radinsky and John Franco	3.00	1.35

1992 Pinnacle Rookies

This 30-card boxed set features top rookies of the 1992 season, with at least one player from each team. A total of 180,000 sets were produced. The fronts feature full-bleed color action player photos except at the bottom where a team-color coded bar carries the player's name (in gold foil lettering) and a black bar has the words "1992 Rookie." The team logo appears in a gold foil circle at the lower right corner.

	MINT	NRMT
COMP.FACT.SET (30)	5.00	2.20
COMMON CARD (1-30)	.15	.07
☐ 1 Luis Mercedes	.15	.07
☐ 2 Scott Cooper	.15	.07
☐ 3 Kenny Lofton	4.00	1.80
☐ 4 John Doherty	.15	.07
☐ 5 Pat Listach	.15	.07
☐ 6 Andy Stankiewicz	.15	.07
☐ 7 Derek Bell	.40	.18
☐ 8 Gary DiSarcina	.15	.07
☐ 9 Roberto Hernandez	.60	.25
☐ 10 Joel Johnston	.15	.07
☐ 11 Pat Mahomes	.15	.07
☐ 12 Todd Van Poppel	.15	.07
☐ 13 Dave Fleming	.15	.07
☐ 14 Monty Fariss	.15	.07
☐ 15 Gary Scott	.15	.07
☐ 16 Moises Alou	.60	.25
☐ 17 Todd Hundley	.40	.18
☐ 18 Kim Batiste	.15	.07
☐ 19 Denny Neagle	.40	.18
☐ 20 Donovan Osborne	.40	.18
☐ 21 Mark Wohlers	.60	.25
☐ 22 Reggie Sanders	.40	.18
☐ 23 Brian Williams	.15	.07
☐ 24 Eric Karros	.75	.35
☐ 25 Frank Seminara	.15	.07
☐ 26 Royce Clayton	.40	.18
☐ 27 Dave Nilsson	.40	.18
☐ 28 Matt Stairs	.15	.07
☐ 29 Chad Curtis	.75	.35
☐ 30 Carlos Hernandez	.15	.07

1992 Pinnacle Mantle

This 30-card standard-size set commemorates the life and career of Mickey Mantle. A total of 180,000 sets were produced. Each set was packaged in a black and blue box that featured a picture of Mantle and a checklist. The fronts feature a mix of black and white, full-color, and colorized photos in a full-bleed design with gold-foil stamping. At the bottom of each photo appears a purple bar bearing his uniform number (7) and name. The horizontal or vertical backs carry a second player photo and summarize chapters from his life and career on a royal blue panel with navy blue borders.

	MINT	NRMT
COMPLETE SET (30)	20.00	9.00
COMMON CARD (1-30)	.75	.35
☐ 1 Mickey Mantle Mutt Mantle Father and Son	1.00	.45
☐ 2 Mickey Mantle High School	.75	.35
☐ 3 Mickey Mantle Commerce Comet	.75	.35
☐ 4 Mickey Mantle Spring Training	.75	.35
☐ 5 Mickey Mantle The Beginning	.75	.35
☐ 6 Mickey Mantle Number 6	.75	.35
☐ 7 Mickey Mantle The Rookie	.75	.35
☐ 8 Mickey Mantle Tape-Measure Shots	.75	.35
☐ 9 Mickey Mantle Shortstop	.75	.35
☐ 10 Mickey Mantle Outfield	.75	.35
☐ 11 Mickey Mantle Speed, Speed, Speed	.75	.35
☐ 12 Mickey Mantle Contracts	.75	.35
☐ 13 Mickey Mantle Three-time MVP	.75	.35
☐ 14 Mickey Mantle Triple Crown	.75	.35
☐ 15 Mickey Mantle Series Slam	.75	.35
☐ 16 Mickey Mantle Series Star	.75	.35
☐ 17 Mickey Mantle Switch Hitter	.75	.35
☐ 18 Mickey Mantle Fan Favorite	.75	.35
☐ 19 Mickey Mantle Milestones	.75	.35
☐ 20 Mickey Mantle Enthusiasm	.75	.35
☐ 21 Mickey Mantle Hitting	.75	.35
☐ 22 Mickey Mantle First Base	.75	.35
☐ 23 Mickey Mantle Courage	.75	.35
☐ 24 Mickey Mantle Stan Musial Mick and Stan	1.50	.70
☐ 25 Whitey Ford Yogi Berra Whitey and Yogi	1.00	.45
☐ 26 Mickey Mantle Billy Martin Mick and Billy	1.00	.45
☐ 27 Mickey Mantle Casey Stengel Mick and Casey	1.00	.45
☐ 28 Mickey Mantle Awards	.75	.35
☐ 29 Mickey Mantle Retirement	.75	.35
☐ 30 Mickey Mantle Cooperstown	1.00	.45

1993 Pinnacle

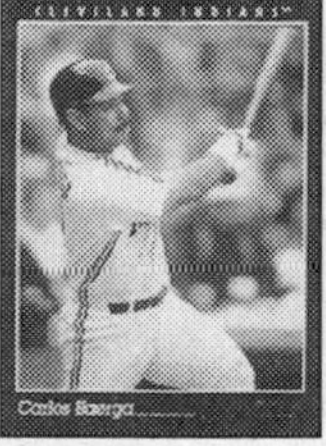

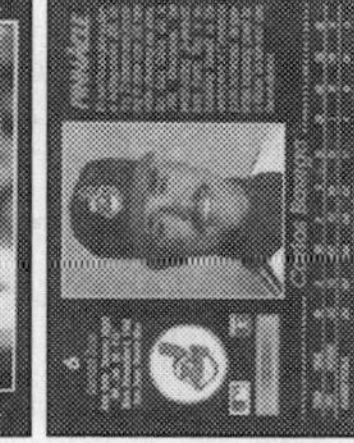

The 1993 Pinnacle set (by Score) contains 620 standard-size cards issued in two series of 310 cards each. Cards were distributed in hobby and retail foil packs and 27-card jumbo superpacks. The fronts feature color action player photos bordered in white and set on a black card face. The player's name appears below the photo, the player's team is above. The set includes the following topical subsets: Rookies (238-288, 575-620), Now and Then (289-296, 470-476), Idols (297-303, 477-483), Hometown Heroes (304-310, 484-490), and Draft Picks (455-469). Rookie Cards in this set include Derek Jeter and Jason Kendall.

	MINT	NRMT
COMPLETE SET (620)	50.00	22.00
COMPLETE SERIES 1 (310)	25.00	11.00
COMPLETE SERIES 2 (310)	25.00	11.00
COMMON CARD (1-620)	.15	.07
☐ 1 Gary Sheffield	.60	.25
☐ 2 Cal Eldred	.15	.07
☐ 3 Larry Walker	.60	.25
☐ 4 Deion Sanders	.60	.25
☐ 5 Dave Fleming	.15	.07
☐ 6 Carlos Baerga	.30	.14
☐ 7 Bernie Williams	.20	.09
☐ 8 John Kruk	.30	.14
☐ 9 Jimmy Key	.30	.14
☐ 10 Jeff Bagwell	1.25	.55
☐ 11 Jim Abbott	.15	.07
☐ 12 Terry Steinbach	.30	.14
☐ 13 Bob Tewksbury	.15	.07
☐ 14 Eric Karros	.30	.14
☐ 15 Ryne Sandberg	.75	.35
☐ 16 Will Clark	.20	.09
☐ 17 Edgar Martinez	.20	.09
☐ 18 Eddie Murray	.60	.25
☐ 19 Andy Van Slyke	.30	.14
☐ 20 Cal Ripken Jr.	2.50	1.10
☐ 21 Ivan Rodriguez	.75	.35
☐ 22 Barry Larkin	.20	.09
☐ 23 Don Mattingly	1.00	.45
☐ 24 Gregg Jefferies	.30	.14
☐ 25 Roger Clemens	1.25	.55
☐ 26 Cecil Fielder	.30	.14
☐ 27 Kent Hrbek	.30	.14
☐ 28 Robin Ventura	.30	.14
☐ 29 Rickey Henderson	.20	.09
☐ 30 Roberto Alomar	.60	.25
☐ 31 Luis Polonia	.15	.07
☐ 32 Andujar Cedeno	.15	.07
☐ 33 Pat Listach	.15	.07
☐ 34 Mark Grace	.20	.09
☐ 35 Otis Nixon	.15	.07
☐ 36 Felix Jose	.15	.07
☐ 37 Mike Sharperson	.15	.07
☐ 38 Dennis Martinez	.30	.14
☐ 39 Willie McGee	.15	.07
☐ 40 Kenny Lofton	1.25	.55
☐ 41 Randy Johnson	.60	.25
☐ 42 Andy Benes	.30	.14
☐ 43 Bobby Bonilla	.30	.14
☐ 44 Mike Mussina	.60	.25
☐ 45 Len Dykstra	.30	.14
☐ 46 Ellis Burks	.30	.14
☐ 47 Chris Sabo	.15	.07
☐ 48 Jay Bell	.30	.14
☐ 49 Jose Canseco	.20	.09
☐ 50 Craig Biggio	.20	.09
☐ 51 Wally Joyner	.30	.14
☐ 52 Mickey Tettleton	.15	.07
☐ 53 Tim Raines	.30	.14
☐ 54 Brian Harper	.15	.07
☐ 55 Rene Gonzales	.15	.07
☐ 56 Mark Langston	.15	.07
☐ 57 Jack Morris	.30	.14
☐ 58 Mark McGwire	1.25	.55
☐ 59 Ken Caminiti	.60	.25
☐ 60 Terry Pendleton	.30	.14
☐ 61 Dave Nilsson	.30	.14
☐ 62 Tom Pagnozzi	.15	.07
☐ 63 Mike Morgan	.15	.07
☐ 64 Darryl Strawberry	.30	.14
☐ 65 Charles Nagy	.30	.14
☐ 66 Ken Hill	.30	.14
☐ 67 Matt Williams	.20	.09
☐ 68 Jay Buhner	.20	.09
☐ 69 Vince Coleman	.15	.07
☐ 70 Brady Anderson	.20	.09
☐ 71 Fred McGriff	.20	.09
☐ 72 Ben McDonald	.15	.07
☐ 73 Terry Mulholland	.15	.07
☐ 74 Randy Tomlin	.15	.07
☐ 75 Nolan Ryan	2.50	1.10
☐ 76 Frank Viola UER (Card incorrectly states he has a surgically repaired elbow)	.15	.07
☐ 77 Jose Rijo	.15	.07
☐ 78 Shane Mack	.15	.07
☐ 79 Travis Fryman	.30	.14
☐ 80 Jack McDowell	.15	.07
☐ 81 Mark Gubicza	.15	.07
☐ 82 Matt Nokes	.15	.07
☐ 83 Bert Blyleven	.30	.14
☐ 84 Eric Anthony	.15	.07
☐ 85 Mike Bordick	.15	.07
☐ 86 John Olerud	.15	.07
☐ 87 B.J.Surhoff	.30	.14
☐ 88 Bernard Gilkey	.30	.14
☐ 89 Shawon Dunston	.15	.07
☐ 90 Tom Glavine	.20	.09
☐ 91 Brett Butler	.30	.14
☐ 92 Moises Alou	.30	.14
☐ 93 Albert Belle	.75	.35
☐ 94 Darren Lewis	.15	.07
☐ 95 Omar Vizquel	.30	.14
☐ 96 Dwight Gooden	.30	.14
☐ 97 Gregg Olson	.15	.07
☐ 98 Tony Gwynn	1.50	.70
☐ 99 Darren Daulton	.30	.14
☐ 100 Dennis Eckersley	.20	.09
☐ 101 Rob Dibble	.15	.07
☐ 102 Mike Greenwell	.15	.07
☐ 103 Jose Lind	.15	.07
☐ 104 Julio Franco	.30	.14
☐ 105 Tom Gordon	.15	.07
☐ 106 Scott Livingstone	.15	.07
☐ 107 Chuck Knoblauch	.60	.25
☐ 108 Frank Thomas	2.50	1.10
☐ 109 Melido Perez	.15	.07
☐ 110 Ken Griffey Jr.	3.00	1.35
☐ 111 Harold Baines	.30	.14
☐ 112 Gary Gaetti	.30	.14
☐ 113 Pete Harnisch	.15	.07
☐ 114 David Wells	.15	.07
☐ 115 Charlie Leibrandt	.15	.07
☐ 116 Ray Lankford	.30	.14
☐ 117 Kevin Seitzer	.15	.07
☐ 118 Robin Yount	.20	.09
☐ 119 Lenny Harris	.15	.07
☐ 120 Chris James	.15	.07
☐ 121 Delino DeShields	.15	.07

☐ 122	Kirt Manwaring	.15	.07
☐ 123	Glenallen Hill	.15	.07
☐ 124	Hensley Meulens	.15	.07
☐ 125	Darrin Jackson	.15	.07
☐ 126	Todd Hundley	.20	.09
☐ 127	Dave Hollins	.15	.07
☐ 128	Sam Horn	.15	.07
☐ 129	Roberto Hernandez	.30	.14
☐ 130	Vicente Palacios	.15	.07
☐ 131	George Brett	1.25	.55
☐ 132	Dave Martinez	.15	.07
☐ 133	Kevin Appier	.30	.14
☐ 134	Pat Kelly	.15	.07
☐ 135	Pedro Munoz	.15	.07
☐ 136	Mark Carreon	.15	.07
☐ 137	Lance Johnson	.30	.14
☐ 138	Devon White	.15	.07
☐ 139	Julio Valera	.15	.07
☐ 140	Eddie Taubensee	.15	.07
☐ 141	Willie Wilson	.15	.07
☐ 142	Stan Belinda	.15	.07
☐ 143	John Smoltz	.20	.09
☐ 144	Darryl Hamilton	.15	.07
☐ 145	Sammy Sosa	.60	.25
☐ 146	Carlos Hernandez	.15	.07
☐ 147	Tom Candiotti	.15	.07
☐ 148	Mike Felder	.15	.07
☐ 149	Rusty Meacham	.15	.07
☐ 150	Ivan Calderon	.15	.07
☐ 151	Pete O'Brien	.15	.07
☐ 152	Erik Hanson	.15	.07
☐ 153	Billy Ripken	.15	.07
☐ 154	Kurt Stillwell	.15	.07
☐ 155	Jeff Kent	.30	.14
☐ 156	Mickey Morandini	.15	.07
☐ 157	Randy Milligan	.15	.07
☐ 158	Reggie Sanders	.30	.14
☐ 159	Luis Rivera	.15	.07
☐ 160	Orlando Merced	.15	.07
☐ 161	Dean Palmer	.30	.14
☐ 162	Mike Perez	.15	.07
☐ 163	Scott Erickson	.15	.07
☐ 164	Kevin McReynolds	.15	.07
☐ 165	Kevin Maas	.15	.07
☐ 166	Ozzie Guillen	.15	.07
☐ 167	Rob Deer	.15	.07
☐ 168	Danny Tartabull	.15	.07
☐ 169	Lee Stevens	.15	.07
☐ 170	Dave Henderson	.15	.07
☐ 171	Derek Bell	.30	.14
☐ 172	Steve Finley	.30	.14
☐ 173	Greg Olson	.15	.07
☐ 174	Geronimo Pena	.15	.07
☐ 175	Paul Quantrill	.15	.07
☐ 176	Steve Buechele	.15	.07
☐ 177	Kevin Gross	.15	.07
☐ 178	Tim Wallach	.15	.07
☐ 179	Dave Valle	.15	.07
☐ 180	Dave Silvestri	.15	.07
☐ 181	Bud Black	.15	.07
☐ 182	Henry Rodriguez	.30	.14
☐ 183	Tim Teufel	.15	.07
☐ 184	Mark McLemore	.15	.07
☐ 185	Bret Saberhagen	.15	.07
☐ 186	Chris Hoiles	.15	.07
☐ 187	Ricky Jordan	.15	.07
☐ 188	Don Slaught	.15	.07
☐ 189	Mo Vaughn	.75	.35
☐ 190	Joe Oliver	.15	.07
☐ 191	Juan Gonzalez	1.50	.70
☐ 192	Scott Leius	.15	.07
☐ 193	Milt Cuyler	.15	.07
☐ 194	Chris Haney	.15	.07
☐ 195	Ron Karkovice	.15	.07
☐ 196	Steve Farr	.15	.07
☐ 197	John Orton	.15	.07
☐ 198	Kelly Gruber	.15	.07
☐ 199	Ron Darling	.15	.07
☐ 200	Ruben Sierra	.15	.07
☐ 201	Chuck Finley	.15	.07
☐ 202	Mike Moore	.15	.07
☐ 203	Pat Borders	.15	.07
☐ 204	Sid Bream	.15	.07
☐ 205	Todd Zeile	.15	.07
☐ 206	Rick Wilkins	.15	.07
☐ 207	Jim Gantner	.15	.07
☐ 208	Frank Castillo	.15	.07
☐ 209	Dave Hansen	.15	.07
☐ 210	Trevor Wilson	.15	.07
☐ 211	Sandy Alomar Jr.	.30	.14
☐ 212	Sean Berry	.15	.07
☐ 213	Tino Martinez	.60	.25
☐ 214	Chito Martinez	.15	.07
☐ 215	Dan Walters	.15	.07
☐ 216	John Franco	.15	.07
☐ 217	Glenn Davis	.15	.07
☐ 218	Mariano Duncan	.15	.07
☐ 219	Mike LaValliere	.15	.07
☐ 220	Rafael Palmeiro	.20	.09
☐ 221	Jack Clark	.15	.07
☐ 222	Hal Morris	.15	.07
☐ 223	Ed Sprague	.15	.07
☐ 224	John Valentin	.30	.14
☐ 225	Sam Militello	.15	.07
☐ 226	Bob Wickman	.15	.07
☐ 227	Damion Easley	.15	.07
☐ 228	John Jaha	.30	.14
☐ 229	Bob Ayrault	.15	.07
☐ 230	Mo Sanford	.15	.07
☐ 231	Walt Weiss	.15	.07
☐ 232	Dante Bichette	.20	.09
☐ 233	Steve Decker	.15	.07
☐ 234	Jerald Clark	.15	.07
☐ 235	Bryan Harvey	.15	.07
☐ 236	Joe Girardi	.15	.07
☐ 237	Dave Magadan	.15	.07
☐ 238	David Nied	.15	.07
☐ 239	Eric Wedge	.15	.07
☐ 240	Rico Brogna	.30	.14
☐ 241	J.T.Bruett	.15	.07
☐ 242	Jonathan Hurst	.15	.07
☐ 243	Bret Boone	.15	.07
☐ 244	Manny Alexander	.15	.07
☐ 245	Scooter Tucker	.15	.07
☐ 246	Troy Neel	.15	.07
☐ 247	Eddie Zosky	.15	.07
☐ 248	Melvin Nieves	.30	.14
☐ 249	Ryan Thompson	.15	.07
☐ 250	Shawn Barton	.15	.07
☐ 251	Ryan Klesko	.75	.35
☐ 252	Mike Piazza	3.00	1.35
☐ 253	Steve Hosey	.15	.07
☐ 254	Shane Reynolds	.30	.14
☐ 255	Dan Wilson	.30	.14
☐ 256	Tom Marsh	.15	.07
☐ 257	Barry Manuel	.15	.07
☐ 258	Paul Miller	.15	.07
☐ 259	Pedro Martinez	.60	.25
☐ 260	Steve Cooke	.15	.07
☐ 261	Johnny Guzman	.15	.07
☐ 262	Mike Butcher	.15	.07
☐ 263	Bien Figueroa	.15	.07
☐ 264	Rich Rowland	.15	.07
☐ 265	Shawn Jeter	.15	.07
☐ 266	Gerald Williams	.15	.07
☐ 267	Derek Parks	.15	.07
☐ 268	Henry Mercedes	.15	.07
☐ 269	David Hulse	.15	.07
☐ 270	Tim Pugh	.15	.07
☐ 271	William Suero	.15	.07
☐ 272	Ozzie Canseco	.15	.07
☐ 273	Fernando Ramsey	.15	.07
☐ 274	Bernardo Brito	.15	.07
☐ 275	Dave Mlicki	.15	.07
☐ 276	Tim Salmon	.75	.35
☐ 277	Mike Raczka	.15	.07
☐ 278	Ken Ryan	.15	.07
☐ 279	Rafael Bournigal	.15	.07
☐ 280	Wil Cordero	.30	.14
☐ 281	Billy Ashley	.15	.07
☐ 282	Paul Wagner	.15	.07
☐ 283	Blas Minor	.15	.07
☐ 284	Rick Trlicek	.15	.07
☐ 285	Willie Greene	.30	.14
☐ 286	Ted Wood	.15	.07
☐ 287	Phil Clark	.15	.07
☐ 288	Jesse Levis	.15	.07
☐ 289	Tony Gwynn NT	.60	.25
☐ 290	Nolan Ryan NT	1.25	.55
☐ 291	Dennis Martinez NT	.15	.07
☐ 292	Eddie Murray NT	.60	.25
☐ 293	Robin Yount NT	.20	.09
☐ 294	George Brett NT	.60	.25
☐ 295	Dave Winfield NT	.20	.09
☐ 296	Bert Blyleven NT	.30	.14
☐ 297	Jeff Bagwell Carl Yastrzemski	.60	.25
☐ 298	John Smoltz Jack Morris	.20	.09
☐ 299	Larry Walker Mike Bossy	.60	.25
☐ 300	Gary Sheffield Barry Larkin	.30	.14
☐ 301	Ivan Rodriguez Carlton Fisk	.30	.14
☐ 302	Delino DeShields Malcolm X	.60	.25
☐ 303	Tim Salmon Dwight Evans	.20	.09
☐ 304	Bernard Gilkey HH	.30	.14
☐ 305	Cal Ripken Jr. HH	1.25	.55
☐ 306	Barry Larkin HH	.20	.09
☐ 307	Kent Hrbek HH	.15	.07
☐ 308	Rickey Henderson HH	.20	.09
☐ 309	Darryl Strawberry HH	.30	.14
☐ 310	John Franco HH	.15	.07
☐ 311	Todd Stottlemyre	.15	.07
☐ 312	Luis Gonzalez	.15	.07
☐ 313	Tommy Greene	.15	.07
☐ 314	Randy Velarde	.15	.07
☐ 315	Steve Avery	.15	.07
☐ 316	Jose Oquendo	.15	.07
☐ 317	Rey Sanchez	.15	.07
☐ 318	Greg Vaughn	.15	.07
☐ 319	Orel Hershiser	.30	.14
☐ 320	Paul Sorrento	.15	.07
☐ 321	Royce Clayton	.15	.07
☐ 322	John Vander Wal	.15	.07
☐ 323	Henry Cotto	.15	.07
☐ 324	Pete Schourek	.15	.07
☐ 325	David Segui	.15	.07
☐ 326	Arthur Rhodes	.15	.07
☐ 327	Bruce Hurst	.15	.07
☐ 328	Wes Chamberlain	.15	.07
☐ 329	Ozzie Smith	.75	.35
☐ 330	Scott Cooper	.15	.07
☐ 331	Felix Fermin	.15	.07
☐ 332	Mike Macfarlane	.15	.07
☐ 333	Dan Gladden	.15	.07
☐ 334	Kevin Tapani	.15	.07
☐ 335	Steve Sax	.15	.07
☐ 336	Jeff Montgomery	.30	.14
☐ 337	Gary DiSarcina	.15	.07
☐ 338	Lance Blankenship	.15	.07
☐ 339	Brian Williams	.15	.07
☐ 340	Duane Ward	.15	.07
☐ 341	Chuck McElroy	.15	.07
☐ 342	Joe Magrane	.15	.07
☐ 343	Jaime Navarro	.15	.07
☐ 344	Dave Justice	.60	.25
☐ 345	Jose Offerman	.15	.07
☐ 346	Marquis Grissom	.30	.14
☐ 347	Bill Swift	.15	.07
☐ 348	Jim Thome	1.25	.55
☐ 349	Archi Cianfrocco	.15	.07
☐ 350	Anthony Young	.15	.07
☐ 351	Leo Gomez	.15	.07
☐ 352	Bill Gullickson	.15	.07
☐ 353	Alan Trammell	.20	.09
☐ 354	Dan Pasqua	.15	.07
☐ 355	Jeff King	.30	.14
☐ 356	Kevin Brown	.30	.14
☐ 357	Tim Belcher	.15	.07
☐ 358	Bip Roberts	.15	.07
☐ 359	Brent Mayne	.15	.07
☐ 360	Rheal Cormier	.15	.07
☐ 361	Mark Guthrie	.15	.07
☐ 362	Craig Grebeck	.15	.07
☐ 363	Andy Stankiewicz	.15	.07
☐ 364	Juan Guzman	.15	.07
☐ 365	Bobby Witt	.15	.07
☐ 366	Mark Portugal	.15	.07
☐ 367	Brian McRae	.15	.07
☐ 368	Mark Lemke	.15	.07
☐ 369	Bill Wegman	.15	.07
☐ 370	Donovan Osborne	.15	.07
☐ 371	Derrick May	.15	.07
☐ 372	Carl Willis	.15	.07
☐ 373	Chris Nabholz	.15	.07
☐ 374	Mark Lewis	.15	.07
☐ 375	John Burkett	.15	.07
☐ 376	Luis Mercedes	.15	.07
☐ 377	Ramon Martinez	.30	.14
☐ 378	Kyle Abbott	.15	.07
☐ 379	Mark Wohlers	.30	.14
☐ 380	Bob Walk	.15	.07
☐ 381	Kenny Rogers	.15	.07
☐ 382	Tim Naehring	.15	.07
☐ 383	Alex Fernandez	.30	.14
☐ 384	Keith Miller	.15	.07
☐ 385	Mike Henneman	.15	.07
☐ 386	Rick Aguilera	.15	.07
☐ 387	George Bell	.15	.07
☐ 388	Mike Gallego	.15	.07
☐ 389	Howard Johnson	.15	.07
☐ 390	Kim Batiste	.15	.07
☐ 391	Jerry Browne	.15	.07
☐ 392	Damon Berryhill	.15	.07
☐ 393	Ricky Bones	.15	.07
☐ 394	Omar Olivares	.15	.07
☐ 395	Mike Harkey	.15	.07
☐ 396	Pedro Astacio	.15	.07
☐ 397	John Wetteland	.30	.14
☐ 398	Rod Beck	.30	.14
☐ 399	Thomas Howard	.15	.07
☐ 400	Mike Devereaux	.15	.07
☐ 401	Tim Wakefield	.30	.14
☐ 402	Curt Schilling	.30	.14
☐ 403	Zane Smith	.15	.07
☐ 404	Bob Zupcic	.15	.07
☐ 405	Tom Browning	.15	.07

☐ 406 Tony Phillips .15 .07
☐ 407 John Doherty .15 .07
☐ 408 Pat Mahomes .15 .07
☐ 409 John Habyan .15 .07
☐ 410 Steve Olin .15 .07
☐ 411 Chad Curtis .30 .14
☐ 412 Joe Grahe .15 .07
☐ 413 John Patterson .15 .07
☐ 414 Brian Hunter .15 .07
☐ 415 Doug Henry .15 .07
☐ 416 Lee Smith .30 .14
☐ 417 Bob Scanlan .15 .07
☐ 418 Kent Mercker .15 .07
☐ 419 Mel Rojas .30 .14
☐ 420 Mark Whiten .15 .07
☐ 421 Carlton Fisk .60 .25
☐ 422 Candy Maldonado .15 .07
☐ 423 Doug Drabek .15 .07
☐ 424 Wade Boggs .60 .25
☐ 425 Mark Davis .15 .07
☐ 426 Kirby Puckett 1.25 .55
☐ 427 Joe Carter .20 .09
☐ 428 Paul Molitor .60 .25
☐ 429 Eric Davis .30 .14
☐ 430 Darryl Kile .30 .14
☐ 431 Jeff Parrett .15 .07
☐ 432 Jeff Blauser .15 .07
☐ 433 Dan Plesac .15 .07
☐ 434 Andres Galarraga .20 .09
☐ 435 Jim Gott .15 .07
☐ 436 Jose Mesa .30 .14
☐ 437 Ben Rivera .15 .07
☐ 438 Dave Winfield .20 .09
☐ 439 Norm Charlton .15 .07
☐ 440 Chris Bosio .15 .07
☐ 441 Wilson Alvarez .30 .14
☐ 442 Dave Stewart .30 .14
☐ 443 Doug Jones .15 .07
☐ 444 Jeff Russell .15 .07
☐ 445 Ron Gant .30 .14
☐ 446 Paul O'Neill .30 .14
☐ 447 Charlie Hayes .15 .07
☐ 448 Joe Hesketh .15 .07
☐ 449 Chris Hammond .15 .07
☐ 450 Hipolito Pichardo .15 .07
☐ 451 Scott Radinsky .15 .07
☐ 452 Bobby Thigpen .15 .07
☐ 453 Xavier Hernandez .15 .07
☐ 454 Lonnie Smith .15 .07
☐ 455 Jamie Arnold DP .30 .14
☐ 456 B.J. Wallace DP .15 .07
☐ 457 Derek Jeter DP 6.00 2.70
☐ 458 Jason Kendall DP 1.00 .45
☐ 459 Rick Helling DP .30 .14
☐ 460 Derek Wallace DP .15 .07
☐ 461 Sean Lowe DP .15 .07
☐ 462 Shannon Stewart DP .75 .35
☐ 463 Benji Grigsby DP .15 .07
☐ 464 Todd Steverson DP .30 .14
☐ 465 Dan Serafini DP .50 .23
☐ 466 Michael Tucker DP .60 .25
☐ 467 Chris Roberts DP .30 .14
☐ 468 Pete Janicki DP .15 .07
☐ 469 Jeff Schmidt DP .15 .07
☐ 470 Don Mattingly NT .60 .25
☐ 471 Cal Ripken Jr. NT 1.25 .55
☐ 472 Jack Morris NT .15 .07
☐ 473 Terry Pendleton NT .15 .07
☐ 474 Dennis Eckersley NT .20 .09
☐ 475 Carlton Fisk NT .60 .25
☐ 476 Wade Boggs NT .60 .25
☐ 477 Len Dykstra .30 .14
Ken Stabler
☐ 478 Danny Tartabull .15 .07
Jose Tartabull
☐ 479 Jeff Conine .30 .14
Dale Murphy
☐ 480 Gregg Jefferies .15 .07
Ron Cey
☐ 481 Paul Molitor .20 .09
Harmon Killebrew
☐ 482 John Valentin .15 .07
Dave Concepcion
☐ 483 Alex Arias .30 .14
Dave Winfield
☐ 484 Barry Bonds HH .60 .25
☐ 485 Doug Drabek HH .15 .07
☐ 486 Dave Winfield HH .20 .09
☐ 487 Brett Butler HH .15 .07
☐ 488 Harold Baines HH .15 .07
☐ 489 David Cone HH .30 .14
☐ 490 Willie McGee HH .15 .07
☐ 491 Robby Thompson .15 .07
☐ 492 Pete Incaviglia .15 .07
☐ 493 Manuel Lee .15 .07
☐ 494 Rafael Belliard .15 .07
☐ 495 Scott Fletcher .15 .07
☐ 496 Jeff Frye .15 .07
☐ 497 Andre Dawson .20 .09
☐ 498 Mike Scioscia .15 .07
☐ 499 Spike Owen .15 .07
☐ 500 Sid Fernandez .15 .07
☐ 501 Joe Orsulak .15 .07
☐ 502 Benito Santiago .15 .07
☐ 503 Dale Murphy .60 .25
☐ 504 Barry Bonds .75 .35
☐ 505 Jose Guzman .15 .07
☐ 506 Tony Pena .15 .07
☐ 507 Greg Swindell .15 .07
☐ 508 Mike Pagliarulo .15 .07
☐ 509 Lou Whitaker .30 .14
☐ 510 Greg Gagne .15 .07
☐ 511 Butch Henry .15 .07
☐ 512 Jeff Brantley .15 .07
☐ 513 Jack Armstrong .15 .07
☐ 514 Danny Jackson .15 .07
☐ 515 Junior Felix .15 .07
☐ 516 Milt Thompson .15 .07
☐ 517 Greg Maddux 2.00 .90
☐ 518 Eric Young .60 .25
☐ 519 Jody Reed .15 .07
☐ 520 Roberto Kelly .15 .07
☐ 521 Darren Holmes .15 .07
☐ 522 Craig Lefferts .15 .07
☐ 523 Charlie Hough .15 .07
☐ 524 Bo Jackson .30 .14
☐ 525 Bill Spiers .15 .07
☐ 526 Orestes Destrade .15 .07
☐ 527 Greg Hibbard .15 .07
☐ 528 Roger McDowell .15 .07
☐ 529 Cory Snyder .15 .07
☐ 530 Harold Reynolds .15 .07
☐ 531 Kevin Reimer .15 .07
☐ 532 Rick Sutcliffe .15 .07
☐ 533 Tony Fernandez .15 .07
☐ 534 Tom Brunansky .15 .07
☐ 535 Jeff Reardon .30 .14
☐ 536 Chili Davis .30 .14
☐ 537 Bob Ojeda .15 .07
☐ 538 Greg Colbrunn .15 .07
☐ 539 Phil Plantier .15 .07
☐ 540 Brian Jordan .20 .09
☐ 541 Pete Smith .15 .07
☐ 542 Frank Tanana .15 .07
☐ 543 John Smiley .15 .07
☐ 544 David Cone .30 .14
☐ 545 Daryl Boston .15 .07
☐ 546 Tom Henke .15 .07
☐ 547 Bill Krueger .15 .07
☐ 548 Freddie Benavides .15 .07
☐ 549 Randy Myers .30 .14
☐ 550 Reggie Jefferson .30 .14
☐ 551 Kevin Mitchell .30 .14
☐ 552 Dave Stieb .15 .07
☐ 553 Bret Barberie .15 .07
☐ 554 Tim Crews .15 .07
☐ 555 Doug Dascenzo .15 .07
☐ 556 Alex Cole .15 .07
☐ 557 Jeff Innis .15 .07
☐ 558 Carlos Garcia .15 .07
☐ 559 Steve Howe .15 .07
☐ 560 Kirk McCaskill .15 .07
☐ 561 Frank Seminara .15 .07
☐ 562 Cris Carpenter .15 .07
☐ 563 Mike Stanley .15 .07
☐ 564 Carlos Quintana .15 .07
☐ 565 Mitch Williams .15 .07
☐ 566 Juan Bell .15 .07
☐ 567 Eric Fox .15 .07
☐ 568 Al Leiter .15 .07
☐ 569 Mike Stanton .15 .07
☐ 570 Scott Kamieniecki .15 .07
☐ 571 Ryan Bowen .15 .07
☐ 572 Andy Ashby .15 .07
☐ 573 Bob Welch .15 .07
☐ 574 Scott Sanderson .15 .07
☐ 575 Joe Kmak .15 .07
☐ 576 Scott Pose .15 .07
☐ 577 Ricky Gutierrez .15 .07
☐ 578 Mike Trombley .15 .07
☐ 579 Sterling Hitchcock .30 .14
☐ 580 Rodney Bolton .15 .07
☐ 581 Tyler Green .15 .07
☐ 582 Tim Costo .15 .07
☐ 583 Tim Laker .15 .07
☐ 584 Steve Reed .15 .07
☐ 585 Tom Kramer .15 .07
☐ 586 Robb Nen .20 .09
☐ 587 Jim Tatum .15 .07
☐ 588 Frank Bolick .15 .07
☐ 589 Kevin Young .15 .07
☐ 590 Matt Whiteside .15 .07
☐ 591 Cesar Hernandez .15 .07
☐ 592 Mike Mohler .15 .07
☐ 593 Alan Embree .15 .07
☐ 594 Terry Jorgensen .15 .07
☐ 595 John Cummings .15 .07
☐ 596 Domingo Martinez .15 .07
☐ 597 Benji Gil .15 .07
☐ 598 Todd Pratt .15 .07
☐ 599 Rene Arocha .15 .07
☐ 600 Dennis Moeller .15 .07
☐ 601 Jeff Conine .30 .14
☐ 602 Trevor Hoffman .20 .09
☐ 603 Daniel Smith .15 .07
☐ 604 Lee Tinsley .30 .14
☐ 605 Dan Peltier .15 .07
☐ 606 Billy Brewer .15 .07
☐ 607 Matt Walbeck .15 .07
☐ 608 Richie Lewis .15 .07
☐ 609 J.T. Snow .75 .35
☐ 610 Pat Gomez .15 .07
☐ 611 Phil Hiatt .15 .07
☐ 612 Alex Arias .15 .07
☐ 613 Kevin Rogers .15 .07
☐ 614 Al Martin .30 .14
☐ 615 Greg Gohr .15 .07
☐ 616 Graeme Lloyd .15 .07
☐ 617 Kent Bottenfield .15 .07
☐ 618 Chuck Carr .15 .07
☐ 619 Darrell Sherman .15 .07
☐ 620 Mike Lansing .30 .14

1993 Pinnacle Expansion Opening Day

This nine-card standard-size dual-sided set was issued to commemorate openning day for the two 1993 expansion teams, the Colorado Rockies and the Florida Marlins. The cards were inserted on top of sealed series two hobby boxes. These cards were also available through a mail-in offer. The full-bleed fronts feature glossy color action player photos. Across the bottom is a team color-coded bar containing the player's name, position, and opening day date. A logo for the Expansion Draft is printed in the lower right corner. An anti-counterfeit device is printed in the bottom black border. The backs carry the same design as the fronts with a player from the Rockies appearing on one side and a Marlin's player on the flip side. The cards are numbered on both sides.

	MINT	NRMT
COMPLETE SET (9)	25.00	11.00
COMMON PAIR (1-9)	1.50	.70
MINOR STARS	4.00	1.80
SEMISTARS	6.00	2.70
UNLISTED STARS	8.00	3.60

☐ 1 Charlie Hough 4.00 1.80
David Nied
☐ 2 Benito Santiago 1.50 .70
Joe Girardi
☐ 3 Orestes Destrade 8.00 3.60
Andres Galarraga
☐ 4 Bret Barberie 4.00 1.80
Eric Young
☐ 5 Dave Magadan 1.50 .70
Charlie Hayes
☐ 6 Walt Weiss 1.50 .70
Freddie Benavides
☐ 7 Jeff Conine 6.00 2.70
Jerald Clark
☐ 8 Scott Pose 1.50 .70
Alex Cole
☐ 9 Junior Felix 8.00 3.60
Dante Bichette

1993 Pinnacle Rookie Team Pinnacle

Cards from this 10-card standard-size set were randomly inserted into one in every 90 series 2 foil packs and each features an American League rookie on one side and a National League rookie on the other. Each double-sided

card displays paintings by artist Christopher Greco encased by a bold black border. The cards are numbered on the front and back.

	MINT	NRMT
COMPLETE SET (10)	100.00	45.00
COMMON PAIR (1-10)	4.00	1.80
☐ 1 Pedro Martinez Mike Trombley	10.00	4.50
☐ 2 Kevin Rogers Sterling Hitchcock	4.00	1.80
☐ 3 Mike Piazza Jesse Levis	50.00	22.00
☐ 4 Ryan Klesko J.T. Snow	12.00	5.50
☐ 5 John Patterson Bret Boone	4.00	1.80
☐ 6 Kevin Young Domingo Martinez	4.00	1.80
☐ 7 Wil Cordero Manny Alexander	4.00	1.80
☐ 8 Steve Hosey Tim Salmon	15.00	6.75
☐ 9 Ryan Thompson Gerald Williams	4.00	1.80
☐ 10 Melvin Nieves David Hulse	6.00	2.70

1993 Pinnacle Slugfest

These 30 standard-size cards salute baseball's top hitters and were inserted one per series 2 jumbo superpacks. The fronts feature color player action shots that are borderless, except at the bottom, where a black stripe carries the player's name in white lettering. The set's title appears below in black lettering within a gold foil stripe.

	MINT	NRMT
COMPLETE SET (30)	60.00	27.00
COMMON CARD (1-30)	1.00	.45
☐ 1 Juan Gonzalez	8.00	3.60
☐ 2 Mark McGwire	5.00	2.20
☐ 3 Cecil Fielder	1.50	.70
☐ 4 Joe Carter	2.00	.90
☐ 5 Fred McGriff	2.00	.90
☐ 6 Barry Bonds	4.00	1.80
☐ 7 Gary Sheffield	3.00	1.35
☐ 8 Dave Hollins	1.00	.45
☐ 9 Frank Thomas	12.00	5.50
☐ 10 Danny Tartabull	1.00	.45
☐ 11 Albert Belle	4.00	1.80
☐ 12 Ruben Sierra	1.00	.45
☐ 13 Larry Walker	3.00	1.35
☐ 14 Jeff Bagwell	6.00	2.70
☐ 15 David Justice	3.00	1.35
☐ 16 Kirby Puckett	6.00	2.70
☐ 17 John Kruk	1.50	.70
☐ 18 Howard Johnson	1.00	.45
☐ 19 Darryl Strawberry	1.50	.70
☐ 20 Will Clark	2.00	.90
☐ 21 Kevin Mitchell	1.00	.45
☐ 22 Mickey Tettleton	1.00	.45
☐ 23 Don Mattingly	6.00	2.70
☐ 24 Jose Canseco	2.00	.90
☐ 25 George Bell	1.00	.45
☐ 26 Andre Dawson	2.00	.90
☐ 27 Ryne Sandberg	4.00	1.80
☐ 28 Ken Griffey Jr.	15.00	6.75
☐ 29 Carlos Baerga	1.50	.70
☐ 30 Travis Fryman	1.50	.70

1993 Pinnacle Team 2001

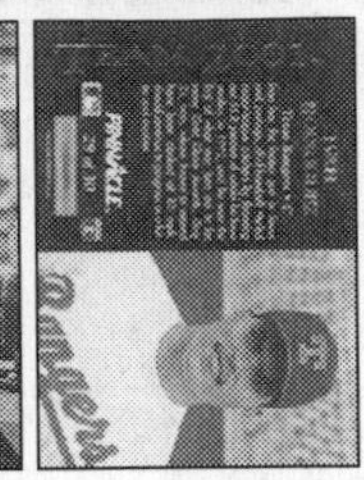

This 30-card standard-size set salutes players expected to be stars in the year 2001. The cards were inserted one per pack in first series jumbo superpacks and feature color player action shots on their fronts. These photos are borderless at the top and right, and black-bordered on the bottom and left. The player's name appears in gold-foil in the bottom margin, and his gold-foil-encircled team logo rests in the bottom left.

	MINT	NRMT
COMPLETE SET (30)	40.00	18.00
COMMON CARD (1-30)	.75	.35
☐ 1 Wil Cordero	.75	.35
☐ 2 Cal Eldred	.75	.35
☐ 3 Mike Mussina	2.50	1.10
☐ 4 Chuck Knoblauch	2.50	1.10
☐ 5 Melvin Nieves	1.00	.45
☐ 6 Tim Wakefield	.75	.35
☐ 7 Carlos Baerga	1.00	.45
☐ 8 Bret Boone	.75	.35
☐ 9 Jeff Bagwell	6.00	2.70
☐ 10 Travis Fryman	1.00	.45
☐ 11 Royce Clayton	.75	.35
☐ 12 Delino DeShields	.75	.35
☐ 13 Juan Gonzalez	8.00	3.60
☐ 14 Pedro Martinez	2.50	1.10
☐ 15 Bernie Williams	1.50	.70
☐ 16 Billy Ashley	.75	.35
☐ 17 Marquis Grissom	1.00	.45
☐ 18 Kenny Lofton	6.00	2.70
☐ 19 Ray Lankford	1.50	.70
☐ 20 Tim Salmon	4.00	1.80
☐ 21 Steve Hosey	.75	.35
☐ 22 Charles Nagy	1.00	.45
☐ 23 Dave Fleming	.75	.35
☐ 24 Reggie Sanders	1.00	.45
☐ 25 Sam Militello	.75	.35
☐ 26 Eric Karros	1.00	.45
☐ 27 Ryan Klesko	4.00	1.80
☐ 28 Dean Palmer	1.00	.45
☐ 29 Ivan Rodriguez	4.00	1.80
☐ 30 Sterling Hitchcock	.75	.35

1993 Pinnacle Team Pinnacle

Cards from this ten-card dual-sided set, featuring a selection of top stars paired of by position, were randomly inserted into one in every 24 first series foil packs. Each double-sided card displays paintings by artist Christopher Greco. A special bonus Team Pinnacle card (11) was available to collectors only through a mail-in offer for ten 1993 Pinnacle baseball wrappers plus 1.50 for shipping and handling. Moreover, hobby dealers who ordered Pinnacle received two bonus cards and an advertisement display promoting the offer.

	MINT	NRMT
COMPLETE SET (10)	90.00	40.00
COMMON PAIR (1-10/B11)	3.00	1.35
☐ 1 Greg Maddux Mike Mussina	25.00	11.00
☐ 2 Tom Glavine John Smiley	6.00	2.70
☐ 3 Darren Daulton Ivan Rodriguez	10.00	4.50
☐ 4 Fred McGriff Frank Thomas	30.00	13.50
☐ 5 Delino DeShields Carlos Baerga	4.00	1.80
☐ 6 Gary Sheffield Edgar Martinez	8.00	3.60
☐ 7 Ozzie Smith Pat Listach	10.00	4.50
☐ 8 Barry Bonds Juan Gonzalez	20.00	9.00
☐ 9 Andy Van Slyke Kirby Puckett	15.00	6.75
☐ 10 Larry Walker Joe Carter	8.00	3.60
☐ B11 Rob Dibble Rick Aguilera	3.00	1.35

1993 Pinnacle Tribute

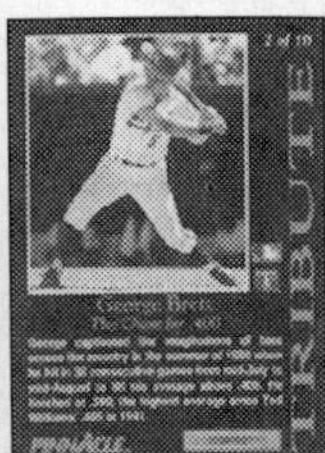

Inserted in second-series packs at a rate of one in 24, these ten standard-size cards pay tribute to two recent retirees from baseball: George Brett (1-5), and Nolan Ryan (6-10). Score estimates that the chances of finding a tribute chase card are not less than one in 24 count good packs. The fronts feature black-bordered color player action shots that are framed by a thin white line. The player's name appears in white lettering within the black bottom margin. Printed vertically, "Tribute" appears in gold foil along the right edge.

	MINT	NRMT
COMPLETE SET (10)	75.00	34.00
COMMON BRETT (1-5)	5.00	2.20
COMMON RYAN (6-10)	10.00	4.50
☐ 1 George Brett Kansas City Royalty	5.00	2.20
☐ 2 George Brett The Chase for .400	5.00	2.20
☐ 3 George Brett Pine Tar Pandemonium	5.00	2.20
☐ 4 George Brett MVP and a World Series, Too	5.00	2.20
☐ 5 George Brett 3,000 or Bust	5.00	2.20
☐ 6 Nolan Ryan The Rookie	10.00	4.50
☐ 7 Nolan Ryan Angel of No Mercy	10.00	4.50
☐ 8 Nolan Ryan Astronomical Success	10.00	4.50
☐ 9 Nolan Ryan 5,000 Ks	10.00	4.50
☐ 10 Nolan Ryan No-Hitter No. 7	10.00	4.50

1993 Pinnacle Cooperstown

This 30-card standard-size set features full-bleed color player photos of possible future HOF inductees. A green and gold foil Cooperstown Card logo overlays the bottom of the picture, and the player's name appears in gold foil within the black stripe that edges the bottom. The borderless back has a second color shot above a black background containing a brief career summary. The Cooperstown Card logo overlays the bottom of the picture.

	MINT	NRMT
COMPLETE SET (30)	8.00	3.60
COMMON CARD (1-30)	.10	.05
DUFEX: 200X BASIC CARDS		
☐ 1 Nolan Ryan	1.50	.70
☐ 2 George Brett	.75	.35
☐ 3 Robin Yount	.35	.16
☐ 4 Carlton Fisk	.50	.23
☐ 5 Dale Murphy	.50	.23
☐ 6 Dennis Eckersley	.35	.16
☐ 7 Rickey Henderson	.50	.23
☐ 8 Ryne Sandberg	.50	.23
☐ 9 Ozzie Smith	.75	.35
☐ 10 Dave Winfield	.50	.23
☐ 11 Andre Dawson	.50	.23
☐ 12 Kirby Puckett	1.00	.45
☐ 13 Wade Boggs	.50	.23
☐ 14 Don Mattingly	1.00	.45
☐ 15 Barry Bonds	.60	.25
☐ 16 Will Clark	.35	.16
☐ 17 Cal Ripken	1.50	.70
☐ 18 Roger Clemens	.75	.35
☐ 19 Dwight Gooden	.20	.09
☐ 20 Tony Gwynn	1.00	.45
☐ 21 Joe Carter	.20	.09
☐ 22 Ken Griffey Jr.	2.00	.90
☐ 23 Paul Molitor	.40	.18
☐ 24 Frank Thomas	1.50	.70
☐ 25 Juan Gonzalez	1.00	.45
☐ 26 Barry Larkin	.35	.16
☐ 27 Eddie Murray	.50	.23
☐ 28 Cecil Fielder	.20	.09
☐ 29 Roberto Alomar	.50	.23
☐ 30 Mark McGwire	.75	.35

1993 Pinnacle DiMaggio

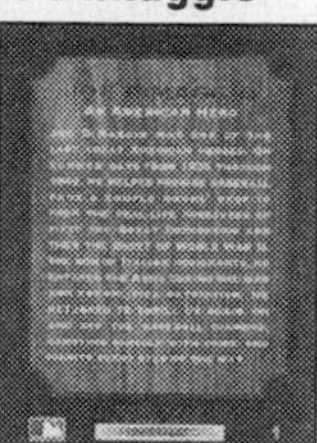

This 30-card set commemorates the life and career of Joe DiMaggio. Production was limited to 209,000 sets, with each set packaged in a black and gold collector's tin that features a color picture of DiMaggio. The black- and gold-bordered cards are standard-size. The fronts feature a mix of black-and-white, full-color, and colorized photos. At the bottom, DiMaggio's name is stamped in gold foil over a wood-grained, gold foil-framed bar. The black backs contain descriptive summaries from chapters in his life printed on a wood-grained background and framed in gold foil. The set includes an authenticator lens that can read the anticounterfeiting pattern at the bottom of the back. A certificate of authenticity card is also included that carries the production number of the set. DiMaggio also signed 9,000 cards for this set. One of 9,000 autographed cards from a special five-card set were randomly inserted into 30-card boxed hobby sets of 1993 Pinnacle Joe DiMaggio.

	MINT	NRMT
COMPLETE SET (30)	20.00	9.00
COMMON CARD (1-30)	.75	.35
☐ 1 Joe DiMaggio An American Hero	.75	.35
☐ 2 Joe DiMaggio San Francisco Seals	.75	.35
☐ 3 Joe DiMaggio Seals Farewell	.75	.35
☐ 4 Joe DiMaggio First Game	.75	.35
☐ 5 Joe DiMaggio The Rookie	.75	.35
☐ 6 Joe DiMaggio Rookie All-Star	.75	.35
☐ 7 Joe DiMaggio Fan Favorite	.75	.35
☐ 8 Joe DiMaggio Teammates' Awe	.75	.35
☐ 9 Joe DiMaggio Classic Swing	.75	.35
☐ 10 Joe DiMaggio Joltin' Power	.75	.35
☐ 11 Joe DiMaggio Bob Feller Rapid Robert Feller vs. Joltin' Joe	1.50	.70
☐ 12 Joe DiMaggio The Complete Hitter	.75	.35
☐ 13 Joe DiMaggio Makin' It Look Easy	.75	.35
☐ 14 Joe DiMaggio Extra Swings	.75	.35
☐ 15 Joe DiMaggio The Run Producer	.75	.35
☐ 16 Joe DiMaggio Quiet Confidence	.75	.35
☐ 17 Joe DiMaggio A Link to the Past	.75	.35
☐ 18 Joe DiMaggio Sticks 'n' Bones	.75	.35
☐ 19 Joe DiMaggio Center of Attention	.75	.35
☐ 20 Joe DiMaggio The DiMaggio Mystique	.75	.35
☐ 21 Joe DiMaggio Joe McCarthy MG	1.00	.45
☐ 22 Joe DiMaggio World War II	.75	.35
☐ 23 Joe DiMaggio Fearless Baserunner	.75	.35
☐ 24 Joe DiMaggio The Summer of '41	.75	.35
☐ 25 Joe DiMaggio Career Statistics	.75	.35
☐ 26 Joe DiMaggio No. 45	.75	.35
☐ 27 Joe DiMaggio Chasing (Babe) Ruth	.75	.35
☐ 28 Joe DiMaggio The Final Season	.75	.35
☐ 29 Joe DiMaggio Retirement	.75	.35
☐ 30 Joe DiMaggio Baseball's Greatest Living Player	.75	.35

1993 Pinnacle DiMaggio Autographs

Joe DiMaggio personally signed a total of 9,000 cards, and one autographed card from this five-card set was randomly inserted in selected 30-card boxed 1993 Pinnacle Joe DiMaggio hobby sets. These five autographed cards are slightly smaller (narrower) than standard size and feature white-bordered black-and-white action shots from DiMaggio's career that place special emphasis on the skills that made him great. DiMaggio's signature appears below the photo within the wide white lower margin.

	MINT	NRMT
COMPLETE SET (5)	1500.00	700.00
COMMON CARD (1-5)	300.00	135.00
☐ 1 Joe DiMaggio Spring 1936	300.00	135.00
☐ 2 Joe DiMaggio Joltin' Joe	300.00	135.00
☐ 3 Joe DiMaggio The Streak	300.00	135.00
☐ 4 Joe DiMaggio Opening Day	300.00	135.00
☐ 5 Joe DiMaggio Ebbets Field	300.00	135.00

1993 Pinnacle Home Run Club

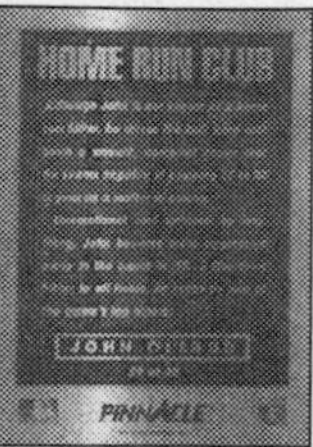

This 48-card boxed standard-size set features players with outstanding home run statistics. Each set contains a certificate of authenticity card that verifies the set is one of 200,000 sets produced and includes the set number printed on a white bar. The checklist is printed on an outer sleeve that encases the black hinged box. The black fronts display an action photo cut-out that is superimposed over the initials "HR" in multi-colored foil. The words "Home Run" are printed over the "H" of the "HR". The card has an inner gold border with the player's name in a gold bordered box over the picture at the bottom. The silver-bordered backs carry descriptive career highlights on a black background with a ghosted HR logo.

	MINT	NRMT
COMPLETE SET (48)	25.00	11.00
COMMON CARD (1-48)	.25	.11
☐ 1 Juan Gonzalez	2.50	1.10
☐ 2 Fred McGriff	.50	.23
☐ 3 Cecil Fielder	.35	.16
☐ 4 Barry Bonds	1.00	.45
☐ 5 Albert Belle	1.50	.70
☐ 6 Gary Sheffield	.75	.35
☐ 7 Joe Carter	.35	.16
☐ 8 Mark McGwire	2.00	.90
☐ 9 Darren Daulton	.35	.16
☐ 10 Jose Canseco	.60	.25
☐ 11 Dave Hollins	.25	.11
☐ 12 Ryne Sandberg	1.50	.70
☐ 13 Ken Griffey Jr.	5.00	2.20
☐ 14 Larry Walker	.75	.35
☐ 15 Rob Deer	.25	.11
☐ 16 Andre Dawson	.50	.23
☐ 17 Frank Thomas	4.00	1.80
☐ 18 Mickey Tettleton	.25	.11
☐ 19 Charlie Hayes	.25	.11
☐ 20 Ron Gant	.35	.16
☐ 21 Rickey Henderson	.75	.35
☐ 22 Matt Williams	.50	.23
☐ 23 Kevin Mitchell	.25	.11
☐ 24 Robin Ventura	.35	.16
☐ 25 Dean Palmer	.35	.16
☐ 26 Mike Piazza	3.00	1.35
☐ 27 J.T. Snow	.75	.35
☐ 28 Jeff Bagwell	2.50	1.10
☐ 29 John Olerud	.35	.16
☐ 30 Greg Vaughn	.25	.11
☐ 31 Dave Justice	.75	.35
☐ 32 Dave Winfield	.75	.35
☐ 33 Danny Tartabull	.25	.11
☐ 34 Eric Anthony	.25	.11
☐ 35 Eddie Murray	1.00	.45
☐ 36 Jay Buhner	.50	.23
☐ 37 Derek Bell	.25	.11
☐ 38 Will Clark	.75	.35
☐ 39 Carlos Baerga	.35	.16
☐ 40 Mo Vaughn	1.25	.55
☐ 41 Bobby Bonilla	.35	.16
☐ 42 Tim Salmon	1.00	.45
☐ 43 Bo Jackson	.35	.16
☐ 44 Howard Johnson	.25	.11
☐ 45 Kent Hrbek	.25	.11
☐ 46 Ruben Sierra	.25	.11
☐ 47 Cal Ripken	4.00	1.80
☐ 48 Travis Fryman	.35	.16

1994 Pinnacle Samples

Sealed in a cello pack, these ten-or 11-card standard-size sample groups were issued to preview the new design of the 1994 Pinnacle baseball set. The fronts feature full-bleed color action player photos. In one of the upper corners the new Pinnacle logo appears, consisting of a gold foil triangular "A" with the brand name immediately below in small white lettering. Toward the bottom, the player's last name in gold foil on a black bar overlays a two-color emblem carrying his first name and his team name. On most of the backs, a ghosted version of the front picture forms the background for a player cutout, biography and statistics. Both sides of the cards have "SAMPLE" stenciled across them. The ten-card set was the retail version whereas the 11-card set was for the hobby. The hobby and retail versions are only distinguishable after opening by "Hobby Edition" or "Retail Edition" printed on the title card and the inclusion of an eleventh card, Paul Molitor in the hobby samples set. The cards are numbered in a baseball icon at the upper right. Also a two-card sample strip consisting of Olerud and Alou cards was issued.

	MINT	NRMT
COMPLETE SET (12)	9.00	4.00
COMMON CARD	.25	.11

	MINT	NRMT
☐ 2 Carlos Baerga	.50	.23
☐ 3 Sammy Sosa	1.00	.45
☐ 5 John Olerud	.50	.23
☐ 7 Moises Alou	.50	.23
☐ 8 Steve Avery	.25	.11
☐ 10 Cecil Fielder	.50	.23
☐ 11 Greg Maddux	2.00	.90
☐ 269 Jeff Granger	.25	.11
☐ TR1 Paul Molitor Tribute	2.00	.90
☐ NNO Title card Hobby Edition (Pinnacle ad)	.25	.11
☐ NNO Title card Retail Edition (Pinnacle ad)	.25	.11
☐ NNO Jeff Granger 1994 Museum Collection	1.00	.45

1994 Pinnacle

The 540-card 1994 Pinnacle standard-size set was issued in two series of 270. Cards were issued in hobby and retail foil-wrapped packs. The card fronts feature full-bleed color action player photos with a small foil logo and players name at the base. Subsets include Rookie Prospects (224-261) and Draft Picks (262-270/430-438). Notable Rookie Cards include Derrek Lee, Chan Ho Park and Billy Wagner. A Carlos Delgado Super Rookie one shot insert was put into packs at a rate of one in 360. It is labeled SR1 and is listed at the end of the set.

	MINT	NRMT
COMPLETE SET (540)	20.00	9.00
COMPLETE SERIES 1 (270)	10.00	4.50
COMPLETE SERIES 2 (270)	10.00	4.50
COMMON CARD (1-540)	.10	.05

	MINT	NRMT
☐ 1 Frank Thomas	2.00	.90
☐ 2 Carlos Baerga	.25	.11
☐ 3 Sammy Sosa	.50	.23
☐ 4 Tony Gwynn	1.25	.55
☐ 5 John Olerud	.10	.05
☐ 6 Ryne Sandberg	.60	.25
☐ 7 Moises Alou	.25	.11
☐ 8 Steve Avery	.10	.05
☐ 9 Tim Salmon	.50	.23
☐ 10 Cecil Fielder	.25	.11
☐ 11 Greg Maddux	1.50	.70
☐ 12 Barry Larkin	.35	.16
☐ 13 Mike Devereaux	.10	.05
☐ 14 Charlie Hayes	.10	.05
☐ 15 Albert Belle	.60	.25
☐ 16 Andy Van Slyke	.25	.11
☐ 17 Mo Vaughn	.60	.25
☐ 18 Brian McRae	.10	.05
☐ 19 Cal Eldred	.10	.05
☐ 20 Craig Biggio	.35	.16
☐ 21 Kirby Puckett	1.00	.45
☐ 22 Derek Bell	.25	.11
☐ 23 Don Mattingly	.75	.35
☐ 24 John Burkett	.10	.05
☐ 25 Roger Clemens	1.00	.45
☐ 26 Barry Bonds	.60	.25
☐ 27 Paul Molitor	.50	.23
☐ 28 Mike Piazza	1.50	.70
☐ 29 Robin Ventura	.25	.11
☐ 30 Jeff Conine	.25	.11
☐ 31 Wade Boggs	.50	.23
☐ 32 Dennis Eckersley	.25	.11
☐ 33 Bobby Bonilla	.25	.11
☐ 34 Lenny Dykstra	.25	.11
☐ 35 Manny Alexander	.10	.05
☐ 36 Ray Lankford	.35	.16
☐ 37 Greg Vaughn	.10	.05
☐ 38 Chuck Finley	.10	.05
☐ 39 Todd Benzinger	.10	.05
☐ 40 Dave Justice	.50	.23
☐ 41 Rob Dibble	.10	.05
☐ 42 Tom Henke	.10	.05
☐ 43 David Nied	.10	.05
☐ 44 Sandy Alomar Jr.	.25	.11
☐ 45 Pete Harnisch	.10	.05
☐ 46 Jeff Russell	.10	.05
☐ 47 Terry Mulholland	.10	.05
☐ 48 Kevin Appier	.25	.11
☐ 49 Randy Tomlin	.10	.05
☐ 50 Cal Ripken Jr.	2.00	.90
☐ 51 Andy Benes	.25	.11
☐ 52 Jimmy Key	.25	.11
☐ 53 Kirt Manwaring	.10	.05
☐ 54 Kevin Tapani	.10	.05
☐ 55 Jose Guzman	.10	.05
☐ 56 Todd Stottlemyre	.10	.05
☐ 57 Jack McDowell	.10	.05
☐ 58 Orel Hershiser	.25	.11
☐ 59 Chris Hammond	.10	.05
☐ 60 Chris Nabholz	.10	.05
☐ 61 Ruben Sierra	.10	.05
☐ 62 Dwight Gooden	.25	.11
☐ 63 John Kruk	.25	.11
☐ 64 Omar Vizquel	.25	.11
☐ 65 Tim Naehring	.10	.05
☐ 66 Dwight Smith	.10	.05
☐ 67 Mickey Tettleton	.10	.05
☐ 68 J.T. Snow	.35	.16
☐ 69 Greg McMichael	.10	.05
☐ 70 Kevin Mitchell	.10	.05
☐ 71 Kevin Brown	.25	.11
☐ 72 Scott Cooper	.10	.05
☐ 73 Jim Thome	.60	.25
☐ 74 Joe Girardi	.10	.05
☐ 75 Eric Anthony	.10	.05
☐ 76 Orlando Merced	.10	.05
☐ 77 Felix Jose	.10	.05
☐ 78 Tommy Greene	.10	.05
☐ 79 Bernard Gilkey	.10	.05
☐ 80 Phil Plantier	.10	.05
☐ 81 Danny Tartabull	.10	.05
☐ 82 Trevor Wilson	.10	.05
☐ 83 Chuck Knoblauch	.50	.23
☐ 84 Rick Wilkins	.10	.05
☐ 85 Devon White	.10	.05
☐ 86 Lance Johnson	.10	.05
☐ 87 Eric Karros	.25	.11
☐ 88 Gary Sheffield	.50	.23
☐ 89 Wil Cordero	.25	.11
☐ 90 Ron Darling	.10	.05
☐ 91 Darren Daulton	.25	.11
☐ 92 Joe Orsulak	.10	.05
☐ 93 Steve Cooke	.10	.05
☐ 94 Darryl Hamilton	.10	.05
☐ 95 Aaron Sele	.10	.05
☐ 96 John Doherty	.10	.05
☐ 97 Gary DiSarcina	.10	.05
☐ 98 Jeff Blauser	.10	.05
☐ 99 John Smiley	.10	.05
☐ 100 Ken Griffey Jr.	2.50	1.10
☐ 101 Dean Palmer	.25	.11
☐ 102 Felix Fermin	.10	.05
☐ 103 Jerald Clark	.10	.05
☐ 104 Doug Drabek	.10	.05
☐ 105 Curt Schilling	.25	.11
☐ 106 Jeff Montgomery	.25	.11
☐ 107 Rene Arocha	.10	.05
☐ 108 Carlos Garcia	.10	.05
☐ 109 Wally Whitehurst	.10	.05
☐ 110 Jim Abbott	.10	.05
☐ 111 Royce Clayton	.25	.11
☐ 112 Chris Hoiles	.10	.05
☐ 113 Mike Morgan	.10	.05
☐ 114 Joe Magrane	.10	.05
☐ 115 Tom Candiotti	.10	.05
☐ 116 Ron Karkovice	.10	.05
☐ 117 Ryan Bowen	.10	.05
☐ 118 Rod Beck	.25	.11
☐ 119 John Wetteland	.25	.11
☐ 120 Terry Steinbach	.25	.11
☐ 121 Dave Hollins	.10	.05
☐ 122 Jeff Kent	.10	.05
☐ 123 Ricky Bones	.10	.05
☐ 124 Brian Jordan	.25	.11
☐ 125 Chad Kreuter	.10	.05
☐ 126 John Valentin	.25	.11
☐ 127 Hilly Hathaway	.10	.05
☐ 128 Wilson Alvarez	.25	.11
☐ 129 Tino Martinez	.50	.23
☐ 130 Rodney Bolton	.10	.05
☐ 131 David Segui	.10	.05
☐ 132 Wayne Kirby	.10	.05
☐ 133 Eric Young	.25	.11
☐ 134 Scott Servais	.10	.05
☐ 135 Scott Radinsky	.10	.05
☐ 136 Bret Barberie	.10	.05
☐ 137 John Roper	.10	.05
☐ 138 Ricky Gutierrez	.10	.05
☐ 139 Bernie Williams	.50	.23
☐ 140 Bud Black	.10	.05
☐ 141 Jose Vizcaino	.10	.05
☐ 142 Gerald Williams	.10	.05
☐ 143 Duane Ward	.10	.05
☐ 144 Danny Jackson	.10	.05
☐ 145 Allen Watson	.10	.05
☐ 146 Scott Fletcher	.10	.05
☐ 147 Delino DeShields	.10	.05
☐ 148 Shane Mack	.10	.05
☐ 149 Jim Eisenreich	.25	.11
☐ 150 Troy Neel	.10	.05
☐ 151 Jay Bell	.25	.11
☐ 152 B.J. Surhoff	.10	.05
☐ 153 Mark Whiten	.10	.05
☐ 154 Mike Henneman	.10	.05
☐ 155 Todd Hundley	.25	.11
☐ 156 Greg Myers	.10	.05
☐ 157 Ryan Klesko	.35	.16
☐ 158 Dave Fleming	.10	.05
☐ 159 Mickey Morandini	.10	.05
☐ 160 Blas Minor	.10	.05
☐ 161 Reggie Jefferson	.25	.11
☐ 162 David Hulse	.10	.05
☐ 163 Greg Swindell	.10	.05
☐ 164 Roberto Hernandez	.25	.11
☐ 165 Brady Anderson	.35	.16
☐ 166 Jack Armstrong	.10	.05
☐ 167 Phil Clark	.10	.05
☐ 168 Melido Perez	.10	.05
☐ 169 Darren Lewis	.10	.05
☐ 170 Sam Horn	.10	.05
☐ 171 Mike Harkey	.10	.05
☐ 172 Juan Guzman	.10	.05
☐ 173 Bob Natal	.10	.05
☐ 174 Deion Sanders	.50	.23
☐ 175 Carlos Quintana	.10	.05
☐ 176 Mel Rojas	.10	.05
☐ 177 Willie Banks	.10	.05
☐ 178 Ben Rivera	.10	.05
☐ 179 Kenny Lofton	.60	.25
☐ 180 Leo Gomez	.10	.05
☐ 181 Roberto Mejia	.10	.05
☐ 182 Mike Perez	.10	.05
☐ 183 Travis Fryman	.25	.11
☐ 184 Ben McDonald	.10	.05
☐ 185 Steve Frey	.10	.05
☐ 186 Kevin Young	.10	.05
☐ 187 Dave Magadan	.10	.05
☐ 188 Bobby Munoz	.10	.05
☐ 189 Pat Rapp	.10	.05
☐ 190 Jose Offerman	.10	.05
☐ 191 Vinny Castilla	.35	.16
☐ 192 Ivan Calderon	.10	.05
☐ 193 Ken Caminiti	.50	.23
☐ 194 Benji Gil	.10	.05
☐ 195 Chuck Carr	.10	.05
☐ 196 Derrick May	.10	.05
☐ 197 Pat Kelly	.10	.05
☐ 198 Jeff Brantley	.10	.05
☐ 199 Jose Lind	.10	.05
☐ 200 Steve Buechele	.10	.05
☐ 201 Wes Chamberlain	.10	.05
☐ 202 Eduardo Perez	.10	.05
☐ 203 Bret Saberhagen	.10	.05
☐ 204 Gregg Jefferies	.25	.11
☐ 205 Darrin Fletcher	.10	.05
☐ 206 Kent Hrbek	.25	.11
☐ 207 Kim Batiste	.10	.05
☐ 208 Jeff King	.25	.11
☐ 209 Donovan Osborne	.10	.05
☐ 210 Dave Nilsson	.25	.11
☐ 211 Al Martin	.10	.05
☐ 212 Mike Moore	.10	.05
☐ 213 Sterling Hitchcock	.25	.11
☐ 214 Geronimo Pena	.10	.05
☐ 215 Kevin Higgins	.10	.05
☐ 216 Norm Charlton	.10	.05
☐ 217 Don Slaught	.10	.05
☐ 218 Mitch Williams	.10	.05
☐ 219 Derek Lilliquist	.10	.05
☐ 220 Armando Reynoso	.10	.05
☐ 221 Kenny Rogers	.10	.05
☐ 222 Doug Jones	.10	.05
☐ 223 Luis Aquino	.10	.05
☐ 224 Mike Oquist	.10	.05
☐ 225 Darryl Scott	.10	.05
☐ 226 Kurt Abbott	.10	.05
☐ 227 Andy Tomberlin	.10	.05
☐ 228 Norberto Martin	.10	.05
☐ 229 Pedro Castellano	.10	.05
☐ 230 Curtis Pride	.25	.11
☐ 231 Jeff McNeely	.10	.05
☐ 232 Scott Lydy	.10	.05

☐ 233 Darren Oliver	.50	.23
☐ 234 Danny Bautista	.10	.05
☐ 235 Butch Huskey	.25	.11
☐ 236 Chipper Jones	1.50	.70
☐ 237 Eddie Zambrano	.10	.05
☐ 238 Domingo Jean	.10	.05
☐ 239 Javier Lopez	.35	.16
☐ 240 Nigel Wilson	.10	.05
☐ 241 Drew Denson	.10	.05
☐ 242 Raul Mondesi	.35	.16
☐ 243 Luis Ortiz	.10	.05
☐ 244 Manny Ramirez	.60	.25
☐ 245 Greg Blosser	.10	.05
☐ 246 Rondell White	.35	.16
☐ 247 Steve Karsay	.10	.05
☐ 248 Scott Stahoviak	.10	.05
☐ 249 Jose Valentin	.25	.11
☐ 250 Marc Newfield	.25	.11
☐ 251 Keith Kessinger	.10	.05
☐ 252 Carl Everett	.10	.05
☐ 253 John O'Donoghue	.10	.05
☐ 254 Turk Wendell	.10	.05
☐ 255 Scott Ruffcorn	.10	.05
☐ 256 Tony Tarasco	.10	.05
☐ 257 Andy Cook	.10	.05
☐ 258 Matt Mieske	.10	.05
☐ 259 Luis Lopez	.10	.05
☐ 260 Ramon Caraballo	.10	.05
☐ 261 Salomon Torres	.10	.05
☐ 262 Brooks Kieschnick	.35	.16
☐ 263 Daron Kirkreit	.25	.11
☐ 264 Bill Wagner	1.00	.45
☐ 265 Matt Drews	.50	.23
☐ 266 Scott Christman	.25	.11
☐ 267 Torii Hunter	.25	.11
☐ 268 Jamey Wright	.50	.23
☐ 269 Jeff Granger	.25	.11
☐ 270 Trot Nixon	.35	.16
☐ 271 Randy Myers	.10	.05
☐ 272 Trevor Hoffman	.25	.11
☐ 273 Bob Wickman	.10	.05
☐ 274 Willie McGee	.10	.05
☐ 275 Hipolito Pichardo	.10	.05
☐ 276 Bobby Witt	.10	.05
☐ 277 Gregg Olson	.10	.05
☐ 278 Randy Johnson	.50	.23
☐ 279 Robb Nen	.25	.11
☐ 280 Paul O'Neill	.25	.11
☐ 281 Lou Whitaker	.25	.11
☐ 282 Chad Curtis	.10	.05
☐ 283 Doug Henry	.10	.05
☐ 284 Tom Glavine	.35	.16
☐ 285 Mike Greenwell	.10	.05
☐ 286 Roberto Kelly	.10	.05
☐ 287 Roberto Alomar	.50	.23
☐ 288 Charlie Hough	.10	.05
☐ 289 Alex Fernandez	.25	.11
☐ 290 Jeff Bagwell	1.00	.45
☐ 291 Wally Joyner	.25	.11
☐ 292 Andujar Cedeno	.10	.05
☐ 293 Rick Aguilera	.10	.05
☐ 294 Darryl Strawberry	.25	.11
☐ 295 Mike Mussina	.50	.23
☐ 296 Jeff Gardner	.10	.05
☐ 297 Chris Gwynn	.10	.05
☐ 298 Matt Williams	.35	.16
☐ 299 Brent Gates	.10	.05
☐ 300 Mark McGwire	1.00	.45
☐ 301 Jim Deshaies	.10	.05
☐ 302 Edgar Martinez	.35	.16
☐ 303 Danny Darwin	.10	.05
☐ 304 Pat Meares	.10	.05
☐ 305 Benito Santiago	.10	.05
☐ 306 Jose Canseco	.35	.16
☐ 307 Jim Gott	.10	.05
☐ 308 Paul Sorrento	.10	.05
☐ 309 Scott Kamieniecki	.10	.05
☐ 310 Larry Walker	.50	.23
☐ 311 Mark Langston	.10	.05
☐ 312 John Jaha	.10	.05
☐ 313 Stan Javier	.10	.05
☐ 314 Hal Morris	.10	.05
☐ 315 Robby Thompson	.10	.05
☐ 316 Pat Hentgen	.25	.11
☐ 317 Tom Gordon	.10	.05
☐ 318 Joey Cora	.10	.05
☐ 319 Luis Alicea	.10	.05
☐ 320 Andre Dawson	.35	.16
☐ 321 Darryl Kile	.25	.11
☐ 322 Jose Rijo	.10	.05
☐ 323 Luis Gonzalez	.10	.05
☐ 324 Billy Ashley	.10	.05
☐ 325 David Cone	.25	.11
☐ 326 Bill Swift	.10	.05
☐ 327 Phil Hiatt	.10	.05
☐ 328 Craig Paquette	.10	.05
☐ 329 Bob Welch	.10	.05
☐ 330 Tony Phillips	.10	.05
☐ 331 Archi Cianfrocco	.10	.05
☐ 332 Dave Winfield	.35	.16
☐ 333 David McCarty	.10	.05
☐ 334 Al Leiter	.10	.05
☐ 335 Tom Browning	.10	.05
☐ 336 Mark Grace	.35	.16
☐ 337 Jose Mesa	.25	.11
☐ 338 Mike Stanley	.10	.05
☐ 339 Roger McDowell	.10	.05
☐ 340 Damion Easley	.10	.05
☐ 341 Angel Miranda	.10	.05
☐ 342 John Smoltz	.35	.16
☐ 343 Jay Buhner	.35	.16
☐ 344 Bryan Harvey	.10	.05
☐ 345 Joe Carter	.35	.16
☐ 346 Dante Bichette	.35	.16
☐ 347 Jason Bere	.10	.05
☐ 348 Frank Viola	.10	.05
☐ 349 Ivan Rodriguez	.60	.25
☐ 350 Juan Gonzalez	1.25	.55
☐ 351 Steve Finley	.25	.11
☐ 352 Mike Felder	.10	.05
☐ 353 Ramon Martinez	.25	.11
☐ 354 Greg Gagne	.10	.05
☐ 355 Ken Hill	.10	.05
☐ 356 Pedro Munoz	.10	.05
☐ 357 Todd Van Poppel	.10	.05
☐ 358 Marquis Grissom	.25	.11
☐ 359 Milt Cuyler	.10	.05
☐ 360 Reggie Sanders	.10	.05
☐ 361 Scott Erickson	.10	.05
☐ 362 Billy Hatcher	.10	.05
☐ 363 Gene Harris	.10	.05
☐ 364 Rene Gonzales	.10	.05
☐ 365 Kevin Rogers	.10	.05
☐ 366 Eric Plunk	.10	.05
☐ 367 Todd Zeile	.10	.05
☐ 368 John Franco	.10	.05
☐ 369 Brett Butler	.25	.11
☐ 370 Bill Spiers	.10	.05
☐ 371 Terry Pendleton	.25	.11
☐ 372 Chris Bosio	.10	.05
☐ 373 Orestes Destrade	.10	.05
☐ 374 Dave Stewart	.25	.11
☐ 375 Darren Holmes	.10	.05
☐ 376 Doug Strange	.10	.05
☐ 377 Brian Turang	.10	.05
☐ 378 Carl Wills	.10	.05
☐ 379 Mark McLemore	.10	.05
☐ 380 Bobby Jones	.25	.11
☐ 381 Scott Sanders	.10	.05
☐ 382 Kirk Rueter	.10	.05
☐ 383 Randy Velarde	.10	.05
☐ 384 Fred McGriff	.35	.16
☐ 385 Charles Nagy	.25	.11
☐ 386 Rich Amaral	.10	.05
☐ 387 Geronimo Berroa	.25	.11
☐ 388 Eric Davis	.25	.11
☐ 389 Ozzie Smith	.60	.25
☐ 390 Alex Arias	.10	.05
☐ 391 Brad Ausmus	.10	.05
☐ 392 Cliff Floyd	.25	.11
☐ 393 Roger Salkeld	.10	.05
☐ 394 Jim Edmonds	.50	.23
☐ 395 Jeromy Burnitz	.25	.11
☐ 396 Dave Staton	.10	.05
☐ 397 Rob Butler	.10	.05
☐ 398 Marcos Armas	.10	.05
☐ 399 Darrell Whitmore	.10	.05
☐ 400 Ryan Thompson	.10	.05
☐ 401 Ross Powell	.10	.05
☐ 402 Joe Oliver	.10	.05
☐ 403 Paul Carey	.10	.05
☐ 404 Bob Hamelin	.10	.05
☐ 405 Chris Turner	.10	.05
☐ 406 Nate Minchey	.10	.05
☐ 407 Lonnie Maclin	.10	.05
☐ 408 Harold Baines	.25	.11
☐ 409 Brian Williams	.10	.05
☐ 410 Johnny Ruffin	.10	.05
☐ 411 Julian Tavarez	.25	.11
☐ 412 Mark Hutton	.10	.05
☐ 413 Carlos Delgado	.35	.16
☐ 414 Chris Gomez	.10	.05
☐ 415 Mike Hampton	.25	.11
☐ 416 Alex Diaz	.10	.05
☐ 417 Jeffrey Hammonds	.25	.11
☐ 418 Jayhawk Owens	.10	.05
☐ 419 J.R. Phillips	.10	.05
☐ 420 Cory Bailey	.10	.05
☐ 421 Denny Hocking	.10	.05
☐ 422 Jon Shave	.10	.05
☐ 423 Damon Buford	.10	.05
☐ 424 Troy O'Leary	.10	.05
☐ 425 Tripp Cromer	.10	.05
☐ 426 Albie Lopez	.10	.05
☐ 427 Tony Fernandez	.10	.05
☐ 428 Ozzie Guillen	.10	.05
☐ 429 Alan Trammell	.35	.16
☐ 430 John Wasdin	.50	.23
☐ 431 Marc Valdes	.25	.11
☐ 432 Brian Anderson	.35	.16
☐ 433 Matt Brunson	.25	.11
☐ 434 Wayne Gomes	.25	.11
☐ 435 Jay Powell	.25	.11
☐ 436 Kirk Presley	.25	.11
☐ 437 Jon Ratliff	.25	.11
☐ 438 Derrek Lee	1.50	.70
☐ 439 Tom Pagnozzi	.10	.05
☐ 440 Kent Mercker	.10	.05
☐ 441 Phil Leftwich	.10	.05
☐ 442 Jamie Moyer	.10	.05
☐ 443 John Flaherty	.10	.05
☐ 444 Mark Wohlers	.25	.11
☐ 445 Jose Bautista	.10	.05
☐ 446 Andres Galarraga	.35	.16
☐ 447 Mark Lemke	.10	.05
☐ 448 Tim Wakefield	.10	.05
☐ 449 Pat Listach	.10	.05
☐ 450 Rickey Henderson	.35	.16
☐ 451 Mike Gallego	.10	.05
☐ 452 Bob Tewksbury	.10	.05
☐ 453 Kirk Gibson	.25	.11
☐ 454 Pedro Astacio	.10	.05
☐ 455 Mike Lansing	.25	.11
☐ 456 Sean Berry	.10	.05
☐ 457 Bob Walk	.10	.05
☐ 458 Chili Davis	.25	.11
☐ 459 Ed Sprague	.10	.05
☐ 460 Kevin Stocker	.10	.05
☐ 461 Mike Stanton	.10	.05
☐ 462 Tim Raines	.10	.05
☐ 463 Mike Bordick	.10	.05
☐ 464 David Wells	.10	.05
☐ 465 Tim Laker	.10	.05
☐ 466 Cory Snyder	.10	.05
☐ 467 Alex Cole	.10	.05
☐ 468 Pete Incaviglia	.10	.05
☐ 469 Roger Pavlik	.10	.05
☐ 470 Greg W. Harris	.10	.05
☐ 471 Xavier Hernandez	.10	.05
☐ 472 Erik Hanson	.10	.05
☐ 473 Jesse Orosco	.10	.05
☐ 474 Greg Colbrunn	.10	.05
☐ 475 Harold Reynolds	.10	.05
☐ 476 Greg A. Harris	.10	.05
☐ 477 Pat Borders	.10	.05
☐ 478 Melvin Nieves	.10	.05
☐ 479 Mariano Duncan	.10	.05
☐ 480 Greg Hibbard	.10	.05
☐ 481 Tim Pugh	.10	.05
☐ 482 Bobby Ayala	.10	.05
☐ 483 Sid Fernandez	.10	.05
☐ 484 Tim Wallach	.10	.05
☐ 485 Randy Milligan	.10	.05
☐ 486 Walt Weiss	.10	.05
☐ 487 Matt Walbeck	.10	.05
☐ 488 Mike Macfarlane	.10	.05
☐ 489 Jerry Browne	.10	.05
☐ 490 Chris Sabo	.10	.05
☐ 491 Tim Belcher	.10	.05
☐ 492 Spike Owen	.10	.05
☐ 493 Rafael Palmeiro	.35	.16
☐ 494 Brian Harper	.10	.05
☐ 495 Eddie Murray	.50	.23
☐ 496 Ellis Burks	.25	.11
☐ 497 Karl Rhodes	.10	.05
☐ 498 Otis Nixon	.25	.11
☐ 499 Lee Smith	.25	.11
☐ 500 Bip Roberts	.10	.05
☐ 501 Pedro Martinez	.50	.23
☐ 502 Brian Hunter	.10	.05
☐ 503 Tyler Green	.10	.05
☐ 504 Bruce Hurst	.10	.05
☐ 505 Alex Gonzalez	.25	.11
☐ 506 Mark Portugal	.10	.05
☐ 507 Bob Ojeda	.10	.05
☐ 508 Dave Henderson	.10	.05
☐ 509 Bo Jackson	.25	.11
☐ 510 Bret Boone	.10	.05
☐ 511 Mark Eichhorn	.10	.05
☐ 512 Luis Polonia	.10	.05
☐ 513 Will Clark	.35	.16
☐ 514 Dave Valle	.10	.05
☐ 515 Dan Wilson	.25	.11
☐ 516 Dennis Martinez	.25	.11
☐ 517 Jim Leyritz	.10	.05
☐ 518 Howard Johnson	.10	.05
☐ 519 Jody Reed	.10	.05
☐ 520 Julio Franco	.25	.11
☐ 521 Jeff Reardon	.25	.11
☐ 522 Willie Greene	.25	.11
☐ 523 Shawon Dunston	.10	.05

☐ 524 Keith Mitchell	.10	.05
☐ 525 Rick Helling	.10	.05
☐ 526 Mark Kiefer	.10	.05
☐ 527 Chan Ho Park	1.50	.70
☐ 528 Tony Longmire	.10	.05
☐ 529 Rich Becker	.25	.11
☐ 530 Tim Hyers	.10	.05
☐ 531 Darrin Jackson	.10	.05
☐ 532 Jack Morris	.25	.11
☐ 533 Rick White	.10	.05
☐ 534 Mike Kelly	.10	.05
☐ 535 James Mouton	.25	.11
☐ 536 Steve Trachsel	.10	.05
☐ 537 Tony Eusebio	.10	.05
☐ 538 Kelly Stinnett	.10	.05
☐ 539 Paul Spoljaric	.10	.05
☐ 540 Darren Dreifort	.10	.05
☐ SR1 C.Delgado Super Rook.	5.00	2.20

1994 Pinnacle Artist's Proofs

Randomly inserted at a rate of one in 26 hobby and retail packs, cards from this 540-card set parallel that of the basic Pinnacle issue. Each card is embossed with a gold-foil-stamped "Artist's Proof" logo just above the player name. The Pinnacle logo is also done in gold foil. Just 1,000 of each card were printed.

	MINT	NRMT
COMPLETE SET (540)	2000.00	900.00
COMPLETE SERIES 1 (270)	1400.00	650.00
COMPLETE SERIES 2 (270)	600.00	275.00
COMMON CARD (1-540)	3.00	1.35

*STARS: 12.5X to 30X BASIC CARDS
*YOUNG STARS: 10X to 25X BASIC CARDS
*ROOKIES: 8X to 20X BASIC CARDS..

1994 Pinnacle Museum Collection

This 540-card set is a parallel dufex to that of the basic Pinnacle issue. They were randomly inserted at a rate of one in four hobby and retail packs. A Museum Collection logo replaces the anti-counterfeit device. Only 6,500 of each card were printed. Five cards (#'s 279, 313, 328, 382 and 387) were available only by mailing in a redemption card randomly seeded into packs.

	MINT	NRMT
COMPLETE SET (540)	600.00	275.00
COMPLETE SERIES 1 (270)	400.00	180.00
COMPLETE SERIES 2 (270)	200.00	90.00
COMMON CARD (1-540)	1.00	.45
TRADE (279/313/328/382/387)	3.00	1.35

*STARS: 6X TO 12X BASIC CARDS....
*YOUNG STARS: 5X TO 10X BASIC CARDS
*ROOKIES: 4X TO 8X BASIC CARDS....

1994 Pinnacle Rookie Team Pinnacle

These nine double-front standard-size cards of the "Rookie Team Pinnacle" set feature a top AL and a top NL rookie prospect by position. The insertion rate for these is one per 48 first series packs. These special portrait cards were painted by artists Christopher Greco and Ron DeFelice. The front features the National League player and card number. Both sides contain a gold Rookie Team Pinnacle logo.

	MINT	NRMT
COMPLETE SET (9)	80.00	36.00
COMMON PAIR (1-9)	5.00	2.20
☐ 1 Carlos Delgado Javier Lopez	12.00	5.50
☐ 2 Bob Hamelin J.R. Phillips	5.00	2.20
☐ 3 Jon Shave Keith Kessinger	5.00	2.20
☐ 4 Luis Ortiz Butch Huskey	8.00	3.60
☐ 5 Kurt Abbott Chipper Jones	40.00	18.00
☐ 6 Manny Ramirez Rondell White	12.00	5.50
☐ 7 Jeffrey Hammonds Cliff Floyd	10.00	4.50
☐ 8 Marc Newfield Nigel Wilson	5.00	2.20
☐ 9 Mark Hutton Salomon Torres	5.00	2.20

1994 Pinnacle Run Creators

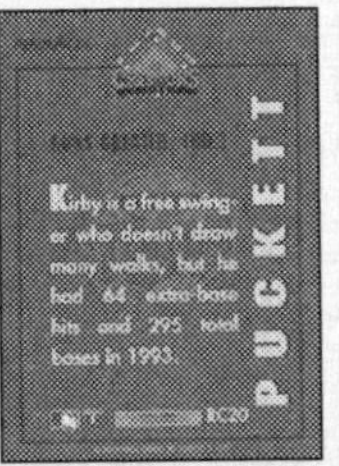

Randomly inserted in either series Pinnacle packs at an approximate rate of one in four jumbo packs, this 44-card standard-size set spotlights top run producers. The player stands out from a solid background on front. His last name and the Pinnacle logo run up the right border in gold foil. The Run Creators logo is at bottom center. A solid colored back contains the team logo as background to statistical highlights including runs created.

	MINT	NRMT
COMPLETE SET (44)	100.00	45.00
COMPLETE SERIES 1 (22)	60.00	27.00
COMPLETE SERIES 2 (22)	40.00	18.00
COMMON CARD (RC1-RC44)	1.00	.45
☐ RC1 John Olerud	1.50	.70
☐ RC2 Frank Thomas	15.00	6.75
☐ RC3 Ken Griffey Jr.	20.00	9.00
☐ RC4 Paul Molitor	4.00	1.80
☐ RC5 Rafael Palmeiro	2.50	1.10
☐ RC6 Roberto Alomar	4.00	1.80
☐ RC7 Juan Gonzalez	10.00	4.50
☐ RC8 Albert Belle	5.00	2.20
☐ RC9 Travis Fryman	1.50	.70
☐ RC10 Rickey Henderson	2.50	1.10
☐ RC11 Tony Phillips	1.00	.45
☐ RC12 Mo Vaughn	5.00	2.20
☐ RC13 Tim Salmon	4.00	1.80
☐ RC14 Kenny Lofton	6.00	2.70
☐ RC15 Carlos Baerga	1.00	.45
☐ RC16 Greg Vaughn	1.00	.45
☐ RC17 Jay Buhner	2.50	1.10
☐ RC18 Chris Hoiles	1.00	.45
☐ RC19 Mickey Tettleton	1.00	.45
☐ RC20 Kirby Puckett	8.00	3.60
☐ RC21 Danny Tartabull	1.00	.45
☐ RC22 Devon White	1.00	.45
☐ RC23 Barry Bonds	5.00	2.20
☐ RC24 Lenny Dykstra	1.50	.70
☐ RC25 John Kruk	1.50	.70
☐ RC26 Fred McGriff	2.50	1.10
☐ RC27 Gregg Jefferies	1.50	.70
☐ RC28 Mike Piazza	12.00	5.50
☐ RC29 Jeff Blauser	1.00	.45
☐ RC30 Andres Galarraga	2.50	1.10
☐ RC31 Darren Daulton	1.50	.70
☐ RC32 Dave Justice	4.00	1.80
☐ RC33 Craig Biggio	2.50	1.10
☐ RC34 Mark Grace	2.50	1.10
☐ RC35 Tony Gwynn	8.00	3.60
☐ RC36 Jeff Bagwell	8.00	3.60
☐ RC37 Jay Bell	1.00	.45
☐ RC38 Marquis Grissom	1.50	.70
☐ RC39 Matt Williams	2.50	1.10
☐ RC40 Charlie Hayes	1.00	.45
☐ RC41 Dante Bichette	2.50	1.10
☐ RC42 Bernard Gilkey	1.00	.45
☐ RC43 Brett Butler	1.50	.70
☐ RC44 Rick Wilkins	1.00	.45

1994 Pinnacle Team Pinnacle

Identical in design to the Rookie Team Pinnacle set, these double-front cards feature top players from each of the nine positions. Randomly inserted in second series hobby and retail packs at a rate of one in 48, these special portrait cards were painted by artists Christopher Greco and Ron DeFelice. The front features the National League

player and card number. Both sides contain a gold Team Pinnacle logo.

	MINT	NRMT
COMPLETE SET (9)	180.00	80.00
COMMON PAIR (1-9)	8.00	3.60
☐ 1 Jeff Bagwell Frank Thomas	40.00	18.00
☐ 2 Carlos Baerga Robby Thompson	8.00	3.60
☐ 3 Matt Williams Dean Palmer	10.00	4.50
☐ 4 Cal Ripken Jr. Jay Bell	30.00	13.50
☐ 5 Ivan Rodriguez Mike Piazza	25.00	11.00
☐ 6 Lenny Dykstra Ken Griffey Jr.	40.00	18.00
☐ 7 Juan Gonzalez Barry Bonds	25.00	11.00
☐ 8 Tim Salmon Dave Justice	20.00	9.00
☐ 9 Greg Maddux Jack McDowell	25.00	11.00

1994 Pinnacle Tribute

Randomly inserted in hobby packs at a rate of one in 18, this 18-card set was issued in two series of nine. Showcasing some of the top superstar veterans, the fronts have a color player photo with "Tribute" up the left border in a black stripe. The player's name appears at the bottom with a notation given to describe the player. The backs are primarily black with a close-up photo of the player. The cards are numbered with a "TR" prefix.

	MINT	NRMT
COMPLETE SET (18)	100.00	45.00
COMPLETE SERIES 1 (9)	30.00	13.50
COMPLETE SERIES 2 (9)	70.00	32.00
COMMON CARD (TR1-TR18)	1.00	.45
☐ TR1 Paul Molitor	4.00	1.80
☐ TR2 Jim Abbott	1.50	.70
☐ TR3 Dave Winfield	2.50	1.10
☐ TR4 Bo Jackson	1.50	.70
☐ TR5 David Justice	4.00	1.80
☐ TR6 Len Dykstra	1.50	.70
☐ TR7 Mike Piazza	12.00	5.50
☐ TR8 Barry Bonds	5.00	2.20
☐ TR9 Randy Johnson	4.00	1.80
☐ TR10 Ozzie Smith	5.00	2.20
☐ TR11 Mark Whiten	1.00	.45
☐ TR12 Greg Maddux	12.00	5.50
☐ TR13 Cal Ripken Jr.	15.00	6.75
☐ TR14 Frank Thomas	15.00	6.75
☐ TR15 Juan Gonzalez	10.00	4.50
☐ TR16 Roberto Alomar	4.00	1.80
☐ TR17 Ken Griffey Jr.	20.00	9.00
☐ TR18 Lee Smith	1.50	.70

1994 Pinnacle The Naturals

These 25 standard-size cards were issued as a boxed set and were printed with Pinnacle's Dufex process, which imparts a metallic appearance to the cards. A certificate of authenticity that carries the set's production number out of 100,000 produced was included with every boxed set.

he borderless fronts feature embossed player photos gainst a textured-foil background. The hand-etched ackground is enhanced with transparent inks. The backs icture the player on a background of nature photography, ıcluding lightning, blue skies and clouds.

	MINT	NRMT
OMPLETE SET (25)	20.00	9.00
OMMON CARD (1-25)	.15	.07
] 1 Frank Thomas	3.00	1.35
] 2 Barry Bonds	1.00	.45
] 3 Ken Griffey Jr.	4.00	1.80
] 4 Juan Gonzalez	2.00	.90
] 5 David Justice	.60	.25
] 6 Albert Belle	1.25	.55
] 7 Kenny Lofton	1.00	.45
] 8 Roberto Alomar	.60	.25
] 9 Tim Salmon	.75	.35
] 10 Randy Johnson	.60	.25
] 11 Kirby Puckett	2.00	.90
] 12 Tony Gwynn	2.00	.90
] 13 Fred McGriff	.40	.18
] 14 Ryne Sandberg	1.00	.45
] 15 Greg Maddux	2.50	1.10
] 16 Matt Williams	.40	.18
] 17 Lenny Dykstra	.15	.07
] 18 Gary Sheffield	.60	.25
] 19 Mike Piazza	2.50	1.10
] 20 Dean Palmer	.15	.07
] 21 Travis Fryman	.25	.11
] 22 Carlos Baerga	.25	.11
] 23 Cal Ripken	2.50	1.10
] 24 John Olerud	.25	.11
] 25 Roger Clemens	1.25	.55
] P18 Gary Sheffield Promo	1.00	.45

994 Pinnacle New Generation

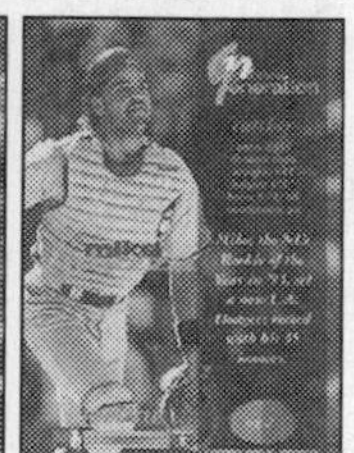

ıis 25-card standard-size set spotlights 25 of the most ominent prospects to hit the major leagues. Just 0,000 sets were produced, and a certificate of thenticity carrying the set serial number was printed on e back of the display box. The fronts feature borderless lor action shots, with the player's name appearing at e bottom along with icons of a baseball and bats. The ck displays another borderless color player action shot, th the player's name appearing across the picture. The cture is ghosted on the left side. This ghosted band rries the player's position, biography, and career ghlights.

	MINT	NRMT
MPLETE SET (25)	5.00	2.20
MMON CARD (NG1-NG25)	.10	.05
NG1 Tim Salmon	.50	.23
NG2 Mike Piazza	2.50	1.10
NG3 Jason Bere	.10	.05
NG4 Jeffrey Hammonds	.20	.09
NG5 Aaron Sele	.10	.05
NG6 Salomon Torres	.10	.05
NG7 Wilfredo Cordero	.10	.05
NG8 Allen Watson	.10	.05
NG9 J.T. Snow	.30	.14
NG10 Cliff Floyd	.20	.09
NG11 Jeff McNeely	.10	.05
NG12 Butch Huskey	.40	.18
NG13 J.R. Phillips	.10	.05
☐ NG14 Bobby Jones	.20	.09
☐ NG15 Javier Lopez	.50	.23
☐ NG16 Scott Ruffcorn	.10	.05
☐ NG17 Manny Ramirez	1.00	.45
☐ NG18 Carlos Delgado	.50	.23
☐ NG19 Rondell White	.40	.18
☐ NG20 Chipper Jones	2.00	.90
☐ NG21 Billy Ashley	.10	.05
☐ NG22 Nigel Wilson	.10	.05
☐ NG23 Jeromy Burnitz	.20	.09
☐ NG24 Danny Bautista	.10	.05
☐ NG25 Darrell Whitmore	.10	.05
☐ PNG10 Cliff Floyd Promo	1.00	.45

1994 Pinnacle Power Surge

These 25 standard-size cards came in a boxed set from Pinnacle and feature on their fronts borderless color action shots. The player's last name appears in gold foil at the top. His team name in white lettering also appears at the top within a marbleized stripe. On the right side, the marbleized back carries a circular player head shot at the top, followed by his name, team name, statistics, and career highlights. On the left are biography and a small action shot.

	MINT	NRMT
COMPLETE SET (25)	5.00	2.20
COMMON CARD (1-25)	.10	.05
☐ PS1 David Justice	.25	.11
☐ PS2 Chris Hoiles	.10	.05
☐ PS3 Mo Vaughn	.40	.18
☐ PS4 Tim Salmon	.25	.11
☐ PS5 J.T. Snow	.10	.05
☐ PS6 Frank Thomas	1.50	.70
☐ PS7 Sammy Sosa	.30	.14
☐ PS8 Rick Wilkins	.10	.05
☐ PS9 Robin Ventura	.25	.11
☐ PS10 Reggie Sanders	.25	.11
☐ PS11 Albert Belle	.75	.35
☐ PS12 Carlos Baerga	.30	.14
☐ PS13 Manny Ramirez	.50	.23
☐ PS14 Travis Fryman	.25	.11
☐ PS15 Gary Sheffield	.30	.14
☐ PS16 Jeff Bagwell	.75	.35
☐ PS17 Mike Piazza	1.00	.45
☐ PS18 Eric Karros	.25	.11
☐ PS19 Cliff Floyd	.10	.05
☐ PS20 Mark Whiten	.10	.05
☐ PS21 Phil Plantier	.10	.05
☐ PS22 Derek Bell	.25	.11
☐ PS23 Ken Griffey Jr.	1.50	.70
☐ PS24 Juan Gonzalez	.75	.35
☐ PS25 Dean Palmer	.10	.05
☐ PS12P Carlos Baerga Promo	1.00	.45

1995 Pinnacle Samples

The 1995 Pinnacle Sample set contains nine standard-size cards. The full-bleed color player photos on the front have gold highlighting that looks like the stitching of a baseball. The horizontal backs feature two color photos, biography, player profile, and statistics. The samples are easily distinguished from their regular issue counterparts by zeros in the stat lines. Also the disclaimer "SAMPLE" is diagonally printed across the front and the back.

	MINT	NRMT
COMPLETE SET (9)	10.00	4.50
COMMON CARD	.50	.23
☐ 16 Mickey Morandini	.50	.23
☐ 119 Gary Sheffield	1.50	.70
☐ 122 Ivan Rodriguez	2.00	.90
☐ 132 Alex Rodriguez	2.50	1.10
☐ 208 Bo Jackson	.75	.35
☐ 223 Jose Rijo	.50	.23
☐ 224 Ryan Klesko	1.00	.45
☐ US22 Wil Cordero	1.50	.70
☐ NNO Title Card	.50	.23

1995 Pinnacle

This 450-card standard-size set was issued in two series of 225 cards. They were released in 12-card packs, 24 packs to a box and 18 boxes in a case. The full-bleed fronts feature action photos. The player's last name is printed in black ink against a dramatic gold foil background at the base of the card. There are no notable Rookie Cards in this set.

	MINT	NRMT
COMPLETE SET (450)	30.00	13.50
COMPLETE SERIES 1 (225)	15.00	6.75
COMPLETE SERIES 2 (225)	15.00	6.75
COMMON CARD (1-450)	.15	.07
☐ 1 Jeff Bagwell	1.25	.55
☐ 2 Roger Clemens	1.25	.55
☐ 3 Mark Whiten	.15	.07
☐ 4 Shawon Dunston	.15	.07
☐ 5 Bobby Bonilla	.30	.14
☐ 6 Kevin Tapani	.15	.07
☐ 7 Eric Karros	.30	.14
☐ 8 Cliff Floyd	.30	.14
☐ 9 Pat Kelly	.15	.07
☐ 10 Jeffrey Hammonds	.30	.14
☐ 11 Jeff Conine	.40	.18
☐ 12 Fred McGriff	.40	.18
☐ 13 Chris Bosio	.15	.07
☐ 14 Mike Mussina	.40	.18
☐ 15 Danny Bautista	.15	.07
☐ 16 Mickey Morandini	.15	.07
☐ 17 Chuck Finley	.30	.14
☐ 18 Jim Thome	.60	.25
☐ 19 Luis Ortiz	.15	.07
☐ 20 Walt Weiss	.15	.07
☐ 21 Don Mattingly	1.00	.45
☐ 22 Bob Hamelin	.15	.07
☐ 23 Melido Perez	.15	.07
☐ 24 Keith Mitchell	.15	.07
☐ 25 John Smoltz	.40	.18
☐ 26 Hector Carrasco	.15	.07
☐ 27 Pat Hentgen	.30	.14
☐ 28 Derrick May	.15	.07
☐ 29 Mike Kingery	.15	.07
☐ 30 Chuck Carr	.15	.07
☐ 31 Billy Ashley	.15	.07
☐ 32 Todd Hundley	.30	.14
☐ 33 Luis Gonzalez	.15	.07
☐ 34 Marquis Grissom	.30	.14
☐ 35 Jeff King	.30	.14
☐ 36 Eddie Williams	.15	.07
☐ 37 Tom Pagnozzi	.15	.07
☐ 38 Chris Hoiles	.15	.07
☐ 39 Sandy Alomar Jr.	.15	.07
☐ 40 Mike Greenwell	.15	.07
☐ 41 Lance Johnson	.15	.07
☐ 42 Junior Felix	.15	.07
☐ 43 Felix Jose	.15	.07
☐ 44 Scott Leius	.15	.07
☐ 45 Ruben Sierra	.15	.07
☐ 46 Kevin Seitzer	.15	.07
☐ 47 Wade Boggs	.60	.25
☐ 48 Reggie Jefferson	.30	.14
☐ 49 Jose Canseco	.40	.18
☐ 50 David Justice	.60	.25
☐ 51 John Smiley	.15	.07
☐ 52 Joe Carter	.30	.14
☐ 53 Rick Wilkins	.15	.07

- ☐ 54 Ellis Burks .30 .14
- ☐ 55 Dave Weathers .15 .07
- ☐ 56 Pedro Astacio .15 .07
- ☐ 57 Ryan Thompson .15 .07
- ☐ 58 James Mouton .15 .07
- ☐ 59 Mel Rojas .15 .07
- ☐ 60 Orlando Merced .15 .07
- ☐ 61 Matt Williams .40 .18
- ☐ 62 Bernard Gilkey .30 .14
- ☐ 63 J.R. Phillips .15 .07
- ☐ 64 Lee Smith .30 .14
- ☐ 65 Jim Edmonds .40 .18
- ☐ 66 Darrin Jackson .15 .07
- ☐ 67 Scott Cooper .15 .07
- ☐ 68 Ron Karkovice .15 .07
- ☐ 69 Chris Gomez .15 .07
- ☐ 70 Kevin Appier .30 .14
- ☐ 71 Bobby Jones .30 .14
- ☐ 72 Doug Drabek .15 .07
- ☐ 73 Matt Mieske .30 .14
- ☐ 74 Sterling Hitchcock .30 .14
- ☐ 75 John Valentin .30 .14
- ☐ 76 Reggie Sanders .15 .07
- ☐ 77 Wally Joyner .30 .14
- ☐ 78 Turk Wendell .15 .07
- ☐ 79 Charlie Hayes .15 .07
- ☐ 80 Bret Barberie .15 .07
- ☐ 81 Troy Neel .15 .07
- ☐ 82 Ken Caminiti .40 .18
- ☐ 83 Milt Thompson .15 .07
- ☐ 84 Paul Sorrento .15 .07
- ☐ 85 Trevor Hoffman .30 .14
- ☐ 86 Jay Bell .30 .14
- ☐ 87 Mark Portugal .15 .07
- ☐ 88 Sid Fernandez .15 .07
- ☐ 89 Charles Nagy .30 .14
- ☐ 90 Jeff Montgomery .30 .14
- ☐ 91 Chuck Knoblauch .60 .25
- ☐ 92 Jeff Frye .15 .07
- ☐ 93 Tony Gwynn 1.50 .70
- ☐ 94 John Olerud .30 .14
- ☐ 95 David Nied .15 .07
- ☐ 96 Chris Hammond .15 .07
- ☐ 97 Edgar Martinez .40 .18
- ☐ 98 Kevin Stocker .15 .07
- ☐ 99 Jeff Fassero .15 .07
- ☐ 100 Curt Schilling .30 .14
- ☐ 101 Dave Clark .15 .07
- ☐ 102 Delino DeShields .15 .07
- ☐ 103 Leo Gomez .15 .07
- ☐ 104 Dave Hollins .15 .07
- ☐ 105 Tim Naehring .15 .07
- ☐ 106 Otis Nixon .30 .14
- ☐ 107 Ozzie Guillen .15 .07
- ☐ 108 Jose Lind .15 .07
- ☐ 109 Stan Javier .15 .07
- ☐ 110 Greg Vaughn .15 .07
- ☐ 111 Chipper Jones 2.00 .90
- ☐ 112 Ed Sprague .15 .07
- ☐ 113 Mike Macfarlane .15 .07
- ☐ 114 Steve Finley .30 .14
- ☐ 115 Ken Hill .15 .07
- ☐ 116 Carlos Garcia .15 .07
- ☐ 117 Lou Whitaker .30 .14
- ☐ 118 Todd Zeile .15 .07
- ☐ 119 Gary Sheffield .60 .25
- ☐ 120 Ben McDonald .15 .07
- ☐ 121 Pete Harnisch .15 .07
- ☐ 122 Ivan Rodriguez .75 .35
- ☐ 123 Wilson Alvarez .30 .14
- ☐ 124 Travis Fryman .30 .14
- ☐ 125 Pedro Munoz .15 .07
- ☐ 126 Mark Lemke .15 .07
- ☐ 127 Jose Valentin .30 .14
- ☐ 128 Ken Griffey Jr. 3.00 1.35
- ☐ 129 Omar Vizquel .30 .14
- ☐ 130 Milt Cuyler .15 .07
- ☐ 131 Steve Trachsel .15 .07
- ☐ 132 Alex Rodriguez 2.50 1.10
- ☐ 133 Garret Anderson .40 .18
- ☐ 134 Armando Benitez .15 .07
- ☐ 135 Shawn Green .30 .14
- ☐ 136 Jorge Fabregas .15 .07
- ☐ 137 Orlando Miller .15 .07
- ☐ 138 Rikkert Faneyte .15 .07
- ☐ 139 Ismael Valdes .30 .14
- ☐ 140 Jose Oliva .15 .07
- ☐ 141 Aaron Small .15 .07
- ☐ 142 Tim Davis .15 .07
- ☐ 143 Ricky Bottalico .30 .14
- ☐ 144 Mike Matheny .15 .07
- ☐ 145 Roberto Petagine .15 .07
- ☐ 146 Fausto Cruz .15 .07
- ☐ 147 Bryce Florie .15 .07
- ☐ 148 Jose Lima .15 .07
- ☐ 149 John Hudek .15 .07
- ☐ 150 Duane Singleton .15 .07
- ☐ 151 John Mabry .40 .18
- ☐ 152 Robert Eenhoorn .15 .07
- ☐ 153 Jon Lieber .15 .07
- ☐ 154 Garey Ingram .15 .07
- ☐ 155 Paul Shuey .15 .07
- ☐ 156 Mike Lieberthal .15 .07
- ☐ 157 Steve Dunn .15 .07
- ☐ 158 Charles Johnson .30 .14
- ☐ 159 Ernie Young .15 .07
- ☐ 160 Jose Martinez .15 .07
- ☐ 161 Kurt Miller .15 .07
- ☐ 162 Joey Eischen .15 .07
- ☐ 163 Dave Stevens .15 .07
- ☐ 164 Brian L.Hunter .40 .18
- ☐ 165 Jeff Cirillo .30 .14
- ☐ 166 Mark Smith .15 .07
- ☐ 167 McKay Christensen .30 .14
- ☐ 168 C.J. Nitkowski .15 .07
- ☐ 169 Antone Williamson .60 .25
- ☐ 170 Paul Konerko 3.00 1.35
- ☐ 171 Scott Elarton .75 .35
- ☐ 172 Jacob Shumate .30 .14
- ☐ 173 Terrence Long .40 .18
- ☐ 174 Mark Johnson .30 .14
- ☐ 175 Ben Grieve 3.00 1.35
- ☐ 176 Jayson Peterson .30 .14
- ☐ 177 Checklist .15 .07
- ☐ 178 Checklist .15 .07
- ☐ 179 Checklist .15 .07
- ☐ 180 Checklist .15 .07
- ☐ 181 Brian Anderson .15 .07
- ☐ 182 Steve Buechele .15 .07
- ☐ 183 Mark Clark .15 .07
- ☐ 184 Cecil Fielder .30 .14
- ☐ 185 Steve Avery .15 .07
- ☐ 186 Devon White .15 .07
- ☐ 187 Craig Shipley .15 .07
- ☐ 188 Brady Anderson .40 .18
- ☐ 189 Kenny Lofton .75 .35
- ☐ 190 Alex Cole .15 .07
- ☐ 191 Brent Gates .15 .07
- ☐ 192 Dean Palmer .30 .14
- ☐ 193 Alex Gonzalez .15 .07
- ☐ 194 Steve Cooke .15 .07
- ☐ 195 Ray Lankford .40 .18
- ☐ 196 Mark McGwire 1.25 .55
- ☐ 197 Marc Newfield .15 .07
- ☐ 198 Pat Rapp .15 .07
- ☐ 199 Darren Lewis .15 .07
- ☐ 200 Carlos Baerga .30 .14
- ☐ 201 Rickey Henderson .40 .18
- ☐ 202 Kurt Abbott .15 .07
- ☐ 203 Kirt Manwaring .15 .07
- ☐ 204 Cal Ripken 2.50 1.10
- ☐ 205 Darren Daulton .30 .14
- ☐ 206 Greg Colbrunn .15 .07
- ☐ 207 Darryl Hamilton .15 .07
- ☐ 208 Bo Jackson .30 .14
- ☐ 209 Tony Phillips .15 .07
- ☐ 210 Geronimo Berroa .15 .07
- ☐ 211 Rich Becker .15 .07
- ☐ 212 Tony Tarasco .15 .07
- ☐ 213 Karl Rhodes .15 .07
- ☐ 214 Phil Plantier .15 .07
- ☐ 215 J.T. Snow .30 .14
- ☐ 216 Mo Vaughn .75 .35
- ☐ 217 Greg Gagne .15 .07
- ☐ 218 Ricky Bones .15 .07
- ☐ 219 Mike Bordick .15 .07
- ☐ 220 Chad Curtis .15 .07
- ☐ 221 Royce Clayton .15 .07
- ☐ 222 Roberto Alomar .60 .25
- ☐ 223 Jose Rijo .15 .07
- ☐ 224 Ryan Klesko .40 .18
- ☐ 225 Mark Langston .15 .07
- ☐ 226 Frank Thomas 2.50 1.10
- ☐ 227 Juan Gonzalez 1.50 .70
- ☐ 228 Ron Gant .30 .14
- ☐ 229 Javier Lopez .40 .18
- ☐ 230 Sammy Sosa .60 .25
- ☐ 231 Kevin Brown .30 .14
- ☐ 232 Gary DiSarcina .15 .07
- ☐ 233 Albert Belle .75 .35
- ☐ 234 Jay Buhner .40 .18
- ☐ 235 Pedro J.Martinez .60 .25
- ☐ 236 Bob Tewksbury .15 .07
- ☐ 237 Mike Piazza 2.00 .90
- ☐ 238 Darryl Kile .30 .14
- ☐ 239 Bryan Harvey .15 .07
- ☐ 240 Andres Galarraga .40 .18
- ☐ 241 Jeff Blauser .15 .07
- ☐ 242 Jeff Kent .15 .07
- ☐ 243 Bobby Munoz .15 .07
- ☐ 244 Greg Maddux 2.00 .90
- ☐ 245 Paul O'Neill .30 .14
- ☐ 246 Lenny Dykstra .30 .14
- ☐ 247 Todd Van Poppel .15 .07
- ☐ 248 Bernie Williams .60 .25
- ☐ 249 Glenallen Hill .15 .07
- ☐ 250 Duane Ward .15 .07
- ☐ 251 Dennis Eckersley .40 .18
- ☐ 252 Pat Mahomes .15 .07
- ☐ 253 Rusty Greer .60 .25
- ☐ 254 Roberto Kelly .15 .07
- ☐ 255 Randy Myers .15 .07
- ☐ 256 Scott Ruffcorn .15 .07
- ☐ 257 Robin Ventura .30 .14
- ☐ 258 Eduardo Perez .15 .07
- ☐ 259 Aaron Sele .15 .07
- ☐ 260 Paul Molitor .60 .25
- ☐ 261 Juan Guzman .15 .07
- ☐ 262 Darren Oliver .30 .14
- ☐ 263 Mike Stanley .15 .07
- ☐ 264 Tom Glavine .40 .18
- ☐ 265 Rico Brogna .15 .07
- ☐ 266 Craig Biggio .40 .18
- ☐ 267 Darrell Whitmore .15 .07
- ☐ 268 Jimmy Key .30 .14
- ☐ 269 Will Clark .40 .18
- ☐ 270 David Cone .30 .14
- ☐ 271 Brian Jordan .30 .14
- ☐ 272 Barry Bonds .75 .35
- ☐ 273 Danny Tartabull .15 .07
- ☐ 274 Ramon J.Martinez .30 .14
- ☐ 275 Al Martin .30 .14
- ☐ 276 Fred McGriff SM .40 .18
- ☐ 277 Carlos Delgado SM .30 .14
- ☐ 278 Juan Gonzalez SM .75 .35
- ☐ 279 Shawn Green SM .30 .14
- ☐ 280 Carlos Baerga SM .30 .14
- ☐ 281 Cliff Floyd SM .15 .07
- ☐ 282 Ozzie Smith SM .60 .25
- ☐ 283 Alex Rodriguez SM 2.00 .90
- ☐ 284 Kenny Lofton SM .40 .18
- ☐ 285 Dave Justice SM .60 .25
- ☐ 286 Tim Salmon SM .60 .25
- ☐ 287 Manny Ramirez SM .60 .25
- ☐ 288 Will Clark SM .40 .18
- ☐ 289 Garret Anderson SM .40 .18
- ☐ 290 Billy Ashley SM .15 .07
- ☐ 291 Tony Gwynn SM .60 .25
- ☐ 292 Raul Mondesi SM .40 .18
- ☐ 293 Rafael Palmeiro SM .40 .18
- ☐ 294 Matt Williams SM .40 .18
- ☐ 295 Don Mattingly SM .60 .25
- ☐ 296 Kirby Puckett SM .60 .25
- ☐ 297 Paul Molitor SM .60 .25
- ☐ 298 Albert Belle SM .60 .25
- ☐ 299 Barry Bonds SM .60 .25
- ☐ 300 Mike Piazza SM 1.00 .45
- ☐ 301 Jeff Bagwell SM .60 .25
- ☐ 302 Frank Thomas SM 1.50 .70
- ☐ 303 Chipper Jones SM 1.00 .45
- ☐ 304 Ken Griffey Jr. SM 1.50 .70
- ☐ 305 Cal Ripken Jr. SM 1.25 .55
- ☐ 306 Eric Anthony .15 .07
- ☐ 307 Todd Benzinger .15 .07
- ☐ 308 Jacob Brumfield .15 .07
- ☐ 309 Wes Chamberlain .15 .07
- ☐ 310 Tino Martinez .60 .25
- ☐ 311 Roberto Mejia .15 .07
- ☐ 312 Jose Offerman .15 .07
- ☐ 313 David Segui .15 .07
- ☐ 314 Eric Young .30 .14
- ☐ 315 Rey Sanchez .15 .07
- ☐ 316 Raul Mondesi .40 .18
- ☐ 317 Bret Boone .15 .07
- ☐ 318 Andre Dawson .40 .18
- ☐ 319 Brian McRae .15 .07
- ☐ 320 Dave Nilsson .30 .14
- ☐ 321 Moises Alou .30 .14
- ☐ 322 Don Slaught .15 .0
- ☐ 323 Dave McCarty .15 .0
- ☐ 324 Mike Huff .15 .0
- ☐ 325 Rick Aguilera .15 .0
- ☐ 326 Rod Beck .15 .0
- ☐ 327 Kenny Rogers .15 .0
- ☐ 328 Andy Benes .15 .0
- ☐ 329 Allen Watson .15 .0
- ☐ 330 Randy Johnson .60 .2
- ☐ 331 Willie Greene .30 .1
- ☐ 332 Hal Morris .15 .0
- ☐ 333 Ozzie Smith .75 .3
- ☐ 334 Jason Bere .15 .0
- ☐ 335 Scott Erickson .15 .0
- ☐ 336 Dante Bichette .40 .1
- ☐ 337 Willie Banks .15 .0
- ☐ 338 Eric Davis .30 .1
- ☐ 339 Rondell White .40 .1
- ☐ 340 Kirby Puckett 1.25 .5
- ☐ 341 Deion Sanders .60 .2
- ☐ 342 Eddie Murray .60 .2
- ☐ 343 Mike Harkey .15 .0
- ☐ 344 Joey Hamilton .30 .1

Card	MINT	NRMT
☐ 345 Roger Salkeld	.15	.07
☐ 346 Wil Cordero	.15	.07
☐ 347 John Wetteland	.30	.14
☐ 348 Geronimo Pena	.15	.07
☐ 349 Kirk Gibson	.30	.14
☐ 350 Manny Ramirez	.60	.25
☐ 351 Wm.VanLandingham	.15	.07
☐ 352 B.J. Surhoff	.30	.14
☐ 353 Ken Ryan	.15	.07
☐ 354 Terry Steinbach	.30	.14
☐ 355 Bret Saberhagen	.15	.07
☐ 356 John Jaha	.15	.07
☐ 357 Joe Girardi	.15	.07
☐ 358 Steve Karsay	.15	.07
☐ 359 Alex Fernandez	.30	.14
☐ 360 Salomon Torres	.15	.07
☐ 361 John Burkett	.15	.07
☐ 362 Derek Bell	.30	.14
☐ 363 Tom Henke	.15	.07
☐ 364 Gregg Jefferies	.30	.14
☐ 365 Jack McDowell	.15	.07
☐ 366 Andujar Cedeno	.15	.07
☐ 367 Dave Winfield	.40	.18
☐ 368 Carl Everett	.15	.07
☐ 369 Danny Jackson	.15	.07
☐ 370 Jeromy Burnitz	.30	.14
☐ 371 Mark Grace	.40	.18
☐ 372 Larry Walker	.60	.25
☐ 373 Bill Swift	.15	.07
☐ 374 Dennis Martinez	.30	.14
☐ 375 Mickey Tettleton	.15	.07
☐ 376 Mel Nieves	.30	.14
☐ 377 Cal Eldred	.15	.07
☐ 378 Orel Hershiser	.30	.14
☐ 379 David Wells	.15	.07
☐ 380 Gary Gaetti	.30	.14
☐ 381 Jeromy Burnitz	.30	.14
☐ 382 Barry Larkin	.40	.18
☐ 383 Jason Jacome	.15	.07
☐ 384 Tim Wallach	.15	.07
☐ 385 Robby Thompson	.15	.07
☐ 386 Frank Viola	.15	.07
☐ 387 Dave Stewart	.30	.14
☐ 388 Bip Roberts	.15	.07
☐ 389 Ron Darling	.15	.07
☐ 390 Carlos Delgado	.30	.14
☐ 391 Tim Salmon	.60	.25
☐ 392 Alan Trammell	.40	.18
☐ 393 Kevin Foster	.15	.07
☐ 394 Jim Abbott	.15	.07
☐ 395 John Kruk	.30	.14
☐ 396 Andy Van Slyke	.30	.14
☐ 397 Dave Magadan	.15	.07
☐ 398 Rafael Palmeiro	.40	.18
☐ 399 Mike Devereaux	.15	.07
☐ 400 Benito Santiago	.15	.07
☐ 401 Brett Butler	.30	.14
☐ 402 John Franco	.30	.14
☐ 403 Matt Walbeck	.15	.07
☐ 404 Terry Pendleton	.30	.14
☐ 405 Chris Sabo	.15	.07
☐ 406 Andrew Lorraine	.30	.14
☐ 407 Dan Wilson	.30	.14
☐ 408 Mike Lansing	.15	.07
☐ 409 Ray McDavid	.30	.14
☐ 410 Shane Andrews	.15	.07
☐ 411 Tom Gordon	.15	.07
☐ 412 Chad Ogea	.15	.07
☐ 413 James Baldwin	.30	.14
☐ 414 Russ Davis	.15	.07
☐ 415 Ray Holbert	.15	.07
☐ 416 Ray Durham	.30	.14
☐ 417 Matt Nokes	.15	.07
☐ 418 Rod Henderson	.15	.07
☐ 419 Gabe White	.15	.07
☐ 420 Todd Hollandsworth	.40	.18
☐ 421 Midre Cummings	.15	.07
☐ 422 Harold Baines	.30	.14
☐ 423 Troy Percival	.15	.07
☐ 424 Joe Vitiello	.15	.07
☐ 425 Andy Ashby	.15	.07
☐ 426 Michael Tucker	.30	.14
☐ 427 Mark Gubicza	.15	.07
☐ 428 Jim Bullinger	.15	.07
☐ 429 Jose Malave	.15	.07
☐ 430 Pete Schourek	.15	.07
☐ 431 Bobby Ayala	.15	.07
☐ 432 Marvin Freeman	.15	.07
☐ 433 Pat Listach	.15	.07
☐ 434 Eddie Taubensee	.15	.07
☐ 435 Steve Howe	.15	.07
☐ 436 Kent Mercker	.15	.07
☐ 437 Hector Fajardo	.15	.07
☐ 438 Scott Kamieniecki	.15	.07
☐ 439 Robb Nen	.15	.07
☐ 440 Mike Kelly	.15	.07
☐ 441 Tom Candiotti	.15	.07
☐ 442 Albie Lopez	.15	.07
☐ 443 Jeff Granger	.15	.07
☐ 444 Rich Aude	.15	.07
☐ 445 Luis Polonia	.15	.07
☐ 446 Frank Thomas CL	1.50	.70
☐ 447 Ken Griffey Jr. CL	1.50	.70
☐ 448 Mike Piazza CL	1.00	.45
☐ 449 Jeff Bagwell CL	.60	.25
☐ 450 Jeff Bagwel CL Frank Thomas Ken Griffey Jr. Mike Piazza	1.50	.70

1995 Pinnacle Artist's Proofs

Inserted one per 36 packs, this is a parallel set to the regular Pinnacle issue. The words "Artist Proof" are clearly labeled in silver on the card front. The name on the bottom is also set against a silver background.

	MINT	NRMT
COMPLETE SET (450)	2000.00	900.00
COMPLETE SERIES 1 (225)	1000.00	450.00
COMPLETE SERIES 2 (225)	1000.00	450.00
COMMON CARD (1-450)	3.00	1.35

*STARS: 10X TO 25X BASIC CARDS ..
*YOUNG STARS: 8X TO 20X BASIC CARDS
*ROOKIES: 6X to 15X BASIC CARDS..

1995 Pinnacle Museum Collection

Inserted one in four packs, this is a parallel to the regular Pinnacle issue. These cards use the Dufex technology on front and are clearly labeled on the back as Museum Collection cards. Seven series 2 cards (#'S 410, 413, 416, 420, 423, 426 and 444) were available only with randomly inserted trade cards. These trade cards expired Dec. 31, 1995.

	MINT	NRMT
COMPLETE SET (450)	500.00	220.00
COMPLETE SERIES 1 (225)	250.00	110.00
COMPLETE SERIES 2 (225)	250.00	110.00
COMMON CARD (1-450)	1.00	.45
TRADE (410/413/416/420)	3.00	1.35
TRADE(423/426/444)	3.00	1.35

*STARS: 4X TO 10X BASIC CARDS ....
*YOUNG STARS: 3X TO 8X BASIC CARDS
*ROOKIES: 2.5X to 6X BASIC CARDS.

1995 Pinnacle ETA

This six-card standard-sized set was randomly inserted approximately one in every 24 first series hobby packs. This set features players who were among the leading prospects for major league stardom. The fronts feature a player photo as well as a quick information bit. The player's name is located on the top. The busy full-bleed backs feature a player photo and some quick comments. On the bottom is the player's name and the card is numbered with an "ETA" prefix in the upper left corner.

	MINT	NRMT
COMPLETE SET (6)	25.00	11.00
COMMON CARD (1-6)	2.00	.90
☐ 1 Ben Grieve	15.00	6.75
☐ 2 Alex Ochoa	2.00	.90
☐ 3 Joe Vitiello	2.00	.90
☐ 4 Johnny Damon	3.00	1.35
☐ 5 Trey Beamon	2.00	.90
☐ 6 Brooks Kieschnick	2.00	.90

1995 Pinnacle Gate Attractions

This 18-card standard-size set was inserted approximately one every 12 second series jumbo packs. The fronts feature two photos, with the words "Gate Attraction" at the bottom left. The player is identified on the top. The horizontal full-bleed backs have the player's name on the left, a player photo in the middle and some career information in the lower right.

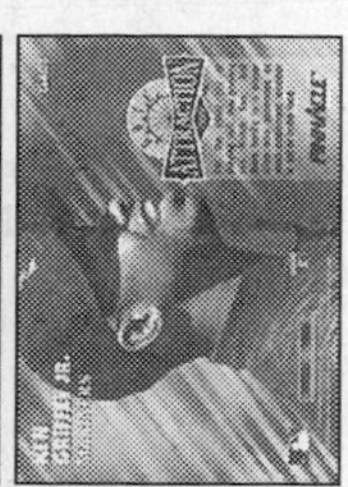

	MINT	NRMT
COMPLETE SET (18)	120.00	55.00
COMMON CARD (GA1-GA18)	2.00	.90
☐ GA1 Ken Griffey Jr.	25.00	11.00
☐ GA2 Frank Thomas	20.00	9.00
☐ GA3 Cal Ripken	20.00	9.00
☐ GA4 Jeff Bagwell	10.00	4.50
☐ GA5 Mike Piazza	15.00	6.75
☐ GA6 Barry Bonds	6.00	2.70
☐ GA7 Kirby Puckett	10.00	4.50
☐ GA8 Albert Belle	6.00	2.70
☐ GA9 Tony Gwynn	10.00	4.50
☐ GA10 Raul Mondesi	3.00	1.35
☐ GA11 Will Clark	3.00	1.35
☐ GA12 Don Mattingly	8.00	3.60
☐ GA13 Roger Clemens	8.00	3.60
☐ GA14 Paul Molitor	4.00	1.80
☐ GA15 Matt Williams	3.00	1.35
☐ GA16 Greg Maddux	15.00	6.75
☐ GA17 Kenny Lofton	6.00	2.70
☐ GA18 Cliff Floyd	2.00	.90

1995 Pinnacle New Blood

This nine-card standard-size set was inserted approximately one in every 90 second series hobby and retail packs. This set features nine players who were leading prospects entering the 1995 season. The Dufex enhanced fronts feature two player photos. One photo is a color shot while the other one is a black and white background photo. The words "New Blood" and player's name are on the bottom. The full-bleed backs feature two more photos. Player information is set against these photos.

	MINT	NRMT
COMPLETE SET (9)	100.00	45.00
COMMON CARD (NB1-NB9)	3.00	1.35
☐ NB1 Alex Rodriguez	40.00	18.00
☐ NB2 Shawn Green	4.00	1.80
☐ NB3 Brian Hunter	6.00	2.70
☐ NB4 Garret Anderson	10.00	4.50
☐ NB5 Charles Johnson	6.00	2.70
☐ NB6 Chipper Jones	30.00	13.50
☐ NB7 Carlos Delgado	10.00	4.50
☐ NB8 Billy Ashley	3.00	1.35
☐ NB9 J.R. Phillips UER Dodgers logo on back Phillips plays for the Giants	3.00	1.35

1995 Pinnacle Performers

These 18 standard-size cards were randomly inserted approximately one in every 12 first series jumbo packs. The full-bleed fronts feature a player photo against a shiny background. The player's name is in white lettering in the upper right corner. The backs have two photos: one a color portrait with the other one being a shaded black and white. There is also some text pertaining to that player.

	MINT	NRMT
COMPLETE SERIES 1 (18)	100.00	45.00
COMMON CARD (1-18)	2.00	.90
☐ PP1 Frank Thomas	30.00	13.50
☐ PP2 Albert Belle	12.00	5.50
☐ PP3 Barry Bonds	8.00	3.60
☐ PP4 Juan Gonzalez	15.00	6.75
☐ PP5 Andres Galarraga		
☐ PP6 Raul Mondesi		
☐ PP7 Paul Molitor	6.00	2.70
☐ PP8 Tim Salmon	6.00	2.70
☐ PP9 Mike Piazza	20.00	9.00
☐ PP10 Gregg Jefferies	2.00	.90
☐ PP11 Will Clark		
☐ PP12 Greg Maddux	20.00	9.00
☐ PP13 Manny Ramirez	6.00	2.70
☐ PP14 Kirby Puckett	12.00	5.50
☐ PP15 Shawn Green	3.00	1.35
☐ PP16 Rafael Palmeiro		
☐ PP17 Paul O'Neill	3.00	1.35
☐ PP18 Jason Bere	2.00	.90

1995 Pinnacle Pin Redemption

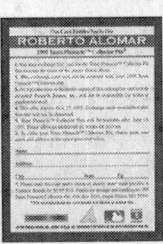

This 18-card standard-size set was randomly inserted in all second series packs. Printed odds indicate that these cards were inserted approximately one every in 48 hobby and retail packs and one in every 36 jumbo packs. The horizontal full-bleed fronts feature an action photo, a team logo and another small player photo. The backs explain the rules for ordering the "Team Pinnacle" Collector Pin. The offer expired on November 15, 1995.

	MINT	NRMT
COMPLETE SET (18)	80.00	36.00
COMMON CARD (1-18)	1.00	.45
☐ 1 Greg Maddux	10.00	4.50
☐ 2 Mike Mussina	3.00	1.35
☐ 3 Mike Piazza	10.00	4.50
☐ 4 Carlos Delgado	1.00	.45
☐ 5 Jeff Bagwell	6.00	2.70
☐ 6 Frank Thomas	12.00	5.50
☐ 7 Craig Biggio	2.00	.90
☐ 8 Roberto Alomar	3.00	1.35
☐ 9 Ozzie Smith	4.00	1.80
☐ 10 Cal Ripken Jr.	12.00	5.50
☐ 11 Matt Williams	2.00	.90
☐ 12 Travis Fryman	1.50	.70
☐ 13 Barry Bonds	4.00	1.80
☐ 14 Ken Griffey Jr.	15.00	6.75
☐ 15 Dave Justice	3.00	1.35
☐ 16 Albert Belle	4.00	1.80
☐ 17 Tony Gwynn	6.00	2.70
☐ 18 Kirby Puckett	6.00	2.70

1995 Pinnacle Pins

These pins were sent to collectors when they redeemed a pin redemption card inserted in series 2 Pinnacle packs. The redemption deadline was November 15, 1995. We have checklisted these pins in the same order as the cards used to redeem for these pins.

	MINT	NRMT
COMPLETE SET (18)	80.00	36.00
COMMON PIN (1-18)	1.00	.45
☐ 1 Greg Maddux	10.00	4.50
☐ 2 Mike Mussina	3.00	1.35
☐ 3 Mike Piazza	10.00	4.50
☐ 4 Carlos Delgado	1.00	.45
☐ 5 Jeff Bagwell	6.00	2.70
☐ 6 Frank Thomas	12.00	5.50
☐ 7 Craig Biggio	2.00	.90
☐ 8 Roberto Alomar	3.00	1.35
☐ 9 Ozzie Smith	4.00	1.80
☐ 10 Cal Ripken Jr.	12.00	5.50
☐ 11 Matt Williams	2.00	.90
☐ 12 Travis Fryman	1.50	.70
☐ 13 Barry Bonds	4.00	1.80
☐ 14 Ken Griffey Jr.	15.00	6.75
☐ 15 Dave Justice	3.00	1.35
☐ 16 Albert Belle	3.00	1.35
☐ 17 Tony Gwynn	6.00	2.70
☐ 18 Kirby Puckett	7.50	3.40

1995 Pinnacle Red Hot

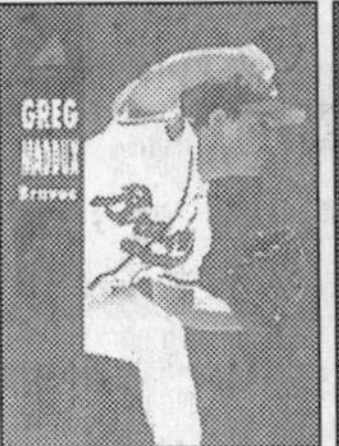

Cards from this 25-card standard-size set were randomly inserted into second series hobby and retail packs. The fronts feature a player photo on the right, with his name, an inset portrait and the words "Red Hot" on the left.

	MINT	NRMT
COMPLETE SET (25)	80.00	36.00
COMMON CARD (RH1-RH25)	1.00	.45
COMP.WHITE SET (25)	300.00	135.00
COMMON WHITE (WH1-WH25)	4.00	1.80
*WHITE HOT: 2X TO 4X RED HOTS		
☐ RH1 Cal Ripken Jr.	12.00	5.50
☐ RH2 Ken Griffey Jr.	15.00	6.75
☐ RH3 Frank Thomas	15.00	6.75
☐ RH4 Jeff Bagwell	6.00	2.70
☐ RH5 Mike Piazza	10.00	4.50
☐ RH6 Barry Bonds	4.00	1.80
☐ RH7 Albert Belle	4.00	1.80
☐ RH8 Tony Gwynn	6.00	2.70
☐ RH9 Kirby Puckett	6.00	2.70
☐ RH10 Don Mattingly	6.00	2.70
☐ RH11 Matt Williams	2.00	.90
☐ RH12 Greg Maddux	10.00	4.50
☐ RH13 Raul Mondesi	2.00	.90
☐ RH14 Paul Molitor	2.50	1.10
☐ RH15 Manny Ramirez	2.50	1.10
☐ RH16 Joe Carter	2.00	.90
☐ RH17 Will Clark	2.00	.90
☐ RH18 Roger Clemens	6.00	2.70
☐ RH19 Tim Salmon	2.50	1.10
☐ RH20 Dave Justice	2.50	1.10
☐ RH21 Kenny Lofton	4.00	1.80
☐ RH22 Deion Sanders	2.50	1.10
☐ RH23 Roberto Alomar	2.50	1.10
☐ RH24 Cliff Floyd	1.00	.45
☐ RH25 Carlos Baerga	1.00	.45

1995 Pinnacle White Hot

Parallel to the more common Red Hot cards, these cards were randomly seeded exclusively into second series hobby packs. A crystal blue foil background and white

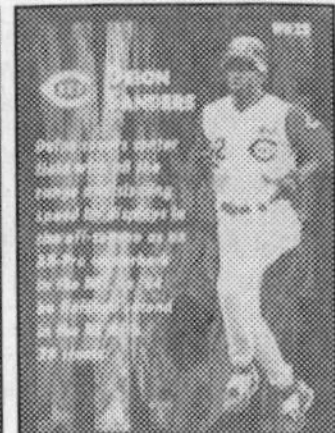

lettering on front differentiate these cards from their more common red counterparts.

	MINT	NRMT
COMPLETE SET (25)	300.00	135.00
COMMON CARD (WH1-WH25)	4.00	1.80
*WHITE: 2X to 4X RED CARDS		

1995 Pinnacle Team Pinnacle

Randomly inserted in series one hobby and retail packs at a rate of one in 90, this nine-card standard-size set showcases the game's top players in an etched-foil design. A player photo is superimposed over the player's team logo. The Team Pinnacle logo, player's name and position are printed in silver foil on a black strip at the bottom left of the card. Cards are numbered with the prefix "TP". All cards were intentionally issued with two variations, whereby one side of the card or the other had the Dufex effect. Regional premiums of up to 25% may exist for the player with the enhanced side.

	MINT	NRMT
COMPLETE SET (9)	250.00	110.00
COMMON CARD (1-9)	5.00	2.20
☐ TP1 Mike Mussina Greg Maddux	30.00	13.50
☐ TP2 Carlos Delgado Mike Piazza	30.00	13.50
☐ TP3 Frank Thomas Jeff Bagwell	40.00	18.00
☐ TP4 Roberto Alomar Craig Biggio	10.00	4.50
☐ TP5 Cal Ripken Ozzie Smith	40.00	18.00
☐ TP6 Travis Fryman Matt Williams	5.00	2.20
☐ TP7 Ken Griffey Jr. Barry Bonds	50.00	22.00
☐ TP8 Albert Belle David Justice	12.00	5.50
☐ TP9 Kirby Puckett Tony Gwynn	30.00	13.50

1995 Pinnacle Upstarts

Top young players are featured in this 30-card standard-size set. The cards were randomly inserted in series one hobby and retail packs at a rate of one in eight. Multi-colored foil fronts feature the player in a action cutout set against a star background. The player's name is wrapped around the "Upstarts" logo which is printed on the lower left of the front. The player's team logo is printed at the top right of the front. Backs are full-bleed color action photos of the player and are numbered at the top right with the prefix "US". A gold polygonal box encloses the player's name and '94 stats along with the team logo. The Pinnacle and '95 Upstarts logo are printed on the top left of the back.

	MINT	NRMT
COMPLETE SET (30)	60.00	27.00
COMMON CARD (US1-US30)	1.00	.45
☐ US1 Frank Thomas	20.00	9.00
☐ US2 Roberto Alomar	4.00	1.80
☐ US3 Mike Piazza	12.00	5.50
☐ US4 Javier Lopez	2.50	1.10
☐ US5 Albert Belle	8.00	3.60
☐ US6 Carlos Delgado	1.50	.70
☐ US7 Brent Gates	1.00	.45
☐ US8 Tim Salmon	4.00	1.80
☐ US9 Raul Mondesi	2.50	1.10
☐ US10 Juan Gonzalez	10.00	4.50
☐ US11 Manny Ramirez	4.00	1.80
☐ US12 Sammy Sosa	4.00	1.80
☐ US13 Jeff Kent	1.00	.45
☐ US14 Melvin Nieves	1.00	.45
☐ US15 Rondell White	1.50	.70
☐ US16 Shawn Green	1.50	.70
☐ US17 Bernie Williams	4.00	1.80
☐ US18 Aaron Sele	1.00	.45
☐ US19 Jason Bere	1.00	.45
☐ US20 Joey Hamilton	1.50	.70
☐ US21 Mike Kelly	1.00	.45
☐ US22 Wil Cordero	1.00	.45
☐ US23 Moises Alou	1.50	.70
☐ US24 Roberto Kelly	1.00	.45
☐ US25 Deion Sanders	4.00	1.80
☐ US26 Steve Karsay	1.00	.45
☐ US27 Bret Boone	1.00	.45
☐ US28 Willie Greene	1.50	.70
☐ US29 Billy Ashley	1.00	.45
☐ US30 Brian Anderson	1.00	.45

1995 Pinnacle FanFest

Available in two-card cello packs, this 30-card standard-size set was issued to commemorate the Pinnacle All-Star FanFest July 7-11 in Arlington, Texas. The fronts feature full-bleed color action photos; at the lower right corner, a gold foil diamond design carries the player's last name and team logo. Between black stripes, the horizontal backs have a player cutout superposed over a photo of The Ballpark in Arlington.

	MINT	NRMT
COMPLETE SET (30)	40.00	18.00
COMMON CARD (1-30)	.40	.18
☐ 1 Cal Ripken	5.00	2.20
☐ 2 Roger Clemens	1.50	.70
☐ 3 Don Mattingly	2.50	1.10
☐ 4 Albert Belle	3.00	1.35
☐ 5 Kirby Puckett	3.00	1.35
☐ 6 Cecil Fielder	.60	.25
☐ 7 Kevin Appier	.60	.25
☐ 8 Will Clark	1.00	.45
☐ 9 Juan Gonzalez	3.00	1.35
☐ 10 Ivan Rodriguez	1.50	.70
☐ 11 Ken Griffey Jr.	6.00	2.70
☐ 12 Tim Salmon	1.00	.45
☐ 13 Frank Thomas	5.00	2.20
☐ 14 Roberto Alomar	1.00	.45
☐ 15 Rickey Henderson	1.00	.45
☐ 16 Raul Mondesi	1.00	.45
☐ 17 Matt Williams	.75	.35
☐ 18 Ozzie Smith	2.00	.90
☐ 19 Deion Sanders	1.00	.45
☐ 20 Tony Gwynn	2.50	1.10
☐ 21 Greg Maddux	4.50	2.00
☐ 22 Sammy Sosa	1.00	.45
☐ 23 Mike Piazza	3.50	1.55
☐ 24 Barry Bonds	1.25	.55
☐ 25 Jeff Bagwell	2.50	1.10
☐ 26 Lenny Dykstra	.60	.25
☐ 27 Rico Brogna	.40	.18
☐ 28 Larry Walker	1.00	.45
☐ 29 Gary Sheffield	1.00	.45
☐ 30 Wil Cordero	.40	.18

1996 Pinnacle Samples

This 9-card set was released to preview the first series of the 1996 Pinnacle set. The fronts feature full-bleed color action photos, with a gold foil triangle across the bottom. The backs have a color closeup photo along with statistics and biography. The disclaimer "SAMPLE" is stamped diagonally across both sides of the card.

	MINT	NRMT
COMPLETE SET (9)	8.00	3.60
COMMON CARD	.25	.11
☐ 1 Greg Maddux	2.50	1.10
☐ 2 Bill Pulsipher	.25	.11
☐ 3 Dante Bichette	.75	.35
☐ 4 Mike Piazza	2.50	1.10
☐ 5 Garret Anderson	.50	.23
☐ 165 Ruben Rivera	.50	.23
☐ 166 Tony Clark	1.00	.45
☐ PP2 Mo Vaughn Pinnacle Power	2.50	1.10
☐ NNO Title Card	.25	.11

1996 Pinnacle

The 1996 Pinnacle set was issued in two separate series of 200 cards each. The 10-card packs retailed for $2.49. On 20-point card stock, the fronts feature full-bleed color action photos, bordered at the bottom by a gold foil triangle. The backs carry a color closeup photo, biography, and statistics. The Series I set features the following topical subsets: The Naturals (134-163), '95 Rookies (164-193) and Checklists (194-200). Series II set features these subsets: Hardball Heroes (30 cards), 300 Series (17 cards), Rookies (25 cards), and Checklists (7 cards). Numbering for the 300 Series subset was based on player's career batting average. At that time, both Paul Molitor and Jeff Bagwell had identical career batting averages of .305, thus Pinnacle numbered both of their 300 Series subset cards as 305. Due to this quirky numbering, the set only runs through card 399, but actually contains 400 cards. A special Cal Ripken Jr. Tribute card was inserted in first series packs at the rate of one in 150.

	MINT	NRMT
COMPLETE SET (400)	30.00	13.50
COMPLETE SERIES 1 (200)	15.00	6.75
COMPLETE SERIES 2 (200)	15.00	6.75
COMMON CARD (1-399)	.15	.07
☐ 1 Greg Maddux	2.00	.90
☐ 2 Bill Pulsipher	.15	.07
☐ 3 Dante Bichette	.30	.14
☐ 4 Mike Piazza	2.00	.90
☐ 5 Garret Anderson	.30	.14
☐ 6 Steve Finley	.30	.14
☐ 7 Andy Benes	.15	.07
☐ 8 Chuck Knoblauch	.60	.25
☐ 9 Tom Gordon	.15	.07
☐ 10 Jeff Bagwell	1.25	.55
☐ 11 Wil Cordero	.15	.07
☐ 12 John Mabry	.30	.14
☐ 13 Jeff Frye	.15	.07
☐ 14 Travis Fryman	.30	.14
☐ 15 John Wetteland	.30	.14
☐ 16 Jason Bates	.15	.07
☐ 17 Danny Tartabull	.15	.07
☐ 18 Charles Nagy	.30	.14
☐ 19 Robin Ventura	.30	.14
☐ 20 Reggie Sanders	.15	.07
☐ 21 Dave Clark	.15	.07
☐ 22 Jaime Navarro	.15	.07
☐ 23 Joey Hamilton	.15	.07
☐ 24 Al Leiter	.15	.07
☐ 25 Deion Sanders	.60	.25
☐ 26 Tim Salmon	.60	.25
☐ 27 Tino Martinez	.60	.25
☐ 28 Mike Greenwell	.15	.07
☐ 29 Phil Plantier	.15	.07
☐ 30 Bobby Bonilla	.30	.14
☐ 31 Kenny Rogers	.15	.07
☐ 32 Chili Davis	.30	.14
☐ 33 Joe Carter	.30	.14
☐ 34 Mike Mussina	.60	.25
☐ 35 Matt Mieske	.15	.07
☐ 36 Jose Canseco	.40	.18
☐ 37 Brad Radke	.30	.14
☐ 38 Juan Gonzalez	1.50	.70
☐ 39 David Segui	.15	.07
☐ 40 Alex Fernandez	.30	.14
☐ 41 Jeff Kent	.15	.07
☐ 42 Todd Zeile	.15	.07
☐ 43 Darryl Strawberry	.30	.14
☐ 44 Jose Rijo	.15	.07
☐ 45 Ramon Martinez	.30	.14
☐ 46 Manny Ramirez	.60	.25
☐ 47 Gregg Jefferies	.30	.14
☐ 48 Bryan Rekar	.15	.07
☐ 49 Jeff King	.30	.14
☐ 50 John Olerud	.15	.07
☐ 51 Marc Newfield	.15	.07
☐ 52 Charles Johnson	.30	.14
☐ 53 Robby Thompson	.15	.07
☐ 54 Brian L. Hunter	.30	.14
☐ 55 Mike Blowers	.15	.07
☐ 56 Keith Lockhart	.15	.07
☐ 57 Ray Lankford	.30	.14
☐ 58 Tim Wallach	.15	.07
☐ 59 Ivan Rodriguez	.75	.35
☐ 60 Ed Sprague	.15	.07
☐ 61 Paul Molitor	.60	.25
☐ 62 Eric Karros	.30	.14
☐ 63 Glenallen Hill	.15	.07
☐ 64 Jay Bell	.30	.14
☐ 65 Tom Pagnozzi	.15	.07
☐ 66 Greg Colbrunn	.15	.07
☐ 67 Edgar Martinez	.40	.18
☐ 68 Paul Sorrento	.15	.07
☐ 69 Kirt Manwaring	.15	.07
☐ 70 Pete Schourek	.15	.07
☐ 71 Orlando Merced	.15	.07
☐ 72 Shawon Dunston	.15	.07
☐ 73 Ricky Bottalico	.15	.07
☐ 74 Brady Anderson	.40	.18
☐ 75 Steve Ontiveros	.15	.07
☐ 76 Jim Abbott	.30	.14
☐ 77 Carl Everett	.15	.07
☐ 78 Mo Vaughn	.75	.35
☐ 79 Pedro Martinez	.60	.25
☐ 80 Harold Baines	.30	.14
☐ 81 Alan Trammell	.40	.18
☐ 82 Steve Avery	.15	.07
☐ 83 Jeff Cirillo	.15	.07
☐ 84 John Valentin	.30	.14
☐ 85 Bernie Williams	.60	.25
☐ 86 Andre Dawson	.60	.25
☐ 87 Dave Winfield	.40	.18
☐ 88 B.J. Surhoff	.15	.07
☐ 89 Jeff Blauser	.15	.07
☐ 90 Barry Larkin	.40	.18
☐ 91 Cliff Floyd	.15	.07
☐ 92 Sammy Sosa	.60	.25
☐ 93 Andres Galarraga	.40	.18
☐ 94 Dave Nilsson	.30	.14
☐ 95 James Mouton	.15	.07
☐ 96 Marquis Grissom	.30	.14
☐ 97 Matt Williams	.40	.18
☐ 98 John Jaha	.15	.07
☐ 99 Don Mattingly	1.00	.45
☐ 100 Tim Naehring	.15	.07
☐ 101 Kevin Appier	.30	.14
☐ 102 Bobby Higginson	.30	.14
☐ 103 Andy Pettitte	.75	.35
☐ 104 Ozzie Smith	.75	.35
☐ 105 Kenny Lofton	.75	.35
☐ 106 Ken Caminiti	.60	.25
☐ 107 Walt Weiss	.15	.07
☐ 108 Jack McDowell	.15	.07
☐ 109 Brian McRae	.15	.07
☐ 110 Gary Gaetti	.30	.14

☐ 111 Curtis Goodwin .15 .07
☐ 112 Dennis Martinez .30 .14
☐ 113 Omar Vizquel .30 .14
☐ 114 Chipper Jones 2.00 .90
☐ 115 Mark Gubicza .15 .07
☐ 116 Ruben Sierra .15 .07
☐ 117 Eddie Murray .60 .25
☐ 118 Chad Curtis .15 .07
☐ 119 Hal Morris .15 .07
☐ 120 Ben McDonald .15 .07
☐ 121 Marty Cordova .15 .07
☐ 122 Ken Griffey Jr. UER 3.00 1.35
Card says Ken homered from both sides
He is only a left hitter
☐ 123 Gary Sheffield .60 .25
☐ 124 Charlie Hayes .15 .07
☐ 125 Shawn Green .30 .14
☐ 126 Jason Giambi .30 .14
☐ 127 Mark Langston .15 .07
☐ 128 Mark Whiten .15 .07
☐ 129 Greg Vaughn .15 .07
☐ 130 Mark McGwire 1.25 .55
☐ 131 Hideo Nomo 1.50 .70
☐ 132 Eric Karros .75 .35
Mike Piazza
Raul Mondesi
Hideo Nomo
☐ 133 Jason Bere .15 .07
☐ 134 Ken Griffey Jr. NAT 1.50 .70
☐ 135 Frank Thomas NAT 1.50 .70
☐ 136 Cal Ripken NAT 1.25 .55
☐ 137 Albert Belle NAT .60 .25
☐ 138 Mike Piazza NAT .60 .25
☐ 139 Dante Bichette NAT .30 .14
☐ 140 Sammy Sosa NAT .60 .25
☐ 141 Mo Vaughn NAT .60 .25
☐ 142 Tim Salmon NAT .60 .25
☐ 143 Reggie Sanders NAT .15 .07
☐ 144 Cecil Fielder NAT .30 .14
☐ 145 Jim Edmonds NAT .60 .25
☐ 146 Rafael Palmeiro NAT .40 .18
☐ 147 Edgar Martinez NAT .40 .18
☐ 148 Barry Bonds NAT .60 .25
☐ 149 Manny Ramirez NAT .60 .25
☐ 150 Larry Walker NAT .60 .25
☐ 151 Jeff Bagwell NAT .60 .25
☐ 152 Ron Gant NAT .30 .14
☐ 153 Andres Galarraga NAT .60 .25
☐ 154 Eddie Murray NAT .60 .25
☐ 155 Kirby Puckett NAT .60 .25
☐ 156 Will Clark NAT .40 .18
☐ 157 Don Mattingly NAT .60 .25
☐ 158 Mark McGwire NAT .60 .25
☐ 159 Dean Palmer NAT .15 .07
☐ 160 Matt Williams NAT .40 .18
☐ 161 Fred McGriff NAT .40 .18
☐ 162 Joe Carter NAT .30 .14
☐ 163 Juan Gonzalez NAT .60 .25
☐ 164 Alex Ochoa .15 .07
☐ 165 Ruben Rivera .30 .14
☐ 166 Tony Clark .60 .25
☐ 167 Brian Barber .15 .07
☐ 168 Matt Lawton .15 .07
☐ 169 Terrell Wade .15 .07
☐ 170 Johnny Damon .30 .14
☐ 171 Derek Jeter 2.00 .90
☐ 172 Phil Nevin .15 .07
☐ 173 Robert Perez .15 .07
☐ 174 C.J. Nitkowski .15 .07
☐ 175 Joe Vitiello .15 .07
☐ 176 Roger Cedeno .30 .14
☐ 177 Ron Coomer .15 .07
☐ 178 Chris Widger .15 .07
☐ 179 Jimmy Haynes .15 .07
☐ 180 Mike Sweeney .60 .25
☐ 181 Howard Battle .15 .07
☐ 182 John Wasdin .15 .07
☐ 183 Jim Pittsley .30 .14
☐ 184 Bob Wolcott .15 .07
☐ 185 LaTroy Hawkins .15 .07
☐ 186 Nigel Wilson .15 .07
☐ 187 Dustin Hermanson .15 .07
☐ 188 Chris Snopek .15 .07
☐ 189 Mariano Rivera .60 .25
☐ 190 Jose Herrera .15 .07
☐ 191 Chris Stynes .15 .07
☐ 192 Larry Thomas .15 .07
☐ 193 David Bell .15 .07
☐ 194 Frank Thomas CL 1.50 .70
☐ 195 Ken Griffey Jr. CL 1.50 .70
☐ 196 Cal Ripken CL 1.25 .55
☐ 197 Jeff Bagwell CL .60 .25
☐ 198 Mike Piazza CL .60 .25
☐ 199 Barry Bonds CL .60 .25
☐ 200 Garret Anderson CL .40 .18
Chipper Jones
☐ 201 Frank Thomas 2.50 1.10
☐ 202 Michael Tucker .30 .14
☐ 203 Kirby Puckett 1.25 .55
☐ 204 Alex Gonzalez .15 .07
☐ 205 Tony Gwynn 1.50 .70
☐ 206 Moises Alou .30 .14
☐ 207 Albert Belle .75 .35
☐ 208 Barry Bonds .75 .35
☐ 209 Fred McGriff .40 .18
☐ 210 Dennis Eckersley .40 .18
☐ 211 Craig Biggio .40 .18
☐ 212 David Cone .30 .14
☐ 213 Will Clark .40 .18
☐ 214 Cal Ripken 2.50 1.10
☐ 215 Wade Boggs .60 .25
☐ 216 Pete Schourek .15 .07
☐ 217 Darren Daulton .30 .14
☐ 218 Carlos Baerga .30 .14
☐ 219 Larry Walker .60 .25
☐ 220 Denny Neagle .30 .14
☐ 221 Jim Edmonds .60 .25
☐ 222 Lee Smith .30 .14
☐ 223 Jason Isringhausen .15 .07
☐ 224 Jay Buhner .40 .18
☐ 225 John Olerud .30 .14
☐ 226 Jeff Conine .30 .14
☐ 227 Dean Palmer .30 .14
☐ 228 Jim Abbott .30 .14
☐ 229 Raul Mondesi .40 .18
☐ 230 Tom Glavine .30 .14
☐ 231 Kevin Seitzer .15 .07
☐ 232 Lenny Dykstra .30 .14
☐ 233 Brian Jordan .30 .14
☐ 234 Rondell White .30 .14
☐ 235 Bret Boone .15 .07
☐ 236 Randy Johnson .60 .25
☐ 237 Paul O'Neill .30 .14
☐ 238 Jim Thome .60 .25
☐ 239 Edgardo Alfonzo .40 .18
☐ 240 Terry Pendleton .30 .14
☐ 241 Harold Baines .30 .14
☐ 242 Roberto Alomar .60 .25
☐ 243 Mark Grace .40 .18
☐ 244 Derek Bell .15 .07
☐ 245 Vinny Castilla .30 .14
☐ 246 Cecil Fielder .30 .14
☐ 247 Roger Clemens 1.25 .55
☐ 248 Orel Hershiser .30 .14
☐ 249 J.T. Snow .30 .14
☐ 250 Rafael Palmeiro .40 .18
☐ 251 Bret Saberhagen .15 .07
☐ 252 Todd Hollandsworth .30 .14
☐ 253 Ryan Klesko .40 .18
☐ 254 Greg Maddux HH .60 .25
☐ 255 Ken Griffey Jr. HH 1.50 .70
☐ 256 Hideo Nomo HH .60 .25
☐ 257 Frank Thomas HH 1.50 .70
☐ 258 Cal Ripken HH 1.25 .55
☐ 259 Jeff Bagwell HH .60 .25
☐ 260 Barry Bonds HH .60 .25
☐ 261 Mo Vaughn HH .60 .25
☐ 262 Albert Belle HH .60 .25
☐ 263 Sammy Sosa HH .60 .25
☐ 264 Reggie Sanders HH .15 .07
☐ 265 Mike Piazza HH .60 .25
☐ 266 Chipper Jones HH .60 .25
☐ 267 Tony Gwynn HH .60 .25
☐ 268 Kirby Puckett HH .60 .25
☐ 269 Wade Boggs HH .60 .25
☐ 270 Will Clark HH .40 .18
☐ 271 Gary Sheffield HH .60 .25
☐ 272 Dante Bichette HH .30 .14
☐ 273 Randy Johnson HH .60 .25
☐ 274 Matt Williams HH .40 .18
☐ 275 Alex Rodriguez HH 1.50 .70
☐ 276 Tim Salmon HH .60 .25
☐ 277 Johnny Damon HH .30 .14
☐ 278 Manny Ramirez HH .60 .25
☐ 279 Derek Jeter HH .60 .25
☐ 280 Eddie Murray HH .60 .25
☐ 281 Ozzie Smith HH .60 .25
☐ 282 Garret Anderson HH .60 .25
☐ 283 Raul Mondesi HH .60 .25
☐ 284 Terry Steinbach .30 .14
☐ 285 Carlos Garcia .15 .07
☐ 286 Dave Justice .60 .25
☐ 287 Eric Anthony .15 .07
☐ 288 Benji Gil .15 .07
☐ 289 Bob Hamelin .15 .07
☐ 290 Dwayne Hosey .15 .07
☐ 291 Andy Pettitte HH .60 .25
☐ 292 Rod Beck .30 .14
☐ 293 Shane Andrews .15 .07
☐ 294 Julian Tavarez .15 .07
☐ 295 Willie Greene .30 .14
☐ 296 Ismael Valdes .30 .14
☐ 297 Glenallen Hill .15 .07
☐ 298 Troy Percival .30 .14
☐ 299 Ray Durham .30 .14
☐ 300 Jeff Conine 300 .30 .14
☐ 301 Ken Griffey Jr. 300 1.50 .70
☐ 302 Will Clark 300 .40 .18
☐ 303 Mike Greenwell 300 .15 .07
☐ 304 Carlos Baerga 300 .30 .14
☐ 305A Paul Molitor 300 .60 .25
☐ 305B Jeff Bagwell 300 .60 .25
☐ 306 Mark Grace 300 .40 .18
☐ 307 Don Mattingly 300 .60 .25
☐ 308 Hal Morris 300 .15 .07
☐ 309 Butch Huskey .30 .14
☐ 310 Ozzie Guillen .15 .07
☐ 311 Erik Hanson .15 .07
☐ 312 Kenny Lofton 300 .60 .25
☐ 313 Edgar Martinez 300 .40 .18
☐ 314 Kurt Abbott .15 .07
☐ 315 John Smoltz .30 .14
☐ 316 Ariel Prieto .15 .07
☐ 317 Mark Carreon .15 .07
☐ 318 Kirby Puckett 300 .60 .25
☐ 319 Carlos Perez .15 .07
☐ 320 Gary DiSarcina .15 .07
☐ 321 Trevor Hoffman .30 .14
☐ 322 Mike Piazza 300 .60 .25
☐ 323 Frank Thomas 300 1.50 .70
☐ 324 Juan Acevedo .15 .07
☐ 325 Bip Roberts .15 .07
☐ 326 Javier Lopez .30 .14
☐ 327 Benito Santiago .15 .07
☐ 328 Mark Lewis .15 .07
☐ 329 Royce Clayton .15 .07
☐ 330 Tom Gordon .15 .07
☐ 331 Ben McDonald .15 .07
☐ 332 Dan Wilson .15 .07
☐ 333 Ron Gant .30 .14
☐ 334 Wade Boggs 300 .60 .25
☐ 335 Paul Molitor .60 .25
☐ 336 Tony Gwynn 300 .60 .25
☐ 337 Sean Berry .15 .07
☐ 338 Rickey Henderson .40 .18
☐ 339 Wil Cordero .15 .07
☐ 340 Kent Mercker .15 .07
☐ 341 Kenny Rogers .15 .07
☐ 342 Ryne Sandberg .75 .35
☐ 343 Charlie Hayes .15 .07
☐ 344 Andy Benes .15 .07
☐ 345 Sterling Hitchcock .15 .07
☐ 346 Bernard Gilkey .30 .14
☐ 347 Julio Franco .30 .14
☐ 348 Ken Hill .15 .07
☐ 349 Russ Davis .15 .07
☐ 350 Mike Blowers .15 .07
☐ 351 B.J. Surhoff .30 .14
☐ 352 Lance Johnson .15 .07
☐ 353 Darryl Hamilton .15 .07
☐ 354 Shawon Dunston .15 .07
☐ 355 Rick Aguilera .15 .07
☐ 356 Danny Tartabull .15 .07
☐ 357 Todd Stottlemyre .15 .07
☐ 358 Mike Bordick .15 .07
☐ 359 Jack McDowell .15 .07
☐ 360 Todd Zeile .15 .07
☐ 361 Tino Martinez .60 .25
☐ 362 Greg Gagne .15 .07
☐ 363 Mike Kelly .15 .07
☐ 364 Tim Raines .15 .07
☐ 365 Ernie Young .15 .07
☐ 366 Mike Stanley .15 .07
☐ 367 Wally Joyner .15 .07
☐ 368 Karim Garcia .60 .25
☐ 369 Paul Wilson .15 .07
☐ 370 Sal Fasano .15 .07
☐ 371 Jason Schmidt .30 .14
☐ 372 Livan Hernandez 1.50 .70
☐ 373 George Arias .15 .07
☐ 374 Steve Gibralter .15 .07
☐ 375 Jermaine Dye .15 .07
☐ 376 Jason Kendall .60 .25
☐ 377 Brooks Kieschnick .30 .14
☐ 378 Jeff Ware .15 .07
☐ 379 Alan Benes .30 .14
☐ 380 Rey Ordonez .30 .14
☐ 381 Jay Powell .15 .07
☐ 382 Osvaldo Fernandez .30 .14
☐ 383 Wilton Guerrero .60 .25
☐ 384 Eric Owens .15 .07
☐ 385 George Williams .15 .07
☐ 386 Chan Ho Park .60 .25
☐ 387 Jeff Suppan .40 .18
☐ 388 F.P. Santangelo .15 .07
☐ 389 Terry Adams .15 .07
☐ 390 Bob Abreu .60 .25
☐ 391 Quinton McCracken .15 .07
☐ 392 Mike Busby .15 .07
☐ 393 Cal Ripken CL 1.25 .55
☐ 394 Ken Griffey Jr. CL 1.50 .70

	MINT	NRMT
☐ 395 Frank Thomas CL	1.50	.70
☐ 396 Chipper Jones CL	.60	.25
☐ 397 Greg Maddux CL	.60	.25
☐ 398 Mike Piazza CL	.60	.25
☐ 399 Ken Griffey Jr CL Cal Ripken Jr. Chipper Jones Frank Thomas Greg Maddux Mike Piazza	1.50	.70
☐ CR1 Cal Ripken Tribute	20.00	9.00

1996 Pinnacle Foil

This 200-card set is a parallel set to the 1996 Pinnacle second series set and was issued in five-card packs which retailed for $2.99. Produced with micro-etched foil fronts, this limited version is similar in design to the regular second series set.

	MINT	NRMT
COMPLETE SET (200)	25.00	11.00
COMMON CARD (201-399)	.15	.07
*STARS: .75 TO 1.5X BASIC CARDS		

1996 Pinnacle Christie Brinkley Collection

Randomly inserted at the rate of one in 23 packs, this 16-card set features the 1995 World Series participants captured by the lens of supermodel and photographer Christie Brinkley. The fronts feature color player photos in various poses with different backgrounds. The backs carry a color portrait of the player and Ms. Brinkley with an explanation as to why she posed them as she did.

	MINT	NRMT
COMPLETE SET (16)	75.00	34.00
COMMON CARD (1-16)	2.00	.90
☐ 1 Greg Maddux	15.00	6.75
☐ 2 Ryan Klesko	3.00	1.35
☐ 3 Dave Justice	5.00	2.20
☐ 4 Tom Glavine	2.00	.90
☐ 5 Chipper Jones	15.00	6.75
☐ 6 Fred McGriff	3.00	1.35
☐ 7 Javier Lopez	2.00	.90
☐ 8 Marquis Grissom	2.00	.90
☐ 9 Jason Schmidt	2.00	.90
☐ 10 Albert Belle	6.00	2.70
☐ 11 Manny Ramirez	5.00	2.20
☐ 12 Carlos Baerga	2.00	.90
☐ 13 Sandy Alomar	2.00	.90
☐ 14 Jim Thome	5.00	2.20
☐ 15 Julio Franco	2.00	.90
☐ 16 Kenny Lofton	6.00	2.70
☐ PCB Christie Brinkley Promo On the Beach	6.00	2.70

1996 Pinnacle Essence of the Game

Randomly inserted in hobby packs only at a rate of one in 23, this 18-card standard-size set takes a unique perspective, photographically capturing the persona of 18 of the game's most popular icons. Using a micro-etched print technology, the fronts display a color player cutout on an acetate card studded with stars, with "Essence of the Game" appearing on a holographic design across the top. On the back, this holographic design carries a highlight.

	MINT	NRMT
COMPLETE SET (18)	150.00	70.00
COMMON CARD (1-18)	2.00	.90
☐ 1 Cal Ripken	20.00	9.00
☐ 2 Greg Maddux	15.00	6.75
☐ 3 Frank Thomas	20.00	9.00
☐ 4 Matt Williams	3.00	1.35
☐ 5 Chipper Jones	15.00	6.75
☐ 6 Reggie Sanders	2.00	.90
☐ 7 Ken Griffey Jr.	25.00	11.00
☐ 8 Kirby Puckett	10.00	4.50
☐ 9 Hideo Nomo	12.00	5.50
☐ 10 Mike Piazza	15.00	6.75
☐ 11 Jeff Bagwell	10.00	4.50
☐ 12 Mo Vaughn	6.00	2.70
☐ 13 Albert Belle	6.00	2.70
☐ 14 Tim Salmon	5.00	2.20
☐ 15 Don Mattingly	8.00	3.60
☐ 16 Will Clark	3.00	1.35
☐ 17 Eddie Murray	5.00	2.20
☐ 18 Barry Bonds	6.00	2.70

1996 Pinnacle First Rate

Randomly inserted in retail packs only at a rate of one in 23, this 18-card set features former first-round draft picks who have become major league superstars done in Dufex print.

	MINT	NRMT
COMPLETE SET (18)	120.00	55.00
COMMON CARD (1-18)	2.00	.90
☐ 1 Ken Griffey Jr.	30.00	13.50
☐ 2 Frank Thomas	25.00	11.00
☐ 3 Mo Vaughn	8.00	3.60
☐ 4 Chipper Jones	20.00	9.00
☐ 5 Alex Rodriguez	20.00	9.00
☐ 6 Kirby Puckett	12.00	5.50
☐ 7 Gary Sheffield	6.00	2.70
☐ 8 Matt Williams	3.00	1.35
☐ 9 Barry Bonds	8.00	3.60
☐ 10 Craig Biggio	3.00	1.35
☐ 11 Robin Ventura	2.50	1.10
☐ 12 Michael Tucker	2.50	1.10
☐ 13 Derek Jeter	15.00	6.75
☐ 14 Manny Ramirez	6.00	2.70
☐ 15 Barry Larkin	2.50	1.10
☐ 16 Shawn Green	2.00	.90
☐ 17 Will Clark	3.00	1.35
☐ 18 Mark McGwire	12.00	5.50

1996 Pinnacle Power

Randomly inserted in packs at a rate of one in 35 retail and hobby packs, or one in 29 jumbo packs, this 20-card set highlights the league's top long-ball hitters in die-cut holographic foil technology. On a black card face, the fronts have a color player cutout superposed over a holographic homeplate. All printing on the front, including the player's name, is stamped in gold foil. The horizontal backs present a color closeup on the left and a player profile on the right.

	MINT	NRMT
COMPLETE SET (20)	125.00	55.00
COMMON CARD (1-20)	2.00	.90
☐ 1 Frank Thomas	25.00	11.00
☐ 2 Mo Vaughn	8.00	3.60
☐ 3 Ken Griffey Jr.	30.00	13.50
☐ 4 Matt Williams	3.00	1.35
☐ 5 Barry Bonds	8.00	3.60
☐ 6 Reggie Sanders	2.00	.90
☐ 7 Mike Piazza	20.00	9.00
☐ 8 Jim Edmonds	6.00	2.70
☐ 9 Dante Bichette	2.50	1.10
☐ 10 Sammy Sosa	6.00	2.70
☐ 11 Jeff Bagwell	12.00	5.50
☐ 12 Fred McGriff	3.00	1.35
☐ 13 Albert Belle	8.00	3.60
☐ 14 Tim Salmon	6.00	2.70
☐ 15 Joe Carter	2.50	1.10
☐ 16 Manny Ramirez	6.00	2.70
☐ 17 Eddie Murray	6.00	2.70
☐ 18 Cecil Fielder	2.50	1.10
☐ 19 Larry Walker	6.00	2.70
☐ 20 Juan Gonzalez	15.00	6.75

1996 Pinnacle Project Stardom

This 18-card set was randomly inserted in hobby packs at the rate of one in 35. The fronts feature a color action player photo on a blue foil background with a player portrait framed by silver foil rays depicting a star shining. The backs carry another player portrait with rays coming from behind his head to give the impression of a shining star, and information about the player is printed on the side.

	MINT	NRMT
COMPLETE SET (18)	150.00	70.00
COMMON CARD (1-18)	3.00	1.35
☐ 1 Paul Wilson	3.00	1.35
☐ 2 Derek Jeter	25.00	11.00
☐ 3 Karim Garcia	4.00	1.80
☐ 4 Johnny Damon	4.00	1.80
☐ 5 Alex Rodriguez	30.00	13.50
☐ 6 Chipper Jones	30.00	13.50
☐ 7 Charles Johnson	4.00	1.80
☐ 8 Bob Abreu	10.00	4.50
☐ 9 Alan Benes	4.00	1.80
☐ 10 Richard Hidalgo	10.00	4.50
☐ 11 Brooks Kieschnick	4.00	1.80
☐ 12 Garret Anderson	6.00	2.70
☐ 13 Livan Hernandez	12.00	5.50
☐ 14 Manny Ramirez	10.00	4.50
☐ 15 Jermaine Dye	3.00	1.35
☐ 16 Todd Hollandsworth	3.00	1.35
☐ 17 Raul Mondesi	6.00	2.70
☐ 18 Ryan Klesko	6.00	2.70

1996 Pinnacle Skylines

Randomly inserted in magazine packs at the rate of one in 29, this 18-card set features baseball's best players pictured against their city's skyline and printed on clear plastic stock. The backs carry the same player portrait with information about the player and the city printed below.

	MINT	NRMT
COMPLETE SET (18)	250.00	110.00
COMMON CARD (1-18)	6.00	2.70
☐ 1 Ken Griffey Jr.	50.00	22.00
☐ 2 Frank Thomas	40.00	18.00
☐ 3 Greg Maddux	30.00	13.50
☐ 4 Cal Ripken	40.00	18.00
☐ 5 Albert Belle	12.00	5.50
☐ 6 Mo Vaughn	12.00	5.50
☐ 7 Mike Piazza	30.00	13.50
☐ 8 Wade Boggs	10.00	4.50
☐ 9 Will Clark	7.00	3.10
☐ 10 Barry Bonds	12.00	5.50
☐ 11 Gary Sheffield	10.00	4.50
☐ 12 Hideo Nomo	25.00	11.00
☐ 13 Tony Gwynn	25.00	11.00
☐ 14 Kirby Puckett	20.00	9.00
☐ 15 Chipper Jones	30.00	13.50
☐ 16 Jeff Bagwell	20.00	9.00
☐ 17 Manny Ramirez	10.00	4.50
☐ 18 Raul Mondesi	6.00	2.70

1996 Pinnacle Slugfest

Randomly inserted exclusively into one in every 35 series 2 retail packs, cards from this 18 cards set feature a selection of baseball's top slugging stars. The fronts carry a color action player photo on a silver foil starburst background. The backs display a color player photo in a wooden bat with player information on the side.

	MINT	NRMT
COMPLETE SET (18)	200.00	90.00
COMMON CARD (1-18)	3.00	1.35
☐ 1 Frank Thomas	30.00	13.50
☐ 2 Ken Griffey Jr.	40.00	18.00
☐ 3 Jeff Bagwell	15.00	6.75
☐ 4 Barry Bonds	10.00	4.50
☐ 5 Mo Vaughn	10.00	4.50
☐ 6 Albert Belle	10.00	4.50
☐ 7 Mike Piazza	25.00	11.00
☐ 8 Matt Williams	5.00	2.20
☐ 9 Dante Bichette	4.00	1.80
☐ 10 Sammy Sosa	8.00	3.60
☐ 11 Gary Sheffield	8.00	3.60
☐ 12 Reggie Sanders	3.00	1.35
☐ 13 Manny Ramlrez	8.00	3.60
☐ 14 Eddie Murray	8.00	3.60
☐ 15 Juan Gonzalez	20.00	9.00
☐ 16 Dean Palmer	3.00	1.35
☐ 17 Rafael Palmeiro	5.00	2.20
☐ 18 Cecil Fielder	4.00	1.80

1996 Pinnacle Starburst

Randomly inserted in first and second series packs at a rate of one in seven, this 200-card quasi-parallel insert set features a select group of major league baseball's hottest superstars derived from the 399-card regular set. Unlike the basic cards, Starburst's are printed on all-foil Dufex card stock. The numbering also differs from the regular issue.

	MINT	NRMT
COMPLETE SET (200)	500.00	220.00
COMPLETE SERIES 1 (100)	250.00	110.00
COMPLETE SERIES 2 (100)	250.00	110.00
COMMON CARD (1-200)	1.00	.45
☐ 1 Greg Maddux	20.00	9.00
☐ 2 Bill Pulsipher	1.00	.45
☐ 3 Dante Bichette	2.00	.90
☐ 4 Mike Piazza	20.00	9.00
☐ 5 Garret Anderson	1.00	.45
☐ 6 Chuck Knoblauch	6.00	2.70
☐ 7 Jeff Bagwell	12.00	5.50
☐ 8 Wil Cordero	1.00	.45
☐ 9 Travis Fryman	2.00	.90
☐ 10 Reggie Sanders	1.00	.45
☐ 11 Deion Sanders	6.00	2.70
☐ 12 Tim Salmon	6.00	2.70
☐ 13 Tino Martinez	6.00	2.70
☐ 14 Bobby Bonilla	2.00	.90
☐ 15 Joe Carter	2.00	.90
☐ 16 Mike Mussina	6.00	2.70
☐ 17 Jose Canseco	2.00	.90
☐ 18 Manny Ramirez	6.00	2.70
☐ 19 Gregg Jefferies	2.00	.90
☐ 20 Charles Johnson	2.00	.90
☐ 21 Brian L. Hunter	2.00	.90
☐ 22 Ray Lankford	2.00	.90
☐ 23 Ivan Rodriguez	8.00	3.60
☐ 24 Paul Molitor	6.00	2.70
☐ 25 Eric Karros	2.00	.90
☐ 26 Edgar Martinez	4.00	1.80
☐ 27 Shawon Dunston	1.00	.45
☐ 28 Mo Vaughn	8.00	3.60
☐ 29 Pedro J. Martinez	6.00	2.70
☐ 30 Marty Cordova	2.00	.90
☐ 31 Ken Caminiti	6.00	2.70
☐ 32 Gary Sheffield	6.00	2.70
☐ 33 Shawn Green	1.00	.45
☐ 34 Cliff Floyd	1.00	.45
☐ 35 Andres Galarraga	6.00	2.70
☐ 36 Matt Williams	4.00	1.80
☐ 37 Don Mattingly	15.00	6.75
☐ 38 Kevin Appier	2.00	.90
☐ 39 Ozzie Smith	8.00	3.60
☐ 40 Kenny Lofton	8.00	3.60
☐ 41 Ken Griffey Jr. UER card mentions him as a swtich-hitter Griffey only bats left	30.00	13.50
☐ 42 Jack McDowell	1.00	.45
☐ 43 Gary Gaetti	1.00	.45
☐ 44 Dennis Martinez	2.00	.90
☐ 45 Chipper Jones	20.00	9.00
☐ 46 Eddie Murray	6.00	2.70
☐ 47 Bernie Williams	6.00	2.70
☐ 48 Andre Dawson	4.00	1.80
☐ 49 Dave Winfield	4.00	1.80
☐ 50 B.J. Surhoff	1.00	.45
☐ 51 Barry Larkin	4.00	1.80
☐ 52 Alan Trammell	4.00	1.80
☐ 53 Sammy Sosa	6.00	2.70
☐ 54 Hideo Nomo	8.00	3.60
☐ 55 Mark McGwire	10.00	4.50
☐ 56 Jay Bell	1.00	.45
☐ 57 Juan Gonzalez	15.00	6.75
☐ 58 Chili Davis	2.00	.90
☐ 59 Robin Ventura	2.00	.90
☐ 60 John Mabry	2.00	.90
☐ 61 Ken Griffey Jr. NAT	15.00	6.75
☐ 62 Frank Thomas NAT	15.00	6.75
☐ 63 Cal Ripken NAT	12.00	5.50
☐ 64 Albert Belle NAT	6.00	2.70
☐ 65 Mike Piazza NAT	6.00	2.70
☐ 66 Dante Bichette NAT	2.00	.90
☐ 67 Sammy Sosa NAT	6.00	2.70
☐ 68 Mo Vaughn NAT	6.00	2.70
☐ 69 Tim Salmon NAT	6.00	2.70
☐ 70 Reggie Sanders NAT	1.00	.45
☐ 71 Cecil Fielder NAT	2.00	.90
☐ 72 Jim Edmonds NAT	6.00	2.70
☐ 73 Rafael Palmeiro NAT	6.00	2.70
☐ 74 Edgar Martinez NAT	4.00	1.80
☐ 75 Barry Bonds NAT	6.00	2.70
☐ 76 Manny Ramirez NAT	6.00	2.70
☐ 77 Larry Walker NAT	6.00	2.70
☐ 78 Jeff Bagwell NAT	6.00	2.70
☐ 79 Ron Gant NAT	2.00	.90
☐ 80 Andres Galarraga NAT	6.00	2.70
☐ 81 Eddie Murray NAT	6.00	2.70
☐ 82 Kirby Puckett NAT	6.00	2.70
☐ 83 Will Clark NAT	4.00	1.80
☐ 84 Don Mattingly NAT	6.00	2.70
☐ 85 Mark McGwire NAT	6.00	2.70
☐ 86 Dean Palmer NAT	2.00	.90
☐ 87 Matt Williams NAT	4.00	1.80
☐ 88 Fred McGriff NAT	4.00	1.80
☐ 89 Joe Carter NAT	2.00	.90
☐ 90 Juan Gonzalez NAT	6.00	2.70
☐ 91 Alex Ochoa	1.00	.45
☐ 92 Ruben Rivera	2.00	.90
☐ 93 Tony Clark	6.00	2.70
☐ 94 Pete Schourek	1.00	.45
☐ 95 Terrell Wade	1.00	.45
☐ 96 Johnny Damon	2.00	.90
☐ 97 Derek Jeter	20.00	9.00
☐ 98 Phil Nevin	1.00	.45
☐ 99 Robert Perez	1.00	.45
☐ 100 Dustin Hermanson	1.00	.45
☐ 101 Frank Thomas	25.00	11.00
☐ 102 Michael Tucker	2.00	.90
☐ 103 Kirby Puckett	12.00	5.50
☐ 104 Alex Gonzalez	1.00	.45
☐ 105 Tony Gwynn	12.00	5.50
☐ 106 Moises Alou	2.00	.90
☐ 107 Albert Belle	12.00	5.50
☐ 108 Barry Bonds	8.00	3.60
☐ 109 Fred McGriff	4.00	1.80
☐ 110 Dennis Eckersley	4.00	1.80
☐ 111 Craig Biggio	4.00	1.80
☐ 112 David Cone	2.00	.90
☐ 113 Will Clark	4.00	1.80
☐ 114 Cal Ripken	25.00	11.00
☐ 115 Wade Boggs	6.00	2.70
☐ 116 Pete Schourek	1.00	.45
☐ 117 Darren Daulton	2.00	.90
☐ 118 Carlos Baerga	2.00	.90
☐ 119 Larry Walker	6.00	2.70
☐ 120 Denny Neagle	2.00	.90
☐ 121 Jim Edmonds	6.00	2.70
☐ 122 Lee Smith	2.00	.90
☐ 123 Jason Isringhausen	1.00	.45
☐ 124 Jay Buhner	4.00	1.80
☐ 125 John Olerud	2.00	.90
☐ 126 Jeff Conine	2.00	.90
☐ 127 Dean Palmer	2.00	.90
☐ 128 Jim Abbott	1.00	.45
☐ 129 Raul Mondesi	4.00	1.80
☐ 130 Tom Glavine	2.00	.90
☐ 131 Kevin Seitzer	1.00	.45
☐ 132 Lenny Dykstra	2.00	.90
☐ 133 Brian Jordan	2.00	.90
☐ 134 Rondell White	2.00	.90
☐ 135 Bret Boone	1.00	.45
☐ 136 Randy Johnson	6.00	2.70
☐ 137 Paul O'Neill	1.00	.45
☐ 138 Jim Thome	6.00	2.70
☐ 139 Edgardo Alfonzo	6.00	2.70
☐ 140 Terry Pendleton	2.00	.90
☐ 141 Harold Baines	2.00	.90
☐ 142 Roberto Alomar	6.00	2.70
☐ 143 Mark Grace	4.00	1.80
☐ 144 Derek Bell	1.00	.45
☐ 145 Vinny Castilla	2.00	.90
☐ 146 Cecil Fielder	2.00	.90
☐ 147 Roger Clemens	6.00	2.70
☐ 148 Orel Hershiser	2.00	.90
☐ 149 J.T. Snow	1.00	.45
☐ 150 Rafael Palmeiro	4.00	1.80
☐ 151 Bret Saberhagen	1.00	.45
☐ 152 Todd Hollandsworth	2.00	.90
☐ 153 Ryan Klesko	4.00	1.80
☐ 154 Greg Maddux HH	6.00	2.70
☐ 155 Ken Griffey Jr. HH	15.00	6.75
☐ 156 Hideo Nomo HH	6.00	2.70
☐ 157 Frank Thomas HH	15.00	6.75
☐ 158 Cal Ripken HH	12.00	5.50
☐ 159 Jeff Bagwell HH	6.00	2.70
☐ 160 Barry Bonds HH	6.00	2.70
☐ 161 Mo Vaughn HH	6.00	2.70
☐ 162 Albert Belle HH	6.00	2.70
☐ 163 Sammy Sosa HH	6.00	2.70
☐ 164 Reggie Sanders HH	2.00	.90
☐ 165 Mike Piazza HH	6.00	2.70
☐ 166 Chipper Jones HH	6.00	2.70
☐ 167 Tony Gwynn HH	6.00	2.70
☐ 168 Kirby Puckett HH	6.00	2.70
☐ 169 Wade Boggs HH	6.00	2.70
☐ 170 Will Clark HH	4.00	1.80
☐ 171 Gary Sheffield HH	6.00	2.70
☐ 172 Dante Bichette HH	4.00	1.80
☐ 173 Randy Johnson HH	6.00	2.70
☐ 174 Matt Williams HH	4.00	1.80
☐ 175 Alex Rodriguez HH	15.00	6.75
☐ 176 Tim Salmon HH	6.00	2.70
☐ 177 Johnny Damon HH	2.00	.90
☐ 178 Manny Ramirez HH	6.00	2.70
☐ 179 Derek Jeter HH	6.00	2.70
☐ 180 Eddie Murray HH	6.00	2.70
☐ 181 Ozzie Smith HH	6.00	2.70
☐ 182 Garret Anderson HH	2.00	.90
☐ 183 Raul Mondesi HH	4.00	1.80
☐ 184 Jeff Conine 300	2.00	.90
☐ 185 Ken Griffey Jr. 300	15.00	6.75
☐ 186 Will Clark 300	4.00	1.80
☐ 187 Mike Greenwell 300	1.00	.45
☐ 188 Carlos Baerga 300	2.00	.90
☐ 189 Paul Molitor 300	6.00	2.70
☐ 190 Jeff Bagwell 300	6.00	2.70
☐ 191 Mark Grace 300	4.00	1.80
☐ 192 Don Mattingly 300	6.00	2.70

	MINT	NRMT
☐ 193 Hal Morris 300	1.00	.45
☐ 194 Kenny Lofton 300	6.00	2.70
☐ 195 Edgar Martinez 300	4.00	1.80
☐ 196 Kirby Puckett 300	6.00	2.70
☐ 197 Mike Piazza 300	6.00	2.70
☐ 198 Frank Thomas 300	15.00	6.75
☐ 199 Wade Boggs 300	4.00	1.80
☐ 200 Tony Gwynn 300	6.00	2.70

1996 Pinnacle Starburst Artist's Proofs

Randomly inserted in packs at a rate of one in 47, this 200-card is a parallel issue to the more common Starburst inserts. The cards are identical to their Starburst counterparts except for the foil "Artist's Proofs" wording on their fronts.

	MINT	NRMT
COMPLETE SET (200)	1500.00	700.00
COMPLETE SERIES 1 (100)	750.00	350.00
COMPLETE SERIES 2 (100)	750.00	350.00
COMMON CARD (1-200)	3.00	1.35

*STARS: 1X TO 2.5X BASIC STARBURST
*YOUNG STARS: .75X TO 2X BASIC STARBURST

1996 Pinnacle Team Pinnacle

Randomly inserted in series one packs at a rate of one in 72, this 9-card set spotlights double-front all-foil Dufex card designs featuring nine top AL and NL players, by position, back-to-back. On a gold foil background displaying a baseball, the fronts present a color player cutout extending beyond the picture frame. "Team Pinnacle," the player's name, and an abbreviation for his position are printed in the bottom border. Only one side of each card is Dufexed.

	MINT	NRMT
COMPLETE SET (9)	150.00	70.00
COMMON CARD (1-9)	4.00	1.80
☐ 1 Frank Thomas Jeff Bagwell	25.00	11.00
☐ 2 Chuck Knoblauch Craig Biggio	7.00	3.10
☐ 3 Jim Thome Matt Williams	4.00	1.80
☐ 4 Barrry Larkin Cal Ripken	25.00	11.00
☐ 5 Barry Bonds Tim Salmon	8.00	3.60
☐ 6 Ken Griffey Jr. Reggie Sanders	30.00	13.50
☐ 7 Albert Belle Sammy Sosa	8.00	3.60
☐ 8 Ivan Rodriguez Mike Piazza	20.00	9.00
☐ 9 Greg Maddux Randy Johnson	20.00	9.00

1996 Pinnacle Team Spirit

Randomly inserted in series two packs at the rate of one in 72, this 12-card set features color action player images in holographic foil stamping over a silver foil ball outlined in baseball stitching. The backs carry two player photos and player information.

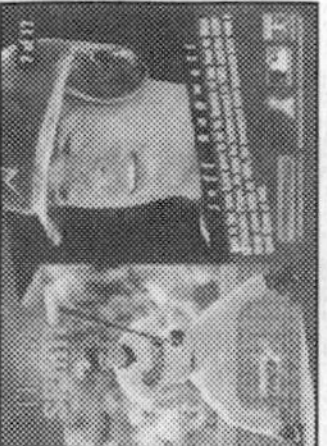

	MINT	NRMT
COMPLETE SET (12)	300.00	135.00
COMMON CARD (1-12)	6.00	2.70
☐ 1 Greg Maddux	30.00	13.50
☐ 2 Ken Griffey Jr.	50.00	22.00
☐ 3 Derek Jeter	25.00	11.00
☐ 4 Mike Piazza	30.00	13.50
☐ 5 Cal Ripken	40.00	18.00
☐ 6 Frank Thomas	40.00	18.00
☐ 7 Jeff Bagwell	20.00	9.00
☐ 8 Mo Vaughn	12.00	5.50
☐ 9 Albert Belle	12.00	5.50
☐ 10 Chipper Jones	30.00	13.50
☐ 11 Johnny Damon	6.00	2.70
☐ 12 Barry Bonds	12.00	5.50

1996 Pinnacle Team Tomorrow

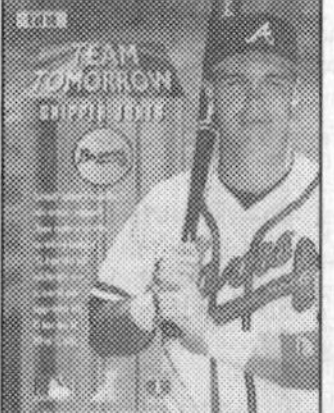

Randomly inserted in series one jumbo packs at a rate of one in 19, this 10-card set is a jumbo exclusive and features the next crop of superstars. The fronts are printed in an all-foil Dufex design with two of the same color player action cutouts--one close up and the other full-length. The backs carry a color player portrait and information about the player.

	MINT	NRMT
COMPLETE SET (10)	100.00	45.00
COMMON CARD (1-10)	3.00	1.35
☐ 1 Ruben Rivera	3.00	1.35
☐ 2 Johnny Damon	4.00	1.80
☐ 3 Raul Mondesi	6.00	2.70
☐ 4 Manny Ramirez	8.00	3.60
☐ 5 Hideo Nomo	20.00	9.00
☐ 6 Chipper Jones	25.00	11.00
☐ 7 Garret Anderson	4.00	1.80
☐ 8 Alex Rodriguez	25.00	11.00
☐ 9 Derek Jeter	20.00	9.00
☐ 10 Karim Garcia	4.00	1.80

1996 Pinnacle FanFest

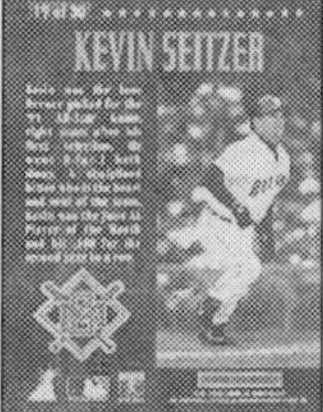

This standard-size set was issued by Pinnacle in conjunction with the 1996 Pinnacle All-Star FanFest held in Philadelphia and was distributed in two-card poly packs. The Daulton card (#30) features Sportflics technology and was inserted at a rate of about 1:60 packs. The Carlton card (#31) was used for the official FanFest badges; apparently, some loose cards also were given to FanFest volunteers. The Carlton card is not considered part of the complete set. Five other cards (with the same design but no foil stamping or UV coating) were also issued by Pinnacle as part of the celebration. These five cards feature different personalities (most of whom are non-baseball related) involved in the show. The set is considered complete at 30 cards with the Daulton SP.

	MINT	NRMT
COMPLETE SET (30)	25.00	11.00
COMMON CARD (1-30)	.25	.11
☐ 1 Cal Ripken	2.50	1.10
☐ 2 Greg Maddux	2.00	.90
☐ 3 Ken Griffey Jr.	3.00	1.35
☐ 4 Frank Thomas	2.50	1.10
☐ 5 Jeff Bagwell	1.25	.55
☐ 6 Hideo Nomo	1.50	.70
☐ 7 Tony Gwynn	1.50	.70
☐ 8 Albert Belle	1.00	.45
☐ 9 Mo Vaughn	1.00	.45
☐ 10 Mike Piazza	2.50	1.10
☐ 11 Dante Bichette	.75	.35
☐ 12 Ryne Sandberg	1.25	.55
☐ 13 Wade Boggs	1.00	.45
☐ 14 Kirby Puckett	1.50	.70
☐ 15 Ozzie Smith	1.25	.55
☐ 16 Barry Bonds	1.25	.55
☐ 17 Gary Sheffield	1.00	.45
☐ 18 Barry Larkin	.75	.35
☐ 19 Kevin Seitzer	.25	.11
☐ 20 Jay Bell	.25	.11
☐ 21 Chipper Jones	2.50	1.10
☐ 22 Ivan Rodriguez	1.25	.55
☐ 23 Cecil Fielder	.50	.23
☐ 24 Manny Ramirez	1.00	.45
☐ 25 Randy Johnson	1.00	.45
☐ 26 Moises Alou	.50	.23
☐ 27 Mark McGwire	1.50	.70
☐ 28 Jason Isringhausen	.25	.11
☐ 29 Joe Carter	.50	.23
☐ 30 Darren Daulton SP	10.00	4.50
☐ 31 Steve Carlton	10.00	4.50
☐ BF1 Ben Franklin	5.00	2.20
☐ BS1 Bud Selig COMM	10.00	4.50
☐ ER1 Ed Rendell Mayor of Philadelphia	5.00	2.20
☐ JS1 John Street City Councilman	5.00	2.20
☐ PP1 Phillie Phanatic	10.00	4.50

1997 Pinnacle

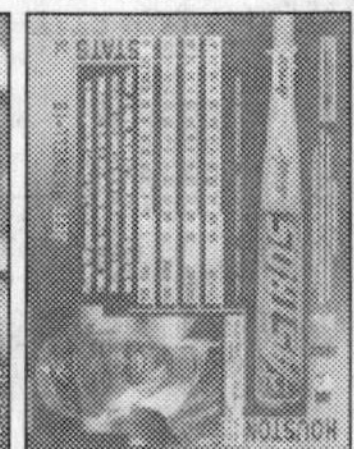

The 1997 Pinnacle set was issued as one series of 200 cards. Cards were distributed in 10-card hobby and retail packs (SRP $2.49) and 7-card magazine packs. This set was released in February, 1997. The set contains the following subsets: Rookies (156-185), Clout (186-197) and Checklists (198-200). Basic card fronts feature full color action shots with dramatic gold foil treatment across the bottom. A conglomeration of legendary players, locales and other regional names of interest related to the specified team of the featured player run in small type within the gold foil borders. Backs feature a small, color mug-shot along with various statistics and information. There are no key Rookie Cards in this set.

	MINT	NRMT
COMPLETE SET (200)	20.00	9.00
COMMON CARD (1-200)	.15	.07
☐ 1 Cecil Fielder	.30	.14
☐ 2 Garret Anderson	.30	.14
☐ 3 Charles Nagy	.30	.14
☐ 4 Darryl Hamilton	.15	.07
☐ 5 Greg Myers	.15	.07
☐ 6 Eric Davis	.30	.14
☐ 7 Jeff Frye	.15	.07
☐ 8 Marquis Grissom	.30	.14
☐ 9 Curt Schilling	.30	.14
☐ 10 Jeff Fassero	.15	.07
☐ 11 Alan Benes	.30	.14
☐ 12 Orlando Miller	.15	.07
☐ 13 Alex Fernandez	.30	.14
☐ 14 Andy Pettitte	.60	.25
☐ 15 Andre Dawson	.40	.18
☐ 16 Mark Grudzielanek	.15	.07

Card	MINT	NRMT
☐ 17 Joe Vitiello	.15	.07
☐ 18 Juan Gonzalez	1.50	.70
☐ 19 Mark Whiten	.15	.07
☐ 20 Lance Johnson	.15	.07
☐ 21 Trevor Hoffman	.30	.14
☐ 22 Marc Newfield	.15	.07
☐ 23 Jim Eisenreich	.30	.14
☐ 24 Joe Carter	.30	.14
☐ 25 Jose Canseco	.40	.18
☐ 26 Bill Swift	.15	.07
☐ 27 Ellis Burks	.30	.14
☐ 28 Ben McDonald	.15	.07
☐ 29 Edgar Martinez	.40	.18
☐ 30 Jamie Moyer	.15	.07
☐ 31 Chan Ho Park	.60	.25
☐ 32 Carlos Delgado	.30	.14
☐ 33 Kevin Mitchell	.15	.07
☐ 34 Carlos Garcia	.15	.07
☐ 35 Darryl Strawberry	.30	.14
☐ 36 Jim Thome	.60	.25
☐ 37 Jose Offerman	.15	.07
☐ 38 Ryan Klesko	.40	.18
☐ 39 Ruben Sierra	.15	.07
☐ 40 Devon White	.15	.07
☐ 41 Brian Jordan	.15	.07
☐ 42 Tony Gwynn	1.50	.70
☐ 43 Rafael Palmeiro	.40	.18
☐ 44 Dante Bichette	.40	.18
☐ 45 Scott Stahoviak	.15	.07
☐ 46 Roger Cedeno	.15	.07
☐ 47 Ivan Rodriguez	.75	.35
☐ 48 Bob Abreu	.60	.25
☐ 49 Darryl Kile	.30	.14
☐ 50 Darren Dreifort	.15	.07
☐ 51 Shawon Dunston	.15	.07
☐ 52 Mark McGwire	1.25	.55
☐ 53 Tim Salmon	.60	.25
☐ 54 Gene Schall	.15	.07
☐ 55 Roger Clemens	1.25	.55
☐ 56 Rondell White	.30	.14
☐ 57 Ed Sprague	.15	.07
☐ 58 Craig Paquette	.15	.07
☐ 59 David Segui	.15	.07
☐ 60 Jaime Navarro	.15	.07
☐ 61 Tom Glavine	.30	.14
☐ 62 Jeff Brantley	.15	.07
☐ 63 Kimera Bartee	.15	.07
☐ 64 Fernando Vina	.15	.07
☐ 65 Eddie Murray	.60	.25
☐ 66 Lenny Dykstra	.30	.14
☐ 67 Kevin Elster	.15	.07
☐ 68 Vinny Castilla	.30	.14
☐ 69 Mike Fetters	.15	.07
☐ 70 Brett Butler	.15	.07
☐ 71 Robby Thompson	.15	.07
☐ 72 Reggie Jefferson	.30	.14
☐ 73 Todd Hundley	.30	.14
☐ 74 Jeff King	.15	.07
☐ 75 Ernie Young	.15	.07
☐ 76 Jeff Bagwell	1.25	.55
☐ 77 Dan Wilson	.15	.07
☐ 78 Paul Molitor	.60	.25
☐ 79 Kevin Seitzer	.15	.07
☐ 80 Kevin Brown	.30	.14
☐ 81 Ron Gant	.30	.14
☐ 82 Dwight Gooden	.30	.14
☐ 83 Todd Stottlemyre	.15	.07
☐ 84 Ken Caminiti	.60	.25
☐ 85 James Baldwin	.15	.07
☐ 86 Jermaine Dye	.15	.07
☐ 87 Harold Baines	.30	.14
☐ 88 Pat Hentgen	.30	.14
☐ 89 Frank Rodriguez	.15	.07
☐ 90 Mark Johnson	.15	.07
☐ 91 Jason Kendall	.30	.14
☐ 92 Alex Rodriguez	2.50	1.10
☐ 93 Alan Trammell	.40	.18
☐ 94 Scott Brosius	.15	.07
☐ 95 Delino DeShields	.15	.07
☐ 96 Chipper Jones	2.00	.90
☐ 97 Barry Bonds	.75	.35
☐ 98 Brady Anderson	.40	.18
☐ 99 Ryne Sandberg	.75	.35
☐ 100 Albert Belle	.75	.35
☐ 101 Jeff Cirillo	.30	.14
☐ 102 Frank Thomas	2.50	1.10
☐ 103 Mike Piazza	2.00	.90
☐ 104 Rickey Henderson	.40	.18
☐ 105 Rey Ordonez	.15	.07
☐ 106 Mark Grace	.40	.18
☐ 107 Terry Steinbach	.30	.14
☐ 108 Ray Durham	.15	.07
☐ 109 Barry Larkin	.40	.18
☐ 110 Tony Clark	.60	.25
☐ 111 Bernie Williams	.60	.25
☐ 112 John Smoltz	.60	.25
☐ 113 Moises Alou	.30	.14
☐ 114 Alex Gonzalez	.15	.07
☐ 115 Rico Brogna	.15	.07
☐ 116 Eric Karros	.30	.14
☐ 117 Jeff Conine	.30	.14
☐ 118 Todd Hollandsworth	.30	.14
☐ 119 Troy Percival	.30	.14
☐ 120 Paul Wilson	.15	.07
☐ 121 Orel Hershiser	.30	.14
☐ 122 Ozzie Smith	.75	.35
☐ 123 Dave Hollins	.15	.07
☐ 124 Ken Hill	.15	.07
☐ 125 Rick Wilkins	.15	.07
☐ 126 Scott Servais	.15	.07
☐ 127 Fernando Valenzuela	.30	.14
☐ 128 Mariano Rivera	.30	.14
☐ 129 Mark Loretta	.15	.07
☐ 130 Shane Reynolds	.15	.07
☐ 131 Darren Oliver	.15	.07
☐ 132 Steve Trachsel	.15	.07
☐ 133 Darren Bragg	.15	.07
☐ 134 Jason Dickson	.30	.14
☐ 135 Darrin Fletcher	.15	.07
☐ 136 Gary Gaetti	.30	.14
☐ 137 Joey Cora	.30	.14
☐ 138 Terry Pendleton	.15	.07
☐ 139 Derek Jeter	2.00	.90
☐ 140 Danny Tartabull	.15	.07
☐ 141 John Flaherty	.15	.07
☐ 142 B.J. Surhoff	.30	.14
☐ 143 Mike Sweeney	.30	.14
☐ 144 Chad Mottola	.15	.07
☐ 145 Andujar Cedeno	.15	.07
☐ 146 Tim Belcher	.15	.07
☐ 147 Mark Thompson	.15	.07
☐ 148 Rafael Bournigal	.15	.07
☐ 149 Marty Cordova	.30	.14
☐ 150 Osvaldo Fernandez	.15	.07
☐ 151 Mike Stanley	.15	.07
☐ 152 Ricky Bottalico	.30	.14
☐ 153 Donne Wall	.15	.07
☐ 154 Omar Vizquel	.30	.14
☐ 155 Mike Mussina	.60	.25
☐ 156 Brant Brown	.15	.07
☐ 157 F.P. Santangelo	.15	.07
☐ 158 Ryan Hancock	.15	.07
☐ 159 Jeff D'Amico	.30	.14
☐ 160 Luis Castillo	.15	.07
☐ 161 Darin Erstad	1.00	.45
☐ 162 Ugueth Urbina	.30	.14
☐ 163 Andruw Jones	1.50	.70
☐ 164 Steve Gibralter	.15	.07
☐ 165 Robin Jennings	.15	.07
☐ 166 Mike Cameron	.30	.14
☐ 167 George Arias	.15	.07
☐ 168 Chris Stynes	.15	.07
☐ 169 Justin Thompson	.30	.14
☐ 170 Jamey Wright	.30	.14
☐ 171 Todd Walker	.15	.07
☐ 172 Nomar Garciaparra	2.00	.90
☐ 173 Jose Paniagua	.15	.07
☐ 174 Marvin Benard	.15	.07
☐ 175 Rocky Coppinger	.30	.14
☐ 176 Quinton McCracken	.15	.07
☐ 177 Amaury Telemaco	.15	.07
☐ 178 Neifi Perez	.30	.14
☐ 179 Todd Greene	.30	.14
☐ 180 Jason Thompson	.15	.07
☐ 181 Wilton Guerrero	.15	.07
☐ 182 Edgar Renteria	.30	.14
☐ 183 Billy Wagner	.30	.14
☐ 184 Alex Ochoa	.15	.07
☐ 185 Dmitri Young	.30	.14
☐ 186 Kenny Lofton CT	.60	.25
☐ 187 Andres Galarraga CT	.40	.18
☐ 188 Chuck Knoblauch CT	.40	.18
☐ 189 Greg Maddux CT	2.00	.90
☐ 190 Mo Vaughn CT	.60	.25
☐ 191 Cal Ripken CT	2.50	1.10
☐ 192 Hideo Nomo CT	1.50	.70
☐ 193 Ken Griffey Jr. CT	3.00	1.35
☐ 194 Sammy Sosa CT	.60	.25
☐ 195 Jay Buhner CT	.40	.18
☐ 196 Manny Ramirez CT	.60	.25
☐ 197 Matt Williams CT	.40	.18
☐ 198 Andruw Jones CL	.75	.35
☐ 199 Darin Erstad CL	.60	.25
☐ 200 Trey Beamon CL	.15	.07

1997 Pinnacle Artist's Proofs

After three years of producing Artist's Proofs cards, Pinnacle decided to add some changes to their line of scarce parallel cards. Instead of the typical one per box parallel with a little foil logo on front the set was completely redesigned in 1997. Following a similar promotion run in the 1996 Finest brand, the 200-card first series set was broken down into three different groups of cards; 125 bronze, 50 silver and 25 gold. One in every 47 first series packs contained either a bronze, silver or gold Artist's Proofs card. The gold cards are scarcest (only 300 of each were produced), and silver cards are scarcer than bronze cards. Print runs for the bronze and silver cards were never announced. Each group of cards is easy to identify by their bold color-specific backgrounds (i.e. gold cards have gold backgrounds). All three groups share the same Artist's Proof logo on front.

	MINT	NRMT
COMPLETE SET (200)	3000.00	1350.00
COMP.BRONZE SET (125)	800.00	350.00
COMMON BRONZE	6.00	2.70
COMP.SILVER SET (50)	1000.00	450.00
COMMON SILVER	8.00	3.60
COMP.GOLD SET (25)	1200.00	550.00
COMMON GOLD	12.00	5.50

Card	MINT	NRMT
☐ 1 Cecil Fielder B	10.00	4.50
☐ 2 Garret Anderson B	10.00	4.50
☐ 3 Charles Nagy B	10.00	4.50
☐ 4 Darryl Hamilton B	6.00	2.70
☐ 5 Greg Myers B	6.00	2.70
☐ 6 Eric Davis B	10.00	4.50
☐ 7 Jeff Frye B	6.00	2.70
☐ 8 Marquis Grissom S	12.00	5.50
☐ 9 Curt Schilling B	10.00	4.50
☐ 10 Jeff Fassero B	6.00	2.70
☐ 11 Alan Benes S	12.00	5.50
☐ 12 Orlando Miller B	6.00	2.70
☐ 13 Alex Fernandez B	10.00	4.50
☐ 14 Andy Pettitte G	40.00	18.00
☐ 15 Andre Dawson B	15.00	6.75
☐ 16 Mark Grudzielanek B	10.00	4.50
☐ 17 Joe Vitiello B	6.00	2.70
☐ 18 Juan Gonzalez G	100.00	45.00
☐ 19 Mark Whiten B	6.00	2.70
☐ 20 Lance Johnson B	6.00	2.70
☐ 21 Trevor Hoffman B	10.00	4.50
☐ 22 Marc Newfield B	6.00	2.70
☐ 23 Jim Eisenreich B	6.00	2.70
☐ 24 Joe Carter S	12.00	5.50
☐ 25 Jose Canseco S	20.00	9.00
☐ 26 Bill Swift B	6.00	2.70
☐ 27 Ellis Burks B	10.00	4.50
☐ 28 Ben McDonald B	6.00	2.70
☐ 29 Edgar Martinez S	20.00	9.00
☐ 30 Jamie Moyer B	6.00	2.70
☐ 31 Chan Ho Park S	30.00	13.50
☐ 32 Carlos Delgado S	12.00	5.50
☐ 33 Kevin Mitchell B	6.00	2.70
☐ 34 Carlos Garcia B	6.00	2.70
☐ 35 Darryl Strawberry G	15.00	6.75
☐ 36 Jim Thome G	40.00	18.00
☐ 37 Jose Offerman B	6.00	2.70
☐ 38 Ryan Klesko S	20.00	9.00
☐ 39 Ruben Sierra B	6.00	2.70
☐ 40 Devon White B	6.00	2.70
☐ 41 Brian Jordan G	15.00	6.75
☐ 42 Tony Gwynn S	80.00	36.00
☐ 43 Rafael Palmeiro S	20.00	9.00
☐ 44 Dante Bichette B	10.00	4.50
☐ 45 Scott Stahoviak B	6.00	2.70
☐ 46 Roger Cedeno B	10.00	4.50
☐ 47 Ivan Rodriguez G	50.00	22.00
☐ 48 Bob Abreu S	12.00	5.50
☐ 49 Darryl Kile B	10.00	4.50
☐ 50 Darren Dreifort B	6.00	2.70
☐ 51 Shawon Dunston B	6.00	2.70
☐ 52 Mark McGwire S	60.00	27.00
☐ 53 Tim Salmon S	30.00	13.50
☐ 54 Gene Schall B	6.00	2.70
☐ 55 Roger Clemens B	50.00	22.00
☐ 56 Rondell White S	12.00	5.50
☐ 57 Ed Sprague B	6.00	2.70
☐ 58 Craig Paquette B	6.00	2.70
☐ 59 David Segui B	6.00	2.70
☐ 60 Jaime Navarro B	6.00	2.70
☐ 61 Tom Glavine S	12.00	5.50
☐ 62 Jeff Brantley B	6.00	2.70
☐ 63 Kimera Bartee B	6.00	2.70
☐ 64 Fernando Vina B	6.00	2.70
☐ 65 Eddie Murray S	30.00	13.50
☐ 66 Lenny Dykstra B	10.00	4.50
☐ 67 Kevin Elster B	6.00	2.70
☐ 68 Vinny Castilla B	10.00	4.50
☐ 69 Mike Fetters S	8.00	3.60
☐ 70 Brett Butler B	10.00	4.50
☐ 71 Robby Thompson B	6.00	2.70
☐ 72 Reggie Jefferson B	10.00	4.50
☐ 73 Todd Hundley S	12.00	5.50
☐ 74 Jeff King B	10.00	4.50
☐ 75 Ernie Young S	8.00	3.60
☐ 76 Jeff Bagwell G	80.00	36.00
☐ 77 Dan Wilson B	10.00	4.50
☐ 78 Paul Molitor G	40.00	18.00
☐ 79 Kevin Seitzer B	6.00	2.70
☐ 80 Kevin Brown S	12.00	5.50

Card	MINT	NRMT
☐ 81 Ron Gant S	12.00	5.50
☐ 82 Dwight Gooden S	12.00	5.50
☐ 83 Todd Stottlemyre B	6.00	2.70
☐ 84 Ken Caminiti G	25.00	11.00
☐ 85 James Baldwin B	6.00	2.70
☐ 86 Jermaine Dye S	12.00	5.50
☐ 87 Harold Baines B	10.00	4.50
☐ 88 Pat Hentgen B	10.00	4.50
☐ 89 Frank Rodriguez B	6.00	2.70
☐ 90 Mark Johnson B	6.00	2.70
☐ 91 Jason Kendall S	12.00	5.50
☐ 92 Alex Rodriguez G	120.00	55.00
☐ 93 Alan Trammell B	10.00	4.50
☐ 94 Scott Brosius B	6.00	2.70
☐ 95 Delino DeShields B	6.00	2.70
☐ 96 Chipper Jones S	80.00	36.00
☐ 97 Barry Bonds S	40.00	18.00
☐ 98 Brady Anderson S	20.00	9.00
☐ 99 Ryne Sandberg S	40.00	18.00
☐ 100 Albert Belle G	50.00	22.00
☐ 101 Jeff Cirillo B	10.00	4.50
☐ 102 Frank Thomas G	150.00	70.00
☐ 103 Mike Piazza S	100.00	45.00
☐ 104 Rickey Henderson B	15.00	6.75
☐ 105 Rey Ordonez S	12.00	5.50
☐ 106 Mark Grace S	20.00	9.00
☐ 107 Terry Steinbach B	10.00	4.50
☐ 108 Ray Durham B	10.00	4.50
☐ 109 Barry Larkin S	20.00	9.00
☐ 110 Tony Clark S	30.00	13.50
☐ 111 Bernie Williams G	40.00	18.00
☐ 112 John Smoltz G	15.00	6.75
☐ 113 Moises Alou B	10.00	4.50
☐ 114 Alex Gonzalez B	6.00	2.70
☐ 115 Rico Brogna B	6.00	2.70
☐ 116 Eric Karros B	10.00	4.50
☐ 117 Jeff Conine S	12.00	5.50
☐ 118 Todd Hollandsworth G	12.00	5.50
☐ 119 Troy Percival S	8.00	3.60
☐ 120 Paul Wilson S	8.00	3.60
☐ 121 Orel Hershiser B	10.00	4.50
☐ 122 Ozzie Smith S	40.00	18.00
☐ 123 Dave Hollins B	6.00	2.70
☐ 124 Ken Hill B	6.00	2.70
☐ 125 Rick Wilkins B	6.00	2.70
☐ 126 Scott Servais B	6.00	2.70
☐ 127 Fernando Valenzuela B	10.00	4.50
☐ 128 Mariano Rivera G	15.00	6.75
☐ 129 Mark Loretta B	6.00	2.70
☐ 130 Shane Reynolds S	8.00	3.60
☐ 131 Darren Oliver B	6.00	2.70
☐ 132 Steve Trachsel B	6.00	2.70
☐ 133 Darren Bragg B	6.00	2.70
☐ 134 Jason Dickson B	10.00	4.50
☐ 135 Darren Fletcher B	6.00	2.70
☐ 136 Gary Gaetti B	6.00	2.70
☐ 137 Joey Cora B	10.00	4.50
☐ 138 Terry Pendleton B	10.00	4.50
☐ 139 Derek Jeter G	100.00	45.00
☐ 140 Danny Tartabull B	6.00	2.70
☐ 141 John Flaherty B	6.00	2.70
☐ 142 B.J. Surhoff B	6.00	2.70
☐ 143 Mark Sweeney B	6.00	2.70
☐ 144 Chad Mottola B	6.00	2.70
☐ 145 Andujar Cedeno B	6.00	2.70
☐ 146 Tim Belcher B	6.00	2.70
☐ 147 Mark Thompson B	6.00	2.70
☐ 148 Rafael Bournigal B	6.00	2.70
☐ 149 Marty Cordova S	12.00	5.50
☐ 150 Osvaldo Fernandez B	6.00	2.70
☐ 151 Mike Stanley B	6.00	2.70
☐ 152 Ricky Bottalico B	10.00	4.50
☐ 153 Donne Wall B	6.00	2.70
☐ 154 Omar Vizquel B	10.00	4.50
☐ 155 Mike Mussina S	30.00	13.50
☐ 156 Brant Brown B	6.00	2.70
☐ 157 F.P. Santangelo S	8.00	3.60
☐ 158 Ryan Hancock B	6.00	2.70
☐ 159 Jeff D'Amico B	10.00	4.50
☐ 160 Luis Castillo B	10.00	4.50
☐ 161 Darin Erstad G	50.00	22.00
☐ 162 Ugueth Urbina B	6.00	2.70
☐ 163 Andruw Jones G	80.00	36.00
☐ 164 Steve Gibralter B	6.00	2.70
☐ 165 Robin Jennings S	8.00	3.60
☐ 166 Mike Cameron B	15.00	6.75
☐ 167 George Arias S	8.00	3.60
☐ 168 Chris Stynes B	6.00	2.70
☐ 169 Justin Thompson B	15.00	6.75
☐ 170 Jamey Wright B	6.00	2.70
☐ 171 Todd Walker G	15.00	6.75
☐ 172 Nomar Garciaparra B	60.00	27.00
☐ 173 Jose Paniagua B	6.00	2.70
☐ 174 Marvin Benard B	6.00	2.70
☐ 175 Rocky Coppinger B	6.00	2.70
☐ 176 Quinton McCracken B	6.00	2.70
☐ 177 Amaury Telemaco B	10.00	4.50
☐ 178 Neifi Perez B	10.00	4.50
☐ 179 Todd Greene B	10.00	4.50
☐ 180 Jason Thompson B	6.00	2.70
☐ 181 Wilton Guerrero B	6.00	2.70
☐ 182 Edgar Renteria S	12.00	5.50
☐ 183 Billy Wagner S	12.00	5.50
☐ 184 Alex Ochoa G	12.00	5.50
☐ 185 Dmitri Young B	10.00	4.50
☐ 186 Kenny Lofton CT B	30.00	13.50
☐ 187 Andres Galarraga CT B	25.00	11.00
☐ 188 Chuck Knoblauch CT G	40.00	18.00
☐ 189 Greg Maddux CT S	100.00	45.00
☐ 190 Mo Vaughn CT S	40.00	18.00
☐ 191 Cal Ripken CT G	150.00	70.00
☐ 192 Hideo Nomo CT S	100.00	45.00
☐ 193 Ken Griffey Jr. CT G	200.00	90.00
☐ 194 Sammy Sosa CT S	30.00	13.50
☐ 195 Jay Buhner CT S	20.00	9.00
☐ 196 Manny Ramirez CT G	40.00	18.00
☐ 197 Matt Williams CT B	15.00	6.75
☐ 198 Andruw Jones CL B	40.00	18.00
☐ 199 Darin Erstad CL B	25.00	11.00
☐ 200 Trey Beamon CL B	6.00	2.70

1997 Pinnacle Museum Collection

Randomly inserted in all packs at a rate of one in nine, these cards parallel the regular issue. Etched foil fronts differentiate them.

	MINT	NRMT
COMPLETE SERIES 1 (200)	600.00	275.00
COMMON CARD (1-200)	1.50	.70
*STARS: 6X TO 12X BASIC CARDS		
*YOUNG STARS: 5X TO 10X BASIC CARDS		

1997 Pinnacle Cardfrontations

Randomly inserted in hobby packs only at a rate of one in 23, this 20-card set displays color player photos on rainbow holographic foil. The card design features a top pitcher on one side with a top home run hitter on the flip side. Both sides are covered with an opaque peel and reveal protective cover.

	MINT	NRMT
COMPLETE SET (20)	250.00	110.00
COMMON CARD (1-20)	5.00	2.20
☐ 1 Greg Maddux Mike Piazza	25.00	11.00
☐ 2 Tom Glavine Ken Caminiti	6.00	2.70
☐ 3 Randy Johnson Cal Ripken	30.00	13.50
☐ 4 Kevin Appier Mark McGwire	15.00	6.75
☐ 5 Andy Pettitte Juan Gonzalez	20.00	9.00
☐ 6 Pat Hentgen Albert Belle	12.00	5.50
☐ 7 Hideo Nomo Chipper Jones	25.00	11.00
☐ 8 Ismael Valdes Sammy Sosa	5.00	2.20
☐ 9 Mike Mussina Manny Ramirez	10.00	4.50
☐ 10 David Cone Jay Buhner	5.00	2.20
☐ 11 Mark Wohlers Gary Sheffield	5.00	2.20
☐ 12 Alan Benes Barry Bonds	10.00	4.50
☐ 13 Roger Clemens Ivan Rodriguez	12.00	5.50
☐ 14 Mariano Rivera Ken Griffey Jr.	40.00	18.00
☐ 15 Dwight Gooden Frank Thomas	30.00	13.50
☐ 16 John Wetteland Darin Erstad	12.00	5.50
☐ 17 John Smoltz Brian Jordan	5.00	2.20
☐ 18 Kevin Brown Jeff Bagwell	15.00	6.75
☐ 19 Jack McDowell Alex Rodriguez	30.00	13.50
☐ 20 Charles Nagy Bernie Williams	6.00	2.70

1997 Pinnacle Home/Away

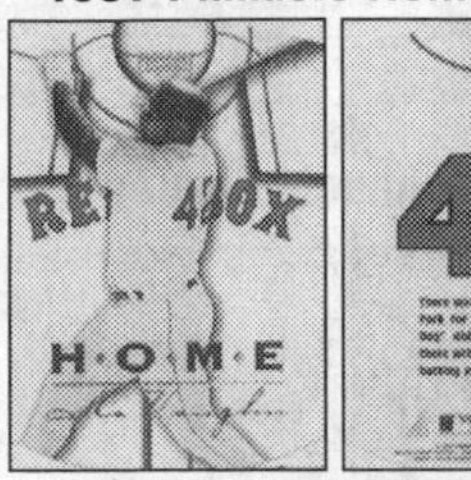

Randomly inserted in only jumbo packs at a rate of one in 33, this 24-card set features color player photos on die-cut cards. The cards were designed and shaped to resemble a player's actual jersey.

	MINT	NRMT
COMPLETE SET (24)	400.00	180.00
COMMON CARD (1-24)	8.00	3.60
☐ 1 Chipper Jones Away	20.00	9.00
☐ 2 Chipper Jones Home	20.00	9.00
☐ 3 Ken Griffey Jr. Away	30.00	13.50
☐ 4 Ken Griffey Jr. Home	30.00	13.50
☐ 5 Mike Piazza Away	20.00	9.00
☐ 6 Mike Piazza Home	20.00	9.00
☐ 7 Frank Thomas Away	25.00	11.00
☐ 8 Frank Thomas Home	25.00	11.00
☐ 9 Jeff Bagwell Away	12.00	5.50
☐ 10 Jeff Bagwell Home	12.00	5.50
☐ 11 Alex Rodriguez Away	20.00	9.00
☐ 12 Alex Rodriguez Home	30.00	13.50
☐ 13 Barry Bonds Away	8.00	3.60
☐ 14 Barry Bonds Home	8.00	3.60
☐ 15 Mo Vaughn Away	8.00	3.60
☐ 16 Mo Vaughn Home	8.00	3.60
☐ 17 Derek Jeter Away	15.00	6.75
☐ 18 Derek Jeter Home	15.00	6.75
☐ 19 Mark McGwire Away	12.00	5.50
☐ 20 Mark McGwire Home	15.00	6.75
☐ 21 Cal Ripken Away	25.00	11.00
☐ 22 Cal Ripken Home	25.00	11.00
☐ 23 Albert Belle Away	8.00	3.60
☐ 24 Albert Belle Home	8.00	3.60

1997 Pinnacle Passport to the Majors

Randomly inserted in all first series packs at a rate of one in 36, this 25-card set features color player photos on a bookfold miniature passport card design and honors the rise to fame of some of the League's most high profile superstars.

	MINT	NRMT
COMPLETE SET (25)	300.00	135.00
COMMON CARD (1-25)	4.00	1.80
☐ 1 Greg Maddux	25.00	11.00
☐ 2 Ken Griffey Jr.	40.00	18.00
☐ 3 Frank Thomas	30.00	13.50
☐ 4 Cal Ripken	30.00	13.50
☐ 5 Mike Piazza	25.00	11.00
☐ 6 Alex Rodriguez	25.00	11.00
☐ 7 Mo Vaughn	10.00	4.50
☐ 8 Chipper Jones	25.00	11.00
☐ 9 Roberto Alomar	8.00	3.60
☐ 10 Edgar Martinez	5.00	2.20
☐ 11 Javier Lopez	4.50	2.00
☐ 12 Ivan Rodriguez	10.00	4.50
☐ 13 Juan Gonzalez	20.00	9.00
☐ 14 Carlos Baerga	4.00	1.80
☐ 15 Sammy Sosa	8.00	3.60

	MINT	NRMT
☐ 16 Manny Ramirez	10.00	4.50
☐ 17 Raul Mondesi	5.00	2.20
☐ 18 Henry Rodriguez	4.00	1.80
☐ 19 Rafael Palmeiro	5.00	2.20
☐ 20 Rey Ordonez	4.00	1.80
☐ 21 Hideo Nomo	20.00	9.00
☐ 22 Mac Suzuki	4.50	2.00
☐ 23 Chan Ho Park	8.00	3.60
☐ 24 Larry Walker	4.00	1.80
☐ 25 Ruben Rivera	4.00	1.80

1997 Pinnacle Shades

Randomly inserted in magazine packs at a rate of one in 23, this 10-card set features color upclose photos of some of the league's best players wearing their favorite pair of sunglasses. The cards have a die-cut design and mirror mylar finish.

	MINT	NRMT
COMPLETE SET (10)	120.00	55.00
COMMON CARD (1-10)	2.50	1.10
☐ 1 Ken Griffey Jr.	25.00	11.00
☐ 2 Juan Gonzalez	12.00	5.50
☐ 3 John Smoltz	2.50	1.10
☐ 4 Gary Sheffield	4.00	1.80
☐ 5 Cal Ripken	20.00	9.00
☐ 6 Mo Vaughn	6.00	2.70
☐ 7 Brian Jordan	2.50	1.10
☐ 8 Mike Piazza	15.00	6.75
☐ 9 Frank Thomas	20.00	9.00
☐ 10 Alex Rodriguez	20.00	9.00

1997 Pinnacle Team Pinnacle

Randomly inserted in packs at a rate of one in 90, this 10-card set matches color player photos of the top American and National League players by position on double-fronted, all-foil Dufex cards. The tenth card is a computer design that makes a full Team Pinnacle picture.

	MINT	NRMT
COMPLETE SET (10)	300.00	135.00
COMMON CARD (1-10)	10.00	4.50
☐ 1 Frank Thomas Jeff Bagwell	40.00	18.00
☐ 2 Chuck Knoblauch Eric Young	10.00	4.50
☐ 3 Ken Caminiti Jim Thome	12.00	5.50
☐ 4 Alex Rodriguez Chipper Jones	50.00	22.00
☐ 5 Mike Piazza Ivan Rodriguez	40.00	18.00
☐ 6 Albert Belle Barry Bonds	20.00	9.00
☐ 7 Ken Griffey Jr. Ellis Burks	50.00	22.00
☐ 8 Juan Gonzalez Gary Sheffield	30.00	13.50
☐ 9 John Smoltz Andy Pettitte	12.00	5.50
☐ 10 Frank Thomas Jeff Bagwell Chuck Knoblauch	40.00	18.00

Eric Young
Ken Caminiti
Jim Thome
Alex Rodriguez
Chipper Jones
Mike Piazza
Ivan Rodriguez
Albert Belle
Barry Bonds
Ken Griffey Jr.
Ellis Burks
Juan Gonzalez
Gary Sheffield
John Smoltz
Andy Pettitte

1997 Pinnacle All-Star FanFest Promos

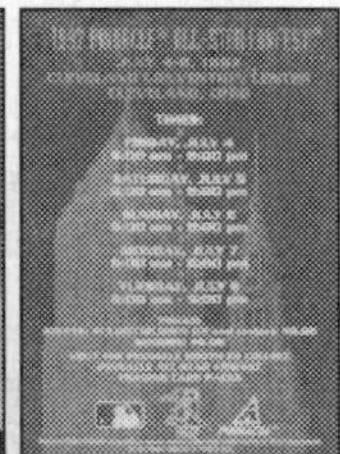

This set of seven cards was issued at the Pinnacle all-Star Fanfest held in Cleveland, Ohio, on July 4-8, 1997. The cards feature the same design as the Pinnacle FanFest set. The fronts display color action player photos with gold foil enhancements. The backs carry a schedule of the times for FanFest. Card #2 differs in that the player photo is in black and White, and the back displays information about the player. The cards are unnumbered and checklisted below alphabetically.

	MINT	NRMT
COMPLETE SET (7)	15.00	6.75
COMMON CARD (1-7)	1.00	.45
☐ 1 Roger Clemens	3.00	1.35
☐ 2 Larry Doby	2.00	.90
☐ 3 Greg Maddux	4.00	1.80
☐ 4 Hideo Nomo	4.00	1.80
☐ 5 Andy Pettitte	1.00	.45
☐ 6 Mike Piazza	4.00	1.80
☐ 7 Ivan Rodriguez	1.50	.70

1997 Pinnacle FanFest

This 21-card set was issued by Pinnacle in conjunction with the 1997 Pinnacle All-Star FanFest held in Cleveland, Ohio, July 4-8, 1997 at the Convention Center. The set was issued in three-card packs and features borderless color action player photos with gold foil stamping. The backs carry a player portrait in a star with player information and statistics printed on a black-and-gray city silhouetted background. Card #21 could only be obtained with a redemption card at the locations listed on the card's back. The Alomar card is not considered part of the complete set. Twelve other cards with the same design were also issued by Pinnacle as part of the celebration. These twelve cards feature different personalities involved in the show or with the Cleveland Indians. These 12 cards are not considered part of the Fan Fest set and are not included in the complete set price.

	MINT	NRMT
COMPLETE SET (20)	25.00	11.00
COMMON CARD (FF1-FF20)	.50	.23
COMMON PC CARD	5.00	2.20
☐ FF1 Frank Thomas	4.00	1.80
☐ FF2 Jeff Bagwell	2.00	.90
☐ FF3 Chuck Knoblauch	1.25	.55
☐ FF4 Craig Biggio	.50	.23
☐ FF5 Alex Rodriguez	4.00	1.80
☐ FF6 Chipper Jones	3.00	1.35
☐ FF7 Cal Ripken	4.00	1.80
☐ FF8 Ken Caminiti	1.25	.55
☐ FF9 Juan Gonzalez	2.00	.90
☐ FF10 Barry Bonds	1.50	.70
☐ FF11 Ken Griffey Jr.	5.00	2.20
☐ FF12 Andruw Jones	1.50	.70
☐ FF13 Manny Ramirez	1.25	.55
☐ FF14 Tony Gwynn	2.50	1.10
☐ FF15 Ivan Rodriguez	1.50	.70
☐ FF16 Mike Piazza	4.00	1.80
☐ FF17 Andy Pettitte	1.25	.55
☐ FF18 Hideo Nomo	2.50	1.10
☐ FF19 Roger Clemens	2.00	.90
☐ FF20 Greg Maddux	3.00	1.35
☐ FF21 Sandy Alomar SP	10.00	4.50
☐ PC1 Macie McInnis	5.00	2.20
☐ PC2 Bill Martin	5.00	2.20
☐ PC3 Dick Goddard	5.00	2.20
☐ PC4 Jack Corrigan ANN	5.00	2.20
☐ PC5 Mike Hegan ANN	7.50	3.40
☐ PC6 Rick Manning ANN	10.00	4.50
☐ PC7 John Sanders ANN	5.00	2.20
☐ PC8 Michael R. White Mayor	5.00	2.20
☐ PC9 Wilma Smith	5.00	2.20
☐ PC10 Tim Taylor	5.00	2.20
☐ PC11 Robin Swoboda	5.00	2.20
☐ PC12 Slider	7.50	3.40

1998 Pinnacle

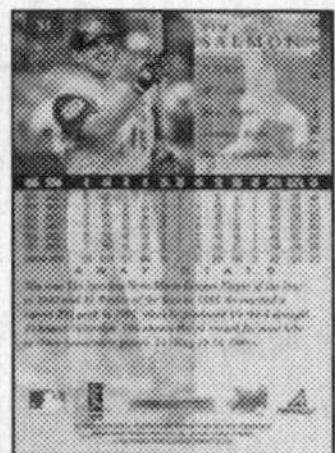

The 1998 Pinnacle set was issued in one series totalling 200 cards and was distributed in 10-card packs with a suggested retail price of $2.99. The fronts feature borderless color player photos with player information on the backs. The set contains the following subsets: Rookies (158-181), Field of Vision (182-187), Goin' Jake (188-197) and Checklists (198-200). Three variations of each card from 1-157 were made. They have home, away and seasonal stats on the back and were all produced in equal quantity.

	MINT	NRMT
COMPLETE SET (200)	30.00	13.50
COMMON CARD (1-200)	.15	.07
☐ 1 Tony Gwynn	1.50	.70
☐ 2 Pedro Martinez	.60	.25
☐ 3 Kenny Lofton	.75	.35
☐ 4 Curt Schilling	.30	.14
☐ 5 Shawn Estes	.30	.14
☐ 6 Tom Glavine	.30	.14
☐ 7 Mike Piazza	2.00	.90
☐ 8 Ray Lankford	.30	.14
☐ 9 Barry Larkin	.40	.18
☐ 10 Tony Womack	.15	.07
☐ 11 Jeff Blauser	.15	.07
☐ 12 Rod Beck	.30	.14
☐ 13 Larry Walker	.60	.25
☐ 14 Greg Maddux	2.00	.90
☐ 15 Mark Grace	.40	.18
☐ 16 Ken Caminiti	.60	.25
☐ 17 Bobby Jones	.30	.14
☐ 18 Chipper Jones	2.00	.90
☐ 19 Javier Lopez	.30	.14
☐ 20 Moises Alou	.30	.14
☐ 21 Royce Clayton	.15	.07
☐ 22 Darryl Kile	.30	.14
☐ 23 Barry Bonds	.75	.35
☐ 24 Steve Finley	.30	.14
☐ 25 Andres Galarraga	.60	.25
☐ 26 Denny Neagle	.30	.14
☐ 27 Todd Hundley	.30	.14
☐ 28 Jeff Bagwell	1.25	.55
☐ 29 Andy Pettitte	.60	.25
☐ 30 Darin Erstad	.75	.35
☐ 31 Carlos Delgado	.30	.14
☐ 32 Matt Williams	.40	.18

☐ 33 Will Clark .40 .18
☐ 34 Vinny Castilla .30 .14
☐ 35 Brad Radke .30 .14
☐ 36 John Olerud .30 .14
☐ 37 Andruw Jones 1.25 .55
☐ 38 Jason Giambi .30 .14
☐ 39 Scott Rolen 1.50 .70
☐ 40 Gary Sheffield .60 .25
☐ 41 Jimmy Key .30 .14
☐ 42 Kevin Appier .30 .14
☐ 43 Wade Boggs .60 .25
☐ 44 Hideo Nomo 1.50 .70
☐ 45 Manny Ramirez .60 .25
☐ 46 Wilton Guerrero .15 .07
☐ 47 Travis Fryman .30 .14
☐ 48 Chili Davis .30 .14
☐ 49 Jeromy Burnitz .30 .14
☐ 50 Craig Biggio .40 .18
☐ 51 Tim Salmon .60 .25
☐ 52 Jose Cruz Jr. 2.50 1.10
☐ 53 Sammy Sosa .60 .25
☐ 54 Hideki Irabu .40 .18
☐ 55 Chan Ho Park .60 .25
☐ 56 Robin Ventura .30 .14
☐ 57 Jose Guillen .30 .14
☐ 58 Deion Sanders .60 .25
☐ 59 Jose Canseco .40 .18
☐ 60 Jay Buhner .40 .18
☐ 61 Rafael Palmeiro .40 .18
☐ 62 Vladimir Guerrero 1.00 .45
☐ 63 Mark McGwire 1.50 .70
☐ 64 Derek Jeter 1.50 .70
☐ 65 Bobby Bonilla .30 .14
☐ 66 Raul Mondesi .60 .25
☐ 67 Paul Molitor .60 .25
☐ 68 Joe Carter .30 .14
☐ 69 Marquis Grissom .30 .14
☐ 70 Juan Gonzalez 1.50 .70
☐ 71 Kevin Orie .30 .14
☐ 72 Rusty Greer .30 .14
☐ 73 Henry Rodriguez .15 .07
☐ 74 Fernando Tatis .30 .14
☐ 75 John Valentin .30 .14
☐ 76 Matt Morris .30 .14
☐ 77 Ray Durham .30 .14
☐ 78 Geronimo Berroa .15 .07
☐ 79 Scott Brosius .15 .07
☐ 80 Willie Greene .30 .14
☐ 81 Rondell White .30 .14
☐ 82 Doug Drabek .15 .07
☐ 83 Derek Bell .15 .07
☐ 84 Butch Huskey .30 .14
☐ 85 Doug Jones .30 .14
☐ 86 Jeff Kent .30 .14
☐ 87 Jim Edmonds .60 .25
☐ 88 Mark McLemore .15 .07
☐ 89 Todd Zeile .30 .14
☐ 90 Edgardo Alfonzo .30 .14
☐ 91 Carlos Baerga .30 .14
☐ 92 Jorge Fabregas .15 .07
☐ 93 Alan Benes .15 .07
☐ 94 Troy Percival .30 .14
☐ 95 Edgar Renteria .30 .14
☐ 96 Jeff Fassero .15 .07
☐ 97 Reggie Sanders .15 .07
☐ 98 Dean Palmer .30 .14
☐ 99 J.T. Snow .30 .14
☐ 100 Dave Nilsson .30 .14
☐ 101 Dan Wilson .15 .07
☐ 102 Robb Nen .30 .14
☐ 103 Damion Easley .15 .07
☐ 104 Kevin Foster .15 .07
☐ 105 Jose Offerman .15 .07
☐ 106 Steve Cooke .15 .07
☐ 107 Matt Stairs .15 .07
☐ 108 Darryl Hamilton .15 .07
☐ 109 Steve Karsay .15 .07
☐ 110 Gary DiSarcina .15 .07
☐ 111 Dante Bichette .30 .14
☐ 112 Billy Wagner .30 .14
☐ 113 David Segui .15 .07
☐ 114 Bobby Higginson .30 .14
☐ 115 Jeffrey Hammonds .30 .14
☐ 116 Kevin Brown .30 .14
☐ 117 Paul Sorrento .15 .07
☐ 118 Mark Leiter .15 .07
☐ 119 Charles Nagy .15 .07
☐ 120 Danny Patterson .15 .07
☐ 121 Brian McRae .15 .07
☐ 122 Jay Bell .15 .07
☐ 123 Jamie Moyer .15 .07
☐ 124 Carl Everett .15 .07
☐ 125 Greg Colbrunn .15 .07
☐ 126 Jason Kendall .15 .07
☐ 127 Luis Sojo .15 .07
☐ 128 Mike Lieberthal .15 .07
☐ 129 Reggie Jefferson .30 .14
☐ 130 Cal Eldred .15 .07
☐ 131 Orel Hershiser .30 .14
☐ 132 Doug Glanville .15 .07
☐ 133 Willie Blair .15 .07
☐ 134 Neifi Perez .15 .07
☐ 135 Sean Berry .15 .07
☐ 136 Chuck Finley .15 .07
☐ 137 Alex Gonzalez .15 .07
☐ 138 Dennis Eckersley .40 .18
☐ 139 Kenny Rogers .15 .07
☐ 140 Troy O'Leary .15 .07
☐ 141 Roger Bailey .15 .07
☐ 142 Yamil Benitez .15 .07
☐ 143 Wally Joyner .30 .14
☐ 144 Bobby Witt .15 .07
☐ 145 Pete Schourek .15 .07
☐ 146 Terry Steinbach .15 .07
☐ 147 B.J. Surhoff .15 .07
☐ 148 Esteban Loaiza .15 .07
☐ 149 Heathcliff Slocumb .15 .07
☐ 150 Ed Sprague .15 .07
☐ 151 Gregg Jefferies .15 .07
☐ 152 Scott Erickson .15 .07
☐ 153 Jaime Navarro .15 .07
☐ 154 David Wells .15 .07
☐ 155 Alex Fernandez .15 .07
☐ 156 Tim Belcher .15 .07
☐ 157 Mark Grudzielanek .15 .07
☐ 158 Scott Hatteberg .15 .07
☐ 159 Paul Konerko 1.00 .45
☐ 160 Ben Grieve 1.25 .55
☐ 161 Abraham Nunez .60 .25
☐ 162 Shannon Stewart .30 .14
☐ 163 Jaret Wright 1.50 .70
☐ 164 Derrek Lee .30 .14
☐ 165 Todd Dunwoody .30 .14
☐ 166 Steve Woodard .15 .07
☐ 167 Ryan McGuire .15 .07
☐ 168 Jeremi Gonzalez .30 .14
☐ 169 Mark Kotsay .40 .18
☐ 170 Brett Tomko .30 .14
☐ 171 Bobby Estalella .30 .14
☐ 172 Livan Hernandez .30 .14
☐ 173 Todd Helton .75 .35
☐ 174 Garrett Stephenson .15 .07
☐ 175 Pokey Reese .15 .07
☐ 176 Tony Saunders .15 .07
☐ 177 Antone Williamson .15 .07
☐ 178 Bartolo Colon .15 .07
☐ 179 Karim Garcia .15 .07
☐ 180 Juan Encarnacion .30 .14
☐ 181 Jacob Cruz .15 .07
☐ 182 Alex Rodriguez FV 1.00 .45
☐ 183 Cal Ripken FV .75 .35
Roberto Alomar
☐ 184 Roger Clemens FV .60 .25
☐ 185 Derek Jeter FV .75 .35
☐ 186 Frank Thomas FV 1.25 .55
☐ 187 Ken Griffey Jr. FV 1.50 .70
☐ 188 Mark McGwire GJ .75 .35
☐ 189 Tino Martinez GJ .40 .18
☐ 190 Larry Walker GJ .60 .25
☐ 191 Brady Anderson GJ .30 .14
☐ 192 Jeff Bagwell GJ .60 .25
☐ 193 Ken Griffey Jr. GJ 1.50 .70
☐ 194 Chipper Jones GJ 1.00 .45
☐ 195 Ray Lankford GJ .30 .14
☐ 196 Jim Thome GJ .60 .25
☐ 197 Nomar Garciaparra GJ 1.00 .45
☐ 198 All-Star Game Home Run Contestants .75 .35
Brady Anderson
Jeff Bagwell
Nomar Garciaparra
Ken Griffey Jr.
Chipper Jones
Ray Lankford
Tino Martinez
Mark McGwire
Jim Thome
Larry Walker
☐ 199 Tino Martinez CL .60 .25
☐ 200 Jacob's Field CL .15 .07
☐ P5 Barry Bonds PROMO 3.00 1.35
☐ P9 Juan Gonzalez PROMO 4.00 1.80
☐ P10 Jeff Bagwell PROMO 4.00 1.80

1998 Pinnacle Artist's Proofs

Only the top 100 cards from the regular issue of the 1998 Pinnacle set were selected for inclusion in this year's Artist's Proofs gold-foil Dufex partial parallel version. The cards were randomly seeded into packs at a rate of 1:39.

	MINT	NRMT
COMPLETE SET (100)	1500.00	700.00
COMMON CARD (PP1-PP100)	5.00	2.20

*STARS: 15X TO 30X BASIC CARDS
*YOUNG STARS: 12.5X TO 25X BASIC CARDS

1998 Pinnacle Museum Collection

Only the top 100 cards from the regular issue 1998 Pinnacle set were selected for inclusion in this year's Museum Collection all-foil Dufex partial parallel version. The cards were randomly seeded into packs at a rate of 1:9.

	MINT	NRMT
COMPLETE SET (100)	600.00	275.00
COMMON CARD (PP1-PP100)	2.00	.90

☐ PP1 Tony Gwynn 20.00 9.00
☐ PP2 Pedro Martinez 8.00 3.60
☐ PP3 Kenny Lofton 10.00 4.50
☐ PP4 Curt Schilling 3.00 1.35
☐ PP5 Shawn Estes 3.00 1.35
☐ PP6 Tom Glavine 3.00 1.35
☐ PP7 Mike Piazza 25.00 11.00
☐ PP8 Ray Lankford 3.00 1.35
☐ PP9 Barry Larkin 5.00 2.20
☐ PP10 Tony Womack 2.00 .90
☐ PP11 Jeff Blauser 3.00 1.35
☐ PP12 Rod Beck 3.00 1.35
☐ PP13 Larry Walker 8.00 3.60
☐ PP14 Greg Maddux 25.00 11.00
☐ PP15 Mark Grace 5.00 2.20
☐ PP16 Ken Caminiti 5.00 2.20
☐ PP17 Bobby Jones 2.00 .90
☐ PP18 Chipper Jones 20.00 9.00
☐ PP19 Javier Lopez 3.00 1.35
☐ PP20 Moises Alou 3.00 1.35
☐ PP21 Royce Clayton 2.00 .90
☐ PP22 Darryl Kile 3.00 1.35
☐ PP23 Barry Bonds 10.00 4.50
☐ PP24 Steve Finley 3.00 1.35
☐ PP25 Andres Galarraga 8.00 3.60
☐ PP26 Denny Neagle 3.00 1.35
☐ PP27 Todd Hundley 3.00 1.35
☐ PP28 Jeff Bagwell 15.00 6.75
☐ PP29 Andy Pettitte 8.00 3.60
☐ PP30 Darin Erstad 8.00 3.60
☐ PP31 Carlos Delgado 3.00 1.35
☐ PP32 Matt Williams 5.00 2.20
☐ PP33 Will Clark 5.00 2.20
☐ PP34 Brad Radke 3.00 1.35
☐ PP35 John Olerud 3.00 1.35
☐ PP36 Andruw Jones 12.00 5.50
☐ PP37 Scott Rolen 15.00 6.75
☐ PP38 Gary Sheffield 8.00 3.60
☐ PP39 Jimmy Key 3.00 1.35
☐ PP40 Wade Boggs 8.00 3.60
☐ PP41 Hideo Nomo 20.00 9.00
☐ PP42 Manny Ramirez 8.00 3.60
☐ PP43 Wilton Guerrero 2.00 .90
☐ PP44 Travis Fryman 3.00 1.35
☐ PP45 Craig Biggio 5.00 2.20
☐ PP46 Tim Salmon 8.00 3.60
☐ PP47 Jose Cruz Jr. 25.00 11.00
☐ PP48 Sammy Sosa 8.00 3.60
☐ PP49 Hideki Irabu 3.00 1.35
☐ PP50 Jose Guillen 8.00 3.60
☐ PP51 Deion Sanders 3.00 1.35
☐ PP52 Jose Canseco 5.00 2.20
☐ PP53 Jay Buhner 5.00 2.20
☐ PP54 Rafael Palmeiro 5.00 2.20
☐ PP55 Vladimir Guerrero 10.00 4.50
☐ PP56 Mark McGwire 15.00 6.75
☐ PP57 Derek Jeter 20.00 9.00
☐ PP58 Bobby Bonilla 3.00 1.35
☐ PP59 Raul Mondesi 5.00 2.20
☐ PP60 Paul Molitor 8.00 3.60
☐ PP61 Joe Carter 3.00 1.35
☐ PP62 Marquis Grissom 3.00 1.35
☐ PP63 Juan Gonzalez 20.00 9.00
☐ PP64 Dante Bichette 3.00 1.35
☐ PP65 Shannon Stewart 3.00 1.35
☐ PP66 Jaret Wright 20.00 9.00
☐ PP67 Derrek Lee 5.00 2.20
☐ PP68 Todd Dunwoody 3.00 1.35
☐ PP69 Steve Woodard 2.00 .90
☐ PP70 Ryan McGuire 2.00 .90
☐ PP71 Jeremi Gonzalez 3.00 1.35
☐ PP72 Mark Kotsay 8.00 3.60
☐ PP73 Brett Tomko 3.00 1.35
☐ PP74 Bobby Estalella 3.00 1.35
☐ PP75 Livan Hernandez 5.00 2.20
☐ PP76 Todd Helton 10.00 4.50
☐ PP77 Garrett Stephenson 2.00 .90
☐ PP78 Pokey Reese 2.00 .90
☐ PP79 Tony Saunders 3.00 1.35
☐ PP80 Antone Williamson 2.00 .90
☐ PP81 Bartolo Colon 3.00 1.35
☐ PP82 Karim Garcia 3.00 1.35
☐ PP83 Juan Encarnacion 8.00 3.60
☐ PP84 Jacob Cruz 3.00 1.35
☐ PP85 Alex Rodriguez FV 12.00 5.50

	MINT	NRMT
☐ PP86 C.Ripken/R.Alomar FV	12.00	5.50
☐ PP87 Roger Clemens FV	8.00	3.60
☐ PP88 Derek Jeter FV	10.00	4.50
☐ PP89 Frank Thomas FV	15.00	6.75
☐ PP90 Ken Griffey Jr. FV	20.00	9.00
☐ PP91 Mark McGwire GJ	8.00	3.60
☐ PP92 Tino Martinez GJ	3.00	1.35
☐ PP93 Larry Walker GJ	4.00	1.80
☐ PP94 Brady Anderson GJ	5.00	2.20
☐ PP95 Jeff Bagwell GJ	8.00	3.60
☐ PP96 Ken Griffey Jr. GJ	20.00	9.00
☐ PP97 Chipper Jones GJ	12.00	5.50
☐ PP98 Ray Lankford GJ	3.00	1.35
☐ PP99 Jim Thome GJ	4.00	1.80
☐ PP100 Nomar Garciaparra GJ	10.00	4.50

1998 Pinnacle Epix

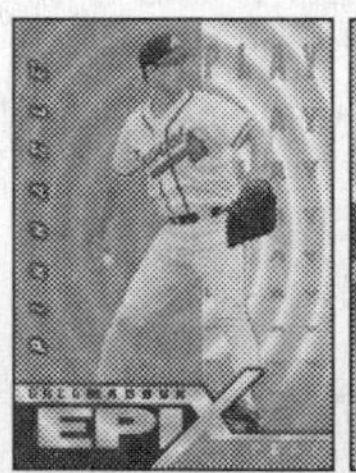

Randomly inserted in Pinnacle packs at the rate of one in 21, this 24-card set features color photos of top players' most memorable games, plays, seasons and moments on Dot Matrix Hologram cards. To obtain all the cards for each player in this fractured insert set, the collector had to open not only Pinnacle Epix packs, but also Score, Pinnacle Certified and Pinnacle Zenith packs.

	MINT	NRMT
COMMON CARD (E1-E24)	6.00	2.70

*PURPLE CARDS: .75X TO 1.5X ORANGE
*EMERALD CARDS: 1.5X TO 3X ORANGE

	MINT	NRMT
☐ E1 Ken Griffey Jr. GAME	50.00	22.00
☐ E2 Juan Gonzalez GAME	25.00	11.00
☐ E3 Jeff Bagwell GAME	20.00	9.00
☐ E4 Ivan Rodriguez GAME	12.00	5.50
☐ E5 Nomar Garciaparra GAME	25.00	11.00
☐ E6 Ryne Sandberg GAME	12.00	5.50
☐ E7 Frank Thomas SEA	80.00	36.00
☐ E8 Derek Jeter SEA	50.00	22.00
☐ E9 Tony Gwynn SEA	50.00	22.00
☐ E10 Albert Belle SEA	25.00	11.00
☐ E11 Scott Rolen SEA	40.00	18.00
☐ E12 Barry Larkin SEA	12.00	5.50
☐ E13 Alex Rodriguez MOM	100.00	45.00
☐ E14 Cal Ripken MOM	120.00	55.00
☐ E15 Chipper Jones MOM	80.00	36.00
☐ E16 Roger Clemens MOM	60.00	27.00
☐ E17 Mo Vaughn MOM	40.00	18.00
☐ E18 Mark McGwire MOM	60.00	27.00
☐ E19 Mike Piazza PLAY	20.00	9.00
☐ E20 Andruw Jones PLAY	10.00	4.50
☐ E21 Greg Maddux PLAY	20.00	9.00
☐ E22 Barry Bonds PLAY	8.00	3.60
☐ E23 Paul Molitor PLAY	6.00	2.70
☐ E24 Eddie Murray PLAY	6.00	2.70

1998 Pinnacle Hit It Here

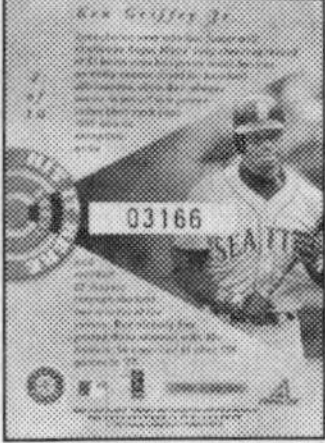

Randomly inserted one in 19 retail and magazine first series packs, and one in 17 first series hobby packs, this 10-card set features color player cut-outs of hot hitters in the league printed on micro-etched silver foil cards with a target in the background. If one of these hitters hit for the cycle on opening day, one lucky collector holding that specific player's card could win $1million. Each card back featured a special serial number that would be entered into a drawing to determine the winner.

	MINT	NRMT
COMPLETE SET (10)	80.00	36.00
COMMON CARD (1-10)	3.00	1.35
☐ 1 Larry Walker	4.00	1.80
☐ 2 Ken Griffey Jr.	20.00	9.00
☐ 3 Mike Piazza	12.00	5.50
☐ 4 Frank Thomas	15.00	6.75
☐ 5 Barry Bonds	5.00	2.20
☐ 6 Albert Belle	5.00	2.20
☐ 7 Tino Martinez	3.00	1.35
☐ 8 Mark McGwire	8.00	3.60
☐ 9 Juan Gonzalez	10.00	4.50
☐ 10 Jeff Bagwell	8.00	3.60

1998 Pinnacle Hit It Here Samples

This 10-card set is a sample parallel version of the 1998 Pinnacle Hit It Here insert set. These cards were distributed along with dealer order forms.

	MINT	NRMT
COMPLETE SET (10)	40.00	18.00
COMMON CARD (1-10)	1.50	.70

*SAMPLES: .5X BASIC HIT IT HERE INSERTS

1998 Pinnacle Spellbound

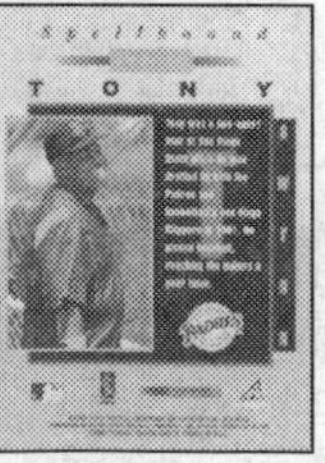

Randomly inserted in hobby packs only at the rate of one in 17, this 50-card set features game action color photos of nine top players printed on full-foil, micro-etched cards and superimposed over one of the letters of the player's name or nickname. All the cards of the same player needed to be collected in order to spell out the player's name when laid side-by-side.

	MINT	NRMT
COMPLETE SET (50)	600.00	275.00
COMMON M.MCGWIRE	12.00	5.50
COMMON R.CLEMENS	10.00	4.50
COMMON F.THOMAS	20.00	9.00
COMMON S.ROLEN	10.00	4.50
COMMON K.GRIFFEY	25.00	11.00
COMMON L.WALKER	5.00	2.20
COMMON N.GARCIAPARRA	12.00	5.50
COMMON C.RIPKEN	20.00	9.00
COMMON T.GWYNN	12.00	5.50

1996 Pinnacle Aficionado Promos

This three-card standard-size set was issued to introduce the new Pinnacle Afficionado brand. The set was distributed to hobby dealers along with promotional information concerning the release.

	MINT	NRMT
COMPLETE SET (3)	5.00	2.20
COMMON CARD	1.00	.45
☐ 9 Roger Clemens	2.00	.90
☐ 107 Ryan Klesko	1.00	.45
☐ MN7 Albert Belle Magic Number	2.00	.90

1996 Pinnacle Aficionado

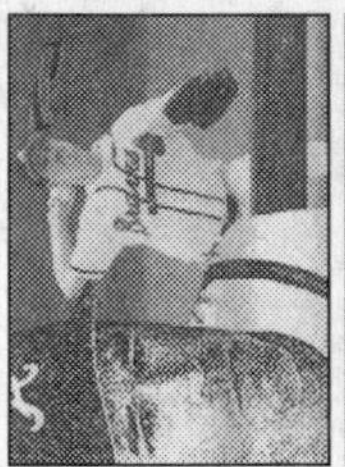
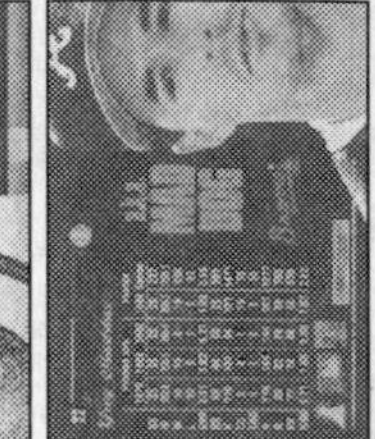

The 1996 Aficionado set was issued in one series totalling 200 cards. The five-card packs retailed for $3.99 and had a special bubble gum scent which was released when the packs were opened. The fronts feature action player photos in sepia tone for players who have played in the Major League for over five years and in color for those who have played less than five years. A heliographic player head print and the player's name printed in gold foil on a wood-look bar round out the front. The backs carry positional comparison statistics between the player and the league average at that position in different eras. Cards numbered 151-160 are a subset titled "Global Reach" and feature color action player cut-outs of international players on a background of a map, a global baseball, and their country's flag.

	MINT	NRMT
COMPLETE SET (200)	50.00	22.00
COMMON CARD (1-200)	.25	.11
☐ 1 Jack McDowell	.25	.11
☐ 2 Jay Bell	.25	.11
☐ 3 Rafael Palmeiro	.75	.35
☐ 4 Wally Joyner	.25	.11
☐ 5 Ozzie Smith	1.25	.55
☐ 6 Mark McGwire	2.00	.90
☐ 7 Kevin Seitzer	.25	.11
☐ 8 Fred McGriff	.75	.35
☐ 9 Roger Clemens	2.00	.90
☐ 10 Randy Johnson	.75	.35
☐ 11 Cecil Fielder	.50	.23
☐ 12 David Cone	.50	.23
☐ 13 Chili Davis	.25	.11
☐ 14 Andres Galarraga	.75	.35
☐ 15 Joe Carter	.50	.23
☐ 16 Ryne Sandberg	1.25	.55
☐ 17 Paul O'Neill	.50	.23
☐ 18 Cal Ripken	4.00	1.80
☐ 19 Wade Boggs	1.00	.45
☐ 20 Greg Gagne	.25	.11
☐ 21 Edgar Martinez	.75	.35
☐ 22 Greg Maddux	3.00	1.35
☐ 23 Ken Caminiti	1.00	.45
☐ 24 Kirby Puckett	2.00	.90
☐ 25 Craig Biggio	.75	.35
☐ 26 Will Clark	.75	.35
☐ 27 Ron Gant	.50	.23
☐ 28 Eddie Murray	1.00	.45
☐ 29 Lance Johnson	.25	.11
☐ 30 Tony Gwynn	2.50	1.10
☐ 31 Dante Bichette	.50	.23
☐ 32 Darren Daulton	.50	.23
☐ 33 Danny Tartabull	.25	.11
☐ 34 Jeff King	.25	.11
☐ 35 Tom Glavine	.50	.23
☐ 36 Rickey Henderson	.75	.35
☐ 37 Jose Canseco	.75	.35
☐ 38 Barry Larkin	.50	.23
☐ 39 Dennis Martinez	.50	.23
☐ 40 Ruben Sierra	.25	.11
☐ 41 Bobby Bonilla	.50	.23
☐ 42 Jeff Conine	.50	.23
☐ 43 Lee Smith	.50	.23
☐ 44 Charlie Hayes	.25	.11
☐ 45 Walt Weiss	.25	.11
☐ 46 Jay Buhner	.75	.35
☐ 47 Kenny Rogers	.25	.11
☐ 48 Paul Molitor	1.00	.45
☐ 49 Hal Morris	.25	.11
☐ 50 Todd Stottlemyre	.25	.11

51 Mike Stanley	.25	.11
52 Mark Grace	.75	.35
53 Lenny Dykstra	.50	.23
54 Andre Dawson	.75	.35
55 Dennis Eckersley	.75	.35
56 Ben McDonald	.25	.11
57 Ray Lankford	.50	.23
58 Mo Vaughn	1.25	.55
59 Frank Thomas	4.00	1.80
60 Julio Franco	.25	.11
61 Jim Abbott	.50	.23
62 Greg Vaughn	.25	.11
63 Marquis Grissom	.50	.23
64 Tino Martinez	1.00	.45
65 Kevin Appier	.50	.23
66 Matt Williams	.75	.35
67 Sammy Sosa	1.00	.45
68 Larry Walker	1.00	.45
69 Ivan Rodriguez	1.25	.55
70 Eric Karros	.50	.23
71 Bernie Williams	1.00	.45
72 Carlos Baerga	.50	.23
73 Jeff Bagwell	2.00	.90
74 Pete Schourek	.25	.11
75 Ken Griffey Jr.	5.00	2.20
76 Bernard Gilkey	.50	.23
77 Albert Belle	1.25	.55
78 Chuck Knoblauch	1.00	.45
79 John Smoltz	.50	.23
80 Barry Bonds	1.25	.55
81 Vinny Castilla	.50	.23
82 John Olerud	.25	.11
83 Mike Mussina	1.00	.45
84 Alex Fernandez	.50	.23
85 Shawon Dunston	.25	.11
86 Travis Fryman	.50	.23
87 Moises Alou	.50	.23
88 Dean Palmer	.50	.23
89 Gregg Jefferies	.50	.23
90 Jim Thome	1.00	.45
91 Dave Justice	1.00	.45
92 B.J. Surhoff	.25	.11
93 Ramon Martinez	.50	.23
94 Gary Sheffield	1.00	.45
95 Andy Benes	.25	.11
96 Reggie Sanders	.25	.11
97 Roberto Alomar	1.00	.45
98 Omar Vizquel	.50	.23
99 Juan Gonzalez	2.50	1.10
100 Robin Ventura	.50	.23
101 Jason Isringhausen	.25	.11
102 Greg Colbrunn	.25	.11
103 Brian Jordan	.50	.23
104 Shawn Green	.25	.11
105 Brian Hunter	.25	.11
106 Rondell White	.50	.23
107 Ryan Klesko	.75	.35
108 Sterling Hitchcock	.25	.11
109 Manny Ramirez	1.00	.45
110 Bret Boone	.25	.11
111 Michael Tucker	.50	.23
112 Julian Tavarez	.25	.11
113 Benji Gil	.25	.11
114 Kenny Lofton	1.25	.55
115 Mike Kelly	.25	.11
116 Ray Durham	.50	.23
117 Trevor Hoffman	.50	.23
118 Butch Huskey	.50	.23
119 Phil Nevin	.25	.11
120 Pedro Martinez	1.00	.45
121 Wil Cordero	.25	.11
122 Tim Salmon	1.00	.45
123 Jim Edmonds	1.00	.45
124 Mike Piazza	3.00	1.35
125 Rico Brogna	.25	.11
126 John Mabry	.50	.23
127 Chipper Jones	3.00	1.35
128 Johnny Damon	.50	.23
129 Raul Mondesi	.75	.35
130 Denny Neagle	.50	.23
131 Marc Newfield	.25	.11
132 Hideo Nomo	2.50	1.10
133 Joe Vitiello	.25	.11
134 Garret Anderson	.50	.23
135 Dave Nilsson	.50	.23
136 Alex Rodriguez	4.00	1.80
137 Russ Davis	.25	.11
138 Frank Rodriguez	.25	.11
139 Royce Clayton	.25	.11
140 John Valentin	.50	.23
141 Marty Cordova	.50	.23
142 Alex Gonzalez	.25	.11
143 Carlos Delgado	.50	.23
144 Willie Greene	.50	.23
145 Cliff Floyd	.25	.11
146 Bobby Higginson	.50	.23
147 J.T. Snow	.50	.23
148 Derek Bell	.25	.11
149 Edgardo Alfonzo	.75	.35
150 Charles Johnson	.50	.23
151 Hideo Nomo GR	1.00	.45
152 Larry Walker GR	1.00	.45
153 Bob Abreu GR	1.00	.45
154 Karim Garcia GR	.50	.23
155 Dave Nilsson GR	.25	.11
156 Chan Ho Park GR	1.00	.45
157 Dennis Martinez GR	.25	.11
158 Sammy Sosa GR	1.00	.45
159 Rey Ordonez GR	.25	.11
160 Roberto Alomar GR	1.00	.45
161 George Arias	.25	.11
162 Jason Schmidt	.50	.23
163 Derek Jeter	3.00	1.35
164 Chris Snopek	.25	.11
165 Todd Hollandsworth	.50	.23
166 Sal Fasano	.25	.11
167 Jay Powell	.25	.11
168 Paul Wilson	.50	.23
169 Jim Pittsley	.50	.23
170 LaTroy Hawkins	.25	.11
171 Bob Abreu	1.00	.45
172 Mike Grace	.25	.11
173 Karim Garcia	.50	.23
174 Richard Hidalgo	1.00	.45
175 Felipe Crespo	.25	.11
176 Terrell Wade	.25	.11
177 Steve Gibralter	.25	.11
178 Jermaine Dye	.25	.11
179 Alan Benes	.50	.23
180 Wilton Guerrero	1.00	.45
181 Brooks Kieschnick	.50	.23
182 Roger Cedeno	.50	.23
183 Osvaldo Fernandez	.50	.23
184 Matt Lawton	.25	.11
185 George Williams	.25	.11
186 Jimmy Haynes	.25	.11
187 Mike Busby	.25	.11
188 Chan Ho Park	1.00	.45
189 Marc Barcelo	.25	.11
190 Jason Kendall	1.00	.45
191 Rey Ordonez	.50	.23
192 Tyler Houston	.25	.11
193 John Wasdin	.25	.11
194 Jeff Suppan	.75	.35
195 Jeff Ware	.25	.11
196 Ken Griffey Jr. CL	2.50	1.10
197 Albert Belle CL	1.00	.45
198 Mike Piazza CL	1.50	.70
199 Greg Maddux CL	1.50	.70
200 Frank Thomas CL	2.50	1.10

1996 Pinnacle Aficionado Artist's Proofs

Randomly inserted in packs at a rate of one in 35, this 200-card set is a parallel set to the regular Pinnacle Aficionado set. A gold foil stamp in the shape of an artist's pen with the words, "Artist's Proof," printed above the wood-grain look bar containing the player's name distinguishes it from the regular set.

	MINT	NRMT
COMPLETE SET (200)	2000.00	900.00
COMMON CARD (1-200)	4.00	1.80
*STARS:15X TO 30X BASIC CARDS		
*YOUNG STARS: 12.5X TO 25X BASIC CARDS		

1996 Pinnacle Aficionado First Pitch Preview

This 100-card set was available through Pinnacle's Web site. Collectors had to answer a series of trivia questions to receive the cards via mail. The set parallels the first 100 cards of the regular issue Aficionado release and thus features only the veteran players that have five or more years of Major League service. The cards are similar in design except for the bronze foil highlights and logo on front designating them as "First Pitch Preview" cards.

	MINT	NRMT
COMPLETE SET (100)	750.00	350.00
COMMON CARD (1-100)	1.00	.45
*STARS: 5X TO 10X BASIC CARDS		

1996 Pinnacle Aficionado Magic Numbers

Randomly inserted in packs at a rate of one in 72, this 10-card set is printed on actual maple wood and features ten of of today's top superstars. The fronts feature an embossed color action player cut-out on a wood background. The backs carry trivia regarding the player's jersey number and those players from the past and present who share this same jersey number.

	MINT	NRMT
COMPLETE SET (10)	250.00	110.00
COMMON CARD (1-10)	6.00	2.70
1 Ken Griffey Jr.	50.00	22.00
2 Greg Maddux	30.00	13.50
3 Frank Thomas	40.00	18.00
4 Mo Vaughn	12.00	5.50
5 Jeff Bagwell	20.00	9.00
6 Chipper Jones	30.00	13.50
7 Albert Belle	12.00	5.50
8 Cal Ripken	40.00	18.00
9 Matt Williams	6.00	2.70
10 Sammy Sosa	8.00	3.60

1996 Pinnacle Aficionado Rivals

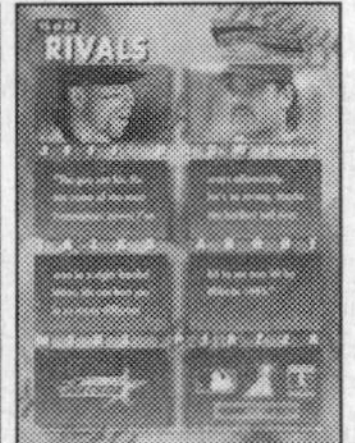

Randomly inserted in packs at a rate of one in 24, this 24-card set features two spot embossed color player photos of rival players. The backs carry a head photo of each and candid player comments on each other.

	MINT	NRMT
COMPLETE SET (24)	300.00	135.00
COMMON CARD (1-24)	10.00	4.50
1 Ken Griffey Frank Thomas	25.00	11.00
2 Frank Thomas Cal Ripken	20.00	9.00
3 Cal Ripken Mo Vaughn	10.00	4.50
4 Mo Vaughn Ken Griffey Jr.	15.00	6.75
5 Ken Griffey Jr. Cal Ripken	25.00	11.00
6 Frank Thomas Mo Vaughn	12.00	5.50
7 Cal Ripken Ken Griffey Jr.	25.00	11.00
8 Mo Vaughn Frank Thomas	12.00	5.50
9 Ken Griffey Jr. Mo Vaughn	15.00	6.75
10 Frank Thomas Ken Griffey Jr.	25.00	11.00
11 Cal Ripken Frank Thomas	20.00	9.00
12 Mo Vaughn Cal Ripken	10.00	4.50
13 Mike Piazza Jeff Bagwell	10.00	4.50
14 Jeff Bagwell Barry Bonds	10.00	4.50
15 Jeff Bagwell Mike Piazza	10.00	4.50
16 Tony Gwynn Mike Piazza	10.00	4.50
17 Mike Piazza Barry Bonds	10.00	4.50
18 Jeff Bagwell Tony Gwynn	10.00	4.50
19 Barry Bonds Mike Piazza	10.00	4.50
20 Tony Gwynn Jeff Bagwell	10.00	4.50
21 Mike Piazza Tony Gwynn	10.00	4.50

	MINT	NRMT
☐ 22 Barry Bonds / Jeff Bagwell	10.00	4.50
☐ 23 Tony Gwynn / Barry Bonds	10.00	4.50
☐ 24 Barry Bonds / Tony Gwynn	10.00	4.50

1996 Pinnacle Aficionado Slick Picks

Randomly inserted in packs at a rate of one in 10, this 32-card set honors 32 draft picks for their future all-star abilities. Printed using a spectroetch print technology, the fronts feature a color action player photo on a black background on one side with a black-and-white player portrait on the other. A small simulated autograph and team name are printed below the portrait. The backs carry another color player portrait on a white background with a three-sided black border and information about when the player was drafted printed over a gray number indicating the round the player was selected in.

	MINT	NRMT
COMPLETE SET (32)	200.00	90.00
COMMON CARD (1-32)	2.00	.90
☐ 1 Mike Piazza	15.00	6.75
☐ 2 Cal Ripken	20.00	9.00
☐ 3 Ken Griffey Jr.	25.00	11.00
☐ 4 Paul Wilson	2.00	.90
☐ 5 Frank Thomas	20.00	9.00
☐ 6 Mo Vaughn	6.00	2.70
☐ 7 Barry Bonds	6.00	2.70
☐ 8 Albert Belle	6.00	2.70
☐ 9 Jeff Bagwell	10.00	4.50
☐ 10 Dante Bichette	2.50	1.10
☐ 11 Hideo Nomo	12.00	5.50
☐ 12 Raul Mondesi	3.00	1.35
☐ 13 Manny Ramirez	5.00	2.20
☐ 14 Greg Maddux	15.00	6.75
☐ 15 Tony Gwynn	10.00	4.50
☐ 16 Ryne Sandberg	6.00	2.70
☐ 17 Reggie Sanders	2.00	.90
☐ 18 Derek Jeter	15.00	6.75
☐ 19 Johnny Damon	2.50	1.10
☐ 20 Alex Rodriguez	20.00	9.00
☐ 21 Ryan Klesko	3.00	1.35
☐ 22 Jim Thome	5.00	2.20
☐ 23 Kenny Lofton	6.00	2.70
☐ 24 Tino Martinez	5.00	2.20
☐ 25 Randy Johnson	5.00	2.20
☐ 26 Wade Boggs	5.00	2.20
☐ 27 Juan Gonzalez	12.00	5.50
☐ 28 Kirby Puckett	10.00	4.50
☐ 29 Tim Salmon	5.00	2.20
☐ 30 Chipper Jones	15.00	6.75
☐ 31 Garret Anderson	2.50	1.10
☐ 32 Eddie Murray	5.00	2.20

1997 Pinnacle Certified

This 150-card set was distributed in six-card hobby only packs with a suggested price of $4.99 and features color action player photos with side triangular silver mylar borders and black-and-white center backgrounds. The backs carry another player photo with player information and statistics. The set is divided into the following subsets: Rookie (106-135) and Certified Stars (136-150) which display a color player image on a background of stars. A Jose Cruz Exchange card was randomly seeded into packs. The deadline to redeem the card was March 31, 1998. Collectors who exchanged this cards received a Cruz card featuring him in a Blue Jay uniform. This #151 card is not considered part of the complete set. Some of these cards are also known to have a "Mirror Black" finish. These cards, while not officially released have surfaced in the secondary market and are very scarce. Please refer to upcoming issues of Beckett Baseball Card Monthly for information as it becomes available on key cards.

	MINT	NRMT
COMPLETE SET (150)	40.00	18.00
COMMON CARD (1-150)	.25	.11
☐ 1 Barry Bonds	1.25	.55
☐ 2 Mo Vaughn	1.25	.55
☐ 3 Matt Williams	.75	.35
☐ 4 Ryne Sandberg	1.25	.55
☐ 5 Jeff Bagwell	2.00	.90
☐ 6 Alan Benes	.25	.11
☐ 7 John Wetteland	.50	.23
☐ 8 Fred McGriff	.75	.35
☐ 9 Craig Biggio	.75	.35
☐ 10 Bernie Williams	1.00	.45
☐ 11 Brian Hunter	.50	.23
☐ 12 Sandy Alomar Jr.	.50	.23
☐ 13 Ray Lankford	.50	.23
☐ 14 Ryan Klesko	.75	.35
☐ 15 Jermaine Dye	.25	.11
☐ 16 Andy Benes	.25	.11
☐ 17 Albert Belle	1.25	.55
☐ 18 Tony Clark	1.00	.45
☐ 19 Dean Palmer	.25	.11
☐ 20 Bernard Gilkey	.25	.11
☐ 21 Ken Caminiti	1.00	.45
☐ 22 Alex Rodriguez	4.00	1.80
☐ 23 Tim Salmon	1.00	.45
☐ 24 Larry Walker	1.00	.45
☐ 25 Barry Larkin	.75	.35
☐ 26 Mike Piazza	3.00	1.35
☐ 27 Brady Anderson	.75	.35
☐ 28 Cal Ripken	4.00	1.80
☐ 29 Charles Nagy	.50	.23
☐ 30 Paul Molitor	1.00	.45
☐ 31 Darin Erstad	1.50	.70
☐ 32 Rey Ordonez	.25	.11
☐ 33 Wally Joyner	.50	.23
☐ 34 David Cone	.50	.23
☐ 35 Sammy Sosa	1.00	.45
☐ 36 Dante Bichette	.50	.23
☐ 37 Eric Karros	.50	.23
☐ 38 Omar Vizquel	.50	.23
☐ 39 Roger Clemens	2.00	.90
☐ 40 Joe Carter	.50	.23
☐ 41 Frank Thomas	4.00	1.80
☐ 42 Javy Lopez	.50	.23
☐ 43 Mike Mussina	1.00	.45
☐ 44 Gary Sheffield	1.00	.45
☐ 45 Tony Gwynn	2.50	1.10
☐ 46 Jason Kendall	.50	.23
☐ 47 Jim Thome	1.00	.45
☐ 48 Andres Galarraga	1.00	.45
☐ 49 Mark McGwire	2.00	.90
☐ 50 Troy Percival	.50	.23
☐ 51 Derek Jeter	3.00	1.35
☐ 52 Todd Hollandsworth	.50	.23
☐ 53 Ken Griffey Jr.	5.00	2.20
☐ 54 Randy Johnson	1.00	.45
☐ 55 Pat Hentgen	.50	.23
☐ 56 Rusty Greer	.50	.23
☐ 57 John Jaha	.25	.11
☐ 58 Kenny Lofton	1.25	.55
☐ 59 Chipper Jones	3.00	1.35
☐ 60 Robb Nen	.25	.11
☐ 61 Rafael Palmeiro	.75	.35
☐ 62 Mariano Rivera	.50	.23
☐ 63 Hideo Nomo	2.50	1.10
☐ 64 Greg Vaughn	.25	.11
☐ 65 Ron Gant	.50	.23
☐ 66 Eddie Murray	1.00	.45
☐ 67 John Smoltz	.50	.23
☐ 68 Manny Ramirez	1.00	.45
☐ 69 Juan Gonzalez	2.50	1.10
☐ 70 F.P. Santangelo	.25	.11
☐ 71 Moises Alou	.50	.23
☐ 72 Alex Ochoa	.25	.11
☐ 73 Chuck Knoblauch	1.00	.45
☐ 74 Raul Mondesi	.75	.35
☐ 75 J.T. Snow	.50	.23
☐ 76 Rickey Henderson	.75	.35
☐ 77 Bobby Bonilla	.50	.23
☐ 78 Wade Boggs	1.00	.45
☐ 79 Ivan Rodriguez	1.25	.55
☐ 80 Brian Jordan	.25	.11
☐ 81 Al Leiter	.25	.11
☐ 82 Jay Buhner	.75	.35
☐ 83 Greg Maddux	3.00	1.35
☐ 84 Edgar Martinez	.75	.35
☐ 85 Kevin Brown	.25	.11
☐ 86 Eric Young	.25	.11
☐ 87 Todd Hundley	.50	.23
☐ 88 Ellis Burks	.50	.23
☐ 89 Marquis Grissom	.50	.23
☐ 90 Jose Canseco	.75	.35
☐ 91 Henry Rodriguez	.25	.11
☐ 92 Andy Pettitte	.50	.23
☐ 93 Mark Grudzielanek	.25	.11
☐ 94 Dwight Gooden	.50	.23
☐ 95 Roberto Alomar	1.00	.45
☐ 96 Paul Wilson	.25	.11
☐ 97 Will Clark	.75	.35
☐ 98 Rondell White	.50	.23
☐ 99 Charles Johnson	.50	.23
☐ 100 Jim Edmonds	1.00	.45
☐ 101 Jason Giambi	.25	.11
☐ 102 Billy Wagner	.50	.23
☐ 103 Edgar Renteria	.50	.23
☐ 104 Johnny Damon	.50	.23
☐ 105 Jason Isringhausen	.25	.11
☐ 106 Andruw Jones	2.50	1.10
☐ 107 Jose Guillen	1.25	.55
☐ 108 Kevin Orie	.25	.11
☐ 109 Brian Giles	.25	.11
☐ 110 Danny Patterson	.25	.11
☐ 111 Vladimir Guerrero	2.00	.90
☐ 112 Scott Rolen	2.50	1.10
☐ 113 Damon Mashore	.25	.11
☐ 114 Nomar Garciaparra	3.00	1.35
☐ 115 Todd Walker	.25	.11
☐ 116 Wilton Guerrero	.25	.11
☐ 117 Bob Abreu	1.00	.45
☐ 118 Brooks Kieschnick	.25	.11
☐ 119 Pokey Reese	.25	.11
☐ 120 Todd Greene	.50	.23
☐ 121 Dmitri Young	.50	.23
☐ 122 Raul Casanova	.25	.11
☐ 123 Glendon Rusch	.25	.11
☐ 124 Jason Dickson	.25	.11
☐ 125 Jorge Posada	.25	.11
☐ 126 Rod Myers	.25	.11
☐ 127 Bubba Trammell	1.00	.45
☐ 128 Scott Spiezio	.25	.11
☐ 129 Hideki Irabu	1.25	.55
☐ 130 Wendell Magee	.25	.11
☐ 131 Bartolo Colon	.50	.23
☐ 132 Chris Holt	.25	.11
☐ 133 Calvin Maduro	.25	.11
☐ 134 Ray Montgomery	.25	.11
☐ 135 Shannon Stewart	.50	.23
☐ 136 Ken Griffey Jr. CERT	2.50	1.10
☐ 137 Vladimir Guerrero CERT	1.00	.45
☐ 138 Roger Clemens CERT	1.00	.45
☐ 139 Mark McGwire CERT	1.00	.45
☐ 140 Albert Belle CERT	1.00	.45
☐ 141 Derek Jeter CERT	1.50	.70
☐ 142 Juan Gonzalez CERT	1.25	.55
☐ 143 Greg Maddux CERT	1.50	.70
☐ 144 Alex Rodriguez CERT	2.00	.90
☐ 145 Jeff Bagwell CERT	1.00	.45
☐ 146 Cal Ripken CERT	2.00	.90
☐ 147 Tony Gwynn CERT	1.25	.55
☐ 148 Frank Thomas CERT	2.00	.90
☐ 149 Hideo Nomo CERT	1.25	.55
☐ 150 Andruw Jones CERT	1.25	.55
☐ 151 Jose Cruz Jr. Blue Jays	30.00	13.50

1997 Pinnacle Certified Mirror Blue

Randomly inserted in packs at the rate of one in 199, this 150-card set is parallel to the base Pinnacle Certified set. The difference is found in the blue design element.

	MINT	NRMT
COMMON CARD (1-150)	25.00	11.00
MINOR STARS	40.00	18.00
SEMISTARS	60.00	27.00
UNLISTED STARS	100.00	45.00

*STARS: 60X TO 100X BASIC CARDS
*YOUNG STARS: 50X TO 80X BASIC CARDS
*ROOKIES: 30X TO 50X BASIC CARDS

	MINT	NRMT
☐ 1 Barry Bonds	150.00	70.00
☐ 2 Mo Vaughn	120.00	55.00
☐ 4 Ryne Sandberg	120.00	55.00
☐ 5 Jeff Bagwell	200.00	90.00
☐ 17 Albert Belle	120.00	55.00
☐ 22 Alex Rodriguez	300.00	135.00
☐ 26 Mike Piazza	300.00	135.00
☐ 28 Cal Ripken	400.00	180.00

	MINT	NRMT
☐ 31 Darin Erstad	120.00	55.00
☐ 39 Roger Clemens	200.00	90.00
☐ 41 Frank Thomas	500.00	220.00
☐ 45 Tony Gwynn	250.00	110.00
☐ 49 Mark McGwire	200.00	90.00
☐ 51 Derek Jeter	250.00	110.00
☐ 53 Ken Griffey Jr.	600.00	275.00
☐ 58 Kenny Lofton	120.00	55.00
☐ 59 Chipper Jones	250.00	110.00
☐ 63 Hideo Nomo	400.00	180.00
☐ 69 Juan Gonzalez	250.00	110.00
☐ 79 Ivan Rodriguez	120.00	55.00
☐ 83 Greg Maddux	300.00	135.00
☐ 106 Andruw Jones	200.00	90.00
☐ 111 Vladimir Guerrero	150.00	70.00
☐ 112 Scott Rolen	200.00	90.00
☐ 114 Nomar Garciaparra	250.00	110.00
☐ 136 Ken Griffey Jr. CERT	250.00	110.00
☐ 143 Greg Maddux CERT	120.00	55.00
☐ 144 Alex Rodriguez CERT	120.00	55.00
☐ 146 Cal Ripken CERT	150.00	70.00
☐ 148 Frank Thomas CERT	200.00	90.00

1997 Pinnacle Certified Mirror Gold

Randomly inserted in packs at the rate of one in 299, this 150-card set is parallel to the base Pinnacle Certified set and is printed on holographic gold mylar.

	MINT	NRMT
COMMON CARD (1-150)	80.00	36.00
MINOR STARS	150.00	70.00
SEMISTARS	250.00	110.00

*STARS: 200X TO 400X BASIC CARDS
*YOUNG STARS: 150X TO 300X BASIC CARDS
*ROOKIES: 100X TO 200X BASIC CARDS

	MINT	NRMT
☐ 1 Barry Bonds	500.00	220.00
☐ 2 Mo Vaughn	400.00	180.00
☐ 4 Ryne Sandberg	500.00	220.00
☐ 5 Jeff Bagwell	800.00	350.00
☐ 10 Bernie Williams	300.00	135.00
☐ 17 Albert Belle	500.00	220.00
☐ 18 Tony Clark	300.00	135.00
☐ 21 Ken Caminiti	300.00	135.00
☐ 22 Alex Rodriguez	1200.00	550.00
☐ 24 Larry Walker	400.00	180.00
☐ 26 Mike Piazza	1200.00	550.00
☐ 28 Cal Ripken	1500.00	700.00
☐ 30 Paul Molitor	400.00	180.00
☐ 31 Darin Erstad	500.00	220.00
☐ 35 Sammy Sosa	300.00	135.00
☐ 39 Roger Clemens	800.00	350.00
☐ 41 Frank Thomas	1800.00	800.00
☐ 43 Mike Mussina	400.00	180.00
☐ 44 Gary Sheffield	300.00	135.00
☐ 45 Tony Gwynn	1000.00	450.00
☐ 47 Jim Thome	400.00	180.00
☐ 49 Mark McGwire	800.00	350.00
☐ 51 Derek Jeter	800.00	350.00
☐ 53 Ken Griffey Jr.	2500.00	1100.00
☐ 54 Randy Johnson	400.00	180.00
☐ 58 Kenny Lofton	400.00	180.00
☐ 59 Chipper Jones	1000.00	450.00
☐ 63 Hideo Nomo	1200.00	550.00
☐ 66 Eddie Murray	400.00	180.00
☐ 68 Manny Ramirez	400.00	180.00
☐ 69 Juan Gonzalez	1000.00	450.00
☐ 73 Chuck Knoblauch	300.00	135.00
☐ 78 Wade Boggs	300.00	135.00
☐ 79 Ivan Rodriguez	500.00	220.00
☐ 83 Greg Maddux	1200.00	550.00
☐ 92 Andy Pettitte	400.00	180.00
☐ 95 Roberto Alomar	400.00	180.00
☐ 106 Andruw Jones	800.00	350.00
☐ 107 Jose Guillen	400.00	180.00
☐ 111 Vladimir Guerrero	600.00	275.00
☐ 112 Scott Rolen	800.00	350.00
☐ 114 Nomar Garciaparra	1000.00	450.00
☐ 129 Hideki Irabu	250.00	110.00
☐ 136 Ken Griffey Jr. CERT	1000.00	450.00
☐ 137 Vladimir Guerrero CERT	250.00	110.00
☐ 138 Roger Clemens CERT	300.00	135.00
☐ 139 Mark McGwire CERT	300.00	135.00
☐ 141 Derek Jeter CERT	300.00	135.00
☐ 142 Juan Gonzalez CERT	400.00	180.00
☐ 143 Greg Maddux CERT	500.00	220.00
☐ 144 Alex Rodriguez CERT	500.00	220.00
☐ 145 Jeff Bagwell CERT	300.00	135.00
☐ 146 Cal Ripken CERT	600.00	275.00
☐ 147 Tony Gwynn CERT	400.00	180.00
☐ 148 Frank Thomas CERT	800.00	350.00
☐ 149 Hideo Nomo CERT	400.00	180.00
☐ 150 Andruw Jones CERT	300.00	135.00

1997 Pinnacle Certified Mirror Red

Randomly inserted in packs at the rate of one in 99, this 150-card set is parallel to the base Pinnacle Certified set. The difference is found in the red design element.

	MINT	NRMT
COMMON CARD (1-150)	12.00	5.50
MINOR STARS	20.00	9.00
SEMISTARS	30.00	13.50
UNLISTED STARS	50.00	22.00

*STARS: 25X TO 50X BASIC CARDS
*YOUNG STARS: 20X TO 40X BASIC CARDS
*ROOKIES: 12.5X TO 25X BASIC CARDS

	MINT	NRMT
☐ 1 Barry Bonds	80.00	36.00
☐ 2 Mo Vaughn	60.00	27.00
☐ 4 Ryne Sandberg	60.00	27.00
☐ 5 Jeff Bagwell	100.00	45.00
☐ 17 Albert Belle	60.00	27.00
☐ 22 Alex Rodriguez	150.00	70.00
☐ 26 Mike Piazza	150.00	70.00
☐ 28 Cal Ripken	200.00	90.00
☐ 31 Darin Erstad	60.00	27.00
☐ 39 Roger Clemens	100.00	45.00
☐ 41 Frank Thomas	250.00	110.00
☐ 45 Tony Gwynn	120.00	55.00
☐ 49 Mark McGwire	100.00	45.00
☐ 51 Derek Jeter	100.00	45.00
☐ 53 Ken Griffey Jr.	300.00	135.00
☐ 58 Kenny Lofton	60.00	27.00
☐ 59 Chipper Jones	120.00	55.00
☐ 63 Hideo Nomo	200.00	90.00
☐ 69 Juan Gonzalez	120.00	55.00
☐ 79 Ivan Rodriguez	60.00	27.00
☐ 83 Greg Maddux	150.00	70.00
☐ 106 Andruw Jones	100.00	45.00
☐ 111 Vladimir Guerrero	80.00	36.00
☐ 112 Scott Rolen	100.00	45.00
☐ 114 Nomar Garciaparra	120.00	55.00
☐ 136 Ken Griffey Jr. CERT	120.00	55.00
☐ 143 Greg Maddux CERT	60.00	27.00
☐ 144 Alex Rodriguez CERT	60.00	27.00
☐ 146 Cal Ripken CERT	80.00	36.00
☐ 148 Frank Thomas CERT	100.00	45.00

1997 Pinnacle Certified Red

Randomly inserted in packs at the rate of one in five, this 150-card set is parallel to the regular set with a solid red tint on the mylar.

	MINT	NRMT
COMPLETE SET (150)	600.00	275.00
COMMON CARD (1-150)	2.00	.90

*STARS: 4X TO 8X BASIC CARDS
*YOUNG STARS: 3X TO 6X BASIC CARDS

1997 Pinnacle Certified Certified Team

Randomly inserted in hobby packs at the rate of one in 19, this 20-card set features color player photos on silver-frosted mirror mylar.

	MINT	NRMT
COMPLETE SET (20)	300.00	135.00
COMMON CARD (1-20)	5.00	2.20
COMP.GOLD SET (20)	1200.00	550.00
COMMON GOLD (1-20)	20.00	9.00

*GOLD TEAM: 2X TO 4X BASIC CARDS
*MIRROR GOLD: 20X TO 50X BASIC CARDS

	MINT	NRMT
☐ 1 Frank Thomas	30.00	13.50
☐ 2 Jeff Bagwell	15.00	6.75
☐ 3 Derek Jeter	20.00	9.00
☐ 4 Chipper Jones	25.00	11.00
☐ 5 Alex Rodriguez	25.00	11.00
☐ 6 Ken Caminiti	6.00	2.70
☐ 7 Cal Ripken	30.00	13.50
☐ 8 Mo Vaughn	10.00	4.50
☐ 9 Ivan Rodriguez	10.00	4.50
☐ 10 Mike Piazza	25.00	11.00
☐ 11 Juan Gonzalez	20.00	9.00
☐ 12 Barry Bonds	10.00	4.50
☐ 13 Ken Griffey Jr.	40.00	18.00
☐ 14 Andruw Jones	15.00	6.75
☐ 15 Albert Belle	10.00	4.50
☐ 16 Gary Sheffield	6.00	2.70
☐ 17 Andy Pettitte	8.00	3.60
☐ 18 Hideo Nomo	25.00	11.00
☐ 19 Greg Maddux	25.00	11.00
☐ 20 John Smoltz	5.00	2.20

1997 Pinnacle Certified Lasting Impressions

Randomly inserted in packs at the rate of one in 19, this 20-card set features color action photos of top veteran stars printed on die-cut Mirror Mylar.

	MINT	NRMT
COMPLETE SET (20)	225.00	100.00
COMMON CARD (1-20)	4.00	1.80

	MINT	NRMT
☐ 1 Cal Ripken	30.00	13.50
☐ 2 Ken Griffey Jr.	40.00	18.00
☐ 3 Mo Vaughn	10.00	4.50
☐ 4 Brian Jordan	4.00	1.80
☐ 5 Mark McGwire	15.00	6.75
☐ 6 Chuck Knoblauch	8.00	3.60
☐ 7 Sammy Sosa	8.00	3.60
☐ 8 Brady Anderson	6.00	2.70
☐ 9 Frank Thomas	30.00	13.50
☐ 10 Tony Gwynn	20.00	9.00
☐ 11 Roger Clemens	15.00	6.75
☐ 12 Alex Rodriguez	25.00	11.00
☐ 13 Paul Molitor	8.00	3.60
☐ 14 Kenny Lofton	10.00	4.50
☐ 15 John Smoltz	4.50	2.00
☐ 16 Roberto Alomar	8.00	3.60
☐ 17 Randy Johnson	8.00	3.60
☐ 18 Ryne Sandberg	10.00	4.50
☐ 19 Manny Ramirez	8.00	3.60
☐ 20 Mike Mussina	8.00	3.60

1997 Pinnacle Inside

The 1997 Pinnacle Inside set was issued in one series totalling 150 cards and was distributed inside 24 different collectible player cans with a suggested retail price of $2.99 for a 10-card can. Printed on 14 pt. stock, the fronts feature a color player photo with a thin black-and-white photo as a side border. The backs carry the black-and-white photo and information about the player's favorite off-the-field activities with a small color player head shot in the center near the top of the card. The set contains a Rookie subset (128-147) and a checklist subset (148-150). The three checklists display black-and-white player photos of American and National League pairings of the 1996 Rookies of the Year, Cy Young winners, and MVPs.

	MINT	NRMT
COMPLETE SET (150)	40.00	18.00
COMMON CARD (1-150)	.20	.09

	MINT	NRMT
☐ 1 David Cone	.40	.18
☐ 2 Sammy Sosa	.75	.35

☐ 3 Joe Carter	.40	.18
☐ 4 Juan Gonzalez	2.00	.90
☐ 5 Hideo Nomo	2.00	.90
☐ 6 Moises Alou	.40	.18
☐ 7 Marc Newfield	.20	.09
☐ 8 Alex Rodriguez	3.00	1.35
☐ 9 Kimera Bartee	.20	.09
☐ 10 Chuck Knoblauch	.75	.35
☐ 11 Jason Isringhausen	.20	.09
☐ 12 Jermaine Allensworth	.20	.09
☐ 13 Frank Thomas	3.00	1.35
☐ 14 Paul Molitor	.75	.35
☐ 15 John Mabry	.20	.09
☐ 16 Greg Maddux	2.50	1.10
☐ 17 Rafael Palmeiro	.60	.25
☐ 18 Brian Jordan	.20	.09
☐ 19 Ken Griffey Jr.	4.00	1.80
☐ 20 Brady Anderson	.60	.25
☐ 21 Ruben Sierra	.20	.09
☐ 22 Travis Fryman	.40	.18
☐ 23 Cal Ripken	3.00	1.35
☐ 24 Will Clark	.60	.25
☐ 25 Todd Hollandsworth	.20	.09
☐ 26 Kevin Brown	.20	.09
☐ 27 Mike Piazza	2.50	1.10
☐ 28 Craig Biggio	.60	.25
☐ 29 Paul Wilson	.20	.09
☐ 30 Andres Galarraga	.75	.35
☐ 31 Chipper Jones	2.50	1.10
☐ 32 Jason Giambi	.40	.18
☐ 33 Ernie Young	.20	.09
☐ 34 Marty Cordova	.20	.09
☐ 35 Albert Belle	1.00	.45
☐ 36 Roger Clemens	1.50	.70
☐ 37 Ryne Sandberg	1.00	.45
☐ 38 Henry Rodriguez	.20	.09
☐ 39 Jay Buhner	.60	.25
☐ 40 Raul Mondesi	.60	.25
☐ 41 Jeff Fassero	.20	.09
☐ 42 Edgar Martinez	.60	.25
☐ 43 Trey Beamon	.20	.09
☐ 44 Mo Vaughn	1.00	.45
☐ 45 Gary Sheffield	.75	.35
☐ 46 Ray Durham	.20	.09
☐ 47 Brett Butler	.40	.18
☐ 48 Ivan Rodriguez	1.00	.45
☐ 49 Fred McGriff	.60	.25
☐ 50 Dean Palmer	.40	.18
☐ 51 Rickey Henderson	.60	.25
☐ 52 Andy Pettitte	.75	.35
☐ 53 Bobby Bonilla	.40	.18
☐ 54 Shawn Green	.40	.18
☐ 55 Tino Martinez	.75	.35
☐ 56 Tony Gwynn	2.00	.90
☐ 57 Tom Glavine	.40	.18
☐ 58 Eric Young	.20	.09
☐ 59 Kevin Appier	.20	.09
☐ 60 Barry Bonds	1.00	.45
☐ 61 Wade Boggs	.75	.35
☐ 62 Jason Kendall	.20	.09
☐ 63 Jeff Bagwell	1.50	.70
☐ 64 Jeff Conine	.40	.18
☐ 65 Greg Vaughn	.20	.09
☐ 66 Eric Karros	.20	.09
☐ 67 Manny Ramirez	.75	.35
☐ 68 John Smoltz	.40	.18
☐ 69 Terrell Wade	.20	.09
☐ 70 John Wetteland	.40	.18
☐ 71 Kenny Lofton	1.00	.45
☐ 72 Jim Thome	.75	.35
☐ 73 Bill Pulsipher	.20	.09
☐ 74 Darryl Strawberry	.40	.18
☐ 75 Roberto Alomar	.75	.35
☐ 76 Bobby Higginson	.40	.18
☐ 77 James Baldwin	.20	.09
☐ 78 Mark McGwire	1.50	.70
☐ 79 Jose Canseco	.60	.25
☐ 80 Mark Grudzielanek	.40	.18
☐ 81 Ryan Klesko	.60	.25
☐ 82 Javy Lopez	.40	.18
☐ 83 Ken Caminiti	.75	.35
☐ 84 Dave Nilsson	.20	.09
☐ 85 Tim Salmon	.75	.35
☐ 86 Cecil Fielder	.40	.18
☐ 87 Derek Jeter	2.50	1.10
☐ 88 Garret Anderson	.40	.18
☐ 89 Dwight Gooden	.40	.18
☐ 90 Carlos Delgado	.40	.18
☐ 91 Ugueth Urbina	.40	.18
☐ 92 Chan Ho Park	.75	.35
☐ 93 Eddie Murray	.75	.35
☐ 94 Alex Ochoa	.20	.09
☐ 95 Rusty Greer	.40	.18
☐ 96 Mark Grace	.60	.25
☐ 97 Pat Hentgen	.40	.18
☐ 98 John Jaha	.20	.09
☐ 99 Charles Johnson	.40	.18
☐ 100 Jermaine Dye	.20	.09
☐ 101 Quinton McCracken	.20	.09
☐ 102 Troy Percival	.40	.18
☐ 103 Shane Reynolds	.20	.09
☐ 104 Rondell White	.40	.18
☐ 105 Charles Nagy	.40	.18
☐ 106 Alan Benes	.20	.09
☐ 107 Tom Goodwin	.20	.09
☐ 108 Ron Gant	.40	.18
☐ 109 Dan Wilson	.20	.09
☐ 110 Darin Erstad	1.25	.55
☐ 111 Matt Williams	.60	.25
☐ 112 Barry Larkin	.60	.25
☐ 113 Mariano Rivera	.40	.18
☐ 114 Larry Walker	.75	.35
☐ 115 Jim Edmonds	.75	.35
☐ 116 Michael Tucker	.40	.18
☐ 117 Todd Hundley	.40	.18
☐ 118 Alex Fernandez	.40	.18
☐ 119 J.T. Snow	.40	.18
☐ 120 Ellis Burks	.40	.18
☐ 121 Steve Finley	.40	.18
☐ 122 Mike Mussina	.75	.35
☐ 123 Curtis Pride	.20	.09
☐ 124 Derek Bell	.20	.09
☐ 125 Dante Bichette	.40	.18
☐ 126 Terry Steinbach	.40	.18
☐ 127 Randy Johnson	.75	.35
☐ 128 Andruw Jones	2.00	.90
☐ 129 Vladimir Guerrero	1.50	.70
☐ 130 Ruben Rivera	.40	.18
☐ 131 Billy Wagner	.40	.18
☐ 132 Scott Rolen	2.00	.90
☐ 133 Rey Ordonez	.20	.09
☐ 134 Karim Garcia	.40	.18
☐ 135 George Arias	.20	.09
☐ 136 Todd Greene	.40	.18
☐ 137 Robin Jennings	.20	.09
☐ 138 Raul Casanova	.20	.09
☐ 139 Steve Gibralter	.20	.09
☐ 140 Edgar Renteria	.40	.18
☐ 141 Chad Mottola	.20	.09
☐ 142 Dmitri Young	.40	.18
☐ 143 Tony Clark	.75	.35
☐ 144 Todd Walker	.20	.09
☐ 145 Kevin Brown	.20	.09
☐ 146 Nomar Garciaparra	2.50	1.10
☐ 147 Neifi Perez	.20	.09
☐ 148 Derek Jeter CL Todd Hollandsworth	.20	.09
☐ 149 Pat Hentgen CL John Smoltz	.20	.09
☐ 150 Juan Gonzalez CL Ken Caminiti	.60	.25

1997 Pinnacle Inside Club Edition

Randomly inserted in packs at a rate of one in seven, this 150-card set is a parallel rendition of the the regular Pinnacle Inside set and is produced on all silver-foil card stock with gold-foil stamping.

	MINT	NRMT
COMPLETE SET (150)	600.00	275.00
COMMON CARD (1-150)	1.50	.70
*STARS: 6X TO 12X BASIC CARDS		
*YOUNG STARS: 5X TO 10X BASIC CARDS		

1997 Pinnacle Inside Diamond Edition

Randomly inserted in packs at a rate of one in 63, this 150-card set is a parallel version of the regular Pinnacle Inside set and is printed on silver foil board with a gold holographic stamp and a die-cut design.

	MINT	NRMT
COMMON CARD (1-150)	20.00	9.00
*STARS: 60X TO 100X BASIC CARDS		
*YOUNG STARS: 50X TO 80X BASIC CARDS		
☐ 4 Juan Gonzalez	200.00	90.00
☐ 5 Hideo Nomo	250.00	110.00
☐ 8 Alex Rodriguez	300.00	135.00
☐ 13 Frank Thomas	400.00	180.00
☐ 16 Greg Maddux	250.00	110.00
☐ 19 Ken Griffey Jr.	500.00	220.00
☐ 23 Cal Ripken	300.00	135.00
☐ 27 Mike Piazza	250.00	110.00
☐ 31 Chipper Jones	200.00	90.00
☐ 35 Albert Belle	100.00	45.00
☐ 36 Roger Clemens	150.00	70.00
☐ 37 Ryne Sandberg	100.00	45.00
☐ 44 Mo Vaughn	100.00	45.00
☐ 48 Ivan Rodriguez	100.00	45.00
☐ 56 Tony Gwynn	200.00	90.00
☐ 60 Barry Bonds	100.00	45.00
☐ 63 Jeff Bagwell	150.00	70.00
☐ 71 Kenny Lofton	100.00	45.00
☐ 78 Mark McGwire	150.00	70.00
☐ 87 Derek Jeter	250.00	110.00
☐ 110 Darin Erstad	100.00	45.00
☐ 128 Andruw Jones	200.00	90.00
☐ 129 Vladimir Guerrero	120.00	55.00
☐ 132 Scott Rolen	150.00	70.00
☐ 146 Nomar Garciaparra	200.00	90.00

1997 Pinnacle Inside 40 Something

Randomly inserted in packs at a rate of one in 47, this 16-card set features color player photos of some of the most powerful hitters in the league who have the best chance of pushing past the 40-homer level.

	MINT	NRMT
COMPLETE SET (16)	400.00	180.00
COMMON CARD (1-16)	8.00	3.60
☐ 1 Juan Gonzalez	50.00	22.00
☐ 2 Barry Bonds	25.00	11.00
☐ 3 Ken Caminiti	15.00	6.75
☐ 4 Mark McGwire	40.00	18.00
☐ 5 Todd Hundley	8.00	3.60
☐ 6 Albert Belle	25.00	11.00
☐ 7 Ellis Burks	10.00	4.50
☐ 8 Jay Buhner	12.00	5.50
☐ 9 Brady Anderson	12.00	5.50
☐ 10 Vinny Castilla	10.00	4.50
☐ 11 Mo Vaughn	25.00	11.00
☐ 12 Ken Griffey Jr.	100.00	45.00
☐ 13 Sammy Sosa	15.00	6.75
☐ 14 Andres Galarraga	15.00	6.75
☐ 15 Gary Sheffield	15.00	6.75
☐ 16 Frank Thomas	80.00	36.00

1997 Pinnacle Inside Cans

This set features replicas of 24 great player cards from the regular Pinnacle Inside set reproduced on the can labels and are painted directly on the metal. Inside each can is information about an opportunity to win a trip to visit a team during their 1998 Spring Training.

	MINT	NRMT
COMPLETE SET (24)	25.00	11.00
COMMON CAN (1-24)	.50	.23
COMMON SEALED CAN	3.00	1.35
☐ 1 Kenny Lofton	.75	.35
☐ 2 Frank Thomas	2.50	1.10
☐ 3 John Smoltz	.50	.23
☐ 4 Manny Ramirez	.60	.25
☐ 5 Alex Rodriguez	2.50	1.10
☐ 6 Barry Bonds	.75	.35
☐ 7 Mo Vaughn	.75	.35
☐ 8 Ken Griffey Jr.	3.00	1.35
☐ 9 Albert Belle	.75	.35
☐ 10 Greg Maddux	2.00	.90
☐ 11 Juan Gonzalez	1.50	.70
☐ 12 Andy Pettitte	.60	.25
☐ 13 Jeff Bagwell	1.25	.55
☐ 14 Ryan Klesko	.60	.25
☐ 15 Chipper Jones	2.00	.90
☐ 16 Derek Jeter	2.00	.90
☐ 17 Ivan Rodriguez	.75	.35
☐ 18 Andruw Jones	2.00	.90
☐ 19 Mike Piazza	2.00	.90
☐ 20 Hideo Nomo	1.50	.70
☐ 21 Ken Caminiti	.60	.25
☐ 22 Cal Ripken	2.50	1.10
☐ 23 Mark McGwire	1.25	.55
☐ 24 Tony Gwynn	1.50	.70

1997 Pinnacle Inside Dueling Dugouts

Randomly inserted in packs at a rate of one in 23, this 20-card set features a color photo of a star player on both

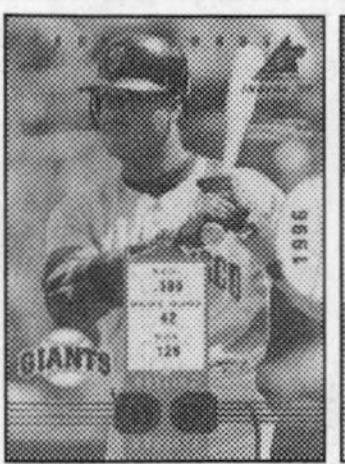

sides of the card with a spinning wheel that lines up to reveal comparative statistics.

	MINT	NRMT
COMPLETE SET (20)	500.00	220.00
COMMON CARD (1-20)	10.00	4.50
☐ 1 Alex Rodriguez Cal Ripken	60.00	27.00
☐ 2 Jeff Bagwell Ken Caminiti	25.00	11.00
☐ 3 Barry Bonds Albert Belle	25.00	11.00
☐ 4 Mike Piazza Ivan Rodriguez	30.00	13.50
☐ 5 Chuck Knoblauch Roberto Alomar	15.00	6.75
☐ 6 Ken Griffey Jr. Andruw Jones	60.00	27.00
☐ 7 Chipper Jones Jim Thome	30.00	13.50
☐ 8 Frank Thomas Mo Vaughn	10.00	4.50
☐ 9 Fred McGriff Mark McGwire	25.00	11.00
☐ 10 Brian Jordan Tony Gwynn	25.00	11.00
☐ 11 Barry Larkin Derek Jeter	25.00	11.00
☐ 12 Kenny Lofton Bernie Williams	15.00	6.75
☐ 13 Juan Gonzalez Manny Ramirez	25.00	11.00
☐ 14 Will Clark Rafael Palmeiro	10.00	4.50
☐ 15 Greg Maddux Roger Clemens	30.00	13.50
☐ 16 John Smoltz Andy Pettitte	10.00	4.50
☐ 17 Mariano Rivera John Wetteland	10.00	4.50
☐ 18 Hideo Nomo Mike Mussina	25.00	11.00
☐ 19 Todd Hollandsworth Darin Erstad	12.00	5.50
☐ 20 Vladimir Guerrero Karim Garcia	15.00	6.75

1997 Pinnacle Mint

The 1997 Pinnacle Mint set was issued in one series totalling 30 cards and was distributed in packs of three cards and two coins for a suggested retail price of $3.99. The challenge was to fit the coins with the die-cut cards that pictured the same player on the minted coin. Two die-cut cards were inserted in each pack. Either one bronze, silver or gold card was also included in each pack. The fronts featured color action player images on a sepia player portrait background and a cut-out area for the matching coin. Ryan Klesko's die cut card was distributed to dealers as a promo. Die cut cards are listed below.

	MINT	NRMT
COMP.DIE CUT SET (30)	20.00	9.00
COMMON DIE CUT (1-30)	.25	.11
☐ 1 Ken Griffey Jr.	2.50	1.10
☐ 2 Frank Thomas	2.00	.90
☐ 3 Alex Rodriguez	2.00	.90
☐ 4 Cal Ripken	2.00	.90
☐ 5 Mo Vaughn	.60	.25
☐ 6 Juan Gonzalez	1.25	.55
☐ 7 Mike Piazza	1.50	.70
☐ 8 Albert Belle	.60	.25
☐ 9 Chipper Jones	1.50	.70
☐ 10 Andruw Jones	1.25	.55
☐ 11 Greg Maddux	1.50	.70
☐ 12 Hideo Nomo	1.25	.55
☐ 13 Jeff Bagwell	1.00	.45
☐ 14 Manny Ramirez	.50	.23
☐ 15 Mark McGwire	1.00	.45
☐ 16 Derek Jeter	1.50	.70
☐ 17 Sammy Sosa	.50	.23
☐ 18 Barry Bonds	.60	.25
☐ 19 Chuck Knoblauch	.50	.23
☐ 20 Dante Bichette	.30	.14
☐ 21 Tony Gwynn	1.25	.55
☐ 22 Ken Caminiti	.50	.23
☐ 23 Gary Sheffield	.50	.23
☐ 24 Tim Salmon	.50	.23
☐ 25 Ivan Rodriguez	.60	.25
☐ 26 Henry Rodriguez	.25	.11
☐ 27 Barry Larkin	.40	.18
☐ 28 Ryan Klesko	.40	.18
☐ 29 Brian Jordan	.25	.11
☐ 30 Jay Buhner	.40	.18
☐ P28 Ryan Klesko Promo	3.00	1.35

1997 Pinnacle Mint Bronze

Each pack contained either one bronze, silver or gold card. The bronze versions are the most common. Each bronze card features color action player images on a sepia player portrait background. The player's team name was embossed in a bronze coin replica placed where the coin was to be inserted in the die-cut version. Ryan Klesko's bronze card was distributed to dealers as a promo.

	MINT	NRMT
COMPLETE SET (30)	40.00	18.00
COMMON CARD (1-30)	.50	.23
*BRONZE: .75X TO 2X DIE CUT CARDS		
☐ P28 Ryan Klesko Promo	3.00	1.35

1997 Pinnacle Mint Gold

Randomly inserted in packs at a rate of one in 48, this 30-card set is parallel to the regular set and is distinguised from the regular set by the use of full Gold-foil dufex print technologies.

	MINT	NRMT
COMPLETE SET (30)	500.00	220.00
COMMON CARD (1-30)	6.00	2.70
*GOLD: 10X TO 25X DIE CUT CARDS.		

1997 Pinnacle Mint Silver

Randomly inserted in packs at a rate of one in 15, this 30-card set is parallel to the regular set and is similar in design. It is distinguised from the regular set by its silver-foil stamping.

	MINT	NRMT
COMPLETE SET (30)	250.00	110.00
COMMON CARD (1-30)	3.00	1.35
*SILVER: 5X TO 12X DIE CUT CARDS		

1997 Pinnacle Mint Coins Brass

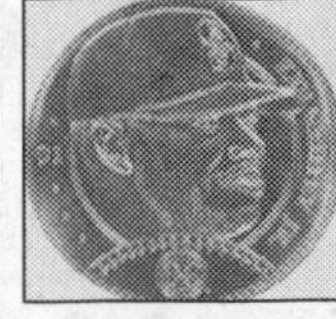

Each pack of Pinnacle Mint contained two coins (a mixture of Brass, Nickel and Gold Plated). The Brass coins were the most common. This set features coins minted in brass with embossed player heads and were made to be matched with the die-cut card version of the same player. Two versions of the Manny Ramirez Brass coin were distributed - an erroneous version with the words "fine silver" printed on back, and a corrected version. Judging from market observations, the "fine silver" version appears to be about four times tougher to find than the corrected. In addition to being inserted in packs, Ryan Klesko's Brass coin was distributed to dealers as a promo.

	MINT	NRMT
COMP.BRASS SET (30)	60.00	27.00
COMMON BRASS (1-30)	.75	.35
COMP.NICKEL SET (30)	300.00	135.00
*NICKEL: 2X TO 5X BASIC CARDS		
COMP.GOLD PLTD.SET (30)	750.00	350.00
*GOLD PLATED: 5X TO 12X BASIC CARDS		
☐ 1 Ken Griffey Jr.	8.00	3.60
☐ 2 Frank Thomas	6.00	2.70
☐ 3 Alex Rodriguez	6.00	2.70
☐ 4 Cal Ripken	6.00	2.70
☐ 5 Mo Vaughn	2.00	.90
☐ 6 Juan Gonzalez	4.00	1.80
☐ 7 Mike Piazza	5.00	2.20
☐ 8 Albert Belle	2.50	1.10
☐ 9 Chipper Jones	5.00	2.20
☐ 10 Andruw Jones	4.00	1.80
☐ 11 Greg Maddux	5.00	2.20
☐ 12 Hideo Nomo	4.00	1.80
☐ 13 Jeff Bagwell	3.00	1.35
☐ 14A Manny Ramirez COR	1.50	.70
☐ 14B Manny Ramirez ERR says "Fine Silver" on back	10.00	4.50
☐ 15 Mark McGwire	3.00	1.35
☐ 16 Derek Jeter	5.00	2.20
☐ 17 Sammy Sosa	1.50	.70
☐ 18 Barry Bonds	2.00	.90
☐ 19 Chuck Knoblauch	1.50	.70
☐ 20 Dante Bichette	1.00	.45
☐ 21 Tony Gwynn	4.00	1.80
☐ 22 Ken Caminiti	1.50	.70
☐ 23 Gary Sheffield	1.50	.70
☐ 24 Tim Salmon	1.50	.70
☐ 25 Ivan Rodriguez	2.00	.90
☐ 26 Henry Rodriguez	.75	.35
☐ 27 Barry Larkin	1.25	.55
☐ 28 Ryan Klesko	1.25	.55
☐ 29 Brian Jordan	.75	.35
☐ 30 Jay Buhner	1.25	.55

1997 Pinnacle Totally Certified Samples

This set was produced to introduce the Pinnacle Totally Certified Platinum Red, Blue, and Gold Sets. One card from each of the three parallel sets was distributed in each version of this preview set.

	MINT	NRMT
COMPLETE SET (5)	12.00	5.50
COMMON CARD	1.00	.45
☐ 18 Tony Clark RED	1.00	.45
☐ 24 Larry Walker BLUE	2.00	.90
☐ 39 Roger Clemens BLUE	3.00	1.35
☐ 41 Frank Thomas GOLD	4.00	1.80
☐ 53 Ken Griffey Jr. GOLD	5.00	2.20

1997 Pinnacle Totally Certified Platinum Blue

This 150-card set is a parallel version of the more-common 1997 Pinnacle Totally Certified Platinum Red set. Platinum Blue cards were seeded at a rate of one per pack. The fronts feature color action player images utilizing full micro-etched, holographic mylar print technology, highlighted with a blue vignette accent and foil stamping. Only 1,999 sets were produced and each card is sequentially numbered on back.

	MINT	NRMT
COMPLETE SET (150)	1000.00	450.00
COMMON CARD (1-150)	3.00	1.35
*BLUE STARS: .75 X TO 2X RED		

1997 Pinnacle Totally Certified Platinum Gold

This 150-card set is a parallel version of the 1997 Pinnacle Totally Certified Platinum Red set. Platinum Gold cards were randomly seeded into one in every 79 packs. The fronts feature color action player images utilizing full micro-etched, holographic mylar foil, highlighted with gold vignette accents and foil stamping. Only 30 sets were produced and each card is sequentially numbered on back.

	MINT	NRMT
COMMON CARD (1-150)	80.00	36.00
MINOR STARS	120.00	55.00

	MINT	NRMT
SEMISTARS	200.00	90.00
UNLISTED STARS	250.00	110.00
☐ 1 Barry Bonds	400.00	180.00
☐ 2 Mo Vaughn	400.00	180.00
☐ 4 Ryne Sandberg	400.00	180.00
☐ 5 Jeff Bagwell	600.00	275.00
☐ 17 Albert Belle	400.00	180.00
☐ 22 Alex Rodriguez	1000.00	450.00
☐ 24 Larry Walker	300.00	135.00
☐ 26 Mike Piazza	1000.00	450.00
☐ 28 Cal Ripken	1200.00	550.00
☐ 30 Paul Molitor	300.00	135.00
☐ 31 Darin Erstad	400.00	180.00
☐ 39 Roger Clemens	600.00	275.00
☐ 41 Frank Thomas	1500.00	700.00
☐ 43 Mike Mussina	300.00	135.00
☐ 45 Tony Gwynn	800.00	350.00
☐ 47 Jim Thome	300.00	135.00
☐ 49 Mark McGwire	600.00	275.00
☐ 51 Derek Jeter	800.00	350.00
☐ 53 Ken Griffey Jr.	2000.00	900.00
☐ 54 Randy Johnson	300.00	135.00
☐ 58 Kenny Lofton	400.00	180.00
☐ 59 Chipper Jones	800.00	350.00
☐ 63 Hideo Nomo	1200.00	550.00
☐ 66 Eddie Murray	300.00	135.00
☐ 68 Manny Ramirez	300.00	135.00
☐ 69 Juan Gonzalez	800.00	350.00
☐ 79 Ivan Rodriguez	400.00	180.00
☐ 83 Greg Maddux	1000.00	450.00
☐ 92 Andy Pettitte	300.00	135.00
☐ 95 Roberto Alomar	300.00	135.00
☐ 106 Andruw Jones	600.00	275.00
☐ 107 Jose Guillen	300.00	135.00
☐ 111 Vladimir Guerrero	500.00	220.00
☐ 112 Scott Rolen	600.00	275.00
☐ 114 Nomar Garciaparra	800.00	350.00
☐ 136 Ken Griffey Jr. CERT	1000.00	450.00
☐ 137 Vladimir Guerrero CERT	250.00	110.00
☐ 138 Roger Clemens CERT	300.00	135.00
☐ 139 Mark McGwire CERT	300.00	135.00
☐ 141 Derek Jeter CERT	400.00	180.00
☐ 142 Juan Gonzalez CERT	400.00	180.00
☐ 143 Greg Maddux CERT	500.00	220.00
☐ 144 Alex Rodriguez CERT	500.00	220.00
☐ 145 Jeff Bagwell CERT	300.00	135.00
☐ 146 Cal Ripken CERT	600.00	275.00
☐ 147 Tony Gwynn CERT	400.00	180.00
☐ 148 Frank Thomas CERT	800.00	350.00
☐ 149 Hideo Nomo CERT	600.00	275.00
☐ 150 Andruw Jones CERT	300.00	135.00

1997 Pinnacle Totally Certified Platinum Red

This 150-card set is a quasi-parallel version of the 1997 Pinnacle Certified set. The checklist and player content is identical, but the photos are all different and the cards are designed a little differently. The fronts feature color action player images utilizing full micro-etched, holographic mylar print technology, highlighted with red vignette accent and foil stamping. The product was distributed in three-card packs with a suggested retail price of $6.99. Platinum Red cards were seeded at a rate of two per pack. Only 3,999 Platinum Red sets were produced and each card is sequentially numbered on back.

	MINT	NRMT
COMPLETE SET (150)	500.00	220.00
COMMON CARD (1-150)	1.50	.70
☐ 1 Barry Bonds	8.00	3.60
☐ 2 Mo Vaughn	8.00	3.60
☐ 3 Matt Williams	4.00	1.80
☐ 4 Ryne Sandberg	8.00	3.60
☐ 5 Jeff Bagwell	12.00	5.50
☐ 6 Alan Benes	3.00	1.35
☐ 7 John Wetteland	3.00	1.35
☐ 8 Fred McGriff	4.00	1.80
☐ 9 Craig Biggio	4.00	1.80
☐ 10 Bernie Williams	6.00	2.70
☐ 11 Brian Hunter	3.00	1.35
☐ 12 Sandy Alomar Jr.	3.00	1.35
☐ 13 Ray Lankford	3.00	1.35
☐ 14 Ryan Klesko	4.00	1.80
☐ 15 Jermaine Dye	1.50	.70
☐ 16 Andy Benes	1.50	.70
☐ 17 Albert Belle	8.00	3.60
☐ 18 Tony Clark	6.00	2.70
☐ 19 Dean Palmer	3.00	1.35
☐ 20 Bernard Gilkey	1.50	.70
☐ 21 Ken Caminiti	6.00	2.70
☐ 22 Alex Rodriguez	20.00	9.00
☐ 23 Tim Salmon	6.00	2.70
☐ 24 Larry Walker	6.00	2.70
☐ 25 Barry Larkin	4.00	1.80
☐ 26 Mike Piazza	20.00	9.00
☐ 27 Brady Anderson	4.00	1.80
☐ 28 Cal Ripken	25.00	11.00
☐ 29 Charles Nagy	3.00	1.35
☐ 30 Paul Molitor	6.00	2.70
☐ 31 Darin Erstad	8.00	3.60
☐ 32 Rey Ordonez	1.50	.70
☐ 33 Wally Joyner	3.00	1.35
☐ 34 David Cone	3.00	1.35
☐ 35 Sammy Sosa	6.00	2.70
☐ 36 Dante Bichette	3.00	1.35
☐ 37 Eric Karros	1.50	.70
☐ 38 Omar Vizquel	3.00	1.35
☐ 39 Roger Clemens	12.00	5.50
☐ 40 Joe Carter	3.00	1.35
☐ 41 Frank Thomas	25.00	11.00
☐ 42 Javy Lopez	3.00	1.35
☐ 43 Mike Mussina	6.00	2.70
☐ 44 Gary Sheffield	6.00	2.70
☐ 45 Tony Gwynn	15.00	6.75
☐ 46 Jason Kendall	3.00	1.35
☐ 47 Jim Thome	6.00	2.70
☐ 48 Andres Galarraga	6.00	2.70
☐ 49 Mark McGwire	12.00	5.50
☐ 50 Troy Percival	3.00	1.35
☐ 51 Derek Jeter	15.00	6.75
☐ 52 Todd Hollandsworth	1.50	.70
☐ 53 Ken Griffey Jr.	30.00	13.50
☐ 54 Randy Johnson	6.00	2.70
☐ 55 Pat Hentgen	3.00	1.35
☐ 56 Rusty Greer	3.00	1.35
☐ 57 John Jaha	1.50	.70
☐ 58 Kenny Lofton	8.00	3.60
☐ 59 Chipper Jones	20.00	9.00
☐ 60 Robb Nen	3.00	1.35
☐ 61 Rafael Palmeiro	4.00	1.80
☐ 62 Mariano Rivera	3.00	1.35
☐ 63 Hideo Nomo	15.00	6.75
☐ 64 Greg Vaughn	1.50	.70
☐ 65 Ron Gant	3.00	1.35
☐ 66 Eddie Murray	6.00	2.70
☐ 67 John Smoltz	3.00	1.35
☐ 68 Manny Ramirez	6.00	2.70
☐ 69 Juan Gonzalez	15.00	6.75
☐ 70 F.P. Santangelo	1.50	.70
☐ 71 Moises Alou	3.00	1.35
☐ 72 Alex Ochoa	1.50	.70
☐ 73 Chuck Knoblauch	6.00	2.70
☐ 74 Raul Mondesi	4.00	1.80
☐ 75 J.T. Snow	3.00	1.35
☐ 76 Rickey Henderson	4.00	1.80
☐ 77 Bobby Bonilla	3.00	1.35
☐ 78 Wade Boggs	6.00	2.70
☐ 79 Ivan Rodriguez	8.00	3.60
☐ 80 Brian Jordan	1.50	.70
☐ 81 Al Leiter	1.50	.70
☐ 82 Jay Buhner	4.00	1.80
☐ 83 Greg Maddux	20.00	9.00
☐ 84 Edgar Martinez	4.00	1.80
☐ 85 Kevin Brown	1.50	.70
☐ 86 Eric Young	1.50	.70
☐ 87 Todd Hundley	3.00	1.35
☐ 88 Ellis Burks	3.00	1.35
☐ 89 Marquis Grissom	3.00	1.35
☐ 90 Jose Canseco	4.00	1.80
☐ 91 Henry Rodriguez	1.50	.70
☐ 92 Andy Pettitte	6.00	2.70
☐ 93 Mark Grudzielanek	1.50	.70
☐ 94 Dwight Gooden	3.00	1.35
☐ 95 Roberto Alomar	6.00	2.70
☐ 96 Paul Wilson	1.50	.70
☐ 97 Will Clark	4.00	1.80
☐ 98 Rondell White	3.00	1.35
☐ 99 Charles Johnson	3.00	1.35
☐ 100 Jim Edmonds	6.00	2.70
☐ 101 Jason Giambi	3.00	1.35
☐ 102 Billy Wagner	3.00	1.35
☐ 103 Edgar Renteria	3.00	1.35
☐ 104 Johnny Damon	3.00	1.35
☐ 105 Jason Isringhausen	1.50	.70
☐ 106 Andruw Jones	12.00	5.50
☐ 107 Jose Guillen	6.00	2.70
☐ 108 Kevin Orie	3.00	1.35
☐ 109 Brian Giles	1.50	.70
☐ 110 Danny Patterson	1.50	.70
☐ 111 Vladimir Guerrero	10.00	4.50
☐ 112 Scott Rolen	12.00	5.50
☐ 113 Damon Mashore	1.50	.70
☐ 114 Nomar Garciaparra	15.00	6.75
☐ 115 Todd Walker	1.50	.70
☐ 116 Wilton Guerrero	1.50	.70
☐ 117 Bob Abreu	6.00	2.70
☐ 118 Brooks Kieschnick	3.00	1.35
☐ 119 Pokey Reese	1.50	.70
☐ 120 Todd Greene	3.00	1.35
☐ 121 Dmitri Young	3.00	1.35
☐ 122 Raul Casanova	1.50	.70
☐ 123 Glendon Rusch	1.50	.70
☐ 124 Jason Dickson	1.50	.70
☐ 125 Jorge Posada	1.50	.70
☐ 126 Rod Myers	1.50	.70
☐ 127 Bubba Trammell	6.00	2.70
☐ 128 Scott Spiezio	1.50	.70
☐ 129 Hideki Irabu	8.00	3.60
☐ 130 Wendell Magee	1.50	.70
☐ 131 Bartolo Colon	3.00	1.35
☐ 132 Chris Holt	1.50	.70
☐ 133 Calvin Maduro	1.50	.70
☐ 134 Ray Montgomery	1.50	.70
☐ 135 Shannon Stewart	1.50	.70
☐ 136 Ken Griffey Jr. CERT	15.00	6.75
☐ 137 Vladimir Guerrero CERT	6.00	2.70
☐ 138 Roger Clemens CERT	6.00	2.70
☐ 139 Mark McGwire CERT	6.00	2.70
☐ 140 Albert Belle CERT	6.00	2.70
☐ 141 Derek Jeter CERT	8.00	3.60
☐ 142 Juan Gonzalez CERT	8.00	3.60
☐ 143 Greg Maddux CERT	10.00	4.50
☐ 144 Alex Rodriguez CERT	10.00	4.50
☐ 145 Jeff Bagwell CERT	6.00	2.70
☐ 146 Cal Ripken CERT	12.00	5.50
☐ 147 Tony Gwynn CERT	8.00	3.60
☐ 148 Frank Thomas CERT	12.00	5.50
☐ 149 Hideo Nomo CERT	6.00	2.70
☐ 150 Andruw Jones CERT	6.00	2.70

1997 Pinnacle X-Press

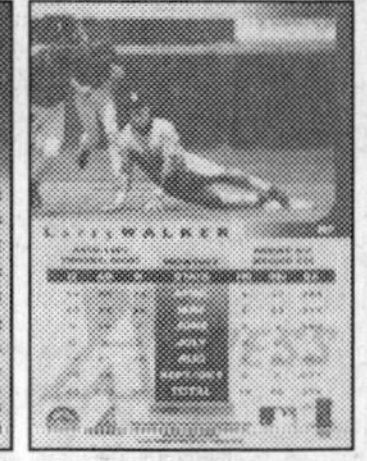

The 1997 Pinnacle X-Press set was issued in one series totalling 150 cards and was distributed in two different kinds of packs. The eight-card packs retailed for $1.99. X-Press Metal Works home plate-shaped retail boxes carried a suggested retail price of $14.99 and contained an eight-card regular pack along with a master deck that had eight more cards, plus one Metal Works card. The set contains the topical subsets: Rookies (116-137), Peak Performers (138-147), and Checklists (148-150).

	MINT	NRMT
COMPLETE SET (150)	20.00	9.00
COMMON CARD (1-150)	.10	.05
☐ 1 Larry Walker	.40	.18
☐ 2 Andy Pettitte	.40	.18
☐ 3 Matt Williams	.30	.14
☐ 4 Juan Gonzalez	1.00	.45
☐ 5 Frank Thomas	1.50	.70
☐ 6 Kenny Lofton	.50	.23
☐ 7 Ken Griffey Jr.	2.00	.90
☐ 8 Andres Galarraga	.40	.18
☐ 9 Greg Maddux	1.25	.55
☐ 10 Hideo Nomo	1.00	.45
☐ 11 Cecil Fielder	.20	.09
☐ 12 Jose Canseco	.30	.14
☐ 13 Tony Gwynn	1.00	.45
☐ 14 Eddie Murray	.40	.18
☐ 15 Alex Rodriguez	1.50	.70
☐ 16 Mike Piazza	1.25	.55
☐ 17 Ken Hill	.10	.05
☐ 18 Chuck Knoblauch	.40	.18
☐ 19 Ellis Burks	.20	.09
☐ 20 Rafael Palmeiro	.30	.14

☐ 21 Vinny Castilla	.20	.09
☐ 22 Rusty Greer	.20	.09
☐ 23 Chipper Jones	1.25	.55
☐ 24 Rey Ordonez	.10	.05
☐ 25 Mariano Rivera	.20	.09
☐ 26 Garret Anderson	.20	.09
☐ 27 Edgar Martinez	.30	.14
☐ 28 Dante Bichette	.20	.09
☐ 29 Todd Hundley	.20	.09
☐ 30 Barry Bonds	.50	.23
☐ 31 Barry Larkin	.20	.09
☐ 32 Derek Jeter	1.25	.55
☐ 33 Marquis Grissom	.20	.09
☐ 34 Dave Justice	.40	.18
☐ 35 Ivan Rodriguez	.50	.23
☐ 36 Jay Buhner	.30	.14
☐ 37 Fred McGriff	.30	.14
☐ 38 Brady Anderson	.30	.14
☐ 39 Tony Clark	.40	.18
☐ 40 Eric Young	.10	.05
☐ 41 Charles Nagy	.20	.09
☐ 42 Mark McGwire	.75	.35
☐ 43 Paul O'Neill	.20	.09
☐ 44 Tino Martinez	.40	.18
☐ 45 Ryne Sandberg	.50	.23
☐ 46 Bernie Williams	.40	.18
☐ 47 Albert Belle	.50	.23
☐ 48 Jeff Cirillo	.20	.09
☐ 49 Tim Salmon	.40	.18
☐ 50 Steve Finley	.20	.09
☐ 51 Lance Johnson	.10	.05
☐ 52 John Smoltz	.20	.09
☐ 53 Javier Lopez	.20	.09
☐ 54 Roger Clemens	.75	.35
☐ 55 Kevin Appier	.20	.09
☐ 56 Ken Caminiti	.40	.18
☐ 57 Cal Ripken	1.50	.70
☐ 58 Moises Alou	.20	.09
☐ 59 Marty Cordova	.10	.05
☐ 60 David Cone	.20	.09
☐ 61 Manny Ramirez	.40	.18
☐ 62 Ray Durham	.10	.05
☐ 63 Jermaine Dye	.10	.05
☐ 64 Craig Biggio	.30	.14
☐ 65 Will Clark	.30	.14
☐ 66 Omar Vizquel	.20	.09
☐ 67 Bernard Gilkey	.10	.05
☐ 68 Greg Vaughn	.10	.05
☐ 69 Wade Boggs	.40	.18
☐ 70 Dave Nilsson	.10	.05
☐ 71 Mark Grace	.30	.14
☐ 72 Dean Palmer	.20	.09
☐ 73 Sammy Sosa	.40	.18
☐ 74 Mike Mussina	.40	.18
☐ 75 Alex Fernandez	.10	.05
☐ 76 Henry Rodriguez	.10	.05
☐ 77 Travis Fryman	.20	.09
☐ 78 Jeff Bagwell	.75	.35
☐ 79 Pat Hentgen	.20	.09
☐ 80 Gary Sheffield	.40	.18
☐ 81 Jim Edmonds	.40	.18
☐ 82 Darin Erstad	.60	.25
☐ 83 Mark Grudzielanek	.10	.05
☐ 84 Jim Thome	.40	.18
☐ 85 Bobby Higginson	.20	.09
☐ 86 Al Martin	.10	.05
☐ 87 Jason Giambi	.20	.09
☐ 88 Mo Vaughn	.50	.23
☐ 89 Jeff Conine	.20	.09
☐ 90 Edgar Renteria	.20	.09
☐ 91 Andy Ashby	.10	.05
☐ 92 Ryan Klesko	.30	.14
☐ 93 John Jaha	.10	.05
☐ 94 Paul Molitor	.40	.18
☐ 95 Brian Hunter	.20	.09
☐ 96 Randy Johnson	.40	.18
☐ 97 Joey Hamilton	.10	.05
☐ 98 Billy Wagner	.20	.09
☐ 99 John Wetteland	.20	.09
☐ 100 Jeff Fassero	.10	.05
☐ 101 Rondell White	.20	.09
☐ 102 Kevin Brown	.20	.09
☐ 103 Andy Benes	.20	.09
☐ 104 Raul Mondesi	.30	.14
☐ 105 Todd Hollandsworth	.10	.05
☐ 106 Alex Ochoa	.10	.05
☐ 107 Bobby Bonilla	.20	.09
☐ 108 Brian Jordan	.10	.05
☐ 109 Tom Glavine	.20	.09
☐ 110 Ron Gant	.20	.09
☐ 111 Jason Kendall	.10	.05
☐ 112 Roberto Alomar	.40	.18
☐ 113 Troy Percival	.10	.05
☐ 114 Michael Tucker	.20	.09
☐ 115 Joe Carter	.20	.09
☐ 116 Andruw Jones	1.00	.45
☐ 117 Nomar Garciaparra	1.25	.55
☐ 118 Todd Walker	.10	.05
☐ 119 Jose Guillen	1.00	.45
☐ 120 Bubba Trammell	.40	.18
☐ 121 Wilton Guerrero	.10	.05
☐ 122 Bob Abreu	.40	.18
☐ 123 Vladimir Guerrero	.75	.35
☐ 124 Dmitri Young	.20	.09
☐ 125 Kevin Orie	.20	.09
☐ 126 Jose Cruz Jr.	3.00	1.35
☐ 127 Brooks Kieschnick	.20	.09
☐ 128 Scott Spiezio	.10	.05
☐ 129 Brian Giles	.10	.05
☐ 130 Jason Dickson	.10	.05
☐ 131 Damon Mashore	.10	.05
☐ 132 Wendell Magee	.10	.05
☐ 133 Matt Morris	.20	.09
☐ 134 Scott Rolen	1.00	.45
☐ 135 Shannon Stewart	.20	.09
☐ 136 Deivi Cruz	.25	.11
☐ 137 Hideki Irabu	.50	.23
☐ 138 Larry Walker PP	.40	.18
☐ 139 Ken Griffey Jr. PP	1.00	.45
☐ 140 Frank Thomas PP	.75	.35
☐ 141 Ivan Rodriguez PP	.40	.18
☐ 142 Randy Johnson PP	.40	.18
☐ 143 Mark McGwire PP	.40	.18
☐ 144 Tino Martinez PP	.40	.18
☐ 145 Tony Clark PP	.40	.18
☐ 146 Mike Piazza PP	.60	.25
☐ 147 Alex Rodriguez PP	.75	.35
☐ 148 Roger Clemens CL	.40	.18
☐ 149 Greg Maddux CL	.60	.25
☐ 150 Hideo Nomo CL	.50	.23

1997 Pinnacle X-Press Men of Summer

Randomly inserted in packs at the rate of one in seven and one in every Master Deck, this 150-card set is parallel to the base set and is printed on full silver foil card stock with foil stamped accents.

	MINT	NRMT
COMPLETE SET (150)	500.00	220.00
COMMON CARD (1-150)	2.00	.90
*STARS: 8X TO 20X BASIC CARDS		
*YOUNG STARS: 6X TO 15X BASIC CARDS		
*ROOKIES: 4X TO 10X BASIC CARDS		

1997 Pinnacle X-Press Far and Away

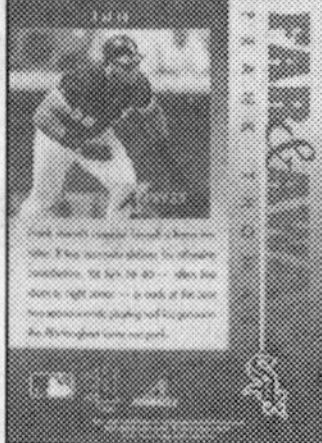

Randomly inserted in regular packs at the rate of one in 19 and one in five in Master Decks, this 18-card set features color photos of the league's top long-ball hitters. The cards are printed with Dufex hand-etched all-foil highlights.

	MINT	NRMT
COMPLETE SET (18)	120.00	55.00
COMMON CARD (1-18)	2.00	.90
☐ 1 Albert Belle	5.00	2.20
☐ 2 Mark McGwire	8.00	3.60
☐ 3 Frank Thomas	15.00	6.75
☐ 4 Mo Vaughn	5.00	2.20
☐ 5 Jeff Bagwell	8.00	3.60
☐ 6 Juan Gonzalez	10.00	4.50
☐ 7 Mike Piazza	12.00	5.50
☐ 8 Andruw Jones	10.00	4.50
☐ 9 Chipper Jones	12.00	5.50
☐ 10 Gary Sheffield	4.00	1.80
☐ 11 Sammy Sosa	4.00	1.80
☐ 12 Darin Erstad	6.00	2.70
☐ 13 Jay Buhner	3.00	1.35
☐ 14 Ken Griffey Jr.	20.00	9.00
☐ 15 Ken Caminiti	4.00	1.80
☐ 16 Brady Anderson	2.00	.90
☐ 17 Manny Ramirez	4.00	1.80
☐ 18 Alex Rodriguez	12.00	5.50

1997 Pinnacle X-Press Melting Pot

Randomly inserted in regular packs at the rate of one in 288 and one in 189 in Master Decks, this 20-card set features color photos of top players. The set tracks the players' origins on foil board with heliogram raised ink printing. The fronts carry a portrait of the player with his country's flag as the background. The backs display another player photo, player information, team logo and his native country. Only 500 of this set were produced and are sequentially numbered.

	MINT	NRMT
COMPLETE SET (20)	800.00	350.00
COMMON CARD (1-20)	8.00	3.60
☐ 1 Jose Guillen	25.00	11.00
☐ 2 Vladimir Guerrero	40.00	18.00
☐ 3 Andruw Jones	50.00	22.00
☐ 4 Larry Walker	25.00	11.00
☐ 5 Manny Ramirez	25.00	11.00
☐ 6 Ken Griffey Jr.	120.00	55.00
☐ 7 Alex Rodriguez	80.00	36.00
☐ 8 Frank Thomas	100.00	45.00
☐ 9 Juan Gonzalez	60.00	27.00
☐ 10 Ivan Rodriguez	30.00	13.50
☐ 11 Hideo Nomo	70.00	32.00
☐ 12 Rafael Palmeiro	15.00	6.75
☐ 13 Dave Nilsson	8.00	3.60
☐ 14 Nomar Garciaparra	60.00	27.00
☐ 15 Wilton Guerrero	8.00	3.60
☐ 16 Sammy Sosa	20.00	9.00
☐ 17 Edgar Renteria	12.00	5.50
☐ 18 Cal Ripken	100.00	45.00
☐ 19 Derek Jeter	60.00	27.00
☐ 20 Rey Ordonez	8.00	3.60
☐ P7 Alex Rodriguez SAMPLE	2.50	1.10

1997 Pinnacle X-Press Melting Pot Samples

These cards were sent out to dealers to indicate what the Pinnacle X-Press Melting Pot set would look like. These cards are numbered the same as the regular cards. The differences are that the word "sample" is printed in large black ink on both the front and the back. In addition, all the cards are numbered 000/500.

	MINT	NRMT
COMPLETE SET (20)	80.00	36.00
*STARS: .1X BASIC MELTING POT		

1997 Pinnacle X-Press Metal Works

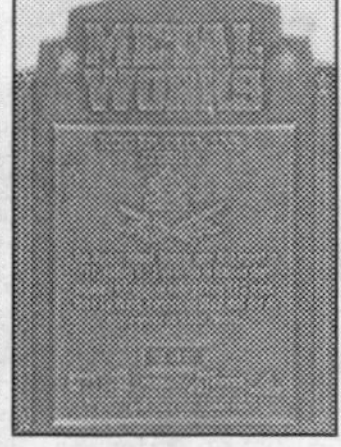

Inserted one in every Home Plate Box, this 20-card bronze set features color photos of top players printed on very thick metal stock. The redemption cards carry no expiration date. They are valid until supplies run out.

	MINT	NRMT
COMPLETE SET (20)	200.00	90.00
COMMON CARD (1-20)	5.00	2.20
*GOLD: 7X TO 15X BASIC INSERT		
*SILVER: 5X TO 8X BASIC INSERT		
☐ 1 Ken Griffey Jr.	25.00	11.00
☐ 2 Frank Thomas	20.00	9.00
☐ 3 Andruw Jones	12.00	5.50
☐ 4 Alex Rodriguez	15.00	6.75
☐ 5 Derek Jeter	15.00	6.75
☐ 6 Cal Ripken	20.00	9.00
☐ 7 Mike Piazza	15.00	6.75
☐ 8 Chipper Jones	15.00	6.75
☐ 9 Juan Gonzalez	12.00	5.50
☐ 10 Greg Maddux	15.00	6.75
☐ 11 Tony Gwynn	12.00	5.50
☐ 12 Jeff Bagwell	10.00	4.50

☐ 13 Albert Belle	6.00	2.70
☐ 14 Mark McGwire	10.00	4.50
☐ 15 Nomar Garciaparra	15.00	6.75
☐ 16 Mo Vaughn	6.00	2.70
☐ 17 Andy Pettitte	5.00	2.20
☐ 18 Manny Ramirez	5.00	2.20
☐ 19 Kenny Lofton	6.00	2.70
☐ 20 Roger Clemens	10.00	4.50
☐ NNO Gold Redemption Card	100.00	45.00
☐ NNO Silver Redemption Card	50.00	22.00

1997 Pinnacle X-Press Swing for the Fences

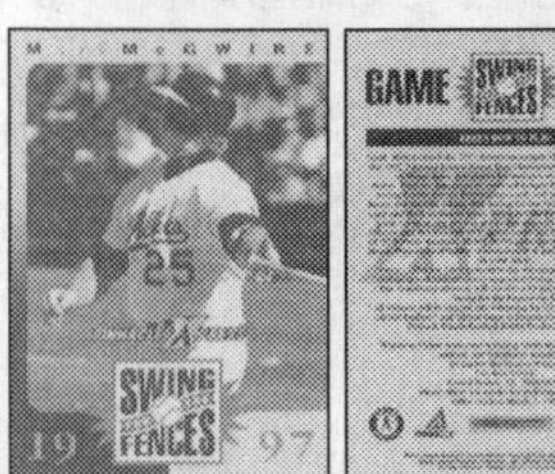

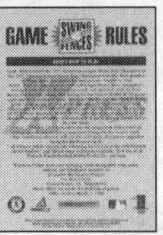

Randomly inserted in packs at the rate of one in two, cards from this 60-card unnumbered set feature color photos of baseball's top long-distance hitters and are the player cards for the Swing for the Fences Game in which collectors accumulated points in order to win prizes. The object was to find the Home Run Champion from either the National or American League and match it with the exact number of home runs hit during the 1997 season by using a combination of Booster Number Point cards and one Base Number Home Run card. A Booster card was inserted one in every two packs and carried a plus or minus point total that allowed collectors to add or subtract points to get the winning homer total. The Base Number Home Run Card was found in the Home Plate Master Deck packs only and carried a predetermined number of Home Runs (between 20 and 42) assigned to each player. The first 1,000 winners received an autographed card of Andruw Jones of the Atlanta Braves. The next 3,000 winners received random 10-card packs of Upgraded Swing For the Fences cards produced on thicker card stock and printed with a special foil prize-winner stamp. After all redemptions were done, a drawing was held for the grand prize of a trip for two to the 1998 Pinnacle All-Star FanFest with tickets to the All-Star Game in Denver, Colorado. Five runner-up winners received a box of all Pinnacle Trading Cards baseball products for a full year. Since Mark McGwire led the majors in homers, his card was also deemed to be a winner although he did not led either league in homers.

	MINT	NRMT
COMPLETE SET (60)	80.00	36.00
COMMON CARD	.25	.11
☐ 1 Sandy Alomar Jr.	.50	.23
☐ 2 Moises Alou	.50	.23
☐ 3 Brady Anderson	.75	.35
☐ 4 Jeff Bagwell	2.00	.90
☐ 5 Derek Bell	.25	.11
☐ 6 Jay Bell	.25	.11
☐ 7 Albert Belle	1.25	.55
☐ 8 Geronimo Berroa	.25	.11
☐ 9 Dante Bichette	.50	.23
☐ 10 Barry Bonds	1.25	.55
☐ 11 Bobby Bonilla	.50	.23
☐ 12 Jay Buhner	.75	.35
☐ 13 Ellis Burks	.50	.23
☐ 14 Ken Caminiti	1.00	.45
☐ 15 Jose Canseco	.50	.23
☐ 16 Joe Carter	.50	.23
☐ 17 Vinny Castilla	.50	.23
☐ 18 Tony Clark	1.00	.45
☐ 19 Carlos Delgado	.50	.23
☐ 20 Jim Edmonds	1.00	.45
☐ 21 Cecil Fielder	.50	.23
☐ 22 Andres Galarraga	1.00	.45
☐ 23 Ron Gant	.25	.11
☐ 24 Bernard Gilkey	.25	.11
☐ 25 Juan Gonzalez	2.50	1.10
☐ 26 Ken Griffey Jr. W	15.00	6.75
☐ 27 Vladimir Guerrero	2.00	.90
☐ 28 Todd Hundley	.50	.23
☐ 29 John Jaha	.25	.11
☐ 30 Andruw Jones	1.00	.45
☐ 31 Chipper Jones	3.00	1.35
☐ 32 David Justice	1.00	.45
☐ 33 Jeff Kent	.25	.11
☐ 34 Ryan Klesko	.75	.35
☐ 35 Barry Larkin	.50	.23
☐ 36 Mike Lieberthal	.25	.11
☐ 37 Javier Lopez	.50	.23
☐ 38 Edgar Martinez	.75	.35
☐ 39 Tino Martinez	1.00	.45
☐ 40 Fred McGriff	.75	.35
☐ 41 Mark McGwire W	10.00	4.50
☐ 42 Raul Mondesi	.75	.35
☐ 43 Tim Naehring	.25	.11
☐ 44 Dave Nilsson	.25	.11
☐ 45 Rafael Palmeiro	.75	.35
☐ 46 Dean Palmer	.25	.11
☐ 47 Mike Piazza	3.00	1.35
☐ 48 Cal Ripken	4.00	1.80
☐ 49 Henry Rodriguez	.25	.11
☐ 50 Tim Salmon	1.00	.45
☐ 51 Gary Sheffield	1.00	.45
☐ 52 Sammy Sosa	1.00	.45
☐ 53 Terry Steinbach	.25	.11
☐ 54 Frank Thomas	4.00	1.80
☐ 55 Jim Thome	1.00	.45
☐ 56 Mo Vaughn	1.25	.55
☐ 57 Larry Walker W	8.00	3.60
☐ 58 Rondell White	.50	.23
☐ 59 Matt Williams	.75	.35
☐ 60 Todd Zeile	.25	.11
☐ NNO A.Jones AU EXCH	50.00	22.00

1997 Pinnacle X-Press Swing for the Fences Upgrade

3,000 lucky winners from the Pinnacle X-Press Swing for the Fences game received special 10-card packs of upgraded Swing For the Fences cards produced on thicker card stock and printed with a special foil prize-winner stamp. Strangely enough, the card backs - containing guidelines for how to mail in winning cards - are identical to the original Swing for the Fences game cards issued in packs. The cards are unnumbered and typically sorted in alphabetical order by player's last name.

	MINT	NRMT
COMPLETE SET (60)	150.00	70.00
COMMON CARD (1-60)	1.00	.45

*STARS: 2X TO 4X BASIC SWING CARDS
*YOUNG STARS: 1.5X TO 3X BASIC SWING CARDS

☐ 26 Ken Griffey Jr.	20.00	9.00
☐ 41 Mark McGwire	8.00	3.60
☐ 57 Larry Walker	4.00	1.80

1939 Play Ball R334

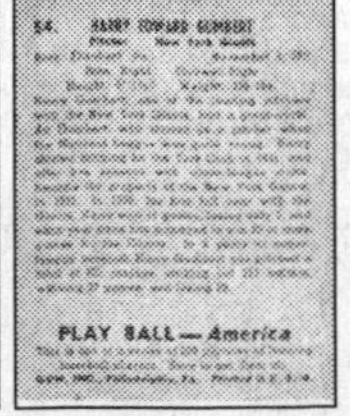

The cards in this 161-card set measure approximately 2 1/2" by 3 1/8". Gum Incorporated introduced a brief (war-shortened) but innovative era of baseball card production with its set of 1939. The combination of actual player photos (black and white), large card size, and extensive biography proved extremely popular. Player names are found either entirely capitalized or with initial caps only, and a "sample card" overprint is not uncommon. The "sample card" overprint variations are valued at double the prices below. Card number 126 was never issued, and cards 116-162 were produced in lesser quantities than cards 1-115. A card of Ted Williams in his rookie season as well as an early card of Joe DiMaggio are the key cards in the set.

	EX-MT	VG-E
COMPLETE SET (162)	12000.00	5400.00
COMMON CARD (1-115)	20.00	9.00
COMMON CARD (116-162)	90.00	40.00
WRAPPER (1-CENT)	200.00	90.00
☐ 1 Jake Powell	75.00	34.00
☐ 2 Lee Grissom	20.00	9.00
☐ 3 Red Ruffing	75.00	34.00
☐ 4 Eldon Auker	20.00	9.00
☐ 5 Luke Sewell	25.00	11.00
☐ 6 Leo Durocher	90.00	40.00
☐ 7 Bobby Doerr	75.00	34.00
☐ 8 Henry Pippen	20.00	9.00
☐ 9 James Tobin	20.00	9.00
☐ 10 James DeShong	20.00	9.00
☐ 11 Johnny Rizzo	20.00	9.00
☐ 12 Hershel Martin	20.00	9.00
☐ 13 Luke Hamlin	20.00	9.00
☐ 14 Jim Tabor	20.00	9.00
☐ 15 Paul Derringer	30.00	13.50
☐ 16 John Peacock	20.00	9.00
☐ 17 Emerson Dickman	20.00	9.00
☐ 18 Harry Danning	20.00	9.00
☐ 19 Paul Dean	30.00	13.50
☐ 20 Joe Heving	20.00	9.00
☐ 21 Dutch Leonard	25.00	11.00
☐ 22 Bucky Walters	25.00	11.00
☐ 23 Burgess Whitehead	20.00	9.00
☐ 24 Richard Coffman	20.00	9.00
☐ 25 George Selkirk	30.00	13.50
☐ 26 Joe DiMaggio	2400.00	1100.00
☐ 27 Fred Ostermueller	20.00	9.00
☐ 28 Sylvester Johnson	20.00	9.00
☐ 29 John(Jack) Wilson	20.00	9.00
☐ 30 Bill Dickey	150.00	70.00
☐ 31 Sam West	20.00	9.00
☐ 32 Bob Seeds	20.00	9.00
☐ 33 Del Young	20.00	9.00
☐ 34 Frank Demaree	20.00	9.00
☐ 35 Bill Jurges	20.00	9.00
☐ 36 Frank McCormick	20.00	9.00
☐ 37 Virgil Davis	20.00	9.00
☐ 38 Billy Myers	20.00	9.00
☐ 39 Rick Ferrell	75.00	34.00
☐ 40 James Bagby Jr.	20.00	9.00
☐ 41 Lon Warneke	20.00	9.00
☐ 42 Arndt Jorgens	20.00	9.00
☐ 43 Melo Almada	20.00	9.00
☐ 44 Don Heffner	20.00	9.00
☐ 45 Merrill May	20.00	9.00
☐ 46 Morris Arnovich	20.00	9.00
☐ 47 Buddy Lewis	20.00	9.00
☐ 48 Lefty Gomez	125.00	55.00
☐ 49 Eddie Miller	20.00	9.00
☐ 50 Charley Gehringer	150.00	70.00
☐ 51 Mel Ott	150.00	70.00
☐ 52 Tommy Henrich	35.00	16.00
☐ 53 Carl Hubbell	125.00	55.00
☐ 54 Harry Gumpert	20.00	9.00
☐ 55 Arky Vaughan	75.00	34.00
☐ 56 Hank Greenberg	200.00	90.00
☐ 57 Buddy Hassett	20.00	9.00
☐ 58 Lou Chiozza	20.00	9.00
☐ 59 Ken Chase	20.00	9.00
☐ 60 Schoolboy Rowe	25.00	11.00
☐ 61 Tony Cuccinello	20.00	9.00
☐ 62 Tom Carey	20.00	9.00
☐ 63 Emmett Mueller	20.00	9.00
☐ 64 Wally Moses	20.00	9.00
☐ 65 Harry Craft	20.00	9.00
☐ 66 Jimmy Ripple	20.00	9.00
☐ 67 Ed Joost	20.00	9.00
☐ 68 Fred Sington	20.00	9.00
☐ 69 Elbie Fletcher	20.00	9.00
☐ 70 Fred Frankhouse	20.00	9.00
☐ 71 Monte Pearson	25.00	11.00
☐ 72 Debs Garms	20.00	9.00
☐ 73 Hal Schumacher	20.00	9.00
☐ 74 Cookie Lavagetto	20.00	9.00
☐ 75 Stan Bordagaray	20.00	9.00
☐ 76 Goody Rosen	20.00	9.00
☐ 77 Lew Riggs	20.00	9.00
☐ 78 Julius Solters	20.00	9.00
☐ 79 Jo Jo Moore	20.00	9.00
☐ 80 Pete Fox	20.00	9.00
☐ 81 Babe Dahlgren	25.00	11.00
☐ 82 Chuck Klein	125.00	55.00
☐ 83 Gus Suhr	20.00	9.00
☐ 84 Skeeter Newsom	20.00	9.00
☐ 85 Johnny Cooney	20.00	9.00
☐ 86 Dolph Camilli	20.00	9.00
☐ 87 Milburn Shoffner	20.00	9.00
☐ 88 Charlie Keller	35.00	16.00

☐ 89 Lloyd Waner	75.00	34.00
☐ 90 Robert Klinger	20.00	9.00
☐ 91 John Knott	20.00	9.00
☐ 92 Ted Williams	2400.00	1100.00
☐ 93 Charles Gelbert	20.00	9.00
☐ 94 Heinie Manush	75.00	34.00
☐ 95 Whit Wyatt	20.00	9.00
☐ 96 Babe Phelps	20.00	9.00
☐ 97 Bob Johnson	25.00	11.00
☐ 98 Pinky Whitney	20.00	9.00
☐ 99 Wally Berger	30.00	13.50
☐ 100 Buddy Myer	20.00	9.00
☐ 101 Roger Cramer	20.00	9.00
☐ 102 Lem Young	20.00	9.00
☐ 103 Moe Berg	175.00	80.00
☐ 104 Tom Bridges	20.00	9.00
☐ 105 Rabbit McNair	20.00	9.00
☐ 106 Dolly Stark UMP	25.00	11.00
☐ 107 Joe Vosmik	20.00	9.00
☐ 108 Frank Hayes	20.00	9.00
☐ 109 Myril Hoag	20.00	9.00
☐ 110 Fred Fitzsimmons	20.00	9.00
☐ 111 Van Lingle Mungo	25.00	11.00
☐ 112 Paul Waner	90.00	40.00
☐ 113 Al Schacht	25.00	11.00
☐ 114 Cecil Travis	20.00	9.00
☐ 115 Ralph Kress	20.00	9.00
☐ 116 Gene Desautels	90.00	40.00
☐ 117 Wayne Ambler	90.00	40.00
☐ 118 Lynn Nelson	90.00	40.00
☐ 119 Will Hershberger	100.00	45.00
☐ 120 Rabbit Warstler	90.00	40.00
☐ 121 Bill Posedel	90.00	40.00
☐ 122 George McQuinn	90.00	40.00
☐ 123 Ray T. Davis	90.00	40.00
☐ 124 Walter Brown	90.00	40.00
☐ 125 Cliff Melton	90.00	40.00
☐ 126 Not issued		
☐ 127 Gil Brack	90.00	40.00
☐ 128 Joe Bowman	90.00	40.00
☐ 129 Bill Swift	90.00	40.00
☐ 130 Bill Brubaker	90.00	40.00
☐ 131 Mort Cooper	100.00	45.00
☐ 132 Jim Brown	90.00	40.00
☐ 133 Lynn Myers	90.00	40.00
☐ 134 Tot Presnell	90.00	40.00
☐ 135 Mickey Owen	100.00	45.00
☐ 136 Roy Bell	90.00	40.00
☐ 137 Pete Appleton	90.00	40.00
☐ 138 George Case	100.00	45.00
☐ 139 Vito Tamulis	90.00	40.00
☐ 140 Ray Hayworth	90.00	40.00
☐ 141 Pete Coscarart	90.00	40.00
☐ 142 Ira Hutchinson	90.00	40.00
☐ 143 Earl Averill	225.00	100.00
☐ 144 Zeke Bonura	100.00	45.00
☐ 145 Hugh Mulcahy	90.00	40.00
☐ 146 Tom Sunkel	90.00	40.00
☐ 147 George Coffman	90.00	40.00
☐ 148 Bill Trotter	90.00	40.00
☐ 149 Max West	90.00	40.00
☐ 150 James Walkup	90.00	40.00
☐ 151 Hugh Casey	100.00	45.00
☐ 152 Roy Weatherly	90.00	40.00
☐ 153 Dizzy Trout	100.00	45.00
☐ 154 Johnny Hudson	90.00	40.00
☐ 155 Jimmy Outlaw	90.00	40.00
☐ 156 Ray Berres	90.00	40.00
☐ 157 Don Padgett	90.00	40.00
☐ 158 Bud Thomas	90.00	40.00
☐ 159 Red Evans	90.00	40.00
☐ 160 Gene Moore	90.00	40.00
☐ 161 Lonnie Frey	90.00	40.00
☐ 162 Whitey Moore	100.00	45.00

1940 Play Ball R335

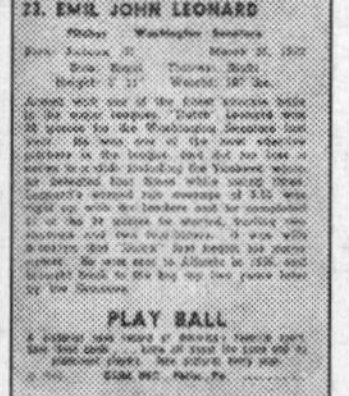

The cards in this 240-card series measure approximately 2 1/2" by 3 1/8". Gum Inc. improved upon its 1939 design by enclosing the 1940 black and white player photo with a frame line and printing the player's name in a panel below the picture (often using a nickname). The set included many Hall of Famers and Old Timers. Cards 1-114 are numbered in team groupings. Cards 181-240 are scarcer than cards 1-180. The backs contain an extensive biography and a dated copyright line. The key cards in the set are the cards of Joe DiMaggio, Shoeless Joe Jackson, and Ted Williams.

	EX-MT	VG-E
COMPLETE SET (240)	18000.00	8100.00
COMMON CARD (1-120)	20.00	9.00
COMMON CARD (121-180)	20.00	9.00
COMMON CARD (181-240)	70.00	32.00
WRAPPER (1-CENT, DIFF. COLORS)	800.00	350.00

Card	EX-MT	VG-E
☐ 1 Joe DiMaggio	2700.00	1200.00
☐ 2 Art Jorgens	22.00	10.00
☐ 3 Babe Dahlgren	22.00	10.00
☐ 4 Tommy Henrich	35.00	16.00
☐ 5 Monte Pearson	22.00	10.00
☐ 6 Lefty Gomez	150.00	70.00
☐ 7 Bill Dickey	175.00	80.00
☐ 8 George Selkirk	22.00	10.00
☐ 9 Charlie Keller	35.00	16.00
☐ 10 Red Ruffing	90.00	40.00
☐ 11 Jake Powell	22.00	10.00
☐ 12 Johnny Schulte	20.00	9.00
☐ 13 Jack Knott	20.00	9.00
☐ 14 Rabbit McNair	20.00	9.00
☐ 15 George Case	22.00	10.00
☐ 16 Cecil Travis	22.00	10.00
☐ 17 Buddy Myer	22.00	10.00
☐ 18 Charlie Gelbert	20.00	9.00
☐ 19 Ken Chase	20.00	9.00
☐ 20 Buddy Lewis	20.00	9.00
☐ 21 Rick Ferrell	80.00	36.00
☐ 22 Sammy West	20.00	9.00
☐ 23 Dutch Leonard	22.00	10.00
☐ 24 Frank Hayes	20.00	9.00
☐ 25 Bob Johnson	22.00	10.00
☐ 26 Wally Moses	22.00	10.00
☐ 27 Ted Williams	1700.00	750.00
☐ 28 Gene Desautels	20.00	9.00
☐ 29 Doc Cramer	22.00	10.00
☐ 30 Moe Berg	150.00	70.00
☐ 31 Jack Wilson	20.00	9.00
☐ 32 Jim Bagby	20.00	9.00
☐ 33 Fritz Ostermueller	20.00	9.00
☐ 34 John Peacock	20.00	9.00
☐ 35 Joe Heving	20.00	9.00
☐ 36 Jim Tabor	20.00	9.00
☐ 37 Emerson Dickman	20.00	9.00
☐ 38 Bobby Doerr	90.00	40.00
☐ 39 Tom Carey	20.00	9.00
☐ 40 Hank Greenberg	250.00	110.00
☐ 41 Charley Gehringer	150.00	70.00
☐ 42 Bud Thomas	20.00	9.00
☐ 43 Pete Fox	20.00	9.00
☐ 44 Dizzy Trout	22.00	10.00
☐ 45 Red Kress	20.00	9.00
☐ 46 Earl Averill	90.00	40.00
☐ 47 Oscar Vitt	20.00	9.00
☐ 48 Luke Sewell	22.00	10.00
☐ 49 Stormy Weatherly	20.00	9.00
☐ 50 Hal Trosky	22.00	10.00
☐ 51 Don Heffner	20.00	9.00
☐ 52 Myril Hoag	20.00	9.00
☐ 53 George McQuinn	22.00	10.00
☐ 54 Bill Trotter	20.00	9.00
☐ 55 Slick Coffman	20.00	9.00
☐ 56 Eddie Miller	22.00	10.00
☐ 57 Max West	20.00	9.00
☐ 58 Bill Posedel	20.00	9.00
☐ 59 Rabbit Warstler	20.00	9.00
☐ 60 John Cooney	20.00	9.00
☐ 61 Tony Cuccinello	22.00	10.00
☐ 62 Buddy Hassett	20.00	9.00
☐ 63 Pete Coscarart	20.00	9.00
☐ 64 Van Lingle Mungo	22.00	10.00
☐ 65 Fred Fitzsimmons	22.00	10.00
☐ 66 Babe Phelps	20.00	9.00
☐ 67 Whit Wyatt	22.00	10.00
☐ 68 Dolph Camilli	22.00	10.00
☐ 69 Cookie Lavagetto	22.00	10.00
☐ 70 Luke Hamlin (Hot Potato)	20.00	9.00
☐ 71 Mel Almada	20.00	9.00
☐ 72 Chuck Dressen	22.00	10.00
☐ 73 Bucky Walters	22.00	10.00
☐ 74 Paul(Duke) Derringer	30.00	13.50
☐ 75 Frank(Buck) McCormick	22.00	10.00
☐ 76 Lonny Frey	20.00	9.00
☐ 77 Willard Hershberger	22.00	10.00
☐ 78 Lew Riggs	20.00	9.00
☐ 79 Harry Craft	22.00	10.00
☐ 80 Billy Myers	20.00	9.00
☐ 81 Wally Berger	22.00	10.00
☐ 82 Hank Gowdy CO	22.00	10.00
☐ 83 Cliff Melton	20.00	9.00
☐ 84 Jo Jo Moore	20.00	9.00
☐ 85 Hal Schumacher	22.00	10.00
☐ 86 Harry Gumbert	20.00	9.00
☐ 87 Carl Hubbell	125.00	55.00
☐ 88 Mel Ott	175.00	80.00
☐ 89 Bill Jurges	20.00	9.00
☐ 90 Frank Demaree	20.00	9.00
☐ 91 Bob Seeds	20.00	9.00
☐ 92 Whitey Whitehead	20.00	9.00
☐ 93 Harry Danning	20.00	9.00
☐ 94 Gus Suhr	20.00	9.00
☐ 95 Hugh Mulcahy	20.00	9.00
☐ 96 Heinie Mueller	20.00	9.00
☐ 97 Morry Arnovich	20.00	9.00
☐ 98 Pinky May	20.00	9.00
☐ 99 Syl Johnson	20.00	9.00
☐ 100 Hersh Martin	20.00	9.00
☐ 101 Del Young	20.00	9.00
☐ 102 Chuck Klein	100.00	45.00
☐ 103 Elbie Fletcher	20.00	9.00
☐ 104 Paul Waner	90.00	40.00
☐ 105 Lloyd Waner	80.00	36.00
☐ 106 Pep Young	20.00	9.00
☐ 107 Arky Vaughan	80.00	36.00
☐ 108 Johnny Rizzo	20.00	9.00
☐ 109 Don Padgett	20.00	9.00
☐ 110 Tom Sunkel	20.00	9.00
☐ 111 Mickey Owen	30.00	13.50
☐ 112 Jimmy Brown	20.00	9.00
☐ 113 Mort Cooper	22.00	10.00
☐ 114 Lon Warneke	22.00	10.00
☐ 115 Mike Gonzalez CO	22.00	10.00
☐ 116 Al Schacht	30.00	13.50
☐ 117 Dolly Stark UMP	22.00	10.00
☐ 118 Waite Hoyt	90.00	40.00
☐ 119 Grover C. Alexander	175.00	80.00
☐ 120 Walter Johnson	250.00	110.00
☐ 121 Atley Donald	25.00	11.00
☐ 122 Sandy Sundra	25.00	11.00
☐ 123 Hildy Hildebrand	25.00	11.00
☐ 124 Earle Combs	100.00	45.00
☐ 125 Art Fletcher	25.00	11.00
☐ 126 Jake Solters	20.00	9.00
☐ 127 Muddy Ruel	20.00	9.00
☐ 128 Pete Appleton	20.00	9.00
☐ 129 Bucky Harris	80.00	36.00
☐ 130 Clyde(Deerfoot) Milan	25.00	11.00
☐ 131 Zeke Bonura	25.00	11.00
☐ 132 Connie Mack MG	200.00	90.00
☐ 133 Jimmie Foxx	250.00	110.00
☐ 134 Joe Cronin	100.00	45.00
☐ 135 Line Drive Nelson	20.00	9.00
☐ 136 Cotton Pippen	20.00	9.00
☐ 137 Bing Miller	20.00	9.00
☐ 138 Beau Bell	20.00	9.00
☐ 139 Elden Auker	20.00	9.00
☐ 140 Dick Coffman	20.00	9.00
☐ 141 Casey Stengel MG	200.00	90.00
☐ 142 George Kelly	90.00	40.00
☐ 143 Gene Moore	20.00	9.00
☐ 144 Joe Vosmik	20.00	9.00
☐ 145 Vito Tamulis	20.00	9.00
☐ 146 Tot Pressnell	20.00	9.00
☐ 147 Johnny Hudson	20.00	9.00
☐ 148 Hugh Casey	25.00	11.00
☐ 149 Pinky Shoffner	20.00	9.00
☐ 150 Whitey Moore	20.00	9.00
☐ 151 Edwin Joost	25.00	11.00
☐ 152 Jimmy Wilson	20.00	9.00
☐ 153 Bill McKechnie MG	80.00	36.00
☐ 154 Jumbo Brown	20.00	9.00
☐ 155 Ray Hayworth	20.00	9.00
☐ 156 Daffy Dean	35.00	16.00
☐ 157 Lou Chiozza	20.00	9.00
☐ 158 Travis Jackson	90.00	40.00
☐ 159 Pancho Snyder	20.00	9.00
☐ 160 Hans Lobert CO	20.00	9.00
☐ 161 Debs Garms	20.00	9.00
☐ 162 Joe Bowman	20.00	9.00
☐ 163 Spud Davis	20.00	9.00
☐ 164 Ray Berres	20.00	9.00
☐ 165 Bob Klinger	20.00	9.00
☐ 166 Bill Brubaker	20.00	9.00
☐ 167 Frankie Frisch MG	90.00	40.00
☐ 168 Honus Wagner CO	250.00	110.00
☐ 169 Gabby Street	20.00	9.00
☐ 170 Tris Speaker	200.00	90.00
☐ 171 Harry Heilmann	90.00	40.00
☐ 172 Chief Bender	90.00	40.00
☐ 173 Napoleon Lajoie	175.00	80.00
☐ 174 Johnny Evers	90.00	40.00
☐ 175 Christy Mathewson	250.00	110.00
☐ 176 Heinie Manush	90.00	40.00
☐ 177 Frank Baker	100.00	45.00
☐ 178 Max Carey	90.00	40.00
☐ 179 George Sisler	150.00	70.00
☐ 180 Mickey Cochrane	150.00	70.00
☐ 181 Spud Chandler	80.00	36.00

☐ 182 Knick Knickerbocker	70.00	32.00
☐ 183 Marvin Breuer	70.00	32.00
☐ 184 Mule Haas	70.00	32.00
☐ 185 Joe Kuhel	70.00	32.00
☐ 186 Taft Wright	70.00	32.00
☐ 187 Jimmy Dykes MG	80.00	36.00
☐ 188 Joe Krakauskas	70.00	32.00
☐ 189 Jim Bloodworth	70.00	32.00
☐ 190 Charley Berry	70.00	32.00
☐ 191 John Babich	70.00	32.00
☐ 192 Dick Siebert	70.00	32.00
☐ 193 Chubby Dean	70.00	32.00
☐ 194 Sam Chapman	70.00	32.00
☐ 195 Dee Miles	70.00	32.00
☐ 196 Red(Nonny) Nonnenkamp	70.00	32.00
☐ 197 Lou Finney	70.00	32.00
☐ 198 Denny Galehouse	70.00	32.00
☐ 199 Pinky Higgins	70.00	32.00
☐ 200 Soup Campbell	70.00	32.00
☐ 201 Barney McCosky	70.00	32.00
☐ 202 Al Milnar	70.00	32.00
☐ 203 Bad News Hale	70.00	32.00
☐ 204 Harry Eisenstat	70.00	32.00
☐ 205 Rollie Hemsley	70.00	32.00
☐ 206 Chet Laabs	70.00	32.00
☐ 207 Gus Mancuso	70.00	32.00
☐ 208 Lee Gamble	70.00	32.00
☐ 209 Hy Vandenberg	70.00	32.00
☐ 210 Bill Lohrman	70.00	32.00
☐ 211 Pop Joiner	70.00	32.00
☐ 212 Babe Young	70.00	32.00
☐ 213 John Rucker	70.00	32.00
☐ 214 Ken O'Dea	70.00	32.00
☐ 215 Johnnie McCarthy	70.00	32.00
☐ 216 Joe Marty	70.00	32.00
☐ 217 Walter Beck	70.00	32.00
☐ 218 Wally Millies	70.00	32.00
☐ 219 Russ Bauers	70.00	32.00
☐ 220 Mace Brown	70.00	32.00
☐ 221 Lee Handley	70.00	32.00
☐ 222 Max Butcher	70.00	32.00
☐ 223 Hughie Jennings	150.00	70.00
☐ 224 Pie Traynor	175.00	80.00
☐ 225 Joe Jackson	2500.00	1100.00
☐ 226 Harry Hooper	150.00	70.00
☐ 227 Jesse Haines	150.00	70.00
☐ 228 Charlie Grimm	80.00	36.00
☐ 229 Buck Herzog	70.00	32.00
☐ 230 Red Faber	150.00	70.00
☐ 231 Dolf Luque	100.00	45.00
☐ 232 Goose Goslin	150.00	70.00
☐ 233 George Earnshaw	80.00	36.00
☐ 234 Frank Chance	150.00	70.00
☐ 235 John McGraw	175.00	80.00
☐ 236 Jim Bottomley	150.00	70.00
☐ 237 Willie Keeler	250.00	110.00
☐ 238 Tony Lazzeri	175.00	80.00
☐ 239 George Uhle	70.00	32.00
☐ 240 Bill Atwood	100.00	45.00

1941 Play Ball R336

The cards in this 72-card set measure approximately 2 1/2" by 3 1/8". Many of the cards in the 1941 Play Ball series are simply color versions of pictures appearing in the 1940 set. This was the only color baseball card set produced by Gum, Inc.. Card numbers 49-72 are slightly more difficult to obtain as they were not issued until 1942. In 1942, numbers 1-48 were also reissued but without the copyright date. The cards were also printed on paper without a cardboard backing; these are generally encountered in sheets or strips. The set features a card of Pee Wee Reese in his rookie year.

	EX-MT	VG-E
COMPLETE SET (72)	10000.00	4500.00
COMMON CARD (1-48)	40.00	18.00
COMMON CARD (49-72)	60.00	27.00
SEMISTARS (49-72)	75.00	34.00
WRAPPER (1-CENT)	800.00	350.00

☐ 1 Eddie Miller	125.00	55.00
☐ 2 Max West	40.00	18.00
☐ 3 Bucky Walters	45.00	20.00
☐ 4 Paul Derringer	55.00	25.00
☐ 5 Frank(Buck) McCormick	45.00	20.00
☐ 6 Carl Hubbell	175.00	80.00
☐ 7 Harry Danning	40.00	18.00
☐ 8 Mel Ott	225.00	100.00
☐ 9 Pinky May	40.00	18.00
☐ 10 Arky Vaughan	100.00	45.00
☐ 11 Debs Garms	40.00	18.00
☐ 12 Jimmy Brown	40.00	18.00
☐ 13 Jimmie Foxx	300.00	135.00
☐ 14 Ted Williams	1600.00	700.00
☐ 15 Joe Cronin	100.00	45.00
☐ 16 Hal Trosky	45.00	20.00
☐ 17 Roy Weatherly	40.00	18.00
☐ 18 Hank Greenberg	300.00	135.00
☐ 19 Charley Gehringer	200.00	90.00
☐ 20 Red Ruffing	100.00	45.00
☐ 21 Charlie Keller	65.00	29.00
☐ 22 Bob Johnson	55.00	25.00
☐ 23 George McQuinn	40.00	18.00
☐ 24 Dutch Leonard	45.00	20.00
☐ 25 Gene Moore	40.00	18.00
☐ 26 Harry Gumpert	40.00	18.00
☐ 27 Babe Young	40.00	18.00
☐ 28 Joe Marty	40.00	18.00
☐ 29 Jack Wilson	40.00	18.00
☐ 30 Lou Finney	40.00	18.00
☐ 31 Joe Kuhel	40.00	18.00
☐ 32 Taft Wright	40.00	18.00
☐ 33 Al Milnar	40.00	18.00
☐ 34 Rollie Hemsley	40.00	18.00
☐ 35 Pinky Higgins	45.00	20.00
☐ 36 Barney McCosky	40.00	18.00
☐ 37 Bruce Campbell	40.00	18.00
☐ 38 Atley Donald	55.00	25.00
☐ 39 Tommy Henrich	65.00	29.00
☐ 40 John Babich	40.00	18.00
☐ 41 Frank(Blimp) Hayes	40.00	18.00
☐ 42 Wally Moses	45.00	20.00
☐ 43 Al Brancato	40.00	18.00
☐ 44 Sam Chapman	40.00	18.00
☐ 45 Eldon Auker	40.00	18.00
☐ 46 Sid Hudson	40.00	18.00
☐ 47 Buddy Lewis	40.00	18.00
☐ 48 Cecil Travis	45.00	20.00
☐ 49 Babe Dahlgren	65.00	29.00
☐ 50 Johnny Cooney	60.00	27.00
☐ 51 Dolph Camilli	65.00	29.00
☐ 52 Kirby Higbe	60.00	27.00
☐ 53 Luke Hamlin	60.00	27.00
☐ 54 Pee Wee Reese	700.00	325.00
☐ 55 Whit Wyatt	65.00	29.00
☐ 56 Johnny VanderMeer	100.00	45.00
☐ 57 Moe Arnovich	60.00	27.00
☐ 58 Frank Demaree	60.00	27.00
☐ 59 Bill Jurges	60.00	27.00
☐ 60 Chuck Klein	225.00	100.00
☐ 61 Vince DiMaggio	250.00	110.00
☐ 62 Elbie Fletcher	60.00	27.00
☐ 63 Dom DiMaggio	250.00	110.00
☐ 64 Bobby Doerr	175.00	80.00
☐ 65 Tommy Bridges	65.00	29.00
☐ 66 Harland Clift	60.00	27.00
☐ 67 Walt Judnich	60.00	27.00
☐ 68 John Knott	60.00	27.00
☐ 69 George Case	65.00	29.00
☐ 70 Bill Dickey	475.00	210.00
☐ 71 Joe DiMaggio	2600.00	1150.00
☐ 72 Lefty Gomez	475.00	210.00

1961 Post

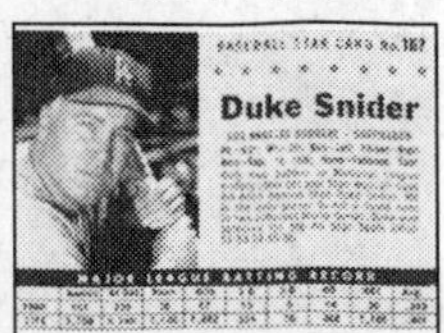

The cards in this 200-card set measure 2 1/2" by 3 1/2". The 1961 Post set was this company's first major set. The cards were available on thick cardbox stock, singly or in various panel sizes from cereal boxes (BOX), or in team sheets, printed on thinner cardboard stock, directly from the Post Cereal Company (COM). It is difficult to differentiate the COM cards from the BOX cards; the thickness of the card stock is the best indicator. Many variations exist and are noted in the checklist below. There are many cards which were produced in lesser quantities; the prices below reflect the relative scarcity of the cards. Cards 10, 23, 70, 73, 94, 113, 135, 163, and 183 are examples of cards printed in limited quantities and hence commanding premium prices. The cards are numbered essentially in team groups, i.e., New York Yankees (1-18), Chicago White Sox (19-34), Detroit (35-46), Boston (47-56), Cleveland (57-67), Baltimore (68-80), Kansas City (81-90), Minnesota (91-100), Milwaukee (101-114), Philadelphia (115-124), Pittsburgh (125-140), San Francisco (141-155), Los Angeles Dodgers (156-170), St. Louis (171-180), Cincinnati (181-190), and Chicago Cubs (191-200). The catalog number is F278-33. The complete set price refers to the set with all variations (357). There was also an album produced by Post to hold the cards.

	NRMT	VG-E
COMPLETE SET (357)	3000.00	1350.00
COMMON CARD (1-200)	3.00	1.35

☐ 1A Yogi Berra COM	30.00	13.50
☐ 1B Yogi Berra BOX	30.00	13.50
☐ 2A Elston Howard COM	5.00	2.20
☐ 2B Elston Howard BOX	5.00	2.20
☐ 3A Bill Skowron COM	5.00	2.20
☐ 3B Bill Skowron BOX	5.00	2.20
☐ 4A Mickey Mantle COM	150.00	70.00
☐ 4B Mickey Mantle BOX	150.00	70.00
☐ 5 Bob Turley COM only	20.00	9.00
☐ 6A Whitey Ford COM	10.00	4.50
☐ 6B Whitey Ford BOX	10.00	4.50
☐ 7A Roger Maris COM	30.00	13.50
☐ 7B Roger Maris BOX	30.00	13.50
☐ 8A Bobby Richardson COM	5.00	2.20
☐ 8B Bobby Richardson BOX	5.00	2.20
☐ 9A Tony Kubek COM	5.00	2.20
☐ 9B Tony Kubek BOX	5.00	2.20
☐ 10 Gil McDougald BOX only	50.00	22.00
☐ 11 Cletis Boyer BOX only	3.00	1.35
☐ 12A Hector Lopez COM	3.00	1.35
☐ 12B Hector Lopez BOX	3.00	1.35
☐ 13 Bob Cerv BOX only	3.00	1.35
☐ 14 Ryne Duren BOX only	3.00	1.35
☐ 15 Bobby Shantz BOX only	3.00	1.35
☐ 16 Art Ditmar BOX only	3.00	1.35
☐ 17 Jim Coates BOX only	3.00	1.35
☐ 18 Johnny Blanchard BOX only	3.00	1.35
☐ 19A Luis Aparicio COM	7.50	3.40
☐ 19B Luis Aparicio BOX	7.50	3.40
☐ 20A Nellie Fox COM	7.50	3.40
☐ 20B Nellie Fox BOX	7.50	3.40
☐ 21A Billy Pierce COM	5.00	2.20
☐ 21B Billy Pierce BOX	5.00	2.20
☐ 22A Early Wynn COM	12.00	5.50
☐ 22B Early Wynn BOX	12.00	5.50
☐ 23 Bob Shaw BOX only	100.00	45.00
☐ 24A Al Smith COM	3.00	1.35
☐ 24B Al Smith BOX	3.00	1.35
☐ 25A Minnie Minoso COM	6.00	2.70
☐ 25B Minnie Minoso BOX	6.00	2.70
☐ 26A Roy Sievers COM	3.00	1.35
☐ 26B Roy Sievers BOX	3.00	1.35
☐ 27A Jim Landis COM	3.00	1.35
☐ 27B Jim Landis BOX	3.00	1.35
☐ 28A Sherm Lollar COM	3.00	1.35
☐ 28B Sherm Lollar BOX	3.00	1.35
☐ 29 Gerry Staley BOX only	3.00	1.35
☐ 30A Gene Freese COM (Reds)	12.00	5.50
☐ 30B Gene Freese BOX (White Sox)	3.00	1.35
☐ 31 Ted Kluszewski BOX only	5.00	2.20
☐ 32 Turk Lown BOX only	3.00	1.35
☐ 33A Jim Rivera COM	3.00	1.35
☐ 33B Jim Rivera BOX	3.00	1.35
☐ 34 Frank Baumann BOX only	3.00	1.35
☐ 35A Al Kaline COM	20.00	9.00
☐ 35B Al Kaline BOX	20.00	9.00
☐ 36A Rocky Colavito COM	7.50	3.40
☐ 36B Rocky Colavito BOX	7.50	3.40
☐ 37A Charlie Maxwell COM	3.00	1.35
☐ 37B Charlie Maxwell BOX	3.00	1.35
☐ 38A Frank Lary COM	3.00	1.35
☐ 38B Frank Lary BOX	3.00	1.35
☐ 39A Jim Bunning COM	7.50	3.40
☐ 39B Jim Bunning BOX	7.50	3.40
☐ 40A Norm Cash COM	5.00	2.20
☐ 40B Norm Cash BOX	5.00	2.20
☐ 41A Frank Bolling COM (Braves, Charlie Gehringer in bio)	5.00	2.20
☐ 41B Frank Bolling BOX (Tigers, Charlie Derringer in bio)	7.50	3.40
☐ 42A Don Mossi COM	3.00	1.35
☐ 42B Don Mossi BOX	3.00	1.35

☐ 43A Lou Berberet COM	3.00	1.35
☐ 43B Lou Berberet BOX	3.00	1.35
☐ 44 Dave Sisler BOX only	3.00	1.35
☐ 45 Eddie Yost BOX only	3.00	1.35
☐ 46 Pete Burnside BOX only	3.00	1.35
☐ 47A Pete Runnels COM	5.00	2.20
☐ 47B Pete Runnels BOX	5.00	2.20
☐ 48A Frank Malzone COM	3.00	1.35
☐ 48B Frank Malzone BOX	3.00	1.35
☐ 49A Vic Wertz COM	5.00	2.20
☐ 49B Vic Wertz BOX	5.00	2.20
☐ 50A Tom Brewer COM	3.00	1.35
☐ 50B Tom Brewer BOX	3.00	1.35
☐ 51A Willie Tasby COM (Sold to Wash.)	6.00	2.70
☐ 51B Willie Tasby BOX (No sale mention)	3.00	1.35
☐ 52A Russ Nixon COM	3.00	1.35
☐ 52B Russ Nixon BOX	3.00	1.35
☐ 53A Don Buddin COM	3.00	1.35
☐ 53B Don Buddin BOX	3.00	1.35
☐ 54A Bill Monbouquette COM	3.00	1.35
☐ 54B Bill Monbouquette BOX	3.00	1.35
☐ 55A Frank Sullivan COM (Phillies)	10.00	4.50
☐ 55B Frank Sullivan BOX (Red Sox)	3.00	1.35
☐ 56A Haywood Sullivan COM	3.00	1.35
☐ 56B Haywood Sullivan BOX	3.00	1.35
☐ 57A Harvey Kuenn COM (Giants)	7.50	3.40
☐ 57B Harvey Kuenn BOX (Indians)	5.00	2.20
☐ 58A Gary Bell COM	5.00	2.20
☐ 58B Gary Bell BOX	5.00	2.20
☐ 59A Jim Perry COM	3.00	1.35
☐ 59B Jim Perry BOX	3.00	1.35
☐ 60A Jim Grant COM	5.00	2.20
☐ 60B Jim Grant BOX	5.00	2.20
☐ 61A Johnny Temple COM	3.00	1.35
☐ 61B Johnny Temple BOX	3.00	1.35
☐ 62A Paul Foytack COM	3.00	1.35
☐ 62B Paul Foytack BOX	3.00	1.35
☐ 63A Vic Power COM	3.00	1.35
☐ 63B Vic Power BOX	3.00	1.35
☐ 64A Tito Francona COM	3.00	1.35
☐ 64B Tito Francona BOX	3.00	1.35
☐ 65A Ken Aspromonte COM (Sold to L.A.)	7.50	3.40
☐ 65B Ken Aspromonte BOX (No sale mention)	7.50	3.40
☐ 66 Bob Wilson BOX only	3.00	1.35
☐ 67A John Romano COM	3.00	1.35
☐ 67B John Romano BOX	3.00	1.35
☐ 68A Jim Gentile COM	5.00	2.20
☐ 68B Jim Gentile BOX	5.00	2.20
☐ 69A Gus Triandos COM	5.00	2.20
☐ 69B Gus Triandos BOX	5.00	2.20
☐ 70 Gene Woodling BOX only	30.00	13.50
☐ 71A Milt Pappas COM	5.00	2.20
☐ 71B Milt Pappas BOX	5.00	2.20
☐ 72A Ron Hansen COM	3.00	1.35
☐ 72B Ron Hansen BOX	3.00	1.35
☐ 73 Chuck Estrada COM only	100.00	45.00
☐ 74A Steve Barber COM	3.00	1.35
☐ 74B Steve Barber BOX	3.00	1.35
☐ 75A Brooks Robinson COM	25.00	11.00
☐ 75B Brooks Robinson BOX	25.00	11.00
☐ 76A Jackie Brandt COM	3.00	1.35
☐ 76B Jackie Brandt BOX	3.00	1.35
☐ 77A Marv Breeding COM	3.00	1.35
☐ 77B Marv Breeding BOX	3.00	1.35
☐ 78 Hal Brown BOX only	3.00	1.35
☐ 79 Billy Klaus BOX only	3.00	1.35
☐ 80A Hoyt Wilhelm COM	7.50	3.40
☐ 80B Hoyt Wilhelm BOX	7.50	3.40
☐ 81A Jerry Lumpe COM	5.00	2.20
☐ 81B Jerry Lumpe BOX	5.00	2.20
☐ 82A Norm Siebern COM	3.00	1.35
☐ 82B Norm Siebern BOX	3.00	1.35
☐ 83A Bud Daley COM	5.00	2.20
☐ 83B Bud Daley BOX	5.00	2.20
☐ 84A Bill Tuttle COM	3.00	1.35
☐ 84B Bill Tuttle BOX	3.00	1.35
☐ 85A Marv Throneberry COM	5.00	2.20
☐ 85B Marv Throneberry BOX	5.00	2.20
☐ 86A Dick Williams COM	5.00	2.20
☐ 86B Dick Williams BOX	5.00	2.20
☐ 87A Ray Herbert COM	3.00	1.35
☐ 87B Ray Herbert BOX	3.00	1.35
☐ 88A Whitey Herzog COM	5.00	2.20
☐ 88B Whitey Herzog BOX	5.00	2.20
☐ 89A Ken Hamlin COM (Sold to L.A.)	20.00	9.00
☐ 89B Ken Hamlin BOX (No sale mention)	3.00	1.35
☐ 90A Hank Bauer COM	5.00	2.20
☐ 90B Hank Bauer BOX	5.00	2.20
☐ 91A Bob Allison COM (Minnesota)	6.00	2.70
☐ 91B Bob Allison BOX (Minneapolis)	6.00	2.70
☐ 92A Harmon Killebrew (Minnesota) COM	40.00	18.00
☐ 92B Harmon Killebrew (Minneapolis) BOX	30.00	13.50
☐ 93A Jim Lemon COM (Minnesota)	20.00	9.00
☐ 93B Jim Lemon BOX (Minneapolis)	60.00	27.00
☐ 94A Chuck Stobbs (Minnesota) COM only	175.00	80.00
☐ 95A Reno Bertoia COM (Minnesota)	5.00	2.20
☐ 95B Reno Bertoia BOX (Minneapolis)	3.00	1.35
☐ 96A Billy Gardner COM (Minnesota)	5.00	2.20
☐ 96B Billy Gardner BOX (Minneapolis)	3.00	1.35
☐ 97A Earl Battey COM (Minnesota)	5.00	2.20
☐ 97B Earl Battey BOX (Minneapolis)	3.00	1.35
☐ 98A Pedro Ramos COM (Minnesota)	5.00	2.20
☐ 98B Pedro Ramos BOX (Minneapolis)	3.00	1.35
☐ 99A Camilo Pascual COM (Minnesota)	5.00	2.20
☐ 99B Camilo Pascual BOX (Minneapolis)	3.00	1.35
☐ 100A Billy Consolo COM (Minnesota)	5.00	2.20
☐ 100B Billy Consolo BOX (Minneapolis)	3.00	1.35
☐ 101A Warren Spahn COM	25.00	11.00
☐ 101B Warren Spahn BOX	25.00	11.00
☐ 102A Lew Burdette COM	5.00	2.20
☐ 102B Lew Burdette BOX	5.00	2.20
☐ 103A Bob Buhl COM	3.00	1.35
☐ 103B Bob Buhl BOX	3.00	1.35
☐ 104A Joe Adcock COM	5.00	2.20
☐ 104B Joe Adcock BOX	5.00	2.20
☐ 105A Johnny Logan COM	5.00	2.20
☐ 105B Johnny Logan BOX	5.00	2.20
☐ 106 Eddie Mathews COM only	30.00	13.50
☐ 107A Hank Aaron COM	30.00	13.50
☐ 107B Hank Aaron BOX	30.00	13.50
☐ 108A Wes Covington COM	3.00	1.35
☐ 108B Wes Covington BOX	3.00	1.35
☐ 109A Bill Bruton COM (Tigers)	6.00	2.70
☐ 109B Bill Bruton BOX (Braves)	6.00	2.70
☐ 110A Del Crandall COM	5.00	2.20
☐ 110B Del Crandall BOX	5.00	2.20
☐ 111 Red Schoendienst BOX only	5.00	2.20
☐ 112 Juan Pizarro BOX only	3.00	1.35
☐ 113 Chuck Cottier BOX only	15.00	6.75
☐ 114 Al Spangler BOX only	3.00	1.35
☐ 115A Dick Farrell COM	5.00	2.20
☐ 115B Dick Farrell BOX	5.00	2.20
☐ 116A Jim Owens COM	5.00	2.20
☐ 116B Jim Owens BOX	5.00	2.20
☐ 117A Robin Roberts COM	7.50	3.40
☐ 117B Robin Roberts BOX	7.50	3.40
☐ 118A Tony Taylor COM	3.00	1.35
☐ 118B Tony Taylor BOX	3.00	1.35
☐ 119A Lee Walls COM	3.00	1.35
☐ 119B Lee Walls BOX	3.00	1.35
☐ 120A Tony Curry COM	3.00	1.35
☐ 120B Tony Curry BOX	3.00	1.35
☐ 121A Pancho Herrera COM	3.00	1.35
☐ 121B Pancho Herrera BOX	3.00	1.35
☐ 122A Ken Walters COM	3.00	1.35
☐ 122B Ken Walters BOX	3.00	1.35
☐ 123A John Callison COM	5.00	2.20
☐ 123B John Callison BOX	5.00	2.20
☐ 124A Gene Conley COM (Red Sox)	12.00	5.50
☐ 124B Gene Conley BOX (Phillies)	3.00	1.35
☐ 125A Bob Friend COM	5.00	2.20
☐ 125B Bob Friend BOX	5.00	2.20
☐ 126A Vern Law COM	5.00	2.20
☐ 126B Vern Law BOX	5.00	2.20
☐ 127A Dick Stuart COM	3.00	1.35
☐ 127B Dick Stuart BOX	3.00	1.35
☐ 128A Bill Mazeroski COM	5.00	2.20
☐ 128B Bill Mazeroski BOX	5.00	2.20
☐ 129A Dick Groat COM	5.00	2.20
☐ 129B Dick Groat BOX	5.00	2.20
☐ 130A Don Hoak COM	3.00	1.35
☐ 130B Don Hoak BOX	3.00	1.35
☐ 131A Bob Skinner COM	3.00	1.35
☐ 131B Bob Skinner BOX	3.00	1.35
☐ 132A Roberto Clemente COM	50.00	22.00
☐ 132B Roberto Clemente BOX	50.00	22.00
☐ 133 Roy Face BOX only	5.00	2.20
☐ 134 Harvey Haddix BOX only	3.00	1.35
☐ 135 Bill Virdon BOX only	40.00	18.00
☐ 136A Gino Cimoli COM	3.00	1.35
☐ 136B Gino Cimoli BOX	3.00	1.35
☐ 137 Rocky Nelson BOX only	3.00	1.35
☐ 138A Smoky Burgess COM	5.00	2.20
☐ 138B Smoky Burgess BOX	5.00	2.20
☐ 139 Hal W. Smith BOX only	3.00	1.35
☐ 140 Wilmer Mizell BOX only	3.00	1.35
☐ 141A Mike McCormick COM	3.00	1.35
☐ 141B Mike McCormick BOX	3.00	1.35
☐ 142A John Antonelli COM (Cleveland)	6.00	2.70
☐ 142B John Antonelli BOX (San Francisco)	5.00	2.20
☐ 143A Sam Jones COM	5.00	2.20
☐ 143B Sam Jones BOX	5.00	2.20
☐ 144A Orlando Cepeda COM	7.50	3.40
☐ 144B Orlando Cepeda BOX	7.50	3.40
☐ 145A Willie Mays COM	35.00	16.00
☐ 145B Willie Mays BOX	35.00	16.00
☐ 146A Willie Kirkland (Cleveland) COM	7.50	3.40
☐ 146B Willie Kirkland (San Francisco) BOX	5.00	2.20
☐ 147A Willie McCovey COM	10.00	4.50
☐ 147B Willie McCovey BOX	10.00	4.50
☐ 148A Don Blasingame COM	3.00	1.35
☐ 148B Don Blasingame BOX	3.00	1.35
☐ 149A Jim Davenport COM	5.00	2.20
☐ 149B Jim Davenport BOX	5.00	2.20
☐ 150A Hobie Landrith COM	3.00	1.35
☐ 150B Hobie Landrith BOX	3.00	1.35
☐ 151 Bob Schmidt BOX only	3.00	1.35
☐ 152A Ed Bressoud COM	3.00	1.35
☐ 152B Ed Bressoud BOX	3.00	1.35
☐ 153A Andre Rodgers (no trade mention) BOX only	20.00	9.00
☐ 153B Andre Rodgers (Traded to Milw.) BOX only	5.00	2.20
☐ 154 Jack Sanford BOX only	3.00	1.35
☐ 155 Billy O'Dell BOX only	3.00	1.35
☐ 156A Norm Larker COM	3.00	1.35
☐ 156B Norm Larker BOX	3.00	1.35
☐ 157A Charlie Neal COM	3.00	1.35
☐ 157B Charlie Neal BOX	3.00	1.35
☐ 158A Jim Gilliam COM	6.00	2.70
☐ 158B Jim Gilliam BOX	6.00	2.70
☐ 159A Wally Moon COM	5.00	2.20
☐ 159B Wally Moon BOX	5.00	2.20
☐ 160A Don Drysdale COM	12.00	5.50
☐ 160B Don Drysdale BOX	12.00	5.50
☐ 161A Larry Sherry COM	5.00	2.20
☐ 161B Larry Sherry BOX	5.00	2.20
☐ 162 Stan Williams BOX only	7.50	3.40
☐ 163 Mel Roach BOX only	90.00	40.00
☐ 164A Maury Wills COM	10.00	4.50
☐ 164B Maury Wills BOX	10.00	4.50
☐ 165 Tommy Davis BOX only	5.00	2.20
☐ 166A John Roseboro COM	3.00	1.35
☐ 166B John Roseboro BOX	3.00	1.35
☐ 167A Duke Snider COM	7.50	3.40
☐ 167B Duke Snider BOX	7.50	3.40
☐ 168A Gil Hodges COM	7.50	3.40
☐ 168B Gil Hodges BOX	7.50	3.40
☐ 169 John Podres BOX only	3.00	1.35
☐ 170 Ed Roebuck BOX only	3.00	1.35
☐ 171A Ken Boyer COM	7.50	3.40
☐ 171B Ken Boyer BOX	7.50	3.40
☐ 172A Joe Cunningham COM	3.00	1.35
☐ 172B Joe Cunningham BOX	3.00	1.35
☐ 173A Daryl Spencer COM	3.00	1.35
☐ 173B Daryl Spencer BOX	3.00	1.35
☐ 174A Larry Jackson COM	3.00	1.35
☐ 174B Larry Jackson BOX	3.00	1.35
☐ 175A Lindy McDaniel COM	3.00	1.35
☐ 175B Lindy McDaniel BOX	3.00	1.35
☐ 176A Bill White COM	5.00	2.20
☐ 176B Bill White BOX	5.00	2.20

□ 177A Alex Grammas COM 3.00 1.35
□ 177B Alex Grammas BOX 3.00 1.35
□ 178A Curt Flood COM 5.00 2.20
□ 178B Curt Flood BOX 5.00 2.20
□ 179A Ernie Broglio COM 3.00 1.35
□ 179B Ernie Broglio BOX 3.00 1.35
□ 180A Hal Smith COM 3.00 1.35
□ 180B Hal Smith BOX 3.00 1.35
□ 181A Vada Pinson COM 5.00 2.20
□ 181B Vada Pinson BOX 5.00 2.20
□ 182A Frank Robinson COM 35.00 16.00
□ 182B Frank Robinson BOX 35.00 16.00
□ 183 Roy McMillan 90.00 40.00
BOX only
□ 184A Bob Purkey COM 3.00 1.35
□ 184B Bob Purkey BOX 3.00 1.35
□ 185A Ed Kasko COM 3.00 1.35
□ 185B Ed Kasko BOX 3.00 1.35
□ 186A Gus Bell COM 3.00 1.35
□ 186B Gus Bell BOX 3.00 1.35
□ 187A Jerry Lynch COM 3.00 1.35
□ 187B Jerry Lynch BOX 3.00 1.35
□ 188A Ed Bailey COM 3.00 1.35
□ 188B Ed Bailey BOX 3.00 1.35
□ 189A Jim O'Toole COM 3.00 1.35
□ 189B Jim O'Toole BOX 3.00 1.35
□ 190A Billy Martin COM 10.00 4.50
(Sold to Milwaukee)
□ 190B Billy Martin BOX 5.00 2.20
(No sale mention)
□ 191A Ernie Banks COM 25.00 11.00
□ 191B Ernie Banks BOX 25.00 11.00
□ 192A Richie Ashburn COM 7.50 3.40
□ 192B Richie Ashburn BOX 7.50 3.40
□ 193A Frank Thomas COM 40.00 18.00
□ 193B Frank Thomas BOX 40.00 18.00
□ 194A Don Cardwell COM 3.00 1.35
□ 194B Don Cardwell BOX 3.00 1.35
□ 195A George Altman COM 3.00 1.35
□ 195B George Altman BOX 3.00 1.35
□ 196A Ron Santo COM 6.00 2.70
□ 196B Ron Santo BOX 6.00 2.70
□ 197A Glen Hobbie COM 3.00 1.35
□ 197B Glen Hobbie BOX 3.00 1.35
□ 198A Sam Taylor COM 3.00 1.35
□ 198B Sam Taylor BOX 3.00 1.35
□ 199A Jerry Kindall COM 3.00 1.35
□ 199B Jerry Kindall BOX 3.00 1.35
□ 200A Don Elston COM 5.00 2.20
□ 200B Don Elston BOX 5.00 2.20

1962 Post

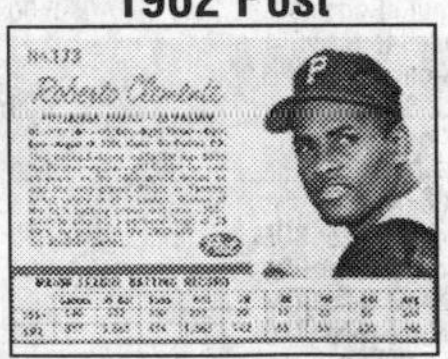

The cards in this 200-player series measure 2 1/2" by 3 1/2" and are oriented horizontally. The 1962 Post set is the easiest of the Post sets to complete. The cards are grouped numerically by team, for example, New York Yankees (1-13), Detroit (14-26), Baltimore (27-36), Cleveland (37-45), Chicago White Sox (46-55), Boston (56-64), Washington (65-73), Los Angeles Angels (74-82), Minnesota (83-91), Kansas City (92-100), Los Angeles Dodgers (101-115), Cincinnati (116-130), San Francisco (131-144), Milwaukee (145-157), St. Louis (158-168), Pittsburgh (169-181), Chicago Cubs (182-191), and Philadelphia (192-200). Cards 5B and 6B were printed on thin stock in a two-card panel and distributed in a Life magazine promotion. The scarce cards are 55, 69, 83, 92, 101, 103, 113, 116, 122, 125, 127, 131, 140, 144, and 158. The checklist for this set is the same as that of 1962 Jello and 1962 Post Canadian, but those sets are considered separate issues. The catalog number for this set is F278-37.

	NRMT	VG-E
COMPLETE SET (210)	2000.00	900.00
COMMON CARD (1-200)	3.00	1.35

□ 1 Bill Skowron 5.00 2.20
□ 2 Bobby Richardson 5.00 2.20
□ 3 Cletis Boyer 4.00 1.80
□ 4 Tony Kubek 5.00 2.20
□ 5A Mickey Mantle 150.00 70.00
□ 5B Mickey Mantle AD 150.00 70.00
□ 6A Roger Maris 25.00 11.00
□ 6B Roger Maris AD 25.00 11.00
□ 7 Yogi Berra 25.00 11.00
□ 8 Elston Howard 5.00 2.20
□ 9 Whitey Ford 10.00 4.50
□ 10 Ralph Terry 3.00 1.35
□ 11 John Blanchard 3.00 1.35
□ 12 Luis Arroyo 3.00 1.35
□ 13 Bill Stafford 3.00 1.35
□ 14A Norm Cash ERR 20.00 9.00
(Throws: right)
□ 14B Norm Cash COR 4.00 1.80
(Throws: left)
□ 15 Jake Wood 3.00 1.35
□ 16 Steve Boros 3.00 1.35
□ 17 Chico Fernandez 3.00 1.35
□ 18 Bill Bruton 3.00 1.35
□ 19 Rocky Colavito 6.00 2.70
□ 20 Al Kaline 15.00 6.75
□ 21 Dick Brown 3.00 1.35
□ 22 Frank Lary 3.00 1.35
□ 23 Don Mossi 3.00 1.35
□ 24 Phil Regan 3.00 1.35
□ 25 Charley Maxwell 3.00 1.35
□ 26 Jim Bunning 7.00 3.10
□ 27A Jim Gentile 4.00 1.80
(Home: Baltimore)
□ 27B Jim Gentile 20.00 9.00
(Home: San Lorenzo)
□ 28 Marv Breeding 3.00 1.35
□ 29 Brooks Robinson 15.00 6.75
□ 30A Ron Hansen 4.00 1.80
(At-Bats)
□ 30B Ron Hansen 4.00 1.80
(At Bats)
□ 31 Jackie Brandt 3.00 1.35
□ 32 Dick Williams 4.00 1.80
□ 33 Gus Triandos 3.00 1.35
□ 34 Milt Pappas 4.00 1.80
□ 35 Hoyt Wilhelm 8.00 3.60
□ 36 Chuck Estrada 7.50 3.40
□ 37 Vic Power 3.00 1.35
□ 38 Johnny Temple 3.00 1.35
□ 39 Bubba Phillips 3.00 1.35
□ 40 Tito Francona 3.00 1.35
□ 41 Willie Kirkland 3.00 1.35
□ 42 John Romano 3.00 1.35
□ 43 Jim Perry 3.00 1.35
□ 44 Woodie Held 3.00 1.35
□ 45 Chuck Essegian 3.00 1.35
□ 46 Roy Sievers 3.00 1.35
□ 47 Nellie Fox 8.00 3.60
□ 48 Al Smith 3.00 1.35
□ 49 Luis Aparicio 7.00 3.10
□ 50 Jim Landis 3.00 1.35
□ 51 Minnie Minoso 5.00 2.20
□ 52 Andy Carey 3.00 1.35
□ 53 Sherman Lollar 3.00 1.35
□ 54 Billy Pierce 4.00 1.80
□ 55 Early Wynn 30.00 13.50
□ 56 Chuck Schilling 3.00 1.35
□ 57 Pete Runnels 3.00 1.35
□ 58 Frank Malzone 3.00 1.35
□ 59 Don Buddin 3.00 1.35
□ 60 Gary Geiger 3.00 1.35
□ 61 Carl Yastrzemski 40.00 18.00
□ 62 Jackie Jensen 4.00 1.80
□ 63 Jim Pagliaroni 3.00 1.35
□ 64 Don Schwall 3.00 1.35
□ 65 Dale Long 3.00 1.35
□ 66 Chuck Cottier 3.00 1.35
□ 67 Billy Klaus 3.00 1.35
□ 68 Coot Veal 3.00 1.35
□ 69 Marty Keough 40.00 18.00
□ 70 Willie Tasby 3.00 1.35
□ 71 Gene Woodling 3.00 1.35
□ 72 Gene Green 3.00 1.35
□ 73 Dick Donovan 3.00 1.35
□ 74 Steve Bilko 3.00 1.35
□ 75 Rocky Bridges 3.00 1.35
□ 76 Eddie Yost 3.00 1.35
□ 77 Leon Wagner 3.00 1.35
□ 78 Albie Pearson 3.00 1.35
□ 79 Ken Hunt 3.00 1.35
□ 80 Earl Averill 3.00 1.35
□ 81 Ryne Duren 3.00 1.35
□ 82 Ted Kluszewski 5.00 2.20
□ 83 Bob Allison 30.00 13.50
□ 84 Billy Martin 5.00 2.20
□ 85 Harmon Killebrew 10.00 4.50
□ 86 Zoilo Versalles 3.00 1.35
□ 87 Lenny Green 3.00 1.35
□ 88 Bill Tuttle 3.00 1.35
□ 89 Jim Lemon 3.00 1.35
□ 90 Earl Battey 3.00 1.35
□ 91 Camilo Pascual 3.00 1.35
□ 92 Norm Siebern 75.00 34.00
□ 93 Jerry Lumpe 3.00 1.35
□ 94 Dick Howser 4.00 1.80
□ 95A Gene Stephens 4.00 1.80
(Born: Jan. 5)
□ 95B Gene Stephens 20.00 9.00
(Born: Jan. 20)
□ 96 Leo Posada 3.00 1.35
□ 97 Joe Pignatano 3.00 1.35
□ 98 Jim Archer 3.00 1.35
□ 99 Haywood Sullivan 3.00 1.35
□ 100 Art Ditmar 3.00 1.35
□ 101 Gil Hodges 100.00 45.00
□ 102 Charlie Neal 3.00 1.35
□ 103 Daryl Spencer 30.00 13.50
□ 104 Maury Wills 6.00 2.70
□ 105 Tommy Davis 4.00 1.80
□ 106 Willie Davis 4.00 1.80
□ 107 John Roseboro 3.00 1.35
□ 108 Johnny Podres 4.00 1.80
□ 109A Sandy Koufax 30.00 13.50
□ 109B Sandy Koufax 100.00 45.00
(With blue lines)
□ 110 Don Drysdale 12.00 5.50
□ 111 Larry Sherry 4.00 1.80
□ 112 Jim Gilliam 5.00 2.20
□ 113 Norm Larker 30.00 13.50
□ 114 Duke Snider 8.00 3.60
□ 115 Stan Williams 3.00 1.35
□ 116 Gordy Coleman 100.00 45.00
□ 117 Don Blasingame 3.00 1.35
□ 118 Gene Freese 3.00 1.35
□ 119 Ed Kasko 3.00 1.35
□ 120 Gus Bell 3.00 1.35
□ 121 Vada Pinson 4.00 1.80
□ 122 Frank Robinson 30.00 13.50
□ 123 Bob Purkey 3.00 1.35
□ 124A Joey Jay 4.00 1.80
□ 124B Joey Jay 20.00 9.00
(With blue lines)
□ 125 Jim Brosnan 30.00 13.50
□ 126 Jim O'Toole 3.00 1.35
□ 127 Jerry Lynch 75.00 34.00
□ 128 Wally Post 3.00 1.35
□ 129 Ken Hunt 3.00 1.35
□ 130 Jerry Zimmerman 3.00 1.35
□ 131 Willie McCovey 100.00 45.00
□ 132 Jose Pagan 3.00 1.35
□ 133 Felipe Alou UER 4.00 1.80
(Misspelled Filipe
in text)
□ 134 Jim Davenport 3.00 1.35
□ 135 Harvey Kuenn 4.00 1.80
□ 136 Orlando Cepeda 5.00 2.20
□ 137 Ed Bailey 3.00 1.35
□ 138 Sam Jones 3.00 1.35
□ 139 Mike McCormick 4.00 1.80
□ 140 Juan Marichal 125.00 55.00
□ 141 Jack Sanford 3.00 1.35
□ 142 Willie Mays 45.00 20.00
□ 143 Stu Miller 7.00 3.10
□ 144 Joe Amalfitano 25.00 11.00
□ 145A Joe Adcock (sic) ERR 75.00 34.00
□ 145B Joe Adcock COR 4.00 1.80
□ 146 Frank Bolling 3.00 1.35
□ 147 Eddie Mathews 12.00 5.50
□ 148 Roy McMillan 3.00 1.35
□ 149 Hank Aaron 40.00 18.00
□ 150 Gino Cimoli 3.00 1.35
□ 151 Frank Thomas 3.00 1.35
□ 152 Joe Torre 6.00 2.70
□ 153 Lew Burdette 4.00 1.80
□ 154 Bob Buhl 3.00 1.35
□ 155 Carlton Willey 3.00 1.35
□ 156 Lee Maye 3.00 1.35
□ 157 Al Spangler 3.00 1.35
□ 158 Bill White 40.00 18.00
□ 159 Ken Boyer 4.00 1.80
□ 160 Joe Cunningham 3.00 1.35
□ 161 Carl Warwick 3.00 1.35
□ 162 Carl Sawatski 3.00 1.35
□ 163 Lindy McDaniel 3.00 1.35
□ 164 Ernie Broglio 3.00 1.35
□ 165 Larry Jackson 3.00 1.35
□ 166 Curt Flood 4.00 1.80
□ 167 Curt Simmons 3.00 1.35
□ 168 Alex Grammas 3.00 1.35
□ 169 Dick Stuart 3.00 1.35
□ 170 Bill Mazeroski UER 5.00 2.20
(Bio reads 1959,
should read 1960)
□ 171 Don Hoak 3.00 1.35
□ 172 Dick Groat 4.00 1.80
□ 173A Roberto Clemente 60.00 27.00
□ 173B Roberto Clemente 175.00 80.00
(With blue lines)
□ 174 Bob Skinner 3.00 1.35
□ 175 Bill Virdon 4.00 1.80
□ 176 Smoky Burgess 3.00 1.35
□ 177 Roy Face 4.00 1.80
□ 178 Bob Friend 3.00 1.35
□ 179 Vernon Law 3.00 1.35

180 Harvey Haddix	3.00	1.35
181 Hal Smith	3.00	1.35
182 Ed Bouchee	3.00	1.35
183 Don Zimmer	3.00	1.35
184 Ron Santo	5.00	2.20
185 Andre Rodgers	3.00	1.35
186 Richie Ashburn	8.00	3.60
187 George Altman	3.00	1.35
188 Ernie Banks	15.00	6.75
189 Sam Taylor	3.00	1.35
190 Don Elston	3.00	1.35
191 Jerry Kindall	3.00	1.35
192 Pancho Herrera	3.00	1.35
193 Tony Taylor	3.00	1.35
194 Ruben Amaro	3.00	1.35
195 Don Demeter	3.00	1.35
196 Bobby Gene Smith	3.00	1.35
197 Clay Dalrymple	3.00	1.35
198 Robin Roberts	8.00	3.60
199 Art Mahaffey	3.00	1.35
200 John Buzhardt	5.00	2.20

1962 Post Canadian

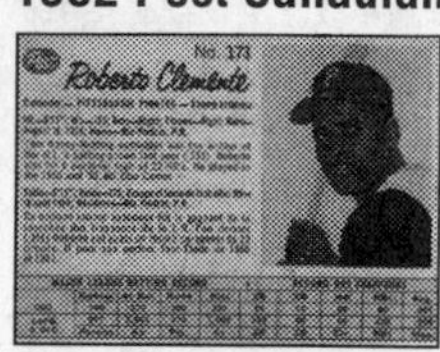

The 200 blank-backed cards comprising the 1962 Post Canadian set measure approximately 2 1/2" by 3 1/2". The set is similar in appearance to the Jell-O set released in the U.S. that same year. The fronts feature a posed color player photo at the upper right. To the left of the photo, the player's name appears in blue cursive lettering, followed below by bilingual biography and career highlights. The cards are numbered on the front. The cards are grouped by team as follows: New York Yankees (1-13), Detroit (14-26), Baltimore (27-36), Cleveland (37-45), Chicago White Sox (46-55), Boston (56-64), Washington (65-73), Los Angeles Angels (74-82), Minnesota (83-91), Kansas City (92-100), Los Angeles Dodgers (101-115), Cincinnati (116-130), San Francisco (131-144), Milwaukee (145-157), St. Louis (158-168), Pittsburgh (169-181), Chicago Cubs (182-191) and Philadelphia (192-200). Maris (6) and Mays (142) are somewhat scarce. Whitey Ford is listed incorrectly with the Dodgers and correctly with the Yankees. The complete set price includes both Whitey Ford variations.

	NRMT	VG-E
COMPLETE SET (201)	2500.00	1100.00
COMMON CARD (1-200)	5.00	2.20
1 Bill Skowron	7.50	3.40
2 Bobby Richardson	7.50	3.40
3 Cletis Boyer	6.00	2.70
4 Tony Kubek	7.50	3.40
5 Mickey Mantle	350.00	160.00
6 Roger Maris	150.00	70.00
7 Yogi Berra	75.00	34.00
8 Elston Howard	7.50	3.40
9A Whitey Ford ERR (Los Angeles Dodgers)	75.00	34.00
9B Whitey Ford COR (New York Yankees)	75.00	34.00
10 Ralph Terry	6.00	2.70
11 John Blanchard	6.00	2.70
12 Luis Arroyo	5.00	2.20
13 Bill Stafford	5.00	2.20
14 Norm Cash	7.50	3.40
15 Jake Wood	5.00	2.20
16 Steve Boros	5.00	2.20
17 Chico Fernandez	5.00	2.20
18 Bill Bruton	5.00	2.20
19 Rocky Colavito	10.00	4.50
20 Al Kaline	40.00	18.00
21 Dick Brown	5.00	2.20
22 Frank Lary	15.00	6.75
23 Don Mossi	6.00	2.70
24 Phil Regan	5.00	2.20
25 Charlie Maxwell	5.00	2.20
26 Jim Bunning	12.50	5.50
27 Jim Gentile	6.00	2.70
28 Marv Breeding	5.00	2.20
29 Brooks Robinson	40.00	18.00
30 Ron Hansen	5.00	2.20
31 Jackie Brandt	5.00	2.20
32 Dick Williams	7.50	3.40
33 Gus Triandos	5.00	2.20
34 Milt Pappas	6.00	2.70
35 Hoyt Wilhelm	50.00	22.00
36 Chuck Estrada	5.00	2.20
37 Vic Power	5.00	2.20
38 Johnny Temple	5.00	2.20
39 Bubba Phillips	5.00	2.20
40 Tito Francona	15.00	6.75
41 Willie Kirkland	5.00	2.20
42 John Romano	5.00	2.20
43 Jim Perry	6.00	2.70
44 Woodie Held	5.00	2.20
45 Chuck Essegian	5.00	2.20
46 Roy Sievers	6.00	2.70
47 Nellie Fox	12.50	5.50
48 Al Smith	5.00	2.20
49 Luis Aparicio	50.00	22.00
50 Jim Landis	5.00	2.20
51 Minnie Minoso	7.50	3.40
52 Andy Carey	5.00	2.20
53 Sherman Lollar	5.00	2.20
54 Bill Pierce	6.00	2.70
55 Early Wynn	12.50	5.50
56 Chuck Schilling	5.00	2.20
57 Pete Runnels	6.00	2.70
58 Frank Malzone	6.00	2.70
59 Don Buddin	5.00	2.20
60 Gary Geiger	5.00	2.20
61 Carl Yastrzemski	100.00	45.00
62 Jackie Jensen	6.00	2.70
63 Jim Pagliaroni	5.00	2.20
64 Don Schwall	15.00	6.75
65 Dale Long	5.00	2.20
66 Chuck Cottier	5.00	2.20
67 Billy Klaus	5.00	2.20
68 Coot Veal	5.00	2.20
69 Marty Keough	5.00	2.20
70 Willie Tasby	5.00	2.20
71 Gene Woodling	6.00	2.70
72 Gene Green	5.00	2.20
73 Dick Donovan	5.00	2.20
74 Steve Bilko	5.00	2.20
75 Rocky Bridges	5.00	2.20
76 Eddie Yost	5.00	2.20
77 Leon Wagner	15.00	6.75
78 Albie Pearson	5.00	2.20
79 Ken L. Hunt	5.00	2.20
80 Earl Averill	5.00	2.20
81 Ryne Duren	6.00	2.70
82 Ted Kluszewski	7.50	3.40
83 Bob Allison	6.00	2.70
84 Billy Martin	7.50	3.40
85 Harmon Killebrew	25.00	11.00
86 Zoilo Versalles	6.00	2.70
87 Lenny Green	15.00	6.75
88 Bill Tuttle	5.00	2.20
89 Jim Lemon	5.00	2.20
90 Earl Battey	5.00	2.20
91 Camilo Pascual	6.00	2.70
92 Norm Siebern	5.00	2.20
93 Jerry Lumpe	5.00	2.20
94 Dick Howser	6.00	2.70
95 Gene Stephens	5.00	2.20
96 Leo Posada	5.00	2.20
97 Joe Pignatano	5.00	2.20
98 Jim Archer	5.00	2.20
99 Haywood Sullivan	5.00	2.20
100 Art Ditmar	5.00	2.20
101 Gil Hodges	25.00	11.00
102 Charlie Neal	5.00	2.20
103 Daryl Spencer	5.00	2.20
104 Maury Wills	10.00	4.50
105 Tommy Davis	20.00	9.00
106 Willie Davis	6.00	2.70
107 John Roseboro	6.00	2.70
108 John Podres	7.50	3.40
109 Sandy Koufax	75.00	34.00
110 Don Drysdale	25.00	11.00
111 Larry Sherry	6.00	2.70
112 Jim Gilliam	25.00	11.00
113 Norm Larker	5.00	2.20
114 Duke Snider	40.00	18.00
115 Stan Williams	5.00	2.20
116 Gordy Coleman	5.00	2.20
117 Don Blasingame	15.00	6.75
118 Gene Freese	5.00	2.20
119 Ed Kasko	5.00	2.20
120 Gus Bell	5.00	2.20
121 Vada Pinson	7.50	3.40
122 Frank Robinson	25.00	11.00
123 Bob Purkey	15.00	6.75
124 Joey Jay	5.00	2.20
125 Jim Brosnan	5.00	2.20
126 Jim O'Toole	5.00	2.20
127 Jerry Lynch	5.00	2.20
128 Wally Post	6.00	2.70
129 Ken R. Hunt	5.00	2.20
130 Jerry Zimmerman	5.00	2.20
131 Willie McCovey	25.00	11.00
132 Jose Pagan	5.00	2.20
133 Felipe Alou	7.50	3.40
134 Jim Davenport	5.00	2.20
135 Harvey Kuenn	5.00	2.20
136 Orlando Cepeda	10.00	4.50
137 Ed Bailey	15.00	6.75
138 Sam Jones	5.00	2.20
139 Mike McCormick	5.00	2.20
140 Juan Marichal	25.00	11.00
141 Jack Sanford	5.00	2.20
142 Willie Mays	125.00	55.00
143 Stu Miller	5.00	2.20
144 Joe Amalfitano	30.00	13.50
145 Joe Adcock	6.00	2.70
146 Frank Bolling	5.00	2.20
147 Eddie Mathews	20.00	9.00
148 Roy McMillan	5.00	2.20
149 Hank Aaron	100.00	45.00
150 Gino Cimoli	5.00	2.20
151 Frank Thomas	6.00	2.70
152 Joe Torre	12.50	5.50
153 Lew Burdette	7.50	3.40
154 Bob Buhl	5.00	2.20
155 Carlton Willey	5.00	2.20
156 Lee Maye	5.00	2.20
157 Al Spangler	5.00	2.20
158 Bill White	7.50	3.40
159 Ken Boyer	10.00	4.50
160 Joe Cunningham	6.00	2.70
161 Carl Warwick	15.00	6.75
162 Carl Sawatski	5.00	2.20
163 Lindy McDaniel	5.00	2.20
164 Ernie Broglio	5.00	2.20
165 Larry Jackson	5.00	2.20
166 Curt Flood	7.50	3.40
167 Curt Simmons	5.00	2.20
168 Alex Grammas	5.00	2.20
169 Dick Stuart	5.00	2.20
170 Bill Mazeroski	10.00	4.50
171 Don Hoak	5.00	2.20
172 Dick Groat	6.00	2.70
173 Roberto Clemente	175.00	80.00
174 Bob Skinner	5.00	2.20
175 Bill Virdon	6.00	2.70
176 Smoky Burgess	15.00	6.75
177 Elroy Face	7.50	3.40
178 Bob Friend	5.00	2.20
179 Vernon Law	6.00	2.70
180 Harvey Haddix	5.00	2.20
181 Hal Smith	5.00	2.20
182 Ed Bouchee	15.00	6.75
183 Don Zimmer	5.00	2.20
184 Ron Santo	7.50	3.40
185 Andre Rodgers	5.00	2.20
186 Richie Ashburn	12.50	5.50
187 George Altman	5.00	2.20
188 Ernie Banks	40.00	18.00
189 Sam Taylor	5.00	2.20
190 Don Elston	5.00	2.20
191 Jerry Kindall	5.00	2.20
192 Pancho Herrera	5.00	2.20
193 Tony Taylor	6.00	2.70
194 Ruben Amaro	5.00	2.20
195 Don Demeter	5.00	2.20
196 Bobby Gene Smith	5.00	2.20
197 Clay Dalrymple	5.00	2.20
198 Robin Roberts	20.00	9.00
199 Art Mahaffey	5.00	2.20
200 John Buzhardt	6.00	2.70

1963 Post

The cards in this 200-card set measure 2 1/2" by 3 1/2". The players are grouped by team with American Leaguers comprising 1-100 and National Leaguers 101-200. The ordering of teams is as follows: Minnesota (1-11), New York Yankees, Los Angeles Angels (24-34), Chicago White Sox (35-45), Detroit (46-56), Baltimore (57-66), Cleveland (67-76), Boston (77-84), Kansas City (85-92), Washington (93-100), San Francisco (101-112), Los Angeles Dodgers (113-124), Cincinnati (125-136), Pittsburgh (137-147), Milwaukee (148-157), St. Louis (158-168), Chicago Cubs (169-176), Philadelphia (177-184), Houston (185-192), and New York Mets (193-200). In contrast to the 1962 issue, the 1963 Post baseball card series is very difficult to complete. There are many card scarcities reflected in the price list below. Cards of the Post set are easily confused with those of the 1963 Jello set, which are 1/4" narrower (a difference which is often eliminated by bad cutting). The catalog designation is F278-38. There was also an album produced by Post to hold the cards.

	NRMT	VG-E
COMPLETE SET (206)	4250.00	1900.00
COMMON CARD (1-200)	3.50	1.55
☐ 1 Vic Power	6.00	2.70
☐ 2 Bernie Allen	3.50	1.55
☐ 3 Zoilo Versalles	3.50	1.55
☐ 4 Rich Rollins	3.50	1.55
☐ 5 Harmon Killebrew	20.00	9.00
☐ 6 Lenny Green	45.00	20.00
☐ 7 Bob Allison	5.00	2.20
☐ 8 Earl Battey	3.50	1.55
☐ 9 Camilo Pascual	3.50	1.55
☐ 10 Jim Kaat	6.00	2.70
☐ 11 Jack Kralick	3.50	1.55
☐ 12 Bill Skowron	5.00	2.20
☐ 13 Bobby Richardson	6.00	2.70
☐ 14 Cletis Boyer	3.50	1.55
☐ 15 Mickey Mantle	350.00	160.00
☐ 16 Roger Maris	175.00	80.00
☐ 17 Yogi Berra ERR	25.00	11.00
Living in Monclair, N.Y.		
☐ 18 Elston Howard	5.00	2.20
☐ 19 Whitey Ford	15.00	6.75
☐ 20 Ralph Terry	3.50	1.55
☐ 21 John Blanchard	3.50	1.55
☐ 22 Bill Stafford	3.50	1.55
☐ 23 Tom Tresh	3.50	1.55
☐ 24 Steve Bilko	3.50	1.55
☐ 25 Bill Moran	3.50	1.55
☐ 26A Joe Koppe	3.50	1.55
(BA: .277)		
☐ 26B Joe Koppe	20.00	9.00
(BA: .227)		
☐ 27 Felix Torres	3.50	1.55
☐ 28A Leon Wagner	3.50	1.55
(BA: .278)		
☐ 28B Leon Wagner	20.00	9.00
(BA: .272)		
☐ 29 Albie Pearson	3.50	1.55
☐ 30 Lee Thomas UER	100.00	45.00
(Photo actually George Thomas)		
☐ 31 Bob Rodgers	3.50	1.55
☐ 32 Dean Chance	3.50	1.55
☐ 33 Ken McBride	3.50	1.55
☐ 34 George Thomas UER	3.50	1.55
(Photo actually Lee Thomas)		
☐ 35 Joe Cunningham	3.50	1.55
☐ 36 Nellie Fox	7.50	3.40
☐ 37 Luis Aparicio	7.50	3.40
☐ 38 Al Smith	45.00	20.00
☐ 39 Floyd Robinson	125.00	55.00
☐ 40 Jim Landis	3.50	1.55
☐ 41 Charlie Maxwell	3.50	1.55
☐ 42 Sherman Lollar	3.50	1.55
☐ 43 Early Wynn	7.50	3.40
☐ 44 Juan Pizarro	3.50	1.55
☐ 45 Ray Herbert	3.50	1.55
☐ 46 Norm Cash	5.00	2.20
☐ 47 Steve Boros	3.50	1.55
☐ 48 Dick McAuliffe	25.00	11.00
☐ 49 Bill Bruton	3.50	1.55
☐ 50 Rocky Colavito	6.00	2.70
☐ 51 Al Kaline	25.00	11.00
☐ 52 Dick Brown	3.50	1.55
☐ 53 Jim Bunning	200.00	90.00
☐ 54 Hank Aguirre	3.50	1.55
☐ 55 Frank Lary	3.50	1.55
☐ 56 Don Mossi	3.50	1.55
☐ 57 Jim Gentile	3.50	1.55
☐ 58 Jackie Brandt	3.50	1.55
☐ 59 Brooks Robinson	25.00	11.00
☐ 60 Ron Hansen	5.00	2.20
☐ 61 Jerry Adair	200.00	90.00
☐ 62 Boog Powell	6.00	2.70
☐ 63 Russ Snyder	3.50	1.55
☐ 64 Steve Barber	3.50	1.55
☐ 65 Milt Pappas	3.50	1.55
☐ 66 Robin Roberts	7.50	3.40
☐ 67 Tito Francona	3.50	1.55
☐ 68 Jerry Kindall	3.50	1.55
☐ 69 Woody Held	3.50	1.55
☐ 70 Bubba Phillips	15.00	6.75
☐ 71 Chuck Essegian	3.50	1.55
☐ 72 Willie Kirkland	3.50	1.55
☐ 73 Al Luplow	3.50	1.55
☐ 74 Ty Cline	3.50	1.55
☐ 75 Dick Donovan	3.50	1.55
☐ 76 John Romano	3.50	1.55
☐ 77 Pete Runnels	3.50	1.55
☐ 78 Ed Bressoud	3.50	1.55
☐ 79 Frank Malzone	3.50	1.55
☐ 80 Carl Yastrzemski	300.00	135.00
☐ 81 Gary Geiger	3.50	1.55
☐ 82 Lou Clinton	3.50	1.55
☐ 83 Earl Wilson	3.50	1.55
☐ 84 Bill Monbouquette	3.50	1.55
☐ 85 Norm Siebern	3.50	1.55
☐ 86 Jerry Lumpe	125.00	55.00
☐ 87 Manny Jimenez	125.00	55.00
☐ 88 Gino Cimoli	3.50	1.55
☐ 89 Ed Charles	3.50	1.55
☐ 90 Ed Rakow	3.50	1.55
☐ 91 Bob Del Greco	3.50	1.55
☐ 92 Haywood Sullivan	3.50	1.55
☐ 93 Chuck Hinton	3.50	1.55
☐ 94 Ken Retzer	3.50	1.55
☐ 95 Harry Bright	3.50	1.55
☐ 96 Bob Johnson	3.50	1.55
☐ 97 Dave Stenhouse	15.00	6.75
☐ 98 Chuck Cottier	25.00	11.00
☐ 99 Tom Cheney	3.50	1.55
☐ 100 Claude Osteen	15.00	6.75
☐ 101 Orlando Cepeda	6.00	2.70
☐ 102 Chuck Hiller	3.50	1.55
☐ 103 Jose Pagan	3.50	1.55
☐ 104 Jim Davenport	3.50	1.55
☐ 105 Harvey Kuenn	5.00	2.20
☐ 106 Willie Mays	50.00	22.00
☐ 107 Felipe Alou	5.00	2.20
☐ 108 Tom Haller	125.00	55.00
☐ 109 Juan Marichal	7.50	3.40
☐ 110 Jack Sanford	3.50	1.55
☐ 111 Bill O'Dell	3.50	1.55
☐ 112 Willie McCovey	10.00	4.50
☐ 113 Lee Walls	3.50	1.55
☐ 114 Jim Gilliam	6.00	2.70
☐ 115 Maury Wills	6.00	2.70
☐ 116 Ron Fairly	3.50	1.55
☐ 117 Tommy Davis	5.00	2.20
☐ 118 Duke Snider	10.00	4.50
☐ 119 Willie Davis	200.00	90.00
☐ 120 John Roseboro	3.50	1.55
☐ 121 Sandy Koufax	35.00	16.00
☐ 122 Stan Williams	3.50	1.55
☐ 123 Don Drysdale	10.00	4.50
☐ 124 Daryl Spencer	3.50	1.55
☐ 125 Gordy Coleman	3.50	1.55
☐ 126 Don Blasingame	3.50	1.55
☐ 127 Leo Cardenas	3.50	1.55
☐ 128 Eddie Kasko	200.00	90.00
☐ 129 Jerry Lynch	15.00	6.75
☐ 130 Vada Pinson	6.00	2.70
☐ 131A Frank Robinson	25.00	11.00
(No stripes)		
☐ 131B Frank Robinson	50.00	22.00
(Stripes on hat)		
☐ 132 John Edwards	3.50	1.55
☐ 133 Joey Jay	3.50	1.55
☐ 134 Bob Purkey	3.50	1.55
☐ 135 Marty Keough	30.00	13.50
☐ 136 Jim O'Toole	3.50	1.55
☐ 137 Dick Stuart	3.50	1.55
☐ 138 Bill Mazeroski	6.00	2.70
☐ 139 Dick Groat	5.00	2.20
☐ 140 Don Hoak	35.00	16.00
☐ 141 Bob Skinner	20.00	9.00
☐ 142 Bill Virdon	5.00	2.20
☐ 143 Roberto Clemente	60.00	27.00
☐ 144 Smoky Burgess	5.00	2.20
☐ 145 Bob Friend	3.50	1.55
☐ 146 Al McBean	3.50	1.55
☐ 147 Roy Face	5.00	2.20
☐ 148 Joe Adcock	5.00	2.20
☐ 149 Frank Bolling	3.50	1.55
☐ 150 Roy McMillan	3.50	1.55
☐ 151 Eddie Mathews	20.00	9.00
☐ 152 Hank Aaron	125.00	55.00
☐ 153 Del Crandall	35.00	16.00
☐ 154A Bob Shaw COR	3.50	1.55
☐ 154B Bob Shaw ERR	15.00	6.75
(Two "in 1959" in same sentence)		
☐ 155 Lew Burdette	5.00	2.20
☐ 156 Joe Torre	6.00	2.70
☐ 157 Tony Cloninger	3.50	1.55
☐ 158A Bill White	5.00	2.20
(Ht. 6'0")		
☐ 158B Bill White	5.00	2.20
(Ht. 6';)		
☐ 159 Julian Javier	3.50	1.55
☐ 160 Ken Boyer	6.00	2.70
☐ 161 Julio Gotay	3.50	1.55
☐ 162 Curt Flood	125.00	55.00
☐ 163 Charlie James	3.50	1.55
☐ 164 Gene Oliver	3.50	1.55
☐ 165 Ernie Broglio	3.50	1.55
☐ 166 Bob Gibson	10.00	4.50
☐ 167A Lindy McDaniel	6.00	2.70
(No asterisk)		
☐ 167B Lindy McDaniel	6.00	2.70
(Asterisk traded line)		
☐ 168 Ray Washburn	3.50	1.55
☐ 169 Ernie Banks	20.00	9.00
☐ 170 Ron Santo	6.00	2.70
☐ 171 George Altman	3.50	1.55
☐ 172 Billy Williams	150.00	70.00
☐ 173 Andre Rodgers	15.00	6.75
☐ 174 Ken Hubbs	30.00	13.50
☐ 175 Don Landrum	3.50	1.55
☐ 176 Dick Bertell	20.00	9.00
☐ 177 Roy Sievers	3.50	1.55
☐ 178 Tony Taylor	3.50	1.55
☐ 179 John Callison	3.50	1.55
☐ 180 Don Demeter	3.50	1.55
☐ 181 Tony Gonzalez	15.00	6.75
☐ 182 Wes Covington	25.00	11.00
☐ 183 Art Mahaffey	3.50	1.55
☐ 184 Clay Dalrymple	3.50	1.55
☐ 185 Al Spangler	3.50	1.55
☐ 186 Roman Mejias	3.50	1.55
☐ 187 Bob Aspromonte	375.00	170.00
☐ 188 Norm Larker	35.00	16.00
☐ 189 Johnny Temple	3.50	1.55
☐ 190 Carl Warwick	3.50	1.55
☐ 191 Bob Lillis	3.50	1.55
☐ 192 Dick Farrell	3.50	1.55
☐ 193 Gil Hodges	10.00	4.50
☐ 194 Marv Throneberry	5.00	2.20
☐ 195 Charlie Neal	10.00	4.50
☐ 196 Frank Thomas	225.00	100.00
☐ 197 Richie Ashburn	30.00	13.50
☐ 198 Felix Mantilla	3.50	1.55
☐ 199 Rod Kanehl	20.00	9.00
☐ 200 Roger Craig	5.00	2.20

1990 Post

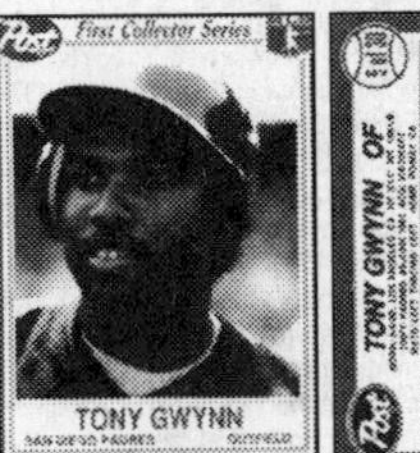

1990 Post Cereal is a 30-card standard-size set issued with the assistance of Mike Schechter Associates. The sets do not have either team logos or other uniform identification on them. There is also a facsimile autograph on the back of the cards. The cards were inserted randomly as a cello pack (with three cards) inside specially marked boxes of Post cereals. The cards feature red, white, and blue fronts with the words, "First Collector Series". Card backs feature a facsimile autograph.

	MINT	NRMT
COMPLETE SET (30)	8.00	3.60
COMMON CARD (1-30)	.05	.02
☐ 1 Don Mattingly	1.25	.55
☐ 2 Roger Clemens	1.00	.45
☐ 3 Kirby Puckett	1.50	.70
☐ 4 George Brett	1.25	.55
☐ 5 Tony Gwynn	1.25	.55
☐ 6 Ozzie Smith	1.00	.45
☐ 7 Will Clark	.50	.23
☐ 8 Orel Hershiser	.10	.05
☐ 9 Ryne Sandberg	1.00	.45
☐ 10 Darryl Strawberry	.10	.05
☐ 11 Nolan Ryan	2.50	1.10
☐ 12 Mark McGwire	1.25	.55
☐ 13 Jim Abbott	.10	.05
☐ 14 Bo Jackson	.10	.05
☐ 15 Kevin Mitchell	.05	.02
☐ 16 Jose Canseco	.50	.23
☐ 17 Wade Boggs	.40	.18
☐ 18 Dale Murphy	.40	.18
☐ 19 Mark Grace	.40	.18
☐ 20 Mike Scott	.05	.02
☐ 21 Cal Ripken	2.50	1.10
☐ 22 Pedro Guerrero	.05	.02
☐ 23 Ken Griffey Jr.	3.00	1.35
☐ 24 Eric Davis	.10	.05
☐ 25 Rickey Henderson	.40	.18
☐ 26 Robin Yount	.40	.18
☐ 27 Von Hayes	.05	.02

☐ 28 Alan Trammell	.25	.11
☐ 29 Dwight Gooden	.10	.05
☐ 30 Joe Carter	.10	.05

Fruity Pebbles, Alpha-Bits, and Marshmallow Alpha-Bits. The fronts feature either posed or action color player photos, with blue and yellow borders. The words "1991 Collector Series" appear in a white stripe at the card top. Some cards (numbers 1, 6, 25, and 30) have a banner at the top that reads "Rookie Star". The player's name is given in a white stripe below the picture. The horizontally oriented backs are printed in aqua and dark blue on white and present complete Major League statistical information and a facsimile autograph on the bottom of the card.

	MINT	NRMT
COMPLETE SET (30)	8.00	3.60
COMMON CARD (1-30)	.05	.02
☐ 1 Dave Justice	.40	.18
☐ 2 Mark McGwire	1.00	.45
☐ 3 Will Clark	.40	.18
☐ 4 Jose Canseco	.25	.11
☐ 5 Vince Coleman	.05	.02
☐ 6 Sandy Alomar Jr.	.10	.05
☐ 7 Darryl Strawberry	.10	.05
☐ 8 Len Dykstra	.10	.05
☐ 9 Gregg Jefferies	.10	.05
☐ 10 Tony Gwynn	1.25	.55
☐ 11 Ken Griffey Jr.	3.00	1.35
☐ 12 Roger Clemens	1.00	.45
☐ 13 Chris Sabo	.05	.02
☐ 14 Bobby Bonilla	.10	.05
☐ 15 Gary Sheffield	.50	.23
☐ 16 Ryne Sandberg	1.00	.45
☐ 17 Nolan Ryan	2.50	1.10
☐ 18 Barry Larkin	.25	.11
☐ 19 Cal Ripken	2.50	1.10
☐ 20 Jim Abbott	.10	.05
☐ 21 Barry Bonds	.50	.23
☐ 22 Mark Grace	.40	.18
☐ 23 Cecil Fielder	.10	.05
☐ 24 Kevin Mitchell	.05	.02
☐ 25 Todd Zeile	.05	.02
☐ 26 George Brett	1.25	.55
☐ 27 Rickey Henderson	.40	.18
☐ 28 Kirby Puckett	1.50	.70
☐ 29 Don Mattingly	1.25	.55
☐ 30 Kevin Maas	.05	.02

1991 Post Canadian

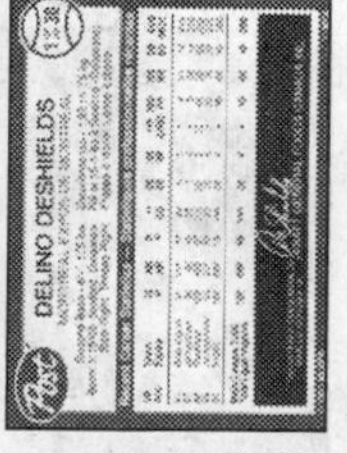

This 30-card Super Stars set was sponsored by Post and features 14 National League and 16 American League players. Two cards were inserted in specially marked boxes of Post Alpha-Bits, Sugar Crisp and Honeycomb sold in Canada. The cards measure the standard size and are bilingual (French and English) on both sides. While all the cards feature color player photos (action or posed) on the fronts, the NL cards (1-14) are accentuated with red stripes while the AL cards (15-30) have royal blue stripes. In a horizontal format, the backs have biography, recent career statistics and a facsimile autograph. The cards are numbered on the back. The side panel also included a checklist, an offer for a baseball player poster-album and an offer to order ten additional cards to complete the set.

	MINT	NRMT
COMPLETE SET (30)	15.00	6.75
COMMON CARD (1-30)	.10	.05
☐ 1 Delino DeShields	.10	.05
☐ 2 Tim Wallach	.10	.05
☐ 3 Andres Galarraga	.50	.23
☐ 4 Dave Magadan	.10	.05
☐ 5 Barry Bonds UER (Career BA .256, should be .265)	1.00	.45
☐ 6 Len Dykstra	.20	.09
☐ 7 Andre Dawson	.35	.16
☐ 8 Ozzie Smith	1.25	.55
☐ 9 Will Clark	.75	.35
☐ 10 Chris Sabo	.10	.05
☐ 11 Eddie Murray	.75	.35
☐ 12 Dave Justice	.50	.23
☐ 13 Benito Santiago	.10	.05
☐ 14 Glenn Davis	.10	.05
☐ 15 Kelly Gruber	.10	.05
☐ 16 Dave Stieb	.10	.05
☐ 17 John Olerud	.20	.09
☐ 18 Roger Clemens	1.50	.70
☐ 19 Cecil Fielder	.20	.09
☐ 20 Kevin Maas	.10	.05
☐ 21 Robin Yount	.50	.23
☐ 22 Cal Ripken	3.00	1.35
☐ 23 Sandy Alomar Jr.	.20	.09
☐ 24 Rickey Henderson	.50	.23
☐ 25 Bobby Thigpen	.10	.05
☐ 26 Ken Griffey Jr.	4.00	1.80
☐ 27 Nolan Ryan	3.00	1.35
☐ 28 Dave Winfield	.50	.23
☐ 29 George Brett	1.50	.70
☐ 30 Kirby Puckett	2.00	.90

1992 Post

This 30-card standard-size set was manufactured by MSA (Michael Schechter Associates) for Post Cereal. Three-card packs were inserted in the following Post cereals: Honeycomb, Super Golden Crisp, Cocoa Pebbles, Fruity Pebbles, Alpha-Bits, Marshmallow Alpha-Bits and, for the first time, Raisin Bran. In the last-mentioned cereal, the cards were protected in cello packs that also had a 50 cent manufacturers coupon good on the next purchase. The other cereals contained tan paper wrapped packs. The complete set could also be obtained via a mail-in offer for 1.00 and five UPC symbols. The fronts feature either posed or action color player photos. A royal blue stripe, which borders the card top, intersects the Post logo at the upper left corner. The player's name and team name appear in a red stripe at the card bottom. The Bagwell and Knoblauch cards display the words "Rookie Star" in a yellow banner at the card top. The horizontally oriented backs show red-bordered posed or action color player photos with biography, statistics and a facsimile autograph on a light-blue box.

	MINT	NRMT
COMPLETE SET (30)	6.00	2.70
COMMON CARD (1-30)	.05	.02
☐ 1 Jeff Bagwell	.75	.35
☐ 2 Ryne Sandberg	.60	.25
☐ 3 Don Mattingly	1.00	.45
☐ 4 Wally Joyner	.05	.02
☐ 5 Dwight Gooden	.10	.05
☐ 6 Chuck Knoblauch	.50	.23
☐ 7 Kirby Puckett	1.00	.45
☐ 8 Ozzie Smith	.60	.25
☐ 9 Cal Ripken	1.50	.70
☐ 10 Darryl Strawberry	.10	.05
☐ 11 George Brett	.75	.35
☐ 12 Joe Carter	.10	.05
☐ 13 Cecil Fielder	.10	.05
☐ 14 Will Clark	.40	.18
☐ 15 Barry Bonds	.40	.18
☐ 16 Roger Clemens	.60	.25
☐ 17 Paul Molitor	.40	.18
☐ 18 Scott Erickson	.05	.02
☐ 19 Wade Boggs	.40	.18
☐ 20 Ken Griffey Jr.	2.00	.90
☐ 21 Bobby Bonilla	.10	.05
☐ 22 Terry Pendleton	.05	.02
☐ 23 Barry Larkin	.25	.11
☐ 24 Frank Thomas	1.50	.70
☐ 25 Jose Canseco	.40	.18
☐ 26 Tony Gwynn	1.00	.45
☐ 27 Nolan Ryan	1.50	.70
☐ 28 Howard Johnson	.05	.02
☐ 29 Dave Justice	.40	.18
☐ 30 Danny Tartabull	.05	.02

1992 Post Canadian

This 18-card Post Super Star II stand-up set was sponsored by Post and measures the standard size. The set features nine American League and nine National League players and is bilingual (French and English) on both sides. The fronts show posed color player photos with team logos airbrushed out. The NL cards (1-9) are accented with a red stripe at the top and bottom of the photo and the AL cards (10-18) are accented with blue stripes. The Post and MLB logos appear in the bottom stripe along with the player's name and team. The backs feature perforated color action player photos that can be displayed standing. As on the front, the NL photos on the back are bordered in red and the AL in blue. The player's name appears in the bottom border.

	MINT	NRMT
COMPLETE SET (18)	15.00	6.75
COMMON CARD (1-18)	.25	.11
☐ 1 Dennis Martinez	.50	.23
☐ 2 Benito Santiago	.25	.11
☐ 3 Will Clark	1.00	.45
☐ 4 Ryne Sandberg	2.50	1.10
☐ 5 Tim Wallach	.25	.11
☐ 6 Ozzie Smith	2.50	1.10
☐ 7 Darryl Strawberry	.50	.23
☐ 8 Brett Butler	.25	.11
☐ 9 Barry Bonds	1.00	.45
☐ 10 Roger Clemens	2.00	.90
☐ 11 Sandy Alomar Jr.	.50	.23
☐ 12 Cecil Fielder	.50	.23
☐ 13 Roberto Alomar	1.00	.45
☐ 14 Kelly Gruber	.25	.11
☐ 15 Cal Ripken	5.00	2.20
☐ 16 Jose Canseco	1.00	.45
☐ 17 Kirby Puckett	2.50	1.10
☐ 18 Rickey Henderson	1.00	.45

1993 Post

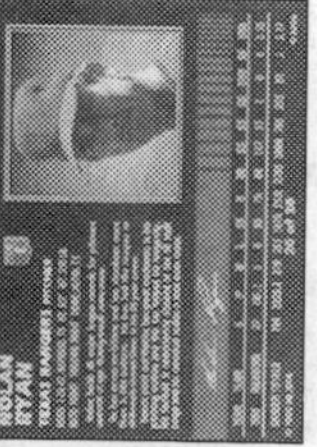

This 30-card standard-size set features full-bleed action color player photos. The pictures are bordered on two sides by a black stripe containing the phrase "1993 Collector Series" and the player's team and position. A red bar across the bottom of the photo is printed with the player's name. The horizontal backs are black and carry biographical information, career highlights, and statistics. A close-up photo appears at the upper right corner. A red bar containing a facsimile autograph divides the statistics from the other information. Three-packs of cards were found in specially marked boxes of Post Cereal during this promotion. In addition, complete sets were available as a mail-in for five proofs of purchase from any Post Cereal plus 1.00.

	MINT	NRMT
COMPLETE SET (30)	6.00	2.70
COMMON CARD (1-30)	.05	.02
☐ 1 Dave Fleming	.05	.02
☐ 2 Will Clark	.40	.18
☐ 3 Kirby Puckett	1.00	.45
☐ 4 Roger Clemens	.75	.35
☐ 5 Fred McGriff	.25	.11
☐ 6 Eric Karros	.10	.05
☐ 7 Ken Griffey Jr.	2.00	.90
☐ 8 Tony Gwynn	1.00	.45
☐ 9 Cal Ripken	1.50	.70
☐ 10 Cecil Fielder	.10	.05
☐ 11 Gary Sheffield	.40	.18
☐ 12 Don Mattingly	1.00	.45
☐ 13 Ryne Sandberg	.60	.25
☐ 14 Frank Thomas	1.50	.70
☐ 15 Barry Bonds	.40	.18
☐ 16 Paul Molitor	.40	.18
☐ 17 Terry Pendleton	.05	.02
☐ 18 Darren Daulton	.10	.05
☐ 19 Mark McGwire	1.00	.45
☐ 20 Nolan Ryan	1.50	.70
☐ 21 Tom Glavine	.10	.05
☐ 22 Roberto Alomar	.40	.18
☐ 23 Juan Gonzalez	1.00	.45
☐ 24 Bobby Bonilla	.10	.05
☐ 25 George Brett	.75	.35
☐ 26 Ozzie Smith	.60	.25
☐ 27 Andy Van Slyke	.10	.05
☐ 28 Barry Larkin	.25	.11
☐ 29 John Kruk	.10	.05
☐ 30 Robin Yount	.40	.18

1993 Post Canadian

This 18-card limited edition stand-up set was sponsored by Post and measures the standard size. The set features American League (1-9) and National League (10-18) players and is printed in French and English. The fronts display color action photos with the team logo airbrushed out. The black borders have the words "Edition Limite, 1993 Limited Edition" printed in gold lettering at the top and the player's name, position and team printed below the photo. The Post logo appears in the lower left corner. The backs carry a second color action photo with the AL players' names on a blue stripe along the left side and the NL players' names on a bright pink stripe. The cards are numbered on the front.

	MINT	NRMT
COMPLETE SET (18)	18.00	8.00
COMMON CARD (1-18)	.15	.07
☐ 1 Pat Borders	.15	.07
☐ 2 Juan Guzman	.15	.07
☐ 3 Roger Clemens	1.50	.70
☐ 4 Joe Carter	.25	.11
☐ 5 Roberto Alomar	.75	.35
☐ 6 Robin Yount	.75	.35
☐ 7 Cal Ripken	3.00	1.35
☐ 8 Kirby Puckett	2.00	.90
☐ 9 Ken Griffey Jr.	4.00	1.80
☐ 10 Darren Daulton	.25	.11
☐ 11 Andy Van Slyke	.25	.11
☐ 12 Bobby Bonilla	.25	.11
☐ 13 Larry Walker	1.00	.45
☐ 14 Ryne Sandberg	1.50	.70
☐ 15 Barry Larkin	.50	.23
☐ 16 Gary Sheffield	.75	.35
☐ 17 Ozzie Smith	1.25	.55
☐ 18 Terry Pendleton	.15	.07

1994 Post

This 30-card standard-size set was sponsored by Post and produced by MSA (Michael Schlechter Associates). The fronts feature color action player photos inside a gold inner border and a forest green marbleized outer border. At the bottom of the picture, a red diagonal stripe with the player's name and team name edges a black triangle that

carries the facsimile autograph in gold ink. On the forest green marbleized background, the backs present player information (biography, player profile, and statistics) on a pastel colored panel alongside a color player cutout. As is customary with an MSA set, the set is devoid of team logos or insignias. The cards are numbered on the back "X of 30."

	MINT	NRMT
COMPLETE SET (30)	5.00	2.20
COMMON CARD (1-30)	.05	.02
☐ 1 Mike Piazza	1.50	.70
☐ 2 Don Mattingly	.75	.35
☐ 3 Juan Gonzalez	1.00	.45
☐ 4 Kirby Puckett	.75	.35
☐ 5 Gary Sheffield	.40	.18
☐ 6 Dave Justice	.40	.18
☐ 7 Jack McDowell	.05	.02
☐ 8 Mo Vaughn	.40	.18
☐ 9 Darren Daulton	.10	.05
☐ 10 Bobby Bonilla	.10	.05
☐ 11 Barry Bonds	.40	.18
☐ 12 Barry Larkin	.25	.11
☐ 13 Tony Gwynn	1.00	.45
☐ 14 Mark Grace	.40	.18
☐ 15 Ken Griffey Jr.	2.00	.90
☐ 16 Tom Glavine	.10	.05
☐ 17 Cecil Fielder	.10	.05
☐ 18 Roberto Alomar	.40	.18
☐ 19 Mark Whiten	.05	.02
☐ 20 Lenny Dykstra	.10	.05
☐ 21 Frank Thomas	1.50	.70
☐ 22 Will Clark	.40	.18
☐ 23 Andres Galarraga	.40	.18
☐ 24 John Olerud	.10	.05
☐ 25 Cal Ripken	1.50	.70
☐ 26 Tim Salmon	.50	.23
☐ 27 Albert Belle	.60	.25
☐ 28 Gregg Jefferies	.10	.05
☐ 29 Jeff Bagwell	.75	.35
☐ 30 Orlando Merced	.05	.02

1994 Post Canadian

This 18-card set was distributed as single cello-wrapped cards in Canadian Post Alpha-Bits, Honeycomb, Sugar-Crisp, and Marshmallow Alpha-Bits. The cards are slightly smaller than standard-size, measuring 2 1/2" by 3 3/8". Randomly inserted throughout the boxes were Joe Carter HERO cards; 1,000 of these were personally signed. Odds of finding a HERO card were about 1 in 16; odds for finding a signed HERO card were 1 in 3,000. The entire set was available through a mail-in offer for 7 UPC's and $3.49 for postage and handling. An album to display the cards was offered for 2 UPC's and $5.99, plus $4.50 for postage and handling. The fronts feature color player action shots on their borderless fronts. The player's name, team name, and position appear in English and French in a purplish banner near the bottom. The back carries a color player head shot at the top, with his name appearing in yellow lettering at the upper right. Team name, position, biography, statistics, and career highlights in English and French round out the card. The cards are numbered on the back as "X of 18."

	MINT	EXC
COMMON PLAYER (1-18)	20.00	9.00

COMMON CARD (1-18)	.25	.11
*GOLD: 4X BASIC CARDS		
☐ 1 Joe Carter	.50	.23
☐ 2 Paul Molitor	1.00	.45
☐ 3 Roberto Alomar	1.00	.45
☐ 4 John Olerud	.50	.23
☐ 5 Dave Stewart	.50	.23
☐ 6 Juan Guzman	.25	.11
☐ 7 Pat Borders	.25	.11
☐ 8 Larry Walker	1.00	.45
☐ 9 Moises Alou	.50	.23
☐ 10 Ken Griffey Jr.	5.00	2.20
☐ 11 Barry Bonds	1.25	.55
☐ 12 Frank Thomas	4.00	1.80
☐ 13 Cal Ripken	4.00	1.80
☐ 14 Mike Piazza	3.00	1.35
☐ 15 Juan Gonzalez	2.50	1.10
☐ 16 Len Dykstra	.50	.23
☐ 17 David Justice	1.00	.45
☐ 18 Kirby Puckett	2.50	1.10
☐ NNO Joe Carter AU Hero Card	20.00	9.00

1995 Post

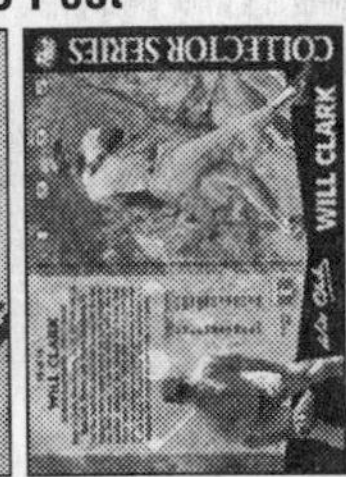

This 16-card standard-size set was distributed solely in limited in-store promotions. Unlike previous years, the cards were not available in cereal boxes nor directly from the company.

	MINT	NRMT
COMPLETE SET (16)	12.00	5.50
COMMON CARD (1-16)	.25	.11
☐ 1 Wade Boggs	1.00	.45
☐ 2 Jeff Bagwell	1.50	.70
☐ 3 Greg Maddux	1.75	.80
☐ 4 Ken Griffey Jr.	3.00	1.35
☐ 5 Roberto Alomar	1.00	.45
☐ 6 Kirby Puckett	1.50	.70
☐ 7 Tony Gwynn	1.50	.70
☐ 8 Cal Ripken, Jr.	2.50	1.10
☐ 9 Matt Williams	.75	.35
☐ 10 David Justice	1.00	.45
☐ 11 Barry Bonds	1.00	.45
☐ 12 Mike Piazza	2.00	.90
☐ 13 Albert Belle	1.25	.55
☐ 14 Frank Thomas	2.50	1.10
☐ 15 Len Dykstra	.25	.11
☐ 16 Will Clark	.75	.35

1995 Post Canadian

This 18-card standard-size set was produced by Upper Deck and issued one per box and was also available via mail-order from the company. The fronts feature color action player photos with the player's name and position printed in a marblized black bar on the side. The backs display another player photo with player information and career statistics. The cards carry both English and French printing and were designed to fit into a marblized design black book with the words "1995 Anniversary Edition" printed in gold foil in English and French on the front.

	MINT	NRMT
COMPLETE SET (18)	40.00	18.00
COMMON CARD (1-18)	1.00	.45
☐ 1 Ken Griffey, Jr.	10.00	4.50
☐ 2 Roberto Alomar	2.50	1.10

	MINT	NRMT
☐ 3 Paul Molitor	2.50	1.10
☐ 4 Devon White	1.00	.45
☐ 5 Moises Alou	1.50	.70
☐ 6 Ken Hill	1.00	.45
☐ 7 Paul O'Neill	1.50	.70
☐ 8 Joe Carter	2.00	.90
☐ 9 Kirby Puckett	5.00	2.20
☐ 10 Jimmy Key	1.00	.45
☐ 11 Frank Thomas	8.00	3.60
☐ 12 David Cone	1.50	.70
☐ 13 Tony Gwynn	5.00	2.20
☐ 14 Matt Williams	2.00	.90
☐ 15 Greg Maddux	6.00	2.70
☐ 16 Jeff Bagwell	5.00	2.20
☐ 17 Barry Bonds	3.00	1.35
☐ 18 Cal Ripken Jr.	8.00	3.60
☐ XX Album	5.00	2.20

1994-95 Pro Mags

1994-95 Pro Mags were distributed in rack packs containing five random player magnets, one team magnet, and a checklist. Each player mag has rounded corners and measures 2 1/8" by 3 3/8" (team mags measure 2 1/8" by 3/4"). Fronts feature borderless color player action shots with name at the bottom and a team logo at upper left. The black magnetized backs are blank. The magnets are numbered on the front. Five hundred Joe Carter autograph magnets were randomly inserted into packs as well.

	MINT	NRMT
COMPLETE SET (140)	80.00	36.00
COMMON CARD (1-140)	.40	.18
☐ 1 Terry Pendleton	.40	.18
☐ 2 Ryan Klesko	1.00	.45
☐ 3 Fred McGriff	1.00	.45
☐ 4 David Justice	1.25	.55
☐ 5 Greg Maddux	3.50	1.55
☐ 6 Brady Anderson	1.00	.45
☐ 7 Ben McDonald	.40	.18
☐ 8 Cal Ripken	5.00	2.20
☐ 9 Mike Mussina	1.25	.55
☐ 10 Jeffrey Hammonds	.40	.18
☐ 11 Roger Clemens	2.00	.90
☐ 12 Andre Dawson	1.00	.45
☐ 13 Mike Greenwell	.40	.18
☐ 14 Mo Vaughn	2.00	.90
☐ 15 Otis Nixon	.75	.35
☐ 16 Chad Curtis	.40	.18
☐ 17 Mark Langston	.40	.18
☐ 18 Tim Salmon	1.25	.55
☐ 19 Chuck Finley	.40	.18
☐ 20 Eduardo Perez	.40	.18
☐ 21 Steve Buechele	.40	.18
☐ 22 Mark Grace	1.50	.70
☐ 23 Sammy Sosa	1.25	.55
☐ 24 Derrick May	.40	.18
☐ 25 Shawon Dunston	.40	.18
☐ 26 Jack McDowell	.40	.18
☐ 27 Tim Raines	.75	.35
☐ 28 Frank Thomas	5.00	2.20
☐ 29 Robin Ventura	.75	.35
☐ 30 Julio Franco	.75	.35
☐ 31 John Smiley	.40	.18
☐ 32 Barry Larkin	1.00	.45
☐ 33 Jose Rijo	.40	.18
☐ 34 Reggie Sanders	.75	.35
☐ 35 Kevin Mitchell	.40	.18
☐ 36 Sandy Alomar	.75	.35
☐ 37 Carlos Baerga	.75	.35
☐ 38 Albert Belle	2.00	.90
☐ 39 Manny Ramirez	1.25	.55
☐ 40 Eddie Murray	1.25	.55
☐ 41 Dante Bichette	.75	.35
☐ 42 Ellis Burks	.75	.35
☐ 43 Andres Galarraga	1.25	.55
☐ 44 Greg Harris	.40	.18
☐ 45 David Nied	.40	.18
☐ 46 Cecil Fielder	.75	.35
☐ 47 Kirk Gibson	.75	.35
☐ 48 Mickey Tettleton	.40	.18
☐ 49 Lou Whitaker	.75	.35
☐ 50 Travis Fryman	.75	.35
☐ 51 Jeff Conine	.75	.35
☐ 52 Charlie Hough	.75	.35
☐ 53 Benito Santiago	.40	.18
☐ 54 Gary Sheffield	1.25	.55
☐ 55 Dave Magadan	.40	.18
☐ 56 Jeff Bagwell	3.00	1.35
☐ 57 Luis Gonzalez	.40	.18
☐ 58 Andujar Cedeno	.40	.18
☐ 59 Craig Biggio	1.00	.45
☐ 60 Doug Drabek	.40	.18
☐ 61 Tom Gordon	.40	.18
☐ 62 Brian McRae	.40	.18
☐ 63 David Cone	.75	.35
☐ 64 Wally Joyner	.75	.35
☐ 65 Jeff Montgomery	.40	.18
☐ 66 Eric Karros	.75	.35
☐ 67 Tom Candiotti	.40	.18
☐ 68 Delino DeShields	.40	.18
☐ 69 Orel Hershiser	.75	.35
☐ 70 Mike Piazza	3.50	1.55
☐ 71 Darryl Hamilton	.40	.18
☐ 72 Kevin Seitzer	.40	.18
☐ 73 B.J. Surhoff	.75	.35
☐ 74 John Jaha	.40	.18
☐ 75 Greg Vaughn	.40	.18
☐ 76 Kent Hrbek	.40	.18
☐ 77 Kirby Puckett	3.00	1.35
☐ 78 Kevin Tapani	.40	.18
☐ 79 Dave Winfield	1.25	.55
☐ 80 Chuck Knoblauch	1.50	.70
☐ 81 Moises Alou	.75	.35
☐ 82 Wil Cordero	.40	.18
☐ 83 Marquis Grissom	.75	.35
☐ 84 Pedro Martinez	.40	.18
☐ 85 Larry Walker	1.25	.55
☐ 86 Jim Abbott	.40	.18
☐ 87 Wade Boggs	1.25	.55
☐ 88 Don Mattingly	3.00	1.35
☐ 89 Luis Polonia	.40	.18
☐ 90 Danny Tartabull	.40	.18
☐ 91 Bobby Bonilla	.75	.35
☐ 92 Todd Hundley	.75	.35
☐ 93 Dwight Gooden	.75	.35
☐ 94 Jeromy Burnitz	.75	.35
☐ 95 Bret Saberhagen	.40	.18
☐ 96 Dennis Eckersley	1.00	.45
☐ 97 Mark McGwire	2.50	1.10
☐ 98 Ruben Sierra	.40	.18
☐ 99 Terry Steinbach	.40	.18
☐ 100 Rickey Henderson	1.50	.70
☐ 101 Darren Daulton	.75	.35
☐ 102 Lenny Dykstra	.75	.35
☐ 103 Dave Hollins	.40	.18
☐ 104 John Kruk	.75	.35
☐ 105 Curt Schilling	.75	.35
☐ 106 Carlos Garcia	.40	.18
☐ 107 Jay Bell	.40	.18
☐ 108 Don Slaught	.40	.18
☐ 109 Andy Van Slyke	.75	.35
☐ 110 Orlando Merced	.40	.18
☐ 111 Ray Lankford	.75	.35
☐ 112 Mark Whiten	.40	.18
☐ 113 Todd Zeile	.40	.18
☐ 114 Ozzie Smith	2.50	1.10
☐ 115 Gregg Jefferies	.75	.35
☐ 116 Derek Bell	.40	.18
☐ 117 Andy Benes	.40	.18
☐ 118 Phil Plantier	.40	.18
☐ 119 Tony Gwynn	3.00	1.35
☐ 120 Bip Roberts	.40	.18
☐ 121 Barry Bonds	2.00	.90
☐ 122 John Burkett	.40	.18
☐ 123 Robby Thompson	.40	.18
☐ 124 Darren Lewis	.40	.18
☐ 125 Willie McGee	.40	.18
☐ 126 Jay Buhner	1.00	.45
☐ 127 Ken Griffey Jr.	6.00	2.70
☐ 128 Randy Johnson	1.25	.55
☐ 129 Eric Anthony	.40	.18
☐ 130 Edgar Martinez	1.00	.45
☐ 131 Kevin Brown	.75	.35
☐ 132 Jose Canseco	1.50	.70
☐ 133 Juan Gonzalez	3.00	1.35
☐ 134 Will Clark	1.50	.70
☐ 135 Ivan Rodriguez	1.50	.70
☐ 136 Roberto Alomar	1.25	.55
☐ 137 Joe Carter	.75	.35
☐ 138 Juan Guzman	.40	.18
☐ 139 Paul Molitor	1.25	.55
☐ 140 John Olerud	.75	.35

1996 Pro Mags All-Stars

These 24 magnet cards measure approximately 2" by 3 1/4". The set was distributed in 12-card packs for each league, including 10 players plus an All-Star Game logo and league logo card. The cards have rounded corners

and the garish fronts feature the players portrait against either the National or American League background. There is also a league logo and a 1996 All-Star game logo on the front of the card. These cards are numbered in very small print in the lower left hand corner. The American League cards are 1-10, while the National League cards are #11-20.

	MINT	NRMT
COMPLETE SET (24)	50.00	22.00
COMMON CARD	.50	.23
☐ 1 Brady Anderson	1.50	.70
☐ 2 Jose Canseco	1.50	.70
☐ 3 Ken Griffey Jr. UER NNO	10.00	4.50
☐ 4 Kenny Lofton	2.50	1.10
☐ 5 Cal Ripken	8.00	3.60
☐ 6 Frank Thomas	8.00	3.60
☐ 7 Ivan Rodriguez	2.50	1.10
☐ 8 Mo Vaughn	2.50	1.10
☐ 9 Albert Belle	4.00	1.80
☐ 10 Alex Rodriguez	8.00	3.60
☐ 11 Hideo Nomo	6.00	2.70
☐ 12 Greg Maddux	6.00	2.70
☐ 13 Jeff Bagwell	5.00	2.20
☐ 14 Barry Bonds	2.50	1.10
☐ 15 Ryan Klesko	1.50	.70
☐ 16 Mike Piazza	6.00	2.70
☐ 17 David Justice	2.00	.90
☐ 18 Dante Bichette	1.00	.45
☐ 19 Barry Larkin	1.50	.70
☐ 20 Tony Gwynn	6.00	2.70
☐ NNO All-Star Game Logo	.50	.23
☐ NNO American League Logo	.50	.23
☐ NNO National League Logo	.50	.23
☐ NNO All-Star Game Logo	.50	.23

1986 Quaker Granola

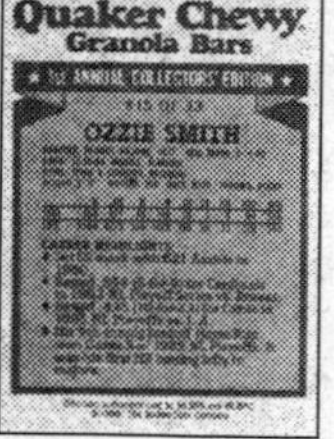

This set of 33 standard-size cards was available in packages of Quaker Oats Chewy Granola, three player cards plus a complete set offer card in each package. The set was also available through a mail-in offer where anyone sending in four UPC seals from Chewy Granola (before 12/31/86) would receive a complete set. The cards were produced by Topps for Quaker Oats. Card backs are printed in red and blue on gray card stock. The cards are numbered on the front and the back. Cards 1-17 feature National League players and cards 18-33 feature American League players. The first three cards in each sequence depict that league's MVP, Cy Young, and Rookie of the Year, respectively. The rest of the cards in each sequence are ordered alphabetically.

	MINT	NRMT
COMPLETE SET (33)	8.00	3.60
COMMON CARD (1-33)	.10	.05
☐ 1 Willie McGee	.25	.11
☐ 2 Dwight Gooden	.40	.18
☐ 3 Vince Coleman	.25	.11
☐ 4 Gary Carter	.60	.25
☐ 5 Jack Clark	.10	.05
☐ 6 Steve Garvey	.40	.18
☐ 7 Tony Gwynn	1.00	.45
☐ 8 Dale Murphy	.60	.25
☐ 9 Dave Parker	.25	.11
☐ 10 Tim Raines	.25	.11
☐ 11 Pete Rose	.75	.35

☐ 12 Nolan Ryan	2.00	.90
☐ 13 Ryne Sandberg	.75	.35
☐ 14 Mike Schmidt	.75	.35
☐ 15 Ozzie Smith	.75	.35
☐ 16 Darryl Strawberry	.25	.11
☐ 17 Fernando Valenzuela	.25	.11
☐ 18 Don Mattingly	1.00	.45
☐ 19 Bret Saberhagen	.25	.11
☐ 20 Ozzie Guillen	.25	.11
☐ 21 Bert Blyleven	.25	.11
☐ 22 Wade Boggs	.75	.35
☐ 23 George Brett	1.00	.45
☐ 24 Darrell Evans	.10	.05
☐ 25 Rickey Henderson	.75	.35
☐ 26 Reggie Jackson	.75	.35
☐ 27 Eddie Murray	.75	.35
☐ 28 Phil Niekro	.60	.25
☐ 29 Dan Quisenberry	.10	.05
☐ 30 Jim Rice	.25	.11
☐ 31 Cal Ripken	2.00	.90
☐ 32 Tom Seaver	.60	.25
☐ 33 Dave Winfield	.60	.25
☐ NNO Offer Card for the complete set	.10	.05

1984 Ralston Purina

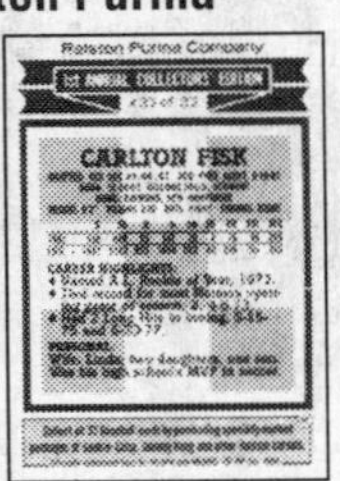

The cards in this 33-card set measure the standard size. In 1984 the Ralston Purina Company issued what it has entitled "The First Annual Collectors Edition of Baseball Cards." The cards feature portrait photos of the players rather than batting action shots. The Topps logo appears along with the Ralston logo on the front of the card. The backs are completely different from the Topps cards of this year; in fact, they contain neither a Topps logo nor a Topps copyright. Large quantities of these cards were obtained by card dealers for direct distribution into the organized hobby, hence the relatively low price of the set.

	MINT	NRMT
COMPLETE SET (33)	5.00	2.20
COMMON CARD (1-33)	.05	.02
☐ 1 Eddie Murray	.50	.23
☐ 2 Ozzie Smith	.75	.35
☐ 3 Ted Simmons	.05	.02
☐ 4 Pete Rose	.50	.23
☐ 5 Greg Luzinski	.05	.02
☐ 6 Andre Dawson	.40	.18
☐ 7 Dave Winfield	.40	.18
☐ 8 Tom Seaver	.40	.18
☐ 9 Jim Rice	.10	.05
☐ 10 Fernando Valenzuela	.10	.05
☐ 11 Wade Boggs	.50	.23
☐ 12 Dale Murphy	.40	.18
☐ 13 George Brett	.75	.35
☐ 14 Nolan Ryan	1.50	.70
☐ 15 Rickey Henderson	.50	.23
☐ 16 Steve Carlton	.40	.18
☐ 17 Rod Carew	.40	.18
☐ 18 Steve Garvey	.25	.11
☐ 19 Reggie Jackson	.40	.18
☐ 20 Dave Concepcion	.10	.05
☐ 21 Robin Yount	.40	.18
☐ 22 Mike Schmidt	.50	.23
☐ 23 Jim Palmer	.40	.18
☐ 24 Bruce Sutter	.05	.02
☐ 25 Dan Quisenberry	.05	.02
☐ 26 Bill Madlock	.10	.05
☐ 27 Cecil Cooper	.10	.05
☐ 28 Gary Carter	.25	.11
☐ 29 Fred Lynn	.10	.05
☐ 30 Pedro Guerrero	.05	.02
☐ 31 Ron Guidry	.10	.05
☐ 32 Keith Hernandez	.10	.05
☐ 33 Carlton Fisk	.40	.18

1987 Ralston Purina

The Ralston Purina Company issued a set of 15 cards picturing players without their respective team logos. The cards measure approximately 2 1/2" by 3 3/8" and are in

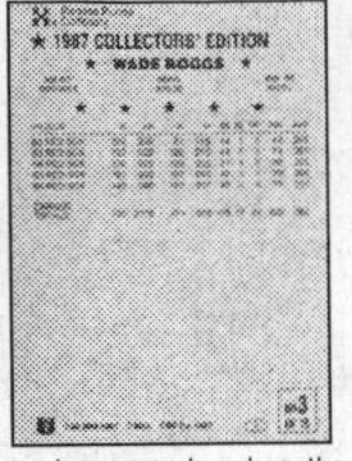

full-color on the front. The cards are numbered on the back in the lower right hand corner; the player's uniform number is prominently displayed on the front. The cards were distributed as inserts inside packages of certain flavors of Ralston Purina's breakfast cereals. Three cards and a contest card were packaged in cellophane and inserted within the cereal box. The set was also available as an uncut sheet through a mail-in offer. Since the uncut sheets are relatively common, the value of the sheet is essentially the same as the value of the sum of the individual cards. In fact there were two uncut sheets issued, one had "Honey Graham Chex" printed at the top and the other had "Cookie Crisp" printed at the top. Also cards were issued with (cards from cereal boxes) and without (cards cut from the uncut sheets) the words "1987 Collectors Edition" printed in blue on the front. Reportedly 100,000 of the uncut sheets were given away free via instant win certificates inserted in with the cereal or collectors could send in two non-winning contest cards plus 1.00 for each uncut sheet.

	MINT	NRMT
COMPLETE SET (15)	18.00	8.00
COMMON CARD (1-15)	.50	.23
☐ 1 Nolan Ryan	5.00	2.20
☐ 2 Steve Garvey	1.00	.45
☐ 3 Wade Boggs	2.00	.90
☐ 4 Dave Winfield	1.50	.70
☐ 5 Don Mattingly	2.50	1.10
☐ 6 Don Sutton	1.50	.70
☐ 7 Dave Parker	.50	.23
☐ 8 Eddie Murray	2.00	.90
☐ 9 Gary Carter	1.00	.45
☐ 10 Roger Clemens	3.00	1.35
☐ 11 Fernando Valenzuela	.75	.35
☐ 12 Cal Ripken	5.00	2.20
☐ 13 Ozzie Smith	2.00	.90
☐ 14 Mike Schmidt	1.50	.70
☐ 15 Ryne Sandberg	2.00	.90

1909 Ramly T204

The cards in this 121-card set measure approximately 2" by 2 1/2". The Ramly baseball series, designated T204 in the catalog, contains unnumbered cards. This set is one of the most distinguished ever produced, containing ornate gold borders around a black and white portrait of each player. There are spelling errors, and two distinct backs, "Ramly" and "TTT", are known. There is a premium of up to 25 percent for the "TTT" back. Much of the obverse card detail is actually embossed. The players have been alphabetized and numbered for reference in the checklist below.

	EX-MT	VG-E
COMPLETE SET (121)	40000.00	18000.00
COMMON CARD (1-121)	250.00	110.00
☐ 1 Whitey Alperman	250.00	110.00
☐ 2 John J. Anderson	250.00	110.00
☐ 3 Jimmy Archer	250.00	110.00
☐ 4 Frank Arrelanes UER	250.00	110.00
☐ 5 Jim Ball (Boston NL)	250.00	110.00
☐ 6 Neal Ball (N.Y. AL)	250.00	110.00
☐ 7 Frank Bancroft	275.00	125.00
☐ 8 Johnny Bates	250.00	110.00
☐ 9 Fred Beebe	250.00	110.00
☐ 10 George Bell	250.00	110.00
☐ 11 Chief Bender	700.00	325.00
☐ 12 Walter Blair	250.00	110.00
☐ 13 Cliff Blankenship	250.00	110.00
☐ 14 Frank Bowerman	250.00	110.00
☐ 15 Kitty Bransfield	250.00	110.00
☐ 16 Roger Bresnahan	700.00	325.00
☐ 17 Al Bridwell	250.00	110.00
☐ 18 Mordecai Brown	700.00	325.00
☐ 19 Fred Burchell	250.00	110.00
☐ 20 Jesse Burkett	800.00	350.00
☐ 21 Bobby Byrnes UER	250.00	110.00
☐ 22 Bill Carrigan	250.00	110.00
☐ 23 Frank Chance	800.00	350.00
☐ 24 Charles Chech	250.00	110.00
☐ 25 Eddie Cicolte	500.00	220.00
☐ 26 Otis Clymer	250.00	110.00
☐ 27 Andrew Coakley	250.00	110.00
☐ 28 Eddie Collins	800.00	350.00
☐ 29 Jimmy Collins	800.00	350.00
☐ 30 Wid Conroy	250.00	110.00
☐ 31 Jack Coombs	300.00	135.00
☐ 32 Doc Crandall	250.00	110.00
☐ 33 Lou Criger	250.00	110.00
☐ 34 Harry Davis	250.00	110.00
☐ 35 Art Devlin	250.00	110.00
☐ 36 Bill Dineen UER	250.00	110.00
☐ 37 Pat Donahue	250.00	110.00
☐ 38 Mike Donlin	275.00	125.00
☐ 39 Bill Donovan	250.00	110.00
☐ 40 Gus Dorner	250.00	110.00
☐ 41 Joe Dunn	250.00	110.00
☐ 42 Kid Elberfield	250.00	110.00
☐ 43 Johnny Evers	800.00	350.00
☐ 44 Bob Ewing	250.00	110.00
☐ 45 George Ferguson	250.00	110.00
☐ 46 Hobe Ferris	250.00	110.00
☐ 47 Jerry Freeman	250.00	110.00
☐ 48 Art Fromme	250.00	110.00
☐ 49 Bob Ganley	250.00	110.00
☐ 50 Doc Gessler	250.00	110.00
☐ 51 Peaches Graham	250.00	110.00
☐ 52 Clark Griffith	600.00	275.00
☐ 53 Roy Hartzell	250.00	110.00
☐ 54 Charlie Hemphill	250.00	110.00
☐ 55 Dick Hoblitzell UER	250.00	110.00
☐ 56 George Howard	250.00	110.00
☐ 57 Harry Howell	250.00	110.00
☐ 58 Miller Huggins	800.00	350.00
☐ 59 John Hummel	250.00	110.00
☐ 60 Walter Johnson	4500.00	2000.00
☐ 61 Tom Jones	250.00	110.00
☐ 62 Mike Kahoe	250.00	110.00
☐ 63 Ed Kargar UER	250.00	110.00
☐ 64 Willie Keeler	1000.00	450.00
☐ 65 Ed Konetchey UER	250.00	110.00
☐ 66 Red Kleinonw	250.00	110.00
☐ 67 John Knight	250.00	110.00
☐ 68 Vive Lindaman	250.00	110.00
☐ 69 Hans Loebert UER	250.00	110.00
☐ 70 Harry Lord	250.00	110.00
☐ 71 Harry Lumley	250.00	110.00
☐ 72 Ernie Lush	250.00	110.00
☐ 73 Rube Manning	250.00	110.00
☐ 74 Jimmy McAleer	250.00	110.00
☐ 75 Amby McConnell	250.00	110.00
☐ 76 Moose McCormick	250.00	110.00
☐ 77 Matty McIntyre	250.00	110.00
☐ 78 Larry McLean	250.00	110.00
☐ 79 Fred Merkle	300.00	135.00
☐ 80 Clyde Milan	275.00	125.00
☐ 81 Mike Mitchell	250.00	110.00
☐ 82 Pat Moran	250.00	110.00
☐ 83 Harry Cy Morgan	250.00	110.00
☐ 84 Tim Murname UER	250.00	110.00
☐ 85 Danny Murphy	250.00	110.00
☐ 86 Red Murray	250.00	110.00
☐ 87 Doc Newton	250.00	110.00
☐ 88 Simon Nichols UER	250.00	110.00
☐ 89 Harry Niles	250.00	110.00
☐ 90 Bill O'Hare UER	250.00	110.00
☐ 91 Charley O'Leary	250.00	110.00
☐ 92 Dode Paskert	250.00	110.00
☐ 93 Barney Pelty	250.00	110.00
☐ 94 Jack Pfeister UER	250.00	110.00
☐ 95 Eddie Plank	1400.00	650.00
☐ 96 Jack Powell	250.00	110.00
☐ 97 Bugs Raymond	275.00	125.00
☐ 98 Tom Reilly	250.00	110.00
☐ 99 Claude Ritchey	250.00	110.00
☐ 100 Nap Rucker	275.00	125.00
☐ 101 Ed Ruelbach UER	275.00	125.00
☐ 102 Slim Sallee	250.00	110.00
☐ 103 Germany Schaefer	275.00	125.00
☐ 104 Jimmy Schekard UER	250.00	110.00
☐ 105 Admiral Schlei	250.00	110.00
☐ 106 Wildfire Schulte	275.00	125.00
☐ 107 Jimmy Sebring	250.00	110.00

☐ 108 Bill Shipke	250.00	110.00
☐ 109 Charlie Smith	250.00	110.00
☐ 110 Tubby Spencer	250.00	110.00
☐ 111 Jake Stahl	300.00	135.00
☐ 112 Harry Stienfeldt UER	300.00	135.00
☐ 113 Jim Stephens	250.00	110.00
☐ 114 Gabby Street	250.00	110.00
☐ 115 Bill Sweeney	250.00	110.00
☐ 116 Fred Tenney	250.00	110.00
☐ 117 Ira Thomas	250.00	110.00
☐ 118 Joe Tinker	800.00	350.00
☐ 119 Bob Unglane UER	250.00	110.00
☐ 120 Heinie Wagner	250.00	110.00
☐ 121 Bobby Wallace	800.00	350.00

1978 Rangers Burger King

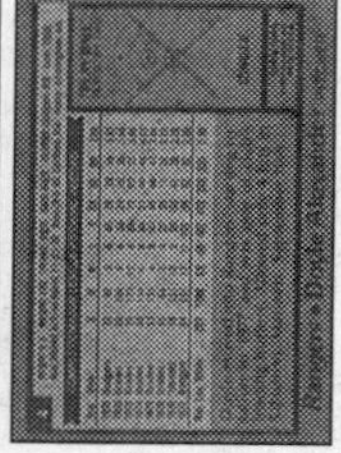

The cards in this 23-card set measure 2 1/2" by 3 1/2". This set of 22 numbered player cards (featuring the Texas Rangers) and one unnumbered checklist was issued regionally by Burger King in 1978. Asterisks denote poses different from those found in the regular Topps cards of this year.

	NRMT	VG-E
COMPLETE SET (23)	15.00	6.75
COMMON CARD (1-22)	.50	.23
☐ 1 Billy Hunter MG	.50	.23
☐ 2 Jim Sundberg	1.00	.45
☐ 3 John Ellis	.50	.23
☐ 4 Doyle Alexander	.75	.35
☐ 5 Jon Matlack *	.75	.35
☐ 6 Dock Ellis	.50	.23
☐ 7 Doc Medich	.50	.23
☐ 8 Fergie Jenkins *	4.00	1.80
☐ 9 Len Barker	.50	.23
☐ 10 Reggie Cleveland *	.50	.23
☐ 11 Mike Hargrove	1.25	.55
☐ 12 Bump Wills	.50	.23
☐ 13 Toby Harrah	1.00	.45
☐ 14 Bert Campaneris	1.00	.45
☐ 15 Sandy Alomar	.75	.35
☐ 16 Kurt Bevacqua	.50	.23
☐ 17 Al Oliver *	1.25	.55
☐ 18 Juan Beniquez	.50	.23
☐ 19 Claudell Washington	1.00	.45
☐ 20 Richie Zisk	.75	.35
☐ 21 John Lowenstein *	.50	.23
☐ 22 Bobby Thompson *	.50	.23
☐ NNO Checklist Card TP	.25	.11

1987 Rangers Mother's

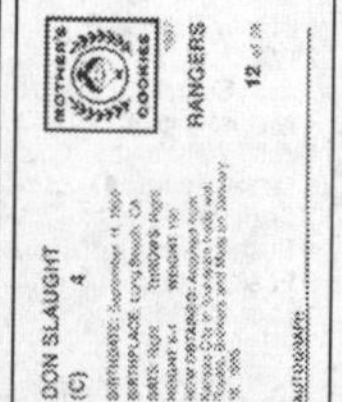

This set consists of 28 full-color, rounded-corner cards each measuring 2 1/2" by 3 1/2". Starter sets (only 20 cards but also including a certificate for eight more cards) were given out at the ballpark and collectors were encouraged to trade to fill in the rest of their set. Cards were originally given out on July 17th during the game against the Yankees. Photos were taken by Barry Colla. The sets were reportedly given out free to the first 25,000 paid admissions at the game.

	MINT	NRMT
COMPLETE SET (28)	12.00	5.50
COMMON CARD (1-28)	.25	.11
☐ 1 Bobby Valentine MG	.50	.23
☐ 2 Pete Incaviglia	.75	.35
☐ 3 Charlie Hough	.75	.35
☐ 4 Oddibe McDowell	.50	.23
☐ 5 Larry Parrish	.50	.23
☐ 6 Scott Fletcher	.25	.11
☐ 7 Steve Buechele	.25	.11
☐ 8 Tom Paciorek	.50	.23
☐ 9 Pete O'Brien	.50	.23
☐ 10 Darrell Porter	.50	.23
☐ 11 Greg A. Harris	.25	.11
☐ 12 Don Slaught	.25	.11
☐ 13 Ruben Sierra	2.00	.90
☐ 14 Curtis Wilkerson	.25	.11
☐ 15 Dale Mohorcic	.25	.11
☐ 16 Ron Meridith	.25	.11
☐ 17 Mitch Williams	1.00	.45
☐ 18 Bob Brower	.25	.11
☐ 19 Edwin Correa	.25	.11
☐ 20 Geno Petralli	.25	.11
☐ 21 Mike Loynd	.25	.11
☐ 22 Jerry Browne	.50	.23
☐ 23 Jose Guzman	.25	.11
☐ 24 Jeff Kunkel	.25	.11
☐ 25 Bobby Witt	1.50	.70
☐ 26 Jeff Russell	.50	.23
☐ 27 Rangers' Trainers	.25	.11
Bill Ziegler		
Danny Wheat		
☐ 28 Checklist Card	.25	.11
Tom Robson CO		
Art Howe CO		
Joe Ferguson CO		
Tim Foli CO		
Tom House CO		
Dave Oliver CO		

1988 Rangers Mother's

This set consists of 28 full-color, rounded-corner cards each measuring 2 1/2" by 3 1/2". Starter sets (only 20 cards but also including a certificate for eight more cards) were given out at the ballpark and collectors were encouraged to trade to fill in the rest of their set. Cards were originally given out on August 7th. Photos were taken by Barry Colla. The sets were reportedly given out free to the first 25,000 paid admissions at the game.

	MINT	NRMT
COMPLETE SET (28)	8.00	3.60
COMMON CARD (1-28)	.25	.11
☐ 1 Bobby Valentine MG	.50	.23
☐ 2 Pete Incaviglia	.50	.23
☐ 3 Charlie Hough	.75	.35
☐ 4 Oddibe McDowell	.50	.23
☐ 5 Larry Parrish	.50	.23
☐ 6 Scott Fletcher	.25	.11
☐ 7 Steve Buechele	.25	.11
☐ 8 Steve Kemp	.25	.11
☐ 9 Pete O'Brien	.50	.23
☐ 10 Ruben Sierra	.75	.35
☐ 11 Mike Stanley	1.00	.45
☐ 12 Jose Cecena	.25	.11
☐ 13 Cecil Espy	.25	.11
☐ 14 Curtis Wilkerson	.25	.11
☐ 15 Dale Mohorcic	.25	.11
☐ 16 Ray Hayward	.25	.11
☐ 17 Mitch Williams	.75	.35
☐ 18 Bob Brower	.25	.11
☐ 19 Paul Kilgus	.25	.11
☐ 20 Geno Petralli	.25	.11
☐ 21 James Steels	.25	.11
☐ 22 Jerry Browne	.25	.11
☐ 23 Jose Guzman	.25	.11
☐ 24 DeWayne Vaughn	.25	.11
☐ 25 Bobby Witt	1.00	.45
☐ 26 Jeff Russell	.50	.23
☐ 27 Rangers' Coaches	.25	.11
Richard Egan		
Tom House		
Art Howe		
Davey Lopes		
David Oliver		
Tom Robson		
☐ 28 Checklist Card	.25	.11
Danny Wheat TR		
Bill Zeigler TR		

1989 Rangers Mother's

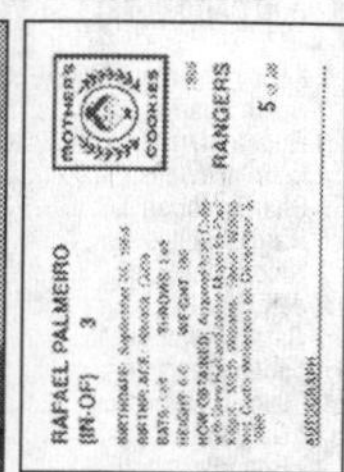

The 1989 Mother's Cookies Texas Rangers set contains 28 standard-size cards with rounded corners. The fronts have borderless color photos, and the horizontally oriented backs have biographical information. Starter sets containing 20 of these cards were given away at a Rangers home game during the 1989 season.

	MINT	NRMT
COMPLETE SET (28)	15.00	6.75
COMMON CARD (1-28)	.25	.11
☐ 1 Bobby Valentine MG	.50	.23
☐ 2 Nolan Ryan	7.50	3.40
☐ 3 Julio Franco	1.00	.45
☐ 4 Charlie Hough	.75	.35
☐ 5 Rafael Palmeiro	2.50	1.10
☐ 6 Jeff Russell	.50	.23
☐ 7 Ruben Sierra	.50	.23
☐ 8 Steve Buechele	.25	.11
☐ 9 Buddy Bell	.75	.35
☐ 10 Pete Incaviglia	.50	.23
☐ 11 Geno Petralli	.25	.11
☐ 12 Cecil Espy	.25	.11
☐ 13 Scott Fletcher	.25	.11
☐ 14 Bobby Witt	.75	.35
☐ 15 Brad Arnsberg	.25	.11
☐ 16 Rick Leach	.25	.11
☐ 17 Jamie Moyer	.50	.23
☐ 18 Kevin Brown	2.00	.90
☐ 19 Jeff Kunkel	.25	.11
☐ 20 Craig McMurtry	.25	.11
☐ 21 Kenny Rogers	.75	.35
☐ 22 Mike Stanley	.75	.35
☐ 23 Cecilio Guante	.25	.11
☐ 24 Jim Sundberg	.50	.23
☐ 25 Jose Guzman	.25	.11
☐ 26 Jeff Stone	.25	.11
☐ 27 Rangers' Coaches	.25	.11
Dick Egan		
Tom House		
Toby Harrah		
Davey Lopes		
Dave Oliver		
Tom Robson		
☐ 28 Checklist Card	.25	.11
Danny Wheat TR		
Bill Ziegler TR		

1990 Rangers Mother's

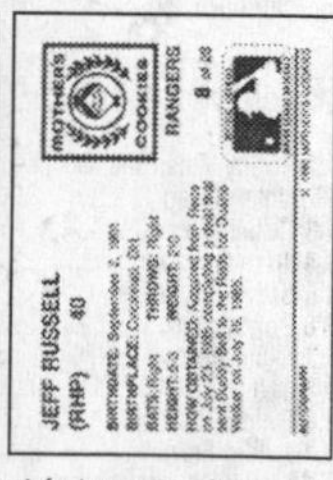

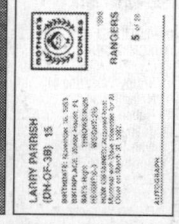

This 28-card, standard-size set features members of the 1990 Texas Rangers. The set has beautiful full-color photos on the front along with biographical information on the back. The set also features the now traditional Mother's Cookies rounded corners. The Rangers cards were distributed on July 22nd to the first 25,000 game attendees in Arlington. They were distributed in 20-card random packets at the game and eight more at the redemption booths. However, both groups of cards were random and there was no guarantee of getting a complete set in the cards. The promotional idea was that the only way one could finish the set was to trade for them. The redemption certificates (for eight more cards) were also able to be redeemed at the 17th Annual Dallas Card Convention on August 18-19, 1990.

	MINT	NRMT
COMPLETE SET (28)	15.00	6.75
COMMON CARD (1-28)	.25	.11

	MINT	NRMT
☐ 1 Bobby Valentine MG	.50	.23
☐ 2 Nolan Ryan	7.50	3.40
☐ 3 Ruben Sierra	.50	.23
☐ 4 Pete Incaviglia	.50	.23
☐ 5 Charlie Hough	.75	.35
☐ 6 Harold Baines	.75	.35
☐ 7 Gino Petralli	.25	.11
☐ 8 Jeff Russell	.50	.23
☐ 9 Rafael Palmeiro	2.00	.90
☐ 10 Julio Franco	1.00	.45
☐ 11 Jack Daugherty	.25	.11
☐ 12 Gary Pettis	.25	.11
☐ 13 Brian Bohanon	.25	.11
☐ 14 Steve Buechele	.25	.11
☐ 15 Bobby Witt	.75	.35
☐ 16 Thad Bosley	.25	.11
☐ 17 Gary Mielke	.25	.11
☐ 18 Jeff Kunkel	.25	.11
☐ 19 Mike Jeffcoat	.25	.11
☐ 20 Mike Stanley	.75	.35
☐ 21 Kevin Brown	1.50	.70
☐ 22 Kenny Rogers	.75	.35
☐ 23 Jeff Huson	.25	.11
☐ 24 Jamie Moyer	.25	.11
☐ 25 Cecil Espy	.25	.11
☐ 26 John Russell	.25	.11
☐ 27 Coaches Card Dave Oliver Davey Lopes Tom Robson Tom House Toby Harrah	.25	.11
☐ 28 Trainers Card Bill Zeigler TR Joe Macko EQ.MG. Marty Stajduhar, Strength and Cond. Danny Wheat ATR	.25	.11

1991 Rangers Mother's

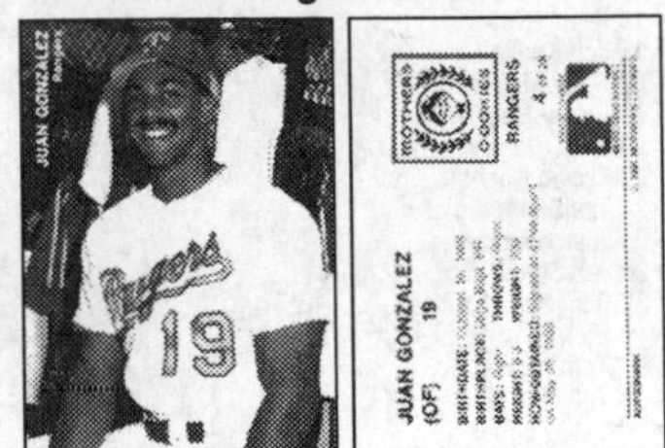

The 1991 Mother's Cookies Texas Rangers set contains 28 cards with rounded corners measuring the standard size. The front design has borderless glossy color player photos, with the locker room as the background. The horizontally oriented backs are printed in red and purple, present biographical information, and have blank slots for player autographs.

	MINT	NRMT
COMPLETE SET (28)	15.00	6.75
COMMON CARD (1-28)	.25	.11

	MINT	NRMT
☐ 1 Bobby Valentine MG	.50	.23
☐ 2 Nolan Ryan	6.00	2.70
☐ 3 Ruben Sierra	.75	.35
☐ 4 Juan Gonzalez	6.00	2.70
☐ 5 Steve Buechele	.25	.11
☐ 6 Bobby Witt	.75	.35
☐ 7 Geno Petralli	.25	.11
☐ 8 Jeff Russell	.50	.23
☐ 9 Rafael Palmeiro	2.00	.90
☐ 10 Julio Franco	.75	.35
☐ 11 Jack Daugherty	.25	.11
☐ 12 Gary Pettis	.25	.11
☐ 13 John Barfield	.25	.11
☐ 14 Scott Chiamparino	.25	.11
☐ 15 Kevin Reimer	.25	.11
☐ 16 Rich Gossage	1.00	.45
☐ 17 Brian Downing	.50	.23
☐ 18 Denny Walling	.25	.11
☐ 19 Mike Jeffcoat	.25	.11
☐ 20 Mike Stanley	.75	.35
☐ 21 Kevin Brown	1.25	.55
☐ 22 Kenny Rogers	.75	.35
☐ 23 Jeff Huson	.25	.11
☐ 24 Mario Diaz	.25	.11
☐ 25 Brad Arnsberg	.25	.11
☐ 26 John Russell	.25	.11
☐ 27 Gerald Alexander	.25	.11
☐ 28 Checklist Card Tom Robson CO Toby Harrah CO Orlando Gomez CO Tom House CO Dave Oliver CO Davey Lopes CO	.25	.11

1992 Rangers Mother's

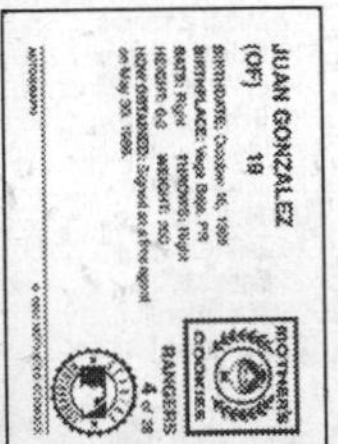

The 1992 Mother's Cookies Rangers set contains 28 cards with rounded corners measuring the standard size. The front design has borderless glossy color player photos in which the players are posed against a blue background. The player's name and team name appear at one of the upper corners. The horizontal backs are printed in red and purple, and present biography and a "how obtained" remark. A blank slot for the player's autograph rounds out the back.

	MINT	NRMT
COMPLETE SET (28)	15.00	6.75
COMMON CARD (1-28)	.25	.11

	MINT	NRMT
☐ 1 Bobby Valentine MG	.50	.23
☐ 2 Nolan Ryan	4.00	1.80
☐ 3 Ruben Sierra	.75	.35
☐ 4 Juan Gonzalez	4.00	1.80
☐ 5 Ivan Rodriguez	3.00	1.35
☐ 6 Bobby Witt	.75	.35
☐ 7 Geno Petralli	.25	.11
☐ 8 Jeff Russell	.50	.23
☐ 9 Rafael Palmeiro	2.00	.90
☐ 10 Julio Franco	.75	.35
☐ 11 Jack Daugherty	.25	.11
☐ 12 Dickie Thon	.25	.11
☐ 13 Floyd Bannister	.25	.11
☐ 14 Scott Chiamparino	.25	.11
☐ 15 Kevin Reimer	.25	.11
☐ 16 Jeff M. Robinson	.25	.11
☐ 17 Brian Downing	.50	.23
☐ 18 Brian Bohanon	.25	.11
☐ 19 Jose Guzman	.25	.11
☐ 20 Terry Mathews	.25	.11
☐ 21 Kevin Brown	1.25	.55
☐ 22 Kenny Rogers	.75	.35
☐ 23 Jeff Huson	.25	.11
☐ 24 Monty Fariss	.25	.11
☐ 25 Al Newman	.25	.11
☐ 26 Dean Palmer	2.00	.90
☐ 27 John Cangelosi	.25	.11
☐ 28 Coaches/Checklist Tom Robson Ray Burris Toby Harrah Dave Oliver Tom House Orlando Gomez	.25	.11

1996 Rangers Mother's

This 28-card set consists of borderless posed color player portraits in stadium settings. The player's and team's names appear in one of the top rounded corners. The backs carry biographical information and the sponsor's logo on a white background in red and purple print. A blank slot for the player's autograph rounds out the back.

	MINT	NRMT
COMPLETE SET (28)	10.00	4.50
COMMON CARD (1-28)	.25	.11

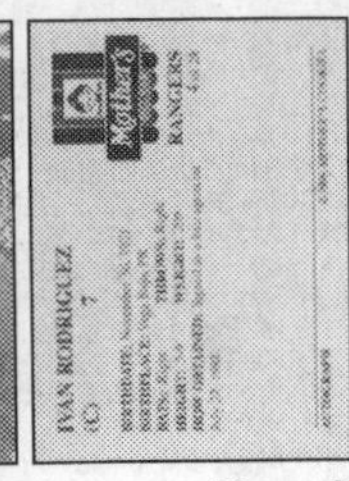

	MINT	NRMT
☐ 1 Johnny Oates MG	.25	.11
☐ 2 Will Clark	1.50	.70
☐ 3 Juan Gonzalez	2.50	1.10
☐ 4 Ivan Rodriguez	2.00	.90
☐ 5 Darryl Hamilton	.50	.23
☐ 6 Dean Palmer	.75	.35
☐ 7 Mickey Tettleton	.50	.23
☐ 8 Craig Worthington	.25	.11
☐ 9 Rusty Greer	2.00	.90
☐ 10 Kevin Gross	.25	.11
☐ 11 Rick Helling	.25	.11
☐ 12 Kevin Elster	.25	.11
☐ 13 Bobby Witt	.50	.23
☐ 14 Mark McLemore	.25	.11
☐ 15 Warren Newson	.25	.11
☐ 16 Mike Henneman	.25	.11
☐ 17 Ken Hill	.75	.35
☐ 18 Gil Heredia	.25	.11
☐ 19 Roger Pavlik	.25	.11
☐ 20 David Valle	.25	.11
☐ 21 Mark Brandenburg	.25	.11
☐ 22 Kurt Stillwell	.25	.11
☐ 23 Ed Vosberg	.25	.11
☐ 24 Dennis Cook	.25	.11
☐ 25 Damon Buford	.25	.11
☐ 26 Benji Gil	.25	.11
☐ 27 Darren Oliver	.50	.23
☐ 28 Coaches Card CL Dick Bosman Bucky Den Larry Hardy Rudy Jaramillo Ed Napoleon Jerry Narron	.25	.11

1997 Rangers Mothers

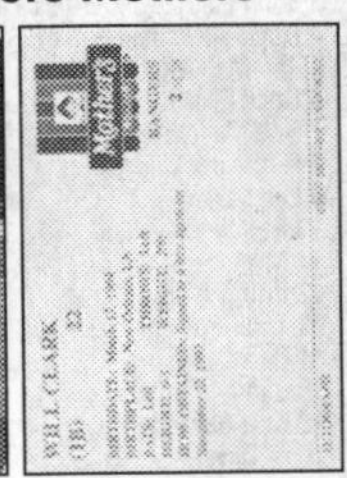

This 28-card set of the Texas Rangers sponsored by Mother's Cookies consists of posed color player photos with rounded corners. The backs carry biographical information and the sponsor's logo on a white background in red and purple print. A blank slot for the player's autograph rounds out the back.

	MINT	NRMT
COMPLETE SET (28)	12.00	5.50
COMMON CARD (1-28)	.25	.11

	MINT	NRMT
☐ 1 Johnny Oates MG	.25	.11
☐ 2 Will Clark	1.25	.55
☐ 3 Juan Gonzalez	2.50	1.10
☐ 4 Ivan Rodriguez	1.50	.70
☐ 5 John Wetteland	1.00	.45
☐ 6 Mickey Tettleton	.50	.23
☐ 7 Dean Palmer	.50	.23
☐ 8 Rusty Greer	1.25	.55
☐ 9 Ed Vosberg	.25	.11
☐ 10 Lee Stevens	.25	.11
☐ 11 Benji Gil	.25	.11
☐ 12 Mike Devereaux	.25	.11
☐ 13 Bobby Witt	.50	.23
☐ 14 Mark McLemore	.25	.11
☐ 15 Warren Newson	.25	.11
☐ 16 Eric Gunderson	.25	.11
☐ 17 Ken Hill	.25	.11
☐ 18 Damon Buford	.25	.11
☐ 19 Roger Pavlik	.25	.11
☐ 20 Bill Ripken	.25	.11
☐ 21 John Burkett	.50	.23
☐ 22 Darren Oliver	.25	.11
☐ 23 Mike Simms	.25	.11
☐ 24 Julio Santana	.25	.11
☐ 25 Henry Mercedes	.25	.11
☐ 26 Xavier Hernandez	.25	.11

☐ 27 Danny Patterson	.25	.11
☐ 28 Coaches Card CL Dick Bosman Bucky Dent Larry Hardy Rudy Jaramillo Ed Napoleon Jerry Narron	.25	.11

1954 Red Heart

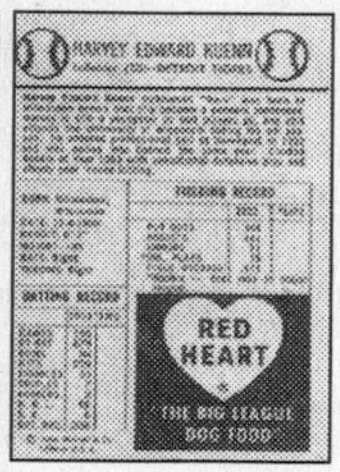

The cards in this 33-card set measure approximately 2 5/8" by 3 3/4". The 1954 Red Heart baseball series was marketed by Red Heart dog food, which, incidentally, was a subsidiary of Morrell Meats. The set consists of three series of eleven unnumbered cards each of which could be ordered from the company via an offer (two can labels plus ten cents for each series) on the can label. Each series has a specific color background (red, green or blue) behind the color player photo. Cards with red backgrounds are considered scarcer and are marked with SP in the checklist (which has been alphabetized and numbered for reference). The catalog designation is F156.

	NRMT	VG-E
COMPLETE SET (33)	2000.00	900.00
COMMON CARD (1-33)	25.00	11.00
COMMON CARD SP	35.00	16.00

☐ 1 Richie Ashburn SP	75.00	34.00
☐ 2 Frank Baumholtz SP	35.00	16.00
☐ 3 Gus Bell	25.00	11.00
☐ 4 Billy Cox	30.00	13.50
☐ 5 Alvin Dark	30.00	13.50
☐ 6 Carl Erskine SP	40.00	18.00
☐ 7 Ferris Fain	25.00	11.00
☐ 8 Dee Fondy	25.00	11.00
☐ 9 Nellie Fox	60.00	27.00
☐ 10 Jim Gilliam	35.00	16.00
☐ 11 Jim Hegan SP	35.00	16.00
☐ 12 George Kell	50.00	22.00
☐ 13 Ralph Kiner SP	75.00	34.00
☐ 14 Ted Kluszewski SP	75.00	34.00
☐ 15 Harvey Kuenn	30.00	13.50
☐ 16 Bob Lemon SP	75.00	34.00
☐ 17 Sherman Lollar	30.00	13.50
☐ 18 Mickey Mantle	500.00	220.00
☐ 19 Billy Martin	50.00	22.00
☐ 20 Gil McDougald SP	40.00	18.00
☐ 21 Roy McMillan	25.00	11.00
☐ 22 Minnie Minoso	35.00	16.00
☐ 23 Stan Musial SP	400.00	180.00
☐ 24 Billy Pierce	30.00	13.50
☐ 25 Al Rosen SP	40.00	18.00
☐ 26 Hank Sauer	25.00	11.00
☐ 27 Red Schoendienst SP	75.00	34.00
☐ 28 Enos Slaughter	50.00	22.00
☐ 29 Duke Snider	150.00	70.00
☐ 30 Warren Spahn	50.00	22.00
☐ 31 Sammy White	25.00	11.00
☐ 32 Eddie Yost	25.00	11.00
☐ 33 Gus Zernial	30.00	13.50

1952 Red Man

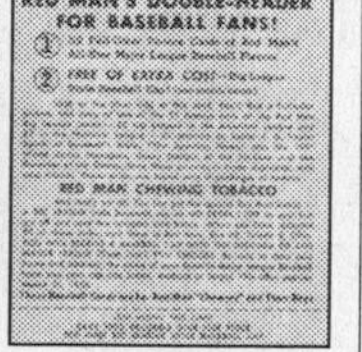

The cards in this 52-card set measure approximately 3 1/2" by 4" (or 3 1/2" by 3 5/8" without the tab). This Red Man issue was the first nationally available tobacco issue since the T cards of the teens early in this century. This 52-card set contains 26 top players from each league. Cards that have the tab (coupon) attached are generally worth a multiplier of cards without tabs. Please refer to multiplier line below. The 1952 Red Man cards are considered to be the most difficult (of the Red Man sets) to find with tabs. Card numbers are located on the tabs. The prices listed below refer to cards without tabs. The numbering of the set is alphabetical by player within league with the exception of the managers who are listed first.

	NRMT	VG-E
COMPLETE SET (52)	750.00	350.00
COMMON CARD	7.50	3.40
CARDS WITH TABS:3X VALUES		

☐ AL1 Casey Stengel MG	25.00	11.00
☐ AL2 Bobby Avila	7.50	3.40
☐ AL3 Yogi Berra	40.00	18.00
☐ AL4 Gil Coan	7.50	3.40
☐ AL5 Dom DiMaggio	15.00	6.75
☐ AL6 Larry Doby	15.00	6.75
☐ AL7 Ferris Fain	7.50	3.40
☐ AL8 Bob Feller	25.00	11.00
☐ AL9 Nellie Fox	20.00	9.00
☐ AL10 Johnny Groth	7.50	3.40
☐ AL11 Jim Hegan	7.50	3.40
☐ AL12 Eddie Joost	7.50	3.40
☐ AL13 George Kell	15.00	6.75
☐ AL14 Gil McDougald	12.50	5.50
☐ AL15 Minnie Minoso	12.50	5.50
☐ AL16 Billy Pierce	10.00	4.50
☐ AL17 Bob Porterfield	7.50	3.40
☐ AL18 Eddie Robinson	7.50	3.40
☐ AL19 Saul Rogovin	7.50	3.40
☐ AL20 Bobby Shantz	10.00	4.50
☐ AL21 Vern Stephens	7.50	3.40
☐ AL22 Vic Wertz	7.50	3.40
☐ AL23 Ted Williams	100.00	45.00
☐ AL24 Early Wynn	15.00	6.75
☐ AL25 Eddie Yost	7.50	3.40
☐ AL26 Gus Zernial	10.00	4.50
☐ NL1 Leo Durocher MG	20.00	9.00
☐ NL2 Richie Ashburn	20.00	9.00
☐ NL3 Ewell Blackwell	7.50	3.40
☐ NL4 Cliff Chambers	7.50	3.40
☐ NL5 Murry Dickson	7.50	3.40
☐ NL6 Sid Gordon	7.50	3.40
☐ NL7 Granny Hamner	10.00	4.50
☐ NL8 Jim Hearn	7.50	3.40
☐ NL9 Monte Irvin	15.00	6.75
☐ NL10 Larry Jansen	7.50	3.40
☐ NL11 Willie Jones	7.50	3.40
☐ NL12 Ralph Kiner	20.00	9.00
☐ NL13 Whitey Lockman	7.50	3.40
☐ NL14 Sal Maglie	10.00	4.50
☐ NL15 Willie Mays	75.00	34.00
☐ NL16 Stan Musial	75.00	34.00
☐ NL17 Pee Wee Reese	25.00	11.00
☐ NL18 Robin Roberts	20.00	9.00
☐ NL19 Red Schoendienst	15.00	6.75
☐ NL20 Enos Slaughter	20.00	9.00
☐ NL21 Duke Snider	45.00	20.00
☐ NL22 Warren Spahn	25.00	11.00
☐ NL23 Eddie Stanky	10.00	4.50
☐ NL24 Bobby Thomson	12.50	5.50
☐ NL25 Earl Torgeson	7.50	3.40
☐ NL26 Wes Westrum	7.50	3.40

1953 Red Man

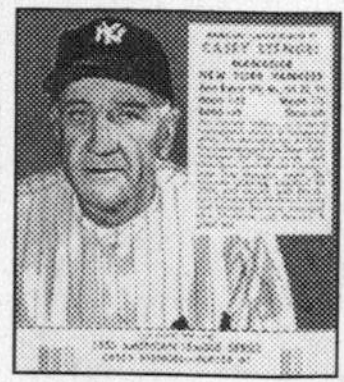

The cards in this 52-card set measure approximately 3 1/2" by 4" (or 3 1/2" by 3 5/8" without the tab). The 1953 Red Man set contains 26 National League stars and 26 American League stars. Card numbers are located both on the write-up of the player and on the tab. Cards that have the tab (coupon) attached are worth a multiplier of cards without tabs. Please refer to the multiplier line below. The prices listed below refer to cards without tabs.

	NRMT	VG-E
COMPLETE SET (52)	600.00	275.00
COMMON CARD (1-52)	6.00	2.70
CARDS WITH TABS: 2.5X VALUES		

☐ AL1 Casey Stengel MG	25.00	11.00
☐ AL2 Hank Bauer	7.50	3.40
☐ AL3 Yogi Berra	40.00	18.00
☐ AL4 Walt Dropo	6.00	2.70
☐ AL5 Nellie Fox	20.00	9.00
☐ AL6 Jackie Jensen	7.50	3.40
☐ AL7 Eddie Joost	6.00	2.70
☐ AL8 George Kell	12.50	5.50
☐ AL9 Dale Mitchell	6.00	2.70
☐ AL10 Phil Rizzuto	25.00	11.00
☐ AL11 Eddie Robinson	6.00	2.70
☐ AL12 Gene Woodling	10.00	4.50
☐ AL13 Gus Zernial	10.00	4.50
☐ AL14 Early Wynn	12.50	5.50
☐ AL15 Joe Dobson	6.00	2.70
☐ AL16 Billy Pierce	10.00	4.50
☐ AL17 Bob Lemon	12.50	5.50
☐ AL18 Johnny Mize	15.00	6.75
☐ AL19 Bob Porterfield	6.00	2.70
☐ AL20 Bobby Shantz	10.00	4.50
☐ AL21 Mickey Vernon	10.00	4.50
☐ AL22 Dom DiMaggio	12.50	5.50
☐ AL23 Gil McDougald	7.50	3.40
☐ AL24 Al Rosen	7.50	3.40
☐ AL25 Mel Parnell	6.00	2.70
☐ AL26 Bobby Avila	6.00	2.70
☐ NL1 Charlie Dressen MG	6.00	2.70
☐ NL2 Bobby Adams	6.00	2.70
☐ NL3 Richie Ashburn	20.00	9.00
☐ NL4 Joe Black	7.50	3.40
☐ NL5 Roy Campanella	45.00	20.00
☐ NL6 Ted Kluszewski	12.50	5.50
☐ NL7 Whitey Lockman	6.00	2.70
☐ NL8 Sal Maglie	7.50	3.40
☐ NL9 Andy Pafko	6.00	2.70
☐ NL10 Pee Wee Reese	25.00	11.00
☐ NL11 Robin Roberts	15.00	6.75
☐ NL12 Red Schoendienst	12.50	5.50
☐ NL13 Enos Slaughter	15.00	6.75
☐ NL14 Duke Snider	45.00	20.00
☐ NL15 Ralph Kiner	15.00	6.75
☐ NL16 Hank Sauer	7.50	3.40
☐ NL17 Del Ennis	7.50	3.40
☐ NL18 Granny Hamner	6.00	2.70
☐ NL19 Warren Spahn	25.00	11.00
☐ NL20 Wes Westrum	6.00	2.70
☐ NL21 Hoyt Wilhelm	12.50	5.50
☐ NL22 Murry Dickson	6.00	2.70
☐ NL23 Warren Hacker	6.00	2.70
☐ NL24 Gerry Staley	6.00	2.70
☐ NL25 Bobby Thomson	12.50	5.50
☐ NL26 Stan Musial	75.00	34.00

1954 Red Man

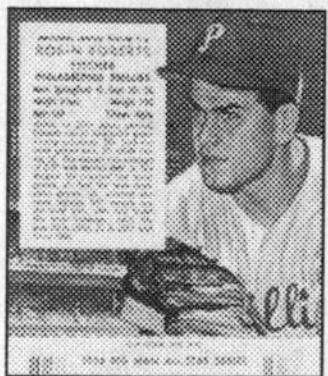

The cards in this 50-card set measure approximately 3 1/2" by 4" (or 3 1/2" by 3 5/8" without the tab). The 1954 Red Man set witnessed a reduction to 25 players from each league. George Kell, Sam Mele, and Dave Philley are known to exist with two different teams. Card number 19 of the National League exists as Enos Slaughter and as Gus Bell. Card numbers are on the write-ups of the players. Cards that have the tab (coupon) attached are worth a multiple of cards without tabs. Please refer to the values below for cards with tabs. The prices listed below refer to cards without tabs. The complete set price below refers to all 54 cards including the four variations.

	NRMT	VG-E
COMPLETE SET (54)	750.00	350.00
COMMON CARD (1-54)	6.00	2.70
*CARDS WITH TABS:2.5X VALUES		

☐ AL1 Bobby Avila	6.00	2.70
☐ AL2 Jim Busby	6.00	2.70
☐ AL3 Nellie Fox	20.00	9.00
☐ AL4A George Kell (Boston)	25.00	11.00
☐ AL4B George Kell (Chicago)	60.00	27.00
☐ AL5 Sherman Lollar	6.00	2.70
☐ AL6A Sam Mele (Baltimore)	12.50	5.50
☐ AL6B Sam Mele (Chicago)	40.00	18.00
☐ AL7 Minnie Minoso	10.00	4.50
☐ AL8 Mel Parnell	6.00	2.70

☐ AL9A Dave Philley (Cleveland)	12.00	5.50
☐ AL9B Dave Philley (Philadelphia)	35.00	16.00
☐ AL10 Billy Pierce	10.00	4.50
☐ AL11 Jimmy Piersall	10.00	4.50
☐ AL12 Al Rosen	10.00	4.50
☐ AL13 Mickey Vernon	10.00	4.50
☐ AL14 Sammy White	6.00	2.70
☐ AL15 Gene Woodling	10.00	4.50
☐ AL16 Whitey Ford	25.00	11.00
☐ AL17 Phil Rizzuto	20.00	9.00
☐ AL18 Bob Porterfield	6.00	2.70
☐ AL19 Chico Carrasquel	6.00	2.70
☐ AL20 Yogi Berra	40.00	18.00
☐ AL21 Bob Lemon	12.50	5.50
☐ AL22 Ferris Fain	6.00	2.70
☐ AL23 Hank Bauer	10.00	4.50
☐ AL24 Jim Delsing	6.00	2.70
☐ AL25 Gil McDougald	10.00	4.50
☐ NL1 Richie Ashburn	20.00	9.00
☐ NL2 Billy Cox	10.00	4.50
☐ NL3 Del Crandall	10.00	4.50
☐ NL4 Carl Erskine	10.00	4.50
☐ NL5 Monte Irvin	12.50	5.50
☐ NL6 Ted Kluszewski	12.50	5.50
☐ NL7 Don Mueller	6.00	2.70
☐ NL8 Andy Pafko	6.00	2.70
☐ NL9 Del Rice	6.00	2.70
☐ NL10 Red Schoendienst	12.50	5.50
☐ NL11 Warren Spahn	20.00	9.00
☐ NL12 Curt Simmons	10.00	4.50
☐ NL13 Roy Campanella	45.00	20.00
☐ NL14 Jim Gilliam	10.00	4.50
☐ NL15 Pee Wee Reese	25.00	11.00
☐ NL16 Duke Snider	45.00	20.00
☐ NL17 Rip Repulski	6.00	2.70
☐ NL18 Robin Roberts	15.00	6.75
☐ NL19A Enos Slaughter	60.00	27.00
☐ NL19B Gus Bell	25.00	11.00
☐ NL20 Johnny Logan	6.00	2.70
☐ NL21 John Antonelli	6.00	2.70
☐ NL22 Gil Hodges	20.00	9.00
☐ NL23 Eddie Mathews	20.00	9.00
☐ NL24 Lew Burdette	10.00	4.50
☐ NL25 Willie Mays	80.00	36.00

1955 Red Man

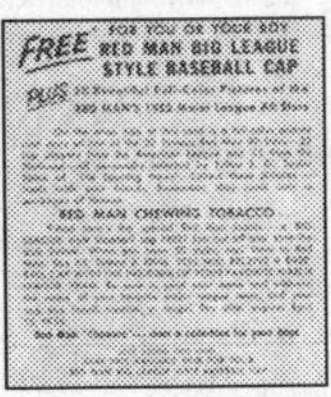

The cards in this 50-card set measure approximately 3 1/2" by 4" (or 3 1/2" by 3 5/8" without the tab). The 1955 Red Man set contains 25 players from each league. Card numbers are on the write-ups of the players. Cards that have the tab (coupon) attached are generally worth a multiple of cards which have had their tabs removed. Please see mulitplier values below. The prices listed below refer to cards without tabs.

	NRMT	VG-E
COMPLETE SET (50)	500.00	220.00
COMMON CARD (1-50)	6.00	2.70
*CARDS WITH TABS:2.5X VALUES		

☐ AL1 Ray Boone	6.00	2.70
☐ AL2 Jim Busby	6.00	2.70
☐ AL3 Whitey Ford	25.00	11.00
☐ AL4 Nellie Fox	20.00	9.00
☐ AL5 Bob Grim	6.00	2.70
☐ AL6 Jack Harshman	6.00	2.70
☐ AL7 Jim Hegan	6.00	2.70
☐ AL8 Bob Lemon	12.50	5.50
☐ AL9 Irv Noren	6.00	2.70
☐ AL10 Bob Porterfield	6.00	2.70
☐ AL11 Al Rosen	8.00	3.60
☐ AL12 Mickey Vernon	10.00	4.50
☐ AL13 Vic Wertz	6.00	2.70
☐ AL14 Early Wynn	12.50	5.50
☐ AL15 Bobby Avila	6.00	2.70
☐ AL16 Yogi Berra	40.00	18.00
☐ AL17 Joe Coleman	6.00	2.70
☐ AL18 Larry Doby	12.50	5.50
☐ AL19 Jackie Jensen	10.00	4.50
☐ AL20 Pete Runnels	6.00	2.70
☐ AL21 Jimmy Piersall	8.00	3.60
☐ AL22 Hank Bauer	8.00	3.60
☐ AL23 Chico Carrasquel	6.00	2.70
☐ AL24 Minnie Minoso	10.00	4.50
☐ AL25 Sandy Consuegra	6.00	2.70
☐ NL1 Richie Ashburn	20.00	9.00
☐ NL2 Del Crandall	6.00	2.70
☐ NL3 Gil Hodges	20.00	9.00
☐ NL4 Brooks Lawrence	6.00	2.70
☐ NL5 Johnny Logan	6.00	2.70
☐ NL6 Sal Maglie	8.00	3.60
☐ NL7 Willie Mays	80.00	36.00
☐ NL8 Don Mueller	6.00	2.70
☐ NL9 Bill Sarni	6.00	2.70
☐ NL10 Warren Spahn	20.00	9.00
☐ NL11 Hank Thompson	6.00	2.70
☐ NL12 Hoyt Wilhelm	12.50	5.50
☐ NL13 John Antonelli	8.00	3.60
☐ NL14 Carl Erskine	10.00	4.50
☐ NL15 Granny Hamner	6.00	2.70
☐ NL16 Ted Kluszewski	12.50	5.50
☐ NL17 Pee Wee Reese	25.00	11.00
☐ NL18 Red Schoendienst	12.50	5.50
☐ NL19 Duke Snider	45.00	20.00
☐ NL20 Frank Thomas	6.00	2.70
☐ NL21 Ray Jablonski	6.00	2.70
☐ NL22 Dusty Rhodes	8.00	3.60
☐ NL23 Gus Bell	8.00	3.60
☐ NL24 Curt Simmons	8.00	3.60
☐ NL25 Marv Grissom	6.00	2.70

1982 Red Sox Coke

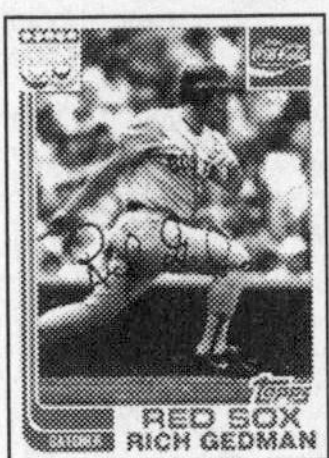

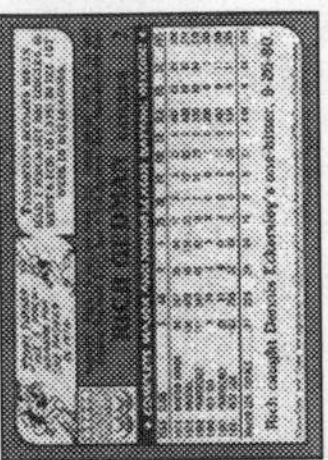

The cards in this 23-card set measure the standard size. This set of Boston Red Sox ballplayers was issued locally in the Boston area as a joint promotion by Brigham's Ice Cream Stores and Coca-Cola. The pictures are identical to those in the Topps regular 1982 issue, except that the colors are brighter and the Brigham and Coke logos appear inside the frame line. The reverses are done in red, black and gray, in contrast to the Topps set, and the number appears to the right of the position listing. The cards were initally distributed in three-card cello packs with an ice cream or Coca-Cola purchase but later became available as sets within the hobby. The unnumbered title or advertising card carries a premium offer on the reverse. The set numbering is in alphabetical order by player's name.

	NRMT	VG-E
COMPLETE SET (23)	8.00	3.60
COMMON CARD (1-22)	.25	.11

☐ 1 Gary Allenson	.25	.11
☐ 2 Tom Burgmeier	.25	.11
☐ 3 Mark Clear	.25	.11
☐ 4 Steve Crawford	.25	.11
☐ 5 Dennis Eckersley	2.00	.90
☐ 6 Dwight Evans	1.25	.55
☐ 7 Rich Gedman	.25	.11
☐ 8 Garry Hancock	.25	.11
☐ 9 Glenn Hoffman	.25	.11
☐ 10 Carney Lansford	.50	.23
☐ 11 Rick Miller	.25	.11
☐ 12 Reid Nichols	.25	.11
☐ 13 Bob Ojeda	.50	.23
☐ 14 Tony Perez	1.50	.70
☐ 15 Chuck Rainey	.25	.11
☐ 16 Jerry Remy	.25	.11
☐ 17 Jim Rice	1.00	.45
☐ 18 Bob Stanley	.50	.23
☐ 19 Dave Stapleton	.25	.11
☐ 20 Mike Torrez	.50	.23
☐ 21 John Tudor	.50	.23
☐ 22 Carl Yastrzemski	3.00	1.35
☐ NNO Title Card	.15	.07

1990 Red Sox Pepsi

The 1990 Pepsi Boston Red Sox set is a 20-card standard-size set, which is checklisted alphabetically below. This set was apparently prepared very early in the 1990 season as Bill Buckner and Lee Smith were still

members of the Red Sox in this set. The top of the front of the card have Boston Red Sox printed while the bottom of the card has the players name surrounded by the Pepsi and the Diet Pepsi logo. The backs of the cards have the Score feel to them except the Pepsi and Diet Pepsi logos are again featured prominently on the back of the cards. The cards were supposedly available as a store promotion with one card per specially marked 12-pack of Pepsi. The cards were difficult to remove from the boxes, thus making perfect mint cards worth an extra premium.

	MINT	NRMT
COMPLETE SET (20)	35.00	16.00
COMMON CARD (1-20)	1.00	.45

☐ 1 Marty Barrett	1.00	.45
☐ 2 Mike Boddicker	1.00	.45
☐ 3 Wade Boggs	10.00	4.50
☐ 4 Bill Buckner	2.00	.90
☐ 5 Ellis Burks	4.00	1.80
☐ 6 Roger Clemens	20.00	9.00
☐ 7 John Dopson	1.00	.45
☐ 8 Dwight Evans	3.00	1.35
☐ 9 Wes Gardner	1.00	.45
☐ 10 Rich Gedman	1.00	.45
☐ 11 Mike Greenwell	2.00	.90
☐ 12 Dennis Lamp	1.00	.45
☐ 13 Rob Murphy	1.00	.45
☐ 14 Tony Pena	1.50	.70
☐ 15 Carlos Quintana	1.00	.45
☐ 16 Jeff Reardon	2.00	.90
☐ 17 Jody Reed	1.50	.70
☐ 18 Luis Rivera	1.00	.45
☐ 19 Kevin Romine	1.00	.45
☐ 20 Lee Smith	3.00	1.35

1991 Red Sox Pepsi

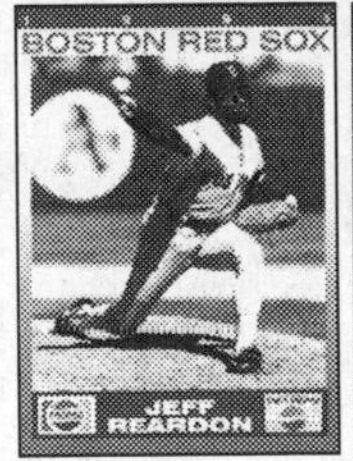

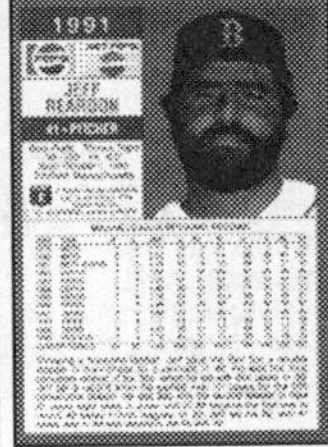

This 20-card set was sponsored by Pepsi and officially licensed by Mike Schechter Associates on behalf of the MLBPA. The 1991 edition consists of 100,000 sets that were available from July 1 through August 10, 1991 in the New England area, with one card per specially marked pack of Pepsi and Diet Pepsi. The promotion also includes a sweepstakes offering a grand prize trip for four to Red Sox Spring training camp. The standard-size cards have color action player photos with a red, white, and blue front design. Two Pepsi logos adorn the card face below the picture. The backs are bordered in red and have a color head shot, biography, professional batting record, and career summary. The cards are unnumbered and checklisted below in alphabetical order.

	MINT	NRMT
COMPLETE SET (20)	20.00	9.00
COMMON CARD (1-20)	.75	.35

☐ 1 Tom Bolton	.75	.35
☐ 2 Tom Brunansky	.75	.35
☐ 3 Ellis Burks	2.50	1.10
☐ 4 Jack Clark	1.00	.45
☐ 5 Roger Clemens	10.00	4.50
☐ 6 Danny Darwin	1.00	.45
☐ 7 Jeff Gray	.75	.35
☐ 8 Mike Greenwell	1.25	.55
☐ 9 Greg A. Harris	.75	.35
☐ 10 Dana Kiecker	.75	.35
☐ 11 Dennis Lamp	.75	.35

☐ 12 John Marzano	.75	.35
☐ 13 Tim Naehring	3.00	1.35
☐ 14 Tony Pena	1.00	.45
☐ 15 Phil Plantier	.75	.35
☐ 16 Carlos Quintana	.75	.35
☐ 17 Jeff Reardon	1.25	.55
☐ 18 Jody Reed	.75	.35
☐ 19 Luis Rivera	.75	.35
☐ 20 Matt Young	.75	.35

1982 Reds Coke

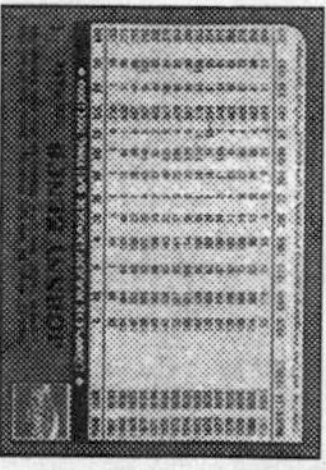

The cards in this 23-card set measure the standard size. The 1982 Coca-Cola Cincinnati Reds set, issued in conjunction with Topps, contains 22 cards of current Reds players. Although the cards of 15 players feature the exact photo used in the Topps' regular issue, the Coke photos have better coloration and appear sharper than their Topps counterparts. Six players, Cedeno, Harris, Hurdle, Kern, Krenchicki, and Trevino are new to the Reds uniform via trades, while Paul Householder had formerly appeared on the Reds' 1982 Topps "Future Stars" card. The cards are numbered 1 to 22 on the red and gray reverse, and the Coke logo appears on both sides of the card. There is an unnumbered title card which contains a premium offer on the reverse. The set numbering is in alphabetical order by player's name.

	NRMT	VG-E
COMPLETE SET (23)	8.00	3.60
COMMON CARD (1-22)	.25	.11
☐ 1 Johnny Bench	3.00	1.35
☐ 2 Bruce Berenyi	.25	.11
☐ 3 Larry Biittner	.25	.11
☐ 4 Cesar Cedeno	.50	.23
☐ 5 Dave Concepcion	.75	.35
☐ 6 Dan Driessen	.25	.11
☐ 7 Greg A. Harris	.50	.23
☐ 8 Paul Householder	.25	.11
☐ 9 Tom Hume	.25	.11
☐ 10 Clint Hurdle	.25	.11
☐ 11 Jim Kern	.25	.11
☐ 12 Wayne Krenchicki	.25	.11
☐ 13 Rafael Landestoy	.25	.11
☐ 14 Charlie Leibrandt	.25	.11
☐ 15 Mike O'Berry	.25	.11
☐ 16 Ron Oester	.25	.11
☐ 17 Frank Pastore	.25	.11
☐ 18 Joe Price	.25	.11
☐ 19 Tom Seaver	3.00	1.35
☐ 20 Mario Soto	.50	.23
☐ 21 Alex Trevino	.25	.11
☐ 22 Mike Vail	.25	.11
☐ NNO Title Card	.15	.07

1987 Reds Kahn's

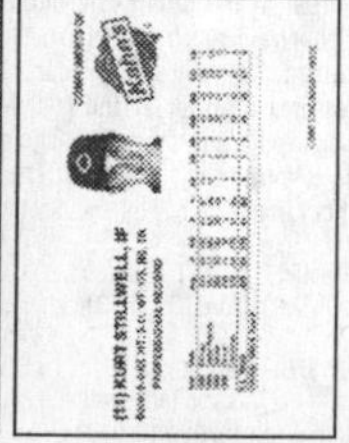

his 28-card standard-size set was issued to the first 0,000 fans at the August 2nd game between the Reds nd the San Francisco Giants at Riverfront Stadium by ahn's Wieners. The cards are unnumbered except for niform number and feature full-color photos bordered in ed and white on the front. The Kahn's logo is printed in ed in the corner of the reverse. The set features a card of arry Larkin in his Rookie Card year.

	MINT	NRMT
COMPLETE SET (28)	25.00	11.00
COMMON CARD	.50	.23
☐ 6 Bo Diaz	.50	.23
☐ 10 Terry Francona	.50	.23
☐ 11 Kurt Stillwell	.50	.23
☐ 12 Nick Esasky	.50	.23
☐ 13 Dave Concepcion	1.50	.70
☐ 15 Barry Larkin	10.00	4.50
☐ 16 Ron Oester	.50	.23
☐ 21 Paul O'Neill	4.00	1.80
☐ 23 Lloyd McClendon	.50	.23
☐ 25 Buddy Bell	1.00	.45
☐ 28 Kal Daniels	.75	.35
☐ 29 Tracy Jones	.50	.23
☐ 30 Guy Hoffman	.50	.23
☐ 31 John Franco	1.50	.70
☐ 32 Tom Browning	.75	.35
☐ 33 Ron Robinson	.50	.23
☐ 34 Bill Gullickson	.50	.23
☐ 35 Pat Pacillo	.50	.23
☐ 39 Dave Parker	1.50	.70
☐ 43 Bill Landrum	.50	.23
☐ 44 Eric Davis	4.00	1.80
☐ 46 Rob Murphy	.50	.23
☐ 47 Frank Williams	.50	.23
☐ 48 Ted Power	.50	.23
☐ NNO Pete Rose MG	4.00	1.80
☐ NNO Coaches Card Scott Breeden Billy DeMars Tommy Helms Bruce Kimm Jim Lett Tony Perez	.75	.35
☐ NNO Ad Card Save 25 cents on Corn Dogs	.25	.11
☐ NNO Ad Card Save 30 cents on Smokeys	.25	.11

1988 Reds Kahn's

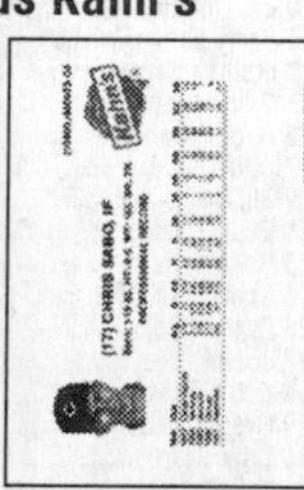

These 26-card standard-size sets were issued to fans at the August 14th game between the Cincinnati Reds and the Atlanta Braves at Riverfront Stadium. The cards are unnumbered except for uniform number and feature full-color photos bordered in red and white on the front. The Kahn's logo is printed in red in the corner of the reverse. The cards are numbered below by uniform number which is listed parenthetically on the front of the cards.

	MINT	NRMT
COMPLETE SET (26)	15.00	6.75
COMMON CARD	.25	.11
☐ 6 Bo Diaz	.25	.11
☐ 8 Terry McGriff	.25	.11
☐ 9 Eddie Milner	.25	.11
☐ 10 Leon Durham	.25	.11
☐ 11 Barry Larkin	5.00	2.20
☐ 12 Nick Esasky	.25	.11
☐ 13 Dave Concepcion	1.25	.55
☐ 14 Pete Rose MG	2.50	1.10
☐ 15 Jeff Treadway	.25	.11
☐ 17 Chris Sabo	1.00	.45
☐ 20 Danny Jackson	.25	.11
☐ 21 Paul O'Neill	1.50	.70
☐ 22 Dave Collins	.25	.11
☐ 27 Jose Rijo	.25	.11
☐ 28 Kal Daniels	.25	.11
☐ 29 Tracy Jones	.25	.11
☐ 30 Lloyd McClendon	.25	.11
☐ 31 John Franco	.75	.35
☐ 32 Tom Browning	.50	.23
☐ 33 Ron Robinson	.25	.11
☐ 40 Jack Armstrong	.25	.11
☐ 44 Eric Davis	1.25	.55
☐ 46 Rob Murphy	.25	.11
☐ 47 Frank Williams	.25	.11
☐ 48 Tim Birtsas	.25	.11
☐ NNO Reds Coaches Lee May Tony Perez Bruce Kimm Tommy Helms Jim Lett Scott Breeden	.75	.35

1989 Reds Kahn's

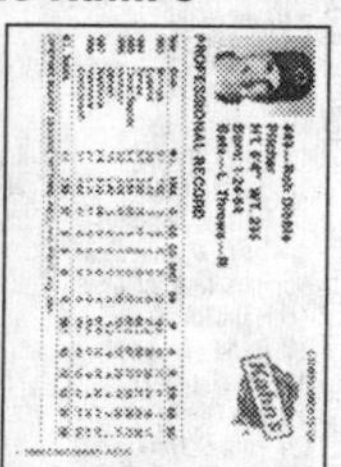

The 1989 Kahn's Reds set contains 28 standard-size cards; each card features a member of the Cincinnati Reds. The fronts have color photos with red borders. The horizontally oriented backs have career stats. The card numbering below is according to uniform number.

	MINT	NRMT
COMPLETE SET (28)	12.00	5.50
COMMON CARD	.25	.11
☐ 6 Bo Diaz	.25	.11
☐ 7 Lenny Harris	.50	.23
☐ 11 Barry Larkin	3.00	1.35
☐ 12 Joel Youngblood	.25	.11
☐ 14 Pete Rose MG	2.00	.90
☐ 16 Ron Oester	.25	.11
☐ 17 Chris Sabo	.50	.23
☐ 20 Danny Jackson	.25	.11
☐ 21 Paul O'Neill	1.00	.45
☐ 25 Todd Benzinger	.25	.11
☐ 27 Jose Rijo	.25	.11
☐ 28 Kal Daniels	.25	.11
☐ 29 Herm Winningham	.25	.11
☐ 30 Ken Griffey	.75	.35
☐ 31 John Franco	.75	.35
☐ 32 Tom Browning	.50	.23
☐ 33 Ron Robinson	.25	.11
☐ 34 Jeff Reed	.25	.11
☐ 36 Rolando Roomes	.25	.11
☐ 37 Norm Charlton	.75	.35
☐ 42 Rick Mahler	.25	.11
☐ 43 Kent Tekulve	.50	.23
☐ 44 Eric Davis	1.25	.55
☐ 48 Tim Birtsas	.25	.11
☐ 49 Rob Dibble	.50	.23
☐ xx Coaches Card Scott Breeden Dave Bristol Tommy Helms Jim Lett Lee May Tony Perez	.50	.23
☐ xx Sponsor Coupon Kahn's Corndogs	.15	.07
☐ xx Sponsor Coupon Kahn's Wieners	.15	.07

1990 Reds Kahn's

This 27-card, standard size set of Cincinnati Reds was issued by Kahn's Meats. This set which continued a more than 30-year tradition of Kahn's issuing Cincinnati Reds cards had the player's photos framed by red and white borders. The front have full-color photos while the back have a small black and white photo in the upper left hand corner and complete career statistics on the back of the card. The set is checklisted alphabetically since the cards are unnumbered.

	MINT	NRMT
COMPLETE SET (27)	10.00	4.50
COMMON CARD (1-27)	.25	.11
☐ 1 Jack Armstrong	.25	.11
☐ 2 Todd Benzinger	.25	.11
☐ 3 Tim Birtsas	.25	.11
☐ 4 Glenn Braggs	.25	.11
☐ 5 Tom Browning	.50	.23
☐ 6 Norm Charlton	.75	.35
☐ 7 Eric Davis	1.25	.55
☐ 8 Rob Dibble	.50	.23
☐ 9 Mariano Duncan	.50	.23
☐ 10 Ken Griffey	.75	.35
☐ 11 Billy Hatcher	.25	.11
☐ 12 Barry Larkin	2.50	1.10
☐ 13 Danny Jackson	.25	.11
☐ 14 Tim Layana	.25	.11
☐ 15 Rick Mahler	.25	.11
☐ 16 Hal Morris	.50	.23
☐ 17 Randy Myers	1.00	.45
☐ 18 Ron Oester	.25	.11
☐ 19 Joe Oliver	.25	.11
☐ 20 Paul O'Neill	1.25	.55
☐ 21 Lou Piniella MG	.75	.35
☐ 22 Luis Quinones	.25	.11
☐ 23 Jeff Reed	.25	.11
☐ 24 Jose Rijo	.25	.11
☐ 25 Chris Sabo	.50	.23
☐ 26 Herm Winningham	.25	.11
☐ 27 Red Coaches Jackie Moore Tony Perez Sam Perlozzo Larry Rothschild Stan Williams	.75	.35

1991 Reds Kahn's

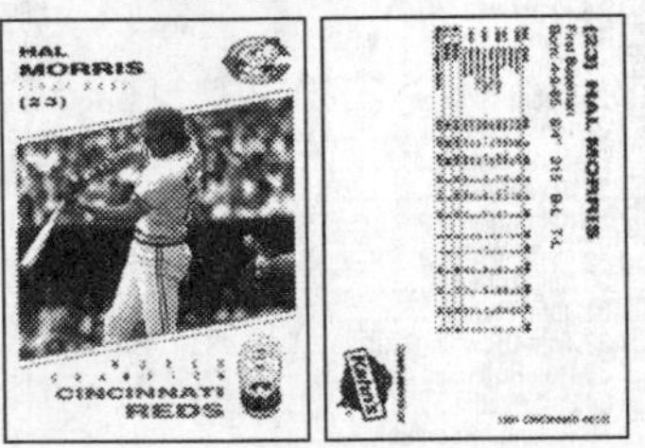

The 1991 Kahn's Cincinnati Reds set contains 28 standard-size cards. The set is skip-numbered by uniform number and includes two Kahn's coupon cards. The front features color action player photos which are mounted diagonally on the card face. Red pinstripe borders frame the picture above and below. The front lettering is printed in red and black on a white background. In a horizontal format the back is printed in red and black, and presents complete statistical information. The Kahn's logo in the lower right corner rounds out the back.

	MINT	NRMT
COMPLETE SET (28)	8.00	3.60
COMMON CARD	.25	.11
☐ 0 Schottzie Mascot	.25	.11
☐ 7 Mariano Duncan	.50	.23
☐ 9 Joe Oliver	.25	.11
☐ 10 Luis Quinones	.25	.11
☐ 11 Barry Larkin	2.50	1.10
☐ 15 Glenn Braggs	.25	.11
☐ 17 Chris Sabo	.25	.11
☐ 19 Bill Doran	.25	.11
☐ 21 Paul O'Neill	1.00	.45
☐ 22 Billy Hatcher	.25	.11
☐ 23 Hal Morris	.50	.23
☐ 25 Todd Benzinger	.25	.11
☐ 27 Jose Rijo	.25	.11
☐ 28 Randy Myers	.75	.35
☐ 29 Herm Winningham	.25	.11
☐ 32 Tom Browning	.50	.23
☐ 34 Jeff Reed	.25	.11
☐ 36 Don Carman	.25	.11
☐ 37 Norm Charlton	.50	.23
☐ 40 Jack Armstrong	.25	.11
☐ 41 Lou Piniella MG	.75	.35
☐ 44 Eric Davis	1.00	.45
☐ 45 Chris Hammond	.25	.11
☐ 47 Scott Scudder	.25	.11
☐ 48 Ted Power	.25	.11
☐ 49 Rob Dibble	.25	.11
☐ 57 Freddie Benavides	.25	.11
☐ NNO Coaches Card Jackie Moore Tony Perez Sam Perlozzo Larry Rothschild Stan Williams	.50	.23

1992 Reds Kahn's

The 1992 Kahn's Cincinnati Reds set consists of 29 standard-size cards. The set included two manufacturer's coupons (one for 50 cents off Kahn's Wieners and another for the same amount off Kahn's Corn Dogs). The fronts feature color action player photos bordered in red. The team name and the player's name appear in white lettering above and below the picture respectively. The team logo overlays the picture at its lower left corner. The horizontally oriented backs have the player's name and sponsor logo in red, while biographical and complete statistical information are printed in black. The cards are skip-numbered by uniform number on both sides and checklisted below accordingly.

	MINT	NRMT
COMPLETE SET (29)	8.00	3.60
COMMON CARD	.25	.11
☐ 2 Schottzie (Mascot)	.25	.11
☐ 9 Joe Oliver	.25	.11
☐ 10 Bip Roberts	.50	.23
☐ 11 Barry Larkin	2.00	.90
☐ 12 Freddie Benavides	.25	.11
☐ 15 Glenn Braggs	.25	.11
☐ 16 Reggie Sanders	.50	.23
☐ 17 Chris Sabo	.25	.11
☐ 19 Bill Doran	.25	.11
☐ 21 Paul O'Neill	1.00	.45
☐ 23 Hal Morris	.50	.23
☐ 25 Scott Bankhead	.25	.11
☐ 26 Darnell Coles	.25	.11
☐ 27 Jose Rijo	.25	.11
☐ 28 Scott Ruskin	.25	.11
☐ 29 Greg Swindell	.25	.11
☐ 30 Dave Martinez	.25	.11
☐ 31 Tim Belcher	.25	.11
☐ 32 Tom Browning	.50	.23
☐ 34 Jeff Reed	.25	.11
☐ 37 Norm Charlton	.75	.35
☐ 38 Troy Afenir	.25	.11
☐ 41 Lou Piniella MG	.75	.35
☐ 45 Chris Hammond	.25	.11
☐ 48 Dwayne Henry	.25	.11
☐ 49 Rob Dibble	.25	.11
☐ NNO Coaches Card Jackie Moore John McLaren Sam Perlozzo Tony Perez Larry Rothschild	.50	.23
☐ NNO Manufacturer's Coupon Kahn's Corn Dogs	.15	.07
☐ NNO Manufacturer's Coupon Kahn's Beef Franks	.15	.07

1993 Reds Kahn's

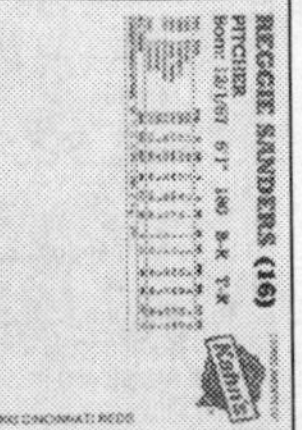

This 27-card standard-size set was issued by Kahn's Meats. The fronts contain an action photo bordered in white with a narrow black inner border. The photo is overlayed on a red pinstriped background with the player's name printed on a red stripe at the top. The set includes two Kahn's coupon cards. In a horizontal format, the backs are printed in red and black and present the player's name, position, number, biography, and statistics. The Kahn's logo in the top right corner rounds out the backs. The cards are unnumbered and checklisted below in alphabetical order.

	MINT	NRMT
COMPLETE SET (30)	8.00	3.60
COMMON CARD (1-28)	.25	.11
☐ 1 Bobby Ayala	.25	.11
☐ 2 Tim Belcher	.50	.23
☐ 3 Jeff Branson	.25	.11
☐ 4 Marty Brennaman ANN Joe Nuxhall ANN	.50	.23
☐ 5 Tom Browning	.50	.23
☐ 6 Jacob Brumfield	.25	.11
☐ 7 Greg Cadaret	.25	.11
☐ 8 Jose Cardenal CO Don Gullett CO Ray Knight CO Dave Miley CO Bobby Valentine CO	.25	.11
☐ 9 Rob Dibble	.50	.23
☐ 10 Davey Johnson MG	.50	.23
☐ 11 Roberto Kelly	.25	.11
☐ 12 Bill Landrum	.25	.11
☐ 13 Barry Larkin	2.00	.90
☐ 14 Randy Milligan	.25	.11
☐ 15 Kevin Mitchell	.50	.23
☐ 16 Hal Morris	.50	.23
☐ 17 Joe Oliver	.25	.11
☐ 18 Tim Pugh	.25	.11
☐ 19 Jeff Reardon	.50	.23
☐ 20 Jose Rijo	.25	.11
☐ 21 Bip Roberts	.50	.23
☐ 22 Chris Sabo	.25	.11
☐ 23 Juan Samuel	.50	.23
☐ 24 Reggie Sanders	.75	.35
☐ 25 Schottzie (mascot) Marge Schott	.25	.11
☐ 26 John Smiley	.50	.23
☐ 27 Gary Varsho	.25	.11
☐ 28 Kevin Wickander	.25	.11
☐ NNO Manufacturer's Coupon (Kahn's hot dogs)	.15	.07
☐ NNO Manufacturer's Coupon (Kahn's corn dogs)	.15	.07

1994 Reds Kahn's

These 33 standard-size cards were handed out at Riverfront Stadium to fans attending a Reds' home game on August 7. The white-bordered fronts feature color player action shots. The player's name and position appear at the upper left within a vertical red bar stripped into the background on the photo's left side. The horizontal white back carries the player's name and uniform number at the top, followed below by position, biography, and statistics. The red Kahn's logo at the upper right rounds out the card. The cards are unnumbered and checklisted below in alphabetical order.

	MINT	NRMT
COMPLETE SET (35)	7.50	3.40
COMMON CARD (1-33)	.25	.11
☐ 1 Bret Boone UER (Misspelled Brett on front and back)	.50	.23
☐ 2 Jeff Branson	.25	.11
☐ 3 Jeff Brantley	.50	.23
☐ 4 Tom Browning	.50	.23
☐ 5 Jacob Brumfield	.25	.11
☐ 6 Hector Carrasco	.25	.11
☐ 7 Rob Dibble	.50	.23
☐ 8 Brian Dorsett	.25	.11
☐ 9 Tony Fernandez	.50	.23
☐ 10 Tim Fortugno UER	.25	.11

(Misspelled Fortungo on back)		
☐ 11 Steve Foster	.25	.11
☐ 12 Ron Gant	1.00	.45
☐ 13 Erik Hanson	.25	.11
☐ 14 Lenny Harris	.25	.11
☐ 15 Thomas Howard	.25	.11
☐ 16 Davey Johnson MG	.75	.35
☐ 17 Barry Larkin	2.00	.90
☐ 18 Chuck McElroy	.25	.11
☐ 19 Kevin Mitchell	.50	.23
☐ 20 Hal Morris	.50	.23
☐ 21 Joe Oliver	.25	.11
☐ 22 Tim Pugh	.25	.11
☐ 23 Jose Rijo	.25	.11
☐ 24 John Roper	.25	.11
☐ 25 Johnny Ruffin	.25	.11
☐ 26 Deion Sanders	1.25	.55
☐ 27 Reggie Sanders	.75	.35
☐ 28 Schottzie (Mascot)	.25	.11
☐ 29 Pete Schourek	.50	.23
☐ 30 John Smiley UER (Front photo is Erik Hanson)	.50	.23
☐ 31 Eddie Taubensee	.25	.11
☐ 32 Jerome Walton	.25	.11
☐ 33 Coaches Bob Boone Don Gullett Grant Jackson Ray Knight Joel Youngblood	.25	.11
☐ NNO Manufacturer's Coupon Kahn's Wieners	.15	.07
☐ NNO Manufacturer's Coupon Kahn's Corn Dogs	.15	.07

1995 Reds Kahn's

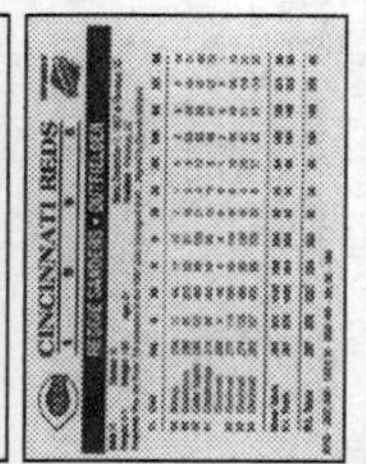

This 34-card standard-size set has white-bordered fronts feature color player action photos. The team name and year appear at the top with the player's name and position printed in a red bar at the bottom. The horizontal white backs carry the team's logo, name and sponsor's logo at the top with the player's name and position in a black bar below. A short player biography and career statistics round out the card. The cards are unnumbered and checklisted below in alphabetical order.

	MINT	NRMT
COMPLETE SET (36)	7.00	3.10
COMMON CARD (1-36)	.10	.05
☐ 1 Eric Anthony	.10	.05
☐ 2 Damon Berryhill	.10	.05
☐ 3 Bret Boone	.25	.11
☐ 4 Jeff Branson	.10	.05
☐ 5 Jeff Brantley	.25	.11
☐ 6 Hector Carrasco	.10	.05
☐ 7 Ron Gant	.60	.25
☐ 8 Willie Greene	.75	.35
☐ 9 Lenny Harris	.10	.05
☐ 10 Xavier Hernandez	.10	.05
☐ 11 Thomas Howard	.10	.05
☐ 12 Brian Hunter	.10	.05
☐ 13 Mike Jackson	.10	.05
☐ 14 Kevin Jarvis	.10	.05
☐ 15 Davey Johnson MG	.40	.18
☐ 16 Barry Larkin	1.50	.70
☐ 17 Mark Lewis	.25	.11
☐ 18 Chuck McElroy	.10	.05
☐ 19 Hal Morris	.25	.11
☐ 20 C.J. Nitkowski	.10	.05
☐ 21 Brad Pennington	.10	.05
☐ 22 Tim Pugh	.10	.05
☐ 23 Jose Rijo	.10	.05
☐ 24 John Roper	.10	.05
☐ 25 Johnny Ruffin	.10	.05
☐ 26 Deion Sanders	.75	.35
☐ 27 Reggie Sanders	.25	.11
☐ 28 Benito Santiago	.25	.11
☐ 29 Schottzie (Mascot)	.10	.05
☐ 30 Pete Schourek	.25	.11
☐ 31 John Smiley	.25	.11
☐ 32 Eddie Taubensee	.10	.05
☐ 33 Jerome Walton	.10	.05
☐ 34 Coaches Ray Knight Don Gullett Grant Jackson Hal McRae Joel Youngblood	.10	.05
☐ NNO Manufacturer's Coupon Kahn's Hot Dogs	.05	.02
☐ NNO Manufacturer's Coupon Kahn's Corn Dogs	.05	.02

1962 Salada Plastic Coins

There are 221 different players in the 1962 plastic baseball coins marketed in Salada Tea and Junket Pudding mixes. Each plastic coin measures 1 3/8" in diameter. The initial production run consisted of 10 representatives from each of the 18 major league teams. A subsequent run added 20 players from the Mets and the Colt 45's and also dropped 21 of the original subjects, who were replaced by 21 new players assigned higher numbers. The "coin" itself is made of one-color plastic (light or dark) blue, black, orange, red or white) which has a color portrait printed on paper inserted into the obverse surface. A 10-coin, shield-like holder was available for each team. The complete set price below includes all variations. Many of the variations in the set are based on whether or not there are red buttons (RB) or white buttons (WB); these variation coin pairs are designated in the checklist below. Some of the tougher variations include Jackie Brandt listed as on the Orioles; Ed Bressoud with his name misspelled; Dick Williams with his name on the right; Gary Geiger with an "O" on the hat.

	NRMT	VG-E
COMPLETE SET (263)	5000.00	2200.00
COMMON COIN (1-180)	1.50	.70
COMMON COIN (181-221)	5.00	2.20
☐ 1 Jim Gentile	2.50	1.10
☐ 2 Billy Pierce	125.00	55.00
☐ 3 Chico Fernandez	1.50	.70
☐ 4 Tom Brewer	25.00	11.00
☐ 5 Woody Held	1.50	.70
☐ 6 Ray Herbert	25.00	11.00
☐ 7A Ken Aspromonte (Angels)	7.50	3.40
☐ 7B Ken Aspromonte (Cleveland)	2.50	1.10
☐ 8 Whitey Ford	25.00	11.00
☐ 9A Jim Lemon RB (does not exist)		
☐ 9B Jim Lemon WB	2.50	1.10
☐ 10 Billy Klaus	1.50	.70
☐ 11 Steve Barber	25.00	11.00
☐ 12 Nellie Fox	7.50	3.40
☐ 13 Jim Bunning	12.00	5.50
☐ 14 Frank Malzone	1.50	.70
☐ 15 Tito Francona	1.50	.70
☐ 16 Bobby Del Greco	1.50	.70
☐ 17A Steve Bilko RB	7.50	3.40
☐ 17B Steve Bilko WB	2.50	1.10
☐ 18 Tony Kubek	60.00	27.00
☐ 19 Earl Battey	1.50	.70
☐ 20 Chuck Cottier	1.50	.70
☐ 21 Willie Tasby	1.50	.70
☐ 22 Bob Allison	2.50	1.10
☐ 23 Roger Maris	35.00	16.00
☐ 24A Earl Averill RB	7.50	3.40
☐ 24B Earl Averill WB	2.50	1.10
☐ 25 Jerry Lumpe	1.50	.70
☐ 26 Jim Grant	25.00	11.00
☐ 27 Carl Yastrzemski	60.00	27.00
☐ 28 Rocky Colavito	5.00	2.20
☐ 29 Al Smith	1.50	.70
☐ 30 Jim Busby	25.00	11.00
☐ 31 Dick Howser	2.50	1.10
☐ 32 Jim Perry	2.50	1.10
☐ 33 Yogi Berra	30.00	13.50
☐ 34A Ken Hamlin RB	7.50	3.40
☐ 34B Ken Hamlin WB	2.50	1.10
☐ 35 Dale Long	1.50	.70
☐ 36 Harmon Killebrew	25.00	11.00
☐ 37 Dick Brown	1.50	.70
☐ 38A Gary Geiger (O on hat)	450.00	200.00
☐ 38B Gary Geiger (no O on hat)	2.50	1.10
☐ 39A Minnie Minoso (White Sox)	50.00	22.00
☐ 39B Minnie Minoso (Cardinals)	25.00	11.00
☐ 40 Brooks Robinson	35.00	16.00
☐ 41 Mickey Mantle	135.00	60.00
☐ 42 Bennie Daniels	1.50	.70
☐ 43 Billy Martin	6.00	2.70
☐ 44 Vic Power	1.50	.70
☐ 45 Joe Pignatano	1.50	.70
☐ 46A Ryne Duren RB	7.50	3.40
☐ 46B Ryne Duren WB	2.50	1.10
☐ 47A Pete Runnels (2nd base)	7.50	3.40
☐ 47B Pete Runnels (1st base)	3.50	1.55
☐ 48A Dick Williams (name right)	900.00	400.00
☐ 48B Dick Williams (name left)	5.00	2.20
☐ 49 Jim Landis	1.50	.70
☐ 50 Steve Boros	1.50	.70
☐ 51A Zoilo Versalles RB	7.50	3.40
☐ 51B Zoilo Versalles WB	2.50	1.10
☐ 52A Johnny Temple (Indians)	10.00	4.50
☐ 52B Johnny Temple (Orioles)	5.00	2.20
☐ 53A Jackie Brandt (Oriole)	5.00	2.20
☐ 53B Jackie Brandt (Orioles)	900.00	400.00
☐ 54 Joe McClain	1.50	.70
☐ 55 Sherman Lollar	1.50	.70
☐ 56 Gene Stephens	1.50	.70
☐ 57A Leon Wagner RB	7.50	3.40
☐ 57B Leon Wagner WB	2.50	1.10
☐ 58 Frank Lary	1.50	.70
☐ 59 Bill Skowron	3.50	1.55
☐ 60 Vic Wertz	25.00	11.00
☐ 61 Willie Kirkland	1.50	.70
☐ 62 Leo Posada	1.50	.70
☐ 63A Albie Pearson RB	7.50	3.40
☐ 63B Albie Pearson WB	2.50	1.10
☐ 64 Bobby Richardson	6.00	2.70
☐ 65A Marv Breeding (Shortstop)	7.50	3.40
☐ 65B Marv Breeding (2nd Base)	3.50	1.55
☐ 66 Roy Sievers	100.00	45.00
☐ 67 Al Kaline	35.00	16.00
☐ 68A Don Buddin (Red Sox)	7.50	3.40
☐ 68B Don Buddin (Colt .45's)	3.50	1.55
☐ 69A Lenny Green RB	7.50	3.40
☐ 69B Lenny Green WB	2.50	1.10
☐ 70 Gene Green	25.00	11.00
☐ 71 Luis Aparicio	15.00	6.75
☐ 72 Norm Cash	3.50	1.55
☐ 73 Jackie Jensen	35.00	16.00
☐ 74 Bubba Phillips	1.50	.70
☐ 75 James Archer	1.50	.70
☐ 76A Ken Hunt RB	7.50	3.40
☐ 76B Ken Hunt WB	2.50	1.10
☐ 77 Ralph Terry	2.50	1.10
☐ 78 Camilo Pascual	1.50	.70
☐ 79 Marty Keough	25.00	11.00
☐ 80 Clete Boyer	2.50	1.10
☐ 81 Jim Pagliaroni	1.50	.70
☐ 82A Gene Leek RB	7.50	3.40
☐ 82B Gene Leek WB	2.50	1.10
☐ 83 Jake Wood	1.50	.70
☐ 84 Coot Veal	25.00	11.00
☐ 85 Norm Siebern	1.50	.70
☐ 86A Andy Carey (White Sox)	35.00	16.00
☐ 86B Andy Carey (Phillies)	3.50	1.55
☐ 87A Bill Tuttle RB	7.50	3.40
☐ 87B Bill Tuttle WB	2.50	1.10
☐ 88A Jimmy Piersall (Indians)	10.00	4.50
☐ 88B Jimmy Piersall (Senators)	5.00	2.20
☐ 89 Ron Hansen	30.00	13.50
☐ 90A Chuck Stobbs RB	7.50	3.40
☐ 90B Chuck Stobbs WB	2.50	1.10
☐ 91A Ken McBride RB	7.50	3.40
☐ 91B Ken McBride WB	2.50	1.10
☐ 92 Bill Bruton	1.50	.70
☐ 93 Gus Triandos	1.50	.70

☐ 94 John Romano 1.50 .70
☐ 95 Elston Howard 6.00 2.70
☐ 96 Gene Woodling 1.50 .70
☐ 97A Early Wynn 50.00 22.00
(pitching)
☐ 97B Early Wynn 25.00 11.00
(portrait)
☐ 98 Milt Pappas 1.50 .70
☐ 99 Bill Monbouquette 1.50 .70
☐ 100 Wayne Causey 1.50 .70
☐ 101 Don Elston 1.50 .70
☐ 102A Charlie Neal 7.50 3.40
(Dodgers)
☐ 102B Charlie Neal 3.50 1.55
(Mets)
☐ 103 Don Blasingame 1.50 .70
☐ 104 Frank Thomas 30.00 13.50
☐ 105 Wes Covington 1.50 .70
☐ 106 Chuck Hiller 1.50 .70
☐ 107 Don Hoak 1.50 .70
☐ 108A Bob Lillis 15.00 6.75
(Cardinals)
☐ 108B Bob Lillis 5.00 2.20
(Colt .45's)
☐ 109 Sandy Koufax 40.00 18.00
☐ 110 Gordy Coleman 1.50 .70
☐ 111 Eddie Matthews 25.00 11.00
(sic, Mathews)
☐ 112 Art Mahaffey 1.50 .70
☐ 113A Ed Bailey (red) 10.00 4.50
☐ 113B Ed Bailey (white) 2.50 1.10
☐ 114 Smoky Burgess 1.50 .70
☐ 115 Bill White 2.50 1.10
☐ 116 Ed Bouchee 25.00 11.00
☐ 117 Bob Buhl 1.50 .70
☐ 118 Vada Pinson 2.50 1.10
☐ 119 Carl Sawatski 1.50 .70
☐ 120 Dick Stuart 2.50 1.10
☐ 121 Harvey Kuenn 35.00 16.00
☐ 122 Pancho Herrera 1.50 .70
☐ 123A Don Zimmer 7.50 3.40
(Cubs)
☐ 123B Don Zimmer 3.50 1.55
(Mets)
☐ 124 Wally Moon 1.50 .70
☐ 125 Joe Adcock 1.50 .70
☐ 126 Joey Jay 1.50 .70
☐ 127A Maury Wills 15.00 6.75
(blue number 3)
☐ 127B Maury Wills 10.00 4.50
(red number 3)
☐ 128 George Altman 1.50 .70
☐ 129A John Buzhardt 10.00 4.50
(Phillies)
☐ 129B John Buzhardt 5.00 2.20
(White Sox)
☐ 130 Felipe Alou 2.50 1.10
☐ 131 Bill Mazeroski 2.50 1.10
☐ 132 Ernie Broglio 1.50 .70
☐ 133 John Roseboro 1.50 .70
☐ 134 Mike McCormick 1.50 .70
☐ 135A Charlie Smith 7.50 3.40
(Philadelphia)
☐ 135B Charlie Smith 3.50 1.55
(White Sox)
☐ 136 Ron Santo 2.50 1.10
☐ 137 Gene Freese 1.50 .70
☐ 138 Dick Groat 2.50 1.10
☐ 139 Curt Flood 2.50 1.10
☐ 140 Frank Bolling 1.50 .70
☐ 141 Clay Dalrymple 1.50 .70
☐ 142 Willie McCovey 30.00 13.50
☐ 143 Bob Skinner 1.50 .70
☐ 144 Lindy McDaniel 1.50 .70
☐ 145 Glen Hobbie 1.50 .70
☐ 146A Gil Hodges 50.00 22.00
(Dodgers)
☐ 146B Gil Hodges 25.00 11.00
(Mets)
☐ 147 Eddie Kasko 1.50 .70
☐ 148 Gino Cimoli 35.00 16.00
☐ 149 Willie Mays 85.00 38.00
☐ 150 Roberto Clemente 90.00 40.00
☐ 151 Red Schoendienst 2.50 1.10
☐ 152 Joe Torre 2.50 1.10
☐ 153 Bob Purkey 1.50 .70
☐ 154A Tommy Davis 7.50 3.40
(Outfield)
☐ 154B Tommy Davis 2.50 1.10
(3rd Base)
☐ 155A Andre Rogers ERR 7.50 3.40
(sic, Rodgers)
☐ 155B Andre Rodgers COR 2.50 1.10
☐ 156 Tony Taylor 1.50 .70
☐ 157 Bob Friend 1.50 .70
☐ 158A Gus Bell 7.50 3.40
(Reds)
☐ 158B Gus Bell 3.50 1.55
(Mets)
☐ 159 Roy McMillan 1.50 .70
☐ 160 Carl Warwick 1.50 .70
☐ 161 Willie Davis 2.50 1.10
☐ 162 Sam Jones 40.00 18.00
☐ 163 Ruben Amaro 1.50 .70
☐ 164 Sammy Taylor 1.50 .70
☐ 165 Frank Robinson 30.00 13.50
☐ 166 Lew Burdette 2.50 1.10
☐ 167 Ken Boyer 3.50 1.55
☐ 168 Bill Virdon 2.50 1.10
☐ 169 Jim Davenport 1.50 .70
☐ 170 Don Demeter 1.50 .70
☐ 171 Richie Ashburn 40.00 18.00
☐ 172 Johnny Podres 2.50 1.10
☐ 173A Joe Cunningham 50.00 22.00
(Cardinals)
☐ 173B Joe Cunningham 20.00 9.00
(White Sox)
☐ 174 Elroy Face 2.50 1.10
☐ 175 Orlando Cepeda 6.00 2.70
☐ 176A Bobby Gene Smith 7.50 3.40
(Philadelphia)
☐ 176B Bobby Gene Smith 3.50 1.55
(Mets)
☐ 177A Ernie Banks 50.00 22.00
(Outfield)
☐ 177B Ernie Banks 25.00 11.00
(Shortstop)
☐ 178A Daryl Spencer 7.50 3.40
(3rd Base)
☐ 178B Daryl Spencer 3.50 1.55
(1st Base)
☐ 179 Bob Schmidt 25.00 11.00
☐ 180 Hank Aaron 75.00 34.00
☐ 181 Hobie Landrith 5.00 2.20
☐ 182A Ed Broussard 400.00 180.00
(sic, Bressoud)
☐ 182B Ed Bressoud 25.00 11.00
(correct)
☐ 183 Felix Mantilla 5.00 2.20
☐ 184 Dick Farrell 5.00 2.20
☐ 185 Bob Miller 5.00 2.20
☐ 186 Don Taussig 5.00 2.20
☐ 187 Pumpsie Green 5.00 2.20
☐ 188 Bobby Shantz 6.00 2.70
☐ 189 Roger Craig 6.00 2.70
☐ 190 Hal Smith 5.00 2.20
☐ 191 Johnny Edwards 5.00 2.20
☐ 192 John DeMerit 5.00 2.20
☐ 193 Joe Amalfitano 5.00 2.20
☐ 194 Norm Larker 5.00 2.20
☐ 195 Al Heist 5.00 2.20
☐ 196 Al Spangler 5.00 2.20
☐ 197 Alex Grammas 5.00 2.20
☐ 198 Jerry Lynch 5.00 2.20
☐ 199 Jim McKnight 5.00 2.20
☐ 200 Jose Pagen 5.00 2.20
(sic, Pagan)
☐ 201 Jim Gilliam 15.00 6.75
☐ 202 Art Ditmar 5.00 2.20
☐ 203 Bud Daley 5.00 2.20
☐ 204 Johnny Callison 6.00 2.70
☐ 205 Stu Miller 5.00 2.20
☐ 206 Russ Snyder 5.00 2.20
☐ 207 Billy Williams 30.00 13.50
☐ 208 Walt Bond 5.00 2.20
☐ 209 Joe Koppe 5.00 2.20
☐ 210 Don Schwall 10.00 4.50
☐ 211 Billy Gardner 6.00 2.70
☐ 212 Chuck Estrada 5.00 2.20
☐ 213 Gary Bell 5.00 2.20
☐ 214 Floyd Robinson 5.00 2.20
☐ 215 Duke Snider 55.00 25.00
☐ 216 Lee Maye 5.00 2.20
☐ 217 Howie Bedell 5.00 2.20
☐ 218 Bob Will 5.00 2.20
☐ 219 Dallas Green 7.50 3.40
☐ 220 Carroll Hardy 5.00 2.20
☐ 221 Danny O'Connell 5.00 2.20

1963 Salada Metal Coins

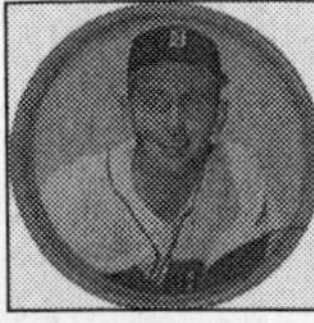

The 1963 baseball coin set distributed by Salada Tea and Junket Pudding marked a drastic change from the set of the previous year. The coins were made of metal, rather than plastic, with conspicuous red rims for National League players and blue rims for their American League counterparts. Each coin measures 1 1/2" in diameter. The subject's portrait was printed in color on the front, with his name, position. team and 1962 statistics listed on the back. Also on the reverse is located the coin number and the line "Save and Trade 63 All Star Baseball Coins."

	NRMT	VG-E
COMPLETE SET (63)	750.00	350.00
COMMON COIN (1-63)	3.50	1.55

☐ 1 Don Drysdale 20.00 9.00
☐ 2 Dick Farrell 3.50 1.55
☐ 3 Bob Gibson 20.00 9.00
☐ 4 Sandy Koufax 40.00 18.00
☐ 5 Juan Marichal 15.00 6.75
☐ 6 Bob Purkey 3.50 1.55
☐ 7 Bob Shaw 3.50 1.55
☐ 8 Warren Spahn 20.00 9.00
☐ 9 Johnny Podres 5.00 2.20
☐ 10 Art Mahaffey 3.50 1.55
☐ 11 Del Crandall 3.50 1.55
☐ 12 John Roseboro 5.00 2.20
☐ 13 Orlando Cepeda 7.50 3.40
☐ 14 Bill Mazeroski 7.50 3.40
☐ 15 Ken Boyer 6.00 2.70
☐ 16 Dick Groat 5.00 2.20
☐ 17 Ernie Banks 30.00 13.50
☐ 18 Frank Bolling 3.50 1.55
☐ 19 Jim Davenport 3.50 1.55
☐ 20 Maury Wills 6.00 2.70
☐ 21 Willie Davis 5.00 2.20
☐ 22 Willie Mays 75.00 34.00
☐ 23 Roberto Clemente 75.00 34.00
☐ 24 Hank Aaron 75.00 34.00
☐ 25 Matty Alou 5.00 2.20
☐ 26 Johnny Callison 5.00 2.20
☐ 27 Richie Ashburn 15.00 6.75
☐ 28 Eddie Mathews 20.00 9.00
☐ 29 Frank Robinson 25.00 11.00
☐ 30 Billy Williams 15.00 6.75
☐ 31 George Altman 3.50 1.55
☐ 32 Hank Aguirre 3.50 1.55
☐ 33 Jim Bunning 15.00 6.75
☐ 34 Dick Donovan 3.50 1.55
☐ 35 Bill Monbouquette 3.50 1.55
☐ 36 Camilo Pascual 5.00 2.20
☐ 37 Dave Stenhouse 3.50 1.55
☐ 38 Ralph Terry 5.00 2.20
☐ 39 Hoyt Wilhelm 15.00 6.75
☐ 40 Jim Kaat 7.50 3.40
☐ 41 Ken McBride 3.50 1.55
☐ 42 Ray Herbert 3.50 1.55
☐ 43 Milt Pappas 5.00 2.20
☐ 44 Earl Battey 3.50 1.55
☐ 45 Elston Howard 6.00 2.70
☐ 46 John Romano 3.50 1.55
☐ 47 Jim Gentile 5.00 2.20
☐ 48 Billy Moran 3.50 1.55
☐ 49 Rich Rollins 3.50 1.55
☐ 50 Luis Aparicio 15.00 6.75
☐ 51 Norm Siebern 3.50 1.55
☐ 52 Bobby Richardson 7.50 3.40
☐ 53 Brooks Robinson 25.00 11.00
☐ 54 Tom Tresh 5.00 2.20
☐ 55 Leon Wagner 3.50 1.55
☐ 56 Mickey Mantle 125.00 55.00
☐ 57 Roger Maris 40.00 18.00
☐ 58 Rocky Colavito 7.50 3.40
☐ 59 Frank Thomas 5.00 2.20
☐ 60 Jim Landis 3.50 1.55
☐ 61 Pete Runnels 5.00 2.20
☐ 62 Yogi Berra 30.00 13.50
☐ 63 Al Kaline 25.00 11.00

1988 Score Samples

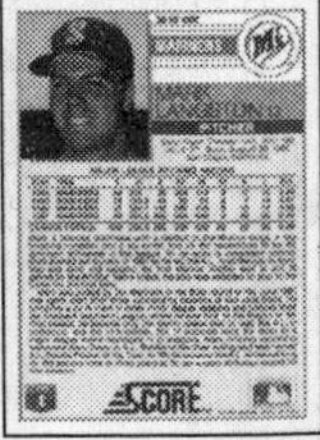

Early in 1988, Score prepared some samples to show prospective dealers and buyers of the new Score cards what they would look like. These sample cards are distinguished by the fact that there is a row of zeroes for the 1987 season statistics since the season was not over when these sample cards were being printed. The cards are standard size and are virtually indistinguishable from the regular 1988 Score cards of the same players except for border color variations in a few instances.

	MINT	NRMT
COMPLETE SET (6)	40.00	18.00
COMMON CARD	5.00	2.20
☐ 30 Mark Langston	8.00	3.60
☐ 48 Tony Pena	5.00	2.20
☐ 71 Keith Moreland	5.00	2.20
☐ 72 Barry Larkin	25.00	11.00
☐ 121 Dennis Boyd	5.00	2.20
☐ 145 Denny Walling	5.00	2.20

1988 Score

This set consists of 660 standard-size cards. The set was distributed by Major League Marketing and features six distinctive border colors on the front. Subsets include Reggie Jackson Tribute (500-504), Highlights (652-660) and Rookie Prospects (623-647). Card number 501, showing Reggie as a member of the Baltimore Orioles, is one of the few opportunities collectors have to visually remember Reggie's one-year stay with the Orioles. The set is distinguished by the fact that each card back shows a full-color picture of the player. Rookie Cards in this set include Ellis Burks, Ken Caminiti, Ron Gant, Tom Glavine, Gregg Jefferies, Jeff Montgomery, and Matt Williams.

	MINT	NRMT
COMPLETE SET (660)	10.00	4.50
COMPLETE FACT.SET (660)	12.00	5.50
COMMON CARD (1-660)	.05	.02
☐ 1 Don Mattingly	.30	.14
☐ 2 Wade Boggs	.20	.09
☐ 3 Tim Raines	.10	.05
☐ 4 Andre Dawson	.10	.05
☐ 5 Mark McGwire	.60	.25
☐ 6 Kevin Seitzer	.10	.05
☐ 7 Wally Joyner	.20	.09
☐ 8 Jesse Barfield	.05	.02
☐ 9 Pedro Guerrero	.10	.05
☐ 10 Eric Davis	.10	.05
☐ 11 George Brett	.40	.18
☐ 12 Ozzie Smith	.25	.11
☐ 13 Rickey Henderson	.20	.09
☐ 14 Jim Rice	.10	.05
☐ 15 Matt Nokes	.05	.02
☐ 16 Mike Schmidt	.25	.11
☐ 17 Dave Parker	.10	.05
☐ 18 Eddie Murray	.20	.09
☐ 19 Andres Galarraga	.20	.09
☐ 20 Tony Fernandez	.05	.02
☐ 21 Kevin McReynolds	.05	.02
☐ 22 B.J. Surhoff	.10	.05
☐ 23 Pat Tabler	.05	.02
☐ 24 Kirby Puckett	.40	.18
☐ 25 Benny Santiago	.05	.02
☐ 26 Ryne Sandberg	.25	.11
☐ 27 Kelly Downs (Will Clark in background, out of focus)	.10	.05
☐ 28 Jose Cruz	.05	.02
☐ 29 Pete O'Brien	.05	.02
☐ 30 Mark Langston	.05	.02
☐ 31 Lee Smith	.10	.05
☐ 32 Juan Samuel	.05	.02
☐ 33 Kevin Bass	.05	.02
☐ 34 R.J. Reynolds	.05	.02
☐ 35 Steve Sax	.05	.02
☐ 36 John Kruk	.10	.05
☐ 37 Alan Trammell	.10	.05
☐ 38 Chris Bosio	.05	.02
☐ 39 Brook Jacoby	.05	.02
☐ 40 Willie McGee UER (Excited misspelled as excitd)	.05	.02
☐ 41 Dave Magadan	.05	.02
☐ 42 Fred Lynn	.05	.02
☐ 43 Kent Hrbek	.10	.05
☐ 44 Brian Downing	.05	.02
☐ 45 Jose Canseco	.20	.09
☐ 46 Jim Presley	.05	.02
☐ 47 Mike Stanley	.10	.05
☐ 48 Tony Pena	.05	.02
☐ 49 David Cone	.20	.09
☐ 50 Rick Sutcliffe	.05	.02
☐ 51 Doug Drabek	.05	.02
☐ 52 Bill Doran	.05	.02
☐ 53 Mike Scioscia	.05	.02
☐ 54 Candy Maldonado	.05	.02
☐ 55 Dave Winfield	.20	.09
☐ 56 Lou Whitaker	.10	.05
☐ 57 Tom Henke	.05	.02
☐ 58 Ken Gerhart	.05	.02
☐ 59 Glenn Braggs	.05	.02
☐ 60 Julio Franco	.10	.05
☐ 61 Charlie Leibrandt	.05	.02
☐ 62 Gary Gaetti	.05	.02
☐ 63 Bob Boone	.10	.05
☐ 64 Luis Polonia	.10	.05
☐ 65 Dwight Evans	.10	.05
☐ 66 Phil Bradley	.05	.02
☐ 67 Mike Boddicker	.05	.02
☐ 68 Vince Coleman	.05	.02
☐ 69 Howard Johnson	.05	.02
☐ 70 Tim Wallach	.05	.02
☐ 71 Keith Moreland	.05	.02
☐ 72 Barry Larkin	.30	.14
☐ 73 Alan Ashby	.05	.02
☐ 74 Rick Rhoden	.05	.02
☐ 75 Darrell Evans	.10	.05
☐ 76 Dave Stieb	.05	.02
☐ 77 Dan Plesac	.05	.02
☐ 78 Will Clark UER (Born 3/17/64, should be 3/13/64)	.25	.11
☐ 79 Frank White	.10	.05
☐ 80 Joe Carter	.20	.09
☐ 81 Mike Witt	.05	.02
☐ 82 Terry Steinbach	.10	.05
☐ 83 Alvin Davis	.05	.02
☐ 84 Tommy Herr (Will Clark shown sliding into second)	.10	.05
☐ 85 Vance Law	.05	.02
☐ 86 Kal Daniels	.05	.02
☐ 87 Rick Honeycutt UER (Wrong years for stats on back)	.05	.02
☐ 88 Alfredo Griffin	.05	.02
☐ 89 Bret Saberhagen	.05	.02
☐ 90 Bert Blyleven	.10	.05
☐ 91 Jeff Reardon	.10	.05
☐ 92 Cory Snyder	.05	.02
☐ 93A Greg Walker ERR (93 of 66)	2.00	.90
☐ 93B Greg Walker COR (93 of 660)	.05	.02
☐ 94 Joe Magrane	.05	.02
☐ 95 Rob Deer	.05	.02
☐ 96 Ray Knight	.10	.05
☐ 97 Casey Candaele	.05	.02
☐ 98 John Cerutti	.05	.02
☐ 99 Buddy Bell	.10	.05
☐ 100 Jack Clark	.10	.05
☐ 101 Eric Bell	.05	.02
☐ 102 Willie Wilson	.05	.02
☐ 103 Dave Schmidt	.05	.02
☐ 104 Dennis Eckersley UER (Complete games stats are wrong)	10.00	4.50
☐ 105 Don Sutton	.20	.09
☐ 106 Danny Tartabull	.05	.02
☐ 107 Fred McGriff	.20	.09
☐ 108 Les Straker	.05	.02
☐ 109 Lloyd Moseby	.05	.02
☐ 110 Roger Clemens	.40	.18
☐ 111 Glenn Hubbard	.05	.02
☐ 112 Ken Williams	.05	.02
☐ 113 Ruben Sierra	.05	.02
☐ 114 Stan Jefferson	.05	.02
☐ 115 Milt Thompson	.05	.02
☐ 116 Bobby Bonilla	.20	.09
☐ 117 Wayne Tolleson	.05	.02
☐ 118 Matt Williams	.60	.25
☐ 119 Chet Lemon	.05	.02
☐ 120 Dale Sveum	.05	.02
☐ 121 Dennis Boyd	.05	.02
☐ 122 Brett Butler	.10	.05
☐ 123 Terry Kennedy	.05	.02
☐ 124 Jack Howell	.05	.02
☐ 125 Curt Young	.05	.02
☐ 126A Dave Valle ERR (Misspelled Dale on card front)	.10	.05
☐ 126B Dave Valle COR	.05	.02
☐ 127 Curt Wilkerson	.05	.02
☐ 128 Tim Teufel	.05	.02
☐ 129 Ozzie Virgil	.05	.02
☐ 130 Brian Fisher	.05	.02
☐ 131 Lance Parrish	.05	.02
☐ 132 Tom Browning	.05	.02
☐ 133A Larry Andersen ERR (Misspelled Anderson on card front)	.10	.05
☐ 133B Larry Andersen COR	.05	.02
☐ 134A Bob Brenly ERR (Misspelled Brenley on card front)	.10	.05
☐ 134B Bob Brenly COR	.05	.02
☐ 135 Mike Marshall	.05	.02
☐ 136 Gerald Perry	.05	.02
☐ 137 Bobby Meacham	.05	.02
☐ 138 Larry Herndon	.05	.02
☐ 139 Fred Manrique	.05	.02
☐ 140 Charlie Hough	.10	.05
☐ 141 Ron Darling	.05	.02
☐ 142 Herm Winningham	.05	.02
☐ 143 Mike Diaz	.05	.02
☐ 144 Mike Jackson	.10	.05
☐ 145 Denny Walling	.05	.02
☐ 146 Robby Thompson	.05	.02
☐ 147 Franklin Stubbs	.05	.02
☐ 148 Albert Hall	.05	.02
☐ 149 Bobby Witt	.05	.02
☐ 150 Lance McCullers	.05	.02
☐ 151 Scott Bradley	.05	.02
☐ 152 Mark McLemore	.05	.02
☐ 153 Tim Laudner	.05	.02
☐ 154 Greg Swindell	.05	.02
☐ 155 Marty Barrett	.05	.02
☐ 156 Mike Heath	.05	.02
☐ 157 Gary Ward	.05	.02
☐ 158A Lee Mazzilli ERR (Misspelled Mazilli on card front)	.10	.05
☐ 158B Lee Mazzilli COR	.05	.02
☐ 159 Tom Foley	.05	.02
☐ 160 Robin Yount	.20	.09
☐ 161 Steve Bedrosian	.05	.02
☐ 162 Bob Walk	.05	.02
☐ 163 Nick Esasky	.05	.02
☐ 164 Ken Caminiti	.75	.35
☐ 165 Jose Uribe	.05	.02
☐ 166 Dave Anderson	.05	.02
☐ 167 Ed Whitson	.05	.02
☐ 168 Ernie Whitt	.05	.02
☐ 169 Cecil Cooper	.10	.05
☐ 170 Mike Pagliarulo	.05	.02
☐ 171 Pat Sheridan	.05	.02
☐ 172 Chris Bando	.05	.02
☐ 173 Lee Lacy	.05	.02
☐ 174 Steve Lombardozzi	.05	.02
☐ 175 Mike Greenwell	.10	.05
☐ 176 Greg Minton	.05	.02
☐ 177 Moose Haas	.05	.02
☐ 178 Mike Kingery	.05	.02
☐ 179 Greg A. Harris	.05	.02
☐ 180 Bo Jackson	.20	.09
☐ 181 Carmelo Martinez	.05	.02
☐ 182 Alex Trevino	.05	.02
☐ 183 Ron Oester	.05	.02
☐ 184 Danny Darwin	.05	.02
☐ 185 Mike Krukow	.05	.02
☐ 186 Rafael Palmeiro	.20	.09
☐ 187 Tim Burke	.05	.02
☐ 188 Roger McDowell	.05	.02
☐ 189 Garry Templeton	.05	.02
☐ 190 Terry Pendleton	.10	.05
☐ 191 Larry Parrish	.05	.02
☐ 192 Rey Quinones	.05	.02
☐ 193 Joaquin Andujar	.05	.02
☐ 194 Tom Brunansky	.05	.02
☐ 195 Donnie Moore	.05	.02
☐ 196 Dan Pasqua	.05	.02
☐ 197 Jim Gantner	.05	.02
☐ 198 Mark Eichhorn	.05	.02
☐ 199 John Grubb	.05	.02
☐ 200 Bill Ripken	.10	.05
☐ 201 Sam Horn	.05	.02
☐ 202 Todd Worrell	.05	.02
☐ 203 Terry Leach	.05	.02
☐ 204 Garth Iorg	.05	.02
☐ 205 Brian Dayett	.05	.02
☐ 206 Bo Diaz	.05	.02
☐ 207 Craig Reynolds	.05	.02
☐ 208 Brian Holton	.05	.02
☐ 209 Marvell Wynne UER (Misspelled Marvelle on card front)	.05	.02
☐ 210 Dave Concepcion	.10	.05
☐ 211 Mike Davis	.05	.02

☐ 212 Devon White	.10	.05
☐ 213 Mickey Brantley	.05	.02
☐ 214 Greg Gagne	.05	.02
☐ 215 Oddibe McDowell	.05	.02
☐ 216 Jimmy Key	.10	.05
☐ 217 Dave Bergman	.05	.02
☐ 218 Calvin Schiraldi	.05	.02
☐ 219 Larry Sheets	.05	.02
☐ 220 Mike Easler	.05	.02
☐ 221 Kurt Stillwell	.05	.02
☐ 222 Chuck Jackson	.05	.02
☐ 223 Dave Martinez	.05	.02
☐ 224 Tim Leary	.05	.02
☐ 225 Steve Garvey	.10	.05
☐ 226 Greg Mathews	.05	.02
☐ 227 Doug Sisk	.05	.02
☐ 228 Dave Henderson (Wearing Red Sox uniform; Red Sox logo on back)	.05	.02
☐ 229 Jimmy Dwyer	.05	.02
☐ 230 Larry Owen	.05	.02
☐ 231 Andre Thornton	.10	.05
☐ 232 Mark Salas	.05	.02
☐ 233 Tom Brookens	.05	.02
☐ 234 Greg Brock	.05	.02
☐ 235 Rance Mulliniks	.05	.02
☐ 236 Bob Brower	.05	.02
☐ 237 Joe Niekro	.05	.02
☐ 238 Scott Bankhead	.05	.02
☐ 239 Doug DeCinces	.05	.02
☐ 240 Tommy John	.10	.05
☐ 241 Rich Gedman	.05	.02
☐ 242 Ted Power	.05	.02
☐ 243 Dave Meads	.05	.02
☐ 244 Jim Sundberg	.05	.02
☐ 245 Ken Oberkfell	.05	.02
☐ 246 Jimmy Jones	.05	.02
☐ 247 Ken Landreaux	.05	.02
☐ 248 Jose Oquendo	.05	.02
☐ 249 John Mitchell	.05	.02
☐ 250 Don Baylor	.10	.05
☐ 251 Scott Fletcher	.05	.02
☐ 252 Al Newman	.05	.02
☐ 253 Carney Lansford	.10	.05
☐ 254 Johnny Ray	.05	.02
☐ 255 Gary Pettis	.05	.02
☐ 256 Ken Phelps	.05	.02
☐ 257 Rick Leach	.05	.02
☐ 258 Tim Stoddard	.05	.02
☐ 259 Ed Romero	.05	.02
☐ 260 Sid Bream	.05	.02
☐ 261A Tom Niedenfuer ERR (Misspelled Neidenfuer on card front)	.10	.05
☐ 261B Tom Niedenfuer COR	.05	.02
☐ 262 Rick Dempsey	.05	.02
☐ 263 Lonnie Smith	.05	.02
☐ 264 Bob Forsch	.05	.02
☐ 265 Barry Bonds	.50	.23
☐ 266 Willie Randolph	.10	.05
☐ 267 Mike Ramsey	.05	.02
☐ 268 Don Slaught	.05	.02
☐ 269 Mickey Tettleton	.10	.05
☐ 270 Jerry Reuss	.05	.02
☐ 271 Marc Sullivan	.05	.02
☐ 272 Jim Morrison	.05	.02
☐ 273 Steve Balboni	.05	.02
☐ 274 Dick Schofield	.05	.02
☐ 275 John Tudor	.05	.02
☐ 276 Gene Larkin	.05	.02
☐ 277 Harold Reynolds	.05	.02
☐ 278 Jerry Browne	.05	.02
☐ 279 Willie Upshaw	.05	.02
☐ 280 Ted Higuera	.05	.02
☐ 281 Terry McGriff	.05	.02
☐ 282 Terry Puhl	.05	.02
☐ 283 Mark Wasinger	.05	.02
☐ 284 Luis Salazar	.05	.02
☐ 285 Ted Simmons	.10	.05
☐ 286 John Shelby	.05	.02
☐ 287 John Smiley	.10	.05
☐ 288 Curt Ford	.05	.02
☐ 289 Steve Crawford	.05	.02
☐ 290 Dan Quisenberry	.05	.02
☐ 291 Alan Wiggins	.05	.02
☐ 292 Randy Bush	.05	.02
☐ 293 John Candelaria	.05	.02
☐ 294 Tony Phillips	.05	.02
☐ 295 Mike Morgan	.05	.02
☐ 296 Bill Wegman	.05	.02
☐ 297A Terry Francona ERR (Misspelled Franconia on card front)	.10	.05
☐ 297B Terry Francona COR	.05	.02
☐ 298 Mickey Hatcher	.05	.02
☐ 299 Andres Thomas	.05	.02
☐ 300 Bob Stanley	.05	.02
☐ 301 Al Pedrique	.05	.02
☐ 302 Jim Lindeman	.05	.02
☐ 303 Wally Backman	.05	.02
☐ 304 Paul O'Neill	.10	.05
☐ 305 Hubie Brooks	.05	.02
☐ 306 Steve Buechele	.05	.02
☐ 307 Bobby Thigpen	.05	.02
☐ 308 George Hendrick	.05	.02
☐ 309 John Moses	.05	.02
☐ 310 Ron Guidry	.05	.02
☐ 311 Bill Schroeder	.05	.02
☐ 312 Jose Nunez	.05	.02
☐ 313 Bud Black	.05	.02
☐ 314 Joe Sambito	.05	.02
☐ 315 Scott McGregor	.05	.02
☐ 316 Rafael Santana	.05	.02
☐ 317 Frank Williams	.05	.02
☐ 318 Mike Fitzgerald	.05	.02
☐ 319 Rick Mahler	.05	.02
☐ 320 Jim Gott	.05	.02
☐ 321 Mariano Duncan	.05	.02
☐ 322 Jose Guzman	.05	.02
☐ 323 Lee Guetterman	.05	.02
☐ 324 Dan Gladden	.05	.02
☐ 325 Gary Carter	.20	.09
☐ 326 Tracy Jones	.05	.02
☐ 327 Floyd Youmans	.05	.02
☐ 328 Bill Dawley	.05	.02
☐ 329 Paul Noce	.05	.02
☐ 330 Angel Salazar	.05	.02
☐ 331 Goose Gossage	.10	.05
☐ 332 George Frazier	.05	.02
☐ 333 Ruppert Jones	.05	.02
☐ 334 Billy Joe Robidoux	.05	.02
☐ 335 Mike Scott	.05	.02
☐ 336 Randy Myers	.10	.05
☐ 337 Bob Sebra	.05	.02
☐ 338 Eric Show	.05	.02
☐ 339 Mitch Williams	.10	.05
☐ 340 Paul Molitor	.20	.09
☐ 341 Gus Polidor	.05	.02
☐ 342 Steve Trout	.05	.02
☐ 343 Jerry Don Gleaton	.05	.02
☐ 344 Bob Knepper	.05	.02
☐ 345 Mitch Webster	.05	.02
☐ 346 John Morris	.05	.02
☐ 347 Andy Hawkins	.05	.02
☐ 348 Dave Leiper	.05	.02
☐ 349 Ernest Riles	.05	.02
☐ 350 Dwight Gooden	.10	.05
☐ 351 Dave Righetti	.10	.05
☐ 352 Pat Dodson	.05	.02
☐ 353 John Habyan	.05	.02
☐ 354 Jim Deshaies	.05	.02
☐ 355 Butch Wynegar	.05	.02
☐ 356 Bryn Smith	.05	.02
☐ 357 Matt Young	.05	.02
☐ 358 Tom Pagnozzi	.10	.05
☐ 359 Floyd Rayford	.05	.02
☐ 360 Darryl Strawberry	.10	.05
☐ 361 Sal Butera	.05	.02
☐ 362 Domingo Ramos	.05	.02
☐ 363 Chris Brown	.05	.02
☐ 364 Jose Gonzalez	.05	.02
☐ 365 Dave Smith	.05	.02
☐ 366 Andy McGaffigan	.05	.02
☐ 367 Stan Javier	.05	.02
☐ 368 Henry Cotto	.05	.02
☐ 369 Mike Birkbeck	.05	.02
☐ 370 Len Dykstra	.10	.05
☐ 371 Dave Collins	.05	.02
☐ 372 Spike Owen	.05	.02
☐ 373 Geno Petralli	.05	.02
☐ 374 Ron Karkovice	.05	.02
☐ 375 Shane Rawley	.05	.02
☐ 376 DeWayne Buice	.05	.02
☐ 377 Bill Pecota	.05	.02
☐ 378 Leon Durham	.05	.02
☐ 379 Ed Olwine	.05	.02
☐ 380 Bruce Hurst	.05	.02
☐ 381 Bob McClure	.05	.02
☐ 382 Mark Thurmond	.05	.02
☐ 383 Buddy Biancalana	.05	.02
☐ 384 Tim Conroy	.05	.02
☐ 385 Tony Gwynn	.50	.23
☐ 386 Greg Gross	.05	.02
☐ 387 Barry Lyons	.05	.02
☐ 388 Mike Felder	.05	.02
☐ 389 Pat Clements	.05	.02
☐ 390 Ken Griffey	.05	.02
☐ 391 Mark Davis	.05	.02
☐ 392 Jose Rijo	.05	.02
☐ 393 Mike Young	.05	.02
☐ 394 Willie Fraser	.05	.02
☐ 395 Dion James	.05	.02
☐ 396 Steve Shields	.05	.02
☐ 397 Randy St.Claire	.05	.02
☐ 398 Danny Jackson	.05	.02
☐ 399 Cecil Fielder	.20	.09
☐ 400 Keith Hernandez	.10	.05
☐ 401 Don Carman	.05	.02
☐ 402 Chuck Crim	.05	.02
☐ 403 Rob Woodward	.05	.02
☐ 404 Junior Ortiz	.05	.02
☐ 405 Glenn Wilson	.05	.02
☐ 406 Ken Howell	.05	.02
☐ 407 Jeff Kunkel	.05	.02
☐ 408 Jeff Reed	.05	.02
☐ 409 Chris James	.05	.02
☐ 410 Zane Smith	.05	.02
☐ 411 Ken Dixon	.05	.02
☐ 412 Ricky Horton	.05	.02
☐ 413 Frank DiPino	.05	.02
☐ 414 Shane Mack	.05	.02
☐ 415 Danny Cox	.05	.02
☐ 416 Andy Van Slyke	.10	.05
☐ 417 Danny Heep	.05	.02
☐ 418 John Cangelosi	.05	.02
☐ 419A John Christensen ERR (Christiansen on card front)	.10	.05
☐ 419B John Christensen COR	.05	.02
☐ 420 Joey Cora	.25	.11
☐ 421 Mike LaValliere	.05	.02
☐ 422 Kelly Gruber	.05	.02
☐ 423 Bruce Benedict	.05	.02
☐ 424 Len Matuszek	.05	.02
☐ 425 Kent Tekulve	.05	.02
☐ 426 Rafael Ramirez	.05	.02
☐ 427 Mike Flanagan	.05	.02
☐ 428 Mike Gallego	.05	.02
☐ 429 Juan Castillo	.05	.02
☐ 430 Neal Heaton	.05	.02
☐ 431 Phil Garner	.05	.02
☐ 432 Mike Dunne	.05	.02
☐ 433 Wallace Johnson	.05	.02
☐ 434 Jack O'Connor	.05	.02
☐ 435 Steve Jeltz	.05	.02
☐ 436 Donell Nixon	.05	.02
☐ 437 Jack Lazorko	.05	.02
☐ 438 Keith Comstock	.05	.02
☐ 439 Jeff D. Robinson	.05	.02
☐ 440 Graig Nettles	.10	.05
☐ 441 Mel Hall	.05	.02
☐ 442 Gerald Young	.05	.02
☐ 443 Gary Redus	.05	.02
☐ 444 Charlie Moore	.05	.02
☐ 445 Bill Madlock	.10	.05
☐ 446 Mark Clear	.05	.02
☐ 447 Greg Booker	.05	.02
☐ 448 Rick Schu	.05	.02
☐ 449 Ron Kittle	.05	.02
☐ 450 Dale Murphy	.20	.09
☐ 451 Bob Dernier	.05	.02
☐ 452 Dale Mohorcic	.05	.02
☐ 453 Rafael Belliard	.05	.02
☐ 454 Charlie Puleo	.05	.02
☐ 455 Dwayne Murphy	.05	.02
☐ 456 Jim Eisenreich	.20	.09
☐ 457 David Palmer	.05	.02
☐ 458 Dave Stewart	.10	.05
☐ 459 Pascual Perez	.05	.02
☐ 460 Glenn Davis	.05	.02
☐ 461 Dan Petry	.05	.02
☐ 462 Jim Winn	.05	.02
☐ 463 Darrell Miller	.05	.02
☐ 464 Mike Moore	.05	.02
☐ 465 Mike LaCoss	.05	.02
☐ 466 Steve Farr	.05	.02
☐ 467 Jerry Mumphrey	.05	.02
☐ 468 Kevin Gross	.05	.02
☐ 469 Bruce Bochy	.05	.02
☐ 470 Orel Hershiser	.10	.05
☐ 471 Eric King	.05	.02
☐ 472 Ellis Burks	.30	.14
☐ 473 Darren Daulton	.10	.05
☐ 474 Mookie Wilson	.10	.05
☐ 475 Frank Viola	.05	.02
☐ 476 Ron Robinson	.05	.02
☐ 477 Bob Melvin	.05	.02
☐ 478 Jeff Musselman	.05	.02
☐ 479 Charlie Kerfeld	.05	.02
☐ 480 Richard Dotson	.05	.02
☐ 481 Kevin Mitchell	.10	.05
☐ 482 Gary Roenicke	.05	.02
☐ 483 Tim Flannery	.05	.02
☐ 484 Rich Yett	.05	.02
☐ 485 Pete Incaviglia	.05	.02
☐ 486 Rick Cerone	.05	.02
☐ 487 Tony Armas	.05	.02
☐ 488 Jerry Reed	.05	.02
☐ 489 Dave Lopes	.10	.05
☐ 490 Frank Tanana	.05	.02
☐ 491 Mike Loynd	.05	.02

☐ 492 Bruce Ruffin .05 .02
☐ 493 Chris Speier .05 .02
☐ 494 Tom Hume .05 .02
☐ 495 Jesse Orosco .05 .02
☐ 496 Robbie Wine UER .05 .02
(Misspelled Robby on card front)
☐ 497 Jeff Montgomery .20 .09
☐ 498 Jeff Dedmon .05 .02
☐ 499 Luis Aguayo .05 .02
☐ 500 Reggie Jackson .20 .09
(Oakland A's)
☐ 501 Reggie Jackson .20 .09
(Baltimore Orioles)
☐ 502 Reggie Jackson .20 .09
(New York Yankees)
☐ 503 Reggie Jackson .20 .09
(California Angels)
☐ 504 Reggie Jackson .20 .09
(Oakland A's)
☐ 505 Billy Hatcher .05 .02
☐ 506 Ed Lynch .05 .02
☐ 507 Willie Hernandez .05 .02
☐ 508 Jose DeLeon .05 .02
☐ 509 Joel Youngblood .05 .02
☐ 510 Bob Welch .05 .02
☐ 511 Steve Ontiveros .05 .02
☐ 512 Randy Ready .05 .02
☐ 513 Juan Nieves .05 .02
☐ 514 Jeff Russell .05 .02
☐ 515 Von Hayes .05 .02
☐ 516 Mark Gubicza .05 .02
☐ 517 Ken Dayley .05 .02
☐ 518 Don Aase .05 .02
☐ 519 Rick Reuschel .05 .02
☐ 520 Mike Henneman .10 .05
☐ 521 Rick Aguilera .10 .05
☐ 522 Jay Howell .05 .02
☐ 523 Ed Correa .05 .02
☐ 524 Manny Trillo .05 .02
☐ 525 Kirk Gibson .10 .05
☐ 526 Wally Ritchie .05 .02
☐ 527 Al Nipper .05 .02
☐ 528 Atlee Hammaker .05 .02
☐ 529 Shawon Dunston .05 .02
☐ 530 Jim Clancy .05 .02
☐ 531 Tom Paciorek .05 .02
☐ 532 Joel Skinner .05 .02
☐ 533 Scott Garrelts .05 .02
☐ 534 Tom O'Malley .05 .02
☐ 535 John Franco .10 .05
☐ 536 Paul Kilgus .05 .02
☐ 537 Darrell Porter .05 .02
☐ 538 Walt Terrell .05 .02
☐ 539 Bill Long .05 .02
☐ 540 George Bell .05 .02
☐ 541 Jeff Sellers .05 .02
☐ 542 Joe Boever .05 .02
☐ 543 Steve Howe .05 .02
☐ 544 Scott Sanderson .05 .02
☐ 545 Jack Morris .20 .09
☐ 546 Todd Benzinger .10 .05
☐ 547 Steve Henderson .05 .02
☐ 548 Eddie Milner .05 .02
☐ 549 Jeff M. Robinson .05 .02
☐ 550 Cal Ripken .75 .35
☐ 551 Jody Davis .05 .02
☐ 552 Kirk McCaskill .05 .02
☐ 553 Craig Lefferts .05 .02
☐ 554 Darnell Coles .05 .02
☐ 555 Phil Niekro .20 .09
☐ 556 Mike Aldrete .05 .02
☐ 557 Pat Perry .05 .02
☐ 558 Juan Agosto .05 .02
☐ 559 Rob Murphy .05 .02
☐ 560 Dennis Rasmussen .05 .02
☐ 561 Manny Lee .05 .02
☐ 562 Jeff Blauser .25 .11
☐ 563 Bob Ojeda .05 .02
☐ 564 Dave Dravecky .10 .05
☐ 565 Gene Garber .05 .02
☐ 566 Ron Roenicke .05 .02
☐ 567 Tommy Hinzo .05 .02
☐ 568 Eric Nolte .05 .02
☐ 569 Ed Hearn .05 .02
☐ 570 Mark Davidson .05 .02
☐ 571 Jim Walewander .05 .02
☐ 572 Donnie Hill UER .05 .02
(84 Stolen Base total listed as 7)
☐ 573 Jamie Moyer .05 .02
☐ 574 Ken Schrom .05 .02
☐ 575 Nolan Ryan .75 .35
☐ 576 Jim Acker .05 .02
☐ 577 Jamie Quirk .05 .02
☐ 578 Jay Aldrich .05 .02
☐ 579 Claudell Washington .05 .02
☐ 580 Jeff Leonard .05 .02
☐ 581 Carmen Castillo .05 .02
☐ 582 Daryl Boston .05 .02
☐ 583 Jeff DeWillis .05 .02
☐ 584 John Marzano .05 .02
☐ 585 Bill Gullickson .05 .02
☐ 586 Andy Allanson .05 .02
☐ 587 Lee Tunnell UER .05 .02
(1987 stat line reads .4.84 ERA)
☐ 588 Gene Nelson .05 .02
☐ 589 Dave LaPoint .05 .02
☐ 590 Harold Baines .10 .05
☐ 591 Bill Buckner .10 .05
☐ 592 Carlton Fisk .20 .09
☐ 593 Rick Manning .05 .02
☐ 594 Doug Jones .10 .05
☐ 595 Tom Candiotti .05 .02
☐ 596 Steve Lake .05 .02
☐ 597 Jose Lind .05 .02
☐ 598 Ross Jones .05 .02
☐ 599 Gary Matthews .05 .02
☐ 600 Fernando Valenzuela .10 .05
☐ 601 Dennis Martinez .10 .05
☐ 602 Les Lancaster .05 .02
☐ 603 Ozzie Guillen .05 .02
☐ 604 Tony Bernazard .05 .02
☐ 605 Chili Davis .10 .05
☐ 606 Roy Smalley .05 .02
☐ 607 Ivan Calderon .05 .02
☐ 608 Jay Tibbs .05 .02
☐ 609 Guy Hoffman .05 .02
☐ 610 Doyle Alexander .05 .02
☐ 611 Mike Bielecki .05 .02
☐ 612 Shawn Hillegas .05 .02
☐ 613 Keith Atherton .05 .02
☐ 614 Eric Plunk .05 .02
☐ 615 Sid Fernandez .05 .02
☐ 616 Dennis Lamp .05 .02
☐ 617 Dave Engle .05 .02
☐ 618 Harry Spilman .05 .02
☐ 619 Don Robinson .05 .02
☐ 620 John Farrell .05 .02
☐ 621 Nelson Liriano .05 .02
☐ 622 Floyd Bannister .05 .02
☐ 623 Randy Milligan .05 .02
☐ 624 Kevin Elster .10 .05
☐ 625 Jody Reed .10 .05
☐ 626 Shawn Abner .05 .02
☐ 627 Kirt Manwaring .10 .05
☐ 628 Pete Stanicek .05 .02
☐ 629 Rob Ducey .05 .02
☐ 630 Steve Kiefer .05 .02
☐ 631 Gary Thurman .05 .02
☐ 632 Darrel Akerfelds .05 .02
☐ 633 Dave Clark .05 .02
☐ 634 Roberto Kelly .20 .09
☐ 635 Keith Hughes .05 .02
☐ 636 John Davis .05 .02
☐ 637 Mike Devereaux .10 .05
☐ 638 Tom Glavine .50 .23
☐ 639 Keith A. Miller .05 .02
☐ 640 Chris Gwynn UER .10 .05
(Wrong batting and throwing on back)
☐ 641 Tim Crews .05 .02
☐ 642 Mackey Sasser .05 .02
☐ 643 Vicente Palacios .05 .02
☐ 644 Kevin Romine .05 .02
☐ 645 Gregg Jefferies .25 .11
☐ 646 Jeff Treadway .05 .02
☐ 647 Ron Gant .15 .07
☐ 648 Mark McGwire and .20 .09
Matt Nokes
(Rookie Sluggers)
☐ 649 Eric Davis and .10 .05
Tim Raines
(Speed and Power)
☐ 650 Don Mattingly and .20 .09
Jack Clark
☐ 651 Tony Fernandez, .25 .11
Alan Trammell, and
Cal Ripken
☐ 652 Vince Coleman HL .05 .02
100 Stolen Bases
☐ 653 Kirby Puckett HL .20 .09
10 Hits in a Row
☐ 654 Benito Santiago HL .05 .02
Hitting Streak
☐ 655 Juan Nieves HL .05 .02
No Hitter
☐ 656 Steve Bedrosian HL .05 .02
Saves Record
☐ 657 Mike Schmidt HL .20 .09
500 Homers
☐ 658 Don Mattingly HL .20 .09
Home Run Streak
☐ 659 Mark McGwire HL .30 .14
Rookie HR Record
☐ 660 Paul Molitor HL .10 .05
Hitting Streak

1988 Score Glossy

This 660 card set is a parallel to the regular 1988 Score set. According to the manufacturer, 5,000 of these sets were produced. These sets are considered glossy as "UV Coating" was added to the fronts of the card. These sets were issued in factory set versions only and released solely through Major League Marketing's hobby accounts.

	MINT	NRMT
COMPLETE FACT.SET (660)	200.00	90.00
COMMON CARD (1-660)	.25	.11
*STARS: 5X to 10X BASIC CARDS		
*ROOKIES: 4X to 8X BASIC CARDS		

1988 Score Box Cards

There are six different wax box bottom panels each featuring three players and a trivia (related to a particular stadium for a given year) question. The players and trivia question cards are individually numbered. The trivia are numbered below with the prefix T in order to avoid confusion. The trivia cards are very unpopular with collectors since they do not picture any players. When panels of four are cut into individuals, the cards are standard size. The card backs of the players feature the respective League logos most prominently.

	MINT	NRMT
COMPLETE SET (24)	10.00	4.50
COMMON CARD (1-18)	.25	.11
COMMON TRIVIA (T1-T6)	.10	.05

☐ 1 Terry Kennedy .25 .11
☐ 2 Don Mattingly 1.50 .70
☐ 3 Willie Randolph .25 .11
☐ 4 Wade Boggs .60 .25
☐ 5 Cal Ripken 3.00 1.35
☐ 6 George Bell .25 .11
☐ 7 Rickey Henderson .60 .25
☐ 8 Dave Winfield .60 .25
☐ 9 Bret Saberhagen .40 .18
☐ 10 Gary Carter .40 .18
☐ 11 Jack Clark .25 .11
☐ 12 Ryne Sandberg 1.25 .55
☐ 13 Mike Schmidt .75 .35
☐ 14 Ozzie Smith 1.25 .55
☐ 15 Eric Davis .40 .18
☐ 16 Andre Dawson .40 .18
☐ 17 Darryl Strawberry .40 .18
☐ 18 Mike Scott .25 .11
☐ T1 Fenway Park '60 .25 .11
Ted Williams Hits
To The End
☐ T2 Comiskey Park '83 .10 .05
Grand Slam
Fred Lynn Breaks Jinx
☐ T3 Anaheim Stadium '87 .25 .11
Old Rookie Record Falls
Mark McGwire
☐ T4 Wrigley Field '38 .10 .05
Gabby Hartnett
Gets Pennant Homer
☐ T5 Comiskey Park '50 .10 .05
Red Schoendienst
Rips Winning HR
☐ T6 County Stadium '87 .10 .05
John Farrell
Stops Hit Streak
Paul Molitor

1988 Score Rookie/Traded

This 110-card standard-size set features traded players (1-65) and rookies (66-110) for the 1988 season. The cards are distinguishable from the regular Score set by the orange borders and by the fact that the numbering on the back has a T suffix. The cards were distributed

exclusively in factory set form along with some trivia cards. Apparently Score's first attempt at a Rookie/Traded set was produced very conservatively, resulting in a set which is now recognized as being much tougher to find than the other Rookie/Traded sets from the other major companies of that year. Extended Rookie Cards in this set include Roberto Alomar, Brady Anderson, Craig Biggio, Jay Buhner, Mark Grace, Darryl Hamilton, Jack McDowell, Todd Stottlemyre and Walt Weiss.

	MINT	NRMT
COMP.FACT.SET (110)	50.00	22.00
COMMON CARD (1T-110T)	.25	.11

☐ 1T Jack Clark	.75	.35
☐ 2T Danny Jackson	.25	.11
☐ 3T Brett Butler	1.50	.70
☐ 4T Kurt Stillwell	.25	.11
☐ 5T Tom Brunansky	.25	.11
☐ 6T Dennis Lamp	.25	.11
☐ 7T Jose DeLeon	.25	.11
☐ 8T Tom Herr	.25	.11
☐ 9T Keith Moreland	.25	.11
☐ 10T Kirk Gibson	3.00	1.35
☐ 11T Bud Black	.25	.11
☐ 12T Rafael Ramirez	.25	.11
☐ 13T Luis Salazar	.25	.11
☐ 14T Goose Gossage	1.50	.70
☐ 15T Bob Welch	.25	.11
☐ 16T Vance Law	.25	.11
☐ 17T Ray Knight	.75	.35
☐ 18T Dan Quisenberry	.25	.11
☐ 19T Don Slaught	.25	.11
☐ 20T Lee Smith	.75	.35
☐ 21T Rick Cerone	.25	.11
☐ 22T Pat Tabler	.25	.11
☐ 23T Larry McWilliams	.25	.11
☐ 24T Ricky Horton	.25	.11
☐ 25T Graig Nettles	.75	.35
☐ 26T Dan Petry	.25	.11
☐ 27T Jose Rijo	.25	.11
☐ 28T Chili Davis	1.50	.70
☐ 29T Dickie Thon	.25	.11
☐ 30T Mackey Sasser	.25	.11
☐ 31T Mickey Tettleton	.75	.35
☐ 32T Rick Dempsey	.25	.11
☐ 33T Ron Hassey	.25	.11
☐ 34T Phil Bradley	.25	.11
☐ 35T Jay Howell	.25	.11
☐ 36T Bill Buckner	.75	.35
☐ 37T Alfredo Griffin	.25	.11
☐ 38T Gary Pettis	.25	.11
☐ 39T Calvin Schiraldi	.25	.11
☐ 40T John Candelaria	.25	.11
☐ 41T Joe Orsulak	.25	.11
☐ 42T Willie Upshaw	.25	.11
☐ 43T Herm Winningham	.25	.11
☐ 44T Ron Kittle	.25	.11
☐ 45T Bob Dernier	.25	.11
☐ 46T Steve Balboni	.25	.11
☐ 47T Steve Shields	.25	.11
☐ 48T Henry Cotto	.25	.11
☐ 49T Dave Henderson	.25	.11
☐ 50T Dave Parker	1.50	.70
☐ 51T Mike Young	.25	.11
☐ 52T Mark Salas	.25	.11
☐ 53T Mike Davis	.25	.11
☐ 54T Rafael Santana	.25	.11
☐ 55T Don Baylor	1.50	.70
☐ 56T Dan Pasqua	.25	.11
☐ 57T Ernest Riles	.25	.11
☐ 58T Glenn Hubbard	.25	.11
☐ 59T Mike Smithson	.25	.11
☐ 60T Richard Dotson	.25	.11
☐ 61T Jerry Reuss	.25	.11
☐ 62T Mike Jackson	.75	.35
☐ 63T Floyd Bannister	.25	.11
☐ 64T Jesse Orosco	.25	.11
☐ 65T Larry Parrish	.25	.11
☐ 66T Jeff Bittiger	.25	.11
☐ 67T Ray Hayward	.25	.11
☐ 68T Ricky Jordan	.75	.35
☐ 69T Tommy Gregg	.25	.11
☐ 70T Brady Anderson	8.00	3.60
☐ 71T Jeff Montgomery	3.00	1.35
☐ 72T Darryl Hamilton	.75	.35
☐ 73T Cecil Espy	.25	.11
☐ 74T Greg Briley	.25	.11
☐ 75T Joey Meyer	.25	.11
☐ 76T Mike Macfarlane	1.50	.70
☐ 77T Oswald Peraza	.25	.11
☐ 78T Jack Armstrong	.25	.11
☐ 79T Don Heinkel	.25	.11
☐ 80T Mark Grace	8.00	3.60
☐ 81T Steve Curry	.25	.11
☐ 82T Damon Berryhill	.25	.11
☐ 83T Steve Ellsworth	.25	.11
☐ 84T Pete Smith	.25	.11
☐ 85T Jack McDowell	3.00	1.35
☐ 86T Rob Dibble	.75	.35
☐ 87T Bryan Harvey UER (Games Pitched 47, Innings 5)	.75	.35
☐ 88T John Dopson	.25	.11
☐ 89T Dave Gallagher	.25	.11
☐ 90T Todd Stottlemyre	3.00	1.35
☐ 91T Mike Schooler	.25	.11
☐ 92T Don Gordon	.25	.11
☐ 93T Sil Campusano	.25	.11
☐ 94T Jeff Pico	.25	.11
☐ 95T Jay Buhner	8.00	3.60
☐ 96T Nelson Santovenia	.25	.11
☐ 97T Al Leiter	3.00	1.35
☐ 98T Luis Alicea	.75	.35
☐ 99T Pat Borders	.75	.35
☐ 100T Chris Sabo	.75	.35
☐ 101T Tim Belcher	.75	.35
☐ 102T Walt Weiss	.75	.35
☐ 103T Craig Biggio	8.00	3.60
☐ 104T Don August	.25	.11
☐ 105T Roberto Alomar	25.00	11.00
☐ 106T Todd Burns	.25	.11
☐ 107T John Costello	.25	.11
☐ 108T Melido Perez	.75	.35
☐ 109T Darrin Jackson	.25	.11
☐ 110T Orestes Destrade	.75	.35

1988 Score Rookie/Traded Glossy

This 110-card standard-size set was issued as a parallel vesion to the regular Score Rookie/Traded set. According to published reports, only 3,000 of these sets were created. The sets were sold solely through Score's dealer's accounts of the time.

	MINT	NRMT
COMPLETE FACT.SET (110)	150.00	70.00
COMMON CARD (1T-110T)	.50	.23
*STARS: 2X to 4X BASIC CARDS		
*ROOKIES: 2X to 4X BASIC CARDS		

1988 Score Young Superstars I

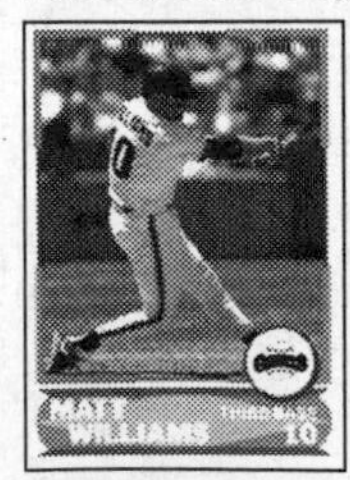

This attractive high-gloss 40-card standard-size set of "Young Superstars" was distributed in a small blue box which had the checklist of the set on a side panel of the box. The cards were also distributed as an insert, one per rack pack. These attractive cards are in full color on the front and also have a full-color small portrait on the card back. The cards in this series are distinguishable from the cards in Series II by the fact that this series has a blue and green border on the card front instead of the (Series II) blue and pink border.

	MINT	NRMT
COMPLETE SET (40)	5.00	2.20
COMMON CARD (1-40)	.05	.02

☐ 1 Mark McGwire	1.50	.70
☐ 2 Benito Santiago	.10	.05
☐ 3 Sam Horn	.05	.02
☐ 4 Chris Bosio	.05	.02
☐ 5 Matt Nokes	.05	.02
☐ 6 Ken Williams	.05	.02
☐ 7 Dion James	.05	.02
☐ 8 B.J. Surhoff	.25	.11
☐ 9 Joe Magrane	.05	.02
☐ 10 Kevin Seitzer	.10	.05
☐ 11 Stanley Jefferson	.05	.02
☐ 12 Devon White	.10	.05
☐ 13 Nelson Liriano	.05	.02
☐ 14 Chris James	.05	.02
☐ 15 Mike Henneman	.10	.05
☐ 16 Terry Steinbach	.25	.11
☐ 17 John Kruk	.25	.11
☐ 18 Matt Williams	1.50	.70
☐ 19 Kelly Downs	.05	.02
☐ 20 Bill Ripken	.05	.02
☐ 21 Ozzie Guillen	.05	.02
☐ 22 Luis Polonia	.10	.05
☐ 23 Dave Magadan	.05	.02
☐ 24 Mike Greenwell	.10	.05
☐ 25 Will Clark	.75	.35
☐ 26 Mike Dunne	.05	.02
☐ 27 Wally Joyner	.40	.18
☐ 28 Robby Thompson	.05	.02
☐ 29 Ken Caminiti	1.00	.45
☐ 30 Jose Canseco	.75	.35
☐ 31 Todd Benzinger	.05	.02
☐ 32 Pete Incaviglia	.05	.02
☐ 33 John Farrell	.05	.02
☐ 34 Casey Candaele	.05	.02
☐ 35 Mike Aldrete	.05	.02
☐ 36 Ruben Sierra	.10	.05
☐ 37 Ellis Burks	.60	.25
☐ 38 Tracy Jones	.05	.02
☐ 39 Kal Daniels	.05	.02
☐ 40 Cory Snyder	.05	.02

1988 Score Young Superstars II

This attractive high-gloss 40-card standard-size set of "Young Superstars" was distributed in a small purple box which had the checklist of the set on a side panel of the box. The cards were not distributed as an insert with rak paks as the first series was, but were only available as a complete set from hobby dealers or through a mail-in offer direct from the company. These attractive cards are in full color on the front and also have a full-color small portrait on the card back. The cards in this series are distinguishable from the cards in Series I by the fact that this series has a blue and pink border on the card front instead of the (Series I) blue and green border.

	MINT	NRMT
COMPLETE SET (40)	5.00	2.20
COMMON CARD (1-40)	.05	.02

☐ 1 Don Mattingly	1.50	.70
☐ 2 Glenn Braggs	.05	.02
☐ 3 Dwight Gooden	.10	.05
☐ 4 Jose Lind	.05	.02
☐ 5 Danny Tartabull	.05	.02
☐ 6 Tony Fernandez	.05	.02
☐ 7 Julio Franco	.10	.05
☐ 8 Andres Galarraga	1.00	.45
☐ 9 Bobby Bonilla	.40	.18
☐ 10 Eric Davis	.25	.11
☐ 11 Gerald Young	.05	.02
☐ 12 Barry Bonds	1.25	.55
☐ 13 Jerry Browne	.05	.02
☐ 14 Jeff Blauser	.10	.05
☐ 15 Mickey Brantley	.05	.02
☐ 16 Floyd Youmans	.05	.02
☐ 17 Bret Saberhagen	.10	.05
☐ 18 Shawon Dunston	.05	.02
☐ 19 Len Dykstra	.10	.05
☐ 20 Darryl Strawberry	.10	.05
☐ 21 Rick Aguilera	.10	.05
☐ 22 Ivan Calderon	.05	.02
☐ 23 Roger Clemens	1.25	.55
☐ 24 Vince Coleman	.05	.02
☐ 25 Gary Thurman	.05	.02
☐ 26 Jeff Treadway	.05	.02

☐ 27 Oddibe McDowell	.05	.02
☐ 28 Fred McGriff	1.00	.45
☐ 29 Mark McLemore	.05	.02
☐ 30 Jeff Musselman	.05	.02
☐ 31 Mitch Williams	.05	.02
☐ 32 Dan Plesac	.05	.02
☐ 33 Juan Nieves	.05	.02
☐ 34 Barry Larkin	1.00	.45
☐ 35 Greg Mathews	.05	.02
☐ 36 Shane Mack	.05	.02
☐ 37 Scott Bankhead	.05	.02
☐ 38 Eric Bell	.05	.02
☐ 39 Greg Swindell	.05	.02
☐ 40 Kevin Elster	.10	.05

1989 Score

This 660-card standard-size set was distributed by Major League Marketing. Cards were issued primarily in fin-wrapped plastic packs and factory sets. Cards feature six distinctive inner border (inside a white outer border) colors on the front. Subsets include Highlights (652-660) and Rookie Prospects (621-651). Rookie Cards in this set include Sandy Alomar Jr., Brady Anderson, Craig Biggio, Charlie Hayes, Randy Johnson, Ramon Martinez, Gary Sheffield, and John Smoltz.

	MINT	NRMT
COMPLETE SET (660)	8.00	3.60
COMPLETE FACT.SET (660)	8.00	3.60
COMMON CARD (1-660)	.05	.02
☐ 1 Jose Canseco	.20	.09
☐ 2 Andre Dawson	.20	.09
☐ 3 Mark McGwire UER	.40	.18
☐ 4 Benito Santiago	.05	.02
☐ 5 Rick Reuschel	.05	.02
☐ 6 Fred McGriff	.20	.09
☐ 7 Kal Daniels	.05	.02
☐ 8 Gary Gaetti	.05	.02
☐ 9 Ellis Burks	.05	.02
☐ 10 Darryl Strawberry	.10	.05
☐ 11 Julio Franco	.10	.05
☐ 12 Lloyd Moseby	.05	.02
☐ 13 Jeff Pico	.05	.02
☐ 14 Johnny Ray	.05	.02
☐ 15 Cal Ripken	.75	.35
☐ 16 Dick Schofield	.05	.02
☐ 17 Mel Hall	.05	.02
☐ 18 Bill Ripken	.05	.02
☐ 19 Brook Jacoby	.05	.02
☐ 20 Kirby Puckett	.40	.18
☐ 21 Bill Doran	.05	.02
☐ 22 Pete O'Brien	.05	.02
☐ 23 Matt Nokes	.05	.02
☐ 24 Brian Fisher	.05	.02
☐ 25 Jack Clark	.10	.05
☐ 26 Gary Pettis	.05	.02
☐ 27 Dave Valle	.05	.02
☐ 28 Willie Wilson	.05	.02
☐ 29 Curt Young	.05	.02
☐ 30 Dale Murphy	.20	.09
☐ 31 Barry Larkin	.20	.09
☐ 32 Dave Stewart	.10	.05
☐ 33 Mike LaValliere	.05	.02
☐ 34 Glenn Hubbard	.05	.02
☐ 35 Ryne Sandberg	.25	.11
☐ 36 Tony Pena	.05	.02
☐ 37 Greg Walker	.05	.02
☐ 38 Von Hayes	.05	.02
☐ 39 Kevin Mitchell	.10	.05
☐ 40 Tim Raines	.10	.05
☐ 41 Keith Hernandez	.10	.05
☐ 42 Keith Moreland	.05	.02
☐ 43 Ruben Sierra	.05	.02
☐ 44 Chet Lemon	.05	.02
☐ 45 Willie Randolph	.10	.05
☐ 46 Andy Allanson	.05	.02
☐ 47 Candy Maldonado	.05	.02
☐ 48 Sid Bream	.05	.02
☐ 49 Denny Walling	.05	.02
☐ 50 Dave Winfield	.20	.09
☐ 51 Alvin Davis	.05	.02
☐ 52 Cory Snyder	.05	.02
☐ 53 Hubie Brooks	.05	.02
☐ 54 Chili Davis	.10	.05
☐ 55 Kevin Seitzer	.05	.02
☐ 56 Jose Uribe	.05	.02
☐ 57 Tony Fernandez	.05	.02
☐ 58 Tim Teufel	.05	.02
☐ 59 Oddibe McDowell	.05	.02
☐ 60 Les Lancaster	.05	.02
☐ 61 Billy Hatcher	.05	.02
☐ 62 Dan Gladden	.05	.02
☐ 63 Marty Barrett	.05	.02
☐ 64 Nick Esasky	.05	.02
☐ 65 Wally Joyner	.10	.05
☐ 66 Mike Greenwell	.05	.02
☐ 67 Ken Williams	.05	.02
☐ 68 Bob Horner	.05	.02
☐ 69 Steve Sax	.05	.02
☐ 70 Rickey Henderson	.20	.09
☐ 71 Mitch Webster	.05	.02
☐ 72 Rob Deer	.05	.02
☐ 73 Jim Presley	.05	.02
☐ 74 Albert Hall	.05	.02
☐ 75 George Brett COR (At age 35)	.40	.18
☐ 75A George Brett ERR (At age 33)	.75	.35
☐ 76 Brian Downing	.05	.02
☐ 77 Dave Martinez	.05	.02
☐ 78 Scott Fletcher	.05	.02
☐ 79 Phil Bradley	.05	.02
☐ 80 Ozzie Smith	.25	.11
☐ 81 Larry Sheets	.05	.02
☐ 82 Mike Aldrete	.05	.02
☐ 83 Darnell Coles	.05	.02
☐ 84 Len Dykstra	.10	.05
☐ 85 Jim Rice	.05	.02
☐ 86 Jeff Treadway	.05	.02
☐ 87 Jose Lind	.05	.02
☐ 88 Willie McGee	.05	.02
☐ 89 Mickey Brantley	.05	.02
☐ 90 Tony Gwynn	.50	.23
☐ 91 R.J. Reynolds	.05	.02
☐ 92 Milt Thompson	.05	.02
☐ 93 Kevin McReynolds	.05	.02
☐ 94 Eddie Murray UER ('86 batting .205, should be .305)	.20	.09
☐ 95 Lance Parrish	.05	.02
☐ 96 Ron Kittle	.05	.02
☐ 97 Gerald Young	.05	.02
☐ 98 Ernie Whitt	.05	.02
☐ 99 Jeff Reed	.05	.02
☐ 100 Don Mattingly	.30	.14
☐ 101 Gerald Perry	.05	.02
☐ 102 Vance Law	.05	.02
☐ 103 John Shelby	.05	.02
☐ 104 Chris Sabo	.05	.02
☐ 105 Danny Tartabull	.05	.02
☐ 106 Glenn Wilson	.05	.02
☐ 107 Mark Davidson	.05	.02
☐ 108 Dave Parker	.10	.05
☐ 109 Eric Davis	.10	.05
☐ 110 Alan Trammell	.05	.02
☐ 111 Ozzie Virgil	.05	.02
☐ 112 Frank Tanana	.05	.02
☐ 113 Rafael Ramirez	.05	.02
☐ 114 Dennis Martinez	.10	.05
☐ 115 Jose DeLeon	.05	.02
☐ 116 Bob Ojeda	.05	.02
☐ 117 Doug Drabek	.05	.02
☐ 118 Andy Hawkins	.05	.02
☐ 119 Greg Maddux	.75	.35
☐ 120 Cecil Fielder UER Reversed Photo on back	.05	.02
☐ 121 Mike Scioscia	.05	.02
☐ 122 Dan Petry	.05	.02
☐ 123 Terry Kennedy	.05	.02
☐ 124 Kelly Downs	.05	.02
☐ 125 Greg Gross UER (Gregg on back)	.05	.02
☐ 126 Fred Lynn	.05	.02
☐ 127 Barry Bonds	.40	.18
☐ 128 Harold Baines	.10	.05
☐ 129 Doyle Alexander	.05	.02
☐ 130 Kevin Elster	.05	.02
☐ 131 Mike Heath	.05	.02
☐ 132 Teddy Higuera	.05	.02
☐ 133 Charlie Leibrandt	.05	.02
☐ 134 Tim Laudner	.05	.02
☐ 135A Ray Knight ERR (Reverse negative)	.20	.09
☐ 135B Ray Knight COR	.05	.02
☐ 136 Howard Johnson	.05	.02
☐ 137 Terry Pendleton	.10	.05
☐ 138 Andy McGaffigan	.05	.02
☐ 139 Ken Oberkfell	.05	.02
☐ 140 Butch Wynegar	.05	.02
☐ 141 Rob Murphy	.05	.02
☐ 142 Rich Renteria	.05	.02
☐ 143 Jose Guzman	.05	.02
☐ 144 Andres Galarraga	.20	.09
☐ 145 Ricky Horton	.05	.02
☐ 146 Frank DiPino	.05	.02
☐ 147 Glenn Braggs	.05	.02
☐ 148 John Kruk	.10	.05
☐ 149 Mike Schmidt	.25	.11
☐ 150 Lee Smith	.10	.05
☐ 151 Robin Yount	.20	.09
☐ 152 Mark Eichhorn	.05	.02
☐ 153 DeWayne Buice	.05	.02
☐ 154 B.J. Surhoff	.10	.05
☐ 155 Vince Coleman	.05	.02
☐ 156 Tony Phillips	.05	.02
☐ 157 Willie Fraser	.05	.02
☐ 158 Lance McCullers	.05	.02
☐ 159 Greg Gagne	.05	.02
☐ 160 Jesse Barfield	.05	.02
☐ 161 Mark Langston	.05	.02
☐ 162 Kurt Stillwell	.05	.02
☐ 163 Dion James	.05	.02
☐ 164 Glenn Davis	.05	.02
☐ 165 Walt Weiss	.05	.02
☐ 166 Dave Concepcion	.10	.05
☐ 167 Alfredo Griffin	.05	.02
☐ 168 Don Heinkel	.05	.02
☐ 169 Luis Rivera	.05	.02
☐ 170 Shane Rawley	.05	.02
☐ 171 Darrell Evans	.10	.05
☐ 172 Robby Thompson	.05	.02
☐ 173 Jody Davis	.05	.02
☐ 174 Andy Van Slyke	.10	.05
☐ 175 Wade Boggs UER (Bio says .364, should be .356)	.20	.09
☐ 176 Garry Templeton ('85 stats off-centered)	.05	.02
☐ 177 Gary Redus	.05	.02
☐ 178 Craig Lefferts	.05	.02
☐ 179 Carney Lansford	.10	.05
☐ 180 Ron Darling	.05	.02
☐ 181 Kirk McCaskill	.05	.02
☐ 182 Tony Armas	.05	.02
☐ 183 Steve Farr	.05	.02
☐ 184 Tom Brunansky	.05	.02
☐ 185 Bryan Harvey UER ('87 games 47, should be 3)	.10	.05
☐ 186 Mike Marshall	.05	.02
☐ 187 Bo Diaz	.05	.02
☐ 188 Willie Upshaw	.05	.02
☐ 189 Mike Pagliarulo	.05	.02
☐ 190 Mike Krukow	.05	.02
☐ 191 Tommy Herr	.05	.02
☐ 192 Jim Pankovits	.05	.02
☐ 193 Dwight Evans	.10	.05
☐ 194 Kelly Gruber	.05	.02
☐ 195 Bobby Bonilla	.05	.02
☐ 196 Wallace Johnson	.05	.02
☐ 197 Dave Stieb	.05	.02
☐ 198 Pat Borders	.10	.05
☐ 199 Rafael Palmeiro	.20	.09
☐ 200 Dwight Gooden	.10	.05
☐ 201 Pete Incaviglia	.10	.05
☐ 202 Chris James	.05	.02
☐ 203 Marvell Wynne	.05	.02
☐ 204 Pat Sheridan	.05	.02
☐ 205 Don Baylor	.05	.02
☐ 206 Paul O'Neill	.05	.02
☐ 207 Pete Smith	.05	.02
☐ 208 Mark McLemore	.05	.02
☐ 209 Henry Cotto	.05	.02
☐ 210 Kirk Gibson	.20	.09
☐ 211 Claudell Washington	.05	.02
☐ 212 Randy Bush	.05	.02
☐ 213 Joe Carter	.20	.09
☐ 214 Bill Buckner	.10	.05
☐ 215 Bert Blyleven UER (Wrong birth year)	.10	.05
☐ 216 Brett Butler	.05	.02
☐ 217 Lee Mazzilli	.05	.02
☐ 218 Spike Owen	.05	.02
☐ 219 Bill Swift	.05	.02
☐ 220 Tim Wallach	.05	.02
☐ 221 David Cone	.20	.09
☐ 222 Don Carman	.05	.02
☐ 223 Rich Gossage	.05	.02
☐ 224 Bob Walk	.05	.02
☐ 225 Dave Righetti	.05	.02
☐ 226 Kevin Bass	.05	.02
☐ 227 Kevin Gross	.05	.02
☐ 228 Tim Burke	.05	.02
☐ 229 Rick Mahler	.05	.02

□ 230 Lou Whitaker UER .10 .05
(252 games in '85, should be 152)
□ 231 Luis Alicea .05 .02
□ 232 Roberto Alomar .30 .14
□ 233 Bob Boone .10 .05
□ 234 Dickie Thon .05 .02
□ 235 Shawon Dunston .05 .02
□ 236 Pete Stanicek .05 .02
□ 237 Craig Biggio .50 .23
(Inconsistent design, portrait on front)
□ 238 Dennis Boyd .05 .02
□ 239 Tom Candiotti .05 .02
□ 240 Gary Carter .20 .09
□ 241 Mike Stanley .05 .02
□ 242 Ken Phelps .05 .02
□ 243 Chris Bosio .05 .02
□ 244 Les Straker .05 .02
□ 245 Dave Smith .05 .02
□ 246 John Candelaria .05 .02
□ 247 Joe Orsulak .05 .02
□ 248 Storm Davis .05 .02
□ 249 Floyd Bannister UER .05 .02
(ML Batting Record)
□ 250 Jack Morris .10 .05
□ 251 Bret Saberhagen .05 .02
□ 252 Tom Niedenfuer .05 .02
□ 253 Neal Heaton .05 .02
□ 254 Eric Show .05 .02
□ 255 Juan Samuel .05 .02
□ 256 Dale Sveum .05 .02
□ 257 Jim Gott .05 .02
□ 258 Scott Garrelts .05 .02
□ 259 Larry McWilliams .05 .02
□ 260 Steve Bedrosian .05 .02
□ 261 Jack Howell .05 .02
□ 262 Jay Tibbs .05 .02
□ 263 Jamie Moyer .05 .02
□ 264 Doug Sisk .05 .02
□ 265 Todd Worrell .05 .02
□ 266 John Farrell .05 .02
□ 267 Dave Collins .05 .02
□ 268 Sid Fernandez .05 .02
□ 269 Tom Brookens .05 .02
□ 270 Shane Mack .05 .02
□ 271 Paul Kilgus .05 .02
□ 272 Chuck Crim .05 .02
□ 273 Bob Knepper .05 .02
□ 274 Mike Moore .05 .02
□ 275 Guillermo Hernandez .05 .02
□ 276 Dennis Eckersley .20 .09
□ 277 Graig Nettles .10 .05
□ 278 Rich Dotson .05 .02
□ 279 Larry Herndon .05 .02
□ 280 Gene Larkin .05 .02
□ 281 Roger McDowell .05 .02
□ 282 Greg Swindell .05 .02
□ 283 Juan Agosto .05 .02
□ 284 Jeff M. Robinson .05 .02
□ 285 Mike Dunne .05 .02
□ 286 Greg Mathews .05 .02
□ 287 Kent Tekulve .05 .02
□ 288 Jerry Mumphrey .05 .02
□ 289 Jack McDowell .05 .02
□ 290 Frank Viola .05 .02
□ 291 Mark Gubicza .05 .02
□ 292 Dave Schmidt .05 .02
□ 293 Mike Henneman .05 .02
□ 294 Jimmy Jones .05 .02
□ 295 Charlie Hough .10 .05
□ 296 Rafael Santana .05 .02
□ 297 Chris Speier .05 .02
□ 298 Mike Witt .05 .02
□ 299 Pascual Perez .05 .02
□ 300 Nolan Ryan .75 .35
□ 301 Mitch Williams .05 .02
□ 302 Mookie Wilson .10 .05
□ 303 Mackey Sasser .05 .02
□ 304 John Cerutti .05 .02
□ 305 Jeff Reardon .10 .05
□ 306 Randy Myers UER .10 .05
(6 hits in '87, should be 61)
□ 307 Greg Brock .05 .02
□ 308 Bob Welch .05 .02
□ 309 Jeff D. Robinson .05 .02
□ 310 Harold Reynolds .05 .02
□ 311 Jim Walewander .05 .02
□ 312 Dave Magadan .05 .02
□ 313 Jim Gantner .05 .02
□ 314 Walt Terrell .05 .02
□ 315 Wally Backman .05 .02
□ 316 Luis Salazar .05 .02
□ 317 Rick Rhoden .05 .02
□ 318 Tom Henke .05 .02
□ 319 Mike Macfarlane .10 .05
□ 320 Dan Plesac .05 .02
□ 321 Calvin Schiraldi .05 .02
□ 322 Stan Javier .05 .02
□ 323 Devon White .05 .02
□ 324 Scott Bradley .05 .02
□ 325 Bruce Hurst .05 .02
□ 326 Manny Lee .05 .02
□ 327 Rick Aguilera .10 .05
□ 328 Bruce Ruffin .05 .02
□ 329 Ed Whitson .05 .02
□ 330 Bo Jackson .20 .09
□ 331 Ivan Calderon .05 .02
□ 332 Mickey Hatcher .05 .02
□ 333 Barry Jones .05 .02
□ 334 Ron Hassey .05 .02
□ 335 Bill Wegman .05 .02
□ 336 Damon Berryhill .05 .02
□ 337 Steve Ontiveros .05 .02
□ 338 Dan Pasqua .05 .02
□ 339 Bill Pecota .05 .02
□ 340 Greg Cadaret .05 .02
□ 341 Scott Bankhead .05 .02
□ 342 Ron Guidry .10 .05
□ 343 Danny Heep .05 .02
□ 344 Bob Brower .05 .02
□ 345 Rich Gedman .05 .02
□ 346 Nelson Santovenia .05 .02
□ 347 George Bell .05 .02
□ 348 Ted Power .05 .02
□ 349 Mark Grant .05 .02
□ 350 Roger Clemens COR .40 .18
(78 career wins)
□ 350A Roger Clemens ERR 2.00 .90
(778 career wins)
□ 351 Bill Long .05 .02
□ 352 Jay Bell .10 .05
□ 353 Steve Balboni .05 .02
□ 354 Bob Kipper .05 .02
□ 355 Steve Jeltz .05 .02
□ 356 Jesse Orosco .05 .02
□ 357 Bob Dernier .05 .02
□ 358 Mickey Tettleton .10 .05
□ 359 Duane Ward .05 .02
□ 360 Darrin Jackson .05 .02
□ 361 Rey Quinones .05 .02
□ 362 Mark Grace .20 .09
□ 363 Steve Lake .05 .02
□ 364 Pat Perry .05 .02
□ 365 Terry Steinbach .10 .05
□ 366 Alan Ashby .05 .02
□ 367 Jeff Montgomery .10 .05
□ 368 Steve Buechele .05 .02
□ 369 Chris Brown .05 .02
□ 370 Orel Hershiser .10 .05
□ 371 Todd Benzinger .05 .02
□ 372 Ron Gant .10 .05
□ 373 Paul Assenmacher .05 .02
□ 374 Joey Meyer .05 .02
□ 375 Neil Allen .05 .02
□ 376 Mike Davis .05 .02
□ 377 Jeff Parrett .05 .02
□ 378 Jay Howell .05 .02
□ 379 Rafael Belliard .05 .02
□ 380 Luis Polonia UER .05 .02
(2 triples in '87, should be 10)
□ 381 Keith Atherton .05 .02
□ 382 Kent Hrbek .10 .05
□ 383 Bob Stanley .05 .02
□ 384 Dave LaPoint .05 .02
□ 385 Rance Mulliniks .05 .02
□ 386 Melido Perez .05 .02
□ 387 Doug Jones .05 .02
□ 388 Steve Lyons .05 .02
□ 389 Alejandro Pena .05 .02
□ 390 Frank White .10 .05
□ 391 Pat Tabler .05 .02
□ 392 Eric Plunk .05 .02
□ 393 Mike Maddux .05 .02
□ 394 Allan Anderson .05 .02
□ 395 Bob Brenly .05 .02
□ 396 Rick Cerone .05 .02
□ 397 Scott Terry .05 .02
□ 398 Mike Jackson .05 .02
□ 399 Bobby Thigpen UER .05 .02
(Bio says 37 saves in '88, should be 34)
□ 400 Don Sutton .20 .09
□ 401 Cecil Espy .05 .02
□ 402 Junior Ortiz .05 .02
□ 403 Mike Smithson .05 .02
□ 404 Bud Black .05 .02
□ 405 Tom Foley .05 .02
□ 406 Andres Thomas .05 .02
□ 407 Rick Sutcliffe .05 .02
□ 408 Brian Harper .05 .02
□ 409 John Smiley .05 .02
□ 410 Juan Nieves .05 .02
□ 411 Shawn Abner .05 .02
□ 412 Wes Gardner .05 .02
□ 413 Darren Daulton .10 .05
□ 414 Juan Berenguer .05 .02
□ 415 Charles Hudson .05 .02
□ 416 Rick Honeycutt .05 .02
□ 417 Greg Booker .05 .02
□ 418 Tim Belcher .05 .02
□ 419 Don August .05 .02
□ 420 Dale Mohorcic .05 .02
□ 421 Steve Lombardozzi .05 .02
□ 422 Atlee Hammaker .05 .02
□ 423 Jerry Don Gleaton .05 .02
□ 424 Scott Bailes .05 .02
□ 425 Bruce Sutter .10 .05
□ 426 Randy Ready .05 .02
□ 427 Jerry Reed .05 .02
□ 428 Bryn Smith .05 .02
□ 429 Tim Leary .05 .02
□ 430 Mark Clear .05 .02
□ 431 Terry Leach .05 .02
□ 432 John Moses .05 .02
□ 433 Ozzie Guillen .05 .02
□ 434 Gene Nelson .05 .02
□ 435 Gary Ward .05 .02
□ 436 Luis Aguayo .05 .02
□ 437 Fernando Valenzuela .10 .05
□ 438 Jeff Russell UER .05 .02
(Saves total does not add up correctly)
□ 439 Cecilio Guante .05 .02
□ 440 Don Robinson .05 .02
□ 441 Rick Anderson .05 .02
□ 442 Tom Glavine .25 .11
□ 443 Daryl Boston .05 .02
□ 444 Joe Price .05 .02
□ 445 Stewart Cliburn .05 .02
□ 446 Manny Trillo .05 .02
□ 447 Joel Skinner .05 .02
□ 448 Charlie Puleo .05 .02
□ 449 Carlton Fisk .20 .09
□ 450 Will Clark .20 .09
□ 451 Otis Nixon .05 .02
□ 452 Rick Schu .05 .02
□ 453 Todd Stottlemyre UER .10 .05
(ML Batting Record)
□ 454 Tim Birtsas .05 .02
□ 455 Dave Gallagher .05 .02
□ 456 Barry Lyons .05 .02
□ 457 Fred Manrique .05 .02
□ 458 Ernest Riles .05 .02
□ 459 Doug Jennings .05 .02
□ 460 Joe Magrane .05 .02
□ 461 Jamie Quirk .05 .02
□ 462 Jack Armstrong .05 .02
□ 463 Bobby Witt .05 .02
□ 464 Keith A. Miller .05 .02
□ 465 Todd Burns .05 .02
□ 466 John Dopson .05 .02
□ 467 Rich Yett .05 .02
□ 468 Craig Reynolds .05 .02
□ 469 Dave Bergman .05 .02
□ 470 Rex Hudler .05 .02
□ 471 Eric King .05 .02
□ 472 Joaquin Andujar .05 .02
□ 473 Sil Campusano .05 .02
□ 474 Terry Mulholland .05 .02
□ 475 Mike Flanagan .05 .02
□ 476 Greg A. Harris .05 .02
□ 477 Tommy John .10 .05
□ 478 Dave Anderson .05 .02
□ 479 Fred Toliver .05 .02
□ 480 Jimmy Key .05 .02
□ 481 Donell Nixon .05 .02
□ 482 Mark Portugal .05 .02
□ 483 Tom Pagnozzi .05 .02
□ 484 Jeff Kunkel .05 .02
□ 485 Frank Williams .05 .02
□ 486 Jody Reed .05 .02
□ 487 Roberto Kelly .10 .05
□ 488 Shawn Hillegas UER .05 .02
(165 innings in '87, should be 165.2)
□ 489 Jerry Reuss .05 .02
□ 490 Mark Davis .05 .02
□ 491 Jeff Sellers .05 .02
□ 492 Zane Smith .05 .02
□ 493 Al Newman .05 .02
□ 494 Mike Young .05 .02
□ 495 Larry Parrish .05 .02
□ 496 Herm Winningham .05 .02
□ 497 Carmen Castillo .05 .02
□ 498 Joe Hesketh .05 .02
□ 499 Darrell Miller .05 .02
□ 500 Mike LaCoss .05 .02
□ 501 Charlie Lea .05 .02

☐ 502 Bruce Benedict .05 .02
☐ 503 Chuck Finley .10 .05
☐ 504 Brad Wellman .05 .02
☐ 505 Tim Crews .05 .02
☐ 506 Ken Gerhart .05 .02
☐ 507A Brian Holton ERR .05 .02
(Born 1/25/65 Denver, should be 11/29/59 in McKeesport)
☐ 507B Brian Holton COR 2.00 .90
☐ 508 Dennis Lamp .05 .02
☐ 509 Bobby Meacham UER .05 .02
('84 games 099)
☐ 510 Tracy Jones .05 .02
☐ 511 Mike R. Fitzgerald .05 .02
☐ 512 Jeff Bittiger .05 .02
☐ 513 Tim Flannery .05 .02
☐ 514 Ray Hayward .05 .02
☐ 515 Dave Leiper .05 .02
☐ 516 Rod Scurry .05 .02
☐ 517 Carmelo Martinez .05 .02
☐ 518 Curtis Wilkerson .05 .02
☐ 519 Stan Jefferson .05 .02
☐ 520 Dan Quisenberry .05 .02
☐ 521 Lloyd McClendon .05 .02
☐ 522 Steve Trout .05 .02
☐ 523 Larry Andersen .05 .02
☐ 524 Don Aase .05 .02
☐ 525 Bob Forsch .05 .02
☐ 526 Geno Petralli .05 .02
☐ 527 Angel Salazar .05 .02
☐ 528 Mike Schooler .05 .02
☐ 529 Jose Oquendo .05 .02
☐ 530 Jay Buhner UER .25 .11
(Wearing 43 on front, listed as 34 on back)
☐ 531 Tom Bolton .05 .02
☐ 532 Al Nipper .05 .02
☐ 533 Dave Henderson .05 .02
☐ 534 John Costello .05 .02
☐ 535 Donnie Moore .05 .02
☐ 536 Mike Laga .05 .02
☐ 537 Mike Gallego .05 .02
☐ 538 Jim Clancy .05 .02
☐ 539 Joel Youngblood .05 .02
☐ 540 Rick Leach .05 .02
☐ 541 Kevin Romine .05 .02
☐ 542 Mark Salas .05 .02
☐ 543 Greg Minton .05 .02
☐ 544 Dave Palmer .05 .02
☐ 545 Dwayne Murphy UER .05 .02
(Game-sinning)
☐ 546 Jim Deshaies .05 .02
☐ 547 Don Gordon .05 .02
☐ 548 Ricky Jordan .10 .05
☐ 549 Mike Boddicker .05 .02
☐ 550 Mike Scott .05 .02
☐ 551 Jeff Ballard .05 .02
☐ 552A Jose Rijo ERR .20 .09
(Uniform listed as 27 on back)
☐ 552B Jose Rijo COR .20 .09
(Uniform listed as 24 on back)
☐ 553 Danny Darwin .05 .02
☐ 554 Tom Browning .05 .02
☐ 555 Danny Jackson .05 .02
☐ 556 Rick Dempsey .05 .02
☐ 557 Jeffrey Leonard .05 .02
☐ 558 Jeff Musselman .05 .02
☐ 559 Ron Robinson .05 .02
☐ 560 John Tudor .05 .02
☐ 561 Don Slaught UER .05 .02
(237 games in 1987)
☐ 562 Dennis Rasmussen .05 .02
☐ 563 Brady Anderson .50 .23
☐ 564 Pedro Guerrero .10 .05
☐ 565 Paul Molitor .20 .09
☐ 566 Terry Clark .05 .02
☐ 567 Terry Puhl .05 .02
☐ 568 Mike Campbell .05 .02
☐ 569 Paul Mirabella .05 .02
☐ 570 Jeff Hamilton .05 .02
☐ 571 Oswald Peraza .05 .02
☐ 572 Bob McClure .05 .02
☐ 573 Jose Bautista .05 .02
☐ 574 Alex Trevino .05 .02
☐ 575 John Franco .10 .05
☐ 576 Mark Parent .05 .02
☐ 577 Nelson Liriano .05 .02
☐ 578 Steve Shields .05 .02
☐ 579 Odell Jones .05 .02
☐ 580 Al Leiter .20 .09
☐ 581 Dave Stapleton .05 .02
☐ 582 World Series '88 .10 .05
Orel Hershiser
Jose Canseco
Kirk Gibson
Dave Stewart
☐ 583 Donnie Hill .05 .02
☐ 584 Chuck Jackson .05 .02
☐ 585 Rene Gonzales .05 .02
☐ 586 Tracy Woodson .05 .02
☐ 587 Jim Adduci .05 .02
☐ 588 Mario Soto .05 .02
☐ 589 Jeff Blauser .10 .05
☐ 590 Jim Traber .05 .02
☐ 591 Jon Perlman .05 .02
☐ 592 Mark Williamson .05 .02
☐ 593 Dave Meads .05 .02
☐ 594 Jim Eisenreich .20 .09
☐ 595A Paul Gibson P1 1.00 .45
☐ 595B Paul Gibson P2 .05 .02
(Airbrushed leg on player in background)
☐ 596 Mike Birkbeck .05 .02
☐ 597 Terry Francona .05 .02
☐ 598 Paul Zuvella .05 .02
☐ 599 Franklin Stubbs .05 .02
☐ 600 Gregg Jefferies .10 .05
☐ 601 John Cangelosi .05 .02
☐ 602 Mike Sharperson .05 .02
☐ 603 Mike Diaz .05 .02
☐ 604 Gary Varsho .05 .02
☐ 605 Terry Blocker .05 .02
☐ 606 Charlie O'Brien .05 .02
☐ 607 Jim Eppard .05 .02
☐ 608 John Davis .05 .02
☐ 609 Ken Griffey Sr. .05 .02
☐ 610 Buddy Bell .10 .05
☐ 611 Ted Simmons UER .10 .05
('78 stats Cardinal)
☐ 612 Matt Williams .25 .11
☐ 613 Danny Cox .05 .02
☐ 614 Al Pedrique .05 .02
☐ 615 Ron Oester .05 .02
☐ 616 John Smoltz .50 .23
☐ 617 Bob Melvin .05 .02
☐ 618 Rob Dibble .10 .05
☐ 619 Kirt Manwaring .05 .02
☐ 620 Felix Fermin .05 .02
☐ 621 Doug Dascenzo .05 .02
☐ 622 Bill Brennan .05 .02
☐ 623 Carlos Quintana .05 .02
☐ 624 Mike Harkey UER .05 .02
(13 and 31 walks in '88, should be 35 and 33)
☐ 625 Gary Sheffield .75 .35
☐ 626 Tom Prince .05 .02
☐ 627 Steve Searcy .05 .02
☐ 628 Charlie Hayes .20 .09
(Listed as outfielder)
☐ 629 Felix Jose UER .05 .02
(Modesto misspelled as Modesta)
☐ 630 Sandy Alomar Jr. .50 .23
(Inconsistent design, portrait on front)
☐ 631 Derek Lilliquist .05 .02
☐ 632 Geronimo Berroa .10 .05
☐ 633 Luis Medina .05 .02
☐ 634 Tom Gordon UER .20 .09
(Height 6'0")
☐ 635 Ramon Martinez .25 .11
☐ 636 Craig Worthington .05 .02
☐ 637 Edgar Martinez .20 .09
☐ 638 Chad Kreuter .05 .02
☐ 639 Ron Jones .05 .02
☐ 640 Van Snider .05 .02
☐ 641 Lance Blankenship .05 .02
☐ 642 Dwight Smith UER .10 .05
(10 HR's in '87, should be 18)
☐ 643 Cameron Drew .05 .02
☐ 644 Jerald Clark .05 .02
☐ 645 Randy Johnson 1.00 .45
☐ 646 Norm Charlton .10 .05
☐ 647 Todd Frohwirth UER .05 .02
(Southpaw on back)
☐ 648 Luis De Los Santos .05 .02
☐ 649 Tim Jones .05 .02
☐ 650 Dave West UER .05 .02
(ML hits 3, should be 6)
☐ 651 Bob Milacki .05 .02
☐ 652 Wrigley Field HL .10 .05
(Let There Be Lights)
☐ 653 Orel Hershiser HL .10 .05
(The Streak)
☐ 654A Wade Boggs HL ERR 1.50 .70
(Wade Whacks 'Em) ("seaason" on back)
☐ 654B Wade Boggs HL COR .20 .09
(Wade Whacks 'Em)
☐ 655 Jose Canseco HL .20 .09
(One of a Kind)
☐ 656 Doug Jones HL .05 .02
(Doug Sets Saves)
☐ 657 Rickey Henderson HL .20 .09
(Rickey Rocks 'Em)
☐ 658 Tom Browning HL .05 .02
(Tom Perfect Pitches)
☐ 659 Mike Greenwell HL .05 .02
(Greenwell Gamers)
☐ 660 Boston Red Sox HL .05 .02
(Joe Morgan MG, Sox Sock 'Em)

1989 Score Rookie/Traded

The 1989 Score Rookie and Traded set contains 110 standard-size cards. The set was issued exclusively in factory set form through hobby dealers. The set was distributed in a blue box with 10 Magic Motion trivia cards. The fronts have coral green borders with pink diamonds at the bottom. Cards 1-80 feature traded players; cards 81-110 feature 1989 rookies. Rookie Cards in this set include Jim Abbott, Joey (Albert) Belle, Ken Griffey Jr., Ken Hill and John Wetteland.

	MINT	NRMT
COMP.FACT.SET (110)	10.00	4.50
COMMON CARD (1T-110T)	.05	.02

☐ 1T Rafael Palmeiro .20 .09
☐ 2T Nolan Ryan 1.50 .70
☐ 3T Jack Clark .10 .05
☐ 4T Dave LaPoint .05 .02
☐ 5T Mike Moore .05 .02
☐ 6T Pete O'Brien .05 .02
☐ 7T Jeffrey Leonard .05 .02
☐ 8T Rob Murphy .05 .02
☐ 9T Tom Herr .05 .02
☐ 10T Claudell Washington .05 .02
☐ 11T Mike Pagliarulo .05 .02
☐ 12T Steve Lake .05 .02
☐ 13T Spike Owen .05 .02
☐ 14T Andy Hawkins .05 .02
☐ 15T Todd Benzinger .05 .02
☐ 16T Mookie Wilson .10 .05
☐ 17T Bert Blyleven .10 .05
☐ 18T Jeff Treadway .05 .02
☐ 19T Bruce Hurst .05 .02
☐ 20T Steve Sax .05 .02
☐ 21T Juan Samuel .05 .02
☐ 22T Jesse Barfield .05 .02
☐ 23T Carmen Castillo .05 .02
☐ 24T Terry Leach .05 .02
☐ 25T Mark Langston .05 .02
☐ 26T Eric King .05 .02
☐ 27T Steve Balboni .05 .02
☐ 28T Len Dykstra .10 .05
☐ 29T Keith Moreland .05 .02
☐ 30T Terry Kennedy .05 .02
☐ 31T Eddie Murray .20 .09
☐ 32T Mitch Williams .05 .02
☐ 33T Jeff Parrett .05 .02
☐ 34T Wally Backman .05 .02
☐ 35T Julio Franco .10 .05
☐ 36T Lance Parrish .05 .02
☐ 37T Nick Esasky .05 .02
☐ 38T Luis Polonia .05 .02
☐ 39T Kevin Gross .05 .02
☐ 40T John Dopson .05 .02
☐ 41T Willie Randolph .10 .05
☐ 42T Jim Clancy .05 .02
☐ 43T Tracy Jones .05 .02
☐ 44T Phil Bradley .05 .02
☐ 45T Milt Thompson .05 .02
☐ 46T Chris James .05 .02
☐ 47T Scott Fletcher .05 .02
☐ 48T Kal Daniels .05 .02
☐ 49T Steve Bedrosian .05 .02
☐ 50T Rickey Henderson .20 .09
☐ 51T Dion James .05 .02
☐ 52T Tim Leary .05 .02
☐ 53T Roger McDowell .05 .02

	MINT	NRMT
54T Mel Hall	.05	.02
55T Dickie Thon	.05	.02
56T Zane Smith	.05	.02
57T Danny Heep	.05	.02
58T Bob McClure	.05	.02
59T Brian Holton	.05	.02
60T Randy Ready	.05	.02
61T Bob Melvin	.05	.02
62T Harold Baines	.10	.05
63T Lance McCullers	.05	.02
64T Jody Davis	.05	.02
65T Darrell Evans	.10	.05
66T Joel Youngblood	.05	.02
67T Frank Viola	.05	.02
68T Mike Aldrete	.05	.02
69T Greg Cadaret	.05	.02
70T John Kruk	.10	.05
71T Pat Sheridan	.05	.02
72T Oddibe McDowell	.05	.02
73T Tom Brookens	.05	.02
74T Bob Boone	.10	.05
75T Walt Terrell	.05	.02
76T Joel Skinner	.05	.02
77T Randy Johnson	1.00	.45
78T Felix Fermin	.05	.02
79T Rick Mahler	.05	.02
80T Richard Dotson	.05	.02
81T Cris Carpenter	.05	.02
82T Bill Spiers	.05	.02
83T Junior Felix	.05	.02
84T Joe Girardi	.20	.09
85T Jerome Walton	.20	.09
86T Greg Litton	.05	.02
87T Greg W.Harris	.05	.02
88T Jim Abbott	.20	.09
89T Kevin Brown	.20	.09
90T John Wetteland	.25	.11
91T Gary Wayne	.05	.02
92T Rich Monteleone	.05	.02
93T Bob Geren	.05	.02
94T Clay Parker	.05	.02
95T Steve Finley	.25	.11
96T Gregg Olson	.10	.05
97T Ken Patterson	.05	.02
98T Ken Hill	.40	.18
99T Scott Scudder	.05	.02
100T Ken Griffey Jr.	6.00	2.70
101T Jeff Brantley	.05	.02
102T Donn Pall	.05	.02
103T Carlos Martinez	.05	.02
104T Joe Oliver	.10	.05
105T Omar Vizquel	.40	.18
106T Joey Belle	2.00	.90
107T Kenny Rogers	.10	.05
108T Mark Carreon	.05	.02
109T Rolando Roomes	.05	.02
110T Pete Harnisch	.10	.05

1989 Score Hottest 100 Rookies

This set was distributed by Publications International in January 1989 through many retail stores and chains; the card set was packaged along with a colorful 48-page book for a suggested retail price of 12.95. Supposedly 225,000 sets were produced. The cards measure the standard size and show full color on both sides of the card. The cards were produced by Score as indicated on the card backs. The set is subtitled "Rising Star" on the reverse. The first six cards (1-6) of a 12-card set of Score's trivia cards, subtitled "Rookies to Remember" is included along with each set. This set is distinguished by the sharp blue borders and the player's first initial inside a yellow triangle in the lower left corner of the obverse. The set features Dave Justice appearing one year before his Rookie Card year.

	MINT	NRMT
COMPLETE SET (100)	10.00	4.50
COMMON CARD (1-100)	.05	.02
1 Gregg Jefferies	.40	.18
2 Vicente Palacios	.05	.02
3 Cameron Drew	.05	.02
4 Doug Dascenzo	.05	.02
5 Luis Medina	.05	.02
6 Craig Worthington	.05	.02
7 Rob Ducey	.05	.02
8 Hal Morris	.10	.05
9 Bill Brennan	.05	.02
10 Gary Sheffield	1.50	.70
11 Mike Devereaux	.05	.02
12 Hensley Meulens	.05	.02
13 Carlos Quintana	.05	.02
14 Todd Frohwirth	.05	.02
15 Scott Lusader	.05	.02
16 Mark Carreon	.05	.02
17 Torey Lovullo	.05	.02
18 Randy Velarde	.05	.02
19 Billy Bean	.05	.02
20 Lance Blankenship	.05	.02
21 Chris Gwynn	.05	.02
22 Felix Jose	.05	.02
23 Derek Lilliquist	.05	.02
24 Gary Thurman	.05	.02
25 Ron Jones	.05	.02
26 Dave Justice	2.00	.90
27 Johnny Paredes	.05	.02
28 Tim Jones	.05	.02
29 Jose Gonzalez	.05	.02
30 Geronimo Berroa	.25	.11
31 Trevor Wilson	.05	.02
32 Morris Madden	.05	.02
33 Lance Johnson	.40	.18
34 Marvin Freeman	.05	.02
35 Jose Cecena	.05	.02
36 Jim Corsi	.05	.02
37 Rolando Roomes	.05	.02
38 Scott Medvin	.05	.02
39 Charlie Hayes	.25	.11
40 Edgar Martinez	.50	.23
41 Van Snider	.05	.02
42 John Fishel	.05	.02
43 Bruce Fields	.05	.02
44 Darryl Hamilton	.15	.07
45 Tom Prince	.05	.02
46 Kirt Manwaring	.05	.02
47 Steve Searcy	.05	.02
48 Mike Harkey	.05	.02
49 German Gonzalez	.05	.02
50 Tony Perezchica	.05	.02
51 Chad Kreuter	.05	.02
52 Luis DeLosSantos	.05	.02
53 Steve Curry	.05	.02
54 Greg Briley	.05	.02
55 Ramon Martinez	.40	.18
56 Ron Tingley	.05	.02
57 Randy Kramer	.05	.02
58 Alex Madrid	.05	.02
59 Kevin Reimer	.05	.02
60 Dave Otto	.05	.02
61 Ken Patterson	.05	.02
62 Keith Miller	.05	.02
63 Randy Johnson	2.00	.90
64 Dwight Smith	.10	.05
65 Eric Yelding	.05	.02
66 Bob Geren	.05	.02
67 Shane Turner	.05	.02
68 Tom Gordon	.30	.14
69 Jeff Huson	.05	.02
70 Marty Brown	.05	.02
71 Nelson Santovenia	.05	.02
72 Roberto Alomar	1.00	.45
73 Mike Schooler	.05	.02
74 Pete Smith	.05	.02
75 John Costello	.05	.02
76 Chris Sabo	.05	.02
77 Damon Berryhill	.05	.02
78 Mark Grace	1.25	.55
79 Melido Perez	.05	.02
80 Al Leiter	.25	.11
81 Todd Stottlemyre	.15	.07
82 Mackey Sasser	.05	.02
83 Don August	.05	.02
84 Jeff Treadway	.05	.02
85 Jody Reed	.05	.02
86 Mike Campbell	.05	.02
87 Ron Gant	.40	.18
88 Ricky Jordan	.05	.02
89 Terry Clark	.05	.02
90 Roberto Kelly	.10	.05
91 Pat Borders	.05	.02
92 Bryan Harvey	.05	.02
93 Joey Meyer	.05	.02
94 Tim Belcher	.05	.02
95 Walt Weiss	.10	.05
96 Dave Gallagher	.05	.02
97 Mike Macfarlane	.05	.02
98 Craig Biggio	1.00	.45
99 Jack Armstrong	.05	.02
100 Todd Burns	.05	.02

1989 Score Hottest 100 Stars

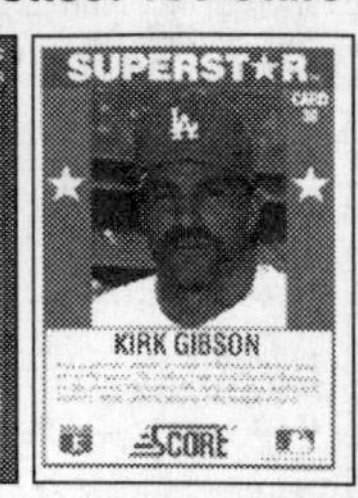

This set was distributed by Publications International in January 1989 through many retail stores and chains; the card set was packaged along with a colorful 48-page book for a suggested retail price of 12.95. Supposedly 225,000 sets were produced. The cards measure the standard size and show full color on both sides of the card. The cards were produced by Score as indicated on the card backs. The set is subtitled "Superstar" on the reverse. The last six cards (7-12) of a 12-card set of Score's trivia cards, subtitled "Rookies to Remember" is included along with each set. This set is distinguished by the sharp red borders and the player's first initial inside a yellow triangle in the upper left corner of the obverse.

	MINT	NRMT
COMPLETE SET (100)	10.00	4.50
COMMON CARD (1-100)	.05	.02
1 Jose Canseco	.30	.14
2 David Cone	.30	.14
3 Dave Winfield	.40	.18
4 George Brett	1.25	.55
5 Frank Viola	.05	.02
6 Cory Snyder	.05	.02
7 Alan Trammell	.15	.07
8 Dwight Evans	.10	.05
9 Tim Leary	.05	.02
10 Don Mattingly	1.25	.55
11 Kirby Puckett	1.25	.55
12 Carney Lansford	.05	.02
13 Dennis Martinez	.10	.05
14 Kent Hrbek	.10	.05
15 Dwight Gooden	.10	.05
16 Dennis Eckersley	.15	.07
17 Kevin Seitzer	.05	.02
18 Lee Smith	.10	.05
19 Danny Tartabull	.05	.02
20 Gerald Perry	.05	.02
21 Gary Gaetti	.10	.05
22 Rick Reuschel	.10	.05
23 Keith Hernandez	.10	.05
24 Jeff Reardon	.10	.05
25 Mark McGwire	1.25	.55
26 Juan Samuel	.05	.02
27 Jack Clark	.05	.02
28 Robin Yount	.40	.18
29 Steve Bedrosian	.05	.02
30 Kirk Gibson	.15	.07
31 Barry Bonds	.50	.23
32 Dan Plesac	.05	.02
33 Steve Sax	.05	.02
34 Jeff M. Robinson	.05	.02
35 Orel Hershiser	.10	.05
36 Julio Franco	.10	.05
37 Dave Righetti	.05	.02
38 Bob Knepper	.05	.02
39 Carlton Fisk	.25	.11
40 Tony Gwynn	1.50	.70
41 Doug Jones	.05	.02
42 Bobby Bonilla	.15	.07
43 Ellis Burks	.15	.07
44 Pedro Guerrero	.05	.02
45 Rickey Henderson	.50	.23
46 Glenn Davis	.05	.02
47 Benito Santiago	.05	.02
48 Greg Maddux	2.00	.90
49 Teddy Higuera	.05	.02
50 Darryl Strawberry	.10	.05
51 Ozzie Guillen	.05	.02
52 Barry Larkin	.60	.25
53 Tony Fernandez	.05	.02
54 Ryne Sandberg	.75	.35
55 Joe Carter	.25	.11
56 Rafael Palmeiro	.50	.23
57 Paul Molitor	.40	.18
58 Eric Davis	.10	.05

Card	MINT	NRMT
☐ 59 Mike Henneman	.05	.02
☐ 60 Mike Scott	.05	.02
☐ 61 Tom Browning	.05	.02
☐ 62 Mark Davis	.05	.02
☐ 63 Tom Henke	.05	.02
☐ 64 Nolan Ryan	2.50	1.10
☐ 65 Fred McGriff	.40	.18
☐ 66 Dale Murphy	.25	.11
☐ 67 Mark Langston	.05	.02
☐ 68 Bobby Thigpen	.05	.02
☐ 69 Mark Gubicza	.05	.02
☐ 70 Mike Greenwell	.10	.05
☐ 71 Ron Darling	.05	.02
☐ 72 Gerald Young	.05	.02
☐ 73 Wally Joyner	.10	.05
☐ 74 Andres Galarraga	.50	.23
☐ 75 Danny Jackson	.05	.02
☐ 76 Mike Schmidt	.60	.25
☐ 77 Cal Ripken	2.00	.90
☐ 78 Alvin Davis	.05	.02
☐ 79 Bruce Hurst	.05	.02
☐ 80 Andre Dawson	.25	.11
☐ 81 Bob Boone	.10	.05
☐ 82 Harold Reynolds	.10	.05
☐ 83 Eddie Murray	.60	.25
☐ 84 Robby Thompson	.05	.02
☐ 85 Will Clark	.60	.25
☐ 86 Vince Coleman	.05	.02
☐ 87 Doug Drabek	.10	.05
☐ 88 Ozzie Smith	.75	.35
☐ 89 Bob Welch	.05	.02
☐ 90 Roger Clemens	1.00	.45
☐ 91 George Bell	.05	.02
☐ 92 Andy Van Slyke	.10	.05
☐ 93 Willie McGee	.10	.05
☐ 94 Todd Worrell	.10	.05
☐ 95 Tim Raines	.10	.05
☐ 96 Kevin McReynolds	.05	.02
☐ 97 John Franco	.10	.05
☐ 98 Jim Gott	.05	.02
☐ 99 Johnny Ray	.05	.02
☐ 100 Wade Boggs	.40	.18

1989 Score Scoremasters

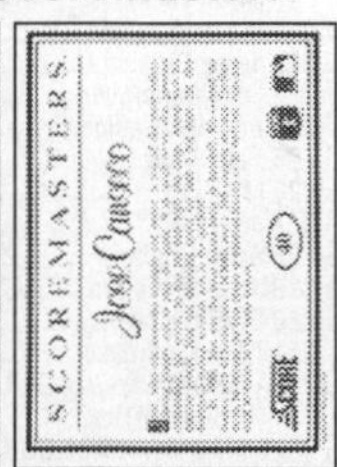

The 1989 Score Scoremasters set contains 42 standard-size cards. The fronts are "pure" with attractively drawn action portraits. The backs feature write-ups of the players' careers. The set was issued in factory set form only.

	MINT	NRMT
COMPLETE FACT. SET (42)	6.00	2.70
COMMON CARD (1-42)	.05	.02
☐ 1 Bo Jackson	.15	.07
☐ 2 Jerome Walton	.05	.02
☐ 3 Cal Ripken	1.50	.70
☐ 4 Mike Scott	.05	.02
☐ 5 Nolan Ryan	1.50	.70
☐ 6 Don Mattingly	.75	.35
☐ 7 Tom Gordon	.05	.02
☐ 8 Jack Morris	.10	.05
☐ 9 Carlton Fisk	.25	.11
☐ 10 Will Clark	.30	.14
☐ 11 George Brett	.60	.25
☐ 12 Kevin Mitchell	.05	.02
☐ 13 Mark Langston	.05	.02
☐ 14 Dave Stewart	.05	.02
☐ 15 Dale Murphy	.25	.11
☐ 16 Gary Gaetti	.10	.05
☐ 17 Wade Boggs	.30	.14
☐ 18 Eric Davis	.10	.05
☐ 19 Kirby Puckett	1.00	.45
☐ 20 Roger Clemens	.75	.35
☐ 21 Orel Hershiser	.10	.05
☐ 22 Mark Grace	.35	.16
☐ 23 Ryne Sandberg	.60	.25
☐ 24 Barry Larkin	.35	.16
☐ 25 Ellis Burks	.25	.11
☐ 26 Dwight Gooden	.10	.05
☐ 27 Ozzie Smith	.60	.25
☐ 28 Andre Dawson	.15	.07
☐ 29 Julio Franco	.10	.05
☐ 30 Ken Griffey Jr.	2.00	.90
☐ 31 Ruben Sierra	.05	.02
☐ 32 Mark McGwire	.60	.25
☐ 33 Andres Galarraga	.25	.11
☐ 34 Joe Carter	.15	.07
☐ 35 Vince Coleman	.05	.02
☐ 36 Mike Greenwell	.05	.02
☐ 37 Tony Gwynn	1.00	.45
☐ 38 Andy Van Slyke	.05	.02
☐ 39 Gregg Jefferies	.25	.11
☐ 40 Jose Canseco	.30	.14
☐ 41 Dave Winfield	.25	.11
☐ 42 Darryl Strawberry	.10	.05

1989 Score Young Superstars I

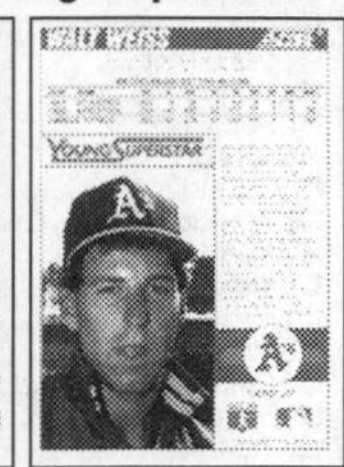

The 1989 Score Young Superstars set I contains 42 standard-size cards. The fronts are pink, white and blue. The vertically oriented backs have color facial shots, 1988 and career stats, and biographical information. One card was included in each 1989 Score rack pack, and the cards were also distributed as a boxed set with five Magic Motion trivia cards.

	MINT	NRMT
COMPLETE SET (42)	5.00	2.20
COMMON CARD (1-42)	.05	.02
☐ 1 Gregg Jefferies	.25	.11
☐ 2 Jody Reed	.05	.02
☐ 3 Mark Grace	.75	.35
☐ 4 Dave Gallagher	.05	.02
☐ 5 Bo Jackson	.15	.07
☐ 6 Jay Buhner	.60	.25
☐ 7 Melido Perez	.05	.02
☐ 8 Bobby Witt	.05	.02
☐ 9 David Cone	.30	.14
☐ 10 Chris Sabo	.05	.02
☐ 11 Pat Borders	.05	.02
☐ 12 Mark Grant	.05	.02
☐ 13 Mike Macfarlane	.05	.02
☐ 14 Mike Jackson	.05	.02
☐ 15 Ricky Jordan	.05	.02
☐ 16 Ron Gant	.25	.11
☐ 17 Al Leiter	.15	.07
☐ 18 Jeff Parrett	.05	.02
☐ 19 Pete Smith	.05	.02
☐ 20 Walt Weiss	.05	.02
☐ 21 Doug Drabek	.10	.05
☐ 22 Kirt Manwaring	.05	.02
☐ 23 Keith Miller	.05	.02
☐ 24 Damon Berryhill	.05	.02
☐ 25 Gary Sheffield	1.00	.45
☐ 26 Brady Anderson	1.00	.45
☐ 27 Mitch Williams	.05	.02
☐ 28 Roberto Alomar	.75	.35
☐ 29 Bobby Thigpen	.05	.02
☐ 30 Bryan Harvey UER (47 games in '87)	.10	.05
☐ 31 Jose Rijo	.05	.02
☐ 32 Dave West	.05	.02
☐ 33 Joey Meyer	.05	.02
☐ 34 Allan Anderson	.05	.02
☐ 35 Rafael Palmeiro	.50	.23
☐ 36 Tim Belcher	.05	.02
☐ 37 John Smiley	.05	.02
☐ 38 Mackey Sasser	.05	.02
☐ 39 Greg Maddux	2.00	.90
☐ 40 Ramon Martinez	.50	.23
☐ 41 Randy Myers	.15	.07
☐ 42 Scott Bankhead	.05	.02

1989 Score Young Superstars II

The 1989 Score Young Superstars II set contains 42 standard-size cards. The fronts are orange, white and purple. The vertically oriented backs have color facial shots, 1988 and career stats, and biographical information. The cards were distributed as a boxed set with five Magic Motion trivia cards.

	MINT	NRMT
COMPLETE SET (42)	4.00	1.80
COMMON CARD (1-42)	.05	.02
☐ 1 Sandy Alomar Jr.	.40	.18
☐ 2 Tom Gordon	.10	.05
☐ 3 Ron Jones	.05	.02
☐ 4 Todd Burns	.05	.02
☐ 5 Paul O'Neill	.25	.11
☐ 6 Gene Larkin	.05	.02
☐ 7 Eric King	.05	.02
☐ 8 Jeff M. Robinson	.05	.02
☐ 9 Bill Wegman	.05	.02
☐ 10 Cecil Espy	.05	.02
☐ 11 Jose Guzman	.05	.02
☐ 12 Kelly Gruber	.05	.02
☐ 13 Duane Ward	.05	.02
☐ 14 Mark Gubicza	.05	.02
☐ 15 Norm Charlton	.10	.05
☐ 16 Jose Oquendo	.05	.02
☐ 17 Geronimo Berroa	.10	.05
☐ 18 Ken Griffey Jr.	3.00	1.35
☐ 19 Lance McCullers	.05	.02
☐ 20 Todd Stottlemyre	.10	.05
☐ 21 Craig Worthington	.05	.02
☐ 22 Mike Devereaux	.05	.02
☐ 23 Tom Glavine	.50	.23
☐ 24 Dale Sveum	.05	.02
☐ 25 Roberto Kelly	.10	.05
☐ 26 Luis Medina	.05	.02
☐ 27 Steve Searcy	.05	.02
☐ 28 Don August	.05	.02
☐ 29 Shawn Hillegas	.05	.02
☐ 30 Mike Campbell	.05	.02
☐ 31 Mike Harkey	.05	.02
☐ 32 Randy Johnson	1.00	.45
☐ 33 Craig Biggio	.75	.35
☐ 34 Mike Schooler	.05	.02
☐ 35 Andres Thomas	.05	.02
☐ 36 Jerome Walton	.05	.02
☐ 37 Cris Carpenter	.05	.02
☐ 38 Kevin Mitchell	.10	.05
☐ 39 Eddie Williams	.05	.02
☐ 40 Chad Kreuter	.05	.02
☐ 41 Danny Jackson	.05	.02
☐ 42 Kurt Stillwell	.05	.02

1990 Score

The 1990 Score set contains 704 standard-size cards. The front borders are red, blue, green or white. The vertically oriented backs are white with borders that match the fronts, and feature color mugshots. Subsets include Draft Picks (661-682) and Dream Team (683-695). Rookie Cards of note include Juan Gonzalez, Marquis Grissom, Dave Justice, Chuck Knoblauch, Ben McDonald, Dean Palmer, Sammy Sosa, Frank Thomas, Mo Vaughn, Larry Walker and Bernie Williams. A ten-card set of Dream Team Rookies was inserted into each hobby factory set, but was not included in retail factory sets.

	MINT	NRMT
COMPLETE SET (704)	10.00	4.50
COMP.RETAIL SET (704)	10.00	4.50
COMP.HOBBY SET (714)	12.00	5.50
COMMON CARD (1-704)	.05	.02
☐ 1 Don Mattingly	.30	.14
☐ 2 Cal Ripken	.75	.35

☐ 3 Dwight Evans .10 .05
☐ 4 Barry Bonds .25 .11
☐ 5 Kevin McReynolds .05 .02
☐ 6 Ozzie Guillen .05 .02
☐ 7 Terry Kennedy .05 .02
☐ 8 Bryan Harvey .05 .02
☐ 9 Alan Trammell .10 .05
☐ 10 Cory Snyder .05 .02
☐ 11 Jody Reed .05 .02
☐ 12 Roberto Alomar .25 .11
☐ 13 Pedro Guerrero .05 .02
☐ 14 Gary Redus .05 .02
☐ 15 Marty Barrett .05 .02
☐ 16 Ricky Jordan .05 .02
☐ 17 Joe Magrane .05 .02
☐ 18 Sid Fernandez .05 .02
☐ 19 Richard Dotson .05 .02
☐ 20 Jack Clark .10 .05
☐ 21 Bob Walk .05 .02
☐ 22 Ron Karkovice .05 .02
☐ 23 Lenny Harris .05 .02
☐ 24 Phil Bradley .05 .02
☐ 25 Andres Galarraga .20 .09
☐ 26 Brian Downing .05 .02
☐ 27 Dave Martinez .05 .02
☐ 28 Eric King .05 .02
☐ 29 Barry Lyons .05 .02
☐ 30 Dave Schmidt .05 .02
☐ 31 Mike Boddicker .05 .02
☐ 32 Tom Foley .05 .02
☐ 33 Brady Anderson .20 .09
☐ 34 Jim Presley .05 .02
☐ 35 Lance Parrish .05 .02
☐ 36 Von Hayes .05 .02
☐ 37 Lee Smith .20 .09
☐ 38 Herm Winningham .05 .02
☐ 39 Alejandro Pena .05 .02
☐ 40 Mike Scott .05 .02
☐ 41 Joe Orsulak .05 .02
☐ 42 Rafael Ramirez .05 .02
☐ 43 Gerald Young .05 .02
☐ 44 Dick Schofield .05 .02
☐ 45 Dave Smith .05 .02
☐ 46 Dave Magadan .05 .02
☐ 47 Dennis Martinez .10 .05
☐ 48 Greg Minton .05 .02
☐ 49 Milt Thompson .05 .02
☐ 50 Orel Hershiser .10 .05
☐ 51 Bip Roberts .05 .02
☐ 52 Jerry Browne .05 .02
☐ 53 Bob Ojeda .05 .02
☐ 54 Fernando Valenzuela .10 .05
☐ 55 Matt Nokes .05 .02
☐ 56 Brook Jacoby .05 .02
☐ 57 Frank Tanana .05 .02
☐ 58 Scott Fletcher .05 .02
☐ 59 Ron Oester .05 .02
☐ 60 Bob Boone .10 .05
☐ 61 Dan Gladden .05 .02
☐ 62 Darnell Coles .05 .02
☐ 63 Gregg Olson .05 .02
☐ 64 Todd Burns .05 .02
☐ 65 Todd Benzinger .05 .02
☐ 66 Dale Murphy .20 .09
☐ 67 Mike Flanagan .05 .02
☐ 68 Jose Oquendo .05 .02
☐ 69 Cecil Espy .05 .02
☐ 70 Chris Sabo .05 .02
☐ 71 Shane Rawley .05 .02
☐ 72 Tom Brunansky .05 .02
☐ 73 Vance Law .05 .02
☐ 74 B.J. Surhoff .10 .05
☐ 75 Lou Whitaker .10 .05
☐ 76 Ken Caminiti UER .20 .09
(Euclid, Ohio should be Hanford, California)
☐ 77 Nelson Liriano .05 .02
☐ 78 Tommy Gregg .05 .02
☐ 79 Don Slaught .05 .02
☐ 80 Eddie Murray .20 .09
☐ 81 Joe Boever .05 .02
☐ 82 Charlie Leibrandt .05 .02
☐ 83 Jose Lind .05 .02
☐ 84 Tony Phillips .05 .02
☐ 85 Mitch Webster .05 .02
☐ 86 Dan Plesac .05 .02
☐ 87 Rick Mahler .05 .02
☐ 88 Steve Lyons .05 .02
☐ 89 Tony Fernandez .05 .02
☐ 90 Ryne Sandberg .25 .11
☐ 91 Nick Esasky .05 .02
☐ 92 Luis Salazar .05 .02
☐ 93 Pete Incaviglia .05 .02
☐ 94 Ivan Calderon .05 .02
☐ 95 Jeff Treadway .05 .02
☐ 96 Kurt Stillwell .05 .02
☐ 97 Gary Sheffield .25 .11
☐ 98 Jeffrey Leonard .05 .02
☐ 99 Andres Thomas .05 .02
☐ 100 Roberto Kelly .05 .02
☐ 101 Alvaro Espinoza .05 .02
☐ 102 Greg Gagne .05 .02
☐ 103 John Farrell .05 .02
☐ 104 Willie Wilson .05 .02
☐ 105 Glenn Braggs .05 .02
☐ 106 Chet Lemon .05 .02
☐ 107A Jamie Moyer ERR .05 .02
(Scintilating)
☐ 107B Jamie Moyer COR .10 .05
(Scintillating)
☐ 108 Chuck Crim .05 .02
☐ 109 Dave Valle .05 .02
☐ 110 Walt Weiss .05 .02
☐ 111 Larry Sheets .05 .02
☐ 112 Don Robinson .05 .02
☐ 113 Danny Heep .05 .02
☐ 114 Carmelo Martinez .05 .02
☐ 115 Dave Gallagher .05 .02
☐ 116 Mike LaValliere .05 .02
☐ 117 Bob McClure .05 .02
☐ 118 Rene Gonzales .05 .02
☐ 119 Mark Parent .05 .02
☐ 120 Wally Joyner .10 .05
☐ 121 Mark Gubicza .05 .02
☐ 122 Tony Pena .05 .02
☐ 123 Carmen Castillo .05 .02
☐ 124 Howard Johnson .05 .02
☐ 125 Steve Sax .05 .02
☐ 126 Tim Belcher .05 .02
☐ 127 Tim Burke .05 .02
☐ 128 Al Newman .05 .02
☐ 129 Dennis Rasmussen .05 .02
☐ 130 Doug Jones .05 .02
☐ 131 Fred Lynn .05 .02
☐ 132 Jeff Hamilton .05 .02
☐ 133 German Gonzalez .05 .02
☐ 134 John Morris .05 .02
☐ 135 Dave Parker .10 .05
☐ 136 Gary Pettis .05 .02
☐ 137 Dennis Boyd .05 .02
☐ 138 Candy Maldonado .05 .02
☐ 139 Rick Cerone .05 .02
☐ 140 George Brett .40 .18
☐ 141 Dave Clark .05 .02
☐ 142 Dickie Thon .05 .02
☐ 143 Junior Ortiz .05 .02
☐ 144 Don August .05 .02
☐ 145 Gary Gaetti .10 .05
☐ 146 Kirt Manwaring .05 .02
☐ 147 Jeff Reed .05 .02
☐ 148 Jose Alvarez .05 .02
☐ 149 Mike Schooler .05 .02
☐ 150 Mark Grace .20 .09
☐ 151 Geronimo Berroa .10 .05
☐ 152 Barry Jones .05 .02
☐ 153 Geno Petralli .05 .02
☐ 154 Jim Deshaies .05 .02
☐ 155 Barry Larkin .20 .09
☐ 156 Alfredo Griffin .05 .02
☐ 157 Tom Henke .05 .02
☐ 158 Mike Jeffcoat .05 .02
☐ 159 Bob Welch .05 .02
☐ 160 Julio Franco .10 .05
☐ 161 Henry Cotto .05 .02
☐ 162 Terry Steinbach .10 .05
☐ 163 Damon Berryhill .05 .02
☐ 164 Tim Crews .05 .02
☐ 165 Tom Browning .05 .02
☐ 166 Fred Manrique .05 .02
☐ 167 Harold Reynolds .05 .02
☐ 168A Ron Hassey ERR .05 .02
(27 on back)
☐ 168B Ron Hassey COR .50 .23
(24 on back)
☐ 169 Shawon Dunston .05 .02
☐ 170 Bobby Bonilla .10 .05
☐ 171 Tommy Herr .05 .02
☐ 172 Mike Heath .05 .02
☐ 173 Rich Gedman .05 .02
☐ 174 Bill Ripken .05 .02
☐ 175 Pete O'Brien .05 .02
☐ 176A Lloyd McClendon ERR .50 .23
(Uniform number on back listed as 1)
☐ 176B Lloyd McClendon COR .05 .02
(Uniform number on back listed as 10)
☐ 177 Brian Holton .05 .02
☐ 178 Jeff Blauser .10 .05
☐ 179 Jim Eisenreich .10 .05
☐ 180 Bert Blyleven .10 .05
☐ 181 Rob Murphy .05 .02
☐ 182 Bill Doran .05 .02
☐ 183 Curt Ford .05 .02
☐ 184 Mike Henneman .05 .02
☐ 185 Eric Davis .10 .05
☐ 186 Lance McCullers .05 .02
☐ 187 Steve Davis .05 .02
☐ 188 Bill Wegman .05 .02
☐ 189 Brian Harper .05 .02
☐ 190 Mike Moore .05 .02
☐ 191 Dale Mohorcic .05 .02
☐ 192 Tim Wallach .05 .02
☐ 193 Keith Hernandez .10 .05
☐ 194 Dave Righetti .05 .02
☐ 195A Bret Saberhagen ERR .10 .05
(Joke)
☐ 195B Bret Saberhagen COR .10 .05
(Joker)
☐ 196 Paul Kilgus .05 .02
☐ 197 Bud Black .05 .02
☐ 198 Juan Samuel .05 .02
☐ 199 Kevin Seitzer .05 .02
☐ 200 Darryl Strawberry .10 .05
☐ 201 Dave Stieb .05 .02
☐ 202 Charlie Hough .05 .02
☐ 203 Jack Morris .10 .05
☐ 204 Rance Mulliniks .05 .02
☐ 205 Alvin Davis .05 .02
☐ 206 Jack Howell .05 .02
☐ 207 Ken Patterson .05 .02
☐ 208 Terry Pendleton .10 .05
☐ 209 Craig Lefferts .05 .02
☐ 210 Kevin Brown UER .20 .09
(First mention of '89 Rangers should be '88)
☐ 211 Dan Petry .05 .02
☐ 212 Dave Leiper .05 .02
☐ 213 Daryl Boston .05 .02
☐ 214 Kevin Hickey .05 .02
☐ 215 Mike Krukow .05 .02
☐ 216 Terry Francona .05 .02
☐ 217 Kirk McCaskill .05 .02
☐ 218 Scott Bailes .05 .02
☐ 219 Bob Forsch .05 .02
☐ 220A Mike Aldrete ERR .05 .02
(25 on back)
☐ 220B Mike Aldrete COR .10 .05
(24 on back)
☐ 221 Steve Buechele .05 .02
☐ 222 Jesse Barfield .05 .02
☐ 223 Juan Berenguer .05 .02
☐ 224 Andy McGaffigan .05 .02
☐ 225 Pete Smith .05 .02
☐ 226 Mike Witt .05 .02
☐ 227 Jay Howell .05 .02
☐ 228 Scott Bradley .05 .02
☐ 229 Jerome Walton .05 .02
☐ 230 Greg Swindell .05 .02
☐ 231 Atlee Hammaker .05 .02
☐ 232A Mike Devereaux ERR .05 .02
(RF on front)
☐ 232B Mike Devereaux COR .50 .23
(CF on front)
☐ 233 Ken Hill .20 .09
☐ 234 Craig Worthington .05 .02
☐ 235 Scott Terry .05 .02
☐ 236 Brett Butler .10 .05
☐ 237 Doyle Alexander .05 .02
☐ 238 Dave Anderson .05 .02
☐ 239 Bob Milacki .05 .02
☐ 240 Dwight Smith .05 .02
☐ 241 Otis Nixon .10 .05
☐ 242 Pat Tabler .05 .02
☐ 243 Derek Lilliquist .05 .02
☐ 244 Danny Tartabull .05 .02
☐ 245 Wade Boggs .20 .09
☐ 246 Scott Garrelts .05 .02
(Should say Relief Pitcher on front)
☐ 247 Spike Owen .05 .02
☐ 248 Norm Charlton .05 .02
☐ 249 Gerald Perry .05 .02
☐ 250 Nolan Ryan .75 .35
☐ 251 Kevin Gross .05 .02
☐ 252 Randy Milligan .05 .02
☐ 253 Mike LaCoss .05 .02
☐ 254 Dave Bergman .05 .02
☐ 255 Tony Gwynn .50 .23
☐ 256 Felix Fermin .05 .02
☐ 257 Greg W. Harris .05 .02
☐ 258 Junior Felix .05 .02
☐ 259 Mark Davis .05 .02
☐ 260 Vince Coleman .05 .02
☐ 261 Paul Gibson .05 .02
☐ 262 Mitch Williams .05 .02
☐ 263 Jeff Russell .05 .02
☐ 264 Omar Vizquel .20 .09
☐ 265 Andre Dawson .20 .09
☐ 266 Storm Davis .05 .02
☐ 267 Guillermo Hernandez .05 .02

☐ 268 Mike Felder .05 .02
☐ 269 Tom Candiotti .05 .02
☐ 270 Bruce Hurst .05 .02
☐ 271 Fred McGriff .20 .09
☐ 272 Glenn Davis .05 .02
☐ 273 John Franco .10 .05
☐ 274 Rich Yett .05 .02
☐ 275 Craig Biggio .20 .09
☐ 276 Gene Larkin .05 .02
☐ 277 Rob Dibble .05 .02
☐ 278 Randy Bush .05 .02
☐ 279 Kevin Bass .05 .02
☐ 280A Bo Jackson ERR .20 .09
(Watham)
☐ 280B Bo Jackson COR .20 .09
(Wathan)
☐ 281 Wally Backman .05 .02
☐ 282 Larry Andersen .05 .02
☐ 283 Chris Bosio .05 .02
☐ 284 Juan Agosto .05 .02
☐ 285 Ozzie Smith .25 .11
☐ 286 George Bell .05 .02
☐ 287 Rex Hudler .05 .02
☐ 288 Pat Borders .05 .02
☐ 289 Danny Jackson .05 .02
☐ 290 Carlton Fisk .20 .09
☐ 291 Tracy Jones .05 .02
☐ 292 Allan Anderson .05 .02
☐ 293 Johnny Ray .05 .02
☐ 294 Lee Guetterman .05 .02
☐ 295 Paul O'Neill .10 .05
☐ 296 Carney Lansford .10 .05
☐ 297 Tom Brookens .05 .02
☐ 298 Claudell Washington .05 .02
☐ 299 Hubie Brooks .05 .02
☐ 300 Will Clark .20 .09
☐ 301 Kenny Rogers .10 .05
☐ 302 Darrell Evans .10 .05
☐ 303 Greg Briley .05 .02
☐ 304 Donn Pall .05 .02
☐ 305 Teddy Higuera .05 .02
☐ 306 Dan Pasqua .05 .02
☐ 307 Dave Winfield .20 .09
☐ 308 Dennis Powell .05 .02
☐ 309 Jose DeLeon .05 .02
☐ 310 Roger Clemens UER .40 .18
(Dominate, should
say dominant)
☐ 311 Melido Perez .05 .02
☐ 312 Devon White .05 .02
☐ 313 Dwight Gooden .10 .05
☐ 314 Carlos Martinez .05 .02
☐ 315 Dennis Eckersley .20 .09
☐ 316 Clay Parker UER .05 .02
(Height 6'11")
☐ 317 Rick Honeycutt .05 .02
☐ 318 Tim Laudner .05 .02
☐ 319 Joe Carter .20 .09
☐ 320 Robin Yount .20 .09
☐ 321 Felix Jose .05 .02
☐ 322 Mickey Tettleton .10 .05
☐ 323 Mike Gallego .05 .02
☐ 324 Edgar Martinez .20 .09
☐ 325 Dave Henderson .05 .02
☐ 326 Chili Davis .10 .05
☐ 327 Steve Balboni .05 .02
☐ 328 Jody Davis .05 .02
☐ 329 Shawn Hillegas .05 .02
☐ 330 Jim Abbott .10 .05
☐ 331 John Dopson .05 .02
☐ 332 Mark Williamson .05 .02
☐ 333 Jeff D. Robinson .05 .02
☐ 334 John Smiley .10 .05
☐ 335 Bobby Thigpen .05 .02
☐ 336 Garry Templeton .05 .02
☐ 337 Marvell Wynne .05 .02
☐ 338A Ken Griffey Sr. ERR .05 .02
(Uniform number on
back listed as 25)
☐ 338B Ken Griffey Sr. COR .50 .23
(Uniform number on
back listed as 30)
☐ 339 Steve Finley .20 .09
☐ 340 Ellis Burks .20 .09
☐ 341 Frank Williams .05 .02
☐ 342 Mike Morgan .05 .02
☐ 343 Kevin Mitchell .10 .05
☐ 344 Joel Youngblood .05 .02
☐ 345 Mike Greenwell .05 .02
☐ 346 Glenn Wilson .05 .02
☐ 347 John Costello .05 .02
☐ 348 Wes Gardner .05 .02
☐ 349 Jeff Ballard .05 .02
☐ 350 Mark Thurmond UER .05 .02
(ERA is 192,
should be 1.92)
☐ 351 Randy Myers .10 .05
☐ 352 Shawn Abner .05 .02
☐ 353 Jesse Orosco .05 .02
☐ 354 Greg Walker .05 .02
☐ 355 Pete Harnisch .05 .02
☐ 356 Steve Farr .05 .02
☐ 357 Dave LaPoint .05 .02
☐ 358 Willie Fraser .05 .02
☐ 359 Mickey Hatcher .05 .02
☐ 360 Rickey Henderson .20 .09
☐ 361 Mike Fitzgerald .05 .02
☐ 362 Bill Schroeder .05 .02
☐ 363 Mark Carreon .05 .02
☐ 364 Ron Jones .05 .02
☐ 365 Jeff Montgomery .10 .05
☐ 366 Bill Krueger .05 .02
☐ 367 John Cangelosi .05 .02
☐ 368 Jose Gonzalez .05 .02
☐ 369 Greg Hibbard .05 .02
☐ 370 John Smoltz .20 .09
☐ 371 Jeff Brantley .10 .05
☐ 372 Frank White .10 .05
☐ 373 Ed Whitson .05 .02
☐ 374 Willie McGee .05 .02
☐ 375 Jose Canseco .20 .09
☐ 376 Randy Ready .05 .02
☐ 377 Don Aase .05 .02
☐ 378 Tony Armas .05 .02
☐ 379 Steve Bedrosian .05 .02
☐ 380 Chuck Finley .10 .05
☐ 381 Kent Hrbek .10 .05
☐ 382 Jim Gantner .05 .02
☐ 383 Mel Hall .05 .02
☐ 384 Mike Marshall .05 .02
☐ 385 Mark McGwire .40 .18
☐ 386 Wayne Tolleson .05 .02
☐ 387 Brian Holman .05 .02
☐ 388 John Wetteland .20 .09
☐ 389 Darren Daulton .10 .05
☐ 390 Rob Deer .05 .02
☐ 391 John Moses .05 .02
☐ 392 Todd Worrell .05 .02
☐ 393 Chuck Cary .05 .02
☐ 394 Stan Javier .05 .02
☐ 395 Willie Randolph .10 .05
☐ 396 Bill Buckner .05 .02
☐ 397 Robby Thompson .05 .02
☐ 398 Mike Scioscia .05 .02
☐ 399 Lonnie Smith .05 .02
☐ 400 Kirby Puckett .40 .18
☐ 401 Mark Langston .05 .02
☐ 402 Danny Darwin .05 .02
☐ 403 Greg Maddux .60 .25
☐ 404 Lloyd Moseby .05 .02
☐ 405 Rafael Palmeiro .20 .09
☐ 406 Chad Kreuter .05 .02
☐ 407 Jimmy Key 1.50 .70
☐ 408 Tim Birtsas .05 .02
☐ 409 Tim Raines 1.50 .70
☐ 410 Dave Stewart .10 .05
☐ 411 Eric Yelding .05 .02
☐ 412 Kent Anderson .05 .02
☐ 413 Les Lancaster .05 .02
☐ 414 Rick Dempsey .05 .02
☐ 415 Randy Johnson .30 .14
☐ 416 Gary Carter .20 .09
☐ 417 Rolando Roomes .05 .02
☐ 418 Dan Schatzeder .05 .02
☐ 419 Bryn Smith .05 .02
☐ 420 Ruben Sierra .05 .02
☐ 421 Steve Jeltz .05 .02
☐ 422 Ken Oberkfell .05 .02
☐ 423 Sid Bream .05 .02
☐ 424 Jim Clancy .05 .02
☐ 425 Kelly Gruber .05 .02
☐ 426 Rick Leach .05 .02
☐ 427 Len Dykstra .10 .05
☐ 428 Jeff Pico .05 .02
☐ 429 John Cerutti .05 .02
☐ 430 David Cone .20 .09
☐ 431 Jeff Kunkel .05 .02
☐ 432 Luis Aquino .05 .02
☐ 433 Ernie Whitt .05 .02
☐ 434 Bo Diaz .05 .02
☐ 435 Steve Lake .05 .02
☐ 436 Pat Perry .05 .02
☐ 437 Mike Davis .05 .02
☐ 438 Cecilio Guante .05 .02
☐ 439 Duane Ward .05 .02
☐ 440 Andy Van Slyke .10 .05
☐ 441 Gene Nelson .05 .02
☐ 442 Luis Polonia .05 .02
☐ 443 Kevin Elster .05 .02
☐ 444 Keith Moreland .05 .02
☐ 445 Roger McDowell .05 .02
☐ 446 Ron Darling .05 .02
☐ 447 Ernest Riles .05 .02
☐ 448 Mookie Wilson .05 .02
☐ 449A Billy Spiers ERR .20 .09
(No birth year)
☐ 449B Billy Spiers COR .05 .02
(Born in 1966)
☐ 450 Rick Sutcliffe .05 .02
☐ 451 Nelson Santovenia .05 .02
☐ 452 Andy Allanson .05 .02
☐ 453 Bob Melvin .05 .02
☐ 454 Benito Santiago .05 .02
☐ 455 Jose Uribe .05 .02
☐ 456 Bill Landrum .05 .02
☐ 457 Bobby Witt .05 .02
☐ 458 Kevin Romine .05 .02
☐ 459 Lee Mazzilli .05 .02
☐ 460 Paul Molitor .20 .09
☐ 461 Ramon Martinez .20 .09
☐ 462 Frank DiPino .05 .02
☐ 463 Walt Terrell .05 .02
☐ 464 Bob Geren .05 .02
☐ 465 Rick Reuschel .05 .02
☐ 466 Mark Grant .05 .02
☐ 467 John Kruk .10 .05
☐ 468 Gregg Jefferies .10 .05
☐ 469 R.J. Reynolds .05 .02
☐ 470 Harold Baines 1.50 .70
☐ 471 Dennis Lamp .05 .02
☐ 472 Tom Gordon .05 .02
☐ 473 Terry Puhl .05 .02
☐ 474 Curt Wilkerson .05 .02
☐ 475 Dan Quisenberry .05 .02
☐ 476 Oddibe McDowell .05 .02
☐ 477A Zane Smith ERR .05 .02
(Career ERA .393)
☐ 477B Zane Smith COR .05 .02
(career ERA 3.93)
☐ 478 Franklin Stubbs .05 .02
☐ 479 Wallace Johnson .05 .02
☐ 480 Jay Tibbs .05 .02
☐ 481 Tom Glavine .20 .09
☐ 482 Manny Lee .05 .02
☐ 483 Joe Hesketh UER .05 .02
(Says Rookiess on back,
should say Rookies)
☐ 484 Mike Bielecki .05 .02
☐ 485 Greg Brock .05 .02
☐ 486 Pascual Perez .05 .02
☐ 487 Kirk Gibson 1.50 .70
☐ 488 Scott Sanderson .05 .02
☐ 489 Domingo Ramos .05 .02
☐ 490 Kal Daniels .05 .02
☐ 491A David Wells ERR .50 .23
(Reverse negative
photo on card back)
☐ 491B David Wells COR .05 .02
☐ 492 Jerry Reed .05 .02
☐ 493 Eric Show .05 .02
☐ 494 Mike Pagliarulo .05 .02
☐ 495 Ron Robinson .05 .02
☐ 496 Brad Komminsk .05 .02
☐ 497 Greg Litton .05 .02
☐ 498 Chris James .05 .02
☐ 499 Luis Quinones .05 .02
☐ 500 Frank Viola .05 .02
☐ 501 Tim Teufel UER .05 .02
(Twins '85, the s is
lower case, should
be upper case)
☐ 502 Terry Leach .05 .02
☐ 503 Matt Williams UER .20 .09
(Wearing 10 on front,
listed as 9 on back)
☐ 504 Tim Leary .05 .02
☐ 505 Doug Drabek .05 .02
☐ 506 Mariano Duncan .05 .02
☐ 507 Charlie Hayes .10 .05
☐ 508 Joey Belle .50 .23
☐ 509 Pat Sheridan .05 .02
☐ 510 Mackey Sasser .05 .02
☐ 511 Jose Rijo .05 .02
☐ 512 Mike Smithson .05 .02
☐ 513 Gary Ward .05 .02
☐ 514 Dion James .05 .02
☐ 515 Jim Gott .05 .02
☐ 516 Drew Hall .05 .02
☐ 517 Doug Bair .05 .02
☐ 518 Scott Scudder .05 .02
☐ 519 Rick Aguilera .10 .05
☐ 520 Rafael Belliard .05 .02
☐ 521 Jay Buhner .20 .09
☐ 522 Jeff Reardon .10 .05
☐ 523 Steve Rosenberg .05 .02
☐ 524 Randy Velarde .05 .02
☐ 525 Jeff Musselman .05 .02
☐ 526 Bill Long .05 .02
☐ 527 Gary Wayne .05 .02
☐ 528 Dave Johnson (P) .05 .02
☐ 529 Ron Kittle .05 .02

Card	Mint	NrMt
☐ 530 Erik Hanson UER (5th line on back says seson, should say season)	.10	.05
☐ 531 Steve Wilson	.05	.02
☐ 532 Joey Meyer	.05	.02
☐ 533 Curt Young	.05	.02
☐ 534 Kelly Downs	.05	.02
☐ 535 Joe Girardi	.10	.05
☐ 536 Lance Blankenship	.05	.02
☐ 537 Greg Mathews	.05	.02
☐ 538 Donell Nixon	.05	.02
☐ 539 Mark Knudson	.05	.02
☐ 540 Jeff Wetherby	.05	.02
☐ 541 Darrin Jackson	.05	.02
☐ 542 Terry Mulholland	.05	.02
☐ 543 Eric Hetzel	.05	.02
☐ 544 Rick Reed	.05	.02
☐ 545 Dennis Cook	.05	.02
☐ 546 Mike Jackson	.05	.02
☐ 547 Brian Fisher	.05	.02
☐ 548 Gene Harris	.05	.02
☐ 549 Jeff King	.10	.05
☐ 550 Dave Dravecky	.20	.09
☐ 551 Randy Kutcher	.05	.02
☐ 552 Mark Portugal	.05	.02
☐ 553 Jim Corsi	.05	.02
☐ 554 Todd Stottlemyre	.10	.05
☐ 555 Scott Bankhead	.05	.02
☐ 556 Ken Dayley	.05	.02
☐ 557 Rick Wrona	.05	.02
☐ 558 Sammy Sosa	.75	.35
☐ 559 Keith Miller	.05	.02
☐ 560 Ken Griffey Jr.	1.50	.70
☐ 561A Ryne Sandberg HL ERR (Position on front listed as 3B)	6.00	2.70
☐ 561B Ryne Sandberg HL COR	.20	.09
☐ 562 Billy Hatcher	.05	.02
☐ 563 Jay Bell	.10	.05
☐ 564 Jack Daugherty	.05	.02
☐ 565 Rich Monteleone	.05	.02
☐ 566 Bo Jackson AS-MVP	.20	.09
☐ 567 Tony Fossas	.05	.02
☐ 568 Roy Smith	.05	.02
☐ 569 Jaime Navarro	.05	.02
☐ 570 Lance Johnson	.10	.05
☐ 571 Mike Dyer	.05	.02
☐ 572 Kevin Ritz	.05	.02
☐ 573 Dave West	.05	.02
☐ 574 Gary Mielke	.05	.02
☐ 575 Scott Lusader	.05	.02
☐ 576 Joe Oliver	.05	.02
☐ 577 Sandy Alomar Jr.	.20	.09
☐ 578 Andy Benes UER (Extra comma between day and year)	.20	.09
☐ 579 Tim Jones	.05	.02
☐ 580 Randy McCament	.05	.02
☐ 581 Curt Schilling	.20	.09
☐ 582 John Orton	.05	.02
☐ 583A Milt Cuyler ERR (998 games)	.50	.23
☐ 583B Milt Cuyler COR (98 games; the extra 9 was ghosted out and may still be visible)	.05	.02
☐ 584 Eric Anthony	.10	.05
☐ 585 Greg Vaughn	.10	.05
☐ 586 Deion Sanders	.20	.09
☐ 587 Jose DeJesus	.05	.02
☐ 588 Chip Hale	.05	.02
☐ 589 John Olerud	.20	.09
☐ 590 Steve Olin	.10	.05
☐ 591 Marquis Grissom	.40	.18
☐ 592 Moises Alou	.50	.23
☐ 593 Mark Lemke	.10	.05
☐ 594 Dean Palmer	.25	.11
☐ 595 Robin Ventura	.20	.09
☐ 596 Tino Martinez	.40	.18
☐ 597 Mike Huff	.05	.02
☐ 598 Scott Hemond	.05	.02
☐ 599 Wally Whitehurst	.05	.02
☐ 600 Todd Zeile	.10	.05
☐ 601 Glenallen Hill	.10	.05
☐ 602 Hal Morris	.10	.05
☐ 603 Juan Bell	.05	.02
☐ 604 Bobby Rose	.05	.02
☐ 605 Matt Merullo	.05	.02
☐ 606 Kevin Maas	.10	.05
☐ 607 Randy Nosek	.05	.02
☐ 608A Billy Bates (Text mentions 12 triples in tenth line)	.05	.02
☐ 608B Billy Bates (Text has no mention of triples)	.05	.02
☐ 609 Mike Stanton	.10	.05
☐ 610 Mauro Gozzo	.05	.02
☐ 611 Charles Nagy	.20	.09
☐ 612 Scott Coolbaugh	.05	.02
☐ 613 Jose Vizcaino	.20	.09
☐ 614 Greg Smith	.05	.02
☐ 615 Jeff Huson	.05	.02
☐ 616 Mickey Weston	.05	.02
☐ 617 John Pawlowski	.05	.02
☐ 618A Joe Skalski ERR (27 on back)	.05	.02
☐ 618B Joe Skalski COR (67 on back)	.50	.23
☐ 619 Bernie Williams	.75	.35
☐ 620 Shawn Holman	.05	.02
☐ 621 Gary Eave	.05	.02
☐ 622 Darrin Fletcher UER (Elmherst, should be Elmhurst)	.10	.05
☐ 623 Pat Combs	.05	.02
☐ 624 Mike Blowers	.20	.09
☐ 625 Kevin Appier	.20	.09
☐ 626 Pat Austin	.05	.02
☐ 627 Kelly Mann	.05	.02
☐ 628 Matt Kinzer	.05	.02
☐ 629 Chris Hammond	.05	.02
☐ 630 Dean Wilkins	.05	.02
☐ 631 Larry Walker UER (Uniform number 55 on front and 33 on back; Home is Maple Ridge, not Maple River)	1.00	.45
☐ 632 Blaine Beatty	.05	.02
☐ 633A Tommy Barrett ERR (29 on back)	.05	.02
☐ 633B Tommy Barrett COR (14 on back)	.50	.23
☐ 634 Stan Belinda	.05	.02
☐ 635 Mike (Tex) Smith	.05	.02
☐ 636 Hensley Meulens	.05	.02
☐ 637 Juan Gonzalez UER (Sarasots on back, should be Sarasota)	2.00	.90
☐ 638 Lenny Webster	.05	.02
☐ 639 Mark Gardner	.05	.02
☐ 640 Tommy Greene	.05	.02
☐ 641 Mike Hartley	.05	.02
☐ 642 Phil Stephenson	.05	.02
☐ 643 Kevin Mmahat	.05	.02
☐ 644 Ed Whited	.05	.02
☐ 645 Delino DeShields	.20	.09
☐ 646 Kevin Blankenship	.05	.02
☐ 647 Paul Sorrento	.20	.09
☐ 648 Mike Roesler	.05	.02
☐ 649 Jason Grimsley	.05	.02
☐ 650 Dave Justice	.75	.35
☐ 651 Scott Cooper	.05	.02
☐ 652 Dave Eiland	.05	.02
☐ 653 Mike Munoz	.05	.02
☐ 654 Jeff Fischer	.05	.02
☐ 655 Terry Jorgensen	.05	.02
☐ 656 George Canale	.05	.02
☐ 657 Brian DuBois UER (Misspelled Dubois on card)	.05	.02
☐ 658 Carlos Quintana	.05	.02
☐ 659 Luis de los Santos	.05	.02
☐ 660 Jerald Clark	.05	.02
☐ 661 Donald Harris DC	.05	.02
☐ 662 Paul Coleman DC	.05	.02
☐ 663 Frank Thomas DC	4.00	1.80
☐ 664 Brent Mayne DC	.05	.02
☐ 665 Eddie Zosky DC	.05	.02
☐ 666 Steve Hosey DC	.05	.02
☐ 667 Scott Bryant DC	.05	.02
☐ 668 Tom Goodwin DC	.20	.09
☐ 669 Cal Eldred DC	.20	.09
☐ 670 Earl Cunningham DC	.05	.02
☐ 671 Alan Zinter DC	.05	.02
☐ 672 Chuck Knoblauch DC	.75	.35
☐ 673 Kyle Abbott DC	.05	.02
☐ 674 Roger Salkeld DC	.05	.02
☐ 675 Maurice Vaughn DC	1.25	.55
☐ 676 Keith(Kiki) Jones DC	.05	.02
☐ 677 Tyler Houston DC	.20	.09
☐ 678 Jeff Jackson DC	.05	.02
☐ 679 Greg Gohr DC	.05	.02
☐ 680 Ben McDonald DC	.20	.09
☐ 681 Greg Blosser DC	.05	.02
☐ 682 Willie Greene DC UER Name spelled as Green	.20	.09
☐ 683A Wade Boggs DT ERR (Text says 215 hits in '89, should be 205)	.20	.09
☐ 683B Wade Boggs DT COR (Text says 205 hits in '89)	.20	.09
☐ 684 Will Clark DT	.20	.09
☐ 685 Tony Gwynn DT UER (Text reads battling instead of batting)	.20	.09
☐ 686 Rickey Henderson DT	.20	.09
☐ 687 Bo Jackson DT	.20	.09
☐ 688 Mark Langston DT	.05	.02
☐ 689 Barry Larkin DT	.10	.05
☐ 690 Kirby Puckett DT	.20	.09
☐ 691 Ryne Sandberg DT	.20	.09
☐ 692 Mike Scott DT	.05	.02
☐ 693A Terry Steinbach DT ERR (cathers)	.05	.02
☐ 693B Terry Steinbach DT COR (catchers)	.05	.02
☐ 694 Bobby Thigpen DT	.05	.02
☐ 695 Mitch Williams DT	.05	.02
☐ 696 Nolan Ryan HL	.40	.18
☐ 697 Bo Jackson FB/BB	.50	.23
☐ 698 Rickey Henderson ALCS-MVP	.20	.09
☐ 699 Will Clark NLCS-MVP	.20	.09
☐ 700 WS Games 1/2 (Dave Stewart Mike Moore)	.10	.05
☐ 701 Lights Out: Candlestick 5:04pm (10/17/89)	.20	.09
☐ 702 WS Game 3 Bashers Blast Giants (Carney Lansford, Rickey Henderson, Jose Canseco, Dave Henderson)	.20	.09
☐ 703 WS Game 4/Wrap-up A's Sweep Battle of of the Bay (A's Celebrate)	.05	.02
☐ 704 Wade Boggs HL Wade Raps 200	.20	.09

1990 Score Rookie Dream Team

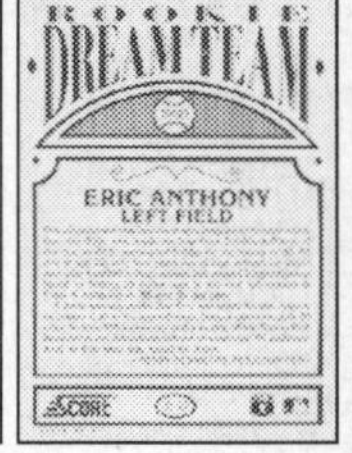

A ten-card set of Dream Team Rookies was inserted only into hobby factory sets.These standard size cards carry a B prefix on the card number and include a player at each position plus a commemorative card honoring the late Baseball Commissioner A. Bartlett Giamatti.

	MINT	NRMT
COMPLETE SET (10)	4.00	1.80
COMMON CARD (B1-B10)	.25	.11
☐ B1 A.Bartlett Giamatti COMM MEM	.50	.23
☐ B2 Pat Combs	.25	.11
☐ B3 Todd Zeile	.35	.16
☐ B4 Luis de los Santos	.25	.11
☐ B5 Mark Lemke	.35	.16
☐ B6 Robin Ventura	.75	.35
☐ B7 Jeff Huson	.25	.11
☐ B8 Greg Vaughn	.35	.16
☐ B9 Marquis Grissom	2.00	.90
☐ B10 Eric Anthony	.25	.11

1990 Score Rookie/Traded

The standard-size 110-card 1990 Score Rookie and Traded set marked the third consecutive year Score had issued an end of the year set to note trades and give rookies early cards. The set was issued through hobby accounts and only in factory set form. The first 66 cards are traded players while the last 44 cards are rookie cards. Hockey star Eric Lindros is included in this set. Rookie Cards in the set include Carlos Baerga, Derek Bell, Todd Hundley and Ray Lankford.

	MINT	NRMT
COMPLETE SET (110)	6.00	2.70
COMMON CARD (1T-110T)	.05	.02

Card	MINT	NRMT
☐ 1T Dave Winfield	.20	.09
☐ 2T Kevin Bass	.05	.02
☐ 3T Nick Esasky	.05	.02
☐ 4T Mitch Webster	.05	.02
☐ 5T Pascual Perez	.05	.02
☐ 6T Gary Pettis	.05	.02
☐ 7T Tony Pena	.05	.02
☐ 8T Candy Maldonado	.05	.02
☐ 9T Cecil Fielder	.10	.05
☐ 10T Carmelo Martinez	.05	.02
☐ 11T Mark Langston	.05	.02
☐ 12T Dave Parker	.10	.05
☐ 13T Don Slaught	.05	.02
☐ 14T Tony Phillips	.05	.02
☐ 15T John Franco	.05	.02
☐ 16T Randy Myers	.10	.05
☐ 17T Jeff Reardon	.10	.05
☐ 18T Sandy Alomar Jr.	.20	.09
☐ 19T Joe Carter	.10	.05
☐ 20T Fred Lynn	.05	.02
☐ 21T Storm Davis	.05	.02
☐ 22T Craig Lefferts	.05	.02
☐ 23T Pete O'Brien	.05	.02
☐ 24T Dennis Boyd	.05	.02
☐ 25T Lloyd Moseby	.05	.02
☐ 26T Mark Davis	.05	.02
☐ 27T Tim Leary	.05	.02
☐ 28T Gerald Perry	.05	.02
☐ 29T Don Aase	.05	.02
☐ 30T Ernie Whitt	.05	.02
☐ 31T Dale Murphy	.20	.09
☐ 32T Alejandro Pena	.05	.02
☐ 33T Juan Samuel	.05	.02
☐ 34T Hubie Brooks	.05	.02
☐ 35T Gary Carter	.20	.09
☐ 36T Jim Presley	.05	.02
☐ 37T Wally Backman	.05	.02
☐ 38T Matt Nokes	.05	.02
☐ 39T Dan Petry	.05	.02
☐ 40T Franklin Stubbs	.05	.02
☐ 41T Jeff Huson	.05	.02
☐ 42T Billy Hatcher	.05	.02
☐ 43T Terry Leach	.05	.02
☐ 44T Phil Bradley	.05	.02
☐ 45T Claudell Washington	.05	.02
☐ 46T Luis Polonia	.05	.02
☐ 47T Daryl Boston	.05	.02
☐ 48T Lee Smith	.10	.05
☐ 49T Tom Brunansky	.05	.02
☐ 50T Mike Witt	.05	.02
☐ 51T Willie Randolph	.10	.05
☐ 52T Stan Javier	.05	.02
☐ 53T Brad Komminsk	.05	.02
☐ 54T John Candelaria	.05	.02
☐ 55T Bryn Smith	.05	.02
☐ 56T Glenn Braggs	.05	.02
☐ 57T Keith Hernandez	.10	.05
☐ 58T Ken Oberkfell	.05	.02
☐ 59T Steve Jeltz	.05	.02
☐ 60T Chris James	.05	.02
☐ 61T Scott Sanderson	.05	.02
☐ 62T Bill Long	.05	.02
☐ 63T Rick Cerone	.05	.02
☐ 64T Scott Bailes	.05	.02
☐ 65T Larry Sheets	.05	.02
☐ 66T Junior Ortiz	.05	.02
☐ 67T Francisco Cabrera	.05	.02
☐ 68T Gary DiSarcina	.20	.09
☐ 69T Greg Olson	.05	.02
☐ 70T Beau Allred	.05	.02
☐ 71T Oscar Azocar	.05	.02
☐ 72T Kent Mercker	.10	.05
☐ 73T John Burkett	.10	.05
☐ 74T Carlos Baerga	.25	.11
☐ 75T Dave Hollins	.20	.09
☐ 76T Todd Hundley	.40	.18
☐ 77T Rick Parker	.05	.02
☐ 78T Steve Cummings	.05	.02
☐ 79T Bill Sampen	.05	.02
☐ 80T Jerry Kutzler	.05	.02
☐ 81T Derek Bell	.25	.11
☐ 82T Kevin Tapani	.10	.05
☐ 83T Jim Leyritz	.20	.09
☐ 84T Ray Lankford	.50	.23
☐ 85T Wayne Edwards	.05	.02
☐ 86T Frank Thomas	4.00	1.80
☐ 87T Tim Naehring	.20	.09
☐ 88T Willie Blair	.05	.02
☐ 89T Alan Mills	.05	.02
☐ 90T Scott Radinsky	.05	.02
☐ 91T Howard Farmer	.05	.02
☐ 92T Julio Machado	.05	.02
☐ 93T Rafael Valdez	.05	.02
☐ 94T Shawn Boskie	.05	.02
☐ 95T David Segui	.20	.09
☐ 96T Chris Hoiles	.20	.09
☐ 97T D.J. Dozier	.10	.05
☐ 98T Hector Villanueva	.05	.02
☐ 99T Eric Gunderson	.05	.02
☐ 100T Eric Lindros	1.50	.70
☐ 101T Dave Otto	.05	.02
☐ 102T Dana Kiecker	.05	.02
☐ 103T Tim Drummond	.05	.02
☐ 104T Mickey Pina	.05	.02
☐ 105T Craig Grebeck	.05	.02
☐ 106T Bernard Gilkey	.25	.11
☐ 107T Tim Layana	.05	.02
☐ 108T Scott Chiamparino	.05	.02
☐ 109T Steve Avery	.10	.05
☐ 110T Terry Shumpert	.05	.02

1990 Score 100 Rising Stars

The 1990 Score Rising Stars set contains 100 standard size cards. The fronts are green, blue and white. The vertically oriented backs feature a large color facial shot and career highlights. The cards were distributed as a set in a blister pack, which also included a full color booklet with more information about each player

	MINT	NRMT
COMPLETE SET (100)	8.00	3.60
COMMON CARD (1-100)	.05	.02
☐ 1 Tom Gordon	.10	.05
☐ 2 Jerome Walton	.05	.02
☐ 3 Ken Griffey Jr.	3.00	1.35
☐ 4 Dwight Smith	.05	.02
☐ 5 Jim Abbott	.25	.11
☐ 6 Todd Zeile	.10	.05
☐ 7 Donn Pall	.05	.02
☐ 8 Rick Reed	.05	.02
☐ 9 Joey Belle	2.00	.90
☐ 10 Gregg Jefferies	.25	.11
☐ 11 Kevin Ritz	.05	.02
☐ 12 Charlie Hayes	.10	.05
☐ 13 Kevin Appier	.15	.07
☐ 14 Jeff Huson	.05	.02
☐ 15 Gary Wayne	.05	.02
☐ 16 Eric Yelding	.05	.02
☐ 17 Clay Parker	.05	.02
☐ 18 Junior Felix	.05	.02
☐ 19 Derek Lilliquist	.05	.02
☐ 20 Gary Sheffield	.75	.35
☐ 21 Craig Worthington	.05	.02
☐ 22 Jeff Brantley	.10	.05
☐ 23 Eric Hetzel	.05	.02
☐ 24 Greg W.Harris	.05	.02
☐ 25 John Wetteland	.15	.07
☐ 26 Joe Oliver	.05	.02
☐ 27 Kevin Maas	.05	.02
☐ 28 Kevin Brown	.25	.11
☐ 29 Mike Stanton	.05	.02
☐ 30 Greg Vaughn	.10	.05
☐ 31 Ron Jones	.05	.02
☐ 32 Gregg Olson	.05	.02
☐ 33 Joe Girardi	.10	.05
☐ 34 Ken Hill	.25	.11
☐ 35 Sammy Sosa	1.00	.45
☐ 36 Geronimo Berroa	.10	.05
☐ 37 Omar Vizquel	.40	.18
☐ 38 Dean Palmer	.50	.23
☐ 39 John Olerud	.50	.23
☐ 40 Deion Sanders	.60	.25
☐ 41 Randy Kramer	.05	.02
☐ 42 Scott Lusader	.05	.02
☐ 43 Dave Johnson (P)	.05	.02
☐ 44 Jeff Wetherby	.05	.02
☐ 45 Eric Anthony	.05	.02
☐ 46 Kenny Rogers	.15	.07
☐ 47 Matt Winters	.05	.02
☐ 48 Mauro Gozzo	.05	.02
☐ 49 Carlos Quintana	.05	.02
☐ 50 Bob Geren	.05	.02
☐ 51 Chad Kreuter	.05	.02
☐ 52 Randy Johnson	1.00	.45
☐ 53 Hensley Meulens	.05	.02
☐ 54 Gene Harris	.05	.02
☐ 55 Bill Spiers	.05	.02
☐ 56 Kelly Mann	.05	.02
☐ 57 Tom McCarthy	.05	.02
☐ 58 Steve Finley	.25	.11
☐ 59 Ramon Martinez	.25	.11
☐ 60 Greg Briley	.05	.02
☐ 61 Jack Daugherty	.05	.02
☐ 62 Tim Jones	.05	.02
☐ 63 Doug Strange	.05	.02
☐ 64 John Orton	.05	.02
☐ 65 Scott Scudder	.05	.02
☐ 66 Mark Gardner	.05	.02
☐ 67 Mark Carreon	.05	.02
☐ 68 Bob Milacki	.05	.02
☐ 69 Andy Benes	.15	.07
☐ 70 Carlos Martinez	.05	.02
☐ 71 Jeff King	.10	.05
☐ 72 Brad Arnsberg	.05	.02
☐ 73 Rick Wrona	.05	.02
☐ 74 Cris Carpenter	.05	.02
☐ 75 Dennis Cook	.05	.02
☐ 76 Pete Harnisch	.05	.02
☐ 77 Greg Hibbard	.05	.02
☐ 78 Ed Whited	.05	.02
☐ 79 Scott Coolbaugh	.05	.02
☐ 80 Billy Bates	.05	.02
☐ 81 German Gonzalez	.05	.02
☐ 82 Lance Blankenship	.05	.02
☐ 83 Lenny Harris	.05	.02
☐ 84 Milt Cuyler	.05	.02
☐ 85 Erik Hanson	.10	.05
☐ 86 Kent Anderson	.05	.02
☐ 87 Hal Morris	.10	.05
☐ 88 Mike Brumley	.05	.02
☐ 89 Ken Patterson	.05	.02
☐ 90 Mike Devereaux	.05	.02
☐ 91 Greg Litton	.05	.02
☐ 92 Rolando Roomes	.05	.02
☐ 93 Ben McDonald	.10	.05
☐ 94 Curt Schilling	.15	.07
☐ 95 Jose DeJesus	.05	.02
☐ 96 Robin Ventura	.25	.11
☐ 97 Steve Searcy	.05	.02
☐ 98 Chip Hale	.05	.02
☐ 99 Marquis Grissom	.75	.35
☐ 100 Luis de los Santos	.05	.02

1990 Score 100 Superstars

The 1990 Score Superstars set contains 100 standard size cards. The fronts are red, white, blue and purple. The vertically oriented backs feature a large color facial shot and career highlights. The cards were distributed as a set in a blister pack, which also included a full color booklet with more information about each player.

	MINT	NRMT
COMPLETE SET (100)	10.00	4.50
COMMON CARD (1-100)	.05	.02
☐ 1 Kirby Puckett	1.50	.70
☐ 2 Steve Sax	.05	.02
☐ 3 Tony Gwynn	1.50	.70
☐ 4 Willie Randolph	.05	.02
☐ 5 Jose Canseco	.30	.14
☐ 6 Ozzie Smith	1.00	.45
☐ 7 Rick Reuschel	.10	.05
☐ 8 Bill Doran	.05	.02
☐ 9 Mickey Tettleton	.05	.02
☐ 10 Don Mattingly	1.25	.55
☐ 11 Greg Swindell	.05	.02

☐ 12 Bert Blyleven	.10	.05
☐ 13 Dave Stewart	.10	.05
☐ 14 Andres Galarraga	.40	.18
☐ 15 Darryl Strawberry	.10	.05
☐ 16 Ellis Burks	.15	.07
☐ 17 Paul O'Neill	.10	.05
☐ 18 Bruce Hurst	.05	.02
☐ 19 Dave Smith	.05	.02
☐ 20 Carney Lansford	.05	.02
☐ 21 Robby Thompson	.05	.02
☐ 22 Gary Gaetti	.10	.05
☐ 23 Jeff Russell	.05	.02
☐ 24 Chuck Finley	.10	.05
☐ 25 Mark McGwire	1.00	.45
☐ 26 Alvin Davis	.05	.02
☐ 27 George Bell	.10	.05
☐ 28 Cory Snyder	.05	.02
☐ 29 Keith Hernandez	.10	.05
☐ 30 Will Clark	.30	.14
☐ 31 Steve Bedrosian	.05	.02
☐ 32 Ryne Sandberg	.75	.35
☐ 33 Tom Browning	.05	.02
☐ 34 Tim Burke	.05	.02
☐ 35 John Smoltz	.40	.18
☐ 36 Phil Bradley	.05	.02
☐ 37 Bobby Bonilla	.10	.05
☐ 38 Kirk McCaskill	.05	.02
☐ 39 Dave Righetti	.05	.02
☐ 40 Bo Jackson	.10	.05
☐ 41 Alan Trammell	.15	.07
☐ 42 Mike Moore UER (Uniform number is 21, not 23 as on front)	.05	.02
☐ 43 Harold Reynolds	.10	.05
☐ 44 Nolan Ryan	2.50	1.10
☐ 45 Fred McGriff	.30	.14
☐ 46 Brian Downing	.05	.02
☐ 47 Brett Butler	.10	.05
☐ 48 Mike Scioscia	.05	.02
☐ 49 John Franco	.10	.05
☐ 50 Kevin Mitchell	.10	.05
☐ 51 Mark Davis	.05	.02
☐ 52 Glenn Davis	.05	.02
☐ 53 Barry Bonds	.50	.23
☐ 54 Dwight Evans	.05	.02
☐ 55 Terry Steinbach	.10	.05
☐ 56 Dave Gallagher	.05	.02
☐ 57 Roberto Kelly	.05	.02
☐ 58 Rafael Palmeiro	.35	.16
☐ 59 Joe Carter	.15	.07
☐ 60 Mark Grace	.30	.14
☐ 61 Pedro Guerrero	.05	.02
☐ 62 Von Hayes	.05	.02
☐ 63 Benito Santiago	.05	.02
☐ 64 Dale Murphy	.25	.11
☐ 65 John Smiley	.05	.02
☐ 66 Cal Ripken	2.00	.90
☐ 67 Mike Greenwell	.10	.05
☐ 68 Devon White	.05	.02
☐ 69 Ed Whitson	.05	.02
☐ 70 Carlton Fisk	.25	.11
☐ 71 Lou Whitaker	.15	.07
☐ 72 Danny Tartabull	.05	.02
☐ 73 Vince Coleman	.05	.02
☐ 74 Andre Dawson	.15	.07
☐ 75 Tim Raines	.10	.05
☐ 76 George Brett	1.50	.70
☐ 77 Tom Herr	.05	.02
☐ 78 Andy Van Slyke	.05	.02
☐ 79 Roger Clemens	.75	.35
☐ 80 Wade Boggs	.30	.14
☐ 81 Wally Joyner	.10	.05
☐ 82 Lonnie Smith	.05	.02
☐ 83 Howard Johnson	.05	.02
☐ 84 Julio Franco	.10	.05
☐ 85 Ruben Sierra	.05	.02
☐ 86 Dan Plesac	.05	.02
☐ 87 Bobby Thigpen	.05	.02
☐ 88 Kevin Seitzer	.05	.02
☐ 89 Dave Stieb	.05	.02
☐ 90 Rickey Henderson	.40	.18
☐ 91 Jeffrey Leonard	.05	.02
☐ 92 Robin Yount	.25	.11
☐ 93 Mitch Williams	.05	.02
☐ 94 Orel Hershiser	.10	.05
☐ 95 Eric Davis	.10	.05
☐ 96 Mark Langston	.05	.02
☐ 97 Mike Scott	.05	.02
☐ 98 Paul Molitor	.50	.23
☐ 99 Dwight Gooden	.10	.05
☐ 100 Kevin Bass	.05	.02

1990 Score McDonald's

This 25-card standard-size set was produced by Score for McDonald's restaurants; included with the set were 15 World Series Trivia cards. The player cards were given

away four to a pack and free with the purchase of fries and a drink, at only 11 McDonald's in the United States (in Idaho and Eastern Oregon) during a special promotion which lasted approximately three weeks. The front has color action player photos, with white and yellow borders on a purple card face that fades as one moves toward the middle of the card. The upper left corner of the picture is cut off to allow space for the McDonald's logo; the player's name and team logo at the bottom round out the card face. The backs have color mugshots, biography, statistics, and career summary.

	MINT	NRMT
COMPLETE SET (25)	500.00	220.00
COMMON CARD (1-25)	5.00	2.20

☐ 1 Will Clark	30.00	13.50
☐ 2 Sandy Alomar Jr.	10.00	4.50
☐ 3 Julio Franco	5.00	2.20
☐ 4 Carlton Fisk	40.00	18.00
☐ 5 Rickey Henderson	25.00	11.00
☐ 6 Matt Williams	25.00	11.00
☐ 7 John Franco	7.50	3.40
☐ 8 Ryne Sandberg	70.00	32.00
☐ 9 Kelly Gruber	5.00	2.20
☐ 10 Andre Dawson	25.00	11.00
☐ 11 Barry Bonds	30.00	13.50
☐ 12 Gary Sheffield	25.00	11.00
☐ 13 Ramon Martinez	10.00	4.50
☐ 14 Len Dykstra	10.00	4.50
☐ 15 Benito Santiago	5.00	2.20
☐ 16 Cecil Fielder	15.00	6.75
☐ 17 John Olerud	15.00	6.75
☐ 18 Roger Clemens	50.00	22.00
☐ 19 George Brett	70.00	32.00
☐ 20 George Bell	5.00	2.20
☐ 21 Ozzie Guillen	5.00	2.20
☐ 22 Steve Sax	5.00	2.20
☐ 23 Dave Stewart	5.00	2.20
☐ 24 Ozzie Smith	70.00	32.00
☐ 25 Robin Yount	25.00	11.00

1990 Score Sportflics Ryan

This standard-size card was issued by Optigraphics (producer of Score and Sportflics) to commemorate the 11th National Sports Card Collectors Convention held in Arlington, Texas in July of 1990. This card featured a Score front similar to the Ryan 1990 Score highlight card except for the 11th National Convention Logo on the bottom right of the card. On the other side a Ryan Sportflics card was printed that stated (reflected) either Sportflics or 1990 National Sports Collectors Convention on the bottom of the card. This issue was limited to a printing of 600 cards with Ryan himself destroying the printing plates.

	MINT	NRMT
COMPLETE SET (1)	450.00	200.00
COMMON CARD (NNO)	450.00	200.00

☐ NNO Nolan Ryan (No number on back; card back is actually another front in Sportflics style)	450.00	200.00

1990 Score Young Superstars I

1990 Score Young Superstars I are glossy full color cards featuring 42 standard-size cards of popular young players. The first series was issued with 1990 Score baseball rack packs while the second series was available only via a mailaway from the company.

	MINT	NRMT
COMPLETE SET (42)	4.00	1.80
COMMON CARD (1-42)	.05	.02

☐ 1 Bo Jackson	.15	.07
☐ 2 Dwight Smith	.05	.02
☐ 3 Joey Belle	2.00	.90
☐ 4 Gregg Olson	.05	.02
☐ 5 Jim Abbott	.15	.07
☐ 6 Felix Fermin	.05	.02
☐ 7 Brian Holman	.05	.02
☐ 8 Clay Parker	.05	.02
☐ 9 Junior Felix	.05	.02
☐ 10 Joe Oliver	.05	.02
☐ 11 Steve Finley	.25	.11
☐ 12 Greg Briley	.05	.02
☐ 13 Greg Vaughn	.15	.07
☐ 14 Bill Spiers	.05	.02
☐ 15 Eric Yelding	.05	.02
☐ 16 Jose Gonzalez	.05	.02
☐ 17 Mark Carreon	.05	.02
☐ 18 Greg W. Harris	.05	.02
☐ 19 Felix Jose	.05	.02
☐ 20 Bob Milacki	.05	.02
☐ 21 Kenny Rogers	.10	.05
☐ 22 Rolando Roomes	.05	.02
☐ 23 Bip Roberts	.10	.05
☐ 24 Jeff Brantley	.10	.05
☐ 25 Jeff Ballard	.05	.02
☐ 26 John Dopson	.05	.02
☐ 27 Ken Patterson	.05	.02
☐ 28 Omar Vizquel	.15	.07
☐ 29 Kevin Brown	.15	.07
☐ 30 Derek Lilliquist	.05	.02
☐ 31 David Wells	.10	.05
☐ 32 Ken Hill	.25	.11
☐ 33 Greg Litton	.05	.02
☐ 34 Rob Ducey	.05	.02
☐ 35 Carlos Martinez	.05	.02
☐ 36 John Smoltz	.40	.18
☐ 37 Lenny Harris	.05	.02
☐ 38 Charlie Hayes	.15	.07
☐ 39 Tommy Gregg	.05	.02
☐ 40 John Wetteland	.25	.11
☐ 41 Jeff Huson	.05	.02
☐ 42 Eric Anthony	.05	.02

1990 Score Young Superstars II

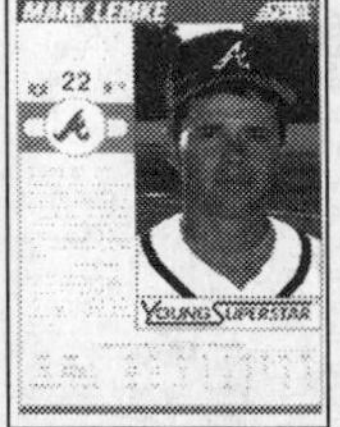

1990 Score Young Superstars II are glossy full color cards featuring 42 standard-size cards of popular young players. Whereas the first series was issued with 1990 Score baseball rack packs, this second series was available only via a mailaway from the company.

	MINT	NRMT
COMPLETE SET (42)	5.00	2.20
COMMON CARD (1-42)	.05	.02

☐ 1 Todd Zeile	.15	.07
☐ 2 Ben McDonald	.10	.05
☐ 3 Delino DeShields	.25	.11
☐ 4 Pat Combs	.05	.02
☐ 5 John Olerud	.30	.14
☐ 6 Marquis Grissom	.50	.23
☐ 7 Mike Stanton	.05	.02
☐ 8 Robin Ventura	.25	.11
☐ 9 Larry Walker	1.00	.45
☐ 10 Dante Bichette	.40	.18
☐ 11 Jack Armstrong	.05	.02
☐ 12 Jay Bell	.10	.05
☐ 13 Andy Benes	.15	.07
☐ 14 Joey Cora	.10	.05
☐ 15 Rob Dibble	.05	.02
☐ 16 Jeff King	.10	.05
☐ 17 Jeff Hamilton	.05	.02
☐ 18 Erik Hanson	.05	.02
☐ 19 Pete Harnisch	.05	.02
☐ 20 Greg Hibbard	.05	.02
☐ 21 Stan Javier	.05	.02
☐ 22 Mark Lemke	.10	.05
☐ 23 Steve Olin	.05	.02
☐ 24 Tommy Greene	.05	.02
☐ 25 Sammy Sosa	1.00	.45
☐ 26 Gary Wayne	.05	.02
☐ 27 Deion Sanders	.75	.35
☐ 28 Steve Wilson	.05	.02
☐ 29 Joe Girardi	.10	.05
☐ 30 John Orton	.05	.02
☐ 31 Kevin Tapani	.25	.11
☐ 32 Carlos Baerga	.25	.11
☐ 33 Glenallen Hill	.10	.05
☐ 34 Mike Blowers	.10	.05
☐ 35 Dave Hollins	.10	.05
☐ 36 Lance Blankenship	.05	.02
☐ 37 Hal Morris	.10	.05
☐ 38 Lance Johnson	.25	.11
☐ 39 Chris Gwynn	.05	.02
☐ 40 Doug Dascenzo	.05	.02
☐ 41 Jerald Clark	.05	.02
☐ 42 Carlos Quintana	.05	.02

1991 Score

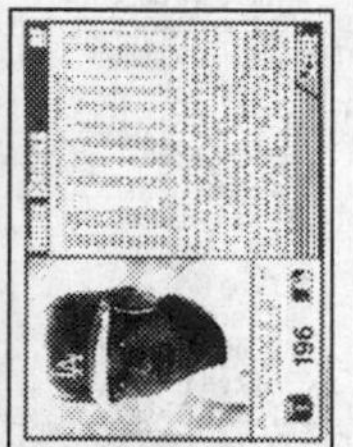

The 1991 Score set contains 893 standard-size cards issued in two separate series of 441 and 452 cards each. This set marks the fourth consecutive year that Score has issued a major set but the first time Score issued the set in two series. Cards were distributed in plastic-wrap packs, blister packs and factory sets. The card fronts feature one of four different solid color borders (black, blue, teal and white) framing the full-color photo of the cards. Subsets include Rookie Prospects (331-379), First Draft Picks (380-391, 671-682), AL All-Stars (392-401), Master Blasters (402-406, 689-693), K-Men (407-411, 684-688), Rifleman (412-416, 694-698), NL All-Stars (661-670), No-Hitters (699-707), Franchise (849-874), Award Winners (875-881) and Dream Team (882-893). An American Flag card (737) was issued to honor the American soldiers involved in Desert Storm. Rookie Cards in the set include Jeff Conine, Chipper Jones, Brian McRae, Mike Mussina and Rondell White. There are a number of pitchers whose card backs show Innings Pitched totals which do not equal the added year-by-year total; the following card numbers were affected, 4, 24, 29, 30, 51, 81, 109, 111, 118, 141, 150, 156, 177, 204, 218, 232, 235, 255, 287, 289, 311, and 328.

	MINT	NRMT
COMPLETE SET (893)	10.00	4.50
COMP.FACT.SET (900)	20.00	9.00
COMMON CARD (1-893)	.05	.02

Card	MINT	NRMT
☐ 1 Jose Canseco	.20	.09
☐ 2 Ken Griffey Jr.	1.50	.70
☐ 3 Ryne Sandberg	.25	.11
☐ 4 Nolan Ryan	.75	.35
☐ 5 Bo Jackson	.20	.09
☐ 6 Bret Saberhagen UER (In bio, missed misspelled as mised)	.05	.02
☐ 7 Will Clark	.20	.09
☐ 8 Ellis Burks	.10	.05
☐ 9 Joe Carter	.20	.09
☐ 10 Rickey Henderson	.20	.09
☐ 11 Ozzie Guillen	.05	.02
☐ 12 Wade Boggs	.20	.09
☐ 13 Jerome Walton	.05	.02
☐ 14 John Franco	.10	.05
☐ 15 Ricky Jordan UER (League misspelled as legue)	.05	.02
☐ 16 Wally Backman	.05	.02
☐ 17 Rob Dibble	.05	.02
☐ 18 Glenn Braggs	.05	.02
☐ 19 Cory Snyder	.05	.02
☐ 20 Kal Daniels	.05	.02
☐ 21 Mark Langston	.05	.02
☐ 22 Kevin Gross	.05	.02
☐ 23 Don Mattingly UER (First line, ' is missing from Yankee)	.30	.14
☐ 24 Dave Righetti	.05	.02
☐ 25 Roberto Alomar	.20	.09
☐ 26 Robby Thompson	.05	.02
☐ 27 Jack McDowell	.05	.02
☐ 28 Bip Roberts UER (Bio reads playd)	.05	.02
☐ 29 Jay Howell	.05	.02
☐ 30 Dave Stieb UER (17 wins in bio, 18 in stats)	.05	.02
☐ 31 Johnny Ray	.05	.02
☐ 32 Steve Sax	.05	.02
☐ 33 Terry Mulholland	.05	.02
☐ 34 Lee Guetterman	.05	.02
☐ 35 Tim Raines	.10	.05
☐ 36 Scott Fletcher	.05	.02
☐ 37 Lance Parrish	.05	.02
☐ 38 Tony Phillips UER (Born 4/15, should be 4/25)	.05	.02
☐ 39 Todd Stottlemyre	.05	.02
☐ 40 Alan Trammell	.20	.09
☐ 41 Todd Burns	.05	.02
☐ 42 Mookie Wilson	.05	.02
☐ 43 Chris Bosio	.05	.02
☐ 44 Jeffrey Leonard	.05	.02
☐ 45 Doug Jones	.05	.02
☐ 46 Mike Scott UER (In first line, dominate should read dominating)	.05	.02
☐ 47 Andy Hawkins	.05	.02
☐ 48 Harold Reynolds	.05	.02
☐ 49 Paul Molitor	.20	.09
☐ 50 John Farrell	.05	.02
☐ 51 Danny Darwin	.05	.02
☐ 52 Jeff Blauser	.05	.02
☐ 53 John Tudor UER (41 wins in '81)	.05	.02
☐ 54 Milt Thompson	.05	.02
☐ 55 Dave Justice	.25	.11
☐ 56 Greg Olson	.05	.02
☐ 57 Willie Blair	.05	.02
☐ 58 Rick Parker	.05	.02
☐ 59 Shawn Boskie	.05	.02
☐ 60 Kevin Tapani	.05	.02
☐ 61 Dave Hollins	.05	.02
☐ 62 Scott Radinsky	.05	.02
☐ 63 Francisco Cabrera	.05	.02
☐ 64 Tim Layana	.05	.02
☐ 65 Jim Leyritz	.10	.05
☐ 66 Wayne Edwards	.05	.02
☐ 67 Lee Stevens	.05	.02
☐ 68 Bill Sampen UER (Fourth line, long is spelled along)	.05	.02
☐ 69 Craig Grebeck UER (Born in Cerritos, not Johnstown)	.05	.02
☐ 70 John Burkett	.10	.05
☐ 71 Hector Villanueva	.05	.02
☐ 72 Oscar Azocar	.05	.02
☐ 73 Alan Mills	.05	.02
☐ 74 Carlos Baerga	.20	.09
☐ 75 Charles Nagy	.20	.09
☐ 76 Tim Drummond	.05	.02
☐ 77 Dana Kiecker	.05	.02
☐ 78 Tom Edens	.05	.02
☐ 79 Kent Mercker	.05	.02
☐ 80 Steve Avery	.05	.02
☐ 81 Lee Smith	.10	.05
☐ 82 Dave Martinez	.05	.02
☐ 83 Dave Winfield	.20	.09
☐ 84 Bill Spiers	.05	.02
☐ 85 Dan Pasqua	.05	.02
☐ 86 Randy Milligan	.05	.02
☐ 87 Tracy Jones	.05	.02
☐ 88 Greg Myers	.05	.02
☐ 89 Keith Hernandez	.10	.05
☐ 90 Todd Benzinger	.05	.02
☐ 91 Mike Jackson	.05	.02
☐ 92 Mike Stanley	.05	.02
☐ 93 Candy Maldonado	.05	.02
☐ 94 John Kruk UER (No decimal point before 1990 BA)	.10	.05
☐ 95 Cal Ripken UER (Genius spelled genuis)	.75	.35
☐ 96 Willie Fraser	.05	.02
☐ 97 Mike Felder	.05	.02
☐ 98 Bill Landrum	.05	.02
☐ 99 Chuck Crim	.05	.02
☐ 100 Chuck Finley	.10	.05
☐ 101 Kirt Manwaring	.05	.02
☐ 102 Jaime Navarro	.05	.02
☐ 103 Dickie Thon	.05	.02
☐ 104 Brian Downing	.05	.02
☐ 105 Jim Abbott	.10	.05
☐ 106 Tom Brookens	.05	.02
☐ 107 Darryl Hamilton UER (Bio info is for Jeff Hamilton)	.10	.05
☐ 108 Bryan Harvey	.05	.02
☐ 109 Greg A. Harris UER (Shown pitching lefty, bio says righty)	.05	.02
☐ 110 Greg Swindell	.05	.02
☐ 111 Juan Berenguer	.05	.02
☐ 112 Mike Heath	.05	.02
☐ 113 Scott Bradley	.05	.02
☐ 114 Jack Morris	.10	.05
☐ 115 Barry Jones	.05	.02
☐ 116 Kevin Romine	.05	.02
☐ 117 Garry Templeton	.05	.02
☐ 118 Scott Sanderson	.05	.02
☐ 119 Roberto Kelly	.05	.02
☐ 120 George Brett	.40	.18
☐ 121 Oddibe McDowell	.05	.02
☐ 122 Jim Acker	.05	.02
☐ 123 Bill Swift UER (Born 12/27/61, should be 10/27)	.05	.02
☐ 124 Eric King	.05	.02
☐ 125 Jay Buhner	.20	.09
☐ 126 Matt Young	.05	.02
☐ 127 Alvaro Espinoza	.05	.02
☐ 128 Greg Hibbard	.05	.02
☐ 129 Jeff M. Robinson	.05	.02
☐ 130 Mike Greenwell	.05	.02
☐ 131 Dion James	.05	.02
☐ 132 Donn Pall UER (1988 ERA in stats 0.00)	.05	.02
☐ 133 Lloyd Moseby	.05	.02
☐ 134 Randy Velarde	.05	.02
☐ 135 Allan Anderson	.05	.02
☐ 136 Mark Davis	.05	.02
☐ 137 Eric Davis	.10	.05
☐ 138 Phil Stephenson	.05	.02
☐ 139 Felix Fermin	.05	.02
☐ 140 Pedro Guerrero	.05	.02
☐ 141 Charlie Hough	.05	.02
☐ 142 Mike Henneman	.05	.02
☐ 143 Jeff Montgomery	.10	.05
☐ 144 Lenny Harris	.05	.02
☐ 145 Bruce Hurst	.05	.02
☐ 146 Eric Anthony	.05	.02
☐ 147 Paul Assenmacher	.05	.02
☐ 148 Jesse Barfield	.05	.02
☐ 149 Carlos Quintana	.05	.02
☐ 150 Dave Stewart	.10	.05
☐ 151 Roy Smith	.05	.02
☐ 152 Paul Gibson	.05	.02
☐ 153 Mickey Hatcher	.05	.02
☐ 154 Jim Eisenreich	.10	.05
☐ 155 Kenny Rogers	.10	.05
☐ 156 Dave Schmidt	.05	.02
☐ 157 Lance Johnson	.05	.02
☐ 158 Dave West	.05	.02
☐ 159 Steve Balboni	.05	.02
☐ 160 Jeff Brantley	.05	.02
☐ 161 Craig Biggio	.20	.09
☐ 162 Brook Jacoby	.05	.02
☐ 163 Dan Gladden	.05	.02
☐ 164 Jeff Reardon UER (Total IP shown as 943.2, should be 943.1)	.10	.05
☐ 165 Mark Carreon	.05	.02
☐ 166 Mel Hall	.05	.02
☐ 167 Gary Mielke	.05	.02
☐ 168 Cecil Fielder	.10	.05
☐ 169 Darrin Jackson	.05	.02
☐ 170 Rick Aguilera	.10	.05
☐ 171 Walt Weiss	.05	.02

☐ 172 Steve Farr	.05	.02
☐ 173 Jody Reed	.05	.02
☐ 174 Mike Jeffcoat	.05	.02
☐ 175 Mark Grace	.20	.09
☐ 176 Larry Sheets	.05	.02
☐ 177 Bill Gullickson	.05	.02
☐ 178 Chris Gwynn	.05	.02
☐ 179 Melido Perez	.05	.02
☐ 180 Sid Fernandez UER (779 runs in 1990)	.05	.02
☐ 181 Tim Burke	.05	.02
☐ 182 Gary Pettis	.05	.02
☐ 183 Rob Murphy	.05	.02
☐ 184 Craig Lefferts	.05	.02
☐ 185 Howard Johnson	.05	.02
☐ 186 Ken Caminiti	.20	.09
☐ 187 Tim Belcher	.05	.02
☐ 188 Greg Cadaret	.05	.02
☐ 189 Matt Williams	.20	.09
☐ 190 Dave Magadan	.05	.02
☐ 191 Geno Petralli	.05	.02
☐ 192 Jeff D. Robinson	.05	.02
☐ 193 Jim Deshaies	.05	.02
☐ 194 Willie Randolph	.10	.05
☐ 195 George Bell	.05	.02
☐ 196 Hubie Brooks	.05	.02
☐ 197 Tom Gordon	.05	.02
☐ 198 Mike Fitzgerald	.05	.02
☐ 199 Mike Pagliarulo	.05	.02
☐ 200 Kirby Puckett	.40	.18
☐ 201 Shawon Dunston	.05	.02
☐ 202 Dennis Boyd	.05	.02
☐ 203 Junior Felix UER (Text has him in NL)	.05	.02
☐ 204 Alejandro Pena	.05	.02
☐ 205 Pete Smith	.05	.02
☐ 206 Tom Glavine UER (Lefty spelled leftie)	.20	.09
☐ 207 Luis Salazar	.05	.02
☐ 208 John Smoltz	.20	.09
☐ 209 Doug Dascenzo	.05	.02
☐ 210 Tim Wallach	.05	.02
☐ 211 Greg Gagne	.05	.02
☐ 212 Mark Gubicza	.05	.02
☐ 213 Mark Parent	.05	.02
☐ 214 Ken Oberkfell	.05	.02
☐ 215 Gary Carter	.20	.09
☐ 216 Rafael Palmeiro	.20	.09
☐ 217 Tom Niedenfuer	.05	.02
☐ 218 Dave LaPoint	.05	.02
☐ 219 Jeff Treadway	.05	.02
☐ 220 Mitch Williams UER ('89 ERA shown as 2.76, should be 2.64)	.05	.02
☐ 221 Jose DeLeon	.05	.02
☐ 222 Mike LaValliere	.05	.02
☐ 223 Darrel Akerfelds	.05	.02
☐ 224A Kent Anderson ERR (First line, flachy should read flashy)	.10	.05
☐ 224B Kent Anderson COR (Corrected in factory sets)	.10	.05
☐ 225 Dwight Evans	.05	.02
☐ 226 Gary Redus	.05	.02
☐ 227 Paul O'Neill	.10	.05
☐ 228 Marty Barrett	.05	.02
☐ 229 Tom Browning	.05	.02
☐ 230 Terry Pendleton	.10	.05
☐ 231 Jack Armstrong	.05	.02
☐ 232 Mike Boddicker	.05	.02
☐ 233 Neal Heaton	.05	.02
☐ 234 Marquis Grissom	.20	.09
☐ 235 Bert Blyleven	.10	.05
☐ 236 Curt Young	.05	.02
☐ 237 Don Carman	.05	.02
☐ 238 Charlie Hayes	.05	.02
☐ 239 Mark Knudson	.05	.02
☐ 240 Todd Zeile	.10	.05
☐ 241 Larry Walker UER (Maple River, should be Maple Ridge)	.30	.14
☐ 242 Jerald Clark	.05	.02
☐ 243 Jeff Ballard	.05	.02
☐ 244 Jeff King	.10	.05
☐ 245 Tom Brunansky	.05	.02
☐ 246 Darren Daulton	.10	.05
☐ 247 Scott Terry	.05	.02
☐ 248 Rob Deer	.05	.02
☐ 249 Brady Anderson UER (1990 Hagerstown 1 hit, should say 13 hits)	.20	.09
☐ 250 Len Dykstra	.10	.05
☐ 251 Greg W. Harris	.05	.02
☐ 252 Mike Hartley	.05	.02
☐ 253 Joey Cora	.10	.05
☐ 254 Ivan Calderon	.05	.02
☐ 255 Ted Power	.05	.02
☐ 256 Sammy Sosa	.25	.11
☐ 257 Steve Buechele	.05	.02
☐ 258 Mike Devereaux UER (No comma between city and state)	.05	.02
☐ 259 Brad Komminsk UER (Last text line, Ba should be BA)	.05	.02
☐ 260 Teddy Higuera	.05	.02
☐ 261 Shawn Abner	.05	.02
☐ 262 Dave Valle	.05	.02
☐ 263 Jeff Huson	.05	.02
☐ 264 Edgar Martinez	.20	.09
☐ 265 Carlton Fisk	.20	.09
☐ 266 Steve Finley	.20	.09
☐ 267 John Wetteland	.20	.09
☐ 268 Kevin Appier	.20	.09
☐ 269 Steve Lyons	.05	.02
☐ 270 Mickey Tettleton	.10	.05
☐ 271 Luis Rivera	.05	.02
☐ 272 Steve Jeltz	.05	.02
☐ 273 R.J. Reynolds	.05	.02
☐ 274 Carlos Martinez	.05	.02
☐ 275 Dan Plesac	.05	.02
☐ 276 Mike Morgan UER (Total IP shown as 1149.1, should be 1149)	.05	.02
☐ 277 Jeff Russell	.05	.02
☐ 278 Pete Incaviglia	.05	.02
☐ 279 Kevin Seitzer UER (Bio has 200 hits twice and .300 four times, should be once and three times)	.05	.02
☐ 280 Bobby Thigpen	.05	.02
☐ 281 Stan Javier UER (Born 1/9, should say 9/1)	.05	.02
☐ 282 Henry Cotto	.05	.02
☐ 283 Gary Wayne	.05	.02
☐ 284 Shane Mack	.05	.02
☐ 285 Brian Holman	.05	.02
☐ 286 Gerald Perry	.05	.02
☐ 287 Steve Crawford	.05	.02
☐ 288 Nelson Liriano	.05	.02
☐ 289 Don Aase	.05	.02
☐ 290 Randy Johnson	.25	.11
☐ 291 Harold Baines	.10	.05
☐ 292 Kent Hrbek	.10	.05
☐ 293A Les Lancaster ERR (No comma between Dallas and Texas)	.05	.02
☐ 293B Les Lancaster COR (Corrected in factory sets)	.05	.02
☐ 294 Jeff Musselman	.05	.02
☐ 295 Kurt Stillwell	.05	.02
☐ 296 Stan Belinda	.05	.02
☐ 297 Lou Whitaker	.10	.05
☐ 298 Glenn Wilson	.05	.02
☐ 299 Omar Vizquel UER (Born 5/15, should be 4/24, there is a decimal before GP total for '90)	.20	.09
☐ 300 Ramon Martinez	.10	.05
☐ 301 Dwight Smith	.05	.02
☐ 302 Tim Crews	.05	.02
☐ 303 Lance Blankenship	.05	.02
☐ 304 Sid Bream	.05	.02
☐ 305 Rafael Ramirez	.05	.02
☐ 306 Steve Wilson	.05	.02
☐ 307 Mackey Sasser	.05	.02
☐ 308 Franklin Stubbs	.05	.02
☐ 309 Jack Daugherty UER (Born 6/3/60, should say July)	.05	.02
☐ 310 Eddie Murray	.20	.09
☐ 311 Bob Welch	.05	.02
☐ 312 Brian Harper	.05	.02
☐ 313 Lance McCullers	.05	.02
☐ 314 Dave Smith	.05	.02
☐ 315 Bobby Bonilla	.10	.05
☐ 316 Jerry Don Gleaton	.05	.02
☐ 317 Greg Maddux	.60	.25
☐ 318 Keith Miller	.05	.02
☐ 319 Mark Portugal	.05	.02
☐ 320 Robin Ventura	.20	.09
☐ 321 Bob Ojeda	.05	.02
☐ 322 Mike Harkey	.05	.02
☐ 323 Jay Bell	.10	.05
☐ 324 Mark McGwire	.40	.18
☐ 325 Gary Gaetti	.10	.05
☐ 326 Jeff Pico	.05	.02
☐ 327 Kevin McReynolds	.05	.02
☐ 328 Frank Tanana	.05	.02
☐ 329 Eric Yelding UER (Listed as 6'3" should be 5'11")	.05	.02
☐ 330 Barry Bonds	.25	.11
☐ 331 Brian McRae UER (No comma between city and state)	.20	.09
☐ 332 Pedro Munoz	.05	.02
☐ 333 Daryl Irvine	.05	.02
☐ 334 Chris Hoiles	.05	.02
☐ 335 Thomas Howard	.05	.02
☐ 336 Jeff Schulz	.05	.02
☐ 337 Jeff Manto	.05	.02
☐ 338 Beau Allred	.05	.02
☐ 339 Mike Bordick	.20	.09
☐ 340 Todd Hundley	.20	.09
☐ 341 Jim Vatcher UER (Height 6'9", should be 5'9")	.05	.02
☐ 342 Luis Sojo	.05	.02
☐ 343 Jose Offerman UER (Born 1969, should say 1968)	.05	.02
☐ 344 Pete Coachman	.05	.02
☐ 345 Mike Benjamin	.05	.02
☐ 346 Ozzie Canseco	.05	.02
☐ 347 Tim McIntosh	.05	.02
☐ 348 Phil Plantier	.10	.05
☐ 349 Terry Shumpert	.05	.02
☐ 350 Darren Lewis	.05	.02
☐ 351 David Walsh	.05	.02
☐ 352A Scott Chiamparino ERR (Bats left, should be right)	.10	.05
☐ 352B Scott Chiamparino COR (corrected in factory sets)	.10	.05
☐ 353 Julio Valera UER (Progressed mis-spelled as progessed)	.05	.02
☐ 354 Anthony Telford	.05	.02
☐ 355 Kevin Wickander	.05	.02
☐ 356 Tim Naehring	.10	.05
☐ 357 Jim Poole	.05	.02
☐ 358 Mark Whiten UER (Shown hitting lefty, bio says righty)	.05	.02
☐ 359 Terry Wells	.05	.02
☐ 360 Rafael Valdez	.05	.02
☐ 361 Mel Stottlemyre Jr.	.05	.02
☐ 362 David Segui	.10	.05
☐ 363 Paul Abbott	.05	.02
☐ 364 Steve Howard	.05	.02
☐ 365 Karl Rhodes	.05	.02
☐ 366 Rafael Novoa	.05	.02
☐ 367 Joe Grahe	.05	.02
☐ 368 Darren Reed	.05	.02
☐ 369 Jeff McKnight	.05	.02
☐ 370 Scott Leius	.05	.02
☐ 371 Mark Dewey	.05	.02
☐ 372 Mark Lee UER (Shown hitting lefty, bio says righty, born in Dakota, should say North Dakota)	.05	.02
☐ 373 Rosario Rodriguez (Shown hitting lefty, bio says righty) UER	.05	.02
☐ 374 Chuck McElroy	.05	.02
☐ 375 Mike Bell	.05	.02
☐ 376 Mickey Morandini	.05	.02
☐ 377 Bill Haselman	.05	.02
☐ 378 Dave Pavlas	.05	.02
☐ 379 Derrick May	.05	.02
☐ 380 Jeromy Burnitz FDP	.20	.09
☐ 381 Donald Peters FDP	.05	.02
☐ 382 Alex Fernandez FDP	.10	.05
☐ 383 Mike Mussina FDP	1.00	.45
☐ 384 Dan Smith FDP	.05	.02
☐ 385 Lance Dickson FDP	.05	.02
☐ 386 Carl Everett FDP	.15	.07
☐ 387 Thomas Nevers FDP	.05	.02
☐ 388 Adam Hyzdu FDP	.05	.02
☐ 389 Todd Van Poppel FDP	.05	.02
☐ 390 Rondell White FDP	.30	.14
☐ 391 Marc Newfield FDP	.15	.07
☐ 392 Julio Franco AS	.05	.02
☐ 393 Wade Boggs AS	.20	.09
☐ 394 Ozzie Guillen AS	.05	.02
☐ 395 Cecil Fielder AS	.10	.05
☐ 396 Ken Griffey Jr. AS	.75	.35
☐ 397 Rickey Henderson AS	.20	.09
☐ 398 Jose Canseco AS	.20	.09
☐ 399 Roger Clemens AS	.20	.09
☐ 400 Sandy Alomar Jr. AS	.05	.02
☐ 401 Bobby Thigpen AS	.05	.02
☐ 402 Bobby Bonilla MB	.10	.05
☐ 403 Eric Davis MB	.10	.05
☐ 404 Fred McGriff MB	.20	.09

☐ 405 Glenn Davis MB	.05	.02
☐ 406 Kevin Mitchell MB	.05	.02
☐ 407 Rob Dibble KM	.05	.02
☐ 408 Ramon Martinez KM	.10	.05
☐ 409 David Cone KM	.10	.05
☐ 410 Bobby Witt KM	.05	.02
☐ 411 Mark Langston KM	.05	.02
☐ 412 Bo Jackson RIF	.10	.05
☐ 413 Shawon Dunston RIF UER (In the baseball, should say in baseball)	.05	.02
☐ 414 Jesse Barfield RIF	.05	.02
☐ 415 Ken Caminiti RIF	.20	.09
☐ 416 Benito Santiago RIF	.05	.02
☐ 417 Nolan Ryan HL	.40	.18
☐ 418 Bobby Thigpen HL UER (Back refers to Hal McRae Jr., should say Brian McRae)	.05	.02
☐ 419 Ramon Martinez HL	.20	.09
☐ 420 Bo Jackson HL	.10	.05
☐ 421 Carlton Fisk HL	.20	.09
☐ 422 Jimmy Key	.05	.02
☐ 423 Junior Noboa	.05	.02
☐ 424 Al Newman	.05	.02
☐ 425 Pat Borders	.05	.02
☐ 426 Von Hayes	.05	.02
☐ 427 Tim Teufel	.05	.02
☐ 428 Eric Plunk UER (Text says Eric's had, no apostrophe needed)	.05	.02
☐ 429 John Moses	.05	.02
☐ 430 Mike Witt	.05	.02
☐ 431 Otis Nixon	.10	.05
☐ 432 Tony Fernandez	.05	.02
☐ 433 Rance Mulliniks	.05	.02
☐ 434 Dan Petry	.05	.02
☐ 435 Bob Geren	.05	.02
☐ 436 Steve Frey	.05	.02
☐ 437 Jamie Moyer	.05	.02
☐ 438 Junior Ortiz	.05	.02
☐ 439 Tom O'Malley	.05	.02
☐ 440 Pat Combs	.05	.02
☐ 441 Jose Canseco DT	.20	.09
☐ 442 Alfredo Griffin	.05	.02
☐ 443 Andres Galarraga	.20	.09
☐ 444 Bryn Smith	.05	.02
☐ 445 Andre Dawson	.20	.09
☐ 446 Juan Samuel	.05	.02
☐ 447 Mike Aldrete	.05	.02
☐ 448 Ron Gant	.10	.05
☐ 449 Fernando Valenzuela	.10	.05
☐ 450 Vince Coleman UER (Should say topped majors in steals four times, not three times)	.05	.02
☐ 451 Kevin Mitchell	.10	.05
☐ 452 Spike Owen	.05	.02
☐ 453 Mike Bielecki	.05	.02
☐ 454 Dennis Martinez	.10	.05
☐ 455 Brett Butler	.05	.02
☐ 456 Ron Darling	.05	.02
☐ 457 Dennis Rasmussen	.05	.02
☐ 458 Ken Howell	.05	.02
☐ 459 Steve Bedrosian	.05	.02
☐ 460 Frank Viola	.05	.02
☐ 461 Jose Lind	.05	.02
☐ 462 Chris Sabo	.05	.02
☐ 463 Dante Bichette	.20	.09
☐ 464 Rick Mahler	.05	.02
☐ 465 John Smiley	.05	.02
☐ 466 Devon White	.05	.02
☐ 467 John Orton	.05	.02
☐ 468 Mike Stanton	.05	.02
☐ 469 Billy Hatcher	.05	.02
☐ 470 Wally Joyner	.10	.05
☐ 471 Gene Larkin	.05	.02
☐ 472 Doug Drabek	.05	.02
☐ 473 Gary Sheffield	.20	.09
☐ 474 David Wells	.05	.02
☐ 475 Andy Van Slyke	.05	.02
☐ 476 Mike Gallego	.05	.02
☐ 477 B.J. Surhoff	.10	.05
☐ 478 Gene Nelson	.05	.02
☐ 479 Mariano Duncan	.05	.02
☐ 480 Fred McGriff	.20	.09
☐ 481 Jerry Browne	.05	.02
☐ 482 Alvin Davis	.05	.02
☐ 483 Bill Wegman	.05	.02
☐ 484 Dave Parker	.10	.05
☐ 485 Dennis Eckersley	.20	.09
☐ 486 Erik Hanson UER (Basketball misspelled as baseketball)	.05	.02
☐ 487 Bill Ripken	.05	.02
☐ 488 Tom Candiotti	.05	.02
☐ 489 Mike Schooler	.05	.02
☐ 490 Gregg Olson	.05	.02
☐ 491 Chris James	.05	.02
☐ 492 Pete Harnisch	.05	.02
☐ 493 Julio Franco	.10	.05
☐ 494 Greg Briley	.05	.02
☐ 495 Ruben Sierra	.05	.02
☐ 496 Steve Olin	.05	.02
☐ 497 Mike Fetters	.05	.02
☐ 498 Mark Williamson	.05	.02
☐ 499 Bob Tewksbury	.05	.02
☐ 500 Tony Gwynn	.50	.23
☐ 501 Randy Myers	.10	.05
☐ 502 Keith Comstock	.05	.02
☐ 503 Craig Worthington UER (DeCinces misspelled DiCinces on back)	.05	.02
☐ 504 Mark Eichhorn UER (Stats incomplete, doesn't have '89 Braves stint)	.05	.02
☐ 505 Barry Larkin	.20	.09
☐ 506 Dave Johnson	.05	.02
☐ 507 Bobby Witt	.05	.02
☐ 508 Joe Orsulak	.05	.02
☐ 509 Pete O'Brien	.05	.02
☐ 510 Brad Arnsberg	.05	.02
☐ 511 Storm Davis	.05	.02
☐ 512 Bob Milacki	.05	.02
☐ 513 Bill Pecota	.05	.02
☐ 514 Glenallen Hill	.05	.02
☐ 515 Danny Tartabull	.05	.02
☐ 516 Mike Moore	.05	.02
☐ 517 Ron Robinson UER (577 K's in 1990)	.05	.02
☐ 518 Mark Gardner	.05	.02
☐ 519 Rick Wrona	.05	.02
☐ 520 Mike Scioscia	.05	.02
☐ 521 Frank Wills	.05	.02
☐ 522 Greg Brock	.05	.02
☐ 523 Jack Clark	.10	.05
☐ 524 Bruce Ruffin	.05	.02
☐ 525 Robin Yount	.20	.09
☐ 526 Tom Foley	.05	.02
☐ 527 Pat Perry	.05	.02
☐ 528 Greg Vaughn	.05	.02
☐ 529 Wally Whitehurst	.05	.02
☐ 530 Norm Charlton	.05	.02
☐ 531 Marvell Wynne	.05	.02
☐ 532 Jim Gantner	.05	.02
☐ 533 Greg Litton	.05	.02
☐ 534 Manny Lee	.05	.02
☐ 535 Scott Bailes	.05	.02
☐ 536 Charlie Leibrandt	.05	.02
☐ 537 Roger McDowell	.05	.02
☐ 538 Andy Benes	.10	.05
☐ 539 Rick Honeycutt	.05	.02
☐ 540 Dwight Gooden	.10	.05
☐ 541 Scott Garrelts	.05	.02
☐ 542 Dave Clark	.05	.02
☐ 543 Lonnie Smith	.05	.02
☐ 544 Rick Reuschel	.05	.02
☐ 545 Delino DeShields UER (Rockford misspelled as Rock Ford in '88)	.05	.02
☐ 546 Mike Sharperson	.05	.02
☐ 547 Mike Kingery	.05	.02
☐ 548 Terry Kennedy	.05	.02
☐ 549 David Cone	.10	.05
☐ 550 Orel Hershiser	.10	.05
☐ 551 Matt Nokes	.05	.02
☐ 552 Eddie Williams	.05	.02
☐ 553 Frank DiPino	.05	.02
☐ 554 Fred Lynn	.05	.02
☐ 555 Alex Cole	.05	.02
☐ 556 Terry Leach	.05	.02
☐ 557 Chet Lemon	.05	.02
☐ 558 Paul Mirabella	.05	.02
☐ 559 Bill Long	.05	.02
☐ 560 Phil Bradley	.05	.02
☐ 561 Duane Ward	.05	.02
☐ 562 Dave Bergman	.05	.02
☐ 563 Eric Show	.05	.02
☐ 564 Xavier Hernandez	.05	.02
☐ 565 Jeff Parrett	.05	.02
☐ 566 Chuck Cary	.05	.02
☐ 567 Ken Hill	.10	.05
☐ 568 Bob Welch Hand (Complement should be compliment) UER	.05	.02
☐ 569 John Mitchell	.05	.02
☐ 570 Travis Fryman	.20	.09
☐ 571 Derek Lilliquist	.05	.02
☐ 572 Steve Lake	.05	.02
☐ 573 John Barfield	.05	.02
☐ 574 Randy Bush	.05	.02
☐ 575 Joe Magrane	.05	.02
☐ 576 Eddie Diaz	.05	.02
☐ 577 Casey Candaele	.05	.02
☐ 578 Jesse Orosco	.05	.02
☐ 579 Tom Henke	.05	.02
☐ 580 Rick Cerone UER (Actually his third go-round with Yankees)	.05	.02
☐ 581 Drew Hall	.05	.02
☐ 582 Tony Castillo	.05	.02
☐ 583 Jimmy Jones	.05	.02
☐ 584 Rick Reed	.05	.02
☐ 585 Joe Girardi	.10	.05
☐ 586 Jeff Gray	.05	.02
☐ 587 Luis Polonia	.05	.02
☐ 588 Joe Klink	.05	.02
☐ 589 Rex Hudler	.05	.02
☐ 590 Kirk McCaskill	.05	.02
☐ 591 Juan Agosto	.05	.02
☐ 592 Wes Gardner	.05	.02
☐ 593 Rich Rodriguez	.05	.02
☐ 594 Mitch Webster	.05	.02
☐ 595 Kelly Gruber	.05	.02
☐ 596 Dale Mohorcic	.05	.02
☐ 597 Willie McGee	.05	.02
☐ 598 Bill Krueger	.05	.02
☐ 599 Bob Walk UER (Cards says he's 33, but actually he's 34)	.05	.02
☐ 600 Kevin Maas	.05	.02
☐ 601 Danny Jackson	.05	.02
☐ 602 Craig McMurtry UER (Anonymously misspelled anonimously)	.05	.02
☐ 603 Curtis Wilkerson	.05	.02
☐ 604 Adam Peterson	.05	.02
☐ 605 Sam Horn	.05	.02
☐ 606 Tommy Gregg	.05	.02
☐ 607 Ken Dayley	.05	.02
☐ 608 Carmelo Castillo	.05	.02
☐ 609 John Shelby	.05	.02
☐ 610 Don Slaught	.05	.02
☐ 611 Calvin Schiraldi	.05	.02
☐ 612 Dennis Lamp	.05	.02
☐ 613 Andres Thomas	.05	.02
☐ 614 Jose Gonzalez	.05	.02
☐ 615 Randy Ready	.05	.02
☐ 616 Kevin Bass	.05	.02
☐ 617 Mike Marshall	.05	.02
☐ 618 Daryl Boston	.05	.02
☐ 619 Andy McGaffigan	.05	.02
☐ 620 Joe Oliver	.05	.02
☐ 621 Jim Gott	.05	.02
☐ 622 Jose Oquendo	.05	.02
☐ 623 Jose DeJesus	.05	.02
☐ 624 Mike Brumley	.05	.02
☐ 625 John Olerud	.10	.05
☐ 626 Ernest Riles	.05	.02
☐ 627 Gene Harris	.05	.02
☐ 628 Jose Uribe	.05	.02
☐ 629 Darnell Coles	.05	.02
☐ 630 Carney Lansford	.10	.05
☐ 631 Tim Leary	.05	.02
☐ 632 Tim Hulett	.05	.02
☐ 633 Kevin Elster	.05	.02
☐ 634 Tony Fossas	.05	.02
☐ 635 Francisco Oliveras	.05	.02
☐ 636 Bob Patterson	.05	.02
☐ 637 Gary Ward	.05	.02
☐ 638 Rene Gonzales	.05	.02
☐ 639 Don Robinson	.05	.02
☐ 640 Darryl Strawberry	.10	.05
☐ 641 Dave Anderson	.05	.02
☐ 642 Scott Scudder	.05	.02
☐ 643 Reggie Harris UER (Hepatitis misspelled as hepititis)	.05	.02
☐ 644 Dave Henderson	.05	.02
☐ 645 Ben McDonald	.10	.05
☐ 646 Bob Kipper	.05	.02
☐ 647 Hal Morris UER (It's should be its)	.05	.02
☐ 648 Tim Birtsas	.05	.02
☐ 649 Steve Searcy	.05	.02
☐ 650 Dale Murphy	.20	.09
☐ 651 Ron Oester	.05	.02
☐ 652 Mike LaCoss	.05	.02
☐ 653 Ron Jones	.05	.02
☐ 654 Kelly Downs	.05	.02
☐ 655 Roger Clemens	.40	.18
☐ 656 Herm Winningham	.05	.02
☐ 657 Trevor Wilson	.05	.02
☐ 658 Jose Rijo	.05	.02
☐ 659 Dann Bilardello UER (Bio has 13 games, 1 hit, and 32 AB, stats show 19, 2, and 37)	.05	.02
☐ 660 Gregg Jefferies	.10	.05
☐ 661 Doug Drabek AS UER	.05	.02

(Through is mis-
spelled though)
☐ 662 Randy Myers AS .05 .02
☐ 663 Benny Santiago AS .05 .02
☐ 664 Will Clark AS .20 .09
☐ 665 Ryne Sandberg AS .20 .09
☐ 666 Barry Larkin AS UER .05 .02
(Line 13, coolly
misspelled cooly)
☐ 667 Matt Williams AS .05 .02
☐ 668 Barry Bonds AS .20 .09
☐ 669 Eric Davis AS .10 .05
☐ 670 Bobby Bonilla AS .10 .05
☐ 671 Chipper Jones FDP 3.00 1.35
☐ 672 Eric Christopherson .05 .02
FDP
☐ 673 Robbie Beckett FDP .05 .02
☐ 674 Shane Andrews FDP .05 .02
☐ 675 Steve Karsay FDP .10 .05
☐ 676 Aaron Holbert FDP .05 .02
☐ 677 Donovan Osborne FDP .10 .05
☐ 678 Todd Ritchie FDP .05 .02
☐ 679 Ron Walden FDP .05 .02
☐ 680 Tim Costo FDP .05 .02
☐ 681 Dan Wilson FDP .25 .11
☐ 682 Kurt Miller FDP .05 .02
☐ 683 Mike Lieberthal FDP .15 .07
☐ 684 Roger Clemens KM .20 .09
☐ 685 Doc Gooden KM .10 .05
☐ 686 Nolan Ryan KM .40 .18
☐ 687 Frank Viola KM .05 .02
☐ 688 Erik Hanson KM .05 .02
☐ 689 Matt Williams MB .20 .09
☐ 690 Jose Canseco MB UER .20 .09
(Mammoth misspelled
as monmouth)
☐ 691 Darryl Strawberry MB .10 .05
☐ 692 Bo Jackson MB .10 .05
☐ 693 Cecil Fielder MB .10 .05
☐ 694 Sandy Alomar Jr. RF .10 .05
☐ 695 Cory Snyder RF .05 .02
☐ 696 Eric Davis RF .10 .05
☐ 697 Ken Griffey Jr. RF .75 .35
☐ 698 Andy Van Slyke RF UER .05 .02
(Line 2, outfielders
does not need)
☐ 699 Mark Langston NH .05 .02
Mike Witt
☐ 700 Randy Johnson NH .20 .09
☐ 701 Nolan Ryan NH .40 .18
☐ 702 Dave Stewart NH .05 .02
☐ 703 Fernando Valenzuela NH .10 .05
☐ 704 Andy Hawkins NH .05 .02
☐ 705 Melido Perez NH .05 .02
☐ 706 Terry Mulholland NH .05 .02
☐ 707 Dave Stieb NH .05 .02
☐ 708 Brian Barnes .05 .02
☐ 709 Bernard Gilkey .10 .05
☐ 710 Steve Decker .05 .02
☐ 711 Paul Faries .05 .02
☐ 712 Paul Marak .05 .02
☐ 713 Wes Chamberlain .05 .02
☐ 714 Kevin Belcher .05 .02
☐ 715 Dan Boone UER .05 .02
(IP adds up to 101,
but card has 101.2)
☐ 716 Steve Adkins .05 .02
☐ 717 Geronimo Pena .05 .02
☐ 718 Howard Farmer .05 .02
☐ 719 Mark Leonard .05 .02
☐ 720 Tom Lampkin .05 .02
☐ 721 Mike Gardiner .05 .02
☐ 722 Jeff Conine .25 .11
☐ 723 Efrain Valdez .05 .02
☐ 724 Chuck Malone .05 .02
☐ 725 Leo Gomez .05 .02
☐ 726 Paul McClellan .05 .02
☐ 727 Mark Leiter .05 .02
☐ 728 Rich DeLucia UER .05 .02
(Line 2, all told
is written alltold)
☐ 729 Mel Rojas .20 .09
☐ 730 Hector Wagner .05 .02
☐ 731 Ray Lankford .20 .09
☐ 732 Turner Ward .05 .02
☐ 733 Gerald Alexander .05 .02
☐ 734 Scott Anderson .05 .02
☐ 735 Tony Perezchica .05 .02
☐ 736 Jimmy Kremers .05 .02
☐ 737 American Flag .20 .09
(Pray for Peace)
☐ 738 Mike York .05 .02
☐ 739 Mike Rochford .05 .02
☐ 740 Scott Aldred .05 .02
☐ 741 Rico Brogna .10 .05
☐ 742 Dave Burba .05 .02
☐ 743 Ray Stephens .05 .02
☐ 744 Eric Gunderson .05 .02
☐ 745 Troy Afenir .05 .02
☐ 746 Jeff Shaw .05 .02
☐ 747 Orlando Merced .10 .05
☐ 748 Omar Olivares UER .05 .02
(Line 9, league is
misspelled legaue)
☐ 749 Jerry Kutzler .05 .02
☐ 750 Mo Vaughn UER .40 .18
(44 SB's in 1990)
☐ 751 Matt Stark .05 .02
☐ 752 Randy Hennis .05 .02
☐ 753 Andujar Cedeno .05 .02
☐ 754 Kelvin Torve .05 .02
☐ 755 Joe Kraemer .05 .02
☐ 756 Phil Clark .05 .02
☐ 757 Ed Vosberg .05 .02
☐ 758 Mike Perez .05 .02
☐ 759 Scott Lewis .05 .02
☐ 760 Steve Chitren .05 .02
☐ 761 Ray Young .05 .02
☐ 762 Andres Santana .05 .02
☐ 763 Rodney McCray .05 .02
☐ 764 Sean Berry UER .10 .05
(Name misspelled
Barry on card front)
☐ 765 Brent Mayne .05 .02
☐ 766 Mike Simms .05 .02
☐ 767 Glenn Sutko .05 .02
☐ 768 Gary DiSarcina .05 .02
☐ 769 George Brett HL .20 .09
☐ 770 Cecil Fielder HL .10 .05
☐ 771 Jim Presley .05 .02
☐ 772 John Dopson .05 .02
☐ 773 Bo Jackson Breaker .20 .09
☐ 774 Brent Knackert UER .05 .02
(Born in 1954, shown
throwing righty, but
bio says lefty)
☐ 775 Bill Doran UER .05 .02
(Reds in NL East)
☐ 776 Dick Schofield .05 .02
☐ 777 Nelson Santovenia .05 .02
☐ 778 Mark Guthrie .05 .02
☐ 779 Mark Lemke .05 .02
☐ 780 Terry Steinbach .10 .05
☐ 781 Tom Bolton .05 .02
☐ 782 Randy Tomlin .05 .02
☐ 783 Jeff Kunkel .05 .02
☐ 784 Felix Jose .05 .02
☐ 785 Rick Sutcliffe .05 .02
☐ 786 John Cerutti .05 .02
☐ 787 Jose Vizcaino UER .05 .02
(Offerman, not Opperman)
☐ 788 Curt Schilling .05 .02
☐ 789 Ed Whitson .05 .02
☐ 790 Tony Pena .05 .02
☐ 791 John Candelaria .05 .02
☐ 792 Carmelo Martinez .05 .02
☐ 793 Sandy Alomar Jr. UER .10 .05
(Indian's should
say Indians')
☐ 794 Jim Neidlinger .05 .02
☐ 795 Barry Larkin WS .20 .09
and Chris Sabo
☐ 796 Paul Sorrento .05 .02
☐ 797 Tom Pagnozzi .05 .02
☐ 798 Tino Martinez .20 .09
☐ 799 Scott Ruskin UER .05 .02
(Text says first three
seasons but lists
averages for four)
☐ 800 Kirk Gibson .10 .05
☐ 801 Walt Terrell .05 .02
☐ 802 John Russell .05 .02
☐ 803 Chili Davis .10 .05
☐ 804 Chris Nabholz .05 .02
☐ 805 Juan Gonzalez .75 .35
☐ 806 Ron Hassey .05 .02
☐ 807 Todd Worrell .05 .02
☐ 808 Tommy Greene .05 .02
☐ 809 Joel Skinner UER .05 .02
(Joel, not Bob, was
drafted in 1979)
☐ 810 Benito Santiago .05 .02
☐ 811 Pat Tabler UER .05 .02
(Line 3, always
misspelled alway)
☐ 812 Scott Erickson UER .10 .05
(Record spelled rcord)
☐ 813 Moises Alou .20 .09
☐ 814 Dale Sveum .05 .02
☐ 815 Ryne Sandberg MANYR .20 .09
☐ 816 Rick Dempsey .05 .02
☐ 817 Scott Bankhead .05 .02
☐ 818 Jason Grimsley .05 .02
☐ 819 Doug Jennings .05 .02
☐ 820 Tom Herr .05 .02
☐ 821 Rob Ducey .05 .02
☐ 822 Luis Quinones .05 .02
☐ 823 Greg Minton .05 .02
☐ 824 Mark Grant .05 .02
☐ 825 Ozzie Smith UER .25 .11
(Shortstop misspelled
shortsop)
☐ 826 Dave Eiland .05 .02
☐ 827 Danny Heep .05 .02
☐ 828 Hensley Meulens .05 .02
☐ 829 Charlie O'Brien .05 .02
☐ 830 Glenn Davis .05 .02
☐ 831 John Marzano UER .05 .02
(International mis-
spelled Internaional)
☐ 832 Steve Ontiveros .05 .02
☐ 833 Ron Karkovice .05 .02
☐ 834 Jerry Goff .05 .02
☐ 835 Ken Griffey Sr. .05 .02
☐ 836 Kevin Reimer .05 .02
☐ 837 Randy Kutcher UER .05 .02
(Infectious mis-
spelled infectous)
☐ 838 Mike Blowers .05 .02
☐ 839 Mike Macfarlane .05 .02
☐ 840 Frank Thomas UER 1.50 .70
(1989 Sarasota stats,
15 games but 188 AB)
☐ 841 The Griffeys .75 .35
Ken Griffey Jr.
Ken Griffey Sr.
☐ 842 Jack Howell .05 .02
☐ 843 Goose Gozzo .05 .02
☐ 844 Gerald Young .05 .02
☐ 845 Zane Smith .05 .02
☐ 846 Kevin Brown .10 .05
☐ 847 Sil Campusano .05 .02
☐ 848 Larry Andersen .05 .02
☐ 849 Cal Ripken FRAN .40 .18
☐ 850 Roger Clemens FRAN .20 .09
☐ 851 Sandy Alomar Jr. FRAN .10 .05
☐ 852 Alan Trammell FRAN .05 .02
☐ 853 George Brett FRAN .20 .09
☐ 854 Robin Yount FRAN .20 .09
☐ 855 Kirby Puckett FRAN .20 .09
☐ 856 Don Mattingly FRAN .20 .09
☐ 857 Rickey Henderson FRAN .20 .09
☐ 858 Ken Griffey Jr. FRAN .75 .35
☐ 859 Ruben Sierra FRAN .05 .02
☐ 860 John Olerud FRAN .10 .05
☐ 861 Dave Justice FRAN .10 .05
☐ 862 Ryne Sandberg FRAN .20 .09
☐ 863 Eric Davis FRAN .10 .05
☐ 864 Darryl Strawberry FRAN .10 .05
☐ 865 Tim Wallach FRAN .05 .02
☐ 866 Doc Gooden FRAN .10 .05
☐ 867 Len Dykstra FRAN .10 .05
☐ 868 Barry Bonds FRAN .20 .09
☐ 869 Todd Zeile FRAN UER .05 .02
(Powerful misspelled
as poweful)
☐ 870 Benito Santiago FRAN .05 .02
☐ 871 Will Clark FRAN .20 .09
☐ 872 Craig Biggio FRAN .20 .09
☐ 873 Wally Joyner FRAN .10 .05
☐ 874 Frank Thomas FRAN 1.00 .45
☐ 875 Rickey Henderson MVP .20 .09
☐ 876 Barry Bonds MVP .20 .09
☐ 877 Bob Welch CY .05 .02
☐ 878 Doug Drabek CY .05 .02
☐ 879 Sandy Alomar Jr ROY .10 .05
☐ 880 Dave Justice ROY .10 .05
☐ 881 Damon Berryhill .05 .02
☐ 882 Frank Viola DT .05 .02
☐ 883 Dave Stewart DT .05 .02
☐ 884 Doug Jones DT .05 .02
☐ 885 Randy Myers DT .05 .02
☐ 886 Will Clark DT .20 .09
☐ 887 Roberto Alomar DT .20 .09
☐ 888 Barry Larkin DT .20 .09
☐ 889 Wade Boggs DT .20 .09
☐ 890 Rickey Henderson DT .20 .09
☐ 891 Kirby Puckett DT .40 .18
☐ 892 Ken Griffey Jr DT 1.50 .70
☐ 893 Benny Santiago DT .05 .02

1991 Score Cooperstown

This seven-card standard-size set was available only in complete set form as an insert with 1991 Score factory sets. The card design is not like the regular 1991 Score cards. The card front features a portrait of the player in an oval on a white background. The words "Cooperstown Card" are prominently displayed on the front. The cards are numbered on the back with a B prefix.

	MINT	NRMT
COMPLETE SET (7)	10.00	4.50
COMMON CARD (B1-B7)	.50	.23
☐ B1 Wade Boggs	1.00	.45
☐ B2 Barry Larkin	.50	.23
☐ B3 Ken Griffey Jr.	5.00	2.20
☐ B4 Rickey Henderson	1.00	.45
☐ B5 George Brett	1.50	.70
☐ B6 Will Clark	1.00	.45
☐ B7 Nolan Ryan	3.00	1.35

1991 Score Hot Rookies

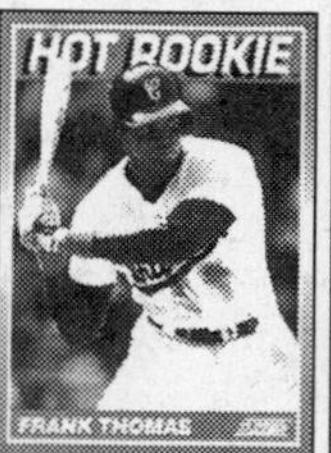

This ten-card standard-size set was inserted in the one per 1991 Score 100-card blister pack. The front features a color action player photo, with white borders and the words "Hot Rookie" in yellow above the picture. The card background shades from orange to yellow to orange as one moves down the card face. In a horizontal format, the left half of the back has a color head shot, while the right half has career summary.

	MINT	NRMT
COMPLETE SET (10)	15.00	6.75
COMMON CARD (1-10)	.50	.23
☐ 1 Dave Justice	2.00	.90
☐ 2 Kevin Maas	.50	.23
☐ 3 Hal Morris	.50	.23
☐ 4 Frank Thomas	10.00	4.50
☐ 5 Jeff Conine	1.50	.70
☐ 6 Sandy Alomar Jr.	1.00	.45
☐ 7 Ray Lankford	1.50	.70
☐ 8 Steve Decker	.50	.23
☐ 9 Juan Gonzalez	5.00	2.20
☐ 10 Jose Offerman	.50	.23

1991 Score Mantle

This seven-card standard-size set features Mickey Mantle at various points in his career. The fronts are full-color glossy shots of Mantle while the backs are in a horizontal format with a full-color photo and some narrative information. The cards were randomly inserted in second series packs. A limited amount of cards were actually signed by Mantle and stamped with certification press. A similar version of this set was also released to dealers and media members on Score's mailing list and was individually to 5,000 numbered on the back. The cards were sent in seven-card packs. The card number and the set serial number appear on the back.

	MINT	NRMT
COMPLETE SET (7)	250.00	110.00
COMMON MANTLE (1-7)	40.00	18.00
*PROMO CARDS: 1X BASIC CARDS		
☐ 1 Mickey Mantle The Rookie (With Billy Martin)	40.00	18.00
☐ 2 Mickey Mantle Triple Crown	40.00	18.00
☐ 3 Mickey Mantle World Series	40.00	18.00
☐ 4 Mickey Mantle Going, Going, Gone	40.00	18.00
☐ 5 Mickey Mantle Speed and Grace	40.00	18.00
☐ 6 Mickey Mantle A True Yankee	40.00	18.00
☐ 7 Mickey Mantle Twilight	40.00	18.00
☐ AU0 Mickey Mantle AU (Autographed with certified signature)	500.00	220.00

1991 Score Rookie/Traded

The 1991 Score Rookie and Traded contains 110 standard-size player cards and was issued exclusively in factory set form along with 10 "World Series II" magic motion trivia cards through hobby dealers. The front design is identical to the regular issue 1991 Score set except for the distinctive mauve borders and T-suffixed numbering. Cards 1T-80T feature traded players, while cards 81T-110T focus on rookies. Rookie Cards in the set inlcude Jeff Bagwell and Ivan Rodriguez.

	MINT	NRMT
COMPLETE SET (110)	4.00	1.80
COMMON CARD (1T-110T)	.05	.02
☐ 1T Bo Jackson	.20	.09
☐ 2T Mike Flanagan	.05	.02
☐ 3T Pete Incaviglia	.05	.02
☐ 4T Jack Clark	.10	.05
☐ 5T Hubie Brooks	.05	.02
☐ 6T Ivan Calderon	.05	.02
☐ 7T Glenn Davis	.05	.02
☐ 8T Wally Backman	.05	.02
☐ 9T Dave Smith	.05	.02
☐ 10T Tim Raines	.10	.05
☐ 11T Joe Carter	.20	.09
☐ 12T Sid Bream	.05	.02
☐ 13T George Bell	.05	.02
☐ 14T Steve Bedrosian	.05	.02
☐ 15T Willie Wilson	.05	.02
☐ 16T Darryl Strawberry	.10	.05
☐ 17T Danny Jackson	.05	.02
☐ 18T Kirk Gibson	.10	.05
☐ 19T Willie McGee	.05	.02
☐ 20T Junior Felix	.05	.02
☐ 21T Steve Farr	.05	.02
☐ 22T Pat Tabler	.05	.02
☐ 23T Brett Butler	.10	.05
☐ 24T Danny Darwin	.05	.02
☐ 25T Mickey Tettleton	.10	.05
☐ 26T Gary Carter	.20	.09
☐ 27T Mitch Williams	.05	.02
☐ 28T Candy Maldonado	.05	.02
☐ 29T Otis Nixon	.10	.05
☐ 30T Brian Downing	.05	.02
☐ 31T Tom Candiotti	.05	.02
☐ 32T John Candelaria	.05	.02
☐ 33T Rob Murphy	.05	.02
☐ 34T Deion Sanders	.20	.09
☐ 35T Willie Randolph	.10	.05
☐ 36T Pete Harnisch	.05	.02
☐ 37T Dante Bichette	.20	.09
☐ 38T Garry Templeton	.05	.02
☐ 39T Gary Gaetti	.10	.05
☐ 40T John Cerutti	.05	.02
☐ 41T Rick Cerone	.05	.02
☐ 42T Mike Pagliarulo	.05	.02
☐ 43T Ron Hassey	.05	.02
☐ 44T Roberto Alomar	.20	.09
☐ 45T Mike Boddicker	.05	.02
☐ 46T Bud Black	.05	.02
☐ 47T Rob Deer	.05	.02
☐ 48T Devon White	.05	.02
☐ 49T Luis Sojo	.05	.02
☐ 50T Terry Pendleton	.10	.05
☐ 51T Kevin Gross	.05	.02
☐ 52T Mike Huff	.05	.02
☐ 53T Dave Righetti	.05	.02
☐ 54T Matt Young	.05	.02
☐ 55T Earnest Riles	.05	.02
☐ 56T Bill Gullickson	.05	.02
☐ 57T Vince Coleman	.05	.02
☐ 58T Fred McGriff	.20	.09
☐ 59T Franklin Stubbs	.05	.02
☐ 60T Eric King	.05	.02
☐ 61T Cory Snyder	.05	.02
☐ 62T Dwight Evans	.10	.05
☐ 63T Gerald Perry	.05	.02
☐ 64T Eric Show	.05	.02
☐ 65T Shawn Hillegas	.05	.02
☐ 66T Tony Fernandez	.05	.02
☐ 67T Tim Teufel	.05	.02
☐ 68T Mitch Webster	.05	.02
☐ 69T Mike Heath	.05	.02
☐ 70T Chili Davis	.10	.05
☐ 71T Larry Andersen	.05	.02
☐ 72T Gary Varsho	.05	.02
☐ 73T Juan Berenguer	.05	.02
☐ 74T Jack Morris	.10	.05
☐ 75T Barry Jones	.05	.02
☐ 76T Rafael Belliard	.05	.02
☐ 77T Steve Buechele	.05	.02
☐ 78T Scott Sanderson	.05	.02
☐ 79T Bob Ojeda	.05	.02
☐ 80T Curt Schilling	.20	.09
☐ 81T Brian Drahman	.05	.02
☐ 82T Ivan Rodriguez	1.50	.70
☐ 83T David Howard	.05	.02
☐ 84T Heathcliff Slocumb	.20	.09
☐ 85T Mike Timlin	.05	.02
☐ 86T Darryl Kile	.20	.09
☐ 87T Pete Schourek	.10	.05
☐ 88T Bruce Walton	.05	.02
☐ 89T Al Osuna	.05	.02
☐ 90T Gary Scott	.05	.02
☐ 91T Doug Simons	.05	.02
☐ 92T Chris Jones	.05	.02
☐ 93T Chuck Knoblauch	.25	.11
☐ 94T Dana Allison	.05	.02
☐ 95T Erik Pappas	.05	.02
☐ 96T Jeff Bagwell	2.50	1.10
☐ 97T Kirk Dressendorfer	.05	.02
☐ 98T Freddie Benavides	.05	.02
☐ 99T Luis Gonzalez	.10	.05
☐ 100T Wade Taylor	.05	.02
☐ 101T Ed Sprague	.05	.02
☐ 102T Bob Scanlan	.05	.02
☐ 103T Rick Wilkins	.05	.02
☐ 104T Chris Donnels	.05	.02
☐ 105T Joe Slusarski	.05	.02
☐ 106T Mark Lewis	.05	.02
☐ 107T Pat Kelly	.10	.05
☐ 108T John Briscoe	.05	.02
☐ 109T Luis Lopez	.05	.02
☐ 110T Jeff Johnson	.05	.02

1991 Score All-Star Fanfest

This 11-card standard-size set was issued with a 3-D 1946 World Series trivia card. The cards feature on the fronts color action player photos, with red borders above and below the pictures. The card face is lime green with miniature yellow baseballs and blue player icons, and it can be seen at the top and bottom of the card front. The backs have a similar pattern on a white background and present biographical information as well as career highlights. The set features young players, who were apparently projected by Score to be future All-Stars. The cards are numbered on the back as "X of 10."

	MINT	NRMT
COMPLETE SET (10)	7.50	3.40
COMMON CARD (1-10)	.25	.11
☐ 1 Ray Lankford	2.00	.90
☐ 2 Steve Decker	.25	.11
☐ 3 Gary Scott	.25	.11
☐ 4 Hensley Meulens	.25	.11
☐ 5 Tim Naehring	.75	.35
☐ 6 Mark Whiten	.25	.11
☐ 7 Ed Sprague	.50	.23
☐ 8 Charles Nagy	1.00	.45
☐ 9 Terry Shumpert	.25	.11
☐ 10 Chuck Knoblauch	3.00	1.35
☐ NNO Title Card	.25	.11

1991 Score 100 Rising Stars

The 1991 Score 100 Rising Stars sets were issued by Score with or without special books which goes with the cards. The standard-size cards feature 100 of the most popular rising stars. The fronts of the cards are beautiful full-color photos surrounded by blue and green borders while the backs have a full color photo on the back and give a brief biography of the player. The sets (with the special book with brief biography on the players) are marketed for retail purposes at a suggested price of 12.95.

	MINT	NRMT
COMPLETE SET (100)	8.00	3.60
COMMON CARD (1-100)	.05	.02
☐ 1 Sandy Alomar Jr.	.15	.07
☐ 2 Tom Edens	.05	.02
☐ 3 Terry Shumpert	.05	.02
☐ 4 Shawn Boskie	.05	.02
☐ 5 Steve Avery	.10	.05
☐ 6 Deion Sanders	.50	.23
☐ 7 John Burkett	.10	.05
☐ 8 Stan Belinda	.05	.02
☐ 9 Thomas Howard	.05	.02
☐ 10 Wayne Edwards	.05	.02
☐ 11 Rick Parker	.05	.02
☐ 12 Randy Veres	.05	.02
☐ 13 Alex Cole	.05	.02
☐ 14 Scott Chiamparino	.05	.02
☐ 15 Greg Olson	.05	.02
☐ 16 Jose DeJesus	.05	.02
☐ 17 Mike Blowers	.05	.02
☐ 18 Jeff Huson	.05	.02
☐ 19 Willie Blair	.05	.02
☐ 20 Howard Farmer	.05	.02
☐ 21 Larry Walker	.40	.18
☐ 22 Scott Hemond	.05	.02
☐ 23 Mel Stottlemyre Jr.	.05	.02
☐ 24 Mark Whiten	.05	.02
☐ 25 Jeff Schulz	.05	.02
☐ 26 Gary DiSarcina	.05	.02
☐ 27 George Canale	.05	.02
☐ 28 Dean Palmer	.25	.11
☐ 29 Jim Leyritz	.10	.05
☐ 30 Carlos Baerga	.30	.14
☐ 31 Rafael Valdez	.05	.02
☐ 32 Derek Bell	.15	.07
☐ 33 Francisco Cabrera	.05	.02
☐ 34 Chris Hoiles	.10	.05
☐ 35 Craig Grebeck	.05	.02
☐ 36 Scott Coolbaugh	.05	.02
☐ 37 Kevin Wickander	.05	.02
☐ 38 Marquis Grissom	.25	.11
☐ 39 Chip Hale	.05	.02
☐ 40 Kevin Maas	.05	.02
☐ 41 Juan Gonzalez	2.00	.90
☐ 42 Eric Anthony	.05	.02
☐ 43 Luis Sojo	.05	.02
☐ 44 Paul Sorrento	.10	.05
☐ 45 Dave Justice	.50	.23
☐ 46 Oscar Azocar	.05	.02
☐ 47 Charles Nagy	.15	.07
☐ 48 Robin Ventura	.25	.11
☐ 49 Reggie Harris	.05	.02
☐ 50 Ben McDonald	.10	.05
☐ 51 Hector Villanueva	.05	.02
☐ 52 Kevin Tapani	.10	.05
☐ 53 Brian Bohanon	.05	.02
☐ 54 Tim Layana	.05	.02
☐ 55 Delino DeShields	.10	.05
☐ 56 Beau Allred	.05	.02
☐ 57 Eric Gunderson	.05	.02
☐ 58 Kent Mercker	.05	.02
☐ 59 Juan Bell	.05	.02
☐ 60 Glenallen Hill	.10	.05
☐ 61 David Segui	.10	.05
☐ 62 Alan Mills	.05	.02
☐ 63 Mike Harkey	.05	.02
☐ 64 Bill Sampen	.05	.02
☐ 65 Greg Vaughn	.05	.02
☐ 66 Alex Fernandez	.15	.07
☐ 67 Mike Hartley	.05	.02
☐ 68 Travis Fryman	.25	.11
☐ 69 Dave Rohde	.05	.02
☐ 70 Tom Lampkin	.05	.02
☐ 71 Mark Gardner	.05	.02
☐ 72 Pat Combs	.05	.02
☐ 73 Kevin Appier	.15	.07
☐ 74 Mike Fetters	.05	.02
☐ 75 Greg Myers	.05	.02
☐ 76 Steve Searcy	.05	.02
☐ 77 Tim Naehring	.25	.11
☐ 78 Frank Thomas	3.00	1.35
☐ 79 Todd Hundley	.25	.11
☐ 80 Ed Vosberg	.05	.02
☐ 81 Todd Zeile	.10	.05
☐ 82 Lee Stevens	.05	.02
☐ 83 Scott Radinsky	.05	.02
☐ 84 Hensley Meulens	.05	.02
☐ 85 Brian DuBois	.05	.02
☐ 86 Steve Olin	.05	.02
☐ 87 Julio Machado	.05	.02
☐ 88 Jose Vizcaino	.10	.05
☐ 89 Mark Lemke	.10	.05
☐ 90 Felix Jose	.05	.02
☐ 91 Wally Whitehurst	.05	.02
☐ 92 Dana Kiecker	.05	.02
☐ 93 Mike Munoz	.05	.02
☐ 94 Adam Peterson	.05	.02
☐ 95 Tim Drummond	.05	.02
☐ 96 Dave Hollins	.05	.02
☐ 97 Craig Wilson	.05	.02
☐ 98 Hal Morris	.10	.05
☐ 99 Jose Offerman	.10	.05
☐ 100 John Olerud	.25	.11

1991 Score 100 Superstars

The 1991 Score 100 Superstars sets were issued by Score with or without special books that came with the cards. The standard-size cards feature 100 of the most popular superstars. The fronts of the cards feature beautiful full-color photos surrounded by red, white and blue borders while the backs are surrounded by red and blue borders and feature a full-color photo on the back along with a brief biography. The sets (with the special book with brief biography on the players) are marketed for retail purposes at a suggested price of 12.95.

	MINT	NRMT
COMPLETE SET (100)	8.00	3.60
COMMON CARD (1-100)	.05	.02
☐ 1 Jose Canseco	.30	.14
☐ 2 Bo Jackson	.10	.05
☐ 3 Wade Boggs	.30	.14
☐ 4 Will Clark	.40	.18
☐ 5 Ken Griffey Jr.	2.00	.90
☐ 6 Doug Drabek	.10	.05
☐ 7 Kirby Puckett	1.00	.45
☐ 8 Joe Orsulak	.05	.02
☐ 9 Eric Davis	.10	.05
☐ 10 Rickey Henderson	.40	.18
☐ 11 Len Dykstra	.15	.07
☐ 12 Ruben Sierra	.05	.02
☐ 13 Paul Molitor	.40	.18
☐ 14 Ron Gant	.10	.05
☐ 15 Ozzie Guillen	.05	.02
☐ 16 Ramon Martinez	.15	.07
☐ 17 Edgar Martinez	.15	.07
☐ 18 Ozzie Smith	.75	.35
☐ 19 Charlie Hayes	.10	.05
☐ 20 Barry Larkin	.30	.14
☐ 21 Cal Ripken	1.50	.70
☐ 22 Andy Van Slyke	.10	.05
☐ 23 Don Mattingly	1.00	.45
☐ 24 Dave Stewart	.10	.05
☐ 25 Nolan Ryan	1.50	.70
☐ 26 Barry Bonds	.40	.18
☐ 27 Gregg Olson	.05	.02
☐ 28 Chris Sabo	.05	.02
☐ 29 John Franco	.10	.05
☐ 30 Gary Sheffield	.40	.18
☐ 31 Jeff Treadway	.05	.02
☐ 32 Tom Browning	.05	.02
☐ 33 Jose Lind	.05	.02
☐ 34 Dave Magadan	.05	.02
☐ 35 Dale Murphy	.25	.11
☐ 36 Tom Candiotti	.05	.02
☐ 37 Willie McGee	.10	.05
☐ 38 Robin Yount	.25	.11
☐ 39 Mark McGwire	1.00	.45
☐ 40 George Bell	.05	.02
☐ 41 Carlton Fisk	.25	.11
☐ 42 Bobby Bonilla	.10	.05
☐ 43 Randy Milligan	.05	.02
☐ 44 Dave Parker	.10	.05
☐ 45 Shawon Dunston	.05	.02
☐ 46 Brian Harper	.05	.02
☐ 47 John Tudor	.05	.02
☐ 48 Ellis Burks	.10	.05
☐ 49 Bob Welch	.10	.05
☐ 50 Roger Clemens	.75	.35
☐ 51 Mike Henneman	.05	.02
☐ 52 Eddie Murray	.50	.23
☐ 53 Kal Daniels	.05	.02
☐ 54 Doug Jones	.05	.02
☐ 55 Craig Biggio	.30	.14
☐ 56 Rafael Palmeiro	.25	.11
☐ 57 Wally Joyner	.10	.05
☐ 58 Tim Wallach	.05	.02
☐ 59 Bret Saberhagen	.05	.02
☐ 60 Ryne Sandberg	.75	.35
☐ 61 Benito Santiago	.05	.02
☐ 62 Darryl Strawberry	.10	.05
☐ 63 Alan Trammell	.15	.07
☐ 64 Kelly Gruber	.05	.02
☐ 65 Dwight Gooden	.10	.05
☐ 66 Dave Winfield	.30	.14
☐ 67 Rick Aguilera	.10	.05
☐ 68 Dave Righetti	.05	.02
☐ 69 Jim Abbott	.10	.05
☐ 70 Frank Viola	.05	.02
☐ 71 Fred McGriff	.25	.11
☐ 72 Steve Sax	.05	.02
☐ 73 Dennis Eckersley	.15	.07
☐ 74 Cory Snyder	.05	.02
☐ 75 Mackey Sasser	.05	.02
☐ 76 Candy Maldonado	.05	.02
☐ 77 Matt Williams	.25	.11
☐ 78 Kent Hrbek	.05	.02
☐ 79 Randy Myers	.10	.05
☐ 80 Gregg Jefferies	.10	.05
☐ 81 Joe Carter	.25	.11
☐ 82 Mike Greenwell	.05	.02
☐ 83 Jack Armstrong	.05	.02
☐ 84 Julio Franco	.10	.05
☐ 85 George Brett	.75	.35
☐ 86 Howard Johnson	.05	.02
☐ 87 Andre Dawson	.15	.07
☐ 88 Cecil Fielder	.10	.05
☐ 89 Tim Raines	.10	.05
☐ 90 Chuck Finley	.10	.05
☐ 91 Mark Grace	.40	.18
☐ 92 Brook Jacoby	.05	.02
☐ 93 Dave Stieb	.05	.02
☐ 94 Tony Gwynn	1.00	.45
☐ 95 Bobby Thigpen	.05	.02
☐ 96 Roberto Kelly	.05	.02
☐ 97 Kevin Seitzer	.05	.02
☐ 98 Kevin Mitchell	.05	.02
☐ 99 Dwight Evans	.10	.05
☐ 100 Roberto Alomar	.40	.18

1991 Score Rookies

This 40-card standard-sized set was distributed with five magic motion trivia cards. The fronts feature high glossy color action player photos, on a blue card face with meandering green lines. The picture has a yellow border on its right side, and red and yellow borders below. The words "1991 Rookie" appear to the left of the picture running the length of the card. The team logo in the lower

right corner rounds out the card face. On a yellow background, the backs have a color head shot, biography, and career highlights.

	MINT	NRMT
COMPLETE SET (40)	5.00	2.20
COMMON CARD (1-40)	.05	.02
☐ 1 Mel Rojas	.10	.05
☐ 2 Ray Lankford	.40	.18
☐ 3 Scott Aldred	.05	.02
☐ 4 Turner Ward	.05	.02
☐ 5 Omar Olivares	.05	.02
☐ 6 Mo Vaughn	2.00	.90
☐ 7 Phil Clark	.05	.02
☐ 8 Brent Mayne	.05	.02
☐ 9 Scott Lewis	.05	.02
☐ 10 Brian Barnes	.05	.02
☐ 11 Bernard Gilkey	.15	.07
☐ 12 Steve Decker	.05	.02
☐ 13 Paul Marak	.05	.02
☐ 14 Wes Chamberlain	.05	.02
☐ 15 Kevin Belcher	.05	.02
☐ 16 Steve Adkins	.05	.02
☐ 17 Geronimo Pena	.05	.02
☐ 18 Mark Leonard	.05	.02
☐ 19 Jeff Conine	.30	.14
☐ 20 Leo Gomez	.05	.02
☐ 21 Chuck Malone	.05	.02
☐ 22 Beau Allred	.05	.02
☐ 23 Todd Hundley	.25	.11
☐ 24 Lance Dickson	.05	.02
☐ 25 Mike Benjamin	.05	.02
☐ 26 Jose Offerman	.10	.05
☐ 27 Terry Shumpert	.05	.02
☐ 28 Darren Lewis	.05	.02
☐ 29 Scott Chiamparino	.05	.02
☐ 30 Tim Naehring	.15	.07
☐ 31 David Segui	.10	.05
☐ 32 Karl Rhodes	.05	.02
☐ 33 Mickey Morandini	.10	.05
☐ 34 Chuck McElroy	.05	.02
☐ 35 Tim McIntosh	.05	.02
☐ 36 Derrick May	.05	.02
☐ 37 Rich DeLucia	.05	.02
☐ 38 Tino Martinez	.75	.35
☐ 39 Hensley Meulens	.05	.02
☐ 40 Andujar Cedeno	.05	.02

1991 Score Ryan Life and Times

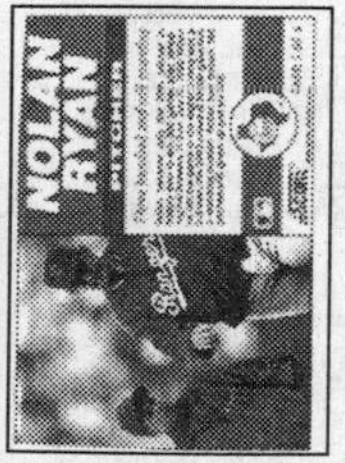

This four-card standard-size set was manufactured by Score to commemorate four significant milestones in Nolan Ryan's illustrious career beginning with his years growing up in Alvin, Texas, his years with the Mets and Angels, with the Astros and Rangers, and his career statistics. Each card commemorates a career milestone (all occur with the Rangers) and features Ryan's color photo on the front. They are part of "The Life and Times of Nolan Ryan," by Tarrant Printing, a special collector set that consists of four volumes (8 1/2" by 11" booklets) along with the cards packaged in a folder. The color action photos on the fronts are full-bleed, except on the left side, where blue and red border stripes run the length of the card. The horizontally oriented backs feature a different color player photo on the left half. The right half is accented with blue and red stripes and has career highlights on a pale yellow background. The cards are numbered on the back.

	MINT	NRMT
COMPLETE SET (4)	30.00	13.50
COMMON CARD (1-4)	7.50	3.40
☐ 1 Nolan Ryan 5,000th Career Strikeout	7.50	3.40
☐ 2 Nolan Ryan 6th Career No-Hitter	7.50	3.40
☐ 3 Nolan Ryan HOR 300th Career Victory	7.50	3.40
☐ 4 Nolan Ryan HOR 7th Career No-Hitter	7.50	3.40

1992 Score Samples

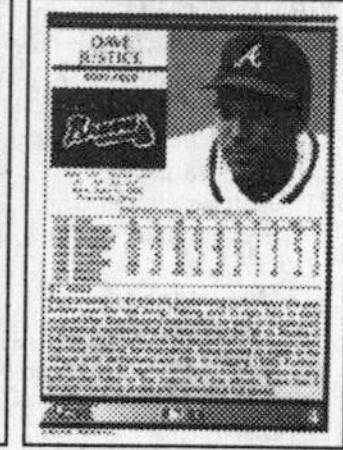

The 1992 Score Preview set contains six standard-size cards done in the same style as the 1992 Score baseball cards. Supposedly the Sandberg and Mack cards are tougher as they were only available at the St. Louis card show that Score attended in November 1991.

	MINT	NRMT
COMPLETE SET (6)	20.00	9.00
COMMON CARD (1-6)	1.00	.45
☐ 1 Ken Griffey Jr.	10.00	4.50
☐ 2 Dave Justice	1.50	.70
☐ 3 Robin Ventura	1.00	.45
☐ 4 Steve Avery	1.00	.45
☐ 5 Ryne Sandberg SP	8.00	3.60
☐ 6 Shane Mack SP	1.00	.45

1992 Score

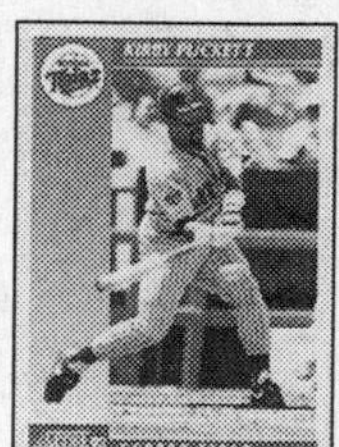

The 1992 Score set marked the second year that Score released their set in two different series. The first series contains 442 cards while the second series contains 451 cards. Cards were distributed in plastic wrapped packs, blister packs, jumbo packs and factory sets. Each pack included a special "World Series II" trivia card. The glossy color action photos on the basic card fronts are bordered above and below by stripes of the same color, and a thicker, different color stripe runs the length of the card to one side of the picture. Topical subsets include Rookie Prospects (395-424/736-772/814-877), No-Hit Club (425-428/784-787), Highlights (429-430), AL All-Stars (431-440; with color montages displaying Chris Greco's player caricatures), Dream Team (441-442/883-893), NL All-Stars (773-782), Highlights (783, 795-797), Draft Picks (799-810), and Memorabilia (878-882). All of the Rookie Prospects (736-772) can be found with or without the Rookie Prospect stripe. Rookie Cards in the set include Vinny Castilla and Manny Ramirez. Chuck Knoblauch, 1991 American League Rookie of the Year, autographed 3,000 of his own 1990 Score Draft Pick cards (card number 672) in gold ink, 2,989 were randomly inserted in Series 2 poly packs, while the other 11 were given away in a sweepstakes. The backs of these Knoblauch autograph cards have special holograms to differentiate them.

	MINT	NRMT
COMPLETE SET (893)	15.00	6.75
COMP.FACT.SET (910)	20.00	9.00
COMPLETE SERIES 1 (442)	8.00	3.60
COMPLETE SERIES 2 (451)	8.00	3.60
COMMON CARD (1-893)	.05	.02
☐ 1 Ken Griffey Jr.	1.25	.55
☐ 2 Nolan Ryan	.75	.35
☐ 3 Will Clark	.05	.02
☐ 4 Dave Justice	.20	.09
☐ 5 Dave Henderson	.05	.02
☐ 6 Bret Saberhagen	.05	.02
☐ 7 Fred McGriff	.05	.02
☐ 8 Erik Hanson	.05	.02
☐ 9 Darryl Strawberry	.10	.05
☐ 10 Dwight Gooden	.10	.05
☐ 11 Juan Gonzalez	.60	.25
☐ 12 Mark Langston	.05	.02
☐ 13 Lonnie Smith	.05	.02
☐ 14 Jeff Montgomery	.10	.05
☐ 15 Roberto Alomar	.20	.09
☐ 16 Delino DeShields	.05	.02
☐ 17 Steve Bedrosian	.05	.02
☐ 18 Terry Pendleton	.10	.05
☐ 19 Mark Carreon	.05	.02
☐ 20 Mark McGwire	.40	.18
☐ 21 Roger Clemens	.40	.18
☐ 22 Chuck Crim	.05	.02
☐ 23 Don Mattingly	.30	.14
☐ 24 Dickie Thon	.05	.02
☐ 25 Ron Gant	.10	.05
☐ 26 Milt Cuyler	.05	.02
☐ 27 Mike Macfarlane	.05	.02
☐ 28 Dan Gladden	.05	.02
☐ 29 Melido Perez	.05	.02
☐ 30 Willie Randolph	.10	.05
☐ 31 Albert Belle	.25	.11
☐ 32 Dave Winfield	.20	.09
☐ 33 Jimmy Jones	.05	.02
☐ 34 Kevin Gross	.05	.02
☐ 35 Andres Galarraga	.20	.09
☐ 36 Mike Devereaux	.05	.02
☐ 37 Chris Bosio	.05	.02
☐ 38 Mike LaValliere	.05	.02
☐ 39 Gary Gaetti	.10	.05
☐ 40 Felix Jose	.05	.02
☐ 41 Alvaro Espinoza	.05	.02
☐ 42 Rick Aguilera	.05	.02
☐ 43 Mike Gallego	.05	.02
☐ 44 Eric Davis	.10	.05
☐ 45 George Bell	.05	.02
☐ 46 Tom Brunansky	.05	.02
☐ 47 Steve Farr	.05	.02
☐ 48 Duane Ward	.05	.02
☐ 49 David Wells	.05	.02
☐ 50 Cecil Fielder	.10	.05
☐ 51 Walt Weiss	.05	.02
☐ 52 Todd Zeile	.05	.02
☐ 53 Doug Jones	.05	.02
☐ 54 Bob Walk	.05	.02
☐ 55 Rafael Palmeiro	.05	.02
☐ 56 Rob Deer	.05	.02
☐ 57 Paul O'Neill	.10	.05
☐ 58 Jeff Reardon	.10	.05
☐ 59 Randy Ready	.05	.02
☐ 60 Scott Erickson	.10	.05
☐ 61 Paul Molitor	.20	.09
☐ 62 Jack McDowell	.05	.02
☐ 63 Jim Acker	.05	.02
☐ 64 Jay Buhner	.05	.02
☐ 65 Travis Fryman	.10	.05
☐ 66 Marquis Grissom	.10	.05
☐ 67 Mike Harkey	.05	.02
☐ 68 Luis Polonia	.05	.02
☐ 69 Ken Caminiti	.20	.09
☐ 70 Chris Sabo	.05	.02
☐ 71 Gregg Olson	.05	.02
☐ 72 Carlton Fisk	.20	.09
☐ 73 Juan Samuel	.05	.02
☐ 74 Todd Stottlemyre	.10	.05
☐ 75 Andre Dawson	.05	.02
☐ 76 Alvin Davis	.05	.02
☐ 77 Bill Doran	.05	.02
☐ 78 B.J. Surhoff	.10	.05
☐ 79 Kirk McCaskill	.05	.02
☐ 80 Dale Murphy	.20	.09
☐ 81 Jose DeLeon	.05	.02
☐ 82 Alex Fernandez	.10	.05
☐ 83 Ivan Calderon	.05	.02
☐ 84 Brent Mayne	.05	.02
☐ 85 Jody Reed	.05	.02
☐ 86 Randy Tomlin	.05	.02
☐ 87 Randy Milligan	.05	.02
☐ 88 Pascual Perez	.05	.02
☐ 89 Hensley Meulens	.05	.02
☐ 90 Joe Carter	.10	.05
☐ 91 Mike Moore	.05	.02
☐ 92 Ozzie Guillen	.05	.02
☐ 93 Shawn Hillegas	.05	.02
☐ 94 Chili Davis	.10	.05

☐ 95 Vince Coleman .05 .02
☐ 96 Jimmy Key .10 .05
☐ 97 Billy Ripken .05 .02
☐ 98 Dave Smith .05 .02
☐ 99 Tom Bolton .05 .02
☐ 100 Barry Larkin .05 .02
☐ 101 Kenny Rogers .05 .02
☐ 102 Mike Boddicker .05 .02
☐ 103 Kevin Elster .05 .02
☐ 104 Ken Hill .10 .05
☐ 105 Charlie Leibrandt .05 .02
☐ 106 Pat Combs .05 .02
☐ 107 Hubie Brooks .05 .02
☐ 108 Julio Franco .10 .05
☐ 109 Vicente Palacios .05 .02
☐ 110 Kal Daniels .05 .02
☐ 111 Bruce Hurst .05 .02
☐ 112 Willie McGee .05 .02
☐ 113 Ted Power .05 .02
☐ 114 Milt Thompson .05 .02
☐ 115 Doug Drabek .05 .02
☐ 116 Rafael Belliard .05 .02
☐ 117 Scott Garrelts .05 .02
☐ 118 Terry Mulholland .05 .02
☐ 119 Jay Howell .05 .02
☐ 120 Danny Jackson .05 .02
☐ 121 Scott Ruskin .05 .02
☐ 122 Robin Ventura .10 .05
☐ 123 Bip Roberts .05 .02
☐ 124 Jeff Russell .05 .02
☐ 125 Hal Morris .05 .02
☐ 126 Teddy Higuera .05 .02
☐ 127 Luis Sojo .05 .02
☐ 128 Carlos Baerga .10 .05
☐ 129 Jeff Ballard .05 .02
☐ 130 Tom Gordon .05 .02
☐ 131 Sid Bream .05 .02
☐ 132 Rance Mulliniks .05 .02
☐ 133 Andy Benes .10 .05
☐ 134 Mickey Tettleton .05 .02
☐ 135 Rich DeLucia .05 .02
☐ 136 Tom Pagnozzi .05 .02
☐ 137 Harold Baines .10 .05
☐ 138 Danny Darwin .05 .02
☐ 139 Kevin Bass .05 .02
☐ 140 Chris Nabholz .05 .02
☐ 141 Pete O'Brien .05 .02
☐ 142 Jeff Treadway .05 .02
☐ 143 Mickey Morandini .05 .02
☐ 144 Eric King .05 .02
☐ 145 Danny Tartabull .05 .02
☐ 146 Lance Johnson .05 .02
☐ 147 Casey Candaele .05 .02
☐ 148 Felix Fermin .05 .02
☐ 149 Rich Rodriguez .05 .02
☐ 150 Dwight Evans .10 .05
☐ 151 Joe Klink .05 .02
☐ 152 Kevin Reimer .05 .02
☐ 153 Orlando Merced .05 .02
☐ 154 Mel Hall .05 .02
☐ 155 Randy Myers .10 .05
☐ 156 Greg A. Harris .05 .02
☐ 157 Jeff Brantley .05 .02
☐ 158 Jim Eisenreich .10 .05
☐ 159 Luis Rivera .05 .02
☐ 160 Cris Carpenter .05 .02
☐ 161 Bruce Ruffin .05 .02
☐ 162 Omar Vizquel .10 .05
☐ 163 Gerald Alexander .05 .02
☐ 164 Mark Guthrie .05 .02
☐ 165 Scott Lewis .05 .02
☐ 166 Bill Sampen .05 .02
☐ 167 Dave Anderson .05 .02
☐ 168 Kevin McReynolds .05 .02
☐ 169 Jose Vizcaino .05 .02
☐ 170 Bob Geren .05 .02
☐ 171 Mike Morgan .05 .02
☐ 172 Jim Gott .05 .02
☐ 173 Mike Pagliarulo .05 .02
☐ 174 Mike Jeffcoat .05 .02
☐ 175 Craig Lefferts .05 .02
☐ 176 Steve Finley .10 .05
☐ 177 Wally Backman .05 .02
☐ 178 Kent Mercker .05 .02
☐ 179 John Cerutti .05 .02
☐ 180 Jay Bell .10 .05
☐ 181 Dale Sveum .05 .02
☐ 182 Greg Gagne .05 .02
☐ 183 Donnie Hill .05 .02
☐ 184 Rex Hudler .05 .02
☐ 185 Pat Kelly .05 .02
☐ 186 Jeff D. Robinson .05 .02
☐ 187 Jeff Gray .05 .02
☐ 188 Jerry Willard .05 .02
☐ 189 Carlos Quintana .05 .02
☐ 190 Dennis Eckersley .20 .09
☐ 191 Kelly Downs .05 .02
☐ 192 Gregg Jefferies .10 .05
☐ 193 Darrin Fletcher .05 .02
☐ 194 Mike Jackson .05 .02
☐ 195 Eddie Murray .20 .09
☐ 196 Bill Landrum .05 .02
☐ 197 Eric Yelding .05 .02
☐ 198 Devon White .05 .02
☐ 199 Larry Walker .20 .09
☐ 200 Ryne Sandberg .25 .11
☐ 201 Dave Magadan .05 .02
☐ 202 Steve Chitren .05 .02
☐ 203 Scott Fletcher .05 .02
☐ 204 Dwayne Henry .05 .02
☐ 205 Scott Coolbaugh .05 .02
☐ 206 Tracy Jones .05 .02
☐ 207 Von Hayes .05 .02
☐ 208 Bob Melvin .05 .02
☐ 209 Scott Scudder .05 .02
☐ 210 Luis Gonzalez .05 .02
☐ 211 Scott Sanderson .05 .02
☐ 212 Chris Donnels .05 .02
☐ 213 Heathcliff Slocumb .05 .02
☐ 214 Mike Timlin .05 .02
☐ 215 Brian Harper .05 .02
☐ 216 Juan Berenguer UER .05 .02
(Decimal point missing
in IP total)
☐ 217 Mike Henneman .05 .02
☐ 218 Bill Spiers .05 .02
☐ 219 Scott Terry .05 .02
☐ 220 Frank Viola .05 .02
☐ 221 Mark Eichhorn .05 .02
☐ 222 Ernest Riles .05 .02
☐ 223 Ray Lankford .20 .09
☐ 224 Pete Harnisch .05 .02
☐ 225 Bobby Bonilla .10 .05
☐ 226 Mike Scioscia .05 .02
☐ 227 Joel Skinner .05 .02
☐ 228 Brian Holman .05 .02
☐ 229 Gilberto Reyes .05 .02
☐ 230 Matt Williams .05 .02
☐ 231 Jaime Navarro .05 .02
☐ 232 Jose Rijo .05 .02
☐ 233 Atlee Hammaker .05 .02
☐ 234 Tim Teufel .05 .02
☐ 235 John Kruk .10 .05
☐ 236 Kurt Stillwell .05 .02
☐ 237 Dan Pasqua .05 .02
☐ 238 Tim Crews .05 .02
☐ 239 Dave Gallagher .05 .02
☐ 240 Leo Gomez .05 .02
☐ 241 Steve Avery .05 .02
☐ 242 Bill Gullickson .05 .02
☐ 243 Mark Portugal .05 .02
☐ 244 Lee Guetterman .05 .02
☐ 245 Benito Santiago .05 .02
☐ 246 Jim Gantner .05 .02
☐ 247 Robby Thompson .05 .02
☐ 248 Terry Shumpert .05 .02
☐ 249 Mike Bell .05 .02
☐ 250 Harold Reynolds .05 .02
☐ 251 Mike Felder .05 .02
☐ 252 Bill Pecota .05 .02
☐ 253 Bill Krueger .05 .02
☐ 254 Alfredo Griffin .05 .02
☐ 255 Lou Whitaker .10 .05
☐ 256 Roy Smith .05 .02
☐ 257 Jerald Clark .05 .02
☐ 258 Sammy Sosa .20 .09
☐ 259 Tim Naehring .10 .05
☐ 260 Dave Righetti .05 .02
☐ 261 Paul Gibson .05 .02
☐ 262 Chris James .05 .02
☐ 263 Larry Andersen .05 .02
☐ 264 Storm Davis .05 .02
☐ 265 Jose Lind .05 .02
☐ 266 Greg Hibbard .05 .02
☐ 267 Norm Charlton .05 .02
☐ 268 Paul Kilgus .05 .02
☐ 269 Greg Maddux .60 .25
☐ 270 Ellis Burks .10 .05
☐ 271 Frank Tanana .05 .02
☐ 272 Gene Larkin .05 .02
☐ 273 Ron Hassey .05 .02
☐ 274 Jeff M. Robinson .05 .02
☐ 275 Steve Howe .05 .02
☐ 276 Daryl Boston .05 .02
☐ 277 Mark Lee .05 .02
☐ 278 Jose Segura .05 .02
☐ 279 Lance Blankenship .05 .02
☐ 280 Don Slaught .05 .02
☐ 281 Russ Swan .05 .02
☐ 282 Bob Tewksbury .05 .02
☐ 283 Geno Petralli .05 .02
☐ 284 Shane Mack .05 .02
☐ 285 Bob Scanlan .05 .02
☐ 286 Tim Leary .05 .02
☐ 287 John Smoltz .05 .02
☐ 288 Pat Borders .05 .02
☐ 289 Mark Davidson .05 .02
☐ 290 Sam Horn .05 .02
☐ 291 Lenny Harris .05 .02
☐ 292 Franklin Stubbs .05 .02
☐ 293 Thomas Howard .05 .02
☐ 294 Steve Lyons .05 .02
☐ 295 Francisco Oliveras .05 .02
☐ 296 Terry Leach .05 .02
☐ 297 Barry Jones .05 .02
☐ 298 Lance Parrish .05 .02
☐ 299 Wally Whitehurst .05 .02
☐ 300 Bob Welch .05 .02
☐ 301 Charlie Hayes .05 .02
☐ 302 Charlie Hough .05 .02
☐ 303 Gary Redus .05 .02
☐ 304 Scott Bradley .05 .02
☐ 305 Jose Oquendo .05 .02
☐ 306 Pete Incaviglia .05 .02
☐ 307 Marvin Freeman .05 .02
☐ 308 Gary Pettis .05 .02
☐ 309 Joe Slusarski .05 .02
☐ 310 Kevin Seitzer .05 .02
☐ 311 Jeff Reed .05 .02
☐ 312 Pat Tabler .05 .02
☐ 313 Mike Maddux .05 .02
☐ 314 Bob Milacki .05 .02
☐ 315 Eric Anthony .05 .02
☐ 316 Dante Bichette .05 .02
☐ 317 Steve Decker .05 .02
☐ 318 Jack Clark .10 .05
☐ 319 Doug Dascenzo .05 .02
☐ 320 Scott Leius .05 .02
☐ 321 Jim Lindeman .05 .02
☐ 322 Bryan Harvey .05 .02
☐ 323 Spike Owen .05 .02
☐ 324 Roberto Kelly .05 .02
☐ 325 Stan Belinda .05 .02
☐ 326 Joey Cora .10 .05
☐ 327 Jeff Innis .05 .02
☐ 328 Willie Wilson .05 .02
☐ 329 Juan Agosto .05 .02
☐ 330 Charles Nagy .10 .05
☐ 331 Scott Bailes .05 .02
☐ 332 Pete Schourek .05 .02
☐ 333 Mike Flanagan .05 .02
☐ 334 Omar Olivares .05 .02
☐ 335 Dennis Lamp .05 .02
☐ 336 Tommy Greene .05 .02
☐ 337 Randy Velarde .05 .02
☐ 338 Tom Lampkin .05 .02
☐ 339 John Russell .05 .02
☐ 340 Bob Kipper .05 .02
☐ 341 Todd Burns .05 .02
☐ 342 Ron Jones .05 .02
☐ 343 Dave Valle .05 .02
☐ 344 Mike Heath .05 .02
☐ 345 John Olerud .10 .05
☐ 346 Gerald Young .05 .02
☐ 347 Ken Patterson .05 .02
☐ 348 Les Lancaster .05 .02
☐ 349 Steve Crawford .05 .02
☐ 350 John Candelaria .05 .02
☐ 351 Mike Aldrete .05 .02
☐ 352 Mariano Duncan .05 .02
☐ 353 Julio Machado .05 .02
☐ 354 Ken Williams .05 .02
☐ 355 Walt Terrell .05 .02
☐ 356 Mitch Williams .05 .02
☐ 357 Al Newman .05 .02
☐ 358 Bud Black .05 .02
☐ 359 Joe Hesketh .05 .02
☐ 360 Paul Assenmacher .05 .02
☐ 361 Bo Jackson .05 .02
☐ 362 Jeff Blauser .05 .02
☐ 363 Mike Brumley .05 .02
☐ 364 Jim Deshaies .05 .02
☐ 365 Brady Anderson .05 .02
☐ 366 Chuck McElroy .05 .02
☐ 367 Matt Merullo .05 .02
☐ 368 Tim Belcher .05 .02
☐ 369 Luis Aquino .05 .02
☐ 370 Joe Oliver .05 .02
☐ 371 Greg Swindell .05 .02
☐ 372 Lee Stevens .05 .02
☐ 373 Mark Knudson .05 .02
☐ 374 Bill Wegman .05 .02
☐ 375 Jerry Don Gleaton .05 .02
☐ 376 Pedro Guerrero .05 .02
☐ 377 Randy Bush .05 .02
☐ 378 Greg W. Harris .05 .02
☐ 379 Eric Plunk .05 .02
☐ 380 Jose DeJesus .05 .02
☐ 381 Bobby Witt .05 .02
☐ 382 Curtis Wilkerson .05 .02
☐ 383 Gene Nelson .05 .02

Card	NRMT	EXC
☐ 384 Wes Chamberlain	.05	.02
☐ 385 Tom Henke	.05	.02
☐ 386 Mark Lemke	.05	.02
☐ 387 Greg Briley	.05	.02
☐ 388 Rafael Ramirez	.05	.02
☐ 389 Tony Fossas	.05	.02
☐ 390 Henry Cotto	.05	.02
☐ 391 Tim Hulett	.05	.02
☐ 392 Dean Palmer	.10	.05
☐ 393 Glenn Braggs	.05	.02
☐ 394 Mark Salas	.05	.02
☐ 395 Rusty Meacham	.05	.02
☐ 396 Andy Ashby	.05	.02
☐ 397 Jose Melendez	.05	.02
☐ 398 Warren Newson	.05	.02
☐ 399 Frank Castillo	.05	.02
☐ 400 Chito Martinez	.05	.02
☐ 401 Bernie Williams	.20	.09
☐ 402 Derek Bell	.10	.05
☐ 403 Javier Ortiz	.05	.02
☐ 404 Tim Sherrill	.05	.02
☐ 405 Rob MacDonald	.05	.02
☐ 406 Phil Plantier	.05	.02
☐ 407 Troy Afenir	.05	.02
☐ 408 Gino Minutelli	.05	.02
☐ 409 Reggie Jefferson	.10	.05
☐ 410 Mike Remlinger	.05	.02
☐ 411 Carlos Rodriguez	.05	.02
☐ 412 Joe Redfield	.05	.02
☐ 413 Alonzo Powell	.05	.02
☐ 414 Scott Livingstone UER (Travis Fryman, not Woody, should be referenced on back)	.05	.02
☐ 415 Scott Kamieniecki	.05	.02
☐ 416 Tim Spehr	.05	.02
☐ 417 Brian Hunter	.05	.02
☐ 418 Ced Landrum	.05	.02
☐ 419 Bret Barberie	.05	.02
☐ 420 Kevin Morton	.05	.02
☐ 421 Doug Henry	.05	.02
☐ 422 Doug Piatt	.05	.02
☐ 423 Pat Rice	.05	.02
☐ 424 Juan Guzman	.05	.02
☐ 425 Nolan Ryan NH	.40	.18
☐ 426 Tommy Greene NH	.05	.02
☐ 427 Bob Milacki and Mike Flanagan NH (Mark Williamson and Gregg Olson)	.05	.02
☐ 428 Wilson Alvarez NH	.10	.05
☐ 429 Otis Nixon HL	.10	.05
☐ 430 Rickey Henderson HL	.05	.02
☐ 431 Cecil Fielder AS	.10	.05
☐ 432 Julio Franco AS	.05	.02
☐ 433 Cal Ripken AS	.40	.18
☐ 434 Wade Boggs AS	.20	.09
☐ 435 Joe Carter AS	.05	.02
☐ 436 Ken Griffey Jr. AS	.75	.35
☐ 437 Ruben Sierra AS	.05	.02
☐ 438 Scott Erickson AS	.05	.02
☐ 439 Tom Henke AS	.05	.02
☐ 440 Terry Steinbach AS	.05	.02
☐ 441 Rickey Henderson DT	.05	.02
☐ 442 Ryne Sandberg DT	.25	.11
☐ 443 Otis Nixon	.10	.05
☐ 444 Scott Radinsky	.05	.02
☐ 445 Mark Grace	.05	.02
☐ 446 Tony Pena	.05	.02
☐ 447 Billy Hatcher	.05	.02
☐ 448 Glenallen Hill	.05	.02
☐ 449 Chris Gwynn	.05	.02
☐ 450 Tom Glavine	.05	.02
☐ 451 John Habyan	.05	.02
☐ 452 Al Osuna	.05	.02
☐ 453 Tony Phillips	.05	.02
☐ 454 Greg Cadaret	.05	.02
☐ 455 Rob Dibble	.05	.02
☐ 456 Rick Honeycutt	.05	.02
☐ 457 Jerome Walton	.05	.02
☐ 458 Mookie Wilson	.05	.02
☐ 459 Mark Gubicza	.05	.02
☐ 460 Craig Biggio	.05	.02
☐ 461 Dave Cochrane	.05	.02
☐ 462 Keith Miller	.05	.02
☐ 463 Alex Cole	.05	.02
☐ 464 Pete Smith	.05	.02
☐ 465 Brett Butler	.05	.02
☐ 466 Jeff Huson	.05	.02
☐ 467 Steve Lake	.05	.02
☐ 468 Lloyd Moseby	.05	.02
☐ 469 Tim McIntosh	.05	.02
☐ 470 Dennis Martinez	.10	.05
☐ 471 Greg Myers	.05	.02
☐ 472 Mackey Sasser	.05	.02
☐ 473 Junior Ortiz	.05	.02
☐ 474 Greg Olson	.05	.02
☐ 475 Steve Sax	.05	.02
☐ 476 Ricky Jordan	.05	.02
☐ 477 Max Venable	.05	.02
☐ 478 Brian McRae	.05	.02
☐ 479 Doug Simons	.05	.02
☐ 480 Rickey Henderson	.05	.02
☐ 481 Gary Varsho	.05	.02
☐ 482 Carl Willis	.05	.02
☐ 483 Rick Wilkins	.05	.02
☐ 484 Donn Pall	.05	.02
☐ 485 Edgar Martinez	.05	.02
☐ 486 Tom Foley	.05	.02
☐ 487 Mark Williamson	.05	.02
☐ 488 Jack Armstrong	.05	.02
☐ 489 Gary Carter	.20	.09
☐ 490 Ruben Sierra	.05	.02
☐ 491 Gerald Perry	.05	.02
☐ 492 Rob Murphy	.05	.02
☐ 493 Zane Smith	.05	.02
☐ 494 Darryl Kile	.05	.02
☐ 495 Kelly Gruber	.05	.02
☐ 496 Jerry Browne	.05	.02
☐ 497 Darryl Hamilton	.05	.02
☐ 498 Mike Stanton	.05	.02
☐ 499 Mark Leonard	.05	.02
☐ 500 Jose Canseco	.05	.02
☐ 501 Dave Martinez	.05	.02
☐ 502 Jose Guzman	.05	.02
☐ 503 Terry Kennedy	.05	.02
☐ 504 Ed Sprague	.05	.02
☐ 505 Frank Thomas UER (His Gulf Coast League stats are wrong)	1.00	.45
☐ 506 Darren Daulton	.10	.05
☐ 507 Kevin Tapani	.05	.02
☐ 508 Luis Salazar	.05	.02
☐ 509 Paul Faries	.05	.02
☐ 510 Sandy Alomar Jr.	.10	.05
☐ 511 Jeff King	.10	.05
☐ 512 Gary Thurman	.05	.02
☐ 513 Chris Hammond	.05	.02
☐ 514 Pedro Munoz	.05	.02
☐ 515 Alan Trammell	.05	.02
☐ 516 Geronimo Pena	.05	.02
☐ 517 Rodney McCray UER (Stole 6 bases in 1990, not 5; career totals are correct at 7)	.05	.02
☐ 518 Manny Lee	.05	.02
☐ 519 Junior Felix	.05	.02
☐ 520 Kirk Gibson	.10	.05
☐ 521 Darrin Jackson	.05	.02
☐ 522 John Burkett	.05	.02
☐ 523 Jeff Johnson	.05	.02
☐ 524 Jim Corsi	.05	.02
☐ 525 Robin Yount	.05	.02
☐ 526 Jamie Quirk	.05	.02
☐ 527 Bob Ojeda	.05	.02
☐ 528 Mark Lewis	.05	.02
☐ 529 Bryn Smith	.05	.02
☐ 530 Kent Hrbek	.10	.05
☐ 531 Dennis Boyd	.05	.02
☐ 532 Ron Karkovice	.05	.02
☐ 533 Don August	.05	.02
☐ 534 Todd Frohwirth	.05	.02
☐ 535 Wally Joyner	.10	.05
☐ 536 Dennis Rasmussen	.05	.02
☐ 537 Andy Allanson	.05	.02
☐ 538 Goose Gossage	.10	.05
☐ 539 John Marzano	.05	.02
☐ 540 Cal Ripken	.75	.35
☐ 541 Bill Swift UER (Brewers logo on front)	.05	.02
☐ 542 Kevin Appier	.10	.05
☐ 543 Dave Bergman	.05	.02
☐ 544 Bernard Gilkey	.10	.05
☐ 545 Mike Greenwell	.05	.02
☐ 546 Jose Uribe	.05	.02
☐ 547 Jesse Orosco	.05	.02
☐ 548 Bob Patterson	.05	.02
☐ 549 Mike Stanley	.05	.02
☐ 550 Howard Johnson	.05	.02
☐ 551 Joe Orsulak	.05	.02
☐ 552 Dick Schofield	.05	.02
☐ 553 Dave Hollins	.05	.02
☐ 554 David Segui	.05	.02
☐ 555 Barry Bonds	.25	.11
☐ 556 Mo Vaughn	.30	.14
☐ 557 Craig Wilson	.05	.02
☐ 558 Bobby Rose	.05	.02
☐ 559 Rod Nichols	.05	.02
☐ 560 Len Dykstra	.10	.05
☐ 561 Craig Grebeck	.05	.02
☐ 562 Darren Lewis	.05	.02
☐ 563 Todd Benzinger	.05	.02
☐ 564 Ed Whitson	.05	.02
☐ 565 Jesse Barfield	.05	.02
☐ 566 Lloyd McClendon	.05	.02
☐ 567 Dan Plesac	.05	.02
☐ 568 Danny Cox	.05	.02
☐ 569 Skeeter Barnes	.05	.02
☐ 570 Bobby Thigpen	.05	.02
☐ 571 Deion Sanders	.20	.09
☐ 572 Chuck Knoblauch	.20	.09
☐ 573 Matt Nokes	.05	.02
☐ 574 Herm Winningham	.05	.02
☐ 575 Tom Candiotti	.05	.02
☐ 576 Jeff Bagwell	.60	.25
☐ 577 Brook Jacoby	.05	.02
☐ 578 Chico Walker	.05	.02
☐ 579 Brian Downing	.05	.02
☐ 580 Dave Stewart	.10	.05
☐ 581 Francisco Cabrera	.05	.02
☐ 582 Rene Gonzales	.05	.02
☐ 583 Stan Javier	.05	.02
☐ 584 Randy Johnson	.20	.09
☐ 585 Chuck Finley	.05	.02
☐ 586 Mark Gardner	.05	.02
☐ 587 Mark Whiten	.05	.02
☐ 588 Garry Templeton	.05	.02
☐ 589 Gary Sheffield	.20	.09
☐ 590 Ozzie Smith	.25	.11
☐ 591 Candy Maldonado	.05	.02
☐ 592 Mike Sharperson	.05	.02
☐ 593 Carlos Martinez	.05	.02
☐ 594 Scott Bankhead	.05	.02
☐ 595 Tim Wallach	.05	.02
☐ 596 Tino Martinez	.20	.09
☐ 597 Roger McDowell	.05	.02
☐ 598 Cory Snyder	.05	.02
☐ 599 Andujar Cedeno	.05	.02
☐ 600 Kirby Puckett	.40	.18
☐ 601 Rick Parker	.05	.02
☐ 602 Todd Hundley	.05	.02
☐ 603 Greg Litton	.05	.02
☐ 604 Dave Johnson	.05	.02
☐ 605 John Franco	.05	.02
☐ 606 Mike Fetters	.05	.02
☐ 607 Luis Alicea	.05	.02
☐ 608 Trevor Wilson	.05	.02
☐ 609 Rob Ducey	.05	.02
☐ 610 Ramon Martinez	.10	.05
☐ 611 Dave Burba	.05	.02
☐ 612 Dwight Smith	.05	.02
☐ 613 Kevin Maas	.05	.02
☐ 614 John Costello	.05	.02
☐ 615 Glenn Davis	.05	.02
☐ 616 Shawn Abner	.05	.02
☐ 617 Scott Hemond	.05	.02
☐ 618 Tom Prince	.05	.02
☐ 619 Wally Ritchie	.05	.02
☐ 620 Jim Abbott	.05	.02
☐ 621 Charlie O'Brien	.05	.02
☐ 622 Jack Daugherty	.05	.02
☐ 623 Tommy Gregg	.05	.02
☐ 624 Jeff Shaw	.05	.02
☐ 625 Tony Gwynn	.50	.23
☐ 626 Mark Leiter	.05	.02
☐ 627 Jim Clancy	.05	.02
☐ 628 Tim Layana	.05	.02
☐ 629 Jeff Schaefer	.05	.02
☐ 630 Lee Smith	.10	.05
☐ 631 Wade Taylor	.05	.02
☐ 632 Mike Simms	.05	.02
☐ 633 Terry Steinbach	.10	.05
☐ 634 Shawon Dunston	.05	.02
☐ 635 Tim Raines	.10	.05
☐ 636 Kirt Manwaring	.05	.02
☐ 637 Warren Cromartie	.05	.02
☐ 638 Luis Quinones	.05	.02
☐ 639 Greg Vaughn	.05	.02
☐ 640 Kevin Mitchell	.10	.05
☐ 641 Chris Hoiles	.05	.02
☐ 642 Tom Browning	.05	.02
☐ 643 Mitch Webster	.05	.02
☐ 644 Steve Olin	.05	.02
☐ 645 Tony Fernandez	.05	.02
☐ 646 Juan Bell	.05	.02
☐ 647 Joe Boever	.05	.02
☐ 648 Carney Lansford	.05	.02
☐ 649 Mike Benjamin	.05	.02
☐ 650 George Brett	.40	.18
☐ 651 Tim Burke	.05	.02
☐ 652 Jack Morris	.10	.05
☐ 653 Orel Hershiser	.05	.02
☐ 654 Mike Schooler	.05	.02
☐ 655 Andy Van Slyke	.10	.05
☐ 656 Dave Stieb	.05	.02
☐ 657 Dave Clark	.05	.02
☐ 658 Ben McDonald	.05	.02
☐ 659 John Smiley	.05	.02
☐ 660 Wade Boggs	.20	.09
☐ 661 Eric Bullock	.05	.02
☐ 662 Eric Show	.05	.02

Card	MINT	NRMT
☐ 663 Lenny Webster	.05	.02
☐ 664 Mike Huff	.05	.02
☐ 665 Rick Sutcliffe	.05	.02
☐ 666 Jeff Manto	.05	.02
☐ 667 Mike Fitzgerald	.05	.02
☐ 668 Matt Young	.05	.02
☐ 669 Dave West	.05	.02
☐ 670 Mike Hartley	.05	.02
☐ 671 Curt Schilling	.10	.05
☐ 672 Brian Bohanon	.05	.02
☐ 673 Cecil Espy	.05	.02
☐ 674 Joe Grahe	.05	.02
☐ 675 Sid Fernandez	.05	.02
☐ 676 Edwin Nunez	.05	.02
☐ 677 Hector Villanueva	.05	.02
☐ 678 Sean Berry	.05	.02
☐ 679 Dave Eiland	.05	.02
☐ 680 Dave Cone	.20	.09
☐ 681 Mike Bordick	.05	.02
☐ 682 Tony Castillo	.05	.02
☐ 683 John Barfield	.05	.02
☐ 684 Jeff Hamilton	.05	.02
☐ 685 Ken Dayley	.05	.02
☐ 686 Carmelo Martinez	.05	.02
☐ 687 Mike Capel	.05	.02
☐ 688 Scott Chiamparino	.05	.02
☐ 689 Rich Gedman	.05	.02
☐ 690 Rich Monteleone	.05	.02
☐ 691 Alejandro Pena	.05	.02
☐ 692 Oscar Azocar	.05	.02
☐ 693 Jim Poole	.05	.02
☐ 694 Mike Gardiner	.05	.02
☐ 695 Steve Buechele	.05	.02
☐ 696 Rudy Seanez	.05	.02
☐ 697 Paul Abbott	.05	.02
☐ 698 Steve Searcy	.05	.02
☐ 699 Jose Offerman	.05	.02
☐ 700 Ivan Rodriguez	.40	.18
☐ 701 Joe Girardi	.05	.02
☐ 702 Tony Perezchica	.05	.02
☐ 703 Paul McClellan	.05	.02
☐ 704 David Howard	.05	.02
☐ 705 Dan Petry	.05	.02
☐ 706 Jack Howell	.05	.02
☐ 707 Jose Mesa	.10	.05
☐ 708 Randy St. Claire	.05	.02
☐ 709 Kevin Brown	.10	.05
☐ 710 Ron Darling	.05	.02
☐ 711 Jason Grimsley	.05	.02
☐ 712 John Orton	.05	.02
☐ 713 Shawn Boskie	.05	.02
☐ 714 Pat Clements	.05	.02
☐ 715 Brian Barnes	.05	.02
☐ 716 Luis Lopez	.05	.02
☐ 717 Bob McClure	.05	.02
☐ 718 Mark Davis	.05	.02
☐ 719 Dann Bilardello	.05	.02
☐ 720 Tom Edens	.05	.02
☐ 721 Willie Fraser	.05	.02
☐ 722 Curt Young	.05	.02
☐ 723 Neal Heaton	.05	.02
☐ 724 Craig Worthington	.05	.02
☐ 725 Mel Rojas	.10	.05
☐ 726 Daryl Irvine	.05	.02
☐ 727 Roger Mason	.05	.02
☐ 728 Kirk Dressendorfer	.05	.02
☐ 729 Scott Aldred	.05	.02
☐ 730 Willie Blair	.05	.02
☐ 731 Allan Anderson	.05	.02
☐ 732 Dana Kiecker	.05	.02
☐ 733 Jose Gonzalez	.05	.02
☐ 734 Brian Drahman	.05	.02
☐ 735 Brad Komminsk	.05	.02
☐ 736 Arthur Rhodes	.05	.02
☐ 737 Terry Mathews	.05	.02
☐ 738 Jeff Fassero	.10	.05
☐ 739 Mike Magnante	.05	.02
☐ 740 Kip Gross	.05	.02
☐ 741 Jim Hunter	.05	.02
☐ 742 Jose Mota	.05	.02
☐ 743 Joe Bitker	.05	.02
☐ 744 Tim Mauser	.05	.02
☐ 745 Ramon Garcia	.05	.02
☐ 746 Rod Beck	.20	.09
☐ 747 Jim Austin	.05	.02
☐ 748 Keith Mitchell	.05	.02
☐ 749 Wayne Rosenthal	.05	.02
☐ 750 Bryan Hickerson	.05	.02
☐ 751 Bruce Egloff	.05	.02
☐ 752 John Wehner	.05	.02
☐ 753 Darren Holmes	.05	.02
☐ 754 Dave Hansen	.05	.02
☐ 755 Mike Mussina	.30	.14
☐ 756 Anthony Young	.05	.02
☐ 757 Ron Tingley	.05	.02
☐ 758 Ricky Bones	.05	.02
☐ 759 Mark Wohlers	.20	.09
☐ 760 Wilson Alvarez	.05	.02
☐ 761 Harvey Pulliam	.05	.02
☐ 762 Ryan Bowen	.05	.02
☐ 763 Terry Bross	.05	.02
☐ 764 Joel Johnston	.05	.02
☐ 765 Terry McDaniel	.05	.02
☐ 766 Esteban Beltre	.05	.02
☐ 767 Rob Maurer	.05	.02
☐ 768 Ted Wood	.05	.02
☐ 769 Mo Sanford	.05	.02
☐ 770 Jeff Carter	.05	.02
☐ 771 Gil Heredia	.05	.02
☐ 772 Monty Fariss	.05	.02
☐ 773 Will Clark AS	.05	.02
☐ 774 Ryne Sandberg AS	.20	.09
☐ 775 Barry Larkin AS	.05	.02
☐ 776 Howard Johnson AS	.05	.02
☐ 777 Barry Bonds AS	.20	.09
☐ 778 Brett Butler AS	.05	.02
☐ 779 Tony Gwynn AS	.20	.09
☐ 780 Ramon Martinez AS	.05	.02
☐ 781 Lee Smith AS	.10	.05
☐ 782 Mike Scioscia AS	.05	.02
☐ 783 Dennis Martinez HL UER (Card has both 13th and 15th perfect game in Major League history)	.05	.02
☐ 784 Dennis Martinez NH	.05	.02
☐ 785 Mark Gardner NH	.05	.02
☐ 786 Bret Saberhagen NH	.05	.02
☐ 787 Kent Mercker NH Mark Wohlers Alejandro Pena	.05	.02
☐ 788 Cal Ripken MVP	.40	.18
☐ 789 Terry Pendleton MVP	.05	.02
☐ 790 Roger Clemens CY	.20	.09
☐ 791 Tom Glavine CY	.10	.05
☐ 792 Chuck Knoblauch ROY	.20	.09
☐ 793 Jeff Bagwell ROY	.30	.14
☐ 794 Cal Ripken MANYR	.40	.18
☐ 795 David Cone HL	.10	.05
☐ 796 Kirby Puckett HL	.20	.09
☐ 797 Steve Avery HL	.05	.02
☐ 798 Jack Morris HL	.10	.05
☐ 799 Allen Watson DC	.10	.05
☐ 800 Manny Ramirez DC	1.25	.55
☐ 801 Cliff Floyd DC	.20	.09
☐ 802 Al Shirley DC	.10	.05
☐ 803 Brian Barber DC	.10	.05
☐ 804 Jon Farrell DC	.05	.02
☐ 805 Brent Gates DC	.05	.02
☐ 806 Scott Ruffcorn DC	.05	.02
☐ 807 Tyrone Hill DC	.05	.02
☐ 808 Benji Gil DC	.10	.05
☐ 809 Aaron Sele DC	.10	.05
☐ 810 Tyler Green DC	.10	.05
☐ 811 Chris Jones	.05	.02
☐ 812 Steve Wilson	.05	.02
☐ 813 Freddie Benavides	.05	.02
☐ 814 Don Wakamatsu	.05	.02
☐ 815 Mike Humphreys	.05	.02
☐ 816 Scott Servais	.05	.02
☐ 817 Rico Rossy	.05	.02
☐ 818 John Ramos	.05	.02
☐ 819 Rob Mallicoat	.05	.02
☐ 820 Milt Hill	.05	.02
☐ 821 Carlos Garcia	.05	.02
☐ 822 Stan Royer	.05	.02
☐ 823 Jeff Plympton	.05	.02
☐ 824 Braulio Castillo	.05	.02
☐ 825 David Haas	.05	.02
☐ 826 Luis Mercedes	.05	.02
☐ 827 Eric Karros	.10	.05
☐ 828 Shawn Hare	.05	.02
☐ 829 Reggie Sanders	.10	.05
☐ 830 Tom Goodwin	.05	.02
☐ 831 Dan Gakeler	.05	.02
☐ 832 Stacy Jones	.05	.02
☐ 833 Kim Batiste	.05	.02
☐ 834 Cal Eldred	.05	.02
☐ 835 Chris George	.05	.02
☐ 836 Wayne Housie	.05	.02
☐ 837 Mike Ignasiak	.05	.02
☐ 838 Josias Manzanillo	.05	.02
☐ 839 Jim Olander	.05	.02
☐ 840 Gary Cooper	.05	.02
☐ 841 Royce Clayton	.10	.05
☐ 842 Hector Fajardo	.05	.02
☐ 843 Blaine Beatty	.05	.02
☐ 844 Jorge Pedre	.05	.02
☐ 845 Kenny Lofton	.75	.35
☐ 846 Scott Brosius	.05	.02
☐ 847 Chris Cron	.05	.02
☐ 848 Denis Boucher	.05	.02
☐ 849 Kyle Abbott	.05	.02
☐ 850 Robert Zupcic	.05	.02
☐ 851 Rheal Cormier	.05	.02
☐ 852 Jim Lewis	.05	.02
☐ 853 Anthony Telford	.05	.02
☐ 854 Cliff Brantley	.05	.02
☐ 855 Kevin Campbell	.05	.02
☐ 856 Craig Shipley	.05	.02
☐ 857 Chuck Carr	.05	.02
☐ 858 Tony Eusebio	.05	.02
☐ 859 Jim Thome	.60	.25
☐ 860 Vinny Castilla	.50	.23
☐ 861 Dann Howitt	.05	.02
☐ 862 Kevin Ward	.05	.02
☐ 863 Steve Wapnick	.05	.02
☐ 864 Rod Brewer	.05	.02
☐ 865 Todd Van Poppel	.05	.02
☐ 866 Jose Hernandez	.05	.02
☐ 867 Amalio Carreno	.05	.02
☐ 868 Calvin Jones	.05	.02
☐ 869 Jeff Gardner	.05	.02
☐ 870 Jarvis Brown	.05	.02
☐ 871 Eddie Taubensee	.05	.02
☐ 872 Andy Mota	.05	.02
☐ 873 Chris Haney	.05	.02
☐ 874 Roberto Hernandez	.10	.05
☐ 875 Laddie Renfroe	.05	.02
☐ 876 Scott Cooper	.05	.02
☐ 877 Armando Reynoso	.05	.02
☐ 878 Ty Cobb MEMO	.25	.11
☐ 879 Babe Ruth MEMO	.40	.18
☐ 880 Honus Wagner MEMO	.20	.09
☐ 881 Lou Gehrig MEMO	.25	.11
☐ 882 Satchel Paige MEMO	.20	.09
☐ 883 Will Clark DT	.05	.02
☐ 884 Cal Ripken DT	2.00	.90
☐ 885 Wade Boggs DT	.20	.09
☐ 886 Kirby Puckett DT	.40	.18
☐ 887 Tony Gwynn DT	.50	.23
☐ 888 Craig Biggio DT	.10	.05
☐ 889 Scott Erickson DT	.05	.02
☐ 890 Tom Glavine DT	.10	.05
☐ 891 Rob Dibble DT	.05	.02
☐ 892 Mitch Williams DT	.05	.02
☐ 893 Frank Thomas DT	1.00	.45
☐ X672 Chuck Knoblauch AU (1990 Score card, autographed with special hologram on back)	60.00	27.00

1992 Score DiMaggio

This five-card standard-size insert set was issued in honor of one of baseball's all-time greats, Joe DiMaggio. These cards were randomly inserted in first series packs. According to sources at Score, 30,000 of each card were produced. On a white card face, the fronts have vintage photos that have been colorized and accented by red, white, and blue border stripes. DiMaggio autographed 2,500 cards for this promotion. 2,495 of these cards were inserted in packs while the other five were used as prizes in a mail-in sweepstakes. The autographed cards are individually numbered out of 2,500.

	MINT	NRMT
COMPLETE SET (5)	150.00	70.00
COMMON DIMAGGIO (1-5)	30.00	13.50
☐ 1 Joe DiMaggio The Minors	30.00	13.50
☐ 2 Joe DiMaggio The Rookie	30.00	13.50
☐ 3 Joe DiMaggio The MVP	30.00	13.50
☐ 4 Joe DiMaggio The Streak	30.00	13.50
☐ 5 Joe DiMaggio The Legend	30.00	13.50
☐ AU0 Joe DiMaggio AU (Autographed with certified signature)	550.00	250.00

1992 Score Factory Inserts

This 17-card insert standard-size set was distributed only in 1992 Score factory sets and consists of four topical

subsets. Cards B1-B7 capture a moment from each game of the 1991 World Series. Cards B8-B11 are Cooperstown cards, honoring future Hall of Famers. Cards B12-B14 form a "Joe D" subset paying tribute to Joe DiMaggio. Cards B15-B17, subtitled "Yaz", conclude the set by commemorating Carl Yastrzemski's heroic feats twenty-five years ago in winning the Triple Crown and lifting the Red Sox to their first American League pennant in 21 years. Each subset displayed a different front design. The World Series cards carry full-bleed color action photos except for a blue stripe at the bottom, while the Cooperstown cards have a color portrait on a white card face. Both the DiMaggio and Yastrzemski subsets have action photos with silver borders; they differ in that the DiMaggio photos are black and white, the Yastrzemski photos color. The DiMaggio and Yastrzemski subsets are numbered on the back within each subset (e.g., "1 of 3") and as a part of the 17-card insert set (e.g., "B1"). In the DiMaggio and Yastrzemski subsets, Score varied the insert set slightly in retail versus hobby factory sets. In the hobby set, the DiMaggio cards display different black-and-white photos that are bordered beneath by a dark blue stripe (the stripe is green in the retail factory insert). On the backs, these hobby inserts have a red stripe at the bottom; the same stripe is dark blue on the retail inserts. The Yastrzemski cards in the hobby set have different color photos on their fronts than the retail inserts.

	MINT	NRMT
COMPLETE SET (17)	6.00	2.70
COMMON WS (B1-B7)	.25	.11
COM.COOPERSTOWN (B8-B11)	.75	.35
COMMON DIMAGGIO (B12-B14)	1.50	.70
COMMON YAZ (B15-B17)	.25	.11
☐ B1 Greg Gagne WS	.25	.11
☐ B2 Scott Leius WS	.25	.11
☐ B3 Mark Lemke WS David Justice	.25	.11
☐ B4 Lonnie Smith WS Brian Harper	.25	.11
☐ B5 David Justice WS	.75	.35
☐ B6 Kirby Puckett WS	3.00	1.35
☐ B7 Gene Larkin WS	.25	.11
☐ B8 Carlton Fisk	.75	.35
☐ B9 Ozzie Smith	2.00	.90
☐ B10 Dave Winfield	.75	.35
☐ B11 Robin Yount	.75	.35
☐ B12 Joe DiMaggio	1.50	.70
☐ B13 Joe DiMaggio	1.50	.70
☐ B14 Joe DiMaggio	1.50	.70
☐ B15 Carl Yastrzemski	.25	.11
☐ B16 Carl Yastrzemski	.25	.11
☐ B17 Carl Yastrzemski	.25	.11

1992 Score Franchise

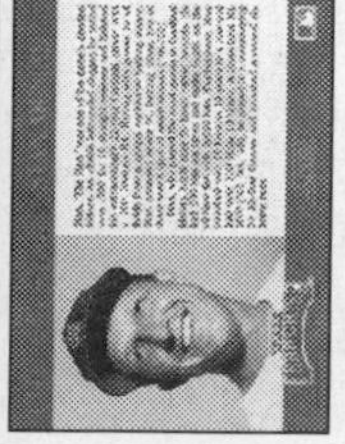

his four-card standard-size set features three all-time reats, Stan Musial, Mickey Mantle, and Carl Yastrzemski. ach former player autographed 2,000 of his 1992 Score ırds, and 500 of the combo cards were signed by all ree. In addition to these signed cards, Score produced 50,000 of each Franchise card, and both signed and ısigned cards were randomly inserted in 1992 Score eries II poly packs, blister packs, and cello packs. The rst three cards feature color action photos of each player. The fourth is horizontally oriented and pictures each player in a batting stance. A forest green stripe borders the top and bottom. The words "The Franchise" and the Score logo appear at the top, and the player's name is printed on the green stripe at the bottom. The backs of the first three cards have a close-up photo and a career summary. The fourth card is a combo card, summarizing the career of all three players.

	MINT	NRMT
COMPLETE SET (4)	30.00	13.50
COMMON CARD (1-4)	5.00	2.20
☐ 1 Stan Musial	5.00	2.20
☐ 2 Mickey Mantle	12.00	5.50
☐ 3 Carl Yastrzemski	5.00	2.20
☐ 4 The Franchise Players Stan Musial Mickey Mantle Carl Yastrzemski	10.00	4.50
☐ AU1 Stan Musial (Autographed with certified signature)	225.00	100.00
☐ AU2 Mickey Mantle (Autographed with certified signature)	550.00	250.00
☐ AU3 Carl Yastrzemski (Autographed with certified signature)	175.00	80.00
☐ AU4 Franchise Players Stan Musial Mickey Mantle Carl Yastrzemski (Autographed with certified signatures of all three)	1600.00	700.00

1992 Score Hot Rookies

This ten-card standard-size set features color action player photos on a white face. These cards were inserted one per blister pack. The words "Hot Rookie" appear in orange and yellow vertically along the left edge of the photo, and the team logo is in the lower left corner. The player's name is printed in yellow on a red box accented with a shadow detail.

	MINT	NRMT
COMPLETE SET (10)	15.00	6.75
COMMON CARD (1-10)	.50	.23
☐ 1 Cal Eldred	.50	.23
☐ 2 Royce Clayton	1.00	.45
☐ 3 Kenny Lofton	10.00	4.50
☐ 4 Todd Van Poppel	.50	.23
☐ 5 Scott Cooper	.50	.23
☐ 6 Todd Hundley	2.00	.90
☐ 7 Tino Martinez	1.50	.70
☐ 8 Anthony Telford	.50	.23
☐ 9 Derek Bell	1.00	.45
☐ 10 Reggie Jefferson	2.00	.90

1992 Score Impact Players

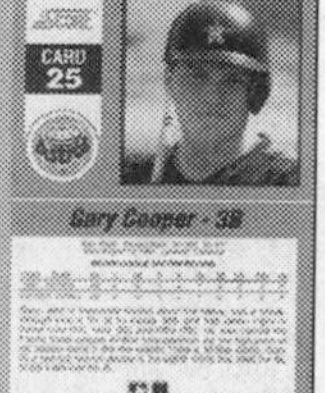

The 1992 Score Impact Players insert set was issued in two series each with 45 standard-size cards with the respective series of the 1992 regular issue Score cards. Five of these cards were inserted in each 1992 Score jumbo pack. The fronts feature full-bleed color action player photos. The pictures are enhanced by a wide vertical stripe running near the left edge containing the words "90's Impact Player" and a narrower stripe at the bottom printed with the player's name.

	MINT	NRMT
COMPLETE SET (90)	20.00	9.00
COMPLETE SERIES 1 (45)	14.00	6.25
COMPLETE SERIES 2 (45)	6.00	2.70
COMMON CARD (1-90)	.10	.05
☐ 1 Chuck Knoblauch	.40	.18
☐ 2 Jeff Bagwell	1.50	.70
☐ 3 Juan Guzman	.10	.05
☐ 4 Milt Cuyler	.10	.05
☐ 5 Ivan Rodriguez	1.00	.45
☐ 6 Rich DeLucia	.10	.05
☐ 7 Orlando Merced	.10	.05
☐ 8 Ray Lankford	.40	.18
☐ 9 Brian Hunter	.10	.05
☐ 10 Roberto Alomar	.40	.18
☐ 11 Wes Chamberlain	.10	.05
☐ 12 Steve Avery	.10	.05
☐ 13 Scott Erickson	.20	.09
☐ 14 Jim Abbott	.10	.05
☐ 15 Mark Whiten	.10	.05
☐ 16 Leo Gomez	.10	.05
☐ 17 Doug Henry	.10	.05
☐ 18 Brent Mayne	.10	.05
☐ 19 Charles Nagy	.20	.09
☐ 20 Phil Plantier	.10	.05
☐ 21 Mo Vaughn	1.00	.45
☐ 22 Craig Biggio	.30	.14
☐ 23 Derek Bell	.20	.09
☐ 24 Royce Clayton	.20	.09
☐ 25 Gary Cooper	.10	.05
☐ 26 Scott Cooper	.10	.05
☐ 27 Juan Gonzalez	1.50	.70
☐ 28 Ken Griffey Jr.	4.00	1.80
☐ 29 Larry Walker	.40	.18
☐ 30 John Smoltz	.40	.18
☐ 31 Todd Hundley	.40	.18
☐ 32 Kenny Lofton	2.00	.90
☐ 33 Andy Mota	.10	.05
☐ 34 Todd Zeile	.10	.05
☐ 35 Arthur Rhodes	.10	.05
☐ 36 Jim Thome	2.50	1.10
☐ 37 Todd Van Poppel	.10	.05
☐ 38 Mark Wohlers	.30	.14
☐ 39 Anthony Young	.10	.05
☐ 40 Sandy Alomar Jr.	.20	.09
☐ 41 John Olerud	.20	.09
☐ 42 Robin Ventura	.20	.09
☐ 43 Frank Thomas	3.00	1.35
☐ 44 Dave Justice	.40	.18
☐ 45 Hal Morris	.10	.05
☐ 46 Ruben Sierra	.10	.05
☐ 47 Travis Fryman	.20	.09
☐ 48 Mike Mussina	.75	.35
☐ 49 Tom Glavine	.30	.14
☐ 50 Barry Larkin	.30	.14
☐ 51 Will Clark UER Career Totals spelled To als	.30	.14
☐ 52 Jose Canseco	.30	.14
☐ 53 Bo Jackson	.20	.09
☐ 54 Dwight Gooden	.20	.09
☐ 55 Barry Bonds	.60	.25
☐ 56 Fred McGriff	.30	.14
☐ 57 Roger Clemens	.40	.18
☐ 58 Benito Santiago	.10	.05
☐ 59 Darryl Strawberry	.20	.09
☐ 60 Cecil Fielder	.20	.09
☐ 61 John Franco	.10	.05
☐ 62 Matt Williams	.30	.14
☐ 63 Marquis Grissom	.20	.09
☐ 64 Danny Tartabull	.10	.05
☐ 65 Ron Gant	.20	.09
☐ 66 Paul O'Neill	.20	.09
☐ 67 Devon White	.10	.05
☐ 68 Rafael Palmeiro	.30	.14
☐ 69 Tom Gordon	.10	.05
☐ 70 Shawon Dunston	.10	.05
☐ 71 Rob Dibble	.10	.05
☐ 72 Eddie Zosky	.10	.05
☐ 73 Jack McDowell	.10	.05
☐ 74 Len Dykstra	.20	.09
☐ 75 Ramon Martinez	.20	.09
☐ 76 Reggie Sanders	.20	.09
☐ 77 Greg Maddux	2.50	1.10
☐ 78 Ellis Burks	.20	.09
☐ 79 John Smiley	.10	.05
☐ 80 Roberto Kelly	.10	.05
☐ 81 Ben McDonald	.10	.05
☐ 82 Mark Lewis	.10	.05
☐ 83 Jose Rijo	.10	.05
☐ 84 Ozzie Guillen	.10	.05
☐ 85 Lance Dickson	.10	.05
☐ 86 Kim Batiste	.10	.05

Card	MINT	NRMT
☐ 87 Gregg Olson	.10	.05
☐ 88 Andy Benes	.20	.09
☐ 89 Cal Eldred	.10	.05
☐ 90 David Cone	.20	.09

1992 Score Rookie/Traded

The 1992 Score Rookie and Traded set contains 110 standard-size cards featuring traded veterans and rookies. This set was issued in complete set form and was released through hobby dealers. The fronts display color action player photos edged on one side by an orange stripe that fades to white as one moves down the card face. The player's name appears in a purple bar above the picture, while his position is printed in a purple bar below the picture. The set is arranged numerically such that cards 1T-79T are traded players and cards 80T-110T feature rookies. The only notable Rookie Card in this set features Brian Jordan.

	MINT	NRMT
COMP.FACT.SET (110)	20.00	9.00
COMMON CARD (1T-110T)	.15	.07

Card	MINT	NRMT
☐ 1T Gary Sheffield	.60	.25
☐ 2T Kevin Seitzer	.15	.07
☐ 3T Danny Tartabull	.15	.07
☐ 4T Steve Sax	.15	.07
☐ 5T Bobby Bonilla	.30	.14
☐ 6T Frank Viola	.15	.07
☐ 7T Dave Winfield	.20	.09
☐ 8T Rick Sutcliffe	.15	.07
☐ 9T Jose Canseco	.20	.09
☐ 10T Greg Swindell	.15	.07
☐ 11T Eddie Murray	.60	.25
☐ 12T Randy Myers	.30	.14
☐ 13T Wally Joyner	.30	.14
☐ 14T Kenny Lofton	8.00	3.60
☐ 15T Jack Morris	.30	.14
☐ 16T Charlie Hayes	.15	.07
☐ 17T Pete Incaviglia	.15	.07
☐ 18T Kevin Mitchell	.30	.14
☐ 19T Kurt Stillwell	.15	.07
☐ 20T Bret Saberhagen	.15	.07
☐ 21T Steve Buechele	.15	.07
☐ 22T John Smiley	.15	.07
☐ 23T Sammy Sosa	.75	.35
☐ 24T George Bell	.15	.07
☐ 25T Curt Schilling	1.00	.45
☐ 26T Dick Schofield	.15	.07
☐ 27T David Cone	.30	.14
☐ 28T Dan Gladden	.15	.07
☐ 29T Kirk McCaskill	.15	.07
☐ 30T Mike Gallego	.15	.07
☐ 31T Kevin McReynolds	.15	.07
☐ 32T Bill Swift	.15	.07
☐ 33T Dave Martinez	.15	.07
☐ 34T Storm Davis	.15	.07
☐ 35T Willie Randolph	.30	.14
☐ 36T Melido Perez	.15	.07
☐ 37T Mark Carreon	.15	.07
☐ 38T Doug Jones	.15	.07
☐ 39T Gregg Jefferies	.30	.14
☐ 40T Mike Jackson	.15	.07
☐ 41T Dickie Thon	.15	.07
☐ 42T Eric King	.15	.07
☐ 43T Herm Winningham	.15	.07
☐ 44T Derek Lilliquist	.15	.07
☐ 45T Dave Anderson	.15	.07
☐ 46T Jeff Reardon	.30	.14
☐ 47T Scott Bankhead	.15	.07
☐ 48T Cory Snyder	.15	.07
☐ 49T Al Newman	.15	.07
☐ 50T Keith Miller	.15	.07
☐ 51T Dave Burba	.15	.07
☐ 52T Bill Pecota	.15	.07
☐ 53T Chuck Crim	.15	.07
☐ 54T Mariano Duncan	.15	.07
☐ 55T Dave Gallagher	.15	.07
☐ 56T Chris Gwynn	.15	.07
☐ 57T Scott Ruskin	.15	.07
☐ 58T Jack Armstrong	.15	.07
☐ 59T Gary Carter	.60	.25
☐ 60T Andres Galarraga	.20	.09
☐ 61T Ken Hill	.30	.14
☐ 62T Eric Davis	.30	.14
☐ 63T Ruben Sierra	.15	.07
☐ 64T Darrin Fletcher	.15	.07
☐ 65T Tim Belcher	.15	.07
☐ 66T Mike Morgan	.15	.07
☐ 67T Scott Scudder	.15	.07
☐ 68T Tom Candiotti	.15	.07
☐ 69T Hubie Brooks	.15	.07
☐ 70T Kal Daniels	.15	.07
☐ 71T Bruce Ruffin	.15	.07
☐ 72T Billy Hatcher	.15	.07
☐ 73T Bob Melvin	.15	.07
☐ 74T Lee Guetterman	.15	.07
☐ 75T Rene Gonzales	.15	.07
☐ 76T Kevin Bass	.15	.07
☐ 77T Tom Bolton	.15	.07
☐ 78T John Wetteland	.30	.14
☐ 79T Bip Roberts	.15	.07
☐ 80T Pat Listach	.15	.07
☐ 81T John Doherty	.15	.07
☐ 82T Sam Militello	.15	.07
☐ 83T Brian Jordan	1.50	.70
☐ 84T Jeff Kent	.75	.35
☐ 85T Dave Fleming	.15	.07
☐ 86T Jeff Tackett	.15	.07
☐ 87T Chad Curtis	.60	.25
☐ 88T Eric Fox	.15	.07
☐ 89T Denny Neagle	1.50	.70
☐ 90T Donovan Osborne	.30	.14
☐ 91T Carlos Hernandez	.15	.07
☐ 92T Tim Wakefield	.60	.25
☐ 93T Tim Salmon	5.00	2.20
☐ 94T Dave Nilsson	.30	.14
☐ 95T Mike Perez	.15	.07
☐ 96T Pat Hentgen	.60	.25
☐ 97T Frank Seminara	.15	.07
☐ 98T Ruben Amaro Jr.	.15	.07
☐ 99T Archi Cianfrocco	.15	.07
☐ 100T Andy Stankiewicz	.15	.07
☐ 101T Jim Bullinger	.15	.07
☐ 102T Pat Mahomes	.15	.07
☐ 103T Hipolito Pichardo	.15	.07
☐ 104T Bret Boone	.30	.14
☐ 105T John Vander Wal	.15	.07
☐ 106T Vince Horsman	.15	.07
☐ 107T James Austin	.15	.07
☐ 108T Brian Williams	.15	.07
☐ 109T Dan Walters	.15	.07
☐ 110T Wil Cordero	.15	.07

1992 Score 100 Rising Stars

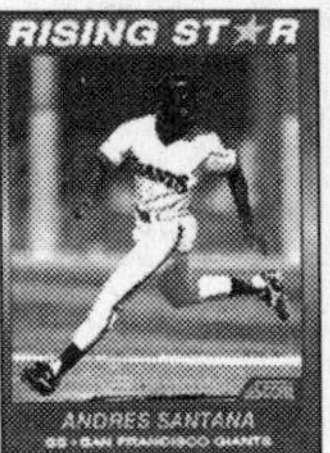

The 1992 Score Rising Stars set contains 100 standard size player cards and six "Magic Motion" trivia cards. The fronts display color action player photos on a card face that shades from green to yellow and back to green. The words "Rising Star" appear above the picture, with the player's name in a blue stripe at the card bottom. The horizontally oriented backs have a color head shot on the left half, with player profile and team logo on the right half.

	MINT	NRMT
COMPLETE SET (100)	8.00	3.60
COMMON CARD (1-100)	.05	.02

Card	MINT	NRMT
☐ 1 Milt Cuyler	.05	.02
☐ 2 David Howard	.05	.02
☐ 3 Brian R. Hunter	.05	.02
☐ 4 Darryl Kile	.25	.11
☐ 5 Pat Kelly	.05	.02
☐ 6 Luis Gonzalez	.10	.05
☐ 7 Mike Benjamin	.05	.02
☐ 8 Eric Anthony	.05	.02
☐ 9 Moises Alou	.40	.18
☐ 10 Darren Lewis	.05	.02
☐ 11 Chuck Knoblauch	1.00	.45
☐ 12 Geronimo Pena	.05	.02
☐ 13 Jeff Plympton	.05	.02
☐ 14 Bret Barberie	.05	.02
☐ 15 Chris Haney	.05	.02
☐ 16 Rick Wilkins	.05	.02
☐ 17 Julio Valera	.05	.02
☐ 18 Joe Slusarski	.05	.02
☐ 19 Jose Melendez	.05	.02
☐ 20 Pete Schourek	.10	.05
☐ 21 Jeff Conine	.40	.18
☐ 22 Paul Faries	.05	.02
☐ 23 Scott Kamieniecki	.05	.02
☐ 24 Bernard Gilkey	.10	.05
☐ 25 Wes Chamberlain	.05	.02
☐ 26 Charles Nagy	.25	.11
☐ 27 Juan Guzman	.05	.02
☐ 28 Heath Slocumb	.10	.05
☐ 29 Eddie Taubensee	.05	.02
☐ 30 Cedric Landrum	.05	.02
☐ 31 Jose Offerman	.05	.02
☐ 32 Andres Santana	.05	.02
☐ 33 David Segui	.10	.05
☐ 34 Bernie Williams	1.00	.45
☐ 35 Jeff Bagwell	2.00	.90
☐ 36 Kevin Morton	.05	.02
☐ 37 Kirk Dressendorfer	.05	.02
☐ 38 Mike Fetters	.05	.02
☐ 39 Darren Holmes	.05	.02
☐ 40 Jeff Johnson	.05	.02
☐ 41 Scott Aldred	.05	.02
☐ 42 Kevin Ward	.05	.02
☐ 43 Ray Lankford	.40	.18
☐ 44 Terry Shumpert	.05	.02
☐ 45 Wade Taylor	.05	.02
☐ 46 Rob MacDonald	.05	.02
☐ 47 Jose Mota	.05	.02
☐ 48 Reggie Harris	.05	.02
☐ 49 Mike Remlinger	.05	.02
☐ 50 Mark Lewis	.10	.05
☐ 51 Tino Martinez	.60	.25
☐ 52 Ed Sprague	.10	.05
☐ 53 Freddie Benavides	.05	.02
☐ 54 Rich DeLucia	.05	.02
☐ 55 Brian Drahman	.05	.02
☐ 56 Steve Decker	.05	.02
☐ 57 Scott Livingstone	.05	.02
☐ 58 Mike Timlin	.05	.02
☐ 59 Bob Scanlan	.05	.02
☐ 60 Dean Palmer	.30	.14
☐ 61 Frank Castillo	.05	.02
☐ 62 Mark Leonard	.05	.02
☐ 63 Chuck McElroy	.05	.02
☐ 64 Derek Bell	.25	.11
☐ 65 Andujar Cedeno	.05	.02
☐ 66 Leo Gomez	.05	.02
☐ 67 Rusty Meacham	.05	.02
☐ 68 Dann Howitt	.05	.02
☐ 69 Chris Jones	.05	.02
☐ 70 Dave Cochrane	.05	.02
☐ 71 Carlos Martinez	.05	.02
☐ 72 Hensley Meulens	.05	.02
☐ 73 Rich Reed	.05	.02
☐ 74 Pedro Munoz	.05	.02
☐ 75 Orlando Merced	.05	.02
☐ 76 Chito Martinez	.05	.02
☐ 77 Ivan Rodriguez	1.50	.70
☐ 78 Brian Barnes	.05	.02
☐ 79 Chris Donnels	.05	.02
☐ 80 Todd Hundley	.25	.11
☐ 81 Gary Scott	.05	.02
☐ 82 John Wehner	.05	.02
☐ 83 Al Osuna	.05	.02
☐ 84 Luis Lopez	.05	.02
☐ 85 Brent Mayne	.05	.02
☐ 86 Phil Plantier	.05	.02
☐ 87 Joe Bitker	.05	.02
☐ 88 Scott Cooper	.05	.02
☐ 89 Chris Hammond	.05	.02
☐ 90 Tim Sherrill	.05	.02
☐ 91 Doug Simons	.05	.02
☐ 92 Kip Gross	.05	.02
☐ 93 Tim McIntosh	.05	.02
☐ 94 Larry Casian	.05	.02
☐ 95 Mike Dalton	.05	.02
☐ 96 Lance Dickson	.05	.02
☐ 97 Joe Grahe	.05	.02
☐ 98 Glenn Sutko	.05	.02
☐ 99 Gerald Alexander	.05	.02
☐ 100 Mo Vaughn	1.25	.55

1992 Score 100 Superstars

The 1992 Score Superstars set contains 100 standard-size player cards and six "Magic Motion" trivia cards. The fronts display color action player photos on a card face that shades from reddish-orange to yellow and back to reddish-orange again. The words "Superstar" appear above the pictures, with the player's name in a purple stripe at the card bottom. The horizontally oriented backs

have a color head shot on the left half, with player profile and team logo on the right half.

	MINT	NRMT
COMPLETE SET (100)	8.00	3.60
COMMON CARD (1-100)	.05	.02
☐ 1 Ken Griffey Jr.	2.00	.90
☐ 2 Scott Erickson	.05	.02
☐ 3 John Smiley	.05	.02
☐ 4 Rick Aguilera	.10	.05
☐ 5 Jeff Reardon	.05	.02
☐ 6 Chuck Finley	.10	.05
☐ 7 Kirby Puckett	1.00	.45
☐ 8 Paul Molitor	.40	.18
☐ 9 Dave Winfield	.25	.11
☐ 10 Mike Greenwell	.05	.02
☐ 11 Bret Saberhagen	.10	.05
☐ 12 Pete Harnisch	.05	.02
☐ 13 Ozzie Guillen	.05	.02
☐ 14 Hal Morris	.05	.02
☐ 15 Tom Glavine	.15	.07
☐ 16 David Cone	.10	.05
☐ 17 Edgar Martinez	.15	.07
☐ 18 Willie McGee	.10	.05
☐ 19 Jim Abbott	.10	.05
☐ 20 Mark Grace	.30	.14
☐ 21 George Brett	.75	.35
☐ 22 Jack McDowell	.05	.02
☐ 23 Don Mattingly	1.00	.45
☐ 24 Will Clark	.30	.14
☐ 25 Dwight Gooden	.10	.05
☐ 26 Barry Bonds	.50	.23
☐ 27 Rafael Palmeiro	.25	.11
☐ 28 Lee Smith	.10	.05
☐ 29 Wally Joyner	.05	.02
☐ 30 Wade Boggs	.30	.14
☐ 31 Tom Henke	.05	.02
☐ 32 Mark Langston	.05	.02
☐ 33 Robin Ventura	.10	.05
☐ 34 Steve Avery	.05	.02
☐ 35 Joe Carter	.25	.11
☐ 36 Benito Santiago	.05	.02
☐ 37 Dave Stieb	.05	.02
☐ 38 Julio Franco	.10	.05
☐ 39 Albert Belle	.50	.23
☐ 40 Dale Murphy	.25	.11
☐ 41 Rob Dibble	.05	.02
☐ 42 Dave Justice	.25	.11
☐ 43 Jose Rijo	.05	.02
☐ 44 Eric Davis	.10	.05
☐ 45 Terry Pendleton	.05	.02
☐ 46 Kevin Maas	.05	.02
☐ 47 Ozzie Smith	.75	.35
☐ 48 Andre Dawson	.25	.11
☐ 49 Sandy Alomar Jr.	.10	.05
☐ 50 Nolan Ryan	1.50	.70
☐ 51 Frank Thomas	1.50	.70
☐ 52 Craig Biggio	.25	.11
☐ 53 Doug Drabek	.05	.02
☐ 54 Bobby Thigpen	.05	.02
☐ 55 Darryl Strawberry	.10	.05
☐ 56 Dennis Eckersley	.15	.07
☐ 57 John Franco	.10	.05
☐ 58 Paul O'Neill	.10	.05
☐ 59 Scott Sanderson	.05	.02
☐ 60 Dave Stewart	.05	.02
☐ 61 Ivan Calderon	.05	.02
☐ 62 Frank Viola	.05	.02
☐ 63 Mark McGwire	1.00	.45
☐ 64 Kelly Gruber	.05	.02
☐ 65 Fred McGriff	.25	.11
☐ 66 Cecil Fielder	.15	.07
☐ 67 Jose Canseco	.30	.14
☐ 68 Howard Johnson	.05	.02
☐ 69 Juan Gonzalez	1.00	.45
☐ 70 Tim Wallach	.05	.02
☐ 71 John Olerud	.10	.05
☐ 72 Carlton Fisk	.25	.11
☐ 73 Otis Nixon	.05	.02
☐ 74 Roger Clemens	.75	.35
☐ 75 Ramon Martinez	.10	.05
☐ 76 Ron Gant	.10	.05
☐ 77 Barry Larkin	.30	.14
☐ 78 Eddie Murray	.50	.23
☐ 79 Vince Coleman	.05	.02
☐ 80 Bobby Bonilla	.10	.05
☐ 81 Tony Gwynn	1.00	.45
☐ 82 Roberto Alomar	.40	.18
☐ 83 Ellis Burks	.10	.05
☐ 84 Robin Yount	.25	.11
☐ 85 Ryne Sandberg	.75	.35
☐ 86 Len Dykstra	.10	.05
☐ 87 Ruben Sierra	.05	.02
☐ 88 George Bell	.05	.02
☐ 89 Cal Ripken	1.50	.70
☐ 90 Danny Tartabull	.05	.02
☐ 91 Gregg Olson	.05	.02
☐ 92 Dave Henderson	.05	.02
☐ 93 Kevin Mitchell	.05	.02
☐ 94 Ben McDonald	.05	.02
☐ 95 Matt Williams	.25	.11
☐ 96 Roberto Kelly	.05	.02
☐ 97 Dennis Martinez	.10	.05
☐ 98 Kent Hrbek	.05	.02
☐ 99 Felix Jose	.05	.02
☐ 100 Rickey Henderson	.25	.11

1992 Score Coke/Hardees Discs

This 24-disc set measures approximately 3" in diameter. The fronts feature color player action photos in different colored fading borders. The white backs carry player career totals. The cards are unnumbered and checklisted below in alphabetical order.

	MINT	NRMT
COMPLETE SET (24)	20.00	9.00
COMMON CARD (1-24)	.25	.11
☐ 1 Roberto Alomar	1.50	.70
☐ 2 Sandy Alomar Jr.	.50	.23
☐ 3 Jeff Bagwell	5.00	2.20
☐ 4 Brett Butler	.50	.23
☐ 5 Roger Clemens	4.00	1.80
☐ 6 Chili Davis	.25	.11
☐ 7 Andre Dawson	1.00	.45
☐ 8 Delino DeShields	.25	.11
☐ 9 Ron Gant	.50	.23
☐ 10 Tom Glavine	.75	.35
☐ 11 Kelly Gruber	.25	.11
☐ 12 Ozzie Guillen	.25	.11
☐ 13 Dave Henderson	.25	.11
☐ 14 Chuck Knoblauch	2.50	1.10
☐ 15 Paul Molitor	1.50	.70
☐ 16 Hal Morris	.50	.23
☐ 17 Rafael Palmeiro	1.50	.70
☐ 18 Terry Pendleton	.25	.11
☐ 19 Benito Santiago	.25	.11
☐ 20 Ozzie Smith	5.00	2.20
☐ 21 Andy Van Slyke	.50	.23
☐ 22 Devon White	.25	.11
☐ 23 Matt Williams	2.00	.90
☐ 24 Robin Yount	1.50	.70
☐ 25 Title Card CL	.25	.11

1992 Score/Pinnacle Promo Panels

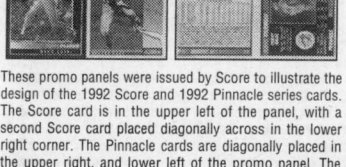

These promo panels were issued by Score to illustrate the design of the 1992 Score and 1992 Pinnacle series cards. The Score card is in the upper left of the panel, with a second Score card placed diagonally across in the lower right corner. The Pinnacle cards are diagonally placed in the upper right, and lower left of the promo panel. The promo panel measures approximately 5" by 7". If cut, each of the four cards would measure the standard size. The Score fronts feature a glossy color action photo bordered above and below by a blue bar. Along the left side is a wider green border. The Score backs carry a close-up shot in the upper right corner, with biography, complete career statistics, and player profile printed on a yellow background. The Pinnacle fronts display a glossy color player photos on a black background accented by thin white borders. On a black background the horizontal backs have a close-up player portrait, statistics, and a player profile. An anti-counterfeit device appears in the bottom border of each back. The cards for each set are numbered on the back as in the regular series; the panels themselves, however, are unnumbered. We have sequenced this set according to the player's card number in the upper left corner.

	MINT	NRMT
COMPLETE SET (25)	75.00	34.00
COMMON PANEL (1-25)	1.50	.70
☐ 1 Nolan Ryan Terry Pendleton Willie McGee Lonnie Smith	10.00	4.50
☐ 2 Will Clark Mark Langston Paul Molitor Devon White	3.00	1.35
☐ 3 Frank Thomas David Justice Mark Carreon Dave Henderson	8.00	3.60
☐ 4 Kirby Puckett Ryne Sandberg Roberto Alomar Dave Henderson	8.00	3.60
☐ 5 Ozzie Smith Darryl Strawberry Kevin Seitzer Jeff Montgomery	3.00	1.35
☐ 6 Robin Yount Jay Buhner Chuck Crim Jimmy Jones	3.00	1.35
☐ 7 Don Mattingly Matt Williams Dave Winfield George Bell	6.00	2.70
☐ 8 Orel Hershiser Wes Chamberlain Gary Gaetti Dickie Thon	1.50	.70
☐ 9 Ron Gant Andres Galarraga Bruce Hurst Alex Fernandez	3.00	1.35
☐ 10 Albert Belle Ellis Burks Melido Perez Kevin Gross	3.00	1.35
☐ 11 Ivan Calderon Bill Doran Rick Aguilera Doug Jones	1.50	.70
☐ 12 Todd Zeile Mike Gallego Lenny Harris Jack Clark	1.50	.70
☐ 13 Harold Baines Walt Weiss Eric Davis Randy Ready	1.50	.70
☐ 14 Nolan Ryan George Brett George Bell Rafael Palmeiro	15.00	6.75
☐ 15 Chili Davis Phil Plantier David Wells Bob Walk	1.50	.70
☐ 16 John Olerud Dave Hollins Jack McDowell Juan Samuel	1.50	.70
☐ 17 Carlton Fisk Kent Hrbek Dennis Martinez Jim Acker	1.50	.70
☐ 18 Jay Buhner Greg Olson Terry Steinbach Kirk McCaskill	1.50	.70
☐ 19 Jeff Bagwell Darryl Strawberry Travis Fryman Andre Dawson	3.00	1.35
☐ 20 Alex Cole Jim Gantner	1.50	.70

Ken Caminiti
Todd Stottlemyre
☐ 21 Alex Fernandez .... 1.50 .70
Bill Gullickson
Jose Guzman
Shawn Hillegas
☐ 22 Beranrd Gilkey .... 1.50 .70
Omar Vizquel
Ivan Calderon
Ozzie Guillen
☐ 23 Gary Gaetti .... 1.50 .70
Doug Drabek
Brent Mayne
Tom Bolton
☐ 24 David Justice .... 1.50 .70
Kevin Maas
Jody Reed
Vince Coleman
☐ 25 Chili Davis .... 1.50 .70
Hensley Meulens
David Howard
Mark Lewis

1992 Score Proctor and Gamble

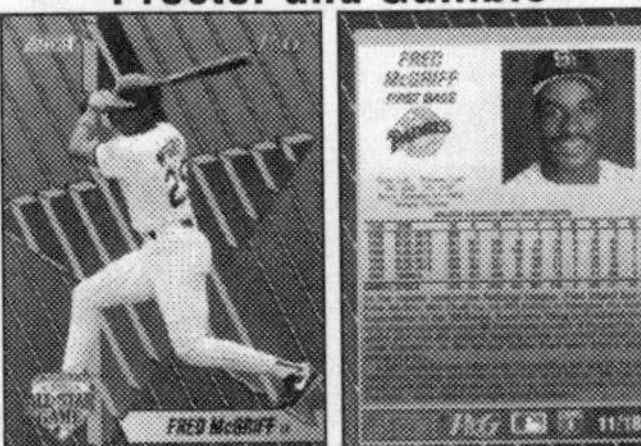

This 18-card standard-size set was produced by Score for Proctor and Gamble as a mail-in premium and contains 18 players from the 1992 All-Star Game line-up. The production run comprised 2,000,000 sets and 25 uncut sheets. A three-card sample set was also produced for sales representatives with a print run of 5,000,000 sets and 25 uncut sheets. The three sample cards, featuring Griffey, Sandberg, and Henderson, are stamped "sample" on the back. Collectors could obtain the set by sending in a required certificate, 99 cents, three UPC symbols from three different Proctor and Gamble products, and 50 cents for postage and handling. The certificate was published in a flyer inserted in Sunday, August 16 newspapers. The card fronts feature color action player cutouts superimposed on a diagonally striped background showing a large star behind the player. Card numbers 1-9 have a blue star on a graded magenta background, while card numbers 10-18 show a red star on blue-green. The backs display a close-up photo, biographical and statistical information, and career summary on a graded yellow-orange background. The cards are numbered "X/18" at the lower right corner.

	MINT	NRMT
COMPLETE SET (18)	6.00	2.70
COMMON CARD (1-18)	.10	.05

☐ 1 Sandy Alomar Jr.	.25	.11
☐ 2 Mark McGwire	.75	.35
☐ 3 Roberto Alomar	.60	.25
☐ 4 Wade Boggs	.60	.25
☐ 5 Cal Ripken	2.00	.90
☐ 6 Kirby Puckett	1.00	.45
☐ 7 Ken Griffey Jr.	2.50	1.10
☐ 8 Jose Canseco	.40	.18
☐ 9 Kevin Brown	.25	.11
☐ 10 Benito Santiago	.10	.05
☐ 11 Fred McGriff	.40	.18
☐ 12 Ryne Sandberg	.75	.35
☐ 13 Terry Pendleton	.10	.05
☐ 14 Ozzie Smith	.75	.35
☐ 15 Barry Bonds	.60	.25
☐ 16 Tony Gwynn	1.25	.55
☐ 17 Andy Van Slyke	.10	.05
☐ 18 Tom Glavine	.40	.18

1992 Score Rookies

This 40-card boxed set measures the standard size and features glossy color action player photos on a kelly green face with meandering purple stripes. The words "1992 Rookie" are printed in white and red along the left edge of the photo. The player's name appears in white on a red banner at the bottom. The banner and the right edge of the picture are edged in canary yellow. The team logo is superimposed on the photo and the red banner. The back design features close-up player photos with kelly green shadow border on a graded royal blue face. The player's

name is printed in red below the picture followed by biography and player profile. The words "1992 Rookie" appear, as on the front, in white and red along the left edge of the card.

	MINT	NRMT
COMPLETE SET (40)	4.00	1.80
COMMON CARD (1-40)	.05	.02

☐ 1 Todd Van Poppel	.05	.02
☐ 2 Kyle Abbott	.05	.02
☐ 3 Derek Bell	.15	.07
☐ 4 Jim Thome	1.50	.70
☐ 5 Mark Wohlers	.25	.11
☐ 6 Todd Hundley	.25	.11
☐ 7 Arthur Lee Rhodes	.05	.02
☐ 8 John Ramos	.05	.02
☐ 9 Chris George	.05	.02
☐ 10 Kenny Lofton	2.00	.90
☐ 11 Ted Wood	.05	.02
☐ 12 Royce Clayton	.10	.05
☐ 13 Scott Cooper	.05	.02
☐ 14 Anthony Young	.05	.02
☐ 15 Joel Johnston	.05	.02
☐ 16 Andy Mota	.05	.02
☐ 17 Lenny Webster	.05	.02
☐ 18 Andy Ashby	.10	.05
☐ 19 Jose Mota	.05	.02
☐ 20 Tim McIntosh	.05	.02
☐ 21 Terry Bross	.05	.02
☐ 22 Harvey Pulliam	.05	.02
☐ 23 Hector Fajardo	.05	.02
☐ 24 Esteban Beltre	.05	.02
☐ 25 Gary DiSarcina	.05	.02
☐ 26 Mike Humphreys	.05	.02
☐ 27 Jarvis Brown	.05	.02
☐ 28 Gary Cooper	.05	.02
☐ 29 Chris Donnels	.05	.02
☐ 30 Monty Fariss	.05	.02
☐ 31 Eric Karros	.40	.18
☐ 32 Braulio Castillo	.05	.02
☐ 33 Cal Eldred	.05	.02
☐ 34 Tom Goodwin	.05	.02
☐ 35 Reggie Sanders	.15	.07
☐ 36 Scott Servais	.05	.02
☐ 37 Kim Batiste	.05	.02
☐ 38 Eric Wedge	.05	.02
☐ 39 Willie Banks	.05	.02
☐ 40 Mo Sanford	.05	.02

1993 Score

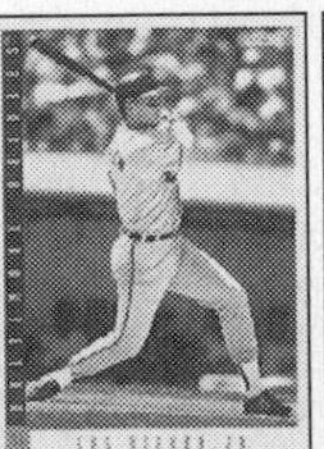

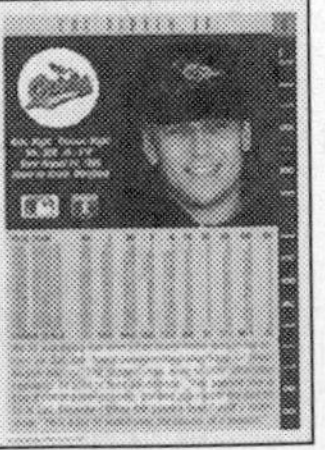

The 1993 Score baseball set consists of 660 standard-size cards issued in one sinle series. The cards were distributed in 16-card poly packs and 35-card jumbo superpacks. The fronts feature color action player photos surrounded by white borders. The player's name appears in the bottom white border, while the team name and position appear in a team color-coded stripe that edges the left side of the picture. Topical subsets featured are Award Winners (481-486), Draft Picks (487-501), All-Star Caricature (502-512 [AL], 522-531 [NL]), Highlights (513-519), World Series Highlights (520-521), Dream Team (532-542) and Rookies (sprinkled throughout the set). Rookie Cards in this set include Derek Jeter and Jason Kendall.

	MINT	NRMT
COMPLETE SET (660)	40.00	18.00
COMMON CARD (1-660)	.10	.05

☐ 1 Ken Griffey Jr.	2.00	.90
☐ 2 Gary Sheffield	.40	.18
☐ 3 Frank Thomas	1.50	.70
☐ 4 Ryne Sandberg	.50	.23
☐ 5 Larry Walker	.40	.18
☐ 6 Cal Ripken Jr.	1.50	.70
☐ 7 Roger Clemens	.75	.35
☐ 8 Bobby Bonilla	.20	.09
☐ 9 Carlos Baerga	.20	.09
☐ 10 Darren Daulton	.20	.09
☐ 11 Travis Fryman	.20	.09
☐ 12 Andy Van Slyke	.20	.09
☐ 13 Jose Canseco	.30	.14
☐ 14 Roberto Alomar	.40	.18
☐ 15 Tom Glavine	.30	.14
☐ 16 Barry Larkin	.30	.14
☐ 17 Gregg Jefferies	.20	.09
☐ 18 Craig Biggio	.30	.14
☐ 19 Shane Mack	.10	.05
☐ 20 Brett Butler	.20	.09
☐ 21 Dennis Eckersley	.30	.14
☐ 22 Will Clark	.30	.14
☐ 23 Don Mattingly	.60	.25
☐ 24 Tony Gwynn	1.00	.45
☐ 25 Ivan Rodriguez	.50	.23
☐ 26 Shawon Dunston	.10	.05
☐ 27 Mike Mussina	.40	.18
☐ 28 Marquis Grissom	.20	.09
☐ 29 Charles Nagy	.20	.09
☐ 30 Len Dykstra	.20	.09
☐ 31 Cecil Fielder	.20	.09
☐ 32 Jay Bell	.20	.09
☐ 33 B.J. Surhoff	.20	.09
☐ 34 Bob Tewksbury	.10	.05
☐ 35 Danny Tartabull	.10	.05
☐ 36 Terry Pendleton	.20	.09
☐ 37 Jack Morris	.20	.09
☐ 38 Hal Morris	.10	.05
☐ 39 Luis Polonia	.10	.05
☐ 40 Ken Caminiti	.40	.18
☐ 41 Robin Ventura	.20	.09
☐ 42 Darryl Strawberry	.20	.09
☐ 43 Wally Joyner	.20	.09
☐ 44 Fred McGriff	.30	.14
☐ 45 Kevin Tapani	.10	.05
☐ 46 Matt Williams	.30	.14
☐ 47 Robin Yount	.30	.14
☐ 48 Ken Hill	.20	.09
☐ 49 Edgar Martinez	.30	.14
☐ 50 Mark Grace	.30	.14
☐ 51 Juan Gonzalez	1.00	.45
☐ 52 Curt Schilling	.20	.09
☐ 53 Dwight Gooden	.20	.09
☐ 54 Chris Hoiles	.10	.05
☐ 55 Frank Viola	.10	.05
☐ 56 Ray Lankford	.20	.09
☐ 57 George Brett	.75	.35
☐ 58 Kenny Lofton	.75	.35
☐ 59 Nolan Ryan	1.50	.70
☐ 60 Mickey Tettleton	.10	.05
☐ 61 John Smoltz	.30	.14
☐ 62 Howard Johnson	.10	.05
☐ 63 Eric Karros	.20	.09
☐ 64 Rick Aguilera	.10	.05
☐ 65 Steve Finley	.20	.09
☐ 66 Mark Langston	.10	.05
☐ 67 Bill Swift	.10	.05
☐ 68 John Olerud	.10	.05
☐ 69 Kevin McReynolds	.10	.05
☐ 70 Jack McDowell	.10	.05
☐ 71 Rickey Henderson	.30	.14
☐ 72 Brian Harper	.10	.05
☐ 73 Mike Morgan	.10	.05
☐ 74 Rafael Palmeiro	.30	.14
☐ 75 Dennis Martinez	.20	.09
☐ 76 Tino Martinez	.40	.18
☐ 77 Eddie Murray	.40	.18
☐ 78 Ellis Burks	.20	.09
☐ 79 John Kruk	.20	.09
☐ 80 Gregg Olson	.10	.05
☐ 81 Bernard Gilkey	.20	.09
☐ 82 Milt Cuyler	.10	.05
☐ 83 Mike LaValliere	.10	.05
☐ 84 Albert Belle	.50	.23
☐ 85 Bip Roberts	.10	.05
☐ 86 Melido Perez	.10	.05
☐ 87 Otis Nixon	.10	.05
☐ 88 Bill Spiers	.10	.05
☐ 89 Jeff Bagwell	.75	.35
☐ 90 Orel Hershiser	.20	.09
☐ 91 Andy Benes	.20	.09
☐ 92 Devon White	.10	.05
☐ 93 Willie McGee	.10	.05
☐ 94 Ozzie Guillen	.10	.05
☐ 95 Ivan Calderon	.10	.05
☐ 96 Keith Miller	.10	.05
☐ 97 Steve Buechele	.10	.05

☐ 98 Kent Hrbek	.20	.09
☐ 99 Dave Hollins	.10	.05
☐ 100 Mike Bordick	.10	.05
☐ 101 Randy Tomlin	.10	.05
☐ 102 Omar Vizquel	.20	.09
☐ 103 Lee Smith	.20	.09
☐ 104 Leo Gomez	.10	.05
☐ 105 Jose Rijo	.10	.05
☐ 106 Mark Whiten	.10	.05
☐ 107 Dave Justice	.40	.18
☐ 108 Eddie Taubensee	.10	.05
☐ 109 Lance Johnson	.20	.09
☐ 110 Felix Jose	.10	.05
☐ 111 Mike Harkey	.10	.05
☐ 112 Randy Milligan	.10	.05
☐ 113 Anthony Young	.10	.05
☐ 114 Rico Brogna	.20	.09
☐ 115 Bret Saberhagen	.10	.05
☐ 116 Sandy Alomar	.20	.09
☐ 117 Terry Mulholland	.10	.05
☐ 118 Darryl Hamilton	.10	.05
☐ 119 Todd Zeile	.10	.05
☐ 120 Bernie Williams	.30	.14
☐ 121 Zane Smith	.10	.05
☐ 122 Derek Bell	.20	.09
☐ 123 Deion Sanders	.40	.18
☐ 124 Luis Sojo	.10	.05
☐ 125 Joe Oliver	.10	.05
☐ 126 Craig Grebeck	.10	.05
☐ 127 Andujar Cedeno	.10	.05
☐ 128 Brian McRae	.10	.05
☐ 129 Jose Offerman	.10	.05
☐ 130 Pedro Munoz	.10	.05
☐ 131 Bud Black	.10	.05
☐ 132 Mo Vaughn	.50	.23
☐ 133 Bruce Hurst	.10	.05
☐ 134 Dave Henderson	.10	.05
☐ 135 Tom Pagnozzi	.10	.05
☐ 136 Erik Hanson	.10	.05
☐ 137 Orlando Merced	.10	.05
☐ 138 Dean Palmer	.20	.09
☐ 139 John Franco	.10	.05
☐ 140 Brady Anderson	.30	.14
☐ 141 Ricky Jordan	.10	.05
☐ 142 Jeff Blauser	.10	.05
☐ 143 Sammy Sosa	.40	.18
☐ 144 Bob Walk	.10	.05
☐ 145 Delino DeShields	.10	.05
☐ 146 Kevin Brown	.20	.09
☐ 147 Mark Lemke	.10	.05
☐ 148 Chuck Knoblauch	.40	.18
☐ 149 Chris Sabo	.10	.05
☐ 150 Bobby Witt	.10	.05
☐ 151 Luis Gonzalez	.10	.05
☐ 152 Ron Karkovice	.10	.05
☐ 153 Jeff Brantley	.10	.05
☐ 154 Kevin Appier	.20	.09
☐ 155 Darrin Jackson	.10	.05
☐ 156 Kelly Gruber	.10	.05
☐ 157 Royce Clayton	.20	.09
☐ 158 Chuck Finley	.10	.05
☐ 159 Jeff King	.20	.09
☐ 160 Greg Vaughn	.10	.05
☐ 161 Geronimo Pena	.10	.05
☐ 162 Steve Farr	.10	.05
☐ 163 Jose Oquendo	.10	.05
☐ 164 Mark Lewis	.10	.05
☐ 165 John Wetteland	.20	.09
☐ 166 Mike Henneman	.10	.05
☐ 167 Todd Hundley	.30	.14
☐ 168 Wes Chamberlain	.10	.05
☐ 169 Steve Avery	.10	.05
☐ 170 Mike Devereaux	.10	.05
☐ 171 Reggie Sanders	.20	.09
☐ 172 Jay Buhner	.30	.14
☐ 173 Eric Anthony	.10	.05
☐ 174 John Burkett	.10	.05
☐ 175 Tom Candiotti	.10	.05
☐ 176 Phil Plantier	.10	.05
☐ 177 Doug Henry	.10	.05
☐ 178 Scott Leius	.10	.05
☐ 179 Kirt Manwaring	.10	.05
☐ 180 Jeff Parrett	.10	.05
☐ 181 Don Slaught	.10	.05
☐ 182 Scott Radinsky	.10	.05
☐ 183 Luis Alicea	.10	.05
☐ 184 Tom Gordon	.10	.05
☐ 185 Rick Wilkins	.10	.05
☐ 186 Todd Stottlemyre	.20	.09
☐ 187 Moises Alou	.20	.09
☐ 188 Joe Grahe	.10	.05
☐ 189 Jeff Kent	.20	.09
☐ 190 Bill Wegman	.10	.05
☐ 191 Kim Batiste	.10	.05
☐ 192 Matt Nokes	.10	.05
☐ 193 Mark Wohlers	.20	.09
☐ 194 Paul Sorrento	.10	.05
☐ 195 Chris Hammond	.10	.05
☐ 196 Scott Livingstone	.10	.05
☐ 197 Doug Jones	.10	.05
☐ 198 Scott Cooper	.10	.05
☐ 199 Ramon Martinez	.20	.09
☐ 200 Dave Valle	.10	.05
☐ 201 Mariano Duncan	.10	.05
☐ 202 Ben McDonald	.10	.05
☐ 203 Darren Lewis	.10	.05
☐ 204 Kenny Rogers	.10	.05
☐ 205 Manuel Lee	.10	.05
☐ 206 Scott Erickson	.10	.05
☐ 207 Dan Gladden	.10	.05
☐ 208 Bob Welch	.10	.05
☐ 209 Greg Olson	.10	.05
☐ 210 Dan Pasqua	.10	.05
☐ 211 Tim Wallach	.10	.05
☐ 212 Jeff Montgomery	.20	.09
☐ 213 Derrick May	.10	.05
☐ 214 Ed Sprague	.10	.05
☐ 215 David Haas	.10	.05
☐ 216 Darrin Fletcher	.10	.05
☐ 217 Brian Jordan	.20	.09
☐ 218 Jaime Navarro	.10	.05
☐ 219 Randy Velarde	.10	.05
☐ 220 Ron Gant	.20	.09
☐ 221 Paul Quantrill	.10	.05
☐ 222 Damion Easley	.10	.05
☐ 223 Charlie Hough	.10	.05
☐ 224 Brad Brink	.10	.05
☐ 225 Barry Manuel	.10	.05
☐ 226 Kevin Koslofski	.10	.05
☐ 227 Ryan Thompson	.10	.05
☐ 228 Mike Munoz	.10	.05
☐ 229 Dan Wilson	.20	.09
☐ 230 Peter Hoy	.10	.05
☐ 231 Pedro Astacio	.10	.05
☐ 232 Matt Stairs	.10	.05
☐ 233 Jeff Reboulet	.10	.05
☐ 234 Manny Alexander	.10	.05
☐ 235 Willie Banks	.10	.05
☐ 236 John Jaha	.20	.09
☐ 237 Scooter Tucker	.10	.05
☐ 238 Russ Springer	.10	.05
☐ 239 Paul Miller	.10	.05
☐ 240 Dan Peltier	.10	.05
☐ 241 Ozzie Canseco	.10	.05
☐ 242 Ben Rivera	.10	.05
☐ 243 John Valentin	.20	.09
☐ 244 Henry Rodriguez	.20	.09
☐ 245 Derek Parks	.10	.05
☐ 246 Carlos Garcia	.10	.05
☐ 247 Tim Pugh	.10	.05
☐ 248 Melvin Nieves	.20	.09
☐ 249 Rich Amaral	.10	.05
☐ 250 Willie Greene	.20	.09
☐ 251 Tim Scott	.10	.05
☐ 252 Dave Silvestri	.10	.05
☐ 253 Rob Mallicoat	.10	.05
☐ 254 Donald Harris	.10	.05
☐ 255 Craig Colbert	.10	.05
☐ 256 Jose Guzman	.10	.05
☐ 257 Domingo Martinez	.10	.05
☐ 258 William Suero	.10	.05
☐ 259 Juan Guerrero	.10	.05
☐ 260 J.T. Snow	.50	.23
☐ 261 Tony Pena	.10	.05
☐ 262 Tim Fortugno	.10	.05
☐ 263 Tom Marsh	.10	.05
☐ 264 Kurt Knudsen	.10	.05
☐ 265 Tim Costo	.10	.05
☐ 266 Steve Shifflett	.10	.05
☐ 267 Billy Ashley	.10	.05
☐ 268 Jerry Nielsen	.10	.05
☐ 269 Pete Young	.10	.05
☐ 270 Johnny Guzman	.10	.05
☐ 271 Greg Colbrunn	.10	.05
☐ 272 Jeff Nelson	.10	.05
☐ 273 Kevin Young	.10	.05
☐ 274 Jeff Frye	.10	.05
☐ 275 J.T. Bruett	.10	.05
☐ 276 Todd Pratt	.10	.05
☐ 277 Mike Butcher	.10	.05
☐ 278 John Flaherty	.10	.05
☐ 279 John Patterson	.10	.05
☐ 280 Eric Hillman	.10	.05
☐ 281 Bien Figueroa	.10	.05
☐ 282 Shane Reynolds	.20	.09
☐ 283 Rich Rowland	.10	.05
☐ 284 Steve Foster	.10	.05
☐ 285 Dave Mlicki	.10	.05
☐ 286 Mike Piazza	2.00	.90
☐ 287 Mike Trombley	.10	.05
☐ 288 Jim Pena	.10	.05
☐ 289 Bob Ayrault	.10	.05
☐ 290 Henry Mercedes	.10	.05
☐ 291 Bob Wickman	.10	.05
☐ 292 Jacob Brumfield	.10	.05
☐ 293 David Hulse	.10	.05
☐ 294 Ryan Klesko	.50	.23
☐ 295 Doug Linton	.10	.05
☐ 296 Steve Cooke	.10	.05
☐ 297 Eddie Zosky	.10	.05
☐ 298 Gerald Williams	.10	.05
☐ 299 Jonathan Hurst	.10	.05
☐ 300 Larry Carter	.10	.05
☐ 301 William Pennyfeather	.10	.05
☐ 302 Cesar Hernandez	.10	.05
☐ 303 Steve Hosey	.10	.05
☐ 304 Blas Minor	.10	.05
☐ 305 Jeff Grotewald	.10	.05
☐ 306 Bernardo Brito	.10	.05
☐ 307 Rafael Bournigal	.10	.05
☐ 308 Jeff Branson	.10	.05
☐ 309 Tom Quinlan	.10	.05
☐ 310 Pat Gomez	.10	.05
☐ 311 Sterling Hitchcock	.20	.09
☐ 312 Kent Bottenfield	.10	.05
☐ 313 Alan Trammell	.30	.14
☐ 314 Cris Colon	.10	.05
☐ 315 Paul Wagner	.10	.05
☐ 316 Matt Maysey	.10	.05
☐ 317 Mike Stanton	.10	.05
☐ 318 Rick Trlicek	.10	.05
☐ 319 Kevin Rogers	.10	.05
☐ 320 Mark Clark	.10	.05
☐ 321 Pedro Martinez	.40	.18
☐ 322 Al Martin	.20	.09
☐ 323 Mike Macfarlane	.10	.05
☐ 324 Rey Sanchez	.10	.05
☐ 325 Roger Pavlik	.10	.05
☐ 326 Troy Neel	.10	.05
☐ 327 Kerry Woodson	.10	.05
☐ 328 Wayne Kirby	.10	.05
☐ 329 Ken Ryan	.10	.05
☐ 330 Jesse Levis	.10	.05
☐ 331 James Austin	.10	.05
☐ 332 Dan Walters	.10	.05
☐ 333 Brian Williams	.10	.05
☐ 334 Wil Cordero	.10	.05
☐ 335 Bret Boone	.10	.05
☐ 336 Hipolito Pichardo	.10	.05
☐ 337 Pat Mahomes	.10	.05
☐ 338 Andy Stankiewicz	.10	.05
☐ 339 Jim Bullinger	.10	.05
☐ 340 Archi Cianfrocco	.10	.05
☐ 341 Ruben Amaro Jr.	.10	.05
☐ 342 Frank Seminara	.10	.05
☐ 343 Pat Hentgen	.30	.14
☐ 344 Dave Nilsson	.20	.09
☐ 345 Mike Perez	.10	.05
☐ 346 Tim Salmon	.50	.23
☐ 347 Tim Wakefield	.20	.09
☐ 348 Carlos Hernandez	.10	.05
☐ 349 Donovan Osborne	.10	.05
☐ 350 Denny Neagle	.20	.09
☐ 351 Sam Militello	.10	.05
☐ 352 Eric Fox	.10	.05
☐ 353 John Doherty	.10	.05
☐ 354 Chad Curtis	.20	.09
☐ 355 Jeff Tackett	.10	.05
☐ 356 Dave Fleming	.10	.05
☐ 357 Pat Listach	.10	.05
☐ 358 Kevin Wickander	.10	.05
☐ 359 John Vander Wal	.10	.05
☐ 360 Arthur Rhodes	.10	.05
☐ 361 Bob Scanlan	.10	.05
☐ 362 Bob Zupcic	.10	.05
☐ 363 Mel Rojas	.20	.09
☐ 364 Jim Thome	.75	.35
☐ 365 Bill Pecota	.10	.05
☐ 366 Mark Carreon	.10	.05
☐ 367 Mitch Williams	.10	.05
☐ 368 Cal Eldred	.10	.05
☐ 369 Stan Belinda	.10	.05
☐ 370 Pat Kelly	.10	.05
☐ 371 Rheal Cormier	.10	.05
☐ 372 Juan Guzman	.10	.05
☐ 373 Damon Berryhill	.10	.05
☐ 374 Gary DiSarcina	.10	.05
☐ 375 Norm Charlton	.10	.05
☐ 376 Roberto Hernandez	.20	.09
☐ 377 Scott Kamieniecki	.10	.05
☐ 378 Rusty Meacham	.10	.05
☐ 379 Kurt Stillwell	.10	.05
☐ 380 Lloyd McClendon	.10	.05
☐ 381 Mark Leonard	.10	.05
☐ 382 Jerry Browne	.10	.05
☐ 383 Glenn Davis	.10	.05
☐ 384 Randy Johnson	.40	.18
☐ 385 Mike Greenwell	.10	.05
☐ 386 Scott Chiamparino	.10	.05
☐ 387 George Bell	.10	.05
☐ 388 Steve Olin	.10	.05

☐ 389 Chuck McElroy .10 .05
☐ 390 Mark Gardner .10 .05
☐ 391 Rod Beck .20 .09
☐ 392 Dennis Rasmussen .10 .05
☐ 393 Charlie Leibrandt .10 .05
☐ 394 Julio Franco .20 .09
☐ 395 Pete Harnisch .10 .05
☐ 396 Sid Bream .10 .05
☐ 397 Milt Thompson .10 .05
☐ 398 Glenallen Hill .10 .05
☐ 399 Chico Walker .10 .05
☐ 400 Alex Cole .10 .05
☐ 401 Trevor Wilson .10 .05
☐ 402 Jeff Conine .20 .09
☐ 403 Kyle Abbott .10 .05
☐ 404 Tom Browning .10 .05
☐ 405 Jerald Clark .10 .05
☐ 406 Vince Horsman .10 .05
☐ 407 Kevin Mitchell .20 .09
☐ 408 Pete Smith .10 .05
☐ 409 Jeff Innis .10 .05
☐ 410 Mike Timlin .10 .05
☐ 411 Charlie Hayes .10 .05
☐ 412 Alex Fernandez .20 .09
☐ 413 Jeff Russell .10 .05
☐ 414 Jody Reed .10 .05
☐ 415 Mickey Morandini .10 .05
☐ 416 Darnell Coles .10 .05
☐ 417 Xavier Hernandez .10 .05
☐ 418 Steve Sax .10 .05
☐ 419 Joe Girardi .10 .05
☐ 420 Mike Fetters .10 .05
☐ 421 Danny Jackson .10 .05
☐ 422 Jim Gott .10 .05
☐ 423 Tim Belcher .10 .05
☐ 424 Jose Mesa .20 .09
☐ 425 Junior Felix .10 .05
☐ 426 Thomas Howard .10 .05
☐ 427 Julio Valera .10 .05
☐ 428 Dante Bichette .30 .14
☐ 429 Mike Sharperson .10 .05
☐ 430 Darryl Kile .10 .05
☐ 431 Lonnie Smith .10 .05
☐ 432 Monty Fariss .10 .05
☐ 433 Reggie Jefferson .20 .09
☐ 434 Bob McClure .10 .05
☐ 435 Craig Lefferts .10 .05
☐ 436 Duane Ward .10 .05
☐ 437 Shawn Abner .10 .05
☐ 438 Roberto Kelly .10 .05
☐ 439 Paul O'Neill .20 .09
☐ 440 Alan Mills .10 .05
☐ 441 Roger Mason .10 .05
☐ 442 Gary Pettis .10 .05
☐ 443 Steve Lake .10 .05
☐ 444 Gene Larkin .10 .05
☐ 445 Larry Andersen .10 .05
☐ 446 Doug Dascenzo .10 .05
☐ 447 Daryl Boston .10 .05
☐ 448 John Candelaria .10 .05
☐ 449 Storm Davis .10 .05
☐ 450 Tom Edens .10 .05
☐ 451 Mike Maddux .10 .05
☐ 452 Tim Naehring .10 .05
☐ 453 John Orton .10 .05
☐ 454 Joey Cora .20 .09
☐ 455 Chuck Crim .10 .05
☐ 456 Dan Plesac .10 .05
☐ 457 Mike Bielecki .10 .05
☐ 458 Terry Jorgensen .10 .05
☐ 459 John Habyan .10 .05
☐ 460 Pete O'Brien .10 .05
☐ 461 Jeff Treadway .10 .05
☐ 462 Frank Castillo .10 .05
☐ 463 Jimmy Jones .10 .05
☐ 464 Tommy Greene .10 .05
☐ 465 Tracy Woodson .10 .05
☐ 466 Rich Rodriguez .10 .05
☐ 467 Joe Hesketh .10 .05
☐ 468 Greg Myers .10 .05
☐ 469 Kirk McCaskill .10 .05
☐ 470 Ricky Bones .10 .05
☐ 471 Lenny Webster .10 .05
☐ 472 Francisco Cabrera .10 .05
☐ 473 Turner Ward .10 .05
☐ 474 Dwayne Henry .10 .05
☐ 475 Al Osuna .10 .05
☐ 476 Craig Wilson .10 .05
☐ 477 Chris Nabholz .10 .05
☐ 478 Rafael Belliard .10 .05
☐ 479 Terry Leach .10 .05
☐ 480 Tim Teufel .10 .05
☐ 481 Dennis Eckersley AW .20 .09
☐ 482 Barry Bonds AW .40 .18
☐ 483 Dennis Eckersley AW .20 .09
☐ 484 Greg Maddux AW .60 .25
☐ 485 Pat Listach AW .10 .05
☐ 486 Eric Karros AW .20 .09
☐ 487 Jamie Arnold DP .20 .09
☐ 488 B.J. Wallace DP .10 .05
☐ 489 Derek Jeter DP 4.00 1.80
☐ 490 Jason Kendall DP .60 .25
☐ 491 Rick Helling DP .20 .09
☐ 492 Derek Wallace DP .10 .05
☐ 493 Sean Lowe DP .10 .05
☐ 494 Shannon Stewart DP .50 .23
☐ 495 Benji Grigsby DP .10 .05
☐ 496 Todd Steverson DP .20 .09
☐ 497 Dan Serafini DP .30 .14
☐ 498 Michael Tucker DP .40 .18
☐ 499 Chris Roberts DP .20 .09
☐ 500 Pete Janicki DP .10 .05
☐ 501 Jeff Schmidt DP .10 .05
☐ 502 Edgar Martinez AS .30 .14
☐ 503 Omar Vizquel AS .20 .09
☐ 504 Ken Griffey Jr. AS 1.00 .45
☐ 505 Kirby Puckett AS .40 .18
☐ 506 Joe Carter AS .30 .14
☐ 507 Ivan Rodriguez AS .40 .18
☐ 508 Jack Morris AS .20 .09
☐ 509 Dennis Eckersley AS .20 .09
☐ 510 Frank Thomas AS 1.00 .45
☐ 511 Roberto Alomar AS .40 .18
☐ 512 Mickey Morandini AS .10 .05
☐ 513 Dennis Eckersley HL .20 .09
☐ 514 Jeff Reardon HL .10 .05
☐ 515 Danny Tartabull HL .10 .05
☐ 516 Bip Roberts HL .10 .05
☐ 517 George Brett HL .40 .18
☐ 518 Robin Yount HL .30 .14
☐ 519 Kevin Gross HL .10 .05
☐ 520 Ed Sprague WS .10 .05
☐ 521 Dave Winfield WS .30 .14
☐ 522 Ozzie Smith AS .40 .18
☐ 523 Barry Bonds AS .40 .18
☐ 524 Andy Van Slyke AS .10 .05
☐ 525 Tony Gwynn AS .40 .18
☐ 526 Darren Daulton AS .20 .09
☐ 527 Greg Maddux AS .60 .25
☐ 528 Fred McGriff AS .30 .14
☐ 529 Lee Smith AS .20 .09
☐ 530 Ryne Sandberg AS .30 .14
☐ 531 Gary Sheffield AS .40 .18
☐ 532 Ozzie Smith DT .40 .18
☐ 533 Kirby Puckett DT .40 .18
☐ 534 Gary Sheffield DT .40 .18
☐ 535 Andy Van Slyke DT .10 .05
☐ 536 Ken Griffey Jr. DT 1.00 .45
☐ 537 Ivan Rodriguez DT .40 .18
☐ 538 Charles Nagy DT .20 .09
☐ 539 Tom Glavine DT .30 .14
☐ 540 Dennis Eckersley DT .20 .09
☐ 541 Frank Thomas DT 1.00 .45
☐ 542 Roberto Alomar DT .30 .14
☐ 543 Sean Berry .10 .05
☐ 544 Mike Schooler .10 .05
☐ 545 Chuck Carr .10 .05
☐ 546 Lenny Harris .10 .05
☐ 547 Gary Scott .10 .05
☐ 548 Derek Lilliquist .10 .05
☐ 549 Brian Hunter .10 .05
☐ 550 Kirby Puckett MOY .40 .18
☐ 551 Jim Eisenreich .20 .09
☐ 552 Andre Dawson .30 .14
☐ 553 David Nied .10 .05
☐ 554 Spike Owen .10 .05
☐ 555 Greg Gagne .10 .05
☐ 556 Sid Fernandez .10 .05
☐ 557 Mark McGwire .75 .35
☐ 558 Bryan Harvey .10 .05
☐ 559 Harold Reynolds .10 .05
☐ 560 Barry Bonds .50 .23
☐ 561 Eric Wedge .10 .05
☐ 562 Ozzie Smith .50 .23
☐ 563 Rick Sutcliffe .10 .05
☐ 564 Jeff Reardon .20 .09
☐ 565 Alex Arias .10 .05
☐ 566 Greg Swindell .10 .05
☐ 567 Brook Jacoby .10 .05
☐ 568 Pete Incaviglia .10 .05
☐ 569 Butch Henry .10 .05
☐ 570 Eric Davis .20 .09
☐ 571 Kevin Seitzer .10 .05
☐ 572 Tony Fernandez .10 .05
☐ 573 Steve Reed .10 .05
☐ 574 Cory Snyder .10 .05
☐ 575 Joe Carter .30 .14
☐ 576 Greg Maddux 1.25 .55
☐ 577 Bert Blyleven UER .20 .09
(Should say 3701
career strikeouts)
☐ 578 Kevin Bass .10 .05
☐ 579 Carlton Fisk .30 .14
☐ 580 Doug Drabek .10 .05
☐ 581 Mark Gubicza .10 .05
☐ 582 Bobby Thigpen .10 .05
☐ 583 Chili Davis .20 .09
☐ 584 Scott Bankhead .10 .05
☐ 585 Harold Baines .20 .09
☐ 586 Eric Young .40 .18
☐ 587 Lance Parrish .10 .05
☐ 588 Juan Bell .10 .05
☐ 589 Bob Ojeda .10 .05
☐ 590 Joe Orsulak .10 .05
☐ 591 Benito Santiago .10 .05
☐ 592 Wade Boggs .40 .18
☐ 593 Robby Thompson .10 .05
☐ 594 Eric Plunk .10 .05
☐ 595 Hensley Meulens .10 .05
☐ 596 Lou Whitaker .20 .09
☐ 597 Dale Murphy .30 .14
☐ 598 Paul Molitor .40 .18
☐ 599 Greg W. Harris .10 .05
☐ 600 Darren Holmes .10 .05
☐ 601 Dave Martinez .10 .05
☐ 602 Tom Henke .10 .05
☐ 603 Mike Benjamin .10 .05
☐ 604 Rene Gonzales .10 .05
☐ 605 Roger McDowell .10 .05
☐ 606 Kirby Puckett .75 .35
☐ 607 Randy Myers .20 .09
☐ 608 Ruben Sierra .10 .05
☐ 609 Wilson Alvarez .20 .09
☐ 610 David Segui .10 .05
☐ 611 Juan Samuel .10 .05
☐ 612 Tom Brunansky .10 .05
☐ 613 Willie Randolph .20 .09
☐ 614 Tony Phillips .10 .05
☐ 615 Candy Maldonado .10 .05
☐ 616 Chris Bosio .10 .05
☐ 617 Bret Barberie .10 .05
☐ 618 Scott Sanderson .10 .05
☐ 619 Ron Darling .10 .05
☐ 620 Dave Winfield .30 .14
☐ 621 Mike Felder .10 .05
☐ 622 Greg Hibbard .10 .05
☐ 623 Mike Scioscia .10 .05
☐ 624 John Smiley .10 .05
☐ 625 Alejandro Pena .10 .05
☐ 626 Terry Steinbach .20 .09
☐ 627 Freddie Benavides .10 .05
☐ 628 Kevin Reimer .10 .05
☐ 629 Braulio Castillo .10 .05
☐ 630 Dave Stieb .10 .05
☐ 631 Dave Magadan .10 .05
☐ 632 Scott Fletcher .10 .05
☐ 633 Cris Carpenter .10 .05
☐ 634 Kevin Maas .10 .05
☐ 635 Todd Worrell .10 .05
☐ 636 Rob Deer .10 .05
☐ 637 Dwight Smith .10 .05
☐ 638 Chito Martinez .10 .05
☐ 639 Jimmy Key .20 .09
☐ 640 Greg A. Harris .10 .05
☐ 641 Mike Moore .10 .05
☐ 642 Pat Borders .10 .05
☐ 643 Bill Gullickson .10 .05
☐ 644 Gary Gaetti .20 .09
☐ 645 David Howard .10 .05
☐ 646 Jim Abbott .10 .05
☐ 647 Willie Wilson .10 .05
☐ 648 David Wells .10 .05
☐ 649 Andres Galarraga .30 .14
☐ 650 Vince Coleman .10 .05
☐ 651 Rob Dibble .10 .05
☐ 652 Frank Tanana .10 .05
☐ 653 Steve Decker .10 .05
☐ 654 David Cone .20 .09
☐ 655 Jack Armstrong .10 .05
☐ 656 Dave Stewart .20 .09
☐ 657 Billy Hatcher .10 .05
☐ 658 Tim Raines .20 .09
☐ 659 Walt Weiss .10 .05
☐ 660 Jose Lind .10 .05

1993 Score Boys of Summer

Randomly inserted exclusively into one in every four 1993 Score 35-card super packs, cards from this standard-size set feature 30 rookies expected to be the best in their class. The fronts are borderless with a color action player photo superimposed over an illustration of the sun. The player's name appears in cursive lettering within a greenish stripe across the bottom. An early Mike Piazza card highlights this set.

	MINT	NRMT
COMPLETE SET (30)	60.00	27.00
COMMON CARD (1-30)	1.00	.45

☐ 1 Billy Ashley 1.00 .45
☐ 2 Tim Salmon 10.00 4.50

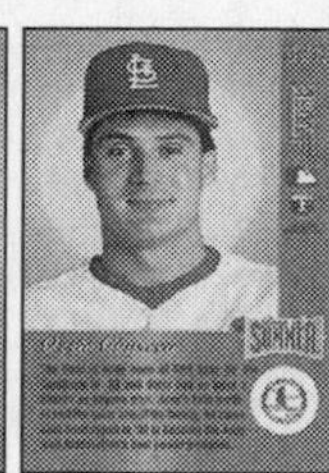

☐ 3 Pedro Martinez	8.00	3.60
☐ 4 Luis Mercedes	1.00	.45
☐ 5 Mike Piazza	30.00	13.50
☐ 6 Troy Neel	1.00	.45
☐ 7 Melvin Nieves	2.00	.90
☐ 8 Ryan Klesko	8.00	3.60
☐ 9 Ryan Thompson	1.00	.45
☐ 10 Kevin Young	1.00	.45
☐ 11 Gerald Williams	1.00	.45
☐ 12 Willie Greene	2.00	.90
☐ 13 John Patterson	1.00	.45
☐ 14 Carlos Garcia	1.00	.45
☐ 15 Ed Zosky	1.00	.45
☐ 16 Sean Berry	1.00	.45
☐ 17 Rico Brogna	2.00	.90
☐ 18 Larry Carter	1.00	.45
☐ 19 Bobby Ayala	1.00	.45
☐ 20 Alan Embree	1.00	.45
☐ 21 Donald Harris	1.00	.45
☐ 22 Sterling Hitchcock	1.00	.45
☐ 23 David Nied	1.00	.45
☐ 24 Henry Mercedes	1.00	.45
☐ 25 Ozzie Canseco	1.00	.45
☐ 26 David Hulse	1.00	.45
☐ 27 Al Martin	2.00	.90
☐ 28 Dan Wilson	2.00	.90
☐ 29 Paul Miller	1.00	.45
☐ 30 Rich Rowland	1.00	.45

1993 Score Franchise

This 28-card set honors the top player on each of the major league teams. These cards were randomly inserted into one in every 24 16-card packs. The full-bleed, color action photos on the fronts have the background darkened so that the player stands out. His name appears in white lettering within a team color-coded bar near the bottom, which conjoins with the set logo in the lower left.

	MINT	NRMT
COMPLETE SET (28)	120.00	55.00
COMMON CARD (1-28)	1.50	.70

☐ 1 Cal Ripken	25.00	11.00
☐ 2 Roger Clemens	10.00	4.50
☐ 3 Mark Langston	1.50	.70
☐ 4 Frank Thomas	25.00	11.00
☐ 5 Carlos Baerga	3.00	1.35
☐ 6 Cecil Fielder	3.00	1.35
☐ 7 Gregg Jefferies	3.00	1.35
☐ 8 Robin Yount	4.00	1.80
☐ 9 Kirby Puckett	12.00	5.50
☐ 10 Don Mattingly	12.00	5.50
☐ 11 Dennis Eckersley	4.00	1.80
☐ 12 Ken Griffey Jr.	30.00	13.50
☐ 13 Juan Gonzalez	15.00	6.75
☐ 14 Roberto Alomar	5.00	2.20
☐ 15 Terry Pendleton	1.50	.70
☐ 16 Ryne Sandberg	6.00	2.70
☐ 17 Barry Larkin	5.00	2.20
☐ 18 Jeff Bagwell	12.00	5.50
☐ 19 Brett Butler	1.50	.70
☐ 20 Larry Walker	5.00	2.20
☐ 21 Bobby Bonilla	3.00	1.35
☐ 22 Darren Daulton	3.00	1.35
☐ 23 Andy Van Slyke	1.50	.70
☐ 24 Ray Lankford	4.00	1.80
☐ 25 Gary Sheffield	5.00	2.20
☐ 26 Will Clark	4.00	1.80
☐ 27 Bryan Harvey	1.50	.70
☐ 28 David Nied	1.50	.70

1993 Score Gold Dream Team

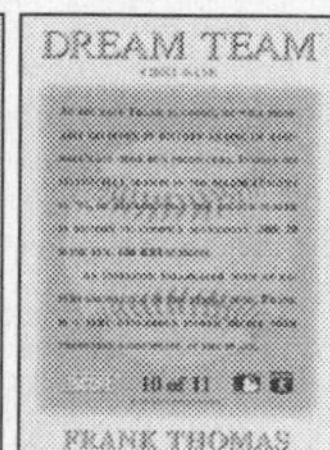

Cards from this 12-card standard-size set feature Score's selection of the best players in baseball at each position. The cards were available only through a mail-in offer. Each card front features sepia tone photos of the players out of uniform, with the exception of Griffey's card (of whom is pictured in his Mariners togs). The photo edges are rounded with an airbrush effect. The words "Dream Team" are printed in gold lettering at the top. The player's name is printed in sepia tones on the bottom edge.

	MINT	NRMT
COMPLETE SET (12)	5.00	2.20
COMMON CARD (1-11)	.20	.09

☐ 1 Ozzie Smith		
☐ 2 Kirby Puckett	.75	.35
☐ 3 Gary Sheffield		
☐ 4 Andy Van Slyke	.20	.09
☐ 5 Ken Griffey Jr.	2.50	1.10
☐ 6 Ivan Rodriguez		
☐ 7 Charles Nagy	.20	.09
☐ 8 Tom Glavine	.30	.14
☐ 9 Dennis Eckersley	.30	.14
☐ 10 Frank Thomas	2.00	.90
☐ 11 Roberto Alomar		
☐ NNO Header Card	.50	.23

1993 Score Proctor and Gamble

This ten-card standard-size set was produced by Score as a promotion for Proctor and Gamble. The set was advertised through store displays; the set could be acquired by sending in three UPC symbols and money to cover postage and handling. The fronts display a color action player photo protruding from a diamond-shaped frame. A wide stripe running from the bottom of the card and intersecting the bottom point of the diamond carries the player's name, position, and a picture of the home stadium. The surrounding card face of the front is olive green and accented with gold foil lettering. The name of the city appears in gold print on the reverse side of the card in the center.

	MINT	NRMT
COMPLETE SET (10)	7.50	3.40
COMMON CARD (1-10)	.25	.11

☐ 1 Wil Cordero	.25	.11
☐ 2 Pedro Martinez	2.00	.90
☐ 3 Bret Boone	.25	.11
☐ 4 Melvin Nieves	.50	.23
☐ 5 Ryan Klesko	3.00	1.35
☐ 6 Ryan Thompson	.25	.11
☐ 7 Kevin Young	.25	.11
☐ 8 Willie Greene	1.00	.45
☐ 9 Eric Wedge	.25	.11
☐ 10 David Nied	.25	.11

1994 Score Samples

This 19-card standard-size promo set features dark blue-bordered color player action shots on its fronts. The player's name appears within a team-colored stripe at the bottom of the photo and his team name appears beneath within a grayish stripe. The horizontal back features a narrow-cropped color player action shot on the left side. The player's name appears at the top within a team color-coded stripe and his position appears beneath in a grayish stripe. His team logo, biography, stats and career highlights follow below. The cards are numbered on the back. Each dealer received one basic promo and one "Gold Rush" promo with their order form. The word "SAMPLE" is printed diagonally across the front and back of each card.

	MINT	NRMT
COMPLETE SET (19)	35.00	16.00
COMMON CARD	.40	.18

☐ 1 Barry Bonds	1.00	.45
☐ 1GR Barry Bonds	3.00	1.35
☐ 2 John Olerud	.40	.18
☐ 2GR John Olerud	1.25	.55
☐ 3 Ken Griffey Jr.	4.00	1.80
☐ 3GR Ken Griffey Jr.	12.00	5.50
☐ 4 Jeff Bagwell	1.50	.70
☐ 4GR Jeff Bagwell	5.00	2.20
☐ 5 John Burkett	.40	.18
☐ 5GR John Burkett	1.25	.55
☐ 6 Jack McDowell	.40	.18
☐ 6GR Jack McDowell	1.25	.55
☐ 7 Albert Belle	2.00	.90
☐ 7GR Albert Belle	6.00	2.70
☐ 8 Andres Galarraga	.75	.35
☐ 8GR Andres Galarraga	2.00	.90
☐ DT5 Barry Larkin	5.00	2.20
☐ NNO Hobby Ad Card	.40	.18
☐ NNO Retail Ad Card	.40	.18

1994 Score

The 1994 Score set of 660 standard-size cards was issued in two series of 330. Cards were distributed in 14-card hobby and retail packs. Each pack contained 13 basic cards plus one Gold Rush parallel card. Cards were also distributed in retail Jumbo packs. 4,875 cases of 1994 Score baseball were printed for the hobby. This figure does not take into account additional product printed for retail outlets. The navy blue bordered card fronts feature color action photos with the player's name and team name appearing on two team color-coded stripes across the bottom. Among the subsets are American League stadiums (317-330) and National League stadiums (647-660). Notable Rookie Cards include Derrek Lee and Billy Wagner.

	MINT	NRMT
COMPLETE SET (660)	24.00	11.00
COMPLETE SERIES 1 (330)	12.00	5.50
COMPLETE SERIES 2 (330)	12.00	5.50
COMMON CARD (1-660)	.10	.05

☐ 1 Barry Bonds	.50	.23
☐ 2 John Olerud	.20	.09
☐ 3 Ken Griffey Jr.	2.00	.90
☐ 4 Jeff Bagwell	.75	.35
☐ 5 John Burkett	.10	.05

☐ 6 Jack McDowell	.10	.05
☐ 7 Albert Belle	.50	.23
☐ 8 Andres Galarraga	.30	.14
☐ 9 Mike Mussina	.40	.18
☐ 10 Will Clark	.30	.14
☐ 11 Travis Fryman	.20	.09
☐ 12 Tony Gwynn	1.00	.45
☐ 13 Robin Yount	.30	.14
☐ 14 Dave Magadan	.10	.05
☐ 15 Paul O'Neill	.20	.09
☐ 16 Ray Lankford	.30	.14
☐ 17 Damion Easley	.10	.05
☐ 18 Andy Van Slyke	.20	.09
☐ 19 Brian McRae	.10	.05
☐ 20 Ryne Sandberg	.50	.23
☐ 21 Kirby Puckett	.75	.35
☐ 22 Dwight Gooden	.20	.09
☐ 23 Don Mattingly	.60	.25
☐ 24 Kevin Mitchell	.10	.05
☐ 25 Roger Clemens	.75	.35
☐ 26 Eric Karros	.20	.09
☐ 27 Juan Gonzalez	1.00	.45
☐ 28 John Kruk	.20	.09
☐ 29 Gregg Jefferies	.20	.09
☐ 30 Tom Glavine	.30	.14
☐ 31 Ivan Rodriguez	.50	.23
☐ 32 Jay Bell	.20	.09
☐ 33 Randy Johnson	.40	.18
☐ 34 Darren Daulton	.20	.09
☐ 35 Rickey Henderson	.30	.14
☐ 36 Eddie Murray	.40	.18
☐ 37 Brian Harper	.10	.05
☐ 38 Delino DeShields	.10	.05
☐ 39 Jose Lind	.10	.05
☐ 40 Benito Santiago	.10	.05
☐ 41 Frank Thomas	1.50	.70
☐ 42 Mark Grace	.30	.14
☐ 43 Roberto Alomar	.40	.18
☐ 44 Andy Benes	.20	.09
☐ 45 Luis Polonia	.10	.05
☐ 46 Brett Butler	.20	.09
☐ 47 Terry Steinbach	.20	.09
☐ 48 Craig Biggio	.30	.14
☐ 49 Greg Vaughn	.10	.05
☐ 50 Charlie Hayes	.10	.05
☐ 51 Mickey Tettleton	.10	.05
☐ 52 Jose Rijo	.10	.05
☐ 53 Carlos Baerga	.20	.09
☐ 54 Jeff Blauser	.10	.05
☐ 55 Leo Gomez	.10	.05
☐ 56 Bob Tewksbury	.10	.05
☐ 57 Mo Vaughn	.50	.23
☐ 58 Orlando Merced	.10	.05
☐ 59 Tino Martinez	.40	.18
☐ 60 Lenny Dykstra	.20	.09
☐ 61 Jose Canseco	.30	.14
☐ 62 Tony Fernandez	.10	.05
☐ 63 Donovan Osborne	.10	.05
☐ 64 Ken Hill	.10	.05
☐ 65 Kent Hrbek	.20	.09
☐ 66 Bryan Harvey	.10	.05
☐ 67 Wally Joyner	.20	.09
☐ 68 Derrick May	.10	.05
☐ 69 Lance Johnson	.10	.05
☐ 70 Willie McGee	.10	.05
☐ 71 Mark Langston	.10	.05
☐ 72 Terry Pendleton	.20	.09
☐ 73 Joe Carter	.30	.14
☐ 74 Barry Larkin	.30	.14
☐ 75 Jimmy Key	.20	.09
☐ 76 Joe Girardi	.10	.05
☐ 77 B.J. Surhoff	.10	.05
☐ 78 Pete Harnisch	.10	.05
☐ 79 Lou Whitaker UER (Milt Cuyler pictured on front)	.20	.09
☐ 80 Cory Snyder	.10	.05
☐ 81 Kenny Lofton	.50	.23
☐ 82 Fred McGriff	.30	.14
☐ 83 Mike Greenwell	.10	.05
☐ 84 Mike Perez	.10	.05
☐ 85 Cal Ripken	1.50	.70
☐ 86 Don Slaught	.10	.05
☐ 87 Omar Vizquel	.20	.09
☐ 88 Curt Schilling	.20	.09
☐ 89 Chuck Knoblauch	.40	.18
☐ 90 Moises Alou	.20	.09
☐ 91 Greg Gagne	.10	.05
☐ 92 Bret Saberhagen	.10	.05
☐ 93 Ozzie Guillen	.10	.05
☐ 94 Matt Williams	.30	.14
☐ 95 Chad Curtis	.10	.05
☐ 96 Mike Harkey	.10	.05
☐ 97 Devon White	.10	.05
☐ 98 Walt Weiss	.10	.05
☐ 99 Kevin Brown	.20	.09
☐ 100 Gary Sheffield	.40	.18
☐ 101 Wade Boggs	.40	.18
☐ 102 Orel Hershiser	.20	.09
☐ 103 Tony Phillips	.10	.05
☐ 104 Andujar Cedeno	.10	.05
☐ 105 Bill Spiers	.10	.05
☐ 106 Otis Nixon	.20	.09
☐ 107 Felix Fermin	.10	.05
☐ 108 Bip Roberts	.10	.05
☐ 109 Dennis Eckersley	.30	.14
☐ 110 Dante Bichette	.30	.14
☐ 111 Ben McDonald	.10	.05
☐ 112 Jim Poole	.10	.05
☐ 113 John Dopson	.10	.05
☐ 114 Rob Dibble	.10	.05
☐ 115 Jeff Treadway	.10	.05
☐ 116 Ricky Jordan	.10	.05
☐ 117 Mike Henneman	.10	.05
☐ 118 Willie Blair	.10	.05
☐ 119 Doug Henry	.10	.05
☐ 120 Gerald Perry	.10	.05
☐ 121 Greg Myers	.10	.05
☐ 122 John Franco	.20	.09
☐ 123 Roger Mason	.10	.05
☐ 124 Chris Hammond	.10	.05
☐ 125 Hubie Brooks	.10	.05
☐ 126 Kent Mercker	.10	.05
☐ 127 Jim Abbott	.10	.05
☐ 128 Kevin Bass	.10	.05
☐ 129 Rick Aguilera	.10	.05
☐ 130 Mitch Webster	.10	.05
☐ 131 Eric Plunk	.10	.05
☐ 132 Mark Carreon	.10	.05
☐ 133 Dave Stewart	.20	.09
☐ 134 Willie Wilson	.10	.05
☐ 135 Dave Fleming	.10	.05
☐ 136 Jeff Tackett	.10	.05
☐ 137 Geno Petralli	.10	.05
☐ 138 Gene Harris	.10	.05
☐ 139 Scott Bankhead	.10	.05
☐ 140 Trevor Wilson	.10	.05
☐ 141 Alvaro Espinoza	.10	.05
☐ 142 Ryan Bowen	.10	.05
☐ 143 Mike Moore	.10	.05
☐ 144 Bill Pecota	.10	.05
☐ 145 Jaime Navarro	.10	.05
☐ 146 Jack Daugherty	.10	.05
☐ 147 Bob Wickman	.10	.05
☐ 148 Chris Jones	.10	.05
☐ 149 Todd Stottlemyre	.10	.05
☐ 150 Brian Williams	.10	.05
☐ 151 Chuck Finley	.10	.05
☐ 152 Lenny Harris	.10	.05
☐ 153 Alex Fernandez	.20	.09
☐ 154 Candy Maldonado	.10	.05
☐ 155 Jeff Montgomery	.20	.09
☐ 156 David West	.10	.05
☐ 157 Mark Williamson	.10	.05
☐ 158 Milt Thompson	.10	.05
☐ 159 Ron Darling	.10	.05
☐ 160 Stan Belinda	.10	.05
☐ 161 Henry Cotto	.10	.05
☐ 162 Mel Rojas	.10	.05
☐ 163 Doug Strange	.10	.05
☐ 164 Rene Arocha	.10	.05
☐ 165 Tim Hulett	.10	.05
☐ 166 Steve Avery	.10	.05
☐ 167 Jim Thome	.50	.23
☐ 168 Tom Browning	.10	.05
☐ 169 Mario Diaz	.10	.05
☐ 170 Steve Reed	.10	.05
☐ 171 Scott Livingstone	.10	.05
☐ 172 Chris Donnels	.10	.05
☐ 173 John Jaha	.10	.05
☐ 174 Carlos Hernandez	.10	.05
☐ 175 Dion James	.10	.05
☐ 176 Bud Black	.10	.05
☐ 177 Tony Castillo	.10	.05
☐ 178 Jose Guzman	.10	.05
☐ 179 Torey Lovullo	.10	.05
☐ 180 John Vander Wal	.10	.05
☐ 181 Mike LaValliere	.10	.05
☐ 182 Sid Fernandez	.10	.05
☐ 183 Brent Mayne	.10	.05
☐ 184 Terry Mulholland	.10	.05
☐ 185 Willie Banks	.10	.05
☐ 186 Steve Cooke	.10	.05
☐ 187 Brent Gates	.10	.05
☐ 188 Erik Pappas	.10	.05
☐ 189 Bill Haselman	.10	.05
☐ 190 Fernando Valenzuela	.20	.09
☐ 191 Gary Redus	.10	.05
☐ 192 Danny Darwin	.10	.05
☐ 193 Mark Portugal	.10	.05
☐ 194 Derek Lilliquist	.10	.05
☐ 195 Charlie O'Brien	.10	.05
☐ 196 Matt Nokes	.10	.05
☐ 197 Danny Sheaffer	.10	.05
☐ 198 Bill Gullickson	.10	.05
☐ 199 Alex Arias	.10	.05
☐ 200 Mike Fetters	.10	.05
☐ 201 Brian Jordan	.20	.09
☐ 202 Joe Grahe	.10	.05
☐ 203 Tom Candiotti	.10	.05
☐ 204 Jeremy Hernandez	.10	.05
☐ 205 Mike Stanton	.10	.05
☐ 206 David Howard	.10	.05
☐ 207 Darren Holmes	.10	.05
☐ 208 Rick Honeycutt	.10	.05
☐ 209 Danny Jackson	.10	.05
☐ 210 Rich Amaral	.10	.05
☐ 211 Blas Minor	.10	.05
☐ 212 Kenny Rogers	.10	.05
☐ 213 Jim Leyritz	.10	.05
☐ 214 Mike Morgan	.10	.05
☐ 215 Dan Gladden	.10	.05
☐ 216 Randy Velarde	.10	.05
☐ 217 Mitch Williams	.10	.05
☐ 218 Hipolito Pichardo	.10	.05
☐ 219 Dave Burba	.10	.05
☐ 220 Wilson Alvarez	.20	.09
☐ 221 Bob Zupcic	.10	.05
☐ 222 Francisco Cabrera	.10	.05
☐ 223 Julio Valera	.10	.05
☐ 224 Paul Assenmacher	.10	.05
☐ 225 Jeff Branson	.10	.05
☐ 226 Todd Frohwirth	.10	.05
☐ 227 Armando Reynoso	.10	.05
☐ 228 Rich Rowland	.10	.05
☐ 229 Freddie Benavides	.10	.05
☐ 230 Wayne Kirby	.10	.05
☐ 231 Darryl Kile	.20	.09
☐ 232 Skeeter Barnes	.10	.05
☐ 233 Ramon Martinez	.20	.09
☐ 234 Tom Gordon	.10	.05
☐ 235 Dave Gallagher	.10	.05
☐ 236 Ricky Bones	.10	.05
☐ 237 Larry Andersen	.10	.05
☐ 238 Pat Meares	.10	.05
☐ 239 Zane Smith	.10	.05
☐ 240 Tim Leary	.10	.05
☐ 241 Phil Clark	.10	.05
☐ 242 Danny Cox	.10	.05
☐ 243 Mike Jackson	.10	.05
☐ 244 Mike Gallego	.10	.05
☐ 245 Lee Smith	.20	.09
☐ 246 Todd Jones	.10	.05
☐ 247 Steve Bedrosian	.10	.05
☐ 248 Troy Neel	.10	.05
☐ 249 Jose Bautista	.10	.05
☐ 250 Steve Frey	.10	.05
☐ 251 Jeff Reardon	.20	.09
☐ 252 Stan Javier	.10	.05
☐ 253 Mo Sanford	.10	.05
☐ 254 Steve Sax	.10	.05
☐ 255 Luis Aquino	.10	.05
☐ 256 Domingo Jean	.10	.05
☐ 257 Scott Servais	.10	.05
☐ 258 Brad Pennington	.10	.05
☐ 259 Dave Hansen	.10	.05
☐ 260 Goose Gossage	.20	.09
☐ 261 Jeff Fassero	.10	.05
☐ 262 Junior Ortiz	.10	.05
☐ 263 Anthony Young	.10	.05
☐ 264 Chris Bosio	.10	.05
☐ 265 Ruben Amaro Jr.	.10	.05
☐ 266 Mark Eichhorn	.10	.05
☐ 267 Dave Clark	.10	.05
☐ 268 Gary Thurman	.10	.05
☐ 269 Les Lancaster	.10	.05
☐ 270 Jamie Moyer	.10	.05
☐ 271 Ricky Gutierrez	.10	.05
☐ 272 Greg A.Harris	.10	.05
☐ 273 Mike Benjamin	.10	.05
☐ 274 Gene Nelson	.10	.05
☐ 275 Damon Berryhill	.10	.05
☐ 276 Scott Radinsky	.10	.05
☐ 277 Mike Aldrete	.10	.05
☐ 278 Jerry DiPoto	.10	.05
☐ 279 Chris Haney	.10	.05
☐ 280 Richie Lewis	.10	.05
☐ 281 Jarvis Brown	.10	.05
☐ 282 Juan Bell	.10	.05
☐ 283 Joe Klink	.10	.05
☐ 284 Graeme Lloyd	.10	.05
☐ 285 Casey Candaele	.10	.05
☐ 286 Bob MacDonald	.10	.05
☐ 287 Mike Sharperson	.10	.05
☐ 288 Gene Larkin	.10	.05
☐ 289 Brian Barnes	.10	.05
☐ 290 David McCarty	.10	.05
☐ 291 Jeff Innis	.10	.05
☐ 292 Bob Patterson	.10	.05
☐ 293 Ben Rivera	.10	.05
☐ 294 John Habyan	.10	.05

☐ 295 Rich Rodriguez	.10	.05
☐ 296 Edwin Nunez	.10	.05
☐ 297 Rod Brewer	.10	.05
☐ 298 Mike Timlin	.10	.05
☐ 299 Jesse Orosco	.10	.05
☐ 300 Gary Gaetti	.20	.09
☐ 301 Todd Benzinger	.10	.05
☐ 302 Jeff Nelson	.10	.05
☐ 303 Rafael Belliard	.10	.05
☐ 304 Matt Whiteside	.10	.05
☐ 305 Vinny Castilla	.30	.14
☐ 306 Matt Turner	.10	.05
☐ 307 Eduardo Perez	.10	.05
☐ 308 Joel Johnston	.10	.05
☐ 309 Chris Gomez	.10	.05
☐ 310 Pat Rapp	.10	.05
☐ 311 Jim Tatum	.10	.05
☐ 312 Kirk Rueter	.10	.05
☐ 313 John Flaherty	.10	.05
☐ 314 Tom Kramer	.10	.05
☐ 315 Mark Whiten	.10	.05
☐ 316 Chris Bosio	.10	.05
☐ 317 Baltimore Orioles CL	.10	.05
☐ 318 Boston Red Sox CL UER (Viola listed as 316; should be 331)	.10	.05
☐ 319 California Angels CL	.10	.05
☐ 320 Chicago White Sox CL	.10	.05
☐ 321 Cleveland Indians CL	.10	.05
☐ 322 Detroit Tigers CL	.10	.05
☐ 323 Kansas City Royals CL	.10	.05
☐ 324 Milwaukee Brewers CL	.10	.05
☐ 325 Minnesota Twins CL	.10	.05
☐ 326 New York Yankees CL	.10	.05
☐ 327 Oakland Athletics CL	.10	.05
☐ 328 Seattle Mariners CL	.10	.05
☐ 329 Texas Rangers CL	.10	.05
☐ 330 Toronto Blue Jays CL	.10	.05
☐ 331 Frank Viola	.10	.05
☐ 332 Ron Gant	.20	.09
☐ 333 Charles Nagy	.10	.05
☐ 334 Roberto Kelly	.10	.05
☐ 335 Brady Anderson	.30	.14
☐ 336 Alex Cole	.10	.05
☐ 337 Alan Trammell	.30	.14
☐ 338 Derek Bell	.20	.09
☐ 339 Bernie Williams	.40	.18
☐ 340 Jose Offerman	.10	.05
☐ 341 Bill Wegman	.10	.05
☐ 342 Ken Caminiti	.40	.18
☐ 343 Pat Borders	.10	.05
☐ 344 Kirt Manwaring	.10	.05
☐ 345 Chili Davis	.20	.09
☐ 346 Steve Buechele	.10	.05
☐ 347 Robin Ventura	.20	.09
☐ 348 Teddy Higuera	.10	.05
☐ 349 Jerry Browne	.10	.05
☐ 350 Scott Kamieniecki	.10	.05
☐ 351 Kevin Tapani	.10	.05
☐ 352 Marquis Grissom	.20	.09
☐ 353 Jay Buhner	.30	.14
☐ 354 Dave Hollins	.10	.05
☐ 355 Dan Wilson	.20	.09
☐ 356 Bob Walk	.10	.05
☐ 357 Chris Hoiles	.10	.05
☐ 358 Todd Zeile	.10	.05
☐ 359 Kevin Appier	.20	.09
☐ 360 Chris Sabo	.10	.05
☐ 361 David Segui	.10	.05
☐ 362 Jerald Clark	.10	.05
☐ 363 Tony Pena	.10	.05
☐ 364 Steve Finley	.20	.09
☐ 365 Roger Pavlik	.10	.05
☐ 366 John Smoltz	.30	.14
☐ 367 Scott Fletcher	.10	.05
☐ 368 Jody Reed	.10	.05
☐ 369 David Wells	.10	.05
☐ 370 Jose Vizcaino	.10	.05
☐ 371 Pat Listach	.10	.05
☐ 372 Orestes Destrade	.10	.05
☐ 373 Danny Tartabull	.10	.05
☐ 374 Greg W. Harris	.10	.05
☐ 375 Juan Guzman	.10	.05
☐ 376 Larry Walker	.40	.18
☐ 377 Gary DiSarcina	.10	.05
☐ 378 Bobby Bonilla	.20	.09
☐ 379 Tim Raines	.10	.05
☐ 380 Tommy Greene	.10	.05
☐ 381 Chris Gwynn	.10	.05
☐ 382 Jeff King	.20	.09
☐ 383 Shane Mack	.10	.05
☐ 384 Ozzie Smith	.50	.23
☐ 385 Eddie Zambrano	.10	.05
☐ 386 Mike Devereaux	.10	.05
☐ 387 Erik Hanson	.10	.05
☐ 388 Scott Cooper	.10	.05
☐ 389 Dean Palmer	.20	.09
☐ 390 John Wetteland	.20	.09
☐ 391 Reggie Jefferson	.20	.09
☐ 392 Mark Lemke	.10	.05
☐ 393 Cecil Fielder	.20	.09
☐ 394 Reggie Sanders	.20	.09
☐ 395 Darryl Hamilton	.10	.05
☐ 396 Daryl Boston	.10	.05
☐ 397 Pat Kelly	.10	.05
☐ 398 Joe Orsulak	.10	.05
☐ 399 Ed Sprague	.10	.05
☐ 400 Eric Anthony	.10	.05
☐ 401 Scott Sanderson	.10	.05
☐ 402 Jim Gott	.10	.05
☐ 403 Ron Karkovice	.10	.05
☐ 404 Phil Plantier	.10	.05
☐ 405 David Cone	.20	.09
☐ 406 Robby Thompson	.10	.05
☐ 407 Dave Winfield	.30	.14
☐ 408 Dwight Smith	.10	.05
☐ 409 Ruben Sierra	.10	.05
☐ 410 Jack Armstrong	.10	.05
☐ 411 Mike Felder	.10	.05
☐ 412 Wil Cordero	.20	.09
☐ 413 Julio Franco	.20	.09
☐ 414 Howard Johnson	.10	.05
☐ 415 Mark McLemore	.10	.05
☐ 416 Pete Incaviglia	.10	.05
☐ 417 John Valentin	.20	.09
☐ 418 Tim Wakefield	.10	.05
☐ 419 Jose Mesa	.20	.09
☐ 420 Bernard Gilkey	.20	.09
☐ 421 Kirk Gibson	.20	.09
☐ 422 Dave Justice	.40	.18
☐ 423 Tom Brunansky	.10	.05
☐ 424 John Smiley	.10	.05
☐ 425 Kevin Maas	.10	.05
☐ 426 Doug Drabek	.10	.05
☐ 427 Paul Molitor	.40	.18
☐ 428 Darryl Strawberry	.20	.09
☐ 429 Tim Naehring	.10	.05
☐ 430 Bill Swift	.10	.05
☐ 431 Ellis Burks	.20	.09
☐ 432 Greg Hibbard	.10	.05
☐ 433 Felix Jose	.10	.05
☐ 434 Bret Barberie	.10	.05
☐ 435 Pedro Munoz	.10	.05
☐ 436 Darrin Fletcher	.10	.05
☐ 437 Bobby Witt	.10	.05
☐ 438 Wes Chamberlain	.10	.05
☐ 439 Mackey Sasser	.10	.05
☐ 440 Mark Whiten	.10	.05
☐ 441 Harold Reynolds	.10	.05
☐ 442 Greg Olson	.10	.05
☐ 443 Billy Hatcher	.10	.05
☐ 444 Joe Oliver	.10	.05
☐ 445 Sandy Alomar Jr.	.20	.09
☐ 446 Tim Wallach	.10	.05
☐ 447 Karl Rhodes	.10	.05
☐ 448 Royce Clayton	.20	.09
☐ 449 Cal Eldred	.10	.05
☐ 450 Rick Wilkins	.10	.05
☐ 451 Mike Stanley	.10	.05
☐ 452 Charlie Hough	.10	.05
☐ 453 Jack Morris	.20	.09
☐ 454 Jon Ratliff	.20	.09
☐ 455 Rene Gonzales	.10	.05
☐ 456 Eddie Taubensee	.10	.05
☐ 457 Roberto Hernandez	.20	.09
☐ 458 Todd Hundley	.20	.09
☐ 459 Mike Macfarlane	.10	.05
☐ 460 Mickey Morandini	.10	.05
☐ 461 Scott Erickson	.10	.05
☐ 462 Lonnie Smith	.10	.05
☐ 463 Dave Henderson	.10	.05
☐ 464 Ryan Klesko	.30	.14
☐ 465 Edgar Martinez	.30	.14
☐ 466 Tom Pagnozzi	.10	.05
☐ 467 Charlie Leibrandt	.10	.05
☐ 468 Brian Anderson	.20	.09
☐ 469 Harold Baines	.20	.09
☐ 470 Tim Belcher	.10	.05
☐ 471 Andre Dawson	.30	.14
☐ 472 Eric Young	.20	.09
☐ 473 Paul Sorrento	.10	.05
☐ 474 Luis Gonzalez	.10	.05
☐ 475 Rob Deer	.10	.05
☐ 476 Mike Piazza	1.25	.55
☐ 477 Kevin Reimer	.10	.05
☐ 478 Jeff Gardner	.10	.05
☐ 479 Melido Perez	.10	.05
☐ 480 Darren Lewis	.10	.05
☐ 481 Duane Ward	.10	.05
☐ 482 Rey Sanchez	.10	.05
☐ 483 Mark Lewis	.10	.05
☐ 484 Jeff Conine	.20	.09
☐ 485 Joey Cora	.20	.09
☐ 486 Trot Nixon	.30	.14
☐ 487 Kevin McReynolds	.10	.05
☐ 488 Mike Lansing	.20	.09
☐ 489 Mike Pagliarulo	.10	.05
☐ 490 Mariano Duncan	.10	.05
☐ 491 Mike Bordick	.10	.05
☐ 492 Kevin Young	.10	.05
☐ 493 Dave Valle	.10	.05
☐ 494 Wayne Gomes	.20	.09
☐ 495 Rafael Palmeiro	.30	.14
☐ 496 Deion Sanders	.40	.18
☐ 497 Rick Sutcliffe	.10	.05
☐ 498 Randy Milligan	.10	.05
☐ 499 Carlos Quintana	.10	.05
☐ 500 Chris Turner	.10	.05
☐ 501 Thomas Howard	.10	.05
☐ 502 Greg Swindell	.10	.05
☐ 503 Chad Kreuter	.10	.05
☐ 504 Eric Davis	.20	.09
☐ 505 Dickie Thon	.10	.05
☐ 506 Matt Drews	.40	.18
☐ 507 Spike Owen	.10	.05
☐ 508 Rod Beck	.20	.09
☐ 509 Pat Hentgen	.20	.09
☐ 510 Sammy Sosa	.40	.18
☐ 511 J.T. Snow	.20	.09
☐ 512 Chuck Carr	.10	.05
☐ 513 Bo Jackson	.20	.09
☐ 514 Dennis Martinez	.20	.09
☐ 515 Phil Hiatt	.10	.05
☐ 516 Jeff Kent	.10	.05
☐ 517 Brooks Kieschnick	.30	.14
☐ 518 Kirk Presley	.20	.09
☐ 519 Kevin Seitzer	.10	.05
☐ 520 Carlos Garcia	.10	.05
☐ 521 Mike Blowers	.10	.05
☐ 522 Luis Alicea	.10	.05
☐ 523 David Hulse	.10	.05
☐ 524 Greg Maddux UER (career strikeout totals listed as 113; should be 1134)	1.25	.55
☐ 525 Gregg Olson	.10	.05
☐ 526 Hal Morris	.10	.05
☐ 527 Daron Kirkreit	.20	.09
☐ 528 David Nied	.10	.05
☐ 529 Jeff Russell	.10	.05
☐ 530 Kevin Gross	.10	.05
☐ 531 John Doherty	.10	.05
☐ 532 Matt Brunson	.20	.09
☐ 533 Dave Nilsson	.20	.09
☐ 534 Randy Myers	.10	.05
☐ 535 Steve Farr	.10	.05
☐ 536 Billy Wagner	.75	.35
☐ 537 Darnell Coles	.10	.05
☐ 538 Frank Tanana	.10	.05
☐ 539 Tim Salmon	.40	.18
☐ 540 Kim Batiste	.10	.05
☐ 541 George Bell	.10	.05
☐ 542 Tom Henke	.10	.05
☐ 543 Sam Horn	.10	.05
☐ 544 Doug Jones	.10	.05
☐ 545 Scott Leius	.10	.05
☐ 546 Al Martin	.10	.05
☐ 547 Bob Welch	.10	.05
☐ 548 Scott Christman	.20	.09
☐ 549 Norm Charlton	.10	.05
☐ 550 Mark McGwire	.75	.35
☐ 551 Greg McMichael	.10	.05
☐ 552 Tim Costo	.10	.05
☐ 553 Rodney Bolton	.10	.05
☐ 554 Pedro Martinez	.40	.18
☐ 555 Marc Valdes	.20	.09
☐ 556 Darrell Whitmore	.10	.05
☐ 557 Tim Bogar	.10	.05
☐ 558 Steve Karsay	.10	.05
☐ 559 Danny Bautista	.10	.05
☐ 560 Jeffrey Hammonds	.20	.09
☐ 561 Aaron Sele	.10	.05
☐ 562 Russ Springer	.10	.05
☐ 563 Jason Bere	.10	.05
☐ 564 Billy Brewer	.10	.05
☐ 565 Sterling Hitchcock	.20	.09
☐ 566 Bobby Munoz	.10	.05
☐ 567 Craig Paquette	.10	.05
☐ 568 Bret Boone	.10	.05
☐ 569 Dan Peltier	.10	.05
☐ 570 Jeromy Burnitz	.20	.09
☐ 571 John Wasdin	.30	.14
☐ 572 Chipper Jones	1.25	.55
☐ 573 Jamey Wright	.40	.18
☐ 574 Jeff Granger	.20	.09
☐ 575 Jay Powell	.20	.09
☐ 576 Ryan Thompson	.10	.05
☐ 577 Lou Frazier	.10	.05
☐ 578 Paul Wagner	.10	.05
☐ 579 Brad Ausmus	.10	.05
☐ 580 Jack Voigt	.10	.05
☐ 581 Kevin Rogers	.10	.05

Card	MINT	NRMT
☐ 582 Damon Buford	.10	.05
☐ 583 Paul Quantrill	.10	.05
☐ 584 Marc Newfield	.20	.09
☐ 585 Derrek Lee	1.25	.55
☐ 586 Shane Reynolds	.20	.09
☐ 587 Cliff Floyd	.20	.09
☐ 588 Jeff Schwarz	.10	.05
☐ 589 Ross Powell	.10	.05
☐ 590 Gerald Williams	.10	.05
☐ 591 Mike Trombley	.10	.05
☐ 592 Ken Ryan	.10	.05
☐ 593 John O'Donoghue	.10	.05
☐ 594 Rod Correia	.10	.05
☐ 595 Darrell Sherman	.10	.05
☐ 596 Steve Scarsone	.10	.05
☐ 597 Sherman Obando	.10	.05
☐ 598 Kurt Abbott	.20	.09
☐ 599 Dave Telgheder	.10	.05
☐ 600 Rick Trlicek	.10	.05
☐ 601 Carl Everett	.10	.05
☐ 602 Luis Ortiz	.10	.05
☐ 603 Larry Luebbers	.10	.05
☐ 604 Kevin Roberson	.10	.05
☐ 605 Butch Huskey	.20	.09
☐ 606 Benji Gil	.10	.05
☐ 607 Todd Van Poppel	.10	.05
☐ 608 Mark Hutton	.10	.05
☐ 609 Chip Hale	.10	.05
☐ 610 Matt Maysey	.10	.05
☐ 611 Scott Ruffcorn	.10	.05
☐ 612 Hilly Hathaway	.10	.05
☐ 613 Allen Watson	.10	.05
☐ 614 Carlos Delgado	.30	.14
☐ 615 Roberto Mejia	.10	.05
☐ 616 Turk Wendell	.10	.05
☐ 617 Tony Tarasco	.10	.05
☐ 618 Raul Mondesi	.30	.14
☐ 619 Kevin Stocker	.10	.05
☐ 620 Javier Lopez	.30	.14
☐ 621 Keith Kessinger	.10	.05
☐ 622 Bob Hamelin	.10	.05
☐ 623 John Roper	.10	.05
☐ 624 Lenny Dykstra WS	.10	.05
☐ 625 Joe Carter WS	.20	.09
☐ 626 Jim Abbott HL	.10	.05
☐ 627 Lee Smith HL	.20	.09
☐ 628 Ken Griffey Jr. HL	1.00	.45
☐ 629 Dave Winfield HL	.30	.14
☐ 630 Darryl Kile HL	.20	.09
☐ 631 Frank Thomas AL MVP	1.00	.45
☐ 632 Barry Bonds NL MVP	.40	.18
☐ 633 Jack McDowell AL CY	.10	.05
☐ 634 Greg Maddux NL CY	.60	.25
☐ 635 Tim Salmon AL ROY	.30	.14
☐ 636 Mike Piazza NL ROY	.60	.25
☐ 637 Brian Turang	.10	.05
☐ 638 Rondell White	.20	.09
☐ 639 Nigel Wilson	.10	.05
☐ 640 Torii Hunter	.20	.09
☐ 641 Salomon Torres	.10	.05
☐ 642 Kevin Higgins	.10	.05
☐ 643 Eric Wedge	.10	.05
☐ 644 Roger Salkeld	.10	.05
☐ 645 Manny Ramirez	.50	.23
☐ 646 Jeff McNeely	.10	.05
☐ 647 Atlanta Braves CL	.10	.05
☐ 648 Chicago Cubs CL	.10	.05
☐ 649 Cincinnati Reds CL	.10	.05
☐ 650 Colorado Rockies CL	.10	.05
☐ 651 Florida Marlins CL	.10	.05
☐ 652 Houston Astros CL	.10	.05
☐ 653 Los Angeles Dodgers CL	.10	.05
☐ 654 Montreal Expos CL	.10	.05
☐ 655 New York Mets CL	.10	.05
☐ 656 Philadelphia Phillies CL	.10	.05
☐ 657 Pittsburgh Pirates CL	.10	.05
☐ 658 St. Louis Cardinals CL	.10	.05
☐ 659 San Diego Padres CL	.10	.05
☐ 660 San Francisco Giants CL	.10	.05

1994 Score Gold Rush

This 660-card standard-size set is parallel to the basic Score issue. This set features metallicized and gold-bordered fronts. Gold Rush cards came one per 14-card pack or super pack. They were also issued two per jumbo. These cards were inserted into both hobby and retail packs.

	MINT	NRMT
COMPLETE SET (660)	160.00	70.00
COMPLETE SERIES 1 (330)	80.00	36.00
COMPLETE SERIES 2 (330)	80.00	36.00
COMMON CARD (1-660)	.25	.11
*STARS: 1.5X to 4X BASIC CARDS		
*YOUNG STARS: 1.25X to 3X BASIC CARDS		

1994 Score Boys of Summer

Randomly inserted in super packs at a rate of one in four, this 60-card set features top young stars and hopefuls. The set was issued in two series of 30 cards. The fronts have a color player photo that is outlined by what resembles static electricity. The backgrounds are blurred and the player's name and Boys of Summer logo appear up the right-hand side. An orange back contains a player photo and text.

	MINT	NRMT
COMPLETE SET (60)	120.00	55.00
COMPLETE SERIES 1 (30)	50.00	22.00
COMPLETE SERIES 2 (30)	70.00	32.00
COMMON CARD (1-60)	1.50	.70
☐ 1 Jeff Conine	3.00	1.35
☐ 2 Aaron Sele	1.50	.70
☐ 3 Kevin Stocker	1.50	.70
☐ 4 Pat Meares	1.50	.70
☐ 5 Jeromy Burnitz	3.00	1.35
☐ 6 Mike Piazza	25.00	11.00
☐ 7 Allen Watson	1.50	.70
☐ 8 Jeffrey Hammonds	3.00	1.35
☐ 9 Kevin Roberson	1.50	.70
☐ 10 Hilly Hathaway	1.50	.70
☐ 11 Kirk Rueter	1.50	.70
☐ 12 Eduardo Perez	1.50	.70
☐ 13 Ricky Gutierrez	1.50	.70
☐ 14 Domingo Jean	1.50	.70
☐ 15 David Nied	1.50	.70
☐ 16 Wayne Kirby	1.50	.70
☐ 17 Mike Lansing	3.00	1.35
☐ 18 Jason Bere	1.50	.70
☐ 19 Brent Gates	1.50	.70
☐ 20 Javier Lopez	5.00	2.20
☐ 21 Greg McMichael	1.50	.70
☐ 22 David Hulse	1.50	.70
☐ 23 Roberto Mejia	1.50	.70
☐ 24 Tim Salmon	6.00	2.70
☐ 25 Rene Arocha	1.50	.70
☐ 26 Bret Boone	1.50	.70
☐ 27 David McCarty	1.50	.70
☐ 28 Todd Van Poppel	1.50	.70
☐ 29 Lance Painter	1.50	.70
☐ 30 Erik Pappas	1.50	.70
☐ 31 Chuck Carr	1.50	.70
☐ 32 Mark Hutton	1.50	.70
☐ 33 Jeff McNeely	1.50	.70
☐ 34 Willie Greene	3.00	1.35
☐ 35 Nigel Wilson	1.50	.70
☐ 36 Rondell White	4.00	1.80
☐ 37 Brian Turang	1.50	.70
☐ 38 Manny Ramirez	10.00	4.50
☐ 39 Salomon Torres	1.50	.70
☐ 40 Melvin Nieves	1.50	.70
☐ 41 Ryan Klesko	6.00	2.70
☐ 42 Keith Kessinger	1.50	.70
☐ 43 Brad Ausmus	1.50	.70
☐ 44 Bob Hamelin	1.50	.70
☐ 45 Carlos Delgado	5.00	2.20
☐ 46 Marc Newfield	3.00	1.35
☐ 47 Raul Mondesi	6.00	2.70
☐ 48 Tim Costo	1.50	.70
☐ 49 Pedro Martinez	4.00	1.80
☐ 50 Steve Karsay	1.50	.70
☐ 51 Danny Bautista	1.50	.70
☐ 52 Butch Huskey	3.00	1.35
☐ 53 Kurt Abbott	1.50	.70
☐ 54 Darrell Sherman	1.50	.70
☐ 55 Damon Buford	1.50	.70
☐ 56 Ross Powell	1.50	.70
☐ 57 Darrell Whitmore	1.50	.70
☐ 58 Chipper Jones	25.00	11.00
☐ 59 Jeff Granger	1.50	.70
☐ 60 Cliff Floyd	3.00	1.35

1994 Score Cycle

This 20-card set was randomly inserted in second series foil at a rate of one in 72 and jumbo packs at a rate of one

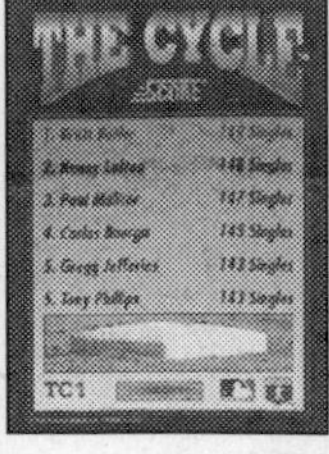

in 36. The set is arranged according to players with the most singles (1-5), doubles (6-10), triples (11-15) and home runs (16-20). The front contains an oval player photo with "The Cycle" at top and the players name at the bottom. Also at the bottom, is the number of of that particular base hit the player accumulated in 1993. A small baseball diamond appears beneath the oval photo. The back lists the top five of the given base hit category. A dark blue border surrounds both sides. The cards are number with a TC prefix.

	MINT	NRMT
COMPLETE SET (20)	150.00	70.00
COMMON CARD (TC1-TC20)	2.50	1.10
☐ TC1 Brett Butler	3.00	1.35
☐ TC2 Kenny Lofton	12.00	5.50
☐ TC3 Paul Molitor	10.00	4.50
☐ TC4 Carlos Baerga	3.00	1.35
☐ TC5 Gregg Jefferies Tony Phillips	2.50	1.10
☐ TC6 John Olerud	2.50	1.10
☐ TC7 Charlie Hayes	2.50	1.10
☐ TC8 Lenny Dykstra	3.00	1.35
☐ TC9 Dante Bichette	5.00	2.20
☐ TC10 Devon White	2.50	1.10
☐ TC11 Lance Johnson	2.50	1.10
☐ TC12 Joey Cora Steve Finley	2.50	1.10
☐ TC13 Tony Fernandez	2.50	1.10
☐ TC14 David Hulse Brett Butler	2.50	1.10
☐ TC15 Jay Bell Brian McRae Mickey Morandini	2.50	1.10
☐ TC16 Juan Gonzalez Barry Bonds	20.00	9.00
☐ TC17 Ken Griffey Jr.	50.00	22.00
☐ TC18 Frank Thomas	40.00	18.00
☐ TC19 Dave Justice	10.00	4.50
☐ TC20 Matt Williams Albert Belle	5.00	2.20

1994 Score Dream Team

Randomly inserted in first series foil and jumbo packs at a rate of one in 72, this ten-card set feature's baseball's Dream Team as selected by Pinnacle Brands. Banded by forest green stripes above and below, the player photos on the fronts feature ten of baseball's best players sporting historical team uniforms from the 1930's. The set title and player's name appear in gold foil lettering on black bars above and below the picture. The backs carry a color head shot and brief player profile.

	MINT	NRMT
COMPLETE SET (10)	60.00	27.00
COMMON CARD (1-10)	2.50	1.10
☐ 1 Mike Mussina	10.00	4.50
☐ 2 Tom Glavine	6.00	2.70
☐ 3 Don Mattingly	15.00	6.75
☐ 4 Carlos Baerga	2.50	1.10
☐ 5 Barry Larkin	6.00	2.70
☐ 6 Matt Williams	6.00	2.70
☐ 7 Juan Gonzalez	25.00	11.00
☐ 8 Andy Van Slyke	2.50	1.10

	MINT	NRMT
☐ 9 Larry Walker	10.00	4.50
☐ 10 Mike Stanley	2.50	1.10

1994 Score Gold Stars

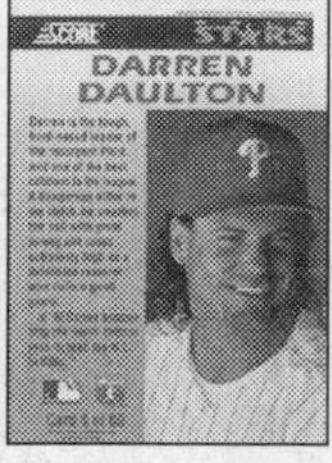

Randomly inserted at a rate of one in every 18 hobby packs, this 60-card set features National and American stars. Split into two series of 30 cards, the first series (1-30) comprises of National League players and the second series (31-60) American Leaguers. The fronts feature a color action player photo cut out and superimposed on a foil background. At the bottom, a navy blue triangle carries the set title and the player's name appears in a white bar. The backs have a color close-up shot and a player profile.

	MINT	NRMT
COMPLETE SET (60)	250.00	110.00
COMPLETE NL SERIES (30)	100.00	45.00
COMPLETE AL SERIES (30)	150.00	70.00
COMMON CARD (1-60)	2.00	.90
☐ 1 Barry Bonds	6.00	2.70
☐ 2 Orlando Merced	2.00	.90
☐ 3 Mark Grace	4.00	1.80
☐ 4 Darren Daulton	3.00	1.35
☐ 5 Jeff Blauser	2.00	.90
☐ 6 Deion Sanders	5.00	2.20
☐ 7 John Kruk	3.00	1.35
☐ 8 Jeff Bagwell	12.00	5.50
☐ 9 Gregg Jefferies	3.00	1.35
☐ 10 Matt Williams	4.00	1.80
☐ 11 Andres Galarraga	4.00	1.80
☐ 12 Jay Bell	2.00	.90
☐ 13 Mike Piazza	20.00	9.00
☐ 14 Ron Gant	3.00	1.35
☐ 15 Barry Larkin	4.00	1.80
☐ 16 Tom Glavine	4.00	1.80
☐ 17 Lenny Dykstra	3.00	1.35
☐ 18 Fred McGriff	4.00	1.80
☐ 19 Andy Van Slyke	3.00	1.35
☐ 20 Gary Sheffield	5.00	2.20
☐ 21 John Burkett	2.00	.90
☐ 22 Dante Bichette	4.00	1.80
☐ 23 Tony Gwynn	12.00	5.50
☐ 24 Dave Justice	5.00	2.20
☐ 25 Marquis Grissom	3.00	1.35
☐ 26 Bobby Bonilla	3.00	1.35
☐ 27 Larry Walker	5.00	2.20
☐ 28 Brett Butler	3.00	1.35
☐ 29 Robby Thompson	2.00	.90
☐ 30 Jeff Conine	3.00	1.35
☐ 31 Joe Carter	4.00	1.80
☐ 32 Ken Griffey Jr.	30.00	13.50
☐ 33 Juan Gonzalez	15.00	6.75
☐ 34 Rickey Henderson	4.00	1.80
☐ 35 Bo Jackson	3.00	1.35
☐ 36 Cal Ripken	25.00	11.00
☐ 37 John Olerud	3.00	1.35
☐ 38 Carlos Baerga	3.00	1.35
☐ 39 Jack McDowell	2.00	.90
☐ 40 Cecil Fielder	3.00	1.35
☐ 41 Kenny Lofton	6.00	2.70
☐ 42 Roberto Alomar	5.00	2.20
☐ 43 Randy Johnson	5.00	2.20
☐ 44 Tim Salmon	5.00	2.20
☐ 45 Frank Thomas	25.00	11.00
☐ 46 Albert Belle	6.00	2.70
☐ 47 Greg Vaughn	2.00	.90
☐ 48 Travis Fryman	3.00	1.35
☐ 49 Don Mattingly	10.00	4.50
☐ 50 Wade Boggs	5.00	2.20
☐ 51 Mo Vaughn	6.00	2.70
☐ 52 Kirby Puckett	12.00	5.50
☐ 53 Devon White	2.00	.90
☐ 54 Tony Phillips	2.00	.90
☐ 55 Brian Harper	2.00	.90
☐ 56 Chad Curtis	2.00	.90
☐ 57 Paul Molitor	5.00	2.20
☐ 58 Ivan Rodriguez	8.00	3.60
☐ 59 Rafael Palmeiro	4.00	1.80
☐ 60 Brian McRae	2.00	.90

1994 Score Rookie/Traded Samples

Issued to preview the designs of Score's 1994 Rookie/Traded set and its inserts, these 11 standard-size cards feature color player action shots on their fronts. The Jackson card is from the one-per-pack Gold Rush insert set. The Palmeiro card represents the randomly inserted Changing Places insert set, and the Ramirez card is an example of the randomly inserted Super Rookies set. Except for the title card, all the cards carry the word "Sample" in diagonal white lettering on their fronts and backs. The cards are numbered on the back with prefixes as shown below.

	MINT	NRMT
COMPLETE SET (11)	12.00	5.50
COMMON CARD	.40	.18
☐ CP2 Rafael Palmeiro	3.00	1.35
☐ RT1 Will Clark	1.00	.45
☐ RT2 Lee Smith	.60	.25
☐ RT3 Bo Jackson	.60	.25
☐ RT4 Ellis Burks	.60	.25
☐ RT5 Eddie Murray	2.00	.90
☐ RT6 Delino DeShields	.40	.18
☐ RT102 Carlos Delgado	1.00	.45
☐ SU2 Manny Ramirez	5.00	2.20
☐ NNO Title Card	.40	.18
☐ NNO September Call-Up Redemption Sample	.40	.18

1994 Score Rookie/Traded

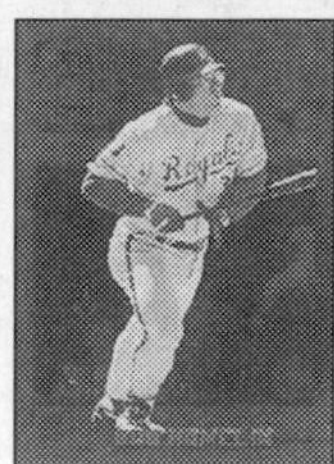

The 1994 Score Rookie and Traded set consists of 165 standard-size cards featuring rookie standouts, traded players, and new young prospects. The set is delineated by traded players (RT1-RT70) and rookies/young prospects (RT71-RT163). The set closes with checklists (RT164-RT165). Each foil pack contained one Gold Rush card. The cards are numbered on the back with an "RT" prefix. Several leading dealers are under the belief that Jose Lima's card (#RT158) was short-printed. A special unnumbered September Call-Up Redemption card could be exchanged for an Alex Rodriguez card. The expiration date was January 31, 1995. Odds of finding a redemption card are approximately one in 240 retail and hobby packs. Rookie Cards include John Mabry and Chan Ho Park.

	MINT	NRMT
COMPLETE SET (165)	10.00	4.50
COMMON CARD (RT1-RT165)	.10	.05
☐ RT1 Will Clark	.30	.14
☐ RT2 Lee Smith	.20	.09
☐ RT3 Bo Jackson	.20	.09
☐ RT4 Ellis Burks	.20	.09
☐ RT5 Eddie Murray	.40	.18
☐ RT6 Delino DeShields	.10	.05
☐ RT7 Erik Hanson	.10	.05
☐ RT8 Rafael Palmeiro	.30	.14
☐ RT9 Luis Polonia	.10	.05
☐ RT10 Omar Vizquel	.20	.09
☐ RT11 Kurt Abbott	.10	.05
☐ RT12 Vince Coleman	.10	.05
☐ RT13 Rickey Henderson	.30	.14
☐ RT14 Terry Mulholland	.10	.05
☐ RT15 Greg Hibbard	.10	.05
☐ RT16 Walt Weiss	.10	.05
☐ RT17 Chris Sabo	.10	.05
☐ RT18 Dave Henderson	.10	.05
☐ RT19 Rick Sutcliffe	.10	.05
☐ RT20 Harold Reynolds	.10	.05
☐ RT21 Jack Morris	.20	.09
☐ RT22 Dan Wilson	.20	.09
☐ RT23 Dave Magadan	.10	.05
☐ RT24 Dennis Martinez	.20	.09
☐ RT25 Wes Chamberlain	.10	.05
☐ RT26 Otis Nixon	.20	.09
☐ RT27 Eric Anthony	.10	.05
☐ RT28 Randy Milligan	.10	.05
☐ RT29 Julio Franco	.20	.09
☐ RT30 Kevin McReynolds	.10	.05
☐ RT31 Anthony Young	.10	.05
☐ RT32 Brian Harper	.10	.05
☐ RT33 Gene Harris	.10	.05
☐ RT34 Eddie Taubensee	.10	.05
☐ RT35 David Segui	.10	.05
☐ RT36 Stan Javier	.10	.05
☐ RT37 Felix Fermin	.10	.05
☐ RT38 Darrin Jackson	.10	.05
☐ RT39 Tony Fernandez	.10	.05
☐ RT40 Jose Vizcaino	.10	.05
☐ RT41 Willie Banks	.10	.05
☐ RT42 Brian Hunter	.10	.05
☐ RT43 Reggie Jefferson	.20	.09
☐ RT44 Junior Felix	.10	.05
☐ RT45 Jack Armstrong	.10	.05
☐ RT46 Bip Roberts	.10	.05
☐ RT47 Jerry Browne	.10	.05
☐ RT48 Marvin Freeman	.10	.05
☐ RT49 Jody Reed	.10	.05
☐ RT50 Alex Cole	.10	.05
☐ RT51 Sid Fernandez	.10	.05
☐ RT52 Pete Smith	.10	.05
☐ RT53 Xavier Hernandez	.10	.05
☐ RT54 Scott Sanderson	.10	.05
☐ RT55 Turner Ward	.10	.05
☐ RT56 Rex Hudler	.10	.05
☐ RT57 Deion Sanders	.40	.18
☐ RT58 Sid Bream	.10	.05
☐ RT59 Tony Pena	.10	.05
☐ RT60 Bret Boone	.10	.05
☐ RT61 Bobby Ayala	.10	.05
☐ RT62 Pedro Martinez	.40	.18
☐ RT63 Howard Johnson	.10	.05
☐ RT64 Mark Portugal	.10	.05
☐ RT65 Roberto Kelly	.10	.05
☐ RT66 Spike Owen	.10	.05
☐ RT67 Jeff Treadway	.10	.05
☐ RT68 Mike Harkey	.10	.05
☐ RT69 Doug Jones	.10	.05
☐ RT70 Steve Farr	.10	.05
☐ RT71 Billy Taylor	.10	.05
☐ RT72 Manny Ramirez	.50	.23
☐ RT73 Bob Hamelin	.10	.05
☐ RT74 Steve Karsay	.10	.05
☐ RT75 Ryan Klesko	.30	.14
☐ RT76 Cliff Floyd	.20	.09
☐ RT77 Jeffrey Hammonds	.20	.09
☐ RT78 Javier Lopez	.30	.14
☐ RT79 Roger Salkeld	.10	.05
☐ RT80 Hector Carrasco	.10	.05
☐ RT81 Gerald Williams	.10	.05
☐ RT82 Raul Mondesi	.30	.14
☐ RT83 Sterling Hitchcock	.20	.09
☐ RT84 Danny Bautista	.10	.05
☐ RT85 Chris Turner	.10	.05
☐ RT86 Shane Reynolds	.10	.05
☐ RT87 Rondell White	.30	.14
☐ RT88 Salomon Torres	.10	.05
☐ RT89 Turk Wendell	.10	.05
☐ RT90 Tony Tarasco	.10	.05
☐ RT91 Shawn Green	.20	.09
☐ RT92 Greg Colbrunn	.10	.05
☐ RT93 Eddie Zambrano	.10	.05
☐ RT94 Rich Becker	.20	.09
☐ RT95 Chris Gomez	.10	.05
☐ RT96 John Patterson	.10	.05
☐ RT97 Derek Parks	.10	.05
☐ RT98 Rich Rowland	.10	.05
☐ RT99 James Mouton	.20	.09
☐ RT100 Tim Hyers	.10	.05
☐ RT101 Jose Valentin	.20	.09
☐ RT102 Carlos Delgado	.30	.14
☐ RT103 Robert Eenhoorn	.10	.05
☐ RT104 John Hudek	.10	.05
☐ RT105 Domingo Cedeno	.10	.05
☐ RT106 Denny Hocking	.10	.05
☐ RT107 Greg Pirkl	.10	.05
☐ RT108 Mark Smith	.10	.05
☐ RT109 Paul Shuey	.10	.05
☐ RT110 Jorge Fabregas	.10	.05
☐ RT111 Rikkert Faneyte	.10	.05

	MINT	NRMT
☐ RT112 Rob Butler	.10	.05
☐ RT113 Darren Oliver	.40	.18
☐ RT114 Troy O'Leary	.10	.05
☐ RT115 Scott Brow	.10	.05
☐ RT116 Tony Eusebio	.10	.05
☐ RT117 Carlos Reyes	.10	.05
☐ RT118 J.R. Phillips	.10	.05
☐ RT119 Alex Diaz	.10	.05
☐ RT120 Charles Johnson	.30	.14
☐ RT121 Nate Minchey	.10	.05
☐ RT122 Scott Sanders	.10	.05
☐ RT123 Daryl Boston	.10	.05
☐ RT124 Joey Hamilton	.20	.09
☐ RT125 Brian Anderson	.30	.14
☐ RT126 Dan Miceli	.10	.05
☐ RT127 Tom Brunansky	.10	.05
☐ RT128 Dave Staton	.10	.05
☐ RT129 Mike Oquist	.10	.05
☐ RT130 John Mabry	.40	.18
☐ RT131 Norberto Martin	.10	.05
☐ RT132 Hector Fajardo	.10	.05
☐ RT133 Mark Hutton	.10	.05
☐ RT134 Fernando Vina	.10	.05
☐ RT135 Lee Tinsley	.10	.05
☐ RT136 Chan Ho Park	1.25	.55
☐ RT137 Paul Spoljaric	.10	.05
☐ RT138 Matias Carrillo	.10	.05
☐ RT139 Mark Kiefer	.10	.05
☐ RT140 Stan Royer	.10	.05
☐ RT141 Bryan Eversgerd	.10	.05
☐ RT142 Brian L.Hunter	.40	.18
☐ RT143 Joe Hall	.10	.05
☐ RT144 Johnny Ruffin	.10	.05
☐ RT145 Alex Gonzalez	.20	.09
☐ RT146 Keith Lockhart	.10	.05
☐ RT147 Tom Marsh	.10	.05
☐ RT148 Tony Longmire	.10	.05
☐ RT149 Keith Mitchell	.10	.05
☐ RT150 Melvin Nieves	.20	.09
☐ RT151 Kelly Stinnett	.10	.05
☐ RT152 Miguel Jimenez	.10	.05
☐ RT153 Jeff Juden	.10	.05
☐ RT154 Matt Walbeck	.10	.05
☐ RT155 Marc Newfield	.20	.09
☐ RT156 Matt Mieske	.10	.05
☐ RT157 Marcus Moore	.10	.05
☐ RT158 Jose Lima SP	1.00	.45
☐ RT159 Mike Kelly	.10	.05
☐ RT160 Jim Edmonds	.40	.18
☐ RT161 Steve Trachsel	.10	.05
☐ RT162 Greg Blosser	.10	.05
☐ RT163 Marc Acre	.10	.05
☐ RT164 AL Checklist	.10	.05
☐ RT165 NL Checklist	.10	.05
☐ HC1 Alex Rodriguez Call-Up Redemption	50.00	22.00

1994 Score Rookie/Traded Gold Rush

Issued one per pack, these cards are a gold foil version of the 165-card Rookie/Traded set. The differences between the basic card and Gold Rush version are the gold foil borders that surround a metallicized player photo. The only difference on the back is a Gold Rush logo.

	MINT	NRMT
COMPLETE SET (165)	50.00	22.00
COMMON CARD (RT1-RT165)	.25	.11

*STARS: 1.5X TO 4X BASIC CARDS...
*YOUNG STARS: 1.25X TO 3X BASIC CARDS

1994 Score Rookie/Traded Changing Places

Randomly inserted in both retail and hobby packs at a rate of one in 36 Rookie/Traded packs, this 10-card standard-size set focuses on ten veteran superstar players who were traded prior to or during the 1994 season. Cards fronts feature a color photo with a slanted design. The backs have a short write-up and a distorted photo.

	MINT	NRMT
COMPLETE SET (10)	30.00	13.50
COMMON CARD (CP1-CP10)	2.50	1.10
☐ CP1 Will Clark	8.00	3.60
☐ CP2 Rafael Palmeiro	8.00	3.60
☐ CP3 Roberto Kelly	2.50	1.10
☐ CP4 Bo Jackson	5.00	2.20
☐ CP5 Otis Nixon	2.50	1.10
☐ CP6 Rickey Henderson	6.00	2.70
☐ CP7 Ellis Burks	5.00	2.20
☐ CP8 Lee Smith	5.00	2.20
☐ CP9 Delino DeShields	2.50	1.10
☐ CP10 Deion Sanders	7.00	3.10

1994 Score Rookie/Traded Super Rookies

Randomly inserted in hobby packs at a rate of one in 36, this 18-card standard-size set focuses on top rookies of 1994. Odds of finding one of these cards is approximately one in 36 hobby packs. Designed much like the Gold Rush, the cards have an all-foil design. The fronts have a player photo and the backs have a photo that serves as background to the Super Rookies logo and text.

	MINT	NRMT
COMPLETE SET (18)	60.00	27.00
COMMON CARD (SU1-SU18)	2.50	1.10
☐ SU1 Carlos Delgado	6.00	2.70
☐ SU2 Manny Ramirez	12.00	5.50
☐ SU3 Ryan Klesko	8.00	3.60
☐ SU4 Raul Mondesi	8.00	3.60
☐ SU5 Bob Hamelin	2.50	1.10
☐ SU6 Steve Karsay	2.50	1.10
☐ SU7 Jeffrey Hammonds	4.00	1.80
☐ SU8 Cliff Floyd	4.00	1.80
☐ SU9 Kurt Abbott	2.50	1.10
☐ SU10 Marc Newfield	4.00	1.80
☐ SU11 Javier Lopez	6.00	2.70
☐ SU12 Rich Becker	2.50	1.10
☐ SU13 Greg Pirkl	2.50	1.10
☐ SU14 Rondell White	5.00	2.20
☐ SU15 James Mouton	2.50	1.10
☐ SU16 Tony Tarasco	2.50	1.10
☐ SU17 Brian Anderson	4.00	1.80
☐ SU18 Jim Edmonds	8.00	3.60

1995 Score Samples

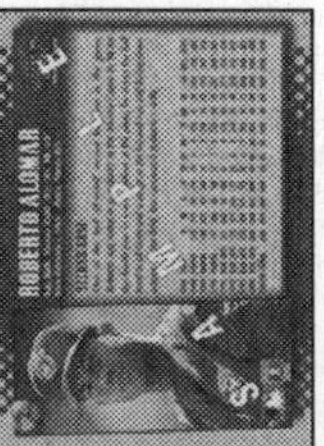

These ten sample cards were issued to herald the release of the 1995 Score baseball series. The standard-size cards feature on their horizontal and vertical fronts color action player shots with irregular dark green and sand brown borders. The player's name, position and the team logo appear in a blue bar under the picture. The word "Sample" is printed diagonally over the photo. The horizontal backs have the same design as the fronts. They carry another small color headshot on the left, with the player's name, short biography, career highlights and statistics on the right. The word "Sample" is also printed diagonally across the backs.

	MINT	NRMT
COMPLETE SET (10)	12.00	5.50
COMMON CARD	.25	.11
☐ 2 Roberto Alomar	1.00	.45
☐ 4 Jose Canseco	.75	.35
☐ 5 Matt Williams	.75	.35
☐ 221 Jeff Bagwell	2.00	.90
☐ 223 Albert Belle	1.50	.70
☐ 224 Chuck Carr	.25	.11
☐ 288 Jorge Fabregas	.25	.11
☐ DP8 McKay Christensen	1.00	.45
☐ HG5 Cal Ripken	6.00	2.70
☐ NNO Title Card	.25	.11

1995 Score

The 1995 Score set consists of 605 standard-size cards issued in hobby, retail and jumbo packs. The horizontal and vertical fronts feature color action player shots with irregular dark green and sand brown borders. The player's name, position and the team logo appear in a blue bar under the photo. The horizontal backs have the same design as the fronts. They carry another small color headshot on the left, with the player's name, short biography, career highlights and statistics on the right. Hobby packs featured a special signed Ryan Klesko (RG1)card. Retail packs also had a Klesko card (SG1) but these were not signed. There are no key Rookie Cards in this set.

	MINT	NRMT
COMPLETE SET (605)	24.00	11.00
COMPLETE SERIES 1 (330)	12.00	5.50
COMPLETE SERIES 2 (275)	12.00	5.50
COMMON CARD (1-605)	.10	.05
☐ 1 Frank Thomas	1.50	.70
☐ 2 Roberto Alomar	.40	.18
☐ 3 Cal Ripken	1.50	.70
☐ 4 Jose Canseco	.30	.14
☐ 5 Matt Williams	.30	.14
☐ 6 Esteban Beltre	.10	.05
☐ 7 Domingo Cedeno	.10	.05
☐ 8 John Valentin	.20	.09
☐ 9 Glenallen Hill	.10	.05
☐ 10 Rafael Belliard	.10	.05
☐ 11 Randy Myers	.10	.05
☐ 12 Mo Vaughn	.50	.23
☐ 13 Hector Carrasco	.10	.05
☐ 14 Chili Davis	.20	.09
☐ 15 Dante Bichette	.30	.14
☐ 16 Darrin Jackson	.10	.05
☐ 17 Mike Piazza	1.25	.55
☐ 18 Junior Felix	.10	.05
☐ 19 Moises Alou	.20	.09
☐ 20 Mark Gubicza	.10	.05
☐ 21 Bret Saberhagen	.10	.05
☐ 22 Lenny Dykstra	.20	.09
☐ 23 Steve Howe	.10	.05
☐ 24 Mark Dewey	.10	.05
☐ 25 Brian Harper	.10	.05
☐ 26 Ozzie Smith	.50	.23
☐ 27 Scott Erickson	.10	.05
☐ 28 Tony Gwynn	1.00	.45
☐ 29 Bob Welch	.10	.05
☐ 30 Barry Bonds	.50	.23
☐ 31 Leo Gomez	.10	.05
☐ 32 Greg Maddux	1.25	.55
☐ 33 Mike Greenwell	.10	.05
☐ 34 Sammy Sosa	.40	.18
☐ 35 Darnell Coles	.10	.05
☐ 36 Tommy Greene	.10	.05
☐ 37 Will Clark	.30	.14
☐ 38 Steve Ontiveros	.10	.05
☐ 39 Stan Javier	.10	.05
☐ 40 Bip Roberts	.10	.05
☐ 41 Paul O'Neill	.20	.09
☐ 42 Bill Haselman	.10	.05
☐ 43 Shane Mack	.10	.05
☐ 44 Orlando Merced	.10	.05
☐ 45 Kevin Seitzer	.10	.05
☐ 46 Trevor Hoffman	.20	.09
☐ 47 Greg Gagne	.10	.05
☐ 48 Jeff Kent	.10	.05
☐ 49 Tony Phillips	.10	.05
☐ 50 Ken Hill	.10	.05

☐ 51 Carlos Baerga	.20	.09
☐ 52 Henry Rodriguez	.10	.05
☐ 53 Scott Sanderson	.10	.05
☐ 54 Jeff Conine	.20	.09
☐ 55 Chris Turner	.10	.05
☐ 56 Ken Caminiti	.40	.18
☐ 57 Harold Baines	.20	.09
☐ 58 Charlie Hayes	.10	.05
☐ 59 Roberto Kelly	.10	.05
☐ 60 John Olerud	.20	.09
☐ 61 Tim Davis	.10	.05
☐ 62 Rich Rowland	.10	.05
☐ 63 Rey Sanchez	.10	.05
☐ 64 Junior Ortiz	.10	.05
☐ 65 Ricky Gutierrez	.10	.05
☐ 66 Rex Hudler	.10	.05
☐ 67 Johnny Ruffin	.10	.05
☐ 68 Jay Buhner	.30	.14
☐ 69 Tom Pagnozzi	.10	.05
☐ 70 Julio Franco	.20	.09
☐ 71 Eric Young	.20	.09
☐ 72 Mike Bordick	.10	.05
☐ 73 Don Slaught	.10	.05
☐ 74 Goose Gossage	.20	.09
☐ 75 Lonnie Smith	.10	.05
☐ 76 Jimmy Key	.20	.09
☐ 77 Dave Hollins	.10	.05
☐ 78 Mickey Tettleton	.10	.05
☐ 79 Luis Gonzalez	.10	.05
☐ 80 Dave Winfield	.30	.14
☐ 81 Ryan Thompson	.10	.05
☐ 82 Felix Jose	.10	.05
☐ 83 Rusty Meacham	.10	.05
☐ 84 Darryl Hamilton	.10	.05
☐ 85 John Wetteland	.20	.09
☐ 86 Tom Brunansky	.10	.05
☐ 87 Mark Lemke	.10	.05
☐ 88 Spike Owen	.10	.05
☐ 89 Shawon Dunston	.10	.05
☐ 90 Wilson Alvarez	.20	.09
☐ 91 Lee Smith	.20	.09
☐ 92 Scott Kamieniecki	.10	.05
☐ 93 Jacob Brumfield	.10	.05
☐ 94 Kirk Gibson	.20	.09
☐ 95 Joe Girardi	.10	.05
☐ 96 Mike Macfarlane	.10	.05
☐ 97 Greg Colbrunn	.10	.05
☐ 98 Ricky Bones	.10	.05
☐ 99 Delino DeShields	.10	.05
☐ 100 Pat Meares	.10	.05
☐ 101 Jeff Fassero	.10	.05
☐ 102 Jim Leyritz	.10	.05
☐ 103 Gary Redus	.10	.05
☐ 104 Terry Steinbach	.20	.09
☐ 105 Kevin McReynolds	.10	.05
☐ 106 Felix Fermin	.10	.05
☐ 107 Danny Jackson	.10	.05
☐ 108 Chris James	.10	.05
☐ 109 Jeff King	.20	.09
☐ 110 Pat Hentgen	.20	.09
☐ 111 Gerald Perry	.10	.05
☐ 112 Tim Raines	.10	.05
☐ 113 Eddie Williams	.10	.05
☐ 114 Jamie Moyer	.10	.05
☐ 115 Bud Black	.10	.05
☐ 116 Chris Gomez	.10	.05
☐ 117 Luis Lopez	.10	.05
☐ 118 Roger Clemens	.75	.35
☐ 119 Javier Lopez	.30	.14
☐ 120 Dave Nilsson	.20	.09
☐ 121 Karl Rhodes	.10	.05
☐ 122 Rick Aguilera	.10	.05
☐ 123 Tony Fernandez	.10	.05
☐ 124 Bernie Williams	.40	.18
☐ 125 James Mouton	.10	.05
☐ 126 Mark Langston	.10	.05
☐ 127 Mike Lansing	.10	.05
☐ 128 Tino Martinez	.40	.18
☐ 129 Joe Orsulak	.10	.05
☐ 130 David Hulse	.10	.05
☐ 131 Pete Incaviglia	.10	.05
☐ 132 Mark Clark	.10	.05
☐ 133 Tony Eusebio	.10	.05
☐ 134 Chuck Finley	.20	.09
☐ 135 Lou Frazier	.10	.05
☐ 136 Craig Grebeck	.10	.05
☐ 137 Kelly Stinnett	.10	.05
☐ 138 Paul Shuey	.10	.05
☐ 139 David Nied	.10	.05
☐ 140 Billy Brewer	.10	.05
☐ 141 Dave Weathers	.10	.05
☐ 142 Scott Leius	.10	.05
☐ 143 Brian Jordan	.20	.09
☐ 144 Melido Perez	.10	.05
☐ 145 Tony Tarasco	.10	.05
☐ 146 Dan Wilson	.20	.09
☐ 147 Rondell White	.30	.14
☐ 148 Mike Henneman	.10	.05
☐ 149 Brian Johnson	.10	.05
☐ 150 Tom Henke	.10	.05
☐ 151 John Patterson	.10	.05
☐ 152 Bobby Witt	.10	.05
☐ 153 Eddie Taubensee	.10	.05
☐ 154 Pat Borders	.10	.05
☐ 155 Ramon Martinez	.20	.09
☐ 156 Mike Kingery	.10	.05
☐ 157 Zane Smith	.10	.05
☐ 158 Benito Santiago	.10	.05
☐ 159 Matias Carrillo	.10	.05
☐ 160 Scott Brosius	.10	.05
☐ 161 Dave Clark	.10	.05
☐ 162 Mark McLemore	.10	.05
☐ 163 Curt Schilling	.20	.09
☐ 164 J.T. Snow	.20	.09
☐ 165 Rod Beck	.10	.05
☐ 166 Scott Fletcher	.10	.05
☐ 167 Bob Tewksbury	.10	.05
☐ 168 Mike LaValliere	.10	.05
☐ 169 Dave Hansen	.10	.05
☐ 170 Pedro Martinez	.40	.18
☐ 171 Kirk Rueter	.10	.05
☐ 172 Jose Lind	.10	.05
☐ 173 Luis Alicea	.10	.05
☐ 174 Mike Moore	.10	.05
☐ 175 Andy Ashby	.10	.05
☐ 176 Jody Reed	.10	.05
☐ 177 Darryl Kile	.20	.09
☐ 178 Carl Willis	.10	.05
☐ 179 Jeromy Burnitz	.20	.09
☐ 180 Mike Gallego	.10	.05
☐ 181 Bill VanLandingham	.10	.05
☐ 182 Sid Fernandez	.10	.05
☐ 183 Kim Batiste	.10	.05
☐ 184 Greg Myers	.10	.05
☐ 185 Steve Avery	.10	.05
☐ 186 Steve Farr	.10	.05
☐ 187 Robb Nen	.10	.05
☐ 188 Dan Pasqua	.10	.05
☐ 189 Bruce Ruffin	.10	.05
☐ 190 Jose Valentin	.20	.09
☐ 191 Willie Banks	.10	.05
☐ 192 Mike Aldrete	.10	.05
☐ 193 Randy Milligan	.10	.05
☐ 194 Steve Karsay	.10	.05
☐ 195 Mike Stanley	.10	.05
☐ 196 Jose Mesa	.10	.05
☐ 197 Tom Browning	.10	.05
☐ 198 John Vander Wal	.10	.05
☐ 199 Kevin Brown	.20	.09
☐ 200 Mike Oquist	.10	.05
☐ 201 Greg Swindell	.10	.05
☐ 202 Eddie Zambrano	.10	.05
☐ 203 Joe Boever	.10	.05
☐ 204 Gary Varsho	.10	.05
☐ 205 Chris Gwynn	.10	.05
☐ 206 David Howard	.10	.05
☐ 207 Jerome Walton	.10	.05
☐ 208 Danny Darwin	.10	.05
☐ 209 Darryl Strawberry	.20	.09
☐ 210 Todd Van Poppel	.10	.05
☐ 211 Scott Livingstone	.10	.05
☐ 212 Dave Fleming	.10	.05
☐ 213 Todd Worrell	.10	.05
☐ 214 Carlos Delgado	.20	.09
☐ 215 Bill Pecota	.10	.05
☐ 216 Jim Lindeman	.10	.05
☐ 217 Rick White	.10	.05
☐ 218 Jose Oquendo	.10	.05
☐ 219 Tony Castillo	.10	.05
☐ 220 Fernando Vina	.10	.05
☐ 221 Jeff Bagwell	.75	.35
☐ 222 Randy Johnson	.40	.18
☐ 223 Albert Belle	.50	.23
☐ 224 Chuck Carr	.10	.05
☐ 225 Mark Leiter	.10	.05
☐ 226 Hal Morris	.10	.05
☐ 227 Robin Ventura	.20	.09
☐ 228 Mike Munoz	.10	.05
☐ 229 Jim Thome	.40	.18
☐ 230 Mario Diaz	.10	.05
☐ 231 John Doherty	.10	.05
☐ 232 Bobby Jones	.20	.09
☐ 233 Raul Mondesi	.30	.14
☐ 234 Ricky Jordan	.10	.05
☐ 235 John Jaha	.10	.05
☐ 236 Carlos Garcia	.10	.05
☐ 237 Kirby Puckett	.75	.35
☐ 238 Orel Hershiser	.20	.09
☐ 239 Don Mattingly	.60	.25
☐ 240 Sid Bream	.10	.05
☐ 241 Brent Gates	.10	.05
☐ 242 Tony Longmire	.10	.05
☐ 243 Robby Thompson	.10	.05
☐ 244 Rick Sutcliffe	.10	.05
☐ 245 Dean Palmer	.20	.09
☐ 246 Marquis Grissom	.20	.09
☐ 247 Paul Molitor	.40	.18
☐ 248 Mark Carreon	.10	.05
☐ 249 Jack Voigt	.10	.05
☐ 250 Greg McMichael UER (photo on front is Mike Stanton)	.10	.05
☐ 251 Damon Berryhill	.10	.05
☐ 252 Brian Dorsett	.10	.05
☐ 253 Jim Edmonds	.40	.18
☐ 254 Barry Larkin	.30	.14
☐ 255 Jack McDowell	.10	.05
☐ 256 Wally Joyner	.20	.09
☐ 257 Eddie Murray	.40	.18
☐ 258 Lenny Webster	.10	.05
☐ 259 Milt Cuyler	.10	.05
☐ 260 Todd Benzinger	.10	.05
☐ 261 Vince Coleman	.10	.05
☐ 262 Todd Stottlemyre	.10	.05
☐ 263 Turner Ward	.10	.05
☐ 264 Ray Lankford	.20	.09
☐ 265 Matt Walbeck	.10	.05
☐ 266 Deion Sanders	.40	.18
☐ 267 Gerald Williams	.10	.05
☐ 268 Jim Gott	.10	.05
☐ 269 Jeff Frye	.10	.05
☐ 270 Jose Rijo	.10	.05
☐ 271 Dave Justice	.40	.18
☐ 272 Ismael Valdes	.20	.09
☐ 273 Ben McDonald	.10	.05
☐ 274 Darren Lewis	.10	.05
☐ 275 Graeme Lloyd	.10	.05
☐ 276 Luis Ortiz	.10	.05
☐ 277 Julian Tavarez	.10	.05
☐ 278 Mark Dalesandro	.10	.05
☐ 279 Brett Merriman	.10	.05
☐ 280 Ricky Bottalico	.20	.09
☐ 281 Robert Eenhoorn	.10	.05
☐ 282 Rikkert Faneyte	.10	.05
☐ 283 Mike Kelly	.10	.05
☐ 284 Mark Smith	.10	.05
☐ 285 Turk Wendell	.10	.05
☐ 286 Greg Blosser	.10	.05
☐ 287 Garey Ingram	.10	.05
☐ 288 Jorge Fabregas	.10	.05
☐ 289 Blaise Ilsley	.10	.05
☐ 290 Joe Hall	.10	.05
☐ 291 Orlando Miller	.10	.05
☐ 292 Jose Lima	.10	.05
☐ 293 Greg O'Halloran	.10	.05
☐ 294 Mark Kiefer	.10	.05
☐ 295 Jose Oliva	.10	.05
☐ 296 Rich Becker	.10	.05
☐ 297 Brian L. Hunter	.30	.14
☐ 298 Dave Silvestri	.10	.05
☐ 299 Armando Benitez	.10	.05
☐ 300 Darren Dreifort	.10	.05
☐ 301 John Mabry	.30	.14
☐ 302 Greg Pirkl	.10	.05
☐ 303 J.R. Phillips	.10	.05
☐ 304 Shawn Green	.20	.09
☐ 305 Roberto Petagine	.10	.05
☐ 306 Keith Lockhart	.10	.05
☐ 307 Jonathan Hurst	.10	.05
☐ 308 Paul Spoljaric	.10	.05
☐ 309 Mike Lieberthal	.10	.05
☐ 310 Garret Anderson	.30	.14
☐ 311 John Johnstone	.10	.05
☐ 312 Alex Rodriguez	1.50	.70
☐ 313 Kent Mercker HL	.10	.05
☐ 314 John Valentin HL	.10	.05
☐ 315 Kenny Rogers HL	.10	.05
☐ 316 Fred McGriff HL	.30	.14
☐ 317 Team Checklists	.10	.05
☐ 318 Team Checklists	.10	.05
☐ 319 Team Checklists	.10	.05
☐ 320 Team Checklists	.10	.05
☐ 321 Team Checklists	.10	.05
☐ 322 Team Checklists	.10	.05
☐ 323 Team Checklists	.10	.05
☐ 324 Team Checklists	.10	.05
☐ 325 Team Checklists	.10	.05
☐ 326 Team Checklists	.10	.05
☐ 327 Team Checklists	.10	.05
☐ 328 Team Checklists	.10	.05
☐ 329 Team Checklists	.10	.05
☐ 330 Team Checklists	.10	.05
☐ 331 Pedro Munoz	.10	.05
☐ 332 Ryan Klesko	.30	.14
☐ 333 Andre Dawson	.30	.14
☐ 334 Derrick May	.10	.05
☐ 335 Aaron Sele	.10	.05
☐ 336 Kevin Mitchell	.10	.05
☐ 337 Steve Trachsel	.10	.05
☐ 338 Andres Galarraga	.30	.14
☐ 339 Terry Pendleton	.20	.09
☐ 340 Gary Sheffield	.40	.18

☐ 341 Travis Fryman .20 .09
☐ 342 Bo Jackson .20 .09
☐ 343 Gary Gaetti .20 .09
☐ 344 Brett Butler .20 .09
☐ 345 B.J. Surhoff .20 .09
☐ 346 Larry Walker .40 .18
☐ 347 Kevin Tapani .10 .05
☐ 348 Rick Wilkins .10 .05
☐ 349 Wade Boggs .40 .18
☐ 350 Mariano Duncan .10 .05
☐ 351 Ruben Sierra .10 .05
☐ 352 Andy Van Slyke .20 .09
☐ 353 Reggie Jefferson .20 .09
☐ 354 Gregg Jefferies .20 .09
☐ 355 Tim Naehring .10 .05
☐ 356 John Roper .10 .05
☐ 357 Joe Carter .30 .14
☐ 358 Kurt Abbott .10 .05
☐ 359 Lenny Harris .10 .05
☐ 360 Lance Johnson .20 .09
☐ 361 Brian Anderson .10 .05
☐ 362 Jim Eisenreich .20 .09
☐ 363 Jerry Browne .10 .05
☐ 364 Mark Grace .30 .14
☐ 365 Devon White .10 .05
☐ 366 Reggie Sanders .10 .05
☐ 367 Ivan Rodriguez .50 .23
☐ 368 Kirt Manwaring .10 .05
☐ 369 Pat Kelly .10 .05
☐ 370 Ellis Burks .20 .09
☐ 371 Charles Nagy .20 .09
☐ 372 Kevin Bass .10 .05
☐ 373 Lou Whitaker .20 .09
☐ 374 Rene Arocha .10 .05
☐ 375 Derek Parks .10 .05
☐ 376 Mark Whiten .10 .05
☐ 377 Mark McGwire .75 .35
☐ 378 Doug Drabek .10 .05
☐ 379 Greg Vaughn .10 .05
☐ 380 Al Martin .20 .09
☐ 381 Ron Darling .10 .05
☐ 382 Tim Wallach .10 .05
☐ 383 Alan Trammell .30 .14
☐ 384 Randy Velarde .10 .05
☐ 385 Chris Sabo .10 .05
☐ 386 Wil Cordero .10 .05
☐ 387 Darrin Fletcher .10 .05
☐ 388 David Segui .10 .05
☐ 389 Steve Buechele .10 .05
☐ 390 Dave Gallagher .10 .05
☐ 391 Thomas Howard .10 .05
☐ 392 Chad Curtis .10 .05
☐ 393 Cal Eldred .10 .05
☐ 394 Jason Bere .10 .05
☐ 395 Bret Barberie .10 .05
☐ 396 Paul Sorrento .10 .05
☐ 397 Steve Finley .20 .09
☐ 398 Cecil Fielder .20 .09
☐ 399 Eric Karros .20 .09
☐ 400 Jeff Montgomery .20 .09
☐ 401 Cliff Floyd .20 .09
☐ 402 Matt Mieske .20 .09
☐ 403 Brian Hunter .10 .05
☐ 404 Alex Cole .10 .05
☐ 405 Kevin Stocker .10 .05
☐ 406 Eric Davis .20 .09
☐ 407 Marvin Freeman .10 .05
☐ 408 Dennis Eckersley .30 .14
☐ 409 Todd Zeile .10 .05
☐ 410 Keith Mitchell .10 .05
☐ 411 Andy Benes .10 .05
☐ 412 Juan Bell .10 .05
☐ 413 Royce Clayton .10 .05
☐ 414 Ed Sprague .10 .05
☐ 415 Mike Mussina .40 .18
☐ 416 Todd Hundley .20 .09
☐ 417 Pat Listach .10 .05
☐ 418 Joe Oliver .10 .05
☐ 419 Rafael Palmeiro .30 .14
☐ 420 Tim Salmon .40 .18
☐ 421 Brady Anderson .30 .14
☐ 422 Kenny Lofton .50 .23
☐ 423 Craig Biggio .30 .14
☐ 424 Bobby Bonilla .20 .09
☐ 425 Kenny Rogers .10 .05
☐ 426 Derek Bell .20 .09
☐ 427 Scott Cooper .10 .05
☐ 428 Ozzie Guillen .10 .05
☐ 429 Omar Vizquel .20 .09
☐ 430 Phil Plantier .10 .05
☐ 431 Chuck Knoblauch .30 .14
☐ 432 Darren Daulton .20 .09
☐ 433 Bob Hamelin .10 .05
☐ 434 Tom Glavine .30 .14
☐ 435 Walt Weiss .10 .05
☐ 436 Jose Vizcaino .10 .05
☐ 437 Ken Griffey Jr. 2.00 .90
☐ 438 Jay Bell .20 .09
☐ 439 Juan Gonzalez 1.00 .45
☐ 440 Jeff Blauser .10 .05
☐ 441 Rickey Henderson .30 .14
☐ 442 Bobby Ayala .10 .05
☐ 443 David Cone .20 .09
☐ 444 Pedro J. Martinez .40 .18
☐ 445 Manny Ramirez .40 .18
☐ 446 Mark Portugal .10 .05
☐ 447 Damion Easley .10 .05
☐ 448 Gary DiSarcina .10 .05
☐ 449 Roberto Hernandez .10 .05
☐ 450 Jeffrey Hammonds .20 .09
☐ 451 Jeff Treadway .10 .05
☐ 452 Jim Abbott .10 .05
☐ 453 Carlos Rodriguez .10 .05
☐ 454 Joey Cora .20 .09
☐ 455 Bret Boone .10 .05
☐ 456 Danny Tartabull .10 .05
☐ 457 John Franco .20 .09
☐ 458 Roger Salkeld .10 .05
☐ 459 Fred McGriff .30 .14
☐ 460 Pedro Astacio .10 .05
☐ 461 Jon Lieber .10 .05
☐ 462 Luis Polonia .10 .05
☐ 463 Geronimo Pena .10 .05
☐ 464 Tom Gordon .10 .05
☐ 465 Brad Ausmus .10 .05
☐ 466 Willie McGee .10 .05
☐ 467 Doug Jones .10 .05
☐ 468 John Smoltz .30 .14
☐ 469 Troy Neel .10 .05
☐ 470 Luis Sojo .10 .05
☐ 471 John Smiley .10 .05
☐ 472 Rafael Bournigal .10 .05
☐ 473 Bill Taylor .10 .05
☐ 474 Juan Guzman .10 .05
☐ 475 Dave Magadan .10 .05
☐ 476 Mike Devereaux .10 .05
☐ 477 Andujar Cedeno .10 .05
☐ 478 Edgar Martinez .30 .14
☐ 479 Milt Thompson .10 .05
☐ 480 Allen Watson .10 .05
☐ 481 Ron Karkovice .10 .05
☐ 482 Joey Hamilton .20 .09
☐ 483 Vinny Castilla .30 .14
☐ 484 Tim Belcher .10 .05
☐ 485 Bernard Gilkey .20 .09
☐ 486 Scott Servais .10 .05
☐ 487 Cory Snyder .10 .05
☐ 488 Mel Rojas .10 .05
☐ 489 Carlos Reyes .10 .05
☐ 490 Chip Hale .10 .05
☐ 491 Bill Swift .10 .05
☐ 492 Pat Rapp .10 .05
☐ 493 Brian McRae .10 .05
☐ 494 Mickey Morandini .10 .05
☐ 495 Tony Pena .10 .05
☐ 496 Danny Bautista .10 .05
☐ 497 Armando Reynoso .10 .05
☐ 498 Ken Ryan .10 .05
☐ 499 Billy Ripken .10 .05
☐ 500 Pat Mahomes .10 .05
☐ 501 Mark Acre .10 .05
☐ 502 Geronimo Berroa .10 .05
☐ 503 Norberto Martin .10 .05
☐ 504 Chad Kreuter .10 .05
☐ 505 Howard Johnson .10 .05
☐ 506 Eric Anthony .10 .05
☐ 507 Mark Wohlers .20 .09
☐ 508 Scott Sanders .10 .05
☐ 509 Pete Harnisch .10 .05
☐ 510 Wes Chamberlain .10 .05
☐ 511 Tom Candiotti .10 .05
☐ 512 Albie Lopez .10 .05
☐ 513 Denny Neagle .20 .09
☐ 514 Sean Berry .10 .05
☐ 515 Billy Hatcher .10 .05
☐ 516 Todd Jones .10 .05
☐ 517 Wayne Kirby .10 .05
☐ 518 Butch Henry .10 .05
☐ 519 Sandy Alomar Jr. .10 .05
☐ 520 Kevin Appier .20 .09
☐ 521 Roberto Mejia .10 .05
☐ 522 Steve Cooke .10 .05
☐ 523 Terry Shumpert .10 .05
☐ 524 Mike Jackson .10 .05
☐ 525 Kent Mercker .10 .05
☐ 526 David Wells .10 .05
☐ 527 Juan Samuel .10 .05
☐ 528 Salomon Torres .10 .05
☐ 529 Duane Ward .10 .05
☐ 530 Rob Dibble .10 .05
☐ 531 Mike Blowers .10 .05
☐ 532 Mark Eichhorn .10 .05
☐ 533 Alex Diaz .10 .05
☐ 534 Dan Miceli .10 .05
☐ 535 Jeff Branson .10 .05
☐ 536 Dave Stevens .10 .05
☐ 537 Charlie O'Brien .10 .05
☐ 538 Shane Reynolds .20 .09
☐ 539 Rich Amaral .10 .05
☐ 540 Rusty Greer .40 .18
☐ 541 Alex Arias .10 .05
☐ 542 Eric Plunk .10 .05
☐ 543 John Hudek .10 .05
☐ 544 Kirk McCaskill .10 .05
☐ 545 Jeff Reboulet .10 .05
☐ 546 Sterling Hitchcock .20 .09
☐ 547 Warren Newson .10 .05
☐ 548 Bryan Harvey .10 .05
☐ 549 Mike Huff .10 .05
☐ 550 Lance Parrish .10 .05
☐ 551 Ken Griffey Jr. HIT 1.00 .45
☐ 552 Matt Williams HIT .30 .14
☐ 553 Roberto Alomar HIT UER .40 .18
(Card says he's a NL All-Star
He plays in the AL)
☐ 554 Jeff Bagwell HIT .40 .18
☐ 555 Dave Justice HIT .40 .18
☐ 556 Cal Ripken Jr. HIT .75 .35
☐ 557 Albert Belle HIT .40 .18
☐ 558 Mike Piazza HIT .60 .25
☐ 559 Kirby Puckett HIT .40 .18
☐ 560 Wade Boggs HIT .40 .18
☐ 561 Tony Gwynn HIT UER .40 .18
card has him winning AL batting titles
he's played whole career in the NL
☐ 562 Barry Bonds HIT .40 .18
☐ 563 Mo Vaughn HIT .40 .18
☐ 564 Don Mattingly HIT .40 .18
☐ 565 Carlos Baerga HIT .10 .05
☐ 566 Paul Molitor HIT .40 .18
☐ 567 Raul Mondesi HIT .30 .14
☐ 568 Manny Ramirez HIT .40 .18
☐ 569 Alex Rodriguez HIT 1.25 .55
☐ 570 Will Clark HIT .30 .14
☐ 571 Frank Thomas HIT 1.00 .45
☐ 572 Moises Alou HIT .20 .09
☐ 573 Jeff Conine HIT .20 .09
☐ 574 Joe Ausanio .10 .05
☐ 575 Charles Johnson .30 .14
☐ 576 Ernie Young .10 .05
☐ 577 Jeff Granger .10 .05
☐ 578 Robert Perez .10 .05
☐ 579 Melvin Nieves .10 .05
☐ 580 Gar Finnvold .10 .05
☐ 581 Duane Singleton .10 .05
☐ 582 Chan Ho Park .40 .18
☐ 583 Fausto Cruz .10 .05
☐ 584 Dave Staton .10 .05
☐ 585 Denny Hocking .10 .05
☐ 586 Nate Minchey .10 .05
☐ 587 Marc Newfield .20 .09
☐ 588 Jayhawk Owens UER .10 .05
Front Photo is Jim Tatum
☐ 589 Darren Bragg .20 .09
☐ 590 Kevin King .10 .05
☐ 591 Kurt Miller .10 .05
☐ 592 Aaron Small .10 .05
☐ 593 Troy O'Leary .10 .05
☐ 594 Phil Stidham .10 .05
☐ 595 Steve Dunn .10 .05
☐ 596 Cory Bailey .10 .05
☐ 597 Alex Gonzalez .20 .09
☐ 598 Jim Bowie .10 .05
☐ 599 Jeff Cirillo .20 .09
☐ 600 Mark Hutton .10 .05
☐ 601 Russ Davis .10 .05
☐ 602 Checklist .10 .05
☐ 603 Checklist .10 .05
☐ 604 Checklist .10 .05
☐ 605 Checklist .10 .05
☐ RG1 R.Klesko Rook.Greatness 4.00 1.80
☐ SG1 Ryan Klesko AU6100 20.00 9.00
☐ NNO Trade Hall of Gold 1.00 .45

1995 Score Gold Rush

Parallel to the basic Score issue, these cards were inserted one per foil pack and two per jumbo pack. The fronts were printed in gold foil and the backs contain the Gold Rush logo. As part of the Gold Rush program, one Platinum Team Redemption card was randomly inserted in Score packs at a rate of one in 36. This redemption card and up to four Gold Rush team sets (and $2) could be redeemed for platinum versions of the team set(s). The Gold Rush sets that were sent in would be returned with a stamp indicating they were already used for redemption purposes. The Platinum Upgrade offer was good through 7/13/95 for series 1, 10/1/95 for series 2.

	MINT	NRMT
COMPLETE SET (605)	120.00	55.00
COMPLETE SERIES 1 (330)	60.00	27.00
COMPLETE SERIES 2 (275)	60.00	27.00
COMMON CARD (1-605)	.15	.07
*STARS: 3X TO 6X BASIC CARDS		
*YOUNG STARS: 2.5X TO 5X BASIC CARDS		

1995 Score Platinum Team Sets

After completing a Score Gold Rush team set in either series, a collector could mail in those cards along with a platinum redemption card. In return, the collector would receive a complete Platinum Team Set. The cards are similar to the gold cards except they have platinum borders and come in a small card case. The top card is the certificate saying this is a platinum team set. Only 4,950 of each platinum team set was produced.

	MINT	NRMT
COMPLETE SET (587)	300.00	135.00
COMPLETE SERIES 1 (316)	200.00	90.00
COMPLETE SERIES 2 (271)	100.00	45.00
COMMON CARD	.25	.11
*STARS: 5X TO 10X BASIC CARDS		
*YOUNG STARS: 4X TO 8X BASIC CARDS		

1995 Score You Trade Em

This skip-numbered 11-card set was available only by redeeming the randomly inserted Score You Trade Em redemption card. The set features a selection of veteran players that were traded to new teams at the beginning of the 1995 season. The numbering and card design parallel the corresponding cards within the regular issue 1995 Score set, but these Trade cards feature the players in their new uniforms.

	MINT	NRMT
COMPLETE SET (11)	1.50	.70
COMMON CARD	.10	.05
☐ 333T Andre Dawson UER position listed as DH	.50	.23
☐ 339T Terry Pendleton	.10	.05
☐ 344T Brett Butler	.25	.11
☐ 346T Larry Walker	.75	.35
☐ 352T Andy Van Slyke	.10	.05
☐ 392T Chad Curtis	.10	.05
☐ 427T Scott Cooper	.10	.05
☐ 443T David Cone	.25	.11
☐ 452T Jim Abbott	.25	.11
☐ 493T Brian McRae	.10	.05
☐ 530T Rob Dibble	.10	.05
☐ NNO Expired Trade Card	.25	.11

1995 Score Airmail

This 18-card set was randomly inserted in series two jumbo packs at a rate of one in 24. The fronts have a color photo of the player in a home run swing with the sky in the background. Broken red and blue inner borders frame the player. A gold stamp with the words "Air Mail" is prominent in upper left. The backs have a color photo with player information including how many home runs per at-bats he averaged. A sunset serves as background.

	MINT	NRMT
COMPLETE SET (18)	50.00	22.00
COMMON CARD (1-18)	2.00	.90
☐ AM1 Bob Hamelin	2.00	.90
☐ AM2 John Mabry	4.00	1.80
☐ AM3 Marc Newfield	3.00	1.35
☐ AM4 Jose Oliva	2.00	.90
☐ AM5 Charles Johnson	4.00	1.80
☐ AM6 Russ Davis	2.00	.90
☐ AM7 Ernie Young	2.00	.90
☐ AM8 Billy Ashley	2.00	.90
☐ AM9 Ryan Klesko	4.00	1.80
☐ AM10 J.R. Phillips	2.00	.90
☐ AM11 Cliff Floyd	3.00	1.35
☐ AM12 Carlos Delgado	4.00	1.80
☐ AM13 Melvin Nieves	3.00	1.35
☐ AM14 Raul Mondesi	4.00	1.80
☐ AM15 Manny Ramirez	6.00	2.70
☐ AM16 Mike Kelly	2.00	.90
☐ AM17 Alex Rodriguez	30.00	13.50
☐ AM18 Rusty Greer	6.00	2.70

1995 Score Contest Redemption

These cards were mailed to collectors who correctly identified intentional errors in two Pinnacle print ads depicting baseball scenes. The Alex Rodriguez card was the prize for the first ad, the Ivan Rodriguez card for the second ad.

	MINT	NRMT
COMPLETE SET (2)	10.00	4.50
COMMON CARD (AD1-AD2)	4.00	1.80
☐ AD1 Alex Rodriguez	6.00	2.70
☐ AD2 Ivan Rodriguez	4.00	1.80

1995 Score Double Gold Champs

This 12-card set was randomly inserted in second series hobby packs at a rate of one in 36. Horizontally-designed fronts have a color action photo with the words "Double Gold Champs" in gold-foil at the bottom above the player's name. The backs have a color photo and a list of the player's accomplishments.

	MINT	NRMT
COMPLETE SET (12)	100.00	45.00
COMMON CARD (1-12)	2.50	1.10
☐ GC1 Frank Thomas	15.00	6.75
☐ GC2 Ken Griffey Jr.	20.00	9.00
☐ GC3 Barry Bonds	5.00	2.20
☐ GC4 Tony Gwynn	10.00	4.50
☐ GC5 Don Mattingly	8.00	3.60
☐ GC6 Greg Maddux	12.00	5.50
☐ GC7 Roger Clemens	6.00	2.70
☐ GC8 Kenny Lofton	5.00	2.20
☐ GC9 Jeff Bagwell	8.00	3.60
☐ GC10 Matt Williams	2.50	1.10
☐ GC11 Kirby Puckett	8.00	3.60
☐ GC12 Cal Ripken	15.00	6.75

1995 Score Draft Picks

Randomly inserted in first series hobby packs at a rate of one in 36, this 18-card set takes a look at top picks selected in June of 1994. Horizontal fronts have two player photos on a white background. Vertical backs have a player photo and 1994 season's highlights. The cards are numbered with a DP prefix.

	MINT	NRMT
COMPLETE SET (18)	50.00	22.00
COMMON CARD (DP1-DP18)	1.00	.45
☐ DP1 McKay Christensen	1.00	.45
☐ DP2 Brett Wagner	1.00	.45
☐ DP3 Paul Wilson	1.50	.70
☐ DP4 C.J. Nitkowski	1.00	.45
☐ DP5 Josh Booty	2.00	.90
☐ DP6 Antone Williamson	1.50	.70
☐ DP7 Paul Konerko	15.00	6.75
☐ DP8 Scott Elarton	2.50	1.10
☐ DP9 Jacob Shumate	1.00	.45
☐ DP10 Terrance Long	1.50	.70
☐ DP11 Mark Johnson	1.00	.45
☐ DP12 Ben Grieve	15.00	6.75
☐ DP13 Doug Million	1.00	.45
☐ DP14 Jayson Peterson	1.00	.45
☐ DP15 Dustin Hermanson	1.50	.70
☐ DP16 Matt Smith	1.00	.45
☐ DP17 Kevin Witt	4.00	1.80
☐ DP18 Brian Buchanan	1.00	.45

1995 Score Dream Team

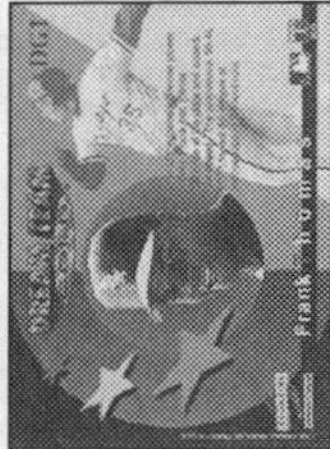

Randomly inserted in first series hobby and retail packs at a rate of one in 72 packs, this 12-card hologram set showcases top performers from the 1994 season. The holographic fronts have two player images. The horizontal backs are not holographic. They are multi-colored with a small player close-up and a brief write-up. The cards are numbered with a DG prefix.

	MINT	NRMT
COMPLETE SET (12)	150.00	70.00
COMMON CARD (DG1-DG12)	2.50	1.10
☐ DG1 Frank Thomas	30.00	13.50
☐ DG2 Roberto Alomar	8.00	3.60
☐ DG3 Cal Ripken	30.00	13.50
☐ DG4 Matt Williams	5.00	2.20
☐ DG5 Mike Piazza	25.00	11.00
☐ DG6 Albert Belle	10.00	4.50
☐ DG7 Ken Griffey Jr.	40.00	18.00
☐ DG8 Tony Gwynn	20.00	9.00
☐ DG9 Paul Molitor	8.00	3.60
☐ DG10 Jimmy Key	3.00	1.35

☐ DG11 Greg Maddux	25.00	11.00
☐ DG12 Lee Smith	2.50	1.10

1995 Score Hall of Gold

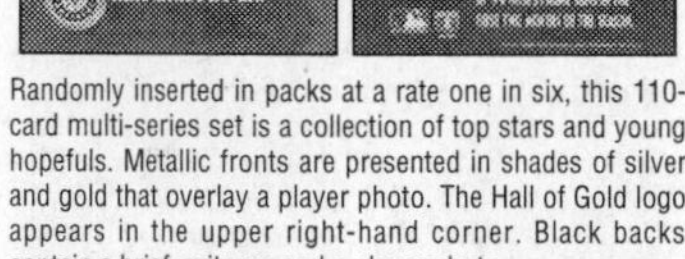

Randomly inserted in packs at a rate one in six, this 110-card multi-series set is a collection of top stars and young hopefuls. Metallic fronts are presented in shades of silver and gold that overlay a player photo. The Hall of Gold logo appears in the upper right-hand corner. Black backs contain a brief write-up and a player photo.

	MINT	NRMT
COMPLETE SET (110)	80.00	36.00
COMPLETE SERIES 1 (55)	50.00	22.00
COMPLETE SERIES 2 (55)	30.00	13.50
COMMON CARD (HG1-HG110)	.50	.23
☐ HG1 Ken Griffey Jr.	12.00	5.50
☐ HG2 Matt Williams	1.50	.70
☐ HG3 Roberto Alomar	2.50	1.10
☐ HG4 Jeff Bagwell	5.00	2.20
☐ HG5 Dave Justice	2.50	1.10
☐ HG6 Cal Ripken	10.00	4.50
☐ HG7 Randy Johnson	2.50	1.10
☐ HG8 Barry Larkin	1.50	.70
☐ HG9 Albert Belle	3.00	1.35
☐ HG10 Mike Piazza	8.00	3.60
☐ HG11 Kirby Puckett	5.00	2.20
☐ HG12 Moises Alou	1.00	.45
☐ HG13 Jose Canseco	1.50	.70
☐ HG14 Tony Gwynn	5.00	2.20
☐ HG15 Roger Clemens	4.00	1.80
☐ HG16 Barry Bonds	3.00	1.35
☐ HG17 Mo Vaughn	3.00	1.35
☐ HG18 Greg Maddux	8.00	3.60
☐ HG19 Dante Bichette	1.50	.70
☐ HG20 Will Clark	1.50	.70
☐ HG21 Lenny Dykstra	1.00	.45
☐ HG22 Don Mattingly	6.00	2.70
☐ HG23 Carlos Baerga	.50	.23
☐ HG24 Ozzie Smith	3.00	1.35
☐ HG25 Paul Molitor	2.50	1.10
☐ HG26 Paul O'Neill	1.00	.45
☐ HG27 Deion Sanders	2.50	1.10
☐ HG28 Jeff Conine	1.00	.45
☐ HG29 John Olerud	1.00	.45
☐ HG30 Jose Rijo	.50	.23
☐ HG31 Sammy Sosa	2.50	1.10
☐ HG32 Robin Ventura	1.00	.45
☐ HG33 Raul Mondesi	1.50	.70
☐ HG34 Eddie Murray	2.50	1.10
☐ HG35 Marquis Grissom	1.00	.45
☐ HG36 Darryl Strawberry	1.00	.45
☐ HG37 Dave Nilsson	.50	.23
☐ HG38 Manny Ramirez	2.50	1.10
☐ HG39 Delino DeShields	.50	.23
☐ HG40 Lee Smith	1.00	.45
☐ HG41 Alex Rodriguez	10.00	4.50
☐ HG42 Julio Franco	.50	.23
☐ HG43 Bret Saberhagen	.50	.23
☐ HG44 Ken Hill	.50	.23
☐ HG45 Roberto Kelly	.50	.23
☐ HG46 Hal Morris	.50	.23
☐ HG47 Jimmy Key	1.00	.45
☐ HG48 Terry Steinbach	.50	.23
☐ HG49 Mickey Tettleton	.50	.23
☐ HG50 Tony Phillips	.50	.23
☐ HG51 Carlos Garcia	.50	.23
☐ HG52 Jim Edmonds	2.50	1.10
☐ HG53 Rod Beck	.50	.23
☐ HG54 Shane Mack	.50	.23
☐ HG55 Ken Caminiti	2.50	1.10
☐ HG56 Frank Thomas	10.00	4.50
☐ HG57 Kenny Lofton	3.00	1.35
☐ HG58 Juan Gonzalez	6.00	2.70
☐ HG59 Jason Bere	.50	.23
☐ HG60 Joe Carter	1.50	.70
☐ HG61 Gary Sheffield	2.50	1.10
☐ HG62 Andres Galarraga	1.50	.70
☐ HG63 Ellis Burks	1.00	.45
☐ HG64 Bobby Bonilla	1.00	.45
☐ HG65 Tom Glavine	1.50	.70
☐ HG66 John Smoltz	1.50	.70
☐ HG67 Fred McGriff	1.50	.70
☐ HG68 Craig Biggio	1.50	.70
☐ HG69 Reggie Sanders	.50	.23
☐ HG70 Kevin Mitchell	.50	.23
☐ HG71 Larry Walker	2.50	1.10
☐ HG72 Carlos Delgado	1.00	.45
☐ HG73 Alex Gonzalez	.50	.23
☐ HG74 Ivan Rodriguez	3.00	1.35
☐ HG75 Ryan Klesko	1.50	.70
☐ HG76 John Kruk	1.00	.45
☐ HG77 Brian McRae	.50	.23
☐ HG78 Tim Salmon	2.50	1.10
☐ HG79 Travis Fryman	1.00	.45
☐ HG80 Chuck Knoblauch	2.50	1.10
☐ HG81 Jay Bell	.50	.23
☐ HG82 Cecil Fielder	1.00	.45
☐ HG83 Cliff Floyd	.50	.23
☐ HG84 Ruben Sierra	.50	.23
☐ HG85 Mike Mussina	1.50	.70
☐ HG86 Mark Grace	1.50	.70
☐ HG87 Dennis Eckersley	1.50	.70
☐ HG88 Dennis Martinez	1.00	.45
☐ HG89 Rafael Palmeiro	1.50	.70
☐ HG90 Ben McDonald	.50	.23
☐ HG91 Dave Hollins	.50	.23
☐ HG92 Steve Avery	.50	.23
☐ HG93 David Cone	1.00	.45
☐ HG94 Darren Daulton	1.00	.45
☐ HG95 Bret Boone	.50	.23
☐ HG96 Wade Boggs	2.50	1.10
☐ HG97 Doug Drabek	.50	.23
☐ HG98 Andy Benes	.50	.23
☐ HG99 Jim Thome	2.50	1.10
☐ HG100 Chili Davis	.50	.23
☐ HG101 Jeffrey Hammonds	.50	.23
☐ HG102 Rickey Henderson	1.50	.70
☐ HG103 Brett Butler	1.00	.45
☐ HG104 Tim Wallach	.50	.23
☐ HG105 Wil Cordero	.50	.23
☐ HG106 Mark Whiten	.50	.23
☐ HG107 Bob Hamelin	.50	.23
☐ HG108 Rondell White	1.00	.45
☐ HG109 Devon White	.50	.23
☐ HG110 Tony Tarasco	.50	.23

1995 Score Hall of Gold You Trade Em

This skip-numbered five-card set was available only by redeeming the randomly inserted Hall of Gold Trade card inserted in second series packs of 1995 Score. The set features a selection of veterans that joined new teams prior to the 1995 season. The design and numbering of the cards parallel the regular Hall of Gold inserts.

	MINT	NRMT
COMPLETE SET (5)	4.00	1.80
COMMON CARD	.50	.23
☐ HG71T Larry Walker	2.50	1.10
☐ HG76T John Kruk	.75	.35
☐ HG77T Brian McRae	.50	.23
☐ HG93T David Cone	1.00	.45
☐ HG110T Tony Tarasco	.50	.23
☐ NNO Exp. Hall of Gold Trade Card..	1.00	.45

1995 Score Rookie Dream Team

This 12-card set was randomly inserted in second series retail and hobby packs at a rate of one in 12. The fronts contain a color photo with a metallic background. The "Rookie Dream Team" title occupy two of the borders. The playerís name is at the bottom in gold-foil. The backs are horizontally designed, have a head shot and player information with the sky serving as a background. The cards are numbered with a RDT prefix.

	MINT	NRMT
COMPLETE SET (12)	60.00	27.00
COMMON CARD (1-12)	2.50	1.10
☐ RDT1 J.R. Phillips	2.50	1.10
☐ RDT2 Alex Gonzalez	2.50	1.10
☐ RDT3 Alex Rodriguez	40.00	18.00
☐ RDT4 Jose Oliva	2.50	1.10
☐ RDT5 Charles Johnson	5.00	2.20
☐ RDT6 Shawn Green	3.50	1.55
☐ RDT7 Brian Hunter	5.00	2.20
☐ RDT8 Garret Anderson	5.00	2.20
☐ RDT9 Julian Tavarez	2.50	1.10
☐ RDT10 Jose Lima	2.50	1.10
☐ RDT11 Armando Benitez	2.50	1.10
☐ RDT12 Ricky Bottalico	3.50	1.55

1995 Score Rules

Randomly inserted in first series jumbo packs, this 30-card standard-size set features top big league players. Card fronts offer a player photo to the left. At right, the player's name is spelled vertically within a green vapor trail left by a baseball that is at the top. A horizontally designed back features three images of the player and a brief write-up. The cards are numbered with an "SR" prefix.

	MINT	NRMT
COMPLETE SET (30)	120.00	55.00
COMMON CARD (SR1-SR30)	1.50	.70
☐ SR1 Ken Griffey Jr.	20.00	9.00
☐ SR2 Frank Thomas	15.00	6.75
☐ SR3 Mike Piazza	12.00	5.50
☐ SR4 Jeff Bagwell	8.00	3.60
☐ SR5 Alex Rodriguez	15.00	6.75
☐ SR6 Albert Belle	5.00	2.20
☐ SR7 Matt Williams	3.00	1.35
☐ SR8 Roberto Alomar	4.00	1.80
☐ SR9 Barry Bonds	5.00	2.20
☐ SR10 Raul Mondesi	3.00	1.35
☐ SR11 Jose Canseco	3.00	1.35
☐ SR12 Kirby Puckett	8.00	3.60
☐ SR13 Fred McGriff	3.00	1.35
☐ SR14 Kenny Lofton	5.00	2.20
☐ SR15 Greg Maddux	12.00	5.50
☐ SR16 Juan Gonzalez	10.00	4.50
☐ SR17 Cliff Floyd	1.50	.70
☐ SR18 Cal Ripken Jr.	15.00	6.75
☐ SR19 Will Clark	3.00	1.35
☐ SR20 Tim Salmon	4.00	1.80
☐ SR21 Paul O'Neill	2.00	.90
☐ SR22 Jason Bere	1.50	.70
☐ SR23 Tony Gwynn	8.00	3.60
☐ SR24 Manny Ramirez	4.00	1.80
☐ SR25 Don Mattingly	8.00	3.60
☐ SR26 Dave Justice	4.00	1.80
☐ SR27 Javier Lopez	3.00	1.35
☐ SR28 Ryan Klesko	3.00	1.35
☐ SR29 Carlos Delgado	2.00	.90
☐ SR30 Mike Mussina	4.00	1.80

1995 Score Rules Jumbos

These 30 cards, measuring 7 1/2" by 10 1/2" were issued one per special Score collector kit. The cards are parallels to the regular Score Rules jumbos and were numbered out of 3,000.

	MINT	NRMT
COMPLETE SET (30)	175.00	80.00
COMMON CARD (SR1-SR30)	2.00	.90
*JUMBOS: 1.25X BASIC CARDS		

1996 Score Samples

This 8-card set was issued to preview the 1996 Score series. Inside white borders, the fronts feature color action photos with the upper left corner torn off to allow space for the "'96 Score" logo. The backs carry a second color closeup photo, biography, statistics, and player profile. The final two cards listed belong to the Rookie subset and have a different front design. All cards have "SAMPLE" stamped diagonally across their front and back.

	MINT	NRMT
COMPLETE SET (8)	6.00	2.70
COMMON CARD	.50	.23
☐ 3 Ryan Klesko	.75	.35
☐ 4 Jim Edmonds	1.00	.45
☐ 5 Barry Larkin	1.00	.45
☐ 6 Jim Thome	1.00	.45
☐ 7 Raul Mondesi	.75	.35
☐ 110 Derek Bell	.50	.23
☐ 240 Derek Jeter	3.00	1.35
☐ 241 Michael Tucker	.60	.25

1996 Score

This set consists of 517 standard-size cards. These cards were issued in packs of 10 that retailed for 99 cents per pack. The fronts feature an action photo surrounded by white borders. The "Score 96" logo is in the upper left, while the player is identified on the bottom. The backs have season and career stats as well as a player photo and some text. A Cal Ripken tribute card was issued at a rate of 1 every 300 packs.

	MINT	NRMT
COMPLETE SET (517)	24.00	11.00
COMPLETE SERIES 1 (275)	12.00	5.50
COMPLETE SERIES 2 (242)	12.00	5.50
COMMON CARD (1-517)	.10	.05
☐ 1 Will Clark	.30	.14
☐ 2 Rich Becker	.20	.09
☐ 3 Ryan Klesko	.30	.14
☐ 4 Jim Edmonds	.30	.14
☐ 5 Barry Larkin	.30	.14
☐ 6 Jim Thome	.40	.18
☐ 7 Raul Mondesi	.30	.14
☐ 8 Don Mattingly	.60	.25
☐ 9 Jeff Conine	.20	.09
☐ 10 Rickey Henderson	.30	.14
☐ 11 Chad Curtis	.10	.05
☐ 12 Darren Daulton	.20	.09
☐ 13 Larry Walker	.40	.18
☐ 14 Carlos Garcia	.10	.05
☐ 15 Carlos Baerga	.20	.09
☐ 16 Tony Gwynn	1.00	.45
☐ 17 Jon Nunnally	.10	.05
☐ 18 Deion Sanders	.40	.18
☐ 19 Mark Grace	.30	.14
☐ 20 Alex Rodriguez	1.50	.70
☐ 21 Frank Thomas	1.50	.70
☐ 22 Brian Jordan	.20	.09
☐ 23 J.T. Snow	.20	.09
☐ 24 Shawn Green	.20	.09
☐ 25 Tim Wakefield	.10	.05
☐ 26 Curtis Goodwin	.10	.05
☐ 27 John Smoltz	.20	.09
☐ 28 Devon White	.10	.05
☐ 29 Johnny Damon	.20	.09
☐ 30 Tim Salmon	.40	.18
☐ 31 Rafael Palmeiro	.30	.14
☐ 32 Bernard Gilkey	.20	.09
☐ 33 John Valentin	.20	.09
☐ 34 Randy Johnson	.40	.18
☐ 35 Garret Anderson	.20	.09
☐ 36 Rikkert Faneyte	.10	.05
☐ 37 Ray Durham	.20	.09
☐ 38 Bip Roberts	.10	.05
☐ 39 Jaime Navarro	.10	.05
☐ 40 Mark Johnson	.10	.05
☐ 41 Darren Lewis	.10	.05
☐ 42 Tyler Green	.10	.05
☐ 43 Bill Pulsipher	.10	.05
☐ 44 Jason Giambi	.20	.09
☐ 45 Kevin Ritz	.10	.05
☐ 46 Jack McDowell	.10	.05
☐ 47 Felipe Lira	.10	.05
☐ 48 Rico Brogna	.10	.05
☐ 49 Terry Pendleton	.20	.09
☐ 50 Rondell White	.20	.09
☐ 51 Andre Dawson	.30	.14
☐ 52 Kirby Puckett	.75	.35
☐ 53 Wally Joyner	.10	.05
☐ 54 B.J. Surhoff	.10	.05
☐ 55 Randy Velarde	.10	.05
☐ 56 Greg Vaughn	.10	.05
☐ 57 Roberto Alomar	.40	.18
☐ 58 David Justice	.40	.18
☐ 59 Kevin Seitzer	.10	.05
☐ 60 Cal Ripken	1.50	.70
☐ 61 Ozzie Smith	.50	.23
☐ 62 Mo Vaughn	.50	.23
☐ 63 Ricky Bones	.10	.05
☐ 64 Gary DiSarcina	.10	.05
☐ 65 Matt Williams	.30	.14
☐ 66 Wilson Alvarez	.30	.14
☐ 67 Lenny Dykstra	.20	.09
☐ 68 Brian McRae	.10	.05
☐ 69 Todd Stottlemyre	.10	.05
☐ 70 Bret Boone	.10	.05
☐ 71 Sterling Hitchcock	.10	.05
☐ 72 Albert Belle	.50	.23
☐ 73 Todd Hundley	.20	.09
☐ 74 Vinny Castilla	.20	.09
☐ 75 Moises Alou	.20	.09
☐ 76 Cecil Fielder	.20	.09
☐ 77 Brad Radke	.20	.09
☐ 78 Quilvio Veras	.10	.05
☐ 79 Eddie Murray	.40	.18
☐ 80 James Mouton	.10	.05
☐ 81 Pat Listach	.10	.05
☐ 82 Mark Gubicza	.10	.05
☐ 83 Dave Winfield	.30	.14
☐ 84 Fred McGriff	.30	.14
☐ 85 Darryl Hamilton	.10	.05
☐ 86 Jeffrey Hammonds	.10	.05
☐ 87 Pedro Munoz	.10	.05
☐ 88 Craig Biggio	.30	.14
☐ 89 Cliff Floyd	.10	.05
☐ 90 Tim Naehring	.10	.05
☐ 91 Brett Butler	.20	.09
☐ 92 Kevin Foster	.10	.05
☐ 93 Pat Kelly	.10	.05
☐ 94 John Smiley	.10	.05
☐ 95 Terry Steinbach	.20	.09
☐ 96 Orel Hershiser	.20	.09
☐ 97 Darrin Fletcher	.10	.05
☐ 98 Walt Weiss	.10	.05
☐ 99 John Wetteland	.20	.09
☐ 100 Alan Trammell	.30	.14
☐ 101 Steve Avery	.10	.05
☐ 102 Tony Eusebio	.10	.05
☐ 103 Sandy Alomar Jr.	.20	.09
☐ 104 Joe Girardi	.10	.05
☐ 105 Rick Aguilera	.10	.05
☐ 106 Tony Tarasco	.10	.05
☐ 107 Chris Hammond	.10	.05
☐ 108 Mike Macfarlane	.10	.05
☐ 109 Doug Drabek	.10	.05
☐ 110 Derek Bell	.10	.05
☐ 111 Ed Sprague	.10	.05
☐ 112 Todd Hollandsworth	.20	.09
☐ 113 Otis Nixon	.10	.05
☐ 114 Keith Lockhart	.10	.05
☐ 115 Donovan Osborne	.10	.05
☐ 116 Dave Magadan	.10	.05
☐ 117 Edgar Martinez	.30	.14
☐ 118 Chuck Carr	.10	.05
☐ 119 J.R. Phillips	.10	.05
☐ 120 Sean Bergman	.10	.05
☐ 121 Andujar Cedeno	.10	.05
☐ 122 Eric Young	.20	.09
☐ 123 Al Martin	.10	.05
☐ 124 Mark Lemke	.10	.05
☐ 125 Jim Eisenreich	.20	.09
☐ 126 Benito Santiago	.10	.05
☐ 127 Ariel Prieto	.10	.05
☐ 128 Jim Bullinger	.10	.05
☐ 129 Russ Davis	.10	.05
☐ 130 Jim Abbott	.20	.09
☐ 131 Jason Isringhausen	.10	.05
☐ 132 Carlos Perez	.10	.05
☐ 133 David Segui	.10	.05
☐ 134 Troy O'Leary	.20	.09
☐ 135 Pat Meares	.10	.05
☐ 136 Chris Hoiles	.10	.05
☐ 137 Ismael Valdes	.20	.09
☐ 138 Jose Oliva	.10	.05
☐ 139 Carlos Delgado	.20	.09
☐ 140 Tom Goodwin	.10	.05
☐ 141 Bob Tewksbury	.10	.05
☐ 142 Chris Gomez	.10	.05
☐ 143 Jose Oquendo	.10	.05
☐ 144 Mark Lewis	.10	.05
☐ 145 Salomon Torres	.10	.05
☐ 146 Luis Gonzalez	.10	.05
☐ 147 Mark Carreon	.10	.05
☐ 148 Lance Johnson	.10	.05
☐ 149 Melvin Nieves	.10	.05
☐ 150 Lee Smith	.20	.09
☐ 151 Jacob Brumfield	.10	.05
☐ 152 Armando Benitez	.10	.05
☐ 153 Curt Schilling	.10	.05
☐ 154 Javier Lopez	.20	.09
☐ 155 Frank Rodriguez	.10	.05
☐ 156 Alex Gonzalez	.10	.05
☐ 157 Todd Worrell	.20	.09
☐ 158 Benji Gil	.10	.05
☐ 159 Greg Gagne	.10	.05
☐ 160 Tom Henke	.20	.09
☐ 161 Randy Myers	.20	.09
☐ 162 Joey Cora	.10	.05
☐ 163 Scott Ruffcorn	.10	.05
☐ 164 W. VanLandingham	.10	.05
☐ 165 Tony Phillips	.10	.05
☐ 166 Eddie Williams	.10	.05
☐ 167 Bobby Bonilla	.20	.09
☐ 168 Denny Neagle	.20	.09
☐ 169 Troy Percival	.20	.09
☐ 170 Billy Ashley	.10	.05
☐ 171 Andy Van Slyke	.20	.09
☐ 172 Jose Offerman	.10	.05
☐ 173 Mark Parent	.10	.05
☐ 174 Edgardo Alfonzo	.30	.14
☐ 175 Trevor Hoffman	.20	.09
☐ 176 David Cone	.20	.09
☐ 177 Dan Wilson	.10	.05
☐ 178 Steve Ontiveros	.10	.05
☐ 179 Dean Palmer	.20	.09
☐ 180 Mike Kelly	.10	.05
☐ 181 Jim Leyritz	.10	.05
☐ 182 Ron Karkovice	.10	.05
☐ 183 Kevin Brown	.20	.09
☐ 184 Jose Valentin	.10	.05
☐ 185 Jorge Fabregas	.10	.05
☐ 186 Jose Mesa	.20	.09
☐ 187 Brent Mayne	.10	.05
☐ 188 Carl Everett	.10	.05
☐ 189 Paul Sorrento	.10	.05
☐ 190 Pete Schourek	.10	.05
☐ 191 Scott Kamieniecki	.10	.05
☐ 192 Roberto Hernandez	.20	.09
☐ 193 Randy Johnson RR	.40	.18
☐ 194 Greg Maddux RR	.40	.18
☐ 195 Hideo Nomo RR	.40	.18
☐ 196 David Cone RR	.20	.09
☐ 197 Mike Mussina RR	.40	.18
☐ 198 Andy Benes RR	.10	.05
☐ 199 Kevin Appier RR	.20	.09
☐ 200 John Smoltz RR	.30	.14
☐ 201 John Wetteland RR	.20	.09
☐ 202 Mark Wohlers RR	.20	.09
☐ 203 Stan Belinda	.10	.05
☐ 204 Brian Anderson	.10	.05
☐ 205 Mike Devereaux	.10	.05
☐ 206 Mark Wohlers	.20	.09
☐ 207 Omar Vizquel	.20	.09
☐ 208 Jose Rijo	.10	.05
☐ 209 Willie Blair	.10	.05
☐ 210 Jamie Moyer	.10	.05
☐ 211 Craig Shipley	.10	.05
☐ 212 Shane Reynolds	.10	.05
☐ 213 Chad Fonville	.10	.05
☐ 214 Jose Vizcaino	.10	.05
☐ 215 Sid Fernandez	.10	.05
☐ 216 Andy Ashby	.10	.05
☐ 217 Frank Castillo	.10	.05
☐ 218 Kevin Tapani	.10	.05
☐ 219 Kent Mercker	.10	.05
☐ 220 Karim Garcia	.20	.09
☐ 221 Antonio Osuna	.10	.05
☐ 222 Tim Unroe	.10	.05
☐ 223 Johnny Damon	.20	.09
☐ 224 LaTroy Hawkins	.10	.05
☐ 225 Mariano Rivera	.40	.18
☐ 226 Jose Alberro	.10	.05
☐ 227 Angel Martinez	.10	.05
☐ 228 Jason Schmidt	.30	.14
☐ 229 Tony Clark	.40	.18
☐ 230 Kevin Jordan UER Ricky Jordan pictured on both sides	.10	.05

☐ 231 Mark Thompson .10 .05
☐ 232 Jim Dougherty .10 .05
☐ 233 Roger Cedeno .20 .09
☐ 234 Ugueth Urbina .10 .05
☐ 235 Ricky Otero .10 .05
☐ 236 Mark Smith .10 .05
☐ 237 Brian Barber .10 .05
☐ 238 Kevin Flora .10 .05
☐ 239 Joe Rosselli .10 .05
☐ 240 Derek Jeter 1.25 .55
☐ 241 Michael Tucker .20 .09
☐ 242 Ben Blomdahl .10 .05
☐ 243 Joe Vitiello .10 .05
☐ 244 Todd Steverson .10 .05
☐ 245 James Baldwin .10 .05
☐ 246 Alan Embree .10 .05
☐ 247 Shannon Penn .10 .05
☐ 248 Chris Stynes .10 .05
☐ 249 Oscar Munoz .10 .05
☐ 250 Jose Herrera .10 .05
☐ 251 Scott Sullivan .10 .05
☐ 252 Reggie Williams .10 .05
☐ 253 Mark Grudzielanek .10 .05
☐ 254 Steve Rodriguez .10 .05
☐ 255 Terry Bradshaw .10 .05
☐ 256 F.P. Santangelo .10 .05
☐ 257 Lyle Mouton .10 .05
☐ 258 George Williams .10 .05
☐ 259 Larry Thomas .10 .05
☐ 260 Rudy Pemberton .10 .05
☐ 261 Jim Pittsley .20 .09
☐ 262 Les Norman .10 .05
☐ 263 Ruben Rivera .20 .09
☐ 264 Cesar Devarez .10 .05
☐ 265 Greg Zaun .10 .05
☐ 266 Dustin Hermanson .10 .05
☐ 267 John Frascatore .10 .05
☐ 268 Joe Randa .10 .05
☐ 269 Jeff Bagwell CL .40 .18
☐ 270 Mike Piazza CL .40 .18
☐ 271 Dante Bichette CL .20 .09
☐ 272 Frank Thomas CL 1.00 .45
☐ 273 Ken Griffey Jr. CL 1.00 .45
☐ 274 Cal Ripken CL .75 .35
☐ 275 Greg Maddux CL .20 .09
Albert Belle
☐ 276 Greg Maddux 1.25 .55
☐ 277 Pedro Martinez .40 .18
☐ 278 Bobby Higginson .20 .09
☐ 279 Ray Lankford .20 .09
☐ 280 Shawon Dunston .10 .05
☐ 281 Gary Sheffield .40 .18
☐ 282 Ken Griffey, Jr. 2.00 .90
☐ 283 Paul Molitor .40 .18
☐ 284 Kevin Appier .20 .09
☐ 285 Chuck Knoblauch .40 .18
☐ 286 Alex Fernandez .20 .09
☐ 287 Steve Finley .20 .09
☐ 288 Jeff Blauser .10 .05
☐ 289 Charles Johnson .20 .09
☐ 290 John Franco .20 .09
☐ 291 Mark Langston .10 .05
☐ 292 Bret Saberhagen .10 .05
☐ 293 John Mabry .20 .09
☐ 294 Ramon Martinez .20 .09
☐ 295 Mike Blowers .10 .05
☐ 296 Paul O'Neill .10 .05
☐ 297 Dave Nilsson .20 .09
☐ 298 Dante Bichette .20 .09
☐ 299 Marty Cordova .10 .05
☐ 300 Jay Bell .20 .09
☐ 301 Mike Mussina .40 .18
☐ 302 Ivan Rodriguez .50 .23
☐ 303 Jose Canseco .30 .14
☐ 304 Jeff Bagwell .75 .35
☐ 305 Manny Ramirez .40 .18
☐ 306 Dennis Martinez .20 .09
☐ 307 Charlie Hayes .10 .05
☐ 308 Joe Carter .20 .09
☐ 309 Travis Fryman .20 .09
☐ 310 Mark McGwire .75 .35
☐ 311 Reggie Sanders UER .10 .05
Photo on front is John Roper
☐ 312 Julian Tavarez .10 .05
☐ 313 Jeff Montgomery .10 .05
☐ 314 Andy Benes .10 .05
☐ 315 John Jaha .10 .05
☐ 316 Jeff Kent .10 .05
☐ 317 Mike Piazza 1.25 .55
☐ 318 Erik Hanson .10 .05
☐ 319 Kenny Rogers .10 .05
☐ 320 Hideo Nomo 1.00 .45
☐ 321 Gregg Jefferies .30 .14
☐ 322 Chipper Jones 1.25 .55
☐ 323 Jay Buhner .30 .14
☐ 324 Dennis Eckersley .30 .14
☐ 325 Kenny Lofton .50 .23
☐ 326 Robin Ventura .20 .09
☐ 327 Tom Glavine .20 .09
☐ 328 Tim Salmon .40 .18
☐ 329 Andres Galarraga .40 .18
☐ 330 Hal Morris .10 .05
☐ 331 Brady Anderson .30 .14
☐ 332 Chili Davis .20 .09
☐ 333 Roger Clemens .75 .35
☐ 334 Marquis Grissom .20 .09
☐ 335 Mike Greenwell UER .10 .05
Name spelled Jeff on Front
☐ 336 Sammy Sosa .40 .18
☐ 337 Ron Gant .20 .09
☐ 338 Ken Caminiti .40 .18
☐ 339 Danny Tartabull .10 .05
☐ 340 Barry Bonds .50 .23
☐ 341 Ben McDonald .10 .05
☐ 342 Ruben Sierra .10 .05
☐ 343 Bernie Williams .40 .18
☐ 344 Wil Cordero .10 .05
☐ 345 Wade Boggs .40 .18
☐ 346 Gary Gaetti .20 .09
☐ 347 Greg Colbrunn .10 .05
☐ 348 Juan Gonzalez 1.00 .45
☐ 349 Marc Newfield .10 .05
☐ 350 Charles Nagy .20 .09
☐ 351 Robby Thompson .10 .05
☐ 352 Roberto Petagine .10 .05
☐ 353 Darryl Strawberry .20 .09
☐ 354 Tino Martinez .40 .18
☐ 355 Eric Karros .20 .09
☐ 356 Cal Ripken SS .75 .35
☐ 357 Cecil Fielder SS .20 .09
☐ 358 Kirby Puckett SS .40 .18
☐ 359 Jim Edmonds SS .40 .18
☐ 360 Matt Williams SS .30 .14
☐ 361 Alex Rodriguez SS 1.00 .45
☐ 362 Barry Larkin SS .30 .14
☐ 363 Rafael Palmeiro SS .30 .14
☐ 364 David Cone SS .20 .09
☐ 365 Roberto Alomar SS .40 .18
☐ 366 Eddie Murray SS .40 .18
☐ 367 Randy Johnson SS .40 .18
☐ 368 Ryan Klesko SS .30 .14
☐ 369 Raul Mondesi SS .30 .14
☐ 370 Mo Vaughn SS .40 .18
☐ 371 Will Clark SS .30 .14
☐ 372 Carlos Baerga SS .10 .05
☐ 373 Frank Thomas SS 1.00 .45
☐ 374 Larry Walker SS .40 .18
☐ 375 Garret Anderson SS .20 .09
☐ 376 Edgar Martinez SS .30 .14
☐ 377 Don Mattingly SS .40 .18
☐ 378 Tony Gwynn SS .40 .18
☐ 379 Albert Belle SS .40 .18
☐ 380 Jason Isringhausen SS .10 .05
☐ 381 Ruben Rivera SS .10 .05
☐ 382 Johnny Damon SS .10 .05
☐ 383 Karim Garcia SS .10 .05
☐ 384 Derek Jeter SS .40 .18
☐ 385 David Justice SS .40 .18
☐ 386 Royce Clayton .10 .05
☐ 387 Mark Whiten .10 .05
☐ 388 Mickey Tettleton .10 .05
☐ 389 Steve Trachsel .10 .05
☐ 390 Danny Bautista .10 .05
☐ 391 Midre Cummings .10 .05
☐ 392 Scott Leius .10 .05
☐ 393 Manny Alexander .10 .05
☐ 394 Brent Gates .10 .05
☐ 395 Rey Sanchez .10 .05
☐ 396 Andy Pettitte .50 .23
☐ 397 Jeff Cirillo .10 .05
☐ 398 Kurt Abbott .10 .05
☐ 399 Lee Tinsley .10 .05
☐ 400 Paul Assenmacher .10 .05
☐ 401 Scott Erickson .10 .05
☐ 402 Todd Zeile .10 .05
☐ 403 Tom Pagnozzi .10 .05
☐ 404 Ozzie Guillen .10 .05
☐ 405 Jeff Frye .10 .05
☐ 406 Kirt Manwaring .10 .05
☐ 407 Chad Ogea .10 .05
☐ 408 Harold Baines .20 .09
☐ 409 Jason Bere .10 .05
☐ 410 Chuck Finley .10 .05
☐ 411 Jeff Fassero .10 .05
☐ 412 Joey Hamilton .20 .09
☐ 413 John Olerud .10 .05
☐ 414 Kevin Stocker .10 .05
☐ 415 Eric Anthony .10 .05
☐ 416 Aaron Sele .10 .05
☐ 417 Chris Bosio .10 .05
☐ 418 Michael Mimbs .10 .05
☐ 419 Orlando Miller .10 .05
☐ 420 Stan Javier .10 .05
☐ 421 Matt Mieske .10 .05
☐ 422 Jason Bates .10 .05
☐ 423 Orlando Merced .10 .05
☐ 424 John Flaherty .10 .05
☐ 425 Reggie Jefferson .10 .05
☐ 426 Scott Stahoviak .10 .05
☐ 427 John Burkett .10 .05
☐ 428 Rod Beck .10 .05
☐ 429 Bill Swift .10 .05
☐ 430 Scott Cooper .10 .05
☐ 431 Mel Rojas .10 .05
☐ 432 Todd Van Poppel .10 .05
☐ 433 Bobby Jones .10 .05
☐ 434 Mike Harkey .10 .05
☐ 435 Sean Berry .10 .05
☐ 436 Glenallen Hill .10 .05
☐ 437 Ryan Thompson .10 .05
☐ 438 Luis Alicea .10 .05
☐ 439 Esteban Loaiza .10 .05
☐ 440 Jeff Reboulet .10 .05
☐ 441 Vince Coleman .10 .05
☐ 442 Ellis Burks .20 .09
☐ 443 Allen Battle .10 .05
☐ 444 Jimmy Key .20 .09
☐ 445 Ricky Bottalico .10 .05
☐ 446 Delino DeShields .10 .05
☐ 447 Albie Lopez .10 .05
☐ 448 Mark Petkovsek .10 .05
☐ 449 Tim Raines .10 .05
☐ 450 Bryan Harvey .10 .05
☐ 451 Pat Hentgen .20 .09
☐ 452 Tim Laker .10 .05
☐ 453 Tom Gordon .10 .05
☐ 454 Phil Plantier .10 .05
☐ 455 Ernie Young .10 .05
☐ 456 Pete Harnisch .10 .05
☐ 457 Roberto Kelly .10 .05
☐ 458 Mark Portugal .10 .05
☐ 459 Mark Leiter .10 .05
☐ 460 Tony Pena .10 .05
☐ 461 Roger Pavlik .10 .05
☐ 462 Jeff King .20 .09
☐ 463 Bryan Rekar .10 .05
☐ 464 Al Leiter .10 .05
☐ 465 Phil Nevin .10 .05
☐ 466 Jose Lima .10 .05
☐ 467 Mike Stanley .10 .05
☐ 468 David McCarty .10 .05
☐ 469 Herb Perry .10 .05
☐ 470 Geronimo Berroa .10 .05
☐ 471 David Wells .10 .05
☐ 472 Vaughn Eshelman .10 .05
☐ 473 Greg Swindell .10 .05
☐ 474 Steve Sparks .10 .05
☐ 475 Luis Sojo .10 .05
☐ 476 Derrick May .10 .05
☐ 477 Joe Oliver .10 .05
☐ 478 Alex Arias .10 .05
☐ 479 Brad Ausmus .10 .05
☐ 480 Gabe White .10 .05
☐ 481 Pat Rapp .10 .05
☐ 482 Damon Buford .10 .05
☐ 483 Turk Wendell .10 .05
☐ 484 Jeff Brantley .10 .05
☐ 485 Curtis Leskanic .10 .05
☐ 486 Robb Nen .10 .05
☐ 487 Lou Whitaker .20 .09
☐ 488 Melido Perez .10 .05
☐ 489 Luis Polonia .10 .05
☐ 490 Scott Brosius .10 .05
☐ 491 Robert Perez .10 .05
☐ 492 Mike Sweeney .40 .18
☐ 493 Mark Loretta .10 .05
☐ 494 Alex Ochoa .20 .09
☐ 495 Matt Lawton .10 .05
☐ 496 Shawn Estes .20 .09
☐ 497 John Wasdin .10 .05
☐ 498 Marc Kroon .10 .05
☐ 499 Chris Snopek .10 .05
☐ 500 Jeff Suppan .30 .14
☐ 501 Terrell Wade .10 .05
☐ 502 Marvin Benard .10 .05
☐ 503 Chris Widger .10 .05
☐ 504 Quinton McCracken .10 .05
☐ 505 Bob Wolcott .10 .05
☐ 506 C.J. Nitkowski .10 .05
☐ 507 Aaron Ledesma .10 .05
☐ 508 Scott Hatteberg .10 .05
☐ 509 Jimmy Haynes .10 .05
☐ 510 Howard Battle .10 .05
☐ 511 Marty Cordova CL .10 .05
☐ 512 Randy Johnson CL .40 .18
☐ 513 Mo Vaughn CL .40 .18
☐ 514 Chan Ho Park CL .40 .18
☐ 515 Greg Maddux CL .40 .18
☐ 516 Barry Larkin CL .30 .14
☐ 517 Tom Glavine CL .20 .09
☐ NNO Cal Ripken 2131 20.00 9.00

1996 Score All-Stars

Randomly inserted in second series jumbo packs at a rate of one in nine, this 20-card set was printed in rainbow holographic prismatic foil.

	MINT	NRMT
COMPLETE SET (20)	80.00	36.00
COMMON CARD (1-20)	1.50	.70
☐ 1 Frank Thomas	12.00	5.50
☐ 2 Albert Belle	4.00	1.80
☐ 3 Ken Griffey Jr.	15.00	6.75
☐ 4 Cal Ripken	12.00	5.50
☐ 5 Mo Vaughn	4.00	1.80
☐ 6 Matt Williams	2.50	1.10
☐ 7 Barry Bonds	4.00	1.80
☐ 8 Dante Bichette	2.00	.90
☐ 9 Tony Gwynn	6.00	2.70
☐ 10 Greg Maddux	10.00	4.50
☐ 11 Randy Johnson	3.00	1.35
☐ 12 Hideo Nomo	7.50	3.40
☐ 13 Tim Salmon	3.00	1.35
☐ 14 Jeff Bagwell	6.00	2.70
☐ 15 Edgar Martinez	2.50	1.10
☐ 16 Reggie Sanders	1.50	.70
☐ 17 Larry Walker	3.00	1.35
☐ 18 Chipper Jones	10.00	4.50
☐ 19 Manny Ramirez	3.00	1.35
☐ 20 Eddie Murray	3.00	1.35

1996 Score Big Bats

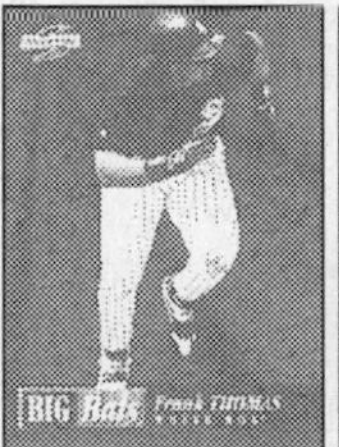

This 20-card set was randomly inserted in retail packs at a rate of approximately one in 31. The fronts feature a player photo set against a gold-foil background. The words "Big Bats" as well as the player's name is printed in white at the bottom. The backs feature a photo against a multi-colored background. The cards are numbered "X" of 20 in the upper left corner.

	MINT	NRMT
COMPLETE SET (20)	120.00	55.00
COMMON CARD (1-20)	2.00	.90
☐ 1 Cal Ripken	20.00	9.00
☐ 2 Ken Griffey Jr.	25.00	11.00
☐ 3 Frank Thomas	20.00	9.00
☐ 4 Jeff Bagwell	10.00	4.50
☐ 5 Mike Piazza	15.00	6.75
☐ 6 Barry Bonds	6.00	2.70
☐ 7 Matt Williams	3.00	1.35
☐ 8 Raul Mondesi	3.00	1.35
☐ 9 Tony Gwynn	10.00	4.50
☐ 10 Albert Belle	6.00	2.70
☐ 11 Manny Ramirez		
☐ 12 Carlos Baerga	2.00	.90
☐ 13 Mo Vaughn	6.00	2.70
☐ 14 Derek Bell	2.00	.90
☐ 15 Larry Walker		
☐ 16 Kenny Lofton	6.00	2.70
☐ 17 Edgar Martinez	3.00	1.35
☐ 18 Reggie Sanders	2.00	.90
☐ 19 Eddie Murray		
☐ 20 Chipper Jones	15.00	6.75

1996 Score Diamond Aces

This 30-card set features some of baseball's best players. These cards were inserted approximately one every eight jumbo packs. The fronts display a color player cutout on a computer-generated background with gold foil accenting. On a similar background, the backs carry a color closeup.

	MINT	NRMT
COMPLETE SET (30)	120.00	55.00
COMMON CARD (1-30)	2.00	.90
☐ 1 Hideo Nomo	12.00	5.50
☐ 2 Brian L.Hunter	3.00	1.35
☐ 3 Ray Durham	3.00	1.35
☐ 4 Frank Thomas	20.00	9.00
☐ 5 Cal Ripken	20.00	9.00
☐ 6 Barry Bonds	6.00	2.70

	MINT	NRMT
☐ 7 Greg Maddux	15.00	6.75
☐ 8 Chipper Jones	15.00	6.75
☐ 9 Raul Mondesi	4.00	1.80
☐ 10 Mike Piazza	15.00	6.75
☐ 11 Derek Jeter	15.00	6.75
☐ 12 Bill Pulsipher	2.00	.90
☐ 13 Larry Walker	4.00	1.80
☐ 14 Ken Griffey Jr.	25.00	11.00
☐ 15 Alex Rodriguez	20.00	9.00
☐ 16 Manny Ramirez	4.00	1.80
☐ 17 Mo Vaughn	6.00	2.70
☐ 18 Reggie Sanders	2.00	.90
☐ 19 Derek Bell	2.00	.90
☐ 20 Jim Edmonds	4.00	1.80
☐ 21 Albert Belle	6.00	2.70
☐ 22 Eddie Murray	4.00	1.80
☐ 23 Tony Gwynn	10.00	4.50
☐ 24 Jeff Bagwell	10.00	4.50
☐ 25 Carlos Baerga	2.00	.90
☐ 26 Matt Williams	4.00	1.80
☐ 27 Garret Anderson	3.00	1.35
☐ 28 Todd Hollandsworth	3.00	1.35
☐ 29 Johnny Damon	2.00	.90
☐ 30 Tim Salmon	4.00	1.80

1996 Score Dream Team

This nine-card set was randomly inserted in approximately one in 72 packs. This set features a leading player at each position. The fronts feature a player photo set against a holographic foil background. The words "1995 Dream Team" as well as his name and team are printed on the bottom of the card. The horizontal backs feature a player photo and some text. The cards are numbered in the upper right as "X" of nine.

	MINT	NRMT
COMPLETE SET (9)	100.00	45.00
COMMON CARD (1-9)	2.00	.90
☐ 1 Cal Ripken	20.00	9.00
☐ 2 Frank Thomas	20.00	9.00
☐ 3 Carlos Baerga	2.00	.90
☐ 4 Matt Williams	3.00	1.35
☐ 5 Mike Piazza	15.00	6.75
☐ 6 Barry Bonds	6.00	2.70
☐ 7 Ken Griffey Jr.	25.00	11.00
☐ 8 Manny Ramirez	4.00	1.80
☐ 9 Greg Maddux	15.00	6.75

1996 Score Dugout Collection

This set is a mini-parallel to the regular issue. Only 110 cards of each Series 1 and Series 2 were selected. Randomly inserted approximately one in every three packs, these cards have all gold foil printing that gives them a shiny copper cast. The words "Dugout Collection" are printed on the back.

	MINT	NRMT
COMPLETE SERIES 1 (110)	50.00	22.00
COMPLETE SERIES 2 (110)	50.00	22.00
COMMON CARD (A1-B110)	.30	.14
☐ A1 Will Clark	.60	.25
☐ A2 Rich Becker	.30	.14
☐ A3 Ryan Klesko	.60	.25
☐ A4 Jim Edmonds	1.50	.70
☐ A5 Barry Larkin	.60	.25
☐ A6 Jim Thome	1.50	.70
☐ A7 Raul Mondesi	.60	.25
☐ A8 Don Mattingly	2.50	1.10
☐ A9 Jeff Conine	.50	.23
☐ A10 Rickey Henderson	.60	.25
☐ A11 Chad Curtis	.30	.14
☐ A12 Darren Daulton	.50	.23
☐ A13 Larry Walker	1.50	.70
☐ A14 Carlos Baerga	.50	.23
☐ A15 Tony Gwynn	4.00	1.80
☐ A16 Jon Nunnally	.30	.14
☐ A17 Deion Sanders	1.50	.70
☐ A18 Mark Grace	.60	.25
☐ A19 Alex Rodriguez	6.00	2.70
☐ A20 Frank Thomas	6.00	2.70
☐ A21 Brian Jordan	.50	.23
☐ A22 J.T. Snow	.50	.23
☐ A23 Shawn Green	.50	.23
☐ A24 Tim Wakefield	.30	.14
☐ A25 Curtis Goodwin	.30	.14
☐ A26 John Smoltz	.50	.23
☐ A27 Devon White	.30	.14
☐ A28 Brian L.Hunter	.50	.23
☐ A29 Rusty Greer	.60	.25
☐ A30 Rafael Palmeiro	.60	.25
☐ A31 Bernard Gilkey	.50	.23
☐ A32 John Valentin	.50	.23
☐ A33 Randy Johnson	1.50	.70
☐ A34 Garret Anderson	.50	.23
☐ A35 Ray Durham	.30	.14
☐ A36 Bip Roberts	.30	.14
☐ A37 Tyler Green	.30	.14
☐ A38 Bill Pulsipher	.30	.14
☐ A39 Jason Giambi	.50	.23
☐ A40 Jack McDowell	.30	.14
☐ A41 Rico Brogna	.50	.23
☐ A42 Terry Pendleton	.30	.14
☐ A43 Rondell White	.50	.23
☐ A44 Andre Dawson	.60	.25
☐ A45 Kirby Puckett	3.00	1.35
☐ A46 Wally Joyner	.50	.23
☐ A47 B.J. Surhoff	.50	.23
☐ A48 Randy Velarde	.30	.14
☐ A49 Greg Vaughn	.30	.14
☐ A50 Roberto Alomar	1.50	.70
☐ A51 David Justice	1.50	.70
☐ A52 Cal Ripken	6.00	2.70
☐ A53 Ozzie Smith	2.00	.90
☐ A54 Mo Vaughn	2.00	.90
☐ A55 Gary DiSarcina	.30	.14
☐ A56 Matt Williams	.60	.25
☐ A57 Lenny Dykstra	.50	.23
☐ A58 Bret Boone	.30	.14
☐ A59 Albert Belle	2.00	.90
☐ A60 Vinny Castilla	.50	.23
☐ A61 Moises Alou	.50	.23
☐ A62 Cecil Fielder	.50	.23
☐ A63 Brad Radke	.50	.23
☐ A64 Quilvio Veras	.30	.14
☐ A65 Eddie Murray	1.50	.70
☐ A66 Dave Winfield	.60	.25
☐ A67 Fred McGriff	.60	.25
☐ A68 Craig Biggio	.60	.25
☐ A69 Cliff Floyd	.30	.14
☐ A70 Tim Naehring	.30	.14
☐ A71 John Wetteland	.50	.23
☐ A72 Alan Trammell	.60	.25
☐ A73 Steve Avery	.30	.14
☐ A74 Rick Aguilera	.50	.23
☐ A75 Derek Bell	.30	.14
☐ A76 Todd Hollandsworth	.50	.23
☐ A77 Edgar Martinez	.60	.25
☐ A78 Mark Lemke	.30	.14
☐ A79 Ariel Prieto	.30	.14
☐ A80 Russ Davis	.30	.14
☐ A81 Jim Abbott	.30	.14
☐ A82 Jason Isringhausen	.30	.14
☐ A83 Carlos Perez	.30	.14
☐ A84 David Segui	.30	.14
☐ A85 Troy O'Leary	.30	.14
☐ A86 Ismael Valdes	.30	.14
☐ A87 Carlos Delgado	.50	.23
☐ A88 Lee Smith	.50	.23

Card	MINT	NRMT
☐ A89 Javier Lopez	.50	.23
☐ A90 Frank Rodriguez	.30	.14
☐ A91 Alex Gonzalez	.30	.14
☐ A92 Benji Gil	.30	.14
☐ A93 Greg Gagne	.30	.14
☐ A94 Randy Myers	.30	.14
☐ A95 Bobby Bonilla	.50	.23
☐ A96 Billy Ashley	.30	.14
☐ A97 Andy Van Slyke	.50	.23
☐ A98 Edgardo Alfonzo	.60	.25
☐ A99 David Cone	.50	.23
☐ A100 Dean Palmer	.50	.23
☐ A101 Jose Mesa	.50	.23
☐ A102 Karim Garcia	.50	.23
☐ A103 Johnny Damon	.50	.23
☐ A104 LaTroy Hawkins	.30	.14
☐ A105 Mark Smith	.30	.14
☐ A106 Derek Jeter	4.00	1.80
☐ A107 Michael Tucker	.50	.23
☐ A108 Joe Vitiello	.30	.14
☐ A109 Ruben Rivera	.50	.23
☐ A110 Greg Zaun	.30	.14
☐ B1 Greg Maddux	5.00	2.20
☐ B2 Pedro Martinez	1.50	.70
☐ B3 Bobby Higginson	.50	.23
☐ B4 Ray Lankford	.50	.23
☐ B5 Shawon Dunston	.30	.14
☐ B6 Gary Sheffield	1.50	.70
☐ B7 Ken Griffey Jr.	8.00	3.60
☐ B8 Paul Molitor	1.50	.70
☐ B9 Kevin Appier	.50	.23
☐ B10 Chuck Knoblauch	1.50	.70
☐ B11 Alex Fernandez	.50	.23
☐ B12 Steve Finley	.50	.23
☐ B13 Jeff Blauser	.30	.14
☐ B14 Charles Johnson	.50	.23
☐ B15 John Franco	.50	.23
☐ B16 Mark Langston	.30	.14
☐ B17 Bret Saberhagen	.30	.14
☐ B18 John Mabry	.50	.23
☐ B19 Ramon Martinez	.50	.23
☐ B20 Mike Blowers	.30	.14
☐ B21 Paul O'Neill	.50	.23
☐ B22 Dave Nilsson	.30	.14
☐ B23 Dante Bichette	.50	.23
☐ B24 Marty Cordova	.30	.14
☐ B25 Jay Bell	.30	.14
☐ B26 Mike Mussina	1.50	.70
☐ B27 Ivan Rodriguez	1.50	.70
☐ B28 Jose Canseco	.60	.25
☐ B29 Jeff Bagwell	3.00	1.35
☐ B30 Manny Ramirez	1.50	.70
☐ B31 Dennis Martinez	.50	.23
☐ B32 Charlie Hayes	.30	.14
☐ B33 Joe Carter	.50	.23
☐ B34 Travis Fryman	.50	.23
☐ B35 Mark McGwire	3.00	1.35
☐ B36 Reggie Sanders	.30	.14
☐ B37 Julian Tavarez	.30	.14
☐ B38 Jeff Montgomery	.30	.14
☐ B39 Andy Benes	.30	.14
☐ B40 John Jaha	.30	.14
☐ B41 Jeff Kent	.30	.14
☐ B42 Mike Piazza	5.00	2.20
☐ B43 Erik Hanson	.30	.14
☐ B44 Kenny Rogers	.30	.14
☐ B45 Hideo Nomo	4.00	1.80
☐ B46 Gregg Jefferies	.50	.23
☐ B47 Chipper Jones	5.00	2.20
☐ B48 Jay Buhner	.60	.25
☐ B49 Dennis Eckersley	.60	.25
☐ B50 Kenny Lofton	2.00	.90
☐ B51 Robin Ventura	.50	.23
☐ B52 Tom Glavine	.50	.23
☐ B53 Tim Salmon	1.50	.70
☐ B54 Andres Galarraga	1.50	.70
☐ B55 Hal Morris	.30	.14
☐ B56 Brady Anderson	.60	.25
☐ B57 Chili Davis	.30	.14
☐ B58 Roger Clemens	3.00	1.35
☐ B59 Marquis Grissom	.50	.23
☐ B60 Mike Greenwell UER	.30	.14
(Front says Jeff Greenwell		
☐ B61 Sammy Sosa	1.50	.70
☐ B62 Ron Gant	.50	.23
☐ B63 Ken Caminiti	1.50	.70
☐ B64 Danny Tartabull	.30	.14
☐ B65 Barry Bonds	2.00	.90
☐ B66 Ben McDonald	.30	.14
☐ B67 Ruben Sierra	.30	.14
☐ B68 Bernie Williams	1.50	.70
☐ B69 Wil Cordero	.30	.14
☐ B70 Wade Boggs	1.50	.70
☐ B71 Gary Gaetti	.50	.23
☐ B72 Greg Colbrunn	.30	.14
☐ B73 Juan Gonzalez	4.00	1.80
☐ B74 Marc Newfield	.30	.14
☐ B75 Charles Nagy	.50	.23
☐ B76 Robby Thompson	.30	.14
☐ B77 Roberto Petagine	.30	.14
☐ B78 Darryl Strawberry	.50	.23
☐ B79 Tino Martinez	1.50	.70
☐ B80 Eric Karros	.50	.23
☐ B81 Cal Ripken SS	3.00	1.35
☐ B82 Cecil Fielder SS	.50	.23
☐ B83 Kirby Puckett SS	1.50	.70
☐ B84 Jim Edmonds SS	1.50	.70
☐ B85 Matt Williams SS	.60	.25
☐ B86 Alex Rodriguez SS	3.00	1.35
☐ B87 Barry Larkin SS	.60	.25
☐ B88 Rafael Palmeiro SS	.60	.25
☐ B89 David Cone SS	.50	.23
☐ B90 Roberto Alomar SS	1.50	.70
☐ B91 Eddie Murray SS	1.50	.70
☐ B92 Randy Johnson SS	1.50	.70
☐ B93 Ryan Klesko SS	.60	.25
☐ B94 Raul Mondesi SS	.60	.25
☐ B95 Mo Vaughn SS	1.50	.70
☐ B96 Will Clark SS	.60	.25
☐ B97 Carlos Baerga SS	.30	.14
☐ B98 Frank Thomas SS	3.00	1.35
☐ B99 Larry Walker SS	1.50	.70
☐ B100 Garret Anderson SS	.50	.23
☐ B101 Edgar Martinez SS	.60	.25
☐ B102 Don Mattingly SS	1.50	.70
☐ B103 Tony Gwynn SS	2.00	.90
☐ B104 Albert Belle SS	1.50	.70
☐ B105 Jason Isringhausen SS	.30	.14
☐ B106 Ruben Rivera SS	.30	.14
☐ B107 Johnny Damon SS	.30	.14
☐ B108 Karim Garcia SS	.30	.14
☐ B109 Derek Jeter SS	4.00	1.80
☐ B110 David Justice SS	1.50	.70

1996 Score Dugout Collection Artist's Proofs

This set is a parallel to the Dugout Collection set. These cards are different from the regular Dugout Collection as they have the words Artist Proof printed on the front. Randomly inserted one in every 36 packs, this set was printed using Gold Rush all gold-foil card technology .

	MINT	NRMT
COMPLETE SER.1 SET (110)	350.00	160.00
COMPLETE SER.2 SET (110)	350.00	160.00
COMMON CARD (1A-110A)	1.50	.70
COMMON CARD (1B-110B)	1.50	.70

*STARS: 1.5X TO 3X BASIC CARDS ...
*YOUNG STARS: 1.25X TO 2.5X BASIC CARDS

1996 Score Future Franchise

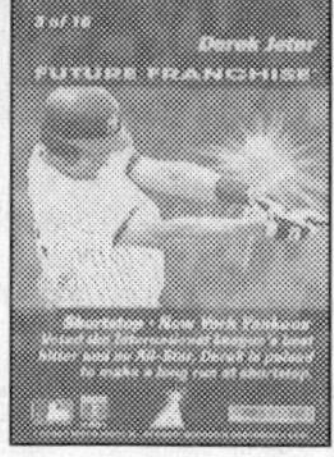

Randomly inserted in retail packs at a rate of one in 72, this 16-card set honors young stars of the game. The fronts feature a color action player cutout on a special holographic foil printed background. The backs carry another player color photo with player information.

	MINT	NRMT
COMPLETE SET (16)	120.00	55.00
COMMON CARD (1-16)	3.00	1.35
☐ 1 Jason Isringhausen	3.00	1.35
☐ 2 Chipper Jones	25.00	11.00
☐ 3 Derek Jeter	20.00	9.00
☐ 4 Alex Rodriguez	25.00	11.00
☐ 5 Alex Ochoa	3.00	1.35
☐ 6 Manny Ramirez	12.00	5.50
☐ 7 Johnny Damon	4.00	1.80
☐ 8 Ruben Rivera	4.00	1.80
☐ 9 Karim Garcia	4.00	1.80
☐ 10 Garret Anderson	5.00	2.20
☐ 11 Marty Cordova	3.00	1.35
☐ 12 Bill Pulsipher	3.00	1.35
☐ 13 Hideo Nomo	20.00	9.00
☐ 14 Marc Newfield	3.00	1.35
☐ 15 Charles Johnson	4.00	1.80
☐ 16 Raul Mondesi	5.00	2.20

1996 Score Gold Stars

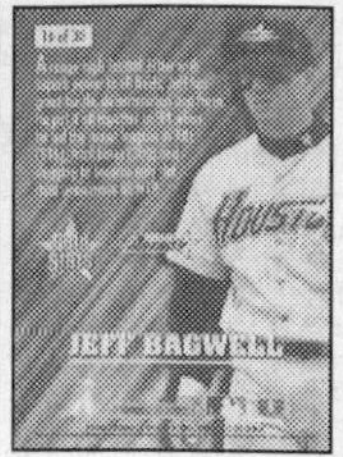

Randomly inserted in packs at a rate of one in 15, this 30-card set features borderless color action player photos with a special sepia player cutout inserted behind a gold foil stamp designating the star player. The backs display another player photo with player information.

	MINT	NRMT
COMPLETE SET (30)	60.00	27.00
COMMON CARD (1-30)	.75	.35
☐ 1 Ken Griffey Jr.	10.00	4.50
☐ 2 Frank Thomas	8.00	3.60
☐ 3 Reggie Sanders	.75	.35
☐ 4 Tim Salmon	1.50	.70
☐ 5 Mike Piazza	6.00	2.70
☐ 6 Tony Gwynn	4.00	1.80
☐ 7 Gary Sheffield	1.50	.70
☐ 8 Matt Williams	1.25	.55
☐ 9 Bernie Williams	1.50	.70
☐ 10 Jason Isringhausen	.75	.35
☐ 11 Albert Belle	4.00	1.80
☐ 12 Chipper Jones	6.00	2.70
☐ 13 Edgar Martinez	1.25	.55
☐ 14 Barry Larkin	1.25	.55
☐ 15 Barry Bonds	2.50	1.10
☐ 16 Jeff Bagwell	4.00	1.80
☐ 17 Greg Maddux	6.00	2.70
☐ 18 Mo Vaughn	2.50	1.10
☐ 19 Ryan Klesko	1.25	.55
☐ 20 Sammy Sosa	1.50	.70
☐ 21 Darren Daulton	1.00	.45
☐ 22 Ivan Rodriguez	2.50	1.10
☐ 23 Dante Bichette	1.00	.45
☐ 24 Hideo Nomo	5.00	2.20
☐ 25 Cal Ripken	8.00	3.60
☐ 26 Rafael Palmeiro	1.25	.55
☐ 27 Larry Walker	1.50	.70
☐ 28 Carlos Baerga	.75	.35
☐ 29 Randy Johnson	1.50	.70
☐ 30 Manny Ramirez	1.50	.70

1996 Score Numbers Game

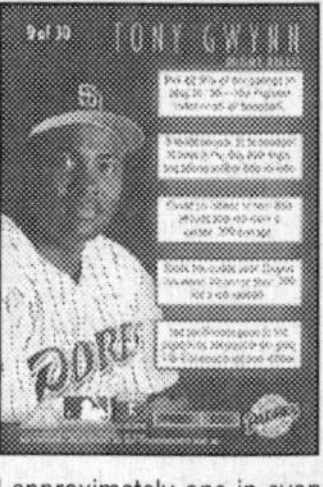

This 30-card set was inserted approximately one in every 15 packs. The fronts feature two player photos. The player's name is spelled vertically on the right while the words "Numbers Game" are printed against a gold-foil background. The backs contain five quick information bytes that feature that player's accomplishments. The cards are numbered as "X" of 30 in the upper left corner.

	MINT	NRMT
COMPLETE SET (30)	60.00	27.00
COMMON CARD (1-30)	.75	.35
☐ 1 Cal Ripken	8.00	3.60
☐ 2 Frank Thomas	8.00	3.60
☐ 3 Ken Griffey Jr.	10.00	4.50
☐ 4 Mike Piazza	6.00	2.70
☐ 5 Barry Bonds	2.50	1.10
☐ 6 Greg Maddux	6.00	2.70
☐ 7 Jeff Bagwell	4.00	1.80
☐ 8 Derek Bell	.75	.35
☐ 9 Tony Gwynn	4.00	1.80
☐ 10 Hideo Nomo	2.50	1.10
☐ 11 Raul Mondesi	1.25	.55
☐ 12 Manny Ramirez	1.50	.70

	MINT	NRMT
☐ 13 Albert Belle	2.50	1.10
☐ 14 Matt Williams	1.25	.55
☐ 15 Jim Edmonds	1.50	.70
☐ 16 Edgar Martinez	1.25	.55
☐ 17 Mo Vaughn	2.50	1.10
☐ 18 Reggie Sanders	.75	.35
☐ 19 Chipper Jones	6.00	2.70
☐ 20 Larry Walker	1.50	.70
☐ 21 Juan Gonzalez	5.00	2.20
☐ 22 Kenny Lofton	2.50	1.10
☐ 23 Don Mattingly	4.00	1.80
☐ 24 Ivan Rodriguez	2.50	1.10
☐ 25 Randy Johnson	1.50	.70
☐ 26 Derek Jeter	6.00	2.70
☐ 27 J.T. Snow	.75	.35
☐ 28 Will Clark	1.25	.55
☐ 29 Rafael Palmeiro	1.25	.55
☐ 30 Alex Rodriguez	8.00	3.60

1996 Score Power Pace

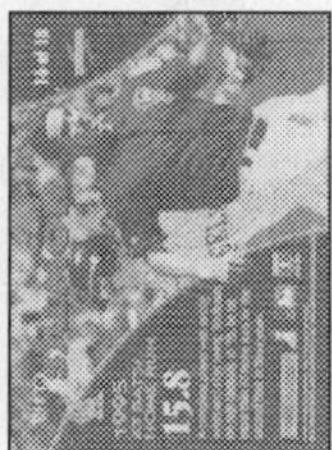

Randomly inserted in retail packs at a rate of one in 31, this 18-card set features homerun hitters. The fronts display color action player cutouts on a gold foil background. The backs carry another player photo with player information including how frequently he can be expected to hit a homerun based on his career at-bats.

	MINT	NRMT
COMPLETE SET (18)	90.00	40.00
COMMON CARD (1-18)	2.00	.90
☐ 1 Mark McGwire	10.00	4.50
☐ 2 Albert Belle	6.00	2.70
☐ 3 Jay Buhner	3.00	1.35
☐ 4 Frank Thomas	20.00	9.00
☐ 5 Matt Williams	3.00	1.35
☐ 6 Gary Sheffield	4.00	1.80
☐ 7 Mike Piazza	15.00	6.75
☐ 8 Larry Walker	4.00	1.80
☐ 9 Mo Vaughn	6.00	2.70
☐ 10 Rafael Palmeiro	3.00	1.35
☐ 11 Dante Bichette	2.50	1.10
☐ 12 Ken Griffey, Jr.	25.00	11.00
☐ 13 Barry Bonds	6.00	2.70
☐ 14 Manny Ramirez	4.00	1.80
☐ 15 Sammy Sosa	4.00	1.80
☐ 16 Tim Salmon	4.00	1.80
☐ 17 Dave Justice	4.00	1.80
☐ 18 Eric Karros	2.00	.90

1996 Score Reflextions

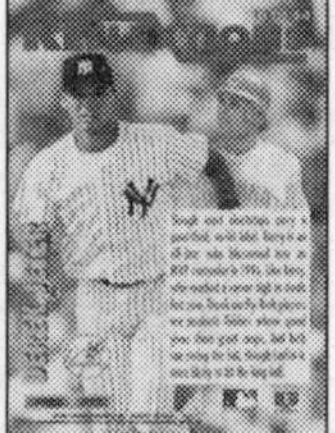

This 20-card set was randomly inserted approximately one in every 31 hobby packs. Two players per card are featured, a veteran player and a younger star playing the same position. These cards feature a mirror effect on the front.

	MINT	NRMT
COMPLETE SET (20)	120.00	55.00
COMMON CARD (1-20)	2.00	.90
☐ 1 Cal Ripken Chipper Jones	25.00	11.00
☐ 2 Ken Griffey Jr. Alex Rodriguez	30.00	13.50
☐ 3 Frank Thomas Mo Vaughn	20.00	9.00
☐ 4 Kenny Lofton Brian L.Hunter	6.00	2.70
☐ 5 Don Mattingly J.T.Snow	6.00	2.70
☐ 6 Manny Ramirez Raul Mondesi	4.00	1.80
☐ 7 Tony Gwynn Garret Anderson	10.00	4.50
☐ 8 Roberto Alomar Carlos Baerga	2.00	.90
☐ 9 Andre Dawson Larry Walker	4.00	1.80
☐ 10 Barry Larkin Derek Jeter	12.00	5.50
☐ 11 Barry Bonds Reggie Sanders	6.00	2.70
☐ 12 Mike Piazza Albert Belle	15.00	6.75
☐ 13 Wade Boggs Edgar Martinez	4.00	1.80
☐ 14 David Cone John Smoltz	2.00	.90
☐ 15 Will Clark Jeff Bagwell	10.00	4.50
☐ 16 Mark McGwire Cecil Fielder	10.00	4.50
☐ 17 Greg Maddux Mike Mussina	15.00	6.75
☐ 18 Randy Johnson Hideo Nomo	12.00	5.50
☐ 19 Jim Thome Dean Palmer	2.00	.90
☐ 20 Chuck Knoblauch Craig Biggio	5.00	2.20

1996 Score Titanic Taters

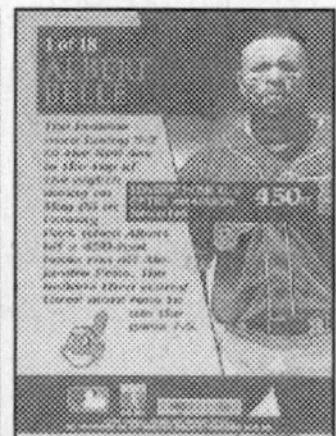

Randomly inserted in hobby packs at a rate of one in 31, this 18-card set features long home run hitters. The fronts display a color action player cutout on a gold foil background of a baseball park. The backs carry another player photo with information about the player's longest home run and the park where it was hit.

	MINT	NRMT
COMPLETE SET (18)	100.00	45.00
COMMON CARD (1-18)	2.00	.90
☐ 1 Albert Belle	6.00	2.70
☐ 2 Frank Thomas	20.00	9.00
☐ 3 Mo Vaughn	6.00	2.70
☐ 4 Ken Griffey Jr.	25.00	11.00
☐ 5 Matt Williams	3.00	1.35
☐ 6 Mark McGwire	10.00	4.50
☐ 7 Dante Bichette	2.50	1.10
☐ 8 Tim Salmon	4.00	1.80
☐ 9 Jeff Bagwell	10.00	4.50
☐ 10 Rafael Palmeiro	3.00	1.35
☐ 11 Mike Piazza	15.00	6.75
☐ 12 Cecil Fielder	2.00	.90
☐ 13 Larry Walker	4.00	1.80
☐ 14 Sammy Sosa	4.00	1.80
☐ 15 Manny Ramirez	4.00	1.80
☐ 16 Gary Sheffield	4.00	1.80
☐ 17 Barry Bonds	6.00	2.70
☐ 18 Jay Buhner	3.00	1.35

1997 Score

The 1997 Score set has a total of 550 cards. The 10-card Series 1 packs and the 12-card Series 2 packs carried a suggested retail price of $.99 each and were distributed exclusively to retail outlets. The fronts feature color player action photos in a white border. The backs carry player information and career statistics. The Hideki Irabu card (#551A and B) is shortprinted (about twice as tough to pull as a basic card). One final note on the Irabu card, in the retail packs and factory sets, the card text is in English. In the Hobby Reserve packs, text is in Japanese.

	MINT	NRMT
COMPLETE SET (551)	40.00	18.00
COMP.FACT.SET (551)	40.00	18.00

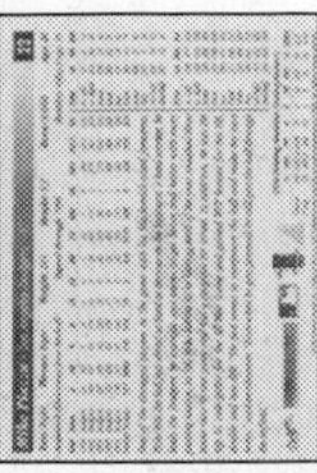

	MINT	NRMT
COMPLETE SERIES 1 (330)	15.00	6.75
COMPLETE SERIES 2 (221)	25.00	11.00
COMMON CARD (1-551)	.10	.05
COMP.SHOW.AP SET (551)	1800.00	825.00
COMP.SHOW.AP SER.1 (330)	1000.00	450.00
COMP.SHOW.AP SER.2 (221)	800.00	360.00
SHOW.AP (1-155)	3.00	1.25

SHOW.AP STARS: 15X TO 30X BASIC CARDS
SHOW.AP YOUNG STARS: 10X TO 20X BASIC CARDS
SHOW.AP ROOKIES: 5X TO 10X BASIC CARDS
SHOW.AP IRABU: 2X TO 4X BASIC CARDS

	MINT	NRMT
☐ 1 Jeff Bagwell	.75	.35
☐ 2 Mickey Tettleton	.10	.05
☐ 3 Johnny Damon	.10	.05
☐ 4 Jeff Conine	.20	.09
☐ 5 Bernie Williams	.40	.18
☐ 6 Will Clark	.30	.14
☐ 7 Ryan Klesko	.30	.14
☐ 8 Cecil Fielder	.20	.09
☐ 9 Paul Wilson	.10	.05
☐ 10 Gregg Jefferies	.20	.09
☐ 11 Chili Davis	.20	.09
☐ 12 Albert Belle	.50	.23
☐ 13 Ken Hill	.10	.05
☐ 14 Cliff Floyd	.10	.05
☐ 15 Jaime Navarro	.10	.05
☐ 16 Ismael Valdes	.20	.09
☐ 17 Jeff King	.10	.05
☐ 18 Chris Bosio	.10	.05
☐ 19 Reggie Sanders	.10	.05
☐ 20 Darren Daulton	.20	.09
☐ 21 Ken Caminiti	.40	.18
☐ 22 Mike Piazza	1.25	.55
☐ 23 Chad Mottola	.10	.05
☐ 24 Darin Erstad	.60	.25
☐ 25 Dante Bichette	.20	.09
☐ 26 Frank Thomas	1.50	.70
☐ 27 Ben McDonald	.10	.05
☐ 28 Raul Casanova	.10	.05
☐ 29 Kevin Ritz	.10	.05
☐ 30 Garret Anderson	.20	.09
☐ 31 Jason Kendall	.20	.09
☐ 32 Billy Wagner	.20	.09
☐ 33 Dave Justice	.40	.18
☐ 34 Marty Cordova	.20	.09
☐ 35 Derek Jeter	1.25	.55
☐ 36 Trevor Hoffman	.20	.09
☐ 37 Geronimo Berroa	.10	.05
☐ 38 Walt Weiss	.10	.05
☐ 39 Kirt Manwaring	.10	.05
☐ 40 Alex Gonzalez	.10	.05
☐ 41 Sean Berry	.10	.05
☐ 42 Kevin Appier	.20	.09
☐ 43 Rusty Greer	.20	.09
☐ 44 Pete Incaviglia	.10	.05
☐ 45 Rafael Palmeiro	.30	.14
☐ 46 Eddie Murray	.40	.18
☐ 47 Moises Alou	.20	.09
☐ 48 Mark Lewis	.10	.05
☐ 49 Hal Morris	.10	.05
☐ 50 Edgar Renteria	.20	.09
☐ 51 Rickey Henderson	.30	.14
☐ 52 Pat Listach	.10	.05
☐ 53 John Wasdin	.10	.05
☐ 54 James Baldwin	.10	.05
☐ 55 Brian Jordan	.20	.09
☐ 56 Edgar Martinez	.30	.14
☐ 57 Wil Cordero	.10	.05
☐ 58 Danny Tartabull	.10	.05
☐ 59 Keith Lockhart	.10	.05
☐ 60 Rico Brogna	.10	.05
☐ 61 Ricky Bottalico	.10	.05
☐ 62 Terry Pendleton	.10	.05
☐ 63 Bret Boone	.10	.05
☐ 64 Charlie Hayes	.10	.05
☐ 65 Marc Newfield	.10	.05
☐ 66 Sterling Hitchcock	.10	.05
☐ 67 Roberto Alomar	.40	.18
☐ 68 John Jaha	.10	.05
☐ 69 Greg Colbrunn	.10	.05
☐ 70 Sal Fasano	.10	.05
☐ 71 Brooks Kieschnick	.20	.09

☐ 72 Pedro Martinez .40 .18
☐ 73 Kevin Elster .10 .05
☐ 74 Ellis Burks .20 .09
☐ 75 Chuck Finley .10 .05
☐ 76 John Olerud .20 .09
☐ 77 Jay Bell .10 .05
☐ 78 Allen Watson .10 .05
☐ 79 Darryl Strawberry .20 .09
☐ 80 Orlando Miller .10 .05
☐ 81 Jose Herrera .10 .05
☐ 82 Andy Pettitte .40 .18
☐ 83 Juan Guzman .10 .05
☐ 84 Alan Benes .20 .09
☐ 85 Jack McDowell .10 .05
☐ 86 Ugueth Urbina .10 .05
☐ 87 Rocky Coppinger .20 .09
☐ 88 Jeff Cirillo .20 .09
☐ 89 Tom Glavine .20 .09
☐ 90 Robby Thompson .10 .05
☐ 91 Barry Bonds .50 .23
☐ 92 Carlos Delgado .20 .09
☐ 93 Mo Vaughn .50 .23
☐ 94 Ryne Sandberg .50 .23
☐ 95 Alex Rodriguez 1.50 .70
☐ 96 Brady Anderson .30 .14
☐ 97 Scott Brosius .10 .05
☐ 98 Dennis Eckersley .30 .14
☐ 99 Brian McRae .10 .05
☐ 100 Rey Ordonez .10 .05
☐ 101 John Valentin .10 .05
☐ 102 Brett Butler .20 .09
☐ 103 Eric Karros .20 .09
☐ 104 Harold Baines .10 .05
☐ 105 Javier Lopez .20 .09
☐ 106 Alan Trammell .30 .14
☐ 107 Jim Thome .40 .18
☐ 108 Frank Rodriguez .10 .05
☐ 109 Bernard Gilkey .10 .05
☐ 110 Reggie Jefferson .20 .09
☐ 111 Scott Stahoviak .10 .05
☐ 112 Steve Gibralter .10 .05
☐ 113 Todd Hollandsworth .20 .09
☐ 114 Ruben Rivera .20 .09
☐ 115 Dennis Martinez .20 .09
☐ 116 Mariano Rivera .20 .09
☐ 117 John Smoltz .20 .09
☐ 118 John Mabry .10 .05
☐ 119 Tom Gordon .10 .05
☐ 120 Alex Ochoa .10 .05
☐ 121 Jamey Wright .20 .09
☐ 122 Dave Nilsson .10 .05
☐ 123 Bobby Bonilla .20 .09
☐ 124 Al Leiter .10 .05
☐ 125 Rick Aguilera .10 .05
☐ 126 Jeff Brantley .10 .05
☐ 127 Kevin Brown .20 .09
☐ 128 George Arias .10 .05
☐ 129 Darren Oliver .10 .05
☐ 130 Bill Pulsipher .10 .05
☐ 131 Roberto Hernandez .10 .05
☐ 132 Delino DeShields .10 .05
☐ 133 Mark Grudzielanek .10 .05
☐ 134 John Wetteland .20 .09
☐ 135 Carlos Baerga .10 .05
☐ 136 Paul Sorrento .10 .05
☐ 137 Leo Gomez .10 .05
☐ 138 Andy Ashby .10 .05
☐ 139 Julio Franco .20 .09
☐ 140 Brian Hunter .10 .05
☐ 141 Jermaine Dye .10 .05
☐ 142 Tony Clark .40 .18
☐ 143 Ruben Sierra .10 .05
☐ 144 Donovan Osborne .10 .05
☐ 145 Mark McLemore .10 .05
☐ 146 Terry Steinbach .10 .05
☐ 147 Bob Wells .10 .05
☐ 148 Chan Ho Park .40 .18
☐ 149 Tim Salmon .40 .18
☐ 150 Paul O'Neill .20 .09
☐ 151 Cal Ripken 1.50 .70
☐ 152 Wally Joyner .10 .05
☐ 153 Omar Vizquel .20 .09
☐ 154 Mike Mussina .40 .18
☐ 155 Andres Galarraga .40 .18
☐ 156 Ken Griffey Jr. 2.00 .90
☐ 157 Kenny Lofton .50 .23
☐ 158 Ray Durham .10 .05
☐ 159 Hideo Nomo 1.00 .45
☐ 160 Ozzie Guillen .10 .05
☐ 161 Roger Pavlik .10 .05
☐ 162 Manny Ramirez .40 .18
☐ 163 Mark Lemke .10 .05
☐ 164 Mike Stanley .10 .05
☐ 165 Chuck Knoblauch .40 .18
☐ 166 Kimera Bartee .10 .05
☐ 167 Wade Boggs .40 .18
☐ 168 Jay Buhner .30 .14
☐ 169 Eric Young .10 .05
☐ 170 Jose Canseco .30 .14
☐ 171 Dwight Gooden .20 .09
☐ 172 Fred McGriff .30 .14
☐ 173 Sandy Alomar Jr. .20 .09
☐ 174 Andy Benes .10 .05
☐ 175 Dean Palmer .10 .05
☐ 176 Larry Walker .40 .18
☐ 177 Charles Nagy .20 .09
☐ 178 David Cone .20 .09
☐ 179 Mark Grace .30 .14
☐ 180 Robin Ventura .20 .09
☐ 181 Roger Clemens .75 .35
☐ 182 Bobby Witt .10 .05
☐ 183 Vinny Castilla .20 .09
☐ 184 Gary Sheffield .40 .18
☐ 185 Dan Wilson .10 .05
☐ 186 Roger Cedeno .10 .05
☐ 187 Mark McGwire .75 .35
☐ 188 Darren Bragg .10 .05
☐ 189 Quinton McCracken .10 .05
☐ 190 Randy Myers .10 .05
☐ 191 Jeromy Burnitz .20 .09
☐ 192 Randy Johnson .40 .18
☐ 193 Chipper Jones 1.25 .55
☐ 194 Greg Vaughn .10 .05
☐ 195 Travis Fryman .20 .09
☐ 196 Tim Naehring .10 .05
☐ 197 B.J. Surhoff .20 .09
☐ 198 Juan Gonzalez 1.00 .45
☐ 199 Terrell Wade .10 .05
☐ 200 Jeff Frye .10 .05
☐ 201 Joey Cora .20 .09
☐ 202 Raul Mondesi .30 .14
☐ 203 Ivan Rodriguez .50 .23
☐ 204 Armando Reynoso .10 .05
☐ 205 Jeffrey Hammonds .10 .05
☐ 206 Darren Dreifort .10 .05
☐ 207 Kevin Seitzer .10 .05
☐ 208 Tino Martinez .40 .18
☐ 209 Jim Bruske .10 .05
☐ 210 Jeff Suppan .20 .09
☐ 211 Mark Carreon .10 .05
☐ 212 Wilson Alvarez .20 .09
☐ 213 John Burkett .10 .05
☐ 214 Tony Phillips .10 .05
☐ 215 Greg Maddux 1.25 .55
☐ 216 Mark Whiten .10 .05
☐ 217 Curtis Pride .10 .05
☐ 218 Lyle Mouton .10 .05
☐ 219 Todd Hundley .20 .09
☐ 220 Greg Gagne .10 .05
☐ 221 Rich Amaral .10 .05
☐ 222 Tom Goodwin .10 .05
☐ 223 Chris Hoiles .10 .05
☐ 224 Jayhawk Owens .10 .05
☐ 225 Kenny Rogers .10 .05
☐ 226 Mike Greenwell .10 .05
☐ 227 Mark Wohlers .10 .05
☐ 228 Henry Rodriguez .10 .05
☐ 229 Robert Perez .10 .05
☐ 230 Jeff Kent .10 .05
☐ 231 Darryl Hamilton .10 .05
☐ 232 Alex Fernandez .20 .09
☐ 233 Ron Karkovice .10 .05
☐ 234 Jimmy Haynes .10 .05
☐ 235 Craig Biggio .30 .14
☐ 236 Ray Lankford .20 .09
☐ 237 Lance Johnson .10 .05
☐ 238 Matt Williams .30 .14
☐ 239 Chad Curtis .10 .05
☐ 240 Mark Thompson .10 .05
☐ 241 Jason Giambi .20 .09
☐ 242 Barry Larkin .30 .14
☐ 243 Paul Molitor .40 .18
☐ 244 Sammy Sosa .40 .18
☐ 245 Kevin Tapani .10 .05
☐ 246 Marquis Grissom .20 .09
☐ 247 Joe Carter .20 .09
☐ 248 Ramon Martinez .20 .09
☐ 249 Tony Gwynn 1.00 .45
☐ 250 Andy Fox .10 .05
☐ 251 Troy O'Leary .10 .05
☐ 252 Warren Newson .10 .05
☐ 253 Troy Percival .20 .09
☐ 254 Jamie Moyer .10 .05
☐ 255 Danny Graves .10 .05
☐ 256 David Wells .10 .05
☐ 257 Todd Zeile .10 .05
☐ 258 Raul Ibanez .10 .05
☐ 259 Tyler Houston .10 .05
☐ 260 LaTroy Hawkins .10 .05
☐ 261 Joey Hamilton .20 .09
☐ 262 Mike Sweeney .20 .09
☐ 263 Brant Brown .10 .05
☐ 264 Pat Hentgen .20 .09
☐ 265 Mark Johnson .10 .05
☐ 266 Robb Nen .10 .05
☐ 267 Justin Thompson .20 .09
☐ 268 Ron Gant .20 .09
☐ 269 Jeff D'Amico .20 .09
☐ 270 Shawn Estes .10 .05
☐ 271 Derek Bell .20 .09
☐ 272 Fernando Valenzuela .20 .09
☐ 273 Tom Pagnozzi .10 .05
☐ 274 John Burke .10 .05
☐ 275 Ed Sprague .10 .05
☐ 276 F.P. Santangelo .10 .05
☐ 277 Todd Greene .10 .05
☐ 278 Butch Huskey .10 .05
☐ 279 Steve Finley .20 .09
☐ 280 Eric Davis .10 .05
☐ 281 Shawn Green .20 .09
☐ 282 Al Martin .10 .05
☐ 283 Michael Tucker .10 .05
☐ 284 Shane Reynolds .10 .05
☐ 285 Matt Mieske .10 .05
☐ 286 Jose Rosado .30 .14
☐ 287 Mark Langston .10 .05
☐ 288 Ralph Milliard .10 .05
☐ 289 Mike Lansing .10 .05
☐ 290 Scott Servais .10 .05
☐ 291 Royce Clayton .10 .05
☐ 292 Mike Grace .10 .05
☐ 293 James Mouton .10 .05
☐ 294 Charles Johnson .20 .09
☐ 295 Gary Gaetti .20 .09
☐ 296 Kevin Mitchell .10 .05
☐ 297 Carlos Garcia .10 .05
☐ 298 Desi Relaford .10 .05
☐ 299 Jason Thompson .10 .05
☐ 300 Osvaldo Fernandez .10 .05
☐ 301 Fernando Vina .10 .05
☐ 302 Jose Offerman .10 .05
☐ 303 Yamil Benitez .10 .05
☐ 304 J.T. Snow .10 .05
☐ 305 Rafael Bournigal .10 .05
☐ 306 Jason Isringhausen .10 .05
☐ 307 Bobby Higginson .20 .09
☐ 308 Nerio Rodriguez .25 .11
☐ 309 Brian Giles .10 .05
☐ 310 Andruw Jones 1.00 .45
☐ 311 Tony Graffanino .10 .05
☐ 312 Arquimedez Pozo .10 .05
☐ 313 Jermaine Allensworth .10 .05
☐ 314 Jeff Darwin .10 .05
☐ 315 George Williams .10 .05
☐ 316 Karim Garcia .20 .09
☐ 317 Trey Beamon .10 .05
☐ 318 Mac Suzuki .20 .09
☐ 319 Robin Jennings .10 .05
☐ 320 Danny Patterson .10 .05
☐ 321 Damon Mashore .10 .05
☐ 322 Wendell Magee .10 .05
☐ 323 Dax Jones .10 .05
☐ 324 Kevin Brown .20 .09
☐ 325 Marvin Benard .10 .05
☐ 326 Mike Cameron .20 .09
☐ 327 Marcus Jensen .10 .05
☐ 328 Eddie Murray CL .40 .18
☐ 329 Paul Molitor CL .40 .18
☐ 330 Todd Hundley CL .20 .09
☐ 331 Norm Charlton .10 .05
☐ 332 Bruce Ruffin .10 .05
☐ 333 John Wetteland .20 .09
☐ 334 Marquis Grissom .20 .09
☐ 335 Sterling Hitchcock .10 .05
☐ 336 John Olerud .20 .09
☐ 337 David Wells .10 .05
☐ 338 Chili Davis .20 .09
☐ 339 Mark Lewis .10 .05
☐ 340 Kenny Lofton .50 .23
☐ 341 Alex Fernandez .20 .09
☐ 342 Ruben Sierra .10 .05
☐ 343 Delino DeShields .10 .05
☐ 344 John Wasdin .10 .05
☐ 345 Dennis Martinez .20 .09
☐ 346 Kevin Elster .10 .05
☐ 347 Bobby Bonilla .20 .09
☐ 348 Jaime Navarro .10 .05
☐ 349 Chad Curtis .10 .05
☐ 350 Terry Steinbach .20 .09
☐ 351 Ariel Prieto .10 .05
☐ 352 Jeff Kent .10 .05
☐ 353 Carlos Garcia .10 .05
☐ 354 Mark Whiten .10 .05
☐ 355 Todd Zeile .10 .05
☐ 356 Eric Davis .20 .09
☐ 357 Greg Colbrunn .10 .05
☐ 358 Moises Alou .20 .09
☐ 359 Allen Watson .10 .05
☐ 360 Jose Canseco .10 .05
☐ 361 Matt Williams .30 .14
☐ 362 Jeff King .10 .05

☐ 363 Darryl Hamilton	.10	.05
☐ 364 Mark Clark	.10	.05
☐ 365 J.T. Snow	.10	.05
☐ 366 Kevin Mitchell	.10	.05
☐ 367 Orlando Miller	.10	.05
☐ 368 Rico Brogna	.10	.05
☐ 369 Mike James	.10	.05
☐ 370 Brad Ausmus	.10	.05
☐ 371 Darryl Kile	.20	.09
☐ 372 Edgardo Alfonzo	.20	.09
☐ 373 Julian Tavarez	.10	.05
☐ 374 Darren Lewis	.10	.05
☐ 375 Steve Karsay	.10	.05
☐ 376 Lee Stevens	.10	.05
☐ 377 Albie Lopez	.10	.05
☐ 378 Orel Hershiser	.20	.09
☐ 379 Lee Smith	.10	.05
☐ 380 Rick Helling	.10	.05
☐ 381 Carlos Perez	.10	.05
☐ 382 Tony Tarasco	.10	.05
☐ 383 Melvin Nieves	.10	.05
☐ 384 Benji Gil	.10	.05
☐ 385 Devon White	.10	.05
☐ 386 Armando Benitez	.10	.05
☐ 387 Bill Swift	.10	.05
☐ 388 John Smiley	.10	.05
☐ 389 Midre Cummings	.10	.05
☐ 390 Tim Belcher	.10	.05
☐ 391 Tim Raines	.20	.09
☐ 392 Todd Worrell	.10	.05
☐ 393 Quilvio Veras	.10	.05
☐ 394 Matt Lawton	.10	.05
☐ 395 Aaron Sele	.10	.05
☐ 396 Bip Roberts	.10	.05
☐ 397 Denny Neagle	.20	.09
☐ 398 Tyler Green	.10	.05
☐ 399 Hipolito Pichardo	.10	.05
☐ 400 Scott Erickson	.10	.05
☐ 401 Bobby Jones	.10	.05
☐ 402 Jim Edmonds	.40	.18
☐ 403 Chad Ogea	.10	.05
☐ 404 Cal Eldred	.10	.05
☐ 405 Pat Listach	.10	.05
☐ 406 Todd Stottlemyre	.10	.05
☐ 407 Phil Nevin	.10	.05
☐ 408 Otis Nixon	.10	.05
☐ 409 Billy Ashley	.10	.05
☐ 410 Jimmy Key	.20	.09
☐ 411 Mike Timlin	.10	.05
☐ 412 Joe Vitiello	.10	.05
☐ 413 Rondell White	.20	.09
☐ 414 Jeff Fassero	.10	.05
☐ 415 Rex Hudler	.10	.05
☐ 416 Curt Schilling	.20	.09
☐ 417 Rich Becker	.10	.05
☐ 418 William Van Landingham	.10	.05
☐ 419 Chris Snopek	.10	.05
☐ 420 David Segui	.10	.05
☐ 421 Eddie Murray	.40	.18
☐ 422 Shane Andrews	.10	.05
☐ 423 Gary DiSarcina	.10	.05
☐ 424 Brian Hunter	.20	.09
☐ 425 Willie Greene	.20	.09
☐ 426 Felipe Crespo	.10	.05
☐ 427 Jason Bates	.10	.05
☐ 428 Albert Belle	.50	.23
☐ 429 Rey Sanchez	.10	.05
☐ 430 Roger Clemens	.75	.35
☐ 431 Deion Sanders	.40	.18
☐ 432 Ernie Young	.10	.05
☐ 433 Jay Bell	.10	.05
☐ 434 Jeff Blauser	.10	.05
☐ 435 Lenny Dykstra	.10	.05
☐ 436 Chuck Carr	.10	.05
☐ 437 Russ Davis	.10	.05
☐ 438 Carl Everett	.10	.05
☐ 439 Damion Easley	.10	.05
☐ 440 Pat Kelly	.10	.05
☐ 441 Pat Rapp	.10	.05
☐ 442 Dave Justice	.40	.18
☐ 443 Graeme Lloyd	.10	.05
☐ 444 Damon Buford	.10	.05
☐ 445 Jose Valentin	.10	.05
☐ 446 Jason Schmidt	.10	.05
☐ 447 Dave Martinez	.10	.05
☐ 448 Danny Tartabull	.10	.05
☐ 449 Jose Vizcaino	.10	.05
☐ 450 Steve Avery	.10	.05
☐ 451 Mike Devereaux	.10	.05
☐ 452 Jim Eisenreich	.20	.09
☐ 453 Mark Leiter	.10	.05
☐ 454 Roberto Kelly	.10	.05
☐ 455 Benito Santiago	.10	.05
☐ 456 Steve Trachsel	.10	.05
☐ 457 Gerald Williams	.10	.05
☐ 458 Pete Schourek	.10	.05
☐ 459 Esteban Loaiza	.10	.05
☐ 460 Mel Rojas	.10	.05
☐ 461 Tim Wakefield	.10	.05
☐ 462 Tony Fernandez	.10	.05
☐ 463 Doug Drabek	.10	.05
☐ 464 Joe Girardi	.10	.05
☐ 465 Mike Bordick	.10	.05
☐ 466 Jim Leyritz	.10	.05
☐ 467 Erik Hanson	.10	.05
☐ 468 Michael Tucker	.10	.05
☐ 469 Tony Womack	.30	.14
☐ 470 Doug Glanville	.10	.05
☐ 471 Rudy Pemberton	.10	.05
☐ 472 Keith Lockhart	.10	.05
☐ 473 Nomar Garciaparra	1.25	.55
☐ 474 Scott Rolen	1.00	.45
☐ 475 Jason Dickson	.10	.05
☐ 476 Glendon Rusch	.10	.05
☐ 477 Todd Walker	.10	.05
☐ 478 Dmitri Young	.20	.09
☐ 479 Rod Myers	.10	.05
☐ 480 Wilton Guerrero	.10	.05
☐ 481 Jorge Posada	.10	.05
☐ 482 Brant Brown	.10	.05
☐ 483 Bubba Trammell	.40	.18
☐ 484 Jose Guillen	.50	.23
☐ 485 Scott Spiezio	.10	.05
☐ 486 Bob Abreu	.40	.18
☐ 487 Chris Holt	.10	.05
☐ 488 Deivi Cruz	.25	.11
☐ 489 Vladimir Guerrero	.75	.35
☐ 490 Julio Santana	.10	.05
☐ 491 Ray Montgomery	.10	.05
☐ 492 Kevin Orie	.10	.05
☐ 493 Todd Hundley GY	.10	.05
☐ 494 Tim Salmon GY	.40	.18
☐ 495 Albert Belle GY	.40	.18
☐ 496 Manny Ramirez GY	.40	.18
☐ 497 Rafael Palmeiro GY	.30	.14
☐ 498 Juan Gonzalez GY	.50	.23
☐ 499 Ken Griffey Jr. GY	1.00	.45
☐ 500 Andruw Jones GY	.60	.25
☐ 501 Mike Piazza GY	.60	.25
☐ 502 Jeff Bagwell GY	.40	.18
☐ 503 Bernie Williams GY	.40	.18
☐ 504 Barry Bonds GY	.40	.18
☐ 505 Ken Caminiti GY	.40	.18
☐ 506 Darin Erstad GY	.40	.18
☐ 507 Alex Rodriguez GY	.75	.35
☐ 508 Frank Thomas GY	.75	.35
☐ 509 Chipper Jones GY	.60	.25
☐ 510 Mo Vaughn GY	.40	.18
☐ 511 Mark McGwire GY	.40	.18
☐ 512 Fred McGriff GY	.30	.14
☐ 513 Jay Buhner GY	.30	.14
☐ 514 Jim Thome GY	.40	.18
☐ 515 Gary Sheffield GY	.40	.18
☐ 516 Dean Palmer GY	.10	.05
☐ 517 Henry Rodriguez GY	.10	.05
☐ 518 Andy Pettitte RF	.40	.18
☐ 519 Mike Mussina RF	.40	.18
☐ 520 Greg Maddux RF	.60	.25
☐ 521 John Smoltz RF	.20	.09
☐ 522 Hideo Nomo RF	.50	.23
☐ 523 Troy Percival RF	.10	.05
☐ 524 John Wetteland RF	.10	.05
☐ 525 Roger Clemens RF	.40	.18
☐ 526 Charles Nagy RF	.10	.05
☐ 527 Mariano Rivera RF	.10	.05
☐ 528 Tom Glavine RF	.10	.05
☐ 529 Randy Johnson RF	.40	.18
☐ 530 Jason Isringhausen RF	.10	.05
☐ 531 Alex Fernandez RF	.10	.05
☐ 532 Kevin Brown RF	.10	.05
☐ 533 Chuck Knoblauch TG	.40	.18
☐ 534 Rusty Greer TG	.20	.09
☐ 535 Tony Gwynn TG	.50	.23
☐ 536 Ryan Klesko TG	.30	.14
☐ 537 Ryne Sandberg TG	.40	.18
☐ 538 Barry Larkin TG	.30	.14
☐ 539 Will Clark TG	.30	.14
☐ 540 Kenny Lofton TG	.40	.18
☐ 541 Paul Molitor TG	.40	.18
☐ 542 Roberto Alomar TG	.40	.18
☐ 543 Rey Ordonez TG	.10	.05
☐ 544 Jason Giambi TG	.10	.05
☐ 545 Derek Jeter TG	.60	.25
☐ 546 Cal Ripken TG	.75	.35
☐ 547 Ivan Rodriguez TG	.40	.18
☐ 548 Ken Griffey Jr. CL	1.00	.45
☐ 549 Frank Thomas CL	.75	.35
☐ 550 Mike Piazza CL	.60	.25
☐ 551A Hideki Irabu SP	10.00	4.50
☐ 551B Hideki Irabu Japanese SP	10.00	4.50

1997 Score Premium Stock

A special Premium Stock version of the base series one set was produced exclusively for hobby outlets. The cards parallel the regular issue set except for a grey border, thicker card stock and a prominent gold foil "Premium Stock" logo on front. The cards were distributed in Premium Stock hobby packs.

	MINT	NRMT
COMPLETE SET (551)	90.00	40.00
COMPLETE SERIES 1 (330)	40.00	18.00
COMPLETE SERIES 2 (221)	50.00	22.00
COMMON CARD (1-551)	.20	.09

*STARS: 1X TO 2X BASIC CARDS
*IRABU: .5X TO 1X BASIC IRABU

1997 Score Reserve Collection

Randomly inserted in second series hobby reserve packs only at a rate of one in 11, this set is parallel to the regular second series set. The cards are printed on thick 20 pt. foil card stock with screen printing for a raised ink effect. A large grey "Reserve Collection" logo is printed on each card back.

	MINT	NRMT
COMPLETE SERIES 2 (221)	600.00	275.00
COMMON CARD (301-551)	2.00	.90

*STARS: 10X TO 20X BASIC CARDS
*YOUNG STARS: 7.5X TO 15X BASIC CARDS
*ROOKIES: 4X TO 8X BASIC CARDS
*IRABU: .5X TO 1X BASIC IRABU

1997 Score Showcase Series

Randomly inserted in first series packs at a rate of 1:7 hobby, 1:2 jumbo, 1:4 magazine and 1:7 retail, and second series packs 1:5 hobby and 1:7 retail, cards from this set are silver-coated parallel versions of the regular Score set.

	MINT	NRMT
COMPLETE SET (551)	450.00	200.00
COMPLETE SERIES 1 (330)	250.00	110.00
COMPLETE SERIES 2 (221)	200.00	90.00
COMMON CARD (1-551)	.75	.35

*STARS: 4X TO 8X BASIC CARDS
*YOUNG STARS: 3X TO 6X BASIC CARDS
*ROOKIES: 2X TO 4X BASIC CARDS
*IRABU: .5X TO 1X BASIC IRABU

1997 Score All-Star Fanfest

This 20-card insert set features players that were involved in the 1996 All-Star game. The cards were available at a rate of 1:29 in special retail Score I boxes.

	MINT	NRMT
COMPLETE SET (20)	200.00	90.00
COMMON CARD (1-20)	2.00	.90
☐ 1 Frank Thomas	25.00	11.00
☐ 2 Jeff Bagwell	12.00	5.50
☐ 3 Chuck Knoblauch	6.00	2.70
☐ 4 Ryne Sandberg	7.50	3.40
☐ 5 Alex Rodriguez	25.00	11.00
☐ 6 Chipper Jones	18.00	8.00
☐ 7 Jim Thome	6.00	2.70
☐ 8 Ken Caminiti	6.00	2.70
☐ 9 Albert Belle	7.50	3.40
☐ 10 Tony Gwynn	15.00	6.75
☐ 11 Ken Griffey Jr.	30.00	13.50
☐ 12 Andruw Jones	12.00	5.50
☐ 13 Juan Gonzalez	15.00	6.75
☐ 14 Brian Jordan	2.00	.90
☐ 15 Ivan Rodriguez	6.00	2.70
☐ 16 Mike Piazza	18.00	8.00
☐ 17 Andy Pettitte	6.00	2.70
☐ 18 John Smoltz	3.00	1.35
☐ 19 John Wetteland	3.00	1.35
☐ 20 Mark Wohlers	3.00	1.35

1997 Score Blast Masters

Randomly inserted in second series packs at a rate of 1:35 (retail) and 1:23 (hobby reserve), this 18-card set features color player photos on a gold prismatic foil card.

	MINT	NRMT
COMPLETE SET (18)	150.00	70.00
COMMON CARD (1-18)	2.50	1.10

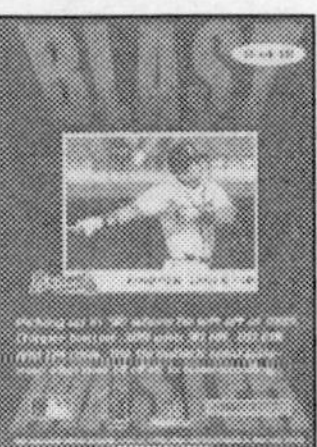

☐ 1 Mo Vaughn	6.00	2.70
☐ 2 Mark McGwire	10.00	4.50
☐ 3 Juan Gonzalez	12.00	5.50
☐ 4 Albert Belle	6.00	2.70
☐ 5 Barry Bonds	6.00	2.70
☐ 6 Ken Griffey Jr.	25.00	11.00
☐ 7 Andruw Jones	12.00	5.50
☐ 8 Chipper Jones	15.00	6.75
☐ 9 Mike Piazza	15.00	6.75
☐ 10 Jeff Bagwell	10.00	4.50
☐ 11 Dante Bichette	3.00	1.35
☐ 12 Alex Rodriguez	15.00	6.75
☐ 13 Gary Sheffield	4.00	1.80
☐ 14 Ken Caminiti	4.00	1.80
☐ 15 Sammy Sosa	4.00	1.80
☐ 16 Vladimir Guerrero	10.00	4.50
☐ 17 Brian Jordan	2.50	1.10
☐ 18 Tim Salmon	4.00	1.80

1997 Score Franchise

Randomly inserted in series one hobby packs only at a rate of one in 72, this nine-card set honors superstar players for their irreplaceable contribution to their team. The fronts display sepia player portraits on a white baseball replica background. The backs carry an action player photo with a sentence about the player which explains why he was selected for this set.

	MINT	NRMT
COMPLETE SET (9)	120.00	55.00
COMMON CARD (1-9)	4.00	1.80
COMP.GLOWING SET (9)	300.00	135.00
COMMON GLOWING (1-9)	12.00	5.50
*GLOWING: 1.25X TO 2X BASIC FRANCHISE		
☐ 1 Ken Griffey Jr.	30.00	13.50
☐ 2 John Smoltz	4.00	1.80
☐ 3 Cal Ripken	25.00	11.00
☐ 4 Chipper Jones	20.00	9.00
☐ 5 Mike Piazza	20.00	9.00
☐ 6 Albert Belle	8.00	3.60
☐ 7 Frank Thomas	25.00	11.00
☐ 8 Sammy Sosa	12.00	5.50
☐ 9 Roberto Alomar	6.00	2.70

1997 Score Heart of the Order

Randomly inserted in packs at a rate of 1:23 (retail) and 1:15 (hobby reserve), this 36-card set features color photos of players on six teams with a panorama of the stadium in the background. Each team's three cards form one collectible unit. Eighteen of these cards are found in retail packs, and eighteen in Hobby Reserve packs.

	MINT	NRMT
COMPLETE SET (36)	120.00	55.00
COMMON CARD (1-36)	1.50	.70
☐ 1 Will Clark	2.50	1.10
☐ 2 Ivan Rodriguez	5.00	2.20
☐ 3 Juan Gonzalez	10.00	4.50
☐ 4 Frank Thomas	15.00	6.75
☐ 5 Albert Belle	5.00	2.20
☐ 6 Robin Ventura	2.00	.90
☐ 7 Alex Rodriguez	12.00	5.50
☐ 8 Jay Buhner	2.50	1.10
☐ 9 Ken Griffey Jr.	20.00	9.00
☐ 10 Rafael Palmeiro	2.50	1.10
☐ 11 Roberto Alomar	4.00	1.80
☐ 12 Cal Ripken	15.00	6.75
☐ 13 Manny Ramirez	4.00	1.80
☐ 14 Matt Williams	2.50	1.10
☐ 15 Jim Thome	4.00	1.80
☐ 16 Derek Jeter	10.00	4.50
☐ 17 Wade Boggs	4.00	1.80
☐ 18 Bernie Williams	4.00	1.80
☐ 19 Chipper Jones	12.00	5.50
☐ 20 Andruw Jones	10.00	4.50
☐ 21 Ryan Klesko	2.50	1.10
☐ 22 Mike Piazza	12.00	5.50
☐ 23 Wilton Guerrero	1.50	.70
☐ 24 Raul Mondesi	2.50	1.10
☐ 25 Tony Gwynn	10.00	4.50
☐ 26 Greg Vaughn	1.50	.70
☐ 27 Ken Caminiti	4.00	1.80
☐ 28 Brian Jordan	1.50	.70
☐ 29 Ron Gant	2.00	.90
☐ 30 Dmitri Young	2.00	.90
☐ 31 Darin Erstad	6.00	2.70
☐ 32 Tim Salmon	4.00	1.80
☐ 33 Jim Edmonds	4.00	1.80
☐ 34 Chuck Knoblauch	4.00	1.80
☐ 35 Paul Molitor	4.00	1.80
☐ 36 Todd Walker	1.50	.70

1997 Score Highlight Zone

Randomly inserted in series one hobby packs only at a rate of one in 35, this 18-card set honors those mega-stars who have the incredible ability to consistently make the highlight films. The set is printed on thicker card stock with special foil stamping and a dot matrix holographic background.

	MINT	NRMT
COMPLETE SET (18)	200.00	90.00
COMMON CARD (1-18)	4.00	1.80
☐ 1 Frank Thomas	25.00	11.00
☐ 2 Ken Griffey Jr.	30.00	13.50
☐ 3 Mo Vaughn	8.00	3.60
☐ 4 Albert Belle	8.00	3.60
☐ 5 Mike Piazza	20.00	9.00
☐ 6 Barry Bonds	8.00	3.60
☐ 7 Greg Maddux	20.00	9.00
☐ 8 Sammy Sosa	6.00	2.70
☐ 9 Jeff Bagwell	12.00	5.50
☐ 10 Alex Rodriguez	20.00	9.00
☐ 11 Chipper Jones	20.00	9.00
☐ 12 Brady Anderson	5.00	2.20
☐ 13 Ozzie Smith	8.00	3.60
☐ 14 Edgar Martinez	5.00	2.20
☐ 15 Cal Ripken	25.00	11.00
☐ 16 Ryan Klesko	4.00	1.80
☐ 17 Randy Johnson	5.00	2.20
☐ 18 Eddie Murray	8.00	3.60

1997 Score Pitcher Perfect

Randomly inserted in series one packs at a rate of one in 23, this 15-card set features players photographed by Randy Johnson in unique poses and foil stamping. The backs carry player information.

	MINT	NRMT
COMPLETE SET (15)	70.00	32.00
COMMON CARD (1-15)	1.50	.70
☐ 1 Cal Ripken	12.00	5.50
☐ 2 Alex Rodriguez	12.00	5.50
☐ 3 Alex Rodriguez Cal Ripken	15.00	6.75
☐ 4 Edgar Martinez	2.00	.90
☐ 5 Ivan Rodriguez	4.00	1.80
☐ 6 Mark McGwire	5.00	2.20
☐ 7 Tim Salmon	2.50	1.10
☐ 8 Chili Davis	1.50	.70
☐ 9 Joe Carter	1.50	.70
☐ 10 Frank Thomas	12.00	5.50
☐ 11 Will Clark	2.00	.90
☐ 12 Mo Vaughn	4.00	1.80
☐ 13 Wade Boggs	2.50	1.10
☐ 14 Ken Griffey Jr.	15.00	6.75
☐ 15 Randy Johnson	2.50	1.10

1997 Score Stand and Deliver

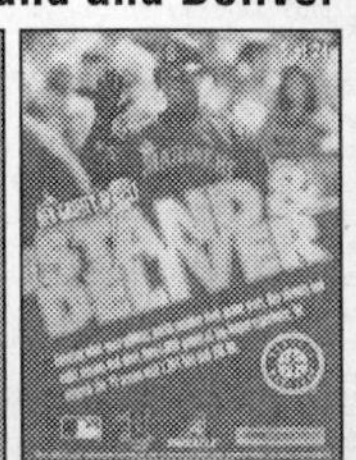

Randomly inserted in series two packs at a rate of 1:71 (retail) and 1:47 (hobby reserve), this 24-card set features color player photos printed on silver foil card stock. The set is broken into six separate 4-card groupings. Groups contain players from the following teams: 1-4 (Braves), 5-8 (Mariners), 9-12 (Yankees), 13-16 (Dodgers), 17-20 (Indians) and 21-24 (Wild Card). The four players featured within the Wild Card group are from "lesser" teams not given a shot at winning the World Series. Each of these cards, unlike cards 1-20, has a "Wild Card" logo stamped on front. Collectors were then supposed to gather up the particular group that won the 1997 World Series, in this case - the Florida Marlins. Since none of the featured teams won, the 4-card Wild Card group was designated as the winner. The winning cards could then be mailed into Pinnacle for a special gold upgrade version of the set, framed in glass.

	MINT	NRMT
COMPLETE SET (24)	350.00	160.00
COMMON CARD (1-24)	4.00	1.80
☐ 1 Andruw Jones	20.00	9.00
☐ 2 Greg Maddux	30.00	13.50
☐ 3 Chipper Jones	30.00	13.50
☐ 4 John Smoltz	6.00	2.70
☐ 5 Ken Griffey Jr.	50.00	22.00
☐ 6 Alex Rodriguez	30.00	13.50
☐ 7 Jay Buhner	8.00	3.60
☐ 8 Randy Johnson	10.00	4.50
☐ 9 Derek Jeter	25.00	11.00
☐ 10 Andy Pettitte		
☐ 11 Bernie Williams	10.00	4.50
☐ 12 Mariano Rivera	6.00	2.70
☐ 13 Mike Piazza	30.00	13.50
☐ 14 Hideo Nomo	25.00	11.00
☐ 15 Raul Mondesi	8.00	3.60
☐ 16 Todd Hollandsworth	4.00	1.80
☐ 17 Manny Ramirez		
☐ 18 Jim Thome		
☐ 19 Dave Justice	10.00	4.50
☐ 20 Matt Williams	8.00	3.60
☐ 21 Juan Gonzalez W	25.00	11.00
☐ 22 Jeff Bagwell W	20.00	9.00
☐ 23 Cal Ripken W	40.00	18.00
☐ 24 Frank Thomas W	40.00	18.00

1997 Score Stellar Season

Randomly inserted in series one pre-priced magazine packs only at a rate of one in 35, this 18-card set features players who had a star season. The cards are printed using dot matrix holographic printing.

	MINT	NRMT
COMPLETE SET (18)	80.00	36.00
COMMON CARD (1-18)	2.00	.90
☐ 1 Juan Gonzalez	10.00	4.50
☐ 2 Chuck Knoblauch	4.00	1.80
☐ 3 Jeff Bagwell	8.00	3.60
☐ 4 John Smoltz	2.50	1.10
☐ 5 Mark McGwire	8.00	3.60
☐ 6 Ken Griffey Jr.	20.00	9.00

	MINT	NRMT
☐ 7 Frank Thomas	15.00	6.75
☐ 8 Alex Rodriguez	12.00	5.50
☐ 9 Mike Piazza	12.00	5.50
☐ 10 Albert Belle	5.00	2.20
☐ 11 Roberto Alomar	4.00	1.80
☐ 12 Sammy Sosa	4.00	1.80
☐ 13 Mo Vaughn	5.00	2.20
☐ 14 Brady Anderson	3.00	1.35
☐ 15 Henry Rodriguez	2.00	.90
☐ 16 Eric Young	2.00	.90
☐ 17 Gary Sheffield	4.00	1.80
☐ 18 Ryan Klesko	3.00	1.35

1997 Score Titanic Taters

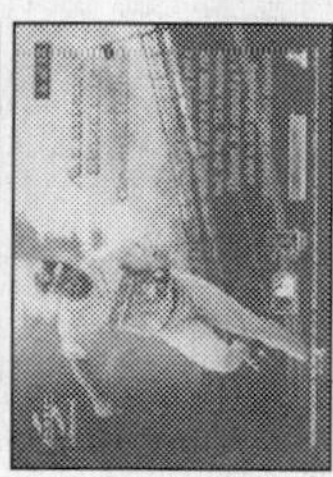

Randomly inserted in series one retail packs only at a rate of one in 35, this 18-card set honors the long-ball ability of some of the league's top sluggers and uses dot matrix holographic printing.

	MINT	NRMT
COMPLETE SET (18)	125.00	55.00
COMMON CARD (1-18)	2.50	1.10
☐ 1 Mark McGwire	10.00	4.50
☐ 2 Mike Piazza	15.00	6.75
☐ 3 Ken Griffey Jr.	25.00	11.00
☐ 4 Juan Gonzalez	12.00	5.50
☐ 5 Frank Thomas	20.00	9.00
☐ 6 Albert Belle	5.00	2.20
☐ 7 Sammy Sosa	4.00	1.80
☐ 8 Jeff Bagwell	10.00	4.50
☐ 9 Todd Hundley	2.50	1.10
☐ 10 Ryan Klesko	3.50	1.55
☐ 11 Brady Anderson	3.50	1.55
☐ 12 Mo Vaughn	6.00	2.70
☐ 13 Jay Buhner	3.50	1.55
☐ 14 Chipper Jones	15.00	6.75
☐ 15 Barry Bonds	6.00	2.70
☐ 16 Gary Sheffield	4.00	1.80
☐ 17 Alex Rodriguez	15.00	6.75
☐ 18 Cecil Fielder	2.50	1.10

1997 Score Braves

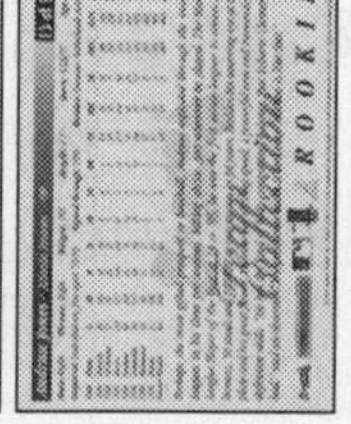

This 15-card set of the Atlanta Braves was issued in five-card packs with a suggested retail of $1.30 each. The fronts feature color player photos with special team specific color foil stamping. The backs carry player information. Only 100 cases were made for each team. Platinum parallel cards were inserted at a rate of 1:6, Premier parallel cards at a rate of 1:31.

	MINT	NRMT
COMPLETE SET (15)	10.00	4.50
COMMON CARD (1-15)	.10	.05
*PLATINUM: 4X BASIC CARDS		
*PREMIER: 20X BASIC CARDS		
☐ 1 Ryan Klesko	.50	.23
☐ 2 Dave Justice	.75	.35
☐ 3 Terry Pendleton	.10	.05
☐ 4 Tom Glavine	.50	.23
☐ 5 Javier Lopez	.25	.11
☐ 6 John Smoltz	.25	.11
☐ 7 Jermaine Dye	.10	.05
☐ 8 Mark Lemke	.10	.05
☐ 9 Fred McGriff	.50	.23
☐ 10 Chipper Jones	3.00	1.35
☐ 11 Terrell Wade	.10	.05
☐ 12 Greg Maddux	3.00	1.35
☐ 13 Mark Wohlers	.25	.11
☐ 14 Marquis Grissom	.25	.11
☐ 15 Andruw Jones	2.00	.90

1997 Score Dodgers

This 15-card set of the Los Angeles Dodgers was issued in five-card packs with a suggested retail price of $1.30 each. The fronts feature color player photos with special team specific color foil stamping. The backs carry player information. Only 100 cases were made for each team. Platinum parallel cards were inserted at a rate of 1:6, Premier parallel cards at a rate of 1:31.

	MINT	NRMT
COMPLETE SET (15)	5.00	2.20
COMMON CARD (1-15)	.10	.05
*PLATINUM: 4X BASIC CARDS		
*PREMIER: 20X BASIC CARDS		
☐ 1 Ismael Valdes	.10	.05
☐ 2 Mike Piazza	2.50	1.10
☐ 3 Todd Hollandsworth	.25	.11
☐ 4 Delino DeShields	.25	.11
☐ 5 Chan Ho Park	1.50	.70
☐ 6 Roger Cedeno	.10	.05
☐ 7 Raul Mondesi	.75	.35
☐ 8 Darren Dreifort	.10	.05
☐ 9 Jim Bruske	.10	.05
☐ 10 Greg Gagne	.10	.05
☐ 11 Chad Curtis	.10	.05
☐ 12 Ramon Martinez	.25	.11
☐ 13 Brett Butler	.25	.11
☐ 14 Eric Karros	.25	.11
☐ 15 Hideo Nomo	2.00	.90

1997 Score Indians

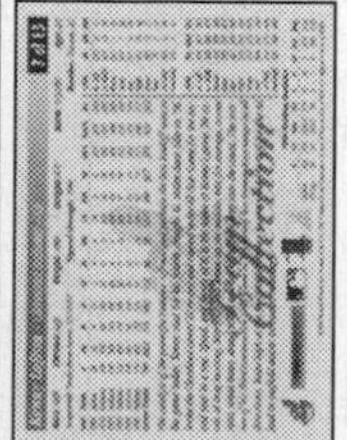

This 15-card set of the Cleveland Indians was issued in five-card packs with a suggested retail price of $1.30 each. The fronts feature color player photos with special team specific color foil stamping. The backs carry player information. Only 100 cases were made for each team. Platinum parallel cards were inserted at a rate of 1:6, Premier parallel cards at a rate of 1:31.

	MINT	NRMT
COMPLETE SET (15)	6.00	2.70
COMMON CARD (1-15)	.10	.05
*PLATINUM: 4X BASIC CARDS		
*PREMIER: 20X BASIC CARDS		
☐ 1 Albert Belle	1.50	.70
☐ 2 Jack McDowell	.10	.05
☐ 3 Jim Thome	1.50	.70
☐ 4 Dennis Martinez	.25	.11
☐ 5 Julio Franco	.25	.11
☐ 6 Omar Vizquel	.75	.35
☐ 7 Kenny Lofton	1.50	.70
☐ 8 Manny Ramirez	1.00	.45
☐ 9 Sandy Alomar Jr.	.50	.23
☐ 10 Charles Nagy	.25	.11
☐ 11 Kevin Seitzer	.10	.05
☐ 12 Mark Carreon	.10	.05
☐ 13 Jeff Kent	.25	.11
☐ 14 Danny Graves	.10	.05
☐ 15 Brian Giles	.10	.05

1997 Score Indians Update

This 15 card set, which is similar in design to the 1997 Score Indians set features some changes from the earlier Indians set. The cards were issued in seven card packs with a suggested retail price of $1.30. An added feature of these packs was that passes to All-Star fanfest were randomly included in the packs. A parallel Tribe collection card was included one every six packs.

	MINT	NRMT
COMPLETE SET (15)	5.00	2.20
COMMON CARD (1-15)	.10	.05
*TRIBE COLLECTION: 4X BASIC CARDS	.10	.05
☐ 1 Matt Williams	1.00	.45
☐ 2 Jack McDowell	.10	.05
☐ 3 Jim Thome	1.25	.55
☐ 4 Chad Ogea	.10	.05
☐ 5 Julio Franco	.25	.11
☐ 6 Omar Vizquel	.75	.35
☐ 7 Kenny Lofton	1.25	.55
☐ 8 Manny Ramirez	1.25	.55
☐ 9 Sandy Alomar Jr	.50	.23
☐ 10 Charles Nagy	.25	.11
☐ 11 Kevin Seitzer	.10	.05
☐ 12 Orel Hershiser	.25	.11
☐ 13 Paul Assenmacher	.10	.05
☐ 14 Eric Plunk	.10	.05
☐ 15 Brian Giles	.10	.05

1997 Score Mariners

This 15-card set of the Seattle Mariners was issued in five-card packs with a suggested retail price of $1.30 each. The fronts feature color player photos with special team specific color foil stamping. The backs carry player information. Only 100 cases were made for each team. Platinum parallel cards were inserted at a rate of 1:6, Premier parallel cards at a rate of 1:31.

	MINT	NRMT
COMPLETE SET (15)	8.00	3.60
COMMON CARD (1-15)	.10	.05
*PLATINUM: 4X BASIC CARDS		
*PREMIER: 20X BASIC CARDS		
☐ 1 Chris Bosio	.10	.05
☐ 2 Edgar Martinez	.50	.23
☐ 3 Alex Rodriguez	3.00	1.35
☐ 4 Paul Sorrento	.10	.05
☐ 5 Bob Wells	.10	.05
☐ 6 Ken Griffey Jr.	4.00	1.80
☐ 7 Jay Buhner	.75	.35
☐ 8 Dan Wilson	.25	.11
☐ 9 Randy Johnson	1.00	.45
☐ 10 Joey Cora	.50	.23

☐ 11 Mark Whiten	.10	.05
☐ 12 Rich Amaral	.10	.05
☐ 13 Raul Ibanez	.10	.05
☐ 14 Jamie Moyer	.10	.05
☐ 15 Mac Suzuki	.10	.05

1997 Score Orioles

This 15-card set of the Baltimore Orioles was issued in five-card packs with a suggested retail price of $1.30 each. The fronts feature color player photos with special team specific color foil stamping. The backs carry player information. Only 100 cases were made for each team. Platinum parallel cards were inserted at a rate of 1:6, Premier parallel cards at a rate of 1:31.

	MINT	NRMT
COMPLETE SET (15)	8.00	3.60
COMMON CARD (1-15)	.10	.05
*PLATINUM: 4X BASIC CARDS		
*PREMIER: 20X BASIC CARDS		

☐ 1 Rafael Palmeiro	.75	.35
☐ 2 Eddie Murray	1.00	.45
☐ 3 Roberto Alomar	1.00	.45
☐ 4 Rocky Coppinger	.10	.05
☐ 5 Brady Anderson	.75	.35
☐ 6 Bobby Bonilla	.25	.11
☐ 7 Cal Ripken	4.00	1.80
☐ 8 Mike Mussina	1.50	.70
☐ 9 Nerio Rodriguez	.10	.05
☐ 10 Randy Myers	.25	.11
☐ 11 B.J. Surhoff	.25	.11
☐ 12 Jeffrey Hammonds	.25	.11
☐ 13 Chris Hoiles	.25	.11
☐ 14 Jimmy Haynes	.10	.05
☐ 15 David Wells	.10	.05

1997 Score Rangers

This 15-card set of the Texas Rangers was issued in five-card packs with a suggested retail price of $1.30 each. The fronts feature color player photos with special team specific color foil stamping. The backs carry player information. Only 100 cases were made for each team. Platinum parallel cards were inserted at a rate of 1:6, Premier parallel cards at a rate of 1:31.

	MINT	NRMT
COMPLETE SET (15)	5.00	2.20
COMMON CARD (1-15)	.10	.05
*PLATINUM: 4X BASIC CARDS		
*PREMIER: 20X BASIC CARDS		

☐ 1 Mickey Tettleton	.25	.11
☐ 2 Will Clark	1.00	.45
☐ 3 Ken Hill	.10	.05
☐ 4 Rusty Greer	1.25	.55
☐ 5 Kevin Elster	.10	.05
☐ 6 Darren Oliver	.25	.11
☐ 7 Mark McLemore	.10	.05
☐ 8 Roger Pavlik	.10	.05
☐ 9 Dean Palmer	.25	.11
☐ 10 Bobby Witt	.10	.05
☐ 11 Juan Gonzalez	3.00	1.35
☐ 12 Ivan Rodriguez	1.50	.70
☐ 13 Darryl Hamilton	.10	.05
☐ 14 John Burkett	.10	.05
☐ 15 Warren Newson	.10	.05

1997 Score Red Sox

This 15-card set of the Boston Red Sox was issued in five-card packs with a suggested retail price of $1.30 each. The fronts feature color player photos with special team specific color foil stamping. The backs carry player information. Only 100 cases were made for each team. Platinum parallel cards were inserted at a rate of 1:6, Premier parallel cards at a rate of 1:31.

	MINT	NRMT
COMPLETE SET (15)	5.00	2.20
COMMON CARD (1-15)	.10	.05

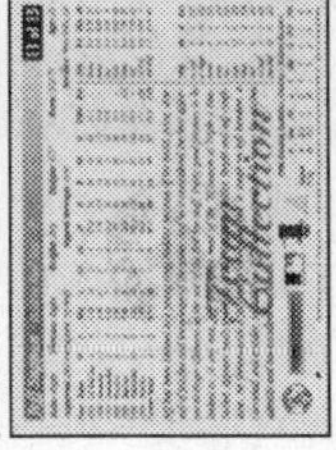

☐ 1 Wil Cordero	.10	.05
☐ 2 Mo Vaughn	2.00	.90
☐ 3 John Valentin	.25	.11
☐ 4 Reggie Jefferson	.10	.05
☐ 5 Tom Gordon	.10	.05
☐ 6 Mike Stanley	.10	.05
☐ 7 Jose Canseco	.75	.35
☐ 8 Roger Clemens	2.00	.90
☐ 9 Darren Bragg	.10	.05
☐ 10 Jeff Frye	.10	.05
☐ 11 Jeff Suppan	.25	.11
☐ 12 Mike Greenwell	.10	.05
☐ 13 Arquimedez Pozo	.10	.05
☐ 14 Tim Naehring	.25	.11
☐ 15 Troy O'Leary	.10	.05

1997 Score Rockies

This 15-card set of the Colorado Rockies was issued in five-card packs with a suggested retail price of $1.30 each. The fronts feature color player photos with special team specific color foil stamping. The backs carry player information. Only 100 cases were made for each team. Platinum parallel cards were inserted at a rate of 1:6, Premier parallel cards at a rate of 1:31.

	MINT	NRMT
COMPLETE SET (15)	5.00	2.20
COMMON CARD (1-15)	.10	.05
*PLATINUM: 4X BASIC CARDS		
*PREMIER: 20X BASIC CARDS		

☐ 1 Dante Bichette	1.00	.45
☐ 2 Kevin Ritz	.10	.05
☐ 3 Walt Weiss	.10	.05
☐ 4 Ellis Burks	.75	.35
☐ 5 Jamey Wright	.25	.11
☐ 6 Andres Galarraga	1.50	.70
☐ 7 Eric Young	.25	.11
☐ 8 Larry Walker	1.50	.70
☐ 9 Vinny Castilla	.75	.35
☐ 10 Quinton McCracken	.10	.05
☐ 11 Armando Reynoso	.10	.05
☐ 12 Jayhawk Owens	.10	.05
☐ 13 Mark Thompson	.10	.05
☐ 14 Bruce Ruffin	.10	.05
☐ 15 John Burke	.10	.05

1997 Score White Sox

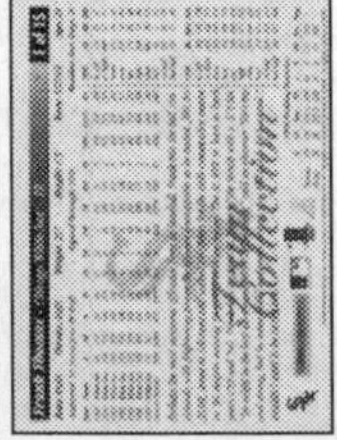

This 15-card set of the Chicago White Sox was issued in five-card packs with a suggested retail price of $1.30 each. The fronts feature color player photos with special team specific color foil stamping. The backs carry player information. Only 100 cases were made for each team. Platinum parallel cards were inserted at a rate of 1:6, Premier parallel cards at a rate of 1:31.

	MINT	NRMT
COMPLETE SET (15)	5.00	2.20
COMMON CARD (1-15)	.10	.05
*PLATINUM: 4X BASIC CARDS	.10	.05
*PREMIER: 20X BASIC CARDS	.10	.05

☐ 1 Frank Thomas	3.50	1.55
☐ 2 James Baldwin	.10	.05
☐ 3 Danny Tartabull	.10	.05
☐ 4 Jeff Darwin	.10	.05
☐ 5 Harold Baines	.50	.23
☐ 6 Roberto Hernandez	.25	.11
☐ 7 Ray Durham	.25	.11
☐ 8 Robin Ventura	.75	.35
☐ 9 Wilson Alvarez	.10	.05
☐ 10 Lyle Mouton	.10	.05
☐ 11 Alex Fernandez	.25	.11
☐ 12 Ron Karkovice	.10	.05
☐ 13 Kevin Tapani	.10	.05
☐ 14 Tony Phillips	.10	.05
☐ 15 Mike Cameron	1.00	.45

1997 Score Yankees

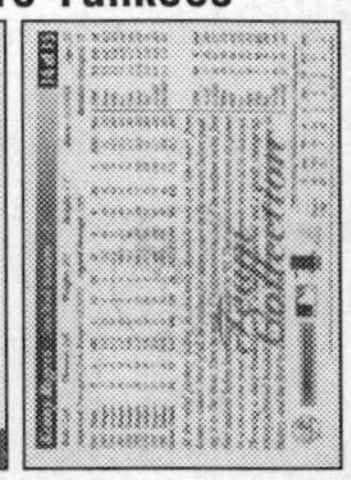

This 15-card set of the New York Yankees was issued in five-card packs with a suggested retail price of $1.30 each. The fronts feature color player photos with special team specific color foil stamping. The backs carry player information. Only 100 cases were made for each team. Platinum parallel cards were inserted at a rate of 1:6, Premier parallel cards at a rate of 1:31.

	MINT	NRMT
COMPLETE SET (15)	8.00	3.60
COMMON CARD (1-15)	.10	.05
*PLATINUM: 4X BASIC CARDS		
*PREMIER: 20X BASIC CARDS		

☐ 1 Bernie Williams	1.50	.70
☐ 2 Cecil Fielder	.25	.11
☐ 3 Derek Jeter	3.00	1.35
☐ 4 Darryl Strawberry	.25	.11
☐ 5 Andy Pettitte	1.50	.70
☐ 6 Ruben Rivera	.25	.11
☐ 7 Mariano Rivera	.75	.35
☐ 8 John Wetteland	.50	.23
☐ 9 Paul O'Neill	.10	.05
☐ 10 Wade Boggs	.75	.35
☐ 11 Dwight Gooden	.25	.11
☐ 12 David Cone	.50	.23
☐ 13 Tino Martinez	1.00	.45
☐ 14 Kenny Rogers	.10	.05
☐ 15 Andy Fox	.10	.05

1998 Score

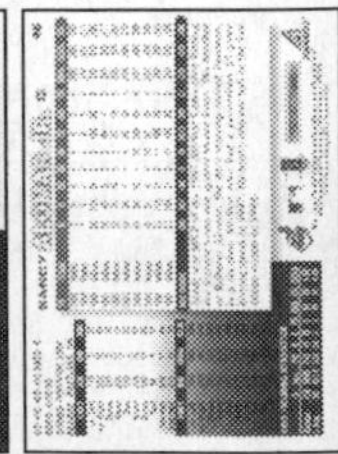

This 270-card set was distributed in 10-card packs exclusively to retail outlets with a suggested retail price of $.99. The fronts feature color player photos in a thin white border. The backs carry player information and statistics.

	MINT	NRMT
COMPLETE SET (270)	20.00	9.00
COMMON CARD (1-270)	.10	.05

☐ 1 Andruw Jones	.75	.35
☐ 2 Dan Wilson	.10	.05
☐ 3 Hideo Nomo	1.00	.45
☐ 4 Chuck Carr	.10	.05

☐ 5 Barry Bonds .50 .23
☐ 6 Jack McDowell .10 .05
☐ 7 Albert Belle .50 .23
☐ 8 Francisco Cordova .10 .05
☐ 9 Greg Maddux 1.25 .55
☐ 10 Alex Rodriguez 1.25 .55
☐ 11 Steve Avery .10 .05
☐ 12 Chuck McElroy .10 .05
☐ 13 Larry Walker .40 .18
☐ 14 Hideki Irabu .30 .14
☐ 15 Roberto Alomar .40 .18
☐ 16 Neifi Perez .10 .05
☐ 17 Jim Thome .40 .18
☐ 18 Rickey Henderson .30 .14
☐ 19 Andres Galarraga .40 .18
☐ 20 Jeff Fassero .10 .05
☐ 21 Kevin Young .10 .05
☐ 22 Derek Jeter 1.00 .45
☐ 23 Andy Benes .10 .05
☐ 24 Mike Piazza 1.25 .55
☐ 25 Todd Stottlemyre .10 .05
☐ 26 Michael Tucker .10 .05
☐ 27 Denny Neagle .10 .05
☐ 28 Javier Lopez .20 .09
☐ 29 Aaron Sele .10 .05
☐ 30 Ryan Klesko .30 .14
☐ 31 Dennis Eckersley .30 .14
☐ 32 Quinton McCracken .10 .05
☐ 33 Brian Anderson .10 .05
☐ 34 Ken Griffey Jr. 2.00 .90
☐ 35 Shawn Estes .10 .05
☐ 36 Tim Wakefield .10 .05
☐ 37 Jimmy Key .20 .09
☐ 38 Jeff Bagwell .75 .35
☐ 39 Edgardo Alfonzo .20 .09
☐ 40 Mike Cameron .20 .09
☐ 41 Mark McGwire 1.00 .45
☐ 42 Tino Martinez .40 .18
☐ 43 Cal Ripken 1.50 .70
☐ 44 Curtis Goodwin .10 .05
☐ 45 Bobby Ayala .10 .05
☐ 46 Sandy Alomar Jr. .20 .09
☐ 47 Bobby Jones .10 .05
☐ 48 Omar Vizquel .20 .09
☐ 49 Roger Clemens .75 .35
☐ 50 Tony Gwynn 1.00 .45
☐ 51 Chipper Jones 1.25 .55
☐ 52 Ron Coomer .10 .05
☐ 53 Dmitri Young .10 .05
☐ 54 Brian Giles .10 .05
☐ 55 Steve Finley .20 .09
☐ 56 David Cone .20 .09
☐ 57 Andy Pettitte .40 .18
☐ 58 Wilton Guerrero .10 .05
☐ 59 Deion Sanders .40 .18
☐ 60 Carlos Delgado .10 .05
☐ 61 Jason Giambi .10 .05
☐ 62 Ozzie Guillen .10 .05
☐ 63 Jay Bell .10 .05
☐ 64 Barry Larkin .30 .14
☐ 65 Sammy Sosa .40 .18
☐ 66 Bernie Williams .40 .18
☐ 67 Terry Steinbach .10 .05
☐ 68 Scott Rolen 1.00 .45
☐ 69 Melvin Nieves .10 .05
☐ 70 Craig Biggio .30 .14
☐ 71 Todd Greene .20 .09
☐ 72 Greg Gagne .10 .05
☐ 73 Shigetoshi Hasegawa .20 .09
☐ 74 Mark McLemore .10 .05
☐ 75 Darren Bragg .10 .05
☐ 76 Brett Butler .20 .09
☐ 77 Ron Gant .20 .09
☐ 78 Mike Difelice .10 .05
☐ 79 Charles Nagy .10 .05
☐ 80 Scott Hatteberg .10 .05
☐ 81 Brady Anderson .30 .14
☐ 82 Jay Buhner .30 .14
☐ 83 Todd Hollandsworth .10 .05
☐ 84 Geronimo Berroa .10 .05
☐ 85 Jeff Suppan .10 .05
☐ 86 Pedro Martinez .40 .18
☐ 87 Roger Cedeno .10 .05
☐ 88 Ivan Rodriguez .50 .23
☐ 89 Jaime Navarro .10 .05
☐ 90 Chris Hoiles .10 .05
☐ 91 Nomar Garciaparra 1.25 .55
☐ 92 Rafael Palmeiro .30 .14
☐ 93 Darin Erstad .50 .23
☐ 94 Kenny Lofton .50 .23
☐ 95 Mike Timlin .10 .05
☐ 96 Chris Clemons .10 .05
☐ 97 Vinny Castilla .20 .09
☐ 98 Charlie Hayes .10 .05
☐ 99 Lyle Mouton .10 .05
☐ 100 Jason Dickson .10 .05
☐ 101 Justin Thompson .10 .05
☐ 102 Pat Kelly .10 .05
☐ 103 Chan Ho Park .40 .18
☐ 104 Ray Lankford .10 .05
☐ 105 Frank Thomas 1.50 .70
☐ 106 Jermaine Allensworth .10 .05
☐ 107 Doug Drabek .10 .05
☐ 108 Todd Hundley .10 .05
☐ 109 Carl Everett .10 .05
☐ 110 Edgar Martinez .30 .14
☐ 111 Robin Ventura .20 .09
☐ 112 John Wetteland .10 .05
☐ 113 Mariano Rivera .20 .09
☐ 114 Jose Rosado .10 .05
☐ 115 Ken Caminiti .40 .18
☐ 116 Paul O'Neill .20 .09
☐ 117 Tim Salmon .40 .18
☐ 118 Eduardo Perez .10 .05
☐ 119 Mike Jackson .10 .05
☐ 120 John Smoltz .20 .09
☐ 121 Brant Brown .10 .05
☐ 122 John Mabry .10 .05
☐ 123 Chuck Knoblauch .40 .18
☐ 124 Reggie Sanders .10 .05
☐ 125 Ken Hill .10 .05
☐ 126 Mike Mussina .40 .18
☐ 127 Chad Curtis .10 .05
☐ 128 Todd Worrell .10 .05
☐ 129 Chris Widger .10 .05
☐ 130 Damon Mashore .10 .05
☐ 131 Kevin Brown .10 .05
☐ 132 Bip Roberts .10 .05
☐ 133 Tim Naehring .10 .05
☐ 134 Dave Martinez .10 .05
☐ 135 Jeff Blauser .10 .05
☐ 136 Dave Justice .30 .14
☐ 137 Dave Hollins .10 .05
☐ 138 Pat Hentgen .20 .09
☐ 139 Darren Daulton .10 .05
☐ 140 Ramon Martinez .10 .05
☐ 141 Raul Casanova .10 .05
☐ 142 Tom Glavine .20 .09
☐ 143 J.T. Snow .20 .09
☐ 144 Tony Graffanino .10 .05
☐ 145 Randy Johnson .40 .18
☐ 146 Orlando Merced .10 .05
☐ 147 Jeff Juden .10 .05
☐ 148 Darryl Kile .20 .09
☐ 149 Ray Durham .10 .05
☐ 150 Alex Fernandez .10 .05
☐ 151 Joey Cora .20 .09
☐ 152 Royce Clayton .10 .05
☐ 153 Randy Myers .10 .05
☐ 154 Charles Johnson .20 .09
☐ 155 Alan Benes .10 .05
☐ 156 Mike Bordick .10 .05
☐ 157 Heathcliff Slocumb .10 .05
☐ 158 Roger Bailey .10 .05
☐ 159 Reggie Jefferson .20 .09
☐ 160 Ricky Bottalico .10 .05
☐ 161 Scott Erickson .10 .05
☐ 162 Matt Williams .30 .14
☐ 163 Robb Nen .10 .05
☐ 164 Matt Stairs .10 .05
☐ 165 Ismael Valdes .10 .05
☐ 166 Lee Stevens .10 .05
☐ 167 Gary DiSarcina .10 .05
☐ 168 Brad Radke .20 .09
☐ 169 Mike Lansing .10 .05
☐ 170 Armando Benitez .10 .05
☐ 171 Mike James .10 .05
☐ 172 Russ Davis .10 .05
☐ 173 Lance Johnson .10 .05
☐ 174 Joey Hamilton .10 .05
☐ 175 John Valentin .10 .05
☐ 176 David Segui .10 .05
☐ 177 David Wells .10 .05
☐ 178 Delino DeShields .10 .05
☐ 179 Eric Karros .10 .05
☐ 180 Jim Leyritz .10 .05
☐ 181 Raul Mondesi .10 .05
☐ 182 Travis Fryman .10 .05
☐ 183 Todd Zeile .10 .05
☐ 184 Brian Jordan .10 .05
☐ 185 Rey Ordonez .10 .05
☐ 186 Jim Edmonds .40 .18
☐ 187 Terrell Wade .10 .05
☐ 188 Marquis Grissom .20 .09
☐ 189 Chris Snopek .10 .05
☐ 190 Shane Reynolds .10 .05
☐ 191 Jeff Frye .10 .05
☐ 192 Paul Sorrento .10 .05
☐ 193 James Baldwin .10 .05
☐ 194 Brian McRae .10 .05
☐ 195 Fred McGriff .30 .14
☐ 196 Troy Percival .10 .05
☐ 197 Rich Amaral .10 .05
☐ 198 Juan Guzman .10 .05
☐ 199 Cecil Fielder .20 .09
☐ 200 Willie Blair .10 .05
☐ 201 Chili Davis .20 .09
☐ 202 Gary Gaetti .20 .09
☐ 203 B.J. Surhoff .20 .09
☐ 204 Steve Cooke .10 .05
☐ 205 Chuck Finley .10 .05
☐ 206 Jeff Kent .10 .05
☐ 207 Ben McDonald .10 .05
☐ 208 Jeffrey Hammonds .20 .09
☐ 209 Tom Goodwin .10 .05
☐ 210 Billy Ashley .10 .05
☐ 211 Wil Cordero .10 .05
☐ 212 Shawon Dunston .10 .05
☐ 213 Tony Phillips .10 .05
☐ 214 Jamie Moyer .10 .05
☐ 215 John Jaha .10 .05
☐ 216 Troy O'Leary .10 .05
☐ 217 Brad Ausmus .10 .05
☐ 218 Garret Anderson .20 .09
☐ 219 Wilson Alvarez .10 .05
☐ 220 Kent Mercker .10 .05
☐ 221 Wade Boggs .40 .18
☐ 222 Mark Wohlers .20 .09
☐ 223 Kevin Appier .10 .05
☐ 224 Tony Fernandez .10 .05
☐ 225 Ugueth Urbina .10 .05
☐ 226 Gregg Jefferies .10 .05
☐ 227 Mo Vaughn .50 .23
☐ 228 Arthur Rhodes .10 .05
☐ 229 Jorge Fabregas .10 .05
☐ 230 Mark Gardner .10 .05
☐ 231 Shane Mack .10 .05
☐ 232 Jorge Posada .10 .05
☐ 233 Jose Cruz Jr. 1.50 .70
☐ 234 Paul Konerko .60 .25
☐ 235 Derrek Lee .20 .09
☐ 236 Steve Woodard .10 .05
☐ 237 Todd Dunwoody .20 .09
☐ 238 Fernando Tatis .40 .18
☐ 239 Jacob Cruz .10 .05
☐ 240 Pokey Reese .10 .05
☐ 241 Mark Kotsay .40 .18
☐ 242 Matt Morris .10 .05
☐ 243 Antone Williamson .10 .05
☐ 244 Ben Grieve .75 .35
☐ 245 Ryan McGuire .10 .05
☐ 246 Lou Collier .10 .05
☐ 247 Shannon Stewart .20 .09
☐ 248 Brett Tomko .20 .09
☐ 249 Bobby Estalella .10 .05
☐ 250 Livan Hernandez .30 .14
☐ 251 Todd Helton .50 .23
☐ 252 Jaret Wright 1.00 .45
☐ 253 Darryl Hamilton IM .10 .05
☐ 254 Stan Javier IM .10 .05
☐ 255 Glenallen Hill IM .10 .05
☐ 256 Mark Gardner IM .10 .05
☐ 257 Cal Ripken IM .75 .35
☐ 258 Mike Mussina IM .40 .18
☐ 259 Mike Piazza IM .60 .25
☐ 260 Sammy Sosa IM .40 .18
☐ 261 Todd Hundley IM .10 .05
☐ 262 Eric Karros IM .20 .09
☐ 263 Denny Neagle IM .10 .05
☐ 264 Jeromy Burnitz IM .10 .05
☐ 265 Greg Maddux IM .60 .25
☐ 266 Tony Clark IM .40 .18
☐ 267 Vladimir Guerrero IM .40 .18
☐ 268 Cal Ripken Jr. CL UER .75 .35
☐ 269 Ken Griffey Jr. CL 1.00 .45
☐ 270 Mark McGwire CL .40 .18

1998 Score Artist's Proofs

Randomly inserted in packs at the rate of one in 35, this 160-card set is a partial parallel to the base set and features color player photos printed on full prismatic foil with the "Artist Proof" stamp on the fronts.

	MINT	NRMT
COMPLETE SET (160)	400.00	180.00
COMMON CARD (1-160)	2.00	.90

*STARS: 10X TO 20X BASIC CARDS ..
*YOUNG STARS: 7.5X TO 15X BASIC CARDS

1998 Score Showcase Series

Randomly inserted in packs at the rate of one in seven, this 160-card set is an all silver-foil partial parallel rendition of the base set.

	MINT	NRMT
COMPLETE SET (160)	100.00	45.00
COMMON CARD (1-160)	.50	.23

*STARS: 2.5X TO 5X BASIC CARDS ...
*YOUNG STARS: 2X TO 4X BASIC CARDS

1998 Score All Score Team

Randomly inserted in packs at the rate of one in 35, this 20-card set features color player images on a metallic foil background. The backs carry a small player head photo with information stating why the player was selected to this appear in this set.

	MINT	NRMT
COMPLETE SET (20)	120.00	55.00
COMMON CARD (1-20)	1.50	.70
☐ 1 Mike Piazza	12.00	5.50
☐ 2 Ivan Rodriguez	5.00	2.20
☐ 3 Frank Thomas	15.00	6.75
☐ 4 Mark McGwire	10.00	4.50
☐ 5 Ryne Sandberg	5.00	2.20
☐ 6 Roberto Alomar	4.00	1.80
☐ 7 Cal Ripken	15.00	6.75
☐ 8 Barry Larkin	2.50	1.10
☐ 9 Paul Molitor	4.00	1.80
☐ 10 Travis Fryman	1.50	.70
☐ 11 Kirby Puckett	8.00	3.60
☐ 12 Tony Gwynn	10.00	4.50
☐ 13 Ken Griffey Jr.	20.00	9.00
☐ 14 Juan Gonzalez	10.00	4.50
☐ 15 Barry Bonds	5.00	2.20
☐ 16 Andruw Jones	6.00	2.70
☐ 17 Roger Clemens	8.00	3.60
☐ 18 Randy Johnson	4.00	1.80
☐ 19 Greg Maddux	12.00	5.50
☐ 20 Dennis Eckersley	1.50	.70

1998 Score All-Score Team Gold Jones Autograph

This special autographed card was created as a prize for Pinnacle's 1998 "Score with Score" hobby shop promotion. Dealers that ordered 1998 Score 1 baseball direct from Pinnacle or through one of their distributors were automatically entered into Pinnacle's hobby shop locator program. In December of 1997, all eligible shops were mailed a "Score with Score" contest ballot box and collector entry forms. Over the next several months, store customers could then fill out and submit forms. In the Spring of 1998, 600 lucky collectors were randomly selected winners. 100 people won actual Interleague game-used baseballs and 500 people won this special Andruw Jones autographed All-Score Team Gold card. The card is easy to differentiate from the more common All-Score Team inserts by it's bold gold (rather than silver) foil front and Jones' black ink signature.

	MINT	NRMT
COMPLETE SET (1)	100.00	45.00
COMMON CARD	100.00	45.00
☐ 1 Andruw Jones Gold AU	100.00	45.00

1998 Score Complete Players

Randomly inserted in packs at the rate of one in 23, this 30-card set features three photos of each of the ten listed players with full holographic foil stamping.

	MINT	NRMT
COMPLETE SET (30)	200.00	90.00
COMMON CARD (1A-10C)	3.00	1.35
☐ 1A Ken Griffey Jr.	15.00	6.75
☐ 1B Ken Griffey Jr.	15.00	6.75
☐ 1C Ken Griffey Jr.	15.00	6.75
☐ 2A Mark McGwire	8.00	3.60
☐ 2B Mark McGwire	8.00	3.60
☐ 2C Mark McGwire	8.00	3.60
☐ 3A Derek Jeter	8.00	3.60
☐ 3B Derek Jeter	8.00	3.60
☐ 3C Derek Jeter	8.00	3.60
☐ 4A Cal Ripken	12.00	5.50
☐ 4B Cal Ripken Jr.	12.00	5.50
☐ 4C Cal Ripken Jr.	12.00	5.50
☐ 5A Mike Piazza	10.00	4.50
☐ 5B Mike Piazza	10.00	4.50
☐ 5C Mike Piazza	10.00	4.50
☐ 6A Darin Erstad	3.00	1.35
☐ 6B Darin Erstad	3.00	1.35
☐ 6C Darin Erstad	3.00	1.35
☐ 7A Frank Thomas	12.00	5.50
☐ 7B Frank Thomas	12.00	5.50
☐ 7C Frank Thomas	12.00	5.50
☐ 8A Andruw Jones	5.00	2.20
☐ 8B Andruw Jones	6.00	2.70
☐ 8C Andruw Jones	6.00	2.70
☐ 9A Nomar Garciaparra	8.00	3.60
☐ 9B Nomar Garciaparra	8.00	3.60
☐ 9C Nomar Garciaparra	8.00	3.60
☐ 10A Manny Ramirez	3.00	1.35
☐ 10B Manny Ramirez	3.00	1.35
☐ 10C Manny Ramirez	3.00	1.35

1998 Score Complete Players Gold

These cards which parallel the regular Complete Player insert set were randomly inserted into the various 1998 Score Team Sets. The reason they are referred to as gold is that the fronts of the cards have a gold sheen to them.

	MINT	NRMT
COMPLETE SET (30)	200.00	90.00
COMMON CARD (1A-10C)	3.00	1.35
*SAME PRICE AS BASIC CARDS		

1998 Score Epix

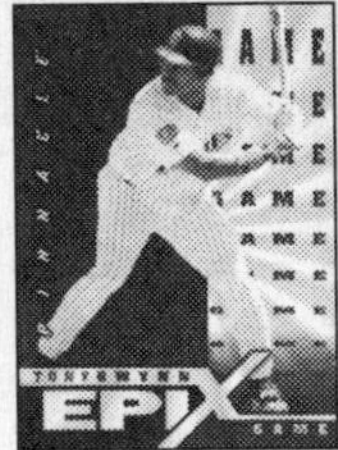

Randomly inserted in Score packs at the rate of one in 61, this 24-card set features color photos of top players' most memorable games, plays, seasons and moments on Dot Matrix Hologram cards. Orange, Purple, and Emerald versions of this set were also produced. To obtain all the cards for each player in this fractured insert set, the collector had to open not only Score packs, but also Pinnacle, Pinnacle Certified and Zenith packs.

	MINT	NRMT
COMMON CARD (E1-E24)	6.00	2.70
*PURPLE CARDS: .75X TO 1.5X ORANGE		
*EMERALD CARDS: 1.5X TO 3X ORANGE		
☐ E1 Ken Griffey Jr. PLAY	30.00	13.50
☐ E2 Juan Gonzalez PLAY	15.00	6.75
☐ E3 Jeff Bagwell PLAY	12.00	5.50
☐ E4 Ivan Rodriguez PLAY	8.00	3.60
☐ E5 Nomar Garciaparra PLAY	15.00	6.75
☐ E6 Ryne Sandberg PLAY	8.00	3.60
☐ E7 Frank Thomas GAME	40.00	18.00
☐ E8 Derek Jeter GAME	25.00	11.00
☐ E9 Tony Gwynn GAME	25.00	11.00
☐ E10 Albert Belle GAME	12.00	5.50
☐ E11 Scott Rolen GAME	20.00	9.00
☐ E12 Barry Larkin GAME	6.00	2.70
☐ E13 Alex Rodriguez SEAS	60.00	27.00
☐ E14 Cal Ripken Jr. SEAS	80.00	36.00
☐ E15 Chipper Jones SEAS	60.00	27.00
☐ E16 Roger Clemens SEAS	40.00	18.00
☐ E17 Mo Vaughn SEAS	25.00	11.00
☐ E18 Mark McGwire SEAS	40.00	18.00
☐ E19 Mike Piazza MOM	100.00	45.00
☐ E20 Andruw Jones MOM	60.00	27.00
☐ E21 Greg Maddux MOM	100.00	45.00
☐ E22 Barry Bonds MOM	40.00	18.00
☐ E23 Paul Molitor MOM	30.00	13.50
☐ E24 Eddie Murray MOM	30.00	13.50

1998 Score Angels

This 15-card set was issued in special retail packs and features color photos of the Anaheim Angels team. The backs carry player information. A special platinum parallel set was also issued and randomly inserted in packs.

	MINT	NRMT
COMPLETE SET (15)	5.00	2.20
COMMON CARD (1-15)	.10	.05
*PLATINUM: 4X BASIC CARDS		
☐ 1 Rickey Henderson	.75	.35
☐ 2 Todd Greene	.25	.11
☐ 3 Shigetoshi Hasegawa	.25	.11
☐ 4 Darin Erstad	.75	.35
☐ 5 Jason Dickson	.25	.11
☐ 6 Tim Salmon	.75	.35
☐ 7 Ken Hill	.10	.05
☐ 8 Dave Hollins	.10	.05
☐ 9 Gary DiSarcina	.10	.05
☐ 10 Mike James	.10	.05
☐ 11 Jim Edmonds	.75	.35
☐ 12 Troy Percival	.25	.11
☐ 13 Chuck Finley	.25	.11
☐ 14 Tony Phillips	.10	.05
☐ 15 Garret Anderson	.50	.23

1998 Score Braves

This 15-card set was issued in special retail packs and features color photos of the Atlanta Braves team. The backs carry player information. A special platinum parallel set was also issued and randomly inserted in packs.

	MINT	NRMT
COMPLETE SET (15)	8.00	3.60
COMMON CARD (1-15)	.10	.05
*PLATINUM: 4X BASIC CARDS		
☐ 1 Andruw Jones	1.50	.70
☐ 2 Greg Maddux	2.50	1.10
☐ 3 Michael Tucker	.25	.11
☐ 4 Denny Neagle	.25	.11
☐ 5 Javier Lopez	.25	.11
☐ 6 Ryan Klesko	.50	.23
☐ 7 Chipper Jones	2.00	.90
☐ 8 Kenny Lofton	1.00	.45
☐ 9 John Smoltz	.25	.11
☐ 10 Jeff Blauser	.10	.05
☐ 11 Tom Glavine	.25	.11
☐ 12 Tony Graffanino	.10	.05
☐ 13 Terrell Wade	.10	.05
☐ 14 Fred McGriff	.50	.23
☐ 15 Mark Wohlers	.25	.11

1998 Score Cardinals

This 15-card set was issued in special retail packs and features color photos of the St. Louis Cardinals team. The backs carry player information. A special platinum parallel set was also issued and randomly inserted in packs.

	MINT	NRMT
COMPLETE SET (15)	4.00	1.80
COMMON CARD (1-15)	.10	.05
*PLATINUM: 4X BASIC CARDS		
☐ 1 Andy Benes	.10	.05
☐ 2 Todd Stottlemyre	.10	.05
☐ 3 Dennis Eckersley	.50	.23
☐ 4 Mark McGwire	1.50	.70
☐ 5 Dmitri Young	.25	.11
☐ 6 Ron Gant	.25	.11
☐ 7 Mike Difelice	.10	.05
☐ 8 Ray Lankford	.50	.23
☐ 9 John Mabry	.10	.05
☐ 10 Royce Clayton	.10	.05
☐ 11 Alan Benes	.25	.11
☐ 12 Delino DeShields	.10	.05
☐ 13 Brian Jordan	.25	.11
☐ 14 Gary Gaetti	.25	.11
☐ 15 Matt Morris	.25	.11

1998 Score Dodgers

This 15-card set was issued in special retail packs and features color photos of the Los Angeles Dodgers team. The backs carry player information. A special platinum parallel set was also issued and randomly inserted in packs.

	MINT	NRMT
COMPLETE SET (15)	7.00	3.10
COMMON CARD (1-15)	.10	.05
*PLATINUM: 4X BASIC CARDS		
☐ 1 Hideo Nomo	2.00	.90
☐ 2 Mike Piazza	2.50	1.10
☐ 3 Wilton Guerrero	.10	.05
☐ 4 Greg Gagne	.10	.05
☐ 5 Brett Butler	.25	.11
☐ 6 Todd Hollandsworth	.25	.11
☐ 7 Roger Cedeno	.10	.05
☐ 8 Chan Ho Park	.75	.35
☐ 9 Todd Worrell	.25	.11
☐ 10 Ramon Martinez	.25	.11
☐ 11 Ismael Valdes	.25	.11
☐ 12 Eric Karros	.25	.11
☐ 13 Raul Mondesi	.50	.23

	MINT	NRMT
☐ 14 Todd Zeile	.25	.11
☐ 15 Billy Ashley	.10	.05

1998 Score Indians

This 15-card set was issued in special retail packs and features color photos of the Cleveland Indians team. The backs carry player information. A special platinum parallel set was also issued and randomly inserted in packs.

	MINT	NRMT
COMPLETE SET (15)	5.00	2.20
COMMON CARD (1-15)	.10	.05
*PLATINUM: 4X BASIC CARDS		
☐ 1 Jack McDowell	.10	.05
☐ 2 Jim Thome	.75	.35
☐ 3 Brian Anderson	.10	.05
☐ 4 Sandy Alomar Jr.	.25	.11
☐ 5 Omar Vizquel	.50	.23
☐ 6 Brian Giles	.10	.05
☐ 7 Charles Nagy	.10	.05
☐ 8 Mike Jackson	.10	.05
☐ 9 David Justice	.75	.35
☐ 10 Jeff Juden	.10	.05
☐ 11 Matt Williams	.50	.23
☐ 12 Marquis Grissom	.25	.11
☐ 13 Tony Fernandez	.10	.05
☐ 14 Bartolo Colon	.25	.11
☐ 15 Jaret Wright	1.50	.70

1998 Score Mariners

This 15-card set was issued in special retail packs and features color photos of the Seattle Mariners team. The backs carry player information. A special platinum parallel set was also issued and randomly inserted in packs.

	MINT	NRMT
COMPLETE SET (15)	8.00	3.60
COMMON CARD (1-15)	.10	.05
*PLATINUM: 4X BASIC CARDS		
☐ 1 Dan Wilson	.25	.11
☐ 2 Alex Rodriguez	2.50	1.10
☐ 3 Jeff Fassero	.10	.05
☐ 4 Ken Griffey Jr.	4.00	1.80
☐ 5 Bobby Ayala	.10	.05
☐ 6 Jay Buhner	.50	.23
☐ 7 Mike Timlin	.10	.05
☐ 8 Edgar Martinez	.50	.23
☐ 9 Randy Johnson	.75	.35
☐ 10 Joey Cora	.25	.11
☐ 11 Heathcliff Slocumb	.10	.05
☐ 12 Russ Davis	.10	.05
☐ 13 Paul Sorrento	.10	.05
☐ 14 Rich Amaral	.10	.05
☐ 15 Jamie Moyer	.10	.05

1998 Score Orioles

This 15-card set was issued in special retail packs and features color photos of the Baltimore Orioles team. The backs carry player information. A special platinum parallel set was also issued and randomly inserted in packs.

	MINT	NRMT
COMPLETE SET (15)	6.00	2.70
COMMON CARD (1-15)	.10	.05
*PLATINUM: 4X BASIC CARDS		
☐ 1 Roberto Alomar	.75	.35
☐ 2 Jimmy Key	.25	.11
☐ 3 Cal Ripken Jr.	3.00	1.35
☐ 4 Brady Anderson	.50	.23
☐ 5 Geronimo Berroa	.10	.05
☐ 6 Chris Hoiles	.10	.05
☐ 7 Rafael Palmeiro	.50	.23
☐ 8 Mike Mussina	.75	.35
☐ 9 Randy Myers	.25	.11
☐ 10 Mike Bordick	.10	.05
☐ 11 Scott Erickson	.25	.11
☐ 12 Armando Benitez	.25	.11
☐ 13 B.J. Surhoff	.10	.05
☐ 14 Jeffrey Hammonds	.25	.11
☐ 15 Arthur Rhodes	.10	.05

1998 Score Red Sox

This 15-card set was issued in special retail packs and features color photos of the Boston Red Sox team. The backs carry player information. A special platinum parallel set was also issued and randomly inserted in packs.

	MINT	NRMT
COMPLETE SET (15)	4.00	1.80
COMMON CARD (1-15)	.10	.05
*PLATINUM: 4X BASIC CARDS		
☐ 1 Steve Avery	.10	.05
☐ 2 Aaron Sele	.10	.05
☐ 3 Tim Wakefield	.10	.05
☐ 4 Darren Bragg	.10	.05
☐ 5 Scott Hatteberg	.10	.05
☐ 6 Jeff Suppan	.10	.05
☐ 7 Nomar Garciaparra	2.50	1.10
☐ 8 Tim Naehring	.10	.05
☐ 9 Reggie Jefferson	.25	.11
☐ 10 John Valentin	.25	.11
☐ 11 Jeff Frye	.10	.05
☐ 12 Wil Cordero	.10	.05
☐ 13 Troy O'Leary	.10	.05
☐ 14 Mo Vaughn	1.00	.45
☐ 15 Shane Mack	.10	.05

1998 Score White Sox

This 15-card set was issued in special retail packs and features color photos of the Chicago White Sox team. The backs carry player information. A special platinum parallel set was also issued and randomly inserted in packs.

	MINT	NRMT
COMPLETE SET (15)	5.00	2.20
COMMON CARD (1-15)	.10	.05
*PLATINUM: 4X BASIC CARDS		
☐ 1 Albert Belle	1.00	.45
☐ 2 Chuck McElroy	.10	.05
☐ 3 Mike Cameron	.25	.11
☐ 4 Ozzie Guillen	.10	.05
☐ 5 Jaime Navarro	.10	.05
☐ 6 Chris Clemons	.10	.05
☐ 7 Lyle Mouton	.10	.05
☐ 8 Frank Thomas	3.00	1.35
☐ 9 Doug Drabek	.10	.05
☐ 10 Robin Ventura	.25	.11
☐ 11 Dave Martinez	.10	.05
☐ 12 Ray Durham	.25	.11
☐ 13 Chris Snopek	.10	.05
☐ 14 James Baldwin	.10	.05
☐ 15 Jorge Fabregas	.10	.05

1998 Score Yankees

This 15-card set was issued in special retail packs and features color photos of the New York Yankees team. The backs carry player information. A special platinum parallel set was also issued and randomly inserted in packs.

	MINT	NRMT
COMPLETE SET (15)	6.00	2.70
COMMON CARD (1-15)	.10	.05
*PLATINUM: 4X BASIC CARDS		
☐ 1 Hideki Irabu	.25	.11
☐ 2 Derek Jeter	2.00	.90
☐ 3 Tino Martinez	.75	.35
☐ 4 David Cone	.25	.11
☐ 5 Andy Pettitte	.75	.35
☐ 6 Bernie Williams	.75	.35
☐ 7 Charlie Hayes	.10	.05
☐ 8 Pat Kelly	.10	.05
☐ 9 Mariano Rivera	.25	.11
☐ 10 Paul O'Neill	.25	.11
☐ 11 Chad Curtis	.10	.05
☐ 12 David Wells	.10	.05
☐ 13 Cecil Fielder	.25	.11
☐ 14 Wade Boggs	.75	.35
☐ 15 Jorge Posada	.10	.05

1997 Scoreboard Mantle

This 75-card set features color and blue-and-white photos of Baseball great Mickey Mantle and some special events that occurred in his life. Cards #1, 6, 7, 70, and 74 are die cut with special gold foil enhancements. Cards #51-69 are replicas of his 1951-1969 trading cards.

	MINT	NRMT
COMPLETE SET (75)	100.00	45.00
COMMON CARD (1-74)	1.00	.45
☐ 1 Mickey Mantle Summary of the Legend	7.50	3.40
☐ 2 Mickey Mantle Triple Crown 1956	1.00	.45
☐ 3 Mickey Mantle MVP 1956	1.00	.45
☐ 4 Mickey Mantle MVP 1957	1.00	.45
☐ 5 Mickey Mantle MVP 1962	1.00	.45
☐ 6 Mickey Mantle Uniform #6	7.50	3.40
☐ 7 Mickey Mantle Uniform #7	7.50	3.40
☐ 8 Mickey Mantle Sparkling Defense	1.00	.45
☐ 9 Mickey Mantle 20-Time All-Star	1.00	.45
☐ 10 Mickey Mantle 4-Time HR Champion	1.00	.45
☐ 11 Mickey Mantle World Series Records	1.00	.45
☐ 12 Mickey Mantle Dirty Dozen	1.00	.45
☐ 13 Mickey Mantle World Champion 1951	1.00	.45
☐ 14 Mickey Mantle World Champion 1952	1.00	.45
☐ 15 Mickey Mantle World Champion 1953	1.00	.45
☐ 16 Mickey Mantle World Champion 1956	1.00	.45
☐ 17 Mickey Mantle World Champion 1958	1.00	.45
☐ 18 Mickey Mantle World Champion 1961	1.00	.45
☐ 19 Mickey Mantle World Champion 1962	1.00	.45
☐ 20 Mickey Mantle Replacing A Legend	1.00	.45
☐ 21 Mickey Mantle Casey On Mantle	1.00	.45
☐ 22 Mickey Mantle Mickey and the Media	1.00	.45
☐ 23 Mickey Mantle Family Man	1.00	.45
☐ 24 Mickey Mantle Fan Favorite	1.00	.45
☐ 25 Mickey Mantle Playing Injured	1.00	.45
☐ 26 Mickey Mantle Clubhouse Leader	1.00	.45
☐ 27 Mickey Mantle Team Leader	1.00	.45
☐ 28 Mickey Mantle Roger Maris Cleanup Hitter	3.00	1.35
☐ 29 Mickey Mantle Legendary Friendships	1.00	.45
☐ 30 Mickey Mantle Time Out	1.00	.45
☐ 31 Mickey Mantle Mantle Is Born	1.00	.45
☐ 32 Mickey Mantle Mutt Mantle	1.00	.45
☐ 33 Mickey Mantle Growing Up	1.00	.45
☐ 34 Mickey Mantle 5-Tool Player-Arm	1.00	.45
☐ 35 Mickey Mantle 5-Tool Player-Defense	1.00	.45
☐ 36 Mickey Mantle 5-Tool Player-Average	1.00	.45
☐ 37 Mickey Mantle 5-Tool Player-Speed	1.00	.45
☐ 38 Mickey Mantle 5-Tool Player-Power	1.00	.45
☐ 39 Mickey Mantle First Home Run	1.00	.45
☐ 40 Mickey Mantle 100th Home Run	1.00	.45
☐ 41 Mickey Mantle 200th Home Run	1.00	.45
☐ 42 Mickey Mantle 300th Home Run	1.00	.45
☐ 43 Mickey Mantle 400th Home Run	1.00	.45
☐ 44 Mickey Mantle 500th Home Run	1.00	.45
☐ 45 Mickey Mantle 536 Career Home Runs	1.00	.45
☐ 46 Mickey Mantle Yankee Stadium Blasts	1.00	.45
☐ 47 Mickey Mantle Switch-Hit Home Runs	1.00	.45
☐ 48 Mickey Mantle 565-ft. Home Run	1.00	.45

Card	MINT	NRMT
☐ 49 Mickey Mantle Signs 1st Pro Contract	1.00	.45
☐ 50 Mickey Mantle Mickey in the Minors	1.00	.45
☐ 51 Mickey Mantle 1951 Trading Card	1.50	.70
☐ 52 Mickey Mantle 1952 Trading Card	1.50	.70
☐ 53 Mickey Mantle 1953 Trading Card	1.50	.70
☐ 54 Mickey Mantle 1954 Trading Card	1.50	.70
☐ 55 Mickey Mantle 1955 Trading Card	1.50	.70
☐ 56A Mickey Mantle 1956 Trading Card Batting left	1.50	.70
☐ 56B Mickey Mantle 1956 Trading Card (Batting right)	1.50	.70
☐ 57 Mickey Mantle 1957 Trading Card	1.50	.70
☐ 58 Mickey Mantle 1958 Trading Card	1.50	.70
☐ 59 Mickey Mantle 1959 Trading Card	1.50	.70
☐ 60 Mickey Mantle 1960 Trading Card	1.50	.70
☐ 61 Mickey Mantle 1961 Trading Card	1.50	.70
☐ 62 Mickey Mantle 1962 Trading Card	1.50	.70
☐ 63 Mickey Mantle 1963 Trading Card	1.50	.70
☐ 64 Mickey Mantle 1964 Trading Card	1.50	.70
☐ 65 Mickey Mantle 1965 Trading Card	1.50	.70
☐ 66 Mickey Mantle 1966 Trading Card	1.50	.70
☐ 67 Mickey Mantle 1967 Trading Card	1.50	.70
☐ 68 Mickey Mantle 1968 Trading Card	1.50	.70
☐ 69 Mickey Mantle 1969 Trading Card	1.50	.70
☐ 70 Mickey Mantle #7 Retired by Yankees	10.00	4.50
☐ 71 Mickey Mantle Bobby Kennedy Mickey Mantle Day 1965	3.00	1.35
☐ 72 Mickey Mantle Mickey Mantle Day 1969	1.00	.45
☐ 73 Mickey Mantle Life After Baseball	1.00	.45
☐ 74 Mickey Mantle Hall of Fame Induction	10.00	4.50
☐ P1 Mickey Mantle Summary of the Legend	3.00	1.35
☐ P7 Mickey Mantle Uniform #7	3.00	1.35

1997 Scoreboard Mantle 7

The first six cards of this seven-card set were randomly inserted in packs of Mickey Mantle Shoe Box Collection cards at the rate of one in 16 with card #7 having an insertion rate of one in 320. The complete set could be mailed in for a chance to win a $7,000 Mickey Mantle prepaid phone card or a $700 one. The fronts feature color photos of Mickey Mantle. The backs display the game rules.

	MINT	NRMT
COMPLETE SET (7)	300.00	135.00
COMMON CARD (1-7)	20.00	9.00
☐ 1 Mickey Mantle (Bat on shoulder)	20.00	9.00
☐ 2 Mickey Mantle (With hat off)	20.00	9.00
☐ 3 Mickey Mantle (Front view while swinging bat)	20.00	9.00
☐ 4 Mickey Mantle (Side view while swinging bat)	20.00	9.00
☐ 5 Mickey Mantle (Head and shoulder view while batting)	30.00	13.50
☐ 6 Mickey Mantle ((Hands on knees)	20.00	9.00
☐ 7 Mickey Mantle (Hand on hip)	200.00	90.00

1993 Select Samples

These eight promo cards were issued to provide dealers with a preview of Score's new Select series cards. The cards measure the standard size feature glossy color

player photos edged on two sides by a two-toned green border area. The back design is similar to the fronts but with a smaller player photo to create space for player profile and statistics. These promo cards are distinguished from the regular issue by the zeroes in the statistic lines.

	MINT	NRMT
COMPLETE SET (8)	25.00	11.00
COMMON CARD	1.00	.45
☐ 22 Robin Yount	4.00	1.80
☐ 24 Don Mattingly	12.00	5.50
☐ 26 Sandy Alomar Jr.	2.00	.90
☐ 41 Gary Sheffield	4.00	1.80
☐ 56 Brady Anderson	3.00	1.35
☐ 65 Rob Dibble	1.00	.45
☐ 75 John Smiley	1.00	.45
☐ 79 Mitch Williams	1.00	.45

1993 Select

Seeking a niche in the premium, mid-price market, Score produced a new 405-card standard-size set entitled Select in 1993. The set includes regular players, rookies, and draft picks, and was sold in 15-card hobby and retail packs and 28-card super packs. The front photos, composed either horizontally or vertically, are ultra-violet coated while the two-toned green borders received a matte finish. The player's name appears in mustard-colored lettering in the bottom border. Subset cards include Draft Picks and Rookies, both sprinkled throughout the latter part of the set. Rookie Cards in this set include Derek Jeter and Jason Kendall.

	MINT	NRMT
COMPLETE SET (405)	30.00	13.50
COMMON CARD (1-405)	.15	.07
☐ 1 Barry Bonds	.75	.35
☐ 2 Ken Griffey Jr.	3.00	1.35
☐ 3 Will Clark	.20	.09
☐ 4 Kirby Puckett	1.25	.55
☐ 5 Tony Gwynn	1.50	.70
☐ 6 Frank Thomas	2.50	1.10
☐ 7 Tom Glavine	.20	.09
☐ 8 Roberto Alomar	.60	.25
☐ 9 Andre Dawson	.20	.09
☐ 10 Ron Darling	.15	.07
☐ 11 Bobby Bonilla	.30	.14
☐ 12 Danny Tartabull	.15	.07
☐ 13 Darren Daulton	.30	.14
☐ 14 Roger Clemens	1.25	.55
☐ 15 Ozzie Smith	.75	.35
☐ 16 Mark McGwire	1.25	.55
☐ 17 Terry Pendleton	.30	.14
☐ 18 Cal Ripken	2.50	1.10
☐ 19 Fred McGriff	.20	.09
☐ 20 Cecil Fielder	.30	.14
☐ 21 Darryl Strawberry	.30	.14
☐ 22 Robin Yount	.20	.09
☐ 23 Barry Larkin	.20	.09
☐ 24 Don Mattingly	1.00	.45
☐ 25 Craig Biggio	.20	.09
☐ 26 Sandy Alomar Jr.	.30	.14
☐ 27 Larry Walker	.60	.25
☐ 28 Junior Felix	.15	.07
☐ 29 Eddie Murray	.60	.25
☐ 30 Robin Ventura	.30	.14
☐ 31 Greg Maddux	2.00	.90
☐ 32 Dave Winfield	.20	.09
☐ 33 John Kruk	.30	.14
☐ 34 Wally Joyner	.30	.14
☐ 35 Andy Van Slyke	.30	.14
☐ 36 Chuck Knoblauch	.60	.25
☐ 37 Tom Pagnozzi	.15	.07
☐ 38 Dennis Eckersley	.20	.09
☐ 39 Dave Justice	.60	.25
☐ 40 Juan Gonzalez	1.50	.70
☐ 41 Gary Sheffield	.60	.25
☐ 42 Paul Molitor	.60	.25
☐ 43 Delino DeShields	.15	.07
☐ 44 Travis Fryman	.30	.14
☐ 45 Hal Morris	.15	.07
☐ 46 Greg Olson	.15	.07
☐ 47 Ken Caminiti	.60	.25
☐ 48 Wade Boggs	.20	.09
☐ 49 Orel Hershiser	.30	.14
☐ 50 Albert Belle	.75	.35
☐ 51 Bill Swift	.15	.07
☐ 52 Mark Langston	.15	.07
☐ 53 Joe Girardi	.15	.07
☐ 54 Keith Miller	.15	.07
☐ 55 Gary Carter	.20	.09
☐ 56 Brady Anderson	.20	.09
☐ 57 Dwight Gooden	.30	.14
☐ 58 Julio Franco	.30	.14
☐ 59 Lenny Dykstra	.30	.14
☐ 60 Mickey Tettleton	.15	.07
☐ 61 Randy Tomlin	.15	.07
☐ 62 B.J. Surhoff	.30	.14
☐ 63 Todd Zeile	.15	.07
☐ 64 Roberto Kelly	.15	.07
☐ 65 Rob Dibble	.15	.07
☐ 66 Leo Gomez	.15	.07
☐ 67 Doug Jones	.15	.07
☐ 68 Ellis Burks	.30	.14
☐ 69 Mike Scioscia	.15	.07
☐ 70 Charles Nagy	.30	.14
☐ 71 Cory Snyder	.15	.07
☐ 72 Devon White	.15	.07
☐ 73 Mark Grace	.20	.09
☐ 74 Luis Polonia	.15	.07
☐ 75 John Smiley 2X	.15	.07
☐ 76 Carlton Fisk	.20	.09
☐ 77 Luis Sojo	.15	.07
☐ 78 George Brett	1.25	.55
☐ 79 Mitch Williams	.15	.07
☐ 80 Kent Hrbek	.30	.14
☐ 81 Jay Bell	.30	.14
☐ 82 Edgar Martinez	.20	.09
☐ 83 Lee Smith	.30	.14
☐ 84 Deion Sanders	.60	.25
☐ 85 Bill Gullickson	.15	.07
☐ 86 Paul O'Neill	.30	.14
☐ 87 Kevin Seitzer	.15	.07
☐ 88 Steve Finley	.30	.14
☐ 89 Mel Hall	.15	.07
☐ 90 Nolan Ryan	2.50	1.10
☐ 91 Eric Davis	.30	.14
☐ 92 Mike Mussina	.60	.25
☐ 93 Tony Fernandez	.15	.07
☐ 94 Frank Viola	.15	.07
☐ 95 Matt Williams	.20	.09
☐ 96 Joe Carter	.30	.14
☐ 97 Ryne Sandberg	.75	.35
☐ 98 Jim Abbott	.15	.07
☐ 99 Marquis Grissom	.30	.14
☐ 100 George Bell	.15	.07
☐ 101 Howard Johnson	.15	.07
☐ 102 Kevin Appier	.30	.14
☐ 103 Dale Murphy	.20	.09
☐ 104 Shane Mack	.15	.07
☐ 105 Jose Lind	.15	.07
☐ 106 Rickey Henderson	.20	.09
☐ 107 Bob Tewksbury	.15	.07
☐ 108 Kevin Mitchell	.30	.14
☐ 109 Steve Avery	.15	.07
☐ 110 Candy Maldonado	.15	.07
☐ 111 Bip Roberts	.15	.07
☐ 112 Lou Whitaker	.30	.14
☐ 113 Jeff Bagwell	1.25	.55
☐ 114 Dante Bichette	.20	.09
☐ 115 Brett Butler	.30	.14
☐ 116 Melido Perez	.15	.07
☐ 117 Andy Benes	.30	.14
☐ 118 Randy Johnson	.20	.09
☐ 119 Willie McGee	.15	.07
☐ 120 Jody Reed	.15	.07
☐ 121 Shawon Dunston	.15	.07
☐ 122 Carlos Baerga	.30	.14
☐ 123 Bret Saberhagen	.15	.07
☐ 124 John Olerud	.15	.07
☐ 125 Ivan Calderon	.15	.07
☐ 126 Bryan Harvey	.15	.07
☐ 127 Terry Mulholland	.15	.07

☐ 128 Ozzie Guillen .15 .07
☐ 129 Steve Buechele .15 .07
☐ 130 Kevin Tapani .15 .07
☐ 131 Felix Jose .15 .07
☐ 132 Terry Steinbach .30 .14
☐ 133 Ron Gant .30 .14
☐ 134 Harold Reynolds .15 .07
☐ 135 Chris Sabo .15 .07
☐ 136 Ivan Rodriguez .75 .35
☐ 137 Eric Anthony .15 .07
☐ 138 Mike Henneman .15 .07
☐ 139 Robby Thompson .15 .07
☐ 140 Scott Fletcher .15 .07
☐ 141 Bruce Hurst .15 .07
☐ 142 Kevin Maas .15 .07
☐ 143 Tom Candiotti .15 .07
☐ 144 Chris Hoiles .15 .07
☐ 145 Mike Morgan .15 .07
☐ 146 Mark Whiten .15 .07
☐ 147 Dennis Martinez .30 .14
☐ 148 Tony Pena .15 .07
☐ 149 Dave Magadan .15 .07
☐ 150 Mark Lewis .15 .07
☐ 151 Mariano Duncan .15 .07
☐ 152 Gregg Jefferies .30 .14
☐ 153 Doug Drabek .15 .07
☐ 154 Brian Harper .15 .07
☐ 155 Ray Lankford .30 .14
☐ 156 Carney Lansford .30 .14
☐ 157 Mike Sharperson .15 .07
☐ 158 Jack Morris .30 .14
☐ 159 Otis Nixon .30 .14
☐ 160 Steve Sax .15 .07
☐ 161 Mark Lemke .15 .07
☐ 162 Rafael Palmeiro .20 .09
☐ 163 Jose Rijo .15 .07
☐ 164 Omar Vizquel .30 .14
☐ 165 Sammy Sosa .60 .25
☐ 166 Milt Cuyler .15 .07
☐ 167 John Franco .15 .07
☐ 168 Darryl Hamilton .15 .07
☐ 169 Ken Hill .30 .14
☐ 170 Mike Devereaux .15 .07
☐ 171 Don Slaught .15 .07
☐ 172 Steve Farr .15 .07
☐ 173 Bernard Gilkey .30 .14
☐ 174 Mike Fetters .15 .07
☐ 175 Vince Coleman .15 .07
☐ 176 Kevin McReynolds .15 .07
☐ 177 John Smoltz .20 .09
☐ 178 Greg Gagne .15 .07
☐ 179 Greg Swindell .15 .07
☐ 180 Juan Guzman .15 .07
☐ 181 Kal Daniels .15 .07
☐ 182 Rick Sutcliffe .15 .07
☐ 183 Orlando Merced .15 .07
☐ 184 Bill Wegman .15 .07
☐ 185 Mark Gardner .15 .07
☐ 186 Rob Deer .15 .07
☐ 187 Dave Hollins .15 .07
☐ 188 Jack Clark .15 .07
☐ 189 Brian Hunter .15 .07
☐ 190 Tim Wallach .15 .07
☐ 191 Tim Belcher .15 .07
☐ 192 Walt Weiss .15 .07
☐ 193 Kurt Stillwell .15 .07
☐ 194 Charlie Hayes .15 .07
☐ 195 Willie Randolph .30 .14
☐ 196 Jack McDowell .15 .07
☐ 197 Jose Offerman .15 .07
☐ 198 Chuck Finley .15 .07
☐ 199 Darrin Jackson .15 .07
☐ 200 Kelly Gruber .15 .07
☐ 201 John Wetteland .30 .14
☐ 202 Jay Buhner .20 .09
☐ 203 Mike LaValliere .15 .07
☐ 204 Kevin Brown .30 .14
☐ 205 Luis Gonzalez .15 .07
☐ 206 Rick Aguilera .15 .07
☐ 207 Norm Charlton .15 .07
☐ 208 Mike Bordick .15 .07
☐ 209 Charlie Leibrandt .15 .07
☐ 210 Tom Brunansky .15 .07
☐ 211 Tom Henke .15 .07
☐ 212 Randy Milligan .15 .07
☐ 213 Ramon Martinez .30 .14
☐ 214 Mo Vaughn .75 .35
☐ 215 Randy Myers .30 .14
☐ 216 Greg Hibbard .15 .07
☐ 217 Wes Chamberlain .15 .07
☐ 218 Tony Phillips .15 .07
☐ 219 Pete Harnisch .15 .07
☐ 220 Mike Gallego .15 .07
☐ 221 Bud Black .15 .07
☐ 222 Greg Vaughn .15 .07
☐ 223 Milt Thompson .15 .07
☐ 224 Ben McDonald .15 .07
☐ 225 Billy Hatcher .15 .07
☐ 226 Paul Sorrento .15 .07
☐ 227 Mark Gubicza .15 .07
☐ 228 Mike Greenwell .15 .07
☐ 229 Curt Schilling .30 .14
☐ 230 Alan Trammell .20 .09
☐ 231 Zane Smith .15 .07
☐ 232 Bobby Thigpen .15 .07
☐ 233 Greg Olson .15 .07
☐ 234 Joe Orsulak .15 .07
☐ 235 Joe Oliver .15 .07
☐ 236 Tim Raines .30 .14
☐ 237 Juan Samuel .15 .07
☐ 238 Chili Davis .30 .14
☐ 239 Spike Owen .15 .07
☐ 240 Dave Stewart .30 .14
☐ 241 Jim Eisenreich .30 .14
☐ 242 Phil Plantier .15 .07
☐ 243 Sid Fernandez .15 .07
☐ 244 Dan Gladden .15 .07
☐ 245 Mickey Morandini .15 .07
☐ 246 Tino Martinez .60 .25
☐ 247 Kirt Manwaring .15 .07
☐ 248 Dean Palmer .30 .14
☐ 249 Tom Browning .15 .07
☐ 250 Brian McRae .30 .14
☐ 251 Scott Leius .15 .07
☐ 252 Bert Blyleven .30 .14
☐ 253 Scott Erickson .15 .07
☐ 254 Bob Welch .15 .07
☐ 255 Pat Kelly .15 .07
☐ 256 Felix Fermin .15 .07
☐ 257 Harold Baines .30 .14
☐ 258 Duane Ward .15 .07
☐ 259 Bill Spiers .15 .07
☐ 260 Jaime Navarro .15 .07
☐ 261 Scott Sanderson .15 .07
☐ 262 Gary Gaetti .30 .14
☐ 263 Bob Ojeda .15 .07
☐ 264 Jeff Montgomery .30 .14
☐ 265 Scott Bankhead .15 .07
☐ 266 Lance Johnson .15 .07
☐ 267 Rafael Belliard .15 .07
☐ 268 Kevin Reimer .15 .07
☐ 269 Benito Santiago .15 .07
☐ 270 Mike Moore .15 .07
☐ 271 Dave Fleming .15 .07
☐ 272 Moises Alou .30 .14
☐ 273 Pat Listach .15 .07
☐ 274 Reggie Sanders .30 .14
☐ 275 Kenny Lofton 1.25 .55
☐ 276 Donovan Osborne .15 .07
☐ 277 Rusty Meacham .15 .07
☐ 278 Eric Karros .30 .14
☐ 279 Andy Stankiewicz .15 .07
☐ 280 Brian Jordan .30 .14
☐ 281 Gary DiSarcina .15 .07
☐ 282 Mark Wohlers .20 .09
☐ 283 Dave Nilsson .30 .14
☐ 284 Anthony Young .15 .07
☐ 285 Jim Bullinger .15 .07
☐ 286 Derek Bell .30 .14
☐ 287 Brian Williams .15 .07
☐ 288 Julio Valera .15 .07
☐ 289 Dan Walters .15 .07
☐ 290 Chad Curtis .30 .14
☐ 291 Michael Tucker DP .60 .25
☐ 292 Bob Zupcic .15 .07
☐ 293 Todd Hundley .20 .09
☐ 294 Jeff Tackett .15 .07
☐ 295 Greg Colbrunn .15 .07
☐ 296 Cal Eldred .15 .07
☐ 297 Chris Roberts DP .30 .14
☐ 298 John Doherty .15 .07
☐ 299 Denny Neagle .30 .14
☐ 300 Arthur Rhodes .15 .07
☐ 301 Mark Clark .15 .07
☐ 302 Scott Cooper .15 .07
☐ 303 Jamie Arnold DP .30 .14
☐ 304 Jim Thome 1.25 .55
☐ 305 Frank Seminara .15 .07
☐ 306 Kurt Knudsen .15 .07
☐ 307 Tim Wakefield .30 .14
☐ 308 John Jaha .30 .14
☐ 309 Pat Hentgen .20 .09
☐ 310 B.J. Wallace DP .15 .07
☐ 311 Roberto Hernandez .30 .14
☐ 312 Hipolito Pichardo .15 .07
☐ 313 Eric Fox .15 .07
☐ 314 Willie Banks .15 .07
☐ 315 Sam Militello .15 .07
☐ 316 Vince Horsman .15 .07
☐ 317 Carlos Hernandez .15 .07
☐ 318 Jeff Kent .30 .14
☐ 319 Mike Perez .15 .07
☐ 320 Scott Livingstone .15 .07
☐ 321 Jeff Conine .30 .14
☐ 322 James Austin .15 .07
☐ 323 John Vander Wal .15 .07
☐ 324 Pat Mahomes .15 .07
☐ 325 Pedro Astacio .15 .07
☐ 326 Bret Boone UER .15 .07
(Misspelled Brett)
☐ 327 Matt Stairs .15 .07
☐ 328 Damion Easley .15 .07
☐ 329 Ben Rivera .15 .07
☐ 330 Reggie Jefferson .30 .14
☐ 331 Luis Mercedes .15 .07
☐ 332 Kyle Abbott .15 .07
☐ 333 Eddie Taubensee .15 .07
☐ 334 Tim McIntosh .15 .07
☐ 335 Phil Clark .15 .07
☐ 336 Wil Cordero .15 .07
☐ 337 Russ Springer .15 .07
☐ 338 Craig Colbert .15 .07
☐ 339 Tim Salmon .75 .35
☐ 340 Braulio Castillo .15 .07
☐ 341 Donald Harris .15 .07
☐ 342 Eric Young .60 .25
☐ 343 Bob Wickman .15 .07
☐ 344 John Valentin .30 .14
☐ 345 Dan Wilson .30 .14
☐ 346 Steve Hosey .15 .07
☐ 347 Mike Piazza 3.00 1.35
☐ 348 Willie Greene .30 .14
☐ 349 Tom Goodwin .15 .07
☐ 350 Eric Hillman .15 .07
☐ 351 Steve Reed .15 .07
☐ 352 Dan Serafini DP .50 .23
☐ 353 Todd Steverson DP .30 .14
☐ 354 Benji Grigsby DP .15 .07
☐ 355 Shannon Stewart DP .75 .35
☐ 356 Sean Lowe DP .15 .07
☐ 357 Derek Wallace DP .15 .07
☐ 358 Rick Helling DP .30 .14
☐ 359 Jason Kendall DP 1.00 .45
☐ 360 Derek Jeter DP 6.00 2.70
☐ 361 David Cone .30 .14
☐ 362 Jeff Reardon .30 .14
☐ 363 Bobby Witt .15 .07
☐ 364 Jose Canseco .20 .09
☐ 365 Jeff Russell .15 .07
☐ 366 Ruben Sierra .15 .07
☐ 367 Alan Mills .15 .07
☐ 368 Matt Nokes .15 .07
☐ 369 Pat Borders .15 .07
☐ 370 Pedro Munoz .15 .07
☐ 371 Danny Jackson .15 .07
☐ 372 Geronimo Pena .15 .07
☐ 373 Craig Lefferts .15 .07
☐ 374 Joe Grahe .15 .07
☐ 375 Roger McDowell .15 .07
☐ 376 Jimmy Key .30 .14
☐ 377 Steve Olin .15 .07
☐ 378 Glenn Davis .15 .07
☐ 379 Rene Gonzales .15 .07
☐ 380 Manuel Lee .15 .07
☐ 381 Ron Karkovice .15 .07
☐ 382 Sid Bream .15 .07
☐ 383 Gerald Williams .15 .07
☐ 384 Lenny Harris .15 .07
☐ 385 J.T. Snow .75 .35
☐ 386 Dave Stieb .15 .07
☐ 387 Kirk McCaskill .15 .07
☐ 388 Lance Parrish .15 .07
☐ 389 Craig Grebeck .15 .07
☐ 390 Rick Wilkins .15 .07
☐ 391 Manny Alexander .15 .07
☐ 392 Mike Schooler .15 .07
☐ 393 Bernie Williams .60 .25
☐ 394 Kevin Koslofski .15 .07
☐ 395 Willie Wilson .15 .07
☐ 396 Jeff Parrett .15 .07
☐ 397 Mike Harkey .15 .07
☐ 398 Frank Tanana .15 .07
☐ 399 Doug Henry .15 .07
☐ 400 Royce Clayton .30 .14
☐ 401 Eric Wedge .15 .07
☐ 402 Derrick May .15 .07
☐ 403 Carlos Garcia .15 .07
☐ 404 Henry Rodriguez .30 .14
☐ 405 Ryan Klesko .75 .35

1993 Select Aces

This 24-card standard-size set features some of the top starting pitchers in both leagues. The cards were randomly inserted into one in every eight 28-card super packs. The fronts display an action player pose cut out and superimposed on a metallic variegated red and silver diamond design. The diamond itself rests on a background consisting of silver metallic streaks that emanate from the center of the card. In imitation of

playing card design, the fronts have a large "A" for Ace in upper left and lower right corners. The player's name in the upper right corner rounds out the card face.

	MINT	NRMT
COMPLETE SET (24)	80.00	36.00
COMMON CARD (1-24)	3.00	1.35
☐ 1 Roger Clemens	20.00	9.00
☐ 2 Tom Glavine	6.00	2.70
☐ 3 Jack McDowell	3.00	1.35
☐ 4 Greg Maddux	30.00	13.50
☐ 5 Jack Morris	4.00	1.80
☐ 6 Dennis Martinez	4.00	1.80
☐ 7 Kevin Brown	4.00	1.80
☐ 8 Dwight Gooden	4.00	1.80
☐ 9 Kevin Appier	4.00	1.80
☐ 10 Mike Morgan	3.00	1.35
☐ 11 Juan Guzman	3.00	1.35
☐ 12 Charles Nagy	4.00	1.80
☐ 13 John Smiley	3.00	1.35
☐ 14 Ken Hill	4.00	1.80
☐ 15 Bob Tewksbury	3.00	1.35
☐ 16 Doug Drabek	3.00	1.35
☐ 17 John Smoltz	6.00	2.70
☐ 18 Greg Swindell	3.00	1.35
☐ 19 Bruce Hurst	3.00	1.35
☐ 20 Mike Mussina	10.00	4.50
☐ 21 Cal Eldred	3.00	1.35
☐ 22 Melido Perez	3.00	1.35
☐ 23 Dave Fleming	3.00	1.35
☐ 24 Kevin Tapani	3.00	1.35

1993 Select Chase Rookies

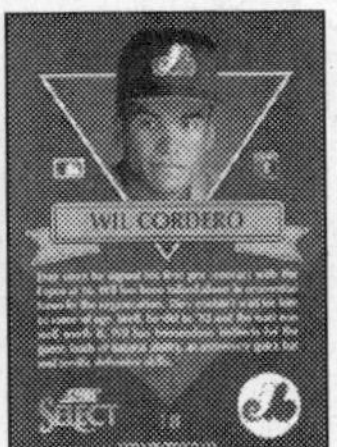

This 21-card standard-size set showcases 1992's best rookies. The cards were randomly inserted into one in every eighteen 15-card hobby packs. The fronts exhibit Score's "dufex" printing process, in which a color photo is printed on a metallic base creating an unusual, three-dimensional look. The pictures are tilted slightly to the left and edged on the left and bottom by red metallic borders.

	MINT	NRMT
COMPLETE SET (21)	120.00	55.00
COMMON CARD (1-21)	2.50	1.10
☐ 1 Pat Listach	2.50	1.10
☐ 2 Moises Alou	5.00	2.20
☐ 3 Reggie Sanders	5.00	2.20
☐ 4 Kenny Lofton	50.00	22.00
☐ 5 Eric Karros	10.00	4.50
☐ 6 Brian Williams	2.50	1.10
☐ 7 Donovan Osborne	2.50	1.10
☐ 8 Sam Militello	2.50	1.10
☐ 9 Chad Curtis	5.00	2.20
☐ 10 Bob Zupcic	2.50	1.10
☐ 11 Tim Salmon	30.00	13.50
☐ 12 Jeff Conine	5.00	2.20
☐ 13 Pedro Astacio	5.00	2.20
☐ 14 Arthur Rhodes	2.50	1.10
☐ 15 Cal Eldred	2.50	1.10
☐ 16 Tim Wakefield	5.00	2.20
☐ 17 Andy Stankiewicz	2.50	1.10
☐ 18 Wil Cordero	2.50	1.10
☐ 19 Todd Hundley	15.00	6.75
☐ 20 Dave Fleming	2.50	1.10
☐ 21 Bret Boone	2.50	1.10

1993 Select Chase Stars

This 24-card standard-size set showcases the top players in Major League Baseball. The cards were randomly inserted into one in every eighteen retail 15-card packs. The fronts exhibit Score's "dufex" printing process, in which a color photo is printed on a metallic base creating an unusual, three-dimensional look. The pictures are tilted slightly to the left and edged on the left and bottom by green metallic borders.

	MINT	NRMT
COMPLETE SET (24)	150.00	70.00
COMMON CARD (1-24)	2.00	.90
☐ 1 Fred McGriff	4.00	1.80
☐ 2 Ryne Sandberg	10.00	4.50
☐ 3 Ozzie Smith	10.00	4.50
☐ 4 Gary Sheffield	4.00	1.80
☐ 5 Darren Daulton	3.00	1.35
☐ 6 Andy Van Slyke	2.00	.90
☐ 7 Barry Bonds	10.00	4.50
☐ 8 Tony Gwynn	20.00	9.00
☐ 9 Greg Maddux	25.00	11.00
☐ 10 Tom Glavine	4.00	1.80
☐ 11 John Franco	2.00	.90
☐ 12 Lee Smith	3.00	1.35
☐ 13 Cecil Fielder	3.00	1.35
☐ 14 Roberto Alomar	8.00	3.60
☐ 15 Cal Ripken	30.00	13.50
☐ 16 Edgar Martinez	4.00	1.80
☐ 17 Ivan Rodriguez	10.00	4.50
☐ 18 Kirby Puckett	15.00	6.75
☐ 19 Ken Griffey Jr.	40.00	18.00
☐ 20 Joe Carter	4.00	1.80
☐ 21 Roger Clemens	15.00	6.75
☐ 22 Dave Fleming	2.00	.90
☐ 23 Paul Molitor	8.00	3.60
☐ 24 Dennis Eckersley	4.00	1.80

1993 Select Stat Leaders

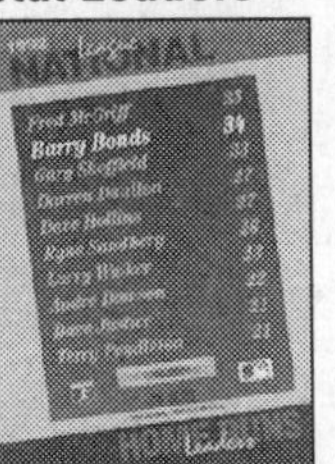

Featuring 45 cards from each league, these 90 Stat Leaders were inserted one per 1993 Score pack in every regular pack and super pack. The fronts feature color player action photos that are borderless on the sides and have oblique green borders at the top and bottom. The player's name appears within an oblique orange stripe across the bottom of the photo. The player's league appears within the top border, and the set's title appears within the bottom border.

	MINT	NRMT
COMPLETE SET (90)	10.00	4.50
COMMON CARD (1-90)	.10	.05
☐ 1 Edgar Martinez	.30	.14
☐ 2 Kirby Puckett	.75	.35
☐ 3 Frank Thomas	1.50	.70
☐ 4 Gary Sheffield	.40	.18
☐ 5 Andy Van Slyke	.20	.09
☐ 6 John Kruk	.20	.09
☐ 7 Kirby Puckett	.75	.35
☐ 8 Carlos Baerga	.20	.09
☐ 9 Paul Molitor	.40	.18
☐ 10 Terry Pendleton	.10	.05
Andy Van Slyke		
☐ 11 Ryne Sandberg	.50	.23
☐ 12 Mark Grace	.30	.14
☐ 13 Frank Thomas	.75	.35
Edgar Martinez		
☐ 14 Don Mattingly	.40	.18
Robin Yount		
☐ 15 Ken Griffey	2.00	.90
☐ 16 Andy Van Slyke	.20	.09
☐ 17 Mariano Duncan	.20	.09
Will Clark		
Ray Lankford		
☐ 18 Marquis Grissom	.20	.09
Terry Pendleton		
☐ 19 Lance Johnson	.10	.05
☐ 20 Mike Devereaux	.10	.05
☐ 21 Brady Anderson	.30	.14
☐ 22 Deion Sanders	.40	.18
☐ 23 Steve Finley	.20	.09
☐ 24 Andy Van Slyke	.20	.09
☐ 25 Juan Gonzalez	1.00	.45
☐ 26 Mark McGwire	.60	.25
☐ 27 Cecil Fielder	.20	.09
☐ 28 Fred McGriff	.30	.14
☐ 29 Barry Bonds	.50	.23
☐ 30 Gary Sheffield	.40	.18
☐ 31 Cecil Fielder	.20	.09
☐ 32 Joe Carter	.20	.09
☐ 33 Frank Thomas	1.50	.70
☐ 34 Darren Daulton	.20	.09
☐ 35 Terry Pendleton	.20	.09
☐ 36 Fred McGriff	.30	.14
☐ 37 Tony Phillips	.10	.05
☐ 38 Frank Thomas	1.50	.70
☐ 39 Roberto Alomar	.40	.18
☐ 40 Barry Bonds	.50	.23
☐ 41 Dave Hollins	.10	.05
☐ 42 Andy Van Slyke	.20	.09
☐ 43 Mark McGwire	.60	.25
☐ 44 Edgar Martinez	.30	.14
☐ 45 Frank Thomas	1.50	.70
☐ 46 Barry Bonds	.50	.23
☐ 47 Gary Sheffield	.40	.18
☐ 48 Fred McGriff	.30	.14
☐ 49 Frank Thomas	1.50	.70
☐ 50 Danny Tartabull	.10	.05
☐ 51 Roberto Alomar	.40	.18
☐ 52 Barry Bonds	.50	.23
☐ 53 John Kruk	.20	.09
☐ 54 Brett Butler	.20	.09
☐ 55 Kenny Lofton	.75	.35
☐ 56 Pat Listach	.10	.05
☐ 57 Brady Anderson	.30	.14
☐ 58 Marquis Grissom	.20	.09
☐ 59 Delino DeShields	.10	.05
☐ 60 Bip Roberts	.10	.05
Steve Finley		
☐ 61 Jack McDowell	.10	.05
☐ 62 Kevin Brown	.40	.18
Roger Clemens		
☐ 63 Charles Nagy	.10	.05
Melido Perez		
☐ 64 Terry Mulholland	.10	.05
☐ 65 Curt Schilling	.10	.05
Doug Drabek		
☐ 66 Greg Maddux	.75	.35
John Smoltz		
☐ 67 Dennis Eckersley	.30	.14
☐ 68 Rick Aguilera	.10	.05
☐ 69 Jeff Montgomery	.20	.09
☐ 70 Lee Smith	.20	.09
☐ 71 Randy Myers	.20	.09
☐ 72 John Wetteland	.20	.09
☐ 73 Randy Johnson	.40	.18
☐ 74 Melido Perez	.10	.05
☐ 75 Roger Clemens	.60	.25
☐ 76 John Smoltz	.30	.14
☐ 77 David Cone	.20	.09
☐ 78 Greg Maddux	1.25	.55
☐ 79 Roger Clemens	.60	.25
☐ 80 Kevin Appier	.20	.09
☐ 81 Mike Mussina	.40	.18
☐ 82 Bill Swift	.10	.05
☐ 83 Bob Tewksbury	.10	.05
☐ 84 Greg Maddux	1.25	.55
☐ 85 Jack Morris	.20	.09
Kevin Brown		
☐ 86 Jack McDowell	.10	.05
☐ 87 Roger Clemens	.40	.18
Mike Mussina		
☐ 88 Tom Glavine	.75	.35
Greg Maddux		
☐ 89 Ken Hill	.10	.05
Bob Tewksbury		
☐ 90 Mike Morgan	.10	.05
Dennis Martinez		

1993 Select Triple Crown

Honoring the three most recent Triple Crown winners since 1993, cards from this 3-card standard-size set were

randomly inserted in 15-card hobby packs. The fronts exhibit Score's "dufex" printing process, in which a color photo is printed on a metallic base creating an unusual, three-dimensional look. The color player photos on the fronts have a forest green metallic border. The player's name and the year he won the Triple Crown appear above the picture, while the words "Triple Crown" are written in script beneath it.

	MINT	NRMT
COMPLETE SET (3)	100.00	45.00
COMMON CARD (1-3)	20.00	9.00
☐ 1 Mickey Mantle	80.00	36.00
☐ 2 Carl Yastrzemski	20.00	9.00
☐ 3 Frank Robinson	20.00	9.00

1993 Select Rookie/Traded

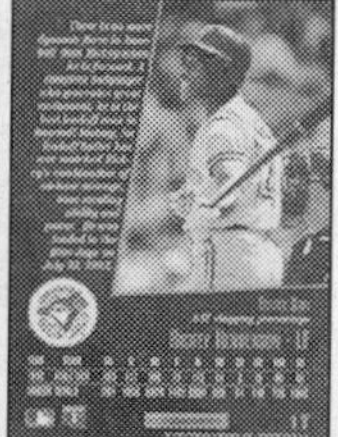

These 150 standard-size cards feature rookies and traded veteran players. The production run comprised 1,950 individually numbered cases. Cards were distributed in foil packs. Card design is similar to the regular 1993 Select cards excpt for the dramatic royal blue borders (instead of emerald green for the regular cards) and T-suffixed numbering. There are no key Rookie Cards in this set. Two Rookie of the Year insert cards and a Nolan Ryan Tribute card were randomly inserted in the foil packs. The chances of finding a Nolan Ryan card was listed at not less than one per 288 packs. The two ROY cards, featuring American League Rookie of the Year, Tim Salmon and National League Rookie of the Year, Mike Piazza were randomly inserted into one in every 576 packs.

	MINT	NRMT
COMPLETE SET (150)	15.00	6.75
COMMON CARD (1T-150T)	.30	.14
☐ 1T Rickey Henderson	.75	.35
☐ 2T Rob Deer	.30	.14
☐ 3T Tim Belcher	.30	.14
☐ 4T Gary Sheffield	1.25	.55
☐ 5T Fred McGriff	.75	.35
☐ 6T Mark Whiten	.30	.14
☐ 7T Jeff Russell	.30	.14
☐ 8T Harold Baines	.50	.23
☐ 9T Dave Winfield	.75	.35
☐ 10T Ellis Burks	.50	.23
☐ 11T Andre Dawson	.75	.35
☐ 12T Gregg Jefferies	.50	.23
☐ 13T Jimmy Key	.50	.23
☐ 14T Harold Reynolds	.30	.14
☐ 15T Tom Henke	.30	.14
☐ 16T Paul Molitor	1.25	.55
☐ 17T Wade Boggs	1.25	.55
☐ 18T David Cone	.50	.23
☐ 19T Tony Fernandez	.30	.14
☐ 20T Roberto Kelly	.30	.14
☐ 21T Paul O'Neill	.50	.23
☐ 22T Jose Lind	.30	.14
☐ 23T Barry Bonds	1.50	.70
☐ 24T Dave Stewart	.50	.23
☐ 25T Randy Myers	.50	.23
☐ 26T Benito Santiago	.30	.14
☐ 27T Tim Wallach	.30	.14
☐ 28T Greg Gagne	.30	.14
☐ 29T Kevin Mitchell	.50	.23
☐ 30T Jim Abbott	.30	.14
☐ 31T Lee Smith	.50	.23
☐ 32T Bobby Munoz	.30	.14
☐ 33T Mo Sanford	.30	.14
☐ 34T John Roper	.30	.14
☐ 35T David Hulse	.30	.14
☐ 36T Pedro Martinez	1.50	.70
☐ 37T Chuck Carr	.30	.14
☐ 38T Armando Reynoso	.30	.14
☐ 39T Ryan Thompson	.30	.14
☐ 40T Carlos Garcia	.30	.14
☐ 41T Matt Whiteside	.30	.14
☐ 42T Benji Gil	.30	.14
☐ 43T Rodney Bolton	.30	.14
☐ 44T J.T. Snow	1.25	.55
☐ 45T David McCarty	.30	.14
☐ 46T Paul Quantrill	.30	.14
☐ 47T Al Martin	.50	.23
☐ 48T Lance Painter	.30	.14
☐ 49T Lou Frazier	.30	.14
☐ 50T Eduardo Perez	.30	.14
☐ 51T Kevin Young	.30	.14
☐ 52T Mike Trombley	.30	.14
☐ 53T Sterling Hitchcock	1.25	.55
☐ 54T Tim Bogar	.30	.14
☐ 55T Hilly Hathaway	.30	.14
☐ 56T Wayne Kirby	.30	.14
☐ 57T Craig Paquette	.30	.14
☐ 58T Bret Boone	.30	.14
☐ 59T Greg McMichael	.30	.14
☐ 60T Mike Lansing	.50	.23
☐ 61T Brent Gates	.30	.14
☐ 62T Rene Arocha	.30	.14
☐ 63T Ricky Gutierrez	.30	.14
☐ 64T Kevin Rogers	.30	.14
☐ 65T Ken Ryan	.30	.14
☐ 66T Phil Hiatt	.30	.14
☐ 67T Pat Meares	.50	.23
☐ 68T Troy Neel	.30	.14
☐ 69T Steve Cooke	.30	.14
☐ 70T Sherman Obando	.30	.14
☐ 71T Blas Minor	.30	.14
☐ 72T Angel Miranda	.30	.14
☐ 73T Tom Kramer	.30	.14
☐ 74T Chip Hale	.30	.14
☐ 75T Brad Pennington	.30	.14
☐ 76T Graeme Lloyd	.30	.14
☐ 77T Darrell Whitmore	.30	.14
☐ 78T David Nied	.30	.14
☐ 79T Todd Van Poppel	.30	.14
☐ 80T Chris Gomez	.50	.23
☐ 81T Jason Bere	.50	.23
☐ 82T Jeffrey Hammonds	1.25	.55
☐ 83T Brad Ausmus	.30	.14
☐ 84T Kevin Stocker	.30	.14
☐ 85T Jeromy Burnitz	.50	.23
☐ 86T Aaron Sele	.50	.23
☐ 87T Roberto Mejia	.30	.14
☐ 88T Kirk Rueter	.30	.14
☐ 89T Kevin Roberson	.30	.14
☐ 90T Allen Watson	.30	.14
☐ 91T Charlie Leibrandt	.30	.14
☐ 92T Eric Davis	.50	.23
☐ 93T Jody Reed	.30	.14
☐ 94T Danny Jackson	.30	.14
☐ 95T Gary Gaetti	.50	.23
☐ 96T Norm Charlton	.30	.14
☐ 97T Doug Drabek	.30	.14
☐ 98T Scott Fletcher	.30	.14
☐ 99T Greg Swindell	.30	.14
☐ 100T John Smiley	.30	.14
☐ 101T Kevin Reimer	.30	.14
☐ 102T Andres Galarraga	.75	.35
☐ 103T Greg Hibbard	.30	.14
☐ 104T Chris Hammond	.30	.14
☐ 105T Darnell Coles	.30	.14
☐ 106T Mike Felder	.30	.14
☐ 107T Jose Guzman	.30	.14
☐ 108T Chris Bosio	.30	.14
☐ 109T Spike Owen	.30	.14
☐ 110T Felix Jose	.30	.14
☐ 111T Cory Snyder	.30	.14
☐ 112T Craig Lefferts	.30	.14
☐ 113T David Wells	.30	.14
☐ 114T Pete Incaviglia	.30	.14
☐ 115T Mike Pagliarulo	.30	.14
☐ 116T Dave Magadan	.30	.14
☐ 117T Charlie Hough	.30	.14
☐ 118T Ivan Calderon	.30	.14
☐ 119T Manuel Lee	.30	.14
☐ 120T Bob Patterson	.30	.14
☐ 121T Bob Ojeda	.30	.14
☐ 122T Scott Bankhead	.30	.14
☐ 123T Greg Maddux	4.00	1.80
☐ 124T Chili Davis	.50	.23
☐ 125T Milt Thompson	.30	.14
☐ 126T Dave Martinez	.30	.14
☐ 127T Frank Tanana	.30	.14
☐ 128T Phil Plantier	.30	.14
☐ 129T Juan Samuel	.30	.14
☐ 130T Eric Young	1.25	.55
☐ 131T Joe Orsulak	.30	.14
☐ 132T Derek Bell	.50	.23
☐ 133T Darrin Jackson	.30	.14
☐ 134T Tom Brunansky	.30	.14
☐ 135T Jeff Reardon	.50	.23
☐ 136T Kevin Higgins	.30	.14
☐ 137T Joel Johnston	.30	.14
☐ 138T Rick Trlicek	.30	.14
☐ 139T Richie Lewis	.30	.14
☐ 140T Jeff Gardner	.30	.14
☐ 141T Jack Voigt	.30	.14
☐ 142T Rod Correia	.30	.14
☐ 143T Billy Brewer	.30	.14
☐ 144T Terry Jorgensen	.30	.14
☐ 145T Rich Amaral	.30	.14
☐ 146T Sean Berry	.30	.14
☐ 147T Dan Peltier	.30	.14
☐ 148T Paul Wagner	.30	.14
☐ 149T Damon Buford	.30	.14
☐ 150T Wil Cordero	.30	.14
☐ NR1 Nolan Ryan Tribute	100.00	45.00
☐ ROY1 Tim Salmon AL ROY	25.00	11.00
☐ ROY2 Mike Piazza NL ROY	80.00	36.00

1993 Select Rookie/Traded All-Star Rookies

This ten-card standard-size set was randomly inserted in foil packs of 1993 Select Rookie and Traded. The insertion rate was reportedly not less than one in 36 packs. The cards feature on their fronts color player action shots that have a grainy metallic appearance. These photos are borderless, except at the top, where the silver-colored player's name is displayed upon red and blue metallic stripes. The set's title appears within a metallic silver-colored stripe near the bottom, which has a star-and-baseball icon emblazoned over its center. This combination of the set's title, stripe, and star-and-baseball icon reappears at the top of the non-metallic back, but in a red, white, and blue design. The player's name, position, and team logo are shown on the red-colored right half of the card. His career highlights appear in white lettering on the blue-colored left half.

	MINT	NRMT
COMPLETE SET (10)	150.00	70.00
COMMON CARD (1-10)	5.00	2.20
UNLISTED STARS	12.00	5.50
☐ 1 Jeff Conine	8.00	3.60
☐ 2 Brent Gates	5.00	2.20
☐ 3 Mike Lansing	5.00	2.20
☐ 4 Kevin Stocker	5.00	2.20
☐ 5 Mike Piazza	80.00	36.00
☐ 6 Jeffrey Hammonds	10.00	4.50
☐ 7 David Hulse	5.00	2.20
☐ 8 Tim Salmon	25.00	11.00
☐ 9 Rene Arocha	5.00	2.20
☐ 10 Greg McMichael	5.00	2.20

1994 Select Samples

Issued to preview the designs of the 1994 Score Select set and its inserts, these nine standard-size cards feature color player action shots on their fronts -- except for the Kruk card (24), which pictures him dozing, and so could hardly qualify as an "action shot." The cards are from the regular series, except for the Dykstra card, the Floyd card, and the Klesko card. Except for the title card, all the cards carry the word "Sample" in diagonal black lettering on their fronts and backs.

	MINT	NRMT
COMPLETE SET (9)	8.00	3.60
COMMON CARD	.25	.11
☐ 3 Paul Molitor	1.00	.45
☐ 17 Kirby Puckett	3.00	1.35
☐ 19 Randy Johnson	1.00	.45
☐ 24 John Kruk	.25	.11
☐ 51 Jose Lind	.25	.11
☐ 197 Ryan Klesko 94 Rookie Prospect	1.50	.70
☐ CC1 Lenny Dykstra Crown Contenders	1.50	.70
☐ RS1 Cliff Floyd Rookie Surge '94	1.50	.70
☐ NNO Title Card	.25	.11

1994 Select

Measuring the standard size, the 1994 Select set consists of 420 cards that were issued in two series of 210. The horizontal fronts feature a color player action photo and a duo-tone player shot. The backs are vertical and contain a photo, 1993 and career statistics and highlights. Special Dave Winfield and Cal Ripken cards were inserted in first series packs. A Paul Molitor MVP card and a Carlos Delgado Rookie of the Year card were inserted in second series packs. The insertion rate for ech card was one in 360 packs. Rookie Cards include Kurt Abbott, Brian Anderson and Chan Ho Park.

	MINT	NRMT
COMPLETE SET (420)	25.00	11.00
COMPLETE SERIES 1 (210)	15.00	6.75
COMPLETE SERIES 2 (210)	10.00	4.50
COMMON CARD (1-420)	.15	.07
☐ 1 Ken Griffey Jr.	3.00	1.35
☐ 2 Greg Maddux	2.00	.90
☐ 3 Paul Molitor	.60	.25
☐ 4 Mike Piazza	2.00	.90
☐ 5 Jay Bell	.30	.14
☐ 6 Frank Thomas	2.50	1.10
☐ 7 Barry Larkin	.40	.18
☐ 8 Paul O'Neill	.30	.14
☐ 9 Darren Daulton	.30	.14
☐ 10 Mike Greenwell	.15	.07
☐ 11 Chuck Carr	.15	.07
☐ 12 Joe Carter	.40	.18
☐ 13 Lance Johnson	.15	.07
☐ 14 Jeff Blauser	.15	.07
☐ 15 Chris Hoiles	.15	.07
☐ 16 Rick Wilkins	.15	.07
☐ 17 Kirby Puckett	1.25	.55
☐ 18 Larry Walker	.60	.25
☐ 19 Randy Johnson	.60	.25
☐ 20 Bernard Gilkey	.30	.14
☐ 21 Devon White	.15	.07
☐ 22 Randy Myers	.15	.07
☐ 23 Don Mattingly	1.00	.45
☐ 24 John Kruk	.30	.14
☐ 25 Ozzie Guillen	.15	.07
☐ 26 Jeff Conine	.30	.14
☐ 27 Mike Macfarlane	.15	.07
☐ 28 Dave Hollins	.15	.07
☐ 29 Chuck Knoblauch	.60	.25
☐ 30 Ozzie Smith	.75	.35
☐ 31 Harold Baines	.30	.14
☐ 32 Ryne Sandberg	.75	.35
☐ 33 Ron Karkovice	.15	.07
☐ 34 Terry Pendleton	.30	.14
☐ 35 Wally Joyner	.30	.14
☐ 36 Mike Mussina	.60	.25
☐ 37 Felix Jose	.15	.07
☐ 38 Derrick May	.15	.07
☐ 39 Scott Cooper	.15	.07
☐ 40 Jose Rijo	.15	.07
☐ 41 Robin Ventura	.30	.14
☐ 42 Charlie Hayes	.15	.07
☐ 43 Jimmy Key	.30	.14
☐ 44 Eric Karros	.30	.14
☐ 45 Ruben Sierra	.15	.07
☐ 46 Ryan Thompson	.15	.07
☐ 47 Brian McRae	.15	.07
☐ 48 Pat Hentgen	.30	.14
☐ 49 John Valentin	.30	.14
☐ 50 Al Martin	.15	.07
☐ 51 Jose Lind	.15	.07
☐ 52 Kevin Stocker	.15	.07
☐ 53 Mike Gallego	.15	.07
☐ 54 Dwight Gooden	.30	.14
☐ 55 Brady Anderson	.40	.18
☐ 56 Jeff King	.30	.14
☐ 57 Mark McGwire	1.25	.55
☐ 58 Sammy Sosa	.60	.25
☐ 59 Ryan Bowen	.15	.07
☐ 60 Mark Lemke	.15	.07
☐ 61 Roger Clemens	1.25	.55
☐ 62 Brian Jordan	.30	.14
☐ 63 Andres Galarraga	.40	.18
☐ 64 Kevin Appier	.30	.14
☐ 65 Don Slaught	.15	.07
☐ 66 Mike Blowers	.15	.07
☐ 67 Wes Chamberlain	.15	.07
☐ 68 Troy Neel	.15	.07
☐ 69 John Wetteland	.30	.14
☐ 70 Joe Girardi	.15	.07
☐ 71 Reggie Sanders	.15	.07
☐ 72 Edgar Martinez	.40	.18
☐ 73 Todd Hundley	.40	.18
☐ 74 Pat Borders	.15	.07
☐ 75 Roberto Mejia	.15	.07
☐ 76 David Cone	.30	.14
☐ 77 Tony Gwynn	1.50	.70
☐ 78 Jim Abbott	.15	.07
☐ 79 Jay Buhner	.40	.18
☐ 80 Mark McLemore	.15	.07
☐ 81 Wil Cordero	.30	.14
☐ 82 Pedro Astacio	.15	.07
☐ 83 Bob Tewksbury	.15	.07
☐ 84 Dave Winfield	.40	.18
☐ 85 Jeff Kent	.15	.07
☐ 86 Todd Van Poppel	.15	.07
☐ 87 Steve Avery	.15	.07
☐ 88 Mike Lansing	.30	.14
☐ 89 Lenny Dykstra	.30	.14
☐ 90 Jose Guzman	.15	.07
☐ 91 Brian R. Hunter	.15	.07
☐ 92 Tim Raines	.15	.07
☐ 93 Andre Dawson	.40	.18
☐ 94 Joe Orsulak	.15	.07
☐ 95 Ricky Jordan	.15	.07
☐ 96 Billy Hatcher	.15	.07
☐ 97 Jack McDowell	.15	.07
☐ 98 Tom Pagnozzi	.15	.07
☐ 99 Darryl Strawberry	.30	.14
☐ 100 Mike Stanley	.15	.07
☐ 101 Bret Saberhagen	.15	.07
☐ 102 Willie Greene	.30	.14
☐ 103 Bryan Harvey	.15	.07
☐ 104 Tim Bogar	.15	.07
☐ 105 Jack Voigt	.15	.07
☐ 106 Brad Ausmus	.15	.07
☐ 107 Ramon Martinez	.30	.14
☐ 108 Mike Perez	.15	.07
☐ 109 Jeff Montgomery	.30	.14
☐ 110 Danny Darwin	.15	.07
☐ 111 Wilson Alvarez	.30	.14
☐ 112 Kevin Mitchell	.30	.14
☐ 113 David Nied	.15	.07
☐ 114 Rich Amaral	.15	.07
☐ 115 Stan Javier	.15	.07
☐ 116 Mo Vaughn	.75	.35
☐ 117 Ben McDonald	.15	.07
☐ 118 Tom Gordon	.15	.07
☐ 119 Carlos Garcia	.15	.07
☐ 120 Phil Plantier	.15	.07
☐ 121 Mike Morgan	.15	.07
☐ 122 Pat Meares	.15	.07
☐ 123 Kevin Young	.15	.07
☐ 124 Jeff Fassero	.15	.07
☐ 125 Gene Harris	.15	.07
☐ 126 Bob Welch	.15	.07
☐ 127 Walt Weiss	.15	.07
☐ 128 Bobby Witt	.15	.07
☐ 129 Andy Van Slyke	.30	.14
☐ 130 Steve Cooke	.15	.07
☐ 131 Mike Devereaux	.15	.07
☐ 132 Joey Cora	.30	.14
☐ 133 Bret Barberie	.15	.07
☐ 134 Orel Hershiser	.30	.14
☐ 135 Ed Sprague	.15	.07
☐ 136 Shawon Dunston	.15	.07
☐ 137 Alex Arias	.15	.07
☐ 138 Archi Cianfrocco	.15	.07
☐ 139 Tim Wallach	.15	.07
☐ 140 Bernie Williams	.60	.25
☐ 141 Karl Rhodes	.15	.07
☐ 142 Pat Kelly	.15	.07
☐ 143 Dave Magadan	.15	.07
☐ 144 Kevin Tapani	.15	.07
☐ 145 Eric Young	.30	.14
☐ 146 Derek Bell	.30	.14
☐ 147 Dante Bichette	.40	.18
☐ 148 Geronimo Pena	.15	.07
☐ 149 Joe Oliver	.15	.07
☐ 150 Orestes Destrade	.15	.07
☐ 151 Tim Naehring	.15	.07
☐ 152 Ray Lankford	.40	.18
☐ 153 Phil Clark	.15	.07
☐ 154 David McCarty	.15	.07
☐ 155 Tommy Greene	.15	.07
☐ 156 Wade Boggs	.60	.25
☐ 157 Kevin Gross	.15	.07
☐ 158 Hal Morris	.15	.07
☐ 159 Moises Alou	.30	.14
☐ 160 Rick Aguilera	.15	.07
☐ 161 Curt Schilling	.30	.14
☐ 162 Chip Hale	.15	.07
☐ 163 Tino Martinez	.60	.25
☐ 164 Mark Whiten	.15	.07
☐ 165 Dave Stewart	.30	.14
☐ 166 Steve Buechele	.15	.07
☐ 167 Bobby Jones	.30	.14
☐ 168 Darrin Fletcher	.15	.07
☐ 169 John Smiley	.15	.07
☐ 170 Cory Snyder	.15	.07
☐ 171 Scott Erickson	.15	.07
☐ 172 Kirk Rueter	.15	.07
☐ 173 Dave Fleming	.15	.07
☐ 174 John Smoltz	.40	.18
☐ 175 Ricky Gutierrez	.15	.07
☐ 176 Mike Bordick	.15	.07
☐ 177 Chan Ho Park	1.50	.70
☐ 178 Alex Gonzalez	.30	.14
☐ 179 Steve Karsay	.15	.07
☐ 180 Jeffrey Hammonds	.30	.14
☐ 181 Manny Ramirez	.75	.35
☐ 182 Salomon Torres	.15	.07
☐ 183 Raul Mondesi	.40	.18
☐ 184 James Mouton	.30	.14
☐ 185 Cliff Floyd	.30	.14
☐ 186 Danny Bautista	.15	.07
☐ 187 Kurt Abbott	.30	.14
☐ 188 Javier Lopez	.40	.18
☐ 189 John Patterson	.15	.07
☐ 190 Greg Blosser	.15	.07
☐ 191 Bob Hamelin	.15	.07
☐ 192 Tony Eusebio	.15	.07
☐ 193 Carlos Delgado	.40	.18
☐ 194 Chris Gomez	.15	.07
☐ 195 Kelly Stinnett	.15	.07
☐ 196 Shane Reynolds	.15	.07
☐ 197 Ryan Klesko	.40	.18
☐ 198 Jim Edmonds UER Mark Dalesandro pictured on front	.60	.25
☐ 199 James Hurst	.15	.07
☐ 200 Dave Staton	.15	.07
☐ 201 Rondell White	.40	.18
☐ 202 Keith Mitchell	.15	.07
☐ 203 Darren Oliver	.60	.25
☐ 204 Mike Matheny	.15	.07
☐ 205 Chris Turner	.15	.07
☐ 206 Matt Mieske	.15	.07
☐ 207 NL Team Checklist	.15	.07
☐ 208 NL Team Checklist	.15	.07
☐ 209 AL Team Checklist	.15	.07
☐ 210 AL Team Checklist	.15	.07
☐ 211 Barry Bonds	.75	.35
☐ 212 Juan Gonzalez	1.50	.70
☐ 213 Jim Eisenreich	.30	.14
☐ 214 Ivan Rodriguez	.75	.35
☐ 215 Tony Phillips	.15	.07
☐ 216 John Jaha	.15	.07
☐ 217 Lee Smith	.30	.14
☐ 218 Bip Roberts	.15	.07
☐ 219 Dave Hansen	.15	.07
☐ 220 Pat Listach	.15	.07
☐ 221 Willie McGee	.15	.07
☐ 222 Damion Easley	.15	.07
☐ 223 Dean Palmer	.30	.14
☐ 224 Mike Moore	.15	.07
☐ 225 Brian Harper	.15	.07
☐ 226 Gary DiSarcina	.15	.07
☐ 227 Delino DeShields	.15	.07
☐ 228 Otis Nixon	.30	.14
☐ 229 Roberto Alomar	.60	.25
☐ 230 Mark Grace	.40	.18
☐ 231 Kenny Lofton	.75	.35
☐ 232 Gregg Jefferies	.30	.14

☐ 233 Cecil Fielder .30 .14
☐ 234 Jeff Bagwell 1.25 .55
☐ 235 Albert Belle .75 .35
☐ 236 Dave Justice .40 .18
☐ 237 Tom Henke .15 .07
☐ 238 Bobby Bonilla .30 .14
☐ 239 John Olerud .30 .14
☐ 240 Robby Thompson .15 .07
☐ 241 Dave Valle .15 .07
☐ 242 Marquis Grissom .30 .14
☐ 243 Greg Swindell .15 .07
☐ 244 Todd Zeile .15 .07
☐ 245 Dennis Eckersley .40 .18
☐ 246 Jose Offerman .15 .07
☐ 247 Greg McMichael .15 .07
☐ 248 Tim Belcher .15 .07
☐ 249 Cal Ripken Jr. 2.50 1.10
☐ 250 Tom Glavine .40 .18
☐ 251 Luis Polonia .15 .07
☐ 252 Bill Swift .15 .07
☐ 253 Juan Guzman .15 .07
☐ 254 Rickey Henderson .40 .18
☐ 255 Terry Mulholland .15 .07
☐ 256 Gary Sheffield .60 .25
☐ 257 Terry Steinbach .30 .14
☐ 258 Brett Butler .30 .14
☐ 259 Jason Bere .15 .07
☐ 260 Doug Strange .15 .07
☐ 261 Kent Hrbek .30 .14
☐ 262 Graeme Lloyd .15 .07
☐ 263 Lou Frazier .15 .07
☐ 264 Charles Nagy .30 .14
☐ 265 Bret Boone .15 .07
☐ 266 Kirk Gibson .30 .14
☐ 267 Kevin Brown .30 .14
☐ 268 Fred McGriff .40 .18
☐ 269 Matt Williams .40 .18
☐ 270 Greg Gagne .15 .07
☐ 271 Mariano Duncan .15 .07
☐ 272 Jeff Russell .15 .07
☐ 273 Eric Davis .30 .14
☐ 274 Shane Mack .15 .07
☐ 275 Jose Vizcaino .15 .07
☐ 276 Jose Canseco .40 .18
☐ 277 Roberto Hernandez .30 .14
☐ 278 Royce Clayton .15 .07
☐ 279 Carlos Baerga .30 .14
☐ 280 Pete Incaviglia .15 .07
☐ 281 Brent Gates .15 .07
☐ 282 Jeromy Burnitz .30 .14
☐ 283 Chili Davis .30 .14
☐ 284 Pete Harnisch .15 .07
☐ 285 Alan Trammell .40 .18
☐ 286 Eric Anthony .15 .07
☐ 287 Ellis Burks .30 .14
☐ 288 Julio Franco .30 .14
☐ 289 Jack Morris .30 .14
☐ 290 Erik Hanson .15 .07
☐ 291 Chuck Finley .15 .07
☐ 292 Reggie Jefferson .30 .14
☐ 293 Kevin McReynolds .15 .07
☐ 294 Greg Hibbard .15 .07
☐ 295 Travis Fryman .30 .14
☐ 296 Craig Biggio .40 .18
☐ 297 Kenny Rogers .15 .07
☐ 298 Dave Henderson .15 .07
☐ 299 Jim Thome .75 .35
☐ 300 Rene Arocha .15 .07
☐ 301 Pedro Munoz .15 .07
☐ 302 David Hulse .15 .07
☐ 303 Greg Vaughn .15 .07
☐ 304 Darren Lewis .15 .07
☐ 305 Deion Sanders .60 .25
☐ 306 Danny Tartabull .15 .07
☐ 307 Darryl Hamilton .15 .07
☐ 308 Andujar Cedeno .15 .07
☐ 309 Tim Salmon .60 .25
☐ 310 Tony Fernandez .15 .07
☐ 311 Alex Fernandez .30 .14
☐ 312 Roberto Kelly .15 .07
☐ 313 Harold Reynolds .15 .07
☐ 314 Chris Sabo .15 .07
☐ 315 Howard Johnson .15 .07
☐ 316 Mark Portugal .15 .07
☐ 317 Rafael Palmeiro .40 .18
☐ 318 Pete Smith .15 .07
☐ 319 Will Clark .40 .18
☐ 320 Henry Rodriguez .15 .07
☐ 321 Omar Vizquel .30 .14
☐ 322 David Segui .15 .07
☐ 323 Lou Whitaker .30 .14
☐ 324 Felix Fermin .15 .07
☐ 325 Spike Owen .15 .07
☐ 326 Darryl Kile .30 .14
☐ 327 Chad Kreuter .15 .07
☐ 328 Rod Beck .30 .14
☐ 329 Eddie Murray .60 .25
☐ 330 B.J. Surhoff .15 .07
☐ 331 Mickey Tettleton .15 .07
☐ 332 Pedro Martinez .60 .25
☐ 333 Roger Pavlik .15 .07
☐ 334 Eddie Taubensee .15 .07
☐ 335 John Doherty .15 .07
☐ 336 Jody Reed .15 .07
☐ 337 Aaron Sele .15 .07
☐ 338 Leo Gomez .15 .07
☐ 339 Dave Nilsson .30 .14
☐ 340 Rob Dibble .15 .07
☐ 341 John Burkett .15 .07
☐ 342 Wayne Kirby .15 .07
☐ 343 Dan Wilson .30 .14
☐ 344 Armando Reynoso .15 .07
☐ 345 Chad Curtis .15 .07
☐ 346 Dennis Martinez .30 .14
☐ 347 Cal Eldred .15 .07
☐ 348 Luis Gonzalez .15 .07
☐ 349 Doug Drabek .15 .07
☐ 350 Jim Leyritz .15 .07
☐ 351 Mark Langston .15 .07
☐ 352 Darrin Jackson .15 .07
☐ 353 Sid Fernandez .15 .07
☐ 354 Benito Santiago .15 .07
☐ 355 Kevin Seitzer .15 .07
☐ 356 Bo Jackson .30 .14
☐ 357 David Wells .15 .07
☐ 358 Paul Sorrento .15 .07
☐ 359 Ken Caminiti .60 .25
☐ 360 Eduardo Perez .15 .07
☐ 361 Orlando Merced .15 .07
☐ 362 Steve Finley .30 .14
☐ 363 Andy Benes .30 .14
☐ 364 Manuel Lee .15 .07
☐ 365 Todd Benzinger .15 .07
☐ 366 Sandy Alomar Jr. .30 .14
☐ 367 Rex Hudler .15 .07
☐ 368 Mike Henneman .15 .07
☐ 369 Vince Coleman .15 .07
☐ 370 Kirt Manwaring .15 .07
☐ 371 Ken Hill .15 .07
☐ 372 Glenallen Hill .15 .07
☐ 373 Sean Berry .15 .07
☐ 374 Geronimo Berroa .30 .14
☐ 375 Duane Ward .15 .07
☐ 376 Allen Watson .15 .07
☐ 377 Marc Newfield .30 .14
☐ 378 Dan Miceli .15 .07
☐ 379 Denny Hocking .15 .07
☐ 380 Mark Kiefer .15 .07
☐ 381 Tony Tarasco .15 .07
☐ 382 Tony Longmire .15 .07
☐ 383 Brian Anderson .40 .18
☐ 384 Fernando Vina .15 .07
☐ 385 Hector Carrasco .15 .07
☐ 386 Mike Kelly .15 .07
☐ 387 Greg Colbrunn .15 .07
☐ 388 Roger Salkeld .15 .07
☐ 389 Steve Trachsel .15 .07
☐ 390 Rich Becker .30 .14
☐ 391 Billy Taylor .15 .07
☐ 392 Rich Rowland .15 .07
☐ 393 Carl Everett .15 .07
☐ 394 Johnny Ruffin .15 .07
☐ 395 Keith Lockhart .15 .07
☐ 396 J.R. Phillips .15 .07
☐ 397 Sterling Hitchcock .30 .14
☐ 398 Jorge Fabregas .15 .07
☐ 399 Jeff Granger .30 .14
☐ 400 Eddie Zambrano .15 .07
☐ 401 Rikkert Faneyte .15 .07
☐ 402 Gerald Williams .15 .07
☐ 403 Joey Hamilton .40 .18
☐ 404 Joe Hall .15 .07
☐ 405 John Hudek .15 .07
☐ 406 Roberto Petagine .15 .07
☐ 407 Charles Johnson .40 .18
☐ 408 Mark Smith .15 .07
☐ 409 Jeff Juden .15 .07
☐ 410 Carlos Pulido .15 .07
☐ 411 Paul Shuey .15 .07
☐ 412 Rob Butler .15 .07
☐ 413 Mark Acre .15 .07
☐ 414 Greg Pirkl .15 .07
☐ 415 Melvin Nieves .30 .14
☐ 416 Tim Hyers .15 .07
☐ 417 NL Checklist .15 .07
☐ 418 NL Checklist .15 .07
☐ 419 AL Checklist .15 .07
☐ 420 AL Checklist .15 .07
☐ RY1 Carlos Delgado 5.00 2.20
☐ SS1 Cal Ripken Jr. Salute 40.00 18.00
☐ SS2 Dave Winfield Salute 5.00 2.20
☐ MVP1 Paul Molitor 8.00 3.60

1994 Select Crown Contenders

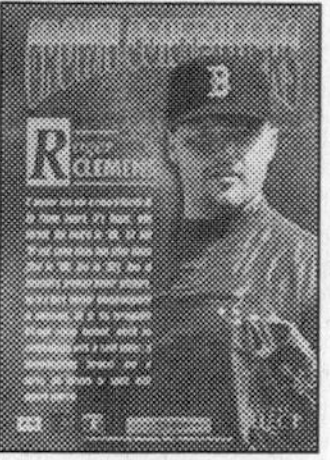

This ten-card set showcases top contenders for various awards such as batting champion, Cy Young Award winner and Most Valuable Player. The cards were inserted in first series packs at a rate of one in 24 and measure the standard size. The horizontal fronts feature color action player shots on a holographic gold foil background. The backs carry a color player close-up photo and highlights. The cards are numbered on the back with a CC prefix.

	MINT	NRMT
COMPLETE SET (10)	80.00	36.00
COMMON CARD (CC1-CC10)	2.00	.90
☐ CC1 Lenny Dykstra	2.00	.90
☐ CC2 Greg Maddux	12.00	5.50
☐ CC3 Roger Clemens	7.50	3.40
☐ CC4 Randy Johnson	5.00	2.20
☐ CC5 Frank Thomas	15.00	6.75
☐ CC6 Barry Bonds	5.00	2.20
☐ CC7 Juan Gonzalez	10.00	4.50
☐ CC8 John Olerud	2.00	.90
☐ CC9 Mike Piazza	12.00	5.50
☐ CC10 Ken Griffey Jr.	20.00	9.00

1994 Select Rookie Surge

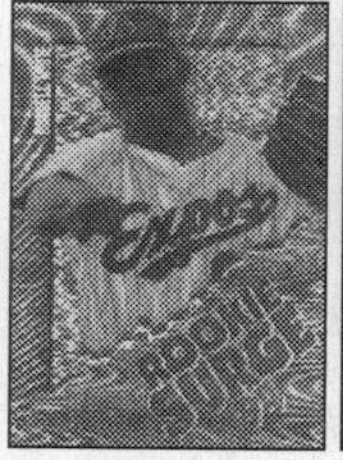

This 18-card standard-size set showcased potential top rookies for 1994. The set was divided into two series of nine cards. The cards were randomly inserted in packs at a rate of one in 48. The fronts exhibit Score's "dufex" printing process, in which a color photo is printed on a metallic base creating an unusual, three-dimensional look. On a multi-colored background, the horizontal backs present a color player headshot. The cards are numbered on the back with an RS prefix.

	MINT	NRMT
COMPLETE SET (18)	80.00	36.00
COMPLETE SERIES 1 (9)	30.00	13.50
COMPLETE SERIES 2 (9)	50.00	22.00
COMMON CARD (RS1-RS18)	2.50	1.10
☐ RS1 Cliff Floyd	5.00	2.20
☐ RS2 Bob Hamelin	2.50	1.10
☐ RS3 Ryan Klesko	12.00	5.50
☐ RS4 Carlos Delgado	10.00	4.50
☐ RS5 Jeffrey Hammonds	5.00	2.20
☐ RS6 Rondell White	6.00	2.70
☐ RS7 Salomon Torres	2.50	1.10
☐ RS8 Steve Karsay	2.50	1.10
☐ RS9 Javier Lopez	10.00	4.50
☐ RS10 Manny Ramirez	20.00	9.00
☐ RS11 Tony Tarasco	2.50	1.10
☐ RS12 Kurt Abbott	2.50	1.10
☐ RS13 Chan Ho Park	20.00	9.00
☐ RS14 Rich Becker	5.00	2.20
☐ RS15 James Mouton	2.50	1.10
☐ RS16 Alex Gonzalez	2.50	1.10
☐ RS17 Raul Mondesi	12.00	5.50
☐ RS18 Steve Trachsel	2.50	1.10

1994 Select Skills

This 10-card standard-size set takes an up close look at the leagues top statistical leaders. The cards were randomly inserted in second series packs at a rate of

approximately one in 24. A foil front has a holographic appearance that allows the player to stand out. The bottom of the front notes the player as being the best at something. For example, the front of Barry Bonds' card notes, "Select's Best Run Producer". The back has a small photo with text. The cards are numbered with an "SK" prefix.

	MINT	NRMT
COMPLETE SET (10)	60.00	27.00
COMMON CARD (SK1-SK10)	4.00	1.80
☐ SK1 Randy Johnson	10.00	4.50
☐ SK2 Barry Larkin	7.50	3.40
☐ SK3 Lenny Dykstra	4.00	1.80
☐ SK4 Kenny Lofton	15.00	6.75
☐ SK5 Juan Gonzalez	25.00	11.00
☐ SK6 Barry Bonds	12.00	5.50
☐ SK7 Marquis Grissom	6.00	2.70
☐ SK8 Ivan Rodriguez	12.00	5.50
☐ SK9 Larry Walker	10.00	4.50
☐ SK10 Travis Fryman	6.00	2.70

1995 Select Samples

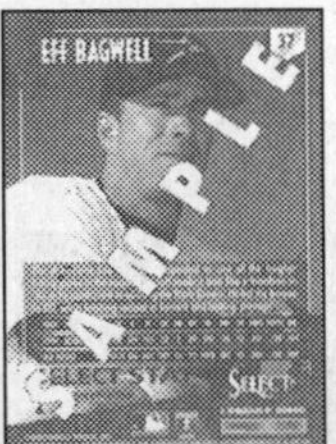

This 4-card set was issued to preview the 1995 Select series. On horizontal fronts, the regular issue cards display a full-bleed color action photo edged on the right by a team color-coded marbleized trapezoid. A color closeup photo is superposed over the trapezoid. The backs carry player profile and statistics printed on a black-and-white closeup photo. Both sides of each card have the disclaimer "SAMPLE" diagonally stamped across the pictures.

	MINT	NRMT
COMPLETE SET (4)	15.00	6.75
COMMON CARD	1.00	.45
☐ 34 Roberto Alomar	2.50	1.10
☐ 37 Jeff Bagwell	4.00	1.80
☐ 241 Alex Rodriguez	10.00	4.50
☐ NNO Title Card	1.00	.45

1995 Select

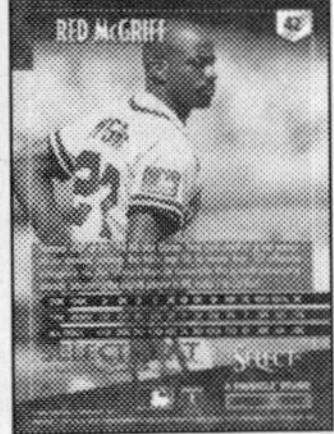

This 250-card set was issued in 12-card packs with 24 packs per box and 24 boxes per case. There was an announced production run of 4,950 cases. These horizontal cards feature an action photo over most of the card with the playerís profile and name on the right side. The "Select 95" logo is in the upper left corner. The vertical backs have a black and white photo on the top. The middle of the card is dedicated to a brief biography as well as seasonal and career stats. A specific important stat is included at the bottom of the card. A special card of Hideo Nomo (#251) was issued to hobby dealers who had bought cases of the Select product.

	MINT	NRMT
COMPLETE SET (250)	15.00	6.75
COMMON CARD (1-250)	.10	.05
☐ 1 Cal Ripken Jr.	1.50	.70
☐ 2 Robin Ventura	.20	.09
☐ 3 Al Martin	.20	.09
☐ 4 Jeff Frye	.10	.05
☐ 5 Darryl Strawberry	.20	.09
☐ 6 Chan Ho Park	.40	.18
☐ 7 Steve Avery	.10	.05
☐ 8 Bret Boone	.10	.05
☐ 9 Danny Tartabull	.10	.05
☐ 10 Dante Bichette	.30	.14
☐ 11 Rondell White	.30	.14
☐ 12 Dave McCarty	.10	.05
☐ 13 Bernard Gilkey	.20	.09
☐ 14 Mark McGwire	.75	.35
☐ 15 Ruben Sierra	.10	.05
☐ 16 Wade Boggs	.30	.14
☐ 17 Mike Piazza	1.25	.55
☐ 18 Jeffrey Hammonds	.20	.09
☐ 19 Mike Mussina	.40	.18
☐ 20 Darryl Kile	.20	.09
☐ 21 Greg Maddux	1.25	.55
☐ 22 Frank Thomas	1.50	.70
☐ 23 Kevin Appier	.20	.09
☐ 24 Jay Bell	.20	.09
☐ 25 Kirk Gibson	.20	.09
☐ 26 Pat Hentgen	.20	.09
☐ 27 Joey Hamilton	.20	.09
☐ 28 Bernie Williams	.40	.18
☐ 29 Aaron Sele	.10	.05
☐ 30 Delino DeShields	.10	.05
☐ 31 Danny Bautista	.10	.05
☐ 32 Jim Thome	.40	.18
☐ 33 Rikkert Faneyte	.10	.05
☐ 34 Roberto Alomar	.40	.18
☐ 35 Paul Molitor	.40	.18
☐ 36 Allen Watson	.10	.05
☐ 37 Jeff Bagwell	.75	.35
☐ 38 Jay Buhner	.30	.14
☐ 39 Marquis Grissom	.20	.09
☐ 40 Jim Edmonds	.40	.18
☐ 41 Ryan Klesko	.30	.14
☐ 42 Fred McGriff	.30	.14
☐ 43 Tony Tarasco	.10	.05
☐ 44 Darren Daulton	.20	.09
☐ 45 Marc Newfield	.20	.09
☐ 46 Barry Bonds	.50	.23
☐ 47 Bobby Bonilla	.20	.09
☐ 48 Greg Pirkl	.10	.05
☐ 49 Steve Karsay	.10	.05
☐ 50 Bob Hamelin	.10	.05
☐ 51 Javier Lopez	.30	.14
☐ 52 Barry Larkin	.30	.14
☐ 53 Kevin Young	.10	.05
☐ 54 Sterling Hitchcock	.20	.09
☐ 55 Tom Glavine	.30	.14
☐ 56 Carlos Delgado	.20	.09
☐ 57 Darren Oliver	.20	.09
☐ 58 Cliff Floyd	.20	.09
☐ 59 Tim Salmon	.40	.18
☐ 60 Albert Belle	.50	.23
☐ 61 Salomon Torres	.10	.05
☐ 62 Gary Sheffield	.40	.18
☐ 63 Ivan Rodriguez	.50	.23
☐ 64 Charles Nagy	.20	.09
☐ 65 Eduardo Perez	.10	.05
☐ 66 Terry Steinbach	.20	.09
☐ 67 Dave Justice	.40	.18
☐ 68 Jason Bere	.10	.05
☐ 69 Dave Nilsson	.20	.09
☐ 70 Brian Anderson	.10	.05
☐ 71 Billy Ashley	.10	.05
☐ 72 Roger Clemens	.75	.35
☐ 73 Jimmy Key	.20	.09
☐ 74 Wally Joyner	.20	.09
☐ 75 Andy Benes	.10	.05
☐ 76 Ray Lankford	.20	.09
☐ 77 Jeff Kent	.10	.05
☐ 78 Moises Alou	.20	.09
☐ 79 Kirby Puckett	.75	.35
☐ 80 Joe Carter	.30	.14
☐ 81 Manny Ramirez	.40	.18
☐ 82 J.R. Phillips	.10	.05
☐ 83 Matt Mieske	.10	.05
☐ 84 John Olerud	.20	.09
☐ 85 Andres Galarraga	.30	.14
☐ 86 Juan Gonzalez	1.00	.45
☐ 87 Pedro Martinez	.40	.18
☐ 88 Dean Palmer	.20	.09
☐ 89 Ken Griffey Jr.	2.00	.90
☐ 90 Brian Jordan	.20	.09
☐ 91 Hal Morris	.10	.05
☐ 92 Lenny Dykstra	.20	.09
☐ 93 Wil Cordero	.10	.05
☐ 94 Tony Gwynn	1.00	.45
☐ 95 Alex Gonzalez	.10	.05
☐ 96 Cecil Fielder	.20	.09
☐ 97 Mo Vaughn	.50	.23
☐ 98 John Valentin	.20	.09
☐ 99 Will Clark	.30	.14
☐ 100 Geronimo Pena	.10	.05
☐ 101 Don Mattingly	.60	.25
☐ 102 Charles Johnson	.20	.09
☐ 103 Raul Mondesi	.30	.14
☐ 104 Reggie Sanders	.10	.05
☐ 105 Royce Clayton	.10	.05
☐ 106 Reggie Jefferson	.20	.09
☐ 107 Craig Biggio	.30	.14
☐ 108 Jack McDowell	.10	.05
☐ 109 James Mouton	.10	.05
☐ 110 Mike Greenwell	.10	.05
☐ 111 David Cone	.20	.09
☐ 112 Matt Williams	.30	.14
☐ 113 Garret Anderson	.30	.14
☐ 114 Carlos Garcia	.10	.05
☐ 115 Alex Fernandez	.10	.05
☐ 116 Deion Sanders	.40	.18
☐ 117 Chili Davis	.20	.09
☐ 118 Mike Kelly	.10	.05
☐ 119 Jeff Conine	.20	.09
☐ 120 Kenny Lofton	.50	.23
☐ 121 Rafael Palmeiro	.30	.14
☐ 122 Chuck Knoblauch	.30	.14
☐ 123 Ozzie Smith	.50	.23
☐ 124 Carlos Baerga	.10	.05
☐ 125 Brett Butler	.20	.09
☐ 126 Sammy Sosa	.40	.18
☐ 127 Ellis Burks	.20	.09
☐ 128 Bret Saberhagen	.10	.05
☐ 129 Doug Drabek	.10	.05
☐ 130 Dennis Martinez	.20	.09
☐ 131 Paul O'Neill	.20	.09
☐ 132 Travis Fryman	.20	.09
☐ 133 Brent Gates	.10	.05
☐ 134 Rickey Henderson	.30	.14
☐ 135 Randy Johnson	.40	.18
☐ 136 Mark Langston	.10	.05
☐ 137 Greg Colbrunn	.10	.05
☐ 138 Jose Rijo	.10	.05
☐ 139 Bryan Harvey	.10	.05
☐ 140 Dennis Eckersley	.20	.09
☐ 141 Ron Gant	.20	.09
☐ 142 Carl Everett	.10	.05
☐ 143 Jeff Granger	.10	.05
☐ 144 Ben McDonald	.10	.05
☐ 145 Kurt Abbott UER (Mariners logo on front	.10	.05
☐ 146 Jim Abbott	.10	.05
☐ 147 Jason Jacome	.10	.05
☐ 148 Rico Brogna	.10	.05
☐ 149 Cal Eldred	.10	.05
☐ 150 Rich Becker	.10	.05
☐ 151 Pete Harnisch	.10	.05
☐ 152 Roberto Petagine	.10	.05
☐ 153 Jacob Brumfield	.10	.05
☐ 154 Todd Hundley	.20	.09
☐ 155 Roger Cedeno	.10	.05
☐ 156 Harold Baines	.20	.09
☐ 157 Steve Dunn	.10	.05
☐ 158 Tim Belk	.10	.05
☐ 159 Marty Cordova	.30	.14
☐ 160 Russ Davis	.10	.05
☐ 161 Jose Malave	.10	.05
☐ 162 Brian Hunter	.30	.14
☐ 163 Andy Pettitte	.60	.25
☐ 164 Brooks Kieschnick	.20	.09
☐ 165 Midre Cummings	.10	.05
☐ 166 Frank Rodriguez	.20	.09
☐ 167 Chad Mottola	.10	.05
☐ 168 Brian Barber	.10	.05
☐ 169 Tim Unroe	.10	.05
☐ 170 Shane Andrews	.10	.05
☐ 171 Kevin Flora	.10	.05
☐ 172 Ray Durham	.30	.14
☐ 173 Chipper Jones	1.25	.55
☐ 174 Butch Huskey	.20	.09
☐ 175 Ray McDavid	.10	.05
☐ 176 Jeff Cirillo	.20	.09
☐ 177 Terry Pendleton	.20	.09
☐ 178 Scott Ruffcorn	.10	.05
☐ 179 Ray Holbert	.10	.05
☐ 180 Joe Randa	.10	.05
☐ 181 Jose Oliva	.10	.05
☐ 182 Andy Van Slyke	.20	.09
☐ 183 Albie Lopez	.10	.05
☐ 184 Chad Curtis	.10	.05
☐ 185 Ozzie Guillen	.10	.05

☐ 186 Chad Ogea	.10	.05
☐ 187 Dan Wilson	.20	.09
☐ 188 Tony Fernandez	.10	.05
☐ 189 John Smoltz	.30	.14
☐ 190 Willie Greene	.20	.09
☐ 191 Darren Lewis	.10	.05
☐ 192 Orlando Miller	.10	.05
☐ 193 Kurt Miller	.10	.05
☐ 194 Andrew Lorraine	.20	.09
☐ 195 Ernie Young	.10	.05
☐ 196 Jimmy Haynes	.20	.09
☐ 197 Raul Casanova	.30	.14
☐ 198 Joe Vitiello	.10	.05
☐ 199 Brad Woodall	.10	.05
☐ 200 Juan Acevedo	.10	.05
☐ 201 Michael Tucker	.20	.09
☐ 202 Shawn Green	.20	.09
☐ 203 Alex Rodriguez	1.50	.70
☐ 204 Julian Tavarez	.10	.05
☐ 205 Jose Lima	.10	.05
☐ 206 Wilson Alvarez	.20	.09
☐ 207 Rich Aude	.10	.05
☐ 208 Armando Benitez	.10	.05
☐ 209 Dwayne Hosey	.10	.05
☐ 210 Gabe White	.10	.05
☐ 211 Joey Eischen	.10	.05
☐ 212 Bill Pulsipher	.20	.09
☐ 213 Robby Thompson	.10	.05
☐ 214 Toby Borland	.10	.05
☐ 215 Rusty Greer	.40	.18
☐ 216 Fausto Cruz	.10	.05
☐ 217 Luis Ortiz	.10	.05
☐ 218 Duane Singleton	.10	.05
☐ 219 Troy Percival	.10	.05
☐ 220 Gregg Jefferies	.20	.09
☐ 221 Mark Grace	.30	.14
☐ 222 Mickey Tettleton	.10	.05
☐ 223 Phil Plantier	.10	.05
☐ 224 Larry Walker	.40	.18
☐ 225 Ken Caminiti	.40	.18
☐ 226 Dave Winfield	.30	.14
☐ 227 Brady Anderson	.30	.14
☐ 228 Kevin Brown	.20	.09
☐ 229 Andujar Cedeno	.10	.05
☐ 230 Roberto Kelly	.10	.05
☐ 231 Jose Canseco	.30	.14
☐ 232 Scott Ruffcorn ST	.10	.05
☐ 233 Billy Ashley ST	.10	.05
☐ 234 J.R. Phillips ST	.10	.05
☐ 235 Chipper Jones ST	.60	.25
☐ 236 Charles Johnson ST	.20	.09
☐ 237 Midre Cummings ST	.10	.05
☐ 238 Brian L.Hunter SH	.20	.09
☐ 239 Garret Anderson ST	.20	.09
☐ 240 Shawn Green SH	.20	.09
☐ 241 Alex Rodriguez ST	1.25	.55
☐ 242 Frank Thomas CL	1.00	.45
☐ 243 Ken Griffey Jr. CL	1.00	.45
☐ 244 Albert Belle CL	.40	.18
☐ 245 Cal Ripken Jr. CL	.75	.35
☐ 246 Barry Bonds CL	.30	.14
☐ 247 Raul Mondesi CL	.30	.14
☐ 248 Mike Piazza CL	.60	.25
☐ 249 Jeff Bagwell CL	.40	.18
☐ 250 Jeff Bagwell Ken Griffey Jr. Frank Thomas Mike Piazza CL	1.25	.55
☐ 251S Hideo Nomo	2.50	1.10

1995 Select Artist's Proofs

This 250-card set is parallel to the regular Select set. These cards were inserted at a rate of one per 24 packs. The only difference between these cards and the regular issue cards are the words "Artist's Proof" printed in the lower left corner. The Hideo Nomo card was randomly distributed directly to hobby dealers and was never inserted in packs.

	MINT	NRMT
COMPLETE SET (250)	2000.00	900.00
COMMON CARD (1-250)	3.00	1.35

*STARS: 35X TO 60X BASIC CARDS..
*YOUNG STARS: 30X TO 50X BASIC CARDS

1995 Select Big Sticks

Randomly inserted in packs, these 12 cards feature leading hitters. The fronts picture the playerís photo against a metallic background. The words "Big Sticks 95" as well as the player's name is on the bottom. The player's team is noted in the middle of the background. The backs contain a player photo, personal information as well as some notes about his career. The cards are numbered in the upper right corner with a "BS" prefix.

	MINT	NRMT
COMPLETE SET (12)	150.00	70.00
COMMON CARD (1-12)	4.00	1.80
☐ BS1 Frank Thomas	25.00	11.00
☐ BS2 Ken Griffey Jr.	30.00	13.50
☐ BS3 Cal Ripken Jr.	25.00	11.00
☐ BS4 Mike Piazza	20.00	9.00
☐ BS5 Don Mattingly	15.00	6.75
☐ BS6 Will Clark	5.00	2.20
☐ BS7 Tony Gwynn	12.00	5.50
☐ BS8 Jeff Bagwell	12.00	5.50
☐ BS9 Barry Bonds	8.00	3.60
☐ BS10 Paul Molitor	6.00	2.70
☐ BS11 Matt Williams	4.00	1.80
☐ BS12 Albert Belle	8.00	3.60

1995 Select Can't Miss

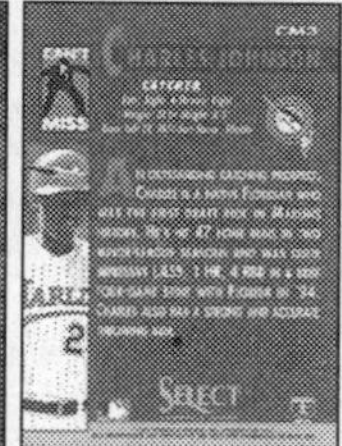

These 12 cards featuring promising young players were inserted one per 24 packs. The player is pictured against a wavy red background. His last name is identified on the bottom left with the "Can't Miss" logo directly above the name. In the middle of the "Can't Miss" logo is a drawing of an umpire signaling safe. The backs have a blue background and include an inset photo, some professional information and biographical data. The cards are numbered with a "CM" prefix in the upper right corner.

	MINT	NRMT
COMPLETE SET (12)	50.00	22.00
COMMON CARD (1-12)	2.00	.90
☐ CM1 Cliff Floyd	2.00	.90
☐ CM2 Ryan Klesko	5.00	2.20
☐ CM3 Charles Johnson	3.00	1.35
☐ CM4 Raul Mondesi	3.00	1.35
☐ CM5 Manny Ramirez	5.00	2.20
☐ CM6 Billy Ashley	2.00	.90
☐ CM7 Alex Gonzalez	2.00	.90
☐ CM8 Carlos Delgado	3.00	1.35
☐ CM9 Garret Anderson	3.00	1.35
☐ CM10 Alex Rodriguez	20.00	9.00
☐ CM11 Chipper Jones	15.00	6.75
☐ CM12 Shawn Green	2.50	1.10

1995 Select Sure Shots

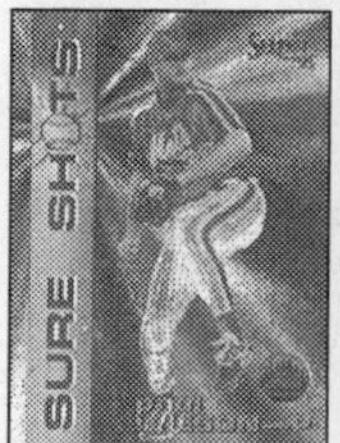

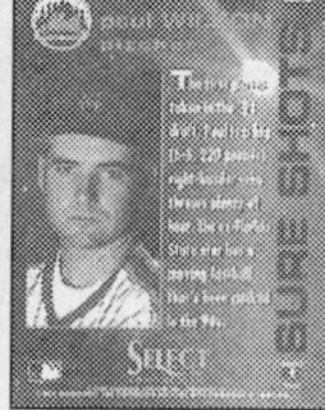

These ten cards were randomly inserted into packs at a rate of one in 90. This set features some of the top 1994 draft picks. The fronts feature the player's photo against a gold metallic background. The phrase "Sure Shots" is printed on gold ink against a blue background on the left. The player is identified in white ink on the bottom. The backs contain some information about the player as well as an inset photo. All this information is set against a blue background with a white light effect. The cards are numbered with an "SS" prefix in the upper right corner.

	MINT	NRMT
COMPLETE SET (10)	80.00	36.00
COMMON CARD (1-10)	2.00	.90
☐ SS1 Ben Grieve	30.00	13.50
☐ SS2 Kevin Witt	8.00	3.60
☐ SS3 Mark Farris	2.00	.90
☐ SS4 Paul Konerko	30.00	13.50
☐ SS5 Dustin Hermanson	2.00	.90
☐ SS6 Ramon Castro	2.00	.90
☐ SS7 McKay Christensen	2.00	.90
☐ SS8 Brian Buchanan	2.00	.90
☐ SS9 Paul Wilson	3.00	1.35
☐ SS10 Terrence Long	6.00	2.70

1996 Select

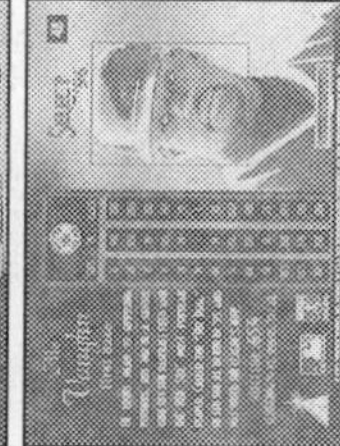

The 1996 Select set was issued in one series totalling 200 cards. The 10-card packs retail for $1.99 each. The fronts feature a color action player photo over most of the card with a small player photo framed and name in gold foil printing. The backs carry another player photo, player information and statistics. The set contains the topical subsets: Lineup Leaders (151-160) and Rookies (161-195).

	MINT	NRMT
COMPLETE SET (200)	15.00	6.75
COMMON CARD (1-200)	.10	.05
☐ 1 Wade Boggs	.40	.18
☐ 2 Shawn Green	.20	.09
☐ 3 Andres Galarraga	.40	.18
☐ 4 Bill Pulsipher	.10	.05
☐ 5 Chuck Knoblauch	.40	.18
☐ 6 Ken Griffey Jr.	2.00	.90
☐ 7 Greg Maddux	1.25	.55
☐ 8 Manny Ramirez	.40	.18
☐ 9 Ivan Rodriguez	.50	.23
☐ 10 Tim Salmon	.40	.18
☐ 11 Frank Thomas	1.50	.70
☐ 12 Jeff Bagwell	.75	.35
☐ 13 Travis Fryman	.20	.09
☐ 14 Kenny Lofton	.50	.23
☐ 15 Matt Williams	.30	.14
☐ 16 Jay Bell	.20	.09
☐ 17 Ken Caminiti	.40	.18
☐ 18 Ray Lankford	.20	.09
☐ 19 Cal Ripken	1.50	.70
☐ 20 Roger Clemens	.75	.35
☐ 21 Carlos Baerga	.20	.09
☐ 22 Mike Piazza	1.25	.55
☐ 23 Gregg Jefferies	.30	.14
☐ 24 Reggie Sanders	.10	.05
☐ 25 Rondell White	.20	.09
☐ 26 Sammy Sosa	.40	.18
☐ 27 Kevin Appier	.20	.09
☐ 28 Kevin Seitzer	.10	.05
☐ 29 Gary Sheffield	.40	.18
☐ 30 Mike Mussina	.40	.18
☐ 31 Mark McGwire	.75	.35
☐ 32 Barry Larkin	.30	.14
☐ 33 Marc Newfield	.10	.05
☐ 34 Ismael Valdes	.20	.09
☐ 35 Marty Cordova	.10	.05
☐ 36 Albert Belle	.50	.23
☐ 37 Johnny Damon	.20	.09
☐ 38 Garret Anderson	.20	.09
☐ 39 Cecil Fielder	.20	.09
☐ 40 John Mabry	.20	.09
☐ 41 Chipper Jones	1.25	.55
☐ 42 Omar Vizquel	.20	.09
☐ 43 Jose Rijo	.10	.05
☐ 44 Charles Johnson	.20	.09
☐ 45 Alex Rodriguez	1.50	.70
☐ 46 Rico Brogna	.10	.05
☐ 47 Joe Carter	.20	.09
☐ 48 Mo Vaughn	.50	.23

☐ 49 Moises Alou	.20	.09
☐ 50 Raul Mondesi	.30	.14
☐ 51 Robin Ventura	.20	.09
☐ 52 Jim Thome	.40	.18
☐ 53 David Justice	.40	.18
☐ 54 Jeff King	.20	.09
☐ 55 Brian L.Hunter	.20	.09
☐ 56 Juan Gonzalez	1.00	.45
☐ 57 John Olerud	.10	.05
☐ 58 Rafael Palmeiro	.30	.14
☐ 59 Tony Gwynn	1.00	.45
☐ 60 Eddie Murray	.40	.18
☐ 61 Jason Isringhausen	.10	.05
☐ 62 Dante Bichette	.20	.09
☐ 63 Randy Johnson	.40	.18
☐ 64 Kirby Puckett	.75	.35
☐ 65 Jim Edmonds	.40	.18
☐ 66 David Cone	.20	.09
☐ 67 Ozzie Smith	.50	.23
☐ 68 Fred McGriff	.30	.14
☐ 69 Darren Daulton	.20	.09
☐ 70 Edgar Martinez	.30	.14
☐ 71 J.T. Snow	.20	.09
☐ 72 Butch Huskey	.20	.09
☐ 73 Hideo Nomo	1.00	.45
☐ 74 Pedro Martinez	.40	.18
☐ 75 Bobby Bonilla	.20	.09
☐ 76 Jeff Conine	.20	.09
☐ 77 Ryan Klesko	.30	.14
☐ 78 Bernie Williams	.40	.18
☐ 79 Andre Dawson	.40	.18
☐ 80 Trevor Hoffman	.20	.09
☐ 81 Mark Grace	.30	.14
☐ 82 Benji Gil	.10	.05
☐ 83 Eric Karros	.20	.09
☐ 84 Pete Schourek	.10	.05
☐ 85 Edgardo Alfonzo	.30	.14
☐ 86 Jay Buhner	.30	.14
☐ 87 Vinny Castilla	.20	.09
☐ 88 Bret Boone	.10	.05
☐ 89 Ray Durham	.20	.09
☐ 90 Brian Jordan	.20	.09
☐ 91 Jose Canseco	.30	.14
☐ 92 Paul O'Neill	.20	.09
☐ 93 Chili Davis	.20	.09
☐ 94 Tom Glavine	.30	.14
☐ 95 Julian Tavarez	.10	.05
☐ 96 Derek Bell	.10	.05
☐ 97 Will Clark	.30	.14
☐ 98 Larry Walker	.40	.18
☐ 99 Denny Neagle	.20	.09
☐ 100 Alex Fernandez	.20	.09
☐ 101 Barry Bonds	.50	.23
☐ 102 Ben McDonald	.10	.05
☐ 103 Andy Pettitte	.50	.23
☐ 104 Tino Martinez	.40	.18
☐ 105 Sterling Hitchcock	.10	.05
☐ 106 Royce Clayton	.10	.05
☐ 107 Jim Abbott	.20	.09
☐ 108 Rickey Henderson	.30	.14
☐ 109 Ramon Martinez	.20	.09
☐ 110 Paul Molitor	.40	.18
☐ 111 Dennis Eckersley	.30	.14
☐ 112 Alex Gonzalez	.10	.05
☐ 113 Marquis Grissom	.20	.09
☐ 114 Greg Vaughn	.10	.05
☐ 115 Lance Johnson	.10	.05
☐ 116 Todd Stottleymyre	.10	.05
☐ 117 Jack McDowell	.10	.05
☐ 118 Ruben Sierra	.10	.05
☐ 119 Brady Anderson	.30	.14
☐ 120 Julio Franco	.20	.09
☐ 121 Brooks Kieschnick	.20	.09
☐ 122 Roberto Alomar	.40	.18
☐ 123 Greg Gagne	.10	.05
☐ 124 Wally Joyner	.10	.05
☐ 125 John Smoltz	.20	.09
☐ 126 John Valentin	.20	.09
☐ 127 Russ Davis	.10	.05
☐ 128 Joe Vitiello	.10	.05
☐ 129 Shawon Dunston	.10	.05
☐ 130 Frank Rodriguez	.10	.05
☐ 131 Charlie Hayes	.10	.05
☐ 132 Andy Benes	.10	.05
☐ 133 B.J. Surhoff	.10	.05
☐ 134 Dave Nilsson	.20	.09
☐ 135 Carlos Delgado	.20	.09
☐ 136 Walt Weiss	.10	.05
☐ 137 Mike Stanley	.10	.05
☐ 138 Greg Colbrunn	.10	.05
☐ 139 Mike Kelly	.10	.05
☐ 140 Ryne Sandberg	.50	.23
☐ 141 Lee Smith	.20	.09
☐ 142 Dennis Martinez	.20	.09
☐ 143 Bernard Gilkey	.20	.09
☐ 144 Lenny Dykstra	.10	.05
☐ 145 Danny Tartabull	.10	.05
☐ 146 Dean Palmer	.20	.09
☐ 147 Craig Biggio	.30	.14
☐ 148 Juan Acevedo	.10	.05
☐ 149 Michael Tucker	.20	.09
☐ 150 Bobby Higginson	.20	.09
☐ 151 Ken Griffey Jr. LUL	1.00	.45
☐ 152 Frank Thomas LUL	1.00	.45
☐ 153 Cal Ripken LUL	.75	.35
☐ 154 Albert Belle LUL	.40	.18
☐ 155 Mike Piazza LUL	.60	.25
☐ 156 Barry Bonds LUL	.40	.18
☐ 157 Sammy Sosa LUL	.40	.18
☐ 158 Mo Vaughn LUL	.40	.18
☐ 159 Greg Maddux LUL	.60	.25
☐ 160 Jeff Bagwell LUL	.40	.18
☐ 161 Derek Jeter	1.25	.55
☐ 162 Paul Wilson	.10	.05
☐ 163 Chris Snopek	.10	.05
☐ 164 Jason Schmidt	.20	.09
☐ 165 Jimmy Haynes	.10	.05
☐ 166 George Arias	.10	.05
☐ 167 Steve Gibralter	.10	.05
☐ 168 Bob Wolcott	.10	.05
☐ 169 Jason Kendall	.20	.09
☐ 170 Greg Zaun	.10	.05
☐ 171 Quinton McCracken	.10	.05
☐ 172 Alan Benes	.20	.09
☐ 173 Rey Ordonez	.20	.09
☐ 174 Livan Hernandez	1.00	.45
☐ 175 Osvaldo Fernandez	.20	.09
☐ 176 Marc Barcelo	.10	.05
☐ 177 Sal Fasano	.10	.05
☐ 178 Mike Grace	.10	.05
☐ 179 Chan Ho Park	.40	.18
☐ 180 Robert Perez	.10	.05
☐ 181 Todd Hollandsworth	.20	.09
☐ 182 Wilton Guerrero	.40	.18
☐ 183 John Wasdin	.10	.05
☐ 184 Jim Pittsley	.20	.09
☐ 185 LaTroy Hawkins	.10	.05
☐ 186 Jay Powell	.10	.05
☐ 187 Felipe Crespo	.10	.05
☐ 188 Jermaine Dye	.10	.05
☐ 189 Bob Abreu	.40	.18
☐ 190 Matt Luke	.10	.05
☐ 191 Richard Hidalgo	.40	.18
☐ 192 Karim Garcia	.20	.09
☐ 193 Marvin Benard	.10	.05
☐ 194 Andy Fox	.10	.05
☐ 195 Terrell Wade	.10	.05
☐ 196 Frank Thomas CL	1.00	.45
☐ 197 Ken Griffey Jr. CL	1.00	.45
☐ 198 Greg Maddux CL	.60	.25
☐ 199 Mike Piazza CL	.60	.25
☐ 200 Cal Ripken CL	.75	.35

1996 Select Artist's Proofs

Randomly inserted one in 35 packs, this 200-card set is parallel and similar in design to the regular set. The difference is the holographic foil-stamped Artist's Proof logo on the card front.

	MINT	NRMT
COMPLETE SET (200)	2000.00	900.00
COMMON CARD (1-200)	3.00	1.35

*STARS: 20X TO 40X BASIC CARDS..
*YOUNG STARS: 15X TO 30X BASIC CARDS

1996 Select Claim To Fame

Randomly inserted in packs at a rate of one in 72, this 20-card set features potential Hall of Famers. The fronts display a color player portrait on a diecut plaque similar to the ones that enshrine Hall of Famers. The backs carry information about the player's claim to fame. Only 2100 of these sets were produced.

	MINT	NRMT
COMPLETE SET (20)	300.00	135.00
COMMON CARD (1-20)	4.00	1.80
☐ 1 Cal Ripken	40.00	18.00
☐ 2 Greg Maddux	30.00	13.50
☐ 3 Ken Griffey Jr.	50.00	22.00
☐ 4 Frank Thomas	40.00	18.00
☐ 5 Mo Vaughn	12.00	5.50
☐ 6 Albert Belle	12.00	5.50
☐ 7 Jeff Bagwell	20.00	9.00
☐ 8 Sammy Sosa	8.00	3.60
☐ 9 Reggie Sanders	4.00	1.80
☐ 10 Hideo Nomo	25.00	11.00
☐ 11 Chipper Jones	30.00	13.50
☐ 12 Mike Piazza	30.00	13.50
☐ 13 Matt Williams	6.00	2.70
☐ 14 Tony Gwynn	25.00	11.00
☐ 15 Johnny Damon	5.00	2.20
☐ 16 Dante Bichette	5.00	2.20
☐ 17 Kirby Puckett	20.00	9.00
☐ 18 Barry Bonds	12.00	5.50
☐ 19 Randy Johnson	8.00	3.60
☐ 20 Eddie Murray	12.00	5.50

1996 Select En Fuego

Randomly inserted in packs at a rate of one in 48, this 25-card set is printed with all-foil Dufex technology, etched highlights and transparent inks that make each card shine. Spanish for "on fire," En Fuego is an expression popularized by ESPN sportscaster Dan Patrick, who provides the commentary for each player on the card back. The fronts feature color action player photos while the backs display more player photos and the commentary.

	MINT	NRMT
COMPLETE SET (25)	300.00	135.00
COMMON CARD (1-25)	3.00	1.35
☐ 1 Ken Griffey Jr.	40.00	18.00
☐ 2 Frank Thomas	30.00	13.50
☐ 3 Cal Ripken	30.00	13.50
☐ 4 Greg Maddux	25.00	11.00
☐ 5 Jeff Bagwell	15.00	6.75
☐ 6 Barry Bonds	10.00	4.50
☐ 7 Mo Vaughn	10.00	4.50
☐ 8 Albert Belle	10.00	4.50
☐ 9 Sammy Sosa	8.00	3.60
☐ 10 Reggie Sanders	3.00	1.35
☐ 11 Mike Piazza	25.00	11.00
☐ 12 Chipper Jones	25.00	11.00
☐ 13 Tony Gwynn	20.00	9.00
☐ 14 Kirby Puckett	15.00	6.75
☐ 15 Wade Boggs	8.00	3.60
☐ 16 Dan Patrick	8.00	3.60
☐ 17 Gary Sheffield	8.00	3.60
☐ 18 Dante Bichette	4.00	1.80
☐ 19 Randy Johnson	8.00	3.60
☐ 20 Matt Williams	5.00	2.20
☐ 21 Alex Rodriguez	25.00	11.00
☐ 22 Tim Salmon	8.00	3.60
☐ 23 Johnny Damon	4.00	1.80
☐ 24 Manny Ramirez	8.00	3.60
☐ 25 Hideo Nomo	20.00	9.00

1996 Select Team Nucleus

Randomly inserted in packs at a rate of one in 18, this 28-card set is printed on clear plastic with holographic and micro-etched highlights and gold foil stamping. The fronts feature color pictures of three team players with the backs displaying the same photos, the players' names, and a sentence stating why these players are special.

	MINT	NRMT
COMPLETE SET (28)	80.00	36.00
COMMON CARD (1-28)	2.00	.90
☐ 1 Albert Belle Manny Ramirez Carlos Baerga	4.00	1.80
☐ 2 Ray Lankford Brian Jordan Ozzie Smith	2.50	1.10
☐ 3 Jay Bell Jeff King Denny Neagle	2.00	.90
☐ 4 Dante Bichette Andres Galarraga Larry Walker	3.00	1.35
☐ 5 Mark McGwire Mike Bordick Terry Steinbach	2.25	1.00
☐ 6 Bernie Williams Wade Boggs David Cone	5.00	2.20
☐ 7 Joe Carter Alex Gonzalez Shawn Green	3.00	1.35
☐ 8 Roger Clemens Mo Vaughn Jose Canseco	6.00	2.70
☐ 9 Ken Griffey Jr. Edgar Martinez Randy Johnson	15.00	6.75
☐ 10 Gregg Jefferies Darren Daulton Len Dykstra	2.00	.90
☐ 11 Mike Piazza Raul Mondesi Hideo Nomo	12.00	5.50
☐ 12 Greg Maddux Chipper Jones Ryan Klesko	15.00	6.75
☐ 13 Cecil Fielder Travis Fryman Phil Nevin	2.00	.90
☐ 14 Ivan Rodriguez Will Clark Juan Gonzalez	8.00	3.60
☐ 15 Ryne Sandberg Sammy Sosa Mark Grace	4.00	1.80
☐ 16 Gary Sheffield Charles Johnson Andre Dawson	2.00	.90
☐ 17 Johnny Damon Michael Tucker Kevin Appier	2.00	.90
☐ 18 Barry Bonds Matt Williams Rod Beck	3.00	1.35
☐ 19 Kirby Puckett Chuck Knoblauch Marty Cordova	6.00	2.70
☐ 20 Cal Ripken Barry Bonilla Mike Mussina	12.00	5.50
☐ 21 Jason Isringhausen Bill Pulsipher Rico Brogna	2.00	.90
☐ 22 Tony Gwynn Ken Caminiti Mark Newfield	6.00	2.70
☐ 23 Tim Salmon Garret Anderson Jim Edmonds	2.50	1.10
☐ 24 Moises Alou Rondell White Cliff Floyd	2.00	.90
☐ 25 Barry Larkin Reggie Sanders Bret Boone	2.00	.90
☐ 26 Jeff Bagwell Craig Biggio Derek Bell	6.00	2.70
☐ 27 Frank Thomas Robin Ventura Alex Fernandez	12.00	5.50
☐ 28 John Jaha Greg Vaughn Kevin Seitzer	2.00	.90

1997 Select

The 1997 Select set was issued in two series totalling 200 cards and was distributed in hobby only six-card packs with a suggested retail price of $2.99. The fronts display a color action player photo over most of the card with a

small player photo at the bottom. The backs carry another player photo, player information and statistics. Each card featues a distinctive silver-foil treatment with either a red or blue foil accent. The red cards are twice as easy to find than the blue cards.

	MINT	NRMT
COMPLETE SET (200)	80.00	36.00
COMPLETE SERIES 1 (150)	50.00	22.00
COMPLETE HI SERIES (50)	30.00	13.50
COMMON RED (1-150)	.15	.07
COMMON BLUE (1-150)	.30	.14
COMMON HI SERIES (151-200)	.30	.14
☐ 1 Juan Gonzalez B	3.00	1.35
☐ 2 Mo Vaughn B	1.50	.70
☐ 3 Tony Gwynn	1.50	.70
☐ 4 Manny Ramirez B	1.25	.55
☐ 5 Jose Canseco R	.40	.18
☐ 6 David Cone R	.30	.14
☐ 7 Chan Ho Park R	.60	.25
☐ 8 Frank Thomas B	5.00	2.20
☐ 9 Todd Hollandsworth R	.15	.07
☐ 10 Marty Cordova R	.15	.07
☐ 11 Gary Sheffield B	1.25	.55
☐ 12 John Smoltz B	.60	.25
☐ 13 Mark Grudzielanek R	.15	.07
☐ 14 Sammy Sosa B	1.25	.55
☐ 15 Paul Molitor R	.60	.25
☐ 16 Kevin Brown R	.30	.14
☐ 17 Albert Belle B	1.50	.70
☐ 18 Eric Young R	.15	.07
☐ 19 John Wetteland R	.15	.07
☐ 20 Ryan Klesko B	1.00	.45
☐ 21 Joe Carter R	.30	.14
☐ 22 Alex Ochoa R	.15	.07
☐ 23 Greg Maddux B	4.00	1.80
☐ 24 Roger Clemens B	2.50	1.10
☐ 25 Ivan Rodriguez B	1.50	.70
☐ 26 Barry Bonds B	1.50	.70
☐ 27 Kenny Lofton B	1.50	.70
☐ 28 Javy Lopez R	.30	.14
☐ 29 Hideo Nomo B	3.00	1.35
☐ 30 Rusty Greer R	.30	.14
☐ 31 Rafael Palmeiro R	.40	.18
☐ 32 Mike Piazza B	4.00	1.80
☐ 33 Ryne Sandberg	.75	.35
☐ 34 Wade Boggs R	.60	.25
☐ 35 Jim Thome B	1.25	.55
☐ 36 Ken Caminiti B	1.25	.55
☐ 37 Mark Grace R	.40	.18
☐ 38 Brian Jordan B	.15	.07
☐ 39 Craig Biggio R	.40	.18
☐ 40 Henry Rodriguez R	.15	.07
☐ 41 Dean Palmer R	.15	.07
☐ 42 Jason Kendall R	.30	.14
☐ 43 Bill Pulsipher R	.15	.07
☐ 44 Tim Salmon B	1.25	.55
☐ 45 Marc Newfield R	.15	.07
☐ 46 Pat Hentgen R	.60	.25
☐ 47 Ken Griffey Jr. B	6.00	2.70
☐ 48 Paul Wilson R	.15	.07
☐ 49 Jay Buhner B	1.00	.45
☐ 50 Rickey Henderson R	.60	.25
☐ 51 Jeff Bagwell B	2.50	1.10
☐ 52 Cecil Fielder R	.30	.14
☐ 53 Alex Rodriguez B	5.00	2.20
☐ 54 John Jaha R	.15	.07
☐ 55 Brady Anderson B	1.00	.45
☐ 56 Andres Galarraga R	.60	.25
☐ 57 Raul Mondesi R	.60	.25
☐ 58 Andy Pettitte R	.60	.25
☐ 59 Roberto Alomar B	1.25	.55
☐ 60 Derek Jeter B	4.00	1.80
☐ 61 Charles Johnson R	.30	.14
☐ 62 Travis Fryman R	.30	.14
☐ 63 Chipper Jones B	4.00	1.80
☐ 64 Edgar Martinez R	.40	.18
☐ 65 Bobby Bonilla R	.30	.14
☐ 66 Greg Vaughn R	.15	.07
☐ 67 Bobby Higginson R	.30	.14
☐ 68 Garret Anderson R	.30	.14
☐ 69 Chuck Knoblauch B	1.25	.55
☐ 70 Jermaine Dye R	.15	.07
☐ 71 Cal Ripken B	5.00	2.20
☐ 72 Jason Giambi R	.30	.14
☐ 73 Trey Beamon R	.15	.07
☐ 74 Shawn Green R	.30	.14
☐ 75 Mark McGwire B	2.50	1.10
☐ 76 Carlos Delgado R	.30	.14
☐ 77 Jason Isringhausen R	.15	.07
☐ 78 Randy Johnson B	1.25	.55
☐ 79 Troy Percival B	.60	.25
☐ 80 Ron Gant R	.15	.07
☐ 81 Ellis Burks R	.30	.14
☐ 82 Mike Mussina B	1.25	.55
☐ 83 Todd Hundley R	.30	.14
☐ 84 Jim Edmonds R	.60	.25
☐ 85 Charles Nagy R	.30	.14
☐ 86 Dante Bichette B	.60	.25
☐ 87 Mariano Rivera R	.30	.14
☐ 88 Matt Williams B	1.00	.45
☐ 89 Rondell White R	.30	.14
☐ 90 Steve Finley R	.30	.14
☐ 91 Alex Fernandez R	.30	.14
☐ 92 Barry Larkin R	.40	.18
☐ 93 Tom Goodwin R	.15	.07
☐ 94 Will Clark R	.40	.18
☐ 95 Michael Tucker R	.30	.14
☐ 96 Derek Bell R	.15	.07
☐ 97 Larry Walker R	.60	.25
☐ 98 Alan Benes R	.15	.07
☐ 99 Tom Glavine R	.30	.14
☐ 100 Darin Erstad B	2.00	.90
☐ 101 Andruw Jones B	3.00	1.35
☐ 102 Scott Rolen	1.50	.70
☐ 103 Todd Walker B	.30	.14
☐ 104 Dmitri Young R	.15	.07
☐ 105 Vladimir Guerrero B	2.50	1.10
☐ 106 Nomar Garciaparra	2.00	.90
☐ 107 Danny Patterson R	.15	.07
☐ 108 Karim Garcia R	.30	.14
☐ 109 Todd Greene R	.30	.14
☐ 110 Ruben Rivera R	.30	.14
☐ 111 Raul Casanova R	.15	.07
☐ 112 Mike Cameron R	.30	.14
☐ 113 Bartolo Colon R	.30	.14
☐ 114 Rod Myers R	.15	.07
☐ 115 Todd Dunn R	.15	.07
☐ 116 Torii Hunter R	.15	.07
☐ 117 Jason Dickson R	.30	.14
☐ 118 Gene Kingsale R	.15	.07
☐ 119 Rafael Medina R	.15	.07
☐ 120 Raul Ibanez R	.15	.07
☐ 121 Bobby Henley R	.15	.07
☐ 122 Scott Spiezio R	.30	.14
☐ 123 Bobby Smith R	.15	.07
☐ 124 J.J. Johnson R	.15	.07
☐ 125 Bubba Trammell R RC	.60	.25
☐ 126 Jeff Abbott R	.15	.07
☐ 127 Neifi Perez R	.15	.07
☐ 128 Derrek Lee R	.30	.14
☐ 129 Kevin Brown C R	.15	.07
☐ 130 Mendy Lopez R	.15	.07
☐ 131 Kevin Orie R	.15	.07
☐ 132 Ryan Jones R	.15	.07
☐ 133 Juan Encarnacion R	.40	.18
☐ 134 Jose Guillen B	1.50	.70
☐ 135 Greg Norton R	.15	.07
☐ 136 Richie Sexson R	.30	.14
☐ 137 Jay Payton R	.15	.07
☐ 138 Bob Abreu R	.60	.25
☐ 139 Ron Belliard R	.15	.07
☐ 140 Wilton Guerrero B	.30	.14
☐ 141 Alex Rodriguez SS B	2.50	1.10
☐ 142 Juan Gonzalez SS B	2.00	.90
☐ 143 Ken Caminiti SS B	1.25	.55
☐ 144 Frank Thomas SS B	2.50	1.10
☐ 145 Ken Griffey Jr. SS B	3.00	1.35
☐ 146 John Smoltz SS B	.60	.25
☐ 147 Mike Piazza SS B	2.00	.90
☐ 148 Derek Jeter SS B	2.00	.90
☐ 149 Frank Thomas CL	1.25	.55
☐ 150 Ken Griffey Jr. CL	1.50	.70
☐ 151 Jose Cruz Jr.	10.00	4.50
☐ 152 Moises Alou	.60	.25
☐ 153 Hideki Irabu	1.50	.70
☐ 154 Glendon Rusch	.30	.14
☐ 155 Ron Coomer	.30	.14
☐ 156 Jeremi Gonzalez	1.00	.45
☐ 157 Fernando Tatis	3.00	1.35
☐ 158 John Olerud	.60	.25
☐ 159 Rickey Henderson	1.00	.45
☐ 160 Shannon Stewart	.30	.14
☐ 161 Kevin Polcovich	.30	.14
☐ 162 Jose Rosado	.30	.14
☐ 163 Ray Lankford	.60	.25
☐ 164 David Justice	1.25	.55
☐ 165 Mark Kotsay	3.00	1.35
☐ 166 Deivi Cruz	.75	.35
☐ 167 Billy Wagner	.60	.25

☐ 168 Jacob Cruz	.30	.14
☐ 169 Matt Morris	.60	.25
☐ 170 Brian Banks	.30	.14
☐ 171 Brett Tomko	.30	.14
☐ 172 Todd Helton	2.00	.90
☐ 173 Eric Young	.30	.14
☐ 174 Bernie Williams	1.25	.55
☐ 175 Jeff Fassero	.30	.14
☐ 176 Ryan McGuire	.30	.14
☐ 177 Darryl Kile	.60	.25
☐ 178 Kelvim Escobar	.50	.23
☐ 179 Dave Nilsson	.30	.14
☐ 180 Geronimo Berroa	.30	.14
☐ 181 Livan Hernandez	1.25	.55
☐ 182 Tony Womack	1.00	.45
☐ 183 Deion Sanders	1.25	.55
☐ 184 Jeff Kent	.60	.25
☐ 185 Brian Hunter	.60	.25
☐ 186 Jose Malave	.30	.14
☐ 187 Steve Woodard	.50	.23
☐ 188 Brad Radke	.60	.25
☐ 189 Todd Dunwoody	.60	.25
☐ 190 Joey Hamilton	.30	.14
☐ 191 Denny Neagle	.60	.25
☐ 192 Bobby Jones	.60	.25
☐ 193 Tony Clark	1.25	.55
☐ 194 Jaret Wright	6.00	2.70
☐ 195 Matt Stairs	.30	.14
☐ 196 Francisco Cordova	.30	.14
☐ 197 Justin Thompson	.60	.25
☐ 198 Pokey Reese	.30	.14
☐ 199 Garrett Stephenson	.30	.14
☐ 200 Carl Everett	.30	.14
☐ P3 Tony Gwynn PROMO	.15	.07
☐ P23 Greg Maddux PROMO	.15	.07
☐ P47 Ken Griffey Jr. PROMO	.15	.07

1997 Select Artist's Proof

Randomly inserted in packs at the rate of one in 71 for red cards and one in 355 for blue cards, this 150-card parallel set is a holographic foil rendition of the Series 1 base set with either red or blue foil treatment and the unique Artist's Proof logo.

	MINT	NRMT
COMPLETE SET (150)	5000.00	2200.00
COMMON RED (1-150)	6.00	2.70
COMMON BLUE (1-150)	15.00	6.75

*STARS: 25X TO 50X BASIC CARDS
*YOUNG STARS: 20X TO 40X BASIC CARDS

1997 Select Company

Randomly inserted one in every Select Hi Series pack, this 200-card set is a fractured parallel version of the Select base set. The difference is found in the full foil card stock with puffed ink accented highlights. The first level features 100 players from the base set with a red bordered design. The second level features the 50 players found only in the Select High Series. The final level features 50 parallel cards of top superstars utilizing a blue puffed ink border.

	MINT	NRMT
COMPLETE SET (200)	250.00	110.00
COMMON CARD (1-200)	.75	.35

*BLUE STARS 1-150: 1.25X TO 2.5X BASIC CARDS
*RED STARS 1-150: 2.5X TO 5X BASIC CARDS
*HI SERIES STARS 151-200: 1.25X TO 2.5X BASIC CARDS

☐ P121 Bobby Henley PROMO	2.00	.90

1997 Select Registered Gold

Randomly inserted in packs at the rate of one in 11 for red cards and one in 47 for blue cards, this 150-card set is parallel to the regular Select Series 1 set. The difference is found in the fractured gold foil treatment which replaces the silver foil treatment of the regular set.

	MINT	NRMT
COMPLETE SET (150)	1000.00	450.00
COMMON RED (1-150)	1.50	.70
COMMON BLUE (1-150)	3.00	1.35

*STARS: 5X TO 10X BASIC CARDS
*YOUNG STARS: 4X TO 8X BASIC CARDS

1997 Select Rookie Autographs

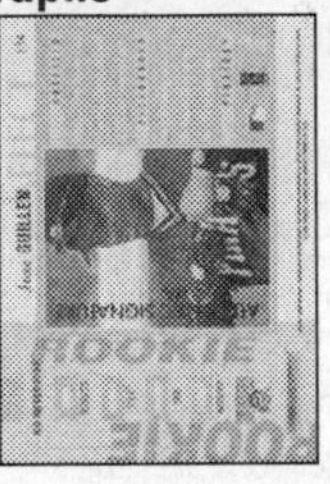

This four-card set features color player photos of four potential Rookie of the Year candidates with their autographs. Each player signed 3000 cards except for Andruw Jones who only signed 2500.

	MINT	NRMT
COMPLETE SET (4)	120.00	55.00
COMMON CARD	12.00	5.50
☐ 1 Jose Guillen	30.00	13.50
☐ 2 Wilton Guerrero	12.00	5.50
☐ 3 Andruw Jones	60.00	27.00
☐ 4 Todd Walker	20.00	9.00

1997 Select Rookie Revolution

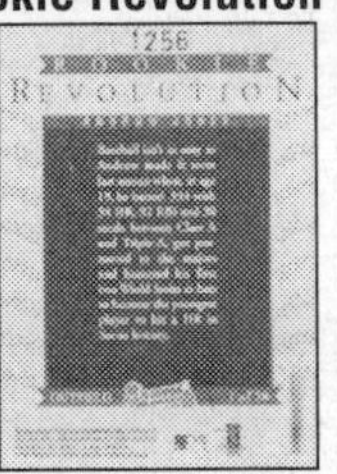

Randomly inserted in packs at a rate of one in 56, this 20-card set features color photos of top rookies on a micro-etched, full mylar card. Each card is sequentially numbered.

	MINT	NRMT
COMPLETE SET (20)	150.00	70.00
COMMON CARD (1-20)	4.00	1.80
☐ 1 Andruw Jones	25.00	11.00
☐ 2 Derek Jeter	30.00	13.50
☐ 3 Todd Hollandsworth	4.00	1.80
☐ 4 Edgar Renteria	5.00	2.20
☐ 5 Jason Kendall	5.00	2.20
☐ 6 Rey Ordonez	4.00	1.80
☐ 7 F.P. Santangelo	4.00	1.80
☐ 8 Jermaine Dye	4.00	1.80
☐ 9 Alex Ochoa	4.00	1.80
☐ 10 Vladimir Guererro	20.00	9.00
☐ 11 Dmitri Young	5.00	2.20
☐ 12 Todd Walker	4.00	1.80
☐ 13 Scott Rolen	25.00	11.00
☐ 14 Nomar Garciaparra	30.00	13.50
☐ 15 Ruben Rivera	4.00	1.80
☐ 16 Darin Erstad	15.00	6.75
☐ 17 Todd Greene	5.00	2.20
☐ 18 Mariano Rivera	5.00	2.20
☐ 19 Trey Beamon	4.00	1.80
☐ 20 Karim Garcia	5.00	2.20

1997 Select Tools of the Trade

Randomly inserted in packs at a rate of one in nine, this 25-card set matches color photos of 25 young players with 25 veteran superstars printed back-to-back on a double-fronted full silver foil card stock with gold foil stamping.

	MINT	NRMT
COMPLETE SET (25)	150.00	70.00
COMMON CARD (1-25)	1.50	.70
COMPLETE MIRROR BLUE (25)	1200.00	540.00
COMMON MIRROR BLUE (1-25)	15.00	6.75

*MIRROR BLUE: 5X TO 10X BASIC TOOLS

☐ 1 Ken Griffey Jr. / Andruw Jones	20.00	9.00
☐ 2 Greg Maddux / Andy Pettitte	10.00	4.50
☐ 3 Cal Ripken / Chipper Jones	15.00	6.75
☐ 4 Mike Piazza / Jason Kendall	10.00	4.50
☐ 5 Albert Belle / Karim Garcia	4.00	1.80
☐ 6 Mo Vaughn / Dmitri Young	4.00	1.80
☐ 7 Juan Gonzalez / Vladimir Guerrero	10.00	4.50
☐ 8 Tony Gwynn / Jermaine Dye	8.00	3.60
☐ 9 Barry Bonds / Alex Ochoa	4.00	1.80
☐ 10 Jeff Bagwell / Jason Giambi	6.00	2.70
☐ 11 Kenny Lofton / Darin Erstad	4.00	1.80
☐ 12 Gary Sheffield / Manny Ramirez	3.00	1.35
☐ 13 Tim Salmon / Todd Hollandsworth	1.50	.70
☐ 14 Sammy Sosa / Ruben Rivera	1.50	.70
☐ 15 Paul Molitor / George Arias	1.50	.70
☐ 16 Jim Thome / Todd Walker	1.50	.70
☐ 17 Wade Boggs / Scott Rolen	6.00	2.70
☐ 18 Ryne Sandberg / Chuck Knoblauch	4.00	1.80
☐ 19 Mark McGwire / Frank Thomas	15.00	6.75
☐ 20 Ivan Rodriguez / Charles Johnson	4.00	1.80
☐ 21 Brian Jordan / Rusty Greer	1.50	.70
☐ 22 Roger Clemens / Troy Percival	6.00	2.70
☐ 23 John Smoltz / Mike Mussina	2.50	1.10
☐ 24 Alex Rodriguez / Rey Ordonez	10.00	4.50
☐ 25 Derek Jeter / Nomar Garciaparra	12.00	5.50

1995 Select Certified Samples

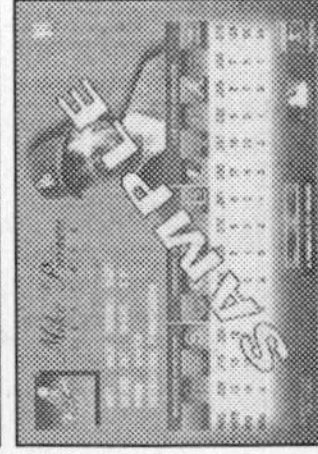

This 8-card set was issued to preview the premier edition of the Select Certified series. This hobby-only issue is distinguished by 24-point cardstock, a metallic sheen, and double lamination. The cards have the word "SAMPLE" stamped diagonally across both sides.

	MINT	NRMT
COMPLETE SET (8)	16.00	7.25
COMMON CARD	.75	.35
☐ 2 Reggie Sanders	.75	.35
☐ 3 Cal Ripken / Gold Team	10.00	4.50
☐ 10 Mo Vaughn	1.25	.55
☐ 39 Mike Piazza	4.00	1.80
☐ 50 Mark McGwire	2.50	1.10
☐ 75 Roberto Alomar	1.25	.55
☐ 89 Larry Walker	1.25	.55
☐ 110 Ray Durham	.75	.35

1995 Select Certified

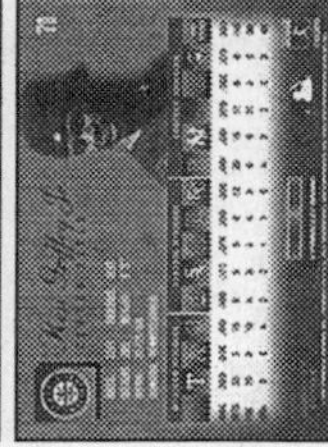

This 135-card standard-size set was issued through hobby outlets only. This product was issued in six-card packs. The cards are made with 24-point stock and are all metallic and double laminated. The fronts feature a player photo, his name in the lower right and the "Select '95 Certified" logo in the upper right. The horizontal backs feature a team by team seasonal summary and a player photo. The cards are numbered in the upper right corner. Rookie Cards in this set include Bobby Higginson and Hideo Nomo. Card #18 was never printed; Cal Ripken is featured on a special card numbered 2131, which is included in the complete set of 135.

	MINT	NRMT
COMPLETE SET (135)	40.00	18.00
COMMON CARD (1-135)	.25	.11

	MINT	NRMT
☐ 1 Barry Bonds	1.25	.55
☐ 2 Reggie Sanders	.25	.11
☐ 3 Terry Steinbach	.50	.23
☐ 4 Eduardo Perez	.25	.11
☐ 5 Frank Thomas	4.00	1.80
☐ 6 Wil Cordero	.25	.11
☐ 7 John Olerud	.50	.23
☐ 8 Deion Sanders	1.00	.45
☐ 9 Mike Mussina	1.00	.45
☐ 10 Mo Vaughn	1.25	.55
☐ 11 Will Clark	.75	.35
☐ 12 Chili Davis	.50	.23
☐ 13 Jimmy Key	.50	.23
☐ 14 Eddie Murray	1.00	.45
☐ 15 Bernard Gilkey	.25	.11
☐ 16 David Cone	.50	.23
☐ 17 Tim Salmon	1.00	.45
☐ 19 Steve Ontiveros	.25	.11
☐ 20 Andres Galarraga	.75	.35
☐ 21 Don Mattingly	1.50	.70
☐ 22 Kevin Appier	.50	.23
☐ 23 Paul Molitor	1.00	.45
☐ 24 Edgar Martinez	.75	.35
☐ 25 Andy Benes	.25	.11
☐ 26 Rafael Palmeiro	.75	.35
☐ 27 Barry Larkin	.75	.35
☐ 28 Gary Sheffield	1.00	.45
☐ 29 Wally Joyner	.50	.23
☐ 30 Wade Boggs	.75	.35
☐ 31 Rico Brogna	.25	.11
☐ 32 Eddie Murray 3000th Hit	1.00	.45
☐ 33 Kirby Puckett	2.00	.90
☐ 34 Bobby Bonilla	.50	.23
☐ 35 Hal Morris	.25	.11
☐ 36 Moises Alou	.50	.23
☐ 37 Javier Lopez	.75	.35
☐ 38 Chuck Knoblauch	1.00	.45
☐ 39 Mike Piazza	3.00	1.35
☐ 40 Travis Fryman	.50	.23
☐ 41 Rickey Henderson	.75	.35
☐ 42 Jim Thome	1.00	.45
☐ 43 Carlos Baerga	.50	.23
☐ 44 Dean Palmer	.50	.23
☐ 45 Kirk Gibson	.50	.23
☐ 46 Bret Saberhagen	.25	.11
☐ 47 Cecil Fielder	.50	.23
☐ 48 Manny Ramirez	1.00	.45
☐ 49 Derek Bell	.50	.23
☐ 50 Mark McGwire	2.00	.90
☐ 51 Jim Edmonds	1.00	.45
☐ 52 Robin Ventura	.50	.23
☐ 53 Ryan Klesko	.75	.35
☐ 54 Jeff Bagwell	2.00	.90
☐ 55 Ozzie Smith	1.25	.55
☐ 56 Albert Belle	1.25	.55
☐ 57 Darren Daulton	.50	.23
☐ 58 Jeff Conine	.50	.23
☐ 59 Greg Maddux	3.00	1.35
☐ 60 Lenny Dykstra	.50	.23
☐ 61 Randy Johnson	1.00	.45
☐ 62 Fred McGriff	.75	.35
☐ 63 Ray Lankford	.50	.23
☐ 64 David Justice	1.00	.45
☐ 65 Paul O'Neill	.50	.23
☐ 66 Tony Gwynn	2.50	1.10
☐ 67 Matt Williams	.75	.35
☐ 68 Dante Bichette	.75	.35
☐ 69 Craig Biggio	.75	.35
☐ 70 Ken Griffey Jr.	5.00	2.20
☐ 71 J.T. Snow	.50	.23
☐ 72 Cal Ripken	4.00	1.80
☐ 73 Jay Bell	.50	.23
☐ 74 Joe Carter	.75	.35
☐ 75 Roberto Alomar	1.00	.45
☐ 76 Benji Gil	.25	.11
☐ 77 Ivan Rodriguez	1.25	.55
☐ 78 Raul Mondesi	.75	.35
☐ 79 Cliff Floyd	.50	.23
☐ 80 Eric Karros	1.00	.45
Mike Piazza		
Raul Mondesi		
☐ 81 Royce Clayton	.25	.11
☐ 82 Billy Ashley	.25	.11
☐ 83 Joey Hamilton	.50	.23
☐ 84 Sammy Sosa	1.00	.45
☐ 85 Jason Bere	.25	.11
☐ 86 Dennis Martinez	.50	.23
☐ 87 Greg Vaughn	.25	.11
☐ 88 Roger Clemens	2.00	.90
☐ 89 Larry Walker	1.00	.45
☐ 90 Mark Grace	.75	.35
☐ 91 Kenny Lofton	1.25	.55
☐ 92 Carlos Perez	.50	.23
☐ 93 Roger Cedeno	.25	.11
☐ 94 Scott Ruffcorn	.25	.11
☐ 95 Jim Pittsley	.50	.23
☐ 96 Andy Pettitte	1.50	.70
☐ 97 James Baldwin	.25	.11
☐ 98 Hideo Nomo	5.00	2.20
☐ 99 Ismael Valdes	.50	.23
☐ 100 Armando Benitez	.25	.11
☐ 101 Jose Malave	.25	.11
☐ 102 Bob Higginson	1.50	.70
☐ 103 LaTroy Hawkins	.25	.11
☐ 104 Russ Davis	.25	.11
☐ 105 Shawn Green	.50	.23
☐ 106 Joe Vitiello	.25	.11
☐ 107 Chipper Jones	3.00	1.35
☐ 108 Shane Andrews	.25	.11
☐ 109 Jose Oliva	.25	.11
☐ 110 Ray Durham	.50	.23
☐ 111 Jon Nunnally	.25	.11
☐ 112 Alex Gonzalez	.25	.11
☐ 113 Vaughn Eshelman	.25	.11
☐ 114 Marty Cordova	.75	.35
☐ 115 Mark Grudzielanek	.75	.35
☐ 116 Brian L.Hunter	.50	.23
☐ 117 Charles Johnson	.75	.35
☐ 118 Alex Rodriguez	4.00	1.80
☐ 119 David Bell	.25	.11
☐ 120 Todd Hollandsworth	.50	.23
☐ 121 Joe Randa	.25	.11
☐ 122 Derek Jeter	3.00	1.35
☐ 123 Frank Rodriguez	.50	.23
☐ 124 Curtis Goodwin	.25	.11
☐ 125 Bill Pulsipher	.25	.11
☐ 126 John Mabry	.75	.35
☐ 127 Julian Tavarez	.25	.11
☐ 128 Edgardo Alfonzo	1.00	.45
☐ 129 Orlando Miller	.25	.11
☐ 130 Juan Acevedo	.25	.11
☐ 131 Jeff Cirillo	.50	.23
☐ 132 Roberto Petagine	.25	.11
☐ 133 Antonio Osuna	.25	.11
☐ 134 Michael Tucker	.75	.35
☐ 135 Garret Anderson	.75	.35
☐ 2131 Cal Ripken TRIB	5.00	2.20

1995 Select Certified Mirror Gold

This 135-card set is a parallel to the regular issue. Pinnacle used their all-holographic foil technology on the fronts. The backs are identical to the regular issue but the words "Mirror Gold" are in the middle. These cards were inserted approximately one every five packs.

	MINT	NRMT
COMPLETE SET (135)	900.00	400.00
COMMON CARD (1-135)	2.50	1.10
*STARS: 6X TO 15X BASIC CARDS		
*YOUNG STARS: 5X TO 12X BASIC CARDS		

1995 Select Certified Checklists

This seven-card standard-size set was inserted one per Select Certified pack. These cards were not made of the same card stock as the regular Certified cards.

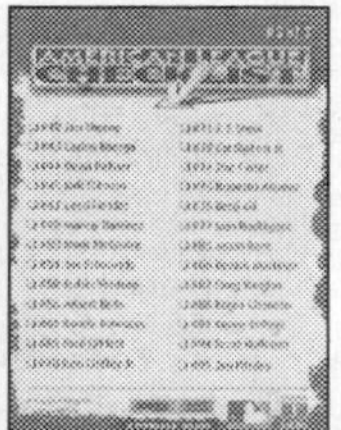

	MINT	NRMT
COMPLETE SET (7)	4.00	1.80
COMMON CARD (1-7)	.25	.11

	MINT	NRMT
☐ 1 Ken Griffey Jr.	1.00	.45
☐ 2 Frank Thomas	.75	.35
☐ 3 Cal Ripken	.75	.35
☐ 4 Jeff Bagwell	.50	.23
☐ 5 Mike Piazza	.60	.25
☐ 6 Barry Bonds	.25	.11
☐ 7 Manny Ramirez	.25	.11
Raul Mondesi		

1995 Select Certified Future

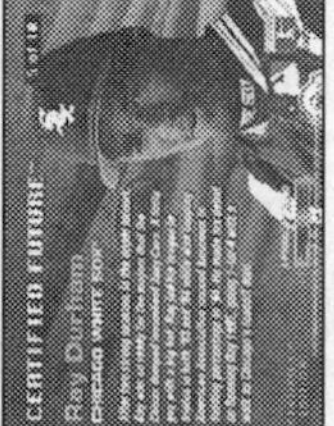

This ten-card set was inserted approximately one in every 19 packs. Ten leading 1995 rookie players are included in this set. These cards were produced using Pinnacle's Dufex technology. The fronts feature a player photo with his name on the bottom. The words "Certified Future" are spelled vertically on the right. The horizontal backs feature some textual information and a player photo.

	MINT	NRMT
COMPLETE SET (10)	60.00	27.00
COMMON CARD (1-10)	2.00	.90

	MINT	NRMT
☐ 1 Chipper Jones	15.00	6.75
☐ 2 Curtis Goodwin	2.00	.90
☐ 3 Hideo Nomo	15.00	6.75
☐ 4 Shawn Green	3.00	1.35
☐ 5 Ray Durham	4.00	1.80
☐ 6 Todd Hollandsworth	3.00	1.35
☐ 7 Brian L.Hunter	4.00	1.80
☐ 8 Carlos Delgado	4.00	1.80
☐ 9 Michael Tucker UER	3.00	1.35
(front photo is Jon Nunnally)		
☐ 10 Alex Rodriguez	20.00	9.00

1995 Select Certified Gold Team

This 12-card was inserted approximately one in every 41 packs. This set features some of the leading players in baseball. These cards feature double-sided all-gold-foil Dufex technology.

	MINT	NRMT
COMPLETE SET (12)	300.00	135.00
COMMON CARD (1-12)	8.00	3.60

	MINT	NRMT
☐ 1 Ken Griffey Jr.	60.00	27.00
☐ 2 Frank Thomas	50.00	22.00
☐ 3 Cal Ripken	50.00	22.00

Card	MINT	NRMT
☐ 4 Jeff Bagwell	25.00	11.00
☐ 5 Mike Piazza	40.00	18.00
☐ 6 Barry Bonds	15.00	6.75
☐ 7 Matt Williams	12.00	5.50
☐ 8 Don Mattingly	20.00	9.00
☐ 9 Will Clark	12.00	5.50
☐ 10 Tony Gwynn	30.00	13.50
☐ 11 Kirby Puckett	25.00	11.00
☐ 12 Jose Canseco	8.00	3.60

1995 Select Certified Potential Unlimited 1975

Cards from this 20-card set were randomly inserted into one in every 29 packs. The cards feature Pinnacle's all-foil Dufex printing technology. The fronts have a player photo in the middle. The words "Potential Unlimited" appear in the upper left and the player's name appears in the bottom left. The horizontal back has a player photo and some text set against a background of a baseball. Only 1,975 sets were made and each card is numbered 1 of 1,975 at the bottom right.

	MINT	NRMT
COMPLETE SET (20)	250.00	110.00
COMMON CARD (1-20)	5.00	2.20
COMPLETE 903 SET (20)	300.00	135.00

*903 CARDS .5X TO 1.2X BASIC 1975 CARDS

Card	MINT	NRMT
☐ 1 Cliff Floyd	5.00	2.20
☐ 2 Manny Ramirez	15.00	6.75
☐ 3 Raul Mondesi	10.00	4.50
☐ 4 Scott Ruffcorn	5.00	2.20
☐ 5 Billy Ashley	5.00	2.20
☐ 6 Alex Gonzalez	5.00	2.20
☐ 7 Midre Cummings	5.00	2.20
☐ 8 Charles Johnson	10.00	4.50
☐ 9 Garret Anderson	10.00	4.50
☐ 10 Hideo Nomo	50.00	22.00
☐ 11 Chipper Jones	50.00	22.00
☐ 12 Curtis Goodwin	5.00	2.20
☐ 13 Frank Rodriguez	5.00	2.20
☐ 14 Shawn Green	7.50	3.40
☐ 15 Ray Durham	10.00	4.50
☐ 16 Todd Hollandsworth	7.50	3.40
☐ 17 Brian L.Hunter	10.00	4.50
☐ 18 Carlos Delgado	10.00	4.50
☐ 19 Michael Tucker	10.00	4.50
☐ 20 Alex Rodriguez	60.00	27.00

1996 Select Certified

The 1996 Select Certified hobby only set was issued in one series totalling 144 cards. Each six-card pack carried a suggested retail price of $4.99. Printed on special 24-point silver mirror mylar card stock, the fronts feature a color player photo on a gray and black background. The backs carry another color player photo with information about his playing abilities.

	MINT	NRMT
COMPLETE SET (144)	40.00	18.00
COMMON CARD (1-144)	.25	.11

Card	MINT	NRMT
☐ 1 Frank Thomas	4.00	1.80
☐ 2 Tino Martinez	1.00	.45
☐ 3 Gary Sheffield	1.00	.45
☐ 4 Kenny Lofton	1.25	.55
☐ 5 Joe Carter	.50	.23
☐ 6 Alex Rodriguez	4.00	1.80
☐ 7 Chipper Jones	3.00	1.35
☐ 8 Roger Clemens	2.00	.90
☐ 9 Jay Bell	.25	.11
☐ 10 Eddie Murray	1.00	.45
☐ 11 Will Clark	.75	.35
☐ 12 Mike Mussina	1.00	.45
☐ 13 Hideo Nomo	2.50	1.10
☐ 14 Andres Galarraga	1.00	.45
☐ 15 Marc Newfield	.25	.11
☐ 16 Jason Isringhausen	.25	.11
☐ 17 Randy Johnson	1.00	.45
☐ 18 Chuck Knoblauch	1.00	.45
☐ 19 J.T. Snow	.50	.23
☐ 20 Mark McGwire	2.00	.90
☐ 21 Tony Gwynn	2.50	1.10
☐ 22 Albert Belle	1.25	.55
☐ 23 Gregg Jefferies	.50	.23
☐ 24 Reggie Sanders	.25	.11
☐ 25 Bernie Williams	1.00	.45
☐ 26 Ray Lankford	.50	.23
☐ 27 Johnny Damon	.50	.23
☐ 28 Ryne Sandberg	1.25	.55
☐ 29 Rondell White	.50	.23
☐ 30 Mike Piazza	3.00	1.35
☐ 31 Barry Bonds	1.25	.55
☐ 32 Greg Maddux	3.00	1.35
☐ 33 Craig Biggio	.75	.35
☐ 34 John Valentin	.50	.23
☐ 35 Ivan Rodriguez	1.25	.55
☐ 36 Rico Brogna	.25	.11
☐ 37 Tim Salmon	1.00	.45
☐ 38 Sterling Hitchcock	.25	.11
☐ 39 Charles Johnson	.50	.23
☐ 40 Travis Fryman	.50	.23
☐ 41 Barry Larkin	.75	.35
☐ 42 Tom Glavine	.50	.23
☐ 43 Marty Cordova	.25	.11
☐ 44 Shawn Green	.25	.11
☐ 45 Ben McDonald	.25	.11
☐ 46 Robin Ventura	.50	.23
☐ 47 Ken Griffey Jr.	5.00	2.20
☐ 48 Orlando Merced	.25	.11
☐ 49 Paul O'Neill	.25	.11
☐ 50 Ozzie Smith	1.25	.55
☐ 51 Manny Ramirez	1.00	.45
☐ 52 Ismael Valdes	.50	.23
☐ 53 Cal Ripken	4.00	1.80
☐ 54 Jeff Bagwell	2.00	.90
☐ 55 Greg Vaughn	.25	.11
☐ 56 Juan Gonzalez	2.50	1.10
☐ 57 Raul Mondesi	.75	.35
☐ 58 Carlos Baerga	.50	.23
☐ 59 Sammy Sosa	1.00	.45
☐ 60 Mike Kelly	.25	.11
☐ 61 Edgar Martinez	.75	.35
☐ 62 Kirby Puckett	2.00	.90
☐ 63 Cecil Fielder	.50	.23
☐ 64 David Cone	.50	.23
☐ 65 Moises Alou	.50	.23
☐ 66 Fred McGriff	.75	.35
☐ 67 Mo Vaughn	1.25	.55
☐ 68 Edgardo Alfonzo	.75	.35
☐ 69 Jim Thome	1.00	.45
☐ 70 Rickey Henderson	.75	.35
☐ 71 Dante Bichette	.50	.23
☐ 72 Lenny Dykstra	.50	.23
☐ 73 Benji Gil	.25	.11
☐ 74 Wade Boggs	1.00	.45
☐ 75 Jim Edmonds	1.00	.45
☐ 76 Michael Tucker	.50	.23
☐ 77 Carlos Delgado	.50	.23
☐ 78 Butch Huskey	.50	.23
☐ 79 Billy Ashley	.25	.11
☐ 80 Dean Palmer	.50	.23
☐ 81 Paul Molitor	1.00	.45
☐ 82 Ryan Klesko	.75	.35
☐ 83 Brian L.Hunter	.50	.23
☐ 84 Jay Buhner	.75	.35
☐ 85 Larry Walker	1.00	.45
☐ 86 Mike Bordick	.25	.11
☐ 87 Matt Williams	.75	.35
☐ 88 Jack McDowell	.25	.11
☐ 89 Hal Morris	.25	.11
☐ 90 Brian Jordan	.50	.23
☐ 91 Andy Pettitte	1.25	.55
☐ 92 Melvin Nieves	.50	.23
☐ 93 Pedro Martinez	1.00	.45
☐ 94 Mark Grace	.75	.35
☐ 95 Garret Anderson	.75	.35
☐ 96 Andre Dawson	1.00	.45
☐ 97 Ray Durham	.50	.23
☐ 98 Jose Canseco	.75	.35
☐ 99 Roberto Alomar	1.00	.45
☐ 100 Derek Jeter	3.00	1.35
☐ 101 Alan Benes	.50	.23
☐ 102 Karim Garcia	.50	.23
☐ 103 Robin Jennings	.25	.11
☐ 104 Bob Abreu	1.00	.45
☐ 105 Sal Fasano UER (name on front is Livan Hernandez)	.25	.11
☐ 106 Steve Gibralter	.25	.11
☐ 107 Jermaine Dye	.25	.11
☐ 108 Jason Kendall	1.00	.45
☐ 109 Mike Grace	.25	.11
☐ 110 Jason Schmidt	.50	.23
☐ 111 Paul Wilson	.25	.11
☐ 112 Rey Ordonez	.50	.23
☐ 113 Wilton Guerrero	1.00	.45
☐ 114 Brooks Kieschnick	.50	.23
☐ 115 George Arias	.25	.11
☐ 116 Osvaldo Fernandez	.25	.11
☐ 117 Todd Hollandsworth	.50	.23
☐ 118 John Wasdin	.25	.11
☐ 119 Eric Owens	.25	.11
☐ 120 Chan Ho Park	1.00	.45
☐ 121 Mark Loretta	.25	.11
☐ 122 Richard Hidalgo	1.00	.45
☐ 123 Jeff Suppan	.50	.23
☐ 124 Jim Pittsley	.50	.23
☐ 125 LaTroy Hawkins	.25	.11
☐ 126 Chris Snopek	.25	.11
☐ 127 Justin Thompson	.50	.23
☐ 128 Jay Powell	.25	.11
☐ 129 Alex Ochoa	.25	.11
☐ 130 Felipe Crespo	.25	.11
☐ 131 Matt Lawton	.25	.11
☐ 132 Jimmy Haynes	.25	.11
☐ 133 Terrell Wade	.25	.11
☐ 134 Ruben Rivera	.50	.23
☐ 135 Frank Thomas PP	2.00	.90
☐ 136 Ken Griffey Jr. PP	2.50	1.10
☐ 137 Greg Maddux PP	1.50	.70
☐ 138 Mike Piazza PP	1.50	.70
☐ 139 Cal Ripken PP	2.00	.90
☐ 140 Albert Belle PP	1.00	.45
☐ 141 Mo Vaughn PP	1.00	.45
☐ 142 Chipper Jones PP	1.50	.70
☐ 143 Hideo Nomo PP	1.25	.55
☐ 144 Ryan Klesko PP	.75	.35

1996 Select Certified Artist's Proofs

Randomly inserted in packs at a rate of one in 12, this 144-card set is parallel to the base set with only 500 sets being produced. The design is similar to the regular set with the exception of a holographic gold foil Artist's proof stamp on the front.

	MINT	NRMT
COMPLETE SET (144)	2000.00	900.00
COMMON CARD (1-144)	3.00	1.35

*STARS: 8X TO 20X BASIC CARDS
*YOUNG STARS: 6X TO 15X BASIC CARDS
*ROOKIES: 3X TO 8X BASIC CARDS

1996 Select Certified Certified Blue

Randomly inserted in packs at a rate of one in 50, this 144-card set is parallel to the base set with only 180 sets being produced. This set is a blue all-foil rendition of the base set.

	MINT	NRMT
COMPLETE SET (144)	5000.00	2200.00
COMMON CARD (1-144)	8.00	3.60

*STARS: 20X to 50X BASIC CARDS
*YOUNG STARS: 15X to 40X BASIC CARDS
*ROOKIES: 8X TO 20X BASIC CARDS

1996 Select Certified Certified Red

Randomly inserted in packs at a rate of one in five, this 144-card set is parallel to the base set with only 1,800 sets being produced. This set is a red all-foil rendition of the base set.

	MINT	NRMT
COMPLETE SET (144)	600.00	275.00
COMMON CARD (1-144)	1.00	.45

*STARS: 3X to 8X BASIC CARDS
*YOUNG STARS: 2.5X to 6X BASIC CARDS
*ROOKIES: 1.25X TO 3X BASIC CARDS

1996 Select Certified Mirror Blue

Randomly inserted in packs at a rate of one in 200, this 144-card set is parallel to the base set with only 45 sets being produced. This set is a blue holographic foil rendition of the base set. No set price has been provided due to scarcity.

	MINT	NRMT
COMMON CARD (1-144)	30.00	13.50
MINOR STARS	50.00	22.00
SEMISTARS	80.00	36.00
STARS	120.00	55.00

*STARS: 60X TO 120X BASIC CARDS
*YOUNG STARS: 50X TO 100X BASIC CARDS
*ROOKIES: 30X TO 60X BASIC CARDS

☐ 1 Frank Thomas	600.00	275.00
☐ 4 Kenny Lofton	150.00	70.00
☐ 6 Alex Rodriguez	600.00	275.00
☐ 7 Chipper Jones	300.00	135.00
☐ 8 Roger Clemens	300.00	135.00
☐ 13 Hideo Nomo	500.00	220.00
☐ 20 Mark McGwire	250.00	110.00
☐ 21 Tony Gwynn	300.00	135.00
☐ 22 Albert Belle	150.00	70.00
☐ 28 Ryne Sandberg	150.00	70.00
☐ 30 Mike Piazza	400.00	180.00
☐ 31 Barry Bonds	200.00	90.00
☐ 32 Greg Maddux	400.00	180.00
☐ 35 Ivan Rodriguez	150.00	70.00
☐ 47 Ken Griffey Jr.	800.00	350.00
☐ 50 Ozzie Smith	150.00	70.00
☐ 53 Cal Ripken	500.00	220.00
☐ 54 Jeff Bagwell	250.00	110.00
☐ 56 Juan Gonzalez	300.00	135.00
☐ 62 Kirby Puckett	250.00	110.00
☐ 67 Mo Vaughn	150.00	70.00
☐ 100 Derek Jeter	300.00	135.00
☐ 135 Frank Thomas PP	250.00	110.00
☐ 136 Ken Griffey Jr. PP	300.00	135.00
☐ 137 Greg Maddux PP	150.00	70.00
☐ 138 Mike Piazza PP	150.00	70.00
☐ 139 Cal Ripken PP	200.00	90.00
☐ 143 Hideo Nomo PP	200.00	90.00

1996 Select Certified Mirror Gold

Randomly inserted in packs at a rate of one in 300, this 144-card set is parallel to the base set with only 30 sets being produced. This set is a gold holographic foil rendition of the base set. No set price has been provided due to scarcity.

	MINT	NRMT
COMMON CARD (1-144)	100.00	45.00
MINOR STARS	200.00	90.00

*STARS: 300X TO 500X BASIC CARDS
*YOUNG STARS: 250X TO 400X BASIC CARDS
*ROOKIES: 125X TO 200X BASIC CARDS

☐ 1 Frank Thomas	2500.00	1100.00
☐ 2 Tino Martinez	500.00	220.00
☐ 3 Gary Sheffield	350.00	160.00
☐ 4 Kenny Lofton	600.00	275.00
☐ 6 Alex Rodriguez	2000.00	900.00
☐ 7 Chipper Jones	1200.00	550.00
☐ 8 Roger Clemens	1500.00	700.00
☐ 10 Eddie Murray	800.00	350.00
☐ 11 Will Clark	300.00	135.00
☐ 12 Mike Mussina	500.00	220.00
☐ 13 Hideo Nomo	1800.00	800.00
☐ 14 Andres Galarraga	300.00	135.00
☐ 17 Randy Johnson	800.00	350.00
☐ 18 Chuck Knoblauch	400.00	180.00
☐ 20 Mark McGwire	1200.00	550.00
☐ 21 Tony Gwynn	1500.00	700.00
☐ 22 Albert Belle	1200.00	550.00
☐ 25 Bernie Williams	350.00	160.00
☐ 28 Ryne Sandberg	600.00	275.00
☐ 30 Mike Piazza	1800.00	800.00
☐ 31 Barry Bonds	900.00	400.00
☐ 32 Greg Maddux	2000.00	900.00
☐ 33 Craig Biggio	250.00	110.00
☐ 35 Ivan Rodriguez	800.00	350.00
☐ 37 Tim Salmon	400.00	180.00
☐ 39 Charles Johnson	250.00	110.00
☐ 41 Barry Larkin	250.00	110.00
☐ 47 Ken Griffey Jr.	4000.00	1800.00
☐ 50 Ozzie Smith	600.00	275.00
☐ 51 Manny Ramirez	500.00	220.00
☐ 53 Cal Ripken	2500.00	1100.00
☐ 54 Jeff Bagwell	1500.00	700.00
☐ 56 Juan Gonzalez	1600.00	700.00
☐ 57 Raul Mondesi	300.00	135.00
☐ 59 Sammy Sosa	350.00	160.00
☐ 61 Edgar Martinez	250.00	110.00
☐ 62 Kirby Puckett	1500.00	700.00
☐ 65 Moises Alou	250.00	110.00
☐ 66 Fred McGriff	250.00	110.00
☐ 67 Mo Vaughn	500.00	220.00
☐ 69 Jim Thome	500.00	220.00
☐ 70 Rickey Henderson	300.00	135.00
☐ 74 Wade Boggs	400.00	180.00
☐ 75 Jim Edmonds	300.00	135.00
☐ 81 Paul Molitor	500.00	220.00
☐ 82 Ryan Klesko	300.00	135.00
☐ 84 Jay Buhner	300.00	135.00
☐ 85 Larry Walker	600.00	275.00
☐ 87 Matt Williams	300.00	135.00
☐ 91 Andy Pettitte	600.00	275.00
☐ 93 Pedro Martinez	350.00	160.00
☐ 94 Mark Grace	250.00	110.00
☐ 98 Jose Canseco	300.00	135.00
☐ 99 Roberto Alomar	500.00	220.00
☐ 100 Derek Jeter	1200.00	550.00
☐ 102 Karim Garcia	250.00	110.00
☐ 120 Chan Ho Park	300.00	135.00
☐ 122 Richard Hidalgo	250.00	110.00
☐ 127 Justin Thompson	250.00	110.00
☐ 134 Ruben Rivera	250.00	110.00
☐ 135 Frank Thomas PP	800.00	350.00
☐ 136 Ken Griffey Jr. PP	3000.00	1350.00
☐ 137 Greg Maddux PP	600.00	275.00
☐ 138 Mike Piazza PP	600.00	275.00
☐ 139 Cal Ripken PP	800.00	350.00
☐ 140 Albert Belle PP	400.00	180.00
☐ 142 Chipper Jones PP	400.00	180.00
☐ 143 Hideo Nomo PP	600.00	275.00

1996 Select Certified Mirror Red

Randomly inserted in packs at a rate of one in 100, this 144-card set is parallel to the base set with only 90 sets being produced. This set is a red holographic foil rendition of the base set. No set price has been provided due to scarcity.

	MINT	NRMT
COMMON CARD (1-144)	15.00	6.75
MINOR STARS	25.00	11.00
SEMISTARS	40.00	18.00
UNLISTED STARS	60.00	27.00

*STARS: 30X TO 60X BASIC CARDS ..
*YOUNG STARS: 25X TO 50X BASIC CARDS
*ROOKIES: 15X TO 30X BASIC CARDS

☐ 1 Frank Thomas	300.00	135.00
☐ 4 Kenny Lofton	80.00	36.00
☐ 6 Alex Rodriguez	300.00	135.00
☐ 7 Chipper Jones	150.00	70.00
☐ 8 Roger Clemens	150.00	70.00
☐ 13 Hideo Nomo	250.00	110.00
☐ 20 Mark McGwire	120.00	55.00
☐ 21 Tony Gwynn	150.00	70.00
☐ 22 Albert Belle	80.00	36.00
☐ 28 Ryne Sandberg	80.00	36.00
☐ 30 Mike Piazza	200.00	90.00
☐ 31 Barry Bonds	100.00	45.00
☐ 32 Greg Maddux	200.00	90.00
☐ 35 Ivan Rodriguez	80.00	36.00
☐ 47 Ken Griffey Jr.	400.00	180.00
☐ 50 Ozzie Smith	80.00	36.00
☐ 53 Cal Ripken	250.00	110.00
☐ 54 Jeff Bagwell	120.00	55.00
☐ 56 Juan Gonzalez	150.00	70.00
☐ 62 Kirby Puckett	120.00	55.00
☐ 67 Mo Vaughn	80.00	36.00
☐ 100 Derek Jeter	150.00	70.00
☐ 135 Frank Thomas PP	120.00	55.00
☐ 136 Ken Griffey Jr. PP	150.00	70.00
☐ 137 Greg Maddux PP	80.00	36.00
☐ 138 Mike Piazza PP	80.00	36.00
☐ 139 Cal Ripken PP	100.00	45.00
☐ 143 Hideo Nomo PP	100.00	45.00

1996 Select Certified Interleague Preview

Randomly inserted in packs at a rate of one in 42, this 25-card set gets ready for the start of interleague play in the 1997 season. Printed on Silver Prime Frost foil stock with gold lettering, the fronts feature color player cutouts of two opposing players. The backs carry another color cutout of the two players with information as to why they are a great matchup.

	MINT	NRMT
COMPLETE SET (25)	300.00	135.00
COMMON CARD (1-25)	6.00	2.70

☐ 1 Ken Griffey Jr. Hideo Nomo	50.00	22.00
☐ 2 Greg Maddux Mo Vaughn	25.00	11.00
☐ 3 Frank Thomas Sammy Sosa	30.00	13.50
☐ 4 Mike Piazza Jim Edmonds	25.00	11.00
☐ 5 Ryan Klesko Roger Clemens	15.00	6.75
☐ 6 Derek Jeter Rey Ordonez	20.00	9.00
☐ 7 Johnny Damon Ray Lankford	6.00	2.70
☐ 8 Manny Ramirez Reggie Sanders	8.00	3.60
☐ 9 Barry Bonds Jay Buhner	10.00	4.50
☐ 10 Jason Isringhausen Wade Boggs	7.00	3.10
☐ 11 David Cone Chipper Jones	25.00	11.00
☐ 12 Jeff Bagwell Will Clark	15.00	6.75
☐ 13 Tony Gwynn Randy Johnson	20.00	9.00
☐ 14 Cal Ripken Tom Glavine	30.00	13.50
☐ 15 Kirby Puckett Andy Benes	15.00	6.75
☐ 16 Gary Sheffield Mike Mussina	9.00	4.00
☐ 17 Raul Mondesi Tim Salmon	9.00	4.00
☐ 18 Rondell White Carlos Delgado	7.00	3.10
☐ 19 Cecil Fielder Ryne Sandberg	10.00	4.50
☐ 20 Kenny Lofton Brian L.Hunter	10.00	4.50
☐ 21 Paul Wilson Paul O'Neill	6.00	2.70
☐ 22 Ismael Valdes Edgar Martinez	6.00	2.70
☐ 23 Matt Williams Mark McGwire	15.00	6.75
☐ 24 Albert Belle Barry Larkin	10.00	4.50
☐ 25 Brady Anderson Marquis Grissom	7.00	3.10
☐ P4 Mike Piazza Jim Edmonds Promo	6.00	2.70

1996 Select Certified Select Few

Randomly inserted in packs at a rate of one in 60, this 18-card set honors superstar athletes with unmatched playing field talents. Utilizing the all-new Dot Matrix hologram technology, the fronts feature color action player cutouts. The backs carry player information. Several of the cards were erroneously printed without player's name on the front. These uncorrected errors are worth the same as the corrected cards.

	MINT	NRMT
COMPLETE SET (18)	250.00	110.00
COMMON CARD (1-18)	5.00	2.20

☐ 1 Sammy Sosa	8.00	3.60
☐ 2 Derek Jeter	20.00	9.00
☐ 3 Ken Griffey Jr.	40.00	18.00

	NRMT	VG-E
☐ 4 Albert Belle	10.00	4.50
☐ 5 Cal Ripken	30.00	13.50
☐ 6 Greg Maddux	25.00	11.00
☐ 7 Frank Thomas	30.00	13.50
☐ 8 Mo Vaughn	10.00	4.50
☐ 9 Chipper Jones	25.00	11.00
☐ 10 Mike Piazza	25.00	11.00
☐ 11 Ryan Klesko	6.00	2.70
☐ 12 Hideo Nomo	20.00	9.00
☐ 13 Alan Benes	6.00	2.70
☐ 14 Manny Ramirez	12.00	5.50
☐ 15 Gary Sheffield	8.00	3.60
☐ 16 Barry Bonds	10.00	4.50
☐ 17 Matt Williams	6.00	2.70
☐ 18 Johnny Damon	5.00	2.20

1983 Seven-Eleven Coins

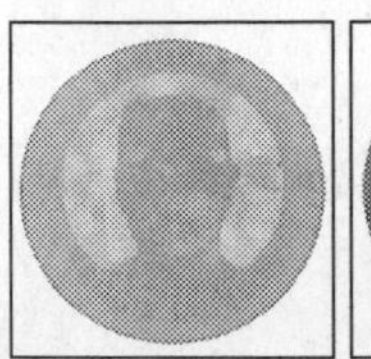

The coins in this 12-coin set measure approximately 1 3/4" diameter. This set of action coins was released by 7-Eleven stores in the Los Angeles area. Given out with large Slurpee drinks, the set features Los Angeles Dodgers (blue background) and California Angels (red background) on plastic discs. The fronts feature two pictures (portrait and action) of each player, each of which can be seen by moving the coin slightly to one side or another. Brief statistics fill the backs of these coins. The coins are numbered by uniform number on the front; in addition, an individual coin number can be found on the back.

	NRMT	VG-E
COMPLETE SET (12)	8.00	3.60
COMMON COIN (1-12)	.25	.11
☐ 1 Rod Carew	2.00	.90
☐ 2 Steve Sax	.40	.18
☐ 3 Fred Lynn	.40	.18
☐ 4 Pedro Guerrero	.60	.25
☐ 5 Reggie Jackson	2.50	1.10
☐ 6 Dusty Baker	.40	.18
☐ 7 Doug DeCinces	.40	.18
☐ 8 Fernando Valenzuela	.75	.35
☐ 9 Tommy John	.60	.25
☐ 10 Rick Monday	.25	.11
☐ 11 Bobby Grich	.40	.18
☐ 12 Greg Brock	.25	.11

1984 Seven-Eleven Coins

The coins in this 72 coin set measure approximately 1 3/4" diameter. For the second year in a row, 7-Eleven issued sets of coins (officially called Slurpee Discs). The fronts feature two pictures (portrait and action) of each player, each of which can be seen by moving the coin slightly to one side or another. There were, in effect, three different sets of 24 coins corresponding to an East, Central and West region. The letter suffix after the number in the checklist below denotes the region of issue, East (E), Central (C), or West (W). Of the total 72 coins, only 60 different players appear. Six players appear in all three sets. The repeat players are Andre Dawson, Robin Yount, Dale Murphy, George Brett, Mike Schmidt and Eddie Murray. Each team is represented by at least one player and as one might expect, players within the three groups favor the teams of the geographical location in which that particular group was issued. Coins are numbered on the back, which is different from the uniform number which is on the front of the coin.

	NRMT	VG-E
COMPLETE SET (72)	80.00	36.00
COMMON COIN	.40	.18
☐ C1 Andre Dawson	1.25	.55
☐ C2 Robin Yount	1.50	.70
☐ C3 Dale Murphy	1.00	.45
☐ C4 Mike Schmidt	3.00	1.35
☐ C5 George Brett	4.00	1.80
☐ C6 Eddie Murray	2.50	1.10
☐ C7 Bruce Sutter	.60	.25
☐ C8 Cecil Cooper	.60	.25
☐ C9 Willie McGee	.75	.35
☐ C10 Mike Hargrove	.60	.25
☐ C11 Kent Hrbek	.60	.25
☐ C12 Carlton Fisk	2.00	.90
☐ C13 Mario Soto	.40	.18
☐ C14 Lonnie Smith	.40	.18
☐ C15 Gary Carter	1.00	.45
☐ C16 Lou Whitaker	.75	.35
☐ C17 Ron Kittle	.40	.18
☐ C18 Paul Molitor	2.00	.90
☐ C19 Ozzie Smith	3.00	1.35
☐ C20 Fergie Jenkins	1.00	.45
☐ C21 Ted Simmons	.60	.25
☐ C22 Pete Rose	4.00	1.80
☐ C23 LaMarr Hoyt	.40	.18
☐ C24 Dan Quisenberry	.40	.18
☐ E1 Andre Dawson	1.25	.55
☐ E2 Robin Yount	1.50	.70
☐ E3 Dale Murphy	1.00	.45
☐ E4 Mike Schmidt	3.00	1.35
☐ E5 George Brett	4.00	1.80
☐ E6 Eddie Murray	2.50	1.10
☐ E7 Dave Winfield	2.00	.90
☐ E8 Tom Seaver	2.50	1.10
☐ E9 Mike Boddicker	.40	.18
☐ E10 Wade Boggs	3.00	1.35
☐ E11 Bill Madlock	.60	.25
☐ E12 Steve Carlton	2.00	.90
☐ E13 Dave Stieb	.40	.18
☐ E14 Cal Ripken	10.00	4.50
☐ E15 Jim Rice	.60	.25
☐ E16 Ron Guidry	.60	.25
☐ E17 Darryl Strawberry	1.50	.70
☐ E18 Tony Pena	.40	.18
☐ E19 John Denny	.40	.18
☐ E20 Tim Raines	.75	.35
☐ E21 Rick Dempsey	.40	.18
☐ E22 Rich Gossage	.75	.35
☐ E23 Gary Matthews	.40	.18
☐ E24 Keith Hernandez	.60	.25
☐ W1 Andre Dawson	1.25	.55
☐ W2 Robin Yount	1.50	.70
☐ W3 Dale Murphy	1.00	.45
☐ W4 Mike Schmidt	3.00	1.35
☐ W5 George Brett	4.00	1.80
☐ W6 Eddie Murray	2.50	1.10
☐ W7 Steve Garvey	1.00	.45
☐ W8 Rod Carew	2.00	.90
☐ W9 Fernando Valenzuela	.60	.25
☐ W10 Bob Horner	.40	.18
☐ W11 Buddy Bell	.60	.25
☐ W12 Reggie Jackson	2.50	1.10
☐ W13 Nolan Ryan	10.00	4.50
☐ W14 Pedro Guerrero	.60	.25
☐ W15 Atlee Hammaker	.40	.18
☐ W16 Fred Lynn	.60	.25
☐ W17 Terry Kennedy	.40	.18
☐ W18 Dusty Baker	.60	.25
☐ W19 Jose Cruz	.60	.25
☐ W20 Steve Rogers	.40	.18
☐ W21 Rickey Henderson	2.00	.90
☐ W22 Steve Sax	.60	.25
☐ W23 Dickie Thon	.40	.18
☐ W24 Matt Young	.40	.18

1985 Seven-Eleven Coins

These "3-D" type coins are very similar to those of the preceding years except that in 1985 7-Eleven issued six subsets. The subsets are Central (C), Detroit (D), Eastern (E), Great Lakes (G), Southeast (S) and Western (W). The letter suffix after the number in the checklist below denotes the region of issue. Each of the six subsets is numbered and contains 16 coins except for the Tigers set which contains only 14 and was distributed in somewhat smaller supply. Each coin measures approximately 1 3/4" in diameter.

	NRMT	VG-E
COMPLETE SET (94)	100.00	45.00
COMMON COIN	.20	.09
☐ C1 Nolan Ryan	10.00	4.50
☐ C2 George Brett	4.00	1.80
☐ C3 Dave Winfield	1.50	.70
☐ C4 Mike Schmidt	3.00	1.35
☐ C5 Bruce Sutter	.40	.18
☐ C6 Joaquin Andujar	.20	.09
☐ C7 Willie Hernandez	.20	.09
☐ C8 Wade Boggs	2.50	1.10
☐ C9 Gary Carter	1.00	.45
☐ C10 Jose Cruz	.20	.09
☐ C11 Kent Hrbek	.75	.35
☐ C12 Reggie Jackson	2.50	1.10
☐ C13 Lance Parrish	.40	.18
☐ C14 Terry Puhl	.20	.09
☐ C15 Dan Quisenberry	.20	.09
☐ C16 Ozzie Smith	2.50	1.10
☐ D1 Lou Whitaker	.75	.35
☐ D2 Sparky Anderson MG	.40	.18
☐ D3 Darrell Evans	.40	.18
☐ D4 Larry Herndon	.20	.09
☐ D5 Dave Rozema	.20	.09
☐ D6 Milt Wilcox	.20	.09
☐ D7 Dan Petry	.20	.09
☐ D8 Alan Trammell	1.00	.45
☐ D9 Aurelio Lopez	.20	.09
☐ D10 Willie Hernandez	.20	.09
☐ D11 Chet Lemon	.20	.09
☐ D12 Jack Morris	.40	.18
☐ D13 Kirk Gibson	.40	.18
☐ D14 Lance Parrish	.40	.18
☐ E1 Eddie Murray	2.00	.90
☐ E2 George Brett	4.00	1.80
☐ E3 Steve Carlton	2.00	.90
☐ E4 Jim Rice	.40	.18
☐ E5 Dave Winfield	1.50	.70
☐ E6 Mike Boddicker	.20	.09
☐ E7 Wade Boggs	2.50	1.10
☐ E8 Dwight Evans	.75	.35
☐ E9 Dwight Gooden	3.00	1.35
☐ E10 Keith Hernandez	.40	.18
☐ E11 Bill Madlock	.40	.18
☐ E12 Don Mattingly	8.00	3.60
☐ E13 Dave Righetti	.40	.18
☐ E14 Cal Ripken	10.00	4.50
☐ E15 Juan Samuel	.20	.09
☐ E16 Mike Schmidt	3.00	1.35
☐ G1 Willie Hernandez	.20	.09
☐ G2 George Brett	4.00	1.80
☐ G3 Dave Winfield	1.50	.70
☐ G4 Eddie Murray	2.00	.90
☐ G5 Bruce Sutter	.40	.18
☐ G6 Harold Baines	.40	.18
☐ G7 Bert Blyleven	.75	.35
☐ G8 Leon Durham	.20	.09
☐ G9 Chet Lemon	.20	.09
☐ G10 Pete Rose	4.00	1.80
☐ G11 Ryne Sandberg	5.00	2.20
☐ G12 Tom Seaver	2.50	1.10
☐ G13 Mario Soto	.20	.09
☐ G14 Rick Sutcliffe	.20	.09
☐ G15 Alan Trammell	1.00	.45
☐ G16 Robin Yount	1.50	.70
☐ S1 Dale Murphy	1.00	.45
☐ S2 Steve Carlton	2.00	.90
☐ S3 Nolan Ryan	8.00	3.60
☐ S4 Bruce Sutter	.40	.18
☐ S5 Dave Winfield	1.50	.70
☐ S6 Steve Bedrosian	.20	.09
☐ S7 Andre Dawson	1.00	.45
☐ S8 Kirk Gibson	.40	.18
☐ S9 Fred Lynn	.40	.18
☐ S10 Gary Matthews	.20	.09
☐ S11 Phil Niekro	1.00	.45
☐ S12 Tim Raines	.40	.18
☐ S13 Darryl Strawberry	.75	.35
☐ S14 Dave Stieb	.40	.18
☐ S15 Willie Upshaw	.20	.09
☐ S16 Lou Whitaker	.75	.35
☐ W1 Mike Schmidt	3.00	1.35
☐ W2 Jim Rice	.40	.18
☐ W3 Dale Murphy	1.00	.45
☐ W4 Eddie Murray	2.00	.90
☐ W5 Dave Winfield	1.50	.70
☐ W6 Rod Carew	2.00	.90
☐ W7 Alvin Davis	.20	.09
☐ W8 Steve Garvey	.75	.35
☐ W9 Rich Gossage	.75	.35
☐ W10 Pedro Guerrero	.40	.18
☐ W11 Tony Gwynn	8.00	3.60
☐ W12 Rickey Henderson	2.00	.90
☐ W13 Reggie Jackson	2.50	1.10
☐ W14 Jeff Leonard	.20	.09
☐ W15 Alejandro Pena	.20	.09
☐ W16 Fernando Valenzuela	.40	.18

1986 Seven-Eleven Coins

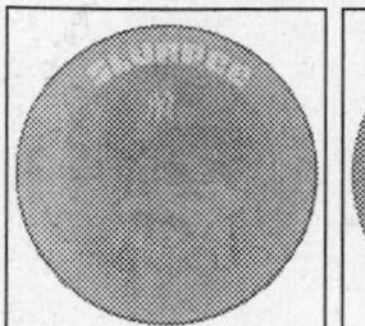

Four subsets of 16 coins each were distributed regionally by the 7-Eleven chain of convenience stores. The letter suffix after the number in the checklist below denotes the region of issue. The regions were Central (C), East (E), South (S) and West (W). The first eight coins in each region are the same; the last eight (9-16) in each region were apparently selected to showcase players from that area. Except for Dwight Gooden all other coins feature three players on each card depending on how you tilt the coin to see one of the three players. The three players are typically related by position. Each coin measures approximately 1 3/4" in diameter.

	MINT	NRMT
COMPLETE SET (64)	60.00	27.00
COMMON COIN	.25	.11
☐ C1 Dwight Gooden	1.50	.70
☐ C2 Wade Boggs	3.00	1.35
George Brett		
Pete Rose		
☐ C3 Keith Hernandez	5.00	2.20
Don Mattingly		
Cal Ripken		
☐ C4 Harold Baines	.35	.16
Pedro Guerrero		
Dave Parker		
☐ C5 Dale Murphy	.60	.25
Jim Rice		
Mike Schmidt		
☐ C6 Ron Guidry	.35	.16
Bret Saberhagen		
Fernando Valenzuela		
☐ C7 Goose Gossage	.35	.16
Dan Quisenberry		
Bruce Sutter		
☐ C8 Steve Carlton	5.00	2.20
Nolan Ryan		
Tom Seaver		
☐ C9 Willie Hernandez	1.50	.70
Ryne Sandberg		
Robin Yount		
☐ C10 Bert Blyleven	.35	.16
Jack Morris		
Rick Sutcliffe		
☐ C11 Rollie Fingers	.35	.16
Bob James		
Lee Smith		
☐ C12 Carlton Fisk	.35	.16
Lance Parrish		
Tony Pena		
☐ C13 Shawon Dunston	.35	.16
Ozzie Guillen		
Earnie Riles		
☐ C14 Brett Butler	.35	.16
Chet Lemon		
Willie Wilson		
☐ C15 Tom Brunansky	.25	.11
Cecil Cooper		
Darrell Evans		
☐ C16 Kirk Gibson	.35	.16
Paul Molitor		
Greg Walker		
☐ E1 Dwight Gooden	1.50	.70
☐ E2 Wade Boggs	3.00	1.35
George Brett		
Pete Rose		
☐ E3 Keith Hernandez	5.00	2.20
Don Mattingly		
Cal Ripken		
☐ E4 Harold Baines	.35	.16
Pedro Guerrero		
Dave Parker		
☐ E5 Dale Murphy	.60	.25
Jim Rice		
Mike Schmidt		
☐ E6 Ron Guidry	.35	.16
Bret Saberhagen		
Fernando Valenzuela		
☐ E7 Goose Gossage	.35	.16
Dan Quisenberry		
Bruce Sutter		
☐ E8 Steve Carlton	5.00	2.20
Nolan Ryan		
Tom Seaver		
☐ E9 Steve Lyons	.25	.11
Rick Schu		
Larry Sheets		
☐ E10 Jeff Reardon	.25	.11
Dave Righetti		
Bob Stanley		
☐ E11 George Bell	1.00	.45
Darryl Strawberry		
Dave Winfield		
☐ E12 Rickey Henderson	.60	.25
Tim Raines		
Juan Samuel		
☐ E13 Andre Dawson	1.50	.70
Dwight Evans		
Eddie Murray		
☐ E14 Mike Boddicker	.25	.11
Ron Darling		
Dave Stieb		
☐ E15 Tim Burke	.25	.11
Brian Fisher		
Roger McDowell		
☐ E16 Jesse Barfield	.35	.16
Gary Carter		
Fred Lynn		
☐ S1 Dwight Gooden	1.50	.70
☐ S2 Wade Boggs	3.00	1.35
George Brett		
Pete Rose		
☐ S3 Keith Hernandez	5.00	2.20
Don Mattingly		
Cal Ripken		
☐ S4 Harold Baines	.35	.16
Pedro Guerrero		
Dave Parker		
☐ S5 Dale Murphy	1.50	.70
Jim Rice		
Mike Schmidt		
☐ S6 Ron Guidry	.35	.16
Bret Saberhagen		
Fernando Valenzuela		
☐ S7 Goose Gossage	.35	.16
Dan Quisenberry		
Bruce Sutter		
☐ S8 Steve Carlton	5.00	2.20
Nolan Ryan		
Tom Seaver		
☐ S9 Vince Coleman	.35	.16
Eric Davis		
Oddibe McDowell		
☐ S10 Buddy Bell	1.50	.70
Ozzie Smith		
Lou Whitaker		
☐ S11 Mike Scott	.25	.11
Mario Soto		
John Tudor		
☐ S12 Jeff Lahti	.25	.11
Ted Power		
Dave Smith		
☐ S13 Jack Clark	.35	.16
Jose Cruz		
Bob Horner		
☐ S14 Bill Doran	.25	.11
Tommy Herr		
Ron Oester		
☐ S15 Tom Browning	.25	.11
Joe Hesketh		
Todd Worrell		
☐ S16 Willie McGee	1.50	.70
Jerry Mumphrey		
Pete Rose		
☐ W1 Dwight Gooden	1.50	.70
☐ W2 Wade Boggs	3.00	1.35
George Brett		
Pete Rose		
☐ W3 Keith Hernandez	5.00	2.20
Don Mattingly		
Cal Ripken		
☐ W4 Harold Baines	.35	.16
Pedro Guerrero		
Dave Parker		
☐ W5 Dale Murphy	1.50	.70
Jim Rice		
Mike Schmidt		
☐ W6 Ron Guidry	.35	.16
Bret Saberhagen		
Fernando Valenzuela		
☐ W7 Goose Gossage	.35	.16
Dan Quisenberry		
Bruce Sutter		
☐ W8 Steve Carlton	5.00	2.20
Nolan Ryan		
Tom Seaver		
☐ W9 Reggie Jackson	.60	.25
Dave Kingman		
Gorman Thomas		
☐ W10 Rod Carew	2.00	.90
Tony Gwynn		
Carney Lansford		
☐ W11 Phil Bradley	.25	.11
Mike Marshall		
Graig Nettles		
☐ W12 Andy Hawkins	.35	.16
Orel Hershiser		
Mike Witt		
☐ W13 Chris Brown	.25	.11
Ivan Calderon		
Mariano Duncan		
☐ W14 Steve Garvey	.35	.16
Bill Madlock		
Jim Presley		
☐ W15 Jay Howell	.25	.11
Donnie Moore		
Edwin Nunez		
☐ W16 Karl Best	.25	.11
Stewart Cliburn		
Steve Ontiveros		

1987 Seven-Eleven Coins

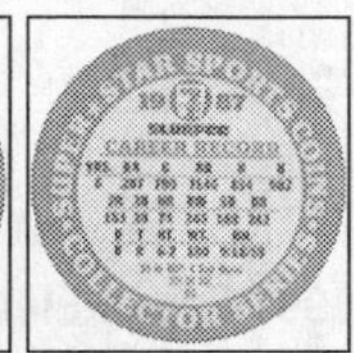

These "3-D" type coins are very similar to those of the preceding years except that in 1987 7-Eleven issued five subsets. The subsets are Detroit (D), East (E), Chicago (C), Mideast (M) and West (W). Each subset has a different color border on the back. The West subset is actually eight Dodgers and eight Angels. The Mideast subset is actually four each from the Mets, Cubs, Red Sox and Orioles. The East subset is actually five each from the Mets, Red Sox and Yankees. The letter prefix before the number in the checklist below denotes the region of issue. Each of the five subsets is numbered and contains between 12 and 16 coins. Each coin measures 1 3/4" in diameter.

	MINT	NRMT
COMPLETE SET (75)	125.00	55.00
COMMON COIN	.50	.23
☐ C1 Harold Baines	1.00	.45
☐ C2 Jody Davis	.50	.23
☐ C3 John Cangelosi	.50	.23
☐ C4 Shawon Dunston	.50	.23
☐ C5 Dave Cochrane	.50	.23
☐ C6 Leon Durham	.50	.23
☐ C7 Carlton Fisk	2.00	.90
☐ C8 Dennis Eckersley	1.25	.55
☐ C9 Ozzie Guillen	.50	.23
☐ C10 Gary Matthews	.50	.23
☐ C11 Ron Karkovice	.50	.23
☐ C12 Keith Moreland	.50	.23
☐ C13 Bobby Thigpen	.50	.23
☐ C14 Ryne Sandberg	5.00	2.20
☐ C15 Greg Walker	.50	.23
☐ C16 Lee Smith	1.25	.55
☐ D1 Darnell Coles	.50	.23
☐ D2 Darrell Evans	1.00	.45
☐ D3 Kirk Gibson	1.25	.55
☐ D4 Willie Hernandez	.50	.23
☐ D5 Larry Herndon	.50	.23
☐ D6 Chet Lemon	.50	.23
☐ D7 Dwight Lowry	.50	.23
☐ D8 Jack Morris	1.00	.45
☐ D9 Dan Petry	.50	.23
☐ D10 Frank Tanana	.50	.23
☐ D11 Alan Trammell	1.25	.55
☐ D12 Lou Whitaker	1.00	.45
☐ E1 Gary Carter	1.50	.70
☐ E2 Don Baylor	1.00	.45
☐ E3 Rickey Henderson	2.00	.90
☐ E4 Lenny Dykstra	1.25	.55
☐ E5 Wade Boggs	2.50	1.10
☐ E6 Mike Pagliarulo	.50	.23
☐ E7 Dwight Gooden	1.50	.70
☐ E8 Roger Clemens	8.00	3.60
☐ E9 Dave Righetti	.50	.23
☐ E10 Keith Hernandez	1.00	.45
☐ E11 Pat Dodson	.50	.23
☐ E12 Don Mattingly	8.00	3.60
☐ E13 Darryl Strawberry	1.25	.55
☐ E14 Jim Rice	1.00	.45
☐ E15 Dave Winfield	2.00	.90
☐ M1 Gary Carter	1.50	.70
☐ M2 Marty Barrett	.50	.23
☐ M3 Jody Davis	.50	.23

☐ M4 Don Aase	.50	.23
☐ M5 Lenny Dykstra	1.25	.55
☐ M6 Wade Boggs	2.00	.90
☐ M7 Keith Moreland	.50	.23
☐ M8 Mike Boddicker	.50	.23
☐ M9 Dwight Gooden	1.50	.70
☐ M10 Roger Clemens	8.00	3.60
☐ M11 Ryne Sandberg	5.00	2.20
☐ M12 Eddie Murray	3.00	1.35
☐ M13 Keith Hernandez	1.00	.45
☐ M14 Jim Rice	1.00	.45
☐ M15 Lee Smith	1.25	.55
☐ M16 Cal Ripken	12.00	5.50
☐ W1 Doug DeCinces	.50	.23
☐ W2 Mariano Duncan	.50	.23
☐ W3 Wally Joyner	2.00	.90
☐ W4 Pedro Guerrero	.50	.23
☐ W5 Kirk McCaskill	.50	.23
☐ W6 Orel Hershiser	1.50	.70
☐ W7 Gary Pettis	.50	.23
☐ W8 Mike Marshall	.50	.23
☐ W9 Dick Schofield	.50	.23
☐ W10 Steve Sax	.50	.23
☐ W11 Don Sutton	1.50	.70
☐ W12 Mike Scioscia	.50	.23
☐ W13 Devon White	1.25	.55
☐ W14 Franklin Stubbs	.50	.23
☐ W15 Mike Witt	.50	.23
☐ W16 Fernando Valenzuela	1.25	.55

1991 Seven-Eleven 3-D Coins National

Measuring 1 3/4" in diameter, these 15 discs have 3-D color player photos on their fronts. Depending on how the disc is tilted, either a head shot or an action photo appears. The player's name, his number and position and the team name are printed in the red border around the photo. The backs carry the player's name, number, position, career record and the words "Superstar Action Coin" in yellow letters in the bottom part of the red border. The discs are numbered on the back as "X of 15."

	MINT	NRMT
COMPLETE SET (15)	8.00	3.60
COMMON COIN (1-15)	.20	.09
☐ 1 Wade Boggs	.60	.25
☐ 2 Barry Bonds	1.00	.45
☐ 3 Roger Clemens	1.00	.45
☐ 4 Lenny Dykstra	.30	.14
☐ 5 Dwight Gooden	.30	.14
☐ 6 Ken Griffey Jr.	4.00	1.80
☐ 7 Rickey Henderson	.60	.25
☐ 8 Gregg Jefferies	.30	.14
☐ 9 Roberto Kelly	.20	.09
☐ 10 Kevin Maas	.20	.09
☐ 11 Don Mattingly	2.00	.90
☐ 12 Mickey Morandini	.20	.09
☐ 13 Dale Murphy	.50	.23
☐ 14 Darryl Strawberry	.30	.14
☐ 15 Frank Viola	.20	.09

1991 Seven-Eleven Coins

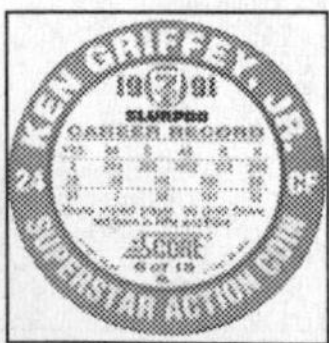

This 120-coin set was produced by Score for 7-Eleven. The Superstar sport coins measure approximately 1 3/4" in diameter and they were attached to the bottom of specially-marked Slurpee cups. The coins were reportedly available through May, or while supplies lasted. These "magic motion" coins have color player pictures on the fronts and different colored borders. The backs have career statistics and brief player profiles. A total of 81 players are featured in the eight regional subsets issued. The subsets are Atlantic (A), Florida (F), Midwest (MW), Northern California (NC), Metro Northeast (NE), Northwest (NW), Southern California (SC) and Texas (T). Ken Griffey Jr. is the only player issued in all eight subsets. The letter suffix before the number in the checklist denotes the region of issue.

	MINT	NRMT
COMPLETE SET (120)	100.00	45.00
COMMON COIN	.35	.16
☐ A1 Glenn Davis	.35	.16
☐ A2 Dwight Evans	.50	.23
☐ A3 Leo Gomez	.35	.16
☐ A4 Ken Griffey Jr.	6.00	2.70
☐ A5 Rickey Henderson	1.00	.45
☐ A6 Jose Canseco	1.00	.45
☐ A7 Dave Justice	.75	.35
☐ A8 Ben McDonald	.35	.16
☐ A9 Randy Milligan	.35	.16
☐ A10 Gregg Olson	.35	.16
☐ A11 Kirby Puckett	2.00	.90
☐ A12 Bill Ripken	.35	.16
☐ A13 Cal Ripken	5.00	2.20
☐ A14 Nolan Ryan	5.00	2.20
☐ A15 David Segui	.35	.16
☐ F1 Barry Bonds	1.50	.70
☐ F2 George Brett	2.00	.90
☐ F3 Roger Clemens	2.00	.90
☐ F4 Glenn Davis	.35	.16
☐ F5 Alex Fernandez	.50	.23
☐ F6 Cecil Fielder	.50	.23
☐ F7 Ken Griffey Jr.	6.00	2.70
☐ F8 Dwight Gooden	.50	.23
☐ F9 Dave Justice	.75	.35
☐ F10 Barry Larkin	.60	.25
☐ F11 Ramon Martinez	.50	.23
☐ F12 Jose Offerman	.35	.16
☐ F13 Kirby Puckett	2.00	.90
☐ F14 Nolan Ryan	5.00	2.20
☐ F15 Terry Shumpert	.35	.16
☐ M1 George Brett	2.00	.90
☐ M2 Andre Dawson	.60	.25
☐ M3 Cecil Fielder	.50	.23
☐ M4 Carlton Fisk	.75	.35
☐ M5 Travis Fryman	.60	.25
☐ M6 Mark Grace	.75	.35
☐ M7 Ken Griffey Jr.	6.00	2.70
☐ M8 Ozzie Guillen	.35	.16
☐ M9 Alex Fernandez	.50	.23
☐ M10 Ray Lankford	.60	.25
☐ M11 Ryne Sandberg	2.00	.90
☐ M12 Ozzie Smith	1.50	.70
☐ M13 Bobby Thigpen	.35	.16
☐ M14 Frank Thomas	6.00	2.70
☐ M15 Alan Trammell	.60	.25
☐ NE4 Lenny Dykstra	.50	.23
☐ NW4 Ken Griffey Jr. Ken Griffey Sr.	1.50	.70
☐ T1 Craig Biggio	.75	.35
☐ T2 Barry Bonds	1.50	.70
☐ T3 Jose Canseco	.75	.35
☐ T4 Roger Clemens	1.50	.70
☐ T5 Glenn Davis	.35	.16
☐ T6 Julio Franco	.50	.23
☐ T7 Juan Gonzalez	3.00	1.35
☐ T8 Ken Griffey Jr.	6.00	2.70
☐ T9 Mike Scott	.35	.16
☐ T10 Rafael Palmeiro	.75	.35
☐ T11 Nolan Ryan	5.00	2.20
☐ T12 Ryne Sandberg	2.00	.90
☐ T13 Ruben Sierra	.35	.16
☐ T14 Todd Van Poppel	.35	.16
☐ T15 Bobby Witt	.35	.16
☐ NC1 John Burkett	.35	.16
☐ NC2 Jose Canseco	.75	.35
☐ NC3 Will Clark	.75	.35
☐ NC4 Steve Decker	.35	.16
☐ NC5 Dennis Eckersley	.60	.25
☐ NC6 Ken Griffey Jr.	6.00	2.70
☐ NC7 Rickey Henderson	.75	.35
☐ NC8 Nolan Ryan	5.00	2.20
☐ NC9 Mark McGwire	2.00	.90
☐ NC10 Kevin Mitchell	.35	.16
☐ NC11 Terry Steinbach	.50	.23
☐ NC12 Dave Stewart	.50	.23
☐ NC13 Todd Van Poppel	.35	.16
☐ NC14 Bob Welch	.35	.16
☐ NC15 Matt Williams	.75	.35
☐ NE1 Wade Boggs	1.00	.45
☐ NE2 Barry Bonds	1.50	.70
☐ NE3 Roger Clemens	2.00	.90
☐ NE5 Dwight Gooden	.50	.23
☐ NE6 Ken Griffey Jr.	6.00	2.70
☐ NE7 Rickey Henderson	.75	.35
☐ NE8 Gregg Jefferies	.50	.23
☐ NE9 Roberto Kelly	.35	.16
☐ NE10 Kevin Maas	.35	.16
☐ NE11 Don Mattingly	3.00	1.35
☐ NE12 Mickey Morandini	.35	.16
☐ NE13 Dale Murphy	.75	.35
☐ NE14 Darryl Strawberry	.50	.23
☐ NE15 Frank Viola	.35	.16
☐ NW1 George Brett	2.00	.90
☐ NW2 Jose Canseco	.75	.35
☐ NW3 Alvin Davis	.35	.16
☐ NW5 Ken Griffey Jr.	6.00	2.70
☐ NW6 Erik Hanson	.35	.16
☐ NW7 Rickey Henderson	.75	.35
☐ NW8 Ryne Sandberg	2.00	.90
☐ NW9 Randy Johnson	1.00	.45
☐ NW10 Dave Justice	.75	.35
☐ NW11 Edgar Martinez	.60	.25
☐ NW12 Tino Martinez	.75	.35
☐ NW13 Harold Reynolds	.50	.23
☐ NW14 Nolan Ryan	5.00	2.20
☐ NW15 Mike Schooler	.35	.16
☐ SC1 Jim Abbott	.50	.23
☐ SC2 Jose Canseco	.75	.35
☐ SC3 Ken Griffey Jr.	6.00	2.70
☐ SC4 Tony Gwynn	3.00	1.35
☐ SC5 Orel Hershiser	.50	.23
☐ SC6 Eric Davis	.35	.16
☐ SC7 Wally Joyner	.50	.23
☐ SC8 Ramon Martinez	.50	.23
☐ SC9 Fred McGriff	.60	.25
☐ SC10 Eddie Murray	1.50	.70
☐ SC11 Jose Offerman	.35	.16
☐ SC12 Nolan Ryan	5.00	2.20
☐ SC13 Benito Santiago	.35	.16
☐ SC14 Darryl Strawberry	.50	.23
☐ SC15 Fernando Valenzuela	.50	.23

1992 Seven-Eleven Coins

These 26 discs, "Superstar Action Coins," measure approximately 1 3/4" in diameter and feature "Magic Motion" plastic-coated photos that alternate between a posed head shot and an action shot as the disc is moved. The photos are encircled by a yellow line and bordered in red. The player's name, team, position and uniform number appear in white lettering within the red border around the photo. The back carries the player's name in yellow lettering within the black border around the statistics table in the central yellow portion.

	MINT	NRMT
COMPLETE SET (26)	12.50	5.50
COMMON COIN (1-26)	.20	.09
☐ 1 Dwight Gooden	.30	.14
☐ 2 Don Mattingly	1.50	.70
☐ 3 Roger Clemens	1.00	.45
☐ 4 Ivan Calderon	.20	.09
☐ 5 Roberto Alomar	.60	.25
☐ 6 Sandy Alomar Jr.	.30	.14
☐ 7 Andy Van Slyke	.30	.14
☐ 8 Lenny Dykstra	.30	.14
☐ 9 Cal Ripken	3.00	1.35
☐ 10 Dave Justice	.50	.23
☐ 11 Nolan Ryan	3.00	1.35
☐ 12 Craig Biggio	.40	.18
☐ 13 Barry Larkin	.40	.18
☐ 14 Ozzie Smith	.75	.35
☐ 15 Ryne Sandberg	1.00	.45
☐ 16 Frank Thomas	3.00	1.35
☐ 17 Robin Yount	.50	.23
☐ 18 Kirby Puckett	1.25	.55
☐ 19 Cecil Fielder	.30	.14
☐ 20 Will Clark	.50	.23
☐ 21 Jose Canseco	.50	.23
☐ 22 Jim Abbott	.20	.09
☐ 23 Tony Gwynn	1.50	.70
☐ 24 Darryl Strawberry	.30	.14
☐ 25 George Brett	1.25	.55
☐ 26 Ken Griffey Jr.	4.00	1.80

1962 Shirriff Plastic Coins

There are 221 different players in this 1962 set of plastic baseball coins marketed in Canada by Shirriff Potato Chips. The set is very similar to the American Salada coin set except for the printing on the reverse of the coin and the relative scarcitites of the coins in the set. Since the Shirriff coins were produced after the Salada coins, there are not the many gradations of scarcities and variations as in the Salada set. Each plastic coin measures approximately 1 3/8" in diameter. The "coin" itself is made of one-color plastic (light or dark) blue, black, orange, red or white) which has a color portrait printed on paper inserted into the obverse surface.

	NRMT	VG-E
COMPLETE SET (221)	1600.00	700.00
COMMON COIN (1-221)	4.00	1.80

	NRMT	VG-E
☐ 1 Jim Gentile	5.00	2.20
☐ 2 Billy Pierce	5.00	2.20
☐ 3 Chico Fernandez	4.00	1.80
☐ 4 Tom Brewer	4.00	1.80
☐ 5 Woody Held	5.00	2.20
☐ 6 Ray Herbert	4.00	1.80
☐ 7 Ken Aspromonte	5.00	2.20
☐ 8 Whitey Ford	25.00	11.00
☐ 9 Jim Lemon	5.00	2.20
☐ 10 Billy Klaus	4.00	1.80
☐ 11 Steve Barber	5.00	2.20
☐ 12 Nellie Fox	15.00	6.75
☐ 13 Jim Bunning	15.00	6.75
☐ 14 Frank Malzone	5.00	2.20
☐ 15 Tito Francona	4.00	1.80
☐ 16 Bobby Del Greco	4.00	1.80
☐ 17 Steve Bilko	4.00	1.80
☐ 18 Tony Kubek	8.00	3.60
☐ 19 Earl Battey	4.00	1.80
☐ 20 Chuck Cottier	4.00	1.80
☐ 21 Willie Tasby	4.00	1.80
☐ 22 Bob Allison	5.00	2.20
☐ 23 Roger Maris	35.00	16.00
☐ 24 Earl Averill	4.00	1.80
☐ 25 Jerry Lumpe	4.00	1.80
☐ 26 Jim Grant	4.00	1.80
☐ 27 Carl Yastrzemski	30.00	13.50
☐ 28 Rocky Colavito	10.00	4.50
☐ 29 Al Smith	4.00	1.80
☐ 30 Jim Busby	5.00	2.20
☐ 31 Dick Howser	5.00	2.20
☐ 32 Jim Perry	5.00	2.20
☐ 33 Yogi Berra	30.00	13.50
☐ 34 Ken Hamlin	4.00	1.80
☐ 35 Dale Long	4.00	1.80
☐ 36 Harmon Killebrew	20.00	9.00
☐ 37 Dick Brown	4.00	1.80
☐ 38 Gary Geiger	5.00	2.20
☐ 39 Minnie Minoso	8.00	3.60
☐ 40 Brooks Robinson	25.00	11.00
☐ 41 Mickey Mantle	150.00	70.00
☐ 42 Bennie Daniels	4.00	1.80
☐ 43 Billy Martin	8.00	3.60
☐ 44 Vic Power	4.00	1.80
☐ 45 Joe Pignatano	4.00	1.80
☐ 46 Ryne Duren	5.00	2.20
☐ 47 Pete Runnels	5.00	2.20
☐ 48 Dick Williams	5.00	2.20
☐ 49 Jim Landis	4.00	1.80
☐ 50 Steve Boros	4.00	1.80
☐ 51 Zoilo Versalles	5.00	2.20
☐ 52 Johnny Temple	5.00	2.20
☐ 53 Jackie Brandt	5.00	2.20
☐ 54 Joe McClain	4.00	1.80
☐ 55 Sherman Lollar	4.00	1.80
☐ 56 Gene Stephens	4.00	1.80
☐ 57 Leon Wagner	4.00	1.80
☐ 58 Frank Lary	5.00	2.20
☐ 59 Bill Skowron	6.00	2.70
☐ 60 Vic Wertz	5.00	2.20
☐ 61 Willie Kirkland	4.00	1.80
☐ 62 Leo Posada	4.00	1.80
☐ 63 Albie Pearson	4.00	1.80
☐ 64 Bobby Richardson	8.00	3.60
☐ 65 Marv Breeding	4.00	1.80
☐ 66 Roy Sievers	5.00	2.20
☐ 67 Al Kaline	30.00	13.50
☐ 68 Don Buddin	4.00	1.80
☐ 69 Lenny Green	4.00	1.80
☐ 70 Gene Green	5.00	2.20
☐ 71 Luis Aparicio	15.00	6.75
☐ 72 Norm Cash	8.00	3.60
☐ 73 Jackie Jensen	6.00	2.70
☐ 74 Bubba Phillips	4.00	1.80
☐ 75 James Archer	4.00	1.80
☐ 76 Ken Hunt	4.00	1.80
☐ 77 Ralph Terry	5.00	2.20
☐ 78 Camilo Pascual	5.00	2.20
☐ 79 Marty Keough	5.00	2.20
☐ 80 Clete Boyer	5.00	2.20
☐ 81 Jim Pagliaroni	4.00	1.80
☐ 82 Gene Leek	4.00	1.80
☐ 83 Jake Wood	4.00	1.80
☐ 84 Coot Veal	4.00	1.80
☐ 85 Norm Siebern	4.00	1.80
☐ 86 Andy Carey	5.00	2.20
☐ 87 Bill Tuttle	5.00	2.20
☐ 88 Jimmy Piersall	6.00	2.70
☐ 89 Ron Hansen	5.00	2.20
☐ 90 Chuck Stobbs	4.00	1.80
☐ 91 Ken McBride	4.00	1.80
☐ 92 Bill Bruton	4.00	1.80
☐ 93 Gus Triandos	5.00	2.20
☐ 94 John Romano	4.00	1.80
☐ 95 Elston Howard	8.00	3.60
☐ 96 Gene Woodling	5.00	2.20
☐ 97 Early Wynn	15.00	6.75
☐ 98 Milt Pappas	5.00	2.20
☐ 99 Bill Monbouquette	4.00	1.80
☐ 100 Wayne Causey	4.00	1.80
☐ 101 Don Elston	4.00	1.80
☐ 102 Charlie Neal	4.00	1.80
☐ 103 Don Blasingame	4.00	1.80
☐ 104 Frank Thomas	5.00	2.20
☐ 105 Wes Covington	4.00	1.80
☐ 106 Chuck Hiller	4.00	1.80
☐ 107 Don Hoak	5.00	2.20
☐ 108 Bob Lillis	4.00	1.80
☐ 109 Sandy Koufax	35.00	16.00
☐ 110 Gordy Coleman	4.00	1.80
☐ 111 Eddie Mathews UER	25.00	11.00
(Misspelled Matthews)		
☐ 112 Art Mahaffey	4.00	1.80
☐ 113 Ed Bailey	4.00	1.80
☐ 114 Smokey Burgess	5.00	2.20
☐ 115 Bill White	6.00	2.70
☐ 116 Ed Bouchee	5.00	2.20
☐ 117 Bob Buhl	4.00	1.80
☐ 118 Vada Pinson	6.00	2.70
☐ 119 Carl Sawatski	4.00	1.80
☐ 120 Dick Stuart	5.00	2.20
☐ 121 Harvey Kuenn	6.00	2.70
☐ 122 Pancho Herrera	4.00	1.80
☐ 123 Don Zimmer	5.00	2.20
☐ 124 Wally Moon	5.00	2.20
☐ 125 Joe Adcock	5.00	2.20
☐ 126 Joey Jay	4.00	1.80
☐ 127 Maury Wills	8.00	3.60
☐ 128 George Altman	4.00	1.80
☐ 129 John Buzhardt	5.00	2.20
☐ 130 Felipe Alou	6.00	2.70
☐ 131 Bill Mazeroski	8.00	3.60
☐ 132 Ernie Broglio	5.00	2.20
☐ 133 John Roseboro	5.00	2.20
☐ 134 Mike McCormick	4.00	1.80
☐ 135 Charlie Smith	4.00	1.80
☐ 136 Ron Santo	8.00	3.60
☐ 137 Gene Freese	4.00	1.80
☐ 138 Dick Groat	6.00	2.70
☐ 139 Curt Flood	6.00	2.70
☐ 140 Frank Bolling	4.00	1.80
☐ 141 Clay Dalrymple	4.00	1.80
☐ 142 Willie McCovey	25.00	11.00
☐ 143 Bob Skinner	4.00	1.80
☐ 144 Lindy McDaniel	4.00	1.80
☐ 145 Glen Hobbie	4.00	1.80
☐ 146 Gil Hodges	15.00	6.75
☐ 147 Eddie Kasko	4.00	1.80
☐ 148 Gino Cimoli	5.00	2.20
☐ 149 Willie Mays	50.00	22.00
☐ 150 Roberto Clemente	75.00	34.00
☐ 151 Red Schoendienst	15.00	6.75
☐ 152 Joe Torre	10.00	4.50
☐ 153 Bob Purkey	4.00	1.80
☐ 154 Tommy Davis	6.00	2.70
☐ 155 Andre Rodgers	4.00	1.80
☐ 156 Tony Taylor	5.00	2.20
☐ 157 Bob Friend	5.00	2.20
☐ 158 Gus Bell	5.00	2.20
☐ 159 Roy McMillan	4.00	1.80
☐ 160 Carl Warwick	4.00	1.80
☐ 161 Willie Davis	5.00	2.20
☐ 162 Sam Jones	5.00	2.20
☐ 163 Ruben Amaro	5.00	2.20
☐ 164 Sammy Taylor	4.00	1.80
☐ 165 Frank Robinson	25.00	11.00
☐ 166 Lew Burdette	5.00	2.20
☐ 167 Ken Boyer	8.00	3.60
☐ 168 Bill Virdon	5.00	2.20
☐ 169 Jim Davenport	4.00	1.80
☐ 170 Don Demeter	4.00	1.80
☐ 171 Richie Ashburn	15.00	6.75
☐ 172 Johnny Podres	5.00	2.20
☐ 173 Joe Cunningham	5.00	2.20
☐ 174 Elroy Face	5.00	2.20
☐ 175 Orlando Cepeda	10.00	4.50
☐ 176 Bobby Gene Smith	4.00	1.80
☐ 177 Ernie Banks	30.00	13.50
☐ 178 Daryl Spencer	4.00	1.80
☐ 179 Bob Schmidt	5.00	2.20
☐ 180 Hank Aaron	50.00	22.00
☐ 181 Hobie Landrith	4.00	1.80
☐ 182 Ed Bressoud	5.00	2.20
☐ 183 Felix Mantilla	4.00	1.80
☐ 184 Dick Farrell	4.00	1.80
☐ 185 Bob Miller	4.00	1.80
☐ 186 Don Taussig	4.00	1.80
☐ 187 Pumpsie Green	4.00	1.80
☐ 188 Bobby Shantz	5.00	2.20
☐ 189 Roger Craig	10.00	4.50
☐ 190 Hal Smith	4.00	1.80
☐ 191 Johnny Edwards	4.00	1.80
☐ 192 John DeMerit	4.00	1.80
☐ 193 Joe Amalfitano	4.00	1.80
☐ 194 Norm Larker	4.00	1.80
☐ 195 Al Heist	4.00	1.80
☐ 196 Al Spangler	4.00	1.80
☐ 197 Alex Grammas	4.00	1.80
☐ 198 Jerry Lynch	4.00	1.80
☐ 199 Jim McKnight	4.00	1.80
☐ 200 Jose Pagan UER	4.00	1.80
(Misspelled Pagen)		
☐ 201 Jim Gilliam	8.00	3.60
☐ 202 Art Ditmar	4.00	1.80
☐ 203 Bud Daley	4.00	1.80
☐ 204 Johnny Callison	5.00	2.20
☐ 205 Stu Miller	4.00	1.80
☐ 206 Russ Snyder	4.00	1.80
☐ 207 Billy Williams	20.00	9.00
☐ 208 Walt Bond	4.00	1.80
☐ 209 Joe Koppe	4.00	1.80
☐ 210 Don Schwall	5.00	2.20
☐ 211 Billy Gardner	5.00	2.20
☐ 212 Chuck Estrada	4.00	1.80
☐ 213 Gary Bell	4.00	1.80
☐ 214 Floyd Robinson	4.00	1.80
☐ 215 Duke Snider	35.00	16.00
☐ 216 Lee Maye	4.00	1.80
☐ 217 Howie Bedell	4.00	1.80
☐ 218 Bob Will	4.00	1.80
☐ 219 Dallas Green	5.00	2.20
☐ 220 Carroll Hardy	4.00	1.80
☐ 221 Danny O'Connell	4.00	1.80

1997 SkyBox E-X2000

This 100-card set was distributed in two-card foil packs with a suggested retail price of $3.99. The fronts feature SkyView insert technology utilizing a die-cut holofoil border with an interior die-cut player image silhouetted in front of a transparent window with a variety of sky patterns. The backs display a modified mirror image of the front with player information and career statistics in a concise, easy-to-read table. An oversized Alex Rodriguez card shipped in its own holder was mailed to dealers who ordered E-X 2000 cases. They are numbered out of 3,000 and priced below. Also priced below is the redemptiokn card for a baseball signed by Rodriguez. 100 of these cards were produced and the redemption deadline was May 1, 1998.

	MINT	NRMT
COMPLETE SET (100)	100.00	45.00
COMMON CARD (1-100)	1.00	.45

	MINT	NRMT
☐ 1 Jim Edmonds	2.00	.90
☐ 2 Darin Erstad	3.00	1.35
☐ 3 Eddie Murray	2.00	.90
☐ 4 Roberto Alomar	2.00	.90
☐ 5 Brady Anderson	1.50	.70
☐ 6 Mike Mussina	2.00	.90
☐ 7 Rafael Palmeiro	1.50	.70
☐ 8 Cal Ripken	8.00	3.60
☐ 9 Steve Avery	1.00	.45
☐ 10 Nomar Garciaparra	6.00	2.70
☐ 11 Mo Vaughn	2.50	1.10
☐ 12 Albert Belle	2.50	1.10
☐ 13 Mike Cameron	1.25	.55
☐ 14 Ray Durham	1.00	.45
☐ 15 Frank Thomas	8.00	3.60
☐ 16 Robin Ventura	1.25	.55
☐ 17 Manny Ramirez	2.00	.90
☐ 18 Jim Thome	2.00	.90
☐ 19 Matt Williams	1.50	.70

☐ 20 Tony Clark	2.00	.90
☐ 21 Travis Fryman	1.25	.55
☐ 22 Bob Higginson	1.25	.55
☐ 23 Kevin Appier	1.25	.55
☐ 24 Johnny Damon	1.25	.55
☐ 25 Jermaine Dye	1.00	.45
☐ 26 Jeff Cirillo	1.25	.55
☐ 27 Ben McDonald	1.00	.45
☐ 28 Chuck Knoblauch	2.00	.90
☐ 29 Paul Molitor	2.00	.90
☐ 30 Todd Walker	1.00	.45
☐ 31 Wade Boggs	2.00	.90
☐ 32 Cecil Fielder	1.25	.55
☐ 33 Derek Jeter	6.00	2.70
☐ 34 Andy Pettitte	2.00	.90
☐ 35 Ruben Rivera	1.00	.45
☐ 36 Bernie Williams	2.00	.90
☐ 37 Jose Canseco	1.50	.70
☐ 38 Mark McGwire	4.00	1.80
☐ 39 Jay Buhner	1.50	.70
☐ 40 Ken Griffey Jr.	10.00	4.50
☐ 41 Randy Johnson	2.00	.90
☐ 42 Edgar Martinez	1.50	.70
☐ 43 Alex Rodriguez	8.00	3.60
☐ 44 Dan Wilson	1.00	.45
☐ 45 Will Clark	1.50	.70
☐ 46 Juan Gonzalez	5.00	2.20
☐ 47 Ivan Rodriguez	2.50	1.10
☐ 48 Joe Carter	1.25	.55
☐ 49 Roger Clemens	4.00	1.80
☐ 50 Juan Guzman	1.00	.45
☐ 51 Pat Hentgen	1.25	.55
☐ 52 Tom Glavine	1.25	.55
☐ 53 Andruw Jones	5.00	2.20
☐ 54 Chipper Jones	6.00	2.70
☐ 55 Ryan Klesko	1.50	.70
☐ 56 Kenny Lofton	2.50	1.10
☐ 57 Greg Maddux	6.00	2.70
☐ 58 Fred McGriff	1.50	.70
☐ 59 John Smoltz	1.25	.55
☐ 60 Mark Wohlers	1.25	.55
☐ 61 Mark Grace	1.50	.70
☐ 62 Ryne Sandberg	2.50	1.10
☐ 63 Sammy Sosa	2.00	.90
☐ 64 Barry Larkin	1.50	.70
☐ 65 Deion Sanders	2.00	.90
☐ 66 Reggie Sanders	1.00	.45
☐ 67 Dante Bichette	1.25	.55
☐ 68 Ellis Burks	1.25	.55
☐ 69 Andres Galarraga	2.00	.90
☐ 70 Moises Alou	1.25	.55
☐ 71 Kevin Brown	1.25	.55
☐ 72 Cliff Floyd	1.00	.45
☐ 73 Edgar Renteria	1.25	.55
☐ 74 Gary Sheffield	2.00	.90
☐ 75 Bob Abreu	2.00	.90
☐ 76 Jeff Bagwell	4.00	1.80
☐ 77 Craig Biggio	1.50	.70
☐ 78 Todd Hollandsworth	1.00	.45
☐ 79 Eric Karros	1.00	.45
☐ 80 Raul Mondesi	1.50	.70
☐ 81 Hideo Nomo	5.00	2.20
☐ 82 Mike Piazza	6.00	2.70
☐ 83 Vladimir Guerrero	4.00	1.80
☐ 84 Henry Rodriguez	1.00	.45
☐ 85 Todd Hundley	1.25	.55
☐ 86 Alex Ochoa	1.00	.45
☐ 87 Rey Ordonez	1.00	.45
☐ 88 Gregg Jefferies	1.25	.55
☐ 89 Scott Rolen	5.00	2.20
☐ 90 Jermaine Allensworth	1.00	.45
☐ 91 Jason Kendall	1.25	.55
☐ 92 Ken Caminiti	2.00	.90
☐ 93 Tony Gwynn	5.00	2.20
☐ 94 Rickey Henderson	1.50	.70
☐ 95 Barry Bonds	2.50	1.10
☐ 96 J.T. Snow	1.00	.45
☐ 97 Dennis Eckersley	1.50	.70
☐ 98 Ron Gant	1.25	.55
☐ 99 Brian Jordan	1.00	.45
☐ 100 Ray Lankford	1.25	.55
☐ 101 Checklist (1-74)	1.00	.45
☐ 102 Checklist (75-102/inserts)	1.00	.45
☐ P43 Alex Rodriguez Three card promo strip	1.00	.45
☐ S43 Alex Rodriguez Mailed to Dealers who ordered Cases Card is numbered out of 3,000	20.00	9.00
☐ NNO Alex Rodriguez Ball Exch 100 produced	200.00	90.00

1997 Skybox E-X2000 Credentials

Randomly inserted in packs at the approximate rate of one in 60, this 100-card set is parallel to the base set with an etched holofoil border. Less than 299 sets were produced and are sequentially numbered in gold foil.

	MINT	NRMT
COMPLETE SET (100)	3000.00	1350.00
COMMON CARD (1-100)	10.00	4.50

*STARS: 10X TO 20X BASIC CARDS ..
*YOUNG STARS: 7.5X TO 15X BASIC CARDS

1997 SkyBox E-X2000 Essential Credentials

Randomly inserted in packs at the rate of one in 200, this 100-card set is parallel to the base set with an etched refractive holographic foil border. Less than 99 sets were produced and are sequentially numbered.

	MINT	NRMT
COMMON CARD (1-100)	30.00	13.50
MINOR STARS	40.00	18.00
SEMISTARS	60.00	27.00
UNLISTED STARS	80.00	36.00

☐ 2 Darin Erstad	150.00	70.00
☐ 3 Eddie Murray	100.00	45.00
☐ 4 Roberto Alomar	120.00	55.00
☐ 6 Mike Mussina	120.00	55.00
☐ 8 Cal Ripken	400.00	180.00
☐ 10 Nomar Garciaparra	300.00	135.00
☐ 11 Mo Vaughn	120.00	55.00
☐ 12 Albert Belle	150.00	70.00
☐ 15 Frank Thomas	400.00	180.00
☐ 17 Manny Ramirez	100.00	45.00
☐ 18 Jim Thome	100.00	45.00
☐ 29 Paul Molitor	100.00	45.00
☐ 33 Derek Jeter	300.00	135.00
☐ 34 Andy Pettitte	120.00	55.00
☐ 38 Mark McGwire	200.00	90.00
☐ 40 Ken Griffey Jr.	500.00	220.00
☐ 41 Randy Johnson	120.00	55.00
☐ 43 Alex Rodriguez	300.00	135.00
☐ 46 Juan Gonzalez	250.00	110.00
☐ 47 Ivan Rodriguez	150.00	70.00
☐ 49 Roger Clemens	200.00	90.00
☐ 53 Andruw Jones	250.00	110.00
☐ 54 Chipper Jones	250.00	110.00
☐ 56 Kenny Lofton	120.00	55.00
☐ 57 Greg Maddux	300.00	135.00
☐ 62 Ryne Sandberg	150.00	70.00
☐ 76 Jeff Bagwell	200.00	90.00
☐ 81 Hideo Nomo	400.00	180.00
☐ 82 Mike Piazza	300.00	135.00
☐ 83 Vladimir Guerrero	200.00	90.00
☐ 89 Scott Rolen	250.00	110.00
☐ 93 Tony Gwynn	250.00	110.00
☐ 95 Barry Bonds	150.00	70.00

1997 SkyBox E-X2000 A Cut Above

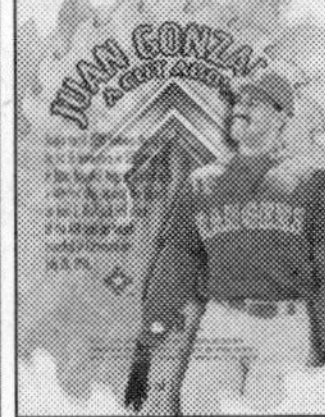

Randomly inserted in packs at the rate of one in 288, this 10-card set features color images of "power hitters" on a holographic foil, die-cut sawblade background.

	MINT	NRMT
COMPLETE SET (10)	500.00	220.00
COMMON CARD (1-10)	15.00	6.75

☐ 1 Frank Thomas	100.00	45.00
☐ 2 Ken Griffey Jr.	120.00	55.00
☐ 3 Alex Rodriguez	80.00	36.00
☐ 4 Albert Belle	30.00	13.50
☐ 5 Juan Gonzalez	60.00	27.00
☐ 6 Mark McGwire	50.00	22.00
☐ 7 Mo Vaughn	30.00	13.50
☐ 8 Manny Ramirez	25.00	11.00
☐ 9 Barry Bonds	30.00	13.50
☐ 10 Fred McGriff	15.00	6.75

1997 SkyBox E-X2000 Emerald Autographs

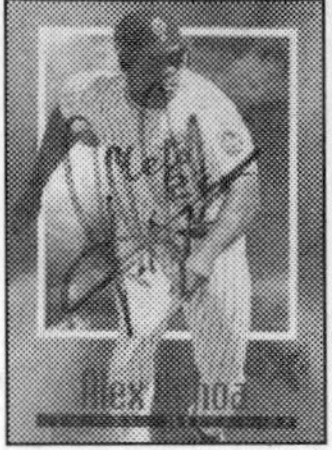

This six-card set features autographed color player photos of some of the hottest young stars in Baseball. These cards were obtained by exchanging a redemption card by mail before the May 1, 1998, deadline.

	MINT	NRMT
COMPLETE SET (6)	400.00	180.00
COMMON CARD	15.00	6.75

☐ 2 Darin Erstad	80.00	36.00
☐ 30 Todd Hollandsworth	20.00	9.00
☐ 43 Alex Ochoa	15.00	6.75
☐ 78 Alex Rodriguez	200.00	90.00
☐ 86 Scott Rolen	100.00	45.00
☐ 89 Todd Walker	25.00	11.00

1997 SkyBox E-X2000 Emerald Autograph Redemptions

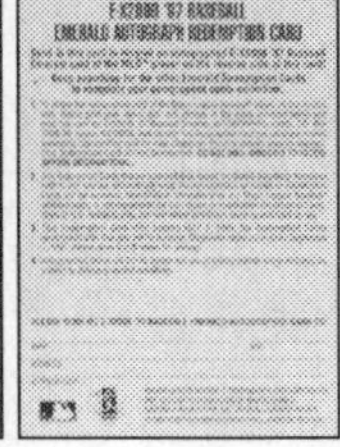

Randomly inserted in packs at the rate of one in 500, this six-card set features redemption cards that could be exchanged via mail before May 1, 1998, for an autographed card of that player.

	MINT	NRMT
COMPLETE SET (6)	80.00	36.00
COMMON CARD	3.00	1.35

☐ AU1 Darin Erstad	15.00	6.75
☐ AU2 Todd Hollandsworth	4.00	1.80
☐ AU3 Alex Ochoa	3.00	1.35
☐ AU4 Alex Rodriguez	40.00	18.00
☐ AU5 Scott Rolen	20.00	9.00
☐ AU6 Todd Walker	5.00	2.20

1997 SkyBox E-X2000 Hall or Nothing

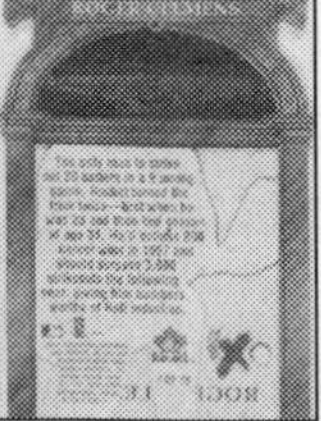

Randomly inserted in packs at the rate of one in 20, this 20-card set features color images of future Cooperstown Hall of Fame candidates printed on 30-pt. acrylic card stock with etched cooper foil borders and gold foil stamping.

	MINT	NRMT
COMPLETE SET (20)	300.00	135.00
COMMON CARD (1-20)	3.00	1.35

☐ 1 Frank Thomas	30.00	13.50
☐ 2 Ken Griffey Jr.	40.00	18.00
☐ 3 Eddie Murray	8.00	3.60
☐ 4 Cal Ripken	30.00	13.50
☐ 5 Ryne Sandberg	10.00	4.50
☐ 6 Wade Boggs	8.00	3.60
☐ 7 Roger Clemens	15.00	6.75
☐ 8 Tony Gwynn	20.00	9.00
☐ 9 Alex Rodriguez	30.00	13.50
☐ 10 Mark McGwire	15.00	6.75
☐ 11 Barry Bonds	10.00	4.50
☐ 12 Greg Maddux	25.00	11.00
☐ 13 Juan Gonzalez	20.00	9.00
☐ 14 Albert Belle	12.00	5.50
☐ 15 Mike Piazza	25.00	11.00
☐ 16 Jeff Bagwell	15.00	6.75
☐ 17 Dennis Eckersley	3.00	1.35
☐ 18 Mo Vaughn	10.00	4.50
☐ 19 Roberto Alomar	8.00	3.60
☐ 20 Kenny Lofton	10.00	4.50

1997 SkyBox E-X2000 Star Date 2000

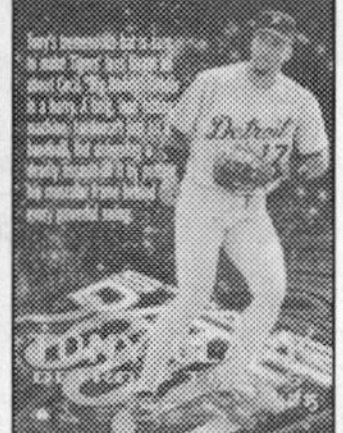

Randomly inserted in packs at the rate of one in nine, this 15-card set features color images of young star players printed on holographic foil with swirls of spot glitter coating.

	MINT	NRMT
COMPLETE SET (15)	60.00	27.00
COMMON CARD (1-15)	1.50	.70
☐ 1 Alex Rodriguez	12.00	5.50
☐ 2 Andruw Jones	10.00	4.50
☐ 3 Andy Pettitte	3.00	1.35
☐ 4 Brooks Kieschnick	1.50	.70
☐ 5 Chipper Jones	10.00	4.50
☐ 6 Darin Erstad	6.00	2.70
☐ 7 Derek Jeter	10.00	4.50
☐ 8 Jason Kendall	2.00	.90
☐ 9 Jermaine Dye	1.50	.70
☐ 10 Neifi Perez	1.50	.70
☐ 11 Scott Rolen	8.00	3.60
☐ 12 Todd Hollandsworth	1.50	.70
☐ 13 Todd Walker	1.50	.70
☐ 14 Tony Clark	3.00	1.35
☐ 15 Vladimir Guerrero	8.00	3.60

1995 Sonic/Pepsi Greats

This 12-card standard-size set was released at Sonic restaurants which served Pepsi products. Some players apparently signed cards for this set. The cards were issued in three-card cello packs. The fronts display color player photos inside red borders. Team logos have been airbrushed off hats and jerseys. In blue print on a white background, the backs present career summary, honors received, player profile, and career statistics. The cards are unnumbered and checklisted below in alphabetical order.

	MINT	NRMT
COMPLETE SET (12)	7.00	3.10
COMMON CARD (1-12)	.50	.23
☐ 1 Bert Campaneris	.50	.23
☐ 2 George Foster	.50	.23
☐ 3 Steve Garvey	.75	.35
☐ 4 Ferguson Jenkins	1.00	.45
☐ 5 Tommy John	.50	.23
☐ 6 Harmon Killebrew	1.00	.45
☐ 7 Sparky Lyle	.50	.23
☐ 8 Fred Lynn	.50	.23
☐ 9 Joe Morgan	1.00	.45
☐ 10 Graig Nettles	.50	.23
☐ 11 Warren Spahn	1.00	.45
☐ 12 Maury Wills	.75	.35

1993 SP

This 290-card standard-size set features fronts with action color player photos. The player's name and position appear within a team-colored stripe at the bottom edge that shades from dark to light, left to right. A team color-checkered stripe is in the upper left and the team name in a gold-lettered arc appears at the top with a gold underline that extends down the right side. The copper foil-stamped SP logo appears at the bottom right. The back displays an action shot of the player in the top half with a team color-checkered stripe in the upper right. The bottom half carries the player's biography, statistics, and career highlights. Special subsets include All Star players (1-18) and Foil Prospects (271-290). Cards 19-270 are in alphabetical order by team nickname. Notable Rookie Cards include Johnny Damon and Derek Jeter.

	MINT	NRMT
COMPLETE SET (290)	80.00	36.00
COMMON CARD (1-270)	.25	.11
☐ 1 Roberto Alomar AS	1.50	.70
☐ 2 Wade Boggs AS	1.50	.70
☐ 3 Joe Carter AS	1.00	.45
☐ 4 Ken Griffey Jr. AS	8.00	3.60
☐ 5 Mark Langston AS	.25	.11
☐ 6 John Olerud AS	.50	.23
☐ 7 Kirby Puckett AS	3.00	1.35
☐ 8 Cal Ripken Jr. AS	6.00	2.70
☐ 9 Ivan Rodriguez AS	2.00	.90
☐ 10 Barry Bonds AS	2.00	.90
☐ 11 Darren Daulton AS	.50	.23
☐ 12 Marquis Grissom AS	.50	.23
☐ 13 David Justice AS	1.50	.70
☐ 14 John Kruk AS	.50	.23
☐ 15 Barry Larkin AS	1.00	.45
☐ 16 Terry Mulholland AS	.25	.11
☐ 17 Ryne Sandberg AS	2.00	.90
☐ 18 Gary Sheffield AS	1.50	.70
☐ 19 Chad Curtis	.50	.23
☐ 20 Chili Davis	.50	.23
☐ 21 Gary DiSarcina	.25	.11
☐ 22 Damion Easley	.25	.11
☐ 23 Chuck Finley	.25	.11
☐ 24 Luis Polonia	.25	.11
☐ 25 Tim Salmon	2.00	.90
☐ 26 J.T. Snow	2.00	.90
☐ 27 Russ Springer	.25	.11
☐ 28 Jeff Bagwell	3.00	1.35
☐ 29 Craig Biggio	1.00	.45
☐ 30 Ken Caminiti	1.50	.70
☐ 31 Andujar Cedeno	.25	.11
☐ 32 Doug Drabek	.25	.11
☐ 33 Steve Finley	.50	.23
☐ 34 Luis Gonzalez	.25	.11
☐ 35 Pete Harnisch	.25	.11
☐ 36 Darryl Kile	.50	.23
☐ 37 Mike Bordick	.25	.11
☐ 38 Dennis Eckersley	1.00	.45
☐ 39 Brent Gates	.25	.11
☐ 40 Rickey Henderson	1.00	.45
☐ 41 Mark McGwire	3.00	1.35
☐ 42 Craig Paquette	.25	.11
☐ 43 Ruben Sierra	.25	.11
☐ 44 Terry Steinbach	.50	.23
☐ 45 Todd Van Poppel	.25	.11
☐ 46 Pat Borders	.25	.11
☐ 47 Tony Fernandez	.25	.11
☐ 48 Juan Guzman	.25	.11
☐ 49 Pat Hentgen	1.00	.45
☐ 50 Paul Molitor	1.50	.70
☐ 51 Jack Morris	.50	.23
☐ 52 Ed Sprague	.25	.11
☐ 53 Duane Ward	.25	.11
☐ 54 Devon White	.25	.11
☐ 55 Steve Avery	.25	.11
☐ 56 Jeff Blauser	.25	.11
☐ 57 Ron Gant	.50	.23
☐ 58 Tom Glavine	1.00	.45
☐ 59 Greg Maddux	5.00	2.20
☐ 60 Fred McGriff	1.00	.45
☐ 61 Terry Pendleton	.50	.23
☐ 62 Deion Sanders	1.50	.70
☐ 63 John Smoltz	1.00	.45
☐ 64 Cal Eldred	.25	.11
☐ 65 Darryl Hamilton	.25	.11
☐ 66 John Jaha	.50	.23
☐ 67 Pat Listach	.25	.11
☐ 68 Jaime Navarro	.25	.11
☐ 69 Kevin Reimer	.25	.11
☐ 70 B.J. Surhoff	.50	.23
☐ 71 Greg Vaughn	.25	.11
☐ 72 Robin Yount	1.00	.45
☐ 73 Rene Arocha	.25	.11
☐ 74 Bernard Gilkey	.50	.23
☐ 75 Gregg Jefferies	.50	.23
☐ 76 Ray Lankford	.50	.23
☐ 77 Tom Pagnozzi	.25	.11
☐ 78 Lee Smith	.50	.23
☐ 79 Ozzie Smith	2.00	.90
☐ 80 Bob Tewksbury	.25	.11
☐ 81 Mark Whiten	.25	.11
☐ 82 Steve Buechele	.25	.11
☐ 83 Mark Grace	1.00	.45
☐ 84 Jose Guzman	.25	.11
☐ 85 Derrick May	.25	.11
☐ 86 Mike Morgan	.25	.11
☐ 87 Randy Myers	.50	.23
☐ 88 Kevin Roberson	.25	.11
☐ 89 Sammy Sosa	1.50	.70
☐ 90 Rick Wilkins	.25	.11
☐ 91 Brett Butler	.50	.23
☐ 92 Eric Davis	.50	.23
☐ 93 Orel Hershiser	.50	.23
☐ 94 Eric Karros	.50	.23
☐ 95 Ramon Martinez	.50	.23
☐ 96 Raul Mondesi	2.00	.90
☐ 97 Jose Offerman	.25	.11
☐ 98 Mike Piazza	8.00	3.60
☐ 99 Darryl Strawberry	.50	.23
☐ 100 Moises Alou	.50	.23
☐ 101 Wil Cordero	.25	.11
☐ 102 Delino DeShields	.25	.11
☐ 103 Darrin Fletcher	.25	.11
☐ 104 Ken Hill	.50	.23
☐ 105 Mike Lansing	.25	.11
☐ 106 Dennis Martinez	.50	.23
☐ 107 Larry Walker	1.50	.70
☐ 108 John Wetteland	.50	.23
☐ 109 Rod Beck	.50	.23
☐ 110 John Burkett	.25	.11
☐ 111 Will Clark	1.00	.45
☐ 112 Royce Clayton	.50	.23
☐ 113 Darren Lewis	.25	.11
☐ 114 Willie McGee	.25	.11
☐ 115 Bill Swift	.25	.11
☐ 116 Robby Thompson	.25	.11
☐ 117 Matt Williams	1.00	.45
☐ 118 Sandy Alomar Jr.	.50	.23
☐ 119 Carlos Baerga	.50	.23
☐ 120 Albert Belle	2.00	.90
☐ 121 Reggie Jefferson	.50	.23
☐ 122 Wayne Kirby	.25	.11
☐ 123 Kenny Lofton	2.50	1.10
☐ 124 Carlos Martinez	.25	.11
☐ 125 Charles Nagy	.50	.23
☐ 126 Paul Sorrento	.25	.11
☐ 127 Rich Amaral	.25	.11
☐ 128 Jay Buhner	1.00	.45
☐ 129 Norm Charlton	.25	.11
☐ 130 Dave Fleming	.25	.11
☐ 131 Erik Hanson	.25	.11
☐ 132 Randy Johnson	1.50	.70
☐ 133 Edgar Martinez	1.00	.45
☐ 134 Tino Martinez	1.50	.70
☐ 135 Omar Vizquel	.50	.23
☐ 136 Bret Barberie	.25	.11
☐ 137 Chuck Carr	.25	.11
☐ 138 Jeff Conine	.50	.23
☐ 139 Orestes Destrade	.25	.11
☐ 140 Chris Hammond	.25	.11
☐ 141 Bryan Harvey	.25	.11
☐ 142 Benito Santiago	.25	.11
☐ 143 Walt Weiss	.25	.11
☐ 144 Darrell Whitmore	.25	.11
☐ 145 Tim Bogar	.25	.11
☐ 146 Bobby Bonilla	.50	.23

Card	MINT	NRMT
☐ 147 Jeromy Burnitz	.25	.11
☐ 148 Vince Coleman	.25	.11
☐ 149 Dwight Gooden	.50	.23
☐ 150 Todd Hundley	1.00	.45
☐ 151 Howard Johnson	.25	.11
☐ 152 Eddie Murray	1.50	.70
☐ 153 Bret Saberhagen	.50	.23
☐ 154 Brady Anderson	1.00	.45
☐ 155 Mike Devereaux	.25	.11
☐ 156 Jeffrey Hammonds	1.00	.45
☐ 157 Chris Hoiles	.25	.11
☐ 158 Ben McDonald	.25	.11
☐ 159 Mark McLemore	.25	.11
☐ 160 Mike Mussina	1.50	.70
☐ 161 Gregg Olson	.25	.11
☐ 162 David Segui	.25	.11
☐ 163 Derek Bell	.50	.23
☐ 164 Andy Benes	.50	.23
☐ 165 Archi Cianfrocco	.25	.11
☐ 166 Ricky Gutierrez	.25	.11
☐ 167 Tony Gwynn	4.00	1.80
☐ 168 Gene Harris	.25	.11
☐ 169 Trevor Hoffman	1.00	.45
☐ 170 Ray McDavid	.25	.11
☐ 171 Phil Plantier	.25	.11
☐ 172 Mariano Duncan	.25	.11
☐ 173 Len Dykstra	.50	.23
☐ 174 Tommy Greene	.25	.11
☐ 175 Dave Hollins	.25	.11
☐ 176 Pete Incaviglia	.25	.11
☐ 177 Mickey Morandini	.25	.11
☐ 178 Curt Schilling	.50	.23
☐ 179 Kevin Stocker	.25	.11
☐ 180 Mitch Williams	.25	.11
☐ 181 Stan Belinda	.25	.11
☐ 182 Jay Bell	.50	.23
☐ 183 Steve Cooke	.25	.11
☐ 184 Carlos Garcia	.25	.11
☐ 185 Jeff King	.50	.23
☐ 186 Orlando Merced	.25	.11
☐ 187 Don Slaught	.25	.11
☐ 188 Andy Van Slyke	.50	.23
☐ 189 Kevin Young	.25	.11
☐ 190 Kevin Brown	.50	.23
☐ 191 Jose Canseco	1.00	.45
☐ 192 Julio Franco	.50	.23
☐ 193 Benji Gil	.25	.11
☐ 194 Juan Gonzalez	4.00	1.80
☐ 195 Tom Henke	.25	.11
☐ 196 Rafael Palmeiro	1.00	.45
☐ 197 Dean Palmer	.50	.23
☐ 198 Nolan Ryan	6.00	2.70
☐ 199 Roger Clemens	3.00	1.35
☐ 200 Scott Cooper	.25	.11
☐ 201 Andre Dawson	1.00	.45
☐ 202 Mike Greenwell	.25	.11
☐ 203 Carlos Quintana	.25	.11
☐ 204 Jeff Russell	.25	.11
☐ 205 Aaron Sele	.50	.23
☐ 206 Mo Vaughn	2.00	.90
☐ 207 Frank Viola	.25	.11
☐ 208 Rob Dibble	.25	.11
☐ 209 Roberto Kelly	.25	.11
☐ 210 Kevin Mitchell	.50	.23
☐ 211 Hal Morris	.25	.11
☐ 212 Joe Oliver	.25	.11
☐ 213 Jose Rijo	.25	.11
☐ 214 Bip Roberts	.25	.11
☐ 215 Chris Sabo	.25	.11
☐ 216 Reggie Sanders	.50	.23
☐ 217 Dante Bichette	1.00	.45
☐ 218 Jerald Clark	.25	.11
☐ 219 Alex Cole	.25	.11
☐ 220 Andres Galarraga	1.00	.45
☐ 221 Joe Girardi	.25	.11
☐ 222 Charlie Hayes	.25	.11
☐ 223 Roberto Mejia	.25	.11
☐ 224 Armando Reynoso	.25	.11
☐ 225 Eric Young	1.50	.70
☐ 226 Kevin Appier	.50	.23
☐ 227 George Brett	3.00	1.35
☐ 228 David Cone	.50	.23
☐ 229 Phil Hiatt	.25	.11
☐ 230 Felix Jose	.25	.11
☐ 231 Wally Joyner	.50	.23
☐ 232 Mike Macfarlane	.25	.11
☐ 233 Brian McRae	.25	.11
☐ 234 Jeff Montgomery	.50	.23
☐ 235 Rob Deer	.25	.11
☐ 236 Cecil Fielder	.50	.23
☐ 237 Travis Fryman	.50	.23
☐ 238 Mike Henneman	.25	.11
☐ 239 Tony Phillips	.25	.11
☐ 240 Mickey Tettleton	.25	.11
☐ 241 Alan Trammell	1.00	.45
☐ 242 David Wells	.25	.11
☐ 243 Lou Whitaker	.50	.23
☐ 244 Rick Aguilera	.25	.11
☐ 245 Scott Erickson	.25	.11
☐ 246 Brian Harper	.25	.11
☐ 247 Kent Hrbek	.50	.23
☐ 248 Chuck Knoblauch	1.50	.70
☐ 249 Shane Mack	.25	.11
☐ 250 David McCarty	.25	.11
☐ 251 Pedro Munoz	.25	.11
☐ 252 Dave Winfield	1.00	.45
☐ 253 Alex Fernandez	.50	.23
☐ 254 Ozzie Guillen	.25	.11
☐ 255 Bo Jackson	.50	.23
☐ 256 Lance Johnson	.25	.11
☐ 257 Ron Karkovice	.25	.11
☐ 258 Jack McDowell	.25	.11
☐ 259 Tim Raines	.50	.23
☐ 260 Frank Thomas	6.00	2.70
☐ 261 Robin Ventura	.50	.23
☐ 262 Jim Abbott	.25	.11
☐ 263 Steve Farr	.25	.11
☐ 264 Jimmy Key	.50	.23
☐ 265 Don Mattingly	2.50	1.10
☐ 266 Paul O'Neill	.50	.23
☐ 267 Mike Stanley	.25	.11
☐ 268 Danny Tartabull	.25	.11
☐ 269 Bob Wickman	.25	.11
☐ 270 Bernie Williams	1.50	.70
☐ 271 Jason Bere FOIL	.50	.23
☐ 272 Roger Cedeno FOIL	1.00	.45
☐ 273 Johnny Damon FOIL	3.00	1.35
☐ 274 Russ Davis FOIL	2.00	.90
☐ 275 Carlos Delgado FOIL	2.00	.90
☐ 276 Carl Everett FOIL	.50	.23
☐ 277 Cliff Floyd FOIL	.50	.23
☐ 278 Alex Gonzalez FOIL	.50	.23
☐ 279 Derek Jeter FOIL	25.00	11.00
☐ 280 Chipper Jones FOIL	10.00	4.50
☐ 281 Javier Lopez FOIL	2.00	.90
☐ 282 Chad Mottola FOIL	.50	.23
☐ 283 Marc Newfield FOIL	.50	.23
☐ 284 Eduardo Perez FOIL	.50	.23
☐ 285 Manny Ramirez FOIL	4.00	1.80
☐ 286 Todd Steverson FOIL	.50	.23
☐ 287 Michael Tucker FOIL	.50	.23
☐ 288 Allen Watson FOIL	.50	.23
☐ 289 Rondell White FOIL	.50	.23
☐ 290 Dmitri Young FOIL	2.00	.90

1993 SP Platinum Power

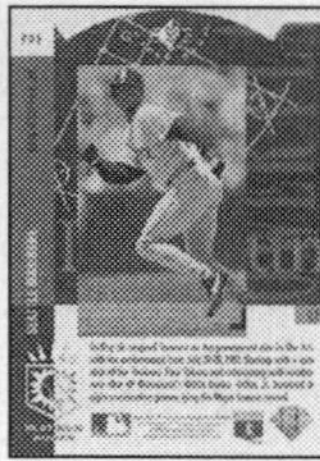

Cards from this 20-card standard-size were inserted one every nine packs and feature power hitters from the American and National Leagues. The color action cut-out shot is superimposed on a royal blue background that contains lettering for Upper Deck Platinum Power and about the player. The top edge of the front is cut out in an arc with a copper foil stripe containing the player's name. The copper foil-stamped Platinum Power logo appears in the lower right. The back displays a color action player photo over the same royal blue background as depicted on the front. On a white background below the player photo is a career summary. The cards are numbered on the back with a "PP" prefix alphabetically by player's name.

	MINT	NRMT
COMPLETE SET (20)	120.00	55.00
COMMON CARD (PP1-PP20)	4.00	1.80
☐ PP1 Albert Belle	10.00	4.50
☐ PP2 Barry Bonds	10.00	4.50
☐ PP3 Joe Carter	6.00	2.70
☐ PP4 Will Clark	6.00	2.70
☐ PP5 Darren Daulton	4.00	1.80
☐ PP6 Cecil Fielder	4.00	1.80
☐ PP7 Ron Gant	4.00	1.80
☐ PP8 Juan Gonzalez	20.00	9.00
☐ PP9 Ken Griffey Jr.	40.00	18.00
☐ PP10 Dave Hollins	4.00	1.80
☐ PP11 David Justice	8.00	3.60
☐ PP12 Fred McGriff	6.00	2.70
☐ PP13 Mark McGwire	12.00	5.50
☐ PP14 Dean Palmer	4.00	1.80
☐ PP15 Mike Piazza	25.00	11.00
☐ PP16 Tim Salmon	8.00	3.60
☐ PP17 Ryne Sandberg	10.00	4.50
☐ PP18 Gary Sheffield	8.00	3.60
☐ PP19 Frank Thomas	40.00	18.00
☐ PP20 Matt Williams	6.00	2.70

1994 SP Previews

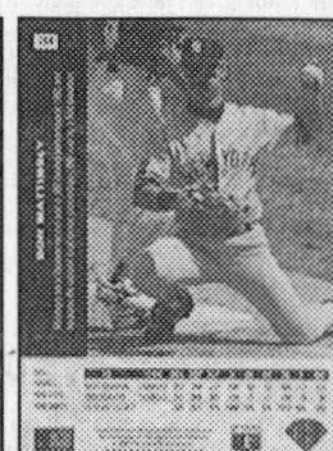

These 15 cards were distributed regionally as inserts in second series Upper Deck hobby packs. They were inserted at a rate of one in 35. The manner of distribution was five cards per Central, East and West region. The cards are nearly identical to the basic SP issue. Card fronts differ in that the region is at bottom right where the team name is located on the SP cards.

	MINT	NRMT
COMPLETE SET (15)	180.00	80.00
COMPLETE CENTRAL (5)	80.00	36.00
COMPLETE EAST (5)	40.00	18.00
COMPLETE WEST (5)	60.00	27.00
COMMON CARD	2.00	.90
☐ CR1 Jeff Bagwell	12.00	5.50
☐ CR2 Michael Jordan	30.00	13.50
☐ CR3 Kirby Puckett	12.00	5.50
☐ CR4 Manny Ramirez	5.00	2.20
☐ CR5 Frank Thomas	25.00	11.00
☐ ER1 Roberto Alomar	5.00	2.20
☐ ER2 Cliff Floyd	2.00	.90
☐ ER3 Javier Lopez	4.00	1.80
☐ ER4 Don Mattingly	12.00	5.50
☐ ER5 Cal Ripken	25.00	11.00
☐ WR1 Barry Bonds	8.00	3.60
☐ WR2 Juan Gonzalez	15.00	6.75
☐ WR3 Ken Griffey Jr.	30.00	13.50
☐ WR4 Mike Piazza	20.00	9.00
☐ WR5 Tim Salmon	5.00	2.20

1994 SP

This 200-card standard-size set primarily contains the game's top players and prospects. The first 20 cards in the set are Foil Prospects which are brighter and more metallic than the rest of the set. Cards 21-200 are in alphabetical order by team nickname. In either case, card fronts have a metallic finish with color player photos and a gold right-hand border. The backs contain a color player photo, 1993, career and best season statistics. The left side has a black border. The Upper Deck hologram on back is gold. Rookie Cards include Brad Fullmer, Derrek Lee, Chan Ho Park and Alex Rodriguez.

	MINT	NRMT
COMPLETE SET (200)	70.00	32.00
COMMON CARD (21-200)	.20	.09
☐ 1 Mike Bell FOIL	1.50	.70
☐ 2 D.J. Boston FOIL	.40	.18
☐ 3 Johnny Damon FOIL	.75	.35
☐ 4 Brad Fullmer FOIL	3.00	1.35
☐ 5 Joey Hamilton FOIL	.40	.18
☐ 6 Todd Hollandsworth FOIL	.40	.18
☐ 7 Brian L. Hunter FOIL	.75	.35

Card	MINT	NRMT
☐ 8 LaTroy Hawkins FOIL	.40	.18
☐ 9 Brooks Kieschnick FOIL	.75	.35
☐ 10 Derrek Lee FOIL	5.00	2.20
☐ 11 Trot Nixon FOIL	.50	.23
☐ 12 Alex Ochoa FOIL	.20	.09
☐ 13 Chan Ho Park FOIL	5.00	2.20
☐ 14 Kirk Presley FOIL	.40	.18
☐ 15 Alex Rodriguez FOIL	35.00	16.00
☐ 16 Jose Silva FOIL	.40	.18
☐ 17 Terrell Wade FOIL	.40	.18
☐ 18 Billy Wagner FOIL	2.50	1.10
☐ 19 Glenn Williams FOIL	.75	.35
☐ 20 Preston Wilson FOIL	.75	.35
☐ 21 Brian Anderson	.75	.35
☐ 22 Chad Curtis	.20	.09
☐ 23 Chili Davis	.40	.18
☐ 24 Bo Jackson	.40	.18
☐ 25 Mark Langston	.20	.09
☐ 26 Tim Salmon	.75	.35
☐ 27 Jeff Bagwell	1.50	.70
☐ 28 Craig Biggio	.50	.23
☐ 29 Ken Caminiti	.75	.35
☐ 30 Doug Drabek	.20	.09
☐ 31 John Hudek	.20	.09
☐ 32 Greg Swindell	.20	.09
☐ 33 Brent Gates	.20	.09
☐ 34 Rickey Henderson	.50	.23
☐ 35 Steve Karsay	.20	.09
☐ 36 Mark McGwire	1.50	.70
☐ 37 Ruben Sierra	.20	.09
☐ 38 Terry Steinbach	.40	.18
☐ 39 Roberto Alomar	.75	.35
☐ 40 Joe Carter	.50	.23
☐ 41 Carlos Delgado	.50	.23
☐ 42 Alex Gonzalez	.40	.18
☐ 43 Juan Guzman	.20	.09
☐ 44 Paul Molitor	.75	.35
☐ 45 John Olerud	.40	.18
☐ 46 Devon White	.20	.09
☐ 47 Steve Avery	.20	.09
☐ 48 Jeff Blauser	.20	.09
☐ 49 Tom Glavine	.50	.23
☐ 50 David Justice	.75	.35
☐ 51 Roberto Kelly	.20	.09
☐ 52 Ryan Klesko	.50	.23
☐ 53 Javier Lopez	.50	.23
☐ 54 Greg Maddux	2.50	1.10
☐ 55 Fred McGriff	.50	.23
☐ 56 Ricky Bones	.20	.09
☐ 57 Cal Eldred	.20	.09
☐ 58 Brian Harper	.20	.09
☐ 59 Pat Listach	.20	.09
☐ 60 B.J. Surhoff	.20	.09
☐ 61 Greg Vaughn	.20	.09
☐ 62 Bernard Gilkey	.40	.18
☐ 63 Gregg Jefferies	.40	.18
☐ 64 Ray Lankford	.50	.23
☐ 65 Ozzie Smith	1.00	.45
☐ 66 Bob Tewksbury	.20	.09
☐ 67 Mark Whiten	.20	.09
☐ 68 Todd Zeile	.20	.09
☐ 69 Mark Grace	.50	.23
☐ 70 Randy Myers	.20	.09
☐ 71 Ryne Sandberg	1.00	.45
☐ 72 Sammy Sosa	.75	.35
☐ 73 Steve Trachsel	.20	.09
☐ 74 Rick Wilkins	.20	.09
☐ 75 Brett Butler	.40	.18
☐ 76 Delino DeShields	.20	.09
☐ 77 Orel Hershiser	.40	.18
☐ 78 Eric Karros	.40	.18
☐ 79 Raul Mondesi	.50	.23
☐ 80 Mike Piazza	2.50	1.10
☐ 81 Tim Wallach	.20	.09
☐ 82 Moises Alou	.40	.18
☐ 83 Cliff Floyd	.40	.18
☐ 84 Marquis Grissom	.40	.18
☐ 85 Pedro J. Martinez	.75	.35
☐ 86 Larry Walker	.75	.35
☐ 87 John Wetteland	.40	.18
☐ 88 Rondell White	.50	.23
☐ 89 Rod Beck	.40	.18
☐ 90 Barry Bonds	1.00	.45
☐ 91 John Burkett	.20	.09
☐ 92 Royce Clayton	.40	.18
☐ 93 Billy Swift	.20	.09
☐ 94 Robby Thompson	.20	.09
☐ 95 Matt Williams	.50	.23
☐ 96 Carlos Baerga	.40	.18
☐ 97 Albert Belle	1.00	.45
☐ 98 Kenny Lofton	1.00	.45
☐ 99 Dennis Martinez	.40	.18
☐ 100 Eddie Murray	.75	.35
☐ 101 Manny Ramirez	1.00	.45
☐ 102 Eric Anthony	.20	.09
☐ 103 Chris Bosio	.20	.09
☐ 104 Jay Buhner	.50	.23
☐ 105 Ken Griffey Jr.	4.00	1.80
☐ 106 Randy Johnson	.75	.35
☐ 107 Edgar Martinez	.50	.23
☐ 108 Chuck Carr	.20	.09
☐ 109 Jeff Conine	.40	.18
☐ 110 Carl Everett	.20	.09
☐ 111 Chris Hammond	.20	.09
☐ 112 Bryan Harvey	.20	.09
☐ 113 Charles Johnson	.50	.23
☐ 114 Gary Sheffield	.75	.35
☐ 115 Bobby Bonilla	.40	.18
☐ 116 Dwight Gooden	.40	.18
☐ 117 Todd Hundley	.40	.18
☐ 118 Bobby Jones	.40	.18
☐ 119 Jeff Kent	.20	.09
☐ 120 Bret Saberhagen	.20	.09
☐ 121 Jeffrey Hammonds	.40	.18
☐ 122 Chris Hoiles	.20	.09
☐ 123 Ben McDonald	.20	.09
☐ 124 Mike Mussina	.75	.35
☐ 125 Rafael Palmeiro	.50	.23
☐ 126 Cal Ripken Jr.	3.00	1.35
☐ 127 Lee Smith	.40	.18
☐ 128 Derek Bell	.40	.18
☐ 129 Andy Benes	.40	.18
☐ 130 Tony Gwynn	2.00	.90
☐ 131 Trevor Hoffman	.40	.18
☐ 132 Phil Plantier	.20	.09
☐ 133 Bip Roberts	.20	.09
☐ 134 Darren Daulton	.40	.18
☐ 135 Lenny Dykstra	.40	.18
☐ 136 Dave Hollins	.20	.09
☐ 137 Danny Jackson	.20	.09
☐ 138 John Kruk	.40	.18
☐ 139 Kevin Stocker	.20	.09
☐ 140 Jay Bell	.40	.18
☐ 141 Carlos Garcia	.20	.09
☐ 142 Jeff King	.40	.18
☐ 143 Orlando Merced	.20	.09
☐ 144 Andy Van Slyke	.40	.18
☐ 145 Rick White	.20	.09
☐ 146 Jose Canseco	.50	.23
☐ 147 Will Clark	.50	.23
☐ 148 Juan Gonzalez	2.00	.90
☐ 149 Rick Helling	.20	.09
☐ 150 Dean Palmer	.40	.18
☐ 151 Ivan Rodriguez	1.00	.45
☐ 152 Roger Clemens	1.50	.70
☐ 153 Scott Cooper	.20	.09
☐ 154 Andre Dawson	.50	.23
☐ 155 Mike Greenwell	.20	.09
☐ 156 Aaron Sele	.20	.09
☐ 157 Mo Vaughn	1.00	.45
☐ 158 Bret Boone	.20	.09
☐ 159 Barry Larkin	.50	.23
☐ 160 Kevin Mitchell	.20	.09
☐ 161 Jose Rijo	.20	.09
☐ 162 Deion Sanders	.75	.35
☐ 163 Reggie Sanders	.40	.18
☐ 164 Dante Bichette	.50	.23
☐ 165 Ellis Burks	.40	.18
☐ 166 Andres Galarraga	.50	.23
☐ 167 Charlie Hayes	.20	.09
☐ 168 David Nied	.20	.09
☐ 169 Walt Weiss	.20	.09
☐ 170 Kevin Appier	.40	.18
☐ 171 David Cone	.40	.18
☐ 172 Jeff Granger	.20	.09
☐ 173 Felix Jose	.20	.09
☐ 174 Wally Joyner	.40	.18
☐ 175 Brian McRae	.20	.09
☐ 176 Cecil Fielder	.40	.18
☐ 177 Travis Fryman	.40	.18
☐ 178 Mike Henneman	.20	.09
☐ 179 Tony Phillips	.20	.09
☐ 180 Mickey Tettleton	.20	.09
☐ 181 Alan Trammell	.50	.23
☐ 182 Rick Aguilera	.20	.09
☐ 183 Rich Becker	.40	.18
☐ 184 Scott Erickson	.20	.09
☐ 185 Chuck Knoblauch	.75	.35
☐ 186 Kirby Puckett	1.50	.70
☐ 187 Dave Winfield	.50	.23
☐ 188 Wilson Alvarez	.40	.18
☐ 189 Jason Bere	.40	.18
☐ 190 Alex Fernandez	.40	.18
☐ 191 Julio Franco	.40	.18
☐ 192 Jack McDowell	.20	.09
☐ 193 Frank Thomas	3.00	1.35
☐ 194 Robin Ventura	.40	.18
☐ 195 Jim Abbott	.20	.09
☐ 196 Wade Boggs	.75	.35
☐ 197 Jimmy Key	.40	.18
☐ 198 Don Mattingly	1.25	.55
☐ 199 Paul O'Neill	.40	.18
☐ 200 Danny Tartabull	.20	.09
☐ P24 Ken Griffey Jr. Promo	3.00	1.35

1994 SP Die Cuts

This 200-card die-cut set is parallel to that of the basic SP issue. The cards were inserted one per SP pack. The difference, of course, is the unique die-cut shape. The backs have a silver Upper Deck hologram as opposed to gold on the basic issue.

	MINT	NRMT
COMPLETE SET (200)	150.00	70.00
COMMON CARD (1-200)	.30	.14

*STARS: 1.5X to 3X BASIC CARDS ....
*YOUNG STARS: 1X to 2X BASIC CARDS

1994 SP Holoviews

Randomly inserted in SP foil packs at a rate of one in five, this 38-card set contains top stars and prospects. Card fronts have a color player photo with a black and blue border to the right with which the player's name appears. A player hologram that runs the width of the card is at the bottom. The backs are primarily blue with a player photo and text.

	MINT	NRMT
COMPLETE SET (38)	150.00	70.00
COMMON CARD (1-38)	2.00	.90

*DIE CUTS: 3X TO 6X BASIC HOLOVIEWS

Card	MINT	NRMT
☐ 1 Roberto Alomar	6.00	2.70
☐ 2 Kevin Appier	3.00	1.35
☐ 3 Jeff Bagwell	12.00	5.50
☐ 4 Jose Canseco	4.00	1.80
☐ 5 Roger Clemens	12.00	5.50
☐ 6 Carlos Delgado	4.00	1.80
☐ 7 Cecil Fielder	3.00	1.35
☐ 8 Cliff Floyd	3.00	1.35
☐ 9 Travis Fryman	3.00	1.35
☐ 10 Andres Galarraga	4.00	1.80
☐ 11 Juan Gonzalez	15.00	6.75
☐ 12 Ken Griffey Jr.	30.00	13.50
☐ 13 Tony Gwynn	15.00	6.75
☐ 14 Jeffrey Hammonds	3.00	1.35
☐ 15 Bo Jackson	3.00	1.35
☐ 16 Michael Jordan	40.00	18.00
☐ 17 David Justice	6.00	2.70
☐ 18 Steve Karsay	2.00	.90
☐ 19 Jeff Kent	2.00	.90
☐ 20 Brooks Kieschnick	3.00	1.35
☐ 21 Ryan Klesko	4.00	1.80
☐ 22 John Kruk	3.00	1.35
☐ 23 Barry Larkin	4.00	1.80
☐ 24 Pat Listach	2.00	.90
☐ 25 Don Mattingly	10.00	4.50
☐ 26 Mark McGwire	12.00	5.50
☐ 27 Raul Mondesi	4.00	1.80
☐ 28 Trot Nixon	3.00	1.35
☐ 29 Mike Piazza	20.00	9.00
☐ 30 Kirby Puckett	12.00	5.50
☐ 31 Manny Ramirez	8.00	3.60
☐ 32 Cal Ripken	25.00	11.00
☐ 33 Alex Rodriguez	30.00	13.50
☐ 34 Tim Salmon	6.00	2.70
☐ 35 Gary Sheffield	6.00	2.70
☐ 36 Ozzie Smith	8.00	3.60
☐ 37 Sammy Sosa	6.00	2.70
☐ 38 Andy Van Slyke	3.00	1.35

1995 SP

This set consists of 207 cards being sold in eight-card, hobby-only packs with a suggested retail price of $3.99. The fronts have full-bleed photos and a large chevron on the left. The chevron consists of red and gold foil for American League players and blue and gold for National Leaguers. The backs have a photo with player information and statistics at the bottom. The backs also have a gold hologram to prevent counterfeiting. Subsets featured are Salute (1-4) and Premier Prospects (5-24). The only notable Rookie Card in this set is Hideo Nomo. Dealers who ordered a certain quantity of Upper Deck baseball cases received as a bonus, a certified autographed SP card of Ken Griffey Jr.

	MINT	NRMT
COMPLETE SET (207)	40.00	18.00
COMMON CARD (1-207)	.20	.09

Card	MINT	NRMT
☐ 1 Cal Ripken Salute	3.00	1.35
☐ 2 Nolan Ryan Salute	3.00	1.35
☐ 3 George Brett Salute	1.50	.70
☐ 4 Mike Schmidt Salute	1.00	.45
☐ 5 Dustin Hermanson FOIL	.40	.18
☐ 6 Antonio Osuna FOIL	.25	.11
☐ 7 Mark Grudzielanek FOIL	.60	.25
☐ 8 Ray Durham FOIL	.50	.23
☐ 9 Ugueth Urbina FOIL	.50	.23
☐ 10 Ruben Rivera FOIL	.75	.35
☐ 11 Curtis Goodwin FOIL	.25	.11
☐ 12 Jimmy Hurst FOIL	.40	.18
☐ 13 Jose Malave FOIL	.40	.18
☐ 14 Hideo Nomo FOIL	4.00	1.80
☐ 15 Juan Acevedo FOIL	.40	.18
☐ 16 Tony Clark FOIL	1.00	.45
☐ 17 Jim Pittsley FOIL	.40	.18
☐ 18 Freddy Garcia FOIL	.40	.18
☐ 19 Carlos Perez FOIL	.40	.18
☐ 20 Raul Casanova FOIL	.50	.23
☐ 21 Quilvio Veras FOIL	.40	.18
☐ 22 Edgardo Alfonzo FOIL	.75	.35
☐ 23 Marty Cordova FOIL	.50	.23
☐ 24 C.J. Nitkowski FOIL	.25	.11
☐ 25 Wade Boggs CL	.75	.35
☐ 26 Dave Winfield CL	.50	.23
☐ 27 Eddie Murray CL	.75	.35
☐ 28 David Justice	.75	.35
☐ 29 Marquis Grissom	.40	.18
☐ 30 Fred McGriff	.50	.23
☐ 31 Greg Maddux	2.50	1.10
☐ 32 Tom Glavine	.50	.23
☐ 33 Steve Avery	.20	.09
☐ 34 Chipper Jones	2.50	1.10
☐ 35 Sammy Sosa	.75	.35
☐ 36 Jaime Navarro	.20	.09
☐ 37 Randy Myers	.20	.09
☐ 38 Mark Grace	.50	.23
☐ 39 Todd Zeile	.20	.09
☐ 40 Brian McRae	.20	.09
☐ 41 Reggie Sanders	.20	.09
☐ 42 Ron Gant	.40	.18
☐ 43 Deion Sanders	.75	.35
☐ 44 Bret Boone	.20	.09
☐ 45 Barry Larkin	.50	.23
☐ 46 Jose Rijo	.20	.09
☐ 47 Jason Bates	.20	.09
☐ 48 Andres Galarraga	.50	.23
☐ 49 Bill Swift	.20	.09
☐ 50 Larry Walker	.75	.35
☐ 51 Vinny Castilla	.50	.23
☐ 52 Dante Bichette	.50	.23
☐ 53 Jeff Conine	.40	.18
☐ 54 John Burkett	.20	.09
☐ 55 Gary Sheffield	.75	.35
☐ 56 Andre Dawson	.50	.23
☐ 57 Terry Pendleton	.40	.18
☐ 58 Charles Johnson	.50	.23
☐ 59 Brian L. Hunter	.50	.23
☐ 60 Jeff Bagwell	1.50	.70
☐ 61 Craig Biggio	.50	.23
☐ 62 Phil Nevin	.20	.09
☐ 63 Doug Drabek	.20	.09
☐ 64 Derek Bell	.40	.18
☐ 65 Raul Mondesi	.50	.23
☐ 66 Eric Karros	.40	.18
☐ 67 Roger Cedeno	.40	.18
☐ 68 Delino DeShields	.20	.09
☐ 69 Ramon Martinez	.40	.18
☐ 70 Mike Piazza	2.50	1.10
☐ 71 Billy Ashley	.20	.09
☐ 72 Jeff Fassero	.20	.09
☐ 73 Shane Andrews	.20	.09
☐ 74 Wil Cordero	.20	.09
☐ 75 Tony Tarasco	.20	.09
☐ 76 Rondell White	.50	.23
☐ 77 Pedro J. Martinez	.75	.35
☐ 78 Moises Alou	.40	.18
☐ 79 Rico Brogna	.20	.09
☐ 80 Bobby Bonilla	.40	.18
☐ 81 Jeff Kent	.20	.09
☐ 82 Brett Butler	.40	.18
☐ 83 Bobby Jones	.40	.18
☐ 84 Bill Pulsipher	.40	.18
☐ 85 Bret Saberhagen	.20	.09
☐ 86 Gregg Jefferies	.40	.18
☐ 87 Lenny Dykstra	.40	.18
☐ 88 Dave Hollins	.20	.09
☐ 89 Charlie Hayes	.20	.09
☐ 90 Darren Daulton	.40	.18
☐ 91 Curt Schilling	.40	.18
☐ 92 Heathcliff Slocumb	.20	.09
☐ 93 Carlos Garcia	.20	.09
☐ 94 Denny Neagle	.40	.18
☐ 95 Jay Bell	.40	.18
☐ 96 Orlando Merced	.20	.09
☐ 97 Dave Clark	.20	.09
☐ 98 Bernard Gilkey	.40	.18
☐ 99 Scott Cooper	.20	.09
☐ 100 Ozzie Smith	1.00	.45
☐ 101 Tom Henke	.20	.09
☐ 102 Ken Hill	.20	.09
☐ 103 Brian Jordan	.50	.23
☐ 104 Ray Lankford	.40	.18
☐ 105 Tony Gwynn	2.00	.90
☐ 106 Andy Benes	.20	.09
☐ 107 Ken Caminiti	.75	.35
☐ 108 Steve Finley	.40	.18
☐ 109 Joey Hamilton	.40	.18
☐ 110 Bip Roberts	.20	.09
☐ 111 Eddie Williams	.20	.09
☐ 112 Rod Beck	.20	.09
☐ 113 Matt Williams	.50	.23
☐ 114 Glenallen Hill	.20	.09
☐ 115 Barry Bonds	1.00	.45
☐ 116 Robby Thompson	.20	.09
☐ 117 Mark Portugal	.20	.09
☐ 118 Brady Anderson	.50	.23
☐ 119 Mike Mussina	.75	.35
☐ 120 Rafael Palmeiro	.50	.23
☐ 121 Chris Hoiles	.20	.09
☐ 122 Harold Baines	.40	.18
☐ 123 Jeffrey Hammonds	.40	.18
☐ 124 Tim Naehring	.20	.09
☐ 125 Mo Vaughn	1.00	.45
☐ 126 Mike Macfarlane	.20	.09
☐ 127 Roger Clemens	1.50	.70
☐ 128 John Valentin	.40	.18
☐ 129 Aaron Sele	.20	.09
☐ 130 Jose Canseco	.50	.23
☐ 131 J.T. Snow	.40	.18
☐ 132 Mark Langston	.20	.09
☐ 133 Chili Davis	.40	.18
☐ 134 Chuck Finley	.40	.18
☐ 135 Tim Salmon	.75	.35
☐ 136 Tony Phillips	.20	.09
☐ 137 Jason Bere	.20	.09
☐ 138 Robin Ventura	.40	.18
☐ 139 Tim Raines	.20	.09
☐ 140 Frank Thomas COR	3.00	1.35
☐ 140A Frank Thomas ERR	8.00	3.60
☐ 141 Alex Fernandez	.40	.18
☐ 142 Jim Abbott	.20	.09
☐ 143 Wilson Alvarez	.40	.18
☐ 144 Carlos Baerga	.40	.18
☐ 145 Albert Belle	1.00	.45
☐ 146 Jim Thome	.75	.35
☐ 147 Dennis Martinez	.40	.18
☐ 148 Eddie Murray	.75	.35
☐ 149 Dave Winfield	.50	.23
☐ 150 Kenny Lofton	1.00	.45
☐ 151 Manny Ramirez	.75	.35
☐ 152 Chad Curtis	.20	.09
☐ 153 Lou Whitaker	.40	.18
☐ 154 Alan Trammell	.50	.23
☐ 155 Cecil Fielder	.40	.18
☐ 156 Kirk Gibson	.40	.18
☐ 157 Michael Tucker	.40	.18
☐ 158 Jon Nunnally	.40	.18
☐ 159 Wally Joyner	.40	.18
☐ 160 Kevin Appier	.40	.18
☐ 161 Jeff Montgomery	.40	.18
☐ 162 Greg Gagne	.20	.09
☐ 163 Ricky Bones	.20	.09
☐ 164 Cal Eldred	.20	.09
☐ 165 Greg Vaughn	.20	.09
☐ 166 Kevin Seitzer	.20	.09
☐ 167 Jose Valentin	.40	.18
☐ 168 Joe Oliver	.20	.09
☐ 169 Rick Aguilera	.20	.09
☐ 170 Kirby Puckett	1.50	.70
☐ 171 Scott Stahoviak	.20	.09
☐ 172 Kevin Tapani	.20	.09
☐ 173 Chuck Knoblauch	.75	.35
☐ 174 Rich Becker	.20	.09
☐ 175 Don Mattingly	1.25	.55
☐ 176 Jack McDowell	.20	.09
☐ 177 Jimmy Key	.40	.18
☐ 178 Paul O'Neill	.40	.18
☐ 179 John Wetteland	.40	.18
☐ 180 Wade Boggs	.75	.35
☐ 181 Derek Jeter	2.50	1.10
☐ 182 Rickey Henderson	.50	.23
☐ 183 Terry Steinbach	.40	.18
☐ 184 Ruben Sierra	.20	.09
☐ 185 Mark McGwire	1.50	.70
☐ 186 Todd Stottlemyre	.20	.09
☐ 187 Dennis Eckersley	.50	.23
☐ 188 Alex Rodriguez	3.00	1.35
☐ 189 Randy Johnson	.75	.35
☐ 190 Ken Griffey Jr.	4.00	1.80
☐ 191 Tino Martinez UER Mike Blowers pictured on back	.40	.18
☐ 192 Jay Buhner	.50	.23
☐ 193 Edgar Martinez	.50	.23
☐ 194 Mickey Tettleton	.20	.09
☐ 195 Juan Gonzalez	2.00	.90
☐ 196 Benji Gil	.20	.09
☐ 197 Dean Palmer	.40	.18
☐ 198 Ivan Rodriguez	1.00	.45
☐ 199 Kenny Rogers	.20	.09
☐ 200 Will Clark	.50	.23
☐ 201 Roberto Alomar	.75	.35
☐ 202 David Cone	.40	.18
☐ 203 Paul Molitor	.75	.35
☐ 204 Shawn Green	.40	.18
☐ 205 Joe Carter	.50	.23
☐ 206 Alex Gonzalez	.20	.09
☐ 207 Pat Hentgen	.40	.18
☐ AU190 Ken Griffey Jr. AU	200.00	90.00

1995 SP Silver

This 207-card set parallels that of the regular SP set and was inserted one per pack. The only difference between the regular 180 cards in the two sets is that the chevron of the parallel version on the left side of the front uses rainbow-colored foil instead of blue or red. The subset cards have a die-cut design to differentiate them from the regular edition cards. The only other difference is the silver (rather than gold) hologram on the back.

	MINT	NRMT
COMPLETE SET (207)	100.00	45.00
COMMON CARD (1-207)	.25	.11

*STARS: 1.5X to 3X BASIC CARDS ....
*YOUNG STARS: 1.25X to 2.5X BASIC CARDS

1995 SP Platinum Power

This 20-card set was randomly inserted in packs at a rate of one in five. This die-cut set is comprised of the top home run hitters in baseball. The fronts have an action photo with a bronze background and rays of light coming out of the "SP" emblem at bottom right. The backs have a player photo in a box at the middle of the card with player statistics at the bottom. The set is sequenced in alphabetical order.

	MINT	NRMT
COMPLETE SET (20)	20.00	9.00
COMMON CARD (PP1-PP20)	.50	.23

Card	MINT	NRMT
☐ PP1 Jeff Bagwell	2.00	.90
☐ PP2 Barry Bonds	1.25	.55
☐ PP3 Ron Gant	.50	.23
☐ PP4 Fred McGriff	.75	.35
☐ PP5 Raul Mondesi	.75	.35
☐ PP6 Mike Piazza	3.00	1.35
☐ PP7 Larry Walker	1.00	.45
☐ PP8 Matt Williams	.75	.35
☐ PP9 Albert Belle	1.25	.55
☐ PP10 Cecil Fielder	.60	.25
☐ PP11 Juan Gonzalez	2.50	1.10
☐ PP12 Ken Griffey Jr.	5.00	2.20
☐ PP13 Mark McGwire	1.50	.70
☐ PP14 Eddie Murray	1.00	.45
☐ PP15 Manny Ramirez	1.00	.45
☐ PP16 Cal Ripken	4.00	1.80

☐ PP17 Tim Salmon	1.00	.45
☐ PP18 Frank Thomas	4.00	1.80
☐ PP19 Jim Thome	1.00	.45
☐ PP20 Mo Vaughn	1.25	.55

1995 SP Special FX

This 48-card set was randomly inserted in packs at a rate of one in 75. The set is comprised of the top names in baseball. The fronts have an action photo on a sky-colored foil background. There is also a hologram of the player's face that allows you to see a 50-degree, 3-D image. The backs have a photo with player information and statistics. The cards are numbered on the back "X/48."

	MINT	NRMT
COMPLETE SET (48)	1000.00	450.00
COMMON CARD (1-48)	8.00	3.60
☐ 1 Jose Canseco	15.00	6.75
☐ 2 Roger Clemens	50.00	22.00
☐ 3 Mo Vaughn	30.00	13.50
☐ 4 Tim Salmon	25.00	11.00
☐ 5 Chuck Finley	8.00	3.60
☐ 6 Robin Ventura	15.00	6.75
☐ 7 Jason Bere	8.00	3.60
☐ 8 Carlos Baerga	8.00	3.60
☐ 9 Albert Belle	30.00	13.50
☐ 10 Kenny Lofton	30.00	13.50
☐ 11 Manny Ramirez	25.00	11.00
☐ 12 Jeff Montgomery	8.00	3.60
☐ 13 Kirby Puckett	50.00	22.00
☐ 14 Wade Boggs	25.00	11.00
☐ 15 Don Mattingly	40.00	18.00
☐ 16 Cal Ripken	100.00	45.00
☐ 17 Ruben Sierra	8.00	3.60
☐ 18 Ken Griffey Jr.	120.00	55.00
☐ 19 Randy Johnson	25.00	11.00
☐ 20 Alex Rodriguez	100.00	45.00
☐ 21 Will Clark	15.00	6.75
☐ 22 Juan Gonzalez	60.00	27.00
☐ 23 Roberto Alomar	25.00	11.00
☐ 24 Joe Carter	15.00	6.75
☐ 25 Alex Gonzalez	8.00	3.60
☐ 26 Paul Molitor	25.00	11.00
☐ 27 Ryan Klesko	15.00	6.75
☐ 28 Fred McGriff	15.00	6.75
☐ 29 Greg Maddux	80.00	36.00
☐ 30 Sammy Sosa	25.00	11.00
☐ 31 Bret Boone	8.00	3.60
☐ 32 Barry Larkin	15.00	6.75
☐ 33 Reggie Sanders	8.00	3.60
☐ 34 Dante Bichette	15.00	6.75
☐ 35 Andres Galarraga	15.00	6.75
☐ 36 Charles Johnson	15.00	6.75
☐ 37 Gary Sheffield	25.00	11.00
☐ 38 Jeff Bagwell	50.00	22.00
☐ 39 Craig Biggio	15.00	6.75
☐ 40 Eric Karros	15.00	6.75
☐ 41 Billy Ashley	8.00	3.60
☐ 42 Raul Mondesi	25.00	11.00
☐ 43 Mike Piazza	80.00	36.00
☐ 44 Rondell White	15.00	6.75
☐ 45 Bret Saberhagen	8.00	3.60
☐ 46 Tony Gwynn	60.00	27.00
☐ 47 Melvin Nieves	8.00	3.60
☐ 48 Matt Williams	15.00	6.75

1996 SP Previews FanFest

These eight standard-size cards were issued to promote the 1996 Upper Deck SP Issue. The fronts feature a color action photo as well as a small inset player shot. The 1996 All-Star game logo as well as the SP logo are on the bottom left corner. The backs have another photo as well as some biographical information.

	MINT	NRMT
COMPLETE SET (8)	40.00	18.00
COMMON CARD (1-8)	1.50	.70
☐ 1 Ken Griffey Jr.	12.00	5.50
☐ 2 Frank Thomas	10.00	4.50
☐ 3 Albert Belle	4.00	1.80
☐ 4 Mo Vaughn	3.00	1.35
☐ 5 Barry Bonds	3.00	1.35
☐ 6 Mike Piazza	8.00	3.60
☐ 7 Matt Williams	1.50	.70
☐ 8 Sammy Sosa	2.00	.90

1996 SP

The 1996 SP set was issued in one series totalling 188 cards. The eight-card packs retail for $4.19 each. Cards number 1-20 feature color action player photos with "Premier Prospects" printed in silver foil across the top and the player's name and team at the bottom in the border. The backs carry player information and statistics. Cards number 21-185 display unique player photos with an outer wood-grain border and inner thin platinum foil border as well as a small inset player shot. The backs carry another color player photo with unique player statistics depending on his position. The only notable Rookie Card in this set is Darin Erstad.

	MINT	NRMT
COMPLETE SET (188)	40.00	18.00
COMMON CARDS (1-188)	.20	.09
☐ 1 Rey Ordonez FOIL	.40	.18
☐ 2 George Arias FOIL	.20	.09
☐ 3 Osvaldo Fernandez FOIL	.40	.18
☐ 4 Darin Erstad FOIL	6.00	2.70
☐ 5 Paul Wilson FOIL	.20	.09
☐ 6 Richard Hidalgo FOIL	.75	.35
☐ 7 Justin Thompson FOIL	.60	.25
☐ 8 Jimmy Haynes FOIL	.20	.09
☐ 9 Edgar Renteria FOIL	.60	.25
☐ 10 Ruben Rivera FOIL	.40	.18
☐ 11 Chris Snopek FOIL	.20	.09
☐ 12 Billy Wagner FOIL	.40	.18
☐ 13 Mike Grace FOIL	.20	.09
☐ 14 Todd Greene FOIL	.60	.25
☐ 15 Karim Garcia FOIL	.40	.18
☐ 16 John Wasdin FOIL	.20	.09
☐ 17 Jason Kendall FOIL	.75	.35
☐ 18 Bob Abreu FOIL	.75	.35
☐ 19 Jermaine Dye FOIL	.20	.09
☐ 20 Jason Schmidt FOIL	.40	.18
☐ 21 Javy Lopez	.40	.18
☐ 22 Ryan Klesko	.60	.25
☐ 23 Tom Glavine	.40	.18
☐ 24 John Smoltz	.40	.18
☐ 25 Greg Maddux	2.50	1.10
☐ 26 Chipper Jones	2.50	1.10
☐ 27 Fred McGriff	.60	.25
☐ 28 David Justice	.75	.35
☐ 29 Roberto Alomar	.75	.35
☐ 30 Cal Ripken	3.00	1.35
☐ 31 B.J. Surhoff	.40	.18
☐ 32 Bobby Bonilla	.40	.18
☐ 33 Mike Mussina	.75	.35
☐ 34 Randy Myers	.40	.18
☐ 35 Rafael Palmeiro	.60	.25
☐ 36 Brady Anderson	.60	.25
☐ 37 Tim Naehring	.20	.09
☐ 38 Jose Canseco	.60	.25
☐ 39 Roger Clemens	1.50	.70
☐ 40 Mo Vaughn	1.00	.45
☐ 41 Jose Valentin	.20	.09
☐ 42 Kevin Mitchell	.20	.09
☐ 43 Chili Davis	.20	.09
☐ 44 Garret Anderson	.40	.18
☐ 45 Tim Salmon	.60	.25
☐ 46 Chuck Finley	.20	.09
☐ 47 Troy Percival	.20	.09
☐ 48 Jim Abbott	.40	.18
☐ 49 J.T. Snow	.20	.09
☐ 50 Jim Edmonds	.60	.25
☐ 51 Sammy Sosa	.75	.35
☐ 52 Brian McRae	.20	.09
☐ 53 Ryne Sandberg	1.00	.45
☐ 54 Jaime Navarro	.20	.09
☐ 55 Mark Grace	.60	.25
☐ 56 Harold Baines	.40	.18
☐ 57 Robin Ventura	.40	.18
☐ 58 Tony Phillips	.20	.09
☐ 59 Alex Fernandez	.40	.18
☐ 60 Frank Thomas	3.00	1.35
☐ 61 Ray Durham	.40	.18
☐ 62 Bret Boone	.20	.09
☐ 63 Reggie Sanders	.20	.09
☐ 64 Pete Schourek	.20	.09
☐ 65 Barry Larkin	.60	.25
☐ 66 John Smiley	.20	.09
☐ 67 Carlos Baerga	.40	.18
☐ 68 Jim Thome	.75	.35
☐ 69 Eddie Murray	.75	.35
☐ 70 Albert Belle	1.00	.45
☐ 71 Dennis Martinez	.40	.18
☐ 72 Jack McDowell	.20	.09
☐ 73 Kenny Lofton	1.00	.45
☐ 74 Manny Ramirez	.75	.35
☐ 75 Dante Bichette	.40	.18
☐ 76 Vinny Castilla	.40	.18
☐ 77 Andres Galarraga	.60	.25
☐ 78 Walt Weiss	.20	.09
☐ 79 Ellis Burks	.40	.18
☐ 80 Larry Walker	.75	.35
☐ 81 Cecil Fielder	.40	.18
☐ 82 Melvin Nieves	.20	.09
☐ 83 Travis Fryman	.40	.18
☐ 84 Chad Curtis	.20	.09
☐ 85 Alan Trammell	.60	.25
☐ 86 Gary Sheffield	.75	.35
☐ 87 Charles Johnson	.40	.18
☐ 88 Andre Dawson	.60	.25
☐ 89 Jeff Conine	.40	.18
☐ 90 Greg Colbrunn	.20	.09
☐ 91 Derek Bell	.20	.09
☐ 92 Brian L.Hunter	.40	.18
☐ 93 Doug Drabek	.20	.09
☐ 94 Craig Biggio	.60	.25
☐ 95 Jeff Bagwell	1.50	.70
☐ 96 Kevin Appier	.40	.18
☐ 97 Jeff Montgomery	.20	.09
☐ 98 Michael Tucker	.40	.18
☐ 99 Bip Roberts	.20	.09
☐ 100 Johnny Damon	.40	.18
☐ 101 Eric Karros	.40	.18
☐ 102 Raul Mondesi	.60	.25
☐ 103 Ramon Martinez	.40	.18
☐ 104 Ismael Valdes	.40	.18
☐ 105 Mike Piazza	2.50	1.10
☐ 106 Hideo Nomo	2.00	.90
☐ 107 Chan Ho Park	.75	.35
☐ 108 Ben McDonald	.20	.09
☐ 109 Kevin Seitzer	.20	.09
☐ 110 Greg Vaughn	.20	.09
☐ 111 Jose Valentin	.20	.09
☐ 112 Rick Aguilera	.40	.18
☐ 113 Marty Cordova	.20	.09
☐ 114 Brad Radke	.40	.18
☐ 115 Kirby Puckett	1.50	.70
☐ 116 Chuck Knoblauch	.75	.35
☐ 117 Paul Molitor	.75	.35
☐ 118 Pedro Martinez	.75	.35
☐ 119 Mike Lansing	.20	.09
☐ 120 Rondell White	.40	.18
☐ 121 Moises Alou	.40	.18
☐ 122 Mark Grudzielanek	.40	.18
☐ 123 Jeff Fassero	.20	.09
☐ 124 Rico Brogna	.20	.09
☐ 125 Jason Isringhausen	.20	.09
☐ 126 Jeff Kent	.20	.09
☐ 127 Bernard Gilkey	.40	.18
☐ 128 Todd Hundley	.40	.18
☐ 129 David Cone	.40	.18
☐ 130 Andy Pettitte	1.00	.45
☐ 131 Wade Boggs	.75	.35
☐ 132 Paul O'Neill	.40	.18
☐ 133 Ruben Sierra	.20	.09
☐ 134 John Wetteland	.40	.18
☐ 135 Derek Jeter	2.50	1.10
☐ 136 Geronimo Berroa	.20	.09
☐ 137 Terry Steinbach	.40	.18
☐ 138 Ariel Prieto	.20	.09
☐ 139 Scott Brosius	.20	.09

☐ 140 Mark McGwire	1.50	.70
☐ 141 Lenny Dykstra	.40	.18
☐ 142 Todd Zeile	.40	.18
☐ 143 Benito Santiago	.20	.09
☐ 144 Mickey Morandini	.20	.09
☐ 145 Gregg Jefferies	.40	.18
☐ 146 Denny Neagle	.40	.18
☐ 147 Orlando Merced	.20	.09
☐ 148 Charlie Hayes	.20	.09
☐ 149 Carlos Garcia	.20	.09
☐ 150 Jay Bell	.40	.18
☐ 151 Ray Lankford	.40	.18
☐ 152 Alan Benes Andy Benes	.40	.18
☐ 153 Dennis Eckersley	.60	.25
☐ 154 Gary Gaetti	.40	.18
☐ 155 Ozzie Smith	1.00	.45
☐ 156 Ron Gant	.40	.18
☐ 157 Brian Jordan	.40	.18
☐ 158 Ken Caminiti	.75	.35
☐ 159 Rickey Henderson	.60	.25
☐ 160 Tony Gwynn	1.50	.70
☐ 161 Wally Joyner	.20	.09
☐ 162 Andy Ashby	.20	.09
☐ 163 Steve Finley	.40	.18
☐ 164 Glenallen Hill	.20	.09
☐ 165 Matt Williams	.60	.25
☐ 166 Barry Bonds	1.00	.45
☐ 167 William VanLandingham	.20	.09
☐ 168 Rod Beck	.40	.18
☐ 169 Randy Johnson	.75	.35
☐ 170 Ken Griffey Jr.	4.00	1.80
☐ 171 Alex Rodriguez	3.00	1.35
☐ 172 Edgar Martinez	.60	.25
☐ 173 Jay Buhner	.60	.25
☐ 174 Russ Davis	.20	.09
☐ 175 Juan Gonzalez	2.00	.90
☐ 176 Mickey Tettleton	.20	.09
☐ 177 Will Clark	.60	.25
☐ 178 Ken Hill	.20	.09
☐ 179 Dean Palmer	.20	.09
☐ 180 Ivan Rodriguez	1.00	.45
☐ 181 Carlos Delgado	.40	.18
☐ 182 Alex Gonzalez	.20	.09
☐ 183 Shawn Green	.20	.09
☐ 184 Juan Guzman	.20	.09
☐ 185 Joe Carter	.40	.18
☐ 186 Hideo Nomo CL	.60	.25
☐ 187 Cal Ripken CL	1.50	.70
☐ 188 Ken Griffey Jr. CL	2.00	.90

1996 SP Baseball Heroes

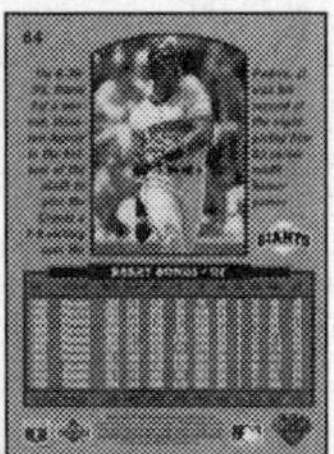

This 10-card set was randomly inserted at the rate of one in 96 packs. It continues the insert set that was started in 1990 featuring ten of the top players in baseball. The fronts feature color action player photos with the team logo on an embossed foil background. The backs carry another color player photo, player information and statistics.

	MINT	NRMT
COMPLETE SET (10)	300.00	135.00
COMMON CARD (82-90/HDR)	12.00	5.50
☐ 82 Frank Thomas	50.00	22.00
☐ 83 Albert Belle	15.00	6.75
☐ 84 Barry Bonds	15.00	6.75
☐ 85 Chipper Jones	40.00	18.00
☐ 86 Hideo Nomo	30.00	13.50
☐ 87 Mike Piazza	40.00	18.00
☐ 88 Manny Ramirez	12.00	5.50
☐ 89 Greg Maddux	40.00	18.00
☐ 90 Ken Griffey Jr.	60.00	27.00
☐ NNO Ken Griffey Jr. HDR	60.00	27.00

1996 SP Marquee Matchups

Randomly inserted at the rate of one in five packs, this 20-card set highlights two superstars' cards with a common matching stadium background photograph in a blue border. Each card features double foil stamping and

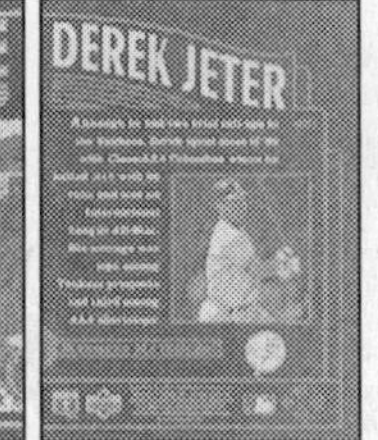

embossed player images. The backs carry player information.

	MINT	NRMT
COMPLETE SET (20)	40.00	18.00
COMMON CARD (MM1-MM20)	1.00	.45
COMP.DIE CUT SET (20)	200.00	90.00

*DIE CUT STARS: 2.5X TO 5X BASIC CARDS

☐ MM1 Ken Griffey Jr.	8.00	3.60
☐ MM2 Hideo Nomo	4.00	1.80
☐ MM3 Derek Jeter	5.00	2.20
☐ MM4 Rey Ordonez	1.00	.45
☐ MM5 Tim Salmon	1.50	.70
☐ MM6 Mike Piazza	5.00	2.20
☐ MM7 Mark McGwire	2.50	1.10
☐ MM8 Barry Bonds	2.00	.90
☐ MM9 Cal Ripken	6.00	2.70
☐ MM10 Greg Maddux	5.00	2.20
☐ MM11 Albert Belle	2.00	.90
☐ MM12 Barry Larkin	1.25	.55
☐ MM13 Jeff Bagwell	3.00	1.35
☐ MM14 Juan Gonzalez	3.00	1.35
☐ MM15 Frank Thomas	6.00	2.70
☐ MM16 Sammy Sosa	1.50	.70
☐ MM17 Mike Mussina	1.50	.70
☐ MM18 Chipper Jones	5.00	2.20
☐ MM19 Roger Clemens	3.00	1.35
☐ MM20 Fred McGriff	1.25	.55

1996 SP Special FX

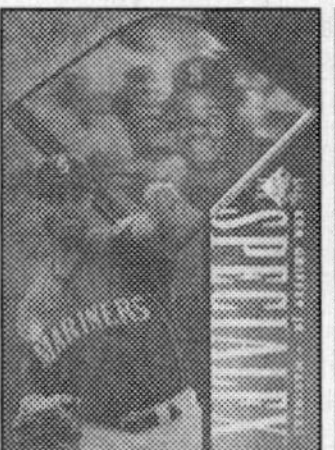

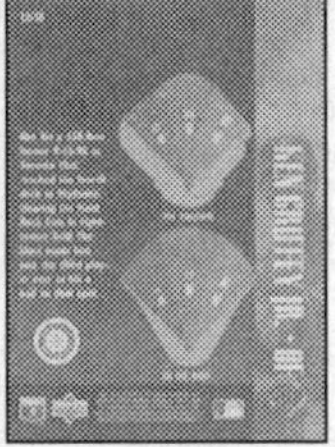

Randomly inserted at the rate of one in 5 packs, this 48-card set features a color action player cutout on a gold foil background with a holoview diamond shaped insert containing a black-and-white player portrait. A wide blue border runs vertically down one side of the card. The backs carry player information and statistics at home and away in baseball field designs on a blue background.

	MINT	NRMT
COMPLETE SET (48)	175.00	80.00
COMMON CARD (1-48)	2.00	.90
COMP.DIE CUT SET (48)	800.00	350.00

*DIE CUT STARS: 2.5X TO 5X BASIC CARDS

☐ 1 Greg Maddux	12.00	5.50
☐ 2 Eric Karros	2.50	1.10
☐ 3 Mike Piazza	12.00	5.50
☐ 4 Raul Mondesi	3.00	1.35
☐ 5 Hideo Nomo	5.00	2.20
☐ 6 Jim Edmonds	4.00	1.80
☐ 7 Jason Isringhausen	2.00	.90
☐ 8 Jay Buhner	3.00	1.35
☐ 9 Barry Larkin	2.50	1.10
☐ 10 Ken Griffey Jr.	20.00	9.00
☐ 11 Gary Sheffield	4.00	1.80
☐ 12 Craig Biggio	3.00	1.35
☐ 13 Paul Wilson	2.00	.90
☐ 14 Rondell White	2.50	1.10
☐ 15 Chipper Jones	12.00	5.50
☐ 16 Kirby Puckett	8.00	3.60
☐ 17 Ron Gant	2.50	1.10
☐ 18 Wade Boggs	4.00	1.80
☐ 19 Fred McGriff	3.00	1.35
☐ 20 Cal Ripken	15.00	6.75
☐ 21 Jason Kendall	4.00	1.80
☐ 22 Johnny Damon	2.50	1.10
☐ 23 Kenny Lofton	5.00	2.20
☐ 24 Roberto Alomar	4.00	1.80
☐ 25 Barry Bonds	5.00	2.20
☐ 26 Dante Bichette	2.50	1.10
☐ 27 Mark McGwire	6.00	2.70
☐ 28 Rafael Palmeiro	3.00	1.35
☐ 29 Juan Gonzalez	10.00	4.50
☐ 30 Albert Belle	8.00	3.60
☐ 31 Randy Johnson	4.00	1.80
☐ 32 Jose Canseco	3.00	1.35
☐ 33 Sammy Sosa	4.00	1.80
☐ 34 Eddie Murray	4.00	1.80
☐ 35 Frank Thomas	20.00	9.00
☐ 36 Tom Glavine	2.50	1.10
☐ 37 Matt Williams	3.00	1.35
☐ 38 Roger Clemens	4.00	1.80
☐ 39 Paul Molitor	4.00	1.80
☐ 40 Tony Gwynn	8.00	3.60
☐ 41 Mo Vaughn	5.00	2.20
☐ 42 Tim Salmon	4.00	1.80
☐ 43 Manny Ramirez	4.00	1.80
☐ 44 Jeff Bagwell	8.00	3.60
☐ 45 Edgar Martinez	3.00	1.35
☐ 46 Rey Ordonez	2.00	.90
☐ 47 Osvaldo Fernandez	2.00	.90
☐ 48 Derek Jeter	12.00	5.50

1997 SP

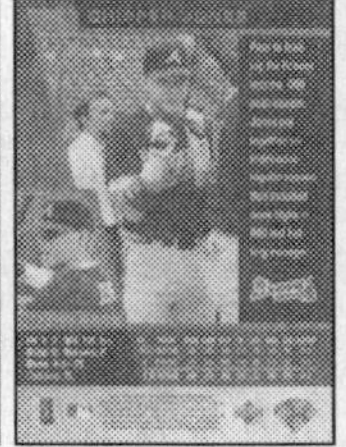

The 1997 SP set was issued in one series totalling 183 cards and was distributed in eight-card packs with a suggested retail of $4.39. The fronts feature color player photos with foil highlights. The backs carry player information and career statistics. Athough unconfirmed by the manufacturer, it is widely perceived in collecting circles that cards numbered between 160 and 180 are in slightly shorter supply. There are Jose Cruz and Hideki Irabu Rookie Cards in this set.

	MINT	NRMT
COMPLETE SET (184)	55.00	25.00
COMMON CARD (1-184)	.20	.09
☐ 1 Andruw Jones FOIL	2.00	.90
☐ 2 Kevin Orie FOIL	.40	.18
☐ 3 Nomar Garciaparra FOIL	2.50	1.10
☐ 4 Jose Guillen FOIL	1.00	.45
☐ 5 Todd Walker FOIL	.20	.09
☐ 6 Derrick Gibson FOIL	.40	.18
☐ 7 Aaron Boone FOIL	.40	.18
☐ 8 Bartolo Colon FOIL	.40	.18
☐ 9 Derrek Lee FOIL	.40	.18
☐ 10 Vladimir Guerrero FOIL	1.50	.70
☐ 11 Wilton Guerrero FOIL	.20	.09
☐ 12 Luis Castillo FOIL	.20	.09
☐ 13 Jason Dickson FOIL	.20	.09
☐ 14 Bubba Trammell FOIL	1.00	.45
☐ 15 Jose Cruz Jr. FOIL	8.00	3.60
☐ 16 Eddie Murray	.75	.35
☐ 17 Darin Erstad	1.25	.55
☐ 18 Garret Anderson	.40	.18
☐ 19 Jim Edmonds	.75	.35
☐ 20 Tim Salmon	.75	.35
☐ 21 Chuck Finley	.20	.09
☐ 22 John Smoltz	.40	.18
☐ 23 Greg Maddux	2.50	1.10
☐ 24 Kenny Lofton	1.00	.45
☐ 25 Chipper Jones	2.50	1.10
☐ 26 Ryan Klesko	.60	.25
☐ 27 Javier Lopez	.40	.18
☐ 28 Fred McGriff	.60	.25
☐ 29 Roberto Alomar	.75	.35
☐ 30 Rafael Palmeiro	.60	.25
☐ 31 Mike Mussina	.75	.35
☐ 32 Brady Anderson	.60	.25
☐ 33 Rocky Coppinger	.20	.09
☐ 34 Cal Ripken	3.00	1.35
☐ 35 Mo Vaughn	1.00	.45
☐ 36 Steve Avery	.20	.09
☐ 37 Tom Gordon	.20	.09
☐ 38 Tim Naehring	.20	.09
☐ 39 Troy O'Leary	.20	.09
☐ 40 Sammy Sosa	.75	.35
☐ 41 Brian McRae	.20	.09
☐ 42 Mel Rojas	.20	.09

Card	MINT	NRMT
☐ 43 Ryne Sandberg	1.00	.45
☐ 44 Mark Grace	.60	.25
☐ 45 Albert Belle	1.00	.45
☐ 46 Robin Ventura	.40	.18
☐ 47 Roberto Hernandez	.40	.18
☐ 48 Ray Durham	.20	.09
☐ 49 Harold Baines	.40	.18
☐ 50 Frank Thomas	3.00	1.35
☐ 51 Bret Boone	.20	.09
☐ 52 Reggie Sanders	.20	.09
☐ 53 Deion Sanders	.75	.35
☐ 54 Hal Morris	.20	.09
☐ 55 Barry Larkin	.60	.25
☐ 56 Jim Thome	.75	.35
☐ 57 Marquis Grissom	.40	.18
☐ 58 David Justice	.75	.35
☐ 59 Charles Nagy	.20	.09
☐ 60 Manny Ramirez	.75	.35
☐ 61 Matt Williams	.60	.25
☐ 62 Jack McDowell	.20	.09
☐ 63 Vinny Castilla	.40	.18
☐ 64 Dante Bichette	.40	.18
☐ 65 Andres Galarraga	.75	.35
☐ 66 Ellis Burks	.40	.18
☐ 67 Larry Walker	.75	.35
☐ 68 Eric Young	.20	.09
☐ 69 Brian L. Hunter	.40	.18
☐ 70 Travis Fryman	.40	.18
☐ 71 Tony Clark	.75	.35
☐ 72 Bobby Higginson	.40	.18
☐ 73 Melvin Nieves	.20	.09
☐ 74 Jeff Conine	.20	.09
☐ 75 Gary Sheffield	.75	.35
☐ 76 Moises Alou	.40	.18
☐ 77 Edgar Renteria	.40	.18
☐ 78 Alex Fernandez	.40	.18
☐ 79 Charles Johnson	.40	.18
☐ 80 Bobby Bonilla	.40	.18
☐ 81 Darryl Kile	.40	.18
☐ 82 Derek Bell	.20	.09
☐ 83 Shane Reynolds	.20	.09
☐ 84 Craig Biggio	.60	.25
☐ 85 Jeff Bagwell	1.50	.70
☐ 86 Billy Wagner	.40	.18
☐ 87 Chili Davis	.40	.18
☐ 88 Kevin Appier	.20	.09
☐ 89 Jay Bell	.40	.18
☐ 90 Johnny Damon	.40	.18
☐ 91 Jeff King	.40	.18
☐ 92 Hideo Nomo	2.00	.90
☐ 93 Todd Hollandsworth	.40	.18
☐ 94 Eric Karros	.40	.18
☐ 95 Mike Piazza	2.50	1.10
☐ 96 Ramon Martinez	.40	.18
☐ 97 Todd Worrell	.40	.18
☐ 98 Raul Mondesi	.60	.25
☐ 99 Dave Nilsson	.20	.09
☐ 100 John Jaha	.20	.09
☐ 101 Jose Valentin	.20	.09
☐ 102 Jeff Cirillo	.40	.18
☐ 103 Jeff D'Amico	.20	.09
☐ 104 Ben McDonald	.20	.09
☐ 105 Paul Molitor	.75	.35
☐ 106 Rich Becker	.20	.09
☐ 107 Frank Rodriguez	.20	.09
☐ 108 Marty Cordova	.20	.09
☐ 109 Terry Steinbach	.40	.18
☐ 110 Chuck Knoblauch	.75	.35
☐ 111 Mark Grudzielanek	.20	.09
☐ 112 Mike Lansing	.20	.09
☐ 113 Pedro J. Martinez	.75	.35
☐ 114 Henry Rodriguez	.20	.09
☐ 115 Rondell White	.40	.18
☐ 116 Rey Ordonez	.20	.09
☐ 117 Carlos Baerga	.40	.18
☐ 118 Lance Johnson	.20	.09
☐ 119 Bernard Gilkey	.20	.09
☐ 120 Todd Hundley	.40	.18
☐ 121 John Franco	.40	.18
☐ 122 Bernie Williams	.75	.35
☐ 123 David Cone	.40	.18
☐ 124 Cecil Fielder	.40	.18
☐ 125 Derek Jeter	2.50	1.10
☐ 126 Tino Martinez	.75	.35
☐ 127 Mariano Rivera	.40	.18
☐ 128 Andy Pettitte	.75	.35
☐ 129 Wade Boggs	.75	.35
☐ 130 Mark McGwire	1.50	.70
☐ 131 Jose Canseco	.60	.25
☐ 132 Geronimo Berroa	.20	.09
☐ 133 Jason Giambi	.40	.18
☐ 134 Ernie Young	.20	.09
☐ 135 Scott Rolen	2.00	.90
☐ 136 Ricky Bottalico	.20	.09
☐ 137 Curt Schilling	.40	.18
☐ 138 Gregg Jefferies	.40	.18
☐ 139 Mickey Morandini	.20	.09
☐ 140 Jason Kendall	.40	.18
☐ 141 Kevin Elster	.20	.09
☐ 142 Al Martin	.20	.09
☐ 143 Joe Randa	.20	.09
☐ 144 Jason Schmidt	.20	.09
☐ 145 Ray Lankford	.40	.18
☐ 146 Brian Jordan	.20	.09
☐ 147 Andy Benes	.20	.09
☐ 148 Alan Benes	.20	.09
☐ 149 Gary Gaetti	.40	.18
☐ 150 Ron Gant	.40	.18
☐ 151 Dennis Eckersley	.60	.25
☐ 152 Rickey Henderson	.60	.25
☐ 153 Joey Hamilton	.20	.09
☐ 154 Ken Caminiti	.75	.35
☐ 155 Tony Gwynn	2.00	.90
☐ 156 Steve Finley	.40	.18
☐ 157 Trevor Hoffman	.40	.18
☐ 158 Greg Vaughn	.20	.09
☐ 159 J.T. Snow	.20	.09
☐ 160 Barry Bonds	1.00	.45
☐ 161 Glenallen Hill	.20	.09
☐ 162 William VanLandingham	.20	.09
☐ 163 Jeff Kent	.20	.09
☐ 164 Jay Buhner	.60	.25
☐ 165 Ken Griffey Jr.	4.00	1.80
☐ 166 Alex Rodriguez	3.00	1.35
☐ 167 Randy Johnson	.75	.35
☐ 168 Edgar Martinez	.60	.25
☐ 169 Dan Wilson	.20	.09
☐ 170 Ivan Rodriguez	1.00	.45
☐ 171 Roger Pavlik	.20	.09
☐ 172 Will Clark	.60	.25
☐ 173 Dean Palmer	.20	.09
☐ 174 Rusty Greer	.40	.18
☐ 175 Juan Gonzalez	2.00	.90
☐ 176 John Wetteland	.40	.18
☐ 177 Joe Carter	.40	.18
☐ 178 Ed Sprague	.20	.09
☐ 179 Carlos Delgado	.20	.09
☐ 180 Roger Clemens	1.50	.70
☐ 181 Juan Guzman	.20	.09
☐ 182 Pat Hentgen	.40	.18
☐ 183 Ken Griffey Jr. CL	.75	.35
☐ 184 Hideki Irabu	1.50	.70

1997 SP Game Film

Randomly inserted in packs, this 10-card set features actual game film that highlights the accomplishments of some of the League's greatest players. Only 500 of each card in this crash numbered, limited edition set were produced.

	MINT	NRMT
COMPLETE SET (10)	1200.00	550.00
COMMON CARD (GF1-GF10)	50.00	22.00
☐ GF1 Alex Rodriguez	120.00	55.00
☐ GF2 Frank Thomas	150.00	70.00
☐ GF3 Andruw Jones	80.00	36.00
☐ GF4 Cal Ripken	150.00	70.00
☐ GF5 Mike Piazza	120.00	55.00
☐ GF6 Derek Jeter	100.00	45.00
☐ GF7 Mark McGwire	80.00	36.00
☐ GF8 Chipper Jones	100.00	45.00
☐ GF9 Barry Bonds	50.00	22.00
☐ GF10 Ken Griffey Jr	200.00	90.00

1997 SP Griffey Heroes

This 10-card continuation insert set pays special tribute to one of the game's most talented players and features color photos of Ken Griffey Jr. Only 2,000 of each card in this crash numbered, limited edition set were produced.

	MINT	NRMT
COMPLETE SET (10)	250.00	110.00
COMMON GRIFFEY (91-100)	30.00	13.50
☐ 91 Ken Griffey Jr.	30.00	13.50
☐ 92 Ken Griffey Jr.	30.00	13.50
☐ 93 Ken Griffey Jr.	30.00	13.50

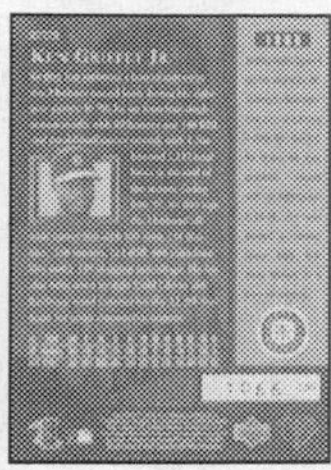

	MINT	NRMT
☐ 94 Ken Griffey Jr.	30.00	13.50
☐ 95 Ken Griffey Jr.	30.00	13.50
☐ 96 Ken Griffey Jr.	30.00	13.50
☐ 97 Ken Griffey Jr.	30.00	13.50
☐ 98 Ken Griffey Jr.	30.00	13.50
☐ 99 Ken Griffey Jr.	30.00	13.50
☐ 100 Ken Griffey Jr.	30.00	13.50

1997 SP Inside Info

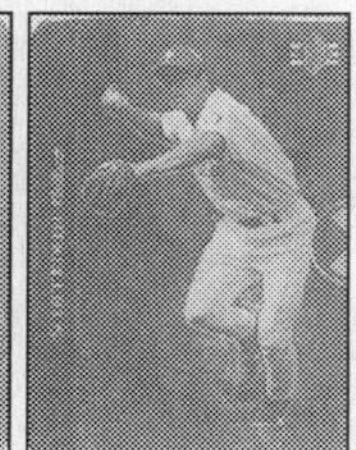

Inserted one in every 30-pack box, this 25-card set features color player photos on original cards with an exclusive pull-out panel that details the accomplishments of the League's brightest stars.

	MINT	NRMT
COMPLETE SET (25)	300.00	135.00
COMMON CARD (1-25)	4.00	1.80
☐ 1 Ken Griffey Jr.	30.00	13.50
☐ 2 Mark McGwire	12.00	5.50
☐ 3 Kenny Lofton	8.00	3.60
☐ 4 Paul Molitor	6.00	2.70
☐ 5 Frank Thomas	25.00	11.00
☐ 6 Greg Maddux	20.00	9.00
☐ 7 Mo Vaughn	8.00	3.60
☐ 8 Cal Ripken	25.00	11.00
☐ 9 Jeff Bagwell	12.00	5.50
☐ 10 Alex Rodriguez	20.00	9.00
☐ 11 John Smoltz	4.00	1.80
☐ 12 Manny Ramirez	6.00	2.70
☐ 13 Sammy Sosa	6.00	2.70
☐ 14 Vladimir Guerrero	10.00	4.50
☐ 15 Albert Belle	8.00	3.60
☐ 16 Mike Piazza	20.00	9.00
☐ 17 Derek Jeter	15.00	6.75
☐ 18 Scott Rolen	12.00	5.50
☐ 19 Tony Gwynn	15.00	6.75
☐ 20 Barry Bonds	8.00	3.60
☐ 21 Ken Caminiti	6.00	2.70
☐ 22 Chipper Jones	20.00	9.00
☐ 23 Juan Gonzalez	15.00	6.75
☐ 24 Roger Clemens	12.00	5.50
☐ 25 Andruw Jones	12.00	5.50

1997 SP Marquee Matchups

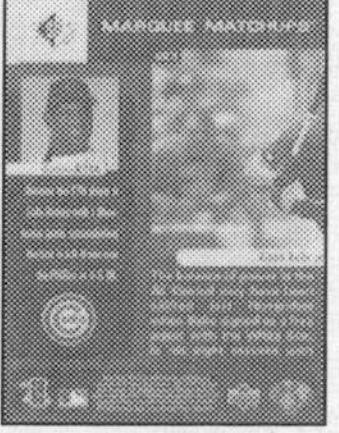

Randomly inserted in packs at a rate of one in five, this 20-card set features color player images on die-cut cards that match-up the best pitchers and hitters from around the League.

	MINT	NRMT
COMPLETE SET (20)	50.00	22.00
COMMON CARD (MM1-MM20)	1.00	.45

□ MM1 Ken Griffey Jr.	8.00	3.60
□ MM2 Andres Galarraga	1.50	.70
□ MM3 Barry Bonds	2.00	.90
□ MM4 Mark McGwire	3.00	1.35
□ MM5 Mike Piazza	5.00	2.20
□ MM6 Tim Salmon	1.50	.70
□ MM7 Tony Gwynn	4.00	1.80
□ MM8 Alex Rodriguez	6.00	2.70
□ MM9 Chipper Jones	5.00	2.20
□ MM10 Derek Jeter	5.00	2.20
□ MM11 Manny Ramirez	1.50	.70
□ MM12 Jeff Bagwell	3.00	1.35
□ MM13 Greg Maddux	5.00	2.20
□ MM14 Cal Ripken	6.00	2.70
□ MM15 Mo Vaughn	2.00	.90
□ MM16 Gary Sheffield	1.50	.70
□ MM17 Jim Thome	1.50	.70
□ MM18 Barry Larkin	1.00	.45
□ MM19 Frank Thomas	6.00	2.70
□ MM20 Sammy Sosa	1.50	.70

1997 SP Special FX

Randomly inserted in packs at a rate of one in nine, this 48-card set features color player photos on Holoview cards with the Special F/X die-cut design. Cards #1-47 are from 1997 with card #49 featuring a design from 1996. There is no card #48.

	MINT	NRMT
COMPLETE SET (48)	300.00	135.00
COMMON CARD (1-47/49)	2.50	1.10

□ 1 Ken Griffey Jr.	25.00	11.00
□ 2 Frank Thomas	20.00	9.00
□ 3 Barry Bonds	6.00	2.70
□ 4 Albert Belle	6.00	2.70
□ 5 Mike Piazza	15.00	6.75
□ 6 Greg Maddux	15.00	6.75
□ 7 Chipper Jones	15.00	6.75
□ 8 Cal Ripken	20.00	9.00
□ 9 Jeff Bagwell	10.00	4.50
□ 10 Alex Rodriguez	15.00	6.75
□ 11 Mark McGwire	10.00	4.50
□ 12 Kenny Lofton	6.00	2.70
□ 13 Juan Gonzalez	12.00	5.50
□ 14 Mo Vaughn	6.00	2.70
□ 15 John Smoltz	3.00	1.35
□ 16 Derek Jeter	12.00	5.50
□ 17 Tony Gwynn	12.00	5.50
□ 18 Ivan Rodriguez	6.00	2.70
□ 19 Barry Larkin	4.00	1.80
□ 20 Sammy Sosa	5.00	2.20
□ 21 Mike Mussina	5.00	2.20
□ 22 Gary Sheffield	5.00	2.20
□ 23 Brady Anderson	4.00	1.80
□ 24 Roger Clemens	10.00	4.50
□ 25 Ken Caminiti	5.00	2.20
□ 26 Roberto Alomar	5.00	2.20
□ 27 Hideo Nomo	12.00	5.50
□ 28 Bernie Williams	5.00	2.20
□ 29 Todd Hundley	3.00	1.35
□ 30 Manny Ramirez	5.00	2.20
□ 31 Eric Karros	3.00	1.35
□ 32 Tim Salmon	5.00	2.20
□ 33 Jay Buhner	4.00	1.80
□ 34 Andy Pettitte	5.00	2.20
□ 35 Jim Thome	5.00	2.20
□ 36 Ryne Sandberg	6.00	2.70
□ 37 Matt Williams	4.00	1.80
□ 38 Ryan Klesko	4.00	1.80
□ 39 Jose Canseco	4.00	1.80
□ 40 Paul Molitor	5.00	2.20
□ 41 Eddie Murray	5.00	2.20
□ 42 Darin Erstad	6.00	2.70
□ 43 Todd Walker	2.50	1.10
□ 44 Wade Boggs	5.00	2.20
□ 45 Andruw Jones	10.00	4.50
□ 46 Scott Rolen	10.00	4.50
□ 47 Vladimir Guerrero	8.00	3.60
□ 49 Alex Rodriguez '96	20.00	9.00

1997 SP SPx Force

Randomly inserted in packs, this 10-card die-cut set features head photos of four of the very best players on each card with an "X" in the background and players' and teams' names on one side. Only 500 of each card in this crash numbered, limited edition set were produced.

	MINT	NRMT
COMPLETE SET (10)	1200.00	550.00
COMMON CARD (1-10)	60.00	27.00

□ 1 Ken Griffey Jr. Jay Buhner Andres Galarraga Dante Bichette	200.00	90.00
□ 2 Albert Belle Brady Anderson Mark McGwire Cecil Fielder	80.00	36.00
□ 3 Mo Vaughn Ken Caminiti Frank Thomas Jeff Bagwell	150.00	70.00
□ 4 Gary Sheffield Sammy Sosa Barry Bonds Jose Canseco	60.00	27.00
□ 5 Greg Maddux Roger Clemens John Smoltz Randy Johnson	150.00	70.00
□ 6 Alex Rodriguez Derek Jeter Chipper Jones Rey Ordonez	150.00	70.00
□ 7 Todd Hollandsworth Mike Piazza Raul Mondesi Hideo Nomo	100.00	45.00
□ 8 Juan Gonzalez Manny Ramirez Roberto Alomar Ivan Rodriguez	100.00	45.00
□ 9 Tony Gwynn Wade Boggs Eddie Murray Paul Molitor	100.00	45.00
□ 10 Andruw Jones Vladimir Guerrero Todd Walker Scott Rolen	100.00	45.00

1997 SP SPx Force Autographs

Randomly inserted in packs, this 10-card set is an autographed parallel version of the regular SPx Force set. Only 100 of each card in this crash numbered, limited edition set were produced.

	MINT	NRMT
COMPLETE SET (10)	3000.00	1350.00
COMMON CARD (1-10)	120.00	55.00

□ 1 Ken Griffey Jr. AU	1000.00	450.00
□ 2 Albert Belle AU	200.00	90.00
□ 3 Mo Vaughn AU EXCH	200.00	90.00
□ 4 Gary Sheffield AU	150.00	70.00
□ 5 Greg Maddux AU	500.00	220.00
□ 6 Alex Rodriguez AU	500.00	220.00
□ 7 Todd Hollandsworth AU	120.00	55.00
□ 8 Roberto Alomar AU	200.00	90.00
□ 9 Tony Gwynn AU	400.00	180.00
□ 10 Andruw Jones AU	250.00	110.00

1997 SP Vintage Autographs

Randomly inserted in packs, this 31-card set features authenticated original 1993-1996 SP cards that have been autographed by the pictured player. The print runs are listed after year following the player's name in the checklist below. Some of the very short printed autographs are listed but not priced.

	MINT	NRMT
COMMON CARD (1-31)	25.00	11.00

□ 1 Jeff Bagwell '93/7		
□ 2 Jeff Bagwell '95/173	200.00	90.00
□ 3 Jeff Bagwell '96/292	150.00	70.00
□ 4 Jeff Bagwell '96 MM/23	500.00	220.00
□ 5 Jay Buhner '95/57	100.00	45.00
□ 6 Jay Buhner '96/79	100.00	45.00
□ 7 Jay Buhner '96 FX/27	150.00	70.00
□ 8 Ken Griffey Jr. '93/16	2500.00	1100.00
□ 9 Ken Griffey Jr. '93 PP/5		
□ 10 Ken Griffey Jr. '94/103	1000.00	450.00
□ 11 Ken Griffey Jr. '95/38	1500.00	700.00
□ 12 Ken Griffey Jr. '96/312	500.00	220.00
□ 13 Tony Gwynn '93/17	800.00	350.00
□ 14 Tony Gwynn '94/367	200.00	90.00
□ 15 Tony Gwynn '94 HV/31	500.00	220.00
□ 16 Tony Gwynn '95/64	400.00	180.00
□ 17 Tony Gwynn '96/20	600.00	275.00
□ 18 Todd Hollandsworth '94/167	25.00	11.00
□ 19 Chipper Jones '93/34	500.00	220.00
□ 20 Chipper Jones '95/60	400.00	180.00
□ 21 Chipper Jones '96/102	300.00	135.00
□ 22 R.Ordonez '96/111	30.00	13.50
□ 23 Rey Ordonez '96 MM/40	50.00	22.00
□ 24 Alex Rodriguez '94/94	400.00	180.00
□ 25 Alex Rodriguez '95/63	500.00	220.00
□ 26 Alex Rodriguez '96/73	500.00	220.00
□ 27 Gary Sheffield '94/130	100.00	45.00
□ 28 Gary Sheffield '94 HVDC/4		
□ 29 Gary Sheffield '95/221	80.00	36.00
□ 30 Gary Sheffield '96/58	120.00	55.00
□ 31 Mo Vaughn '97 EXCH/250	80.00	36.00

1995 SP Championship

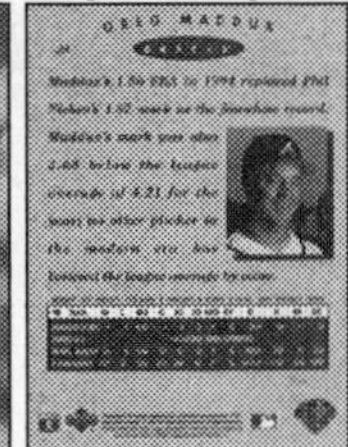

This set contains 200 cards that were sold in six-card retail packs for a suggested price of $2.99. The fronts have a full-bleed action photo with the words "SP Championship Series" in gold-foil in the bottom left-hand corner. In the bottom right-hand corner is the team's name in blue (National League) and red (American League) foil. The backs have a small head shot and player information. Statistics and team name are also on the back in blue or red just like on the front. Subsets featured are Diamonds in the Rough (1-20), October Legends (100-114) and Major League Profiles. Rookie Cards in this set include Bobby Higginson and Hideo Nomo.

	MINT	NRMT
COMPLETE SET (200)	40.00	18.00
COMMON CARD (1-200)	.20	.09

□ 1 Hideo Nomo	4.00	1.80
□ 2 Roger Cedeno	.40	.18
□ 3 Curtis Goodwin	.20	.09
□ 4 Jon Nunnally	.40	.18
□ 5 Bill Pulsipher	.40	.18
□ 6 Garret Anderson	.50	.23
□ 7 Dustin Hermanson	.40	.18
□ 8 Marty Cordova	.50	.23
□ 9 Ruben Rivera	.75	.35
□ 10 Ariel Prieto	.40	.18
□ 11 Edgardo Alfonzo	.75	.35
□ 12 Ray Durham	.50	.23
□ 13 Quilvio Veras	.40	.18
□ 14 Ugueth Urbina	.40	.18
□ 15 Carlos Perez	.40	.18
□ 16 Glenn Dishman	.40	.18

Card	MINT	NRMT
☐ 17 Jeff Suppan	.50	.23
☐ 18 Jason Bates	.20	.09
☐ 19 Jason Isringhausen	.40	.18
☐ 20 Derek Jeter	2.50	1.10
☐ 21 Fred McGriff MLP	.50	.23
☐ 22 Marquis Grissom	.40	.18
☐ 23 Fred McGriff	.50	.23
☐ 24 Tom Glavine	.50	.23
☐ 25 Greg Maddux	2.50	1.10
☐ 26 Chipper Jones	2.50	1.10
☐ 27 Sammy Sosa MLP	.75	.35
☐ 28 Randy Myers	.20	.09
☐ 29 Mark Grace	.50	.23
☐ 30 Sammy Sosa	.75	.35
☐ 31 Todd Zeile	.20	.09
☐ 32 Brian McRae	.20	.09
☐ 33 Ron Gant MLP	.40	.18
☐ 34 Reggie Sanders	.20	.09
☐ 35 Ron Gant	.40	.18
☐ 36 Barry Larkin	.50	.23
☐ 37 Bret Boone	.20	.09
☐ 38 John Smiley	.20	.09
☐ 39 Larry Walker MLP	.75	.35
☐ 40 Andres Galarraga	.50	.23
☐ 41 Bill Swift	.20	.09
☐ 42 Larry Walker	.75	.35
☐ 43 Vinny Castilla	.50	.23
☐ 44 Dante Bichette	.50	.23
☐ 45 Jeff Conine MLP	.40	.18
☐ 46 Charles Johnson	.50	.23
☐ 47 Gary Sheffield	.50	.23
☐ 48 Andre Dawson	.50	.23
☐ 49 Jeff Conine	.40	.18
☐ 50 Jeff Bagwell MLP	.75	.35
☐ 51 Phil Nevin	.20	.09
☐ 52 Craig Biggio	.50	.23
☐ 53 Brian L. Hunter	.40	.18
☐ 54 Doug Drabek	.20	.09
☐ 55 Jeff Bagwell	1.50	.70
☐ 56 Derek Bell	.40	.18
☐ 57 Mike Piazza MLP	1.25	.55
☐ 58 Raul Mondesi	.50	.23
☐ 59 Eric Karros	.40	.18
☐ 60 Mike Piazza	2.50	1.10
☐ 61 Ramon Martinez	.40	.18
☐ 62 Billy Ashley	.20	.09
☐ 63 Rondell White MLP	.50	.23
☐ 64 Jeff Fassero	.20	.09
☐ 65 Moises Alou	.40	.18
☐ 66 Tony Tarasco	.20	.09
☐ 67 Rondell White	.50	.23
☐ 68 Pedro J. Martinez	.75	.35
☐ 69 Bobby Jones MLP	.40	.18
☐ 70 Bobby Bonilla	.40	.18
☐ 71 Bobby Jones	.40	.18
☐ 72 Bret Saberhagen	.20	.09
☐ 73 Darren Daulton MLP	.40	.18
☐ 74 Darren Daulton	.40	.18
☐ 75 Gregg Jefferies	.40	.18
☐ 76 Tyler Green	.20	.09
☐ 77 Heathcliff Slocumb	.20	.09
☐ 78 Lenny Dykstra	.40	.18
☐ 79 Jay Bell MLP	.40	.18
☐ 80 Denny Neagle	.40	.18
☐ 81 Orlando Merced	.20	.09
☐ 82 Jay Bell	.40	.18
☐ 83 Ozzie Smith MLP	.75	.35
☐ 84 Ken Hill	.20	.09
☐ 85 Ozzie Smith	1.00	.45
☐ 86 Bernard Gilkey	.40	.18
☐ 87 Ray Lankford	.50	.23
☐ 88 Tony Gwynn MLP	.75	.35
☐ 89 Ken Caminiti	.75	.35
☐ 90 Tony Gwynn	2.00	.90
☐ 91 Joey Hamilton	.40	.18
☐ 92 Bip Roberts	.20	.09
☐ 93 Deion Sanders MLP	.75	.35
☐ 94 Glenallen Hill	.20	.09
☐ 95 Matt Williams	.50	.23
☐ 96 Barry Bonds	1.00	.45
☐ 97 Rod Beck	.20	.09
☐ 98 Eddie Murray CL	.75	.35
☐ 99 Cal Ripken Jr. CL	1.50	.70
☐ 100 Roberto Alomar OL	.75	.35
☐ 101 George Brett OL	1.00	.45
☐ 102 Joe Carter OL	.50	.23
☐ 103 Will Clark OL	.50	.23
☐ 104 Dennis Eckersley OL	.50	.23
☐ 105 Whitey Ford OL	.75	.35
☐ 106 Steve Garvey OL	.40	.18
☐ 107 Kirk Gibson OL	.40	.18
☐ 108 Orel Hershiser OL	.40	.18
☐ 109 Reggie Jackson OL	.75	.35
☐ 110 Paul Molitor OL	.75	.35
☐ 111 Kirby Puckett OL	.75	.35
☐ 112 Mike Schmidt OL	.75	.35
☐ 113 Dave Stewart OL	.20	.09
☐ 114 Alan Trammell OL	.50	.23
☐ 115 Cal Ripken Jr. MLP	1.50	.70
☐ 116 Brady Anderson	.50	.23
☐ 117 Mike Mussina	.50	.23
☐ 118 Rafael Palmeiro	.50	.23
☐ 119 Chris Hoiles	.20	.09
☐ 120 Cal Ripken	3.00	1.35
☐ 121 Mo Vaughn MLP	.75	.35
☐ 122 Roger Clemens	1.50	.70
☐ 123 Tim Naehring	.20	.09
☐ 124 John Valentin	.40	.18
☐ 125 Mo Vaughn	1.00	.45
☐ 126 Tim Wakefield	.20	.09
☐ 127 Jose Canseco	.50	.23
☐ 128 Rick Aguilera	.20	.09
☐ 129 Chili Davis MLP	.40	.18
☐ 130 Lee Smith	.40	.18
☐ 131 Jim Edmonds	.75	.35
☐ 132 Chuck Finley	.40	.18
☐ 133 Chili Davis	.40	.18
☐ 134 J.T. Snow	.40	.18
☐ 135 Tim Salmon	.75	.35
☐ 136 Frank Thomas MLP	2.00	.90
☐ 137 Jason Bere	.20	.09
☐ 138 Robin Ventura	.40	.18
☐ 139 Tim Raines	.20	.09
☐ 140 Frank Thomas	3.00	1.35
☐ 141 Alex Fernandez	.40	.18
☐ 142 Eddie Murray MLP	.75	.35
☐ 143 Carlos Baerga	.40	.18
☐ 144 Eddie Murray	.75	.35
☐ 145 Albert Belle	1.00	.45
☐ 146 Jim Thome	.75	.35
☐ 147 Dennis Martinez	.40	.18
☐ 148 Dave Winfield	.50	.23
☐ 149 Kenny Lofton	1.00	.45
☐ 150 Manny Ramirez	.75	.35
☐ 151 Cecil Fielder MLP	.40	.18
☐ 152 Lou Whitaker	.40	.18
☐ 153 Alan Trammell	.50	.23
☐ 154 Kirk Gibson	.40	.18
☐ 155 Cecil Fielder	.40	.18
☐ 156 Bobby Higginson	1.25	.55
☐ 157 Kevin Appier MLP	.40	.18
☐ 158 Wally Joyner	.40	.18
☐ 159 Jeff Montgomery	.40	.18
☐ 160 Kevin Appier	.40	.18
☐ 161 Gary Gaetti	.40	.18
☐ 162 Greg Gagne	.20	.09
☐ 163 Ricky Bones MLP	.20	.09
☐ 164 Greg Vaughn	.20	.09
☐ 165 Kevin Seitzer	.20	.09
☐ 166 Ricky Bones	.20	.09
☐ 167 Kirby Puckett MLP	.75	.35
☐ 168 Pedro Munoz	.20	.09
☐ 169 Chuck Knoblauch	.75	.35
☐ 170 Kirby Puckett	1.50	.70
☐ 171 Don Mattingly MLP	.75	.35
☐ 172 Wade Boggs	.75	.35
☐ 173 Paul O'Neill	.40	.18
☐ 174 John Wetteland	.40	.18
☐ 175 Don Mattingly	1.25	.55
☐ 176 Jack McDowell	.20	.09
☐ 177 Mark McGwire MLP	.75	.35
☐ 178 Rickey Henderson	.50	.23
☐ 179 Terry Steinbach	.40	.18
☐ 180 Ruben Sierra	.20	.09
☐ 181 Mark McGwire	1.50	.70
☐ 182 Dennis Eckersley	.50	.23
☐ 183 Ken Griffey Jr. MLP	2.00	.90
☐ 184 Alex Rodriguez	3.00	1.35
☐ 185 Ken Griffey Jr.	4.00	1.80
☐ 186 Randy Johnson	.75	.35
☐ 187 Jay Buhner	.50	.23
☐ 188 Edgar Martinez	.50	.23
☐ 189 Will Clark MLP	.50	.23
☐ 190 Juan Gonzalez	2.00	.90
☐ 191 Benji Gil	.20	.09
☐ 192 Ivan Rodriguez	1.00	.45
☐ 193 Kenny Rogers	.20	.09
☐ 194 Will Clark	.50	.23
☐ 195 Paul Molitor MLP	.75	.35
☐ 196 Roberto Alomar	.75	.35
☐ 197 David Cone	.40	.18
☐ 198 Paul Molitor	.75	.35
☐ 199 Shawn Green	.40	.18
☐ 200 Joe Carter	.50	.23
☐ CR1 Cal Ripken, Jr. Tribute	25.00	11.00
☐ CR1 Cal Ripken 2131 DC	80.00	36.00

1995 SP Championship Die Cuts

This 200-card set parallels the regular SP Championship set and was inserted one per pack. The only difference between the sets is the die-cut bordered design.

	MINT	NRMT
COMPLETE SET (200)	150.00	70.00
COMMON CARD (1-200)	.30	.14
*STARS: 1.5X to 3X BASIC CARDS		
*YOUNG STARS: 1.25X to 2.5X BASIC CARDS		

1995 SP Championship Classic Performances

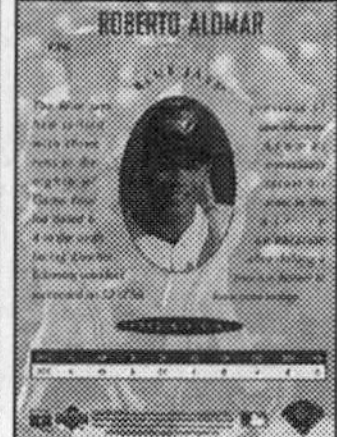

Cards from this 10-card set were randomly inserted in packs at a rate of one in 15. The set consists of 10 of the most memorable highlights since the 1969 Miracle Mets. The fronts have a series action photo highlighted with the words "Classic Performances" at the top in gold-foil enclosed by red. The backs have a color head shot with information and statistics from the series.

	MINT	NRMT
COMPLETE SET (10)	40.00	18.00
COMMON CARD (CP1-CP10)	2.00	.90
COMP.DIE CUT SET (10)	200.00	90.00
*DIE CUTS: 2X TO 5X BASIC CARDS		
☐ CP1 Reggie Jackson	5.00	2.20
☐ CP2 Nolan Ryan	15.00	6.75
☐ CP3 Kirk Gibson	3.00	1.35
☐ CP4 Joe Carter	3.50	1.55
☐ CP5 George Brett	8.00	3.60
☐ CP6 Roberto Alomar	4.00	1.80
☐ CP7 Ozzie Smith	5.00	2.20
☐ CP8 Kirby Puckett	8.00	3.60
☐ CP9 Bret Saberhagen	2.00	.90
☐ CP10 Steve Garvey	3.00	1.35

1995 SP Championship Fall Classic

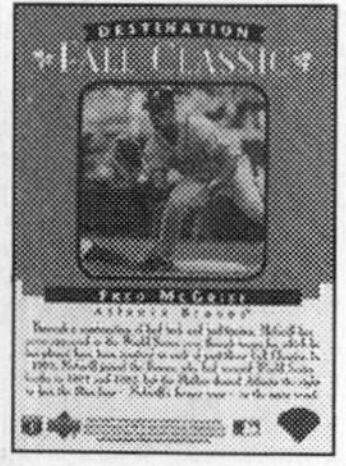

This nine-card set was randomly inserted in packs at a rate of one in 40. The set is comprised of players who had never been to the World Series prior to the 1995 Fall Classic. The fronts have a color-action photo with the game background in foil. There is a grain-colored border with the word "Destination" at the top in bronze-foil and "Fall Classic" underneath in black. The backs have a small, color picture inside a black box with player information underneath. Diecut versions were inserted at a rate of one in 72 packs and are valued at 1.5X to 3X the prices below.

	MINT	NRMT
COMPLETE SET (9)	120.00	55.00
COMMON CARD (1-9)	4.00	1.80
COMP.DIE CUT SET (9)	250.00	110.00
*DIECUTS: .75X TO 2X BASIC CARDS		
☐ 1 Ken Griffey Jr.	30.00	13.50
☐ 2 Frank Thomas	30.00	13.50
☐ 3 Albert Belle	12.00	5.50
☐ 4 Mike Piazza	20.00	9.00
☐ 5 Don Mattingly	15.00	6.75
☐ 6 Hideo Nomo	15.00	6.75
☐ 7 Greg Maddux	20.00	9.00
☐ 8 Fred McGriff	4.00	1.80
☐ 9 Barry Bonds	6.00	2.70

1985-86 Sportflics Prototypes

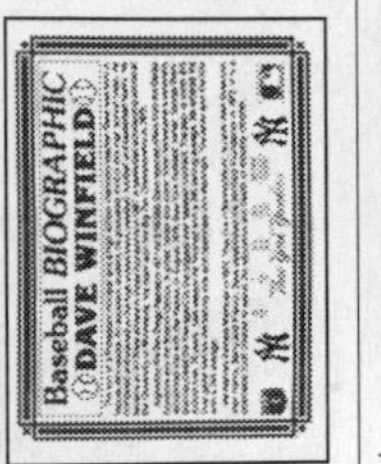

The 1985-86 Sportflics Proof set contains four standard-size unnumbered cards, one mini (1 5/16" by 1 5/16") Joe DiMaggio card, and one trivia card (1 3/4" by 2"). The standard-size cards resemble regular 1986 Sportflics cards, but have different photos and stats only through 1984. One of the Winfield cards has a bio only; unfortunately the biographical statements on the back are incorrect in several instances. The DiMaggio card has black and white photos on the front, and career totals on the back. The trivia card is the same as those distributed with 1986 Sportflics, except it shows the major league baseball logo on the front. These test cards were apparently produced in limited quantity to show Major League Baseball and the Major League Baseball Players Association what Sportflics was proposing in order to be a new licensee for producing cards. These cards are very difficult to find and are considerably rarer than the Sportflics Test cards which were given out after the Sportflics license had been granted.

	NRMT	VG-E
COMPLETE SET (5)	150.00	70.00
COMMON CARD (1-5)	5.00	2.20
☐ 1 Joe DiMaggio (Small size)	75.00	34.00
☐ 2 Mike Schmidt (Stats on back)	50.00	22.00
☐ 3 Bruce Sutter (Stats on back)	5.00	2.20
☐ 4 Dave Winfield (Biographical back)	15.00	6.75
☐ 5 Dave Winfield (Stats on back)	25.00	11.00

1985-86 Sportflics Samples

This three-card pack was a test, distributed freely by salesmen to potential buyers to show them what the new Sportflics product would look like. The set is sometimes referred to as the Vendor Sample Kit. Some of these packs even found their way to the retail counters. They are not rare although they are obviously much less common than the regular issue of Sportflics. The cards show statistics only up through 1984. The copyright date on the card backs shows 1986. The cards are standard size.

	NRMT	VG-E
COMPLETE SET (3)	40.00	18.00
COMMON CARD	15.00	6.75
☐ 1 RBI Sluggers	15.00	6.75
Mike Schmidt		
Dale Murphy		
Jim Rice		
☐ 43 Pete Rose (Pictured with batting helmet; Pete is number 50 in regular 1986 set)	15.00	6.75
☐ 45 Tom Seaver (Tom is number 25 in regular 1986 set)	15.00	6.75

1986 Sportflics

This 200-card standard-size set was marketed with 133 small trivia cards. This inaugural set for Sportflics was initially fairly well received by collectors. Sportflics was distributed by Major League Marketing; the company also maintained distribution agreements with Wrigley and Amurol. The set features 139 single player "magic motion" cards (which can be tilted to show three different pictures of the same player), 50 "Tri-Stars" (which show three different players), 10 "Big Six" cards (which show six players who share similar achievements), and one World Champs card featuring 12 members of the victorious Kansas City Royals. Some of the cards also have (limited production and rarely seen) proof versions with some player selection differences; a proof version of number 178 includes Jim Wilson instead of Mark Funderburk. Also a proof of number 179 with Karl Best, Mark Funderburk, Andres Galarraga, Dwayne Henry, Pete Incaviglia, and Todd Worrell was produced. The following sequences can be found to be in alphabetical order, 26-49, 76-99, 101-124, 151-174, and 187-199. Cards 1-24 seem to be Sportflics' selection of top players and cards 25, 50, 100, 125, and 175 all set milestones or records during the 1985 season. The Robin Yount Yankee error (#42A) is not considered part of the complete set.

	MINT	NRMT
COMPLETE SET (200)	20.00	9.00
COMPLETE FACT.SET (200)	20.00	9.00
COMMON CARD (1-200)	.05	.02
☐ 1 George Brett	1.00	.45
☐ 2 Don Mattingly	1.25	.55
☐ 3 Wade Boggs	.40	.18
☐ 4 Eddie Murray	.60	.25
☐ 5 Dale Murphy	.25	.11
☐ 6 Rickey Henderson	.30	.14
☐ 7 Harold Baines	.10	.05
☐ 8 Cal Ripken	2.50	1.10
☐ 9 Orel Hershiser	.15	.07
☐ 10 Bret Saberhagen	.15	.07
☐ 11 Tim Raines	.10	.05
☐ 12 Fernando Valenzuela	.10	.05
☐ 13 Tony Gwynn	1.50	.70
☐ 14 Pedro Guerrero	.05	.02
☐ 15 Keith Hernandez	.10	.05
☐ 16 Earnie Riles	.05	.02
☐ 17 Jim Rice	.10	.05
☐ 18 Ron Guidry	.10	.05
☐ 19 Willie McGee	.10	.05
☐ 20 Ryne Sandberg	1.00	.45
☐ 21 Kirk Gibson	.10	.05
☐ 22 Ozzie Guillen	.10	.05
☐ 23 Dave Parker	.10	.05
☐ 24 Vince Coleman	.15	.07
☐ 25 Tom Seaver	.60	.25
☐ 26 Brett Butler	.10	.05
☐ 27 Steve Carlton	.50	.23
☐ 28 Gary Carter	.15	.07
☐ 29 Cecil Cooper	.10	.05
☐ 30 Jose Cruz	.10	.05
☐ 31 Alvin Davis	.05	.02
☐ 32 Dwight Evans	.10	.05
☐ 33 Julio Franco	.10	.05
☐ 34 Damaso Garcia	.05	.02
☐ 35 Steve Garvey	.15	.07
☐ 36 Kent Hrbek	.10	.05
☐ 37 Reggie Jackson	.60	.25
☐ 38 Fred Lynn	.10	.05
☐ 39 Paul Molitor	.75	.35
☐ 40 Jim Presley	.05	.02
☐ 41 Dave Righetti	.05	.02
☐ 42A Robin Yount ERR New York Yankees	20.00	9.00
☐ 42B Robin Yount COR Milwaukee Brewers	.40	.18
☐ 43 Nolan Ryan	2.50	1.10
☐ 44 Mike Schmidt	.75	.35
☐ 45 Lee Smith	.15	.07
☐ 46 Rick Sutcliffe	.05	.02
☐ 47 Bruce Sutter	.10	.05
☐ 48 Lou Whitaker	.10	.05
☐ 49 Dave Winfield	.25	.11
☐ 50 Pete Rose	.75	.35
☐ 51 NL MVP's	.75	.35
Ryne Sandberg		
Steve Garvey		
Pete Rose		
☐ 52 Slugging Stars	.75	.35
George Brett		
Harold Baines		
Jim Rice		
☐ 53 No-Hitters	.15	.07
Phil Niekro		
Jerry Reuss		
Mike Witt		
☐ 54 Big Hitters	2.00	.90
Don Mattingly		
Cal Ripken		
Robin Yount		
☐ 55 Bullpen Aces	.15	.07
Dan Quisenberry		
Goose Gossage		
Lee Smith		
☐ 56 Rookies of The Year	.75	.35
Darryl Strawberry		
Steve Sax		
Pete Rose		
☐ 57 AL MVP's	1.50	.70
Cal Ripken		
Don Baylor		
Reggie Jackson		
☐ 58 Repeat Batting Champs	.75	.35
Dave Parker		
Bill Madlock		
Pete Rose		
☐ 59 Cy Young Winners	.15	.07
LaMarr Hoyt		
Mike Flanagan		
Ron Guidry		
☐ 60 Double Award Winners	.25	.11
Fernando Valenzuela		
Rick Sutcliffe		
Tom Seaver		
☐ 61 Home Run Champs	.50	.23
Reggie Jackson		
Jim Rice		
Tony Armas		
☐ 62 NL MVP's	.50	.23
Keith Hernandez		
Dale Murphy		
Mike Schmidt		
☐ 63 AL MVP's	.75	.35
Robin Yount		
George Brett		
Fred Lynn		
☐ 64 Comeback Players	.05	.02
Bert Blyleven		
Jerry Koosman		
John Denny		
☐ 65 Cy Young Relievers	.15	.07
Willie Hernandez		
Rollie Fingers		
Bruce Sutter		
☐ 66 Rookies of The Year	.15	.07
Bob Horner		
Andre Dawson		
Gary Matthews		
☐ 67 Rookies of The Year	.50	.23
Ron Kittle		
Carlton Fisk		
Tom Seaver		
☐ 68 Home Run Champs	.25	.11
Mike Schmidt		
George Foster		
Dave Kingman		
☐ 69 Double Award Winners	1.50	.70
Cal Ripken		
Rod Carew		
Pete Rose		
☐ 70 Cy Young Winners	.50	.23
Rick Sutcliffe		
Steve Carlton		
Tom Seaver		
☐ 71 Top Sluggers	.50	.23
Reggie Jackson		
Fred Lynn		
Robin Yount		
☐ 72 Rookies of The Year	.15	.07
Dave Righetti		
Fernando Valenzuela		
Rick Sutcliffe		
☐ 73 Rookies of The Year	1.50	.70
Fred Lynn		
Eddie Murray		
Cal Ripken		
☐ 74 Rookies of The Year	.15	.07
Alvin Davis		

Lou Whitaker		
Rod Carew		
☐ 75 Batting Champs	1.00	.45
Don Mattingly		
Wade Boggs		
Carney Lansford		
☐ 76 Jesse Barfield	.05	.02
☐ 77 Phil Bradley	.05	.02
☐ 78 Chris Brown	.05	.02
☐ 79 Tom Browning	.05	.02
☐ 80 Tom Brunansky	.05	.02
☐ 81 Bill Buckner	.10	.05
☐ 82 Chili Davis	.10	.05
☐ 83 Mike Davis	.05	.02
☐ 84 Rich Gedman	.05	.02
☐ 85 Willie Hernandez	.05	.02
☐ 86 Ron Kittle	.05	.02
☐ 87 Lee Lacy	.05	.02
☐ 88 Bill Madlock	.05	.02
☐ 89 Mike Marshall	.05	.02
☐ 90 Keith Moreland	.05	.02
☐ 91 Graig Nettles	.10	.05
☐ 92 Lance Parrish	.05	.02
☐ 93 Kirby Puckett	1.25	.55
☐ 94 Juan Samuel	.05	.02
☐ 95 Steve Sax	.05	.02
☐ 96 Dave Stieb	.05	.02
☐ 97 Darryl Strawberry	.15	.07
☐ 98 Willie Upshaw	.05	.02
☐ 99 Frank Viola	.10	.05
☐ 100 Dwight Gooden	.50	.23
☐ 101 Joaquin Andujar	.05	.02
☐ 102 George Bell	.05	.02
☐ 103 Bert Blyleven	.10	.05
☐ 104 Mike Boddicker	.05	.02
☐ 105 Britt Burns	.05	.02
☐ 106 Rod Carew	.50	.23
☐ 107 Jack Clark	.10	.05
☐ 108 Danny Cox	.05	.02
☐ 109 Ron Darling	.05	.02
☐ 110 Andre Dawson	.25	.11
☐ 111 Leon Durham	.05	.02
☐ 112 Tony Fernandez	.05	.02
☐ 113 Tommy Herr	.05	.02
☐ 114 Teddy Higuera	.05	.02
☐ 115 Bob Horner	.05	.02
☐ 116 Dave Kingman	.10	.05
☐ 117 Jack Morris	.10	.05
☐ 118 Dan Quisenberry	.05	.02
☐ 119 Jeff Reardon	.10	.05
☐ 120 Bryn Smith	.05	.02
☐ 121 Ozzie Smith	1.00	.45
☐ 122 John Tudor	.05	.02
☐ 123 Tim Wallach	.05	.02
☐ 124 Willie Wilson	.05	.02
☐ 125 Carlton Fisk	.40	.18
☐ 126 RBI Sluggers	.15	.07
Gary Carter		
Al Oliver		
George Foster		
☐ 127 Run Scorers	.75	.35
Tim Raines		
Ryne Sandberg		
Keith Hernandez		
☐ 128 Run Scorers	1.50	.70
Paul Molitor		
Cal Ripken		
Willie Wilson		
☐ 129 No-Hitters	.15	.07
John Candelaria		
Dennis Eckersley		
Bob Forsch		
☐ 130 World Series MVP's	.75	.35
Pete Rose		
Ron Cey		
Rollie Fingers		
☐ 131 All-Star Game MVP's	.15	.07
Dave Concepcion		
George Foster		
Bill Madlock		
☐ 132 Cy Young Winners	.10	.05
John Denny		
Fernando Valenzuela		
Vida Blue		
☐ 133 Comeback Players	.10	.05
Rich Dotson		
Joaquin Andujar		
Doyle Alexander		
☐ 134 Big Winners	.15	.07
Rick Sutcliffe		
Tom Seaver		
John Denny		
☐ 135 Veteran Pitchers	.50	.23
Tom Seaver		
Phil Niekro		
Don Sutton		
☐ 136 Rookies of The Year	.15	.07
Dwight Gooden		
Vince Coleman		
Alfredo Griffin		
☐ 137 All-Star Game MVP's	.15	.07
Gary Carter		
Fred Lynn		
Steve Garvey		
☐ 138 Veteran Hitters	.75	.35
Tony Perez		
Rusty Staub		
Pete Rose		
☐ 139 Power Hitters	.50	.23
Mike Schmidt		
Jim Rice		
George Foster		
☐ 140 Batting Champs	.75	.35
Tony Gwynn		
Al Oliver		
Bill Buckner		
☐ 141 No-Hitters	1.50	.70
Nolan Ryan		
Jack Morris		
Dave Righetti		
☐ 142 No-Hitters	.25	.11
Tom Seaver		
Bert Blyleven		
Vida Blue		
☐ 143 Strikeout Kings	1.50	.70
Nolan Ryan		
Fernando Valenzuela		
Dwight Gooden		
☐ 144 Base Stealers	.15	.07
Tim Raines		
Willie Wilson		
Davey Lopes		
☐ 145 RBI Sluggers	.15	.07
Tony Armas		
Cecil Cooper		
Eddie Murray		
☐ 146 AL MVP's	.50	.23
Rod Carew		
Jim Rice		
Rollie Fingers		
☐ 147 World Series MVP's	.25	.11
Alan Trammell		
Rick Dempsey		
Reggie Jackson		
☐ 148 World Series MVP's	.25	.11
Darrell Porter		
Pedro Guerrero		
Mike Schmidt		
☐ 149 ERA Leaders	.10	.05
Mike Boddicker		
Rick Sutcliffe		
Ron Guidry		
☐ 150 Comeback Players	.25	.11
Reggie Jackson		
Dave Kingman		
Fred Lynn		
☐ 151 Buddy Bell	.10	.05
☐ 152 Dennis Boyd	.05	.02
☐ 153 Dave Concepcion	.10	.05
☐ 154 Brian Downing	.05	.02
☐ 155 Shawon Dunston	.10	.05
☐ 156 John Franco	.15	.07
☐ 157 Scott Garrelts	.05	.02
☐ 158 Bob James	.05	.02
☐ 159 Charlie Leibrandt	.05	.02
☐ 160 Oddibe McDowell	.05	.02
☐ 161 Roger McDowell	.05	.02
☐ 162 Mike Moore	.05	.02
☐ 163 Phil Niekro	.25	.11
☐ 164 Al Oliver	.10	.05
☐ 165 Tony Pena	.05	.02
☐ 166 Ted Power	.05	.02
☐ 167 Mike Scioscia	.05	.02
☐ 168 Mario Soto	.05	.02
☐ 169 Bob Stanley	.05	.02
☐ 170 Garry Templeton	.05	.02
☐ 171 Andre Thornton	.05	.02
☐ 172 Alan Trammell	.15	.07
☐ 173 Doug DeCinces	.05	.02
☐ 174 Greg Walker	.05	.02
☐ 175 Don Sutton	.25	.11
☐ 176 1985 Award Winners	1.00	.45
Ozzie Guillen		
Bret Saberhagen		
Don Mattingly		
Vince Coleman		
Dwight Gooden		
Willie McGee		
☐ 177 1985 Hot Rookies	.10	.05
Stew Cliburn		
Brian Fisher UER		
(Photo actually		
Mike Pagliarulo)		
Joe Hesketh		
Joe Orsulak		
Mark Salas		
Larry Sheets		
☐ 178 1986 Rookies To Watch	4.00	1.80
Jose Canseco		
Mark Funderburk		
Mike Greenwell		
Steve Lombardozzi UER		
(Photo actually		
Mark Salas)		
Billy Joe Robidoux		
Danny Tartabull		
☐ 179 1985 Gold Glovers	1.00	.45
George Brett		
Ron Guidry		
Keith Hernandez		
Don Mattingly		
Willie McGee		
Dale Murphy		
☐ 180 Active Lifetime .300	1.00	.45
Wade Boggs		
George Brett		
Rod Carew		
Cecil Cooper		
Don Mattingly		
Willie Wilson		
☐ 181 Active Lifetime .300	.75	.35
Tony Gwynn		
Bill Madlock		
Pedro Guerrero		
Dave Parker		
Pete Rose		
Keith Hernandez		
☐ 182 1985 Milestones	1.00	.45
Rod Carew		
Phil Niekro		
Pete Rose		
Nolan Ryan		
Tom Seaver		
Matt Tallman (fan)		
☐ 183 1985 Triple Crown	1.00	.45
Wade Boggs		
Darrell Evans		
Don Mattingly		
Willie McGee		
Dale Murphy		
Dave Parker		
☐ 184 1985 Highlights	1.00	.45
Wade Boggs		
Dwight Gooden		
Rickey Henderson		
Don Mattingly		
Willie McGee		
John Tudor		
☐ 185 1985 20 Game Winners	.15	.07
Dwight Gooden		
Ron Guidry		
John Tudor		
Joaquin Andujar		
Bret Saberhagen		
Tom Browning		
☐ 186 World Series Champs	.25	.11
Lonnie Smith		
Dane Iorg		
Willie Wilson		
Charlie Leibrandt		
George Brett		
Bret Saberhagen		
Darryl Motley		
Dan Quisenberry		
Danny Jackson		
Jim Sundberg		
Steve Balboni		
Frank White		
☐ 187 Hubie Brooks	.05	.02
☐ 188 Glenn Davis	.05	.02
☐ 189 Darrell Evans	.10	.05
☐ 190 Rich Gossage	.10	.05
☐ 191 Andy Hawkins	.05	.02
☐ 192 Jay Howell	.05	.02
☐ 193 LaMarr Hoyt	.05	.02
☐ 194 Davey Lopes	.05	.02
☐ 195 Mike Scott	.05	.02
☐ 196 Ted Simmons	.10	.05
☐ 197 Gary Ward	.05	.02
☐ 198 Bob Welch	.05	.02
☐ 199 Mike Young	.05	.02
☐ 200 Buddy Biancalana	.05	.02

1986 Sportflics Rookies

This set of 50 three-phase "animated" standard-size cards features top rookies of 1986 as well as a few outstanding rookies from the past. These "Magic Motion" cards feature a distinctive light blue border on the front of the card. Cards were distributed in a light blue box, which also contained 34 trivia cards, each measuring 1 3/4" by 2". There are 47 single player cards along with two Tri-Stars

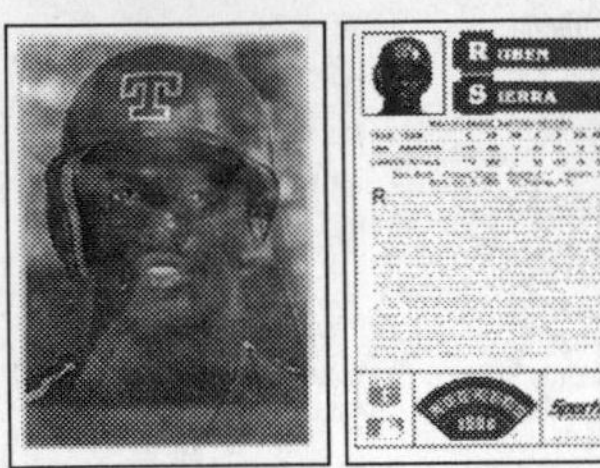

and one Big Six. The statistics on the card backs are inclusive up through the just-completed 1986 season.

	MINT	NRMT
COMPLETE SET (50)	10.00	4.50
COMPLETE FACT.SET (50)	10.00	4.50
COMMON CARD (1-50)	.10	.05
☐ 1 John Kruk	.60	.25
☐ 2 Edwin Correa	.10	.05
☐ 3 Pete Incaviglia	.20	.09
☐ 4 Dale Sveum	.10	.05
☐ 5 Juan Nieves	.10	.05
☐ 6 Will Clark	1.50	.70
☐ 7 Wally Joyner	1.00	.45
☐ 8 Lance McCullers	.10	.05
☐ 9 Scott Bailes	.10	.05
☐ 10 Dan Plesac	.10	.05
☐ 11 Jose Canseco	2.00	.90
☐ 12 Bobby Witt	.20	.09
☐ 13 Barry Bonds	3.00	1.35
☐ 14 Andres Thomas	.10	.05
☐ 15 Jim Deshaies	.10	.05
☐ 16 Ruben Sierra	.50	.23
☐ 17 Steve Lombardozzi	.10	.05
☐ 18 Cory Snyder	.10	.05
☐ 19 Reggie Williams	.10	.05
☐ 20 Mitch Williams	.20	.09
☐ 21 Glenn Braggs	.10	.05
☐ 22 Danny Tartabull	.20	.09
☐ 23 Charlie Kerfeld	.10	.05
☐ 24 Paul Assenmacher	.20	.09
☐ 25 Robby Thompson	.10	.05
☐ 26 Bobby Bonilla	.60	.25
☐ 27 Andres Galarraga	2.00	.90
☐ 28 Billy Joe Robidoux	.10	.05
☐ 29 Bruce Ruffin	.10	.05
☐ 30 Greg Swindell	.20	.09
☐ 31 John Cangelosi	.10	.05
☐ 32 Jim Traber	.10	.05
☐ 33 Russ Morman	.10	.05
☐ 34 Barry Larkin	2.00	.90
☐ 35 Todd Worrell	.50	.23
☐ 36 John Cerutti	.10	.05
☐ 37 Mike Kingery	.10	.05
☐ 38 Mark Eichhorn	.10	.05
☐ 39 Scott Bankhead	.10	.05
☐ 40 Bo Jackson	.75	.35
☐ 41 Greg Mathews	.10	.05
☐ 42 Eric King	.10	.05
☐ 43 Kal Daniels	.10	.05
☐ 44 Calvin Schiraldi	.10	.05
☐ 45 Mickey Brantley	.10	.05
☐ 46 Tri-Stars	.75	.35
Willie Mays		
Pete Rose		
Fred Lynn		
☐ 47 Tri-Stars	.50	.23
Tom Seaver		
Fernando Valenzuela		
Dwight Gooden		
☐ 48 Big Six	1.00	.45
Eddie Murray		
Lou Whitaker		
Dave Righetti		
Steve Sax		
Cal Ripken		
Darryl Strawberry		
☐ 49 Kevin Mitchell	.35	.16
☐ 50 Mike Diaz	.10	.05

1986 Sportflics Decade Greats

This set of 75 three-phase "animated" standard-size cards was produced by Sportflics and manufactured by Opti-Graphics of Arlington, Texas. The cards feature both sepia (players of the '30s and '40s) and full color cards. The concept of the set was that the best players at each position for each decade (from the '30s to the '80s) were chosen. The bios were written by Les Woodcock. Also included with the set in the specially designed collector box are 51 trivia cards with historical questions about the six decades of All-Star games. Sample cards of Dwight Gooden and Mel Ott, which are blank backed except for being stamped "Sample" on the back, also exist.

	MINT	NRMT
COMPLETE SET (75)	20.00	9.00
COMPLETE FACT.SET (75)	20.00	9.00
COMMON CARD (1-75)	.10	.05
☐ 1 Babe Ruth	3.00	1.35
☐ 2 Jimmie Foxx	.60	.25
☐ 3 Lefty Grove	.60	.25
☐ 4 Hank Greenberg	.60	.25
☐ 5 Al Simmons	.25	.11
☐ 6 Carl Hubbell	.40	.18
☐ 7 Joe Cronin	.25	.11
☐ 8 Mel Ott	.60	.25
☐ 9 Lefty Gomez	.60	.25
☐ 10 Lou Gehrig	3.00	1.35
(Best '30s Player)		
☐ 11 Pie Traynor	.40	.18
☐ 12 Charlie Gehringer	.40	.18
☐ 13 Best '30s Catchers	.25	.11
Bill Dickey		
Mickey Cochrane		
Gabby Hartnett		
☐ 14 Best '30s Pitchers	.40	.18
Dizzy Dean		
Red Ruffing		
Paul Derringer		
☐ 15 Best '30s Outfielders	.25	.11
Paul Waner		
Joe Medwick		
Earl Averill		
☐ 16 Bob Feller	.75	.35
☐ 17 Lou Boudreau	.40	.18
☐ 18 Enos Slaughter	.40	.18
☐ 19 Hal Newhouser	.40	.18
☐ 20 Joe DiMaggio	3.00	1.35
☐ 21 Pee Wee Reese	.60	.25
☐ 22 Phil Rizzuto	.60	.25
☐ 23 Ernie Lombardi	.25	.11
☐ 24 Best '40s Infielders	.40	.18
Johnny Mize		
Joe Gordon		
George Kell		
☐ 25 Ted Williams	3.00	1.35
(Best '40s Player)		
☐ 26 Mickey Mantle	4.00	1.80
☐ 27 Warren Spahn	.60	.25
☐ 28 Jackie Robinson	1.50	.70
☐ 29 Ernie Banks	.60	.25
☐ 30 Stan Musial	1.00	.45
(Best '50s Player)		
☐ 31 Yogi Berra	.75	.35
☐ 32 Duke Snider	.75	.35
☐ 33 Roy Campanella	1.00	.45
☐ 34 Eddie Mathews	.60	.25
☐ 35 Ralph Kiner	.40	.18
☐ 36 Early Wynn	.40	.18
☐ 37 Double Play Duo	.60	.25
Nellie Fox		
Luis Aparicio		
☐ 38 Best '50s First Base	.10	.05
Gil Hodges		
Ted Kluszewski		
Mickey Vernon		
☐ 39 Best '50s Pitchers	.25	.11
Bob Lemon		
Don Newcombe		
Robin Roberts		
☐ 40 Henry Aaron	1.50	.70
☐ 41 Frank Robinson	.40	.18
☐ 42 Bob Gibson	.40	.18
☐ 43 Roberto Clemente	2.00	.90
☐ 44 Whitey Ford	.60	.25
☐ 45 Brooks Robinson	.75	.35
☐ 46 Juan Marichal	.40	.18
☐ 47 Carl Yastrzemski	.75	.35
☐ 48 Best '60s First Base	.40	.18
Willie McCovey		
Harmon Killebrew		
Orlando Cepeda		
☐ 49 Best '60s Catchers	.10	.05
Joe Torre		
Elston Howard		
Bill Freehan		
☐ 50 Willie Mays	1.50	.70
(Best '50s Player)		
☐ 51 Best '60s Outfielders	.40	.18
Al Kaline		
Tony Oliva		
Billy Williams		
☐ 52 Tom Seaver	.75	.35
☐ 53 Reggie Jackson	.75	.35
☐ 54 Steve Carlton	.60	.25
☐ 55 Mike Schmidt	1.50	.70
☐ 56 Joe Morgan	.60	.25
☐ 57 Jim Rice	.25	.11
☐ 58 Jim Palmer	.60	.25
☐ 59 Lou Brock	.40	.18
☐ 60 Pete Rose	1.50	.70
(Best '70s Player)		
☐ 61 Steve Garvey	.40	.18
☐ 62 Best '70s Catchers	.60	.25
Thurman Munson		
Carlton Fisk		
Ted Simmons		
☐ 63 Best '70s Pitchers	1.50	.70
Vida Blue		
Catfish Hunter		
Nolan Ryan		
☐ 64 George Brett	2.00	.90
☐ 65 Don Mattingly	2.50	1.10
☐ 66 Fernando Valenzuela	.10	.05
☐ 67 Dale Murphy	.60	.25
☐ 68 Wade Boggs	.75	.35
☐ 69 Rickey Henderson	.75	.35
☐ 70 Eddie Murray	.75	.35
(Best '80s Player)		
☐ 71 Ron Guidry	.10	.05
☐ 72 Best '80s Catchers	.25	.11
Gary Carter		
Lance Parrish		
Tony Pena		
☐ 73 Best '80s Infielders	2.00	.90
Cal Ripken		
Lou Whitaker		
Robin Yount		
☐ 74 Best '80s Outfielders	.40	.18
Pedro Guerrero		
Tim Raines		
Dave Winfield		
☐ 75 Dwight Gooden	.60	.25

1987 Sportflics

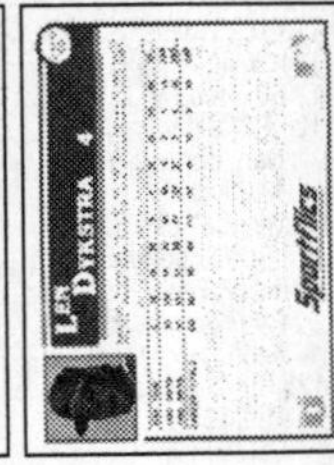

This 200-card standard-size color set was produced by Sportflics and again features three sequence action pictures on each card. Also included with the cards were 136 small team logo and trivia cards. There are 165 individual players, 20 Tri-Stars (the top three players in each league at each position), and 15 other miscellaneous multi-player cards. The cards feature a red border on the front. A full-color face shot of the player is printed on the back of the card. Cards are numbered on the back in the upper right corner. The cards in the factory-collated sets are copyrighted 1986, while the cards in the wax packs are copyrighted 1987 or show no copyright year on the back. Cards from wax packs with 1987 copyright are 1-35, 41-75, 81-115, 121-155, and 161-195; the rest of the numbers (when taken from wax packs) are found without a copyright year.

	MINT	NRMT
COMPLETE SET (200)	25.00	11.00
COMPLETE FACT.SET (200)	30.00	13.50
COMMON CARD (1-200)	.10	.05
☐ 1 Don Mattingly	1.50	.70
☐ 2 Wade Boggs	.50	.23
☐ 3 Dale Murphy	.40	.18
☐ 4 Rickey Henderson	.50	.23
☐ 5 George Brett	1.25	.55
☐ 6 Eddie Murray	.75	.35
☐ 7 Kirby Puckett	1.50	.70
☐ 8 Ryne Sandberg	1.25	.55

☐ 9 Cal Ripken	3.00	1.35
☐ 10 Roger Clemens	1.50	.70
☐ 11 Ted Higuera	.10	.05
☐ 12 Steve Sax	.10	.05
☐ 13 Chris Brown	.10	.05
☐ 14 Jesse Barfield	.10	.05
☐ 15 Kent Hrbek	.20	.09
☐ 16 Robin Yount	.40	.18
☐ 17 Glenn Davis	.10	.05
☐ 18 Hubie Brooks	.10	.05
☐ 19 Mike Scott	.10	.05
☐ 20 Darryl Strawberry	.30	.14
☐ 21 Alvin Davis	.10	.05
☐ 22 Eric Davis	.20	.09
☐ 23 Danny Tartabull	.10	.05
☐ 24A Cory Snyder ERR '86 (Photo on front is Pat Tabler)	1.00	.45
☐ 24B Cory Snyder ERR '87 (Photos on front and back are Pat Tabler)	.50	.23
☐ 24C Cory Snyder COR '86	.50	.23
☐ 25 Pete Rose	1.00	.45
☐ 26 Wally Joyner	.60	.25
☐ 27 Pedro Guerrero	.10	.05
☐ 28 Tom Seaver	.75	.35
☐ 29 Bob Knepper	.10	.05
☐ 30 Mike Schmidt	.75	.35
☐ 31 Tony Gwynn	2.00	.90
☐ 32 Don Slaught	.10	.05
☐ 33 Todd Worrell	.20	.09
☐ 34 Tim Raines	.20	.09
☐ 35 Dave Parker	.20	.09
☐ 36 Bob Ojeda	.10	.05
☐ 37 Pete Incaviglia	.20	.09
☐ 38 Bruce Hurst	.10	.05
☐ 39 Bobby Witt	.30	.14
☐ 40 Steve Garvey	.20	.09
☐ 41 Dave Winfield	.40	.18
☐ 42 Jose Cruz	.20	.09
☐ 43 Orel Hershiser	.20	.09
☐ 44 Reggie Jackson	.75	.35
☐ 45 Chili Davis	.20	.09
☐ 46 Robby Thompson	.20	.09
☐ 47 Dennis Boyd	.10	.05
☐ 48 Kirk Gibson	.20	.09
☐ 49 Fred Lynn	.20	.09
☐ 50 Gary Carter	.30	.14
☐ 51 George Bell	.10	.05
☐ 52 Pete O'Brien	.10	.05
☐ 53 Ron Darling	.10	.05
☐ 54 Paul Molitor	1.00	.45
☐ 55 Mike Pagliarulo	.10	.05
☐ 56 Mike Boddicker	.10	.05
☐ 57 Dave Righetti	.10	.05
☐ 58 Len Dykstra	.30	.14
☐ 59 Mike Witt	.10	.05
☐ 60 Tony Bernazard	.10	.05
☐ 61 John Kruk	.40	.18
☐ 62 Mike Krukow	.10	.05
☐ 63 Sid Fernandez	.10	.05
☐ 64 Gary Gaetti	.20	.09
☐ 65 Vince Coleman	.10	.05
☐ 66 Pat Tabler	.10	.05
☐ 67 Mike Scioscia	.10	.05
☐ 68 Scott Garrelts	.10	.05
☐ 69 Brett Butler	.20	.09
☐ 70 Bill Buckner	.20	.09
☐ 71A Dennis Rasmussen ERR '86 copyright (Photo on back is John Montefusco)	.50	.23
☐ 71B Dennis Rasmussen COR '87 copyright (Photo with mustache)	.20	.09
☐ 72 Tim Wallach	.10	.05
☐ 73 Bob Horner	.10	.05
☐ 74 Willie McGee	.20	.09
☐ 75 Tri-Stars: Don Mattingly, Wally Joyner, Eddie Murray	.60	.25
☐ 76A Jesse Orosco COR '86 copyright	.20	.09
☐ 76B Jesse Orosco ERR '87 copyright (Number on back is 96)	.10	.05
☐ 77 Tri-Stars: Todd Worrell, Jeff Reardon, Dave Smith	.20	.09
☐ 78 Candy Maldonado	.10	.05
☐ 79 Tri-Stars: Ozzie Smith, Hubie Brooks, Shawon Dunston	.30	.14
☐ 80 Tri-Stars: George Bell, Jose Canseco, Jim Rice	.40	.18
☐ 81 Bert Blyleven	.20	.09
☐ 82 Mike Marshall	.10	.05
☐ 83 Ron Guidry	.20	.09
☐ 84 Julio Franco	.20	.09
☐ 85 Willie Wilson	.20	.09
☐ 86 Lee Lacy	.10	.05
☐ 87 Jack Morris	.20	.09
☐ 88 Ray Knight	.10	.05
☐ 89 Phil Bradley	.10	.05
☐ 90 Jose Canseco	1.00	.45
☐ 91 Gary Ward	.10	.05
☐ 92 Mike Easler	.10	.05
☐ 93 Tony Pena	.10	.05
☐ 94 Dave Smith	.10	.05
☐ 95 Will Clark	1.00	.45
☐ 96 Lloyd Moseby (See also 76B)	.10	.05
☐ 97 Jim Rice	.20	.09
☐ 98 Shawon Dunston	.10	.05
☐ 99 Don Sutton	.40	.18
☐ 100 Dwight Gooden	.30	.14
☐ 101 Lance Parrish	.10	.05
☐ 102 Mark Langston	.10	.05
☐ 103 Floyd Youmans	.10	.05
☐ 104 Lee Smith	.30	.14
☐ 105 Willie Hernandez	.10	.05
☐ 106 Doug DeCinces	.10	.05
☐ 107 Ken Schrom	.10	.05
☐ 108 Don Carman	.10	.05
☐ 109 Brook Jacoby	.10	.05
☐ 110 Steve Bedrosian	.10	.05
☐ 111 Tri-Stars: Roger Clemens, Jack Morris, Ted Higuera	.40	.18
☐ 112 Tri-Stars: Marty Barrett, Tony Bernazard, Lou Whitaker	.30	.14
☐ 113 Tri-Stars: Cal Ripken, Scott Fletcher, Tony Fernandez	2.00	.90
☐ 114 Tri-Stars: Wade Boggs, George Brett, Gary Gaetti	.75	.35
☐ 115 Tri-Stars: Mike Schmidt, Chris Brown, Tim Wallach	.40	.18
☐ 116 Tri-Stars: Ryne Sandberg, Johnny Ray, Bill Doran	.40	.18
☐ 117 Tri-Stars: Dave Parker, Tony Gwynn, Kevin Bass	.75	.35
☐ 118 Big Six Rookies: Ty Gainey, Terry Steinbach, Dave Clark, Pat Dodson, Phil Lombardi, Benito Santiago	.30	.14
☐ 119 Hi-Lite Tri-Stars: Dave Righetti, Fernando Valenzuela, Mike Scott	.20	.09
☐ 120 Tri-Stars: Fernando Valenzuela, Mike Scott, Dwight Gooden	.30	.14
☐ 121 Johnny Ray	.10	.05
☐ 122 Keith Moreland	.10	.05
☐ 123 Juan Samuel	.10	.05
☐ 124 Wally Backman	.10	.05
☐ 125 Nolan Ryan	3.00	1.35
☐ 126 Greg A. Harris	.10	.05
☐ 127 Kirk McCaskill	.10	.05
☐ 128 Dwight Evans	.20	.09
☐ 129 Rick Rhoden	.10	.05
☐ 130 Bill Madlock	.20	.09
☐ 131 Oddibe McDowell	.10	.05
☐ 132 Darrell Evans	.20	.09
☐ 133 Keith Hernandez	.20	.09
☐ 134 Tom Brunansky	.10	.05
☐ 135 Kevin McReynolds	.10	.05
☐ 136 Scott Fletcher	.10	.05
☐ 137 Lou Whitaker	.20	.09
☐ 138 Carney Lansford	.20	.09
☐ 139 Andre Dawson	.40	.18
☐ 140 Carlton Fisk	.40	.18
☐ 141 Buddy Bell	.20	.09
☐ 142 Ozzie Smith	1.25	.55
☐ 143 Dan Pasqua	.10	.05
☐ 144 Kevin Mitchell	.30	.14
☐ 145 Bret Saberhagen	.20	.09
☐ 146 Charlie Kerfeld	.10	.05
☐ 147 Phil Niekro	.40	.18
☐ 148 John Candelaria	.10	.05
☐ 149 Rich Gedman	.10	.05
☐ 150 Fernando Valenzuela	.20	.09
☐ 151 Tri-Stars: Gary Carter, Mike Scioscia, Tony Pena	.30	.14
☐ 152 Tri-Stars: Tim Raines, Jose Cruz, Vince Coleman	.30	.14
☐ 153 Tri-Stars: Jesse Barfield, Harold Baines, Dave Winfield	.30	.14
☐ 154 Tri-Stars: Lance Parrish, Don Slaught, Rich Gedman	.20	.09
☐ 155 Tri-Stars: Dale Murphy, Kevin McReynolds, Eric Davis	.30	.14
☐ 156 Hi-Lite Tri-Stars: Don Sutton, Mike Schmidt, Jim Deshaies	.40	.18
☐ 157 Speedburners: Rickey Henderson, John Cangelosi, Gary Pettis	.30	.14
☐ 158 Big Six Rookies: Randy Asadoor, Casey Candaele, Kevin Seitzer, Rafael Palmeiro, Tim Pyznarski, Dave Cochrane	2.00	.90
☐ 159 Big Six: Don Mattingly, Rickey Henderson, Roger Clemens, Dale Murphy, Eddie Murray, Dwight Gooden	1.00	.45
☐ 160 Roger McDowell	.10	.05
☐ 161 Brian Downing	.10	.05
☐ 162 Bill Doran	.10	.05
☐ 163 Don Baylor	.20	.09
☐ 164A Alfredo Griffin ERR (No uniform number on card back) '87	.20	.09
☐ 164B Alfredo Griffin COR '86	.20	.09
☐ 165 Don Aase	.10	.05
☐ 166 Glenn Wilson	.10	.05
☐ 167 Dan Quisenberry	.10	.05
☐ 168 Frank White	.20	.09
☐ 169 Cecil Cooper	.20	.09
☐ 170 Jody Davis	.10	.05
☐ 171 Harold Baines	.20	.09
☐ 172 Rob Deer	.10	.05
☐ 173 John Tudor	.10	.05
☐ 174 Larry Parrish	.10	.05
☐ 175 Kevin Bass	.10	.05
☐ 176 Joe Carter	.40	.18
☐ 177 Mitch Webster	.10	.05
☐ 178 Dave Kingman	.20	.09
☐ 179 Jim Presley	.10	.05
☐ 180 Mel Hall	.10	.05
☐ 181 Shane Rawley	.10	.05
☐ 182 Marty Barrett	.10	.05
☐ 183 Damaso Garcia	.10	.05
☐ 184 Bobby Grich	.10	.05
☐ 185 Leon Durham	.10	.05
☐ 186 Ozzie Guillen	.10	.05
☐ 187 Tony Fernandez	.10	.05
☐ 188 Alan Trammell	.30	.14
☐ 189 Jim Clancy	.10	.05
☐ 190 Bo Jackson	.50	.23
☐ 191 Bob Forsch	.10	.05
☐ 192 John Franco	.20	.09
☐ 193 Von Hayes	.10	.05
☐ 194 Tri-Stars: Don Aase, Dave Righetti, Mark Eichhorn	.20	.09
☐ 195 Tri-Stars: Keith Hernandez, Will Clark, Glenn Davis	.75	.35

	MINT	NRMT
☐ 196 Hi-Lite Tri-Stars Roger Clemens Joe Cowley Bob Horner	.40	.18
☐ 197 Big Six George Brett Hubie Brooks Tony Gwynn Ryne Sandberg Tim Raines Wade Boggs	1.00	.45
☐ 198 Tri-Stars Kirby Puckett Rickey Henderson Fred Lynn	1.00	.45
☐ 199 Speedburners Tim Raines Vince Coleman Eric Davis	.30	.14
☐ 200 Steve Carlton	.60	.25

1987 Sportflics Dealer Panels

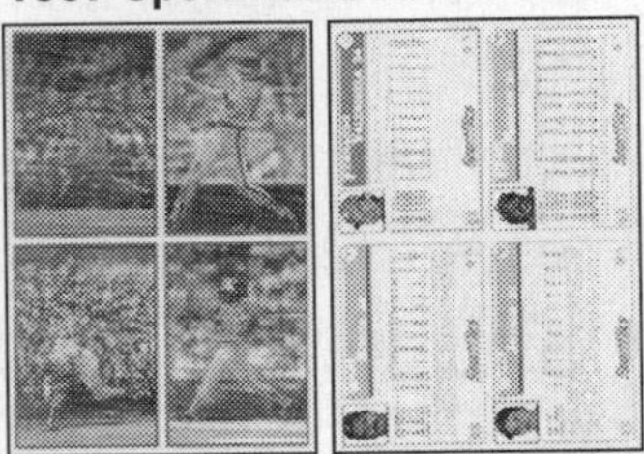

These "Magic Motion" card panels of four were issued only to dealers who were ordering other Sportflics product in quantity. If cut into individual cards, the interior white borders will be slightly narrower than the regular issue Sportflics since the panels of four measure a shade under 4 7/8" by 6 7/8". The cards have a 1986 copyright on the back same as the factory collated sets. Other than the slight difference in size, these cards are essentially styled the same as the regular issue of 1987 Sportflics. This set of sixteen top players was accompanied by the inclusion of four smaller panels of four team logo/team fact cards. The 16 small team cards correspond directly to the 16 players in the sets. The checklist below prices the panels and gives the card number for each player, which is the same as the player's card number in the Sportflics regular set.

	MINT	NRMT
COMPLETE SET (4)	28.00	12.50
COMMON PANEL (1-4)	5.00	2.20
☐ 1 Don Mattingly 1 Roger Clemens 10 Mike Schmidt 30 Tim Raines 34	10.00	4.50
☐ 2 Wade Boggs 2 Eddie Murray 6 Wally Joyner 26 Fernando Valenzuela 150	5.00	2.20
☐ 3 Dale Murphy 3 Tony Gwynn 31 Jim Rice 97 Keith Hernandez 133	6.00	2.70
☐ 4 Rickey Henderson 4 George Brett 5 Cal Ripken 9 Dwight Gooden 100	12.00	5.50

1987 Sportflics Rookies I

These "Magic Motion" cards were issued as a series of 25 cards packaged in its own complete set box, along with 17 trivia cards. Cards are standard sized. The three front photos show the player in two action poses and one portrait pose. The card backs also provide a full-color photo (1 3/8" by 2 1/4") of the player as well as the usual statistics and biographical notes. The front photos are framed by a wide, round-cornered, red border and have the player's name and uniform number at the bottom. The cards in the set are numbered essentially in alphabetical order by player's name.

	MINT	NRMT
COMPLETE SET (25)	6.00	2.70
COMPLETE FACT.SET (25)	6.00	2.70
COMMON CARD (1-25)	.10	.05
☐ 1 Eric Bell	.10	.05
☐ 2 Chris Bosio	.20	.09
☐ 3 Bob Brower	.10	.05
☐ 4 Jerry Browne	.10	.05
☐ 5 Ellis Burks	1.00	.45
☐ 6 Casey Candaele	.10	.05
☐ 7 Ken Gerhart	.10	.05
☐ 8 Mike Greenwell	.20	.09
☐ 9 Stan Jefferson	.10	.05
☐ 10 Dave Magadan	.10	.05
☐ 11 Joe Magrane	.10	.05
☐ 12 Fred McGriff	1.50	.70
☐ 13 Mark McGwire	1.50	.70
☐ 14 Mark McLemore	.20	.09
☐ 15 Jeff Musselman	.10	.05
☐ 16 Matt Nokes	.10	.05
☐ 17 Paul O'Neill	.50	.23
☐ 18 Luis Polonia	.20	.09
☐ 19 Benito Santiago	.20	.09
☐ 20 Kevin Seitzer	.50	.23
☐ 21 John Smiley	.20	.09
☐ 22 Terry Steinbach	.50	.23
☐ 23 B.J. Surhoff	.60	.25
☐ 24 Devon White	.50	.23
☐ 25 Matt Williams	2.00	.90

1987 Sportflics Rookies II

These "Magic Motion" cards were issued as a series of 25 cards packaged in its own complete set box along with 17 trivia cards. Cards are standard sized. In this second set the card numbering begins with number 26. The three front photos show the player in two action poses and one portrait pose. The card backs also provide a full-color photo (approximately 1 3/8" by 2 1/4") of the player as well as the usual statistics and biographical notes. The front photos are framed by a wide, round-cornered, red border and have the player's name and uniform number at the bottom.

	MINT	NRMT
COMPLETE SET (25)	5.00	2.20
COMPLETE FACT.SET (25)	5.00	2.20
COMMON CARD (26-50)	.10	.05
☐ 26 DeWayne Buice	.10	.05
☐ 27 Willie Fraser	.10	.05
☐ 28 Billy Ripken	.10	.05
☐ 29 Mike Henneman	.20	.09
☐ 30 Shawn Hillegas	.10	.05
☐ 31 Shane Mack	.10	.05
☐ 32 Rafael Palmeiro	2.50	1.10
☐ 33 Mike Jackson	.10	.05
☐ 34 Gene Larkin	.10	.05
☐ 35 Jimmy Jones	.10	.05
☐ 36 Gerald Young	.10	.05
☐ 37 Ken Caminiti	2.50	1.10
☐ 38 Sam Horn	.10	.05
☐ 39 David Cone	1.50	.70
☐ 40 Mike Dunne	.10	.05
☐ 41 Ken Williams	.10	.05
☐ 42 John Morris	.10	.05
☐ 43 Jim Lindeman	.10	.05
☐ 44 Mike Stanley	.30	.14
☐ 45 Les Straker	.10	.05
☐ 46 Jeff M. Robinson	.10	.05
☐ 47 Todd Benzinger	.10	.05
☐ 48 Jeff Blauser	.40	.18
☐ 49 John Marzano	.10	.05
☐ 50 Keith Miller	.10	.05

1987 Sportflics Rookie Packs

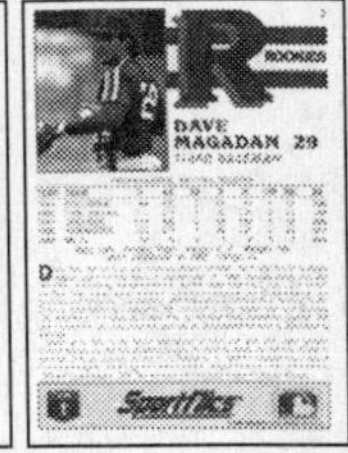

This two pack-set consists of ten "rookie" players and two trivia cards. Each of the two different packs had half the set and the outside of the wrapper told which cards were inside. Each card below has the pack number indicated by P1 or P2. The cards measure the standard size. Dealers received one rookie pack with every Team Preview set they ordered. The card backs also feature a full-color small photo of the player.

	MINT	NRMT
COMPLETE SET (10)	8.00	3.60
COMMON CARD (1-10)	.40	.18
☐ 1 Terry Steinbach P2	.75	.35
☐ 2 Rafael Palmeiro P1	4.00	1.80
☐ 3 Dave Magadan P2	.60	.25
☐ 4 Marvin Freeman P2	.40	.18
☐ 5 Brick Smith P2	.40	.18
☐ 6 B.J. Surhoff P1	1.00	.45
☐ 7 John Smiley P1	.60	.25
☐ 8 Alonzo Powell P2	.40	.18
☐ 9 Benito Santiago P1	.75	.35
☐ 10 Devon White P1	1.00	.45

1987 Sportflics Superstar Discs

These 18 discs, measuring approximately 4 5/8" in diameter, featured leading players. The player's photo was surrounded by a red border. Player information is located on the back

	MINT	EXC
COMPLETE SET (18)	40.00	18.00
COMMON DISC (1-18)	1.00	.45
☐ 1 Joe Carter	2.00	.90
☐ 2 Mike Scott	1.00	.45
☐ 3 Ryne Sandberg	5.00	2.20
☐ 4 Mike Schmidt	3.00	1.35
☐ 5 Dale Murphy	2.50	1.10
☐ 6 Fernando Valenzuela	1.50	.70
☐ 7 Tony Gwynn	6.00	2.70
☐ 8 Cal Ripken Jr.	10.00	4.50
☐ 9 Gary Carter	3.00	1.35
☐ 10 Cory Snyder	1.00	.45
☐ 11 Kirby Puckett	5.00	2.20
☐ 12 George Brett	5.00	2.20
☐ 13 Keith Hernandez	1.50	.70
☐ 14 Rickey Henderson	3.00	1.35
☐ 15 Tim Raines	1.50	.70
☐ 16 Bo Jackson	1.50	.70
☐ 17 Pete Rose	5.00	2.20
☐ 18 Eric Davis	1.50	.70

1987 Sportflics Team Preview

This 26-card standard-size set features a card for each Major League team. Each card shows 12 different players on that team via four "Magic Motion" trios. The narrative on the back gives Outlook, Newcomers to Watch, and Summary for each team. The list of players appearing on the front is given at the bottom of the reverse of each card. The was distributed as a complete set in its own box along with 26 team logo trivia cards measuring approximately 1 3/4" by 2".

	MINT	NRMT
COMPLETE SET (26)	10.00	4.50
COMMON CARD (1-26)	.30	.14

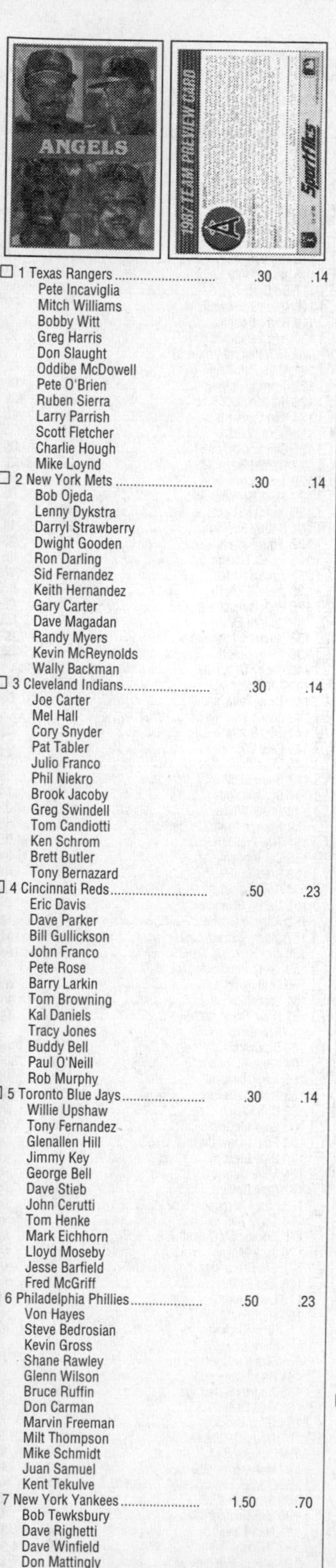

□ 1 Texas Rangers .30 .14
Pete Incaviglia
Mitch Williams
Bobby Witt
Greg Harris
Don Slaught
Oddibe McDowell
Pete O'Brien
Ruben Sierra
Larry Parrish
Scott Fletcher
Charlie Hough
Mike Loynd

□ 2 New York Mets .30 .14
Bob Ojeda
Lenny Dykstra
Darryl Strawberry
Dwight Gooden
Ron Darling
Sid Fernandez
Keith Hernandez
Gary Carter
Dave Magadan
Randy Myers
Kevin McReynolds
Wally Backman

□ 3 Cleveland Indians .30 .14
Joe Carter
Mel Hall
Cory Snyder
Pat Tabler
Julio Franco
Phil Niekro
Brook Jacoby
Greg Swindell
Tom Candiotti
Ken Schrom
Brett Butler
Tony Bernazard

□ 4 Cincinnati Reds .50 .23
Eric Davis
Dave Parker
Bill Gullickson
John Franco
Pete Rose
Barry Larkin
Tom Browning
Kal Daniels
Tracy Jones
Buddy Bell
Paul O'Neill
Rob Murphy

□ 5 Toronto Blue Jays .30 .14
Willie Upshaw
Tony Fernandez
Glenallen Hill
Jimmy Key
George Bell
Dave Stieb
John Cerutti
Tom Henke
Mark Eichhorn
Lloyd Moseby
Jesse Barfield
Fred McGriff

□ 6 Philadelphia Phillies .50 .23
Von Hayes
Steve Bedrosian
Kevin Gross
Shane Rawley
Glenn Wilson
Bruce Ruffin
Don Carman
Marvin Freeman
Milt Thompson
Mike Schmidt
Juan Samuel
Kent Tekulve

□ 7 New York Yankees 1.50 .70
Bob Tewksbury
Dave Righetti
Dave Winfield
Don Mattingly
Dennis Rasmussen
Mike Pagliarulo
Rickey Henderson
Dan Pasqua
Joel Skinner
Willie Randolph
Phil Lombardi
Rick Rhoden

□ 8 Houston Astros 1.50 .70
Glenn Davis
Bob Knepper
Kevin Bass
Nolan Ryan
Jose Cruz
Ty Gainey
Mike Scott
Charlie Kerfeld
Dave Smith
Bill Doran
Robby Wine
Jim Deshaies

□ 9 Boston Red Sox .50 .23
Wade Boggs
Roger Clemens
Dennis Boyd
Dwight Evans
Pat Dodson
Dave Henderson
Bruce Hurst
Don Baylor
Marty Barrett
Calvin Schiraldi
Mike Greenwell
Jim Rice

□ 10 San Francisco Giants .50 .23
Chris Brown
Mike Krukow
Will Clark
Chili Davis
Robby Thompson
Kelly Downs
Jeff Leonard
Terry Mulholland
Bob Brenly
Scott Garrelts
Candy Maldonado
Mark Grant

□ 11 California Angels .30 .14
Don Sutton
Mike Witt
Donnie Moore
Wally Joyner
John Candelaria
Doug DeCinces
Brian Downing
Kirk McCaskill
Devon White
Gary Pettis
Ruppert Jones
Darrell Miller

□ 12 St. Louis Cardinals .50 .23
Terry Pendleton
Tom Herr
Todd Worrell
Jack Clark
John Tudor
Bob Forsch
Danny Cox
Vince Coleman
Willie McGee
Ozzie Smith
Joe Magrane
Andy Van Slyke

□ 13 Kansas City Royals 1.00 .45
Bo Jackson
Danny Tartabull
George Brett
Mark Gubicza
Bret Saberhagen
Willie Wilson
Kevin Seitzer
Frank White
Charlie Leibrandt
Dan Quisenberry
Hal McRae
Lonnie Smith

□ 14 Los Angeles Dodgers .30 .14
Mike Scioscia
Steve Sax
Fernando Valenzuela
Reggie Williams
Mike Marshall
Mariano Duncan
Orel Hershiser
Franklin Stubbs
Matt Young
Pedro Guerrero
Jose Gonzalez
Ralph Bryant

□ 15 Detroit Tigers .50 .23
Lou Whitaker
Dan Petry
Alan Trammell
Chet Lemon
Jack Morris
Frank Tanana
Darnell Coles
Darrell Evans
Dwight Lowry
Kirk Gibson
Willie Hernandez
Eric King

□ 16 San Diego Padres .50 .23
Tony Gwynn
John Kruk
Kevin Mitchell
Lance McCullers
Shane Mack
Craig Lefferts
Steve Garvey
Benny Santiago
Randy Asadoor
Andy Hawkins
Jim Jones
Ed Wojna

□ 17 Minnesota Twins 1.00 .45
Gary Gaetti
Roy Smalley
Kirby Puckett
Frank Viola
Mark Salas
Bert Blyleven
Tom Brunansky
Kent Hrbek
Joe Klink
Steve Lombardozzi
Greg Gagne
Jeff Reardon

□ 18 Pittsburgh Pirates .50 .23
John Smiley
Sid Bream
Mike Diaz
Tony Pena
Johnny Ray
Jim Morrison
R.J. Reynolds
Barry Bonds
Joe Orsulak
Bobby Bonilla
Bob Patterson
Brian Fisher

□ 19 Milwaukee Brewers .50 .23
Ernest Riles
Rob Deer
Billy Jo Robidoux
Dan Plesac
Dale Sveum
Teddy Higuera
Robin Yount
Glenn Braggs
B.J. Surhoff
Paul Molitor
Juan Nieves
Tim Pyznarski

□ 20 Montreal Expos .30 .14
Floyd Youmans
Tim Burke
Casey Candaele
Randy St. Claire
Tim Wallach
Alonzo Powell
Mitch Webster
Mike Fitzgerald
Dave Collins
Andres Galarraga
Hubie Brooks
Billy More

□ 21 Baltimore Orioles 2.00 .90
Don Aase
Mike Boddicker
Eric Bell
Larry Sheets
Jim Traber
Terry Kennedy
Fred Lynn
Cal Ripken Jr.
Eddie Murray
Lee Lacy
Ray Knight
Ken Gerhart

□ 22 Chicago Cubs 1.50 .70
Ryne Sandberg
Leon Durham
Rafael Palmeiro
Jody Davis
Keith Moreland

	MINT	NRMT
Scott Sanderson		
Shawon Dunston		
Lee Smith		
Jerry Mumphrey		
Dave Martinez		
Greg Maddux		
Dennis Eckersley		
☐ 23 Oakland Athletics	.50	.23
Terry Steinbach		
Mike Davis		
Carney Lansford		
Jose Canseco		
Mark McGwire		
Rob Nelson		
Jose Rijo		
Dwayne Murphy		
Curt Young		
Tony Phillips		
Alfredo Griffin		
Reggie Jackson		
☐ 24 Atlanta Braves	.30	.14
Rick Mahler		
Ken Oberkfell		
Gene Garber		
Andres Thomas		
Dale Murphy		
Ken Griffey		
David Palmer		
Paul Assenmacher		
Dion James		
Zane Smith		
Tom Glavine		
Glenn Hubbard		
☐ 25 Seattle Mariners	.30	.14
Dave Valle		
Donell Nixon		
Scott Bradley		
Ken Phelps		
Mike Moore		
Mark Langston		
Alvin Davis		
Mickey Brantley		
Scott Bankhead		
Jim Presley		
Phil Bradley		
Steve Fireovid		
☐ 26 Chicago White Sox	.30	.14
Carlton Fisk		
Harold Baines		
Joe Cowley		
John Cangelosi		
Ozzie Guillen		
Bobby Thigpen		
Greg Walker		
Ron Hassey		
Bob James		
Ron Karkovice		
Dave Cochrane		
Russ Morman		

1988 Sportflics

This 225-card standard-size full-color set was produced by Sportflics and again features three sequence action pictures on each card. There are 219 individual players, three Highlights trios, and three Rookie Prospect trio cards. The cards feature a red border on the front. A full-color action picture of the player is printed on the back of the card.

	MINT	NRMT
COMPLETE SET (225)	30.00	13.50
COMPLETE FACT.SET (225)	30.00	13.50
COMMON CARD (1-225)	.10	.05

	MINT	NRMT
☐ 1 Don Mattingly	1.50	.70
☐ 2 Tim Raines	.20	.09
☐ 3 Andre Dawson	.40	.18
☐ 4 George Bell	.10	.05
☐ 5 Joe Carter	.30	.14
☐ 6 Matt Nokes	.10	.05
☐ 7 Dave Winfield	.40	.18
☐ 8 Kirby Puckett	1.50	.70
☐ 9 Will Clark	.50	.23
☐ 10 Eric Davis	.20	.09
☐ 11 Rickey Henderson	.50	.23
☐ 12 Ryne Sandberg	1.25	.55
☐ 13 Jesse Barfield UER (Misspelled Jessie on card back)	.10	.05
☐ 14 Ozzie Guillen	.10	.05
☐ 15 Bret Saberhagen	.10	.05
☐ 16 Tony Gwynn	2.00	.90
☐ 17 Kevin Seitzer	.20	.09
☐ 18 Jack Clark	.20	.09
☐ 19 Danny Tartabull	.10	.05
☐ 20 Ted Higuera	.10	.05
☐ 21 Charlie Leibrandt UER (Misspelled Liebrandt on card front)	.10	.05
☐ 22 Benito Santiago	.10	.05
☐ 23 Fred Lynn	.10	.05
☐ 24 Robby Thompson	.10	.05
☐ 25 Alan Trammell	.30	.14
☐ 26 Tony Fernandez	.10	.05
☐ 27 Rick Sutcliffe	.10	.05
☐ 28 Gary Carter	.30	.14
☐ 29 Cory Snyder	.10	.05
☐ 30 Lou Whitaker	.20	.09
☐ 31 Keith Hernandez	.20	.09
☐ 32 Mike Witt	.10	.05
☐ 33 Harold Baines	.20	.09
☐ 34 Robin Yount	.40	.18
☐ 35 Mike Schmidt	.75	.35
☐ 36 Dion James	.10	.05
☐ 37 Tom Candiotti	.10	.05
☐ 38 Tracy Jones	.10	.05
☐ 39 Nolan Ryan	3.00	1.35
☐ 40 Fernando Valenzuela	.20	.09
☐ 41 Vance Law	.10	.05
☐ 42 Roger McDowell	.10	.05
☐ 43 Carlton Fisk	.40	.18
☐ 44 Scott Garrelts	.10	.05
☐ 45 Lee Guetterman	.10	.05
☐ 46 Mark Langston	.10	.05
☐ 47 Willie Randolph	.20	.09
☐ 48 Bill Doran	.10	.05
☐ 49 Larry Parrish	.10	.05
☐ 50 Wade Boggs	.50	.23
☐ 51 Shane Rawley	.10	.05
☐ 52 Alvin Davis	.10	.05
☐ 53 Jeff Reardon	.20	.09
☐ 54 Jim Presley	.10	.05
☐ 55 Kevin Bass	.10	.05
☐ 56 Kevin McReynolds	.10	.05
☐ 57 B.J. Surhoff	.20	.09
☐ 58 Julio Franco	.20	.09
☐ 59 Eddie Murray	.75	.35
☐ 60 Jody Davis	.10	.05
☐ 61 Todd Worrell	.20	.09
☐ 62 Von Hayes	.10	.05
☐ 63 Billy Hatcher	.10	.05
☐ 64 John Kruk	.30	.14
☐ 65 Tom Henke	.10	.05
☐ 66 Mike Scott	.10	.05
☐ 67 Vince Coleman	.10	.05
☐ 68 Ozzie Smith	1.25	.55
☐ 69 Ken Williams	.10	.05
☐ 70 Steve Bedrosian	.10	.05
☐ 71 Luis Polonia	.10	.05
☐ 72 Brook Jacoby	.10	.05
☐ 73 Ron Darling	.10	.05
☐ 74 Lloyd Moseby	.10	.05
☐ 75 Wally Joyner	.30	.14
☐ 76 Dan Quisenberry	.10	.05
☐ 77 Scott Fletcher	.10	.05
☐ 78 Kirk McCaskill	.10	.05
☐ 79 Paul Molitor	1.00	.45
☐ 80 Mike Aldrete	.10	.05
☐ 81 Neal Heaton	.10	.05
☐ 82 Jeffrey Leonard	.10	.05
☐ 83 Dave Magadan	.10	.05
☐ 84 Danny Cox	.10	.05
☐ 85 Lance McCullers	.10	.05
☐ 86 Jay Howell	.10	.05
☐ 87 Charlie Hough	.20	.09
☐ 88 Gene Garber	.20	.09
☐ 89 Jesse Orosco	.10	.05
☐ 90 Don Robinson	.10	.05
☐ 91 Willie McGee	.20	.09
☐ 92 Bert Blyleven	.20	.09
☐ 93 Phil Bradley	.10	.05
☐ 94 Terry Kennedy	.10	.05
☐ 95 Kent Hrbek	.20	.09
☐ 96 Juan Samuel	.10	.05
☐ 97 Pedro Guerrero	.10	.05
☐ 98 Sid Bream	.10	.05
☐ 99 Devon White	.20	.09
☐ 100 Mark McGwire	1.50	.70
☐ 101 Dave Parker	.20	.09
☐ 102 Glenn Davis	.10	.05
☐ 103 Greg Walker	.10	.05
☐ 104 Rick Rhoden	.10	.05
☐ 105 Mitch Webster	.10	.05
☐ 106 Len Dykstra	.20	.09
☐ 107 Gene Larkin	.10	.05
☐ 108 Floyd Youmans	.10	.05
☐ 109 Andy Van Slyke	.20	.09
☐ 110 Mike Scioscia	.10	.05
☐ 111 Kirk Gibson	.20	.09
☐ 112 Kal Daniels	.10	.05
☐ 113 Ruben Sierra	.20	.09
☐ 114 Sam Horn	.10	.05
☐ 115 Ray Knight	.10	.05
☐ 116 Jimmy Key	.20	.09
☐ 117 Bo Diaz	.10	.05
☐ 118 Mike Greenwell	.20	.09
☐ 119 Barry Bonds	1.25	.55
☐ 120 Reggie Jackson UER (463 lifetime homers)	.75	.35
☐ 121 Mike Pagliarulo	.10	.05
☐ 122 Tommy John	.20	.09
☐ 123 Bill Madlock	.20	.09
☐ 124 Ken Caminiti	1.00	.45
☐ 125 Gary Ward	.10	.05
☐ 126 Candy Maldonado	.10	.05
☐ 127 Harold Reynolds	.20	.09
☐ 128 Joe Magrane	.10	.05
☐ 129 Mike Henneman	.10	.05
☐ 130 Jim Gantner	.10	.05
☐ 131 Bobby Bonilla	.30	.14
☐ 132 John Farrell	.10	.05
☐ 133 Frank Tanana	.10	.05
☐ 134 Zane Smith	.10	.05
☐ 135 Dave Righetti	.10	.05
☐ 136 Rick Reuschel	.20	.09
☐ 137 Dwight Evans	.20	.09
☐ 138 Howard Johnson	.10	.05
☐ 139 Terry Leach	.10	.05
☐ 140 Casey Candaele	.10	.05
☐ 141 Tom Herr	.10	.05
☐ 142 Tony Pena	.10	.05
☐ 143 Lance Parrish	.10	.05
☐ 144 Ellis Burks	.60	.25
☐ 145 Pete O'Brien	.10	.05
☐ 146 Mike Boddicker	.10	.05
☐ 147 Buddy Bell	.20	.09
☐ 148 Bo Jackson	.30	.14
☐ 149 Frank White	.20	.09
☐ 150 George Brett	1.25	.55
☐ 151 Tim Wallach	.10	.05
☐ 152 Cal Ripken	3.00	1.35
☐ 153 Brett Butler	.20	.09
☐ 154 Gary Gaetti	.20	.09
☐ 155 Darryl Strawberry	.20	.09
☐ 156 Alfredo Griffin	.10	.05
☐ 157 Marty Barrett	.10	.05
☐ 158 Jim Rice	.30	.14
☐ 159 Terry Pendleton	.20	.09
☐ 160 Orel Hershiser	.20	.09
☐ 161 Larry Sheets	.10	.05
☐ 162 Dave Stewart UER (Braves logo)	.20	.09
☐ 163 Shawon Dunston	.10	.05
☐ 164 Keith Moreland	.10	.05
☐ 165 Ken Oberkfell	.10	.05
☐ 166 Ivan Calderon	.10	.05
☐ 167 Bob Welch	.20	.09
☐ 168 Fred McGriff	.50	.23
☐ 169 Pete Incaviglia	.10	.05
☐ 170 Dale Murphy	.40	.18
☐ 171 Mike Dunne	.10	.05
☐ 172 Chili Davis	.20	.09
☐ 173 Milt Thompson	.10	.05
☐ 174 Terry Steinbach	.30	.14
☐ 175 Oddibe McDowell	.10	.05
☐ 176 Jack Morris	.20	.09
☐ 177 Sid Fernandez	.10	.05
☐ 178 Ken Griffey	.20	.09
☐ 179 Lee Smith	.20	.09
☐ 180 Highlights 1987	.40	.18
Kirby Puckett		
Juan Nieves		
Mike Schmidt		
☐ 181 Brian Downing	.10	.05
☐ 182 Andres Galarraga	.50	.23
☐ 183 Rob Deer	.10	.05
☐ 184 Greg Brock	.10	.05
☐ 185 Doug DeCinces	.10	.05
☐ 186 Johnny Ray	.10	.05
☐ 187 Hubie Brooks	.10	.05
☐ 188 Darrell Evans	.20	.09
☐ 189 Mel Hall	.10	.05
☐ 190 Jim Deshaies	.10	.05
☐ 191 Dan Plesac	.10	.05
☐ 192 Willie Wilson	.20	.09
☐ 193 Mike LaValliere	.10	.05

☐ 194 Tom Brunansky	.10	.05
☐ 195 John Franco	.20	.09
☐ 196 Frank Viola	.10	.05
☐ 197 Bruce Hurst	.10	.05
☐ 198 John Tudor	.10	.05
☐ 199 Bob Forsch	.10	.05
☐ 200 Dwight Gooden	.20	.09
☐ 201 Jose Canseco	.50	.23
☐ 202 Carney Lansford	.20	.09
☐ 203 Kelly Downs	.10	.05
☐ 204 Glenn Wilson	.10	.05
☐ 205 Pat Tabler	.10	.05
☐ 206 Mike Davis	.10	.05
☐ 207 Roger Clemens	1.00	.45
☐ 208 Dave Smith	.10	.05
☐ 209 Curt Young	.10	.05
☐ 210 Mark Eichhorn	.10	.05
☐ 211 Juan Nieves	.10	.05
☐ 212 Bob Boone	.20	.09
☐ 213 Don Sutton	.40	.18
☐ 214 Willie Upshaw	.10	.05
☐ 215 Jim Clancy	.10	.05
☐ 216 Bill Ripken	.10	.05
☐ 217 Ozzie Virgil	.10	.05
☐ 218 Dave Concepcion	.20	.09
☐ 219 Alan Ashby	.10	.05
☐ 220 Mike Marshall	.10	.05
☐ 221 Highlights 1987 Mark McGwire Paul Molitor Vince Coleman	.20	.09
☐ 222 Highlights 1987 Benito Santiago Steve Bedrosian Don Mattingly	.60	.25
☐ 223 Rookie Prospects Shawn Abner Jay Buhner Gary Thurman	1.50	.70
☐ 224 Rookie Prospects Tim Crews Vicente Palacios John Davis	.10	.05
☐ 225 Rookie Prospects Jody Reed Jeff Treadway Keith Miller	.20	.09

1988 Sportflics Gamewinners

his 25-card set of "Gamewinners" was distributed in a reen and yellow box along with 17 trivia cards by Weiser ard Company of New Jersey. The 25 players selected for ie set show a strong New York preference. The set was stensibly produced for use as a youth organizational und raiser. The cards are the standard size and are done ı the typical Sportflics' Magic Motion (three picture) tyle.

	MINT	NRMT
OMPLETE FACT.SET (25)	6.00	2.70
OMMON CARD (1-25)	.10	.05
☐ 1 Don Mattingly	3.00	1.35
☐ 2 Mark McGwire	3.00	1.35
☐ 3 Wade Boggs	.75	.35
☐ 4 Will Clark	1.50	.70
☐ 5 Eric Davis	.25	.11
☐ 6 Willie Randolph	.10	.05
☐ 7 Dave Winfield	.75	.35
☐ 8 Rickey Henderson	.75	.35
☐ 9 Dwight Gooden	.25	.11
☐ 10 Benito Santiago	.25	.11
☐ 11 Keith Hernandez	.25	.11
☐ 12 Juan Samuel	.10	.05
☐ 13 Kevin Seitzer	.25	.11
☐ 14 Gary Carter	.50	.23
☐ 15 Darryl Strawberry	.25	.11
☐ 16 Rick Rhoden	.10	.05
☐ 17 Howard Johnson	.10	.05
☐ 18 Matt Nokes	.10	.05
☐ 19 Dave Righetti	.10	.05
☐ 20 Roger Clemens	1.50	.70
☐ 21 Mike Schmidt	1.00	.45
☐ 22 Kevin McReynolds	.10	.05
☐ 23 Mike Pagliarulo	.10	.05
☐ 24 Kevin Elster	.10	.05
☐ 25 Jack Clark	.25	.11

1989 Sportflics

This 225-card standard-size full-color set was produced by Sportflics (distributed by Major League Marketing) and again features three sequence action pictures on each card. There are 220 individual players, two Highlights trios, and three Rookie Prospect trio cards. The cards feature a white border on the front with red and blue inner trim colors. A full-color action picture of the player is printed on the back of the card.

	MINT	NRMT
COMPLETE SET (225)	30.00	13.50
COMPLETE FACT.SET (225)	30.00	13.50
COMMON CARD (1-225)	.10	.05
☐ 1 Jose Canseco	.50	.23
☐ 2 Wally Joyner	.20	.09
☐ 3 Roger Clemens	1.00	.45
☐ 4 Greg Swindell	.10	.05
☐ 5 Jack Morris	.20	.09
☐ 6 Mickey Brantley	.10	.05
☐ 7 Jim Presley	.10	.05
☐ 8 Pete O'Brien	.10	.05
☐ 9 Jesse Barfield	.10	.05
☐ 10 Frank Viola	.10	.05
☐ 11 Kevin Bass	.10	.05
☐ 12 Glenn Wilson	.10	.05
☐ 13 Chris Sabo	.10	.05
☐ 14 Fred McGriff	.35	.16
☐ 15 Mark Grace	.75	.35
☐ 16 Devon White	.20	.09
☐ 17 Juan Samuel	.10	.05
☐ 18 Lou Whitaker UER (Card back says Bats: Right and Throws: Left)	.20	.09
☐ 19 Greg Walker	.10	.05
☐ 20 Roberto Alomar	1.00	.45
☐ 21 Mike Schmidt	.75	.35
☐ 22 Benito Santiago	.10	.05
☐ 23 Dave Stewart	.20	.09
☐ 24 Dave Winfield	.40	.18
☐ 25 George Bell	.10	.05
☐ 26 Jack Clark	.20	.09
☐ 27 Doug Drabek	.10	.05
☐ 28 Ron Gant	.35	.16
☐ 29 Glenn Braggs	.10	.05
☐ 30 Rafael Palmeiro	.50	.23
☐ 31 Brett Butler	.20	.09
☐ 32 Ron Darling	.10	.05
☐ 33 Alvin Davis	.10	.05
☐ 34 Bob Walk	.10	.05
☐ 35 Dave Stieb	.10	.05
☐ 36 Orel Hershiser	.20	.09
☐ 37 John Farrell	.10	.05
☐ 38 Doug Jones	.10	.05
☐ 39 Kelly Downs	.10	.05
☐ 40 Bob Boone	.20	.09
☐ 41 Gary Sheffield UER (7 career triples, should be 0)	2.00	.90
☐ 42 Doug Dascenzo	.10	.05
☐ 43 Chad Kreuter	.10	.05
☐ 44 Ricky Jordan	.10	.05
☐ 45 Dave West	.10	.05
☐ 46 Danny Tartabull	.10	.05
☐ 47 Teddy Higuera	.10	.05
☐ 48 Gary Gaetti	.20	.09
☐ 49 Dave Parker	.20	.09
☐ 50 Don Mattingly	1.50	.70
☐ 51 David Cone	.20	.09
☐ 52 Kal Daniels	.10	.05
☐ 53 Carney Lansford	.20	.09
☐ 54 Mike Marshall	.10	.05
☐ 55 Kevin Seitzer	.10	.05
☐ 56 Mike Henneman	.10	.05
☐ 57 Bill Doran	.10	.05
☐ 58 Steve Sax	.10	.05
☐ 59 Lance Parrish	.10	.05
☐ 60 Keith Hernandez	.20	.09
☐ 61 Jose Uribe	.10	.05
☐ 62 Jose Lind	.10	.05
☐ 63 Steve Bedrosian	.10	.05
☐ 64 George Brett UER (Text says .380 in 1980, should be .390)	1.25	.55
☐ 65 Kirk Gibson	.35	.16
☐ 66 Cal Ripken	3.00	1.35
☐ 67 Mitch Webster	.10	.05
☐ 68 Fred Lynn	.10	.05
☐ 69 Eric Davis	.20	.09
☐ 70 Bo Jackson	.20	.09
☐ 71 Kevin Elster	.10	.05
☐ 72 Rick Reuschel	.20	.09
☐ 73 Tim Burke	.10	.05
☐ 74 Mark Davis	.10	.05
☐ 75 Claudell Washington	.10	.05
☐ 76 Lance McCullers	.10	.05
☐ 77 Mike Moore	.10	.05
☐ 78 Robby Thompson	.10	.05
☐ 79 Roger McDowell	.10	.05
☐ 80 Danny Jackson	.10	.05
☐ 81 Tim Leary	.10	.05
☐ 82 Bobby Witt	.10	.05
☐ 83 Jim Gott	.10	.05
☐ 84 Andy Hawkins	.10	.05
☐ 85 Ozzie Guillen	.10	.05
☐ 86 John Tudor	.10	.05
☐ 87 Todd Burns	.10	.05
☐ 88 Dave Gallagher	.10	.05
☐ 89 Jay Buhner	.75	.35
☐ 90 Gregg Jefferies	.35	.16
☐ 91 Bob Welch	.20	.09
☐ 92 Charlie Hough	.20	.09
☐ 93 Tony Fernandez	.10	.05
☐ 94 Ozzie Virgil	.10	.05
☐ 95 Andre Dawson	.50	.23
☐ 96 Hubie Brooks	.10	.05
☐ 97 Kevin McReynolds	.10	.05
☐ 98 Mike LaValliere	.10	.05
☐ 99 Terry Pendleton	.20	.09
☐ 100 Wade Boggs	.60	.25
☐ 101 Dennis Eckersley	.35	.16
☐ 102 Mark Gubicza	.10	.05
☐ 103 Frank Tanana	.10	.05
☐ 104 Joe Carter	.35	.16
☐ 105 Ozzie Smith	1.25	.55
☐ 106 Dennis Martinez	.20	.09
☐ 107 Jeff Treadway	.10	.05
☐ 108 Greg Maddux	3.00	1.35
☐ 109 Bret Saberhagen	.20	.09
☐ 110 Dale Murphy	.50	.23
☐ 111 Rob Deer	.10	.05
☐ 112 Pete Incaviglia	.10	.05
☐ 113 Vince Coleman	.10	.05
☐ 114 Tim Wallach	.10	.05
☐ 115 Nolan Ryan	3.00	1.35
☐ 116 Walt Weiss	.10	.05
☐ 117 Brian Downing	.10	.05
☐ 118 Melido Perez	.10	.05
☐ 119 Terry Steinbach	.20	.09
☐ 120 Mike Scott	.10	.05
☐ 121 Tim Belcher	.10	.05
☐ 122 Mike Boddicker	.10	.05
☐ 123 Len Dykstra	.20	.09
☐ 124 Fernando Valenzuela	.20	.09
☐ 125 Gerald Young	.10	.05
☐ 126 Tom Henke	.20	.09
☐ 127 Dave Henderson	.10	.05
☐ 128 Dan Plesac	.10	.05
☐ 129 Chili Davis	.20	.09
☐ 130 Bryan Harvey	.10	.05
☐ 131 Don August	.10	.05
☐ 132 Mike Harkey	.10	.05
☐ 133 Luis Polonia	.10	.05
☐ 134 Craig Worthington	.10	.05
☐ 135 Joey Meyer	.10	.05
☐ 136 Barry Larkin	.50	.23
☐ 137 Glenn Davis	.10	.05
☐ 138 Mike Scioscia	.10	.05
☐ 139 Andres Galarraga	.50	.23
☐ 140 Dwight Gooden	.20	.09
☐ 141 Keith Moreland	.10	.05
☐ 142 Kevin Mitchell	.10	.05
☐ 143 Mike Greenwell	.10	.05
☐ 144 Mel Hall	.10	.05
☐ 145 Rickey Henderson	.50	.23
☐ 146 Barry Bonds	.75	.35
☐ 147 Eddie Murray	.75	.35
☐ 148 Lee Smith	.20	.09
☐ 149 Julio Franco	.20	.09
☐ 150 Tim Raines	.20	.09
☐ 151 Mitch Williams	.10	.05

□ 152 Tim Laudner .10 .05
□ 153 Mike Pagliarulo .10 .05
□ 154 Floyd Bannister .10 .05
□ 155 Gary Carter .35 .16
□ 156 Kirby Puckett 1.50 .70
□ 157 Harold Baines .20 .09
□ 158 Dave Righetti .10 .05
□ 159 Mark Langston .10 .05
□ 160 Tony Gwynn 1.50 .70
□ 161 Tom Brunansky .10 .05
□ 162 Vance Law .10 .05
□ 163 Kelly Gruber .10 .05
□ 164 Gerald Perry .10 .05
□ 165 Harold Reynolds .10 .05
□ 166 Andy Van Slyke .20 .09
□ 167 Jimmy Key .20 .09
□ 168 Jeff Reardon .20 .09
□ 169 Milt Thompson .10 .05
□ 170 Will Clark .50 .23
□ 171 Chet Lemon .10 .05
□ 172 Pat Tabler .10 .05
□ 173 Jim Rice .35 .16
□ 174 Billy Hatcher .10 .05
□ 175 Bruce Hurst .10 .05
□ 176 John Franco .20 .09
□ 177 Van Snider .10 .05
□ 178 Ron Jones .10 .05
□ 179 Jerald Clark .10 .05
□ 180 Tom Browning .10 .05
□ 181 Von Hayes .10 .05
□ 182 Bobby Bonilla .35 .16
□ 183 Todd Worrell .10 .05
□ 184 John Kruk .20 .09
□ 185 Scott Fletcher .10 .05
□ 186 Willie Wilson .20 .09
□ 187 Jody Davis .10 .05
□ 188 Kent Hrbek .20 .09
□ 189 Ruben Sierra .10 .05
□ 190 Shawon Dunston .10 .05
□ 191 Ellis Burks .35 .16
□ 192 Brook Jacoby .10 .05
□ 193 Jeff M. Robinson .10 .05
□ 194 Rich Dotson .10 .05
□ 195 Johnny Ray .10 .05
□ 196 Cory Snyder .10 .05
□ 197 Mike Witt .10 .05
□ 198 Marty Barrett .10 .05
□ 199 Robin Yount .50 .23
□ 200 Mark McGwire 1.25 .55
□ 201 Ryne Sandberg 1.25 .55
□ 202 John Candelaria .10 .05
□ 203 Matt Nokes .10 .05
□ 204 Dwight Evans .20 .09
□ 205 Darryl Strawberry .20 .09
□ 206 Willie McGee .20 .09
□ 207 Bobby Thigpen .10 .05
□ 208 B.J. Surhoff .20 .09
□ 209 Paul Molitor 1.00 .45
□ 210 Jody Reed .10 .05
□ 211 Doyle Alexander .10 .05
□ 212 Dennis Rasmussen .10 .05
□ 213 Kevin Gross .10 .05
□ 214 Kirk McCaskill .10 .05
□ 215 Alan Trammell .35 .16
□ 216 Damon Berryhill .10 .05
□ 217 Rick Sutcliffe .10 .05
□ 218 Don Slaught .10 .05
□ 219 Carlton Fisk .50 .23
□ 220 Allan Anderson .10 .05
□ 221 Jose Canseco .35 .16
Wade Boggs
Mike Greenwell
□ 222 Orel Hershiser .20 .09
Dennis Eckersley
Tom Browning
□ 223 Gary Sheffield 2.00 .90
Gregg Jefferies
Sandy Alomar Jr.
□ 224 Bob Milacki 3.00 1.35
Randy Johnson
Ramon Martinez
□ 225 Cameron Drew .35 .16
Geronimo Berroa
Ron Jones

1990 Sportflics

The 1990 Sportflics set contains 225 standard-size cards. On the fronts, the black, white, orange, and yellow borders surround two photos, which can each be seen depending on the angle. The set is considered an improvement over the previous years' versions by many collectors due to the increased clarity of the fronts, caused by having two images rather than three. The backs are dominated by large color photos.

	MINT	NRMT
COMPLETE SET (225)	30.00	13.50
COMPLETE FACT.SET (225)	30.00	13.50
COMMON CARD (1-225)	.10	.05

□ 1 Kevin Mitchell .10 .05
□ 2 Wade Boggs .60 .25
□ 3 Cory Snyder .10 .05
□ 4 Paul O'Neill .20 .09
□ 5 Will Clark .50 .23
□ 6 Tony Fernandez .10 .05
□ 7 Ken Griffey Jr. 5.00 2.20
□ 8 Nolan Ryan 4.00 1.80
□ 9 Rafael Palmeiro .50 .23
□ 10 Jesse Barfield .10 .05
□ 11 Kirby Puckett 1.50 .70
□ 12 Steve Sax .10 .05
□ 13 Fred McGriff .35 .16
□ 14 Gregg Jefferies .20 .09
□ 15 Mark Grace .60 .25
□ 16 Ozzie Smith 1.25 .55
□ 17 George Bell .10 .05
□ 18 Robin Yount .50 .23
□ 19 Glenn Davis .10 .05
□ 20 Jeffrey Leonard .10 .05
□ 21 Chili Davis .20 .09
□ 22 Craig Biggio .35 .16
□ 23 Jose Canseco .50 .23
□ 24 Derek Lilliquist .10 .05
□ 25 Chris Bosio .10 .05
□ 26 Dave Stieb .10 .05
□ 27 Bobby Thigpen .10 .05
□ 28 Jack Clark .20 .09
□ 29 Kevin Ritz .10 .05
□ 30 Tom Gordon .10 .05
□ 31 Bryan Harvey .10 .05
□ 32 Jim Deshaies .10 .05
□ 33 Terry Steinbach .20 .09
□ 34 Tom Glavine .35 .16
□ 35 Bob Welch .20 .09
□ 36 Charlie Hayes .10 .05
□ 37 Jeff Reardon .20 .09
□ 38 Joe Orsulak .10 .05
□ 39 Scott Garrelts .10 .05
□ 40 Bob Boone .20 .09
□ 41 Scott Bankhead .10 .05
□ 42 Tom Henke .20 .09
□ 43 Greg Briley .10 .05
□ 44 Teddy Higuera .10 .05
□ 45 Pat Borders .10 .05
□ 46 Kevin Seitzer .10 .05
□ 47 Bruce Hurst .10 .05
□ 48 Ozzie Guillen .10 .05
□ 49 Wally Joyner .20 .09
□ 50 Mike Greenwell .10 .05
□ 51 Gary Gaetti .20 .09
□ 52 Gary Sheffield UER .60 .25
(Uniform listed as 21, should be 1)
□ 53 Dennis Martinez .20 .09
□ 54 Ryne Sandberg 1.25 .55
□ 55 Mike Scott .10 .05
□ 56 Todd Benzinger .10 .05
□ 57 Kelly Gruber .10 .05
□ 58 Jose Lind .10 .05
□ 59 Allan Anderson .10 .05
□ 60 Robby Thompson .10 .05
□ 61 John Smoltz .60 .25
□ 62 Mark Davis .10 .05
□ 63 Tom Herr .10 .05
□ 64 Randy Johnson 1.00 .45
□ 65 Lonnie Smith .10 .05
□ 66 Pedro Guerrero .10 .05
□ 67 Jerome Walton .10 .05
□ 68 Ramon Martinez .35 .16
□ 69 Tim Raines .20 .09
□ 70 Matt Williams .50 .23
□ 71 Joe Oliver .10 .05
□ 72 Nick Esasky .10 .05
□ 73 Kevin Brown .35 .16
□ 74 Walt Weiss .10 .05
□ 75 Roger McDowell .10 .05
□ 76 Jose DeLeon .10 .05
□ 77 Brian Downing .10 .05
□ 78 Jay Howell .10 .05
□ 79 Jose Uribe .10 .05
□ 80 Ellis Burks .35 .16
□ 81 Sammy Sosa 2.00 .90
□ 82 Johnny Ray .10 .05
□ 83 Danny Darwin .10 .05
□ 84 Carney Lansford .20 .09
□ 85 Jose Oquendo .10 .05
□ 86 John Cerutti .10 .05
□ 87 Dave Winfield .50 .23
□ 88 Dave Righetti .10 .05
□ 89 Danny Jackson .10 .05
□ 90 Andy Benes .35 .16
□ 91 Tom Browning .10 .05
□ 92 Pete O'Brien .10 .05
□ 93 Roberto Alomar .75 .35
□ 94 Bret Saberhagen .20 .09
□ 95 Phil Bradley .10 .05
□ 96 Doug Jones .10 .05
□ 97 Eric Davis .20 .09
□ 98 Tony Gwynn 2.00 .90
□ 99 Jim Abbott .20 .09
□ 100 Cal Ripken 4.00 1.80
□ 101 Andy Van Slyke .20 .09
□ 102 Dan Plesac .10 .05
□ 103 Lou Whitaker .20 .09
□ 104 Steve Bedrosian .10 .05
□ 105 Dave Gallagher .10 .05
□ 106 Keith Hernandez .20 .09
□ 107 Duane Ward .10 .05
□ 108 Andre Dawson .50 .23
□ 109 Howard Johnson .10 .05
□ 110 Mark Langston .10 .05
□ 111 Jerry Browne .10 .05
□ 112 Alvin Davis .10 .05
□ 113 Sid Fernandez .10 .05
□ 114 Mike Devereaux .10 .05
□ 115 Benito Santiago .10 .05
□ 116 Bip Roberts .10 .05
□ 117 Craig Worthington .10 .05
□ 118 Kevin Elster .10 .05
□ 119 Harold Reynolds .20 .09
□ 120 Joe Carter .20 .09
□ 121 Brian Harper .10 .05
□ 122 Frank Viola .10 .05
□ 123 Jeff Ballard .10 .05
□ 124 John Kruk .20 .09
□ 125 Harold Baines .20 .09
□ 126 Tom Candiotti .10 .05
□ 127 Kevin McReynolds .10 .05
□ 128 Mookie Wilson .20 .09
□ 129 Danny Tartabull .10 .05
□ 130 Craig Lefferts .10 .05
□ 131 Jose DeJesus .10 .05
□ 132 John Orton .10 .05
□ 133 Curt Schilling .50 .23
□ 134 Marquis Grissom 1.25 .55
□ 135 Greg Vaughn .10 .05
□ 136 Brett Butler .20 .09
□ 137 Rob Deer .10 .05
□ 138 John Franco .20 .09
□ 139 Keith Moreland .10 .05
□ 140 Dave Smith .10 .05
□ 141 Mark McGwire 1.50 .70
□ 142 Vince Coleman .10 .05
□ 143 Barry Bonds .75 .35
□ 144 Mike Henneman .10 .05
□ 145 Dwight Gooden .20 .09
□ 146 Darryl Strawberry .20 .09
□ 147 Von Hayes .10 .05
□ 148 Andres Galarraga .50 .23
□ 149 Roger Clemens 1.25 .55
□ 150 Don Mattingly 1.50 .70
□ 151 Joe Magrane .10 .05
□ 152 Dwight Smith .10 .05
□ 153 Ricky Jordan .10 .05
□ 154 Alan Trammell .35 .16
□ 155 Brook Jacoby .10 .05
□ 156 Len Dykstra .20 .09
□ 157 Mike LaValliere .10 .05
□ 158 Julio Franco .20 .09
□ 159 Joey Belle 2.00 .90
□ 160 Barry Larkin .50 .23
□ 161 Rick Reuschel .20 .09
□ 162 Nelson Santovenia .10 .05
□ 163 Mike Scioscia .10 .05
□ 164 Damon Berryhill .10 .05
□ 165 Todd Worrell .20 .09
□ 166 Jim Eisenreich .20 .09
□ 167 Ivan Calderon .10 .0
□ 168 Mauro Gozzo .10 .0
□ 169 Kirk McCaskill .10 .0
□ 170 Dennis Eckersley .35 .1
□ 171 Mickey Tettleton .20 .0
□ 172 Chuck Finley .20 .0
□ 173 Dave Magadan .10 .0

☐ 174 Terry Pendleton	.20	.09
☐ 175 Willie Randolph	.20	.09
☐ 176 Jeff Huson	.10	.05
☐ 177 Todd Zeile	.20	.09
☐ 178 Steve Olin	.10	.05
☐ 179 Eric Anthony	.10	.05
☐ 180 Scott Coolbaugh	.10	.05
☐ 181 Rick Sutcliffe	.10	.05
☐ 182 Tim Wallach	.10	.05
☐ 183 Paul Molitor	1.00	.45
☐ 184 Roberto Kelly	.10	.05
☐ 185 Mike Moore	.10	.05
☐ 186 Junior Felix	.10	.05
☐ 187 Mike Schooler	.10	.05
☐ 188 Ruben Sierra	.10	.05
☐ 189 Dale Murphy	.50	.23
☐ 190 Dan Gladden	.10	.05
☐ 191 John Smiley	.10	.05
☐ 192 Jeff Russell	.10	.05
☐ 193 Bert Blyleven	.20	.09
☐ 194 Dave Stewart	.20	.09
☐ 195 Bobby Bonilla	.20	.09
☐ 196 Mitch Williams	.20	.09
☐ 197 Orel Hershiser	.20	.09
☐ 198 Kevin Bass	.10	.05
☐ 199 Tim Burke	.10	.05
☐ 200 Bo Jackson	.20	.09
☐ 201 David Cone	.35	.16
☐ 202 Gary Pettis	.10	.05
☐ 203 Kent Hrbek	.20	.09
☐ 204 Carlton Fisk	.50	.23
☐ 205 Bob Geren	.10	.05
☐ 206 Bill Spiers	.10	.05
☐ 207 Oddibe McDowell	.10	.05
☐ 208 Rickey Henderson	.60	.25
☐ 209 Ken Caminiti	.50	.23
☐ 210 Devon White	.20	.09
☐ 211 Greg Maddux	3.00	1.35
☐ 212 Ed Whitson	.10	.05
☐ 213 Carlos Martinez	.10	.05
☐ 214 George Brett	1.50	.70
☐ 215 Gregg Olson	.10	.05
☐ 216 Kenny Rogers	.20	.09
☐ 217 Dwight Evans	.20	.09
☐ 218 Pat Tabler	.10	.05
☐ 219 Jeff Treadway	.10	.05
☐ 220 Scott Fletcher	.10	.05
☐ 221 Deion Sanders	.75	.35
☐ 222 Robin Ventura	.50	.23
☐ 223 Chip Hale	.10	.05
☐ 224 Tommy Greene	.10	.05
☐ 225 Dean Palmer	.75	.35

1994 Sportflics Samples

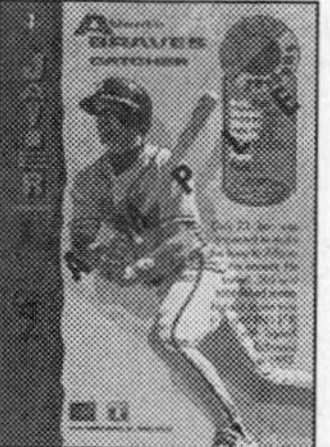

Enclosed in a cello pack, this four-card standard-size set was issued to give dealers a preview of the design of the forthcoming 1994 Sportflics 2000 series. The fronts feature two images that alternate when the card is tilted slightly. The design of the backs varies slightly, but all have a second color player photo and player information. The disclaimer "SAMPLE" is stenciled diagonally across the front and back of each card. In addition to the whole set being sent to dealers, all Wal-Mart greeters were given Len Dykstra cards to give out to promote this product.

	MINT	NRMT
COMPLETE SET (4)	6.00	2.70
COMMON CARD (1-4)	.50	.23
☐ 1 Len Dykstra	.75	.35
☐ 7 Javier Lopez	1.50	.70
☐ 193 Greg Maddux	5.00	2.20
☐ NNO Sportflics 2000 '94 Hobby Baseball (Ad card)	.50	.23

1994 Sportflics

After a three-year hiatus, Pinnacle resumed producing these lenticular "three-dimensional" cards, issued in hobby and retail packs. Each of the 193 "Magic Motion" cards features two images, which alternate when the card is viewed from different angles and creates the illusion of movement. Cards 176-193 are Starflics featuring top stars. The two commemorative cards, featuring Cliff Floyd and Paul Molitor, were inserted at a rate of one in every 360 packs.

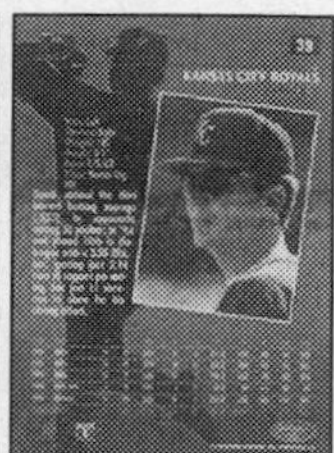

	MINT	NRMT
COMPLETE SET (193)	25.00	11.00
COMMON CARD (1-193)	.15	.07
☐ 1 Lenny Dykstra	.30	.14
☐ 2 Mike Stanley	.15	.07
☐ 3 Alex Fernandez	.30	.14
☐ 4 Mark McGwire UER (name spelled McGuire on front)	1.25	.55
☐ 5 Eric Karros	.30	.14
☐ 6 Dave Justice	.60	.25
☐ 7 Jeff Bagwell	1.25	.55
☐ 8 Darren Lewis	.15	.07
☐ 9 David McCarty	.15	.07
☐ 10 Albert Belle	.75	.35
☐ 11 Ben McDonald	.15	.07
☐ 12 Joe Carter	.40	.18
☐ 13 Benito Santiago	.15	.07
☐ 14 Rob Dibble	.15	.07
☐ 15 Roger Clemens	1.25	.55
☐ 16 Travis Fryman	.30	.14
☐ 17 Doug Drabek	.15	.07
☐ 18 Jay Buhner	.40	.18
☐ 19 Orlando Merced	.15	.07
☐ 20 Ryan Klesko	.40	.18
☐ 21 Chuck Finley	.15	.07
☐ 22 Dante Bichette	.40	.18
☐ 23 Wally Joyner	.30	.14
☐ 24 Robin Yount	.40	.18
☐ 25 Tony Gwynn	1.50	.70
☐ 26 Allen Watson	.15	.07
☐ 27 Rick Wilkins	.15	.07
☐ 28 Gary Sheffield	.60	.25
☐ 29 John Burkett	.15	.07
☐ 30 Randy Johnson	.60	.25
☐ 31 Roberto Alomar	.60	.25
☐ 32 Fred McGriff	.40	.18
☐ 33 Ozzie Guillen	.15	.07
☐ 34 Jimmy Key	.30	.14
☐ 35 Juan Gonzalez	1.50	.70
☐ 36 Wil Cordero	.30	.14
☐ 37 Aaron Sele	.15	.07
☐ 38 Mark Langston	.15	.07
☐ 39 David Cone	.30	.14
☐ 40 John Jaha	.15	.07
☐ 41 Ozzie Smith	.75	.35
☐ 42 Kirby Puckett	1.25	.55
☐ 43 Kenny Lofton	.75	.35
☐ 44 Mike Mussina	.60	.25
☐ 45 Ryne Sandberg	.75	.35
☐ 46 Robby Thompson	.15	.07
☐ 47 Bryan Harvey	.15	.07
☐ 48 Marquis Grissom	.30	.14
☐ 49 Bobby Bonilla	.30	.14
☐ 50 Dennis Eckersley	.40	.18
☐ 51 Curt Schilling	.30	.14
☐ 52 Andy Benes	.30	.14
☐ 53 Greg Maddux	2.00	.90
☐ 54 Bill Swift	.15	.07
☐ 55 Andres Galarraga	.40	.18
☐ 56 Tony Phillips	.15	.07
☐ 57 Darryl Hamilton	.15	.07
☐ 58 Duane Ward	.15	.07
☐ 59 Bernie Williams	.60	.25
☐ 60 Steve Avery	.15	.07
☐ 61 Eduardo Perez	.15	.07
☐ 62 Jeff Conine	.30	.14
☐ 63 Dave Winfield	.40	.18
☐ 64 Phil Plantier	.15	.07
☐ 65 Ray Lankford	.40	.18
☐ 66 Robin Ventura	.30	.14
☐ 67 Mike Piazza	2.00	.90
☐ 68 Jason Bere	.15	.07
☐ 69 Cal Ripken	2.50	1.10
☐ 70 Frank Thomas	2.50	1.10
☐ 71 Carlos Baerga	.30	.14
☐ 72 Darryl Kile	.30	.14
☐ 73 Ruben Sierra	.15	.07
☐ 74 Gregg Jefferies UER (Name spelled Jeffries on front)	.30	.14
☐ 75 John Olerud	.30	.14
☐ 76 Andy Van Slyke	.30	.14
☐ 77 Larry Walker	.60	.25
☐ 78 Cecil Fielder	.30	.14
☐ 79 Andre Dawson	.40	.18
☐ 80 Tom Glavine	.40	.18
☐ 81 Sammy Sosa	.40	.18
☐ 82 Charlie Hayes	.15	.07
☐ 83 Chuck Knoblauch	.60	.25
☐ 84 Kevin Appier	.30	.14
☐ 85 Dean Palmer	.30	.14
☐ 86 Royce Clayton	.30	.14
☐ 87 Moises Alou	.30	.14
☐ 88 Ivan Rodriguez	.75	.35
☐ 89 Tim Salmon	.60	.25
☐ 90 Ron Gant	.30	.14
☐ 91 Barry Bonds	.75	.35
☐ 92 Jack McDowell	.15	.07
☐ 93 Alan Trammell	.40	.18
☐ 94 Doc Gooden	.30	.14
☐ 95 Jay Bell	.30	.14
☐ 96 Devon White	.15	.07
☐ 97 Wilson Alvarez	.30	.14
☐ 98 Jim Thome	.75	.35
☐ 99 Ramon Martinez	.30	.14
☐ 100 Kent Hrbek	.30	.14
☐ 101 John Kruk	.30	.14
☐ 102 Wade Boggs	.60	.25
☐ 103 Greg Vaughn	.15	.07
☐ 104 Tom Henke	.15	.07
☐ 105 Brian Jordan	.40	.18
☐ 106 Paul Molitor	.60	.25
☐ 107 Cal Eldred	.15	.07
☐ 108 Deion Sanders	.60	.25
☐ 109 Barry Larkin	.40	.18
☐ 110 Mike Greenwell	.15	.07
☐ 111 Jeff Blauser	.15	.07
☐ 112 Jose Rijo	.15	.07
☐ 113 Pete Harnisch	.15	.07
☐ 114 Chris Hoiles	.15	.07
☐ 115 Edgar Martinez	.40	.18
☐ 116 Juan Guzman	.15	.07
☐ 117 Todd Zeile	.15	.07
☐ 118 Danny Tartabull	.15	.07
☐ 119 Chad Curtis	.15	.07
☐ 120 Mark Grace	.40	.18
☐ 121 J.T. Snow	.15	.07
☐ 122 Mo Vaughn	.75	.35
☐ 123 Lance Johnson	.15	.07
☐ 124 Eric Davis	.30	.14
☐ 125 Orel Hershiser	.30	.14
☐ 126 Kevin Mitchell	.15	.07
☐ 127 Don Mattingly	1.00	.45
☐ 128 Darren Daulton	.30	.14
☐ 129 Rod Beck	.30	.14
☐ 130 Charles Nagy	.30	.14
☐ 131 Mickey Tettleton	.15	.07
☐ 132 Kevin Brown	.30	.14
☐ 133 Pat Hentgen	.30	.14
☐ 134 Terry Mulholland	.15	.07
☐ 135 Steve Finley	.30	.14
☐ 136 John Smoltz	.40	.18
☐ 137 Frank Viola	.15	.07
☐ 138 Jim Abbott	.15	.07
☐ 139 Matt Williams	.40	.18
☐ 140 Bernard Gilkey	.30	.14
☐ 141 Jose Canseco	.40	.18
☐ 142 Mark Whiten	.15	.07
☐ 143 Ken Griffey Jr.	3.00	1.35
☐ 144 Rafael Palmeiro	.40	.18
☐ 145 Dave Hollins	.15	.07
☐ 146 Will Clark	.40	.18
☐ 147 Paul O'Neill	.30	.14
☐ 148 Bobby Jones	.30	.14
☐ 149 Butch Huskey	.30	.14
☐ 150 Jeffrey Hammonds	.30	.14
☐ 151 Manny Ramirez	.75	.35
☐ 152 Bob Hamelin	.15	.07
☐ 153 Kurt Abbott	.15	.07
☐ 154 Scott Stahoviak	.15	.07
☐ 155 Steve Hosey	.15	.07
☐ 156 Salomon Torres	.15	.07
☐ 157 Sterling Hitchcock	.30	.14
☐ 158 Nigel Wilson	.15	.07
☐ 159 Luis Lopez	.15	.07
☐ 160 Chipper Jones	2.00	.90
☐ 161 Norberto Martin	.15	.07
☐ 162 Raul Mondesi	.40	.18
☐ 163 Steve Karsay	.15	.07
☐ 164 J.R. Phillips	.15	.07
☐ 165 Marc Newfield	.30	.14
☐ 166 Mark Hutton	.15	.07
☐ 167 Curtis Pride	.30	.14
☐ 168 Carl Everett	.15	.07

Card	MINT	NRMT
☐ 169 Scott Ruffcorn	.15	.07
☐ 170 Turk Wendell	.15	.07
☐ 171 Jeff McNeely	.15	.07
☐ 172 Javier Lopez	.40	.18
☐ 173 Cliff Floyd	.30	.14
☐ 174 Rondell White	.40	.18
☐ 175 Scott Lydy	.15	.07
☐ 176 Frank Thomas AS	1.50	.70
☐ 177 Roberto Alomar AS	.40	.18
☐ 178 Travis Fryman AS	.30	.14
☐ 179 Cal Ripken AS	1.25	.55
☐ 180 Chris Hoiles AS	.15	.07
☐ 181 Ken Griffey Jr. AS	1.50	.70
☐ 182 Juan Gonzalez AS	.60	.25
☐ 183 Joe Carter AS	.30	.14
☐ 184 Jack McDowell AS	.15	.07
☐ 185 Fred McGriff AS	.40	.18
☐ 186 Robby Thompson AS	.15	.07
☐ 187 Matt Williams AS	.40	.18
☐ 188 Jay Bell AS	.15	.07
☐ 189 Mike Piazza AS	1.00	.45
☐ 190 Barry Bonds AS	.60	.25
☐ 191 Lenny Dykstra AS	.15	.07
☐ 192 Dave Justice AS	.60	.25
☐ 193 Greg Maddux AS	1.00	.45
☐ NNO0 Cliff Floyd Special	2.00	.90
☐ NNO0 Paul Molitor Special	10.00	4.50

1994 Sportflics Movers

These 12 standard-size chase cards were randomly inserted in retail foil packs and picture the game's top veterans. The insertion rate was one in every 24 packs. Fronts feature the dual image effect with the player's name appearing in dual image. The name "Movers" appears in a circular design off to the left of the player's name.

	MINT	NRMT
COMPLETE SET (12)	50.00	22.00
COMMON CARD (MM1-MM12)	1.50	.70
☐ MM1 Gregg Jefferies	1.50	.70
☐ MM2 Ryne Sandberg	8.00	3.60
☐ MM3 Cecil Fielder	2.00	.90
☐ MM4 Kirby Puckett	10.00	4.50
☐ MM5 Tony Gwynn	10.00	4.50
☐ MM6 Andres Galarraga	5.00	2.20
☐ MM7 Sammy Sosa	5.00	2.20
☐ MM8 Rickey Henderson	5.00	2.20
☐ MM9 Don Mattingly	12.00	5.50
☐ MM10 Joe Carter	5.00	2.20
☐ MM11 Carlos Baerga	1.50	.70
☐ MM12 Lenny Dykstra	1.50	.70

1994 Sportflics Shakers

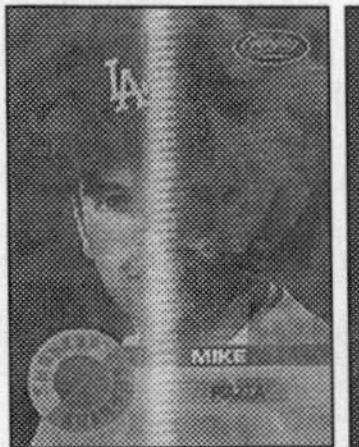
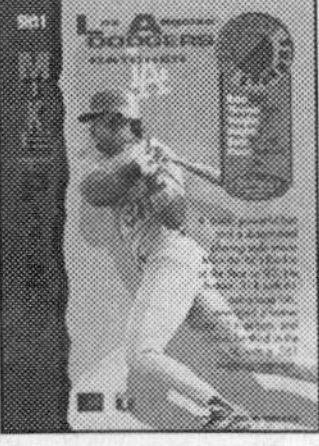

These 12 standard-size chase cards were randomly inserted in hobby foil packs and picture baseball's elite young players. The insertion rate was one in every 24 packs. Fronts feature the dual image effect with the player's name also appearing as dual image. The name "Shakers" appears in a circular design off to the left of the player's name.

	MINT	NRMT
COMPLETE SET (12)	70.00	32.00
COMMON CARD (SH1-SH12)	2.00	.90
☐ SH1 Kenny Lofton	12.00	5.50
☐ SH2 Tim Salmon	6.00	2.70
☐ SH3 Jeff Bagwell	15.00	6.75
☐ SH4 Jason Bere	2.00	.90
☐ SH5 Salomon Torres	2.00	.90
☐ SH6 Rondell White	3.00	1.35
☐ SH7 Javier Lopez	3.00	1.35
☐ SH8 Dean Palmer	3.00	1.35
☐ SH9 Jim Thome	8.00	3.60
☐ SH10 J.T. Snow	3.00	1.35
☐ SH11 Mike Piazza	20.00	9.00
☐ SH12 Manny Ramirez	10.00	4.50

1994 Sportflics Rookie/Traded Samples

This set of nine standard-size sample cards previews the 1994 Sportflics Rookie/Traded series. On the fronts, two color game-action photos are overlayed to create a multi-dimensional card that changes images when the card is rotated. On a red and black geometric design, the backs carry a color head shot, biography, and statistics. Both sides have the word "SAMPLE" running diagonally from the lower left to the upper right corner.

	MINT	NRMT
COMPLETE SET (9)	8.00	3.60
COMMON CARD	.50	.23
☐ 1 Will Clark	2.00	.90
☐ 14 Bret Boone	.50	.23
☐ 20 Ellis Burks	1.00	.45
☐ 25 Deion Sanders	2.50	1.10
☐ 65 Chris Turner	.50	.23
☐ 82 Tony Tarasco	.50	.23
☐ 102 Rich Becker	.50	.23
☐ GG1 Gary Sheffield Going, Going, Gone	2.50	1.10
☐ NNO Title Card	.50	.23

1994 Sportflics Rookie/Traded

This set of 150 standard-size cards was distributed in five-card retail packs at a suggested price of $1.89. The set features top rookies and traded players. This set was released only through retail (non-hobby) outlets. The fronts feature the "Magic Motion" printing with two action views of the player which change with the tilting of the card. The playerís name is printed in red and expands and contracts with the tilting of the card. Numbered backs include a player biography and career stats and the 1994 performance of the rookie or how the player was acquired in a trade. A full-color photo of the player is framed at an angle with a red and black background. Rookie Cards in this set include Chan Ho Park and Alex Rodriguez.

	MINT	NRMT
COMPLETE SET (150)	25.00	11.00
COMMON CARD (1-150)	.25	.11
☐ 1 Will Clark	.75	.35
☐ 2 Sid Fernandez	.25	.11
☐ 3 Joe Magrane	.25	.11
☐ 4 Pete Smith	.25	.11
☐ 5 Roberto Kelly	.25	.11
☐ 6 Delino DeShields	.25	.11
☐ 7 Brian Harper	.25	.11
☐ 8 Darrin Jackson	.25	.11
☐ 9 Omar Vizquel	.50	.23
☐ 10 Luis Polonia	.25	.11
☐ 11 Reggie Jefferson	.50	.23
☐ 12 Geronimo Berroa	.50	.23
☐ 13 Mike Harkey	.25	.11
☐ 14 Bret Boone	.25	.11
☐ 15 Dave Henderson	.25	.11
☐ 16 Pedro J.Martinez	1.00	.45
☐ 17 Jose Vizcaino	.25	.11
☐ 18 Xavier Hernandez	.25	.11
☐ 19 Eddie Taubensee	.25	.11
☐ 20 Ellis Burks	.50	.23
☐ 21 Turner Ward	.25	.11
☐ 22 Terry Mulholland	.25	.11
☐ 23 Howard Johnson	.25	.11
☐ 24 Vince Coleman	.25	.11
☐ 25 Deion Sanders	1.00	.45
☐ 26 Rafael Palmeiro	.75	.35
☐ 27 Dave Weathers	.25	.11
☐ 28 Kent Mercker	.25	.11
☐ 29 Gregg Olson	.25	.11
☐ 30 Cory Bailey	.25	.11
☐ 31 Brian L.Hunter	1.00	.45
☐ 32 Garey Ingram	.25	.11
☐ 33 Daniel Smith	.25	.11
☐ 34 Denny Hocking	.25	.11
☐ 35 Charles Johnson	.75	.35
☐ 36 Otis Nixon	.50	.23
☐ 37 Hector Fajardo	.25	.11
☐ 38 Lee Smith	.50	.23
☐ 39 Phil Stidham	.25	.11
☐ 40 Melvin Nieves	.50	.23
☐ 41 Julio Franco	.50	.23
☐ 42 Greg Gohr	.25	.11
☐ 43 Steve Dunn	.25	.11
☐ 44 Tony Fernandez	.25	.11
☐ 45 Toby Borland	.25	.11
☐ 46 Paul Shuey	.25	.11
☐ 47 Shawn Hare	.25	.11
☐ 48 Shawn Green	.50	.23
☐ 49 Julian Tavarez	.50	.23
☐ 50 Ernie Young	.25	.11
☐ 51 Chris Sabo	.25	.11
☐ 52 Greg O'Halloran	.25	.11
☐ 53 Donnie Elliott	.25	.11
☐ 54 Jim Converse	.25	.11
☐ 55 Ray Holbert	.25	.11
☐ 56 Keith Lockhart	.25	.11
☐ 57 Tony Longmire	.25	.11
☐ 58 Jorge Fabregas	.25	.11
☐ 59 Ravelo Manzanillo	.25	.11
☐ 60 Marcus Moore	.25	.11
☐ 61 Carlos Rodriguez	.25	.11
☐ 62 Mark Portugal	.25	.11
☐ 63 Yorkis Perez	.25	.11
☐ 64 Dan Miceli	.25	.11
☐ 65 Chris Turner	.25	.11
☐ 66 Mike Oquist	.25	.11
☐ 67 Tom Quinlan	.25	.11
☐ 68 Matt Walbeck	.25	.11
☐ 69 Dave Staton	.25	.11
☐ 70 Wm.VanLandingham	.25	.11
☐ 71 Dave Stevens	.25	.11
☐ 72 Domingo Cedeno	.25	.11
☐ 73 Alex Diaz	.25	.11
☐ 74 Darren Bragg	.50	.23
☐ 75 James Hurst	.25	.11
☐ 76 Alex Gonzalez	.50	.23
☐ 77 Steve Dreyer	.25	.11
☐ 78 Robert Eenhoorn	.25	.11
☐ 79 Derek Parks	.25	.11
☐ 80 Jose Valentin	.50	.23
☐ 81 Wes Chamberlain	.25	.11
☐ 82 Tony Tarasco	.25	.11
☐ 83 Steve Traschel	.25	.11
☐ 84 Willie Banks	.25	.11
☐ 85 Rob Butler	.25	.11
☐ 86 Miguel Jimenez	.25	.11
☐ 87 Gerald Williams	.25	.11
☐ 88 Aaron Small	.25	.11
☐ 89 Matt Mieske	.25	.11
☐ 90 Tim Hyers	.25	.11
☐ 91 Eddie Murray	1.00	.45
☐ 92 Dennis Martinez	.50	.23
☐ 93 Tony Eusebio	.25	.11
☐ 94 Brian Anderson	.75	.35
☐ 95 Blaise Ilsley	.25	.11
☐ 96 Johnny Ruffin	.25	.11
☐ 97 Carlos Reyes	.25	.11
☐ 98 Greg Pirkl	.25	.11
☐ 99 Jack Morris	.50	.23
☐ 100 John Mabry	.75	.35
☐ 101 Mike Kelly	.25	.11

☐ 102 Rich Becker	.50	.23
☐ 103 Chris Gomez	.25	.11
☐ 104 Jim Edmonds	1.00	.45
☐ 105 Rich Rowland	.25	.11
☐ 106 Damon Buford	.25	.11
☐ 107 Mark Kiefer	.25	.11
☐ 108 Matias Carrillo	.25	.11
☐ 109 James Mouton	.50	.23
☐ 110 Kelly Stinnett	.25	.11
☐ 111 Billy Ashley	.25	.11
☐ 112 Fausto Cruz	.25	.11
☐ 113 Roberto Petagine	.25	.11
☐ 114 Joe Hall	.25	.11
☐ 115 Brian Johnson	.25	.11
☐ 116 Kevin Jarvis	.25	.11
☐ 117 Tim Davis	.25	.11
☐ 118 John Patterson	.25	.11
☐ 119 Stan Royer	.25	.11
☐ 120 Jeff Juden	.25	.11
☐ 121 Bryan Eversgerd	.25	.11
☐ 122 Chan Ho Park	2.50	1.10
☐ 123 Shane Reynolds	.50	.23
☐ 124 Danny Bautista	.25	.11
☐ 125 Rikkert Faneyte	.25	.11
☐ 126 Carlos Pulido	.25	.11
☐ 127 Mike Matheny	.25	.11
☐ 128 Hector Carrasco	.25	.11
☐ 129 Eddie Zambrano	.25	.11
☐ 130 Lee Tinsley	.50	.23
☐ 131 Roger Salkeld	.25	.11
☐ 132 Carlos Delgado	.75	.35
☐ 133 Troy O'Leary	.25	.11
☐ 134 Keith Mitchell	.25	.11
☐ 135 Lance Painter	.25	.11
☐ 136 Nate Minchey	.25	.11
☐ 137 Eric Anthony	.25	.11
☐ 138 Rafael Bournigal	.25	.11
☐ 139 Joey Hamilton	.50	.23
☐ 140 Bobby Munoz	.25	.11
☐ 141 Rex Hudler	.25	.11
☐ 142 Alex Cole	.25	.11
☐ 143 Stan Javier	.25	.11
☐ 144 Jose Oliva	.25	.11
☐ 145 Tom Brunansky	.25	.11
☐ 146 Greg Colbrunn	.25	.11
☐ 147 Luis S.Lopez	.25	.11
☐ 148 Alex Rodriguez	10.00	4.50
☐ 149 Darryl Strawberry	.50	.23
☐ 150 Bo Jackson	.50	.23
☐ RO1 R.Klesko ROY M.Ramirez	8.00	3.60

1994 Sportflics Rookie/Traded Artist's Proofs

This set of cards parallels the 150 regular issue Rookie/Traded cards and are embellished with the gold foil "Artist's Proof" stamp. They were randomly inserted in at a rate of one in 24 packs.

	MINT	NRMT
COMPLETE SET (150)	2000.00	900.00
COMMON CARD (1-150)	10.00	4.50
MINOR STARS	20.00	9.00
*STARS: 40X TO 80X BASIC CARDS		
*YOUNG STARS: 25X TO 50X BASIC CARDS		
☐ 1 Will Clark	50.00	22.00
☐ 16 Pedro Martinez	60.00	27.00
☐ 26 Rafael Palmeiro	40.00	18.00
☐ 31 Brian L.Hunter	40.00	18.00
☐ 91 Eddie Murray	80.00	36.00
☐ 104 Jim Edmonds	60.00	27.00
☐ 122 Chan Ho Park	100.00	45.00
☐ 132 Carlos Delgado	40.00	18.00
☐ 139 Joey Hamilton	40.00	18.00
☐ 148 Alex Rodriguez	400.00	180.00

1994 Sportflics Rookie/Traded Going Going Gone

Randomly inserted in packs at a rate of one in 18, this 12-card set features big hitters. Sportflics used its "Magic Mirror" technology to produce two images when the card is tilted. The Going, Going, Gone logo is placed at the top left of the front and a gold strip runs vertically on the left side. The player's name is printed in black on top of the gold strip. It expands and contracts when the card is moved. Borderless backs are numbered with the prefix "GG" and have a dark background containing a blurred stadium. The player's close-up picture is bordered with a biography box and name on the left. The playerís slugging percentage, number of home runs and RBI totals are printed on the right side of the back with a shadow effect.

	MINT	NRMT
COMPLETE SET (12)	90.00	40.00
COMMON CARD (GG1-GG12)	3.00	1.35
☐ GG1 Gary Sheffield	5.00	2.20
☐ GG2 Matt Williams	4.00	1.80
☐ GG3 Juan Gonzalez	12.00	5.50
☐ GG4 Ken Griffey Jr.	25.00	11.00
☐ GG5 Mike Piazza	15.00	6.75
☐ GG6 Frank Thomas	20.00	9.00
☐ GG7 Tim Salmon	5.00	2.20
☐ GG8 Barry Bonds	6.00	2.70
☐ GG9 Fred McGriff	4.00	1.80
☐ GG10 Cecil Fielder	3.00	1.35
☐ GG11 Albert Belle	6.00	2.70
☐ GG12 Joe Carter	4.00	1.80

1994 Sportflics Rookie/Traded Rookie Starflics

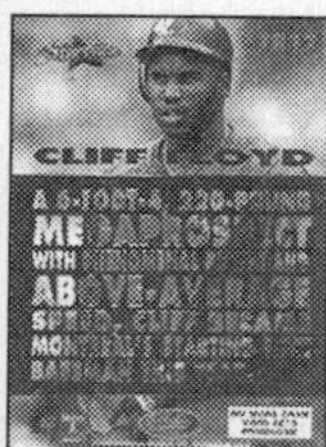

Randomly inserted in packs at a rate of one in 36, these 3-D cards highlight the rookie sensations of 1994. Horizontal fronts feature the player in a full-color action shot with a smaller, mirror image of the player set off in the blue background. The Starflics logo, player's name and team logo are printed on the left side of the front. Backs are borderless and carry full-color action shots of the player. The player's name is printed in gold foil and a player background is printed with reverse type on gold foil.

	MINT	NRMT
COMPLETE SET (18)	150.00	70.00
COMMON CARD (TR1-TR18)	5.00	2.20
☐ TR1 John Hudek	5.00	2.20
☐ TR2 Manny Ramirez	25.00	11.00
☐ TR3 Jeffrey Hammonds	8.00	3.60
☐ TR4 Carlos Delgado	12.00	5.50
☐ TR5 Javier Lopez	12.00	5.50
☐ TR6 Alex Gonzalez	8.00	3.60
☐ TR7 Raul Mondesi	15.00	6.75
☐ TR8 Bob Hamelin	5.00	2.20
☐ TR9 Ryan Klesko	15.00	6.75
☐ TR10 Brian Anderson	5.00	2.20
☐ TR11 Alex Rodriguez	80.00	36.00
☐ TR12 Cliff Floyd	8.00	3.60
☐ TR13 Chan Ho Park	20.00	9.00
☐ TR14 Steve Karsay	5.00	2.20
☐ TR15 Rondell White	10.00	4.50
☐ TR16 Shawn Green	8.00	3.60
☐ TR17 Rich Becker	5.00	2.20
☐ TR18 Charles Johnson	10.00	4.50

1994 Sportflics FanFest All-Stars

At Fanfest, collectors received redemption coupons at various locations. These redemption coupons could be turned in at certain distribution centers for the Sportflics cards. It is noted on the backs that 10,000 sets were produced. The cards measure the standard size. The borderless fronts carry two-dimensional color action photos featuring an American League player and a National League player. The player's names appear in the

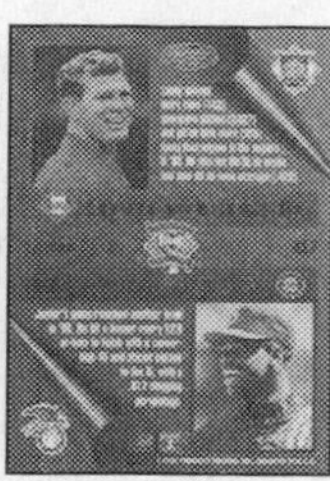

upper left and bottom right corners. The backs carry headshots and statistics for each player. According to reports, between 10-20 percent of the mintage of this set was destroyed at the end of fanfest.

	MINT	NRMT
COMPLETE SET (9)	175.00	80.00
COMMON CARD (AS1-AS9)	5.00	2.20
☐ AS1 Fred McGriff / Frank Thomas	20.00	9.00
☐ AS2 Ryne Sandberg / Roberto Alomar	30.00	13.50
☐ AS3 Matt Williams / Travis Fryman	5.00	2.20
☐ AS4 Ozzie Smith / Cal Ripken Jr.	40.00	18.00
☐ AS5 Mike Piazza / Ivan Rodriguez	25.00	11.00
☐ AS6 Barry Bonds / Juan Gonzalez	20.00	9.00
☐ AS7 Lenny Dykstra / Ken Griffey Jr.	25.00	11.00
☐ AS8 Gary Sheffield / Kirby Puckett	15.00	6.75
☐ AS9 Greg Maddux / Mike Mussina	20.00	9.00

1995 Sportflix Samples

This nine-card set features samples of the 1995 Sportlix series. The cards are numbered below according to their numbers in the regular series. This apparently is one of the scarcest promo sets in recent years -- it is rumored that only 200 to 300 of each card were produced.

	MINT	NRMT
COMPLETE SET (9)	300.00	135.00
COMMON CARD	10.00	4.50
☐ 3 Fred McGriff	20.00	9.00
☐ 20 Frank Thomas	100.00	45.00
☐ 105 Manny Ramirez	30.00	13.50
☐ 122 Cal Ripken	100.00	45.00
☐ 128 Roberto Alomar	30.00	13.50
☐ 152 Russ Davis	10.00	4.50
☐ 162 Chipper Jones	75.00	34.00
☐ DE2 Matt Williams (Detonator)	20.00	9.00
☐ NNO Title card	10.00	4.50

1995 Sportflix

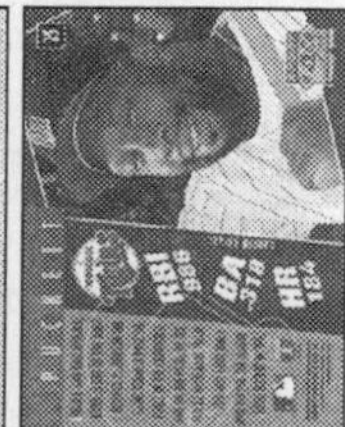

This 170 card standard-size set was released by Pinnacle brands. The set was issued in 5 card packs that had a suggested retail price of $1.89 per pack. Thirty-six of these packs are contained in a full box. Jumbo packs were also issued: these packs contained 8 cards per pack and had 36 packs in a box. Card fronts feature Pinnacle's "Magic Motion" printing which shows the player in two different action shots when the card is tilted. The player's position is printed diagonally on the top right with the team logo underneath. Horizontal backs feature a full-color player photo on the right. Subsets include a rookies section (141-165) and a checklist grouping (166-170). There are no key Rookie Cards in this set.

	MINT	NRMT
COMPLETE SET (170)	20.00	9.00
COMMON CARD (1-170)	.15	.07

	MINT	NRMT
☐ 1 Ken Griffey Jr.	3.00	1.35
☐ 2 Jeffrey Hammonds	.30	.14
☐ 3 Fred McGriff	.40	.18
☐ 4 Rickey Henderson	.40	.18
☐ 5 Derrick May	.15	.07
☐ 6 Robin Ventura	.30	.14
☐ 7 Royce Clayton	.15	.07
☐ 8 Paul Molitor	.60	.25
☐ 9 Charlie Hayes	.15	.07
☐ 10 David Nied	.15	.07
☐ 11 Ellis Burks	.30	.14
☐ 12 Bernard Gilkey	.30	.14
☐ 13 Don Mattingly	1.00	.45
☐ 14 Albert Belle	.75	.35
☐ 15 Doug Drabek	.15	.07
☐ 16 Tony Gwynn	1.50	.70
☐ 17 Delino DeShields	.15	.07
☐ 18 Bobby Bonilla	.30	.14
☐ 19 Cliff Floyd	.30	.14
☐ 20 Frank Thomas	2.50	1.10
☐ 21 Raul Mondesi	.40	.18
☐ 22 Dave Nilsson	.30	.14
☐ 23 Todd Zeile	.15	.07
☐ 24 Bernie Williams	.60	.25
☐ 25 Kirby Puckett	1.25	.55
☐ 26 David Cone	.30	.14
☐ 27 Darren Daulton	.30	.14
☐ 28 Marquis Grissom	.30	.14
☐ 29 Randy Johnson	.40	.18
☐ 30 Jeff Kent	.15	.07
☐ 31 Orlando Merced	.15	.07
☐ 32 Dave Justice	.60	.25
☐ 33 Ivan Rodriguez	.75	.35
☐ 34 Kirk Gibson	.30	.14
☐ 35 Alex Fernandez	.30	.14
☐ 36 Rick Wilkins	.15	.07
☐ 37 Andy Benes	.15	.07
☐ 38 Bret Saberhagen	.15	.07
☐ 39 Billy Ashley	.15	.07
☐ 40 Jose Rijo	.15	.07
☐ 41 Matt Williams	.40	.18
☐ 42 Lenny Dykstra	.30	.14
☐ 43 Jay Bell	.30	.14
☐ 44 Reggie Jefferson	.30	.14
☐ 45 Greg Maddux	2.00	.90
☐ 46 Gary Sheffield	.60	.25
☐ 47 Bret Boone	.15	.07
☐ 48 Jeff Bagwell	1.25	.55
☐ 49 Ben McDonald	.15	.07
☐ 50 Eric Karros	.30	.14
☐ 51 Roger Clemens	1.25	.55
☐ 52 Sammy Sosa	.60	.25
☐ 53 Barry Bonds	.75	.35
☐ 54 Joey Hamilton	.30	.14
☐ 55 Brian Jordan	.30	.14
☐ 56 Wil Cordero	.15	.07
☐ 57 Aaron Sele	.15	.07
☐ 58 Paul O'Neill	.30	.14
☐ 59 Carlos Garcia	.15	.07
☐ 60 Mike Mussina	.60	.25
☐ 61 John Olerud	.30	.14
☐ 62 Kevin Appier	.30	.14
☐ 63 Matt Mieske	.30	.14
☐ 64 Carlos Baerga	.30	.14
☐ 65 Ryan Klesko	.40	.18
☐ 66 Jimmy Key	.30	.14
☐ 67 James Mouton	.15	.07
☐ 68 Tim Salmon	.60	.25
☐ 69 Hal Morris	.15	.07
☐ 70 Albie Lopez	.15	.07
☐ 71 Dave Hollins	.15	.07
☐ 72 Greg Colbrunn	.15	.07
☐ 73 Juan Gonzalez	1.50	.70
☐ 74 Wally Joyner	.30	.14
☐ 75 Bob Hamelin	.15	.07
☐ 76 Brady Anderson	.40	.18
☐ 77 Deion Sanders	.60	.25
☐ 78 Javier Lopez	.40	.18
☐ 79 Brian McRae	.15	.07
☐ 80 Craig Biggio	.40	.18
☐ 81 Kenny Lofton	.75	.35
☐ 82 Cecil Fielder	.30	.14
☐ 83 Mike Piazza	2.00	.90
☐ 84 Rafael Palmeiro	.40	.18
☐ 85 Jim Thome	.60	.25
☐ 86 Ruben Sierra	.15	.07
☐ 87 Mark Langston	.15	.07
☐ 88 John Valentin	.30	.14
☐ 89 Shawon Dunston	.15	.07
☐ 90 Travis Fryman	.30	.14
☐ 91 Chuck Knoblauch	.60	.25
☐ 92 Dean Palmer	.30	.14
☐ 93 Robby Thompson	.15	.07
☐ 94 Barry Larkin	.40	.18
☐ 95 Darren Lewis	.15	.07
☐ 96 Andres Galarraga	.40	.18
☐ 97 Tony Phillips	.15	.07
☐ 98 Mo Vaughn	.75	.35
☐ 99 Pedro Martinez	.60	.25
☐ 100 Chad Curtis	.15	.07
☐ 101 Brent Gates	.15	.07
☐ 102 Pat Hentgen	.30	.14
☐ 103 Rico Brogna	.15	.07
☐ 104 Carlos Delgado	.30	.14
☐ 105 Manny Ramirez	.60	.25
☐ 106 Mike Greenwell	.15	.07
☐ 107 Wade Boggs	.60	.25
☐ 108 Ozzie Smith	.75	.35
☐ 109 Rusty Greer	.60	.25
☐ 110 Willie Greene	.15	.07
☐ 111 Chili Davis	.30	.14
☐ 112 Reggie Sanders	.15	.07
☐ 113 Roberto Kelly	.15	.07
☐ 114 Tom Glavine	.40	.18
☐ 115 Moises Alou	.30	.14
☐ 116 Dennis Eckersley	.40	.18
☐ 117 Danny Tartabull	.15	.07
☐ 118 Jeff Conine	.30	.14
☐ 119 Will Clark	.40	.18
☐ 120 Joe Carter	.40	.18
☐ 121 Mark McGwire	1.25	.55
☐ 122 Cal Ripken Jr.	2.50	1.10
☐ 123 Danny Jackson	.15	.07
☐ 124 Phil Plantier	.15	.07
☐ 125 Dante Bichette	.40	.18
☐ 126 Jack McDowell	.15	.07
☐ 127 Jose Canseco	.40	.18
☐ 128 Roberto Alomar	.60	.25
☐ 129 Rondell White	.30	.14
☐ 130 Ray Lankford	.40	.18
☐ 131 Ryan Thompson	.15	.07
☐ 132 Ken Caminiti	.60	.25
☐ 133 Gregg Jefferies	.30	.14
☐ 134 Omar Vizquel	.30	.14
☐ 135 Mark Grace	.40	.18
☐ 136 Derek Bell	.30	.14
☐ 137 Mickey Tettleton	.15	.07
☐ 138 Wilson Alvarez	.30	.14
☐ 139 Larry Walker	.60	.25
☐ 140 Bo Jackson	.30	.14
☐ 141 Alex Rodriguez	2.50	1.10
☐ 142 Orlando Miller	.15	.07
☐ 143 Shawn Green	.30	.14
☐ 144 Steve Dunn	.15	.07
☐ 145 Midre Cummings	.15	.07
☐ 146 Chan Ho Park	.60	.25
☐ 147 Jose Oliva	.15	.07
☐ 148 Armando Benitez	.15	.07
☐ 149 J.R. Phillips	.15	.07
☐ 150 Charles Johnson	.30	.14
☐ 151 Garret Anderson	.40	.18
☐ 152 Russ Davis	.15	.07
☐ 153 Brian L.Hunter	.30	.14
☐ 154 Ernie Young	.15	.07
☐ 155 Marc Newfield	.30	.14
☐ 156 Greg Pirkl	.15	.07
☐ 157 Scott Ruffcorn	.15	.07
☐ 158 Rikkert Faneyte	.15	.07
☐ 159 Duane Singleton	.15	.07
☐ 160 Gabe White	.15	.07
☐ 161 Alex Gonzalez	.30	.14
☐ 162 Chipper Jones	2.00	.90
☐ 163 Mike Kelly	.15	.07
☐ 164 Kurt Miller	.15	.07
☐ 165 Roberto Petagine	.15	.07
☐ 166 Jeff Bagwell CL	.60	.25
☐ 167 Mike Piazza CL	1.00	.45
☐ 168 Ken Griffey Jr. CL	1.50	.70
☐ 169 Frank Thomas CL	1.50	.70
☐ 170 Barry Bonds CL Cal Ripken	1.25	.55

1995 Sportflix Artist's Proofs

Cards from this 170-card parallel set were randomly inserted in packs at a rate of one in 36. Only 700 sets were printed. The "Artist's Proof" logo is printed in gold foil at the bottom right and the player's last name expands and contracts with the tilting of the card.

	MINT	NRMT
COMPLETE SET (170)	1000.00	450.00
COMMON CARD (1-170)	2.50	1.10

*STARS: 10X TO 25X BASIC CARDS ..
*YOUNG STARS: 8X TO 20X BASIC CARDS

1995 Sportflix Detonators

Randomly inserted in packs at a rate of one in 16, this nine-card set highlights power hitters. The player is featured in a full-color cutout action shot atop a gold column with his name inscribed. The background is set back and is lit up with fireworks. The player's team logo and a rocket with the word "Detonators" is printed along the bottom of the card. A blue-sky with a Greek column serves as a backdrop for the borderless backs. A full-color shot of the player is pictured in the column and a short synopsis of the playerís '94 performance is printed in black type on the right side of the back. Backs are numbered with the prefix "DE".

	MINT	NRMT
COMPLETE SET (9)	30.00	13.50
COMMON CARD (1-9)	1.00	.45

	MINT	NRMT
☐ DE1 Jeff Bagwell	4.00	1.80
☐ DE2 Matt Williams	1.50	.70
☐ DE3 Ken Griffey Jr.	10.00	4.50
☐ DE4 Frank Thomas	8.00	3.60
☐ DE5 Mike Piazza	6.00	2.70
☐ DE6 Barry Bonds	2.50	1.10
☐ DE7 Albert Belle	2.50	1.10
☐ DE8 Cliff Floyd	1.00	.45
☐ DE9 Juan Gonzalez	5.00	2.20

1995 Sportflix Double Take

Randomly inserted in packs at a rate of one in 48, this 12-card set features two stars in one see-through 3-D card. Fronts feature the Sportflix "Magic Motion" process that allows the viewer to see two different images when the card is tilted. The players' names are reverse-printed across a red bar with the corresponding team logo on the bottom right. When the card is titled, the player's picture, name and team logo appear. "Double Take" is printed vertically on the left side of the card. Backs are see through and contain only the card number.

	MINT	NRMT
COMPLETE SET (12)	150.00	70.00
COMMON CARD (1-12)	4.00	1.80

	MINT	NRMT
☐ 1 Jeff Bagwell Frank Thomas	25.00	11.00
☐ 2 Will Clark Fred McGriff	4.00	1.80
☐ 3 Roberto Alomar Jeff Kent	4.00	1.80
☐ 4 Matt Williams Wade Boggs	4.00	1.80
☐ 5 Cal Ripken Jr. Ozzie Smith	20.00	9.00
☐ 6 Alex Rodriguez Wil Cordero	20.00	9.00
☐ 7 Mike Piazza Carlos Delgado	15.00	6.75
☐ 8 Kenny Lofton Dave Justice	6.00	2.70
☐ 9 Barry Bonds	25.00	11.00

Card	MINT	NRMT
Ken Griffey Jr.		
☐ 10 Albert Belle	6.00	2.70
Raul Mondesi		
☐ 11 Tony Gwynn	15.00	6.75
Kirby Puckett		
☐ 12 Jimmy Key	12.00	5.50
Greg Maddux		

1995 Sportflix Hammer Team

This 18-card set was inserted randomly in packs at a rate of one in 48 and looks at the league's top hitters. The 3-D fronts feature a full-color cutout of the player in action set against a backdrop of blue sky and basepaths. Sledgehammers are placed in the foreground and background of the fronts, while the player's name is printed at the bottom of the card against a green grass background. Full-bleed, horizontal backs are numbered with the prefix "HT" and picture the player in full color. A swinging sledgehammer is in motion against a backdrop of green grass while a 1994 player synopsis is printed in white type underneath the hammer.

	MINT	NRMT
COMPLETE SET (18)	25.00	11.00
COMMON CARD (1-18)	.50	.23
☐ HT1 Ken Griffey Jr.	5.00	2.20
☐ HT2 Frank Thomas	4.00	1.80
☐ HT3 Jeff Bagwell	2.00	.90
☐ HT4 Mike Piazza	3.00	1.35
☐ HT5 Cal Ripken Jr.	4.00	1.80
☐ HT6 Albert Belle	1.25	.55
☐ HT7 Barry Bonds	1.25	.55
☐ HT8 Don Mattingly	2.00	.90
☐ HT9 Will Clark	.75	.35
☐ HT10 Tony Gwynn	2.00	.90
☐ HT11 Matt Williams	.50	.23
☐ HT12 Kirby Puckett	2.00	.90
☐ HT13 Manny Ramirez		
☐ HT14 Fred McGriff	.75	.35
☐ HT15 Juan Gonzalez	2.50	1.10
☐ HT16 Kenny Lofton	1.25	.55
☐ HT17 Raul Mondesi	.75	.35
☐ HT18 Tim Salmon		

1995 Sportflix ProMotion

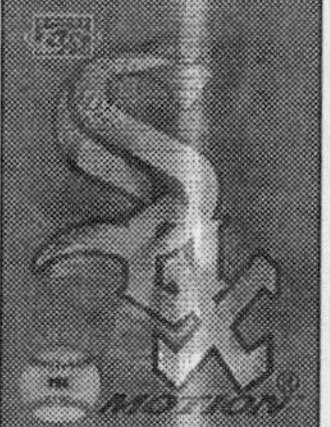

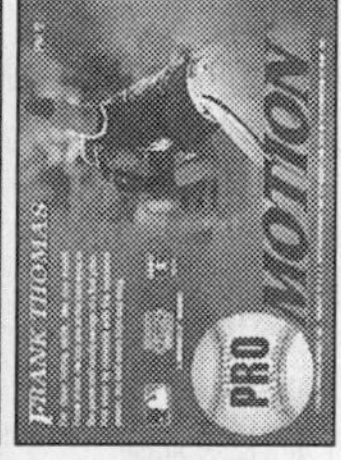

Randomly inserted in jumbo packs at a rate of one in 18, this 12-card set features top stars in the "Magic Motion" technology. Card fronts are coordinated in team colors and depict the player in a full-color action photo. The player's team logo is displayed when tilted. The horizontal backs feature the player in an action shot and are numbered with the prefix "PM". The player's name appears in white type across the top while the "Pro-Motion" logo is printed in black across the bottom of the back.

	MINT	NRMT
COMPLETE SET (12)	150.00	70.00
COMMPN CARD (PM1-PM12)	5.00	2.20
☐ PM1 Ken Griffey Jr.	40.00	18.00
☐ PM2 Frank Thomas	30.00	13.50
☐ PM3 Cal Ripken Jr.	30.00	13.50
☐ PM4 Jeff Bagwell	15.00	6.75
☐ PM5 Mike Piazza	25.00	11.00
☐ PM6 Matt Williams	7.00	3.10
☐ PM7 Albert Belle	10.00	4.50
☐ PM8 Jose Canseco	5.00	2.20
☐ PM9 Don Mattingly	12.00	5.50
☐ PM10 Barry Bonds	10.00	4.50
☐ PM11 Will Clark	7.00	3.10
☐ PM12 Kirby Puckett	15.00	6.75

1996 Sportflix

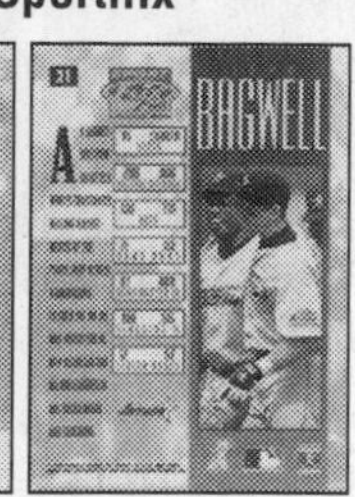

With retail only distribution, this 144 card set comes in five card packs that retail for $1.99. Regular cards picture two different pieces of photography. By flicking the wrist, one image disappears and another appears. Some cards use two different photos, and others use sequence action photography to create the illusion of animation. The wording in the bottom border also changes with movement. The set contains the UC3 Subset (97-120), Rookies Subset (121-141), and Checklists (142-144). The UC3 Subset features veteran superstars in 3-D animation. The 21-card Rookie subset carries color player photos on a background of part of a baseball that changes into a wooden baseball bat section when moved. Eight of the Rookies subset cards were made in jumbo (5 X 7") format, renumbered out of eight, and inserted as "chiptoppers" in retail boxes. These cards are valued at 15 times the corresponding basic card.

	MINT	NRMT
COMPLETE SET (144)	25.00	11.00
COMMON CARD (1-144)	.15	.07
☐ 1 Wade Boggs	.60	.25
☐ 2 Tim Salmon	.60	.25
☐ 3 Will Clark	.40	.18
☐ 4 Dante Bichette	.30	.14
☐ 5 Barry Bonds	.75	.35
☐ 6 Kirby Puckett	1.25	.55
☐ 7 Albert Belle	.75	.35
☐ 8 Greg Maddux	2.00	.90
☐ 9 Tony Gwynn	1.50	.70
☐ 10 Mike Piazza	2.00	.90
☐ 11 Ivan Rodriguez	.75	.35
☐ 12 Marty Cordova	.15	.07
☐ 13 Frank Thomas	2.50	1.10
☐ 14 Raul Mondesi	.40	.18
☐ 15 Johnny Damon	.30	.14
☐ 16 Mark McGwire	1.25	.55
☐ 17 Len Dykstra	.30	.14
☐ 18 Ken Griffey Jr.	3.00	1.35
☐ 19 Chipper Jones	2.00	.90
☐ 20 Alex Rodriguez	2.50	1.10
☐ 21 Jeff Bagwell	1.25	.55
☐ 22 Jim Edmonds	.60	.25
☐ 23 Edgar Martinez	.40	.18
☐ 24 David Cone	.30	.14
☐ 25 Tom Glavine	.30	.14
☐ 26 Eddie Murray	.60	.25
☐ 27 Paul Molitor	.60	.25
☐ 28 Ryan Klesko	.40	.18
☐ 29 Rafael Palmeiro	.40	.18
☐ 30 Manny Ramirez	.60	.25
☐ 31 Mo Vaughn	.75	.35
☐ 32 Rico Brogna	.15	.07
☐ 33 Marc Newfield	.15	.07
☐ 34 J.T. Snow	.30	.14
☐ 35 Reggie Sanders	.15	.07
☐ 36 Fred McGriff	.40	.18
☐ 37 Craig Biggio	.40	.18
☐ 38 Jeff King	.30	.14
☐ 39 Kenny Lofton	.75	.35
☐ 40 Gary Gaetti	.30	.14
☐ 41 Eric Karros	.30	.14
☐ 42 Jason Isringhausen	.15	.07
☐ 43 B.J. Surhoff	.30	.14
☐ 44 Michael Tucker	.30	.14
☐ 45 Gary Sheffield	.60	.25
☐ 46 Chili Davis	.30	.14
☐ 47 Bobby Bonilla	.30	.14
☐ 48 Hideo Nomo	1.50	.70
☐ 49 Ray Durham	.30	.14
☐ 50 Phil Nevin	.15	.07
☐ 51 Randy Johnson	.60	.25
☐ 52 Bill Pulsipher	.15	.07
☐ 53 Ozzie Smith	.75	.35
☐ 54 Cal Ripken	2.50	1.10
☐ 55 Cecil Fielder	.30	.14
☐ 56 Matt Williams	.40	.18
☐ 57 Sammy Sosa	.60	.25
☐ 58 Roger Clemens	1.25	.55
☐ 59 Brian L.Hunter	.30	.14
☐ 60 Barry Larkin	.40	.18
☐ 61 Charles Johnson	.30	.14
☐ 62 David Justice	.60	.25
☐ 63 Garret Anderson	.30	.14
☐ 64 Rondell White	.30	.14
☐ 65 Derek Bell	.15	.07
☐ 66 Andres Galarraga	.40	.18
☐ 67 Moises Alou	.30	.14
☐ 68 Travis Fryman	.30	.14
☐ 69 Pedro J. Martinez	.60	.25
☐ 70 Carlos Baerga	.30	.14
☐ 71 John Valentin	.30	.14
☐ 72 Larry Walker	.60	.25
☐ 73 Roberto Alomar	.60	.25
☐ 74 Mike Mussina	.60	.25
☐ 75 Kevin Appier	.30	.14
☐ 76 Bernie Williams	.60	.25
☐ 77 Ray Lankford	.30	.14
☐ 78 Gregg Jefferies	.30	.14
☐ 79 Robin Ventura	.30	.14
☐ 80 Kenny Rogers	.15	.07
☐ 81 Paul O'Neill	.15	.07
☐ 82 Mark Grace	.40	.18
☐ 83 Deion Sanders	.60	.25
☐ 84 Tino Martinez	.60	.25
☐ 85 Joe Carter	.30	.14
☐ 86 Pete Schourek	.15	.07
☐ 87 Jack McDowell	.15	.07
☐ 88 John Mabry	.30	.14
☐ 89 Darren Daulton	.30	.14
☐ 90 Jim Thome	.60	.25
☐ 91 Jay Buhner	.40	.18
☐ 92 Jay Bell	.15	.07
☐ 93 Kevin Seitzer	.15	.07
☐ 94 Jose Canseco	.40	.18
☐ 95 Juan Gonzalez	1.50	.70
☐ 96 Jeff Conine	.30	.14
☐ 97 Chipper Jones UC3	1.00	.45
☐ 98 Ken Griffey Jr. UC3	1.50	.70
☐ 99 Frank Thomas UC3	1.50	.70
☐ 100 Cal Ripken UC3	1.25	.55
☐ 101 Albert Belle UC3	.60	.25
☐ 102 Mike Piazza UC3	1.00	.45
☐ 103 Dante Bichette UC3	.30	.14
☐ 104 Sammy Sosa UC3	.60	.25
☐ 105 Mo Vaughn UC3	.60	.25
☐ 106 Tim Salmon UC3	.60	.25
☐ 107 Reggie Sanders UC3	.15	.07
☐ 108 Gary Sheffield UC3	.60	.25
☐ 109 Ruben Rivera UC3	.15	.07
☐ 110 Rafael Palmeiro UC3	.40	.18
☐ 111 Edgar Martinez UC3	.40	.18
☐ 112 Barry Bonds UC3	.60	.25
☐ 113 Manny Ramirez UC3	.60	.25
☐ 114 Larry Walker UC3	.60	.25
☐ 115 Jeff Bagwell UC3	.60	.25
☐ 116 Matt Williams UC3	.40	.18
☐ 117 Mark McGwire UC3	.60	.25
☐ 118 Johnny Damon UC3	.15	.07
☐ 119 Eddie Murray UC3	.60	.25
☐ 120 Jay Buhner UC3	.40	.18
☐ 121 Tim Unroe	.15	.07
☐ 122 Todd Hollandsworth	.30	.14
☐ 123 Tony Clark	.60	.25
☐ 124 Roger Cedeno	.30	.14
☐ 125 Jim Pittsley	.30	.14
☐ 126 Ruben Rivera	.30	.14
☐ 127 Bob Wolcott	.15	.07
☐ 128 Chan Ho Park	.60	.25
☐ 129 Chris Snopek	.15	.07
☐ 130 Alex Ochoa	.15	.07
☐ 131 Yamil Benitez	.30	.14
☐ 132 Jimmy Haynes	.15	.07
☐ 133 Dustin Hermanson	.15	.07
☐ 134 Shawn Estes	.30	.14
☐ 135 Howard Battle	.15	.07
☐ 136 Matt Lawton	.15	.07
☐ 137 Terrell Wade	.15	.07
☐ 138 Jason Schmidt	.30	.14
☐ 139 Derek Jeter	2.00	.90
☐ 140 Shannon Stewart	.15	.07
☐ 141 Chris Stynes	.15	.07
☐ 142 Ken Griffey Jr. CL	1.50	.70
☐ 143 Greg Maddux CL	.60	.25
☐ 144 Cal Ripken CL	1.25	.55

1996 Sportflix Artist's Proofs

Inserted at the rate of one in 30, cards from this 144-card set are parallel to the regular set. A gold-foil stamped

Artist's Proof logo distinguish them from their regular issue counterparts.

	MINT	NRMT
COMPLETE SET (144)	1000.00	450.00
COMMON CARD (1-144)	3.00	1.35

*STARS: 15X TO 30X BASIC CARDS..
*YOUNG STARS: 12.5X TO 25X BASIC CARDS

1996 Sportflix Double Take

Randomly inserted in jumbo packs, this 12-card set features color player photos of 2 players per card that play the same position.

	MINT	NRMT
COMPLETE SET (12)	120.00	55.00
COMMON CARD (1-12)	5.00	2.20
☐ 1 Barry Larkin Cal Ripken	15.00	6.75
☐ 2 Roberto Alomar Craig Biggio	5.00	2.20
☐ 3 Chipper Jones Matt Williams	12.00	5.50
☐ 4 Ken Griffey Ruben Rivera	20.00	9.00
☐ 5 Greg Maddux Hideo Nomo	12.00	5.50
☐ 6 Frank Thomas Mo Vaughn	15.00	6.75
☐ 7 Ivan Rodriguez Mike Piazza	12.00	5.50
☐ 8 Albert Belle Barry Bonds	6.00	2.70
☐ 9 Alex Rodriguez Derek Jeter	20.00	9.00
☐ 10 Kirby Puckett Tony Gwynn	15.00	6.75
☐ 11 Manny Ramirez Sammy Sosa	5.00	2.20
☐ 12 Jeff Bagwell Rico Brogna	6.00	2.70

1996 Sportflix Hit Parade

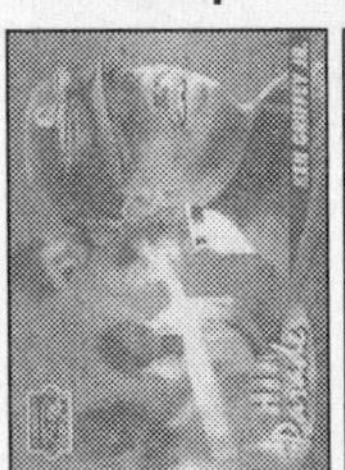

With an insertion rate of one in 35, this 16-card set features color player photos of hitters in 3D with a background scene in full-motion animation.

	MINT	NRMT
COMPLETE SET (16)	120.00	55.00
COMMON CARD (1-16)	2.50	1.10
☐ 1 Ken Griffey Jr.	20.00	9.00
☐ 2 Cal Ripken	15.00	6.75
☐ 3 Frank Thomas	15.00	6.75
☐ 4 Mike Piazza	12.00	5.50
☐ 5 Mo Vaughn	5.00	2.20
☐ 6 Albert Belle	5.00	2.20
☐ 7 Jeff Bagwell	8.00	3.60
☐ 8 Matt Williams	3.50	1.55
☐ 9 Sammy Sosa	4.00	1.80
☐ 10 Kirby Puckett	8.00	3.60
☐ 11 Dante Bichette	2.50	1.10
☐ 12 Gary Sheffield	4.00	1.80
☐ 13 Tony Gwynn	8.00	3.60
☐ 14 Wade Boggs	4.00	1.80
☐ 15 Chipper Jones	12.00	5.50
☐ 16 Barry Bonds	5.00	2.20

1996 Sportflix Power Surge

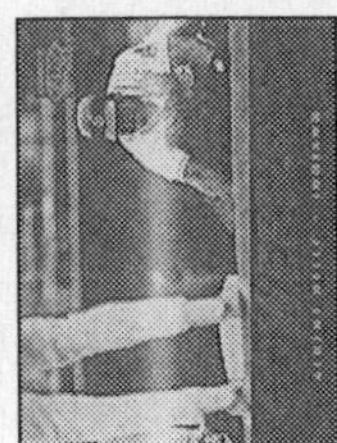

With an insertion rate of one in 35, this retail only 24-card set is pinted on clear plastic and is a 3-D parallel rendition of the UC3 subset found in the regular Sportflix set.

	MINT	NRMT
COMPLETE SET (24)	200.00	90.00
COMMON CARD (1-24)	3.00	1.35
☐ 1 Chipper Jones	25.00	11.00
☐ 2 Ken Griffey Jr.	40.00	18.00
☐ 3 Frank Thomas	30.00	13.50
☐ 4 Cal Ripken	30.00	13.50
☐ 5 Albert Belle	10.00	4.50
☐ 6 Mike Piazza	25.00	11.00
☐ 7 Dante Bichette	4.00	1.80
☐ 8 Sammy Sosa	6.00	2.70
☐ 9 Mo Vaughn	10.00	4.50
☐ 10 Tim Salmon	5.00	2.20
☐ 11 Reggie Sanders	3.00	1.35
☐ 12 Gary Sheffield	6.00	2.70
☐ 13 Ruben Rivera	4.00	1.80
☐ 14 Rafael Palmeiro	6.00	2.70
☐ 15 Edgar Martinez	6.00	2.70
☐ 16 Barry Bonds	10.00	4.50
☐ 17 Manny Ramirez	8.00	3.60
☐ 18 Larry Walker	8.00	3.60
☐ 19 Jeff Bagwell	15.00	6.75
☐ 20 Matt Williams	6.00	2.70
☐ 21 Mark McGwire	15.00	6.75
☐ 22 Johnny Damon	4.00	1.80
☐ 23 Eddie Murray	8.00	3.60
☐ 24 Jay Buhner	6.00	2.70

1996 Sportflix ProMotion

Inserted at the rate of one in 17, this 20-card set uses morphing technology and multi-phase animation to turn a player's photo into a bat, a ball, a glove, or a catcher's mask.

	MINT	NRMT
COMPLETE SET (20)	100.00	45.00
COMMON CARD (1-20)	1.00	.45
☐ 1 Cal Ripken	12.00	5.50
☐ 2 Greg Maddux	10.00	4.50
☐ 3 Mo Vaughn	4.00	1.80
☐ 4 Albert Belle	4.00	1.80
☐ 5 Mike Piazza	10.00	4.50
☐ 6 Ken Griffey Jr.	15.00	6.75
☐ 7 Frank Thomas	12.00	5.50
☐ 8 Jeff Bagwell	6.00	2.70
☐ 9 Hideo Nomo	8.00	3.60
☐ 10 Chipper Jones	10.00	4.50
☐ 11 Tony Gwynn	6.00	2.70
☐ 12 Don Mattingly	8.00	3.60
☐ 13 Dante Bichette	1.50	.70
☐ 14 Matt Williams	2.00	.90
☐ 15 Manny Ramirez		
☐ 16 Barry Bonds	4.00	1.80
☐ 17 Reggie Sanders	1.00	.45
☐ 18 Tim Salmon		
☐ 19 Ruben Rivera	1.00	.45
☐ 20 Garret Anderson	1.50	.70

1911 Sporting Life M116

The cards in this 288-card set measure approximately 1 1/2" by 2 5/8". The Sporting Life set was offered as a premium to the publication's subscribers in 1911. Each of the 24 series of 12 cards came in an envelope printed with a list of the players within. Cards marked with an asterisk are also found with a special blue background and are worth double the listed price. McConnell appears with both Boston AL (common) and Chicago White Sox (scarce); McQuillan appears with Phillies (common) and Cincinnati (scarce). Cards are numbered in the checklist below alphabetically within team. Teams are ordered alphabetically within league: Boston AL (1-19), Chicago AL (20-36), Cleveland (37-52), Detroit (53-73), New York AL (74-84), Philadelphia AL (85-105), St. Louis AL (106-120), Washington (121-134), Boston NL (135-147), Brooklyn (148-164), Chicago NL (165-185), Cincinnati (186-203), New York NL (204-223), Philadelphia NL (224-242), Pittsburgh (243-261), and St. Louis (262-279). Cards 280-288 feature minor leaguers and are somewhat more difficult to find since most are from the tougher higher series.

	EX-MT	VG-E
COMPLETE SET (290)	30000.00	13500.00
COMMON MAJOR (1-279)	50.00	22.00
COMMON MINOR (280-288)	50.00	22.00
COMMON S19-S24	100.00	45.00
☐ 1 Frank Arellanes	50.00	22.00
☐ 2 Bill Carrigan	50.00	22.00
☐ 3 Ed Cicotte	125.00	55.00
☐ 4 Ray Collins S24	100.00	45.00
☐ 5 Pat Donahue	50.00	22.00
☐ 6 Patsy Donovan MG S21	100.00	45.00
☐ 7 Arthur Engle	50.00	22.00
☐ 8 Larry Gardner S24	100.00	45.00
☐ 9 Charles Hall	50.00	22.00
☐ 10 Harry Hooper S23	300.00	135.00
☐ 11 Edwin Karger	50.00	22.00
☐ 12 Harry Lord *	50.00	22.00
☐ 13 Thomas Madden S24	100.00	45.00
☐ 14A Amby McConnell (Boston AL)	50.00	22.00
☐ 14B Amby McConnell (Chicago AL)	2000.00	900.00
☐ 15 Tris Speaker S23	600.00	275.00
☐ 16 Jake Stahl	60.00	27.00
☐ 17 John Thoney	50.00	22.00
☐ 18 Heinie Wagner	60.00	27.00
☐ 19 Joe Wood S23	200.00	90.00
☐ 20 Lena Blackburn UER (Sic, Blackburne)	50.00	22.00
☐ 21 James J. Block S21	100.00	45.00
☐ 22 Patsy Dougherty	50.00	22.00
☐ 23 Hugh Duffy MG	125.00	55.00
☐ 24 Ed Hahn	50.00	22.00
☐ 25 Paul Meloan S24	100.00	45.00
☐ 26 Fred Parent	50.00	22.00
☐ 27 Frederick Payne S21	100.00	45.00
☐ 28 William Purtell	50.00	22.00
☐ 29 James Scott S23	100.00	45.00
☐ 30 Frank Smith	50.00	22.00
☐ 31 Billy Sullivan	60.00	27.00
☐ 32 Lee Tannehill	50.00	22.00
☐ 33 Ed Walsh	125.00	55.00
☐ 34 Guy(Doc) White	50.00	22.00
☐ 35 Irv Young	50.00	22.00
☐ 36 Dutch Zwilling S24	100.00	45.00
☐ 37 Harry Bemis	50.00	22.00
☐ 38 Charles Berger	50.00	22.00
☐ 39 Joseph Birmingham	50.00	22.00
☐ 40 Hugh Bradley	50.00	22.00
☐ 41 Nig Clarke	50.00	22.00
☐ 42 Cy Falkenberg	50.00	22.00
☐ 43 Elmer Flick	150.00	70.00
☐ 44 Addie Joss	200.00	90.00
☐ 45 Napoleon Lajoie *	300.00	135.00
☐ 46 Frederick Linke S20	100.00	45.00
☐ 47 B.(Bris) Lord	50.00	22.00
☐ 48 Deacon McGuire MG	50.00	22.00

Card	Price	Price
☐ 49 Harry Niles	50.00	22.00
☐ 50 George Stovall	50.00	22.00
☐ 51 Terry Turner	50.00	22.00
☐ 52 Cy Young	400.00	180.00
☐ 53 Heine Beckendorf	50.00	22.00
☐ 54 Donie Bush	50.00	22.00
☐ 55 Ty Cobb *	2000.00	900.00
☐ 56 Sam Crawford *	150.00	70.00
☐ 57 Jim Delehanty	60.00	27.00
☐ 58 Bill Donovan	50.00	22.00
☐ 59 Hugh Jennings MG *	125.00	55.00
☐ 60 Davy Jones	50.00	22.00
☐ 61 Tom Jones	50.00	22.00
☐ 62 Chick Lathers S21	100.00	45.00
☐ 63 Matty McIntyre	50.00	22.00
☐ 64 George Moriarty	60.00	27.00
☐ 65 George Mullin	50.00	22.00
☐ 66 Charley O'Leary	50.00	22.00
☐ 67 Hub Pernoll S23	100.00	45.00
☐ 68 Boss Schmidt	50.00	22.00
☐ 69 Oscar Stanage	50.00	22.00
☐ 70 Sailor Stroud S21	100.00	45.00
☐ 71 Ed Summers	50.00	22.00
☐ 72 Ed Willett	50.00	22.00
☐ 73 Ralph Works	50.00	22.00
☐ 74 Jimmy Austin S19	100.00	45.00
☐ 75 Hal Chase *	100.00	45.00
☐ 76 Birdie Cree	50.00	22.00
☐ 77 Lou Criger	50.00	22.00
☐ 78 Russ Ford S23	100.00	45.00
☐ 79 Earle Gardner S23	100.00	45.00
☐ 80 John Knight S19	100.00	45.00
☐ 81 Frank LaPorte	50.00	22.00
☐ 82 George Stallings MG	50.00	22.00
☐ 83 Jeff Sweeney S19	100.00	45.00
☐ 84 Harry Wolter	50.00	22.00
☐ 85 Tommy Atkins S24	100.00	45.00
☐ 86 Frank Baker	150.00	70.00
☐ 87 Jack Barry	60.00	27.00
☐ 88 Chief Bender *	100.00	45.00
☐ 89 Eddie Collins *	150.00	70.00
☐ 90 Jack Coombs	100.00	45.00
☐ 91 Harry Davis *	50.00	22.00
☐ 92 Jimmy Dygert	50.00	22.00
☐ 93 Topsy Hartsel	50.00	22.00
☐ 94 Heinie Heitmuller	50.00	22.00
☐ 95 Harry Krause	50.00	22.00
☐ 96 Jack Lapp S24	100.00	45.00
☐ 97 Paddy Livingstone	50.00	22.00
☐ 98 Connie Mack MG	250.00	110.00
☐ 99 Stuffy McInnis S24 UER (Misspelled McInnes on card)	100.00	45.00
☐ 100 Cy Morgan	50.00	22.00
☐ 101 Danny Murphy	50.00	22.00
☐ 102 Rube Oldring	50.00	22.00
☐ 103 Eddie Plank	300.00	135.00
☐ 104 Amos Strunk S24	100.00	45.00
☐ 105 Ira Thomas *	50.00	22.00
☐ 106 Bill Bailey	50.00	22.00
☐ 107 Dode Criss S19	100.00	45.00
☐ 108 Bert Graham	50.00	22.00
☐ 109 Roy Hartzell	50.00	22.00
☐ 110 Danny Hoffman	50.00	22.00
☐ 111 Harry Howell	50.00	22.00
☐ 112 Joe Lake S19	100.00	45.00
☐ 113 Jack O'Conner	50.00	22.00
☐ 114 Barney Pelty	50.00	22.00
☐ 115 Jack Powell	50.00	22.00
☐ 116 Al Schweitzer	50.00	22.00
☐ 117 Jim Stephens	50.00	22.00
☐ 118 George Stone	50.00	22.00
☐ 119 Rube Waddell	150.00	70.00
☐ 120 Bobby Wallace	100.00	45.00
☐ 121 Wid Conroy	50.00	22.00
☐ 122 Kid Elberfeld	50.00	22.00
☐ 123 Eddie Foster	50.00	22.00
☐ 124 Doc Gessler	50.00	22.00
☐ 125 Walter Johnson	700.00	325.00
☐ 126 Red Killifer S22	100.00	45.00
☐ 127 Jimmy McAleer MG	50.00	22.00
☐ 128 George McBride S21	100.00	45.00
☐ 129 Clyde Milan	60.00	27.00
☐ 130 Warren Miller S23	100.00	45.00
☐ 131 Doc Reisling	50.00	22.00
☐ 132 Germany Schaefer	60.00	27.00
☐ 133 Gabby Street	50.00	22.00
☐ 134 Bob Unglaub	50.00	22.00
☐ 135 Fred Beck	50.00	22.00
☐ 136 Buster Brown	50.00	22.00
☐ 137 Cliff Curtis S23	100.00	45.00
☐ 138 George Ferguson	50.00	22.00
☐ 139 Samuel Frock S20	100.00	45.00
☐ 140 Peaches Graham	50.00	22.00
☐ 141 Buck Herzog	50.00	22.00
☐ 142 Fred Lake MG	50.00	22.00
☐ 143 Bayard Sharpe S23	100.00	45.00
☐ 144 David Shean S20	100.00	45.00
☐ 145 Charlie Smith S22	100.00	45.00
☐ 146 Harry Smith	50.00	22.00
☐ 147 Bill Sweeney	50.00	22.00
☐ 148 Cy Barger	50.00	22.00
☐ 149 George Bell	50.00	22.00
☐ 150 Bill Bergen	50.00	22.00
☐ 151 Al Burch	50.00	22.00
☐ 152 Bill Dahlen MG	60.00	27.00
☐ 153 William Davidson S21	100.00	45.00
☐ 154 Frank Dessau S21	100.00	45.00
☐ 155 Tex Erwin S20	100.00	45.00
☐ 156 John Hummel	50.00	22.00
☐ 157 George Hunter	50.00	22.00
☐ 158 Tim Jordan *	50.00	22.00
☐ 159 Ed Lennox	50.00	22.00
☐ 160 Pryor McElveen	50.00	22.00
☐ 161 Tommy McMillan	50.00	22.00
☐ 162 Nap Rucker	60.00	27.00
☐ 163 Doc Scanlon UER (Sic, Scanlan)	50.00	22.00
☐ 164 Kaiser Wilhelm	50.00	22.00
☐ 165 Jimmy Archer S22	100.00	45.00
☐ 166 Ginger Beaumont	50.00	22.00
☐ 167 Mordecai Brown *	150.00	70.00
☐ 168 Frank Chance *	200.00	90.00
☐ 169 Johnny Evers	150.00	70.00
☐ 170 Solly Hofman	50.00	22.00
☐ 171 John Kane	50.00	22.00
☐ 172 Johnny Kling	50.00	22.00
☐ 173 Rube Kroh	50.00	22.00
☐ 174 Harry McIntire	50.00	22.00
☐ 175 Tom Needham	50.00	22.00
☐ 176 Orvie Overall	50.00	22.00
☐ 177 Big Jeff Pfeffer S23	100.00	45.00
☐ 178 Jack Pfiester	50.00	22.00
☐ 179 Ed Reulbach	60.00	27.00
☐ 180 Lew Richie	50.00	22.00
☐ 181 Frank Schulte	50.00	22.00
☐ 182 Jimmy Sheckard	50.00	22.00
☐ 183 Harry Steinfeldt	60.00	27.00
☐ 184 Joe Tinker	150.00	70.00
☐ 185 Heinie Zimmerman S19	100.00	45.00
☐ 186 Fred Beebe	50.00	22.00
☐ 187 Bob Bescher	50.00	22.00
☐ 188 Chappy Charles	50.00	22.00
☐ 189 Tommy Clarke S20	100.00	45.00
☐ 190 Tom Downey	50.00	22.00
☐ 191 Jim Doyle	50.00	22.00
☐ 192 Dick Eagan UER (Sic, Egan)	50.00	22.00
☐ 193 Art Fromme	50.00	22.00
☐ 194 Harry Gaspar S19	100.00	45.00
☐ 195 Clark Griffith MG	125.00	55.00
☐ 196 Doc Hoblitzel	50.00	22.00
☐ 197 Hans Lobert	50.00	22.00
☐ 198 Larry McLean	50.00	22.00
☐ 199 Mike Mitchell	50.00	22.00
☐ 200 Art Phelan S23	100.00	45.00
☐ 201 Jack Rowan	50.00	22.00
☐ 202 Bob Space UER (Sic, Spade)	50.00	22.00
☐ 203 George Suggs	50.00	22.00
☐ 204 Red Ames S22	100.00	45.00
☐ 205 Al Bridwell	50.00	22.00
☐ 206 Doc Crandall	50.00	22.00
☐ 207 Art Devlin	50.00	22.00
☐ 208 Josh Devore S19	100.00	45.00
☐ 209 Larry Doyle *	60.00	27.00
☐ 210 Art Fletcher S22	100.00	45.00
☐ 211 Christy Mathewson *	700.00	325.00
☐ 212 John McGraw MG	200.00	90.00
☐ 213 Fred Merkle	60.00	27.00
☐ 214 Red Murray	50.00	22.00
☐ 215 Chief Meyers S23 UER (Misspelled Myers on card)	100.00	45.00
☐ 216 Bugs Raymond	60.00	27.00
☐ 217 Admiral Schlei	50.00	22.00
☐ 218 Cy Seymour	50.00	22.00
☐ 219 Tillie Shafer S19	100.00	45.00
☐ 220 Fred Snodgrass	60.00	27.00
☐ 221 Fred Tenney *	50.00	22.00
☐ 222 Art Wilson S23	100.00	45.00
☐ 223 Hooks Wiltse	50.00	22.00
☐ 224 Johnny Bates	50.00	22.00
☐ 225 Kitty Bransfeld	50.00	22.00
☐ 226 Red Dooin *	50.00	22.00
☐ 227 Mickey Doolan	50.00	22.00
☐ 228 Bob Ewing	50.00	22.00
☐ 229 Bill Foxen	50.00	22.00
☐ 230 Eddie Grant	50.00	22.00
☐ 231 Fred Jacklitsch	50.00	22.00
☐ 232 Otto Knabe	50.00	22.00
☐ 233 Sherry Magee	50.00	22.00
☐ 234A Geo.McQuillan * (Philadelphia NL)	50.00	22.00
☐ 234B Geo.McQuillan (Cincinnati NL)	2000.00	900.00
☐ 235 Earl Moore	50.00	22.00
☐ 236 Pat Moran	50.00	22.00
☐ 237 Lew Moren	50.00	22.00
☐ 238 Dode Paskert S19	100.00	45.00
☐ 239 Lou Schettler S20	100.00	45.00
☐ 240 Tully Sparks	50.00	22.00
☐ 241 John Titus S23	100.00	45.00
☐ 242A Jimmy Walsh S20 (Dark background)	150.00	70.00
☐ 242B Jimmy Walsh S22 (White background)	150.00	70.00
☐ 243 Ed Abbaticchio	50.00	22.00
☐ 244 Babe Adams	60.00	27.00
☐ 245 Bobby Byrne	50.00	22.00
☐ 246 Howie Camnitz	50.00	22.00
☐ 247 Vin Campbell S21	100.00	45.00
☐ 248 Fred Clarke	125.00	55.00
☐ 249 John Flynn S20	100.00	45.00
☐ 250 George Gibson *	50.00	22.00
☐ 251 Ham Hyatt	50.00	22.00
☐ 252 Fred Leach *	50.00	22.00
☐ 253 Sam Leever	50.00	22.00
☐ 254 Lefty Leifield	50.00	22.00
☐ 255 Nick Maddox	50.00	22.00
☐ 256 Dots Miller	50.00	22.00
☐ 257 Paddy O'Connor	50.00	22.00
☐ 258 Deacon Phillipe	60.00	27.00
☐ 259 Mike Simon S21	100.00	45.00
☐ 260 Hans Wagner *	700.00	325.00
☐ 261 Chief Wilson	50.00	22.00
☐ 262 Les Bachman UER (Sic, Backman)	50.00	22.00
☐ 263 Jack Bliss S21	100.00	45.00
☐ 264 Roger Bresnahan *	125.00	55.00
☐ 265 Frank Corridon	50.00	22.00
☐ 266 Ray Demmitt S22	100.00	45.00
☐ 267 Rube Ellis	50.00	22.00
☐ 268 Steve Evans S23	100.00	45.00
☐ 269 Bob Harmon S20	100.00	45.00
☐ 270 Miller Huggins	125.00	55.00
☐ 271 Rudy Hulswitt	50.00	22.00
☐ 272 Ed Konetchy	50.00	22.00
☐ 273 Johnny Lush	50.00	22.00
☐ 274 Al Mattern	50.00	22.00
☐ 275 Mike Mowery S21	100.00	45.00
☐ 276 Rebel Oakes S24	100.00	45.00
☐ 277 Ed Phelps	50.00	22.00
☐ 278 Slim Sallee	50.00	22.00
☐ 279 Vic Willis	125.00	55.00
☐ 280 Coveleski: Louisville S22 UER (Misspelled Coveleskie on card)	150.00	70.00
☐ 281 Foster: Rochester S19	100.00	45.00
☐ 282 Frill: Jersey City S20	100.00	45.00
☐ 283 Hughes: Rochester S23	100.00	45.00
☐ 284 Krueger: Sacramento S20	100.00	45.00
☐ 285 Mitchell: Rochester S19	100.00	45.00
☐ 286 O'Hara: Toronto	50.00	22.00
☐ 287 Perring: Columbus S20	100.00	45.00
☐ 288 Ray: Western League S24	100.00	45.00

1915 Sporting News M101-5

The cards in this 200-card set measure approximately 1 5/8 by 3". The 1915 M101-5 series of black and white, numbered baseball cards is very similar in style to M101-4. The set was offered as a marketing promotion by C.C. Spink and Son, publishers of The Sporting News ("The Baseball Paper of the World"). Most of the players in this also appear in the M101-4 set. Those cards which are asterisked in the checklist below are those cards which do not appear in the companion M101-4 set issued the next year.

	EX-MT	VG-E
COMPLETE SET (200)	25000.00	11200.00
COMMON CARD (1-200)	45.00	20.00

Card	EX-MT	VG-E
☐ 1 Babe Adams	60.00	27.00
☐ 2 Sam Agnew	45.00	20.00
☐ 3 Ed Ainsmith	45.00	20.00
☐ 4 Grover Cleveland Alexander	250.00	110.00
☐ 5 Leon Ames	45.00	20.00
☐ 6 Jimmy Archer	45.00	20.00
☐ 7 Jimmy Austin	45.00	20.00
☐ 8 Frank Baker	100.00	45.00
☐ 9 Dave Bancroft	100.00	45.00
☐ 10 Jack Barry	60.00	27.00
☐ 11 Zinn Beck	45.00	20.00
☐ 12 Luke Boone *	60.00	27.00
☐ 13 Joe Benz	45.00	20.00
☐ 14 Bob Bescher	45.00	20.00
☐ 15 Al Betzel	45.00	20.00
☐ 16 Roger Bresnahan *	100.00	45.00
☐ 17 Eddie Burns	45.00	20.00
☐ 18 George J. Burns	45.00	20.00
☐ 19 Joe Bush	60.00	27.00
☐ 20 Owen Bush *	60.00	27.00
☐ 21 Art Butler	45.00	20.00
☐ 22 Bobby Byrne	45.00	20.00
☐ 23 Mordecai Brown	100.00	45.00
☐ 24 Jimmy Callahan	45.00	20.00
☐ 25 Ray Caldwell	45.00	20.00
☐ 26 Max Carey	100.00	45.00
☐ 27 George Chalmers	45.00	20.00
☐ 28 Frank Chance MG *	150.00	70.00
☐ 29 Ray Chapman	60.00	27.00
☐ 30 Larry Cheney	45.00	20.00
☐ 31 Ed Cicotte	125.00	55.00
☐ 32 Tommy Clarke	45.00	20.00
☐ 33 Eddie Collins	100.00	45.00
☐ 34 Shano Collins	45.00	20.00
☐ 35 Charles Comiskey OWN	100.00	45.00
☐ 36 Joe Connolly	45.00	20.00
☐ 37 L.(Doc) Cook *	60.00	27.00
☐ 38 Jack Coombs *	100.00	45.00
☐ 39 Dan Costello *	60.00	27.00
☐ 40 Harry Coveleskie	60.00	27.00
☐ 41 Gavvy Cravath	60.00	27.00
☐ 42 Sam Crawford	100.00	45.00
☐ 43 Jean Dale	45.00	20.00
☐ 44 Jake Daubert	60.00	27.00
☐ 45 G.A. Davis Jr. *	60.00	27.00
☐ 46 Charles Deal	45.00	20.00
☐ 47 Frank Demaree	45.00	20.00
☐ 48 Bill Doak	45.00	20.00
☐ 49 Bill Donovan	45.00	20.00
☐ 50 Red Dooin	45.00	20.00
☐ 51 Mike Doolan	45.00	20.00
☐ 52 Larry Doyle	60.00	27.00
☐ 53 Jean Dubuc	45.00	20.00
☐ 54 Oscar Dugey	45.00	20.00
☐ 55 John Evers	100.00	45.00
☐ 56 Red Faber	100.00	45.00
☐ 57 Happy Felsch	125.00	55.00
☐ 58 Bill Fischer	45.00	20.00
☐ 59 Ray Fisher	45.00	20.00
☐ 60 Max Flack	45.00	20.00
☐ 61 Art Fletcher	45.00	20.00
☐ 62 Eddie Foster	45.00	20.00
☐ 63 Jacques Fournier	45.00	20.00
☐ 64 Del Gainer	45.00	20.00
☐ 65 Larry Gardner	45.00	20.00
☐ 66 Joe Gedeon	45.00	20.00
☐ 67 Gus Getz	45.00	20.00
☐ 68 George Gibson	45.00	20.00
☐ 69 Wilbur Good	45.00	20.00
☐ 70 Hank Gowdy	60.00	27.00
☐ 71 Jack Graney	60.00	27.00
☐ 72 Tommy Griffith	45.00	20.00
☐ 73 Heinie Groh	60.00	27.00
☐ 74 Earl Hamilton	45.00	20.00
☐ 75 Bob Harmon	45.00	20.00
☐ 76 Roy Hartzell	45.00	20.00
☐ 77 Claude Hendrix	45.00	20.00
☐ 78 Olaf Henriksen	45.00	20.00
☐ 79 John Henry	45.00	20.00
☐ 80 Buck Herzog	45.00	20.00
☐ 81 Hugh High	45.00	20.00
☐ 82 Dick Hoblitzell	45.00	20.00
☐ 83 Harry Hooper	100.00	45.00
☐ 84 Ivan Howard	45.00	20.00
☐ 85 Miller Huggins	100.00	45.00
☐ 86 Joe Jackson	4500.00	2000.00
☐ 87 William James	45.00	20.00
☐ 88 Harold Janvrin	45.00	20.00
☐ 89 Hughie Jennings MG	100.00	45.00
☐ 90 Walter Johnson	650.00	300.00
☐ 91 Fielder Jones	45.00	20.00
☐ 92 Benny Kauff	45.00	20.00
☐ 93 Bill Killefer	45.00	20.00
☐ 94 Ed Konetchy	45.00	20.00
☐ 95 Napoleon Lajoie	300.00	135.00
☐ 96 Jack Lapp	45.00	20.00
☐ 97 John Lavan	45.00	20.00
☐ 98 Jimmy Lavender	45.00	20.00
☐ 99 Nemo Leibold	45.00	20.00
☐ 100 Hub Leonard	60.00	27.00
☐ 101 Duffy Lewis	60.00	27.00
☐ 102 Hans Lobert	45.00	20.00
☐ 103 Tom Long	45.00	20.00
☐ 104 Fred Luderus	45.00	20.00
☐ 105 Connie Mack MG	200.00	90.00
☐ 106 Lee Magee	45.00	20.00
☐ 107 Al Mamaux	45.00	20.00
☐ 108 Leslie Mann	45.00	20.00
☐ 109 Rabbit Maranville	100.00	45.00
☐ 110 Rube Marquard	100.00	45.00
☐ 111 Armando Marsans *	60.00	27.00
☐ 112 J.E.(Erskine) Mayer	45.00	20.00
☐ 113 George McBride	45.00	20.00
☐ 114 John McGraw	150.00	70.00
☐ 115 Jack McInnis	60.00	27.00
☐ 116 Fred Merkle	60.00	27.00
☐ 117 Chief Meyers	45.00	20.00
☐ 118 Clyde Milan	60.00	27.00
☐ 119 Otto Miller	45.00	20.00
☐ 120 Willie Mitchell	45.00	20.00
☐ 121 Fred Mollwitz	45.00	20.00
☐ 122 J.H.(Herbie) Moran *	60.00	27.00
☐ 123 Pat Moran MG	45.00	20.00
☐ 124 Ray Morgan	45.00	20.00
☐ 125 George Moriarty	45.00	20.00
☐ 126 Guy Morton	45.00	20.00
☐ 127 Eddie Murphy	45.00	20.00
☐ 128 Jack Murray *	60.00	27.00
☐ 129 Hy Myers	45.00	20.00
☐ 130 Bert Niehoff	45.00	20.00
☐ 131 Les Nunamaker *	60.00	27.00
☐ 132 Rube Oldring	45.00	20.00
☐ 133 Oliver O'Mara	45.00	20.00
☐ 134 Steve O'Neill	60.00	27.00
☐ 135 Dode Paskert	45.00	20.00
☐ 136 Roger Peckinpaugh	60.00	27.00
☐ 137 E.J.(Jeff) Pfeffer *	60.00	27.00
☐ 138 George Pierce *	60.00	27.00
☐ 139 Wally Pipp	60.00	27.00
☐ 140 Del Pratt	45.00	20.00
☐ 141 Bill Rariden	45.00	20.00
☐ 142 Eppa Rixey	100.00	45.00
☐ 143 Davey Robertson	45.00	20.00
☐ 144 Wilbert Robinson MG	150.00	70.00
☐ 145 Bob Roth	45.00	20.00
☐ 146 Eddie Roush	100.00	45.00
☐ 147 Clarence Rowland MG	45.00	20.00
☐ 148 Nap Rucker	60.00	27.00
☐ 149 Dick Rudolph	45.00	20.00
☐ 150 Reb Russell	45.00	20.00
☐ 151 Babe Ruth	6000.00	2700.00
☐ 152 Vic Saier	45.00	20.00
☐ 153 Slim Sallee	45.00	20.00
☐ 154 Germany Schaefer *	60.00	27.00
☐ 155 Ray Schalk	100.00	45.00
☐ 156 Wally Schang	60.00	27.00
☐ 157 Charles Schmidt *	60.00	27.00
☐ 158 Frank Schulte	45.00	20.00
☐ 159 Jim Scott	45.00	20.00
☐ 160 Everett Scott	60.00	27.00
☐ 161 Tom Seaton	45.00	20.00
☐ 162 Howard Shanks	45.00	20.00
☐ 163 Bob Shawkey	60.00	27.00
☐ 164 Ernie Shore	60.00	27.00
☐ 165 Bert Shotton	45.00	20.00
☐ 166 George Sisler	150.00	70.00
☐ 167 Red Smith	45.00	20.00
☐ 168 Fred Snodgrass	60.00	27.00
☐ 169 George Stallings MG	45.00	20.00
☐ 170 Oscar Stanage	45.00	20.00
☐ 171 Charles Stengel	650.00	300.00
☐ 172 Milton Stock	45.00	20.00
☐ 173 Amos Strunk	45.00	20.00
☐ 174 Billy Sullivan	60.00	27.00
☐ 175 Jeff Tesreau	45.00	20.00
☐ 176 Jim Thorpe *	4000.00	1800.00
☐ 177 Joe Tinker	100.00	45.00
☐ 178 Fred Toney	45.00	20.00
☐ 179 Terry Turner	45.00	20.00
☐ 180 Jim Vaughn	45.00	20.00
☐ 181 Bobby Veach	45.00	20.00
☐ 182 James Viox	45.00	20.00
☐ 183 Oscar Vitt	45.00	20.00
☐ 184 Honus Wagner	650.00	300.00
☐ 185 Clarence Walker	45.00	20.00
☐ 186 Zack Wheat	100.00	45.00
☐ 187 Ed Walsh	100.00	45.00
☐ 188 Buck Weaver	150.00	70.00
☐ 189 Carl Weilman	45.00	20.00
☐ 190 George Whitted	45.00	20.00
☐ 191 Fred Williams	45.00	20.00
☐ 192 Arthur Wilson	45.00	20.00
☐ 193 Chief Wilson	45.00	20.00
☐ 194 Ivy Wingo	45.00	20.00
☐ 195 Meldon Wolfgang	45.00	20.00
☐ 196 Joe Wood	100.00	45.00
☐ 197 Steve Yerkes	45.00	20.00
☐ 198 Rollie Zeider	45.00	20.00
☐ 199 Heinie Zimmerman	45.00	20.00
☐ 200 Dutch Zwilling	45.00	20.00

1916 Sporting News M101-4

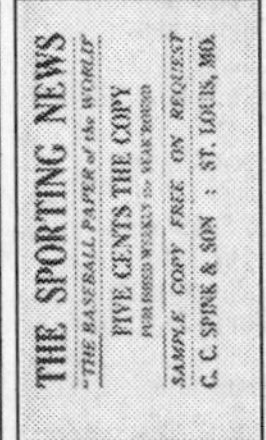

The cards in this 200-card set measure approximately 1 5/8" by 3". Issued in 1916 as a premium offer, the M101-4 set features black and white photos of current ballplayers. Each card is numbered and the reverse carries Sporting News advertising. The fronts are the same as D329, H801-9 and the unclassified Famous and Barr set. Most of the players in this also appear in the M101-5 set. Those cards which are asterisked in the checklist below are those cards which do not appear in the companion M101-5 set issued the year before.

	EX-MT	VG-E
COMPLETE SET (200)	20000.00	9000.00
COMMON CARD (1-200)	40.00	18.00

Card	EX-MT	VG-E
☐ 1 Babe Adams	50.00	22.00
☐ 2 Sam Agnew	50.00	22.00
☐ 3 Eddie Ainsmith	40.00	18.00
☐ 4 Grover Cleveland Alexander	250.00	110.00
☐ 5 Leon Ames	50.00	22.00
☐ 6 Jimmy Archer	50.00	22.00
☐ 7 Jimmy Austin	50.00	22.00
☐ 8 H.D.(Doug) Baird *	50.00	22.00
☐ 9 Frank Baker	100.00	45.00
☐ 10 Dave Bancroft	75.00	34.00
☐ 11 Jack Barry	50.00	22.00
☐ 12 Zinn Beck	40.00	18.00
☐ 13 Chief Bender *	100.00	45.00
☐ 14 Joe Benz	40.00	18.00
☐ 15 Bob Bescher	40.00	18.00
☐ 16 Al Betzel	40.00	18.00
☐ 17 Mordecai Brown	75.00	34.00
☐ 18 Eddie Burns	40.00	18.00
☐ 19 George H. Burns *	50.00	22.00
☐ 20 George J. Burns	40.00	18.00
☐ 21 Joe Bush	50.00	22.00
☐ 22 Donie Bush *	50.00	22.00
☐ 23 Art Butler	40.00	18.00
☐ 24 Bobbie Byrne	40.00	18.00
☐ 25 Forrest Cady *	50.00	22.00
☐ 26 Jim Callahan	40.00	18.00
☐ 27 Ray Caldwell	40.00	18.00
☐ 28 Max Carey	75.00	34.00
☐ 29 George Chalmers	40.00	18.00
☐ 30 Ray Chapman	50.00	22.00
☐ 31 Larry Cheney	40.00	18.00
☐ 32 Ed Cicotte	125.00	55.00
☐ 33 Tommy Clarke	40.00	18.00
☐ 34 Eddie Collins	100.00	45.00
☐ 35 Shano Collins	40.00	18.00
☐ 36 Charles Comiskey OWN	100.00	45.00
☐ 37 Joe Connolly	40.00	18.00
☐ 38 Ty Cobb *	2000.00	900.00
☐ 39 Harry Coveleskie	40.00	18.00
☐ 40 Gavvy Cravath	50.00	22.00
☐ 41 Sam Crawford	75.00	34.00
☐ 42 Jean Dale	40.00	18.00
☐ 43 Jake Daubert	50.00	22.00
☐ 44 Charles Deal	40.00	18.00
☐ 45 Frank Demaree	40.00	18.00
☐ 46 Josh Devore *	50.00	22.00
☐ 47 William Doak	40.00	18.00
☐ 48 Bill Donovan	40.00	18.00
☐ 49 Red Dooin	40.00	18.00
☐ 50 Mike Doolan	50.00	22.00
☐ 51 Larry Doyle	50.00	22.00
☐ 52 Jean Dubuc	40.00	18.00

☐ 53 Oscar J. Dugey	40.00	18.00
☐ 54 John Evers	100.00	45.00
☐ 55 Red Faber	75.00	34.00
☐ 56 Happy Felsch	125.00	55.00
☐ 57 Bill Fischer	40.00	18.00
☐ 58 Ray Fisher	40.00	18.00
☐ 59 Max Flack	40.00	18.00
☐ 60 Art Fletcher	40.00	18.00
☐ 61 Eddie Foster	40.00	18.00
☐ 62 Jacques Fournier	40.00	18.00
☐ 63 Del Gainer	40.00	18.00
☐ 64 Chick Gandil *	150.00	70.00
☐ 65 Larry Gardner	50.00	22.00
☐ 66 Joe Gedeon	50.00	22.00
☐ 67 Gus Getz	50.00	22.00
☐ 68 George Gibson	50.00	22.00
☐ 69 Wilbur Good	40.00	18.00
☐ 70 Hank Gowdy	50.00	22.00
☐ 71 Jack Graney	50.00	22.00
☐ 72 Clark Griffith *	100.00	45.00
☐ 73 Tommy Griffith	40.00	18.00
☐ 74 Heinie Groh	50.00	22.00
☐ 75 Earl Hamilton	40.00	18.00
☐ 76 Bob Harmon	40.00	18.00
☐ 77 Topsy Hartzell	40.00	18.00
☐ 78 Claude Hendrix	40.00	18.00
☐ 79 Olaf Henriksen	40.00	18.00
☐ 80 John Henry	40.00	18.00
☐ 81 Buck Herzog	40.00	18.00
☐ 82 Hugh High	40.00	18.00
☐ 83 Dick Hoblitzell	40.00	18.00
☐ 84 Harry Hooper	75.00	34.00
☐ 85 Ivan Howard	40.00	18.00
☐ 86 Miller Huggins	75.00	34.00
☐ 87 Joe Jackson	4500.00	2000.00
☐ 88 William James	40.00	18.00
☐ 89 Harold Janvrin	40.00	18.00
☐ 90 Hughie Jennings MG	75.00	34.00
☐ 91 Walter Johnson	600.00	275.00
☐ 92 Fielder Jones	40.00	18.00
☐ 93 Joe Judge *	50.00	22.00
☐ 94 Benny Kauff	40.00	18.00
☐ 95 Bill Killifer	40.00	18.00
☐ 96 Ed Konetchy	40.00	18.00
☐ 97 Nap Lajoie	250.00	110.00
☐ 98 Jack Lapp	40.00	18.00
☐ 99 John Lavan	40.00	18.00
☐ 100 Jimmy Lavender	40.00	18.00
☐ 101 Nemo Leibold	40.00	18.00
☐ 102 Hub Leonard	50.00	22.00
☐ 103 Duffy Lewis	50.00	22.00
☐ 104 Hans Lobert	40.00	18.00
☐ 105 Tom Long	40.00	18.00
☐ 106 Fred Luderus	40.00	18.00
☐ 107 Connie Mack MG	200.00	90.00
☐ 108 Lee Magee	40.00	18.00
☐ 109 Sherry Magee *	50.00	22.00
☐ 110 Al Mamaux	40.00	18.00
☐ 111 Leslie Mann	40.00	18.00
☐ 112 Rabbit Maranville	75.00	34.00
☐ 113 Rube Marquard	75.00	34.00
☐ 114 J.E.(Erskine) Mayer	40.00	18.00
☐ 115 George McBride	40.00	18.00
☐ 116 John McGraw MG	150.00	70.00
☐ 117 Jack McInnis	50.00	22.00
☐ 118 Fred Merkle	50.00	22.00
☐ 119 Chief Meyers	50.00	22.00
☐ 120 Clyde Milan	40.00	18.00
☐ 121 John Miller *	50.00	22.00
☐ 122 Otto Miller	40.00	18.00
☐ 123 Willie Mitchell	40.00	18.00
☐ 124 Fred Mollwitz	40.00	18.00
☐ 125 Pat Moran MG	40.00	18.00
☐ 126 Ray Morgan	40.00	18.00
☐ 127 George Moriarty	40.00	18.00
☐ 128 Guy Morton	40.00	18.00
☐ 129 Mike Mowrey *	50.00	22.00
☐ 130 Eddie Murphy	40.00	18.00
☐ 131 Hy Myers	40.00	18.00
☐ 132 Bert Niehoff	40.00	18.00
☐ 133 Rube Oldring	40.00	18.00
☐ 134 Oliver O'Mara	40.00	18.00
☐ 135 Steve O'Neill	50.00	22.00
☐ 136 Dode Paskert	40.00	18.00
☐ 137 Roger Peckinpaugh	50.00	22.00
☐ 138 Wally Pipp	50.00	22.00
☐ 139 Del Pratt	40.00	18.00
☐ 140 Pat Ragan *	50.00	22.00
☐ 141 Bill Rariden	40.00	18.00
☐ 142 Eppa Rixey	75.00	34.00
☐ 143 Davey Robertson	40.00	18.00
☐ 144 Wilbert Robinson MG	150.00	70.00
☐ 145 Bob Roth	40.00	18.00
☐ 146 Eddie Roush	100.00	45.00
☐ 147 Clarence Rowland MG	40.00	18.00
☐ 148 Nap Rucker	50.00	22.00
☐ 149 Dick Rudolph	50.00	22.00
☐ 150 Reb Russell	40.00	18.00
☐ 151 Babe Ruth	6000.00	2700.00
☐ 152 Vic Saier	40.00	18.00
☐ 153 Slim Sallee	50.00	22.00
☐ 154 Ray Schalk	75.00	34.00
☐ 155 Wally Schang	50.00	22.00
☐ 156 Frank Schulte	40.00	18.00
☐ 157 Everett Scott	50.00	22.00
☐ 158 Jim Scott	40.00	18.00
☐ 159 Tom Seaton	40.00	18.00
☐ 160 Howard Shanks	40.00	18.00
☐ 161 Bob Shawkey	50.00	22.00
☐ 162 Ernie Shore	50.00	22.00
☐ 163 Burt Shotton	40.00	18.00
☐ 164 George Sisler	150.00	70.00
☐ 165 Red Smith	40.00	18.00
☐ 166 Fred Snodgrass	50.00	22.00
☐ 167 George Stallings MG	40.00	18.00
☐ 168 Oscar Stanage	40.00	18.00
☐ 169 Casey Stengel	600.00	275.00
☐ 170 Milton Stock	40.00	18.00
☐ 171 Amos Strunk	40.00	18.00
☐ 172 Billy Sullivan	50.00	22.00
☐ 173 Jeff Tesreau	40.00	18.00
☐ 174 Joe Tinker	100.00	45.00
☐ 175 Fred Toney	40.00	18.00
☐ 176 Terry Turner	40.00	18.00
☐ 177 George Tyler *	50.00	22.00
☐ 178 Jim Vaughn	40.00	18.00
☐ 179 Bobby Veach	40.00	18.00
☐ 180 James Viox	40.00	18.00
☐ 181 Oscar Vitt	40.00	18.00
☐ 182 Honus Wagner	600.00	275.00
☐ 183 Clarence Walker	40.00	18.00
☐ 184 Ed Walsh	75.00	34.00
☐ 185 Bill Wambsganss *	50.00	22.00
☐ 186 Buck Weaver	150.00	70.00
☐ 187 Carl Weilman	40.00	18.00
☐ 188 Zack Wheat	75.00	34.00
☐ 189 George Whitted	40.00	18.00
☐ 190 Fred Williams	40.00	18.00
☐ 191 Arthur Wilson	40.00	18.00
☐ 192 Chief Wilson	40.00	18.00
☐ 193 Ivy Wingo	40.00	18.00
☐ 194 Meldon Wolfgang	40.00	18.00
☐ 195 Joe Wood	75.00	34.00
☐ 196 Steve Yerkes	40.00	18.00
☐ 197 Pep Young * (Detroit Tigers)	50.00	22.00
☐ 198 Rollie Zeider	50.00	22.00
☐ 199 Heinie Zimmerman	50.00	22.00
☐ 200 Dutch Zwilling	50.00	22.00

1997 Sports Illustrated

The 1997 Sports Illustrated set was issued in one series totalling 180 cards. Each pack contained six cards and carried a $1.99 SRP. The fronts feature Sports Illustrated action player photos with player stories on the backs. The set contains the topical subsets: Fresh Faces (1-27), Season Highlights (28-36), Inside Baseball (37-54), S.I.BER Vision 55-72) and Classic Covers (169-180). An unnumbered Jose Cruz Jr. foldout checklist was also seeded in approximately 1:4 packs.

	MINT	NRMT
COMPLETE SET (180)	40.00	18.00
COMMON CARD (1-180)	.15	.07
☐ 1 Bob Abreu	.60	.25
☐ 2 Jaime Bluma	.15	.07
☐ 3 Emil Brown	.40	.18
☐ 4 Jose Cruz Jr.	5.00	2.20
☐ 5 Jason Dickson	.30	.14
☐ 6 Nomar Garciaparra	2.00	.90
☐ 7 Todd Greene	.30	.14
☐ 8 Vladimir Guerrero	1.25	.55
☐ 9 Wilton Guerrero	.15	.07
☐ 10 Jose Guillen	.75	.35
☐ 11 Hideki Irabu	.75	.35
☐ 12 Russ Johnson	.15	.07
☐ 13 Andruw Jones	1.50	.70
☐ 14 Damon Mashore	.15	.07
☐ 15 Jason McDonald	.15	.07
☐ 16 Ryan McGuire	.15	.07
☐ 17 Matt Morris	.30	.14
☐ 18 Kevin Orie	.15	.07
☐ 19 Dante Powell	.15	.07
☐ 20 Pokey Reese	.15	.07
☐ 21 Joe Roa	.15	.07
☐ 22 Scott Rolen	1.50	.70
☐ 23 Glendon Rusch	.15	.07
☐ 24 Scott Spiezio	.15	.07
☐ 25 Bubba Trammell	.60	.25
☐ 26 Todd Walker	.15	.07
☐ 27 Jamey Wright	.15	.07
☐ 28 Ken Griffey Jr. SH	1.50	.70
☐ 29 Tino Martinez SH	.60	.25
☐ 30 Roger Clemens SH	.60	.25
☐ 31 Hideki Irabu SH	.60	.25
☐ 32 Kevin Brown SH	.15	.07
☐ 33 Chipper Jones SH Cal Ripken	1.25	.55
☐ 34 Sandy Alomar SH	.30	.14
☐ 35 Ken Caminiti SH	.60	.25
☐ 36 Randy Johnson SH	.60	.25
☐ 37 Andy Ashby IB	.15	.07
☐ 38 Jay Buhner IB	.40	.18
☐ 39 Joe Carter IB	.30	.14
☐ 40 Darren Daulton IB	.30	.14
☐ 41 Jeff Fassero IB	.15	.07
☐ 42 Andres Galarraga IB	.60	.25
☐ 43 Rusty Greer IB	.30	.14
☐ 44 Marquis Grissom IB	.30	.14
☐ 45 Joey Hamilton IB	.15	.07
☐ 46 Jimmy Key IB	.30	.14
☐ 47 Ryan Klesko IB	.40	.18
☐ 48 Eddie Murray IB	.60	.25
☐ 49 Charles Nagy IB	.15	.07
☐ 50 Dave Nilsson IB	.15	.07
☐ 51 Ricardo Rincon IB	.15	.07
☐ 52 Billy Wagner IB	.30	.14
☐ 53 Dan Wilson IB	.15	.07
☐ 54 Dmitri Young IB	.30	.14
☐ 55 Roberto Alomar SIV	.60	.25
☐ 56 Sandy Alomar Jr. SIV	.30	.14
☐ 57 Scott Brosius SIV	.15	.07
☐ 58 Tony Clark SIV	.60	.25
☐ 59 Carlos Delgado SIV	.30	.14
☐ 60 Jermaine Dye SIV	.15	.07
☐ 61 Darin Erstad SIV	.60	.25
☐ 62 Derek Jeter SIV	1.00	.45
☐ 63 Jason Kendall SIV	.30	.14
☐ 64 Hideo Nomo SIV	.75	.35
☐ 65 Rey Ordonez SIV	.15	.07
☐ 66 Andy Pettitte SIV	.60	.25
☐ 67 Manny Ramirez SIV	.60	.25
☐ 68 Edgar Renteria SIV	.30	.14
☐ 69 Shane Reynolds SIV	.15	.07
☐ 70 Alex Rodriguez SIV	1.25	.55
☐ 71 Ivan Rodriguez SIV	.60	.25
☐ 72 Jose Rosado SIV	.15	.07
☐ 73 John Smoltz	.30	.14
☐ 74 Tom Glavine	.30	.14
☐ 75 Greg Maddux	2.00	.90
☐ 76 Chipper Jones	2.00	.90
☐ 77 Kenny Lofton	.75	.35
☐ 78 Fred McGriff	.40	.18
☐ 79 Kevin Brown	.15	.07
☐ 80 Alex Fernandez	.30	.14
☐ 81 Al Leiter	.15	.07
☐ 82 Bobby Bonilla	.30	.14
☐ 83 Gary Sheffield	.60	.25
☐ 84 Moises Alou	.30	.14
☐ 85 Henry Rodriguez	.15	.07
☐ 86 Mark Grudzielanek	.15	.07
☐ 87 Pedro Martinez	.60	.25
☐ 88 Todd Hundley	.30	.14
☐ 89 Bernard Gilkey	.15	.07
☐ 90 Bobby Jones	.15	.07
☐ 91 Curt Schilling	.30	.14
☐ 92 Ricky Bottalico	.30	.14
☐ 93 Mike Lieberthal	.15	.07
☐ 94 Sammy Sosa	.60	.25
☐ 95 Ryne Sandberg	.75	.35
☐ 96 Mark Grace	.40	.18
☐ 97 Deion Sanders	.60	.25
☐ 98 Reggie Sanders	.15	.07
☐ 99 Barry Larkin	.40	.18
☐ 100 Craig Biggio	.40	.18
☐ 101 Jeff Bagwell	1.25	.55
☐ 102 Derek Bell	.15	.07
☐ 103 Brian Jordan	.15	.07
☐ 104 Ray Lankford	.30	.14
☐ 105 Ron Gant	.30	.14
☐ 106 Al Martin	.15	.07
☐ 107 Kevin Elster	.15	.07
☐ 108 Jermaine Allensworth	.15	.07
☐ 109 Vinny Castilla	.30	.14
☐ 110 Dante Bichette	.30	.14

☐ 111 Larry Walker	.60	.25
☐ 112 Mike Piazza	2.00	.90
☐ 113 Eric Karros	.15	.07
☐ 114 Todd Hollandsworth	.15	.07
☐ 115 Raul Mondesi	.40	.18
☐ 116 Hideo Nomo	1.50	.70
☐ 117 Ramon Martinez	.30	.14
☐ 118 Ken Caminiti	.60	.25
☐ 119 Tony Gwynn	1.50	.70
☐ 120 Steve Finley	.30	.14
☐ 121 Barry Bonds	.75	.35
☐ 122 J.T. Snow	.15	.07
☐ 123 Rod Beck	.15	.07
☐ 124 Cal Ripken	2.50	1.10
☐ 125 Mike Mussina	.60	.25
☐ 126 Brady Anderson	.40	.18
☐ 127 Bernie Williams	.60	.25
☐ 128 Derek Jeter	2.00	.90
☐ 129 Tino Martinez	.60	.25
☐ 130 Andy Pettitte	.60	.25
☐ 131 David Cone	.30	.14
☐ 132 Mariano Rivera	.30	.14
☐ 133 Roger Clemens	1.25	.55
☐ 134 Pat Hentgen	.30	.14
☐ 135 Juan Guzman	.15	.07
☐ 136 Bob Higginson	.30	.14
☐ 137 Tony Clark	.60	.25
☐ 138 Travis Fryman	.30	.14
☐ 139 Mo Vaughn	.75	.35
☐ 140 Tim Naehring	.15	.07
☐ 141 John Valentin	.15	.07
☐ 142 Matt Williams	.30	.14
☐ 143 David Justice	.60	.25
☐ 144 Jim Thome	.60	.25
☐ 145 Chuck Knoblauch	.60	.25
☐ 146 Paul Molitor	.60	.25
☐ 147 Marty Cordova	.15	.07
☐ 148 Frank Thomas	2.50	1.10
☐ 149 Albert Belle	.75	.35
☐ 150 Robin Ventura	.30	.14
☐ 151 John Jaha	.15	.07
☐ 152 Jeff Cirillo	.30	.14
☐ 153 Jose Valentin	.15	.07
☐ 154 Jay Bell	.15	.07
☐ 155 Jeff King	.30	.14
☐ 156 Kevin Appier	.15	.07
☐ 157 Ken Griffey Jr.	3.00	1.35
☐ 158 Alex Rodriguez	2.50	1.10
☐ 159 Randy Johnson	.60	.25
☐ 160 Juan Gonzalez	1.50	.70
☐ 161 Will Clark	.40	.18
☐ 162 Dean Palmer	.30	.14
☐ 163 Tim Salmon	.60	.25
☐ 164 Jim Edmonds	.60	.25
☐ 165 Jim Leyritz	.15	.07
☐ 166 Jose Canseco	.40	.18
☐ 167 Jason Giambi	.15	.07
☐ 168 Mark McGwire	1.25	.55
☐ 169 Barry Bonds CC	.60	.25
☐ 170 Alex Rodriguez CC	1.25	.55
☐ 171 Roger Clemens CC	.60	.25
☐ 172 Ken Griffey Jr. CC	1.50	.70
☐ 173 Greg Maddux CC	1.00	.45
☐ 174 Mike Piazza CC	1.00	.45
☐ 175 Will Clark CC Mark McGwire	.60	.25
☐ 176 Hideo Nomo CC	.75	.35
☐ 177 Cal Ripken CC	1.25	.55
☐ 178 Ken Griffey Jr. CC Frank Thomas	1.25	.55
☐ 179 Alex Rodriguez CC Derek Jeter	1.25	.55
☐ 180 John Wetteland CC	.15	.07
☐ P158 Alex Rodriguez Promo	1.00	.45
☐ NNO Jose Cruz Jr. CL	.50	.23

1997 Sports Illustrated Extra Edition

Randomly inserted in packs, this 180-card set if parallel to the base set with etched holofoil accents. Only 500 of each card were produced and are sequentially numbered.

	MINT	NRMT
COMPLETE SET (180)	2500.00	1100.00
COMMON CARD (1-180)	5.00	2.20
MINOR STARS	8.00	3.60
SEMISTARS	12.00	5.50
UNLISTED STARS	20.00	9.00

*STARS: 15X TO 30X BASIC CARDS
*YOUNG STARS: 12.5X TO 25X BASIC CARDS
*ROOKIES: 7.5X TO 15X BASIC CARDS

☐ 4 Jose Cruz Jr.	80.00	36.00
☐ 6 Nomar Garciaparra	50.00	22.00
☐ 13 Andruw Jones	40.00	18.00
☐ 22 Scott Rolen	40.00	18.00
☐ 28 Ken Griffey Jr.SH	60.00	27.00
☐ 33 Chipper Jones SH Cal Ripken	50.00	22.00
☐ 70 Alex Rodriguez SIV	40.00	18.00
☐ 75 Greg Maddux	60.00	27.00
☐ 76 Chipper Jones	60.00	27.00
☐ 101 Jeff Bagwell	40.00	18.00
☐ 112 Mike Piazza	60.00	27.00
☐ 116 Hideo Nomo	50.00	22.00
☐ 119 Tony Gwynn	50.00	22.00
☐ 124 Cal Ripken	80.00	36.00
☐ 128 Derek Jeter	50.00	22.00
☐ 133 Roger Clemens	40.00	18.00
☐ 148 Frank Thomas	80.00	36.00
☐ 157 Ken Griffey Jr.	100.00	45.00
☐ 158 Alex Rodriguez	60.00	27.00
☐ 160 Juan Gonzalez	50.00	22.00
☐ 168 Mark McGwire	40.00	18.00
☐ 170 Alex Rodriguez CC	40.00	18.00
☐ 172 Ken Griffey Jr. CC	60.00	27.00
☐ 173 Greg Maddux CC	40.00	18.00
☐ 174 Mike Piazza CC	40.00	18.00
☐ 177 Cal Ripken CC	50.00	22.00
☐ 178 Ken Griffey Jr. CC Frank Thomas	100.00	45.00
☐ 179 Alex Rodriguez CC Derek Jeter	50.00	22.00

1997 Sports Illustrated Autographed Mini-Covers

Randomly inserted in packs, this six-card set features color photos of three current and three retired players on miniature SI covers. Only 250 of each card was produced and serially numbered and autographed.

	MINT	NRMT
COMPLETE SET (6)	1000.00	450.00
COMMON CARD (1-6)	80.00	36.00
☐ 1 Alex Rodriguez	250.00	110.00
☐ 2 Cal Ripken	300.00	135.00
☐ 3 Kirby Puckett	150.00	70.00
☐ 4 Willie Mays	200.00	90.00
☐ 5 Frank Robinson	80.00	36.00
☐ 6 Hank Aaron	150.00	70.00

1997 Sports Illustrated Cooperstown Collection

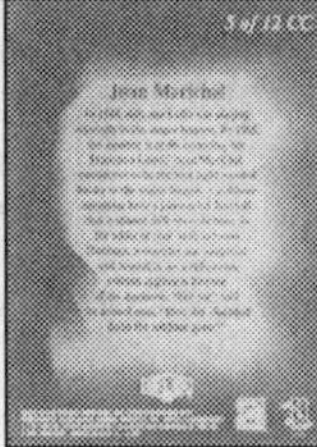

Randomly inserted in packs at the rate of one in 12, this 12-card set features classic Sports Illustrated baseball covers with a description of the issue on the back.

	MINT	NRMT
COMPLETE SET (12)	60.00	27.00
COMMON CARD (1-12)	5.00	2.20
☐ 1 Hank Aaron	10.00	4.50
☐ 2 Yogi Berra	6.00	2.70
☐ 3 Lou Brock	5.00	2.20
☐ 4 Rod Carew	5.00	2.20
☐ 5 Juan Marichal	5.00	2.20
☐ 6 Al Kaline	6.00	2.70
☐ 7 Joe Morgan	5.00	2.20
☐ 8 Brooks Robinson	5.00	2.20
☐ 9 Willie Stargell	5.00	2.20
☐ 10 Kirby Puckett	10.00	4.50
☐ 11 Willie Mays	12.00	5.50
☐ 12 Frank Robinson	5.00	2.20

1997 Sports Illustrated Great Shots

Randomly inserted one per pack, this 25-card set showcases some of the greatest photography in Sports Illustrated history and features color player photos that unfold into mini posters. When unfolded, the posters measure 5" by 7".

	MINT	NRMT
COMPLETE SET (25)	8.00	3.60
COMMON CARD (1-25)	.25	.11
☐ 1 Chipper Jones	1.25	.55
☐ 2 Ryan Klesko	.35	.16
☐ 3 Kenny Lofton	.50	.23
☐ 4 Greg Maddux	1.25	.55
☐ 5 John Smoltz	.30	.14
☐ 6 Roberto Alomar	.40	.18
☐ 7 Cal Ripken	1.50	.70
☐ 8 Mo Vaughn	.50	.23
☐ 9 Albert Belle	.50	.23
☐ 10 Frank Thomas	1.50	.70
☐ 11 Ryne Sandberg	.50	.23
☐ 12 Deion Sanders	.40	.18
☐ 13 Vinny Castilla Andres Galarraga	.40	.18
☐ 14 Eric Karros	.25	.11
☐ 15 Mike Piazza	1.25	.55
☐ 16 Derek Jeter	1.25	.55
☐ 17 Mark McGwire	.75	.35
☐ 18 Darren Daulton	.30	.14
☐ 19 Andy Ashby	.25	.11
☐ 20 Barry Bonds	.50	.23
☐ 21 Jay Buhner	.35	.16
☐ 22 Randy Johnson	.40	.18
☐ 23 Alex Rodriguez	1.50	.70
☐ 24 Juan Gonzalez	1.00	.45
☐ 25 Ken Griffey Jr.	2.00	.90

1977-79 Sportscaster

This listing just covers the baseball cards covered in this 2,194 card set. The cards have rounded corners and measure 4 11/16" by 6 1/4". The color action photos are full-bleed except at the top, where a color stripe carries the sport, card title and various emblems. In a two-column format, the backs provide copious commentary. All cards are numbered on the back with a distributor's number (e.g. 01 021), followed by the pack number and individual card number (02-08 means the eighth card in the second set). A complete set listing as well as complete pricing can be found in our basketball annual.

	NRMT	VG-E
COMPLETE BB SUBSET (142)	600.00	275.00
COMMON CARD	1.00	.45
☐ 121 Tom Seaver Baseball	4.00	1.80
☐ 208 Joe DiMaggio Baseball	10.00	4.50
☐ 216 1969 Mets Mets Win Nolan Ryan Baseball	8.00	3.60
☐ 316 Henry Aaron Baseball	5.00	2.20
☐ 422 Johnny Bench Baseball	4.00	1.80
☐ 511 Babe Ruth Baseball	8.00	3.60
☐ 514 Bobby Thomson Baseball	1.50	.70
☐ 522 The 1927 Yankees Baseball	2.50	1.10
☐ 624 Johnny Vander Meer Baseball	1.50	.70
☐ 716 Roger Maris Mickey Mantle Baseball	12.00	5.50
☐ 804 Pete Rose	6.00	2.70

Baseball
☐ 923 Jackie Robinson 10.00 4.50
Baseball
☐ 1007 Rod Carew 2.50 1.10
Baseball
☐ 10122 400-Homer Club 10.00 4.50
Duke Snider
Baseball
☐ 10201 Mike Flanagan 8.00 3.60
Baseball
☐ 10210 Boston's Fenway 8.00 3.60
Fenway Park
Baseball
☐ 10224 Jim Piersall 10.00 4.50
Baseball
☐ 1106 Willie Mays 6.00 2.70
Baseball
☐ 1109 The Rules 3.00 1.35
Hank Aaron
Baseball
☐ 1207 Ernie Banks 3.00 1.35
Baseball
☐ 1303 Ted Williams 10.00 4.50
Baseball
☐ 1409 The Oakland A's 3.00 1.35
1971-75
Four A's Stars
Catfish Hunter
Rollie Fingers
Reggie Jackson
Sal Bando
Baseball
☐ 1410 Jim Hunter 3.00 1.35
Baseball
☐ 1411 Maury Wills 2.50 1.10
Baseball
☐ 1509 A Century and a 2.50 1.10
Half of BB
Johnny Bench
Baseball
☐ 1607 Brooks Robinson 2.50 1.10
Baseball
☐ 1704 Randy Jones .... 1.00 .45
Baseball
☐ 1805 Joe Morgan 2.50 1.10
Baseball
☐ 1811 Mark Fidrych 2.50 1.10
Baseball
☐ 1816 Lingo II .... 1.50 .70
Earl Weaver
Baseball
☐ 1920 Gaylord Perry .... 1.50 .70
Baseball
☐ 2005 Thurman Munson 4.00 1.80
Baseball
☐ 2104 Lingo I .... 1.00 .45
Dodger Pitcher
Baseball
☐ 2105 Joe Rudi .... 1.00 .45
Baseball
☐ 2109 Vada Pinson .... 1.50 .70
Baseball
☐ 2116 Stan Musial 5.00 2.20
Baseball
☐ 2304 Nolan Ryan 25.00 11.00
Baseball
☐ 2323 Warren Spahn 3.00 1.35
Baseball
☐ 2416 Lou Brock 2.50 1.10
Baseball
☐ 2518 Frank Tanana .... 1.50 .70
Baseball
☐ 2615 Jim Palmer 4.00 1.80
Baseball
☐ 2702 Steve Carlton 3.00 1.35
Baseball
☐ 2721 Dave Kingman .... 1.50 .70
Baseball
☐ 2902 The Perfect Game 4.00 1.80
Sandy Koufax
Baseball
☐ 2922 At-A-Glance 2.50 1.10
Reference
Tom Seaver
Ball Sports
☐ 3003 Triple Crown 3.00 1.35
Carl Yastrzemski
Baseball
☐ 3016 Ron Cey .... 1.50 .70
Baseball
☐ 3101 Instruction 3.00 1.35
Rod Carew
Baseball
☐ 3201 The 3000 Hit Club 20.00 9.00
Roberto Clemente
Baseball
☐ 3204 Tommy John 2.50 1.10
Baseball
☐ 3217 Cy Young Awards 3.00 1.35
Tom Seaver
Baseball
☐ 3305 Keeping Score .... 1.00 .45
Fan Scorekeeping
Baseball
☐ 3402 Four Home Runs in 8.00 3.60
A Game
Mike Schmidt
Baseball
☐ 3419 All-Star Game 2.50 1.10
Joe Morgan
Steve Garvey
Baseball
☐ 3424 Greg Luzinski .... 1.50 .70
Baseball
☐ 3502 Infield Fly Rule .... 1.50 .70
Bobby Grich
Baseball
☐ 3504 John Candelaria .... 1.50 .70
Baseball
☐ 3515 Interference 3.00 1.35
Johnny Bench
Baseball
☐ 3601 Ron LeFlore .... 1.50 .70
Baseball
☐ 3709 Pickoff .... 1.50 .70
Luis Tiant
Baseball
☐ 3722 NCAA Tournament .... 1.00 .45
Texas A,M/Texas
Baseball
☐ 3809 George Brett 20.00 9.00
Baseball
☐ 3810 Jim Rice 2.50 1.10
Baseball
☐ 3902 Rundown .... 1.50 .70
Mets vs. Astros
Baseball
☐ 3904 Measurements .... 1.00 .45
Memorial Stadium
Baseball
☐ 4001 Garry Templeton .... 1.50 .70
Baseball
☐ 4002 Jeff Burroughs .... 1.50 .70
Baseball
☐ 4103 Relief Pitching .... 1.50 .70
Mike Marshall
Baseball
☐ 4107 Triple Play .... 1.50 .70
Bill Wambsganss
Baseball
☐ 4208 Dave Parker 2.50 1.10
Dave Kingman
Baseball
☐ 4209 Bert Blyleven .... 1.50 .70
Baseball
☐ 4307 Rick Reuschel .... 1.50 .70
Baseball
☐ 4417 Hidden Ball Trick .... 1.50 .70
A's/Red Sox
Baseball
☐ 4517 Hit and Run 2.50 1.10
George Foster
Baseball
☐ 4522 Hitting the Cutoff .... 1.50 .70
Man: Red Sox Player
Baseball
☐ 4622 Amateur Draft .... 1.50 .70
Rick Monday
Baseball
☐ 4702 Great Moments 2.50 1.10
Ferguson Jenkins
Baseball
☐ 4705 Great Moments 3.00 1.35
Bob Gibson
Baseball
☐ 5007 Dennis Eckersley 4.00 1.80
Baseball
☐ 5102 The Double Steal .... 1.50 .70
Davey Lopes
Baseball
☐ 5103 Cy Young 3.00 1.35
Baseball
☐ 5202 Gene Tenace .... 1.50 .70
Baseball
☐ 5209 Great Moments 2.50 1.10
Mickey Lolich
Baseball
☐ 5307 Andre Thornton .... 1.50 .70
Baseball
☐ 5408 Great Moments 2.50 1.10
Carl Yastrzemski
Baseball
☐ 5409 Freddie Patek .... 1.50 .70
Baseball
☐ 5503 Lyman Bostock .... 1.50 .70
Baseball
☐ 5613 Carlton Fisk 12.00 5.50
Baseball
☐ 5702 Dave Winfield 15.00 6.75
Baseball
☐ 5801 Shea Stadium 2.50 1.10
Baseball
☐ 5802 Busch Memorial 2.50 1.10
Stadium
Baseball
☐ 5805 Fenway Park 5.00 2.20
Baseball
☐ 5812 Baltimore Memorial 2.50 1.10
Stadium
Baseball
☐ 5814 Yankee Stadium 5.00 2.20
Baseball
☐ 5818 Candlestick Park 4.00 1.80
Baseball
☐ 5821 Veterans Stadium 2.50 1.10
Baseball
☐ 5823 Dodger Stadium 2.50 1.10
Baseball
☐ 5920 Frank Robinson 8.00 3.60
Baseball
☐ 6023 Sandy Koufax 10.00 4.50
Baseball
☐ 6102 Ron Guidry 2.50 1.10
Baseball
☐ 6116 Roberto Clemente 30.00 13.50
Baseball
☐ 6204 Don Larsen's 5.00 2.20
Perfect Game
Baseball
☐ 6318 Gil Hodges 8.00 3.60
Baseball
☐ 6518 Vida Blue 4.00 1.80
Baseball
☐ 6615 Designated Hitter 5.00 2.20
Rusty Staub
Baseball
☐ 6701 Steve Garvey 5.00 2.20
Baseball
☐ 6715 The Presidential Ball 5.00 2.20
Pres.William Taft
Baseball
☐ 6810 7th Game of the 4.00 1.80
World Series
Bert Campaneris
Baseball
☐ 6818 Babe Ruth Baseball 4.00 1.80
Ed Figueroa
Baseball
☐ 6906 Roy Campanella 10.00 4.50
Baseball
☐ 6917 Little League To 4.00 1.80
Big Leagues
Hector Torres
Baseball
☐ 7013 Daffy Dean 5.00 2.20
Dizzy Dean
Baseball
☐ 7103 J.R. Richard 4.00 1.80
Baseball
☐ 7213 Hitting Pitchers 8.00 3.60
Don Drysdale
Baseball
☐ 7315 Emmett Ashford 4.00 1.80
Baseball
☐ 7401 Forever Blowing 5.00 2.20
Bubbles
Davey Lopes
Baseball
☐ 7410 Phil Niekro 8.00 3.60
Baseball
☐ 7423 Ken Forsch 4.00 1.80
Bob Forsch
Baseball
☐ 7509 Tommy Lasorda 8.00 3.60
Baseball
☐ 7515 Hack Wilson 5.00 2.20
Baseball
☐ 7524 The Firemen 8.00 3.60
Goose Gossage
Baseball
☐ 7611 Iron Mike 2.50 1.10
Pitching Machine
Baseball
☐ 7619 Training Camps 2.50 1.10
Spring Training
Baseball
☐ 7708 Monty Stratton 5.00 2.20
Baseball
☐ 7713 Ron Taylor 4.00 1.80
Baseball
☐ 7816 Willie McCovey 8.00 3.60
Baseball
☐ 7911 Craig Swan 4.00 1.80

Baseball		
☐ 8021 Umpires Strike	6.00	2.70
Ump Picket Line		
Ron Luciano and others		
Baseball		
☐ 8124 Wrigley Marathlon	20.00	9.00
Mike Schmidt		
Baseball		
☐ 8219 Bobby Bonds	8.00	3.60
Baseball		
☐ 8309 Billy Martin	10.00	4.50
Baseball		
☐ 8321 Brother vs. Brother	8.00	3.60
Joe Niekro		
Baseball		
☐ 8408 Triple Play	8.00	3.60
Rick Burleson		
Baseball		
☐ 8415 The Money Game	10.00	4.50
Dennis Eckersley		
Baseball		
☐ 8418 Clemente Award	8.00	3.60
Andre Thornton		
Beyond Sports		
☐ 8504 Like Father	8.00	3.60
Like Son		
Roy Smalley		
Baseball		
☐ 8608 Danny Ainge	60.00	27.00
Baseball/Basketball		
☐ 8712 Lee Mazzilli	8.00	3.60
Baseball		
☐ 8718 Steve Dembrowski	5.00	2.20
Baseball		
☐ 8720 Hutch Award	20.00	9.00
Al Kaline		
Beyond Sports		
☐ 8803 Dave Winfield	20.00	9.00
Baseball		
☐ 8824 Cape Cod League	6.00	2.70
Jim Beattie		
Baseball		

1996 SPx

This 1996 SPx set was issued in one series totalling 60 cards. The one-card packs had a suggested retail price of $3.49. Printed on 32 pt. card stock with Holoview technology and a perimeter diecut design, the set features color player photos with a Holography background on the fronts and decorative foil stamping on the back. Two special cards are included in the set: a Ken Griffey Jr. Commemorative card was inserted one in every 75 packs and a Mike Piazza Tribute card inserted one in every 95 packs. An autographed version of each of these cards was inserted at the rate of one in 2,000.

	MINT	NRMT
COMPLETE SET (60)	80.00	36.00
COMMON CARD (1-60)	1.00	.45
☐ 1 Greg Maddux	6.00	2.70
☐ 2 Chipper Jones	6.00	2.70
☐ 3 Fred McGriff	1.50	.70
☐ 4 Tom Glavine	1.25	.55
☐ 5 Cal Ripken	8.00	3.60
☐ 6 Roberto Alomar	2.00	.90
☐ 7 Rafael Palmeiro	1.50	.70
☐ 8 Jose Canseco	1.50	.70
☐ 9 Roger Clemens	4.00	1.80
☐ 10 Mo Vaughn	2.50	1.10
☐ 11 Jim Edmonds	2.00	.90
☐ 12 Tim Salmon	2.00	.90
☐ 13 Sammy Sosa	2.00	.90
☐ 14 Ryne Sandberg	2.50	1.10
☐ 15 Mark Grace	1.50	.70
☐ 16 Frank Thomas	8.00	3.60
☐ 17 Barry Larkin	1.50	.70
☐ 18 Kenny Lofton	2.50	1.10
☐ 19 Albert Belle	2.50	1.10
☐ 20 Eddie Murray	2.00	.90
☐ 21 Manny Ramirez	2.00	.90
☐ 22 Dante Bichette	1.25	.55
☐ 23 Larry Walker	2.00	.90
☐ 24 Vinny Castilla	1.25	.55
☐ 25 Andres Galarraga	2.00	.90
☐ 26 Cecil Fielder	1.25	.55
☐ 27 Gary Sheffield	2.00	.90
☐ 28 Craig Biggio	1.50	.70
☐ 29 Jeff Bagwell	4.00	1.80
☐ 30 Derek Bell	1.00	.45
☐ 31 Johnny Damon	1.25	.55
☐ 32 Eric Karros	1.25	.55
☐ 33 Mike Piazza	6.00	2.70
☐ 34 Raul Mondesi	1.50	.70
☐ 35 Hideo Nomo	5.00	2.20
☐ 36 Kirby Puckett	4.00	1.80
☐ 37 Paul Molitor	2.00	.90
☐ 38 Marty Cordova	1.00	.45
☐ 39 Rondell White	1.25	.55
☐ 40 Jason Isringhausen	1.00	.45
☐ 41 Paul Wilson	1.00	.45
☐ 42 Rey Ordonez	1.25	.55
☐ 43 Derek Jeter	6.00	2.70
☐ 44 Wade Boggs	2.00	.90
☐ 45 Mark McGwire	4.00	1.80
☐ 46 Jason Kendall	2.00	.90
☐ 47 Ron Gant	1.25	.55
☐ 48 Ozzie Smith	2.50	1.10
☐ 49 Tony Gwynn	5.00	2.20
☐ 50 Ken Caminiti	2.00	.90
☐ 51 Barry Bonds	2.50	1.10
☐ 52 Matt Williams	1.50	.70
☐ 53 Osvaldo Fernandez	1.25	.55
☐ 54 Jay Buhner	1.50	.70
☐ 55 Ken Griffey Jr.	10.00	4.50
☐ 56 Randy Johnson	2.00	.90
☐ 57 Alex Rodriguez	8.00	3.60
☐ 58 Juan Gonzalez	5.00	2.20
☐ 59 Joe Carter	1.25	.55
☐ 60 Carlos Delgado	1.25	.55
☐ KG1 Ken Griffey Jr. Comm.	15.00	6.75
☐ MP1 Mike Piazza Trib.	8.00	3.60
☐ KGAU Ken Griffey Jr. Auto.	350.00	160.00
☐ MPAU Mike Piazza Auto.	225.00	100.00

1996 SPx Gold

Parallel to the regular version, this 60-card set was randomly inserted in hobby packs only at a rate of one in 7. The design is similar to the regular set with the exception being the gold foil borders on front.

	MINT	NRMT
COMPLETE SET (60)	300.00	135.00
COMMON CARD (1-60)	4.00	1.80
*STARS: 1.5X TO 4X BASIC CARDS		

1996 SPx Bound for Glory

Randomly inserted in packs at a rate of one in 24, this 10-card set features players with a chance to be long remembered. The fronts display color player photos with a diecut perimeter design and a Holography background. The words, "Bound for Glory" are printed at the top. The backs carry decorative foil stamping.

	MINT	NRMT
COMPLETE SET (10)	150.00	70.00
COMMON CARD (1-10)	6.00	2.70
☐ 1 Ken Griffey Jr.	30.00	13.50
☐ 2 Frank Thomas	25.00	11.00
☐ 3 Barry Bonds	8.00	3.60
☐ 4 Cal Ripken	25.00	11.00
☐ 5 Greg Maddux	20.00	9.00
☐ 6 Chipper Jones	20.00	9.00
☐ 7 Roberto Alomar	6.00	2.70
☐ 8 Manny Ramirez	6.00	2.70
☐ 9 Tony Gwynn	15.00	6.75
☐ 10 Mike Piazza	20.00	9.00

1997 SPx

The 1997 SPx set was issued in one series totalling 50 cards and was distributed in three-card hobby only packs

with a suggested retail price of $5.99. The fronts feature color player images on a Holoview perimeter die cut design. The backs carry a player photo, player information, and career statistics.

	MINT	NRMT
COMPLETE SET (50)	60.00	27.00
COMMON CARD (1-50)	.50	.23
☐ 1 Eddie Murray	1.25	.55
☐ 2 Darin Erstad	2.00	.90
☐ 3 Tim Salmon	1.25	.55
☐ 4 Andruw Jones	3.00	1.35
☐ 5 Chipper Jones	4.00	1.80
☐ 6 John Smoltz	.75	.35
☐ 7 Greg Maddux	4.00	1.80
☐ 8 Kenny Lofton	1.50	.70
☐ 9 Roberto Alomar	1.25	.55
☐ 10 Rafael Palmeiro	1.00	.45
☐ 11 Brady Anderson	1.00	.45
☐ 12 Cal Ripken	5.00	2.20
☐ 13 Nomar Garciaparra	4.00	1.80
☐ 14 Mo Vaughn	1.50	.70
☐ 15 Ryne Sandberg	1.50	.70
☐ 16 Sammy Sosa	1.25	.55
☐ 17 Frank Thomas	5.00	2.20
☐ 18 Albert Belle	1.50	.70
☐ 19 Barry Larkin	1.00	.45
☐ 20 Deion Sanders	1.25	.55
☐ 21 Manny Ramirez	1.25	.55
☐ 22 Jim Thome	1.25	.55
☐ 23 Dante Bichette	.75	.35
☐ 24 Andres Galarraga	1.25	.55
☐ 25 Larry Walker	1.25	.55
☐ 26 Gary Sheffield	1.25	.55
☐ 27 Jeff Bagwell	2.50	1.10
☐ 28 Raul Mondesi	1.00	.45
☐ 29 Hideo Nomo	3.00	1.35
☐ 30 Mike Piazza	4.00	1.80
☐ 31 Paul Molitor	1.25	.55
☐ 32 Todd Walker	.50	.23
☐ 33 Vladimir Guerrero	2.50	1.10
☐ 34 Todd Hundley	.75	.35
☐ 35 Andy Pettitte	1.25	.55
☐ 36 Derek Jeter	4.00	1.80
☐ 37 Jose Canseco	1.00	.45
☐ 38 Mark McGwire	2.50	1.10
☐ 39 Scott Rolen	3.00	1.35
☐ 40 Ron Gant	.75	.35
☐ 41 Ken Caminiti	1.25	.55
☐ 42 Tony Gwynn	3.00	1.35
☐ 43 Barry Bonds	1.50	.70
☐ 44 Jay Buhner	1.00	.45
☐ 45 Ken Griffey Jr.	6.00	2.70
☐ 46 Alex Rodriguez	5.00	2.20
☐ 47 Jose Cruz Jr.	12.00	5.50
☐ 48 Juan Gonzalez	3.00	1.35
☐ 49 Ivan Rodriguez	1.50	.70
☐ 50 Roger Clemens	2.50	1.10
☐ S45 Ken Griffey Jr. SAMPLE	3.00	1.35

1997 SPx Bronze

Randomly inserted in packs at the approximate rate of one in three, cards from this 50-card set are a parallel version of the base set with bronze foil enhancements.

	MINT	NRMT
COMPLETE SET (50)	200.00	90.00
COMMON CARD (1-50)	1.50	.70
*BRONZE STARS: 1.5X TO 3X BASIC CARDS		
*BRONZE ROOKIES: 1X TO 2X BASIC CARDS		

1997 SPx Gold

Randomly inserted in packs at the rate of one in 17, This 50-card set is parallel to the base set and features gold foil enhancements.

	MINT	NRMT
COMPLETE SET (50)	800.00	350.00
COMMON CARD (1-50)	5.00	2.20
*GOLD STARS: 5X TO 10X BASIC CARDS		
*GOLD ROOKIES: 3X TO 6X BASIC CARDS		

1997 SPx Grand Finale

Randomly inserted in packs, cards from this 50-card set are an extremely limited edition parallel version of the base set and features an all gold holoview image. Only 50 of each card was produced.The set was entitled Grand Finale to signify the fact that this would be the last baseball product Upper Deck would ever use the holoview technology on.

	MINT	NRMT
COMPLETE SET (50)	7500.00	3400.00
COMMON CARD (1-50)	25.00	11.00
MINOR STARS	40.00	18.00
SEMISTARS	60.00	27.00
UNLISTED STARS	100.00	45.00

☐ 2 Darin Erstad	120.00	55.00
☐ 4 Andruw Jones	200.00	90.00
☐ 5 Chipper Jones	250.00	110.00
☐ 7 Greg Maddux	300.00	135.00
☐ 8 Kenny Lofton	120.00	55.00
☐ 12 Cal Ripken	400.00	180.00
☐ 13 Nomar Garciaparra	250.00	110.00
☐ 14 Mo Vaughn	120.00	55.00
☐ 15 Ryne Sandberg	120.00	55.00
☐ 17 Frank Thomas	500.00	220.00
☐ 18 Albert Belle	120.00	55.00
☐ 27 Jeff Bagwell	200.00	90.00
☐ 29 Hideo Nomo	300.00	135.00
☐ 30 Mike Piazza	300.00	135.00
☐ 33 Vladimir Guerrero	150.00	70.00
☐ 36 Derek Jeter	250.00	110.00
☐ 38 Mark McGwire	200.00	90.00
☐ 39 Scott Rolen	200.00	90.00
☐ 42 Tony Gwynn	250.00	110.00
☐ 43 Barry Bonds	120.00	55.00
☐ 45 Ken Griffey Jr.	600.00	275.00
☐ 46 Alex Rodriguez	300.00	135.00
☐ 47 Jose Cruz Jr.	300.00	135.00
☐ 48 Juan Gonzalez	250.00	110.00
☐ 49 Ivan Rodriguez	120.00	55.00
☐ 50 Roger Clemens	200.00	90.00

1997 SPx Silver

Randomly inserted in packs at an approximate rate of one in six, cards from this 50-card set are a parallel version of the base set with silver foil enhancements.

	MINT	NRMT
COMPLETE SET (50)	300.00	135.00
COMMON CARD (1-50)	2.50	1.10

*SILVER STARS: 2.5X TO 5X BASIC CARDS
*SILVER ROOKIES: 1.5X TO 3X BASIC CARDS

1997 SPx Steel

Randomly inserted one in approximately one in every two packs, cards from this 50-card set are a parallel version of the base set with foil enhancements. Many dealers and collectors believe that cards 25-50 were printed in shorter supply.

	MINT	NRMT
COMPLETE SET (50)	120.00	55.00
COMMON CARD (1-50)	1.00	.45

*STEEL STARS: 1X TO 2X BASIC CARDS
*STEEL ROOKIES: .75X TO 1.5X BASIC CARDS

1997 SPx Bound for Glory

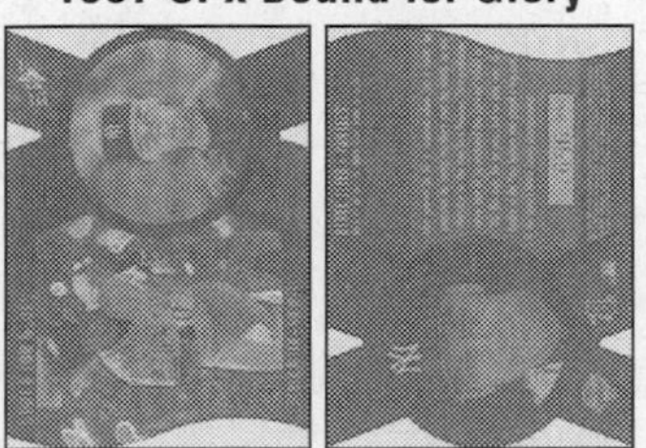

Randomly inserted in packs, this 20-card set features color photos of promising great players on a Holoview die cut card design. Only 1,500 of each card was produced and are sequentially numbered.

	MINT	NRMT
COMPLETE SET (20)	500.00	220.00
COMMON CARD (1-20)	10.00	4.50

☐ 1 Andruw Jones	25.00	11.00
☐ 2 Chipper Jones	40.00	18.00
☐ 3 Greg Maddux	40.00	18.00
☐ 4 Kenny Lofton	15.00	6.75
☐ 5 Cal Ripken	50.00	22.00
☐ 6 Mo Vaughn	15.00	6.75
☐ 7 Frank Thomas	50.00	22.00
☐ 8 Albert Belle	15.00	6.75
☐ 9 Manny Ramirez	12.00	5.50
☐ 10 Gary Sheffield	12.00	5.50
☐ 11 Jeff Bagwell	25.00	11.00
☐ 12 Mike Piazza	40.00	18.00
☐ 13 Derek Jeter	30.00	13.50
☐ 14 Mark McGwire	25.00	11.00
☐ 15 Tony Gwynn	30.00	13.50
☐ 16 Ken Caminiti	10.00	4.50
☐ 17 Barry Bonds	15.00	6.75
☐ 18 Alex Rodriguez	40.00	18.00
☐ 19 Ken Griffey Jr.	60.00	27.00
☐ 20 Juan Gonzalez	30.00	13.50

1997 SPx Bound for Glory Supreme Signatures

Randomly inserted in packs, this five-card set features autographed Bound for Glory cards. Only 250 of each card was produced and signed and are sequentially numbered.

	MINT	NRMT
COMPLETE SET (5)	1200.00	550.00
COMMON CARD (1-5)	80.00	36.00

☐ 1 Jeff Bagwell	200.00	90.00
☐ 2 Ken Griffey Jr.	500.00	220.00
☐ 3 Andruw Jones	200.00	90.00
☐ 4 Alex Rodriguez	300.00	135.00
☐ 5 Gary Sheffield	80.00	36.00

1997 SPx Cornerstones of the Game

Randomly inserted in packs, cards from this 10-card set display color photos of 20 top players. Two players are featured on each card using double Holoview technology. Only 500 of each card was produced and each is sequentially numbered on back.

	MINT	NRMT
COMPLETE SET (10)	700.00	325.00
COMMON CARD (1-10)	50.00	22.00

☐ 1 Ken Griffey Jr. Barry Bonds	120.00	55.00
☐ 2 Frank Thomas Albert Belle	100.00	45.00
☐ 3 Chipper Jones Greg Maddux	80.00	36.00
☐ 4 Tony Gwynn Paul Molitor	50.00	22.00
☐ 5 Andruw Jones Vladimir Guerrero	50.00	22.00
☐ 6 Jeff Bagwell Ryne Sandberg	50.00	22.00
☐ 7 Mike Piazza Ivan Rodriguez	60.00	27.00
☐ 8 Cal Ripken Eddie Murray	80.00	36.00
☐ 9 Mo Vaughn Mark McGwire	50.00	22.00
☐ 10 Alex Rodriguez Derek Jeter	80.00	36.00

1981 Squirt

The cards in this 22-panel set consist of 33 different individual cards, each measuring the standard-size. The set was also available as two-card panels measuring approximately 2 1/2" by 10 1/2". Cards numbered 1-11 appear twice, whereas cards 12-33 appear only once in the 22-panel set. The pattern for pairings was 1/12 and 1/23, 2/13 and 2/24, 3/14 and 3/25, and so forth on up to 11/22 and 11/33. Two card panels have a value equal to the sum of the individual cards on the panel. Supposedly panels 4/15, 4/26, 5/27, and 6/28 are more difficult to find than the other panels and are marked as SP in the checklist below.

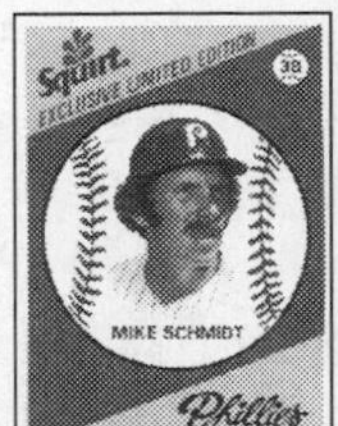

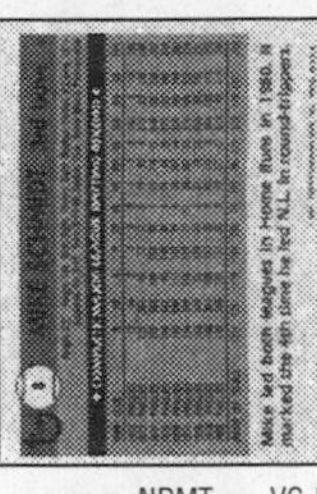

	NRMT	VG-E
COMPLETE PANEL SET	25.00	11.00
COMPLETE IND. SET	15.00	6.75
COMMON PANEL	.50	.23
COMMON CARD (1-11) DP	.25	.11
COMMON CARD (12-33)	.25	.11

☐ 1 George Brett DP	3.00	1.35
☐ 2 George Foster DP	.25	.11
☐ 3 Ben Oglivie DP	.25	.11
☐ 4 Steve Garvey DP	.50	.23
☐ 5 Reggie Jackson DP	1.00	.45
☐ 6 Bill Buckner DP	.25	.11
☐ 7 Jim Rice DP	.50	.23
☐ 8 Mike Schmidt DP	2.00	.90
☐ 9 Rod Carew DP	.75	.35
☐ 10 Dave Parker DP	.40	.18
☐ 11 Pete Rose DP	2.00	.90
☐ 12 Garry Templeton	.25	.11
☐ 13 Rick Burleson	.25	.11
☐ 14 Dave Kingman	.25	.11
☐ 15 Eddie Murray SP	8.00	3.60
☐ 16 Don Sutton	.75	.35
☐ 17 Dusty Baker	.50	.23
☐ 18 Jack Clark	.25	.11
☐ 19 Dave Winfield	1.25	.55
☐ 20 Johnny Bench	1.50	.70
☐ 21 Lee Mazzilli	.25	.11
☐ 22 Al Oliver	.50	.23
☐ 23 Jerry Mumphrey	.25	.11
☐ 24 Tony Armas	.25	.11
☐ 25 Fred Lynn	.50	.23
☐ 26 Ron LeFlore SP	1.00	.45
☐ 27 Steve Kemp SP	1.00	.45
☐ 28 Rickey Henderson SP	8.00	3.60
☐ 29 John Castino	.25	.11
☐ 30 Cecil Cooper	.25	.11
☐ 31 Bruce Bochte	.25	.11
☐ 32 Joe Charboneau	.25	.11
☐ 33 Chet Lemon	.25	.11

1982 Squirt

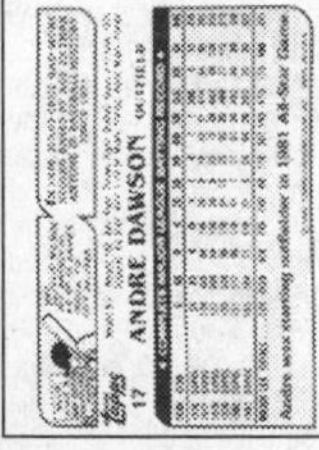

The cards in this 22-card set measure the standard size. Although the 1982 "Exclusive Limited Edition" was prepared for Squirt by Topps, the format and pictures are completely different from the regular Topps cards of this year. Each color picture is obliquely cut and the word Squirt is printed in red in the top left corner. The cards are numbered 1 through 22 and the reverses are yellow and black on white. The cards were issued on four types of panels: (1) yellow attachment card at top with picture card in center and scratch-off game at bottom; (2) yellow attachment card at top with scratch-off game in center and picture card at bottom; (3) white attachment card at top with "Collect all 22" panel in center and picture card at bottom; (4) two card panel with attachment card at top. The two card panels have parallel cards; that is, numbers 1 and 12 together, numbers 2 and 13 together, etc. Two card panels have a value equal to the sum of the individual cards on the panel. The two types (1 and 2) with the scratch-off games are more slightly difficult to obtain than the other two types and hence command prices double those below.

	NRMT	VG-E
COMPLETE SET (22)	7.50	3.40
COMMON CARD (1-22)	.25	.11

Card	NRMT	VG-E
☐ 1 Cecil Cooper	.50	.23
☐ 2 Jerry Remy	.25	.11
☐ 3 George Brett	3.00	1.35
☐ 4 Alan Trammell	.75	.35
☐ 5 Reggie Jackson	1.25	.55
☐ 6 Kirk Gibson	.75	.35
☐ 7 Dave Winfield	1.00	.45
☐ 8 Carlton Fisk	1.00	.45
☐ 9 Ron Guidry	.50	.23
☐ 10 Dennis Leonard	.25	.11
☐ 11 Rollie Fingers	1.00	.45
☐ 12 Pete Rose	2.00	.90
☐ 13 Phil Garner	.25	.11
☐ 14 Mike Schmidt	2.00	.90
☐ 15 Dave Concepcion	.50	.23
☐ 16 George Hendrick	.25	.11
☐ 17 Andre Dawson	1.00	.45
☐ 18 George Foster	.50	.23
☐ 19 Gary Carter	.75	.35
☐ 20 Fernando Valenzuela	.50	.23
☐ 21 Tom Seaver	1.00	.45
☐ 22 Bruce Sutter	.50	.23

1976 SSPC

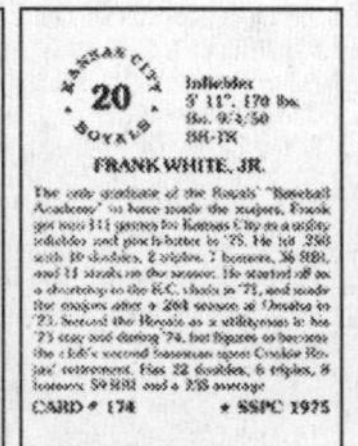

The cards in this 630-card set measure 2 1/2" by 3 1/2". The 1976 "Pure Card" set issued by TCMA derives its name from the lack of borders, logos, signatures, etc., which often clutter up the picture areas of some baseball sets. It differs from other sets produced by this company in that it cannot be re-issued due to an agreement entered into by the manufacturer. Thus, while not technically a legitimate issue, it is significant because it cannot be reprinted, unlike other collector issues. The cards are numbered in team groups, i.e., Atlanta (1-21), Cincinnati (22-46), Houston (47-65), Los Angeles (66-91), San Francisco (92-113), San Diego (114-133), Chicago White Sox (134-158), Kansas City (159-185), California (186-204), Minnesota (205-225), Milwaukee (226-251), Texas (252-273), St. Louis (274-300), Chicago Cubs (301-321), Montreal (322-351), Detroit (352-373), Baltimore (374-401), Boston (402-424), New York Yankees (425-455), Philadelphia (456-477), Oakland (478-503), Cleveland (504-532), New York Mets (533-560), and Pittsburgh (561-586). The rest of the numbers are filled in with checklists (589-595), miscellaneous players, and a heavy dose of coaches. There are a few instances in the set where the team identified on the back is different from the team shown on the front due to trades made after the completion of the 1975 season. The set features rookie year cards of Dennis Eckersley and Willie Randolph as well as early cards of George Brett, Gary Carter, and Robin Yount. The card backs were edited by Keith Olbermann, prior to his MSNBC broaddcasting days.

	NRMT	VG-E
COMPLETE SET (630)	90.00	40.00
COMMON CARD (1-630)	.10	.05

Card	NRMT	VG-E
☐ 1 Buzz Capra	.10	.05
☐ 2 Tom House	.10	.05
☐ 3 Max Leon	.10	.05
☐ 4 Carl Morton	.10	.05
☐ 5 Phil Niekro	4.00	1.80
☐ 6 Mike Thompson	.10	.05
☐ 7 Elias Sosa	.10	.05
☐ 8 Larvell Blanks	.10	.05
☐ 9 Darrell Evans	.35	.16
☐ 10 Rod Gilbreath	.10	.05
☐ 11 Mike Lum	.10	.05
☐ 12 Craig Robinson	.10	.05
☐ 13 Earl Williams	.10	.05
☐ 14 Vic Correll	.10	.05
☐ 15 Biff Pocoroba	.10	.05
☐ 16 Dusty Baker	.50	.23
☐ 17 Ralph Garr	.20	.09
☐ 18 Cito Gaston	.35	.16
☐ 19 Dave May	.10	.05
☐ 20 Rowland Office	.10	.05
☐ 21 Bob Beall	.10	.05
☐ 22 Sparky Anderson MG	1.00	.45
☐ 23 Jack Billingham	.10	.05
☐ 24 Pedro Borbon	.10	.05
☐ 25 Clay Carroll	.10	.05
☐ 26 Pat Darcy	.10	.05
☐ 27 Don Gullett	.20	.09
☐ 28 Clay Kirby	.10	.05
☐ 29 Gary Nolan	.20	.09
☐ 30 Fred Norman	.10	.05
☐ 31 Johnny Bench	6.00	2.70
☐ 32 Bill Plummer	.10	.05
☐ 33 Darrel Chaney	.10	.05
☐ 34 Dave Concepcion	.50	.23
☐ 35 Terry Crowley	.10	.05
☐ 36 Dan Driessen	.20	.09
☐ 37 Doug Flynn	.10	.05
☐ 38 Joe Morgan	4.00	1.80
☐ 39 Tony Perez	2.00	.90
☐ 40 Ken Griffey	1.25	.55
☐ 41 Pete Rose	10.00	4.50
☐ 42 Ed Armbrister	.10	.05
☐ 43 John Vukovich	.10	.05
☐ 44 George Foster	1.00	.45
☐ 45 Cesar Geronimo	.10	.05
☐ 46 Merv Rettenmund	.10	.05
☐ 47 Jim Crawford	.10	.05
☐ 48 Ken Forsch	.10	.05
☐ 49 Doug Konieczny	.10	.05
☐ 50 Joe Niekro	.35	.16
☐ 51 Cliff Johnson	.10	.05
☐ 52 Skip Jutze	.10	.05
☐ 53 Milt May	.10	.05
☐ 54 Rob Andrews	.10	.05
☐ 55 Ken Boswell	.10	.05
☐ 56 Tommy Helms	.10	.05
☐ 57 Roger Metzger	.10	.05
☐ 58 Larry Milbourne	.10	.05
☐ 59 Doug Rader	.20	.09
☐ 60 Bob Watson	.50	.23
☐ 61 Enos Cabell	.10	.05
☐ 62 Jose Cruz	.35	.16
☐ 63 Cesar Cedeno	.35	.16
☐ 64 Greg Gross	.10	.05
☐ 65 Wilbur Howard	.10	.05
☐ 66 Al Downing	.10	.05
☐ 67 Burt Hooton	.10	.05
☐ 68 Charlie Hough	.50	.23
☐ 69 Tommy John	1.00	.45
☐ 70 Andy Messersmith	.20	.09
☐ 71 Doug Rau	.10	.05
☐ 72 Rick Rhoden	.20	.09
☐ 73 Don Sutton	3.00	1.35
☐ 74 Rick Auerbach	.10	.05
☐ 75 Ron Cey	.50	.23
☐ 76 Ivan DeJesus	.10	.05
☐ 77 Steve Garvey	2.00	.90
☐ 78 Lee Lacy	.10	.05
☐ 79 Dave Lopes	.20	.09
☐ 80 Ken McMullen	.10	.05
☐ 81 Joe Ferguson	.10	.05
☐ 82 Paul Powell	.10	.05
☐ 83 Steve Yeager	.10	.05
☐ 84 Willie Crawford	.10	.05
☐ 85 Henry Cruz	.10	.05
☐ 86 Charlie Manuel	.10	.05
☐ 87 Manny Mota	.20	.09
☐ 88 Tom Paciorek	.35	.16
☐ 89 Jim Wynn	.20	.09
☐ 90 Walt Alston MG	1.00	.45
☐ 91 Bill Buckner	.50	.23
☐ 92 Jim Barr	.10	.05
☐ 93 Mike Caldwell	.10	.05
☐ 94 John D'Acquisto	.10	.05
☐ 95 Dave Heaverlo	.10	.05
☐ 96 Gary Lavelle	.10	.05
☐ 97 John Montefusco	.20	.09
☐ 98 Charlie Williams	.10	.05
☐ 99 Chris Arnold	.10	.05
☐ 100 Marc Hill	.10	.05
☐ 101 Dave Rader	.10	.05
☐ 102 Bruce Miller	.10	.05
☐ 103 Willie Montanez	.10	.05
☐ 104 Steve Ontiveros	.10	.05
☐ 105 Chris Speier	.10	.05
☐ 106 Derrel Thomas	.10	.05
☐ 107 Gary Thomasson	.10	.05
☐ 108 Glenn Adams	.10	.05
☐ 109 Von Joshua	.10	.05
☐ 110 Gary Matthews	.20	.09
☐ 111 Bobby Murcer	.50	.23
☐ 112 Horace Speed	.10	.05
☐ 113 Wes Westrum MG	.10	.05
☐ 114 Rich Folkers	.10	.05
☐ 115 Alan Foster	.10	.05
☐ 116 Dave Freisleben	.10	.05
☐ 117 Dan Frisella	.10	.05
☐ 118 Randy Jones	.20	.09
☐ 119 Dan Spillner	.10	.05
☐ 120 Larry Hardy	.10	.05
☐ 121 Randy Hundley	.20	.09
☐ 122 Fred Kendall	.10	.05
☐ 123 John McNamara MG	.10	.05
☐ 124 Tito Fuentes	.10	.05
☐ 125 Enzo Hernandez	.10	.05
☐ 126 Steve Huntz	.10	.05
☐ 127 Mike Ivie	.10	.05
☐ 128 Hector Torres	.10	.05
☐ 129 Ted Kubiak	.10	.05
☐ 130 John Grubb	.10	.05
☐ 131 John Scott	.10	.05
☐ 132 Bob Tolan	.20	.09
☐ 133 Dave Winfield	15.00	6.75
☐ 134 Bill Gogolewski	.10	.05
☐ 135 Dan Osborn	.10	.05
☐ 136 Jim Kaat	1.00	.45
☐ 137 Claude Osteen	.20	.09
☐ 138 Cecil Upshaw	.10	.05
☐ 139 Wilbur Wood	.20	.09
☐ 140 Lloyd Allen	.10	.05
☐ 141 Brian Downing	.35	.16
☐ 142 Jim Essian	.10	.05
☐ 143 Bucky Dent	.20	.09
☐ 144 Jorge Orta	.10	.05
☐ 145 Lee Richard	.10	.05
☐ 146 Bill Stein	.10	.05
☐ 147 Ken Henderson	.10	.05
☐ 148 Carlos May	.10	.05
☐ 149 Nyls Nyman	.10	.05
☐ 150 Bob Coluccio	.10	.05
☐ 151 Chuck Tanner MG	.20	.09
☐ 152 Pat Kelly	.10	.05
☐ 153 Jerry Hairston	.10	.05
☐ 154 Pete Varney	.10	.05
☐ 155 Bill Melton	.10	.05
☐ 156 Rich Gossage	1.50	.70
☐ 157 Terry Forster	.20	.09
☐ 158 Rich Hinton	.10	.05
☐ 159 Nelson Briles	.10	.05
☐ 160 Al Fitzmorris	.10	.05
☐ 161 Steve Mingori	.10	.05
☐ 162 Marty Pattin	.10	.05
☐ 163 Paul Splittorff	.10	.05
☐ 164 Dennis Leonard	.20	.09
☐ 165 Buck Martinez	.20	.09
☐ 166 Bob Stinson	.10	.05
☐ 167 George Brett	25.00	11.00
☐ 168 Harmon Killebrew	4.00	1.80
☐ 169 John Mayberry	.20	.09
☐ 170 Fred Patek	.20	.09
☐ 171 Cookie Rojas	.20	.09
☐ 172 Rodney Scott	.10	.05
☐ 173 Tony Solaita	.10	.05
☐ 174 Frank White	.50	.23
☐ 175 Al Cowens	.10	.05
☐ 176 Hal McRae	.50	.23
☐ 177 Amos Otis	.35	.16
☐ 178 Vada Pinson	.50	.23
☐ 179 Jim Wohlford	.10	.05
☐ 180 Doug Bird	.10	.05
☐ 181 Mark Littell	.10	.05
☐ 182 Bob McClure	.10	.05
☐ 183 Steve Busby	.20	.09
☐ 184 Fran Healy	.10	.05
☐ 185 Whitey Herzog MG	.35	.16
☐ 186 Andy Hassler	.10	.05
☐ 187 Nolan Ryan	30.00	13.50
☐ 188 Bill Singer	.10	.05
☐ 189 Frank Tanana	.50	.23
☐ 190 Ed Figueroa	.10	.05
☐ 191 Dave Collins	.20	.09
☐ 192 Dick Williams MG	.20	.09
☐ 193 Ellie Rodriguez	.10	.05
☐ 194 Dave Chalk	.10	.05
☐ 195 Winston Llenas	.10	.05
☐ 196 Rudy Meoli	.10	.05
☐ 197 Orlando Ramirez	.10	.05
☐ 198 Jerry Remy	.10	.05
☐ 199 Billy Smith	.10	.05
☐ 200 Bruce Bochte	.10	.05
☐ 201 Joe Lahoud	.10	.05
☐ 202 Morris Nettles	.10	.05
☐ 203 Mickey Rivers	.20	.09
☐ 204 Leroy Stanton	.10	.05
☐ 205 Vic Albury	.10	.05
☐ 206 Tom Burgmeier	.10	.05
☐ 207 Bill Butler	.10	.05
☐ 208 Bill Campbell	.10	.05
☐ 209 Ray Corbin	.10	.05
☐ 210 Joe Decker	.10	.05
☐ 211 Jim Hughes	.10	.05
☐ 212 Ed Bane UER (Photo actually Mike Pazik)	.10	.05
☐ 213 Glenn Borgmann	.10	.05
☐ 214 Rod Carew	6.00	2.70

☐ 215 Steve Brye .10 .05
☐ 216 Dan Ford .10 .05
☐ 217 Tony Oliva 1.00 .45
☐ 218 Dave Goltz .10 .05
☐ 219 Bert Blyleven .75 .35
☐ 220 Larry Hisle .20 .09
☐ 221 Steve Braun .10 .05
☐ 222 Jerry Terrell .10 .05
☐ 223 Eric Soderholm .10 .05
☐ 224 Phil Roof .10 .05
☐ 225 Danny Thompson .10 .05
☐ 226 Jim Colborn .10 .05
☐ 227 Tom Murphy .10 .05
☐ 228 Ed Rodriguez .10 .05
☐ 229 Jim Slaton .10 .05
☐ 230 Ed Sprague .10 .05
☐ 231 Charlie Moore .10 .05
☐ 232 Darrell Porter .20 .09
☐ 233 Kurt Bevacqua .20 .09
☐ 234 Pedro Garcia .10 .05
☐ 235 Mike Hegan .20 .09
☐ 236 Don Money .20 .09
☐ 237 George Scott .20 .09
☐ 238 Robin Yount 15.00 6.75
☐ 239 Hank Aaron 15.00 6.75
☐ 240 Rob Ellis .10 .05
☐ 241 Sixto Lezcano .20 .09
☐ 242 Bob Mitchell .10 .05
☐ 243 Gorman Thomas .20 .09
☐ 244 Bill Travers .10 .05
☐ 245 Pete Broberg .10 .05
☐ 246 Bill Sharp .10 .05
☐ 247 Bobby Darwin .10 .05
☐ 248 Rick Austin UER .10 .05
(Photo actually
Larry Anderson)
☐ 249 Larry Anderson UER .10 .05
(Photo actually
Rick Austin)
☐ 250 Tom Bianco .10 .05
☐ 251 Lafayette Currence .10 .05
☐ 252 Steve Foucault .10 .05
☐ 253 Bill Hands .10 .05
☐ 254 Steve Hargan .10 .05
☐ 255 Fergie Jenkins 4.00 1.80
☐ 256 Bob Sheldon .10 .05
☐ 257 Jim Umbarger .10 .05
☐ 258 Clyde Wright .10 .05
☐ 259 Bill Fahey .10 .05
☐ 260 Jim Sundberg .35 .16
☐ 261 Leo Cardenas .10 .05
☐ 262 Jim Fregosi .35 .16
☐ 263 Mike Hargrove .20 .09
☐ 264 Toby Harrah .20 .09
☐ 265 Roy Howell .10 .05
☐ 266 Lenny Randle .10 .05
☐ 267 Roy Smalley .20 .09
☐ 268 Jim Spencer .10 .05
☐ 269 Jeff Burroughs .20 .09
☐ 270 Tom Grieve .20 .09
☐ 271 Joe Lovitto .10 .05
☐ 272 Frank Lucchesi MG .10 .05
☐ 273 Dave Nelson .10 .05
☐ 274 Ted Simmons 1.00 .45
☐ 275 Lou Brock 5.00 2.20
☐ 276 Ron Fairly .20 .09
☐ 277 Bake McBride .10 .05
☐ 278 Reggie Smith .35 .16
☐ 279 Willie Davis .20 .09
☐ 280 Ken Reitz .10 .05
☐ 281 Buddy Bradford .10 .05
☐ 282 Luis Melendez .10 .05
☐ 283 Mike Tyson .10 .05
☐ 284 Ted Sizemore .10 .05
☐ 285 Mario Guerrero .10 .05
☐ 286 Larry Lintz .10 .05
☐ 287 Ken Rudolph .10 .05
☐ 288 Dick Billings .10 .05
☐ 289 Jerry Mumphrey .20 .09
☐ 290 Mike Wallace .10 .05
☐ 291 Al Hrabosky .20 .09
☐ 292 Ken Reynolds .10 .05
☐ 293 Mike Garman .10 .05
☐ 294 Bob Forsch .20 .09
☐ 295 John Denny .20 .09
☐ 296 Harry Rasmussen .10 .05
☐ 297 Lynn McGlothen .10 .05
☐ 298 Mike Barlow .10 .05
☐ 299 Greg Terlecky .10 .05
☐ 300 Red Schoendienst MG .75 .35
☐ 301 Rick Reuschel .35 .16
☐ 302 Steve Stone .20 .09
☐ 303 Bill Bonham .10 .05
☐ 304 Oscar Zamora .10 .05
☐ 305 Ken Frailing .10 .05
☐ 306 Milt Wilcox .10 .05
☐ 307 Darold Knowles .10 .05
☐ 308 Jim Marshall MG .10 .05
☐ 309 Bill Madlock .75 .35
☐ 310 Jose Cardenal .20 .09
☐ 311 Rick Monday .20 .09
☐ 312 Jerry Morales .10 .05
☐ 313 Tim Hosley .10 .05
☐ 314 Gene Hiser .10 .05
☐ 315 Don Kessinger .20 .09
☐ 316 Manny Trillo .20 .09
☐ 317 Pete LaCock .10 .05
☐ 318 George Mitterwald .10 .05
☐ 319 Steve Swisher .10 .05
☐ 320 Rob Sperring .10 .05
☐ 321 Vic Harris .10 .05
☐ 322 Ron Dunn .10 .05
☐ 323 Jose Morales .10 .05
☐ 324 Pete Mackanin .10 .05
☐ 325 Jim Cox .10 .05
☐ 326 Larry Parrish .20 .09
☐ 327 Mike Jorgensen .10 .05
☐ 328 Tim Foli .10 .05
☐ 329 Hal Breeden .10 .05
☐ 330 Nate Colbert .20 .09
☐ 331 Pepe Frias .10 .05
☐ 332 Pat Scanlon .10 .05
☐ 333 Bob Bailey .10 .05
☐ 334 Gary Carter 6.00 2.70
☐ 335 Pepe Mangual .10 .05
☐ 336 Larry Biittner .10 .05
☐ 337 Jim Lyttle .10 .05
☐ 338 Gary Roenicke .35 .16
☐ 339 Tony Scott .10 .05
☐ 340 Jerry White .10 .05
☐ 341 Jim Dwyer .10 .05
☐ 342 Ellis Valentine .20 .09
☐ 343 Fred Scherman .10 .05
☐ 344 Dennis Blair .10 .05
☐ 345 Woodie Fryman .10 .05
☐ 346 Chuck Taylor .10 .05
☐ 347 Dan Warthen .10 .05
☐ 348 Dan Carrithers .10 .05
☐ 349 Steve Rogers .20 .09
☐ 350 Dale Murray .10 .05
☐ 351 Duke Snider CO 3.00 1.35
☐ 352 Ralph Houk MG .20 .09
☐ 353 John Hiller .10 .05
☐ 354 Mickey Lolich .50 .23
☐ 355 Dave Lemancyzk .10 .05
☐ 356 Lerrin LaGrow .10 .05
☐ 357 Fred Arroyo .10 .05
☐ 358 Joe Coleman .10 .05
☐ 359 Ben Oglivie .20 .09
☐ 360 Willie Horton .20 .09
☐ 361 John Knox .10 .05
☐ 362 Leon Roberts .10 .05
☐ 363 Ron LeFlore .20 .09
☐ 364 Gary Sutherland .10 .05
☐ 365 Dan Meyer .10 .05
☐ 366 Aurelio Rodriguez .10 .05
☐ 367 Tom Veryzer .10 .05
☐ 368 Jack Pierce .10 .05
☐ 369 Gene Michael .20 .09
☐ 370 Billy Baldwin .10 .05
☐ 371 Gates Brown .10 .05
☐ 372 Mickey Stanley .20 .09
☐ 373 Terry Humphrey .10 .05
☐ 374 Doyle Alexander .20 .09
☐ 375 Mike Cuellar .35 .16
☐ 376 Wayne Garland .10 .05
☐ 377 Ross Grimsley .10 .05
☐ 378 Grant Jackson .10 .05
☐ 379 Dyar Miller .10 .05
☐ 380 Jim Palmer 5.00 2.20
☐ 381 Mike Torrez .20 .09
☐ 382 Mike Willis .10 .05
☐ 383 Dave Duncan .20 .09
☐ 384 Ellie Hendricks .10 .05
☐ 385 Jim Hutto .10 .05
☐ 386 Bob Bailor .10 .05
☐ 387 Doug DeCinces .35 .16
☐ 388 Bob Grich .35 .16
☐ 389 Lee May .35 .16
☐ 390 Tony Muser .10 .05
☐ 391 Tim Nordbrook .10 .05
☐ 392 Brooks Robinson 5.00 2.20
☐ 393 Royle Stillman .10 .05
☐ 394 Don Baylor 1.00 .45
☐ 395 Paul Blair .20 .09
☐ 396 Al Bumbry .10 .05
☐ 397 Larry Harlow .10 .05
☐ 398 Tommy Davis .20 .09
☐ 399 Jim Northrup .20 .09
☐ 400 Ken Singleton .20 .09
☐ 401 Tom Shopay .10 .05
☐ 402 Fred Lynn 1.25 .55
☐ 403 Carlton Fisk 6.00 2.70
☐ 404 Cecil Cooper .50 .23
☐ 405 Jim Rice 3.00 1.35
☐ 406 Juan Beniquez .10 .05
☐ 407 Denny Doyle .10 .05
☐ 408 Dwight Evans 1.25 .55
☐ 409 Carl Yastrzemski 6.00 2.70
☐ 410 Rick Burleson .10 .05
☐ 411 Bernie Carbo .10 .05
☐ 412 Doug Griffin .10 .05
☐ 413 Rico Petrocelli .20 .09
☐ 414 Bob Montgomery .10 .05
☐ 415 Tim Blackwell .10 .05
☐ 416 Rick Miller .10 .05
☐ 417 Darrell Johnson MG .10 .05
☐ 418 Jim Burton .10 .05
☐ 419 Jim Willoughby .10 .05
☐ 420 Rogelio Moret .10 .05
☐ 421 Bill Lee .20 .09
☐ 422 Dick Drago .10 .05
☐ 423 Diego Segui .10 .05
☐ 424 Luis Tiant .50 .23
☐ 425 Jim Hunter 4.00 1.80
☐ 426 Rick Sawyer .10 .05
☐ 427 Rudy May .10 .05
☐ 428 Dick Tidrow .10 .05
☐ 429 Sparky Lyle .50 .23
☐ 430 Doc Medich .10 .05
☐ 431 Pat Dobson .10 .05
☐ 432 Dave Pagan .10 .05
☐ 433 Thurman Munson 3.00 1.35
☐ 434 Chris Chambliss .50 .23
☐ 435 Roy White .20 .09
☐ 436 Walt Williams .10 .05
☐ 437 Graig Nettles .75 .35
☐ 438 Rick Dempsey .20 .09
☐ 439 Bobby Bonds 1.00 .45
☐ 440 Ed Herrmann .10 .05
☐ 441 Sandy Alomar .20 .09
☐ 442 Fred Stanley .10 .05
☐ 443 Terry Whitfield .10 .05
☐ 444 Rich Bladt .10 .05
☐ 445 Lou Piniella .75 .35
☐ 446 Rich Coggins .10 .05
☐ 447 Ed Brinkman .10 .05
☐ 448 Jim Mason .10 .05
☐ 449 Larry Murray .10 .05
☐ 450 Ron Blomberg .10 .05
☐ 451 Elliott Maddox .10 .05
☐ 452 Kerry Dineen .10 .05
☐ 453 Billy Martin MG 1.25 .55
☐ 454 Dave Bergman .10 .05
☐ 455 Otto Velez .10 .05
☐ 456 Joe Hoerner .10 .05
☐ 457 Tug McGraw .50 .23
☐ 458 Gene Garber .20 .09
☐ 459 Steve Carlton 6.00 2.70
☐ 460 Larry Christenson .10 .05
☐ 461 Tom Underwood .10 .05
☐ 462 Jim Lonborg .20 .09
☐ 463 Jay Johnstone .35 .16
☐ 464 Larry Bowa .35 .16
☐ 465 Dave Cash .10 .05
☐ 466 Ollie Brown .10 .05
☐ 467 Greg Luzinski .50 .23
☐ 468 Johnny Oates .50 .23
☐ 469 Mike Anderson .10 .05
☐ 470 Mike Schmidt 20.00 9.00
☐ 471 Bob Boone .75 .35
☐ 472 Tom Hutton .10 .05
☐ 473 Rich Allen 1.00 .45
☐ 474 Tony Taylor .20 .09
☐ 475 Jerry Martin .10 .05
☐ 476 Danny Ozark MG .10 .05
☐ 477 Dick Ruthven .10 .05
☐ 478 Jim Todd .10 .05
☐ 479 Paul Lindblad .10 .05
☐ 480 Rollie Fingers 4.00 1.80
☐ 481 Vida Blue .35 .16
☐ 482 Ken Holtzman .20 .09
☐ 483 Dick Bosman .10 .05
☐ 484 Sonny Siebert .10 .05
☐ 485 Glenn Abbott .10 .05
☐ 486 Stan Bahnsen .10 .05
☐ 487 Mike Norris .20 .09
☐ 488 Alvin Dark MG .20 .09
☐ 489 Claudell Washington .20 .09
☐ 490 Joe Rudi .20 .09
☐ 491 Bill North .10 .05
☐ 492 Bert Campaneris .20 .09
☐ 493 Gene Tenace .20 .09
☐ 494 Reggie Jackson 10.00 4.50
☐ 495 Phil Garner .20 .09
☐ 496 Billy Williams 4.00 1.80
☐ 497 Sal Bando .20 .09
☐ 498 Jim Holt .10 .05
☐ 499 Ted Martinez .10 .05
☐ 500 Ray Fosse .10 .05
☐ 501 Matt Alexander .10 .05

☐ 502 Larry Haney	.10	.05
☐ 503 Angel Mangual	.10	.05
☐ 504 Fred Beene	.10	.05
☐ 505 Tom Buskey	.10	.05
☐ 506 Dennis Eckersley	15.00	6.75
☐ 507 Roric Harrison	.10	.05
☐ 508 Don Hood	.10	.05
☐ 509 Jim Kern	.10	.05
☐ 510 Dave LaRoche	.10	.05
☐ 511 Fritz Peterson	.10	.05
☐ 512 Jim Strickland	.10	.05
☐ 513 Rick Waits	.10	.05
☐ 514 Alan Ashby	.35	.16
☐ 515 John Ellis	.10	.05
☐ 516 Rick Cerone	.35	.16
☐ 517 Buddy Bell	.35	.16
☐ 518 Jack Brohamer	.10	.05
☐ 519 Rico Carty	.20	.09
☐ 520 Ed Crosby	.10	.05
☐ 521 Frank Duffy	.10	.05
☐ 522 Duane Kuiper UER (Photo actually Rick Manning)	.10	.05
☐ 523 Joe Lis	.10	.05
☐ 524 Boog Powell	1.00	.45
☐ 525 Frank Robinson	5.00	2.20
☐ 526 Oscar Gamble	.20	.09
☐ 527 George Hendrick	.20	.09
☐ 528 John Lowenstein	.10	.05
☐ 529 Rick Manning UER (Photo actually Duane Kuiper)	.20	.09
☐ 530 Tommy Smith	.10	.05
☐ 531 Charlie Spikes	.10	.05
☐ 532 Steve Kline	.10	.05
☐ 533 Ed Kranepool	.20	.09
☐ 534 Mike Vail	.10	.05
☐ 535 Del Unser	.10	.05
☐ 536 Felix Millan	.10	.05
☐ 537 Rusty Staub	.50	.23
☐ 538 Jesus Alou	.10	.05
☐ 539 Wayne Garrett	.10	.05
☐ 540 Mike Phillips	.10	.05
☐ 541 Joe Torre	.75	.35
☐ 542 Dave Kingman	.75	.35
☐ 543 Gene Clines	.10	.05
☐ 544 Jack Heidemann	.10	.05
☐ 545 Bud Harrelson	.20	.09
☐ 546 John Stearns	.20	.09
☐ 547 John Milner	.10	.05
☐ 548 Bob Apodaca	.10	.05
☐ 549 Skip Lockwood	.10	.05
☐ 550 Ken Sanders	.10	.05
☐ 551 Tom Seaver	7.50	3.40
☐ 552 Rick Baldwin	.10	.05
☐ 553 Hank Webb	.10	.05
☐ 554 Jon Matlack	.10	.05
☐ 555 Randy Tate	.10	.05
☐ 556 Tom Hall	.10	.05
☐ 557 George Stone	.10	.05
☐ 558 Craig Swan	.10	.05
☐ 559 Jerry Cram	.10	.05
☐ 560 Roy Staiger	.10	.05
☐ 561 Kent Tekulve	.20	.09
☐ 562 Jerry Reuss	.20	.09
☐ 563 John Candelaria	.35	.16
☐ 564 Larry Demery	.10	.05
☐ 565 Dave Giusti	.10	.05
☐ 566 Jim Rooker	.10	.05
☐ 567 Ramon Hernandez	.10	.05
☐ 568 Bruce Kison	.10	.05
☐ 569 Ken Brett	.10	.05
☐ 570 Bob Moose	.10	.05
☐ 571 Manny Sanguillen	.20	.09
☐ 572 Dave Parker	3.00	1.35
☐ 573 Willie Stargell	4.00	1.80
☐ 574 Richie Zisk	.20	.09
☐ 575 Rennie Stennett	.10	.05
☐ 576 Al Oliver	.75	.35
☐ 577 Bill Robinson	.20	.09
☐ 578 Bob Robertson	.10	.05
☐ 579 Rich Hebner	.20	.09
☐ 580 Ed Kirkpatrick	.10	.05
☐ 581 Duffy Dyer	.10	.05
☐ 582 Craig Reynolds	.10	.05
☐ 583 Frank Taveras	.10	.05
☐ 584 Willie Randolph	3.00	1.35
☐ 585 Art Howe	.35	.16
☐ 586 Danny Murtaugh MG	.20	.09
☐ 587 Rick McKinney	.10	.05
☐ 588 Ed Goodson	.10	.05
☐ 589 Checklist 1 George Brett Al Cowens	5.00	2.20
☐ 590 Checklist 2 Keith Hernandez Lou Brock	1.25	.55
☐ 591 Checklist 3 Jerry Koosman Duke Snider	1.50	.70
☐ 592 Checklist 4 Maury Wills John Knox	.20	.09
☐ 593A Checklist 5 ERR Jim Hunter Nolan Ryan (Noland on front)	20.00	9.00
☐ 593B Checklist 5 COR Jim Hunter Nolan Ryan	10.00	4.50
☐ 594 Checklist 6 Ralph Branca Carl Erskine Pee Wee Reese	.35	.16
☐ 595 Checklist 7 Willie Mays Herb Score	2.00	.90
☐ 596 Larry Cox	.10	.05
☐ 597 Gene Mauch MG	.20	.09
☐ 598 Whitey Wietelmann CO	.10	.05
☐ 599 Wayne Simpson	.10	.05
☐ 600 Mel Thomason	.10	.05
☐ 601 Ike Hampton	.10	.05
☐ 602 Ken Crosby	.10	.05
☐ 603 Ralph Rowe	.10	.05
☐ 604 Jim Tyrone	.10	.05
☐ 605 Mick Kelleher	.10	.05
☐ 606 Mario Mendoza	.10	.05
☐ 607 Mike Rogodzinski	.10	.05
☐ 608 Bob Gallagher	.10	.05
☐ 609 Jerry Koosman	.35	.16
☐ 610 Joe Frazier MG	.10	.05
☐ 611 Karl Kuehl MG	.10	.05
☐ 612 Frank LaCorte	.10	.05
☐ 613 Ray Bare	.10	.05
☐ 614 Billy Muffett CO	.10	.05
☐ 615 Bill Laxton	.10	.05
☐ 616 Willie Mays CO	10.00	4.50
☐ 617 Phil Cavarretta CO	.20	.09
☐ 618 Ted Kluszewski CO	.50	.23
☐ 619 Elston Howard CO	.35	.16
☐ 620 Alex Grammas CO	.10	.05
☐ 621 Mickey Vernon CO	.20	.09
☐ 622 Dick Sisler CO	.10	.05
☐ 623 Harvey Haddix CO	.10	.05
☐ 624 Bobby Winkles CO	.10	.05
☐ 625 John Pesky CO	.20	.09
☐ 626 Jim Davenport CO	.10	.05
☐ 627 Dave Tomlin	.10	.05
☐ 628 Roger Craig CO	.20	.09
☐ 629 Joe Amalfitano CO	.10	.05
☐ 630 Jim Reese CO	.50	.23

1978 SSPC 270

This 270-card set was issued as magazine (All-Star Gallery) inserts in sets of three panels, with each panel measuring approximately 7 1/4" by 10 3/4". Each of the three panels contains nine cards. If cut, the individual cards would measure the standard size (2 1/2" by 3 1/2"). The fronts display color posed and action player photos with thin black inner borders and white outer borders. The backs carry the player's name, biographical information, and career summary. The cards are checklisted below alphabetically according to teams as follows: New York Yankees (1-27)), Philadelphia Phillie (28-54), Los Angeles Dodgers (55-81), Texas Rangers (82-108), Cincinnati Reds (109-135), Chicago White Sox (136-162), Boston Red Sox (163-189), California Angels (190-216), Kansas City Royals (217-243), and Chicago Cubs (244-270). The pricing below is for individual cards.

	NRMT	VG-E
COMPLETE SET (270)	50.00	22.00
COMMON CARD (1-270)	.10	.05

☐ 1 Thurman Munson	1.50	.70
☐ 2 Cliff Johnson	.10	.05
☐ 3 Lou Piniella	.50	.23
☐ 4 Dell Alston	.10	.05
☐ 5 Yankee Stadium	.10	.05
☐ 6 Ken Holtzman	.20	.09
☐ 7 Chris Chambliss	.35	.16
☐ 8 Roy White	.20	.09
☐ 9 Ed Figueroa	.10	.05
☐ 10 Dick Tidrow	.10	.05
☐ 11 Sparky Lyle	.35	.16
☐ 12 Fred Stanley	.10	.05
☐ 13 Mickey Rivers	.20	.09
☐ 14 Billy Martin MG	.50	.23
☐ 15 George Zeber	.10	.05
☐ 16 Ken Clay	.10	.05
☐ 17 Ron Guidry	.35	.16
☐ 18 Don Gullett	.20	.09
☐ 19 Fran Healy	.10	.05
☐ 20 Paul Blair	.10	.05
☐ 21 Mickey Klutts	.10	.05
☐ 22 Yankees Team Photo	.20	.09
☐ 23 Catfish Hunter	1.50	.70
☐ 24 Bucky Dent	.20	.09
☐ 25 Graig Nettles	.50	.23
☐ 26 Reggie Jackson	3.00	1.35
☐ 27 Willie Randolph	.35	.16
☐ 28 Garry Maddox	.20	.09
☐ 29 Steve Carlton	2.00	.90
☐ 30 Ron Reed	.10	.05
☐ 31 Greg Luzinski	.35	.16
☐ 32 Bobby Wine CO	.10	.05
☐ 33 Bob Boone	.35	.16
☐ 34 Carroll Beringer CO	.10	.05
☐ 35 Richie Hebner	.20	.09
☐ 36 Ray Rippelmeyer CO	.10	.05
☐ 37 Terry Harmon	.10	.05
☐ 38 Gene Garber	.20	.09
☐ 39 Ted Sizemore	.10	.05
☐ 40 Barry Foote	.10	.05
☐ 41 Tony Taylor CO	.10	.05
☐ 42 Tug McGraw	.50	.23
☐ 43 Jay Johnstone	.35	.16
☐ 44 Randy Lerch	.10	.05
☐ 45 Billy DeMars CO	.10	.05
☐ 46 Mike Schmidt	5.00	2.20
☐ 47 Larry Christenson	.10	.05
☐ 48 Tim McCarver	.50	.23
☐ 49 Larry Bowa	.35	.16
☐ 50 Danny Ozark MG	.10	.05
☐ 51 Jerry Martin	.10	.05
☐ 52 Jim Lonborg	.20	.09
☐ 53 Bake McBride	.10	.05
☐ 54 Warren Brusstar	.10	.05
☐ 55 Burt Hooton	.20	.09
☐ 56 Bill Russell	.20	.09
☐ 57 Dusty Baker	.35	.16
☐ 58 Reggie Smith	.35	.16
☐ 59 Rick Rhoden	.10	.05
☐ 60 Jerry Grote	.10	.05
☐ 61 Bill Butler	.10	.05
☐ 62 Ron Cey	.35	.16
☐ 63 Tom Lasorda MG	.60	.25
☐ 64 Teddy Martinez	.10	.05
☐ 65 Ed Goodson	.10	.05
☐ 66 Vic Davalillo	.10	.05
☐ 67 Davey Lopes	.20	.09
☐ 68 Terry Forster	.10	.05
☐ 69 Lee Lacy	.10	.05
☐ 70 Mike Garman	.10	.05
☐ 71 Steve Garvey	.75	.35
☐ 72 Johnny Oates	.35	.16
☐ 73 Steve Yeager	.10	.05
☐ 74 Rafael Landestoy	.10	.05
☐ 75 Tommy John	.50	.23
☐ 76 Glenn Burke	.10	.05
☐ 77 Rick Monday	.20	.09
☐ 78 Doug Rau	.10	.05
☐ 79 Manny Mota	.20	.09
☐ 80 Don Sutton	1.00	.45
☐ 81 Charlie Hough	.35	.16
☐ 82 Mike Hargrove	.20	.09
☐ 83 Jim Sundberg	.20	.09
☐ 84 Fergie Jenkins	1.50	.70
☐ 85 Paul Lindblad	.10	.05
☐ 86 Sandy Alomar	.10	.05
☐ 87 John Lowenstein	.10	.05
☐ 88 Claudell Washington	.20	.09
☐ 89 Toby Harrah	.20	.09
☐ 90 Jim Umbarger	.10	.05
☐ 91 Len Barker	.10	.05
☐ 92 Dave May	.10	.05
☐ 93 Kurt Bevacqua	.10	.05
☐ 94 Jim Mason	.10	.05
☐ 95 Bump Wills	.10	.05
☐ 96 Dock Ellis	.10	.05
☐ 97 Bill Fahey	.10	.05
☐ 98 Richie Zisk	.10	.05
☐ 99 Jon Matlack	.10	.05
☐ 100 John Ellis	.10	.05

Card	MINT	NRMT
☐ 101 Bert Campaneris	.20	.09
☐ 102 Doc Medich	.10	.05
☐ 103 Juan Beniquez	.10	.05
☐ 104 Billy Hunter MG	.10	.05
☐ 105 Doyle Alexander	.20	.09
☐ 106 Roger Moret	.10	.05
☐ 107 Mike Jorgensen	.10	.05
☐ 108 Al Oliver	.35	.16
☐ 109 Fred Norman	.10	.05
☐ 110 Ray Knight	.60	.25
☐ 111 Pedro Borbon	.10	.05
☐ 112 Bill Bonham	.10	.05
☐ 113 George Foster	.50	.23
☐ 114 Doug Bair	.10	.05
☐ 115 Cesar Geronimo	.10	.05
☐ 116 Tom Seaver	2.00	.90
☐ 117 Mario Soto	.20	.09
☐ 118 Ken Griffey	.35	.16
☐ 119 Mike Lum	.10	.05
☐ 120 Tom Hume	.10	.05
☐ 121 Joe Morgan	1.50	.70
☐ 122 Manny Sarmiento	.10	.05
☐ 123 Dan Driessen	.20	.09
☐ 124 Ed Armbrister	.10	.05
☐ 125 Champ Summers	.10	.05
☐ 126 Rick Auerbach	.10	.05
☐ 127 Doug Capilla	.10	.05
☐ 128 Johnny Bench	2.00	.90
☐ 129 Sparky Anderson MG	.50	.23
☐ 130 Raul Ferreyra	.10	.05
☐ 131 Dale Murray	.10	.05
☐ 132 Pete Rose	3.00	1.35
☐ 133 Dave Concepcion	.35	.16
☐ 134 Junior Kennedy	.10	.05
☐ 135 Dave Collins	.20	.09
☐ 136 Mike Eden	.10	.05
☐ 137 Lamar Johnson	.10	.05
☐ 138 Ron Schueler	.10	.05
☐ 139 Bob Lemon MG	.50	.23
☐ 140 Bobby Bonds	.50	.23
☐ 141 Thad Bosley	.10	.05
☐ 142 Jorge Orta	.10	.05
☐ 143 Wilbur Wood	.10	.05
☐ 144 Francisco Barrios	.10	.05
☐ 145 Greg Prior	.10	.05
☐ 146 Chet Lemon	.20	.09
☐ 147 Mike Squires	.10	.05
☐ 148 Eric Soderholm	.10	.05
☐ 149 Reggie Sanders	.10	.05
☐ 150 Kevin Bell	.10	.05
☐ 151 Alan Bannister	.10	.05
☐ 152 Henry Cruz	.10	.05
☐ 153 Larry Doby CO	.35	.16
☐ 154 Don Kessinger	.20	.09
☐ 155 Ralph Garr	.20	.09
☐ 156 Bill Nahorodny	.10	.05
☐ 157 Ron Blomberg	.10	.05
☐ 158 Bob Molinaro	.10	.05
☐ 159 Junior Moore	.10	.05
☐ 160 Minnie Minoso CO	.35	.16
☐ 161 Lerrin LaGrow	.10	.05
☐ 162 Wayne Nordhagen	.10	.05
☐ 163 Ramon Aviles	.10	.05
☐ 164 Bob Stanley	.35	.16
☐ 165 Reggie Cleveland	.10	.05
☐ 166 Jack Brohamer	.10	.05
☐ 167 Bill Lee	.20	.09
☐ 168 Jim Burton	.10	.05
☐ 169 Bill Campbell	.10	.05
☐ 170 Mike Torrez	.10	.05
☐ 171 Dick Drago	.10	.05
☐ 172 Butch Hobson	.10	.05
☐ 173 Bob Bailey	.10	.05
☐ 174 Fred Lynn	.20	.09
☐ 175 Rick Burleson	.20	.09
☐ 176 Luis Tiant	.35	.16
☐ 177 Ted Williams CO	5.00	2.20
☐ 178 Dennis Eckersley	1.50	.70
☐ 179 Don Zimmer MG	.10	.05
☐ 180 Carlton Fisk	1.50	.70
☐ 181 Dwight Evans	.50	.23
☐ 182 Fred Kendall	.10	.05
☐ 183 George Scott	.20	.09
☐ 184 Frank Duffy	.10	.05
☐ 185 Bernie Carbo	.10	.05
☐ 186 Jerry Remy	.10	.05
☐ 187 Carl Yastrzemski	2.00	.90
☐ 188 Allen Ripley	.10	.05
☐ 189 Jim Rice	.75	.35
☐ 190 Ken Landreaux	.10	.05
☐ 191 Paul Hartzell	.10	.05
☐ 192 Ken Brett	.10	.05
☐ 193 Dave Garcia MG	.10	.05
☐ 194 Dobby Grich	.35	.16
☐ 195 Lyman Bostock Jr.	.35	.16
☐ 196 Ike Hampton	.10	.05
☐ 197 Dave LaRoche	.10	.05
☐ 198 Dave Chalk	.10	.05
☐ 199 Rick Miller	.10	.05
☐ 200 Floyd Rayford	.10	.05
☐ 201 Willie Aikens	.20	.09
☐ 202 Balor Moore	.10	.05
☐ 203 Nolan Ryan	15.00	6.75
☐ 204 Danny Goodwin	.10	.05
☐ 205 Ron Fairly	.20	.09
☐ 206 Dyar Miller	.10	.05
☐ 207 Carney Lansford	.60	.25
☐ 208 Don Baylor	.50	.23
☐ 209 Gil Flores	.10	.05
☐ 210 Terry Humphrey	.10	.05
☐ 211 Frank Tanana	.50	.23
☐ 212 Chris Knapp	.10	.05
☐ 213 Ron Jackson	.10	.05
☐ 214 Joe Rudi	.20	.09
☐ 215 Tony Solaita	.10	.05
☐ 216 Rance Mulliniks	.10	.05
☐ 217 George Brett	12.50	5.50
☐ 218 Doug Bird	.10	.05
☐ 219 Hal McRae	.50	.23
☐ 220 Dennis Leonard	.20	.09
☐ 221 Darrell Porter	.20	.09
☐ 222 Randy McGilberry	.10	.05
☐ 223 Pete LaCock	.10	.05
☐ 224 Whitey Herzog MG	.35	.16
☐ 225 Andy Hassler	.10	.05
☐ 226 Joe Lahoud	.10	.05
☐ 227 Amos Otis	.20	.09
☐ 228 Al Hrabosky	.20	.09
☐ 229 Clint Hurdle	.10	.05
☐ 230 Paul Splittorff	.10	.05
☐ 231 Marty Pattin	.10	.05
☐ 232 Frank White	.35	.16
☐ 233 John Wathan	.10	.05
☐ 234 Freddie Patek	.20	.09
☐ 235 Rich Gale	.10	.05
☐ 236 U.L. Washington	.10	.05
☐ 237 Larry Gura	.10	.05
☐ 238 Jim Colborn	.10	.05
☐ 239 Tom Poquette	.10	.05
☐ 240 Al Cowens	.10	.05
☐ 241 Willie Wilson	.50	.23
☐ 242 Steve Mingori	.10	.05
☐ 243 Jerry Terrell	.10	.05
☐ 244 Larry Biittner	.10	.05
☐ 245 Rick Reuschel	.20	.09
☐ 246 Dave Rader	.10	.05
☐ 247 Paul Reuschel	.10	.05
☐ 248 Heity Cruz	.10	.05
☐ 249 Woodie Fryman	.10	.05
☐ 250 Steve Ontiveros	.10	.05
☐ 251 Mike Gordon	.10	.05
☐ 252 Dave Kingman	.50	.23
☐ 253 Gene Clines	.10	.05
☐ 254 Bruce Sutter	.35	.16
☐ 255 Willie Hernandez	.20	.09
☐ 256 Ivan DeJesus	.10	.05
☐ 257 Greg Gross	.10	.05
☐ 258 Larry Cox	.10	.05
☐ 259 Joe Wallis	.10	.05
☐ 260 Dennis Lamp	.10	.05
☐ 261 Ray Burris	.10	.05
☐ 262 Bill Caudill	.10	.05
☐ 263 Donnie Moore	.10	.05
☐ 264 Bill Buckner	.35	.16
☐ 265 Bobby Murcer	.35	.16
☐ 266 Dave Roberts	.10	.05
☐ 267 Mike Krukow	.10	.05
☐ 268 Herman Franks MG	.10	.05
☐ 269 Mick Kelleher	.10	.05
☐ 270 Rudy Meoli	.10	.05

1991 Stadium Club

This 600-card standard size set marked Topps first premium quality set. The set was issued in two separate series of 300 cards each. Cards were distributed in plastic wrapped packs. Series II cards were also available at McDonald's restaurants in the Northeast at three cards per pack. The set created a stir in the hobby upon release with dazzling full-color borderless photos and slick, glossy card stock. The back of each card has the basic biographical information as well as making use of the Fastball BARS system and an inset photo of the player's Topps rookie card. Rookie Cards include Jeff Bagwell, Jeff Conine and Brian McRae.

	MINT	NRMT
COMPLETE SET (600)	100.00	45.00
COMPLETE SERIES 1 (300)	60.00	27.00
COMPLETE SERIES 2 (300)	40.00	18.00
COMMON CARD (1-600)	.25	.11

Card	MINT	NRMT
☐ 1 Dave Stewart TUX	.30	.14
☐ 2 Wally Joyner	.50	.23
☐ 3 Shawon Dunston	.25	.11
☐ 4 Darren Daulton	.50	.23
☐ 5 Will Clark	1.00	.45
☐ 6 Sammy Sosa	1.25	.55
☐ 7 Dan Plesac	.25	.11
☐ 8 Marquis Grissom	1.00	.45
☐ 9 Erik Hanson	.25	.11
☐ 10 Geno Petralli	.25	.11
☐ 11 Jose Rijo	.25	.11
☐ 12 Carlos Quintana	.25	.11
☐ 13 Junior Ortiz	.25	.11
☐ 14 Bob Walk	.25	.11
☐ 15 Mike Macfarlane	.25	.11
☐ 16 Eric Yelding	.25	.11
☐ 17 Bryn Smith	.25	.11
☐ 18 Bip Roberts	.25	.11
☐ 19 Mike Scioscia	.25	.11
☐ 20 Mark Williamson	.25	.11
☐ 21 Don Mattingly	1.50	.70
☐ 22 John Franco	.25	.11
☐ 23 Chet Lemon	.25	.11
☐ 24 Tom Henke	.25	.11
☐ 25 Jerry Browne	.25	.11
☐ 26 Dave Justice	1.25	.55
☐ 27 Mark Langston	.25	.11
☐ 28 Damon Berryhill	.25	.11
☐ 29 Kevin Bass	.25	.11
☐ 30 Scott Fletcher	.25	.11
☐ 31 Moises Alou	2.00	.90
☐ 32 Dave Valle	.25	.11
☐ 33 Jody Reed	.25	.11
☐ 34 Dave West	.25	.11
☐ 35 Kevin McReynolds	.25	.11
☐ 36 Pat Combs	.25	.11
☐ 37 Eric Davis	.50	.23
☐ 38 Bret Saberhagen	.25	.11
☐ 39 Stan Javier	.25	.11
☐ 40 Chuck Cary	.25	.11
☐ 41 Tony Phillips	.25	.11
☐ 42 Lee Smith	.50	.23
☐ 43 Tim Teufel	.25	.11
☐ 44 Lance Dickson	.25	.11
☐ 45 Greg Litton	.25	.11
☐ 46 Teddy Higuera	.25	.11
☐ 47 Edgar Martinez	1.00	.45
☐ 48 Steve Avery	.50	.23
☐ 49 Walt Weiss	.25	.11
☐ 50 David Segui	.50	.23
☐ 51 Andy Benes	.50	.23
☐ 52 Karl Rhodes	.25	.11
☐ 53 Neal Heaton	.25	.11
☐ 54 Danny Gladden	.25	.11
☐ 55 Luis Rivera	.25	.11
☐ 56 Kevin Brown	.30	.14
☐ 57 Frank Thomas	8.00	3.60
☐ 58 Terry Mulholland	.25	.11
☐ 59 Dick Schofield	.25	.11
☐ 60 Ron Darling	.25	.11
☐ 61 Sandy Alomar Jr.	.30	.14
☐ 62 Dave Stieb	.25	.11
☐ 63 Alan Trammell	1.00	.45
☐ 64 Matt Nokes	.25	.11
☐ 65 Lenny Harris	.25	.11
☐ 66 Milt Thompson	.25	.11
☐ 67 Storm Davis	.25	.11
☐ 68 Joe Oliver	.25	.11
☐ 69 Andres Galarraga	1.00	.45
☐ 70 Ozzie Guillen	.25	.11
☐ 71 Ken Howell	.25	.11
☐ 72 Garry Templeton	.25	.11
☐ 73 Derrick May	.25	.11
☐ 74 Xavier Hernandez	.25	.11
☐ 75 Dave Parker	.50	.23
☐ 76 Rick Aguilera	.50	.23
☐ 77 Robby Thompson	.25	.11
☐ 78 Pete Incaviglia	.25	.11
☐ 79 Bob Welch	.25	.11
☐ 80 Randy Milligan	.25	.11
☐ 81 Chuck Finley	.50	.23
☐ 82 Alvin Davis	.25	.11
☐ 83 Tim Naehring	.50	.23
☐ 84 Jay Bell	.50	.23
☐ 85 Joe Magrane	.25	.11

☐ 86 Howard Johnson .25 .11
☐ 87 Jack McDowell .25 .11
☐ 88 Kevin Seitzer .25 .11
☐ 89 Bruce Ruffin .25 .11
☐ 90 Fernando Valenzuela .50 .23
☐ 91 Terry Kennedy .25 .11
☐ 92 Barry Larkin 1.00 .45
☐ 93 Larry Walker 1.50 .70
☐ 94 Luis Salazar .25 .11
☐ 95 Gary Sheffield 1.00 .45
☐ 96 Bobby Witt .25 .11
☐ 97 Lonnie Smith .25 .11
☐ 98 Bryan Harvey .25 .11
☐ 99 Mookie Wilson .50 .23
☐ 100 Dwight Gooden .50 .23
☐ 101 Lou Whitaker .30 .14
☐ 102 Ron Karkovice .25 .11
☐ 103 Jesse Barfield .25 .11
☐ 104 Jose DeJesus .25 .11
☐ 105 Benito Santiago .25 .11
☐ 106 Brian Holman .25 .11
☐ 107 Rafael Ramirez .25 .11
☐ 108 Ellis Burks .50 .23
☐ 109 Mike Bielecki .25 .11
☐ 110 Kirby Puckett 2.00 .90
☐ 111 Terry Shumpert .25 .11
☐ 112 Chuck Crim .25 .11
☐ 113 Todd Benzinger .25 .11
☐ 114 Brian Barnes .25 .11
☐ 115 Carlos Baerga 1.00 .45
☐ 116 Kal Daniels .25 .11
☐ 117 Dave Johnson .25 .11
☐ 118 Andy Van Slyke .50 .23
☐ 119 John Burkett .25 .11
☐ 120 Rickey Henderson 1.00 .45
☐ 121 Tim Jones .25 .11
☐ 122 Daryl Irvine .25 .11
☐ 123 Ruben Sierra .25 .11
☐ 124 Jim Abbott .50 .23
☐ 125 Daryl Boston .25 .11
☐ 126 Greg Maddux 3.00 1.35
☐ 127 Von Hayes .25 .11
☐ 128 Mike Fitzgerald .25 .11
☐ 129 Wayne Edwards .25 .11
☐ 130 Greg Briley .25 .11
☐ 131 Rob Dibble .25 .11
☐ 132 Gene Larkin .25 .11
☐ 133 David Wells .25 .11
☐ 134 Steve Balboni .25 .11
☐ 135 Greg Vaughn .50 .23
☐ 136 Mark Davis .25 .11
☐ 137 Dave Rhode .25 .11
☐ 138 Eric Show .25 .11
☐ 139 Bobby Bonilla .50 .23
☐ 140 Dana Kiecker .25 .11
☐ 141 Gary Pettis .25 .11
☐ 142 Dennis Boyd .25 .11
☐ 143 Mike Benjamin .25 .11
☐ 144 Luis Polonia .25 .11
☐ 145 Doug Jones .25 .11
☐ 146 Al Newman .25 .11
☐ 147 Alex Fernandez 1.50 .70
☐ 148 Bill Doran .25 .11
☐ 149 Kevin Elster .25 .11
☐ 150 Len Dykstra .50 .23
☐ 151 Mike Gallego .25 .11
☐ 152 Tim Belcher .25 .11
☐ 153 Jay Buhner 1.00 .45
☐ 154 Ozzie Smith UER 1.25 .55
(Rookie card is 1979, but card back says '78)
☐ 155 Jose Canseco 1.00 .45
☐ 156 Gregg Olson .25 .11
☐ 157 Charlie O'Brien .25 .11
☐ 158 Frank Tanana .25 .11
☐ 159 George Brett 2.00 .90
☐ 160 Jeff Huson .25 .11
☐ 161 Kevin Tapani .25 .11
☐ 162 Jerome Walton .25 .11
☐ 163 Charlie Hayes .25 .11
☐ 164 Chris Bosio .25 .11
☐ 165 Chris Sabo .25 .11
☐ 166 Lance Parrish .25 .11
☐ 167 Don Robinson .25 .11
☐ 168 Manny Lee .25 .11
☐ 169 Dennis Rasmussen .25 .11
☐ 170 Wade Boggs 1.00 .45
☐ 171 Bob Geren .25 .11
☐ 172 Mackey Sasser .25 .11
☐ 173 Julio Franco .50 .23
☐ 174 Otis Nixon .50 .23
☐ 175 Bert Blyleven .50 .23
☐ 176 Craig Biggio 1.00 .45
☐ 177 Eddie Murray 1.00 .45
☐ 178 Randy Tomlin .25 .11
☐ 179 Tino Martinez 1.00 .45
☐ 180 Carlton Fisk 1.00 .45
☐ 181 Dwight Smith .25 .11
☐ 182 Scott Garrelts .25 .11
☐ 183 Jim Gantner .25 .11
☐ 184 Dickie Thon .25 .11
☐ 185 John Farrell .25 .11
☐ 186 Cecil Fielder .50 .23
☐ 187 Glenn Braggs .25 .11
☐ 188 Allan Anderson .25 .11
☐ 189 Kurt Stillwell .25 .11
☐ 190 Jose Oquendo .25 .11
☐ 191 Joe Orsulak .25 .11
☐ 192 Ricky Jordan .25 .11
☐ 193 Kelly Downs .25 .11
☐ 194 Delino DeShields .25 .11
☐ 195 Omar Vizquel 1.00 .45
☐ 196 Mark Carreon .25 .11
☐ 197 Mike Harkey .25 .11
☐ 198 Jack Howell .25 .11
☐ 199 Lance Johnson .50 .23
☐ 200 Nolan Ryan TUX 4.00 1.80
☐ 201 John Marzano .25 .11
☐ 202 Doug Drabek .25 .11
☐ 203 Mark Lemke .25 .11
☐ 204 Steve Sax .25 .11
☐ 205 Greg Harris .25 .11
☐ 206 B.J. Surhoff .50 .23
☐ 207 Todd Burns .25 .11
☐ 208 Jose Gonzalez .25 .11
☐ 209 Mike Scott .25 .11
☐ 210 Dave Magadan .25 .11
☐ 211 Dante Bichette 1.00 .45
☐ 212 Trevor Wilson .25 .11
☐ 213 Hector Villanueva .25 .11
☐ 214 Dan Pasqua .25 .11
☐ 215 Greg Colbrunn .25 .11
☐ 216 Mike Jeffcoat .25 .11
☐ 217 Harold Reynolds .25 .11
☐ 218 Paul O'Neill .50 .23
☐ 219 Mark Guthrie .25 .11
☐ 220 Barry Bonds 1.25 .55
☐ 221 Jimmy Key .30 .14
☐ 222 Billy Ripken .25 .11
☐ 223 Tom Pagnozzi .25 .11
☐ 224 Bo Jackson .30 .14
☐ 225 Sid Fernandez .25 .11
☐ 226 Mike Marshall .25 .11
☐ 227 John Kruk .50 .23
☐ 228 Mike Fetters .25 .11
☐ 229 Eric Anthony .25 .11
☐ 230 Ryne Sandberg 1.25 .55
☐ 231 Carney Lansford .50 .23
☐ 232 Melido Perez .25 .11
☐ 233 Jose Lind .25 .11
☐ 234 Darryl Hamilton .25 .11
☐ 235 Tom Browning .25 .11
☐ 236 Spike Owen .25 .11
☐ 237 Juan Gonzalez 8.00 3.60
☐ 238 Felix Fermin .25 .11
☐ 239 Keith Miller .25 .11
☐ 240 Mark Gubicza .25 .11
☐ 241 Kent Anderson .25 .11
☐ 242 Alvaro Espinoza .25 .11
☐ 243 Dale Murphy 1.00 .45
☐ 244 Orel Hershiser .50 .23
☐ 245 Paul Molitor 1.00 .45
☐ 246 Eddie Whitson .25 .11
☐ 247 Joe Girardi .50 .23
☐ 248 Kent Hrbek .50 .23
☐ 249 Bill Sampen .25 .11
☐ 250 Kevin Mitchell .50 .23
☐ 251 Mariano Duncan .25 .11
☐ 252 Scott Bradley .25 .11
☐ 253 Mike Greenwell .25 .11
☐ 254 Tom Gordon .25 .11
☐ 255 Todd Zeile .50 .23
☐ 256 Bobby Thigpen .25 .11
☐ 257 Gregg Jefferies .50 .23
☐ 258 Kenny Rogers .25 .11
☐ 259 Shane Mack .25 .11
☐ 260 Zane Smith .25 .11
☐ 261 Mitch Williams .25 .11
☐ 262 Jim Deshaies .25 .11
☐ 263 Dave Winfield 1.00 .45
☐ 264 Ben McDonald .50 .23
☐ 265 Randy Ready .25 .11
☐ 266 Pat Borders .25 .11
☐ 267 Jose Uribe .25 .11
☐ 268 Derek Lilliquist .25 .11
☐ 269 Greg Brock .25 .11
☐ 270 Ken Griffey Jr. 8.00 3.60
☐ 271 Jeff Gray .25 .11
☐ 272 Danny Tartabull .25 .11
☐ 273 Denny Martinez .50 .23
☐ 274 Robin Ventura 1.00 .45
☐ 275 Randy Myers .50 .23
☐ 276 Jack Daugherty .25 .11
☐ 277 Greg Gagne .25 .11
☐ 278 Jay Howell .25 .11
☐ 279 Mike LaValliere .25 .11
☐ 280 Rex Hudler .25 .11
☐ 281 Mike Simms .25 .11
☐ 282 Kevin Maas .25 .11
☐ 283 Jeff Ballard .25 .11
☐ 284 Dave Henderson .25 .11
☐ 285 Pete O'Brien .25 .11
☐ 286 Brook Jacoby .25 .11
☐ 287 Mike Henneman .25 .11
☐ 288 Greg Olson .25 .11
☐ 289 Greg Myers .25 .11
☐ 290 Mark Grace 1.00 .45
☐ 291 Shawn Abner .25 .11
☐ 292 Frank Viola .25 .11
☐ 293 Lee Stevens .25 .11
☐ 294 Jason Grimsley .25 .11
☐ 295 Matt Williams 1.00 .45
☐ 296 Ron Robinson .25 .11
☐ 297 Tom Brunansky .25 .11
☐ 298 Checklist 1-100 .25 .11
☐ 299 Checklist 101-200 .25 .11
☐ 300 Checklist 201-300 .25 .11
☐ 301 Darryl Strawberry .50 .23
☐ 302 Bud Black .25 .11
☐ 303 Harold Baines .50 .23
☐ 304 Roberto Alomar 1.00 .45
☐ 305 Norm Charlton .25 .11
☐ 306 Gary Thurman .25 .11
☐ 307 Mike Felder .25 .11
☐ 308 Tony Gwynn 2.50 1.10
☐ 309 Roger Clemens 2.00 .90
☐ 310 Andre Dawson 1.00 .45
☐ 311 Scott Radinsky .25 .11
☐ 312 Bob Melvin .25 .11
☐ 313 Kirk McCaskill .25 .11
☐ 314 Pedro Guerrero .25 .11
☐ 315 Walt Terrell .25 .11
☐ 316 Sam Horn .25 .11
☐ 317 Wes Chamberlain UER .25 .11
(Card listed as 1989 Debut card, should be 1990)
☐ 318 Pedro Munoz .25 .11
☐ 319 Roberto Kelly .25 .11
☐ 320 Mark Portugal .25 .11
☐ 321 Tim McIntosh .25 .11
☐ 322 Jesse Orosco .25 .11
☐ 323 Gary Green .25 .11
☐ 324 Greg Harris .25 .11
☐ 325 Hubie Brooks .25 .11
☐ 326 Chris Nabholz .25 .11
☐ 327 Terry Pendleton .50 .23
☐ 328 Eric King .25 .11
☐ 329 Chili Davis .50 .23
☐ 330 Anthony Telford .25 .11
☐ 331 Kelly Gruber .25 .11
☐ 332 Dennis Eckersley .30 .14
☐ 333 Mel Hall .25 .11
☐ 334 Bob Kipper .25 .11
☐ 335 Willie McGee .25 .11
☐ 336 Steve Olin .25 .11
☐ 337 Steve Buechele .25 .11
☐ 338 Scott Leius .25 .11
☐ 339 Hal Morris .25 .11
☐ 340 Jose Offerman .25 .11
☐ 341 Kent Mercker .25 .11
☐ 342 Ken Griffey Sr. .25 .11
☐ 343 Pete Harnisch .25 .11
☐ 344 Kirk Gibson .50 .23
☐ 345 Dave Smith .25 .11
☐ 346 Dave Martinez .25 .11
☐ 347 Atlee Hammaker .25 .11
☐ 348 Brian Downing .25 .11
☐ 349 Todd Hundley 1.50 .70
☐ 350 Candy Maldonado .25 .11
☐ 351 Dwight Evans .50 .23
☐ 352 Steve Searcy .25 .11
☐ 353 Gary Gaetti .50 .23
☐ 354 Jeff Reardon .50 .23
☐ 355 Travis Fryman 1.50 .70
☐ 356 Dave Righetti .25 .11
☐ 357 Fred McGriff 1.00 .45
☐ 358 Don Slaught .25 .11
☐ 359 Gene Nelson .25 .11
☐ 360 Billy Spiers .25 .11
☐ 361 Lee Guetterman .25 .11
☐ 362 Darren Lewis .25 .11
☐ 363 Duane Ward .25 .11
☐ 364 Lloyd Moseby .25 .11
☐ 365 John Smoltz 1.00 .45
☐ 366 Felix Jose .25 .11
☐ 367 David Cone .50 .23
☐ 368 Wally Backman .25 .11
☐ 369 Jeff Montgomery .50 .23
☐ 370 Rich Garces .25 .11
☐ 371 Billy Hatcher .25 .11
☐ 372 Bill Swift .25 .11

☐ 373 Jim Eisenreich	.50	.23
☐ 374 Rob Ducey	.25	.11
☐ 375 Tim Crews	.25	.11
☐ 376 Steve Finley	.50	.23
☐ 377 Jeff Blauser	.25	.11
☐ 378 Willie Wilson	.25	.11
☐ 379 Gerald Perry	.25	.11
☐ 380 Jose Mesa	.50	.23
☐ 381 Pat Kelly	.25	.11
☐ 382 Matt Merullo	.25	.11
☐ 383 Ivan Calderon	.25	.11
☐ 384 Scott Chiamparino	.25	.11
☐ 385 Lloyd McClendon	.25	.11
☐ 386 Dave Bergman	.25	.11
☐ 387 Ed Sprague	.25	.11
☐ 388 Jeff Bagwell	6.00	2.70
☐ 389 Brett Butler	.30	.14
☐ 390 Larry Andersen	.25	.11
☐ 391 Glenn Davis	.25	.11
☐ 392 Alex Cole UER	.25	.11
(Front photo actually Otis Nixon)		
☐ 393 Mike Heath	.25	.11
☐ 394 Danny Darwin	.25	.11
☐ 395 Steve Lake	.25	.11
☐ 396 Tim Layana	.25	.11
☐ 397 Terry Leach	.25	.11
☐ 398 Bill Wegman	.25	.11
☐ 399 Mark McGwire	2.00	.90
☐ 400 Mike Boddicker	.25	.11
☐ 401 Steve Howe	.25	.11
☐ 402 Bernard Gilkey	.50	.23
☐ 403 Thomas Howard	.25	.11
☐ 404 Rafael Belliard	.25	.11
☐ 405 Tom Candiotti	.25	.11
☐ 406 Rene Gonzales	.25	.11
☐ 407 Chuck McElroy	.25	.11
☐ 408 Paul Sorrento	.50	.23
☐ 409 Randy Johnson	1.25	.55
☐ 410 Brady Anderson	1.00	.45
☐ 411 Dennis Cook	.25	.11
☐ 412 Mickey Tettleton	.50	.23
☐ 413 Mike Stanton	.25	.11
☐ 414 Ken Oberkfell	.25	.11
☐ 415 Rick Honeycutt	.25	.11
☐ 416 Nelson Santovenia	.25	.11
☐ 417 Bob Tewksbury	.25	.11
☐ 418 Brent Mayne	.25	.11
☐ 419 Steve Farr	.25	.11
☐ 420 Phil Stephenson	.25	.11
☐ 421 Jeff Russell	.25	.11
☐ 422 Chris James	.25	.11
☐ 423 Tim Leary	.25	.11
☐ 424 Gary Carter	1.00	.45
☐ 425 Glenallen Hill	.25	.11
☐ 426 Matt Young UER	.25	.11
(Card mentions 83T/Tr as RC, but 84T shown)		
☐ 427 Sid Bream	.25	.11
☐ 428 Greg Swindell	.25	.11
☐ 429 Scott Aldred	.25	.11
☐ 430 Cal Ripken	4.00	1.80
☐ 431 Bill Landrum	.25	.11
☐ 432 Earnest Riles	.25	.11
☐ 433 Danny Jackson	.25	.11
☐ 434 Casey Candaele	.25	.11
☐ 435 Ken Hill	.50	.23
☐ 436 Jaime Navarro	.25	.11
☐ 437 Lance Blankenship	.25	.11
☐ 438 Randy Velarde	.25	.11
☐ 439 Frank DiPino	.25	.11
☐ 440 Carl Nichols	.25	.11
☐ 441 Jeff M. Robinson	.25	.11
☐ 442 Deion Sanders	1.00	.45
☐ 443 Vicente Palacios	.25	.11
☐ 444 Devon White	.50	.23
☐ 445 John Cerutti	.25	.11
☐ 446 Tracy Jones	.25	.11
☐ 447 Jack Morris	.50	.23
☐ 448 Mitch Webster	.25	.11
☐ 449 Bob Ojeda	.25	.11
☐ 450 Oscar Azocar	.25	.11
☐ 451 Luis Aquino	.25	.11
☐ 452 Mark Whiten	.25	.11
☐ 453 Stan Belinda	.25	.11
☐ 454 Ron Gant	.50	.23
☐ 455 Jose DeLeon	.25	.11
☐ 456 Mark Salas UER	.25	.11
(Back has 85T photo, but calls it 86T)		
☐ 457 Junior Felix	.25	.11
☐ 458 Wally Whitehurst	.25	.11
☐ 459 Phil Plantier	.50	.23
☐ 460 Juan Berenguer	.25	.11
☐ 461 Franklin Stubbs	.25	.11
☐ 462 Joe Boever	.25	.11
☐ 463 Tim Wallach	.25	.11
☐ 464 Mike Moore	.25	.11
☐ 465 Albert Belle	1.50	.70
☐ 466 Mike Witt	.25	.11
☐ 467 Craig Worthington	.25	.11
☐ 468 Jerald Clark	.25	.11
☐ 469 Scott Terry	.25	.11
☐ 470 Milt Cuyler	.25	.11
☐ 471 John Smiley	.25	.11
☐ 472 Charles Nagy	1.00	.45
☐ 473 Alan Mills	.25	.11
☐ 474 John Russell	.25	.11
☐ 475 Bruce Hurst	.25	.11
☐ 476 Andujar Cedeno	.25	.11
☐ 477 Dave Eiland	.25	.11
☐ 478 Brian McRae	.75	.35
☐ 479 Mike LaCoss	.25	.11
☐ 480 Chris Gwynn	.25	.11
☐ 481 Jamie Moyer	.25	.11
☐ 482 John Olerud	.50	.23
☐ 483 Efrain Valdez	.25	.11
☐ 484 Sil Campusano	.25	.11
☐ 485 Pascual Perez	.25	.11
☐ 486 Gary Redus	.25	.11
☐ 487 Andy Hawkins	.25	.11
☐ 488 Cory Snyder	.25	.11
☐ 489 Chris Hoiles	.25	.11
☐ 490 Ron Hassey	.25	.11
☐ 491 Gary Wayne	.25	.11
☐ 492 Mark Lewis	.25	.11
☐ 493 Scott Coolbaugh	.25	.11
☐ 494 Gerald Young	.25	.11
☐ 495 Juan Samuel	.25	.11
☐ 496 Willie Fraser	.25	.11
☐ 497 Jeff Treadway	.25	.11
☐ 498 Vince Coleman	.25	.11
☐ 499 Cris Carpenter	.25	.11
☐ 500 Jack Clark	.50	.23
☐ 501 Kevin Appier	1.00	.45
☐ 502 Rafael Palmeiro	1.00	.45
☐ 503 Hensley Meulens	.25	.11
☐ 504 George Bell	.25	.11
☐ 505 Tony Pena	.25	.11
☐ 506 Roger McDowell	.25	.11
☐ 507 Luis Sojo	.25	.11
☐ 508 Mike Schooler	.25	.11
☐ 509 Robin Yount	1.00	.45
☐ 510 Jack Armstrong	.25	.11
☐ 511 Rick Cerone	.25	.11
☐ 512 Curt Wilkerson	.25	.11
☐ 513 Joe Carter	1.00	.45
☐ 514 Tim Burke	.25	.11
☐ 515 Tony Fernandez	.25	.11
☐ 516 Ramon Martinez	.30	.14
☐ 517 Tim Hulett	.25	.11
☐ 518 Terry Steinbach	.50	.23
☐ 519 Pete Smith	.25	.11
☐ 520 Ken Caminiti	1.00	.45
☐ 521 Shawn Boskie	.25	.11
☐ 522 Mike Pagliarulo	.25	.11
☐ 523 Tim Raines	.50	.23
☐ 524 Alfredo Griffin	.25	.11
☐ 525 Henry Cotto	.25	.11
☐ 526 Mike Stanley	.25	.11
☐ 527 Charlie Leibrandt	.25	.11
☐ 528 Jeff King	.50	.23
☐ 529 Eric Plunk	.25	.11
☐ 530 Tom Lampkin	.25	.11
☐ 531 Steve Bedrosian	.25	.11
☐ 532 Tom Herr	.25	.11
☐ 533 Craig Lefferts	.25	.11
☐ 534 Jeff Reed	.25	.11
☐ 535 Mickey Morandini	.25	.11
☐ 536 Greg Cadaret	.25	.11
☐ 537 Ray Lankford	2.00	.90
☐ 538 John Candelaria	.25	.11
☐ 539 Rob Deer	.25	.11
☐ 540 Brad Arnsberg	.25	.11
☐ 541 Mike Sharperson	.25	.11
☐ 542 Jeff D. Robinson	.25	.11
☐ 543 Mo Vaughn	5.00	2.20
☐ 544 Jeff Parrett	.25	.11
☐ 545 Willie Randolph	.50	.23
☐ 546 Herm Winningham	.25	.11
☐ 547 Jeff Innis	.25	.11
☐ 548 Chuck Knoblauch	3.00	1.35
☐ 549 Tommy Greene UER	.25	.11
(Born in North Carolina, not South Carolina)		
☐ 550 Jeff Hamilton	.25	.11
☐ 551 Barry Jones	.25	.11
☐ 552 Ken Dayley	.25	.11
☐ 553 Rick Dempsey	.25	.11
☐ 554 Greg Smith	.25	.11
☐ 555 Mike Devereaux	.25	.11
☐ 556 Keith Comstock	.25	.11
☐ 557 Paul Faries	.25	.11
☐ 558 Tom Glavine	1.00	.45
☐ 559 Craig Grebeck	.25	.11
☐ 560 Scott Erickson	.50	.23
☐ 561 Joel Skinner	.25	.11
☐ 562 Mike Morgan	.25	.11
☐ 563 Dave Gallagher	.25	.11
☐ 564 Todd Stottlemyre	.25	.11
☐ 565 Rich Rodriguez	.25	.11
☐ 566 Craig Wilson	.25	.11
☐ 567 Jeff Brantley	.25	.11
☐ 568 Scott Kamieniecki	.25	.11
☐ 569 Steve Decker	.25	.11
☐ 570 Juan Agosto	.25	.11
☐ 571 Tommy Gregg	.25	.11
☐ 572 Kevin Wickander	.25	.11
☐ 573 Jamie Quirk UER	.25	.11
(Rookie card is 1976, but card back is 1990)		
☐ 574 Jerry Don Gleaton	.25	.11
☐ 575 Chris Hammond	.25	.11
☐ 576 Luis Gonzalez	.50	.23
☐ 577 Russ Swan	.25	.11
☐ 578 Jeff Conine	1.00	.45
☐ 579 Charlie Hough	.25	.11
☐ 580 Jeff Kunkel	.25	.11
☐ 581 Darrel Akerfelds	.25	.11
☐ 582 Jeff Manto	.25	.11
☐ 583 Alejandro Pena	.25	.11
☐ 584 Mark Davidson	.25	.11
☐ 585 Bob MacDonald	.25	.11
☐ 586 Paul Assenmacher	.25	.11
☐ 587 Dan Wilson	1.00	.45
☐ 588 Tom Bolton	.25	.11
☐ 589 Brian Harper	.25	.11
☐ 590 John Habyan	.25	.11
☐ 591 John Orton	.25	.11
☐ 592 Mark Gardner	.25	.11
☐ 593 Turner Ward	.25	.11
☐ 594 Bob Patterson	.25	.11
☐ 595 Ed Nunez	.25	.11
☐ 596 Gary Scott UER	.25	.11
(Major League Batting Record should be Minor League)		
☐ 597 Scott Bankhead	.25	.11
☐ 598 Checklist 301-400	.25	.11
☐ 599 Checklist 401-500	.25	.11
☐ 600 Checklist 501-600	.25	.11

1992 Stadium Club Dome

The 1992 Stadium Club Dome set (issued by Topps) features 100 top draft picks, 56 1991 All-Star Game cards, 25 1991 Team U.S.A. cards, and 19 1991 Championship and World Series cards, all packaged in a factory set box inside a molded-plastic SkyDome display. Topps actually references this set as a 1991 set and the copyright lines on the card backs say 1991, but the set was released well into 1992. The standard-size cards display full-bleed glossy player photos on the fronts. The player's name appears in an sky-blue stripe that is accented by parallel gold stripes. Rookie Cards in this set include Shawn Green, Todd Hollandsworth, Alex Ochoa and Manny Ramirez.

	MINT	NRMT
COMP.FACT.SET (200)	10.00	4.50
COMMON CARD (1-200)	.10	.05
☐ 1 Terry Adams	.20	.09
☐ 2 Tommy Adams	.10	.05
☐ 3 Rick Aguilera	.10	.05
☐ 4 Ron Allen	.10	.05
☐ 5 Roberto Alomar	.40	.18
☐ 6 Sandy Alomar	.20	.09
☐ 7 Greg Anthony	.10	.05
☐ 8 James Austin	.10	.05
☐ 9 Steve Avery	.10	.05
☐ 10 Harold Baines	.20	.09
☐ 11 Brian Barber	.20	.09
☐ 12 Jon Barnes	.10	.05
☐ 13 George Bell	.10	.0

☐ 14 Doug Bennett	.10	.05
☐ 15 Sean Bergman	.20	.09
☐ 16 Craig Biggio	.15	.07
☐ 17 Bill Bliss	.10	.05
☐ 18 Wade Boggs	.40	.18
☐ 19 Bobby Bonilla	.20	.09
☐ 20 Russell Brock	.10	.05
☐ 21 Tarrik Brock	.10	.05
☐ 22 Tom Browning	.10	.05
☐ 23 Brett Butler	.20	.09
☐ 24 Ivan Calderon	.10	.05
☐ 25 Joe Carter	.15	.07
☐ 26 Joe Caruso	.10	.05
☐ 27 Dan Cholowsky	.10	.05
☐ 28 Will Clark	.15	.07
☐ 29 Roger Clemens	.75	.35
☐ 30 Shawn Curran	.10	.05
☐ 31 Chris Curtis	.10	.05
☐ 32 Chili Davis	.20	.09
☐ 33 Andre Dawson	.15	.07
☐ 34 Joe DeBerry	.10	.05
☐ 35 John Dettmer	.10	.05
☐ 36 Rob Dibble	.10	.05
☐ 37 John Donati	.10	.05
☐ 38 Dave Doorneweerd	.10	.05
☐ 39 Darren Dreifort	.20	.09
☐ 40 Mike Durant	.10	.05
☐ 41 Chris Durkin	.10	.05
☐ 42 Dennis Eckersley	.15	.07
☐ 43 Brian Edmondson	.10	.05
☐ 44 Vaughn Eshelman	.10	.05
☐ 45 Shawn Estes	.75	.35
☐ 46 Jorge Fabregas	.10	.05
☐ 47 Jon Farrell	.10	.05
☐ 48 Cecil Fielder	.20	.09
☐ 49 Carlton Fisk	.15	.07
☐ 50 Tim Flannelly	.10	.05
☐ 51 Cliff Floyd	.40	.18
☐ 52 Julio Franco	.20	.09
☐ 53 Greg Gagne	.10	.05
☐ 54 Chris Gambs	.10	.05
☐ 55 Ron Gant	.20	.09
☐ 56 Brent Gates	.20	.09
☐ 57 Dwayne Gerald	.10	.05
☐ 58 Jason Giambi	.75	.35
☐ 59 Benji Gil	.20	.09
☐ 60 Mark Gipner	.10	.05
☐ 61 Danny Gladden	.10	.05
☐ 62 Tom Glavine	.15	.07
☐ 63 Jimmy Gonzalez	.10	.05
☐ 64 Jeff Granger	.20	.09
☐ 65 Dan Grapenthien	.10	.05
☐ 66 Dennis Gray	.10	.05
☐ 67 Shawn Green	.50	.23
☐ 68 Tyler Green	.20	.09
☐ 69 Todd Greene	.75	.35
☐ 70 Ken Griffey Jr.	2.00	.90
☐ 71 Kelly Gruber	.10	.05
☐ 72 Ozzie Guillen	.10	.05
☐ 73 Tony Gwynn	1.00	.45
☐ 74 Shane Halter	.10	.05
☐ 75 Jeffrey Hammonds	.40	.18
☐ 76 Larry Hanlon	.10	.05
☐ 77 Pete Harnisch	.10	.05
☐ 78 Mike Harrison	.10	.05
☐ 79 Bryan Harvey	.10	.05
☐ 80 Scott Hatteberg	.10	.05
☐ 81 Rick Helling	.10	.05
☐ 82 Dave Henderson	.10	.05
☐ 83 Rickey Henderson	.15	.07
☐ 84 Tyrone Hill	.10	.05
☐ 85 Todd Hollandsworth	.50	.23
☐ 86 Brian Holliday	.10	.05
☐ 87 Terry Horn	.10	.05
☐ 88 Jeff Hostetler	.10	.05
☐ 89 Kent Hrbek	.20	.09
☐ 90 Mark Hubbard	.10	.05
☐ 91 Charles Johnson	1.00	.45
☐ 92 Howard Johnson	.10	.05
☐ 93 Todd Johnson	.10	.05
☐ 94 Bobby Jones	.40	.18
☐ 95 Dan Jones	.10	.05
☐ 96 Felix Jose	.10	.05
☐ 97 David Justice	.40	.18
☐ 98 Jimmy Key	.20	.09
☐ 99 Marc Kroon	.10	.05
☐ 100 John Kruk	.20	.09
☐ 101 Mark Langston	.10	.05
☐ 102 Barry Larkin	.15	.07
☐ 103 Mike LaValliere	.10	.05
☐ 104 Scott Leius	.10	.05
☐ 105 Mark Lemke	.10	.05
☐ 106 Donnie Leshnock	.10	.05
☐ 107 Jimmy Lewis	.10	.05
[illegible] Shane Livesy	.10	.05
[illegible]n Long	.10	.05
[illegible] Mallory	.10	.05

☐ 111 Denny Martinez	.20	.09
☐ 112 Justin Mashore	.10	.05
☐ 113 Jason McDonald	.20	.09
☐ 114 Jack McDowell	.20	.09
☐ 115 Tom McKinnon	.10	.05
☐ 116 Billy McMillon	.20	.09
☐ 117 Buck McNabb	.20	.09
☐ 118 Jim Mecir	.10	.05
☐ 119 Dan Melendez	.10	.05
☐ 120 Shawn Miller	.20	.09
☐ 121 Trever Miller	.10	.05
☐ 122 Paul Molitor	.40	.18
☐ 123 Vincent Moore	.10	.05
☐ 124 Mike Morgan	.10	.05
☐ 125 Jack Morris WS	.20	.09
☐ 126 Jack Morris AS	.10	.05
☐ 127 Sean Mulligan	.10	.05
☐ 128 Eddie Murray AS	.40	.18
☐ 129 Mike Neill	.10	.05
☐ 130 Phil Nevin	.20	.09
☐ 131 Mark O'Brien	.10	.05
☐ 132 Alex Ochoa	.40	.18
☐ 133 Chad Ogea	.50	.23
☐ 134 Greg Olson	.10	.05
☐ 135 Paul O'Neill	.20	.09
☐ 136 Jared Osentowski	.10	.05
☐ 137 Mike Pagliarulo	.10	.05
☐ 138 Rafael Palmeiro	.15	.07
☐ 139 Rodney Pedraza	.10	.05
☐ 140 Tony Phillips (P)	.10	.05
☐ 141 Scott Pisciotta	.20	.09
☐ 142 Christopher Pritchett	.10	.05
☐ 143 Jason Pruitt	.10	.05
☐ 144 Kirby Puckett WS UER (Championship series AB and BA is wrong)	.75	.35
☐ 145 Kirby Puckett AS	.75	.35
☐ 146 Manny Ramirez	2.50	1.10
☐ 147 Eddie Ramos	.10	.05
☐ 148 Mark Ratekin	.10	.05
☐ 149 Jeff Reardon	.20	.09
☐ 150 Sean Rees	.10	.05
☐ 151 Calvin Reese	.15	.07
☐ 152 Desmond Relaford	.40	.18
☐ 153 Eric Richardson	.10	.05
☐ 154 Cal Ripken	1.50	.70
☐ 155 Chris Roberts	.20	.09
☐ 156 Mike Robertson	.10	.05
☐ 157 Steve Rodriguez	.10	.05
☐ 158 Mike Rossiter	.10	.05
☐ 159 Scott Ruffcorn	.10	.05
☐ 160 Chris Sabo	.10	.05
☐ 161 Juan Samuel	.10	.05
☐ 162 Ryne Sandberg UER (On 5th line, prior misspelled as prilor)	.50	.23
☐ 163 Scott Sanderson	.10	.05
☐ 164 Benny Santiago	.10	.05
☐ 165 Gene Schall	.10	.05
☐ 166 Chad Schoenvogel	.10	.05
☐ 167 Chris Seelbach	.20	.09
☐ 168 Aaron Sele	.15	.07
☐ 169 Basil Shabazz	.10	.05
☐ 170 Al Shirley	.20	.09
☐ 171 Paul Shuey	.10	.05
☐ 172 Ruben Sierra	.10	.05
☐ 173 John Smiley	.10	.05
☐ 174 Lee Smith	.20	.09
☐ 175 Ozzie Smith	.50	.23
☐ 176 Tim Smith	.10	.05
☐ 177 Zane Smith	.10	.05
☐ 178 John Smoltz	.15	.07
☐ 179 Scott Stahoviak	.20	.09
☐ 180 Kennie Steenstra	.10	.05
☐ 181 Kevin Stocker	.10	.05
☐ 182 Chris Stynes	.40	.18
☐ 183 Danny Tartabull	.10	.05
☐ 184 Brien Taylor	.20	.09
☐ 185 Todd Taylor	.10	.05
☐ 186 Larry Thomas	.10	.05
☐ 187 Ozzie Timmons (See also 188)	.20	.09
☐ 188 David Tuttle UER (Mistakenly numbered as 187 on card)	.10	.05
☐ 189 Andy Van Slyke	.20	.09
☐ 190 Frank Viola	.10	.05
☐ 191 Michael Walkden	.10	.05
☐ 192 Jeff Ware	.10	.05
☐ 193 Allen Watson	.20	.09
☐ 194 Steve Whitaker	.10	.05
☐ 195 Jerry Willard	.10	.05
☐ 196 Craig Wilson	.10	.05
☐ 197 Chris Wimmer	.10	.05
☐ 198 Steve Wojciechowski	.10	.05
☐ 199 Joel Wolfe	.10	.05
☐ 200 Ivan Zweig	.10	.05

1992 Stadium Club

The 1992 Stadium Club baseball card set consists of 900 standard-size cards issued in three series of 300 cards each. Cards were issued in plastic wrapped packs. A card-like application form for membership in Topps Stadium Club was inserted in each pack. The glossy color player photos on the fronts are full-bleed. The "Topps Stadium Club" logo is superimposed at the bottom of the card face, with the player's name appearing immediately below the logo. Some cards in the set have the Stadium Club logo printed upside down. The backs display a mini reprint of the player's rookie card and "BARS" (Baseball Analysis and Reporting System) statistics. Card numbers 591-610 form a "Members Choice" subset. The only notable Rookie Card in this set features Bill Pulsipher.

	MINT	NRMT
COMPLETE SET (900)	50.00	22.00
COMPLETE SERIES 1 (300)	18.00	8.00
COMPLETE SERIES 2 (300)	18.00	8.00
COMPLETE SERIES 3 (300)	18.00	8.00
COMMON CARD (1-900)	.10	.05

☐ 1 Cal Ripken UER (Misspelled Ripkin on card back)	1.50	.70
☐ 2 Eric Yelding	.10	.05
☐ 3 Geno Petralli	.10	.05
☐ 4 Wally Backman	.10	.05
☐ 5 Milt Cuyler	.10	.05
☐ 6 Kevin Bass	.10	.05
☐ 7 Dante Bichette	.10	.05
☐ 8 Ray Lankford	.40	.18
☐ 9 Mel Hall	.10	.05
☐ 10 Joe Carter	.10	.05
☐ 11 Juan Samuel	.10	.05
☐ 12 Jeff Montgomery	.20	.09
☐ 13 Glenn Braggs	.10	.05
☐ 14 Henry Cotto	.10	.05
☐ 15 Deion Sanders	.40	.18
☐ 16 Dick Schofield	.10	.05
☐ 17 David Cone	.20	.09
☐ 18 Chili Davis	.20	.09
☐ 19 Tom Foley	.10	.05
☐ 20 Ozzie Guillen	.10	.05
☐ 21 Luis Salazar	.10	.05
☐ 22 Terry Steinbach	.20	.09
☐ 23 Chris James	.10	.05
☐ 24 Jeff King	.20	.09
☐ 25 Carlos Quintana	.10	.05
☐ 26 Mike Maddux	.10	.05
☐ 27 Tommy Greene	.10	.05
☐ 28 Jeff Russell	.10	.05
☐ 29 Steve Finley	.20	.09
☐ 30 Mike Flanagan	.10	.05
☐ 31 Darren Lewis	.10	.05
☐ 32 Mark Lee	.10	.05
☐ 33 Willie Fraser	.10	.05
☐ 34 Mike Henneman	.10	.05
☐ 35 Kevin Maas	.10	.05
☐ 36 Dave Hansen	.10	.05
☐ 37 Erik Hanson	.10	.05
☐ 38 Bill Doran	.10	.05
☐ 39 Mike Boddicker	.10	.05
☐ 40 Vince Coleman	.10	.05
☐ 41 Devon White	.10	.05
☐ 42 Mark Gardner	.10	.05
☐ 43 Scott Lewis	.10	.05
☐ 44 Juan Berenguer	.10	.05
☐ 45 Carney Lansford	.20	.09
☐ 46 Curt Wilkerson	.10	.05
☐ 47 Shane Mack	.10	.05
☐ 48 Bip Roberts	.10	.05
☐ 49 Greg A. Harris	.10	.05
☐ 50 Ryne Sandberg	.50	.23
☐ 51 Mark Whiten	.10	.05
☐ 52 Jack McDowell	.10	.05
☐ 53 Jimmy Jones	.10	.05
☐ 54 Steve Lake	.10	.05
☐ 55 Bud Black	.10	.05
☐ 56 Dave Valle	.10	.05

☐ 57 Kevin Reimer .10 .05
☐ 58 Rich Gedman UER .10 .05
(Wrong BARS chart used)
☐ 59 Travis Fryman .20 .09
☐ 60 Steve Avery .10 .05
☐ 61 Francisco de la Rosa .10 .05
☐ 62 Scott Hemond .10 .05
☐ 63 Hal Morris .10 .05
☐ 64 Hensley Meulens .10 .05
☐ 65 Frank Castillo .20 .09
☐ 66 Gene Larkin .10 .05
☐ 67 Jose DeLeon .10 .05
☐ 68 Al Osuna .10 .05
☐ 69 Dave Cochrane .10 .05
☐ 70 Robin Ventura .20 .09
☐ 71 John Cerutti .10 .05
☐ 72 Kevin Gross .10 .05
☐ 73 Ivan Calderon .10 .05
☐ 74 Mike Macfarlane .10 .05
☐ 75 Stan Belinda .10 .05
☐ 76 Shawn Hillegas .10 .05
☐ 77 Pat Borders .10 .05
☐ 78 Jim Vatcher .10 .05
☐ 79 Bobby Rose .10 .05
☐ 80 Roger Clemens .75 .35
☐ 81 Craig Worthington .10 .05
☐ 82 Jeff Treadway .10 .05
☐ 83 Jamie Quirk .10 .05
☐ 84 Randy Bush .10 .05
☐ 85 Anthony Young .10 .05
☐ 86 Trevor Wilson .10 .05
☐ 87 Jaime Navarro .10 .05
☐ 88 Les Lancaster .10 .05
☐ 89 Pat Kelly .10 .05
☐ 90 Alvin Davis .10 .05
☐ 91 Larry Andersen .10 .05
☐ 92 Rob Deer .10 .05
☐ 93 Mike Sharperson .10 .05
☐ 94 Lance Parrish .10 .05
☐ 95 Cecil Espy .10 .05
☐ 96 Tim Spehr .10 .05
☐ 97 Dave Stieb .10 .05
☐ 98 Terry Mulholland .10 .05
☐ 99 Dennis Boyd .10 .05
☐ 100 Barry Larkin .10 .05
☐ 101 Ryan Bowen .10 .05
☐ 102 Felix Fermin .10 .05
☐ 103 Luis Alicea .10 .05
☐ 104 Tim Hulett .10 .05
☐ 105 Rafael Belliard .10 .05
☐ 106 Mike Gallego .10 .05
☐ 107 Dave Righetti .10 .05
☐ 108 Jeff Schaefer .10 .05
☐ 109 Ricky Bones .10 .05
☐ 110 Scott Erickson .20 .09
☐ 111 Matt Nokes .10 .05
☐ 112 Bob Scanlan .10 .05
☐ 113 Tom Candiotti .10 .05
☐ 114 Sean Berry .10 .05
☐ 115 Kevin Morton .10 .05
☐ 116 Scott Fletcher .10 .05
☐ 117 B.J. Surhoff .20 .09
☐ 118 Dave Magadan UER .10 .05
(Born Tampa, not Tamps)
☐ 119 Bill Gullickson .10 .05
☐ 120 Marquis Grissom .20 .09
☐ 121 Lenny Harris .10 .05
☐ 122 Wally Joyner .20 .09
☐ 123 Kevin Brown .20 .09
☐ 124 Braulio Castillo .10 .05
☐ 125 Eric King .10 .05
☐ 126 Mark Portugal .10 .05
☐ 127 Calvin Jones .10 .05
☐ 128 Mike Heath .10 .05
☐ 129 Todd Van Poppel .10 .05
☐ 130 Benny Santiago .10 .05
☐ 131 Gary Thurman .10 .05
☐ 132 Joe Girardi .10 .05
☐ 133 Dave Eiland .10 .05
☐ 134 Orlando Merced .10 .05
☐ 135 Joe Orsulak .10 .05
☐ 136 John Burkett .10 .05
☐ 137 Ken Dayley .10 .05
☐ 138 Ken Hill .20 .09
☐ 139 Walt Terrell .10 .05
☐ 140 Mike Scioscia .10 .05
☐ 141 Junior Felix .10 .05
☐ 142 Ken Caminiti .40 .18
☐ 143 Carlos Baerga .20 .09
☐ 144 Tony Fossas .10 .05
☐ 145 Craig Grebeck .10 .05
☐ 146 Scott Bradley .10 .05
☐ 147 Kent Mercker .10 .05
☐ 148 Derrick May .10 .05
☐ 149 Jerald Clark .10 .05
☐ 150 George Brett .75 .35
☐ 151 Luis Quinones .10 .05
☐ 152 Mike Pagliarulo .10 .05
☐ 153 Jose Guzman .10 .05
☐ 154 Charlie O'Brien .10 .05
☐ 155 Darren Holmes .10 .05
☐ 156 Joe Boever .10 .05
☐ 157 Rich Monteleone .10 .05
☐ 158 Reggie Harris .10 .05
☐ 159 Roberto Alomar .40 .18
☐ 160 Robby Thompson .10 .05
☐ 161 Chris Hoiles .10 .05
☐ 162 Tom Pagnozzi .10 .05
☐ 163 Omar Vizquel .20 .09
☐ 164 John Candelaria .10 .05
☐ 165 Terry Shumpert .10 .05
☐ 166 Andy Mota .10 .05
☐ 167 Scott Bailes .10 .05
☐ 168 Jeff Blauser .10 .05
☐ 169 Steve Olin .10 .05
☐ 170 Doug Drabek .10 .05
☐ 171 Dave Bergman .10 .05
☐ 172 Eddie Whitson .10 .05
☐ 173 Gilberto Reyes .10 .05
☐ 174 Mark Grace .10 .05
☐ 175 Paul O'Neill .20 .09
☐ 176 Greg Cadaret .10 .05
☐ 177 Mark Williamson .10 .05
☐ 178 Casey Candaele .10 .05
☐ 179 Candy Maldonado .10 .05
☐ 180 Lee Smith .20 .09
☐ 181 Harold Reynolds .10 .05
☐ 182 David Justice .40 .18
☐ 183 Lenny Webster .10 .05
☐ 184 Donn Pall .10 .05
☐ 185 Gerald Alexander .10 .05
☐ 186 Jack Clark .20 .09
☐ 187 Stan Javier .10 .05
☐ 188 Ricky Jordan .10 .05
☐ 189 Franklin Stubbs .10 .05
☐ 190 Dennis Eckersley .10 .05
☐ 191 Danny Tartabull .10 .05
☐ 192 Pete O'Brien .10 .05
☐ 193 Mark Lewis .10 .05
☐ 194 Mike Felder .10 .05
☐ 195 Mickey Tettleton .10 .05
☐ 196 Dwight Smith .10 .05
☐ 197 Shawn Abner .10 .05
☐ 198 Jim Leyritz UER .10 .05
(Career totals less
than 1991 totals)
☐ 199 Mike Devereaux .10 .05
☐ 200 Craig Biggio .10 .05
☐ 201 Kevin Elster .10 .05
☐ 202 Rance Mulliniks .10 .05
☐ 203 Tony Fernandez .10 .05
☐ 204 Allan Anderson .10 .05
☐ 205 Herm Winningham .10 .05
☐ 206 Tim Jones .10 .05
☐ 207 Ramon Martinez .20 .09
☐ 208 Teddy Higuera .10 .05
☐ 209 John Kruk .20 .09
☐ 210 Jim Abbott .10 .05
☐ 211 Dean Palmer .20 .09
☐ 212 Mark Davis .10 .05
☐ 213 Jay Buhner .10 .05
☐ 214 Jesse Barfield .10 .05
☐ 215 Kevin Mitchell .20 .09
☐ 216 Mike LaValliere .10 .05
☐ 217 Mark Wohlers .10 .05
☐ 218 Dave Henderson .10 .05
☐ 219 Dave Smith .10 .05
☐ 220 Albert Belle .50 .23
☐ 221 Spike Owen .10 .05
☐ 222 Jeff Gray .10 .05
☐ 223 Paul Gibson .10 .05
☐ 224 Bobby Thigpen .10 .05
☐ 225 Mike Mussina .60 .25
☐ 226 Darrin Jackson .10 .05
☐ 227 Luis Gonzalez .10 .05
☐ 228 Greg Briley .10 .05
☐ 229 Brent Mayne .10 .05
☐ 230 Paul Molitor .40 .18
☐ 231 Al Leiter .20 .09
☐ 232 Andy Van Slyke .20 .09
☐ 233 Ron Tingley .10 .05
☐ 234 Bernard Gilkey .20 .09
☐ 235 Kent Hrbek .20 .09
☐ 236 Eric Karros .20 .09
☐ 237 Randy Velarde .10 .05
☐ 238 Andy Allanson .10 .05
☐ 239 Willie McGee .10 .05
☐ 240 Juan Gonzalez 1.25 .55
☐ 241 Karl Rhodes .10 .05
☐ 242 Luis Mercedes .10 .05
☐ 243 Billy Swift .10 .05
☐ 244 Tommy Gregg .10 .05
☐ 245 David Howard .10 .05
☐ 246 Dave Hollins .10 .05
☐ 247 Kip Gross .10 .05
☐ 248 Walt Weiss .10 .05
☐ 249 Mackey Sasser .10 .05
☐ 250 Cecil Fielder .20 .09
☐ 251 Jerry Browne .10 .05
☐ 252 Doug Dascenzo .10 .05
☐ 253 Darryl Hamilton .10 .05
☐ 254 Dann Bilardello .10 .05
☐ 255 Luis Rivera .10 .05
☐ 256 Larry Walker .40 .18
☐ 257 Ron Karkovice .10 .05
☐ 258 Bob Tewksbury .10 .05
☐ 259 Jimmy Key .20 .09
☐ 260 Bernie Williams .40 .18
☐ 261 Gary Wayne .10 .05
☐ 262 Mike Simms UER .10 .05
(Reversed negative)
☐ 263 John Orton .10 .05
☐ 264 Marvin Freeman .10 .05
☐ 265 Mike Jeffcoat .10 .05
☐ 266 Roger Mason .10 .05
☐ 267 Edgar Martinez .10 .05
☐ 268 Henry Rodriguez .40 .18
☐ 269 Sam Horn .10 .05
☐ 270 Brian McRae .10 .05
☐ 271 Kirt Manwaring .10 .05
☐ 272 Mike Bordick .10 .05
☐ 273 Chris Sabo .10 .05
☐ 274 Jim Olander .10 .05
☐ 275 Greg W. Harris .10 .05
☐ 276 Dan Gakeler .10 .05
☐ 277 Bill Sampen .10 .05
☐ 278 Joel Skinner .10 .05
☐ 279 Curt Schilling .40 .18
☐ 280 Dale Murphy .10 .05
☐ 281 Lee Stevens .10 .05
☐ 282 Lonnie Smith .10 .05
☐ 283 Manuel Lee .10 .05
☐ 284 Shawn Boskie .10 .05
☐ 285 Kevin Seitzer .10 .05
☐ 286 Stan Royer .10 .05
☐ 287 John Dopson .10 .05
☐ 288 Scott Bullett .10 .05
☐ 289 Ken Patterson .10 .05
☐ 290 Todd Hundley .10 .05
☐ 291 Tim Leary .10 .05
☐ 292 Brett Butler .20 .09
☐ 293 Gregg Olson .10 .05
☐ 294 Jeff Brantley .10 .05
☐ 295 Brian Holman .10 .05
☐ 296 Brian Harper .10 .05
☐ 297 Brian Bohanon .10 .05
☐ 298 Checklist 1-100 .10 .05
☐ 299 Checklist 101-200 .10 .05
☐ 300 Checklist 201-300 .10 .05
☐ 301 Frank Thomas 2.00 .90
☐ 302 Lloyd McClendon .10 .05
☐ 303 Brady Anderson .10 .05
☐ 304 Julio Valera .10 .05
☐ 305 Mike Aldrete .10 .05
☐ 306 Joe Oliver .10 .05
☐ 307 Todd Stottlemyre .20 .09
☐ 308 Rey Sanchez .10 .05
☐ 309 Gary Sheffield UER .40 .18
(Listed as 5'1",
should be 5'11")
☐ 310 Andujar Cedeno .10 .05
☐ 311 Kenny Rogers .10 .05
☐ 312 Bruce Hurst .10 .05
☐ 313 Mike Schooler .10 .05
☐ 314 Mike Benjamin .10 .05
☐ 315 Chuck Finley .10 .05
☐ 316 Mark Lemke .10 .05
☐ 317 Scott Livingstone .10 .05
☐ 318 Chris Nabholz .10 .05
☐ 319 Mike Humphreys .10 .05
☐ 320 Pedro Guerrero .10 .05
☐ 321 Willie Banks .10 .05
☐ 322 Tom Goodwin .20 .09
☐ 323 Hector Wagner .10 .05
☐ 324 Wally Ritchie .10 .05
☐ 325 Mo Vaughn .60 .25
☐ 326 Joe Klink .10 .05
☐ 327 Cal Eldred .10 .05
☐ 328 Daryl Boston .10 .05
☐ 329 Mike Huff .10 .05
☐ 330 Jeff Bagwell 1.25 .55
☐ 331 Bob Milacki .10 .05
☐ 332 Tom Prince .10 .05
☐ 333 Pat Tabler .10 .05
☐ 334 Ced Landrum .10 .05
☐ 335 Reggie Jefferson .20 .09
☐ 336 Mo Sanford .10 .05
☐ 337 Kevin Ritz .10 .05
☐ 338 Gerald Perry .10 .05
☐ 339 Jeff Hamilton .10 .05
☐ 340 Tim Wallach .10 .05

☐ 341 Jeff Huson .10 .05
☐ 342 Jose Melendez .10 .05
☐ 343 Willie Wilson .10 .05
☐ 344 Mike Stanton .10 .05
☐ 345 Joel Johnston .10 .05
☐ 346 Lee Guetterman .10 .05
☐ 347 Francisco Oliveras .10 .05
☐ 348 Dave Burba .10 .05
☐ 349 Tim Crews .10 .05
☐ 350 Scott Leius .10 .05
☐ 351 Danny Cox .10 .05
☐ 352 Wayne Housie .10 .05
☐ 353 Chris Donnels .10 .05
☐ 354 Chris George .10 .05
☐ 355 Gerald Young .10 .05
☐ 356 Roberto Hernandez .20 .09
☐ 357 Neal Heaton .10 .05
☐ 358 Todd Frohwirth .10 .05
☐ 359 Jose Vizcaino .10 .05
☐ 360 Jim Thome 1.25 .55
☐ 361 Craig Wilson .10 .05
☐ 362 Dave Haas .10 .05
☐ 363 Billy Hatcher .10 .05
☐ 364 John Barfield .10 .05
☐ 365 Luis Aquino .10 .05
☐ 366 Charlie Leibrandt .10 .05
☐ 367 Howard Farmer .10 .05
☐ 368 Bryn Smith .10 .05
☐ 369 Mickey Morandini .10 .05
☐ 370 Jose Canseco .10 .05
(See also 597)
☐ 371 Jose Uribe .10 .05
☐ 372 Bob MacDonald .10 .05
☐ 373 Luis Sojo .10 .05
☐ 374 Craig Shipley .10 .05
☐ 375 Scott Bankhead .10 .05
☐ 376 Greg Gagne .10 .05
☐ 377 Scott Cooper .10 .05
☐ 378 Jose Offerman .10 .05
☐ 379 Billy Spiers .10 .05
☐ 380 John Smiley .10 .05
☐ 381 Jeff Carter .10 .05
☐ 382 Heathcliff Slocumb .10 .05
☐ 383 Jeff Tackett .10 .05
☐ 384 John Kiely .10 .05
☐ 385 John Vander Wal .10 .05
☐ 386 Omar Olivares .10 .05
☐ 387 Ruben Sierra .10 .05
☐ 388 Tom Gordon .10 .05
☐ 389 Charles Nagy .20 .09
☐ 390 Dave Stewart .20 .09
☐ 391 Pete Harnisch .10 .05
☐ 392 Tim Burke .10 .05
☐ 393 Roberto Kelly .10 .05
☐ 394 Freddie Benavides .10 .05
☐ 395 Tom Glavine .10 .05
☐ 396 Wes Chamberlain .10 .05
☐ 397 Eric Gunderson .10 .05
☐ 398 Dave West .10 .05
☐ 399 Ellis Burks .20 .09
☐ 400 Ken Griffey Jr. 2.50 1.10
☐ 401 Thomas Howard .10 .05
☐ 402 Juan Guzman .10 .05
☐ 403 Mitch Webster .10 .05
☐ 404 Matt Merullo .10 .05
☐ 405 Steve Buechele .10 .05
☐ 406 Danny Jackson .10 .05
☐ 407 Felix Jose .10 .05
☐ 408 Doug Piatt .10 .05
☐ 409 Jim Eisenreich .20 .09
☐ 410 Bryan Harvey .10 .05
☐ 411 Jim Austin .10 .05
☐ 412 Jim Poole .10 .05
☐ 413 Glenallen Hill .10 .05
☐ 414 Gene Nelson .10 .05
☐ 415 Ivan Rodriguez .75 .35
☐ 416 Frank Tanana .10 .05
☐ 417 Steve Decker .10 .05
☐ 418 Jason Grimsley .10 .05
☐ 419 Tim Layana .10 .05
☐ 420 Don Mattingly .60 .25
☐ 421 Jerome Walton .10 .05
☐ 422 Rob Ducey .10 .05
☐ 423 Andy Benes .20 .09
☐ 424 John Marzano .10 .05
☐ 425 Gene Harris .10 .05
☐ 426 Tim Raines .20 .09
☐ 427 Bret Barberie .10 .05
☐ 428 Harvey Pulliam .10 .05
☐ 429 Cris Carpenter .10 .05
☐ 430 Howard Johnson .10 .05
☐ 431 Orel Hershiser .20 .09
☐ 432 Brian Hunter .10 .05
☐ 433 Kevin Tapani .10 .05
☐ 434 Rick Reed .10 .05
☐ 435 Ron Witmeyer .20 .09
☐ 436 Gary Gaetti .20 .09
☐ 437 Alex Cole .10 .05
☐ 438 Chito Martinez .10 .05
☐ 439 Greg Litton .10 .05
☐ 440 Julio Franco .20 .09
☐ 441 Mike Munoz .10 .05
☐ 442 Erik Pappas .10 .05
☐ 443 Pat Combs .10 .05
☐ 444 Lance Johnson .20 .09
☐ 445 Ed Sprague .20 .09
☐ 446 Mike Greenwell .10 .05
☐ 447 Milt Thompson .10 .05
☐ 448 Mike Magnante .10 .05
☐ 449 Chris Haney .10 .05
☐ 450 Robin Yount .10 .05
☐ 451 Rafael Ramirez .10 .05
☐ 452 Gino Minutelli .10 .05
☐ 453 Tom Lampkin .10 .05
☐ 454 Tony Perezchica .10 .05
☐ 455 Dwight Gooden .20 .09
☐ 456 Mark Guthrie .10 .05
☐ 457 Jay Howell .10 .05
☐ 458 Gary DiSarcina .10 .05
☐ 459 John Smoltz .10 .05
☐ 460 Will Clark .10 .05
☐ 461 Dave Otto .10 .05
☐ 462 Rob Maurer .10 .05
☐ 463 Dwight Evans .20 .09
☐ 464 Tom Brunansky .10 .05
☐ 465 Shawn Hare .10 .05
☐ 466 Geronimo Pena .10 .05
☐ 467 Alex Fernandez .20 .09
☐ 468 Greg Myers .10 .05
☐ 469 Jeff Fassero .20 .09
☐ 470 Len Dykstra .20 .09
☐ 471 Jeff Johnson .10 .05
☐ 472 Russ Swan .10 .05
☐ 473 Archie Corbin .10 .05
☐ 474 Chuck McElroy .10 .05
☐ 475 Mark McGwire .75 .35
☐ 476 Wally Whitehurst .10 .05
☐ 477 Tim McIntosh .10 .05
☐ 478 Sid Bream .10 .05
☐ 479 Jeff Juden .10 .05
☐ 480 Carlton Fisk .40 .18
☐ 481 Jeff Plympton .10 .05
☐ 482 Carlos Martinez .10 .05
☐ 483 Jim Gott .10 .05
☐ 484 Bob McClure .10 .05
☐ 485 Tim Teufel .10 .05
☐ 486 Vicente Palacios .10 .05
☐ 487 Jeff Reed .10 .05
☐ 488 Tony Phillips .10 .05
☐ 489 Mel Rojas .20 .09
☐ 490 Ben McDonald .10 .05
☐ 491 Andres Santana .10 .05
☐ 492 Chris Beasley .10 .05
☐ 493 Mike Timlin .10 .05
☐ 494 Brian Downing .10 .05
☐ 495 Kirk Gibson .20 .09
☐ 496 Scott Sanderson .10 .05
☐ 497 Nick Esasky .10 .05
☐ 498 Johnny Guzman .10 .05
☐ 499 Mitch Williams .10 .05
☐ 500 Kirby Puckett .75 .35
☐ 501 Mike Harkey .10 .05
☐ 502 Jim Gantner .10 .05
☐ 503 Bruce Egloff .10 .05
☐ 504 Josias Manzanillo .10 .05
☐ 505 Delino DeShields .10 .05
☐ 506 Rheal Cormier .10 .05
☐ 507 Jay Bell .20 .09
☐ 508 Rich Rowland .10 .05
☐ 509 Scott Servais .10 .05
☐ 510 Terry Pendleton .20 .09
☐ 511 Rich DeLucia .10 .05
☐ 512 Warren Newson .10 .05
☐ 513 Paul Faries .10 .05
☐ 514 Kal Daniels .10 .05
☐ 515 Jarvis Brown .10 .05
☐ 516 Rafael Palmeiro .10 .05
☐ 517 Kelly Downs .10 .05
☐ 518 Steve Chitren .10 .05
☐ 519 Moises Alou .20 .09
☐ 520 Wade Boggs .40 .18
☐ 521 Pete Schourek .10 .05
☐ 522 Scott Terry .10 .05
☐ 523 Kevin Appier .20 .09
☐ 524 Gary Redus .10 .05
☐ 525 George Bell .10 .05
☐ 526 Jeff Kaiser .10 .05
☐ 527 Alvaro Espinoza .10 .05
☐ 528 Luis Polonia .10 .05
☐ 529 Darren Daulton .20 .09
☐ 530 Norm Charlton .10 .05
☐ 531 John Olerud .20 .09
☐ 532 Dan Plesac .10 .05
☐ 533 Billy Ripken .10 .05
☐ 534 Rod Nichols .10 .05
☐ 535 Joey Cora .20 .09
☐ 536 Harold Baines .20 .09
☐ 537 Bob Ojeda .10 .05
☐ 538 Mark Leonard .10 .05
☐ 539 Danny Darwin .10 .05
☐ 540 Shawon Dunston .10 .05
☐ 541 Pedro Munoz .10 .05
☐ 542 Mark Gubicza .10 .05
☐ 543 Kevin Baez .10 .05
☐ 544 Todd Zeile .10 .05
☐ 545 Don Slaught .10 .05
☐ 546 Tony Eusebio .10 .05
☐ 547 Alonzo Powell .10 .05
☐ 548 Gary Pettis .10 .05
☐ 549 Brian Barnes .10 .05
☐ 550 Lou Whitaker .20 .09
☐ 551 Keith Mitchell .10 .05
☐ 552 Oscar Azocar .10 .05
☐ 553 Stu Cole .10 .05
☐ 554 Steve Wapnick .10 .05
☐ 555 Derek Bell .20 .09
☐ 556 Luis Lopez .10 .05
☐ 557 Anthony Telford .10 .05
☐ 558 Tim Mauser .10 .05
☐ 559 Glen Sutko .10 .05
☐ 560 Darryl Strawberry .20 .09
☐ 561 Tom Bolton .10 .05
☐ 562 Cliff Young .10 .05
☐ 563 Bruce Walton .10 .05
☐ 564 Chico Walker .10 .05
☐ 565 John Franco .10 .05
☐ 566 Paul McClellan .10 .05
☐ 567 Paul Abbott .10 .05
☐ 568 Gary Varsho .10 .05
☐ 569 Carlos Maldonado .10 .05
☐ 570 Kelly Gruber .10 .05
☐ 571 Jose Oquendo .10 .05
☐ 572 Steve Frey .10 .05
☐ 573 Tino Martinez .40 .18
☐ 574 Bill Haselman .10 .05
☐ 575 Eric Anthony .10 .05
☐ 576 John Habyan .10 .05
☐ 577 Jeff McNeely .10 .05
☐ 578 Chris Bosio .10 .05
☐ 579 Joe Grahe .10 .05
☐ 580 Fred McGriff .10 .05
☐ 581 Rick Honeycutt .10 .05
☐ 582 Matt Williams .10 .05
☐ 583 Cliff Brantley .10 .05
☐ 584 Rob Dibble .10 .05
☐ 585 Skeeter Barnes .10 .05
☐ 586 Greg Hibbard .10 .05
☐ 587 Randy Milligan .10 .05
☐ 588 Checklist 301-400 .10 .05
☐ 589 Checklist 401-500 .10 .05
☐ 590 Checklist 501-600 .10 .05
☐ 591 Frank Thomas MC 1.50 .70
☐ 592 David Justice MC .40 .18
☐ 593 Roger Clemens MC .40 .18
☐ 594 Steve Avery MC .10 .05
☐ 595 Cal Ripken MC 1.00 .45
☐ 596 Barry Larkin MC UER .10 .05
(Ranked in AL, should be NL)
☐ 597 Jose Canseco MC UER .10 .05
(Mistakenly numbered 370 on card back)
☐ 598 Will Clark MC .10 .05
☐ 599 Cecil Fielder MC .20 .09
☐ 600 Ryne Sandberg MC .10 .05
☐ 601 Chuck Knoblauch MC .40 .18
☐ 602 Dwight Gooden MC .20 .09
☐ 603 Ken Griffey Jr. MC 1.50 .70
☐ 604 Barry Bonds MC .40 .18
☐ 605 Nolan Ryan MC 1.00 .45
☐ 606 Jeff Bagwell MC .60 .25
☐ 607 Robin Yount MC .10 .05
☐ 608 Bobby Bonilla MC .20 .09
☐ 609 George Brett MC .40 .18
☐ 610 Howard Johnson MC .10 .05
☐ 611 Esteban Beltre .10 .05
☐ 612 Mike Christopher .10 .05
☐ 613 Troy Afenir .10 .05
☐ 614 Mariano Duncan .10 .05
☐ 615 Doug Henry .10 .05
☐ 616 Doug Jones .10 .05
☐ 617 Alvin Davis .10 .05
☐ 618 Craig Lefferts .10 .05
☐ 619 Kevin McReynolds .10 .05
☐ 620 Barry Bonds .50 .23
☐ 621 Turner Ward .10 .05
☐ 622 Joe Magrane .10 .05
☐ 623 Mark Parent .10 .05
☐ 624 Tom Browning .10 .05
☐ 625 John Smiley .10 .05
☐ 626 Steve Wilson .10 .05

☐ 627 Mike Gallego .10 .05
☐ 628 Sammy Sosa .40 .18
☐ 629 Rico Rossy .10 .05
☐ 630 Royce Clayton .20 .09
☐ 631 Clay Parker .10 .05
☐ 632 Pete Smith .10 .05
☐ 633 Jeff McKnight .10 .05
☐ 634 Jack Daugherty .10 .05
☐ 635 Steve Sax .10 .05
☐ 636 Joe Hesketh .10 .05
☐ 637 Vince Horsman .10 .05
☐ 638 Eric King .10 .05
☐ 639 Joe Boever .10 .05
☐ 640 Jack Morris .20 .09
☐ 641 Arthur Rhodes .10 .05
☐ 642 Bob Melvin .10 .05
☐ 643 Rick Wilkins .10 .05
☐ 644 Scott Scudder .10 .05
☐ 645 Bip Roberts .10 .05
☐ 646 Julio Valera .10 .05
☐ 647 Kevin Campbell .10 .05
☐ 648 Steve Searcy .10 .05
☐ 649 Scott Kamieniecki .10 .05
☐ 650 Kurt Stillwell .10 .05
☐ 651 Bob Welch .10 .05
☐ 652 Andres Galarraga .10 .05
☐ 653 Mike Jackson .10 .05
☐ 654 Bo Jackson .20 .09
☐ 655 Sid Fernandez .10 .05
☐ 656 Mike Bielecki .10 .05
☐ 657 Jeff Reardon .20 .09
☐ 658 Wayne Rosenthal .10 .05
☐ 659 Eric Bullock .10 .05
☐ 660 Eric Davis .20 .09
☐ 661 Randy Tomlin .10 .05
☐ 662 Tom Edens .10 .05
☐ 663 Rob Murphy .10 .05
☐ 664 Leo Gomez .10 .05
☐ 665 Greg Maddux 1.25 .55
☐ 666 Greg Vaughn .10 .05
☐ 667 Wade Taylor .10 .05
☐ 668 Brad Arnsberg .10 .05
☐ 669 Mike Moore .10 .05
☐ 670 Mark Langston .10 .05
☐ 671 Barry Jones .10 .05
☐ 672 Bill Landrum .10 .05
☐ 673 Greg Swindell .10 .05
☐ 674 Wayne Edwards .10 .05
☐ 675 Greg Olson .10 .05
☐ 676 Bill Pulsipher .40 .18
☐ 677 Bobby Witt .10 .05
☐ 678 Mark Carreon .10 .05
☐ 679 Patrick Lennon .10 .05
☐ 680 Ozzie Smith .50 .23
☐ 681 John Briscoe .10 .05
☐ 682 Matt Young .10 .05
☐ 683 Jeff Conine .40 .18
☐ 684 Phil Stephenson .10 .05
☐ 685 Ron Darling .10 .05
☐ 686 Bryan Hickerson .10 .05
☐ 687 Dale Sveum .10 .05
☐ 688 Kirk McCaskill .10 .05
☐ 689 Rich Amaral .10 .05
☐ 690 Danny Tartabull .10 .05
☐ 691 Donald Harris .10 .05
☐ 692 Doug Davis .10 .05
☐ 693 John Farrell .10 .05
☐ 694 Paul Gibson .10 .05
☐ 695 Kenny Lofton 1.50 .70
☐ 696 Mike Fetters .10 .05
☐ 697 Rosario Rodriguez .10 .05
☐ 698 Chris Jones .10 .05
☐ 699 Jeff Manto .10 .05
☐ 700 Rick Sutcliffe .10 .05
☐ 701 Scott Bankhead .10 .05
☐ 702 Donnie Hill .10 .05
☐ 703 Todd Worrell .10 .05
☐ 704 Rene Gonzales .10 .05
☐ 705 Rick Cerone .10 .05
☐ 706 Tony Pena .10 .05
☐ 707 Paul Sorrento .10 .05
☐ 708 Gary Scott .10 .05
☐ 709 Junior Noboa .10 .05
☐ 710 Wally Joyner .20 .09
☐ 711 Charlie Hayes .10 .05
☐ 712 Rich Rodriguez .10 .05
☐ 713 Rudy Seanez .10 .05
☐ 714 Jim Bullinger .10 .05
☐ 715 Jeff M. Robinson .10 .05
☐ 716 Jeff Branson .10 .05
☐ 717 Andy Ashby .10 .05
☐ 718 Dave Burba .10 .05
☐ 719 Rich Gossage .20 .09
☐ 720 Randy Johnson .40 .18
☐ 721 David Wells .10 .05
☐ 722 Paul Kilgus .10 .05
☐ 723 Dave Martinez .10 .05
☐ 724 Denny Neagle .20 .09
☐ 725 Andy Stankiewicz .10 .05
☐ 726 Rick Aguilera .10 .05
☐ 727 Junior Ortiz .10 .05
☐ 728 Storm Davis .10 .05
☐ 729 Don Robinson .10 .05
☐ 730 Ron Gant .20 .09
☐ 731 Paul Assenmacher .10 .05
☐ 732 Mike Gardiner .10 .05
☐ 733 Milt Hill .10 .05
☐ 734 Jeremy Hernandez .10 .05
☐ 735 Ken Hill .20 .09
☐ 736 Xavier Hernandez .10 .05
☐ 737 Gregg Jefferies .20 .09
☐ 738 Dick Schofield .10 .05
☐ 739 Ron Robinson .10 .05
☐ 740 Sandy Alomar .20 .09
☐ 741 Mike Stanley .10 .05
☐ 742 Butch Henry .10 .05
☐ 743 Floyd Bannister .10 .05
☐ 744 Brian Drahman .10 .05
☐ 745 Dave Winfield .10 .05
☐ 746 Bob Walk .10 .05
☐ 747 Chris James .10 .05
☐ 748 Don Prybylinski .10 .05
☐ 749 Dennis Rasmussen .10 .05
☐ 750 Rickey Henderson .10 .05
☐ 751 Chris Hammond .10 .05
☐ 752 Bob Kipper .10 .05
☐ 753 Dave Rohde .10 .05
☐ 754 Hubie Brooks .10 .05
☐ 755 Bret Saberhagen .10 .05
☐ 756 Jeff D. Robinson .10 .05
☐ 757 Pat Listach .10 .05
☐ 758 Bill Wegman .10 .05
☐ 759 John Wetteland .20 .09
☐ 760 Phil Plantier .10 .05
☐ 761 Wilson Alvarez .20 .09
☐ 762 Scott Aldred .10 .05
☐ 763 Armando Reynoso .10 .05
☐ 764 Todd Benzinger .10 .05
☐ 765 Kevin Mitchell .20 .09
☐ 766 Gary Sheffield .40 .18
☐ 767 Allan Anderson .10 .05
☐ 768 Rusty Meacham .10 .05
☐ 769 Rick Parker .10 .05
☐ 770 Nolan Ryan 1.50 .70
☐ 771 Jeff Ballard .10 .05
☐ 772 Cory Snyder .10 .05
☐ 773 Denis Boucher .10 .05
☐ 774 Jose Gonzalez .10 .05
☐ 775 Juan Guerrero .10 .05
☐ 776 Ed Nunez .10 .05
☐ 777 Scott Ruskin .10 .05
☐ 778 Terry Leach .10 .05
☐ 779 Carl Willis .10 .05
☐ 780 Bobby Bonilla .20 .09
☐ 781 Duane Ward .10 .05
☐ 782 Joe Slusarski .10 .05
☐ 783 David Segui .10 .05
☐ 784 Kirk Gibson .20 .09
☐ 785 Frank Viola .10 .05
☐ 786 Keith Miller .10 .05
☐ 787 Mike Morgan .10 .05
☐ 788 Kim Batiste .10 .05
☐ 789 Sergio Valdez .10 .05
☐ 790 Eddie Taubensee .10 .05
☐ 791 Jack Armstrong .10 .05
☐ 792 Scott Fletcher .10 .05
☐ 793 Steve Farr .10 .05
☐ 794 Dan Pasqua .10 .05
☐ 795 Eddie Murray .40 .18
☐ 796 John Morris .10 .05
☐ 797 Francisco Cabrera .10 .05
☐ 798 Mike Perez .10 .05
☐ 799 Ted Wood .10 .05
☐ 800 Jose Rijo .10 .05
☐ 801 Danny Gladden .10 .05
☐ 802 Archi Cianfrocco .10 .05
☐ 803 Monty Fariss .10 .05
☐ 804 Roger McDowell .10 .05
☐ 805 Randy Myers .20 .09
☐ 806 Kirk Dressendorfer .10 .05
☐ 807 Zane Smith .10 .05
☐ 808 Glenn Davis .10 .05
☐ 809 Torey Lovullo .10 .05
☐ 810 Andre Dawson .10 .05
☐ 811 Bill Pecota .10 .05
☐ 812 Ted Power .10 .05
☐ 813 Willie Blair .10 .05
☐ 814 Dave Fleming .10 .05
☐ 815 Chris Gwynn .10 .05
☐ 816 Jody Reed .10 .05
☐ 817 Mark Dewey .10 .05
☐ 818 Kyle Abbott .10 .05
☐ 819 Tom Henke .10 .05
☐ 820 Kevin Seitzer .10 .05
☐ 821 Al Newman .10 .05
☐ 822 Tim Sherrill .10 .05
☐ 823 Chuck Crim .10 .05
☐ 824 Darren Reed .10 .05
☐ 825 Tony Gwynn 1.00 .45
☐ 826 Steve Foster .10 .05
☐ 827 Steve Howe .10 .05
☐ 828 Brook Jacoby .10 .05
☐ 829 Rodney McCray .10 .05
☐ 830 Chuck Knoblauch .40 .18
☐ 831 John Wehner .10 .05
☐ 832 Scott Garrelts .10 .05
☐ 833 Alejandro Pena .10 .05
☐ 834 Jeff Parrett UER .10 .05
(Kentucy)
☐ 835 Juan Bell .10 .05
☐ 836 Lance Dickson .10 .05
☐ 837 Darryl Kile .10 .05
☐ 838 Efrain Valdez .10 .05
☐ 839 Bob Zupcic .10 .05
☐ 840 George Bell .10 .05
☐ 841 Dave Gallagher .10 .05
☐ 842 Tim Belcher .10 .05
☐ 843 Jeff Shaw .10 .05
☐ 844 Mike Fitzgerald .10 .05
☐ 845 Gary Carter .10 .05
☐ 846 John Russell .10 .05
☐ 847 Eric Hillman .10 .05
☐ 848 Mike Witt .10 .05
☐ 849 Curt Wilkerson .10 .05
☐ 850 Alan Trammell .20 .09
☐ 851 Rex Hudler .10 .05
☐ 852 Mike Walkden .10 .05
☐ 853 Kevin Ward .10 .05
☐ 854 Tim Naehring .20 .09
☐ 855 Bill Swift .10 .05
☐ 856 Damon Berryhill .10 .05
☐ 857 Mark Eichhorn .10 .05
☐ 858 Hector Villanueva .10 .05
☐ 859 Jose Lind .10 .05
☐ 860 Denny Martinez .20 .09
☐ 861 Bill Krueger .10 .05
☐ 862 Mike Kingery .10 .05
☐ 863 Jeff Innis .10 .05
☐ 864 Derek Lilliquist .10 .05
☐ 865 Reggie Sanders .20 .09
☐ 866 Ramon Garcia .10 .05
☐ 867 Bruce Ruffin .10 .05
☐ 868 Dickie Thon .10 .05
☐ 869 Melido Perez .10 .05
☐ 870 Ruben Amaro .10 .05
☐ 871 Alan Mills .10 .05
☐ 872 Matt Sinatro .10 .05
☐ 873 Eddie Zosky .10 .05
☐ 874 Pete Incaviglia .10 .05
☐ 875 Tom Candiotti .10 .05
☐ 876 Bob Patterson .10 .05
☐ 877 Neal Heaton .10 .05
☐ 878 Terrel Hansen .10 .05
☐ 879 Dave Eiland .10 .05
☐ 880 Von Hayes .10 .05
☐ 881 Tim Scott .10 .05
☐ 882 Otis Nixon .20 .09
☐ 883 Herm Winningham .10 .05
☐ 884 Dion James .10 .05
☐ 885 Dave Wainhouse .10 .05
☐ 886 Frank DiPino .10 .05
☐ 887 Dennis Cook .10 .05
☐ 888 Jose Mesa .20 .09
☐ 889 Mark Leiter .10 .05
☐ 890 Willie Randolph .20 .09
☐ 891 Craig Colbert .10 .05
☐ 892 Dwayne Henry .10 .05
☐ 893 Jim Lindeman .10 .05
☐ 894 Charlie Hough .10 .05
☐ 895 Gil Heredia .10 .05
☐ 896 Scott Chiamparino .10 .05
☐ 897 Lance Blankenship .10 .05
☐ 898 Checklist 601-700 .10 .05
☐ 899 Checklist 701-800 .10 .05
☐ 900 Checklist 801-900 .10 .05

1992 Stadium Club First Draft Picks

This three-card standard-size set, featuring Major League Baseball's Number 1 draft pick for 1990, 1991, and 1992, was randomly inserted into 1992 Stadium Club Series III packs at an approximate rate of 1:72. One card also was mailed to each member of Topps Stadium Club. The cards feature on the fronts full-bleed posed color player photos. The player's draft year is printed on an orange circle in the upper right corner and is accented by gold foil stripes of varying lengths that run vertically down the right edge of the card. The player's name appears on the Stadium Club

logo at the bottom. The number "1" is gold-foil stamped in a black diamond at the lower left and is followed by a red stripe gold-foil stamped with the words "Draft Pick of the '90s". The back design features color photos on a black and red background with the player's signature gold-foil stamped across the bottom of the photo and gold foil bars running down the right edge of the picture. The team name and biographical information is included in a yellow and white box.

	MINT	NRMT
COMPLETE SET (3)	16.00	7.25
COMMON CARD (1-3)	1.00	.45
☐ 1 Chipper Jones	15.00	6.75
☐ 2 Brien Taylor	1.00	.45
☐ 3 Phil Nevin	2.00	.90

1992 Stadium Club Master Photos

In the first package of materials sent to 1992 Topps Stadium Club members, along with an 11-card boxed set, members received a randomly chosen "Master Photo" printed on (approximately) 5" by 7" white card stock to demonstrate how the photos are cropped to create a borderless design. Each master photo has the Topps Stadium Club logo and the words "Master Photo" above a gold foil picture frame enclosing the color player photo. The backs are blank. The cards are unnumbered and checklisted below alphabetically. Master photos were also available through a special promotion at Walmart as an insert one-per-box in specially marked wax boxes of regular Topps Stadium Club cards.

	MINT	NRMT
COMPLETE SET (15)	25.00	11.00
COMMON CARD (1-15)	.50	.23
☐ 1 Wade Boggs	1.00	.45
☐ 2 Barry Bonds	1.25	.55
☐ 3 Jose Canseco	1.00	.45
☐ 4 Will Clark	1.00	.45
☐ 5 Cecil Fielder	.60	.25
☐ 6 Dwight Gooden	.60	.25
☐ 7 Ken Griffey Jr.	5.00	2.20
☐ 8 Rickey Henderson	1.00	.45
☐ 9 Lance Johnson	.50	.23
☐ 10 Cal Ripken	5.00	2.20
☐ 11 Nolan Ryan	5.00	2.20
☐ 12 Deion Sanders	1.00	.45
☐ 13 Darryl Strawberry	.60	.25
☐ 14 Danny Tartabull	.50	.23
☐ 15 Frank Thomas	5.00	2.20

1992 Stadium Club East Coast National

These cards were selected from the regular Stadium Club series and were printed for the Gloria Rothstein's East Coast National Convention. The fronts feature borderless color player photos with the East Coast National Convention logo printed in gold foil in a top corner while the backs display a mini reprint of the player's rookie card and "BARS" (Baseball Analysis and Reporting System) statistics. The cards are checklisted below according to their numbers in the regular series.

	MINT	NRMT
COMPLETE SET (100)	150.00	70.00
COMMON CARD	1.00	.45
☐ 601 Chuck Knoblauch MC	7.50	3.40
☐ 602 Doc Gooden MC	2.00	.90
☐ 603 Ken Griffey Jr. MC	40.00	18.00
☐ 604 Barry Bonds MC	7.50	3.40
☐ 605 Nolan Ryan MC	40.00	18.00
☐ 606 Jeff Bagwell MC	20.00	9.00
☐ 607 Robin Yount MC	6.00	2.70
☐ 608 Bobby Bonilla MC	2.00	.90
☐ 609 George Brett MC	20.00	9.00
☐ 610 Howard Johnson MC	1.00	.45
☐ 611 Esteban Beltre	1.00	.45
☐ 612 Mike Christopher	1.00	.45
☐ 613 Troy Afenir	1.00	.45
☐ 619 Kevin McReynolds	1.00	.45
☐ 620 Barry Bonds	15.00	6.75
☐ 622 Joe Magrane	1.00	.45
☐ 623 Mark Parent	1.00	.45
☐ 626 Steve Wilson	1.00	.45
☐ 629 Rico Rossy	1.00	.45
☐ 631 Clay Parker	1.00	.45
☐ 633 Jeff McKnight	1.00	.45
☐ 637 Vince Horsman	1.00	.45
☐ 638 Eric King	1.00	.45
☐ 639 Joe Boever	1.00	.45
☐ 641 Arthur Rhodes	2.00	.90
☐ 647 Kevin Campbell	1.00	.45
☐ 653 Mike Jackson	1.00	.45
☐ 661 Randy Tomlin	1.00	.45
☐ 665 Greg Maddux	25.00	11.00
☐ 668 Brad Arnsberg	1.00	.45
☐ 671 Barry Jones	1.00	.45
☐ 672 Bill Landrum	1.00	.45
☐ 673 Greg Swindell	1.00	.45
☐ 676 Bill Pulsipher	4.00	1.80
☐ 679 Patrick Lennon	1.00	.45
☐ 681 John Briscoe	1.00	.45
☐ 684 Phil Stephenson	1.00	.45
☐ 685 Ron Darling	1.00	.45
☐ 686 Bryan Hickerson	1.00	.45
☐ 688 Kirk McCaskill	1.00	.45
☐ 689 Rich Amaral	1.00	.45
☐ 692 Doug Davis	1.00	.45
☐ 693 John Farrell	1.00	.45
☐ 700 Rick Sutcliffe	2.00	.90
☐ 704 Rene Gonzalez	1.00	.45
☐ 713 Rudy Seanez	1.00	.45
☐ 714 Jim Bullinger	1.00	.45
☐ 716 Jeff Branson	1.00	.45
☐ 717 Andy Ashby	2.00	.90
☐ 725 Andy Stankiewicz	1.00	.45
☐ 733 Milt Hill	1.00	.45
☐ 739 Ron Robinson	1.00	.45
☐ 742 Butch Henry	1.00	.45
☐ 747 Chris James	1.00	.45
☐ 749 Dennis Rasmussen	1.00	.45
☐ 753 Dave Rohde	1.00	.45
☐ 757 Pat Listach	2.00	.90
☐ 758 Bill Wegman	1.00	.45
☐ 763 Armando Reynoso	1.00	.45
☐ 765 Kevin Mitchell	2.00	.90
☐ 766 Gary Sheffield	6.00	2.70
☐ 769 Rick Parker	1.00	.45
☐ 771 Jeff Ballard	1.00	.45
☐ 772 Cory Snyder	1.00	.45
☐ 774 Jose Gonzalez	1.00	.45
☐ 775 Juan Guerrero	1.00	.45
☐ 776 Ed Nunez	1.00	.45
☐ 778 Terry Leach	1.00	.45
☐ 782 Joe Slusarski	1.00	.45
☐ 784 Kirk Gibson	2.00	.90
☐ 788 Kim Batiste	1.00	.45
☐ 802 Archi Cianfrocco	1.00	.45
☐ 806 Kirk Dressendorfer	1.00	.45
☐ 807 Zane Smith	1.00	.45
☐ 814 Dave Fleming	1.00	.45
☐ 815 Chris Gwynn	1.00	.45
☐ 817 Mark Dewey	1.00	.45
☐ 819 Tom Henke	2.00	.90
☐ 822 Tim Sherrill	1.00	.45
☐ 826 Steve Foster	1.00	.45
☐ 831 John Wehner	1.00	.45
☐ 832 Scott Garrelts	1.00	.45
☐ 840 George Bell	2.00	.90
☐ 841 Dave Gallagher	1.00	.45
☐ 846 John Russell	1.00	.45
☐ 847 Eric Hillman	1.00	.45
☐ 852 Mike Walkden	1.00	.45
☐ 855 Bill Swift	1.00	.45
☐ 864 Derek Lilliquist	1.00	.45
☐ 876 Bob Patterson	1.00	.45
☐ 878 Terrel Hansen	1.00	.45
☐ 881 Tim Scott	1.00	.45
☐ 886 Frank DiPino	1.00	.45
☐ 891 Craig Colbert	1.00	.45
☐ 892 Dwayne Henry	1.00	.45
☐ 893 Jim Lindeman	1.00	.45
☐ 895 Gil Heredia	1.00	.45
☐ 898 Checklist	1.00	.45
☐ 899 Checklist	1.00	.45
☐ 900 Checklist	1.00	.45

1992 Stadium Club National Convention

These cards were selected from the regular Stadium Club series and were printed for the National Convention in Atlanta. The fronts feature borderless color player photos with the National Convention logo printed in gold foil in a top corner while the backs display a mini reprint of the player's rookie card and "BARS" (Baseball Analysis and Reporting System) statistics. The cards are checklisted below according to their numbers in the regular series.

	MINT	NRMT
COMPLETE SET (100)	150.00	70.00
COMMON CARD	1.00	.45
☐ 616 Doug Jones	2.00	.90
☐ 617 Alvin Davis	1.00	.45
☐ 618 Craig Lefferts	1.00	.45
☐ 621 Turner Ward	1.00	.45
☐ 625 John Smiley	1.00	.45
☐ 627 Mike Gallego	1.00	.45
☐ 630 Royce Clayton	4.00	1.80
☐ 634 Jack Daugherty	1.00	.45
☐ 635 Steve Sax	1.00	.45
☐ 636 Joe Hesketh	1.00	.45
☐ 643 Rick Wilkins	1.00	.45
☐ 644 Scott Scudder	1.00	.45
☐ 645 Bip Roberts	1.00	.45
☐ 650 Kurt Stillwell	1.00	.45
☐ 652 Andres Galarraga	6.00	2.70
☐ 657 Jeff Reardon	2.00	.90
☐ 660 Eric Davis	2.00	.90
☐ 662 Tom Edens	1.00	.45
☐ 675 Greg Olson	1.00	.45
☐ 678 Mark Carreon	1.00	.45
☐ 680 Ozzie Smith	40.00	18.00
☐ 682 Matt Young	1.00	.45
☐ 690 Danny Tartabull	1.00	.45
☐ 691 Donald Harris	1.00	.45
☐ 695 Kenny Lofton	25.00	11.00
☐ 697 Rosario Rodriguez	1.00	.45
☐ 701 Scott Bankhead	1.00	.45
☐ 705 Rick Cerone	1.00	.45
☐ 706 Tony Pena	1.00	.45
☐ 709 Junior Noboa	1.00	.45
☐ 710 Wally Joyner	2.00	.90
☐ 711 Charlie Hayes	1.00	.45
☐ 712 Rich Rodriguez	1.00	.45
☐ 721 David Wells	1.00	.45
☐ 723 Dave Martinez	1.00	.45
☐ 726 Rick Aguilera	2.00	.90
☐ 727 Junior Ortiz	1.00	.45
☐ 729 Don Robinson	1.00	.45
☐ 730 Ron Gant	2.00	.90
☐ 731 Paul Assenmacher	1.00	.45
☐ 732 Mark Gardiner	1.00	.45
☐ 735 Ken Hill	2.00	.90
☐ 736 Xavier Hernandez	1.00	.45
☐ 737 Gregg Jefferies	2.00	.90
☐ 740 Sandy Alomar	2.00	.90
☐ 741 Mike Stanley	1.00	.45
☐ 744 Brian Drahman	1.00	.45
☐ 746 Bob Walk	1.00	.45
☐ 751 Chris Hammond	1.00	.45
☐ 759 John Wetteland	4.00	1.80
☐ 760 Phil Plantier	1.00	.45
☐ 761 Wilson Alvarez	2.00	.90
☐ 773 Dennis Boucher	1.00	.45
☐ 777 Scott Ruskin	1.00	.45
☐ 779 Carl Willis	1.00	.45
☐ 783 David Segui	2.00	.90
☐ 786 Keith Miller	1.00	.45
☐ 790 Eddie Taubensee	1.00	.45
☐ 791 Jack Armstrong	1.00	.45
☐ 792 Scott Fletcher	1.00	.45
☐ 793 Steve Farr	1.00	.45
☐ 794 Dan Pasqua	1.00	.45
☐ 797 Francisco Cabrera	1.00	.45
☐ 798 Mike Perez	1.00	.45
☐ 801 Danny Gladden	1.00	.45
☐ 803 Monty Fariss	1.00	.45
☐ 804 Roger McDowell	1.00	.45
☐ 805 Randy Myers	2.00	.90
☐ 808 Glenn Davis	1.00	.45
☐ 809 Torey Lovullo	1.00	.45

	MINT	NRMT
☐ 816 Jody Reed	1.00	.45
☐ 825 Tony Gwynn	50.00	22.00
☐ 827 Steve Howe	1.00	.45
☐ 828 Brook Jacoby	1.00	.45
☐ 829 Rodney McCray	1.00	.45
☐ 830 Chuck Knoblauch	15.00	6.75
☐ 835 Juan Bell	1.00	.45
☐ 836 Lance Dickson	1.00	.45
☐ 837 Darryl Kile	6.00	2.70
☐ 842 Tim Belcher	1.00	.45
☐ 843 Jeff Shaw	1.00	.45
☐ 844 Mike Fitzgerald	1.00	.45
☐ 845 Gary Carter	6.00	2.70
☐ 850 Alan Trammell	4.00	1.80
☐ 851 Rex Hudler	1.00	.45
☐ 856 Damon Berryhill	1.00	.45
☐ 857 Mark Eichhorn	1.00	.45
☐ 858 Hector Villanueva	1.00	.45
☐ 860 Denny Martinez	2.00	.90
☐ 865 Reggie Sanders	2.00	.90
☐ 869 Melido Perez	1.00	.45
☐ 874 Pete Incaviglia	1.00	.45
☐ 875 Tom Candiotti	1.00	.45
☐ 877 Neal Heaton	1.00	.45
☐ 879 Dave Eiland	1.00	.45
☐ 882 Otis Nixon	2.00	.90
☐ 883 Herm Winningham	1.00	.45
☐ 884 Dion James	1.00	.45
☐ 887 Dennis Cook	1.00	.45
☐ 894 Charlie Hough	2.00	.90

1993 Stadium Club Murphy

This 200-card boxed set features 1992 All-Star Game cards, 1992 Team USA cards, and 1992 Championship and World Series cards. Topps actually refers to this set as a 1992 issue, but the set was released in 1993. The standard-size cards display full-bleed posed and action color player shots on the fronts. The player's name appears below the Topps Stadium Club logo in the lower right with parallel gold foil stripes intersecting the logo. The horizontal back presents the player's biography, statistics, and highlights on a ghosted photo. This set is housed in a replica of San Diego's Jack Murphy Stadium, site of the 1992 All-Star Game. Production was limited to 8,000 cases, with 16 boxes per case. The set includes 100 Draft Pick cards, 56 All-Star cards, 25 Team USA cards, and 19 cards commemorating the 1992 National and American League Championship Series and the World Series. Notable Rookie Cards in this set include Derek Jeter, Jason Kendall and Preston Wilson.

	MINT	NRMT
COMP.FACT.SET (212)	30.00	13.50
COMPLETE SET (200)	25.00	11.00
COMMON CARD (1-200)	.15	.07
☐ 1 Dave Winfield	.20	.09
☐ 2 Juan Guzman	.15	.07
☐ 3 Tony Gwynn	1.50	.70
☐ 4 Chris Roberts	.30	.14
☐ 5 Benny Santiago	.15	.07
☐ 6 Sherard Clinkscales	.15	.07
☐ 7 Jon Nunnally	.30	.14
☐ 8 Chuck Knoblauch	.60	.25
☐ 9 Bob Wolcott	.30	.14
☐ 10 Steve Rodriguez	.15	.07
☐ 11 Mark Williams	.15	.07
☐ 12 Danny Clyburn	1.25	.55
☐ 13 Darren Dreifort	.15	.07
☐ 14 Andy Van Slyke	.30	.14
☐ 15 Wade Boggs	.20	.09
☐ 16 Scott Patton	.15	.07
☐ 17 Gary Sheffield	.60	.25
☐ 18 Ron Villone	.15	.07
☐ 19 Roberto Alomar	.60	.25
☐ 20 Marc Valdes	.15	.07
☐ 21 Daron Kirkreit	.15	.07
☐ 22 Jeff Granger	.15	.07
☐ 23 Levon Largusa	.15	.07
☐ 24 Jimmy Key	.30	.14
☐ 25 Kevin Pearson	.15	.07
☐ 26 Michael Moore	.15	.07
☐ 27 Preston Wilson	1.50	.70
☐ 28 Kirby Puckett	1.25	.55
☐ 29 Tim Crabtree	.15	.07
☐ 30 Bip Roberts	.15	.07
☐ 31 Kelly Gruber	.15	.07
☐ 32 Tony Fernandez	.15	.07
☐ 33 Jason Angel	.15	.07
☐ 34 Calvin Murray	.15	.07
☐ 35 Chad McConnell	.15	.07
☐ 36 Jason Moler	.15	.07
☐ 37 Mark Lemke	.15	.07
☐ 38 Tom Knauss	.15	.07
☐ 39 Larry Mitchell	.15	.07
☐ 40 Doug Mirabelli	.15	.07
☐ 41 Everett Stull II	.15	.07
☐ 42 Chris Wimmer	.15	.07
☐ 43 Dan Serafini	.50	.23
☐ 44 Ryne Sandberg	.75	.35
☐ 45 Steve Lyons	.15	.07
☐ 46 Ryan Freeburg	.15	.07
☐ 47 Ruben Sierra	.15	.07
☐ 48 David Mysel	.15	.07
☐ 49 Joe Hamilton	.15	.07
☐ 50 Steve Rodriguez	.15	.07
☐ 51 Tim Wakefield	.30	.14
☐ 52 Scott Gentile	.15	.07
☐ 53 Doug Jones	.15	.07
☐ 54 Willie Brown	.15	.07
☐ 55 Chad Mottola	.30	.14
☐ 56 Ken Griffey Jr.	3.00	1.35
☐ 57 Jon Lieber	.15	.07
☐ 58 Denny Martinez	.30	.14
☐ 59 Joe Petcka	.15	.07
☐ 60 Benji Simonton	.15	.07
☐ 61 Brett Backlund	.15	.07
☐ 62 Damon Berryhill	.15	.07
☐ 63 Juan Guzman	.15	.07
☐ 64 Doug Hecker	.15	.07
☐ 65 Jamie Arnold	.15	.07
☐ 66 Bob Tewksbury	.15	.07
☐ 67 Tim Leger	.15	.07
☐ 68 Todd Etler	.15	.07
☐ 69 Lloyd McClendon	.15	.07
☐ 70 Kurt Ehmann	.15	.07
☐ 71 Rick Magdaleno	.30	.14
☐ 72 Tom Pagnozzi	.15	.07
☐ 73 Jeffrey Hammonds	.60	.25
☐ 74 Joe Carter	.20	.09
☐ 75 Chris Holt	.15	.07
☐ 76 Charles Johnson	1.00	.45
☐ 77 Bob Walk	.15	.07
☐ 78 Fred McGriff	.20	.09
☐ 79 Tom Evans	.50	.23
☐ 80 Scott Klingenbeck	.15	.07
☐ 81 Chad McConnell	.15	.07
☐ 82 Chris Eddy	.15	.07
☐ 83 Phil Nevin	.15	.07
☐ 84 John Kruk	.30	.14
☐ 85 Tony Sheffield	.15	.07
☐ 86 John Smoltz	.20	.09
☐ 87 Trevor Humphry	.15	.07
☐ 88 Charles Nagy	.30	.14
☐ 89 Sean Runyan	.15	.07
☐ 90 Mike Gulan	.15	.07
☐ 91 Darren Daulton	.30	.14
☐ 92 Otis Nixon	.30	.14
☐ 93 Nomar Garciaparra	10.00	4.50
☐ 94 Larry Walker	.60	.25
☐ 95 Hut Smith	.15	.07
☐ 96 Rick Helling	.15	.07
☐ 97 Roger Clemens	1.25	.55
☐ 98 Ron Gant	.30	.14
☐ 99 Kenny Felder	.15	.07
☐ 100 Steve Murphy	.15	.07
☐ 101 Mike Smith	.15	.07
☐ 102 Terry Pendleton	.30	.14
☐ 103 Tim Davis	.15	.07
☐ 104 Jeff Patzke	.20	.09
☐ 105 Craig Wilson	.15	.07
☐ 106 Tom Glavine	.20	.09
☐ 107 Mark Langston	.15	.07
☐ 108 Mark Thompson	.15	.07
☐ 109 Eric Owens	.15	.07
☐ 110 Keith Johnson	.15	.07
☐ 111 Robin Ventura	.30	.14
☐ 112 Ed Sprague	.15	.07
☐ 113 Jeff Schmidt	.15	.07
☐ 114 Don Wengert	.15	.07
☐ 115 Craig Biggio	.20	.09
☐ 116 Kenny Carlyle	.15	.07
☐ 117 Derek Jeter	8.00	3.60
☐ 118 Manuel Lee	.15	.07
☐ 119 Jeff Haas	.15	.07
☐ 120 Roger Bailey	.15	.07
☐ 121 Sean Lowe	.15	.07
☐ 122 Rick Aguilera	.15	.07
☐ 123 Sandy Alomar	.30	.14
☐ 124 Derek Wallace	.15	.07
☐ 125 B.J. Wallace	.15	.07
☐ 126 Greg Maddux	2.00	.90
☐ 127 Tim Moore	.15	.07
☐ 128 Lee Smith	.30	.14
☐ 129 Todd Steverson	.15	.07
☐ 130 Chris Widger	.15	.07
☐ 131 Paul Molitor	.60	.25
☐ 132 Chris Smith	.15	.07
☐ 133 Chris Gomez	.20	.09
☐ 134 Jimmy Baron	.15	.07
☐ 135 John Smoltz	.20	.09
☐ 136 Pat Borders	.15	.07
☐ 137 Donnie Leshnock	.15	.07
☐ 138 Gus Gandarillos	.15	.07
☐ 139 Will Clark	.20	.09
☐ 140 Ryan Luzinski	.15	.07
☐ 141 Cal Ripken	2.50	1.10
☐ 142 B.J. Wallace	.15	.07
☐ 143 Trey Beamon	.50	.23
☐ 144 Norm Charlton	.15	.07
☐ 145 Mike Mussina	.60	.25
☐ 146 Billy Owens	.15	.07
☐ 147 Ozzie Smith	.75	.35
☐ 148 Jason Kendall	2.00	.90
☐ 149 Mike Matthews	.30	.14
☐ 150 David Spykstra	.15	.07
☐ 151 Benji Grigsby	.15	.07
☐ 152 Sean Smith	.30	.14
☐ 153 Mark McGwire	1.25	.55
☐ 154 David Cone	.30	.14
☐ 155 Shon Walker	.30	.14
☐ 156 Jason Giambi	.60	.25
☐ 157 Jack McDowell	.15	.07
☐ 158 Paxton Briley	.15	.07
☐ 159 Edgar Martinez	.20	.09
☐ 160 Brian Sackinsky	.15	.07
☐ 161 Barry Bonds	.75	.35
☐ 162 Roberto Kelly	.15	.07
☐ 163 Jeff Alkire	.15	.07
☐ 164 Mike Sharperson	.15	.07
☐ 165 Jamie Taylor	.15	.07
☐ 166 John Saffer	.15	.07
☐ 167 Jerry Browne	.15	.07
☐ 168 Travis Fryman	.30	.14
☐ 169 Brady Anderson	.20	.09
☐ 170 Chris Roberts	.30	.14
☐ 171 Lloyd Peever	.15	.07
☐ 172 Francisco Cabrera	.15	.07
☐ 173 Ramiro Martinez	.15	.07
☐ 174 Jeff Alkire	.15	.07
☐ 175 Ivan Rodriguez	.75	.35
☐ 176 Kevin Brown	.30	.14
☐ 177 Chad Roper	.15	.07
☐ 178 Rod Henderson	.15	.07
☐ 179 Dennis Eckersley	.20	.09
☐ 180 Shannon Stewart	1.50	.70
☐ 181 DeShawn Warren	.30	.14
☐ 182 Lonnie Smith	.15	.07
☐ 183 Willie Adams	.15	.07
☐ 184 Jeff Montgomery	.30	.14
☐ 185 Damon Hollins	.50	.23
☐ 186 Byron Mathews	.15	.07
☐ 187 Harold Baines	.30	.14
☐ 188 Rick Greene	.15	.07
☐ 189 Carlos Baerga	.30	.14
☐ 190 Brandon Cromer	.15	.07
☐ 191 Roberto Alomar	.60	.25
☐ 192 Rich Ireland	.15	.07
☐ 193 Steve Montgomery	.15	.07
☐ 194 Brant Brown	.50	.23
☐ 195 Ritchie Moody	.15	.07
☐ 196 Michael Tucker	.60	.25
☐ 197 Jason Varitek	.60	.25
☐ 198 David Manning	.15	.07
☐ 199 Marquis Riley	.15	.07
☐ 200 Jason Giambi	.60	.25

1993 Stadium Club Murphy Master Photos

One Murphy Master Photo was included in each 1993 Stadium Club Murphy Special factory set. Each of these twelve uncropped Murphy Master Photos is inlaid in a 5" by 7" white frame and bordered with a prismatic foil trim. The photo within parallels the corresponding player's regular issue Murphy card. The cards are unnumbered and checklisted below in alphabetical order.

	MINT	NRMT
COMPLETE SET (12)	5.00	2.20
COMMON MASTER PHOTO	.10	.05
☐ 1 Sandy Alomar AS	.10	.05
☐ 2 Tom Glavine AS	.25	.11

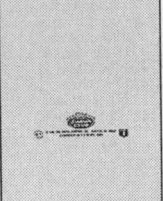

Card	MINT	NRMT
☐ 3 Ken Griffey Jr. AS	4.00	1.80
☐ 4 Tony Gwynn AS	2.00	.90
☐ 5 Chuck Knoblauch AS	1.00	.45
☐ 6 Chad Mottola '92	.10	.05
☐ 7 Kirby Puckett AS	1.50	.70
☐ 8 Chris Roberts USA	.10	.05
☐ 9 Ryne Sandberg AS	1.25	.55
☐ 10 Gary Sheffield AS	.75	.35
☐ 11 Larry Walker AS	1.00	.45
☐ 12 Preston Wilson '92	1.50	.70

1993 Stadium Club

The 1993 Stadium Club baseball set consists of 750 standard-size cards issued in three series of 300, 300, and 150 cards respectively. The fronts display full-bleed glossy color player photos. A red stripe carrying the player's name and edged on the bottom by a gold stripe cuts across the bottom of the picture. A white baseball icon with gold motion streaks rounds out the front. Award Winner and League Leader cards are studded with gold foil stars. On a background consisting of an artistic drawing of a baseball player's arm extended with ball in glove, the backs carry a second color action photo, biographical information, 1992 Stats Player Profile, the player's ranking (either on his team and/or the AL or NL), statistics, and a miniature reproduction of his Topps rookie card. Each series closes with a Members Choice subset (291-300, 591-600, and 746-750.

	MINT	NRMT
COMPLETE SET (750)	60.00	27.00
COMPLETE SERIES 1 (300)	20.00	9.00
COMPLETE SERIES 2 (300)	25.00	11.00
COMPLETE SERIES 3 (150)	15.00	6.75
COMMON CARD (1-750)	.15	.07

Card	MINT	NRMT
☐ 1 Pat Borders	.15	.07
☐ 2 Greg Maddux	2.00	.90
☐ 3 Daryl Boston	.15	.07
☐ 4 Bob Ayrault	.15	.07
☐ 5 Tony Phillips IF	.15	.07
☐ 6 Damion Easley	.15	.07
☐ 7 Kip Gross	.15	.07
☐ 8 Jim Thome	1.25	.55
☐ 9 Tim Belcher	.15	.07
☐ 10 Gary Wayne	.15	.07
☐ 11 Sam Militello	.15	.07
☐ 12 Mike Magnante	.15	.07
☐ 13 Tim Wakefield	.30	.14
☐ 14 Tim Hulett	.15	.07
☐ 15 Rheal Cormier	.15	.07
☐ 16 Juan Guerrero	.15	.07
☐ 17 Rich Gossage	.30	.14
☐ 18 Tim Laker	.15	.07
☐ 19 Darrin Jackson	.15	.07
☐ 20 Jack Clark	.15	.07
☐ 21 Roberto Hernandez	.30	.14
☐ 22 Dean Palmer	.30	.14
☐ 23 Harold Reynolds	.15	.07
☐ 24 Dan Plesac	.15	.07
☐ 25 Brent Mayne	.15	.07
☐ 26 Pat Hentgen	.20	.09
☐ 27 Luis Sojo	.15	.07
☐ 28 Ron Gant	.30	.14
☐ 29 Paul Gibson	.15	.07
☐ 30 Bip Roberts	.15	.07
☐ 31 Mickey Tettleton	.15	.07
☐ 32 Randy Velarde	.15	.07
☐ 33 Brian McRae	.15	.07
☐ 34 Wes Chamberlain	.15	.07
☐ 35 Wayne Kirby	.15	.07
☐ 36 Rey Sanchez	.15	.07
☐ 37 Jesse Orosco	.15	.07
☐ 38 Mike Stanton	.15	.07
☐ 39 Royce Clayton	.30	.14
☐ 40 Cal Ripken UER (Place of birth Havre de Grave; should be Havre de Grace)	2.50	1.10
☐ 41 John Dopson	.15	.07
☐ 42 Gene Larkin	.15	.07
☐ 43 Tim Raines	.30	.14
☐ 44 Randy Myers	.30	.14
☐ 45 Clay Parker	.15	.07
☐ 46 Mike Scioscia	.15	.07
☐ 47 Pete Incaviglia	.15	.07
☐ 48 Todd Van Poppel	.15	.07
☐ 49 Ray Lankford	.20	.09
☐ 50 Eddie Murray	.60	.25
☐ 51 Barry Bonds COR	.75	.35
☐ 51A Barry Bonds ERR (Missing four stars over name to indicate NL MVP)	.75	.35
☐ 52 Gary Thurman	.15	.07
☐ 53 Bob Wickman	.15	.07
☐ 54 Joey Cora	.30	.14
☐ 55 Kenny Rogers	.15	.07
☐ 56 Mike Devereaux	.15	.07
☐ 57 Kevin Seitzer	.15	.07
☐ 58 Rafael Belliard	.15	.07
☐ 59 David Wells	.15	.07
☐ 60 Mark Clark	.15	.07
☐ 61 Carlos Baerga	.30	.14
☐ 62 Scott Brosius	.15	.07
☐ 63 Jeff Grotewold	.15	.07
☐ 64 Rick Wrona	.15	.07
☐ 65 Kurt Knudsen	.15	.07
☐ 66 Lloyd McClendon	.15	.07
☐ 67 Omar Vizquel	.30	.14
☐ 68 Jose Vizcaino	.15	.07
☐ 69 Rob Ducey	.15	.07
☐ 70 Casey Candaele	.15	.07
☐ 71 Ramon Martinez	.30	.14
☐ 72 Todd Hundley	.20	.09
☐ 73 John Marzano	.15	.07
☐ 74 Derek Parks	.15	.07
☐ 75 Jack McDowell	.15	.07
☐ 76 Tim Scott	.15	.07
☐ 77 Mike Mussina	.60	.25
☐ 78 Delino DeShields	.15	.07
☐ 79 Chris Bosio	.15	.07
☐ 80 Mike Bordick	.15	.07
☐ 81 Rod Beck	.30	.14
☐ 82 Ted Power	.15	.07
☐ 83 John Kruk	.30	.14
☐ 84 Steve Shifflett	.15	.07
☐ 85 Danny Tartabull	.15	.07
☐ 86 Mike Greenwell	.15	.07
☐ 87 Jose Melendez	.15	.07
☐ 88 Craig Wilson	.15	.07
☐ 89 Melvin Nieves	.30	.14
☐ 90 Ed Sprague	.15	.07
☐ 91 Willie McGee	.15	.07
☐ 92 Joe Orsulak	.15	.07
☐ 93 Jeff King	.30	.14
☐ 94 Dan Pasqua	.15	.07
☐ 95 Brian Harper	.15	.07
☐ 96 Joe Oliver	.15	.07
☐ 97 Shane Turner	.15	.07
☐ 98 Lenny Harris	.15	.07
☐ 99 Jeff Parrett	.15	.07
☐ 100 Luis Polonia	.15	.07
☐ 101 Kent Bottenfield	.15	.07
☐ 102 Albert Belle	.75	.35
☐ 103 Mike Maddux	.15	.07
☐ 104 Randy Tomlin	.15	.07
☐ 105 Andy Stankiewicz	.15	.07
☐ 106 Rico Rossy	.15	.07
☐ 107 Joe Hesketh	.15	.07
☐ 108 Dennis Powell	.15	.07
☐ 109 Derrick May	.15	.07
☐ 110 Pete Harnisch	.15	.07
☐ 111 Kent Mercker	.15	.07
☐ 112 Scott Fletcher	.15	.07
☐ 113 Rex Hudler	.15	.07
☐ 114 Chico Walker	.15	.07
☐ 115 Rafael Palmeiro	.20	.09
☐ 116 Mark Leiter	.15	.07
☐ 117 Pedro Munoz	.15	.07
☐ 118 Jim Bullinger	.15	.07
☐ 119 Ivan Calderon	.15	.07
☐ 120 Mike Timlin	.15	.07
☐ 121 Rene Gonzales	.15	.07
☐ 122 Greg Vaughn	.15	.07
☐ 123 Mike Flanagan	.15	.07
☐ 124 Mike Hartley	.15	.07
☐ 125 Jeff Montgomery	.30	.14
☐ 126 Mike Gallego	.15	.07
☐ 127 Don Slaught	.15	.07
☐ 128 Charlie O'Brien	.15	.07
☐ 129 Jose Offerman (Can be found with home town missing on back)	.15	.07
☐ 130 Mark Wohlers	.30	.14
☐ 131 Eric Fox	.15	.07
☐ 132 Doug Strange	.15	.07
☐ 133 Jeff Frye	.15	.07
☐ 134 Wade Boggs UER (Redundantly lists lefty breakdown)	.20	.09
☐ 135 Lou Whitaker	.30	.14
☐ 136 Craig Grebeck	.15	.07
☐ 137 Rich Rodriguez	.15	.07
☐ 138 Jay Bell	.30	.14
☐ 139 Felix Fermin	.15	.07
☐ 140 Denny Martinez	.30	.14
☐ 141 Eric Anthony	.15	.07
☐ 142 Roberto Alomar	.60	.25
☐ 143 Darren Lewis	.15	.07
☐ 144 Mike Blowers	.15	.07
☐ 145 Scott Bankhead	.15	.07
☐ 146 Jeff Reboulet	.15	.07
☐ 147 Frank Viola	.15	.07
☐ 148 Bill Pecota	.15	.07
☐ 149 Carlos Hernandez	.15	.07
☐ 150 Bobby Witt	.15	.07
☐ 151 Sid Bream	.15	.07
☐ 152 Todd Zeile	.15	.07
☐ 153 Dennis Cook	.15	.07
☐ 154 Brian Bohanon	.15	.07
☐ 155 Pat Kelly	.15	.07
☐ 156 Milt Cuyler	.15	.07
☐ 157 Juan Bell	.15	.07
☐ 158 Randy Milligan	.15	.07
☐ 159 Mark Gardner	.15	.07
☐ 160 Pat Tabler	.15	.07
☐ 161 Jeff Reardon	.30	.14
☐ 162 Ken Patterson	.15	.07
☐ 163 Bobby Bonilla	.30	.14
☐ 164 Tony Pena	.15	.07
☐ 165 Greg Swindell	.15	.07
☐ 166 Kirk McCaskill	.15	.07
☐ 167 Doug Drabek	.15	.07
☐ 168 Franklin Stubbs	.15	.07
☐ 169 Ron Tingley	.15	.07
☐ 170 Willie Banks	.15	.07
☐ 171 Sergio Valdez	.15	.07
☐ 172 Mark Lemke	.15	.07
☐ 173 Robin Yount	.20	.09
☐ 174 Storm Davis	.15	.07
☐ 175 Dan Walters	.15	.07
☐ 176 Steve Farr	.15	.07
☐ 177 Curt Wilkerson	.15	.07
☐ 178 Luis Alicea	.15	.07
☐ 179 Russ Swan	.15	.07
☐ 180 Mitch Williams	.15	.07
☐ 181 Wilson Alvarez	.30	.14
☐ 182 Carl Willis	.15	.07
☐ 183 Craig Biggio	.20	.09
☐ 184 Sean Berry	.15	.07
☐ 185 Trevor Wilson	.15	.07
☐ 186 Jeff Tackett	.15	.07
☐ 187 Ellis Burks	.30	.14
☐ 188 Jeff Branson	.15	.07
☐ 189 Matt Nokes	.15	.07
☐ 190 John Smiley	.15	.07
☐ 191 Danny Gladden	.15	.07
☐ 192 Mike Boddicker	.15	.07
☐ 193 Roger Pavlik	.15	.07
☐ 194 Paul Sorrento	.15	.07
☐ 195 Vince Coleman	.15	.07
☐ 196 Gary DiSarcina	.15	.07
☐ 197 Rafael Bournigal	.15	.07
☐ 198 Mike Schooler	.15	.07
☐ 199 Scott Ruskin	.15	.07
☐ 200 Frank Thomas	2.50	1.10
☐ 201 Kyle Abbott	.15	.07
☐ 202 Mike Perez	.15	.07
☐ 203 Andre Dawson	.20	.09
☐ 204 Bill Swift	.15	.07
☐ 205 Alejandro Pena	.15	.07
☐ 206 Dave Winfield	.60	.25
☐ 207 Andujar Cedeno	.15	.07
☐ 208 Terry Steinbach	.30	.14
☐ 209 Chris Hammond	.15	.07
☐ 210 Todd Burns	.15	.07
☐ 211 Hipolito Pichardo	.15	.07
☐ 212 John Kiely	.15	.07
☐ 213 Tim Teufel	.15	.07
☐ 214 Lee Guetterman	.15	.07
☐ 215 Geronimo Pena	.15	.07
☐ 216 Brett Butler	.30	.1

☐ 217 Bryan Hickerson	.15	.07
☐ 218 Rick Trlicek	.15	.07
☐ 219 Lee Stevens	.15	.07
☐ 220 Roger Clemens	1.25	.55
☐ 221 Carlton Fisk	.20	.09
☐ 222 Chili Davis	.30	.14
☐ 223 Walt Terrell	.15	.07
☐ 224 Jim Eisenreich	.30	.14
☐ 225 Ricky Bones	.15	.07
☐ 226 Henry Rodriguez	.30	.14
☐ 227 Ken Hill	.30	.14
☐ 228 Rick Wilkins	.15	.07
☐ 229 Ricky Jordan	.15	.07
☐ 230 Bernard Gilkey	.30	.14
☐ 231 Tim Fortugno	.15	.07
☐ 232 Geno Petralli	.15	.07
☐ 233 Jose Rijo	.15	.07
☐ 234 Jim Leyritz	.15	.07
☐ 235 Kevin Campbell	.15	.07
☐ 236 Al Osuna	.15	.07
☐ 237 Pete Smith	.15	.07
☐ 238 Pete Schourek	.15	.07
☐ 239 Moises Alou	.30	.14
☐ 240 Donn Pall	.15	.07
☐ 241 Denny Neagle	.30	.14
☐ 242 Dan Peltier	.15	.07
☐ 243 Scott Scudder	.15	.07
☐ 244 Juan Guzman	.30	.14
☐ 245 Dave Burba	.15	.07
☐ 246 Rick Sutcliffe	.15	.07
☐ 247 Tony Fossas	.15	.07
☐ 248 Mike Munoz	.15	.07
☐ 249 Tim Salmon	.75	.35
☐ 250 Rob Murphy	.15	.07
☐ 251 Roger McDowell	.15	.07
☐ 252 Lance Parrish	.15	.07
☐ 253 Cliff Brantley	.15	.07
☐ 254 Scott Leius	.15	.07
☐ 255 Carlos Martinez	.15	.07
☐ 256 Vince Horsman	.15	.07
☐ 257 Oscar Azocar	.15	.07
☐ 258 Craig Shipley	.15	.07
☐ 259 Ben McDonald	.15	.07
☐ 260 Jeff Brantley	.15	.07
☐ 261 Damon Berryhill	.15	.07
☐ 262 Joe Grahe	.15	.07
☐ 263 Dave Hansen	.15	.07
☐ 264 Rich Amaral	.15	.07
☐ 265 Tim Pugh	.15	.07
☐ 266 Dion James	.15	.07
☐ 267 Frank Tanana	.15	.07
☐ 268 Stan Belinda	.15	.07
☐ 269 Jeff Kent	.30	.14
☐ 270 Bruce Ruffin	.15	.07
☐ 271 Xavier Hernandez	.15	.07
☐ 272 Darrin Fletcher	.15	.07
☐ 273 Tino Martinez	.60	.25
☐ 274 Benny Santiago	.15	.07
☐ 275 Scott Radinsky	.15	.07
☐ 276 Mariano Duncan	.15	.07
☐ 277 Kenny Lofton	1.25	.55
☐ 278 Dwight Smith	.15	.07
☐ 279 Joe Carter	.20	.09
☐ 280 Tim Jones	.15	.07
☐ 281 Jeff Huson	.15	.07
☐ 282 Phil Plantier	.15	.07
☐ 283 Kirby Puckett	1.25	.55
☐ 284 Johnny Guzman	.15	.07
☐ 285 Mike Morgan	.15	.07
☐ 286 Chris Sabo	.15	.07
☐ 287 Matt Williams	.20	.09
☐ 288 Checklist 1-100	.15	.07
☐ 289 Checklist 101-200	.15	.07
☐ 290 Checklist 201-300	.15	.07
☐ 291 Dennis Eckersley MC	.20	.09
☐ 292 Eric Karros MC	.30	.14
☐ 293 Pat Listach MC	.15	.07
☐ 294 Andy Van Slyke MC	.15	.07
☐ 295 Robin Ventura MC	.30	.14
☐ 296 Tom Glavine MC	.20	.09
☐ 297 Juan Gonzalez MC UER (Misspelled Gonzales)	.75	.35
☐ 298 Travis Fryman MC	.30	.14
☐ 299 Larry Walker MC	.60	.25
☐ 300 Gary Sheffield MC	.60	.25
☐ 301 Chuck Finley	.15	.07
☐ 302 Luis Gonzalez	.15	.07
☐ 303 Darryl Hamilton	.15	.07
☐ 304 Bien Figueroa	.15	.07
☐ 305 Ron Darling	.15	.07
☐ 306 Jonathan Hurst	.15	.07
☐ 307 Mike Sharperson	.15	.07
☐ 308 Mike Christopher	.15	.07
☐ 309 Marvin Freeman	.15	.07
☐ 310 Jay Buhner	.20	.09
☐ 311 Butch Henry	.15	.07
☐ 312 Greg W. Harris	.15	.07
☐ 313 Darren Daulton	.30	.14
☐ 314 Chuck Knoblauch	.60	.25
☐ 315 Greg A. Harris	.15	.07
☐ 316 John Franco	.15	.07
☐ 317 John Wehner	.15	.07
☐ 318 Donald Harris	.15	.07
☐ 319 Benny Santiago	.15	.07
☐ 320 Larry Walker	.60	.25
☐ 321 Randy Knorr	.15	.07
☐ 322 Ramon Martinez	.30	.14
☐ 323 Mike Stanley	.15	.07
☐ 324 Bill Wegman	.15	.07
☐ 325 Tom Candiotti	.15	.07
☐ 326 Glenn Davis	.15	.07
☐ 327 Chuck Crim	.15	.07
☐ 328 Scott Livingstone	.15	.07
☐ 329 Eddie Taubensee	.15	.07
☐ 330 George Bell	.15	.07
☐ 331 Edgar Martinez	.20	.09
☐ 332 Paul Assenmacher	.15	.07
☐ 333 Steve Hosey	.15	.07
☐ 334 Mo Vaughn	.75	.35
☐ 335 Bret Saberhagen	.15	.07
☐ 336 Mike Trombley	.15	.07
☐ 337 Mark Lewis	.15	.07
☐ 338 Terry Pendleton	.30	.14
☐ 339 Dave Hollins	.15	.07
☐ 340 Jeff Conine	.30	.14
☐ 341 Bob Tewksbury	.15	.07
☐ 342 Billy Ashley	.15	.07
☐ 343 Zane Smith	.15	.07
☐ 344 John Wetteland	.30	.14
☐ 345 Chris Hoiles	.15	.07
☐ 346 Frank Castillo	.15	.07
☐ 347 Bruce Hurst	.15	.07
☐ 348 Kevin McReynolds	.15	.07
☐ 349 Dave Henderson	.15	.07
☐ 350 Ryan Bowen	.15	.07
☐ 351 Sid Fernandez	.15	.07
☐ 352 Mark Whiten	.15	.07
☐ 353 Nolan Ryan	2.50	1.10
☐ 354 Rick Aguilera	.15	.07
☐ 355 Mark Langston	.15	.07
☐ 356 Jack Morris	.30	.14
☐ 357 Rob Deer	.15	.07
☐ 358 Dave Fleming	.15	.07
☐ 359 Lance Johnson	.30	.14
☐ 360 Joe Millette	.15	.07
☐ 361 Wil Cordero	.15	.07
☐ 362 Chito Martinez	.15	.07
☐ 363 Scott Servais	.15	.07
☐ 364 Bernie Williams	.60	.25
☐ 365 Pedro Martinez	.60	.25
☐ 366 Ryne Sandberg	.75	.35
☐ 367 Brad Ausmus	.15	.07
☐ 368 Scott Cooper	.15	.07
☐ 369 Rob Dibble	.15	.07
☐ 370 Walt Weiss	.15	.07
☐ 371 Mark Davis	.15	.07
☐ 372 Orlando Merced	.15	.07
☐ 373 Mike Jackson	.15	.07
☐ 374 Kevin Appier	.30	.14
☐ 375 Esteban Beltre	.15	.07
☐ 376 Joe Slusarski	.15	.07
☐ 377 William Suero	.15	.07
☐ 378 Pete O'Brien	.15	.07
☐ 379 Alan Embree	.15	.07
☐ 380 Lenny Webster	.15	.07
☐ 381 Eric Davis	.30	.14
☐ 382 Duane Ward	.15	.07
☐ 383 John Habyan	.15	.07
☐ 384 Jeff Bagwell	1.25	.55
☐ 385 Ruben Amaro	.15	.07
☐ 386 Julio Valera	.15	.07
☐ 387 Robin Ventura	.30	.14
☐ 388 Archi Cianfrocco	.15	.07
☐ 389 Skeeter Barnes	.15	.07
☐ 390 Tim Costo	.15	.07
☐ 391 Luis Mercedes	.15	.07
☐ 392 Jeremy Hernandez	.15	.07
☐ 393 Shawon Dunston	.15	.07
☐ 394 Andy Van Slyke	.30	.14
☐ 395 Kevin Maas	.15	.07
☐ 396 Kevin Brown	.30	.14
☐ 397 J.T. Bruett	.15	.07
☐ 398 Darryl Strawberry	.30	.14
☐ 399 Tom Pagnozzi	.15	.07
☐ 400 Sandy Alomar Jr.	.30	.14
☐ 401 Keith Miller	.15	.07
☐ 402 Rich DeLucia	.15	.07
☐ 403 Shawn Abner	.15	.07
☐ 404 Howard Johnson	.15	.07
☐ 405 Mike Benjamin	.15	.07
☐ 406 Roberto Mejia	.15	.07
☐ 407 Mike Butcher	.15	.07
☐ 408 Deion Sanders UER (Braves on front and Yankees on back)	.60	.25
☐ 409 Todd Stottlemyre	.15	.07
☐ 410 Scott Kamieniecki	.15	.07
☐ 411 Doug Jones	.15	.07
☐ 412 John Burkett	.15	.07
☐ 413 Lance Blankenship	.15	.07
☐ 414 Jeff Parrett	.15	.07
☐ 415 Barry Larkin	.20	.09
☐ 416 Alan Trammell	.20	.09
☐ 417 Mark Kiefer	.15	.07
☐ 418 Gregg Olson	.15	.07
☐ 419 Mark Grace	.20	.09
☐ 420 Shane Mack	.15	.07
☐ 421 Bob Walk	.15	.07
☐ 422 Curt Schilling	.15	.07
☐ 423 Erik Hanson	.15	.07
☐ 424 George Brett	1.25	.55
☐ 425 Reggie Jefferson	.30	.14
☐ 426 Mark Portugal	.15	.07
☐ 427 Ron Karkovice	.15	.07
☐ 428 Matt Young	.15	.07
☐ 429 Troy Neel	.15	.07
☐ 430 Hector Fajardo	.15	.07
☐ 431 Dave Righetti	.15	.07
☐ 432 Pat Listach	.15	.07
☐ 433 Jeff Innis	.15	.07
☐ 434 Bob MacDonald	.15	.07
☐ 435 Brian Jordan	.20	.09
☐ 436 Jeff Blauser	.15	.07
☐ 437 Mike Myers	.15	.07
☐ 438 Frank Seminara	.15	.07
☐ 439 Rusty Meacham	.15	.07
☐ 440 Greg Briley	.15	.07
☐ 441 Derek Lilliquist	.15	.07
☐ 442 John Vander Wal	.15	.07
☐ 443 Scott Erickson	.15	.07
☐ 444 Bob Scanlan	.15	.07
☐ 445 Todd Frohwirth	.15	.07
☐ 446 Tom Goodwin	.15	.07
☐ 447 William Pennyfeather	.15	.07
☐ 448 Travis Fryman	.30	.14
☐ 449 Mickey Morandini	.15	.07
☐ 450 Greg Olson	.15	.07
☐ 451 Trevor Hoffman	.20	.09
☐ 452 Dave Magadan	.15	.07
☐ 453 Shawn Jeter	.15	.07
☐ 454 Andres Galarraga	.20	.09
☐ 455 Ted Wood	.15	.07
☐ 456 Freddie Benavides	.15	.07
☐ 457 Junior Felix	.15	.07
☐ 458 Alex Cole	.15	.07
☐ 459 John Orton	.15	.07
☐ 460 Eddie Zosky	.15	.07
☐ 461 Dennis Eckersley	.20	.09
☐ 462 Lee Smith	.30	.14
☐ 463 John Smoltz	.20	.09
☐ 464 Ken Caminiti	.60	.25
☐ 465 Melido Perez	.15	.07
☐ 466 Tom Marsh	.15	.07
☐ 467 Jeff Nelson	.15	.07
☐ 468 Jesse Levis	.15	.07
☐ 469 Chris Nabholz	.15	.07
☐ 470 Mike Macfarlane	.15	.07
☐ 471 Reggie Sanders	.30	.14
☐ 472 Chuck McElroy	.15	.07
☐ 473 Kevin Gross	.15	.07
☐ 474 Matt Whiteside	.15	.07
☐ 475 Cal Eldred	.15	.07
☐ 476 Dave Gallagher	.15	.07
☐ 477 Len Dykstra	.30	.14
☐ 478 Mark McGwire	1.25	.55
☐ 479 David Segui	.15	.07
☐ 480 Mike Henneman	.15	.07
☐ 481 Bret Barberie	.15	.07
☐ 482 Steve Sax	.15	.07
☐ 483 Dave Valle	.15	.07
☐ 484 Danny Darwin	.15	.07
☐ 485 Devon White	.15	.07
☐ 486 Eric Plunk	.15	.07
☐ 487 Jim Gott	.15	.07
☐ 488 Scooter Tucker	.15	.07
☐ 489 Omar Olivares	.15	.07
☐ 490 Greg Myers	.15	.07
☐ 491 Brian Hunter	.15	.07
☐ 492 Kevin Tapani	.15	.07
☐ 493 Rich Monteleone	.15	.07
☐ 494 Steve Buechele	.15	.07
☐ 495 Bo Jackson	.30	.14
☐ 496 Mike LaValliere	.15	.07
☐ 497 Mark Leonard	.15	.07
☐ 498 Daryl Boston	.15	.07
☐ 499 Jose Canseco	.20	.09
☐ 500 Brian Barnes	.15	.07
☐ 501 Randy Johnson	.60	.25
☐ 502 Tim McIntosh	.15	.07
☐ 503 Cecil Fielder	.30	.14
☐ 504 Derek Bell	.30	.14
☐ 505 Kevin Koslofski	.15	.07

☐ 506 Darren Holmes .15 .07
☐ 507 Brady Anderson .20 .09
☐ 508 John Valentin .30 .14
☐ 509 Jerry Browne .15 .07
☐ 510 Fred McGriff .20 .09
☐ 511 Pedro Astacio .15 .07
☐ 512 Gary Gaetti .30 .14
☐ 513 John Burke .15 .07
☐ 514 Dwight Gooden .30 .14
☐ 515 Thomas Howard .15 .07
☐ 516 Darrell Whitmore UER .15 .07
(11 games played in 1992; should be 121)
☐ 517 Ozzie Guillen .15 .07
☐ 518 Darryl Kile .30 .14
☐ 519 Rich Rowland .15 .07
☐ 520 Carlos Delgado .20 .09
☐ 521 Doug Henry .15 .07
☐ 522 Greg Colbrunn .15 .07
☐ 523 Tom Gordon .15 .07
☐ 524 Ivan Rodriguez .75 .35
☐ 525 Kent Hrbek .30 .14
☐ 526 Eric Young .20 .09
☐ 527 Rod Brewer .15 .07
☐ 528 Eric Karros .30 .14
☐ 529 Marquis Grissom .30 .14
☐ 530 Rico Brogna .20 .09
☐ 531 Sammy Sosa .60 .25
☐ 532 Bret Boone .30 .14
☐ 533 Luis Rivera .15 .07
☐ 534 Hal Morris .15 .07
☐ 535 Monty Fariss .15 .07
☐ 536 Leo Gomez .15 .07
☐ 537 Wally Joyner .30 .14
☐ 538 Tony Gwynn 1.50 .70
☐ 539 Mike Williams .15 .07
☐ 540 Juan Gonzalez 1.50 .70
☐ 541 Ryan Klesko .75 .35
☐ 542 Ryan Thompson .15 .07
☐ 543 Chad Curtis .30 .14
☐ 544 Orel Hershiser .30 .14
☐ 545 Carlos Garcia .15 .07
☐ 546 Bob Welch .15 .07
☐ 547 Vinny Castilla .60 .25
☐ 548 Ozzie Smith .75 .35
☐ 549 Luis Salazar .15 .07
☐ 550 Mark Guthrie .15 .07
☐ 551 Charles Nagy .30 .14
☐ 552 Alex Fernandez .30 .14
☐ 553 Mel Rojas .30 .14
☐ 554 Orestes Destrade .15 .07
☐ 555 Mark Gubicza .15 .07
☐ 556 Steve Finley .30 .14
☐ 557 Don Mattingly 1.00 .45
☐ 558 Rickey Henderson .20 .09
☐ 559 Tommy Greene .15 .07
☐ 560 Arthur Rhodes .15 .07
☐ 561 Alfredo Griffin .15 .07
☐ 562 Will Clark .20 .09
☐ 563 Bob Zupcic .15 .07
☐ 564 Chuck Carr .15 .07
☐ 565 Henry Cotto .15 .07
☐ 566 Billy Spiers .15 .07
☐ 567 Jack Armstrong .15 .07
☐ 568 Kurt Stillwell .15 .07
☐ 569 David McCarty .15 .07
☐ 570 Joe Vitiello .15 .07
☐ 571 Gerald Williams .15 .07
☐ 572 Dale Murphy .60 .25
☐ 573 Scott Aldred .15 .07
☐ 574 Bill Gullickson .15 .07
☐ 575 Bobby Thigpen .15 .07
☐ 576 Glenallen Hill .15 .07
☐ 577 Dwayne Henry .15 .07
☐ 578 Calvin Jones .15 .07
☐ 579 Al Martin .30 .14
☐ 580 Ruben Sierra .15 .07
☐ 581 Andy Benes .30 .14
☐ 582 Anthony Young .15 .07
☐ 583 Shawn Boskie .15 .07
☐ 584 Scott Pose .15 .07
☐ 585 Mike Piazza 3.00 1.35
☐ 586 Donovan Osborne .15 .07
☐ 587 James Austin .15 .07
☐ 588 Checklist 301-400 .15 .07
☐ 589 Checklist 401-500 .15 .07
☐ 590 Checklist 501-600 .15 .07
☐ 591 Ken Griffey Jr. MC 1.50 .70
☐ 592 Ivan Rodriguez MC .60 .25
☐ 593 Carlos Baerga MC .30 .14
☐ 594 Fred McGriff MC .20 .09
☐ 595 Mark McGwire MC .60 .25
☐ 596 Roberto Alomar MC .30 .14
☐ 597 Kirby Puckett MC .60 .25
☐ 598 Marquis Grissom MC .30 .14
☐ 599 John Smoltz MC .20 .09
☐ 600 Ryne Sandberg MC .20 .09
☐ 601 Wade Boggs .60 .25
☐ 602 Jeff Reardon .30 .14
☐ 603 Billy Ripken .15 .07
☐ 604 Bryan Harvey .15 .07
☐ 605 Carlos Quintana .15 .07
☐ 606 Greg Hibbard .15 .07
☐ 607 Ellis Burks .30 .14
☐ 608 Greg Swindell .15 .07
☐ 609 Dave Winfield .20 .09
☐ 610 Charlie Hough .15 .07
☐ 611 Chili Davis .30 .14
☐ 612 Jody Reed .15 .07
☐ 613 Mark Williamson .15 .07
☐ 614 Phil Plantier .15 .07
☐ 615 Jim Abbott .15 .07
☐ 616 Dante Bichette .20 .09
☐ 617 Mark Eichhorn .15 .07
☐ 618 Gary Sheffield .60 .25
☐ 619 Richie Lewis .15 .07
☐ 620 Joe Girardi .15 .07
☐ 621 Jaime Navarro .15 .07
☐ 622 Willie Wilson .15 .07
☐ 623 Scott Fletcher .15 .07
☐ 624 Bud Black .15 .07
☐ 625 Tom Brunansky .15 .07
☐ 626 Steve Avery .15 .07
☐ 627 Paul Molitor .60 .25
☐ 628 Gregg Jefferies .30 .14
☐ 629 Dave Stewart .30 .14
☐ 630 Javier Lopez .60 .25
☐ 631 Greg Gagne .15 .07
☐ 632 Roberto Kelly .15 .07
☐ 633 Mike Fetters .15 .07
☐ 634 Ozzie Canseco .15 .07
☐ 635 Jeff Russell .15 .07
☐ 636 Pete Incaviglia .15 .07
☐ 637 Tom Henke .15 .07
☐ 638 Chipper Jones 3.00 1.35
☐ 639 Jimmy Key .30 .14
☐ 640 Dave Martinez .15 .07
☐ 641 Dave Stieb .15 .07
☐ 642 Milt Thompson .15 .07
☐ 643 Alan Mills .15 .07
☐ 644 Tony Fernandez .15 .07
☐ 645 Randy Bush .15 .07
☐ 646 Joe Magrane .15 .07
☐ 647 Ivan Calderon .15 .07
☐ 648 Jose Guzman .15 .07
☐ 649 John Olerud .15 .07
☐ 650 Tom Glavine .60 .25
☐ 651 Julio Franco .30 .14
☐ 652 Armando Reynoso .15 .07
☐ 653 Felix Jose .15 .07
☐ 654 Ben Rivera .15 .07
☐ 655 Andre Dawson .20 .09
☐ 656 Mike Harkey .15 .07
☐ 657 Kevin Seitzer .15 .07
☐ 658 Lonnie Smith .15 .07
☐ 659 Norm Charlton .15 .07
☐ 660 David Justice .60 .25
☐ 661 Fernando Valenzuela .30 .14
☐ 662 Dan Wilson .30 .14
☐ 663 Mark Gardner .15 .07
☐ 664 Doug Dascenzo .15 .07
☐ 665 Greg Maddux 2.00 .90
☐ 666 Harold Baines .30 .14
☐ 667 Randy Myers .30 .14
☐ 668 Harold Reynolds .15 .07
☐ 669 Candy Maldonado .15 .07
☐ 670 Al Leiter .15 .07
☐ 671 Jerald Clark .15 .07
☐ 672 Doug Drabek .15 .07
☐ 673 Kirk Gibson .30 .14
☐ 674 Steve Reed .15 .07
☐ 675 Mike Felder .15 .07
☐ 676 Ricky Gutierrez .15 .07
☐ 677 Spike Owen .15 .07
☐ 678 Otis Nixon .30 .14
☐ 679 Scott Sanderson .15 .07
☐ 680 Mark Carreon .15 .07
☐ 681 Troy Percival .30 .14
☐ 682 Kevin Stocker .15 .07
☐ 683 Jim Converse .15 .07
☐ 684 Barry Bonds .75 .35
☐ 685 Greg Gohr .15 .07
☐ 686 Tim Wallach .15 .07
☐ 687 Matt Mieske .30 .14
☐ 688 Robby Thompson .15 .07
☐ 689 Brien Taylor .15 .07
☐ 690 Kirt Manwaring .15 .07
☐ 691 Mike Lansing .30 .14
☐ 692 Steve Decker .15 .07
☐ 693 Mike Moore .15 .07
☐ 694 Kevin Mitchell .30 .14
☐ 695 Phil Hiatt .15 .07
☐ 696 Tony Tarasco .15 .07
☐ 697 Benji Gil .15 .07
☐ 698 Jeff Juden .15 .07
☐ 699 Kevin Reimer .15 .07
☐ 700 Andy Ashby .15 .07
☐ 701 John Jaha .30 .14
☐ 702 Tim Bogar .15 .07
☐ 703 David Cone .30 .14
☐ 704 Willie Greene .30 .14
☐ 705 David Hulse .15 .07
☐ 706 Cris Carpenter .15 .07
☐ 707 Ken Griffey Jr. 3.00 1.35
☐ 708 Steve Bedrosian .15 .07
☐ 709 Dave Nilsson .30 .14
☐ 710 Paul Wagner .15 .07
☐ 711 B.J. Surhoff .30 .14
☐ 712 Rene Arocha .15 .07
☐ 713 Manuel Lee .15 .07
☐ 714 Brian Williams .15 .07
☐ 715 Sherman Obando .15 .07
☐ 716 Terry Mulholland .15 .07
☐ 717 Paul O'Neill .30 .14
☐ 718 David Nied .15 .07
☐ 719 J.T. Snow .75 .35
☐ 720 Nigel Wilson .15 .07
☐ 721 Mike Bielecki .15 .07
☐ 722 Kevin Young .15 .07
☐ 723 Charlie Leibrandt .15 .07
☐ 724 Frank Bolick .15 .07
☐ 725 Jon Shave .15 .07
☐ 726 Steve Cooke .15 .07
☐ 727 Domingo Martinez .15 .07
☐ 728 Todd Worrell .15 .07
☐ 729 Jose Lind .15 .07
☐ 730 Jim Tatum .15 .07
☐ 731 Mike Hampton .30 .14
☐ 732 Mike Draper .15 .07
☐ 733 Henry Mercedes .15 .07
☐ 734 John Johnstone .15 .07
☐ 735 Mitch Webster .15 .07
☐ 736 Russ Springer .15 .07
☐ 737 Rob Natal .15 .07
☐ 738 Steve Howe .15 .07
☐ 739 Darrell Sherman .15 .07
☐ 740 Pat Mahomes .15 .07
☐ 741 Alex Arias .15 .07
☐ 742 Damon Buford .15 .07
☐ 743 Charlie Hayes .15 .07
☐ 744 Guillermo Velasquez .15 .07
☐ 745 Checklist 601-750 UER .15 .07
(650 Tom Glavine)
☐ 746 Frank Thomas MC 1.50 .70
☐ 747 Barry Bonds MC .60 .25
☐ 748 Roger Clemens MC .60 .25
☐ 749 Joe Carter MC .20 .09
☐ 750 Greg Maddux MC 1.00 .45

1993 Stadium Club First Day Issue

Two thousand of each 1993 Stadium Club baseball card were produced on the first day and then randomly inserted in packs at a rate of 1:24. These standard-size cards are identical to the regular-issue 1993 Stadium Club cards, except for the embossed prismatic-foil "1st Day Production" logo stamped in an upper corner. Some of the logos have been transferred from "common" 1st day cards to the fronts of better players.

	MINT	NRMT
COMPLETE SET (750)	2000.00	900.00
COMPLETE SERIES 1 (300)	700.00	325.00
COMPLETE SERIES 2 (300)	800.00	350.00
COMPLETE SERIES 3 (150)	500.00	220.00
COMMON CARD (1-750)	1.00	.45

*STARS: 10X to 25X BASIC CARDS
*YOUNG STARS: 8X to 20X BASIC CARDS
*ROOKIES: 6X to 15X BASIC CARDS

1993 Stadium Club Members Only Parallel

These standard-sized cards were issued in complete set form only through Topps' Stadium Club. These cards are the same as the regular Stadium Club cards except they are imprinted with the Stadium Club logo on the front. The set includes parallel versions of both the basic cards and the insert cards. Only the inserts cards have been priced below. Please use the multiplier for values on the basic cards. These sets were issued at an approximate cost of $200 to Stadium Club members. Even though, the set was issued at $200, the current market conditions makes this set available at less than original issue cost.

	MINT	NRMT
COMPLETE FACT.SET (760)	150.00	70.00
COMMON CARD (1-750)	.25	.11
*STARS: 3X to 6X BASIC CARDS	1.00	.45

*YOUNG STARS: 2X to 4X BASIC CARDS

*ROOKIES: 2X to 4X BASIC CARDS....

☐ MA1 Robin Yount	3.00	1.35
☐ MA2 George Brett	8.00	3.60
☐ MA3 David Nied	1.00	.45
☐ MA4 Nigel Wilson	1.00	.45
☐ MB1 Will Clark Mark McGwire	2.00	.90
☐ MB2 Dwight Gooden Don Mattingly	3.00	1.35
☐ MB3 Ryne Sandberg Frank Thomas	10.00	4.50
☐ MB4 Darryl Strawberry Ken Griffey	8.00	3.60
☐ MC1 David Nied	1.00	.45
☐ MC2 Charlie Hough	1.00	.45

1993 Stadium Club Inserts

This 10-card set was randomly inserted in all series of Stadium Club packs, the first four in series 1, the second four in series 2 and the last two in series 3. The themes of the standard-size cards differ from series to series, but the basic design -- borderless color action shots on the fronts -- remains the same throughout. The series 1 and 3 cards are numbered on the back, the series 2 cards are unnumbered. No matter what series, all of these inserts were included one every 15 packs.

	MINT	NRMT
COMPLETE SET (10)	16.00	7.25
COMPLETE SERIES 1 (4)	5.00	2.20
COMPLETE SERIES 2 (4)	10.00	4.50
COMPLETE SERIES 3 (2)	2.00	.90
COMMON SER.1 CARD (A1-A4)	.50	.23
COMMON SER.2 CARD (B1-B4)	1.25	.55
COMMON SER.3 CARD (C1-C2)	.50	.23

☐ A1 Robin Yount 3000 Hit Club	1.25	.55
☐ A2 George Brett 3000 Hit Club	4.00	1.80
☐ A3 David Nied First Draft Pick of the Rockies	.50	.23
☐ A4 Nigel Wilson 1st DP Marlins	.50	.23
☐ B1 Will Clark Mark McGwire Pacific Terrific	1.25	.55
☐ B2 Dwight Gooden Don Mattingly Broadway Stars NY	1.25	.55
☐ B3 Ryne Sandberg Frank Thomas Second City Sluggers	4.00	1.80
☐ B4 Darryl Strawberry Ken Griffey Jr. Pacific Terrific	4.00	1.80
☐ C1 David Nied UER Colorado Rockies Firsts (Misspelled pitch- hitter on back)	.50	.23
☐ C2 Charlie Hough Florida Marlins Firsts	.50	.23

1993 Stadium Club Master Photos

ach of the three Stadium Club series features Master hotos, uncropped versions of the regular Stadium Club ards. Each Master Photo is inlaid in a 5" by 7" white ame and bordered with a prismatic foil trim. The Master hotos were made available to the public in two ways. irst, one in every 24 packs included a Master Photo inner card redeemable for a group of three Master hotos until Jan. 31, 1994. Second, each hobby box ontained one Master Photo. The cards are unnumbered nd checklisted below in alphabetical order within series I -12), II (13-24), and III (25-30). Two different versions f these master photos were issued, one with and one

without the "Members Only" gold foil seal at the upper right corner. The "Members Only" Master Photos were only available with the direct-mail solicited 750-card Stadium Club Members Only set.

	MINT	NRMT
COMPLETE SET (30)	24.00	11.00
COMPLETE SERIES 1 (12)	6.00	2.70
COMPLETE SERIES 2 (12)	8.00	3.60
COMPLETE SERIES 3 (6)	10.00	4.50
COMMON CARD	.25	.11

☐ 1 Carlos Baerga	.35	.16
☐ 2 Delino DeShields	.25	.11
☐ 3 Brian McRae	.25	.11
☐ 4 Sam Militello	.25	.11
☐ 5 Joe Oliver	.25	.11
☐ 6 Kirby Puckett	2.00	.90
☐ 7 Cal Ripken	4.00	1.80
☐ 8 Bip Roberts	.25	.11
☐ 9 Mike Scioscia	.25	.11
☐ 10 Rick Sutcliffe	.25	.11
☐ 11 Danny Tartabull	.25	.11
☐ 12 Tim Wakefield	.25	.11
☐ 13 George Brett	2.00	.90
☐ 14 Jose Canseco	.50	.23
☐ 15 Will Clark	.50	.23
☐ 16 Travis Fryman	.35	.16
☐ 17 Dwight Gooden	.35	.16
☐ 18 Mark Grace	.50	.23
☐ 19 Rickey Henderson	.50	.23
☐ 20 Mark McGwire MC	1.50	.70
☐ 21 Nolan Ryan	4.00	1.80
☐ 22 Ruben Sierra	.25	.11
☐ 23 Darryl Strawberry	.35	.16
☐ 24 Larry Walker	1.25	.55
☐ 25 Barry Bonds	1.25	.55
☐ 26 Ken Griffey Jr.	5.00	2.20
☐ 27 Greg Maddux	3.00	1.35
☐ 28 David Nied	.25	.11
☐ 29 J.T. Snow	.35	.16
☐ 30 Brien Taylor	.25	.11

1993 Stadium Club Angels

This 30-card standard-size set features the 1993 California Angels. The full-bleed color fronts display primarily color player action photos with a few posed. Along the top left edge the player's name is printed in purple on an orange bar, with the words "Team Angels" appearing on a gray bar across the lower right edge. The right edge has a wide green bar with a gold foil-stamped baseball icon at the top. The horizontal backs are green and present a close-up photo of the player on the left with biography and statistics on the right. The set was issued in hobby (plastic box) and retail (blister) form.

	MINT	NRMT
COMPLETE SET (30)	5.00	2.20
COMMON CARD (1-30)	.10	.05

☐ 1 J.T. Snow	1.00	.45
☐ 2 Chuck Crim	.10	.05
☐ 3 Chili Davis	.25	.11
☐ 4 Mark Langston	.10	.05
☐ 5 Ron Tingley	.10	.05
☐ 6 Eduardo Perez	.10	.05
☐ 7 Scott Sanderson	.10	.05
☐ 8 Jorge Fabregas	.25	.11
☐ 9 Troy Percival	.50	.23
☐ 10 Rod Correia	.10	.05
☐ 11 Greg Myers	.10	.05
☐ 12 Steve Frey	.10	.05
☐ 13 Tim Salmon	3.00	1.35
☐ 14 Scott Lewis	.10	.05
☐ 15 Rene Gonzales	.10	.05
☐ 16 Chuck Finley	.25	.11
☐ 17 John Orton	.10	.05
☐ 18 Joe Grahe	.10	.05
☐ 19 Luis Polonia	.10	.05
☐ 20 John Farrell	.10	.05
☐ 21 Damion Easley	.10	.05
☐ 22 Gene Nelson	.10	.05
☐ 23 Chad Curtis	.50	.23
☐ 24 Russ Springer	.25	.11
☐ 25 DeShawn Warren	.10	.05
☐ 26 Darryl Scott	.10	.05
☐ 27 Gary DiSarcina	.10	.05
☐ 28 Jerry Nielsen	.10	.05
☐ 29 Torey Lovullo	.10	.05
☐ 30 Julio Valera	.10	.05

1993 Stadium Club Astros

This 30-card standard-size set features the 1993 Houston Astros. The full-bleed color fronts display primarily color player action photos with a few posed. Along the top left edge the player's name is printed in blue on an orange bar, with the words "Team Astros" appearing on a gray bar across the lower right edge. The right edge has a wide green bar with a gold foil-stamped baseball icon at the top. The horizontal backs are green and present a close-up photo of the player on the left with biography and statistics on the right. The set was issued in hobby (plastic box) and retail (blister) form.

	MINT	NRMT
COMPLETE SET (30)	5.00	2.20
COMMON CARD (1-30)	.10	.05

☐ 1 Doug Drabek	.25	.11
☐ 2 Eddie Taubensee	.25	.11
☐ 3 James Mouton	.50	.23
☐ 4 Ken Caminiti	.75	.35
☐ 5 Chris James	.10	.05
☐ 6 Jeff Juden	.10	.05
☐ 7 Eric Anthony	.10	.05
☐ 8 Jeff Bagwell	2.00	.90
☐ 9 Greg Swindell	.10	.05
☐ 10 Steve Finley	.50	.23
☐ 11 Al Osuna	.10	.05
☐ 12 Gary Mota	.10	.05
☐ 13 Scott Servais	.10	.05
☐ 14 Craig Biggio	.75	.35
☐ 15 Doug Jones	.10	.05
☐ 16 Rob Mallicoat	.10	.05
☐ 17 Darryl Kile	.50	.23
☐ 18 Kevin Bass	.10	.05
☐ 19 Pete Harnisch	.10	.05
☐ 20 Andujar Cedeno	.10	.05
☐ 21 Brian L.Hunter	1.00	.45
☐ 22 Brian Williams	.10	.05
☐ 23 Chris Donnels	.10	.05
☐ 24 Xavier Hernandez	.10	.05
☐ 25 Todd Jones	.25	.11
☐ 26 Luis Gonzalez	.25	.11
☐ 27 Rick Parker	.10	.05
☐ 28 Casey Candaele	.10	.05
☐ 29 Tony Eusebio	.10	.05
☐ 30 Mark Portugal	.10	.05

1993 Stadium Club Athletics

This 30-card standard-size set features the 1993 Oakland Athletics. The full-bleed color fronts display primarily color player action photos with a few posed. Along the top left edge the player's name is printed in green on an orange bar, with the words "Team Athletics" appearing on a gray bar across the lower right edge. The right edge has a wide green bar with a gold foil-stamped baseball icon at the top. The horizontal backs are green and present a

close-up photo of the player on the left with biography and statistics on the right. The set was issued in hobby (plastic box) and retail (blister) form.

	MINT	NRMT
COMPLETE SET (30)	4.00	1.80
COMMON CARD (1-30)	.10	.05

	MINT	NRMT
☐ 1 Dennis Eckersley	.50	.23
☐ 2 Lance Blankenship	.10	.05
☐ 3 Mike Mohler	.10	.05
☐ 4 Jerry Browne	.10	.05
☐ 5 Kevin Seitzer	.25	.11
☐ 6 Storm Davis	.10	.05
☐ 7 Mark McGwire	2.00	.90
☐ 8 Rickey Henderson	.75	.35
☐ 9 Terry Steinbach	.10	.05
☐ 10 Ruben Sierra	.10	.05
☐ 11 Dave Henderson	.10	.05
☐ 12 Bob Welch	.25	.11
☐ 13 Rick Honeycutt	.10	.05
☐ 14 Ron Darling	.10	.05
☐ 15 Joe Boever	.10	.05
☐ 16 Bobby Witt	.10	.05
☐ 17 Izzy Molina	.10	.05
☐ 18 Mike Bordick	.25	.11
☐ 19 Brent Gates	.10	.05
☐ 20 Shawn Hillegas	.10	.05
☐ 21 Scott Hemond	.10	.05
☐ 22 Todd Van Poppel	.10	.05
☐ 23 Johnny Guzman	.10	.05
☐ 24 Scott Lydy	.10	.05
☐ 25 Scott Baker	.10	.05
☐ 26 Todd Revenig	.10	.05
☐ 27 Scott Brosius	.25	.11
☐ 28 Troy Neel	.10	.05
☐ 29 Dale Sveum	.10	.05
☐ 30 Mike Neill	.10	.05

1993 Stadium Club Braves

This 30-card standard-size set features the 1993 Atlanta Braves. The full-bleed color fronts display primarily color player action photos with a few posed. Along the top left edge the player's name is printed in red on a blue bar, with the words "Team Braves" appearing on a gray bar across the lower right edge. The right edge has a wide green bar with a gold foil-stamped baseball icon at the top. The horizontal backs are green and present a close-up photo of the player on the left with biography and statistics on the right. The set was issued in hobby (plastic box) and retail (blister) form.

	MINT	NRMT
COMPLETE SET (30)	8.00	3.60
COMMON CARD (1-30)	.10	.05

	MINT	NRMT
☐ 1 Tom Glavine	.50	.23
☐ 2 Bill Pecota	.10	.05
☐ 3 David Justice	.75	.35
☐ 4 Mark Lemke	.10	.05
☐ 5 Jeff Blauser	.25	.11
☐ 6 Ron Gant	.25	.11
☐ 7 Greg Olson	.10	.05
☐ 8 Francisco Cabrera	.10	.05
☐ 9 Chipper Jones	3.00	1.35
☐ 10 Steve Avery	.10	.05
☐ 11 Kent Mercker	.10	.05
☐ 12 John Smoltz	.50	.23
☐ 13 Pete Smith	.10	.05
☐ 14 Damon Berryhill	.10	.05
☐ 15 Sid Bream	.10	.05
☐ 16 Otis Nixon	.25	.11
☐ 17 Mike Stanton	.10	.05
☐ 18 Greg Maddux	3.00	1.35
☐ 19 Jay Howell	.10	.05
☐ 20 Rafael Belliard	.10	.05
☐ 21 Terry Pendleton	.25	.11
☐ 22 Deion Sanders	.75	.35
☐ 23 Brian R. Hunter	.10	.05
☐ 24 Marvin Freeman	.10	.05
☐ 25 Mark Wohlers	.25	.11
☐ 26 Ryan Klesko	1.00	.45
☐ 27 Javier Lopez	.75	.35
☐ 28 Melvin Nieves	.25	.11
☐ 29 Tony Tarasco	.10	.05
☐ 30 Ramon Caraballo	.10	.05

1993 Stadium Club Cardinals

This 30-card standard-size set features the 1993 St. Louis Cardinals. The full-bleed color fronts display primarily color player action photos with a few posed. Along the top left edge the player's name is printed in red on a gray bar, with the words "Team Cardinals" appearing on a gray bar across the lower right edge. The right edge has a wide green bar with a gold foil-stamped baseball icon at the top. The horizontal backs are green and present a close-up photo of the player on the left with biography and statistics on the right. The set was issued in hobby (plastic box) and retail (blister) form.

	MINT	NRMT
COMPLETE SET (30)	4.00	1.80
COMMON CARD (1-30)	.10	.05

	MINT	NRMT
☐ 1 Ozzie Smith	2.00	.90
☐ 2 Rene Arocha	.10	.05
☐ 3 Bernard Gilkey	.25	.11
☐ 4 Jose Oquendo	.10	.05
☐ 5 Mike Perez	.10	.05
☐ 6 Tom Pagnozzi	.10	.05
☐ 7 Rod Brewer	.10	.05
☐ 8 Joe Magrane	.10	.05
☐ 9 Todd Zeile	.25	.11
☐ 10 Bob Tewksbury	.10	.05
☐ 11 Darrel Deak	.10	.05
☐ 12 Gregg Jefferies	.25	.11
☐ 13 Lee Smith	.25	.11
☐ 14 Ozzie Canseco	.10	.05
☐ 15 Tom Urbani	.10	.05
☐ 16 Donovan Osborne	.25	.11
☐ 17 Ray Lankford	.50	.23
☐ 18 Rheal Cormier	.10	.05
☐ 19 Allen Watson	.25	.11
☐ 20 Geronimo Pena	.10	.05
☐ 21 Rob Murphy	.10	.05
☐ 22 Tracy Woodson	.10	.05
☐ 23 Basil Shabazz	.10	.05
☐ 24 Omar Olivares	.10	.05
☐ 25 Brian Jordan	.25	.11
☐ 26 Les Lancaster	.10	.05
☐ 27 Sean Lowe	.10	.05
☐ 28 Hector Villanueva	.10	.05
☐ 29 Brian Barber	.25	.11
☐ 30 Aaron Holbert	.10	.05

1993 Stadium Club Cubs

This 30-card standard-size set features the 1993 Chicago Cubs. The full-bleed color fronts display primarily color player action photos with a few posed. Along the top left edge the player's name is printed in red on a light blue bar, with the words "Team Cubs" appearing on a gray bar across the lower right edge. The right edge has a wide green bar with a gold foil-stamped baseball icon at the top. The horizontal backs are green and present a close-up photo of the player on the left with biography and statistics on the right. The set was issued in hobby (plastic box) and retail (blister) form.

	MINT	NRMT
COMPLETE SET (30)	4.00	1.80
COMMON CARD (1-30)	.10	.05

	MINT	NRMT
☐ 1 Ryne Sandberg	2.00	.90
☐ 2 Sammy Sosa	.75	.35
☐ 3 Greg Hibbard	.10	.05
☐ 4 Candy Maldonado	.10	.05
☐ 5 Willie Wilson	.25	.11
☐ 6 Dan Plesac	.10	.05
☐ 7 Steve Buechele	.10	.05
☐ 8 Mark Grace	1.00	.45
☐ 9 Shawon Dunston	.25	.11
☐ 10 Steve Lake	.10	.05
☐ 11 Dwight Smith	.10	.05
☐ 12 Derrick May	.10	.05
☐ 13 Paul Assenmacher	.10	.05
☐ 14 Mike Harkey	.10	.05
☐ 15 Lance Dickson	.10	.05
☐ 16 Randy Myers	.25	.11
☐ 17 Mike Morgan	.10	.05
☐ 18 Chuck McElroy	.10	.05
☐ 19 Jose Guzman	.10	.05
☐ 20 Jose Vizcaino	.25	.11
☐ 21 Frank Castillo	.10	.05
☐ 22 Bob Scanlan	.10	.05
☐ 23 Rick Wilkins	.10	.05
☐ 24 Rey Sanchez	.10	.05
☐ 25 Phil Dauphin	.10	.05
☐ 26 Jim Bullinger	.10	.05
☐ 27 Jessie Hollins	.10	.05
☐ 28 Matt Walbeck	.10	.05
☐ 29 Fernando Ramsey	.10	.05
☐ 30 Jose Bautista	.10	.05

1993 Stadium Club Dodgers

This 30-card standard-size set features the 1993 Los Angeles Dodgers. The full-bleed color fronts display primarily color player action photos with a few posed. Along the top left edge the player's name is printed in blue on a red bar, with the words "Team Dodgers" appearing on a gray bar across the lower right edge. The right edge has a wide green bar with a gold foil-stamped baseball icon at the top. The horizontal backs are green and present a close-up photo of the player on the left with biography and statistics on the right. The set was issued in hobby (plastic box) and retail (blister) form.

	MINT	NRMT
COMPLETE SET (30)	8.00	3.60
COMMON CARD (1-30)	.10	.05

	MINT	NRMT
☐ 1 Darryl Strawberry	.25	.11
☐ 2 Pedro Martinez	1.00	.45
☐ 3 Jody Reed	.10	.05
☐ 4 Carlos Hernandez	.10	.05
☐ 5 Kevin Gross	.10	.05
☐ 6 Mike Piazza	3.00	1.35
☐ 7 Jim Gott	.10	.05
☐ 8 Eric Karros	.75	.35
☐ 9 Mike Sharperson	.10	.05
☐ 10 Ramon Martinez	.25	.11
☐ 11 Tim Wallach	.10	.05
☐ 12 Pedro Astacio	.25	.11
☐ 13 Lenny Harris	.10	.05
☐ 14 Brett Butler	.25	.11
☐ 15 Raul Mondesi	1.00	.45

☐ 16 Todd Worrell	.25	.11
☐ 17 Jose Offerman	.10	.05
☐ 18 Mitch Webster	.10	.05
☐ 19 Tom Candiotti	.10	.05
☐ 20 Eric Davis	.25	.11
☐ 21 Michael Moore	.10	.05
☐ 22 Billy Ashley	.10	.05
☐ 23 Orel Hershiser	.25	.11
☐ 24 Roger Cedeno	.25	.11
☐ 25 Roger McDowell	.10	.05
☐ 26 Mike James	.10	.05
☐ 27 Steve Wilson	.10	.05
☐ 28 Todd Hollandsworth	1.00	.45
☐ 29 Cory Snyder	.10	.05
☐ 30 Todd Williams	.10	.05

1993 Stadium Club Giants

This 30-card standard-size set features the 1993 San Francisco Giants. The full-bleed color fronts display primarily color player action photos with a few posed. Along the top left edge the player's name is printed in yellow on an orange bar, with the words "Team Giants" appearing on a gray bar across the lower right edge. The right edge has a wide green bar with a gold foil-stamped baseball icon at the top. The horizontal backs are green and present a close-up photo of the player on the left with biography and statistics on the right. The set was issued in hobby (plastic box) and retail (blister) form.

	MINT	NRMT
COMPLETE SET (30)	4.00	1.80
COMMON CARD (1-30)	.10	.05
☐ 1 Barry Bonds	1.25	.55
☐ 2 Dave Righetti	.10	.05
☐ 3 Matt Williams	.75	.35
☐ 4 Royce Clayton	.25	.11
☐ 5 Salomon Torres	.10	.05
☐ 6 Kirt Manwaring	.10	.05
☐ 7 J.R. Phillips	.10	.05
☐ 8 Kevin Rogers	.10	.05
☐ 9 Will Clark	1.00	.45
☐ 10 John Burkett	.10	.05
☐ 11 Willie McGee	.25	.11
☐ 12 Rod Beck	.25	.11
☐ 13 Jeff Reed	.10	.05
☐ 14 Jeff Brantley	.10	.05
☐ 15 Steve Hosey	.10	.05
☐ 16 Chris Hancock	.10	.05
☐ 17 Adell Davenport	.10	.05
☐ 18 Mike Jackson	.10	.05
☐ 19 Dave Martinez	.10	.05
☐ 20 Bill Swift	.10	.05
☐ 21 Steve Scarsone	.10	.05
☐ 22 Trevor Wilson	.10	.05
☐ 23 Mark Carreon	.10	.05
☐ 24 Bud Black	.10	.05
☐ 25 Darren Lewis	.10	.05
☐ 26 Dan Carlson	.10	.05
☐ 27 Craig Colbert	.10	.05
☐ 28 Greg Brummett	.10	.05
☐ 29 Bryan Hickerson	.10	.05
☐ 30 Robby Thompson	.10	.05

1993 Stadium Club Mariners

This 30-card standard-size set features the 1993 Seattle Mariners. The full-bleed color fronts display primarily color player action photos with a few posed. Along the top left edge the player's name is printed in yellow on a blue bar, with the words "Team Mariners" appearing on a gray bar across the lower right edge. The right edge has a wide green bar with a gold foil-stamped baseball icon at the top. The horizontal backs are green and present a close-up photo of the player on the left with biography and statistics on the right. The set was issued in hobby (plastic box) and retail (blister) form.

	MINT	NRMT
COMPLETE SET (30)	8.00	3.60
COMMON CARD (1-30)	.10	.05
☐ 1 Ken Griffey Jr.	4.00	1.80
☐ 2 Desi Relaford	.25	.11
☐ 3 Dave Wainhouse	.10	.05
☐ 4 Rich Amaral	.10	.05
☐ 5 Brian Deak	.10	.05
☐ 6 Bret Boone	.10	.05
☐ 7 Bill Haselman	.10	.05
☐ 8 Dave Fleming	.10	.05
☐ 9 Fernando Vina	.25	.11
☐ 10 Greg Litton	.10	.05
☐ 11 Mackey Sasser	.10	.05
☐ 12 Lee Tinsley	.10	.05
☐ 13 Norm Charlton	.10	.05
☐ 14 Russ Swan	.10	.05
☐ 15 Brian Holman	.10	.05
☐ 16 Randy Johnson	1.00	.45
☐ 17 Erik Hanson	.10	.05
☐ 18 Tino Martinez	1.00	.45
☐ 19 Marc Newfield	.25	.11
☐ 20 Dave Valle	.10	.05
☐ 21 John Cummings	.10	.05
☐ 22 Mike Hampton	.50	.23
☐ 23 Jay Buhner	.75	.35
☐ 24 Edgar Martinez	.75	.35
☐ 25 Omar Vizquel	.50	.23
☐ 26 Pete O'Brien	.10	.05
☐ 27 Brian Turang	.10	.05
☐ 28 Chris Bosio	.10	.05
☐ 29 Mike Felder	.10	.05
☐ 30 Shawn Estes	.75	.35

1993 Stadium Club Marlins

This 30-card standard-size set features the 1993 Florida Marlins. The full-bleed color fronts display primarily color player action photos with a few posed. Along the top left edge the player's name is printed in orange on a sea green bar, with the words "Team Marlins" appearing on a gray bar across the lower right edge. The right edge has a wide green bar with a gold foil-stamped baseball icon at the top. The horizontal backs are green and present a close-up photo of the player on the left with biography and statistics on the right. The set was issued in hobby (plastic box) and retail (blister) form as well as being distributed in shrinkwrapped cardboard boxes with a manager card pictured on it.

	MINT	NRMT
COMPLETE SET (30)	4.00	1.80
COMMON CARD (1-30)	.10	.05
☐ 1 Nigel Wilson	.10	.05
☐ 2 Bryan Harvey	.10	.05
☐ 3 Bob McClure	.10	.05
☐ 4 Alex Arias	.10	.05
☐ 5 Walt Weiss	.25	.11
☐ 6 Charlie Hough	.25	.11
☐ 7 Scott Chiamparino	.10	.05
☐ 8 Junior Felix	.10	.05
☐ 9 Jack Armstrong	.10	.05
☐ 10 Dave Magadan	.10	.05
☐ 11 Cris Carpenter	.10	.05
☐ 12 Benito Santiago	.10	.05
☐ 13 Jeff Conine	.75	.35
☐ 14 Jerry Don Gleaton	.10	.05
☐ 15 Steve Decker	.10	.05
☐ 16 Ryan Bowen	.10	.05
☐ 17 Ramon Martinez	.10	.05
☐ 18 Bret Barberie	.10	.05
☐ 19 Monty Fariss	.10	.05
☐ 20 Trevor Hoffman	.50	.23
☐ 21 Scott Pose	.10	.05
☐ 22 Mike Myers	.10	.05
☐ 23 Geronimo Berroa	.25	.11
☐ 24 Darrell Whitmore	.10	.05
☐ 25 Chuck Carr	.10	.05
☐ 26 Dave Weathers	.10	.05
☐ 27 Matt Turner	.10	.05
☐ 28 Jose Martinez	.10	.05
☐ 29 Orestes Destrade	.10	.05
☐ 30 Carl Everett	.25	.11

1993 Stadium Club Phillies

This 30-card standard-size set features the 1993 Philadelphia Phillies. The full-bleed color fronts display primarily color player action photos with a few posed. Along the top left edge the player's name is printed in blue on a coral bar, with the words "Team Phillies" appearing on a gray bar across the lower right edge. The right edge has a wide green bar with a gold foil-stamped baseball icon at the top. The horizontal backs are green and present a close-up photo of the player on the left with biography and statistics on the right. The set was issued in hobby (plastic box) and retail (blister) form.

	MINT	NRMT
COMPLETE SET (30)	4.00	1.80
COMMON CARD (1-30)	.10	.05
☐ 1 Darren Daulton	.75	.35
☐ 2 Larry Andersen	.10	.05
☐ 3 Kyle Abbott	.10	.05
☐ 4 Chad McConnell	.10	.05
☐ 5 Danny Jackson	.10	.05
☐ 6 Kevin Stocker	.25	.11
☐ 7 Jim Eisenreich	.50	.23
☐ 8 Mickey Morandini	.25	.11
☐ 9 Bob Ayrault	.10	.05
☐ 10 Doug Lindsey	.10	.05
☐ 11 Dave Hollins	.10	.05
☐ 12 Dave West	.10	.05
☐ 13 Wes Chamberlain	.10	.05
☐ 14 Curt Schilling	.75	.35
☐ 15 Len Dykstra	.50	.23
☐ 16 Trevor Humphry	.10	.05
☐ 17 Terry Mulholland	.10	.05
☐ 18 Gene Schall	.25	.11
☐ 19 Mike Lieberthal	.50	.23
☐ 20 Ben Rivera	.10	.05
☐ 21 Mariano Duncan	.10	.05
☐ 22 Pete Incaviglia	.25	.11
☐ 23 Ron Blazier	.10	.05
☐ 24 Jeff Jackson	.10	.05
☐ 25 Jose DeLeon	.10	.05
☐ 26 Ron Lockett	.10	.05
☐ 27 Tommy Greene	.10	.05
☐ 28 Milt Thompson	.10	.05
☐ 29 Mitch Williams	.25	.11
☐ 30 John Kruk	.50	.23

1993 Stadium Club Rangers

This 30-card standard-size set features the 1993 Texas Rangers. The full-bleed color fronts display primarily color player action photos with a few posed. Along the top left edge the player's name is printed in blue on a coral red bar, with the words "Team Rangers" appearing on a gray bar across the lower right edge. The right edge has a wide green bar with a gold foil-stamped baseball icon at the top. The horizontal backs are green and present a close-up photo of the player on the left with biography and statistics on the right. The set was issued in hobby (plastic box) and retail (blister) form.

	MINT	NRMT
COMPLETE SET (30)	8.00	3.60
COMMON CARD (1-30)	.10	.05
☐ 1 Nolan Ryan	4.00	1.80
☐ 2 Ritchie Moody	.10	.05
☐ 3 Matt Whiteside	.10	.05
☐ 4 David Hulse	.10	.05
☐ 5 Roger Pavlik	.10	.05
☐ 6 Dan Smith	.10	.05
☐ 7 Donald Harris	.10	.05
☐ 8 Butch Davis	.10	.05
☐ 9 Benji Gil	.10	.05
☐ 10 Ivan Rodriguez	1.25	.55
☐ 11 Dean Palmer	.50	.23
☐ 12 Jeff Huson	.10	.05
☐ 13 Rob Maurer	.10	.05
☐ 14 Gary Redus	.10	.05
☐ 15 Doug Dascenzo	.10	.05
☐ 16 Charlie Leibrandt	.10	.05
☐ 17 Tom Henke	.25	.11
☐ 18 Manuel Lee	.10	.05
☐ 19 Kenny Rogers	.25	.11
☐ 20 Kevin Brown	.50	.23
☐ 21 Juan Gonzalez	2.00	.90
☐ 22 Geno Petralli	.10	.05
☐ 23 John Russell	.10	.05
☐ 24 Robb Nen	.50	.23
☐ 25 Julio Franco	.25	.11
☐ 26 Rafael Palmeiro	.50	.23
☐ 27 Todd Burns	.10	.05
☐ 28 Jose Canseco	1.00	.45
☐ 29 Billy Ripken	.10	.05
☐ 30 Dan Peltier	.10	.05

1993 Stadium Club Rockies

This 30-card standard-size set features the 1993 Colorado Rockies. The full-bleed color fronts display primarily color player action photos with a few posed. Along the top left edge the player's name is printed in gray on a purple bar, with the words "Team Rockies" appearing on a gray bar across the lower right edge. The right edge has a wide green bar with a gold foil-stamped baseball icon at the top. The horizontal backs are green and present a close-up photo of the player on the left with biography and statistics on the right. The set was issued in hobby (plastic box) and retail (blister) form as well as being distributed in shrinkwrapped cardboard boxes with a manager card pictured on it.

	MINT	NRMT
COMPLETE SET (30)	5.00	2.20
COMMON CARD (1-30)	.10	.05
☐ 1 David Nied	.10	.05
☐ 2 Quinton McCracken	.10	.05
☐ 3 Charlie Hayes	.25	.11
☐ 4 Bryn Smith	.10	.05
☐ 5 Dante Bichette	1.00	.45
☐ 6 Alex Cole	.10	.05
☐ 7 Scott Aldred	.10	.05
☐ 8 Roberto Mejia	.10	.05
☐ 9 Jeff Parrett	.10	.05
☐ 10 Joe Girardi	.25	.11
☐ 11 Andres Galarraga	1.25	.55
☐ 12 Daryl Boston	.10	.05
☐ 13 Jerald Clark	.10	.05
☐ 14 Gerald Young	.10	.05
☐ 15 Bruce Ruffin	.10	.05
☐ 16 Rudy Seanez	.10	.05
☐ 17 Darren Holmes	.10	.05
☐ 18 Andy Ashby	.25	.11
☐ 19 Chris Jones	.10	.05
☐ 20 Mark Thompson	.25	.11
☐ 21 Freddie Benavides	.10	.05
☐ 22 Eric Wedge	.10	.05
☐ 23 Vinny Castilla	.75	.35
☐ 24 Butch Henry	.10	.05
☐ 25 Jim Tatum	.10	.05
☐ 26 Steve Reed	.10	.05
☐ 27 Eric Young	.50	.23
☐ 28 Danny Sheaffer	.10	.05
☐ 29 Roger Bailey	.10	.05
☐ 30 Brad Ausmus	.25	.11

1993 Stadium Club Royals

This 30-card standard-size set features the 1993 Kansas City Royals. The full-bleed color fronts display primarily color player action photos with a few posed. Along the top left edge the player's name is printed in yellow on a blue bar, with the words "Team Royals" appearing on a gray bar across the lower right edge. The right edge has a wide green bar with a gold foil-stamped baseball icon at the top. The horizontal backs are green and present a close-up photo of the player on the left with biography and statistics on the right. The set was issued in hobby (plastic box) and retail (blister) form.

	MINT	NRMT
COMPLETE SET (30)	4.00	1.80
COMMON CARD (1-30)	.10	.05
☐ 1 George Brett	2.00	.90
☐ 2 Mike Macfarlane	.10	.05
☐ 3 Tom Gordon	.25	.11
☐ 4 Wally Joyner	.25	.11
☐ 5 Kevin Appier	.50	.23
☐ 6 Phil Hiatt	.10	.05
☐ 7 Keith Miller	.10	.05
☐ 8 Hipolito Pichardo	.10	.05
☐ 9 Chris Gwynn	.10	.05
☐ 10 Jose Lind	.10	.05
☐ 11 Mark Gubicza	.10	.05
☐ 12 Dennis Rasmussen	.10	.05
☐ 13 Mike Magnante	.10	.05
☐ 14 Joe Vitiello	.10	.05
☐ 15 Kevin McReynolds	.10	.05
☐ 16 Greg Gagne	.10	.05
☐ 17 David Cone	.50	.23
☐ 18 Brent Mayne	.10	.05
☐ 19 Jeff Montgomery	.25	.11
☐ 20 Joe Randa	.10	.05
☐ 21 Felix Jose	.10	.05
☐ 22 Bill Sampen	.10	.05
☐ 23 Curt Wilkerson	.10	.05
☐ 24 Mark Gardner	.10	.05
☐ 25 Brian McRae	.10	.05
☐ 26 Hubie Brooks	.10	.05
☐ 27 Chris Eddy	.10	.05
☐ 28 Harvey Pulliam	.10	.05
☐ 29 Rusty Meacham	.10	.05
☐ 30 Danny Miceli	.10	.05

1993 Stadium Club White Sox

This 30-card standard-size set features the 1993 Chicago White Sox. The full-bleed color fronts display primarily color player action photos with a few posed. Along the top left edge the player's name is printed in light blue on a gray bar, with the words "Team White Sox" appearing on a gray bar across the lower right edge. The right edge has a wide green bar with a gold foil-stamped baseball icon at the top. The horizontal backs are green and present a close-up photo of the player on the left with biography and statistics on the right. The set was issued in hobby (plastic box) and retail (blister) form.

	MINT	NRMT
COMPLETE SET (30)	8.00	3.60
COMMON CARD (1-30)	.10	.05
☐ 1 Frank Thomas	3.00	1.35
☐ 2 Bo Jackson	.25	.11
☐ 3 Rod Bolton	.10	.05
☐ 4 Dave Stieb	.10	.05
☐ 5 Tim Raines	.50	.23
☐ 6 Joey Cora	.25	.11
☐ 7 Warren Newson	.10	.05
☐ 8 Roberto Hernandez	.50	.23
☐ 9 Brandon Wilson	.10	.05
☐ 10 Wilson Alvarez	.25	.11
☐ 11 Dan Pasqua	.10	.05
☐ 12 Ozzie Guillen	.25	.11
☐ 13 Robin Ventura	.50	.23
☐ 14 Craig Grebeck	.10	.05
☐ 15 Lance Johnson	.25	.11
☐ 16 Carlton Fisk	.75	.35
☐ 17 Ron Karkovice	.10	.05
☐ 18 Jack McDowell	.25	.11
☐ 19 Scott Radinsky	.10	.05
☐ 20 Bobby Thigpen	.10	.05
☐ 21 Donn Pall	.10	.05
☐ 22 George Bell	.10	.05
☐ 23 Alex Fernandez	.50	.23
☐ 24 Mike Huff	.10	.05
☐ 25 Jason Bere	.25	.11
☐ 26 Johnny Ruffin	.10	.05
☐ 27 Ellis Burks	.25	.11
☐ 28 Kirk McCaskill	.10	.05
☐ 29 Terry Leach	.10	.05
☐ 30 Shawn Gilbert	.10	.05

1993 Stadium Club Yankees

This 30-card standard-size set features the 1993 New York Yankees. The full-bleed color fronts display primarily color player action photos with a few posed. Along the top left edge the player's name is printed in gray on a purple bar, with the words "Team Yankees" appearing on a gray bar across the lower right edge. The right edge has a wide green bar with a gold foil-stamped baseball icon at the top. The horizontal backs are green and present a close-up photo of the player on the left with biography and statistics on the right. The set was issued in hobby (plastic box) and retail (blister) form.

	MINT	NRMT
COMPLETE SET (30)	6.00	2.70
COMMON CARD (1-30)	.10	.05
☐ 1 Don Mattingly	2.00	.90
☐ 2 Jim Abbott	.25	.11
☐ 3 Matt Nokes	.10	.05
☐ 4 Danny Tartabull	.25	.11
☐ 5 Wade Boggs	1.00	.45
☐ 6 Melido Perez	.10	.05
☐ 7 Steve Farr	.10	.05
☐ 8 Kevin Maas	.10	.05
☐ 9 Randy Velarde	.10	.05
☐ 10 Mike Humphreys	.10	.05
☐ 11 Mike Gallego	.10	.05
☐ 12 Mike Stanley	.25	.11
☐ 13 Jimmy Key	.50	.23
☐ 14 Paul O'Neill	.50	.23
☐ 15 Spike Owen	.10	.05
☐ 16 Pat Kelly	.10	.05
☐ 17 Sterling Hitchcock	.25	.11
☐ 18 Mike Witt	.10	.05
☐ 19 Scott Kamieniecki	.10	.05
☐ 20 John Habyan	.10	.05
☐ 21 Bernie Williams	1.00	.45

☐ 22 Brien Taylor	.10	.05
☐ 23 Rick Monteleone	.10	.05
☐ 24 Mark Hutton	.10	.05
☐ 25 Robert Eenhoorn	.10	.05
☐ 26 Gerald Williams	.10	.05
☐ 27 Sam Militello	.10	.05
☐ 28 Bob Wickman	.10	.05
☐ 29 Andy Stankiewicz	.10	.05
☐ 30 Domingo Jean	.10	.05

1993 Stadium Club Ultra-Pro

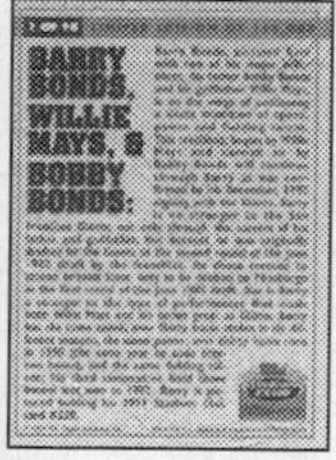

The ten cards in this set measure the standard size and were available singly as limited edition random inserts in the Topps Stadium Club Ultra-Pro Platinum collector pages refill packs (1-6) and individual semi-rigid card protector packs (7-10). The cards feature full-bleed posed color player photos. A red stripe across the bottom is accented with a prismatic gold-foil stripe and contains the player's name in prismatic gold-foil lettering. This stripe design intersects the Stadium Club/Ultra-Pro logo. The backs carry player profile within an aqua outline against a stucco-textured background. The cards are numbered on the back. In light of a marketing partnership with the Rembrandt Company, this ten-card set was produced by Stadium Club to mark the launch of a new accessory line of premium card storage accessory products. Reportedly no more than 150,000 sets were produced. Willie Mays is Barry Bonds' godfather.

	MINT	NRMT
COMPLETE SET (10)	20.00	9.00
COMMON CARD (1-10)	1.00	.45
☐ 1 Barry Bonds	2.50	1.10
Willie Mays		
Bobby Bonds		
☐ 2 Willie Mays	3.00	1.35
Leaning on bat		
☐ 3 Bobby Bonds	1.00	.45
Kneeling, leaning on bat		
☐ 4 Barry Bonds	2.00	.90
Bat extended		
☐ 5 Barry Bonds	2.00	.90
Bobby Bonds		
☐ 6 Willie Mays	3.00	1.35
Squatting posture, glove in hand		
☐ 7 Barry Bonds	2.00	.90
Dressed in suit		
☐ 8 Bobby Bonds	2.00	.90
Willie Mays		
☐ 9 Willie Mays	3.00	1.35
Kneeling, bat in right hand		
☐ 10 Barry Bonds	2.00	.90
Dressed in tuxedo		

1994 Stadium Club Pre-Production

Issued to herald the release of 1994 Stadium Club Series I, the nine standard-size cards comprising this promo set feature on their fronts borderless color player action shots. The player's last name appears in white lettering within a red foil-stamped rectangle at the bottom; his first name appears alongside in black "typewritten" lettering within a division color-coded "tearaway." The red foil-stamped Stadium Club logo appears in an upper corner. The back carries a color player action cutout superposed upon a blue and black background. The player's name, team, biography, career highlights, and statistics appear in lettering of several different colors and typefaces. The cards have the disclaimer "Pre-Production Sample" printed vertically running down the left edge of the back.

	MINT	NRMT
COMPLETE SET (9)	6.00	2.70
COMMON CARD	.50	.23
☐ 6 Al Martin	.75	.35
☐ 15 Junior Ortiz	.50	.23
☐ 36 Tim Salmon	1.50	.70
☐ 56 Jerry Spradlin	.50	.23
☐ 122 Tom Pagnozzi	.50	.23
☐ 123 Ron Gant	.75	.35
☐ 125 Dennis Eckersley	1.00	.45
☐ 135 Jose Lind	.50	.23
☐ 238 Barry Bonds	2.00	.90

1994 Stadium Club

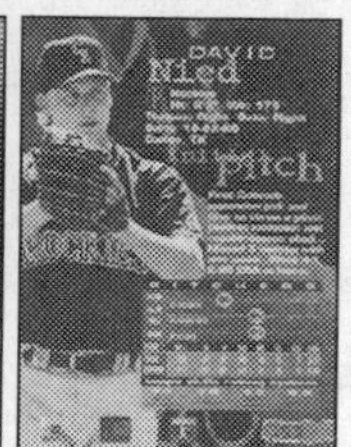

The 720 standard-size cards comprising this set were issued two series of 270 and a third series of 180. Card fronts feature borderless color player action photos. The player's last name appears in white lettering within a red-foil-stamped rectangle at the bottom. His first name appears alongside in black "typewritten" lettering within a division color-coded "tearaway." The red-foil-stamped Stadium Club logo appears in an upper corner. The back carries a color player action cutout superimposed upon a blue and black background. The player's name, team, biography, career highlights and statistics appear in lettering of several different colors and typefaces. There are a number of subsets including Home Run Club (258-268), Tale of Two Players (525/526), Division Leaders (527-532), Quick Starts (533-538), Career Contributors (541-543), Rookie Rocker (626-630), Rookie Rocket (631-634) and Fantastic Finishes (714-719). The only notable Rookie Card is Chan Ho Park.

	MINT	NRMT
COMPLETE SET (720)	55.00	25.00
COMPLETE SERIES 1 (270)	20.00	9.00
COMPLETE SERIES 2 (270)	20.00	9.00
COMPLETE SERIES 3 (180)	15.00	6.75
COMMON CARD (1-720)	.15	.07
☐ 1 Robin Yount	.40	.18
☐ 2 Rick Wilkins	.15	.07
☐ 3 Steve Scarsone	.15	.07
☐ 4 Gary Sheffield	.60	.25
☐ 5 George Brett UER	1.25	.55
(birthdate listed as 1963; should be 1953)		
☐ 6 Al Martin	.15	.07
☐ 7 Joe Oliver	.15	.07
☐ 8 Stan Belinda	.15	.07
☐ 9 Denny Hocking	.15	.07
☐ 10 Roberto Alomar	.60	.25
☐ 11 Luis Polonia	.15	.07
☐ 12 Scott Hemond	.15	.07
☐ 13 Jody Reed	.15	.07
☐ 14 Mel Rojas	.15	.07
☐ 15 Junior Ortiz	.15	.07
☐ 16 Harold Baines	.30	.14
☐ 17 Brad Pennington	.15	.07
☐ 18 Jay Bell	.30	.14
☐ 19 Tom Henke	.15	.07
☐ 20 Jeff Branson	.15	.07
☐ 21 Roberto Mejia	.15	.07
☐ 22 Pedro Munoz	.15	.07
☐ 23 Matt Nokes	.15	.07
☐ 24 Jack McDowell	.15	.07
☐ 25 Cecil Fielder	.30	.14
☐ 26 Tony Fossas	.15	.07
☐ 27 Jim Eisenreich	.30	.14
☐ 28 Anthony Young	.15	.07
☐ 29 Chuck Carr	.15	.07
☐ 30 Jeff Treadway	.15	.07
☐ 31 Chris Nabholz	.15	.07
☐ 32 Tom Candiotti	.15	.07
☐ 33 Mike Maddux	.15	.07
☐ 34 Nolan Ryan	2.50	1.10
☐ 35 Luis Gonzalez	.15	.07
☐ 36 Tim Salmon	.60	.25
☐ 37 Mark Whiten	.15	.07
☐ 38 Roger McDowell	.15	.07
☐ 39 Royce Clayton	.30	.14
☐ 40 Troy Neel	.15	.07
☐ 41 Mike Harkey	.15	.07
☐ 42 Darrin Fletcher	.15	.07
☐ 43 Wayne Kirby	.15	.07
☐ 44 Rich Amaral	.15	.07
☐ 45 Robb Nen UER	.30	.14
(Nenn on back)		
☐ 46 Tim Teufel	.15	.07
☐ 47 Steve Cooke	.15	.07
☐ 48 Jeff McNeely	.15	.07
☐ 49 Jeff Montgomery	.30	.14
☐ 50 Skeeter Barnes	.15	.07
☐ 51 Scott Stahoviak	.15	.07
☐ 52 Pat Kelly	.15	.07
☐ 53 Brady Anderson	.40	.18
☐ 54 Mariano Duncan	.15	.07
☐ 55 Brian Bohanon	.15	.07
☐ 56 Jerry Spradlin	.15	.07
☐ 57 Ron Karkovice	.15	.07
☐ 58 Jeff Gardner	.15	.07
☐ 59 Bobby Bonilla	.30	.14
☐ 60 Tino Martinez	.60	.25
☐ 61 Todd Benzinger	.15	.07
☐ 62 Steve Trachsel	.15	.07
☐ 63 Brian Jordan	.30	.14
☐ 64 Steve Bedrosian	.15	.07
☐ 65 Brent Gates	.15	.07
☐ 66 Shawn Green	.30	.14
☐ 67 Sean Berry	.15	.07
☐ 68 Joe Klink	.15	.07
☐ 69 Fernando Valenzuela	.30	.14
☐ 70 Andy Tomberlin	.15	.07
☐ 71 Tony Pena	.15	.07
☐ 72 Eric Young	.30	.14
☐ 73 Chris Gomez	.15	.07
☐ 74 Paul O'Neill	.30	.14
☐ 75 Ricky Gutierrez	.15	.07
☐ 76 Brad Holman	.15	.07
☐ 77 Lance Painter	.15	.07
☐ 78 Mike Butcher	.15	.07
☐ 79 Sid Bream	.15	.07
☐ 80 Sammy Sosa	.60	.25
☐ 81 Felix Fermin	.15	.07
☐ 82 Todd Hundley	.30	.14
☐ 83 Kevin Higgins	.15	.07
☐ 84 Todd Pratt	.15	.07
☐ 85 Ken Griffey Jr.	3.00	1.35
☐ 86 John O'Donoghue	.15	.07
☐ 87 Rick Renteria	.15	.07
☐ 88 John Burkett	.15	.07
☐ 89 Jose Vizcaino	.15	.07
☐ 90 Kevin Seitzer	.15	.07
☐ 91 Bobby Witt	.15	.07
☐ 92 Chris Turner	.15	.07
☐ 93 Omar Vizquel	.30	.14
☐ 94 David Justice	.60	.25
☐ 95 David Segui	.15	.07
☐ 96 Dave Hollins	.15	.07
☐ 97 Doug Strange	.15	.07
☐ 98 Jerald Clark	.15	.07
☐ 99 Mike Moore	.15	.07
☐ 100 Joey Cora	.30	.14
☐ 101 Scott Kamieniecki	.15	.07
☐ 102 Andy Benes	.30	.14
☐ 103 Chris Bosio	.15	.07
☐ 104 Rey Sanchez	.15	.07
☐ 105 John Jaha	.15	.07
☐ 106 Otis Nixon	.30	.14
☐ 107 Rickey Henderson	.40	.18
☐ 108 Jeff Bagwell	1.25	.55
☐ 109 Gregg Jefferies	.30	.14
☐ 110 Roberto Alomar	.40	.18
Paul Molitor		
John Olerud		
☐ 111 Ron Gant	.40	.18
David Justice		
Fred McGriff		
☐ 112 Juan Gonzalez	.40	.18
Rafael Palmeiro		
Dean Palmer		
☐ 113 Greg Swindell	.15	.07
☐ 114 Bill Haselman	.15	.07
☐ 115 Phil Plantier	.15	.07
☐ 116 Ivan Rodriguez	.75	.35
☐ 117 Kevin Tapani	.15	.07
☐ 118 Mike LaValliere	.15	.07
☐ 119 Tim Costo	.15	.07
☐ 120 Mickey Morandini	.15	.07
☐ 121 Brett Butler	.30	.14

□ 122 Tom Pagnozzi .15 .07
□ 123 Ron Gant .30 .14
□ 124 Damion Easley .15 .07
□ 125 Dennis Eckersley .40 .18
□ 126 Matt Mieske .15 .07
□ 127 Cliff Floyd .30 .14
□ 128 Julian Tavarez .30 .14
□ 129 Arthur Rhodes .15 .07
□ 130 Dave West .15 .07
□ 131 Tim Naehring .15 .07
□ 132 Freddie Benavides .15 .07
□ 133 Paul Assenmacher .15 .07
□ 134 David McCarty .15 .07
□ 135 Jose Lind .15 .07
□ 136 Reggie Sanders .15 .07
□ 137 Don Slaught .15 .07
□ 138 Andujar Cedeno .15 .07
□ 139 Rob Deer .15 .07
□ 140 Mike Piazza UER 2.00 .90
(listed as outfielder)
□ 141 Moises Alou .30 .14
□ 142 Tom Foley .15 .07
□ 143 Benito Santiago .15 .07
□ 144 Sandy Alomar .30 .14
□ 145 Carlos Hernandez .15 .07
□ 146 Luis Alicea .15 .07
□ 147 Tom Lampkin .15 .07
□ 148 Ryan Klesko .40 .18
□ 149 Juan Guzman .15 .07
□ 150 Scott Servais .15 .07
□ 151 Tony Gwynn 1.50 .70
□ 152 Tim Wakefield .15 .07
□ 153 David Nied .15 .07
□ 154 Chris Haney .15 .07
□ 155 Danny Bautista .15 .07
□ 156 Randy Velarde .15 .07
□ 157 Darrin Jackson .15 .07
□ 158 J.R. Phillips .15 .07
□ 159 Greg Gagne .15 .07
□ 160 Luis Aquino .15 .07
□ 161 John Vander Wal .15 .07
□ 162 Randy Myers .15 .07
□ 163 Ted Power .15 .07
□ 164 Scott Brosius .15 .07
□ 165 Len Dykstra .30 .14
□ 166 Jacob Brumfield .15 .07
□ 167 Bo Jackson .30 .14
□ 168 Eddie Taubensee .15 .07
□ 169 Carlos Baerga .30 .14
□ 170 Tim Bogar .15 .07
□ 171 Jose Canseco .40 .18
□ 172 Greg Blosser UER .15 .07
(Gregg on front)
□ 173 Chili Davis .30 .14
□ 174 Randy Knorr .15 .07
□ 175 Mike Perez .15 .07
□ 176 Henry Rodriguez .15 .07
□ 177 Brian Turang .15 .07
□ 178 Roger Pavlik .15 .07
□ 179 Aaron Sele .15 .07
□ 180 Fred McGriff .40 .18
Gary Sheffield
□ 181 J.T. Snow .40 .18
Tim Salmon
□ 182 Roberto Hernandez .30 .14
□ 183 Jeff Reboulet .15 .07
□ 184 John Doherty .15 .07
□ 185 Danny Sheaffer .15 .07
□ 186 Bip Roberts .15 .07
□ 187 Denny Martinez .30 .14
□ 188 Darryl Hamilton .15 .07
□ 189 Eduardo Perez .15 .07
□ 190 Pete Harnisch .15 .07
□ 191 Rich Gossage .30 .14
□ 192 Mickey Tettleton .15 .07
□ 193 Lenny Webster .15 .07
□ 194 Lance Johnson .15 .07
□ 195 Don Mattingly 1.00 .45
□ 196 Gregg Olson .15 .07
□ 197 Mark Gubicza .15 .07
□ 198 Scott Fletcher .15 .07
□ 199 Jon Shave .15 .07
□ 200 Tim Mauser .15 .07
□ 201 Jeromy Burnitz .30 .14
□ 202 Rob Dibble .15 .07
□ 203 Will Clark .40 .18
□ 204 Steve Buechele .15 .07
□ 205 Brian Williams .15 .07
□ 206 Carlos Garcia .15 .07
□ 207 Mark Clark .15 .07
□ 208 Rafael Palmeiro .40 .18
□ 209 Eric Davis .30 .14
□ 210 Pat Meares .15 .07
□ 211 Chuck Finley .15 .07
□ 212 Jason Bere .15 .07
□ 213 Gary DiSarcina .15 .07
□ 214 Tony Fernandez .15 .07
□ 215 B.J. Surhoff .15 .07
□ 216 Lee Guetterman .15 .07
□ 217 Tim Wallach .15 .07
□ 218 Kirt Manwaring .15 .07
□ 219 Albert Belle .75 .35
□ 220 Doc Gooden .30 .14
□ 221 Archi Cianfrocco .15 .07
□ 222 Terry Mulholland .15 .07
□ 223 Hipolito Pichardo .15 .07
□ 224 Kent Hrbek .30 .14
□ 225 Craig Grebeck .15 .07
□ 226 Todd Jones .15 .07
□ 227 Mike Bordick .15 .07
□ 228 John Olerud .30 .14
□ 229 Jeff Blauser .15 .07
□ 230 Alex Arias .15 .07
□ 231 Bernard Gilkey .30 .14
□ 232 Denny Neagle .30 .14
□ 233 Pedro Borbon .15 .07
□ 234 Dick Schofield .15 .07
□ 235 Matias Carrillo .15 .07
□ 236 Juan Bell .15 .07
□ 237 Mike Hampton .30 .14
□ 238 Barry Bonds .75 .35
□ 239 Cris Carpenter .15 .07
□ 240 Eric Karros .30 .14
□ 241 Greg McMichael .15 .07
□ 242 Pat Hentgen .30 .14
□ 243 Tim Pugh .15 .07
□ 244 Vinny Castilla .40 .18
□ 245 Charlie Hough .15 .07
□ 246 Bobby Munoz .15 .07
□ 247 Kevin Baez .15 .07
□ 248 Todd Frohwirth .15 .07
□ 249 Charlie Hayes .15 .07
□ 250 Mike Macfarlane .15 .07
□ 251 Danny Darwin .15 .07
□ 252 Ben Rivera .15 .07
□ 253 Dave Henderson .15 .07
□ 254 Steve Avery .15 .07
□ 255 Tim Belcher .15 .07
□ 256 Dan Plesac .15 .07
□ 257 Jim Thome .75 .35
□ 258 Albert Belle HR .60 .25
□ 259 Barry Bonds HR .60 .25
□ 260 Ron Gant HR .30 .14
□ 261 Juan Gonzalez HR .75 .35
□ 262 Ken Griffey Jr. HR 1.50 .70
□ 263 David Justice HR .40 .18
□ 264 Fred McGriff HR .30 .14
□ 265 Rafael Palmeiro HR .30 .14
□ 266 Mike Piazza HR 1.00 .45
□ 267 Frank Thomas HR 1.50 .70
□ 268 Matt Williams HR .30 .14
□ 269 Checklist 1-135 .15 .07
□ 270 Checklist 136-270 .15 .07
□ 271 Mike Stanley .15 .07
□ 272 Tony Tarasco .15 .07
□ 273 Teddy Higuera .15 .07
□ 274 Ryan Thompson .15 .07
□ 275 Rick Aguilera .15 .07
□ 276 Ramon Martinez .30 .14
□ 277 Orlando Merced .15 .07
□ 278 Guillermo Velasquez .15 .07
□ 279 Mark Hutton .15 .07
□ 280 Larry Walker .60 .25
□ 281 Kevin Gross .15 .07
□ 282 Jose Offerman .15 .07
□ 283 Jim Leyritz .15 .07
□ 284 Jamie Moyer .15 .07
□ 285 Frank Thomas 2.50 1.10
□ 286 Derek Bell .30 .14
□ 287 Derrick May .15 .07
□ 288 Dave Winfield .40 .18
□ 289 Curt Schilling .30 .14
□ 290 Carlos Quintana .15 .07
□ 291 Bob Natal .15 .07
□ 292 David Cone .30 .14
□ 293 Al Osuna .15 .07
□ 294 Bob Hamelin .15 .07
□ 295 Chad Curtis .15 .07
□ 296 Danny Jackson .15 .07
□ 297 Bob Welch .15 .07
□ 298 Felix Jose .15 .07
□ 299 Jay Buhner .40 .18
□ 300 Joe Carter .40 .18
□ 301 Kenny Lofton .75 .35
□ 302 Kirk Rueter .15 .07
□ 303 Kim Batiste .15 .07
□ 304 Mike Morgan .15 .07
□ 305 Pat Borders .15 .07
□ 306 Rene Arocha .15 .07
□ 307 Ruben Sierra .15 .07
□ 308 Steve Finley .30 .14
□ 309 Travis Fryman .30 .14
□ 310 Zane Smith .15 .07
□ 311 Willie Wilson .15 .07
□ 312 Trevor Hoffman .30 .14
□ 313 Terry Pendleton .30 .14
□ 314 Salomon Torres .15 .07
□ 315 Robin Ventura .30 .14
□ 316 Randy Tomlin .15 .07
□ 317 Dave Stewart .30 .14
□ 318 Mike Benjamin .15 .07
□ 319 Matt Turner .15 .07
□ 320 Manny Ramirez .75 .35
□ 321 Kevin Young .15 .07
□ 322 Ken Caminiti .60 .25
□ 323 Joe Girardi .15 .07
□ 324 Jeff McKnight .15 .07
□ 325 Gene Harris .15 .07
□ 326 Devon White .15 .07
□ 327 Darryl Kile .30 .14
□ 328 Craig Paquette .15 .07
□ 329 Cal Eldred .15 .07
□ 330 Bill Swift .15 .07
□ 331 Alan Trammell .40 .18
□ 332 Armando Reynoso .15 .07
□ 333 Brent Mayne .15 .07
□ 334 Chris Donnels .15 .07
□ 335 Darryl Strawberry .30 .14
□ 336 Dean Palmer .30 .14
□ 337 Frank Castillo .15 .07
□ 338 Jeff King .30 .14
□ 339 John Franco .30 .14
□ 340 Kevin Appier .30 .14
□ 341 Lance Blankenship .15 .07
□ 342 Mark McLemore .15 .07
□ 343 Pedro Astacio .15 .07
□ 344 Rich Batchelor .15 .07
□ 345 Ryan Bowen .15 .07
□ 346 Terry Steinbach .30 .14
□ 347 Troy O'Leary .15 .07
□ 348 Willie Blair .15 .07
□ 349 Wade Boggs .60 .25
□ 350 Tim Raines .15 .07
□ 351 Scott Livingstone .15 .07
□ 352 Rod Correia .15 .07
□ 353 Ray Lankford .40 .18
□ 354 Pat Listach .15 .07
□ 355 Milt Thompson .15 .07
□ 356 Miguel Jimenez .15 .07
□ 357 Marc Newfield .30 .14
□ 358 Mark McGwire 1.25 .55
□ 359 Kirby Puckett 1.25 .55
□ 360 Kent Mercker .15 .07
□ 361 John Kruk .30 .14
□ 362 Jeff Kent .15 .07
□ 363 Hal Morris .15 .07
□ 364 Edgar Martinez .40 .18
□ 365 Dave Magadan .15 .07
□ 366 Dante Bichette .40 .18
□ 367 Chris Hammond .15 .07
□ 368 Bret Saberhagen .15 .07
□ 369 Billy Ripken .15 .07
□ 370 Bill Gullickson .15 .07
□ 371 Andre Dawson .40 .18
□ 372 Roberto Kelly .15 .07
□ 373 Cal Ripken 2.50 1.10
□ 374 Craig Biggio .40 .18
□ 375 Dan Pasqua .15 .07
□ 376 Dave Nilsson .30 .14
□ 377 Duane Ward .15 .07
□ 378 Greg Vaughn .15 .07
□ 379 Jeff Fassero .15 .07
□ 380 Jerry DiPoto .15 .07
□ 381 John Patterson .15 .07
□ 382 Kevin Brown .30 .14
□ 383 Kevin Roberson .15 .07
□ 384 Joe Orsulak .15 .07
□ 385 Hilly Hathaway .15 .07
□ 386 Mike Greenwell .15 .07
□ 387 Orestes Destrade .15 .07
□ 388 Mike Gallego .15 .07
□ 389 Ozzie Guillen .15 .07
□ 390 Raul Mondesi .40 .18
□ 391 Scott Lydy .15 .07
□ 392 Tom Urbani .15 .07
□ 393 Wil Cordero .30 .14
□ 394 Tony Longmire .15 .07
□ 395 Todd Zeile .15 .07
□ 396 Scott Cooper .15 .07
□ 397 Ryne Sandberg .75 .35
□ 398 Ricky Bones .15 .07
□ 399 Phil Clark .15 .07
□ 400 Orel Hershiser .30 .14
□ 401 Mike Henneman .15 .07
□ 402 Mark Lemke .15 .07
□ 403 Mark Grace .40 .18
□ 404 Ken Ryan .15 .07
□ 405 John Smoltz .40 .18
□ 406 Jeff Conine .30 .14
□ 407 Greg Harris .15 .07
□ 408 Doug Drabek .15 .07

☐ 409 Dave Fleming	.15	.07
☐ 410 Danny Tartabull	.15	.07
☐ 411 Chad Kreuter	.15	.07
☐ 412 Brad Ausmus	.15	.07
☐ 413 Ben McDonald	.15	.07
☐ 414 Barry Larkin	.40	.18
☐ 415 Bret Barberie	.15	.07
☐ 416 Chuck Knoblauch	.60	.25
☐ 417 Ozzie Smith	.75	.35
☐ 418 Ed Sprague	.15	.07
☐ 419 Matt Williams	.40	.18
☐ 420 Jeremy Hernandez	.15	.07
☐ 421 Jose Bautista	.15	.07
☐ 422 Kevin Mitchell	.30	.14
☐ 423 Manuel Lee	.15	.07
☐ 424 Mike Devereaux	.15	.07
☐ 425 Omar Olivares	.15	.07
☐ 426 Rafael Belliard	.15	.07
☐ 427 Richie Lewis	.15	.07
☐ 428 Ron Darling	.15	.07
☐ 429 Shane Mack	.15	.07
☐ 430 Tim Hulett	.15	.07
☐ 431 Wally Joyner	.30	.14
☐ 432 Wes Chamberlain	.15	.07
☐ 433 Tom Browning	.15	.07
☐ 434 Scott Radinsky	.15	.07
☐ 435 Rondell White	.40	.18
☐ 436 Rod Beck	.30	.14
☐ 437 Rheal Cormier	.15	.07
☐ 438 Randy Johnson	.60	.25
☐ 439 Pete Schourek	.15	.07
☐ 440 Mo Vaughn	.75	.35
☐ 441 Mike Timlin	.15	.07
☐ 442 Mark Langston	.15	.07
☐ 443 Lou Whitaker	.30	.14
☐ 444 Kevin Stocker	.15	.07
☐ 445 Ken Hill	.15	.07
☐ 446 John Wetteland	.30	.14
☐ 447 J.T. Snow	.30	.14
☐ 448 Erik Pappas	.15	.07
☐ 449 David Hulse	.15	.07
☐ 450 Darren Daulton	.30	.14
☐ 451 Chris Hoiles	.15	.07
☐ 452 Bryan Harvey	.15	.07
☐ 453 Darren Lewis	.15	.07
☐ 454 Andres Galarraga	.40	.18
☐ 455 Joe Hesketh	.15	.07
☐ 456 Jose Valentin	.30	.14
☐ 457 Dan Peltier	.15	.07
☐ 458 Joe Boever	.15	.07
☐ 459 Kevin Rogers	.15	.07
☐ 460 Craig Shipley	.15	.07
☐ 461 Alvaro Espinoza	.15	.07
☐ 462 Wilson Alvarez	.30	.14
☐ 463 Cory Snyder	.15	.07
☐ 464 Candy Maldonado	.15	.07
☐ 465 Blas Minor	.15	.07
☐ 466 Rod Bolton	.15	.07
☐ 467 Kenny Rogers	.15	.07
☐ 468 Greg Myers	.15	.07
☐ 469 Jimmy Key	.30	.14
☐ 470 Tony Castillo	.15	.07
☐ 471 Mike Stanton	.15	.07
☐ 472 Deion Sanders	.60	.25
☐ 473 Tito Navarro	.15	.07
☐ 474 Mike Gardiner	.15	.07
☐ 475 Steve Reed	.15	.07
☐ 476 John Roper	.15	.07
☐ 477 Mike Trombley	.15	.07
☐ 478 Charles Nagy	.30	.14
☐ 479 Larry Casian	.15	.07
☐ 480 Eric Hillman	.15	.07
☐ 481 Bill Wertz	.15	.07
☐ 482 Jeff Schwarz	.15	.07
☐ 483 John Valentin	.30	.14
☐ 484 Carl Willis	.15	.07
☐ 485 Gary Gaetti	.30	.14
☐ 486 Bill Pecota	.15	.07
☐ 487 John Smiley	.15	.07
☐ 488 Mike Mussina	.60	.25
☐ 489 Mike Ignasiak	.15	.07
☐ 490 Billy Brewer	.15	.07
☐ 491 Jack Voigt	.15	.07
☐ 492 Mike Munoz	.15	.07
☐ 493 Lee Tinsley	.30	.14
☐ 494 Bob Wickman	.15	.07
☐ 495 Roger Salkeld	.15	.07
☐ 496 Thomas Howard	.15	.07
☐ 497 Mark Davis	.15	.07
☐ 498 Dave Clark	.15	.07
☐ 499 Turk Wendell	.15	.07
☐ 500 Rafael Bournigal	.15	.07
☐ 501 Chip Hale	.15	.07
☐ 502 Matt Whiteside	.15	.07
☐ 503 Brian Koelling	.15	.07
☐ 504 Jeff Reed	.15	.07
☐ 505 Paul Wagner	.15	.07
☐ 506 Torey Lovullo	.15	.07
☐ 507 Curtis Leskanic	.15	.07
☐ 508 Derek Lilliquist	.15	.07
☐ 509 Joe Magrane	.15	.07
☐ 510 Mackey Sasser	.15	.07
☐ 511 Lloyd McClendon	.15	.07
☐ 512 Jayhawk Owens	.15	.07
☐ 513 Woody Williams	.15	.07
☐ 514 Gary Redus	.15	.07
☐ 515 Tim Spehr	.15	.07
☐ 516 Jim Abbott	.15	.07
☐ 517 Lou Frazier	.15	.07
☐ 518 Erik Plantenberg	.15	.07
☐ 519 Tim Worrell	.15	.07
☐ 520 Brian McRae	.15	.07
☐ 521 Chan Ho Park	2.00	.90
☐ 522 Mark Wohlers	.30	.14
☐ 523 Geronimo Pena	.15	.07
☐ 524 Andy Ashby	.15	.07
☐ 525 Tim Raines TALE	.15	.07
☐ 526 Paul Molitor TALE	.60	.25
☐ 527 Joe Carter DL	.30	.14
☐ 528 Frank Thomas DL UER (listed as third in RBI in 1993; was actually second)	1.50	.70
☐ 529 Ken Griffey Jr. DL	1.50	.70
☐ 530 David Justice DL	.30	.14
☐ 531 Gregg Jefferies DL	.15	.07
☐ 532 Barry Bonds DL	.60	.25
☐ 533 John Kruk QS	.15	.07
☐ 534 Roger Clemens QS	.60	.25
☐ 535 Cecil Fielder QS	.30	.14
☐ 536 Ruben Sierra QS	.15	.07
☐ 537 Tony Gwynn QS	.60	.25
☐ 538 Tom Glavine QS	.30	.14
☐ 539 Checklist 271-405 UER (number on back is 269)	.15	.07
☐ 540 Checklist 406-540 UER (numbered 270 on back)	.15	.07
☐ 541 Ozzie Smith ATL	.60	.25
☐ 542 Eddie Murray ATL	.60	.25
☐ 543 Lee Smith ATL	.30	.14
☐ 544 Greg Maddux	2.00	.90
☐ 545 Denis Boucher	.15	.07
☐ 546 Mark Gardner	.15	.07
☐ 547 Bo Jackson	.30	.14
☐ 548 Eric Anthony	.15	.07
☐ 549 Delino DeShields	.15	.07
☐ 550 Turner Ward	.15	.07
☐ 551 Scott Sanderson	.15	.07
☐ 552 Hector Carrasco	.15	.07
☐ 553 Tony Phillips	.15	.07
☐ 554 Melido Perez	.15	.07
☐ 555 Mike Felder	.15	.07
☐ 556 Jack Morris	.30	.14
☐ 557 Rafael Palmeiro	.40	.18
☐ 558 Shane Reynolds	.15	.07
☐ 559 Pete Incaviglia	.15	.07
☐ 560 Greg Harris	.15	.07
☐ 561 Matt Walbeck	.15	.07
☐ 562 Todd Van Poppel	.15	.07
☐ 563 Todd Stottlemyre	.15	.07
☐ 564 Ricky Bones	.15	.07
☐ 565 Mike Jackson	.15	.07
☐ 566 Kevin McReynolds	.15	.07
☐ 567 Melvin Nieves	.15	.07
☐ 568 Juan Gonzalez	1.50	.70
☐ 569 Frank Viola	.15	.07
☐ 570 Vince Coleman	.15	.07
☐ 571 Brian Anderson	.30	.14
☐ 572 Omar Vizquel	.30	.14
☐ 573 Bernie Williams	.60	.25
☐ 574 Tom Glavine	.40	.18
☐ 575 Mitch Williams	.15	.07
☐ 576 Shawon Dunston	.15	.07
☐ 577 Mike Lansing	.30	.14
☐ 578 Greg Pirkl	.15	.07
☐ 579 Sid Fernandez	.15	.07
☐ 580 Doug Jones	.15	.07
☐ 581 Walt Weiss	.15	.07
☐ 582 Tim Belcher	.15	.07
☐ 583 Alex Fernandez	.30	.14
☐ 584 Alex Cole	.15	.07
☐ 585 Greg Cadaret	.15	.07
☐ 586 Bob Tewksbury	.15	.07
☐ 587 Dave Hansen	.15	.07
☐ 588 Kurt Abbott	.30	.14
☐ 589 Rick White	.15	.07
☐ 590 Kevin Bass	.15	.07
☐ 591 Geronimo Berroa	.30	.14
☐ 592 Jaime Navarro	.15	.07
☐ 593 Steve Farr	.15	.07
☐ 594 Jack Armstrong	.15	.07
☐ 595 Steve Howe	.15	.07
☐ 596 Jose Rijo	.15	.07
☐ 597 Otis Nixon	.30	.14
☐ 598 Robby Thompson	.15	.07
☐ 599 Kelly Stinnett	.15	.07
☐ 600 Carlos Delgado	.40	.18
☐ 601 Brian Johnson	.15	.07
☐ 602 Gregg Olson	.15	.07
☐ 603 Jim Edmonds	.60	.25
☐ 604 Mike Blowers	.15	.07
☐ 605 Lee Smith	.30	.14
☐ 606 Pat Rapp	.15	.07
☐ 607 Mike Magnante	.15	.07
☐ 608 Karl Rhodes	.15	.07
☐ 609 Jeff Juden	.15	.07
☐ 610 Rusty Meacham	.15	.07
☐ 611 Pedro Martinez	.60	.25
☐ 612 Todd Worrell	.15	.07
☐ 613 Stan Javier	.15	.07
☐ 614 Mike Hampton	.30	.14
☐ 615 Jose Guzman	.15	.07
☐ 616 Xavier Hernandez	.15	.07
☐ 617 David Wells	.15	.07
☐ 618 John Habyan	.15	.07
☐ 619 Chris Nabholz	.15	.07
☐ 620 Bobby Jones	.30	.14
☐ 621 Chris James	.15	.07
☐ 622 Ellis Burks	.30	.14
☐ 623 Erik Hanson	.15	.07
☐ 624 Pat Meares	.15	.07
☐ 625 Harold Reynolds	.15	.07
☐ 626 Bob Hamelin RR	.15	.07
☐ 627 Manny Ramirez RR	.60	.25
☐ 628 Ryan Klesko RR	.30	.14
☐ 629 Carlos Delgado RR	.30	.14
☐ 630 Javier Lopez RR	.30	.14
☐ 631 Steve Karsay RR	.15	.07
☐ 632 Rick Helling RR	.15	.07
☐ 633 Steve Trachsel RR	.15	.07
☐ 634 Hector Carrasco RR	.15	.07
☐ 635 Andy Stankiewicz	.15	.07
☐ 636 Paul Sorrento	.15	.07
☐ 637 Scott Erickson	.15	.07
☐ 638 Chipper Jones	2.00	.90
☐ 639 Luis Polonia	.15	.07
☐ 640 Howard Johnson	.15	.07
☐ 641 John Dopson	.15	.07
☐ 642 Jody Reed	.15	.07
☐ 643 Lonnie Smith	.15	.07
☐ 644 Mark Portugal	.15	.07
☐ 645 Paul Molitor	.60	.25
☐ 646 Paul Assenmacher	.15	.07
☐ 647 Hubie Brooks	.15	.07
☐ 648 Gary Wayne	.15	.07
☐ 649 Sean Berry	.15	.07
☐ 650 Roger Clemens	1.25	.55
☐ 651 Brian L.Hunter	.60	.25
☐ 652 Wally Whitehurst	.15	.07
☐ 653 Allen Watson	.15	.07
☐ 654 Rickey Henderson	.40	.18
☐ 655 Sid Bream	.15	.07
☐ 656 Dan Wilson	.30	.14
☐ 657 Ricky Jordan	.15	.07
☐ 658 Sterling Hitchcock	.30	.14
☐ 659 Darrin Jackson	.15	.07
☐ 660 Junior Felix	.15	.07
☐ 661 Tom Brunansky	.15	.07
☐ 662 Jose Vizcaino	.15	.07
☐ 663 Mark Leiter	.15	.07
☐ 664 Gil Heredia	.15	.07
☐ 665 Fred McGriff	.40	.18
☐ 666 Will Clark	.40	.18
☐ 667 Al Leiter	.15	.07
☐ 668 James Mouton	.15	.07
☐ 669 Billy Bean	.15	.07
☐ 670 Scott Leius	.15	.07
☐ 671 Bret Boone	.15	.07
☐ 672 Darren Holmes	.15	.07
☐ 673 Dave Weathers	.15	.07
☐ 674 Eddie Murray	.60	.25
☐ 675 Felix Fermin	.15	.07
☐ 676 Chris Sabo	.15	.07
☐ 677 Billy Spiers	.15	.07
☐ 678 Aaron Sele	.30	.14
☐ 679 Juan Samuel	.15	.07
☐ 680 Julio Franco	.30	.14
☐ 681 Heathcliff Slocumb	.30	.14
☐ 682 Denny Martinez	.30	.14
☐ 683 Jerry Browne	.15	.07
☐ 684 Pedro Martinez	.60	.25
☐ 685 Rex Hudler	.15	.07
☐ 686 Willie McGee	.15	.07
☐ 687 Andy Van Slyke	.30	.14
☐ 688 Pat Mahomes	.15	.07
☐ 689 Dave Henderson	.15	.07
☐ 690 Tony Eusebio	.15	.07
☐ 691 Rick Sutcliffe	.15	.07
☐ 692 Willie Banks	.15	.07
☐ 693 Alan Mills	.15	.07
☐ 694 Jeff Treadway	.15	.07
☐ 695 Alex Gonzalez	.30	.14

☐ 696 David Segui	.15	.07
☐ 697 Rick Helling	.15	.07
☐ 698 Bip Roberts	.15	.07
☐ 699 Jeff Cirillo	.50	.23
☐ 700 Terry Mulholland	.15	.07
☐ 701 Marvin Freeman	.15	.07
☐ 702 Jason Bere	.30	.14
☐ 703 Javier Lopez	.40	.18
☐ 704 Greg Hibbard	.15	.07
☐ 705 Tommy Greene	.15	.07
☐ 706 Marquis Grissom	.30	.14
☐ 707 Brian Harper	.15	.07
☐ 708 Steve Karsay	.15	.07
☐ 709 Jeff Brantley	.15	.07
☐ 710 Jeff Russell	.15	.07
☐ 711 Bryan Hickerson	.15	.07
☐ 712 Jim Pittsley	.50	.23
☐ 713 Bobby Ayala	.15	.07
☐ 714 John Smoltz	.40	.18
☐ 715 Jose Rijo	.15	.07
☐ 716 Greg Maddux	1.00	.45
☐ 717 Matt Williams	.40	.18
☐ 718 Frank Thomas	1.50	.70
☐ 719 Ryne Sandberg	.60	.25
☐ 720 Checklist	.15	.07

1994 Stadium Club First Day Issue

Randomly inserted in one of every 24 packs, these First Day Production cards are identical to the regular issues except for a special 1st Day foil stamp engraved on the front of each card. No more than 2,000 of each Stadium Club card was issued as First Day Issue. Some FDI logos have been transferred from "common" players to the front of "star" players.

	MINT	NRMT
COMPLETE SET (720)	2700.00	1200.00
COMPLETE SERIES 1 (270)	1200.00	550.00
COMPLETE SERIES 2 (270)	1000.00	450.00
COMPLETE SERIES 3 (180)	500.00	220.00
COMMON CARD (1-720)	2.00	.90

*STARS: 15X to 30X BASIC CARDS ...
*YOUNG STARS: 12.5X to 25X BASIC CARDS

1994 Stadium Club Golden Rainbow

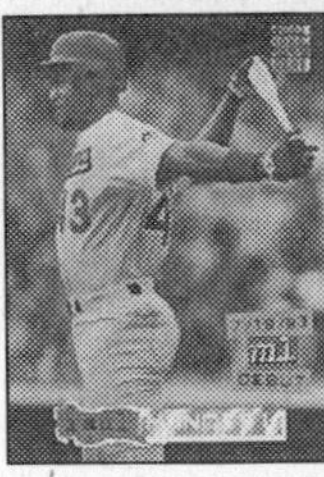

Parallel to the basic Stadium Club set, Golden Rainbows differ in that the player's last name on front has gold refracting foil over it. The cards were inserted one per Stadium Club foil pack and two per jumbo.

	MINT	NRMT
COMPLETE SET (720)	170.00	75.00
COMPLETE SERIES 1 (270)	65.00	29.00
COMPLETE SERIES 2 (270)	65.00	29.00
COMPLETE SERIES 3 (180)	40.00	18.00
COMMON CARD (1-720)	.25	.11

*STARS: 2X to 4X BASIC CARDS ....
*YOUNG STARS: 1.5X to 3X BASIC CARDS

1994 Stadium Club Members Only Parallel

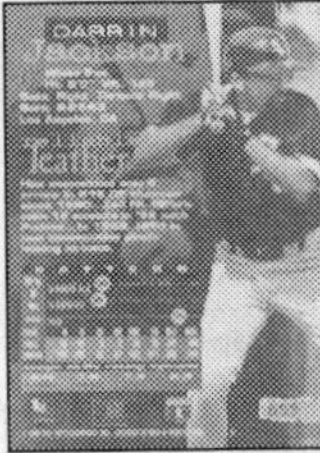

This set, issued only to Topps Stadium Club Members, is a parallel of the regular Stadium Club set. This set was issued in factory set form only and includes parallel versions of both the basic issue and insert cards from the 1994 Stadium Club set. According to Topps, 5,000 sets were produced. Only the insert cards have been listed below. Please use the multiplier for values on the basic issue cards.

	MINT	NRMT
COMPLETE FACT.SET (770)	200.00	90.00
COMMON CARD (1-720)	.25	.11

*MEMBERS ONLY: 3X TO 6X BASIC CARDS

☐ F1 Jeff Bagwell	4.00	1.80
☐ F2 Albert Belle	5.00	2.20
☐ F3 Barry Bonds	2.50	1.10
☐ F4 Juan Gonzalez	5.00	2.20
☐ F5 Ken Griffey Jr.	10.00	4.50
☐ F6 Marquis Grissom	1.00	.45
☐ F7 David Justice	1.00	.45
☐ F8 Mike Piazza	8.00	3.60
☐ F9 Tim Salmon	2.50	1.10
☐ F10 Frank Thomas	10.00	4.50
☐ DD1 Mike Piazza	12.00	5.50
☐ DD2 Dave Winfield	1.50	.70
☐ DD3 John Kruk	1.00	.45
☐ DD4 Cal Ripken	15.00	6.75
☐ DD5 Kirby Puckett	8.00	3.60
☐ DD6 Barry Bonds	4.00	1.80
☐ DD7 Ken Griffey Jr.	15.00	6.75
☐ DD8 Tim Salmon	2.50	1.10
☐ DD9 Frank Thomas	15.00	6.75
☐ DD10 Jeff Kent	1.00	.45
☐ DD11 Randy Johnson	3.00	1.35
☐ DD12 Darren Daulton	1.00	.45
☐ ST1 Atlanta Braves (Jeff Blauser Terry Pendleton)	8.00	3.60
☐ ST2 Chicago Cubs (Sammy Sosa Derrick May)	1.50	.70
☐ ST3 Cincinnati Reds (Reggie Sanders Barry Larkin)	2.00	.90
☐ ST4 Colorado Rockies (Vinny Castilla Eric Young)	1.50	.70
☐ ST5 Florida Marlins (Alex Arias)	1.50	.70
☐ ST6 Houston Astros (Eric Anthony Steve Finley)	1.50	.70
☐ ST7 Los Angeles Dodgers (Mike Piazza)	2.00	.90
☐ ST8 Montreal Expos (Marquis Grissom)	1.50	.70
☐ ST9 New York Mets (Bobby Bonilla)	1.50	.70
☐ ST10 Philadelphia Phillies (Mickey Morandini)	1.50	.70
☐ ST11 Pittsburgh Pirates (Andy Van Slyke Jay Bell)	1.50	.70
☐ ST12 St. Louis Cardinals (Todd Zeile Gregg Jefferies)	1.50	.70
☐ ST13 San Diego Padres (Ricky Gutierrez)	1.50	.70
☐ ST14 San Francisco Giants (Matt Williams Kirt Manwaring)	2.00	.90
☐ ST15 Baltimore Orioles (Cal Ripken)	4.00	1.80
☐ ST16 Boston Red Sox (Luis Rivera John Valentin)	4.00	1.80
☐ ST17 California Angels (Tim Salmon)	1.50	.70
☐ ST18 Chicago White Sox (Joey Cora)	1.50	.70
☐ ST19 Cleveland Indians (Kenny Lofton Carlos Baerga Albert Belle)	4.00	1.80
☐ ST20 Detroit Tigers (Alan Trammell Tony Phillips)	1.50	.70
☐ ST21 Kansas City Royals Jose Lind Curt Wilkerson)	1.50	.70
☐ ST22 Milwaukee Brewers (Julio Navarro John Jaha Cal Eldred)	1.50	.70
☐ ST23 Minnesota Twins (Kirby Puckett Kent Hrbek)	1.50	.70
☐ ST24 New York Yankees Don Mattingly Bernie Williams)	2.00	.90
☐ ST25 Oakland Athletics (Mike Bordick Brent Gates)	1.50	.70
☐ ST26 Seattle Mariners (Jay Buhner Mike Blowers)	4.00	1.80
☐ ST27 Texas Rangers (Ivan Rodriguez Dean Palmer Jose Canseco Juan Gonzalez)	2.00	.90
☐ ST28 Toronto Blue Jays (John Olerud)	1.50	.70

1994 Stadium Club Dugout Dirt

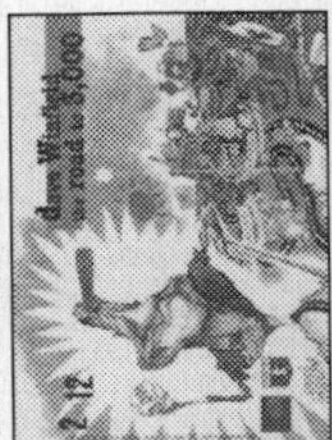

Randomly inserted at a rate of one per six packs, these standard-size cards feature some of baseball's most popular and colorful players by sports cartoonists Daniel Guidera and Steve Benson. The cards resemble basic Stadium Club cards except for a Dugout Dirt logo at the bottom. Backs contain a cartoon. Cards 1-4 were found in first series packs with cards 5-8 and 9-12 were inserted in second series and third series packs respectively.

	MINT	NRMT
COMPLETE SET (12)	10.00	4.50
COMPLETE SERIES 1 (4)	5.00	2.20
COMPLETE SERIES 2 (4)	3.00	1.35
COMPLETE SERIES 3 (4)	3.00	1.35
COMMON CARD (DD1-DD12)	.25	.11

☐ DD1 Mike Piazza	2.00	.90
☐ DD2 Dave Winfield	.40	.18
☐ DD3 John Kruk	.25	.11
☐ DD4 Cal Ripken	2.50	1.10
☐ DD5 Jack McDowell	.25	.11
☐ DD6 Barry Bonds	.75	.35
☐ DD7 Ken Griffey Jr.	3.00	1.35
☐ DD8 Tim Salmon	.50	.23
☐ DD9 Frank Thomas	2.50	1.10
☐ DD10 Jeff Kent	.25	.11
☐ DD11 Randy Johnson	.50	.23
☐ DD12 Darren Daulton	.25	.11

1994 Stadium Club Finest

This set contains 10 standard-size metallic cards of top players. They were randomly inserted one in 6 third series packs. The fronts feature a color player photo with a red and yellow background. Backs contain a color player photo with 1993 and career statistics. Jumbo versions measuring approximately five inches by seven inches were issued for retail repacks.

	MINT	NRMT
COMPLETE SET (10)	35.00	16.00
COMMON CARD (F1-F10)	1.00	.45

*JUMBOS: 2X TO 5X BASIC JUMBOS

☐ F1 Jeff Bagwell	4.00	1.80
☐ F2 Albert Belle	2.50	1.10
☐ F3 Barry Bonds	2.50	1.10
☐ F4 Juan Gonzalez	5.00	2.20
☐ F5 Ken Griffey Jr.	10.00	4.50
☐ F6 Marquis Grissom	1.00	.45
☐ F7 David Justice	2.00	.90
☐ F8 Mike Piazza	6.00	2.70
☐ F9 Tim Salmon	2.00	.90
☐ F10 Frank Thomas	8.00	3.60

1994 Stadium Club Super Teams

Randomly inserted at a rate of one per 24 first series packs only, this 28-card standard-size features one card for each of the 28 MLB teams. Collectors holding team cards could redeem them for special prizes if those teams won a division title, a league championship, or the World Series. But, since the strike affected the 1994 season, Topps postponed the promotion until the 1995 season. The expiration was pushed back to January 31, 1996.

	MINT	NRMT
COMPLETE SET (28)	50.00	22.00
COMMON TEAM (1-28)	1.00	.45
☐ ST1 Atlanta Braves (Jeff Blauser, Terry Pendleton)	10.00	4.50
☐ ST2 Chicago Cubs (Sammy Sosa, Derrick May)	1.00	.45
☐ ST3 Cincinnati Reds (Reggie Sanders, Barry Larkin)	2.00	.90
☐ ST4 Colorado Rockies (Vinny Castilla, Eric Young)	1.00	.45
☐ ST5 Florida Marlins (Alex Arias)	1.00	.45
☐ ST6 Houston Astros (Eric Anthony, Steve Finley)	1.00	.45
☐ ST7 Los Angeles Dodgers (Mike Piazza)	6.00	2.70
☐ ST8 Montreal Expos (Marquis Grissom)	1.00	.45
☐ ST9 New York Mets (Bobby Bonilla)	1.00	.45
☐ ST10 Philadelphia Phillies (Mickey Morandini)	1.00	.45
☐ ST11 Pittsburgh Pirates (Andy Van Slyke, Jay Bell)	1.00	.45
☐ ST12 St. Louis Cardinals (Todd Zeile, Gregg Jefferies)	1.00	.45
☐ ST13 San Diego Padres (Ricky Gutierrez)	1.00	.45
☐ ST14 San Francisco Giants (Matt Williams, Kirt Manwaring)	2.00	.90
☐ ST15 Baltimore Orioles (Cal Ripken)	8.00	3.60
☐ ST16 Boston Red Sox (Luis Rivera, John Valentin)	2.00	.90
☐ ST17 California Angels (Tim Salmon)	1.00	.45
☐ ST18 Chicago White Sox (Joey Cora)	1.00	.45
☐ ST19 Cleveland Indians (Kenny Lofton, Carlos Baerga, Albert Belle)	5.00	2.20
☐ ST20 Detroit Tigers (Alan Trammell, Tony Phillips)	1.00	.45
☐ ST21 Kansas City Royals (Jose Lind, Curt Wilkerson)	1.00	.45
☐ ST22 Milwaukee Brewers (Julio Navarro, John Jaha, Cal Eldred)	1.00	.45
☐ ST23 Minnesota Twins (Kirby Puckett, Kent Hrbek)	4.00	1.80
☐ ST24 New York Yankees (Don Mattingly, Bernie Williams)	3.00	1.35
☐ ST25 Oakland Athletics (Mike Bordick, Brent Gates)	1.00	.45
☐ ST26 Seattle Mariners (Jay Buhner, Mike Blowers)	2.00	.90
☐ ST27 Texas Rangers (Ivan Rodriguez, Dean Palmer, Jose Canseco, Juan Gonzalez)	5.00	2.20
☐ ST28 Toronto Blue Jays (John Olerud)	1.00	.45

1994 Stadium Club Members Only

Issued to Stadium Club members, this 50-card standard-size set features 45 regular Stadium Club cards as well as five Stadium Club Finest cards. The fronts have full-bleed color action player photos. The player's name is printed in the bottom left corner, and the words "Topps Stadium Club Members Only" appear in one of the top corners. On a black background, the horizontal backs carry a color player close-up shot, and a player profile.

	MINT	NRMT
COMPLETE SET (50)	20.00	9.00
COMMON CARD (1-50)	.10	.05
☐ 1 Juan Gonzalez	2.00	.90
☐ 2 Tom Henke	.10	.05
☐ 3 John Kruk	.20	.09
☐ 4 Paul Molitor	.50	.23
☐ 5 David Justice	.50	.23
☐ 6 Rafael Palmeiro	.35	.16
☐ 7 John Smoltz	.20	.09
☐ 8 Matt Williams	.35	.16
☐ 9 John Olerud	.10	.05
☐ 10 Mark Grace	.50	.23
☐ 11 Joe Carter	.20	.09
☐ 12 Wilson Alvarez	.10	.05
☐ 13 Len Dykstra	.20	.09
☐ 14 Kevin Appier	.20	.09
☐ 15 Andres Galarraga	.50	.23
☐ 16 Mark Langston	.10	.05
☐ 17 Ken Griffey Jr.	3.00	1.35
☐ 18 Albert Belle	.75	.35
☐ 19 Gregg Jefferies	.10	.05
☐ 20 Duane Ward	.10	.05
☐ 21 Jack McDowell	.10	.05
☐ 22 Randy Johnson	.50	.23
☐ 23 Tom Glavine	.20	.09
☐ 24 Barry Bonds	.75	.35
☐ 25 Chuck Carr	.10	.05
☐ 26 Ron Gant	.20	.09
☐ 27 Kenny Lofton	.75	.35
☐ 28 Mike Piazza	2.50	1.10
☐ 29 Frank Thomas	2.50	1.10
☐ 30 Fred McGriff	.35	.16
☐ 31 Bryan Harvey	.10	.05
☐ 32 John Burkett	.10	.05
☐ 33 Roberto Alomar	.50	.23
☐ 34 Cecil Fielder	.20	.09
☐ 35 Marquis Grissom	.20	.09
☐ 36 Randy Myers	.10	.05
☐ 37 Tony Phillips	.10	.05
☐ 38 Rickey Henderson	.35	.16
☐ 39 Luis Polonia	.10	.05
☐ 40 Jose Rijo	.10	.05
☐ 41 Jeff Montgomery	.10	.05
☐ 42 Greg Maddux	2.50	1.10
☐ 43 Tony Gwynn	2.00	.90
☐ 44 Rod Beck	.10	.05
☐ 45 Carlos Baerga	.20	.09
☐ 46 Wil Cordero FIN	.10	.05
☐ 47 Tim Salmon FIN	1.50	.70
☐ 48 Mike Lansing FIN	.20	.09
☐ 49 J.T. Snow FIN	.20	.09
☐ 50 Jeff Conine FIN	.20	.09

1994 Stadium Club Members Only Finest Bronze

Available only to members who purchase the Members Only baseball set, this 3-card set is the first edition of Topps Finest Bronze cards. Measuring 2 3/4" by 3 3/4", the cards are mounted on bronze and factory sealed in clear resin. On a colorful reflective background, the fronts display a player cutout that is highlighted by a circle design. In black lettering, the horizontal backs present biography as well as major and minor league batting record.

	MINT	NRMT
COMPLETE SET (3)	60.00	27.00
COMMON CARD (1-3)	10.00	4.50
☐ 1 Barry Bonds	10.00	4.50
☐ 2 Ken Griffey Jr.	30.00	13.50
☐ 3 Frank Thomas	25.00	11.00

1994 Stadium Club Team

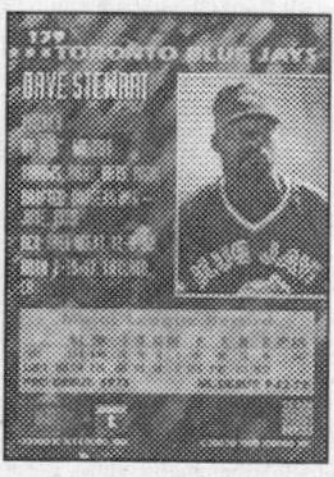

This 360-card standard-size set features 30 players from 12 teams. The fronts feature full-bleed color action photos that are edged on the bottom and right by a gradated black-and-green pattern. The player's name is printed in gold foil in the bottom stripe, while a line of gold squares accents the right stripe and intersects the team name (also in gold foil). On a gradated green and black background, the backs carry a color head shot, biogaphy, and statistics. The cards are numbered on the back and checklisted below alphabetically according to teams.

	MINT	NRMT
COMPLETE SET (360)	30.00	13.50
COMMON CARD (1-360)	.05	.02
☐ 1 Barry Bonds	.75	.35
☐ 2 Royce Clayton	.10	.05
☐ 3 Kirt Manwaring	.05	.02
☐ 4 J.R. Phillips	.05	.02
☐ 5 Robby Thompson	.05	.02
☐ 6 Willie McGee	.10	.05

☐ 7 Steve Hosey .05 .02
☐ 8 Dave Burba .05 .02
☐ 9 Steve Scarsone .05 .02
☐ 10 Salomon Torres .05 .02
☐ 11 Bryan Hickerson .05 .02
☐ 12 Mike Benjamin .05 .02
☐ 13 Mark Carreon .05 .02
☐ 14 Rich Monteleone .05 .02
☐ 15 Dave Martinez .05 .02
☐ 16 Bill Swift .05 .02
☐ 17 Jeff Reed .05 .02
☐ 18 John Patterson .05 .02
☐ 19 Darren Lewis .05 .02
☐ 20 Mark Portugal .05 .02
☐ 21 Trevor Wilson .05 .02
☐ 22 Matt Williams .40 .18
☐ 23 Kevin Rogers .05 .02
☐ 24 Luis Mercedes .05 .02
☐ 25 Mike Jackson .05 .02
☐ 26 Steve Frey .05 .02
☐ 27 Tony Menendez .05 .02
☐ 28 John Burkett .05 .02
☐ 29 Todd Benzinger .05 .02
☐ 30 Rod Beck .10 .05
☐ 31 Greg Maddux 2.00 .90
☐ 32 Steve Avery .05 .02
☐ 33 Milt Hill .05 .02
☐ 34 Charlie O'Brien .05 .02
☐ 35 John Smoltz .10 .05
☐ 36 Jarvis Brown .05 .02
☐ 37 Dave Gallagher .05 .02
☐ 38 Ryan Klesko .75 .35
☐ 39 Kent Mercker .05 .02
☐ 40 Terry Pendleton .10 .05
☐ 41 Ron Gant .10 .05
☐ 42 Pedro Borbon Jr. .05 .02
☐ 43 Steve Bedrosian .05 .02
☐ 44 Ramon Caraballo .05 .02
☐ 45 Tyler Houston .10 .05
☐ 46 Mark Lemke .05 .02
☐ 47 Fred McGriff .40 .18
☐ 48 Jose Oliva .05 .02
☐ 49 David Justice .40 .18
☐ 50 Chipper Jones 2.50 1.10
☐ 51 Tony Tarasco .05 .02
☐ 52 Javier Lopez .50 .23
☐ 53 Mark Wohlers .10 .05
☐ 54 Deion Sanders .50 .23
☐ 55 Greg McMichael .05 .02
☐ 56 Tom Glavine .25 .11
☐ 57 Bill Pecota .05 .02
☐ 58 Mike Stanton .05 .02
☐ 59 Rafael Belliard .05 .02
☐ 60 Jeff Blauser .10 .05
☐ 61 Bryan Harvey .05 .02
☐ 62 Bret Barberie .05 .02
☐ 63 Rick Renteria .05 .02
☐ 64 Chris Hammond .05 .02
☐ 65 Pat Rapp .05 .02
☐ 66 Nigel Wilson .05 .02
☐ 67 Gary Sheffield .40 .18
☐ 68 Jerry Browne .05 .02
☐ 69 Charlie Hough .10 .05
☐ 70 Orestes Destrade .05 .02
☐ 71 Mario Diaz .05 .02
☐ 72 Ryan Bowen .05 .02
☐ 73 Carl Everett .10 .05
☐ 74 Richie Lewis .05 .02
☐ 75 Bob Natal .05 .02
☐ 76 Rich Rodriguez .05 .02
☐ 77 Darrell Whitmore .05 .02
☐ 78 Matt Turner .05 .02
☐ 79 Benito Santiago .10 .05
☐ 80 Robb Nen .10 .05
☐ 81 Dave Magadan .05 .02
☐ 82 Brian Drahman .05 .02
☐ 83 Mark Gardner .05 .02
☐ 84 Chuck Carr .05 .02
☐ 85 Alex Arias .05 .02
☐ 86 Kurt Abbott .10 .05
☐ 87 Joe Klink .05 .02
☐ 88 Jeff Mutis .05 .02
☐ 89 Dave Weathers .05 .02
☐ 90 Jeff Conine .10 .05
☐ 91 Andres Galarraga .50 .23
☐ 92 Vinny Castilla .25 .11
☐ 93 Roberto Mejia .05 .02
☐ 94 Darrell Sherman .05 .02
☐ 95 Mike Harkey .05 .02
☐ 96 Danny Sheaffer .05 .02
☐ 97 Pedro Castellano .05 .02
☐ 98 Walt Weiss .10 .05
☐ 99 Greg W. Harris .05 .02
☐ 100 Jayhawk Owens .05 .02
☐ 101 Bruce Ruffin .05 .02
☐ 102 Mike Munoz .05 .02
☐ 103 Armando Reynoso .05 .02
☐ 104 Eric Young .10 .05
☐ 105 Dante Bichette .40 .18
☐ 106 Marvin Freeman .05 .02
☐ 107 Joe Girardi .05 .02
☐ 108 Kent Bottenfield .05 .02
☐ 109 Howard Johnson .05 .02
☐ 110 Nelson Liriano .05 .02
☐ 111 David Nied .05 .02
☐ 112 Steve Reed .05 .02
☐ 113 Eric Wedge .05 .02
☐ 114 Charlie Hayes .10 .05
☐ 115 Ellis Burks .10 .05
☐ 116 Willie Blair .05 .02
☐ 117 Darren Holmes .05 .02
☐ 118 Curtis Leskanic .05 .02
☐ 119 Lance Painter .05 .02
☐ 120 Jim Tatum .05 .02
☐ 121 Frank Thomas 2.50 1.10
☐ 122 Jack McDowell .10 .05
☐ 123 Ron Karkovice .05 .02
☐ 124 Mike LaValliere .05 .02
☐ 125 Scott Radinsky .05 .02
☐ 126 Robin Ventura .25 .11
☐ 127 Scott Ruffcorn .05 .02
☐ 128 Steve Sax .05 .02
☐ 129 Roberto Hernandez .10 .05
☐ 130 Jose DeLeon .05 .02
☐ 131 Rod Bolton .05 .02
☐ 132 Wilson Alvarez .25 .11
☐ 133 Craig Grebeck .05 .02
☐ 134 Lance Johnson .10 .05
☐ 135 Kirk McCaskill .05 .02
☐ 136 Tim Raines .10 .05
☐ 137 Jeff Schwarz .05 .02
☐ 138 Warren Newson .05 .02
☐ 139 Norberto Martin .05 .02
☐ 140 Mike Huff .05 .02
☐ 141 Ozzie Guillen .10 .05
☐ 142 Alex Fernandez .10 .05
☐ 143 Joey Cora .10 .05
☐ 144 Jason Bere .10 .05
☐ 145 James Baldwin .10 .05
☐ 146 Esteban Beltre .05 .02
☐ 147 Julio Franco .10 .05
☐ 148 Matt Merullo .05 .02
☐ 149 Dan Pasqua .05 .02
☐ 150 Darrin Jackson .05 .02
☐ 151 Joe Carter .25 .11
☐ 152 Danny Cox .05 .02
☐ 153 Roberto Alomar .50 .23
☐ 154 Woody Williams .05 .02
☐ 155 Duane Ward .05 .02
☐ 156 Ed Sprague .10 .05
☐ 157 Domingo Martinez .05 .02
☐ 158 Pat Hentgen .40 .18
☐ 159 Shawn Green .25 .11
☐ 160 Dick Schofield .05 .02
☐ 161 Paul Molitor .50 .23
☐ 162 Darnell Coles .05 .02
☐ 163 Willie Canate .05 .02
☐ 164 Domingo Cedeno .05 .02
☐ 165 Pat Borders .05 .02
☐ 166 Greg Cadaret .05 .02
☐ 167 Tony Castillo .05 .02
☐ 168 Carlos Delgado .50 .23
☐ 169 Scott Brow .05 .02
☐ 170 Juan Guzman .10 .05
☐ 171 Al Leiter .10 .05
☐ 172 John Olerud .10 .05
☐ 173 Todd Stottlemyre .10 .05
☐ 174 Devon White .05 .02
☐ 175 Paul Spoljaric .05 .02
☐ 176 Randy Knorr .05 .02
☐ 177 Huck Flener .05 .02
☐ 178 Rob Butler .05 .02
☐ 179 Dave Stewart .10 .05
☐ 180 Mike Timlin .10 .05
☐ 181 Don Mattingly 1.50 .70
☐ 182 Mark Hutton .05 .02
☐ 183 Mike Gallego .05 .02
☐ 184 Jim Abbott .10 .05
☐ 185 Paul Gibson .05 .02
☐ 186 Scott Kamieniecki .05 .02
☐ 187 Sam Horn .05 .02
☐ 188 Melido Perez .05 .02
☐ 189 Randy Velarde .05 .02
☐ 190 Gerald Williams .05 .02
☐ 191 Dave Silvestri .05 .02
☐ 192 Jim Leyritz .10 .05
☐ 193 Steve Howe .05 .02
☐ 194 Russ Davis .40 .18
☐ 195 Paul Assenmacher .05 .02
☐ 196 Pat Kelly .05 .02
☐ 197 Mike Stanley .10 .05
☐ 198 Bernie Williams .50 .23
☐ 199 Paul O'Neill .25 .11
☐ 200 Donn Pall .05 .02
☐ 201 Xavier Hernandez .05 .02
☐ 202 James Austin .05 .02
☐ 203 Sterling Hitchcock .10 .05
☐ 204 Wade Boggs .50 .23
☐ 205 Jimmy Key .10 .05
☐ 206 Matt Nokes .05 .02
☐ 207 Terry Mulholland .05 .02
☐ 208 Luis Polonia .05 .02
☐ 209 Danny Tartabull .10 .05
☐ 210 Bob Wickman .05 .02
☐ 211 Len Dykstra .10 .05
☐ 212 Kim Batiste .05 .02
☐ 213 Tony Longmire .05 .02
☐ 214 Bobby Munoz .05 .02
☐ 215 Pete Incaviglia .05 .02
☐ 216 Doug Jones .10 .05
☐ 217 Mariano Duncan .05 .02
☐ 218 Jeff Juden .05 .02
☐ 219 Milt Thompson .05 .02
☐ 220 Dave West .05 .02
☐ 221 Roger Mason .05 .02
☐ 222 Tommy Greene .05 .02
☐ 223 Larry Andersen .05 .02
☐ 224 Jim Eisenreich .10 .05
☐ 225 Dave Hollins .05 .02
☐ 226 John Kruk .10 .05
☐ 227 Todd Pratt .05 .02
☐ 228 Ricky Jordan .05 .02
☐ 229 Curt Schilling .25 .11
☐ 230 Mike Williams .05 .02
☐ 231 Heathcliff Slocumb .10 .05
☐ 232 Ben Rivera .05 .02
☐ 233 Mike Lieberthal .05 .02
☐ 234 Mickey Morandini .05 .02
☐ 235 Danny Jackson .05 .02
☐ 236 Kevin Foster .05 .02
☐ 237 Darren Daulton .10 .05
☐ 238 Wes Chamberlain .05 .02
☐ 239 Tyler Green .05 .02
☐ 240 Kevin Stocker .10 .05
☐ 241 Juan Gonzalez 1.50 .70
☐ 242 Rick Honeycutt .05 .02
☐ 243 Bruce Hurst .05 .02
☐ 244 Steve Dreyer .05 .02
☐ 245 Brian Bohanon .05 .02
☐ 246 Benji Gil .05 .02
☐ 247 Jon Shave .05 .02
☐ 248 Manuel Lee .05 .02
☐ 249 Donald Harris .05 .02
☐ 250 Jose Canseco .50 .23
☐ 251 David Hulse .05 .02
☐ 252 Kenny Rogers .10 .05
☐ 253 Jeff Huson .05 .02
☐ 254 Dan Peltier .05 .02
☐ 255 Mike Scioscia .05 .02
☐ 256 Jack Armstrong .05 .02
☐ 257 Rob Ducey .05 .02
☐ 258 Will Clark .50 .23
☐ 259 Cris Carpenter .05 .02
☐ 260 Kevin Brown .10 .05
☐ 261 Jeff Frye .05 .02
☐ 262 Jay Howell .05 .02
☐ 263 Roger Pavlik .05 .02
☐ 264 Gary Redus .05 .02
☐ 265 Ivan Rodriguez .75 .35
☐ 266 Matt Whiteside .05 .02
☐ 267 Doug Strange .05 .02
☐ 268 Billy Ripken .05 .02
☐ 269 Dean Palmer .25 .11
☐ 270 Tom Henke .10 .05
☐ 271 Cal Ripken 3.00 1.35
☐ 272 Mark McLemore .05 .02
☐ 273 Sid Fernandez .05 .02
☐ 274 Sherman Obando .05 .02
☐ 275 Paul Carey .05 .02
☐ 276 Mike Oquist .05 .02
☐ 277 Alan Mills .05 .02
☐ 278 Harold Baines .10 .05
☐ 279 Mike Mussina .50 .23
☐ 280 Arthur Rhodes .05 .02
☐ 281 Kevin McGehee .05 .02
☐ 282 Mark Eichhorn .05 .02
☐ 283 Damon Buford .05 .02
☐ 284 Ben McDonald .10 .05
☐ 285 David Segui .10 .05
☐ 286 Brad Pennington .05 .02
☐ 287 Jamie Moyer .05 .02
☐ 288 Chris Hoiles .10 .05
☐ 289 Mike Cook .05 .02
☐ 290 Brady Anderson .40 .18
☐ 291 Chris Sabo .05 .02
☐ 292 Jack Voigt .05 .02
☐ 293 Jim Poole .05 .02
☐ 294 Jeff Tackett .05 .02
☐ 295 Rafael Palmeiro .40 .18
☐ 296 Alex Ochoa .10 .05
☐ 297 John O'Donoghue .05 .02

	MINT	NRMT
☐ 298 Tim Hulett	.05	.02
☐ 299 Mike Devereaux	.05	.02
☐ 300 Manny Alexander	.05	.02
☐ 301 Ozzie Smith	1.25	.55
☐ 302 Omar Olivares	.05	.02
☐ 303 Rheal Cormier	.05	.02
☐ 304 Donovan Osborne	.10	.05
☐ 305 Mark Whiten	.05	.02
☐ 306 Todd Zeile	.10	.05
☐ 307 Geronimo Pena	.05	.02
☐ 308 Brian Jordan	.10	.05
☐ 309 Luis Alicea	.05	.02
☐ 310 Ray Lankford	.25	.11
☐ 311 Stan Royer	.05	.02
☐ 312 Bob Tewksbury	.05	.02
☐ 313 Jose Oquendo	.05	.02
☐ 314 Steve Dixon	.05	.02
☐ 315 Rene Arocha	.05	.02
☐ 316 Bernard Gilkey	.25	.11
☐ 317 Gregg Jefferies	.25	.11
☐ 318 Rob Murphy	.05	.02
☐ 319 Tom Pagnozzi	.05	.02
☐ 320 Mike Perez	.05	.02
☐ 321 Tom Urbani	.05	.02
☐ 322 Allen Watson	.10	.05
☐ 323 Erik Pappas	.05	.02
☐ 324 Paul Kilgus	.05	.02
☐ 325 John Habyan	.05	.02
☐ 326 Rod Brewer	.05	.02
☐ 327 Rich Batchelor	.05	.02
☐ 328 Tripp Cromer	.05	.02
☐ 329 Gerald Perry	.05	.02
☐ 330 Les Lancaster	.05	.02
☐ 331 Ryne Sandberg	1.25	.55
☐ 332 Derrick May	.05	.02
☐ 333 Steve Buechele	.05	.02
☐ 334 Willie Banks	.05	.02
☐ 335 Larry Luebbers	.05	.02
☐ 336 Tommy Shields	.05	.02
☐ 337 Eric Yelding	.05	.02
☐ 338 Rey Sanchez	.05	.02
☐ 339 Mark Grace	.50	.23
☐ 340 Jose Bautista	.05	.02
☐ 341 Frank Castillo	.05	.02
☐ 342 Jose Guzman	.05	.02
☐ 343 Rafael Novoa	.05	.02
☐ 344 Karl Rhodes	.05	.02
☐ 345 Steve Trachsel	.05	.02
☐ 346 Rick Wilkins	.05	.02
☐ 347 Sammy Sosa	.50	.23
☐ 348 Kevin Roberson	.05	.02
☐ 349 Mark Parent	.05	.02
☐ 350 Randy Myers	.10	.05
☐ 351 Glenallen Hill	.05	.02
☐ 352 Lance Dickson	.05	.02
☐ 353 Shawn Boskie	.05	.02
☐ 354 Shawon Dunston	.05	.02
☐ 355 Dan Plesac	.05	.02
☐ 356 Jose Vizcaino	.05	.02
☐ 357 Willie Wilson	.05	.02
☐ 358 Turk Wendell	.05	.02
☐ 359 Mike Morgan	.05	.02
☐ 360 Jim Bullinger	.05	.02

1994 Stadium Club Team First Day Issue

This 360-card standard-size set features 30 players from 12 teams. First Day Issue cards were randomly packed one in every six 12-card packs; the odds of finding these insert cards in 20-card jumbo packs are one in three. Also one 1st Day Issue card was included in the 30-card team sets sold in blister packs. They are identical in design with the regular Stadium Club Team cards except for a holographic "1st Day Issue" emblem on the fronts.

	MINT	NRMT
COMPLETE SET (360)	600.00	275.00
COMMON CARD (1-360)	2.00	.90

*STARS: 10X to 20X BASIC CARDS ...
*YOUNG STARS: 7.5X to 15X BASIC CARDS

1994 Stadium Club Team Finest

This 12-card standard-size set consists of one player from each of the 12 teams featured in the 1994 Stadium Club team series. The cards were randomly inserted in 12-card foil packs. Also one card was included in the 30-card team sets sold in blister packs. The cards are identical in design with the regular series, except for the metallic sheen characteristic of the Finest series.

	MINT	NRMT
COMPLETE SET (12)	30.00	13.50
COMMON CARD (1-12)	1.00	.45

	MINT	NRMT
☐ 1 Roberto Alomar	2.00	.90
☐ 2 Barry Bonds	2.50	1.10
☐ 3 Len Dykstra	1.25	.55
☐ 4 Andres Galarraga	2.00	.90
☐ 5 Juan Gonzalez	5.00	2.20
☐ 6 David Justice	2.00	.90
☐ 7 Don Mattingly	4.00	1.80
☐ 8 Cal Ripken	8.00	3.60
☐ 9 Ryne Sandberg	4.00	1.80
☐ 10 Gary Sheffield	2.00	.90
☐ 11 Ozzie Smith	4.00	1.80
☐ 12 Frank Thomas	8.00	3.60

1995 Stadium Club

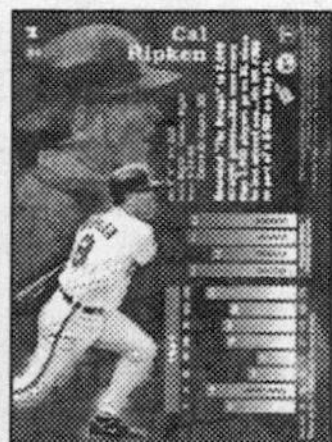

The 1995 Stadium Club baseball card collection was issued in three series of 270, 225 and 135 standard-size cards for a total of 630. The cards were distributed in 14-card packs at a suggested retail price of $2.50 and contained 24 packs per box. Cards feature players in full-bleed action photos with team logo and player's name in gold foil at the bottom of the card. Backs feature statistical bar graphs and action photos of players. Notable Rookie Cards include Mark Grudzielanek, Bobby Higginson and Hideo Nomo.

	MINT	NRMT
COMPLETE SET (630)	60.00	27.00
COMPLETE SERIES 1 (270)	25.00	11.00
COMPLETE SERIES 2 (225)	20.00	9.00
COMPLETE SERIES 3 (135)	15.00	6.75
COMMON CARD (1-630)	.15	.07

	MINT	NRMT
☐ 1 Cal Ripken	2.50	1.10
☐ 2 Bo Jackson	.30	.14
☐ 3 Bryan Harvey	.15	.07
☐ 4 Curt Schilling	.30	.14
☐ 5 Bruce Ruffin	.15	.07
☐ 6 Travis Fryman	.30	.14
☐ 7 Jim Abbott	.15	.07
☐ 8 David McCarty	.15	.07
☐ 9 Gary Gaetti	.30	.14
☐ 10 Roger Clemens	1.25	.55
☐ 11 Carlos Garcia	.15	.07
☐ 12 Lee Smith	.30	.14
☐ 13 Bobby Ayala	.15	.07
☐ 14 Charles Nagy	.30	.14
☐ 15 Lou Frazier	.15	.07
☐ 16 Rene Arocha	.15	.07
☐ 17 Carlos Delgado	.40	.18
☐ 18 Steve Finley	.30	.14
☐ 19 Ryan Klesko	.40	.18
☐ 20 Cal Eldred	.15	.07
☐ 21 Rey Sanchez	.15	.07
☐ 22 Ken Hill	.15	.07
☐ 23 Benito Santiago	.15	.07
☐ 24 Julian Tavarez	.15	.07
☐ 25 Jose Vizcaino	.15	.07
☐ 26 Andy Benes	.15	.07
☐ 27 Mariano Duncan	.15	.07
☐ 28 Checklist A	.15	.07
☐ 29 Shawon Dunston	.15	.07
☐ 30 Rafael Palmeiro	.40	.18
☐ 31 Dean Palmer	.30	.14
☐ 32 Andres Galarraga	.40	.18
☐ 33 Joey Cora	.30	.14
☐ 34 Mickey Tettleton	.15	.07
☐ 35 Barry Larkin	.40	.18
☐ 36 Carlos Baerga	.30	.14
☐ 37 Orel Hershiser	.30	.14
☐ 38 Jody Reed	.15	.07
☐ 39 Paul Molitor	.60	.25
☐ 40 Jim Edmonds	.60	.25
☐ 41 Bob Tewksbury	.15	.07
☐ 42 John Patterson	.15	.07
☐ 43 Ray McDavid	.15	.07
☐ 44 Zane Smith	.15	.07
☐ 45 Bret Saberhagen SE	.15	.07
☐ 46 Greg Maddux SE	1.00	.45
☐ 47 Frank Thomas SE	1.50	.70
☐ 48 Carlos Baerga SE	.30	.14
☐ 49 Billy Spiers	.15	.07
☐ 50 Stan Javier	.15	.07
☐ 51 Rex Hudler	.15	.07
☐ 52 Denny Hocking	.15	.07
☐ 53 Todd Worrell	.15	.07
☐ 54 Mark Clark	.15	.07
☐ 55 Hipolito Pichardo	.15	.07
☐ 56 Bob Wickman	.15	.07
☐ 57 Raul Mondesi	.40	.18
☐ 58 Steve Cooke	.15	.07
☐ 59 Rod Beck	.15	.07
☐ 60 Tim Davis	.15	.07
☐ 61 Jeff Kent	.15	.07
☐ 62 John Valentin	.30	.14
☐ 63 Alex Arias	.15	.07
☐ 64 Steve Reed	.15	.07
☐ 65 Ozzie Smith	.75	.35
☐ 66 Terry Pendleton	.30	.14
☐ 67 Kenny Rogers	.15	.07
☐ 68 Vince Coleman	.15	.07
☐ 69 Tom Pagnozzi	.15	.07
☐ 70 Roberto Alomar	.60	.25
☐ 71 Darrin Jackson	.15	.07
☐ 72 Dennis Eckersley	.40	.18
☐ 73 Jay Buhner	.40	.18
☐ 74 Darren Lewis	.15	.07
☐ 75 Dave Weathers	.15	.07
☐ 76 Matt Walbeck	.15	.07
☐ 77 Brad Ausmus	.15	.07
☐ 78 Danny Bautista	.15	.07
☐ 79 Bob Hamelin	.15	.07
☐ 80 Steve Trachsel	.15	.07
☐ 81 Ken Ryan	.15	.07
☐ 82 Chris Turner	.15	.07
☐ 83 David Segui	.15	.07
☐ 84 Ben McDonald	.15	.07
☐ 85 Wade Boggs	.60	.25
☐ 86 John VanderWal	.15	.07
☐ 87 Sandy Alomar Jr.	.30	.14
☐ 88 Ron Karkovice	.15	.07
☐ 89 Doug Jones	.15	.07
☐ 90 Gary Sheffield	.60	.25
☐ 91 Ken Caminiti	.60	.25
☐ 92 Chris Bosio	.15	.07
☐ 93 Kevin Tapani	.15	.07
☐ 94 Walt Weiss	.15	.07
☐ 95 Erik Hanson	.15	.07
☐ 96 Ruben Sierra	.15	.07
☐ 97 Nomar Garciaparra	4.00	1.80
☐ 98 Terrence Long	.60	.25
☐ 99 Jacob Shumate	.30	.14
☐ 100 Paul Wilson	.30	.14
☐ 101 Kevin Witt	.75	.35
☐ 102 Paul Konerko	3.00	1.35
☐ 103 Ben Grieve	3.00	1.35
☐ 104 Mark Johnson	.30	.14
☐ 105 Cade Gaspar	.30	.14
☐ 106 Mark Farris	.30	.14
☐ 107 Dustin Hermanson	.30	.14
☐ 108 Scott Elarton	.75	.35
☐ 109 Doug Million	.15	.07
☐ 110 Matt Smith	.30	.14
☐ 111 Brian Buchanan	.30	.14
☐ 112 Jayson Peterson	.30	.14
☐ 113 Bret Wagner	.30	.14
☐ 114 C.J. Nitkowski	.15	.07
☐ 115 Ramon Castro	.30	.14
☐ 116 Rafael Bournigal	.15	.07
☐ 117 Jeff Fassero	.15	.07
☐ 118 Bobby Bonilla	.30	.14
☐ 119 Ricky Gutierrez	.15	.07
☐ 120 Roger Pavlik	.15	.07
☐ 121 Mike Greenwell	.15	.07
☐ 122 Deion Sanders	.60	.25
☐ 123 Charlie Hayes	.15	.07
☐ 124 Paul O'Neill	.30	.14
☐ 125 Jay Bell	.30	.14
☐ 126 Royce Clayton	.15	.07
☐ 127 Willie Banks	.15	.07
☐ 128 Mark Wohlers	.30	.14
☐ 129 Todd Jones	.15	.07
☐ 130 Todd Stottlemyre	.15	.07
☐ 131 Will Clark	.40	.18
☐ 132 Wilson Alvarez	.30	.14
☐ 133 Chili Davis	.30	.14

☐ 134 Dave Burba .15 .07
☐ 135 Chris Hoiles .15 .07
☐ 136 Jeff Blauser .15 .07
☐ 137 Jeff Reboulet .15 .07
☐ 138 Bret Saberhagen .15 .07
☐ 139 Kirk Rueter .15 .07
☐ 140 Dave Nilsson .30 .14
☐ 141 Pat Borders .15 .07
☐ 142 Ron Darling .15 .07
☐ 143 Derek Bell .30 .14
☐ 144 Dave Hollins .15 .07
☐ 145 Juan Gonzalez 1.50 .70
☐ 146 Andre Dawson .40 .18
☐ 147 Jim Thome .60 .25
☐ 148 Larry Walker .60 .25
☐ 149 Mike Piazza 2.00 .90
☐ 150 Mike Perez .15 .07
☐ 151 Steve Avery .15 .07
☐ 152 Dan Wilson .30 .14
☐ 153 Andy Van Slyke .30 .14
☐ 154 Junior Felix .15 .07
☐ 155 Jack McDowell .15 .07
☐ 156 Danny Tartabull .15 .07
☐ 157 Willie Blair .15 .07
☐ 158 Wm.VanLandingham .15 .07
☐ 159 Robb Nen .15 .07
☐ 160 Lee Tinsley .15 .07
☐ 161 Ismael Valdes .30 .14
☐ 162 Juan Guzman .30 .14
☐ 163 Scott Servais .15 .07
☐ 164 Cliff Floyd .30 .14
☐ 165 Allen Watson .15 .07
☐ 166 Eddie Taubensee .15 .07
☐ 167 Scott Hemond .15 .07
☐ 168 Jeff Tackett .15 .07
☐ 169 Chad Curtis .15 .07
☐ 170 Rico Brogna .15 .07
☐ 171 Luis Polonia .15 .07
☐ 172 Checklist B .15 .07
☐ 173 Lance Johnson .30 .14
☐ 174 Sammy Sosa .40 .18
☐ 175 Mike Macfarlane .15 .07
☐ 176 Darryl Hamilton .15 .07
☐ 177 Rick Aguilera .15 .07
☐ 178 Dave West .15 .07
☐ 179 Mike Gallego .15 .07
☐ 180 Marc Newfield .30 .14
☐ 181 Steve Buechele .15 .07
☐ 182 David Wells .15 .07
☐ 183 Tom Glavine .40 .18
☐ 184 Joe Girardi .15 .07
☐ 185 Craig Biggio .40 .18
☐ 186 Eddie Murray .60 .25
☐ 187 Kevin Gross .15 .07
☐ 188 Sid Fernandez .15 .07
☐ 189 John Franco .30 .14
☐ 190 Bernard Gilkey .30 .14
☐ 191 Matt Williams .40 .18
☐ 192 Darrin Fletcher .15 .07
☐ 193 Jeff Conine .30 .14
☐ 194 Ed Sprague .15 .07
☐ 195 Eduardo Perez .15 .07
☐ 196 Scott Livingstone .15 .07
☐ 197 Ivan Rodriguez .75 .35
☐ 198 Orlando Merced .15 .07
☐ 199 Ricky Bones .15 .07
☐ 200 Javier Lopez .40 .18
☐ 201 Miguel Jimenez .15 .07
☐ 202 Terry McGriff .15 .07
☐ 203 Mike Lieberthal .15 .07
☐ 204 David Cone .30 .14
☐ 205 Todd Hundley .30 .14
☐ 206 Ozzie Guillen .15 .07
☐ 207 Alex Cole .15 .07
☐ 208 Tony Phillips .15 .07
☐ 209 Jim Eisenreich .30 .14
☐ 210 Greg Vaughn BES .15 .07
☐ 211 Barry Larkin BES .40 .18
☐ 212 Don Mattingly BES .60 .25
☐ 213 Mark Grace BES .40 .18
☐ 214 Jose Canseco BES .40 .18
☐ 215 Joe Carter BES .30 .14
☐ 216 David Cone BES .30 .14
☐ 217 Sandy Alomar Jr. BES .30 .14
☐ 218 Al Martin BES .15 .07
☐ 219 Roberto Kelly BES .15 .07
☐ 220 Paul Sorrento .15 .07
☐ 221 Tony Fernandez .15 .07
☐ 222 Stan Belinda .15 .07
☐ 223 Mike Stanley .15 .07
☐ 224 Doug Drabek .15 .07
☐ 225 Todd Van Poppel .15 .07
☐ 226 Matt Mieske .30 .14
☐ 227 Tino Martinez .60 .25
☐ 228 Andy Ashby .15 .07
☐ 229 Midre Cummings .15 .07
☐ 230 Jeff Frye .15 .07
☐ 231 Hal Morris .15 .07
☐ 232 Jose Lind .15 .07
☐ 233 Shawn Green .30 .14
☐ 234 Rafael Belliard .15 .07
☐ 235 Randy Myers .15 .07
☐ 236 Frank Thomas CE 1.50 .70
☐ 237 Darren Daulton CE .15 .07
☐ 238 Sammy Sosa CE .60 .25
☐ 239 Cal Ripken CE 1.25 .55
☐ 240 Jeff Bagwell CE .60 .25
☐ 241 Ken Griffey Jr. 3.00 1.35
☐ 242 Brett Butler .30 .14
☐ 243 Derrick May .15 .07
☐ 244 Pat Listach .15 .07
☐ 245 Mike Bordick .15 .07
☐ 246 Mark Langston .15 .07
☐ 247 Randy Velarde .15 .07
☐ 248 Julio Franco .30 .14
☐ 249 Chuck Knoblauch .40 .18
☐ 250 Bill Gullickson .15 .07
☐ 251 Dave Henderson .15 .07
☐ 252 Bret Boone .15 .07
☐ 253 Al Martin .30 .14
☐ 254 Armando Benitez .15 .07
☐ 255 Wil Cordero .15 .07
☐ 256 Al Leiter .30 .14
☐ 257 Luis Gonzalez .15 .07
☐ 258 Charlie O'Brien .15 .07
☐ 259 Tim Wallach .15 .07
☐ 260 Scott Sanders .15 .07
☐ 261 Tom Henke .15 .07
☐ 262 Otis Nixon .30 .14
☐ 263 Darren Daulton .30 .14
☐ 264 Manny Ramirez .60 .25
☐ 265 Bret Barberie .15 .07
☐ 266 Mel Rojas .15 .07
☐ 267 John Burkett .15 .07
☐ 268 Brady Anderson .40 .18
☐ 269 John Roper .15 .07
☐ 270 Shane Reynolds .15 .07
☐ 271 Barry Bonds .75 .35
☐ 272 Alex Fernandez .30 .14
☐ 273 Brian McRae .15 .07
☐ 274 Todd Zeile .15 .07
☐ 275 Greg Swindell .15 .07
☐ 276 Johnny Ruffin .15 .07
☐ 277 Troy Neel .15 .07
☐ 278 Eric Karros .30 .14
☐ 279 John Hudek .15 .07
☐ 280 Thomas Howard .15 .07
☐ 281 Joe Carter .40 .18
☐ 282 Mike Devereaux .15 .07
☐ 283 Butch Henry .15 .07
☐ 284 Reggie Jefferson .30 .14
☐ 285 Mark Lemke .15 .07
☐ 286 Jeff Montgomery .30 .14
☐ 287 Ryan Thompson .15 .07
☐ 288 Paul Shuey .15 .07
☐ 289 Mark McGwire 1.25 .55
☐ 290 Bernie Williams .60 .25
☐ 291 Mickey Morandini .15 .07
☐ 292 Scott Leius .15 .07
☐ 293 David Hulse .15 .07
☐ 294 Greg Gagne .15 .07
☐ 295 Moises Alou .30 .14
☐ 296 Geronimo Berroa .15 .07
☐ 297 Eddie Zambrano .15 .07
☐ 298 Alan Trammell .40 .18
☐ 299 Don Slaught .15 .07
☐ 300 Jose Rijo .15 .07
☐ 301 Joe Ausanio .15 .07
☐ 302 Tim Raines .15 .07
☐ 303 Melido Perez .15 .07
☐ 304 Kent Mercker .15 .07
☐ 305 James Mouton .15 .07
☐ 306 Luis Lopez .15 .07
☐ 307 Mike Kingery .15 .07
☐ 308 Willie Greene .15 .07
☐ 309 Cecil Fielder .30 .14
☐ 310 Scott Kamieniecki .15 .07
☐ 311 Mike Greenwell BES .15 .07
☐ 312 Bobby Bonilla BES .30 .14
☐ 313 Andres Galarraga BES .40 .18
☐ 314 Cal Ripken BES 1.25 .55
☐ 315 Matt Williams BES .40 .18
☐ 316 Tom Pagnozzi BES .15 .07
☐ 317 Len Dykstra BES .30 .14
☐ 318 Frank Thomas BES 1.50 .70
☐ 319 Kirby Puckett BES .60 .25
☐ 320 Mike Piazza BES 1.00 .45
☐ 321 Jason Jacome .15 .07
☐ 322 Brian Hunter .15 .07
☐ 323 Brent Gates .15 .07
☐ 324 Jim Converse .15 .07
☐ 325 Damion Easley .15 .07
☐ 326 Dante Bichette .40 .18
☐ 327 Kurt Abbott .15 .07
☐ 328 Scott Cooper .15 .07
☐ 329 Mike Henneman .15 .07
☐ 330 Orlando Miller .15 .07
☐ 331 John Kruk .30 .14
☐ 332 Jose Oliva .15 .07
☐ 333 Reggie Sanders .15 .07
☐ 334 Omar Vizquel .30 .14
☐ 335 Devon White .15 .07
☐ 336 Mike Morgan .15 .07
☐ 337 J.R. Phillips .15 .07
☐ 338 Gary DiSarcina .15 .07
☐ 339 Joey Hamilton .15 .07
☐ 340 Randy Johnson .60 .25
☐ 341 Jim Leyritz .15 .07
☐ 342 Bobby Jones .30 .14
☐ 343 Jaime Navarro .15 .07
☐ 344 Bip Roberts .15 .07
☐ 345 Steve Karsay .15 .07
☐ 346 Kevin Stocker .15 .07
☐ 347 Jose Canseco .40 .18
☐ 348 Bill Wegman .15 .07
☐ 349 Rondell White .40 .18
☐ 350 Mo Vaughn .75 .35
☐ 351 Joe Orsulak .15 .07
☐ 352 Pat Meares .15 .07
☐ 353 Albie Lopez .15 .07
☐ 354 Edgar Martinez .40 .18
☐ 355 Brian Jordan .30 .14
☐ 356 Tommy Greene .15 .07
☐ 357 Chuck Carr .15 .07
☐ 358 Pedro Astacio .15 .07
☐ 359 Russ Davis .15 .07
☐ 360 Chris Hammond .15 .07
☐ 361 Gregg Jefferies .30 .14
☐ 362 Shane Mack .15 .07
☐ 363 Fred McGriff .40 .18
☐ 364 Pat Rapp .15 .07
☐ 365 Bill Swift .15 .07
☐ 366 Checklist .15 .07
☐ 367 Robin Ventura .30 .14
☐ 368 Bobby Witt .15 .07
☐ 369 Karl Rhodes .15 .07
☐ 370 Eddie Williams .15 .07
☐ 371 John Jaha .15 .07
☐ 372 Steve Howe .15 .07
☐ 373 Leo Gomez .15 .07
☐ 374 Hector Fajardo .15 .07
☐ 375 Jeff Bagwell 1.25 .55
☐ 376 Mark Acre .15 .07
☐ 377 Wayne Kirby .15 .07
☐ 378 Mark Portugal .15 .07
☐ 379 Jesus Tavarez .15 .07
☐ 380 Jim Lindeman .15 .07
☐ 381 Don Mattingly 1.00 .45
☐ 382 Trevor Hoffman .30 .14
☐ 383 Chris Gomez .15 .07
☐ 384 Garret Anderson .40 .18
☐ 385 Bobby Munoz .15 .07
☐ 386 Jon Lieber .15 .07
☐ 387 Rick Helling .15 .07
☐ 388 Marvin Freeman .15 .07
☐ 389 Juan Castillo .15 .07
☐ 390 Jeff Cirillo .30 .14
☐ 391 Sean Berry .15 .07
☐ 392 Hector Carrasco .15 .07
☐ 393 Mark Grace .40 .18
☐ 394 Pat Kelly .15 .07
☐ 395 Tim Naehring .15 .07
☐ 396 Greg Pirkl .15 .07
☐ 397 John Smoltz .40 .18
☐ 398 Robby Thompson .15 .07
☐ 399 Rick White .15 .07
☐ 400 Frank Thomas 2.50 1.10
☐ 401 Jeff Conine CS .30 .14
☐ 402 Jose Valentin CS .15 .07
☐ 403 Carlos Baerga CS .30 .14
☐ 404 Rick Aguilera CS .15 .07
☐ 405 Wilson Alvarez CS .15 .07
☐ 406 Juan Gonzalez CS .75 .35
☐ 407 Barry Larkin CS .40 .18
☐ 408 Ken Hill CS .15 .07
☐ 409 Chuck Carr CS .15 .07
☐ 410 Tim Raines CS .15 .07
☐ 411 Bryan Eversgerd .15 .07
☐ 412 Phil Plantier .15 .07
☐ 413 Josias Manzanillo .15 .07
☐ 414 Roberto Kelly .15 .07
☐ 415 Rickey Henderson .40 .18
☐ 416 John Smiley .15 .07
☐ 417 Kevin Brown .30 .14
☐ 418 Jimmy Key .30 .14
☐ 419 Wally Joyner .30 .14
☐ 420 Roberto Hernandez .15 .07
☐ 421 Felix Fermin .15 .07
☐ 422 Checklist .15 .07
☐ 423 Greg Vaughn .15 .07
☐ 424 Ray Lankford .40 .18

☐ 425 Greg Maddux 2.00 .90
☐ 426 Mike Mussina .40 .18
☐ 427 Geronimo Pena .15 .07
☐ 428 David Nied .15 .07
☐ 429 Scott Erickson .15 .07
☐ 430 Kevin Mitchell .30 .14
☐ 431 Mike Lansing .15 .07
☐ 432 Brian Anderson .15 .07
☐ 433 Jeff King .30 .14
☐ 434 Ramon Martinez .30 .14
☐ 435 Kevin Seitzer .15 .07
☐ 436 Salomon Torres .15 .07
☐ 437 Brian L.Hunter .40 .18
☐ 438 Melvin Nieves .15 .07
☐ 439 Mike Kelly .15 .07
☐ 440 Marquis Grissom .30 .14
☐ 441 Chuck Finley .30 .14
☐ 442 Len Dykstra .30 .14
☐ 443 Ellis Burks .30 .14
☐ 444 Harold Baines .30 .14
☐ 445 Kevin Appier .30 .14
☐ 446 David Justice .60 .25
☐ 447 Darryl Kile .30 .14
☐ 448 John Olerud .30 .14
☐ 449 Greg McMichael .15 .07
☐ 450 Kirby Puckett 1.25 .55
☐ 451 Jose Valentin .30 .14
☐ 452 Rick Wilkins .15 .07
☐ 453 Arthur Rhodes .15 .07
☐ 454 Pat Hentgen .30 .14
☐ 455 Tom Gordon .15 .07
☐ 456 Tom Candiotti .15 .07
☐ 457 Jason Bere .15 .07
☐ 458 Wes Chamberlain .15 .07
☐ 459 Greg Colbrunn .15 .07
☐ 460 John Doherty .15 .07
☐ 461 Kevin Foster .15 .07
☐ 462 Mark Whiten .15 .07
☐ 463 Terry Steinbach .30 .14
☐ 464 Aaron Sele .15 .07
☐ 465 Kirt Manwaring .15 .07
☐ 466 Darren Hall .15 .07
☐ 467 Delino DeShields .15 .07
☐ 468 Andujar Cedeno .15 .07
☐ 469 Billy Ashley .15 .07
☐ 470 Kenny Lofton .75 .35
☐ 471 Pedro Munoz .15 .07
☐ 472 John Wetteland .30 .14
☐ 473 Tim Salmon .60 .25
☐ 474 Denny Neagle .30 .14
☐ 475 Tony Gwynn 1.50 .70
☐ 476 Vinny Castilla .40 .18
☐ 477 Steve Dreyer .15 .07
☐ 478 Jeff Shaw .15 .07
☐ 479 Chad Ogea .15 .07
☐ 480 Scott Ruffcorn .15 .07
☐ 481 Lou Whitaker .30 .14
☐ 482 J.T. Snow .30 .14
☐ 483 Rich Rowland .15 .07
☐ 484 Denny Martinez .30 .14
☐ 485 Pedro Martinez .60 .25
☐ 486 Rusty Greer .60 .25
☐ 487 Dave Fleming .15 .07
☐ 488 John Dettmer .15 .07
☐ 489 Albert Belle .75 .35
☐ 490 Ravelo Manzanillo .15 .07
☐ 491 Henry Rodriguez .15 .07
☐ 492 Andrew Lorraine .15 .07
☐ 493 Dwayne Hosey .15 .07
☐ 494 Mike Blowers .15 .07
☐ 495 Turner Ward .15 .07
☐ 496 Fred McGriff EC .40 .18
☐ 497 Sammy Sosa EC .60 .25
☐ 498 Barry Larkin EC .40 .18
☐ 499 Andres Galarraga EC .40 .18
☐ 500 Gary Sheffield EC .60 .25
☐ 501 Jeff Bagwell EC .60 .25
☐ 502 Mike Piazza EC 1.00 .45
☐ 503 Moises Alou EC .30 .14
☐ 504 Bobby Bonilla EC .30 .14
☐ 505 Darren Daulton EC .30 .14
☐ 506 Jeff King EC .30 .14
☐ 507 Ray Lankford EC .40 .18
☐ 508 Tony Gwynn EC .60 .25
☐ 509 Barry Bonds EC .40 .18
☐ 510 Cal Ripken EC 1.25 .55
☐ 511 Mo Vaughn EC .40 .18
☐ 512 Tim Salmon EC .60 .25
☐ 513 Frank Thomas EC 1.50 .70
☐ 514 Albert Belle EC .60 .25
☐ 515 Cecil Fielder EC .30 .14
☐ 516 Kevin Appier EC .30 .14
☐ 517 Greg Vaughn EC .15 .07
☐ 518 Kirby Puckett EC .60 .25
☐ 519 Paul O'Neill EC .15 .07
☐ 520 Ruben Sierra EC .15 .07
☐ 521 Ken Griffey Jr. EC 1.50 .70
☐ 522 Will Clark EC .40 .18
☐ 523 Joe Carter EC .40 .18
☐ 524 Antonio Osuna .15 .07
☐ 525 Glenallen Hill .15 .07
☐ 526 Alex Gonzalez .30 .14
☐ 527 Dave Stewart .30 .14
☐ 528 Ron Gant .30 .14
☐ 529 Jason Bates .15 .07
☐ 530 Mike Macfarlane .15 .07
☐ 531 Esteban Loaiza .15 .07
☐ 532 Joe Randa .15 .07
☐ 533 Dave Winfield .40 .18
☐ 534 Danny Darwin .15 .07
☐ 535 Pete Harnisch .15 .07
☐ 536 Joey Cora .30 .14
☐ 537 Jaime Navarro .15 .07
☐ 538 Marty Cordova .40 .18
☐ 539 Andujar Cedeno .15 .07
☐ 540 Mickey Tettleton .15 .07
☐ 541 Andy Van Slyke .30 .14
☐ 542 Carlos Perez .30 .14
☐ 543 Chipper Jones 2.00 .90
☐ 544 Tony Fernandez .15 .07
☐ 545 Tom Henke .15 .07
☐ 546 Pat Borders .15 .07
☐ 547 Chad Curtis .15 .07
☐ 548 Ray Durham .30 .14
☐ 549 Joe Oliver .15 .07
☐ 550 Jose Mesa .15 .07
☐ 551 Steve Finley .30 .14
☐ 552 Otis Nixon .30 .14
☐ 553 Jacob Brumfield .15 .07
☐ 554 Bill Swift .15 .07
☐ 555 Quilvio Veras .15 .07
☐ 556 Hideo Nomo UER 3.00 1.35
Wins and IP totals reversed
☐ 557 Joe Vitiello .15 .07
☐ 558 Mike Perez .15 .07
☐ 559 Charlie Hayes .15 .07
☐ 560 Brad Radke .75 .35
☐ 561 Darren Bragg .30 .14
☐ 562 Orel Hershiser .30 .14
☐ 563 Edgardo Alfonzo .60 .25
☐ 564 Doug Jones .15 .07
☐ 565 Andy Pettitte 1.00 .45
☐ 566 Benito Santiago .15 .07
☐ 567 John Burkett .15 .07
☐ 568 Brad Clontz .15 .07
☐ 569 Jim Abbott .15 .07
☐ 570 Joe Rosselli .15 .07
☐ 571 Mark Grudzielanek .50 .23
☐ 572 Dustin Hermanson .15 .07
☐ 573 Benji Gil .15 .07
☐ 574 Mark Whiten .15 .07
☐ 575 Mike Ignasiak .15 .07
☐ 576 Kevin Ritz .15 .07
☐ 577 Paul Quantrill .15 .07
☐ 578 Andre Dawson .40 .18
☐ 579 Jerald Clark .15 .07
☐ 580 Frank Rodriguez .15 .07
☐ 581 Mark Kiefer .15 .07
☐ 582 Trevor Wilson .15 .07
☐ 583 Gary Wilson .15 .07
☐ 584 Andy Stankiewicz .15 .07
☐ 585 Felipe Lira .15 .07
☐ 586 Mike Mimbs .15 .07
☐ 587 Jon Nunnally .30 .14
☐ 588 Tomas Perez .30 .14
☐ 589 Checklist .15 .07
☐ 590 Todd Hollandsworth .30 .14
☐ 591 Roberto Petagine .15 .07
☐ 592 Mariano Rivera .60 .25
☐ 593 Mark McLemore .15 .07
☐ 594 Bobby Witt .15 .07
☐ 595 Jose Offerman .15 .07
☐ 596 Jason Christiansen .15 .07
☐ 597 Jeff Manto .15 .07
☐ 598 Jim Dougherty .15 .07
☐ 599 Juan Acevedo .15 .07
☐ 600 Troy O'Leary .15 .07
☐ 601 Ron Villone .15 .07
☐ 602 Tripp Cromer .15 .07
☐ 603 Steve Scarsone .15 .07
☐ 604 Lance Parrish .15 .07
☐ 605 Ozzie Timmons .15 .07
☐ 606 Ray Holbert .15 .07
☐ 607 Tony Phillips .15 .07
☐ 608 Phil Plantier .15 .07
☐ 609 Shane Andrews .15 .07
☐ 610 Heathcliff Slocumb .15 .07
☐ 611 Bobby Higginson 1.00 .45
☐ 612 Bob Tewksbury .15 .07
☐ 613 Terry Pendleton .30 .14
☐ 614 Scott Cooper TA .15 .07
☐ 615 John Wetteland TA .30 .14
☐ 616 Ken Hill TA .15 .07
☐ 617 Marquis Grissom TA .30 .14
☐ 618 Larry Walker TA .60 .25
☐ 619 Derek Bell TA .15 .07
☐ 620 David Cone TA .30 .14
☐ 621 Ken Caminiti TA .60 .25
☐ 622 Jack McDowell TA .15 .07
☐ 623 Vaughn Eshelman TA .15 .07
☐ 624 Brian McRae TA .15 .07
☐ 625 Gregg Jefferies TA .15 .07
☐ 626 Kevin Brown TA .30 .14
☐ 627 Lee Smith TA .30 .14
☐ 628 Tony Tarasco TA .15 .07
☐ 629 Brett Butler TA .30 .14
☐ 630 Jose Canseco TA .40 .18

1995 Stadium Club First Day Issue

Parallel to the basic first series Stadium Club issue, these cards, were primarily inserted in second series Topps packs. They were also inserted at a rate of ten per Topps factory set. Some logos have been transferred from "common" players to the fronts of "star" players. Nine double printed cards were issued in both first and second series Topps packs. Those cards are as follows: 29, 39, 79, 96, 131, 149, 153, 168 and 197.

	MINT	NRMT
COMPLETE SET (270)	275.00	125.00
COMMON CARD (1-270)	1.00	.45
COMMON DP (29/39/79/96)	.50	.23
COMMON DP (153/168/197)	.50	.23

*STARS: 7.5X to 15X BASIC CARDS ..
*YOUNG STARS: 6X to 12X BASIC CARDS
*DOUBLE PRINT STARS: 2X to 4X BASIC CARDS

1995 Stadium Club Members Only Parallel

This set is a parallel to the regular 1995 Stadium Club set.These cards are identical to their regular issue counterparts except for the distinctive "Members Only" logo. According to Topps, only 4,000 factory sets were issued through the Topps Stadium Club at a price of $200 each. A certificate of authenicity carrying the serial number accompanied each set. In addition to the 630 regular cards, the factory set includes Members Only versions of the following inserts: Crystal Ball, Clear Cut, Power Zone, Ring Leaders, Super Skills, Virtual Extremists and Virtual Reality (listed separately). Only the insert cards are listed below. Please use the multipliers for values on the basic cards.

	MINT	NRMT
SET W/O VIRTUAL REALITY (755)	250.00	110.00
COMMON REG.CARD (1-630)	.25	.11

*MEMBERS ONLY: 3X TO 6X BASIC CARDS

☐ CB1 Chipper Jones 15.00 6.75
☐ CB2 Dustin Hermanson 2.00 .90
☐ CB3 Ray Durham 2.00 .90
☐ CB4 Phil Nevin 1.00 .45
☐ CB5 Billy Ashley 1.00 .45
☐ CB6 Shawn Green 2.00 .90
☐ CB7 Jason Bates 1.00 .45
☐ CB8 Benji Gil 1.00 .45
☐ CB9 Marty Cordova 2.00 .90
☐ CB10 Quilvio Veras 2.00 .90
☐ CB11 Mark Grudzielanek 3.00 1.35
☐ CB12 Ruben Rivera 4.00 1.80
☐ CB13 Bill Pulsipher 2.00 .90
☐ CB14 Derek Jeter 15.00 6.75
☐ CB15 LaTroy Hawkins 1.00 .45
☐ CC1 Mike Piazza 12.00 5.50
☐ CC2 Ruben Sierra 1.00 .45
☐ CC3 Tony Gwynn 8.00 3.60
☐ CC4 Frank Thomas 15.00 6.75
☐ CC5 Fred McGriff 2.00 .90
☐ CC6 Rafael Palmeiro 1.00 .45
☐ CC7 Bobby Bonilla 1.00 .45
☐ CC8 Chili Davis 1.00 .45
☐ CC9 Hal Morris 1.00 .45
☐ CC10 Jose Canseco 2.50 1.10
☐ CC11 Jay Bell 1.00 .45
☐ CC12 Kirby Puckett 8.00 3.60
☐ CC13 Gary Sheffield 3.00 1.35
☐ CC14 Bob Hamelin 1.00 .45
☐ CC15 Jeff Bagwell 6.00 2.70
☐ CC16 Albert Belle 5.00 2.20
☐ CC17 Sammy Sosa 3.00 1.35
☐ CC18 Ken Griffey Jr. 15.00 6.75
☐ CC19 Todd Zeile 1.00 .45
☐ CC20 Mo Vaughn 4.00 1.80
☐ CC21 Moises Alou 1.50 .70
☐ CC22 Paul O'Neill 1.50 .70
☐ CC23 Andres Galarraga 1.00 .45

☐ CC24 Greg Vaughn	1.50	.70
☐ CC25 Len Dykstra	1.50	.70
☐ CC26 Joe Carter	.50	.23
☐ CC27 Barry Bonds	4.00	1.80
☐ CC28 Cecil Fielder	1.50	.70
☐ PZ1 Jeff Bagwell	6.00	2.70
☐ PZ2 Albert Belle	8.00	3.60
☐ PZ3 Barry Bonds	4.00	1.80
☐ PZ4 Joe Carter	2.00	.90
☐ PZ5 Cecil Fielder	1.50	.70
☐ PZ6 Andres Galarraga	2.00	.90
☐ PZ7 Ken Griffey Jr.	15.00	6.75
☐ PZ8 Paul Molitor	4.00	1.80
☐ PZ9 Fred McGriff	2.00	.90
☐ PZ10 Rafael Palmeiro	2.00	.90
☐ PZ11 Frank Thomas	15.00	6.75
☐ PZ12 Matt Williams	2.00	.90
☐ RL1 Jeff Bagwell	6.00	2.70
☐ RL2 Mark McGwire	5.00	2.20
☐ RL3 Ozzie Smith	4.00	1.80
☐ RL4 Paul Molitor	4.00	1.80
☐ RL5 Darryl Strawberry	.50	.23
☐ RL6 Eddie Murray	4.00	1.80
☐ RL7 Tony Gwynn	8.00	3.60
☐ RL8 Jose Canseco	2.50	1.10
☐ RL9 Howard Johnson	1.00	.45
☐ RL10 Andre Dawson	2.00	.90
☐ RL11 Matt Williams	2.00	.90
☐ RL12 Tim Raines	1.50	.70
☐ RL13 Fred McGriff	2.00	.90
☐ RL14 Ken Griffey Jr.	15.00	6.75
☐ RL15 Gary Sheffield	3.00	1.35
☐ RL16 Dennis Eckersley	1.50	.70
☐ RL17 Kevin Mitchell	1.00	.45
☐ RL18 Will Clark	2.50	1.10
☐ RL19 Darren Daulton	1.00	.45
☐ RL20 Paul O'Neill	1.50	.70
☐ RL21 Julio Franco	1.00	.45
☐ RL22 Albert Belle	8.00	3.60
☐ RL23 Juan Gonzalez	8.00	3.60
☐ RL24 Kirby Puckett	8.00	3.60
☐ RL25 Joe Carter	2.00	.90
☐ RL26 Frank Thomas	15.00	6.75
☐ RL27 Cal Ripken	15.00	6.75
☐ RL28 John Olerud	1.00	.45
☐ RL29 Ruben Sierra	1.00	.45
☐ RL30 Barry Bonds	4.00	1.80
☐ RL31 Cecil Fielder	1.50	.70
☐ RL32 Roger Clemens	3.00	1.35
☐ RL33 Don Mattingly	8.00	3.60
☐ RL34 Terry Pendleton	1.50	.70
☐ RL35 Rickey Henderson	2.00	.90
☐ RL36 Dave Winfield	2.00	.90
☐ RL37 Edgar Martinez	2.00	.90
☐ RL38 Wade Boggs	1.00	.45
☐ RL39 Willie McGee	1.00	.45
☐ RL40 Andres Galarraga	2.00	.90
☐ SS1 Roberto Alomar	4.00	1.80
☐ SS2 Barry Bonds	4.00	1.80
☐ SS3 Jay Buhner	1.00	.45
☐ SS4 Chuck Carr	1.00	.45
☐ SS5 Don Mattingly	8.00	3.60
☐ SS6 Raul Mondesi	2.00	.90
☐ SS7 Tim Salmon	2.00	.90
☐ SS8 Deion Sanders	2.00	.90
☐ SS9 Devon White	1.00	.45
☐ SS10 Mark Whiten	1.00	.45
☐ SS11 Ken Griffey Jr.	15.00	6.75
☐ SS12 Marquis Grissom	1.50	.70
☐ SS13 Paul O'Neill	1.50	.70
☐ SS14 Kenny Lofton	4.00	1.80
☐ SS15 Larry Walker	3.00	1.35
☐ SS16 Scott Cooper	1.00	.45
☐ SS17 Barry Larkin	2.00	.90
☐ SS18 Matt Williams	2.00	.90
☐ SS19 John Wetteland	1.50	.70
☐ SS20 Randy Johnson	3.00	1.35
☐ VRE1 Barry Bonds	4.00	1.80
☐ VRE2 Ken Griffey Jr.	15.00	6.75
☐ VRE3 Jeff Bagwell	6.00	2.70
☐ VRE4 Albert Belle	8.00	3.60
☐ VRE5 Frank Thomas	15.00	6.75
☐ VRE6 Tony Gwynn	8.00	3.60
☐ VRE7 Kenny Lofton	4.00	1.80
☐ VRE8 Deion Sanders	2.00	.90
☐ VRE9 Ken Hill	1.00	.45
☐ VRE10 Jimmy Key	1.50	.70

1995 Stadium Club Super Team Division Winners

Each of these six team sets was available exclusively by mailing in the corresponding winning 1994 Super Team card. Each team set was distributed in a clear plastic sealed wrapper and included ten player cards and a Super Team card (of which was stamped "REDEEMED" on back). The card design and numbering for the player cards parallels regular issue 1995 Stadium Club cards. In fact, the only way to tell these cards apart is by the gold foil "Division Winner" logo on each card front. The cards are listed below alphabetically by team; the prefixes B, D, I, M, R and RS have been added to denote Braves, Dodgers, Indians, Mariners, Reds and Red Sox.

	MINT	NRMT
COMP.BRAVES SET (11)	8.00	3.60
COMP.DODGERS SET (11)	8.00	3.60
COMP.INDIANS SET (11)	6.00	2.70
COMP.MARINERS SET (11)	6.00	2.70
COMP.REDS SET (11)	3.00	1.35
COMP.RED SOX SET (11)	4.00	1.80
COMMON CARD	.25	.11
MINOR STARS	.40	.18
☐ B1T Braves DW Super Team	.50	.23
Jeff Blauser		
Terry Pendleton		
☐ B19 Ryan Klesko	.75	.35
☐ B128 Mark Wohlers	.25	.11
☐ B151 Steve Avery	.25	.11
☐ B183 Tom Glavine	.40	.18
☐ B200 Javy Lopez	.60	.25
☐ B393 Fred McGriff	.60	.25
☐ B397 John Smoltz	.40	.18
☐ B425 Greg Maddux	3.00	1.35
☐ B446 Dave Justice	.75	.35
☐ B543 Chipper Jones	3.00	1.35
☐ D7T Dodgers DW Super Team	1.00	.45
Mike Piazza		
☐ D57 Raul Mondesi	.75	.35
☐ D149 Mike Piazza	3.00	1.35
☐ D161 Ismael Valdez	.40	.18
☐ D242 Brett Butler	.40	.18
☐ D259 Tim Wallach	.25	.11
☐ D278 Eric Karros	.40	.18
☐ D434 Ramon Martinez	.40	.18
☐ D456 Tom Candiotti	.25	.11
☐ D467 Delino DeShields	.25	.11
☐ D556 Hideo Nomo	5.00	2.20
☐ I19T Indians DW Super Team	1.00	.45
Carlos Baerga		
Albert Belle		
Kenny Lofton		
☐ I36 Carlos Baerga	.40	.18
☐ I147 Jim Thome	1.00	.45
☐ I186 Eddie Murray	.75	.35
☐ I264 Manny Ramirez	1.00	.45
☐ I334 Omar Vizquel	.75	.35
☐ I470 Kenny Lofton	1.00	.45
☐ I484 Dennis Martinez	.40	.18
☐ I489 Albert Belle	1.50	.70
☐ I550 Jose Mesa	.40	.18
☐ I562 Orel Hershiser	.40	.18
☐ M26T Mariners DW Super Team	.60	.25
Mike Blowers		
Jay Buhner		
☐ M73 Jay Buhner	.60	.25
☐ M92 Chris Bosio	.25	.11
☐ M152 Dan Wilson	.40	.18
☐ M227 Tino Martinez	.75	.35
☐ M241 Ken Griffey Jr.	5.00	2.20
☐ M340 Randy Johnson	.75	.35
☐ M354 Edgar Martinez	.60	.25
☐ M421 Felix Fermin	.25	.11
☐ M494 Mike Blowers	.25	.11
☐ M536 Joey Cora	.25	.11
☐ RE3T Reds DW Super Team	.75	.35
Barry Larkin		
Reggie Sanders		
☐ RE35 Barry Larkin	.60	.25
☐ RE231 Hal Morris	.25	.11
☐ RE252 Bret Boone	.25	.11
☐ RE280 Thomas Howard	.25	.11
☐ RE300 Jose Rijo	.25	.11
☐ RE333 Reggie Sanders	.40	.18
☐ RE392 Hector Carrasco	.25	.11
☐ RE416 John Smiley	.25	.11
☐ RE528 Ron Gant	.40	.18
☐ RE566 Benito Santiago	.25	.11
☐ RS1T Red Sox DW Super Team	.60	.25
Luis Rivera		
John Valentin		
☐ RS10 Roger Clemens	1.50	.70
☐ RS62 John Valentin	.25	.11
☐ RS121 Mike Greenwell	.25	.11
☐ RS160 Lee Tinsley	.25	.11
☐ RS347 Jose Canseco	.75	.35
☐ RS350 Mo Vaughn	1.25	.55
☐ RS395 Tim Naehring	.25	.11
☐ RS464 Aaron Sele	.25	.11
☐ RS530 Mike Macfarlane	.25	.11
☐ RS600 Troy O'Leary	.25	.11

1995 Stadium Club Super Team World Series

Because of the strike-interrupted season, the 1994 Stadium Club Super Team insert program had to be finished up with the 1995 product. Collectors who redeemed the 1994 Atlanta Braves Super Team card received: 1) a complete 630-card 1995 Stadium Club parallel set stamped with a special gold foil World Series logo (of which was mailed in two separate series of 585 and 45 cards) 2) a Division Winner parallel Braves team set along with the winner card stamped "redeemed" on its back 3) a jumbo-sized (3" by 5") parallel Master Photo Braves team set. Collectors who redeemed the 1994 Cleveland Indians Super Team card got parallel Indians Division Winner and Master Photo team sets. Collectors who redeemed the 1994 Super Team card of a division winner (Dodgers, Mariners, Red Sox and Reds) received a Division Winner parallel team set of the respective team that they sent in. All of these winner cards parallel the 1995 Stadium Club regular series cards.

	MINT	NRMT
COMP.WORLD SERIES SET (585)	100.00	45.00
COMP.SER.3 EC AND TA SET (45)	15.00	6.75
COMMON CARD (1-630)	.15	.07
*STARS: 1X to 2X BASIC CARDS		
*YOUNG STARS: .75X to 1.5X BASIC CARDS		

1995 Stadium Club Super Team Master Photos

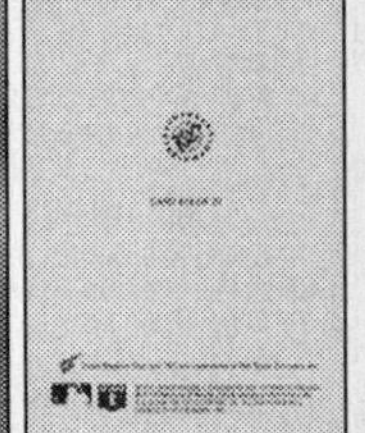

This 20-card set was distributed in two separate 10-card sealed team bags. The cards were available exclusively by mailing in a Braves or Indians 1994 Super Team card. These oversized cards (5" by 7") feature a reproduction of the player's standard 1995 Stadium Club card enframed around a shining blue background. Unlike the standard issue cards they parallel, these are numbered X of 20.

	MINT	NRMT
COMPLETE SET (20)	22.00	10.00
COMP.BRAVES SET (10)	12.00	5.50
COMP.INDIANS SET (10)	10.00	4.50
COMMON CARD (1-20)	.50	.23
☐ 1 Steve Avery	.50	.23
☐ 2 Tom Glavine	.75	.35
☐ 3 Chipper Jones	5.00	2.20
☐ 4 Dave Justice	1.50	.70
☐ 5 Ryan Klesko	1.00	.45
☐ 6 Javy Lopez	1.00	.45
☐ 7 Greg Maddux	5.00	2.20
☐ 8 Fred McGriff	1.00	.45
☐ 9 John Smoltz	.75	.35
☐ 10 Mark Wohlers	.75	.35
☐ 11 Carlos Baerga	.75	.35
☐ 12 Albert Belle	2.00	.90
☐ 13 Orel Hershiser	.75	.35
☐ 14 Kenny Lofton	2.00	.90
☐ 15 Dennis Martinez	.75	.35
☐ 16 Jose Mesa	.75	.35
☐ 17 Eddie Murray	1.50	.70
☐ 18 Manny Ramirez	1.50	.70
☐ 19 Jim Thome	1.50	.70
☐ 20 Omar Vizquel	1.00	.45

1995 Stadium Club Clear Cut

Randomly inserted at a rate of one in 24 hobby and retail packs, this 28-card set features a full color action photo of the player against a clear acetate background with the player's name printed vertically. Backs highlight the season achievement of the player on a thin horizontal strip.

	MINT	NRMT
COMPLETE SET (28)	80.00	36.00
COMPLETE SET (14)	40.00	18.00
COMPLETE SERIES 2 (14)	40.00	18.00
COMMON CARD (CC1-CC28)	1.50	.70

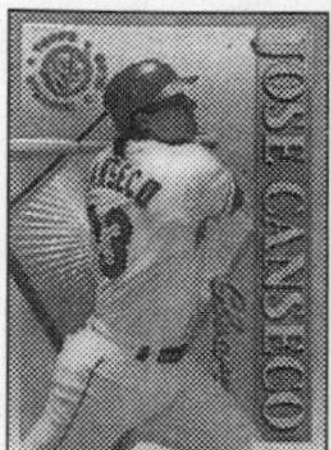

Card	MINT	NRMT
☐ CC1 Mike Piazza	15.00	6.75
☐ CC2 Ruben Sierra	1.50	.70
☐ CC3 Tony Gwynn	10.00	4.50
☐ CC4 Frank Thomas	20.00	9.00
☐ CC5 Fred McGriff	2.50	1.10
☐ CC6 Rafael Palmeiro	2.50	1.10
☐ CC7 Bobby Bonilla	2.00	.90
☐ CC8 Chili Davis	2.00	.90
☐ CC9 Hal Morris	1.50	.70
☐ CC10 Jose Canseco	2.50	1.10
☐ CC11 Jay Bell	1.50	.70
☐ CC12 Kirby Puckett	10.00	4.50
☐ CC13 Gary Sheffield	3.00	1.35
☐ CC14 Bob Hamelin	1.50	.70
☐ CC15 Jeff Bagwell	10.00	4.50
☐ CC16 Albert Belle	6.00	2.70
☐ CC17 Sammy Sosa	3.00	1.35
☐ CC18 Ken Griffey Jr.	25.00	11.00
☐ CC19 Todd Zeile	1.50	.70
☐ CC20 Mo Vaughn	6.00	2.70
☐ CC21 Moises Alou	2.00	.90
☐ CC22 Paul O'Neill	2.00	.90
☐ CC23 Andres Galarraga	2.50	1.10
☐ CC24 Greg Vaughn	1.50	.70
☐ CC25 Len Dykstra	2.00	.90
☐ CC26 Joe Carter	2.50	1.10
☐ CC27 Barry Bonds	6.00	2.70
☐ CC28 Cecil Fielder	2.00	.90

1995 Stadium Club Crunch Time

This 20-card standard-size set features home run hitters and was randomly inserted in first series rack packs. Fronts are action illustrations of players on gold foil paper with the Crunch Time logo and player's name printed in gold foil at the bottom of the card. The horizontal backs include a pie chart and statistics of player offensive output and player action photos. The cards are numbered as "X" of 20 in the upper right corner.

	MINT	NRMT
COMPLETE SET (20)	40.00	18.00
COMMON CARD (1-20)	.75	.35
☐ 1 Jeff Bagwell	4.00	1.80
☐ 2 Kirby Puckett	4.00	1.80
☐ 3 Frank Thomas	8.00	3.60
☐ 4 Albert Belle	2.50	1.10
☐ 5 Julio Franco	.75	.35
☐ 6 Jose Canseco	1.25	.55
☐ 7 Paul Molitor		
☐ 8 Joe Carter	1.25	.55
☐ 9 Ken Griffey Jr.	10.00	4.50
☐ 10 Larry Walker		
☐ 11 Dante Bichette	1.25	.55
☐ 12 Carlos Baerga	.75	.35
☐ 13 Fred McGriff	1.25	.55
☐ 14 Ruben Sierra	.75	.35
☐ 15 Will Clark	1.25	.55
☐ 16 Moises Alou	.75	.35
☐ 17 Rafael Palmeiro	1.25	.55
☐ 18 Travis Fryman	.75	.35
☐ 19 Barry Bonds	2.50	1.10
☐ 20 Cal Ripken	8.00	3.60

1995 Stadium Club Crystal Ball

This 15-card standard-size set was inserted into series three packs at a rate of one in 24. Fifteen leading 1995 rookies and prospects were featured in this set. The fronts feature a player photo in the middle with the words "Crystal Ball" on the top with the player's name on the bottom. The backs have season-by-season stats with a sentence about the player's accomplishments during that season. A player photo in the upper right is set in a crystal ball. The player is identified on the top and the cards are numbered with a "CB" prefix in the upper left corner.

	MINT	NRMT
COMPLETE SET (15)	60.00	27.00
COMMON CARD (CB1-CB15)	2.00	.90
☐ CB1 Chipper Jones	25.00	11.00
☐ CB2 Dustin Hermanson	2.00	.90
☐ CB3 Ray Durham	4.00	1.80
☐ CB4 Phil Nevin	2.00	.90
☐ CB5 Billy Ashley	2.00	.90
☐ CB6 Shawn Green	3.00	1.35
☐ CB7 Jason Bates	2.00	.90
☐ CB8 Benji Gil	2.00	.90
☐ CB9 Marty Cordova	4.00	1.80
☐ CB10 Quilvio Veras	2.00	.90
☐ CB11 Mark Grudzielanek	4.00	1.80
☐ CB12 Ruben Rivera	6.00	2.70
☐ CB13 Bill Pulsipher	2.00	.90
☐ CB14 Derek Jeter	25.00	11.00
☐ CB15 LaTroy Hawkins	2.00	.90

1995 Stadium Club Phone Cards

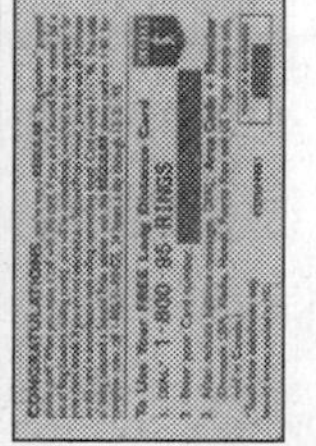

These phone cards were randomly inserted into packs. The prizes for these cards were as follows. The Gold Winner card was redeemable for the ring depicted on the front of the card. The silver winner card was redeemable for a set of all 39 phone cards. The regular winner card was redeemable for a ring leaders set. The fronts feature a photo of a specific ring while the backs have game information. If the card was not a winner for any of the prizes, it was still good for three minutes of time. The phone cards expired on January 1, 1996. If the PIN number is revealed the value is a percentage of an untouched card.

	MINT	NRMT
COMPLETE REGULAR SET (13)	10.00	4.50
COMMON REGULAR CARD	1.00	.45
COMPLETE SILVER SET (13)	20.00	9.00
COMMON SILVER CARD	2.00	.90
COMPLETE GOLD SET (13)	30.00	13.50
COMMON GOLD CARD	3.00	1.35

*PIN NUMBER REVEALED: .25X to .50X BASIC CARDS

1995 Stadium Club Power Zone

This 12-card standard-size set was inserted into series three packs at a rate of one in 24. The fronts feature a player photo and his name on the right. The left side of

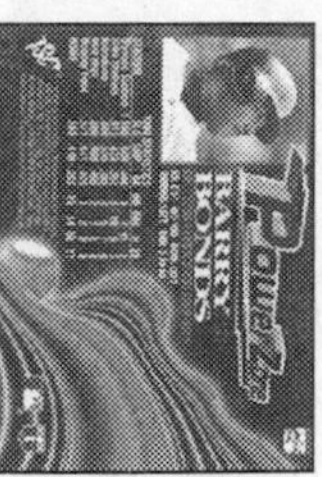

the card has the bat powering through an explosion. The words "Power Zone" are on the bottom. The horizontal backs feature a close-up photo, some vital information as well as some seasonal highlights. The cards are numbered in the upper right corner with a "PZ" prefix. The set is sequenced in alphabetical order.

	MINT	NRMT
COMPLETE SET (12)	90.00	40.00
COMMON CARD (PZ1-PZ12)	2.00	.90
☐ PZ1 Jeff Bagwell	12.00	5.50
☐ PZ2 Albert Belle	6.00	2.70
☐ PZ3 Barry Bonds	8.00	3.60
☐ PZ4 Joe Carter	4.00	1.80
☐ PZ5 Cecil Fielder	2.00	.90
☐ PZ6 Andres Galarraga	4.00	1.80
☐ PZ7 Ken Griffey Jr.	30.00	13.50
☐ PZ8 Paul Molitor	5.00	2.20
☐ PZ9 Fred McGriff	4.00	1.80
☐ PZ10 Rafael Palmeiro	4.00	1.80
☐ PZ11 Frank Thomas	25.00	11.00
☐ PZ12 Matt Williams	4.00	1.80

1995 Stadium Club Ring Leaders

Randomly inserted in packs, this set features players who have won various awards or titles. This set was also redeemable as a prize with winning regular phone cards. This set features Stadium Club's "Power Matrix Technology," which makes the cards shine and glow. The horizontal fronts feature a player photo, rings in both upper corners as well as other designs that make for a very busy front. The backs have information on how the player earned his rings, along with a player photo and some other pertinent information.

	MINT	NRMT
COMPLETE SET (40)	175.00	80.00
COMPLETE SERIES 1 (20)	65.00	29.00
COMPLETE SERIES 2 (20)	100.00	45.00
COMMON CARD (RL1-RL40)	2.00	.90
☐ RL1 Jeff Bagwell	12.00	5.50
☐ RL2 Mark McGwire	10.00	4.50
☐ RL3 Ozzie Smith	8.00	3.60
☐ RL4 Paul Molitor	5.00	2.20
☐ RL5 Darryl Strawberry	3.00	1.35
☐ RL6 Eddie Murray	5.00	2.20
☐ RL7 Tony Gwynn	12.00	5.50
☐ RL8 Jose Canseco	4.00	1.80
☐ RL9 Howard Johnson	2.00	.90
☐ RL10 Andre Dawson	4.00	1.80
☐ RL11 Matt Williams	4.00	1.80
☐ RL12 Tim Raines	2.00	.90
☐ RL13 Fred McGriff	4.00	1.80
☐ RL14 Ken Griffey Jr.	30.00	13.50
☐ RL15 Gary Sheffield	5.00	2.20
☐ RL16 Dennis Eckersley	4.00	1.80
☐ RL17 Kevin Mitchell	2.00	.90
☐ RL18 Will Clark	4.00	1.80
☐ RL19 Darren Daulton	3.00	1.35
☐ RL20 Paul O'Neill	3.00	1.35
☐ RL21 Julio Franco	2.00	.90
☐ RL22 Albert Belle	12.00	5.50
☐ RL23 Juan Gonzalez	15.00	6.75
☐ RL24 Kirby Puckett	12.00	5.50

☐ RL25 Joe Carter	4.00	1.80
☐ RL26 Frank Thomas	25.00	11.00
☐ RL27 Cal Ripken	25.00	11.00
☐ RL28 John Olerud	2.00	.90
☐ RL29 Ruben Sierra	2.00	.90
☐ RL30 Barry Bonds	6.00	2.70
☐ RL31 Cecil Fielder	3.00	1.35
☐ RL32 Roger Clemens	10.00	4.50
☐ RL33 Don Mattingly	12.00	5.50
☐ RL34 Terry Pendleton	2.00	.90
☐ RL35 Rickey Henderson	4.00	1.80
☐ RL36 Dave Winfield	4.00	1.80
☐ RL37 Edgar Martinez	4.00	1.80
☐ RL38 Wade Boggs	5.00	2.20
☐ RL39 Willie McGee	2.00	.90
☐ RL40 Andres Galarraga	4.00	1.80

1995 Stadium Club Super Skills

This 20-card set was randomly inserted into hobby packs. The full-bleed front features a player photo against a multi-colored background. The background was enhanced using Stadium Club's "Power Matrix" Technology. The "Super Skills" logo is in the lower left corner. The backs have a full-bleed photo with a description of the player's special skill. The cards are numbered in the upper left as "X" of 9.

	MINT	NRMT
COMPLETE SET (20)	70.00	32.00
COMPLETE SERIES 1 (9)	30.00	13.50
COMPLETE SERIES 2 (11)	40.00	18.00
COMMON CARD (SS1-SS20)	1.50	.70
☐ SS1 Roberto Alomar	4.00	1.80
☐ SS2 Barry Bonds	6.00	2.70
☐ SS3 Jay Buhner	3.00	1.35
☐ SS4 Chuck Carr	1.50	.70
☐ SS5 Don Mattingly	12.00	5.50
☐ SS6 Raul Mondesi	3.00	1.35
☐ SS7 Tim Salmon	4.00	1.80
☐ SS8 Deion Sanders	4.00	1.80
☐ SS9 Devon White	1.50	.70
☐ SS10 Mark Whiten	1.50	.70
☐ SS11 Ken Griffey Jr.	25.00	11.00
☐ SS12 Marquis Grissom	2.00	.90
☐ SS13 Paul O'Neill	2.00	.90
☐ SS14 Kenny Lofton	6.00	2.70
☐ SS15 Larry Walker	4.00	1.80
☐ SS16 Scott Cooper	1.50	.70
☐ SS17 Barry Larkin	3.00	1.35
☐ SS18 Matt Williams	3.00	1.35
☐ SS19 John Wetteland	2.00	.90
☐ SS20 Randy Johnson	4.00	1.80

1995 Stadium Club Virtual Extremists

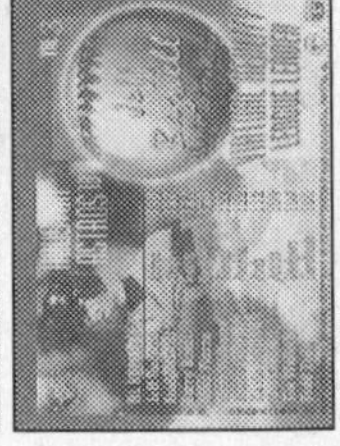

This 10-card set was inserted randomly into second series rack packs. The fronts feature a player photo against a baseball backdrop. The words "VR Extremist" are spelled vertically down the right side while the player name is in silver foil on the bottom. All of this is surrounded by blue and purple borders. The horizontal backs feature projected full-season 1994 stats. The cards are numbered with a "VRE" prefix in the upper right corner.

	MINT	NRMT
COMPLETE SET (10)	120.00	55.00
COMMON CARD (VRE1-VRE10)	2.50	1.10
☐ VRE1 Barry Bonds	10.00	4.50
☐ VRE2 Ken Griffey Jr.	40.00	18.00
☐ VRE3 Jeff Bagwell	15.00	6.75
☐ VRE4 Albert Belle	10.00	4.50
☐ VRE5 Frank Thomas	30.00	13.50
☐ VRE6 Tony Gwynn	20.00	9.00
☐ VRE7 Kenny Lofton	10.00	4.50
☐ VRE8 Deion Sanders	8.00	3.60
☐ VRE9 Ken Hill	2.50	1.10
☐ VRE10 Jimmy Key	3.00	1.35

1995 Stadium Club Virtual Reality

This 270-card standard-size set parallels a selection of cards from the regular 1995 Stadium Club set. Differences include the words "Virtual Reality" printed above the player's name and the numbering on the back. These cards were inserted in the first two Stadium Club series on a one per pack, two per rack pack basis.

	MINT	NRMT
COMPLETE SET (270)	90.00	40.00
COMPLETE SERIES 1 (135)	45.00	20.00
COMPLETE SERIES 2 (135)	45.00	20.00
COMMON CARD (1-270)	.25	.11
☐ 1 Cal Ripken	5.00	2.20
☐ 2 Travis Fryman	.50	.23
☐ 3 Jim Abbott	.35	.16
☐ 4 Gary Gaetti	.35	.16
☐ 5 Roger Clemens	2.50	1.10
☐ 6 Carlos Garcia	.25	.11
☐ 7 Lee Smith	.35	.16
☐ 8 Bobby Ayala	.25	.11
☐ 9 Charles Nagy	.35	.16
☐ 10 Rene Arocha	.25	.11
☐ 11 Carlos Delgado	.50	.23
☐ 12 Steve Finley	.35	.16
☐ 13 Ryan Klesko	.75	.35
☐ 14 Cal Eldred	.25	.11
☐ 15 Rey Sanchez	.25	.11
☐ 16 Ken Hill	.25	.11
☐ 17 Jose Vizcaino	.25	.11
☐ 18 Andy Benes	.35	.16
☐ 19 Shawon Dunston	.25	.11
☐ 20 Rafael Palmeiro	.50	.23
☐ 21 Dean Palmer	.35	.16
☐ 22 Joey Cora	.35	.16
☐ 23 Mickey Tettleton	.25	.11
☐ 24 Barry Larkin	.50	.23
☐ 25 Carlos Baerga	.35	.16
☐ 26 Orel Hershiser	.35	.16
☐ 27 Jody Reed	.25	.11
☐ 28 Paul Molitor	.75	.35
☐ 29 Jim Edmonds	.75	.35
☐ 30 Bob Tewksbury	.25	.11
☐ 31 Ray McDavid	.25	.11
☐ 32 Stan Javier	.25	.11
☐ 33 Todd Worrell	.25	.11
☐ 34 Bob Wickman	.25	.11
☐ 35 Raul Mondesi	.75	.35
☐ 36 Rod Beck	.25	.11
☐ 37 Jeff Kent	.25	.11
☐ 38 John Valentin	.35	.16
☐ 39 Ozzie Smith	1.50	.70
☐ 40 Terry Pendleton	.35	.16
☐ 41 Kenny Rogers	.25	.11
☐ 42 Vince Coleman	.25	.11
☐ 43 Roberto Alomar	.75	.35
☐ 44 Darrin Jackson	.25	.11
☐ 45 Dennis Eckersley	.50	.23
☐ 46 Jay Buhner	.50	.23
☐ 47 Dave Weathers	.25	.11
☐ 48 Danny Bautista	.25	.11
☐ 49 Bob Hamelin	.25	.11
☐ 50 Steve Trachsel	.25	.11
☐ 51 Ben McDonald	.25	.11
☐ 52 Wade Boggs	.75	.35
☐ 53 Sandy Alomar Jr.	.25	.11
☐ 54 Ron Karkovice	.25	.11
☐ 55 Doug Jones	.25	.11
☐ 56 Gary Sheffield	.75	.35
☐ 57 Ken Caminiti	.75	.35
☐ 58 Kevin Tapani	.25	.11
☐ 59 Ruben Sierra	.25	.11
☐ 60 Bobby Bonilla	.35	.16
☐ 61 Deion Sanders	.75	.35
☐ 62 Charlie Hayes	.25	.11
☐ 63 Paul O'Neill	.35	.16
☐ 64 Jay Bell	.25	.11
☐ 65 Todd Jones	.25	.11
☐ 66 Todd Stottlemyre	.25	.11
☐ 67 Will Clark	.50	.23
☐ 68 Wilson Alvarez	.25	.11
☐ 69 Chili Davis	.35	.16
☐ 70 Chris Hoiles	.25	.11
☐ 71 Bret Saberhagen	.25	.11
☐ 72 Dave Nilsson	.25	.11
☐ 73 Derek Bell	.25	.11
☐ 74 Juan Gonzalez	3.00	1.35
☐ 75 Andre Dawson	.75	.35
☐ 76 Jim Thome	1.25	.55
☐ 77 Larry Walker	.75	.35
☐ 78 Mike Piazza	4.00	1.80
☐ 79 Dan Wilson	.25	.11
☐ 80 Junior Felix	.25	.11
☐ 81 Jack McDowell	.25	.11
☐ 82 Danny Tartabull	.25	.11
☐ 83 William Van Landingham	.25	.11
☐ 84 Robb Nen	.35	.16
☐ 85 Ismael Valdes	.25	.11
☐ 86 Juan Guzman	.25	.11
☐ 87 Cliff Floyd	.25	.11
☐ 88 Rico Brogna	.25	.11
☐ 89 Luis Polonia	.25	.11
☐ 90 Lance Johnson	.25	.11
☐ 91 Sammy Sosa	.75	.35
☐ 92 Dave West	.25	.11
☐ 93 Tom Glavine	.50	.23
☐ 94 Joe Girardi	.25	.11
☐ 95 Craig Biggio	.50	.23
☐ 96 Eddie Murray	.75	.35
☐ 97 Kevin Gross	.25	.11
☐ 98 John Franco	.35	.16
☐ 99 Matt Williams	.50	.23
☐ 100 Darrin Fletcher	.25	.11
☐ 101 Jeff Conine	.35	.16
☐ 102 Ed Sprague	.25	.11
☐ 103 Ivan Rodriguez	1.50	.70
☐ 104 Orlando Merced	.25	.11
☐ 105 Ricky Bones	.25	.11
☐ 106 David Cone	.35	.16
☐ 107 Todd Hundley	.35	.16
☐ 108 Alex Cole	.25	.11
☐ 109 Tony Phillips	.25	.11
☐ 110 Jim Eisenreich	.35	.16
☐ 111 Paul Sorrento	.25	.11
☐ 112 Mike Stanley	.25	.11
☐ 113 Doug Drabek	.25	.11
☐ 114 Matt Mieske	.25	.11
☐ 115 Tino Martinez	.75	.35
☐ 116 Midre Cummings	.25	.11
☐ 117 Hal Morris	.25	.11
☐ 118 Shawn Green	.35	.16
☐ 119 Randy Myers	.25	.11
☐ 120 Ken Griffey Jr.	6.00	2.70
☐ 121 Brett Butler	.35	.16
☐ 122 Julio Franco	.35	.16
☐ 123 Chuck Knoblauch	.75	.35
☐ 124 Bret Boone	.25	.11
☐ 125 Wil Cordero	.25	.11
☐ 126 Luis Gonzalez	.25	.11
☐ 127 Tim Wallach	.25	.11
☐ 128 Scott Sanders	.25	.11
☐ 129 Tom Henke	.25	.11
☐ 130 Otis Nixon	.25	.11
☐ 131 Darren Daulton	.35	.16
☐ 132 Manny Ramirez	1.50	.70
☐ 133 Bret Barberie	.25	.11
☐ 134 Brady Anderson	.50	.23
☐ 135 Shane Reynolds	.25	.11
☐ 136 Barry Bonds	1.50	.70
☐ 137 Alex Fernandez	.35	.16
☐ 138 Brian McRae	.25	.11
☐ 139 Todd Zeile	.25	.11
☐ 140 Greg Swindell	.25	.11
☐ 141 Troy Neel	.25	.11
☐ 142 Eric Karros	.35	.16
☐ 143 John Hudek	.25	.11
☐ 144 Joe Carter	.35	.16
☐ 145 Mike Devereaux	.25	.11
☐ 146 Butch Henry	.25	.11

☐ 147 Mark Lemke .25 .11
☐ 148 Jeff Montgomery .25 .11
☐ 149 Ryan Thompson .25 .11
☐ 150 Bernie Williams .75 .35
☐ 151 Scott Leius .25 .11
☐ 152 Greg Gagne .25 .11
☐ 153 Moises Alou .35 .16
☐ 154 Geronimo Berroa .25 .11
☐ 155 Alan Trammell .50 .23
☐ 156 Don Slaught .25 .11
☐ 157 Jose Rijo .25 .11
☐ 158 Tim Raines .35 .16
☐ 159 Melido Perez .25 .11
☐ 160 Kent Mercker .25 .11
☐ 161 James Mouton .25 .11
☐ 162 Luis Lopez .25 .11
☐ 163 Mike Kingery .25 .11
☐ 164 Cecil Fielder .35 .16
☐ 165 Scott Kamieniecki .25 .11
☐ 166 Brent Gates .25 .11
☐ 167 Jason Jacome .25 .11
☐ 168 Dante Bichette .50 .23
☐ 169 Kurt Abbott .25 .11
☐ 170 Mike Henneman .25 .11
☐ 171 John Kruk .35 .16
☐ 172 Jose Oliva .25 .11
☐ 173 Reggie Sanders .25 .11
☐ 174 Omar Vizquel .35 .16
☐ 175 Devon White .25 .11
☐ 176 Mark McGwire 2.00 .90
☐ 177 Gary DiSarcina .25 .11
☐ 178 Joey Hamilton .35 .16
☐ 179 Randy Johnson .75 .35
☐ 180 Jim Leyritz .25 .11
☐ 181 Bobby Jones .25 .11
☐ 182 Bip Roberts .25 .11
☐ 183 Jose Canseco .50 .23
☐ 184 Mo Vaughn 1.50 .70
☐ 185 Edgar Martinez .50 .23
☐ 186 Tommy Greene .25 .11
☐ 187 Chuck Carr .25 .11
☐ 188 Pedro Astacio .25 .11
☐ 189 Shane Mack .25 .11
☐ 190 Fred McGriff .50 .23
☐ 191 Pat Rapp .25 .11
☐ 192 Bill Swift .25 .11
☐ 193 Robin Ventura .35 .16
☐ 194 Bobby Witt .25 .11
☐ 195 Steve Howe .25 .11
☐ 196 Leo Gomez .25 .11
☐ 197 Hector Fajardo .25 .11
☐ 198 Jeff Bagwell 2.50 1.10
☐ 199 Rondell White .35 .16
☐ 200 Don Mattingly 2.00 .90
☐ 201 Trevor Hoffman .35 .16
☐ 202 Chris Gomez .25 .11
☐ 203 Bobby Munoz .25 .11
☐ 204 Marvin Freeman .25 .11
☐ 205 Sean Berry .25 .11
☐ 206 Mark Grace .50 .23
☐ 207 Pat Kelly .25 .11
☐ 208 Eddie Williams .25 .11
☐ 209 Frank Thomas 5.00 2.20
☐ 210 Bryan Eversgerd .25 .11
☐ 211 Phil Plantier .25 .11
☐ 212 Roberto Kelly .25 .11
☐ 213 Rickey Henderson .50 .23
☐ 214 John Smiley .25 .11
☐ 215 Kevin Brown .35 .16
☐ 216 Jimmy Key .25 .11
☐ 217 Wally Joyner .35 .16
☐ 218 Roberto Hernandez .25 .11
☐ 219 Felix Fermin .25 .11
☐ 220 Greg Vaughn .25 .11
☐ 221 Ray Lankford .35 .16
☐ 222 Greg Maddux 4.00 1.80
☐ 223 Mike Mussina .75 .35
☐ 224 David Nied .25 .11
☐ 225 Scott Erickson .25 .11
☐ 226 Kevin Mitchell .25 .11
☐ 227 Brian Anderson .25 .11
☐ 228 Jeff King .25 .11
☐ 229 Ramon Martinez .35 .16
☐ 230 Kevin Seitzer .25 .11
☐ 231 Marquis Grissom .35 .16
☐ 232 Chuck Finley .25 .11
☐ 233 Len Dykstra .35 .16
☐ 234 Ellis Burks .35 .16
☐ 235 Harold Baines .35 .16
☐ 236 Kevin Appier .35 .16
☐ 237 David Justice .75 .35
☐ 238 Darryl Kile .35 .16
☐ 239 John Olerud .35 .16
☐ 240 Greg McMichael .25 .11
☐ 241 Kirby Puckett 2.50 1.10
☐ 242 Jose Valentin .25 .11
☐ 243 Rick Wilkins .25 .11
☐ 244 Pat Hentgen .50 .23
☐ 245 Tom Gordon .25 .11
☐ 246 Tom Candiotti .25 .11
☐ 247 Jason Bere .25 .11
☐ 248 Wes Chamberlain .25 .11
☐ 249 Jeff Cirillo .25 .11
☐ 250 Kevin Foster .25 .11
☐ 251 Mark Whiten .25 .11
☐ 252 Terry Steinbach .35 .16
☐ 253 Aaron Sele .25 .11
☐ 254 Kirt Manwaring .25 .11
☐ 255 Delino DeShields .25 .11
☐ 256 Andujar Cedeno .25 .11
☐ 257 Kenny Lofton 1.50 .70
☐ 258 John Wetteland .35 .16
☐ 259 Tim Salmon .75 .35
☐ 260 Denny Neagle .35 .16
☐ 261 Tony Gwynn 3.00 1.35
☐ 262 Lou Whitaker .35 .16
☐ 263 J.T. Snow .35 .16
☐ 264 Denny Martinez .35 .16
☐ 265 Pedro Martinez .75 .35
☐ 266 Rusty Greer .50 .23
☐ 267 Dave Fleming .25 .11
☐ 268 John Dettmer .25 .11
☐ 269 Albert Belle 3.00 1.35
☐ 270 Henry Rodriguez .25 .11

1995 Stadium Club Virtual Reality Members Only

These cards parallel the regular 1995 Stadium Club Stadium Club Virtual Reality cards. The only difference is that they all have a Stadium Club Members Only logo imprinted on the front. These cards were distributed as part of the package of material that members of the "Stadium Club Members Only" club received when they ordered the 1995 parallel master set.

	MINT	NRMT
COMPLETE FACT.SET (270)	100.00	45.00
COMMON CARD (1-270)	.25	.11

*MEMBERS ONLY: 2X BASIC CARDS.

1995 Stadium Club Members Only

Topps produced a 50-card boxed set for each of the four major sports. With their club membership, members received one set of their choice and had the option of purchasing additional sets for $10.00 each. Player section was based on 1994 leaders from both leagues in various statistical categories. The five Finest cards (46-50) represent Topps' selection of the top rookies of 1994. The color action photos on the fronts have brightly-colored backgrounds and carry the distinctive Topps Stadium Club Members Only gold foil seal. The backs present a second color photo and player profile.

	MINT	NRMT
COMPLETE SET (50)	20.00	9.00
COMMON CARD (1-50)	.10	.05

☐ 1 Moises Alou .20 .09
☐ 2 Jeff Bagwell 2.00 .90
☐ 3 Albert Belle 1.25 .55
☐ 4 Andy Benes .10 .05
☐ 5 Dante Bichette .35 .16
☐ 6 Craig Biggio .35 .16
☐ 7 Wade Boggs .50 .23
☐ 8 Barry Bonds .60 .25
☐ 9 Brett Butler .20 .09
☐ 10 Jose Canseco .35 .16
☐ 11 Joe Carter .20 .09
☐ 12 Vince Coleman .10 .05
☐ 13 Jeff Conine .20 .09
☐ 14 Cecil Fielder .20 .09
☐ 15 John Franco .20 .09
☐ 16 Julio Franco .20 .09
☐ 17 Travis Fryman .20 .09
☐ 18 Andres Galarraga .50 .23
☐ 19 Ken Griffey Jr. 4.00 1.80
☐ 20 Marquis Grissom .20 .09
☐ 21 Tony Gwynn 1.50 .70
☐ 22 Ken Hill .10 .05
☐ 23 Randy Johnson .60 .25
☐ 24 Lance Johnson .10 .05
☐ 25 Jimmy Key .20 .09
☐ 26 Chuck Knoblauch .50 .23
☐ 27 Ray Lankford .20 .09
☐ 28 Darren Lewis .10 .05
☐ 29 Kenny Lofton .60 .25
☐ 30 Greg Maddux 2.50 1.10
☐ 31 Fred McGriff .35 .16
☐ 32 Kevin Mitchell .10 .05
☐ 33 Paul Molitor .60 .25
☐ 34 Hal Morris .10 .05
☐ 35 Paul O'Neill .20 .09
☐ 36 Rafael Palmeiro .35 .16
☐ 37 Tony Phillips .10 .05
☐ 38 Mike Piazza 2.50 1.10
☐ 39 Kirby Puckett 1.50 .70
☐ 40 Cal Ripken 3.00 1.35
☐ 41 Deion Sanders .50 .23
☐ 42 Lee Smith .20 .09
☐ 43 Frank Thomas 3.00 1.35
☐ 44 Larry Walker .50 .23
☐ 45 Matt Williams .35 .16
☐ 46 Manny Ramirez .50 .23
☐ 47 Joey Hamilton .20 .09
☐ 48 Raul Mondesi .50 .23
☐ 49 Bob Hamelin .10 .05
☐ 50 Ryan Klesko .35 .16

1995 Stadium Club Members Only Finest Bronze

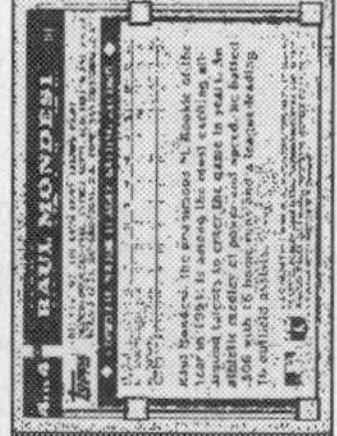

As a special bonus along with the complete 1995 Stadium Club Members Only factory set, members received these four cards featuring the 1994 Rookie of the Year and Cy Young Award Winners. The first shipment included series 1 and 2 cards as well as two of the Finest Bronze cards. The second shipment included series 3 cards and the remaining two Finest Bronze cards. The cards feature chromium metallized graphics, mounted on bronze and factory sealed in clear resin. Also, collectors got one of thsese cards if they only ordered one series. Bob Hamelin (series 1), Greg Maddux (Series 2) and David Cone (series 3). Mondesi was only available if one bought a complete set.

	MINT	NRMT
COMPLETE SET (4)	50.00	22.00
COMMON CARD (1-4)	3.00	1.35

☐ 1 Bob Hamelin 3.00 1.35
☐ 2 Greg Maddux 40.00 18.00
☐ 3 David Cone 5.00 2.20
☐ 4 Raul Mondesi 10.00 4.50

1996 Stadium Club

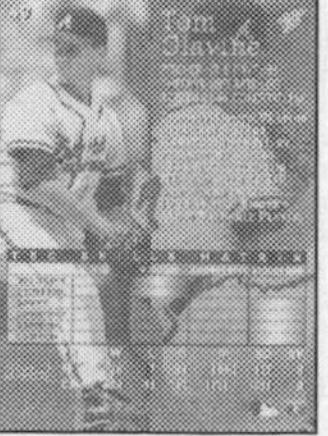

The 1996 Stadium Club set consists of 450 cards. The product was primarily distributed in first and second series foil-wrapped packs.There was also a factory set, which included the Mantle insert cards, packaged in cereal box type cartons and made available through retail outlets. Card fronts feature glossy, full-bleed color action photos. At the bottom, the player's name is gold foil stamped on a team color-coded nameplate that is highlighted by gold foil stamping. The colorful backs carry biography, highlights, and the TSC Skills Matrix. The set includes a Team TSC subset (181-270). These subset cards were slightly shortprinted in comparison to the other cards in the set.

	MINT	NRMT
COMPLETE SET (450)	70.00	32.00
COMP.CEREAL SET (454)	80.00	36.00
COMPLETE SERIES 1 (225)	35.00	16.00
COMPLETE SERIES 2 (225)	35.00	16.00
COMMON (1-180/271-450)	.15	.07
COMMON TSC SP (181-270)	.25	.11

Card	MINT	NRMT
☐ 1 Hideo Nomo	1.50	.70
☐ 2 Paul Molitor	.60	.25
☐ 3 Garret Anderson	.30	.14
☐ 4 Jose Mesa	.30	.14
☐ 5 Vinny Castilla	.30	.14
☐ 6 Mike Mussina	.60	.25
☐ 7 Ray Durham	.30	.14
☐ 8 Jack McDowell	.15	.07
☐ 9 Juan Gonzalez	1.50	.70
☐ 10 Chipper Jones	2.00	.90
☐ 11 Deion Sanders	.60	.25
☐ 12 Rondell White	.30	.14
☐ 13 Tom Henke	.30	.14
☐ 14 Derek Bell	.15	.07
☐ 15 Randy Myers	.15	.07
☐ 16 Randy Johnson	.60	.25
☐ 17 Len Dykstra	.30	.14
☐ 18 Bill Pulsipher	.15	.07
☐ 19 Greg Colbrunn	.15	.07
☐ 20 David Wells	.15	.07
☐ 21 Chad Curtis	.15	.07
☐ 22 Roberto Hernandez	.30	.14
☐ 23 Kirby Puckett	1.25	.55
☐ 24 Joe Vitiello	.15	.07
☐ 25 Roger Clemens	1.25	.55
☐ 26 Al Martin	.15	.07
☐ 27 Chad Ogea	.15	.07
☐ 28 David Segui	.15	.07
☐ 29 Joey Hamilton	.30	.14
☐ 30 Dan Wilson	.15	.07
☐ 31 Chad Fonville	.15	.07
☐ 32 Bernard Gilkey	.30	.14
☐ 33 Kevin Seitzer	.15	.07
☐ 34 Shawn Green	.30	.14
☐ 35 Rick Aguilera	.15	.07
☐ 36 Gary DiSarcina	.15	.07
☐ 37 Jaime Navarro	.15	.07
☐ 38 Doug Jones	.15	.07
☐ 39 Brent Gates	.15	.07
☐ 40 Dean Palmer	.30	.14
☐ 41 Pat Rapp	.15	.07
☐ 42 Tony Clark	.60	.25
☐ 43 Bill Swift	.15	.07
☐ 44 Randy Velarde	.15	.07
☐ 45 Matt Williams	.40	.18
☐ 46 John Mabry	.30	.14
☐ 47 Mike Fetters	.15	.07
☐ 48 Orlando Miller	.15	.07
☐ 49 Tom Glavine	.30	.14
☐ 50 Delino DeShields	.15	.07
☐ 51 Scott Erickson	.15	.07
☐ 52 Andy Van Slyke	.30	.14
☐ 53 Jim Bullinger	.15	.07
☐ 54 Lyle Mouton	.15	.07
☐ 55 Bret Saberhagen	.15	.07
☐ 56 Benito Santiago	.15	.07
☐ 57 Dan Miceli	.15	.07
☐ 58 Carl Everett	.15	.07
☐ 59 Rod Beck	.15	.07
☐ 60 Phil Nevin	.15	.07
☐ 61 Jason Giambi	.30	.14
☐ 62 Paul Menhart	.15	.07
☐ 63 Eric Karros	.30	.14
☐ 64 Allen Watson	.15	.07
☐ 65 Jeff Cirillo	.30	.14
☐ 66 Lee Smith	.30	.14
☐ 67 Sean Berry	.15	.07
☐ 68 Luis Sojo	.15	.07
☐ 69 Jeff Montgomery	.15	.07
☐ 70 Todd Hundley	.30	.14
☐ 71 John Burkett	.15	.07
☐ 72 Mark Gubicza	.15	.07
☐ 73 Don Mattingly	1.00	.45
☐ 74 Jeff Brantley	.15	.07
☐ 75 Matt Walbeck	.15	.07
☐ 76 Steve Parris	.15	.07
☐ 77 Ken Caminiti	.60	.25
☐ 78 Kirt Manwaring	.15	.07
☐ 79 Greg Vaughn	.15	.07
☐ 80 Pedro Martinez	.60	.25
☐ 81 Benji Gil	.15	.07
☐ 82 Heathcliff Slocumb	.15	.07
☐ 83 Joe Girardi	.15	.07
☐ 84 Sean Bergman	.15	.07
☐ 85 Matt Karchner	.15	.07
☐ 86 Butch Huskey	.30	.14
☐ 87 Mike Morgan	.15	.07
☐ 88 Todd Worrell	.30	.14
☐ 89 Mike Bordick	.15	.07
☐ 90 Bip Roberts	.15	.07
☐ 91 Mike Hampton	.15	.07
☐ 92 Troy O'Leary	.15	.07
☐ 93 Wally Joyner	.15	.07
☐ 94 Dave Stevens	.15	.07
☐ 95 Cecil Fielder	.30	.14
☐ 96 Wade Boggs	.60	.25
☐ 97 Hal Morris	.15	.07
☐ 98 Mickey Tettleton	.15	.07
☐ 99 Jeff Kent	.15	.07
☐ 100 Denny Martinez	.30	.14
☐ 101 Luis Gonzalez	.15	.07
☐ 102 John Jaha	.15	.07
☐ 103 Javier Lopez	.30	.14
☐ 104 Mark McGwire	1.25	.55
☐ 105 Ken Griffey Jr.	3.00	1.35
☐ 106 Darren Daulton	.30	.14
☐ 107 Bryan Rekar	.15	.07
☐ 108 Mike Macfarlane	.15	.07
☐ 109 Gary Gaetti	.30	.14
☐ 110 Shane Reynolds	.15	.07
☐ 111 Pat Meares	.15	.07
☐ 112 Jason Schmidt	.30	.14
☐ 113 Otis Nixon	.15	.07
☐ 114 John Franco	.30	.14
☐ 115 Marc Newfield	.15	.07
☐ 116 Andy Benes	.15	.07
☐ 117 Ozzie Guillen	.15	.07
☐ 118 Brian Jordan	.30	.14
☐ 119 Terry Pendleton	.15	.07
☐ 120 Chuck Finley	.15	.07
☐ 121 Scott Stahoviak	.15	.07
☐ 122 Sid Fernandez	.15	.07
☐ 123 Derek Jeter	2.00	.90
☐ 124 John Smiley	.15	.07
☐ 125 David Bell	.15	.07
☐ 126 Brett Butler	.15	.07
☐ 127 Doug Drabek	.15	.07
☐ 128 J.T. Snow	.30	.14
☐ 129 Joe Carter	.30	.14
☐ 130 Dennis Eckersley	.40	.18
☐ 131 Marty Cordova	.30	.14
☐ 132 Greg Maddux	2.00	.90
☐ 133 Tom Goodwin	.15	.07
☐ 134 Andy Ashby	.15	.07
☐ 135 Paul Sorrento	.15	.07
☐ 136 Ricky Bones	.15	.07
☐ 137 Shawon Dunston	.15	.07
☐ 138 Moises Alou	.30	.14
☐ 139 Mickey Morandini	.15	.07
☐ 140 Ramon Martinez	.30	.14
☐ 141 Royce Clayton	.15	.07
☐ 142 Brad Ausmus	.15	.07
☐ 143 Kenny Rogers	.15	.07
☐ 144 Tim Naehring	.15	.07
☐ 145 Chris Gomez	.15	.07
☐ 146 Bobby Bonilla	.30	.14
☐ 147 Wilson Alvarez	.30	.14
☐ 148 Johnny Damon	.30	.14
☐ 149 Pat Hentgen	.30	.14
☐ 150 Andres Galarraga	.60	.25
☐ 151 David Cone	.30	.14
☐ 152 Lance Johnson	.15	.07
☐ 153 Carlos Garcia	.15	.07
☐ 154 Doug Johns	.15	.07
☐ 155 Midre Cummings	.15	.07
☐ 156 Steve Sparks	.15	.07
☐ 157 Sandy Martinez	.15	.07
☐ 158 Wm. Van Landingham	.15	.07
☐ 159 David Justice	.60	.25
☐ 160 Mark Grace	.40	.18
☐ 161 Robb Nen	.15	.07
☐ 162 Mike Greenwell	.15	.07
☐ 163 Brad Radke	.30	.14
☐ 164 Edgardo Alfonzo	.40	.18
☐ 165 Mark Leiter	.15	.07
☐ 166 Walt Weiss	.15	.07
☐ 167 Mel Rojas	.30	.14
☐ 168 Bret Boone	.15	.07
☐ 169 Ricky Bottalico	.15	.07
☐ 170 Bobby Higginson	.30	.14
☐ 171 Trevor Hoffman	.30	.14
☐ 172 Jay Bell	.15	.07
☐ 173 Gabe White	.15	.07
☐ 174 Curtis Goodwin	.15	.07
☐ 175 Tyler Green	.15	.07
☐ 176 Roberto Alomar	.60	.25
☐ 177 Sterling Hitchcock	.15	.07
☐ 178 Ryan Klesko	.40	.18
☐ 179 Donne Wall	.15	.07
☐ 180 Brian McRae	.15	.07
☐ 181 Will Clark TSC SP	.40	.18
☐ 182 Frank Thomas TSC SP	3.00	1.35
☐ 183 Jeff Bagwell TSC SP	1.50	.70
☐ 184 Mo Vaughn TSC SP	1.00	.45
☐ 185 Tino Martinez TSC SP	.60	.25
☐ 186 Craig Biggio TSC SP	.40	.18
☐ 187 Chuck Knoblauch TSC SP	.60	.25
☐ 188 Carlos Baerga TSC SP	.30	.14
☐ 189 Quilvio Veras TSC SP	.25	.11
☐ 190 Luis Alicea TSC SP	.25	.11
☐ 191 Jim Thome TSC SP	.75	.35
☐ 192 Mike Blowers TSC SP	.25	.11
☐ 193 Robin Ventura TSC SP	.30	.14
☐ 194 Jeff King TSC SP	.25	.11
☐ 195 Tony Phillips TSC SP	.25	.11
☐ 196 John Valentin TSC SP	.30	.14
☐ 197 Barry Larkin TSC SP	.40	.18
☐ 198 Cal Ripken TSC SP	3.00	1.35
☐ 199 Omar Vizquel TSC SP	.25	.11
☐ 200 Kurt Abbott TSC SP	.25	.11
☐ 201 Albert Belle TSC SP	1.00	.45
☐ 202 Barry Bonds TSC SP	1.00	.45
☐ 203 Ron Gant TSC SP	.30	.14
☐ 204 Dante Bichette TSC SP	.30	.14
☐ 205 Jeff Conine TSC SP	.30	.14
☐ 206 Jim Edmonds TSC SP UER Greg Myers pictured on front	.60	.25
☐ 207 Stan Javier TSC SP	.25	.11
☐ 208 Kenny Lofton TSC SP	1.00	.45
☐ 209 Ray Lankford TSC SP	.30	.14
☐ 210 Bernie Williams TSC SP	.60	.25
☐ 211 Jay Buhner TSC SP	.40	.18
☐ 212 Paul O'Neill TSC SP	.30	.14
☐ 213 Tim Salmon TSC SP	.60	.25
☐ 214 Reggie Sanders TSC SP	.25	.11
☐ 215 Manny Ramirez TSC SP	.75	.35
☐ 216 Mike Piazza TSC SP	2.50	1.10
☐ 217 Mike Stanley TSC SP	.25	.11
☐ 218 Tony Eusebio TSC SP	.25	.11
☐ 219 Chris Hoiles TSC SP	.25	.11
☐ 220 Ron Karkovice TSC SP	.25	.11
☐ 221 Edgar Martinez TSC SP	.40	.18
☐ 222 Chili Davis TSC SP	.30	.14
☐ 223 Jose Canseco TSC SP	.40	.18
☐ 224 Eddie Murray TSC SP	.75	.35
☐ 225 Geronimo Berroa TSC SP	.25	.11
☐ 226 Chipper Jones TSC SP	2.50	1.10
☐ 227 Garret Anderson TSC SP	.30	.14
☐ 228 Marty Cordova TSC SP	.25	.11
☐ 229 Jon Nunnally TSC SP	.25	.11
☐ 230 Brian L.Hunter TSC SP	.30	.14
☐ 231 Shawn Green TSC SP	.30	.14
☐ 232 Ray Durham TSC SP	.30	.14
☐ 233 Alex Gonzalez TSC SP	.25	.11
☐ 234 Bobby Higginson TSC SP	.30	.14
☐ 235 Randy Johnson TSC SP	.60	.25
☐ 236 Al Leiter TSC SP	.25	.11
☐ 237 Tom Glavine TSC SP	.30	.14
☐ 238 Kenny Rogers TSC SP	.25	.11
☐ 239 Mike Hampton TSC SP	.25	.11
☐ 240 David Wells TSC SP	.25	.11
☐ 241 Jim Abbott TSC SP	.30	.14
☐ 242 Denny Neagle TSC SP	.25	.11
☐ 243 Wilson Alvarez TSC SP	.30	.14
☐ 244 John Smiley TSC SP	.25	.11
☐ 245 Greg Maddux TSC SP	2.50	1.10
☐ 246 Andy Ashby TSC SP	.25	.11
☐ 247 Hideo Nomo TSC SP	2.00	.90
☐ 248 Pat Rapp TSC SP	.25	.11
☐ 249 Tim Wakefield TSC SP	.25	.11
☐ 250 John Smoltz TSC SP	.30	.14
☐ 251 Joey Hamilton TSC SP	.25	.11
☐ 252 Frank Castillo TSC SP	.25	.11
☐ 253 Denny Martinez TSC SP	.30	.14
☐ 254 Jaime Navarro TSC SP	.25	.11
☐ 255 Karim Garcia TSC SP	.30	.14
☐ 256 Bob Abreu TSC SP	.60	.25
☐ 257 Butch Huskey TSC SP	.30	.14
☐ 258 Ruben Rivera TSC SP	.30	.14
☐ 259 Johnny Damon TSC SP	.30	.14
☐ 260 Derek Jeter TSC SP	2.50	1.10
☐ 261 Dennis Eckersley TSC SP	.40	.18
☐ 262 Jose Mesa TSC SP	.30	.14
☐ 263 Tom Henke TSC SP	.30	.14
☐ 264 Rick Aguilera TSC SP	.30	.14
☐ 265 Randy Myers TSC SP	.30	.14
☐ 266 John Franco TSC SP	.30	.14
☐ 267 Jeff Brantley TSC SP	.25	.11
☐ 268 John Wetteland TSC SP	.30	.14
☐ 269 Mark Wohlers TSC SP	.30	.14
☐ 270 Rod Beck TSC SP	.30	.14
☐ 271 Barry Larkin	.40	.18
☐ 272 Paul O'Neill	.30	.14
☐ 273 Bobby Jones	.15	.07
☐ 274 Will Clark	.40	.18

Card	MINT	NRMT
☐ 275 Steve Avery	.15	.07
☐ 276 Jim Edmonds	.60	.25
☐ 277 John Olerud	.30	.14
☐ 278 Carlos Perez	.15	.07
☐ 279 Chris Hoiles	.15	.07
☐ 280 Jeff Conine	.30	.14
☐ 281 Jim Eisenreich	.30	.14
☐ 282 Jason Jacome	.15	.07
☐ 283 Ray Lankford	.30	.14
☐ 284 John Wasdin	.15	.07
☐ 285 Frank Thomas	2.50	1.10
☐ 286 Jason Isringhausen	.15	.07
☐ 287 Glenallen Hill	.15	.07
☐ 288 Esteban Loaiza	.15	.07
☐ 289 Bernie Williams	.60	.25
☐ 290 Curtis Leskanic	.15	.07
☐ 291 Scott Cooper	.15	.07
☐ 292 Curt Schilling	.30	.14
☐ 293 Eddie Murray	.60	.25
☐ 294 Rick Krivda	.15	.07
☐ 295 Domingo Cedeno	.15	.07
☐ 296 Jeff Fassero	.15	.07
☐ 297 Albert Belle	.75	.35
☐ 298 Craig Biggio	.40	.18
☐ 299 Fernando Vina	.15	.07
☐ 300 Edgar Martinez	.40	.18
☐ 301 Tony Gwynn	1.50	.70
☐ 302 Felipe Lira	.15	.07
☐ 303 Mo Vaughn	.75	.35
☐ 304 Alex Fernandez	.30	.14
☐ 305 Keith Lockhart	.15	.07
☐ 306 Roger Pavlik	.15	.07
☐ 307 Lee Tinsley	.15	.07
☐ 308 Omar Vizquel	.30	.14
☐ 309 Scott Servais	.15	.07
☐ 310 Danny Tartabull	.15	.07
☐ 311 Chili Davis	.30	.14
☐ 312 Cal Eldred	.15	.07
☐ 313 Roger Cedeno	.15	.07
☐ 314 Chris Hammond	.15	.07
☐ 315 Rusty Greer	.40	.18
☐ 316 Brady Anderson	.40	.18
☐ 317 Ron Villone	.15	.07
☐ 318 Mark Carreon	.15	.07
☐ 319 Larry Walker	.60	.25
☐ 320 Pete Harnisch	.15	.07
☐ 321 Robin Ventura	.30	.14
☐ 322 Tim Belcher	.15	.07
☐ 323 Tony Tarasco	.15	.07
☐ 324 Juan Guzman	.15	.07
☐ 325 Kenny Lofton	.75	.35
☐ 326 Kevin Foster	.15	.07
☐ 327 Wil Cordero	.15	.07
☐ 328 Troy Percival	.30	.14
☐ 329 Turk Wendell	.15	.07
☐ 330 Thomas Howard	.15	.07
☐ 331 Carlos Baerga	.30	.14
☐ 332 B.J. Surhoff	.15	.07
☐ 333 Jay Buhner	.40	.18
☐ 334 Andujar Cedeno	.15	.07
☐ 335 Jeff King	.30	.14
☐ 336 Dante Bichette	.30	.14
☐ 337 Alan Trammell	.40	.18
☐ 338 Scott Leius	.15	.07
☐ 339 Chris Snopek	.15	.07
☐ 340 Roger Bailey	.15	.07
☐ 341 Jacob Brumfield	.15	.07
☐ 342 Jose Canseco	.40	.18
☐ 343 Rafael Palmeiro	.40	.18
☐ 344 Quilvio Veras	.15	.07
☐ 345 Darrin Fletcher	.15	.07
☐ 346 Carlos Delgado	.30	.14
☐ 347 Tony Eusebio	.15	.07
☐ 348 Ismael Valdes	.30	.14
☐ 349 Terry Steinbach	.30	.14
☐ 350 Orel Hershiser	.30	.14
☐ 351 Kurt Abbott	.15	.07
☐ 352 Jody Reed	.15	.07
☐ 353 David Howard	.15	.07
☐ 354 Ruben Sierra	.15	.07
☐ 355 John Ericks	.15	.07
☐ 356 Buck Showalter MG	.15	.07
☐ 357 Jim Thome	.60	.25
☐ 358 Geronimo Berroa	.15	.07
☐ 359 Robby Thompson	.15	.07
☐ 360 Jose Vizcaino	.15	.07
☐ 361 Jeff Frye	.15	.07
☐ 362 Kevin Appier	.30	.14
☐ 363 Pat Kelly	.15	.07
☐ 364 Ron Gant	.30	.14
☐ 365 Luis Alicea	.15	.07
☐ 366 Armando Benitez	.15	.07
☐ 367 Rico Brogna	.15	.07
☐ 368 Manny Ramirez	.60	.25
☐ 369 Mike Lansing	.15	.07
☐ 370 Sammy Sosa	.60	.25
☐ 371 Don Wengert	.15	.07
☐ 372 Dave Nilsson	.30	.14
☐ 373 Sandy Alomar	.30	.14
☐ 374 Joey Cora	.30	.14
☐ 375 Larry Thomas	.15	.07
☐ 376 John Valentin	.30	.14
☐ 377 Kevin Ritz	.15	.07
☐ 378 Steve Finley	.30	.14
☐ 379 Frank Rodriguez	.15	.07
☐ 380 Ivan Rodriguez	.75	.35
☐ 381 Alex Ochoa	.15	.07
☐ 382 Mark Lemke	.15	.07
☐ 383 Scott Brosius	.15	.07
☐ 384 James Mouton	.15	.07
☐ 385 Mark Langston	.15	.07
☐ 386 Ed Sprague	.15	.07
☐ 387 Joe Oliver	.15	.07
☐ 388 Steve Ontiveros	.15	.07
☐ 389 Rey Sanchez	.15	.07
☐ 390 Mike Henneman	.15	.07
☐ 391 Jose Valentin	.15	.07
☐ 392 Tom Candiotti	.15	.07
☐ 393 Damon Buford	.15	.07
☐ 394 Erik Hanson	.15	.07
☐ 395 Mark Smith	.15	.07
☐ 396 Pete Schourek	.15	.07
☐ 397 John Flaherty	.15	.07
☐ 398 Dave Martinez	.15	.07
☐ 399 Tommy Greene	.15	.07
☐ 400 Gary Sheffield	.60	.25
☐ 401 Glenn Dishman	.15	.07
☐ 402 Barry Bonds	.75	.35
☐ 403 Tom Pagnozzi	.15	.07
☐ 404 Todd Stottlemyre	.15	.07
☐ 405 Tim Salmon	.60	.25
☐ 406 John Hudek	.15	.07
☐ 407 Fred McGriff	.40	.18
☐ 408 Orlando Merced	.15	.07
☐ 409 Brian Barber	.15	.07
☐ 410 Ryan Thompson	.15	.07
☐ 411 Mariano Rivera	.60	.25
☐ 412 Eric Young	.30	.14
☐ 413 Chris Bosio	.15	.07
☐ 414 Chuck Knoblauch	.60	.25
☐ 415 Jamie Moyer	.15	.07
☐ 416 Chan Ho Park	.60	.25
☐ 417 Mark Portugal	.15	.07
☐ 418 Tim Raines	.15	.07
☐ 419 Antonio Osuna	.15	.07
☐ 420 Todd Zeile	.15	.07
☐ 421 Steve Wojciechowski	.15	.07
☐ 422 Marquis Grissom	.30	.14
☐ 423 Norm Charlton	.15	.07
☐ 424 Cal Ripken	2.50	1.10
☐ 425 Gregg Jefferies	.30	.14
☐ 426 Mike Stanton	.15	.07
☐ 427 Tony Fernandez	.15	.07
☐ 428 Jose Rijo	.15	.07
☐ 429 Jeff Bagwell	1.25	.55
☐ 430 Raul Mondesi	.40	.18
☐ 431 Travis Fryman	.30	.14
☐ 432 Ron Karkovice	.15	.07
☐ 433 Alan Benes	.30	.14
☐ 434 Tony Phillips	.15	.07
☐ 435 Reggie Sanders	.15	.07
☐ 436 Andy Pettitte	.75	.35
☐ 437 Matt Lawton	.15	.07
☐ 438 Jeff Blauser	.15	.07
☐ 439 Michael Tucker	.30	.14
☐ 440 Mark Loretta	.15	.07
☐ 441 Charlie Hayes	.15	.07
☐ 442 Mike Piazza	2.00	.90
☐ 443 Shane Andrews	.15	.07
☐ 444 Jeff Suppan	.40	.18
☐ 445 Steve Rodriguez	.15	.07
☐ 446 Mike Matheny	.15	.07
☐ 447 Trenidad Hubbard	.15	.07
☐ 448 Denny Hocking	.15	.07
☐ 449 Mark Grudzielanek	.30	.14
☐ 450 Joe Randa	.15	.07

1996 Stadium Club Members Only Parallel

This set, of which only 750 were produced is a parallel to the regular 1996 Stadium Club set. The cards are embossed with a "Members Only" logo and were available only to members of Topps' Stadium Club. The set includes a parallel of the complete 450-card basic set plus the following inserts: Bash and Burn, Mickey Mantle Heroes, Megaheroes, Metalists, Midsummer Matchups, Power Packed, Power Streak, Prime Cuts and TSC Awards. Only the inserts cards are priced below. Please refer to the multiplier for value on parallels to the basic issue cards.

	MINT	NRMT
COMP.SET W/INSERTS (555)	500.00	220.00
COMPLETE BASE SET (450)	200.00	90.00
COMMON CARD (1-450)	.25	.11
COMMON MANTLE (M1-M19)	5.00	2.20
*MEMBERS ONLY: 6X BASIC CARDS.		
☐ M1 Jeff Bagwell	8.00	3.60
☐ M2 Barry Bonds	5.00	2.20
☐ M3 Jose Canseco	2.50	1.10
☐ M4 Roger Clemens	4.00	1.80
☐ M5 Dennis Eckersley	1.00	.45
☐ M6 Greg Maddux	20.00	9.00
☐ M7 Cal Ripken	20.00	9.00
☐ M8 Frank Thomas	20.00	9.00
☐ BB1 Sammy Sosa	3.00	1.35
☐ BB2 Barry Bonds	5.00	2.20
☐ BB3 Reggie Sanders	1.50	.70
☐ BB4 Craig Biggio	1.50	.70
☐ BB5 Raul Mondesi	1.50	.70
☐ BB6 Ron Gant	1.50	.70
☐ BB7 Ray Lankford	1.50	.70
☐ BB8 Glenallen Hill	1.00	.45
☐ BB9 Chad Curtis	1.00	.45
☐ BB10 John Valentin	1.00	.45
☐ MH1 Frank Thomas	20.00	9.00
☐ MH2 Ken Griffey Jr.	20.00	9.00
☐ MH3 Hideo Nomo	5.00	2.20
☐ MH4 Ozzie Smith	8.00	3.60
☐ MH5 Will Clark	2.50	1.10
☐ MH6 Jack McDowell	1.00	.45
☐ MH7 Andres Galarraga	2.00	.90
☐ MH8 Roger Clemens	4.00	1.80
☐ MH9 Deion Sanders	2.00	.90
☐ MH10 Mo Vaughn	5.00	2.20
☐ MM1 Hideo Nomo Randy Johnson	6.00	2.70
☐ MM2 Mike Piazza Ivan Rodriguez	12.00	5.50
☐ MM3 Fred McGriff Frank Thomas	20.00	9.00
☐ MM4 Craig Biggio Carlos Baerga	2.00	.90
☐ MM5 Vinny Castilla Wade Boggs	2.50	1.10
☐ MM6 Barry Larkin Cal Ripken	20.00	9.00
☐ MM7 Barry Bonds Albert Belle	12.00	5.50
☐ MM8 Len Dykstra Kenny Lofton	5.00	2.20
☐ MM9 Tony Gwynn Kirby Puckett	12.00	5.50
☐ MM10 Ron Gant Edgar Martinez	2.00	.90
☐ PC1 Albert Belle	10.00	4.50
☐ PC2 Barry Bonds	5.00	2.20
☐ PC3 Ken Griffey Jr.	20.00	9.00
☐ PC4 Tony Gwynn	10.00	4.50
☐ PC5 Edgar Martinez	1.50	.70
☐ PC6 Rafael Palmeiro	2.00	.90
☐ PC7 Mike Piazza	12.00	5.50
☐ PC8 Frank Thomas	20.00	9.00
☐ PP1 Albert Belle	10.00	4.50
☐ PP2 Mark McGwire	6.00	2.70
☐ PP3 Jose Canseco	2.50	1.10
☐ PP4 Mike Piazza	12.00	5.50
☐ PP5 Ron Gant	1.50	.70
☐ PP6 Ken Griffey Jr.	20.00	9.00
☐ PP7 Mo Vaughn	5.00	2.20
☐ PP8 Cecil Fielder	1.50	.70
☐ PP9 Tim Salmon	2.00	.90
☐ PP10 Frank Thomas	20.00	9.00
☐ PP11 Juan Gonzalez	10.00	4.50
☐ PP12 Andres Galarraga	2.00	.90
☐ PP13 Fred McGriff	2.00	.90
☐ PP14 Jay Buhner	2.00	.90
☐ PP15 Dante Bichette	2.00	.90
☐ PS1 Randy Johnson	4.00	1.80
☐ PS2 Hideo Nomo	5.00	2.20
☐ PS3 Albert Belle	10.00	4.50
☐ PS4 Dante Bichette	2.00	.90
☐ PS5 Jay Buhner	2.00	.90
☐ PS6 Frank Thomas	20.00	9.00
☐ PS7 Mark McGwire	6.00	2.70
☐ PS8 Rafael Palmeiro	2.00	.90
☐ PS9 Mo Vaughn	5.00	2.20
☐ PS10 Sammy Sosa	3.00	1.35
☐ PS11 Larry Walker	2.50	1.10
☐ PS12 Gary Gaetti	1.00	.45
☐ PS13 Tim Salmon	2.00	.90
☐ PS14 Barry Bonds	5.00	2.20
☐ PS15 Jim Edmonds	1.50	.70
☐ TSCA1 Cal Ripken	20.00	9.00
☐ TSCA2 Albert Belle	10.00	4.50
☐ TSCA3 Tom Glavine	2.00	.90
☐ TSCA4 Jeff Conine	1.50	.70
☐ TSCA5 Ken Griffey Jr.	20.00	9.00

	MINT	NRMT
☐ TSCA6 Hideo Nomo	5.00	2.20
☐ TSCA7 Greg Maddux	15.00	6.75
☐ TSCA8 Chipper Jones	15.00	6.75
☐ TSCA9 Randy Johnson	4.00	1.80
☐ TSCA10 Jose Mesa	1.00	.45

1996 Stadium Club Bash and Burn

Randomly inserted in packs at a rate of one in 29 (retail) and one in 48 (hobby), this ten card set features power/speed players. The fronts carry photos of the players hitting with a baseball background. The backs display photos of the same players running down the baseline on a background of flames.

	MINT	NRMT
COMPLETE SET (10)	30.00	13.50
COMMON CARD (BB1-BB10)	2.00	.90
☐ BB1 Sammy Sosa	8.00	3.60
☐ BB2 Barry Bonds	12.00	5.50
☐ BB3 Reggie Sanders	2.00	.90
☐ BB4 Craig Biggio	4.00	1.80
☐ BB5 Raul Mondesi	4.00	1.80
☐ BB6 Ron Gant	3.00	1.35
☐ BB7 Ray Lankford	3.00	1.35
☐ BB8 Glenallen Hill	2.00	.90
☐ BB9 Chad Curtis	2.00	.90
☐ BB10 John Valentin	3.00	1.35

1996 Stadium Club Extreme Players Bronze

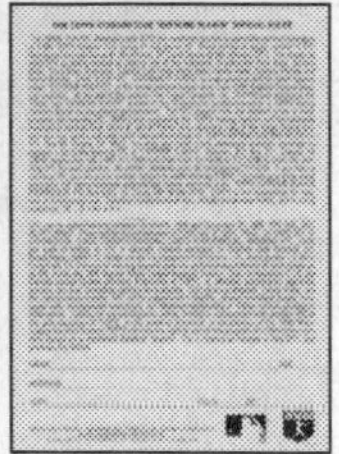

One hundred and seventy nine different players were featured on Extreme Player game cards randomly issued in 1996 Stadium Club first and second series packs. Each player has three versions: Bronze, Silver and Gold. All of these cards parallel their corresponding regular issue card except for the Bronze foil "Extreme Players" logo on each card front and the "EP" suffix on the card number, thus creating a skip-numbered set. The Bronze cards listed below were seeded at a rate of 1:12 packs. At the conclusion of the 1996 regular season, an Extreme Player from each of ten positions was identified as a winner based on scores calculated from their actual playing statistics. The 10 winning players are noted with a "W" below. Prior to the December 31st, 1996 deadline, each of the ten winning Extreme Players Bronze cards was redeemable for a 10-card set of Extreme Winners Bronze.

	MINT	NRMT
COMP.BRONZE SET (179)	250.00	110.00
COMP.BRONZE SER.1 (90)	125.00	55.00
COMP.BRONZE SER.2 (89)	125.00	55.00
COMMON BRONZE	.75	.35
BRONZE MINOR STARS	1.50	.70
BRONZE SEMISTARS	2.00	.90
BRONZE UNLISTED STARS	3.00	1.35

*SILVER SINGLES: 1.5X VALUE
*SILVER WIN: .75X TO 1.5X BRONZE WIN
*GOLD SINGLES: 3X VALUE
*GOLD WIN: 1.5X TO 3X BRONZE WIN

	MINT	NRMT
☐ 1 Hideo Nomo	4.00	1.80
☐ 3 Garret Anderson	1.50	.70
☐ 4 Jose Mesa	1.50	.70
☐ 5 Vinny Castilla	1.50	.70
☐ 6 Mike Mussina	3.00	1.35
☐ 7 Ray Durham	1.50	.70
☐ 8 Jack McDowell	.75	.35
☐ 9 Juan Gonzalez	8.00	3.60
☐ 10 Chipper Jones	10.00	4.50
☐ 11 Deion Sanders	3.00	1.35
☐ 12 Rondell White	1.50	.70
☐ 13 Tom Henke	1.50	.70
☐ 14 Derek Bell	.75	.35
☐ 15 Randy Myers	1.50	.70
☐ 16 Randy Johnson	3.00	1.35
☐ 17 Len Dykstra	1.50	.70
☐ 18 Bill Pulsipher	.75	.35
☐ 21 Chad Curtis	.75	.35
☐ 22 Roberto Hernandez	.75	.35
☐ 23 Kirby Puckett	6.00	2.70
☐ 25 Roger Clemens	3.00	1.35
☐ 31 Chad Fonville	.75	.35
☐ 32 Bernard Gilkey	1.50	.70
☐ 34 Shawn Green	.75	.35
☐ 35 Rick Aguilera	.75	.35
☐ 40 Dean Palmer	1.50	.70
☐ 45 Matt Williams	2.00	.90
☐ 49 Tom Glavine	1.50	.70
☐ 50 Delino DeShields	.75	.35
☐ 56 Benito Santiago	.75	.35
☐ 59 Rod Beck	.75	.35
☐ 63 Eric Karros	1.50	.70
☐ 66 Lee Smith	1.50	.70
☐ 69 Jeff Montgomery	1.50	.70
☐ 70 Todd Hundley	1.50	.70
☐ 73 Don Mattingly	8.00	3.60
☐ 77 Ken Caminiti W	5.00	2.20
☐ 80 Pedro Martinez	3.00	1.35
☐ 82 Heathcliff Slocumb	.75	.35
☐ 83 Joe Girardi	.75	.35
☐ 88 Todd Worrell W	1.50	.70
☐ 90 Bip Roberts	.75	.35
☐ 95 Cecil Fielder	1.50	.70
☐ 96 Wade Boggs	3.00	1.35
☐ 98 Mickey Tettleton	.75	.35
☐ 99 Jeff Kent	.75	.35
☐ 100 Denny Martinez	1.50	.70
☐ 101 Luis Gonzalez	.75	.35
☐ 103 Javy Lopez	1.50	.70
☐ 104 Mark McGwire	5.00	2.20
☐ 105 Ken Griffey Jr. W	30.00	13.50
☐ 106 Darren Daulton	1.50	.70
☐ 108 Mike Macfarlane	.75	.35
☐ 110 Shane Reynolds	.75	.35
☐ 114 John Franco	1.50	.70
☐ 116 Andy Benes	.75	.35
☐ 118 Brian Jordan	1.50	.70
☐ 119 Terry Pendleton	1.50	.70
☐ 120 Chuck Finley	.75	.35
☐ 123 Derek Jeter	10.00	4.50
☐ 124 John Smiley	.75	.35
☐ 126 Brett Butler	1.50	.70
☐ 127 Doug Drabek	.75	.35
☐ 128 J.T. Snow	.75	.35
☐ 129 Joe Carter	1.50	.70
☐ 130 Dennis Eckersley	2.00	.90
☐ 131 Marty Cordova	.75	.35
☐ 132 Greg Maddux W	25.00	11.00
☐ 135 Paul Sorrento	.75	.35
☐ 137 Shawon Dunston	.75	.35
☐ 138 Moises Alou	1.50	.70
☐ 140 Ramon Martinez	.75	.35
☐ 141 Royce Clayton	.75	.35
☐ 143 Kenny Rogers	.75	.35
☐ 144 Tim Naehring	.75	.35
☐ 145 Chris Gomez	.75	.35
☐ 146 Bobby Bonilla	1.50	.70
☐ 148 Johnny Damon	1.50	.70
☐ 150 Andres Galarraga W	4.00	1.80
☐ 151 David Cone	1.50	.70
☐ 152 Lance Johnson	.75	.35
☐ 159 David Justice	3.00	1.35
☐ 160 Mark Grace	2.00	.90
☐ 161 Robb Nen	.75	.35
☐ 162 Mike Greenwell	.75	.35
☐ 167 Mel Rojas	.75	.35
☐ 168 Bret Boone	.75	.35
☐ 172 Jay Bell	.75	.35
☐ 176 Roberto Alomar	3.00	1.35
☐ 178 Ryan Klesko	2.00	.90
☐ 271 Barry Larkin W	4.00	1.80
☐ 272 Paul O'Neill	.75	.35
☐ 274 Will Clark	2.00	.90
☐ 275 Steve Avery	.75	.35
☐ 276 Jim Edmonds	3.00	1.35
☐ 277 John Olerud	1.50	.70
☐ 279 Chris Hoiles	.75	.35
☐ 280 Jeff Conine	1.50	.70
☐ 283 Ray Lankford	1.50	.70
☐ 285 Frank Thomas	15.00	6.75
☐ 286 Jason Isringhausen	.75	.35
☐ 287 Glenallen Hill	.75	.35
☐ 289 Bernie Williams	3.00	1.35
☐ 290 Eddie Murray	3.00	1.35
☐ 296 Jeff Fassero	.75	.35
☐ 297 Albert Belle	6.00	2.70
☐ 298 Craig Biggio	2.00	.90
☐ 300 Edgar Martinez	2.00	.90
☐ 301 Tony Gwynn	6.00	2.70
☐ 303 Mo Vaughn	4.00	1.80
☐ 304 Alex Fernandez	1.50	.70
☐ 308 Omar Vizquel	1.50	.70
☐ 310 Danny Tartabull	.75	.35
☐ 316 Brady Anderson	2.00	.90
☐ 319 Larry Walker	3.00	1.35
☐ 321 Robin Ventura	1.50	.70
☐ 325 Kenny Lofton	4.00	1.80
☐ 327 Wil Cordero	.75	.35
☐ 328 Troy Percival	.75	.35
☐ 331 Carlos Baerga	1.50	.70
☐ 333 Jay Buhner	2.00	.90
☐ 335 Jeff King	.75	.35
☐ 336 Dante Bichette	1.50	.70
☐ 337 Alan Trammell	2.00	.90
☐ 342 Jose Canseco	2.00	.90
☐ 343 Rafael Palmeiro	2.00	.90
☐ 344 Quilvio Veras	.75	.35
☐ 345 Darrin Fletcher	.75	.35
☐ 347 Tony Eusebio	.75	.35
☐ 348 Ismael Valdes	1.50	.70
☐ 349 Terry Steinbach	1.50	.70
☐ 350 Orel Hershiser	1.50	.70
☐ 351 Kurt Abbott	.75	.35
☐ 354 Ruben Sierra	.75	.35
☐ 357 Jim Thome	3.00	1.35
☐ 358 Geronimo Berroa	.75	.35
☐ 359 Robby Thompson	.75	.35
☐ 360 Jose Vizcaino	.75	.35
☐ 362 Kevin Appier	1.50	.70
☐ 364 Ron Gant	1.50	.70
☐ 367 Rico Brogna	.75	.35
☐ 368 Manny Ramirez	3.00	1.35
☐ 370 Sammy Sosa	3.00	1.35
☐ 373 Sandy Alomar	1.50	.70
☐ 378 Steve Finley	1.50	.70
☐ 380 Ivan Rodriguez	3.00	1.35
☐ 382 Mark Lemke	.75	.35
☐ 385 Mark Langston	.75	.35
☐ 386 Ed Sprague	.75	.35
☐ 388 Steve Ontiveros	.75	.35
☐ 392 Tom Candiotti	.75	.35
☐ 394 Erik Hanson	.75	.35
☐ 396 Pete Schourek	.75	.35
☐ 400 Gary Sheffield W	5.00	2.20
☐ 402 Barry Bonds W	8.00	3.60
☐ 403 Tom Pagnozzi	.75	.35
☐ 404 Todd Stottlemyre	.75	.35
☐ 405 Tim Salmon	3.00	1.35
☐ 407 Fred McGriff	2.00	.90
☐ 408 Orlando Merced	.75	.35
☐ 412 Eric Young	1.50	.70
☐ 414 Chuck Knoblauch W	5.00	2.20
☐ 417 Mark Portugal	.75	.35
☐ 418 Tim Raines	.75	.35
☐ 420 Todd Zeile	.75	.35
☐ 422 Marquis Grissom	1.50	.70
☐ 423 Norm Charlton	.75	.35
☐ 424 Cal Ripken	12.00	5.50
☐ 425 Gregg Jefferies	1.50	.70
☐ 428 Jose Rijo	.75	.35
☐ 429 Jeff Bagwell	6.00	2.70
☐ 430 Raul Mondesi	2.00	.90
☐ 431 Travis Fryman	1.50	.70
☐ 434 Tony Phillips	.75	.35
☐ 435 Reggie Sanders	.75	.35
☐ 436 Andy Pettitte	5.00	2.20
☐ 438 Jeff Blauser	.75	.35
☐ 441 Charlie Hayes	.75	.35
☐ 442 Mike Piazza W	20.00	9.00

1996 Stadium Club Extreme Winners Bronze

This 10-card skip-numbered set was only available to collectors who redeemed one of the ten winning Bronze Extreme Players cards before the December 31st, 1996 deadline. The cards parallel the Extreme Players cards inserted in Stadium Club packs except for their distinctive diffraction foil fronts.

	MINT	NRMT
COMPLETE SET (10)	25.00	11.00
COMMON CARD (EW1-EW10)	.50	.23
MINOR STARS	.75	.35

*SILVER SINGLES: 3X VALUE
*GOLD SINGLES: 15X VALUE

	MINT	NRMT
☐ EW1 Greg Maddux	6.00	2.70
☐ EW2 Mike Piazza	6.00	2.70

Card	MINT	NRMT
☐ EW3 Andres Galarraga	1.25	.55
☐ EW4 Chuck Knoblauch	1.50	.70
☐ EW5 Ken Caminiti	1.50	.70
☐ EW6 Barry Larkin	1.00	.45
☐ EW7 Barry Bonds	2.50	1.10
☐ EW8 Ken Griffey Jr.	10.00	4.50
☐ EW9 Gary Sheffield	1.50	.70
☐ EW10 Todd Worrell	.50	.23

1996 Stadium Club Mantle

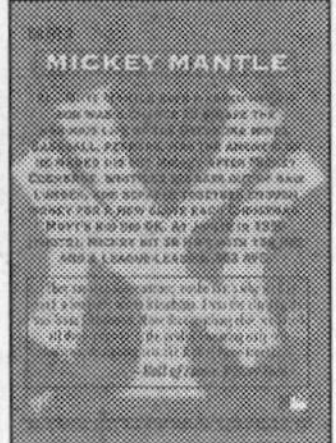

Randomly inserted at a rate of one card in every 24 packs in series 1, one in 12 packs in series 2, this 19-card retrospective set chronicles Mantle's career with classic photography, celebrity quotes and highlights from each year. The cards are double foil-stamped. The series 1 cards feature black-and-white photos, series 2 color photos. Mantle's name is printed across a silver foil facade of Yankee Stadium on each card top. The retail cereal box sets contain gold-foil stamped Mantles. They are valued the same as the regular cards.

	MINT	NRMT
COMPLETE SET (19)	170.00	75.00
COMPLETE SERIES 1 (9)	110.00	50.00
COMPLETE SERIES 2 (10)	60.00	27.00
COMMON MANTLE (MM1-MM9)	14.00	6.25
COMMON MANTLE (MM10-MM-19)	8.00	3.60
☐ MM1 Mickey Mantle Batting Follow Through, 1950	14.00	6.25
☐ MM2 Mickey Mantle	14.00	6.25
☐ MM3 Mickey Mantle Locker room shot, 1951	14.00	6.25
☐ MM4 Mickey Mantle	14.00	6.25
☐ MM5 Mickey Mantle	14.00	6.25
☐ MM6 Mickey Mantle	14.00	6.25
☐ MM7 Mickey Mantle	14.00	6.25
☐ MM8 Mickey Mantle	14.00	6.25
☐ MM9 Mickey Mantle Batting both ways, 1959	14.00	6.25
☐ MM10 Mickey Mantle	8.00	3.60
☐ MM11 Mickey Mantle Beating out hit, 1961	8.00	3.60
☐ MM12 Mickey Mantle Roger Maris 1961	8.00	3.60
☐ MM13 Mickey Mantle	8.00	3.60
☐ MM14 Mickey Mantle	8.00	3.60
☐ MM15 Mickey Mantle Smiling Pose, 1964	8.00	3.60
☐ MM16 Mickey Mantle	8.00	3.60
☐ MM17 Mickey Mantle	8.00	3.60
☐ MM18 Mickey Mantle	8.00	3.60
☐ MM19 Mickey Mantle	8.00	3.60

1996 Stadium Club Megaheroes

Randomly inserted at a rate of one in every 48 hobby and 24 retail packs, this 10-card set features super-heroic players matched with a comic book-style illustration depicting their nicknames. The fronts display a color player cutout superposed on diffraction foilboard illustrating the player's nickname. On a textured background, the backs present a closeup photo (in an oval

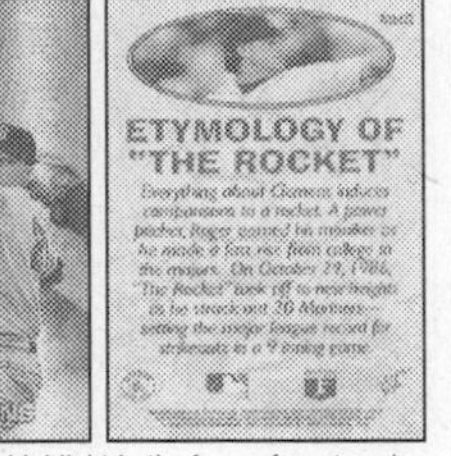

format) and a career highlight in the form of an etymology of his nickname.

	MINT	NRMT
COMPLETE SET (10)	50.00	22.00
COMMON CARD (MH1-MH10)	1.50	.70
☐ MH1 Frank Thomas	15.00	6.75
☐ MH2 Ken Griffey Jr.	20.00	9.00
☐ MH3 Hideo Nomo	10.00	4.50
☐ MH4 Ozzie Smith	5.00	2.20
☐ MH5 Will Clark	2.50	1.10
☐ MH6 Jack McDowell	1.50	.70
☐ MH7 Andres Galarraga	2.50	1.10
☐ MH8 Roger Clemens	6.00	2.70
☐ MH9 Deion Sanders	3.00	1.35
☐ MH10 Mo Vaughn	5.00	2.20

1996 Stadium Club Metalists

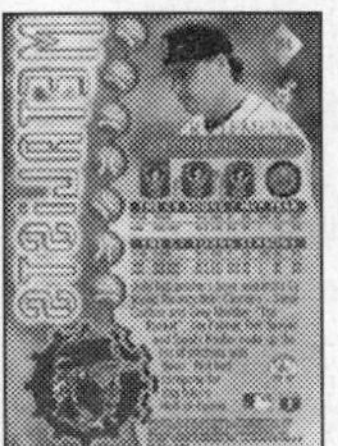

Randomly inserted in packs at a rate of one in 96 (retail) and one in 48 (hobby), this eight-card set features players with two or more MLB awards and is printed on laser-cut foil board.

	MINT	NRMT
COMPLETE SET (8)	50.00	22.00
COMMON CARD (M1-M8)	2.00	.90
☐ M1 Jeff Bagwell	8.00	3.60
☐ M2 Barry Bonds	5.00	2.20
☐ M3 Jose Canseco		
☐ M4 Roger Clemens	6.00	2.70
☐ M5 Dennis Eckersley	2.00	.90
☐ M6 Greg Maddux	12.00	5.50
☐ M7 Cal Ripken	15.00	6.75
☐ M8 Frank Thomas	15.00	6.75

1996 Stadium Club Midsummer Matchups

Randomly inserted at a rate of one in every 48 hobby and 24 retail packs, this 10-card set salutes 1995 National League and American League All-Stars as they are matched back-to-back by position on these two-sided etched foil cards. Each side features a color player cutout on a screened background of 1995 All-Star game emblems. On each side, the lower right corner is peeled back to reveal space for the American or National League logo.

	MINT	NRMT
COMPLETE SET (10)	60.00	27.00
COMMON CARD (M1-M10)	2.00	.90
☐ MM1 Hideo Nomo Randy Johnson	10.00	4.50
☐ MM2 Mike Piazza Ivan Rodriguez	12.00	5.50
☐ MM3 Fred McGriff Frank Thomas	15.00	6.75
☐ MM4 Craig Biggio Carlos Baerga	2.00	.90
☐ MM5 Vinny Castilla Wade Boggs	2.50	1.10
☐ MM6 Barry Larkin Cal Ripken	15.00	6.75
☐ MM7 Barry Bonds Albert Belle	8.00	3.60
☐ MM8 Len Dykstra Kenny Lofton	5.00	2.20
☐ MM9 Tony Gwynn Kirby Puckett	15.00	6.75
☐ MM10 Ron Gant Edgar Martinez	2.50	1.10

1996 Stadium Club Power Packed

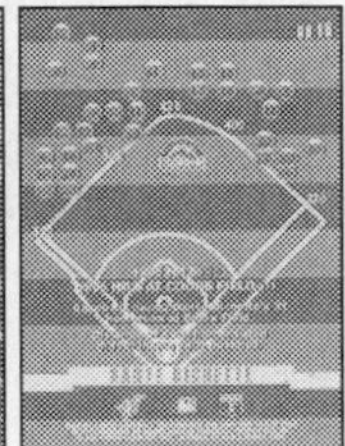

Randomly inserted in packs at a rate of one in 48, this 15-card set features the biggest, most powerful hitters in the League. Printed on Power Matrix, the cards carry diagrams showing where the players hit the ball over the fence and how far.

	MINT	NRMT
COMPLETE SET (15)	80.00	36.00
COMMON CARD (PP1-PP15)	2.00	.90
☐ PP1 Albert Belle	6.00	2.70
☐ PP2 Mark McGwire	8.00	3.60
☐ PP3 Jose Canseco	3.00	1.35
☐ PP4 Mike Piazza	15.00	6.75
☐ PP5 Ron Gant	2.00	.90
☐ PP6 Ken Griffey Jr.	25.00	11.00
☐ PP7 Mo Vaughn	6.00	2.70
☐ PP8 Cecil Fielder	2.50	1.10
☐ PP9 Tim Salmon	4.00	1.80
☐ PP10 Frank Thomas	20.00	9.00
☐ PP11 Juan Gonzalez	12.00	5.50
☐ PP12 Andres Galarraga	3.00	1.35
☐ PP13 Fred McGriff	3.00	1.35
☐ PP14 Jay Buhner	3.00	1.35
☐ PP15 Dante Bichette	2.50	1.10

1996 Stadium Club Power Streak

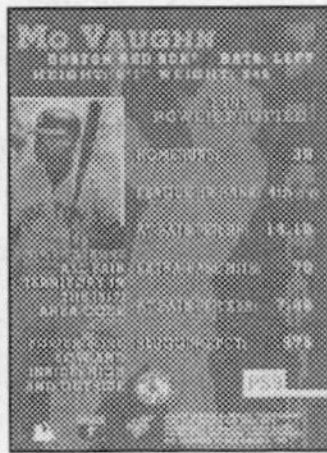

Randomly inserted at a rate of one in every 24 hobby packs and 48 retail packs, this 15-card set spotlights baseball's most awesome power hitters and strikeout artists. The cards feature Topps' Power Matrix technology. The fronts display a color player cutout on a silver metallic and holographic background featuring a baseball. The backs carry a small color photo and biography; in addition, the player's batting prowess is presented under three topics: 1995 Power Profile, Power Stroke, and Power Zone.

	MINT	NRMT
COMPLETE SET (15)	60.00	27.00
COMMON CARD (PS1-PS15)	1.50	.70

☐ PS1 Randy Johnson	4.00	1.80
☐ PS2 Hideo Nomo	12.00	5.50
☐ PS3 Albert Belle	6.00	2.70
☐ PS4 Dante Bichette	2.00	.90
☐ PS5 Jay Buhner	3.00	1.35
☐ PS6 Frank Thomas	25.00	11.00
☐ PS7 Mark McGwire	8.00	3.60
☐ PS8 Rafael Palmeiro	3.00	1.35
☐ PS9 Mo Vaughn	6.00	2.70
☐ PS10 Sammy Sosa	4.00	1.80
☐ PS11 Larry Walker	4.00	1.80
☐ PS12 Gary Gaetti	1.50	.70
☐ PS13 Tim Salmon	4.00	1.80
☐ PS14 Barry Bonds	6.00	2.70
☐ PS15 Jim Edmonds	4.00	1.80

1996 Stadium Club Prime Cuts

Randomly inserted at a rate of one in every 36 hobby and 72 retail packs, this 8-card set this set highlights eight hitters with the purest swings. These laser-cut cards feature diffraction gold foil. The cards are numbered on the back with a "PC" prefix.

	MINT	NRMT
COMPLETE SET (8)	60.00	27.00
COMMON CARD (PC1-PC8)	2.00	.90
☐ PC1 Albert Belle	5.00	2.20
☐ PC2 Barry Bonds	5.00	2.20
☐ PC3 Ken Griffey Jr.	20.00	9.00
☐ PC4 Tony Gwynn	8.00	3.60
☐ PC5 Edgar Martinez	2.00	.90
☐ PC6 Rafael Palmeiro	3.00	1.35
☐ PC7 Mike Piazza	12.00	5.50
☐ PC8 Frank Thomas	15.00	6.75

1996 Stadium Club TSC Awards

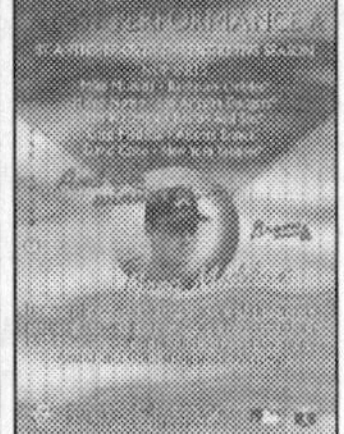

Randomly inserted in packs at a rate of one in 24 (retail) and one in 48 (hobby), this ten-card set features players whom TSC baseball experts voted to win various awards and is printed on diffraction foil.

	MINT	NRMT
COMPLETE SET (10)	40.00	18.00
COMMON CARD (1-10)	1.50	.70
☐ 1 Cal Ripken	12.00	5.50
☐ 2 Albert Belle	6.00	2.70
☐ 3 Tom Glavine	2.00	.90
☐ 4 Jeff Conine	1.50	.70
☐ 5 Ken Griffey Jr.	15.00	6.75
☐ 6 Hideo Nomo	4.00	1.80
☐ 7 Greg Maddux	10.00	4.50
☐ 8 Chipper Jones	10.00	4.50
☐ 9 Randy Johnson	3.00	1.35
☐ 10 Jose Mesa	1.50	.70

1996 Stadium Club Members Only

This 50-card set features color player photos of Topps' selection of 45 (#1-45) of the top 1995 American and National League players. The set includes five Finest

Cards (#46-50) which represent Topps' selection of the top rookies from 1995. The backs carry information about the player.

	MINT	NRMT
COMPLETE SET (50)	20.00	9.00
COMMON CARD (1-50)	.10	.05
☐ 1 Carlos Baerga	.35	.16
☐ 2 Derek Bell	.10	.05
☐ 3 Albert Belle	1.25	.55
☐ 4 Dante Bichette	.50	.23
☐ 5 Craig Biggio	.50	.23
☐ 6 Wade Boggs	.50	.23
☐ 7 Barry Bonds	.75	.35
☐ 8 Jay Buhner	.35	.16
☐ 9 Vinny Castilla	.20	.09
☐ 10 Jeff Conine	.20	.09
☐ 11 Jim Edmonds	.50	.23
☐ 12 Steve Finley	.20	.09
☐ 13 Andres Galarraga	.50	.23
☐ 14 Mark Grace	.35	.16
☐ 15 Tony Gwynn	1.50	.70
☐ 16 Lance Johnson	.10	.05
☐ 17 Randy Johnson	.50	.23
☐ 18 Eric Karros	.20	.09
☐ 19 Chuck Knoblauch	.50	.23
☐ 20 Barry Larkin	.35	.16
☐ 21 Kenny Lofton	.60	.25
☐ 22 Greg Maddux	2.50	1.10
☐ 23 Edgar Martinez	.35	.16
☐ 24 Tino Martinez	.50	.23
☐ 25 Mark McGwire	1.25	.55
☐ 26 Brian McRae	.10	.05
☐ 27 Jose Mesa	.10	.05
☐ 28 Eddie Murray	.50	.23
☐ 29 Mike Mussina	.50	.23
☐ 30 Randy Myers	.20	.09
☐ 31 Hideo Nomo	1.25	.55
☐ 32 Rafael Palmeiro	.35	.16
☐ 33 Tony Phillips	.10	.05
☐ 34 Mike Piazza	2.50	1.10
☐ 35 Kirby Puckett	1.50	.70
☐ 36 Manny Ramirez	.50	.23
☐ 37 Tim Salmon	.50	.23
☐ 38 Reggie Sanders	.10	.05
☐ 39 Sammy Sosa	.50	.23
☐ 40 Frank Thomas	2.50	1.10
☐ 41 Jim Thome	.50	.23
☐ 42 John Valentin	.10	.05
☐ 43 Mo Vaughn	.75	.35
☐ 44 Quilvio Veras	.10	.05
☐ 45 Larry Walker	.50	.23
☐ 46 Hideo Nomo FIN	2.00	.90
☐ 47 Marty Cordova FIN	.20	.09
☐ 48 Chipper Jones FIN	3.00	1.35
☐ 49 Garret Anderson FIN	.30	.14
☐ 50 Andy Pettitte FIN	2.00	.90

1997 Stadium Club Pre-Production

Each Topps wholesale account received one of these three Pre-Production sample cards along with their order forms for 1997 Stadium Club Series 1 baseball. The cards were designed to provide wholesale customers with a sneak preview of the upcoming Stadium Club release. The design parallels the regular issue cards excpt for the PP-prefixed numbering. In addition, the term "Pre-Production Sample" replaces the line of 1996 statistics on back.

	MINT	NRMT
COMPLETE SET (3)	5.00	2.20
COMMON CARD (PP1-PP3)	1.00	.45
☐ PP1 Chipper Jones	3.00	1.35
☐ PP2 Kenny Lofton	2.00	.90
☐ PP3 Gary Sheffield	1.00	.45

1997 Stadium Club

Cards from this 390 card set were distributed in eight-card hobby and retail packs (SRP $3) and 13-card hobby collector packs (SRP $5). Card fronts feature color action player photos printed on 20 pt. card stock with Topps Super Color processing, Hi-gloss laminating, embossing and double foil stamping. The backs carry player information and statistics. In addition to the standard selection of major leaguers, the set contains a 15-card TSC 2000 subset (181-195) featuring a selection of top young prospects. These subset cards were inserted one in every two eight-card first series packs and one per 13-card first series pack. First series cards were released in February, 1997. The 195-card Series 2 set was issued in six-card retail packs with a suggested retail price of $2 and in nine-card hobby packs with a suggested retail price of $3. The second series set features a 15-card Stadium Sluggers subset (376-390) with an insertion rate of one in every two hobby and three retail Series 2 packs. Second series cards were released in April, 1997.

	MINT	NRMT
COMPLETE SET (390)	80.00	36.00
COMPLETE SERIES 1 (195)	40.00	18.00
COMPLETE SERIES 2 (195)	40.00	18.00
COMMON CARD (1-390)	.15	.07
☐ 1 Chipper Jones	2.00	.90
☐ 2 Gary Sheffield	.60	.25
☐ 3 Kenny Lofton	.75	.35
☐ 4 Brian Jordan	.30	.14
☐ 5 Mark McGwire	1.25	.55
☐ 6 Charles Nagy	.30	.14
☐ 7 Tim Salmon	.40	.18
☐ 8 Cal Ripken	2.50	1.10
☐ 9 Jeff Conine	.30	.14
☐ 10 Paul Molitor	.60	.25
☐ 11 Mariano Rivera	.30	.14
☐ 12 Pedro Martinez	.60	.25
☐ 13 Jeff Bagwell	1.25	.55
☐ 14 Bobby Bonilla	.30	.14
☐ 15 Barry Bonds	.75	.35
☐ 16 Ryan Klesko	.40	.18
☐ 17 Barry Larkin	.40	.18
☐ 18 Jim Thome	.60	.25
☐ 19 Jay Buhner	.40	.18
☐ 20 Juan Gonzalez	1.50	.70
☐ 21 Mike Mussina	.60	.25
☐ 22 Kevin Appier	.30	.14
☐ 23 Eric Karros	.30	.14
☐ 24 Steve Finley	.30	.14
☐ 25 Ed Sprague	.15	.07
☐ 26 Bernard Gilkey	.15	.07
☐ 27 Tony Phillips	.15	.07
☐ 28 Henry Rodriguez	.15	.07
☐ 29 John Smoltz	.30	.14
☐ 30 Dante Bichette	.40	.18
☐ 31 Mike Piazza	2.00	.90
☐ 32 Paul O'Neill	.30	.14
☐ 33 Billy Wagner	.30	.14
☐ 34 Reggie Sanders	.15	.07
☐ 35 John Jaha	.15	.07
☐ 36 Eddie Murray	.60	.25
☐ 37 Eric Young	.30	.14
☐ 38 Roberto Hernandez	.15	.07
☐ 39 Pat Hentgen	.30	.14
☐ 40 Sammy Sosa	.60	.25
☐ 41 Todd Hundley	.30	.14
☐ 42 Mo Vaughn	.75	.35
☐ 43 Robin Ventura	.30	.14
☐ 44 Mark Grudzielanek	.15	.07

☐ 45 Shane Reynolds	.15	.07
☐ 46 Andy Pettitte	.60	.25
☐ 47 Fred McGriff	.40	.18
☐ 48 Rey Ordonez	.15	.07
☐ 49 Will Clark	.40	.18
☐ 50 Ken Griffey Jr.	3.00	1.35
☐ 51 Todd Worrell	.30	.14
☐ 52 Rusty Greer	.30	.14
☐ 53 Mark Grace	.40	.18
☐ 54 Tom Glavine	.30	.14
☐ 55 Derek Jeter	2.00	.90
☐ 56 Rafael Palmeiro	.40	.18
☐ 57 Bernie Williams	.60	.25
☐ 58 Marty Cordova	.30	.14
☐ 59 Andres Galarraga	.60	.25
☐ 60 Ken Caminiti	.60	.25
☐ 61 Garret Anderson	.30	.14
☐ 62 Denny Martinez	.30	.14
☐ 63 Mike Greenwell	.15	.07
☐ 64 David Segui	.15	.07
☐ 65 Julio Franco	.30	.14
☐ 66 Rickey Henderson	.40	.18
☐ 67 Ozzie Guillen	.15	.07
☐ 68 Pete Harnisch	.15	.07
☐ 69 Chan Ho Park	.60	.25
☐ 70 Harold Baines	.30	.14
☐ 71 Mark Clark	.15	.07
☐ 72 Steve Avery	.15	.07
☐ 73 Brian Hunter	.30	.14
☐ 74 Pedro Astacio	.15	.07
☐ 75 Jack McDowell	.15	.07
☐ 76 Gregg Jefferies	.30	.14
☐ 77 Jason Kendall	.30	.14
☐ 78 Todd Walker	.15	.07
☐ 79 B.J. Surhoff	.15	.07
☐ 80 Moises Alou	.30	.14
☐ 81 Fernando Vina	.15	.07
☐ 82 Darryl Strawberry	.30	.14
☐ 83 Jose Rosado	.30	.14
☐ 84 Chris Gomez	.15	.07
☐ 85 Chili Davis	.30	.14
☐ 86 Alan Benes	.30	.14
☐ 87 Todd Hollandsworth	.30	.14
☐ 88 Jose Vizcaino	.15	.07
☐ 89 Edgardo Alfonzo	.30	.14
☐ 90 Ruben Rivera	.30	.14
☐ 91 Donovan Osborne	.15	.07
☐ 92 Doug Glanville	.15	.07
☐ 93 Gary DiSarcina	.15	.07
☐ 94 Brooks Kieschnick	.30	.14
☐ 95 Bobby Jones	.15	.07
☐ 96 Raul Casanova	.15	.07
☐ 97 Jermaine Allensworth	.15	.07
☐ 98 Kenny Rogers	.15	.07
☐ 99 Mark McLemore	.15	.07
☐ 100 Jeff Fassero	.15	.07
☐ 101 Sandy Alomar Jr.	.30	.14
☐ 102 Chuck Finley	.15	.07
☐ 103 Eric Owens	.15	.07
☐ 104 Billy McMillon	.15	.07
☐ 105 Dwight Gooden	.30	.14
☐ 106 Sterling Hitchcock	.15	.07
☐ 107 Doug Drabek	.30	.14
☐ 108 Paul Wilson	.15	.07
☐ 109 Chris Snopek	.15	.07
☐ 110 Al Leiter	.15	.07
☐ 111 Bob Tewksbury	.15	.07
☐ 112 Todd Greene	.30	.14
☐ 113 Jose Valentin	.15	.07
☐ 114 Delino DeShields	.15	.07
☐ 115 Mike Bordick	.15	.07
☐ 116 Pat Meares	.15	.07
☐ 117 Mariano Duncan	.15	.07
☐ 118 Steve Trachsel	.15	.07
☐ 119 Luis Castillo	.30	.14
☐ 120 Andy Benes	.30	.14
☐ 121 Donne Wall	.15	.07
☐ 122 Alex Gonzalez	.15	.07
☐ 123 Dan Wilson	.15	.07
☐ 124 Omar Vizquel	.30	.14
☐ 125 Devon White	.15	.07
☐ 126 Darryl Hamilton	.15	.07
☐ 127 Orlando Merced	.15	.07
☐ 128 Royce Clayton	.15	.07
☐ 129 William VanLandingham	.15	.07
☐ 130 Terry Steinbach	.15	.07
☐ 131 Jeff Blauser	.15	.07
☐ 132 Jeff Cirillo	.30	.14
☐ 133 Roger Pavlik	.15	.07
☐ 134 Danny Tartabull	.15	.07
☐ 135 Jeff Montgomery	.15	.07
☐ 136 Bobby Higginson	.30	.14
☐ 137 Mike Grace	.15	.07
☐ 138 Kevin Elster	.15	.07
☐ 139 Brian Giles	.15	.07
☐ 140 Rod Beck	.15	.07
☐ 141 Ismael Valdes	.30	.14
☐ 142 Scott Brosius	.15	.07
☐ 143 Mike Fetters	.15	.07
☐ 144 Gary Gaetti	.30	.14
☐ 145 Mike Lansing	.15	.07
☐ 146 Glenallen Hill	.15	.07
☐ 147 Shawn Green	.15	.07
☐ 148 Mel Rojas	.15	.07
☐ 149 Joey Cora	.30	.14
☐ 150 John Smiley	.15	.07
☐ 151 Marvin Benard	.15	.07
☐ 152 Curt Schilling	.30	.14
☐ 153 Dave Nilsson	.15	.07
☐ 154 Edgar Renteria	.30	.14
☐ 155 Joey Hamilton	.30	.14
☐ 156 Carlos Garcia	.15	.07
☐ 157 Nomar Garciaparra	2.00	.90
☐ 158 Kevin Ritz	.15	.07
☐ 159 Keith Lockhart	.15	.07
☐ 160 Justin Thompson	.30	.14
☐ 161 Terry Adams	.15	.07
☐ 162 Jamey Wright	.30	.14
☐ 163 Otis Nixon	.30	.14
☐ 164 Michael Tucker	.15	.07
☐ 165 Mike Stanley	.15	.07
☐ 166 Ben McDonald	.15	.07
☐ 167 John Mabry	.15	.07
☐ 168 Troy O'Leary	.15	.07
☐ 169 Mel Nieves	.15	.07
☐ 170 Bret Boone	.15	.07
☐ 171 Mike Timlin	.15	.07
☐ 172 Scott Rolen	1.50	.70
☐ 173 Reggie Jefferson	.30	.14
☐ 174 Neifi Perez	.30	.14
☐ 175 Brian McRae	.15	.07
☐ 176 Tom Goodwin	.15	.07
☐ 177 Aaron Sele	.15	.07
☐ 178 Benito Santiago	.15	.07
☐ 179 Frank Rodriguez	.15	.07
☐ 180 Eric Davis	.15	.07
☐ 181 Andruw Jones 2000 SP	3.00	1.35
☐ 182 Todd Walker 2000 SP	1.00	.45
☐ 183 Wes Helms 2000 SP	.75	.35
☐ 184 Nelson Figueroa 2000 SP	.50	.23
☐ 185 Vladimir Guerrero 2000 SP	2.50	1.10
☐ 186 Billy McMillon 2000	.30	.14
☐ 187 Todd Helton 2000 SP	2.50	1.10
☐ 188 Nomar Garciaparra 2000 SP	4.00	1.80
☐ 189 Katsuhiro Maeda 2000	.40	.18
☐ 190 Russell Branyan 2000 SP	2.00	.90
☐ 191 Glendon Rusch 2000	.30	.14
☐ 192 Bartolo Colon 2000	.40	.18
☐ 193 Scott Rolen 2000 SP	3.00	1.35
☐ 194 Angel Echevarria 2000	.30	.14
☐ 195 Bob Abreu 2000	.60	.25
☐ 196 Greg Maddux	2.00	.90
☐ 197 Joe Carter	.30	.14
☐ 198 Alex Ochoa	.15	.07
☐ 199 Ellis Burks	.30	.14
☐ 200 Ivan Rodriguez	.75	.35
☐ 201 Marquis Grissom	.30	.14
☐ 202 Trevor Hoffman	.30	.14
☐ 203 Matt Williams	.40	.18
☐ 204 Carlos Delgado	.30	.14
☐ 205 Ramon Martinez	.30	.14
☐ 206 Chuck Knoblauch	.60	.25
☐ 207 Juan Guzman	.15	.07
☐ 208 Derek Bell	.15	.07
☐ 209 Roger Clemens	1.25	.55
☐ 210 Vladimir Guerrero	1.25	.55
☐ 211 Cecil Fielder	.30	.14
☐ 212 Hideo Nomo	1.25	.55
☐ 213 Frank Thomas	2.50	1.10
☐ 214 Greg Vaughn	.15	.07
☐ 215 Javy Lopez	.30	.14
☐ 216 Raul Mondesi	.40	.18
☐ 217 Wade Boggs	.60	.25
☐ 218 Carlos Baerga	.30	.14
☐ 219 Tony Gwynn	1.50	.70
☐ 220 Tino Martinez	.60	.25
☐ 221 Vinny Castilla	.30	.14
☐ 222 Lance Johnson	.15	.07
☐ 223 David Justice	.60	.25
☐ 224 Rondell White	.30	.14
☐ 225 Dean Palmer	.30	.14
☐ 226 Jim Edmonds	.60	.25
☐ 227 Albert Belle	1.00	.45
☐ 228 Alex Fernandez	.15	.07
☐ 229 Ryne Sandberg	.75	.35
☐ 230 Jose Mesa	.30	.14
☐ 231 David Cone	.30	.14
☐ 232 Troy Percival	.30	.14
☐ 233 Edgar Martinez	.40	.18
☐ 234 Jose Canseco	.40	.18
☐ 235 Kevin Brown	.30	.14
☐ 236 Ray Lankford	.30	.14
☐ 237 Karim Garcia	.30	.14
☐ 238 J.T. Snow	.30	.14
☐ 239 Dennis Eckersley	.40	.18
☐ 240 Roberto Alomar	.60	.25
☐ 241 John Valentin	.15	.07
☐ 242 Ron Gant	.30	.14
☐ 243 Geronimo Berroa	.15	.07
☐ 244 Manny Ramirez	.60	.25
☐ 245 Travis Fryman	.30	.14
☐ 246 Denny Neagle	.30	.14
☐ 247 Randy Johnson	.60	.25
☐ 248 Darin Erstad	1.00	.45
☐ 249 Mark Wohlers	.30	.14
☐ 250 Ken Hill	.15	.07
☐ 251 Larry Walker	.60	.25
☐ 252 Craig Biggio	.40	.18
☐ 253 Brady Anderson	.40	.18
☐ 254 John Wetteland	.30	.14
☐ 255 Andruw Jones	1.50	.70
☐ 256 Turk Wendell	.15	.07
☐ 257 Jason Isringhausen	.15	.07
☐ 258 Jaime Navarro	.15	.07
☐ 259 Sean Berry	.15	.07
☐ 260 Albie Lopez	.15	.07
☐ 261 Jay Bell	.30	.14
☐ 262 Bobby Witt	.15	.07
☐ 263 Tony Clark	.60	.25
☐ 264 Tim Wakefield	.15	.07
☐ 265 Brad Radke	.30	.14
☐ 266 Tim Belcher	.15	.07
☐ 267 Nerio Rodriguez	.50	.23
☐ 268 Roger Cedeno	.15	.07
☐ 269 Tim Naehring	.15	.07
☐ 270 Kevin Tapani	.15	.07
☐ 271 Joe Randa	.15	.07
☐ 272 Randy Myers	.30	.14
☐ 273 Dave Burba	.15	.07
☐ 274 Mike Sweeney	.15	.07
☐ 275 Danny Graves	.15	.07
☐ 276 Chad Mottola	.15	.07
☐ 277 Ruben Sierra	.15	.07
☐ 278 Norm Charlton	.15	.07
☐ 279 Scott Servais	.15	.07
☐ 280 Jacob Cruz	.15	.07
☐ 281 Mike Macfarlane	.15	.07
☐ 282 Rich Becker	.15	.07
☐ 283 Shannon Stewart	.30	.14
☐ 284 Gerald Williams	.15	.07
☐ 285 Jody Reed	.15	.07
☐ 286 Jeff D'Amico	.15	.07
☐ 287 Walt Weiss	.15	.07
☐ 288 Jim Leyritz	.15	.07
☐ 289 Francisco Cordova	.15	.07
☐ 290 F.P. Santangelo	.15	.07
☐ 291 Scott Erickson	.15	.07
☐ 292 Hal Morris	.15	.07
☐ 293 Ray Durham	.15	.07
☐ 294 Andy Ashby	.15	.07
☐ 295 Darryl Kile	.30	.14
☐ 296 Jose Paniagua	.15	.07
☐ 297 Mickey Tettleton	.30	.14
☐ 298 Joe Girardi	.15	.07
☐ 299 Rocky Coppinger	.15	.07
☐ 300 Bob Abreu	.60	.25
☐ 301 John Olerud	.30	.14
☐ 302 Paul Shuey	.15	.07
☐ 303 Jeff Brantley	.15	.07
☐ 304 Bob Wells	.15	.07
☐ 305 Kevin Seitzer	.15	.07
☐ 306 Shawon Dunston	.15	.07
☐ 307 Jose Herrera	.15	.07
☐ 308 Butch Huskey	.30	.14
☐ 309 Jose Offerman	.15	.07
☐ 310 Rick Aguilera	.30	.14
☐ 311 Greg Gagne	.15	.07
☐ 312 John Burkett	.15	.07
☐ 313 Mark Thompson	.15	.07
☐ 314 Alvaro Espinoza	.15	.07
☐ 315 Todd Stottlemyre	.15	.07
☐ 316 Al Martin	.15	.07
☐ 317 James Baldwin	.15	.07
☐ 318 Cal Eldred	.15	.07
☐ 319 Sid Fernandez	.15	.07
☐ 320 Mickey Morandini	.15	.07
☐ 321 Robb Nen	.15	.07
☐ 322 Mark Lemke	.15	.07
☐ 323 Pete Schourek	.15	.07
☐ 324 Marcus Jensen	.15	.07
☐ 325 Rich Aurilla	.15	.07
☐ 326 Jeff King	.30	.14
☐ 327 Scott Stahoviak	.15	.07
☐ 328 Ricky Otero	.15	.07
☐ 329 Antonio Osuna	.15	.07
☐ 330 Chris Hoiles	.15	.07
☐ 331 Luis Gonzalez	.15	.07
☐ 332 Wil Cordero	.15	.07
☐ 333 Johnny Damon	.30	.14
☐ 334 Mark Langston	.15	.07
☐ 335 Orlando Miller	.15	.07

	MINT	NRMT
☐ 336 Jason Giambi	.15	.07
☐ 337 Damian Jackson	.15	.07
☐ 338 David Wells	.15	.07
☐ 339 Bip Roberts	.15	.07
☐ 340 Matt Ruebel	.15	.07
☐ 341 Tom Candiotti	.15	.07
☐ 342 Wally Joyner	.15	.07
☐ 343 Jimmy Key	.30	.14
☐ 344 Tony Batista	.30	.14
☐ 345 Paul Sorrento	.15	.07
☐ 346 Ron Karkovice	.15	.07
☐ 347 Wilson Alvarez	.30	.14
☐ 348 John Flaherty	.15	.07
☐ 349 Rey Sanchez	.15	.07
☐ 350 John Vander Wal	.15	.07
☐ 351 Jermaine Dye	.15	.07
☐ 352 Mike Hampton	.15	.07
☐ 353 Greg Colbrunn	.15	.07
☐ 354 Heathcliff Slocumb	.15	.07
☐ 355 Ricky Bottalico	.30	.14
☐ 356 Marty Janzen	.15	.07
☐ 357 Orel Hershiser	.30	.14
☐ 358 Rex Hudler	.15	.07
☐ 359 Amaury Telemaco	.15	.07
☐ 360 Darrin Fletcher	.15	.07
☐ 361 Brant Brown UER Card numbered 351	.15	.07
☐ 362 Russ Davis	.15	.07
☐ 363 Allen Watson	.15	.07
☐ 364 Mike Lieberthal	.15	.07
☐ 365 Dave Stevens	.15	.07
☐ 366 Jay Powell	.15	.07
☐ 367 Tony Fossas	.15	.07
☐ 368 Bob Wolcott	.15	.07
☐ 369 Mark Loretta	.15	.07
☐ 370 Shawn Estes	.30	.14
☐ 371 Sandy Martinez	.15	.07
☐ 372 Wendell Magee Jr.	.15	.07
☐ 373 John Franco	.30	.14
☐ 374 Tom Pagnozzi UER misnumbered as 274	.15	.07
☐ 375 Willie Adams	.15	.07
☐ 376 Chipper Jones SS SP	4.00	1.80
☐ 377 Mo Vaughn SS SP	.60	.25
☐ 378 Frank Thomas SS SP	5.00	2.20
☐ 379 Albert Belle SS SP	1.50	.70
☐ 380 Andres Galarraga SS SP	.60	.25
☐ 381 Gary Sheffield SS SP	.60	.25
☐ 382 Jeff Bagwell SS SP	2.50	1.10
☐ 383 Mike Piazza SS SP	4.00	1.80
☐ 384 Mark McGwire SS SP	2.50	1.10
☐ 385 Ken Griffey Jr. SS SP	6.00	2.70
☐ 386 Barry Bonds SS SP	1.50	.70
☐ 387 Juan Gonzalez SS SP	3.00	1.35
☐ 388 Brady Anderson SS SP	.40	.18
☐ 389 Ken Caminiti SS SP	.40	.18
☐ 390 Jay Buhner SS SP	.40	.18

1997 Stadium Club Matrix

Randomly inserted in first and second series eight-card packs at a rate of one in 12 and in 13-card packs at a rate of one in six, this 120-card set is parallel to the first 60 cards of both the series one and series two of the regular set. Each Matrix card was reproduced with Power Matrix technology, giving the card fronts a glittering effect.

	MINT	NRMT
COMPLETE SET (120)	500.00	220.00
COMPLETE SERIES 1 (60)	250.00	110.00
COMPLETE SERIES 2 (60)	250.00	110.00
COMMON CARD (1-60)	1.25	.55
COMMON CARD (196-255)	1.25	.55

*STARS: 6X TO 12X BASIC CARDS ....
*YOUNG STARS: 5X TO 10X BASIC CARDS

1997 Stadium Club Co-Signers

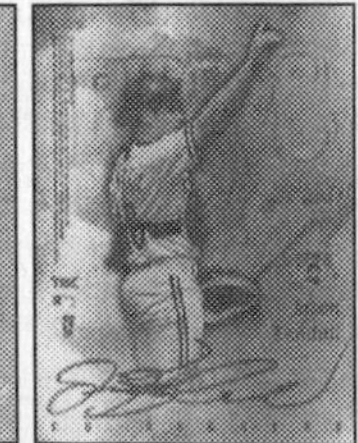

Randomly inserted in first series eight-card hobby packs at a rate of one in 168 and first series 13-card hobby collector packs at a rate of one in 96, cards (CO1-CO5) from this dual-sided, dual-player set feature color action player photos printed on 20pt. card stock with authentic signatures of two major league stand-outs per card. The last five cards (CO6-CO10) were randomly inserted in second series 10-card hobby packs with a rate of one in 168 and inserted with a rate of one in 96 hobby collector packs.

	MINT	NRMT
COMPLETE SET (10)	750.00	350.00
COMPLETE SERIES 1 (5)	400.00	180.00
COMPLETE SERIES 2 (5)	350.00	160.00
COMMON CARD (CO1-CO10)	40.00	18.00
☐ CO1 Andy Pettitte Derek Jeter	150.00	70.00
☐ CO2 Paul Wilson Todd Hundley	40.00	18.00
☐ CO3 Jermaine Dye Mark Wohlers	50.00	22.00
☐ CO4 Scott Rolen Gregg Jefferies	100.00	45.00
☐ CO5 Todd Hollandsworth Jason Kendall	60.00	27.00
☐ CO6 Alan Benes Robin Ventura	60.00	27.00
☐ CO7 Eric Karros Raul Mondesi	60.00	27.00
☐ CO8 Rey Ordonez Nomar Garciaparra	120.00	55.00
☐ CO9 Rondell White Marty Cordova	50.00	22.00
☐ CO10 Tony Gwynn Karim Garcia	120.00	55.00

1997 Stadium Club Firebrand Redemption

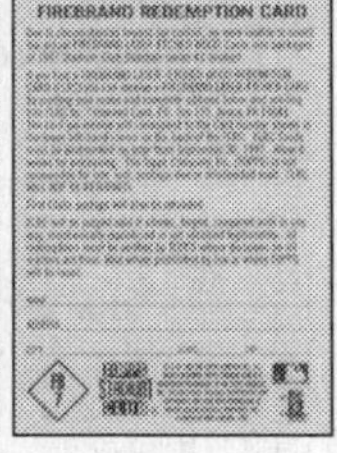

Randomly inserted exclusively into first series eight-card retail packs at a rate of one in 36, these redemption cards feature a selection of the leagues top sluggers. Due to circumstances beyond the manufacturers control, they were not able to insert the actual etched-wood cards into packs and had to resort to these redemption cards.

	MINT	NRMT
COMPLETE SET (12)	150.00	70.00
COMMON CARD (F1-F12)	4.00	1.80

*WOOD CARDS: 1.25X BASIC CARDS

	MINT	NRMT
☐ F1 Jeff Bagwell	12.00	5.50
☐ F2 Albert Belle	8.00	3.60
☐ F3 Barry Bonds	8.00	3.60
☐ F4 Andres Galarraga	5.00	2.20
☐ F5 Ken Griffey Jr.	30.00	13.50
☐ F6 Brady Anderson	4.00	1.80
☐ F7 Mark McGwire	12.00	5.50
☐ F8 Chipper Jones	20.00	9.00
☐ F9 Frank Thomas	25.00	11.00
☐ F10 Mike Piazza	20.00	9.00
☐ F11 Mo Vaughn	8.00	3.60
☐ F12 Juan Gonzalez	15.00	6.75

1997 Stadium Club Instavision

The first ten cards of this 22-card set were randomly inserted in first series eight-card packs at a rate of one in 24 and first series 13-card packs at a rate of 1:12. The last 12 cards were inserted in series two packs at the rate of one in 24 and one in 12 in hobby collector packs. The set highlights some of the 1996 season's most exciting moments through exclusive holographic video action.

	MINT	NRMT
COMPLETE SET (22)	80.00	36.00
COMPLETE SERIES 1 (10)	30.00	13.50
COMPLETE SERIES 2 (12)	50.00	22.00
COMMON CARD (I1-I22)	2.50	1.10
☐ I1 Eddie Murray	5.00	2.20
☐ I2 Paul Molitor	5.00	2.20
☐ I3 Todd Hundley	2.50	1.10
☐ I4 Roger Clemens	10.00	4.50
☐ I5 Barry Bonds	6.00	2.70
☐ I6 Mark McGwire	10.00	4.50
☐ I7 Brady Anderson	4.00	1.80
☐ I8 Barry Larkin	4.00	1.80
☐ I9 Ken Caminiti	5.00	2.20
☐ I10 Hideo Nomo	12.00	5.50

1997 Stadium Club Millennium

Randomly inserted in first and second series eight-card packs at a rate of one in 24 and 13-card packs at a rate of 1:12, this 40-card set features color player photos of 40 breakthrough stars of Major League Baseball reproduced using state-of-the-art advanced embossed holographic technology.

	MINT	NRMT
COMPLETE SET (40)	250.00	110.00
COMPLETE SERIES 1 (20)	100.00	45.00
COMPLETE SERIES 2 (20)	150.00	70.00
COMMON CARD (M1-M40)	3.00	1.35
☐ M1 Derek Jeter	20.00	9.00
☐ M2 Mark Grudzielanek	3.00	1.35
☐ M3 Jacob Cruz	3.00	1.35
☐ M4 Ray Durham	4.00	1.80
☐ M5 Tony Clark	8.00	3.60
☐ M6 Chipper Jones	25.00	11.00
☐ M7 Luis Castillo	4.00	1.80
☐ M8 Carlos Delgado	4.00	1.80
☐ M9 Brant Brown	3.00	1.35
☐ M10 Jason Kendall	4.00	1.80
☐ M11 Alan Benes	4.00	1.80
☐ M12 Rey Ordonez	4.00	1.80
☐ M13 Justin Thompson	4.00	1.80
☐ M14 Jermaine Allensworth	4.00	1.80
☐ M15 Brian Hunter	3.00	1.35
☐ M16 Marty Cordova	4.00	1.80
☐ M17 Edgar Renteria	4.00	1.80
☐ M18 Karim Garcia	3.00	1.35
☐ M19 Todd Greene	4.00	1.80
☐ M20 Paul Wilson	3.00	1.35

1997 Stadium Club Patent Leather

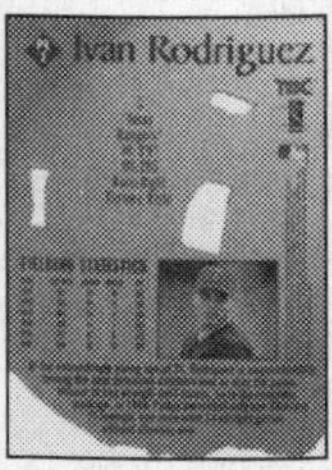

Randomly inserted in second series retail packs only at a rate of one in 36, this 13-card set features action player images standing in a baseball glove and with an inner die-cut glove background printed on leather card stock.

	MINT	NRMT
COMPLETE SET (13)	125.00	55.00
COMMON CARD (PL1-PL13)	3.00	1.35

☐ PL1 Ivan Rodriguez	10.00	4.50
☐ PL2 Ken Caminiti	8.00	3.60
☐ PL3 Barry Bonds	10.00	4.50
☐ PL4 Ken Griffey Jr.	40.00	18.00
☐ PL5 Greg Maddux	25.00	11.00
☐ PL6 Craig Biggio	5.00	2.20
☐ PL7 Andres Galarraga	8.00	3.60
☐ PL8 Kenny Lofton	10.00	4.50
☐ PL9 Barry Larkin	5.00	2.20
☐ PL10 Mark Grace	5.00	2.20
☐ PL11 Rey Ordonez	3.00	1.35
☐ PL12 Roberto Alomar	8.00	3.60
☐ PL13 Derek Jeter	20.00	9.00

1997 Stadium Club Pure Gold

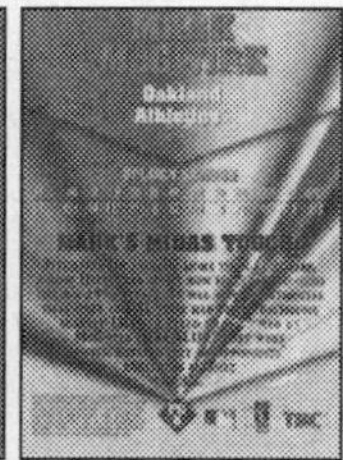

Randomly inserted in first and second series eight-card packs at a rate of one in 72 and 13-card packs at a rate of one in 36, this 20-card set features color action star player photos reproduced on 20 pt. embossed gold mirror foilboard.

	MINT	NRMT
COMPLETE SET (20)	450.00	200.00
COMPLETE SERIES 1 (10)	200.00	90.00
COMPLETE SERIES 2 (10)	250.00	110.00
COMMON CARD (PG1-PG20)	8.00	3.60
☐ PG1 Brady Anderson	8.00	3.60
☐ PG2 Albert Belle	15.00	6.75
☐ PG3 Dante Bichette	8.00	3.60
☐ PG4 Barry Bonds	15.00	6.75
☐ PG5 Jay Buhner	8.00	3.60
☐ PG6 Tony Gwynn	30.00	13.50
☐ PG7 Chipper Jones	40.00	18.00
☐ PG8 Mark McGwire	25.00	11.00
☐ PG9 Gary Sheffield	10.00	4.50
☐ PG10 Frank Thomas	50.00	22.00
☐ PG11 Juan Gonzalez	30.00	13.50
☐ PG12 Ken Caminiti	10.00	4.50
☐ PG13 Kenny Lofton	15.00	6.75
☐ PG14 Jeff Bagwell	25.00	11.00
☐ PG15 Ken Griffey Jr.	60.00	27.00
☐ PG16 Cal Ripken	50.00	22.00
☐ PG17 Mo Vaughn	15.00	6.75
☐ PG18 Mike Piazza	40.00	18.00
☐ PG19 Derek Jeter	30.00	13.50
☐ PG20 Andres Galarraga	10.00	4.50

1997 Stadium Club Members Only Parallel

These cards are a parallel issue to the 1997 Stadium Club Series 1 and Series 2 sets and the following insert sets: Millennium, Instavision, Firebrand, and Pure Gold. No first series Co-Signers insert cards are in this set, but it does contain the second series Patent Leather insert set. The only difference between the regular issue cards and these parallels are the words "TSC Members Only" printed lightly in the background. The cards all come together in factory set form and one must be a member of Topps Stadium Club to order these cards.

	MINT	NRMT
COMPLETE SET (497)	400.00	180.00
COMPLETE SERIES 1 (235)	200.00	90.00
COMPLETE SERIES 2 (242)	200.00	90.00
COMMON CARD (1-390)	.25	.11
*MEMBERS ONLY: 6X BASIC CARDS.		
☐ I1 Eddie Murray	4.00	1.80
☐ I2 Paul Molitor	4.00	1.80
☐ I3 Todd Hundley	1.50	.70
☐ I4 Roger Clemens	7.50	3.40
☐ I5 Barry Bonds	5.00	2.20
☐ I6 Mark McGwire	8.00	3.60
☐ I7 Brady Anderson	3.00	1.35
☐ I8 Barry Larkin	3.00	1.35
☐ I9 Ken Caminiti	3.00	1.35
☐ I10 Hideo Nomo	10.00	4.50
☐ I11 Bernie Williams	3.00	1.35
☐ I12 Juan Gonzalez	10.00	4.50
☐ I13 Andy Pettitte	3.00	1.35
☐ I14 Albert Belle	6.00	2.70
☐ I15 John Smoltz	2.00	.90
☐ I16 Brian Jordan	1.00	.45
☐ I17 Derek Jeter	12.50	5.50
☐ I18 Ken Caminiti	3.00	1.35
☐ I19 John Wetteland	2.00	.90
☐ I20 Brady Anderson	3.00	1.35
☐ I21 Andruw Jones	8.00	3.60
☐ I22 Jim Leyritz	1.00	.45
☐ M1 Derek Jeter	12.50	5.50
☐ M2 Mark Grudzielanek	2.50	1.10
☐ M3 Jacob Cruz	2.00	.90
☐ M4 Ray Durham	2.50	1.10
☐ M5 Tony Clark	6.00	2.70
☐ M6 Chipper Jones	12.50	5.50
☐ M7 Luis Castillo	2.00	.90
☐ M8 Carlos Delgado	2.50	1.10
☐ M9 Brant Brown	2.00	.90
☐ M10 Jason Kendall	2.50	1.10
☐ M11 Alan Benes	2.00	.90
☐ M12 Rey Ordonez	1.00	.45
☐ M13 Justin Thompson	2.00	.90
☐ M14 Jermaine Allensworth	2.00	.90
☐ M15 Brian L. Hunter	2.00	.90
☐ M16 Marty Cordova	2.50	1.10
☐ M17 Edgar Renteria	2.00	.90
☐ M18 Karim Garcia	2.00	.90
☐ M19 Todd Greene	1.00	.45
☐ M20 Paul Wilson	2.00	.90
☐ M21 Andruw Jones	8.00	3.60
☐ M22 Todd Walker	1.00	.45
☐ M23 Alex Ochoa	.25	.11
☐ M24 Bartolo Colon	.25	.11
☐ M25 Wendell Magee Jr.	1.00	.45
☐ M26 Jose Rosado	1.00	.45
☐ M27 Katsuhiro Maeda	2.00	.90
☐ M28 Bob Abreu	2.00	.90
☐ M29 Brooks Kieschnick	1.00	.45
☐ M30 Derrick Gibson	2.00	.90
☐ M31 Mike Sweeney	1.00	.45
☐ M32 Jeff D'Amico	1.00	.45
☐ M33 Chad Mottola	1.00	.45
☐ M34 Chris Snopek	1.00	.45
☐ M35 Jaime Bluma	1.00	.45
☐ M36 Vladimir Guerrero	5.00	2.20
☐ M37 Nomar Garciaparra	15.00	6.75
☐ M38 Scott Rolen	7.50	3.40
☐ M39 Dmitri Young	1.00	.45
☐ M40 Neifi Perez	1.00	.45
☐ FB1 Jeff Bagwell	6.00	2.70
☐ FB2 Albert Belle	6.00	2.70
☐ FB3 Barry Bonds	5.00	2.20
☐ FB4 Andres Galarraga	4.00	1.80
☐ FB5 Ken Griffey Jr.	25.00	11.00
☐ FB6 Brady Anderson	3.00	1.35
☐ FB7 Mark McGwire	8.00	3.60
☐ FB8 Chipper Jones	12.50	5.50
☐ FB9 Frank Thomas	20.00	9.00
☐ FB10 Mike Piazza	12.50	5.50
☐ FB11 Mo Vaughn	5.00	2.20
☐ FB12 Juan Gonzalez	10.00	4.50
☐ PG1 Brady Anderson	3.00	1.35
☐ PG2 Albert Belle	6.00	2.70
☐ PG3 Dante Bichette	2.50	1.10
☐ PG4 Barry Bonds	5.00	2.20
☐ PG5 Jay Buhner	2.50	1.10
☐ PG6 Tony Gwynn	8.00	3.60
☐ PG7 Chipper Jones	12.50	5.50
☐ PG8 Mark McGwire	8.00	3.60
☐ PG9 Gary Sheffield	3.00	1.35
☐ PG10 Frank Thomas	20.00	9.00
☐ PG11 Juan Gonzalez	10.00	4.50
☐ PG12 Ken Caminiti	3.00	1.35
☐ PG13 Kenny Lofton	5.00	2.20
☐ PG14 Jeff Bagwell	6.00	2.70
☐ PG15 Ken Griffey Jr.	25.00	11.00
☐ PG16 Cal Ripken	20.00	9.00
☐ PG17 Mo Vaughn	5.00	2.20
☐ PG18 Mike Piazza	12.50	5.50
☐ PG19 Derek Jeter	12.50	5.50
☐ PG20 Andres Galarraga	4.00	1.80
☐ PL1 Ivan Rodriguez	6.00	2.70
☐ PL2 Ken Caminiti	3.00	1.35
☐ PL3 Barry Bonds	5.00	2.20
☐ PL4 Ken Griffey Jr.	25.00	11.00
☐ PL5 Greg Maddux	15.00	6.75
☐ PL6 Craig Biggio	4.00	1.80
☐ PL7 Andres Galarraga	4.00	1.80
☐ PL8 Kenny Lofton	5.00	2.20
☐ PL9 Barry Larkin	3.00	1.35
☐ PL10 Mark Grace	3.00	1.35
☐ PL11 Rey Ordonez	1.00	.45
☐ PL12 Roberto Alomar	3.00	1.35
☐ PL13 Derek Jeter	12.50	5.50

1953 Stahl Meyer

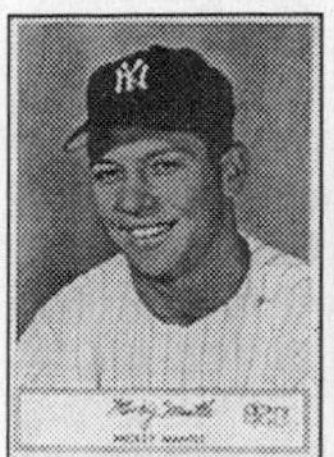

The cards in this nine-card set measure approximately 3 1/4" by 4 1/2". The 1953 Stahl Meyer set of full color, unnumbered cards includes three players from each of the three New York teams. The cards have white borders. The Lockman card is the most plentiful of any card in the set. Some batting and fielding statistics and short biography are included on the back. The cards are ordered in the checklist below by alphabetical order without regard to team affiliation.

	NRMT	VG-E
COMPLETE SET	4500.00	2000.00
COMMON CARD (1-9)	125.00	55.00
☐ 1 Hank Bauer	150.00	70.00
☐ 2 Roy Campanella	600.00	275.00
☐ 3 Gil Hodges	300.00	135.00
☐ 4 Monte Irvin	200.00	90.00
☐ 5 Whitey Lockman	125.00	55.00
☐ 6 Mickey Mantle	2500.00	1100.00
☐ 7 Phil Rizzuto	300.00	135.00
☐ 8 Duke Snider	600.00	275.00
☐ 9 Bobby Thomson	150.00	70.00

1954 Stahl Meyer

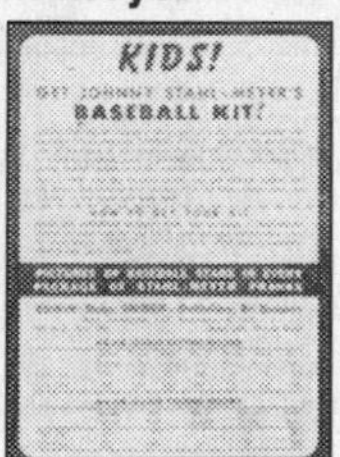

The cards in this 12-card set measure approximately 3 1/4" by 4 1/2". The 1954 Stahl Meyer set of full color, unnumbered cards includes four players from each of the three New York teams. The cards have yellow borders and the backs, oriented horizontally, include an ad for a baseball kit and the player's statistics. No player biography is included on the back. The cards are ordered in the checklist below by alphabetical order without regard to team affiliation.

	NRMT	VG-E
COMPLETE SET (12)	6750.00	3000.00
COMMON CARD (1-12)	150.00	70.00
☐ 1 Hank Bauer	175.00	80.00
☐ 2 Carl Erskine	175.00	80.00
☐ 3 Gil Hodges	325.00	145.00
☐ 4 Monte Irvin	225.00	100.00
☐ 5 Whitey Lockman	150.00	70.00
☐ 6 Mickey Mantle	3000.00	1350.00
☐ 7 Willie Mays	1500.00	700.00
☐ 8 Gil McDougald	175.00	80.00
☐ 9 Don Mueller	150.00	70.00
☐ 10 Don Newcombe	175.00	80.00
☐ 11 Phil Rizzuto	300.00	135.00
☐ 12 Duke Snider	600.00	275.00

1955 Stahl Meyer

The cards in this 12-card set measure approximately 3 1/4" by 4 1/2". The 1955 Stahl Meyer set of full color, unnumbered cards contains four players each from the three New York teams. As in the 1954 set, the cards have yellow borders; however, the back of the cards contain a sketch of Mickey Mantle with an ad for a baseball cap or a pennant. The cards are ordered in the checklist below by alphabetical order without regard to team affiliation.

	NRMT	VG-E
COMPLETE SET (12)	5500.00	2500.00
COMMON CARD (1-12)	150.00	70.00

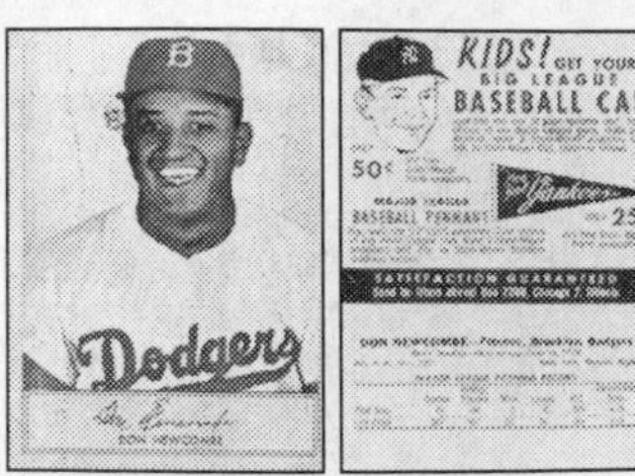

☐ 1 Hank Bauer	175.00	80.00
☐ 2 Carl Erskine	175.00	80.00
☐ 3 Gil Hodges	325.00	145.00
☐ 4 Monte Irvin	225.00	100.00
☐ 5 Whitey Lockman	150.00	70.00
☐ 6 Mickey Mantle	3000.00	1350.00
☐ 7 Gil McDougald	175.00	80.00
☐ 8 Don Mueller	150.00	70.00
☐ 9 Don Newcombe	175.00	80.00
☐ 10 Dusty Rhodes	150.00	70.00
☐ 11 Phil Rizzuto	325.00	145.00
☐ 12 Duke Snider	600.00	275.00

1990 Starline Long John Silver

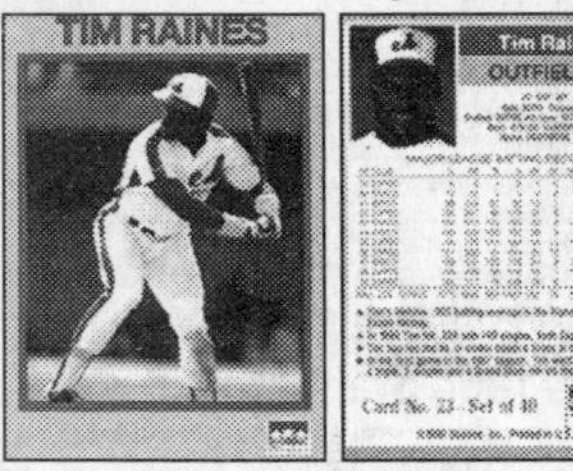

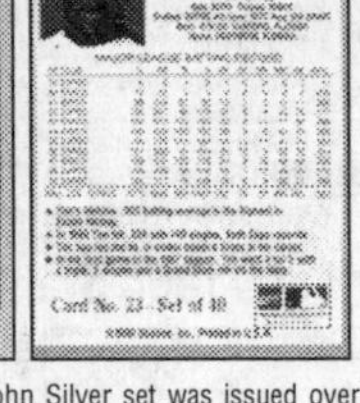

The 1990 Starline Long John Silver set was issued over an eight-week promotion, five cards at a time within a cello pack. The set was initially available only through the Long John Silver seafood fast-food chain with one pack being given to each customer who ordered a meal with a 32-ounce Coke. This 40-card, standard-size set featured the best of today's players. There are several cards for some of the players in the set. After the promotion at Long John Silver had been completed, there were reportedly more than 100,000 sets left over that were released into the organized hobby.

	MINT	NRMT
COMPLETE SET (40)	6.00	2.70
COMMON CARD (1-40)	.10	.05
☐ 1 Don Mattingly	.50	.23
☐ 2 Mark Grace	.40	.18
☐ 3 Eric Davis	.20	.09
☐ 4 Tony Gwynn	.60	.25
☐ 5 Bobby Bonilla	.20	.09
☐ 6 Wade Boggs	.30	.14
☐ 7 Frank Viola	.10	.05
☐ 8 Ruben Sierra	.10	.05
☐ 9 Mark McGwire	.75	.35
☐ 10 Alan Trammell	.30	.14
☐ 11 Mark McGwire	.50	.23
☐ 12 Gregg Jefferies	.20	.09
☐ 13 Nolan Ryan	1.00	.45
☐ 14 John Smoltz	.20	.09
☐ 15 Glenn Davis	.10	.05
☐ 16 Mark Grace	.30	.14
☐ 17 Wade Boggs	.40	.18
☐ 18 Frank Viola	.10	.05
☐ 19 Bret Saberhagen	.10	.05
☐ 20 Chris Sabo	.10	.05
☐ 21 Darryl Strawberry	.20	.09
☐ 22 Wade Boggs	.30	.14
☐ 23 Tim Raines	.10	.05
☐ 24 Alan Trammell	.20	.09
☐ 25 Chris Sabo	.10	.05
☐ 26 Nolan Ryan	1.00	.45
☐ 27 Mark McGwire	.75	.35
☐ 28 Don Mattingly	.50	.23
☐ 29 Tony Gwynn	.60	.25
☐ 30 Glenn Davis	.10	.05
☐ 31 Bobby Bonilla	.20	.09
☐ 32 Gregg Jefferies	.20	.09
☐ 33 Ruben Sierra	.10	.05
☐ 34 John Smoltz	.20	.09
☐ 35 Don Mattingly	.50	.23
☐ 36 Bret Saberhagen	.10	.05
☐ 37 Darryl Strawberry	.20	.09
☐ 38 Eric Davis	.10	.05
☐ 39 Tim Raines	.10	.05
☐ 40 Mark Grace	.30	.14

1991 Studio Previews

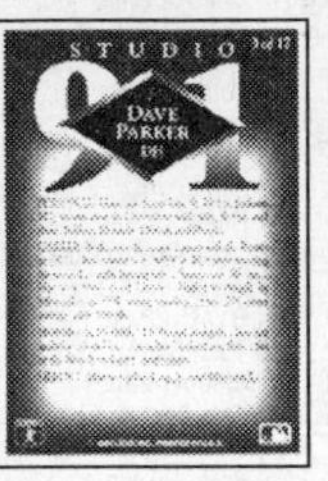

This 18-card preview set was issued four at a time within 1991 Donruss retail factory sets in order to show dealers and collectors the look of their new Studio cards. The standard-size cards are exactly the same style as those in the Studio series, with black and white player photos bordered in mauve and player information on the backs.

	MINT	NRMT
COMPLETE SET (18)	20.00	9.00
COMMON CARD (1-17)	1.00	.45
☐ 1 Juan Bell	1.00	.45
☐ 2 Roger Clemens	10.00	4.50
☐ 3 Dave Parker	2.00	.90
☐ 4 Tim Raines	2.00	.90
☐ 5 Kevin Seitzer	1.00	.45
☐ 6 Ted Higuera	1.00	.45
☐ 7 Bernie Williams	8.00	3.60
☐ 8 Harold Baines	2.00	.90
☐ 9 Gary Pettis	1.00	.45
☐ 10 Dave Justice	5.00	2.20
☐ 11 Eric Davis	2.00	.90
☐ 12 Andujar Cedeno	1.00	.45
☐ 13 Tom Foley	1.00	.45
☐ 14 Dwight Gooden	2.00	.90
☐ 15 Doug Drabek	1.00	.45
☐ 16 Steve Decker	1.00	.45
☐ 17 Joe Torre MG	2.00	.90
☐ NNO Title card	1.00	.45

1991 Studio

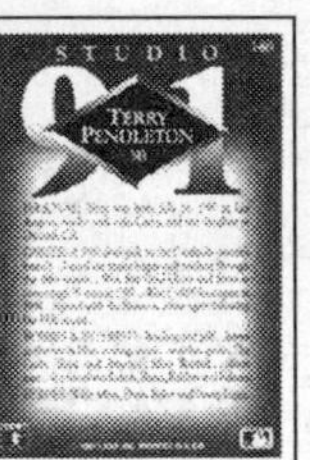

The 1991 Studio set, issued by Donruss/Leaf, contains 264 standard-size cards issued in one series. Cards were distributed in foil packs each of which contained one of 21 different Rod Carew puzzle panels. The Studio card fronts feature posed black and white head-and-shoulders player photos with mauve borders. The team logo, player's name, and position appear along the bottom of the card face. The cards are ordered alphabetically within and according to teams for each league with American League teams preceding National League. Rookie Cards in the set include Jeff Bagwell, Jeff Conine and Brian McRae.

	MINT	NRMT
COMPLETE SET (264)	15.00	6.75
COMMON CARD (1-263)	.10	.05
☐ 1 Glenn Davis	.10	.05
☐ 2 Dwight Evans	.20	.09
☐ 3 Leo Gomez	.10	.05
☐ 4 Chris Hoiles	.10	.05
☐ 5 Sam Horn	.10	.05
☐ 6 Ben McDonald	.20	.09
☐ 7 Randy Milligan	.10	.05
☐ 8 Gregg Olson	.10	.05
☐ 9 Cal Ripken	1.50	.70
☐ 10 David Segui	.20	.09
☐ 11 Wade Boggs	.40	.18
☐ 12 Ellis Burks	.10	.05
☐ 13 Jack Clark	.20	.09
☐ 14 Roger Clemens	.75	.35
☐ 15 Mike Greenwell	.10	.05
☐ 16 Tim Naehring	.20	.09
☐ 17 Tony Pena	.10	.05
☐ 18 Phil Plantier	.20	.09
☐ 19 Jeff Reardon	.20	.09
☐ 20 Mo Vaughn	.75	.35
☐ 21 Jimmy Reese CO	.20	.09
☐ 22 Jim Abbott UER (Born in 1967, not 1969)	.20	.09
☐ 23 Bert Blyleven	.20	.09
☐ 24 Chuck Finley	.20	.09
☐ 25 Gary Gaetti	.20	.09
☐ 26 Wally Joyner	.20	.09
☐ 27 Mark Langston	.10	.05
☐ 28 Kirk McCaskill	.10	.05
☐ 29 Lance Parrish	.10	.05
☐ 30 Dave Winfield	.40	.18
☐ 31 Alex Fernandez	.20	.09
☐ 32 Carlton Fisk	.40	.18
☐ 33 Scott Fletcher	.10	.05
☐ 34 Greg Hibbard	.10	.05
☐ 35 Charlie Hough	.10	.05
☐ 36 Jack McDowell	.10	.05
☐ 37 Tim Raines	.20	.09
☐ 38 Sammy Sosa	.50	.23
☐ 39 Bobby Thigpen	.10	.05
☐ 40 Frank Thomas	3.00	1.35
☐ 41 Sandy Alomar Jr.	.10	.05
☐ 42 John Farrell	.10	.05
☐ 43 Glenallen Hill	.10	.05
☐ 44 Brook Jacoby	.10	.05
☐ 45 Chris James	.10	.05
☐ 46 Doug Jones	.10	.05
☐ 47 Eric King	.10	.05
☐ 48 Mark Lewis	.10	.05
☐ 49 Greg Swindell UER (Photo actually Turner Ward)	.10	.05
☐ 50 Mark Whiten	.10	.05
☐ 51 Milt Cuyler	.10	.05
☐ 52 Rob Deer	.10	.05
☐ 53 Cecil Fielder	.20	.09
☐ 54 Travis Fryman	.40	.18
☐ 55 Bill Gullickson	.10	.05
☐ 56 Lloyd Moseby	.10	.05
☐ 57 Frank Tanana	.10	.05
☐ 58 Mickey Tettleton	.20	.09
☐ 59 Alan Trammell	.40	.18
☐ 60 Lou Whitaker	.10	.05
☐ 61 Mike Boddicker	.10	.05
☐ 62 George Brett	.75	.35
☐ 63 Jeff Conine	.50	.23
☐ 64 Warren Cromartie	.10	.05
☐ 65 Storm Davis	.10	.05
☐ 66 Kirk Gibson	.20	.09
☐ 67 Mark Gubicza	.10	.05
☐ 68 Brian McRae	.40	.18
☐ 69 Bret Saberhagen	.10	.05
☐ 70 Kurt Stillwell	.10	.05
☐ 71 Tim McIntosh	.10	.05
☐ 72 Candy Maldonado	.10	.05
☐ 73 Paul Molitor	.40	.18
☐ 74 Willie Randolph	.20	.09
☐ 75 Ron Robinson	.10	.05
☐ 76 Gary Sheffield	.40	.18
☐ 77 Franklin Stubbs	.10	.05
☐ 78 B.J. Surhoff	.20	.09
☐ 79 Greg Vaughn	.20	.09
☐ 80 Robin Yount	.40	.18
☐ 81 Rick Aguilera	.20	.09
☐ 82 Steve Bedrosian	.10	.05
☐ 83 Scott Erickson	.20	.09
☐ 84 Greg Gagne	.10	.05
☐ 85 Dan Gladden	.10	.05
☐ 86 Brian Harper	.10	.05
☐ 87 Kent Hrbek	.20	.09
☐ 88 Shane Mack	.10	.05
☐ 89 Jack Morris	.20	.09
☐ 90 Kirby Puckett	.75	.35
☐ 91 Jesse Barfield	.10	.05
☐ 92 Steve Farr	.10	.05
☐ 93 Steve Howe	.10	.05
☐ 94 Roberto Kelly	.10	.05
☐ 95 Tim Leary	.10	.05
☐ 96 Kevin Maas	.10	.05
☐ 97 Don Mattingly	.60	.25
☐ 98 Hensley Meulens	.10	.05
☐ 99 Scott Sanderson	.10	.05
☐ 100 Steve Sax	.10	.05
☐ 101 Jose Canseco	.40	.18
☐ 102 Dennis Eckersley	.10	.05
☐ 103 Dave Henderson	.10	.05
☐ 104 Rickey Henderson	.40	.18
☐ 105 Rick Honeycutt	.10	.05
☐ 106 Mark McGwire	.75	.35
☐ 107 Dave Stewart UER (No-hitter against	.20	.09

Toronto, not Texas)
☐ 108 Eric Show .10 .05
☐ 109 Todd Van Poppel .10 .05
☐ 110 Bob Welch .10 .05
☐ 111 Alvin Davis .10 .05
☐ 112 Ken Griffey Jr. 3.00 1.35
☐ 113 Ken Griffey Sr. .10 .05
☐ 114 Erik Hanson UER .10 .05
(Misspelled Eric)
☐ 115 Brian Holman .10 .05
☐ 116 Randy Johnson .50 .23
☐ 117 Edgar Martinez .40 .18
☐ 118 Tino Martinez .40 .18
☐ 119 Harold Reynolds .10 .05
☐ 120 David Valle .10 .05
☐ 121 Kevin Belcher .10 .05
☐ 122 Scott Chiamparino .10 .05
☐ 123 Julio Franco .20 .09
☐ 124 Juan Gonzalez 1.50 .70
☐ 125 Rich Gossage .20 .09
☐ 126 Jeff Kunkel .10 .05
☐ 127 Rafael Palmeiro .40 .18
☐ 128 Nolan Ryan 1.50 .70
☐ 129 Ruben Sierra .10 .05
☐ 130 Bobby Witt .10 .05
☐ 131 Roberto Alomar .40 .18
☐ 132 Tom Candiotti .10 .05
☐ 133 Joe Carter .20 .09
☐ 134 Ken Dayley .10 .05
☐ 135 Kelly Gruber .10 .05
☐ 136 John Olerud .20 .09
☐ 137 Dave Stieb .10 .05
☐ 138 Turner Ward .10 .05
☐ 139 Devon White .10 .05
☐ 140 Mookie Wilson .10 .05
☐ 141 Steve Avery .20 .09
☐ 142 Sid Bream .10 .05
☐ 143 Nick Esasky UER .10 .05
(Homers abbreviated RH)
☐ 144 Ron Gant .20 .09
☐ 145 Tom Glavine .40 .18
☐ 146 David Justice .50 .23
☐ 147 Kelly Mann .10 .05
☐ 148 Terry Pendleton .20 .09
☐ 149 John Smoltz .40 .18
☐ 150 Jeff Treadway .10 .05
☐ 151 George Bell .10 .05
☐ 152 Shawn Boskie .10 .05
☐ 153 Andre Dawson .20 .09
☐ 154 Lance Dickson .10 .05
☐ 155 Shawon Dunston .10 .05
☐ 156 Joe Girardi .20 .09
☐ 157 Mark Grace .10 .05
☐ 158 Ryne Sandberg .50 .23
☐ 159 Gary Scott .10 .05
☐ 160 Dave Smith .10 .05
☐ 161 Tom Browning .10 .05
☐ 162 Eric Davis .20 .09
☐ 163 Rob Dibble .10 .05
☐ 164 Mariano Duncan .10 .05
☐ 165 Chris Hammond .10 .05
☐ 166 Billy Hatcher .10 .05
☐ 167 Barry Larkin .40 .18
☐ 168 Hal Morris .10 .05
☐ 169 Paul O'Neill .20 .09
☐ 170 Chris Sabo .10 .05
☐ 171 Eric Anthony .10 .05
☐ 172 Jeff Bagwell 3.00 1.35
☐ 173 Craig Biggio .40 .18
☐ 174 Ken Caminiti .40 .18
☐ 175 Jim Deshaies .10 .05
☐ 176 Steve Finley .20 .09
☐ 177 Pete Harnisch .10 .05
☐ 178 Darryl Kile .40 .18
☐ 179 Curt Schilling .10 .05
☐ 180 Mike Scott .10 .05
☐ 181 Brett Butler .20 .09
☐ 182 Gary Carter .40 .18
☐ 183 Orel Hershiser .20 .09
☐ 184 Ramon Martinez .10 .05
☐ 185 Eddie Murray .40 .18
☐ 186 Jose Offerman .10 .05
☐ 187 Bob Ojeda .10 .05
☐ 188 Juan Samuel .10 .05
☐ 189 Mike Scioscia .10 .05
☐ 190 Darryl Strawberry .20 .09
☐ 191 Moises Alou .40 .18
☐ 192 Brian Barnes .10 .05
☐ 193 Oil Can Boyd .10 .05
☐ 194 Ivan Calderon .10 .05
☐ 195 Delino DeShields .10 .05
☐ 196 Mike Fitzgerald .10 .05
☐ 197 Andres Galarraga .40 .18
☐ 198 Marquis Grissom .40 .18
☐ 199 Bill Sampen .10 .05
☐ 200 Tim Wallach .10 .05
☐ 201 Daryl Boston .10 .05
☐ 202 Vince Coleman .10 .05
☐ 203 John Franco .10 .05
☐ 204 Dwight Gooden .20 .09
☐ 205 Tom Herr .10 .05
☐ 206 Gregg Jefferies .20 .09
☐ 207 Howard Johnson .10 .05
☐ 208 Dave Magadan UER .10 .05
(Born 1862,
should be 1962)
☐ 209 Kevin McReynolds .10 .05
☐ 210 Frank Viola .10 .05
☐ 211 Wes Chamberlain .10 .05
☐ 212 Darren Daulton .20 .09
☐ 213 Len Dykstra .20 .09
☐ 214 Charlie Hayes .10 .05
☐ 215 Ricky Jordan .10 .05
☐ 216 Steve Lake .20 .09
(Pictured with parrot
on his shoulder)
☐ 217 Roger McDowell .10 .05
☐ 218 Mickey Morandini .10 .05
☐ 219 Terry Mulholland .10 .05
☐ 220 Dale Murphy .40 .18
☐ 221 Jay Bell .20 .09
☐ 222 Barry Bonds .50 .23
☐ 223 Bobby Bonilla .10 .05
☐ 224 Doug Drabek .10 .05
☐ 225 Bill Landrum .10 .05
☐ 226 Mike LaValliere .10 .05
☐ 227 Jose Lind .10 .05
☐ 228 Don Slaught .10 .05
☐ 229 John Smiley .10 .05
☐ 230 Andy Van Slyke .20 .09
☐ 231 Bernard Gilkey .20 .09
☐ 232 Pedro Guerrero .10 .05
☐ 233 Rex Hudler .10 .05
☐ 234 Ray Lankford .40 .18
☐ 235 Joe Magrane .10 .05
☐ 236 Jose Oquendo .10 .05
☐ 237 Lee Smith .40 .18
☐ 238 Ozzie Smith .50 .23
☐ 239 Milt Thompson .10 .05
☐ 240 Todd Zeile .20 .09
☐ 241 Larry Andersen .10 .05
☐ 242 Andy Benes .20 .09
☐ 243 Paul Faries .10 .05
☐ 244 Tony Fernandez .10 .05
☐ 245 Tony Gwynn 1.00 .45
☐ 246 Atlee Hammaker .10 .05
☐ 247 Fred McGriff .40 .18
☐ 248 Bip Roberts .10 .05
☐ 249 Bentio Santiago .10 .05
☐ 250 Ed Whitson .10 .05
☐ 251 Dave Anderson .10 .05
☐ 252 Mike Benjamin .10 .05
☐ 253 John Burkett UER .20 .09
(Front photo actually
Trevor Wilson)
☐ 254 Will Clark .40 .18
☐ 255 Scott Garrelts .10 .05
☐ 256 Willie McGee .10 .05
☐ 257 Kevin Mitchell .20 .09
☐ 258 Dave Righetti .10 .05
☐ 259 Matt Williams .40 .18
☐ 260 Bud Black .10 .05
Steve Decker
☐ 261 Sparky Anderson MG CL .20 .09
☐ 262 Tom Lasorda MG CL .10 .05
☐ 263 Tony LaRussa MG CL .20 .09
☐ NNO Title Card .10 .05

1992 Studio Previews

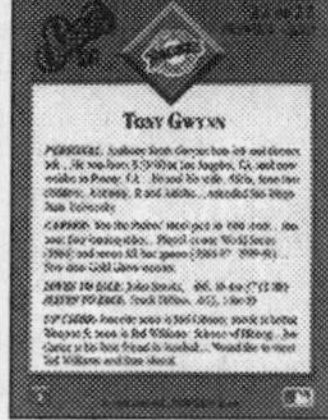

This 22-card standard-sized set was issued by Leaf to preview the design of the 1992 Leaf Studio series. A color posed player photo has been cut out and superimposed against the background of a black and white action shot of the player. These pictures are framed in black on a gold card face. The player's name and team name appear in the bottom gold border. On a white panel bordered in gold, the backs feature player information under five headings (Personal, Career, Loves to face, Hates to face, and Up Close). The cards are numbered on the back. These Preview cards were distributed on a limited basis to members of the Donruss Dealer Network to show them the new Studio design, and are among the tougher promos to obtain from the 1990s. Unlike the 1991 set of the same name, the 1992 set was not inserted in 1992 Donruss factory sets. It appears that Roberto Alomar and Ozzie Smith are a little more difficult to find than the other 20 cards; they are designated SP in the checklist below.

	MINT	NRMT
COMPLETE SET (22)	225.00	100.00
COMMON CARD (1-22)	2.50	1.10

☐ 1 Ruben Sierra 2.50 1.10
☐ 2 Kirby Puckett 15.00 6.75
☐ 3 Ryne Sandberg 15.00 6.75
☐ 4 John Kruk 2.50 1.10
☐ 5 Cal Ripken 30.00 13.50
☐ 6 Robin Yount 6.00 2.70
☐ 7 Dwight Gooden 4.00 1.80
☐ 8 David Justice 8.00 3.60
☐ 9 Don Mattingly 20.00 9.00
☐ 10 Wally Joyner 4.00 1.80
☐ 11 Will Clark 6.00 2.70
☐ 12 Rob Dibble 2.50 1.10
☐ 13 Roberto Alomar SP 20.00 9.00
☐ 14 Wade Boggs 8.00 3.60
☐ 15 Barry Bonds 10.00 4.50
☐ 16 Jeff Bagwell 20.00 9.00
☐ 17 Mark McGwire 12.50 5.50
☐ 18 Frank Thomas 40.00 18.00
☐ 19 Brett Butler 4.00 1.80
☐ 20 Ozzie Smith SP 25.00 11.00
☐ 21 Jim Abbott 2.50 1.10
☐ 22 Tony Gwynn 20.00 9.00

1992 Studio

The 1992 Studio set consists of ten players from each of the 26 major league teams, three checklists, and an introduction card for a total of 264 standard-size cards. Inside champagne color metallic borders, the fronts carry a color close-up shot superimposed on a black and white action player photo. The backs focus on the personal side of each player by providing an up-close look, and unusual statistics show the batter or pitcher each player "Loves to Face" or "Hates to Face". The key Rookie Cards in this set are Chad Curtis and Brian Jordan.

	MINT	NRMT
COMPLETE SET (264)	15.00	6.75
COMMON CARD (1-264)	.05	.02

☐ 1 Steve Avery .05 .02
☐ 2 Sid Bream .05 .02
☐ 3 Ron Gant .10 .05
☐ 4 Tom Glavine .10 .05
☐ 5 David Justice .30 .14
☐ 6 Mark Lemke .05 .02
☐ 7 Greg Olson .05 .02
☐ 8 Terry Pendleton .10 .05
☐ 9 Deion Sanders .30 .14
☐ 10 John Smoltz .10 .05
☐ 11 Doug Dascenzo .05 .02
☐ 12 Andre Dawson .10 .05
☐ 13 Joe Girardi .05 .02
☐ 14 Mark Grace .10 .05
☐ 15 Greg Maddux 1.00 .45
☐ 16 Chuck McElroy .05 .02
☐ 17 Mike Morgan .05 .02
☐ 18 Ryne Sandberg .40 .18
☐ 19 Gary Scott .05 .02
☐ 20 Sammy Sosa .30 .14
☐ 21 Norm Charlton .05 .02
☐ 22 Rob Dibble .05 .02
☐ 23 Barry Larkin .10 .05
☐ 24 Hal Morris .05 .02
☐ 25 Paul O'Neill .10 .05
☐ 26 Jose Rijo .05 .02
☐ 27 Bip Roberts .05 .02
☐ 28 Chris Sabo .05 .02
☐ 29 Reggie Sanders .10 .05
☐ 30 Greg Swindell .05 .02
☐ 31 Jeff Bagwell 1.00 .45

☐ 32 Craig Biggio .10 .05
☐ 33 Ken Caminiti .30 .14
☐ 34 Andujar Cedeno .05 .02
☐ 35 Steve Finley .10 .05
☐ 36 Pete Harnisch .05 .02
☐ 37 Butch Henry .05 .02
☐ 38 Doug Jones .05 .02
☐ 39 Darryl Kile .10 .05
☐ 40 Eddie Taubensee .05 .02
☐ 41 Brett Butler .10 .05
☐ 42 Tom Candiotti .05 .02
☐ 43 Eric Davis .10 .05
☐ 44 Orel Hershiser .10 .05
☐ 45 Eric Karros .10 .05
☐ 46 Ramon Martinez .10 .05
☐ 47 Jose Offerman .05 .02
☐ 48 Mike Scioscia .05 .02
☐ 49 Mike Sharperson .05 .02
☐ 50 Darryl Strawberry .10 .05
☐ 51 Bret Barberie .05 .02
☐ 52 Ivan Calderon .05 .02
☐ 53 Gary Carter .10 .05
☐ 54 Delino DeShields .05 .02
☐ 55 Marquis Grissom .10 .05
☐ 56 Ken Hill .10 .05
☐ 57 Dennis Martinez .10 .05
☐ 58 Spike Owen .05 .02
☐ 59 Larry Walker .30 .14
☐ 60 Tim Wallach .05 .02
☐ 61 Bobby Bonilla .10 .05
☐ 62 Tim Burke .05 .02
☐ 63 Vince Coleman .05 .02
☐ 64 John Franco .05 .02
☐ 65 Dwight Gooden .10 .05
☐ 66 Todd Hundley .10 .05
☐ 67 Howard Johnson .05 .02
☐ 68 Eddie Murray UER .30 .14
(He's not all-time switch homer leader, but he has most games with homers from both sides)
☐ 69 Bret Saberhagen .05 .02
☐ 70 Anthony Young .05 .02
☐ 71 Kim Batiste .05 .02
☐ 72 Wes Chamberlain .05 .02
☐ 73 Darren Daulton .10 .05
☐ 74 Mariano Duncan .05 .02
☐ 75 Len Dykstra .10 .05
☐ 76 John Kruk .10 .05
☐ 77 Mickey Morandini .05 .02
☐ 78 Terry Mulholland .05 .02
☐ 79 Dale Murphy .30 .14
☐ 80 Mitch Williams .05 .02
☐ 81 Jay Bell .10 .05
☐ 82 Barry Bonds .40 .18
☐ 83 Steve Buechele .05 .02
☐ 84 Doug Drabek .05 .02
☐ 85 Mike LaValliere .05 .02
☐ 86 Jose Lind .05 .02
☐ 87 Denny Neagle .10 .05
☐ 88 Randy Tomlin .05 .02
☐ 89 Andy Van Slyke .10 .05
☐ 90 Gary Varsho .05 .02
☐ 91 Pedro Guerrero .05 .02
☐ 92 Rex Hudler .05 .02
☐ 93 Brian Jordan .40 .18
☐ 94 Felix Jose .05 .02
☐ 95 Donovan Osborne .10 .05
☐ 96 Tom Pagnozzi .05 .02
☐ 97 Lee Smith .10 .05
☐ 98 Ozzie Smith .40 .18
☐ 99 Todd Worrell .05 .02
☐ 100 Todd Zeile .05 .02
☐ 101 Andy Benes .10 .05
☐ 102 Jerald Clark .05 .02
☐ 103 Tony Fernandez .05 .02
☐ 104 Tony Gwynn .75 .35
☐ 105 Greg W. Harris .05 .02
☐ 106 Fred McGriff .10 .05
☐ 107 Benito Santiago .05 .02
☐ 108 Gary Sheffield .10 .05
☐ 109 Kurt Stillwell .05 .02
☐ 110 Tim Teufel .05 .02
☐ 111 Kevin Bass .05 .02
☐ 112 Jeff Brantley .05 .02
☐ 113 John Burkett .05 .02
☐ 114 Will Clark .10 .05
☐ 115 Royce Clayton .10 .05
☐ 116 Mike Jackson .05 .02
☐ 117 Darren Lewis .05 .02
☐ 118 Bill Swift .05 .02
☐ 119 Robby Thompson .05 .02
☐ 120 Matt Williams .10 .05
☐ 121 Brady Anderson .10 .05
☐ 122 Glenn Davis .05 .02
☐ 123 Mike Devereaux .05 .02
☐ 124 Chris Hoiles .05 .02
☐ 125 Sam Horn .05 .02
☐ 126 Ben McDonald .05 .02
☐ 127 Mike Mussina .50 .23
☐ 128 Gregg Olson .05 .02
☐ 129 Cal Ripken Jr. 1.25 .55
☐ 130 Rick Sutcliffe .05 .02
☐ 131 Wade Boggs .30 .14
☐ 132 Roger Clemens .60 .25
☐ 133 Greg A. Harris .05 .02
☐ 134 Tim Naehring .10 .05
☐ 135 Tony Pena .05 .02
☐ 136 Phil Plantier .05 .02
☐ 137 Jeff Reardon .10 .05
☐ 138 Jody Reed .05 .02
☐ 139 Mo Vaughn .50 .23
☐ 140 Frank Viola .05 .02
☐ 141 Jim Abbott .05 .02
☐ 142 Hubie Brooks .05 .02
☐ 143 Chad Curtis .30 .14
☐ 144 Gary DiSarcina .05 .02
☐ 145 Chuck Finley .05 .02
☐ 146 Bryan Harvey .05 .02
☐ 147 Von Hayes .05 .02
☐ 148 Mark Langston .05 .02
☐ 149 Lance Parrish .05 .02
☐ 150 Lee Stevens .05 .02
☐ 151 George Bell .05 .02
☐ 152 Alex Fernandez .10 .05
☐ 153 Greg Hibbard .05 .02
☐ 154 Lance Johnson .10 .05
☐ 155 Kirk McCaskill .05 .02
☐ 156 Tim Raines .10 .05
☐ 157 Steve Sax .05 .02
☐ 158 Bobby Thigpen .05 .02
☐ 159 Frank Thomas 1.50 .70
☐ 160 Robin Ventura .10 .05
☐ 161 Sandy Alomar Jr. .10 .05
☐ 162 Jack Armstrong .05 .02
☐ 163 Carlos Baerga .10 .05
☐ 164 Albert Belle .40 .18
☐ 165 Alex Cole .05 .02
☐ 166 Glenallen Hill .05 .02
☐ 167 Mark Lewis .05 .02
☐ 168 Kenny Lofton 1.25 .55
☐ 169 Paul Sorrento .05 .02
☐ 170 Mark Whiten .05 .02
☐ 171 Milt Cuyler .05 .02
☐ 172 Rob Deer .05 .02
☐ 173 Cecil Fielder .10 .05
☐ 174 Travis Fryman .10 .05
☐ 175 Mike Henneman .05 .02
☐ 176 Tony Phillips .05 .02
☐ 177 Frank Tanana .05 .02
☐ 178 Mickey Tettleton .05 .02
☐ 179 Alan Trammell .10 .05
☐ 180 Lou Whitaker .10 .05
☐ 181 George Brett .60 .25
☐ 182 Tom Gordon .05 .02
☐ 183 Mark Gubicza .05 .02
☐ 184 Gregg Jefferies .10 .05
☐ 185 Wally Joyner .10 .05
☐ 186 Brent Mayne .05 .02
☐ 187 Brian McRae .05 .02
☐ 188 Kevin McReynolds .05 .02
☐ 189 Keith Miller .05 .02
☐ 190 Jeff Montgomery .10 .05
☐ 191 Dante Bichette .10 .05
☐ 192 Ricky Bones .05 .02
☐ 193 Scott Fletcher .05 .02
☐ 194 Paul Molitor .30 .14
☐ 195 Jaime Navarro .05 .02
☐ 196 Franklin Stubbs .05 .02
☐ 197 B.J. Surhoff .10 .05
☐ 198 Greg Vaughn .05 .02
☐ 199 Bill Wegman .05 .02
☐ 200 Robin Yount .30 .14
☐ 201 Rick Aguilera .05 .02
☐ 202 Scott Erickson .10 .05
☐ 203 Greg Gagne .05 .02
☐ 204 Brian Harper .05 .02
☐ 205 Kent Hrbek .10 .05
☐ 206 Scott Leius .05 .02
☐ 207 Shane Mack .05 .02
☐ 208 Pat Mahomes .05 .02
☐ 209 Kirby Puckett .60 .25
☐ 210 John Smiley .05 .02
☐ 211 Mike Gallego .05 .02
☐ 212 Charlie Hayes .05 .02
☐ 213 Pat Kelly .05 .02
☐ 214 Roberto Kelly .05 .02
☐ 215 Kevin Maas .05 .02
☐ 216 Don Mattingly .50 .23
☐ 217 Matt Nokes .05 .02
☐ 218 Melido Perez .05 .02
☐ 219 Scott Sanderson .05 .02
☐ 220 Danny Tartabull .05 .02
☐ 221 Harold Baines .10 .05
☐ 222 Jose Canseco .10 .05
☐ 223 Dennis Eckersley .10 .05
☐ 224 Dave Henderson .05 .02
☐ 225 Carney Lansford .10 .05
☐ 226 Mark McGwire .60 .25
☐ 227 Mike Moore .05 .02
☐ 228 Randy Ready .05 .02
☐ 229 Terry Steinbach .10 .05
☐ 230 Dave Stewart .10 .05
☐ 231 Jay Buhner .10 .05
☐ 232 Ken Griffey Jr. 2.00 .90
☐ 233 Erik Hanson .05 .02
☐ 234 Randy Johnson .30 .14
☐ 235 Edgar Martinez .10 .05
☐ 236 Tino Martinez .30 .14
☐ 237 Kevin Mitchell .10 .05
☐ 238 Pete O'Brien .05 .02
☐ 239 Harold Reynolds .05 .02
☐ 240 David Valle .05 .02
☐ 241 Julio Franco .10 .05
☐ 242 Juan Gonzalez 1.00 .45
☐ 243 Jose Guzman .05 .02
☐ 244 Rafael Palmeiro .30 .14
☐ 245 Dean Palmer .10 .05
☐ 246 Ivan Rodriguez .60 .25
☐ 247 Jeff Russell .05 .02
☐ 248 Nolan Ryan 1.25 .55
☐ 249 Ruben Sierra .05 .02
☐ 250 Dickie Thon .05 .02
☐ 251 Roberto Alomar .30 .14
☐ 252 Derek Bell .10 .05
☐ 253 Pat Borders .05 .02
☐ 254 Joe Carter .10 .05
☐ 255 Kelly Gruber .05 .02
☐ 256 Juan Guzman .05 .02
☐ 257 Jack Morris .10 .05
☐ 258 John Olerud .10 .05
☐ 259 Devon White .05 .02
☐ 260 Dave Winfield .10 .05
☐ 261 Checklist .05 .02
☐ 262 Checklist .05 .02
☐ 263 Checklist .05 .02
☐ 264 History Card .05 .02

1992 Studio Heritage

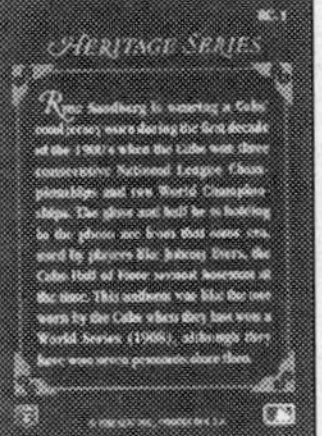

The 1992 Studio Heritage standard-size insert set presents today's star players dressed in vintage uniforms. Cards numbered 1-8 were randomly inserted in 12-card foil packs while cards numbered 9-14 were inserted one per pack in 28-card jumbo packs. The fronts display sepia-toned portraits of the players dressed in vintage uniforms of their current teams. The pictures are bordered by dark turquoise and have bronze foil picture holders at each corner. The set title "Heritage Series" also appears in bronze foil lettering above the pictures. Within a bronze picture frame design on dark turquoise, the backs give a brief history of the team with special reference to the year of the vintage uniform. The cards are numbered on the back with a "BC" prefix.

	MINT	NRMT
COMPLETE SET (14)	25.00	11.00
COMP.FOIL SET (8)	15.00	6.75
COMP.JUMBO SET (6)	10.00	4.50
COMMON CARD (BC1-BC14)	.75	.35
☐ BC1 Ryne Sandberg	2.00	.90
☐ BC2 Carlton Fisk	1.50	.70
☐ BC3 Wade Boggs	1.25	.55
☐ BC4 Jose Canseco	1.25	.55
☐ BC5 Don Mattingly	4.00	1.80
☐ BC6 Darryl Strawberry	.75	.35
☐ BC7 Cal Ripken	8.00	3.60
☐ BC8 Will Clark	1.25	.55
☐ BC9 Andre Dawson		
☐ BC10 Andy Van Slyke	.75	.35
☐ BC11 Paul Molitor		
☐ BC12 Jeff Bagwell	5.00	2.20
☐ BC13 Darren Daulton		
☐ BC14 Kirby Puckett	3.00	1.35

1993 Studio

The 220 standard-size cards comprising this set feature borderless fronts with posed color player photos that are cut out and superposed upon a closeup of an embroidered team logo. A facsimile player autograph appears in prismatic gold foil across the lower portion of the photo. The borderless black backs carry another posed color player photo shunted to the right side, with the player's name, position, team, biography, and personal profile appearing in white lettering on the left side. The key Rookie Card in this set is J.T. Snow.

	MINT	NRMT
COMPLETE SET (220)	20.00	9.00
COMMON CARD (1-220)	.10	.05
☐ 1 Dennis Eckersley	.20	.09
☐ 2 Chad Curtis	.25	.11
☐ 3 Eric Anthony	.10	.05
☐ 4 Roberto Alomar	.50	.23
☐ 5 Steve Avery	.10	.05
☐ 6 Cal Eldred	.10	.05
☐ 7 Bernard Gilkey	.25	.11
☐ 8 Steve Buechele	.10	.05
☐ 9 Brett Butler	.25	.11
☐ 10 Terry Mulholland	.10	.05
☐ 11 Moises Alou	.25	.11
☐ 12 Barry Bonds	.60	.25
☐ 13 Sandy Alomar Jr.	.25	.11
☐ 14 Chris Bosio	.10	.05
☐ 15 Scott Sanderson	.10	.05
☐ 16 Bobby Bonilla	.25	.11
☐ 17 Brady Anderson	.20	.09
☐ 18 Derek Bell	.25	.11
☐ 19 Wes Chamberlain	.10	.05
☐ 20 Jay Bell	.25	.11
☐ 21 Kevin Brown	.25	.11
☐ 22 Roger Clemens	1.00	.45
☐ 23 Roberto Kelly	.10	.05
☐ 24 Dante Bichette	.20	.09
☐ 25 George Brett	1.00	.45
☐ 26 Rob Deer	.10	.05
☐ 27 Brian Harper	.10	.05
☐ 28 George Bell	.10	.05
☐ 29 Jim Abbott	.10	.05
☐ 30 Dave Henderson	.10	.05
☐ 31 Wade Boggs	.20	.09
☐ 32 Chili Davis	.25	.11
☐ 33 Ellis Burks	.25	.11
☐ 34 Jeff Bagwell	1.00	.45
☐ 35 Kent Hrbek	.25	.11
☐ 36 Pat Borders	.10	.05
☐ 37 Cecil Fielder	.25	.11
☐ 38 Sid Bream	.10	.05
☐ 39 Greg Gagne	.10	.05
☐ 40 Darryl Hamilton	.10	.05
☐ 41 Jerald Clark	.10	.05
☐ 42 Mark Grace	.20	.09
☐ 43 Barry Larkin	.20	.09
☐ 44 John Burkett	.10	.05
☐ 45 Scott Cooper	.10	.05
☐ 46 Mike Lansing	.25	.11
☐ 47 Jose Canseco	.20	.09
☐ 48 Will Clark	.20	.09
☐ 49 Carlos Garcia	.10	.05
☐ 50 Carlos Baerga	.25	.11
☐ 51 Darren Daulton	.25	.11
☐ 52 Jay Buhner	.20	.09
☐ 53 Andy Benes	.25	.11
☐ 54 Jeff Conine	.25	.11
☐ 55 Mike Devereaux	.10	.05
☐ 56 Vince Coleman	.10	.05
☐ 57 Terry Steinbach	.25	.11
☐ 58 J.T. Snow	.60	.25
☐ 59 Greg Swindell	.10	.05
☐ 60 Devon White	.10	.05
☐ 61 John Smoltz	.20	.09
☐ 62 Todd Zeile	.10	.05
☐ 63 Rick Wilkins	.10	.05
☐ 64 Tim Wallach	.10	.05
☐ 65 John Wetteland	.25	.11
☐ 66 Matt Williams	.20	.09
☐ 67 Paul Sorrento	.10	.05
☐ 68 David Valle	.10	.05
☐ 69 Walt Weiss	.10	.05
☐ 70 John Franco	.10	.05
☐ 71 Nolan Ryan	2.00	.90
☐ 72 Frank Viola	.10	.05
☐ 73 Chris Sabo	.10	.05
☐ 74 David Nied	.10	.05
☐ 75 Kevin McReynolds	.10	.05
☐ 76 Lou Whitaker	.25	.11
☐ 77 Dave Winfield	.20	.09
☐ 78 Robin Ventura	.25	.11
☐ 79 Spike Owen	.10	.05
☐ 80 Cal Ripken Jr.	2.00	.90
☐ 81 Dan Walters	.10	.05
☐ 82 Mitch Williams	.10	.05
☐ 83 Tim Wakefield	.25	.11
☐ 84 Rickey Henderson	.20	.09
☐ 85 Gary DiSarcina	.10	.05
☐ 86 Craig Biggio	.20	.09
☐ 87 Joe Carter	.20	.09
☐ 88 Ron Gant	.25	.11
☐ 89 John Jaha	.25	.11
☐ 90 Gregg Jefferies	.25	.11
☐ 91 Jose Guzman	.10	.05
☐ 92 Eric Karros	.20	.09
☐ 93 Wil Cordero	.25	.11
☐ 94 Royce Clayton	.25	.11
☐ 95 Albert Belle	.60	.25
☐ 96 Ken Griffey Jr.	2.50	1.10
☐ 97 Orestes Destrade	.10	.05
☐ 98 Tony Fernandez	.10	.05
☐ 99 Leo Gomez	.10	.05
☐ 100 Tony Gwynn	1.25	.55
☐ 101 Len Dykstra	.25	.11
☐ 102 Jeff King	.25	.11
☐ 103 Julio Franco	.25	.11
☐ 104 Andre Dawson	.20	.09
☐ 105 Randy Milligan	.10	.05
☐ 106 Alex Cole	.10	.05
☐ 107 Phil Hiatt	.10	.05
☐ 108 Travis Fryman	.25	.11
☐ 109 Chuck Knoblauch	.50	.23
☐ 110 Bo Jackson	.25	.11
☐ 111 Pat Kelly	.10	.05
☐ 112 Bret Saberhagen	.25	.11
☐ 113 Ruben Sierra	.10	.05
☐ 114 Tim Salmon	.60	.25
☐ 115 Doug Jones	.10	.05
☐ 116 Ed Sprague	.10	.05
☐ 117 Terry Pendleton	.25	.11
☐ 118 Robin Yount	.20	.09
☐ 119 Mark Whiten	.10	.05
☐ 120 Checklist 1-110	.10	.05
☐ 121 Sammy Sosa	.50	.23
☐ 122 Darryl Strawberry	.25	.11
☐ 123 Larry Walker	.50	.23
☐ 124 Robby Thompson	.10	.05
☐ 125 Carlos Martinez	.10	.05
☐ 126 Edgar Martinez	.20	.09
☐ 127 Benito Santiago	.10	.05
☐ 128 Howard Johnson	.10	.05
☐ 129 Harold Reynolds	.10	.05
☐ 130 Craig Shipley	.10	.05
☐ 131 Curt Schilling	.25	.11
☐ 132 Andy Van Slyke	.25	.11
☐ 133 Ivan Rodriguez	.60	.25
☐ 134 Mo Vaughn	.60	.25
☐ 135 Bip Roberts	.10	.05
☐ 136 Charlie Hayes	.10	.05
☐ 137 Brian McRae	.10	.05
☐ 138 Mickey Tettleton	.10	.05
☐ 139 Frank Thomas	2.00	.90
☐ 140 Paul O'Neill	.25	.11
☐ 141 Mark McGwire	1.00	.45
☐ 142 Damion Easley	.10	.05
☐ 143 Ken Caminiti	.50	.23
☐ 144 Juan Guzman	.25	.11
☐ 145 Tom Glavine	.20	.09
☐ 146 Pat Listach	.10	.05
☐ 147 Lee Smith	.25	.11
☐ 148 Derrick May	.10	.05
☐ 149 Ramon Martinez	.25	.11
☐ 150 Delino DeShields	.10	.05
☐ 151 Kirt Manwaring	.10	.05
☐ 152 Reggie Jefferson	.25	.11
☐ 153 Randy Johnson	.50	.23
☐ 154 Dave Magadan	.10	.05
☐ 155 Dwight Gooden	.25	.11
☐ 156 Chris Hoiles	.10	.05
☐ 157 Fred McGriff	.20	.09
☐ 158 Dave Hollins	.10	.05
☐ 159 Al Martin	.25	.11
☐ 160 Juan Gonzalez	1.25	.55
☐ 161 Mike Greenwell	.10	.05
☐ 162 Kevin Mitchell	.25	.11
☐ 163 Andres Galarraga	.20	.09
☐ 164 Wally Joyner	.25	.11
☐ 165 Kirk Gibson	.25	.11
☐ 166 Pedro Munoz	.10	.05
☐ 167 Ozzie Guillen	.10	.05
☐ 168 Jimmy Key	.25	.11
☐ 169 Kevin Seitzer	.10	.05
☐ 170 Luis Polonia	.10	.05
☐ 171 Luis Gonzalez	.10	.05
☐ 172 Paul Molitor	.50	.23
☐ 173 David Justice	.50	.23
☐ 174 B.J. Surhoff	.25	.11
☐ 175 Ray Lankford	.20	.09
☐ 176 Ryne Sandberg	.60	.25
☐ 177 Jody Reed	.10	.05
☐ 178 Marquis Grissom	.25	.11
☐ 179 Willie McGee	.10	.05
☐ 180 Kenny Lofton	1.00	.45
☐ 181 Junior Felix	.10	.05
☐ 182 Jose Offerman	.10	.05
☐ 183 John Kruk	.25	.11
☐ 184 Orlando Merced	.10	.05
☐ 185 Rafael Palmeiro	.20	.09
☐ 186 Billy Hatcher	.10	.05
☐ 187 Joe Oliver	.10	.05
☐ 188 Joe Girardi	.10	.05
☐ 189 Jose Lind	.10	.05
☐ 190 Harold Baines	.25	.11
☐ 191 Mike Pagliarulo	.10	.05
☐ 192 Lance Johnson	.10	.05
☐ 193 Don Mattingly	.75	.35
☐ 194 Doug Drabek	.10	.05
☐ 195 John Olerud	.10	.05
☐ 196 Greg Maddux	1.50	.70
☐ 197 Greg Vaughn	.10	.05
☐ 198 Tom Pagnozzi	.10	.05
☐ 199 Willie Wilson	.10	.05
☐ 200 Jack McDowell	.10	.05
☐ 201 Mike Piazza	2.50	1.10
☐ 202 Mike Mussina	.50	.23
☐ 203 Charles Nagy	.25	.11
☐ 204 Tino Martinez	.50	.23
☐ 205 Charlie Hough	.10	.05
☐ 206 Todd Hundley	.20	.09
☐ 207 Gary Sheffield	.50	.23
☐ 208 Mickey Morandini	.10	.05
☐ 209 Don Slaught	.10	.05
☐ 210 Dean Palmer	.25	.11
☐ 211 Jose Rijo	.10	.05
☐ 212 Vinny Castilla	.50	.23
☐ 213 Tony Phillips	.10	.05
☐ 214 Kirby Puckett	1.00	.45
☐ 215 Tim Raines	.25	.11
☐ 216 Otis Nixon	.25	.11
☐ 217 Ozzie Smith	.60	.25
☐ 218 Jose Vizcaino	.10	.05
☐ 219 Randy Tomlin	.10	.05
☐ 220 Checklist 111-220	.10	.05

1993 Studio Heritage

This 12-card standard-size set was randomly inserted in all 1993 Leaf Studio foil packs, and features sepia-toned portraits of current players in vintage team uniforms. The pictures are bordered in turquoise blue and have bronze-foil simulated picture holders at each corner. The set title appears in white lettering above the picture, and the player's name is printed in white below. The horizontal and turquoise-blue-bordered back shades from beige to red from top to bottom, and carries a posed sepia-toned player picture on the right within an oval set off by red and black lines. His name appears in white lettering at the top within a black arc. A brief story of the team represented by the player's vintage uniform follows below.

	MINT	NRMT
COMPLETE SET (12)	30.00	13.50
COMMON CARD (1-12)	1.00	.45
☐ 1 George Brett	6.00	2.70
☐ 2 Juan Gonzalez	8.00	3.60
☐ 3 Roger Clemens	3.00	1.35
☐ 4 Mark McGwire	5.00	2.20

Card	MINT	NRMT
☐ 5 Mark Grace	1.50	.70
☐ 6 Ozzie Smith	4.00	1.80
☐ 7 Barry Larkin	1.50	.70
☐ 8 Frank Thomas	15.00	6.75
☐ 9 Carlos Baerga	1.00	.45
☐ 10 Eric Karros	1.25	.55
☐ 11 J.T. Snow	1.25	.55
☐ 12 John Kruk	1.00	.45

1993 Studio Silhouettes

The 1993 Studio Silhouettes 10-card standard-size set was inserted one per 20-card Studio jumbo pack. Full-bleed grayish fronts display posed color photos of star players against action silhouettes. The set's title is printed across the top and the player's name appears along the bottom in copper foil within a darker gray area. The borderless and grayish back features a color player action photo on one side and a personal profile on the other.

	MINT	NRMT
COMPLETE SET (10)	25.00	11.00
COMMON CARD (1-10)	.50	.23
☐ 1 Frank Thomas	8.00	3.60
☐ 2 Barry Bonds	2.00	.90
☐ 3 Jeff Bagwell	3.00	1.35
☐ 4 Juan Gonzalez	4.00	1.80
☐ 5 Travis Fryman	.75	.35
☐ 6 J.T. Snow	1.00	.45
☐ 7 John Kruk	.75	.35
☐ 8 Jeff Blauser	.50	.23
☐ 9 Mike Piazza	5.00	2.20
☐ 10 Nolan Ryan	8.00	3.60

1993 Studio Superstars on Canvas

This ten-card standard-size set was randomly inserted in 1993 Studio hobby and retail foil packs. The set features players in gray-bordered portraits that blend photography and artwork. The design of each front simulates a canvas painting of a player displayed on an artist's easel. The player's name appears in copper foil across the easel's base near the bottom. The set's title appears in white lettering beneath. The horizontal back carries a cutout color action player photo on one side and the player's name and career highlights within a black rectangle on the other, all superposed upon an abstract team color-coded design.

	MINT	NRMT
COMPLETE SET (10)	35.00	16.00
COMMON CARD (1-10)	1.00	.45
☐ 1 Ken Griffey Jr.	15.00	6.75
☐ 2 Jose Canseco	2.00	.90
☐ 3 Mark McGwire	5.00	2.20
☐ 4 Mike Mussina	3.00	1.35
☐ 5 Joe Carter	2.00	.90
☐ 6 Frank Thomas	12.00	5.50
☐ 7 Darren Daulton	1.00	.45
☐ 8 Mark Grace	2.00	.90
☐ 9 Andres Galarraga	2.00	.90
☐ 10 Barry Bonds	4.00	1.80

1993 Studio Thomas

The 1993 Studio Frank Thomas five-card standard-size set was randomly inserted in all 1993 Studio packs. The cards feature borderless posed black-and-white portraits of the Chicago White Sox slugging first baseman

	MINT	NRMT
COMPLETE SET (5)	30.00	13.50
COMMON THOMAS (1-5)	6.00	2.70
☐ 1 Frank Thomas Childhood	6.00	2.70
☐ 2 Frank Thomas Baseball Memories	6.00	2.70
☐ 3 Frank Thomas Family	6.00	2.70
☐ 4 Frank Thomas Performance	6.00	2.70
☐ 5 Frank Thomas Role Model	6.00	2.70

1994 Studio

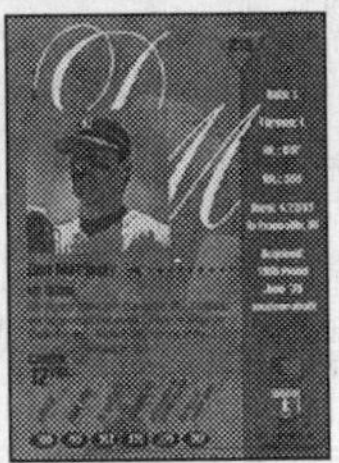

The 1994 Studio set consists of 220 full-bleed, standard-size cards. Card fronts offer a player photo with his jersey hanging in a locker room setting in the background. Backs contain statistics and a small photo. The set is grouped alphabetically within teams.

	MINT	NRMT
COMPLETE SET (220)	15.00	6.75
COMMON CARD (1-220)	.15	.07
☐ 1 Dennis Eckersley	.40	.18
☐ 2 Brent Gates	.15	.07
☐ 3 Rickey Henderson	.40	.18
☐ 4 Mark McGwire	1.25	.55
☐ 5 Troy Neel	.15	.07
☐ 6 Ruben Sierra	.15	.07
☐ 7 Terry Steinbach	.30	.14
☐ 8 Chad Curtis	.15	.07
☐ 9 Chili Davis	.30	.14
☐ 10 Gary DiSarcina	.15	.07
☐ 11 Damion Easley	.15	.07
☐ 12 Bo Jackson	.30	.14
☐ 13 Mark Langston	.15	.07
☐ 14 Eduardo Perez	.15	.07
☐ 15 Tim Salmon	.60	.25
☐ 16 Jeff Bagwell	1.25	.55
☐ 17 Craig Biggio	.40	.18
☐ 18 Ken Caminiti	.60	.25
☐ 19 Andujar Cedeno	.15	.07
☐ 20 Doug Drabek	.15	.07
☐ 21 Steve Finley	.30	.14
☐ 22 Luis Gonzalez	.15	.07
☐ 23 Darryl Kile	.30	.14
☐ 24 Roberto Alomar	.60	.25
☐ 25 Pat Borders	.15	.07
☐ 26 Joe Carter	.40	.18
☐ 27 Carlos Delgado	.40	.18
☐ 28 Pat Hentgen	.30	.14
☐ 29 Paul Molitor	.60	.25
☐ 30 John Olerud	.30	.14
☐ 31 Ed Sprague	.15	.07
☐ 32 Devon White	.15	.07
☐ 33 Steve Avery	.15	.07
☐ 34 Tom Glavine	.40	.18
☐ 35 David Justice	.60	.25
☐ 36 Roberto Kelly	.15	.07
☐ 37 Ryan Klesko	.40	.18
☐ 38 Javier Lopez	.40	.18
☐ 39 Greg Maddux	2.00	.90
☐ 40 Fred McGriff	.40	.18
☐ 41 Terry Pendleton	.30	.14
☐ 42 Ricky Bones	.15	.07
☐ 43 Darryl Hamilton	.15	.07
☐ 44 Brian Harper	.15	.07
☐ 45 John Jaha	.15	.07
☐ 46 Dave Nilsson	.30	.14
☐ 47 Kevin Seitzer	.15	.07
☐ 48 Greg Vaughn	.15	.07
☐ 49 Turner Ward	.15	.07
☐ 50 Bernard Gilkey	.30	.14
☐ 51 Gregg Jefferies	.30	.14
☐ 52 Ray Lankford	.30	.14
☐ 53 Tom Pagnozzi	.15	.07
☐ 54 Ozzie Smith	.75	.35
☐ 55 Bob Tewksbury	.15	.07
☐ 56 Mark Whiten	.15	.07
☐ 57 Todd Zeile	.15	.07
☐ 58 Steve Buechele	.15	.07
☐ 59 Shawon Dunston	.15	.07
☐ 60 Mark Grace	.40	.18
☐ 61 Derrick May	.15	.07
☐ 62 Karl Rhodes	.15	.07
☐ 63 Ryne Sandberg	.75	.35
☐ 64 Sammy Sosa	.60	.25
☐ 65 Rick Wilkins	.15	.07
☐ 66 Brett Butler	.30	.14
☐ 67 Delino DeShields	.15	.07
☐ 68 Orel Hershiser	.30	.14
☐ 69 Eric Karros	.30	.14
☐ 70 Raul Mondesi	.40	.18
☐ 71 Jose Offerman	.15	.07
☐ 72 Mike Piazza	2.00	.90
☐ 73 Tim Wallach	.15	.07
☐ 74 Moises Alou	.30	.14
☐ 75 Sean Berry	.15	.07
☐ 76 Wil Cordero	.30	.14
☐ 77 Cliff Floyd	.30	.14
☐ 78 Marquis Grissom	.30	.14
☐ 79 Ken Hill	.15	.07
☐ 80 Larry Walker	.60	.25
☐ 81 John Wetteland	.30	.14
☐ 82 Rod Beck	.30	.14
☐ 83 Barry Bonds	.75	.35
☐ 84 Royce Clayton	.30	.14
☐ 85 Darren Lewis	.15	.07
☐ 86 Willie McGee	.15	.07
☐ 87 Bill Swift	.15	.07
☐ 88 Robby Thompson	.15	.07
☐ 89 Matt Williams	.40	.18
☐ 90 Sandy Alomar Jr.	.30	.14
☐ 91 Carlos Baerga	.30	.14
☐ 92 Albert Belle	.75	.35
☐ 93 Kenny Lofton	.75	.35
☐ 94 Eddie Murray	.60	.25
☐ 95 Manny Ramirez	.75	.35
☐ 96 Paul Sorrento	.15	.07
☐ 97 Jim Thome	.75	.35
☐ 98 Rich Amaral	.15	.07
☐ 99 Eric Anthony	.15	.07
☐ 100 Jay Buhner	.40	.18
☐ 101 Ken Griffey Jr.	3.00	1.35
☐ 102 Randy Johnson	.60	.25
☐ 103 Edgar Martinez	.40	.18
☐ 104 Tino Martinez	.60	.25
☐ 105 Kurt Abbott	.15	.07
☐ 106 Bret Barberie	.15	.07
☐ 107 Chuck Carr	.15	.07
☐ 108 Jeff Conine	.30	.14
☐ 109 Chris Hammond	.15	.07
☐ 110 Bryan Harvey	.15	.07
☐ 111 Benito Santiago	.15	.07
☐ 112 Gary Sheffield	.60	.25
☐ 113 Bobby Bonilla	.30	.14
☐ 114 Dwight Gooden	.30	.14
☐ 115 Todd Hundley	.30	.14
☐ 116 Bobby Jones	.30	.14
☐ 117 Jeff Kent	.15	.07
☐ 118 Kevin McReynolds	.15	.07
☐ 119 Bret Saberhagen	.15	.07
☐ 120 Ryan Thompson	.15	.07
☐ 121 Harold Baines	.30	.14
☐ 122 Mike Devereaux	.15	.07
☐ 123 Jeffrey Hammonds	.30	.14
☐ 124 Ben McDonald	.15	.07
☐ 125 Mike Mussina	.40	.18
☐ 126 Rafael Palmeiro	.40	.18
☐ 127 Cal Ripken Jr.	2.50	1.10
☐ 128 Lee Smith	.30	.14
☐ 129 Brad Ausmus	.15	.07
☐ 130 Derek Bell	.30	.14
☐ 131 Andy Benes	.30	.14
☐ 132 Tony Gwynn	1.50	.70

	MINT	NRMT
☐ 133 Trevor Hoffman	.30	.14
☐ 134 Scott Livingstone	.15	.07
☐ 135 Phil Plantier	.15	.07
☐ 136 Darren Daulton	.30	.14
☐ 137 Mariano Duncan	.15	.07
☐ 138 Lenny Dykstra	.30	.14
☐ 139 Dave Hollins	.15	.07
☐ 140 Pete Incaviglia	.15	.07
☐ 141 Danny Jackson	.15	.07
☐ 142 John Kruk	.30	.14
☐ 143 Kevin Stocker	.15	.07
☐ 144 Jay Bell	.30	.14
☐ 145 Carlos Garcia	.15	.07
☐ 146 Jeff King	.30	.14
☐ 147 Al Martin	.15	.07
☐ 148 Orlando Merced	.15	.07
☐ 149 Don Slaught	.15	.07
☐ 150 Andy Van Slyke	.30	.14
☐ 151 Kevin Brown	.30	.14
☐ 152 Jose Canseco	.40	.18
☐ 153 Will Clark	.40	.18
☐ 154 Juan Gonzalez	1.50	.70
☐ 155 David Hulse	.15	.07
☐ 156 Dean Palmer	.30	.14
☐ 157 Ivan Rodriguez	.75	.35
☐ 158 Kenny Rogers	.15	.07
☐ 159 Roger Clemens	1.25	.55
☐ 160 Scott Cooper	.15	.07
☐ 161 Andre Dawson	.40	.18
☐ 162 Mike Greenwell	.15	.07
☐ 163 Otis Nixon	.15	.07
☐ 164 Aaron Sele	.15	.07
☐ 165 John Valentin	.30	.14
☐ 166 Mo Vaughn	.75	.35
☐ 167 Bret Boone	.15	.07
☐ 168 Barry Larkin	.40	.18
☐ 169 Kevin Mitchell	.15	.07
☐ 170 Hal Morris	.15	.07
☐ 171 Jose Rijo	.15	.07
☐ 172 Deion Sanders	.60	.25
☐ 173 Reggie Sanders	.15	.07
☐ 174 John Smiley	.15	.07
☐ 175 Dante Bichette	.40	.18
☐ 176 Ellis Burks	.30	.14
☐ 177 Andres Galarraga	.40	.18
☐ 178 Joe Girardi	.15	.07
☐ 179 Charlie Hayes	.15	.07
☐ 180 Roberto Mejia	.15	.07
☐ 181 Walt Weiss	.15	.07
☐ 182 David Cone	.30	.14
☐ 183 Gary Gaetti	.30	.14
☐ 184 Greg Gagne	.15	.07
☐ 185 Felix Jose	.15	.07
☐ 186 Wally Joyner	.30	.14
☐ 187 Mike Macfarlane	.15	.07
☐ 188 Brian McRae	.15	.07
☐ 189 Eric Davis	.30	.14
☐ 190 Cecil Fielder	.30	.14
☐ 191 Travis Fryman	.30	.14
☐ 192 Tony Phillips	.15	.07
☐ 193 Mickey Tettleton	.15	.07
☐ 194 Alan Trammell	.30	.14
☐ 195 Lou Whitaker	.40	.18
☐ 196 Kent Hrbek	.30	.14
☐ 197 Chuck Knoblauch	.60	.25
☐ 198 Shane Mack	.15	.07
☐ 199 Pat Meares	.15	.07
☐ 200 Kirby Puckett	1.25	.55
☐ 201 Matt Walbeck	.15	.07
☐ 202 Dave Winfield	.40	.18
☐ 203 Wilson Alvarez	.30	.14
☐ 204 Alex Fernandez	.30	.14
☐ 205 Julio Franco	.30	.14
☐ 206 Ozzie Guillen	.15	.07
☐ 207 Jack McDowell	.15	.07
☐ 208 Tim Raines	.15	.07
☐ 209 Frank Thomas	2.50	1.10
☐ 210 Robin Ventura	.30	.14
☐ 211 Jim Abbott	.15	.07
☐ 212 Wade Boggs	.60	.25
☐ 213 Pat Kelly	.15	.07
☐ 214 Jimmy Key	.30	.14
☐ 215 Don Mattingly	1.00	.45
☐ 216 Paul O'Neill	.30	.14
☐ 217 Mike Stanley	.15	.07
☐ 218 Danny Tartabull	.15	.07
☐ 219 Checklist	.15	.07
☐ 220 Checklist	.15	.07

1994 Studio Editor's Choice

This eight-card standard-sized set was randomly inserted in foil packs at a rate of one in 36. These cards are acetate and were designed much like a film strip with black borders. The fronts have various stop-action shots of the player and no back.

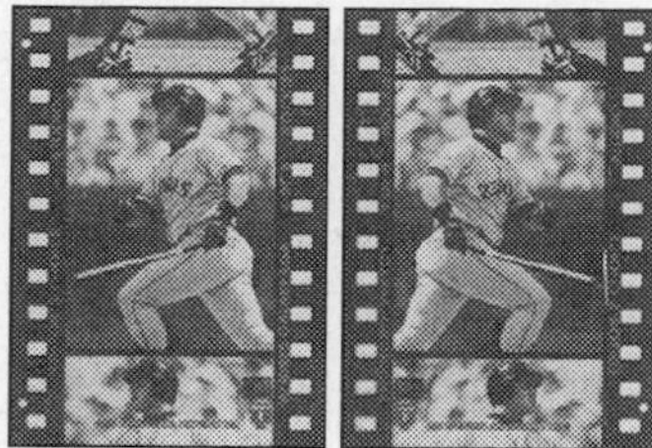

	MINT	NRMT
COMPLETE SET (8)	40.00	18.00
COMMON CARD (1-8)	1.50	.70
☐ 1 Barry Bonds	4.00	1.80
☐ 2 Frank Thomas	12.00	5.50
☐ 3 Ken Griffey Jr.	15.00	6.75
☐ 4 Andres Galarraga	2.50	1.10
☐ 5 Juan Gonzalez	8.00	3.60
☐ 6 Tim Salmon	3.00	1.35
☐ 7 Paul O'Neill	1.50	.70
☐ 8 Mike Piazza	10.00	4.50

1994 Studio Heritage

Each player in this eight-card insert set (randomly inserted in foil packs at a rate of one in nine) is modelling a vintage uniform of his team. The year of the uniform is noted in gold lettering at the top with a gold Heritage Collection logo at the bottom. A black and white photo of the stadium that the team used from the era of the depicted uniform serves as background. The back has a small photo a team highlight from that year.

	MINT	NRMT
COMPLETE SET (8)	15.00	6.75
COMMON CARD (1-8)	.50	.23
☐ 1 Barry Bonds	2.00	.90
☐ 2 Frank Thomas	8.00	3.60
☐ 3 Joe Carter	2.00	.90
☐ 4 Don Mattingly	4.00	1.80
☐ 5 Ryne Sandberg	2.00	.90
☐ 6 Javier Lopez	2.00	.90
☐ 7 Gregg Jefferies	.50	.23
☐ 8 Mike Mussina	1.50	.70

1994 Studio Series Stars

This 10-card acetate set showcases top stars and was limited to 10,000 of each card. They were randomly inserted in foil packs at a rate of one in 60. The player cutout is surrounded by a small circle of stars with the player's name at the top. The team name, limited edition notation and the Series Stars logo are at the bottom. The back of the cutout contains a photo. Gold versions of this set were more difficult to obtain in packs (one in 120, 5,000 total).

	MINT	NRMT
COMPLETE SET (10)	150.00	70.00
COMMON CARD (1-10)	4.00	1.80
COMP.GOLD SET (10)	300.00	135.00

*GOLD: 1X TO 2X BASIC SERIES STARS

	MINT	NRMT
☐ 1 Tony Gwynn	12.00	5.50
☐ 2 Barry Bonds	8.00	3.60
☐ 3 Frank Thomas	25.00	11.00
☐ 4 Ken Griffey Jr.	30.00	13.50
☐ 5 Joe Carter	4.00	1.80
☐ 6 Mike Piazza	20.00	9.00
☐ 7 Cal Ripken Jr.	25.00	11.00
☐ 8 Greg Maddux	20.00	9.00
☐ 9 Juan Gonzalez	15.00	6.75
☐ 10 Don Mattingly	12.00	5.50

1995 Studio

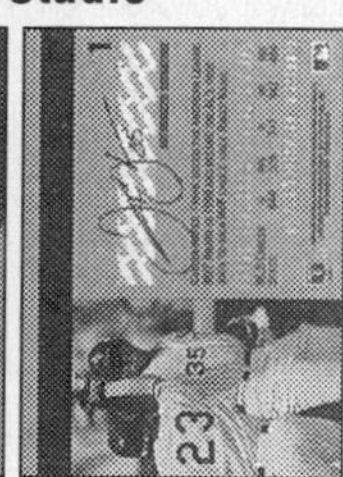

This 200-card horizontal set was issued by Donruss for the fifth consecutive year. Using a different design than past Studio issues, these cards were designed similarly to credit cards. The cards were issued in five-card packs with a suggested retail price of $1.49. The fronts have a player photo on the right with holographic team logo in the right corner. The rest of the card has the player identified in the upper left. Underneath that information are 1994 stats as well as various vital statistics. There is also the "Studio" logo in the upper left corner. The horizontal backs have an action photo on the left. The right has the player's signature along with a pertinent fact and his career statistics. There are no Rookie Cards in this set.

	MINT	NRMT
COMPLETE SET (200)	60.00	27.00
COMMON CARD (1-200)	.20	.09
☐ 1 Frank Thomas	3.00	1.35
☐ 2 Jeff Bagwell	1.50	.70
☐ 3 Don Mattingly	1.25	.55
☐ 4 Mike Piazza	2.50	1.10
☐ 5 Ken Griffey Jr.	4.00	1.80
☐ 6 Greg Maddux	2.50	1.10
☐ 7 Barry Bonds	1.00	.45
☐ 8 Cal Ripken Jr.	3.00	1.35
☐ 9 Jose Canseco	.50	.23
☐ 10 Paul Molitor	.75	.35
☐ 11 Kenny Lofton	1.00	.45
☐ 12 Will Clark	.50	.23
☐ 13 Tim Salmon	.75	.35
☐ 14 Joe Carter	.50	.23
☐ 15 Albert Belle	1.00	.45
☐ 16 Roger Clemens	1.50	.70
☐ 17 Roberto Alomar	.75	.35
☐ 18 Alex Rodriguez	3.00	1.35
☐ 19 Raul Mondesi	.50	.23
☐ 20 Deion Sanders	.50	.23
☐ 21 Juan Gonzalez	2.00	.90
☐ 22 Kirby Puckett	1.50	.70
☐ 23 Fred McGriff	.50	.23
☐ 24 Matt Williams	.50	.23
☐ 25 Tony Gwynn	2.00	.90
☐ 26 Cliff Floyd	.20	.09
☐ 27 Travis Fryman	.40	.18
☐ 28 Shawn Green	.40	.18
☐ 29 Mike Mussina	.75	.35
☐ 30 Bob Hamelin	.20	.09
☐ 31 David Justice	.75	.35
☐ 32 Manny Ramirez	.75	.35
☐ 33 David Cone	.40	.18
☐ 34 Marquis Grissom	.40	.18
☐ 35 Moises Alou	.40	.18
☐ 36 Carlos Baerga	.40	.18
☐ 37 Barry Larkin	.50	.23
☐ 38 Robin Ventura	.40	.18
☐ 39 Mo Vaughn	1.00	.45
☐ 40 Jeffrey Hammonds	.40	.18
☐ 41 Ozzie Smith	1.00	.45
☐ 42 Andres Galarraga	.50	.23
☐ 43 Carlos Delgado	.40	.18
☐ 44 Lenny Dykstra	.40	.18
☐ 45 Cecil Fielder	.40	.18
☐ 46 Wade Boggs	.50	.23
☐ 47 Gregg Jefferies	.40	.18
☐ 48 Randy Johnson	.75	.35
☐ 49 Rafael Palmeiro	.50	.23
☐ 50 Craig Biggio	.50	.23

☐ 51 Steve Avery	.20	.09
☐ 52 Ricky Bottalico	.40	.18
☐ 53 Chris Gomez	.20	.09
☐ 54 Carlos Garcia	.20	.09
☐ 55 Brian Anderson	.20	.09
☐ 56 Wilson Alvarez	.40	.18
☐ 57 Roberto Kelly	.20	.09
☐ 58 Larry Walker	.75	.35
☐ 59 Dean Palmer	.40	.18
☐ 60 Rick Aguilera	.20	.09
☐ 61 Javier Lopez	.50	.23
☐ 62 Shawon Dunston	.20	.09
☐ 63 Wm. VanLandingham	.20	.09
☐ 64 Jeff Kent	.20	.09
☐ 65 David McCarty	.20	.09
☐ 66 Armando Benitez	.20	.09
☐ 67 Brett Butler	.40	.18
☐ 68 Bernard Gilkey	.40	.18
☐ 69 Joey Hamilton	.40	.18
☐ 70 Chad Curtis	.20	.09
☐ 71 Dante Bichette	.50	.23
☐ 72 Chuck Carr	.20	.09
☐ 73 Pedro Martinez	.75	.35
☐ 74 Ramon Martinez	.40	.18
☐ 75 Rondell White	.50	.23
☐ 76 Alex Fernandez	.40	.18
☐ 77 Dennis Martinez	.40	.18
☐ 78 Sammy Sosa	.75	.35
☐ 79 Bernie Williams	.75	.35
☐ 80 Lou Whitaker	.40	.18
☐ 81 Kurt Abbott	.20	.09
☐ 82 Tino Martinez	.75	.35
☐ 83 Willie Greene	.20	.09
☐ 84 Garret Anderson	.50	.23
☐ 85 Jose Rijo	.20	.09
☐ 86 Jeff Montgomery	.40	.18
☐ 87 Mark Langston	.20	.09
☐ 88 Reggie Sanders	.20	.09
☐ 89 Rusty Greer	.75	.35
☐ 90 Delino DeShields	.20	.09
☐ 91 Jason Bere	.20	.09
☐ 92 Lee Smith	.40	.18
☐ 93 Devon White	.40	.18
☐ 94 John Wetteland	.40	.18
☐ 95 Luis Gonzalez	.20	.09
☐ 96 Greg Vaughn	.20	.09
☐ 97 Lance Johnson	.40	.18
☐ 98 Alan Trammell	.50	.23
☐ 99 Bret Saberhagen	.20	.09
☐ 100 Jack McDowell	.20	.09
☐ 101 Trevor Hoffman	.40	.18
☐ 102 Dave Nilsson	.40	.18
☐ 103 Bryan Harvey	.20	.09
☐ 104 Chuck Knoblauch	.75	.35
☐ 105 Bobby Bonilla	.40	.18
☐ 106 Hal Morris	.20	.09
☐ 107 Mark Whiten	.20	.09
☐ 108 Phil Plantier	.20	.09
☐ 109 Ryan Klesko	.50	.23
☐ 110 Greg Gagne	.20	.09
☐ 111 Ruben Sierra	.20	.09
☐ 112 J.R. Phillips	.20	.09
☐ 113 Terry Steinbach	.40	.18
☐ 114 Jay Buhner	.50	.23
☐ 115 Ken Caminiti	.75	.35
☐ 116 Gary DiSarcina	.20	.09
☐ 117 Ivan Rodriguez	1.00	.45
☐ 118 Bip Roberts	.20	.09
☐ 119 Jay Bell	.40	.18
☐ 120 Ken Hill	.20	.09
☐ 121 Mike Greenwell	.20	.09
☐ 122 Rick Wilkins	.20	.09
☐ 123 Rickey Henderson	.50	.23
☐ 124 Dave Hollins	.20	.09
☐ 125 Terry Pendleton	.40	.18
☐ 126 Rich Becker	.20	.09
☐ 127 Billy Ashley	.20	.09
☐ 128 Derek Bell	.40	.18
☐ 129 Dennis Eckersley	.50	.23
☐ 130 Andujar Cedeno	.20	.09
☐ 131 John Jaha	.20	.09
☐ 132 Chuck Finley	.40	.18
☐ 133 Steve Finley	.40	.18
☐ 134 Danny Tartabull	.20	.09
☐ 135 Jeff Conine	.40	.18
☐ 136 Jon Lieber	.20	.09
☐ 137 Jim Abbott	.20	.09
☐ 138 Steve Trachsel	.20	.09
☐ 139 Bret Boone	.20	.09
☐ 140 Charles Johnson	.40	.18
☐ 141 Mark McGwire	1.50	.70
☐ 142 Eddie Murray	.75	.35
☐ 143 Doug Drabek	.20	.09
☐ 144 Steve Cooke	.20	.09
☐ 145 Kevin Seitzer	.20	.09
☐ 146 Rod Beck	.20	.09
☐ 147 Eric Karros	.40	.18
☐ 148 Tim Raines	.20	.09
☐ 149 Joe Girardi	.20	.09
☐ 150 Aaron Sele	.20	.09
☐ 151 Robby Thompson	.20	.09
☐ 152 Chan Ho Park	.75	.35
☐ 153 Ellis Burks	.40	.18
☐ 154 Brian McRae	.20	.09
☐ 155 Jimmy Key	.40	.18
☐ 156 Rico Brogna	.20	.09
☐ 157 Ozzie Guillen	.20	.09
☐ 158 Chili Davis	.40	.18
☐ 159 Darren Daulton	.40	.18
☐ 160 Chipper Jones	2.50	1.10
☐ 161 Walt Weiss	.20	.09
☐ 162 Paul O'Neill	.40	.18
☐ 163 Al Martin	.40	.18
☐ 164 John Valentin	.40	.18
☐ 165 Tim Wallach	.20	.09
☐ 166 Scott Erickson	.20	.09
☐ 167 Ryan Thompson	.20	.09
☐ 168 Todd Zeile	.20	.09
☐ 169 Scott Cooper	.20	.09
☐ 170 Matt Mieske	.40	.18
☐ 171 Allen Watson	.20	.09
☐ 172 Brian L.Hunter	.50	.23
☐ 173 Kevin Stocker	.20	.09
☐ 174 Cal Eldred	.20	.09
☐ 175 Tony Phillips	.20	.09
☐ 176 Ben McDonald	.20	.09
☐ 177 Mark Grace	.50	.23
☐ 178 Midre Cummings	.20	.09
☐ 179 Orlando Merced	.20	.09
☐ 180 Jeff King	.40	.18
☐ 181 Gary Sheffield	.75	.35
☐ 182 Tom Glavine	.50	.23
☐ 183 Edgar Martinez	.50	.23
☐ 184 Steve Karsay	.20	.09
☐ 185 Pat Listach	.20	.09
☐ 186 Wil Cordero	.20	.09
☐ 187 Brady Anderson	.50	.23
☐ 188 Bobby Jones	.40	.18
☐ 189 Andy Benes	.20	.09
☐ 190 Ray Lankford	.40	.18
☐ 191 John Doherty	.20	.09
☐ 192 Wally Joyner	.40	.18
☐ 193 Jim Thome	.75	.35
☐ 194 Royce Clayton	.20	.09
☐ 195 John Olerud	.40	.18
☐ 196 Steve Buechele	.20	.09
☐ 197 Harold Baines	.40	.18
☐ 198 Geronimo Berroa	.20	.09
☐ 199 Checklist	.20	.09
☐ 200 Checklist	.20	.09

1995 Studio Gold Series

This 50-card set was inserted one per packs. This set parallels the first 50 cards of the regular studio set. The only differences between these cards and the regular issue are they were printed with a gold background and are numbered in the right corner as "X" of 50. Also the words "Studio Gold" are printed in the upper front left corner.

	MINT	NRMT
COMPLETE SET (50)	40.00	18.00
COMMON CARD (1-50)	.50	.23
*GOLD: 1.5X BASIC CARDS		

1995 Studio Platinum Series

This 25-card set was randomly inserted into packs at a rate of one in 10 packs. This set parallels the first 25 cards of the regular issue. These cards are different from the regular issue in that they have a platinum background, the words "Studio Platinum" in the upper left corner and are numbered on the back as "X" of 25.

	MINT	NRMT
COMPLETE SET (25)	150.00	70.00
COMMON CARD (1-25)	2.00	.90
*PLATINUM: 6X BASIC CARDS		

1996 Studio

The 1996 Studio set was issued in one series totalling 150 cards. and distributed in seven-card packs. The fronts feature color action player photos with a player portrait in the background. The backs carry another player photo, biographical information, with a head photo and vital statistics printed on the letters of the card's name.

	MINT	NRMT
COMPLETE SET (150)	15.00	6.75
COMMON CARD (1-150)	.15	.07

☐ 1 Cal Ripken	2.00	.90
☐ 2 Alex Gonzalez	.15	.07

☐ 3 Roger Cedeno	.25	.11
☐ 4 Todd Hollandsworth	.25	.11
☐ 5 Gregg Jefferies	.15	.07
☐ 6 Ryne Sandberg	.60	.25
☐ 7 Eric Karros	.25	.11
☐ 8 Jeff Conine	.25	.11
☐ 9 Rafael Palmeiro	.40	.18
☐ 10 Bip Roberts	.15	.07
☐ 11 Roger Clemens	1.00	.45
☐ 12 Tom Glavine	.25	.11
☐ 13 Jason Giambi	.25	.11
☐ 14 Rey Ordonez	.25	.11
☐ 15 Chan Ho Park	.50	.23
☐ 16 Vinny Castilla	.25	.11
☐ 17 Butch Huskey	.25	.11
☐ 18 Greg Maddux	1.50	.70
☐ 19 Bernard Gilkey	.25	.11
☐ 20 Marquis Grissom	.25	.11
☐ 21 Chuck Knoblauch	.50	.23
☐ 22 Ozzie Smith	.60	.25
☐ 23 Garret Anderson	.25	.11
☐ 24 J.T. Snow	.25	.11
☐ 25 John Valentin	.25	.11
☐ 26 Barry Larkin	.40	.18
☐ 27 Bobby Bonilla	.25	.11
☐ 28 Todd Zeile	.25	.11
☐ 29 Roberto Alomar	.50	.23
☐ 30 Ramon Martinez	.25	.11
☐ 31 Jeff King	.25	.11
☐ 32 Dennis Eckersley	.50	.23
☐ 33 Derek Jeter	1.50	.70
☐ 34 Edgar Martinez	.40	.18
☐ 35 Geronimo Berroa	.15	.07
☐ 36 Hal Morris	.15	.07
☐ 37 Troy Percival	.25	.11
☐ 38 Jason Isringhausen	.15	.07
☐ 39 Greg Vaughn	.15	.07
☐ 40 Robin Ventura	.25	.11
☐ 41 Craig Biggio	.40	.18
☐ 42 Will Clark	.40	.18
☐ 43 Sammy Sosa	.50	.23
☐ 44 Bernie Williams	.50	.23
☐ 45 Kenny Lofton	.60	.25
☐ 46 Wade Boggs	.50	.23
☐ 47 Javy Lopez	.25	.11
☐ 48 Reggie Sanders	.25	.11
☐ 49 Jeff Bagwell	1.00	.45
☐ 50 Fred McGriff	.40	.18
☐ 51 Charles Johnson	.25	.11
☐ 52 Darren Daulton	.25	.11
☐ 53 Jose Canseco	.40	.18
☐ 54 Cecil Fielder	.25	.11
☐ 55 Hideo Nomo	1.25	.55
☐ 56 Tim Salmon	.50	.23
☐ 57 Carlos Delgado	.25	.11
☐ 58 David Cone	.25	.11
☐ 59 Tim Raines	.15	.07
☐ 60 Lyle Mouton	.15	.07
☐ 61 Wally Joyner	.15	.07
☐ 62 Bret Boone	.15	.07
☐ 63 Raul Mondesi	.40	.18
☐ 64 Gary Sheffield	.50	.23
☐ 65 Alex Rodriguez	2.00	.90
☐ 66 Russ Davis	.15	.07
☐ 67 Checklist	.15	.07
☐ 68 Marty Cordova	.25	.11
☐ 69 Ruben Sierra	.15	.07
☐ 70 Jose Mesa	.25	.11
☐ 71 Matt Williams	.40	.18
☐ 72 Chipper Jones	1.50	.70
☐ 73 Randy Johnson	.50	.23
☐ 74 Kirby Puckett	1.00	.45
☐ 75 Jim Edmonds	.50	.23
☐ 76 Barry Bonds	.60	.25
☐ 77 David Segui	.15	.07
☐ 78 Larry Walker	.50	.23
☐ 79 Jason Kendall	.50	.23
☐ 80 Mike Piazza	1.50	.70
☐ 81 Brian L.Hunter	.25	.11
☐ 82 Julio Franco	.25	.11
☐ 83 Jay Bell	.25	.11
☐ 84 Kevin Seitzer	.15	.07
☐ 85 John Smoltz	.25	.11

☐ 86 Joe Carter	.25	.11
☐ 87 Ray Durham	.25	.11
☐ 88 Carlos Baerga	.25	.11
☐ 89 Ron Gant	.25	.11
☐ 90 Orlando Merced	.15	.07
☐ 91 Lee Smith	.25	.11
☐ 92 Pedro Martinez	.50	.23
☐ 93 Frank Thomas	2.00	.90
☐ 94 Al Martin	.15	.07
☐ 95 Chad Curtis	.15	.07
☐ 96 Eddie Murray	.50	.23
☐ 97 Rusty Greer	.40	.18
☐ 98 Jay Buhner	.40	.18
☐ 99 Rico Brogna	.15	.07
☐ 100 Todd Hundley	.25	.11
☐ 101 Moises Alou	.25	.11
☐ 102 Chili Davis	.25	.11
☐ 103 Ismael Valdes	.25	.11
☐ 104 Mo Vaughn	.60	.25
☐ 105 Juan Gonzalez	1.25	.55
☐ 106 Mark Grudzielanek	.25	.11
☐ 107 Derek Bell	.15	.07
☐ 108 Shawn Green	.15	.07
☐ 109 David Justice	.50	.23
☐ 110 Paul O'Neill	.25	.11
☐ 111 Kevin Appier	.25	.11
☐ 112 Ray Lankford	.25	.11
☐ 113 Travis Fryman	.25	.11
☐ 114 Manny Ramirez	.50	.23
☐ 115 Brooks Kieschnick	.25	.11
☐ 116 Ken Griffey Jr.	2.50	1.10
☐ 117 Jeffrey Hammonds	.15	.07
☐ 118 Mark McGwire	1.00	.45
☐ 119 Denny Neagle	.25	.11
☐ 120 Quilvio Veras	.15	.07
☐ 121 Alan Benes	.25	.11
☐ 122 Rondell White	.25	.11
☐ 123 Osvaldo Fernandez	.25	.11
☐ 124 Andres Galarraga	.50	.23
☐ 125 Johnny Damon	.25	.11
☐ 126 Lenny Dykstra	.25	.11
☐ 127 Jason Schmidt	.25	.11
☐ 128 Mike Mussina	.50	.23
☐ 129 Ken Caminiti	.50	.23
☐ 130 Michael Tucker	.25	.11
☐ 131 LaTroy Hawkins	.15	.07
☐ 132 Checklist	.15	.07
☐ 133 Delino DeShields	.15	.07
☐ 134 Dave Nilsson	.25	.11
☐ 135 Jack McDowell	.15	.07
☐ 136 Joey Hamilton	.25	.11
☐ 137 Dante Bichette	.40	.18
☐ 138 Paul Molitor	.50	.23
☐ 139 Ivan Rodriguez	.60	.25
☐ 140 Mark Grace	.40	.18
☐ 141 Paul Wilson	.15	.07
☐ 142 Orel Hershiser	.25	.11
☐ 143 Albert Belle	.60	.25
☐ 144 Tino Martinez	.50	.23
☐ 145 Tony Gwynn	1.25	.55
☐ 146 George Arias	.15	.07
☐ 147 Brian Jordan	.25	.11
☐ 148 Brian McRae	.15	.07
☐ 149 Rickey Henderson	.40	.18
☐ 150 Ryan Klesko	.40	.18

1996 Studio Press Proofs Bronze

Randomly inserted in packs, this 150-card Bronze set is parallel to the regular set and is similar in design with bronze foil stamping. Only 2,000 sets were produced. Prices below refer to Bronze cards.

	MINT	NRMT
COMPLETE SET (150)	400.00	180.00
COMMON CARD (1-150)	1.00	.45

STARS: 5X TO 12X BASIC CARDS
YOUNG STARS: 4X TO 10X BASIC CARDS

1996 Studio Press Proofs Gold

Randomly inserted in packs, this 150-card set is parallel to the regular set and is similar in design with gold foil stamping. Only 500 sets were produced.

	MINT	NRMT
COMPLETE SET (150)	1500.00	700.00
COMMON CARD (1-150)	4.00	1.80

STARS: 25X TO 50X BASIC CARDS
YOUNG STARS: 20X TO 40X BASIC CARDS

1996 Studio Press Proofs Silver

Randomly inserted in magazine packs, this 150-card set is parallel to the regular set and is similar in design with silver foil stamping. Only 100 sets were produced.

	MINT	NRMT
COMPLETE SET (150)	3500.00	1600.00
COMMON CARD (1-150)	10.00	4.50

*STARS: 50X TO 100X BASIC CARDS
*YOUNG STARS: 40X TO 80X BASIC CARDS

1996 Studio Hit Parade

Randomly inserted in packs at a rate of 1:48, cards from this ten-card set feature some of the League's top long-ball hitters. The fronts feature color action player photos on a die-cut record design in the background. The backs carry the player's batting average breakdown. Each card is serial numbered of 5,000 on back.

	MINT	NRMT
COMPLETE SET (10)	100.00	45.00
COMMON CARD (1-10)	3.00	1.35
☐ 1 Tony Gwynn	10.00	4.50
☐ 2 Ken Griffey Jr.	25.00	11.00
☐ 3 Frank Thomas	20.00	9.00
☐ 4 Jeff Bagwell	10.00	4.50
☐ 5 Kirby Puckett	10.00	4.50
☐ 6 Mike Piazza	15.00	6.75
☐ 7 Barry Bonds	6.00	2.70
☐ 8 Albert Belle	6.00	2.70
☐ 9 Tim Salmon	3.00	1.35
☐ 10 Mo Vaughn	6.00	2.70

1996 Studio Masterstrokes

Randomly inserted in packs, this eight-card set features some of the League's most popular stars. Printed with brushed embossed technologies, the cards display color action player images in simulated oil painting detail. Each card from this set was also produced in a promo form.

	MINT	NRMT
COMPLETE SET (8)	150.00	70.00
COMMON CARD (1-8)	8.00	3.60
☐ 1 Tony Gwynn	20.00	9.00
☐ 2 Mike Piazza	25.00	11.00
☐ 3 Jeff Bagwell	15.00	6.75
☐ 4 Manny Ramirez	8.00	3.60
☐ 5 Cal Ripken	30.00	13.50
☐ 6 Frank Thomas	30.00	13.50
☐ 7 Ken Griffey Jr.	40.00	18.00
☐ 8 Greg Maddux	25.00	11.00
☐ P2 Mike Piazza Promo	5.00	2.20

1996 Studio Stained Glass Stars

Randomly inserted in packs, this 12-card set honors some of the league's hottest superstars. The cards feature color player images on a genuine-look stained glass background and were printed with a clear plastic, die-cut technology.

	MINT	NRMT
COMPLETE SET (12)	100.00	45.00
COMMON CARD (1-12)	4.00	1.80
☐ 1 Cal Ripken	12.00	5.50
☐ 2 Ken Griffey Jr.	15.00	6.75
☐ 3 Frank Thomas	12.00	5.50
☐ 4 Greg Maddux	10.00	4.50

☐ 5 Chipper Jones	10.00	4.50
☐ 6 Mike Piazza	10.00	4.50
☐ 7 Albert Belle	4.00	1.80
☐ 8 Jeff Bagwell	6.00	2.70
☐ 9 Hideo Nomo	8.00	3.60
☐ 10 Barry Bonds	4.00	1.80
☐ 11 Manny Ramirez	4.00	1.80
☐ 12 Kenny Lofton	4.00	1.80

1997 Studio

The 1997 Studio set was issued in one series totalling 165 cards and was distributed in five-card packs with an 8x10 Studio Portrait for a suggested retail price of $2.49. The fronts feature color player portraits, while the backs carry player information. It is believed that the following cards: 112, 133, 137, 147 and 161 were short printed.

	MINT	NRMT
COMPLETE SET (165)	55.00	25.00
COMMON CARD (1-165)	.15	.07
☐ 1 Frank Thomas	2.50	1.10
☐ 2 Gary Sheffield	.60	.25
☐ 3 Jason Isringhausen	.15	.07
☐ 4 Ron Gant	.15	.07
☐ 5 Andy Pettitte	.60	.25
☐ 6 Todd Hollandsworth	.15	.07
☐ 7 Troy Percival	.15	.07
☐ 8 Mark McGwire	1.25	.55
☐ 9 Barry Larkin	.30	.14
☐ 10 Ken Caminiti	.60	.25
☐ 11 Paul Molitor	.60	.25
☐ 12 Travis Fryman	.15	.07
☐ 13 Kevin Brown	.15	.07
☐ 14 Robin Ventura	.15	.07
☐ 15 Andres Galarraga	.60	.25
☐ 16 Ken Griffey Jr.	3.00	1.35
☐ 17 Roger Clemens	1.25	.55
☐ 18 Alan Benes	.15	.07
☐ 19 Dave Justice	.60	.25
☐ 20 Damon Buford	.15	.07
☐ 21 Mike Piazza	2.00	.90
☐ 22 Ray Durham	.15	.07
☐ 23 Billy Wagner	.15	.07
☐ 24 Dean Palmer	.15	.07
☐ 25 David Cone	.15	.07
☐ 26 Ruben Sierra	.15	.07
☐ 27 Henry Rodriguez	.15	.07
☐ 28 Ray Lankford	.15	.07
☐ 29 Jamey Wright	.15	.07
☐ 30 Brady Anderson	.30	.14
☐ 31 Tino Martinez	.60	.25
☐ 32 Manny Ramirez	.60	.25
☐ 33 Jeff Conine	.15	.07
☐ 34 Dante Bichette	.15	.07
☐ 35 Jose Canseco	.30	.14
☐ 36 Mo Vaughn	.75	.35
☐ 37 Sammy Sosa	.60	.25
☐ 38 Mark Grudzielanek	.15	.07
☐ 39 Mike Mussina	.60	.25
☐ 40 Bill Pulsipher	.15	.07
☐ 41 Ryne Sandberg	.75	.35
☐ 42 Rickey Henderson	.30	.14
☐ 43 Alex Rodriguez	2.50	1.10
☐ 44 Eddie Murray	.60	.25
☐ 45 Ernie Young	.15	.07
☐ 46 Joey Hamilton	.15	.07
☐ 47 Wade Boggs	.60	.25

☐ 48 Rusty Greer .15 .07
☐ 49 Carlos Delgado .15 .07
☐ 50 Ellis Burks .15 .07
☐ 51 Cal Ripken 2.50 1.10
☐ 52 Alex Fernandez .15 .07
☐ 53 Wally Joyner .15 .07
☐ 54 James Baldwin .15 .07
☐ 55 Juan Gonzalez 1.50 .70
☐ 56 John Smoltz .15 .07
☐ 57 Omar Vizquel .15 .07
☐ 58 Shane Reynolds .15 .07
☐ 59 Barry Bonds .75 .35
☐ 60 Jason Kendall .15 .07
☐ 61 Marty Cordova .15 .07
☐ 62 Charles Johnson .15 .07
☐ 63 John Jaha .15 .07
☐ 64 Chan Ho Park .60 .25
☐ 65 Jermaine Allensworth .15 .07
☐ 66 Mark Grace .30 .14
☐ 67 Tim Salmon .60 .25
☐ 68 Edgar Martinez .30 .14
☐ 69 Marquis Grissom .15 .07
☐ 70 Craig Biggio .30 .14
☐ 71 Bobby Higginson .15 .07
☐ 72 Kevin Seitzer .15 .07
☐ 73 Hideo Nomo 1.50 .70
☐ 74 Dennis Eckersley .30 .14
☐ 75 Bobby Bonilla .15 .07
☐ 76 Dwight Gooden .15 .07
☐ 77 Jeff Cirillo .15 .07
☐ 78 Brian McRae .15 .07
☐ 79 Chipper Jones 2.00 .90
☐ 80 Jeff Fassero .15 .07
☐ 81 Fred McGriff .30 .14
☐ 82 Garret Anderson .15 .07
☐ 83 Eric Karros .15 .07
☐ 84 Derek Bell .15 .07
☐ 85 Kenny Lofton .75 .35
☐ 86 John Mabry .15 .07
☐ 87 Pat Hentgen .15 .07
☐ 88 Greg Maddux 2.00 .90
☐ 89 Jason Giambi .15 .07
☐ 90 Al Martin .15 .07
☐ 91 Derek Jeter 2.00 .90
☐ 92 Rey Ordonez .15 .07
☐ 93 Will Clark .30 .14
☐ 94 Kevin Appier .15 .07
☐ 95 Roberto Alomar .60 .25
☐ 96 Joe Carter .15 .07
☐ 97 Bernie Williams .60 .25
☐ 98 Albert Belle .75 .35
☐ 99 Greg Vaughn .15 .07
☐ 100 Tony Clark .60 .25
☐ 101 Matt Williams .30 .14
☐ 102 Jeff Bagwell 1.25 .55
☐ 103 Reggie Sanders .15 .07
☐ 104 Mariano Rivera .15 .07
☐ 105 Larry Walker .60 .25
☐ 106 Shawn Green .15 .07
☐ 107 Alex Ochoa .15 .07
☐ 108 Ivan Rodriguez .75 .35
☐ 109 Eric Young .15 .07
☐ 110 Javier Lopez .15 .07
☐ 111 Brian Hunter .15 .07
☐ 112 Raul Mondesi SP 2.50 1.10
☐ 113 Randy Johnson .60 .25
☐ 114 Tony Phillips .15 .07
☐ 115 Carlos Garcia .15 .07
☐ 116 Moises Alou .15 .07
☐ 117 Paul O'Neill .15 .07
☐ 118 Jim Thome .60 .25
☐ 119 Jermaine Dye .15 .07
☐ 120 Wilson Alvarez .15 .07
☐ 121 Rondell White .15 .07
☐ 122 Michael Tucker .15 .07
☐ 123 Mike Lansing .15 .07
☐ 124 Tony Gwynn 1.50 .70
☐ 125 Ryan Klesko .30 .14
☐ 126 Jim Edmonds .60 .25
☐ 127 Chuck Knoblauch .60 .25
☐ 128 Rafael Palmeiro .30 .14
☐ 129 Jay Buhner .30 .14
☐ 130 Tom Glavine .15 .07
☐ 131 Julio Franco .15 .07
☐ 132 Cecil Fielder .15 .07
☐ 133 Paul Wilson SP 2.00 .90
☐ 134 Deion Sanders .60 .25
☐ 135 Alex Gonzalez .15 .07
☐ 136 Charles Nagy .15 .07
☐ 137 Andy Ashby SP 2.00 .90
☐ 138 Edgar Renteria .15 .07
☐ 139 Pedro Martinez .60 .25
☐ 140 Brian Jordan .15 .07
☐ 141 Todd Hundley .15 .07
☐ 142 Marc Newfield .15 .07
☐ 143 Darryl Strawberry .15 .07
☐ 144 Dan Wilson .15 .07
☐ 145 Brian Giles .15 .07
☐ 146 F.P. Santangelo .15 .07
☐ 147 Shannon Stewart SP 2.00 .90
☐ 148 Scott Spiezio .15 .07
☐ 149 Andruw Jones 1.50 .70
☐ 150 Karim Garcia .15 .07
☐ 151 Vladimir Guerrero 1.25 .55
☐ 152 George Arias .15 .07
☐ 153 Brooks Kieschnick .15 .07
☐ 154 Todd Walker .15 .07
☐ 155 Scott Rolen 1.50 .70
☐ 156 Todd Greene .15 .07
☐ 157 Dmitri Young .15 .07
☐ 158 Ruben Rivera .15 .07
☐ 159 Bartolo Colon .15 .07
☐ 160 Nomar Garciaparra 2.00 .90
☐ 161 Bob Abreu SP 2.00 .90
☐ 162 Darin Erstad 1.00 .45
☐ 163 Ken Griffey Jr. CL .60 .25
☐ 164 Frank Thomas CL .60 .25
☐ 165 Alex Rodriguez CL .60 .25

1997 Studio Press Proof Gold

Randomly inserted in packs, this 165-card set is parallel to the regular Studio set. The difference is found in the special micro-etched border with gold holographic foil stamping. Only 500 of each card was produced.

	MINT	NRMT
COMPLETE SET (165)	2000.00	900.00
COMMON CARD (1-165)	5.00	2.20

*STARS: 15X TO 30X BASIC CARDS ..
*YOUNG STARS: 12.5X TO 25X BASIC CARDS

1997 Studio Press Proof Silver

Randomly inserted in packs, this 165-card set is parallel to the regular Studio set. The difference is found in the special micro-etched border with silver holographic foil stamping. Only 1500 of each card was produced.

	MINT	NRMT
COMPLETE SET (165)	600.00	275.00
COMMON CARD (1-165)	2.00	.90

*STARS: 6X TO 12X BASIC CARDS ....
*YOUNG STARS: 5X TO 10X BASIC CARDS

1997 Studio Autographs

Randonly inserted in packs, this three-card set features autographed 8x10 Studio Portraits of the three players checklisted below. Only a limited number of portraits were signed by each player. The amount each player signed is listed next to his name.

	MINT	NRMT
COMPLETE SET (3)	250.00	110.00
COMMON CARD (1-3)	30.00	13.50

☐ 1 Vladimir Guerrero/500 125.00 55.00
☐ 2 Scott Rolen/1000 100.00 45.00
☐ 3 Todd Walker/1250 30.00 13.50

1997 Studio Hard Hats

Randomly inserted in packs, this 24-card set features color player images of 24 major league superstars on a unique clear plastic, foil-stamped, die cut batting helmet design. Only 5000 of each card was produced and are sequentially numbered.

	MINT	NRMT
COMPLETE SET (24)	250.00	110.00
COMMON CARD (1-24)	2.50	1.10

☐ 1 Ivan Rodriguez 8.00 3.60
☐ 2 Albert Belle 8.00 3.60
☐ 3 Ken Griffey Jr. 30.00 13.50
☐ 4 Chuck Knoblauch 6.00 2.70
☐ 5 Frank Thomas 25.00 11.00
☐ 6 Cal Ripken 25.00 11.00
☐ 7 Todd Walker 2.50 1.10
☐ 8 Alex Rodriguez 20.00 9.00
☐ 9 Jim Thome 6.00 2.70
☐ 10 Mike Piazza 20.00 9.00
☐ 11 Barry Larkin 4.00 1.80
☐ 12 Chipper Jones 20.00 9.00
☐ 13 Derek Jeter 15.00 6.75
☐ 14 Matt Williams 4.00 1.80
☐ 15 Jason Giambi 3.00 1.35
☐ 16 Tim Salmon 6.00 2.70
☐ 17 Brady Anderson 4.00 1.80
☐ 18 Rondell White 3.00 1.35
☐ 19 Bernie Williams 6.00 2.70
☐ 20 Juan Gonzalez 15.00 6.75
☐ 21 Karim Garcia 2.50 1.10
☐ 22 Scott Rolen 15.00 6.75
☐ 23 Darin Erstad 10.00 4.50
☐ 24 Brian Jordan 2.50 1.10

1997 Studio Master Strokes

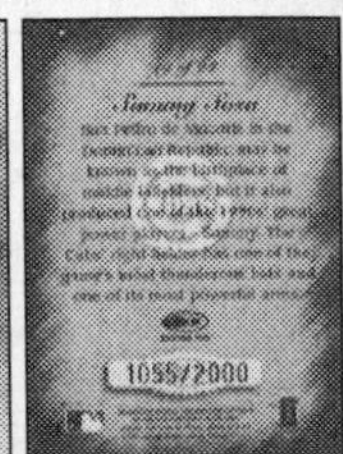

Randomly inserted in packs, this 24-card set features color photos of superstar players on all canvas card stock with gold foil stamping. Only 2,000 of each card was produced and is sequentially numbered.

	MINT	NRMT
COMPLETE SET (24)	600.00	275.00
COMMON CARD (1-24)	10.00	4.50
COMP. 8 X 10 SET (24)	250.00	110.00
COMMON 8 X 10 (1-24)	4.00	1.80

*8 X 10'S: .2X TO .4X BASIC MASTER STROKE

☐ 1 Derek Jeter 30.00 13.50
☐ 2 Jeff Bagwell 25.00 11.00
☐ 3 Ken Griffey Jr. 60.00 27.00
☐ 4 Barry Bonds 15.00 6.75
☐ 5 Frank Thomas 50.00 22.00
☐ 6 Andy Pettitte 10.00 4.50
☐ 7 Mo Vaughn 15.00 6.75
☐ 8 Alex Rodriguez 40.00 18.00
☐ 9 Andruw Jones 25.00 11.00
☐ 10 Kenny Lofton 15.00 6.75
☐ 11 Cal Ripken 50.00 22.00
☐ 12 Greg Maddux 40.00 18.00
☐ 13 Manny Ramirez 10.00 4.50
☐ 14 Mike Piazza 40.00 18.00
☐ 15 Vladimir Guerrero 20.00 9.00
☐ 16 Albert Belle 20.00 9.00
☐ 17 Chipper Jones 40.00 18.00
☐ 18 Hideo Nomo 30.00 13.50
☐ 19 Sammy Sosa 10.00 4.50
☐ 20 Tony Gwynn 30.00 13.50
☐ 21 Gary Sheffield 10.00 4.50
☐ 22 Mark McGwire 25.00 11.00
☐ 23 Juan Gonzalez 30.00 13.50
☐ 24 Paul Molitor 10.00 4.50

1997 Studio Portraits 8x10

Randomly inserted one in every pack, this 24-card set features 8x10 portraits of star players printed on super premium, 20 pt. card stock highlighted by a signable UV coating.

	MINT	NRMT
COMPLETE SET (24)	25.00	11.00
COMMON CARD (1-24)	.75	.35

☐ 1 Ken Griffey Jr. 6.00 2.70
☐ 2 Frank Thomas 5.00 2.20
☐ 3 Alex Rodriguez 5.00 2.20

☐ 4 Andruw Jones	3.00	1.35
☐ 5 Cal Ripken	5.00	2.20
☐ 6 Greg Maddux	4.00	1.80
☐ 7 Mike Piazza	4.00	1.80
☐ 8 Chipper Jones	4.00	1.80
☐ 9 Albert Belle	1.25	.55
☐ 10 Derek Jeter	4.00	1.80
☐ 11 Juan Gonzalez	3.00	1.35
☐ 12 Todd Walker	.75	.35
☐ 13 Mark McGwire	2.50	1.10
☐ 14 Barry Bonds	1.25	.55
☐ 15 Jeff Bagwell	2.50	1.10
☐ 16 Manny Ramirez	1.00	.45
☐ 17 Kenny Lofton	1.25	.55
☐ 18 Mo Vaughn	1.25	.55
☐ 19 Hideo Nomo	2.50	1.10
☐ 20 Tony Gwynn	2.50	1.10
☐ 21 Vladimir Guerrero	2.50	1.10
☐ 22 Gary Sheffield	1.00	.45
☐ 23 Ryne Sandberg	1.25	.55
☐ 24 Scott Rolen	3.00	1.35

1994 Sucker Saver

hese sucker saver lollipops were produced by Innovative onfections. The actual discs were issued by Michael chechter Associates, and one disc was included with ach sucker. It is reported that sales of this confectionary roduct were so poor that it was discontinued. Each disc easures 2 5/8" in diameter. Inside a red ring, the fronts isplay a color player headshot within a diamond design. he player's name appears in black lettering on a yellow ripe across the top of the disc. The backs of the discs e printed in blue and are numbered "X of 20."

	MINT	NRMT
OMPLETE SET (20)	35.00	16.00
OMMON CARD (1-20)	.75	.35
1 Rickey Henderson	2.00	.90
2 Ken Caminiti	2.00	.90
3 Terry Pendleton	.75	.35
4 Tim Raines	.75	.35
5 Joe Carter	1.00	.45
6 Benito Santiago	.75	.35
7 Jim Abbott	.75	.35
8 Ozzie Smith	3.00	1.35
9 Don Slaught	.75	.35
10 Tony Gwynn	4.00	1.80
11 Mark Langston	.75	.35
12 Darryl Strawberry	1.00	.45
13 Dave Justice	2.00	.90
14 Cecil Fielder	1.00	.45
15 Cal Ripken	6.00	2.70
16 Jeff Bagwell	3.00	1.35
17 Mike Piazza	5.00	2.20
18 Bobby Bonilla	1.00	.45
19 Barry Bonds	2.00	.90
20 Roger Clemens	3.00	1.35

1995 Summit Samples

s 9-card standard-sized set was issued in an 8 1/2" by 1/2" black portfolio. The fronts freature color action -out player photos on a background that is partly white d partly game action. The player's name and team logo gold-foil stamped on a black bar below. The backs ry a color closeup photo that partially overlays a seball diamond containing 1994 monthly statistics. The yer's name, sponsors' logos and card number round the back. The disclaimer "sample" is printed diagonally oss both sides of the card.

	MINT	NRMT
MPLETE SET (9)	15.00	6.75
MMON CARD	.25	.11
10 Barry Larkin	1.25	.55
11 Albert Belle	3.00	1.35
79 Cal Ripken	6.00	2.70
80 David Cone	.75	.35
125 Alex Gonzalez	.75	.35
☐ 130 Charles Johnson	.75	.35
☐ BB12 Jose Canseco	3.00	1.35
☐ BB17 Fred McGriff	3.00	1.35
☐ NNO Title Card	.25	.11

1995 Summit

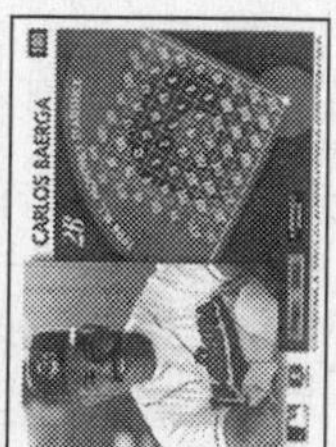

This set contains 200 standard-size cards and was sold in seven-card retail packs for a suggested price of $1.99. This set is a premium product issued by Pinnacle Brands and produced on thicker paper than the regular set. The fronts have an action photo on a white background with the player's name and team emblem at the bottom in gold-foil. The backs have a player color photo on the left side with a baseball diamond on the right that gives the player's statistics month by month for the season. Subsets featured are Rookies (112-173), Bat Speed (174-188) and Special Delivery (189-193). Notable Rookie Cards in this set include Bobby Higginson and Hideo Nomo.

	MINT	NRMT
COMPLETE SET (200)	20.00	9.00
COMMON CARD (1-200)	.10	.05
☐ 1 Ken Griffey Jr.	2.50	1.10
☐ 2 Alex Fernandez	.25	.11
☐ 3 Fred McGriff	.40	.18
☐ 4 Ben McDonald	.10	.05
☐ 5 Rafael Palmeiro	.40	.18
☐ 6 Tony Gwynn	1.25	.55
☐ 7 Jim Thome	.50	.23
☐ 8 Ken Hill	.10	.05
☐ 9 Barry Bonds	.60	.25
☐ 10 Barry Larkin	.40	.18
☐ 11 Albert Belle	.60	.25
☐ 12 Billy Ashley	.10	.05
☐ 13 Matt Williams	.40	.18
☐ 14 Andy Benes	.10	.05
☐ 15 Midre Cummings	.10	.05
☐ 16 J.R. Phillips	.10	.05
☐ 17 Edgar Martinez	.40	.18
☐ 18 Manny Ramirez	.50	.23
☐ 19 Jose Canseco	.40	.18
☐ 20 Chili Davis	.25	.11
☐ 21 Don Mattingly	.75	.35
☐ 22 Bernie Williams	.50	.23
☐ 23 Tom Glavine	.40	.18
☐ 24 Robin Ventura	.25	.11
☐ 25 Jeff Conine	.25	.11
☐ 26 Mark Grace	.40	.18
☐ 27 Mark McGwire	1.00	.45
☐ 28 Carlos Delgado	.40	.18
☐ 29 Greg Colbrunn	.10	.05
☐ 30 Greg Maddux	1.50	.70
☐ 31 Craig Biggio	.40	.18
☐ 32 Kirby Puckett	1.00	.45
☐ 33 Derek Bell	.25	.11
☐ 34 Lenny Dykstra	.25	.11
☐ 35 Tim Salmon	.50	.23
☐ 36 Deion Sanders	.50	.23
☐ 37 Moises Alou	.25	.11
☐ 38 Ray Lankford	.25	.11
☐ 39 Willie Greene	.10	.05
☐ 40 Ozzie Smith	.60	.25
☐ 41 Roger Clemens	1.00	.45
☐ 42 Andres Galarraga	.40	.18
☐ 43 Gary Sheffield	.40	.18
☐ 44 Sammy Sosa	.50	.23
☐ 45 Larry Walker	.50	.23
☐ 46 Kevin Appier	.25	.11
☐ 47 Raul Mondesi	.40	.18
☐ 48 Kenny Lofton	.60	.25
☐ 49 Darryl Hamilton	.10	.05
☐ 50 Roberto Alomar	.50	.23
☐ 51 Hal Morris	.10	.05
☐ 52 Cliff Floyd	.25	.11
☐ 53 Brent Gates	.10	.05
☐ 54 Rickey Henderson	.50	.23
☐ 55 John Olerud	.25	.11
☐ 56 Gregg Jefferies	.25	.11
☐ 57 Cecil Fielder	.25	.11
☐ 58 Paul Molitor	.50	.23
☐ 59 Bret Boone	.10	.05
☐ 60 Greg Vaughn	.10	.05
☐ 61 Wally Joyner	.25	.11
☐ 62 Jeffrey Hammonds	.25	.11
☐ 63 James Mouton	.10	.05
☐ 64 Omar Vizquel	.25	.11
☐ 65 Wade Boggs	.40	.18
☐ 66 Terry Steinbach	.25	.11
☐ 67 Wil Cordero	.10	.05
☐ 68 Joey Hamilton	.25	.11
☐ 69 Rico Brogna	.10	.05
☐ 70 Darren Daulton	.25	.11
☐ 71 Chuck Knoblauch	.50	.23
☐ 72 Bob Hamelin	.10	.05
☐ 73 Carl Everett	.10	.05
☐ 74 Joe Carter	.40	.18
☐ 75 Dave Winfield	.50	.23
☐ 76 Bobby Bonilla	.25	.11
☐ 77 Paul O'Neill	.25	.11
☐ 78 Javier Lopez	.40	.18
☐ 79 Cal Ripken	2.00	.90
☐ 80 David Cone	.25	.11
☐ 81 Bernard Gilkey	.25	.11
☐ 82 Ivan Rodriguez	.60	.25
☐ 83 Dean Palmer	.25	.11
☐ 84 Jason Bere	.10	.05
☐ 85 Will Clark	.40	.18
☐ 86 Scott Cooper	.10	.05
☐ 87 Royce Clayton	.10	.05
☐ 88 Mike Piazza	1.50	.70
☐ 89 Ryan Klesko	.40	.18
☐ 90 Juan Gonzalez	1.25	.55
☐ 91 Travis Fryman	.25	.11
☐ 92 Frank Thomas	2.00	.90
☐ 93 Eduardo Perez	.10	.05
☐ 94 Mo Vaughn	.60	.25
☐ 95 Jay Bell	.25	.11
☐ 96 Jeff Bagwell	1.00	.45
☐ 97 Randy Johnson	.40	.18
☐ 98 Jimmy Key	.25	.11
☐ 99 Dennis Eckersley	.40	.18
☐ 100 Carlos Baerga	.25	.11
☐ 101 Eddie Murray	.50	.23
☐ 102 Mike Mussina	.50	.23
☐ 103 Brian Anderson	.10	.05
☐ 104 Jeff Cirillo	.25	.11
☐ 105 Dante Bichette	.40	.18
☐ 106 Bret Saberhagen	.10	.05
☐ 107 Jeff Kent	.10	.05
☐ 108 Ruben Sierra	.10	.05
☐ 109 Kirk Gibson	.25	.11
☐ 110 Steve Karsay	.10	.05
☐ 111 David Justice	.50	.23
☐ 112 Benji Gil	.10	.05
☐ 113 Vaughn Eshelman	.10	.05
☐ 114 Carlos Perez	.25	.11
☐ 115 Chipper Jones	1.50	.70
☐ 116 Shane Andrews	.10	.05
☐ 117 Orlando Miller	.10	.05
☐ 118 Scott Ruffcorn	.10	.05
☐ 119 Jose Oliva	.10	.05
☐ 120 Joe Vitiello	.10	.05
☐ 121 Jon Nunnally	.25	.11
☐ 122 Garret Anderson	.40	.18
☐ 123 Curtis Goodwin	.10	.05
☐ 124 Mark Grudzielanek	.40	.18
☐ 125 Alex Gonzalez	.10	.05
☐ 126 David Bell	.10	.05
☐ 127 Dustin Hermanson	.25	.11
☐ 128 Dave Nilsson	.25	.11
☐ 129 Wilson Heredia	.10	.05
☐ 130 Charles Johnson	.40	.18
☐ 131 Frank Rodriguez	.25	.11
☐ 132 Alex Ochoa	.10	.05
☐ 133 Alex Rodriguez	2.00	.90
☐ 134 Bobby Higginson	.75	.35
☐ 135 Edgardo Alfonzo	.50	.23
☐ 136 Armando Benitez	.10	.05
☐ 137 Rich Aude	.10	.05
☐ 138 Tim Naehring	.10	.05
☐ 139 Joe Randa	.10	.05
☐ 140 Quilvio Veras	.10	.05
☐ 141 Hideo Nomo	2.50	1.10
☐ 142 Ray Holbert	.10	.05
☐ 143 Michael Tucker	.25	.11
☐ 144 Chad Mottola	.10	.05
☐ 145 John Valentin	.25	.11
☐ 146 James Baldwin	.25	.11
☐ 147 Esteban Loaiza	.10	.05
☐ 148 Marty Cordova	.40	.18
☐ 149 Juan Acevedo	.10	.05
☐ 150 Tim Unroe UER Cardinals logo	.10	.05
☐ 151 Brad Clontz UER A's logo	.10	.05
☐ 152 Steve Rodriguez UER	.10	.05

Card	MINT	NRMT
Yankees logo		
☐ 153 Rudy Pemberton UER	.10	.05
Dodgers logo		
☐ 154 Ozzie Timmons UER	.10	.05
Tigers logo		
☐ 155 Ricky Otero	.10	.05
☐ 156 Allen Battle	.10	.05
☐ 157 Joe Rosselli	.10	.05
☐ 158 Roberto Petagine	.10	.05
☐ 159 Todd Hollandsworth	.25	.11
☐ 160 Shannon Penn UER	.10	.05
Cubs logo		
☐ 161 Antonio Osuna UER	.10	.05
Tigers logo		
☐ 162 Russ Davis UER	.10	.05
Red Sox logo		
☐ 163 Jason Giambi UER	.40	.18
two errors: front photo actually Brent Gates		
also Braves logo		
☐ 164 Terry Bradshaw UER	.10	.05
Brewers logo		
☐ 165 Ray Durham	.40	.18
☐ 166 Todd Steverson	.10	.05
☐ 167 Tim Belk	.10	.05
☐ 168 Andy Pettitte	.75	.35
☐ 169 Roger Cedeno	.10	.05
☐ 170 Jose Parra	.25	.11
☐ 171 Scott Sullivan	.10	.05
☐ 172 LaTroy Hawkins	.10	.05
☐ 173 Jeff McCurry	.10	.05
☐ 174 Ken Griffey Jr. BS	1.25	.55
☐ 175 Frank Thomas BS	1.25	.55
☐ 176 Cal Ripken Jr. BS	1.00	.45
☐ 177 Jeff Bagwell BS	.50	.23
☐ 178 Mike Piazza BS	.75	.35
☐ 179 Barry Bonds BS	.50	.23
☐ 180 Matt Williams BS	.40	.18
☐ 181 Don Mattingly BS	.50	.23
☐ 182 Will Clark BS	.40	.18
☐ 183 Tony Gwynn BS	.50	.23
☐ 184 Kirby Puckett BS	.50	.23
☐ 185 Jose Canseco BS	.40	.18
☐ 186 Paul Molitor BS	.50	.23
☐ 187 Albert Belle BS	.50	.23
☐ 188 Joe Carter BS	.40	.18
☐ 189 Greg Maddux SD	.75	.35
☐ 190 Roger Clemens SD	.50	.23
☐ 191 David Cone SD	.25	.11
☐ 192 Mike Mussina SD	.50	.23
☐ 193 Randy Johnson SD	.50	.23
☐ 194 Frank Thomas CL	1.25	.55
☐ 195 Ken Griffey Jr. CL	1.25	.55
☐ 196 Cal Ripken CL	1.00	.45
☐ 197 Jeff Bagwell CL	.50	.23
☐ 198 Mike Piazza CL	.75	.35
☐ 199 Barry Bonds CL	.50	.23
☐ 200 Mo Vaughn CL	.25	.11
Matt Williams		

1995 Summit Nth Degree

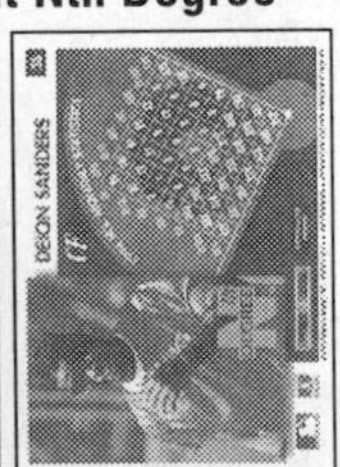

This set is a parallel of the 200 regular cards from the Summit set and inserted one per four packs. The only difference between these cards and the regular set is that "Nth degree" card fronts have a prismatic foil background.

	MINT	NRMT
COMPLETE SET (200)	400.00	180.00
COMMON CARD (1-200)	1.00	.45
*STARS: 6X to 12X BASIC CARDS		
*YOUNG STARS: 5X to 10X BASIC CARDS		

1995 Summit Big Bang

This 20-card set was randomly inserted in packs at a rate of one in 72. The set is comprised of the best home run hitters in the game. The set uses a process called "Spectrotech" which allows the card to be made of foil and have a holographic image. The fronts have an action photo with a game background which also shows the player. The backs have a player photo and information on his power exploits.

	MINT	NRMT
COMPLETE SET (20)	400.00	180.00
COMMON CARD (BB1-BB20)	4.00	1.80
☐ BB1 Ken Griffey Jr.	60.00	27.00
☐ BB2 Frank Thomas	50.00	22.00
☐ BB3 Cal Ripken	50.00	22.00
☐ BB4 Jeff Bagwell	25.00	11.00
☐ BB5 Mike Piazza	40.00	18.00
☐ BB6 Barry Bonds	15.00	6.75
☐ BB7 Matt Williams	4.00	1.80
☐ BB8 Don Mattingly	20.00	9.00
☐ BB9 Will Clark	8.00	3.60
☐ BB10 Tony Gwynn	30.00	13.50
☐ BB11 Kirby Puckett	25.00	11.00
☐ BB12 Jose Canseco	8.00	3.60
☐ BB13 Paul Molitor	12.00	5.50
☐ BB14 Albert Belle	15.00	6.75
☐ BB15 Joe Carter	8.00	3.60
☐ BB16 Rafael Palmeiro	8.00	3.60
☐ BB17 Fred McGriff	8.00	3.60
☐ BB18 David Justice	12.00	5.50
☐ BB19 Tim Salmon	12.00	5.50
☐ BB20 Mo Vaughn	15.00	6.75

1995 Summit New Age

This 15-card set was randomly inserted in packs at a rate of one in 18. The set is comprised 15 of the best young players in baseball. The fronts are horizontally designed and have a color-action photo with a background of a baseball stadium with a red and gray background. The backs have a photo with player information and the words "New Age" at the bottom in red and white.

	MINT	NRMT
COMPLETE SET (15)	60.00	27.00
COMMON CARD (NA1-NA15)	1.50	.70
☐ NA1 Cliff Floyd	2.00	.90
☐ NA2 Manny Ramirez	6.00	2.70
☐ NA3 Raul Mondesi	3.00	1.35
☐ NA4 Alex Rodriguez	25.00	11.00
☐ NA5 Billy Ashley	1.50	.70
☐ NA6 Alex Gonzalez	1.50	.70
☐ NA7 Michael Tucker	3.00	1.35
☐ NA8 Charles Johnson	3.00	1.35
☐ NA9 Carlos Delgado	3.00	1.35
☐ NA10 Benji Gil	1.50	.70
☐ NA11 Chipper Jones	20.00	9.00
☐ NA12 Todd Hollandsworth	2.00	.90
☐ NA13 Frankie Rodriguez	1.50	.70
☐ NA14 Shawn Green	2.00	.90
☐ NA15 Ray Durham	3.00	1.35

1995 Summit 21 Club

This nine-card set was randomly inserted in packs at a rate of one in 36. The set is comprised of young players with bright futures. Both sides of the card are done in foil with the front having a color photo with a gold background with "21 Club" in gray and red in the bottom right hand corner. The backs are laid out horizontally with a player head shot and information done in foil.

	MINT	NRMT
COMPLETE SET (9)	30.00	13.50
COMMON CARD (TC1-TC9)	3.00	1.35
☐ TC1 Bob Abreu	5.00	2.20
☐ TC2 Pokey Reese	3.00	1.35
☐ TC3 Edgardo Alfonzo	4.00	1.80
☐ TC4 Jim Pittsley	3.00	1.35
☐ TC5 Ruben Rivera	8.00	3.60
☐ TC6 Chan Ho Park	4.00	1.80
☐ TC7 Julian Tavarez	3.00	1.35
☐ TC8 Ismael Valdes	3.50	1.55
☐ TC9 Dmitri Young	3.50	1.55

1996 Summit

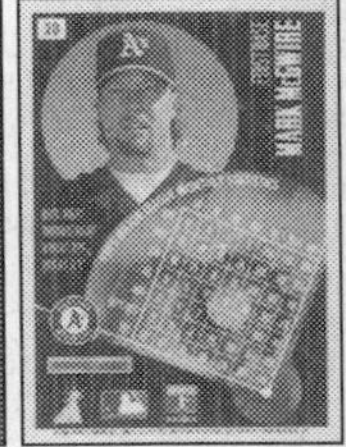

The 1996 Summit set was issued in one series totalling 200 cards. The seven-card packs had a suggested retail of $2.99 each. The fronts feature color player photos on a gold striped black background. The backs carry another player photo with player information and statistics.

	MINT	NRMT
COMPLETE SET (200)	25.00	11.00
COMMON CARD (1-200)	.15	.07
☐ 1 Mike Piazza	2.00	.90
☐ 2 Matt Williams	.40	.18
☐ 3 Tino Martinez	.60	.25
☐ 4 Reggie Sanders	.15	.07
☐ 5 Ray Durham	.30	.14
☐ 6 Brad Radke	.30	.14
☐ 7 Jeff Bagwell	1.25	.55
☐ 8 Ron Gant	.30	.14
☐ 9 Lance Johnson	.15	.07
☐ 10 Kevin Seitzer	.15	.07
☐ 11 Dante Bichette	.30	.14
☐ 12 Ivan Rodriguez	.75	.35
☐ 13 Jim Abbott	.30	.14
☐ 14 Greg Colbrunn	.15	.07
☐ 15 Rondell White	.30	.14
☐ 16 Shawn Green	.30	.14
☐ 17 Gregg Jefferies	.30	.14
☐ 18 Omar Vizquel	.30	.14
☐ 19 Cal Ripken	2.50	1.10
☐ 20 Mark McGwire	1.25	.55
☐ 21 Wally Joyner	.15	.0
☐ 22 Chili Davis	.15	.0
☐ 23 Jose Canseco	.30	.1
☐ 24 Royce Clayton	.15	.0
☐ 25 Jay Bell	.15	.0
☐ 26 Travis Fryman	.30	.1
☐ 27 Jeff King	.15	.0
☐ 28 Todd Hundley	.30	.1
☐ 29 Joe Vitiello	.15	.0
☐ 30 Russ Davis	.15	.0
☐ 31 Mo Vaughn	.75	.3
☐ 32 Raul Mondesi	.40	.1
☐ 33 Ray Lankford	.30	.1
☐ 34 Mike Stanley	.15	.0
☐ 35 B.J. Surhoff	.30	.1
☐ 36 Greg Vaughn	.15	.0
☐ 37 Todd Stottleymyre	.15	.0
☐ 38 Carlos Delgado	.30	.1
☐ 39 Kenny Lofton	.75	.3
☐ 40 Hideo Nomo	1.50	.7
☐ 41 Sterling Hitchcock	.15	.0
☐ 42 Pete Schourek	.15	.0
☐ 43 Edgardo Alfonzo	.60	.2
☐ 44 Ken Hill	.30	.1
☐ 45 Ken Caminiti	.60	.2
☐ 46 Bobby Higginson	.30	.1

☐ 47 Michael Tucker	.30	.14
☐ 48 David Cone	.30	.14
☐ 49 Cecil Fielder	.30	.14
☐ 50 Brian L. Hunter	.30	.14
☐ 51 Charles Johnson	.30	.14
☐ 52 Bobby Bonilla	.30	.14
☐ 53 Eddie Murray	.60	.25
☐ 54 Kenny Rogers	.15	.07
☐ 55 Jim Edmonds	.60	.25
☐ 56 Trevor Hoffman	.30	.14
☐ 57 Kevin Mtchell UER	.15	.07
☐ 58 Ruben Sierra	.15	.07
☐ 59 Benji Gil	.15	.07
☐ 60 Juan Gonzalez	1.50	.70
☐ 61 Larry Walker	.60	.25
☐ 62 Jack McDowell	.15	.07
☐ 63 Shawon Dunston	.15	.07
☐ 64 Andy Benes	.15	.07
☐ 65 Jay Buhner	.40	.18
☐ 66 Rickey Henderson	.40	.18
☐ 67 Alex Gonzalez	.15	.07
☐ 68 Mike Kelly	.15	.07
☐ 69 Fred McGriff	.40	.18
☐ 70 Ryne Sandberg	.75	.35
☐ 71 Ernie Young	.15	.07
☐ 72 Kevin Appier	.30	.14
☐ 73 Moises Alou	.30	.14
☐ 74 John Jaha	.15	.07
☐ 75 J.T. Snow	.15	.07
☐ 76 Jim Thome	.60	.25
☐ 77 Kirby Puckett	1.25	.55
☐ 78 Hal Morris	.15	.07
☐ 79 Robin Ventura	.30	.14
☐ 80 Ben McDonald	.15	.07
☐ 81 Tim Salmon	.60	.25
☐ 82 Albert Belle	.75	.35
☐ 83 Marquis Grissom	.30	.14
☐ 84 Alex Rodriguez	2.50	1.10
☐ 85 Manny Ramirez	.60	.25
☐ 86 Ken Griffey Jr.	3.00	1.35
☐ 87 Sammy Sosa	.60	.25
☐ 88 Frank Thomas	2.50	1.10
☐ 89 Lee Smith	.30	.14
☐ 90 Marty Cordova	.15	.07
☐ 91 Greg Maddux	2.00	.90
☐ 92 Lenny Dykstra	.30	.14
☐ 93 Butch Huskey	.30	.14
☐ 94 Garret Anderson	.30	.14
☐ 95 Mike Bordick	.15	.07
☐ 96 Dave Justice	.60	.25
☐ 97 Chad Curtis	.15	.07
☐ 98 Carlos Baerga	.30	.14
☐ 99 Jason Isringhausen	.15	.07
☐ 100 Gary Sheffield	.60	.25
☐ 101 Roger Clemens	1.25	.55
☐ 102 Ozzie Smith	.75	.35
☐ 103 Ramon Martinez	.30	.14
☐ 104 Paul O'Neill	.30	.14
☐ 105 Will Clark	.40	.18
☐ 106 Tom Glavine	.30	.14
☐ 107 Barry Bonds	.75	.35
☐ 108 Barry Larkin	.40	.18
☐ 109 Derek Bell	.30	.14
☐ 110 Randy Johnson	.60	.25
☐ 111 Jeff Conine	.30	.14
☐ 112 John Mabry	.30	.14
☐ 113 Julian Tavarez	.15	.07
☐ 114 Gary DiSarcina	.15	.07
☐ 115 Andres Galarraga	.40	.18
☐ 116 Marc Newfield	.15	.07
☐ 117 Frank Rodriguez	.15	.07
☐ 118 Brady Anderson	.40	.18
☐ 119 Mike Mussina	.60	.25
☐ 120 Orlando Merced	.15	.07
☐ 121 Melvin Nieves	.15	.07
☐ 122 Brian Jordan	.15	.07
☐ 123 Rafael Palmeiro	.40	.18
☐ 124 Johnny Damon	.30	.14
☐ 125 Wil Cordero	.15	.07
☐ 126 Chipper Jones	2.00	.90
☐ 127 Eric Karros	.30	.14
☐ 128 Darren Daulton	.30	.14
☐ 129 Vinny Castilla	.30	.14
☐ 130 Joe Carter	.30	.14
☐ 131 Bernie Williams	.60	.25
☐ 132 Bernard Gilkey	.30	.14
☐ 133 Bret Boone	.15	.07
☐ 134 Tony Gwynn	1.50	.70
☐ 135 Dave Nilsson	.30	.14
☐ 136 Ryan Klesko	.40	.18
☐ 137 Paul Molitor	.60	.25
☐ 138 John Olerud	.30	.14
☐ 139 Craig Biggio	.40	.18
☐ 140 John Valentin	.30	.14
☐ 141 Chuck Knoblauch	.60	.25
☐ 142 Edgar Martinez	.40	.18
☐ 143 Rico Brogna	.15	.07
☐ 144 Dean Palmer	.30	.14
☐ 145 Mark Grace	.40	.18
☐ 146 Roberto Alomar	.60	.25
☐ 147 Alex Fernandez	.30	.14
☐ 148 Andre Dawson	.40	.18
☐ 149 Wade Boggs	.60	.25
☐ 150 Mark Lewis	.15	.07
☐ 151 Gary Gaetti	.25	.11
☐ 152 Paul Wilson Roger Clemens	.30	.14
☐ 153 Rey Ordonez Ozzie Smith	.30	.14
☐ 154 Derek Jeter Cal Ripken	1.00	.45
☐ 155 Andy Benes Alan Benes	.15	.07
☐ 156 Jason Kendall Mike Piazza	.75	.35
☐ 157 Ryan Klesko Frank Thomas	.75	.35
☐ 158 Johnny Damon Ken Griffey Jr.	1.00	.45
☐ 159 Karim Garcia Sammy Sosa	.30	.14
☐ 160 Raul Mondesi Tim Salmon	.60	.25
☐ 161 Chipper Jones Matt Williams	.75	.35
☐ 162 Rey Ordonez	.30	.14
☐ 163 Bob Wolcott	.15	.07
☐ 164 Brooks Kieschnick	.30	.14
☐ 165 Steve Gibralter	.15	.07
☐ 166 Bob Abreu	.60	.25
☐ 167 Greg Zaun	.15	.07
☐ 168 Tavo Alvarez	.15	.07
☐ 169 Sal Fasano	.15	.07
☐ 170 George Arias	.15	.07
☐ 171 Derek Jeter	2.00	.90
☐ 172 Livan Hernandez	1.50	.70
☐ 173 Alan Benes	.30	.14
☐ 174 George Williams	.15	.07
☐ 175 John Wasdin	.15	.07
☐ 176 Chan Ho Park	.60	.25
☐ 177 Paul Wilson	.15	.07
☐ 178 Jeff Suppan	.40	.18
☐ 179 Quinton McCracken	.15	.07
☐ 180 Wilton Guerrero	.60	.25
☐ 181 Eric Owens	.15	.07
☐ 182 Felipe Crespo	.15	.07
☐ 183 LaTroy Hawkins	.15	.07
☐ 184 Jason Schmidt	.30	.14
☐ 185 Terrell Wade	.15	.07
☐ 186 Mike Grace	.15	.07
☐ 187 Chris Snopek	.15	.07
☐ 188 Jason Kendall	.60	.25
☐ 189 Todd Hollandsworth	.30	.14
☐ 190 Jim Pittsley	.30	.14
☐ 191 Jermaine Dye	.15	.07
☐ 192 Mike Busby	.15	.07
☐ 193 Richard Hidalgo	.60	.25
☐ 194 Tyler Houston	.15	.07
☐ 195 Jimmy Haynes	.15	.07
☐ 196 Karim Garcia	.30	.14
☐ 197 Ken Griffey Jr. CL	1.50	.70
☐ 198 Frank Thomas CL	1.50	.70
☐ 199 Greg Maddux CL	1.00	.45
☐ 200 Cal Ripken CL	1.25	.55

1996 Summit Above and Beyond

Randomly inserted in packs at a rate of one in four, this 200-card set is parallel to the regular set and is similar in design. The prismatic foil background distinguishes it from the regular set.

	MINT	NRMT
COMPLETE SET (200)	500.00	220.00
COMMON CARD (1-200)	1.50	.70

*STARS: 6X to 12X BASIC CARDS

*YOUNG STARS: 5X to 10X BASIC CARDS

1996 Summit Artist's Proofs

Randomly inserted in packs at a rate of one in 36, this 200-card set is parallel to the regular set and is similar in design with the foil stamped Artist's Proof logo on the front.

	MINT	NRMT
COMPLETE SET (200)	2500.00	1100.00
COMMON CARD (1-200)	4.00	1.80

*STARS: 20X TO 40X BASIC CARDS

*YOUNG STARS: 15X TO 30X BASIC CARDS

1996 Summit Foil

Available exclusively through seven-card retail Super Packs (SRP $2.99), these foil cards parallel the basic 200-card Summit set. The micro-etched foil card fronts distinguishes them from basic cards.

	MINT	NRMT
COMPLETE SET (200)	50.00	22.00
COMMON CARD (1-200)	.15	.07

*STARS: 1.5X BASIC CARDS

*YOUNG STARS: 1.5X BASIC CARDS.

1996 Summit Ballparks

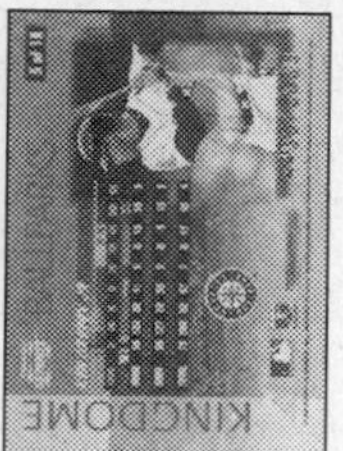

Randomly inserted in packs at a rate of one in seven, this 18-card set features color action player photos on picture backgrounds of their home ballparks. The backs carry the name of the ballparks and players statistics. Eight thousand of these sets were produced and each card was serial numbered on the back.

	MINT	NRMT
COMPLETE SET (18)	150.00	70.00
COMMON CARD (1-18)	3.00	1.35
☐ 1 Cal Ripken	20.00	9.00
☐ 2 Albert Belle	10.00	4.50
☐ 3 Dante Bichette	3.50	1.55
☐ 4 Mo Vaughn	6.00	2.70
☐ 5 Ken Griffey Jr.	25.00	11.00
☐ 6 Derek Jeter	15.00	6.75
☐ 7 Juan Gonzalez	12.00	5.50
☐ 8 Greg Maddux	15.00	6.75
☐ 9 Frank Thomas	25.00	11.00
☐ 10 Ryne Sandberg	6.00	2.70
☐ 11 Mike Piazza	15.00	6.75
☐ 12 Johnny Damon	3.50	1.55
☐ 13 Barry Bonds	6.00	2.70
☐ 14 Jeff Bagwell	10.00	4.50
☐ 15 Paul Wilson	3.00	1.35
☐ 16 Tim Salmon	5.00	2.20
☐ 17 Kirby Puckett	10.00	4.50
☐ 18 Tony Gwynn	10.00	4.50

1996 Summit Big Bang

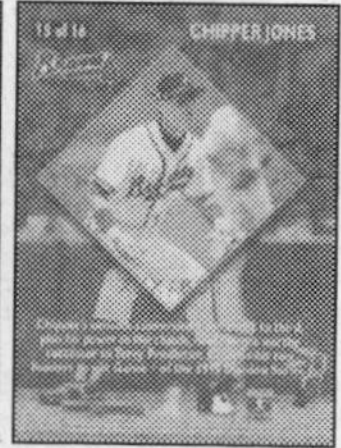

Randomly inserted in packs at a rate of one in 72, this 16-card set features the League's big hitters on Spectroetched backgrounds with etched foil highlights. Only 600 sets were produced and each card is individually numbered of 600 on back.The backs carry a player portrait in a diamond with a faded version of the front as a background and information about the player.

	MINT	NRMT
COMPLETE SET (16)	750.00	350.00
COMMON CARD (1-16)	10.00	4.50

	MINT	NRMT
COMPLETE MIRAGE SET (16)	750.00	350.00
*MIRAGE: 1X BASIC CARDS		
☐ 1 Frank Thomas	100.00	45.00
☐ 2 Ken Griffey Jr.	120.00	55.00
☐ 3 Albert Belle	30.00	13.50
☐ 4 Mo Vaughn	30.00	13.50
☐ 5 Barry Bonds	30.00	13.50
☐ 6 Cal Ripken	100.00	45.00
☐ 7 Jeff Bagwell	50.00	22.00
☐ 8 Mike Piazza	80.00	36.00
☐ 9 Ryan Klesko	15.00	6.75
☐ 10 Manny Ramirez	25.00	11.00
☐ 11 Tim Salmon	25.00	11.00
☐ 12 Dante Bichette	15.00	6.75
☐ 13 Sammy Sosa	25.00	11.00
☐ 14 Raul Mondesi	25.00	11.00
☐ 15 Chipper Jones	80.00	36.00
☐ 16 Garret Anderson	10.00	4.50

1996 Summit Hitters Inc.

Randomly inserted in packs at a rate of one in 36, this 16-card set features color action player images with embossed highlights on an enlarged photo of the player's eyes for background. The backs carry information about the player's batting ability. Four thousand of these sets were produced and individually serially numbered on the back.

	MINT	NRMT
COMPLETE SET (16)	250.00	110.00
COMMON CARD (1-16)	5.00	2.20
☐ 1 Tony Gwynn	20.00	9.00
☐ 2 Mo Vaughn	10.00	4.50
☐ 3 Tim Salmon	8.00	3.60
☐ 4 Ken Griffey Jr.	40.00	18.00
☐ 5 Sammy Sosa	6.00	2.70
☐ 6 Frank Thomas	30.00	13.50
☐ 7 Wade Boggs	8.00	3.60
☐ 8 Albert Belle	10.00	4.50
☐ 9 Cal Ripken	30.00	13.50
☐ 10 Manny Ramirez	10.00	4.50
☐ 11 Ryan Klesko	7.00	3.10
☐ 12 Dante Bichette	5.00	2.20
☐ 13 Mike Piazza	25.00	11.00
☐ 14 Chipper Jones	25.00	11.00
☐ 15 Ryne Sandberg	10.00	4.50
☐ 16 Matt Williams	7.00	3.10

1996 Summit Positions

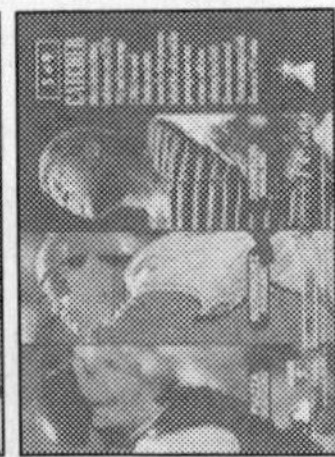

Randomly inserted in Magazine packs only at the rate of one in 50, this nine-card set honors the best players at each playing position. The fronts feature color action player images on a baseball diamond background with head photos of the players at the bottom. The backs carry information about how well the players perform at their position.

	MINT	NRMT
COMPLETE SET (9)	325.00	145.00
COMMON CARD (1-9)	20.00	9.00
☐ 1 Jeff Bagwell Mo Vaughn Frank Thomas	50.00	22.00
☐ 2 Roberto Alomar Craig Biggio Chuck Knoblauch	20.00	9.00
☐ 3 Matt Williams Jim Thome Chipper Jones	40.00	18.00
☐ 4 Barry Larkin Cal Ripken Alex Rodriguez	80.00	36.00
☐ 5 Mike Piazza Ivan Rodriguez Charles Johnson	40.00	18.00
☐ 6 Hideo Nomo Greg Maddux Randy Johnson	50.00	22.00
☐ 7 Barry Bonds Albert Belle Ryan Klesko	25.00	11.00
☐ 8 Johnny Damon Jim Edmonds Ken Griffey Jr.	50.00	22.00
☐ 9 Manny Ramirez Gary Sheffield Sammy Sosa	20.00	9.00

1990 Sunflower Seeds

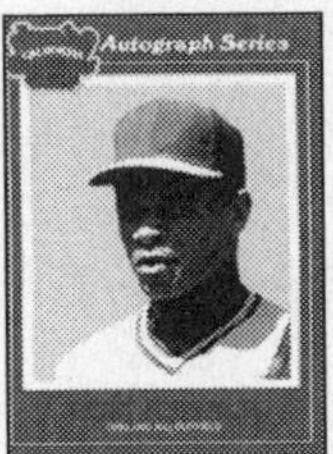

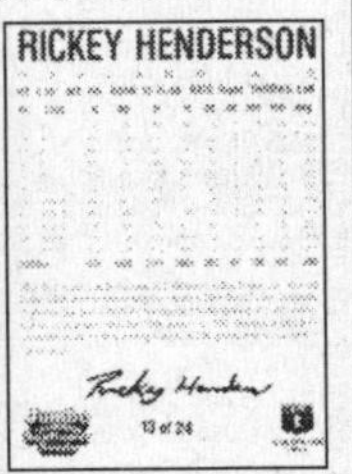

This 24-card, standard-size set is an attractive set which frames the players photo by solid blue borders. In the upper left hand of the card the description, Jumbo California Sunflower Seeds, was placed and underneath the photo is the player's name in red and the team name in very small printing in white. The back of the card features the complete major league record of the player and a short write up as well. This set was issued by Stagi and Scriven Farms Inc. with the cooperation of Michael Schechter Associates (MSA) and features some of the big-name stars in baseball at the time of printing of the set. The set was an attempt by the company to promote sunflower seeds as an alternative to chewing tobacco in the dugout. Three cards were available as an insert in each specially marked bag of Jumbo California Sunflower Seeds.

	MINT	NRMT
COMPLETE SET (24)	15.00	6.75
COMMON CARD (1-24)	.25	.11
☐ 1 Kevin Mitchell	.25	.11
☐ 2 Ken Griffey Jr.	5.00	2.20
☐ 3 Howard Johnson	.25	.11
☐ 4 Bo Jackson	.50	.23
☐ 5 Kirby Puckett	3.00	1.35
☐ 6 Robin Yount	.75	.35
☐ 7 Dave Stieb	.25	.11
☐ 8 Don Mattingly	3.00	1.35
☐ 9 Barry Bonds	1.25	.55
☐ 10 Pedro Guerrero	.25	.11
☐ 11 Tony Gwynn	3.00	1.35
☐ 12 Von Hayes	.25	.11
☐ 13 Rickey Henderson	.75	.35
☐ 14 Tim Raines	.50	.23
☐ 15 Alan Trammell	.75	.35
☐ 16 Dave Stewart	.25	.11
☐ 17 Will Clark	1.50	.70
☐ 18 Roger Clemens	2.00	.90
☐ 19 Wally Joyner	.50	.23
☐ 20 Ryne Sandberg	2.50	1.10
☐ 21 Eric Davis	.50	.23
☐ 22 Mike Scott	.25	.11
☐ 23 Cal Ripken	4.00	1.80
☐ 24 Eddie Murray	1.00	.45

1991 Sunflower Seeds

This 24-card, standard-size set was sponsored by Jumbo California Sunflower Seeds. The posed color player photos are framed by white and yellow borders on a red background. The company logo and the words "Autograph Series II" appear above the photo, with the player's name, team, and position given below the picture. A facsimile autograph is inscribed across the picture. The backs are printed in red on white and present Major League

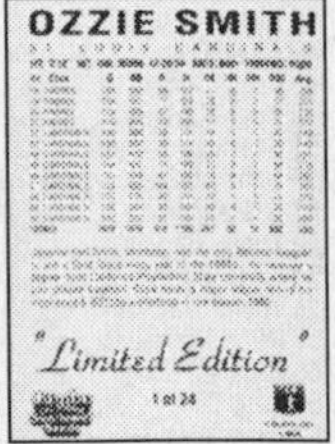

statistics and career highlights. The set was again issued by Stagi and Scriven Farms Inc. with the cooperation of Michael Schechter Associates (MSA). The set was another attempt by the company to promote sunflower seeds as an alternative to chewing tobacco in the dugout. Two cards were available as an insert in each specially marked bag of Jumbo California Sunflower Seeds.

	MINT	NRMT
COMPLETE SET (24)	10.00	4.50
COMMON CARD (1-24)	.25	.11
☐ 1 Ozzie Smith	1.50	.70
☐ 2 Wade Boggs	1.00	.45
☐ 3 Bobby Bonilla	.50	.23
☐ 4 George Brett	1.50	.70
☐ 5 Kal Daniels	.25	.11
☐ 6 Glenn Davis	.25	.11
☐ 7 Chuck Finley	.25	.11
☐ 8 Cecil Fielder	.50	.23
☐ 9 Len Dykstra	.50	.23
☐ 10 Dwight Gooden	.50	.23
☐ 11 Ken Griffey Jr.	3.00	1.35
☐ 12 Kelly Gruber	.25	.11
☐ 13 Kent Hrbek	.25	.11
☐ 14 Andre Dawson	.75	.35
☐ 15 Dave Justice	1.00	.45
☐ 16 Barry Larkin	.75	.35
☐ 17 Ben McDonald	.25	.11
☐ 18 Mark McGwire	1.50	.70
☐ 19 Roberto Alomar	1.00	.45
☐ 20 Nolan Ryan	2.50	1.10
☐ 21 Sandy Alomar Jr.	.50	.23
☐ 22 Bobby Thigpen	.25	.11
☐ 23 Tim Wallach	.25	.11
☐ 24 Matt Williams	.75	.35

1992 Sunflower Seeds

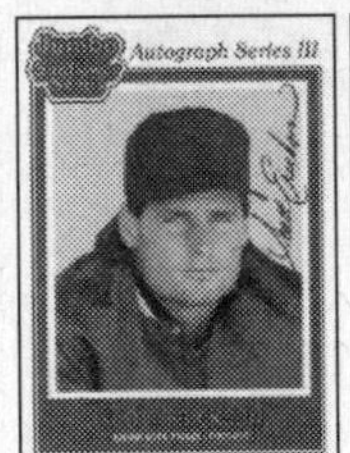

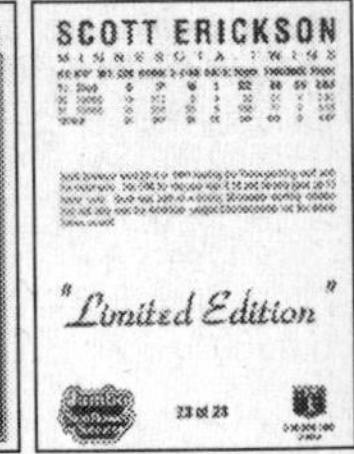

This 24-card, standard-size set was sponsored by Jumbo California Sunflower Seeds and produced by Michael Schechter Associates (MSA). The posed color player photos are framed in white and bright blue on a white background. The company log appears in the upper left corner. The words "Autograph Series III" are printed in red at the top. The player's name, team, and position are given in the blue border below the picture. A facsimile autograph is inscribed across the picture. The backs feature statistical information and career highlights printed in blue on a white background.

	MINT	NRMT
COMPLETE SET (24)	10.00	4.50
COMMON CARD (1-24)	.25	.11
☐ 1 Jeff Reardon	.25	.11
☐ 2 Bill Gullickson	.25	.11
☐ 3 Todd Zeile	.25	.11
☐ 4 Terry Mulholland	.25	.11
☐ 5 Kirby Puckett	1.50	.70
☐ 6 Howard Johnson	.25	.11
☐ 7 Terry Pendleton	.25	.11
☐ 8 Will Clark	.75	.35
☐ 9 Cal Ripken	2.50	1.10
☐ 10 Chris Sabo	.25	.11
☐ 11 Jim Abbott	.25	.11
☐ 12 Joe Carter	.50	.23
☐ 13 Paul Molitor	1.00	.45
☐ 14 Ken Griffey Jr.	3.00	1.35

☐ 15 Randy Johnson	1.00	.45
☐ 16 Bobby Bonilla	.50	.23
☐ 17 John Smiley	.25	.11
☐ 18 Jose Canseco	.75	.35
☐ 19 Tom Glavine	.50	.23
☐ 20 Darryl Strawberry	.50	.23
☐ 21 Brett Butler	.50	.23
☐ 22 Devon White	.25	.11
☐ 23 Scott Erickson	.25	.11
☐ 24 Willie McGee	.50	.23

1948 Swell Sport Thrills

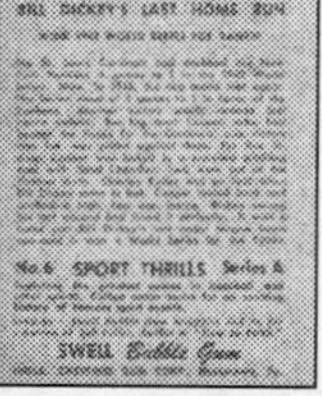

The cards in this 20-card set measure approximately 2 7/16" by 3". The 1948 Swell Gum Sports Thrills set of black and white, numbered cards highlights events from baseball history. The cards have picture framed borders with the title "Sports Thrills Highlights in the World of Sport" on the front. The backs of the cards give the story of the event pictured on the front. Cards numbered 9, 11, 16, and 20 are more difficult to obtain than the other cards in this set. The catalog designation is R448.

	NRMT	VG-E
COMPLETE SET (20)	1000.00	450.00
COMMON CARD (1-20)	25.00	11.00
☐ 1 Greatest Single Inning Athletics' 10 Run Rally	25.00	11.00
☐ 2 Pete Reiser Amazing Record Debut With Dodgers	25.00	11.00
☐ 3 Jackie Robinson Dramatic Debut ROY	150.00	70.00
☐ 4 Walter Johnson Greatest Pitcher of Them All	60.00	27.00
☐ 5 Three Strikes Not Out: Lost Third Strike Changes Tide of 1941 World Series	25.00	11.00
☐ 6 Bill Dickey Last Home Run Wins Series	40.00	18.00
☐ 7 Hal Schumacher Never Say Die Pitcher	25.00	11.00
☐ 8 Carl Hubbell Five Strikeouts Nationals Lose All-Star Game	40.00	18.00
☐ 9 Al Gionfriddo Greatest Catch	30.00	13.50
☐ 10 Johnny VanderMeer No Hits No Runs	30.00	13.50
☐ 11 Grover C. Alexander Bases Loaded	50.00	22.00
☐ 12 Babe Ruth Points Most Dramatic Homer	200.00	90.00
☐ 13 Tommy Bridges Goose Goslin Winning Run: 1935 World Series	25.00	11.00
☐ 14 Lou Gehrig Four Homers	125.00	55.00
☐ 15 Joe DiMaggio Four Men To Stop Him Bat Streak	100.00	45.00
☐ 16 Ted Williams Three Run Homer in Ninth	175.00	80.00
☐ 17 Johnny Lindell Football Block Paves Way For Yank's Series Victory	25.00	11.00
☐ 18 Pee Wee Reese Home Run To Fame Grand Slam	50.00	22.00
☐ 19 Bob Feller Strikeout Record Whiffs Five	50.00	22.00
☐ 20 Carl Furillo Rifle Arm	35.00	16.00

1911 T205 Gold Border

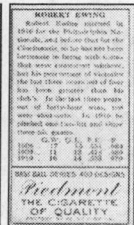

The cards in this 209-card set measure approximately 1 1/2" by 2 5/8". The T205 set (catalog designation), also known as the "Gold Border" set, was issued in 1911 in packages of the following cigarette brands: American Beauty, Broadleaf, Cycle, Drum, Hassan, Honest Long Cut, Piedmont, Polar Bear, Sovereign and Sweet Caporal. All the above were products of the American Tobacco Company, and the ads for the various brands appear below the biographical section on the back of each card. There are pose variations noted in the checklist (which is alphabetized and numbered for reference) and there are 12 minor league cards of a more ornate design which are somewhat scarce. The numbers below correspond to alphabetical order within category, i.e., major leaguers and minor leaguers are alphabetized separately. The gold borders of T205 cards chip easily and they are hard to find in "Mint" or even "Near Mint" condition, due to this there is a high premium on these high condition cards.

	EX-MT	VG-E
COMPLETE SET (209)	30000.00	13500.00
COMMON MAJORS (1-186)	75.00	34.00
COMMON MINORS (187-198)	200.00	90.00
☐ 1 Ed Abbaticchio	75.00	34.00
☐ 2 Red Ames	75.00	34.00
☐ 3 Jimmy Archer	75.00	34.00
☐ 4 Jimmy Austin	75.00	34.00
☐ 5 Bill Bailey	75.00	34.00
☐ 6 Frank "Homerun" Baker	250.00	110.00
☐ 7 Neal Ball	75.00	34.00
☐ 8A Cy Barger (Full B)	75.00	34.00
☐ 8B Cy Barger Part B	300.00	135.00
☐ 9 Jack Barry	75.00	34.00
☐ 10 Johnny Bates	75.00	34.00
☐ 11 Fred Beck	75.00	34.00
☐ 12 Beals Becker	75.00	34.00
☐ 13 George Bell	75.00	34.00
☐ 14 Chief Bender	200.00	90.00
☐ 15 Bill Bergen	75.00	34.00
☐ 16 Bob Bescher	75.00	34.00
☐ 17 Joe Birmingham	75.00	34.00
☐ 18 Russ Blackburne	75.00	34.00
☐ 19 Kitty Bransfield	75.00	34.00
☐ 20A Roger Bresnahan (Mouth closed)	200.00	90.00
☐ 20B Roger Bresnahan (Mouth open)	400.00	180.00
☐ 21 Al Bridwell	75.00	34.00
☐ 22 Mordecai Brown	200.00	90.00
☐ 23 Bobby Byrne	75.00	34.00
☐ 24 Howie Camnitz	75.00	34.00
☐ 25 Bill Carrigan	75.00	34.00
☐ 26 Frank Chance	225.00	100.00
☐ 27A Hal Chase (Chase only)	350.00	160.00
☐ 27B Hal Chase (Hal Chase)	150.00	70.00
☐ 28 Eddie Cicotte	150.00	70.00
☐ 29 Fred Clarke	200.00	90.00
☐ 30 Ty Cobb	3000.00	1350.00
☐ 31A Edward T. Collins (Mouth closed)	200.00	90.00
☐ 31B Edward T. Collins (Mouth open)	400.00	180.00
☐ 32 Frank Corridon	75.00	34.00
☐ 33 Otis Crandall	75.00	34.00
☐ 34 Lou Criger	75.00	34.00
☐ 35 Bill Dahlen	200.00	90.00
☐ 36 Jake Daubert	90.00	40.00
☐ 37 Jim Delahanty	75.00	34.00
☐ 38 Art Devlin	75.00	34.00
☐ 39 Josh Devore	75.00	34.00
☐ 40 Walt Dickson	75.00	34.00
☐ 41 Jiggs Donahue UER (Misspelled Donohue on card)	225.00	100.00
☐ 42 Red Dooin	75.00	34.00
☐ 43 Mickey Doolan	75.00	34.00
☐ 44A Patsy Dougherty (White stocking)	200.00	90.00
☐ 44B Patsy Dougherty (Red stocking)	75.00	34.00
☐ 45 Tom Downey	75.00	34.00
☐ 46 Larry Doyle	90.00	40.00
☐ 47 Hugh Duffy	300.00	135.00
☐ 48 Jimmy Dygert	75.00	34.00
☐ 49 Dick Egan	75.00	34.00
☐ 50 Kid Elberfeld	75.00	34.00
☐ 51 Clyde Engle	75.00	34.00
☐ 52 Steve Evans	75.00	34.00
☐ 53 Johnny Evers	250.00	110.00
☐ 54 Bob Ewing	75.00	34.00
☐ 55 George Ferguson	75.00	34.00
☐ 56 Ray Fisher	200.00	90.00
☐ 57 Art Fletcher	75.00	34.00
☐ 58 John Flynn	75.00	34.00
☐ 59A Russell Ford (Dark cap)	75.00	34.00
☐ 59B Russell Ford (Light cap)	200.00	90.00
☐ 60 Bill Foxen	75.00	34.00
☐ 61 Art Fromme	75.00	34.00
☐ 62 Earl Gardner	75.00	34.00
☐ 63 Harry Gaspar	75.00	34.00
☐ 64 George Gibson	75.00	34.00
☐ 65 Wilbur Good	75.00	34.00
☐ 66A George F. Graham (Boston Rustlers)	75.00	34.00
☐ 66B George F. Graham (Chicago Cubs)	400.00	180.00
☐ 67 Eddie Grant	200.00	90.00
☐ 68 Dolly Gray	75.00	34.00
☐ 69 Clark Griffith	200.00	90.00
☐ 70 Bob Groom	75.00	34.00
☐ 71A Robert Harmon (Both ears)	75.00	34.00
☐ 71B Robert Harmon (Left ear only)	300.00	135.00
☐ 72 Topsy Hartsel	75.00	34.00
☐ 73 Arnold Hauser	75.00	34.00
☐ 74 Charlie Hemphill	75.00	34.00
☐ 75 Buck Herzog	75.00	34.00
☐ 76 Dick Hoblitzell	75.00	34.00
☐ 77 Danny Hoffman	75.00	34.00
☐ 78 Miller Huggins	200.00	90.00
☐ 79 John Hummell	75.00	34.00
☐ 80 Fred Jacklitsch	75.00	34.00
☐ 81 Hughie Jennings	200.00	90.00
☐ 82 Walter Johnson	1200.00	550.00
☐ 83 Davy Jones	75.00	34.00
☐ 84 Tom Jones	75.00	34.00
☐ 85 Addie Joss	600.00	275.00
☐ 86 Ed Karger	250.00	110.00
☐ 87 Ed Killian	75.00	34.00
☐ 88 Red Kleinow	250.00	110.00
☐ 89 John Kling	75.00	34.00
☐ 90 John Knight	75.00	34.00
☐ 91 Ed Konetchy	75.00	34.00
☐ 92 Harry Krause	75.00	34.00
☐ 93 Rube Kroh	75.00	34.00
☐ 94 Frank Lang	75.00	34.00
☐ 95 Frank LaPorte	75.00	34.00
☐ 96 Arlie Latham	75.00	34.00
☐ 97 Tommy Leach	75.00	34.00
☐ 98 Sam Leever	75.00	34.00
☐ 99 Lefty Leifield	75.00	34.00
☐ 100 Ed Lennox	75.00	34.00
☐ 101 Paddy Livingston	75.00	34.00
☐ 102 Hans Lobert	75.00	34.00
☐ 103 Bris Lord	75.00	34.00
☐ 104 Harry Lord	75.00	34.00
☐ 105 John Lush	75.00	34.00
☐ 106 Nick Maddox	75.00	34.00
☐ 107 Sherry Magee	75.00	34.00
☐ 108 Rube Marquard	200.00	90.00
☐ 109 Christy Mathewson	900.00	400.00
☐ 110 Al Mattern	75.00	34.00
☐ 111 George McBride	75.00	34.00
☐ 112 Amby McConnell	75.00	34.00
☐ 113 Pryor McElveen	75.00	34.00
☐ 114 John McGraw MG	300.00	135.00
☐ 115 Harry McIntire	75.00	34.00
☐ 116 Matty McIntyre	75.00	34.00
☐ 117 Larry McLean	75.00	34.00
☐ 118 Fred Merkle	90.00	40.00
☐ 119 Chief Meyers	75.00	34.00
☐ 120 Clyde Milan	90.00	40.00
☐ 121 Dots Miller	75.00	34.00
☐ 122 Mike Mitchell	75.00	34.00
☐ 123 Pat Moran	75.00	34.00
☐ 124 George Moriarty	75.00	34.00
☐ 125 George Mullin	75.00	34.00
☐ 126 Danny Murphy	75.00	34.00
☐ 127 Red Murray	75.00	34.00

☐ 128 Tom Needham 75.00 34.00
☐ 129 Rebel Oakes 75.00 34.00
☐ 130 Rube Oldring 75.00 34.00
☐ 131 Charley O'Leary 75.00 34.00
☐ 132 Fred Olmstead 75.00 34.00
☐ 133 Orval Overall 75.00 34.00
☐ 134 Freddy Parent 75.00 34.00
☐ 135 Dode Paskert 75.00 34.00
☐ 136 Fred Payne 75.00 34.00
☐ 137 Barney Pelty 75.00 34.00
☐ 138 Jack Pfiester 75.00 34.00
☐ 139 Ed Phelps 75.00 34.00
☐ 140 Decon Phillippe 90.00 40.00
☐ 141 Jack Quinn 75.00 34.00
☐ 142 Bugs Raymond 250.00 110.00
☐ 143 Ed Reulbach 75.00 34.00
☐ 144 Lewis Richie 75.00 34.00
☐ 145 Jack Rowan 200.00 90.00
☐ 146 Nap Rucker 90.00 40.00
☐ 147 Doc Scanlan 200.00 90.00
☐ 148 Germany Schaefer 75.00 34.00
☐ 149 Admiral Schlei 75.00 34.00
☐ 150 Boss Schmidt 75.00 34.00
☐ 151 Wildfire Schulte 75.00 34.00
☐ 152 Jim Scott 75.00 34.00
☐ 153 Bayard Sharpe 75.00 34.00
☐ 154A David Shean 75.00 34.00
(Boston Rustlers)
☐ 154B David Shean 400.00 180.00
(Chicago Cubs)
☐ 155 Jimmy Sheckard 75.00 34.00
☐ 156 Hack Simmons 75.00 34.00
☐ 157 Tony Smith 75.00 34.00
☐ 158 Fred Snodgrass 75.00 34.00
☐ 159 Tris Speaker 500.00 220.00
☐ 160 Jake Stahl 90.00 40.00
☐ 161 Oscar Stanage 75.00 34.00
☐ 162 Harry Steinfeldt 90.00 40.00
☐ 163 George Stone 75.00 34.00
☐ 164 George Stovall 75.00 34.00
☐ 165 Gabby Street 75.00 34.00
☐ 166 George Suggs 250.00 110.00
☐ 167 Ed Summers 75.00 34.00
☐ 168 Jeff Sweeney 200.00 90.00
☐ 169 Lee Tannehill 75.00 34.00
☐ 170 Ira Thomas 75.00 34.00
☐ 171 Joe Tinker 250.00 110.00
☐ 172 John Titus 75.00 34.00
☐ 173 Terry Turner 300.00 135.00
☐ 174 Hippo Vaughn 200.00 90.00
☐ 175 Heinie Wagner 200.00 90.00
☐ 176A Roderick J. Wallace 175.00 80.00
(With cap)
☐ 176B Roderick J. Wallace 400.00 180.00
(Without cap)
☐ 177 Ed Walsh 400.00 180.00
☐ 178 Zach Wheat 200.00 90.00
☐ 179 Doc White 75.00 34.00
☐ 180 Kirby White 200.00 90.00
☐ 181 Kaiser Wilhelm 200.00 90.00
☐ 182 Ed Willett 75.00 34.00
☐ 183A George Wiltse 75.00 34.00
(Both ears)
☐ 183B George Wiltse 300.00 135.00
(Right ear only)
☐ 184 Owen Wilson 75.00 34.00
☐ 185 Harry Wolter 75.00 34.00
☐ 186 Cy Young 800.00 350.00
☐ 187 Dr.Merle T. Adkins: 200.00 90.00
Baltimore
☐ 188 Jack Dunn 250.00 110.00
☐ 189 George Merritt 200.00 90.00
☐ 190 Charles Hanford 200.00 90.00
☐ 191 Hick Cady 200.00 90.00
☐ 192 James Frick 200.00 90.00
☐ 193 Wyatt Lee 200.00 90.00
☐ 194 Lewis McAllister 200.00 90.00
☐ 195 John Nee 200.00 90.00
☐ 196 Jimmy Collins 450.00 200.00
☐ 197 James Phelan 200.00 90.00
☐ 198 Emil Batch 200.00 90.00

1909-11 T206 White Border

The T206 set was and is the most popular of all the tobacco issues. The set was issued from 1909 to 1911 with nineteen different brands of cigarettes: American Beauty, Broadleaf, Cycle, Carolina Brights, Coupon, Drum, El Principe de Gales, Hindu, Hustler, Lenox, Old Mill, Piedmont, Polar Bear, Red Cross, Sovereign, Sweet Caporal, Tolstoi, and Uzit. There was also a Ty Cobb back version that was a promotional issue and is very scarce. Only Cobb appears on cards with Ty Cobb backs. The minor league cards are supposedly slightly more difficult to obtain than the cards of the major leaguers, with the Southern League player cards being the most difficult.

Minor League players were obtained from the American Association and the Eastern league. Southern League players were obtained from a variety of leagues including the following: South Atlantic League, Southern League, Texas League, and Virginia League. Series 150 was issued between February 1909 thru the end of May, 1909. Series 350 was issued from the end of May, 1909 thru April, 1910. The last series 350-to-406 was issued in late December 1910 thur early 1991. The set price below does not include ultra-expensive Wagner, Plank, Magie error, or Doyle variation. The Wagner card is one of the most sought after cards in the hobby. This card (#366 in the checklist below) was pulled from circulation almost immediately after being issued. While estimates of how many Wagners are in existence vary, the card is considered by many collectors the ultimate card to own. Perhaps the best conditioned example of this card was sold in a public auction in 1991 for $451,000 to hockey great Wayne Gretzky and Bruce McNall. That same card was later used in a major giveaway sponsored by most of the card companies, Treat products and Wal-Mart. That card sold for more than $640,500 in 1996.

	EX-MT	VG-E
COMPLETE SET (520)	55000.00	24800.00
COMMON MAJORS (1-389)	50.00	22.00
COMMON MINORS (390-475)	40.00	18.00
COMMON SOUTHERN(476-523)	100.00	45.00

☐ 1 Ed Abbaticchio: 50.00 22.00
Pitt
Batting follow thru
☐ 2 Ed Abbaticchio: 60.00 27.00
Pitt.
Batting waiting pitch
☐ 3 Bill Abstein: Pitt. 50.00 22.00
☐ 4 Whitey Alperman: 60.00 27.00
Brooklyn
☐ 5 Red Ames: N.Y. NL 60.00 27.00
Portrait
☐ 6 Red Ames: N.Y. NL 50.00 22.00
Hands over head
☐ 7 Red Ames: N.Y. NL 60.00 27.00
Hands in front of chest
☐ 8 Frank Arellanes: 50.00 22.00
Boston AL
☐ 9 Jake Atz: Chicago AL 50.00 22.00
☐ 10 Frank Baker: 200.00 90.00
Phila. AL
☐ 11 Neal Ball: N.Y. AL 60.00 27.00
☐ 12 Neal Ball: Cleveland 50.00 22.00
☐ 13 Jap Barbeau: 50.00 22.00
St. Louis NL
☐ 14 Jack Barry: 50.00 22.00
Phila. AL
☐ 15 Johnny Bates: 60.00 27.00
Boston NL
☐ 16 Ginger Beaumont: 60.00 27.00
Boston NL
☐ 17 Fred Beck: Boston NL 50.00 22.00
☐ 18 Beals Becker: 50.00 22.00
Boston NL
☐ 19 George Bell: 50.00 22.00
Brooklyn
pitching follow thru
☐ 20 George Bell: 60.00 27.00
Brooklyn
Hands
over head
☐ 21 Chief Bender 225.00 100.00
Phila. AL
Portrait
☐ 22 Chief Bender 200.00 90.00
Phila. AL
pitching, trees
☐ 23 Chief Bender 200.00 90.00
Phila AL
pitching, no trees
☐ 24 Bill Bergen: 50.00 22.00
Brooklyn
Catching
☐ 25 Bill Bergen: 60.00 27.00
Brooklyn
Batting
☐ 26 Heinie Berger: 50.00 22.00
Cleveland
☐ 27 Bob Bescher: Cinc. 50.00 22.00
Catching fly ball
☐ 28 Bob Bescher: Cinc. 50.00 22.00
Portrait
☐ 29 Joe Birmingham: 60.00 27.00
Cleveland
☐ 30 Jack Bliss: St.L. NL 50.00 22.00
☐ 31 Frank Bowerman: 60.00 27.00
Boston NL
☐ 32 Bill Bradley: 60.00 27.00
Cleveland
Portrait
☐ 33 Bill Bradley: 50.00 22.00
Cleveland
Batting
☐ 34 Kitty Bransfield: 60.00 27.00
Phila. NL
☐ 35 Roger Bresnahan: 225.00 100.00
St.L. NL
Portrait
☐ 36 Roger Bresnahan: 200.00 90.00
St.L. NL
Batting
☐ 37 Al Bridwell: N.Y. 60.00 27.00
NL
Portrait
☐ 38 Al Bridwell: N.Y. 50.00 22.00
NL
Wearing sweater
☐ 39 George Brown: 100.00 45.00
Chicago NL
(Sic& Browne)
☐ 40 George Brown: 500.00 220.00
Washington
(Sic& Browne)
☐ 41 Mordecai Brown: 250.00 110.00
Chicago NL
Portrait
☐ 42 Mordecai Brown: 175.00 80.00
Chicago NL
Chicago down front of shirt
☐ 43 Mordecai Brown: 300.00 135.00
Chicago NL
Cubs across chest
☐ 44 Al Burch: Brooklyn 50.00 22.00
Fielding
☐ 45 Al Burch: Brooklyn 125.00 55.00
Batting
☐ 46 Bill Burns: Chicago 50.00 22.00
AL
☐ 47 Donie Bush: Detroit 60.00 27.00
☐ 48 Bobby Byrne: 50.00 22.00
St. Louis NL
☐ 49 Howie Camnitz: 60.00 27.00
Pitt
Arms folded over chest
☐ 50 Howie Camnitz: 50.00 22.00
Pitt
Hands over head
☐ 51 Howie Camnitz: 50.00 22.00
Pitt.
Throwing
☐ 52 Billy Campbell: 50.00 22.00
Cincinnati
☐ 53 Bill Carrigan: 50.00 22.00
Boston AL
☐ 54 Frank Chance: 300.00 135.00
Chicago NL
Cubs across chest
☐ 55 Frank Chance: 200.00 90.00
Chicago NL
Chicago down front of shirt
☐ 56 Frank Chance: 200.00 90.00
Chicago NL
Batting
☐ 57 Chappy Charles: 50.00 22.00
St. Louis NL
☐ 58 Hal Chase: N.Y. AL 100.00 45.00
Port. blue bkgd.
☐ 59 Hal Chase: N.Y. AL 200.00 90.00
Port., pink bkgd.
☐ 60 Hal Chase: N.Y. AL 75.00 34.00
Holding cup
☐ 61 Hal Chase: N.Y. AL 75.00 34.00
Throwing, dark cap
☐ 62 Hal Chase: N.Y. AL 125.00 55.00
Throwing, white cap
☐ 63 Jack Chesbro: 250.00 110.00
New York AL
☐ 64 Eddie Cicotte: 175.00 80.00
Boston AL
☐ 65 Fred Clarke: Pitt. 200.00 90.00
Portrait
☐ 66 Fred Clarke: Pitt. 175.00 80.00

☐ 67 Josh Clarke: Cleve.	60.00	27.00
☐ 68 Ty Cobb: Detroit Port., red bkgd.	1600.00	700.00
☐ 69 Ty Cobb: Detroit Port., green background	2500.00	1100.00
☐ 70 Ty Cobb: Detroit Bat on shoulder	1600.00	700.00
☐ 71 Ty Cobb: Detroit Bat away from shoulder	1400.00	650.00
☐ 72 Eddie Collins: Phila. AL	200.00	90.00
☐ 73 Wid Conroy: Washington Fielding	60.00	27.00
☐ 74 Wid Conroy: Wash. Bat on shoulder	50.00	22.00
☐ 75 Harry Covaleski: Phila. NL	60.00	27.00
☐ 76 Doc Crandall N.Y. NL, without cap	50.00	22.00
☐ 77 Doc Crandall N.Y. NL sweater and cap	50.00	22.00
☐ 78 Sam Crawford: Detroit Batting	175.00	80.00
☐ 79 Sam Crawford: Detroit, Throwing	225.00	100.00
☐ 80 Birdie Cree: N.Y. AL	50.00	22.00
☐ 81 Lou Criger: St.L. AL	60.00	27.00
☐ 82 Dode Criss: St.L. AL	60.00	27.00
☐ 83 Bill Dahlen: Boston NL	100.00	45.00
☐ 84 Bill Dahlen: Brooklyn	225.00	100.00
☐ 85 George Davis: Chicago AL	60.00	27.00
☐ 86 Harry Davis Phila. AL Davis on card	50.00	22.00
☐ 87 Harry Davis Phila. AL H.Davis on card	60.00	27.00
☐ 88 Jim Delehanty: Wash.	60.00	27.00
☐ 89 Ray Demmitt: St.L. AL	3500.00	1600.00
☐ 90 Ray Demmitt: N.Y. AL	60.00	27.00
☐ 91 Art Devlin: N.Y. NL	60.00	27.00
☐ 92 Josh Devore: N.Y. NL	50.00	22.00
☐ 93 Bill Dineen: St. Louis AL	50.00	22.00
☐ 94 Mike Donlin N.Y. NL Fielding	125.00	55.00
☐ 95 Mike Donlin N.Y. NL Sitting	75.00	34.00
☐ 96 Mike Donlin: N.Y.NL Batting	60.00	27.00
☐ 97 Jiggs Donohue: Chicago AL	60.00	27.00
☐ 98 Bill Donovan: Detroit Portrait	60.00	27.00
☐ 99 Bill Donovan: Detroit Throwing	50.00	22.00
☐ 100 Red Dooin: Phila. NL	60.00	27.00
☐ 101 Mickey Doolan: Phila. NL Fielding	50.00	22.00
☐ 102 Mickey Doolan: Phila. NL Batting	50.00	22.00
☐ 103 Mickey Doolin (Sic, Doolan): Phila. NL	60.00	27.00
☐ 104 Patsy Dougherty: Chicago AL Portrait	60.00	27.00
☐ 105 Patsy Dougherty: Chicago AL Fielding	50.00	22.00
☐ 106 Tom Downey: Cinc. Batting	50.00	22.00
☐ 107 Tom Downey: Cinc. Fielding	50.00	22.00
☐ 108A Larry Doyle: N.Y. Hands over head	70.00	32.00
☐ 108B Larry Doyle: N.Y. NAT'L hands over head)	18000.00	8100.00
☐ 109 Larry Doyle: N.Y. NL Sweater	60.00	27.00
☐ 110 Larry Doyle: N.Y. NL Throwing	75.00	34.00
☐ 111 Larry Doyle: N.Y. NL Bat on shoulder	60.00	27.00
☐ 112 Jean Dubuc: Cin.	50.00	22.00
☐ 113 Hugh Duffy: Chicago AL	200.00	90.00
☐ 114 Joe Dunn: Brooklyn	50.00	22.00
☐ 115 Bull Durham: N.Y. NL	60.00	27.00
☐ 116 Jimmy Dygert: Phila. AL	50.00	22.00
☐ 117 Ted Easterly: Cleveland	50.00	22.00
☐ 118 Dick Egan: Cinc.	50.00	22.00
☐ 119 Kid Elberfeld: Wash. Fielding	50.00	22.00
☐ 120 Kid Elberfeld: Wash. Portrait	1000.00	450.00
☐ 121 Kid Elberfeld: N.Y. AL Portrait	60.00	27.00
☐ 122 Clyde Engle: N.Y. AL	50.00	22.00
☐ 123 Steve Evans: St. Louis NL	50.00	22.00
☐ 124 Johnny Evers: Chicago NL Portrait	250.00	110.00
☐ 125 Johnny Evers: Chicago NL Cubs across chest	300.00	135.00
☐ 126 Johnny Evers: Chicago NL Chicago down front of shirt	200.00	90.00
☐ 127 Bob Ewing: Cinc.	60.00	27.00
☐ 128 George Ferguson: Boston NL	50.00	22.00
☐ 129 Hobe Ferris: St. Louis AL	60.00	27.00
☐ 130 Lou Fiene: Chicago AL Portrait	50.00	22.00
☐ 131 Lou Fiene: Chicago AL Throwing	50.00	22.00
☐ 132 Art Fletcher: New York NL	50.00	22.00
☐ 133 Elmer Flick: Cleveland	225.00	100.00
☐ 134 Russ Ford: N.Y. AL	50.00	22.00
☐ 135 John Frill: N.Y. AL	50.00	22.00
☐ 136 Art Fromme: Cinc.	50.00	22.00
☐ 137 Chick Gandil: Chicago AL	250.00	110.00
☐ 138 Bob Ganley: Washington	60.00	27.00
☐ 139 Harry Gasper: Cinc. (Sic, Gaspar)	50.00	22.00
☐ 140 Rube Geyer: St.L. NL	50.00	22.00
☐ 141 George Gibson: Pitt.	60.00	27.00
☐ 142 Billy Gilbert: St. Louis NL	60.00	27.00
☐ 143 Wilbur Goode (Sic, Good): Cleve.	60.00	27.00
☐ 144 Bill Graham: St. Louis AL	50.00	22.00
☐ 145 Peaches Graham: Boston NL	50.00	22.00
☐ 146 Dolly Gray: Washington	60.00	27.00
☐ 147 Clark Griffith: Cinc. Portrait	200.00	90.00
☐ 148 Clark Griffith: Cinc. Batting	150.00	70.00
☐ 149 Bob Groom: Washington	50.00	22.00
☐ 150 Ed Hahn: Chicago AL	60.00	27.00
☐ 151 Topsy Hartsel: Phila. AL	50.00	22.00
☐ 152 Charlie Hemphill: N.Y. AL	60.00	27.00
☐ 153 Buck Herzog: N.Y. NL	60.00	27.00
☐ 154 Buck Herzog: Boston NL	50.00	22.00
☐ 155 Bill Hinchman: Cleveland	60.00	27.00
☐ 156 Doc Hoblitzell: Cincinnati	50.00	22.00
☐ 157 Danny Hoffman: St. Louis AL	50.00	22.00
☐ 158 Solly Hofman: Chicago NL	50.00	22.00
☐ 159 Del Howard: Chicago NL	50.00	22.00
☐ 160 Harry Howell: St.L. AL Portrait	50.00	22.00
☐ 161 Harry Howell: St.L. AL Left hand on hip	50.00	22.00
☐ 162 Miller Huggins: Cinc. Portrait	225.00	100.00
☐ 163 Miller Huggins: Cinc. Hands to mouth	150.00	70.00
☐ 164 Rudy Hulswitt: St. Louis NL	50.00	22.00
☐ 165 John Hummel: Brooklyn	50.00	22.00
☐ 166 George Hunter: Brooklyn	50.00	22.00
☐ 167 Frank Isbell: Chicago AL	60.00	27.00
☐ 168 Fred Jacklitsch: Phila. NL	60.00	27.00
☐ 169 Hughie Jennings MG: Detroit Portrait	225.00	100.00
☐ 170 Hughie Jennings MG: Detroit Yelling	150.00	70.00
☐ 171 Hugh Jennings MG: Detroit Dancing for joy	150.00	70.00
☐ 172 Walter Johnson: Washington Portrait	900.00	400.00
☐ 173 Walter Johnson: Washington Ready to pitch	750.00	350.00
☐ 174 Tom Jones: St.L. AL	60.00	27.00
☐ 175 Tom Jones: Detroit	50.00	22.00
☐ 176 Fielder Jones: Chic. AL Portrait	60.00	27.00
☐ 177 Fielder Jones: Chic. AL Hands on hips	60.00	27.00
☐ 178 Tim Jordan: Brooklyn Portrait	60.00	27.00
☐ 179 Tim Jordan: Brooklyn Batting	50.00	22.00
☐ 180 Addie Joss: Cleveland Portrait	350.00	160.00
☐ 181 Addie Joss: Cleveland Ready to pitch	200.00	90.00
☐ 182 Ed Karger: Cinc.	60.00	27.00
☐ 183 Willie Keeler: N.Y. AL Portrait	350.00	160.00
☐ 184 Willie Keeler: N.Y. AL Batting	300.00	135.00
☐ 185 Ed Killian: Detroit Portrait	60.00	27.00
☐ 186 Ed Killian: Detroit Pitching	50.00	22.00
☐ 187 Red Kleinow: N.Y. AL Batting	60.00	27.00
☐ 188 Red Kleinow: N.Y. AL Catching	50.00	22.00
☐ 189 Red Kleinow: Boston AL Catching	300.00	135.00
☐ 190 Johnny Kling: Chicago NL	60.00	27.00
☐ 191 Otto Knabe: Phila. NL	50.00	22.00
☐ 192 John Knight: N.Y. AL Portrait	50.00	22.00
☐ 193 John Knight: N.Y. AL Batting	50.00	22.00
☐ 194 Ed Konetchy: St.L. NL Awaiting low ball	50.00	22.00
☐ 195 Ed Konetchy: St.L. NL Glove above head	60.00	27.00
☐ 196 Harry Krause: Phila.	50.00	22.00

AL Portrait		
☐ 197 Harry Krause: Phila. AL Pitching	50.00	22.00
☐ 198 Rube Kroh: Chicago NL	50.00	22.00
☐ 199 Nap Lajoie: Cleveland Portrait	450.00	200.00
☐ 200 Nap Lajoie: Cleveland Batting	350.00	160.00
☐ 201 Nap Lajoie: Cleveland Throwing	350.00	160.00
☐ 202 Joe Lake: N.Y. AL	60.00	27.00
☐ 203 Joe Lake: St.L. AL Hands over head	50.00	22.00
☐ 204 Joe Lake: St.L. AL Throwing	50.00	22.00
☐ 205 Frank LaPorte: N.Y. AL	50.00	22.00
☐ 206 Arlie Latham: N.Y. NL	50.00	22.00
☐ 207 Fred Leach: Pitt. Portrait	60.00	27.00
☐ 208 Fred Leach: Pitt. In fielding position	50.00	22.00
☐ 209 Lefty Leifield: Pitt. Batting	50.00	22.00
☐ 210 Lefty Leifield: Pitt. Hands behind head	60.00	27.00
☐ 211 Ed Lennox: Brooklyn	50.00	22.00
☐ 212 Glenn Liebhardt: Cleveland	60.00	27.00
☐ 213 Vive Lindaman: Boston NL	100.00	45.00
☐ 214 Paddy Livingstone: Phila. AL	50.00	22.00
☐ 215 Hans Lobert: Cinc.	60.00	27.00
☐ 216 Harry Lord: Bost. AL	50.00	22.00
☐ 217 Harry Lumley: Brooklyn	60.00	27.00
☐ 218 Carl Lundgren: Chicago NL	300.00	135.00
☐ 219 Nick Maddox: Pitt.	50.00	22.00
☐ 220 Sherry Magee: Phila. NL Portrait	75.00	34.00
☐ 221 Sherry Magee: Phila. NL Batting	50.00	22.00
☐ 222 Sherry Magie: Phila. NL, (Sic, Magee) Portrait, name misspelled	15000.00	6800.00
☐ 223 Rube Manning: N.Y. AL Batting	60.00	27.00
☐ 224 Rube Manning: N.Y. AL Hands over head	50.00	22.00
☐ 225 Rube Marquard: N.Y. NL Portrait	225.00	100.00
☐ 226 Rube Marquard: N.Y. NL Pitching	175.00	80.00
☐ 227 Rube Marquard: N.Y. NL Standing	200.00	90.00
☐ 228 Doc Marshall: Brooklyn	50.00	22.00
☐ 229 Christy Mathewson: N.Y. NL Portrait	900.00	400.00
☐ 230 Christy Mathewson: N.Y. NL Pitching, white cap	700.00	325.00
☐ 231 Christy Mathewson: N.Y. NL Pitching, dark cap	700.00	325.00
☐ 232 Al Mattern: Boston NL	50.00	22.00
☐ 233 Jack McAleese: St. Louis AL	50.00	22.00
☐ 234 George McBride: Washington	50.00	22.00
☐ 235 Moose McCormick: N.Y. NL	50.00	22.00
☐ 236 Pryor McElveen: Brooklyn	50.00	22.00
☐ 237 John McGraw: N.Y. NL Portrait, no cap	350.00	160.00
☐ 238 John McGraw: N.Y. NL Wearing sweater	200.00	90.00
☐ 239 John McGraw: N.Y. NL pointing	225.00	100.00
☐ 240 John McGraw: N.Y. NL Glove on hip	225.00	100.00
☐ 241 Matty McIntyre: Brooklyn	60.00	27.00
☐ 242 Matty McIntyre: Brooklyn and Chicago NL	50.00	22.00
☐ 243 Mike McIntyre: Detroit	50.00	22.00
☐ 244 Larry McLean: Cinc.	50.00	22.00
☐ 245 George McQuillan: Phila. NL Throwing	60.00	27.00
☐ 246 George McQuillan: Phila. NL Batting	50.00	22.00
☐ 247 Fred Merkle: N.Y. NL Portrait	75.00	34.00
☐ 248 Fred Merkle: N.Y. NL Throwing	75.00	34.00
☐ 249 Chief Meyers: New York NL	50.00	22.00
☐ 250 Clyde Milan: Washington	50.00	22.00
☐ 251 Dots Miller: Pitt.	50.00	22.00
☐ 252 Mike Mitchell: Cinc.	50.00	22.00
☐ 253 Pat Moran: Chicago NL	50.00	22.00
☐ 254 George Moriarty: Detroit	50.00	22.00
☐ 255 Mike Mowrey: Cinc.	50.00	22.00
☐ 256 George Mullen: Detroit (Sic, Mullin)	50.00	22.00
☐ 257 George Mullin: Detroit Throwing	60.00	27.00
☐ 258 George Mullin: Detroit Batting	50.00	22.00
☐ 259 Danny Murphy: Phila. AL Throwing	60.00	27.00
☐ 260 Danny Murphy: Phila. AL Bat on shoulder	50.00	22.00
☐ 261 Red Murray: N.Y. NL Sweater	50.00	22.00
☐ 262 Red Murray: N.Y. NL Bat on shoulder	50.00	22.00
☐ 263 Chief Myers (Sic, Meyers): N.Y. NL Fielding	50.00	22.00
☐ 264 Chief Myers (Sic, Meyers): N.Y. NL Batting	50.00	22.00
☐ 265 Tom Needham: Chicago NL	50.00	22.00
☐ 266 Simon Nicholls: Phila. AL	60.00	27.00
☐ 267 Simon Nichols (Sic& Nicholls): Phila. AL	50.00	22.00
☐ 268 Harry Niles: Boston AL	60.00	27.00
☐ 269 Rebel Oakes: Cinc.	50.00	22.00
☐ 270 Bill O'Hara: N.Y. NL	50.00	22.00
☐ 271 Bill O'Hara: St. Louis NL	3500.00	1600.00
☐ 272 Rube Oldring: Phila. AL Fielding	60.00	27.00
☐ 273 Rube Oldring: Phila. AL Bat on shoulder	60.00	27.00
☐ 274 Charley O'Leary: Detroit Portrait	60.00	27.00
☐ 275 Charley O'Leary: Detroit Hands on knees	50.00	22.00
☐ 276 Orval Overall: Chicago NL Portrait	60.00	27.00
☐ 277 Orval Overall: Chicago NL Pitching follow thru	50.00	22.00
☐ 278 Orval Overall: Chicago NL, Pitching hiding ball in glove	50.00	22.00
☐ 279 Frank Owen: Chicago AL (Sic& Owens)	60.00	27.00
☐ 280 Freddy Parent: Chicago AL	60.00	27.00
☐ 281 Dode Paskert: Cinc.	50.00	22.00
☐ 282 Jim Pastorius: Brooklyn	60.00	27.00
☐ 283 Harry Pattee: Brooklyn	150.00	70.00
☐ 284 Fred Payne: Chicago AL	50.00	22.00
☐ 285 Barney Pelty: St.L. AL HOR	100.00	45.00
☐ 286 Barney Pelty: St.L. AL VERT	50.00	22.00
☐ 287 George Perring: Cleveland	50.00	22.00
☐ 288 Jeff Pfeffer: Chicago NL	50.00	22.00
☐ 289 Jack Pfeister: Chic. NL Sitting	50.00	22.00
☐ 290 Jack Pfeister: Chic. NL Pitching	50.00	22.00
☐ 291 Ed Phelps: St.L. NL	50.00	22.00
☐ 292 Deacon Phillippe: Pitt.	75.00	34.00
☐ 293 Eddie Plank: Phila. AL	25000.00	11200.00
☐ 294 Jack Powell: St. Louis AL	60.00	27.00
☐ 295 Mike Powers: Phila. AL	125.00	55.00
☐ 296 Billy Purtell: Chicago AL	50.00	22.00
☐ 297 Jack Quinn: N.Y. AL	50.00	22.00
☐ 298 Bugs Raymond: New York NL	60.00	27.00
☐ 299 Ed Reulbach: Chicago NL Pitching	75.00	34.00
☐ 300 Ed Reulbach: Chicago NL Hands at side	125.00	55.00
☐ 301 Bob Rhoades: sic, Rhoads, Cleveland, Hand in air	50.00	22.00
☐ 302 Bob Rhoades: sic, Rhoads, Cleveland, Ready to pitch	50.00	22.00
☐ 303 Charlie Rhodes: St. Louis NL	50.00	22.00
☐ 304 Claude Ritchey: Boston NL	60.00	27.00
☐ 305 Claude Rossman: Detroit	50.00	22.00
☐ 306 Nap Rucker: Brooklyn Portrait	75.00	34.00
☐ 307 Nap Rucker: Brooklyn Pitching	60.00	27.00
☐ 308 Germany Schaefer: Washington	60.00	27.00
☐ 309 Germany Schaefer: Detroit	60.00	27.00
☐ 310 Admiral Schlei: N.Y. NL Sweater	50.00	22.00
☐ 311 Admiral Schlei: N.Y. NL Batting	50.00	22.00
☐ 312 Admiral Schlei: N.Y. NL Fielding	60.00	27.00
☐ 313 Boss Schmidt: Detroit Portrait	50.00	22.00
☐ 314 Boss Schmidt: Detroit Throwing	60.00	27.00
☐ 315 Frank Schulte: Chicago NL Batting, back turned	50.00	22.00
☐ 316 Frank Schulte: Chicago NL Batting, front pose	60.00	27.00

☐ 317 Jim Scott: Chicago AL	50.00	22.00
☐ 318 Cy Seymour: N.Y. NL Portrait	50.00	22.00
☐ 319 Cy Seymour: N.Y. NL Throwing	50.00	22.00
☐ 320 Cy Seymour: N.Y. NL Batting	60.00	27.00
☐ 321 Al Shaw: St.L. NL	60.00	27.00
☐ 322 Jimmy Sheckard: Chicago NL Throwing	50.00	22.00
☐ 323 Jimmy Sheckard: Chicago NL Side view	60.00	27.00
☐ 324 Bill Shipke: Washington	60.00	27.00
☐ 325 Frank Smith: Chicago AL& Listed as Smith	50.00	22.00
☐ 326 Frank Smith: Chicago and Boston AL	400.00	180.00
☐ 327 Frank Smith: Chicago AL (Listed as F.Smith)	60.00	27.00
☐ 328 Happy Smith: Brk.	50.00	22.00
☐ 329 Fred Snodgrass: N.Y. NL Batting	60.00	27.00
☐ 330 Fred Snodgrass: N.Y. NL Catching	60.00	27.00
☐ 331 Bob Spade: Cinc.	60.00	27.00
☐ 332 Tris Speaker: Boston AL	450.00	200.00
☐ 333 Tubby Spencer: Boston AL	60.00	27.00
☐ 334 Jake Stahl: Boston AL Catching fly ball	60.00	27.00
☐ 335 Jake Stahl: Boston AL Standing, arms down	60.00	27.00
☐ 336 Oscar Stanage: Detroit	50.00	22.00
☐ 337 Charlie Starr: Boston NL	50.00	22.00
☐ 338 Harry Steinfeldt: Chicago NL Portrait	75.00	34.00
☐ 339 Harry Steinfeldt: Chicago NL Batting	60.00	27.00
☐ 340 Jim Stephens: St.L. AL	50.00	22.00
☐ 341 George Stone: St.L. AL	60.00	27.00
☐ 342 George Stovall: Cleveland Portrait	60.00	27.00
☐ 343 George Stovall: Cleveland Batting	50.00	22.00
☐ 344 Gabby Street: Washington Portrait	60.00	27.00
☐ 345 Gabby Street: Washington Catching	50.00	22.00
☐ 346 Billy Sullivan: Chicago AL	60.00	27.00
☐ 347 Ed Summers: Detroit	50.00	22.00
☐ 348 Jeff Sweeney: New York AL	50.00	22.00
☐ 349 Bill Sweeney: Boston NL	50.00	22.00
☐ 350 Jesse Tannehill: Washington	50.00	22.00
☐ 351 Lee Tannehill: Chicago AL (Listed as L.Tannehill)	60.00	27.00
☐ 352 Lee Tannehill: Chicago AL (Listed as Tannehill)	50.00	22.00
☐ 353 Fred Tenney: N.Y. NL	60.00	27.00
☐ 354 Ira Thomas: Phila. AL	50.00	22.00
☐ 355 Joe Tinker: Chicago NL Ready to hit	175.00	80.00
☐ 356 Joe Tinker: Chicago NL Bat on shoulder	200.00	90.00
☐ 357 Joe Tinker: Chicago NL Portrait	250.00	110.00
☐ 358 Joe Tinker: Chicago NL Hands on knees	225.00	100.00
☐ 359 John Titus: Phila. NL	50.00	22.00
☐ 360 Terry Turner: Cleveland	60.00	27.00
☐ 361 Bob Unglaub: Washington	50.00	22.00
☐ 362 Rube Waddell: St.L. AL Portrait	275.00	125.00
☐ 363 Rube Waddell: St.L. AL Pitching	175.00	80.00
☐ 364 Heinie Wagner: Boston AL Bat on left shoulder	100.00	45.00
☐ 365 Heinie Wagner: Boston AL Bat on right shoulder	60.00	27.00
☐ 366 Honus Wagner: Pitt.	225000.00	100000.00
☐ 367 Bobby Wallace: St. Louis AL	175.00	80.00
☐ 368 Ed Walsh: Chicago AL	225.00	100.00
☐ 369 Jack Warhop: N.Y. AL	50.00	22.00
☐ 370 Jake Weimer: N.Y. NL	60.00	27.00
☐ 371 Zach Wheat: Brooklyn	200.00	90.00
☐ 372 Doc White: Chicago AL Portrait	60.00	27.00
☐ 373 Doc White: Chicago AL Pitching	50.00	22.00
☐ 374 Kaiser Wilhelm: Brooklyn Batting	50.00	22.00
☐ 375 Kaiser Wilhelm: Brooklyn Hands to chest	60.00	27.00
☐ 376 Ed Willett: Detroit Batting	50.00	22.00
☐ 377 Ed Willetts (Sic& Willett): Detroit Pitching	50.00	22.00
☐ 378 Jimmy Williams: St. Louis AL	60.00	27.00
☐ 379 Vic Willis: Pitt.	250.00	110.00
☐ 380 Vic Willis: St.L. NL Pitching	200.00	90.00
☐ 381 Vic Willis: St.L. NL Batting	200.00	90.00
☐ 382 Chief Wilson: Pitt.	50.00	22.00
☐ 383 Hooks Wiltse: N.Y. NL Portrait	60.00	27.00
☐ 384 Hooks Wiltse: N.Y. NL Sweater	50.00	22.00
☐ 385 Hooks Wiltse: N.Y. NL Pitching	50.00	22.00
☐ 386 Cy Young: Cleveland Portrait	700.00	325.00
☐ 387 Cy Young: Cleveland Pitch, front view	500.00	220.00
☐ 388 Cy Young: Cleveland Pitch, side view	500.00	220.00
☐ 389 Heinie Zimmerman: Chicago NL	50.00	22.00
☐ 390 Fred Abbott: Toledo	40.00	18.00
☐ 391 Merle(Doc) Adkins: Baltimore	40.00	18.00
☐ 392 John Anderson: Providence	40.00	18.00
☐ 393 Herman Armbruster: St. Paul	40.00	18.00
☐ 394 Harry Arndt: Prov.	40.00	18.00
☐ 395 Cy Barger: Rochester	50.00	22.00
☐ 396 John Barry: Milwaukee	40.00	18.00
☐ 397 Emil H. Batch: Rochester	40.00	18.00
☐ 398 Jake Beckley: K.C.	200.00	90.00
☐ 399 Russell Blackburne (Lena): Providence	40.00	18.00
☐ 400 David Brain: Buffalo	40.00	18.00
☐ 401 Roy Brashear: K.C.	40.00	18.00
☐ 402 Fred Burchell: Buffalo	40.00	18.00
☐ 403 Jimmy Burke: Ind.	40.00	18.00
☐ 404 John Butler: Roch.	40.00	18.00
☐ 405 Charles Carr: Ind.	40.00	18.00
☐ 406 James Peter Casey (Doc): Montreal	40.00	18.00
☐ 407 Peter Cassidy: Baltimore	40.00	18.00
☐ 408 Wm. Chappelle: Rochester	50.00	22.00
☐ 409 Wm. Clancy: Buffalo	40.00	18.00
☐ 410 Joshua Clark: Col.	40.00	18.00
☐ 411 William Clymer: Columbus	40.00	18.00
☐ 412 Jimmy Collins: Minneapolis	250.00	110.00
☐ 413 Bunk Congalton: Columbus	40.00	18.00
☐ 414 Gavvy Cravath: Minneapolis	60.00	27.00
☐ 415 Monte Cross: Ind.	50.00	22.00
☐ 416 Paul Davidson: Ind.	40.00	18.00
☐ 417 Frank Delehanty: Louisville	50.00	22.00
☐ 418 Rube Dessau: Balt.	40.00	18.00
☐ 419 Gus Dorner: K.C.	40.00	18.00
☐ 420 Jerome Downs: Minn.	40.00	18.00
☐ 421 Jack Dunn: Baltimore	50.00	22.00
☐ 422 James Flanagan: Buffalo	40.00	18.00
☐ 423 James Freeman: Tol.	40.00	18.00
☐ 424 John Ganzel: Roch.	40.00	18.00
☐ 425 Myron Grimshaw: Toronto	40.00	18.00
☐ 426 Robert Hall: Balt.	40.00	18.00
☐ 427 William Hallman: Kansas City	50.00	22.00
☐ 428 John Hannifan: J.C.	40.00	18.00
☐ 429 Jack Hayden: Ind.	40.00	18.00
☐ 430 Harry Hinchman: Toledo	40.00	18.00
☐ 431 Harry C. Hoffman (Izzy): Providence	40.00	18.00
☐ 432 James B. Jackson: Baltimore	50.00	22.00
☐ 433 Joe Kelley: Tor.	200.00	90.00
☐ 434 Rube Kisinger: Buffalo& (Sic) Kissinger	50.00	22.00
☐ 435 Otto Kruger: Col. (Sic) Krueger	40.00	18.00
☐ 436 Wm. Lattimore: Tol.	40.00	18.00
☐ 437 James Lavender: Providence	40.00	18.00
☐ 438 Carl Lundgren: K.C.	40.00	18.00
☐ 439 Wm. Malarkey: Buff.	50.00	22.00
☐ 440 Wm. Maloney: Roch.	40.00	18.00
☐ 441 Dennis McGann: Milwaukee	40.00	18.00
☐ 442 James McGinley: Toronto	40.00	18.00
☐ 443 Joe McGinnity: New.	225.00	100.00
☐ 444 Ulysses McGlynn: Milwaukee	40.00	18.00
☐ 445 George Merritt: Jersey City	40.00	18.00
☐ 446 Wm. Milligan: J.C.	40.00	18.00
☐ 447 Fred Mitchell: Tor.	40.00	18.00
☐ 448 Dan Moeller: J.C.	40.00	18.00
☐ 449 Joseph Herbert Moran: Providence	40.00	18.00
☐ 450 Wm. Nattress: Buffalo	40.00	18.00
☐ 451 Frank Oberlin: Minneapolis	40.00	18.00
☐ 452 Peter O'Brien: St. Paul	40.00	18.00
☐ 453 Wm. O'Neil: Minn.	40.00	18.00
☐ 454 James Phelan: Prov.	40.00	18.00
☐ 455 Oliver Pickering: Minneapolis.	40.00	18.00
☐ 456 Philip Poland: Baltimore	40.00	18.00
☐ 457 Ambrose Puttman: Louisville	40.00	18.00
☐ 458 Lee Quillen: Minn.	40.00	18.00
☐ 459 Newton Randall: Milwaukee	40.00	18.00
☐ 460 Louis Ritter: K.C.	40.00	18.00
☐ 461 Dick Rudolph: Tor.	40.00	18.00
☐ 462 George Schirm: Buffalo	40.00	18.00
☐ 463 Larry Schlafly: Newark	40.00	18.00
☐ 464 Ossie Schreck: Col. (Sic) Schreckengost	50.00	22.00
☐ 465 William Shannon: Kansas City	40.00	18.00
☐ 466 Bayard Sharpe: Newark	40.00	18.00
☐ 467 Royal Shaw: Prov.	40.00	18.00
☐ 468 James Slagle: Balt.	40.00	18.00

☐ 469 George Henry Smith: Buffalo	40.00	18.00
☐ 470 Samuel Strang: Baltimore	40.00	18.00
☐ 471 Luther Taylor: (Dummy): Buffalo	100.00	45.00
☐ 472 John Thielman: Louisville	40.00	18.00
☐ 473 John F. White: Buffalo	40.00	18.00
☐ 474 William Wright: Toledo	40.00	18.00
☐ 475 Irving M. Young: Minneapolis	50.00	22.00
☐ 476 Jack Bastian: San Antonio	100.00	45.00
☐ 477 Harry Bay: Nashv.	100.00	45.00
☐ 478 Wm. Bernhard: Nashville	100.00	45.00
☐ 479 Ted Breitenstein: New Orleans	100.00	45.00
☐ 480 George Carey: (Scoops): Memphis	100.00	45.00
☐ 481 Cad Coles: Augusta	100.00	45.00
☐ 482 Wm. Cranston: Memphis	100.00	45.00
☐ 483 Roy Ellam: Nashville	100.00	45.00
☐ 484 Edward Foster: Charleston	100.00	45.00
☐ 485 Charles Fritz: N.O.	100.00	45.00
☐ 486 Ed Greminger: Montgomery	100.00	45.00
☐ 487 Guiheen: Portsmouth	100.00	45.00
☐ 488 William F. Hart Little Rock	100.00	45.00
☐ 489 James Henry Hart: Montgomery	100.00	45.00
☐ 490 J.R. Helm: Columbus (Georgia)	100.00	45.00
☐ 491 Gordon Hickman: Mobile	100.00	45.00
☐ 492 Buck Hooker: Lynchburg	100.00	45.00
☐ 493 Ernie Howard: Sav.	100.00	45.00
☐ 494 A.O. Jordan: Atlanta	100.00	45.00
☐ 495 J.F. Kiernan: Columbia	100.00	45.00
☐ 496 Frank King: Danville	100.00	45.00
☐ 497 James LaFitte: Macon	100.00	45.00
☐ 498 Harry Lentz: Little Rock (Sic) Sentz	100.00	45.00
☐ 499 Perry Lipe: Richmond	100.00	45.00
☐ 500 George Manion: Columbia	100.00	45.00
☐ 501 McCauley: Portsmouth	100.00	45.00
☐ 502 Charles B. Miller: Dallas	100.00	45.00
☐ 503 Carlton Molesworth: Birmingham	100.00	45.00
☐ 504 Dominic Mullaney: Jacksonville	100.00	45.00
☐ 505 Albert Orth: Lynchburg	100.00	45.00
☐ 506 William Otey: Norf.	100.00	45.00
☐ 507 George Paige: Charleston	100.00	45.00
☐ 508 Hub Perdue: Nashv.	125.00	55.00
☐ 509 Archie Persons: Montgomery	100.00	45.00
☐ 510 Edward Reagan: N.O.	100.00	45.00
☐ 511 R.H. Revelle: Richmond	100.00	45.00
☐ 512 Isaac Rockenfeld: Montgomery	100.00	45.00
☐ 513 Ray Ryan: Roanoke	100.00	45.00
☐ 514 Charles Seitz: Norfolk	100.00	45.00
☐ 515 Frank Shaughnessy (Shag): Roanoke	125.00	55.00
☐ 516 Carlos Smith: Shreveport	100.00	45.00
☐ 517 Sid Smith: Atlanta	100.00	45.00
☐ 518 M.R.(Dolly) Stark: San Antonio	125.00	55.00
☐ 519 Tony Thebo: Waco	100.00	45.00
☐ 520 Woodie Thornton: Mobile	100.00	45.00
☐ 521 Juan Violat: Jacksonville: (Sic) Viola	100.00	45.00
☐ 522 James Westlake: Danville	100.00	45.00
☐ 523 Foley White: Houston	100.00	45.00

1912 T207 Brown Background

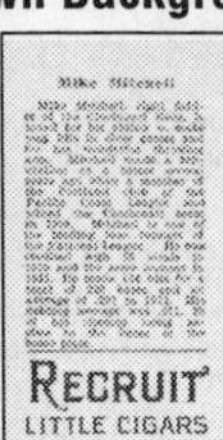

The cards in this 207-card set measure approximately 1 1/2" by 2 5/8". The T207 set, also known as the "Brown Background" set was issued beginning in May with Broadleaf, Cycle, Napoleon, Recruit and anonymous (Factories no. 2, 3 or 25) backs in 1912. Broadleaf, Cycle and anonymous backs are difficult to obtain. Although many scarcities and cards with varying degrees of difficulty to obtain exist (see prices below), the Loudermilk, Lewis (Boston NL) and Miller (Chicago NL) cards are the rarest, followed by Saier and Tyler. The cards are numbered below for reference in alphabetical order by player's name. The complete set price below does include the Lewis variation missing the Braves patch on the sleeve.

	EX-MT	VG-E
COMPLETE SET (208)	28000.00	12600.00
COMMON CARD (1-207)	60.00	27.00
☐ 1 Bert Adams: Cleve	80.00	36.00
☐ 2 Eddie Ainsmith: Wash	60.00	27.00
☐ 3 Rafael Almeida: Cinc	80.00	36.00
☐ 4 Jimmy Austin: StL AL with StL on shirt	60.00	27.00
☐ 5 Jimmy Austin: StL AL without StL on shirt	125.00	55.00
☐ 6 Neal Ball: Cleve	60.00	27.00
☐ 7 Cy Barger: Brk	60.00	27.00
☐ 8 Jack Barry: Phil AL	60.00	27.00
☐ 9 Paddy Bauman: Det	125.00	55.00
☐ 10 Beals Becker: NY NL	60.00	27.00
☐ 11 Chief Bender: Phil AL	200.00	90.00
☐ 12 Joe Benz: Chi AL	80.00	36.00
☐ 13 Bob Bescher: Cinc	60.00	27.00
☐ 14 Joe Birmingham: Cleve	80.00	36.00
☐ 15 Lena Blackburne: Chi AL	80.00	36.00
☐ 16 Fred Blanding: Cleve	80.00	36.00
☐ 17 Bruno Block: Chi AL	60.00	27.00
☐ 18 Ping Bodie: Chi AL	60.00	27.00
☐ 19 Hugh Bradley: Bos AL	60.00	27.00
☐ 20 Roger Bresnahan: StL NL	200.00	90.00
☐ 21 Jack Bushelman: Bos AL	80.00	36.00
☐ 22 Hank Butcher: Cleve	80.00	36.00
☐ 23 Bobby Byrne: Pitt	60.00	27.00
☐ 24 Nixey Callahan: Chi AL	60.00	27.00
☐ 25 Howie Camnitz: Pitt	60.00	27.00
☐ 26 Max Carey: Pitt	150.00	70.00
☐ 27 Bill Carrigan: Bos AL correct back	60.00	27.00
☐ 28 Bill Carrigan: Bos AL Wagner back	150.00	70.00
☐ 29 George Chalmers: Phil NL	60.00	27.00
☐ 30 Frank Chance: Chi NL	250.00	110.00
☐ 31 Eddie Cicotte: Bos AL	175.00	80.00
☐ 32 Tommy Clarke: Cinc	60.00	27.00
☐ 33 King Cole: Chi NL	60.00	27.00
☐ 34 Shano Collins: Chi AL	60.00	27.00
☐ 35 Bob Coulson: Brk	60.00	27.00
☐ 36 Tex Covington: Det	60.00	27.00
☐ 37 Doc Crandall: NY NL	60.00	27.00
☐ 38 Bill Cunningham: Wash	80.00	36.00
☐ 39 Dave Danforth: Phil AL	60.00	27.00
☐ 40 Bert Daniels: NY AL	60.00	27.00
☐ 41 Jake Daubert: Brk	80.00	36.00
☐ 42 Harry Davis: Cleve	60.00	27.00
☐ 43 Jim Delahanty: Det	70.00	32.00
☐ 44 Claud Derrick: Phil AL	60.00	27.00
☐ 45 Art Devlin: Bos NL	60.00	27.00
☐ 46 Josh Devore: NY NL	60.00	27.00
☐ 47 Mike Donlin: Pitt	80.00	36.00
☐ 48 Ed Donnelly: Bos NL	80.00	36.00
☐ 49 Red Dooin: Phil NL	60.00	27.00
☐ 50 Tom Downey: Phil NL	80.00	36.00
☐ 51 Larry Doyle: NY NL	70.00	32.00
☐ 52 Dellos Drake: Det	60.00	27.00
☐ 53 Ted Easterly: Cleve	60.00	27.00
☐ 54 Rube Ellis: StL NL	60.00	27.00
☐ 55 Clyde Engle: Bos AL	60.00	27.00
☐ 56 Tex Erwin: Brk	60.00	27.00
☐ 57 Steve Evans: StL NL	60.00	27.00
☐ 58 Jack Ferry: Pitt	60.00	27.00
☐ 59 Ray Fisher: NY AL white cap	150.00	70.00
☐ 60 Ray Fisher: NY AL blue cap	80.00	36.00
☐ 61 Art Fletcher: NY NL	60.00	27.00
☐ 62 Jack Fournier: Chi AL	80.00	36.00
☐ 63 Art Fromme: Cinc	60.00	27.00
☐ 64 Del Gainor: Det	60.00	27.00
☐ 65 Larry Gardner: Bos AL	60.00	27.00
☐ 66 Lefty George: Cleve	60.00	27.00
☐ 67 Roy Golden: StL NL	60.00	27.00
☐ 68 Hank Gowdy: Bos NL	70.00	32.00
☐ 69 Peaches Graham; Phil NL	80.00	36.00
☐ 70 Jack Graney: Cleve	70.00	32.00
☐ 71 Vean Gregg: Cleve	80.00	36.00
☐ 72 Casey Hageman: Bos AL	60.00	27.00
☐ 73 Sea Lion Hall: Bos AL	60.00	27.00
☐ 74 Ed Hallinan: St.L. AL	60.00	27.00
☐ 75 Earl Hamilton: St.L. AL	60.00	27.00
☐ 76 Bob Harmon: St.L. NL	60.00	27.00
☐ 77 Grover Hartley: NY NL	80.00	36.00
☐ 78 Olaf Henriksen: Bos AL	60.00	27.00
☐ 79 John Henry: Wash	80.00	36.00
☐ 80 Buck Herzog: NY NL	80.00	36.00
☐ 81 Bob Higgins: Brk	60.00	27.00
☐ 82 Red Hoff: NY AL	80.00	36.00
☐ 83 Willie Hogan: StL AL	60.00	27.00
☐ 84 Harry Hooper: Bos AL	400.00	180.00
☐ 85 Ben Houser: Bos NL	80.00	36.00
☐ 86 Ham Hyatt: Pitt	80.00	36.00
☐ 87 Walter Johnson: Wash	1000.00	450.00
☐ 88 George Kahler: Cleve	60.00	27.00
☐ 89 Billy Kelly: Pitt	80.00	36.00
☐ 90 Jay Kirke: Bos NL	80.00	36.00
☐ 91 Johnny Kling: Bos NL	60.00	27.00
☐ 92 Otto Knabe: Phil NL	60.00	27.00
☐ 93 Elmer Knetzer: Brk	60.00	27.00
☐ 94 Ed Konetchy: StL NL	60.00	27.00
☐ 95 Harry Krause: Phil AL	60.00	27.00
☐ 96 Walt Kuhn: Chi AL	80.00	36.00
☐ 97 Joe Kutina: StL AL	80.00	36.00
☐ 98 Frank Lange: Chi AL	80.00	36.00
☐ 99 Jack Lapp: Phil AL	60.00	27.00
☐ 100 Arlie Latham: NY NL	60.00	27.00
☐ 101 Tommy Leach: Pitt	60.00	27.00
☐ 102 Lefty Leifield: Pitt	60.00	27.00
☐ 103 Ed Lennox: Chi NL	60.00	27.00
☐ 104 Duffy Lewis: Bos AL	60.00	27.00
☐ 105A Irving Lewis: Bos NL Braves patch on sleeve	2000.00	900.00
☐ 105B Irving Lewis: Bos NL Nothing on sleeve	2500.00	1100.00
☐ 106 Jack Lively: Det	60.00	27.00
☐ 107 Paddy Livingston: Cleve "A" shirt	250.00	110.00
☐ 108 Paddy Livingston: Cleve "C" shirt	250.00	110.00
☐ 109 Paddy Livingston: Cleve "c" shirt	80.00	36.00
☐ 110 Bris Lord: Phil AL	60.00	27.00
☐ 111 Harry Lord: Chi AL	60.00	27.00
☐ 112 Louis Lowdermilk: StL NL	2500.00	1100.00
☐ 113 Rube Marquard: NY NL	200.00	90.00
☐ 114 Armando Marsans: Cinc	60.00	27.00
☐ 115 George McBride: Wash	60.00	27.00
☐ 116 Alex McCarthy: Pitt	150.00	70.00
☐ 117 Ed McDonald: Bos NL	60.00	27.00
☐ 118 John McGraw: NY NL	250.00	110.00
☐ 119 Harry McIntire: Chi NL	60.00	27.00
☐ 120 Matty McIntyre: Chi AL	60.00	27.00
☐ 121 Bill McKechnie: Pitt	350.00	160.00
☐ 122 Larry McLean: Cinc	60.00	27.00
☐ 123 Clyde Milan: Wash	70.00	32.00
☐ 124 Dots Miller: Pitt	60.00	27.00
☐ 125 Ward Miller: Chi NL	1500.00	700.00
☐ 126 Otto Miller: Brk	80.00	36.00
☐ 127 Doc Miller: Bos NL	80.00	36.00
☐ 128 Mike Mitchell: Cinc	60.00	27.00
☐ 129 Willie Mitchell: Cleve	80.00	36.00
☐ 130 George Mogridge:	80.00	36.00

Chi AL		
☐ 131 Earl Moore: Phil NL	80.00	36.00
☐ 132 Pat Moran: Phil NL	60.00	27.00
☐ 133 Cy Morgan: Phil AL	60.00	27.00
☐ 134 Ray Morgan: Wash	60.00	27.00
☐ 135 George Moriarity: Det	80.00	36.00
☐ 136 George Mullin: Det With "D" on cap)	80.00	36.00
☐ 137 George Mullin: Det Without "D" on cap	200.00	90.00
☐ 138 Tom Needham: Chi NL	60.00	27.00
☐ 139 Red Nelson: StL AL	80.00	36.00
☐ 140 Hub Northen: Brk	60.00	27.00
☐ 141 Les Nunamaker: Bos AL	60.00	27.00
☐ 142 Rebel Oakes: StL NL	60.00	27.00
☐ 143 Buck O'Brien: Bos AL	60.00	27.00
☐ 144 Rube Oldring: Phil AL	70.00	32.00
☐ 145 Ivy Olson: Cleve	60.00	27.00
☐ 146 Marty O'Toole: Pitt	60.00	27.00
☐ 147 Dode Paskert: Phil NL	60.00	27.00
☐ 148 Barney Pelty: StL AL	80.00	36.00
☐ 149 Hub Perdue: Bos NL	70.00	32.00
☐ 150 Rube Peters: Chi AL	80.00	36.00
☐ 151 Art Phelan: Cinc	80.00	36.00
☐ 152 Jack Quinn: NY AL	70.00	32.00
☐ 153 Pat Ragan: Brk	400.00	180.00
☐ 154 Rasmussen: Phil NL	350.00	160.00
☐ 155 Morrie Rath: Chi AL	80.00	36.00
☐ 156 Ed Reulbach: Chi NL	70.00	32.00
☐ 157 Nap Rucker: Brk	70.00	32.00
☐ 158 Ryan: Cleve	80.00	36.00
☐ 159 Vic Saier: Chi NL	900.00	400.00
☐ 160 Scanlon: Phil NL	60.00	27.00
☐ 161 Germany Schaefer: Wash	70.00	32.00
☐ 162 Bill Schardt: Brk	60.00	27.00
☐ 163 Frank Schulte: Chi NL	60.00	27.00
☐ 164 Jim Scott: Chi AL	60.00	27.00
☐ 165 Hank Severeid: Cinc	60.00	27.00
☐ 166 Mike Simon: Pitt NL	60.00	27.00
☐ 167 Wally Smith: StL NL	60.00	27.00
☐ 168 Frank Smith: Cinc	60.00	27.00
☐ 169 Fred Snodgrass: NY NL	80.00	36.00
☐ 170 Tris Speaker: Bos AL	1200.00	550.00
☐ 171 Harry Spratt: Bos NL	60.00	27.00
☐ 172 Eddie Stack: Brk	60.00	27.00
☐ 173 Oscar Stanage: Det	60.00	27.00
☐ 174 Bill Steele: StL NL	60.00	27.00
☐ 175 Harry Steinfeldt: StL NL	70.00	32.00
☐ 176 George Stovall: StL AL	60.00	27.00
☐ 177 Gabby Street: NY AL	70.00	32.00
☐ 178 Amos Strunk: Phil AL	60.00	27.00
☐ 179 Billy Sullivan: Chi AL	70.00	32.00
☐ 180 Bill Sweeney: Bos NL	150.00	70.00
☐ 181 Lee Tannehill: Chi AL	60.00	27.00
☐ 182 Claude Thomas: Bos AL	60.00	27.00
☐ 183 Joe Tinker: Chi NL	250.00	110.00
☐ 184 Bert Tooley: Brk	60.00	27.00
☐ 185 Terry Turner: Cleve	60.00	27.00
☐ 186 Lefty Tyler: Bos NL	600.00	275.00
☐ 187 Hippo Vaughn: NY AL	60.00	27.00
☐ 188 Heine Wagner: Bos AL correct back	80.00	36.00
☐ 189 Heine Wagner: Bos AL Carrigan back	200.00	90.00
☐ 190 Tilly Walker: Wash	60.00	27.00
☐ 191 Bobby Wallace: StL AL	175.00	80.00
☐ 192 Jack Warhop: NY AL	60.00	27.00
☐ 193 Buck Weaver: Chi AL	600.00	275.00
☐ 194 Zack Wheat: Brk	200.00	90.00
☐ 195 Doc White: Chi AL	80.00	36.00
☐ 196 Dewey Wilie: StL NL	80.00	36.00
☐ 197 Bob Williams: NY AL	60.00	27.00
☐ 198 Art Wilson: NY NL	60.00	27.00
☐ 199 Chief Wilson: Pitt	80.00	36.00
☐ 200 Hooks Wiltse: NY NL	60.00	27.00
☐ 201 Ivey Wingo: StL NL	60.00	27.00
☐ 202 Harry Wolverton: NY AL	60.00	27.00
☐ 203 Joe Wood: Bos AL	175.00	80.00
☐ 204 Gene Woodburn: StL NL	100.00	45.00
☐ 205 Ralph Works: Det	300.00	135.00
☐ 206 Steve Yerkes: Bos AL	60.00	27.00
☐ 207 Rollie Zeider: Chi AL	100.00	45.00

1933 Tatoo Orbit R305

The cards in this 60-card set measure 2" by 2 1/4". The 1933 Tatoo Orbit set contains unnumbered, color cards. Blaeholder and Hadley, and to a lesser degree Andrews and Hornsby are considered more difficult to obtain than the other cards in this set. The cards are ordered and numbered below alphabetically by the player's name.

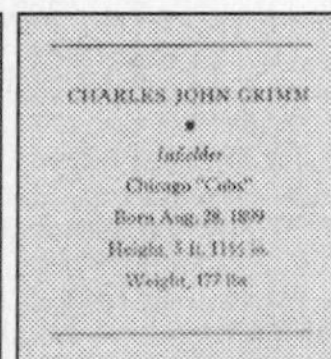

	EX-MT	VG-E
COMPLETE SET (60)	3500.00	1600.00
COMMON CARD (1-60)	40.00	18.00
☐ 1 Dale Alexander	40.00	18.00
☐ 2 Ivy Andrews	125.00	55.00
☐ 3 Earl Averill	75.00	34.00
☐ 4 Dick Bartell	40.00	18.00
☐ 5 Wally Berger	40.00	18.00
☐ 6 George Blaeholder	175.00	80.00
☐ 7 Irving Burns	40.00	18.00
☐ 8 Guy Bush	40.00	18.00
☐ 9 Bruce Campbell	40.00	18.00
☐ 10 Chalmers Cissell	40.00	18.00
☐ 11 Watson Clark	40.00	18.00
☐ 12 Mickey Cochrane	125.00	55.00
☐ 13 Phil Collins	40.00	18.00
☐ 14 Kiki Cuyler	75.00	34.00
☐ 15 Dizzy Dean	200.00	90.00
☐ 16 Jimmy Dykes	40.00	18.00
☐ 17 George Earnshaw	40.00	18.00
☐ 18 Woody English	40.00	18.00
☐ 19 Lou Fonseca	40.00	18.00
☐ 20 Jimmy Foxx	150.00	70.00
☐ 21 Burleigh Grimes	75.00	34.00
☐ 22 Charlie Grimm	60.00	27.00
☐ 23 Lefty Grove	125.00	55.00
☐ 24 Frank Grube	40.00	18.00
☐ 25 George Haas	40.00	18.00
☐ 26 Bump Hadley	175.00	80.00
☐ 27 Chick Hafey	75.00	34.00
☐ 28 Jess Haines	75.00	34.00
☐ 29 Bill Hallahan	40.00	18.00
☐ 30 Mel Harder	50.00	22.00
☐ 31 Gabby Hartnett	75.00	34.00
☐ 32 Babe Herman	60.00	27.00
☐ 33 Billy Herman	75.00	34.00
☐ 34 Rogers Hornsby	250.00	110.00
☐ 35 Roy Johnson	40.00	18.00
☐ 36 Smead Jolley	40.00	18.00
☐ 37 Billy Jurges	40.00	18.00
☐ 38 Willie Kamm	40.00	18.00
☐ 39 Mark Koenig	40.00	18.00
☐ 40 Jim Levey	40.00	18.00
☐ 41 Ernie Lombardi	75.00	34.00
☐ 42 Red Lucas	40.00	18.00
☐ 43 Ted Lyons	75.00	34.00
☐ 44 Connie Mack MG	100.00	45.00
☐ 45 Pat Malone	40.00	18.00
☐ 46 Pepper Martin	60.00	27.00
☐ 47 Marty McManus	40.00	18.00
☐ 48 Lefty O'Doul	60.00	27.00
☐ 49 Dick Porter	40.00	18.00
☐ 50 Carl N. Reynolds	40.00	18.00
☐ 51 Charlie Root	50.00	22.00
☐ 52 Bob Seeds	40.00	18.00
☐ 53 Al Simmons	75.00	34.00
☐ 54 Riggs Stephenson	50.00	22.00
☐ 55 Lyle Tinning	40.00	18.00
☐ 56 Joe Vosmik	40.00	18.00
☐ 57 Rube Walberg	40.00	18.00
☐ 58 Paul Waner	75.00	34.00
☐ 59 Lon Warneke	40.00	18.00
☐ 60 Arthur Whitney	40.00	18.00

1996 Team Out

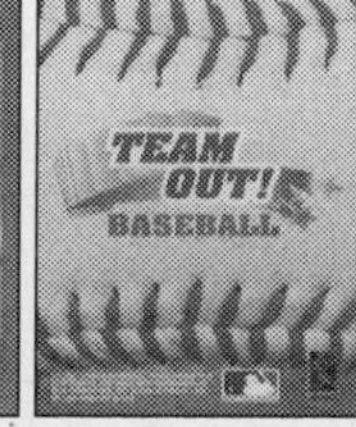

This 101-card set makes up a Baseball card game and is distributed in boxes of 60-card decks with a suggested retail of $12.95 a box. Each deck contains 37 player photo cards and 23 cartoon player cards. A total of 91 different player cards and 10 cartoon cards are available. The backs carry the name of the card game printed on a picture of a section of a baseball. The cards are unnumbered and checklisted below in alphabetical order with the last 10 cards being the cartoon cards and listed with a "C" prefix.

	MINT	NRMT
COMPLETE SET (101)	75.00	34.00
COMMON CARD (1-91)	.25	.11
COMMON CARTOON (C92-C101)	.10	.05
☐ 1 Roberto Alomar	1.00	.45
☐ 2 Brady Anderson	.75	.35
☐ 3 Kevin Appier	.50	.23
☐ 4 Carlos Baerga	.25	.11
☐ 5 Jeff Bagwell	2.50	1.10
☐ 6 Albert Belle	1.25	.55
☐ 7 Dante Bichette	.50	.23
☐ 8 Craig Biggio	.75	.35
☐ 9 Wade Boggs	1.00	.45
☐ 10 Barry Bonds	1.25	.55
☐ 11 Kevin Brown	.50	.23
☐ 12 Jay Buhner	.75	.35
☐ 13 Ellis Burks	.50	.23
☐ 14 Ken Caminiti	1.00	.45
☐ 15 Joe Carter	.50	.23
☐ 16 Vinny Castilla	.50	.23
☐ 17 Jeff Cirillo	.25	.11
☐ 18 Will Clark	.75	.35
☐ 19 Jeff Conine	.50	.23
☐ 20 Joey Cora	.50	.23
☐ 21 Marty Cordova	.50	.23
☐ 22 Eric Davis	.50	.23
☐ 23 Ray Durham	.25	.11
☐ 24 Jim Edmonds	1.00	.45
☐ 25 Cecil Fielder	.50	.23
☐ 26 Travis Fryman	.50	.23
☐ 27 Jason Giambi	.75	.35
☐ 28 Bernard Gilkey	.25	.11
☐ 29 Tom Glavine	.50	.23
☐ 30 Juan Gonzalez	2.50	1.10
☐ 31 Mark Grace	.75	.35
☐ 32 Ken Griffey Jr.	5.00	2.20
☐ 33 Marquis Grissom	.50	.23
☐ 34 Mark Grudzielanek	.50	.23
☐ 35 Ozzie Guillen	.25	.11
☐ 36 Tony Gwynn	2.00	.90
☐ 37 Bobby Higginson	.50	.23
☐ 38 Todd Hundley	.50	.23
☐ 39 Derek Jeter	3.00	1.35
☐ 40 Lance Johnson	.25	.11
☐ 41 Randy Johnson	1.00	.45
☐ 42 Chipper Jones	3.00	1.35
☐ 43 Brian Jordan	.50	.23
☐ 44 Wally Joyner	.50	.23
☐ 45 Jason Kendall	.25	.11
☐ 46 Chuck Knoblauch	1.00	.45
☐ 47 Ray Lankford	.50	.23
☐ 48 Mike Lansing	.25	.11
☐ 49 Barry Larkin	.75	.35
☐ 50 Kenny Lofton	1.25	.55
☐ 51 Javier Lopez	.50	.23
☐ 52 Mike Macfarlane	.25	.11
☐ 53 Greg Maddux	3.00	1.35
☐ 54 Al Martin	.25	.11
☐ 55 Mark McGwire	2.00	.90
☐ 56 Brian McRae	.25	.11
☐ 57 Raul Mondesi	1.00	.45
☐ 58 Denny Neagle	.50	.23
☐ 59 Hideo Nomo	2.00	.90
☐ 60 John Olerud	.50	.23
☐ 61 Rey Ordonez	.25	.11
☐ 62 Troy Percival	.25	.11
☐ 63 Andy Pettitte	1.00	.45
☐ 64 Mike Piazza	3.00	1.35
☐ 65 Manny Ramirez	1.00	.45
☐ 66 Cal Ripken	4.00	1.80
☐ 67 Alex Rodriguez	4.00	1.80
☐ 68 Ivan Rodriguez	1.25	.55
☐ 69 Tim Salmon	1.00	.45
☐ 70 Ryne Sandberg	2.00	.90
☐ 71 Benito Santiago	.25	.11
☐ 72 Kevin Seitzer	.25	.11
☐ 73 Scott Servais	.25	.11
☐ 74 Gary Sheffield	1.00	.45
☐ 75 Ozzie Smith	2.00	.90
☐ 76 John Smoltz	.50	.23
☐ 77 Sammy Sosa	1.00	.45
☐ 78 Mike Stanley	.25	.11
☐ 79 Terry Steinbach	.25	.11
☐ 80 Frank Thomas	4.00	1.80
☐ 81 Steve Trachsel	.25	.11
☐ 82 Jose Valentin	.25	.11
☐ 83 Mo Vaughn	1.25	.55
☐ 84 Robin Ventura	.50	.23
☐ 85 Jose Vizcaino	.25	.11
☐ 86 Larry Walker	1.00	.45

☐ 87 Walt Weiss	.25	.11
☐ 88 Bernie Williams	1.00	.45
☐ 89 Matt Williams	.75	.35
☐ 90 Eric Young	.25	.11
☐ 91 Todd Zeile	.25	.11
☐ C92 Roberto Alomar	.25	.11
☐ C93 Albert Belle Raul Mondesi	.25	.11
☐ C94 Barry Bonds	.25	.11
☐ C95 Ken Griffey Sammy Sosa	1.25	.55
☐ C96 Greg Maddux	1.00	.45
☐ C97 Mark McGwire Ozzie Smith Mo Vaughn	.75	.35
☐ C98 Mike Piazza Matt Williams	.50	.23
☐ C99 Alex Rodriguez Cal Ripken	1.50	.70
☐ C100 Frank Thomas	2.00	.90
☐ C101 G.T. Roped	.10	.05

1993 Ted Williams Promos

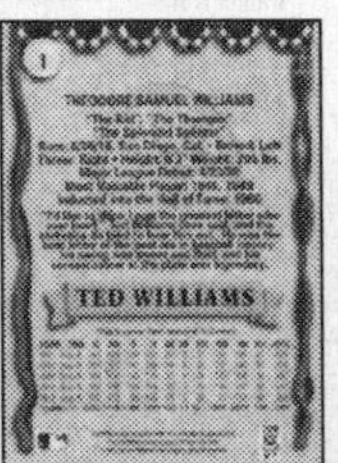

These three standard-size promo cards were issued to preview the design of the forthcoming 1993 Ted Williams baseball set. Though the cards differ from the corresponding numbered cards in the regular series, the promos are not marked as such. Promo card 1 features a different action photo on its front as well as a different ghosted background picture. Also the lettering of Ted Williams' name differs slightly in color, lime green on the promo, orange on the regular issue card. The layout of the backs is identical, but close inspection reveals that the career summaries on each card are slightly different. The promo is easily distinguished by the fact that the career summary begins with a quote by Williams himself. Promo cards 115 and 160 are easily distinguished from their counterparts in the regular issue; in the promo set, player cards have replaced the checklist cards from the regular series. The cards are unnumbered and checklisted below in alphabetical order.

	MINT	NRMT
COMPLETE SET (3)	30.00	13.50
COMMON CARD	6.00	2.70
☐ 1 Ted Williams	15.00	6.75
☐ 115 Satchell Paige	6.00	2.70
☐ 160 Juan Gonzalez The Measure of a Hitter	10.00	4.50

1993 Ted Williams

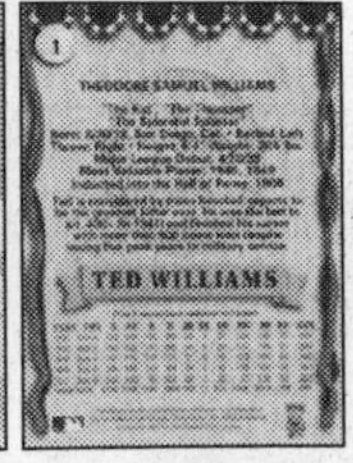

This set of 160 cards marks the inaugural effort of the Ted Williams Card Company. The standard-size cards are UV-coated, and bear the company's embossed logo. The card designs vary from subset to subset, and since the borderless cards feature players of the past (with only two exceptions), some of the photos on the fronts are black-and-white, some are color, and still others are sepia-toned. Generally, the backs carry Williams' comments on each player's abilities and career highlights. All the cards are numbered on the back and are grouped according to team and subset as follows: Boston Red Sox (1-7), Brooklyn/Los Angeles Dodgers (8-17), California Angels (18, 19), Chicago Cubs (20-24), Chicago White Sox (25-27), Cincinnati Reds (28-30), Cleveland Indians (31-35), Detroit Tigers (36-40), Houston Astros (41), Kansas City/Oakland Athletics (42-45), Milwaukee/Atlanta Braves (46-48), Milwaukee Brewers (49), Minnesota Twins (50), New York/San Francisco Giants (51-55), New York Mets (56, 57), New York Yankees (58-69), Philadelphia Phillies (70-73), Pittsburgh Pirates (74-81), Baltimore Orioles (82-85), St. Louis Cardinals (86-93), San Diego Padres (94), The Negro Leagues (97-115), All-American Girls' Professional Baseball League (116-120), Ted's Greatest Hitters (121-130), Barrier Breakers (131-140), Goin' North (141-150), and Dawning of a Legacy (151-160), which features cards of Juan Gonzalez and Jeff Bagwell, the only two current players in the set. Ted Williams personally signed 406 of his Locklear Collection insert card for this set and Juan Gonzalez signed 172 cards (43 each of his four different regular cards in this set) as well. Also, two POGs, or milk bottle caps, were inserted in each pack. These feature illustrations of former major and Negro league players, logos of their teams, and reproductions of selected signatures of former major league players.

	MINT	NRMT
COMPLETE SET (160)	15.00	6.75
COMMON CARD (1-160)	.05	.02
☐ 1 Ted Williams	2.00	.90
☐ 2 Rick Ferrell	.25	.11
☐ 3 Jim Lonborg	.05	.02
☐ 4 Mel Parnell	.05	.02
☐ 5 Jim Piersall	.10	.05
☐ 6 Luis Tiant	.10	.05
☐ 7 Carl Yastrzemski	.50	.23
☐ 8 Ralph Branca	.10	.05
☐ 9 Roy Campanella	.75	.35
☐ 10 Ron Cey	.10	.05
☐ 11 Tommy Davis	.10	.05
☐ 12 Don Drysdale	.35	.16
☐ 13 Carl Erskine	.10	.05
☐ 14 Steve Garvey	.15	.07
☐ 15 Don Newcombe	.15	.07
☐ 16 Duke Snider	.75	.35
☐ 17 Maury Wills	.15	.07
☐ 18 Jim Fregosi	.10	.05
☐ 19 Bobby Grich	.10	.05
☐ 20 Bill Buckner	.10	.05
☐ 21 Billy Herman UER (Ted Williams stats on back)	.25	.11
☐ 22 Ferguson Jenkins	.25	.11
☐ 23 Ron Santo	.15	.07
☐ 24 Billy Williams	.25	.11
☐ 25 Luis Aparicio	.25	.11
☐ 26 Luke Appling	.25	.11
☐ 27 Minnie Minoso	.15	.07
☐ 28 Johnny Bench	.50	.23
☐ 29 George Foster	.10	.05
☐ 30 Joe Morgan	.25	.11
☐ 31 Buddy Bell	.10	.05
☐ 32 Lou Boudreau	.25	.11
☐ 33 Rocky Colavito	.15	.07
☐ 34 Jim(Mudcat) Grant	.05	.02
☐ 35 Tris Speaker	.25	.11
☐ 36 Ray Boone	.05	.02
☐ 37 Darrell Evans	.10	.05
☐ 38 Al Kaline	.50	.23
☐ 39 George Kell	.25	.11
☐ 40 Mickey Lolich	.15	.07
☐ 41 Cesar Cedeno	.10	.05
☐ 42 Sal Bando	.05	.02
☐ 43 Vida Blue	.10	.05
☐ 44 Bert Campaneris	.05	.02
☐ 45 Ken Holtzman	.05	.02
☐ 46 Lew Burdette	.10	.05
☐ 47 Bob Horner	.05	.02
☐ 48 Warren Spahn	.25	.11
☐ 49 Cecil Cooper	.10	.05
☐ 50 Tony Oliva	.15	.07
☐ 51 Bobby Bonds	.15	.07
☐ 52 Alvin Dark	.10	.05
☐ 53 Dave Dravecky	.10	.05
☐ 54 Monte Irvin	.25	.11
☐ 55 Willie Mays	1.00	.45
☐ 56 Bud Harrelson	.10	.05
☐ 57 Dave Kingman UER (Darrell Evans has 414 homers and is not in HOF)	.10	.05
☐ 58 Yogi Berra	.50	.23
☐ 59 Don Baylor	.15	.07
☐ 60 Jim Bouton	.10	.05
☐ 61 Bobby Brown	.10	.05
☐ 62 Whitey Ford	.50	.23
☐ 63 Lou Gehrig	1.50	.70
☐ 64 Charlie Keller	.10	.05
☐ 65 Eddie Lopat	.10	.05
☐ 66 Johnny Mize	.25	.11
☐ 67 Bobby Murcer	.10	.05
☐ 68 Graig Nettles	.15	.07
☐ 69 Bobby Shantz	.05	.02
☐ 70 Richie Ashburn	.25	.11
☐ 71 Larry Bowa	.10	.05
☐ 72 Steve Carlton	.40	.18
☐ 73 Robin Roberts	.25	.11
☐ 74 Matty Alou	.05	.02
☐ 75 Harvey Haddix	.05	.02
☐ 76 Ralph Kiner	.25	.11
☐ 77 Bill Madlock	.10	.05
☐ 78 Bill Mazeroski	.15	.07
☐ 79 Al Oliver	.10	.05
☐ 80 Manny Sanguillen	.05	.02
☐ 81 Willie Stargell	.25	.11
☐ 82 Al Bumbry	.05	.02
☐ 83 Davey Johnson	.10	.05
☐ 84 Boog Powell	.15	.07
☐ 85 Earl Weaver MG	.15	.07
☐ 86 Lou Brock	.25	.11
☐ 87 Orlando Cepeda UER (Born in Puerto Rico& not Dominican Republic)	.15	.07
☐ 88 Curt Flood	.10	.05
☐ 89 Joe Garagiola	.15	.07
☐ 90 Bob Gibson	.25	.11
☐ 91 Rogers Hornsby UER (Misspelled Rodgers on card front)	.25	.11
☐ 92 Enos Slaughter	.25	.11
☐ 93 Joe Torre	.15	.07
☐ 94 Gaylord Perry	.25	.11
☐ 95 Checklist	.05	.02
☐ 96 Checklist	.05	.02
☐ 97 Cool Papa Bell	.30	.14
☐ 98 Garnett Blair	.10	.05
☐ 99 Gene Benson	.15	.07
☐ 100 Lyman Bostock Sr.	.10	.05
☐ 101 Marlin Carter	.10	.05
☐ 102 Oscar Charleston	.25	.11
☐ 103 Ray Dandridge	.25	.11
☐ 104 Mahlon Duckett	.10	.05
☐ 105 Josh Gibson	.75	.35
☐ 106 Cowan(Bubber) Hyde	.10	.05
☐ 107 William(Judy) Johnson	.25	.11
☐ 108 Buck Leonard	.25	.11
☐ 109 John Henry Lloyd	.25	.11
☐ 110 Lester Lockett	.10	.05
☐ 111 Max Manning	.10	.05
☐ 112 Satchel Paige	.75	.35
☐ 113 Armando Vazquez	.10	.05
☐ 114 Joe(Smokey) Williams	.25	.11
☐ 115 Checklist	.05	.02
☐ 116 Alice(Lefty) Hohlmeyer	.25	.11
☐ 117 Dotty Kamenshek	.25	.11
☐ 118 Lavonne(Pepper) Davis	.25	.11
☐ 119 Marge Wenzell	.25	.11
☐ 120 Checklist	.05	.02
☐ 121 Babe Ruth	2.50	1.10
☐ 122 Lou Gehrig	1.50	.70
☐ 123 Jimmie Foxx	.50	.23
☐ 124 Rogers Hornsby	.50	.23
☐ 125 Ty Cobb	1.50	.70
☐ 126 Willie Mays	1.00	.45
☐ 127 Ralph Kiner	.40	.18
☐ 128 Tris Speaker	.40	.18
☐ 129 Johnny Mize	.35	.16
☐ 130 Checklist	.05	.02
☐ 131 Satchel Paige	.50	.23
☐ 132 Joe Black	.10	.05
☐ 133 Roy Campanella	.50	.23
☐ 134 Larry Doby UER (Misspelled Dolby on card back)	.15	.07
☐ 135 Jim Gilliam	.15	.07
☐ 136 Monte Irvin	.40	.18
☐ 137 Sam Jethroe	.10	.05
☐ 138 Willie Mays	1.00	.45
☐ 139 Don Newcombe	.10	.05
☐ 140 Checklist	.05	.02
☐ 141 Roy Campanella	.50	.23
☐ 142 Bob Gibson	.25	.11
☐ 143 Boog Powell	.15	.07
☐ 144 Willie Mays	1.00	.45
☐ 145 Johnny Mize	.25	.11
☐ 146 Monte Irvin	.25	.11
☐ 147 Earl Weaver MG	.15	.07
☐ 148 Ted Williams	1.50	.70
☐ 149 Jim Gilliam	.10	.05
☐ 150 Checklist	.05	.02
☐ 151 Juan Gonzalez Footsteps to Greatness	.75	.35
☐ 152 Juan Gonzalez Sign 'em Up	.75	.35
☐ 153 Juan Gonzalez	.75	.35

Card	MINT	NRMT
The Road to Success		
☐ 154 Juan Gonzalez	.75	.35
Looking Ahead		
☐ 155 Checklist 151-155	.05	.02
☐ 156 Jeff Bagwell	.50	.23
Born with Red Sox Blood		
☐ 157 Jeff Bagwell	.50	.23
Movin' Up Then Out		
☐ 158 Jeff Bagwell	.50	.23
Year 1		
☐ 159 Jeff Bagwell	.50	.23
Year 2		
☐ 160 Checklist 156-160	.05	.02
☐ AU151 Juan Gonzalez AU	250.00	110.00
(Certified autograph)		
Footsteps to Greatness		
☐ AU152 Juan Gonzalez AU	250.00	110.00
(Certified autograph)		
Sign 'em Up		
☐ AU153 Juan Gonzalez AU	250.00	110.00
(Certified autograph)		
The Road to Success		
☐ AU154 Juan Gonzalez AU	250.00	110.00
(Certified autograph)		
Looking Ahead		

1993 Ted Williams Brooks Robinson

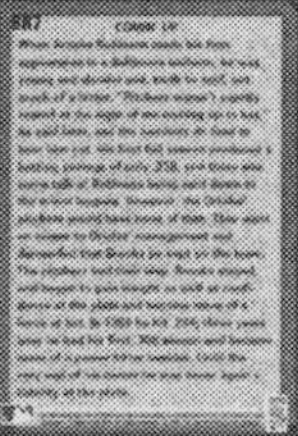

Randomly inserted in retail packs, this ten-card standard-size set features on its fronts borderless photos of Brooks Robinson. His name is stamped in gold foil, the set's logo appears in one corner, and the embossed company logo appears in another. The back carries Williams' comments on Robinson's outstanding career within a simulated embroidery panel. Autographed cards of Robinson were randomly inserted into retail packs. These cards are certified but have been rarely seen in the marketplace

	MINT	NRMT
COMPLETE SET (10)	15.00	6.75
COMMON CARD (1-10)	1.50	.70
☐ 1 Brooks Robinson	1.50	.70
Salad Days		
☐ 2 Brooks Robinson	1.50	.70
Brooks Calbert Robinson		
☐ 3 Brooks Robinson	1.50	.70
'66 Series		
☐ 4 Brooks Robinson	1.50	.70
Fielding Stats		
☐ 5 Brooks Robinson	1.50	.70
'70 Series 2		
☐ 6 Brooks Robinson	1.50	.70
'70 Series 1		
☐ 7 Brooks Robinson	1.50	.70
Comin' Up		
☐ 8 Brooks Robinson	1.50	.70
All-Star Games		
☐ 9 Brooks Robinson	1.50	.70
1964		
☐ 10 Checklist Card	1.50	.70

1993 Ted Williams Locklear Collection

This ten-card standard-size set features the artwork of noted artist and former major league player Gene Locklear. The set includes famous players from the past. The white-edged fronts carry the player's name, vertically presented along the left edge, in blue print. A logo for Gene Locklear is overlaid on the lower right corner. The backs have descriptive career summaries superimposed over a ghosted collage of all the players in the set. The cards are numbered on the back with an "LC" prefix with the order of players being alphabetical.

	MINT	NRMT
COMPLETE SET (10)	35.00	16.00
COMMON CARD (1-10)	3.00	1.35

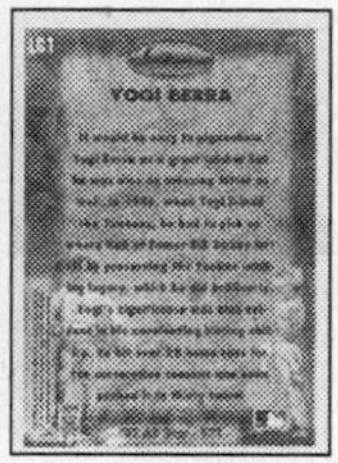

	MINT	NRMT
☐ 1 Yogi Berra	6.00	2.70
☐ 2 Lou Brock	3.00	1.35
☐ 3 Willie Mays	7.50	3.40
☐ 4 Johnny Mize	3.00	1.35
☐ 5 Satchel Paige	6.00	2.70
☐ 6 Babe Ruth	10.00	4.50
☐ 7 Enos Slaughter	3.00	1.35
☐ 8 Carl Yastrzemski	5.00	2.20
☐ 9 Ted Williams	7.50	3.40
☐ 10 Checklist	3.00	1.35
☐ AU9 Ted Williams AU	500.00	220.00
(Certified autograph)		

1993 Ted Williams Memories

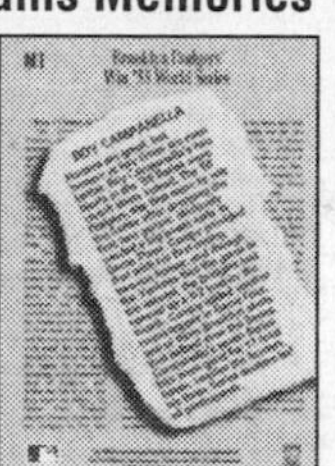

Individual cards from this special 20-card standard-size set were regionally but otherwise randomly inserted in foil hobby packs. For example, the 1973 Oakland A's cards were randomly inserted only in packs destined for shipment to the West Coast while the 1955 Brooklyn Dodgers cards were available only on the East Coast. The fronts feature borderless action player photos that have dimmed edges. The player's name appears in white lettering at the bottom and the embossed company logo is displayed in an upper corner. The set logo, along with the year, rests in the lower left. Ted Williams' comments on each player are printed obliquely within a ragged-edged white rectangle that resembles a newspaper article cutout. This is superposed upon text that resembles a newspaper article. The cards are numbered on the back with an "M" prefix.

	MINT	NRMT
COMPLETE SET (20)	40.00	18.00
COMMON CARD (1-20)	1.50	.70
☐ 1 Roy Campanella	5.00	2.20
☐ 2 Jim Gilliam	2.00	.90
☐ 3 Gil Hodges	4.00	1.80
☐ 4 Duke Snider	5.00	2.20
☐ 5 1955 Brooklyn	1.50	.70
Dodgers Checklist		
☐ 6 Don Drysdale	4.00	1.80
☐ 7 Tommy Davis	1.50	.70
☐ 8 Johnny Podres	1.50	.70
☐ 9 Maury Wills	35.00	16.00
☐ 10 1963 Los Angeles	1.50	.70
Dodgers Checklist		
☐ 11 Roberto Clemente	7.00	3.10
☐ 12 Al Oliver	2.00	.90
☐ 13 Manny Sanguillen	1.50	.70
☐ 14 Willie Stargell	3.00	1.35
☐ 15 1971 Pittsburgh	1.50	.70
Pirates Checklist		
☐ 16 Johnny Bench	3.00	1.35
☐ 17 George Foster	2.00	.90
☐ 18 Joe Morgan	3.00	1.35
☐ 19 Tony Perez	3.00	1.35
☐ 20 1975 Cincinnati	1.50	.70
Reds Checklist		

1993 Ted Williams POG Cards

This set of 52 POGs was issued in pairs on 26 cards. The cards measure approximately 2 9/16" by 3 9/16" and are printed on a thick cardboard stock. Each POG measures 1 5/8" in diameter and is perforated for punch out. The

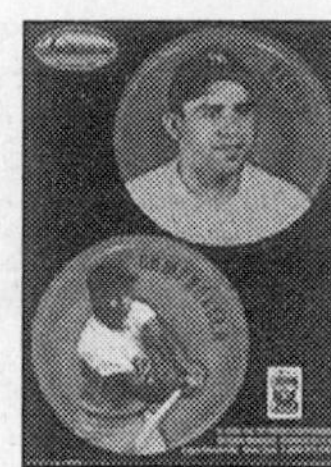

fronts of the cards are black and the backs are white. The POGs consist of team logos, various special logos, and some players. The POGs are unnumbered and checklisted below alphabetically according to non-player cards (1-20) and cards which feature at least one player (21-26).

	MINT	NRMT
COMPLETE SET (26)	6.00	2.70
COMMON CARD (1-26)	.25	.11
☐ 1 Atlanta Black Crackers	.25	.11
Baltimore Elite Giants		
☐ 2 Atlanta Braves	.25	.11
New York Mets		
☐ 3 Baltimore Orioles	.25	.11
1993 All-Star Game		
1993 World Series		
☐ 4 Birmingham Black Barons	.25	.11
New York Cuban Stars		
☐ 5 Chicago Cubs	.25	.11
Detroit Tigers		
☐ 6 Cincinnati Reds	.25	.11
Kansas City Royals		
1969-1993		
☐ 7 Classic Teams	.25	.11
The Negro Leagues		
Negro League		
Baseball Players Assoc.		
☐ 8 Cleveland Buckeyes	.25	.11
Detroit Stars		
☐ 9 Cleveland Indians	.25	.11
Kansas City Athletics		
☐ 10 Houston Colt .45s	.25	.11
New York Yankees		
☐ 11 Florida Marlins	.25	.11
1993 Inaugural Year		
Colorado Rockies		
1993 Inaugural Year		
☐ 12 Indianapolis ABCs	.25	.11
New York Harlem Stars		
☐ 13 Louisville Black Caps	.25	.11
Philadelphia Stars		
☐ 14 Minnesota Twins	.25	.11
Boston Red Sox		
☐ 15 Montreal Expos	.25	.11
1969-1993		
San Diego Padres		
1969-1993		
☐ 16 New York Black Yankees	.25	.11
Homestead Grays		
☐ 17 New York Giants	.25	.11
Milwaukee Braves		
☐ 18 Oakland A's	.25	.11
21 (Clemente's number)		
☐ 19 Pittsburgh Pirates	.25	.11
St. Louis Cardinals		
☐ 20 St. Louis Browns	.25	.11
Brooklyn Dodgers		
☐ 21 Yogi Berra	1.00	.45
Roy Campanella		
☐ 22 Brooklyn Dodgers	.75	.35
Roy Campanella		
☐ 23 Lou Gehrig	2.00	.90
Ted Williams		
☐ 24 Lou Gehrig	1.50	.70
New York Yankees		
☐ 25 Tommy Davis	.40	.18
George Foster		
☐ 26 Ted Williams	1.50	.70
1941 - .406		
Ted Williams		

1993 Ted Williams Roberto Clemente

Randomly inserted in foil packs and subtitled "Etched in Stone," this ten-card standard-size set features on its fronts borderless photos of Roberto Clemente. His name and the set subtitle are "graven" in the upper right, and the company logo, along with the words "Tribute '93" within gold foil bars, are embossed in the lower left. On the back, Ted Williams' comments on Clemente's illustrious career

appear within a simulated glazed stone tablet. The cards are numbered on the back with an "ES" prefix. The card numbering follows chronological order.

	MINT	NRMT
COMPLETE SET (10)	20.00	9.00
COMMON CARD (1-10)	2.00	.90
☐ 1 Roberto Clemente Youth	2.00	.90
☐ 2 Roberto Clemente Sign Up	2.00	.90
☐ 3 Roberto Clemente Try-Out	2.00	.90
☐ 4 Roberto Clemente Playing Mad	2.00	.90
☐ 5 Roberto Clemente Minor Leagues	2.00	.90
☐ 6 Roberto Clemente 1955-1959	2.00	.90
☐ 7 Roberto Clemente 1960	2.00	.90
☐ 8 Roberto Clemente 1963	2.00	.90
☐ 9 Roberto Clemente 1970	2.00	.90
☐ 10 Roberto Clemente Checklist	2.00	.90

1994 Ted Williams

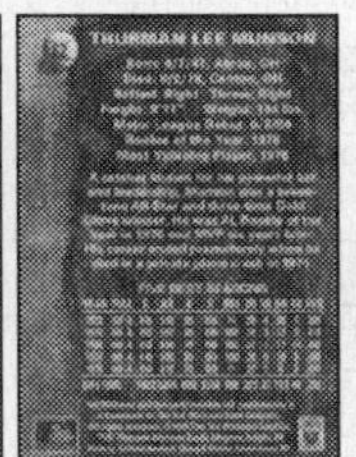

The 1994 Ted Williams set comprises 162 standard-size cards distributed in 12-card packs. The series features former major league baseball players, players from the All-American Girls Professional Baseball League, 17 Negro League stars, and 17 current top prospects. The fronts feature color action player photos that are full-bleed, except at the right where a rugged and textured rock edges the picture. The backs have a similar design, only that the photo is replaced by biography, player profile, and statistics superposed on a wooden simulation of the team's logo. Topical subsets featured are Women in Baseball (93-99), The Negro League (100-117), The Campaign (118-135), Goin' North (136-144), Swinging for the Fences (145-153), and Dawning of a Legacy (154-162).The cards are numbered on the back. A red foil version of the Ted Williams (LP1) and Larry Bird (LP2) insert cards were produced. The values are the same as those listed below. Leon Day signed some cards for release in the packs.

	MINT	NRMT
COMPLETE SET (162)	10.00	4.50
COMMON CARD (1-162)	.05	.02
☐ 1 Ted Williams	1.00	.45
☐ 2 Bernie Carbo	.05	.02
☐ 3 Bobby Doerr	.25	.11
☐ 4 Fred Lynn	.10	.05
☐ 5 John Pesky	.10	.05
☐ 6 Rico Petrocelli	.10	.05
☐ 7 Cy Young	.25	.11
☐ 8 Paul Blair	.05	.02
☐ 9 Andy Etchebarren	.05	.02
☐ 10 Brooks Robinson	.25	.11
☐ 11 Gil Hodges	.15	.07
☐ 12 Tommy John	.10	.05
☐ 13 Rick Monday	.05	.02
☐ 14 Dean Chance	.05	.02
☐ 15 Doug DeCinces	.05	.02
☐ 16 Gabby Hartnett	.25	.11
☐ 17 Don Kessinger	.05	.02
☐ 18 Bruce Sutter	.10	.05
☐ 19 Eddie Collins Sr.	.15	.07
☐ 20 Nellie Fox	.25	.11
☐ 21 Carlos May	.05	.02
☐ 22 Ted Kluszewski	.15	.07
☐ 23 Vada Pinson	.10	.05
☐ 24 Johnny Vander Meer	.10	.05
☐ 25 Bob Feller	.25	.11
☐ 26 Mike Garcia	.05	.02
☐ 27 Sam McDowell	.05	.02
☐ 28 Al Rosen	.10	.05
☐ 29 Norm Cash	.10	.05
☐ 30 Ty Cobb	.75	.35
☐ 31 Mark Fidrych	.10	.05
☐ 32 Hank Greenberg	.25	.11
☐ 33 Dennis McLain	.10	.05
☐ 34 Virgil Trucks	.05	.02
☐ 35 Enos Cabell	.05	.02
☐ 36 Mike Scott	.05	.02
☐ 37 Bob Watson	.10	.05
☐ 38 Amos Otis	.05	.02
☐ 39 Frank White	.05	.02
☐ 40 Joe Adcock	.10	.05
☐ 41 Rico Carty	.05	.02
☐ 42 Ralph Garr	.05	.02
☐ 43 Ed Mathews	.25	.11
☐ 44 Ben Oglivie	.05	.02
☐ 45 Gorman Thomas	.05	.02
☐ 46 Earl Battey	.05	.02
☐ 47 Rod Carew	.25	.11
☐ 48 Jim Kaat	.10	.05
☐ 49 Harmon Killebrew	.25	.11
☐ 50 Gary Carter	.15	.07
☐ 51 Steve Rogers	.05	.02
☐ 52 Rusty Staub	.10	.05
☐ 53 Sal Maglie	.10	.05
☐ 54 Juan Marichal	.25	.11
☐ 55 Mel Ott	.25	.11
☐ 56 Bobby Thomson	.15	.07
☐ 57 Tommie Agee	.05	.02
☐ 58 Tug McGraw	.10	.05
☐ 59 Elston Howard	.15	.07
☐ 60 Sparky Lyle	.10	.05
☐ 61 Billy Martin	.10	.05
☐ 62 Thurman Munson	.15	.07
☐ 63 Bobby Richardson	.10	.05
☐ 64 Bill Skowron	.10	.05
☐ 65 Mickey Cochrane	.25	.11
☐ 66 Rollie Fingers	.25	.11
☐ 67 Lefty Grove	.25	.11
☐ 68 James Hunter	.25	.11
☐ 69 Connie Mack MG	.25	.11
☐ 70 Al Simmons	.10	.05
☐ 71 Dick Allen	.15	.07
☐ 72 Bob Boone	.10	.05
☐ 73 Del Ennis	.05	.02
☐ 74 Chuck Klein	.25	.11
☐ 75 Mike Schmidt	.35	.16
☐ 76 Dock Ellis	.05	.02
☐ 77 Elroy Face	.05	.02
☐ 78 Phil Garner	.05	.02
☐ 79 Bill Mazeroski	.15	.07
☐ 80 Pie Traynor	.25	.11
☐ 81 Honus Wagner	.35	.16
☐ 82 Dizzy Dean	.25	.11
☐ 83 Red Schoendienst	.25	.11
☐ 84 Randy Jones	.05	.02
☐ 85 Nate Colbert	.05	.02
☐ 86 Jeff Burroughs	.05	.02
☐ 87 Jim Sundberg	.05	.02
☐ 88 Frank Howard	.10	.05
☐ 89 Walter Johnson	.25	.11
☐ 90 Eddie Yost	.05	.02
☐ 91 Checklist 1	.05	.02
☐ 92 Checklist 2	.05	.02
☐ 93 Faye Dancer	.15	.07
☐ 94 Snookie Dayle	.10	.05
☐ 95 Maddy English	.10	.05
☐ 96 Nickie Fox	.10	.05
☐ 97 Sophie Kurys	.25	.11
☐ 98 Alma Ziegler	.10	.05
☐ 99 Checklist	.05	.02
☐ 100 Newton Allen	.10	.05
☐ 101 Willard Brown	.10	.05
☐ 102 Larry Brown	.10	.05
☐ 103 Leon Day	.25	.11
☐ 104 John Donaldson	.10	.05
☐ 105 Rube Foster	.15	.07
☐ 106 John Fowler	.10	.05
☐ 107 Elander Harris	.10	.05
☐ 108 Webster McDonald	.10	.05
☐ 109 Buck O'Neil	.25	.11
☐ 110 Ted "Double Duty" Radcliffe	.15	.07
☐ 111 Wilber Rogan	.10	.05
☐ 112 Marcenia Stone	.10	.05
☐ 113 James Taylor	.10	.05
☐ 114 Fleetwood Walker	.15	.07
☐ 115 George Wilson	.10	.05
☐ 116 Judson Wilson	.10	.05
☐ 117 Checklist	.05	.02
☐ 118 Howard Battle	.10	.05
☐ 119 John Burke	.05	.02
☐ 120 Brian Dubose	.05	.02
☐ 121 Alex Gonzalez	.10	.05
☐ 122 Jose Herrera	.10	.05
☐ 123 Jason Giambi	.25	.11
☐ 124 Derek Jeter	1.00	.45
☐ 125 Charles Johnson	.50	.23
☐ 126 Daron Kirkreit	.10	.05
☐ 127 Jason Moler	.10	.05
☐ 128 Vince Moore	.10	.05
☐ 129 Chad Mottola	.05	.02
☐ 130 Jose Silva	.05	.02
☐ 131 Mac Suzuki	.15	.07
☐ 132 Brien Taylor	.05	.02
☐ 133 Michael Tucker	.25	.11
☐ 134 Billy Wagner	.40	.18
☐ 135 Checklist	.05	.02
☐ 136 Gary Carter	.15	.07
☐ 137 Tony Conigliaro	.10	.05
☐ 138 Sparky Lyle	.10	.05
☐ 139 Roger Maris	.15	.07
☐ 140 Vada Pinson	.10	.05
☐ 141 Mike Schmidt	.25	.11
☐ 142 Frank White	.05	.02
☐ 143 Ted Williams	.75	.35
☐ 144 Checklist	.05	.02
☐ 145 Joe Adcock	.05	.02
☐ 146 Rocky Colavito	.15	.07
☐ 147 Lou Gehrig	1.00	.45
☐ 148 Gil Hodges	.10	.05
☐ 149 Bob Horner	.05	.02
☐ 150 Willie Mays	1.00	.45
☐ 151 Mike Schmidt	.25	.11
☐ 152 Pat Seerey	.05	.02
☐ 153 Checklist	.05	.02
☐ 154 Cliff Floyd The Honors Begin	.10	.05
☐ 155 Cliff Floyd The Top Polecat	.10	.05
☐ 156 Cliff Floyd Minor League Team of the Year	.10	.05
☐ 157 Cliff Floyd Major League Debut	.10	.05
☐ 158 Tim Salmon Award Winner	.30	.14
☐ 159 Tim Salmon Early Professional Career	.30	.14
☐ 160 Tim Salmon An MVP Season	.30	.14
☐ 161 Tim Salmon Rookie of the Year	.30	.14
☐ 162 Checklist	.05	.02
☐ P1 Ted Williams Promo	2.00	.90
☐ LP1 Larry Bird	5.00	2.20
☐ LP2 Ted Williams	5.00	2.20
☐ NNO Leon Day AU Certified Autograph	25.00	11.00

1994 Ted Williams 500 Club

Randomly inserted in foil packs, this nine-card standard-size set profiles members of baseball's elite 500 home run club. The fronts display full-bleed color action shots that have a ribbed appearance. The words "The 500 Club" appear on a sign in the lower left corner, with the player's name following the curve of the sign. On a wood plaque hung on a simulated wooden wall, the backs summarize the player's outstanding achievement. Cards numbers are prefixed with a "5C." A red foil version of this set was produced. The values are the same as those listed below.

	MINT	NRMT
COMPLETE SET (9)	20.00	9.00
COMMON CARD (1-8)	1.00	.45

☐ 1 Hank Aaron	4.00	1.80
☐ 2 Reggie Jackson	3.00	1.35
☐ 3 Harmon Killebrew	1.25	.55
☐ 4 Mickey Mantle	8.00	3.60
☐ 5 Jimmie Foxx	3.00	1.35
☐ 6 Babe Ruth	6.00	2.70
☐ 7 Mike Schmidt	5.00	2.20
☐ 8 Ted Williams	6.00	2.70
☐ 9 Checklist	1.00	.45

1994 Ted Williams Dan Gardiner Collection

Randomly inserted in foil packs, this nine-card standard-size set presents top minor league prospects. Both sides display color paintings by noted artist Dan Gardiner. The backs also include a brief player profile.

	MINT	NRMT
COMPLETE SET (9)	20.00	9.00
COMMON CARD (DG1-DG9)	.75	.35
☐ DG1 Michael Jordan	15.00	6.75
☐ DG2 Michael Tucker	2.50	1.10
☐ DG3 Derek Jeter	8.00	3.60
☐ DG4 Charles Johnson	3.00	1.35
☐ DG5 Howard Battle	.75	.35
☐ DG6 Quilvio Veras	1.50	.70
☐ DG7 Brian L. Hunter	2.00	.90
☐ DG8 Brien Taylor	.75	.35
☐ DG9 Checklist	2.00	.90

1994 Ted Williams Locklear Collection

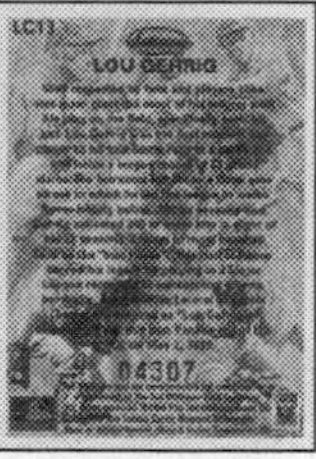

Randomly inserted in foil packs, this nine-card standard-size set again features the work of noted artist Gene Locklear. Inside white borders, the fronts display full-color paintings of former major league greats. The player's name is printed vertically along the left edge. The backs have descriptive career summaries superposed over a collage of all the players portrayed in the set. The numbering on the backs is in continuation of last year's Locklear Collection insert series.

	MINT	NRMT
COMPLETE SET (9)	20.00	9.00
COMMON CARD (LC11-LC19)	1.50	.70
☐ LC11 Ty Cobb	5.00	2.20
☐ LC12 Bob Feller	2.50	1.10
☐ LC13 Lou Gehrig	8.00	3.60
☐ LC14 Josh Gibson	3.00	1.35
☐ LC15 Walter Johnson	3.00	1.35
☐ LC16 Casey Stengel	3.00	1.35
☐ LC17 Honus Wagner	6.00	2.70
☐ LC18 Cy Young	4.00	1.80
☐ LC19 Checklist	1.50	.70

1994 Ted Williams Memories

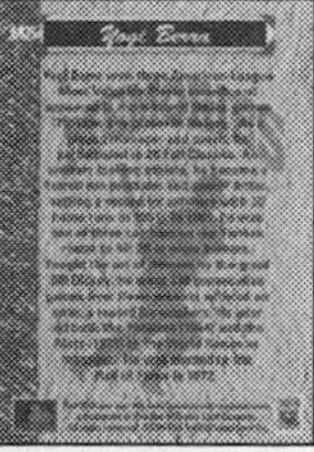

Randomly inserted only in hobby packs, this special regional insert set was sold on a regional basis, highlighting four great teams of the past. This year's set captures the 1954 New York Giants (M21-M24), the 1961 New York Yankees (M25-M28), the 1968 Detroit Tigers (M29-M32), and the 1975 Boston Red Sox (M33-M36). The numbering on the backs is in continuation of last year's Memories insert series.

	MINT	NRMT
COMPLETE SET (17)	40.00	18.00
COMMON CARD (M21-M37)	1.00	.45
☐ M21 Monte Irvin	3.00	1.35
☐ M22 Sal Maglie	2.50	1.10
☐ M23 Dusty Rhodes	1.50	.70
☐ M24 Hank Thompson	1.50	.70
☐ M25 Yogi Berra	5.00	2.20
☐ M26 Elston Howard	4.00	1.80
☐ M27 Roger Maris	6.00	2.70
☐ M28 Bobby Richardson	2.50	1.10
☐ M29 Norm Cash	2.50	1.10
☐ M30 Al Kaline	6.00	2.70
☐ M31 Mickey Lolich	2.00	.90
☐ M32 Denny McLain	2.50	1.10
☐ M33 Bernie Carbo	1.50	.70
☐ M34 Fred Lynn	2.00	.90
☐ M35 Rico Petrocelli	2.00	.90
☐ M36 Luis Tiant	2.00	.90
☐ M37 Checklist	1.00	.45

1994 Ted Williams Mike Schmidt

Randomly inserted one per jumbo pack, this nine-card standard-size set highlights the career of Mike Schmidt. The fronts display full-bleed color player photos that have a textured appearance. On a background consisting of a red, white, and blue flag, a ghosted panel summarizes his career by presenting various highlights.

	MINT	NRMT
COMPLETE SET (9)	6.00	2.70
COMMON CARD (MS1-MS8)	.75	.35
☐ MS1 Mike Schmidt Mike	.75	.35
☐ MS2 Mike Schmidt The White House	.75	.35
☐ MS3 Mike Schmidt Soaping Up	.75	.35
☐ MS4 Mike Schmidt The Promised Land	.75	.35
☐ MS5 Mike Schmidt Who is Who	.75	.35
☐ MS6 Mike Schmidt The Call	.75	.35
☐ MS7 Mike Schmidt Leading The Way	.75	.35
☐ MS8 Mike Schmidt Award Winner	.75	.35
☐ MS9 Checklist	.50	.23

1994 Ted Williams Roger Maris

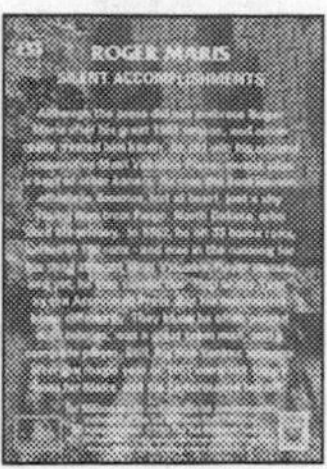

Randomly inserted in foil packs, this nine-card standard-size set highlights the career of Roger Maris. The full-color photos on the fronts are partly full-bleed and partly edged by jagged bronze borders. When placed in a 9-card plastic sheet, the background on the backs form a composite "Etched in Stone" logo. The text overprinted on the backs summarize Maris' career from amateur baseball until his untimely death in 1985. A red foil version of this set was also produced. The values are the same as those listed below.

	MINT	NRMT
COMPLETE SET (9)	12.00	5.50
COMMON CARD (ES1-ES8)	1.50	.70
☐ ES1 Roger Maris Scouting Report	1.50	.70
☐ ES2 Roger Maris Traded	1.50	.70
☐ ES3 Roger Maris Career Year	1.50	.70
☐ ES4 Roger Maris 1961	1.50	.70
☐ ES5 Roger Maris Silent Accomplishments	1.50	.70
☐ ES6 Roger Maris Team Player	1.50	.70
☐ ES7 Roger Maris Reborn	1.50	.70
☐ ES8 Roger Maris Hero's Welcome	1.50	.70
☐ ES9 Roger Maris Checklist	1.00	.45

1994 Ted Williams Trade for Babe

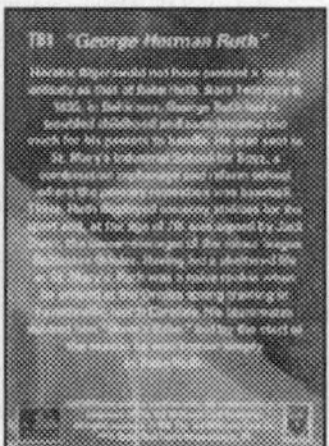

A special "Trade for Babe" chase card was randomly inserted throughout the packs. By mailing in the trade card plus 4.50 for shipping and handling, the collector received this nine-card standard-size set. The fronts display full-bleed colorized photos while the text on the backs highlight various turning points in his career or aspects of his personality.

	MINT	NRMT
COMPLETE SET (9)	40.00	18.00
COMMON CARD (T1-T8)	5.00	2.20
☐ T1 Babe Ruth German Herman Ruth	5.00	2.20
☐ T2 Babe Ruth King of the Hill	5.00	2.20
☐ T3 Babe Ruth On to New York	5.00	2.20
☐ T4 Babe Ruth Called Shot?	5.00	2.20
☐ T5 Babe Ruth The Bambino and The Iron Horse	5.00	2.20
☐ T6 Babe Ruth Larger Than Life	5.00	2.20
☐ T7 Babe Ruth Always a Yankee	5.00	2.20
☐ T8 Babe Ruth The Babe	5.00	2.20
☐ T9 Babe Ruth Checklist	4.00	1.80
☐ NNO0 Trade Card	4.00	1.80

1978 Tigers Burger King

The cards in this 23-card set measure 2 1/2" by 3 1/2". Twenty-three color cards, 22 players and one numbered

checklist, comprise the 1978 Burger King Tigers set issued in the Detroit area. The cards marked with an asterisk contain photos different from those appearing on the Topps regular issue cards of that year. For example, Jack Morris, Alan Trammell, and Lou Whitaker (in the 1978 Topps regular issue cards) each appear on rookie prospect cards with three other young players; whereas in this Burger King set, each has his own individual card.

	NRMT	VG-E
COMPLETE SET (23)	50.00	22.00
COMMON CARD (1-22)	.25	.11
☐ 1 Ralph Houk MG	.75	.35
☐ 2 Milt May	.25	.11
☐ 3 John Wockenfuss	.25	.11
☐ 4 Mark Fidrych	.75	.35
☐ 5 Dave Rozema	.25	.11
☐ 6 Jack Billingham *	.25	.11
☐ 7 Jim Slaton *	.25	.11
☐ 8 Jack Morris *	7.50	3.40
☐ 9 John Hiller	.50	.23
☐ 10 Steve Foucault	.25	.11
☐ 11 Milt Wilcox	.25	.11
☐ 12 Jason Thompson	.75	.35
☐ 13 Lou Whitaker *	12.50	5.50
☐ 14 Aurelio Rodriguez	.25	.11
☐ 15 Alan Trammell *	25.00	11.00
☐ 16 Steve Dillard *	.25	.11
☐ 17 Phil Mankowski	.25	.11
☐ 18 Steve Kemp	.50	.23
☐ 19 Ron LeFlore	.75	.35
☐ 20 Tim Corcoran	.25	.11
☐ 21 Mickey Stanley	.75	.35
☐ 22 Rusty Staub	1.25	.55
☐ NNO Checklist Card TP	.15	.07

1985 Tigers Wendy's/Coke

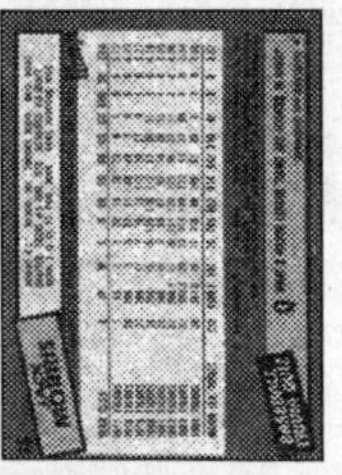

This 22-card standard-size set features Detroit Tigers. The set was co-sponsored by Wendy's and Coca-Cola and was distributed in the Detroit metropolitan area. Coca-Cola purchasers were given a pack which contained three Tiger cards plus a header card. The orange-bordered player photos are different from those used by Topps in their regular set. The cards were produced by Topps as evidenced by the similarity of the card backs with the Topps regular set backs. The set is numbered on the back; the order corresponds to the alphabetical order of the player's names.

	NRMT	VG-E
COMPLETE SET (22)	6.00	2.70
COMMON CARD (1-22)	.10	.05
☐ 1 Sparky Anderson MG (Checklist back)	.50	.23
☐ 2 Doug Bair	.10	.05
☐ 3 Juan Berenguer	.10	.05
☐ 4 Dave Bergman	.10	.05
☐ 5 Tom Brookens	.10	.05
☐ 6 Marty Castillo	.10	.05
☐ 7 Darrell Evans	.35	.16
☐ 8 Barbaro Garbey	.10	.05
☐ 9 Kirk Gibson	1.25	.55
☐ 10 Johnny Grubb	.10	.05
☐ 11 Willie Hernandez	.20	.09
☐ 12 Larry Herndon	.10	.05
☐ 13 Rusty Kuntz	.10	.05
☐ 14 Chet Lemon	.20	.09
☐ 15 Aurelio Lopez	.10	.05
☐ 16 Jack Morris	1.25	.55
☐ 17 Lance Parrish	.50	.23
☐ 18 Dan Petry	.20	.09
☐ 19 Bill Scherrer	.10	.05
☐ 20 Alan Trammell	2.50	1.10
☐ 21 Lou Whitaker	1.50	.70
☐ 22 Milt Wilcox	.10	.05

1947 Tip Top

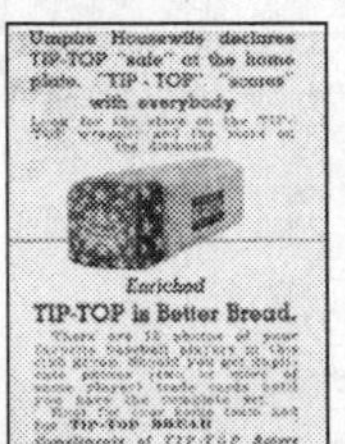

The cards in this 163-card set measure approximately 2 1/4" by 3". The 1947 Tip Top Bread issue contains unnumbered cards with black and white player photos. The set is of interest to baseball historians in that it contains cards of many players not appearing in any other card sets. The cards were issued locally for the eleven following teams: Red Sox (1-15), White Sox (16-30), Tigers (31-45), Yankees (46-60), Browns (61-75), Braves (76-90), Dodgers (91-104), Cubs (105-119), Giants (120-135), Pirates (136-149), and Cardinals (150-164). Players of the Red Sox, Tigers, White Sox, Braves, and the Cubs are scarcer than those of the other teams; players from these tougher teams are marked by SP below to indicate their scarcity. The catalog designation is D323. These unnumbered cards are listed in alphabetical order within teams (with teams also alphabetized within league) for convenience.

	EX-MT	VG-E
COMPLETE SET (163)	9000.00	4000.00
COMMON CARD (1-164)	25.00	11.00
COMMON SP PLAYER	75.00	34.00
☐ 1 Leon Culberson SP	75.00	34.00
☐ 2 Dom DiMaggio SP	150.00	70.00
☐ 3 Joe Dobson SP	75.00	34.00
☐ 4 Bob Doerr SP	300.00	135.00
☐ 5 Dave(Boo) Ferris SP	75.00	34.00
☐ 6 Mickey Harris SP	75.00	34.00
☐ 7 Frank Hayes SP	75.00	34.00
☐ 8 Cecil Hughson SP	75.00	34.00
☐ 9 Earl Johnson SP	75.00	34.00
☐ 10 Roy Partee SP	75.00	34.00
☐ 11 Johnny Pesky SP	90.00	40.00
☐ 12 Rip Russell SP	75.00	34.00
☐ 13 Hal Wagner SP	75.00	34.00
☐ 14 Rudy York SP	90.00	40.00
☐ 15 Bill Zuber SP	75.00	34.00
☐ 16 Floyd Baker SP	75.00	34.00
☐ 17 Earl Caldwell SP	75.00	34.00
☐ 18 Loyd Christopher SP	75.00	34.00
☐ 19 George Dickey SP	75.00	34.00
☐ 20 Ralph Hodgin SP	75.00	34.00
☐ 21 Bob Kennedy SP	75.00	34.00
☐ 22 Joe Kuhel SP	75.00	34.00
☐ 23 Thornton Lee SP	75.00	34.00
☐ 24 Ed Lopat SP	125.00	55.00
☐ 25 Cass Michaels SP	75.00	34.00
☐ 26 John Rigney SP	75.00	34.00
☐ 27 Mike Tresh SP	75.00	34.00
☐ 28 Thurman Tucker SP	75.00	34.00
☐ 29 Jack Wallasca SP	75.00	34.00
☐ 30 Taft Wright SP	75.00	34.00
☐ 31 Walter(Hoot)Evers SP	75.00	34.00
☐ 32 John Gorsica SP	75.00	34.00
☐ 33 Fred Hutchinson SP	90.00	40.00
☐ 34 George Kell SP	400.00	180.00
☐ 35 Eddie Lake SP	75.00	34.00
☐ 36 Ed Mayo SP	75.00	34.00
☐ 37 Arthur Mills SP	75.00	34.00
☐ 38 Pat Mullin SP	75.00	34.00
☐ 39 James Outlaw SP	75.00	34.00
☐ 40 Frank Overmire SP	75.00	34.00
☐ 41 Bob Swift SP	75.00	34.00
☐ 42 Birdie Tebbetts SP	75.00	34.00
☐ 43 Dizzy Trout SP	90.00	40.00
☐ 44 Virgil Trucks SP	90.00	40.00
☐ 45 Dick Wakefield SP	75.00	34.00
☐ 46 Yogi Berra (Listed as Larry on card)	400.00	180.00
☐ 47 Floyd(Bill) Bevans	25.00	11.00
☐ 48 Bobby Brown	30.00	13.50
☐ 49 Thomas Byrne	25.00	11.00
☐ 50 Frank Crosetti	35.00	16.00
☐ 51 Tom Henrich	35.00	16.00
☐ 52 Charlie Keller	35.00	16.00
☐ 53 Johnny Lindell	25.00	11.00
☐ 54 Joe Page	30.00	13.50
☐ 55 Mel Queen	25.00	11.00
☐ 56 Allie Reynolds	35.00	16.00
☐ 57 Phil Rizzuto	150.00	70.00
☐ 58 Aaron Robinson	25.00	11.00
☐ 59 George Stirnweiss	25.00	11.00
☐ 60 Charles Wensloff	25.00	11.00
☐ 61 John Berardino	35.00	16.00
☐ 62 Clifford Fannin	25.00	11.00
☐ 63 Dennis Galehouse	25.00	11.00
☐ 64 Jeff Heath	25.00	11.00
☐ 65 Walter Judnich	25.00	11.00
☐ 66 Jack Kramer	25.00	11.00
☐ 67 Paul Lehner	25.00	11.00
☐ 68 Lester Moss	25.00	11.00
☐ 69 Bob Muncrief	25.00	11.00
☐ 70 Nelson Potter	25.00	11.00
☐ 71 Fred Sanford	25.00	11.00
☐ 72 Joe Schultz	25.00	11.00
☐ 73 Vern Stephens	30.00	13.50
☐ 74 Jerry Witte	25.00	11.00
☐ 75 Al Zarilla	25.00	11.00
☐ 76 Charles Barrett SP	75.00	34.00
☐ 77 Hank Camelli SP	75.00	34.00
☐ 78 Dick Culler SP	75.00	34.00
☐ 79 Nanny Fernandez SP	75.00	34.00
☐ 80 Si Johnson SP	75.00	34.00
☐ 81 Danny Litwhiler SP	75.00	34.00
☐ 82 Phil Masi SP	75.00	34.00
☐ 83 Carvel Rowell SP	75.00	34.00
☐ 84 Connie Ryan SP	75.00	34.00
☐ 85 John Sain SP	125.00	55.00
☐ 86 Ray Sanders SP	75.00	34.00
☐ 87 Sibby Sisti SP	75.00	34.00
☐ 88 Billy Southworth SP MG	90.00	40.00
☐ 89 Warren Spahn SP	500.00	220.00
☐ 90 Ed Wright SP	75.00	34.00
☐ 91 Bob Bragan	30.00	13.50
☐ 92 Ralph Branca	30.00	13.50
☐ 93 Hugh Casey	25.00	11.00
☐ 94 Bruce Edwards	25.00	11.00
☐ 95 Hal Gregg	25.00	11.00
☐ 96 Joe Hatten	25.00	11.00
☐ 97 Gene Hermanski	25.00	11.00
☐ 98 John Jorgensen	25.00	11.00
☐ 99 Harry Lavagetto	30.00	13.50
☐ 100 Vic Lombardi	25.00	11.00
☐ 101 Frank Melton	25.00	11.00
☐ 102 Ed Miksis	25.00	11.00
☐ 103 Marv Rackley	25.00	11.00
☐ 104 Ed Stevens	25.00	11.00
☐ 105 Phil Cavarretta SP	125.00	55.00
☐ 106 Bob Chipman SP	75.00	34.00
☐ 107 Stan Hack SP	90.00	40.00
☐ 108 Don Johnson SP	75.00	34.00
☐ 109 Emil Kush SP	75.00	34.00
☐ 110 Bill Lee SP	90.00	40.00
☐ 111 Mickey Livingston SP	75.00	34.00
☐ 112 Harry Lowrey SP	75.00	34.00
☐ 113 Clyde McCullough SP	75.00	34.00
☐ 114 Andy Pafko SP	90.00	40.00
☐ 115 Marv Rickert SP	75.00	34.00
☐ 116 John Schmitz SP	75.00	34.00
☐ 117 Bobby Sturgeon SP	75.00	34.00
☐ 118 Ed Waitkus SP	90.00	40.00
☐ 119 Henry Wyse SP	75.00	34.00
☐ 120 Bill Ayers	25.00	11.00
☐ 121 Buddy Blattner	25.00	11.00
☐ 122 Mike Budnick	25.00	11.00
☐ 123 Sid Gordon	25.00	11.00
☐ 124 Clint Hartung	25.00	11.00
☐ 125 Monte Kennedy	25.00	11.00
☐ 126 Dave Koslo	25.00	11.00
☐ 127 Whitey Lockman	30.00	13.50
☐ 128 Jack Lohrke	25.00	11.00
☐ 129 Ernie Lombardi	75.00	34.00
☐ 130 Willard Marshall	25.00	11.00
☐ 131 John Mize	125.00	55.00
☐ 132 Eugene Thompson (Does not exist)		
☐ 133 Ken Trinkle	25.00	11.00
☐ 134 Bill Voiselle	25.00	11.00
☐ 135 Mickey Witek	25.00	11.00
☐ 136 Eddie Basinski	25.00	11.00
☐ 137 Ernie Bonham	25.00	11.00
☐ 138 Billy Cox	30.00	13.50
☐ 139 Elbie Fletcher	25.00	11.00
☐ 140 Frank Gustine	25.00	11.00

☐ 141 Kirby Higbe	25.00	11.00
☐ 142 Leroy Jarvis	25.00	11.00
☐ 143 Ralph Kiner	125.00	55.00
☐ 144 Fred Ostermueller	25.00	11.00
☐ 145 Preacher Roe	35.00	16.00
☐ 146 Jim Russell	25.00	11.00
☐ 147 Rip Sewell	25.00	11.00
☐ 148 Nick Strincevich	25.00	11.00
☐ 149 Honus Wagner CO	125.00	55.00
☐ 150 Alpha Brazle	25.00	11.00
☐ 151 Ken Burkhart	25.00	11.00
☐ 152 Bernard Creger	25.00	11.00
☐ 153 Joffre Cross	25.00	11.00
☐ 154 Chuck Diering	25.00	11.00
☐ 155 Ervin Dusak	25.00	11.00
☐ 156 Joe Garagiola	75.00	34.00
☐ 157 Tony Kaufmann	25.00	11.00
☐ 158 Whitey Kurowski	25.00	11.00
☐ 159 Marty Marion	35.00	16.00
☐ 160 George Munger	25.00	11.00
☐ 161 Del Rice	25.00	11.00
☐ 162 Dick Sisler	30.00	13.50
☐ 163 Enos Slaughter	125.00	55.00
☐ 164 Ted Wilks	25.00	11.00

1994 Tombstone Pizza

Produced by Michael Schlechter Associates for Pinnacle and sponsored by Tombstone Pizza, this 30-card standard-size set showcases 15 of the hottest players from the National (1-15) and American (16-30) Leagues. The promotion ran from May 15 to July 4, 1994, or while supplies lasted. One card was packaged in each Tombstone pizza. Collectors could obtain the complete set by sending in five proofs-of-purchase and 1.00 for shipping and handling. The fronts feature color action player photos on a black background with thin green borders. The words "'94 Tombstone Super-Pro Series" are printed in orange letters above the picture, while the player's name and team name along with the sponsor's logo appear under the picture. The horizontal backs carry a color player portrait with the player's name and position, biography and statistics, and a facsimile autograph. Like most MSA sets, the team logos have been airbrushed away. The cards are arranged alphabetically within each league.

	MINT	NRMT
COMPLETE SET (30)	18.00	8.00
COMMON CARD (1-30)	.15	.07
☐ 1 Jeff Bagwell	1.25	.55
☐ 2 Jay Bell	.15	.07
☐ 3 Barry Bonds	.75	.35
☐ 4 Bobby Bonilla	.25	.11
☐ 5 Andres Galarraga	.60	.25
☐ 6 Mark Grace	.60	.25
☐ 7 Marquis Grissom	.25	.11
☐ 8 Tony Gwynn	1.50	.70
☐ 9 Bryan Harvey	.15	.07
☐ 10 Gregg Jefferies	.15	.07
☐ 11 David Justice	.60	.25
☐ 12 John Kruk	.25	.11
☐ 13 Barry Larkin	.40	.18
☐ 14 Greg Maddux	2.50	1.10
☐ 15 Mike Piazza	2.50	1.10
☐ 16 Jim Abbott	.15	.07
☐ 17 Albert Belle	1.25	.55
☐ 18 Cecil Fielder	.25	.11
☐ 19 Juan Gonzalez	2.00	.90
☐ 20 Mike Greenwell	.15	.07
☐ 21 Ken Griffey Jr.	4.00	1.80
☐ 22 Jack McDowell	.15	.07
☐ 23 Jeff Montgomery	.15	.07
☐ 24 John Olerud	.25	.11
☐ 25 Kirby Puckett	1.50	.70
☐ 26 Cal Ripken	3.00	1.35
☐ 27 Tim Salmon	.75	.35
☐ 28 Ruben Sierra	.15	.07
☐ 29 Frank Thomas	3.00	1.35
☐ 30 Robin Yount	.60	.25

1995 Tombstone Pizza

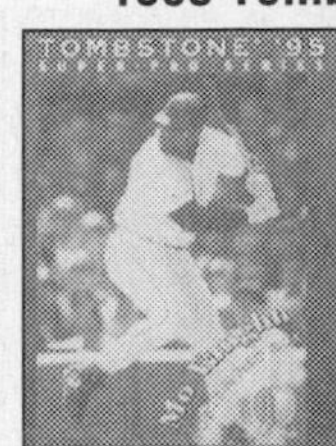

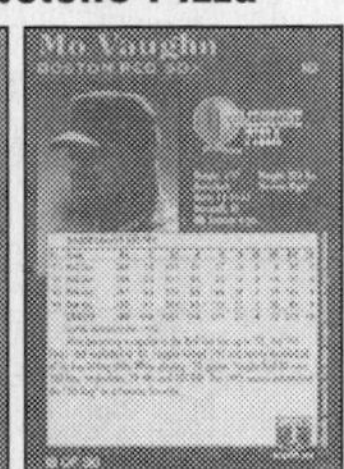

This 30-card standard-size set features 15 of the hottest players each from the National and the American Leagues. One card was packaged in each Tombstone Pizza. Six thousand classic player cards, autographed by Johnny Bench, George Brett or Bob Gibson, were randomly packed. Collectors who pulled one of these autograph cards could receive an 8 1/2" by 11" certificate of authenticity through a mail-in offer. Also collectors could obtain the complete set by sending in five proofs-of-purchase. The limit was two sets per family or address, and the offer expired December 31, 1995, or while supplies lasted. The cards are numbered on the back "X of 30."

	MINT	NRMT
COMPLETE SET (30)	15.00	6.75
COMMON CARD (1-30)	.15	.07
☐ 1 Frank Thomas	3.00	1.35
☐ 2 David Cone	.30	.14
☐ 3 Bob Hamelin	.15	.07
☐ 4 Jeff Bagwell	1.50	.70
☐ 5 Greg Maddux	2.50	1.10
☐ 6 Raul Mondesi	.75	.35
☐ 7 Chili Davis	.30	.14
☐ 8 Cecil Fielder	.30	.14
☐ 9 Ken Griffey Jr.	4.00	1.80
☐ 10 Jimmy Key	.30	.14
☐ 11 Kenny Lofton	.75	.35
☐ 12 Paul Molitor	.75	.35
☐ 13 Kirby Puckett	2.00	.90
☐ 14 Cal Ripken	3.00	1.35
☐ 15 Ivan Rodriguez	.75	.35
☐ 16 Kevin Seitzer	.15	.07
☐ 17 Ruben Sierra	.15	.07
☐ 18 Mo Vaughn	.75	.35
☐ 19 Moises Alou	.30	.14
☐ 20 Barry Bonds	1.00	.45
☐ 21 Jeff Conine	.30	.14
☐ 22 Lenny Dykstra	.30	.14
☐ 23 Andres Galarraga	.75	.35
☐ 24 Tony Gwynn	1.50	.70
☐ 25 Barry Larkin	.50	.23
☐ 26 Fred McGriff	.50	.23
☐ 27 Orlando Merced	.15	.07
☐ 28 Bret Saberhagen	.15	.07
☐ 29 Ozzie Smith	1.00	.45
☐ 30 Sammy Sosa	.75	.35

1951 Topps Blue Backs

The cards in this 52-card set measure approximately 2" by 2 5/8". The 1951 Topps series of blue-backed baseball cards could be used to play a baseball game by shuffling the cards and drawing them from a pile. These cards (packaged two adjoined in a penny pack) were marketed with a piece of caramel candy, which often melted or was squashed in such a way as to damage the card and wrapper (despite the fact that a paper shield was inserted between candy and card). Blue Backs are more difficult to obtain than the similarly styled Red Backs. The set is denoted on the cards as "Set B" and the Red Back set is correspondingly Set A. The only notable Rookie Card in the set is Billy Pierce.

	NRMT	VG-E
COMPLETE SET (52)	1700.00	750.00
COMMON CARD (1-52)	30.00	13.50
WRAPPER (1-CENT)	200.00	90.00
☐ 1 Eddie Yost	60.00	18.00
☐ 2 Hank Majeski	30.00	13.50
☐ 3 Richie Ashburn	225.00	100.00
☐ 4 Del Ennis	35.00	16.00
☐ 5 Johnny Pesky	35.00	16.00
☐ 6 Red Schoendienst	100.00	45.00
☐ 7 Gerry Staley	30.00	13.50
☐ 8 Dick Sisler	30.00	13.50
☐ 9 Johnny Sain	50.00	22.00
☐ 10 Joe Page	35.00	16.00
☐ 11 Johnny Groth	30.00	13.50
☐ 12 Sam Jethroe	35.00	16.00
☐ 13 Mickey Vernon	35.00	16.00
☐ 14 Red Munger	30.00	13.50
☐ 15 Eddie Joost	30.00	13.50
☐ 16 Murry Dickson	30.00	13.50
☐ 17 Roy Smalley	30.00	13.50
☐ 18 Ned Garver	30.00	13.50
☐ 19 Phil Masi	30.00	13.50
☐ 20 Ralph Branca	50.00	22.00
☐ 21 Billy Johnson	30.00	13.50
☐ 22 Bob Kuzava	30.00	13.50
☐ 23 Dizzy Trout	35.00	16.00
☐ 24 Sherman Lollar	35.00	16.00
☐ 25 Sam Mele	30.00	13.50
☐ 26 Chico Carrasquel	35.00	16.00
☐ 27 Andy Pafko	35.00	16.00
☐ 28 Harry Brecheen	35.00	16.00
☐ 29 Granville Hamner	30.00	13.50
☐ 30 Enos Slaughter	100.00	45.00
☐ 31 Lou Brissie	30.00	13.50
☐ 32 Bob Elliott	35.00	16.00
☐ 33 Don Lenhardt	30.00	13.50
☐ 34 Earl Torgeson	30.00	13.50
☐ 35 Tommy Byrne	30.00	13.50
☐ 36 Cliff Fannin	30.00	13.50
☐ 37 Bobby Doerr	90.00	40.00
☐ 38 Irv Noren	35.00	16.00
☐ 39 Ed Lopat	45.00	20.00
☐ 40 Vic Wertz	35.00	16.00
☐ 41 Johnny Schmitz	30.00	13.50
☐ 42 Bruce Edwards	30.00	13.50
☐ 43 Willie Jones	30.00	13.50
☐ 44 Johnny Wyrostek	30.00	13.50
☐ 45 Billy Pierce	50.00	22.00
☐ 46 Gerry Priddy	30.00	13.50
☐ 47 Herman Wehmeier	30.00	13.50
☐ 48 Billy Cox	30.00	13.50
☐ 49 Hank Sauer	35.00	16.00
☐ 50 Johnny Mize	100.00	45.00
☐ 51 Eddie Waitkus	35.00	16.00
☐ 52 Sam Chapman	40.00	13.50

1951 Topps Red Backs

The cards in this 52-card set measure approximately 2" by 2 5/8". The 1951 Topps Red Back set is identical in style to the Blue Back set of the same year. The cards have rounded corners and were designed to be used as a baseball game. Zernial, number 36, is listed with either the White Sox or Athletics, and Holmes, number 52, with either the Braves or Hartford. The set is denoted on the cards as "Set A" and the Blue Back set is correspondingly Set B. The cards were packaged as two connected cards along with a piece of caramel in a penny pack. The most notable Rookie Card in the set is Monte Irvin.

	NRMT	VG-E
COMPLETE SET (54)	850.00	375.00
COMMON CARD (1-52)	10.00	4.50
WRAPPER (1-CENT)	5.00	2.20
☐ 1 Yogi Berra	125.00	45.00
☐ 2 Sid Gordon	10.00	4.50
☐ 3 Ferris Fain	12.00	5.50
☐ 4 Vern Stephens	12.00	5.50
☐ 5 Phil Rizzuto	60.00	27.00
☐ 6 Allie Reynolds	18.00	8.00
☐ 7 Howie Pollet	10.00	4.50

☐ 8 Early Wynn	25.00	11.00
☐ 9 Roy Sievers	12.00	5.50
☐ 10 Mel Parnell	12.00	5.50
☐ 11 Gene Hermanski	10.00	4.50
☐ 12 Jim Hegan	12.00	5.50
☐ 13 Dale Mitchell	12.00	5.50
☐ 14 Wayne Terwilliger	10.00	4.50
☐ 15 Ralph Kiner	25.00	11.00
☐ 16 Preacher Roe	12.00	5.50
☐ 17 Gus Bell	15.00	6.75
☐ 18 Jerry Coleman	15.00	6.75
☐ 19 Dick Kokos	10.00	4.50
☐ 20 Dom DiMaggio	18.00	8.00
☐ 21 Larry Jansen	12.00	5.50
☐ 22 Bob Feller	60.00	27.00
☐ 23 Ray Boone	15.00	6.75
☐ 24 Hank Bauer	18.00	8.00
☐ 25 Cliff Chambers	10.00	4.50
☐ 26 Luke Easter	12.00	5.50
☐ 27 Wally Westlake	10.00	4.50
☐ 28 Elmer Valo	10.00	4.50
☐ 29 Bob Kennedy	12.00	5.50
☐ 30 Warren Spahn	60.00	27.00
☐ 31 Gil Hodges	40.00	18.00
☐ 32 Henry Thompson	12.00	5.50
☐ 33 William Werle	10.00	4.50
☐ 34 Grady Hatton	10.00	4.50
☐ 35 Al Rosen	12.00	5.50
☐ 36A Gus Zernial (Chicago)	40.00	18.00
☐ 36B Gus Zernial (Philadelphia)	20.00	9.00
☐ 37 Wes Westrum	12.00	5.50
☐ 38 Duke Snider	60.00	27.00
☐ 39 Ted Kluszewski	20.00	9.00
☐ 40 Mike Garcia	12.00	5.50
☐ 41 Whitey Lockman	12.00	5.50
☐ 42 Ray Scarborough	10.00	4.50
☐ 43 Maurice McDermott	10.00	4.50
☐ 44 Sid Hudson	10.00	4.50
☐ 45 Andy Seminick	10.00	4.50
☐ 46 Billy Goodman	12.00	5.50
☐ 47 Tommy Glaviano	10.00	4.50
☐ 48 Eddie Stanky	12.00	5.50
☐ 49 Al Zarilla	10.00	4.50
☐ 50 Monte Irvin	40.00	18.00
☐ 51 Eddie Robinson	10.00	4.50
☐ 52A Tommy Holmes (Boston)	40.00	10.00
☐ 52B Tommy Holmes (Hartford)	25.00	6.25

1951 Topps Connie Mack All-Stars

The cards in this 11-card set measure approximately 2 1/16" by 5 1/4". The series of die-cut cards which comprise the set entitled Connie Mack All-Stars was one of Topps' most distinctive and fragile card designs. Printed on thin cardboard, these elegant cards were protected in the wrapper by panels of accompanying Red Backs, but once removed were easily damaged (after all, they were intended to be folded and used as toy figures). Cards without tops have a value less than one-half of that listed below. The cards are unnumbered and are listed below in alphabetical order.

	NRMT	VG-E
COMPLETE SET (11)	7000.00	3200.00
COMMON CARD (1-11)	150.00	70.00
WRAPPER (1-CENT)	350.00	160.00

☐ 1 Grover C. Alexander	400.00	180.00
☐ 2 Mickey Cochrane	300.00	135.00
☐ 3 Eddie Collins	150.00	70.00
☐ 4 Jimmy Collins	150.00	70.00
☐ 5 Lou Gehrig	2000.00	900.00
☐ 6 Walter Johnson	650.00	300.00
☐ 7 Connie Mack	350.00	160.00
☐ 8 Christy Mathewson	425.00	190.00
☐ 9 Babe Ruth	2500.00	1100.00
☐ 10 Tris Speaker	150.00	70.00
☐ 11 Honus Wagner	400.00	180.00

1951 Topps Current All-Stars

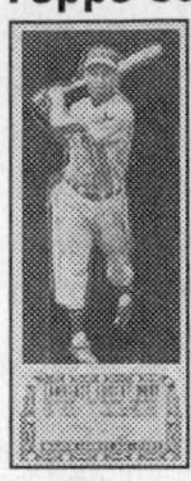

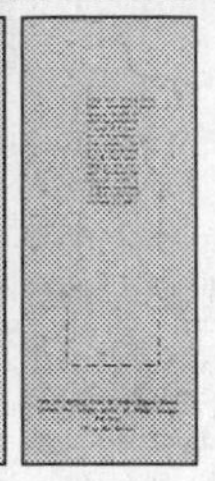

The cards in this 11-card set measure approximately 2 1/16" by 5 1/4". The 1951 Topps Current All-Star series is probably the rarest of all legitimate, nationally issued, post war baseball issues. The set price listed below does not include the prices for the cards of Konstanty, Roberts and Stanky, which likely never were released to the public in gum packs. These three cards (SP in the checklist below) were probably obtained directly from the company and exist in extremely limited numbers. As with the Connie Mack set, cards without the die-cut background are worth half of the value listed below. The cards are unnumbered and are listed below in alphabetical order. These cards were issued in two card packs (one being a Current AS the other being a Topps Team card).

	NRMT	VG-E
COMPLETE SET (8)	4500.00	2000.00
COMMON CARD (1-11)	250.00	110.00
WRAPPER (1-CENT)	500.00	220.00

☐ 1 Yogi Berra	1500.00	700.00
☐ 2 Larry Doby	325.00	145.00
☐ 3 Walt Dropo	250.00	110.00
☐ 4 Hoot Evers	250.00	110.00
☐ 5 George Kell	600.00	275.00
☐ 6 Ralph Kiner	750.00	350.00
☐ 7 Jim Konstanty SP	12500.00	5600.00
☐ 8 Bob Lemon	600.00	275.00
☐ 9 Phil Rizzuto	750.00	350.00
☐ 10 Robin Roberts SP	15000.00	6800.00
☐ 11 Eddie Stanky SP	12500.00	5600.00

1951 Topps Teams

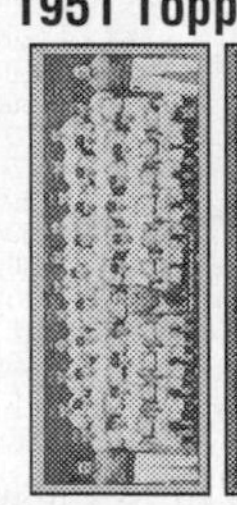

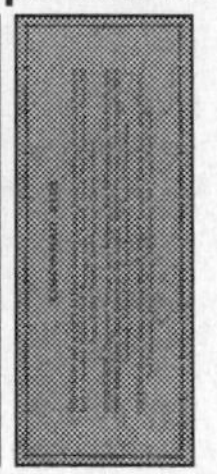

The cards in this nine-card set measure approximately 2 1/16" by 5 1/4". These unnumbered team cards issued by Topps in 1951 carry black and white photographs framed by a yellow border. These cards were issued in the same five-cent wrapper as the Connie Mack and Current All Stars. They have been assigned reference numbers in the checklist alphabetically by team city and name. They are found with or without "1950" printed in the name panel before the team name. Although the dated variations are slightly more difficult to find, there is usually no difference in value.

	NRMT	VG-E
COMPLETE SET (9)	2250.00	1000.00
COMMON TEAM (1-9)	200.00	90.00

☐ 1 Boston Red Sox	400.00	180.00
☐ 2 Brooklyn Dodgers	375.00	170.00
☐ 3 Chicago White Sox	200.00	90.00
☐ 4 Cincinnati Reds	200.00	90.00
☐ 5 New York Giants	250.00	110.00
☐ 6 Philadelphia Athletics	200.00	90.00
☐ 7 Philadelphia Phillies	200.00	90.00
☐ 8 St. Louis Cardinals	350.00	160.00
☐ 9 Washington Senators	200.00	90.00

1952 Topps

The cards in this 407-card set measure approximately 2 5/8" by 3 3/4". The 1952 Topps set is Topps' first truly major set. Card numbers 1 to 80 were issued with red or black backs, both of which are less plentiful than card numbers 81 to 250. In fact, the first series is considered the most difficult with respect to finding perfect condition cards. Card number 48 (Joe Page) and number 49 (Johnny Sain) can be found with each other's write-up on their back. However, many dealers today believe that all cards numbered 1-250 are valued the same. Card numbers 251 to 310 are somewhat scarce and numbers 311 to 407 are quite scarce. Cards 281-300 were single printed compared to the other cards in the next to last series. Cards 311-313 were double printed on the last high number printing sheet. The key card in the set is obviously Mickey Mantle, number 311, Mickey's first of many Topps cards. A really obscure variation on cards from 311 through 313 is that they exist with the stitching on the number circle in the back either clockwise or counter clockwise. There is no price differential for either variation. Card #307, Frank Campos has been discovered to have a black star next to the words "Topps Baseball" on the back. This card is very scarce but since it is rarely traded in the secondary market -- no value can be established at this time. Many collectors are not aware of this variation. In the early 1980's, Topps issued a standard-size reprint set of the 52 Topps set. These cards were issued only as a factory set and have a current market value of between two and three hundred dollars. Five people portrayed in the regular set: Billy Loes (#20), Dom DiMaggio (#22), Saul Rogovin (#159), Solly Hemus (#196) and Tommy Holmes (#289) are not in the reprint set. Although rarely seen, there exist salesman sample panels of three cards containing the fronts of regular cards with ad information on the back. Two such panels seen are Bob Mahoney/Robin Roberts/Sid Hudson and Wally Westlake/Dizzy Trout/Irv Noren. The cards were issued in one-card penny packs and six-card nickle packs. The key Rookie Cards in this set are Billy Martin, Eddie Mathews (the last card in the set), and Hoyt Wilhelm.

	NRMT	VG-E
COMPLETE SET (407)	65000.00	29200.00
COMMON CARD (1-80)	50.00	22.00
*RED/BLACK BACKS 1-80 SAME VALUE		
COMMON CARD (81-250)	35.00	16.00
COMMON CARD (251-310)	50.00	22.00
COMMON CARD (311-407)	250.00	110.00
WRAPPER (1-cent)	250.00	110.00
WRAPPER (5-cent)	100.00	45.00

☐ 1 Andy Pafko	1200.00	120.00
☐ 2 Pete Runnels	100.00	45.00
☐ 3 Hank Thompson	60.00	27.00
☐ 4 Don Lenhardt	50.00	22.00
☐ 5 Larry Jansen	60.00	27.00
☐ 6 Grady Hatton	50.00	22.00
☐ 7 Wayne Terwilliger	50.00	22.00
☐ 8 Fred Marsh	50.00	22.00
☐ 9 Robert Hogue	50.00	22.00
☐ 10 Al Rosen	60.00	27.00
☐ 11 Phil Rizzuto	200.00	90.00
☐ 12 Monty Basgall	50.00	22.00
☐ 13 Johnny Wyrostek	50.00	22.00
☐ 14 Bob Elliott	60.00	27.00
☐ 15 Johnny Pesky	60.00	27.00
☐ 16 Gene Hermanski	50.00	22.00
☐ 17 Jim Hegan	60.00	27.00
☐ 18 Merrill Combs	50.00	22.00
☐ 19 Johnny Bucha	50.00	22.00
☐ 20 Billy Loes	120.00	55.00
☐ 21 Ferris Fain	60.00	27.00
☐ 22 Dom DiMaggio	80.00	36.00
☐ 23 Billy Goodman	60.00	27.00
☐ 24 Luke Easter	60.00	27.00
☐ 25 Johnny Groth	50.00	22.00
☐ 26 Monte Irvin	100.00	45.00
☐ 27 Sam Jethroe	60.00	27.00
☐ 28 Jerry Priddy	50.00	22.00
☐ 29 Ted Kluszewski	100.00	45.00
☐ 30 Mel Parnell	60.00	27.00
☐ 31 Gus Zernial Posed with seven baseballs	80.00	36.00

☐ 32 Eddie Robinson	50.00	22.00
☐ 33 Warren Spahn	200.00	90.00
☐ 34 Elmer Valo	50.00	22.00
☐ 35 Hank Sauer	60.00	27.00
☐ 36 Gil Hodges	175.00	80.00
☐ 37 Duke Snider	250.00	110.00
☐ 38 Wally Westlake	50.00	22.00
☐ 39 Dizzy Trout	60.00	27.00
☐ 40 Irv Noren	60.00	27.00
☐ 41 Bob Wellman	50.00	22.00
☐ 42 Lou Kretlow	50.00	22.00
☐ 43 Ray Scarborough	50.00	22.00
☐ 44 Con Dempsey	50.00	22.00
☐ 45 Eddie Joost	50.00	22.00
☐ 46 Gordon Goldsberry	50.00	22.00
☐ 47 Willie Jones	60.00	27.00
☐ 48A Joe Page COR	75.00	34.00
☐ 48B Joe Page ERR	275.00	125.00
(Bio for Sain)		
☐ 49A Johnny Sain COR	75.00	34.00
☐ 49B Johnny Sain ERR	275.00	125.00
(Bio for Page)		
☐ 50 Marv Rickert	50.00	22.00
☐ 51 Jim Russell	50.00	22.00
☐ 52 Don Mueller	60.00	27.00
☐ 53 Chris Van Cuyk	50.00	22.00
☐ 54 Leo Kiely	50.00	22.00
☐ 55 Ray Boone	60.00	27.00
☐ 56 Tommy Glaviano	50.00	22.00
☐ 57 Ed Lopat	80.00	36.00
☐ 58 Bob Mahoney	50.00	22.00
☐ 59 Robin Roberts	150.00	70.00
☐ 60 Sid Hudson	50.00	22.00
☐ 61 Tookie Gilbert	50.00	22.00
☐ 62 Chuck Stobbs	50.00	22.00
☐ 63 Howie Pollet	50.00	22.00
☐ 64 Roy Sievers	60.00	27.00
☐ 65 Enos Slaughter	150.00	70.00
☐ 66 Preacher Roe	80.00	36.00
☐ 67 Allie Reynolds	80.00	36.00
☐ 68 Cliff Chambers	50.00	22.00
☐ 69 Virgil Stallcup	50.00	22.00
☐ 70 Al Zarilla	50.00	22.00
☐ 71 Tom Upton	50.00	22.00
☐ 72 Karl Olson	50.00	22.00
☐ 73 Bill Werle	50.00	22.00
☐ 74 Andy Hansen	50.00	22.00
☐ 75 Wes Westrum	60.00	27.00
☐ 76 Eddie Stanky	60.00	27.00
☐ 77 Bob Kennedy	60.00	27.00
☐ 78 Ellis Kinder	50.00	22.00
☐ 79 Gerry Staley	50.00	22.00
☐ 80 Herman Wehmeier	50.00	22.00
☐ 81 Vernon Law	50.00	22.00
☐ 82 Duane Pillette	35.00	16.00
☐ 83 Billy Johnson	35.00	16.00
☐ 84 Vern Stephens	50.00	22.00
☐ 85 Bob Kuzava	50.00	22.00
☐ 86 Ted Gray	35.00	16.00
☐ 87 Dale Coogan	35.00	16.00
☐ 88 Bob Feller	200.00	90.00
☐ 89 Johnny Lipon	35.00	16.00
☐ 90 Mickey Grasso	35.00	16.00
☐ 91 Red Schoendienst	80.00	36.00
☐ 92 Dale Mitchell	50.00	22.00
☐ 93 Al Sima	35.00	16.00
☐ 94 Sam Mele	35.00	16.00
☐ 95 Ken Holcombe	35.00	16.00
☐ 96 Willard Marshall	35.00	16.00
☐ 97 Earl Torgeson	35.00	16.00
☐ 98 Billy Pierce	50.00	22.00
☐ 99 Gene Woodling	60.00	27.00
☐ 100 Del Rice	35.00	16.00
☐ 101 Max Lanier	35.00	16.00
☐ 102 Bill Kennedy	35.00	16.00
☐ 103 Cliff Mapes	35.00	16.00
☐ 104 Don Kolloway	35.00	16.00
☐ 105 Johnny Pramesa	35.00	16.00
☐ 106 Mickey Vernon	60.00	27.00
☐ 107 Connie Ryan	35.00	16.00
☐ 108 Jim Konstanty	60.00	27.00
☐ 109 Ted Wilks	35.00	16.00
☐ 110 Dutch Leonard	35.00	16.00
☐ 111 Peanuts Lowrey	35.00	16.00
☐ 112 Hank Majeski	35.00	16.00
☐ 113 Dick Sisler	50.00	22.00
☐ 114 Willard Ramsdell	35.00	16.00
☐ 115 Red Munger	35.00	16.00
☐ 116 Carl Scheib	35.00	16.00
☐ 117 Sherm Lollar	50.00	22.00
☐ 118 Ken Raffensberger	35.00	16.00
☐ 119 Mickey McDermott	35.00	16.00
☐ 120 Bob Chakales	35.00	16.00
☐ 121 Gus Niarhos	35.00	16.00
☐ 122 Jackie Jensen	80.00	36.00
☐ 123 Eddie Yost	50.00	22.00
☐ 124 Monte Kennedy	35.00	16.00
☐ 125 Bill Rigney	35.00	16.00
☐ 126 Fred Hutchinson	50.00	22.00
☐ 127 Paul Minner	35.00	16.00
☐ 128 Don Bollweg	35.00	16.00
☐ 129 Johnny Mize	90.00	40.00
☐ 130 Sheldon Jones	35.00	16.00
☐ 131 Morrie Martin	35.00	16.00
☐ 132 Clyde Kluttz	35.00	16.00
☐ 133 Al Widmar	35.00	16.00
☐ 134 Joe Tipton	35.00	16.00
☐ 135 Dixie Howell	35.00	16.00
☐ 136 Johnny Schmitz	35.00	16.00
☐ 137 Roy McMillan	50.00	22.00
☐ 138 Bill MacDonald	35.00	16.00
☐ 139 Ken Wood	35.00	16.00
☐ 140 Johnny Antonelli	50.00	22.00
☐ 141 Clint Hartung	35.00	16.00
☐ 142 Harry Perkowski	35.00	16.00
☐ 143 Les Moss	35.00	16.00
☐ 144 Ed Blake	35.00	16.00
☐ 145 Joe Haynes	35.00	16.00
☐ 146 Frank House	35.00	16.00
☐ 147 Bob Young	35.00	16.00
☐ 148 Johnny Klippstein	35.00	16.00
☐ 149 Dick Kryhoski	35.00	16.00
☐ 150 Ted Beard	35.00	16.00
☐ 151 Wally Post	50.00	22.00
☐ 152 Al Evans	35.00	16.00
☐ 153 Bob Rush	35.00	16.00
☐ 154 Joe Muir	35.00	16.00
☐ 155 Frank Overmire	35.00	16.00
☐ 156 Frank Hiller	35.00	16.00
☐ 157 Bob Usher	35.00	16.00
☐ 158 Eddie Waitkus	35.00	16.00
☐ 159 Saul Rogovin	35.00	16.00
☐ 160 Owen Friend	35.00	16.00
☐ 161 Bud Byerly	35.00	16.00
☐ 162 Del Crandall	50.00	22.00
☐ 163 Stan Rojek	35.00	16.00
☐ 164 Walt Dubiel	35.00	16.00
☐ 165 Eddie Kazak	35.00	16.00
☐ 166 Paul LaPalme	35.00	16.00
☐ 167 Bill Howerton	35.00	16.00
☐ 168 Charlie Silvera	60.00	27.00
☐ 169 Howie Judson	35.00	16.00
☐ 170 Gus Bell	50.00	22.00
☐ 171 Ed Erautt	35.00	16.00
☐ 172 Eddie Miksis	35.00	16.00
☐ 173 Roy Smalley	35.00	16.00
☐ 174 Clarence Marshall	35.00	16.00
☐ 175 Billy Martin	300.00	135.00
☐ 176 Hank Edwards	35.00	16.00
☐ 177 Bill Wight	35.00	16.00
☐ 178 Cass Michaels	35.00	16.00
☐ 179 Frank Smith	35.00	16.00
☐ 180 Charlie Maxwell	50.00	22.00
☐ 181 Bob Swift	35.00	16.00
☐ 182 Billy Hitchcock	35.00	16.00
☐ 183 Erv Dusak	35.00	16.00
☐ 184 Bob Ramazzotti	35.00	16.00
☐ 185 Bill Nicholson	50.00	22.00
☐ 186 Walt Masterson	35.00	16.00
☐ 187 Bob Miller	35.00	16.00
☐ 188 Clarence Podbielan	35.00	16.00
☐ 189 Pete Reiser	60.00	27.00
☐ 190 Don Johnson	35.00	16.00
☐ 191 Yogi Berra	350.00	160.00
☐ 192 Myron Ginsberg	35.00	16.00
☐ 193 Harry Simpson	50.00	22.00
☐ 194 Joe Hatton	35.00	16.00
☐ 195 Minnie Minoso	150.00	70.00
☐ 196 Solly Hemus	60.00	27.00
☐ 197 George Strickland	35.00	16.00
☐ 198 Phil Haugstad	35.00	16.00
☐ 199 George Zuverink	35.00	16.00
☐ 200 Ralph Houk	80.00	36.00
☐ 201 Alex Kellner	35.00	16.00
☐ 202 Joe Collins	65.00	29.00
☐ 203 Curt Simmons	60.00	27.00
☐ 204 Ron Northey	35.00	16.00
☐ 205 Clyde King	60.00	27.00
☐ 206 Joe Ostrowski	35.00	16.00
☐ 207 Mickey Harris	35.00	16.00
☐ 208 Marlin Stuart	35.00	16.00
☐ 209 Howie Fox	35.00	16.00
☐ 210 Dick Fowler	35.00	16.00
☐ 211 Ray Coleman	35.00	16.00
☐ 212 Ned Garver	35.00	16.00
☐ 213 Nippy Jones	35.00	16.00
☐ 214 Johnny Hopp	50.00	22.00
☐ 215 Hank Bauer	65.00	29.00
☐ 216 Richie Ashburn	175.00	80.00
☐ 217 Snuffy Stirnweiss	50.00	22.00
☐ 218 Clyde McCullough	35.00	16.00
☐ 219 Bobby Shantz	60.00	27.00
☐ 220 Joe Presko	35.00	16.00
☐ 221 Granny Hamner	35.00	16.00
☐ 222 Hoot Evers	35.00	16.00
☐ 223 Del Ennis	50.00	22.00
☐ 224 Bruce Edwards	35.00	16.00
☐ 225 Frank Baumholtz	35.00	16.00
☐ 226 Dave Philley	35.00	16.00
☐ 227 Joe Garagiola	80.00	36.00
☐ 228 Al Brazle	35.00	16.00
☐ 229 Gene Bearden UER	35.00	16.00
(Misspelled Beardon)		
☐ 230 Matt Batts	35.00	16.00
☐ 231 Sam Zoldak	35.00	16.00
☐ 232 Billy Cox	50.00	22.00
☐ 233 Bob Friend	60.00	27.00
☐ 234 Steve Souchock	35.00	16.00
☐ 235 Walt Dropo	35.00	16.00
☐ 236 Ed Fitzgerald	35.00	16.00
☐ 237 Jerry Coleman	65.00	29.00
☐ 238 Art Houtteman	35.00	16.00
☐ 239 Rocky Bridges	50.00	22.00
☐ 240 Jack Phillips	35.00	16.00
☐ 241 Tommy Byrne	35.00	16.00
☐ 242 Tom Poholsky	35.00	16.00
☐ 243 Larry Doby	80.00	36.00
☐ 244 Vic Wertz	35.00	16.00
☐ 245 Sherry Robertson	35.00	16.00
☐ 246 George Kell	80.00	36.00
☐ 247 Randy Gumpert	35.00	16.00
☐ 248 Frank Shea	35.00	16.00
☐ 249 Bobby Adams	35.00	16.00
☐ 250 Carl Erskine	90.00	40.00
☐ 251 Chico Carrasquel	50.00	22.00
☐ 252 Vern Bickford	50.00	22.00
☐ 253 Johnny Berardino	75.00	34.00
☐ 254 Joe Dobson	50.00	22.00
☐ 255 Clyde Vollmer	50.00	22.00
☐ 256 Pete Suder	50.00	22.00
☐ 257 Bobby Avila	60.00	27.00
☐ 258 Steve Gromek	50.00	22.00
☐ 259 Bob Addis	50.00	22.00
☐ 260 Pete Castiglione	50.00	22.00
☐ 261 Willie Mays	2500.00	1100.00
☐ 262 Virgil Trucks	60.00	27.00
☐ 263 Harry Brecheen	60.00	27.00
☐ 264 Roy Hartsfield	50.00	22.00
☐ 265 Chuck Diering	50.00	22.00
☐ 266 Murry Dickson	50.00	22.00
☐ 267 Sid Gordon	60.00	27.00
☐ 268 Bob Lemon	150.00	70.00
☐ 269 Willard Nixon	50.00	22.00
☐ 270 Lou Brissie	50.00	22.00
☐ 271 Jim Delsing	50.00	22.00
☐ 272 Mike Garcia	60.00	27.00
☐ 273 Erv Palica	50.00	22.00
☐ 274 Ralph Branca	120.00	55.00
☐ 275 Pat Mullin	50.00	22.00
☐ 276 Jim Wilson	50.00	22.00
☐ 277 Early Wynn	150.00	70.00
☐ 278 Allie Clark	50.00	22.00
☐ 279 Eddie Stewart	50.00	22.00
☐ 280 Cloyd Boyer	60.00	27.00
☐ 281 Tommy Brown SP	60.00	27.00
☐ 282 Birdie Tebbetts SP	80.00	36.00
☐ 283 Phil Masi SP	60.00	27.00
☐ 284 Hank Arft SP	60.00	27.00
☐ 285 Cliff Fannin SP	60.00	27.00
☐ 286 Joe DeMaestri SP	60.00	27.00
☐ 287 Steve Bilko SP	60.00	27.00
☐ 288 Chet Nichols SP	60.00	27.00
☐ 289 Tommy Holmes SP	75.00	34.00
☐ 290 Joe Astroth SP	60.00	27.00
☐ 291 Gil Coan SP	60.00	27.00
☐ 292 Floyd Baker SP	60.00	27.00
☐ 293 Sibby Sisti SP	60.00	27.00
☐ 294 Walker Cooper SP	60.00	27.00
☐ 295 Phil Cavarretta SP	75.00	34.00
☐ 296 Red Rolfe MG SP	60.00	27.00
☐ 297 Andy Seminick SP	60.00	27.00
☐ 298 Bob Ross SP	60.00	27.00
☐ 299 Ray Murray SP	60.00	27.00
☐ 300 Barney McCosky SP	60.00	27.00
☐ 301 Bob Porterfield	50.00	22.00
☐ 302 Max Surkont	50.00	22.00
☐ 303 Harry Dorish	50.00	22.00
☐ 304 Sam Dente	50.00	22.00
☐ 305 Paul Richards MG	60.00	27.00
☐ 306 Lou Sleater	50.00	22.00
☐ 307 Frank Campos	50.00	22.00
☐ 308 Luis Aloma	50.00	22.00
☐ 309 Jim Busby	50.00	22.00
☐ 310 George Metkovich	60.00	27.00
☐ 311 Mickey Mantle	23000.00	10400.00
☐ 312 Jackie Robinson DP	1400.00	650.00
☐ 313 Bobby Thomson DP	300.00	135.00
☐ 314 Roy Campanella	2000.00	900.00
☐ 315 Leo Durocher MG	375.00	170.00
☐ 316 Dave Williams	300.00	135.00
☐ 317 Conrado Marrero	300.00	135.00

☐ 318 Harold Gregg	250.00	110.00
☐ 319 Al Walker	250.00	110.00
☐ 320 John Rutherford	300.00	135.00
☐ 321 Joe Black	350.00	160.00
☐ 322 Randy Jackson	250.00	110.00
☐ 323 Bubba Church	250.00	110.00
☐ 324 Warren Hacker	250.00	110.00
☐ 325 Bill Serena	250.00	110.00
☐ 326 George Shuba	400.00	180.00
☐ 327 Al Wilson	250.00	110.00
☐ 328 Bob Borkowski	250.00	110.00
☐ 329 Ike Delock	250.00	110.00
☐ 330 Turk Lown	250.00	110.00
☐ 331 Tom Morgan	250.00	110.00
☐ 332 Anthony Bartirome	250.00	110.00
☐ 333 Pee Wee Reese	1400.00	650.00
☐ 334 Wilmer Mizell	300.00	135.00
☐ 335 Ted Lepcio	250.00	110.00
☐ 336 Dave Koslo	250.00	110.00
☐ 337 Jim Hearn	250.00	110.00
☐ 338 Sal Yvars	250.00	110.00
☐ 339 Russ Meyer	250.00	110.00
☐ 340 Bob Hooper	250.00	110.00
☐ 341 Hal Jeffcoat	250.00	110.00
☐ 342 Clem Labine	400.00	180.00
☐ 343 Dick Gernert	250.00	110.00
☐ 344 Ewell Blackwell	300.00	135.00
☐ 345 Sammy White	250.00	110.00
☐ 346 George Spencer	250.00	110.00
☐ 347 Joe Adcock	300.00	135.00
☐ 348 Robert Kelly	250.00	110.00
☐ 349 Bob Cain	250.00	110.00
☐ 350 Cal Abrams	250.00	110.00
☐ 351 Alvin Dark	300.00	135.00
☐ 352 Karl Drews	250.00	110.00
☐ 353 Bobby Del Greco	250.00	110.00
☐ 354 Fred Hatfield	250.00	110.00
☐ 355 Bobby Morgan	250.00	110.00
☐ 356 Toby Atwell	250.00	110.00
☐ 357 Smoky Burgess	300.00	135.00
☐ 358 John Kucab	250.00	110.00
☐ 359 Dee Fondy	250.00	110.00
☐ 360 George Crowe	300.00	135.00
☐ 361 William Posedel CO	250.00	110.00
☐ 362 Ken Heintzelman	250.00	110.00
☐ 363 Dick Rozek	250.00	110.00
☐ 364 Clyde Sukeforth CO	250.00	110.00
☐ 365 Cookie Lavagetto CO	375.00	170.00
☐ 366 Dave Madison	250.00	110.00
☐ 367 Ben Thorpe	250.00	110.00
☐ 368 Ed Wright	250.00	110.00
☐ 369 Dick Groat	350.00	160.00
☐ 370 Billy Hoeft	300.00	135.00
☐ 371 Bobby Hofman	250.00	110.00
☐ 372 Gil McDougald	375.00	170.00
☐ 373 Jim Turner CO	400.00	180.00
☐ 374 John Benton	250.00	110.00
☐ 375 John Merson	250.00	110.00
☐ 376 Faye Throneberry	250.00	110.00
☐ 377 Chuck Dressen MG	375.00	170.00
☐ 378 Leroy Fusselman	250.00	110.00
☐ 379 Joe Rossi	250.00	110.00
☐ 380 Clem Koshorek	250.00	110.00
☐ 381 Milton Stock CO	250.00	110.00
☐ 382 Sam Jones	350.00	160.00
☐ 383 Del Wilber	250.00	110.00
☐ 384 Frank Crosetti CO	400.00	180.00
☐ 385 Herman Franks CO	250.00	110.00
☐ 386 John Yuhas	250.00	110.00
☐ 387 Billy Meyer MG	250.00	110.00
☐ 388 Bob Chipman	250.00	110.00
☐ 389 Ben Wade	250.00	110.00
☐ 390 Glenn Nelson	250.00	110.00
☐ 391 Ben Chapman UER CO (Photo actually Sam Chapman)	250.00	110.00
☐ 392 Hoyt Wilhelm	700.00	325.00
☐ 393 Ebba St.Claire	250.00	110.00
☐ 394 Billy Herman CO	400.00	180.00
☐ 395 Jake Pitler CO	325.00	145.00
☐ 396 Dick Williams	400.00	180.00
☐ 397 Forrest Main	250.00	110.00
☐ 398 Hal Rice	250.00	110.00
☐ 399 Jim Fridley	250.00	110.00
☐ 400 Bill Dickey CO	800.00	350.00
☐ 401 Bob Schultz	250.00	110.00
☐ 402 Earl Harrist	250.00	110.00
☐ 403 Bill Miller	250.00	110.00
☐ 404 Dick Brodowski	250.00	110.00
☐ 405 Eddie Pellagrini	250.00	110.00
☐ 406 Joe Nuxhall	350.00	160.00
☐ 407 Eddie Mathews	3800.00	950.00

1953 Topps

The cards in this 274-card set measure 2 5/8" by 3 3/4". Although the last card is numbered 280, there are only

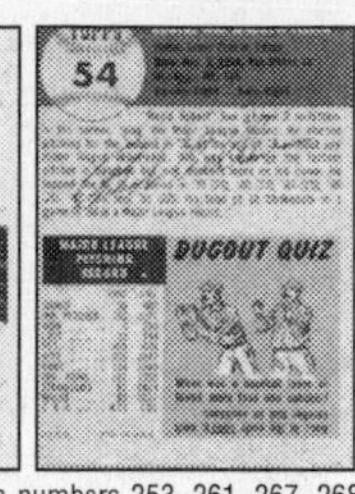

274 cards in the set since numbers 253, 261, 267, 268, 271, and 275 were never issued. The 1953 Topps series contains line drawings of players in full color. The name and team panel at the card base is easily damaged, making it very difficult to complete a mint set. The high number series, 221 to 280, was produced in shorter supply late in the year and hence is more difficult to complete than the lower numbers. The key cards in the set are Mickey Mantle (82) and Willie Mays (244). The key Rookie Cards in this set are Roy Face, Jim Gilliam, and Johnny Podres, all from the last series. There are a number of double-printed cards (actually not double but 50 percent more of each of these numbers were printed compared to the other cards in the series) indicated by DP in the checklist below. There were five players (10 Smoky Burgess, 44 Ellis Kinder, 61 Early Wynn, 72 Fred Hutchinson, and 81 Joe Black) held out of the first run of 1-85 (but printed in with numbers 86-165), who are each marked by SP in the checklist below. In addition, there are five numbers which were printed with the more plentiful series 166-220; these cards (94, 107, 131, 145, and 156) are also indicated by DP in the checklist below. The cards were issued in one-card penny packs or six-card nickle packs. There were some three-card advertising panels produced by Topps; the players include Johnny Mize/Clem Koshorek/Toby Atwell and Mickey Mantle/Johnny Wyrostek/Sal Yvars. When cut apart, these advertising cards are distinguished by the non-standard card back, i.e., part of an advertisement for the 1953 Topps set instead of the typical statistics and biographical information about the player pictured.

	NRMT	VG-E
COMPLETE SET (274)	13500.00	6100.00
COMMON CARD (1-165)	30.00	13.50
COMMON CARD (166-220)	25.00	11.00
COMMON DP (1-220)	15.00	6.75
COMMON CARD (221-280)	100.00	45.00
UNLISTED STARS 221-280	175.00	80.00
WRAPPER (1-cent, dated)	200.00	90.00
WRAPPER (1-cent, undated)	300.00	135.00
WRAPPER (5-cent, dated)	400.00	180.00
WRAPPER (5-cent, undated)	350.00	160.00

☐ 1 Jackie Robinson DP	450.00	125.00
☐ 2 Luke Easter DP	20.00	9.00
☐ 3 George Crowe	30.00	13.50
☐ 4 Ben Wade	30.00	13.50
☐ 5 Joe Dobson	30.00	13.50
☐ 6 Sam Jones	40.00	18.00
☐ 7 Bob Borkowski DP	15.00	6.75
☐ 8 Clem Koshorek DP	15.00	6.75
☐ 9 Joe Collins	40.00	18.00
☐ 10 Smoky Burgess SP	70.00	32.00
☐ 11 Sal Yvars	30.00	13.50
☐ 12 Howie Judson DP	15.00	6.75
☐ 13 Conrado Marrero DP	15.00	6.75
☐ 14 Clem Labine DP	20.00	9.00
☐ 15 Bobo Newsom DP	30.00	13.50
☐ 16 Peanuts Lowrey DP	15.00	6.75
☐ 17 Billy Hitchcock	30.00	13.50
☐ 18 Ted Lepcio DP	30.00	13.50
☐ 19 Mel Parnell DP	30.00	13.50
☐ 20 Hank Thompson	40.00	18.00
☐ 21 Billy Johnson	30.00	13.50
☐ 22 Howie Fox	30.00	13.50
☐ 23 Toby Atwell DP	15.00	6.75
☐ 24 Ferris Fain	40.00	18.00
☐ 25 Ray Boone	40.00	18.00
☐ 26 Dale Mitchell DP	20.00	9.00
☐ 27 Roy Campanella DP	175.00	80.00
☐ 28 Eddie Pellagrini	30.00	13.50
☐ 29 Hal Jeffcoat	30.00	13.50
☐ 30 Willard Nixon	30.00	13.50
☐ 31 Ewell Blackwell	50.00	22.00
☐ 32 Clyde Vollmer	30.00	13.50
☐ 33 Bob Kennedy DP	15.00	6.75
☐ 34 George Shuba	40.00	18.00
☐ 35 Irv Noren DP	15.00	6.75
☐ 36 Johnny Groth DP	15.00	6.75
☐ 37 Eddie Mathews DP	100.00	45.00
☐ 38 Jim Hearn DP	15.00	6.75
☐ 39 Eddie Miksis	30.00	13.50
☐ 40 John Lipon	30.00	13.50
☐ 41 Enos Slaughter	80.00	36.00
☐ 42 Gus Zernial DP	30.00	13.50
☐ 43 Gil McDougald	50.00	22.00
☐ 44 Ellis Kinder SP	35.00	16.00
☐ 45 Grady Hatton DP	15.00	6.75
☐ 46 Johnny Klippstein DP	15.00	6.75
☐ 47 Bubba Church DP	15.00	6.75
☐ 48 Bob Del Greco DP	15.00	6.75
☐ 49 Faye Throneberry DP	15.00	6.75
☐ 50 Chuck Dressen MG DP	22.50	10.00
☐ 51 Frank Campos DP	15.00	6.75
☐ 52 Ted Gray DP	15.00	6.75
☐ 53 Sherm Lollar DP	30.00	13.50
☐ 54 Bob Feller DP	100.00	45.00
☐ 55 Maurice McDermott DP	15.00	6.75
☐ 56 Gerry Staley DP	15.00	6.75
☐ 57 Carl Scheib	30.00	13.50
☐ 58 George Metkovich	30.00	13.50
☐ 59 Karl Drews DP	15.00	6.75
☐ 60 Cloyd Boyer DP	15.00	6.75
☐ 61 Early Wynn SP	90.00	40.00
☐ 62 Monte Irvin DP	35.00	16.00
☐ 63 Gus Niarhos DP	15.00	6.75
☐ 64 Dave Philley	30.00	13.50
☐ 65 Earl Harrist	30.00	13.50
☐ 66 Minnie Minoso	50.00	22.00
☐ 67 Roy Sievers DP	30.00	13.50
☐ 68 Del Rice	30.00	13.50
☐ 69 Dick Brodowski	30.00	13.50
☐ 70 Ed Yuhas	30.00	13.50
☐ 71 Tony Bartirome	30.00	13.50
☐ 72 Fred Hutchinson MG SP	50.00	22.00
☐ 73 Eddie Robinson	30.00	13.50
☐ 74 Joe Rossi	30.00	13.50
☐ 75 Mike Garcia	40.00	18.00
☐ 76 Pee Wee Reese	150.00	70.00
☐ 77 Johnny Mize DP	50.00	22.00
☐ 78 Red Schoendienst	60.00	27.00
☐ 79 Johnny Wyrostek	30.00	13.50
☐ 80 Jim Hegan	40.00	18.00
☐ 81 Joe Black SP	70.00	32.00
☐ 82 Mickey Mantle	3000.00	1350.00
☐ 83 Howie Pollet	30.00	13.50
☐ 84 Bob Hooper DP	15.00	6.75
☐ 85 Bobby Morgan DP	15.00	6.75
☐ 86 Billy Martin	125.00	55.00
☐ 87 Ed Lopat	50.00	22.00
☐ 88 Willie Jones DP	15.00	6.75
☐ 89 Chuck Stobbs DP	15.00	6.75
☐ 90 Hank Edwards DP	15.00	6.75
☐ 91 Ebba St.Claire DP	15.00	6.75
☐ 92 Paul Minner DP	15.00	6.75
☐ 93 Hal Rice DP	15.00	6.75
☐ 94 Bill Kennedy DP	15.00	6.75
☐ 95 Willard Marshall DP	15.00	6.75
☐ 96 Virgil Trucks	40.00	18.00
☐ 97 Don Kolloway DP	15.00	6.75
☐ 98 Cal Abrams DP	15.00	6.75
☐ 99 Dave Madison	30.00	13.50
☐ 100 Bill Miller	30.00	13.50
☐ 101 Ted Wilks	30.00	13.50
☐ 102 Connie Ryan DP	15.00	6.75
☐ 103 Joe Astroth DP	15.00	6.75
☐ 104 Yogi Berra	200.00	90.00
☐ 105 Joe Nuxhall DP	30.00	13.50
☐ 106 Johnny Antonelli	40.00	18.00
☐ 107 Danny O'Connell DP	15.00	6.75
☐ 108 Bob Porterfield DP	15.00	6.75
☐ 109 Alvin Dark	40.00	18.00
☐ 110 Herman Wehmeier DP	15.00	6.75
☐ 111 Hank Sauer DP	20.00	9.00
☐ 112 Ned Garver DP	15.00	6.75
☐ 113 Jerry Priddy	30.00	13.50
☐ 114 Phil Rizzuto	160.00	70.00
☐ 115 George Spencer	30.00	13.50
☐ 116 Frank Smith DP	15.00	6.75
☐ 117 Sid Gordon DP	15.00	6.75
☐ 118 Gus Bell DP	20.00	9.00
☐ 119 Johnny Sain SP	50.00	22.00
☐ 120 Davey Williams	40.00	18.00
☐ 121 Walt Dropo	40.00	18.00
☐ 122 Elmer Valo	30.00	13.50
☐ 123 Tommy Byrne DP	15.00	6.75
☐ 124 Sibby Sisti DP	15.00	6.75
☐ 125 Dick Williams DP	22.50	10.00
☐ 126 Bill Connelly DP	15.00	6.75
☐ 127 Clint Courtney DP	15.00	6.75
☐ 128 Wilmer Mizell DP (Inconsistent design, logo on front with black birds)	20.00	9.00
☐ 129 Keith Thomas	30.00	13.50
☐ 130 Turk Lown DP	15.00	6.75
☐ 131 Harry Byrd DP	15.00	6.75
☐ 132 Tom Morgan	30.00	13.50

☐ 133 Gil Coan	30.00	13.50
☐ 134 Rube Walker	40.00	18.00
☐ 135 Al Rosen DP	25.00	11.00
☐ 136 Ken Heintzelman DP	15.00	6.75
☐ 137 John Rutherford DP	15.00	6.75
☐ 138 George Kell	60.00	27.00
☐ 139 Sammy White	30.00	13.50
☐ 140 Tommy Glaviano	30.00	13.50
☐ 141 Allie Reynolds DP	25.00	11.00
☐ 142 Vic Wertz	40.00	18.00
☐ 143 Billy Pierce !	50.00	22.00
☐ 144 Bob Schultz DP	15.00	6.75
☐ 145 Harry Dorish DP	15.00	6.75
☐ 146 Granny Hamner	30.00	13.50
☐ 147 Warren Spahn	150.00	70.00
☐ 148 Mickey Grasso	30.00	13.50
☐ 149 Dom DiMaggio DP	35.00	16.00
☐ 150 Harry Simpson DP	15.00	6.75
☐ 151 Hoyt Wilhelm	80.00	36.00
☐ 152 Bob Adams DP	15.00	6.75
☐ 153 Andy Seminick DP	15.00	6.75
☐ 154 Dick Groat	40.00	18.00
☐ 155 Dutch Leonard	30.00	13.50
☐ 156 Jim Rivera DP	30.00	13.50
☐ 157 Bob Addis DP	15.00	6.75
☐ 158 Johnny Logan	35.00	16.00
☐ 159 Wayne Terwilliger DP	15.00	6.75
☐ 160 Bob Young	30.00	13.50
☐ 161 Vern Bickford DP	15.00	6.75
☐ 162 Ted Kluszewski	50.00	22.00
☐ 163 Fred Hatfield DP	15.00	6.75
☐ 164 Frank Shea DP	15.00	6.75
☐ 165 Billy Hoeft	30.00	13.50
☐ 166 Billy Hunter	25.00	11.00
☐ 167 Art Schult	25.00	11.00
☐ 168 Willard Schmidt	25.00	11.00
☐ 169 Dizzy Trout	40.00	18.00
☐ 170 Bill Werle	25.00	11.00
☐ 171 Bill Glynn	25.00	11.00
☐ 172 Rip Repulski	25.00	11.00
☐ 173 Preston Ward	25.00	11.00
☐ 174 Billy Loes	40.00	18.00
☐ 175 Ron Kline	25.00	11.00
☐ 176 Don Hoak	40.00	18.00
☐ 177 Jim Dyck	25.00	11.00
☐ 178 Jim Waugh	25.00	11.00
☐ 179 Gene Hermanski	25.00	11.00
☐ 180 Virgil Stallcup	25.00	11.00
☐ 181 Al Zarilla	25.00	11.00
☐ 182 Bobby Hofman	25.00	11.00
☐ 183 Stu Miller	40.00	18.00
☐ 184 Hal Brown	25.00	11.00
☐ 185 Jim Pendleton	25.00	11.00
☐ 186 Charlie Bishop	25.00	11.00
☐ 187 Jim Fridley	25.00	11.00
☐ 188 Andy Carey	40.00	18.00
☐ 189 Ray Jablonski	25.00	11.00
☐ 190 Dixie Walker CO	40.00	18.00
☐ 191 Ralph Kiner	80.00	36.00
☐ 192 Wally Westlake	25.00	11.00
☐ 193 Mike Clark	25.00	11.00
☐ 194 Eddie Kazak	25.00	11.00
☐ 195 Ed McGhee	25.00	11.00
☐ 196 Bob Keegan	25.00	11.00
☐ 197 Del Crandall	40.00	18.00
☐ 198 Forrest Main	25.00	11.00
☐ 199 Marion Fricano	25.00	11.00
☐ 200 Gordon Goldsberry	25.00	11.00
☐ 201 Paul LaPalme	25.00	11.00
☐ 202 Carl Sawatski	25.00	11.00
☐ 203 Cliff Fannin	25.00	11.00
☐ 204 Dick Bokelman	25.00	11.00
☐ 205 Vern Benson	25.00	11.00
☐ 206 Ed Bailey	25.00	11.00
☐ 207 Whitey Ford	160.00	70.00
☐ 208 Jim Wilson	25.00	11.00
☐ 209 Jim Greengrass	25.00	11.00
☐ 210 Bob Cerv	40.00	18.00
☐ 211 J.W. Porter	25.00	11.00
☐ 212 Jack Dittmer	25.00	11.00
☐ 213 Ray Scarborough	25.00	11.00
☐ 214 Bill Bruton	40.00	18.00
☐ 215 Gene Conley	40.00	18.00
☐ 216 Jim Hughes	25.00	11.00
☐ 217 Murray Wall	25.00	11.00
☐ 218 Les Fusselman	25.00	11.00
☐ 219 Pete Runnels UER (Photo actually Don Johnson)	40.00	18.00
☐ 220 Satchel Paige UER (Misspelled Satchell on card front)	450.00	200.00
☐ 221 Bob Milliken	100.00	45.00
☐ 222 Vic Janowicz DP	60.00	27.00
☐ 223 Johnny O'Brien DP	50.00	22.00
☐ 224 Lou Sleater DP	100.00	45.00
☐ 225 Bobby Shantz	120.00	55.00
☐ 226 Ed Erautt	100.00	45.00
☐ 227 Morrie Martin	100.00	45.00
☐ 228 Hal Newhouser	150.00	70.00
☐ 229 Rocky Krsnich	100.00	45.00
☐ 230 Johnny Lindell DP	50.00	22.00
☐ 231 Solly Hemus DP	50.00	22.00
☐ 232 Dick Kokos	100.00	45.00
☐ 233 Al Aber	100.00	45.00
☐ 234 Ray Murray DP	50.00	22.00
☐ 235 John Hetki DP	50.00	22.00
☐ 236 Harry Perkowski DP	50.00	22.00
☐ 237 Bud Podbielan DP	50.00	22.00
☐ 238 Cal Hogue DP	50.00	22.00
☐ 239 Jim Delsing	100.00	45.00
☐ 240 Fred Marsh	100.00	45.00
☐ 241 Al Sima DP	50.00	22.00
☐ 242 Charlie Silvera	120.00	55.00
☐ 243 Carlos Bernier DP	50.00	22.00
☐ 244 Willie Mays	2700.00	1200.00
☐ 245 Bill Norman CO	100.00	45.00
☐ 246 Roy Face DP	80.00	36.00
☐ 247 Mike Sandlock DP	50.00	22.00
☐ 248 Gene Stephens DP	50.00	22.00
☐ 249 Eddie O'Brien	100.00	45.00
☐ 250 Bob Wilson	100.00	45.00
☐ 251 Sid Hudson	100.00	45.00
☐ 252 Hank Foiles	100.00	45.00
☐ 253 Does not exist		
☐ 254 Preacher Roe DP	80.00	36.00
☐ 255 Dixie Howell	100.00	45.00
☐ 256 Les Peden	100.00	45.00
☐ 257 Bob Boyd	100.00	45.00
☐ 258 Jim Gilliam	300.00	135.00
☐ 259 Roy McMillan DP	100.00	45.00
☐ 260 Sam Calderone	100.00	45.00
☐ 261 Does not exist		
☐ 262 Bob Oldis	100.00	45.00
☐ 263 Johnny Podres	275.00	125.00
☐ 264 Gene Woodling DP	100.00	45.00
☐ 265 Jackie Jensen	125.00	55.00
☐ 266 Bob Cain	100.00	45.00
☐ 267 Does not exist		
☐ 268 Does not exist		
☐ 269 Duane Pillette	100.00	45.00
☐ 270 Vern Stephens	120.00	55.00
☐ 271 Does not exist		
☐ 272 Bill Antonello	100.00	45.00
☐ 273 Harvey Haddix	125.00	55.00
☐ 274 John Riddle CO	100.00	45.00
☐ 275 Does not exist		
☐ 276 Ken Raffensberger	100.00	45.00
☐ 277 Don Lund	100.00	45.00
☐ 278 Willie Miranda	100.00	45.00
☐ 279 Joe Coleman DP	50.00	22.00
☐ 280 Milt Bolling	300.00	50.00

1954 Topps

The cards in this 250-card set measure approximately 2 5/8" by 3 3/4". Each of the cards in the 1954 Topps set contains a large "head" shot of the player in color plus a smaller full-length photo in black and white set against a color background. The cards were issued in one-card penny packs or five-card nickle packs. This set contains the Rookie Cards of Hank Aaron, Ernie Banks, and Al Kaline and two separate cards of Ted Williams (number 1 and number 250). Conspicuous by his absence is Mickey Mantle who apparently was the exclusive property of Bowman during 1954 (and 1955). The first two issues of Sports Illustrated magazine contained "card" inserts on regular paper stock. The first issue showed actual cards in the set in color, while the second issue showed some created cards of New York Yankees players in black and white, including Mickey Mantle.

	NRMT	VG-E
COMPLETE SET (250)	7500.00	3400.00
COMMON CARD (51-75)	25.00	11.00
WRAPPER (1-CENT, DATED)	200.00	90.00
WRAPPER (1-CENT, UNDATED)	150.00	70.00
WRAPPER (5-CENT, DATED)	300.00	135.00
WRAPPER (5-CENT, UNDATED)	250.00	110.00

☐ 1 Ted Williams	650.00	230.00
☐ 2 Gus Zernial	25.00	11.00
☐ 3 Monte Irvin	40.00	18.00
☐ 4 Hank Sauer	25.00	11.00
☐ 5 Ed Lopat	25.00	11.00
☐ 6 Pete Runnels	25.00	11.00
☐ 7 Ted Kluszewski	40.00	18.00
☐ 8 Bob Young	15.00	6.75
☐ 9 Harvey Haddix	25.00	11.00
☐ 10 Jackie Robinson	300.00	135.00
☐ 11 Paul Leslie Smith	15.00	6.75
☐ 12 Del Crandall	25.00	11.00
☐ 13 Billy Martin	60.00	27.00
☐ 14 Preacher Roe	25.00	11.00
☐ 15 Al Rosen	25.00	11.00
☐ 16 Vic Janowicz	25.00	11.00
☐ 17 Phil Rizzuto	75.00	34.00
☐ 18 Walt Dropo	25.00	11.00
☐ 19 Johnny Lipon	15.00	6.75
☐ 20 Warren Spahn	75.00	34.00
☐ 21 Bobby Shantz	25.00	11.00
☐ 22 Jim Greengrass	15.00	6.75
☐ 23 Luke Easter	25.00	11.00
☐ 24 Granny Hamner	15.00	6.75
☐ 25 Harvey Kuenn	40.00	18.00
☐ 26 Ray Jablonski	15.00	6.75
☐ 27 Ferris Fain	25.00	11.00
☐ 28 Paul Minner	15.00	6.75
☐ 29 Jim Hegan	25.00	11.00
☐ 30 Eddie Mathews	75.00	34.00
☐ 31 Johnny Klippstein	15.00	6.75
☐ 32 Duke Snider	125.00	55.00
☐ 33 Johnny Schmitz	15.00	6.75
☐ 34 Jim Rivera	15.00	6.75
☐ 35 Jim Gilliam	40.00	18.00
☐ 36 Hoyt Wilhelm	50.00	22.00
☐ 37 Whitey Ford	100.00	45.00
☐ 38 Eddie Stanky MG	25.00	11.00
☐ 39 Sherm Lollar	25.00	11.00
☐ 40 Mel Parnell	25.00	11.00
☐ 41 Willie Jones	15.00	6.75
☐ 42 Don Mueller	25.00	11.00
☐ 43 Dick Groat	25.00	11.00
☐ 44 Ned Garver	15.00	6.75
☐ 45 Richie Ashburn	70.00	32.00
☐ 46 Ken Raffensberger	15.00	6.75
☐ 47 Ellis Kinder	15.00	6.75
☐ 48 Billy Hunter	25.00	11.00
☐ 49 Ray Murray	15.00	6.75
☐ 50 Yogi Berra	150.00	70.00
☐ 51 Johnny Lindell	25.00	11.00
☐ 52 Vic Power	35.00	16.00
☐ 53 Jack Dittmer	25.00	11.00
☐ 54 Vern Stephens	30.00	13.50
☐ 55 Phil Cavarretta MG	30.00	13.50
☐ 56 Willie Miranda	25.00	11.00
☐ 57 Luis Aloma	25.00	11.00
☐ 58 Bob Wilson	25.00	11.00
☐ 59 Gene Conley	30.00	13.50
☐ 60 Frank Baumholtz	25.00	11.00
☐ 61 Bob Cain	25.00	11.00
☐ 62 Eddie Robinson	25.00	11.00
☐ 63 Johnny Pesky	30.00	13.50
☐ 64 Hank Thompson	25.00	11.00
☐ 65 Bob Swift CO	25.00	11.00
☐ 66 Ted Lepcio	25.00	11.00
☐ 67 Jim Willis	25.00	11.00
☐ 68 Sam Calderone	25.00	11.00
☐ 69 Bud Podbielan	25.00	11.00
☐ 70 Larry Doby	50.00	22.00
☐ 71 Frank Smith	25.00	11.00
☐ 72 Preston Ward	25.00	11.00
☐ 73 Wayne Terwilliger	25.00	11.00
☐ 74 Bill Taylor	25.00	11.00
☐ 75 Fred Haney MG	25.00	11.00
☐ 76 Bob Scheffing CO	15.00	6.75
☐ 77 Ray Boone	25.00	11.00
☐ 78 Ted Kazanski	15.00	6.75
☐ 79 Andy Pafko	25.00	11.00
☐ 80 Jackie Jensen	25.00	11.00
☐ 81 Dave Hoskins	15.00	6.75
☐ 82 Milt Bolling	15.00	6.75
☐ 83 Joe Collins	25.00	11.00
☐ 84 Dick Cole	15.00	6.75
☐ 85 Bob Turley	30.00	13.50
☐ 86 Billy Herman CO	25.00	11.00
☐ 87 Roy Face	25.00	11.00
☐ 88 Matt Batts	15.00	6.75
☐ 89 Howie Pollet	15.00	6.75
☐ 90 Willie Mays	500.00	220.00
☐ 91 Bob Oldis	15.00	6.75
☐ 92 Wally Westlake	15.00	6.75
☐ 93 Sid Hudson	15.00	6.75
☐ 94 Ernie Banks	750.00	350.00
☐ 95 Hal Rice	15.00	6.75
☐ 96 Charlie Silvera	25.00	11.00
☐ 97 Jerald Hal Lane	15.00	6.75

98 Joe Black	30.00	13.50
99 Bobby Hofman	15.00	6.75
100 Bob Keegan	15.00	6.75
101 Gene Woodling	25.00	11.00
102 Gil Hodges	70.00	32.00
103 Jim Lemon	15.00	6.75
104 Mike Sandlock	15.00	6.75
105 Andy Carey	25.00	11.00
106 Dick Kokos	15.00	6.75
107 Duane Pillette	15.00	6.75
108 Thornton Kipper	15.00	6.75
109 Bill Bruton	25.00	11.00
110 Harry Dorish	15.00	6.75
111 Jim Delsing	15.00	6.75
112 Bill Renna	15.00	6.75
113 Bob Boyd	15.00	6.75
114 Dean Stone	15.00	6.75
115 Rip Repulski	15.00	6.75
116 Steve Bilko	15.00	6.75
117 Solly Hemus	15.00	6.75
118 Carl Scheib	15.00	6.75
119 Johnny Antonelli	25.00	11.00
120 Roy McMillan	25.00	11.00
121 Clem Labine	25.00	11.00
122 Johnny Logan	25.00	11.00
123 Bobby Adams	15.00	6.75
124 Marion Fricano	15.00	6.75
125 Harry Perkowski	15.00	6.75
126 Ben Wade	15.00	6.75
127 Steve O'Neill MG	15.00	6.75
128 Hank Aaron	1500.00	700.00
129 Forrest Jacobs	15.00	6.75
130 Hank Bauer	25.00	11.00
131 Reno Bertoia	15.00	6.75
132 Tommy Lasorda	200.00	90.00
133 Dave Baker CO	15.00	6.75
134 Cal Hogue	15.00	6.75
135 Joe Presko	15.00	6.75
136 Connie Ryan	15.00	6.75
137 Wally Moon	30.00	13.50
138 Bob Borkowski	15.00	6.75
139 The O'Briens Johnny O'Brien Eddie O'Brien	40.00	18.00
140 Tom Wright	15.00	6.75
141 Joey Jay	25.00	11.00
142 Tom Poholsky	15.00	6.75
143 Rollie Hemsley CO	15.00	6.75
144 Bill Werle	15.00	6.75
145 Elmer Valo	15.00	6.75
146 Don Johnson	15.00	6.75
147 Johnny Riddle CO	15.00	6.75
148 Bob Trice	15.00	6.75
149 Al Robertson	15.00	6.75
150 Dick Kryhoski	15.00	6.75
151 Alex Grammas	15.00	6.75
152 Michael Blyzka	15.00	6.75
153 Al Walker	15.00	6.75
154 Mike Fornieles	15.00	6.75
155 Bob Kennedy	25.00	11.00
156 Joe Coleman	15.00	6.75
157 Don Lenhardt	15.00	6.75
158 Peanuts Lowrey	15.00	6.75
159 Dave Philley	15.00	6.75
160 Ralph Kress CO	15.00	6.75
161 John Hetki	15.00	6.75
162 Herman Wehmeier	15.00	6.75
163 Frank House	15.00	6.75
164 Stu Miller	25.00	11.00
165 Jim Pendleton	15.00	6.75
166 Johnny Podres	30.00	13.50
167 Don Lund	15.00	6.75
168 Morrie Martin	15.00	6.75
169 Jim Hughes	25.00	11.00
170 James(Dusty) Rhodes	25.00	11.00
171 Leo Kiely	15.00	6.75
172 Harold Brown	15.00	6.75
173 Jack Harshman	15.00	6.75
174 Tom Qualters	15.00	6.75
175 Frank Leja	25.00	11.00
176 Robert Keely CO	15.00	6.75
177 Bob Milliken	15.00	6.75
178 Bill Glynn	15.00	6.75
179 Gair Allie	15.00	6.75
180 Wes Westrum	25.00	11.00
181 Mel Roach	15.00	6.75
182 Chuck Harmon	15.00	6.75
183 Earle Combs CO	25.00	11.00
184 Ed Bailey	15.00	6.75
185 Chuck Stobbs	15.00	6.75
186 Karl Olson	15.00	6.75
187 Heinie Manush CO	25.00	11.00
188 Dave Jolly	15.00	6.75
189 Bob Ross	15.00	6.75
190 Ray Herbert	15.00	6.75
191 John(Dick) Schofield	25.00	11.00
192 Ellis Deal CO	15.00	6.75
193 Johnny Hopp CO	25.00	11.00
194 Bill Sarni	15.00	6.75
195 Billy Consolo	15.00	6.75
196 Stan Jok	15.00	6.75
197 Lynwood Rowe CO ("Schoolboy")	25.00	11.00
198 Carl Sawatski	15.00	6.75
199 Glenn(Rocky) Nelson	15.00	6.75
200 Larry Jansen	25.00	11.00
201 Al Kaline	750.00	350.00
202 Bob Purkey	25.00	11.00
203 Harry Brecheen CO	25.00	11.00
204 Angel Scull	15.00	6.75
205 Johnny Sain	30.00	13.50
206 Ray Crone	15.00	6.75
207 Tom Oliver CO	15.00	6.75
208 Grady Hatton	15.00	6.75
209 Chuck Thompson	15.00	6.75
210 Bob Buhl	25.00	11.00
211 Don Hoak	25.00	11.00
212 Bob Micelotta	15.00	6.75
213 Johnny Fitzpatrick CO	15.00	6.75
214 Arnie Portocarrero	15.00	6.75
215 Ed McGhee	15.00	6.75
216 Al Sima	15.00	6.75
217 Paul Schreiber CO	15.00	6.75
218 Fred Marsh	15.00	6.75
219 Chuck Kress	15.00	6.75
220 Ruben Gomez	25.00	11.00
221 Dick Brodowski	15.00	6.75
222 Bill Wilson	15.00	6.75
223 Joe Haynes CO	15.00	6.75
224 Dick Weik	15.00	6.75
225 Don Liddle	15.00	6.75
226 Jehosie Heard	15.00	6.75
227 Colonel Mills CO	15.00	6.75
228 Gene Hermanski	15.00	6.75
229 Bob Talbot	15.00	6.75
230 Bob Kuzava	25.00	11.00
231 Roy Smalley	15.00	6.75
232 Lou Limmer	15.00	6.75
233 Augie Galan CO	15.00	6.75
234 Jerry Lynch	15.00	6.75
235 Vern Law	25.00	11.00
236 Paul Penson	15.00	6.75
237 Mike Ryba CO	15.00	6.75
238 Al Aber	15.00	6.75
239 Bill Skowron	100.00	45.00
240 Sam Mele	25.00	11.00
241 Robert Miller	15.00	6.75
242 Curt Roberts	15.00	6.75
243 Ray Blades CO	15.00	6.75
244 Leroy Wheat	15.00	6.75
245 Roy Sievers	25.00	11.00
246 Howie Fox	15.00	6.75
247 Ed Mayo CO	15.00	6.75
248 Al Smith	25.00	11.00
249 Wilmer Mizell	25.00	11.00
250 Ted Williams	750.00	300.00

1955 Topps

The cards in this 206-card set measure approximately 2 5/8" by 3 3/4". Both the large "head" shot and the smaller full-length photos used on each card of the 1955 Topps set are in color. The card fronts were designed horizontally for the first time in Topps' history. The first card features Dusty Rhodes, hitting star and MVP in the New York Giants' 1954 World Series sweep over the Cleveland Indians. A "high" series, 161 to 210, is more difficult to find than cards 1 to 160. Numbers 175, 186, 203, and 209 were never issued. To fill in for the four cards not issued in the high number series, Topps double printed four players, those appearing on cards 170, 172, 184, and 188. Cards were issued in one-card penny packs or six-card nickle packs. Although rarely seen, there exist salesman sample panels of three cards containing the fronts of regular cards with ad information for the 1955 Topps regular and the 1955 Topps Doubleheaders on the back. One such ad panel depicts (from top to bottom) Danny Schell, Jake Thies, and Howie Pollet. The key Rookie Cards in this set are Ken Boyer, Roberto Clemente, Harmon Killebrew, and Sandy Koufax.

	NRMT	VG-E
COMPLETE SET (206)	7200.00	3200.00
COMMON CARD (1-150)	12.00	5.50
COMMON CARD (151-160)	20.00	9.00
COMMON CARD (161-210)	30.00	13.50
WRAPPER (1-CENT, DATED)	150.00	70.00
WRAPPER (1-CENT, UNDATED)	50.00	22.00
WRAPPER (5-CENT, DATED)	150.00	70.00
WRAPPER (5-CENT, DATED)	100.00	45.00
1 Dusty Rhodes	50.00	10.00
2 Ted Williams	450.00	200.00
3 Art Fowler	15.00	6.75
4 Al Kaline	175.00	80.00
5 Jim Gilliam	25.00	11.00
6 Stan Hack MG	18.00	8.00
7 Jim Hegan	15.00	6.75
8 Harold Smith	12.00	5.50
9 Robert Miller	12.00	5.50
10 Bob Keegan	12.00	5.50
11 Ferris Fain	15.00	6.75
12 Vernon(Jake) Thies	12.00	5.50
13 Fred Marsh	12.00	5.50
14 Jim Finigan	12.00	5.50
15 Jim Pendleton	12.00	5.50
16 Roy Sievers	15.00	6.75
17 Bobby Hofman	12.00	5.50
18 Russ Kemmerer	12.00	5.50
19 Billy Herman CO	18.00	8.00
20 Andy Carey	15.00	6.75
21 Alex Grammas	12.00	5.50
22 Bill Skowron	20.00	9.00
23 Jack Parks	12.00	5.50
24 Hal Newhouser	18.00	8.00
25 Johnny Podres	20.00	9.00
26 Dick Groat	18.00	8.00
27 Billy Gardner	15.00	6.75
28 Ernie Banks	175.00	80.00
29 Herman Wehmeier	12.00	5.50
30 Vic Power	15.00	6.75
31 Warren Spahn	90.00	40.00
32 Warren McGhee	12.00	5.50
33 Tom Qualters	12.00	5.50
34 Wayne Terwilliger	12.00	5.50
35 Dave Jolly	12.00	5.50
36 Leo Kiely	12.00	5.50
37 Joe Cunningham	15.00	6.75
38 Bob Turley	18.00	8.00
39 Bill Glynn	12.00	5.50
40 Don Hoak	15.00	6.75
41 Chuck Stobbs	12.00	5.50
42 John(Windy) McCall	12.00	5.50
43 Harvey Haddix	18.00	8.00
44 Harold Valentine	12.00	5.50
45 Hank Sauer	18.00	8.00
46 Ted Kazanski	12.00	5.50
47 Hank Aaron UER (Birth incorrectly listed as 2/10)	350.00	160.00
48 Bob Kennedy	15.00	6.75
49 J.W. Porter	12.00	5.50
50 Jackie Robinson	300.00	135.00
51 Jim Hughes	15.00	6.75
52 Bill Tremel	12.00	5.50
53 Bill Taylor	12.00	5.50
54 Lou Limmer	12.00	5.50
55 Rip Repulski	12.00	5.50
56 Ray Jablonski	12.00	5.50
57 Billy O'Dell	12.00	5.50
58 Jim Rivera	12.00	5.50
59 Gair Allie	12.00	5.50
60 Dean Stone	12.00	5.50
61 Forrest Jacobs	12.00	5.50
62 Thornton Kipper	12.00	5.50
63 Joe Collins	15.00	6.75
64 Gus Triandos	18.00	8.00
65 Ray Boone	18.00	8.00
66 Ron Jackson	12.00	5.50
67 Wally Moon	18.00	8.00
68 Jim Davis	12.00	5.50
69 Ed Bailey	15.00	6.75
70 Al Rosen	18.00	8.00
71 Ruben Gomez	12.00	5.50
72 Karl Olson	12.00	5.50
73 Jack Shepard	12.00	5.50
74 Bob Borkowski	12.00	5.50
75 Sandy Amoros	30.00	13.50
76 Howie Pollet	12.00	5.50
77 Arnie Portocarrero	12.00	5.50
78 Gordon Jones	12.00	5.50
79 Clyde(Danny) Schell	12.00	5.50
80 Bob Grim	18.00	8.00
81 Gene Conley	15.00	6.75
82 Chuck Harmon	12.00	5.50
83 Tom Brewer	12.00	5.50

Card	NRMT	VG-E
☐ 84 Camilo Pascual	18.00	8.00
☐ 85 Don Mossi	18.00	8.00
☐ 86 Bill Wilson	12.00	5.50
☐ 87 Frank House	12.00	5.50
☐ 88 Bob Skinner	18.00	8.00
☐ 89 Joe Frazier	15.00	6.75
☐ 90 Karl Spooner	15.00	6.75
☐ 91 Milt Bolling	12.00	5.50
☐ 92 Don Zimmer	30.00	13.50
☐ 93 Steve Bilko	12.00	5.50
☐ 94 Reno Bertoia	12.00	5.50
☐ 95 Preston Ward	12.00	5.50
☐ 96 Chuck Bishop	12.00	5.50
☐ 97 Carlos Paula	12.00	5.50
☐ 98 John Riddle CO	12.00	5.50
☐ 99 Frank Leja	12.00	5.50
☐ 100 Monte Irvin	35.00	16.00
☐ 101 Johnny Gray	12.00	5.50
☐ 102 Wally Westlake	12.00	5.50
☐ 103 Chuck White	12.00	5.50
☐ 104 Jack Harshman	12.00	5.50
☐ 105 Chuck Diering	12.00	5.50
☐ 106 Frank Sullivan	12.00	5.50
☐ 107 Curt Roberts	12.00	5.50
☐ 108 Al Walker	15.00	6.75
☐ 109 Ed Lopat	18.00	8.00
☐ 110 Gus Zernial	15.00	6.75
☐ 111 Bob Milliken	15.00	6.75
☐ 112 Nelson King	12.00	5.50
☐ 113 Harry Brecheen CO	15.00	6.75
☐ 114 Louis Ortiz	12.00	5.50
☐ 115 Ellis Kinder	12.00	5.50
☐ 116 Tom Hurd	12.00	5.50
☐ 117 Mel Roach	12.00	5.50
☐ 118 Bob Purkey	12.00	5.50
☐ 119 Bob Lennon	12.00	5.50
☐ 120 Ted Kluszewski	40.00	18.00
☐ 121 Bill Renna	12.00	5.50
☐ 122 Carl Sawatski	12.00	5.50
☐ 123 Sandy Koufax	900.00	400.00
☐ 124 Harmon Killebrew	250.00	110.00
☐ 125 Ken Boyer	60.00	27.00
☐ 126 Dick Hall	12.00	5.50
☐ 127 Dale Long	18.00	8.00
☐ 128 Ted Lepcio	12.00	5.50
☐ 129 Elvin Tappe	12.00	5.50
☐ 130 Mayo Smith MG	12.00	5.50
☐ 131 Grady Hatton	12.00	5.50
☐ 132 Bob Trice	12.00	5.50
☐ 133 Dave Hoskins	12.00	5.50
☐ 134 Joey Jay	15.00	6.75
☐ 135 Johnny O'Brien	15.00	6.75
☐ 136 Veston(Bunky) Stewart	12.00	5.50
☐ 137 Harry Elliott	12.00	5.50
☐ 138 Ray Herbert	12.00	5.50
☐ 139 Steve Kraly	12.00	5.50
☐ 140 Mel Parnell	15.00	6.75
☐ 141 Tom Wright	12.00	5.50
☐ 142 Jerry Lynch	15.00	6.75
☐ 143 John(Dick) Schofield	15.00	6.75
☐ 144 John(Joe) Amalfitano	12.00	5.50
☐ 145 Elmer Valo	12.00	5.50
☐ 146 Dick Donovan	12.00	5.50
☐ 147 Hugh Pepper	12.00	5.50
☐ 148 Hector Brown	12.00	5.50
☐ 149 Ray Crone	12.00	5.50
☐ 150 Mike Higgins MG	12.00	5.50
☐ 151 Ralph Kress CO	20.00	9.00
☐ 152 Harry Agganis	70.00	32.00
☐ 153 Bud Podbielan	20.00	9.00
☐ 154 Willie Miranda	20.00	9.00
☐ 155 Eddie Mathews	90.00	40.00
☐ 156 Joe Black	35.00	16.00
☐ 157 Robert Miller	20.00	9.00
☐ 158 Tommy Carroll	20.00	9.00
☐ 159 Johnny Schmitz	20.00	9.00
☐ 160 Ray Narleski	20.00	9.00
☐ 161 Chuck Tanner	35.00	16.00
☐ 162 Joe Coleman	30.00	13.50
☐ 163 Faye Throneberry	30.00	13.50
☐ 164 Roberto Clemente	2200.00	1000.00
☐ 165 Don Johnson	30.00	13.50
☐ 166 Hank Bauer	45.00	20.00
☐ 167 Thomas Casagrande	30.00	13.50
☐ 168 Duane Pillette	30.00	13.50
☐ 169 Bob Oldis	30.00	13.50
☐ 170 Jim Pearce DP	15.00	6.75
☐ 171 Dick Brodowski	30.00	13.50
☐ 172 Frank Baumholtz DP	15.00	6.75
☐ 173 Bob Kline	30.00	13.50
☐ 174 Rudy Minarcin	30.00	13.50
☐ 175 Does not exist		
☐ 176 Norm Zauchin	30.00	13.50
☐ 177 Al Robertson	30.00	13.50
☐ 178 Bobby Adams	30.00	13.50
☐ 179 Jim Bolger	30.00	13.50
☐ 180 Clem Labine	45.00	20.00
☐ 181 Roy McMillan	40.00	18.00
☐ 182 Humberto Robinson	30.00	13.50
☐ 183 Anthony Jacobs	30.00	13.50
☐ 184 Harry Perkowski DP	15.00	6.75
☐ 185 Don Ferrarese	30.00	13.50
☐ 186 Does not exist		
☐ 187 Gil Hodges	125.00	55.00
☐ 188 Charlie Silvera DP	15.00	6.75
☐ 189 Phil Rizzuto	125.00	55.00
☐ 190 Gene Woodling	40.00	18.00
☐ 191 Eddie Stanky MG	40.00	18.00
☐ 192 Jim Delsing	30.00	13.50
☐ 193 Johnny Sain	45.00	20.00
☐ 194 Willie Mays	400.00	180.00
☐ 195 Ed Roebuck	45.00	20.00
☐ 196 Gale Wade	30.00	13.50
☐ 197 Al Smith	40.00	18.00
☐ 198 Yogi Berra	200.00	90.00
☐ 199 Odbert Hamric	40.00	18.00
☐ 200 Jackie Jensen	35.00	16.00
☐ 201 Sherman Lollar !	40.00	18.00
☐ 202 Jim Owens	30.00	13.50
☐ 203 Does not exist		
☐ 204 Frank Smith	30.00	13.50
☐ 205 Gene Freese	30.00	13.50
☐ 206 Pete Daley	30.00	13.50
☐ 207 Billy Consolo	30.00	13.50
☐ 208 Ray Moore	30.00	13.50
☐ 209 Does not exist		
☐ 210 Duke Snider	450.00	135.00

1955 Topps Double Header

The cards in this 66-card set measure approximately 2 1/16" by 4 7/8". Borrowing a design from the T201 Mecca series, Topps issued a 132-player "Double Header" set in a separate wrapper in 1955. Each player is numbered in the biographical section on the reverse. When open, with perforated flap up, one player is revealed; when the flap is lowered, or closed, the player design on top incorporates a portion of the inside player artwork. When the cards are placed side by side, a continuous ballpark background is formed. Some cards have been found without perforations, and all players pictured appear in the low series of the 1955 regular issue. The cards were issued in one-card penny packs with a piece of bubble gum.

	NRMT	VG-E
COMPLETE SET (66)	4000.00	1800.00
COMMON CARD (1-132)	40.00	18.00
WRAPPER (1-CENT)	200.00	90.00

Card	NRMT	VG-E
☐ 1 Al Rosen and 2 Chuck Diering	50.00	22.00
☐ 3 Monte Irvin and 4 Russ Kemmerer	75.00	34.00
☐ 5 Ted Kazanski and 6 Gordon Jones	40.00	18.00
☐ 7 Bill Taylor and 8 Billy O'Dell	40.00	18.00
☐ 9 J.W. Porter and 10 Thornton Kipper	40.00	18.00
☐ 11 Curt Roberts and 12 Arnie Portocarrero	40.00	18.00
☐ 13 Wally Westlake and 14 Frank House	40.00	18.00
☐ 15 Rube Walker and 16 Lou Limmer	40.00	18.00
☐ 17 Dean Stone and 18 Charlie White	40.00	18.00
☐ 19 Karl Spooner and 20 Jim Hughes	40.00	18.00
☐ 21 Bill Skowron and 22 Frank Sullivan	50.00	22.00
☐ 23 Jack Shepard and 24 Stan Hack MG	40.00	18.00
☐ 25 Jackie Robinson and 26 Don Hoak	300.00	135.00
☐ 27 Dusty Rhodes and 28 Jim Davis	40.00	18.00
☐ 29 Vic Power and 30 Ed Bailey	40.00	18.00
☐ 31 Howie Pollet and 32 Ernie Banks	225.00	100.00
☐ 33 Jim Pendleton and 34 Gene Conley	40.00	18.00
☐ 35 Karl Olson and 36 Andy Carey	40.00	18.00
☐ 37 Wally Moon and 38 Joe Cunningham	50.00	22.00
☐ 39 Freddie Marsh and 40 Vernon Thies	40.00	18.00
☐ 41 Eddie Lopat and 42 Harvey Haddix	50.00	22.00
☐ 43 Leo Kiely and 44 Chuck Stobbs	40.00	18.00
☐ 45 Al Kaline and 46 Harold Valentine	225.00	100.00
☐ 47 Forrest Jacobs and 48 Johnny Gray	40.00	18.00
☐ 49 Ron Jackson and 50 Jim Finigan	40.00	18.00
☐ 51 Ray Jablonski and 52 Bob Keegan	40.00	18.00
☐ 53 Billy Herman CO and 54 Sandy Amoros	75.00	34.00
☐ 55 Chuck Harmon and 56 Bob Skinner	40.00	18.00
☐ 57 Dick Hall and 58 Bob Grim	40.00	18.00
☐ 59 Billy Glynn and 60 Bob Miller	40.00	18.00
☐ 61 Billy Gardner and 62 John Hetki	40.00	18.00
☐ 63 Bob Borkowski and 64 Bob Turley	40.00	18.00
☐ 65 Joe Collins and 66 Jack Harshman	40.00	18.00
☐ 67 Jim Hegan and 68 Jack Parks	40.00	18.00
☐ 69 Ted Williams and 70 Mayo Smith MG	400.00	180.00
☐ 71 Gair Allie and 72 Grady Hatton	40.00	18.00
☐ 73 Jerry Lynch and 74 Harry Brecheen CO	40.00	18.00
☐ 75 Tom Wright and 76 Vernon Stewart	40.00	18.00
☐ 77 Dave Hoskins and 78 Warren McGhee	40.00	18.00
☐ 79 Roy Sievers and 80 Art Fowler	40.00	18.00
☐ 81 Danny Schell and 82 Gus Triandos	40.00	18.00
☐ 83 Joe Frazier and 84 Don Mossi	40.00	18.00
☐ 85 Elmer Valo and 86 Hector Brown	40.00	18.00
☐ 87 Bob Kennedy and 88 Windy McCall	40.00	18.00
☐ 89 Ruben Gomez and 90 Jim Rivera	40.00	18.00
☐ 91 Louis Ortiz and 92 Milt Bolling	40.00	18.00
☐ 93 Carl Sawatski and 94 El Tappe	40.00	18.00
☐ 95 Dave Jolly and 96 Bobby Hofman	40.00	18.00
☐ 97 Preston Ward and 98 Don Zimmer	50.00	22.00
☐ 99 Bill Renna and 100 Dick Groat	50.00	22.00
☐ 101 Bill Wilson and 102 Bill Tremel	40.00	18.00
☐ 103 Hank Sauer and 104 Camilo Pascual	50.00	22.00
☐ 105 Hank Aaron and 106 Ray Herbert	500.00	220.00
☐ 107 Alex Grammas and 108 Tom Qualters	40.00	18.00
☐ 109 Hal Newhouser and 110 Chuck Bishop	75.00	34.00
☐ 111 Harmon Killebrew and 112 John Podres	200.00	90.00
☐ 113 Ray Boone and 114 Bob Purkey	40.00	18.00
☐ 115 Dale Long and 116 Ferris Fain	40.00	18.00
☐ 117 Steve Bilko and 118 Bob Milliken	40.00	18.00
☐ 119 Mel Parnell and 120 Tom Hurd	40.00	18.00
☐ 121 Ted Kluszewski and 122 Jim Owens	75.00	34.00
☐ 123 Gus Zernial and 124 Bob Trice	40.00	18.00
☐ 125 Rip Repulski and 126 Ted Lepcio	40.00	18.00
☐ 127 Warren Spahn and	200.00	90.00

Card	NRMT	VG-E
128 Tom Brewer		
☐ 129 Jim Gilliam and	75.00	34.00
130 Ellis Kinder		
☐ 131 Herm Wehmeier and	40.00	18.00
132 Wayne Terwilliger		

1956 Topps

The cards in this 340-card set measure approximately 2 5/8" by 3 3/4". Following up with another horizontally oriented card in 1956, Topps improved the format by layering the color "head" shot onto an actual action sequence involving the player. Cards 1 to 180 come with either white or gray backs: in the 1 to 100 sequence, gray backs are less common (worth about 10 percent more) and in the 101 to 180 sequence, white backs are less common (worth 30 percent more). The team cards, used for the first time in a regular set by Topps, are found dated 1955, or undated, with the team name appearing on either side. The dated team cards in the first series were not printed on the gray stock. The two unnumbered checklist cards are highly prized (must be unmarked to qualify as excellent or mint). The complete set price below does not include the unnumbered checklist cards or any of the variations. The set was issued in one-card penny packs or six-card nickle packs. Both types of packs included a piece of bubble gum. The key Rookie Cards in this set are Walt Alston, Luis Aparicio, and Roger Craig. There are ten double-printed cards in the first series as evidenced by the discovery of an uncut sheet of 110 cards (10 by 11); these DP's are listed below.

	NRMT	VG-E
COMPLETE SET (340)	7000.00	3200.00
COMMON CARD (1-100)	10.00	4.50
COMMON CARD (101-180)	12.00	5.50
COMMON CARD (261-340)	12.00	5.50
COMMON CARD (181-260)	15.00	6.75
WRAPPER (1-CENT)	250.00	110.00
WRAPPER (1-CENT, REPEAT)	100.00	45.00
WRAPPER (5-CENT)	200.00	90.00

Card	NRMT	VG-E
☐ 1 William Harridge PRES	100.00	28.00
☐ 2 Warren Giles PRES	25.00	11.00
☐ 3 Elmer Valo	10.00	4.50
☐ 4 Carlos Paula	10.00	4.50
☐ 5 Ted Williams	325.00	145.00
☐ 6 Ray Boone	16.00	7.25
☐ 7 Ron Negray	10.00	4.50
☐ 8 Walter Alston MG	40.00	18.00
☐ 9 Ruben Gomez DP	9.00	4.00
☐ 10 Warren Spahn	70.00	32.00
☐ 11A Chicago Cubs	30.00	13.50
(Centered)		
☐ 11B Cubs Team	80.00	36.00
(Dated 1955)		
☐ 11C Cubs Team	30.00	13.50
(Name at far left)		
☐ 12 Andy Carey	15.00	6.75
☐ 13 Roy Face	16.00	7.25
☐ 14 Ken Boyer DP	16.00	7.25
☐ 15 Ernie Banks DP	80.00	36.00
☐ 16 Hector Lopez	16.00	7.25
☐ 17 Gene Conley	15.00	6.75
☐ 18 Dick Donovan	10.00	4.50
☐ 19 Chuck Diering	10.00	4.50
☐ 20 Al Kaline	90.00	40.00
☐ 21 Joe Collins DP	15.00	6.75
☐ 22 Jim Finigan	10.00	4.50
☐ 23 Fred Marsh	10.00	4.50
☐ 24 Dick Groat	16.00	7.25
☐ 25 Ted Kluszewski	35.00	16.00
☐ 26 Grady Hatton	10.00	4.50
☐ 27 Nelson Burbrink	10.00	4.50
☐ 28 Bobby Hofman	10.00	4.50
☐ 29 Jack Harshman	10.00	4.50
☐ 30 Jackie Robinson DP	175.00	80.00
☐ 31 Hank Aaron UER	275.00	125.00
(Small photo		
actually Willie Mays)		
☐ 32 Frank House	10.00	4.50
☐ 33 Roberto Clemente	450.00	200.00
☐ 34 Tom Brewer	10.00	4.50
☐ 35 Al Rosen	16.00	7.25
☐ 36 Rudy Minarcin	10.00	4.50
☐ 37 Alex Grammas	10.00	4.50
☐ 38 Bob Kennedy	15.00	6.75
☐ 39 Don Mossi	15.00	6.75
☐ 40 Bob Turley	16.00	7.25
☐ 41 Hank Sauer	16.00	7.25
☐ 42 Sandy Amoros	16.00	7.25
☐ 43 Ray Moore	10.00	4.50
☐ 44 Windy McCall	10.00	4.50
☐ 45 Gus Zernial	15.00	6.75
☐ 46 Gene Freese DP	9.00	4.00
☐ 47 Art Fowler	10.00	4.50
☐ 48 Jim Hegan	15.00	6.75
☐ 49 Pedro Ramos	10.00	4.50
☐ 50 Dusty Rhodes	16.00	7.25
☐ 51 Ernie Oravetz	10.00	4.50
☐ 52 Bob Grim	15.00	6.75
☐ 53 Arnie Portocarrero	10.00	4.50
☐ 54 Bob Keegan	10.00	4.50
☐ 55 Wally Moon	16.00	7.25
☐ 56 Dale Long	15.00	6.75
☐ 57 Duke Maas	10.00	4.50
☐ 58 Ed Roebuck	15.00	6.75
☐ 59 Jose Santiago	10.00	4.50
☐ 60 Mayo Smith MG DP	9.00	4.00
☐ 61 Bill Skowron	16.00	7.25
☐ 62 Hal Smith	10.00	4.50
☐ 63 Roger Craig	16.00	7.25
☐ 64 Luis Arroyo	10.00	4.50
☐ 65 Johnny O'Brien	15.00	6.75
☐ 66 Bob Speake	10.00	4.50
☐ 67 Vic Power	15.00	6.75
☐ 68 Chuck Stobbs	10.00	4.50
☐ 69 Chuck Tanner	16.00	7.25
☐ 70 Jim Rivera	10.00	4.50
☐ 71 Frank Sullivan	10.00	4.50
☐ 72A Phillies Team	30.00	13.50
(Centered)		
☐ 72B Phillies Team	80.00	36.00
(Dated 1955)		
☐ 72C Phillies Team	30.00	13.50
(Name at far left)		
☐ 73 Wayne Terwilliger	10.00	4.50
☐ 74 Jim King	10.00	4.50
☐ 75 Roy Sievers DP	15.00	6.75
☐ 76 Ray Crone	10.00	4.50
☐ 77 Harvey Haddix	16.00	7.25
☐ 78 Herman Wehmeier	10.00	4.50
☐ 79 Sandy Koufax	350.00	160.00
☐ 80 Gus Triandos DP	10.00	4.50
☐ 81 Wally Westlake	10.00	4.50
☐ 82 Bill Renna	10.00	4.50
☐ 83 Karl Spooner	15.00	6.75
☐ 84 Babe Birrer	10.00	4.50
☐ 85A Cleveland Indians	30.00	13.50
(Centered)		
☐ 85B Indians Team	80.00	36.00
(Dated 1955)		
☐ 85C Indians Team	30.00	13.50
(Name at far left)		
☐ 86 Ray Jablonski DP	9.00	4.00
☐ 87 Dean Stone	10.00	4.50
☐ 88 Johnny Kucks	15.00	6.75
☐ 89 Norm Zauchin	10.00	4.50
☐ 90A Cincinnati Redlegs	30.00	13.50
Team (Centered)		
☐ 90B Reds Team	80.00	36.00
(Dated 1955)		
☐ 90C Reds Team	30.00	13.50
(Name at far left)		
☐ 91 Gail Harris	10.00	4.50
☐ 92 Bob(Red) Wilson	10.00	4.50
☐ 93 George Susce	10.00	4.50
☐ 94 Ron Kline	10.00	4.50
☐ 95A Milwaukee Braves	42.00	19.00
Team (Centered)		
☐ 95B Braves Team	80.00	36.00
(Dated 1955)		
☐ 95C Braves Team	42.00	19.00
(Name at far left)		
☐ 96 Bill Tremel	10.00	4.50
☐ 97 Jerry Lynch	15.00	6.75
☐ 98 Camilo Pascual	15.00	6.75
☐ 99 Don Zimmer	15.00	6.75
☐ 100A Baltimore Orioles	35.00	16.00
Team (centered)		
☐ 100B Orioles Team	80.00	36.00
(Dated 1955)		
☐ 100C Orioles Team	35.00	16.00
(Name at far left)		
☐ 101 Roy Campanella	150.00	70.00
☐ 102 Jim Davis	12.00	5.50
☐ 103 Willie Miranda	12.00	5.50
☐ 104 Bob Lennon	12.00	5.50
☐ 105 Al Smith	12.00	5.50
☐ 106 Joe Astroth	12.00	5.50
☐ 107 Eddie Mathews	60.00	27.00
☐ 108 Laurin Pepper	12.00	5.50
☐ 109 Enos Slaughter	35.00	16.00
☐ 110 Yogi Berra	125.00	55.00
☐ 111 Boston Red Sox	40.00	18.00
Team Card		
☐ 112 Dee Fondy	12.00	5.50
☐ 113 Phil Rizzuto	90.00	40.00
☐ 114 Jim Owens	12.00	5.50
☐ 115 Jackie Jensen	15.00	6.75
☐ 116 Eddie O'Brien	12.00	5.50
☐ 117 Virgil Trucks	15.00	6.75
☐ 118 Nellie Fox	50.00	22.00
☐ 119 Larry Jackson	15.00	6.75
☐ 120 Richie Ashburn	50.00	22.00
☐ 121 Pittsburgh Pirates	25.00	11.00
Team Card		
☐ 122 Willard Nixon	12.00	5.50
☐ 123 Roy McMillan	15.00	6.75
☐ 124 Don Kaiser	12.00	5.50
☐ 125 Minnie Minoso	35.00	16.00
☐ 126 Jim Brady	12.00	5.50
☐ 127 Willie Jones	15.00	6.75
☐ 128 Eddie Yost	15.00	6.75
☐ 129 Jake Martin	12.00	5.50
☐ 130 Willie Mays	300.00	135.00
☐ 131 Bob Roselli	12.00	5.50
☐ 132 Bobby Avila	12.00	5.50
☐ 133 Ray Narleski	12.00	5.50
☐ 134 St. Louis Cardinals	25.00	11.00
Team Card		
☐ 135 Mickey Mantle	1400.00	650.00
☐ 136 Johnny Logan	15.00	6.75
☐ 137 Al Silvera	12.00	5.50
☐ 138 Johnny Antonelli	15.00	6.75
☐ 139 Tommy Carroll	12.00	5.50
☐ 140 Herb Score	60.00	27.00
☐ 141 Joe Frazier	12.00	5.50
☐ 142 Gene Baker	12.00	5.50
☐ 143 Jim Piersall	15.00	6.75
☐ 144 Leroy Powell	12.00	5.50
☐ 145 Gil Hodges	50.00	22.00
☐ 146 Washington Nationals	25.00	11.00
Team Card		
☐ 147 Earl Torgeson	12.00	5.50
☐ 148 Alvin Dark	16.00	7.25
☐ 149 Dixie Howell	12.00	5.50
☐ 150 Duke Snider	90.00	40.00
☐ 151 Spook Jacobs	15.00	6.75
☐ 152 Billy Hoeft	15.00	6.75
☐ 153 Frank Thomas	15.00	6.75
☐ 154 Dave Pope	12.00	5.50
☐ 155 Harvey Kuenn	16.00	7.25
☐ 156 Wes Westrum	15.00	6.75
☐ 157 Dick Brodowski	12.00	5.50
☐ 158 Wally Post	15.00	6.75
☐ 159 Clint Courtney	12.00	5.50
☐ 160 Billy Pierce	15.00	6.75
☐ 161 Joe DeMaestri	12.00	5.50
☐ 162 Dave(Gus) Bell	15.00	6.75
☐ 163 Gene Woodling	15.00	6.75
☐ 164 Harmon Killebrew	100.00	45.00
☐ 165 Red Schoendienst	35.00	16.00
☐ 166 Brooklyn Dodgers	250.00	110.00
Team Card		
☐ 167 Harry Dorish	12.00	5.50
☐ 168 Sammy White	12.00	5.50
☐ 169 Bob Nelson	12.00	5.50
☐ 170 Bill Virdon	15.00	6.75
☐ 171 Jim Wilson	12.00	5.50
☐ 172 Frank Torre	15.00	6.75
☐ 173 Johnny Podres	22.50	10.00
☐ 174 Glen Gorbous	12.00	5.50
☐ 175 Del Crandall	15.00	6.75
☐ 176 Alex Kellner	12.00	5.50
☐ 177 Hank Bauer	22.50	10.00
☐ 178 Joe Black	16.00	7.25
☐ 179 Harry Chiti	12.00	5.50
☐ 180 Robin Roberts	40.00	18.00
☐ 181 Billy Martin	60.00	27.00
☐ 182 Paul Minner	15.00	6.75
☐ 183 Stan Lopata	15.00	6.75
☐ 184 Don Bessent	15.00	6.75
☐ 185 Bill Bruton	20.00	9.00
☐ 186 Ron Jackson	15.00	6.75
☐ 187 Early Wynn	40.00	18.00
☐ 188 Chicago White Sox	40.00	18.00
Team Card		
☐ 189 Ned Garver	15.00	6.75
☐ 190 Carl Furillo	35.00	16.00
☐ 191 Frank Lary	20.00	9.00
☐ 192 Smoky Burgess	20.00	9.00
☐ 193 Wilmer Mizell	20.00	9.00
☐ 194 Monte Irvin	35.00	16.00
☐ 195 George Kell	35.00	16.00
☐ 196 Tom Poholsky	15.00	6.75

☐ 197 Granny Hamner 15.00 6.75
☐ 198 Ed Fitzgerald 15.00 6.75
☐ 199 Hank Thompson 20.00 9.00
☐ 200 Bob Feller 100.00 45.00
☐ 201 Rip Repulski 15.00 6.75
☐ 202 Jim Hearn 15.00 6.75
☐ 203 Bill Tuttle 15.00 6.75
☐ 204 Art Swanson 15.00 6.75
☐ 205 Whitey Lockman 20.00 9.00
☐ 206 Erv Palica 15.00 6.75
☐ 207 Jim Small 15.00 6.75
☐ 208 Elston Howard 50.00 22.00
☐ 209 Max Surkont 15.00 6.75
☐ 210 Mike Garcia 20.00 9.00
☐ 211 Murry Dickson 15.00 6.75
☐ 212 Johnny Temple 15.00 6.75
☐ 213 Detroit Tigers Team Card 60.00 27.00
☐ 214 Bob Rush 15.00 6.75
☐ 215 Tommy Byrne 20.00 9.00
☐ 216 Jerry Schoonmaker 15.00 6.75
☐ 217 Billy Klaus 15.00 6.75
☐ 218 Joe Nuxhall UER (Misspelled Nuxall) 20.00 9.00
☐ 219 Lew Burdette 20.00 9.00
☐ 220 Del Ennis 20.00 9.00
☐ 221 Bob Friend 20.00 9.00
☐ 222 Dave Philley 15.00 6.75
☐ 223 Randy Jackson 15.00 6.75
☐ 224 Bud Podbielan 15.00 6.75
☐ 225 Gil McDougald 30.00 13.50
☐ 226 New York Giants Team Card 80.00 36.00
☐ 227 Russ Meyer 15.00 6.75
☐ 228 Mickey Vernon 20.00 9.00
☐ 229 Harry Brecheen CO 20.00 9.00
☐ 230 Chico Carrasquel 15.00 6.75
☐ 231 Bob Hale 15.00 6.75
☐ 232 Toby Atwell 15.00 6.75
☐ 233 Carl Erskine 35.00 16.00
☐ 234 Pete Runnels 15.00 6.75
☐ 235 Don Newcombe 50.00 22.00
☐ 236 Kansas City Athletics Team Card 30.00 13.50
☐ 237 Jose Valdivielso 15.00 6.75
☐ 238 Walt Dropo 20.00 9.00
☐ 239 Harry Simpson 15.00 6.75
☐ 240 Whitey Ford 100.00 45.00
☐ 241 Don Mueller UER (6" tall) 20.00 9.00
☐ 242 Hershell Freeman 15.00 6.75
☐ 243 Sherm Lollar 20.00 9.00
☐ 244 Bob Buhl 20.00 9.00
☐ 245 Billy Goodman 20.00 9.00
☐ 246 Tom Gorman 15.00 6.75
☐ 247 Bill Sarni 15.00 6.75
☐ 248 Bob Porterfield 15.00 6.75
☐ 249 Johnny Klippstein 15.00 6.75
☐ 250 Larry Doby 35.00 16.00
☐ 251 New York Yankees Team Card UER (Don Larsen misspelled as Larson on front) 275.00 125.00
☐ 252 Vern Law 20.00 9.00
☐ 253 Irv Noren 15.00 6.75
☐ 254 George Crowe 15.00 6.75
☐ 255 Bob Lemon 35.00 16.00
☐ 256 Tom Hurd 15.00 6.75
☐ 257 Bobby Thomson 35.00 16.00
☐ 258 Art Ditmar 15.00 6.75
☐ 259 Sam Jones 20.00 9.00
☐ 260 Pee Wee Reese 120.00 55.00
☐ 261 Bobby Shantz 15.00 6.75
☐ 262 Howie Pollet 12.00 5.50
☐ 263 Bob Miller 12.00 5.50
☐ 264 Ray Monzant 12.00 5.50
☐ 265 Sandy Consuegra 12.00 5.50
☐ 266 Don Ferrarese 12.00 5.50
☐ 267 Bob Nieman 12.00 5.50
☐ 268 Dale Mitchell 16.00 7.25
☐ 269 Jack Meyer 12.00 5.50
☐ 270 Billy Loes 15.00 6.75
☐ 271 Foster Castleman 12.00 5.50
☐ 272 Danny O'Connell 12.00 5.50
☐ 273 Walker Cooper 12.00 5.50
☐ 274 Frank Baumholtz 12.00 5.50
☐ 275 Jim Greengrass 12.00 5.50
☐ 276 George Zuverink 12.00 5.50
☐ 277 Daryl Spencer 12.00 5.50
☐ 278 Chet Nichols 12.00 5.50
☐ 279 Johnny Groth 12.00 5.50
☐ 280 Jim Gilliam 35.00 16.00
☐ 281 Art Houtteman 12.00 5.50
☐ 282 Warren Hacker 12.00 5.50
☐ 283 Hal Smith 12.00 5.50
☐ 284 Ike Delock 12.00 5.50
☐ 285 Eddie Miksis 12.00 5.50
☐ 286 Bill Wight 12.00 5.50
☐ 287 Bobby Adams 12.00 5.50
☐ 288 Bob Cerv 40.00 18.00
☐ 289 Hal Jeffcoat 12.00 5.50
☐ 290 Curt Simmons 15.00 6.75
☐ 291 Frank Kellert 12.00 5.50
☐ 292 Luis Aparicio 125.00 55.00
☐ 293 Stu Miller 15.00 6.75
☐ 294 Ernie Johnson 15.00 6.75
☐ 295 Clem Labine 18.00 8.00
☐ 296 Andy Seminick 12.00 5.50
☐ 297 Bob Skinner 15.00 6.75
☐ 298 Johnny Schmitz 12.00 5.50
☐ 299 Charlie Neal 35.00 16.00
☐ 300 Vic Wertz 16.00 7.25
☐ 301 Marv Grissom 12.00 5.50
☐ 302 Eddie Robinson 12.00 5.50
☐ 303 Jim Dyck 12.00 5.50
☐ 304 Frank Malzone 16.00 7.25
☐ 305 Brooks Lawrence 12.00 5.50
☐ 306 Curt Roberts 12.00 5.50
☐ 307 Hoyt Wilhelm 35.00 16.00
☐ 308 Chuck Harmon 12.00 5.50
☐ 309 Don Blasingame 16.00 7.25
☐ 310 Steve Gromek 12.00 5.50
☐ 311 Hal Naragon 12.00 5.50
☐ 312 Andy Pafko 16.00 7.25
☐ 313 Gene Stephens 12.00 5.50
☐ 314 Hobie Landrith 12.00 5.50
☐ 315 Milt Bolling 12.00 5.50
☐ 316 Jerry Coleman 18.00 8.00
☐ 317 Al Aber 12.00 5.50
☐ 318 Fred Hatfield 12.00 5.50
☐ 319 Jack Crimian 12.00 5.50
☐ 320 Joe Adcock 16.00 7.25
☐ 321 Jim Konstanty 15.00 6.75
☐ 322 Karl Olson 12.00 5.50
☐ 323 Willard Schmidt 12.00 5.50
☐ 324 Rocky Bridges 15.00 6.75
☐ 325 Don Liddle 12.00 5.50
☐ 326 Connie Johnson 12.00 5.50
☐ 327 Bob Wiesler 12.00 5.50
☐ 328 Preston Ward 12.00 5.50
☐ 329 Lou Berberet 12.00 5.50
☐ 330 Jim Busby 12.00 5.50
☐ 331 Dick Hall 12.00 5.50
☐ 332 Don Larsen 60.00 27.00
☐ 333 Rube Walker 12.00 5.50
☐ 334 Bob Miller 12.00 5.50
☐ 335 Don Hoak 15.00 6.75
☐ 336 Ellis Kinder 12.00 5.50
☐ 337 Bobby Morgan 12.00 5.50
☐ 338 Jim Delsing 12.00 5.50
☐ 339 Rance Pless 12.00 5.50
☐ 340 Mickey McDermott 60.00 12.00
☐ NNO Checklist 1/3 300.00 95.00
☐ NNO Checklist 2/4 300.00 95.00

1956 Topps Pins

This set of 60 full-color pins was Topps first and only baseball player pin set. Each pin measures 1 3/16" in diameter. Although the set was advertised to contain 90 pins, only 60 were issued. The checklist below lists the players in alphabetical order within team, e.g., Baltimore Orioles (1-4), Chicago Cubs (5-7), Cleveland Indians (8-11), Kansas City A's (12-15), Milwaukee Braves (16-19), Philadelphia Phillies (20-22), Boston Red Sox (23-26), New York Yankees (27-31), Chicago White Sox (32-35), Detroit Tigers (36-38), New York Giants (39-41), Pittsburgh Pirates (42-44), St. Louis Cardinals (45-48), Brooklyn Dodgers (49-53), Cincinnati Redlegs (54-57) and Washington Senators (58-60). Chuck Diering, Hector Lopez and Chuck Stobbs (noted below with SP) are more difficult to obtain than other pins in the set.

	NRMT	VG-E
COMPLETE SET (60)	2250.00	1000.00
COMMON PIN (1-60)	15.00	6.75
PIN BOX (5-CENT)	200.00	90.00

☐ 1 Chuck Diering SP 250.00 110.00
☐ 2 Willie Miranda 15.00 6.75
☐ 3 Hal Smith 15.00 6.75
☐ 4 Gus Triandos 20.00 9.00
☐ 5 Ernie Banks 75.00 34.00
☐ 6 Hank Sauer 20.00 9.00
☐ 7 Bill Tremel 15.00 6.75
☐ 8 Jim Hegan 15.00 6.75
☐ 9 Don Mossi 15.00 6.75
☐ 10 Al Rosen 25.00 11.00
☐ 11 Al Smith 15.00 6.75
☐ 12 Jim Finigan 15.00 6.75
☐ 13 Hector Lopez SP 200.00 90.00
☐ 14 Vic Power 15.00 6.75
☐ 15 Gus Zernial 20.00 9.00
☐ 16 Hank Aaron 125.00 55.00
☐ 17 Gene Conley 15.00 6.75
☐ 18 Eddie Mathews 75.00 34.00
☐ 19 Warren Spahn 75.00 34.00
☐ 20 Ron Negray 15.00 6.75
☐ 21 Mayo Smith MG 15.00 6.75
☐ 22 Herman Wehmeier 15.00 6.75
☐ 23 Grady Hatton 15.00 6.75
☐ 24 Jackie Jensen 25.00 11.00
☐ 25 Frank Sullivan 15.00 6.75
☐ 26 Ted Williams 150.00 70.00
☐ 27 Yogi Berra 100.00 45.00
☐ 28 Joe Collins 20.00 9.00
☐ 29 Phil Rizzuto 50.00 22.00
☐ 30 Bill Skowron 25.00 11.00
☐ 31 Bob Turley 25.00 11.00
☐ 32 Dick Donovan 15.00 6.75
☐ 33 Jack Harshman 15.00 6.75
☐ 34 Bob Kennedy 15.00 6.75
☐ 35 Jim Rivera 15.00 6.75
☐ 36 Ray Boone 20.00 9.00
☐ 37 Frank House 15.00 6.75
☐ 38 Al Kaline 75.00 34.00
☐ 39 Ruben Gomez 15.00 6.75
☐ 40 Bobby Hofman 15.00 6.75
☐ 41 Willie Mays 135.00 60.00
☐ 42 Dick Groat 25.00 11.00
☐ 43 Dale Long 20.00 9.00
☐ 44 Johnny O'Brien 15.00 6.75
☐ 45 Luis Arroyo 15.00 6.75
☐ 46 Ken Boyer 25.00 11.00
☐ 47 Harvey Haddix 15.00 6.75
☐ 48 Wally Moon 15.00 6.75
☐ 49 Sandy Amoros 15.00 6.75
☐ 50 Gil Hodges 50.00 22.00
☐ 51 Jackie Robinson 150.00 70.00
☐ 52 Duke Snider 75.00 34.00
☐ 53 Karl Spooner 15.00 6.75
☐ 54 Joe Black 25.00 11.00
☐ 55 Art Fowler 15.00 6.75
☐ 56 Ted Kluszewski 30.00 13.50
☐ 57 Roy McMillan 15.00 6.75
☐ 58 Carlos Paula 15.00 6.75
☐ 59 Roy Sievers 15.00 6.75
☐ 60 Chuck Stobbs SP 200.00 90.00

1957 Topps

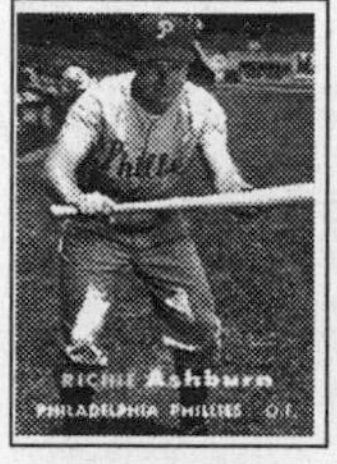

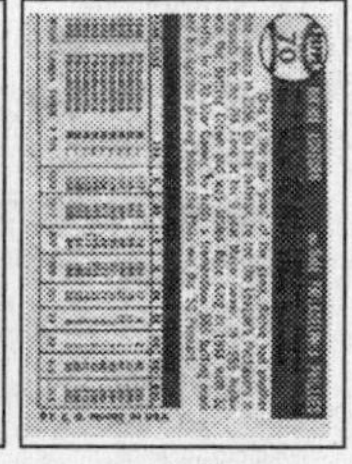

The cards in this 407-card set measure 2 1/2" by 3 1/2". In 1957, Topps returned to the vertical obverse, adopted what we now call the standard card size, and used a large, uncluttered color photo for the first time since 1952. Cards in the series 265 to 352 and the unnumbered checklist cards are scarcer than other cards in the set. However within this scarce series (265-352) there are 22 cards which were printed in double the quantity of the other cards in the series; these 22 double prints are indicated by DP in the checklist below. The first star combination cards, cards 400 and 407, are quite popular with collectors. They feature the big stars of the previous season's World Series teams, the Dodgers (Furillo, Hodges, Campanella, and Snider) and Yankees (Berra and Mantle). The complete set price below does not include the unnumbered checklist cards. Confirmed packaging includes one-cent penny packs and six-card nickle packs. Cello packs are definately known to exist and some collectors remember buyikng rack packs of 57's as well. The key Rookie Cards in this set are Jim Bunning, Rocky Colavito, Don Drysdale, Whitey Herzog, Tony Kubek, Bill Mazeroski, Bobby Richardson, Brooks Robinson, and Frank Robinson.

	NRMT	VG-E
COMPLETE SET (407)	7000.00	3200.00
COMMON CARD (1-88)	10.00	4.50
COMMON CARD (89-176)	8.00	3.60
COMMON CARD (177-264)	8.00	3.60
COMMON CARD (265-352)	20.00	9.00
COMMON CARD (353-407)	8.00	3.60
COMMON DP 265-352	14.00	6.25
WRAPPER (1-CENT)	300.00	135.00
WRAPPER (5-CENT)	200.00	90.00

	NRMT	VG-E
☐ 1 Ted Williams	500.00	150.00
☐ 2 Yogi Berra	125.00	55.00
☐ 3 Dale Long	15.00	6.75
☐ 4 Johnny Logan	15.00	6.75
☐ 5 Sal Maglie	18.00	8.00
☐ 6 Hector Lopez	15.00	6.75
☐ 7 Luis Aparicio	35.00	16.00
☐ 8 Don Mossi	15.00	6.75
☐ 9 Johnny Temple	15.00	6.75
☐ 10 Willie Mays	225.00	100.00
☐ 11 George Zuverink	10.00	4.50
☐ 12 Dick Groat	14.00	6.25
☐ 13 Wally Burnette	10.00	4.50
☐ 14 Bob Nieman	10.00	4.50
☐ 15 Robin Roberts	35.00	16.00
☐ 16 Walt Moryn	10.00	4.50
☐ 17 Billy Gardner	10.00	4.50
☐ 18 Don Drysdale	200.00	90.00
☐ 19 Bob Wilson	10.00	4.50
☐ 20 Hank Aaron UER (Reverse negative photo on front)	200.00	90.00
☐ 21 Frank Sullivan	10.00	4.50
☐ 22 Jerry Snyder UER (Photo actually Ed Fitzgerald)	10.00	4.50
☐ 23 Sherm Lollar	15.00	6.75
☐ 24 Bill Mazeroski	75.00	34.00
☐ 25 Whitey Ford	70.00	32.00
☐ 26 Bob Boyd	10.00	4.50
☐ 27 Ted Kazanski	10.00	4.50
☐ 28 Gene Conley	15.00	6.75
☐ 29 Whitey Herzog	25.00	11.00
☐ 30 Pee Wee Reese	65.00	29.00
☐ 31 Ron Northey	10.00	4.50
☐ 32 Hershell Freeman	10.00	4.50
☐ 33 Jim Small	10.00	4.50
☐ 34 Tom Sturdivant	15.00	6.75
☐ 35 Frank Robinson	200.00	90.00
☐ 36 Bob Grim	10.00	4.50
☐ 37 Frank Torre	15.00	6.75
☐ 38 Nellie Fox	45.00	20.00
☐ 39 Al Worthington	10.00	4.50
☐ 40 Early Wynn	30.00	13.50
☐ 41 Hal W. Smith	10.00	4.50
☐ 42 Dee Fondy	10.00	4.50
☐ 43 Connie Johnson	10.00	4.50
☐ 44 Joe DeMaestri	10.00	4.50
☐ 45 Carl Furillo	20.00	9.00
☐ 46 Robert J. Miller	10.00	4.50
☐ 47 Don Blasingame	10.00	4.50
☐ 48 Bill Bruton	15.00	6.75
☐ 49 Daryl Spencer	10.00	4.50
☐ 50 Herb Score	20.00	9.00
☐ 51 Clint Courtney	10.00	4.50
☐ 52 Lee Walls	10.00	4.50
☐ 53 Clem Labine	18.00	8.00
☐ 54 Elmer Valo	10.00	4.50
☐ 55 Ernie Banks	120.00	55.00
☐ 56 Dave Sisler	10.00	4.50
☐ 57 Jim Lemon	15.00	6.75
☐ 58 Ruben Gomez	10.00	4.50
☐ 59 Dick Williams	14.00	6.25
☐ 60 Billy Hoeft	15.00	6.75
☐ 61 Dusty Rhodes	14.00	6.25
☐ 62 Billy Martin	45.00	20.00
☐ 63 Ike Delock	10.00	4.50
☐ 64 Pete Runnels	15.00	6.75
☐ 65 Wally Moon	14.00	6.25
☐ 66 Brooks Lawrence	10.00	4.50
☐ 67 Chico Carrasquel	10.00	4.50
☐ 68 Ray Crone	10.00	4.50
☐ 69 Roy McMillan	15.00	6.75
☐ 70 Richie Ashburn	45.00	20.00
☐ 71 Murry Dickson	10.00	4.50
☐ 72 Bill Tuttle	10.00	4.50
☐ 73 George Crowe	10.00	4.50
☐ 74 Vito Valentinetti	10.00	4.50
☐ 75 Jimmy Piersall	14.00	6.25
☐ 76 Roberto Clemente	300.00	135.00
☐ 77 Paul Foytack	10.00	4.50
☐ 78 Vic Wertz	14.00	6.25
☐ 79 Lindy McDaniel	14.00	6.25
☐ 80 Gil Hodges	45.00	20.00
☐ 81 Herman Wehmeier	10.00	4.50
☐ 82 Elston Howard	20.00	9.00
☐ 83 Lou Skizas	10.00	4.50
☐ 84 Moe Drabowsky	15.00	6.75
☐ 85 Larry Doby	20.00	9.00
☐ 86 Bill Sarni	10.00	4.50
☐ 87 Tom Gorman	10.00	4.50
☐ 88 Harvey Kuenn	14.00	6.25
☐ 89 Roy Sievers	15.00	6.75
☐ 90 Warren Spahn	70.00	32.00
☐ 91 Mack Burk	8.00	3.60
☐ 92 Mickey Vernon	15.00	6.75
☐ 93 Hal Jeffcoat	8.00	3.60
☐ 94 Bobby Del Greco	8.00	3.60
☐ 95 Mickey Mantle	1000.00	450.00
☐ 96 Hank Aguirre	8.00	3.60
☐ 97 New York Yankees Team Card	80.00	36.00
☐ 98 Alvin Dark	14.00	6.25
☐ 99 Bob Keegan	8.00	3.60
☐ 100 League Presidents Warren Giles Will Harridge	14.00	6.25
☐ 101 Chuck Stobbs	8.00	3.60
☐ 102 Ray Boone	14.00	6.25
☐ 103 Joe Nuxhall	14.00	6.25
☐ 104 Hank Foiles	8.00	3.60
☐ 105 Johnny Antonelli	14.00	6.25
☐ 106 Ray Moore	8.00	3.60
☐ 107 Jim Rivera	8.00	3.60
☐ 108 Tommy Byrne	15.00	6.75
☐ 109 Hank Thompson	8.00	3.60
☐ 110 Bill Virdon	15.00	6.75
☐ 111 Hal R. Smith	8.00	3.60
☐ 112 Tom Brewer	8.00	3.60
☐ 113 Wilmer Mizell	15.00	6.75
☐ 114 Milwaukee Braves Team Card	22.00	10.00
☐ 115 Jim Gilliam	14.00	6.25
☐ 116 Mike Fornieles	8.00	3.60
☐ 117 Joe Adcock	14.00	6.25
☐ 118 Bob Porterfield	8.00	3.60
☐ 119 Stan Lopata	8.00	3.60
☐ 120 Bob Lemon	25.00	11.00
☐ 121 Clete Boyer	20.00	9.00
☐ 122 Ken Boyer	18.00	8.00
☐ 123 Steve Ridzik	8.00	3.60
☐ 124 Dave Philley	8.00	3.60
☐ 125 Al Kaline	100.00	45.00
☐ 126 Bob Wiesler	8.00	3.60
☐ 127 Bob Buhl	15.00	6.75
☐ 128 Ed Bailey	15.00	6.75
☐ 129 Saul Rogovin	8.00	3.60
☐ 130 Don Newcombe	20.00	9.00
☐ 131 Milt Bolling	8.00	3.60
☐ 132 Art Ditmar	15.00	6.75
☐ 133 Del Crandall	15.00	6.75
☐ 134 Don Kaiser	8.00	3.60
☐ 135 Bill Skowron	18.00	8.00
☐ 136 Jim Hegan	15.00	6.75
☐ 137 Bob Rush	8.00	3.60
☐ 138 Minnie Minoso	20.00	9.00
☐ 139 Lou Kretlow	8.00	3.60
☐ 140 Frank Thomas	15.00	6.75
☐ 141 Al Aber	8.00	3.60
☐ 142 Charley Thompson	8.00	3.60
☐ 143 Andy Pafko	14.00	6.25
☐ 144 Ray Narleski	8.00	3.60
☐ 145 Al Smith	8.00	3.60
☐ 146 Don Ferrarese	8.00	3.60
☐ 147 Al Walker	8.00	3.60
☐ 148 Don Mueller	15.00	6.75
☐ 149 Bob Kennedy	15.00	6.75
☐ 150 Bob Friend	14.00	6.25
☐ 151 Willie Miranda	8.00	3.60
☐ 152 Jack Harshman	8.00	3.60
☐ 153 Karl Olson	8.00	3.60
☐ 154 Red Schoendienst	25.00	11.00
☐ 155 Jim Brosnan	15.00	6.75
☐ 156 Gus Triandos	15.00	6.75
☐ 157 Wally Post	15.00	6.75
☐ 158 Curt Simmons	15.00	6.75
☐ 159 Solly Drake	8.00	3.60
☐ 160 Billy Pierce	15.00	6.75
☐ 161 Pittsburgh Pirates Team Card	20.00	9.00
☐ 162 Jack Meyer	8.00	3.60
☐ 163 Sammy White	8.00	3.60
☐ 164 Tommy Carroll	8.00	3.60
☐ 165 Ted Kluszewski	50.00	22.00
☐ 166 Roy Face	15.00	6.75
☐ 167 Vic Power	15.00	6.75
☐ 168 Frank Lary	15.00	6.75
☐ 169 Herb Plews	8.00	3.60
☐ 170 Duke Snider	100.00	45.00
☐ 171 Boston Red Sox Team Card	20.00	9.00
☐ 172 Gene Woodling	15.00	6.75
☐ 173 Roger Craig	14.00	6.25
☐ 174 Willie Jones	8.00	3.60
☐ 175 Don Larsen	25.00	11.00
☐ 176A Gene Baker ERR (Misspelled Bakep on card back)	350.00	160.00
☐ 176B Gene Baker COR	15.00	6.75
☐ 177 Eddie Yost	15.00	6.75
☐ 178 Don Bessent	8.00	3.60
☐ 179 Ernie Oravetz	8.00	3.60
☐ 180 Gus Bell	15.00	6.75
☐ 181 Dick Donovan	8.00	3.60
☐ 182 Hobie Landrith	8.00	3.60
☐ 183 Chicago Cubs Team Card	20.00	9.00
☐ 184 Tito Francona	8.00	3.60
☐ 185 Johnny Kucks	15.00	6.75
☐ 186 Jim King	8.00	3.60
☐ 187 Virgil Trucks	15.00	6.75
☐ 188 Felix Mantilla	15.00	6.75
☐ 189 Willard Nixon	8.00	3.60
☐ 190 Randy Jackson	8.00	3.60
☐ 191 Joe Margoneri	8.00	3.60
☐ 192 Jerry Coleman	15.00	6.75
☐ 193 Del Rice	8.00	3.60
☐ 194 Hal Brown	8.00	3.60
☐ 195 Bobby Avila	8.00	3.60
☐ 196 Larry Jackson	15.00	6.75
☐ 197 Hank Sauer	15.00	6.75
☐ 198 Detroit Tigers Team Card	20.00	9.00
☐ 199 Vern Law	15.00	6.75
☐ 200 Gil McDougald	18.00	8.00
☐ 201 Sandy Amoros	15.00	6.75
☐ 202 Dick Gernert	8.00	3.60
☐ 203 Hoyt Wilhelm	25.00	11.00
☐ 204 Kansas City Athletics Team Card	20.00	9.00
☐ 205 Charlie Maxwell	15.00	6.75
☐ 206 Willard Schmidt	8.00	3.60
☐ 207 Gordon(Billy) Hunter	8.00	3.60
☐ 208 Lou Burdette	14.00	6.25
☐ 209 Bob Skinner	15.00	6.75
☐ 210 Roy Campanella	125.00	55.00
☐ 211 Camilo Pascual	15.00	6.75
☐ 212 Rocky Colavito	160.00	70.00
☐ 213 Les Moss	8.00	3.60
☐ 214 Philadelphia Phillies Team Card	20.00	9.00
☐ 215 Enos Slaughter	25.00	11.00
☐ 216 Marv Grissom	8.00	3.60
☐ 217 Gene Stephens	8.00	3.60
☐ 218 Ray Jablonski	8.00	3.60
☐ 219 Tom Acker	8.00	3.60
☐ 220 Jackie Jensen	15.00	6.75
☐ 221 Dixie Howell	8.00	3.60
☐ 222 Alex Grammas	8.00	3.60
☐ 223 Frank House	8.00	3.60
☐ 224 Marv Blaylock	8.00	3.60
☐ 225 Harry Simpson	8.00	3.60
☐ 226 Preston Ward	8.00	3.60
☐ 227 Gerry Staley	8.00	3.60
☐ 228 Smoky Burgess UER (Misspelled Smokey on card back)	15.00	6.75
☐ 229 George Susce	8.00	3.60
☐ 230 George Kell	25.00	11.00
☐ 231 Solly Hemus	8.00	3.60
☐ 232 Whitey Lockman	15.00	6.75
☐ 233 Art Fowler	8.00	3.60
☐ 234 Dick Cole	8.00	3.60
☐ 235 Tom Poholsky	8.00	3.60
☐ 236 Joe Ginsberg	8.00	3.60
☐ 237 Foster Castleman	8.00	3.60
☐ 238 Eddie Robinson	8.00	3.60
☐ 239 Tom Morgan	8.00	3.60
☐ 240 Hank Bauer	14.00	6.25
☐ 241 Joe Lonnett	8.00	3.60
☐ 242 Charlie Neal	14.00	6.25
☐ 243 St. Louis Cardinals Team Card	20.00	9.00
☐ 244 Billy Loes	15.00	6.75
☐ 245 Rip Repulski	8.00	3.60
☐ 246 Jose Valdivielso	8.00	3.60
☐ 247 Turk Lown	8.00	3.60
☐ 248 Jim Finigan	8.00	3.60
☐ 249 Dave Pope	8.00	3.60
☐ 250 Eddie Mathews	45.00	20.00
☐ 251 Baltimore Orioles Team Card	15.00	6.75
☐ 252 Carl Erskine	14.00	6.25
☐ 253 Gus Zernial	15.00	6.75
☐ 254 Ron Negray	8.00	3.60
☐ 255 Charlie Silvera	15.00	6.75
☐ 256 Ron Kline	8.00	3.60
☐ 257 Walt Dropo	8.00	3.60
☐ 258 Steve Gromek	8.00	3.60
☐ 259 Eddie O'Brien	8.00	3.60
☐ 260 Del Ennis	15.00	6.75

☐ 261 Bob Chakales 8.00 3.60
☐ 262 Bobby Thomson 15.00 6.75
☐ 263 George Strickland 8.00 3.60
☐ 264 Bob Turley 15.00 6.75
☐ 265 Harvey Haddix DP 14.00 6.25
☐ 266 Ken Kuhn DP 14.00 6.25
☐ 267 Danny Kravitz 20.00 9.00
☐ 268 Jack Collum 20.00 9.00
☐ 269 Bob Cerv 25.00 11.00
☐ 270 Washington Senators 50.00 22.00
Team Card
☐ 271 Danny O'Connell DP 14.00 6.25
☐ 272 Bobby Shantz 25.00 11.00
☐ 273 Jim Davis 20.00 9.00
☐ 274 Don Hoak 20.00 9.00
☐ 275 Cleveland Indians 50.00 22.00
Team Card UER
(Text on back credits Tribe
with winning AL title in '28.
The Yankees won that year.)
☐ 276 Jim Pyburn 20.00 9.00
☐ 277 Johnny Podres DP 45.00 20.00
☐ 278 Fred Hatfield DP 14.00 6.25
☐ 279 Bob Thurman 20.00 9.00
☐ 280 Alex Kellner 20.00 9.00
☐ 281 Gail Harris 20.00 9.00
☐ 282 Jack Dittmer DP 14.00 6.25
☐ 283 Wes Covington DP 14.00 6.25
☐ 284 Don Zimmer 35.00 16.00
☐ 285 Ned Garver 20.00 9.00
☐ 286 Bobby Richardson 120.00 55.00
☐ 287 Sam Jones 20.00 9.00
☐ 288 Ted Lepcio 20.00 9.00
☐ 289 Jim Bolger DP 14.00 6.25
☐ 290 Andy Carey DP 30.00 13.50
☐ 291 Windy McCall 20.00 9.00
☐ 292 Billy Klaus 20.00 9.00
☐ 293 Ted Abernathy 20.00 9.00
☐ 294 Rocky Bridges DP 14.00 6.25
☐ 295 Joe Collins DP 30.00 13.50
☐ 296 Johnny Klippstein 20.00 9.00
☐ 297 Jack Crimian 20.00 9.00
☐ 298 Irv Noren DP 14.00 6.25
☐ 299 Chuck Harmon 20.00 9.00
☐ 300 Mike Garcia 30.00 13.50
☐ 301 Sammy Esposito DP 20.00 9.00
☐ 302 Sandy Koufax DP 250.00 110.00
☐ 303 Billy Goodman 30.00 13.50
☐ 304 Joe Cunningham 30.00 13.50
☐ 305 Chico Fernandez 20.00 9.00
☐ 306 Darrell Johnson DP 14.00 6.25
☐ 307 Jack D. Phillips DP 14.00 6.25
☐ 308 Dick Hall 20.00 9.00
☐ 309 Jim Busby DP 14.00 6.25
☐ 310 Max Surkont DP 14.00 6.25
☐ 311 Al Pilarcik DP 14.00 6.25
☐ 312 Tony Kubek DP 65.00 29.00
☐ 313 Mel Parnell 15.00 6.75
☐ 314 Ed Bouchee DP 14.00 6.25
☐ 315 Lou Berberet DP 14.00 6.25
☐ 316 Billy O'Dell 20.00 9.00
☐ 317 New York Giants 50.00 22.00
Team Card
☐ 318 Mickey McDermott 20.00 9.00
☐ 319 Gino Cimoli 20.00 9.00
☐ 320 Neil Chrisley 20.00 9.00
☐ 321 John(Red) Murff 20.00 9.00
☐ 322 Cincinnati Reds 50.00 22.00
Team Card
☐ 323 Wes Westrum 30.00 13.50
☐ 324 Brooklyn Dodgers 125.00 55.00
Team Card
☐ 325 Frank Bolling 20.00 9.00
☐ 326 Pedro Ramos 20.00 9.00
☐ 327 Jim Pendleton 20.00 9.00
☐ 328 Brooks Robinson 400.00 180.00
☐ 329 Chicago White Sox 50.00 22.00
Team Card
☐ 330 Jim Wilson 20.00 9.00
☐ 331 Ray Katt 20.00 9.00
☐ 332 Bob Bowman 20.00 9.00
☐ 333 Ernie Johnson 20.00 9.00
☐ 334 Jerry Schoonmaker 20.00 9.00
☐ 335 Granny Hamner 20.00 9.00
☐ 336 Haywood Sullivan 25.00 11.00
☐ 337 Rene Valdes 20.00 9.00
☐ 338 Jim Bunning 130.00 57.50
☐ 339 Bob Speake 20.00 9.00
☐ 340 Bill Wight 20.00 9.00
☐ 341 Don Gross 20.00 9.00
☐ 342 Gene Mauch 25.00 11.00
☐ 343 Taylor Phillips 20.00 9.00
☐ 344 Paul LaPalme 20.00 9.00
☐ 345 Paul Smith 20.00 9.00
☐ 346 Dick Littlefield 20.00 9.00
☐ 347 Hal Naragon 20.00 9.00
☐ 348 Jim Hearn 20.00 9.00

☐ 349 Nellie King 20.00 9.00
☐ 350 Eddie Miksis 20.00 9.00
☐ 351 Dave Hillman 20.00 9.00
☐ 352 Ellis Kinder 20.00 9.00
☐ 353 Cal Neeman 8.00 3.60
☐ 354 W. (Rip) Coleman 8.00 3.60
☐ 355 Frank Malzone 15.00 6.75
☐ 356 Faye Throneberry 8.00 3.60
☐ 357 Earl Torgeson 8.00 3.60
☐ 358 Jerry Lynch 15.00 6.75
☐ 359 Tom Cheney 8.00 3.60
☐ 360 Johnny Groth 8.00 3.60
☐ 361 Curt Barclay 8.00 3.60
☐ 362 Roman Mejias 15.00 6.75
☐ 363 Eddie Kasko 8.00 3.60
☐ 364 Cal McLish 15.00 6.75
☐ 365 Ozzie Virgil 8.00 3.60
☐ 366 Ken Lehman 8.00 3.60
☐ 367 Ed Fitzgerald 8.00 3.60
☐ 368 Bob Purkey 8.00 3.60
☐ 369 Milt Graff 8.00 3.60
☐ 370 Warren Hacker 8.00 3.60
☐ 371 Bob Lennon 8.00 3.60
☐ 372 Norm Zauchin 8.00 3.60
☐ 373 Pete Whisenant 8.00 3.60
☐ 374 Don Cardwell 8.00 3.60
☐ 375 Jim Landis 15.00 6.75
☐ 376 Don Elston 8.00 3.60
☐ 377 Andre Rodgers 8.00 3.60
☐ 378 Elmer Singleton 8.00 3.60
☐ 379 Don Lee 8.00 3.60
☐ 380 Walker Cooper 8.00 3.60
☐ 381 Dean Stone 8.00 3.60
☐ 382 Jim Brideweser 8.00 3.60
☐ 383 Juan Pizarro 8.00 3.60
☐ 384 Bobby G. Smith 8.00 3.60
☐ 385 Art Houtteman 8.00 3.60
☐ 386 Lyle Luttrell 8.00 3.60
☐ 387 Jack Sanford 15.00 6.75
☐ 388 Pete Daley 8.00 3.60
☐ 389 Dave Jolly 8.00 3.60
☐ 390 Reno Bertoia 8.00 3.60
☐ 391 Ralph Terry 15.00 6.75
☐ 392 Chuck Tanner 14.00 6.25
☐ 393 Raul Sanchez 8.00 3.60
☐ 394 Luis Arroyo 15.00 6.75
☐ 395 Bubba Phillips 8.00 3.60
☐ 396 Casey Wise 8.00 3.60
☐ 397 Roy Smalley 8.00 3.60
☐ 398 Al Cicotte 15.00 6.75
☐ 399 Billy Consolo 8.00 3.60
☐ 400 Dodgers' Sluggers 250.00 110.00
Carl Furillo
Gil Hodges
Roy Campanella
Duke Snider
☐ 401 Earl Battey 14.00 6.25
☐ 402 Jim Pisoni 8.00 3.60
☐ 403 Dick Hyde 8.00 3.60
☐ 404 Harry Anderson 8.00 3.60
☐ 405 Duke Maas 8.00 3.60
☐ 406 Bob Hale 8.00 3.60
☐ 407 Yankee Power Hitters 500.00 150.00
Mickey Mantle
Yogi Berra
☐ NNO1 Checklist 1/2 250.00 75.00
☐ NNO2 Checklist 2/3 400.00 100.00
☐ NNO3 Checklist 3/4 750.00 170.00
☐ NNO4 Checklist 4/5 900.00 200.00
☐ NNO5 Saturday, May 4th 80.00 20.00
Boston Red Sox
vs. Cleveland Indians
Cincinnati Redlegs
vs. New York Giants
☐ NNO6 Saturday, May 25th 80.00 20.00
Detroit Tigers
vs. Kansas City Athletics
Pittsburgh Pirates
vs. Philadelphia Phillies
☐ NNO7 Saturday, June 22nd 100.00 25.00
Brooklyn Dodgers
vs. St. Louis Cardinals
Chicago White Sox
vs. New York Yankees
☐ NNO8 Saturday, July 19th 100.00 25.00
Milwaukee Braves
vs. New York Giants
Baltimore Orioles
vs. Kansas City Athletics
☐ NNO9 Lucky Penny Charm 80.00 36.00
and Key Chain
offer card

1958 Topps

This is a 494-card standard-size set. Card number 145, which was supposedly to be Ed Bouchee, was not issued.

The 1958 Topps set contains the first Sport Magazine All-Star Selection series (475-495) and expanded use of combination cards. For the first time team cards carried series checklists on back (Milwaukee, Detroit, Baltimore, and Cincinnati are also found with players listed alphabetically). In the first series some cards were issued with yellow name (YL) or team (YT) lettering, as opposed to the common white lettering. They are explicity noted below. Cards were issued in one-card penny packs or six-card nickle packs. In the last series, All-Star cards of Stan Musial and Mickey Mantle were triple printed; the cards they replaced (443, 446, 450, and 462) on the printing sheet were hence printed in shorter supply than other cards in the last series and are marked with an SP in the list below. The All-Star card of Musial marked his first appearence on a Topps card. Technically the New York Giants team card (19) is an error as the Giants had already moved to San Francisco. The key Rookie Cards in this set are Orlando Cepeda, Curt Flood, Roger Maris, and Vada Pinson.

	NRMT	VG-E
COMPLETE SET (494)	4800.00	2200.00
COMMON CARD (1-110)	12.00	5.50
COMMON CARD (111-495)	8.00	3.60
WRAPPER (1-CENT)	100.00	45.00
WRAPPER (5-CENT)	125.00	55.00

☐ 1 Ted Williams 425.00 150.00
☐ 2A Bob Lemon 35.00 16.00
☐ 2B Bob Lemon YT 60.00 27.00
☐ 3 Alex Kellner 12.00 5.50
☐ 4 Hank Foiles 12.00 5.50
☐ 5 Willie Mays 225.00 100.00
☐ 6 George Zuverink 12.00 5.50
☐ 7 Dale Long 15.00 6.75
☐ 8A Eddie Kasko 12.00 5.50
☐ 8B Eddie Kasko YL 45.00 20.00
☐ 9 Hank Bauer 15.00 6.75
☐ 10 Lou Burdette 15.00 6.75
☐ 11A Jim Rivera 12.00 5.50
☐ 11B Jim Rivera YT 45.00 20.00
☐ 12 George Crowe 12.00 5.50
☐ 13A Billy Hoeft 12.00 5.50
☐ 13B Billy Hoeft YL 45.00 20.00
☐ 14 Rip Repulski 12.00 5.50
☐ 15 Jim Lemon 15.00 6.75
☐ 16 Charlie Neal 15.00 6.75
☐ 17 Felix Mantilla 12.00 5.50
☐ 18 Frank Sullivan 12.00 5.50
☐ 19 New York Giants 40.00 8.00
Team Card
(Checklist on back)
☐ 20A Gil McDougald 18.00 8.00
☐ 20B Gil McDougald YL 60.00 27.00
☐ 21 Curt Barclay 12.00 5.50
☐ 22 Hal Naragon 12.00 5.50
☐ 23A Bill Tuttle 12.00 5.50
☐ 23B Bill Tuttle YL 45.00 20.00
☐ 24A Hobie Landrith 12.00 5.50
☐ 24B Hobie Landrith YL 45.00 20.00
☐ 25 Don Drysdale 85.00 38.00
☐ 26 Ron Jackson 12.00 5.50
☐ 27 Bud Freeman 12.00 5.50
☐ 28 Jim Busby 12.00 5.50
☐ 29 Ted Lepcio 12.00 5.50
☐ 30A Hank Aaron 200.00 90.00
☐ 30B Hank Aaron YL 425.00 190.00
☐ 31 Tex Clevenger 12.00 5.50
☐ 32A J.W. Porter 12.00 5.50
☐ 32B J.W. Porter YL 45.00 20.00
☐ 33A Cal Neeman 12.00 5.50
☐ 33B Cal Neeman YT 45.00 20.00
☐ 34 Bob Thurman 12.00 5.50
☐ 35A Don Mossi 15.00 6.75
☐ 35B Don Mossi YT 45.00 20.00
☐ 36 Ted Kazanski 12.00 5.50
☐ 37 Mike McCormick UER 15.00 6.75
(Photo actually
Ray Monzant)
☐ 38 Dick Gernert 12.00 5.50
☐ 39 Bob Martyn 12.00 5.50
☐ 40 George Kell 18.00 8.00

☐ 41 Dave Hillman	12.00	5.50
☐ 42 John Roseboro	24.00	11.00
☐ 43 Sal Maglie	15.00	6.75
☐ 44 Washington Senators Team Card (Checklist on back)	20.00	4.00
☐ 45 Dick Groat	15.00	6.75
☐ 46A Lou Sleater	12.00	5.50
☐ 46B Lou Sleater YL	45.00	20.00
☐ 47 Roger Maris	425.00	190.00
☐ 48 Chuck Harmon	12.00	5.50
☐ 49 Smoky Burgess	15.00	6.75
☐ 50A Billy Pierce	15.00	6.75
☐ 50B Billy Pierce YT	50.00	22.00
☐ 51 Del Rice	12.00	5.50
☐ 52A Bob Clemente	275.00	125.00
☐ 52B Bob Clemente YT	450.00	200.00
☐ 53A Morrie Martin	12.00	5.50
☐ 53B Morrie Martin YL	45.00	20.00
☐ 54 Norm Siebern	20.00	9.00
☐ 55 Chico Carrasquel	12.00	5.50
☐ 56 Bill Fischer	12.00	5.50
☐ 57A Tim Thompson	12.00	5.50
☐ 57B Tim Thompson YL	45.00	20.00
☐ 58A Art Schult	12.00	5.50
☐ 58B Art Schult YT	45.00	20.00
☐ 59 Dave Sisler	12.00	5.50
☐ 60A Del Ennis	15.00	6.75
☐ 60B Del Ennis YL	50.00	22.00
☐ 61A Darrell Johnson	12.00	5.50
☐ 61B Darrell Johnson YL	45.00	20.00
☐ 62 Joe DeMaestri	12.00	5.50
☐ 63 Joe Nuxhall	15.00	6.75
☐ 64 Joe Lonnett	12.00	5.50
☐ 65A Von McDaniel	12.00	5.50
☐ 65B Von McDaniel YL	45.00	20.00
☐ 66 Lee Walls	12.00	5.50
☐ 67 Joe Ginsberg	12.00	5.50
☐ 68 Daryl Spencer	12.00	5.50
☐ 69 Wally Burnette	12.00	5.50
☐ 70A Al Kaline	100.00	45.00
☐ 70B Al Kaline YL	180.00	80.00
☐ 71 Dodgers Team (Checklist on back)	60.00	12.00
☐ 72 Bud Byerly	12.00	5.50
☐ 73 Pete Daley	12.00	5.50
☐ 74 Roy Face	15.00	6.75
☐ 75 Gus Bell	15.00	6.75
☐ 76A Dick Farrell	12.00	5.50
☐ 76B Dick Farrell YT	45.00	20.00
☐ 77A Don Zimmer	15.00	6.75
☐ 77B Don Zimmer YT	50.00	22.00
☐ 78A Ernie Johnson	15.00	6.75
☐ 78B Ernie Johnson YL	50.00	22.00
☐ 79A Dick Williams	15.00	6.75
☐ 79B Dick Williams YT	50.00	22.00
☐ 80 Dick Drott	12.00	5.50
☐ 81A Steve Boros	12.00	5.50
☐ 81B Steve Boros YT	45.00	20.00
☐ 82 Ron Kline	12.00	5.50
☐ 83 Bob Hazle	12.00	5.50
☐ 84 Billy O'Dell	12.00	5.50
☐ 85A Luis Aparicio	30.00	13.50
☐ 85B Luis Aparicio YT	70.00	32.00
☐ 86 Valmy Thomas	12.00	5.50
☐ 87 Johnny Kucks	12.00	5.50
☐ 88 Duke Snider	75.00	34.00
☐ 89 Billy Klaus	12.00	5.50
☐ 90 Robin Roberts	30.00	13.50
☐ 91 Chuck Tanner	15.00	6.75
☐ 92A Clint Courtney	12.00	5.50
☐ 92B Clint Courtney YL	45.00	20.00
☐ 93 Sandy Amoros	15.00	6.75
☐ 94 Bob Skinner	15.00	6.75
☐ 95 Frank Bolling	12.00	5.50
☐ 96 Joe Durham	12.00	5.50
☐ 97A Larry Jackson	12.00	5.50
☐ 97B Larry Jackson YL	45.00	20.00
☐ 98A Billy Hunter	12.00	5.50
☐ 98B Billy Hunter YL	45.00	20.00
☐ 99 Bobby Adams	12.00	5.50
☐ 100A Early Wynn	25.00	11.00
☐ 100B Early Wynn YT	60.00	27.00
☐ 101A Bobby Richardson	24.00	11.00
☐ 101B Bobby Richardson YL	55.00	25.00
☐ 102 George Strickland	12.00	5.50
☐ 103 Jerry Lynch	15.00	6.75
☐ 104 Jim Pendleton	12.00	5.50
☐ 105 Billy Gardner	12.00	5.50
☐ 106 Dick Schofield	15.00	6.75
☐ 107 Ossie Virgil	12.00	5.50
☐ 108A Jim Landis	12.00	5.50
☐ 108B Jim Landis YT	45.00	20.00
☐ 109 Herb Plews	12.00	5.50
☐ 110 Johnny Logan	15.00	6.75
☐ 111 Stu Miller	10.00	4.50
☐ 112 Gus Zernial	10.00	4.50
☐ 113 Jerry Walker	8.00	3.60
☐ 114 Irv Noren	10.00	4.50
☐ 115 Jim Bunning	25.00	11.00
☐ 116 Dave Philley	8.00	3.60
☐ 117 Frank Torre	10.00	4.50
☐ 118 Harvey Haddix	10.00	4.50
☐ 119 Harry Chiti	8.00	3.60
☐ 120 Johnny Podres	12.00	5.50
☐ 121 Eddie Miksis	8.00	3.60
☐ 122 Walt Moryn	8.00	3.60
☐ 123 Dick Tomanek	8.00	3.60
☐ 124 Bobby Usher	8.00	3.60
☐ 125 Alvin Dark	10.00	4.50
☐ 126 Stan Palys	8.00	3.60
☐ 127 Tom Sturdivant	10.00	4.50
☐ 128 Willie Kirkland	8.00	3.60
☐ 129 Jim Derrington	8.00	3.60
☐ 130 Jackie Jensen	10.00	4.50
☐ 131 Bob Henrich	8.00	3.60
☐ 132 Vern Law	10.00	4.50
☐ 133 Russ Nixon	8.00	3.60
☐ 134 Philadelphia Phillies Team Card (Checklist on back)	15.00	3.00
☐ 135 Mike(Moe) Drabowsky	10.00	4.50
☐ 136 Jim Finigan	8.00	3.60
☐ 137 Russ Kemmerer	8.00	3.60
☐ 138 Earl Torgeson	8.00	3.60
☐ 139 George Brunet	8.00	3.60
☐ 140 Wes Covington	10.00	4.50
☐ 141 Ken Lehman	8.00	3.60
☐ 142 Enos Slaughter	25.00	11.00
☐ 143 Billy Muffett	8.00	3.60
☐ 144 Bobby Morgan	8.00	3.60
☐ 145 Never issued		
☐ 146 Dick Gray	8.00	3.60
☐ 147 Don McMahon	8.00	3.60
☐ 148 Billy Consolo	8.00	3.60
☐ 149 Tom Acker	8.00	3.60
☐ 150 Mickey Mantle	800.00	350.00
☐ 151 Buddy Pritchard	8.00	3.60
☐ 152 Johnny Antonelli	10.00	4.50
☐ 153 Les Moss	8.00	3.60
☐ 154 Harry Byrd	8.00	3.60
☐ 155 Hector Lopez	10.00	4.50
☐ 156 Dick Hyde	8.00	3.60
☐ 157 Dee Fondy	8.00	3.60
☐ 158 Cleveland Indians Team Card (Checklist on back)	15.00	3.00
☐ 159 Taylor Phillips	8.00	3.60
☐ 160 Don Hoak	10.00	4.50
☐ 161 Don Larsen	14.00	6.25
☐ 162 Gil Hodges	30.00	13.50
☐ 163 Jim Wilson	8.00	3.60
☐ 164 Bob Taylor	8.00	3.60
☐ 165 Bob Nieman	8.00	3.60
☐ 166 Danny O'Connell	8.00	3.60
☐ 167 Frank Baumann	8.00	3.60
☐ 168 Joe Cunningham	8.00	3.60
☐ 169 Ralph Terry	10.00	4.50
☐ 170 Vic Wertz	10.00	4.50
☐ 171 Harry Anderson	8.00	3.60
☐ 172 Don Gross	8.00	3.60
☐ 173 Eddie Yost	8.00	3.60
☐ 174 Athletics Team (Checklist on back)	15.00	3.00
☐ 175 Marv Throneberry	16.00	7.25
☐ 176 Bob Buhl	10.00	4.50
☐ 177 Al Smith	8.00	3.60
☐ 178 Ted Kluszewski	16.00	7.25
☐ 179 Willie Miranda	8.00	3.60
☐ 180 Lindy McDaniel	10.00	4.50
☐ 181 Willie Jones	8.00	3.60
☐ 182 Joe Caffie	8.00	3.60
☐ 183 Dave Jolly	8.00	3.60
☐ 184 Elvin Tappe	8.00	3.60
☐ 185 Ray Boone	10.00	4.50
☐ 186 Jack Meyer	8.00	3.60
☐ 187 Sandy Koufax	225.00	100.00
☐ 188 Milt Bolling UER (Photo actually Lou Berberet)	8.00	3.60
☐ 189 George Susce	8.00	3.60
☐ 190 Red Schoendienst	18.00	8.00
☐ 191 Art Ceccarelli	8.00	3.60
☐ 192 Milt Graff	8.00	3.60
☐ 193 Jerry Lumpe	8.00	3.60
☐ 194 Roger Craig	10.00	4.50
☐ 195 Whitey Lockman	10.00	4.50
☐ 196 Mike Garcia	10.00	4.50
☐ 197 Haywood Sullivan	10.00	4.50
☐ 198 Bill Virdon	10.00	4.50
☐ 199 Don Blasingame	8.00	3.60
☐ 200 Bob Keegan	8.00	3.60
☐ 201 Jim Bolger	8.00	3.60
☐ 202 Woody Held	8.00	3.60
☐ 203 Al Walker	8.00	3.60
☐ 204 Leo Kiely	8.00	3.60
☐ 205 Johnny Temple	10.00	4.50
☐ 206 Bob Shaw	8.00	3.60
☐ 207 Solly Hemus	8.00	3.60
☐ 208 Cal McLish	8.00	3.60
☐ 209 Bob Anderson	8.00	3.60
☐ 210 Wally Moon	10.00	4.50
☐ 211 Pete Burnside	8.00	3.60
☐ 212 Bubba Phillips	8.00	3.60
☐ 213 Red Wilson	8.00	3.60
☐ 214 Willard Schmidt	8.00	3.60
☐ 215 Jim Gilliam	14.00	6.25
☐ 216 St. Louis Cardinals Team Card (Checklist on back)	15.00	3.00
☐ 217 Jack Harshman	8.00	3.60
☐ 218 Dick Rand	8.00	3.60
☐ 219 Camilo Pascual	10.00	4.50
☐ 220 Tom Brewer	8.00	3.60
☐ 221 Jerry Kindall	8.00	3.60
☐ 222 Bud Daley	8.00	3.60
☐ 223 Andy Pafko	10.00	4.50
☐ 224 Bob Grim	10.00	4.50
☐ 225 Billy Goodman	10.00	4.50
☐ 226 Bob Smith	8.00	3.60
☐ 227 Gene Stephens	8.00	3.60
☐ 228 Duke Maas	8.00	3.60
☐ 229 Frank Zupo	8.00	3.60
☐ 230 Richie Ashburn	30.00	13.50
☐ 231 Lloyd Merritt	8.00	3.60
☐ 232 Reno Bertoia	8.00	3.60
☐ 233 Mickey Vernon	10.00	4.50
☐ 234 Carl Sawatski	8.00	3.60
☐ 235 Tom Gorman	8.00	3.60
☐ 236 Ed Fitzgerald	8.00	3.60
☐ 237 Bill Wight	8.00	3.60
☐ 238 Bill Mazeroski	24.00	11.00
☐ 239 Chuck Stobbs	8.00	3.60
☐ 240 Bill Skowron	16.00	7.25
☐ 241 Dick Littlefield	8.00	3.60
☐ 242 Johnny Klippstein	8.00	3.60
☐ 243 Larry Raines	8.00	3.60
☐ 244 Don Demeter	8.00	3.60
☐ 245 Frank Lary	10.00	4.50
☐ 246 New York Yankees Team Card (Checklist on back)	90.00	18.00
☐ 247 Casey Wise	8.00	3.60
☐ 248 Herman Wehmeier	8.00	3.60
☐ 249 Ray Moore	8.00	3.60
☐ 250 Roy Sievers	10.00	4.50
☐ 251 Warren Hacker	8.00	3.60
☐ 252 Bob Trowbridge	8.00	3.60
☐ 253 Don Mueller	10.00	4.50
☐ 254 Alex Grammas	8.00	3.60
☐ 255 Bob Turley	10.00	4.50
☐ 256 Chicago White Sox Team Card (Checklist on back)	15.00	3.00
☐ 257 Hal Smith	8.00	3.60
☐ 258 Carl Erskine	14.00	6.25
☐ 259 Al Pilarcik	8.00	3.60
☐ 260 Frank Malzone	10.00	4.50
☐ 261 Turk Lown	8.00	3.60
☐ 262 Johnny Groth	8.00	3.60
☐ 263 Eddie Bressoud	10.00	4.50
☐ 264 Jack Sanford	10.00	4.50
☐ 265 Pete Runnels	10.00	4.50
☐ 266 Connie Johnson	8.00	3.60
☐ 267 Sherm Lollar	10.00	4.50
☐ 268 Granny Hamner	8.00	3.60
☐ 269 Paul Smith	8.00	3.60
☐ 270 Warren Spahn	50.00	22.00
☐ 271 Billy Martin	30.00	13.50
☐ 272 Ray Crone	8.00	3.60
☐ 273 Hal Smith	8.00	3.60
☐ 274 Rocky Bridges	8.00	3.60
☐ 275 Elston Howard	16.00	7.25
☐ 276 Bobby Avila	8.00	3.60
☐ 277 Virgil Trucks	10.00	4.50
☐ 278 Mack Burk	8.00	3.60
☐ 279 Bob Boyd	8.00	3.60
☐ 280 Jim Piersall	10.00	4.50
☐ 281 Sammy Taylor	8.00	3.60
☐ 282 Paul Foytack	8.00	3.60
☐ 283 Ray Shearer	8.00	3.60
☐ 284 Ray Katt	8.00	3.60
☐ 285 Frank Robinson	100.00	45.00
☐ 286 Gino Cimoli	8.00	3.60
☐ 287 Sam Jones	10.00	4.50
☐ 288 Harmon Killebrew	85.00	38.00
☐ 289 Lou Burdette Bobby Shantz	10.00	4.50
☐ 290 Dick Donovan	8.00	3.60
☐ 291 Don Landrum	8.00	3.60
☐ 292 Ned Garver	8.00	3.60

☐ 293 Gene Freese 8.00 3.60
☐ 294 Hal Jeffcoat 8.00 3.60
☐ 295 Minnie Minoso 14.00 6.25
☐ 296 Ryne Duren 16.00 7.25
☐ 297 Don Buddin 8.00 3.60
☐ 298 Jim Hearn 8.00 3.60
☐ 299 Harry Simpson 8.00 3.60
☐ 300 Will Harridge PRES 14.00 6.25
Warren Giles
☐ 301 Randy Jackson 8.00 3.60
☐ 302 Mike Baxes 8.00 3.60
☐ 303 Neil Chrisley 8.00 3.60
☐ 304 Harvey Kuenn 20.00 9.00
Al Kaline
☐ 305 Clem Labine 10.00 4.50
☐ 306 Whammy Douglas 8.00 3.60
☐ 307 Brooks Robinson 100.00 45.00
☐ 308 Paul Giel 10.00 4.50
☐ 309 Gail Harris 8.00 3.60
☐ 310 Ernie Banks 100.00 45.00
☐ 311 Bob Purkey 8.00 3.60
☐ 312 Boston Red Sox 15.00 3.00
Team Card
(Checklist on back)
☐ 313 Bob Rush 8.00 3.60
☐ 314 Duke Snider 30.00 13.50
Walt Alston MG
☐ 315 Bob Friend 10.00 4.50
☐ 316 Tito Francona 10.00 4.50
☐ 317 Albie Pearson 10.00 4.50
☐ 318 Frank House 8.00 3.60
☐ 319 Lou Skizas 8.00 3.60
☐ 320 Whitey Ford 50.00 22.00
☐ 321 Sluggers Supreme 70.00 32.00
Ted Kluszewski
Ted Williams
☐ 322 Harding Peterson 10.00 4.50
☐ 323 Elmer Valo 8.00 3.60
☐ 324 Hoyt Wilhelm 18.00 8.00
☐ 325 Joe Adcock 10.00 4.50
☐ 326 Bob Miller 8.00 3.60
☐ 327 Chicago Cubs 15.00 3.00
Team Card
(Checklist on back)
☐ 328 Ike Delock 8.00 3.60
☐ 329 Bob Cerv 10.00 4.50
☐ 330 Ed Bailey 10.00 4.50
☐ 331 Pedro Ramos 8.00 3.60
☐ 332 Jim King 8.00 3.60
☐ 333 Andy Carey 10.00 4.50
☐ 334 Bob Friend 10.00 4.50
Billy Pierce
☐ 335 Ruben Gomez 8.00 3.60
☐ 336 Bert Hamric 8.00 3.60
☐ 337 Hank Aguirre 8.00 3.60
☐ 338 Walt Dropo 10.00 4.50
☐ 339 Fred Hatfield 8.00 3.60
☐ 340 Don Newcombe 14.00 6.25
☐ 341 Pittsburgh Pirates 15.00 3.00
Team Card
(Checklist on back)
☐ 342 Jim Brosnan 10.00 4.50
☐ 343 Orlando Cepeda 90.00 40.00
☐ 344 Bob Porterfield 8.00 3.60
☐ 345 Jim Hegan 10.00 4.50
☐ 346 Steve Bilko 8.00 3.60
☐ 347 Don Rudolph 8.00 3.60
☐ 348 Chico Fernandez 8.00 3.60
☐ 349 Murry Dickson 8.00 3.60
☐ 350 Ken Boyer 16.00 7.25
☐ 351 Braves Fence Busters 35.00 16.00
Del Crandall
Eddie Mathews
Hank Aaron
Joe Adcock
☐ 352 Herb Score 14.00 6.25
☐ 353 Stan Lopata 8.00 3.60
☐ 354 Art Ditmar 10.00 4.50
☐ 355 Bill Bruton 10.00 4.50
☐ 356 Bob Malkmus 8.00 3.60
☐ 357 Danny McDevitt 8.00 3.60
☐ 358 Gene Baker 8.00 3.60
☐ 359 Billy Loes 10.00 4.50
☐ 360 Roy McMillan 10.00 4.50
☐ 361 Mike Fornieles 8.00 3.60
☐ 362 Ray Jablonski 8.00 3.60
☐ 363 Don Elston 8.00 3.60
☐ 364 Earl Battey 8.00 3.60
☐ 365 Tom Morgan 8.00 3.60
☐ 366 Gene Green 8.00 3.60
☐ 367 Jack Urban 8.00 3.60
☐ 368 Rocky Colavito 50.00 22.00
☐ 369 Ralph Lumenti 8.00 3.60
☐ 370 Yogi Berra 90.00 40.00
☐ 371 Marty Keough 8.00 3.60
☐ 372 Don Cardwell 8.00 3.60
☐ 373 Joe Pignatano 8.00 3.60
☐ 374 Brooks Lawrence 8.00 3.60
☐ 375 Pee Wee Reese 50.00 22.00
☐ 376 Charley Rabe 8.00 3.60
☐ 377A Milwaukee Braves 15.00 6.75
Team Card
(Alphabetical)
☐ 377B Milwaukee Team 100.00 20.00
numerical checklist
☐ 378 Hank Sauer 10.00 4.50
☐ 379 Ray Herbert 8.00 3.60
☐ 380 Charlie Maxwell 10.00 4.50
☐ 381 Hal Brown 8.00 3.60
☐ 382 Al Cicotte 8.00 3.60
☐ 383 Lou Berberet 8.00 3.60
☐ 384 John Goryl 8.00 3.60
☐ 385 Wilmer Mizell 10.00 4.50
☐ 386 Birdie's Sluggers 14.00 6.25
Ed Bailey
Birdie Tebbetts MG
Frank Robinson
☐ 387 Wally Post 10.00 4.50
☐ 388 Billy Moran 8.00 3.60
☐ 389 Bill Taylor 8.00 3.60
☐ 390 Del Crandall 10.00 4.50
☐ 391 Dave Melton 8.00 3.60
☐ 392 Bennie Daniels 8.00 3.60
☐ 393 Tony Kubek 18.00 8.00
☐ 394 Jim Grant 8.00 3.60
☐ 395 Willard Nixon 8.00 3.60
☐ 396 Dutch Dotterer 8.00 3.60
☐ 397A Detroit Tigers 15.00 6.75
Team Card
(Alphabetical)
☐ 397B Detroit Team 100.00 20.00
numerical checklist
☐ 398 Gene Woodling 10.00 4.50
☐ 399 Marv Grissom 8.00 3.60
☐ 400 Nellie Fox 30.00 13.50
☐ 401 Don Bessent 8.00 3.60
☐ 402 Bobby Gene Smith 8.00 3.60
☐ 403 Steve Korcheck 8.00 3.60
☐ 404 Curt Simmons 10.00 4.50
☐ 405 Ken Aspromonte 8.00 3.60
☐ 406 Vic Power 10.00 4.50
☐ 407 Carlton Willey 10.00 4.50
☐ 408A Baltimore Orioles 15.00 6.75
Team Card
(Alphabetical)
☐ 408B Baltimore Team 100.00 20.00
numerical checklist
☐ 409 Frank Thomas 10.00 4.50
☐ 410 Murray Wall 8.00 3.60
☐ 411 Tony Taylor 10.00 4.50
☐ 412 Gerry Staley 8.00 3.60
☐ 413 Jim Davenport 8.00 3.60
☐ 414 Sammy White 8.00 3.60
☐ 415 Bob Bowman 8.00 3.60
☐ 416 Foster Castleman 8.00 3.60
☐ 417 Carl Furillo 14.00 6.25
☐ 418 Mickey Mantle 275.00 125.00
Hank Aaron
☐ 419 Bobby Shantz 10.00 4.50
☐ 420 Vada Pinson 40.00 18.00
☐ 421 Dixie Howell 8.00 3.60
☐ 422 Norm Zauchin 8.00 3.60
☐ 423 Phil Clark 8.00 3.60
☐ 424 Larry Doby 14.00 6.25
☐ 425 Sammy Esposito 8.00 3.60
☐ 426 Johnny O'Brien 10.00 4.50
☐ 427 Al Worthington 8.00 3.60
☐ 428A Cincinnati Reds 15.00 6.75
Team Card
(Alphabetical)
☐ 428B Cincinnati Team 100.00 20.00
numerical checklist
☐ 429 Gus Triandos 10.00 4.50
☐ 430 Bobby Thomson 10.00 4.50
☐ 431 Gene Conley 10.00 4.50
☐ 432 John Powers 8.00 3.60
☐ 433A Pancho Herrer ERR 650.00 300.00
☐ 433B Pancho Herrera COR 10.00 4.50
☐ 434 Harvey Kuenn 10.00 4.50
☐ 435 Ed Roebuck 10.00 4.50
☐ 436 Willie Mays 75.00 34.00
Duke Snider
☐ 437 Bob Speake 8.00 3.60
☐ 438 Whitey Herzog 10.00 4.50
☐ 439 Ray Narleski 8.00 3.60
☐ 440 Eddie Mathews 40.00 18.00
☐ 441 Jim Marshall 10.00 4.50
☐ 442 Phil Paine 8.00 3.60
☐ 443 Billy Harrell SP 20.00 9.00
☐ 444 Danny Kravitz 8.00 3.60
☐ 445 Bob Smith 8.00 3.60
☐ 446 Carroll Hardy SP 20.00 9.00
☐ 447 Ray Monzant 8.00 3.60
☐ 448 Charlie Lau 12.00 5.50
☐ 449 Gene Fodge 8.00 3.60
☐ 450 Preston Ward SP 20.00 9.00
☐ 451 Joe Taylor 8.00 3.60
☐ 452 Roman Mejias 8.00 3.60
☐ 453 Tom Qualters 8.00 3.60
☐ 454 Harry Hanebrink 8.00 3.60
☐ 455 Hal Griggs 8.00 3.60
☐ 456 Dick Brown 8.00 3.60
☐ 457 Milt Pappas 12.00 5.50
☐ 458 Julio Becquer 8.00 3.60
☐ 459 Ron Blackburn 8.00 3.60
☐ 460 Chuck Essegian 8.00 3.60
☐ 461 Ed Mayer 8.00 3.60
☐ 462 Gary Geiger SP 20.00 9.00
☐ 463 Vito Valentinetti 8.00 3.60
☐ 464 Curt Flood 30.00 13.50
☐ 465 Arnie Portocarrero 8.00 3.60
☐ 466 Pete Whisenant 8.00 3.60
☐ 467 Glen Hobbie 8.00 3.60
☐ 468 Bob Schmidt 8.00 3.60
☐ 469 Don Ferrarese 8.00 3.60
☐ 470 R.C. Stevens 8.00 3.60
☐ 471 Lenny Green 8.00 3.60
☐ 472 Joey Jay 10.00 4.50
☐ 473 Bill Renna 8.00 3.60
☐ 474 Roman Semproch 8.00 3.60
☐ 475 Fred Haney AS MG and 20.00 6.00
Casey Stengel AS MG
(Checklist back)
☐ 476 Stan Musial AS TP 40.00 18.00
☐ 478 Johnny Temple AS 8.00 3.60
☐ 479 Nellie Fox AS 18.00 8.00
☐ 480 Eddie Mathews AS 20.00 9.00
☐ 481 Frank Malzone AS 8.00 3.60
☐ 482 Ernie Banks AS 35.00 16.00
☐ 483 Luis Aparicio AS 18.00 8.00
☐ 484 Frank Robinson AS 24.00 11.00
☐ 485 Ted Williams AS 125.00 55.00
☐ 486 Willie Mays AS 50.00 22.00
☐ 487 Mickey Mantle AS TP 200.00 90.00
☐ 488 Hank Aaron AS 50.00 22.00
☐ 489 Jackie Jensen AS 10.00 4.50
☐ 490 Ed Bailey AS 8.00 3.60
☐ 491 Sherm Lollar AS 8.00 3.60
☐ 492 Bob Friend AS 8.00 3.60
☐ 493 Bob Turley AS 10.00 4.50
☐ 494 Warren Spahn AS 24.00 11.00
☐ 495 Herb Score AS 16.00 3.20
☐ xx Contest Cards 50.00 22.00

1959 Topps

The cards in this 572-card set measure 2 1/2" by 3 1/2". The 1959 Topps set contains bust pictures of the players in a colored circle. Card numbers 551 to 572 are Sporting News All-Star Selections. High numbers 507 to 572 have the card number in a black background on the reverse rather than a green background as in the lower numbers. The high numbers are more difficult to obtain. Several cards in the 300s exist with or without an extra traded or option line on the back of the card. Cards 199 to 286 exist with either white or gray backs. There is no price differential for either colored back. Cards 461 to 470 contain "Highlights" while cards 116 to 146 give an alphabetically ordered listing of "Rookie Prospects." These Rookie Prospects (RP) were Topps' first organized inclusion of untested "Rookie" cards. Card 440 features Lew Burdette erroneously posing as a left-handed pitcher. Cards were issued in one-card penny packs or six-card nickle packs. There were some three-card advertising panels produced by Topps; the players included are from the first series. One advertising panel shows Don McMahon, Red Wilson and Bob Boyd on the front with Ted Kluszewski's card back on the back of the panel. Other panels are: Joe Pignatano, Sam Jones and Jack Urban also with Kluszewski's card back on back, Billy Hunter, Chuck Stobbs and Carl Sawatski on the front with the back of Nellie Fox's card on the back, Vito Valentinetti, Ken Lehman and Ed Bouchee on the front with Fox's card back on back and Mel Roach, Brooks Lawrence and Warren Spahn also with Fox on back. When separated, these advertising cards are distinguished by the non-standard card back, i.e., part of an advertisement for the 1959 Topps set instead of the typical statistics and biographical information about the player pictured. The key Rookie Cards in this set are Felipe Alou, Sparky Anderson (called George on the card), Norm Cash, Bob Gibson, and Bill White.

	NRMT	VG-E
COMPLETE SET (572)	4500.00	2000.00
COMMON CARD (1-110)	6.00	2.70
COMMON CARD (111-506)	4.00	1.80
COMMON CARD (507-572)	16.00	7.25
WRAPPER (1-CENT)	125.00	55.00
WRAPPER (5-CENT)	100.00	45.00

Card	NRMT	VG-E
☐ 1 Ford Frick COMM	50.00	13.50
☐ 2 Eddie Yost	8.00	3.60
☐ 3 Don McMahon	8.00	3.60
☐ 4 Albie Pearson	8.00	3.60
☐ 5 Dick Donovan	8.00	3.60
☐ 6 Alex Grammas	6.00	2.70
☐ 7 Al Pilarcik	6.00	2.70
☐ 8 Phillies Team	65.00	13.00
(Checklist on back)		
☐ 9 Paul Giel	8.00	3.60
☐ 10 Mickey Mantle	600.00	275.00
☐ 11 Billy Hunter	8.00	3.60
☐ 12 Vern Law	8.00	3.60
☐ 13 Dick Gernert	6.00	2.70
☐ 14 Pete Whisenant	6.00	2.70
☐ 15 Dick Drott	6.00	2.70
☐ 16 Joe Pignatano	6.00	2.70
☐ 17 Frank Thomas	8.00	3.60
Danny Murtaugh MG		
Ted Kluszewski		
☐ 18 Jack Urban	6.00	2.70
☐ 19 Eddie Bressoud	6.00	2.70
☐ 20 Duke Snider	50.00	22.00
☐ 21 Connie Johnson	6.00	2.70
☐ 22 Al Smith	8.00	3.60
☐ 23 Murry Dickson	8.00	3.60
☐ 24 Red Wilson	6.00	2.70
☐ 25 Don Hoak	8.00	3.60
☐ 26 Chuck Stobbs	6.00	2.70
☐ 27 Andy Pafko	8.00	3.60
☐ 28 Al Worthington	6.00	2.70
☐ 29 Jim Bolger	6.00	2.70
☐ 30 Nellie Fox	30.00	13.50
☐ 31 Ken Lehman	6.00	2.70
☐ 32 Don Buddin	6.00	2.70
☐ 33 Ed Fitzgerald	6.00	2.70
☐ 34 Al Kaline	20.00	9.00
Charley Maxwell		
☐ 35 Ted Kluszewski	16.00	7.25
☐ 36 Hank Aguirre	6.00	2.70
☐ 37 Gene Green	6.00	2.70
☐ 38 Morrie Martin	6.00	2.70
☐ 39 Ed Bouchee	6.00	2.70
☐ 40A Warren Spahn ERR	75.00	34.00
(Born 1931)		
☐ 40B Warren Spahn ERR	100.00	45.00
(Born 1931, but three is partially obscured)		
☐ 40C Warren Spahn COR	50.00	22.00
(Born 1921)		
☐ 41 Bob Martyn	6.00	2.70
☐ 42 Murray Wall	6.00	2.70
☐ 43 Steve Bilko	6.00	2.70
☐ 44 Vito Valentinetti	6.00	2.70
☐ 45 Andy Carey	8.00	3.60
☐ 46 Bill R. Henry	6.00	2.70
☐ 47 Jim Finigan	6.00	2.70
☐ 48 Orioles Team	25.00	5.00
(Checklist on back)		
☐ 49 Bill Hall	6.00	2.70
☐ 50 Willie Mays	125.00	55.00
☐ 51 Rip Coleman	6.00	2.70
☐ 52 Coot Veal	6.00	2.70
☐ 53 Stan Williams	8.00	3.60
☐ 54 Mel Roach	6.00	2.70
☐ 55 Tom Brewer	6.00	2.70
☐ 56 Carl Sawatski	6.00	2.70
☐ 57 Al Cicotte	6.00	2.70
☐ 58 Eddie Miksis	6.00	2.70
☐ 59 Irv Noren	8.00	3.60
☐ 60 Bob Turley	8.00	3.60
☐ 61 Dick Brown	6.00	2.70
☐ 62 Tony Taylor	8.00	3.60
☐ 63 Jim Hearn	6.00	2.70
☐ 64 Joe DeMaestri	6.00	2.70
☐ 65 Frank Torre	8.00	3.60
☐ 66 Joe Ginsberg	6.00	2.70
☐ 67 Brooks Lawrence	6.00	2.70
☐ 68 Dick Schofield	8.00	3.60
☐ 69 Giants Team	25.00	5.00
(Checklist on back)		
☐ 70 Harvey Kuenn	8.00	3.60
☐ 71 Don Bessent	6.00	2.70
☐ 72 Bill Renna	6.00	2.70
☐ 73 Ron Jackson	8.00	3.60
☐ 74 Jim Lemon	8.00	3.60
Cookie Lavagetto MG		
Roy Sievers		
☐ 75 Sam Jones	8.00	3.60
☐ 76 Bobby Richardson	20.00	9.00
☐ 77 John Goryl	6.00	2.70
☐ 78 Pedro Ramos	6.00	2.70
☐ 79 Harry Chiti	6.00	2.70
☐ 80 Minnie Minoso	10.00	4.50
☐ 81 Hal Jeffcoat	6.00	2.70
☐ 82 Bob Boyd	6.00	2.70
☐ 83 Bob Smith	6.00	2.70
☐ 84 Reno Bertoia	6.00	2.70
☐ 85 Harry Anderson	6.00	2.70
☐ 86 Bob Keegan	8.00	3.60
☐ 87 Danny O'Connell	6.00	2.70
☐ 88 Herb Score	10.00	4.50
☐ 89 Billy Gardner	6.00	2.70
☐ 90 Bill Skowron	16.00	7.25
☐ 91 Herb Moford	6.00	2.70
☐ 92 Dave Philley	6.00	2.70
☐ 93 Julio Becquer	6.00	2.70
☐ 94 White Sox Team	40.00	8.00
(Checklist on back)		
☐ 95 Carl Willey	6.00	2.70
☐ 96 Lou Berberet	6.00	2.70
☐ 97 Jerry Lynch	8.00	3.60
☐ 98 Arnie Portocarrero	6.00	2.70
☐ 99 Ted Kazanski	6.00	2.70
☐ 100 Bob Cerv	8.00	3.60
☐ 101 Alex Kellner	6.00	2.70
☐ 102 Felipe Alou	30.00	13.50
☐ 103 Billy Goodman	8.00	3.60
☐ 104 Del Rice	8.00	3.60
☐ 105 Lee Walls	6.00	2.70
☐ 106 Hal Woodeshick	6.00	2.70
☐ 107 Norm Larker	8.00	3.60
☐ 108 Zack Monroe	8.00	3.60
☐ 109 Bob Schmidt	6.00	2.70
☐ 110 George Witt	8.00	3.60
☐ 111 Redlegs Team	12.00	2.40
(Checklist on back)		
☐ 112 Billy Consolo	4.00	1.80
☐ 113 Taylor Phillips	4.00	1.80
☐ 114 Earl Battey	8.00	3.60
☐ 115 Mickey Vernon	8.00	3.60
☐ 116 Bob Allison RP	12.00	5.50
☐ 117 John Blanchard RP	8.00	3.60
☐ 118 John Buzhardt RP	4.00	1.80
☐ 119 John Callison RP	12.00	5.50
☐ 120 Chuck Coles RP	4.00	1.80
☐ 121 Bob Conley RP	4.00	1.80
☐ 122 Bennie Daniels RP	4.00	1.80
☐ 123 Don Dillard RP	4.00	1.80
☐ 124 Dan Dobbek RP	4.00	1.80
☐ 125 Ron Fairly RP	8.00	3.60
☐ 126 Ed Haas RP	4.00	1.80
☐ 127 Kent Hadley RP	4.00	1.80
☐ 128 Bob Hartman RP	4.00	1.80
☐ 129 Frank Herrera RP	4.00	1.80
☐ 130 Lou Jackson RP	4.00	1.80
☐ 131 Deron Johnson RP	8.00	3.60
☐ 132 Don Lee RP	4.00	1.80
☐ 133 Bob Lillis RP	4.00	1.80
☐ 134 Jim McDaniel RP	4.00	1.80
☐ 135 Gene Oliver RP	4.00	1.80
☐ 136 Jim O'Toole RP	4.00	1.80
☐ 137 Dick Ricketts RP	4.00	1.80
☐ 138 John Romano RP	4.00	1.80
☐ 139 Ed Sadowski RP	4.00	1.80
☐ 140 Charlie Secrest RP	4.00	1.80
☐ 141 Joe Shipley RP	4.00	1.80
☐ 142 Dick Stigman RP	4.00	1.80
☐ 143 Willie Tasby RP	4.00	1.80
☐ 144 Jerry Walker RP	4.00	1.80
☐ 145 Dom Zanni RP	4.00	1.80
☐ 146 Jerry Zimmerman RP	4.00	1.80
☐ 147 Cubs Clubbers	25.00	11.00
Dale Long		
Ernie Banks		
Walt Moryn		
☐ 148 Mike McCormick	8.00	3.60
☐ 149 Jim Bunning	20.00	9.00
☐ 150 Stan Musial	125.00	55.00
☐ 151 Bob Malkmus	4.00	1.80
☐ 152 Johnny Klippstein	4.00	1.80
☐ 153 Jim Marshall	4.00	1.80
☐ 154 Ray Herbert	4.00	1.80
☐ 155 Enos Slaughter	20.00	9.00
☐ 156 Ace Hurlers	12.00	5.50
Billy Pierce		
Robin Roberts		
☐ 157 Felix Mantilla	4.00	1.80
☐ 158 Walt Dropo	4.00	1.80
☐ 159 Bob Shaw	8.00	3.60
☐ 160 Dick Groat	8.00	3.60
☐ 161 Frank Baumann	4.00	1.80
☐ 162 Bobby G. Smith	4.00	1.80
☐ 163 Sandy Koufax	150.00	70.00
☐ 164 Johnny Groth	4.00	1.80
☐ 165 Bill Bruton	4.00	1.80
☐ 166 Destruction Crew	25.00	11.00
Minnie Minoso		
Rocky Colavito		
(Misspelled Colovito on card back)		
Larry Doby		
☐ 167 Duke Maas	4.00	1.80
☐ 168 Carroll Hardy	4.00	1.80
☐ 169 Ted Abernathy	4.00	1.80
☐ 170 Gene Woodling	8.00	3.60
☐ 171 Willard Schmidt	4.00	1.80
☐ 172 Athletics Team	12.00	2.40
(Checklist on back)		
☐ 173 Bill Monbouquette	8.00	3.60
☐ 174 Jim Pendleton	4.00	1.80
☐ 175 Dick Farrell	8.00	3.60
☐ 176 Preston Ward	4.00	1.80
☐ 177 John Briggs	4.00	1.80
☐ 178 Ruben Amaro	8.00	3.60
☐ 179 Don Rudolph	4.00	1.80
☐ 180 Yogi Berra	75.00	34.00
☐ 181 Bob Porterfield	4.00	1.80
☐ 182 Milt Graff	4.00	1.80
☐ 183 Stu Miller	8.00	3.60
☐ 184 Harvey Haddix	8.00	3.60
☐ 185 Jim Busby	4.00	1.80
☐ 186 Mudcat Grant	8.00	3.60
☐ 187 Bubba Phillips	8.00	3.60
☐ 188 Juan Pizarro	4.00	1.80
☐ 189 Neil Chrisley	4.00	1.80
☐ 190 Bill Virdon	8.00	3.60
☐ 191 Russ Kemmerer	4.00	1.80
☐ 192 Charlie Beamon	4.00	1.80
☐ 193 Sammy Taylor	4.00	1.80
☐ 194 Jim Brosnan	8.00	3.60
☐ 195 Rip Repulski	4.00	1.80
☐ 196 Billy Moran	4.00	1.80
☐ 197 Ray Semproch	4.00	1.80
☐ 198 Jim Davenport	8.00	3.60
☐ 199 Leo Kiely	4.00	1.80
☐ 200 Warren Giles NL PRES	8.00	3.60
☐ 201 Tom Acker	4.00	1.80
☐ 202 Roger Maris	100.00	45.00
☐ 203 Ossie Virgil	4.00	1.80
☐ 204 Casey Wise	4.00	1.80
☐ 205 Don Larsen	8.00	3.60
☐ 206 Carl Furillo	8.00	3.60
☐ 207 George Strickland	4.00	1.80
☐ 208 Willie Jones	4.00	1.80
☐ 209 Lenny Green	4.00	1.80
☐ 210 Ed Bailey	4.00	1.80
☐ 211 Bob Blaylock	4.00	1.80
☐ 212 Hank Aaron	75.00	34.00
Eddie Mathews		
☐ 213 Jim Rivera	8.00	3.60
☐ 214 Marcelino Solis	4.00	1.80
☐ 215 Jim Lemon	8.00	3.60
☐ 216 Andre Rodgers	4.00	1.80
☐ 217 Carl Erskine	8.00	3.60
☐ 218 Roman Mejias	4.00	1.80
☐ 219 George Zuverink	4.00	1.80
☐ 220 Frank Malzone	8.00	3.60
☐ 221 Bob Bowman	4.00	1.80
☐ 222 Bobby Shantz	4.00	1.80
☐ 223 Cardinals Team	12.00	2.40
(Checklist on back)		
☐ 224 Claude Osteen	8.00	3.60
☐ 225 Johnny Logan	8.00	3.60
☐ 226 Art Ceccarelli	4.00	1.80
☐ 227 Hal W. Smith	4.00	1.80
☐ 228 Don Gross	4.00	1.80
☐ 229 Vic Power	8.00	3.60
☐ 230 Bill Fischer	4.00	1.80
☐ 231 Ellis Burton	4.00	1.80
☐ 232 Eddie Kasko	4.00	1.80
☐ 233 Paul Foytack	4.00	1.80
☐ 234 Chuck Tanner	8.00	3.60
☐ 235 Valmy Thomas	4.00	1.80
☐ 236 Ted Bowsfield	4.00	1.80
☐ 237 Run Preventers	12.00	5.50
Gil McDougald		
Bob Turley		
Bobby Richardson		
☐ 238 Gene Baker	4.00	1.80
☐ 239 Bob Trowbridge	4.00	1.80
☐ 240 Hank Bauer	8.00	3.60
☐ 241 Billy Muffett	4.00	1.80

☐ 242 Ron Samford	4.00	1.80
☐ 243 Marv Grissom	4.00	1.80
☐ 244 Ted Gray	4.00	1.80
☐ 245 Ned Garver	4.00	1.80
☐ 246 J.W. Porter	4.00	1.80
☐ 247 Don Ferrarese	4.00	1.80
☐ 248 Red Sox Team (Checklist on back)	12.00	2.40
☐ 249 Bobby Adams	4.00	1.80
☐ 250 Billy O'Dell	4.00	1.80
☐ 251 Clete Boyer	8.00	3.60
☐ 252 Ray Boone	8.00	3.60
☐ 253 Seth Morehead	4.00	1.80
☐ 254 Zeke Bella	4.00	1.80
☐ 255 Del Ennis	8.00	3.60
☐ 256 Jerry Davie	4.00	1.80
☐ 257 Leon Wagner	8.00	3.60
☐ 258 Fred Kipp	4.00	1.80
☐ 259 Jim Pisoni	4.00	1.80
☐ 260 Early Wynn UER (1957 Cleveland)	16.00	7.25
☐ 261 Gene Stephens	4.00	1.80
☐ 262 Johnny Podres Clem Labine Don Drysdale	16.00	7.25
☐ 263 Bud Daley	4.00	1.80
☐ 264 Chico Carrasquel	4.00	1.80
☐ 265 Ron Kline	4.00	1.80
☐ 266 Woody Held	4.00	1.80
☐ 267 John Romonosky	4.00	1.80
☐ 268 Tito Francona	8.00	3.60
☐ 269 Jack Meyer	4.00	1.80
☐ 270 Gil Hodges	25.00	11.00
☐ 271 Orlando Pena	4.00	1.80
☐ 272 Jerry Lumpe	4.00	1.80
☐ 273 Joey Jay	8.00	3.60
☐ 274 Jerry Kindall	8.00	3.60
☐ 275 Jack Sanford	8.00	3.60
☐ 276 Pete Daley	4.00	1.80
☐ 277 Turk Lown	8.00	3.60
☐ 278 Chuck Essegian	4.00	1.80
☐ 279 Ernie Johnson	4.00	1.80
☐ 280 Frank Bolling	4.00	1.80
☐ 281 Walt Craddock	4.00	1.80
☐ 282 R.C. Stevens	4.00	1.80
☐ 283 Russ Heman	4.00	1.80
☐ 284 Steve Korcheck	4.00	1.80
☐ 285 Joe Cunningham	4.00	1.80
☐ 286 Dean Stone	4.00	1.80
☐ 287 Don Zimmer	8.00	3.60
☐ 288 Dutch Dotterer	4.00	1.80
☐ 289 Johnny Kucks	8.00	3.60
☐ 290 Wes Covington	4.00	1.80
☐ 291 Pedro Ramos Camilo Pascual	4.00	1.80
☐ 292 Dick Williams	8.00	3.60
☐ 293 Ray Moore	4.00	1.80
☐ 294 Hank Foiles	4.00	1.80
☐ 295 Billy Martin	25.00	11.00
☐ 296 Ernie Broglio	4.00	1.80
☐ 297 Jackie Brandt	4.00	1.80
☐ 298 Tex Clevenger	4.00	1.80
☐ 299 Billy Klaus	4.00	1.80
☐ 300 Richie Ashburn	25.00	11.00
☐ 301 Earl Averill	4.00	1.80
☐ 302 Don Mossi	8.00	3.60
☐ 303 Marty Keough	4.00	1.80
☐ 304 Cubs Team (Checklist on back)	12.00	2.40
☐ 305 Curt Raydon	4.00	1.80
☐ 306 Jim Gilliam	8.00	3.60
☐ 307 Curt Barclay	4.00	1.80
☐ 308 Norm Siebern	4.00	1.80
☐ 309 Sal Maglie	8.00	3.60
☐ 310 Luis Aparicio	20.00	9.00
☐ 311 Norm Zauchin	4.00	1.80
☐ 312 Don Newcombe	8.00	3.60
☐ 313 Frank House	4.00	1.80
☐ 314 Don Cardwell	4.00	1.80
☐ 315 Joe Adcock	8.00	3.60
☐ 316A Ralph Lumenti UER (Option) (Photo actually Camilo Pascual)	4.00	1.80
☐ 316B Ralph Lumenti UER (No option) (Photo actually Camilo Pascual)	80.00	36.00
☐ 317 Willie Mays Richie Ashburn	70.00	32.00
☐ 318 Rocky Bridges	4.00	1.80
☐ 319 Dave Hillman	4.00	1.80
☐ 320 Bob Skinner	8.00	3.60
☐ 321A Bob Giallombardo (Option)	4.00	1.80
☐ 321B Bob Giallombardo (No option)	80.00	36.00
☐ 322A Harry Hanebrink (Traded)	4.00	1.80
☐ 322B Harry Hanebrink (No trade)	80.00	36.00
☐ 323 Frank Sullivan	4.00	1.80
☐ 324 Don Demeter	4.00	1.80
☐ 325 Ken Boyer	10.00	4.50
☐ 326 Marv Throneberry	8.00	3.60
☐ 327 Gary Bell	4.00	1.80
☐ 328 Lou Skizas	4.00	1.80
☐ 329 Tigers Team (Checklist on back)	12.00	2.40
☐ 330 Gus Triandos	8.00	3.60
☐ 331 Steve Boros	4.00	1.80
☐ 332 Ray Monzant	4.00	1.80
☐ 333 Harry Simpson	4.00	1.80
☐ 334 Glen Hobbie	4.00	1.80
☐ 335 Johnny Temple	8.00	3.60
☐ 336A Billy Loes (With traded line)	8.00	3.60
☐ 336B Billy Loes (No trade)	80.00	36.00
☐ 337 George Crowe	4.00	1.80
☐ 338 Sparky Anderson	65.00	29.00
☐ 339 Roy Face	8.00	3.60
☐ 340 Roy Sievers	8.00	3.60
☐ 341 Tom Qualters	4.00	1.80
☐ 342 Ray Jablonski	4.00	1.80
☐ 343 Billy Hoeft	4.00	1.80
☐ 344 Russ Nixon	4.00	1.80
☐ 345 Gil McDougald	8.00	3.60
☐ 346 Dave Sisler Tom Brewer	4.00	1.80
☐ 347 Bob Buhl	4.00	1.80
☐ 348 Ted Lepcio	4.00	1.80
☐ 349 Hoyt Wilhelm	16.00	7.25
☐ 350 Ernie Banks	75.00	34.00
☐ 351 Earl Torgeson	4.00	1.80
☐ 352 Robin Roberts	20.00	9.00
☐ 353 Curt Flood	8.00	3.60
☐ 354 Pete Burnside	4.00	1.80
☐ 355 Jimmy Piersall	8.00	3.60
☐ 356 Bob Mabe	4.00	1.80
☐ 357 Dick Stuart	8.00	3.60
☐ 358 Ralph Terry	8.00	3.60
☐ 359 Bill White	20.00	9.00
☐ 360 Al Kaline	65.00	29.00
☐ 361 Willard Nixon	4.00	1.80
☐ 362A Dolan Nichols (With option line)	4.00	1.80
☐ 362B Dolan Nichols (No option)	80.00	36.00
☐ 363 Bobby Avila	4.00	1.80
☐ 364 Danny McDevitt	4.00	1.80
☐ 365 Gus Bell	8.00	3.60
☐ 366 Humberto Robinson	4.00	1.80
☐ 367 Cal Neeman	4.00	1.80
☐ 368 Don Mueller	8.00	3.60
☐ 369 Dick Tomanek	4.00	1.80
☐ 370 Pete Runnels	8.00	3.60
☐ 371 Dick Brodowski	4.00	1.80
☐ 372 Jim Hegan	8.00	3.60
☐ 373 Herb Plews	4.00	1.80
☐ 374 Art Ditmar	8.00	3.60
☐ 375 Bob Nieman	4.00	1.80
☐ 376 Hal Naragon	4.00	1.80
☐ 377 John Antonelli	8.00	3.60
☐ 378 Gail Harris	4.00	1.80
☐ 379 Bob Miller	4.00	1.80
☐ 380 Hank Aaron	125.00	55.00
☐ 381 Mike Baxes	4.00	1.80
☐ 382 Curt Simmons	8.00	3.60
☐ 383 Words of Wisdom Don Larsen Casey Stengel MG	14.00	6.25
☐ 384 Dave Sisler	4.00	1.80
☐ 385 Sherm Lollar	8.00	3.60
☐ 386 Jim Delsing	4.00	1.80
☐ 387 Don Drysdale	35.00	16.00
☐ 388 Bob Will	4.00	1.80
☐ 389 Joe Nuxhall	8.00	3.60
☐ 390 Orlando Cepeda	16.00	7.25
☐ 391 Milt Pappas	8.00	3.60
☐ 392 Whitey Herzog	8.00	3.60
☐ 393 Frank Lary	8.00	3.60
☐ 394 Randy Jackson	4.00	1.80
☐ 395 Elston Howard	10.00	4.50
☐ 396 Bob Rush	4.00	1.80
☐ 397 Senators Team (Checklist on back)	12.00	2.40
☐ 398 Wally Post	8.00	3.60
☐ 399 Larry Jackson	4.00	1.80
☐ 400 Jackie Jensen	8.00	3.60
☐ 401 Ron Blackburn	4.00	1.80
☐ 402 Hector Lopez	8.00	3.60
☐ 403 Clem Labine	8.00	3.60
☐ 404 Hank Sauer	8.00	3.60
☐ 405 Roy McMillan	8.00	3.60
☐ 406 Solly Drake	4.00	1.80
☐ 407 Moe Drabowsky	8.00	3.60
☐ 408 Nellie Fox Luis Aparicio	35.00	16.00
☐ 409 Gus Zernial	8.00	3.60
☐ 410 Billy Pierce	8.00	3.60
☐ 411 Whitey Lockman	8.00	3.60
☐ 412 Stan Lopata	4.00	1.80
☐ 413 Camilo Pascual UER (Listed as Camillo on front and Pasqual on back)	8.00	3.60
☐ 414 Dale Long	8.00	3.60
☐ 415 Bill Mazeroski	12.00	5.50
☐ 416 Haywood Sullivan	8.00	3.60
☐ 417 Virgil Trucks	8.00	3.60
☐ 418 Gino Cimoli	4.00	1.80
☐ 419 Braves Team (Checklist on back)	12.00	2.40
☐ 420 Rocky Colavito	30.00	13.50
☐ 421 Herman Wehmeier	4.00	1.80
☐ 422 Hobie Landrith	4.00	1.80
☐ 423 Bob Grim	8.00	3.60
☐ 424 Ken Aspromonte	4.00	1.80
☐ 425 Del Crandall	8.00	3.60
☐ 426 Gerry Staley	8.00	3.60
☐ 427 Charlie Neal	8.00	3.60
☐ 428 Ron Kline Bob Friend Vernon Law Roy Face	4.00	1.80
☐ 429 Bobby Thomson	8.00	3.60
☐ 430 Whitey Ford	50.00	22.00
☐ 431 Whammy Douglas	4.00	1.80
☐ 432 Smoky Burgess	8.00	3.60
☐ 433 Billy Harrell	4.00	1.80
☐ 434 Hal Griggs	4.00	1.80
☐ 435 Frank Robinson	50.00	22.00
☐ 436 Granny Hamner	4.00	1.80
☐ 437 Ike Delock	4.00	1.80
☐ 438 Sammy Esposito	4.00	1.80
☐ 439 Brooks Robinson	50.00	22.00
☐ 440 Lou Burdette (Posing as if lefthanded)	8.00	3.60
☐ 441 John Roseboro	8.00	3.60
☐ 442 Ray Narleski	4.00	1.80
☐ 443 Daryl Spencer	4.00	1.80
☐ 444 Ron Hansen	8.00	3.60
☐ 445 Cal McLish	4.00	1.80
☐ 446 Rocky Nelson	4.00	1.80
☐ 447 Bob Anderson	4.00	1.80
☐ 448 Vada Pinson UER (Born: 8/8/38 should be 8/11/38)	10.00	4.50
☐ 449 Tom Gorman	4.00	1.80
☐ 450 Eddie Mathews	35.00	16.00
☐ 451 Jimmy Constable	4.00	1.80
☐ 452 Chico Fernandez	4.00	1.80
☐ 453 Les Moss	4.00	1.80
☐ 454 Phil Clark	4.00	1.80
☐ 455 Larry Doby	8.00	3.60
☐ 456 Jerry Casale	4.00	1.80
☐ 457 Dodgers Team (Checklist on back)	30.00	6.00
☐ 458 Gordon Jones	4.00	1.80
☐ 459 Bill Tuttle	4.00	1.80
☐ 460 Bob Friend	8.00	3.60
☐ 461 Mickey Mantle HL	130.00	57.50
☐ 462 Rocky Colavito HL	16.00	7.25
☐ 463 Al Kaline HL	25.00	11.00
☐ 464 Willie Mays HL 54 World Series Catch	40.00	18.00
☐ 465 Roy Sievers HL	8.00	3.60
☐ 466 Billy Pierce HL	8.00	3.60
☐ 467 Hank Aaron HL	30.00	13.50
☐ 468 Duke Snider HL	18.00	8.00
☐ 469 Ernie Banks HL	18.00	8.00
☐ 470 Stan Musial HL 3,000 Hits	25.00	11.00
☐ 471 Tom Sturdivant	4.00	1.80
☐ 472 Gene Freese	4.00	1.80
☐ 473 Mike Fornieles	4.00	1.80
☐ 474 Moe Thacker	4.00	1.80
☐ 475 Jack Harshman	4.00	1.80
☐ 476 Indians Team (Checklist on back)	12.00	2.40
☐ 477 Barry Latman	4.00	1.80
☐ 478 Bob Clemente	225.00	100.00
☐ 479 Lindy McDaniel	8.00	3.60
☐ 480 Red Schoendienst	16.00	7.25
☐ 481 Charlie Maxwell	8.00	3.60
☐ 482 Russ Meyer	4.00	1.80
☐ 483 Clint Courtney	4.00	1.80
☐ 484 Willie Kirkland	4.00	1.80
☐ 485 Ryne Duren	8.00	3.60

☐ 486 Sammy White 4.00 1.80
☐ 487 Hal Brown 4.00 1.80
☐ 488 Walt Moryn 4.00 1.80
☐ 489 John Powers 4.00 1.80
☐ 490 Frank Thomas 8.00 3.60
☐ 491 Don Blasingame 4.00 1.80
☐ 492 Gene Conley 8.00 3.60
☐ 493 Jim Landis 8.00 3.60
☐ 494 Don Pavletich 4.00 1.80
☐ 495 Johnny Podres 8.00 3.60
☐ 496 Wayne Terwilliger UER 4.00 1.80
(Athlftics on front)
☐ 497 Hal R. Smith 4.00 1.80
☐ 498 Dick Hyde 4.00 1.80
☐ 499 Johnny O'Brien 8.00 3.60
☐ 500 Vic Wertz 8.00 3.60
☐ 501 Bob Tiefenauer 4.00 1.80
☐ 502 Alvin Dark 8.00 3.60
☐ 503 Jim Owens 4.00 1.80
☐ 504 Ossie Alvarez 4.00 1.80
☐ 505 Tony Kubek 12.00 5.50
☐ 506 Bob Purkey 4.00 1.80
☐ 507 Bob Hale 16.00 7.25
☐ 508 Art Fowler 16.00 7.25
☐ 509 Norm Cash 65.00 29.00
☐ 510 Yankees Team 125.00 25.00
(Checklist on back)
☐ 511 George Susce 16.00 7.25
☐ 512 George Altman 16.00 7.25
☐ 513 Tommy Carroll 16.00 7.25
☐ 514 Bob Gibson 250.00 110.00
☐ 515 Harmon Killebrew 125.00 55.00
☐ 516 Mike Garcia 20.00 9.00
☐ 517 Joe Koppe 16.00 7.25
☐ 518 Mike Cueller UER 30.00 13.50
(Sic, Cuellar)
☐ 519 Pete Runnels 20.00 9.00
Dick Gernert
Frank Malzone
☐ 520 Don Elston 16.00 7.25
☐ 521 Gary Geiger 16.00 7.25
☐ 522 Gene Snyder 16.00 7.25
☐ 523 Harry Bright 16.00 7.25
☐ 524 Larry Osborne 16.00 7.25
☐ 525 Jim Coates 20.00 9.00
☐ 526 Bob Speake 16.00 7.25
☐ 527 Solly Hemus 16.00 7.25
☐ 528 Pirates Team 65.00 13.00
(Checklist on back)
☐ 529 George Bamberger 25.00 11.00
☐ 530 Wally Moon 20.00 9.00
☐ 531 Ray Webster 16.00 7.25
☐ 532 Mark Freeman 16.00 7.25
☐ 533 Darrell Johnson 20.00 9.00
☐ 534 Faye Throneberry 16.00 7.25
☐ 535 Ruben Gomez 16.00 7.25
☐ 536 Danny Kravitz 16.00 7.25
☐ 537 Rudolph Arias 16.00 7.25
☐ 538 Chick King 16.00 7.25
☐ 539 Gary Blaylock 16.00 7.25
☐ 540 Willie Miranda 16.00 7.25
☐ 541 Bob Thurman 16.00 7.25
☐ 542 Jim Perry 30.00 13.50
☐ 543 Bob Skinner 175.00 80.00
Bill Virdon
Roberto Clemente
☐ 544 Lee Tate 16.00 7.25
☐ 545 Tom Morgan 16.00 7.25
☐ 546 Al Schroll 16.00 7.25
☐ 547 Jim Baxes 16.00 7.25
☐ 548 Elmer Singleton 16.00 7.25
☐ 549 Howie Nunn 16.00 7.25
☐ 550 Roy Campanella 160.00 70.00
(Symbol of Courage)
☐ 551 Fred Haney AS MG 16.00 7.25
☐ 552 Casey Stengel AS MG 30.00 13.50
☐ 553 Orlando Cepeda AS 25.00 11.00
☐ 554 Bill Skowron AS 25.00 11.00
☐ 555 Bill Mazeroski AS 25.00 11.00
☐ 556 Nellie Fox AS 40.00 18.00
☐ 557 Ken Boyer AS 25.00 11.00
☐ 558 Frank Malzone AS 16.00 7.25
☐ 559 Ernie Banks AS 65.00 29.00
☐ 560 Luis Aparicio AS 30.00 13.50
☐ 561 Hank Aaron AS 125.00 55.00
☐ 562 Al Kaline AS 65.00 29.00
☐ 563 Willie Mays AS 125.00 55.00
☐ 564 Mickey Mantle AS 300.00 135.00
☐ 565 Wes Covington AS 16.00 7.25
☐ 566 Roy Sievers AS 16.00 7.25
☐ 567 Del Crandall AS 16.00 7.25
☐ 568 Gus Triandos AS 16.00 7.25
☐ 569 Bob Friend AS 16.00 7.25
☐ 570 Bob Turley AS 16.00 7.25
☐ 571 Warren Spahn AS 40.00 18.00
☐ 572 Billy Pierce AS 30.00 9.50

1960 Topps

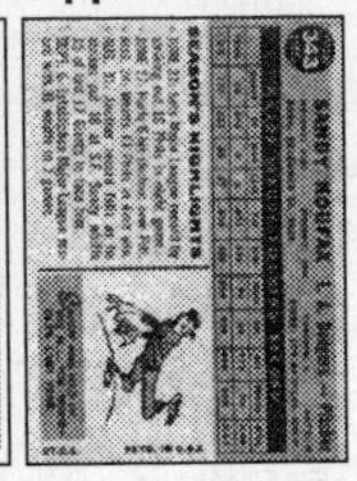

The cards in this 572-card set measure 2 1/2" by 3 1/2". The 1960 Topps set is the only Topps standard size issue to use a horizontally oriented front. World Series cards appeared for the first time (385 to 391), and there is a Rookie Prospect (RP) series (117-148), the most famous of which is Carl Yastrzemski, and a Sport Magazine All-Star Selection (AS) series (553-572). There are 16 manager cards listed alphabetically from 212 through 227. The 1959 Topps All-Rookie team is featured on cards 316-325. The coaching staff of each team was also afforded their own card in a 16-card subset (455-470). Cards 375 to 440 come with either gray or white backs. There is no price differential for either color back. The high series (507-572) were printed on a more limited basis than the rest of the set. The team cards have series checklists on the reverse. Cards were issued in one-card penny packs and six-card nickle packs. The key Rookie Cards in this set are Jim Kaat, Willie McCovey and Carl Yastrzemski.

	NRMT	VG-E
COMPLETE SET (572)	3500.00	1600.00
COMMON CARD (1-440)	4.00	1.80
COMMON CARD (441-506)	7.00	3.10
COMMON CARD (507-572)	16.00	7.25
WRAPPER (1-CENT)	900.00	400.00
WRAPPER (1-CENT REPEAT)	500.00	220.00
WRAPPER (5-CENT)	40.00	18.00

☐ 1 Early Wynn 30.00 7.50
☐ 2 Roman Mejias 4.00 1.80
☐ 3 Joe Adcock 6.00 2.70
☐ 4 Bob Purkey 4.00 1.80
☐ 5 Wally Moon 6.00 2.70
☐ 6 Lou Berberet 4.00 1.80
☐ 7 Master and Mentor 25.00 11.00
Willie Mays
Bill Rigney MG
☐ 8 Bud Daley 4.00 1.80
☐ 9 Faye Throneberry 4.00 1.80
☐ 10 Ernie Banks 50.00 22.00
☐ 11 Norm Siebern 4.00 1.80
☐ 12 Milt Pappas 6.00 2.70
☐ 13 Wally Post 6.00 2.70
☐ 14 Jim Grant 6.00 2.70
☐ 15 Pete Runnels 6.00 2.70
☐ 16 Ernie Broglio 6.00 2.70
☐ 17 Johnny Callison 6.00 2.70
☐ 18 Dodgers Team 50.00 10.00
(Checklist on back)
☐ 19 Felix Mantilla 4.00 1.80
☐ 20 Roy Face 6.00 2.70
☐ 21 Dutch Dotterer 4.00 1.80
☐ 22 Rocky Bridges 4.00 1.80
☐ 23 Eddie Fisher 4.00 1.80
☐ 24 Dick Gray 4.00 1.80
☐ 25 Roy Sievers 6.00 2.70
☐ 26 Wayne Terwilliger 4.00 1.80
☐ 27 Dick Drott 4.00 1.80
☐ 28 Brooks Robinson 50.00 22.00
☐ 29 Clem Labine 6.00 2.70
☐ 30 Tito Francona 4.00 1.80
☐ 31 Sammy Esposito 4.00 1.80
☐ 32 Sophomore Stalwarts 4.00 1.80
Jim O'Toole
Vada Pinson
☐ 33 Tom Morgan 4.00 1.80
☐ 34 Sparky Anderson 14.00 6.25
☐ 35 Whitey Ford 50.00 22.00
☐ 36 Russ Nixon 4.00 1.80
☐ 37 Bill Bruton 4.00 1.80
☐ 38 Jerry Casale 4.00 1.80
☐ 39 Earl Averill 4.00 1.80
☐ 40 Joe Cunningham 4.00 1.80
☐ 41 Barry Latman 4.00 1.80
☐ 42 Hobie Landrith 4.00 1.80
☐ 43 Senators Team 9.00 1.80
(Checklist on back)
☐ 44 Bobby Locke 4.00 1.80
☐ 45 Roy McMillan 6.00 2.70
☐ 46 Jerry Fisher 4.00 1.80
☐ 47 Don Zimmer 6.00 2.70
☐ 48 Hal W. Smith 4.00 1.80
☐ 49 Curt Raydon 4.00 1.80
☐ 50 Al Kaline 50.00 22.00
☐ 51 Jim Coates 6.00 2.70
☐ 52 Dave Philley 4.00 1.80
☐ 53 Jackie Brandt 4.00 1.80
☐ 54 Mike Fornieles 4.00 1.80
☐ 55 Bill Mazeroski 10.00 4.50
☐ 56 Steve Korcheck 4.00 1.80
☐ 57 Win Savers 4.00 1.80
Turk Lown
Gerry Staley
☐ 58 Gino Cimoli 4.00 1.80
☐ 59 Juan Pizarro 4.00 1.80
☐ 60 Gus Triandos 6.00 2.70
☐ 61 Eddie Kasko 4.00 1.80
☐ 62 Roger Craig 6.00 2.70
☐ 63 George Strickland 4.00 1.80
☐ 64 Jack Meyer 4.00 1.80
☐ 65 Elston Howard 7.00 3.10
☐ 66 Bob Trowbridge 4.00 1.80
☐ 67 Jose Pagan 4.00 1.80
☐ 68 Dave Hillman 4.00 1.80
☐ 69 Billy Goodman 6.00 2.70
☐ 70 Lew Burdette 6.00 2.70
☐ 71 Marty Keough 4.00 1.80
☐ 72 Tigers Team 20.00 4.00
(Checklist on back)
☐ 73 Bob Gibson 50.00 22.00
☐ 74 Walt Moryn 4.00 1.80
☐ 75 Vic Power 6.00 2.70
☐ 76 Bill Fischer 4.00 1.80
☐ 77 Hank Foiles 4.00 1.80
☐ 78 Bob Grim 4.00 1.80
☐ 79 Walt Dropo 4.00 1.80
☐ 80 Johnny Antonelli 6.00 2.70
☐ 81 Russ Snyder 4.00 1.80
☐ 82 Ruben Gomez 4.00 1.80
☐ 83 Tony Kubek 7.00 3.10
☐ 84 Hal R. Smith 4.00 1.80
☐ 85 Frank Lary 6.00 2.70
☐ 86 Dick Gernert 4.00 1.80
☐ 87 John Romonosky 4.00 1.80
☐ 88 John Roseboro 6.00 2.70
☐ 89 Hal Brown 4.00 1.80
☐ 90 Bobby Avila 4.00 1.80
☐ 91 Bennie Daniels 4.00 1.80
☐ 92 Whitey Herzog 6.00 2.70
☐ 93 Art Schult 4.00 1.80
☐ 94 Leo Kiely 4.00 1.80
☐ 95 Frank Thomas 6.00 2.70
☐ 96 Ralph Terry 6.00 2.70
☐ 97 Ted Lepcio 4.00 1.80
☐ 98 Gordon Jones 4.00 1.80
☐ 99 Lenny Green 4.00 1.80
☐ 100 Nellie Fox 20.00 9.00
☐ 101 Bob Miller 4.00 1.80
☐ 102 Kent Hadley 4.00 1.80
☐ 103 Dick Farrell 6.00 2.70
☐ 104 Dick Schofield 6.00 2.70
☐ 105 Larry Sherry 6.00 2.70
☐ 106 Billy Gardner 4.00 1.80
☐ 107 Carlton Willey 4.00 1.80
☐ 108 Pete Daley 4.00 1.80
☐ 109 Clete Boyer 6.00 2.70
☐ 110 Cal McLish 4.00 1.80
☐ 111 Vic Wertz 6.00 2.70
☐ 112 Jack Harshman 4.00 1.80
☐ 113 Bob Skinner 4.00 1.80
☐ 114 Ken Aspromonte 4.00 1.80
☐ 115 Fork and Knuckler 7.00 3.10
Roy Face
Hoyt Wilhelm
☐ 116 Jim Rivera 4.00 1.80
☐ 117 Tom Borland RP 4.00 1.80
☐ 118 Bob Bruce RP 4.00 1.80
☐ 119 Chico Cardenas RP 6.00 2.70
☐ 120 Duke Carmel RP 4.00 1.80
☐ 121 Camilo Carreon RP 4.00 1.80
☐ 122 Don Dillard RP 4.00 1.80
☐ 123 Dan Dobbek RP 4.00 1.80
☐ 124 Jim Donohue RP 4.00 1.80
☐ 125 Dick Ellsworth RP 6.00 2.70
☐ 126 Chuck Estrada RP 4.00 1.80
☐ 127 Ron Hansen RP 6.00 2.70
☐ 128 Bill Harris RP 4.00 1.80
☐ 129 Bob Hartman RP 4.00 1.80
☐ 130 Frank Herrera RP 4.00 1.80
☐ 131 Ed Hobaugh RP 4.00 1.80
☐ 132 Frank Howard RP 25.00 11.00
☐ 133 Manuel Javier RP 6.00 2.70
(Sic, Julian)
☐ 134 Deron Johnson RP 6.00 2.70
☐ 135 Ken Johnson RP 4.00 1.80
☐ 136 Jim Kaat RP 40.00 18.00

Card		
☐ 137 Lou Klimchock RP	4.00	1.80
☐ 138 Art Mahaffey RP	6.00	2.70
☐ 139 Carl Mathias RP	4.00	1.80
☐ 140 Julio Navarro RP	4.00	1.80
☐ 141 Jim Proctor RP	4.00	1.80
☐ 142 Bill Short RP	4.00	1.80
☐ 143 Al Spangler RP	4.00	1.80
☐ 144 Al Stieglitz RP	4.00	1.80
☐ 145 Jim Umbricht RP	4.00	1.80
☐ 146 Ted Wieand RP	4.00	1.80
☐ 147 Bob Will RP	4.00	1.80
☐ 148 Carl Yastrzemski RP	125.00	55.00
☐ 149 Bob Nieman	4.00	1.80
☐ 150 Billy Pierce	6.00	2.70
☐ 151 Giants Team	9.00	1.80
(Checklist on back)		
☐ 152 Gail Harris	4.00	1.80
☐ 153 Bobby Thomson	6.00	2.70
☐ 154 Jim Davenport	6.00	2.70
☐ 155 Charlie Neal	6.00	2.70
☐ 156 Art Ceccarelli	4.00	1.80
☐ 157 Rocky Nelson	6.00	2.70
☐ 158 Wes Covington	6.00	2.70
☐ 159 Jim Piersall	6.00	2.70
☐ 160 Rival All-Stars	140.00	65.00
Mickey Mantle		
Ken Boyer		
☐ 161 Ray Narleski	4.00	1.80
☐ 162 Sammy Taylor	4.00	1.80
☐ 163 Hector Lopez	6.00	2.70
☐ 164 Reds Team	9.00	1.80
(Checklist on back)		
☐ 165 Jack Sanford	6.00	2.70
☐ 166 Chuck Essegian	4.00	1.80
☐ 167 Valmy Thomas	4.00	1.80
☐ 168 Alex Grammas	4.00	1.80
☐ 169 Jake Striker	4.00	1.80
☐ 170 Del Crandall	6.00	2.70
☐ 171 Johnny Groth	4.00	1.80
☐ 172 Willie Kirkland	4.00	1.80
☐ 173 Billy Martin	20.00	9.00
☐ 174 Indians Team	9.00	1.80
(Checklist on back)		
☐ 175 Pedro Ramos	4.00	1.80
☐ 176 Vada Pinson	6.00	2.70
☐ 177 Johnny Kucks	4.00	1.80
☐ 178 Woody Held	4.00	1.80
☐ 179 Rip Coleman	4.00	1.80
☐ 180 Harry Simpson	4.00	1.80
☐ 181 Billy Loes	6.00	2.70
☐ 182 Glen Hobbie	4.00	1.80
☐ 183 Eli Grba	4.00	1.80
☐ 184 Gary Geiger	4.00	1.80
☐ 185 Jim Owens	4.00	1.80
☐ 186 Dave Sisler	4.00	1.80
☐ 187 Jay Hook	4.00	1.80
☐ 188 Dick Williams	6.00	2.70
☐ 189 Don McMahon	4.00	1.80
☐ 190 Gene Woodling	6.00	2.70
☐ 191 Johnny Klippstein	4.00	1.80
☐ 192 Danny O'Connell	4.00	1.80
☐ 193 Dick Hyde	4.00	1.80
☐ 194 Bobby Gene Smith	4.00	1.80
☐ 195 Lindy McDaniel	6.00	2.70
☐ 196 Andy Carey	6.00	2.70
☐ 197 Ron Kline	4.00	1.80
☐ 198 Jerry Lynch	6.00	2.70
☐ 199 Dick Donovan	6.00	2.70
☐ 200 Willie Mays	90.00	40.00
☐ 201 Larry Osborne	4.00	1.80
☐ 202 Fred Kipp	4.00	1.80
☐ 203 Sammy White	4.00	1.80
☐ 204 Ryne Duren	6.00	2.70
☐ 205 Johnny Logan	6.00	2.70
☐ 206 Claude Osteen	6.00	2.70
☐ 207 Bob Boyd	4.00	1.80
☐ 208 White Sox Team	9.00	1.80
(Checklist on back)		
☐ 209 Ron Blackburn	4.00	1.80
☐ 210 Harmon Killebrew	25.00	11.00
☐ 211 Taylor Phillips	4.00	1.80
☐ 212 Walter Alston MG	12.00	5.50
☐ 213 Chuck Dressen MG	6.00	2.70
☐ 214 Jimmy Dykes MG	6.00	2.70
☐ 215 Bob Elliott MG	6.00	2.70
☐ 216 Joe Gordon MG	6.00	2.70
☐ 217 Charlie Grimm MG	6.00	2.70
☐ 218 Solly Hemus MG	4.00	1.80
☐ 219 Fred Hutchinson MG	6.00	2.70
☐ 220 Billy Jurges MG	4.00	1.80
☐ 221 Cookie Lavagetto MG	4.00	1.80
☐ 222 Al Lopez MG	6.00	2.70
☐ 223 Danny Murtaugh MG	6.00	2.70
☐ 224 Paul Richards MG	6.00	2.70
☐ 225 Bill Rigney MG	4.00	1.80
☐ 226 Eddie Sawyer MG	4.00	1.80
☐ 227 Casey Stengel MG	15.00	6.75
☐ 228 Ernie Johnson	6.00	2.70
☐ 229 Joe M. Morgan	4.00	1.80
☐ 230 Mound Magicians	12.00	5.50
Lou Burdette		
Warren Spahn		
Bob Buhl		
☐ 231 Hal Naragon	4.00	1.80
☐ 232 Jim Busby	4.00	1.80
☐ 233 Don Elston	4.00	1.80
☐ 234 Don Demeter	4.00	1.80
☐ 235 Gus Bell	6.00	2.70
☐ 236 Dick Ricketts	4.00	1.80
☐ 237 Elmer Valo	4.00	1.80
☐ 238 Danny Kravitz	4.00	1.80
☐ 239 Joe Shipley	4.00	1.80
☐ 240 Luis Aparicio	15.00	6.75
☐ 241 Albie Pearson	6.00	2.70
☐ 242 Cardinals Team	9.00	1.80
(Checklist on back)		
☐ 243 Bubba Phillips	4.00	1.80
☐ 244 Hal Griggs	4.00	1.80
☐ 245 Eddie Yost	6.00	2.70
☐ 246 Lee Maye	6.00	2.70
☐ 247 Gil McDougald	6.00	2.70
☐ 248 Del Rice	4.00	1.80
☐ 249 Earl Wilson	6.00	2.70
☐ 250 Stan Musial	80.00	36.00
☐ 251 Bob Malkmus	4.00	1.80
☐ 252 Ray Herbert	4.00	1.80
☐ 253 Eddie Bressoud	4.00	1.80
☐ 254 Arnie Portocarrero	4.00	1.80
☐ 255 Jim Gilliam	6.00	2.70
☐ 256 Dick Brown	4.00	1.80
☐ 257 Gordy Coleman	4.00	1.80
☐ 258 Dick Groat	6.00	2.70
☐ 259 George Altman	4.00	1.80
☐ 260 Power Plus	14.00	6.25
Rocky Colavito		
Tito Francona		
☐ 261 Pete Burnside	4.00	1.80
☐ 262 Hank Bauer	6.00	2.70
☐ 263 Darrell Johnson	4.00	1.80
☐ 264 Robin Roberts	15.00	6.75
☐ 265 Rip Repulski	4.00	1.80
☐ 266 Joey Jay	6.00	2.70
☐ 267 Jim Marshall	4.00	1.80
☐ 268 Al Worthington	4.00	1.80
☐ 269 Gene Green	4.00	1.80
☐ 270 Bob Turley	6.00	2.70
☐ 271 Julio Becquer	4.00	1.80
☐ 272 Fred Green	6.00	2.70
☐ 273 Neil Chrisley	4.00	1.80
☐ 274 Tom Acker	4.00	1.80
☐ 275 Curt Flood	6.00	2.70
☐ 276 Ken McBride	4.00	1.80
☐ 277 Harry Bright	4.00	1.80
☐ 278 Stan Williams	6.00	2.70
☐ 279 Chuck Tanner	6.00	2.70
☐ 280 Frank Sullivan	4.00	1.80
☐ 281 Ray Boone	6.00	2.70
☐ 282 Joe Nuxhall	6.00	2.70
☐ 283 John Blanchard	6.00	2.70
☐ 284 Don Gross	4.00	1.80
☐ 285 Harry Anderson	4.00	1.80
☐ 286 Ray Semproch	4.00	1.80
☐ 287 Felipe Alou	6.00	2.70
☐ 288 Bob Mabe	4.00	1.80
☐ 289 Willie Jones	4.00	1.80
☐ 290 Jerry Lumpe	4.00	1.80
☐ 291 Bob Keegan	4.00	1.80
☐ 292 Dodger Backstops	6.00	2.70
Joe Pignatano		
John Roseboro		
☐ 293 Gene Conley	6.00	2.70
☐ 294 Tony Taylor	6.00	2.70
☐ 295 Gil Hodges	20.00	9.00
☐ 296 Nelson Chittum	4.00	1.80
☐ 297 Reno Bertoia	4.00	1.80
☐ 298 George Witt	4.00	1.80
☐ 299 Earl Torgeson	4.00	1.80
☐ 300 Hank Aaron	80.00	36.00
☐ 301 Jerry Davie	4.00	1.80
☐ 302 Phillies Team	9.00	1.80
(Checklist on back)		
☐ 303 Billy O'Dell	4.00	1.80
☐ 304 Joe Ginsberg	4.00	1.80
☐ 305 Richie Ashburn	20.00	9.00
☐ 306 Frank Baumann	4.00	1.80
☐ 307 Gene Oliver	4.00	1.80
☐ 308 Dick Hall	4.00	1.80
☐ 309 Bob Hale	4.00	1.80
☐ 310 Frank Malzone	6.00	2.70
☐ 311 Raul Sanchez	4.00	1.80
☐ 312 Charley Lau	6.00	2.70
☐ 313 Turk Lown	4.00	1.80
☐ 314 Chico Fernandez	4.00	1.80
☐ 315 Bobby Shantz	6.00	2.70
☐ 316 Willie McCovey	115.00	52.50
☐ 317 Pumpsie Green	6.00	2.70
☐ 318 Jim Baxes	6.00	2.70
☐ 319 Joe Koppe	6.00	2.70
☐ 320 Bob Allison	6.00	2.70
☐ 321 Ron Fairly	6.00	2.70
☐ 322 Willie Tasby	6.00	2.70
☐ 323 John Romano	6.00	2.70
☐ 324 Jim Perry	6.00	2.70
☐ 325 Jim O'Toole	6.00	2.70
☐ 326 Bob Clemente	225.00	100.00
☐ 327 Ray Sadecki	4.00	1.80
☐ 328 Earl Battey	4.00	1.80
☐ 329 Zack Monroe	4.00	1.80
☐ 330 Harvey Kuenn	6.00	2.70
☐ 331 Henry Mason	4.00	1.80
☐ 332 Yankees Team	80.00	16.00
(Checklist on back)		
☐ 333 Danny McDevitt	4.00	1.80
☐ 334 Ted Abernathy	4.00	1.80
☐ 335 Red Schoendienst	12.00	5.50
☐ 336 Ike Delock	4.00	1.80
☐ 337 Cal Neeman	4.00	1.80
☐ 338 Ray Monzant	4.00	1.80
☐ 339 Harry Chiti	4.00	1.80
☐ 340 Harvey Haddix	6.00	2.70
☐ 341 Carroll Hardy	4.00	1.80
☐ 342 Casey Wise	4.00	1.80
☐ 343 Sandy Koufax	175.00	80.00
☐ 344 Clint Courtney	4.00	1.80
☐ 345 Don Newcombe	6.00	2.70
☐ 346 J.C. Martin UER	6.00	2.70
(Face actually		
Gary Peters)		
☐ 347 Ed Bouchee	4.00	1.80
☐ 348 Barry Shetrone	4.00	1.80
☐ 349 Moe Drabowsky	6.00	2.70
☐ 350 Mickey Mantle	475.00	210.00
☐ 351 Don Nottebart	4.00	1.80
☐ 352 Cincy Clouters	8.00	3.60
Gus Bell		
Frank Robinson		
Jerry Lynch		
☐ 353 Don Larsen	6.00	2.70
☐ 354 Bob Lillis	4.00	1.80
☐ 355 Bill White	6.00	2.70
☐ 356 Joe Amalfitano	4.00	1.80
☐ 357 Al Schroll	4.00	1.80
☐ 358 Joe DeMaestri	4.00	1.80
☐ 359 Buddy Gilbert	4.00	1.80
☐ 360 Herb Score	6.00	2.70
☐ 361 Bob Oldis	4.00	1.80
☐ 362 Russ Kemmerer	4.00	1.80
☐ 363 Gene Stephens	4.00	1.80
☐ 364 Paul Foytack	4.00	1.80
☐ 365 Minnie Minoso	7.00	3.10
☐ 366 Dallas Green	8.00	3.60
☐ 367 Bill Tuttle	4.00	1.80
☐ 368 Daryl Spencer	4.00	1.80
☐ 369 Billy Hoeft	4.00	1.80
☐ 370 Bill Skowron	7.00	3.10
☐ 371 Bud Byerly	4.00	1.80
☐ 372 Frank House	4.00	1.80
☐ 373 Don Hoak	6.00	2.70
☐ 374 Bob Buhl	6.00	2.70
☐ 375 Dale Long	6.00	2.70
☐ 376 John Briggs	4.00	1.80
☐ 377 Roger Maris	80.00	36.00
☐ 378 Stu Miller	6.00	2.70
☐ 379 Red Wilson	4.00	1.80
☐ 380 Bob Shaw	4.00	1.80
☐ 381 Braves Team	9.00	1.80
(Checklist on back)		
☐ 382 Ted Bowsfield	4.00	1.80
☐ 383 Leon Wagner	4.00	1.80
☐ 384 Don Cardwell	4.00	1.80
☐ 385 Charlie Neal WS	6.00	2.70
☐ 386 Charlie Neal WS	6.00	2.70
☐ 387 Carl Furillo WS	6.00	2.70
☐ 388 Gil Hodges WS	10.00	4.50
☐ 389 Luis Aparicio WS	12.00	5.50
Maury Wills		
☐ 390 World Series Game 6	6.00	2.70
☐ 391 World Series Summary	6.00	2.70
The Champs Celebrate		
☐ 392 Tex Clevenger	4.00	1.80
☐ 393 Smoky Burgess	6.00	2.70
☐ 394 Norm Larker	6.00	2.70
☐ 395 Hoyt Wilhelm	15.00	6.75
☐ 396 Steve Bilko	4.00	1.80
☐ 397 Don Blasingame	4.00	1.80
☐ 398 Mike Cuellar	6.00	2.70
☐ 399 Young Hill Stars	6.00	2.70
Milt Pappas		
Jack Fisher		
Jerry Walker		
☐ 400 Rocky Colavito	20.00	9.00

☐ 401 Bob Duliba	4.00	1.80
☐ 402 Dick Stuart	6.00	2.70
☐ 403 Ed Sadowski	4.00	1.80
☐ 404 Bob Rush	4.00	1.80
☐ 405 Bobby Richardson	14.00	6.25
☐ 406 Billy Klaus	4.00	1.80
☐ 407 Gary Peters UER	6.00	2.70
(Face actually		
J.C. Martin)		
☐ 408 Carl Furillo	6.00	2.70
☐ 409 Ron Samford	4.00	1.80
☐ 410 Sam Jones	6.00	2.70
☐ 411 Ed Bailey	4.00	1.80
☐ 412 Bob Anderson	4.00	1.80
☐ 413 Athletics Team	9.00	1.80
(Checklist on back)		
☐ 414 Don Williams	4.00	1.80
☐ 415 Bob Cerv	4.00	1.80
☐ 416 Humberto Robinson	4.00	1.80
☐ 417 Chuck Cottier	4.00	1.80
☐ 418 Don Mossi	6.00	2.70
☐ 419 George Crowe	4.00	1.80
☐ 420 Eddie Mathews	30.00	13.50
☐ 421 Duke Maas	4.00	1.80
☐ 422 John Powers	4.00	1.80
☐ 423 Ed Fitzgerald	4.00	1.80
☐ 424 Pete Whisenant	4.00	1.80
☐ 425 Johnny Podres	6.00	2.70
☐ 426 Ron Jackson	4.00	1.80
☐ 427 Al Grunwald	4.00	1.80
☐ 428 Al Smith	4.00	1.80
☐ 429 AL Kings	12.00	5.50
Nellie Fox		
Harvey Kuenn		
☐ 430 Art Ditmar	4.00	1.80
☐ 431 Andre Rodgers	4.00	1.80
☐ 432 Chuck Stobbs	4.00	1.80
☐ 433 Irv Noren	4.00	1.80
☐ 434 Brooks Lawrence	4.00	1.80
☐ 435 Gene Freese	4.00	1.80
☐ 436 Marv Throneberry	6.00	2.70
☐ 437 Bob Friend	6.00	2.70
☐ 438 Jim Coker	4.00	1.80
☐ 439 Tom Brewer	4.00	1.80
☐ 440 Jim Lemon	6.00	2.70
☐ 441 Gary Bell	7.00	3.10
☐ 442 Joe Pignatano	7.00	3.10
☐ 443 Charlie Maxwell	7.00	3.10
☐ 444 Jerry Kindall	7.00	3.10
☐ 445 Warren Spahn	50.00	22.00
☐ 446 Ellis Burton	7.00	3.10
☐ 447 Ray Moore	7.00	3.10
☐ 448 Jim Gentile	20.00	9.00
☐ 449 Jim Brosnan	7.00	3.10
☐ 450 Orlando Cepeda	18.00	8.00
☐ 451 Curt Simmons	7.00	3.10
☐ 452 Ray Webster	7.00	3.10
☐ 453 Vern Law	10.00	4.50
☐ 454 Hal Woodeshick	7.00	3.10
☐ 455 Baltimore Coaches	7.00	3.10
Eddie Robinson		
Harry Brecheen		
Luman Harris		
☐ 456 Red Sox Coaches	10.00	4.50
Rudy York		
Billy Herman		
Sal Maglie		
Del Baker		
☐ 457 Cubs Coaches	7.00	3.10
Charlie Root		
Lou Klein		
Elvin Tappe		
☐ 458 White Sox Coaches	7.00	3.10
Johnny Cooney		
Don Gutteridge		
Tony Cuccinello		
Ray Berres		
☐ 459 Reds Coaches	7.00	3.10
Reggie Otero		
Cot Deal		
Wally Moses		
☐ 460 Indians Coaches	10.00	4.50
Mel Harder		
Jo-Jo White		
Bob Lemon		
Ralph(Red) Kress		
☐ 461 Tigers Coaches	10.00	4.50
Tom Ferrick		
Luke Appling		
Billy Hitchcock		
☐ 462 Athletics Coaches	7.00	3.10
Fred Fitzsimmons		
Don Heffner		
Walker Cooper		
☐ 463 Dodgers Coaches	7.00	3.10
Bobby Bragan		
Pete Reiser		
Joe Becker		
Greg Mulleavy		
☐ 464 Braves Coaches	7.00	3.10
Bob Scheffing		
Whitlow Wyatt		
Andy Pafko		
George Myatt		
☐ 465 Yankees Coaches	12.00	5.50
Bill Dickey		
Ralph Houk		
Frank Crosetti		
Ed Lopat		
☐ 466 Phillies Coaches	7.00	3.10
Ken Silvestri		
Dick Carter		
Andy Cohen		
☐ 467 Pirates Coaches	7.00	3.10
Mickey Vernon		
Frank Oceak		
Sam Narron		
Bill Burwell		
☐ 468 Cardinals Coaches	7.00	3.10
Johnny Keane		
Howie Pollet		
Ray Katt		
Harry Walker		
☐ 469 Giants Coaches	7.00	3.10
Wes Westrum		
Salty Parker		
Bill Posedel		
☐ 470 Senators Coaches	7.00	3.10
Bob Swift		
Ellis Clary		
Sam Mele		
☐ 471 Ned Garver	7.00	3.10
☐ 472 Alvin Dark	7.00	3.10
☐ 473 Al Cicotte	7.00	3.10
☐ 474 Haywood Sullivan	7.00	3.10
☐ 475 Don Drysdale	35.00	16.00
☐ 476 Lou Johnson	7.00	3.10
☐ 477 Don Ferrarese	7.00	3.10
☐ 478 Frank Torre	7.00	3.10
☐ 479 Georges Maranda	7.00	3.10
☐ 480 Yogi Berra	70.00	32.00
☐ 481 Wes Stock	7.00	3.10
☐ 482 Frank Bolling	7.00	3.10
☐ 483 Camilo Pascual	7.00	3.10
☐ 484 Pirates Team	50.00	10.00
(Checklist on back)		
☐ 485 Ken Boyer	14.00	6.25
☐ 486 Bobby Del Greco	7.00	3.10
☐ 487 Tom Sturdivant	7.00	3.10
☐ 488 Norm Cash	20.00	9.00
☐ 489 Steve Ridzik	7.00	3.10
☐ 490 Frank Robinson	50.00	22.00
☐ 491 Mel Roach	7.00	3.10
☐ 492 Larry Jackson	7.00	3.10
☐ 493 Duke Snider	50.00	22.00
☐ 494 Orioles Team	25.00	5.00
(Checklist on back)		
☐ 495 Sherm Lollar	7.00	3.10
☐ 496 Bill Virdon	10.00	4.50
☐ 497 John Tsitouris	7.00	3.10
☐ 498 Al Pilarcik	7.00	3.10
☐ 499 Johnny James	7.00	3.10
☐ 500 Johnny Temple	7.00	3.10
☐ 501 Bob Schmidt	7.00	3.10
☐ 502 Jim Bunning	20.00	9.00
☐ 503 Don Lee	7.00	3.10
☐ 504 Seth Morehead	7.00	3.10
☐ 505 Ted Kluszewski	20.00	9.00
☐ 506 Lee Walls	7.00	3.10
☐ 507 Dick Stigman	16.00	7.25
☐ 508 Billy Consolo	16.00	7.25
☐ 509 Tommy Davis	25.00	11.00
☐ 510 Gerry Staley	16.00	7.25
☐ 511 Ken Walters	16.00	7.25
☐ 512 Joe Gibbon	16.00	7.25
☐ 513 Chicago Cubs	30.00	6.00
Team Card		
(Checklist on back)		
☐ 514 Steve Barber	16.00	7.25
☐ 515 Stan Lopata	16.00	7.25
☐ 516 Marty Kutyna	16.00	7.25
☐ 517 Charlie James	16.00	7.25
☐ 518 Tony Gonzalez	16.00	7.25
☐ 519 Ed Roebuck	16.00	7.25
☐ 520 Don Buddin	16.00	7.25
☐ 521 Mike Lee	16.00	7.25
☐ 522 Ken Hunt	20.00	9.00
☐ 523 Clay Dalrymple	16.00	7.25
☐ 524 Bill Henry	16.00	7.25
☐ 525 Marv Breeding	16.00	7.25
☐ 526 Paul Giel	16.00	7.25
☐ 527 Jose Valdivielso	16.00	7.25
☐ 528 Ben Johnson	16.00	7.25
☐ 529 Norm Sherry	20.00	9.00
☐ 530 Mike McCormick	16.00	7.25
☐ 531 Sandy Amoros	16.00	7.25
☐ 532 Mike Garcia	16.00	7.25
☐ 533 Lu Clinton	16.00	7.25
☐ 534 Ken MacKenzie	16.00	7.25
☐ 535 Whitey Lockman	16.00	7.25
☐ 536 Wynn Hawkins	16.00	7.25
☐ 537 Boston Red Sox	30.00	6.00
Team Card		
(Checklist on back)		
☐ 538 Frank Barnes	16.00	7.25
☐ 539 Gene Baker	16.00	7.25
☐ 540 Jerry Walker	16.00	7.25
☐ 541 Tony Curry	16.00	7.25
☐ 542 Ken Hamlin	16.00	7.25
☐ 543 Elio Chacon	16.00	7.25
☐ 544 Bill Monbouquette	16.00	7.25
☐ 545 Carl Sawatski	16.00	7.25
☐ 546 Hank Aguirre	16.00	7.25
☐ 547 Bob Aspromonte	16.00	7.25
☐ 548 Don Mincher	16.00	7.25
☐ 549 John Buzhardt	16.00	7.25
☐ 550 Jim Landis	16.00	7.25
☐ 551 Ed Rakow	16.00	7.25
☐ 552 Walt Bond	16.00	7.25
☐ 553 Bill Skowron AS	20.00	9.00
☐ 554 Willie McCovey AS	30.00	13.50
☐ 555 Nellie Fox AS	30.00	13.50
☐ 556 Charlie Neal AS	16.00	7.25
☐ 557 Frank Malzone AS	16.00	7.25
☐ 558 Eddie Mathews AS	30.00	13.50
☐ 559 Luis Aparicio AS	30.00	13.50
☐ 560 Ernie Banks AS	60.00	27.00
☐ 561 Al Kaline AS	60.00	27.00
☐ 562 Joe Cunningham AS	16.00	7.25
☐ 563 Mickey Mantle AS	325.00	145.00
☐ 564 Willie Mays AS	125.00	55.00
☐ 565 Roger Maris AS	80.00	36.00
☐ 566 Hank Aaron AS	115.00	52.50
☐ 567 Sherm Lollar AS	16.00	7.25
☐ 568 Del Crandall AS	16.00	7.25
☐ 569 Camilo Pascual AS	16.00	7.25
☐ 570 Don Drysdale AS	30.00	13.50
☐ 571 Billy Pierce AS	16.00	7.25
☐ 572 Johnny Antonelli AS	30.00	9.00
☐ NNO Iron-on team transfer	4.00	1.80

1960 Topps Tattoos

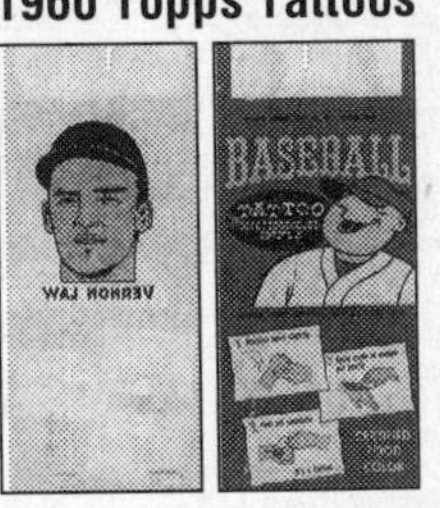

In 1960 this tattoo set was issued separately by both Topps and O-Pee-Chee. They are actually the reverses (inside surfaces) of the wrappers in which the (one cent) product "Tattoo Bubble Gum" was packaged. The dimensions given (1 9/16" by 3 1/2") are for the entire wrapper. The wrapper lists instructions on how to apply the tattoo. The "tattoos" were to be applied by moistening the skin and then pressing the tattoo to the moistened spot. The tattoos are unnumbered and are colored. There are 96 tattoos in the set: 55 players, 16 team logos, 15 action shots and ten autographed balls. In the checklist below the player tattoos are numbered 1-55 in alphabetical order, the team tattoos (56-71) are numbered in alphabetical team order (within league), the action photos (72-86) are numbered in alphabetical order by title and the facsimile autographed ball tattoos (87-96) are numbered in alphabetical order according to the autographing player.

	NRMT	VG-E
COMPLETE SET (96)	1800.00	800.00
COMMON TATTOO (1-55)	7.00	3.10
COMMON TEAM (56-71)	5.00	2.20
COMMON ACTION (72-86)	2.50	1.10
COMMON BALL (87-96)	2.50	1.10
WRAPPER	10.00	4.50

☐ 1 Hank Aaron	125.00	55.00
☐ 2 Bob Allison	8.50	3.80
☐ 3 Johnny Antonelli	8.50	3.80
☐ 4 Richie Ashburn	30.00	13.50
☐ 5 Ernie Banks	50.00	22.00
☐ 6 Yogi Berra	100.00	45.00
☐ 7 Lew Burdette	8.50	3.80

Card	NRMT	VG-E
☐ 8 Orlando Cepeda	20.00	9.00
☐ 9 Rocky Colavito	20.00	9.00
☐ 10 Joe Cunningham	8.50	3.80
☐ 11 Bud Daley	7.00	3.10
☐ 12 Don Drysdale	40.00	18.00
☐ 13 Ryne Duren	10.00	4.50
☐ 14 Roy Face	10.00	4.50
☐ 15 Whitey Ford	40.00	18.00
☐ 16 Nellie Fox	30.00	13.50
☐ 17 Tito Francona	7.00	3.10
☐ 18 Gene Freese	7.00	3.10
☐ 19 Jim Gilliam	15.00	6.75
☐ 20 Dick Groat	10.00	4.50
☐ 21 Ray Herbert	7.00	3.10
☐ 22 Glen Hobbie	7.00	3.10
☐ 23 Jackie Jensen	15.00	6.75
☐ 24 Sam Jones	7.00	3.10
☐ 25 Al Kaline	50.00	22.00
☐ 26 Harmon Killebrew	35.00	16.00
☐ 27 Harvey Kuenn	15.00	6.75
☐ 28 Frank Lary	8.50	3.80
☐ 29 Vern Law	10.00	4.50
☐ 30 Frank Malzone	8.50	3.80
☐ 31 Mickey Mantle	400.00	180.00
☐ 32 Roger Maris	50.00	22.00
☐ 33 Eddie Mathews	35.00	16.00
☐ 34 Willie Mays	135.00	60.00
☐ 35 Cal McLish	7.00	3.10
☐ 36 Wally Moon	8.50	3.80
☐ 37 Walt Moryn	7.00	3.10
☐ 38 Don Mossi	8.50	3.80
☐ 39 Stan Musial	75.00	34.00
☐ 40 Charlie Neal	8.50	3.80
☐ 41 Don Newcombe	10.00	4.50
☐ 42 Milt Pappas	8.50	3.80
☐ 43 Camilo Pascual	8.50	3.80
☐ 44 Billy Pierce	8.50	3.80
☐ 45 Robin Roberts	30.00	13.50
☐ 46 Frank Robinson	35.00	16.00
☐ 47 Pete Runnels	8.50	3.80
☐ 48 Herb Score	10.00	4.50
☐ 49 Warren Spahn	40.00	18.00
☐ 50 Johnny Temple	8.50	3.80
☐ 51 Gus Triandos	8.50	3.80
☐ 52 Jerry Walker	7.00	3.10
☐ 53 Bill White	15.00	6.75
☐ 54 Gene Woodling	8.50	3.80
☐ 55 Early Wynn	30.00	13.50
☐ 56 Chicago Cubs	5.00	2.20
☐ 57 Cincinnati Reds	5.00	2.20
☐ 58 Los Angeles Dodgers	5.00	2.20
☐ 59 Milwaukee Braves	5.00	2.20
☐ 60 Philadelphia Phillies	5.00	2.20
☐ 61 Pittsburgh Pirates	5.00	2.20
☐ 62 St. Louis Cardinals	5.00	2.20
☐ 63 San Francisco Giants	5.00	2.20
☐ 64 Baltimore Orioles	5.00	2.20
☐ 65 Boston Red Sox	7.00	3.10
☐ 66 Chicago White Sox	5.00	2.20
☐ 67 Cleveland Indians	5.00	2.20
☐ 68 Detroit Tigers	5.00	2.20
☐ 69 Kansas City Athletics	5.00	2.20
☐ 70 New York Yankees	8.50	3.80
☐ 71 Washington Senators	5.00	2.20
☐ 72 Circus Catch	2.50	1.10
☐ 73 Double Play	2.50	1.10
☐ 74 Grand Slam Homer	2.50	1.10
☐ 75 Great Catch	2.50	1.10
☐ 76 Left Hand Batter	2.50	1.10
☐ 77 Left Hand Pitcher	2.50	1.10
☐ 78 Out at First	2.50	1.10
☐ 79 Out at Home	2.50	1.10
☐ 80 Right Hand Batter	2.50	1.10
☐ 81 Right Hand Pitcher	2.50	1.10
☐ 82 Right Hand Pitcher	2.50	1.10
(Different pose)		
☐ 83 Run Down	2.50	1.10
☐ 84 Stolen Base	2.50	1.10
☐ 85 The Final Word	2.50	1.10
☐ 86 Twisting Foul	2.50	1.10
☐ 87 Richie Ashburn	8.50	3.80
(Autographed ball)		
☐ 88 Rocky Colavito	8.50	3.80
(Autographed ball)		
☐ 89 Roy Face	2.50	1.10
(Autographed ball)		
☐ 90 Jackie Jensen	4.00	1.80
(Autographed ball)		
☐ 91 Harmon Killebrew	10.00	4.50
(Autographed ball)		
☐ 92 Mickey Mantle	175.00	80.00
(Autographed ball)		
☐ 93 Willie Mays	35.00	16.00
(Autographed ball)		
☐ 94 Stan Musial	25.00	11.00
(Autographed ball)		
☐ 95 Billy Pierce	4.00	1.80
(Autographed ball)		
☐ 96 Jerry Walker	2.50	1.10
(Autographed ball)		

1961 Topps

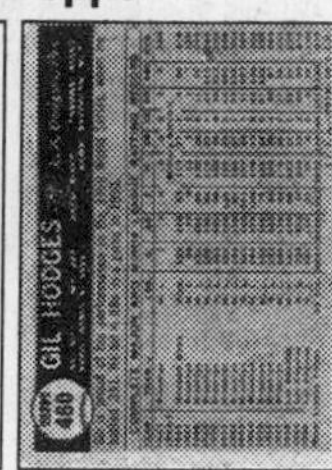

The cards in this 587-card set measure 2 1/2" by 3 1/2". In 1961, Topps returned to the vertical obverse format. Introduced for the first time were "League Leaders" (41-50) and separate, numbered checklist cards. Two number 463s exist: the Braves team card carrying that number was meant to be number 426. There are three versions of the second series checklist card number 98; the variations are distinguished by the color of the "CHECKLIST" headline on the front of the card, the color of the printing of the card number on the bottom of the reverse, and the presence of the copyright notice running vertically on the card back. There are two groups of managers (131-139/219-226) as well as separate subsets of World Series cards (306-313), Baseball Thrills (401-410), MVP's of the 1950's (AL 471-478/NL 479-486) and Sporting News All-Stars (566-589). The usual last series scarcity (523-589) exists. Some collectors believe that 61 high numbers are the toughest of all the Topps hi numbers. The set actually totals 587 cards since numbers 587 and 588 were never issued. Cards were issued in one-card penny packs as well as five-card nickle packs. The key Rookie Cards in this set are Juan Marichal, Ron Santo and Billy Williams.

	NRMT	VG-E
COMPLETE SET (587)	4800.00	2200.00
COMMON CARD (1-370)	3.00	1.35
COMMON CARD (371-446)	4.00	1.80
COMMON CARD (447-522)	7.00	3.10
COMMON CARD (523-589)	30.00	13.50
WRAPPER (1-CENT)	200.00	90.00
WRAPPER (1-CENT, REPEAT)	100.00	45.00
WRAPPER (5-CENT)	40.00	18.00
☐ 1 Dick Groat	30.00	6.00
☐ 2 Roger Maris	150.00	70.00
☐ 3 John Buzhardt	3.00	1.35
☐ 4 Lenny Green	3.00	1.35
☐ 5 John Romano	3.00	1.35
☐ 6 Ed Roebuck	3.00	1.35
☐ 7 White Sox Team	8.00	3.60
☐ 8 Dick Williams	6.00	2.70
☐ 9 Bob Purkey	3.00	1.35
☐ 10 Brooks Robinson	40.00	18.00
☐ 11 Curt Simmons	6.00	2.70
☐ 12 Moe Thacker	3.00	1.35
☐ 13 Chuck Cottier	3.00	1.35
☐ 14 Don Mossi	6.00	2.70
☐ 15 Willie Kirkland	3.00	1.35
☐ 16 Billy Muffett	3.00	1.35
☐ 17 Checklist 1	12.00	2.40
☐ 18 Jim Grant	6.00	2.70
☐ 19 Clete Boyer	7.00	3.10
☐ 20 Robin Roberts	15.00	6.75
☐ 21 Zorro Versalles UER	7.00	3.10
(First name should be Zoilo)		
☐ 22 Clem Labine	6.00	2.70
☐ 23 Don Demeter	3.00	1.35
☐ 24 Ken Johnson	3.00	1.35
☐ 25 Reds' Heavy Artillery	8.00	3.60
Vada Pinson		
Gus Bell		
Frank Robinson		
☐ 26 Wes Stock	3.00	1.35
☐ 27 Jerry Kindall	3.00	1.35
☐ 28 Hector Lopez	6.00	2.70
☐ 29 Don Nottebart	3.00	1.35
☐ 30 Nellie Fox	16.00	7.25
☐ 31 Bob Schmidt	3.00	1.35
☐ 32 Ray Sadecki	3.00	1.35
☐ 33 Gary Geiger	3.00	1.35
☐ 34 Wynn Hawkins	3.00	1.35
☐ 35 Ron Santo	40.00	18.00
☐ 36 Jack Kralick	3.00	1.35
☐ 37 Charley Maxwell	6.00	2.70
☐ 38 Bob Lillis	3.00	1.35
☐ 39 Leo Posada	3.00	1.35
☐ 40 Bob Turley	6.00	2.70
☐ 41 NL Batting Leaders	35.00	16.00
Dick Groat		
Norm Larker		
Willie Mays		
Roberto Clemente		
☐ 42 AL Batting Leaders	8.00	3.60
Pete Runnels		
Al Smith		
Minnie Minoso		
Bill Skowron		
☐ 43 NL Home Run Leaders	30.00	13.50
Ernie Banks		
Hank Aaron		
Ed Mathews		
Ken Boyer		
☐ 44 AL Home Run Leaders	120.00	55.00
Mickey Mantle		
Roger Maris		
Jim Lemon		
Rocky Colavito		
☐ 45 NL ERA Leaders	8.00	3.60
Mike McCormick		
Ernie Broglio		
Don Drysdale		
Bob Friend		
Stan Williams		
☐ 46 AL ERA Leaders	8.00	3.60
Frank Baumann		
Jim Bunning		
Art Ditmar		
Hal Brown		
☐ 47 NL Pitching Leaders	8.00	3.60
Ernie Broglio		
Warren Spahn		
Vern Law		
Lou Burdette		
☐ 48 AL Pitching Leaders	8.00	3.60
Chuck Estrada		
Jim Perry UER		
(Listed as an Oriole)		
Bud Daley		
Art Ditmar		
Frank Lary		
Milt Pappas		
☐ 49 NL Strikeout Leaders	20.00	9.00
Don Drysdale		
Sandy Koufax		
Sam Jones		
Ernie Broglio		
☐ 50 AL Strikeout Leaders	8.00	3.60
Jim Bunning		
Pedro Ramos		
Early Wynn		
Frank Lary		
☐ 51 Detroit Tigers	8.00	3.60
Team Card		
☐ 52 George Crowe	3.00	1.35
☐ 53 Russ Nixon	3.00	1.35
☐ 54 Earl Francis	3.00	1.35
☐ 55 Jim Davenport	6.00	2.70
☐ 56 Russ Kemmerer	3.00	1.35
☐ 57 Marv Throneberry	7.00	3.10
☐ 58 Joe Schaffernoth	3.00	1.35
☐ 59 Jim Woods	3.00	1.35
☐ 60 Woody Held	3.00	1.35
☐ 61 Ron Piche	3.00	1.35
☐ 62 Al Pilarcik	3.00	1.35
☐ 63 Jim Kaat	8.00	3.60
☐ 64 Alex Grammas	3.00	1.35
☐ 65 Ted Kluszewski	8.00	3.60
☐ 66 Bill Henry	3.00	1.35
☐ 67 Ossie Virgil	3.00	1.35
☐ 68 Deron Johnson	6.00	2.70
☐ 69 Earl Wilson	6.00	2.70
☐ 70 Bill Virdon	6.00	2.70
☐ 71 Jerry Adair	3.00	1.35
☐ 72 Stu Miller	6.00	2.70
☐ 73 Al Spangler	3.00	1.35
☐ 74 Joe Pignatano	3.00	1.35
☐ 75 Lindy Shows Larry	6.00	2.70
Lindy McDaniel		
Larry Jackson		
☐ 76 Harry Anderson	3.00	1.35
☐ 77 Dick Stigman	3.00	1.35
☐ 78 Lee Walls	3.00	1.35
☐ 79 Joe Ginsberg	3.00	1.35
☐ 80 Harmon Killebrew	20.00	9.00
☐ 81 Tracy Stallard	3.00	1.35
☐ 82 Joe Christopher	3.00	1.35
☐ 83 Bob Bruce	3.00	1.35
☐ 84 Lee Maye	3.00	1.35
☐ 85 Jerry Walker	3.00	1.35
☐ 86 Los Angeles Dodgers	8.00	3.60
Team Card		
☐ 87 Joe Amalfitano	3.00	1.35

Card		
☐ 88 Richie Ashburn	16.00	7.25
☐ 89 Billy Martin	16.00	7.25
☐ 90 Gerry Staley	3.00	1.35
☐ 91 Walt Moryn	3.00	1.35
☐ 92 Hal Naragon	3.00	1.35
☐ 93 Tony Gonzalez	3.00	1.35
☐ 94 Johnny Kucks	3.00	1.35
☐ 95 Norm Cash	7.00	3.10
☐ 96 Billy O'Dell	3.00	1.35
☐ 97 Jerry Lynch	6.00	2.70
☐ 98A Checklist 2 (Red "Checklist" 98 black on white)	70.00	14.00
☐ 98B Checklist 2 (Yellow "Checklist" 98 black on white)	70.00	14.00
☐ 98C Checklist 2 (Yellow "Checklist" 98 white on black no copyright)	70.00	14.00
☐ 99 Don Buddin UER (66 HR's)	3.00	1.35
☐ 100 Harvey Haddix	7.00	3.10
☐ 101 Bubba Phillips	3.00	1.35
☐ 102 Gene Stephens	3.00	1.35
☐ 103 Ruben Amaro	3.00	1.35
☐ 104 John Blanchard	6.00	2.70
☐ 105 Carl Willey	3.00	1.35
☐ 106 Whitey Herzog	3.00	1.35
☐ 107 Seth Morehead	3.00	1.35
☐ 108 Dan Dobbek	3.00	1.35
☐ 109 Johnny Podres	7.00	3.10
☐ 110 Vada Pinson	7.00	3.10
☐ 111 Jack Meyer	3.00	1.35
☐ 112 Chico Fernandez	3.00	1.35
☐ 113 Mike Fornieles	3.00	1.35
☐ 114 Hobie Landrith	3.00	1.35
☐ 115 Johnny Antonelli	6.00	2.70
☐ 116 Joe DeMaestri	3.00	1.35
☐ 117 Dale Long	6.00	2.70
☐ 118 Chris Cannizzaro	3.00	1.35
☐ 119 A's Big Armor Norm Siebern Hank Bauer Jerry Lumpe	6.00	2.70
☐ 120 Eddie Mathews	30.00	13.50
☐ 121 Eli Grba	6.00	2.70
☐ 122 Chicago Cubs Team Card	8.00	3.60
☐ 123 Billy Gardner	3.00	1.35
☐ 124 J.C. Martin	3.00	1.35
☐ 125 Steve Barber	3.00	1.35
☐ 126 Dick Stuart	6.00	2.70
☐ 127 Ron Kline	3.00	1.35
☐ 128 Rip Repulski	3.00	1.35
☐ 129 Ed Hobaugh	3.00	1.35
☐ 130 Norm Larker	3.00	1.35
☐ 131 Paul Richards MG	6.00	2.70
☐ 132 Al Lopez MG	6.00	2.70
☐ 133 Ralph Houk MG	6.00	2.70
☐ 134 Mickey Vernon MG	6.00	2.70
☐ 135 Fred Hutchinson MG	6.00	2.70
☐ 136 Walter Alston MG	7.00	3.10
☐ 137 Chuck Dressen MG	6.00	2.70
☐ 138 Danny Murtaugh MG	7.00	3.10
☐ 139 Solly Hemus MG	6.00	2.70
☐ 140 Gus Triandos	6.00	2.70
☐ 141 Billy Williams	60.00	27.00
☐ 142 Luis Arroyo	6.00	2.70
☐ 143 Russ Snyder	3.00	1.35
☐ 144 Jim Coker	3.00	1.35
☐ 145 Bob Buhl	6.00	2.70
☐ 146 Marty Keough	3.00	1.35
☐ 147 Ed Rakow	3.00	1.35
☐ 148 Julian Javier	6.00	2.70
☐ 149 Bob Oldis	3.00	1.35
☐ 150 Willie Mays	100.00	45.00
☐ 151 Jim Donohue	3.00	1.35
☐ 152 Earl Torgeson	3.00	1.35
☐ 153 Don Lee	3.00	1.35
☐ 154 Bobby Del Greco	3.00	1.35
☐ 155 Johnny Temple	6.00	2.70
☐ 156 Ken Hunt	6.00	2.70
☐ 157 Cal McLish	3.00	1.35
☐ 158 Pete Daley	3.00	1.35
☐ 159 Orioles Team	8.00	3.60
☐ 160 Whitey Ford UER (Incorrectly listed as 5'0" tall)	40.00	18.00
☐ 161 Sherman Jones UER (Photo actually Eddie Fisher)	3.00	1.35
☐ 162 Jay Hook	3.00	1.35
☐ 163 Ed Sadowski	3.00	1.35
☐ 164 Felix Mantilla	3.00	1.35
☐ 165 Gino Cimoli	3.00	1.35
☐ 166 Danny Kravitz	3.00	1.35
☐ 167 San Francisco Giants Team Card	8.00	3.60
☐ 168 Tommy Davis	7.00	3.10
☐ 169 Don Elston	3.00	1.35
☐ 170 Al Smith	3.00	1.35
☐ 171 Paul Foytack	3.00	1.35
☐ 172 Don Dillard	3.00	1.35
☐ 173 Beantown Bombers Frank Malzone Vic Wertz Jackie Jensen	6.00	2.70
☐ 174 Ray Semproch	3.00	1.35
☐ 175 Gene Freese	3.00	1.35
☐ 176 Ken Aspromonte	3.00	1.35
☐ 177 Don Larsen	7.00	3.10
☐ 178 Bob Nieman	3.00	1.35
☐ 179 Joe Koppe	3.00	1.35
☐ 180 Bobby Richardson	12.00	5.50
☐ 181 Fred Green	3.00	1.35
☐ 182 Dave Nicholson	3.00	1.35
☐ 183 Andre Rodgers	3.00	1.35
☐ 184 Steve Bilko	6.00	2.70
☐ 185 Herb Score	7.00	3.10
☐ 186 Elmer Valo	6.00	2.70
☐ 187 Billy Klaus	3.00	1.35
☐ 188 Jim Marshall	3.00	1.35
☐ 189A Checklist 3 (Copyright symbol almost adjacent to 263 Ken Hamlin)	70.00	14.00
☐ 189B Checklist 3 (Copyright symbol adjacent to 264 Glen Hobbie)	70.00	14.00
☐ 190 Stan Williams	6.00	2.70
☐ 191 Mike de la Hoz	3.00	1.35
☐ 192 Dick Brown	3.00	1.35
☐ 193 Gene Conley	6.00	2.70
☐ 194 Gordy Coleman	6.00	2.70
☐ 195 Jerry Casale	3.00	1.35
☐ 196 Ed Bouchee	3.00	1.35
☐ 197 Dick Hall	3.00	1.35
☐ 198 Carl Sawatski	3.00	1.35
☐ 199 Bob Boyd	3.00	1.35
☐ 200 Warren Spahn	30.00	13.50
☐ 201 Pete Whisenant	3.00	1.35
☐ 202 Al Neiger	3.00	1.35
☐ 203 Eddie Bressoud	3.00	1.35
☐ 204 Bob Skinner	6.00	2.70
☐ 205 Billy Pierce	6.00	2.70
☐ 206 Gene Green	3.00	1.35
☐ 207 Dodger Southpaws Sandy Koufax Johnny Podres	30.00	13.50
☐ 208 Larry Osborne	3.00	1.35
☐ 209 Ken McBride	3.00	1.35
☐ 210 Pete Runnels	6.00	2.70
☐ 211 Bob Gibson	40.00	18.00
☐ 212 Haywood Sullivan	6.00	2.70
☐ 213 Bill Stafford	3.00	1.35
☐ 214 Danny Murphy	3.00	1.35
☐ 215 Gus Bell	6.00	2.70
☐ 216 Ted Bowsfield	3.00	1.35
☐ 217 Mel Roach	3.00	1.35
☐ 218 Hal Brown	3.00	1.35
☐ 219 Gene Mauch MG	6.00	2.70
☐ 220 Alvin Dark MG	6.00	2.70
☐ 221 Mike Higgins MG	3.00	1.35
☐ 222 Jimmy Dykes MG	6.00	2.70
☐ 223 Bob Scheffing MG	3.00	1.35
☐ 224 Joe Gordon MG	6.00	2.70
☐ 225 Bill Rigney MG	6.00	2.70
☐ 226 Cookie Lavagetto MG	6.00	2.70
☐ 227 Juan Pizarro	3.00	1.35
☐ 228 New York Yankees Team Card	70.00	32.00
☐ 229 Rudy Hernandez	3.00	1.35
☐ 230 Don Hoak	6.00	2.70
☐ 231 Dick Drott	3.00	1.35
☐ 232 Bill White	7.00	3.10
☐ 233 Joey Jay	6.00	2.70
☐ 234 Ted Lepcio	3.00	1.35
☐ 235 Camilo Pascual	6.00	2.70
☐ 236 Don Gile	3.00	1.35
☐ 237 Billy Loes	6.00	2.70
☐ 238 Jim Gilliam	7.00	3.10
☐ 239 Dave Sisler	3.00	1.35
☐ 240 Ron Hansen	3.00	1.35
☐ 241 Al Cicotte	3.00	1.35
☐ 242 Hal Smith	3.00	1.35
☐ 243 Frank Lary	6.00	2.70
☐ 244 Chico Cardenas	6.00	2.70
☐ 245 Joe Adcock	7.00	3.10
☐ 246 Bob Davis	3.00	1.35
☐ 247 Billy Goodman	6.00	2.70
☐ 248 Ed Keegan	3.00	1.35
☐ 249 Cincinnati Reds Team Card	6.00	2.70
☐ 250 Buc Hill Aces Vern Law Roy Face	6.00	2.70
☐ 251 Bill Bruton	3.00	1.35
☐ 252 Bill Short	3.00	1.35
☐ 253 Sammy Taylor	3.00	1.35
☐ 254 Ted Sadowski	3.00	1.35
☐ 255 Vic Power	6.00	2.70
☐ 256 Billy Hoeft	3.00	1.35
☐ 257 Carroll Hardy	3.00	1.35
☐ 258 Jack Sanford	6.00	2.70
☐ 259 John Schaive	3.00	1.35
☐ 260 Don Drysdale	30.00	13.50
☐ 261 Charlie Lau	6.00	2.70
☐ 262 Tony Curry	3.00	1.35
☐ 263 Ken Hamlin	3.00	1.35
☐ 264 Glen Hobbie	3.00	1.35
☐ 265 Tony Kubek	8.00	3.60
☐ 266 Lindy McDaniel	6.00	2.70
☐ 267 Norm Siebern	3.00	1.35
☐ 268 Ike Delock	3.00	1.35
☐ 269 Harry Chiti	3.00	1.35
☐ 270 Bob Friend	7.00	3.10
☐ 271 Jim Landis	3.00	1.35
☐ 272 Tom Morgan	3.00	1.35
☐ 273A Checklist 4 (Copyright symbol adjacent to 336 Don Mincher)	16.00	3.20
☐ 273B Checklist 4 (Copyright symbol adjacent to 339 Gene Baker)	16.00	3.20
☐ 274 Gary Bell	3.00	1.35
☐ 275 Gene Woodling	6.00	2.70
☐ 276 Ray Rippelmeyer	3.00	1.35
☐ 277 Hank Foiles	3.00	1.35
☐ 278 Don McMahon	3.00	1.35
☐ 279 Jose Pagan	3.00	1.35
☐ 280 Frank Howard	8.00	3.60
☐ 281 Frank Sullivan	3.00	1.35
☐ 282 Faye Throneberry	3.00	1.35
☐ 283 Bob Anderson	3.00	1.35
☐ 284 Dick Gernert	3.00	1.35
☐ 285 Sherm Lollar	6.00	2.70
☐ 286 George Witt	3.00	1.35
☐ 287 Carl Yastrzemski	50.00	22.00
☐ 288 Albie Pearson	6.00	2.70
☐ 289 Ray Moore	3.00	1.35
☐ 290 Stan Musial	100.00	45.00
☐ 291 Tex Clevenger	3.00	1.35
☐ 292 Jim Baumer	3.00	1.35
☐ 293 Tom Sturdivant	3.00	1.35
☐ 294 Don Blasingame	3.00	1.35
☐ 295 Milt Pappas	6.00	2.70
☐ 296 Wes Covington	6.00	2.70
☐ 297 Athletics Team	16.00	7.25
☐ 298 Jim Golden	3.00	1.35
☐ 299 Clay Dalrymple	3.00	1.35
☐ 300 Mickey Mantle	475.00	210.00
☐ 301 Chet Nichols	3.00	1.35
☐ 302 Al Heist	3.00	1.35
☐ 303 Gary Peters	6.00	2.70
☐ 304 Rocky Nelson	3.00	1.35
☐ 305 Mike McCormick	6.00	2.70
☐ 306 Bill Virdon WS	8.00	3.60
☐ 307 Mickey Mantle WS	100.00	45.00
☐ 308 Bobby Richardson WS	12.00	5.50
☐ 309 Gino Cimoli WS	8.00	3.60
☐ 310 Roy Face WS	8.00	3.60
☐ 311 Whitey Ford WS	16.00	7.25
☐ 312 Bill Mazeroski WS Mazeroski Homer Wins it	20.00	9.00
☐ 313 World Series Summary Pirates Celebrate	16.00	7.25
☐ 314 Bob Miller	3.00	1.35
☐ 315 Earl Battey	6.00	2.70
☐ 316 Bobby Gene Smith	3.00	1.35
☐ 317 Jim Brewer	3.00	1.35
☐ 318 Danny O'Connell	3.00	1.35
☐ 319 Valmy Thomas	3.00	1.35
☐ 320 Lou Burdette	7.00	3.10
☐ 321 Marv Breeding	3.00	1.35
☐ 322 Bill Kunkel	6.00	2.70
☐ 323 Sammy Esposito	3.00	1.35
☐ 324 Hank Aguirre	3.00	1.35
☐ 325 Wally Moon	6.00	2.70
☐ 326 Dave Hillman	3.00	1.35
☐ 327 Matty Alou	10.00	4.50
☐ 328 Jim O'Toole	6.00	2.70
☐ 329 Julio Becquer	3.00	1.35
☐ 330 Rocky Colavito	20.00	9.00
☐ 331 Ned Garver	3.00	1.35
☐ 332 Dutch Dotterer UER (Photo actually Tommy Dotterer Dutch's brother)	3.00	1.35

- ☐ 333 Fritz Brickell 3.00 1.35
- ☐ 334 Walt Bond 3.00 1.35
- ☐ 335 Frank Bolling 3.00 1.35
- ☐ 336 Don Mincher 6.00 2.70
- ☐ 337 Al's Aces 7.00 3.10
  Early Wynn
  Al Lopez
  Herb Score
- ☐ 338 Don Landrum 3.00 1.35
- ☐ 339 Gene Baker 3.00 1.35
- ☐ 340 Vic Wertz 6.00 2.70
- ☐ 341 Jim Owens 3.00 1.35
- ☐ 342 Clint Courtney 3.00 1.35
- ☐ 343 Earl Robinson 3.00 1.35
- ☐ 344 Sandy Koufax 125.00 55.00
- ☐ 345 Jimmy Piersall 7.00 3.10
- ☐ 346 Howie Nunn 3.00 1.35
- ☐ 347 St. Louis Cardinals 6.00 2.70
  Team Card
- ☐ 348 Steve Boros 3.00 1.35
- ☐ 349 Danny McDevitt 3.00 1.35
- ☐ 350 Ernie Banks 45.00 20.00
- ☐ 351 Jim King 3.00 1.35
- ☐ 352 Bob Shaw 3.00 1.35
- ☐ 353 Howie Bedell 3.00 1.35
- ☐ 354 Billy Harrell 3.00 1.35
- ☐ 355 Bob Allison 7.00 3.10
- ☐ 356 Ryne Duren 3.00 1.35
- ☐ 357 Daryl Spencer 3.00 1.35
- ☐ 358 Earl Averill 6.00 2.70
- ☐ 359 Dallas Green 3.00 1.35
- ☐ 360 Frank Robinson 40.00 18.00
- ☐ 361A Checklist 5 10.00 2.00
  (No ad on back)
- ☐ 361B Checklist 5 10.00 2.00
  (Special Feature
  ad on back)
- ☐ 362 Frank Funk 3.00 1.35
- ☐ 363 John Roseboro 7.00 3.10
- ☐ 364 Moe Drabowsky 6.00 2.70
- ☐ 365 Jerry Lumpe 3.00 1.35
- ☐ 366 Eddie Fisher 3.00 1.35
- ☐ 367 Jim Rivera 3.00 1.35
- ☐ 368 Bennie Daniels 3.00 1.35
- ☐ 369 Dave Philley 3.00 1.35
- ☐ 370 Roy Face 6.00 2.70
- ☐ 371 Bill Skowron SP 60.00 27.00
- ☐ 372 Bob Hendley 4.00 1.80
- ☐ 373 Boston Red Sox 6.00 2.70
  Team Card
- ☐ 374 Paul Giel 4.00 1.80
- ☐ 375 Ken Boyer 10.00 4.50
- ☐ 376 Mike Roarke 4.00 1.80
- ☐ 377 Ruben Gomez 4.00 1.80
- ☐ 378 Wally Post 6.00 2.70
- ☐ 379 Bobby Shantz 4.00 1.80
- ☐ 380 Minnie Minoso 8.00 3.60
- ☐ 381 Dave Wickersham 4.00 1.80
- ☐ 382 Frank Thomas 6.00 2.70
- ☐ 383 Frisco First Liners 6.00 2.70
  Mike McCormick
  Jack Sanford
  Billy O'Dell
- ☐ 384 Chuck Essegian 4.00 1.80
- ☐ 385 Jim Perry 6.00 2.70
- ☐ 386 Joe Hicks 4.00 1.80
- ☐ 387 Duke Maas 4.00 1.80
- ☐ 388 Bob Clemente 180.00 80.00
- ☐ 389 Ralph Terry 6.00 2.70
- ☐ 390 Del Crandall 6.00 2.70
- ☐ 391 Winston Brown 4.00 1.80
- ☐ 392 Reno Bertoia 4.00 1.80
- ☐ 393 Batter Bafflers 4.00 1.80
  Don Cardwell
  Glen Hobbie
- ☐ 394 Ken Walters 4.00 1.80
- ☐ 395 Chuck Estrada 6.00 2.70
- ☐ 396 Bob Aspromonte 4.00 1.80
- ☐ 397 Hal Woodeshick 4.00 1.80
- ☐ 398 Hank Bauer 7.00 3.10
- ☐ 399 Cliff Cook 4.00 1.80
- ☐ 400 Vern Law 6.00 2.70
- ☐ 401 Babe Ruth HL 50.00 22.00
  60th HR
- ☐ 402 Don Larsen HL SP 30.00 13.50
  WS Perfect Game
- ☐ 403 Joe Oeschger HL 6.00 2.70
  Leon Cadore
  26 Inning Tie
- ☐ 404 Rogers Hornsby HL 10.00 4.50
  .424 Season BA
- ☐ 405 Lou Gehrig HL 80.00 36.00
  Consecutive Game Streak
- ☐ 406 Mickey Mantle HL 100.00 45.00
  565 foot HR
- ☐ 407 Jack Chesbro HL 6.00 2.70
  41 victories
- ☐ 408 Christy Mathewson HL SP 20.00 9.00
  267 Strikeouts
- ☐ 409 Walter Johnson SL 12.00 5.50
  3 Shutouts in 4 days
- ☐ 410 Harvey Haddix HL 6.00 2.70
  12 Perfect Innings
- ☐ 411 Tony Taylor 6.00 2.70
- ☐ 412 Larry Sherry 6.00 2.70
- ☐ 413 Eddie Yost 6.00 2.70
- ☐ 414 Dick Donovan 6.00 2.70
- ☐ 415 Hank Aaron 90.00 40.00
- ☐ 416 Dick Howser 10.00 4.50
- ☐ 417 Juan Marichal SP 125.00 55.00
- ☐ 418 Ed Bailey 6.00 2.70
- ☐ 419 Tom Borland 4.00 1.80
- ☐ 420 Ernie Broglio 6.00 2.70
- ☐ 421 Ty Cline SP 9.00 4.00
- ☐ 422 Bud Daley 4.00 1.80
- ☐ 423 Charlie Neal SP 9.00 4.00
- ☐ 424 Turk Lown 4.00 1.80
- ☐ 425 Yogi Berra 80.00 36.00
- ☐ 426 Milwaukee Braves 12.00 5.50
  Team Card
  (Back numbered 463)
- ☐ 427 Dick Ellsworth 6.00 2.70
- ☐ 428 Ray Barker SP 9.00 4.00
- ☐ 429 Al Kaline 45.00 20.00
- ☐ 430 Bill Mazeroski SP 60.00 27.00
- ☐ 431 Chuck Stobbs 4.00 1.80
- ☐ 432 Coot Veal 6.00 2.70
- ☐ 433 Art Mahaffey 4.00 1.80
- ☐ 434 Tom Brewer 4.00 1.80
- ☐ 435 Orlando Cepeda UER 14.00 6.25
  (San Francis on
  card front)
- ☐ 436 Jim Maloney SP 20.00 9.00
- ☐ 437A Checklist 6 10.00 2.00
  440 Louis Aparicio
- ☐ 437B Checklist 6 10.00 2.00
  440 Luis Aparicio
- ☐ 438 Curt Flood 8.00 3.60
- ☐ 439 Phil Regan 6.00 2.70
- ☐ 440 Luis Aparicio 15.00 6.75
- ☐ 441 Dick Bertell 4.00 1.80
- ☐ 442 Gordon Jones 4.00 1.80
- ☐ 443 Duke Snider 40.00 18.00
- ☐ 444 Joe Nuxhall 6.00 2.70
- ☐ 445 Frank Malzone 6.00 2.70
- ☐ 446 Bob Taylor 4.00 1.80
- ☐ 447 Harry Bright 7.00 3.10
- ☐ 448 Del Rice 7.00 3.10
- ☐ 449 Bob Bolin 7.00 3.10
- ☐ 450 Jim Lemon 7.00 3.10
- ☐ 451 Power for Ernie 7.00 3.10
  Daryl Spencer
  Bill White
  Ernie Broglio
- ☐ 452 Bob Allen 7.00 3.10
- ☐ 453 Dick Schofield 7.00 3.10
- ☐ 454 Pumpsie Green 7.00 3.10
- ☐ 455 Early Wynn 15.00 6.75
- ☐ 456 Hal Bevan 7.00 3.10
- ☐ 457 Johnny James 7.00 3.10
  (Listed as Angel,
  but wearing Yankee
  uniform and cap)
- ☐ 458 Willie Tasby 7.00 3.10
- ☐ 459 Terry Fox 7.00 3.10
- ☐ 460 Gil Hodges 20.00 9.00
- ☐ 461 Smoky Burgess 10.00 4.50
- ☐ 462 Lou Klimchock 7.00 3.10
- ☐ 463 Jack Fisher 7.00 3.10
  (See also 426)
- ☐ 464 Lee Thomas 10.00 4.50
  (Pictured with Yankee
  cap but listed as
  Los Angeles Angel)
- ☐ 465 Roy McMillan 7.00 3.10
- ☐ 466 Ron Moeller 7.00 3.10
- ☐ 467 Cleveland Indians 7.50 3.40
  Team Card
- ☐ 468 John Callison 10.00 4.50
- ☐ 469 Ralph Lumenti 7.00 3.10
- ☐ 470 Roy Sievers 10.00 4.50
- ☐ 471 Phil Rizzuto MVP 20.00 9.00
- ☐ 472 Yogi Berra MVP 60.00 27.00
- ☐ 473 Bob Shantz MVP 7.00 3.10
- ☐ 474 Al Rosen MVP 10.00 4.50
- ☐ 475 Mickey Mantle MVP 200.00 90.00
- ☐ 476 Jackie Jensen MVP 10.00 4.50
- ☐ 477 Nellie Fox MVP 18.00 8.00
- ☐ 478 Roger Maris MVP 50.00 22.00
- ☐ 479 Jim Konstanty MVP 7.00 3.10
- ☐ 480 Roy Campanella MVP 35.00 16.00
- ☐ 481 Hank Sauer MVP 7.00 3.10
- ☐ 482 Willie Mays MVP 50.00 22.00
- ☐ 483 Don Newcombe MVP 10.00 4.50
- ☐ 484 Hank Aaron MVP 50.00 22.00
- ☐ 485 Ernie Banks MVP 35.00 16.00
- ☐ 486 Dick Groat MVP 10.00 4.50
- ☐ 487 Gene Oliver 7.00 3.10
- ☐ 488 Joe McClain 10.00 4.50
- ☐ 489 Walt Dropo 7.00 3.10
- ☐ 490 Jim Bunning 16.00 7.25
- ☐ 491 Philadelphia Phillies 7.50 3.40
  Team Card
- ☐ 492 Ron Fairly 10.00 4.50
- ☐ 493 Don Zimmer UER 10.00 4.50
  (Brooklyn A.L.)
- ☐ 494 Tom Cheney 7.00 3.10
- ☐ 495 Elston Howard 12.00 5.50
- ☐ 496 Ken MacKenzie 7.00 3.10
- ☐ 497 Willie Jones 7.00 3.10
- ☐ 498 Ray Herbert 7.00 3.10
- ☐ 499 Chuck Schilling 7.00 3.10
- ☐ 500 Harvey Kuenn 10.00 4.50
- ☐ 501 John DeMerit 7.00 3.10
- ☐ 502 Clarence Coleman 10.00 4.50
- ☐ 503 Tito Francona 7.00 3.10
- ☐ 504 Billy Consolo 7.00 3.10
- ☐ 505 Red Schoendienst 14.00 6.25
- ☐ 506 Willie Davis 16.00 7.25
- ☐ 507 Pete Burnside 7.00 3.10
- ☐ 508 Rocky Bridges 7.00 3.10
- ☐ 509 Camilo Carreon 7.00 3.10
- ☐ 510 Art Ditmar 7.00 3.10
- ☐ 511 Joe M. Morgan 7.00 3.10
- ☐ 512 Bob Will 7.00 3.10
- ☐ 513 Jim Brosnan 7.00 3.10
- ☐ 514 Jake Wood 7.00 3.10
- ☐ 515 Jackie Brandt 7.00 3.10
- ☐ 516 Checklist 7 10.00 2.00
- ☐ 517 Willie McCovey 50.00 22.00
- ☐ 518 Andy Carey 7.00 3.10
- ☐ 519 Jim Pagliaroni 7.00 3.10
- ☐ 520 Joe Cunningham 7.00 3.10
- ☐ 521 Brother Battery 7.00 3.10
  Norm Sherry
  Larry Sherry
- ☐ 522 Dick Farrell UER 7.00 3.10
  (Phillies cap but
  listed on Dodgers)
- ☐ 523 Joe Gibbon 30.00 13.50
- ☐ 524 Johnny Logan 30.00 13.50
- ☐ 525 Ron Perranoski 40.00 18.00
- ☐ 526 R.C. Stevens 30.00 13.50
- ☐ 527 Gene Leek 30.00 13.50
- ☐ 528 Pedro Ramos 30.00 13.50
- ☐ 529 Bob Roselli 30.00 13.50
- ☐ 530 Bob Malkmus 30.00 13.50
- ☐ 531 Jim Coates 40.00 18.00
- ☐ 532 Bob Hale 30.00 13.50
- ☐ 533 Jack Curtis 30.00 13.50
- ☐ 534 Eddie Kasko 30.00 13.50
- ☐ 535 Larry Jackson 30.00 13.50
- ☐ 536 Bill Tuttle 30.00 13.50
- ☐ 537 Bobby Locke 30.00 13.50
- ☐ 538 Chuck Hiller 30.00 13.50
- ☐ 539 Johnny Klippstein 30.00 13.50
- ☐ 540 Jackie Jensen 40.00 18.00
- ☐ 541 Roland Sheldon 40.00 18.00
- ☐ 542 Minnesota Twins 70.00 32.00
  Team Card
- ☐ 543 Roger Craig 40.00 18.00
- ☐ 544 George Thomas 30.00 13.50
- ☐ 545 Hoyt Wilhelm 50.00 22.00
- ☐ 546 Marty Kutyna 30.00 13.50
- ☐ 547 Leon Wagner 30.00 13.50
- ☐ 548 Ted Wills 30.00 13.50
- ☐ 549 Hal R. Smith 30.00 13.50
- ☐ 550 Frank Baumann 30.00 13.50
- ☐ 551 George Altman 30.00 13.50
- ☐ 552 Jim Archer 30.00 13.50
- ☐ 553 Bill Fischer 30.00 13.50
- ☐ 554 Pittsburgh Pirates 70.00 32.00
  Team Card
- ☐ 555 Sam Jones 30.00 13.50
- ☐ 556 Ken R. Hunt 30.00 13.50
- ☐ 557 Jose Valdivielso 30.00 13.50
- ☐ 558 Don Ferrarese 30.00 13.50
- ☐ 559 Jim Gentile 60.00 27.00
- ☐ 560 Barry Latman 30.00 13.50
- ☐ 561 Charley James 30.00 13.50
- ☐ 562 Bill Monbouquette 30.00 13.50
- ☐ 563 Bob Cerv 45.00 20.00
- ☐ 564 Don Cardwell 30.00 13.50
- ☐ 565 Felipe Alou 40.00 18.00
- ☐ 566 Paul Richards AS MG 30.00 13.50
- ☐ 567 Danny Murtaugh AS MG 30.00 13.50
- ☐ 568 Bill Skowron AS 40.00 18.00
- ☐ 569 Frank Herrera AS 30.00 13.50
- ☐ 570 Nellie Fox AS 50.00 22.00
- ☐ 571 Bill Mazeroski AS 40.00 18.00
- ☐ 572 Brooks Robinson AS 90.00 40.00

☐ 573 Ken Boyer AS	40.00	18.00
☐ 574 Luis Aparicio AS	45.00	20.00
☐ 575 Ernie Banks AS	90.00	40.00
☐ 576 Roger Maris AS	160.00	70.00
☐ 577 Hank Aaron AS	160.00	70.00
☐ 578 Mickey Mantle AS	425.00	190.00
☐ 579 Willie Mays AS	160.00	70.00
☐ 580 Al Kaline AS	90.00	40.00
☐ 581 Frank Robinson AS	90.00	40.00
☐ 582 Earl Battey AS	30.00	13.50
☐ 583 Del Crandall AS	30.00	13.50
☐ 584 Jim Perry AS	30.00	13.50
☐ 585 Bob Friend AS	30.00	13.50
☐ 586 Whitey Ford AS	90.00	40.00
☐ 589 Warren Spahn AS	100.00	30.00

1961 Topps Magic Rub-Offs

There are 36 "Magic Rub-Offs" in this set of inserts also marketed in packages of 1961 Topps baseball cards. Each rub off measures 2 1/16" by 3 1/16". Of this number, 18 are team designs (numbered 1-18 below), while the remaining 18 depict players (numbered 19-36 below). The latter, one from each team, were apparently selected for their unusual nicknames. Note: The Duke Maas insert is misspelled "Mass".

	NRMT	VG-E
COMPLETE SET (36)	140.00	65.00
COMMON RUB-OFF (1-18)	2.00	.90
COMMON CARD (19-36)	4.00	1.80

☐ 1 Detroit Tigers	3.00	1.35
☐ 2 New York Yankees	4.00	1.80
☐ 3 Minnesota Twins	2.00	.90
☐ 4 Washington Senators	2.00	.90
☐ 5 Boston Red Sox	3.00	1.35
☐ 6 Los Angeles Angels	2.00	.90
☐ 7 Kansas City A's	2.00	.90
☐ 8 Baltimore Orioles	2.00	.90
☐ 9 Chicago White Sox	2.00	.90
☐ 10 Cleveland Indians	2.00	.90
☐ 11 Pittsburgh Pirates	2.00	.90
☐ 12 San Francisco Giants	2.00	.90
☐ 13 Los Angeles Dodgers	4.00	1.80
☐ 14 Philadelphia Phillies	2.00	.90
☐ 15 Cincinnati Redlegs	2.00	.90
☐ 16 St. Louis Cardinals	2.00	.90
☐ 17 Chicago Cubs	2.00	.90
☐ 18 Milwaukee Braves	2.00	.90
☐ 19 John Romano	2.00	.90
☐ 20 Ray Moore	2.00	.90
☐ 21 Ernie Banks	25.00	11.00
☐ 22 Charlie Maxwell	4.00	1.80
☐ 23 Yogi Berra	25.00	11.00
☐ 24 Henry "Dutch" Dotterer	4.00	1.80
☐ 25 Jim Brosnan	4.00	1.80
☐ 26 Billy Martin	10.00	4.50
☐ 27 Jackie Brandt	4.00	1.80
☐ 28 Duke Maas sic, Mass	5.00	2.20
☐ 29 Pete Runnels	5.00	2.20
☐ 30 Joe Gordon MG	5.00	2.20
☐ 31 Sam Jones	4.00	1.80
☐ 32 Walt Moryn	4.00	1.80
☐ 33 Harvey Haddix	5.00	2.20
☐ 34 Frank Howard	6.00	2.70
☐ 35 Turk Lown	4.00	1.80
☐ 36 Frank Herrera	4.00	1.80

1961 Topps Stamps Inserts

There are 207 different baseball players depicted in this stamp series, which was issued as an insert in packages of the regular Topps cards of 1961. The set is actually comprised of 208 stamps: 104 players are pictured on brown stamps and 104 players appear on green stamps, with Kaline found in both colors. The stamps were issued in attached pairs and an album was sold separately (10 cents) at retail outlets. Each stamp measures 1 3/8" by 1 3/16". Stamps are unnumbered but are presented here in alphabetical order by team, Chicago Cubs (1-12),

Cincinnati Reds (13-24), Los Angeles Dodgers (25-36), Milwaukee Braves (37-48), Philadelphia Phillies (49-60), Pittsburgh Pirates (61-72), San Francisco Giants (73-84), St. Louis Cardinals (85-96), Baltimore Orioles AL (97-107), Boston Red Sox (108-119), Chicago White Sox (120-131), Cleveland Indians (132-143), Detroit Tigers (144-155), Kansas City A's (156-168), Los Angeles Angels (169-175), Minnesota Twins (176-187), New York Yankees (188-200) and Washington Senators (201-207).

	NRMT	VG-E
COMPLETE SET (207)	350.00	160.00
COMMON STAMP (1-207)	.80	.35

☐ 1 George Altman	.80	.35
☐ 2 Bob Anderson (brown)	.80	.35
☐ 3 Richie Ashburn	6.00	2.70
☐ 4 Ernie Banks	10.00	4.50
☐ 5 Ed Bouchee	.80	.35
☐ 6 Jim Brewer	.80	.35
☐ 7 Dick Ellsworth	.80	.35
☐ 8 Don Elston	.80	.35
☐ 10 Sammy Taylor	.80	.35
☐ 11 Bob Will	.80	.35
☐ 12 Billy Williams	5.00	2.20
☐ 13 Ed Bailey	.80	.35
☐ 14 Gus Bell	.80	.35
☐ 15 Jim Brosnan (brown)	.80	.35
☐ 16 Chico Cardenas	.80	.35
☐ 17 Gene Freese	.80	.35
☐ 18 Eddie Kasko	.80	.35
☐ 19 Jerry Lynch	.80	.35
☐ 21 Jim O'Toole	.80	.35
☐ 22 Vada Pinson	1.50	.70
☐ 23 Wally Post	.80	.35
☐ 24 Frank Robinson	10.00	4.50
☐ 25 Tommy Davis	1.25	.55
☐ 26 Don Drysdale	6.00	2.70
☐ 27 Frank Howard (brown)	1.50	.70
☐ 28 Norm Larker	.80	.35
☐ 29 Wally Moon	1.00	.45
☐ 31 Johnny Podres	1.50	.70
☐ 32 Ed Roebuck	.80	.35
☐ 33 Johnny Roseboro	.80	.35
☐ 34 Larry Sherry	.80	.35
☐ 37 Hank Aaron	15.00	6.75
☐ 38 Joe Adcock	1.00	.45
☐ 39 Bill Bruton	.80	.35
☐ 40 Bob Buhl	.80	.35
☐ 41 Wes Covington (brown)	.80	.35
☐ 42 Del Crandall	1.00	.45
☐ 43 Joey Jay	.80	.35
☐ 44 Felix Mantilla	.80	.35
☐ 45 Eddie Mathews	6.00	2.70
☐ 46 Roy McMillan	.80	.35
☐ 47 Warren Spahn	8.00	3.60
☐ 48 Carlton Willey	.80	.35
☐ 49 John Buzhardt	.80	.35
☐ 50 Johnny Callison	1.00	.45
☐ 51 Tony Curry	.80	.35
☐ 52 Clay Dalrymple (brown)	.80	.35
☐ 53 Bobby Del Greco	.80	.35
☐ 54 Dick Farrell	.80	.35
☐ 55 Tony Gonzalez	.80	.35
☐ 56 Pancho Herrera	.80	.35
☐ 57 Art Mahaffey	.80	.35
☐ 58 Robin Roberts	5.00	2.20
☐ 59 Tony Taylor	1.00	.45
☐ 60 Lee Walls	.80	.35
☐ 61 Smoky Burgess	1.00	.45
☐ 62 Roy Face (brown)	1.25	.55
☐ 64 Dick Groat	1.25	.55
☐ 65 Don Hoak	.80	.35
☐ 66 Vern Law	1.25	.55
☐ 67 Bill Mazeroski	1.50	.70
☐ 68 Rocky Nelson	.80	.35
☐ 69 Bob Skinner	.80	.35
☐ 70 Hal Smith	.80	.35
☐ 71 Dick Stuart	1.00	.45
☐ 72 Bill Virdon	1.25	.55
☐ 73 Don Blasingame	.80	.35
☐ 74 Eddie Bressoud (brown)	.80	.35
☐ 75 Orlando Cepeda	3.00	1.35
☐ 76 Jim Davenport	.80	.35
☐ 77 Harvey Kuenn	1.50	.70
☐ 78 Hobie Landrith	.80	.35
☐ 79 Juan Marichal	6.00	2.70
☐ 81 Mike McCormick	1.00	.45
☐ 82 Willie McCovey	8.00	3.60
☐ 83 Billy O'Dell	.80	.35
☐ 84 Jack Sanford	.80	.35
☐ 85 Ken Boyer	1.50	.70
☐ 86 Curt Flood	1.25	.55
☐ 87 Alex Grammas (brown)	.80	.35
☐ 88 Larry Jackson	.80	.35
☐ 89 Julian Javier	.80	.35
☐ 90 Ron Kline	.80	.35
☐ 91 Lindy McDaniel	.80	.35
☐ 92 Stan Musial	15.00	6.75
☐ 93 Curt Simmons	.80	.35
☐ 94 Hal Smith	.80	.35
☐ 95 Daryl Spencer	.80	.35
☐ 96 Bill White	1.25	.55
☐ 97 Steve Barber	.80	.35
☐ 98 Jackie Brandt (brown)	.80	.35
☐ 99 Marv Breeding	.80	.35
☐ 100 Chuck Estrada	.80	.35
☐ 101 Jim Gentile	1.25	.55
☐ 102 Ron Hansen	.80	.35
☐ 103 Milt Pappas	1.00	.45
☐ 104 Brooks Robinson	10.00	4.50
☐ 105 Gene Stephens	.80	.35
☐ 106 Gus Triandos	1.00	.45
☐ 107 Hoyt Wilhelm	5.00	2.20
☐ 108 Tom Brewer	.80	.35
☐ 110 Ike Delock	.80	.35
☐ 111 Gary Geiger	.80	.35
☐ 112 Jackie Jensen	1.50	.70
☐ 113 Frank Malzone	1.00	.45
☐ 114 Bill Monbouquette	.80	.35
☐ 115 Russ Nixon	.80	.35
☐ 116 Pete Runnels	1.00	.45
☐ 117 Willie Tasby	.80	.35
☐ 118 Vic Wertz	1.00	.45
☐ 119 Gene Conley (brown)	.80	.35
☐ 119 Carl Yastrzemski	12.50	5.50
☐ 120 Luis Aparicio	5.00	2.20
☐ 121 Russ Kemmerer (brown)	.80	.35
☐ 122 Jim Landis	.80	.35
☐ 123 Sherman Lollar	.80	.35
☐ 124 J.C. Martin	.80	.35
☐ 125 Minnie Minoso	1.50	.70
☐ 126 Billy Pierce	1.25	.55
☐ 127 Bob Shaw	.80	.35
☐ 128 Roy Sievers	1.25	.55
☐ 129 Al Smith	.80	.35
☐ 130 Gerry Staley	.80	.35
☐ 131 Early Wynn	5.00	2.20
☐ 132 Johnny Antonelli (brown)	1.00	.45
☐ 133 Ken Aspromonte	.80	.35
☐ 134 Tito Francona	.80	.35
☐ 135 Jim Grant	.80	.35
☐ 136 Woody Held	.80	.35
☐ 137 Barry Latman	.80	.35
☐ 138 Jim Perry	1.00	.45
☐ 139 Jimmy Piersall	1.50	.70
☐ 140 Bubba Phillips	.80	.35
☐ 142 John Romano	.80	.35
☐ 143 Johnny Temple	.80	.35
☐ 144 Hank Aguirre (brown)	.80	.35
☐ 145 Frank Bolling	.80	.35
☐ 146 Steve Boros	1.00	.45
☐ 147 Jim Bunning	5.00	2.20
☐ 148 Norm Cash	1.50	.70
☐ 149 Harry Chiti	.80	.35
☐ 150 Chico Fernandez	.80	.35
☐ 151 Dick Gernert	.80	.35
☐ 152A Al Kaline (green)	10.00	4.50
☐ 152B Al Kaline (brown)	10.00	4.50
☐ 153 Frank Lary	1.00	.45
☐ 154 Charlie Maxwell	.80	.35
☐ 155 Dave Sisler	.80	.35
☐ 156 Hank Bauer	1.00	.45
☐ 157 Bob Boyd (brown)	.80	.35
☐ 158 Andy Carey	.80	.35
☐ 159 Bud Daley	.80	.35
☐ 160 Dick Hall	.80	.35
☐ 161 J.C. Hartman	.80	.35
☐ 162 Ray Herbert	.80	.35
☐ 163 Whitey Herzog	2.00	.90
☐ 164 Jerry Lumpe	.80	.35
☐ 165 Norm Siebern	.80	.35
☐ 166 Marv Throneberry	1.50	.70
☐ 167 Bill Tuttle	.80	.35

☐ 168 Dick Williams	1.25	.55
☐ 169 Jerry Casale (brown)	.80	.35
☐ 170 Bob Cerv	1.00	.45
☐ 171 Ned Garver	.80	.35
☐ 172 Ron Hunt	.80	.35
☐ 173 Ted Kluszewski	3.00	1.35
☐ 174 Bob Sadowski	.80	.35
☐ 175 Eddie Yost	.80	.35
☐ 176 Bob Allison	1.25	.55
☐ 177 Earl Battey (brown)	.80	.35
☐ 178 Reno Bertoia	.80	.35
☐ 179 Billy Gardner	1.00	.45
☐ 180 Jim Kaat	3.00	1.35
☐ 181 Harmon Killebrew	6.00	2.70
☐ 182 Jim Lemon	1.00	.45
☐ 183 Camilo Pascual	1.00	.45
☐ 184 Pedro Ramos	.80	.35
☐ 185 Chuck Stobbs	.80	.35
☐ 186 Zoilo Versalles	.80	.35
☐ 187 Pete Whisenant	.80	.35
☐ 188 Luis Arroyo (brown)	1.00	.45
☐ 189 Yogi Berra	12.50	5.50
☐ 190 John Blanchard	1.00	.45
☐ 191 Clete Boyer	1.25	.55
☐ 192 Art Ditmar	.80	.35
☐ 193 Whitey Ford	12.50	5.50
☐ 194 Elston Howard	2.50	1.10
☐ 195 Tony Kubek	2.50	1.10
☐ 196 Mickey Mantle	60.00	27.00
☐ 197 Roger Maris	15.00	6.75
☐ 198 Bobby Shantz	1.00	.45
☐ 199 Bill Stafford	.80	.35
☐ 200 Bob Turley	1.00	.45
☐ 201 Bud Daley (brown)	.80	.35
☐ 202 Dick Donovan	.80	.35
☐ 203 Bobby Klaus	.80	.35
☐ 204 Johnny Klippstein	.80	.35
☐ 205 Dale Long	1.00	.45
☐ 206 Ray Semproch	.80	.35
☐ 207 Gene Woodling	1.00	.45
☐ XX Stamp Album	20.00	9.00

1962 Topps

The cards in this 598-card set measure 2 1/2" by 3 1/2". The 1962 Topps set contains a mini-series spotlighting Babe Ruth (135-144). Other subsets in the set include League Leaders (51-60), World Series cards (232-237), In Action cards (311-319), NL All Stars (390-399), AL All Stars (466-475), and Rookie Prospects (591-598). The All-Star selections were again provided by Sport Magazine, as in 1958 and 1960. The second series had two distinct printings which are distinguishable by numerous color and pose variations. Those cards with a distinctive "green tint" are valued at a slight premuim as they are basically the result of a flawed printing process occurring early in the second series run. Card number 139 exists as A: Babe Ruth Special card, B: Hal Reniff with arms over head, or C: Hal Reniff in the same pose as card number 159. In addition, two poses exist for these cards: 129, 132, 134, 147, 174, 176, and 190. The high number series, 523 to 598, is somewhat more difficult to obtain than other cards in the set. Within the last series (523-598) there are 43 cards which were printed in lesser quantities; these are marked SP in the checklist below. In particular, the Rookie Parade subset (591-598) of this last series is even more difficult. This was the first year Topps produced multi-player Rookie Cards. The set price listed does not include the pose variations (see checklist below for individual values). Cards were issued in one-card penny packs as well as five-card nickle packs. The key Rookie Cards in this set are Lou Brock, Tim McCarver, Gaylord Perry, and Bob Uecker.

	NRMT	VG-E
COMPLETE SET (598)	4600.00	2100.00
COMMON CARD (1-370)	5.00	2.20
COMMON CARD (371-446)	6.00	2.70
COMMON CARD (447-522)	12.00	5.50
COMMON CARD (523-598)	20.00	9.00
WRAPPER (1-CENT)	100.00	45.00
WRAPPER (5-CENT)	30.00	13.50
☐ 1 Roger Maris	200.00	50.00
☐ 2 Jim Brosnan	5.00	2.20
☐ 3 Pete Runnels	5.00	2.20
☐ 4 John DeMerit	8.00	3.60
☐ 5 Sandy Koufax UER	175.00	80.00
(Struck ou 18)		
☐ 6 Marv Breeding	5.00	2.20
☐ 7 Frank Thomas	10.00	4.50
☐ 8 Ray Herbert	5.00	2.20
☐ 9 Jim Davenport	8.00	3.60
☐ 10 Bob Clemente	225.00	100.00
☐ 11 Tom Morgan	5.00	2.20
☐ 12 Harry Craft MG	8.00	3.60
☐ 13 Dick Howser	8.00	3.60
☐ 14 Bill White	8.00	3.60
☐ 15 Dick Donovan	5.00	2.20
☐ 16 Darrell Johnson	5.00	2.20
☐ 17 Johnny Callison	8.00	3.60
☐ 18 Managers' Dream	200.00	90.00
Mickey Mantle		
Willie Mays		
☐ 19 Ray Washburn	5.00	2.20
☐ 20 Rocky Colavito	15.00	6.75
☐ 21 Jim Kaat	8.00	3.60
☐ 22A Checklist 1 ERR	12.00	2.40
(121-176 on back)		
☐ 22B Checklist 1 COR	12.00	2.40
☐ 23 Norm Larker	5.00	2.20
☐ 24 Tigers Team	10.00	4.50
☐ 25 Ernie Banks	45.00	20.00
☐ 26 Chris Cannizzaro	8.00	3.60
☐ 27 Chuck Cottier	5.00	2.20
☐ 28 Minnie Minoso	10.00	4.50
☐ 29 Casey Stengel MG	20.00	9.00
☐ 30 Eddie Mathews	25.00	11.00
☐ 31 Tom Tresh	20.00	9.00
☐ 32 John Roseboro	8.00	3.60
☐ 33 Don Larsen	8.00	3.60
☐ 34 Johnny Temple	8.00	3.60
☐ 35 Don Schwall	8.00	3.60
☐ 36 Don Leppert	5.00	2.20
☐ 37 Tribe Hill Trio	5.00	2.20
Barry Latman		
Dick Stigman		
Jim Perry		
☐ 38 Gene Stephens	5.00	2.20
☐ 39 Joe Koppe	5.00	2.20
☐ 40 Orlando Cepeda	14.00	6.25
☐ 41 Cliff Cook	5.00	2.20
☐ 42 Jim King	5.00	2.20
☐ 43 Los Angeles Dodgers	10.00	4.50
Team Card		
☐ 44 Don Taussig	5.00	2.20
☐ 45 Brooks Robinson	45.00	20.00
☐ 46 Jack Baldschun	5.00	2.20
☐ 47 Bob Will	5.00	2.20
☐ 48 Ralph Terry	8.00	3.60
☐ 49 Hal Jones	5.00	2.20
☐ 50 Stan Musial	100.00	45.00
☐ 51 AL Batting Leaders	8.00	3.60
Norm Cash		
Jim Piersall		
Al Kaline		
Elston Howard		
☐ 52 NL Batting Leaders	18.00	8.00
Bob Clemente		
Vada Pinson		
Ken Boyer		
Wally Moon		
☐ 53 AL Home Run Leaders	110.00	50.00
Roger Maris		
Mickey Mantle		
Jim Gentile		
Harmon Killebrew		
☐ 54 NL Home Run Leaders	18.00	8.00
Orlando Cepeda		
Willie Mays		
Frank Robinson		
☐ 55 AL ERA Leaders	8.00	3.60
Dick Donovan		
Bill Stafford		
Don Mossi		
Milt Pappas		
☐ 56 NL ERA Leaders	8.00	3.60
Warren Spahn		
Jim O'Toole		
Curt Simmons		
Mike McCormick		
☐ 57 AL Wins Leaders	8.00	3.60
Whitey Ford		
Frank Lary		
Steve Barber		
Jim Bunning		
☐ 58 NL Wins Leaders	8.00	3.60
Warren Spahn		
Joe Jay		
Jim O'Toole		
☐ 59 AL Strikeout Leaders	8.00	3.60
Camilo Pascual		
Whitey Ford		
Jim Bunning		
Juan Pizzaro		
☐ 60 NL Strikeout Leaders	18.00	8.00
Sandy Koufax		
Stan Williams		
Don Drysdale		
Jim O'Toole		
☐ 61 Cardinals Team	10.00	4.50
☐ 62 Steve Boros	5.00	2.20
☐ 63 Tony Cloninger	8.00	3.60
☐ 64 Russ Snyder	5.00	2.20
☐ 65 Bobby Richardson	12.00	5.50
☐ 66 Cuno Barragan	5.00	2.20
☐ 67 Harvey Haddix	8.00	3.60
☐ 68 Ken Hunt	5.00	2.20
☐ 69 Phil Ortega	5.00	2.20
☐ 70 Harmon Killebrew	25.00	11.00
☐ 71 Dick LeMay	5.00	2.20
☐ 72 Bob's Pupils	5.00	2.20
Steve Boros		
Bob Scheffing MG		
Jake Wood		
☐ 73 Nellie Fox	20.00	9.00
☐ 74 Bob Lillis	8.00	3.60
☐ 75 Milt Pappas	8.00	3.60
☐ 76 Howie Bedell	5.00	2.20
☐ 77 Tony Taylor	8.00	3.60
☐ 78 Gene Green	5.00	2.20
☐ 79 Ed Hobaugh	5.00	2.20
☐ 80 Vada Pinson	8.00	3.60
☐ 81 Jim Pagliaroni	5.00	2.20
☐ 82 Deron Johnson	8.00	3.60
☐ 83 Larry Jackson	5.00	2.20
☐ 84 Lenny Green	5.00	2.20
☐ 85 Gil Hodges	20.00	9.00
☐ 86 Donn Clendenon	8.00	3.60
☐ 87 Mike Roarke	5.00	2.20
☐ 88 Ralph Houk MG	8.00	3.60
(Berra in background)		
☐ 89 Barney Schultz	5.00	2.20
☐ 90 Jimmy Piersall	8.00	3.60
☐ 91 J.C. Martin	5.00	2.20
☐ 92 Sam Jones	5.00	2.20
☐ 93 John Blanchard	8.00	3.60
☐ 94 Jay Hook	8.00	3.60
☐ 95 Don Hoak	8.00	3.60
☐ 96 Eli Grba	5.00	2.20
☐ 97 Tito Francona	5.00	2.20
☐ 98 Checklist 2	12.00	2.40
☐ 99 John (Boog) Powell	30.00	13.50
☐ 100 Warren Spahn	30.00	13.50
☐ 101 Carroll Hardy	5.00	2.20
☐ 102 Al Schroll	5.00	2.20
☐ 103 Don Blasingame	5.00	2.20
☐ 104 Ted Savage	5.00	2.20
☐ 105 Don Mossi	8.00	3.60
☐ 106 Carl Sawatski	5.00	2.20
☐ 107 Mike McCormick	8.00	3.60
☐ 108 Willie Davis	8.00	3.60
☐ 109 Bob Shaw	5.00	2.20
☐ 110 Bill Skowron	8.00	3.60
☐ 111 Dallas Green	8.00	3.60
☐ 112 Hank Foiles	5.00	2.20
☐ 113 Chicago White Sox	10.00	4.50
Team Card		
☐ 114 Howie Koplitz	5.00	2.20
☐ 115 Bob Skinner	8.00	3.60
☐ 116 Herb Score	8.00	3.60
☐ 117 Gary Geiger	5.00	2.20
☐ 118 Julian Javier	8.00	3.60
☐ 119 Danny Murphy	5.00	2.20
☐ 120 Bob Purkey	5.00	2.20
☐ 121 Billy Hitchcock MG	5.00	2.20
☐ 122 Norm Bass	5.00	2.20
☐ 123 Mike de la Hoz	5.00	2.20
☐ 124 Bill Pleis	5.00	2.20
☐ 125 Gene Woodling	8.00	3.60
☐ 126 Al Cicotte	5.00	2.20
☐ 127 Pride of A's	5.00	2.20
Norm Siebern		
Hank Bauer MG		
Jerry Lumpe		
☐ 128 Art Fowler	5.00	2.20
☐ 129A Lee Walls	5.00	2.20
(Facing right)		
☐ 129B Lee Walls	25.00	11.00
(Facing left)		
☐ 130 Frank Bolling	5.00	2.20
☐ 131 Pete Richert	5.00	2.20
☐ 132A Angels Team	10.00	4.50
(Without photo)		
☐ 132B Angels Team	25.00	11.00
(With photo)		
☐ 133 Felipe Alou	8.00	3.60

Card		
☐ 134A Billy Hoeft	5.00	2.20
(Facing right)		
☐ 134B Billy Hoeft	25.00	11.00
(Facing straight)		
☐ 135 Babe Ruth Special 1	20.00	9.00
Babe as a Boy		
☐ 136 Babe Ruth Special 2	20.00	9.00
Babe Joins Yanks		
☐ 137 Babe Ruth Special 3	20.00	9.00
With Miller Huggins		
☐ 138 Babe Ruth Special 4	20.00	9.00
Famous Slugger		
☐ 139A Babe Ruth Special 5	30.00	13.50
Babe Hits 60		
☐ 139B Hal Reniff PORT	12.00	5.50
☐ 139C Hal Reniff	65.00	29.00
(Pitching)		
☐ 140 Babe Ruth Special 6	50.00	22.00
With Lou Gehrig		
☐ 141 Babe Ruth Special 7	20.00	9.00
Twilight Years		
☐ 142 Babe Ruth Special 8	20.00	9.00
Coaching Dodgers		
☐ 143 Babe Ruth Special 9	20.00	9.00
Greatest Sports Hero		
☐ 144 Babe Ruth Special 10	20.00	9.00
Farewell Speech		
☐ 145 Barry Latman	5.00	2.20
☐ 146 Don Demeter	5.00	2.20
☐ 147A Bill Kunkel PORT	5.00	2.20
☐ 147B Bill Kunkel	25.00	11.00
(Pitching pose)		
☐ 148 Wally Post	5.00	2.20
☐ 149 Bob Duliba	5.00	2.20
☐ 150 Al Kaline	45.00	20.00
☐ 151 Johnny Klippstein	5.00	2.20
☐ 152 Mickey Vernon MG	8.00	3.60
☐ 153 Pumpsie Green	6.00	2.70
☐ 154 Lee Thomas	6.00	2.70
☐ 155 Stu Miller	6.00	2.70
☐ 156 Merritt Ranew	5.00	2.20
☐ 157 Wes Covington	8.00	3.60
☐ 158 Braves Team	10.00	4.50
☐ 159 Hal Reniff	8.00	3.60
☐ 160 Dick Stuart	8.00	3.60
☐ 161 Frank Baumann	5.00	2.20
☐ 162 Sammy Drake	5.00	2.20
☐ 163 Hot Corner Guard	8.00	3.60
Billy Gardner		
Cletis Boyer		
☐ 164 Hal Naragon	5.00	2.20
☐ 165 Jackie Brandt	5.00	2.20
☐ 166 Don Lee	5.00	2.20
☐ 167 Tim McCarver	30.00	13.50
☐ 168 Leo Posada	5.00	2.20
☐ 169 Bob Cerv	8.00	3.60
☐ 170 Ron Santo	14.00	6.25
☐ 171 Dave Sisler	5.00	2.20
☐ 172 Fred Hutchinson MG	8.00	3.60
☐ 173 Chico Fernandez	5.00	2.20
☐ 174A Carl Willey	5.00	2.20
(Capless)		
☐ 174B Carl Willey	25.00	11.00
(With cap)		
☐ 175 Frank Howard	8.00	3.60
☐ 176A Eddie Yost PORT	5.00	2.20
☐ 176B Eddie Yost BATTING	25.00	11.00
☐ 177 Bobby Shantz	8.00	3.60
☐ 178 Camilo Carreon	5.00	2.20
☐ 179 Tom Sturdivant	5.00	2.20
☐ 180 Bob Allison	8.00	3.60
☐ 181 Paul Brown	5.00	2.20
☐ 182 Bob Nieman	5.00	2.20
☐ 183 Roger Craig	8.00	3.60
☐ 184 Haywood Sullivan	8.00	3.60
☐ 185 Roland Sheldon	8.00	3.60
☐ 186 Mack Jones	5.00	2.20
☐ 187 Gene Conley	5.00	2.20
☐ 188 Chuck Hiller	5.00	2.20
☐ 189 Dick Hall	5.00	2.20
☐ 190A Wally Moon PORT	5.00	2.20
☐ 190B Wally Moon BATTING	28.00	12.50
☐ 191 Jim Brewer	5.00	2.20
☐ 192A Checklist 3	12.00	2.40
(Without comma)		
☐ 192B Checklist 3	16.00	3.20
(Comma after		
Checklist)		
☐ 193 Eddie Kasko	5.00	2.20
☐ 194 Dean Chance	8.00	3.60
☐ 195 Joe Cunningham	5.00	2.20
☐ 196 Terry Fox	5.00	2.20
☐ 197 Daryl Spencer	5.00	2.20
☐ 198 Johnny Keane MG	5.00	2.20
☐ 199 Gaylord Perry	80.00	36.00
☐ 200 Mickey Mantle	450.00	200.00
☐ 201 Ike Delock	5.00	2.20
☐ 202 Carl Warwick	5.00	2.20
☐ 203 Jack Fisher	5.00	2.20
☐ 204 Johnny Weekly	5.00	2.20
☐ 205 Gene Freese	5.00	2.20
☐ 206 Senators Team	10.00	4.50
☐ 207 Pete Burnside	5.00	2.20
☐ 208 Billy Martin	20.00	9.00
☐ 209 Jim Fregosi	14.00	6.25
☐ 210 Roy Face	8.00	3.60
☐ 211 Midway Masters	5.00	2.20
Frank Bolling		
Roy McMillan		
☐ 212 Jim Owens	5.00	2.20
☐ 213 Richie Ashburn	20.00	9.00
☐ 214 Dom Zanni	5.00	2.20
☐ 215 Woody Held	5.00	2.20
☐ 216 Ron Kline	5.00	2.20
☐ 217 Walter Alston MG	8.00	3.60
☐ 218 Joe Torre	40.00	18.00
☐ 219 Al Downing	8.00	3.60
☐ 220 Roy Sievers	8.00	3.60
☐ 221 Bill Short	5.00	2.20
☐ 222 Jerry Zimmerman	5.00	2.20
☐ 223 Alex Grammas	5.00	2.20
☐ 224 Don Rudolph	5.00	2.20
☐ 225 Frank Malzone	8.00	3.60
☐ 226 San Francisco Giants	10.00	4.50
Team Card		
☐ 227 Bob Tiefenauer	5.00	2.20
☐ 228 Dale Long	8.00	3.60
☐ 229 Jesus McFarlane	5.00	2.20
☐ 230 Camilo Pascual	8.00	3.60
☐ 231 Ernie Bowman	5.00	2.20
☐ 232 World Series Game 1	10.00	4.50
Yanks win opener		
☐ 233 Joey Jay WS	10.00	4.50
☐ 234 Roger Maris WS	20.00	9.00
☐ 235 Whitey Ford WS	10.00	4.50
sets new mark		
☐ 236 World Series Game 5	10.00	4.50
Yanks crush Reds		
☐ 237 World Series Summary	10.00	4.50
Yanks celebrate		
☐ 238 Norm Sherry	5.00	2.20
☐ 239 Cecil Butler	5.00	2.20
☐ 240 George Altman	5.00	2.20
☐ 241 Johnny Kucks	5.00	2.20
☐ 242 Mel McGaha MG	5.00	2.20
☐ 243 Robin Roberts	15.00	6.75
☐ 244 Don Gile	5.00	2.20
☐ 245 Ron Hansen	5.00	2.20
☐ 246 Art Ditmar	5.00	2.20
☐ 247 Joe Pignatano	5.00	2.20
☐ 248 Bob Aspromonte	8.00	3.60
☐ 249 Ed Keegan	5.00	2.20
☐ 250 Norm Cash	8.00	3.60
☐ 251 New York Yankees	60.00	27.00
Team Card		
☐ 252 Earl Francis	5.00	2.20
☐ 253 Harry Chiti MG	5.00	2.20
☐ 254 Gordon Windhorn	5.00	2.20
☐ 255 Juan Pizarro	5.00	2.20
☐ 256 Elio Chacon	8.00	3.60
☐ 257 Jack Spring	5.00	2.20
☐ 258 Marty Keough	5.00	2.20
☐ 259 Lou Klimchock	5.00	2.20
☐ 260 Billy Pierce	8.00	3.60
☐ 261 George Alusik	5.00	2.20
☐ 262 Bob Schmidt	5.00	2.20
☐ 263 The Right Pitch	5.00	2.20
Bob Purkey		
Jim Turner CO		
Joe Jay		
☐ 264 Dick Ellsworth	8.00	3.60
☐ 265 Joe Adcock	8.00	3.60
☐ 266 John Anderson	5.00	2.20
☐ 267 Dan Dobbek	5.00	2.20
☐ 268 Ken McBride	5.00	2.20
☐ 269 Bob Oldis	5.00	2.20
☐ 270 Dick Groat	8.00	3.60
☐ 271 Ray Rippelmeyer	5.00	2.20
☐ 272 Earl Robinson	5.00	2.20
☐ 273 Gary Bell	5.00	2.20
☐ 274 Sammy Taylor	5.00	2.20
☐ 275 Norm Siebern	5.00	2.20
☐ 276 Hal Kolstad	5.00	2.20
☐ 277 Checklist 4	16.00	3.20
☐ 278 Ken Johnson	8.00	3.60
☐ 279 Hobie Landrith UER	8.00	3.60
(Wrong birthdate)		
☐ 280 Johnny Podres	8.00	3.60
☐ 281 Jake Gibbs	8.00	3.60
☐ 282 Dave Hillman	5.00	2.20
☐ 283 Charlie Smith	5.00	2.20
☐ 284 Ruben Amaro	5.00	2.20
☐ 285 Curt Simmons	8.00	3.60
☐ 286 Al Lopez MG	8.00	3.60
☐ 287 George Witt	5.00	2.20
☐ 288 Billy Williams	30.00	13.50
☐ 289 Mike Krsnich	5.00	2.20
☐ 290 Jim Gentile	8.00	3.60
☐ 291 Hal Stowe	5.00	2.20
☐ 292 Jerry Kindall	5.00	2.20
☐ 293 Bob Miller	8.00	3.60
☐ 294 Phillies Team	10.00	4.50
☐ 295 Vern Law	8.00	3.60
☐ 296 Ken Hamlin	5.00	2.20
☐ 297 Ron Perranoski	8.00	3.60
☐ 298 Bill Tuttle	5.00	2.20
☐ 299 Don Wert	5.00	2.20
☐ 300 Willie Mays	150.00	70.00
☐ 301 Galen Cisco	5.00	2.20
☐ 302 Johnny Edwards	5.00	2.20
☐ 303 Frank Torre	8.00	3.60
☐ 304 Dick Farrell	8.00	3.60
☐ 305 Jerry Lumpe	5.00	2.20
☐ 306 Redbird Rippers	5.00	2.20
Lindy McDaniel		
Larry Jackson		
☐ 307 Jim Grant	8.00	3.60
☐ 308 Neil Chrisley	8.00	3.60
☐ 309 Moe Morhardt	5.00	2.20
☐ 310 Whitey Ford	45.00	20.00
☐ 311 Tony Kubek IA	8.00	3.60
☐ 312 Warren Spahn IA	14.00	6.25
☐ 313 Roger Maris IA	35.00	16.00
Blasts 61th		
☐ 314 Rocky Colavito IA	12.00	5.50
☐ 315 Whitey Ford IA	15.00	6.75
☐ 316 Harmon Killebrew IA	15.00	6.75
☐ 317 Stan Musial IA	20.00	9.00
☐ 318 Mickey Mantle IA	175.00	80.00
☐ 319 Mike McCormick IA	5.00	2.20
☐ 320 Hank Aaron	140.00	65.00
☐ 321 Lee Stange	5.00	2.20
☐ 322 Alvin Dark MG	8.00	3.60
☐ 323 Don Landrum	5.00	2.20
☐ 324 Joe McClain	5.00	2.20
☐ 325 Luis Aparicio	15.00	6.75
☐ 326 Tom Parsons	5.00	2.20
☐ 327 Ozzie Virgil	5.00	2.20
☐ 328 Ken Walters	5.00	2.20
☐ 329 Bob Bolin	5.00	2.20
☐ 330 John Romano	5.00	2.20
☐ 331 Moe Drabowsky	8.00	3.60
☐ 332 Don Buddin	5.00	2.20
☐ 333 Frank Cipriani	5.00	2.20
☐ 334 Boston Red Sox	10.00	4.50
Team Card		
☐ 335 Bill Bruton	5.00	2.20
☐ 336 Billy Muffett	5.00	2.20
☐ 337 Jim Marshall	8.00	3.60
☐ 338 Billy Gardner	5.00	2.20
☐ 339 Jose Valdivielso	5.00	2.20
☐ 340 Don Drysdale	35.00	16.00
☐ 341 Mike Hershberger	5.00	2.20
☐ 342 Ed Rakow	5.00	2.20
☐ 343 Albie Pearson	8.00	3.60
☐ 344 Ed Bauta	5.00	2.20
☐ 345 Chuck Schilling	5.00	2.20
☐ 346 Jack Kralick	5.00	2.20
☐ 347 Chuck Hinton	5.00	2.20
☐ 348 Larry Burright	8.00	3.60
☐ 349 Paul Foytack	5.00	2.20
☐ 350 Frank Robinson	45.00	20.00
☐ 351 Braves' Backstops	8.00	3.60
Joe Torre		
Del Crandall		
☐ 352 Frank Sullivan	5.00	2.20
☐ 353 Bill Mazeroski	10.00	4.50
☐ 354 Roman Mejias	8.00	3.60
☐ 355 Steve Barber	5.00	2.20
☐ 356 Tom Haller	5.00	2.20
☐ 357 Jerry Walker	5.00	2.20
☐ 358 Tommy Davis	8.00	3.60
☐ 359 Bobby Locke	5.00	2.20
☐ 360 Yogi Berra	75.00	34.00
☐ 361 Bob Hendley	5.00	2.20
☐ 362 Ty Cline	5.00	2.20
☐ 363 Bob Roselli	5.00	2.20
☐ 364 Ken Hunt	5.00	2.20
☐ 365 Charlie Neal	8.00	3.60
☐ 366 Phil Regan	8.00	3.60
☐ 367 Checklist 5	16.00	3.20
☐ 368 Bob Tillman	5.00	2.20
☐ 369 Ted Bowsfield	5.00	2.20
☐ 370 Ken Boyer	8.00	3.60
☐ 371 Earl Battey	6.00	2.70
☐ 372 Jack Curtis	6.00	2.70
☐ 373 Al Heist	6.00	2.70
☐ 374 Gene Mauch MG	10.00	4.50
☐ 375 Ron Fairly	10.00	4.50
☐ 376 Bud Daley	8.00	3.60
☐ 377 John Orsino	6.00	2.70

☐ 378 Bennie Daniels	6.00	2.70
☐ 379 Chuck Essegian	6.00	2.70
☐ 380 Lou Burdette	10.00	4.50
☐ 381 Chico Cardenas	10.00	4.50
☐ 382 Dick Williams	8.00	3.60
☐ 383 Ray Sadecki	6.00	2.70
☐ 384 K.C. Athletics Team Card	10.00	4.50
☐ 385 Early Wynn	15.00	6.75
☐ 386 Don Mincher	8.00	3.60
☐ 387 Lou Brock	125.00	55.00
☐ 388 Ryne Duren	8.00	3.60
☐ 389 Smoky Burgess	10.00	4.50
☐ 390 Orlando Cepeda AS	10.00	4.50
☐ 391 Bill Mazeroski AS	10.00	4.50
☐ 392 Ken Boyer AS	8.00	3.60
☐ 393 Roy McMillan AS	6.00	2.70
☐ 394 Hank Aaron AS	45.00	20.00
☐ 395 Willie Mays AS	50.00	22.00
☐ 396 Frank Robinson AS	16.00	7.25
☐ 397 John Roseboro AS	6.00	2.70
☐ 398 Don Drysdale AS	16.00	7.25
☐ 399 Warren Spahn AS	16.00	7.25
☐ 400 Elston Howard	10.00	4.50
☐ 401 AL/NL Homer Kings Roger Maris Orlando Cepeda	60.00	27.00
☐ 402 Gino Cimoli	6.00	2.70
☐ 403 Chet Nichols	6.00	2.70
☐ 404 Tim Harkness	8.00	3.60
☐ 405 Jim Perry	8.00	3.60
☐ 406 Bob Taylor	6.00	2.70
☐ 407 Hank Aguirre	6.00	2.70
☐ 408 Gus Bell	8.00	3.60
☐ 409 Pittsburgh Pirates Team Card	10.00	4.50
☐ 410 Al Smith	6.00	2.70
☐ 411 Danny O'Connell	6.00	2.70
☐ 412 Charlie James	6.00	2.70
☐ 413 Matty Alou	10.00	4.50
☐ 414 Joe Gaines	6.00	2.70
☐ 415 Bill Virdon	10.00	4.50
☐ 416 Bob Scheffing MG	6.00	2.70
☐ 417 Joe Azcue	6.00	2.70
☐ 418 Andy Carey	6.00	2.70
☐ 419 Bob Bruce	8.00	3.60
☐ 420 Gus Triandos	8.00	3.60
☐ 421 Ken MacKenzie	8.00	3.60
☐ 422 Steve Bilko	6.00	2.70
☐ 423 Rival League Relief Aces: Roy Face Hoyt Wilhelm	10.00	4.50
☐ 424 Al McBean	6.00	2.70
☐ 425 Carl Yastrzemski	125.00	55.00
☐ 426 Bob Farley	6.00	2.70
☐ 427 Jake Wood	6.00	2.70
☐ 428 Joe Hicks	6.00	2.70
☐ 429 Billy O'Dell	6.00	2.70
☐ 430 Tony Kubek	10.00	4.50
☐ 431 Bob Rodgers	8.00	3.60
☐ 432 Jim Pendleton	6.00	2.70
☐ 433 Jim Archer	6.00	2.70
☐ 434 Clay Dalrymple	6.00	2.70
☐ 435 Larry Sherry	8.00	3.60
☐ 436 Felix Mantilla	8.00	3.60
☐ 437 Ray Moore	6.00	2.70
☐ 438 Dick Brown	6.00	2.70
☐ 439 Jerry Buchek	6.00	2.70
☐ 440 Joey Jay	6.00	2.70
☐ 441 Checklist 6	16.00	7.25
☐ 442 Wes Stock	6.00	2.70
☐ 443 Del Crandall	8.00	3.60
☐ 444 Ted Wills	6.00	2.70
☐ 445 Vic Power	8.00	3.60
☐ 446 Don Elston	6.00	2.70
☐ 447 Willie Kirkland	12.00	5.50
☐ 448 Joe Gibbon	12.00	5.50
☐ 449 Jerry Adair	12.00	5.50
☐ 450 Jim O'Toole	15.00	6.75
☐ 451 Jose Tartabull	16.00	7.25
☐ 452 Earl Averill Jr.	12.00	5.50
☐ 453 Cal McLish	12.00	5.50
☐ 454 Floyd Robinson	12.00	5.50
☐ 455 Luis Arroyo	15.00	6.75
☐ 456 Joe Amalfitano	15.00	6.75
☐ 457 Lou Clinton	12.00	5.50
☐ 458A Bob Buhl (Braves emblem on cap)	15.00	6.75
☐ 458B Bob Buhl (No emblem on cap)	50.00	22.00
☐ 459 Ed Bailey	12.00	5.50
☐ 460 Jim Bunning	18.00	8.00
☐ 461 Ken Hubbs	35.00	16.00
☐ 462A Willie Tasby (Senators emblem on cap)	12.00	5.50
☐ 462B Willie Tasby (No emblem on cap)	50.00	22.00
☐ 463 Hank Bauer MG	16.00	7.25
☐ 464 Al Jackson	12.00	5.50
☐ 465 Reds Team	20.00	9.00
☐ 466 Norm Cash AS	15.00	6.75
☐ 467 Chuck Schilling AS	12.00	5.50
☐ 468 Brooks Robinson AS	25.00	11.00
☐ 469 Luis Aparicio AS	16.00	7.25
☐ 470 Al Kaline AS	25.00	11.00
☐ 471 Mickey Mantle AS	200.00	90.00
☐ 472 Rocky Colavito AS	16.00	7.25
☐ 473 Elston Howard AS	20.00	9.00
☐ 474 Frank Lary AS	12.00	5.50
☐ 475 Whitey Ford AS	16.00	7.25
☐ 476 Orioles Team	20.00	9.00
☐ 477 Andre Rodgers	12.00	5.50
☐ 478 Don Zimmer (Shown with Mets cap, but listed as with Cincinnati)	20.00	9.00
☐ 479 Joel Horlen	12.00	5.50
☐ 480 Harvey Kuenn	16.00	7.25
☐ 481 Vic Wertz	16.00	7.25
☐ 482 Sam Mele MG	12.00	5.50
☐ 483 Don McMahon	12.00	5.50
☐ 484 Dick Schofield	12.00	5.50
☐ 485 Pedro Ramos	12.00	5.50
☐ 486 Jim Gilliam	16.00	7.25
☐ 487 Jerry Lynch	12.00	5.50
☐ 488 Hal Brown	12.00	5.50
☐ 489 Julio Gotay	12.00	5.50
☐ 490 Clete Boyer UER Reversed Negative	16.00	7.25
☐ 491 Leon Wagner	12.00	5.50
☐ 492 Hal W. Smith	15.00	6.75
☐ 493 Danny McDevitt	12.00	5.50
☐ 494 Sammy White	12.00	5.50
☐ 495 Don Cardwell	12.00	5.50
☐ 496 Wayne Causey	12.00	5.50
☐ 497 Ed Bouchee	15.00	6.75
☐ 498 Jim Donohue	12.00	5.50
☐ 499 Zoilo Versalles	15.00	6.75
☐ 500 Duke Snider	50.00	22.00
☐ 501 Claude Osteen	15.00	6.75
☐ 502 Hector Lopez	15.00	6.75
☐ 503 Danny Murtaugh MG	15.00	6.75
☐ 504 Eddie Bressoud	12.00	5.50
☐ 505 Juan Marichal	45.00	20.00
☐ 506 Charlie Maxwell	15.00	6.75
☐ 507 Ernie Broglio	15.00	6.75
☐ 508 Gordy Coleman	15.00	6.75
☐ 509 Dave Giusti	16.00	7.25
☐ 510 Jim Lemon	12.00	5.50
☐ 511 Bubba Phillips	12.00	5.50
☐ 512 Mike Fornieles	12.00	5.50
☐ 513 Whitey Herzog	16.00	7.25
☐ 514 Sherm Lollar	15.00	6.75
☐ 515 Stan Williams	15.00	6.75
☐ 516 Checklist 7	45.00	9.00
☐ 517 Dave Wickersham	12.00	5.50
☐ 518 Lee Maye	12.00	5.50
☐ 519 Bob Johnson	12.00	5.50
☐ 520 Bob Friend	16.00	7.25
☐ 521 Jacke Davis UER (Listed as OF on front and P on back)	12.00	5.50
☐ 522 Lindy McDaniel	15.00	6.75
☐ 523 Russ Nixon SP	32.00	14.50
☐ 524 Howie Nunn SP	32.00	14.50
☐ 525 George Thomas	20.00	9.00
☐ 526 Hal Woodeshick SP	32.00	14.50
☐ 527 Dick McAuliffe	25.00	11.00
☐ 528 Turk Lown	20.00	9.00
☐ 529 John Schaive SP	32.00	14.50
☐ 530 Bob Gibson SP	150.00	70.00
☐ 531 Bobby G. Smith	20.00	9.00
☐ 532 Dick Stigman	20.00	9.00
☐ 533 Charley Lau SP	35.00	16.00
☐ 534 Tony Gonzalez SP	32.00	14.50
☐ 535 Ed Roebuck	20.00	9.00
☐ 536 Dick Gernert	20.00	9.00
☐ 537 Cleveland Indians Team Card	50.00	22.00
☐ 538 Jack Sanford	20.00	9.00
☐ 539 Billy Moran	20.00	9.00
☐ 540 Jim Landis SP	32.00	14.50
☐ 541 Don Nottebart SP	32.00	14.50
☐ 542 Dave Philley	20.00	9.00
☐ 543 Bob Allen SP	32.00	14.50
☐ 544 Willie McCovey SP	115.00	52.50
☐ 545 Hoyt Wilhelm SP	50.00	22.00
☐ 546 Moe Thacker SP	32.00	14.50
☐ 547 Don Ferrarese	20.00	9.00
☐ 548 Bobby Del Greco	20.00	9.00
☐ 549 Bill Rigney MG SP	32.00	14.50
☐ 550 Art Mahaffey SP	32.00	14.50
☐ 551 Harry Bright	20.00	9.00
☐ 552 Chicago Cubs SP Team Card	60.00	27.00
☐ 553 Jim Coates	20.00	9.00
☐ 554 Bubba Morton SP	32.00	14.50
☐ 555 John Buzhardt SP	32.00	14.50
☐ 556 Al Spangler	20.00	9.00
☐ 557 Bob Anderson SP	32.00	14.50
☐ 558 John Goryl	20.00	9.00
☐ 559 Mike Higgins MG	20.00	9.00
☐ 560 Chuck Estrada SP	32.00	14.50
☐ 561 Gene Oliver SP	32.00	14.50
☐ 562 Bill Henry	20.00	9.00
☐ 563 Ken Aspromonte	20.00	9.00
☐ 564 Bob Grim	20.00	9.00
☐ 565 Jose Pagan	20.00	9.00
☐ 566 Marty Kutyna SP	32.00	14.50
☐ 567 Tracy Stallard SP	32.00	14.50
☐ 568 Jim Golden	20.00	9.00
☐ 569 Ed Sadowski SP	32.00	14.50
☐ 570 Bill Stafford SP	32.00	14.50
☐ 571 Billy Klaus SP	32.00	14.50
☐ 572 Bob G. Miller SP	35.00	16.00
☐ 573 Johnny Logan	20.00	9.00
☐ 574 Dean Stone	20.00	9.00
☐ 575 Red Schoendienst SP	50.00	22.00
☐ 576 Russ Kemmerer SP	32.00	14.50
☐ 577 Dave Nicholson SP	32.00	14.50
☐ 578 Jim Duffalo	20.00	9.00
☐ 579 Jim Schaffer SP	32.00	14.50
☐ 580 Bill Monbouquette	20.00	9.00
☐ 581 Mel Roach	20.00	9.00
☐ 582 Ron Piche	20.00	9.00
☐ 583 Larry Osborne	20.00	9.00
☐ 584 Minnesota Twins SP Team Card	60.00	27.00
☐ 585 Glen Hobbie SP	32.00	14.50
☐ 586 Sammy Esposito SP	32.00	14.50
☐ 587 Frank Funk SP	32.00	14.50
☐ 588 Birdie Tebbetts MG	20.00	9.00
☐ 589 Bob Turley	30.00	13.50
☐ 590 Curt Flood	30.00	13.50
☐ 591 Rookie Pitchers SP Sam McDowell Ron Taylor Ron Nischwitz Art Quirk Dick Radatz	70.00	32.00
☐ 592 Rookie Pitchers SP Dan Pfister Bo Belinsky Dave Stenhouse Jim Bouton Joe Bonikowski	70.00	32.00
☐ 593 Rookie Pitchers SP Jack Lamabe Craig Anderson Jack Hamilton Bob Moorhead Bob Veale	40.00	18.00
☐ 594 Rookie Catchers SP Doc Edwards Ken Retzer Bob Uecker Doug Camilli Don Pavletich	75.00	34.00
☐ 595 Rookie Infielders SP Bob Sadowski Felix Torres Marlan Coughtry Ed Charles	40.00	18.00
☐ 596 Rookie Infielders SP Bernie Allen Joe Pepitone Phil Linz Rich Rollins	70.00	32.00
☐ 597 Rookie Infielders SP Jim McKnight Rod Kanehl Amado Samuel Denis Menke	40.00	18.00
☐ 598 Rookie Outfielders SP Al Luplow Manny Jimenez Howie Goss Jim Hickman Ed Olivares	80.00	23.00

1962 Topps Bucks

There are 96 "Baseball Bucks" in this unusual set released in its own one-cent package in 1962. Each "buck" measures 1 3/4" by 4 1/8". Each depicts a player with accompanying biography and facsimile autograph to the left. To the right is found a drawing of the player's home stadium. His team and position are listed under the ribbon

design containing his name. The team affiliation and league are also indicated within circles on the reverse.

	NRMT	VG-E
COMPLETE SET (96)	1250.00	550.00
COMMON BUCK (1-96)	4.50	2.00
WRAPPER (1-CENT)	50.00	22.00

	NRMT	VG-E
☐ 1 Hank Aaron	60.00	27.00
☐ 2 Joe Adcock	6.00	2.70
☐ 3 George Altman	4.50	2.00
☐ 4 Jim Archer	4.50	2.00
☐ 5 Richie Ashburn	25.00	11.00
☐ 6 Ernie Banks	35.00	16.00
☐ 7 Earl Battey	4.50	2.00
☐ 8 Gus Bell	4.50	2.00
☐ 9 Yogi Berra	40.00	18.00
☐ 10 Ken Boyer	8.00	3.60
☐ 11 Jackie Brandt	4.50	2.00
☐ 12 Jim Bunning	25.00	11.00
☐ 13 Lew Burdette	6.00	2.70
☐ 14 Don Cardwell	4.50	2.00
☐ 15 Norm Cash	8.00	3.60
☐ 16 Orlando Cepeda	15.00	6.75
☐ 17 Roberto Clemente	100.00	45.00
☐ 18 Rocky Colavito	15.00	6.75
☐ 19 Chuck Cottier	4.50	2.00
☐ 20 Roger Craig	6.00	2.70
☐ 21 Bennie Daniels	4.50	2.00
☐ 22 Don Demeter	4.50	2.00
☐ 23 Don Drysdale	30.00	13.50
☐ 24 Chuck Estrada	4.50	2.00
☐ 25 Dick Farrell	4.50	2.00
☐ 26 Whitey Ford	40.00	18.00
☐ 27 Nellie Fox	25.00	11.00
☐ 28 Tito Francona	4.50	2.00
☐ 29 Bob Friend	4.50	2.00
☐ 30 Jim Gentile	6.00	2.70
☐ 31 Dick Gernert	4.50	2.00
☐ 32 Lenny Green	4.50	2.00
☐ 33 Dick Groat	6.00	2.70
☐ 34 Woodie Held	4.50	2.00
☐ 35 Don Hoak	4.50	2.00
☐ 36 Gil Hodges	25.00	11.00
☐ 37 Elston Howard	15.00	6.75
☐ 38 Frank Howard	8.00	3.60
☐ 39 Dick Howser	6.00	2.70
☐ 40 Ken Hunt	4.50	2.00
☐ 41 Larry Jackson	4.50	2.00
☐ 42 Joey Jay	4.50	2.00
☐ 43 Al Kaline	35.00	16.00
☐ 44 Harmon Killebrew	25.00	11.00
☐ 45 Sandy Koufax	60.00	27.00
☐ 46 Harvey Kuenn	6.00	2.70
☐ 47 Jim Landis	4.50	2.00
☐ 48 Norm Larker	4.50	2.00
☐ 49 Frank Lary	4.50	2.00
☐ 50 Jerry Lumpe	4.50	2.00
☐ 51 Art Mahaffey	4.50	2.00
☐ 52 Frank Malzone	4.50	2.00
☐ 53 Felix Mantilla	4.50	2.00
☐ 54 Mickey Mantle	200.00	90.00
☐ 55 Roger Maris	50.00	22.00
☐ 56 Eddie Mathews	25.00	11.00
☐ 57 Willie Mays	65.00	29.00
☐ 58 Ken McBride	4.50	2.00
☐ 59 Mike McCormick	4.50	2.00
☐ 60 Stu Miller	4.50	2.00
☐ 61 Minnie Minoso	8.00	3.60
☐ 62 Wally Moon	6.00	2.70
☐ 63 Stan Musial	60.00	27.00
☐ 64 Danny O'Connell	4.50	2.00
☐ 65 Jim O'Toole	4.50	2.00
☐ 66 Camilo Pascual	4.50	2.00
☐ 67 Jim Perry	6.00	2.70
☐ 68 Jimmy Piersall	6.00	2.70
☐ 69 Vada Pinson	8.00	3.60
☐ 70 Juan Pizarro	4.50	2.00
☐ 71 Johnny Podres	6.00	2.70
☐ 72 Vic Power	4.50	2.00
☐ 73 Bob Purkey	4.50	2.00
☐ 74 Pedro Ramos	4.50	2.00
☐ 75 Brooks Robinson	35.00	16.00
☐ 76 Floyd Robinson	4.50	2.00
☐ 77 Frank Robinson	35.00	16.00
☐ 78 John Romano	4.50	2.00
☐ 79 Pete Runnels	4.50	2.00
☐ 80 Don Schwall	4.50	2.00
☐ 81 Bobby Shantz	4.50	2.00
☐ 82 Norm Siebern	4.50	2.00
☐ 83 Roy Sievers	4.50	2.00
☐ 84 Hal Smith	4.50	2.00
☐ 85 Warren Spahn	25.00	11.00
☐ 86 Dick Stuart	6.00	2.70
☐ 87 Tony Taylor	4.50	2.00
☐ 88 Leroy Thomas	6.00	2.70
☐ 89 Gus Triandos	4.50	2.00
☐ 90 Leon Wagner	4.50	2.00
☐ 91 Jerry Walker	4.50	2.00
☐ 92 Bill White	8.00	3.60
☐ 93 Billy Williams	25.00	11.00
☐ 94 Gene Woodling	6.00	2.70
☐ 95 Early Wynn	25.00	11.00
☐ 96 Carl Yastrzemski	35.00	16.00

1962 Topps Stamps Inserts

The 201 baseball player stamps inserted into the Topps regular issue of 1962 are color photos set upon red or yellow backgrounds (100 players for each color). They came in two-stamp panels with a small additional strip which contained advertising for an album. Roy Sievers appears with Kansas City or Philadelphia; the set price includes both versions. Each stamp measures 1 3/8" by 1 7/8". Stamps are unnumbered but are presented here in alphabetical order by team, Baltimore Orioles AL (1-10), Boston Red Sox (11-20), Chicago White Sox (21-30), Cleveland Indians (31-40), Detroit Tigers (41-50), Kansas City A's (51-61), Los Angeles Angels (62-71), Minnesota Twins (72-81), New York Yankees (82-91), Washington Senators (92-101), Chicago Cubs NL (102-111), Cincinnati Reds (112-121), Houston Colt .45's (122-131), Los Angeles Dodgers (132-141), Milwaukee Braves (142-151), New York Mets (152-161), Philadelphia Phillies (162-171), Pittsburgh Pirates (172-181), St. Louis Cardinals (182-191) and San Francisco Giants (192-201).

	NRMT	VG-E
COMPLETE SET (201)	350.00	160.00
COMMON STAMP (1-201)	.80	.35

	NRMT	VG-E
☐ 1 Baltimore Emblem	.80	.35
☐ 2 Jerry Adair	.80	.35
☐ 3 Jackie Brandt	.80	.35
☐ 4 Chuck Estrada	.80	.35
☐ 5 Jim Gentile	1.00	.45
☐ 6 Ron Hansen	.80	.35
☐ 7 Milt Pappas	1.00	.45
☐ 8 Brooks Robinson	8.00	3.60
☐ 9 Gus Triandos	1.00	.45
☐ 10 Hoyt Wilhelm	5.00	2.20
☐ 11 Boston Emblem	.80	.35
☐ 12 Mike Fornieles	.80	.35
☐ 13 Gary Geiger	.80	.35
☐ 14 Frank Malzone	1.00	.45
☐ 15 Bill Monbouquette	.80	.35
☐ 16 Russ Nixon	.80	.35
☐ 17 Pete Runnels	1.00	.45
☐ 18 Chuck Schilling	.80	.35
☐ 19 Don Schwall	.80	.35
☐ 20 Carl Yastrzemski	12.50	5.50
☐ 21 Chicago Emblem	.80	.35
☐ 22 Luis Aparicio	5.00	2.20
☐ 23 Camilo Carreon	.80	.35
☐ 24 Nellie Fox	6.00	2.70
☐ 25 Ray Herbert	.80	.35
☐ 26 Jim Landis	.80	.35
☐ 27 J.C. Martin	.80	.35
☐ 28 Juan Pizzaro	.80	.35
☐ 29 Floyd Robinson	.80	.35
☐ 30 Early Wynn	5.00	2.20
☐ 31 Cleveland Emblem	.80	.35
☐ 32 Ty Cline	.80	.35
☐ 33 Dick Donovan	.80	.35
☐ 34 Tito Francona	.80	.35
☐ 35 Woody Held	.80	.35
☐ 36 Barry Latman	.80	.35
☐ 37 Jim Perry	1.00	.45
☐ 38 Bubba Phillips	.80	.35
☐ 39 Vic Power	.80	.35
☐ 40 Johnny Romano	.80	.35
☐ 41 Detroit Emblem	.80	.35
☐ 42 Steve Boros	1.00	.45
☐ 43 Bill Bruton	.80	.35
☐ 44 Jim Bunning	5.00	2.20
☐ 45 Norm Cash	1.25	.55
☐ 46 Rocky Colavito	4.00	1.80
☐ 47 Al Kaline	8.00	3.60
☐ 48 Frank Lary	1.00	.45
☐ 49 Don Mossi	1.00	.45
☐ 50 Jake Wood	.80	.35
☐ 51 Kansas City Emblem	.80	.35
☐ 52 Jim Archer	.80	.35
☐ 53 Dick Howser	1.50	.70
☐ 54 Jerry Lumpe	.80	.35
☐ 55 Leo Posada	.80	.35
☐ 56 Bob Shaw	.80	.35
☐ 57 Norm Siebern	.80	.35
☐ 58 Roy Sievers (see also 169)	1.50	.70
☐ 59 Gene Stephens	.80	.35
☐ 60 Haywood Sullivan	.80	.35
☐ 61 Jerry Walker	.80	.35
☐ 62 Los Angeles Emblem	.80	.35
☐ 63 Steve Bilko	.80	.35
☐ 64 Ted Bowsfield	.80	.35
☐ 65 Ken Hunt	.80	.35
☐ 66 Ken McBride	.80	.35
☐ 67 Albie Pearson	.80	.35
☐ 68 Bob Rodgers	1.25	.55
☐ 69 George Thomas	.80	.35
☐ 70 Lee Thomas	1.00	.45
☐ 71 Leon Wagner	.80	.35
☐ 72 Minnesota Emblem	.80	.35
☐ 73 Bob Allison	1.00	.45
☐ 74 Earl Battey	.80	.35
☐ 75 Lenny Green	.80	.35
☐ 76 Harmon Killebrew	6.00	2.70
☐ 77 Jack Kralick	.80	.35
☐ 78 Camilo Pascual	1.00	.45
☐ 79 Pedro Ramos	.80	.35
☐ 80 Bill Tuttle	.80	.35
☐ 81 Zoilo Versailles	.80	.35
☐ 82 New York Emblem	1.00	.45
☐ 83 Yogi Berra	12.50	5.50
☐ 84 Clete Boyer	1.25	.55
☐ 85 Whitey Ford	10.00	4.50
☐ 86 Elston Howard	2.50	1.10
☐ 87 Tony Kubek	2.50	1.10
☐ 88 Mickey Mantle	60.00	27.00
☐ 89 Roger Maris	20.00	9.00
☐ 90 Bobby Richardson	2.50	1.10
☐ 91 Bill Skowron	1.50	.70
☐ 92 Washington Emblem	.80	.35
☐ 93 Chuck Cottier	.80	.35
☐ 94 Pete Daley	.80	.35
☐ 95 Bennie Daniels	.80	.35
☐ 96 Chuck Hinton	.80	.35
☐ 97 Bob Johnson	.80	.35
☐ 98 Joe McClain	.80	.35
☐ 99 Danny O'Connell	.80	.35
☐ 100 Jimmy Piersall	1.50	.70
☐ 101 Gene Woodling	1.00	.45
☐ 102 Chicago Emblem	.80	.35
☐ 103 George Altman	.80	.35
☐ 104 Ernie Banks	8.00	3.60
☐ 105 Dick Bertell	.80	.35
☐ 106 Don Cardwell	.80	.35
☐ 107 Dick Ellsworth	.80	.35
☐ 108 Glen Hobbie	.80	.35
☐ 109 Ron Santo	1.50	.70
☐ 110 Barney Schultz	.80	.35
☐ 111 Billy Williams	4.00	1.80
☐ 112 Cincinnati Emblem	.80	.35
☐ 113 Gordon Coleman	.80	.35
☐ 114 Johnny Edwards	.80	.35
☐ 115 Gene Freese	.80	.35
☐ 116 Joey Jay	.80	.35
☐ 117 Eddie Kasko	.80	.35
☐ 118 Jim O'Toole	.80	.35
☐ 119 Vada Pinson	1.50	.70
☐ 120 Bob Purkey	.80	.35
☐ 121 Frank Robinson	8.00	3.60
☐ 122 Houston Emblem	.80	.35
☐ 123 Joe Amalfitano	.80	.35
☐ 124 Bob Aspromonte	.80	.35
☐ 125 Dick Farrell	.80	.35
☐ 126 Al Heist	.80	.35
☐ 127 Sam Jones	.80	.35
☐ 128 Bobby Shantz	1.00	.45
☐ 129 Hal W. Smith	.80	.35
☐ 130 Al Spangler	.80	.35
☐ 131 Bob Tiefenauer	.80	.35

Card	NRMT	VG-E
☐ 132 Los Angeles Emblem	.80	.35
☐ 133 Don Drysdale	6.00	2.70
☐ 134 Ron Fairly	1.00	.45
☐ 135 Frank Howard	1.25	.55
☐ 136 Sandy Koufax	15.00	6.75
☐ 137 Wally Moon	1.00	.45
☐ 138 Johnny Podres	1.50	.70
☐ 139 John Roseboro	.80	.35
☐ 140 Duke Snider	10.00	4.50
☐ 141 Daryl Spencer	.80	.35
☐ 142 Milwaukee Emblem	.80	.35
☐ 143 Hank Aaron	15.00	6.75
☐ 144 Joe Adcock	1.00	.45
☐ 145 Frank Bolling	1.00	.45
☐ 146 Lou Burdette	1.25	.55
☐ 147 Del Crandall	1.00	.45
☐ 148 Eddie Mathews	6.00	2.70
☐ 149 Roy McMillan	.80	.35
☐ 150 Warren Spahn	8.00	3.60
☐ 151 Joe Torre	3.00	1.35
☐ 152 New York Emblem	1.00	.45
☐ 153 Gus Bell	1.00	.45
☐ 154 Roger Craig	1.50	.70
☐ 155 Gil Hodges	6.00	2.70
☐ 156 Jay Hook	1.00	.45
☐ 157 Hobie Landrith	1.00	.45
☐ 158 Felix Mantilla	1.00	.45
☐ 159 Bob L. Miller	1.00	.45
☐ 160 Lee Walls	1.00	.45
☐ 161 Don Zimmer	1.50	.70
☐ 162 Philadelphia Emblem	.80	.35
☐ 163 Ruben Amaro	.80	.35
☐ 164 Jack Baldschun	.80	.35
☐ 165 Johnny Callison UER Name spelled Callizon	1.00	.45
☐ 166 Clay Dalrymple	.80	.35
☐ 167 Don Demeter	.80	.35
☐ 168 Tony Gonzalez	.80	.35
☐ 169 Roy Sievers (see also 58)	1.50	.70
☐ 170 Tony Taylor	1.00	.45
☐ 171 Art Mahaffey	.80	.35
☐ 172 Pittsburgh Emblem	.80	.35
☐ 173 Smoky Burgess	1.00	.45
☐ 174 Roberto Clemente	40.00	18.00
☐ 175 Roy Face	1.25	.55
☐ 176 Bob Friend	1.00	.45
☐ 177 Dick Groat	1.25	.55
☐ 178 Don Hoak	.80	.35
☐ 179 Bill Mazeroski	1.50	.70
☐ 180 Dick Stuart	1.00	.45
☐ 181 Bill Virdon	1.25	.55
☐ 182 St. Louis Emblem	.80	.35
☐ 183 Ken Boyer	1.50	.70
☐ 184 Larry Jackson	.80	.35
☐ 185 Julian Javier	.80	.35
☐ 186 Tim McCarver	2.00	.90
☐ 187 Lindy McDaniel	.80	.35
☐ 188 Minnie Minoso	1.50	.70
☐ 189 Stan Musial	15.00	6.75
☐ 190 Ray Sadecki	.80	.35
☐ 191 Bill White	1.25	.55
☐ 192 San Francisco Emblem	.80	.35
☐ 193 Felipe Alou	1.25	.55
☐ 194 Ed Bailey	.80	.35
☐ 195 Orlando Cepeda	2.00	.90
☐ 196 Jim Davenport	.80	.35
☐ 197 Harvey Kuenn	1.50	.70
☐ 198 Juan Marichal	5.00	2.20
☐ 199 Willie Mays	18.00	8.00
☐ 200 Mike McCormick	1.00	.45
☐ 201 Stu Miller	.80	.35
☐ XX Stamp Album	20.00	9.00

1963 Topps

The cards in this 576-card set measure 2 1/2" by 3 1/2". The sharp color photographs of the 1963 set are a vivid contrast to the drab pictures of 1962. In addition to the "League Leaders" series (1-10) and World Series cards (142-148), the seventh and last series of cards (523-576) contains seven rookie cards (each depicting four players). Cards were issued, among other ways, in one-card penny packs and five-card nickle packs. There were some three-card advertising panels produced by Topps; the players included are from the first series; one panel shows Hoyt Wilhelm, Don Lock, and Bob Duliba on the front with a Stan Musial ad/endorsement on one of the backs. Key Rookie Cards in this set are Bill Freehan, Tony Oliva, Pete Rose, Willie Stargell and Rusty Staub.

	NRMT	VG-E
COMPLETE SET (576)	5000.00	2200.00
COMMON CARD (1-196)	4.00	1.80
COMMON CARD (197-283)	5.00	2.20
COMMON CARD (284-370)	5.00	2.20
COMMON CARD (371-446)	5.00	2.20
COMMON CARD (447-522)	25.00	11.00
COMMON CARD (523-576)	15.00	6.75
WRAPPER (1-CENT)	40.00	18.00
WRAPPER (5-CENT)	30.00	13.50
☐ 1 NL Batting Leaders Tommy Davis Frank Robinson Stan Musial Hank Aaron Bill White	40.00	8.00
☐ 2 AL Batting Leaders Pete Runnels Mickey Mantle Floyd Robinson Norm Siebern Chuck Hinton	50.00	22.00
☐ 3 NL Home Run Leaders Willie Mays Hank Aaron Frank Robinson Orlando Cepeda Ernie Banks	30.00	13.50
☐ 4 AL Home Run Leaders Harmon Killebrew Norm Cash Rocky Colavito Roger Maris Jim Gentile Leon Wagner	18.00	8.00
☐ 5 NL ERA Leaders Sandy Koufax Bob Shaw Bob Purkey Bob Gibson Don Drysdale	20.00	9.00
☐ 6 AL ERA Leaders Hank Aguirre Robin Roberts Whitey Ford Eddie Fisher Dean Chance	10.00	4.50
☐ 7 NL Pitching Leaders Don Drysdale Jack Sanford Bob Purkey Billy O'Dell Art Mahaffey Joe Jay	10.00	4.50
☐ 8 AL Pitching Leaders Ralph Terry Dick Donovan Ray Herbert Jim Bunning Camilo Pascual	8.00	3.60
☐ 9 NL Strikeout Leaders Don Drysdale Sandy Koufax Bob Gibson Billy O'Dell Dick Farrell	20.00	9.00
☐ 10 AL Strikeout Leaders Camilo Pascual Jim Bunning Ralph Terry Juan Pizarro Jim Kaat	8.00	3.60
☐ 11 Lee Walls	4.00	1.80
☐ 12 Steve Barber	4.00	1.80
☐ 13 Philadelphia Phillies Team Card	8.00	3.60
☐ 14 Pedro Ramos	4.00	1.80
☐ 15 Ken Hubbs UER (No position listed on front of card)	10.00	4.50
☐ 16 Al Smith	4.00	1.80
☐ 17 Ryne Duren	8.00	3.60
☐ 18 Buc Blasters Smoky Burgess Dick Stuart Bob Clemente Bob Skinner	70.00	32.00
☐ 19 Pete Burnside	4.00	1.80
☐ 20 Tony Kubek	8.00	3.60
☐ 21 Marty Keough	4.00	1.80
☐ 22 Curt Simmons	8.00	3.60
☐ 23 Ed Lopat MG	8.00	3.60
☐ 24 Bob Bruce	4.00	1.80
☐ 25 Al Kaline	45.00	20.00
☐ 26 Ray Moore	4.00	1.80
☐ 27 Choo Choo Coleman	8.00	3.60
☐ 28 Mike Fornieles	4.00	1.80
☐ 29A 1962 Rookie Stars Sammy Ellis Ray Culp John Boozer Jesse Gonder	8.00	3.60
☐ 29B 1963 Rookie Stars Sammy Ellis Ray Culp John Boozer Jesse Gonder	4.00	1.80
☐ 30 Harvey Kuenn	8.00	3.60
☐ 31 Cal Koonce	4.00	1.80
☐ 32 Tony Gonzalez	4.00	1.80
☐ 33 Bo Belinsky	8.00	3.60
☐ 34 Dick Schofield	4.00	1.80
☐ 35 John Buzhardt	4.00	1.80
☐ 36 Jerry Kindall	4.00	1.80
☐ 37 Jerry Lynch	4.00	1.80
☐ 38 Bud Daley	8.00	3.60
☐ 39 Angels Team	8.00	3.60
☐ 40 Vic Power	8.00	3.60
☐ 41 Charley Lau	8.00	3.60
☐ 42 Stan Williams (Listed as Yankee on card but LA cap)	8.00	3.60
☐ 43 Veteran Masters Casey Stengel MG Gene Woodling	8.00	3.60
☐ 44 Terry Fox	4.00	1.80
☐ 45 Bob Aspromonte	4.00	1.80
☐ 46 Tommie Aaron	8.00	3.60
☐ 47 Don Lock	4.00	1.80
☐ 48 Birdie Tebbetts MG	8.00	3.60
☐ 49 Dal Maxvill	8.00	3.60
☐ 50 Billy Pierce	8.00	3.60
☐ 51 George Alusik	4.00	1.80
☐ 52 Chuck Schilling	4.00	1.80
☐ 53 Joe Moeller	8.00	3.60
☐ 54A 1962 Rookie Stars Nelson Mathews Harry Fanok Jack Cullen Dave DeBusschere	15.00	6.75
☐ 54B 1963 Rookie Stars Nelson Mathews Harry Fanok Jack Cullen Dave DeBusschere	8.00	3.60
☐ 55 Bill Virdon	8.00	3.60
☐ 56 Dennis Bennett	4.00	1.80
☐ 57 Billy Moran	4.00	1.80
☐ 58 Bob Will	4.00	1.80
☐ 59 Craig Anderson	4.00	1.80
☐ 60 Elston Howard	8.00	3.60
☐ 61 Ernie Bowman	4.00	1.80
☐ 62 Bob Hendley	4.00	1.80
☐ 63 Reds Team	8.00	3.60
☐ 64 Dick McAuliffe	8.00	3.60
☐ 65 Jackie Brandt	4.00	1.80
☐ 66 Mike Joyce	4.00	1.80
☐ 67 Ed Charles	4.00	1.80
☐ 68 Friendly Foes Duke Snider Gil Hodges	25.00	11.00
☐ 69 Bud Zipfel	4.00	1.80
☐ 70 Jim O'Toole	8.00	3.60
☐ 71 Bobby Wine	8.00	3.60
☐ 72 Johnny Romano	4.00	1.80
☐ 73 Bobby Bragan MG	8.00	3.60
☐ 74 Denny Lemaster	4.00	1.80
☐ 75 Bob Allison	8.00	3.60
☐ 76 Earl Wilson	8.00	3.60
☐ 77 Al Spangler	4.00	1.80
☐ 78 Marv Throneberry	8.00	3.60
☐ 79 Checklist 1	10.00	2.00
☐ 80 Jim Gilliam	8.00	3.60
☐ 81 Jim Schaffer	4.00	1.80
☐ 82 Ed Rakow	4.00	1.80
☐ 83 Charley James	4.00	1.80
☐ 84 Ron Kline	4.00	1.80
☐ 85 Tom Haller	8.00	3.60
☐ 86 Charley Maxwell	8.00	3.60
☐ 87 Bob Veale	8.00	3.60
☐ 88 Ron Hansen	4.00	1.80
☐ 89 Dick Stigman	4.00	1.80
☐ 90 Gordy Coleman	8.00	3.60
☐ 91 Dallas Green	8.00	3.60
☐ 92 Hector Lopez	8.00	3.60

Card		
☐ 93 Galen Cisco	4.00	1.80
☐ 94 Bob Schmidt	4.00	1.80
☐ 95 Larry Jackson	4.00	1.80
☐ 96 Lou Clinton	4.00	1.80
☐ 97 Bob Duliba	4.00	1.80
☐ 98 George Thomas	4.00	1.80
☐ 99 Jim Umbricht	4.00	1.80
☐ 100 Joe Cunningham	4.00	1.80
☐ 101 Joe Gibbon	4.00	1.80
☐ 102A Checklist 2	10.00	2.00
(Red on yellow)		
☐ 102B Checklist 2	10.00	2.00
(White on red)		
☐ 103 Chuck Essegian	4.00	1.80
☐ 104 Lew Krausse	4.00	1.80
☐ 105 Ron Fairly	8.00	3.60
☐ 106 Bobby Bolin	4.00	1.80
☐ 107 Jim Hickman	8.00	3.60
☐ 108 Hoyt Wilhelm	10.00	4.50
☐ 109 Lee Maye	4.00	1.80
☐ 110 Rich Rollins	8.00	3.60
☐ 111 Al Jackson	4.00	1.80
☐ 112 Dick Brown	4.00	1.80
☐ 113 Don Landrum UER	4.00	1.80
(Photo actually		
Ron Santo)		
☐ 114 Dan Osinski	4.00	1.80
☐ 115 Carl Yastrzemski	40.00	18.00
☐ 116 Jim Brosnan	8.00	3.60
☐ 117 Jacke Davis	4.00	1.80
☐ 118 Sherm Lollar	4.00	1.80
☐ 119 Bob Lillis	4.00	1.80
☐ 120 Roger Maris	45.00	20.00
☐ 121 Jim Hannan	4.00	1.80
☐ 122 Julio Gotay	4.00	1.80
☐ 123 Frank Howard	8.00	3.60
☐ 124 Dick Howser	8.00	3.60
☐ 125 Robin Roberts	14.00	6.25
☐ 126 Bob Uecker	14.00	6.25
☐ 127 Bill Tuttle	4.00	1.80
☐ 128 Matty Alou	8.00	3.60
☐ 129 Gary Bell	4.00	1.80
☐ 130 Dick Groat	8.00	3.60
☐ 131 Washington Senators	8.00	3.60
Team Card		
☐ 132 Jack Hamilton	4.00	1.80
☐ 133 Gene Freese	4.00	1.80
☐ 134 Bob Scheffing MG	4.00	1.80
☐ 135 Richie Ashburn	20.00	9.00
☐ 136 Ike Delock	4.00	1.80
☐ 137 Mack Jones	4.00	1.80
☐ 138 Pride of NL	70.00	32.00
Willie Mays		
Stan Musial		
☐ 139 Earl Averill	4.00	1.80
☐ 140 Frank Lary	8.00	3.60
☐ 141 Manny Mota	8.00	3.60
☐ 142 Whitey Ford WS	10.00	4.50
☐ 143 Jack Sanford WS	8.00	3.60
☐ 144 Roger Maris WS	12.00	5.50
☐ 145 Chuck Hiller WS	8.00	3.60
☐ 146 Tom Tresh WS	8.00	3.60
☐ 147 Billy Pierce WS	8.00	3.60
☐ 148 Ralph Terry WS	8.00	3.60
☐ 149 Marv Breeding	4.00	1.80
☐ 150 Johnny Podres	8.00	3.60
☐ 151 Pirates Team	8.00	3.60
☐ 152 Ron Nischwitz	4.00	1.80
☐ 153 Hal Smith	4.00	1.80
☐ 154 Walter Alston MG	8.00	3.60
☐ 155 Bill Stafford	4.00	1.80
☐ 156 Roy McMillan	8.00	3.60
☐ 157 Diego Segui	8.00	3.60
☐ 158 Rookie Stars	8.00	3.60
Rogelio Alvares		
Dave Roberts		
Tommy Harper		
Bob Saverine		
☐ 159 Jim Pagliaroni	4.00	1.80
☐ 160 Juan Pizarro	4.00	1.80
☐ 161 Frank Torre	8.00	3.60
☐ 162 Twins Team	8.00	3.60
☐ 163 Don Larsen	8.00	3.60
☐ 164 Bubba Morton	4.00	1.80
☐ 165 Jim Kaat	8.00	3.60
☐ 166 Johnny Keane MG	4.00	1.80
☐ 167 Jim Fregosi	8.00	3.60
☐ 168 Russ Nixon	4.00	1.80
☐ 169 Rookie Stars	25.00	11.00
Dick Egan		
Julio Navarro		
Tommie Sisk		
Gaylord Perry		
☐ 170 Joe Adcock	8.00	3.60
☐ 171 Steve Hamilton	4.00	1.80
☐ 172 Gene Oliver	4.00	1.80
☐ 173 Bombers' Best	200.00	90.00
Tom Tresh		
Mickey Mantle		
Bobby Richardson		
☐ 174 Larry Burright	4.00	1.80
☐ 175 Bob Buhl	8.00	3.60
☐ 176 Jim King	4.00	1.80
☐ 177 Bubba Phillips	4.00	1.80
☐ 178 Johnny Edwards	4.00	1.80
☐ 179 Ron Piche	4.00	1.80
☐ 180 Bill Skowron	8.00	3.60
☐ 181 Sammy Esposito	4.00	1.80
☐ 182 Albie Pearson	8.00	3.60
☐ 183 Joe Pepitone	8.00	3.60
☐ 184 Vern Law	8.00	3.60
☐ 185 Chuck Hiller	4.00	1.80
☐ 186 Jerry Zimmerman	4.00	1.80
☐ 187 Willie Kirkland	4.00	1.80
☐ 188 Eddie Bressoud	4.00	1.80
☐ 189 Dave Giusti	8.00	3.60
☐ 190 Minnie Minoso	8.00	3.60
☐ 191 Checklist 3	10.00	2.00
☐ 192 Clay Dalrymple	4.00	1.80
☐ 193 Andre Rodgers	4.00	1.80
☐ 194 Joe Nuxhall	8.00	3.60
☐ 195 Manny Jimenez	4.00	1.80
☐ 196 Doug Camilli	4.00	1.80
☐ 197 Roger Craig	8.00	3.60
☐ 198 Lenny Green	5.00	2.20
☐ 199 Joe Amalfitano	5.00	2.20
☐ 200 Mickey Mantle	550.00	250.00
☐ 201 Cecil Butler	5.00	2.20
☐ 202 Boston Red Sox	8.00	3.60
Team Card		
☐ 203 Chico Cardenas	8.00	3.60
☐ 204 Don Nottebart	5.00	2.20
☐ 205 Luis Aparicio	15.00	6.75
☐ 206 Ray Washburn	5.00	2.20
☐ 207 Ken Hunt	5.00	2.20
☐ 208 Rookie Stars	5.00	2.20
Ron Herbel		
John Miller		
Wally Wolf		
Ron Taylor		
☐ 209 Hobie Landrith	5.00	2.20
☐ 210 Sandy Koufax !	175.00	80.00
☐ 211 Fred Whitfield	5.00	2.20
☐ 212 Glen Hobbie	5.00	2.20
☐ 213 Billy Hitchcock MG	5.00	2.20
☐ 214 Orlando Pena	5.00	2.20
☐ 215 Bob Skinner	8.00	3.60
☐ 216 Gene Conley	8.00	3.60
☐ 217 Joe Christopher	5.00	2.20
☐ 218 Tiger Twirlers	8.00	3.60
Frank Lary		
Don Mossi		
Jim Bunning		
☐ 219 Chuck Cottier	5.00	2.20
☐ 220 Camilo Pascual	8.00	3.60
☐ 221 Cookie Rojas	8.00	3.60
☐ 222 Cubs Team	8.00	3.60
☐ 223 Eddie Fisher	5.00	2.20
☐ 224 Mike Roarke	5.00	2.20
☐ 225 Joey Jay	5.00	2.20
☐ 226 Julian Javier	8.00	3.60
☐ 227 Jim Grant	8.00	3.60
☐ 228 Rookie Stars	40.00	18.00
Max Alvis		
Bob Bailey		
Tony Oliva		
(Listed as Pedro)		
Ed Kranepool		
☐ 229 Willie Davis	8.00	3.60
☐ 230 Pete Runnels	8.00	3.60
☐ 231 Eli Grba UER	5.00	2.20
(Large photo is		
Ryne Duren)		
☐ 232 Frank Malzone	8.00	3.60
☐ 233 Casey Stengel MG	20.00	9.00
☐ 234 Dave Nicholson	5.00	2.20
☐ 235 Billy O'Dell	5.00	2.20
☐ 236 Bill Bryan	5.00	2.20
☐ 237 Jim Coates	8.00	3.60
☐ 238 Lou Johnson	5.00	2.20
☐ 239 Harvey Haddix	8.00	3.60
☐ 240 Rocky Colavito	15.00	6.75
☐ 241 Bob Smith	5.00	2.20
☐ 242 Power Plus	60.00	27.00
Ernie Banks		
Hank Aaron		
☐ 243 Don Leppert	5.00	2.20
☐ 244 John Tsitouris	5.00	2.20
☐ 245 Gil Hodges	20.00	9.00
☐ 246 Lee Stange	5.00	2.20
☐ 247 Yankees Team	40.00	18.00
☐ 248 Tito Francona	5.00	2.20
☐ 249 Leo Burke	5.00	2.20
☐ 250 Stan Musial	125.00	55.00
☐ 251 Jack Lamabe	5.00	2.20
☐ 252 Ron Santo	10.00	4.50
☐ 253 Rookie Stars	5.00	2.20
Len Gabrielson		
Pete Jernigan		
John Wojcik		
Deacon Jones		
☐ 254 Mike Hershberger	5.00	2.20
☐ 255 Bob Shaw	5.00	2.20
☐ 256 Jerry Lumpe	5.00	2.20
☐ 257 Hank Aguirre	5.00	2.20
☐ 258 Alvin Dark MG	8.00	3.60
☐ 259 Johnny Logan	8.00	3.60
☐ 260 Jim Gentile	8.00	3.60
☐ 261 Bob Miller	5.00	2.20
☐ 262 Ellis Burton	5.00	2.20
☐ 263 Dave Stenhouse	5.00	2.20
☐ 264 Phil Linz	5.00	2.20
☐ 265 Vada Pinson	8.00	3.60
☐ 266 Bob Allen	5.00	2.20
☐ 267 Carl Sawatski	5.00	2.20
☐ 268 Don Demeter	5.00	2.20
☐ 269 Don Mincher	5.00	2.20
☐ 270 Felipe Alou	8.00	3.60
☐ 271 Dean Stone	5.00	2.20
☐ 272 Danny Murphy	5.00	2.20
☐ 273 Sammy Taylor	5.00	2.20
☐ 274 Checklist 4	10.00	2.00
☐ 275 Eddie Mathews	20.00	9.00
☐ 276 Barry Shetrone	5.00	2.20
☐ 277 Dick Farrell	5.00	2.20
☐ 278 Chico Fernandez	5.00	2.20
☐ 279 Wally Moon	8.00	3.60
☐ 280 Bob Rodgers	5.00	2.20
☐ 281 Tom Sturdivant	5.00	2.20
☐ 282 Bobby Del Greco	5.00	2.20
☐ 283 Roy Sievers	8.00	3.60
☐ 284 Dave Sisler	5.00	2.20
☐ 285 Dick Stuart	8.00	3.60
☐ 286 Stu Miller	8.00	3.60
☐ 287 Dick Bertell	5.00	2.20
☐ 288 Chicago White Sox	8.00	3.60
Team Card		
☐ 289 Hal Brown	5.00	2.20
☐ 290 Bill White	8.00	3.60
☐ 291 Don Rudolph	5.00	2.20
☐ 292 Pumpsie Green	8.00	3.60
☐ 293 Bill Pleis	5.00	2.20
☐ 294 Bill Rigney MG	5.00	2.20
☐ 295 Ed Roebuck	5.00	2.20
☐ 296 Doc Edwards	5.00	2.20
☐ 297 Jim Golden	5.00	2.20
☐ 298 Don Dillard	5.00	2.20
☐ 299 Rookie Stars	8.00	3.60
Dave Morehead		
Bob Dustal		
Tom Butters		
Dan Schneider		
☐ 300 Willie Mays	135.00	60.00
☐ 301 Bill Fischer	5.00	2.20
☐ 302 Whitey Herzog	8.00	3.60
☐ 303 Earl Francis	5.00	2.20
☐ 304 Harry Bright	5.00	2.20
☐ 305 Don Hoak	5.00	2.20
☐ 306 Star Receivers	8.00	3.60
Earl Battey		
Elston Howard		
☐ 307 Chet Nichols	5.00	2.20
☐ 308 Camilo Carreon	5.00	2.20
☐ 309 Jim Brewer	5.00	2.20
☐ 310 Tommy Davis	8.00	3.60
☐ 311 Joe McClain	5.00	2.20
☐ 312 Houston Colts	25.00	11.00
Team Card		
☐ 313 Ernie Broglio	5.00	2.20
☐ 314 John Goryl	5.00	2.20
☐ 315 Ralph Terry	8.00	3.60
☐ 316 Norm Sherry	8.00	3.60
☐ 317 Sam McDowell	8.00	3.60
☐ 318 Gene Mauch MG	8.00	3.60
☐ 319 Joe Gaines	5.00	2.20
☐ 320 Warren Spahn	40.00	18.00
☐ 321 Gino Cimoli	5.00	2.20
☐ 322 Bob Turley	8.00	3.60
☐ 323 Bill Mazeroski	10.00	4.50
☐ 324 Rookie Stars	8.00	3.60
George Williams		
Pete Ward		
Phil Roof		
Vic Davalillo		
☐ 325 Jack Sanford	5.00	2.20
☐ 326 Hank Foiles	5.00	2.20
☐ 327 Paul Foytack	5.00	2.20
☐ 328 Dick Williams	8.00	3.60
☐ 329 Lindy McDaniel	8.00	3.60
☐ 330 Chuck Hinton	5.00	2.20
☐ 331 Series Foes	8.00	3.60
Bill Stafford		

Bill Pierce
☐ 332 Joel Horlen 8.00 3.60
☐ 333 Carl Warwick 5.00 2.20
☐ 334 Wynn Hawkins 5.00 2.20
☐ 335 Leon Wagner 5.00 2.20
☐ 336 Ed Bauta 5.00 2.20
☐ 337 Dodgers Team 25.00 11.00
☐ 338 Russ Kemmerer 5.00 2.20
☐ 339 Ted Bowsfield 5.00 2.20
☐ 340 Yogi Berra P/CO 70.00 32.00
☐ 341 Jack Baldschun 5.00 2.20
☐ 342 Gene Woodling 8.00 3.60
☐ 343 Johnny Pesky MG 8.00 3.60
☐ 344 Don Schwall 5.00 2.20
☐ 345 Brooks Robinson 60.00 27.00
☐ 346 Billy Hoeft 5.00 2.20
☐ 347 Joe Torre 14.00 6.25
☐ 348 Vic Wertz 8.00 3.60
☐ 349 Zoilo Versalles 8.00 3.60
☐ 350 Bob Purkey 5.00 2.20
☐ 351 Al Luplow 5.00 2.20
☐ 352 Ken Johnson 5.00 2.20
☐ 353 Billy Williams 30.00 13.50
☐ 354 Dom Zanni 5.00 2.20
☐ 355 Dean Chance 8.00 3.60
☐ 356 John Schaive 5.00 2.20
☐ 357 George Altman 5.00 2.20
☐ 358 Milt Pappas 8.00 3.60
☐ 359 Haywood Sullivan 8.00 3.60
☐ 360 Don Drysdale 40.00 18.00
☐ 361 Clete Boyer 8.00 3.60
☐ 362 Checklist 5 10.00 2.00
☐ 363 Dick Radatz 8.00 3.60
☐ 364 Howie Goss 5.00 2.20
☐ 365 Jim Bunning 15.00 6.75
☐ 366 Tony Taylor 8.00 3.60
☐ 367 Tony Cloninger 5.00 2.20
☐ 368 Ed Bailey 5.00 2.20
☐ 369 Jim Lemon 5.00 2.20
☐ 370 Dick Donovan 5.00 2.20
☐ 371 Rod Kanehl 8.00 3.60
☐ 372 Don Lee 5.00 2.20
☐ 373 Jim Campbell 5.00 2.20
☐ 374 Claude Osteen 8.00 3.60
☐ 375 Ken Boyer 8.00 3.60
☐ 376 John Wyatt 5.00 2.20
☐ 377 Baltimore Orioles 10.00 4.50
Team Card
☐ 378 Bill Henry 5.00 2.20
☐ 379 Bob Anderson 5.00 2.20
☐ 380 Ernie Banks UER 75.00 34.00
(Back has career Major
and Minor, but he
never played in Minors)
☐ 381 Frank Baumann 5.00 2.20
☐ 382 Ralph Houk MG 8.00 3.60
☐ 383 Pete Richert 5.00 2.20
☐ 384 Bob Tillman 5.00 2.20
☐ 385 Art Mahaffey 5.00 2.20
☐ 386 Rookie Stars 5.00 2.20
Ed Kirkpatrick
John Bateman
Larry Bearnarth
Garry Roggenburk
☐ 387 Al McBean 5.00 2.20
☐ 388 Jim Davenport 8.00 3.60
☐ 389 Frank Sullivan 5.00 2.20
☐ 390 Hank Aaron 125.00 55.00
☐ 391 Bill Dailey 5.00 2.20
☐ 392 Tribe Thumpers 5.00 2.20
Johnny Romano
Tito Francona
☐ 393 Ken MacKenzie 8.00 3.60
☐ 394 Tim McCarver 14.00 6.25
☐ 395 Don McMahon 5.00 2.20
☐ 396 Joe Koppe 5.00 2.20
☐ 397 Kansas City Athletics 8.00 3.60
Team Card
☐ 398 Boog Powell 25.00 11.00
☐ 399 Dick Ellsworth 5.00 2.20
☐ 400 Frank Robinson 60.00 27.00
☐ 401 Jim Bouton 14.00 6.25
☐ 402 Mickey Vernon MG 8.00 3.60
☐ 403 Ron Perranoski 8.00 3.60
☐ 404 Bob Oldis 5.00 2.20
☐ 405 Floyd Robinson 5.00 2.20
☐ 406 Howie Koplitz 5.00 2.20
☐ 407 Rookie Stars 5.00 2.20
Frank Kostro
Chico Ruiz
Larry Elliot
Dick Simpson
☐ 408 Billy Gardner 5.00 2.20
☐ 409 Roy Face 8.00 3.60
☐ 410 Earl Battey 5.00 2.20
☐ 411 Jim Constable 5.00 2.20
☐ 412 Dodger Big Three 40.00 18.00
Johnny Podres
Don Drysdale
Sandy Koufax
☐ 413 Jerry Walker 5.00 2.20
☐ 414 Ty Cline 5.00 2.20
☐ 415 Bob Gibson 60.00 27.00
☐ 416 Alex Grammas 5.00 2.20
☐ 417 Giants Team 8.00 3.60
☐ 418 John Orsino 5.00 2.20
☐ 419 Tracy Stallard 5.00 2.20
☐ 420 Bobby Richardson 14.00 6.25
☐ 421 Tom Morgan 5.00 2.20
☐ 422 Fred Hutchinson MG 8.00 3.60
☐ 423 Ed Hobaugh 5.00 2.20
☐ 424 Charlie Smith 5.00 2.20
☐ 425 Smoky Burgess 8.00 3.60
☐ 426 Barry Latman 5.00 2.20
☐ 427 Bernie Allen 5.00 2.20
☐ 428 Carl Boles 5.00 2.20
☐ 429 Lou Burdette 8.00 3.60
☐ 430 Norm Siebern 5.00 2.20
☐ 431A Checklist 6 10.00 2.00
(White on red)
☐ 431B Checklist 6 30.00 6.00
(Black on orange)
☐ 432 Roman Mejias 5.00 2.20
☐ 433 Denis Menke 5.00 2.20
☐ 434 John Callison 8.00 3.60
☐ 435 Woody Held 5.00 2.20
☐ 436 Tim Harkness 8.00 3.60
☐ 437 Bill Bruton 5.00 2.20
☐ 438 Wes Stock 5.00 2.20
☐ 439 Don Zimmer 8.00 3.60
☐ 440 Juan Marichal 30.00 13.50
☐ 441 Lee Thomas 8.00 3.60
☐ 442 J.C. Hartman 5.00 2.20
☐ 443 Jimmy Piersall 8.00 3.60
☐ 444 Jim Maloney 8.00 3.60
☐ 445 Norm Cash 8.00 3.60
☐ 446 Whitey Ford 40.00 18.00
☐ 447 Felix Mantilla 25.00 11.00
☐ 448 Jack Kralick 25.00 11.00
☐ 449 Jose Tartabull 25.00 11.00
☐ 450 Bob Friend 30.00 13.50
☐ 451 Indians Team 40.00 18.00
☐ 452 Barney Schultz 25.00 11.00
☐ 453 Jake Wood 25.00 11.00
☐ 454A Art Fowler 25.00 11.00
(Card number on
white background)
☐ 454B Art Fowler 30.00 13.50
(Card number on
orange background)
☐ 455 Ruben Amaro 25.00 11.00
☐ 456 Jim Coker 25.00 11.00
☐ 457 Tex Clevenger 25.00 11.00
☐ 458 Al Lopez MG 30.00 13.50
☐ 459 Dick LeMay 25.00 11.00
☐ 460 Del Crandall 30.00 13.50
☐ 461 Norm Bass 25.00 11.00
☐ 462 Wally Post 25.00 11.00
☐ 463 Joe Schaffernoth 25.00 11.00
☐ 464 Ken Aspromonte 25.00 11.00
☐ 465 Chuck Estrada 25.00 11.00
☐ 466 Rookie Stars SP 60.00 27.00
Nate Oliver
Tony Martinez
Bill Freehan
Jerry Robinson
☐ 467 Phil Ortega 25.00 11.00
☐ 468 Carroll Hardy 30.00 13.50
☐ 469 Jay Hook 30.00 13.50
☐ 470 Tom Tresh SP 60.00 27.00
☐ 471 Ken Retzer 25.00 11.00
☐ 472 Lou Brock 100.00 45.00
☐ 473 New York Mets 100.00 45.00
Team Card
☐ 474 Jack Fisher 25.00 11.00
☐ 475 Gus Triandos 30.00 13.50
☐ 476 Frank Funk 25.00 11.00
☐ 477 Donn Clendenon 30.00 13.50
☐ 478 Paul Brown 25.00 11.00
☐ 479 Ed Brinkman 25.00 11.00
☐ 480 Bill Monbouquette 25.00 11.00
☐ 481 Bob Taylor 25.00 11.00
☐ 482 Felix Torres 25.00 11.00
☐ 483 Jim Owens UER 25.00 11.00
(Stat column for Wins
has an R instead)
☐ 484 Dale Long SP 30.00 13.50
☐ 485 Jim Landis 25.00 11.00
☐ 486 Ray Sadecki 25.00 11.00
☐ 487 John Roseboro 30.00 13.50
☐ 488 Jerry Adair 25.00 11.00
☐ 489 Paul Toth 25.00 11.00
☐ 490 Willie McCovey 125.00 55.00
☐ 491 Harry Craft MG 25.00 11.00
☐ 492 Dave Wickersham 25.00 11.00
☐ 493 Walt Bond 25.00 11.00
☐ 494 Phil Regan 25.00 11.00
☐ 495 Frank Thomas SP 30.00 13.50
☐ 496 Rookie Stars 30.00 13.50
Steve Dalkowski
Fred Newman
Jack Smith
Carl Bouldin
☐ 497 Bennie Daniels 25.00 11.00
☐ 498 Eddie Kasko 25.00 11.00
☐ 499 J.C. Martin 25.00 11.00
☐ 500 Harmon Killebrew SP 150.00 70.00
☐ 501 Joe Azcue 25.00 11.00
☐ 502 Daryl Spencer 25.00 11.00
☐ 503 Braves Team 40.00 18.00
☐ 504 Bob Johnson 25.00 11.00
☐ 505 Curt Flood 30.00 13.50
☐ 506 Gene Green 25.00 11.00
☐ 507 Roland Sheldon 30.00 13.50
☐ 508 Ted Savage 25.00 11.00
☐ 509A Checklist 7 40.00 8.00
(Copyright centered)
☐ 509B Checklist 7 40.00 8.00
(Copyright to right)
☐ 510 Ken McBride 25.00 11.00
☐ 511 Charlie Neal 30.00 13.50
☐ 512 Cal McLish 25.00 11.00
☐ 513 Gary Geiger 25.00 11.00
☐ 514 Larry Osborne 25.00 11.00
☐ 515 Don Elston 25.00 11.00
☐ 516 Purnell Goldy 25.00 11.00
☐ 517 Hal Woodeshick 25.00 11.00
☐ 518 Don Blasingame 25.00 11.00
☐ 519 Claude Raymond 25.00 11.00
☐ 520 Orlando Cepeda 30.00 13.50
☐ 521 Dan Pfister 25.00 11.00
☐ 522 Rookie Stars 30.00 13.50
Mel Nelson
Gary Peters
Jim Roland
Art Quirk
☐ 523 Bill Kunkel 15.00 6.75
☐ 524 Cardinals Team 30.00 13.50
☐ 525 Nellie Fox 50.00 22.00
☐ 526 Dick Hall 15.00 6.75
☐ 527 Ed Sadowski 15.00 6.75
☐ 528 Carl Willey 15.00 6.75
☐ 529 Wes Covington 15.00 6.75
☐ 530 Don Mossi 20.00 9.00
☐ 531 Sam Mele MG 15.00 6.75
☐ 532 Steve Boros 15.00 6.75
☐ 533 Bobby Shantz 20.00 9.00
☐ 534 Ken Walters 15.00 6.75
☐ 535 Jim Perry 20.00 9.00
☐ 536 Norm Larker 15.00 6.75
☐ 537 Rookie Stars 1000.00 450.00
Pedro Gonzalez
Ken McMullen
Al Weis
Pete Rose
☐ 538 George Brunet 15.00 6.75
☐ 539 Wayne Causey 15.00 6.75
☐ 540 Bob Clemente 375.00 170.00
☐ 541 Ron Moeller 15.00 6.75
☐ 542 Lou Klimchock 15.00 6.75
☐ 543 Russ Snyder 15.00 6.75
☐ 544 Rookie Stars 40.00 18.00
Duke Carmel
Bill Haas
Rusty Staub
Dick Phillips
☐ 545 Jose Pagan 15.00 6.75
☐ 546 Hal Reniff 20.00 9.00
☐ 547 Gus Bell 15.00 6.75
☐ 548 Tom Satriano 15.00 6.75
☐ 549 Rookie Stars 15.00 6.75
Marcelino Lopez
Pete Lovrich
Paul Ratliff
Elmo Plaskett
☐ 550 Duke Snider 75.00 34.00
☐ 551 Billy Klaus 15.00 6.75
☐ 552 Detroit Tigers 50.00 22.00
Team Card
☐ 553 Rookie Stars 125.00 55.00
Brock Davis
Jim Gosger
Willie Stargell
John Herrnstein
☐ 554 Hank Fischer 15.00 6.75
☐ 555 John Blanchard 20.00 9.00
☐ 556 Al Worthington 15.00 6.75
☐ 557 Cuno Barragan 15.00 6.75
☐ 558 Rookie Stars 20.00 9.00
Bill Faul
Ron Hunt
Al Moran
Bob Lipski

Card	NRMT	VG-E
☐ 559 Danny Murtaugh MG	15.00	6.75
☐ 560 Ray Herbert	15.00	6.75
☐ 561 Mike De La Hoz	15.00	6.75
☐ 562 Rookie Stars	25.00	11.00
Randy Cardinal		
Dave McNally		
Ken Rowe		
Don Rowe		
☐ 563 Mike McCormick	15.00	6.75
☐ 564 George Banks	15.00	6.75
☐ 565 Larry Sherry	15.00	6.75
☐ 566 Cliff Cook	15.00	6.75
☐ 567 Jim Duffalo	15.00	6.75
☐ 568 Bob Sadowski	15.00	6.75
☐ 569 Luis Arroyo	20.00	9.00
☐ 570 Frank Bolling	15.00	6.75
☐ 571 Johnny Klippstein	15.00	6.75
☐ 572 Jack Spring	15.00	6.75
☐ 573 Coot Veal	15.00	6.75
☐ 574 Hal Kolstad	15.00	6.75
☐ 575 Don Cardwell	15.00	6.75
☐ 576 Johnny Temple	25.00	9.50

1963 Topps Stick-Ons Inserts

Stick-on inserts were found in several series of the 1963 Topps cards. Each sticker measures 1 1/4" by 2 3/4". They are found either with blank backs or with instructions on the reverse. Stick-ons with the instruction backs are a little tougher to find. The player photo is in color inside an oval with name, team and postion below. Since these inserts were unnumbered, they are ordered below alphabetically.

	NRMT	VG-E
COMPLETE SET (46)	300.00	135.00
COMMON STICKER (1-46)	2.50	1.10
☐ 1 Hank Aaron	30.00	13.50
☐ 2 Luis Aparicio	10.00	4.50
☐ 3 Richie Ashburn	12.00	5.50
☐ 4 Bob Aspromonte	2.50	1.10
☐ 5 Ernie Banks	15.00	6.75
☐ 6 Ken Boyer	5.00	2.20
☐ 7 Jim Bunning	10.00	4.50
☐ 8 Johnny Callison	2.50	1.10
☐ 9 Roberto Clemente	50.00	22.00
☐ 10 Orlando Cepeda	7.50	3.40
☐ 11 Rocky Colavito	7.50	3.40
☐ 12 Tommy Davis	3.50	1.55
☐ 13 Dick Donovan	2.50	1.10
☐ 14 Don Drysdale	12.00	5.50
☐ 15 Dick Farrell	2.50	1.10
☐ 16 Jim Gentile	3.50	1.55
☐ 17 Ray Herbert	2.50	1.10
☐ 18 Chuck Hinton	2.50	1.10
☐ 19 Ken Hubbs	3.50	1.55
☐ 20 Al Jackson	2.50	1.10
☐ 21 Al Kaline	15.00	6.75
☐ 22 Harmon Killebrew	10.00	4.50
☐ 23 Sandy Koufax	25.00	11.00
☐ 24 Jerry Lumpe	2.50	1.10
☐ 25 Art Mahaffey	2.50	1.10
☐ 26 Mickey Mantle	80.00	36.00
☐ 27 Willie Mays	35.00	16.00
☐ 28 Bill Mazeroski	5.00	2.20
☐ 29 Bill Monbouquette	2.50	1.10
☐ 30 Stan Musial	25.00	11.00
☐ 31 Camilo Pascual	2.50	1.10
☐ 32 Bob Purkey	2.50	1.10
☐ 33 Bobby Richardson	5.00	2.20
☐ 34 Brooks Robinson	15.00	6.75
☐ 35 Floyd Robinson	2.50	1.10
☐ 36 Frank Robinson	15.00	6.75
☐ 37 Bob Rodgers	2.50	1.10
☐ 38 Johnny Romano	2.50	1.10
☐ 39 Jack Sanford	2.50	1.10
☐ 40 Norm Siebern	2.50	1.10
☐ 41 Warren Spahn	10.00	4.50
☐ 42 Dave Stenhouse	2.50	1.10
☐ 43 Ralph Terry	2.50	1.10
☐ 44 Lee Thomas	3.50	1.55
☐ 45 Bill White	5.00	2.20
☐ 46 Carl Yastrzemski	20.00	9.00

1964 Topps

The cards in this 587-card set measure 2 1/2" by 3 1/2". Players in the 1964 Topps baseball series were easy to sort by team due to the giant block lettering found at the top of each card. The name and position of the player are found underneath the picture, and the card is numbered in a ball design on the orange-colored back. The usual last series scarcity holds for this set (523 to 587). Subsets within this set include League Leaders (1-12) and World Series cards (136-140). Among other vehicles, cards were issued in one-card penny packs as well as five-card nickle packs. There were some three-card advertising panels produced by Topps; the players included are from the first series; one panel shows Walt Alston, Bill Henry, and Vada Pinson on the front with a Mickey Mantle card back on one of the backs. Another panel shows Carl Willey, White Sox Rookies, and Bob Friend on the front with a Mickey Mantle card back on one of the backs. The key Rookie Cards in this set are Richie Allen, Tony Conigliaro, Tommy John, Tony LaRussa, Phil Niekro and Lou Piniella.

	NRMT	VG-E
COMPLETE SET (587)	3000.00	1350.00
COMMON CARD (1-196)	3.00	1.35
COMMON CARD (197-370)	4.00	1.80
COMMON CARD (371-522)	7.00	3.10
COMMON CARD (523-587)	16.00	7.25
WRAPPER (1-CENT)	100.00	45.00
WRAPPER (1-CENT, REPEAT)	125.00	55.00
WRAPPER (5-CENT)	30.00	13.50
WRAPPER (5-CENT, COIN)	40.00	18.00
☐ 1 NL ERA Leaders	30.00	9.00
Sandy Koufax		
Dick Ellsworth		
Bob Friend		
☐ 2 AL ERA Leaders	6.00	2.70
Gary Peters		
Juan Pizarro		
Camilo Pascual		
☐ 3 NL Pitching Leaders	18.00	8.00
Sandy Koufax		
Juan Marichal		
Warren Spahn		
Jim Maloney		
☐ 4 AL Pitching Leaders	10.00	4.50
Whitey Ford		
Camilo Pascual		
Jim Bouton		
☐ 5 NL Strikeout Leaders	15.00	6.75
Sandy Koufax		
Jim Maloney		
Don Drysdale		
☐ 6 AL Strikeout Leaders	6.00	2.70
Camilo Pascual		
Jim Bunning		
Dick Stigman		
☐ 7 NL Batting Leaders	20.00	9.00
Tommy Davis		
Bob Clemente		
Dick Groat		
Hank Aaron		
☐ 8 AL Batting Leaders	15.00	6.75
Carl Yastrzemski		
Al Kaline		
Rich Rollins		
☐ 9 NL Home Run Leaders	30.00	13.50
Hank Aaron		
Willie McCovey		
Willie Mays		
Orlando Cepeda		
☐ 10 AL Home Run Leaders	10.00	4.50
Harmon Killebrew		
Dick Stuart		
Bob Allison		
☐ 11 NL RBI Leaders	15.00	6.75
Hank Aaron		
Ken Boyer		
Bill White		
☐ 12 AL RBI Leaders	10.00	4.50
Dick Stuart		
Al Kaline		
Harmon Killebrew		
☐ 13 Hoyt Wilhelm	10.00	4.50
☐ 14 Dodgers Rookies	3.00	1.35
Dick Nen		
Nick Willhite		
☐ 15 Zoilo Versalles	6.00	2.70
☐ 16 John Boozer	3.00	1.35
☐ 17 Willie Kirkland	3.00	1.35
☐ 18 Billy O'Dell	3.00	1.35
☐ 19 Don Wert	3.00	1.35
☐ 20 Bob Friend	6.00	2.70
☐ 21 Yogi Berra MG	30.00	13.50
☐ 22 Jerry Adair	3.00	1.35
☐ 23 Chris Zachary	3.00	1.35
☐ 24 Carl Sawatski	3.00	1.35
☐ 25 Bill Monbouquette	3.00	1.35
☐ 26 Gino Cimoli	3.00	1.35
☐ 27 New York Mets	8.00	3.60
Team Card		
☐ 28 Claude Osteen	6.00	2.70
☐ 29 Lou Brock	35.00	16.00
☐ 30 Ron Perranoski	6.00	2.70
☐ 31 Dave Nicholson	3.00	1.35
☐ 32 Dean Chance	6.00	2.70
☐ 33 Reds Rookies	6.00	2.70
Sammy Ellis		
Mel Queen		
☐ 34 Jim Perry	6.00	2.70
☐ 35 Eddie Mathews	20.00	9.00
☐ 36 Hal Reniff	3.00	1.35
☐ 37 Smoky Burgess	6.00	2.70
☐ 38 Jim Wynn	7.00	3.10
☐ 39 Hank Aguirre	3.00	1.35
☐ 40 Dick Groat	6.00	2.70
☐ 41 Friendly Foes	8.00	3.60
Willie McCovey		
Leon Wagner		
☐ 42 Moe Drabowsky	6.00	2.70
☐ 43 Roy Sievers	6.00	2.70
☐ 44 Duke Carmel	3.00	1.35
☐ 45 Milt Pappas	6.00	2.70
☐ 46 Ed Brinkman	3.00	1.35
☐ 47 Giants Rookies	6.00	2.70
Jesus Alou		
Ron Herbel		
☐ 48 Bob Perry	3.00	1.35
☐ 49 Bill Henry	3.00	1.35
☐ 50 Mickey Mantle	300.00	135.00
☐ 51 Pete Richert	3.00	1.35
☐ 52 Chuck Hinton	3.00	1.35
☐ 53 Denis Menke	3.00	1.35
☐ 54 Sam Mele MG	3.00	1.35
☐ 55 Ernie Banks	35.00	16.00
☐ 56 Hal Brown	3.00	1.35
☐ 57 Tim Harkness	3.00	1.35
☐ 58 Don Demeter	3.00	1.35
☐ 59 Ernie Broglio	3.00	1.35
☐ 60 Frank Malzone	6.00	2.70
☐ 61 Angel Backstops	6.00	2.70
Bob Rodgers		
Ed Sadowski		
☐ 62 Ted Savage	3.00	1.35
☐ 63 John Orsino	3.00	1.35
☐ 64 Ted Abernathy	3.00	1.35
☐ 65 Felipe Alou	6.00	2.70
☐ 66 Eddie Fisher	3.00	1.35
☐ 67 Tigers Team	8.00	3.60
☐ 68 Willie Davis	6.00	2.70
☐ 69 Clete Boyer	6.00	2.70
☐ 70 Joe Torre	8.00	3.60
☐ 71 Jack Spring	3.00	1.35
☐ 72 Chico Cardenas	6.00	2.70
☐ 73 Jimmie Hall	6.00	2.70
☐ 74 Pirates Rookies	3.00	1.35
Bob Priddy		
Tom Butters		
☐ 75 Wayne Causey	3.00	1.35
☐ 76 Checklist 1	8.00	1.60
☐ 77 Jerry Walker	3.00	1.35
☐ 78 Merritt Ranew	3.00	1.35
☐ 79 Bob Heffner	3.00	1.35
☐ 80 Vada Pinson	6.00	2.70
☐ 81 All-Star Vets	10.00	4.50
Nellie Fox		
Harmon Killebrew		
☐ 82 Jim Davenport	6.00	2.70
☐ 83 Gus Triandos	6.00	2.70
☐ 84 Carl Willey	3.00	1.35
☐ 85 Pete Ward	3.00	1.35
☐ 86 Al Downing	6.00	2.70
☐ 87 St. Louis Cardinals	8.00	3.60
Team Card		
☐ 88 John Roseboro	6.00	2.70
☐ 89 Boog Powell	6.00	2.70

☐ 90 Earl Battey 3.00 1.35
☐ 91 Bob Bailey 6.00 2.70
☐ 92 Steve Ridzik 3.00 1.35
☐ 93 Gary Geiger 3.00 1.35
☐ 94 Braves Rookies 3.00 1.35
Jim Britton
Larry Maxie
☐ 95 George Altman 3.00 1.35
☐ 96 Bob Buhl 6.00 2.70
☐ 97 Jim Fregosi 6.00 2.70
☐ 98 Bill Bruton 3.00 1.35
☐ 99 Al Stanek 3.00 1.35
☐ 100 Elston Howard 6.00 2.70
☐ 101 Walt Alston MG 6.00 2.70
☐ 102 Checklist 2 8.00 1.60
☐ 103 Curt Flood 6.00 2.70
☐ 104 Art Mahaffey 6.00 2.70
☐ 105 Woody Held 3.00 1.35
☐ 106 Joe Nuxhall 6.00 2.70
☐ 107 White Sox Rookies 3.00 1.35
Bruce Howard
Frank Kreutzer
☐ 108 John Wyatt 3.00 1.35
☐ 109 Rusty Staub 6.00 2.70
☐ 110 Albie Pearson 6.00 2.70
☐ 111 Don Elston 3.00 1.35
☐ 112 Bob Tillman 3.00 1.35
☐ 113 Grover Powell 3.00 1.35
☐ 114 Don Lock 3.00 1.35
☐ 115 Frank Bolling 3.00 1.35
☐ 116 Twins Rookies 12.00 5.50
Jay Ward
Tony Oliva
☐ 117 Earl Francis 3.00 1.35
☐ 118 John Blanchard 6.00 2.70
☐ 119 Gary Kolb 3.00 1.35
☐ 120 Don Drysdale 20.00 9.00
☐ 121 Pete Runnels 6.00 2.70
☐ 122 Don McMahon 3.00 1.35
☐ 123 Jose Pagan 3.00 1.35
☐ 124 Orlando Pena 3.00 1.35
☐ 125 Pete Rose 150.00 70.00
☐ 126 Russ Snyder 3.00 1.35
☐ 127 Angels Rookies 3.00 1.35
Aubrey Gatewood
Dick Simpson
☐ 128 Mickey Lolich 20.00 9.00
☐ 129 Amado Samuel 3.00 1.35
☐ 130 Gary Peters 6.00 2.70
☐ 131 Steve Boros 3.00 1.35
☐ 132 Braves Team 8.00 3.60
☐ 133 Jim Grant 6.00 2.70
☐ 134 Don Zimmer 6.00 2.70
☐ 135 Johnny Callison 6.00 2.70
☐ 136 Sandy Koufax WS 18.00 8.00
strikes out 15
☐ 137 Tommy Davis WS 8.00 3.60
☐ 138 Ron Fairly WS 8.00 3.60
☐ 139 Frank Howard WS 8.00 3.60
☐ 140 World Series Summary 8.00 3.60
Dodgers celebrate
☐ 141 Danny Murtaugh MG 6.00 2.70
☐ 142 John Bateman 3.00 1.35
☐ 143 Bubba Phillips 3.00 1.35
☐ 144 Al Worthington 3.00 1.35
☐ 145 Norm Siebern 3.00 1.35
☐ 146 Indians Rookies 30.00 13.50
Tommy John
Bob Chance
☐ 147 Ray Sadecki 3.00 1.35
☐ 148 J.C. Martin 3.00 1.35
☐ 149 Paul Foytack 3.00 1.35
☐ 150 Willie Mays 100.00 45.00
☐ 151 Athletics Team 8.00 3.60
☐ 152 Denny Lemaster 3.00 1.35
☐ 153 Dick Williams 6.00 2.70
☐ 154 Dick Tracewski 6.00 2.70
☐ 155 Duke Snider 30.00 13.50
☐ 156 Bill Dailey 3.00 1.35
☐ 157 Gene Mauch MG 6.00 2.70
☐ 158 Ken Johnson 3.00 1.35
☐ 159 Charlie Dees 3.00 1.35
☐ 160 Ken Boyer 6.00 2.70
☐ 161 Dave McNally 6.00 2.70
☐ 162 Hitting Area 6.00 2.70
Dick Sisler CO
Vada Pinson
☐ 163 Donn Clendenon 6.00 2.70
☐ 164 Bud Daley 3.00 1.35
☐ 165 Jerry Lumpe 3.00 1.35
☐ 166 Marty Keough 3.00 1.35
☐ 167 Senators Rookies 30.00 13.50
Mike Brumley
Lou Piniella
☐ 168 Al Weis 3.00 1.35
☐ 169 Del Crandall 6.00 2.70
☐ 170 Dick Radatz 6.00 2.70
☐ 171 Ty Cline 3.00 1.35
☐ 172 Indians Team 8.00 3.60
☐ 173 Ryne Duren 6.00 2.70
☐ 174 Doc Edwards 3.00 1.35
☐ 175 Billy Williams 12.00 5.50
☐ 176 Tracy Stallard 3.00 1.35
☐ 177 Harmon Killebrew 20.00 9.00
☐ 178 Hank Bauer MG 6.00 2.70
☐ 179 Carl Warwick 3.00 1.35
☐ 180 Tommy Davis 6.00 2.70
☐ 181 Dave Wickersham 3.00 1.35
☐ 182 Sox Sockers 15.00 6.75
Carl Yastrzemski
Chuck Schilling
☐ 183 Ron Taylor 3.00 1.35
☐ 184 Al Luplow 3.00 1.35
☐ 185 Jim O'Toole 6.00 2.70
☐ 186 Roman Mejias 3.00 1.35
☐ 187 Ed Roebuck 3.00 1.35
☐ 188 Checklist 3 8.00 1.60
☐ 189 Bob Hendley 3.00 1.35
☐ 190 Bobby Richardson 8.00 3.60
☐ 191 Clay Dalrymple 6.00 2.70
☐ 192 Cubs Rookies 3.00 1.35
John Boccabella
Billy Cowan
☐ 193 Jerry Lynch 3.00 1.35
☐ 194 John Goryl 3.00 1.35
☐ 195 Floyd Robinson 3.00 1.35
☐ 196 Jim Gentile 3.00 1.35
☐ 197 Frank Lary 6.00 2.70
☐ 198 Len Gabrielson 4.00 1.80
☐ 199 Joe Azcue 4.00 1.80
☐ 200 Sandy Koufax 100.00 45.00
☐ 201 Orioles Rookies 6.00 2.70
Sam Bowens
Wally Bunker
☐ 202 Galen Cisco 6.00 2.70
☐ 203 John Kennedy 6.00 2.70
☐ 204 Matty Alou 6.00 2.70
☐ 205 Nellie Fox 14.00 6.25
☐ 206 Steve Hamilton 6.00 2.70
☐ 207 Fred Hutchinson MG 6.00 2.70
☐ 208 Wes Covington 6.00 2.70
☐ 209 Bob Allen 4.00 1.80
☐ 210 Carl Yastrzemski 35.00 16.00
☐ 211 Jim Coker 4.00 1.80
☐ 212 Pete Lovrich 4.00 1.80
☐ 213 Angels Team 8.00 3.60
☐ 214 Ken McMullen 6.00 2.70
☐ 215 Ray Herbert 4.00 1.80
☐ 216 Mike de la Hoz 4.00 1.80
☐ 217 Jim King 4.00 1.80
☐ 218 Hank Fischer 4.00 1.80
☐ 219 Young Aces 6.00 2.70
Al Downing
Jim Bouton
☐ 220 Dick Ellsworth 6.00 2.70
☐ 221 Bob Saverine 4.00 1.80
☐ 222 Billy Pierce 6.00 2.70
☐ 223 George Banks 4.00 1.80
☐ 224 Tommie Sisk 4.00 1.80
☐ 225 Roger Maris 50.00 22.00
☐ 226 Colts Rookies 7.00 3.10
Jerry Grote
Larry Yellen
☐ 227 Barry Latman 4.00 1.80
☐ 228 Felix Mantilla 4.00 1.80
☐ 229 Charley Lau 6.00 2.70
☐ 230 Brooks Robinson 35.00 16.00
☐ 231 Dick Calmus 4.00 1.80
☐ 232 Al Lopez MG 6.00 2.70
☐ 233 Hal Smith 4.00 1.80
☐ 234 Gary Bell 4.00 1.80
☐ 235 Ron Hunt 4.00 1.80
☐ 236 Bill Faul 4.00 1.80
☐ 237 Cubs Team 8.00 3.60
☐ 238 Roy McMillan 6.00 2.70
☐ 239 Herm Starrette 4.00 1.80
☐ 240 Bill White 6.00 2.70
☐ 241 Jim Owens 4.00 1.80
☐ 242 Harvey Kuenn 6.00 2.70
☐ 243 Phillies Rookies 30.00 13.50
Richie Allen
John Herrnstein
☐ 244 Tony LaRussa 30.00 13.50
☐ 245 Dick Stigman 4.00 1.80
☐ 246 Manny Mota 6.00 2.70
☐ 247 Dave DeBusschere 6.00 2.70
☐ 248 Johnny Pesky MG 6.00 2.70
☐ 249 Doug Camilli 4.00 1.80
☐ 250 Al Kaline 40.00 18.00
☐ 251 Choo Choo Coleman 6.00 2.70
☐ 252 Ken Aspromonte 4.00 1.80
☐ 253 Wally Post 6.00 2.70
☐ 254 Don Hoak 6.00 2.70
☐ 255 Lee Thomas 6.00 2.70
☐ 256 Johnny Weekly 4.00 1.80
☐ 257 San Francisco Giants 8.00 3.60
Team Card
☐ 258 Garry Roggenburk 4.00 1.80
☐ 259 Harry Bright 4.00 1.80
☐ 260 Frank Robinson 35.00 16.00
☐ 261 Jim Hannan 4.00 1.80
☐ 262 Cards Rookies 8.00 3.60
Mike Shannon
Harry Fanok
☐ 263 Chuck Estrada 4.00 1.80
☐ 264 Jim Landis 4.00 1.80
☐ 265 Jim Bunning 14.00 6.25
☐ 266 Gene Freese 4.00 1.80
☐ 267 Wilbur Wood 7.00 3.10
☐ 268 Bill's Got It 6.00 2.70
Danny Murtaugh MG
Bill Virdon
☐ 269 Ellis Burton 4.00 1.80
☐ 270 Rich Rollins 6.00 2.70
☐ 271 Bob Sadowski 4.00 1.80
☐ 272 Jake Wood 4.00 1.80
☐ 273 Mel Nelson 4.00 1.80
☐ 274 Checklist 4 8.00 1.60
☐ 275 John Tsitouris 4.00 1.80
☐ 276 Jose Tartabull 6.00 2.70
☐ 277 Ken Retzer 4.00 1.80
☐ 278 Bobby Shantz 6.00 2.70
☐ 279 Joe Koppe UER 4.00 1.80
(Glove on wrong hand)
☐ 280 Juan Marichal 12.00 5.50
☐ 281 Yankees Rookies 6.00 2.70
Jake Gibbs
Tom Metcalf
☐ 282 Bob Bruce 4.00 1.80
☐ 283 Tom McCraw 4.00 1.80
☐ 284 Dick Schofield 4.00 1.80
☐ 285 Robin Roberts 14.00 6.25
☐ 286 Don Landrum 4.00 1.80
☐ 287 Red Sox Rookies 50.00 22.00
Tony Conigliaro
Bill Spanswick
☐ 288 Al Moran 4.00 1.80
☐ 289 Frank Funk 4.00 1.80
☐ 290 Bob Allison 6.00 2.70
☐ 291 Phil Ortega 4.00 1.80
☐ 292 Mike Roarke 4.00 1.80
☐ 293 Phillies Team 8.00 3.60
☐ 294 Ken L. Hunt 4.00 1.80
☐ 295 Roger Craig 6.00 2.70
☐ 296 Ed Kirkpatrick 4.00 1.80
☐ 297 Ken MacKenzie 4.00 1.80
☐ 298 Harry Craft MG 4.00 1.80
☐ 299 Bill Stafford 4.00 1.80
☐ 300 Hank Aaron 90.00 40.00
☐ 301 Larry Brown 4.00 1.80
☐ 302 Dan Pfister 4.00 1.80
☐ 303 Jim Campbell 4.00 1.80
☐ 304 Bob Johnson 4.00 1.80
☐ 305 Jack Lamabe 4.00 1.80
☐ 306 Giant Gunners 35.00 16.00
Willie Mays
Orlando Cepeda
☐ 307 Joe Gibbon 4.00 1.80
☐ 308 Gene Stephens 4.00 1.80
☐ 309 Paul Toth 4.00 1.80
☐ 310 Jim Gilliam 6.00 2.70
☐ 311 Tom Brown 6.00 2.70
☐ 312 Tigers Rookies 4.00 1.80
Fritz Fisher
Fred Gladding
☐ 313 Chuck Hiller 4.00 1.80
☐ 314 Jerry Buchek 4.00 1.80
☐ 315 Bo Belinsky 6.00 2.70
☐ 316 Gene Oliver 4.00 1.80
☐ 317 Al Smith 4.00 1.80
☐ 318 Minnesota Twins 8.00 3.60
Team Card
☐ 319 Paul Brown 4.00 1.80
☐ 320 Rocky Colavito 14.00 6.25
☐ 321 Bob Lillis 4.00 1.80
☐ 322 George Brunet 4.00 1.80
☐ 323 John Buzhardt 4.00 1.80
☐ 324 Casey Stengel MG 15.00 6.75
☐ 325 Hector Lopez 6.00 2.70
☐ 326 Ron Brand 4.00 1.80
☐ 327 Don Blasingame 4.00 1.80
☐ 328 Bob Shaw 4.00 1.80
☐ 329 Russ Nixon 4.00 1.80
☐ 330 Tommy Harper 6.00 2.70
☐ 331 AL Bombers 175.00 80.00
Roger Maris
Norm Cash
Mickey Mantle
Al Kaline
☐ 332 Ray Washburn 4.00 1.80
☐ 333 Billy Moran 4.00 1.80

☐ 334 Lew Krausse 4.00 1.80
☐ 335 Don Mossi 6.00 2.70
☐ 336 Andre Rodgers 4.00 1.80
☐ 337 Dodgers Rookies 6.00 2.70
Al Ferrara
Jeff Torborg
☐ 338 Jack Kralick 4.00 1.80
☐ 339 Walt Bond 4.00 1.80
☐ 340 Joe Cunningham 4.00 1.80
☐ 341 Jim Roland 4.00 1.80
☐ 342 Willie Stargell 30.00 13.50
☐ 343 Senators Team 8.00 3.60
☐ 344 Phil Linz 6.00 2.70
☐ 345 Frank Thomas 6.00 2.70
☐ 346 Joey Jay 4.00 1.80
☐ 347 Bobby Wine 6.00 2.70
☐ 348 Ed Lopat MG 6.00 2.70
☐ 349 Art Fowler 4.00 1.80
☐ 350 Willie McCovey 20.00 9.00
☐ 351 Dan Schneider 4.00 1.80
☐ 352 Eddie Bressoud 4.00 1.80
☐ 353 Wally Moon 6.00 2.70
☐ 354 Dave Giusti 4.00 1.80
☐ 355 Vic Power 6.00 2.70
☐ 356 Reds Rookies 6.00 2.70
Bill McCool
Chico Ruiz
☐ 357 Charley James 4.00 1.80
☐ 358 Ron Kline 4.00 1.80
☐ 359 Jim Schaffer 4.00 1.80
☐ 360 Joe Pepitone 7.00 3.10
☐ 361 Jay Hook 4.00 1.80
☐ 362 Checklist 5 8.00 1.60
☐ 363 Dick McAuliffe 6.00 2.70
☐ 364 Joe Gaines 4.00 1.80
☐ 365 Cal McLish 6.00 2.70
☐ 366 Nelson Mathews 4.00 1.80
☐ 367 Fred Whitfield 4.00 1.80
☐ 368 White Sox Rookies 6.00 2.70
Fritz Ackley
Don Buford
☐ 369 Jerry Zimmerman 4.00 1.80
☐ 370 Hal Woodeshick 4.00 1.80
☐ 371 Frank Howard 10.00 4.50
☐ 372 Howie Koplitz 7.00 3.10
☐ 373 Pirates Team 15.00 6.75
☐ 374 Bobby Bolin 7.00 3.10
☐ 375 Ron Santo 10.00 4.50
☐ 376 Dave Morehead 7.00 3.10
☐ 377 Bob Skinner 7.00 3.10
☐ 378 Braves Rookies 10.00 4.50
Woody Woodward
Jack Smith
☐ 379 Tony Gonzalez 7.00 3.10
☐ 380 Whitey Ford 35.00 16.00
☐ 381 Bob Taylor 7.00 3.10
☐ 382 Wes Stock 7.00 3.10
☐ 383 Bill Rigney MG 7.00 3.10
☐ 384 Ron Hansen 7.00 3.10
☐ 385 Curt Simmons 10.00 4.50
☐ 386 Lenny Green 7.00 3.10
☐ 387 Terry Fox 7.00 3.10
☐ 388 A's Rookies 10.00 4.50
John O'Donoghue
George Williams
☐ 389 Jim Umbricht 10.00 4.50
(Card back mentions
his death)
☐ 390 Orlando Cepeda 10.00 4.50
☐ 391 Sam McDowell 10.00 4.50
☐ 392 Jim Pagliaroni 7.00 3.10
☐ 393 Casey Teaches 10.00 4.50
Casey Stengel MG
Ed Kranepool
☐ 394 Bob Miller 7.00 3.10
☐ 395 Tom Tresh 10.00 4.50
☐ 396 Dennis Bennett 7.00 3.10
☐ 397 Chuck Cottier 7.00 3.10
☐ 398 Mets Rookies 7.00 3.10
Bill Haas
Dick Smith
☐ 399 Jackie Brandt 7.00 3.10
☐ 400 Warren Spahn 40.00 18.00
☐ 401 Charlie Maxwell 7.00 3.10
☐ 402 Tom Sturdivant 7.00 3.10
☐ 403 Reds Team 15.00 6.75
☐ 404 Tony Martinez 7.00 3.10
☐ 405 Ken McBride 7.00 3.10
☐ 406 Al Spangler 7.00 3.10
☐ 407 Bill Freehan 10.00 4.50
☐ 408 Cubs Rookies 7.00 3.10
Jim Stewart
Fred Burdette
☐ 409 Bill Fischer 7.00 3.10
☐ 410 Dick Stuart 10.00 4.50
☐ 411 Lee Walls 7.00 3.10
☐ 412 Ray Culp 10.00 4.50
☐ 413 Johnny Keane MG 7.00 3.10
☐ 414 Jack Sanford 7.00 3.10
☐ 415 Tony Kubek 10.00 4.50
☐ 416 Lee Maye 7.00 3.10
☐ 417 Don Cardwell 7.00 3.10
☐ 418 Orioles Rookies 10.00 4.50
Darold Knowles
Les Narum
☐ 419 Ken Harrelson 14.00 6.25
☐ 420 Jim Maloney 10.00 4.50
☐ 421 Camilo Carreon 7.00 3.10
☐ 422 Jack Fisher 7.00 3.10
☐ 423 Tops in NL 125.00 55.00
Hank Aaron
Willie Mays
☐ 424 Dick Bertell 7.00 3.10
☐ 425 Norm Cash 10.00 4.50
☐ 426 Bob Rodgers 7.00 3.10
☐ 427 Don Rudolph 7.00 3.10
☐ 428 Red Sox Rookies 7.00 3.10
Archie Skeen
Pete Smith
(Back states Archie
has retired)
☐ 429 Tim McCarver 10.00 4.50
☐ 430 Juan Pizarro 7.00 3.10
☐ 431 George Alusik 7.00 3.10
☐ 432 Ruben Amaro 10.00 4.50
☐ 433 Yankees Team 40.00 18.00
☐ 434 Don Nottebart 7.00 3.10
☐ 435 Vic Davalillo 7.00 3.10
☐ 436 Charlie Neal 10.00 4.50
☐ 437 Ed Bailey 7.00 3.10
☐ 438 Checklist 6 25.00 5.00
☐ 439 Harvey Haddix 10.00 4.50
☐ 440 Bob Clemente UER 250.00 110.00
(1960 Pittsburfh)
☐ 441 Bob Duliba 7.00 3.10
☐ 442 Pumpsie Green 10.00 4.50
☐ 443 Chuck Dressen MG 10.00 4.50
☐ 444 Larry Jackson 7.00 3.10
☐ 445 Bill Skowron 10.00 4.50
☐ 446 Julian Javier 10.00 4.50
☐ 447 Ted Bowsfield 7.00 3.10
☐ 448 Cookie Rojas 10.00 4.50
☐ 449 Deron Johnson 10.00 4.50
☐ 450 Steve Barber 7.00 3.10
☐ 451 Joe Amalfitano 7.00 3.10
☐ 452 Giants Rookies 10.00 4.50
Gil Garrido
Jim Ray Hart
☐ 453 Frank Baumann 7.00 3.10
☐ 454 Tommie Aaron 10.00 4.50
☐ 455 Bernie Allen 7.00 3.10
☐ 456 Dodgers Rookies 10.00 4.50
Wes Parker
John Werhas
☐ 457 Jesse Gonder 7.00 3.10
☐ 458 Ralph Terry 10.00 4.50
☐ 459 Red Sox Rookies 7.00 3.10
Pete Charton
Dalton Jones
☐ 460 Bob Gibson 35.00 16.00
☐ 461 George Thomas 7.00 3.10
☐ 462 Birdie Tebbetts MG 7.00 3.10
☐ 463 Don Leppert 7.00 3.10
☐ 464 Dallas Green 10.00 4.50
☐ 465 Mike Hershberger 7.00 3.10
☐ 466 A's Rookies 10.00 4.50
Dick Green
Aurelio Monteagudo
☐ 467 Bob Aspromonte 7.00 3.10
☐ 468 Gaylord Perry 40.00 18.00
☐ 469 Cubs Rookies 10.00 4.50
Fred Norman
Sterling Slaughter
☐ 470 Jim Bouton 10.00 4.50
☐ 471 Gates Brown 10.00 4.50
☐ 472 Vern Law 10.00 4.50
☐ 473 Baltimore Orioles 15.00 6.75
Team Card
☐ 474 Larry Sherry 10.00 4.50
☐ 475 Ed Charles 7.00 3.10
☐ 476 Braves Rookies 14.00 6.25
Rico Carty
Dick Kelley
☐ 477 Mike Joyce 7.00 3.10
☐ 478 Dick Howser 10.00 4.50
☐ 479 Cardinals Rookies 7.00 3.10
Dave Bakenhaster
Johnny Lewis
☐ 480 Bob Purkey 7.00 3.10
☐ 481 Chuck Schilling 7.00 3.10
☐ 482 Phillies Rookies 10.00 4.50
John Briggs
Danny Cater
☐ 483 Fred Valentine 7.00 3.10
☐ 484 Bill Pleis 7.00 3.10
☐ 485 Tom Haller 7.00 3.10
☐ 486 Bob Kennedy MG 7.00 3.10
☐ 487 Mike McCormick 7.00 3.10
☐ 488 Yankees Rookies 10.00 4.50
Pete Mikkelsen
Bob Meyer
☐ 489 Julio Navarro 7.00 3.10
☐ 490 Ron Fairly 10.00 4.50
☐ 491 Ed Rakow 7.00 3.10
☐ 492 Colts Rookies 7.00 3.10
Jim Beauchamp
Mike White
☐ 493 Don Lee 7.00 3.10
☐ 494 Al Jackson 7.00 3.10
☐ 495 Bill Virdon 10.00 4.50
☐ 496 White Sox Team 15.00 6.75
☐ 497 Jeoff Long 7.00 3.10
☐ 498 Dave Stenhouse 7.00 3.10
☐ 499 Indians Rookies 7.00 3.10
Chico Salmon
Gordon Seyfried
☐ 500 Camilo Pascual 10.00 4.50
☐ 501 Bob Veale 10.00 4.50
☐ 502 Angels Rookies 7.00 3.10
Bobby Knoop
Bob Lee
☐ 503 Earl Wilson 7.00 3.10
☐ 504 Claude Raymond 7.00 3.10
☐ 505 Stan Williams 7.00 3.10
☐ 506 Bobby Bragan MG 7.00 3.10
☐ 507 Johnny Edwards 7.00 3.10
☐ 508 Diego Segui 7.00 3.10
☐ 509 Pirates Rookies 10.00 4.50
Gene Alley
Orlando McFarlane
☐ 510 Lindy McDaniel 10.00 4.50
☐ 511 Lou Jackson 10.00 4.50
☐ 512 Tigers Rookies 14.00 6.25
Willie Horton
Joe Sparma
☐ 513 Don Larsen 10.00 4.50
☐ 514 Jim Hickman 10.00 4.50
☐ 515 Johnny Romano 7.00 3.10
☐ 516 Twins Rookies 7.00 3.10
Jerry Arrigo
Dwight Siebler
☐ 517A Checklist 7 ERR 25.00 5.00
(Incorrect numbering
sequence on back)
☐ 517B Checklist 7 COR 15.00 3.00
(Correct numbering
on back)
☐ 518 Carl Bouldin 7.00 3.10
☐ 519 Charlie Smith 7.00 3.10
☐ 520 Jack Baldschun 10.00 4.50
☐ 521 Tom Satriano 7.00 3.10
☐ 522 Bob Tiefenauer 7.00 3.10
☐ 523 Lou Burdette UER 20.00 9.00
(Pitching lefty)
☐ 524 Reds Rookies 16.00 7.25
Jim Dickson
Bobby Klaus
☐ 525 Al McBean 16.00 7.25
☐ 526 Lou Clinton 16.00 7.25
☐ 527 Larry Bearnarth 16.00 7.25
☐ 528 A's Rookies 20.00 9.00
Dave Duncan
Tommie Reynolds
☐ 529 Alvin Dark MG 20.00 9.00
☐ 530 Leon Wagner 16.00 7.25
☐ 531 Los Angeles Dodgers 25.00 11.00
Team Card
☐ 532 Twins Rookies 16.00 7.25
Bud Bloomfield
(Bloomfield photo
actually Jay Ward)
Joe Nossek
☐ 533 Johnny Klippstein 16.00 7.25
☐ 534 Gus Bell 16.00 7.25
☐ 535 Phil Regan 16.00 7.25
☐ 536 Mets Rookies 16.00 7.25
Larry Elliot
John Stephenson
☐ 537 Dan Osinski 16.00 7.25
☐ 538 Minnie Minoso 20.00 9.00
☐ 539 Roy Face 20.00 9.00
☐ 540 Luis Aparicio 25.00 11.00
☐ 541 Braves Rookies 100.00 45.00
Phil Roof
Phil Niekro
☐ 542 Don Mincher 16.00 7.25
☐ 543 Bob Uecker 40.00 18.00
☐ 544 Colts Rookies 16.00 7.25
Steve Hertz
Joe Hoerner
☐ 545 Max Alvis 16.00 7.25

☐ 546 Joe Christopher	16.00	7.25
☐ 547 Gil Hodges MG	25.00	11.00
☐ 548 NL Rookies	16.00	7.25
Wayne Schurr		
Paul Speckenbach		
☐ 549 Joe Moeller	16.00	7.25
☐ 550 Ken Hubbs MEM	35.00	16.00
☐ 551 Billy Hoeft	16.00	7.25
☐ 552 Indians Rookies	16.00	7.25
Tom Kelley		
Sonny Siebert		
☐ 553 Jim Brewer	16.00	7.25
☐ 554 Hank Foiles	16.00	7.25
☐ 555 Lee Stange	16.00	7.25
☐ 556 Mets Rookies	16.00	7.25
Steve Dillon		
Ron Locke		
☐ 557 Leo Burke	16.00	7.25
☐ 558 Don Schwall	16.00	7.25
☐ 559 Dick Phillips	16.00	7.25
☐ 560 Dick Farrell	16.00	7.25
☐ 561 Phillies Rookies UER	20.00	9.00
Dave Bennett		
(19 ... is 18)		
Rick Wise		
☐ 562 Pedro Ramos	16.00	7.25
☐ 563 Dal Maxvill	16.00	7.25
☐ 564 AL Rookies	16.00	7.25
Joe McCabe		
Jerry McNertney		
☐ 565 Stu Miller	16.00	7.25
☐ 566 Ed Kranepool	20.00	9.00
☐ 567 Jim Kaat	20.00	9.00
☐ 568 NL Rookies	16.00	7.25
Phil Gagliano		
Cap Peterson		
☐ 569 Fred Newman	16.00	7.25
☐ 570 Bill Mazeroski	20.00	9.00
☐ 571 Gene Conley	16.00	7.25
☐ 572 AL Rookies	16.00	7.25
Dave Gray		
Dick Egan		
☐ 573 Jim Duffalo	16.00	7.25
☐ 574 Manny Jimenez	16.00	7.25
☐ 575 Tony Cloninger	16.00	7.25
☐ 576 Mets Rookies	16.00	7.25
Jerry Hinsley		
Bill Wakefield		
☐ 577 Gordy Coleman	16.00	7.25
☐ 578 Glen Hobbie	16.00	7.25
☐ 579 Red Sox Team	25.00	11.00
☐ 580 Johnny Podres	20.00	9.00
☐ 581 Yankees Rookies	20.00	9.00
Pedro Gonzalez		
Archie Moore		
☐ 582 Rod Kanehl	20.00	9.00
☐ 583 Tito Francona	16.00	7.25
☐ 584 Joel Horlen	16.00	7.25
☐ 585 Tony Taylor	20.00	9.00
☐ 586 Jimmy Piersall	20.00	9.00
☐ 587 Bennie Daniels !	20.00	8.00

1964 Topps Coins Inserts

This set of 164 unnumbered coins issued in 1964 is sometimes divided into two sets -- the regular series (1-120) and the all-star series (121-164). Each metal coin is approximately 1 1/2" in diameter. The regular series features gold and silver coins with a full color photo of the player, including the background of the photo. The player's name, team and position are delineated on the coin front. The back includes the line "Collect the entire set of 120 all-stars". The all-star series (denoted AS in the checklist below) contains a full color cutout photo of the player on a solid background. The fronts feature the line "1964 All-stars" along with the name only of the player. The backs contain the line "Collect all 44 special stars". Mantle, Causey and Hinton appear in two variations each. The complete set price below includes all variations. Some dealers believe the following coins are short printed: Callison, Tresh, Rollins, Santo, Pappas, Freehan, Hendley, Staub, Bateman and O'Dell.

	NRMT	VG-E
COMPLETE SET (167)	600.00	275.00
COMMON COIN (1-164)	1.00	.45
☐ 1 Don Zimmer	1.50	.70
☐ 2 Jim Wynn	1.50	.70
☐ 3 Johnny Orsino	1.00	.45
☐ 4 Jim Bouton	1.50	.70
☐ 5 Dick Groat	1.50	.70
☐ 6 Leon Wagner	1.00	.45
☐ 7 Frank Malzone	1.00	.45
☐ 8 Steve Barber	1.00	.45
☐ 9 Johnny Romano	1.00	.45
☐ 10 Tom Tresh	1.50	.70
☐ 11 Felipe Alou	1.50	.70
☐ 12 Dick Stuart	1.50	.70
☐ 13 Claude Osteen	1.00	.45
☐ 14 Juan Pizarro	1.00	.45
☐ 15 Donn Clendenon	1.00	.45
☐ 16 Jimmie Hall	1.00	.45
☐ 17 Al Jackson	1.00	.45
☐ 18 Brooks Robinson	15.00	6.75
☐ 19 Bob Allison	1.50	.70
☐ 20 Ed Roebuck	1.00	.45
☐ 21 Pete Ward	1.00	.45
☐ 22 Willie McCovey	8.00	3.60
☐ 23 Elston Howard	2.00	.90
☐ 24 Diego Segui	1.00	.45
☐ 25 Ken Boyer	1.50	.70
☐ 26 Carl Yastrzemski	15.00	6.75
☐ 27 Bill Mazeroski	2.00	.90
☐ 28 Jerry Lumpe	1.00	.45
☐ 29 Woody Held	1.00	.45
☐ 30 Dick Radatz	1.00	.45
☐ 31 Luis Aparicio	6.00	2.70
☐ 32 Dave Nicholson	1.00	.45
☐ 33 Eddie Mathews	10.00	4.50
☐ 34 Don Drysdale	10.00	4.50
☐ 35 Ray Culp	1.00	.45
☐ 36 Juan Marichal	8.00	3.60
☐ 37 Frank Robinson	15.00	6.75
☐ 38 Chuck Hinton	1.00	.45
☐ 39 Floyd Robinson	1.00	.45
☐ 40 Tommy Harper	1.50	.70
☐ 41 Ron Hansen	1.00	.45
☐ 42 Ernie Banks	15.00	6.75
☐ 43 Jesse Gonder	1.00	.45
☐ 44 Billy Williams	5.00	2.20
☐ 45 Vada Pinson	2.00	.90
☐ 46 Rocky Colavito	3.00	1.35
☐ 47 Bill Monbouquette	1.00	.45
☐ 48 Max Alvis	1.00	.45
☐ 49 Norm Siebern	1.00	.45
☐ 50 Johnny Callison	1.50	.70
☐ 51 Rich Rollins	1.00	.45
☐ 52 Ken McBride	1.00	.45
☐ 53 Don Lock	1.00	.45
☐ 54 Ron Fairly	1.50	.70
☐ 55 Roberto Clemente	40.00	18.00
☐ 56 Dick Ellsworth	1.00	.45
☐ 57 Tommy Davis	1.50	.70
☐ 58 Tony Gonzalez	1.00	.45
☐ 59 Bob Gibson	8.00	3.60
☐ 60 Jim Maloney	1.50	.70
☐ 61 Frank Howard	2.00	.90
☐ 62 Jim Pagliaroni	1.00	.45
☐ 63 Orlando Cepeda	3.00	1.35
☐ 64 Ron Perranoski	1.00	.45
☐ 65 Curt Flood	2.00	.90
☐ 66 Alvin McBean	1.00	.45
☐ 67 Dean Chance	1.00	.45
☐ 68 Ron Santo	3.00	1.35
☐ 69 Jack Baldschun	1.00	.45
☐ 70 Milt Pappas	1.50	.70
☐ 71 Gary Peters	1.00	.45
☐ 72 Bobby Richardson	2.00	.90
☐ 73 Frank Thomas	1.00	.45
☐ 74 Hank Aguirre	1.00	.45
☐ 75 Carlton Willey	1.00	.45
☐ 76 Camilo Pascual	1.00	.45
☐ 77 Bob Friend	1.00	.45
☐ 78 Bill White	1.50	.70
☐ 79 Norm Cash	2.00	.90
☐ 80 Willie Mays	30.00	13.50
☐ 81 Leon Carmel	1.00	.45
☐ 82 Pete Rose	25.00	11.00
☐ 83 Hank Aaron	25.00	11.00
☐ 84 Bob Aspromonte	1.00	.45
☐ 85 Jim O'Toole	1.00	.45
☐ 86 Vic Davalillo	1.00	.45
☐ 87 Bill Freehan	1.50	.70
☐ 88 Warren Spahn	10.00	4.50
☐ 89 Ken Hunt	1.00	.45
☐ 90 Denis Menke	1.00	.45
☐ 91 Dick Farrell	1.00	.45
☐ 92 Jim Hickman	1.00	.45
☐ 93 Jim Bunning	6.00	2.70
☐ 94 Bob Hendley	1.00	.45
☐ 95 Ernie Broglio	1.00	.45
☐ 96 Rusty Staub	2.00	.90
☐ 97 Lou Brock	8.00	3.60
☐ 98 Jim Fregosi	2.00	.90
☐ 99 Jim Grant	1.00	.45
☐ 100 Al Kaline	10.00	4.50
☐ 101 Earl Battey	1.00	.45
☐ 102 Wayne Causey	1.00	.45
☐ 103 Chuck Schilling	1.00	.45
☐ 104 Boog Powell	2.00	.90
☐ 105 Dave Wickersham	1.00	.45
☐ 106 Sandy Koufax	20.00	9.00
☐ 107 John Bateman	1.00	.45
☐ 108 Ed Brinkman	1.00	.45
☐ 109 Al Downing	1.00	.45
☐ 110 Joe Azcue	1.00	.45
☐ 111 Albie Pearson	1.00	.45
☐ 112 Harmon Killebrew	8.00	3.60
☐ 113 Tony Taylor	1.50	.70
☐ 114 Larry Jackson	1.00	.45
☐ 115 Billy O'Dell	1.00	.45
☐ 116 Don Demeter	1.00	.45
☐ 117 Ed Charles	1.00	.45
☐ 118 Joe Torre	3.00	1.35
☐ 119 Don Nottebart	1.00	.45
☐ 120 Mickey Mantle	80.00	36.00
☐ 121 Joe Pepitone AS	1.50	.70
☐ 122 Dick Stuart AS	1.00	.45
☐ 123 Bobby Richardson AS	2.00	.90
☐ 124 Jerry Lumpe AS	1.00	.45
☐ 125 Brooks Robinson AS	10.00	4.50
☐ 126 Frank Malzone AS	1.00	.45
☐ 127 Luis Aparicio AS	5.00	2.20
☐ 128 Jim Fregosi AS	1.50	.70
☐ 129 Al Kaline AS	10.00	4.50
☐ 130 Leon Wagner AS	1.00	.45
☐ 131A Mickey Mantle AS	60.00	27.00
(right handed)		
☐ 131B Mickey Mantle AS	60.00	27.00
(left handed)		
☐ 132 Albie Pearson AS	1.00	.45
☐ 133 Harmon Killebrew AS	10.00	4.50
☐ 134 Carl Yastrzemski AS	10.00	4.50
☐ 135 Elston Howard AS	2.00	.90
☐ 136 Earl Battey AS	1.00	.45
☐ 137 Camilo Pascual AS	1.00	.45
☐ 138 Jim Bouton AS	1.50	.70
☐ 139 Whitey Ford AS	10.00	4.50
☐ 140 Gary Peters AS	1.00	.45
☐ 141 Bill White AS	1.50	.70
☐ 142 Orlando Cepeda AS	2.00	.90
☐ 143 Bill Mazeroski AS	2.00	.90
☐ 144 Tony Taylor AS	1.00	.45
☐ 145 Ken Boyer AS	2.00	.90
☐ 146 Ron Santo AS	2.00	.90
☐ 147 Dick Groat AS	1.50	.70
☐ 148 Roy McMillan AS	1.00	.45
☐ 149 Hank Aaron AS	20.00	9.00
☐ 150 Roberto Clemente AS	30.00	13.50
☐ 151 Willie Mays AS	25.00	11.00
☐ 152 Vada Pinson AS	1.50	.70
☐ 153 Tommy Davis AS	1.50	.70
☐ 154 Frank Robinson AS	10.00	4.50
☐ 155 Joe Torre AS	2.00	.90
☐ 156 Tim McCarver AS	3.00	1.35
☐ 157 Juan Marichal AS	5.00	2.20
☐ 158 Jim Maloney AS	1.50	.70
☐ 159 Sandy Koufax AS	15.00	6.75
☐ 160 Warren Spahn AS	6.00	2.70
☐ 161A Wayne Causey AS	10.00	4.50
National League		
☐ 161B Wayne Causey AS	1.50	.70
American League		
☐ 162A Chuck Hinton AS	10.00	4.50
National League		
☐ 162B Chuck Hinton AS	1.50	.70
American League		
☐ 163 Bob Aspromonte AS	1.00	.45
☐ 164 Ron Hunt AS	1.00	.45

1964 Topps Giants

The cards in this 60-card set measure approximately 3 1/8" by 5 1/4". The 1964 Topps Giants are postcard size cards containing color player photographs. They are numbered on the backs, which also contain biographical information presented in a newspaper format. These "giant size" cards were distributed in both cellophane and waxed gum packs apart from the Topps regular issue of 1964. The gum packs contain three cards. The Cards 3, 28, 42, 45, 47, 51 and 60 are more difficult to find and are indicated by SP in the checklist below.

	NRMT	VG-E
COMPLETE SET (60)	200.00	90.00
COMMON CARD (1-60)	.50	.23
WRAPPER (5-CENT)	35.00	16.00
☐ 1 Gary Peters	.75	.35
☐ 2 Ken Johnson	.50	.23
☐ 3 Sandy Koufax SP	40.00	18.00
☐ 4 Bob Bailey	.50	.23
☐ 5 Milt Pappas	.75	.35
☐ 6 Ron Hunt	.50	.23
☐ 7 Whitey Ford	4.00	1.80
☐ 8 Roy McMillan	.50	.23
☐ 9 Rocky Colavito	1.25	.55
☐ 10 Jim Bunning	3.00	1.35
☐ 11 Roberto Clemente	15.00	6.75
☐ 12 Al Kaline	5.00	2.20
☐ 13 Nellie Fox	3.00	1.35
☐ 14 Tony Gonzalez	.50	.23
☐ 15 Jim Gentile	.50	.23
☐ 16 Dean Chance	.75	.35
☐ 17 Dick Ellsworth	.75	.35
☐ 18 Jim Fregosi	.75	.35
☐ 19 Dick Groat	.75	.35
☐ 20 Chuck Hinton	.50	.23
☐ 21 Elston Howard	.75	.35
☐ 22 Dick Farrell	.50	.23
☐ 23 Albie Pearson	.50	.23
☐ 24 Frank Howard	.75	.35
☐ 25 Mickey Mantle	30.00	13.50
☐ 26 Joe Torre	1.25	.55
☐ 27 Eddie Brinkman	.50	.23
☐ 28 Bob Friend SP	10.00	4.50
☐ 29 Frank Robinson	5.00	2.20
☐ 30 Bill Freehan	.75	.35
☐ 31 Warren Spahn	4.00	1.80
☐ 32 Camilo Pascual	.75	.35
☐ 33 Pete Ward	.50	.23
☐ 34 Jim Maloney	.75	.35
☐ 35 Dave Wickersham	.50	.23
☐ 36 Johnny Callison	.75	.35
☐ 37 Juan Marichal	4.00	1.80
☐ 38 Harmon Killebrew	4.00	1.80
☐ 39 Luis Aparicio	3.00	1.35
☐ 40 Dick Radatz	.50	.23
☐ 41 Bob Gibson	4.00	1.80
☐ 42 Dick Stuart SP	10.00	4.50
☐ 43 Tommy Davis	.75	.35
☐ 44 Tony Oliva	1.25	.55
☐ 45 Wayne Causey SP	10.00	4.50
☐ 46 Max Alvis	.50	.23
☐ 47 Galen Cisco SP	10.00	4.50
☐ 48 Carl Yastrzemski	5.00	2.20
☐ 49 Hank Aaron	10.00	4.50
☐ 50 Brooks Robinson	5.00	2.20
☐ 51 Willie Mays SP	50.00	22.00
☐ 52 Billy Williams	3.00	1.35
☐ 53 Juan Pizarro	.50	.23
☐ 54 Leon Wagner	.50	.23
☐ 55 Orlando Cepeda	1.25	.55
☐ 56 Vada Pinson	.75	.35
☐ 57 Ken Boyer	.75	.35
☐ 58 Ron Santo	1.25	.55
☐ 59 John Romano	.50	.23
☐ 60 Bill Skowron SP	15.00	6.75

1964 Topps Stand Ups

In 1964 Topps produced a die-cut "Stand-Up" card design for the first time since their Connie Mack and Current All Stars of 1951. The cards have full-length, color player photos set against a green and yellow background. Of the 77 cards in the set, 22 were single printed and these are marked in the checklist below with an SP. These unnumbered cards are standard-size (2 1/2" by 3 1/2"), blank backed, and have been numbered here for reference in alphabetical order of players.

	NRMT	VG-E
COMPLETE SET (77)	2500.00	1100.00
COMMON CARD (1-77)	7.50	3.40
COMMON CARD SP	30.00	13.50
WRAPPER (1-CENT)	150.00	70.00
WRAPPER (5-CENT)	325.00	145.00
☐ 1 Hank Aaron	150.00	70.00
☐ 2 Hank Aguirre	7.50	3.40
☐ 3 George Altman	7.50	3.40
☐ 4 Max Alvis	7.50	3.40
☐ 5 Bob Aspromonte	7.50	3.40
☐ 6 Jack Baldschun SP	30.00	13.50
☐ 7 Ernie Banks	60.00	27.00
☐ 8 Steve Barber	7.50	3.40
☐ 9 Earl Battey	7.50	3.40
☐ 10 Ken Boyer	10.00	4.50
☐ 11 Ernie Broglio	7.50	3.40
☐ 12 John Callison	10.00	4.50
☐ 13 Norm Cash SP	35.00	16.00
☐ 14 Wayne Causey	7.50	3.40
☐ 15 Orlando Cepeda	15.00	6.75
☐ 16 Ed Charles	7.50	3.40
☐ 17 Roberto Clemente	225.00	100.00
☐ 18 Donn Clendenon SP	30.00	13.50
☐ 19 Rocky Colavito	15.00	6.75
☐ 20 Ray Culp SP	30.00	13.50
☐ 21 Tommy Davis	10.00	4.50
☐ 22 Don Drysdale SP	100.00	45.00
☐ 23 Dick Ellsworth	7.50	3.40
☐ 24 Dick Farrell	7.50	3.40
☐ 25 Jim Fregosi	10.00	4.50
☐ 26 Bob Friend	7.50	3.40
☐ 27 Jim Gentile	10.00	4.50
☐ 28 Jesse Gonder SP	30.00	13.50
☐ 29 Tony Gonzalez SP	30.00	13.50
☐ 30 Dick Groat	10.00	4.50
☐ 31 Woody Held	7.50	3.40
☐ 32 Chuck Hinton	7.50	3.40
☐ 33 Elston Howard	10.00	4.50
☐ 34 Frank Howard SP	35.00	16.00
☐ 35 Ron Hunt	7.50	3.40
☐ 36 Al Jackson	7.50	3.40
☐ 37 Ken Johnson	7.50	3.40
☐ 38 Al Kaline	60.00	27.00
☐ 39 Harmon Killebrew	50.00	22.00
☐ 40 Sandy Koufax	100.00	45.00
☐ 41 Don Lock SP	30.00	13.50
☐ 42 Jerry Lumpe SP	30.00	13.50
☐ 43 Jim Maloney	10.00	4.50
☐ 44 Frank Malzone	7.50	3.40
☐ 45 Mickey Mantle	550.00	250.00
☐ 46 Juan Marichal SP	100.00	45.00
☐ 47 Eddie Mathews SP	100.00	45.00
☐ 48 Willie Mays	160.00	70.00
☐ 49 Bill Mazeroski	15.00	6.75
☐ 50 Ken McBride	7.50	3.40
☐ 51 Willie McCovey SP	100.00	45.00
☐ 52 Claude Osteen	10.00	4.50
☐ 53 Jim O'Toole	7.50	3.40
☐ 54 Camilo Pascual	10.00	4.50
☐ 55 Albie Pearson SP	30.00	13.50
☐ 56 Gary Peters	7.50	3.40
☐ 57 Vada Pinson	10.00	4.50
☐ 58 Juan Pizarro	7.50	3.40
☐ 59 Boog Powell	12.00	5.50
☐ 60 Bobby Richardson	10.00	4.50
☐ 61 Brooks Robinson	60.00	27.00
☐ 62 Floyd Robinson	7.50	3.40
☐ 63 Frank Robinson	60.00	27.00
☐ 64 Ed Roebuck SP	30.00	13.50
☐ 65 Rich Rollins	7.50	3.40
☐ 66 John Romano	7.50	3.40
☐ 67 Ron Santo SP	35.00	16.00
☐ 68 Norm Siebern	7.50	3.40
☐ 69 Warren Spahn SP	100.00	45.00
☐ 70 Dick Stuart SP	30.00	13.50
☐ 71 Lee Thomas	7.50	3.40
☐ 72 Joe Torre	12.00	5.50
☐ 73 Pete Ward	7.50	3.40
☐ 74 Bill White SP	35.00	16.00
☐ 75 Billy Williams SP	75.00	34.00
☐ 76 Hal Woodeshick SP	30.00	13.50
☐ 77 Carl Yastrzemski SP	400.00	180.00

1965 Topps

The cards in this 598-card set measure 2 1/2" by 3 1/2". The cards comprising the 1965 Topps set have team names located within a distinctive pennant design below the picture. The cards have blue borders on the reverse and were issued by series. Within this last series (523-598) there are 44 cards that were printed in lesser quantities than the other cards in that series; these shorter-printed cards are marked by SP in the checklist

below. Featured subsets within this set include League Leaders (1-12) and World Series cards (132-139). This was the last year Topps issued one-card penny packs. Card were also issued in five-card nickle packs. The key Rookie Cards in this set are Steve Carlton, Jim "Catfish" Hunter, Joe Morgan, Mansori Murakami and Tony Perez.

	NRMT	VG-E
COMPLETE SET (598)	3500.00	1600.00
COMMON CARD (1-196)	2.00	.90
COMMON CARD (197-283)	2.50	1.10
COMMON CARD (284-370)	4.00	1.80
COMMON CARD (371-598)	7.00	3.10
WRAPPER (1-CENT)	125.00	55.00
WRAPPER (5-CENT)	100.00	45.00
☐ 1 AL Batting Leaders Tony Oliva Elston Howard Brooks Robinson	20.00	6.00
☐ 2 NL Batting Leaders Bob Clemente Hank Aaron Rico Carty	25.00	11.00
☐ 3 AL Home Run Leaders Harmon Killebrew Mickey Mantle Boog Powell	40.00	18.00
☐ 4 NL Home Run Leaders Willie Mays Billy Williams Jim Ray Hart Orlando Cepeda Johnny Callison	15.00	6.75
☐ 5 AL RBI Leaders Brooks Robinson Harmon Killebrew Mickey Mantle Dick Stuart	40.00	18.00
☐ 6 NL RBI Leaders Ken Boyer Willie Mays Ron Santo	12.00	5.50
☐ 7 AL ERA Leaders Dean Chance Joel Horlen	4.00	1.80
☐ 8 NL ERA Leaders Sandy Koufax Don Drysdale	20.00	9.00
☐ 9 AL Pitching Leaders Dean Chance Gary Peters Dave Wickersham Juan Pizarro Wally Bunker	4.00	1.80
☐ 10 NL Pitching Leaders Larry Jackson Ray Sadecki Juan Marichal	4.00	1.80
☐ 11 AL Strikeout Leaders Al Downing Dean Chance Camilo Pascual	4.00	1.80
☐ 12 NL Strikeout Leaders Bob Veale Don Drysdale Bob Gibson	8.00	3.60
☐ 13 Pedro Ramos	4.00	1.80
☐ 14 Len Gabrielson	2.00	.90
☐ 15 Robin Roberts	10.00	4.50
☐ 16 Houston Rookie DP Joe Morgan Sonny Jackson	70.00	32.00
☐ 17 Johnny Romano	2.00	.90
☐ 18 Bill McCool	2.00	.90
☐ 19 Gates Brown	4.00	1.80
☐ 20 Jim Bunning	10.00	4.50
☐ 21 Don Blasingame	2.00	.90
☐ 22 Charlie Smith	2.00	.90
☐ 23 Bob Tiefenauer	2.00	.90
☐ 24 Minnesota Twins Team Card	4.00	1.80
☐ 25 Al McBean	2.00	.90
☐ 26 Bobby Knoop	2.00	.90

☐ 27 Dick Bertell 2.00 .90
☐ 28 Barney Schultz 2.00 .90
☐ 29 Felix Mantilla 2.00 .90
☐ 30 Jim Bouton 6.00 2.70
☐ 31 Mike White 2.00 .90
☐ 32 Herman Franks MG 2.00 .90
☐ 33 Jackie Brandt 2.00 .90
☐ 34 Cal Koonce 2.00 .90
☐ 35 Ed Charles 2.00 .90
☐ 36 Bobby Wine 2.00 .90
☐ 37 Fred Gladding 2.00 .90
☐ 38 Jim King 2.00 .90
☐ 39 Gerry Arrigo 2.00 .90
☐ 40 Frank Howard 5.00 2.20
☐ 41 White Sox Rookies 2.00 .90
Bruce Howard
Marv Staehle
☐ 42 Earl Wilson 4.00 1.80
☐ 43 Mike Shannon 4.00 1.80
(Name in red, other
Cardinals in yellow)
☐ 44 Wade Blasingame 2.00 .90
☐ 45 Roy McMillan 4.00 1.80
☐ 46 Bob Lee 2.00 .90
☐ 47 Tommy Harper 4.00 1.80
☐ 48 Claude Raymond 4.00 1.80
☐ 49 Orioles Rookies 4.00 1.80
Curt Blefary
John Miller
☐ 50 Juan Marichal 10.00 4.50
☐ 51 Bill Bryan 2.00 .90
☐ 52 Ed Roebuck 2.00 .90
☐ 53 Dick McAuliffe 4.00 1.80
☐ 54 Joe Gibbon 2.00 .90
☐ 55 Tony Conigliaro 15.00 6.75
☐ 56 Ron Kline 2.00 .90
☐ 57 Cardinals Team 4.00 1.80
☐ 58 Fred Talbot 2.00 .90
☐ 59 Nate Oliver 2.00 .90
☐ 60 Jim O'Toole 4.00 1.80
☐ 61 Chris Cannizzaro 2.00 .90
☐ 62 Jim Kaat UER DP 6.00 2.70
(Misspelled Katt)
☐ 63 Ty Cline 2.00 .90
☐ 64 Lou Burdette 5.00 2.20
☐ 65 Tony Kubek 5.00 2.20
☐ 66 Bill Rigney MG 2.00 .90
☐ 67 Harvey Haddix 4.00 1.80
☐ 68 Del Crandall 4.00 1.80
☐ 69 Bill Virdon 4.00 1.80
☐ 70 Bill Skowron 5.00 2.20
☐ 71 John O'Donoghue 2.00 .90
☐ 72 Tony Gonzalez 2.00 .90
☐ 73 Dennis Ribant 2.00 .90
☐ 74 Red Sox Rookies 10.00 4.50
Rico Petrocelli
Jerry Stephenson
☐ 75 Deron Johnson 4.00 1.80
☐ 76 Sam McDowell 4.00 1.80
☐ 77 Doug Camilli 2.00 .90
☐ 78 Dal Maxvill 2.00 .90
☐ 79A Checklist 1 10.00 2.00
(61 Cannizzaro)
☐ 79B Checklist 1 10.00 2.00
(61 C.Cannizzaro)
☐ 80 Turk Farrell 2.00 .90
☐ 81 Don Buford 4.00 1.80
☐ 82 Braves Rookies 6.00 2.70
Santos Alomar
John Braun
☐ 83 George Thomas 2.00 .90
☐ 84 Ron Herbel 2.00 .90
☐ 85 Willie Smith 2.00 .90
☐ 86 Les Narum 2.00 .90
☐ 87 Nelson Mathews 2.00 .90
☐ 88 Jack Lamabe 2.00 .90
☐ 89 Mike Hershberger 2.00 .90
☐ 90 Rich Rollins 4.00 1.80
☐ 91 Cubs Team 4.00 1.80
☐ 92 Dick Howser 4.00 1.80
☐ 93 Jack Fisher 2.00 .90
☐ 94 Charlie Lau 4.00 1.80
☐ 95 Bill Mazeroski DP 5.00 2.20
☐ 96 Sonny Siebert 4.00 1.80
☐ 97 Pedro Gonzalez 2.00 .90
☐ 98 Bob Miller 2.00 .90
☐ 99 Gil Hodges MG 7.00 3.10
☐ 100 Ken Boyer 5.00 2.20
☐ 101 Fred Newman 2.00 .90
☐ 102 Steve Boros 2.00 .90
☐ 103 Harvey Kuenn 4.00 1.80
☐ 104 Checklist 2 10.00 2.00
☐ 105 Chico Salmon 2.00 .90
☐ 106 Gene Oliver 2.00 .90
☐ 107 Phillies Rookies 4.00 1.80
Pat Corrales
Costen Shockley

☐ 108 Don Mincher 2.00 .90
☐ 109 Walt Bond 2.00 .90
☐ 110 Ron Santo 6.00 2.70
☐ 111 Lee Thomas 4.00 1.80
☐ 112 Derrell Griffith 2.00 .90
☐ 113 Steve Barber 2.00 .90
☐ 114 Jim Hickman 4.00 1.80
☐ 115 Bobby Richardson 6.00 2.70
☐ 116 Cardinals Rookies 4.00 1.80
Dave Dowling
Bob Tolan
☐ 117 Wes Stock 2.00 .90
☐ 118 Hal Lanier 4.00 1.80
☐ 119 John Kennedy 2.00 .90
☐ 120 Frank Robinson 35.00 16.00
☐ 121 Gene Alley 4.00 1.80
☐ 122 Bill Pleis 2.00 .90
☐ 123 Frank Thomas 4.00 1.80
☐ 124 Tom Satriano 2.00 .90
☐ 125 Juan Pizarro 2.00 .90
☐ 126 Dodgers Team 6.00 2.70
☐ 127 Frank Lary 2.00 .90
☐ 128 Vic Davalillo 2.00 .90
☐ 129 Bennie Daniels 2.00 .90
☐ 130 Al Kaline 35.00 16.00
☐ 131 Johnny Keane MG 2.00 .90
☐ 132 Mike Shannon WS 6.00 2.70
☐ 133 Mel Stottlemyre WS 6.00 2.70
☐ 134 Mickey Mantle WS 75.00 34.00
Mantle's Clutch HR
☐ 135 Ken Boyer WS 6.00 2.70
☐ 136 Tim McCarver WS 6.00 2.70
☐ 137 Jim Bouton WS 6.00 2.70
☐ 138 Bob Gibson WS 12.00 5.50
☐ 139 World Series Summary 4.00 1.80
Cards celebrate
☐ 140 Dean Chance 5.00 2.20
☐ 141 Charlie James 2.00 .90
☐ 142 Bill Monbouquette 2.00 .90
☐ 143 Pirates Rookies 2.00 .90
John Gelnar
Jerry May
☐ 144 Ed Kranepool 4.00 1.80
☐ 145 Luis Tiant 12.00 5.50
☐ 146 Ron Hansen 2.00 .90
☐ 147 Dennis Bennett 2.00 .90
☐ 148 Willie Kirkland 2.00 .90
☐ 149 Wayne Schurr 2.00 .90
☐ 150 Brooks Robinson 35.00 16.00
☐ 151 Athletics Team 4.00 1.80
☐ 152 Phil Ortega 2.00 .90
☐ 153 Norm Cash 5.00 2.20
☐ 154 Bob Humphreys 2.00 .90
☐ 155 Roger Maris 40.00 18.00
☐ 156 Bob Sadowski 2.00 .90
☐ 157 Zoilo Versalles 4.00 1.80
☐ 158 Dick Sisler 2.00 .90
☐ 159 Jim Duffalo 2.00 .90
☐ 160 Bob Clemente UER 160.00 70.00
(1960 Pittsburfh)
☐ 161 Frank Baumann 2.00 .90
☐ 162 Russ Nixon 2.00 .90
☐ 163 Johnny Briggs 2.00 .90
☐ 164 Al Spangler 2.00 .90
☐ 165 Dick Ellsworth 2.00 .90
☐ 166 Indians Rookies 5.00 2.20
George Culver
Tommie Agee
☐ 167 Bill Wakefield 2.00 .90
☐ 168 Dick Green 2.00 .90
☐ 169 Dave Vineyard 2.00 .90
☐ 170 Hank Aaron 90.00 40.00
☐ 171 Jim Roland 2.00 .90
☐ 172 Jimmy Piersall 5.00 2.20
☐ 173 Detroit Tigers 4.00 1.80
Team Card
☐ 174 Joey Jay 2.00 .90
☐ 175 Bob Aspromonte 2.00 .90
☐ 176 Willie McCovey 20.00 9.00
☐ 177 Pete Mikkelsen 2.00 .90
☐ 178 Dalton Jones 2.00 .90
☐ 179 Hal Woodeshick 2.00 .90
☐ 180 Bob Allison 4.00 1.80
☐ 181 Senators Rookies 2.00 .90
Don Loun
Joe McCabe
☐ 182 Mike de la Hoz 2.00 .90
☐ 183 Dave Nicholson 2.00 .90
☐ 184 John Boozer 2.00 .90
☐ 185 Max Alvis 2.00 .90
☐ 186 Billy Cowan 2.00 .90
☐ 187 Casey Stengel MG 15.00 6.75
☐ 188 Sam Bowens 2.00 .90
☐ 189 Checklist 3 10.00 2.00
☐ 190 Bill White 5.00 2.20
☐ 191 Phil Regan 4.00 1.80
☐ 192 Jim Coker 2.00 .90

☐ 193 Gaylord Perry 18.00 8.00
☐ 194 Rookie Stars 2.00 .90
Bill Kelso
Rick Reichardt
☐ 195 Bob Veale 4.00 1.80
☐ 196 Ron Fairly 5.00 2.20
☐ 197 Diego Segui 2.50 1.10
☐ 198 Smoky Burgess 4.00 1.80
☐ 199 Bob Heffner 2.50 1.10
☐ 200 Joe Torre 6.00 2.70
☐ 201 Twins Rookies 4.00 1.80
Sandy Valdespino
Cesar Tovar
☐ 202 Leo Burke 2.50 1.10
☐ 203 Dallas Green 4.00 1.80
☐ 204 Russ Snyder 2.50 1.10
☐ 205 Warren Spahn 30.00 13.50
☐ 206 Willie Horton 4.00 1.80
☐ 207 Pete Rose 140.00 65.00
☐ 208 Tommy John 8.00 3.60
☐ 209 Pirates Team 6.00 2.70
☐ 210 Jim Fregosi 5.00 2.20
☐ 211 Steve Ridzik 2.50 1.10
☐ 212 Ron Brand 2.50 1.10
☐ 213 Jim Davenport 2.50 1.10
☐ 214 Bob Purkey 2.50 1.10
☐ 215 Pete Ward 2.50 1.10
☐ 216 Al Worthington 2.50 1.10
☐ 217 Walter Alston MG 5.00 2.20
☐ 218 Dick Schofield 2.50 1.10
☐ 219 Bob Meyer 2.50 1.10
☐ 220 Billy Williams 10.00 4.50
☐ 221 John Tsitouris 2.50 1.10
☐ 222 Bob Tillman 2.50 1.10
☐ 223 Dan Osinski 2.50 1.10
☐ 224 Bob Chance 2.50 1.10
☐ 225 Bo Belinsky 4.00 1.80
☐ 226 Yankees Rookies 4.00 1.80
Elvio Jimenez
Jake Gibbs
☐ 227 Bobby Klaus 2.50 1.10
☐ 228 Jack Sanford 2.50 1.10
☐ 229 Lou Clinton 2.50 1.10
☐ 230 Ray Sadecki 2.50 1.10
☐ 231 Jerry Adair 2.50 1.10
☐ 232 Steve Blass 4.00 1.80
☐ 233 Don Zimmer 4.00 1.80
☐ 234 White Sox Team 4.00 1.80
☐ 235 Chuck Hinton 2.50 1.10
☐ 236 Denny McLain 30.00 13.50
☐ 237 Bernie Allen 2.50 1.10
☐ 238 Joe Moeller 2.50 1.10
☐ 239 Doc Edwards 2.50 1.10
☐ 240 Bob Bruce 2.50 1.10
☐ 241 Mack Jones 2.50 1.10
☐ 242 George Brunet 2.50 1.10
☐ 243 Reds Rookies 4.00 1.80
Ted Davidson
Tommy Helms
☐ 244 Lindy McDaniel 4.00 1.80
☐ 245 Joe Pepitone 3.50 1.55
☐ 246 Tom Butters 4.00 1.80
☐ 247 Wally Moon 4.00 1.80
☐ 248 Gus Triandos 4.00 1.80
☐ 249 Dave McNally 4.00 1.80
☐ 250 Willie Mays 100.00 45.00
☐ 251 Billy Herman MG 5.00 2.20
☐ 252 Pete Richert 2.50 1.10
☐ 253 Danny Cater 2.50 1.10
☐ 254 Roland Sheldon 2.50 1.10
☐ 255 Camilo Pascual 4.00 1.80
☐ 256 Tito Francona 2.50 1.10
☐ 257 Jim Wynn 5.00 2.20
☐ 258 Larry Bearnarth 2.50 1.10
☐ 259 Tigers Rookies 7.00 3.10
Jim Northrup
Ray Oyler
☐ 260 Don Drysdale 20.00 9.00
☐ 261 Duke Carmel 2.50 1.10
☐ 262 Bud Daley 2.50 1.10
☐ 263 Marty Keough 2.50 1.10
☐ 264 Bob Buhl 4.00 1.80
☐ 265 Jim Pagliaroni 2.50 1.10
☐ 266 Bert Campaneris 10.00 4.50
☐ 267 Senators Team 4.00 1.80
☐ 268 Ken McBride 2.50 1.10
☐ 269 Frank Bolling 2.50 1.10
☐ 270 Milt Pappas 4.00 1.80
☐ 271 Don Wert 2.50 1.10
☐ 272 Chuck Schilling 2.50 1.10
☐ 273 Checklist 4 10.00 2.00
☐ 274 Lum Harris MG 2.50 1.10
☐ 275 Dick Groat 5.00 2.20
☐ 276 Hoyt Wilhelm 10.00 4.50
☐ 277 Johnny Lewis 2.50 1.10
☐ 278 Ken Retzer 2.50 1.10
☐ 279 Dick Tracewski 2.50 1.10

☐ 280 Dick Stuart 4.00 1.80
☐ 281 Bill Stafford 2.50 1.10
☐ 282 Giants Rookies 40.00 18.00
Dick Estelle
Masanori Murakami
☐ 283 Fred Whitfield 2.50 1.10
☐ 284 Nick Willhite 4.00 1.80
☐ 285 Ron Hunt 4.00 1.80
☐ 286 Athletics Rookies 4.00 1.80
Jim Dickson
Aurelio Monteagudo
☐ 287 Gary Kolb 4.00 1.80
☐ 288 Jack Hamilton 4.00 1.80
☐ 289 Gordy Coleman 6.00 2.70
☐ 290 Wally Bunker 6.00 2.70
☐ 291 Jerry Lynch 4.00 1.80
☐ 292 Larry Yellen 4.00 1.80
☐ 293 Angels Team 10.00 4.50
☐ 294 Tim McCarver 8.00 3.60
☐ 295 Dick Radatz 6.00 2.70
☐ 296 Tony Taylor 6.00 2.70
☐ 297 Dave DeBusschere 8.00 3.60
☐ 298 Jim Stewart 4.00 1.80
☐ 299 Jerry Zimmerman 4.00 1.80
☐ 300 Sandy Koufax 120.00 55.00
☐ 301 Birdie Tebbetts MG 6.00 2.70
☐ 302 Al Stanek 4.00 1.80
☐ 303 John Orsino 4.00 1.80
☐ 304 Dave Stenhouse 4.00 1.80
☐ 305 Rico Carty 6.00 2.70
☐ 306 Bubba Phillips 4.00 1.80
☐ 307 Barry Latman 4.00 1.80
☐ 308 Mets Rookies 6.00 2.70
Cleon Jones
Tom Parsons
☐ 309 Steve Hamilton 6.00 2.70
☐ 310 Johnny Callison 6.00 2.70
☐ 311 Orlando Pena 4.00 1.80
☐ 312 Joe Nuxhall 4.00 1.80
☐ 313 Jim Schaffer 4.00 1.80
☐ 314 Sterling Slaughter 4.00 1.80
☐ 315 Frank Malzone 6.00 2.70
☐ 316 Reds Team 10.00 4.50
☐ 317 Don McMahon 4.00 1.80
☐ 318 Matty Alou 8.00 3.60
☐ 319 Ken McMullen 4.00 1.80
☐ 320 Bob Gibson 40.00 18.00
☐ 321 Rusty Staub 8.00 3.60
☐ 322 Rick Wise 6.00 2.70
☐ 323 Hank Bauer MG 6.00 2.70
☐ 324 Bobby Locke 4.00 1.80
☐ 325 Donn Clendenon 6.00 2.70
☐ 326 Dwight Siebler 4.00 1.80
☐ 327 Denis Menke 4.00 1.80
☐ 328 Eddie Fisher 4.00 1.80
☐ 329 Hawk Taylor 4.00 1.80
☐ 330 Whitey Ford 35.00 16.00
☐ 331 Dodgers Rookies 6.00 2.70
Al Ferrara
John Purdin
☐ 332 Ted Abernathy 4.00 1.80
☐ 333 Tom Reynolds 4.00 1.80
☐ 334 Vic Roznovsky 4.00 1.80
☐ 335 Mickey Lolich 8.00 3.60
☐ 336 Woody Held 4.00 1.80
☐ 337 Mike Cuellar 6.00 2.70
☐ 338 Philadelphia Phillies 10.00 4.50
Team Card
☐ 339 Ryne Duren 6.00 2.70
☐ 340 Tony Oliva 20.00 9.00
☐ 341 Bob Bolin 4.00 1.80
☐ 342 Bob Rodgers 6.00 2.70
☐ 343 Mike McCormick 6.00 2.70
☐ 344 Wes Parker 6.00 2.70
☐ 345 Floyd Robinson 4.00 1.80
☐ 346 Bobby Bragan MG 4.00 1.80
☐ 347 Roy Face 6.00 2.70
☐ 348 George Banks 4.00 1.80
☐ 349 Larry Miller 4.00 1.80
☐ 350 Mickey Mantle 550.00 250.00
☐ 351 Jim Perry 6.00 2.70
☐ 352 Alex Johnson 6.00 2.70
☐ 353 Jerry Lumpe 4.00 1.80
☐ 354 Cubs Rookies 4.00 1.80
Billy Ott
Jack Warner
☐ 355 Vada Pinson 8.00 3.60
☐ 356 Bill Spanswick 4.00 1.80
☐ 357 Carl Warwick 4.00 1.80
☐ 358 Albie Pearson 6.00 2.70
☐ 359 Ken Johnson 4.00 1.80
☐ 360 Orlando Cepeda 8.00 3.60
☐ 361 Checklist 5 15.00 3.00
☐ 362 Don Schwall 4.00 1.80
☐ 363 Bob Johnson 4.00 1.80
☐ 364 Galen Cisco 4.00 1.80
☐ 365 Jim Gentile 6.00 2.70
☐ 366 Dan Schneider 4.00 1.80
☐ 367 Leon Wagner 4.00 1.80
☐ 368 White Sox Rookies 6.00 2.70
Ken Berry
Joel Gibson
☐ 369 Phil Linz 6.00 2.70
☐ 370 Tommy Davis 6.00 2.70
☐ 371 Frank Kreutzer 7.00 3.10
☐ 372 Clay Dalrymple 7.00 3.10
☐ 373 Curt Simmons 7.00 3.10
☐ 374 Angels Rookies 7.00 3.10
Jose Cardenal
Dick Simpson
☐ 375 Dave Wickersham 7.00 3.10
☐ 376 Jim Landis 7.00 3.10
☐ 377 Willie Stargell 30.00 13.50
☐ 378 Chuck Estrada 7.00 3.10
☐ 379 Giants Team 15.00 6.75
☐ 380 Rocky Colavito 18.00 8.00
☐ 381 Al Jackson 7.00 3.10
☐ 382 J.C. Martin 7.00 3.10
☐ 383 Felipe Alou 10.00 4.50
☐ 384 Johnny Klippstein 7.00 3.10
☐ 385 Carl Yastrzemski 70.00 32.00
☐ 386 Cubs Rookies 7.00 3.10
Paul Jaeckel
Fred Norman
☐ 387 Johnny Podres 10.00 4.50
☐ 388 John Blanchard 15.00 6.75
☐ 389 Don Larsen 10.00 4.50
☐ 390 Bill Freehan 10.00 4.50
☐ 391 Mel McGaha MG 7.00 3.10
☐ 392 Bob Friend 15.00 6.75
☐ 393 Ed Kirkpatrick 7.00 3.10
☐ 394 Jim Hannan 7.00 3.10
☐ 395 Jim Ray Hart 7.00 3.10
☐ 396 Frank Bertaina 7.00 3.10
☐ 397 Jerry Buchek 7.00 3.10
☐ 398 Reds Rookies 15.00 6.75
Dan Neville
Art Shamsky
☐ 399 Ray Herbert 7.00 3.10
☐ 400 Harmon Killebrew 40.00 18.00
☐ 401 Carl Willey 7.00 3.10
☐ 402 Joe Amalfitano 7.00 3.10
☐ 403 Boston Red Sox 15.00 6.75
Team Card
☐ 404 Stan Williams 7.00 3.10
(Listed as Indian
but Yankee cap)
☐ 405 John Roseboro 15.00 6.75
☐ 406 Ralph Terry 15.00 6.75
☐ 407 Lee Maye 7.00 3.10
☐ 408 Larry Sherry 7.00 3.10
☐ 409 Astros Rookies 10.00 4.50
Jim Beauchamp
Larry Dierker
☐ 410 Luis Aparicio 12.00 5.50
☐ 411 Roger Craig 15.00 6.75
☐ 412 Bob Bailey 7.00 3.10
☐ 413 Hal Reniff 7.00 3.10
☐ 414 Al Lopez MG 10.00 4.50
☐ 415 Curt Flood 10.00 4.50
☐ 416 Jim Brewer 7.00 3.10
☐ 417 Ed Brinkman 7.00 3.10
☐ 418 Johnny Edwards 7.00 3.10
☐ 419 Ruben Amaro 7.00 3.10
☐ 420 Larry Jackson 7.00 3.10
☐ 421 Twins Rookies 7.00 3.10
Gary Dotter
Jay Ward
☐ 422 Aubrey Gatewood 7.00 3.10
☐ 423 Jesse Gonder 7.00 3.10
☐ 424 Gary Bell 7.00 3.10
☐ 425 Wayne Causey 7.00 3.10
☐ 426 Braves Team 25.00 11.00
☐ 427 Bob Saverine 7.00 3.10
☐ 428 Bob Shaw 7.00 3.10
☐ 429 Don Demeter 7.00 3.10
☐ 430 Gary Peters 7.00 3.10
☐ 431 Cards Rookies 10.00 4.50
Nelson Briles
Wayne Spiezio
☐ 432 Jim Grant 15.00 6.75
☐ 433 John Bateman 7.00 3.10
☐ 434 Dave Morehead 7.00 3.10
☐ 435 Willie Davis 10.00 4.50
☐ 436 Don Elston 7.00 3.10
☐ 437 Chico Cardenas 15.00 6.75
☐ 438 Harry Walker MG 7.00 3.10
☐ 439 Moe Drabowsky 15.00 6.75
☐ 440 Tom Tresh 10.00 4.50
☐ 441 Denny Lemaster 7.00 3.10
☐ 442 Vic Power 7.00 3.10
☐ 443 Checklist 6 25.00 5.00
☐ 444 Bob Hendley 7.00 3.10
☐ 445 Don Lock 7.00 3.10
☐ 446 Art Mahaffey 7.00 3.10
☐ 447 Julian Javier 15.00 6.75
☐ 448 Lee Stange 7.00 3.10
☐ 449 Mets Rookies 7.00 3.10
Jerry Hinsley
Gary Kroll
☐ 450 Elston Howard 10.00 4.50
☐ 451 Jim Owens 7.00 3.10
☐ 452 Gary Geiger 7.00 3.10
☐ 453 Dodgers Rookies 15.00 6.75
Willie Crawford
John Werhas
☐ 454 Ed Rakow 7.00 3.10
☐ 455 Norm Siebern 7.00 3.10
☐ 456 Bill Henry 7.00 3.10
☐ 457 Bob Kennedy MG 15.00 6.75
☐ 458 John Buzhardt 7.00 3.10
☐ 459 Frank Kostro 7.00 3.10
☐ 460 Richie Allen 40.00 18.00
☐ 461 Braves Rookies 60.00 27.00
Clay Carroll
Phil Niekro
☐ 462 Lew Krausse UER 7.00 3.10
(Photo actually
Pete Lovrich)
☐ 463 Manny Mota 10.00 4.50
☐ 464 Ron Piche 7.00 3.10
☐ 465 Tom Haller 15.00 6.75
☐ 466 Senators Rookies 7.00 3.10
Pete Craig
Dick Nen
☐ 467 Ray Washburn 7.00 3.10
☐ 468 Larry Brown 7.00 3.10
☐ 469 Don Nottebart 7.00 3.10
☐ 470 Yogi Berra P/CO 50.00 22.00
☐ 471 Billy Hoeft 7.00 3.10
☐ 472 Don Pavletich UER 7.00 3.10
Listed as a pitcher
☐ 473 Orioles Rookies 16.00 7.25
Paul Blair
Dave Johnson
☐ 474 Cookie Rojas 15.00 6.75
☐ 475 Clete Boyer 10.00 4.50
☐ 476 Billy O'Dell 7.00 3.10
☐ 477 Cards Rookies 250.00 110.00
Fritz Ackley
Steve Carlton
☐ 478 Wilbur Wood 10.00 4.50
☐ 479 Ken Harrelson 10.00 4.50
☐ 480 Joel Horlen 7.00 3.10
☐ 481 Cleveland Indians 25.00 11.00
Team Card
☐ 482 Bob Priddy 7.00 3.10
☐ 483 George Smith 7.00 3.10
☐ 484 Ron Perranoski 15.00 6.75
☐ 485 Nellie Fox P/CO 16.00 7.25
☐ 486 Angels Rookies 7.00 3.10
Tom Egan
Pat Rogan
☐ 487 Woody Woodward 15.00 6.75
☐ 488 Ted Wills 7.00 3.10
☐ 489 Gene Mauch MG 15.00 6.75
☐ 490 Earl Battey 7.00 3.10
☐ 491 Tracy Stallard 7.00 3.10
☐ 492 Gene Freese 7.00 3.10
☐ 493 Tigers Rookies 7.00 3.10
Bill Roman
Bruce Brubaker
☐ 494 Jay Ritchie 7.00 3.10
☐ 495 Joe Christopher 7.00 3.10
☐ 496 Joe Cunningham 7.00 3.10
☐ 497 Giants Rookies 15.00 6.75
Ken Henderson
Jack Hiatt
☐ 498 Gene Stephens 7.00 3.10
☐ 499 Stu Miller 15.00 6.75
☐ 500 Eddie Mathews 35.00 16.00
☐ 501 Indians Rookies 7.00 3.10
Ralph Gagliano
Jim Rittwage
☐ 502 Don Cardwell 7.00 3.10
☐ 503 Phil Gagliano 7.00 3.10
☐ 504 Jerry Grote 15.00 6.75
☐ 505 Ray Culp 7.00 3.10
☐ 506 Sam Mele MG 7.00 3.10
☐ 507 Sammy Ellis 7.00 3.10
☐ 508 Checklist 7 25.00 5.00
☐ 509 Red Sox Rookies 7.00 3.10
Bob Guindon
Gerry Vezendy
☐ 510 Ernie Banks 80.00 36.00
☐ 511 Ron Locke 7.00 3.10
☐ 512 Cap Peterson 7.00 3.10
☐ 513 New York Yankees 40.00 18.00
Team Card
☐ 514 Joe Azcue 7.00 3.10
☐ 515 Vern Law 15.00 6.75

Card	NRMT	VG-E
☐ 516 Al Weis	7.00	3.10
☐ 517 Angels Rookies	15.00	6.75
Paul Schaal		
Jack Warner		
☐ 518 Ken Rowe	7.00	3.10
☐ 519 Bob Uecker UER	30.00	13.50
(Posing as a left-handed batter)		
☐ 520 Tony Cloninger	7.00	3.10
☐ 521 Phillies Rookies	7.00	3.10
Dave Bennett		
Morrie Stevens		
☐ 522 Hank Aguirre	7.00	3.10
☐ 523 Mike Brumley SP	12.00	5.50
☐ 524 Dave Giusti SP	12.00	5.50
☐ 525 Eddie Bressoud	7.00	3.10
☐ 526 Athletics Rookies SP	80.00	36.00
Rene Lachemann		
Johnny Odom		
Jim Hunter UER		
(Tim on back)		
Skip Lockwood		
☐ 527 Jeff Torborg SP	16.00	7.25
☐ 528 George Altman	7.00	3.10
☐ 529 Jerry Fosnow SP	12.00	5.50
☐ 530 Jim Maloney	15.00	6.75
☐ 531 Chuck Hiller	7.00	3.10
☐ 532 Hector Lopez	15.00	6.75
☐ 533 Mets Rookies SP	25.00	11.00
Dan Napoleon		
Ron Swoboda		
Tug McGraw		
Jim Bethke		
☐ 534 John Herrnstein	7.00	3.10
☐ 535 Jack Kralick SP	12.00	5.50
☐ 536 Andre Rodgers SP	12.00	5.50
☐ 537 Angels Rookies	7.00	3.10
Marcelino Lopez		
Phil Roof		
Rudy May		
☐ 538 Chuck Dressen SP MG	15.00	6.75
☐ 539 Herm Starrette	7.00	3.10
☐ 540 Lou Brock SP	50.00	22.00
☐ 541 White Sox Rookies	7.00	3.10
Greg Bollo		
Bob Locker		
☐ 542 Lou Klimchock	7.00	3.10
☐ 543 Ed Connolly SP	12.00	5.50
☐ 544 Howie Reed	7.00	3.10
☐ 545 Jesus Alou SP	14.00	6.25
☐ 546 Indians Rookies	7.00	3.10
Bill Davis		
Mike Hedlund		
Ray Barker		
Floyd Weaver		
☐ 547 Jake Wood SP	12.00	5.50
☐ 548 Dick Stigman	7.00	3.10
☐ 549 Cubs Rookies SP	20.00	9.00
Roberto Pena		
Glenn Beckert		
☐ 550 Mel Stottlemyre SP	30.00	13.50
☐ 551 New York Mets SP	30.00	13.50
Team Card		
☐ 552 Julio Gotay	7.00	3.10
☐ 553 Astros Rookies	7.00	3.10
Dan Coombs		
Gene Ratliff		
Jack McClure		
☐ 554 Chico Ruiz SP	12.00	5.50
☐ 555 Jack Baldschun SP	12.00	5.50
☐ 556 Red Schoendienst SP MG	24.00	11.00
☐ 557 Jose Santiago	7.00	3.10
☐ 558 Tommie Sisk	7.00	3.10
☐ 559 Ed Bailey SP	12.00	5.50
☐ 560 Boog Powell SP	24.00	11.00
☐ 561 Dodgers Rookies	10.00	4.50
Dennis Daboll		
Mike Kekich		
Hector Valle		
Jim Lefebvre		
☐ 562 Billy Moran	7.00	3.10
☐ 563 Julio Navarro	7.00	3.10
☐ 564 Mel Nelson	7.00	3.10
☐ 565 Ernie Broglio SP	12.00	5.50
☐ 566 Yankees Rookies SP	15.00	6.75
Gil Blanco		
Ross Moschitto		
Art Lopez		
☐ 567 Tommie Aaron	7.00	3.10
☐ 568 Ron Taylor SP	12.00	5.50
☐ 569 Gino Cimoli SP	12.00	5.50
☐ 570 Claude Osteen SP	15.00	6.75
☐ 571 Ossie Virgil SP	12.00	5.50
☐ 572 Baltimore Orioles SP	30.00	13.50
Team Card		
☐ 573 Red Sox Rookies SP	24.00	11.00
Jim Lonborg		
Gerry Moses		
Bill Schlesinger		
Mike Ryan		
☐ 574 Roy Sievers	15.00	6.75
☐ 575 Jose Pagan	7.00	3.10
☐ 576 Terry Fox SP	12.00	5.50
☐ 577 AL Rookie Stars SP	15.00	6.75
Darold Knowles		
Don Buschhorn		
Richie Scheinblum		
☐ 578 Camilo Carreon SP	12.00	5.50
☐ 579 Dick Smith SP	12.00	5.50
☐ 580 Jimmie Hall SP	12.00	5.50
☐ 581 NL Rookie Stars SP	100.00	45.00
Tony Perez		
Dave Ricketts		
Kevin Collins		
☐ 582 Bob Schmidt SP	12.00	5.50
☐ 583 Wes Covington SP	12.00	5.50
☐ 584 Harry Bright	15.00	6.75
☐ 585 Hank Fischer	7.00	3.10
☐ 586 Tom McCraw SP	12.00	5.50
☐ 587 Joe Sparma	7.00	3.10
☐ 588 Lenny Green	7.00	3.10
☐ 589 Giants Rookies SP	12.00	5.50
Frank Linzy		
Bob Schroder		
☐ 590 John Wyatt	7.00	3.10
☐ 591 Bob Skinner SP	12.00	5.50
☐ 592 Frank Bork SP	12.00	5.50
☐ 593 Tigers Rookies SP	12.00	5.50
Jackie Moore		
John Sullivan		
☐ 594 Joe Gaines	7.00	3.10
☐ 595 Don Lee	7.00	3.10
☐ 596 Don Landrum SP	12.00	5.50
☐ 597 Twins Rookies	7.00	3.10
Joe Nossek		
John Sevcik		
Dick Reese		
☐ 598 Al Downing SP	24.00	7.25

1965 Topps Embossed Inserts

The cards in this 72-card set measure approximately 2 1/8" by 3 1/2". The 1965 Topps Embossed set contains gold foil cameo player portraits. Each league had 36 representatives set on blue backgrounds for the AL and red backgrounds for the NL. The Topps embossed set was distributed as inserts in packages of the regular 1965 baseball series.

	NRMT	VG-E
COMPLETE SET (72)	180.00	80.00
COMMON CARD (1-72)	1.00	.45
☐ 1 Carl Yastrzemski	7.00	3.10
☐ 2 Ron Fairly	1.00	.45
☐ 3 Max Alvis	1.00	.45
☐ 4 Jim Ray Hart	1.00	.45
☐ 5 Bill Skowron	1.00	.45
☐ 6 Ed Kranepool	.75	.35
☐ 7 Tim McCarver	1.00	.45
☐ 8 Sandy Koufax	12.00	5.50
☐ 9 Donn Clendenon	.75	.35
☐ 10 John Romano	1.00	.45
☐ 11 Mickey Mantle	60.00	27.00
☐ 12 Joe Torre	1.50	.70
☐ 13 Al Kaline	7.00	3.10
☐ 14 Al McBean	1.00	.45
☐ 15 Don Drysdale	5.00	2.20
☐ 16 Brooks Robinson	7.00	3.10
☐ 17 Jim Bunning	4.00	1.80
☐ 18 Gary Peters	1.00	.45
☐ 19 Roberto Clemente	25.00	11.00
☐ 20 Milt Pappas	1.00	.45
☐ 21 Wayne Causey	1.00	.45
☐ 22 Frank Robinson	7.00	3.10
☐ 23 Bill Mazeroski	1.00	.45
☐ 24 Diego Segui	1.00	.45
☐ 25 Jim Bouton	1.00	.45
☐ 26 Eddie Mathews	4.00	1.80
☐ 27 Willie Mays	18.00	8.00
☐ 28 Ron Santo	1.00	.45
☐ 29 Boog Powell	1.00	.45
☐ 30 Ken McBride	1.00	.45
☐ 31 Leon Wagner	1.00	.45
☐ 32 Johnny Callison	.75	.35
☐ 33 Zoilo Versalles	.75	.35
☐ 34 Jack Baldschun	1.00	.45
☐ 35 Ron Hunt	1.00	.45
☐ 36 Richie Allen	1.00	.45
☐ 37 Frank Malzone	1.00	.45
☐ 38 Bob Allison	.75	.35
☐ 39 Jim Fregosi	1.00	.45
☐ 40 Billy Williams	3.00	1.35
☐ 41 Bill Freehan	1.00	.45
☐ 42 Vada Pinson	1.00	.45
☐ 43 Bill White	1.00	.45
☐ 44 Roy McMillan	1.00	.45
☐ 45 Orlando Cepeda	3.00	1.35
☐ 46 Rocky Colavito	3.00	1.35
☐ 47 Ken Boyer	1.00	.45
☐ 48 Dick Radatz	1.00	.45
☐ 49 Tommy Davis	.75	.35
☐ 50 Walt Bond	.75	.35
☐ 51 John Orsino	1.00	.45
☐ 52 Joe Christopher	1.00	.45
☐ 53 Al Spangler	1.00	.45
☐ 54 Jim King	1.00	.45
☐ 55 Mickey Lolich	1.00	.45
☐ 56 Harmon Killebrew	4.00	1.80
☐ 57 Bob Shaw	1.00	.45
☐ 58 Ernie Banks	7.00	3.10
☐ 59 Hank Aaron	15.00	6.75
☐ 60 Chuck Hinton	1.00	.45
☐ 61 Bob Aspromonte	1.00	.45
☐ 62 Lee Maye	1.00	.45
☐ 63 Joe Cunningham	1.00	.45
☐ 64 Pete Ward	1.00	.45
☐ 65 Bobby Richardson	1.00	.45
☐ 66 Dean Chance	.75	.35
☐ 67 Dick Ellsworth	1.00	.45
☐ 68 Jim Maloney	.75	.35
☐ 69 Bob Gibson	4.00	1.80
☐ 70 Earl Battey	1.00	.45
☐ 71 Tony Kubek	1.00	.45
☐ 72 Jack Kralick	1.00	.45

1965 Topps Transfers Inserts

The 1965 Topps transfers (2" by 3") were issued in series of 24 each as inserts in three of the regular 1965 Topps cards series. Thirty-six of the transfers feature blue bands at the top and bottom while 36 feature red bands at the top and bottom. The team name and position are listed in the top band while the player's name is listed in the bottom band. Transfers 1-36 have blue panels whereas 37-72 have red panels. These unnumbered transfers are ordered below alphabetically by player's name within each color group. Transfers of Bob Veale and Carl Yastrzemski are supposedly tougher to find than the others in the set; they are marked below by SP.

	NRMT	VG-E
COMPLETE SET (72)	400.00	180.00
COMMON TRANSFER (1-72)	1.50	.70
☐ 1 Bob Allison	1.50	.70
☐ 2 Max Alvis	1.50	.70
☐ 3 Luis Aparicio	6.00	2.70
☐ 4 Walt Bond	1.50	.70
☐ 5 Jim Bouton	2.00	.90
☐ 6 Jim Bunning	6.00	2.70
☐ 7 Rico Carty	2.00	.90
☐ 8 Wayne Causey	1.50	.70
☐ 9 Orlando Cepeda	5.00	2.20
☐ 10 Dean Chance	1.50	.70
☐ 11 Tony Conigliaro	2.00	.90
☐ 12 Bill Freehan	2.00	.90
☐ 13 Jim Fregosi	2.00	.90
☐ 14 Bob Gibson	10.00	4.50
☐ 15 Dick Groat	2.00	.90
☐ 16 Tom Haller	1.50	.70

☐ 17 Al Jackson	1.50	.70
☐ 18 Bobby Knoop	1.50	.70
☐ 19 Jim Maloney	2.00	.90
☐ 20 Juan Marichal	6.00	2.70
☐ 21 Lee Maye	1.50	.70
☐ 22 Jim O'Toole	1.50	.70
☐ 23 Camilo Pascual	1.50	.70
☐ 24 Vada Pinson	2.00	.90
☐ 25 Juan Pizarro	1.50	.70
☐ 26 Bobby Richardson	3.00	1.35
☐ 27 Bob Rodgers	1.50	.70
☐ 28 John Roseboro	1.50	.70
☐ 29 Dick Stuart	2.00	.90
☐ 30 Luis Tiant	2.00	.90
☐ 31 Joe Torre	2.00	.90
☐ 32 Bob Veale SP	10.00	4.50
☐ 33 Leon Wagner	1.50	.70
☐ 34 Dave Wickersham	1.50	.70
☐ 35 Billy Williams	5.00	2.20
☐ 36 Carl Yastrzemski SP	40.00	18.00
☐ 37 Hank Aaron	30.00	13.50
☐ 38 Richie Allen	4.00	1.80
☐ 39 Ken Aspromonte	1.50	.70
☐ 40 Ken Boyer	3.00	1.35
☐ 41 Johnny Callison	2.00	.90
☐ 42 Dean Chance	1.50	.70
☐ 43 Joe Christopher	1.50	.70
☐ 44 Roberto Clemente	50.00	22.00
☐ 45 Rocky Colavito	5.00	2.20
☐ 46 Tommy Davis	2.00	.90
☐ 47 Don Drysdale	12.00	5.50
☐ 48 Chuck Hinton	1.50	.70
☐ 49 Frank Howard	2.00	.90
☐ 50 Ron Hunt	1.50	.70
☐ 51 Al Kaline	15.00	6.75
☐ 52 Harmon Killebrew	10.00	4.50
☐ 53 Jim King	1.50	.70
☐ 54 Ron Kline	1.50	.70
☐ 55 Sandy Koufax	25.00	11.00
☐ 56 Ed Kranepool	1.50	.70
☐ 57 Mickey Mantle	100.00	45.00
☐ 58 Willie Mays	35.00	16.00
☐ 59 Bill Mazeroski	3.00	1.35
☐ 60 Tony Oliva	4.00	1.80
☐ 61 Milt Pappas	1.50	.70
☐ 62 Gary Peters	1.50	.70
☐ 63 Boog Powell	3.00	1.35
☐ 64 Dick Radatz	1.50	.70
☐ 65 Brooks Robinson	15.00	6.75
☐ 66 Frank Robinson	15.00	6.75
☐ 67 Ron Santo	3.00	1.35
☐ 68 Diego Segui	1.50	.70
☐ 69 Bill Skowron	2.00	.90
☐ 70 Al Spangler	1.50	.70
☐ 71 Pete Ward	1.50	.70
☐ 72 Bill White	2.00	.90

1966 Topps

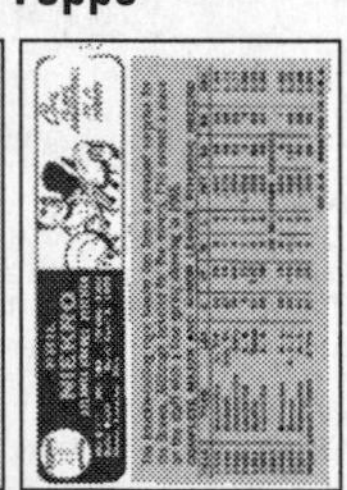

The cards in this 598-card set measure 2 1/2" by 3 1/2". There are the same number of cards as in the 1965 set. Once again, the seventh series cards (523 to 598) are considered more difficult to obtain than the cards of any other series in the set. Within this last series there are 43 cards that were printed in lesser quantities than the other cards in that series; these shorter-printed cards are marked by SP in the checklist below. Among other ways, cards were issued in five-card nickle packs. The only featured subset within this set is League Leaders (215-226). Noteworthy Rookie Cards in the set include Jim Palmer (126), Ferguson Jenkins (254), and Don Sutton (288). Jim Palmer is described in the bio (on his card back) as a left-hander.

	NRMT	VG-E
COMPLETE SET (598)	4000.00	1800.00
COMMON CARD (1-109)	1.50	.70
COMMON CARD (110-283)	2.00	.90
COMMON CARD (284-370)	3.00	1.35
COMMON CARD (371-446)	5.00	2.20
COMMON CARD (447-522)	9.00	4.00
COMMON CARD (523-598)	15.00	6.75
COMMON SP 523-598	30.00	13.50
WRAPPER (5-CENT)	25.00	11.00

☐ 1 Willie Mays	135.00	42.50
☐ 2 Ted Abernathy	1.50	.70
☐ 3 Sam Mele MG	1.50	.70
☐ 4 Ray Culp	1.50	.70
☐ 5 Jim Fregosi	4.00	1.80
☐ 6 Chuck Schilling	1.50	.70
☐ 7 Tracy Stallard	1.50	.70
☐ 8 Floyd Robinson	1.50	.70
☐ 9 Clete Boyer	4.00	1.80
☐ 10 Tony Cloninger	1.50	.70
☐ 11 Senators Rookies Brant Alyea Pete Craig	1.50	.70
☐ 12 John Tsitouris	1.50	.70
☐ 13 Lou Johnson	4.00	1.80
☐ 14 Norm Siebern	1.50	.70
☐ 15 Vern Law	4.00	1.80
☐ 16 Larry Brown	1.50	.70
☐ 17 John Stephenson	1.50	.70
☐ 18 Roland Sheldon	1.50	.70
☐ 19 San Francisco Giants Team Card	6.00	2.70
☐ 20 Willie Horton	4.00	1.80
☐ 21 Don Nottebart	1.50	.70
☐ 22 Joe Nossek	1.50	.70
☐ 23 Jack Sanford	1.50	.70
☐ 24 Don Kessinger	6.00	2.70
☐ 25 Pete Ward	1.50	.70
☐ 26 Ray Sadecki	1.50	.70
☐ 27 Orioles Rookies Darold Knowles Andy Etchebarren	1.50	.70
☐ 28 Phil Niekro	20.00	9.00
☐ 29 Mike Brumley	1.50	.70
☐ 30 Pete Rose DP	35.00	16.00
☐ 31 Jack Cullen	4.00	1.80
☐ 32 Adolfo Phillips	1.50	.70
☐ 33 Jim Pagliaroni	1.50	.70
☐ 34 Checklist 1	6.00	1.20
☐ 35 Ron Swoboda	4.00	1.80
☐ 36 Jim Hunter UER (Stats say 1963 and 1964, should be 1964 and 1965)	20.00	9.00
☐ 37 Billy Herman MG	4.00	1.80
☐ 38 Ron Nischwitz	1.50	.70
☐ 39 Ken Henderson	1.50	.70
☐ 40 Jim Grant	1.50	.70
☐ 41 Don LeJohn	1.50	.70
☐ 42 Aubrey Gatewood	1.50	.70
☐ 43A Don Landrum (Dark button on pants showing)	4.00	1.80
☐ 43B Don Landrum (Button on pants partially airbrushed)	20.00	9.00
☐ 43C Don Landrum (Button on pants not showing)	4.00	1.80
☐ 44 Indians Rookies Bill Davis Tom Kelley	1.50	.70
☐ 45 Jim Gentile	4.00	1.80
☐ 46 Howie Koplitz	1.50	.70
☐ 47 J.C. Martin	1.50	.70
☐ 48 Paul Blair	4.00	1.80
☐ 49 Woody Woodward	4.00	1.80
☐ 50 Mickey Mantle DP	200.00	90.00
☐ 51 Gordon Richardson	1.50	.70
☐ 52 Power Plus Wes Covington Johnny Callison	4.00	1.80
☐ 53 Bob Duliba	1.50	.70
☐ 54 Jose Pagan	1.50	.70
☐ 55 Ken Harrelson	4.00	1.80
☐ 56 Sandy Valdespino	1.50	.70
☐ 57 Jim Lefebvre	4.00	1.80
☐ 58 Dave Wickersham	1.50	.70
☐ 59 Reds Team	6.00	2.70
☐ 60 Curt Flood	4.00	1.80
☐ 61 Bob Bolin	1.50	.70
☐ 62A Merritt Ranew (With sold line)	4.00	1.80
☐ 62B Merritt Ranew (Without sold line)	30.00	13.50
☐ 63 Jim Stewart	1.50	.70
☐ 64 Bob Bruce	1.50	.70
☐ 65 Leon Wagner	1.50	.70
☐ 66 Al Weis	1.50	.70
☐ 67 Mets Rookies Cleon Jones Dick Selma	4.00	1.80
☐ 68 Hal Reniff	1.50	.70
☐ 69 Ken Hamlin	1.50	.70
☐ 70 Carl Yastrzemski	25.00	11.00
☐ 71 Frank Carpin	1.50	.70
☐ 72 Tony Perez	25.00	11.00
☐ 73 Jerry Zimmerman	1.50	.70
☐ 74 Don Mossi	4.00	1.80
☐ 75 Tommy Davis	4.00	1.80
☐ 76 Red Schoendienst MG	4.00	1.80
☐ 77 John Orsino	1.50	.70
☐ 78 Frank Linzy	1.50	.70
☐ 79 Joe Pepitone	2.50	1.10
☐ 80 Richie Allen	5.00	2.20
☐ 81 Ray Oyler	1.50	.70
☐ 82 Bob Hendley	1.50	.70
☐ 83 Albie Pearson	4.00	1.80
☐ 84 Braves Rookies Jim Beauchamp Dick Kelley	1.50	.70
☐ 85 Eddie Fisher	1.50	.70
☐ 86 John Bateman	1.50	.70
☐ 87 Dan Napoleon	1.50	.70
☐ 88 Fred Whitfield	1.50	.70
☐ 89 Ted Davidson	1.50	.70
☐ 90 Luis Aparicio	7.00	3.10
☐ 91A Bob Uecker TR	12.00	5.50
☐ 91B Bob Uecker NTR	40.00	18.00
☐ 92 Yankees Team	14.00	6.25
☐ 93 Jim Lonborg	4.00	1.80
☐ 94 Matty Alou	4.00	1.80
☐ 95 Pete Richert	1.50	.70
☐ 96 Felipe Alou	4.00	1.80
☐ 97 Jim Merritt	1.50	.70
☐ 98 Don Demeter	1.50	.70
☐ 99 Buc Belters Willie Stargell Donn Clendenon	6.00	2.70
☐ 100 Sandy Koufax	75.00	34.00
☐ 101A Checklist 2 (115 W. Spahn) ERR	16.00	3.20
☐ 101B Checklist 2 (115 Bill Henry) COR	10.00	2.00
☐ 102 Ed Kirkpatrick	1.50	.70
☐ 103A Dick Groat TR	4.00	1.80
☐ 103B Dick Groat NTR	40.00	18.00
☐ 104A Alex Johnson TR	4.00	1.80
☐ 104B Alex Johnson NTR	30.00	13.50
☐ 105 Milt Pappas	4.00	1.80
☐ 106 Rusty Staub	4.00	1.80
☐ 107 A's Rookies Larry Stahl Ron Tompkins	1.50	.70
☐ 108 Bobby Klaus	1.50	.70
☐ 109 Ralph Terry	4.00	1.80
☐ 110 Ernie Banks	30.00	13.50
☐ 111 Gary Peters	2.00	.90
☐ 112 Manny Mota	4.00	1.80
☐ 113 Hank Aguirre	2.00	.90
☐ 114 Jim Gosger	2.00	.90
☐ 115 Bill Henry	2.00	.90
☐ 116 Walter Alston MG	4.00	1.80
☐ 117 Jake Gibbs	4.00	1.80
☐ 118 Mike McCormick	4.00	1.80
☐ 119 Art Shamsky	2.00	.90
☐ 120 Harmon Killebrew	16.00	7.25
☐ 121 Ray Herbert	2.00	.90
☐ 122 Joe Gaines	2.00	.90
☐ 123 Pirates Rookies Frank Bork Jerry May	2.00	.90
☐ 124 Tug McGraw	4.00	1.80
☐ 125 Lou Brock	20.00	9.00
☐ 126 Jim Palmer UER (Described as a lefthander on card back)	100.00	45.00
☐ 127 Ken Berry	2.00	.90
☐ 128 Jim Landis	2.00	.90
☐ 129 Jack Kralick	2.00	.90
☐ 130 Joe Torre	4.00	1.80
☐ 131 Angels Team	6.00	2.70
☐ 132 Orlando Cepeda	5.00	2.20
☐ 133 Don McMahon	2.00	.90
☐ 134 Wes Parker	4.00	1.80
☐ 135 Dave Morehead	2.00	.90
☐ 136 Woody Held	2.00	.90
☐ 137 Pat Corrales	4.00	1.80
☐ 138 Roger Repoz	2.00	.90
☐ 139 Cubs Rookies Byron Browne Don Young	2.00	.90
☐ 140 Jim Maloney	4.00	1.80
☐ 141 Tom McCraw	2.00	.90
☐ 142 Don Dennis	2.00	.90
☐ 143 Jose Tartabull	4.00	1.80
☐ 144 Don Schwall	2.00	.90
☐ 145 Bill Freehan	4.00	1.80
☐ 146 George Altman	2.00	.90
☐ 147 Lum Harris MG	2.00	.90
☐ 148 Bob Johnson	2.00	.90

☐ 149 Dick Nen .... 2.00 .90
☐ 150 Rocky Colavito 8.00 3.60
☐ 151 Gary Wagner .... 2.00 .90
☐ 152 Frank Malzone 4.00 1.80
☐ 153 Rico Carty 4.00 1.80
☐ 154 Chuck Hiller .... 2.00 .90
☐ 155 Marcelino Lopez .... 2.00 .90
☐ 156 Double Play Combo .... 2.00 .90
Dick Schofield
Hal Lanier
☐ 157 Rene Lachemann .... 2.00 .90
☐ 158 Jim Brewer .... 2.00 .90
☐ 159 Chico Ruiz .... 2.00 .90
☐ 160 Whitey Ford 25.00 11.00
☐ 161 Jerry Lumpe .... 2.00 .90
☐ 162 Lee Maye .... 2.00 .90
☐ 163 Tito Francona .... 2.00 .90
☐ 164 White Sox Rookies 4.00 1.80
Tommie Agee
Marv Staehle
☐ 165 Don Lock .... 2.00 .90
☐ 166 Chris Krug .... 2.00 .90
☐ 167 Boog Powell 5.00 2.20
☐ 168 Dan Osinski .... 2.00 .90
☐ 169 Duke Sims .... 2.00 .90
☐ 170 Cookie Rojas 4.00 1.80
☐ 171 Nick Willhite .... 2.00 .90
☐ 172 Mets Team 6.00 2.70
☐ 173 Al Spangler .... 2.00 .90
☐ 174 Ron Taylor .... 2.00 .90
☐ 175 Bert Campaneris 4.00 1.80
☐ 176 Jim Davenport .... 2.00 .90
☐ 177 Hector Lopez .... 2.00 .90
☐ 178 Bob Tillman .... 2.00 .90
☐ 179 Cards Rookies 4.00 1.80
Dennis Aust
Bob Tolan
☐ 180 Vada Pinson 4.00 1.80
☐ 181 Al Worthington .... 2.00 .90
☐ 182 Jerry Lynch .... 2.00 .90
☐ 183A Checklist 3 .... 8.00 1.60
(Large print
on front)
☐ 183B Checklist 3 .... 8.00 1.60
(Small print
on front)
☐ 184 Denis Menke .... 2.00 .90
☐ 185 Bob Buhl 4.00 1.80
☐ 186 Ruben Amaro .... 2.00 .90
☐ 187 Chuck Dressen MG 4.00 1.80
☐ 188 Al Luplow .... 2.00 .90
☐ 189 John Roseboro 4.00 1.80
☐ 190 Jimmie Hall .... 2.00 .90
☐ 191 Darrell Sutherland .... 2.00 .90
☐ 192 Vic Power 4.00 1.80
☐ 193 Dave McNally 4.00 1.80
☐ 194 Senators Team 6.00 2.70
☐ 195 Joe Morgan 14.00 6.25
☐ 196 Don Pavletich .... 2.00 .90
☐ 197 Sonny Siebert .... 2.00 .90
☐ 198 Mickey Stanley 4.00 1.80
☐ 199 Chisox Clubbers 4.00 1.80
Bill Skowron
Johnny Romano
Floyd Robinson
☐ 200 Eddie Mathews 14.00 6.25
☐ 201 Jim Dickson .... 2.00 .90
☐ 202 Clay Dalrymple .... 2.00 .90
☐ 203 Jose Santiago .... 2.00 .90
☐ 204 Cubs Team 6.00 2.70
☐ 205 Tom Tresh 4.00 1.80
☐ 206 Al Jackson .... 2.00 .90
☐ 207 Frank Quilici .... 2.00 .90
☐ 208 Bob Miller .... 2.00 .90
☐ 209 Tigers Rookies 4.00 1.80
Fritz Fisher
John Hiller
☐ 210 Bill Mazeroski 5.00 2.20
☐ 211 Frank Kreutzer .... 2.00 .90
☐ 212 Ed Kranepool 4.00 1.80
☐ 213 Fred Newman .... 2.00 .90
☐ 214 Tommy Harper 4.00 1.80
☐ 215 NL Batting Leaders 50.00 22.00
Bob Clemente
Hank Aaron
Willie Mays
☐ 216 AL Batting Leaders 6.00 2.70
Tony Oliva
Carl Yastrzemski
Vic Davalillo
☐ 217 NL Home Run Leaders 20.00 9.00
Willie Mays
Willie McCovey
Billy Williams
☐ 218 AL Home Run Leaders 4.00 1.80
Tony Conigliaro
Norm Cash
Willie Horton
☐ 219 NL RBI Leaders 12.00 5.50
Deron Johnson
Frank Robinson
Willie Mays
☐ 220 AL RBI Leaders 4.00 1.80
Rocky Colavito
Willie Horton
Tony Oliva
☐ 221 NL ERA Leaders 12.00 5.50
Sandy Koufax
Juan Marichal
Vern Law
☐ 222 AL ERA Leaders 4.00 1.80
Sam McDowell
Eddie Fisher
Sonny Siebert
☐ 223 NL Pitching Leaders 12.00 5.50
Sandy Koufax
Tony Cloninger
Don Drysdale
☐ 224 AL Pitching Leaders 4.00 1.80
Jim Grant
Mel Stottlemyre
Jim Kaat
☐ 225 NL Strikeout Leaders 12.00 5.50
Sandy Koufax
Bob Veale
Bob Gibson
☐ 226 AL Strikeout Leaders 4.00 1.80
Sam McDowell
Mickey Lolich
Dennis McLain
Sonny Siebert
☐ 227 Russ Nixon .... 2.00 .90
☐ 228 Larry Dierker 4.00 1.80
☐ 229 Hank Bauer MG 4.00 1.80
☐ 230 Johnny Callison 4.00 1.80
☐ 231 Floyd Weaver .... 2.00 .90
☐ 232 Glenn Beckert 4.00 1.80
☐ 233 Dom Zanni .... 2.00 .90
☐ 234 Yankees Rookies 8.00 3.60
Rich Beck
Roy White
☐ 235 Don Cardwell .... 2.00 .90
☐ 236 Mike Hershberger .... 2.00 .90
☐ 237 Billy O'Dell .... 2.00 .90
☐ 238 Dodgers Team 6.00 2.70
☐ 239 Orlando Pena .... 2.00 .90
☐ 240 Earl Battey .... 2.00 .90
☐ 241 Dennis Ribant .... 2.00 .90
☐ 242 Jesus Alou .... 2.00 .90
☐ 243 Nelson Briles 4.00 1.80
☐ 244 Astros Rookies .... 2.00 .90
Chuck Harrison
Sonny Jackson
☐ 245 John Buzhardt .... 2.00 .90
☐ 246 Ed Bailey .... 2.00 .90
☐ 247 Carl Warwick .... 2.00 .90
☐ 248 Pete Mikkelsen .... 2.00 .90
☐ 249 Bill Rigney MG .... 2.00 .90
☐ 250 Sammy Ellis .... 2.00 .90
☐ 251 Ed Brinkman .... 2.00 .90
☐ 252 Denny Lemaster .... 2.00 .90
☐ 253 Don Wert .... 2.00 .90
☐ 254 Phillies Rookies 80.00 36.00
Ferguson Jenkins
Bill Sorrell
☐ 255 Willie Stargell 20.00 9.00
☐ 256 Lew Krausse .... 2.00 .90
☐ 257 Jeff Torborg 4.00 1.80
☐ 258 Dave Giusti .... 2.00 .90
☐ 259 Boston Red Sox 6.00 2.70
Team Card
☐ 260 Bob Shaw .... 2.00 .90
☐ 261 Ron Hansen .... 2.00 .90
☐ 262 Jack Hamilton .... 2.00 .90
☐ 263 Tom Egan .... 2.00 .90
☐ 264 Twins Rookies .... 2.00 .90
Andy Kosco
Ted Uhlaender
☐ 265 Stu Miller 4.00 1.80
☐ 266 Pedro Gonzalez UER .... 2.00 .90
(Misspelled Gonzales
on card back)
☐ 267 Joe Sparma .... 2.00 .90
☐ 268 John Blanchard .... 2.00 .90
☐ 269 Don Heffner MG .... 2.00 .90
☐ 270 Claude Osteen 4.00 1.80
☐ 271 Hal Lanier .... 2.00 .90
☐ 272 Jack Baldschun .... 2.00 .90
☐ 273 Astro Aces 4.00 1.80
Bob Aspromonte
Rusty Staub
☐ 274 Buster Narum .... 2.00 .90
☐ 275 Tim McCarver 4.00 1.80
☐ 276 Jim Bouton 4.00 1.80
☐ 277 George Thomas .... 2.00 .90
☐ 278 Cal Koonce .... 2.00 .90
☐ 279A Checklist 4 .... 8.00 1.60
(Player's cap black)
☐ 279B Checklist 4 .... 8.00 1.60
(Player's cap red)
☐ 280 Bobby Knoop .... 2.00 .90
☐ 281 Bruce Howard .... 2.00 .90
☐ 282 Johnny Lewis .... 2.00 .90
☐ 283 Jim Perry 4.00 1.80
☐ 284 Bobby Wine 3.00 1.35
☐ 285 Luis Tiant 6.00 2.70
☐ 286 Gary Geiger 3.00 1.35
☐ 287 Jack Aker 3.00 1.35
☐ 288 Dodgers Rookies 50.00 22.00
Bill Singer
Don Sutton
☐ 289 Larry Sherry 3.00 1.35
☐ 290 Ron Santo 6.00 2.70
☐ 291 Moe Drabowsky 5.00 2.20
☐ 292 Jim Coker 3.00 1.35
☐ 293 Mike Shannon 5.00 2.20
☐ 294 Steve Ridzik 3.00 1.35
☐ 295 Jim Ray Hart 5.00 2.20
☐ 296 Johnny Keane MG 5.00 2.20
☐ 297 Jim Owens 3.00 1.35
☐ 298 Rico Petrocelli 6.00 2.70
☐ 299 Lou Burdette 6.00 2.70
☐ 300 Bob Clemente 150.00 70.00
☐ 301 Greg Bollo 3.00 1.35
☐ 302 Ernie Bowman 3.00 1.35
☐ 303 Cleveland Indians 5.00 2.20
Team Card
☐ 304 John Herrnstein 3.00 1.35
☐ 305 Camilo Pascual 5.00 2.20
☐ 306 Ty Cline 3.00 1.35
☐ 307 Clay Carroll 5.00 2.20
☐ 308 Tom Haller 5.00 2.20
☐ 309 Diego Segui 3.00 1.35
☐ 310 Frank Robinson 30.00 13.50
☐ 311 Reds Rookies 5.00 2.20
Tommy Helms
Dick Simpson
☐ 312 Bob Saverine 3.00 1.35
☐ 313 Chris Zachary 3.00 1.35
☐ 314 Hector Valle 3.00 1.35
☐ 315 Norm Cash 6.00 2.70
☐ 316 Jack Fisher 3.00 1.35
☐ 317 Dalton Jones 3.00 1.35
☐ 318 Harry Walker MG 3.00 1.35
☐ 319 Gene Freese 3.00 1.35
☐ 320 Bob Gibson 25.00 11.00
☐ 321 Rick Reichardt 3.00 1.35
☐ 322 Bill Faul 3.00 1.35
☐ 323 Ray Barker 3.00 1.35
☐ 324 John Boozer 3.00 1.35
☐ 325 Vic Davalillo 3.00 1.35
☐ 326 Braves Team 5.00 2.20
☐ 327 Bernie Allen 3.00 1.35
☐ 328 Jerry Grote 5.00 2.20
☐ 329 Pete Charton 3.00 1.35
☐ 330 Ron Fairly 5.00 2.20
☐ 331 Ron Herbel 3.00 1.35
☐ 332 Bill Bryan 3.00 1.35
☐ 333 Senators Rookies 3.00 1.35
Joe Coleman
Jim French
☐ 334 Marty Keough 3.00 1.35
☐ 335 Juan Pizarro 3.00 1.35
☐ 336 Gene Alley 5.00 2.20
☐ 337 Fred Gladding 3.00 1.35
☐ 338 Dal Maxvill 3.00 1.35
☐ 339 Del Crandall 5.00 2.20
☐ 340 Dean Chance 5.00 2.20
☐ 341 Wes Westrum MG 5.00 2.20
☐ 342 Bob Humphreys 3.00 1.35
☐ 343 Joe Christopher 3.00 1.35
☐ 344 Steve Blass 5.00 2.20
☐ 345 Bob Allison 5.00 2.20
☐ 346 Mike de la Hoz 3.00 1.35
☐ 347 Phil Regan 5.00 2.20
☐ 348 Orioles Team 8.00 3.60
☐ 349 Cap Peterson 3.00 1.35
☐ 350 Mel Stottlemyre 6.00 2.70
☐ 351 Fred Valentine 3.00 1.35
☐ 352 Bob Aspromonte 3.00 1.35
☐ 353 Al McBean 3.00 1.35
☐ 354 Smoky Burgess 5.00 2.20
☐ 355 Wade Blasingame 3.00 1.35
☐ 356 Red Sox Rookies 3.00 1.35
Owen Johnson
Ken Sanders
☐ 357 Gerry Arrigo 3.00 1.35
☐ 358 Charlie Smith 3.00 1.35
☐ 359 Johnny Briggs 3.00 1.35
☐ 360 Ron Hunt 3.00 1.35
☐ 361 Tom Satriano 3.00 1.35
☐ 362 Gates Brown 5.00 2.20

☐ 363 Checklist 5 8.00 1.60
☐ 364 Nate Oliver 3.00 1.35
☐ 365 Roger Maris 35.00 16.00
☐ 366 Wayne Causey 3.00 1.35
☐ 367 Mel Nelson 3.00 1.35
☐ 368 Charlie Lau 5.00 2.20
☐ 369 Jim King 3.00 1.35
☐ 370 Chico Cardenas 3.00 1.35
☐ 371 Lee Stange 5.00 2.20
☐ 372 Harvey Kuenn 8.00 3.60
☐ 373 Giants Rookies 8.00 3.60
Jack Hiatt
Dick Estelle
☐ 374 Bob Locker 5.00 2.20
☐ 375 Donn Clendenon 8.00 3.60
☐ 376 Paul Schaal 5.00 2.20
☐ 377 Turk Farrell 5.00 2.20
☐ 378 Dick Tracewski 5.00 2.20
☐ 379 Cardinal Team 10.00 4.50
☐ 380 Tony Conigliaro 10.00 4.50
☐ 381 Hank Fischer 5.00 2.20
☐ 382 Phil Roof 5.00 2.20
☐ 383 Jackie Brandt 5.00 2.20
☐ 384 Al Downing 8.00 3.60
☐ 385 Ken Boyer 8.00 3.60
☐ 386 Gil Hodges MG 8.00 3.60
☐ 387 Howie Reed 5.00 2.20
☐ 388 Don Mincher 5.00 2.20
☐ 389 Jim O'Toole 8.00 3.60
☐ 390 Brooks Robinson 45.00 20.00
☐ 391 Chuck Hinton 5.00 2.20
☐ 392 Cubs Rookies 8.00 3.60
Bill Hands
Randy Hundley
☐ 393 George Brunet 5.00 2.20
☐ 394 Ron Brand 5.00 2.20
☐ 395 Len Gabrielson 5.00 2.20
☐ 396 Jerry Stephenson 5.00 2.20
☐ 397 Bill White 8.00 3.60
☐ 398 Danny Cater 5.00 2.20
☐ 399 Ray Washburn 5.00 2.20
☐ 400 Zoilo Versalles 8.00 3.60
☐ 401 Ken McMullen 5.00 2.20
☐ 402 Jim Hickman 5.00 2.20
☐ 403 Fred Talbot 5.00 2.20
☐ 404 Pittsburgh Pirates 10.00 4.50
Team Card
☐ 405 Elston Howard 8.00 3.60
☐ 406 Joey Jay 5.00 2.20
☐ 407 John Kennedy 5.00 2.20
☐ 408 Lee Thomas 8.00 3.60
☐ 409 Billy Hoeft 5.00 2.20
☐ 410 Al Kaline 35.00 16.00
☐ 411 Gene Mauch MG 5.00 2.20
☐ 412 Sam Bowens 5.00 2.20
☐ 413 Johnny Romano 5.00 2.20
☐ 414 Dan Coombs 5.00 2.20
☐ 415 Max Alvis 5.00 2.20
☐ 416 Phil Ortega 5.00 2.20
☐ 417 Angels Rookies 5.00 2.20
Jim McGlothlin
Ed Sukla
☐ 418 Phil Gagliano 5.00 2.20
☐ 419 Mike Ryan 5.00 2.20
☐ 420 Juan Marichal 14.00 6.25
☐ 421 Roy McMillan 8.00 3.60
☐ 422 Ed Charles 5.00 2.20
☐ 423 Ernie Broglio 5.00 2.20
☐ 424 Reds Rookies 10.00 4.50
Lee May
Darrell Osteen
☐ 425 Bob Veale 8.00 3.60
☐ 426 White Sox Team 8.00 3.60
☐ 427 John Miller 5.00 2.20
☐ 428 Sandy Alomar 8.00 3.60
☐ 429 Bill Monbouquette 5.00 2.20
☐ 430 Don Drysdale 20.00 9.00
☐ 431 Walt Bond 5.00 2.20
☐ 432 Bob Heffner 5.00 2.20
☐ 433 Alvin Dark MG 8.00 3.60
☐ 434 Willie Kirkland 5.00 2.20
☐ 435 Jim Bunning 14.00 6.25
☐ 436 Julian Javier 8.00 3.60
☐ 437 Al Stanek 5.00 2.20
☐ 438 Willie Smith 5.00 2.20
☐ 439 Pedro Ramos 5.00 2.20
☐ 440 Deron Johnson 8.00 3.60
☐ 441 Tommie Sisk 5.00 2.20
☐ 442 Orioles Rookies 5.00 2.20
Ed Barnowski
Eddie Watt
☐ 443 Bill Wakefield 5.00 2.20
☐ 444 Checklist 6 8.00 1.60
☐ 445 Jim Kaat 10.00 4.50
☐ 446 Mack Jones 5.00 2.20
☐ 447 Dick Ellsworth UER 12.00 5.50
(Photo actually
Ken Hubbs)
☐ 448 Eddie Stanky MG 9.00 4.00
☐ 449 Joe Moeller 9.00 4.00
☐ 450 Tony Oliva 12.00 5.50
☐ 451 Barry Latman 9.00 4.00
☐ 452 Joe Azcue 9.00 4.00
☐ 453 Ron Kline 9.00 4.00
☐ 454 Jerry Buchek 9.00 4.00
☐ 455 Mickey Lolich 12.00 5.50
☐ 456 Red Sox Rookies 9.00 4.00
Darrell Brandon
Joe Foy
☐ 457 Joe Gibbon 9.00 4.00
☐ 458 Manny Jiminez 9.00 4.00
☐ 459 Bill McCool 9.00 4.00
☐ 460 Curt Blefary 9.00 4.00
☐ 461 Roy Face 15.00 6.75
☐ 462 Bob Rodgers 9.00 4.00
☐ 463 Philadelphia Phillies 15.00 6.75
Team Card
☐ 464 Larry Bearnarth 9.00 4.00
☐ 465 Don Buford 9.00 4.00
☐ 466 Ken Johnson 9.00 4.00
☐ 467 Vic Roznovsky 9.00 4.00
☐ 468 Johnny Podres 12.00 5.50
☐ 469 Yankees Rookies 25.00 11.00
Bobby Murcer
Dooley Womack
☐ 470 Sam McDowell 15.00 6.75
☐ 471 Bob Skinner 9.00 4.00
☐ 472 Terry Fox 9.00 4.00
☐ 473 Rich Rollins 9.00 4.00
☐ 474 Dick Schofield 9.00 4.00
☐ 475 Dick Radatz 9.00 4.00
☐ 476 Bobby Bragan MG 9.00 4.00
☐ 477 Steve Barber 9.00 4.00
☐ 478 Tony Gonzalez 9.00 4.00
☐ 479 Jim Hannan 9.00 4.00
☐ 480 Dick Stuart 9.00 4.00
☐ 481 Bob Lee 9.00 4.00
☐ 482 Cubs Rookies 9.00 4.00
John Boccabella
Dave Dowling
☐ 483 Joe Nuxhall 9.00 4.00
☐ 484 Wes Covington 9.00 4.00
☐ 485 Bob Bailey 9.00 4.00
☐ 486 Tommy John 12.00 5.50
☐ 487 Al Ferrara 9.00 4.00
☐ 488 George Banks 9.00 4.00
☐ 489 Curt Simmons 9.00 4.00
☐ 490 Bobby Richardson 12.00 5.50
☐ 491 Dennis Bennett 9.00 4.00
☐ 492 Athletics Team 15.00 6.75
☐ 493 Johnny Klippstein 9.00 4.00
☐ 494 Gordy Coleman 9.00 4.00
☐ 495 Dick McAuliffe 15.00 6.75
☐ 496 Lindy McDaniel 9.00 4.00
☐ 497 Chris Cannizzaro 9.00 4.00
☐ 498 Pirates Rookies 9.00 4.00
Luke Walker
Woody Fryman
☐ 499 Wally Bunker 9.00 4.00
☐ 500 Hank Aaron 125.00 55.00
☐ 501 John O'Donoghue 9.00 4.00
☐ 502 Lenny Green UER 9.00 4.00
(Born: aJn. 6, 1933)
☐ 503 Steve Hamilton 15.00 6.75
☐ 504 Grady Hatton MG 9.00 4.00
☐ 505 Jose Cardenal 9.00 4.00
☐ 506 Bo Belinsky 15.00 6.75
☐ 507 Johnny Edwards 9.00 4.00
☐ 508 Steve Hargan 9.00 4.00
☐ 509 Jake Wood 9.00 4.00
☐ 510 Hoyt Wilhelm 16.00 7.25
☐ 511 Giants Rookies 9.00 4.00
Bob Barton
Tito Fuentes
☐ 512 Dick Stigman 9.00 4.00
☐ 513 Camilo Carreon 9.00 4.00
☐ 514 Hal Woodeshick 9.00 4.00
☐ 515 Frank Howard 14.00 6.25
☐ 516 Eddie Bressoud 9.00 4.00
☐ 517A Checklist 7 15.00 3.00
529 White Sox Rookies
544 Cardinals Rookies
☐ 517B Checklist 7 15.00 3.00
529 W. Sox Rookies
544 Cards Rookies
☐ 518 Braves Rookies 9.00 4.00
Herb Hippauf
Arnie Umbach
☐ 519 Bob Friend 15.00 6.75
☐ 520 Jim Wynn 15.00 6.75
☐ 521 John Wyatt 9.00 4.00
☐ 522 Phil Linz 9.00 4.00
☐ 523 Bob Sadowski 15.00 6.75
☐ 524 Giants Rookies SP 30.00 13.50
Ollie Brown
Don Mason
☐ 525 Gary Bell SP 30.00 13.50
☐ 526 Twins Team SP 100.00 45.00
☐ 527 Julio Navarro 15.00 6.75
☐ 528 Jesse Gonder SP 30.00 13.50
☐ 529 White Sox Rookies 15.00 6.75
Lee Elia
Dennis Higgins
Bill Voss
☐ 530 Robin Roberts 60.00 27.00
☐ 531 Joe Cunningham 15.00 6.75
☐ 532 Aurelio Monteagudo SP 30.00 13.50
☐ 533 Jerry Adair SP 30.00 13.50
☐ 534 Mets Rookies 15.00 6.75
Dave Eilers
Rob Gardner
☐ 535 Willie Davis SP 40.00 18.00
☐ 536 Dick Egan 15.00 6.75
☐ 537 Herman Franks MG 15.00 6.75
☐ 538 Bob Allen SP 30.00 13.50
☐ 539 Astros Rookies 15.00 6.75
Bill Heath
Carroll Sembera
☐ 540 Denny McLain SP 80.00 36.00
☐ 541 Gene Oliver SP 30.00 13.50
☐ 542 George Smith 15.00 6.75
☐ 543 Roger Craig SP 35.00 16.00
☐ 544 Cardinals Rookies SP 30.00 13.50
Joe Hoerner
George Kernek
Jimy Williams UER
(Misspelled Jimmy
on card)
☐ 545 Dick Green SP 30.00 13.50
☐ 546 Dwight Siebler 15.00 6.75
☐ 547 Horace Clarke SP 40.00 18.00
☐ 548 Gary Kroll SP 30.00 13.50
☐ 549 Senators Rookies 15.00 6.75
Al Closter
Casey Cox
☐ 550 Willie McCovey SP 90.00 40.00
☐ 551 Bob Purkey SP 30.00 13.50
☐ 552 Birdie Tebbetts 30.00 13.50
MG SP
☐ 553 Rookie Stars 15.00 6.75
Pat Garrett
Jackie Warner
☐ 554 Jim Northrup SP 30.00 13.50
☐ 555 Ron Perranoski SP 30.00 13.50
☐ 556 Mel Queen SP 30.00 13.50
☐ 557 Felix Mantilla SP 30.00 13.50
☐ 558 Red Sox Rookies 20.00 9.00
Guido Grilli
Pete Magrini
George Scott
☐ 559 Roberto Pena SP 30.00 13.50
☐ 560 Joel Horlen 8.00 3.60
☐ 561 ChooChoo Coleman SP 35.00 16.00
☐ 562 Russ Snyder 15.00 6.75
☐ 563 Twins Rookies 15.00 6.75
Pete Cimino
Cesar Tovar
☐ 564 Bob Chance SP 30.00 13.50
☐ 565 Jimmy Piersall SP 40.00 18.00
☐ 566 Mike Cuellar SP 35.00 16.00
☐ 567 Dick Howser SP 40.00 18.00
☐ 568 Athletics Rookies 15.00 6.75
Paul Lindblad
Ron Stone
☐ 569 Orlando McFarlane SP 30.00 13.50
☐ 570 Art Mahaffey SP 30.00 13.50
☐ 571 Dave Roberts SP 30.00 13.50
☐ 572 Bob Priddy 15.00 6.75
☐ 573 Derrell Griffith 15.00 6.75
☐ 574 Mets Rookies 15.00 6.75
Bill Hepler
Bill Murphy
☐ 575 Earl Wilson 15.00 6.75
☐ 576 Dave Nicholson SP 30.00 13.50
☐ 577 Jack Lamabe SP 30.00 13.50
☐ 578 Chi Chi Olivo SP 30.00 13.50
☐ 579 Orioles Rookies 20.00 9.00
Frank Bertaina
Gene Brabender
Dave Johnson
☐ 580 Billy Williams SP 70.00 32.00
☐ 581 Tony Martinez 15.00 6.75
☐ 582 Garry Roggenburk 15.00 6.75
☐ 583 Tigers Team SP UER 125.00 55.00
(Text on back states Tigers
finished third in 1966 instead
of fourth.)
☐ 584 Yankees Rookies 15.00 6.75
Frank Fernandez
Fritz Peterson
☐ 585 Tony Taylor 25.00 11.00
☐ 586 Claude Raymond SP 30.00 13.50
☐ 587 Dick Bertell 15.00 6.75

Card	NRMT	VG-E
☐ 588 Athletics Rookies	15.00	6.75
Chuck Dobson		
Ken Suarez		
☐ 589 Lou Klimchock SP	35.00	16.00
☐ 590 Bill Skowron SP	40.00	18.00
☐ 591 NL Rookies SP	40.00	18.00
Bart Shirley		
Grant Jackson		
☐ 592 Andre Rodgers	15.00	6.75
☐ 593 Doug Camilli SP	30.00	13.50
☐ 594 Chico Salmon	15.00	6.75
☐ 595 Larry Jackson	15.00	6.75
☐ 596 Astros Rookies SP	35.00	16.00
Nate Colbert		
Greg Sims		
☐ 597 John Sullivan	15.00	6.75
☐ 598 Gaylord Perry SP	190.00	55.00

1966 Topps Rub-Offs Inserts

There are 120 "rub-offs" in the Topps insert set of 1966, of which 100 depict players and the remaining 20 show team pennants. Each rub off measures 2 1/16" by 3". The color player photos are vertical while the team pennants are horizontal; both types of transfer have a large black printer's mark. These rub-offs were originally printed in rolls of 20 and are frequently still found this way. Since these rub-offs are unnumbered, they are ordered below alphabetically within type, players (1-100) and team pennants (101-120).

	NRMT	VG-E
COMPLETE SET (120)	375.00	170.00
COMMON RUB-OFF (1-100)	1.00	.45
COMMON PENNANT (101-120)	.80	.35
☐ 1 Hank Aaron	15.00	6.75
☐ 2 Jerry Adair	1.00	.45
☐ 3 Richie Allen	2.00	.90
☐ 4 Jesus Alou	1.50	.70
☐ 5 Max Alvis	1.00	.45
☐ 6 Bob Aspromonte	1.00	.45
☐ 7 Ernie Banks	10.00	4.50
☐ 8 Earl Battey	1.00	.45
☐ 9 Curt Blefary	1.00	.45
☐ 10 Ken Boyer	1.50	.70
☐ 11 Bob Bruce	1.00	.45
☐ 12 Jim Bunning	5.00	2.20
☐ 13 Johnny Callison	1.50	.70
☐ 14 Bert Campaneris	1.50	.70
☐ 15 Jose Cardenal	1.00	.45
☐ 16 Dean Chance	1.50	.70
☐ 17 Ed Charles	1.00	.45
☐ 18 Roberto Clemente	50.00	22.00
☐ 19 Tony Cloninger	1.00	.45
☐ 20 Rocky Colavito	3.00	1.35
☐ 21 Tony Conigliaro	2.00	.90
☐ 22 Vic Davalillo	1.00	.45
☐ 23 Willie Davis	1.50	.70
☐ 24 Don Drysdale	7.00	3.10
☐ 25 Sammy Ellis	1.00	.45
☐ 26 Dick Ellsworth	1.00	.45
☐ 27 Ron Fairly	1.50	.70
☐ 28 Dick Farrell	1.00	.45
☐ 29 Eddie Fisher	1.00	.45
☐ 30 Jack Fisher	1.00	.45
☐ 31 Curt Flood	2.00	.90
☐ 32 Whitey Ford	6.00	2.70
☐ 33 Bill Freehan	1.50	.70
☐ 34 Jim Fregosi	1.50	.70
☐ 35 Bob Gibson	5.00	2.20
☐ 36 Jim Grant	1.00	.45
☐ 37 Jimmie Hall	1.00	.45
☐ 38 Ken Harrelson	1.50	.70
☐ 39 Jim Ray Hart	1.00	.45
☐ 40 Joel Horlen	1.00	.45
☐ 41 Willie Horton	1.50	.70
☐ 42 Frank Howard	2.00	.90
☐ 43 Deron Johnson	1.00	.45
☐ 44 Al Kaline	10.00	4.50
☐ 45 Harmon Killebrew	6.00	2.70
☐ 46 Bobby Knoop	1.00	.45
☐ 47 Sandy Koufax	15.00	6.75
☐ 48 Ed Kranepool	1.00	.45
☐ 49 Gary Kroll	1.00	.45
☐ 50 Don Landrum	1.00	.45
☐ 51 Vern Law	1.50	.70
☐ 52 Johnny Lewis	1.00	.45
☐ 53 Don Lock	1.00	.45
☐ 54 Mickey Lolich	2.00	.90
☐ 55 Jim Maloney	1.50	.70
☐ 56 Felix Mantilla	1.00	.45
☐ 57 Mickey Mantle	75.00	34.00
☐ 58 Juan Marichal	5.00	2.20
☐ 59 Eddie Mathews	5.00	2.20
☐ 60 Willie Mays	18.00	8.00
☐ 61 Bill Mazeroski	2.00	.90
☐ 62 Dick McAuliffe	1.00	.45
☐ 63 Tim McCarver	2.00	.90
☐ 64 Willie McCovey	4.00	1.80
☐ 65 Sam McDowell	1.50	.70
☐ 66 Ken McMullen	1.00	.45
☐ 67 Denis Menke	1.00	.45
☐ 68 Bill Monbouquette	1.00	.45
☐ 69 Joe Morgan	6.00	2.70
☐ 70 Fred Newman	1.00	.45
☐ 71 John O'Donoghue	1.00	.45
☐ 72 Tony Oliva	3.00	1.35
☐ 73 Johnny Orsino	1.00	.45
☐ 74 Phil Ortega	1.00	.45
☐ 75 Milt Pappas	1.50	.70
☐ 76 Dick Radatz	1.50	.70
☐ 77 Bobby Richardson	3.00	1.35
☐ 78 Pete Richert	1.00	.45
☐ 79 Brooks Robinson	10.00	4.50
☐ 80 Floyd Robinson	1.00	.45
☐ 81 Frank Robinson	10.00	4.50
☐ 82 Cookie Rojas	2.00	.90
☐ 83 Pete Rose	30.00	13.50
☐ 84 John Roseboro	1.50	.70
☐ 85 Ron Santo	2.00	.90
☐ 86 Bill Skowron	2.00	.90
☐ 87 Willie Stargell	6.00	2.70
☐ 88 Mel Stottlemyre	2.00	.90
☐ 89 Dick Stuart	1.00	.45
☐ 90 Ron Swoboda	1.50	.70
☐ 91 Fred Talbot	1.00	.45
☐ 92 Ralph Terry	1.50	.70
☐ 93 Joe Torre	3.00	1.35
☐ 94 Tom Tresh	2.00	.90
☐ 95 Bob Veale	1.00	.45
☐ 96 Pete Ward	1.00	.45
☐ 97 Bill White	1.50	.70
☐ 98 Billy Williams	4.00	1.80
☐ 99 Jim Wynn	1.50	.70
☐ 100 Carl Yastrzemski	10.00	4.50
☐ 101 Baltimore Orioles	1.50	.70
☐ 102 Boston Red Sox	1.00	.45
☐ 103 California Angels	.80	.35
☐ 104 Chicago Cubs	.80	.35
☐ 105 Chicago White Sox	.80	.35
☐ 106 Cincinnati Reds	.80	.35
☐ 107 Cleveland Indians	.80	.35
☐ 108 Detroit Tigers	1.00	.45
☐ 109 Houston Astros	.80	.35
☐ 110 Kansas City Athletics	.80	.35
☐ 111 Los Angeles Dodgers	1.50	.70
☐ 112 Milwaukee Braves	.80	.35
☐ 113 Minnesota Twins	.80	.35
☐ 114 New York Mets	1.00	.45
☐ 115 New York Yankees	2.00	.90
☐ 116 Philadelphia Phillies	.80	.35
☐ 117 Pittsburgh Pirates	.80	.35
☐ 118 San Francisco Giants	.80	.35
☐ 119 St. Louis Cardinals	.80	.35
☐ 120 Washington Senators	1.50	.70

1967 Topps

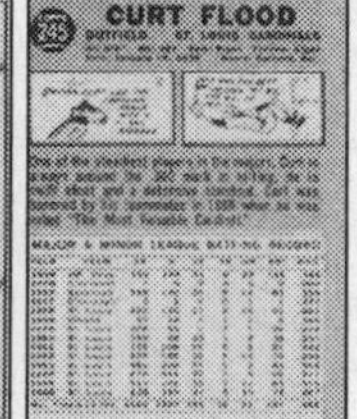

The cards in this 609-card set measure 2 1/2" by 3 1/2". The 1967 Topps series is considered by some collectors to be one of the company's finest accomplishments in baseball card production. Excellent color photographs are combined with easy-to-read backs. Cards 458 to 533 are slightly harder to find than numbers 1 to 457, and the inevitable high series (534 to 609) exists. Each checklist card features a small circular picture of a popular player included in that series. Printing discrepancies resulted in some high series cards being in shorter supply. The checklist below identifies (by DP) 22 double-printed high numbers; of the 76 cards in the last series, 54 cards were short printed and the other 22 cards are much more plentiful. Featured subsets within this set include World Series cards (151-155) and League Leaders (233-244). A limited number of "proof" Roger Maris cards were produced. These cards are blank backed and Maris is listed as a New York Yankee on it. The Maris card is currently valued between $500 and $1000. Some Bob Bolin cards: #252 have a white smear in between his names. Another tough variation that has been recently discovered is a variation on card #58 Paul Schaal. The tough version has a green bat above his name. The key Rookie Cards in the set are high number cards of Rod Carew and Tom Seaver. Confirmed methods of selling these cards include five-card nickle wax packs. Although rarely seen, there exists a salesman's sample panel of three cards that pictures Earl Battey, Manny Mota, and Gene Brabender with ad information on the back about the "new" Topps cards.

	NRMT	VG-E
COMPLETE SET (609)	4600.00	2100.00
COMMON CARD (1-109)	1.50	.70
COMMON CARD (110-283)	2.00	.90
COMMON CARD (284-370)	2.50	1.10
COMMON CARD (371-457)	4.00	1.80
COMMON CARD (458-533)	6.00	2.70
COMMON CARD (534-609)	16.00	7.25
COMMON DP 534-609	9.00	4.00
WRAPPER (5-CENT)	25.00	11.00
☐ 1 The Champs DP	20.00	6.00
Frank Robinson		
Hank Bauer MG		
Brooks Robinson		
☐ 2 Jack Hamilton	1.50	.70
☐ 3 Duke Sims	1.50	.70
☐ 4 Hal Lanier	1.50	.70
☐ 5 Whitey Ford UER	20.00	9.00
(1953 listed as		
1933 in stats on back)		
☐ 6 Dick Simpson	1.50	.70
☐ 7 Don McMahon	1.50	.70
☐ 8 Chuck Harrison	1.50	.70
☐ 9 Ron Hansen	1.50	.70
☐ 10 Matty Alou	2.50	1.10
☐ 11 Barry Moore	1.50	.70
☐ 12 Dodgers Rookies	2.50	1.10
Jim Campanis		
Bill Singer		
☐ 13 Joe Sparma	1.50	.70
☐ 14 Phil Linz	4.00	1.80
☐ 15 Earl Battey	1.50	.70
☐ 16 Bill Hands	1.50	.70
☐ 17 Jim Gosger	1.50	.70
☐ 18 Gene Oliver	1.50	.70
☐ 19 Jim McGlothlin	1.50	.70
☐ 20 Orlando Cepeda	6.00	2.70
☐ 21 Dave Bristol MG	1.50	.70
☐ 22 Gene Brabender	1.50	.70
☐ 23 Larry Elliot	1.50	.70
☐ 24 Bob Allen	1.50	.70
☐ 25 Elston Howard	4.00	1.80
☐ 26A Bob Priddy NTR	30.00	13.50
☐ 26B Bob Priddy TR	4.00	1.80
☐ 27 Bob Saverine	1.50	.70
☐ 28 Barry Latman	1.50	.70
☐ 29 Tom McCraw	1.50	.70
☐ 30 Al Kaline DP	16.00	7.25
☐ 31 Jim Brewer	1.50	.70
☐ 32 Bob Bailey	4.00	1.80
☐ 33 Athletic Rookies	5.00	2.20
Sal Bando		
Randy Schwartz		
☐ 34 Pete Cimino	1.50	.70
☐ 35 Rico Carty	4.00	1.80
☐ 36 Bob Tillman	1.50	.70
☐ 37 Rick Wise	4.00	1.80
☐ 38 Bob Johnson	1.50	.70
☐ 39 Curt Simmons	2.50	1.10
☐ 40 Rick Reichardt	1.50	.70
☐ 41 Joe Hoerner	1.50	.70
☐ 42 Mets Team	10.00	4.50
☐ 43 Chico Salmon	1.50	.70
☐ 44 Joe Nuxhall	4.00	1.80
☐ 45 Roger Maris	30.00	13.50
☐ 46 Lindy McDaniel	4.00	1.80
☐ 47 Ken McMullen	1.50	.70
☐ 48 Bill Freehan	2.50	1.10
☐ 49 Roy Face	2.50	1.10
☐ 50 Tony Oliva	6.00	2.70
☐ 51 Astros Rookies	1.50	.70

Dave Adlesh
Wes Bales
☐ 52 Dennis Higgins 1.50 .70
☐ 53 Clay Dalrymple 1.50 .70
☐ 54 Dick Green 1.50 .70
☐ 55 Don Drysdale 16.00 7.25
☐ 56 Jose Tartabull 4.00 1.80
☐ 57 Pat Jarvis 1.50 .70
☐ 58 Paul Schaal 1.50 .70
☐ 59 Ralph Terry 4.00 1.80
☐ 60 Luis Aparicio 6.00 2.70
☐ 61 Gordy Coleman 4.00 1.80
☐ 62 Frank Robinson CL 30.00 6.00
☐ 63 Cards' Clubbers 10.00 4.50
Lou Brock
Curt Flood
☐ 64 Fred Valentine 1.50 .70
☐ 65 Tom Haller 4.00 1.80
☐ 66 Manny Mota 2.50 1.10
☐ 67 Ken Berry 1.50 .70
☐ 68 Bob Buhl 4.00 1.80
☐ 69 Vic Davalillo 1.50 .70
☐ 70 Ron Santo 4.00 1.80
☐ 71 Camilo Pascual 2.50 1.10
☐ 72 Tigers Rookies 1.50 .70
George Korince
(Photo actually
James Murray Brown)
John (Tom) Matchick
☐ 73 Rusty Staub 4.00 1.80
☐ 74 Wes Stock 1.50 .70
☐ 75 George Scott 2.50 1.10
☐ 76 Jim Barbieri 1.50 .70
☐ 77 Dooley Womack 4.00 1.80
☐ 78 Pat Corrales 4.00 1.80
☐ 79 Bubba Morton 1.50 .70
☐ 80 Jim Maloney 4.00 1.80
☐ 81 Eddie Stanky MG 2.50 1.10
☐ 82 Steve Barber 1.50 .70
☐ 83 Ollie Brown 1.50 .70
☐ 84 Tommie Sisk 1.50 .70
☐ 85 Johnny Callison 2.50 1.10
☐ 86A Mike McCormick NTR 30.00 13.50
(Senators on front
and Senators on back)
☐ 86B Mike McCormick TR 4.00 1.80
(Traded line
at end of bio;
Senators on front,
but Giants on back)
☐ 87 George Altman 1.50 .70
☐ 88 Mickey Lolich 4.00 1.80
☐ 89 Felix Millan 2.50 1.10
☐ 90 Jim Nash 1.50 .70
☐ 91 Johnny Lewis 1.50 .70
☐ 92 Ray Washburn 1.50 .70
☐ 93 Yankees Rookies 4.00 1.80
Stan Bahnsen
Bobby Murcer
☐ 94 Ron Fairly 2.50 1.10
☐ 95 Sonny Siebert 1.50 .70
☐ 96 Art Shamsky 1.50 .70
☐ 97 Mike Cuellar 4.00 1.80
☐ 98 Rich Rollins 1.50 .70
☐ 99 Lee Stange 1.50 .70
☐ 100 Frank Robinson DP 14.00 6.25
☐ 101 Ken Johnson 1.50 .70
☐ 102 Philadelphia Phillies 4.00 1.80
Team Card
☐ 103 Mickey Mantle CL 16.00 3.20
☐ 104 Minnie Rojas 1.50 .70
☐ 105 Ken Boyer 2.50 1.10
☐ 106 Randy Hundley 4.00 1.80
☐ 107 Joel Horlen 1.50 .70
☐ 108 Alex Johnson 4.00 1.80
☐ 109 Tribe Thumpers 5.00 2.20
Rocky Colavito
Leon Wagner
☐ 110 Jack Aker 4.00 1.80
☐ 111 John Kennedy 2.00 .90
☐ 112 Dave Wickersham 2.00 .90
☐ 113 Dave Nicholson 2.00 .90
☐ 114 Jack Baldschun 2.00 .90
☐ 115 Paul Casanova 2.00 .90
☐ 116 Herman Franks MG 2.00 .90
☐ 117 Darrell Brandon 2.00 .90
☐ 118 Bernie Allen 2.00 .90
☐ 119 Wade Blasingame 2.00 .90
☐ 120 Floyd Robinson 2.00 .90
☐ 121 Eddie Bressoud 2.00 .90
☐ 122 George Brunet 2.00 .90
☐ 123 Pirates Rookies 2.00 .90
Jim Price
Luke Walker
☐ 124 Jim Stewart 2.00 .90
☐ 125 Moe Drabowsky 4.00 1.80
☐ 126 Tony Taylor 2.00 .90
☐ 127 John O'Donoghue 2.00 .90
☐ 128 Ed Spiezio 2.00 .90
☐ 129 Phil Roof 2.00 .90
☐ 130 Phil Regan 4.00 1.80
☐ 131 Yankees Team 10.00 4.50
☐ 132 Ozzie Virgil 2.00 .90
☐ 133 Ron Kline 2.00 .90
☐ 134 Gates Brown 3.00 1.35
☐ 135 Deron Johnson 4.00 1.80
☐ 136 Carroll Sembera 2.00 .90
☐ 137 Twins Rookies 2.00 .90
Ron Clark
Jim Ollum
☐ 138 Dick Kelley 2.00 .90
☐ 139 Dalton Jones 4.00 1.80
☐ 140 Willie Stargell 20.00 9.00
☐ 141 John Miller 2.00 .90
☐ 142 Jackie Brandt 2.00 .90
☐ 143 Sox Sockers 2.00 .90
Pete Ward
Don Buford
☐ 144 Bill Hepler 2.00 .90
☐ 145 Larry Brown 2.00 .90
☐ 146 Steve Carlton 70.00 32.00
☐ 147 Tom Egan 2.00 .90
☐ 148 Adolfo Phillips 2.00 .90
☐ 149 Joe Moeller 2.00 .90
☐ 150 Mickey Mantle 300.00 135.00
☐ 151 Moe Drabowsky WS 4.00 1.80
☐ 152 Jim Palmer WS 8.00 3.60
☐ 153 Paul Blair WS 4.00 1.80
☐ 154 Brooks Robinson WS 4.00 1.80
Dave McNally
☐ 155 World Series Summary 4.00 1.80
Winners celebrate
☐ 156 Ron Herbel 2.00 .90
☐ 157 Danny Cater 2.00 .90
☐ 158 Jimmie Coker 2.00 .90
☐ 159 Bruce Howard 2.00 .90
☐ 160 Willie Davis 3.00 1.35
☐ 161 Dick Williams MG 3.00 1.35
☐ 162 Billy O'Dell 2.00 .90
☐ 163 Vic Roznovsky 2.00 .90
☐ 164 Dwight Siebler UER 2.00 .90
(Last line of stats
shows 1960 Minnesota)
☐ 165 Cleon Jones 4.00 1.80
☐ 166 Eddie Mathews 16.00 7.25
☐ 167 Senators Rookies 2.00 .90
Joe Coleman
Tim Cullen
☐ 168 Ray Culp 2.00 .90
☐ 169 Horace Clarke 4.00 1.80
☐ 170 Dick McAuliffe 3.00 1.35
☐ 171 Cal Koonce 2.00 .90
☐ 172 Bill Heath 2.00 .90
☐ 173 St. Louis Cardinals 4.00 1.80
Team Card
☐ 174 Dick Radatz 4.00 1.80
☐ 175 Bobby Knoop 2.00 .90
☐ 176 Sammy Ellis 2.00 .90
☐ 177 Tito Fuentes 2.00 .90
☐ 178 John Buzhardt 2.00 .90
☐ 179 Braves Rookies 2.00 .90
Charles Vaughan
Cecil Upshaw
☐ 180 Curt Blefary 2.00 .90
☐ 181 Terry Fox 2.00 .90
☐ 182 Ed Charles 2.00 .90
☐ 183 Jim Pagliaroni 2.00 .90
☐ 184 George Thomas 2.00 .90
☐ 185 Ken Holtzman 3.00 1.35
☐ 186 Mets Maulers 3.00 1.35
Ed Kranepool
Ron Swoboda
☐ 187 Pedro Ramos 2.00 .90
☐ 188 Ken Harrelson 3.00 1.35
☐ 189 Chuck Hinton 2.00 .90
☐ 190 Turk Farrell 2.00 .90
☐ 191A Willie Mays CL 10.00 2.00
214 Tom Kelley
☐ 191B Willie Mays CL 12.00 2.40
214 Dick Kelley
☐ 192 Fred Gladding 2.00 .90
☐ 193 Jose Cardenal 3.00 1.35
☐ 194 Bob Allison 3.00 1.35
☐ 195 Al Jackson 2.00 .90
☐ 196 Johnny Romano 2.00 .90
☐ 197 Ron Perranoski 3.00 1.35
☐ 198 Chuck Hiller 2.00 .90
☐ 199 Billy Hitchcock MG 2.00 .90
☐ 200 Willie Mays UER 85.00 38.00
('63 Sna Francisco
on card back stats)
☐ 201 Hal Reniff 4.00 1.80
☐ 202 Johnny Edwards 2.00 .90
☐ 203 Al McBean 2.00 .90
☐ 204 Orioles Rookies 3.00 1.35
Mike Epstein
Tom Phoebus
☐ 205 Dick Groat 3.00 1.35
☐ 206 Dennis Bennett 2.00 .90
☐ 207 John Orsino 2.00 .90
☐ 208 Jack Lamabe 2.00 .90
☐ 209 Joe Nossek 2.00 .90
☐ 210 Bob Gibson 20.00 9.00
☐ 211 Twins Team 4.00 1.80
☐ 212 Chris Zachary 2.00 .90
☐ 213 Jay Johnstone 3.00 1.35
☐ 214 Dick Kelley 2.00 .90
☐ 215 Ernie Banks 20.00 9.00
☐ 216 Bengal Belters 10.00 4.50
Norm Cash
Al Kaline
☐ 217 Rob Gardner 2.00 .90
☐ 218 Wes Parker 3.00 1.35
☐ 219 Clay Carroll 4.00 1.80
☐ 220 Jim Ray Hart 3.00 1.35
☐ 221 Woody Fryman 4.00 1.80
☐ 222 Reds Rookies 3.00 1.35
Darrell Osteen
Lee May
☐ 223 Mike Ryan 4.00 1.80
☐ 224 Walt Bond 2.00 .90
☐ 225 Mel Stottlemyre 3.00 1.35
☐ 226 Julian Javier 3.00 1.35
☐ 227 Paul Lindblad 2.00 .90
☐ 228 Gil Hodges MG 5.00 2.20
☐ 229 Larry Jackson 2.00 .90
☐ 230 Boog Powell 6.00 2.70
☐ 231 John Bateman 2.00 .90
☐ 232 Don Buford 2.00 .90
☐ 233 AL ERA Leaders 4.00 1.80
Gary Peters
Joel Horlen
Steve Hargan
☐ 234 NL ERA Leaders 15.00 6.75
Sandy Koufax
Mike Cuellar
Juan Marichal
☐ 235 AL Pitching Leaders 6.00 2.70
Jim Kaat
Denny McLain
Earl Wilson
☐ 236 NL Pitching Leaders 25.00 11.00
Sandy Koufax
Juan Marichal
Bob Gibson
Gaylord Perry
☐ 237 AL Strikeout Leaders 6.00 2.70
Sam McDowell
Jim Kaat
Earl Wilson
☐ 238 NL Strikeout Leaders 12.00 5.50
Sandy Koufax
Jim Bunning
Bob Veale
☐ 239 AL Batting Leaders 9.00 4.00
Frank Robinson
Tony Oliva
Al Kaline
☐ 240 NL Batting Leaders 6.00 2.70
Matty Alou
Felipe Alou
Rico Carty
☐ 241 AL RBI Leaders 9.00 4.00
Frank Robinson
Harmon Killebrew
Boog Powell
☐ 242 NL RBI Leaders 24.00 11.00
Hank Aaron
Bob Clemente
Richie Allen
☐ 243 AL Home Run Leaders 9.00 4.00
Frank Robinson
Harmon Killebrew
Boog Powell
☐ 244 NL Home Run Leaders 20.00 9.00
Hank Aaron
Richie Allen
Willie Mays
☐ 245 Curt Flood 3.00 1.35
☐ 246 Jim Perry 3.00 1.35
☐ 247 Jerry Lumpe 2.00 .90
☐ 248 Gene Mauch MG 3.00 1.35
☐ 249 Nick Willhite 2.00 .90
☐ 250 Hank Aaron UER 80.00 36.00
(Second 1961 in stats
should be 1962)
☐ 251 Woody Held 2.00 .90
☐ 252 Bob Bolin 2.00 .90
☐ 253 Indians Rookies 2.00 .90
Bill Davis
Gus Gil
☐ 254 Milt Pappas 3.00 1.35
(No facsimile auto-

graph on card front)
□ 255 Frank Howard 4.00 1.80
□ 256 Bob Hendley 2.00 .90
□ 257 Charlie Smith 2.00 .90
□ 258 Lee Maye 2.00 .90
□ 259 Don Dennis 2.00 .90
□ 260 Jim Lefebvre 3.00 1.35
□ 261 John Wyatt 2.00 .90
□ 262 Athletics Team 4.00 1.80
□ 263 Hank Aguirre 2.00 .90
□ 264 Ron Swoboda 3.00 1.35
□ 265 Lou Burdette 3.00 1.35
□ 266 Pitt Power 5.00 2.20
Willie Stargell
Donn Clendenon
□ 267 Don Schwall 2.00 .90
□ 268 Johnny Briggs 2.00 .90
□ 269 Don Nottebart 2.00 .90
□ 270 Zoilo Versalles 2.00 .90
□ 271 Eddie Watt 2.00 .90
□ 272 Cubs Rookies 4.00 1.80
Bill Connors
Dave Dowling
□ 273 Dick Lines 2.00 .90
□ 274 Bob Aspromonte 2.00 .90
□ 275 Fred Whitfield 2.00 .90
□ 276 Bruce Brubaker 2.00 .90
□ 277 Steve Whitaker 4.00 1.80
□ 278 Jim Kaat CL 30.00 6.00
□ 279 Frank Linzy 2.00 .90
□ 280 Tony Conigliaro 10.00 4.50
□ 281 Bob Rodgers 2.00 .90
□ 282 John Odom 2.00 .90
□ 283 Gene Alley 4.00 1.80
□ 284 Johnny Podres 3.00 1.35
□ 285 Lou Brock 20.00 9.00
□ 286 Wayne Causey 2.50 1.10
□ 287 Mets Rookies 2.50 1.10
Greg Goossen
Bart Shirley
□ 288 Denny Lemaster 2.50 1.10
□ 289 Tom Tresh 3.50 1.55
□ 290 Bill White 3.00 1.35
□ 291 Jim Hannan 2.50 1.10
□ 292 Don Pavletich 2.50 1.10
□ 293 Ed Kirkpatrick 2.50 1.10
□ 294 Walter Alston MG 4.00 1.80
□ 295 Sam McDowell 5.00 2.20
□ 296 Glenn Beckert 5.00 2.20
□ 297 Dave Morehead 5.00 2.20
□ 298 Ron Davis 2.50 1.10
□ 299 Norm Siebern 2.50 1.10
□ 300 Jim Kaat 6.00 2.70
□ 301 Jesse Gonder 2.50 1.10
□ 302 Orioles Team 6.00 2.70
□ 303 Gil Blanco 2.50 1.10
□ 304 Phil Gagliano 2.50 1.10
□ 305 Earl Wilson 5.00 2.20
□ 306 Bud Harrelson 6.00 2.70
□ 307 Jim Beauchamp 2.50 1.10
□ 308 Al Downing 5.00 2.20
□ 309 Hurlers Beware 5.00 2.20
Johnny Callison
Richie Allen
□ 310 Gary Peters 2.50 1.10
□ 311 Ed Brinkman 2.50 1.10
□ 312 Don Mincher 2.50 1.10
□ 313 Bob Lee 2.50 1.10
□ 314 Red Sox Rookies 8.00 3.60
Mike Andrews
Reggie Smith
□ 315 Billy Williams 10.00 4.50
□ 316 Jack Kralick 2.50 1.10
□ 317 Cesar Tovar 3.00 1.35
□ 318 Dave Giusti 2.50 1.10
□ 319 Paul Blair 5.00 2.20
□ 320 Gaylord Perry 14.00 6.25
□ 321 Mayo Smith MG 2.50 1.10
□ 322 Jose Pagan 2.50 1.10
□ 323 Mike Hershberger 2.50 1.10
□ 324 Hal Woodeshick 2.50 1.10
□ 325 Chico Cardenas 5.00 2.20
□ 326 Bob Uecker 10.00 4.50
□ 327 California Angels 6.00 2.70
Team Card
□ 328 Clete Boyer UER 5.00 2.20
(Stats only go up
through 1965)
□ 329 Charlie Lau 5.00 2.20
□ 330 Claude Osteen 5.00 2.20
□ 331 Joe Foy 5.00 2.20
□ 332 Jesus Alou 2.50 1.10
□ 333 Ferguson Jenkins 18.00 8.00
□ 334 Twin Terrors 6.00 2.70
Bob Allison
Harmon Killebrew
□ 335 Bob Veale 5.00 2.20
□ 336 Joe Azcue 2.50 1.10
□ 337 Joe Morgan 14.00 6.25
□ 338 Bob Locker 2.50 1.10
□ 339 Chico Ruiz 2.50 1.10
□ 340 Joe Pepitone 3.50 1.55
□ 341 Giants Rookies 2.50 1.10
Dick Dietz
Bill Sorrell
□ 342 Hank Fischer 2.50 1.10
□ 343 Tom Satriano 2.50 1.10
□ 344 Ossie Chavarria 2.50 1.10
□ 345 Stu Miller 5.00 2.20
□ 346 Jim Hickman 2.50 1.10
□ 347 Grady Hatton MG 2.50 1.10
□ 348 Tug McGraw 3.00 1.35
□ 349 Bob Chance 2.50 1.10
□ 350 Joe Torre 5.00 2.20
□ 351 Vern Law 5.00 2.20
□ 352 Ray Oyler 2.50 1.10
□ 353 Bill McCool 2.50 1.10
□ 354 Cubs Team 6.00 2.70
□ 355 Carl Yastrzemski 50.00 22.00
□ 356 Larry Jaster 2.50 1.10
□ 357 Bill Skowron 3.00 1.35
□ 358 Ruben Amaro 2.50 1.10
□ 359 Dick Ellsworth 2.50 1.10
□ 360 Leon Wagner 2.50 1.10
□ 361 Roberto Clemente CL 14.00 2.80
□ 362 Darold Knowles 2.50 1.10
□ 363 Dave Johnson 5.00 2.20
□ 364 Claude Raymond 2.50 1.10
□ 365 John Roseboro 5.00 2.20
□ 366 Andy Kosco 2.50 1.10
□ 367 Angels Rookies 2.50 1.10
Bill Kelso
Don Wallace
□ 368 Jack Hiatt 2.50 1.10
□ 369 Jim Hunter 18.00 8.00
□ 370 Tommy Davis 3.00 1.35
□ 371 Jim Lonborg 8.00 3.60
□ 372 Mike de la Hoz 4.00 1.80
□ 373 White Sox Rookies DP 4.00 1.80
Duane Josephson
Fred Klages
□ 374A Mel Queen ERR DP 20.00 9.00
(Incomplete stat
line on back)
□ 374B Mel Queen COR DP 4.00 1.80
(Complete stat
line on back)
□ 375 Jake Gibbs 8.00 3.60
□ 376 Don Lock DP 4.00 1.80
□ 377 Luis Tiant 8.00 3.60
□ 378 Detroit Tigers 8.00 3.60
Team Card UER
(Willie Horton with
262 RBI's in 1966)
□ 379 Jerry May DP 4.00 1.80
□ 380 Dean Chance DP 4.00 1.80
□ 381 Dick Schofield DP 4.00 1.80
□ 382 Dave McNally 8.00 3.60
□ 383 Ken Henderson DP 4.00 1.80
□ 384 Cardinals Rookies 4.00 1.80
Jim Cosman
Dick Hughes
□ 385 Jim Fregosi 8.00 3.60
(Batting wrong)
□ 386 Dick Selma DP 4.00 1.80
□ 387 Cap Peterson DP 4.00 1.80
□ 388 Arnold Earley DP 4.00 1.80
□ 389 Alvin Dark MG DP 8.00 3.60
□ 390 Jim Wynn DP 8.00 3.60
□ 391 Wilbur Wood DP 8.00 3.60
□ 392 Tommy Harper DP 8.00 3.60
□ 393 Jim Bouton DP 8.00 3.60
□ 394 Jake Wood DP 4.00 1.80
□ 395 Chris Short 8.00 3.60
□ 396 Atlanta Aces 4.00 1.80
Denis Menke
Tony Cloninger
□ 397 Willie Smith DP 4.00 1.80
□ 398 Jeff Torborg 8.00 3.60
□ 399 Al Worthington DP 4.00 1.80
□ 400 Bob Clemente DP 100.00 45.00
□ 401 Jim Coates 4.00 1.80
□ 402A Phillies Rookies DP 20.00 9.00
Grant Jackson
Billy Wilson
Incomplete stat line
□ 402B Phillies Rookies DP 8.00 3.60
Grant Jackson
Billy Wilson
□ 403 Dick Nen 4.00 1.80
□ 404 Nelson Briles 8.00 3.60
□ 405 Russ Snyder 4.00 1.80
□ 406 Lee Elia DP 4.00 1.80
□ 407 Reds Team 8.00 3.60
□ 408 Jim Northrup DP 8.00 3.60
□ 409 Ray Sadecki 4.00 1.80
□ 410 Lou Johnson DP 4.00 1.80
□ 411 Dick Howser DP 4.00 1.80
□ 412 Astros Rookies 8.00 3.60
Norm Miller
Doug Rader
□ 413 Jerry Grote 4.00 1.80
□ 414 Casey Cox 4.00 1.80
□ 415 Sonny Jackson 4.00 1.80
□ 416 Roger Repoz 4.00 1.80
□ 417A Bob Bruce ERR DP 30.00 13.50
(RBAVES on back)
□ 417B Bob Bruce COR DP 4.00 1.80
□ 418 Sam Mele MG 4.00 1.80
□ 419 Don Kessinger DP 8.00 3.60
□ 420 Denny McLain 6.00 2.70
□ 421 Dal Maxvill DP 4.00 1.80
□ 422 Hoyt Wilhelm 10.00 4.50
□ 423 Fence Busters DP 25.00 11.00
Willie Mays
Willie McCovey
□ 424 Pedro Gonzalez 4.00 1.80
□ 425 Pete Mikkelsen 4.00 1.80
□ 426 Lou Clinton 4.00 1.80
□ 427A Ruben Gomez ERR DP 20.00 9.00
(Incomplete stat
line on back)
□ 427B Ruben Gomez COR DP 4.00 1.80
(Complete stat
line on back)
□ 428 Dodgers Rookies DP 8.00 3.60
Tom Hutton
Gene Michael
□ 429 Garry Roggenburk DP 4.00 1.80
□ 430 Pete Rose 80.00 36.00
□ 431 Ted Uhlaender 4.00 1.80
□ 432 Jimmie Hall DP 4.00 1.80
□ 433 Al Luplow DP 4.00 1.80
□ 434 Eddie Fisher DP 4.00 1.80
□ 435 Mack Jones DP 4.00 1.80
□ 436 Pete Ward 4.00 1.80
□ 437 Senators Team 8.00 3.60
□ 438 Chuck Dobson 4.00 1.80
□ 439 Byron Browne 4.00 1.80
□ 440 Steve Hargan 4.00 1.80
□ 441 Jim Davenport 4.00 1.80
□ 442 Yankees Rookies DP 8.00 3.60
Bill Robinson
Joe Verbanic
□ 443 Tito Francona DP 4.00 1.80
□ 444 George Smith 4.00 1.80
□ 445 Don Sutton 25.00 11.00
□ 446 Russ Nixon DP 4.00 1.80
□ 447A Bo Belinsky ERR DP 5.00 2.20
(Incomplete stat
line on back)
□ 447B Bo Belinsky COR DP 8.00 3.60
(Complete stat
line on back)
□ 448 Harry Walker DP MG 4.00 1.80
□ 449 Orlando Pena 4.00 1.80
□ 450 Richie Allen 9.00 4.00
□ 451 Fred Newman DP 4.00 1.80
□ 452 Ed Kranepool 8.00 3.60
□ 453 Aurelio Monteagudo DP 4.00 1.80
□ 454A Juan Marichal CL 8.00 1.60
Missing left ear
□ 454B Juan Marichal CL 8.00 1.60
left ear showing
□ 455 Tommie Agee 8.00 3.60
□ 456 Phil Niekro 16.00 7.25
□ 457 Andy Etchebarren DP 8.00 3.60
□ 458 Lee Thomas 6.00 2.70
□ 459 Senators Rookies 6.00 2.70
Dick Bosman
Pete Craig
□ 460 Harmon Killebrew 60.00 27.00
□ 461 Bob Miller 6.00 2.70
□ 462 Bob Barton 6.00 2.70
□ 463 Hill Aces 12.00 5.50
Sam McDowell
Sonny Siebert
□ 464 Dan Coombs 6.00 2.70
□ 465 Willie Horton 12.00 5.50
□ 466 Bobby Wine 6.00 2.70
□ 467 Jim O'Toole 6.00 2.70
□ 468 Ralph Houk MG 6.00 2.70
□ 469 Len Gabrielson 6.00 2.70
□ 470 Bob Shaw 6.00 2.70
□ 471 Rene Lachemann 6.00 2.70
□ 472 Rookies Pirates 6.00 2.70
John Gelnar
George Spriggs
□ 473 Jose Santiago 6.00 2.70
□ 474 Bob Tolan 6.00 2.70
□ 475 Jim Palmer 90.00 40.00
□ 476 Tony Perez SP 70.00 32.00

☐ 477 Braves Team 15.00 6.75
☐ 478 Bob Humphreys 6.00 2.70
☐ 479 Gary Bell 6.00 2.70
☐ 480 Willie McCovey 35.00 16.00
☐ 481 Leo Durocher MG 15.00 6.75
☐ 482 Bill Monbouquette 6.00 2.70
☐ 483 Jim Landis 6.00 2.70
☐ 484 Jerry Adair 6.00 2.70
☐ 485 Tim McCarver 20.00 9.00
☐ 486 Twins Rookies 6.00 2.70
Rich Reese
Bill Whitby
☐ 487 Tommie Reynolds 6.00 2.70
☐ 488 Gerry Arrigo 6.00 2.70
☐ 489 Doug Clemens 6.00 2.70
☐ 490 Tony Cloninger 6.00 2.70
☐ 491 Sam Bowens 6.00 2.70
☐ 492 Pittsburgh Pirates 15.00 6.75
Team Card
☐ 493 Phil Ortega 6.00 2.70
☐ 494 Bill Rigney MG 6.00 2.70
☐ 495 Fritz Peterson 6.00 2.70
☐ 496 Orlando McFarlane 6.00 2.70
☐ 497 Ron Campbell 6.00 2.70
☐ 498 Larry Dierker 12.00 5.50
☐ 499 Indians Rookies 6.00 2.70
George Culver
Jose Vidal
☐ 500 Juan Marichal 25.00 11.00
☐ 501 Jerry Zimmerman 6.00 2.70
☐ 502 Derrell Griffith 6.00 2.70
☐ 503 Los Angeles Dodgers 15.00 6.75
Team Card
☐ 504 Orlando Martinez 6.00 2.70
☐ 505 Tommy Helms 12.00 5.50
☐ 506 Smoky Burgess 6.00 2.70
☐ 507 Orioles Rookies 6.00 2.70
Ed Barnowski
Larry Haney
☐ 508 Dick Hall 6.00 2.70
☐ 509 Jim King 6.00 2.70
☐ 510 Bill Mazeroski 15.00 6.75
☐ 511 Don Wert 6.00 2.70
☐ 512 Red Schoendienst MG 15.00 6.75
☐ 513 Marcelino Lopez 6.00 2.70
☐ 514 John Werhas 6.00 2.70
☐ 515 Bert Campaneris 9.00 4.00
☐ 516 Giants Team 15.00 6.75
☐ 517 Fred Talbot 6.00 2.70
☐ 518 Denis Menke 6.00 2.70
☐ 519 Ted Davidson 6.00 2.70
☐ 520 Max Alvis 6.00 2.70
☐ 521 Bird Bombers 12.00 5.50
Boog Powell
Curt Blefary
☐ 522 John Stephenson 6.00 2.70
☐ 523 Jim Merritt 6.00 2.70
☐ 524 Felix Mantilla 6.00 2.70
☐ 525 Ron Hunt 6.00 2.70
☐ 526 Tigers Rookies 6.00 2.70
Pat Dobson
George Korince
(See 67T-72)
☐ 527 Dennis Ribant 6.00 2.70
☐ 528 Rico Petrocelli 10.00 4.50
☐ 529 Gary Wagner 6.00 2.70
☐ 530 Felipe Alou 12.00 5.50
☐ 531 Brooks Robinson CL 14.00 2.80
☐ 532 Jim Hicks 6.00 2.70
☐ 533 Jack Fisher 6.00 2.70
☐ 534 Hank Bauer MG DP 9.00 4.00
☐ 535 Donn Clendenon 18.00 8.00
☐ 536 Cubs Rookies 35.00 16.00
Joe Niekro
Paul Popovich
☐ 537 Chuck Estrada DP 9.00 4.00
☐ 538 J.C. Martin 16.00 7.25
☐ 539 Dick Egan DP 9.00 4.00
☐ 540 Norm Cash 35.00 16.00
☐ 541 Joe Gibbon 16.00 7.25
☐ 542 Athletics Rookies DP 15.00 6.75
Rick Monday
Tony Pierce
☐ 543 Dan Schneider 16.00 7.25
☐ 544 Cleveland Indians 30.00 13.50
Team Card
☐ 545 Jim Grant 16.00 7.25
☐ 546 Woody Woodward 18.00 8.00
☐ 547 Red Sox Rookies DP 9.00 4.00
Russ Gibson
Bill Rohr
☐ 548 Tony Gonzalez DP 9.00 4.00
☐ 549 Jack Sanford 16.00 7.25
☐ 550 Vada Pinson DP 10.00 4.50
☐ 551 Doug Camilli DP 9.00 4.00
☐ 552 Ted Savage 16.00 7.25
☐ 553 Yankees Rookies 30.00 13.50
Mike Hegan
Thad Tillotson
☐ 554 Andre Rodgers DP 9.00 4.00
☐ 555 Don Cardwell 18.00 8.00
☐ 556 Al Weis DP 9.00 4.00
☐ 557 Al Ferrara 16.00 7.25
☐ 558 Orioles Rookies 50.00 22.00
Mark Belanger
Bill Dillman
☐ 559 Dick Tracewski DP 9.00 4.00
☐ 560 Jim Bunning 70.00 32.00
☐ 561 Sandy Alomar 20.00 9.00
☐ 562 Steve Blass DP 9.00 4.00
☐ 563 Joe Adcock 20.00 9.00
☐ 564 Astros Rookies DP 9.00 4.00
Alonzo Harris
Aaron Pointer
☐ 565 Lew Krausse 16.00 7.25
☐ 566 Gary Geiger DP 9.00 4.00
☐ 567 Steve Hamilton 25.00 11.00
☐ 568 John Sullivan 25.00 11.00
☐ 569 AL Rookies DP 250.00 110.00
Rod Carew
Hank Allen
☐ 570 Maury Wills 85.00 38.00
☐ 571 Larry Sherry 16.00 7.25
☐ 572 Don Demeter 16.00 7.25
☐ 573 Chicago White Sox 30.00 13.50
Team Card UER
(Indians team
stats on back)
☐ 574 Jerry Buchek 16.00 7.25
☐ 575 Dave Boswell 16.00 7.25
☐ 576 NL Rookies 25.00 11.00
Ramon Hernandez
Norm Gigon
☐ 577 Bill Short 16.00 7.25
☐ 578 John Boccabella 16.00 7.25
☐ 579 Bill Henry 16.00 7.25
☐ 580 Rocky Colavito 100.00 45.00
☐ 581 Mets Rookies 850.00 375.00
Bill Denehy
Tom Seaver
☐ 582 Jim Owens DP 9.00 4.00
☐ 583 Ray Barker 25.00 11.00
☐ 584 Jimmy Piersall 35.00 16.00
☐ 585 Wally Bunker 16.00 7.25
☐ 586 Manny Jimenez 16.00 7.25
☐ 587 NL Rookies 35.00 16.00
Don Shaw
Gary Sutherland
☐ 588 Johnny Klippstein DP 9.00 4.00
☐ 589 Dave Ricketts DP 9.00 4.00
☐ 590 Pete Richert 16.00 7.25
☐ 591 Ty Cline 16.00 7.25
☐ 592 NL Rookies 25.00 11.00
Jim Shellenback
Ron Willis
☐ 593 Wes Westrum MG 25.00 11.00
☐ 594 Dan Osinski 18.00 8.00
☐ 595 Cookie Rojas 18.00 8.00
☐ 596 Galen Cisco DP 10.00 4.50
☐ 597 Ted Abernathy 16.00 7.25
☐ 598 White Sox Rookies 18.00 8.00
Walt Williams
Ed Stroud
☐ 599 Bob Duliba DP 9.00 4.00
☐ 600 Brooks Robinson 275.00 125.00
☐ 601 Bill Bryan DP 9.00 4.00
☐ 602 Juan Pizarro 25.00 11.00
☐ 603 Athletics Rookies 25.00 11.00
Tim Talton
Ramon Webster
☐ 604 Red Sox Team 125.00 55.00
☐ 605 Mike Shannon 50.00 22.00
☐ 606 Ron Taylor 18.00 8.00
☐ 607 Mickey Stanley 40.00 18.00
☐ 608 Cubs Rookies DP 9.00 4.00
Rich Nye
John Upham
☐ 609 Tommy John 70.00 23.00

1967 Topps Posters Inserts

The wrappers of the 1967 Topps cards have this 32-card set advertised as follows: 'Extra -- All Star Pin-Up Inside." Printed on (5" by 7") paper in full color, these "All-Star" inserts have fold lines which are generally not very noticeable when stored carefully. They are numbered, blank-backed, and carry a facsimile autograph.

	NRMT	VG-E
COMPLETE SET (32)	60.00	27.00
COMMON CARD (1-32)	.80	.35

☐ 1 Boog Powell 1.00 .45
☐ 2 Bert Campaneris .80 .35
☐ 3 Brooks Robinson 4.00 1.80

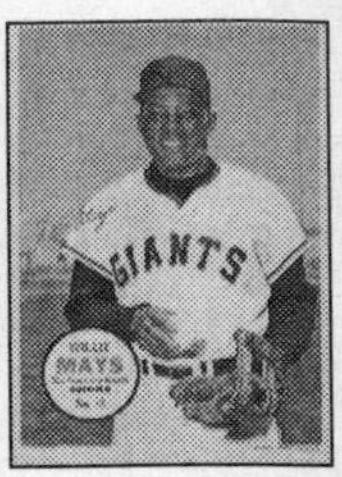

☐ 4 Tommie Agee .80 .35
☐ 5 Carl Yastrzemski 4.00 1.80
☐ 6 Mickey Mantle 20.00 9.00
☐ 7 Frank Howard 1.00 .45
☐ 8 Sam McDowell .80 .35
☐ 9 Orlando Cepeda 1.00 .45
☐ 10 Chico Cardenas .80 .35
☐ 11 Roberto Clemente 10.00 4.50
☐ 12 Willie Mays 8.00 3.60
☐ 13 Cleon Jones .80 .35
☐ 14 Johnny Callison 1.00 .45
☐ 15 Hank Aaron 6.00 2.70
☐ 16 Don Drysdale 3.00 1.35
☐ 17 Bobby Knoop .80 .35
☐ 18 Tony Oliva 1.00 .45
☐ 19 Frank Robinson 4.00 1.80
☐ 20 Denny McLain 1.00 .45
☐ 21 Al Kaline 4.00 1.80
☐ 22 Joe Pepitone 1.00 .45
☐ 23 Harmon Killebrew 3.00 1.35
☐ 24 Leon Wagner .80 .35
☐ 25 Joe Morgan 2.50 1.10
☐ 26 Ron Santo 1.00 .45
☐ 27 Joe Torre 1.00 .45
☐ 28 Juan Marichal 3.00 1.35
☐ 29 Matty Alou .80 .35
☐ 30 Felipe Alou 1.00 .45
☐ 31 Ron Hunt .80 .35
☐ 32 Willie McCovey 2.50 1.10

1968 Topps

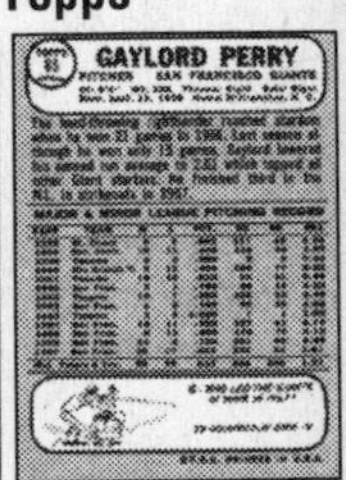

The cards in this 598-card set measure 2 1/2" by 3 1/2". The 1968 Topps set includes Sporting News All-Star Selections as card numbers 361 to 380. Other subsets in the set include League Leaders (1-12) and World Series cards (151-158). The front of each checklist card features a picture of a popular player inside a circle. Higher numbers 458 to 598 are slightly more difficult to obtain. The first series looks different from the other series, as it has a lighter, wider mesh background on the card front. The later series all had a much darker, finer mesh pattern. Among other fashions, cards were issued in five-card nickle packs. The key Rookie Cards in the set are Johnny Bench and Nolan Ryan.

	NRMT	VG-E
COMPLETE SET (598)	3000.00	1350.00
COMMON CARD (1-457)	1.75	.80
COMMON CARD (458-598)	3.50	1.55
WRAPPER (5-CENT)	25.00	11.00

☐ 1 NL Batting Leaders 30.00 12.00
Bob Clemente
Tony Gonzalez
Matty Alou
☐ 2 AL Batting Leaders 14.00 6.25
Carl Yastrzemski
Frank Robinson
Al Kaline
☐ 3 NL RBI Leaders 20.00 9.00
Orlando Cepeda
Bob Clemente
Hank Aaron
☐ 4 AL RBI Leaders 12.00 5.50
Carl Yastrzemski
Harmon Killebrew
Frank Robinson

☐ 5 NL Home Run Leaders	8.00	3.60
Hank Aaron		
Jim Wynn		
Ron Santo		
Willie McCovey		
☐ 6 AL Home Run Leaders	8.00	3.60
Carl Yastrzemski		
Harmon Killebrew		
Frank Howard		
☐ 7 NL ERA Leaders	3.50	1.55
Phil Niekro		
Jim Bunning		
Chris Short		
☐ 8 AL ERA Leaders	3.50	1.55
Joel Horlen		
Gary Peters		
Sonny Siebert		
☐ 9 NL Pitching Leaders	5.00	2.20
Mike McCormick		
Ferguson Jenkins		
Jim Bunning		
Claude Osteen		
☐ 10A AL Pitching Leaders	4.00	1.80
Jim Lonborg ERR		
(Misspelled Lonberg		
on card back)		
Earl Wilson		
Dean Chance		
☐ 10B AL Pitching Leaders	4.00	1.80
Jim Lonborg COR		
Earl Wilson		
Dean Chance		
☐ 11 NL Strikeout Leaders	6.00	2.70
Jim Bunning		
Ferguson Jenkins		
Gaylord Perry		
☐ 12 AL Strikeout Leaders	3.50	1.55
Jim Lonborg UER		
(Misspelled Longberg		
on card back)		
Sam McDowell		
Dean Chance		
☐ 13 Chuck Hartenstein	1.75	.80
☐ 14 Jerry McNertney	1.75	.80
☐ 15 Ron Hunt	1.75	.80
☐ 16 Indians Rookies	5.00	2.20
Lou Piniella		
Richie Scheinblum		
☐ 17 Dick Hall	1.75	.80
☐ 18 Mike Hershberger	1.75	.80
☐ 19 Juan Pizarro	1.75	.80
☐ 20 Brooks Robinson	25.00	11.00
☐ 21 Ron Davis	1.75	.80
☐ 22 Pat Dobson	4.00	1.80
☐ 23 Chico Cardenas	4.00	1.80
☐ 24 Bobby Locke	1.75	.80
☐ 25 Julian Javier	4.00	1.80
☐ 26 Darrell Brandon	1.75	.80
☐ 27 Gil Hodges MG	8.00	3.60
☐ 28 Ted Uhlaender	1.75	.80
☐ 29 Joe Verbanic	1.75	.80
☐ 30 Joe Torre	5.00	2.20
☐ 31 Ed Stroud	1.75	.80
☐ 32 Joe Gibbon	1.75	.80
☐ 33 Pete Ward	1.75	.80
☐ 34 Al Ferrara	1.75	.80
☐ 35 Steve Hargan	1.75	.80
☐ 36 Pirates Rookies	4.00	1.80
Bob Moose		
Bob Robertson		
☐ 37 Billy Williams	8.00	3.60
☐ 38 Tony Pierce	1.75	.80
☐ 39 Cookie Rojas	4.00	1.80
☐ 40 Denny McLain	10.00	4.50
☐ 41 Julio Gotay	1.75	.80
☐ 42 Larry Haney	1.75	.80
☐ 43 Gary Bell	1.75	.80
☐ 44 Frank Kostro	1.75	.80
☐ 45 Tom Seaver	50.00	22.00
☐ 46 Dave Ricketts	1.75	.80
☐ 47 Ralph Houk MG	4.00	1.80
☐ 48 Ted Davidson	1.75	.80
☐ 49A Eddie Brinkman	1.75	.80
(White team name)		
☐ 49B Eddie Brinkman	50.00	22.00
(Yellow team name)		
☐ 50 Willie Mays	65.00	29.00
☐ 51 Bob Locker	1.75	.80
☐ 52 Hawk Taylor	1.75	.80
☐ 53 Gene Alley	4.00	1.80
☐ 54 Stan Williams	4.00	1.80
☐ 55 Felipe Alou	5.00	2.20
☐ 56 Orioles Rookies	1.75	.80
Dave Leonhard		
Dave May		
☐ 57 Dan Schneider	1.75	.80
☐ 58 Eddie Mathews	16.00	7.25
☐ 59 Don Lock	1.75	.80
☐ 60 Ken Holtzman	4.00	1.80
☐ 61 Reggie Smith	3.00	1.35
☐ 62 Chuck Dobson	1.75	.80
☐ 63 Dick Kenworthy	1.75	.80
☐ 64 Jim Merritt	1.75	.80
☐ 65 John Roseboro	4.00	1.80
☐ 66A Casey Cox	1.75	.80
(White team name)		
☐ 66B Casey Cox	100.00	45.00
(Yellow team name)		
☐ 67 Jim Kaat CL	6.00	1.20
☐ 68 Ron Willis	1.75	.80
☐ 69 Tom Tresh	2.50	1.10
☐ 70 Bob Veale	4.00	1.80
☐ 71 Vern Fuller	1.75	.80
☐ 72 Tommy John	6.00	2.70
☐ 73 Jim Ray Hart	4.00	1.80
☐ 74 Milt Pappas	4.00	1.80
☐ 75 Don Mincher	1.75	.80
☐ 76 Braves Rookies	4.00	1.80
Jim Britton		
Ron Reed		
☐ 77 Don Wilson	4.00	1.80
☐ 78 Jim Northrup	5.00	2.20
☐ 79 Ted Kubiak	1.75	.80
☐ 80 Rod Carew	50.00	22.00
☐ 81 Larry Jackson	1.75	.80
☐ 82 Sam Bowens	1.75	.80
☐ 83 John Stephenson	1.75	.80
☐ 84 Bob Tolan	4.00	1.80
☐ 85 Gaylord Perry	8.00	3.60
☐ 86 Willie Stargell	8.00	3.60
☐ 87 Dick Williams MG	4.00	1.80
☐ 88 Phil Regan	4.00	1.80
☐ 89 Jake Gibbs	4.00	1.80
☐ 90 Vada Pinson	3.00	1.35
☐ 91 Jim Ollom	1.75	.80
☐ 92 Ed Kranepool	4.00	1.80
☐ 93 Tony Cloninger	1.75	.80
☐ 94 Lee Maye	1.75	.80
☐ 95 Bob Aspromonte	1.75	.80
☐ 96 Senator Rookies	1.75	.80
Frank Coggins		
Dick Nold		
☐ 97 Tom Phoebus	1.75	.80
☐ 98 Gary Sutherland	1.75	.80
☐ 99 Rocky Colavito	8.00	3.60
☐ 100 Bob Gibson	25.00	11.00
☐ 101 Glenn Beckert	4.00	1.80
☐ 102 Jose Cardenal	4.00	1.80
☐ 103 Don Sutton	6.00	2.70
☐ 104 Dick Dietz	1.75	.80
☐ 105 Al Downing	4.00	1.80
☐ 106 Dalton Jones	1.75	.80
☐ 107A Juan Marichal CL	6.00	1.20
Tan wide mesh		
☐ 107B Juan Marichal CL	6.00	1.20
Brown fine mesh		
☐ 108 Don Pavletich	1.75	.80
☐ 109 Bert Campaneris	4.00	1.80
☐ 110 Hank Aaron	60.00	27.00
☐ 111 Rich Reese	1.75	.80
☐ 112 Woody Fryman	1.75	.80
☐ 113 Tigers Rookies	2.50	1.10
Tom Matchick		
Daryl Patterson		
☐ 114 Ron Swoboda	4.00	1.80
☐ 115 Sam McDowell	4.00	1.80
☐ 116 Ken McMullen	1.75	.80
☐ 117 Larry Jaster	1.75	.80
☐ 118 Mark Belanger	4.00	1.80
☐ 119 Ted Savage	1.75	.80
☐ 120 Mel Stottlemyre	5.00	2.20
☐ 121 Jimmie Hall	1.75	.80
☐ 122 Gene Mauch MG	4.00	1.80
☐ 123 Jose Santiago	1.75	.80
☐ 124 Nate Oliver	1.75	.80
☐ 125 Joel Horlen	1.75	.80
☐ 126 Bobby Etheridge	1.75	.80
☐ 127 Paul Lindblad	1.75	.80
☐ 128 Astros Rookies	1.75	.80
Tom Dukes		
Alonzo Harris		
☐ 129 Mickey Stanley	5.00	2.20
☐ 130 Tony Perez	8.00	3.60
☐ 131 Frank Bertaina	1.75	.80
☐ 132 Bud Harrelson	4.00	1.80
☐ 133 Fred Whitfield	1.75	.80
☐ 134 Pat Jarvis	1.75	.80
☐ 135 Paul Blair	4.00	1.80
☐ 136 Randy Hundley	4.00	1.80
☐ 137 Twins Team	4.00	1.80
☐ 138 Ruben Amaro	1.75	.80
☐ 139 Chris Short	1.75	.80
☐ 140 Tony Conigliaro	8.00	3.60
☐ 141 Dal Maxvill	1.75	.80
☐ 142 White Sox Rookies	1.75	.80
Buddy Bradford		
Bill Voss		
☐ 143 Pete Cimino	1.75	.80
☐ 144 Joe Morgan	12.00	5.50
☐ 145 Don Drysdale	12.00	5.50
☐ 146 Sal Bando	4.00	1.80
☐ 147 Frank Linzy	1.75	.80
☐ 148 Dave Bristol MG	1.75	.80
☐ 149 Bob Saverine	1.75	.80
☐ 150 Bob Clemente	70.00	32.00
☐ 151 Lou Brock WS	10.00	4.50
☐ 152 Carl Yastrzemski WS	10.00	4.50
☐ 153 Nellie Briles WS	4.50	2.00
☐ 154 Bob Gibson WS	10.00	4.50
☐ 155 Jim Lonborg WS	4.50	2.00
☐ 156 Rico Petrocelli WS	4.50	2.00
☐ 157 World Series Game 7	4.50	2.00
St. Louis wins it		
☐ 158 World Series Summary	4.50	2.00
Cardinals celebrate		
☐ 159 Don Kessinger	4.00	1.80
☐ 160 Earl Wilson	4.00	1.80
☐ 161 Norm Miller	1.75	.80
☐ 162 Cards Rookies	4.00	1.80
Hal Gilson		
Mike Torrez		
☐ 163 Gene Brabender	1.75	.80
☐ 164 Ramon Webster	1.75	.80
☐ 165 Tony Oliva	5.00	2.20
☐ 166 Claude Raymond	1.75	.80
☐ 167 Elston Howard	5.00	2.20
☐ 168 Dodgers Team	4.00	1.80
☐ 169 Bob Bolin	1.75	.80
☐ 170 Jim Fregosi	4.00	1.80
☐ 171 Don Nottebart	1.75	.80
☐ 172 Walt Williams	1.75	.80
☐ 173 John Boozer	1.75	.80
☐ 174 Bob Tillman	1.75	.80
☐ 175 Maury Wills	6.00	2.70
☐ 176 Bob Allen	1.75	.80
☐ 177 Mets Rookies	900.00	400.00
Jerry Koosman		
Nolan Ryan		
☐ 178 Don Wert	4.00	1.80
☐ 179 Bill Stoneman	1.75	.80
☐ 180 Curt Flood	3.00	1.35
☐ 181 Jerry Zimmerman	1.75	.80
☐ 182 Dave Giusti	1.75	.80
☐ 183 Bob Kennedy MG	4.00	1.80
☐ 184 Lou Johnson	4.00	1.80
☐ 185 Tom Haller	1.75	.80
☐ 186 Eddie Watt	1.75	.80
☐ 187 Sonny Jackson	1.75	.80
☐ 188 Cap Peterson	1.75	.80
☐ 189 Bill Landis	1.75	.80
☐ 190 Bill White	3.00	1.35
☐ 191 Dan Frisella	1.75	.80
☐ 192A Carl Yastrzemski CL	8.00	1.60
Special Baseball Playing Card		
☐ 192B Carl Yastrzemski CL	8.00	1.60
Special Baseball		
Playing Card Game		
☐ 193 Jack Hamilton	1.75	.80
☐ 194 Don Buford	1.75	.80
☐ 195 Joe Pepitone	2.50	1.10
☐ 196 Gary Nolan	4.00	1.80
☐ 197 Larry Brown	1.75	.80
☐ 198 Roy Face	4.00	1.80
☐ 199 A's Rookies	1.75	.80
Roberto Rodriquez		
Darrell Osteen		
☐ 200 Orlando Cepeda	6.00	2.70
☐ 201 Mike Marshall	3.00	1.35
☐ 202 Adolfo Phillips	1.75	.80
☐ 203 Dick Kelley	1.75	.80
☐ 204 Andy Etchebarren	1.75	.80
☐ 205 Juan Marichal	8.00	3.60
☐ 206 Cal Ermer MG	1.75	.80
☐ 207 Carroll Sembera	1.75	.80
☐ 208 Willie Davis	2.50	1.10
☐ 209 Tim Cullen	1.75	.80
☐ 210 Gary Peters	1.75	.80
☐ 211 J.C. Martin	1.75	.80
☐ 212 Dave Morehead	1.75	.80
☐ 213 Chico Ruiz	1.75	.80
☐ 214 Yankees Rookies	4.00	1.80
Stan Bahnsen		
Frank Fernandez		
☐ 215 Jim Bunning	7.00	3.10
☐ 216 Bubba Morton	1.75	.80
☐ 217 Dick Farrell	1.75	.80
☐ 218 Ken Suarez	1.75	.80
☐ 219 Rob Gardner	1.75	.80
☐ 220 Harmon Killebrew	14.00	6.25
☐ 221 Braves Team	4.00	1.80
☐ 222 Jim Hardin	1.75	.80

☐ 223 Ollie Brown 1.75 .80
☐ 224 Jack Aker 1.75 .80
☐ 225 Richie Allen 6.00 2.70
☐ 226 Jimmie Price 1.75 .80
☐ 227 Joe Hoerner 1.75 .80
☐ 228 Dodgers Rookies 4.00 1.80
Jack Billingham
Jim Fairey
☐ 229 Fred Klages 1.75 .80
☐ 230 Pete Rose 35.00 16.00
☐ 231 Dave Baldwin 1.75 .80
☐ 232 Denis Menke 1.75 .80
☐ 233 George Scott 4.00 1.80
☐ 234 Bill Monbouquette 1.75 .80
☐ 235 Ron Santo 5.00 2.20
☐ 236 Tug McGraw 5.00 2.20
☐ 237 Alvin Dark MG 4.00 1.80
☐ 238 Tom Satriano 1.75 .80
☐ 239 Bill Henry 1.75 .80
☐ 240 Al Kaline 25.00 11.00
☐ 241 Felix Millan 1.75 .80
☐ 242 Moe Drabowsky 4.00 1.80
☐ 243 Rich Rollins 1.75 .80
☐ 244 John Donaldson 1.75 .80
☐ 245 Tony Gonzalez 1.75 .80
☐ 246 Fritz Peterson 4.00 1.80
☐ 247 Reds Rookies 125.00 55.00
Johnny Bench
Ron Tompkins
☐ 248 Fred Valentine 1.75 .80
☐ 249 Bill Singer 1.75 .80
☐ 250 Carl Yastrzemski 25.00 11.00
☐ 251 Manny Sanguillen 6.00 2.70
☐ 252 Angels Team 4.00 1.80
☐ 253 Dick Hughes 1.75 .80
☐ 254 Cleon Jones 4.00 1.80
☐ 255 Dean Chance 4.00 1.80
☐ 256 Norm Cash 6.00 2.70
☐ 257 Phil Niekro 8.00 3.60
☐ 258 Cubs Rookies 1.75 .80
Jose Arcia
Bill Schlesinger
☐ 259 Ken Boyer 3.00 1.35
☐ 260 Jim Wynn 4.00 1.80
☐ 261 Dave Duncan 4.00 1.80
☐ 262 Rick Wise 4.00 1.80
☐ 263 Horace Clarke 4.00 1.80
☐ 264 Ted Abernathy 1.75 .80
☐ 265 Tommy Davis 4.00 1.80
☐ 266 Paul Popovich 1.75 .80
☐ 267 Herman Franks MG 1.75 .80
☐ 268 Bob Humphreys 1.75 .80
☐ 269 Bob Tiefenauer 1.75 .80
☐ 270 Matty Alou 4.00 1.80
☐ 271 Bobby Knoop 1.75 .80
☐ 272 Ray Culp 1.75 .80
☐ 273 Dave Johnson 4.00 1.80
☐ 274 Mike Cuellar 4.00 1.80
☐ 275 Tim McCarver 5.00 2.20
☐ 276 Jim Roland 1.75 .80
☐ 277 Jerry Buchek 1.75 .80
☐ 278 Orlando Cepeda CL 6.00 1.20
☐ 279 Bill Hands 1.75 .80
☐ 280 Mickey Mantle 250.00 110.00
☐ 281 Jim Campanis 1.75 .80
☐ 282 Rick Monday 4.00 1.80
☐ 283 Mel Queen 1.75 .80
☐ 284 Johnny Briggs 1.75 .80
☐ 285 Dick McAuliffe 4.00 1.80
☐ 286 Cecil Upshaw 1.75 .80
☐ 287 White Sox Rookies 1.75 .80
Mickey Abarbanel
Cisco Carlos
☐ 288 Dave Wickersham 1.75 .80
☐ 289 Woody Held 1.75 .80
☐ 290 Willie McCovey 12.00 5.50
☐ 291 Dick Lines 1.75 .80
☐ 292 Art Shamsky 1.75 .80
☐ 293 Bruce Howard 1.75 .80
☐ 294 Red Schoendienst MG 5.00 2.20
☐ 295 Sonny Siebert 1.75 .80
☐ 296 Byron Browne 1.75 .80
☐ 297 Russ Gibson 1.75 .80
☐ 298 Jim Brewer 1.75 .80
☐ 299 Gene Michael 4.00 1.80
☐ 300 Rusty Staub 3.00 1.35
☐ 301 Twins Rookies 1.75 .80
George Mitterwald
Rick Renick
☐ 302 Gerry Arrigo 1.75 .80
☐ 303 Dick Green 4.00 1.80
☐ 304 Sandy Valdespino 1.75 .80
☐ 305 Minnie Rojas 1.75 .80
☐ 306 Mike Ryan 1.75 .80
☐ 307 John Hiller 4.00 1.80
☐ 308 Pirates Team 4.00 1.80
☐ 309 Ken Henderson 1.75 .80

☐ 310 Luis Aparicio 7.00 3.10
☐ 311 Jack Lamabe 1.75 .80
☐ 312 Curt Blefary 1.75 .80
☐ 313 Al Weis 1.75 .80
☐ 314 Red Sox Rookies 1.75 .80
Bill Rohr
George Spriggs
☐ 315 Zoilo Versalles 1.75 .80
☐ 316 Steve Barber 1.75 .80
☐ 317 Ron Brand 1.75 .80
☐ 318 Chico Salmon 1.75 .80
☐ 319 George Culver 1.75 .80
☐ 320 Frank Howard 5.00 2.20
☐ 321 Leo Durocher MG 5.00 2.20
☐ 322 Dave Boswell 1.75 .80
☐ 323 Deron Johnson 4.00 1.80
☐ 324 Jim Nash 1.75 .80
☐ 325 Manny Mota 4.00 1.80
☐ 326 Dennis Ribant 1.75 .80
☐ 327 Tony Taylor 4.00 1.80
☐ 328 Angels Rookies 1.75 .80
Chuck Vinson
Jim Weaver
☐ 329 Duane Josephson 1.75 .80
☐ 330 Roger Maris 30.00 13.50
☐ 331 Dan Osinski 1.75 .80
☐ 332 Doug Rader 4.00 1.80
☐ 333 Ron Herbel 1.75 .80
☐ 334 Orioles Team 4.00 1.80
☐ 335 Bob Allison 4.00 1.80
☐ 336 John Purdin 1.75 .80
☐ 337 Bill Robinson 4.00 1.80
☐ 338 Bob Johnson 1.75 .80
☐ 339 Rich Nye 1.75 .80
☐ 340 Max Alvis 1.75 .80
☐ 341 Jim Lemon MG 1.75 .80
☐ 342 Ken Johnson 1.75 .80
☐ 343 Jim Gosger 1.75 .80
☐ 344 Donn Clendenon 4.00 1.80
☐ 345 Bob Hendley 1.75 .80
☐ 346 Jerry Adair 1.75 .80
☐ 347 George Brunet 1.75 .80
☐ 348 Phillies Rookies 1.75 .80
Larry Colton
Dick Thoenen
☐ 349 Ed Spiezio 1.75 .80
☐ 350 Hoyt Wilhelm 7.00 3.10
☐ 351 Bob Barton 1.75 .80
☐ 352 Jackie Hernandez 1.75 .80
☐ 353 Mack Jones 1.75 .80
☐ 354 Pete Richert 1.75 .80
☐ 355 Ernie Banks 25.00 11.00
☐ 356A Ken Holtzman CL 6.00 1.20
Head centered within circle
☐ 356B Ken Holtzman 6.00 1.20
Head shifted right
within circle
☐ 357 Len Gabrielson 1.75 .80
☐ 358 Mike Epstein 1.75 .80
☐ 359 Joe Moeller 1.75 .80
☐ 360 Willie Horton 5.00 2.20
☐ 361 Harmon Killebrew AS 8.00 3.60
☐ 362 Orlando Cepeda AS 4.00 1.80
☐ 363 Rod Carew AS 8.00 3.60
☐ 364 Joe Morgan AS 8.00 3.60
☐ 365 Brooks Robinson AS 8.00 3.60
☐ 366 Ron Santo AS 3.00 1.35
☐ 367 Jim Fregosi AS 4.00 1.80
☐ 368 Gene Alley AS 4.00 1.80
☐ 369 Carl Yastrzemski AS 10.00 4.50
☐ 370 Hank Aaron AS 20.00 9.00
☐ 371 Tony Oliva AS 3.00 1.35
☐ 372 Lou Brock AS 8.00 3.60
☐ 373 Frank Robinson AS 8.00 3.60
☐ 374 Bob Clemente AS 30.00 13.50
☐ 375 Bill Freehan AS 3.00 1.35
☐ 376 Tim McCarver AS 4.00 1.80
☐ 377 Joel Horlen AS 4.00 1.80
☐ 378 Bob Gibson AS 8.00 3.60
☐ 379 Gary Peters AS 4.00 1.80
☐ 380 Ken Holtzman AS 4.00 1.80
☐ 381 Boog Powell 5.00 2.20
☐ 382 Ramon Hernandez 1.75 .80
☐ 383 Steve Whitaker 1.75 .80
☐ 384 Reds Rookies 6.00 2.70
Bill Henry
Hal McRae
☐ 385 Jim Hunter 12.00 5.50
☐ 386 Greg Goossen 1.75 .80
☐ 387 Joe Foy 1.75 .80
☐ 388 Ray Washburn 1.75 .80
☐ 389 Jay Johnstone 4.00 1.80
☐ 390 Bill Mazeroski 5.00 2.20
☐ 391 Bob Priddy 1.75 .80
☐ 392 Grady Hatton MG 1.75 .80
☐ 393 Jim Perry 4.00 1.80
☐ 394 Tommie Aaron 4.00 1.80

☐ 395 Camilo Pascual 4.00 1.80
☐ 396 Bobby Wine 1.75 .80
☐ 397 Vic Davalillo 1.75 .80
☐ 398 Jim Grant 1.75 .80
☐ 399 Ray Oyler 4.00 1.80
☐ 400A Mike McCormick 4.00 1.80
(Yellow letters)
☐ 400B Mike McCormick 150.00 70.00
(Team name in
white letters)
☐ 401 Mets Team 3.50 1.55
☐ 402 Mike Hegan 4.00 1.80
☐ 403 John Buzhardt 1.75 .80
☐ 404 Floyd Robinson 1.75 .80
☐ 405 Tommy Helms 4.00 1.80
☐ 406 Dick Ellsworth 1.75 .80
☐ 407 Gary Kolb 1.75 .80
☐ 408 Steve Carlton 30.00 13.50
☐ 409 Orioles Rookies 1.75 .80
Frank Peters
Ron Stone
☐ 410 Ferguson Jenkins 10.00 4.50
☐ 411 Ron Hansen 1.75 .80
☐ 412 Clay Carroll 4.00 1.80
☐ 413 Tom McCraw 1.75 .80
☐ 414 Mickey Lolich 8.00 3.60
☐ 415 Johnny Callison 4.00 1.80
☐ 416 Bill Rigney MG 1.75 .80
☐ 417 Willie Crawford 1.75 .80
☐ 418 Eddie Fisher 1.75 .80
☐ 419 Jack Hiatt 1.75 .80
☐ 420 Cesar Tovar 1.75 .80
☐ 421 Ron Taylor 1.75 .80
☐ 422 Rene Lachemann 1.75 .80
☐ 423 Fred Gladding 1.75 .80
☐ 424 Chicago White Sox 3.50 1.55
Team Card
☐ 425 Jim Maloney 4.00 1.80
☐ 426 Hank Allen 1.75 .80
☐ 427 Dick Calmus 1.75 .80
☐ 428 Vic Roznovsky 1.75 .80
☐ 429 Tommie Sisk 1.75 .80
☐ 430 Rico Petrocelli 4.00 1.80
☐ 431 Dooley Womack 1.75 .80
☐ 432 Indians Rookies 1.75 .80
Bill Davis
Jose Vidal
☐ 433 Bob Rodgers 1.75 .80
☐ 434 Ricardo Joseph 1.75 .80
☐ 435 Ron Perranoski 4.00 1.80
☐ 436 Hal Lanier 1.75 .80
☐ 437 Don Cardwell 1.75 .80
☐ 438 Lee Thomas 4.00 1.80
☐ 439 Lum Harris MG 1.75 .80
☐ 440 Claude Osteen 4.00 1.80
☐ 441 Alex Johnson 4.00 1.80
☐ 442 Dick Bosman 1.75 .80
☐ 443 Joe Azcue 1.75 .80
☐ 444 Jack Fisher 1.75 .80
☐ 445 Mike Shannon 4.00 1.80
☐ 446 Ron Kline 1.75 .80
☐ 447 Tigers Rookies 4.00 1.80
George Korince
Fred Lasher
☐ 448 Gary Wagner 1.75 .80
☐ 449 Gene Oliver 1.75 .80
☐ 450 Jim Kaat 6.00 2.70
☐ 451 Al Spangler 1.75 .80
☐ 452 Jesus Alou 1.75 .80
☐ 453 Sammy Ellis 1.75 .80
☐ 454A Frank Robinson CL 6.00 1.20
Cap complete within circle
☐ 454B Frank Robinson CL 6.00 1.20
Cap partially within circle
☐ 455 Rico Carty 4.00 1.80
☐ 456 John O'Donoghue 1.75 .80
☐ 457 Jim Lefebvre 4.00 1.80
☐ 458 Lew Krausse 6.00 2.70
☐ 459 Dick Simpson 3.50 1.55
☐ 460 Jim Lonborg 6.00 2.70
☐ 461 Chuck Hiller 3.50 1.55
☐ 462 Barry Moore 3.50 1.55
☐ 463 Jim Schaffer 3.50 1.55
☐ 464 Don McMahon 3.50 1.55
☐ 465 Tommie Agee 4.00 1.80
☐ 466 Bill Dillman 3.50 1.55
☐ 467 Dick Howser 6.00 2.70
☐ 468 Larry Sherry 3.50 1.55
☐ 469 Ty Cline 3.50 1.55
☐ 470 Bill Freehan 6.00 2.70
☐ 471 Orlando Pena 3.50 1.55
☐ 472 Walter Alston MG 6.00 2.70
☐ 473 Al Worthington 3.50 1.55
☐ 474 Paul Schaal 3.50 1.55
☐ 475 Joe Niekro 5.00 2.20
☐ 476 Woody Woodward 3.50 1.55
☐ 477 Philadelphia Phillies 6.00 2.70

Card	NRMT	VG-E
Team Card		
☐ 478 Dave McNally	6.00	2.70
☐ 479 Phil Gagliano	3.50	1.55
☐ 480 Manager's Dream	80.00	36.00
Tony Oliva		
Chico Cardenas		
Bob Clemente		
☐ 481 John Wyatt	3.50	1.55
☐ 482 Jose Pagan	3.50	1.55
☐ 483 Darold Knowles	3.50	1.55
☐ 484 Phil Roof	3.50	1.55
☐ 485 Ken Berry	3.50	1.55
☐ 486 Cal Koonce	3.50	1.55
☐ 487 Lee May	4.00	1.80
☐ 488 Dick Tracewski	4.50	2.00
☐ 489 Wally Bunker	3.50	1.55
☐ 490 Super Stars	175.00	80.00
Harmon Killebrew		
Willie Mays		
Mickey Mantle		
☐ 491 Denny Lemaster	3.50	1.55
☐ 492 Jeff Torborg	6.00	2.70
☐ 493 Jim McGlothlin	3.50	1.55
☐ 494 Ray Sadecki	3.50	1.55
☐ 495 Leon Wagner	3.50	1.55
☐ 496 Steve Hamilton	6.00	2.70
☐ 497 Cardinals Team	7.00	3.10
☐ 498 Bill Bryan	3.50	1.55
☐ 499 Steve Blass	6.00	2.70
☐ 500 Frank Robinson	30.00	13.50
☐ 501 John Odom	6.00	2.70
☐ 502 Mike Andrews	3.50	1.55
☐ 503 Al Jackson	3.50	1.55
☐ 504 Russ Snyder	3.50	1.55
☐ 505 Joe Sparma	10.00	4.50
☐ 506 Clarence Jones	4.00	1.80
☐ 507 Wade Blasingame	3.50	1.55
☐ 508 Duke Sims	3.50	1.55
☐ 509 Dennis Higgins	3.50	1.55
☐ 510 Ron Fairly	4.00	1.80
☐ 511 Bill Kelso	3.50	1.55
☐ 512 Grant Jackson	3.50	1.55
☐ 513 Hank Bauer MG	6.00	2.70
☐ 514 Al McBean	3.50	1.55
☐ 515 Russ Nixon	3.50	1.55
☐ 516 Pete Mikkelsen	3.50	1.55
☐ 517 Diego Segui	6.00	2.70
☐ 518A Clete Boyer CL ERR	12.00	2.40
539 AL Rookies		
☐ 518B Clete Boyer CL COR	12.00	2.40
539 ML Rookies		
☐ 519 Jerry Stephenson	3.50	1.55
☐ 520 Lou Brock	25.00	11.00
☐ 521 Don Shaw	3.50	1.55
☐ 522 Wayne Causey	3.50	1.55
☐ 523 John Tsitouris	3.50	1.55
☐ 524 Andy Kosco	3.50	1.55
☐ 525 Jim Davenport	3.50	1.55
☐ 526 Bill Denehy	3.50	1.55
☐ 527 Tito Francona	3.50	1.55
☐ 528 Tigers Team	70.00	32.00
☐ 529 Bruce Von Hoff	3.50	1.55
☐ 530 Bird Belters	40.00	18.00
Brooks Robinson		
Frank Robinson		
☐ 531 Chuck Hinton	3.50	1.55
☐ 532 Luis Tiant	6.00	2.70
☐ 533 Wes Parker	4.50	2.00
☐ 534 Bob Miller	3.50	1.55
☐ 535 Danny Cater	6.00	2.70
☐ 536 Bill Short	3.50	1.55
☐ 537 Norm Siebern	3.50	1.55
☐ 538 Manny Jimenez	3.50	1.55
☐ 539 Major League Rookies	3.50	1.55
Jim Ray		
Mike Ferraro		
☐ 540 Nelson Briles	6.00	2.70
☐ 541 Sandy Alomar	6.00	2.70
☐ 542 John Boccabella	3.50	1.55
☐ 543 Bob Lee	3.50	1.55
☐ 544 Mayo Smith MG	8.00	3.60
☐ 545 Lindy McDaniel	6.00	2.70
☐ 546 Roy White	4.50	2.00
☐ 547 Dan Coombs	3.50	1.55
☐ 548 Bernie Allen	3.50	1.55
☐ 549 Orioles Rookies	3.50	1.55
Curt Motton		
Roger Nelson		
☐ 550 Clete Boyer	6.00	2.70
☐ 551 Darrell Sutherland	3.50	1.55
☐ 552 Ed Kirkpatrick	3.50	1.55
☐ 553 Hank Aguirre	3.50	1.55
☐ 554 A's Team	8.00	3.60
☐ 555 Jose Tartabull	6.00	2.70
☐ 556 Dick Selma	3.50	1.55
☐ 557 Frank Quilici	3.50	1.55
☐ 558 Johnny Edwards	3.50	1.55
☐ 559 Pirates Rookies	3.50	1.55
Carl Taylor		
Luke Walker		
☐ 560 Paul Casanova	3.50	1.55
☐ 561 Lee Elia	3.50	1.55
☐ 562 Jim Bouton	6.00	2.70
☐ 563 Ed Charles	3.50	1.55
☐ 564 Eddie Stanky MG	6.00	2.70
☐ 565 Larry Dierker	6.00	2.70
☐ 566 Ken Harrelson	6.00	2.70
☐ 567 Clay Dalrymple	3.50	1.55
☐ 568 Willie Smith	3.50	1.55
☐ 569 NL Rookies	3.50	1.55
Ivan Murrell		
Les Rohr		
☐ 570 Rick Reichardt	3.50	1.55
☐ 571 Tony LaRussa	12.00	5.50
☐ 572 Don Bosch	3.50	1.55
☐ 573 Joe Coleman	3.50	1.55
☐ 574 Cincinnati Reds	8.00	3.60
Team Card		
☐ 575 Jim Palmer	35.00	16.00
☐ 576 Dave Adlesh	3.50	1.55
☐ 577 Fred Talbot	3.50	1.55
☐ 578 Orlando Martinez	3.50	1.55
☐ 579 NL Rookies	6.00	2.70
Larry Hisle		
Mike Lum		
☐ 580 Bob Bailey	3.50	1.55
☐ 581 Garry Roggenburk	3.50	1.55
☐ 582 Jerry Grote	6.00	2.70
☐ 583 Gates Brown	8.00	3.60
☐ 584 Larry Shepard MG	3.50	1.55
☐ 585 Wilbur Wood	6.00	2.70
☐ 586 Jim Pagliaroni	6.00	2.70
☐ 587 Roger Repoz	3.50	1.55
☐ 588 Dick Schofield	3.50	1.55
☐ 589 Twins Rookies	3.50	1.55
Ron Clark		
Moe Ogier		
☐ 590 Tommy Harper	4.00	1.80
☐ 591 Dick Nen	3.50	1.55
☐ 592 John Bateman	3.50	1.55
☐ 593 Lee Stange	3.50	1.55
☐ 594 Phil Linz	6.00	2.70
☐ 595 Phil Ortega	3.50	1.55
☐ 596 Charlie Smith	3.50	1.55
☐ 597 Bill McCool	3.50	1.55
☐ 598 Jerry May	7.00	2.20

1968 Topps Game Card Inserts

The cards in this 33-card set measure approximately 2 1/4" by 3 1/4". This "Game" card set of players, issued as inserts with the regular third series 1968 Topps baseball cards, was patterned directly after the Red Back and Blue Back sets of 1951. Each card has a color player photo set upon a pure white background, with a facsimile autograph underneath the picture. The cards have blue backs, and were also sold in boxed sets on a limited basis.

	NRMT	VG-E
COMPLETE SET (33)	125.00	55.00
COMMON CARD (1-33)	.80	.35
☐ 1 Matty Alou	1.00	.45
☐ 2 Mickey Mantle	40.00	18.00
☐ 3 Carl Yastrzemski	4.00	1.80
☐ 4 Hank Aaron	15.00	6.75
☐ 5 Harmon Killebrew	3.00	1.35
☐ 6 Roberto Clemente	25.00	11.00
☐ 7 Frank Robinson	5.00	2.20
☐ 8 Willie Mays	18.00	8.00
☐ 9 Brooks Robinson	5.00	2.20
☐ 10 Tommy Davis	.80	.35
☐ 11 Bill Freehan	1.00	.45
☐ 12 Claude Osteen	.80	.35
☐ 13 Gary Peters	.80	.35
☐ 14 Jim Lonborg	.80	.35
☐ 15 Steve Hargan	.80	.35
☐ 16 Dean Chance	.80	.35
☐ 17 Mike McCormick	.80	.35
☐ 18 Tim McCarver	1.00	.45
☐ 19 Ron Santo	1.00	.45
☐ 20 Tony Gonzalez	.80	.35
☐ 21 Frank Howard	1.00	.45
☐ 22 George Scott	.80	.35
☐ 23 Richie Allen	1.00	.45
☐ 24 Jim Wynn	1.00	.45
☐ 25 Gene Alley	.80	.35
☐ 26 Rick Monday	.80	.35
☐ 27 Al Kaline	5.00	2.20
☐ 28 Rusty Staub	1.00	.45
☐ 29 Rod Carew	5.00	2.20
☐ 30 Pete Rose	15.00	6.75
☐ 31 Joe Torre	1.50	.70
☐ 32 Orlando Cepeda	1.50	.70
☐ 33 Jim Fregosi	1.00	.45

1968 Topps 3-D

The cards in this 12-card set measure 2 1/4" by 3 1/2". Topps' experiment with "3-D" cards came two years before Kellogg's inaugural set. These cards are considered to be quite rare. This was a "test set" sold in a plain white wrapper with a sticker attached as a design, a device used by Topps for limited marketing. The cards employ a sharp foreground picture set against an indistinct background, covered by a layer of plastic to produce the "3-D" effect. The checklist below is ordered alphabetically.

	NRMT	VG-E
COMPLETE SET (12)	12500.00	5600.00
COMMON CARD (1-12)	750.00	350.00
WRAPPERS (10-CENTS)	1000.00	450.00
☐ 1 Roberto Clemente	6000.00	2700.00
☐ 2 Willie Davis	1200.00	550.00
☐ 3 Ron Fairly	750.00	350.00
☐ 4 Curt Flood	1200.00	550.00
☐ 5 Jim Lonborg	1200.00	550.00
☐ 6 Jim Maloney	1200.00	550.00
☐ 7 Tony Perez	2000.00	900.00
☐ 8 Boog Powell	1200.00	550.00
☐ 9 Bill Robinson	750.00	350.00
☐ 10 Rusty Staub	1200.00	550.00
☐ 11 Mel Stottlemyre	1200.00	550.00
☐ 12 Ron Swoboda	750.00	350.00

1968 Topps Posters

This 1968 color poster set is not an "insert" but was issued separately with a piece of gum and in its own wrapper. The posters are numbered at the lower left and the player's name and team appear in a large star. The poster was folded six times to fit into the package, so fold lines are a factor in grading. Each poster measures 9 3/4" by 18 1/8".

	NRMT	VG-E
COMPLETE SET (24)	300.00	135.00
COMMON CARD (1-24)	2.50	1.10
☐ 1 Dean Chance	3.50	1.55
☐ 2 Max Alvis	2.50	1.10
☐ 3 Frank Howard	3.50	1.55
☐ 4 Jim Fregosi	3.50	1.55
☐ 5 Jim Hunter	10.00	4.50
☐ 6 Bob Clemente	60.00	27.00
☐ 7 Don Drysdale	10.00	4.50
☐ 8 Jim Wynn	2.50	1.10
☐ 9 Al Kaline	15.00	6.75

Card	NRMT	VG-E
☐ 10 Harmon Killebrew	12.00	5.50
☐ 11 Jim Lonborg	3.50	1.55
☐ 12 Orlando Cepeda	5.00	2.20
☐ 13 Gary Peters	2.50	1.10
☐ 14 Hank Aaron	20.00	9.00
☐ 15 Richie Allen	3.50	1.55
☐ 16 Carl Yastrzemski	15.00	6.75
☐ 17 Ron Swoboda	2.50	1.10
☐ 18 Mickey Mantle	75.00	34.00
☐ 19 Tim McCarver	3.50	1.55
☐ 20 Willie Mays	20.00	9.00
☐ 21 Ron Santo	3.50	1.55
☐ 22 Rusty Staub	3.50	1.55
☐ 23 Pete Rose	40.00	18.00
☐ 24 Frank Robinson	15.00	6.75

1969 Topps

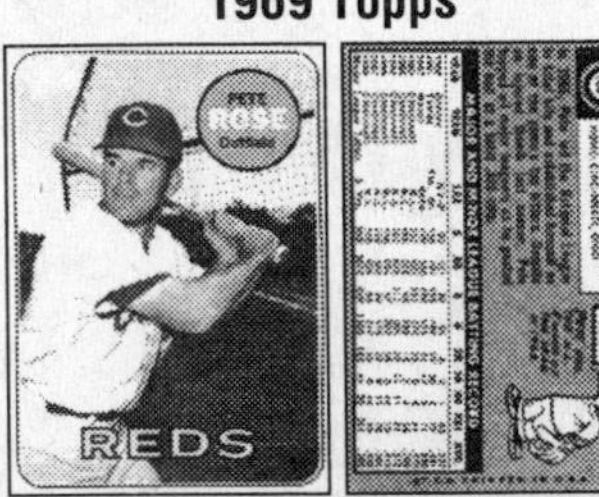

The cards in this 664-card set measure 2 1/2" by 3 1/2". The 1969 Topps set includes Sporting News All-Star Selections as card numbers 416 to 435. Other popular subsets within this set include League Leaders (1-12) and World Series cards (162-169). The fifth series contains several variations; the more difficult variety consists of cards with the player's first name, last name, and/or position in white letters instead of lettering in some other color. These are designated in the checklist below by WL (white letters). Each checklist card features a different popular player's picture inside a circle on the front of the checklist card. Two different team identifications of Clay Dalrymple and Donn Clendenon exist, as indicated in the checklist. The key Rookie Cards in this set are Rollie Fingers, Reggie Jackson, and Graig Nettles. This was the last year that Topps issued multi-player special star cards, ending a 13-year tradition, which they had begun in 1957. There were cropping differences in checklist cards 57, 214, and 412, due to their each being printed with two different series. The differences are difficult to explain and have not been greatly sought by collectors; hence they are not listed explicitly in the list below. The All-Star cards 426-435, when turned over and placed together, form a puzzle back of Pete Rose. This would turn out to be the final year that Topps issued cards in five-card nickle wax packs.

	NRMT	VG-E
COMPLETE SET (664)	2200.00	1000.00
COMMON (1-218/328-512)	1.50	.70
COMMON CARD (219-327)	2.50	1.10
COMMON CARD (513-588)	2.00	.90
COMMON CARD (589-664)	3.00	1.35
WRAPPER (5-CENT)	20.00	9.00

Card	NRMT	VG-E
☐ 1 AL Batting Leaders	14.00	5.00
Carl Yastrzemski		
Danny Cater		
Tony Oliva		
☐ 2 NL Batting Leaders	7.00	3.10
Pete Rose		
Matty Alou		
Felipe Alou		
☐ 3 AL RBI Leaders	3.50	1.55
Ken Harrelson		
Frank Howard		
Jim Northrup		
☐ 4 NL RBI Leaders	6.00	2.70
Willie McCovey		
Ron Santo		
Billy Williams		
☐ 5 AL Home Run Leaders	3.50	1.55
Frank Howard		
Willie Horton		
Ken Harrelson		
☐ 6 NL Home Run Leaders	6.00	2.70
Willie McCovey		
Richie Allen		
Ernie Banks		
☐ 7 AL ERA Leaders	3.50	1.55
Luis Tiant		
Sam McDowell		
Dave McNally		
☐ 8 NL ERA Leaders	5.00	2.20
Bob Gibson		
Bobby Bolin		
Bob Veale		
☐ 9 AL Pitching Leaders	3.50	1.55
Denny McLain		
Dave McNally		
Luis Tiant		
Mel Stottlemyre		
☐ 10 NL Pitching Leaders	7.00	3.10
Juan Marichal		
Bob Gibson		
Fergie Jenkins		
☐ 11 AL Strikeout Leaders	3.50	1.55
Sam McDowell		
Denny McLain		
Luis Tiant		
☐ 12 NL Strikeout Leaders	4.00	1.80
Bob Gibson		
Fergie Jenkins		
Bill Singer		
☐ 13 Mickey Stanley	2.50	1.10
☐ 14 Al McBean	1.50	.70
☐ 15 Boog Powell	3.50	1.55
☐ 16 Giants Rookies	1.50	.70
Cesar Gutierrez		
Rich Robertson		
☐ 17 Mike Marshall	2.50	1.10
☐ 18 Dick Schofield	1.50	.70
☐ 19 Ken Suarez	1.50	.70
☐ 20 Ernie Banks	18.00	8.00
☐ 21 Jose Santiago	1.50	.70
☐ 22 Jesus Alou	2.50	1.10
☐ 23 Lew Krausse	1.50	.70
☐ 24 Walt Alston MG	4.00	1.80
☐ 25 Roy White	2.50	1.10
☐ 26 Clay Carroll	2.50	1.10
☐ 27 Bernie Allen	1.50	.70
☐ 28 Mike Ryan	1.50	.70
☐ 29 Dave Morehead	1.50	.70
☐ 30 Bob Allison	2.50	1.10
☐ 31 Mets Rookies	2.50	1.10
Gary Gentry		
Amos Otis		
☐ 32 Sammy Ellis	1.50	.70
☐ 33 Wayne Causey	1.50	.70
☐ 34 Gary Peters	1.50	.70
☐ 35 Joe Morgan	10.00	4.50
☐ 36 Luke Walker	1.50	.70
☐ 37 Curt Motton	1.50	.70
☐ 38 Zoilo Versalles	2.50	1.10
☐ 39 Dick Hughes	1.50	.70
☐ 40 Mayo Smith MG	1.50	.70
☐ 41 Bob Barton	1.50	.70
☐ 42 Tommy Harper	2.50	1.10
☐ 43 Joe Niekro	2.50	1.10
☐ 44 Danny Cater	1.50	.70
☐ 45 Maury Wills	3.00	1.35
☐ 46 Fritz Peterson	2.50	1.10
☐ 47A Paul Popovich	1.50	.70
(No helmet emblem)		
☐ 47B Paul Popovich	25.00	11.00
(C emblem on helmet)		
☐ 48 Brant Alyea	1.50	.70
☐ 49A Royals Rookies ERR	25.00	11.00
Steve Jones		
E. Rodriquez		
☐ 49B Royals Rookies COR	1.50	.70
Steve Jones		
E. Rodriguez		
☐ 50 Bob Clemente UER	50.00	22.00
(Bats Right		
listed twice)		
☐ 51 Woody Fryman	1.50	.70
☐ 52 Mike Andrews	1.50	.70
☐ 53 Sonny Jackson	1.50	.70
☐ 54 Cisco Carlos	1.50	.70
☐ 55 Jerry Grote	2.50	1.10
☐ 56 Rich Reese	1.50	.70
☐ 57 Denny McLain CL	6.00	1.20
☐ 58 Fred Gladding	1.50	.70
☐ 59 Jay Johnstone	2.50	1.10
☐ 60 Nelson Briles	2.50	1.10
☐ 61 Jimmie Hall	1.50	.70
☐ 62 Chico Salmon	1.50	.70
☐ 63 Jim Hickman	2.50	1.10
☐ 64 Bill Monbouquette	1.50	.70
☐ 65 Willie Davis	2.50	1.10
☐ 66 Orioles Rookies	1.50	.70
Mike Adamson		
Merv Rettenmund		
☐ 67 Bill Stoneman	2.50	1.10
☐ 68 Dave Duncan	2.50	1.10
☐ 69 Steve Hamilton	2.50	1.10
☐ 70 Tommy Helms	2.50	1.10
☐ 71 Steve Whitaker	2.50	1.10
☐ 72 Ron Taylor	1.50	.70
☐ 73 Johnny Briggs	1.50	.70
☐ 74 Preston Gomez MG	2.50	1.10
☐ 75 Luis Aparicio	5.00	2.20
☐ 76 Norm Miller	1.50	.70
☐ 77A Ron Perranoski	2.50	1.10
(No emblem on cap)		
☐ 77B Ron Perranoski	25.00	11.00
(LA on cap)		
☐ 78 Tom Satriano	1.50	.70
☐ 79 Milt Pappas	2.50	1.10
☐ 80 Norm Cash	2.50	1.10
☐ 81 Mel Queen	1.50	.70
☐ 82 Pirates Rookies	8.00	3.60
Rich Hebner		
Al Oliver		
☐ 83 Mike Ferraro	2.50	1.10
☐ 84 Bob Humphreys	1.50	.70
☐ 85 Lou Brock	18.00	8.00
☐ 86 Pete Richert	1.50	.70
☐ 87 Horace Clarke	2.50	1.10
☐ 88 Rich Nye	1.50	.70
☐ 89 Russ Gibson	1.50	.70
☐ 90 Jerry Koosman	2.50	1.10
☐ 91 Alvin Dark MG	2.50	1.10
☐ 92 Jack Billingham	2.50	1.10
☐ 93 Joe Foy	2.50	1.10
☐ 94 Hank Aguirre	1.50	.70
☐ 95 Johnny Bench	45.00	20.00
☐ 96 Denny Lemaster	1.50	.70
☐ 97 Buddy Bradford	1.50	.70
☐ 98 Dave Giusti	1.50	.70
☐ 99A Twins Rookies	16.00	7.25
Danny Morris		
Graig Nettles		
(No loop)		
☐ 99B Twins Rookies	16.00	7.25
Danny Morris		
Graig Nettles		
(Errant loop in		
upper left corner		
of obverse)		
☐ 100 Hank Aaron	35.00	16.00
☐ 101 Daryl Patterson	1.50	.70
☐ 102 Jim Davenport	1.50	.70
☐ 103 Roger Repoz	1.50	.70
☐ 104 Steve Blass	2.50	1.10
☐ 105 Rick Monday	2.50	1.10
☐ 106 Jim Hannan	1.50	.70
☐ 107A Bob Gibson CL ERR	6.00	1.20
161 Jim Purdin		
☐ 107B Bob Gibson CL COR	7.50	1.50
161 John Purdin		
☐ 108 Tony Taylor	2.50	1.10
☐ 109 Jim Lonborg	2.50	1.10
☐ 110 Mike Shannon	2.50	1.10
☐ 111 Johnny Morris	1.50	.70
☐ 112 J.C. Martin	2.50	1.10
☐ 113 Dave May	1.50	.70
☐ 114 Yankees Rookies	2.50	1.10
Alan Closter		
John Cumberland		
☐ 115 Bill Hands	1.50	.70
☐ 116 Chuck Harrison	1.50	.70
☐ 117 Jim Fairey	1.50	.70
☐ 118 Stan Williams	1.50	.70
☐ 119 Doug Rader	2.50	1.10
☐ 120 Pete Rose	18.00	8.00
☐ 121 Joe Grzenda	1.50	.70
☐ 122 Ron Fairly	2.50	1.10
☐ 123 Wilbur Wood	2.50	1.10
☐ 124 Hank Bauer MG	2.50	1.10
☐ 125 Ray Sadecki	1.50	.70
☐ 126 Dick Tracewski	1.50	.70
☐ 127 Kevin Collins	2.50	1.10
☐ 128 Tommie Aaron	2.50	1.10
☐ 129 Bill McCool	1.50	.70
☐ 130 Carl Yastrzemski	18.00	8.00
☐ 131 Chris Cannizzaro	1.50	.70
☐ 132 Dave Baldwin	1.50	.70
☐ 133 Johnny Callison	2.50	1.10
☐ 134 Jim Weaver	1.50	.70
☐ 135 Tommy Davis	2.50	1.10
☐ 136 Cards Rookies	1.50	.70
Steve Huntz		
Mike Torrez		
☐ 137 Wally Bunker	1.50	.70
☐ 138 John Bateman	1.50	.70
☐ 139 Andy Kosco	1.50	.70
☐ 140 Jim Lefebvre	2.50	1.10
☐ 141 Bill Dillman	1.50	.70
☐ 142 Woody Woodward	2.50	1.10
☐ 143 Joe Nossek	1.50	.70
☐ 144 Bob Hendley	2.50	1.10
☐ 145 Max Alvis	1.50	.70
☐ 146 Jim Perry	2.50	1.10
☐ 147 Leo Durocher MG	4.00	1.80
☐ 148 Lee Stange	1.50	.70

☐ 149 Ollie Brown	2.50	1.10
☐ 150 Denny McLain	4.00	1.80
☐ 151A Clay Dalrymple	1.50	.70
Portrait, Orioles		
☐ 151B Clay Dalrymple	16.00	7.25
Catching, Phillies		
☐ 152 Tommie Sisk	1.50	.70
☐ 153 Ed Brinkman	1.50	.70
☐ 154 Jim Britton	1.50	.70
☐ 155 Pete Ward	1.50	.70
☐ 156 Houston Rookies	1.50	.70
Hal Gilson		
Leon McFadden		
☐ 157 Bob Rodgers	2.50	1.10
☐ 158 Joe Gibbon	1.50	.70
☐ 159 Jerry Adair	1.50	.70
☐ 160 Vada Pinson	2.50	1.10
☐ 161 John Purdin	1.50	.70
☐ 162 Bob Gibson WS	8.00	3.60
Fans 17		
☐ 163 Willie Horton WS	6.00	2.70
☐ 164 Tim McCarver WS	8.00	3.60
Roger Maris		
☐ 165 Lou Brock WS	8.00	3.60
☐ 166 Al Kaline WS	8.00	3.60
☐ 167 Jim Northrup WS	6.00	2.70
☐ 168 Mickey Lolich WS	8.00	3.60
Bob Gibson		
☐ 169 Dick McAuliffe WS	6.00	2.70
Denny McLain		
Willie Horton		
☐ 170 Frank Howard	3.00	1.35
☐ 171 Glenn Beckert	2.50	1.10
☐ 172 Jerry Stephenson	1.50	.70
☐ 173 White Sox Rookies	1.50	.70
Bob Christian		
Gerry Nyman		
☐ 174 Grant Jackson	1.50	.70
☐ 175 Jim Bunning	7.00	3.10
☐ 176 Joe Azcue	1.50	.70
☐ 177 Ron Reed	1.50	.70
☐ 178 Ray Oyler	2.50	1.10
☐ 179 Don Pavletich	1.50	.70
☐ 180 Willie Horton	2.50	1.10
☐ 181 Mel Nelson	1.50	.70
☐ 182 Bill Rigney MG	1.50	.70
☐ 183 Don Shaw	1.50	.70
☐ 184 Roberto Pena	1.50	.70
☐ 185 Tom Phoebus	1.50	.70
☐ 186 Johnny Edwards	1.50	.70
☐ 187 Leon Wagner	1.50	.70
☐ 188 Rick Wise	2.50	1.10
☐ 189 Red Sox Rookies	1.50	.70
Joe Lahoud		
John Thibodeau		
☐ 190 Willie Mays	45.00	20.00
☐ 191 Lindy McDaniel	2.50	1.10
☐ 192 Jose Pagan	1.50	.70
☐ 193 Don Cardwell	2.50	1.10
☐ 194 Ted Uhlaender	1.50	.70
☐ 195 John Odom	1.50	.70
☐ 196 Lum Harris MG	1.50	.70
☐ 197 Dick Selma	1.50	.70
☐ 198 Willie Smith	1.50	.70
☐ 199 Jim French	1.50	.70
☐ 200 Bob Gibson	12.00	5.50
☐ 201 Russ Snyder	1.50	.70
☐ 202 Don Wilson	2.50	1.10
☐ 203 Dave Johnson	2.50	1.10
☐ 204 Jack Hiatt	1.50	.70
☐ 205 Rick Reichardt	1.50	.70
☐ 206 Phillies Rookies	2.50	1.10
Larry Hisle		
Barry Lersch		
☐ 207 Roy Face	2.50	1.10
☐ 208A Donn Clendenon	2.50	1.10
Houston		
☐ 208B Donn Clendenon	16.00	7.25
Expos		
☐ 209 Larry Haney UER	1.50	.70
(Reverse negative)		
☐ 210 Felix Millan	1.50	.70
☐ 211 Galen Cisco	1.50	.70
☐ 212 Tom Tresh	2.50	1.10
☐ 213 Gerry Arrigo	1.50	.70
☐ 214 Checklist 3	6.00	1.20
With 69T deckle CL		
on back (no player)		
☐ 215 Rico Petrocelli	2.50	1.10
☐ 216 Don Sutton	6.00	2.70
☐ 217 John Donaldson	1.50	.70
☐ 218 John Roseboro	2.50	1.10
☐ 219 Freddie Patek	3.00	1.35
☐ 220 Sam McDowell	4.00	1.80
☐ 221 Art Shamsky	4.00	1.80
☐ 222 Duane Josephson	2.50	1.10
☐ 223 Tom Dukes	4.00	1.80

☐ 224 Angels Rookies	2.50	1.10
Bill Harrelson		
Steve Kealey		
☐ 225 Don Kessinger	4.00	1.80
☐ 226 Bruce Howard	2.50	1.10
☐ 227 Frank Johnson	2.50	1.10
☐ 228 Dave Leonhard	2.50	1.10
☐ 229 Don Lock	2.50	1.10
☐ 230 Rusty Staub UER	4.00	1.80
For 1966 stats, Houston spelled Huoston		
☐ 231 Pat Dobson	4.00	1.80
☐ 232 Dave Ricketts	2.50	1.10
☐ 233 Steve Barber	4.00	1.80
☐ 234 Dave Bristol MG	2.50	1.10
☐ 235 Jim Hunter	10.00	4.50
☐ 236 Manny Mota	4.00	1.80
☐ 237 Bobby Cox	10.00	4.50
☐ 238 Ken Johnson	2.50	1.10
☐ 239 Bob Taylor	4.00	1.80
☐ 240 Ken Harrelson	4.00	1.80
☐ 241 Jim Brewer	2.50	1.10
☐ 242 Frank Kostro	2.50	1.10
☐ 243 Ron Kline	2.50	1.10
☐ 244 Indians Rookies	3.00	1.35
Ray Fosse		
George Woodson		
☐ 245 Ed Charles	4.00	1.80
☐ 246 Joe Coleman	2.50	1.10
☐ 247 Gene Oliver	2.50	1.10
☐ 248 Bob Priddy	2.50	1.10
☐ 249 Ed Spiezio	4.00	1.80
☐ 250 Frank Robinson	20.00	9.00
☐ 251 Ron Herbel	2.50	1.10
☐ 252 Chuck Cottier	2.50	1.10
☐ 253 Jerry Johnson	2.50	1.10
☐ 254 Joe Schultz MG	4.00	1.80
☐ 255 Steve Carlton	30.00	13.50
☐ 256 Gates Brown	4.00	1.80
☐ 257 Jim Ray	2.50	1.10
☐ 258 Jackie Hernandez	4.00	1.80
☐ 259 Bill Short	2.50	1.10
☐ 260 Reggie Jackson	350.00	160.00
☐ 261 Bob Johnson	2.50	1.10
☐ 262 Mike Kekich	4.00	1.80
☐ 263 Jerry May	2.50	1.10
☐ 264 Bill Landis	2.50	1.10
☐ 265 Chico Cardenas	4.00	1.80
☐ 266 Dodger Rookies	4.00	1.80
Tom Hutton		
Alan Foster		
☐ 267 Vicente Romo	2.50	1.10
☐ 268 Al Spangler	2.50	1.10
☐ 269 Al Weis	4.00	1.80
☐ 270 Mickey Lolich	3.00	1.35
☐ 271 Larry Stahl	4.00	1.80
☐ 272 Ed Stroud	2.50	1.10
☐ 273 Ron Willis	2.50	1.10
☐ 274 Clyde King MG	2.50	1.10
☐ 275 Vic Davalillo	2.50	1.10
☐ 276 Gary Wagner	2.50	1.10
☐ 277 Elrod Hendricks	2.50	1.10
☐ 278 Gary Geiger UER	2.50	1.10
(Batting wrong)		
☐ 279 Roger Nelson	4.00	1.80
☐ 280 Alex Johnson	4.00	1.80
☐ 281 Ted Kubiak	2.50	1.10
☐ 282 Pat Jarvis	2.50	1.10
☐ 283 Sandy Alomar	4.00	1.80
☐ 284 Expos Rookies	4.00	1.80
Jerry Robertson		
Mike Wegener		
☐ 285 Don Mincher	4.00	1.80
☐ 286 Dock Ellis	3.00	1.35
☐ 287 Jose Tartabull	4.00	1.80
☐ 288 Ken Holtzman	4.00	1.80
☐ 289 Bart Shirley	2.50	1.10
☐ 290 Jim Kaat	4.00	1.80
☐ 291 Vern Fuller	2.50	1.10
☐ 292 Al Downing	4.00	1.80
☐ 293 Dick Dietz	2.50	1.10
☐ 294 Jim Lemon MG	2.50	1.10
☐ 295 Tony Perez	12.00	5.50
☐ 296 Andy Messersmith	4.00	1.80
☐ 297 Deron Johnson	2.50	1.10
☐ 298 Dave Nicholson	4.00	1.80
☐ 299 Mark Belanger	4.00	1.80
☐ 300 Felipe Alou	4.00	1.80
☐ 301 Darrell Brandon	4.00	1.80
☐ 302 Jim Pagliaroni	2.50	1.10
☐ 303 Cal Koonce	4.00	1.80
☐ 304 Padres Rookies	8.00	3.60
Bill Davis		
Clarence Gaston		
☐ 305 Dick McAuliffe	4.00	1.80
☐ 306 Jim Grant	4.00	1.80
☐ 307 Gary Kolb	2.50	1.10
☐ 308 Wade Blasingame	2.50	1.10

☐ 309 Walt Williams	2.50	1.10
☐ 310 Tom Haller	2.50	1.10
☐ 311 Sparky Lyle	8.00	3.60
☐ 312 Lee Elia	2.50	1.10
☐ 313 Bill Robinson	4.00	1.80
☐ 314 Don Drysdale CL	6.00	1.20
☐ 315 Eddie Fisher	2.50	1.10
☐ 316 Hal Lanier	2.50	1.10
☐ 317 Bruce Look	2.50	1.10
☐ 318 Jack Fisher	2.50	1.10
☐ 319 Ken McMullen UER	2.50	1.10
(Headings on back		
are for a pitcher)		
☐ 320 Dal Maxvill	2.50	1.10
☐ 321 Jim McAndrew	4.00	1.80
☐ 322 Jose Vidal	4.00	1.80
☐ 323 Larry Miller	2.50	1.10
☐ 324 Tiger Rookies	4.00	1.80
Les Cain		
Dave Campbell		
☐ 325 Jose Cardenal	4.00	1.80
☐ 326 Gary Sutherland	4.00	1.80
☐ 327 Willie Crawford	2.50	1.10
☐ 328 Joel Horlen	1.50	.70
☐ 329 Rick Joseph	1.50	.70
☐ 330 Tony Conigliaro	5.00	2.20
☐ 331 Braves Rookies	2.50	1.10
Gil Garrido		
Tom House		
☐ 332 Fred Talbot	1.50	.70
☐ 333 Ivan Murrell	1.50	.70
☐ 334 Phil Roof	1.50	.70
☐ 335 Bill Mazeroski	3.00	1.35
☐ 336 Jim Roland	1.50	.70
☐ 337 Marty Martinez	1.50	.70
☐ 338 Del Unser	1.50	.70
☐ 339 Reds Rookies	1.50	.70
Steve Mingori		
Jose Pena		
☐ 340 Dave McNally	2.50	1.10
☐ 341 Dave Adlesh	1.50	.70
☐ 342 Bubba Morton	1.50	.70
☐ 343 Dan Frisella	1.50	.70
☐ 344 Tom Matchick	1.50	.70
☐ 345 Frank Linzy	1.50	.70
☐ 346 Wayne Comer	1.50	.70
☐ 347 Randy Hundley	2.50	1.10
☐ 348 Steve Hargan	1.50	.70
☐ 349 Dick Williams MG	2.50	1.10
☐ 350 Richie Allen	4.00	1.80
☐ 351 Carroll Sembera	1.50	.70
☐ 352 Paul Schaal	2.50	1.10
☐ 353 Jeff Torborg	2.50	1.10
☐ 354 Nate Oliver	1.50	.70
☐ 355 Phil Niekro	7.00	3.10
☐ 356 Frank Quilici	1.50	.70
☐ 357 Carl Taylor	1.50	.70
☐ 358 Athletics Rookies	1.50	.70
George Lauzerique		
Roberto Rodriquez		
☐ 359 Dick Kelley	1.50	.70
☐ 360 Jim Wynn	2.50	1.10
☐ 361 Gary Holman	1.50	.70
☐ 362 Jim Maloney	2.50	1.10
☐ 363 Russ Nixon	1.50	.70
☐ 364 Tommie Agee	4.00	1.80
☐ 365 Jim Fregosi	2.50	1.10
☐ 366 Bo Belinsky	2.50	1.10
☐ 367 Lou Johnson	2.50	1.10
☐ 368 Vic Roznovsky	1.50	.70
☐ 369 Bob Skinner MG	2.50	1.10
☐ 370 Juan Marichal	8.00	3.60
☐ 371 Sal Bando	2.50	1.10
☐ 372 Adolfo Phillips	1.50	.70
☐ 373 Fred Lasher	1.50	.70
☐ 374 Bob Tillman	1.50	.70
☐ 375 Harmon Killebrew	16.00	7.25
☐ 376 Royals Rookies	1.50	.70
Mike Fiore		
Jim Rooker		
☐ 377 Gary Bell	2.50	1.10
☐ 378 Jose Herrera	1.50	.70
☐ 379 Ken Boyer	2.50	1.10
☐ 380 Stan Bahnsen	2.50	1.10
☐ 381 Ed Kranepool	2.50	1.10
☐ 382 Pat Corrales	2.50	1.10
☐ 383 Casey Cox	1.50	.70
☐ 384 Larry Shepard MG	1.50	.70
☐ 385 Orlando Cepeda	3.50	1.55
☐ 386 Jim McGlothlin	1.50	.70
☐ 387 Bobby Klaus	1.50	.70
☐ 388 Tom McCraw	1.50	.70
☐ 389 Dan Coombs	1.50	.70
☐ 390 Bill Freehan	2.50	1.10
☐ 391 Ray Culp	1.50	.70
☐ 392 Bob Burda	1.50	.70
☐ 393 Gene Brabender	2.50	1.10

☐ 394 Pilots Rookies 5.00 2.20
Lou Piniella
Marv Staehle
☐ 395 Chris Short 1.50 .70
☐ 396 Jim Campanis 1.50 .70
☐ 397 Chuck Dobson 1.50 .70
☐ 398 Tito Francona 1.50 .70
☐ 399 Bob Bailey 2.50 1.10
☐ 400 Don Drysdale 15.00 6.75
☐ 401 Jake Gibbs 2.50 1.10
☐ 402 Ken Boswell 2.50 1.10
☐ 403 Bob Miller 1.50 .70
☐ 404 Cubs Rookies 2.50 1.10
Vic LaRose
Gary Ross
☐ 405 Lee May 2.50 1.10
☐ 406 Phil Ortega 1.50 .70
☐ 407 Tom Egan 1.50 .70
☐ 408 Nate Colbert 1.50 .70
☐ 409 Bob Moose 1.50 .70
☐ 410 Al Kaline 25.00 11.00
☐ 411 Larry Dierker 2.50 1.10
☐ 412 Mickey Mantle CL DP 12.00 2.40
☐ 413 Roland Sheldon 2.50 1.10
☐ 414 Duke Sims 1.50 .70
☐ 415 Ray Washburn 1.50 .70
☐ 416 Willie McCovey AS 7.00 3.10
☐ 417 Ken Harrelson AS 2.50 1.10
☐ 418 Tommy Helms AS 2.50 1.10
☐ 419 Rod Carew AS 10.00 4.50
☐ 420 Ron Santo AS 4.00 1.80
☐ 421 Brooks Robinson AS 7.00 3.10
☐ 422 Don Kessinger AS 2.50 1.10
☐ 423 Bert Campaneris AS 4.00 1.80
☐ 424 Pete Rose AS 14.00 6.25
☐ 425 Carl Yastrzemski AS 10.00 4.50
☐ 426 Curt Flood AS 4.00 1.80
☐ 427 Tony Oliva AS 4.00 1.80
☐ 428 Lou Brock AS 6.00 2.70
☐ 429 Willie Horton AS 2.50 1.10
☐ 430 Johnny Bench AS 10.00 4.50
☐ 431 Bill Freehan AS 4.00 1.80
☐ 432 Bob Gibson AS 6.00 2.70
☐ 433 Denny McLain AS 2.50 1.10
☐ 434 Jerry Koosman AS 3.00 1.35
☐ 435 Sam McDowell AS 2.50 1.10
☐ 436 Gene Alley 2.50 1.10
☐ 437 Luis Alcaraz 1.50 .70
☐ 438 Gary Waslewski 1.50 .70
☐ 439 White Sox Rookies 1.50 .70
Ed Herrmann
Dan Lazar
☐ 440A Willie McCovey 18.00 8.00
☐ 440B Willie McCovey WL 100.00 45.00
(McCovey white)
☐ 441A Dennis Higgins 1.50 .70
☐ 441B Dennis Higgins WL 20.00 9.00
(Higgins white)
☐ 442 Ty Cline 1.50 .70
☐ 443 Don Wert 1.50 .70
☐ 444A Joe Moeller 1.50 .70
☐ 444B Joe Moeller WL 20.00 9.00
(Moeller white)
☐ 445 Bobby Knoop 1.50 .70
☐ 446 Claude Raymond 1.50 .70
☐ 447A Ralph Houk MG 2.50 1.10
☐ 447B Ralph Houk WL 22.00 10.00
MG (Houk white)
☐ 448 Bob Tolan 2.50 1.10
☐ 449 Paul Lindblad 1.50 .70
☐ 450 Billy Williams 7.00 3.10
☐ 451A Rich Rollins 2.50 1.10
☐ 451B Rich Rollins WL 20.00 9.00
(Rich and 3B white)
☐ 452A Al Ferrara 1.50 .70
☐ 452B Al Ferrara WL 20.00 9.00
(Al and OF white)
☐ 453 Mike Cuellar 2.50 1.10
☐ 454A Phillies Rookies 2.50 1.10
Larry Colton
Don Money
☐ 454B Phillies Rookies WL 22.00 10.00
Larry Colton
Don Money
(Names in white)
☐ 455 Sonny Siebert 1.50 .70
☐ 456 Bud Harrelson 2.50 1.10
☐ 457 Dalton Jones 1.50 .70
☐ 458 Curt Blefary 1.50 .70
☐ 459 Dave Boswell 1.50 .70
☐ 460 Joe Torre 3.50 1.55
☐ 461A Mike Epstein 1.50 .70
☐ 461B Mike Epstein WL 20.00 9.00
(Epstein white)
☐ 462 Red Schoendienst 2.50 1.10
MG
☐ 463 Dennis Ribant 1.50 .70
☐ 464A Dave Marshall 1.50 .70
☐ 464B Dave Marshall WL 20.00 9.00
(Marshall white)
☐ 465 Tommy John 4.00 1.80
☐ 466 John Boccabella 2.50 1.10
☐ 467 Tommie Reynolds 1.50 .70
☐ 468A Pirates Rookies 1.50 .70
Bruce Dal Canton
Bob Robertson
☐ 468B Pirates Rookies WL 20.00 9.00
Bruce Dal Canton
Bob Robertson
(Names in white)
☐ 469 Chico Ruiz 1.50 .70
☐ 470A Mel Stottlemyre 2.50 1.10
☐ 470B Mel Stottlemyre WL 30.00 13.50
(Stottlemyre white)
☐ 471A Ted Savage 1.50 .70
☐ 471B Ted Savage WL 20.00 9.00
(Savage white)
☐ 472 Jim Price 1.50 .70
☐ 473A Jose Arcia 1.50 .70
☐ 473B Jose Arcia WL 20.00 9.00
(Jose and 2B white)
☐ 474 Tom Murphy 1.50 .70
☐ 475 Tim McCarver 3.00 1.35
☐ 476A Boston Rookies 3.00 1.35
Ken Brett
Gerry Moses
☐ 476B Boston Rookies WL 30.00 13.50
Ken Brett
Gerry Moses
(Names in white)
☐ 477 Jeff James 1.50 .70
☐ 478 Don Buford 1.50 .70
☐ 479 Richie Scheinblum 1.50 .70
☐ 480 Tom Seaver 80.00 36.00
☐ 481 Bill Melton 2.50 1.10
☐ 482A Jim Gosger 1.50 .70
☐ 482B Jim Gosger WL 20.00 9.00
(Jim and OF white)
☐ 483 Ted Abernathy 1.50 .70
☐ 484 Joe Gordon MG 2.50 1.10
☐ 485A Gaylord Perry 10.00 4.50
☐ 485B Gaylord Perry WL 85.00 38.00
(Perry white)
☐ 486A Paul Casanova 1.50 .70
☐ 486B Paul Casanova WL 20.00 9.00
(Casanova white)
☐ 487 Denis Menke 1.50 .70
☐ 488 Joe Sparma 1.50 .70
☐ 489 Clete Boyer 2.50 1.10
☐ 490 Matty Alou 2.50 1.10
☐ 491A Twins Rookies 1.50 .70
Jerry Crider
George Mitterwald
☐ 491B Twins Rookies WL 20.00 9.00
Jerry Crider
George Mitterwald
(Names in white)
☐ 492 Tony Cloninger 1.50 .70
☐ 493A Wes Parker 2.50 1.10
☐ 493B Wes Parker WL 22.00 10.00
(Parker white)
☐ 494 Ken Berry 1.50 .70
☐ 495 Bert Campaneris 2.50 1.10
☐ 496 Larry Jaster 1.50 .70
☐ 497 Julian Javier 2.50 1.10
☐ 498 Juan Pizarro 2.50 1.10
☐ 499 Astro Rookies 1.50 .70
Don Bryant
Steve Shea
☐ 500A Mickey Mantle UER 350.00 160.00
(No Topps copy-
right on card back)
☐ 500B Mickey Mantle WL 1000.00 450.00
(Mantle in white;
no Topps copyright
on card back) UER
☐ 501A Tony Gonzalez 2.50 1.10
☐ 501B Tony Gonzalez WL 22.00 10.00
(Tony and OF white)
☐ 502 Minnie Rojas 1.50 .70
☐ 503 Larry Brown 1.50 .70
☐ 504 Brooks Robinson CL 7.00 1.40
☐ 505A Bobby Bolin 1.50 .70
☐ 505B Bobby Bolin WL 22.00 10.00
(Bolin white)
☐ 506 Paul Blair 2.50 1.10
☐ 507 Cookie Rojas 2.50 1.10
☐ 508 Moe Drabowsky 2.50 1.10
☐ 509 Manny Sanguillen 2.50 1.10
☐ 510 Rod Carew 35.00 16.00
☐ 511A Diego Segui 2.50 1.10
☐ 511B Diego Segui WL 22.00 10.00
(Diego and P white)
☐ 512 Cleon Jones 2.50 1.10
☐ 513 Camilo Pascual 3.00 1.35
☐ 514 Mike Lum 2.00 .90
☐ 515 Dick Green 2.00 .90
☐ 516 Earl Weaver MG 18.00 8.00
☐ 517 Mike McCormick 3.00 1.35
☐ 518 Fred Whitfield 2.00 .90
☐ 519 Yankees Rookies 2.00 .90
Jerry Kenney
Len Boehmer
☐ 520 Bob Veale 3.00 1.35
☐ 521 George Thomas 2.00 .90
☐ 522 Joe Hoerner 2.00 .90
☐ 523 Bob Chance 2.00 .90
☐ 524 Expos Rookies 3.00 1.35
Jose Laboy
Floyd Wicker
☐ 525 Earl Wilson 3.00 1.35
☐ 526 Hector Torres 2.00 .90
☐ 527 Al Lopez MG 4.00 1.80
☐ 528 Claude Osteen 3.00 1.35
☐ 529 Ed Kirkpatrick 3.00 1.35
☐ 530 Cesar Tovar 2.00 .90
☐ 531 Dick Farrell 2.00 .90
☐ 532 Bird Hill Aces 3.00 1.35
Tom Phoebus
Jim Hardin
Dave McNally
Mike Cuellar
☐ 533 Nolan Ryan 425.00 190.00
☐ 534 Jerry McNertney 3.00 1.35
☐ 535 Phil Regan 3.00 1.35
☐ 536 Padres Rookies 2.00 .90
Danny Breeden
Dave Roberts
☐ 537 Mike Paul 2.00 .90
☐ 538 Charlie Smith 2.00 .90
☐ 539 Ted Shows How 10.00 4.50
Mike Epstein
Ted Williams MG
☐ 540 Curt Flood 3.00 1.35
☐ 541 Joe Verbanic 2.00 .90
☐ 542 Bob Aspromonte 2.00 .90
☐ 543 Fred Newman 2.00 .90
☐ 544 Tigers Rookies 2.00 .90
Mike Kilkenny
Ron Woods
☐ 545 Willie Stargell 12.00 5.50
☐ 546 Jim Nash 2.00 .90
☐ 547 Billy Martin MG 6.00 2.70
☐ 548 Bob Locker 2.00 .90
☐ 549 Ron Brand 2.00 .90
☐ 550 Brooks Robinson 30.00 13.50
☐ 551 Wayne Granger 2.00 .90
☐ 552 Dodgers Rookies 3.00 1.35
Ted Sizemore
Bill Sudakis
☐ 553 Ron Davis 2.00 .90
☐ 554 Frank Bertaina 2.00 .90
☐ 555 Jim Ray Hart 3.00 1.35
☐ 556 A's Stars 3.00 1.35
Sal Bando
Bert Campaneris
Danny Cater
☐ 557 Frank Fernandez 2.00 .90
☐ 558 Tom Burgmeier 3.00 1.35
☐ 559 Cardinals Rookies 2.00 .90
Joe Hague
Jim Hicks
☐ 560 Luis Tiant 3.00 1.35
☐ 561 Ron Clark 2.00 .90
☐ 562 Bob Watson 7.00 3.10
☐ 563 Marty Pattin 3.00 1.35
☐ 564 Gil Hodges MG 10.00 4.50
☐ 565 Hoyt Wilhelm 7.00 3.10
☐ 566 Ron Hansen 2.00 .90
☐ 567 Pirates Rookies 2.00 .90
Elvio Jimenez
Jim Shellenback
☐ 568 Cecil Upshaw 2.00 .90
☐ 569 Billy Harris 2.00 .90
☐ 570 Ron Santo 7.00 3.10
☐ 571 Cap Peterson 2.00 .90
☐ 572 Giants Heroes 16.00 7.25
Willie McCovey
Juan Marichal
☐ 573 Jim Palmer 35.00 16.00
☐ 574 George Scott 3.00 1.35
☐ 575 Bill Singer 3.00 1.35
☐ 576 Phillies Rookies 2.00 .90
Ron Stone
Bill Wilson
☐ 577 Mike Hegan 3.00 1.35
☐ 578 Don Bosch 2.00 .90
☐ 579 Dave Nelson 2.00 .90
☐ 580 Jim Northrup 3.00 1.35
☐ 581 Gary Nolan 3.00 1.35
☐ 582A Tony Oliva CL 5.00 1.00

Card	NRMT	VG-E
White circle on back		
☐ 582B Tony Oliva CL	8.00	1.60
Red circle on back		
☐ 583 Clyde Wright	2.00	.90
☐ 584 Don Mason	2.00	.90
☐ 585 Ron Swoboda	3.00	1.35
☐ 586 Tim Cullen	2.00	.90
☐ 587 Joe Rudi	7.00	3.10
☐ 588 Bill White	3.00	1.35
☐ 589 Joe Pepitone	4.00	1.80
☐ 590 Rico Carty	5.00	2.20
☐ 591 Mike Hedlund	3.00	1.35
☐ 592 Padres Rookies	5.00	2.20
Rafael Robles		
Al Santorini		
☐ 593 Don Nottebart	3.00	1.35
☐ 594 Dooley Womack	3.00	1.35
☐ 595 Lee Maye	3.00	1.35
☐ 596 Chuck Hartenstein	3.00	1.35
☐ 597 A.L. Rookies	35.00	16.00
Bob Floyd		
Larry Burchart		
Rollie Fingers		
☐ 598 Ruben Amaro	3.00	1.35
☐ 599 John Boozer	3.00	1.35
☐ 600 Tony Oliva	6.00	2.70
☐ 601 Tug McGraw	7.00	3.10
☐ 602 Cubs Rookies	5.00	2.20
Alec Distaso		
Don Young		
Jim Qualls		
☐ 603 Joe Keough	3.00	1.35
☐ 604 Bobby Etheridge	3.00	1.35
☐ 605 Dick Ellsworth	3.00	1.35
☐ 606 Gene Mauch MG	5.00	2.20
☐ 607 Dick Bosman	3.00	1.35
☐ 608 Dick Simpson	3.00	1.35
☐ 609 Phil Gagliano	3.00	1.35
☐ 610 Jim Hardin	3.00	1.35
☐ 611 Braves Rookies	5.00	2.20
Bob Didier		
Walt Hriniak		
Gary Neibauer		
☐ 612 Jack Aker	5.00	2.20
☐ 613 Jim Beauchamp	3.00	1.35
☐ 614 Houston Rookies	3.00	1.35
Tom Griffin		
Skip Guinn		
☐ 615 Len Gabrielson	3.00	1.35
☐ 616 Don McMahon	3.00	1.35
☐ 617 Jesse Gonder	3.00	1.35
☐ 618 Ramon Webster	3.00	1.35
☐ 619 Royals Rookies	4.00	1.80
Bill Butler		
Pat Kelly		
Juan Rios		
☐ 620 Dean Chance	4.00	1.80
☐ 621 Bill Voss	3.00	1.35
☐ 622 Dan Osinski	3.00	1.35
☐ 623 Hank Allen	3.00	1.35
☐ 624 NL Rookies	4.00	1.80
Darrel Chaney		
Duffy Dyer		
Terry Harmon		
☐ 625 Mack Jones UER	5.00	2.20
(Batting wrong)		
☐ 626 Gene Michael	5.00	2.20
☐ 627 George Stone	3.00	1.35
☐ 628 Red Sox Rookies	4.00	1.80
Bill Conigliaro		
Syd O'Brien		
Fred Wenz		
☐ 629 Jack Hamilton	3.00	1.35
☐ 630 Bobby Bonds	35.00	16.00
☐ 631 John Kennedy	5.00	2.20
☐ 632 Jon Warden	3.00	1.35
☐ 633 Harry Walker MG	3.00	1.35
☐ 634 Andy Etchebarren	3.00	1.35
☐ 635 George Culver	3.00	1.35
☐ 636 Woody Held	3.00	1.35
☐ 637 Padres Rookies	4.00	1.80
Jerry DaVanon		
Frank Reberger		
Clay Kirby		
☐ 638 Ed Sprague	3.00	1.35
☐ 639 Barry Moore	3.00	1.35
☐ 640 Ferguson Jenkins	20.00	9.00
☐ 641 NL Rookies	4.00	1.80
Bobby Darwin		
John Miller		
Tommy Dean		
☐ 642 John Hiller	3.00	1.35
☐ 643 Billy Cowan	3.00	1.35
☐ 644 Chuck Hinton	3.00	1.35
☐ 645 George Brunet	3.00	1.35
☐ 646 Expos Rookies	5.00	2.20
Dan McGinn		
Carl Morton		
☐ 647 Dave Wickersham	3.00	1.35
☐ 648 Bobby Wine	5.00	2.20
☐ 649 Al Jackson	3.00	1.35
☐ 650 Ted Williams MG	18.00	8.00
☐ 651 Gus Gil	5.00	2.20
☐ 652 Eddie Watt	3.00	1.35
☐ 653 Aurelio Rodriguez UER	5.00	2.20
(Photo actually		
Angels' batboy)		
☐ 654 White Sox Rookies	5.00	2.20
Carlos May		
Don Secrist		
Rich Morales		
☐ 655 Mike Hershberger	3.00	1.35
☐ 656 Dan Schneider	3.00	1.35
☐ 657 Bobby Murcer	6.00	2.70
☐ 658 AL Rookies	3.00	1.35
Tom Hall		
Bill Burbach		
Jim Miles		
☐ 659 Johnny Podres	4.00	1.80
☐ 660 Reggie Smith	6.00	2.70
☐ 661 Jim Merritt	3.00	1.35
☐ 662 Royals Rookies	5.00	2.20
Dick Drago		
George Spriggs		
Bob Oliver		
☐ 663 Dick Radatz	5.00	2.20
☐ 664 Ron Hunt	5.00	1.35

1969 Topps Decals Inserts

The 1969 Topps Decal Inserts are a set of 48 unnumbered decals issued as inserts in packages of 1969 Topps regular issue cards. Each decal is approximately 1" by 1 1/2" although including the plain backing the measurement is 1 3/4" by 2 1/8". The decals appear to be miniature versions of the Topps regular issue of that year. The copyright notice on the side indicates that these decals were produced in the United Kingdom. Most of the players on the decals are stars.

	NRMT	VG-E
COMPLETE SET (48)	450.00	200.00
COMMON DECAL (1-48)	2.50	1.10
☐ 1 Hank Aaron	50.00	22.00
☐ 2 Richie Allen	5.00	2.20
☐ 3 Felipe Alou	3.00	1.35
☐ 4 Matty Alou	3.00	1.35
☐ 5 Luis Aparicio	6.00	2.70
☐ 6 Roberto Clemente	60.00	27.00
☐ 7 Donn Clendenon	2.50	1.10
☐ 8 Tommy Davis	3.00	1.35
☐ 9 Don Drysdale	10.00	4.50
☐ 10 Joe Foy	2.50	1.10
☐ 11 Jim Fregosi	3.00	1.35
☐ 12 Bob Gibson	10.00	4.50
☐ 13 Tony Gonzalez	2.50	1.10
☐ 14 Tom Haller	2.50	1.10
☐ 15 Ken Harrelson	3.00	1.35
☐ 16 Tommy Helms	2.50	1.10
☐ 17 Willie Horton	3.00	1.35
☐ 18 Frank Howard	3.00	1.35
☐ 19 Reggie Jackson	50.00	22.00
☐ 20 Ferguson Jenkins	6.00	2.70
☐ 21 Harmon Killebrew	6.00	2.70
☐ 22 Jerry Koosman	3.00	1.35
☐ 23 Mickey Mantle	125.00	55.00
☐ 24 Willie Mays	50.00	22.00
☐ 25 Tim McCarver	5.00	2.20
☐ 26 Willie McCovey	10.00	4.50
☐ 27 Sam McDowell	3.00	1.35
☐ 28 Denny McLain	3.00	1.35
☐ 29 Dave McNally	3.00	1.35
☐ 30 Don Mincher	2.50	1.10
☐ 31 Rick Monday	3.00	1.35
☐ 32 Tony Oliva	3.50	1.55
☐ 33 Camilo Pascual	2.50	1.10
☐ 34 Rick Reichardt	2.50	1.10
☐ 35 Frank Robinson	10.00	4.50
☐ 36 Pete Rose	35.00	16.00
☐ 37 Ron Santo	5.00	2.20
☐ 38 Tom Seaver	25.00	11.00
☐ 39 Dick Selma	2.50	1.10
☐ 40 Chris Short	2.50	1.10
☐ 41 Rusty Staub	3.50	1.55
☐ 42 Mel Stottlemyre	3.00	1.35
☐ 43 Luis Tiant	3.00	1.35
☐ 44 Pete Ward	2.50	1.10
☐ 45 Hoyt Wilhelm	7.50	3.40
☐ 46 Maury Wills	5.00	2.20
☐ 47 Jim Wynn	1.25	.55
☐ 48 Carl Yastrzemski	15.00	6.75

1969 Topps Deckle Inserts

The cards in this 33-card set measure approximately 2 1/4" by 3 1/4". This unusual black and white insert set derives its name from the serrated border, or edge, of the cards. The cards were included as inserts in the regularly issued Topps baseball third series of 1969. Card number 11 is found with either Hoyt Wilhelm or Jim Wynn, and number 22 with either Rusty Staub or Joe Foy. The set price below does include all variations. The set numbering is arranged in team order by league except for cards 11 and 22.

	NRMT	VG-E
COMPLETE SET (35)	100.00	45.00
COMMON CARD (1-33)	.80	.35
☐ 1 Brooks Robinson	7.50	3.40
☐ 2 Boog Powell	2.00	.90
☐ 3 Ken Harrelson	.80	.35
☐ 4 Carl Yastrzemski	6.00	2.70
☐ 5 Jim Fregosi	1.25	.55
☐ 6 Luis Aparicio	3.00	1.35
☐ 7 Luis Tiant	1.25	.55
☐ 8 Denny McLain	1.25	.55
☐ 9 Willie Horton	1.25	.55
☐ 10 Bill Freehan	1.25	.55
☐ 11A Hoyt Wilhelm	7.50	3.40
☐ 11B Jim Wynn	12.00	5.50
☐ 12 Rod Carew	5.00	2.20
☐ 13 Mel Stottlemyre	1.25	.55
☐ 14 Rick Monday	.80	.35
☐ 15 Tommy Davis	1.25	.55
☐ 16 Frank Howard	1.25	.55
☐ 17 Felipe Alou	1.25	.55
☐ 18 Don Kessinger	.80	.35
☐ 19 Ron Santo	2.00	.90
☐ 20 Tommy Helms	.80	.35
☐ 21 Pete Rose	10.00	4.50
☐ 22A Rusty Staub	3.00	1.35
☐ 22B Joe Foy	12.00	5.50
☐ 23 Tom Haller	.80	.35
☐ 24 Maury Wills	1.25	.55
☐ 25 Jerry Koosman	1.25	.55
☐ 26 Richie Allen	2.00	.90
☐ 27 Roberto Clemente	20.00	9.00
☐ 28 Curt Flood	1.25	.55
☐ 29 Bob Gibson	5.00	2.20
☐ 30 Al Ferrara	.80	.35
☐ 31 Willie McCovey	4.00	1.80
☐ 32 Juan Marichal	4.00	1.80
☐ 33 Willie Mays	12.00	5.50

1969 Topps Four-in-One

This was a test issue consisting of 25 sticker cards (blank back). Each card measures 2 1/2" by 3 1/2" and features four mini-stickers. These unnumbered stickers are ordered in the checklist below alphabetically by the upper left player's name on each card. Each mini-card featured is from the 1969 Topps second series. Five of the cards were double printed (technically 50 percent more were printed) compared to the others in the set; these are marked below by DP.

	NRMT	VG-E
COMPLETE SET (25)	900.00	400.00
COMMON CARD (1-25)	12.00	5.50
☐ 1 Jerry Adair	100.00	45.00
Don Wilson		

Willie Mays		
Johnny Morris		
☐ 2 Astros Rookies	12.00	5.50
(Gilson/McFadden)		
Wally Bunker		
Joe Gibbon		
Don Cardwell		
☐ 3 Donn Clendenon	12.00	5.50
Woody Woodward		
Tommie Aaron		
Jim Britton		
☐ 4 Tommy Davis	20.00	9.00
Don Pavletich		
W.S. Game 4		
(Brock homer)		
Vada Pinson		
☐ 5 Ron Fairly	12.00	5.50
Rick Wise		
Max Alvis		
Glenn Beckert		
☐ 6 Jim French	12.00	5.50
Dick Selma		
Johnny Callison		
Lum Harris MG		
☐ 7 Bob Gibson DP	40.00	18.00
W.S. Game 3		
(McCarver homer)		
Rick Reichardt		
Larry Haney		
☐ 8 Andy Kosco	15.00	6.75
Ron Reed		
Jim Bunning		
Ollie Brown		
☐ 9 Jim Lefebvre	12.00	5.50
John Purdin		
Bill Dillman		
John Roseboro		
☐ 10 Felix Millan DP	12.00	5.50
Bill Hands		
Lindy McDaniel		
Chuck Harrison		
☐ 11 Mel Nelson	15.00	6.75
Dave Johnson		
Jack Hiatt		
Tommie Sisk		
☐ 12 John Odom	15.00	6.75
Leo Durocher MG		
Wilbur Wood		
Clay Dalrymple		
☐ 13 Ray Oyler DP	12.00	5.50
Hank Bauer MG		
Kevin Collins		
Russ Snyder		
☐ 14 Jim Perry	15.00	6.75
W.S. Game 7		
(Lolich/B.Gibson)		
Gerry Arrigo		
Red Sox Rookies		
(Lahoud/Thibodeau)		
☐ 15 Doug Rader	12.00	5.50
Bill McCool		
Roberto Pena		
W.S. Game 2		
(Tiger homers)		
☐ 16 Bob Rodgers	15.00	6.75
Willie Horton		
Roy Face		
Ed Brinkman		
☐ 17 Ray Sadecki	12.00	5.50
Dave Baldwin		
J.C. Martin		
Dave May		
☐ 18 Mike Shannon DP	15.00	6.75
W.S. Game 1		
(Gibson fans 17)		
Jose Pagan		
Tom Phoebus		
☐ 19 Lee Stange	300.00	135.00
Don Sutton		
Ted Uhlaender		
Pete Rose		
☐ 20 Jim Weaver	12.00	5.50
Dick Tracewski		
Joe Grzenda		
Frank Howard		
☐ 21 White Sox Rookies	15.00	6.75
(Christian/Nyman)		
Denny McLain		
Grant Jackson		
Joe Azcue		
☐ 22 Stan Williams	12.00	5.50
John Edwards		
Jim Fairey		
Phillies Rookies		
(Hisle/Lersch)		
☐ 23 W.S. Celebration	12.00	5.50
(Tigers celebrate)		
Leon Wagner		
John Bateman		
Willie Smith		
☐ 24 Yankees Rookies	12.00	5.50
(Closter/Cumberland)		
Chris Cannizzaro		
W.S. Game 5		
(Kaline's hit)		
Bob Hendley		
☐ 25 Carl Yastrzemski DP	175.00	80.00
Rico Petrocelli		
Joe Nossek		
Cards Rookies		
(Huntz/Torrez)		

1969 Topps Super

The cards in this 66-card set measure approximately 2 1/4" by 3 1/4". This beautiful Topps set was released independently of the regular baseball series of 1969. It is referred to as "Super Baseball" on the back of the card, a title which was also used for the postcard-size cards issued in 1970 and 1971. Complete sheets, and cards with square corners cut from these sheets, are sometimes encountered. The set numbering is in alphabetical order by teams within league. Cards from the far right of each row are usually found with a white line on the right edge. Although rarely seen, this set was issued in 3-card cello packs. The set features Reggie Jackson in his Rookie Card year.

	NRMT	VG-E
COMPLETE SET (66)	5500.00	2500.00
COMMON CARD (1-66)	12.00	5.50
☐ 1 Dave McNally	12.00	5.50
☐ 2 Frank Robinson	200.00	90.00
☐ 3 Brooks Robinson	200.00	90.00
☐ 4 Ken Harrelson	15.00	6.75
☐ 5 Carl Yastrzemski	250.00	110.00
☐ 6 Ray Culp	12.00	5.50
☐ 7 Jim Fregosi	15.00	6.75
☐ 8 Rick Reichardt	12.00	5.50
☐ 9 Vic Davalillo	12.00	5.50
☐ 10 Luis Aparicio	75.00	34.00
☐ 11 Pete Ward	12.00	5.50
☐ 12 Joel Horlen	12.00	5.50
☐ 13 Luis Tiant	15.00	6.75
☐ 14 Sam McDowell	12.00	5.50
☐ 15 Jose Cardenal	12.00	5.50
☐ 16 Willie Horton	15.00	6.75
☐ 17 Denny McLain	20.00	9.00
☐ 18 Bill Freehan	15.00	6.75
☐ 19 Harmon Killebrew	150.00	70.00
☐ 20 Tony Oliva	30.00	13.50
☐ 21 Dean Chance	12.00	5.50
☐ 22 Joe Foy	12.00	5.50
☐ 23 Roger Nelson	12.00	5.50
☐ 24 Mickey Mantle	1000.00	450.00
☐ 25 Mel Stottlemyre	15.00	6.75
☐ 26 Roy White	15.00	6.75
☐ 27 Rick Monday	12.00	5.50
☐ 28 Reggie Jackson	450.00	200.00
☐ 29 Bert Campaneris	15.00	6.75
☐ 30 Frank Howard	20.00	9.00
☐ 31 Camilo Pascual	12.00	5.50
☐ 32 Tommy Davis	15.00	6.75
☐ 33 Don Mincher	12.00	5.50
☐ 34 Hank Aaron	450.00	200.00
☐ 35 Felipe Alou	20.00	9.00
☐ 36 Joe Torre	40.00	18.00
☐ 37 Ferguson Jenkins	75.00	34.00
☐ 38 Ron Santo	30.00	13.50
☐ 39 Billy Williams	75.00	34.00
☐ 40 Tommy Helms	12.00	5.50
☐ 41 Pete Rose	400.00	180.00
☐ 42 Joe Morgan	125.00	55.00
☐ 43 Jim Wynn	12.00	5.50
☐ 44 Curt Blefary	12.00	5.50
☐ 45 Willie Davis	12.00	5.50
☐ 46 Don Drysdale	100.00	45.00
☐ 47 Tom Haller	12.00	5.50
☐ 48 Rusty Staub	20.00	9.00
☐ 49 Maury Wills	25.00	11.00
☐ 50 Cleon Jones	12.00	5.50
☐ 51 Jerry Koosman	20.00	9.00
☐ 52 Tom Seaver	400.00	180.00
☐ 53 Richie Allen	20.00	9.00
☐ 54 Chris Short	12.00	5.50
☐ 55 Cookie Rojas	12.00	5.50
☐ 56 Matty Alou	12.00	5.50
☐ 57 Steve Blass	12.00	5.50
☐ 58 Roberto Clemente	600.00	275.00
☐ 59 Curt Flood	20.00	9.00
☐ 60 Bob Gibson	150.00	70.00
☐ 61 Tim McCarver	25.00	11.00
☐ 62 Dick Selma	12.00	5.50
☐ 63 Ollie Brown	12.00	5.50
☐ 64 Juan Marichal	100.00	45.00
☐ 65 Willie Mays	475.00	210.00
☐ 66 Willie McCovey	100.00	45.00

1969 Topps Team Posters

This set was issued as a separate set by Topps, but was apparently not widely distributed. It was folded many times to fit the packaging and hence is typically found with relatively heavy fold creases. Each team poster measures approximately 12" by 20". These posters are in full color with a blank back. Each team features nine or ten individual players; a complete list is listed in the checklist below. Each player photo is accompanied by a facsimile autograph. The posters are numbered in the bottom left corner.

	NRMT	VG-E
COMPLETE SET (24)	1200.00	550.00
COMMON TEAM (1-24)	20.00	9.00
☐ 1 Detroit Tigers	40.00	18.00
Norm Cash		
Al Kaline		
Mickey Lolich		
Denny McLain		
Bill Freehan		
Willie Horton		
Dick McAuliffe		
Jim Northrup		
Mickey Stanley		
Don Wert		
Earl Wilson		
☐ 2 Atlanta Braves	60.00	27.00
Hank Aaron		
Phil Niekro		
Joe Torre		
Felipe Alou		
Clete Boyer		
Rico Carty		
Tito Francona		
Sonny Jackson		
Pat Jarvis		
Felix Millan		
Milt Pappas		
☐ 3 Boston Red Sox	60.00	27.00
Carl Yastrzemski		
Mike Andrews		
Tony Conigliaro		
Ray Culp		
Russ Gibson		
Ken Harrelson		
Jim Lonborg		
Rico Petrocelli		

Jose Santiago
George Scott
Reggie Smith

☐ 4 Chicago Cubs 50.00 22.00
Ernie Banks
Billy Williams
Glenn Beckert
Bill Hands
Jim Hickman
Ken Holtzman
Randy Hundley
Fergie Jenkins
Don Kessinger
Adolpho Phillips
Ron Santo

☐ 5 Baltimore Orioles 60.00 27.00
Boog Powell
Brooks Robinson
Frank Robinson
Mark Belanger
Paul Blair
Don Buford
Andy Etchebarren
Jim Hardin
Dave Johnson
Dave McNally
Tom Phoebus

☐ 6 Houston Astros 20.00 9.00
Joe Morgan
Curt Blefary
Donn Clendenon
Larry Dierker
John Edwards
Denny Lemaster
Denis Menke
Norm Miller
Doug Rader
Don Wilson
Jim Wynn

☐ 7 Kansas City Royals 20.00 9.00
Wally Bunker
Jerry Adair
Mike Fiore
Joe Foy
Jackie Hernandez
Pat Kelly
Dave Morehead
Roger Nelson
Dave Nicholson
Ellie Rodriguez
Steve Whitaker

☐ 8 Philadelphia Phillies 20.00 9.00
Richie Allen
John Callison
Woodie Fryman
Larry Hisle
Don Money
Cookie Rojas
Mike Ryan
Chris Short
Tony Taylor
Bill White
Rick Wise

☐ 9 Seattle Pilots 40.00 18.00
Tommy Davis
Jack Aker
Steve Barber
Gary Bell
Jim Gosger
Tommy Harper
Jerry McNertney
Don Mincher
Ray Oyler
Rich Rollins
Chico Salmon

☐ 10 Montreal Expos 20.00 9.00
Rusty Staub
Maury Wills
Bob Bailey
John Bateman
Jack Billingham
Jim Grant
Larry Jaster
Mack Jones
Manny Mota
Gary Sutherland
Jimy Williams

☐ 11 Chicago White Sox 20.00 9.00
Luis Aparicio
Tommy John
Sandy Alomar
Ken Berry
Buddy Bradford
Joel Horlen
Duane Josephson
Tom McCraw
Bill Melton
Pete Ward
Wilbur Wood

☐ 12 San Diego Padres 20.00 9.00
Ollie Brown
Jose Arcia
Danny Breeden
Bill Davis
Ron Davis
Tony Gonzalez
Dick Kelley
Al McBean
Roberto Pena
Dick Selma
Ed Spiezio

☐ 13 Cleveland Indians 20.00 9.00
Luis Tiant
Max Alvis
Joe Azcue
Jose Cardenal
Vern Fuller
Lou Johnson
Sam McDowell
Sonny Siebert
Duke Sims
Russ Snyder
Zoilo Versalles

☐ 14 San Francisco Giants 50.00 22.00
Juan Marichal
Willie Mays
Willie McCovey
Gaylord Perry
Bobby Bolin
Jim Davenport
Dick Dietz
Jim Ray Hart
Ron Hunt
Hal Lanier
Charley Smith

☐ 15 Minnesota Twins 30.00 13.50
Rod Carew
Harmon Killebrew
Bob Allison
Chico Cardenas
Dean Chance
Jim Kaat
Tony Oliva
Jim Perry
John Roseboro
Cesar Tovar
Ted Uhlaender

☐ 16 Pittsburgh Pirates 125.00 55.00
Roberto Clemente
Willie Stargell
Gene Alley
Matty Alou
Steve Blass
Jim Bunning
Richie Hebner
Jerry May
Bill Mazeroski
Bob Robertson
Bob Veale

☐ 17 California Angels 20.00 9.00
Hoyt Wilhelm
Ruben Amaro
George Brunet
Bob Chance
Vic Davallilo
Jim Fregosi
Bobby Knoop
Jim McGlothlin
Rick Reichardt
Roger Repoz
Bob Rodgers

☐ 18 St. Louis Cardinals 40.00 18.00
Lou Brock
Orlando Cepeda
Curt Flood
Bob Gibson
Nellie Briles
Julian Javier
Dal Maxvill
Tim McCarver
Vada Pinson
Mike Shannon
Ray Washburn

☐ 19 New York Yankees 175.00 80.00
Mickey Mantle
Mel Stottlemyre
Tom Tresh
Stan Bahnsen
Horace Clarke
Bobby Cox
Jake Gibbs
Joe Pepitone
Fritz Peterson
Bill Robinson
Roy White

☐ 20 Cincinnati Reds 100.00 45.00
Johnny Bench
Tony Perez
Pete Rose
Gerry Arrigo
Tommy Helms
Alex Johnson
Jim Maloney
Lee May
Gary Nolan
Bob Tolan
Woody Woodward

☐ 21 Oakland A's 100.00 45.00
Jim Hunter
Reggie Jackson
Sal Bando
Bert Campaneris
Danny Cater
Dick Green
Mike Hershberger
Rick Monday
Jim Nash
John Odom
Jim Pagliaroni

☐ 22 Los Angeles Dodgers 30.00 13.50
Don Drysdale
Willie Crawford
Willie Davis
Ron Fairly
Tom Haller
Andy Kosco
Jim Lefevre
Claude Osteen
Paul Popovich
Bill Singer
Bill Sudakis

☐ 23 Washington Senators 20.00 9.00
Frank Howard
Bernie Allen
Brant Alyea
Ed Brinkman
Paul Casanova
Joe Coleman
Mike Epstein
Jim Hannan
Ken McMullen
Camilo Pascual
Del Unser

☐ 24 New York Mets 100.00 45.00
Tom Seaver
Tommie Agee
Ken Boswell
Ed Charles
Jerry Grote
Bud Harrelson
Cleon Jones
Jerry Koosman
Ed Kranepool
Jim McAndrew
Ron Swoboda

1970 Topps

The cards in this 720-card set measure 2 1/2" by 3 1/2". The Topps set for 1970 has color photos surrounded by white frame lines and gray borders. The backs have a blue biographical section and a yellow record section. All-Star selections are featured on cards 450 to 469. Other topical subsets within this set include League Leaders (61-72), Playoffs cards (195-202), and World Series cards (305-310). There are graduations of scarcity, terminating in the high series (634-720), which are outlined in the value summary. Cards were issued in ten-card dime packs as well as thirty-three card cello packs encased in a small Topps box. The key Rookie Card in this set is Thurman Munson.

	NRMT	VG-E
COMPLETE SET (720)	1800.00	800.00
COMMON CARD (1-372)	1.00	.45
COMMON CARD (373-459)	1.50	.70
COMMON CARD (460-546)	2.00	.90
COMMON CARD (547-633)	4.00	1.80

COMMON CARD (634-720) 10.00 4.50
WRAPPER (10-CENT) 20.00 9.00

☐ 1 New York Mets 16.00 5.00
Team Card
☐ 2 Diego Segui 2.00 .90
☐ 3 Darrel Chaney 1.00 .45
☐ 4 Tom Egan 1.00 .45
☐ 5 Wes Parker 1.50 .70
☐ 6 Grant Jackson 1.00 .45
☐ 7 Indians Rookies 1.00 .45
Gary Boyd
Russ Nagelson
☐ 8 Jose Martinez 1.00 .45
☐ 9 Checklist 1 12.00 2.40
☐ 10 Carl Yastrzemski 14.00 6.25
☐ 11 Nate Colbert 1.00 .45
☐ 12 John Hiller 1.00 .45
☐ 13 Jack Hiatt 1.00 .45
☐ 14 Hank Allen 1.00 .45
☐ 15 Larry Dierker 1.00 .45
☐ 16 Charlie Metro MG 1.00 .45
☐ 17 Hoyt Wilhelm 5.00 2.20
☐ 18 Carlos May 1.00 .45
☐ 19 John Boccabella 1.00 .45
☐ 20 Dave McNally 1.00 .45
☐ 21 A's Rookies 6.00 2.70
Vida Blue
Gene Tenace
☐ 22 Ray Washburn 1.00 .45
☐ 23 Bill Robinson 2.00 .90
☐ 24 Dick Selma 1.00 .45
☐ 25 Cesar Tovar 1.00 .45
☐ 26 Tug McGraw 2.00 .90
☐ 27 Chuck Hinton 1.00 .45
☐ 28 Billy Wilson 1.00 .45
☐ 29 Sandy Alomar 2.00 .90
☐ 30 Matty Alou 2.00 .90
☐ 31 Marty Pattin 2.00 .90
☐ 32 Harry Walker MG 1.00 .45
☐ 33 Don Wert 1.00 .45
☐ 34 Willie Crawford 1.00 .45
☐ 35 Joel Horlen 1.00 .45
☐ 36 Red Rookies 2.00 .90
Danny Breeden
Bernie Carbo
☐ 37 Dick Drago 1.00 .45
☐ 38 Mack Jones 1.00 .45
☐ 39 Mike Nagy 1.00 .45
☐ 40 Rich Allen 2.00 .90
☐ 41 George Lauzerique 1.00 .45
☐ 42 Tito Fuentes 1.00 .45
☐ 43 Jack Aker 1.00 .45
☐ 44 Roberto Pena 1.00 .45
☐ 45 Dave Johnson 2.00 .90
☐ 46 Ken Rudolph 1.00 .45
☐ 47 Bob Miller 1.00 .45
☐ 48 Gil Garrido 1.00 .45
☐ 49 Tim Cullen 1.00 .45
☐ 50 Tommie Agee 2.00 .90
☐ 51 Bob Christian 1.00 .45
☐ 52 Bruce Dal Canton 1.00 .45
☐ 53 John Kennedy 1.00 .45
☐ 54 Jeff Torborg 2.00 .90
☐ 55 John Odom 1.00 .45
☐ 56 Phillies Rookies 1.00 .45
Joe Lis
Scott Reid
☐ 57 Pat Kelly 1.00 .45
☐ 58 Dave Marshall 1.00 .45
☐ 59 Dick Ellsworth 1.00 .45
☐ 60 Jim Wynn 2.00 .90
☐ 61 NL Batting Leaders 12.00 5.50
Pete Rose
Bob Clemente
Cleon Jones
☐ 62 AL Batting Leaders 3.50 1.55
Rod Carew
Reggie Smith
Tony Oliva
☐ 63 NL RBI Leaders 4.00 1.80
Willie McCovey
Ron Santo
Tony Perez
☐ 64 AL RBI Leaders 6.00 2.70
Harmon Killebrew
Boog Powell
Reggie Jackson
☐ 65 NL Home Run Leaders 6.00 2.70
Willie McCovey
Hank Aaron
Lee May
☐ 66 AL Home Run Leaders 6.00 2.70
Harmon Killebrew
Frank Howard
Reggie Jackson
☐ 67 NL ERA Leaders 7.00 3.10
Juan Marichal
Steve Carlton
Bob Gibson
☐ 68 AL ERA Leaders 2.00 .90
Dick Bosman
Jim Palmer
Mike Cuellar
☐ 69 NL Pitching Leaders 7.00 3.10
Tom Seaver
Phil Niekro
Fergie Jenkins
Juan Marichal
☐ 70 AL Pitching Leaders 2.00 .90
Dennis McLain
Mike Cuellar
Dave Boswell
Dave McNally
Jim Perry
Mel Stottlemyre
☐ 71 NL Strikeout Leaders 4.00 1.80
Fergie Jenkins
Bob Gibson
Bill Singer
☐ 72 AL Strikeout Leaders 2.00 .90
Sam McDowell
Mickey Lolich
Andy Messersmith
☐ 73 Wayne Granger 1.00 .45
☐ 74 Angels Rookies 1.00 .45
Greg Washburn
Wally Wolf
☐ 75 Jim Kaat 2.00 .90
☐ 76 Carl Taylor 1.00 .45
☐ 77 Frank Linzy 1.00 .45
☐ 78 Joe Lahoud 1.00 .45
☐ 79 Clay Kirby 1.00 .45
☐ 80 Don Kessinger 2.00 .90
☐ 81 Dave May 1.00 .45
☐ 82 Frank Fernandez 1.00 .45
☐ 83 Don Cardwell 1.00 .45
☐ 84 Paul Casanova 1.00 .45
☐ 85 Max Alvis 1.00 .45
☐ 86 Lum Harris MG 1.00 .45
☐ 87 Steve Renko 1.00 .45
☐ 88 Pilots Rookies 2.00 .90
Miguel Fuentes
Dick Baney
☐ 89 Juan Rios 1.00 .45
☐ 90 Tim McCarver 2.00 .90
☐ 91 Rich Morales 1.00 .45
☐ 92 George Culver 1.00 .45
☐ 93 Rick Renick 1.00 .45
☐ 94 Freddie Patek 2.00 .90
☐ 95 Earl Wilson 2.00 .90
☐ 96 Cardinals Rookies 2.00 .90
Leron Lee
Jerry Reuss
☐ 97 Joe Moeller 1.00 .45
☐ 98 Gates Brown 2.00 .90
☐ 99 Bobby Pfeil 1.00 .45
☐ 100 Mel Stottlemyre 2.00 .90
☐ 101 Bobby Floyd 1.00 .45
☐ 102 Joe Rudi 2.00 .90
☐ 103 Frank Reberger 1.00 .45
☐ 104 Gerry Moses 1.00 .45
☐ 105 Tony Gonzalez 1.00 .45
☐ 106 Darold Knowles 1.00 .45
☐ 107 Bobby Etheridge 1.00 .45
☐ 108 Tom Burgmeier 1.00 .45
☐ 109 Expos Rookies 1.00 .45
Garry Jestadt
Carl Morton
☐ 110 Bob Moose 1.00 .45
☐ 111 Mike Hegan 2.00 .90
☐ 112 Dave Nelson 1.00 .45
☐ 113 Jim Ray 1.00 .45
☐ 114 Gene Michael 1.00 .45
☐ 115 Alex Johnson 2.00 .90
☐ 116 Sparky Lyle 2.00 .90
☐ 117 Don Young 1.00 .45
☐ 118 George Mitterwald 1.00 .45
☐ 119 Chuck Taylor 1.00 .45
☐ 120 Sal Bando 2.00 .90
☐ 121 Orioles Rookies 1.00 .45
Fred Beene
Terry Crowley
☐ 122 George Stone 1.00 .45
☐ 123 Don Gutteridge MG 1.00 .45
☐ 124 Larry Jaster 1.00 .45
☐ 125 Deron Johnson 1.00 .45
☐ 126 Marty Martinez 1.00 .45
☐ 127 Joe Coleman 1.00 .45
☐ 128A Checklist 2 ERR 6.00 1.20
(226 R Perranoski)
☐ 128B Checklist 2 COR 6.00 1.20
(226 R. Perranoski)
☐ 129 Jimmie Price 1.00 .45
☐ 130 Ollie Brown 1.00 .45
☐ 131 Dodgers Rookies 1.00 .45
Ray Lamb
Bob Stinson
☐ 132 Jim McGlothlin 1.00 .45
☐ 133 Clay Carroll 1.00 .45
☐ 134 Danny Walton 1.00 .45
☐ 135 Dick Dietz 1.00 .45
☐ 136 Steve Hargan 1.00 .45
☐ 137 Art Shamsky 1.00 .45
☐ 138 Joe Foy 1.00 .45
☐ 139 Rich Nye 1.00 .45
☐ 140 Reggie Jackson 50.00 22.00
☐ 141 Pirates Rookies 2.00 .90
Dave Cash
Johnny Jeter
☐ 142 Fritz Peterson 1.00 .45
☐ 143 Phil Gagliano 1.00 .45
☐ 144 Ray Culp 1.00 .45
☐ 145 Rico Carty 2.00 .90
☐ 146 Danny Murphy 1.00 .45
☐ 147 Angel Hermoso 1.00 .45
☐ 148 Earl Weaver MG 3.00 1.35
☐ 149 Billy Champion 1.00 .45
☐ 150 Harmon Killebrew 8.00 3.60
☐ 151 Dave Roberts 1.00 .45
☐ 152 Ike Brown 1.00 .45
☐ 153 Gary Gentry 1.00 .45
☐ 154 Senators Rookies 1.00 .45
Jim Miles
Jan Dukes
☐ 155 Denis Menke 1.00 .45
☐ 156 Eddie Fisher 1.00 .45
☐ 157 Manny Mota 2.00 .90
☐ 158 Jerry McNertney 2.00 .90
☐ 159 Tommy Helms 2.00 .90
☐ 160 Phil Niekro 5.00 2.20
☐ 161 Richie Scheinblum 1.00 .45
☐ 162 Jerry Johnson 1.00 .45
☐ 163 Syd O'Brien 1.00 .45
☐ 164 Ty Cline 1.00 .45
☐ 165 Ed Kirkpatrick 1.00 .45
☐ 166 Al Oliver 2.00 .90
☐ 167 Bill Burbach 1.00 .45
☐ 168 Dave Watkins 1.00 .45
☐ 169 Tom Hall 1.00 .45
☐ 170 Billy Williams 7.00 3.10
☐ 171 Jim Nash 1.00 .45
☐ 172 Braves Rookies 2.00 .90
Garry Hill
Ralph Garr
☐ 173 Jim Hicks 1.00 .45
☐ 174 Ted Sizemore 2.00 .90
☐ 175 Dick Bosman 1.00 .45
☐ 176 Jim Ray Hart 2.00 .90
☐ 177 Jim Northrup 2.00 .90
☐ 178 Denny Lemaster 1.00 .45
☐ 179 Ivan Murrell 1.00 .45
☐ 180 Tommy John 2.00 .90
☐ 181 Sparky Anderson MG 5.00 2.20
☐ 182 Dick Hall 1.00 .45
☐ 183 Jerry Grote 1.00 .45
☐ 184 Ray Fosse 1.00 .45
☐ 185 Don Mincher 2.00 .90
☐ 186 Rick Joseph 1.00 .45
☐ 187 Mike Hedlund 1.00 .45
☐ 188 Manny Sanguillen 2.00 .90
☐ 189 Yankees Rookies 50.00 22.00
Thurman Munson
Dave McDonald
☐ 190 Joe Torre 2.00 .90
☐ 191 Vicente Romo 1.00 .45
☐ 192 Jim Qualls 1.00 .45
☐ 193 Mike Wegener 1.00 .45
☐ 194 Chuck Manuel 1.00 .45
☐ 195 Tom Seaver NLCS 15.00 6.75
☐ 196 Ken Boswell NLCS 2.00 .90
☐ 197 Nolan Ryan NLCS 30.00 13.50
☐ 198 NL Playoff Summary 15.00 6.75
Mets celebrate
(Nolan Ryan)
☐ 199 Mike Cuellar ALCS 2.00 .90
☐ 200 Boog Powell ALCS 4.00 1.80
☐ 201 Boog Powell ALCS 2.00 .90
Andy Etchebarren)
☐ 202 AL Playoff Summary 2.00 .90
Orioles celebrate
☐ 203 Rudy May 1.00 .45
☐ 204 Len Gabrielson 1.00 .45
☐ 205 Bert Campaneris 2.00 .90
☐ 206 Clete Boyer 2.00 .90
☐ 207 Tigers Rookies 1.00 .45
Norman McRae
Bob Reed
☐ 208 Fred Gladding 1.00 .45
☐ 209 Ken Suarez 1.00 .45
☐ 210 Juan Marichal 7.00 3.10
☐ 211 Ted Williams MG 12.00 5.50
☐ 212 Al Santorini 1.00 .45
☐ 213 Andy Etchebarren 1.00 .45

☐ 214 Ken Boswell	1.00	.45
☐ 215 Reggie Smith	2.00	.90
☐ 216 Chuck Hartenstein	1.00	.45
☐ 217 Ron Hansen	1.00	.45
☐ 218 Ron Stone	1.00	.45
☐ 219 Jerry Kenney	1.00	.45
☐ 220 Steve Carlton	15.00	6.75
☐ 221 Ron Brand	1.00	.45
☐ 222 Jim Rooker	2.00	.90
☐ 223 Nate Oliver	1.00	.45
☐ 224 Steve Barber	2.00	.90
☐ 225 Lee May	2.00	.90
☐ 226 Ron Perranoski	1.50	.70
☐ 227 Astros Rookies	1.50	.70
John Mayberry		
Bob Watkins		
☐ 228 Aurelio Rodriguez	1.00	.45
☐ 229 Rich Robertson	1.00	.45
☐ 230 Brooks Robinson	14.00	6.25
☐ 231 Luis Tiant	1.50	.70
☐ 232 Bob Didier	1.00	.45
☐ 233 Lew Krausse	1.00	.45
☐ 234 Tommy Dean	1.00	.45
☐ 235 Mike Epstein	1.00	.45
☐ 236 Bob Veale	1.00	.45
☐ 237 Russ Gibson	1.00	.45
☐ 238 Jose Laboy	1.00	.45
☐ 239 Ken Berry	1.00	.45
☐ 240 Ferguson Jenkins	7.00	3.10
☐ 241 Royals Rookies	1.00	.45
Al Fitzmorris		
Scott Northey		
☐ 242 Walter Alston MG	2.00	.90
☐ 243 Joe Sparma	1.00	.45
☐ 244A Checklist 3	6.00	1.20
(Red bat on front)		
☐ 244B Checklist 3	6.00	1.20
(Brown bat on front)		
☐ 245 Leo Cardenas	1.00	.45
☐ 246 Jim McAndrew	1.00	.45
☐ 247 Lou Klimchock	1.00	.45
☐ 248 Jesus Alou	1.00	.45
☐ 249 Bob Locker	1.00	.45
☐ 250 Willie McCovey UER	10.00	4.50
(1963 San Francisci)		
☐ 251 Dick Schofield	1.00	.45
☐ 252 Lowell Palmer	1.00	.45
☐ 253 Ron Woods	1.00	.45
☐ 254 Camilo Pascual	1.00	.45
☐ 255 Jim Spencer	1.00	.45
☐ 256 Vic Davalillo	1.00	.45
☐ 257 Dennis Higgins	1.00	.45
☐ 258 Paul Popovich	1.00	.45
☐ 259 Tommie Reynolds	1.00	.45
☐ 260 Claude Osteen	1.00	.45
☐ 261 Curt Motton	1.00	.45
☐ 262 Padres Rookies	1.00	.45
Jerry Morales		
Jim Williams		
☐ 263 Duane Josephson	1.00	.45
☐ 264 Rich Hebner	1.00	.45
☐ 265 Randy Hundley	1.00	.45
☐ 266 Wally Bunker	1.00	.45
☐ 267 Twins Rookies	1.00	.45
Herman Hill		
Paul Ratliff		
☐ 268 Claude Raymond	1.00	.45
☐ 269 Cesar Gutierrez	1.00	.45
☐ 270 Chris Short	1.00	.45
☐ 271 Greg Goossen	1.00	.45
☐ 272 Hector Torres	1.00	.45
☐ 273 Ralph Houk MG	1.50	.70
☐ 274 Gerry Arrigo	1.00	.45
☐ 275 Duke Sims	1.00	.45
☐ 276 Ron Hunt	1.00	.45
☐ 277 Paul Doyle	1.00	.45
☐ 278 Tommie Aaron	1.00	.45
☐ 279 Bill Lee	2.00	.90
☐ 280 Donn Clendenon	1.00	.45
☐ 281 Casey Cox	1.00	.45
☐ 282 Steve Huntz	1.00	.45
☐ 283 Angel Bravo	1.00	.45
☐ 284 Jack Baldschun	1.00	.45
☐ 285 Paul Blair	2.00	.90
☐ 286 Dodgers Rookies	6.00	2.70
Jack Jenkins		
Bill Buckner		
☐ 287 Fred Talbot	1.00	.45
☐ 288 Larry Hisle	1.00	.45
☐ 289 Gene Brabender	1.00	.45
☐ 290 Rod Carew	18.00	8.00
☐ 291 Leo Durocher MG	3.00	1.35
☐ 292 Eddie Leon	1.00	.45
☐ 293 Bob Bailey	1.00	.45
☐ 294 Jose Azcue	1.00	.45
☐ 295 Cecil Upshaw	1.00	.45
☐ 296 Woody Woodward	1.00	.45
☐ 297 Curt Blefary	1.00	.45
☐ 298 Ken Henderson	1.00	.45
☐ 299 Buddy Bradford	1.00	.45
☐ 300 Tom Seaver	40.00	18.00
☐ 301 Chico Salmon	1.00	.45
☐ 302 Jeff James	1.00	.45
☐ 303 Brant Alyea	1.00	.45
☐ 304 Bill Russell	6.00	2.70
☐ 305 Don Buford WS	4.00	1.80
☐ 306 Donn Clendenon WS	4.00	1.80
☐ 307 Tommie Agee WS	4.00	1.80
☐ 308 J.C. Martin WS	4.00	1.80
☐ 309 Jerry Koosman WS	4.00	1.80
☐ 310 World Series Summary	5.00	2.20
Mets whoop it up		
☐ 311 Dick Green	1.00	.45
☐ 312 Mike Torrez	1.00	.45
☐ 313 Mayo Smith MG	1.00	.45
☐ 314 Bill McCool	1.00	.45
☐ 315 Luis Aparicio	5.00	2.20
☐ 316 Skip Guinn	1.00	.45
☐ 317 Red Sox Rookies	1.00	.45
Billy Conigliaro		
Luis Alvarado		
☐ 318 Willie Smith	1.00	.45
☐ 319 Clay Dalrymple	1.00	.45
☐ 320 Jim Maloney	1.00	.45
☐ 321 Lou Piniella	2.00	.90
☐ 322 Luke Walker	1.00	.45
☐ 323 Wayne Comer	1.00	.45
☐ 324 Tony Taylor	1.00	.45
☐ 325 Dave Boswell	1.00	.45
☐ 326 Bill Voss	1.00	.45
☐ 327 Hal King	1.00	.45
☐ 328 George Brunet	1.00	.45
☐ 329 Chris Cannizzaro	1.00	.45
☐ 330 Lou Brock	10.00	4.50
☐ 331 Chuck Dobson	1.00	.45
☐ 332 Bobby Wine	1.00	.45
☐ 333 Bobby Murcer	2.00	.90
☐ 334 Phil Regan	1.00	.45
☐ 335 Bill Freehan	2.00	.90
☐ 336 Del Unser	1.00	.45
☐ 337 Mike McCormick	1.00	.45
☐ 338 Paul Schaal	1.00	.45
☐ 339 Johnny Edwards	1.00	.45
☐ 340 Tony Conigliaro	3.00	1.35
☐ 341 Bill Sudakis	1.00	.45
☐ 342 Wilbur Wood	1.50	.70
☐ 343A Checklist 4	6.00	1.20
(Red bat on front)		
☐ 343B Checklist 4	6.00	1.20
(Brown bat on front)		
☐ 344 Marcelino Lopez	1.00	.45
☐ 345 Al Ferrara	1.00	.45
☐ 346 Red Schoendienst MG	2.00	.90
☐ 347 Russ Snyder	1.00	.45
☐ 348 Mets Rookies	1.50	.70
Mike Jorgensen		
Jesse Hudson		
☐ 349 Steve Hamilton	1.00	.45
☐ 350 Roberto Clemente	70.00	32.00
☐ 351 Tom Murphy	1.00	.45
☐ 352 Bob Barton	1.00	.45
☐ 353 Stan Williams	1.00	.45
☐ 354 Amos Otis	1.50	.70
☐ 355 Doug Rader	1.00	.45
☐ 356 Fred Lasher	1.00	.45
☐ 357 Bob Burda	1.00	.45
☐ 358 Pedro Borbon	1.50	.70
☐ 359 Phil Roof	1.00	.45
☐ 360 Curt Flood	2.00	.90
☐ 361 Ray Jarvis	1.00	.45
☐ 362 Joe Hague	1.00	.45
☐ 363 Tom Shopay	1.00	.45
☐ 364 Dan McGinn	1.00	.45
☐ 365 Zoilo Versalles	1.00	.45
☐ 366 Barry Moore	1.00	.45
☐ 367 Mike Lum	1.00	.45
☐ 368 Ed Herrmann	1.00	.45
☐ 369 Alan Foster	1.00	.45
☐ 370 Tommy Harper	2.00	.90
☐ 371 Rod Gaspar	1.00	.45
☐ 372 Dave Giusti	1.50	.70
☐ 373 Roy White	2.00	.90
☐ 374 Tommie Sisk	1.50	.70
☐ 375 Johnny Callison	2.00	.90
☐ 376 Lefty Phillips MG	1.50	.70
☐ 377 Bill Butler	1.00	.45
☐ 378 Jim Davenport	1.50	.70
☐ 379 Tom Tischinski	1.50	.70
☐ 380 Tony Perez	7.00	3.10
☐ 381 Athletics Rookies	1.50	.70
Bobby Brooks		
Mike Olivo		
☐ 382 Jack DiLauro	1.50	.70
☐ 383 Mickey Stanley	2.00	.90
☐ 384 Gary Neibauer	1.50	.70
☐ 385 George Scott	2.00	.90
☐ 386 Bill Dillman	1.50	.70
☐ 387 Baltimore Orioles	4.00	1.80
Team Card		
☐ 388 Byron Browne	1.50	.70
☐ 389 Jim Shellenback	1.50	.70
☐ 390 Willie Davis	2.00	.90
☐ 391 Larry Brown	1.50	.70
☐ 392 Walt Hriniak	2.00	.90
☐ 393 John Gelnar	1.50	.70
☐ 394 Gil Hodges MG	5.00	2.20
☐ 395 Walt Williams	1.50	.70
☐ 396 Steve Blass	2.00	.90
☐ 397 Roger Repoz	1.50	.70
☐ 398 Bill Stoneman	1.50	.70
☐ 399 New York Yankees	4.00	1.80
Team Card		
☐ 400 Denny McLain	2.00	.90
☐ 401 Giants Rookies	1.50	.70
John Harrell		
Bernie Williams		
☐ 402 Ellie Rodriguez	1.50	.70
☐ 403 Jim Bunning	5.00	2.20
☐ 404 Rich Reese	1.50	.70
☐ 405 Bill Hands	1.50	.70
☐ 406 Mike Andrews	1.50	.70
☐ 407 Bob Watson	2.00	.90
☐ 408 Paul Lindblad	1.50	.70
☐ 409 Bob Tolan	2.00	.90
☐ 410 Boog Powell	4.00	1.80
☐ 411 Los Angeles Dodgers	4.00	1.80
Team Card		
☐ 412 Larry Burchart	1.50	.70
☐ 413 Sonny Jackson	1.50	.70
☐ 414 Paul Edmondson	1.50	.70
☐ 415 Julian Javier	2.00	.90
☐ 416 Joe Verbanic	1.50	.70
☐ 417 John Bateman	1.50	.70
☐ 418 John Donaldson	1.50	.70
☐ 419 Ron Taylor	1.50	.70
☐ 420 Ken McMullen	2.00	.90
☐ 421 Pat Dobson	2.00	.90
☐ 422 Royals Team	4.00	1.80
☐ 423 Jerry May	1.50	.70
☐ 424 Mike Kilkenny	1.50	.70
(Inconsistent design		
card number in		
white circle)		
☐ 425 Bobby Bonds	6.00	2.70
☐ 426 Bill Rigney MG	1.50	.70
☐ 427 Fred Norman	1.50	.70
☐ 428 Don Buford	1.50	.70
☐ 429 Cubs Rookies	1.50	.70
Randy Bobb		
Jim Cosman		
☐ 430 Andy Messersmith	2.00	.90
☐ 431 Ron Swoboda	2.00	.90
☐ 432A Checklist 5	6.00	1.20
(Baseball in		
yellow letters)		
☐ 432B Checklist 5	6.00	1.20
(Baseball in		
white letters)		
☐ 433 Ron Bryant	1.50	.70
☐ 434 Felipe Alou	2.00	.90
☐ 435 Nelson Briles	2.00	.90
☐ 436 Philadelphia Phillies	4.00	1.80
Team Card		
☐ 437 Danny Cater	1.50	.70
☐ 438 Pat Jarvis	1.50	.70
☐ 439 Lee Maye	1.50	.70
☐ 440 Bill Mazeroski	3.00	1.35
☐ 441 John O'Donoghue	1.50	.70
☐ 442 Gene Mauch MG	2.00	.90
☐ 443 Al Jackson	1.50	.70
☐ 444 White Sox Rookies	1.50	.70
Billy Farmer		
John Matias		
☐ 445 Vada Pinson	2.00	.90
☐ 446 Billy Grabarkewitz	1.50	.70
☐ 447 Lee Stange	1.50	.70
☐ 448 Houston Astros	4.00	1.80
Team Card		
☐ 449 Jim Palmer	12.00	5.50
☐ 450 Willie McCovey AS	7.00	3.10
☐ 451 Boog Powell AS	4.00	1.80
☐ 452 Felix Millan AS	2.00	.90
☐ 453 Rod Carew AS	7.00	3.10
☐ 454 Ron Santo AS	4.00	1.80
☐ 455 Brooks Robinson AS	7.00	3.10
☐ 456 Don Kessinger AS	2.00	.90
☐ 457 Rico Petrocelli AS	4.00	1.80
☐ 458 Pete Rose AS	14.00	6.25
☐ 459 Reggie Jackson AS	14.00	6.25
☐ 460 Matty Alou AS	3.00	1.35
☐ 461 Carl Yastrzemski AS	10.00	4.50

☐ 462 Hank Aaron AS	15.00	6.75
☐ 463 Frank Robinson AS	7.00	3.10
☐ 464 Johnny Bench AS	14.00	6.25
☐ 465 Bill Freehan AS	3.00	1.35
☐ 466 Juan Marichal AS	4.00	1.80
☐ 467 Denny McLain AS	3.00	1.35
☐ 468 Jerry Koosman AS	3.00	1.35
☐ 469 Sam McDowell AS	3.00	1.35
☐ 470 Willie Stargell	10.00	4.50
☐ 471 Chris Zachary	2.00	.90
☐ 472 Braves Team	3.00	1.35
☐ 473 Don Bryant	2.00	.90
☐ 474 Dick Kelley	2.00	.90
☐ 475 Dick McAuliffe	3.00	1.35
☐ 476 Don Shaw	2.00	.90
☐ 477 Orioles Rookies Al Severinsen Roger Freed	2.00	.90
☐ 478 Bobby Heise	2.00	.90
☐ 479 Dick Woodson	2.00	.90
☐ 480 Glenn Beckert	3.00	1.35
☐ 481 Jose Tartabull	3.00	1.35
☐ 482 Tom Hilgendorf	2.00	.90
☐ 483 Gail Hopkins	2.00	.90
☐ 484 Gary Nolan	3.00	1.35
☐ 485 Jay Johnstone	3.00	1.35
☐ 486 Terry Harmon	2.00	.90
☐ 487 Cisco Carlos	2.00	.90
☐ 488 J.C. Martin	2.00	.90
☐ 489 Eddie Kasko MG	2.00	.90
☐ 490 Bill Singer	3.00	1.35
☐ 491 Graig Nettles	6.00	2.70
☐ 492 Astros Rookies Keith Lampard Scipio Spinks	2.00	.90
☐ 493 Lindy McDaniel	3.00	1.35
☐ 494 Larry Stahl	2.00	.90
☐ 495 Dave Morehead	2.00	.90
☐ 496 Steve Whitaker	2.00	.90
☐ 497 Eddie Watt	2.00	.90
☐ 498 Al Weis	2.00	.90
☐ 499 Skip Lockwood	3.00	1.35
☐ 500 Hank Aaron	50.00	22.00
☐ 501 Chicago White Sox Team Card	5.00	2.20
☐ 502 Rollie Fingers	10.00	4.50
☐ 503 Dal Maxvill	2.00	.90
☐ 504 Don Pavletich	2.00	.90
☐ 505 Ken Holtzman	3.00	1.35
☐ 506 Ed Stroud	2.00	.90
☐ 507 Pat Corrales	3.00	1.35
☐ 508 Joe Niekro	3.00	1.35
☐ 509 Montreal Expos Team Card	3.00	1.35
☐ 510 Tony Oliva	3.00	1.35
☐ 511 Joe Hoerner	2.00	.90
☐ 512 Billy Harris	2.00	.90
☐ 513 Preston Gomez MG	2.00	.90
☐ 514 Steve Hovley	2.00	.90
☐ 515 Don Wilson	3.00	1.35
☐ 516 Yankees Rookies John Ellis Jim Lyttle	2.00	.90
☐ 517 Joe Gibbon	2.00	.90
☐ 518 Bill Melton	2.00	.90
☐ 519 Don McMahon	2.00	.90
☐ 520 Willie Horton	3.00	1.35
☐ 521 Cal Koonce	2.00	.90
☐ 522 Angels Team	5.00	2.20
☐ 523 Jose Pena	2.00	.90
☐ 524 Alvin Dark MG	3.00	1.35
☐ 525 Jerry Adair	2.00	.90
☐ 526 Ron Herbel	2.00	.90
☐ 527 Don Bosch	2.00	.90
☐ 528 Elrod Hendricks	2.00	.90
☐ 529 Bob Aspromonte	2.00	.90
☐ 530 Bob Gibson	14.00	6.25
☐ 531 Ron Clark	2.00	.90
☐ 532 Danny Murtaugh MG	3.00	1.35
☐ 533 Buzz Stephen	2.00	.90
☐ 534 Minnesota Twins Team Card	5.00	2.20
☐ 535 Andy Kosco	2.00	.90
☐ 536 Mike Kekich	2.00	.90
☐ 537 Joe Morgan	10.00	4.50
☐ 538 Bob Humphreys	2.00	.90
☐ 539 Phillies Rookies Denny Doyle Larry Bowa	6.00	2.70
☐ 540 Gary Peters	2.00	.90
☐ 541 Bill Heath	2.00	.90
☐ 542 Checklist 6	8.00	1.60
☐ 543 Clyde Wright	2.00	.90
☐ 544 Cincinnati Reds Team Card	2.50	1.10
☐ 545 Ken Harrelson	3.00	1.35
☐ 546 Ron Reed	2.00	.90
☐ 547 Rick Monday	6.00	2.70
☐ 548 Howie Reed	4.00	1.80
☐ 549 St. Louis Cardinals Team Card	8.00	3.60
☐ 550 Frank Howard	6.00	2.70
☐ 551 Dock Ellis	6.00	2.70
☐ 552 Royals Rookies Don O'Riley Dennis Paepke Fred Rico	4.00	1.80
☐ 553 Jim Lefebvre	6.00	2.70
☐ 554 Tom Timmermann	4.00	1.80
☐ 555 Orlando Cepeda	6.00	2.70
☐ 556 Dave Bristol MG	6.00	2.70
☐ 557 Ed Kranepool	6.00	2.70
☐ 558 Vern Fuller	4.00	1.80
☐ 559 Tommy Davis	6.00	2.70
☐ 560 Gaylord Perry	10.00	4.50
☐ 561 Tom McCraw	4.00	1.80
☐ 562 Ted Abernathy	4.00	1.80
☐ 563 Boston Red Sox Team Card	8.00	3.60
☐ 564 Johnny Briggs	4.00	1.80
☐ 565 Jim Hunter	10.00	4.50
☐ 566 Gene Alley	6.00	2.70
☐ 567 Bob Oliver	4.00	1.80
☐ 568 Stan Bahnsen	6.00	2.70
☐ 569 Cookie Rojas	6.00	2.70
☐ 570 Jim Fregosi	6.00	2.70
☐ 571 Jim Brewer	4.00	1.80
☐ 572 Frank Quilici MG	4.00	1.80
☐ 573 Padres Rookies Mike Corkins Rafael Robles Ron Slocum	4.00	1.80
☐ 574 Bobby Bolin	6.00	2.70
☐ 575 Cleon Jones	6.00	2.70
☐ 576 Milt Pappas	6.00	2.70
☐ 577 Bernie Allen	4.00	1.80
☐ 578 Tom Griffin	4.00	1.80
☐ 579 Detroit Tigers Team Card	8.00	3.60
☐ 580 Pete Rose	50.00	22.00
☐ 581 Tom Satriano	4.00	1.80
☐ 582 Mike Paul	4.00	1.80
☐ 583 Hal Lanier	4.00	1.80
☐ 584 Al Downing	6.00	2.70
☐ 585 Rusty Staub	8.00	3.60
☐ 586 Rickey Clark	4.00	1.80
☐ 587 Jose Arcia	4.00	1.80
☐ 588A Checklist 7 ERR (666 Adolfo)	12.00	2.40
☐ 588B Checklist 7 COR (666 Adolpho)	12.00	2.40
☐ 589 Joe Keough	4.00	1.80
☐ 590 Mike Cuellar	6.00	2.70
☐ 591 Mike Ryan UER (Pitching Record header on card back)	4.00	1.80
☐ 592 Daryl Patterson	4.00	1.80
☐ 593 Chicago Cubs Team Card	8.00	3.60
☐ 594 Jake Gibbs	4.00	1.80
☐ 595 Maury Wills	8.00	3.60
☐ 596 Mike Hershberger	6.00	2.70
☐ 597 Sonny Siebert	4.00	1.80
☐ 598 Joe Pepitone	6.00	2.70
☐ 599 Senators Rookies Dick Stelmaszek Gene Martin Dick Such	4.00	1.80
☐ 600 Willie Mays	70.00	32.00
☐ 601 Pete Richert	4.00	1.80
☐ 602 Ted Savage	4.00	1.80
☐ 603 Ray Oyler	4.00	1.80
☐ 604 Clarence Gaston	6.00	2.70
☐ 605 Rick Wise	6.00	2.70
☐ 606 Chico Ruiz	4.00	1.80
☐ 607 Gary Waslewski	4.00	1.80
☐ 608 Pittsburgh Pirates Team Card	8.00	3.60
☐ 609 Buck Martinez (Inconsistent design card number in white circle)	6.00	2.70
☐ 610 Jerry Koosman	8.00	3.60
☐ 611 Norm Cash	5.00	2.20
☐ 612 Jim Hickman	6.00	2.70
☐ 613 Dave Baldwin	6.00	2.70
☐ 614 Mike Shannon	6.00	2.70
☐ 615 Mark Belanger	6.00	2.70
☐ 616 Jim Merritt	4.00	1.80
☐ 617 Jim French	4.00	1.80
☐ 618 Billy Wynne	4.00	1.80
☐ 619 Norm Miller	4.00	1.80
☐ 620 Jim Perry	6.00	2.70
☐ 621 Braves Rookies Mike McQueen Darrell Evans Rick Kester	10.00	4.50
☐ 622 Don Sutton	10.00	4.50
☐ 623 Horace Clarke	6.00	2.70
☐ 624 Clyde King MG	4.00	1.80
☐ 625 Dean Chance	4.00	1.80
☐ 626 Dave Ricketts	4.00	1.80
☐ 627 Gary Wagner	4.00	1.80
☐ 628 Wayne Garrett	4.00	1.80
☐ 629 Merv Rettenmund	4.00	1.80
☐ 630 Ernie Banks	50.00	22.00
☐ 631 Oakland Athletics Team Card	8.00	3.60
☐ 632 Gary Sutherland	4.00	1.80
☐ 633 Roger Nelson	4.00	1.80
☐ 634 Bud Harrelson	15.00	6.75
☐ 635 Bob Allison	15.00	6.75
☐ 636 Jim Stewart	10.00	4.50
☐ 637 Cleveland Indians Team Card	15.00	6.75
☐ 638 Frank Bertaina	10.00	4.50
☐ 639 Dave Campbell	10.00	4.50
☐ 640 Al Kaline	50.00	22.00
☐ 641 Al McBean	10.00	4.50
☐ 642 Angels Rookies Greg Garrett Gordon Lund Jarvis Tatum	10.00	4.50
☐ 643 Jose Pagan	10.00	4.50
☐ 644 Gerry Nyman	10.00	4.50
☐ 645 Don Money	15.00	6.75
☐ 646 Jim Britton	10.00	4.50
☐ 647 Tom Matchick	10.00	4.50
☐ 648 Larry Haney	10.00	4.50
☐ 649 Jimmie Hall	10.00	4.50
☐ 650 Sam McDowell	15.00	6.75
☐ 651 Jim Gosger	10.00	4.50
☐ 652 Rich Rollins	15.00	6.75
☐ 653 Moe Drabowsky	10.00	4.50
☐ 654 NL Rookies Oscar Gamble Boots Day Angel Mangual	12.00	5.50
☐ 655 John Roseboro	15.00	6.75
☐ 656 Jim Hardin	10.00	4.50
☐ 657 San Diego Padres Team Card	15.00	6.75
☐ 658 Ken Tatum	10.00	4.50
☐ 659 Pete Ward	10.00	4.50
☐ 660 Johnny Bench	100.00	45.00
☐ 661 Jerry Robertson	10.00	4.50
☐ 662 Frank Lucchesi MG	10.00	4.50
☐ 663 Tito Francona	10.00	4.50
☐ 664 Bob Robertson	10.00	4.50
☐ 665 Jim Lonborg	15.00	6.75
☐ 666 Adolpho Phillips	10.00	4.50
☐ 667 Bob Meyer	15.00	6.75
☐ 668 Bob Tillman	10.00	4.50
☐ 669 White Sox Rookies Bart Johnson Dan Lazar Mickey Scott	10.00	4.50
☐ 670 Ron Santo	12.00	5.50
☐ 671 Jim Campanis	10.00	4.50
☐ 672 Leon McFadden	10.00	4.50
☐ 673 Ted Uhlaender	10.00	4.50
☐ 674 Dave Leonhard	10.00	4.50
☐ 675 Jose Cardenal	15.00	6.75
☐ 676 Washington Senators Team Card	20.00	9.00
☐ 677 Woodie Fryman	10.00	4.50
☐ 678 Dave Duncan	15.00	6.75
☐ 679 Ray Sadecki	10.00	4.50
☐ 680 Rico Petrocelli	15.00	6.75
☐ 681 Bob Garibaldi	10.00	4.50
☐ 682 Dalton Jones	10.00	4.50
☐ 683 Reds Rookies Vern Geishert Hal McRae Wayne Simpson	15.00	6.75
☐ 684 Jack Fisher	10.00	4.50
☐ 685 Tom Haller	10.00	4.50
☐ 686 Jackie Hernandez	10.00	4.50
☐ 687 Bob Priddy	10.00	4.50
☐ 688 Ted Kubiak	15.00	6.75
☐ 689 Frank Tepedino	10.00	4.50
☐ 690 Ron Fairly	15.00	6.75
☐ 691 Joe Grzenda	10.00	4.50
☐ 692 Duffy Dyer	10.00	4.50
☐ 693 Bob Johnson	10.00	4.50
☐ 694 Gary Ross	10.00	4.50
☐ 695 Bobby Knoop	10.00	4.50
☐ 696 San Francisco Giants Team Card	15.00	6.75
☐ 697 Jim Hannan	10.00	4.50
☐ 698 Tom Tresh	15.00	6.75
☐ 699 Hank Aguirre	10.00	4.50

☐ 700 Frank Robinson	50.00	22.00
☐ 701 Jack Billingham	10.00	4.50
☐ 702 AL Rookies	10.00	4.50
Bob Johnson		
Ron Klimkowski		
Bill Zepp		
☐ 703 Lou Marone	10.00	4.50
☐ 704 Frank Baker	10.00	4.50
☐ 705 Tony Cloninger UER	10.00	4.50
(Batter headings		
on card back)		
☐ 706 John McNamara MG	10.00	4.50
☐ 707 Kevin Collins	10.00	4.50
☐ 708 Jose Santiago	10.00	4.50
☐ 709 Mike Fiore	10.00	4.50
☐ 710 Felix Millan	10.00	4.50
☐ 711 Ed Brinkman	10.00	4.50
☐ 712 Nolan Ryan	375.00	170.00
☐ 713 Seattle Pilots	25.00	11.00
Team Card		
☐ 714 Al Spangler	10.00	4.50
☐ 715 Mickey Lolich	15.00	6.75
☐ 716 Cardinals Rookies	15.00	6.75
Sal Campisi		
Reggie Cleveland		
Santiago Guzman		
☐ 717 Tom Phoebus	10.00	4.50
☐ 718 Ed Spiezio	10.00	4.50
☐ 719 Jim Roland	10.00	4.50
☐ 720 Rick Reichardt	14.00	4.70

1970 Topps Booklets

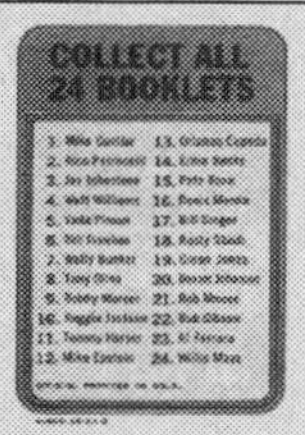

Inserted into packages of the 1970 Topps (and O-Pee-Chee) regular issue of cards, there are 24 miniature biographies of ballplayers in the set. Each numbered paper booklet contains six pages of comic book style story and a checklist of the booklet is available on the back page. These little booklets measure approximately 2 1/2" by 3 7/16".

	NRMT	VG-E
COMPLETE SET (24)	40.00	18.00
COMMON CARD (1-16)	.50	.23
COMMON CARD (17-24)	.60	.25
☐ 1 Mike Cuellar	.50	.23
☐ 2 Rico Petrocelli	.60	.25
☐ 3 Jay Johnstone	.60	.25
☐ 4 Walt Williams	.50	.23
☐ 5 Vada Pinson	.75	.35
☐ 6 Bill Freehan	.75	.35
☐ 7 Wally Bunker	.50	.23
☐ 8 Tony Oliva	1.00	.45
☐ 9 Bobby Murcer	.75	.35
☐ 10 Reggie Jackson	6.00	2.70
☐ 11 Tommy Harper	.50	.23
☐ 12 Mike Epstein	.50	.23
☐ 13 Orlando Cepeda	1.50	.70
☐ 14 Ernie Banks	5.00	2.20
☐ 15 Pete Rose	6.00	2.70
☐ 16 Denis Menke	.50	.23
☐ 17 Bill Singer	.60	.25
☐ 18 Rusty Staub	1.00	.45
☐ 19 Cleon Jones	.60	.25
☐ 20 Deron Johnson	.60	.25
☐ 21 Bob Moose	.60	.25
☐ 22 Bob Gibson	5.00	2.20
☐ 23 Al Ferrara	.60	.25
☐ 24 Willie Mays	7.50	3.40

1970 Topps Posters Inserts

In 1970 Topps raised its price per package of cards to ten cents, and a series of 24 color posters was included as a bonus to the collector. Each thin-paper poster is numbered and features a large portrait and a smaller black and white action pose. It was folded five times to fit in the packaging. Each poster measures 8 11/16" by 9 5/8".

	NRMT	VG-E
COMPLETE SET (24)	50.00	22.00
COMMON POSTER (1-24)	.75	.35

☐ 1 Joe Horlen	.75	.35
☐ 2 Phil Niekro	3.00	1.35
☐ 3 Willie Davis	1.25	.55
☐ 4 Lou Brock	4.00	1.80
☐ 5 Ron Santo	1.00	.45
☐ 6 Ken Harrelson	1.25	.55
☐ 7 Willie McCovey	4.00	1.80
☐ 8 Rick Wise	.75	.35
☐ 9 Andy Messersmith	.75	.35
☐ 10 Ron Fairly	.75	.35
☐ 11 Johnny Bench	6.00	2.70
☐ 12 Frank Robinson	4.00	1.80
☐ 13 Tommie Agee	.75	.35
☐ 14 Roy White	.75	.35
☐ 15 Larry Dierker	.75	.35
☐ 16 Rod Carew	4.00	1.80
☐ 17 Don Mincher	.75	.35
☐ 18 Ollie Brown	.75	.35
☐ 19 Ed Kirkpatrick	.75	.35
☐ 20 Reggie Smith	1.25	.55
☐ 21 Roberto Clemente	20.00	9.00
☐ 22 Frank Howard	1.25	.55
☐ 23 Bert Campaneris	.75	.35
☐ 24 Denny McLain	1.00	.45

1970-71 Topps Scratchoffs

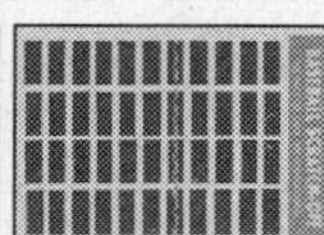

The 1970-71 Topps Scratch-off inserts are heavy cardboard, folded inserts issued with the regular card series of those years. Unfolded, they form a game board upon which a baseball game is played by means of rubbing off black ink from the playing squares to reveal moves. Inserts with white centers were issued in 1970 and inserts with red centers in 1971. Unfolded, these inserts measure 3 3/8" by 5".

	NRMT	VG-E
COMPLETE SET (24)	40.00	18.00
COMMON CARD (1-24)	.60	.25
☐ 1 Hank Aaron	6.00	2.70
☐ 2 Rich Allen	1.25	.55
☐ 3 Luis Aparicio	3.00	1.35
☐ 4 Sal Bando	.60	.25
☐ 5 Glenn Beckert	.60	.25
☐ 6 Dick Bosman	.60	.25
☐ 7 Nate Colbert	.60	.25
☐ 8 Mike Hegan	.60	.25
☐ 9 Mack Jones	.60	.25
☐ 10 Al Kaline	4.00	1.80
☐ 11 Harmon Killebrew	4.00	1.80
☐ 12 Juan Marichal	3.00	1.35
☐ 13 Tim McCarver	1.25	.55
☐ 14 Sam McDowell	.75	.35
☐ 15 Claude Osteen	.60	.25
☐ 16 Tony Perez	2.00	.90
☐ 17 Lou Piniella	1.25	.55
☐ 18 Boog Powell	1.25	.55
☐ 19 Tom Seaver	5.00	2.20
☐ 20 Jim Spencer	.60	.25
☐ 21 Willie Stargell	4.00	1.80
☐ 22 Mel Stottlemyre	.75	.35
☐ 23 Jim Wynn	.75	.35
☐ 24 Carl Yastrzemski	4.00	1.80

1970 Topps Super

The cards in this 42-card set measure approximately 3 1/8" by 5 1/4". The 1970 Topps Super set was a separate Topps issue printed on heavy stock and marketed in its own wrapper with gum. The blue and yellow backs are identical to the respective player's backs in the 1970 Topps regular issue. Cards 38, Boog Powell, is the key card of the set; other short print run cards are listed in the checklist with SP. The obverse pictures are borderless and contain a facsimile autograph. The set was issued in three-card wax packs.

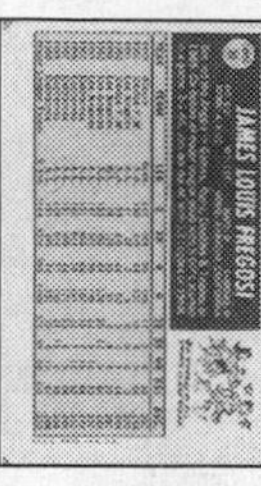

	NRMT	VG-E
COMPLETE SET (42)	200.00	90.00
COMMON CARD (1-42)	1.00	.45
☐ 1 Claude Osteen SP	3.00	1.35
☐ 2 Sal Bando SP	3.00	1.35
☐ 3 Luis Aparicio	3.00	1.35
☐ 4 Harmon Killebrew	5.00	2.20
☐ 5 Tom Seaver SP	20.00	9.00
☐ 6 Larry Dierker	1.25	.55
☐ 7 Bill Freehan	1.25	.55
☐ 8 Johnny Bench	10.00	4.50
☐ 9 Tommy Harper	1.00	.45
☐ 10 Sam McDowell	1.00	.45
☐ 11 Lou Brock	5.00	2.20
☐ 12 Roberto Clemente	30.00	13.50
☐ 13 Willie McCovey	5.00	2.20
☐ 14 Rico Petrocelli	1.00	.45
☐ 15 Phil Niekro	4.00	1.80
☐ 16 Frank Howard	1.25	.55
☐ 17 Denny McLain	1.25	.55
☐ 18 Willie Mays	15.00	6.75
☐ 19 Willie Stargell	5.00	2.20
☐ 20 Joel Horlen	1.00	.45
☐ 21 Ron Santo	1.50	.70
☐ 22 Dick Bosman	1.00	.45
☐ 23 Tim McCarver	1.50	.70
☐ 24 Hank Aaron	15.00	6.75
☐ 25 Andy Messersmith	1.00	.45
☐ 26 Tony Oliva	1.50	.70
☐ 27 Mel Stottlemyre	1.25	.55
☐ 28 Reggie Jackson	15.00	6.75
☐ 29 Carl Yastrzemski	7.50	3.40
☐ 30 Jim Fregosi	1.25	.55
☐ 31 Vada Pinson	1.25	.55
☐ 32 Lou Piniella	1.50	.70
☐ 33 Bob Gibson	4.00	1.80
☐ 34 Pete Rose	15.00	6.75
☐ 35 Jim Wynn	1.25	.55
☐ 36 Ollie Brown SP	6.00	2.70
☐ 37 Frank Robinson SP	20.00	9.00
☐ 38 Boog Powell SP	50.00	22.00
☐ 39 Willie Davis SP	3.00	1.35
☐ 40 Billy Williams SP	7.50	3.40
☐ 41 Rusty Staub	1.50	.70
☐ 42 Tommie Agee	1.00	.45

1971 Topps

The cards in this 752-card set measure 2 1/2" by 3 1/2". The 1971 Topps set is a challenge to complete in strict mint condition because the black obverse border is easily scratched and damaged. An unusual feature of this set is that the player is also pictured in black and white on the back of the card. Featured subsets within this set include League Leaders (61-72), Playoffs cards (195-202), and World Series cards (327-332). Cards 524-643 and the last series (644-752) are somewhat scarce. The last series was printed in two sheets of 132. On the printing sheets 44 cards were printed in 50 percent greater quantity than the other 66 cards. These 66 (slightly) shorter-printed numbers are identified in the checklist below by SP. The key Rookie Cards in this set are the multi-player Rookie Card of Dusty Baker and Don Baylor and the individual cards of Bert Blyleven, Dave Concepcion, Steve Garvey, and Ted Simmons.

	NRMT	VG-E
COMPLETE SET (752)	2000.00	900.00
COMMON CARD (1-393)	1.50	.70
COMMON CARD (394-523)	2.50	1.10
COMMON CARD (524-643)	4.00	1.80
COMMON CARD (644-752)	8.00	3.60
COMMON SP (644-752)	12.00	5.50
WRAPPER (10-CENT)	15.00	6.75
☐ 1 Baltimore Orioles	15.00	5.00
Team Card		
☐ 2 Dock Ellis	1.50	.70
☐ 3 Dick McAuliffe	1.50	.70
☐ 4 Vic Davalillo	1.50	.70
☐ 5 Thurman Munson	18.00	8.00
☐ 6 Ed Spiezio	1.50	.70
☐ 7 Jim Holt	1.50	.70
☐ 8 Mike McQueen	1.50	.70
☐ 9 George Scott	2.00	.90
☐ 10 Claude Osteen	1.50	.70
☐ 11 Elliott Maddox	2.00	.90
☐ 12 Johnny Callison	2.00	.90
☐ 13 White Sox Rookies	1.50	.70
Charlie Brinkman		
Dick Moloney		
☐ 14 Dave Concepcion	18.00	8.00
☐ 15 Andy Messersmith	2.00	.90
☐ 16 Ken Singleton	4.00	1.80
☐ 17 Billy Sorrell	1.50	.70
☐ 18 Norm Miller	1.50	.70
☐ 19 Skip Pitlock	1.50	.70
☐ 20 Reggie Jackson	25.00	11.00
☐ 21 Dan McGinn	1.50	.70
☐ 22 Phil Roof	1.50	.70
☐ 23 Oscar Gamble	1.50	.70
☐ 24 Rich Hand	1.50	.70
☐ 25 Clarence Gaston	2.50	1.10
☐ 26 Bert Blyleven	8.00	3.60
☐ 27 Pirates Rookies	1.50	.70
Fred Cambria		
Gene Clines		
☐ 28 Ron Klimkowski	1.50	.70
☐ 29 Don Buford	1.50	.70
☐ 30 Phil Niekro	5.00	2.20
☐ 31 Eddie Kasko MG	1.50	.70
☐ 32 Jerry DaVanon	1.50	.70
☐ 33 Del Unser	1.50	.70
☐ 34 Sandy Vance	1.50	.70
☐ 35 Lou Piniella	2.50	1.10
☐ 36 Dean Chance	1.50	.70
☐ 37 Rich McKinney	1.50	.70
☐ 38 Jim Colborn	1.50	.70
☐ 39 Tiger Rookies	1.50	.70
Lerrin LaGrow		
Gene Lamont		
☐ 40 Lee May	2.00	.90
☐ 41 Rick Austin	1.50	.70
☐ 42 Boots Day	1.50	.70
☐ 43 Steve Kealey	1.50	.70
☐ 44 Johnny Edwards	1.50	.70
☐ 45 Jim Hunter	7.00	3.10
☐ 46 Dave Campbell	1.50	.70
☐ 47 Johnny Jeter	1.50	.70
☐ 48 Dave Baldwin	1.50	.70
☐ 49 Don Money	1.50	.70
☐ 50 Willie McCovey	8.00	3.60
☐ 51 Steve Kline	1.50	.70
☐ 52 Braves Rookies	1.50	.70
Oscar Brown		
Earl Williams		
☐ 53 Paul Blair	2.00	.90
☐ 54 Checklist 1	6.00	1.20
☐ 55 Steve Carlton	15.00	6.75
☐ 56 Duane Josephson	1.50	.70
☐ 57 Von Joshua	1.50	.70
☐ 58 Bill Lee	2.00	.90
☐ 59 Gene Mauch MG	2.00	.90
☐ 60 Dick Bosman	1.50	.70
☐ 61 AL Batting Leaders	3.50	1.55
Alex Johnson		
Carl Yastrzemski		
Tony Oliva		
☐ 62 NL Batting Leaders	2.00	.90
Rico Carty		
Joe Torre		
Manny Sanguillen		
☐ 63 AL RBI Leaders	2.50	1.10
Frank Howard		
Tony Conigliaro		
Boog Powell		
☐ 64 NL RBI Leaders	5.00	2.20
Johnny Bench		
Tony Perez		
Billy Williams		
☐ 65 AL HR Leaders	4.00	1.80
Frank Howard		
Harmon Killebrew		
Carl Yastrzemski		
☐ 66 NL HR Leaders	6.00	2.70
Johnny Bench		
Billy Williams		
Tony Perez		
☐ 67 AL ERA Leaders	3.50	1.55
Diego Segui		
Jim Palmer		
Clyde Wright		
☐ 68 NL ERA Leaders	3.50	1.55
Tom Seaver		
Wayne Simpson		
Luke Walker		
☐ 69 AL Pitching Leaders	2.00	.90
Mike Cuellar		
Dave McNally		
Jim Perry		
☐ 70 NL Pitching Leaders	6.00	2.70
Bob Gibson		
Gaylord Perry		
Fergie Jenkins		
☐ 71 AL Strikeout Leaders	2.00	.90
Sam McDowell		
Mickey Lolich		
Bob Johnson		
☐ 72 NL Strikeout Leaders	7.00	3.10
Tom Seaver		
Bob Gibson		
Fergie Jenkins		
☐ 73 George Brunet	1.50	.70
☐ 74 Twins Rookies	1.50	.70
Pete Hamm		
Jim Nettles		
☐ 75 Gary Nolan	2.00	.90
☐ 76 Ted Savage	1.50	.70
☐ 77 Mike Compton	1.50	.70
☐ 78 Jim Spencer	1.50	.70
☐ 79 Wade Blasingame	1.50	.70
☐ 80 Bill Melton	1.50	.70
☐ 81 Felix Millan	1.50	.70
☐ 82 Casey Cox	1.50	.70
☐ 83 Met Rookies	1.50	.70
Tim Foli		
Randy Bobb		
☐ 84 Marcel Lachemann	1.50	.70
☐ 85 Billy Grabarkewitz	1.50	.70
☐ 86 Mike Kilkenny	1.50	.70
☐ 87 Jack Heidemann	1.50	.70
☐ 88 Hal King	1.50	.70
☐ 89 Ken Brett	1.50	.70
☐ 90 Joe Pepitone	2.50	1.10
☐ 91 Bob Lemon MG	2.50	1.10
☐ 92 Fred Wenz	1.50	.70
☐ 93 Senators Rookies	1.50	.70
Norm McRae		
Denny Riddleberger		
☐ 94 Don Hahn	1.50	.70
☐ 95 Luis Tiant	2.50	1.10
☐ 96 Joe Hague	1.50	.70
☐ 97 Floyd Wicker	1.50	.70
☐ 98 Joe Decker	1.50	.70
☐ 99 Mark Belanger	2.00	.90
☐ 100 Pete Rose	25.00	11.00
☐ 101 Les Cain	1.50	.70
☐ 102 Astros Rookies	2.00	.90
Ken Forsch		
Larry Howard		
☐ 103 Rich Severson	1.50	.70
☐ 104 Dan Frisella	1.50	.70
☐ 105 Tony Conigliaro	2.50	1.10
☐ 106 Tom Dukes	1.50	.70
☐ 107 Roy Foster	1.50	.70
☐ 108 John Cumberland	1.50	.70
☐ 109 Steve Hovley	1.50	.70
☐ 110 Bill Mazeroski	2.50	1.10
☐ 111 Yankee Rookies	1.50	.70
Loyd Colson		
Bobby Mitchell		
☐ 112 Manny Mota	2.00	.90
☐ 113 Jerry Crider	1.50	.70
☐ 114 Billy Conigliaro	2.00	.90
☐ 115 Donn Clendenon	2.00	.90
☐ 116 Ken Sanders	1.50	.70
☐ 117 Ted Simmons	8.00	3.60
☐ 118 Cookie Rojas	2.00	.90
☐ 119 Frank Lucchesi MG	1.50	.70
☐ 120 Willie Horton	2.50	1.10
☐ 121 Cubs Rookies	1.50	.70
Jim Dunegan		
Roe Skidmore		
☐ 122 Eddie Watt	1.50	.70
☐ 123A Checklist 2	6.00	1.20
(Card number		
at bottom right)		
☐ 123B Checklist 2	6.00	1.20
(Card number		
centered)		
☐ 124 Don Gullett	2.00	.90
☐ 125 Ray Fosse	2.00	.90
☐ 126 Danny Coombs	1.50	.70
☐ 127 Danny Thompson	2.00	.90
☐ 128 Frank Johnson	1.50	.70
☐ 129 Aurelio Monteagudo	1.50	.70
☐ 130 Denis Menke	1.50	.70
☐ 131 Curt Blefary	1.50	.70
☐ 132 Jose Laboy	1.50	.70
☐ 133 Mickey Lolich	2.50	1.10
☐ 134 Jose Arcia	1.50	.70
☐ 135 Rick Monday	2.50	1.10
☐ 136 Duffy Dyer	1.50	.70
☐ 137 Marcelino Lopez	1.50	.70
☐ 138 Phillies Rookies	2.00	.90
Joe Lis		
Willie Montanez		
☐ 139 Paul Casanova	1.50	.70
☐ 140 Gaylord Perry	7.00	3.10
☐ 141 Frank Quilici	1.50	.70
☐ 142 Mack Jones	1.50	.70
☐ 143 Steve Blass	2.00	.90
☐ 144 Jackie Hernandez	1.50	.70
☐ 145 Bill Singer	2.00	.90
☐ 146 Ralph Houk MG	2.00	.90
☐ 147 Bob Priddy	1.50	.70
☐ 148 John Mayberry	2.00	.90
☐ 149 Mike Hershberger	1.50	.70
☐ 150 Sam McDowell	2.50	1.10
☐ 151 Tommy Davis	2.00	.90
☐ 152 Angels Rookies	1.50	.70
Lloyd Allen		
Winston Llenas		
☐ 153 Gary Ross	1.50	.70
☐ 154 Cesar Gutierrez	1.50	.70
☐ 155 Ken Henderson	1.50	.70
☐ 156 Bart Johnson	1.50	.70
☐ 157 Bob Bailey	1.50	.70
☐ 158 Jerry Reuss	2.00	.90
☐ 159 Jarvis Tatum	1.50	.70
☐ 160 Tom Seaver	18.00	8.00
☐ 161 Coin Checklist	6.00	1.20
☐ 162 Jack Billingham	1.50	.70
☐ 163 Buck Martinez	2.00	.90
☐ 164 Reds Rookies	2.00	.90
Frank Duffy		
Milt Wilcox		
☐ 165 Cesar Tovar	1.50	.70
☐ 166 Joe Hoerner	1.50	.70
☐ 167 Tom Grieve	2.50	1.10
☐ 168 Bruce Dal Canton	1.50	.70
☐ 169 Ed Herrmann	1.50	.70
☐ 170 Mike Cuellar	2.00	.90
☐ 171 Bobby Wine	1.50	.70
☐ 172 Duke Sims	1.50	.70
☐ 173 Gil Garrido	1.50	.70
☐ 174 Dave LaRoche	1.50	.70
☐ 175 Jim Hickman	1.50	.70
☐ 176 Red Sox Rookies	2.00	.90
Bob Montgomery		
Doug Griffin		
☐ 177 Hal McRae	2.50	1.10
☐ 178 Dave Duncan	1.50	.70
☐ 179 Mike Corkins	1.50	.70
☐ 180 Al Kaline UER	18.00	8.00
(Home instead		
of Birth)		
☐ 181 Hal Lanier	1.50	.70
☐ 182 Al Downing	2.00	.90
☐ 183 Gil Hodges MG	4.00	1.80
☐ 184 Stan Bahnsen	1.50	.70
☐ 185 Julian Javier	2.00	.90
☐ 186 Bob Spence	1.50	.70
☐ 187 Ted Abernathy	1.50	.70
☐ 188 Dodgers Rookies	3.00	1.35
Bob Valentine		
Mike Strahler		
☐ 189 George Mitterwald	1.50	.70
☐ 190 Bob Tolan	2.00	.90
☐ 191 Mike Andrews	1.50	.70
☐ 192 Billy Wilson	1.50	.70
☐ 193 Bob Grich	4.00	1.80
☐ 194 Mike Lum	1.50	.70
☐ 195 Boog Powell ALCS	3.00	1.35
☐ 196 Dave McNally ALCS	3.00	1.35
☐ 197 Jim Palmer ALCS	5.00	2.20
☐ 198 AL Playoff Summary	2.50	1.10
Orioles celebrate		
☐ 199 Ty Cline NLCS	2.50	1.10
☐ 200 Bobby Tolan NLCS	2.50	1.10
☐ 201 Ty Cline NLCS	2.50	1.10
☐ 202 NL Playoff Summary	2.50	1.10
Reds celebrate		
☐ 203 Larry Gura	2.00	.90
☐ 204 Brewers Rookies	1.50	.70
Bernie Smith		
George Kopacz		
☐ 205 Gerry Moses	1.50	.70

☐ 206 Checklist 3	6.00	1.20
☐ 207 Alan Foster	1.50	.70
☐ 208 Billy Martin MG	4.00	1.80
☐ 209 Steve Renko	1.50	.70
☐ 210 Rod Carew	18.00	8.00
☐ 211 Phil Hennigan	1.50	.70
☐ 212 Rich Hebner	2.00	.90
☐ 213 Frank Baker	1.50	.70
☐ 214 Al Ferrara	1.50	.70
☐ 215 Diego Segui	1.50	.70
☐ 216 Cards Rookies Reggie Cleveland Luis Melendez	1.50	.70
☐ 217 Ed Stroud	1.50	.70
☐ 218 Tony Cloninger	1.50	.70
☐ 219 Elrod Hendricks	1.50	.70
☐ 220 Ron Santo	2.50	1.10
☐ 221 Dave Morehead	1.50	.70
☐ 222 Bob Watson	2.50	1.10
☐ 223 Cecil Upshaw	1.50	.70
☐ 224 Alan Gallagher	1.50	.70
☐ 225 Gary Peters	1.50	.70
☐ 226 Bill Russell	2.50	1.10
☐ 227 Floyd Weaver	1.50	.70
☐ 228 Wayne Garrett	1.50	.70
☐ 229 Jim Hannan	1.50	.70
☐ 230 Willie Stargell	8.00	3.60
☐ 231 Indians Rookies Vince Colbert John Lowenstein	1.50	.70
☐ 232 John Strohmayer	1.50	.70
☐ 233 Larry Bowa	2.50	1.10
☐ 234 Jim Lyttle	1.50	.70
☐ 235 Nate Colbert	1.50	.70
☐ 236 Bob Humphreys	1.50	.70
☐ 237 Cesar Cedeno	3.00	1.35
☐ 238 Chuck Dobson	1.50	.70
☐ 239 Red Schoendienst MG	2.50	1.10
☐ 240 Clyde Wright	1.50	.70
☐ 241 Dave Nelson	1.50	.70
☐ 242 Jim Ray	1.50	.70
☐ 243 Carlos May	2.00	.90
☐ 244 Bob Tillman	1.50	.70
☐ 245 Jim Kaat	2.50	1.10
☐ 246 Tony Taylor	2.00	.90
☐ 247 Royals Rookies Jerry Cram Paul Splittorff	2.00	.90
☐ 248 Hoyt Wilhelm	4.00	1.80
☐ 249 Chico Salmon	1.50	.70
☐ 250 Johnny Bench	18.00	8.00
☐ 251 Frank Reberger	1.50	.70
☐ 252 Eddie Leon	1.50	.70
☐ 253 Bill Sudakis	1.50	.70
☐ 254 Cal Koonce	1.50	.70
☐ 255 Bob Robertson	2.00	.90
☐ 256 Tony Gonzalez	1.50	.70
☐ 257 Nelson Briles	1.50	.70
☐ 258 Dick Green	1.50	.70
☐ 259 Dave Marshall	1.50	.70
☐ 260 Tommy Harper	2.00	.90
☐ 261 Darold Knowles	1.50	.70
☐ 262 Padres Rookies Jim Williams Dave Robinson	1.50	.70
☐ 263 John Ellis	1.50	.70
☐ 264 Joe Morgan	8.00	3.60
☐ 265 Jim Northrup	2.00	.90
☐ 266 Bill Stoneman	1.50	.70
☐ 267 Rich Morales	1.50	.70
☐ 268 Philadelphia Phillies Team Card	4.00	1.80
☐ 269 Gail Hopkins	1.50	.70
☐ 270 Rico Carty	2.50	1.10
☐ 271 Bill Zepp	1.50	.70
☐ 272 Tommy Helms	2.00	.90
☐ 273 Pete Richert	1.50	.70
☐ 274 Ron Slocum	1.50	.70
☐ 275 Vada Pinson	2.50	1.10
☐ 276 Giants Rookies Mike Davison George Foster	8.00	3.60
☐ 277 Gary Waslewski	1.50	.70
☐ 278 Jerry Grote	1.50	.70
☐ 279 Lefty Phillips MG	1.50	.70
☐ 280 Ferguson Jenkins	7.00	3.10
☐ 281 Danny Walton	1.50	.70
☐ 282 Jose Pagan	1.50	.70
☐ 283 Dick Such	1.50	.70
☐ 284 Jim Gosger	1.50	.70
☐ 285 Sal Bando	2.50	1.10
☐ 286 Jerry McNertney	1.50	.70
☐ 287 Mike Fiore	1.50	.70
☐ 288 Joe Moeller	1.50	.70
☐ 289 Chicago White Sox Team Card	2.00	.90
☐ 290 Tony Oliva	2.50	1.10
☐ 291 George Culver	1.50	.70
☐ 292 Jay Johnstone	2.00	.90
☐ 293 Pat Corrales	2.00	.90
☐ 294 Steve Dunning	1.50	.70
☐ 295 Bobby Bonds	5.00	2.20
☐ 296 Tom Timmermann	1.50	.70
☐ 297 Johnny Briggs	1.50	.70
☐ 298 Jim Nelson	1.50	.70
☐ 299 Ed Kirkpatrick	1.50	.70
☐ 300 Brooks Robinson	18.00	8.00
☐ 301 Earl Wilson	1.50	.70
☐ 302 Phil Gagliano	1.50	.70
☐ 303 Lindy McDaniel	2.00	.90
☐ 304 Ron Brand	1.50	.70
☐ 305 Reggie Smith	2.50	1.10
☐ 306 Jim Nash	1.50	.70
☐ 307 Don Wert	1.50	.70
☐ 308 St. Louis Cardinals Team Card	2.00	.90
☐ 309 Dick Ellsworth	1.50	.70
☐ 310 Tommie Agee	2.50	1.10
☐ 311 Lee Stange	1.50	.70
☐ 312 Harry Walker MG	1.50	.70
☐ 313 Tom Hall	1.50	.70
☐ 314 Jeff Torborg	2.00	.90
☐ 315 Ron Fairly	2.50	1.10
☐ 316 Fred Scherman	1.50	.70
☐ 317 Athletic Rookies Jim Driscoll Angel Mangual	1.50	.70
☐ 318 Rudy May	1.50	.70
☐ 319 Ty Cline	1.50	.70
☐ 320 Dave McNally	2.00	.90
☐ 321 Tom Matchick	1.50	.70
☐ 322 Jim Beauchamp	1.50	.70
☐ 323 Billy Champion	1.50	.70
☐ 324 Graig Nettles	2.50	1.10
☐ 325 Juan Marichal	7.00	3.10
☐ 326 Richie Scheinblum	1.50	.70
☐ 327 Boog Powell WS	2.50	1.10
☐ 328 Don Buford WS	2.50	1.10
☐ 329 Frank Robinson WS	5.00	2.20
☐ 330 World Series Game 4 Reds stay alive	2.50	1.10
☐ 331 Brooks Robinson WS commits robbery	6.00	2.70
☐ 332 World Series Summary Orioles celebrate	2.50	1.10
☐ 333 Clay Kirby	1.50	.70
☐ 334 Roberto Pena	1.50	.70
☐ 335 Jerry Koosman	2.50	1.10
☐ 336 Detroit Tigers Team Card	2.00	.90
☐ 337 Jesus Alou	1.50	.70
☐ 338 Gene Tenace	2.00	.90
☐ 339 Wayne Simpson	1.50	.70
☐ 340 Rico Petrocelli	2.50	1.10
☐ 341 Steve Garvey	25.00	11.00
☐ 342 Frank Tepedino	1.50	.70
☐ 343 Pirates Rookies Ed Acosta Milt May	1.50	.70
☐ 344 Ellie Rodriguez	1.50	.70
☐ 345 Joel Horlen	1.50	.70
☐ 346 Lum Harris MG	1.50	.70
☐ 347 Ted Uhlaender	1.50	.70
☐ 348 Fred Norman	1.50	.70
☐ 349 Rich Reese	1.50	.70
☐ 350 Billy Williams	7.00	3.10
☐ 351 Jim Shellenback	1.50	.70
☐ 352 Denny Doyle	1.50	.70
☐ 353 Carl Taylor	1.50	.70
☐ 354 Don McMahon	1.50	.70
☐ 355 Bud Harrelson (Nolan Ryan in photo)	3.50	1.55
☐ 356 Bob Locker	1.50	.70
☐ 357 Cincinnati Reds Team Card	2.00	.90
☐ 358 Danny Cater	1.50	.70
☐ 359 Ron Reed	1.50	.70
☐ 360 Jim Fregosi	2.00	.90
☐ 361 Don Sutton	7.00	3.10
☐ 362 Orioles Rookies Mike Adamson Roger Freed	1.50	.70
☐ 363 Mike Nagy	1.50	.70
☐ 364 Tommy Dean	1.50	.70
☐ 365 Bob Johnson	1.50	.70
☐ 366 Ron Stone	1.50	.70
☐ 367 Dalton Jones	1.50	.70
☐ 368 Bob Veale	2.00	.90
☐ 369 Checklist 4	6.00	1.20
☐ 370 Joe Torre	2.50	1.10
☐ 371 Jack Hiatt	1.50	.70
☐ 372 Lew Krausse	1.50	.70
☐ 373 Tom McCraw	1.50	.70
☐ 374 Clete Boyer	2.00	.90
☐ 375 Steve Hargan	1.50	.70
☐ 376 Expos Rookies Clyde Mashore Ernie McAnally	1.50	.70
☐ 377 Greg Garrett	1.50	.70
☐ 378 Tito Fuentes	1.50	.70
☐ 379 Wayne Granger	1.50	.70
☐ 380 Ted Williams MG	10.00	4.50
☐ 381 Fred Gladding	1.50	.70
☐ 382 Jake Gibbs	1.50	.70
☐ 383 Rod Gaspar	1.50	.70
☐ 384 Rollie Fingers	6.00	2.70
☐ 385 Maury Wills	2.50	1.10
☐ 386 Boston Red Sox Team Card	2.00	.90
☐ 387 Ron Herbel	1.50	.70
☐ 388 Al Oliver	2.50	1.10
☐ 389 Ed Brinkman	1.50	.70
☐ 390 Glenn Beckert	2.00	.90
☐ 391 Twins Rookies Steve Brye Cotton Nash	2.00	.90
☐ 392 Grant Jackson	1.50	.70
☐ 393 Merv Rettenmund	2.00	.90
☐ 394 Clay Carroll	2.50	1.10
☐ 395 Roy White	3.00	1.35
☐ 396 Dick Schofield	2.50	1.10
☐ 397 Alvin Dark MG	3.00	1.35
☐ 398 Howie Reed	2.50	1.10
☐ 399 Jim French	2.50	1.10
☐ 400 Hank Aaron	50.00	22.00
☐ 401 Tom Murphy	2.50	1.10
☐ 402 Los Angeles Dodgers Team Card	5.00	2.20
☐ 403 Joe Coleman	2.50	1.10
☐ 404 Astros Rookies Buddy Harris Roger Metzger	2.50	1.10
☐ 405 Leo Cardenas	2.50	1.10
☐ 406 Ray Sadecki	2.50	1.10
☐ 407 Joe Rudi	3.00	1.35
☐ 408 Rafael Robles	2.50	1.10
☐ 409 Don Pavletich	2.50	1.10
☐ 410 Ken Holtzman	4.00	1.80
☐ 411 George Spriggs	2.50	1.10
☐ 412 Jerry Johnson	2.50	1.10
☐ 413 Pat Kelly	2.50	1.10
☐ 414 Woodie Fryman	2.50	1.10
☐ 415 Mike Hegan	2.50	1.10
☐ 416 Gene Alley	2.50	1.10
☐ 417 Dick Hall	2.50	1.10
☐ 418 Adolfo Phillips	2.50	1.10
☐ 419 Ron Hansen	2.50	1.10
☐ 420 Jim Merritt	2.50	1.10
☐ 421 John Stephenson	2.50	1.10
☐ 422 Frank Bertaina	2.50	1.10
☐ 423 Tigers Rookies Dennis Saunders Tim Marting	2.50	1.10
☐ 424 Roberto Rodriquez	2.50	1.10
☐ 425 Doug Rader	2.50	1.10
☐ 426 Chris Cannizzaro	2.50	1.10
☐ 427 Bernie Allen	2.50	1.10
☐ 428 Jim McAndrew	2.50	1.10
☐ 429 Chuck Hinton	2.50	1.10
☐ 430 Wes Parker	2.50	1.10
☐ 431 Tom Burgmeier	2.50	1.10
☐ 432 Bob Didier	2.50	1.10
☐ 433 Skip Lockwood	2.50	1.10
☐ 434 Gary Sutherland	2.50	1.10
☐ 435 Jose Cardenal	4.00	1.80
☐ 436 Wilbur Wood	2.50	1.10
☐ 437 Danny Murtaugh MG	3.00	1.35
☐ 438 Mike McCormick	4.00	1.80
☐ 439 Phillies Rookies Greg Luzinski Scott Reid	6.00	2.70
☐ 440 Bert Campaneris	3.00	1.35
☐ 441 Milt Pappas	4.00	1.80
☐ 442 California Angels Team Card	4.00	1.80
☐ 443 Rich Robertson	2.50	1.10
☐ 444 Jimmie Price	2.50	1.10
☐ 445 Art Shamsky	2.50	1.10
☐ 446 Bobby Bolin	2.50	1.10
☐ 447 Cesar Geronimo	4.00	1.80
☐ 448 Dave Roberts	2.50	1.10
☐ 449 Brant Alyea	2.50	1.10
☐ 450 Bob Gibson	18.00	8.00
☐ 451 Joe Keough	2.50	1.10
☐ 452 John Boccabella	2.50	1.10
☐ 453 Terry Crowley	2.50	1.10
☐ 454 Mike Paul	2.50	1.10
☐ 455 Don Kessinger	3.00	1.35
☐ 456 Bob Meyer	2.50	1.10
☐ 457 Willie Smith	2.50	1.10
☐ 458 White Sox Rookies	2.50	1.10

Ron Lolich
Dave Lemonds
☐ 459 Jim Lefebvre 2.50 1.10
☐ 460 Fritz Peterson 2.50 1.10
☐ 461 Jim Ray Hart 2.50 1.10
☐ 462 Washington Senators 5.00 2.20
Team Card
☐ 463 Tom Kelley 2.50 1.10
☐ 464 Aurelio Rodriguez 2.50 1.10
☐ 465 Tim McCarver 6.00 2.70
☐ 466 Ken Berry 2.50 1.10
☐ 467 Al Santorini 2.50 1.10
☐ 468 Frank Fernandez 2.50 1.10
☐ 469 Bob Aspromonte 2.50 1.10
☐ 470 Bob Oliver 2.50 1.10
☐ 471 Tom Griffin 2.50 1.10
☐ 472 Ken Rudolph 2.50 1.10
☐ 473 Gary Wagner 2.50 1.10
☐ 474 Jim Fairey 2.50 1.10
☐ 475 Ron Perranoski 2.50 1.10
☐ 476 Dal Maxvill 2.50 1.10
☐ 477 Earl Weaver MG 4.00 1.80
☐ 478 Bernie Carbo 2.50 1.10
☐ 479 Dennis Higgins 2.50 1.10
☐ 480 Manny Sanguillen 3.00 1.35
☐ 481 Daryl Patterson 2.50 1.10
☐ 482 San Diego Padres 5.00 2.20
Team Card
☐ 483 Gene Michael 4.00 1.80
☐ 484 Don Wilson 2.50 1.10
☐ 485 Ken McMullen 2.50 1.10
☐ 486 Steve Huntz 2.50 1.10
☐ 487 Paul Schaal 2.50 1.10
☐ 488 Jerry Stephenson 2.50 1.10
☐ 489 Luis Alvarado 2.50 1.10
☐ 490 Deron Johnson 4.00 1.80
☐ 491 Jim Hardin 2.50 1.10
☐ 492 Ken Boswell 2.50 1.10
☐ 493 Dave May 2.50 1.10
☐ 494 Braves Rookies 4.00 1.80
Ralph Garr
Rick Kester
☐ 495 Felipe Alou 4.00 1.80
☐ 496 Woody Woodward 2.50 1.10
☐ 497 Horacio Pina 2.50 1.10
☐ 498 John Kennedy 2.50 1.10
☐ 499 Checklist 5 6.00 1.20
☐ 500 Jim Perry 4.00 1.80
☐ 501 Andy Etchebarren 2.50 1.10
☐ 502 Chicago Cubs 5.00 2.20
Team Card
☐ 503 Gates Brown 4.00 1.80
☐ 504 Ken Wright 2.50 1.10
☐ 505 Ollie Brown 2.50 1.10
☐ 506 Bobby Knoop 2.50 1.10
☐ 507 George Stone 2.50 1.10
☐ 508 Roger Repoz 2.50 1.10
☐ 509 Jim Grant 2.50 1.10
☐ 510 Ken Harrelson 3.00 1.35
☐ 511 Chris Short 4.00 1.80
(Pete Rose leading off second)
☐ 512 Red Sox Rookies 2.50 1.10
Dick Mills
Mike Garman
☐ 513 Nolan Ryan 250.00 110.00
☐ 514 Ron Woods 2.50 1.10
☐ 515 Carl Morton 2.50 1.10
☐ 516 Ted Kubiak 2.50 1.10
☐ 517 Charlie Fox MG 2.50 1.10
☐ 518 Joe Grzenda 2.50 1.10
☐ 519 Willie Crawford 2.50 1.10
☐ 520 Tommy John 5.00 2.20
☐ 521 Leron Lee 2.50 1.10
☐ 522 Minnesota Twins 5.00 2.20
Team Card
☐ 523 John Odom 2.50 1.10
☐ 524 Mickey Stanley 5.00 2.20
☐ 525 Ernie Banks 50.00 22.00
☐ 526 Ray Jarvis 4.00 1.80
☐ 527 Cleon Jones 6.00 2.70
☐ 528 Wally Bunker 4.00 1.80
☐ 529 NL Rookie Infielders 5.00 2.20
Enzo Hernandez
Bill Buckner
Marty Perez
☐ 530 Carl Yastrzemski 40.00 18.00
☐ 531 Mike Torrez 4.00 1.80
☐ 532 Bill Rigney MG 4.00 1.80
☐ 533 Mike Ryan 4.00 1.80
☐ 534 Luke Walker 4.00 1.80
☐ 535 Curt Flood 5.00 2.20
☐ 536 Claude Raymond 5.00 2.20
☐ 537 Tom Egan 4.00 1.80
☐ 538 Angel Bravo 4.00 1.80
☐ 539 Larry Brown 4.00 1.80
☐ 540 Larry Dierker 6.00 2.70
☐ 541 Bob Burda 4.00 1.80
☐ 542 Bob Miller 4.00 1.80
☐ 543 New York Yankees 10.00 4.50
Team Card
☐ 544 Vida Blue 6.00 2.70
☐ 545 Dick Dietz 4.00 1.80
☐ 546 John Matias 4.00 1.80
☐ 547 Pat Dobson 6.00 2.70
☐ 548 Don Mason 4.00 1.80
☐ 549 Jim Brewer 5.00 2.20
☐ 550 Harmon Killebrew 25.00 11.00
☐ 551 Frank Linzy 4.00 1.80
☐ 552 Buddy Bradford 4.00 1.80
☐ 553 Kevin Collins 4.00 1.80
☐ 554 Lowell Palmer 4.00 1.80
☐ 555 Walt Williams 4.00 1.80
☐ 556 Jim McGlothlin 4.00 1.80
☐ 557 Tom Satriano 4.00 1.80
☐ 558 Hector Torres 4.00 1.80
☐ 559 AL Rookie Pitchers 4.00 1.80
Terry Cox
Bill Gogolewski
Gary Jones
☐ 560 Rusty Staub 5.00 2.20
☐ 561 Syd O'Brien 4.00 1.80
☐ 562 Dave Giusti 4.00 1.80
☐ 563 San Francisco Giants 8.00 3.60
Team Card
☐ 564 Al Fitzmorris 4.00 1.80
☐ 565 Jim Wynn 5.00 2.20
☐ 566 Tim Cullen 4.00 1.80
☐ 567 Walt Alston MG 6.00 2.70
☐ 568 Sal Campisi 4.00 1.80
☐ 569 Ivan Murrell 4.00 1.80
☐ 570 Jim Palmer 30.00 13.50
☐ 571 Ted Sizemore 4.00 1.80
☐ 572 Jerry Kenney 4.00 1.80
☐ 573 Ed Kranepool 5.00 2.20
☐ 574 Jim Bunning 7.00 3.10
☐ 575 Bill Freehan 5.00 2.20
☐ 576 Cubs Rookies 4.00 1.80
Adrian Garrett
Brock Davis
Garry Jestadt
☐ 577 Jim Lonborg 5.00 2.20
☐ 578 Ron Hunt 4.00 1.80
☐ 579 Marty Pattin 4.00 1.80
☐ 580 Tony Perez 18.00 8.00
☐ 581 Roger Nelson 4.00 1.80
☐ 582 Dave Cash 6.00 2.70
☐ 583 Ron Cook 4.00 1.80
☐ 584 Cleveland Indians 8.00 3.60
Team Card
☐ 585 Willie Davis 5.00 2.20
☐ 586 Dick Woodson 4.00 1.80
☐ 587 Sonny Jackson 4.00 1.80
☐ 588 Tom Bradley 4.00 1.80
☐ 589 Bob Barton 4.00 1.80
☐ 590 Alex Johnson 6.00 2.70
☐ 591 Jackie Brown 4.00 1.80
☐ 592 Randy Hundley 6.00 2.70
☐ 593 Jack Aker 4.00 1.80
☐ 594 Cards Rookies 5.00 2.20
Bob Chlupsa
Bob Stinson
Al Hrabosky
☐ 595 Dave Johnson 6.00 2.70
☐ 596 Mike Jorgensen 4.00 1.80
☐ 597 Ken Suarez 4.00 1.80
☐ 598 Rick Wise 6.00 2.70
☐ 599 Norm Cash 5.00 2.20
☐ 600 Willie Mays 90.00 40.00
☐ 601 Ken Tatum 4.00 1.80
☐ 602 Marty Martinez 4.00 1.80
☐ 603 Pittsburgh Pirates 8.00 3.60
Team Card
☐ 604 John Gelnar 4.00 1.80
☐ 605 Orlando Cepeda 6.00 2.70
☐ 606 Chuck Taylor 4.00 1.80
☐ 607 Paul Ratliff 4.00 1.80
☐ 608 Mike Wegener 4.00 1.80
☐ 609 Leo Durocher MG 7.00 3.10
☐ 610 Amos Otis 6.00 2.70
☐ 611 Tom Phoebus 4.00 1.80
☐ 612 Indians Rookies 4.00 1.80
Lou Camilli
Ted Ford
Steve Mingori
☐ 613 Pedro Borbon 4.00 1.80
☐ 614 Billy Cowan 4.00 1.80
☐ 615 Mel Stottlemyre 5.00 2.20
☐ 616 Larry Hisle 6.00 2.70
☐ 617 Clay Dalrymple 4.00 1.80
☐ 618 Tug McGraw 5.00 2.20
☐ 619A Checklist 6 ERR 8.00 1.60
(No copyright)
☐ 619B Checklist 6 COR 12.00 2.40
(Copyright on back)
☐ 620 Frank Howard 5.00 2.20
☐ 621 Ron Bryant 4.00 1.80
☐ 622 Joe Lahoud 4.00 1.80
☐ 623 Pat Jarvis 4.00 1.80
☐ 624 Oakland Athletics 8.00 3.60
Team Card
☐ 625 Lou Brock 30.00 13.50
☐ 626 Freddie Patek 6.00 2.70
☐ 627 Steve Hamilton 4.00 1.80
☐ 628 John Bateman 4.00 1.80
☐ 629 John Hiller 6.00 2.70
☐ 630 Roberto Clemente 110.00 50.00
☐ 631 Eddie Fisher 4.00 1.80
☐ 632 Darrel Chaney 4.00 1.80
☐ 633 AL Rookie Outfielders 4.00 1.80
Bobby Brooks
Pete Koegel
Scott Northey
☐ 634 Phil Regan 6.00 2.70
☐ 635 Bobby Murcer 6.00 2.70
☐ 636 Denny Lemaster 4.00 1.80
☐ 637 Dave Bristol MG 4.00 1.80
☐ 638 Stan Williams 4.00 1.80
☐ 639 Tom Haller 4.00 1.80
☐ 640 Frank Robinson 40.00 18.00
☐ 641 New York Mets 15.00 6.75
Team Card
☐ 642 Jim Roland 4.00 1.80
☐ 643 Rick Reichardt 6.00 2.70
☐ 644 Jim Stewart SP 12.00 5.50
☐ 645 Jim Maloney SP 14.00 6.25
☐ 646 Bobby Floyd SP 12.00 5.50
☐ 647 Juan Pizarro 8.00 3.60
☐ 648 Mets Rookies SP 25.00 11.00
Rich Folkers
Ted Martinez
John Matlack
☐ 649 Sparky Lyle SP 18.00 8.00
☐ 650 Rich Allen SP 40.00 18.00
☐ 651 Jerry Robertson SP 12.00 5.50
☐ 652 Atlanta Braves 8.00 3.60
Team Card
☐ 653 Russ Snyder SP 12.00 5.50
☐ 654 Don Shaw SP 12.00 5.50
☐ 655 Mike Epstein SP 12.00 5.50
☐ 656 Gerry Nyman SP 12.00 5.50
☐ 657 Jose Azcue 8.00 3.60
☐ 658 Paul Lindblad SP 12.00 5.50
☐ 659 Byron Browne SP 12.00 5.50
☐ 660 Ray Culp 8.00 3.60
☐ 661 Chuck Tanner MG SP 14.00 6.25
☐ 662 Mike Hedlund SP 12.00 5.50
☐ 663 Marv Staehle 8.00 3.60
☐ 664 Rookie Pitchers SP 14.00 6.25
Archie Reynolds
Bob Reynolds
Ken Reynolds
☐ 665 Ron Swoboda SP 18.00 8.00
☐ 666 Gene Brabender SP 12.00 5.50
☐ 667 Pete Ward 8.00 3.60
☐ 668 Gary Neibauer 8.00 3.60
☐ 669 Ike Brown SP 14.00 6.25
☐ 670 Bill Hands 8.00 3.60
☐ 671 Bill Voss SP 12.00 5.50
☐ 672 Ed Crosby SP 12.00 5.50
☐ 673 Gerry Janeski SP 12.00 5.50
☐ 674 Montreal Expos 12.00 5.50
Team Card
☐ 675 Dave Boswell 8.00 3.60
☐ 676 Tommie Reynolds 8.00 3.60
☐ 677 Jack DiLauro SP 12.00 5.50
☐ 678 George Thomas 8.00 3.60
☐ 679 Don O'Riley 8.00 3.60
☐ 680 Don Mincher SP 12.00 5.50
☐ 681 Bill Butler 8.00 3.60
☐ 682 Terry Harmon 8.00 3.60
☐ 683 Bill Burbach SP 12.00 5.50
☐ 684 Curt Motton 8.00 3.60
☐ 685 Moe Drabowsky 8.00 3.60
☐ 686 Chico Ruiz SP 12.00 5.50
☐ 687 Ron Taylor SP 12.00 5.50
☐ 688 Sparky Anderson MG SP 40.00 18.00
☐ 689 Frank Baker 8.00 3.60
☐ 690 Bob Moose 8.00 3.60
☐ 691 Bobby Heise 8.00 3.60
☐ 692 AL Rookie Pitchers SP 12.00 5.50
Hal Haydel
Rogelio Moret
Wayne Twitchell
☐ 693 Jose Pena SP 12.00 5.50
☐ 694 Rick Renick SP 12.00 5.50
☐ 695 Joe Niekro 9.00 4.00
☐ 696 Jerry Morales 8.00 3.60
☐ 697 Rickey Clark SP 12.00 5.50
☐ 698 Milwaukee Brewers SP 20.00 9.00
Team Card
☐ 699 Jim Britton 8.00 3.60
☐ 700 Boog Powell SP 30.00 13.50

☐ 701 Bob Garibaldi	8.00	3.60
☐ 702 Milt Ramirez	8.00	3.60
☐ 703 Mike Kekich	8.00	3.60
☐ 704 J.C. Martin SP	12.00	5.50
☐ 705 Dick Selma SP	12.00	5.50
☐ 706 Joe Foy SP	12.00	5.50
☐ 707 Fred Lasher	8.00	3.60
☐ 708 Russ Nagelson SP	12.00	5.50
☐ 709 Rookie Outfielders SP Dusty Baker Don Baylor Tom Paciorek	90.00	40.00
☐ 710 Sonny Siebert	8.00	3.60
☐ 711 Larry Stahl SP	12.00	5.50
☐ 712 Jose Martinez	8.00	3.60
☐ 713 Mike Marshall SP	14.00	6.25
☐ 714 Dick Williams MG SP	14.00	6.25
☐ 715 Horace Clarke SP	14.00	6.25
☐ 716 Dave Leonhard	8.00	3.60
☐ 717 Tommie Aaron SP	12.00	5.50
☐ 718 Billy Wynne	8.00	3.60
☐ 719 Jerry May SP	12.00	5.50
☐ 720 Matty Alou	9.00	4.00
☐ 721 John Morris	8.00	3.60
☐ 722 Houston Astros SP Team Card	20.00	9.00
☐ 723 Vicente Romo SP	12.00	5.50
☐ 724 Tom Tischinski SP	12.00	5.50
☐ 725 Gary Gentry SP	12.00	5.50
☐ 726 Paul Popovich	8.00	3.60
☐ 727 Ray Lamb SP	12.00	5.50
☐ 728 NL Rookie Outfielders Wayne Redmond Keith Lampard Bernie Williams	8.00	3.60
☐ 729 Dick Billings	8.00	3.60
☐ 730 Jim Rooker	8.00	3.60
☐ 731 Jim Qualls SP	12.00	5.50
☐ 732 Bob Reed	8.00	3.60
☐ 733 Lee Maye SP	12.00	5.50
☐ 734 Rob Gardner SP	12.00	5.50
☐ 735 Mike Shannon SP	14.00	6.25
☐ 736 Mel Queen SP	12.00	5.50
☐ 737 Preston Gomez SP MG	12.00	5.50
☐ 738 Russ Gibson SP	12.00	5.50
☐ 739 Barry Lersch SP	12.00	5.50
☐ 740 Luis Aparicio SP UER (Led AL in steals from 1965 to 1964, should be 1956 to 1964)	30.00	13.50
☐ 741 Skip Guinn	8.00	3.60
☐ 742 Kansas City Royals Team Card	12.00	5.50
☐ 743 John O'Donoghue SP	12.00	5.50
☐ 744 Chuck Manuel SP	12.00	5.50
☐ 745 Sandy Alomar SP	12.00	5.50
☐ 746 Andy Kosco	8.00	3.60
☐ 747 NL Rookie Pitchers Al Severinsen Scipio Spinks Balor Moore	8.00	3.60
☐ 748 John Purdin SP	12.00	5.50
☐ 749 Ken Szotkiewicz	8.00	3.60
☐ 750 Denny McLain SP	25.00	11.00
☐ 751 Al Weis SP	15.00	6.75
☐ 752 Dick Drago	12.00	2.90

1971 Topps Coins Inserts

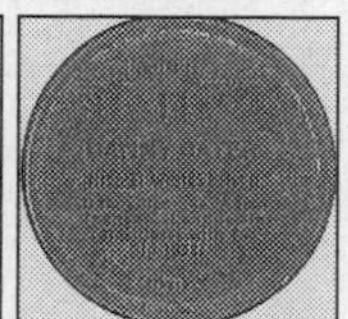

This full-color set of 153 coins, which were inserted into packs, contains the photo of the player surrounded by a colored band, which contains the player's name, his team, his position and several stars. The backs contain the coin number, short biographical data and the line "Collect the entire set of 153 coins." The set was evidently produced in three groups of 51 as coins 1-51 have brass backs, coins 52-102 have chrome backs and coins 103-153 have blue backs. In fact it has been verified that the coins were printed in three sheets of 51 coins comprised of three rows of 17 coins. Each coin measures approximately 1 1/2" in diameter.

	NRMT	VG-E
COMPLETE SET (153)	300.00	135.00
COMMON COIN (1-153)	.75	.35

☐ 1 Clarence Gaston	1.00	.45
☐ 2 Dave Johnson	1.00	.45
☐ 3 Jim Bunning	4.00	1.80
☐ 4 Jim Spencer	.75	.35
☐ 5 Felix Millan	.75	.35
☐ 6 Gerry Moses	.75	.35
☐ 7 Ferguson Jenkins	4.00	1.80
☐ 8 Felipe Alou	1.00	.45
☐ 9 Jim McGlothlin	.75	.35
☐ 10 Dick McAuliffe	.75	.35
☐ 11 Joe Torre	3.00	1.35
☐ 12 Jim Perry	1.00	.45
☐ 13 Bobby Bonds	2.00	.90
☐ 14 Danny Cater	.75	.35
☐ 15 Bill Mazeroski	1.50	.70
☐ 16 Luis Aparicio	4.00	1.80
☐ 17 Doug Rader	.75	.35
☐ 18 Vada Pinson	1.50	.70
☐ 19 John Bateman	.75	.35
☐ 20 Lew Krausse	.75	.35
☐ 21 Billy Grabarkewitz	.75	.35
☐ 22 Frank Howard	1.50	.70
☐ 23 Jerry Koosman	1.50	.70
☐ 24 Rod Carew	6.00	2.70
☐ 25 Al Ferrara	.75	.35
☐ 26 Dave McNally	1.00	.45
☐ 27 Jim Hickman	.75	.35
☐ 28 Sandy Alomar	1.00	.45
☐ 29 Lee May	1.00	.45
☐ 30 Rico Petrocelli	1.00	.45
☐ 31 Don Money	.75	.35
☐ 32 Jim Rooker	.75	.35
☐ 33 Dick Dietz	.75	.35
☐ 34 Roy White	1.00	.45
☐ 35 Carl Morton	.75	.35
☐ 36 Walt Williams	.75	.35
☐ 37 Phil Niekro	4.00	1.80
☐ 38 Bill Freehan	1.00	.45
☐ 39 Julian Javier	.75	.35
☐ 40 Rick Monday	1.00	.45
☐ 41 Don Wilson	.75	.35
☐ 42 Ray Fosse	1.00	.45
☐ 43 Art Shamsky	.75	.35
☐ 44 Ted Savage	.75	.35
☐ 45 Claude Osteen	1.00	.45
☐ 46 Ed Brinkman	.75	.35
☐ 47 Matty Alou	1.00	.45
☐ 48 Bob Oliver	.75	.35
☐ 49 Danny Coombs	.75	.35
☐ 50 Frank Robinson	8.00	3.60
☐ 51 Randy Hundley	.75	.35
☐ 52 Cesar Tovar	1.00	.45
☐ 53 Wayne Simpson	.75	.35
☐ 54 Bobby Murcer	1.50	.70
☐ 55 Carl Taylor	.75	.35
☐ 56 Tommy John	2.00	.90
☐ 57 Willie McCovey	6.00	2.70
☐ 58 Carl Yastrzemski	8.00	3.60
☐ 59 Bob Bailey	.75	.35
☐ 60 Clyde Wright	.75	.35
☐ 61 Orlando Cepeda	2.00	.90
☐ 62 Al Kaline	8.00	3.60
☐ 63 Bob Gibson	8.00	3.60
☐ 64 Bert Campaneris	1.00	.45
☐ 65 Ted Sizemore	.75	.35
☐ 66 Duke Sims	.75	.35
☐ 67 Bud Harrelson	.75	.35
☐ 68 Gerald McNertney	.75	.35
☐ 69 Jim Wynn	1.00	.45
☐ 70 Dick Bosman	.75	.35
☐ 71 Roberto Clemente	20.00	9.00
☐ 72 Rich Reese	.75	.35
☐ 73 Gaylord Perry	4.00	1.80
☐ 74 Boog Powell	2.00	.90
☐ 75 Billy Williams	4.00	1.80
☐ 76 Bill Melton	.75	.35
☐ 77 Nate Colbert	.75	.35
☐ 78 Reggie Smith	1.00	.45
☐ 79 Deron Johnson	.75	.35
☐ 80 Jim Hunter	4.00	1.80
☐ 81 Bobby Tolan	1.00	.45
☐ 82 Jim Northrup	.75	.35
☐ 83 Ron Fairly	1.00	.45
☐ 84 Alex Johnson	.75	.35
☐ 85 Pat Jarvis	.75	.35
☐ 86 Sam McDowell	1.00	.45
☐ 87 Lou Brock	6.00	2.70
☐ 88 Danny Walton	.75	.35
☐ 89 Denis Menke	.75	.35
☐ 90 Jim Palmer	6.00	2.70
☐ 91 Tommy Agee	1.00	.45
☐ 92 Duane Josephson	.75	.35
☐ 93 Willie Davis	1.00	.45
☐ 94 Mel Stottlemyre	1.00	.45
☐ 95 Ron Santo	1.50	.70
☐ 96 Amos Otis	1.00	.45
☐ 97 Ken Henderson	.75	.35
☐ 98 George Scott	1.00	.45
☐ 99 Dock Ellis	1.00	.45
☐ 100 Harmon Killebrew	6.00	2.70
☐ 101 Pete Rose	10.00	4.50
☐ 102 Rick Reichardt	.75	.35
☐ 103 Cleon Jones	.75	.35
☐ 104 Ron Perranoski	.75	.35
☐ 105 Tony Perez	2.00	.90
☐ 106 Mickey Lolich	2.00	.90
☐ 107 Tim McCarver	1.50	.70
☐ 108 Reggie Jackson	10.00	4.50
☐ 109 Chris Cannizzaro	.75	.35
☐ 110 Steve Hargan	.75	.35
☐ 111 Rusty Staub	2.00	.90
☐ 112 Andy Messersmith	1.00	.45
☐ 113 Rico Carty	1.00	.45
☐ 114 Brooks Robinson	8.00	3.60
☐ 115 Steve Carlton	8.00	3.60
☐ 116 Mike Hegan	.75	.35
☐ 117 Joe Morgan	6.00	2.70
☐ 118 Thurman Munson	6.00	2.70
☐ 119 Don Kessinger	.75	.35
☐ 120 Joel Horlen	.75	.35
☐ 121 Wes Parker	1.00	.45
☐ 122 Sonny Siebert	.75	.35
☐ 123 Willie Stargell	6.00	2.70
☐ 124 Aurelio Rodriguez	.75	.35
☐ 125 Juan Marichal	6.00	2.70
☐ 126 Mike Epstein	.75	.35
☐ 127 Tom Seaver	10.00	4.50
☐ 128 Tony Oliva	2.00	.90
☐ 129 Jim Merritt	.75	.35
☐ 130 Willie Horton	1.00	.45
☐ 131 Rick Wise	.75	.35
☐ 132 Sal Bando	1.00	.45
☐ 133 Ollie Brown	.75	.35
☐ 134 Ken Harrelson	1.00	.45
☐ 135 Mack Jones	.75	.35
☐ 136 Jim Fregosi	1.00	.45
☐ 137 Hank Aaron	12.50	5.50
☐ 138 Fritz Peterson	.75	.35
☐ 139 Joe Hague	.75	.35
☐ 140 Tommy Harper	.75	.35
☐ 141 Larry Dierker	.75	.35
☐ 142 Tony Conigliaro	1.50	.70
☐ 143 Glenn Beckert	.75	.35
☐ 144 Carlos May	.75	.35
☐ 145 Don Sutton	3.00	1.35
☐ 146 Paul Casanova	.75	.35
☐ 147 Bob Moose	.75	.35
☐ 148 Chico Cardenas	.75	.35
☐ 149 Johnny Bench	10.00	4.50
☐ 150 Mike Cuellar	1.00	.45
☐ 151 Donn Clendenon	.75	.35
☐ 152 Lou Piniella	2.00	.90
☐ 153 Willie Mays	15.00	6.75

1971 Topps Greatest Moments

The cards in this 55-card set measure 2 1/2" by 4 3/4". The 1971 Topps Greatest Moments set contains numbered cards depicting specific career highlights of current players. The obverses are black bordered and contain a small cameo picture of the left side; a deckle-bordered black and white action photo dominates the rest of the card. The backs are designed in newspaper style. Sometimes found in uncut sheets, this test set was retailed in gum packs on a very limited basis. Double prints (DP) are listed in the checklist below; there were 22 double prints and 33 single prints.

	NRMT	VG-E
COMPLETE SET (55)	1350.00	600.00
COMMON CARD (1-55)	20.00	9.00
COMMON DP	5.00	2.20

☐ 1 Thurman Munson DP	30.00	13.50
☐ 2 Hoyt Wilhelm	30.00	13.50
☐ 3 Rico Carty	20.00	9.00
☐ 4 Carl Morton DP	5.00	2.20
☐ 5 Sal Bando DP	5.00	2.20
☐ 6 Bert Campaneris DP	5.00	2.20
☐ 7 Jim Kaat	25.00	11.00

☐ 8 Harmon Killebrew	50.00	22.00
☐ 9 Brooks Robinson	75.00	34.00
☐ 10 Jim Perry	20.00	9.00
☐ 11 Tony Oliva	25.00	11.00
☐ 12 Vada Pinson	25.00	11.00
☐ 13 Johnny Bench	125.00	55.00
☐ 14 Tony Perez	30.00	13.50
☐ 15 Pete Rose DP	75.00	34.00
☐ 16 Jim Fregosi DP	5.00	2.20
☐ 17 Alex Johnson DP	5.00	2.20
☐ 18 Clyde Wright DP	5.00	2.20
☐ 19 Al Kaline DP	30.00	13.50
☐ 20 Denny McLain	25.00	11.00
☐ 21 Jim Northrup	20.00	9.00
☐ 22 Bill Freehan	20.00	9.00
☐ 23 Mickey Lolich	25.00	11.00
☐ 24 Bob Gibson DP	20.00	9.00
☐ 25 Tim McCarver DP	5.00	2.20
☐ 26 Orlando Cepeda DP	7.50	3.40
☐ 27 Lou Brock DP	20.00	9.00
☐ 28 Nate Colbert DP	5.00	2.20
☐ 29 Maury Wills	25.00	11.00
☐ 30 Wes Parker	20.00	9.00
☐ 31 Jim Wynn	20.00	9.00
☐ 32 Larry Dierker	20.00	9.00
☐ 33 Bill Melton	20.00	9.00
☐ 34 Joe Morgan	35.00	16.00
☐ 35 Rusty Staub	25.00	11.00
☐ 36 Ernie Banks DP	30.00	13.50
☐ 37 Billy Williams	35.00	16.00
☐ 38 Lou Piniella	25.00	11.00
☐ 39 Rico Petrocelli DP	5.00	2.20
☐ 40 Carl Yastrzemski DP	50.00	22.00
☐ 41 Willie Mays DP	75.00	34.00
☐ 42 Tommy Harper	20.00	9.00
☐ 43 Jim Bunning DP	15.00	6.75
☐ 44 Fritz Peterson	20.00	9.00
☐ 45 Roy White	20.00	9.00
☐ 46 Bobby Murcer	20.00	9.00
☐ 47 Reggie Jackson	125.00	55.00
☐ 48 Frank Howard	25.00	11.00
☐ 49 Dick Bosman	20.00	9.00
☐ 50 Sam McDowell DP	5.00	2.20
☐ 51 Luis Aparicio DP	15.00	6.75
☐ 52 Willie McCovey DP	20.00	9.00
☐ 53 Joe Pepitone	20.00	9.00
☐ 54 Jerry Grote	20.00	9.00
☐ 55 Bud Harrelson	20.00	9.00

1971 Topps Super

The cards in this 63-card set measure 3 1/8" by 5 1/4". The obverse format of the Topps Super set of 1971 is identical to that of the 1970 set, that is, a borderless color photograph with a facsimile autograph printed on it. The backs are enlargements of the respective player's cards of the 1971 regular baseball issue. There are no reported scarcities in the set. Just as in 1970, this set was issued in three-card wax packs.

	NRMT	VG-E
COMPLETE SET (63)	200.00	90.00
COMMON CARD (1-63)	1.00	.45
☐ 1 Reggie Smith	1.50	.70
☐ 2 Gaylord Perry	3.00	1.35
☐ 3 Ted Savage	1.00	.45
☐ 4 Donn Clendenon	1.00	.45
☐ 5 Boog Powell	2.00	.90
☐ 6 Tony Perez	3.00	1.35
☐ 7 Dick Bosman	1.00	.45
☐ 8 Alex Johnson	1.00	.45
☐ 9 Rusty Staub	2.00	.90
☐ 10 Mel Stottlemyre	1.25	.55
☐ 11 Tony Oliva	2.00	.90
☐ 12 Bill Freehan	1.50	.70
☐ 13 Fritz Peterson	1.00	.45
☐ 14 Wes Parker	1.25	.55
☐ 15 Cesar Cedeno	1.25	.55
☐ 16 Sam McDowell	1.00	.45
☐ 17 Frank Howard	1.50	.70
☐ 18 Dave McNally	1.25	.55
☐ 19 Rico Petrocelli	1.25	.55
☐ 20 Pete Rose	25.00	11.00
☐ 21 Luke Walker	1.00	.45
☐ 22 Nate Colbert	1.00	.45
☐ 23 Luis Aparicio	3.00	1.35
☐ 24 Jim Perry	1.25	.55
☐ 25 Lou Brock	5.00	2.20
☐ 26 Roy White	1.00	.45
☐ 27 Claude Osteen	1.00	.45
☐ 28 Carl Morton	1.00	.45
☐ 29 Rico Carty	1.25	.55
☐ 30 Larry Dierker	1.00	.45
☐ 31 Bert Campaneris	1.00	.45
☐ 32 Johnny Bench	10.00	4.50
☐ 33 Felix Millan	1.00	.45
☐ 34 Tim McCarver	2.00	.90
☐ 35 Ron Santo	2.00	.90
☐ 36 Tommie Agee	1.00	.45
☐ 37 Roberto Clemente	35.00	16.00
☐ 38 Reggie Jackson	15.00	6.75
☐ 39 Clyde Wright	1.00	.45
☐ 40 Rich Allen	2.00	.90
☐ 41 Curt Flood	1.25	.55
☐ 42 Ferguson Jenkins	3.00	1.35
☐ 43 Willie Stargell	4.00	1.80
☐ 44 Hank Aaron	15.00	6.75
☐ 45 Amos Otis	1.25	.55
☐ 46 Willie McCovey	4.00	1.80
☐ 47 Bill Melton	1.00	.45
☐ 48 Bob Gibson	4.00	1.80
☐ 49 Carl Yastrzemski	10.00	4.50
☐ 50 Glenn Beckert	1.00	.45
☐ 51 Ray Fosse	1.00	.45
☐ 52 Cito Gaston	1.50	.70
☐ 53 Tom Seaver	10.00	4.50
☐ 54 Al Kaline	8.00	3.60
☐ 55 Jim Northrup	1.00	.45
☐ 56 Willie Mays	18.00	8.00
☐ 57 Sal Bando	1.00	.45
☐ 58 Deron Johnson	1.00	.45
☐ 59 Brooks Robinson	8.00	3.60
☐ 60 Harmon Killebrew	4.00	1.80
☐ 61 Joe Torre	3.00	1.35
☐ 62 Lou Piniella	1.50	.70
☐ 63 Tommy Harper	1.00	.45

1972 Topps

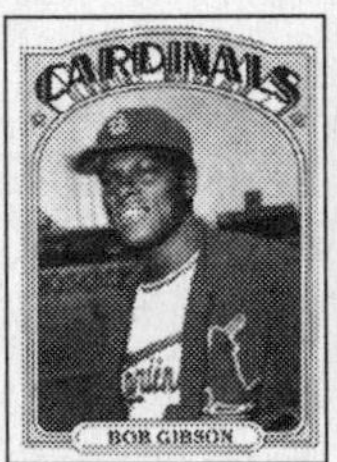

The cards in this 787-card set measure 2 1/2" by 3 1/2". The 1972 Topps set contained the most cards ever for a Topps set to that point in time. Features appearing for the first time were "Boyhood Photos" (341-348/491-498), Awards and Trophy cards (621-626), "In Action" (distributed throughout the set), and "Traded Cards" (751-757). Other subsets included League Leaders (85-96), Playoffs cards (221-222), and World Series cards (223-230). The curved lines of the color picture are a departure from the rectangular designs of other years. There is a series of intermediate scarcity (526-656) and the usual high numbers (657-787). The backs of cards 692, 694, 696, 700, 706 and 710 form a picture back of Tom Seaver. The backs of cards 698, 702, 704, 708, 712, 714 form a picture back of Tony Oliva. As in previous years, cards were issued in a variety of ways including ten-card dime wax packs. The key Rookie Card in this set is Carlton Fisk.

	NRMT	VG-E
COMPLETE SET (787)	1700.00	750.00
COMMON CARD (1-132)	.60	.25
COMMON CARD (133-263)	1.00	.45
COMMON CARD (264-394)	1.25	.55
COMMON CARD (395-525)	1.50	.70
COMMON CARD (526-656)	4.00	1.80
COMMON CARD (657-787)	12.00	5.50
WRAPPER (10-CENT)	15.00	6.75
☐ 1 Pittsburgh Pirates Team Card	8.00	2.90
☐ 2 Ray Culp	.60	.25
☐ 3 Bob Tolan	.60	.25
☐ 4 Checklist 1-132	4.00	.80
☐ 5 John Bateman	.60	.25
☐ 6 Fred Scherman	.60	.25
☐ 7 Enzo Hernandez	.60	.25
☐ 8 Ron Swoboda	1.25	.55
☐ 9 Stan Williams	.60	.25
☐ 10 Amos Otis	1.25	.55
☐ 11 Bobby Valentine	1.00	.45
☐ 12 Jose Cardenal	.60	.25
☐ 13 Joe Grzenda	.60	.25
☐ 14 Phillies Rookies	.60	.25
Pete Koegel		
Mike Anderson		
Wayne Twitchell		
☐ 15 Walt Williams	.60	.25
☐ 16 Mike Jorgensen	.60	.25
☐ 17 Dave Duncan	.60	.25
☐ 18A Juan Pizarro (Yellow underline C and S of Cubs)	.60	.25
☐ 18B Juan Pizarro (Green underline C and S of Cubs)	5.00	2.20
☐ 19 Billy Cowan	.60	.25
☐ 20 Don Wilson	.60	.25
☐ 21 Atlanta Braves Team Card	1.25	.55
☐ 22 Rob Gardner	.60	.25
☐ 23 Ted Kubiak	.60	.25
☐ 24 Ted Ford	.60	.25
☐ 25 Bill Singer	.60	.25
☐ 26 Andy Etchebarren	.60	.25
☐ 27 Bob Johnson	.60	.25
☐ 28 Twins Rookies	.60	.25
Bob Gebhard		
Steve Brye		
Hal Haydel		
☐ 29A Bill Bonham (Yellow underline C and S of Cubs)	.60	.25
☐ 29B Bill Bonham (Green underline C and S of Cubs)	5.00	2.20
☐ 30 Rico Petrocelli	1.00	.45
☐ 31 Cleon Jones	1.25	.55
☐ 32 Cleon Jones IA	.60	.25
☐ 33 Billy Martin MG	4.00	1.80
☐ 34 Billy Martin IA	2.00	.90
☐ 35 Jerry Johnson	.60	.25
☐ 36 Jerry Johnson IA	.60	.25
☐ 37 Carl Yastrzemski	10.00	4.50
☐ 38 Carl Yastrzemski IA	6.00	2.70
☐ 39 Bob Barton	.60	.25
☐ 40 Bob Barton IA	.60	.25
☐ 41 Tommy Davis	1.00	.45
☐ 42 Tommy Davis IA	.60	.25
☐ 43 Rick Wise	1.25	.55
☐ 44 Rick Wise IA	.60	.25
☐ 45A Glenn Beckert (Yellow underline C and S of Cubs)	1.25	.55
☐ 45B Glenn Beckert (Green underline C and S of Cubs)	5.00	2.20
☐ 46 Glenn Beckert IA	.60	.25
☐ 47 John Ellis	.60	.25
☐ 48 John Ellis IA	.60	.25
☐ 49 Willie Mays	25.00	11.00
☐ 50 Willie Mays IA	14.00	6.25
☐ 51 Harmon Killebrew	7.00	3.10
☐ 52 Harmon Killebrew IA	3.50	1.55
☐ 53 Bud Harrelson	1.00	.45
☐ 54 Bud Harrelson IA	.60	.25
☐ 55 Clyde Wright	.60	.25
☐ 56 Rich Chiles	.60	.25
☐ 57 Bob Oliver	.60	.25
☐ 58 Ernie McAnally	.60	.25
☐ 59 Fred Stanley	.60	.25
☐ 60 Manny Sanguillen	1.00	.45
☐ 61 Cubs Rookies	1.00	.45
Burt Hooton		
Gene Hiser		
Earl Stephenson		
☐ 62 Angel Mangual	.60	.25
☐ 63 Duke Sims	.60	.25
☐ 64 Pete Broberg	.60	.25
☐ 65 Cesar Cedeno	1.00	.45
☐ 66 Ray Corbin	.60	.25
☐ 67 Red Schoendienst MG	1.00	.45
☐ 68 Jim York	.60	.25
☐ 69 Roger Freed	.60	.25
☐ 70 Mike Cuellar	1.25	.55
☐ 71 California Angels Team Card	1.50	.70
☐ 72 Bruce Kison	.60	.25
☐ 73 Steve Huntz	.60	.25
☐ 74 Cecil Upshaw	.60	.25
☐ 75 Bert Campaneris	1.00	.45
☐ 76 Don Carrithers	.60	.25

☐ 77 Ron Theobald .60 .25
☐ 78 Steve Arlin .60 .25
☐ 79 Red Sox Rookies 60.00 27.00
Mike Garman
Cecil Cooper
Carlton Fisk
☐ 80 Tony Perez 4.00 1.80
☐ 81 Mike Hedlund .60 .25
☐ 82 Ron Woods .60 .25
☐ 83 Dalton Jones .60 .25
☐ 84 Vince Colbert .60 .25
☐ 85 NL Batting Leaders 1.75 .80
Joe Torre
Ralph Garr
Glenn Beckert
☐ 86 AL Batting Leaders 1.75 .80
Tony Oliva
Bobby Murcer
Merv Rettenmund
☐ 87 NL RBI Leaders 3.50 1.55
Joe Torre
Willie Stargell
Hank Aaron
☐ 88 AL RBI Leaders 3.00 1.35
Harmon Killebrew
Frank Robinson
Reggie Smith
☐ 89 NL Home Run Leaders 3.00 1.35
Willie Stargell
Hank Aaron
Lee May
☐ 90 AL Home Run Leaders 2.50 1.10
Bill Melton
Norm Cash
Reggie Jackson
☐ 91 NL ERA Leaders 2.50 1.10
Tom Seaver
Dave Roberts UER
(Photo actually
Danny Coombs)
Don Wilson
☐ 92 AL ERA Leaders 2.50 1.10
Vida Blue
Wilbur Wood
Jim Palmer
☐ 93 NL Pitching Leaders 4.00 1.80
Fergie Jenkins
Steve Carlton
Al Downing
Tom Seaver
☐ 94 AL Pitching Leaders 1.75 .80
Mickey Lolich
Vida Blue
Wilbur Wood
☐ 95 NL Strikeout Leaders 3.00 1.35
Tom Seaver
Fergie Jenkins
Bill Stoneman
☐ 96 AL Strikeout Leaders 1.75 .80
Mickey Lolich
Vida Blue
Joe Coleman
☐ 97 Tom Kelley .60 .25
☐ 98 Chuck Tanner MG 1.00 .45
☐ 99 Ross Grimsley .60 .25
☐ 100 Frank Robinson 8.00 3.60
☐ 101 Astros Rookies 1.50 .70
Bill Greif
J.R. Richard
Ray Busse
☐ 102 Lloyd Allen .60 .25
☐ 103 Checklist 133-263 4.00 .80
☐ 104 Toby Harrah 1.50 .70
☐ 105 Gary Gentry .60 .25
☐ 106 Milwaukee Brewers 1.25 .55
Team Card
☐ 107 Jose Cruz 1.50 .70
☐ 108 Gary Waslewski .60 .25
☐ 109 Jerry May .60 .25
☐ 110 Ron Hunt .60 .25
☐ 111 Jim Grant .60 .25
☐ 112 Greg Luzinski 1.50 .70
☐ 113 Rogelio Moret .60 .25
☐ 114 Bill Buckner 1.50 .70
☐ 115 Jim Fregosi 1.00 .45
☐ 116 Ed Farmer .60 .25
☐ 117A Cleo James .60 .25
(Yellow underline
C and S of Cubs)
☐ 117B Cleo James 5.00 2.20
(Green underline
C and S of Cubs)
☐ 118 Skip Lockwood .60 .25
☐ 119 Marty Perez .60 .25
☐ 120 Bill Freehan 1.00 .45
☐ 121 Ed Sprague .60 .25
☐ 122 Larry Biittner .60 .25
☐ 123 Ed Acosta .60 .25
☐ 124 Yankees Rookies .60 .25
Alan Closter
Rusty Torres
Roger Hambright
☐ 125 Dave Cash 1.25 .55
☐ 126 Bart Johnson .60 .25
☐ 127 Duffy Dyer .60 .25
☐ 128 Eddie Watt .60 .25
☐ 129 Charlie Fox MG .60 .25
☐ 130 Bob Gibson 8.00 3.60
☐ 131 Jim Nettles .60 .25
☐ 132 Joe Morgan 6.00 2.70
☐ 133 Joe Keough 1.00 .45
☐ 134 Carl Morton 1.00 .45
☐ 135 Vada Pinson 1.50 .70
☐ 136 Darrel Chaney 1.00 .45
☐ 137 Dick Williams MG 1.50 .70
☐ 138 Mike Kekich 1.00 .45
☐ 139 Tim McCarver 2.00 .90
☐ 140 Pat Dobson 2.00 .90
☐ 141 Mets Rookies 2.00 .90
Buzz Capra
Lee Stanton
Jon Matlack
☐ 142 Chris Chambliss 4.00 1.80
☐ 143 Garry Jestadt 1.00 .45
☐ 144 Marty Pattin 1.00 .45
☐ 145 Don Kessinger 1.50 .70
☐ 146 Steve Kealey 1.00 .45
☐ 147 Dave Kingman 5.00 2.20
☐ 148 Dick Billings 1.00 .45
☐ 149 Gary Neibauer 1.00 .45
☐ 150 Norm Cash 2.00 .90
☐ 151 Jim Brewer 1.00 .45
☐ 152 Gene Clines 1.00 .45
☐ 153 Rick Auerbach 1.00 .45
☐ 154 Ted Simmons 3.00 1.35
☐ 155 Larry Dierker 2.00 .90
☐ 156 Minnesota Twins 2.00 .90
Team Card
☐ 157 Don Gullett 1.00 .45
☐ 158 Jerry Kenney 1.00 .45
☐ 159 John Boccabella 1.00 .45
☐ 160 Andy Messersmith 2.00 .90
☐ 161 Brock Davis 1.00 .45
☐ 162 Brewers Rookies UER 2.00 .90
Jerry Bell
Darrell Porter
Bob Reynolds
(Porter and Bell
photos switched)
☐ 163 Tug McGraw 2.00 .90
☐ 164 Tug McGraw IA 2.00 .90
☐ 165 Chris Speier 2.00 .90
☐ 166 Chris Speier IA 2.00 .90
☐ 167 Deron Johnson 1.00 .45
☐ 168 Deron Johnson IA 1.00 .45
☐ 169 Vida Blue 2.00 .90
☐ 170 Vida Blue IA 2.00 .90
☐ 171 Darrell Evans 2.00 .90
☐ 172 Darrell Evans IA 2.00 .90
☐ 173 Clay Kirby 1.00 .45
☐ 174 Clay Kirby IA 1.00 .45
☐ 175 Tom Haller 1.00 .45
☐ 176 Tom Haller IA 1.00 .45
☐ 177 Paul Schaal 1.00 .45
☐ 178 Paul Schaal IA 1.00 .45
☐ 179 Dock Ellis 1.00 .45
☐ 180 Dock Ellis IA 1.00 .45
☐ 181 Ed Kranepool 1.00 .45
☐ 182 Ed Kranepool IA 1.00 .45
☐ 183 Bill Melton 1.00 .45
☐ 184 Bill Melton IA 1.00 .45
☐ 185 Ron Bryant 1.00 .45
☐ 186 Ron Bryant IA 1.00 .45
☐ 187 Gates Brown 1.00 .45
☐ 188 Frank Lucchesi MG 1.00 .45
☐ 189 Gene Tenace 1.50 .70
☐ 190 Dave Giusti 1.00 .45
☐ 191 Jeff Burroughs 2.00 .90
☐ 192 Chicago Cubs 2.00 .90
Team Card
☐ 193 Kurt Bevacqua 1.00 .45
☐ 194 Fred Norman 1.00 .45
☐ 195 Orlando Cepeda 2.00 .90
☐ 196 Mel Queen 1.00 .45
☐ 197 Johnny Briggs 1.00 .45
☐ 198 Dodgers Rookies 4.00 1.80
Charlie Hough
Bob O'Brien
Mike Strahler
☐ 199 Mike Fiore 1.00 .45
☐ 200 Lou Brock 7.00 3.10
☐ 201 Phil Roof 1.00 .45
☐ 202 Scipio Spinks 1.00 .45
☐ 203 Ron Blomberg 1.00 .45
☐ 204 Tommy Helms 1.00 .45
☐ 205 Dick Drago 1.00 .45
☐ 206 Dal Maxvill 1.00 .45
☐ 207 Tom Egan 1.00 .45
☐ 208 Milt Pappas 2.00 .90
☐ 209 Joe Rudi 1.50 .70
☐ 210 Denny McLain 1.50 .70
☐ 211 Gary Sutherland 1.00 .45
☐ 212 Grant Jackson 1.00 .45
☐ 213 Angels Rookies 1.00 .45
Billy Parker
Art Kusnyer
Tom Silverio
☐ 214 Mike McQueen 1.00 .45
☐ 215 Alex Johnson 2.00 .90
☐ 216 Joe Niekro 2.00 .90
☐ 217 Roger Metzger 1.00 .45
☐ 218 Eddie Kasko MG 1.00 .45
☐ 219 Rennie Stennett 2.00 .90
☐ 220 Jim Perry 2.00 .90
☐ 221 NL Playoffs 1.50 .70
Bucs champs
☐ 222 Brooks Robinson ALCS 3.00 1.35
☐ 223 Dave McNally WS 1.75 .80
☐ 224 Dave Johnson WS 1.75 .80
Mark Belanger
☐ 225 Manny Sanguillen WS 1.75 .80
☐ 226 Roberto Clemente WS 8.00 3.60
☐ 227 Nellie Briles WS 1.75 .80
☐ 228 Frank Robinson WS 2.50 1.10
Manny Sanguillen
☐ 229 Steve Blass WS 1.75 .80
☐ 230 World Series Summary 1.75 .80
(Pirates celebrate)
☐ 231 Casey Cox 1.00 .45
☐ 232 Giants Rookies 1.00 .45
Chris Arnold
Jim Barr
Dave Rader
☐ 233 Jay Johnstone 2.00 .90
☐ 234 Ron Taylor 1.00 .45
☐ 235 Merv Rettenmund 1.00 .45
☐ 236 Jim McGlothlin 1.00 .45
☐ 237 New York Yankees 2.00 .90
Team Card
☐ 238 Leron Lee 1.00 .45
☐ 239 Tom Timmermann 1.00 .45
☐ 240 Rich Allen 2.00 .90
☐ 241 Rollie Fingers 5.00 2.20
☐ 242 Don Mincher 2.00 .90
☐ 243 Frank Linzy 1.00 .45
☐ 244 Steve Braun 1.00 .45
☐ 245 Tommie Agee 1.50 .70
☐ 246 Tom Burgmeier 1.00 .45
☐ 247 Milt May 1.00 .45
☐ 248 Tom Bradley 1.00 .45
☐ 249 Harry Walker MG 1.00 .45
☐ 250 Boog Powell 2.00 .90
☐ 251 Checklist 264-394 6.00 1.20
☐ 252 Ken Reynolds 1.00 .45
☐ 253 Sandy Alomar 1.50 .70
☐ 254 Boots Day 1.00 .45
☐ 255 Jim Lonborg 2.00 .90
☐ 256 George Foster 2.50 1.10
☐ 257 Tigers Rookies 1.00 .45
Jim Foor
Tim Hosley
Paul Jata
☐ 258 Randy Hundley 1.50 .70
☐ 259 Sparky Lyle 2.00 .90
☐ 260 Ralph Garr 2.00 .90
☐ 261 Steve Mingori 1.00 .45
☐ 262 San Diego Padres 2.00 .90
Team Card
☐ 263 Felipe Alou 1.50 .70
☐ 264 Tommy John 1.50 .70
☐ 265 Wes Parker 1.50 .70
☐ 266 Bobby Bolin 1.25 .55
☐ 267 Dave Concepcion 3.00 1.35
☐ 268 A's Rookies 1.25 .55
Dwain Anderson
Chris Floethe
☐ 269 Don Hahn 1.25 .55
☐ 270 Jim Palmer 8.00 3.60
☐ 271 Ken Rudolph 1.25 .55
☐ 272 Mickey Rivers 1.50 .70
☐ 273 Bobby Floyd 1.25 .55
☐ 274 Al Severinsen 1.25 .55
☐ 275 Cesar Tovar 1.25 .55
☐ 276 Gene Mauch MG 2.00 .90
☐ 277 Elliott Maddox 1.25 .55
☐ 278 Dennis Higgins 1.25 .55
☐ 279 Larry Brown 1.25 .55
☐ 280 Willie McCovey 7.00 3.10
☐ 281 Bill Parsons 1.25 .55
☐ 282 Houston Astros 2.00 .90
Team Card

☐ 283 Darrell Brandon 1.25 .55
☐ 284 Ike Brown 1.25 .55
☐ 285 Gaylord Perry 6.00 2.70
☐ 286 Gene Alley 2.00 .90
☐ 287 Jim Hardin 1.25 .55
☐ 288 Johnny Jeter 1.25 .55
☐ 289 Syd O'Brien 1.25 .55
☐ 290 Sonny Siebert 1.25 .55
☐ 291 Hal McRae 1.50 .70
☐ 292 Hal McRae IA 2.00 .90
☐ 293 Dan Frisella 1.25 .55
☐ 294 Dan Frisella IA 1.25 .55
☐ 295 Dick Dietz 1.25 .55
☐ 296 Dick Dietz IA 1.25 .55
☐ 297 Claude Osteen 2.00 .90
☐ 298 Claude Osteen IA 1.25 .55
☐ 299 Hank Aaron 40.00 18.00
☐ 300 Hank Aaron IA 20.00 9.00
☐ 301 George Mitterwald 1.25 .55
☐ 302 George Mitterwald IA 1.25 .55
☐ 303 Joe Pepitone 1.50 .70
☐ 304 Joe Pepitone IA 1.25 .55
☐ 305 Ken Boswell 1.25 .55
☐ 306 Ken Boswell IA 1.25 .55
☐ 307 Steve Renko 1.25 .55
☐ 308 Steve Renko IA 1.25 .55
☐ 309 Roberto Clemente 50.00 22.00
☐ 310 Roberto Clemente IA 25.00 11.00
☐ 311 Clay Carroll 1.25 .55
☐ 312 Clay Carroll IA 1.25 .55
☐ 313 Luis Aparicio 4.00 1.80
☐ 314 Luis Aparicio IA 1.75 .80
☐ 315 Paul Splittorff 1.25 .55
☐ 316 Cardinals Rookies 2.00 .90
Jim Bibby
Jorge Roque
Santiago Guzman
☐ 317 Rich Hand 1.25 .55
☐ 318 Sonny Jackson 1.25 .55
☐ 319 Aurelio Rodriguez 1.25 .55
☐ 320 Steve Blass 2.00 .90
☐ 321 Joe Lahoud 1.25 .55
☐ 322 Jose Pena 1.25 .55
☐ 323 Earl Weaver MG 1.50 .70
☐ 324 Mike Ryan 1.25 .55
☐ 325 Mel Stottlemyre 1.50 .70
☐ 326 Pat Kelly 1.25 .55
☐ 327 Steve Stone 1.50 .70
☐ 328 Boston Red Sox 2.00 .90
Team Card
☐ 329 Roy Foster 1.25 .55
☐ 330 Jim Hunter 4.00 1.80
☐ 331 Stan Swanson 1.25 .55
☐ 332 Buck Martinez 1.25 .55
☐ 333 Steve Barber 1.25 .55
☐ 334 Rangers Rookies 1.25 .55
Bill Fahey
Jim Mason
Tom Ragland
☐ 335 Bill Hands 1.25 .55
☐ 336 Marty Martinez 1.25 .55
☐ 337 Mike Kilkenny 1.25 .55
☐ 338 Bob Grich 1.50 .70
☐ 339 Ron Cook 1.25 .55
☐ 340 Roy White 1.50 .70
☐ 341 Joe Torre KP 1.25 .55
☐ 342 Wilbur Wood KP 1.25 .55
☐ 343 Willie Stargell KP 1.50 .70
☐ 344 Dave McNally KP 1.25 .55
☐ 345 Rick Wise KP 1.25 .55
☐ 346 Jim Fregosi KP 1.25 .55
☐ 347 Tom Seaver KP 3.00 1.35
☐ 348 Sal Bando KP 1.25 .55
☐ 349 Al Fitzmorris 1.25 .55
☐ 350 Frank Howard 1.50 .70
☐ 351 Braves Rookies 2.00 .90
Tom House
Rick Kester
Jimmy Britton
☐ 352 Dave LaRoche 1.25 .55
☐ 353 Art Shamsky 1.25 .55
☐ 354 Tom Murphy 1.25 .55
☐ 355 Bob Watson 2.00 .90
☐ 356 Gerry Moses 1.25 .55
☐ 357 Woody Fryman 1.25 .55
☐ 358 Sparky Anderson MG 3.00 1.35
☐ 359 Don Pavletich 1.25 .55
☐ 360 Dave Roberts 1.25 .55
☐ 361 Mike Andrews 1.25 .55
☐ 362 New York Mets 2.00 .90
Team Card
☐ 363 Ron Klimkowski 1.25 .55
☐ 364 Johnny Callison 2.00 .90
☐ 365 Dick Bosman 2.00 .90
☐ 366 Jimmy Rosario 1.25 .55
☐ 367 Ron Perranoski 2.00 .90
☐ 368 Danny Thompson 1.25 .55
☐ 369 Jim Lefebvre 2.00 .90
☐ 370 Don Buford 1.25 .55
☐ 371 Denny Lemaster 1.25 .55
☐ 372 Royals Rookies 1.25 .55
Lance Clemons
Monty Montgomery
☐ 373 John Mayberry 2.00 .90
☐ 374 Jack Heidemann 1.25 .55
☐ 375 Reggie Cleveland 1.25 .55
☐ 376 Andy Kosco 1.25 .55
☐ 377 Terry Harmon 1.25 .55
☐ 378 Checklist 395-525 4.00 .80
☐ 379 Ken Berry 1.25 .55
☐ 380 Earl Williams 1.25 .55
☐ 381 Chicago White Sox 2.00 .90
Team Card
☐ 382 Joe Gibbon 1.25 .55
☐ 383 Brant Alyea 1.25 .55
☐ 384 Dave Campbell 2.00 .90
☐ 385 Mickey Stanley 2.00 .90
☐ 386 Jim Colborn 1.25 .55
☐ 387 Horace Clarke 2.00 .90
☐ 388 Charlie Williams 1.25 .55
☐ 389 Bill Rigney MG 1.25 .55
☐ 390 Willie Davis 1.50 .70
☐ 391 Ken Sanders 1.25 .55
☐ 392 Pirates Rookies 2.00 .90
Fred Cambria
Richie Zisk
☐ 393 Curt Motton 1.25 .55
☐ 394 Ken Forsch 2.00 .90
☐ 395 Matty Alou 1.75 .80
☐ 396 Paul Lindblad 1.50 .70
☐ 397 Philadelphia Phillies 2.00 .90
Team Card
☐ 398 Larry Hisle 2.00 .90
☐ 399 Milt Wilcox 1.50 .70
☐ 400 Tony Oliva 1.75 .80
☐ 401 Jim Nash 1.50 .70
☐ 402 Bobby Heise 1.50 .70
☐ 403 John Cumberland 1.50 .70
☐ 404 Jeff Torborg 2.00 .90
☐ 405 Ron Fairly 2.00 .90
☐ 406 George Hendrick 1.75 .80
☐ 407 Chuck Taylor 1.00 .45
☐ 408 Jim Northrup 2.00 .90
☐ 409 Frank Baker 1.00 .45
☐ 410 Ferguson Jenkins 6.00 2.70
☐ 411 Bob Montgomery 1.00 .45
☐ 412 Dick Kelley 1.00 .45
☐ 413 White Sox Rookies 1.00 .45
Don Eddy
Dave Lemonds
☐ 414 Bob Miller 1.00 .45
☐ 415 Cookie Rojas 2.00 .90
☐ 416 Johnny Edwards 1.00 .45
☐ 417 Tom Hall 1.00 .45
☐ 418 Tom Shopay 1.00 .45
☐ 419 Jim Spencer 1.00 .45
☐ 420 Steve Carlton 18.00 8.00
☐ 421 Ellie Rodriguez 1.00 .45
☐ 422 Ray Lamb 1.00 .45
☐ 423 Oscar Gamble 2.00 .90
☐ 424 Bill Gogolewski 1.00 .45
☐ 425 Ken Singleton 2.00 .90
☐ 426 Ken Singleton IA 1.00 .45
☐ 427 Tito Fuentes 1.00 .45
☐ 428 Tito Fuentes IA 1.00 .45
☐ 429 Bob Robertson 1.00 .45
☐ 430 Bob Robertson IA 1.00 .45
☐ 431 Clarence Gaston 1.75 .80
☐ 432 Clarence Gaston IA 2.00 .90
☐ 433 Johnny Bench 25.00 11.00
☐ 434 Johnny Bench IA 14.00 6.25
☐ 435 Reggie Jackson 25.00 11.00
☐ 436 Reggie Jackson IA 14.00 6.25
☐ 437 Maury Wills 1.75 .80
☐ 438 Maury Wills IA 2.00 .90
☐ 439 Billy Williams 6.00 2.70
☐ 440 Billy Williams IA 3.00 1.35
☐ 441 Thurman Munson 15.00 6.75
☐ 442 Thurman Munson IA 8.00 3.60
☐ 443 Ken Henderson 1.50 .70
☐ 444 Ken Henderson IA 1.50 .70
☐ 445 Tom Seaver 30.00 13.50
☐ 446 Tom Seaver IA 15.00 6.75
☐ 447 Willie Stargell 8.00 3.60
☐ 448 Willie Stargell IA 3.00 1.35
☐ 449 Bob Lemon MG 1.75 .80
☐ 450 Mickey Lolich 1.75 .80
☐ 451 Tony LaRussa 3.00 1.35
☐ 452 Ed Herrmann 1.50 .70
☐ 453 Barry Lersch 1.50 .70
☐ 454 Oakland A's 2.00 .90
Team Card
☐ 455 Tommy Harper 2.00 .90
☐ 456 Mark Belanger 2.00 .90
☐ 457 Padres Rookies 1.50 .70
Darcy Fast
Derrel Thomas
Mike Ivie
☐ 458 Aurelio Monteagudo 1.50 .70
☐ 459 Rick Renick 1.50 .70
☐ 460 Al Downing 1.50 .70
☐ 461 Tim Cullen 1.50 .70
☐ 462 Rickey Clark 1.50 .70
☐ 463 Bernie Carbo 1.50 .70
☐ 464 Jim Roland 1.50 .70
☐ 465 Gil Hodges MG 4.00 1.80
☐ 466 Norm Miller 1.50 .70
☐ 467 Steve Kline 1.50 .70
☐ 468 Richie Scheinblum 1.50 .70
☐ 469 Ron Herbel 1.50 .70
☐ 470 Ray Fosse 1.50 .70
☐ 471 Luke Walker 1.50 .70
☐ 472 Phil Gagliano 1.50 .70
☐ 473 Dan McGinn 1.50 .70
☐ 474 Orioles Rookies 15.00 6.75
Don Baylor
Roric Harrison
Johnny Oates
☐ 475 Gary Nolan 2.00 .90
☐ 476 Lee Richard 1.50 .70
☐ 477 Tom Phoebus 1.50 .70
☐ 478 Checklist 526-656 6.00 1.20
☐ 479 Don Shaw 1.50 .70
☐ 480 Lee May 2.00 .90
☐ 481 Billy Conigliaro 1.75 .80
☐ 482 Joe Hoerner 1.50 .70
☐ 483 Ken Suarez 1.50 .70
☐ 484 Lum Harris MG 1.50 .70
☐ 485 Phil Regan 2.00 .90
☐ 486 John Lowenstein 1.50 .70
☐ 487 Detroit Tigers 2.00 .90
Team Card
☐ 488 Mike Nagy 1.50 .70
☐ 489 Expos Rookies 1.50 .70
Terry Humphrey
Keith Lampard
☐ 490 Dave McNally 2.00 .90
☐ 491 Lou Piniella KP 2.00 .90
☐ 492 Mel Stottlemyre KP 2.00 .90
☐ 493 Bob Bailey KP 2.00 .90
☐ 494 Willie Horton KP 2.00 .90
☐ 495 Bill Melton KP 2.00 .90
☐ 496 Bud Harrelson KP 2.00 .90
☐ 497 Jim Perry KP 2.00 .90
☐ 498 Brooks Robinson KP 3.00 1.35
☐ 499 Vicente Romo 1.50 .70
☐ 500 Joe Torre 1.75 .80
☐ 501 Pete Hamm 1.50 .70
☐ 502 Jackie Hernandez 1.50 .70
☐ 503 Gary Peters 1.50 .70
☐ 504 Ed Spiezio 1.50 .70
☐ 505 Mike Marshall 1.75 .80
☐ 506 Indians Rookies 1.50 .70
Terry Ley
Jim Moyer
Dick Tidrow
☐ 507 Fred Gladding 1.50 .70
☐ 508 Elrod Hendricks 1.50 .70
☐ 509 Don McMahon 1.50 .70
☐ 510 Ted Williams MG 10.00 4.50
☐ 511 Tony Taylor 2.00 .90
☐ 512 Paul Popovich 1.50 .70
☐ 513 Lindy McDaniel 2.00 .90
☐ 514 Ted Sizemore 1.50 .70
☐ 515 Bert Blyleven 3.00 1.35
☐ 516 Oscar Brown 1.00 .45
☐ 517 Ken Brett 1.00 .45
☐ 518 Wayne Garrett 1.00 .45
☐ 519 Ted Abernathy 1.00 .45
☐ 520 Larry Bowa 1.75 .80
☐ 521 Alan Foster 1.00 .45
☐ 522 Los Angeles Dodgers 3.00 1.35
Team Card
☐ 523 Chuck Dobson 1.00 .45
☐ 524 Reds Rookies 1.00 .45
Ed Armbrister
Mel Behney
☐ 525 Carlos May 2.00 .90
☐ 526 Bob Bailey 6.00 2.70
☐ 527 Dave Leonhard 4.00 1.80
☐ 528 Ron Stone 4.00 1.80
☐ 529 Dave Nelson 6.00 2.70
☐ 530 Don Sutton 7.00 3.10
☐ 531 Freddie Patek 6.00 2.70
☐ 532 Fred Kendall 4.00 1.80
☐ 533 Ralph Houk MG 4.50 2.00
☐ 534 Jim Hickman 6.00 2.70
☐ 535 Ed Brinkman 4.00 1.80
☐ 536 Doug Rader 6.00 2.70
☐ 537 Bob Locker 4.00 1.80
☐ 538 Charlie Sands 4.00 1.80

☐ 539 Terry Forster 4.50 2.00
☐ 540 Felix Millan 4.00 1.80
☐ 541 Roger Repoz 4.00 1.80
☐ 542 Jack Billingham 4.00 1.80
☐ 543 Duane Josephson 4.00 1.80
☐ 544 Ted Martinez 4.00 1.80
☐ 545 Wayne Granger 4.00 1.80
☐ 546 Joe Hague 4.00 1.80
☐ 547 Cleveland Indians 8.00 3.60
Team Card
☐ 548 Frank Reberger 4.00 1.80
☐ 549 Dave May 4.00 1.80
☐ 550 Brooks Robinson 25.00 11.00
☐ 551 Ollie Brown 4.00 1.80
☐ 552 Ollie Brown IA 4.00 1.80
☐ 553 Wilbur Wood 4.50 2.00
☐ 554 Wilbur Wood IA 4.00 1.80
☐ 555 Ron Santo 4.50 2.00
☐ 556 Ron Santo IA 6.00 2.70
☐ 557 John Odom 4.00 1.80
☐ 558 John Odom IA 4.00 1.80
☐ 559 Pete Rose 40.00 18.00
☐ 560 Pete Rose IA 20.00 9.00
☐ 561 Leo Cardenas 4.00 1.80
☐ 562 Leo Cardenas IA 4.00 1.80
☐ 563 Ray Sadecki 4.00 1.80
☐ 564 Ray Sadecki IA 4.00 1.80
☐ 565 Reggie Smith 4.50 2.00
☐ 566 Reggie Smith IA 4.00 1.80
☐ 567 Juan Marichal 12.00 5.50
☐ 568 Juan Marichal IA 6.00 2.70
☐ 569 Ed Kirkpatrick 4.00 1.80
☐ 570 Ed Kirkpatrick IA 4.00 1.80
☐ 571 Nate Colbert 4.00 1.80
☐ 572 Nate Colbert IA 4.00 1.80
☐ 573 Fritz Peterson 4.00 1.80
☐ 574 Fritz Peterson IA 4.00 1.80
☐ 575 Al Oliver 4.50 2.00
☐ 576 Leo Durocher MG 5.00 2.20
☐ 577 Mike Paul 6.00 2.70
☐ 578 Billy Grabarkewitz 4.00 1.80
☐ 579 Doyle Alexander 4.50 2.00
☐ 580 Lou Piniella 5.00 2.20
☐ 581 Wade Blasingame 4.00 1.80
☐ 582 Montreal Expos 8.00 3.60
Team Card
☐ 583 Darold Knowles 4.00 1.80
☐ 584 Jerry McNertney 4.00 1.80
☐ 585 George Scott 4.50 2.00
☐ 586 Denis Menke 4.00 1.80
☐ 587 Billy Wilson 4.00 1.80
☐ 588 Jim Holt 4.00 1.80
☐ 589 Hal Lanier 4.00 1.80
☐ 590 Graig Nettles 4.50 2.00
☐ 591 Paul Casanova 4.00 1.80
☐ 592 Lew Krausse 4.00 1.80
☐ 593 Rich Morales 4.00 1.80
☐ 594 Jim Beauchamp 4.00 1.80
☐ 595 Nolan Ryan 225.00 100.00
☐ 596 Manny Mota 4.50 2.00
☐ 597 Jim Magnuson 4.00 1.80
☐ 598 Hal King 6.00 2.70
☐ 599 Billy Champion 4.00 1.80
☐ 600 Al Kaline 25.00 11.00
☐ 601 George Stone 4.00 1.80
☐ 602 Dave Bristol MG 4.00 1.80
☐ 603 Jim Ray 4.00 1.80
☐ 604A Checklist 657-787 12.00 2.40
(Copyright on back
bottom right)
☐ 604B Checklist 657-787 12.00 2.40
(Copyright on back
bottom left)
☐ 605 Nelson Briles 6.00 2.70
☐ 606 Luis Melendez 4.00 1.80
☐ 607 Frank Duffy 4.00 1.80
☐ 608 Mike Corkins 4.00 1.80
☐ 609 Tom Grieve 6.00 2.70
☐ 610 Bill Stoneman 6.00 2.70
☐ 611 Rich Reese 4.00 1.80
☐ 612 Joe Decker 4.00 1.80
☐ 613 Mike Ferraro 4.00 1.80
☐ 614 Ted Uhlaender 4.00 1.80
☐ 615 Steve Hargan 4.00 1.80
☐ 616 Joe Ferguson 6.00 2.70
☐ 617 Kansas City Royals 8.00 3.60
Team Card
☐ 618 Rich Robertson 4.00 1.80
☐ 619 Rich McKinney 4.00 1.80
☐ 620 Phil Niekro 10.00 4.50
☐ 621 Commissioners Award 5.00 2.20
☐ 622 MVP Award 5.00 2.20
☐ 623 Cy Young Award 5.00 2.20
☐ 624 Minor League Player 5.00 2.20
of the Year
☐ 625 Rookie of the Year 5.00 2.20
☐ 626 Babe Ruth Award 5.00 2.20
☐ 627 Moe Drabowsky 4.00 1.80
☐ 628 Terry Crowley 4.00 1.80
☐ 629 Paul Doyle 4.00 1.80
☐ 630 Rich Hebner 6.00 2.70
☐ 631 John Strohmayer 4.00 1.80
☐ 632 Mike Hegan 4.00 1.80
☐ 633 Jack Hiatt 4.00 1.80
☐ 634 Dick Woodson 4.00 1.80
☐ 635 Don Money 6.00 2.70
☐ 636 Bill Lee 6.00 2.70
☐ 637 Preston Gomez MG 4.00 1.80
☐ 638 Ken Wright 4.00 1.80
☐ 639 J.C. Martin 4.00 1.80
☐ 640 Joe Coleman 4.00 1.80
☐ 641 Mike Lum 4.00 1.80
☐ 642 Dennis Riddleberger 4.00 1.80
☐ 643 Russ Gibson 4.00 1.80
☐ 644 Bernie Allen 4.00 1.80
☐ 645 Jim Maloney 6.00 2.70
☐ 646 Chico Salmon 4.00 1.80
☐ 647 Bob Moose 4.00 1.80
☐ 648 Jim Lyttle 4.00 1.80
☐ 649 Pete Richert 4.00 1.80
☐ 650 Sal Bando 4.50 2.00
☐ 651 Cincinnati Reds 7.00 3.10
Team Card
☐ 652 Marcelino Lopez 4.00 1.80
☐ 653 Jim Fairey 4.00 1.80
☐ 654 Horacio Pina 6.00 2.70
☐ 655 Jerry Grote 4.00 1.80
☐ 656 Rudy May 4.00 1.80
☐ 657 Bobby Wine 12.00 5.50
☐ 658 Steve Dunning 12.00 5.50
☐ 659 Bob Aspromonte 12.00 5.50
☐ 660 Paul Blair 15.00 6.75
☐ 661 Bill Virdon MG 13.00 5.75
☐ 662 Stan Bahnsen 12.00 5.50
☐ 663 Fran Healy 15.00 6.75
☐ 664 Bobby Knoop 12.00 5.50
☐ 665 Chris Short 12.00 5.50
☐ 666 Hector Torres 12.00 5.50
☐ 667 Ray Newman 12.00 5.50
☐ 668 Texas Rangers 30.00 13.50
Team Card
☐ 669 Willie Crawford 12.00 5.50
☐ 670 Ken Holtzman 15.00 6.75
☐ 671 Donn Clendenon 15.00 6.75
☐ 672 Archie Reynolds 12.00 5.50
☐ 673 Dave Marshall 12.00 5.50
☐ 674 John Kennedy 12.00 5.50
☐ 675 Pat Jarvis 12.00 5.50
☐ 676 Danny Cater 12.00 5.50
☐ 677 Ivan Murrell 12.00 5.50
☐ 678 Steve Luebber 12.00 5.50
☐ 679 Astros Rookies 12.00 5.50
Bob Fenwick
Bob Stinson
☐ 680 Dave Johnson 15.00 6.75
☐ 681 Bobby Pfeil 12.00 5.50
☐ 682 Mike McCormick 15.00 6.75
☐ 683 Steve Hovley 12.00 5.50
☐ 684 Hal Breeden 12.00 5.50
☐ 685 Joel Horlen 12.00 5.50
☐ 686 Steve Garvey 40.00 18.00
☐ 687 Del Unser 12.00 5.50
☐ 688 St. Louis Cardinals 20.00 9.00
Team Card
☐ 689 Eddie Fisher 12.00 5.50
☐ 690 Willie Montanez 15.00 6.75
☐ 691 Curt Blefary 12.00 5.50
☐ 692 Curt Blefary IA 12.00 5.50
☐ 693 Alan Gallagher 12.00 5.50
☐ 694 Alan Gallagher IA 12.00 5.50
☐ 695 Rod Carew 75.00 34.00
☐ 696 Rod Carew IA 35.00 16.00
☐ 697 Jerry Koosman 15.00 6.75
☐ 698 Jerry Koosman IA 13.00 5.75
☐ 699 Bobby Murcer 15.00 6.75
☐ 700 Bobby Murcer IA 13.00 5.75
☐ 701 Jose Pagan 12.00 5.50
☐ 702 Jose Pagan IA 12.00 5.50
☐ 703 Doug Griffin 12.00 5.50
☐ 704 Doug Griffin IA 12.00 5.50
☐ 705 Pat Corrales 15.00 6.75
☐ 706 Pat Corrales IA 12.00 5.50
☐ 707 Tim Foli 12.00 5.50
☐ 708 Tim Foli IA 12.00 5.50
☐ 709 Jim Kaat 16.00 7.25
☐ 710 Jim Kaat IA 14.00 6.25
☐ 711 Bobby Bonds 20.00 9.00
☐ 712 Bobby Bonds IA 14.00 6.25
☐ 713 Gene Michael 20.00 9.00
☐ 714 Gene Michael IA 15.00 6.75
☐ 715 Mike Epstein 12.00 5.50
☐ 716 Jesus Alou 12.00 5.50
☐ 717 Bruce Dal Canton 12.00 5.50
☐ 718 Del Rice MG 12.00 5.50
☐ 719 Cesar Geronimo 12.00 5.50
☐ 720 Sam McDowell 15.00 6.75
☐ 721 Eddie Leon 12.00 5.50
☐ 722 Bill Sudakis 12.00 5.50
☐ 723 Al Santorini 12.00 5.50
☐ 724 AL Rookie Pitchers 12.00 5.50
John Curtis
Rich Hinton
Mickey Scott
☐ 725 Dick McAuliffe 15.00 6.75
☐ 726 Dick Selma 12.00 5.50
☐ 727 Jose Laboy 12.00 5.50
☐ 728 Gail Hopkins 12.00 5.50
☐ 729 Bob Veale 15.00 6.75
☐ 730 Rick Monday 13.00 5.75
☐ 731 Baltimore Orioles 20.00 9.00
Team Card
☐ 732 George Culver 12.00 5.50
☐ 733 Jim Ray Hart 15.00 6.75
☐ 734 Bob Burda 12.00 5.50
☐ 735 Diego Segui 12.00 5.50
☐ 736 Bill Russell 13.00 5.75
☐ 737 Len Randle 15.00 6.75
☐ 738 Jim Merritt 12.00 5.50
☐ 739 Don Mason 12.00 5.50
☐ 740 Rico Carty 15.00 6.75
☐ 741 Rookie First Basemen 13.00 5.75
Tom Hutton
John Milner
Rick Miller
☐ 742 Jim Rooker 12.00 5.50
☐ 743 Cesar Gutierrez 12.00 5.50
☐ 744 Jim Slaton 12.00 5.50
☐ 745 Julian Javier 15.00 6.75
☐ 746 Lowell Palmer 12.00 5.50
☐ 747 Jim Stewart 12.00 5.50
☐ 748 Phil Hennigan 12.00 5.50
☐ 749 Walter Alston MG 14.00 6.25
☐ 750 Willie Horton 12.00 5.50
☐ 751 Steve Carlton TR 50.00 22.00
☐ 752 Joe Morgan TR 45.00 20.00
☐ 753 Denny McLain TR 20.00 9.00
☐ 754 Frank Robinson TR 45.00 20.00
☐ 755 Jim Fregosi TR 13.00 5.75
☐ 756 Rick Wise TR 15.00 6.75
☐ 757 Jose Cardenal TR 15.00 6.75
☐ 758 Gil Garrido 12.00 5.50
☐ 759 Chris Cannizzaro 12.00 5.50
☐ 760 Bill Mazeroski 18.00 8.00
☐ 761 Rookie Outfielders 25.00 11.00
Ben Oglivie
Ron Cey
Bernie Williams
☐ 762 Wayne Simpson 12.00 5.50
☐ 763 Ron Hansen 12.00 5.50
☐ 764 Dusty Baker 20.00 9.00
☐ 765 Ken McMullen 12.00 5.50
☐ 766 Steve Hamilton 12.00 5.50
☐ 767 Tom McCraw 15.00 6.75
☐ 768 Denny Doyle 12.00 5.50
☐ 769 Jack Aker 12.00 5.50
☐ 770 Jim Wynn 13.00 5.75
☐ 771 San Francisco Giants 20.00 9.00
Team Card
☐ 772 Ken Tatum 12.00 5.50
☐ 773 Ron Brand 12.00 5.50
☐ 774 Luis Alvarado 12.00 5.50
☐ 775 Jerry Reuss 15.00 6.75
☐ 776 Bill Voss 12.00 5.50
☐ 777 Hoyt Wilhelm 25.00 11.00
☐ 778 Twins Rookies 18.00 8.00
Vic Albury
Rick Dempsey
Jim Strickland
☐ 779 Tony Cloninger 12.00 5.50
☐ 780 Dick Green 12.00 5.50
☐ 781 Jim McAndrew 12.00 5.50
☐ 782 Larry Stahl 12.00 5.50
☐ 783 Les Cain 12.00 5.50
☐ 784 Ken Aspromonte 12.00 5.50
☐ 785 Vic Davalillo 12.00 5.50
☐ 786 Chuck Brinkman 12.00 5.50
☐ 787 Ron Reed 16.00 5.50

1973 Topps

The cards in this 660-card set measure 2 1/2" by 3 1/2". The 1973 Topps set marked the last year in which Topps marketed baseball cards in consecutive series. The last series (529-660) is more difficult to obtain. In some parts of the country, however, all five series were distributed together. Beginning in 1974, all Topps cards were printed at the same time, thus eliminating the "high number" factor. The set features team leader cards with small individual pictures of the coaching staff members and a larger picture of the manager. The "background" variations

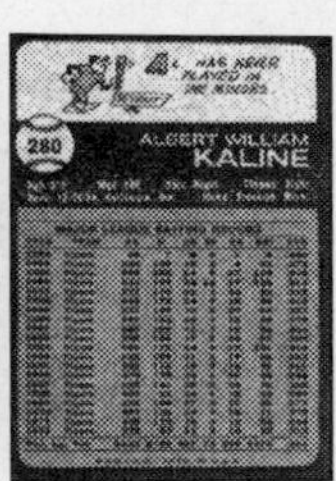

below with respect to these leader cards are subtle and are best understood after a side-by-side comparison of the two varieties. An "All-Time Leaders" series (471-478) appeared for the first time in this set. Kid Pictures appeared again for the second year in a row (341-346). Other topical subsets within the set included League Leaders (61-68), Playoffs cards (201-202), World Series cards (203-210), and Rookie Prospects (601-616). For the fourth and final time, cards were issued in ten-card dime packs, cards were also released in 54-card rack packs. The key Rookie Cards in this set are all in the Rookie Prospect series: Bob Boone, Dwight Evans, and Mike Schmidt.

	NRMT	VG-E
COMPLETE SET (660)	750.00	350.00
COMMON CARD (1-264)	.50	.23
COMMON CARD (265-396)	.75	.35
COMMON CARD (397-528)	1.25	.55
COMMON CARD (529-660)	3.50	1.55
WRAPPER (10-CENT, BATTER)	15.00	6.75
WRAPPER (10-CENT)	15.00	6.75

□ 1 All-Time HR Leaders 40.00 11.50
Babe Ruth 714
Hank Aaron 673
Willie Mays 654
□ 2 Rich Hebner 1.25 .55
□ 3 Jim Lonborg 1.25 .55
□ 4 John Milner .50 .23
□ 5 Ed Brinkman .50 .23
□ 6 Mac Scarce .50 .23
□ 7 Texas Rangers 1.25 .55
Team Card
□ 8 Tom Hall .50 .23
□ 9 Johnny Oates .50 .23
□ 10 Don Sutton 1.00 .45
□ 11 Chris Chambliss .75 .35
□ 12A Padres Leaders 1.25 .55
Don Zimmer MG
Dave Garcia CO
Johnny Podres CO
Bob Skinner CO
Whitey Wietelmann CO
(Podres no right ear)
□ 12B Padres Leaders 2.50 1.10
(Podres has right ear)
□ 13 George Hendrick 1.25 .55
□ 14 Sonny Siebert .50 .23
□ 15 Ralph Garr 1.25 .55
□ 16 Steve Braun .50 .23
□ 17 Fred Gladding .50 .23
□ 18 Leroy Stanton .50 .23
□ 19 Tim Foli .50 .23
□ 20 Stan Bahnsen .50 .23
□ 21 Randy Hundley 1.25 .55
□ 22 Ted Abernathy .50 .23
□ 23 Dave Kingman 1.00 .45
□ 24 Al Santorini .50 .23
□ 25 Roy White .75 .35
□ 26 Pittsburgh Pirates 1.25 .55
Team Card
□ 27 Bill Gogolewski .50 .23
□ 28 Hal McRae 1.00 .45
□ 29 Tony Taylor 1.25 .55
□ 30 Tug McGraw .75 .35
□ 31 Buddy Bell 3.00 1.35
□ 32 Fred Norman .50 .23
□ 33 Jim Breazeale .50 .23
□ 34 Pat Dobson .50 .23
□ 35 Willie Davis .75 .35
□ 36 Steve Barber .50 .23
□ 37 Bill Robinson 1.25 .55
□ 38 Mike Epstein .50 .23
□ 39 Dave Roberts .50 .23
□ 40 Reggie Smith .75 .35
□ 41 Tom Walker .50 .23
□ 42 Mike Andrews .50 .23
□ 43 Randy Moffitt .50 .23
□ 44 Rick Monday .75 .35
□ 45 Ellie Rodriguez UER .50 .23
(Photo actually
John Felske)
□ 46 Lindy McDaniel 1.25 .55
□ 47 Luis Melendez .50 .23
□ 48 Paul Splittorff .50 .23
□ 49A Twins Leaders 1.25 .55
Frank Quilici MG
Vern Morgan CO
Bob Rodgers CO
Ralph Rowe CO
Al Worthington CO
(Solid backgrounds)
□ 49B Twins Leaders 2.50 1.10
(Natural backgrounds)
□ 50 Roberto Clemente 60.00 27.00
□ 51 Chuck Seelbach .50 .23
□ 52 Denis Menke .50 .23
□ 53 Steve Dunning .50 .23
□ 54 Checklist 1-132 4.00 .80
□ 55 Jon Matlack 1.25 .55
□ 56 Merv Rettenmund .50 .23
□ 57 Derrel Thomas .50 .23
□ 58 Mike Paul .50 .23
□ 59 Steve Yeager 1.25 .55
□ 60 Ken Holtzman 1.25 .55
□ 61 Batting Leaders 3.00 1.35
Billy Williams
Rod Carew
□ 62 Home Run Leaders 2.50 1.10
Johnny Bench
Dick Allen
□ 63 RBI Leaders 2.50 1.10
Johnny Bench
Dick Allen
□ 64 Stolen Base Leaders 2.00 .90
Lou Brock
Bert Campaneris
□ 65 ERA Leaders 2.00 .90
Steve Carlton
Luis Tiant
□ 66 Victory Leaders 2.00 .90
Steve Carlton
Gaylord Perry
Wilbur Wood
□ 67 Strikeout Leaders 30.00 13.50
Steve Carlton
Nolan Ryan
□ 68 Leading Firemen 1.25 .55
Clay Carroll
Sparky Lyle
□ 69 Phil Gagliano .50 .23
□ 70 Milt Pappas 1.25 .55
□ 71 Johnny Briggs .50 .23
□ 72 Ron Reed .50 .23
□ 73 Ed Herrmann .50 .23
□ 74 Billy Champion .50 .23
□ 75 Vada Pinson 1.00 .45
□ 76 Doug Rader .50 .23
□ 77 Mike Torrez 1.25 .55
□ 78 Richie Scheinblum .50 .23
□ 79 Jim Willoughby .50 .23
□ 80 Tony Oliva UER 1.00 .45
(Minnseota on front)
□ 81A Cubs Leaders 1.50 .70
Whitey Lockman MG
Hank Aguirre CO
Ernie Banks CO
Larry Jansen CO
Pete Reiser CO
(Solid backgrounds)
□ 81B Cubs Leaders 2.00 .90
(Natural backgrounds)
□ 82 Fritz Peterson .50 .23
□ 83 Leron Lee .50 .23
□ 84 Rollie Fingers 5.00 2.20
□ 85 Ted Simmons 1.00 .45
□ 86 Tom McCraw .50 .23
□ 87 Ken Boswell .50 .23
□ 88 Mickey Stanley 1.25 .55
□ 89 Jack Billingham .50 .23
□ 90 Brooks Robinson 7.00 3.10
□ 91 Los Angeles Dodgers 1.25 .55
Team Card
□ 92 Jerry Bell .50 .23
□ 93 Jesus Alou .50 .23
□ 94 Dick Billings .50 .23
□ 95 Steve Blass 1.25 .55
□ 96 Doug Griffin .50 .23
□ 97 Willie Montanez 1.25 .55
□ 98 Dick Woodson .50 .23
□ 99 Carl Taylor .50 .23
□ 100 Hank Aaron 25.00 11.00
□ 101 Ken Henderson .50 .23
□ 102 Rudy May .50 .23
□ 103 Celerino Sanchez .50 .23
□ 104 Reggie Cleveland .50 .23
□ 105 Carlos May .50 .23
□ 106 Terry Humphrey .50 .23
□ 107 Phil Hennigan .50 .23
□ 108 Bill Russell .75 .35
□ 109 Doyle Alexander 1.25 .55
□ 110 Bob Watson 1.25 .55
□ 111 Dave Nelson .50 .23
□ 112 Gary Ross .50 .23
□ 113 Jerry Grote .50 .23
□ 114 Lynn McGlothen .50 .23
□ 115 Ron Santo 1.00 .45
□ 116A Yankees Leaders 1.25 .55
Ralph Houk MG
Jim Hegan CO
Elston Howard CO
Dick Howser CO
Jim Turner CO
(Solid backgrounds)
□ 116B Yankees Leaders 2.50 1.10
(Natural backgrounds)
□ 117 Ramon Hernandez .50 .23
□ 118 John Mayberry 1.25 .55
□ 119 Larry Bowa .75 .35
□ 120 Joe Coleman .50 .23
□ 121 Dave Rader .50 .23
□ 122 Jim Strickland .50 .23
□ 123 Sandy Alomar 1.25 .55
□ 124 Jim Hardin .50 .23
□ 125 Ron Fairly 1.25 .55
□ 126 Jim Brewer .50 .23
□ 127 Milwaukee Brewers 1.25 .55
Team Card
□ 128 Ted Sizemore .50 .23
□ 129 Terry Forster 1.25 .55
□ 130 Pete Rose 15.00 6.75
□ 131A Red Sox Leaders 1.25 .55
Eddie Kasko MG
Doug Camilli CO
Don Lenhardt CO
Eddie Popowski CO
(No right ear)
Lee Stange CO
□ 131B Red Sox Leaders 2.50 1.10
(Popowski has right
ear showing)
□ 132 Matty Alou .75 .35
□ 133 Dave Roberts .50 .23
□ 134 Milt Wilcox .50 .23
□ 135 Lee May UER 1.25 .55
(Career average .000)
□ 136A Orioles Leaders 2.00 .90
Earl Weaver MG
George Bamberger CO
Jim Frey CO
Billy Hunter CO
George Staller CO
(Orange backgrounds)
□ 136B Orioles Leaders 3.00 1.35
(Dark pale
backgrounds)
□ 137 Jim Beauchamp .50 .23
□ 138 Horacio Pina .50 .23
□ 139 Carmen Fanzone .50 .23
□ 140 Lou Piniella 1.00 .45
□ 141 Bruce Kison .50 .23
□ 142 Thurman Munson 6.00 2.70
□ 143 John Curtis .50 .23
□ 144 Marty Perez .50 .23
□ 145 Bobby Bonds 1.00 .45
□ 146 Woodie Fryman .50 .23
□ 147 Mike Anderson .50 .23
□ 148 Dave Goltz .50 .23
□ 149 Ron Hunt .50 .23
□ 150 Wilbur Wood 1.25 .55
□ 151 Wes Parker 1.25 .55
□ 152 Dave May .50 .23
□ 153 Al Hrabosky 1.25 .55
□ 154 Jeff Torborg 1.25 .55
□ 155 Sal Bando 1.25 .55
□ 156 Cesar Geronimo .50 .23
□ 157 Denny Riddleberger .50 .23
□ 158 Houston Astros 1.25 .55
Team Card
□ 159 Clarence Gaston 1.00 .45
□ 160 Jim Palmer 7.00 3.10
□ 161 Ted Martinez .50 .23
□ 162 Pete Broberg .50 .23
□ 163 Vic Davalillo .50 .23
□ 164 Monty Montgomery .50 .23
□ 165 Luis Aparicio 3.00 1.35
□ 166 Terry Harmon .50 .23
□ 167 Steve Stone 1.25 .55
□ 168 Jim Northrup 1.25 .55
□ 169 Ron Schueler .50 .23
□ 170 Harmon Killebrew 5.00 2.20
□ 171 Bernie Carbo .50 .23
□ 172 Steve Kline .50 .23
□ 173 Hal Breeden .50 .23
□ 174 Rich Gossage 6.00 2.70
□ 175 Frank Robinson 7.00 3.10

☐ 176 Chuck Taylor	.50	.23
☐ 177 Bill Plummer	.50	.23
☐ 178 Don Rose	.50	.23
☐ 179A A's Leaders	1.25	.55
Dick Williams MG		
Jerry Adair CO		
Vern Hoscheit CO		
Irv Noren CO		
Wes Stock CO		
(Hoscheit left ear		
showing)		
☐ 179B A's Leaders	2.50	1.10
(Hoscheit left ear		
not showing)		
☐ 180 Ferguson Jenkins	5.00	2.20
☐ 181 Jack Brohamer	.50	.23
☐ 182 Mike Caldwell	1.25	.55
☐ 183 Don Buford	.50	.23
☐ 184 Jerry Koosman	1.00	.45
☐ 185 Jim Wynn	.75	.35
☐ 186 Bill Fahey	.50	.23
☐ 187 Luke Walker	.50	.23
☐ 188 Cookie Rojas	1.25	.55
☐ 189 Greg Luzinski	1.00	.45
☐ 190 Bob Gibson	7.00	3.10
☐ 191 Detroit Tigers	1.25	.55
Team Card		
☐ 192 Pat Jarvis	.50	.23
☐ 193 Carlton Fisk	7.00	3.10
☐ 194 Jorge Orta	.50	.23
☐ 195 Clay Carroll	.50	.23
☐ 196 Ken McMullen	.50	.23
☐ 197 Ed Goodson	.50	.23
☐ 198 Horace Clarke	.50	.23
☐ 199 Bert Blyleven	1.00	.45
☐ 200 Billy Williams	5.00	2.20
☐ 201 George Hendrick ALCS	1.25	.55
☐ 202 George Foster NLCS	1.25	.55
☐ 203 Gene Tenace WS	1.25	.55
☐ 204 World Series Game 2	1.25	.55
A's two straight		
☐ 205 Tony Perez WS	2.50	1.10
☐ 206 Gene Tenace WS	1.25	.55
☐ 207 John "Blue Moon" Odom WS	1.25	.55
☐ 208 Johnny Bench WS6	5.00	2.20
☐ 209 Bert Campaneris WS	1.25	.55
☐ 210 World Series Summary	.50	.23
World champions:		
A's Win		
☐ 211 Balor Moore	.50	.23
☐ 212 Joe Lahoud	.50	.23
☐ 213 Steve Garvey	5.00	2.20
☐ 214 Steve Hamilton	.50	.23
☐ 215 Dusty Baker	1.00	.45
☐ 216 Toby Harrah	1.25	.55
☐ 217 Don Wilson	.50	.23
☐ 218 Aurelio Rodriguez	.50	.23
☐ 219 St. Louis Cardinals	1.25	.55
Team Card		
☐ 220 Nolan Ryan	100.00	45.00
☐ 221 Fred Kendall	.50	.23
☐ 222 Rob Gardner	.50	.23
☐ 223 Bud Harrelson	1.25	.55
☐ 224 Bill Lee	1.25	.55
☐ 225 Al Oliver	1.00	.45
☐ 226 Ray Fosse	.50	.23
☐ 227 Wayne Twitchell	.50	.23
☐ 228 Bobby Darwin	.50	.23
☐ 229 Roric Harrison	.50	.23
☐ 230 Joe Morgan	6.00	2.70
☐ 231 Bill Parsons	.50	.23
☐ 232 Ken Singleton	1.25	.55
☐ 233 Ed Kirkpatrick	.50	.23
☐ 234 Bill North	.50	.23
☐ 235 Jim Hunter	4.00	1.80
☐ 236 Tito Fuentes	.50	.23
☐ 237A Braves Leaders	1.50	.70
Eddie Mathews MG		
Lew Burdette CO		
Jim Busby CO		
Roy Hartsfield CO		
Ken Silvestri CO		
(Burdette right ear		
showing)		
☐ 237B Braves Leaders	3.00	1.35
(Burdette right ear		
not showing)		
☐ 238 Tony Muser	.50	.23
☐ 239 Pete Richert	.50	.23
☐ 240 Bobby Murcer	.75	.35
☐ 241 Dwain Anderson	.50	.23
☐ 242 George Culver	.50	.23
☐ 243 California Angels	1.25	.55
Team Card		
☐ 244 Ed Acosta	.50	.23
☐ 245 Carl Yastrzemski	8.00	3.60
☐ 246 Ken Sanders	.50	.23
☐ 247 Del Unser	.50	.23
☐ 248 Jerry Johnson	.50	.23
☐ 249 Larry Biittner	.50	.23
☐ 250 Manny Sanguillen	1.25	.55
☐ 251 Roger Nelson	.50	.23
☐ 252A Giants Leaders	1.25	.55
Charlie Fox MG		
Joe Amalfitano CO		
Andy Gilbert CO		
Don McMahon CO		
John McNamara CO		
(Orange backgrounds)		
☐ 252B Giants Leaders	2.50	1.10
(Dark pale		
backgrounds)		
☐ 253 Mark Belanger	1.25	.55
☐ 254 Bill Stoneman	.50	.23
☐ 255 Reggie Jackson	15.00	6.75
☐ 256 Chris Zachary	.50	.23
☐ 257A Mets Leaders	2.50	1.10
Yogi Berra MG		
Roy McMillan CO		
Joe Pignatano CO		
Rube Walker CO		
Eddie Yost CO		
(Orange backgrounds)		
☐ 257B Mets Leaders	5.00	2.20
(Dark pale		
backgrounds)		
☐ 258 Tommy John	1.00	.45
☐ 259 Jim Holt	.50	.23
☐ 260 Gary Nolan	1.25	.55
☐ 261 Pat Kelly	.50	.23
☐ 262 Jack Aker	.50	.23
☐ 263 George Scott	1.25	.55
☐ 264 Checklist 133-264	4.00	.80
☐ 265 Gene Michael	1.25	.55
☐ 266 Mike Lum	.50	.23
☐ 267 Lloyd Allen	.50	.23
☐ 268 Jerry Morales	.50	.23
☐ 269 Tim McCarver	1.00	.45
☐ 270 Luis Tiant	1.00	.45
☐ 271 Tom Hutton	.50	.23
☐ 272 Ed Farmer	.50	.23
☐ 273 Chris Speier	.50	.23
☐ 274 Darold Knowles	.50	.23
☐ 275 Tony Perez	4.00	1.80
☐ 276 Joe Lovitto	.50	.23
☐ 277 Bob Miller	.50	.23
☐ 278 Baltimore Orioles	1.25	.55
Team Card		
☐ 279 Mike Strahler	.50	.23
☐ 280 Al Kaline	7.00	3.10
☐ 281 Mike Jorgensen	.50	.23
☐ 282 Steve Hovley	.50	.23
☐ 283 Ray Sadecki	.50	.23
☐ 284 Glenn Borgmann	.50	.23
☐ 285 Don Kessinger	.50	.23
☐ 286 Frank Linzy	.50	.23
☐ 287 Eddie Leon	.50	.23
☐ 288 Gary Gentry	.50	.23
☐ 289 Bob Oliver	.50	.23
☐ 290 Cesar Cedeno	1.00	.45
☐ 291 Rogelio Moret	.50	.23
☐ 292 Jose Cruz	1.25	.55
☐ 293 Bernie Allen	.50	.23
☐ 294 Steve Arlin	.50	.23
☐ 295 Bert Campaneris	1.00	.45
☐ 296 Reds Leaders	2.50	1.10
Sparky Anderson MG		
Alex Grammas CO		
Ted Kluszewski CO		
George Scherger CO		
Larry Shepard CO		
☐ 297 Walt Williams	.50	.23
☐ 298 Ron Bryant	.50	.23
☐ 299 Ted Ford	.50	.23
☐ 300 Steve Carlton	10.00	4.50
☐ 301 Billy Grabarkewitz	.50	.23
☐ 302 Terry Crowley	.50	.23
☐ 303 Nelson Briles	.50	.23
☐ 304 Duke Sims	.50	.23
☐ 305 Willie Mays	35.00	16.00
☐ 306 Tom Burgmeier	.50	.23
☐ 307 Boots Day	.50	.23
☐ 308 Skip Lockwood	.50	.23
☐ 309 Paul Popovich	.50	.23
☐ 310 Dick Allen	1.50	.70
☐ 311 Joe Decker	.50	.23
☐ 312 Oscar Brown	.50	.23
☐ 313 Jim Ray	.50	.23
☐ 314 Ron Swoboda	.50	.23
☐ 315 John Odom	.50	.23
☐ 316 San Diego Padres	1.25	.55
Team Card		
☐ 317 Danny Cater	.50	.23
☐ 318 Jim McGlothlin	.50	.23
☐ 319 Jim Spencer	.50	.23
☐ 320 Lou Brock	6.00	2.70
☐ 321 Rich Hinton	.50	.23
☐ 322 Garry Maddox	1.00	.45
☐ 323 Tigers Leaders	1.50	.70
Billy Martin MG		
Art Fowler CO		
Charlie Silvera CO		
Dick Tracewski CO		
☐ 324 Al Downing	.50	.23
☐ 325 Boog Powell	1.00	.45
☐ 326 Darrell Brandon	.50	.23
☐ 327 John Lowenstein	.50	.23
☐ 328 Bill Bonham	.50	.23
☐ 329 Ed Kranepool	.50	.23
☐ 330 Rod Carew	7.00	3.10
☐ 331 Carl Morton	.50	.23
☐ 332 John Felske	.50	.23
☐ 333 Gene Clines	.50	.23
☐ 334 Freddie Patek	.50	.23
☐ 335 Bob Tolan	.50	.23
☐ 336 Tom Bradley	.50	.23
☐ 337 Dave Duncan	.50	.23
☐ 338 Checklist 265-396	4.00	.80
☐ 339 Dick Tidrow	.50	.23
☐ 340 Nate Colbert	.50	.23
☐ 341 Jim Palmer KP	1.50	.70
☐ 342 Sam McDowell KP	.50	.23
☐ 343 Bobby Murcer KP	.50	.23
☐ 344 Jim Hunter KP	1.50	.70
☐ 345 Chris Speier KP	.50	.23
☐ 346 Gaylord Perry KP	1.25	.55
☐ 347 Kansas City Royals	1.25	.55
Team Card		
☐ 348 Rennie Stennett	.50	.23
☐ 349 Dick McAuliffe	.50	.23
☐ 350 Tom Seaver	12.00	5.50
☐ 351 Jimmy Stewart	.50	.23
☐ 352 Don Stanhouse	.50	.23
☐ 353 Steve Brye	.50	.23
☐ 354 Billy Parker	.50	.23
☐ 355 Mike Marshall	1.25	.55
☐ 356 White Sox Leaders	.50	.23
Chuck Tanner MG		
Joe Lonnett CO		
Jim Mahoney CO		
Al Monchak CO		
Johnny Sain CO		
☐ 357 Ross Grimsley	.50	.23
☐ 358 Jim Nettles	.50	.23
☐ 359 Cecil Upshaw	.50	.23
☐ 360 Joe Rudi UER	1.25	.55
(Photo actually		
Gene Tenace)		
☐ 361 Fran Healy	.50	.23
☐ 362 Eddie Watt	.50	.23
☐ 363 Jackie Hernandez	.50	.23
☐ 364 Rick Wise	.50	.23
☐ 365 Rico Petrocelli	1.25	.55
☐ 366 Brock Davis	.50	.23
☐ 367 Burt Hooton	.50	.23
☐ 368 Bill Buckner	1.00	.45
☐ 369 Lerrin LaGrow	.50	.23
☐ 370 Willie Stargell	5.00	2.20
☐ 371 Mike Kekich	.50	.23
☐ 372 Oscar Gamble	.50	.23
☐ 373 Clyde Wright	.50	.23
☐ 374 Darrell Evans	1.00	.45
☐ 375 Larry Dierker	1.25	.55
☐ 376 Frank Duffy	.50	.23
☐ 377 Expos Leaders	.50	.23
Gene Mauch MG		
Dave Bristol CO		
Larry Doby CO		
Cal McLish CO		
Jerry Zimmerman CO		
☐ 378 Len Randle	.50	.23
☐ 379 Cy Acosta	.50	.23
☐ 380 Johnny Bench	12.00	5.50
☐ 381 Vicente Romo	.50	.23
☐ 382 Mike Hegan	.50	.23
☐ 383 Diego Segui	.50	.23
☐ 384 Don Baylor	4.00	1.80
☐ 385 Jim Perry	1.25	.55
☐ 386 Don Money	.50	.23
☐ 387 Jim Barr	.50	.23
☐ 388 Ben Oglivie	1.25	.55
☐ 389 New York Mets	3.00	1.35
Team Card		
☐ 390 Mickey Lolich	1.00	.45
☐ 391 Lee Lacy	.50	.23
☐ 392 Dick Drago	.50	.23
☐ 393 Jose Cardenal	.50	.23
☐ 394 Sparky Lyle	1.00	.45
☐ 395 Roger Metzger	.50	.23
☐ 396 Grant Jackson	.50	.23
☐ 397 Dave Cash	1.25	.55

☐ 398 Rich Hand 1.25 .55
☐ 399 George Foster 2.00 .90
☐ 400 Gaylord Perry 5.00 2.20
☐ 401 Clyde Mashore 1.25 .55
☐ 402 Jack Hiatt 1.25 .55
☐ 403 Sonny Jackson 1.25 .55
☐ 404 Chuck Brinkman 1.25 .55
☐ 405 Cesar Tovar 1.25 .55
☐ 406 Paul Lindblad 1.25 .55
☐ 407 Felix Millan 1.25 .55
☐ 408 Jim Colborn 1.25 .55
☐ 409 Ivan Murrell 1.25 .55
☐ 410 Willie McCovey 6.00 2.70
(Bench behind plate)
☐ 411 Ray Corbin 1.25 .55
☐ 412 Manny Mota 2.00 .90
☐ 413 Tom Timmermann 1.25 .55
☐ 414 Ken Rudolph 1.25 .55
☐ 415 Marty Pattin 1.25 .55
☐ 416 Paul Schaal 1.25 .55
☐ 417 Scipio Spinks 1.25 .55
☐ 418 Bob Grich 2.00 .90
☐ 419 Casey Cox 1.25 .55
☐ 420 Tommie Agee 1.25 .55
☐ 421A Angels Leaders 2.00 .90
Bobby Winkles MG
Tom Morgan CO
Salty Parker CO
Jimmie Reese CO
John Roseboro CO
(Orange backgrounds)
☐ 421B Angels Leaders 3.00 1.35
(Dark pale
backgrounds)
☐ 422 Bob Robertson 1.25 .55
☐ 423 Johnny Jeter 1.25 .55
☐ 424 Denny Doyle 1.25 .55
☐ 425 Alex Johnson 1.25 .55
☐ 426 Dave LaRoche 1.25 .55
☐ 427 Rick Auerbach 1.25 .55
☐ 428 Wayne Simpson 1.25 .55
☐ 429 Jim Fairey 1.25 .55
☐ 430 Vida Blue 2.00 .90
☐ 431 Gerry Moses 1.25 .55
☐ 432 Dan Frisella 1.25 .55
☐ 433 Willie Horton 2.00 .90
☐ 434 San Francisco Giants 3.00 1.35
Team Card
☐ 435 Rico Carty 2.00 .90
☐ 436 Jim McAndrew 1.25 .55
☐ 437 John Kennedy 1.25 .55
☐ 438 Enzo Hernandez 1.25 .55
☐ 439 Eddie Fisher 1.25 .55
☐ 440 Glenn Beckert 1.25 .55
☐ 441 Gail Hopkins 1.25 .55
☐ 442 Dick Dietz 1.25 .55
☐ 443 Danny Thompson 1.25 .55
☐ 444 Ken Brett 1.25 .55
☐ 445 Ken Berry 1.25 .55
☐ 446 Jerry Reuss 2.00 .90
☐ 447 Joe Hague 1.25 .55
☐ 448 John Hiller 1.25 .55
☐ 449A Indians Leaders 4.00 1.80
Ken Aspromonte MG
Rocky Colavito CO
Joe Lutz CO
Warren Spahn CO
(Spahn's right
ear pointed)
☐ 449B Indians Leaders 4.00 1.80
(Spahn's right
ear round)
☐ 450 Joe Torre 2.00 .90
☐ 451 John Vukovich 1.25 .55
☐ 452 Paul Casanova 1.25 .55
☐ 453 Checklist 397-528 3.00 .60
☐ 454 Tom Haller 1.25 .55
☐ 455 Bill Melton 1.25 .55
☐ 456 Dick Green 1.25 .55
☐ 457 John Strohmayer 1.25 .55
☐ 458 Jim Mason 1.25 .55
☐ 459 Jimmy Howarth 1.25 .55
☐ 460 Bill Freehan 2.00 .90
☐ 461 Mike Corkins 1.25 .55
☐ 462 Ron Blomberg 1.25 .55
☐ 463 Ken Tatum 1.25 .55
☐ 464 Chicago Cubs 3.00 1.35
Team Card
☐ 465 Dave Giusti 1.25 .55
☐ 466 Jose Arcia 1.25 .55
☐ 467 Mike Ryan 1.25 .55
☐ 468 Tom Griffin 1.25 .55
☐ 469 Dan Monzon 1.25 .55
☐ 470 Mike Cuellar 2.00 .90
☐ 471 Ty Cobb ATL 8.00 3.60
4191 Hits
☐ 472 Lou Gehrig ATL 14.00 6.25
23 Grand Slams
☐ 473 Hank Aaron ATL 10.00 4.50
6172 Total Bases
☐ 474 Babe Ruth ATL 16.00 7.25
2209 RBI
☐ 475 Ty Cobb ATL 8.00 3.60
.367 Batting Average
☐ 476 Walter Johnson ATL 3.00 1.35
113 Shutouts
☐ 477 Cy Young ATL 3.00 1.35
511 Victories
☐ 478 Walter Johnson ATL 3.00 1.35
3508 Strikeouts
☐ 479 Hal Lanier 1.25 .55
☐ 480 Juan Marichal 5.00 2.20
☐ 481 Chicago White Sox 3.00 1.35
Team Card
☐ 482 Rick Reuschel 3.00 1.35
☐ 483 Dal Maxvill 1.25 .55
☐ 484 Ernie McAnally 1.25 .55
☐ 485 Norm Cash 2.00 .90
☐ 486A Phillies Leaders 2.00 .90
Danny Ozark MG
Carroll Beringer CO
Billy DeMars CO
Ray Rippelmeyer CO
Bobby Wine CO
(Orange backgrounds)
☐ 486B Phillies Leaders 3.00 1.35
(Dark pale
backgrounds)
☐ 487 Bruce Dal Canton 1.25 .55
☐ 488 Dave Campbell 2.00 .90
☐ 489 Jeff Burroughs 2.00 .90
☐ 490 Claude Osteen 1.25 .55
☐ 491 Bob Montgomery 1.25 .55
☐ 492 Pedro Borbon 1.25 .55
☐ 493 Duffy Dyer 1.25 .55
☐ 494 Rich Morales 1.25 .55
☐ 495 Tommy Helms 1.25 .55
☐ 496 Ray Lamb 1.25 .55
☐ 497A Cardinals Leaders 2.00 .90
Red Schoendienst MG
Vern Benson CO
George Kissell CO
Barney Schultz CO
(Orange backgrounds)
☐ 497B Cardinals Leaders 3.00 1.35
(Dark pale
backgrounds)
☐ 498 Graig Nettles 3.00 1.35
☐ 499 Bob Moose 1.25 .55
☐ 500 Oakland A's 3.00 1.35
Team Card
☐ 501 Larry Gura 1.25 .55
☐ 502 Bobby Valentine 2.00 .90
☐ 503 Phil Niekro 5.00 2.20
☐ 504 Earl Williams 1.25 .55
☐ 505 Bob Bailey 1.25 .55
☐ 506 Bart Johnson 1.25 .55
☐ 507 Darrel Chaney 1.25 .55
☐ 508 Gates Brown 1.25 .55
☐ 509 Jim Nash 1.25 .55
☐ 510 Amos Otis 2.00 .90
☐ 511 Sam McDowell 2.00 .90
☐ 512 Dalton Jones 1.25 .55
☐ 513 Dave Marshall 1.25 .55
☐ 514 Jerry Kenney 1.25 .55
☐ 515 Andy Messersmith 2.00 .90
☐ 516 Danny Walton 1.25 .55
☐ 517A Pirates Leaders 2.00 .90
Bill Virdon MG
Don Leppert CO
Bill Mazeroski CO
Dave Ricketts CO
Mel Wright CO
(Mazeroski has
no right ear)
☐ 517B Pirates Leaders 3.00 1.35
(Mazeroski has
right ear)
☐ 518 Bob Veale 1.25 .55
☐ 519 Johnny Edwards 1.25 .55
☐ 520 Mel Stottlemyre 2.00 .90
☐ 521 Atlanta Braves 3.00 1.35
Team Card
☐ 522 Leo Cardenas 1.25 .55
☐ 523 Wayne Granger 1.25 .55
☐ 524 Gene Tenace 2.00 .90
☐ 525 Jim Fregosi 2.00 .90
☐ 526 Ollie Brown 1.25 .55
☐ 527 Dan McGinn 1.25 .55
☐ 528 Paul Blair 1.25 .55
☐ 529 Milt May 3.50 1.55
☐ 530 Jim Kaat 5.00 2.20
☐ 531 Ron Woods 3.50 1.55
☐ 532 Steve Mingori 3.50 1.55
☐ 533 Larry Stahl 3.50 1.55
☐ 534 Dave Lemonds 3.50 1.55
☐ 535 Johnny Callison 5.00 2.20
☐ 536 Philadelphia Phillies 5.00 2.20
Team Card
☐ 537 Bill Slayback 3.50 1.55
☐ 538 Jim Ray Hart 5.00 2.20
☐ 539 Tom Murphy 3.50 1.55
☐ 540 Cleon Jones 5.00 2.20
☐ 541 Bob Bolin 3.50 1.55
☐ 542 Pat Corrales 5.00 2.20
☐ 543 Alan Foster 3.50 1.55
☐ 544 Von Joshua 3.50 1.55
☐ 545 Orlando Cepeda 5.00 2.20
☐ 546 Jim York 3.50 1.55
☐ 547 Bobby Heise 3.50 1.55
☐ 548 Don Durham 3.50 1.55
☐ 549 Rangers Leaders 5.00 2.20
Whitey Herzog MG
Chuck Estrada CO
Chuck Hiller CO
Jackie Moore CO
☐ 550 Dave Johnson 5.00 2.20
☐ 551 Mike Kilkenny 3.50 1.55
☐ 552 J.C. Martin 3.50 1.55
☐ 553 Mickey Scott 3.50 1.55
☐ 554 Dave Concepcion 5.00 2.20
☐ 555 Bill Hands 3.50 1.55
☐ 556 New York Yankees 8.00 3.60
Team Card
☐ 557 Bernie Williams 3.50 1.55
☐ 558 Jerry May 3.50 1.55
☐ 559 Barry Lersch 3.50 1.55
☐ 560 Frank Howard 4.00 1.80
☐ 561 Jim Geddes 3.50 1.55
☐ 562 Wayne Garrett 3.50 1.55
☐ 563 Larry Haney 3.50 1.55
☐ 564 Mike Thompson 3.50 1.55
☐ 565 Jim Hickman 3.50 1.55
☐ 566 Lew Krausse 3.50 1.55
☐ 567 Bob Fenwick 3.50 1.55
☐ 568 Ray Newman 3.50 1.55
☐ 569 Dodgers Leaders 5.00 2.20
Walt Alston MG
Red Adams CO
Monty Basgall CO
Jim Gilliam CO
Tom Lasorda CO
☐ 570 Bill Singer 5.00 2.20
☐ 571 Rusty Torres 3.50 1.55
☐ 572 Gary Sutherland 3.50 1.55
☐ 573 Fred Beene 3.50 1.55
☐ 574 Bob Didier 3.50 1.55
☐ 575 Dock Ellis 3.50 1.55
☐ 576 Montreal Expos 6.00 2.70
Team Card
☐ 577 Eric Soderholm 3.50 1.55
☐ 578 Ken Wright 3.50 1.55
☐ 579 Tom Grieve 5.00 2.20
☐ 580 Joe Pepitone 5.00 2.20
☐ 581 Steve Kealey 3.50 1.55
☐ 582 Darrell Porter 5.00 2.20
☐ 583 Bill Grief 3.50 1.55
☐ 584 Chris Arnold 3.50 1.55
☐ 585 Joe Niekro 5.00 2.20
☐ 586 Bill Sudakis 3.50 1.55
☐ 587 Rich McKinney 3.50 1.55
☐ 588 Checklist 529-660 24.00 4.80
☐ 589 Ken Forsch 3.50 1.55
☐ 590 Deron Johnson 5.00 2.20
☐ 591 Mike Hedlund 3.50 1.55
☐ 592 John Boccabella 3.50 1.55
☐ 593 Royals Leaders 3.50 1.55
Jack McKeon MG
Galen Cisco CO
Harry Dunlop CO
Charlie Lau CO
☐ 594 Vic Harris 3.50 1.55
☐ 595 Don Gullett 5.00 2.20
☐ 596 Boston Red Sox 8.00 3.60
Team Card
☐ 597 Mickey Rivers 4.00 1.80
☐ 598 Phil Roof 3.50 1.55
☐ 599 Ed Crosby 3.50 1.55
☐ 600 Dave McNally 5.00 2.20
☐ 601 Rookie Catchers 5.00 2.20
Sergio Robles
George Pena
Rick Stelmaszek
☐ 602 Rookie Pitchers 5.00 2.20
Mel Behney
Ralph Garcia
Doug Rau
☐ 603 Rookie 3rd Basemen 5.00 2.20
Terry Hughes
Bill McNulty
Ken Reitz
☐ 604 Rookie Pitchers 5.00 2.20

Jesse Jefferson		
Dennis O'Toole		
Bob Strampe		
☐ 605 Rookie 1st Basemen	5.00	2.20
Enos Cabell		
Pat Bourque		
Gonzalo Marquez		
☐ 606 Rookie Outfielders	5.00	2.20
Gary Matthews		
Tom Paciorek		
Jorge Roque		
☐ 607 Rookie Shortstops	5.00	2.20
Pepe Frias		
Ray Busse		
Mario Guerrero		
☐ 608 Rookie Pitchers	5.00	2.20
Steve Busby		
Dick Colpaert		
George Medich		
☐ 609 Rookie 2nd Basemen	6.00	2.70
Larvell Blanks		
Pedro Garcia		
Dave Lopes		
☐ 610 Rookie Pitchers	5.00	2.20
Jimmy Freeman		
Charlie Hough		
Hank Webb		
☐ 611 Rookie Outfielders	5.00	2.20
Rich Coggins		
Jim Wohlford		
Richie Zisk		
☐ 612 Rookie Pitchers	5.00	2.20
Steve Lawson		
Bob Reynolds		
Brent Strom		
☐ 613 Rookie Catchers	16.00	7.25
Bob Boone		
Skip Jutze		
Mike Ivie		
☐ 614 Rookie Outfielders	16.00	7.25
Al Bumbry		
Dwight Evans		
Charlie Spikes		
☐ 615 Rookie 3rd Basemen	300.00	135.00
Ron Cey		
John Hilton		
Mike Schmidt		
☐ 616 Rookie Pitchers	5.00	2.20
Norm Angelini		
Steve Blateric		
Mike Garman		
☐ 617 Rich Chiles	3.50	1.55
☐ 618 Andy Etchebarren	3.50	1.55
☐ 619 Billy Wilson	3.50	1.55
☐ 620 Tommy Harper	5.00	2.20
☐ 621 Joe Ferguson	5.00	2.20
☐ 622 Larry Hisle	5.00	2.20
☐ 623 Steve Renko	3.50	1.55
☐ 624 Astros Leaders	6.00	2.70
Leo Durocher MG		
Preston Gomez CO		
Grady Hatton CO		
Hub Kittle CO		
Jim Owens CO		
☐ 625 Angel Mangual	3.50	1.55
☐ 626 Bob Barton	3.50	1.55
☐ 627 Luis Alvarado	3.50	1.55
☐ 628 Jim Slaton	3.50	1.55
☐ 629 Cleveland Indians Team Card	6.00	2.70
☐ 630 Denny McLain	8.00	3.60
☐ 631 Tom Matchick	3.50	1.55
☐ 632 Dick Selma	3.50	1.55
☐ 633 Ike Brown	3.50	1.55
☐ 634 Alan Closter	3.50	1.55
☐ 635 Gene Alley	5.00	2.20
☐ 636 Rickey Clark	3.50	1.55
☐ 637 Norm Miller	3.50	1.55
☐ 638 Ken Reynolds	3.50	1.55
☐ 639 Willie Crawford	3.50	1.55
☐ 640 Dick Bosman	3.50	1.55
☐ 641 Cincinnati Reds Team Card	8.00	3.60
☐ 642 Jose Laboy	3.50	1.55
☐ 643 Al Fitzmorris	3.50	1.55
☐ 644 Jack Heidemann	3.50	1.55
☐ 645 Bob Locker	3.50	1.55
☐ 646 Brewers Leaders	3.50	1.55
Del Crandall MG		
Harvey Kuenn CO		
Joe Nossek CO		
Bob Shaw CO		
Jim Walton CO		
☐ 647 George Stone	3.50	1.55
☐ 648 Tom Egan	3.50	1.55
☐ 649 Rich Folkers	3.50	1.55
☐ 650 Felipe Alou	4.00	1.80
☐ 651 Don Carrithers	3.50	1.55
☐ 652 Ted Kubiak	3.50	1.55
☐ 653 Joe Hoerner	3.50	1.55
☐ 654 Minnesota Twins Team Card	5.00	2.20
☐ 655 Clay Kirby	3.50	1.55
☐ 656 John Ellis	3.50	1.55
☐ 657 Bob Johnson	3.50	1.55
☐ 658 Elliott Maddox	3.50	1.55
☐ 659 Jose Pagan	3.50	1.55
☐ 660 Fred Scherman	4.00	1.55

1973 Topps Blue Team Checklists

This 24-card standard-size set is rather difficult to find. These blue-bordered team checklist cards are very similar in design to the mass produced red trim team checklist cards issued by Topps the next year. Reportedly these were inserts only found in the test packs that included all series.

	NRMT	VG-E
COMPLETE SET (24)	175.00	80.00
COMMON TEAM (1-24)	8.00	3.60
☐ 1 Atlanta Braves	8.00	3.60
☐ 2 Baltimore Orioles	8.00	3.60
☐ 3 Boston Red Sox	8.00	3.60
☐ 4 California Angels	8.00	3.60
☐ 5 Chicago Cubs	8.00	3.60
☐ 6 Chicago White Sox	8.00	3.60
☐ 7 Cincinnati Reds	8.00	3.60
☐ 8 Cleveland Indians	8.00	3.60
☐ 9 Detroit Tigers	8.00	3.60
☐ 10 Houston Astros	8.00	3.60
☐ 11 Kansas City Royals	8.00	3.60
☐ 12 Los Angeles Dodgers	8.00	3.60
☐ 13 Milwaukee Brewers	8.00	3.60
☐ 14 Minnesota Twins	8.00	3.60
☐ 15 Montreal Expos	8.00	3.60
☐ 16 New York Mets	10.00	4.50
☐ 17 New York Yankees	10.00	4.50
☐ 18 Oakland A's	8.00	3.60
☐ 19 Philadelphia Phillies	8.00	3.60
☐ 20 Pittsburgh Pirates	8.00	3.60
☐ 21 San Diego Padres	8.00	3.60
☐ 22 San Francisco Giants	8.00	3.60
☐ 23 St. Louis Cardinals	8.00	3.60
☐ 24 Texas Rangers	8.00	3.60

1973 Topps Candy Lids

One of Topps' most unusual test sets is this series of 55 color portraits of baseball players printed on the bottom of candy lids. These lids measure 1 7/8" in diameter. The product was called "Baseball Stars Bubble Gum" and consisted of a small tub of candy-coated gum kernels. Issued in 1973, the lids are unnumbered and each has a small tab. Underneath the picture is a small ribbon design which contains the player's name, team and position.

	NRMT	VG-E
COMPLETE SET (55)	600.00	275.00
COMMON LID (1-55)	3.00	1.35
☐ 1 Hank Aaron	35.00	16.00
☐ 2 Dick Allen	5.00	2.20
☐ 3 Dusty Baker	5.00	2.20
☐ 4 Sal Bando	3.00	1.35
☐ 5 Johnny Bench	25.00	11.00
☐ 6 Bobby Bonds	5.00	2.20
☐ 7 Dick Bosman	3.00	1.35
☐ 8 Lou Brock	15.00	6.75
☐ 9 Rod Carew	15.00	6.75
☐ 10 Steve Carlton	15.00	6.75
☐ 11 Nate Colbert	3.00	1.35
☐ 12 Willie Davis	3.00	1.35
☐ 13 Larry Dierker	3.00	1.35
☐ 14 Mike Epstein	3.00	1.35
☐ 15 Carlton Fisk	15.00	6.75
☐ 16 Tim Foli	3.00	1.35
☐ 17 Ray Fosse	3.00	1.35
☐ 18 Bill Freehan	3.00	1.35
☐ 19 Bob Gibson	15.00	6.75
☐ 20 Bud Harrelson	3.00	1.35
☐ 21 Jim Hunter	10.00	4.50
☐ 22 Reggie Jackson	25.00	11.00
☐ 23 Ferguson Jenkins	10.00	4.50
☐ 24 Al Kaline	15.00	6.75
☐ 25 Harmon Killebrew	15.00	6.75
☐ 26 Clay Kirby	3.00	1.35
☐ 27 Mickey Lolich	5.00	2.20
☐ 28 Greg Luzinski	5.00	2.20
☐ 29 Willie McCovey	15.00	6.75
☐ 30 Mike Marshall	3.00	1.35
☐ 31 Lee May	3.00	1.35
☐ 32 John Mayberry	3.00	1.35
☐ 33 Willie Mays	35.00	16.00
☐ 34 Thurman Munson	10.00	4.50
☐ 35 Bobby Murcer	5.00	2.20
☐ 36 Gary Nolan	3.00	1.35
☐ 37 Amos Otis	3.00	1.35
☐ 38 Jim Palmer	15.00	6.75
☐ 39 Gaylord Perry	10.00	4.50
☐ 40 Lou Piniella	5.00	2.20
☐ 41 Brooks Robinson	15.00	6.75
☐ 42 Frank Robinson	15.00	6.75
☐ 43 Ellie Rodriguez	3.00	1.35
☐ 44 Pete Rose	35.00	16.00
☐ 45 Nolan Ryan	100.00	45.00
☐ 46 Manny Sanguillen	3.00	1.35
☐ 47 George Scott	3.00	1.35
☐ 48 Tom Seaver	25.00	11.00
☐ 49 Chris Speier	3.00	1.35
☐ 50 Willie Stargell	15.00	6.75
☐ 51 Don Sutton	10.00	4.50
☐ 52 Joe Torre	5.00	2.20
☐ 53 Billy Williams	10.00	4.50
☐ 54 Wilbur Wood	3.00	1.35
☐ 55 Carl Yastrzemski	25.00	11.00

1974 Topps

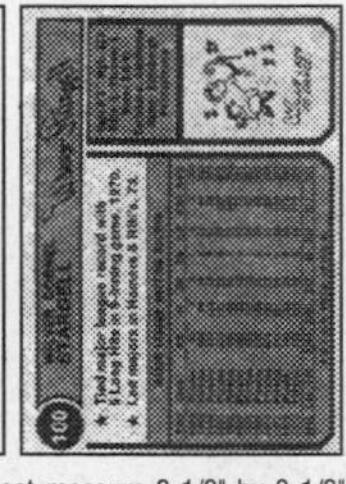

The cards in this 660-card set measure 2 1/2" by 3 1/2". This year marked the first time Topps issued all the cards of its baseball set at the same time rather than in series. Among other methods, cards were issued in eight-card dime wax packs and 42 card rack packs. For the first time, factory sets were issued through the JC Penny's catalog. Sales were probably disappointing for it would be several years before factory sets were issued again. Some interesting variations were created by the rumored move of the San Diego Padres to Washington. Fifteen cards (13 players, the team card, and the rookie card (599) of the Padres were printed either as "San Diego" (SD) or "Washington." The latter are the scarcer variety and are denoted in the checklist below by WAS. Each team's manager and his coaches again have a combined card with small pictures of each coach below the larger photo of the team's manager. The first six cards in the set (1-6) feature Hank Aaron and his illustrious career. Other topical subsets included in the set are League Leaders (201-208), All-Star selections (331-339), Playoffs cards (470-471), World Series cards (472-479), and Rookie Prospects (596-608). The card backs for the All-Stars (331-339) have no statistics, but form a picture puzzle of Bobby Bonds, the 1973 All-Star Game MVP. The key Rookie Cards in this set are Ken Griffey Sr., Dave Parker, and Dave Winfield.

	NRMT	VG-E
COMPLETE SET (660)	600.00	275.00
COMPLETE FACT.SET (660)	625.00	275.00
COMMON CARD (1-660)	.50	.23
WRAPPERS (10-CENTS)	10.00	4.50
☐ 1 Hank Aaron	40.00	12.00
All-Time Home Run King		
(Complete ML record)		
☐ 2 Aaron Special 54-57	7.00	3.10
(Records on back)		
☐ 3 Aaron Special 58-61	7.00	3.10
(Memorable homers)		
☐ 4 Aaron Special 62-65	7.00	3.10
(Life in ML's 1954-63)		
☐ 5 Aaron Special 66-69	7.00	3.10
(Life in ML's 1964-73)		
☐ 6 Aaron Special 70-73	7.00	3.10
(Milestone homers)		
☐ 7 Jim Hunter	3.00	1.35
☐ 8 George Theodore	.50	.23
☐ 9 Mickey Lolich	1.00	.45
☐ 10 Johnny Bench	12.00	5.50
☐ 11 Jim Bibby	.50	.23
☐ 12 Dave May	.50	.23
☐ 13 Tom Hilgendorf	.50	.23
☐ 14 Paul Popovich	.50	.23
☐ 15 Joe Torre	2.00	.90
☐ 16 Baltimore Orioles	1.00	.45
Team Card		
☐ 17 Doug Bird	.50	.23
☐ 18 Gary Thomasson	.50	.23
☐ 19 Gerry Moses	.50	.23
☐ 20 Nolan Ryan	70.00	32.00
☐ 21 Bob Gallagher	.50	.23
☐ 22 Cy Acosta	.50	.23
☐ 23 Craig Robinson	.50	.23
☐ 24 John Hiller	1.00	.45
☐ 25 Ken Singleton	1.00	.45
☐ 26 Bill Campbell	.50	.23
☐ 27 George Scott	1.00	.45
☐ 28 Manny Sanguillen	1.00	.45
☐ 29 Phil Niekro	3.00	1.35
☐ 30 Bobby Bonds	2.00	.90
☐ 31 Astros Leaders	1.00	.45
Preston Gomez MG		
Roger Craig CO		
Hub Kittle CO		
Grady Hatton CO		
Bob Lillis CO		
☐ 32A Johnny Grubb SD	1.00	.45
☐ 32B Johnny Grubb WAS	6.00	2.70
☐ 33 Don Newhauser	.50	.23
☐ 34 Andy Kosco	.50	.23
☐ 35 Gaylord Perry	3.00	1.35
☐ 36 St. Louis Cardinals	1.00	.45
Team Card		
☐ 37 Dave Sells	.50	.23
☐ 38 Don Kessinger	1.00	.45
☐ 39 Ken Suarez	.50	.23
☐ 40 Jim Palmer	5.00	2.20
☐ 41 Bobby Floyd	.50	.23
☐ 42 Claude Osteen	1.00	.45
☐ 43 Jim Wynn	1.00	.45
☐ 44 Mel Stottlemyre	1.00	.45
☐ 45 Dave Johnson	1.00	.45
☐ 46 Pat Kelly	.50	.23
☐ 47 Dick Ruthven	.50	.23
☐ 48 Dick Sharon	.50	.23
☐ 49 Steve Renko	.50	.23
☐ 50 Rod Carew	5.00	2.20
☐ 51 Bobby Heise	.50	.23
☐ 52 Al Oliver	.50	.23
☐ 53A Fred Kendall SD	1.00	.45
☐ 53B Fred Kendall WAS	6.00	2.70
☐ 54 Elias Sosa	.50	.23
☐ 55 Frank Robinson	6.00	2.70
☐ 56 New York Mets	1.00	.45
Team Card		
☐ 57 Darold Knowles	.50	.23
☐ 58 Charlie Spikes	.50	.23
☐ 59 Ross Grimsley	.50	.23
☐ 60 Lou Brock	5.00	2.20
☐ 61 Luis Aparicio	3.00	1.35
☐ 62 Bob Locker	.50	.23
☐ 63 Bill Sudakis	.50	.23
☐ 64 Doug Rau	.50	.23
☐ 65 Amos Otis	1.00	.45
☐ 66 Sparky Lyle	1.00	.45
☐ 67 Tommy Helms	.50	.23
☐ 68 Grant Jackson	.50	.23
☐ 69 Del Unser	.50	.23
☐ 70 Dick Allen	2.00	.90
☐ 71 Dan Frisella	.50	.23
☐ 72 Aurelio Rodriguez	.50	.23
☐ 73 Mike Marshall	2.00	.90
☐ 74 Minnesota Twins	1.00	.45
Team Card		
☐ 75 Jim Colborn	.50	.23
☐ 76 Mickey Rivers	1.00	.45
☐ 77A Rich Troedson SD	6.00	2.70
☐ 77B Rich Troedson WAS	1.00	.45
☐ 78 Giants Leaders	.75	.35
Charlie Fox MG		
John McNamara CO		
Joe Amalfitano CO		
Andy Gilbert CO		
Don McMahon CO		
☐ 79 Gene Tenace	1.00	.45
☐ 80 Tom Seaver	12.00	5.50
☐ 81 Frank Duffy	.50	.23
☐ 82 Dave Giusti	.50	.23
☐ 83 Orlando Cepeda	2.00	.90
☐ 84 Rick Wise	.50	.23
☐ 85 Joe Morgan	5.00	2.20
☐ 86 Joe Ferguson	1.00	.45
☐ 87 Fergie Jenkins	3.00	1.35
☐ 88 Freddie Patek	1.00	.45
☐ 89 Jackie Brown	.50	.23
☐ 90 Bobby Murcer	1.00	.45
☐ 91 Ken Forsch	.50	.23
☐ 92 Paul Blair	1.00	.45
☐ 93 Rod Gilbreath	.50	.23
☐ 94 Detroit Tigers	1.00	.45
Team Card		
☐ 95 Steve Carlton	6.00	2.70
☐ 96 Jerry Hairston	.50	.23
☐ 97 Bob Bailey	.50	.23
☐ 98 Bert Blyleven	2.00	.90
☐ 99 Brewers Leaders	1.00	.45
Del Crandall MG		
Harvey Kuenn CO		
Joe Nossek CO		
Jim Walton CO		
Al Widmar CO		
☐ 100 Willie Stargell	4.00	1.80
☐ 101 Bobby Valentine	1.00	.45
☐ 102A Bill Greif SD	1.00	.45
☐ 102B Bill Greif WAS	6.00	2.70
☐ 103 Sal Bando	1.00	.45
☐ 104 Ron Bryant	.50	.23
☐ 105 Carlton Fisk	12.00	5.50
☐ 106 Harry Parker	.50	.23
☐ 107 Alex Johnson	.50	.23
☐ 108 Al Hrabosky	1.00	.45
☐ 109 Bob Grich	1.00	.45
☐ 110 Billy Williams	3.00	1.35
☐ 111 Clay Carroll	.50	.23
☐ 112 Dave Lopes	2.00	.90
☐ 113 Dick Drago	.50	.23
☐ 114 Angels Team	1.00	.45
☐ 115 Willie Horton	1.00	.45
☐ 116 Jerry Reuss	1.00	.45
☐ 117 Ron Blomberg	.50	.23
☐ 118 Bill Lee	1.00	.45
☐ 119 Phillies Leaders	1.00	.45
Danny Ozark MG		
Ray Ripplemeyer CO		
Bobby Wine CO		
Carroll Beringer CO		
Billy DeMars CO		
☐ 120 Wilbur Wood	.50	.23
☐ 121 Larry Lintz	.50	.23
☐ 122 Jim Holt	.50	.23
☐ 123 Nelson Briles	1.00	.45
☐ 124 Bobby Coluccio	.50	.23
☐ 125A Nate Colbert SD	1.00	.45
☐ 125B Nate Colbert WAS	6.00	2.70
☐ 126 Checklist 1-132	3.00	.60
☐ 127 Tom Paciorek	1.00	.45
☐ 128 John Ellis	.50	.23
☐ 129 Chris Speier	.50	.23
☐ 130 Reggie Jackson	15.00	6.75
☐ 131 Bob Boone	2.00	.90
☐ 132 Felix Millan	.50	.23
☐ 133 David Clyde	1.00	.45
☐ 134 Denis Menke	.50	.23
☐ 135 Roy White	1.00	.45
☐ 136 Rick Reuschel	1.00	.45
☐ 137 Al Bumbry	1.00	.45
☐ 138 Eddie Brinkman	.50	.23
☐ 139 Aurelio Monteagudo	.50	.23
☐ 140 Darrell Evans	2.00	.90
☐ 141 Pat Bourque	.50	.23
☐ 142 Pedro Garcia	.50	.23
☐ 143 Dick Woodson	.50	.23
☐ 144 Dodgers Leaders	2.00	.90
Walter Alston MG		
Tom Lasorda CO		
Jim Gilliam CO		
Red Adams CO		
Monty Basgall CO		
☐ 145 Dock Ellis	.50	.23
☐ 146 Ron Fairly	1.00	.45
☐ 147 Bart Johnson	.50	.23
☐ 148A Dave Hilton SD	1.00	.45
☐ 148B Dave Hilton WAS	6.00	2.70
☐ 149 Mac Scarce	.50	.23
☐ 150 John Mayberry	1.00	.45
☐ 151 Diego Segui	.50	.23
☐ 152 Oscar Gamble	1.00	.45
☐ 153 Jon Matlack	1.00	.45
☐ 154 Houston Astros	1.00	.45
Team Card		
☐ 155 Bert Campaneris	1.00	.45
☐ 156 Randy Moffitt	.50	.23
☐ 157 Vic Harris	.50	.23
☐ 158 Jack Billingham	.50	.23
☐ 159 Jim Ray Hart	1.00	.45
☐ 160 Brooks Robinson	6.00	2.70
☐ 161 Ray Burris UER	1.00	.45
(Card number is		
printed sideways)		
☐ 162 Bill Freehan	1.00	.45
☐ 163 Ken Berry	.50	.23
☐ 164 Tom House	.50	.23
☐ 165 Willie Davis	1.00	.45
☐ 166 Royals Leaders	1.00	.45
Jack McKeon MG		
Charlie Lau CO		
Harry Dunlop CO		
Galen Cisco CO		
☐ 167 Luis Tiant	2.00	.90
☐ 168 Danny Thompson	.50	.23
☐ 169 Steve Rogers	2.00	.90
☐ 170 Bill Melton	.50	.23
☐ 171 Eduardo Rodriguez	.50	.23
☐ 172 Gene Clines	.50	.23
☐ 173A Randy Jones SD	2.00	.90
☐ 173B Randy Jones WAS	10.00	4.50
☐ 174 Bill Robinson	1.00	.45
☐ 175 Reggie Cleveland	.50	.23
☐ 176 John Lowenstein	.50	.23
☐ 177 Dave Roberts	.50	.23
☐ 178 Garry Maddox	1.00	.45
☐ 179 Mets Leaders	3.00	1.35
Yogi Berra MG		
Rube Walker CO		
Eddie Yost CO		
Roy McMillan CO		
Joe Pignatano CO		
☐ 180 Ken Holtzman	1.00	.45
☐ 181 Cesar Geronimo	.50	.23
☐ 182 Lindy McDaniel	1.00	.45
☐ 183 Johnny Oates	1.00	.45
☐ 184 Texas Rangers	1.00	.45
Team Card		
☐ 185 Jose Cardenal	.50	.23
☐ 186 Fred Scherman	.50	.23
☐ 187 Don Baylor	2.00	.90
☐ 188 Rudy Meoli	.50	.23
☐ 189 Jim Brewer	.50	.23
☐ 190 Tony Oliva	2.00	.90
☐ 191 Al Fitzmorris	.50	.23
☐ 192 Mario Guerrero	.50	.23
☐ 193 Tom Walker	.50	.23
☐ 194 Darrell Porter	1.00	.45
☐ 195 Carlos May	.50	.23
☐ 196 Jim Fregosi	1.00	.45
☐ 197A Vicente Romo SD	1.00	.45
☐ 197B Vicente Romo WAS	6.00	2.70
☐ 198 Dave Cash	.50	.23
☐ 199 Mike Kekich	.50	.23
☐ 200 Cesar Cedeno	1.00	.45
☐ 201 Batting Leaders	5.00	2.20
Rod Carew		
Pete Rose		
☐ 202 Home Run Leaders	5.00	2.20
Reggie Jackson		
Willie Stargell		
☐ 203 RBI Leaders	5.00	2.20
Reggie Jackson		
Willie Stargell		
☐ 204 Stolen Base Leaders	2.00	.90
Tommy Harper		
Lou Brock		
☐ 205 Victory Leaders	1.00	.45
Wilbur Wood		
Ron Bryant		
☐ 206 ERA Leaders	5.00	2.20
Jim Palmer		
Tom Seaver		
☐ 207 Strikeout Leaders	20.00	9.00
Nolan Ryan		
Tom Seaver		
☐ 208 Leading Firemen	1.00	.45
John Hiller		
Mike Marshall		
☐ 209 Ted Sizemore	.50	.23
☐ 210 Bill Singer	.50	.23
☐ 211 Chicago Cubs Team	1.00	.45
☐ 212 Rollie Fingers	3.00	1.35

☐ 213 Dave Rader	.50	.23
☐ 214 Billy Grabarkewitz	.50	.23
☐ 215 Al Kaline UER	5.00	2.20
(No copyright on back)		
☐ 216 Ray Sadecki	.50	.23
☐ 217 Tim Foli	.50	.23
☐ 218 Johnny Briggs	.50	.23
☐ 219 Doug Griffin	.50	.23
☐ 220 Don Sutton	3.00	1.35
☐ 221 White Sox Leaders	1.00	.45
Chuck Tanner MG		
Jim Mahoney CO		
Alex Monchak CO		
Johnny Sain CO		
Joe Lonnett CO		
☐ 222 Ramon Hernandez	.50	.23
☐ 223 Jeff Burroughs	1.00	.45
☐ 224 Roger Metzger	.50	.23
☐ 225 Paul Splittorff	.50	.23
☐ 226A Padres Team SD	2.00	.90
☐ 226B Padres Team WAS	10.00	4.50
☐ 227 Mike Lum	.50	.23
☐ 228 Ted Kubiak	.50	.23
☐ 229 Fritz Peterson	.50	.23
☐ 230 Tony Perez	3.00	1.35
☐ 231 Dick Tidrow	.50	.23
☐ 232 Steve Brye	.50	.23
☐ 233 Jim Barr	.50	.23
☐ 234 John Milner	.50	.23
☐ 235 Dave McNally	1.00	.45
☐ 236 Cardinals Leaders	2.00	.90
Red Schoendienst MG		
Barney Schultz CO		
George Kissell CO		
Johnny Lewis CO		
Vern Benson CO		
☐ 237 Ken Brett	.50	.23
☐ 238 Fran Healy HOR	2.00	.90
(Munson sliding		
in background)		
☐ 239 Bill Russell	2.00	.90
☐ 240 Joe Coleman	.50	.23
☐ 241A Glenn Beckert SD	.75	.35
☐ 241B Glenn Beckert WAS	6.00	2.70
☐ 242 Bill Gogolewski	.50	.23
☐ 243 Bob Oliver	.50	.23
☐ 244 Carl Morton	.50	.23
☐ 245 Cleon Jones	6.00	2.70
☐ 246 Oakland Athletics	2.00	.90
Team Card		
☐ 247 Rick Miller	.50	.23
☐ 248 Tom Hall	.50	.23
☐ 249 George Mitterwald	.50	.23
☐ 250A Willie McCovey SD	6.00	2.70
☐ 250B Willie McCovey WAS	30.00	13.50
☐ 251 Graig Nettles	2.00	.90
☐ 252 Dave Parker	10.00	4.50
☐ 253 John Boccabella	.50	.23
☐ 254 Stan Bahnsen	.50	.23
☐ 255 Larry Bowa	1.00	.45
☐ 256 Tom Griffin	.50	.23
☐ 257 Buddy Bell	2.00	.90
☐ 258 Jerry Morales	.50	.23
☐ 259 Bob Reynolds	.50	.23
☐ 260 Ted Simmons	2.00	.90
☐ 261 Jerry Bell	.50	.23
☐ 262 Ed Kirkpatrick	.50	.23
☐ 263 Checklist 133-264	2.50	.50
☐ 264 Joe Rudi	1.00	.45
☐ 265 Tug McGraw	2.00	.90
☐ 266 Jim Northrup	1.00	.45
☐ 267 Andy Messersmith	1.00	.45
☐ 268 Tom Grieve	1.00	.45
☐ 269 Bob Johnson	.50	.23
☐ 270 Ron Santo	2.00	.90
☐ 271 Bill Hands	.50	.23
☐ 272 Paul Casanova	.50	.23
☐ 273 Checklist 265-396	3.00	.60
☐ 274 Fred Beene	.50	.23
☐ 275 Ron Hunt	.50	.23
☐ 276 Angels Leaders	1.00	.45
Bobby Winkles MG		
John Roseboro CO		
Tom Morgan CO		
Jimmie Reese CO		
Salty Parker CO		
☐ 277 Gary Nolan	1.00	.45
☐ 278 Cookie Rojas	1.00	.45
☐ 279 Jim Crawford	.50	.23
☐ 280 Carl Yastrzemski	6.00	2.70
☐ 281 San Francisco Giants	1.00	.45
Team Card		
☐ 282 Doyle Alexander	1.00	.45
☐ 283 Mike Schmidt	50.00	22.00
☐ 284 Dave Duncan	1.00	.45
☐ 285 Reggie Smith	1.00	.45
☐ 286 Tony Muser	.50	.23
☐ 287 Clay Kirby	.50	.23
☐ 288 Gorman Thomas	2.00	.90
☐ 289 Rick Auerbach	.50	.23
☐ 290 Vida Blue	1.00	.45
☐ 291 Don Hahn	.50	.23
☐ 292 Chuck Seelbach	.50	.23
☐ 293 Milt May	.50	.23
☐ 294 Steve Foucault	.50	.23
☐ 295 Rick Monday	1.00	.45
☐ 296 Ray Corbin	.50	.23
☐ 297 Hal Breeden	.50	.23
☐ 298 Roric Harrison	.50	.23
☐ 299 Gene Michael	1.00	.45
☐ 300 Pete Rose	15.00	6.75
☐ 301 Bob Montgomery	.50	.23
☐ 302 Rudy May	.50	.23
☐ 303 George Hendrick	1.00	.45
☐ 304 Don Wilson	.50	.23
☐ 305 Tito Fuentes	.50	.23
☐ 306 Orioles Leaders	2.00	.90
Earl Weaver MG		
Jim Frey CO		
George Bamberger CO		
Billy Hunter CO		
George Staller CO		
☐ 307 Luis Melendez	.50	.23
☐ 308 Bruce Dal Canton	.50	.23
☐ 309A Dave Roberts SD	1.00	.45
☐ 309B Dave Roberts WAS	7.00	3.10
☐ 310 Terry Forster	1.00	.45
☐ 311 Jerry Grote	.50	.23
☐ 312 Deron Johnson	1.00	.45
☐ 313 Barry Lersch	.50	.23
☐ 314 Milwaukee Brewers	1.00	.45
Team Card		
☐ 315 Ron Cey	2.00	.90
☐ 316 Jim Perry	1.00	.45
☐ 317 Richie Zisk	1.00	.45
☐ 318 Jim Merritt	.50	.23
☐ 319 Randy Hundley	1.00	.45
☐ 320 Dusty Baker	2.00	.90
☐ 321 Steve Braun	.50	.23
☐ 322 Ernie McAnally	.50	.23
☐ 323 Richie Scheinblum	.50	.23
☐ 324 Steve Kline	.50	.23
☐ 325 Tommy Harper	2.00	.90
☐ 326 Reds Leaders	3.00	1.35
Sparky Anderson MG		
Larry Shepard CO		
George Scherger CO		
Alex Grammas CO		
Ted Kluszewski CO		
☐ 327 Tom Timmermann	.50	.23
☐ 328 Skip Jutze	.50	.23
☐ 329 Mark Belanger	1.00	.45
☐ 330 Juan Marichal	3.00	1.35
☐ 331 All-Star Catchers	5.00	2.20
Carlton Fisk		
Johnny Bench		
☐ 332 All-Star 1B	5.00	2.20
Dick Allen		
Hank Aaron		
☐ 333 All-Star 2B	3.00	1.35
Rod Carew		
Joe Morgan		
☐ 334 All-Star 3B	3.00	1.35
Brooks Robinson		
Ron Santo		
☐ 335 All-Star SS	1.00	.45
Bert Campaneris		
Chris Speier		
☐ 336 All-Star LF	3.00	1.35
Bobby Murcer		
Pete Rose		
☐ 337 All-Star CF	1.00	.45
Amos Otis		
Cesar Cedeno		
☐ 338 All-Star RF	5.00	2.20
Reggie Jackson		
Billy Williams		
☐ 339 All-Star Pitchers	3.00	1.35
Jim Hunter		
Rick Wise		
☐ 340 Thurman Munson	6.00	2.70
☐ 341 Dan Driessen	1.00	.45
☐ 342 Jim Lonborg	1.00	.45
☐ 343 Royals Team	1.00	.45
☐ 344 Mike Caldwell	.50	.23
☐ 345 Bill North	.50	.23
☐ 346 Ron Reed	.50	.23
☐ 347 Sandy Alomar	1.00	.45
☐ 348 Pete Richert	.50	.23
☐ 349 John Vukovich	.50	.23
☐ 350 Bob Gibson	5.00	2.20
☐ 351 Dwight Evans	3.00	1.35
☐ 352 Bill Stoneman	.50	.23
☐ 353 Rich Coggins	.50	.23
☐ 354 Cubs Leaders	1.00	.45
Whitey Lockman MG		
J.C. Martin CO		
Hank Aguirre CO		
Al Spangler CO		
Jim Marshall CO		
☐ 355 Dave Nelson	.50	.23
☐ 356 Jerry Koosman	1.00	.45
☐ 357 Buddy Bradford	.50	.23
☐ 358 Dal Maxvill	.50	.23
☐ 359 Brent Strom	.50	.23
☐ 360 Greg Luzinski	2.00	.90
☐ 361 Don Carrithers	.50	.23
☐ 362 Hal King	.50	.23
☐ 363 New York Yankees	2.00	.90
Team Card		
☐ 364A Cito Gaston SD	2.00	.90
☐ 364B Cito Gaston WAS	8.00	3.60
☐ 365 Steve Busby	1.00	.45
☐ 366 Larry Hisle	1.00	.45
☐ 367 Norm Cash	2.00	.90
☐ 368 Manny Mota	1.00	.45
☐ 369 Paul Lindblad	.50	.23
☐ 370 Bob Watson	1.00	.45
☐ 371 Jim Slaton	.50	.23
☐ 372 Ken Reitz	.50	.23
☐ 373 John Curtis	.50	.23
☐ 374 Marty Perez	.50	.23
☐ 375 Earl Williams	.50	.23
☐ 376 Jorge Orta	.50	.23
☐ 377 Ron Woods	.50	.23
☐ 378 Burt Hooton	1.00	.45
☐ 379 Rangers Leaders	2.00	.90
Billy Martin MG		
Frank Lucchesi CO		
Art Fowler CO		
Charlie Silvera CO		
Jackie Moore CO		
☐ 380 Bud Harrelson	1.00	.45
☐ 381 Charlie Sands	.50	.23
☐ 382 Bob Moose	.50	.23
☐ 383 Philadelphia Phillies	1.00	.45
Team Card		
☐ 384 Chris Chambliss	1.00	.45
☐ 385 Don Gullett	1.00	.45
☐ 386 Gary Matthews	2.00	.90
☐ 387A Rich Morales SD	1.00	.45
☐ 387B Rich Morales WAS	7.00	3.10
☐ 388 Phil Roof	.50	.23
☐ 389 Gates Brown	.50	.23
☐ 390 Lou Piniella	2.00	.90
☐ 391 Billy Champion	.50	.23
☐ 392 Dick Green	.50	.23
☐ 393 Orlando Pena	.50	.23
☐ 394 Ken Henderson	.50	.23
☐ 395 Doug Rader	.50	.23
☐ 396 Tommy Davis	1.00	.45
☐ 397 George Stone	.50	.23
☐ 398 Duke Sims	.50	.23
☐ 399 Mike Paul	.50	.23
☐ 400 Harmon Killebrew	5.00	2.20
☐ 401 Elliott Maddox	.50	.23
☐ 402 Jim Rooker	.50	.23
☐ 403 Red Sox Leaders	1.00	.45
Darrell Johnson MG		
Eddie Popowski CO		
Lee Stange CO		
Don Zimmer CO		
Don Bryant CO		
☐ 404 Jim Howarth	.50	.23
☐ 405 Ellie Rodriguez	.50	.23
☐ 406 Steve Arlin	.50	.23
☐ 407 Jim Wohlford	.50	.23
☐ 408 Charlie Hough	2.00	.90
☐ 409 Ike Brown	.50	.23
☐ 410 Pedro Borbon	.50	.23
☐ 411 Frank Baker	.50	.23
☐ 412 Chuck Taylor	.50	.23
☐ 413 Don Money	1.00	.45
☐ 414 Checklist 397-528	3.00	.60
☐ 415 Gary Gentry	.50	.23
☐ 416 Chicago White Sox	1.00	.45
Team Card		
☐ 417 Rich Folkers	.50	.23
☐ 418 Walt Williams	.50	.23
☐ 419 Wayne Twitchell	.50	.23
☐ 420 Ray Fosse	.50	.23
☐ 421 Dan Fife	.50	.23
☐ 422 Gonzalo Marquez	.50	.23
☐ 423 Fred Stanley	.50	.23
☐ 424 Jim Beauchamp	.50	.23
☐ 425 Pete Broberg	.50	.23
☐ 426 Rennie Stennett	.50	.23
☐ 427 Bobby Bolin	.50	.23
☐ 428 Gary Sutherland	.50	.23
☐ 429 Dick Lange	.50	.23
☐ 430 Matty Alou	1.00	.45

☐ 431 Gene Garber	1.00	.45
☐ 432 Chris Arnold	.50	.23
☐ 433 Lerrin LaGrow	.50	.23
☐ 434 Ken McMullen	.50	.23
☐ 435 Dave Concepcion	2.00	.90
☐ 436 Don Hood	.50	.23
☐ 437 Jim Lyttle	.50	.23
☐ 438 Ed Herrmann	.50	.23
☐ 439 Norm Miller	.50	.23
☐ 440 Jim Kaat	2.00	.90
☐ 441 Tom Ragland	.50	.23
☐ 442 Alan Foster	.50	.23
☐ 443 Tom Hutton	.50	.23
☐ 444 Vic Davalillo	.50	.23
☐ 445 George Medich	.50	.23
☐ 446 Len Randle	.50	.23
☐ 447 Twins Leaders	1.00	.45
Frank Quilici MG		
Ralph Rowe CO		
Bob Rodgers CO		
Vern Morgan CO		
☐ 448 Ron Hodges	.50	.23
☐ 449 Tom McCraw	.50	.23
☐ 450 Rich Hebner	1.00	.45
☐ 451 Tommy John	2.00	.90
☐ 452 Gene Hiser	.50	.23
☐ 453 Balor Moore	.50	.23
☐ 454 Kurt Bevacqua	.50	.23
☐ 455 Tom Bradley	.50	.23
☐ 456 Dave Winfield	100.00	45.00
☐ 457 Chuck Goggin	.50	.23
☐ 458 Jim Ray	.50	.23
☐ 459 Cincinnati Reds	2.00	.90
Team Card		
☐ 460 Boog Powell	2.00	.90
☐ 461 John Odom	.50	.23
☐ 462 Luis Alvarado	.50	.23
☐ 463 Pat Dobson	.50	.23
☐ 464 Jose Cruz	2.00	.90
☐ 465 Dick Bosman	.50	.23
☐ 466 Dick Billings	.50	.23
☐ 467 Winston Llenas	.50	.23
☐ 468 Pepe Frias	.50	.23
☐ 469 Joe Decker	.50	.23
☐ 470 Reggie Jackson ALCS	6.00	2.70
☐ 471 Jon Matlack NLCS	1.00	.45
☐ 472 Darold Knowles WS	1.00	.45
☐ 473 Willie Mays WS	8.00	3.60
☐ 474 Bert Campaneris WS	1.00	.45
☐ 475 Rusty Staub WS	1.00	.45
☐ 476 Cleon Jones WS	1.00	.45
☐ 477 Reggie Jackson WS	6.00	2.70
☐ 478 Bert Campaneris WS	1.00	.45
☐ 479 World Series Summary	1.00	.45
A's celebrate; win		
2nd consecutive		
championship		
☐ 480 Willie Crawford	.50	.23
☐ 481 Jerry Terrell	.50	.23
☐ 482 Bob Didier	.50	.23
☐ 483 Atlanta Braves	1.00	.45
Team Card		
☐ 484 Carmen Fanzone	.50	.23
☐ 485 Felipe Alou	2.00	.90
☐ 486 Steve Stone	1.00	.45
☐ 487 Ted Martinez	.50	.23
☐ 488 Andy Etchebarren	.50	.23
☐ 489 Pirates Leaders	1.00	.45
Danny Murtaugh MG		
Don Osborn CO		
Don Leppert CO		
Bill Mazeroski CO		
Bob Skinner CO		
☐ 490 Vada Pinson	2.00	.90
☐ 491 Roger Nelson	.50	.23
☐ 492 Mike Rogodzinski	.50	.23
☐ 493 Joe Hoerner	.50	.23
☐ 494 Ed Goodson	.50	.23
☐ 495 Dick McAuliffe	1.00	.45
☐ 496 Tom Murphy	.50	.23
☐ 497 Bobby Mitchell	.50	.23
☐ 498 Pat Corrales	1.00	.45
☐ 499 Rusty Torres	.50	.23
☐ 500 Lee May	1.00	.45
☐ 501 Eddie Leon	.50	.23
☐ 502 Dave LaRoche	.50	.23
☐ 503 Eric Soderholm	.50	.23
☐ 504 Joe Niekro	1.00	.45
☐ 505 Bill Buckner	1.00	.45
☐ 506 Ed Farmer	.50	.23
☐ 507 Larry Stahl	.50	.23
☐ 508 Montreal Expos	1.00	.45
Team Card		
☐ 509 Jesse Jefferson	.50	.23
☐ 510 Wayne Garrett	.50	.23
☐ 511 Toby Harrah	1.00	.45
☐ 512 Joe Lahoud	.50	.23
☐ 513 Jim Campanis	.50	.23
☐ 514 Paul Schaal	.50	.23
☐ 515 Willie Montanez	.50	.23
☐ 516 Horacio Pina	.50	.23
☐ 517 Mike Hegan	.50	.23
☐ 518 Derrel Thomas	.50	.23
☐ 519 Bill Sharp	.50	.23
☐ 520 Tim McCarver	2.00	.90
☐ 521 Indians Leaders	1.00	.45
Ken Aspromonte MG		
Clay Bryant CO		
Tony Pacheco CO		
☐ 522 J.R. Richard	2.00	.90
☐ 523 Cecil Cooper	2.00	.90
☐ 524 Bill Plummer	.50	.23
☐ 525 Clyde Wright	.50	.23
☐ 526 Frank Tepedino	.50	.23
☐ 527 Bobby Darwin	.50	.23
☐ 528 Bill Bonham	.50	.23
☐ 529 Horace Clarke	1.00	.45
☐ 530 Mickey Stanley	1.00	.45
☐ 531 Expos Leaders	1.00	.45
Gene Mauch MG		
Dave Bristol CO		
Cal McLish CO		
Larry Doby CO		
Jerry Zimmerman CO		
☐ 532 Skip Lockwood	.50	.23
☐ 533 Mike Phillips	.50	.23
☐ 534 Eddie Watt	.50	.23
☐ 535 Bob Tolan	.50	.23
☐ 536 Duffy Dyer	.50	.23
☐ 537 Steve Mingori	.50	.23
☐ 538 Cesar Tovar	.50	.23
☐ 539 Lloyd Allen	.50	.23
☐ 540 Bob Robertson	.50	.23
☐ 541 Cleveland Indians	1.00	.45
Team Card		
☐ 542 Rich Gossage	2.00	.90
☐ 543 Danny Cater	.50	.23
☐ 544 Ron Schueler	.50	.23
☐ 545 Billy Conigliaro	1.00	.45
☐ 546 Mike Corkins	.50	.23
☐ 547 Glenn Borgmann	.50	.23
☐ 548 Sonny Siebert	.50	.23
☐ 549 Mike Jorgensen	.50	.23
☐ 550 Sam McDowell	1.00	.45
☐ 551 Von Joshua	.50	.23
☐ 552 Denny Doyle	.50	.23
☐ 553 Jim Willoughby	.50	.23
☐ 554 Tim Johnson	.50	.23
☐ 555 Woodie Fryman	.50	.23
☐ 556 Dave Campbell	.50	.23
☐ 557 Jim McGlothlin	.50	.23
☐ 558 Bill Fahey	.50	.23
☐ 559 Darrel Chaney	.50	.23
☐ 560 Mike Cuellar	1.00	.45
☐ 561 Ed Kranepool	1.00	.45
☐ 562 Jack Aker	.50	.23
☐ 563 Hal McRae	1.00	.45
☐ 564 Mike Ryan	.50	.23
☐ 565 Milt Wilcox	.50	.23
☐ 566 Jackie Hernandez	.50	.23
☐ 567 Boston Red Sox	1.00	.45
Team Card		
☐ 568 Mike Torrez	1.00	.45
☐ 569 Rick Dempsey	1.00	.45
☐ 570 Ralph Garr	1.00	.45
☐ 571 Rich Hand	.50	.23
☐ 572 Enzo Hernandez	.50	.23
☐ 573 Mike Adams	.50	.23
☐ 574 Bill Parsons	.50	.23
☐ 575 Steve Garvey	4.00	1.80
☐ 576 Scipio Spinks	.50	.23
☐ 577 Mike Sadek	.50	.23
☐ 578 Ralph Houk MG	1.00	.45
☐ 579 Cecil Upshaw	.50	.23
☐ 580 Jim Spencer	.50	.23
☐ 581 Fred Norman	.50	.23
☐ 582 Bucky Dent	4.00	1.80
☐ 583 Marty Pattin	.50	.23
☐ 584 Ken Rudolph	.50	.23
☐ 585 Merv Rettenmund	.50	.23
☐ 586 Jack Brohamer	.50	.23
☐ 587 Larry Christenson	.50	.23
☐ 588 Hal Lanier	.50	.23
☐ 589 Boots Day	.50	.23
☐ 590 Roger Moret	.50	.23
☐ 591 Sonny Jackson	.50	.23
☐ 592 Ed Bane	.50	.23
☐ 593 Steve Yeager	1.00	.45
☐ 594 Leroy Stanton	.50	.23
☐ 595 Steve Blass	1.00	.45
☐ 596 Rookie Pitchers	.50	.23
Wayne Garland		
Fred Holdsworth		
Mark Littell		
Dick Pole		
☐ 597 Rookie Shortstops	.75	.35
Dave Chalk		
John Gamble		
Pete MacKanin		
Manny Trillo		
☐ 598 Rookie Outfielders	12.00	5.50
Dave Augustine		
Ken Griffey		
Steve Ontiveros		
Jim Tyrone		
☐ 599A Rookie Pitchers WAS	2.00	.90
Ron Diorio		
Dave Freisleben		
Frank Riccelli		
Greg Shanahan		
☐ 599B Rookie Pitchers SD	3.00	1.35
(SD in large print)		
☐ 599C Rookie Pitchers SD	5.00	2.20
(SD in small print)		
☐ 600 Rookie Infielders	5.00	2.20
Ron Cash		
Jim Cox		
Bill Madlock		
Reggie Sanders		
☐ 601 Rookie Outfielders	3.00	1.35
Ed Armbrister		
Rich Bladt		
Brian Downing		
Bake McBride		
☐ 602 Rookie Pitchers	1.00	.45
Glen Abbott		
Rick Henninger		
Craig Swan		
Dan Vossler		
☐ 603 Rookie Catchers	1.00	.45
Barry Foote		
Tom Lundstedt		
Charlie Moore		
Sergio Robles		
☐ 604 Rookie Infielders	5.00	2.20
Terry Hughes		
John Knox		
Andre Thornton		
Frank White		
☐ 605 Rookie Pitchers	4.00	1.80
Vic Albury		
Ken Frailing		
Kevin Kobel		
Frank Tanana		
☐ 606 Rookie Outfielders	1.00	.45
Jim Fuller		
Wilbur Howard		
Tommy Smith		
Otto Velez		
☐ 607 Rookie Shortstops	1.00	.45
Leo Foster		
Tom Heintzelman		
Dave Rosello		
Frank Taveras		
☐ 608A Rookie Pitchers: ERR	2.00	.90
Bob Apodaco (sic)		
Dick Baney		
John D'Acquisto		
Mike Wallace		
☐ 608B Rookie Pitchers: COR	1.00	.45
Bob Apodaca		
Dick Baney		
John D'Acquisto		
Mike Wallace		
☐ 609 Rico Petrocelli	1.00	.45
☐ 610 Dave Kingman	2.00	.90
☐ 611 Rich Stelmaszek	.50	.23
☐ 612 Luke Walker	.50	.23
☐ 613 Dan Monzon	.50	.23
☐ 614 Adrian Devine	.50	.23
☐ 615 Johnny Jeter UER	.50	.23
(Misspelled Johnnie		
on card back)		
☐ 616 Larry Gura	.50	.23
☐ 617 Ted Ford	.50	.23
☐ 618 Jim Mason	.50	.23
☐ 619 Mike Anderson	.50	.23
☐ 620 Al Downing	.50	.23
☐ 621 Bernie Carbo	.50	.23
☐ 622 Phil Gagliano	.50	.23
☐ 623 Celerino Sanchez	.50	.23
☐ 624 Bob Miller	.50	.23
☐ 625 Ollie Brown	.50	.23
☐ 626 Pittsburgh Pirates	1.00	.45
Team Card		
☐ 627 Carl Taylor	.50	.23
☐ 628 Ivan Murrell	.50	.23
☐ 629 Rusty Staub	2.00	.90
☐ 630 Tommie Agee	1.00	.45
☐ 631 Steve Barber	.50	.23
☐ 632 George Culver	.50	.23
☐ 633 Dave Hamilton	.50	.23

Card	NRMT	VG-E
☐ 634 Braves Leaders	2.00	.90
Eddie Mathews MG		
Herm Starrette CO		
Connie Ryan CO		
Jim Busby CO		
Ken Silvestri CO		
☐ 635 Johnny Edwards	.50	.23
☐ 636 Dave Goltz	.50	.23
☐ 637 Checklist 529-660	3.00	.60
☐ 638 Ken Sanders	.50	.23
☐ 639 Joe Lovitto	.50	.23
☐ 640 Milt Pappas	1.00	.45
☐ 641 Chuck Brinkman	.50	.23
☐ 642 Terry Harmon	.50	.23
☐ 643 Dodgers Team	1.00	.45
☐ 644 Wayne Granger	.50	.23
☐ 645 Ken Boswell	.50	.23
☐ 646 George Foster	2.00	.90
☐ 647 Juan Beniquez	.50	.23
☐ 648 Terry Crowley	.50	.23
☐ 649 Fernando Gonzalez	.50	.23
☐ 650 Mike Epstein	.50	.23
☐ 651 Leron Lee	.50	.23
☐ 652 Gail Hopkins	.50	.23
☐ 653 Bob Stinson	.50	.23
☐ 654A Jesus Alou ERR (No position)	1.00	.45
☐ 654B Jesus Alou COR (Outfield)	5.00	2.20
☐ 655 Mike Tyson	.50	.23
☐ 656 Adrian Garrett	.50	.23
☐ 657 Jim Shellenback	.50	.23
☐ 658 Lee Lacy	.50	.23
☐ 659 Joe Lis	.50	.23
☐ 660 Larry Dierker	2.00	.50

1974 Topps Traded

The cards in this 44-card set measure 2 1/2" by 3 1/2". The 1974 Topps Traded set contains 43 player cards and one unnumbered checklist card. The fronts have the word "traded" in block letters and the backs are designed in newspaper style. Card numbers are the same as in the regular set except they are followed by a "T." No known scarcities exist for this set. The cards were inserted in all packs toward the end of the production run. They were produced in large enough quantity that they are no scarcer than the regular Topps cards.

	NRMT	VG-E
COMPLETE SET (44)	15.00	6.75
COMMON CARD	.50	.23

Card	NRMT	VG-E
☐ 23T Craig Robinson	.50	.23
☐ 42T Claude Osteen	.75	.35
☐ 43T Jim Wynn	.75	.35
☐ 51T Bobby Heise	.50	.23
☐ 59T Ross Grimsley	.50	.23
☐ 62T Bob Locker	.50	.23
☐ 63T Bill Sudakis	.50	.23
☐ 73T Mike Marshall	.75	.35
☐ 123T Nelson Briles	.75	.35
☐ 139T Aurelio Monteagudo	.50	.23
☐ 151T Diego Segui	.50	.23
☐ 165T Willie Davis	.75	.35
☐ 175T Reggie Cleveland	.50	.23
☐ 182T Lindy McDaniel	.75	.35
☐ 186T Fred Scherman	.50	.23
☐ 249T George Mitterwald	.50	.23
☐ 262T Ed Kirkpatrick	.50	.23
☐ 269T Bob Johnson	.50	.23
☐ 270T Ron Santo	1.00	.45
☐ 313T Barry Lersch	.50	.23
☐ 319T Randy Hundley	.75	.35
☐ 330T Juan Marichal	2.00	.90
☐ 348T Pete Richert	.50	.23
☐ 373T John Curtis	.50	.23
☐ 390T Lou Piniella	1.00	.45
☐ 428T Gary Sutherland	.50	.23
☐ 454T Kurt Bevacqua	.50	.23
☐ 458T Jim Ray	.50	.23
☐ 485T Felipe Alou	1.00	.45
☐ 486T Steve Stone	.75	.35
☐ 496T Tom Murphy	.50	.23
☐ 516T Horacio Pina	.50	.23
☐ 534T Eddie Watt	.50	.23
☐ 538T Cesar Tovar	.50	.23
☐ 544T Ron Schueler	.50	.23
☐ 579T Cecil Upshaw	.50	.23
☐ 585T Merv Rettenmund	.50	.23
☐ 612T Luke Walker	.50	.23
☐ 616T Larry Gura	.75	.35
☐ 618T Jim Mason	.50	.23
☐ 630T Tommie Agee	.75	.35
☐ 648T Terry Crowley	.50	.23
☐ 649T Fernando Gonzalez	.50	.23
☐ NNO Traded Checklist	1.50	.30

1974 Topps Team Checklists

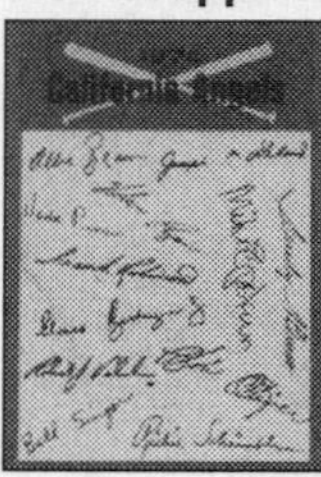

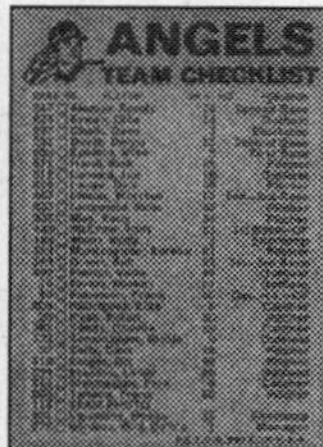

The cards in this 24-card set measure 2 1/2" by 3 1/2". The 1974 series of checklists was issued in packs with the regular cards for that year. The cards are unnumbered (arbitrarily numbered below alphabetically by team name) and have bright red borders. The year and team name appear in a green panel decorated by a crossed bats design, below which is a white area containing facsimile autographs of various players. The mustard-yellow and gray-colored backs list team members alphabetically, along with their card number, uniform number and position. Uncut sheets of these cards were also available through a wrapper mail-in offer. The uncut sheet value in NR/Mt or better condition is approximately $150.

	NRMT	VG-E
COMPLETE SET (24)	20.00	9.00
COMMON TEAM (1-24)	1.00	.30

Card	NRMT	VG-E
☐ 1 Atlanta Braves	1.00	.30
☐ 2 Baltimore Orioles	1.00	.30
☐ 3 Boston Red Sox	1.00	.30
☐ 4 California Angels	1.00	.30
☐ 5 Chicago Cubs	1.00	.30
☐ 6 Chicago White Sox	1.00	.30
☐ 7 Cincinnati Reds	1.00	.30
☐ 8 Cleveland Indians	1.00	.30
☐ 9 Detroit Tigers	1.00	.30
☐ 10 Houston Astros	1.00	.30
☐ 11 Kansas City Royals	1.00	.30
☐ 12 Los Angeles Dodgers	1.00	.30
☐ 13 Milwaukee Brewers	1.00	.30
☐ 14 Minnesota Twins	1.00	.30
☐ 15 Montreal Expos	1.00	.30
☐ 16 New York Mets	1.00	.30
☐ 17 New York Yankees	1.00	.30
☐ 18 Oakland A's	1.00	.30
☐ 19 Philadelphia Phillies	1.00	.30
☐ 20 Pittsburgh Pirates	1.00	.30
☐ 21 San Diego Padres	1.00	.30
☐ 22 San Francisco Giants	1.00	.30
☐ 23 St. Louis Cardinals	1.00	.30
☐ 24 Texas Rangers	1.00	.30

1974 Topps Deckle Edge

The cards in this 72-card set measure 2 7/8" by 5". Returning to a format first used in 1969, Topps produced a set of black and white photo cards in 1974 bearing an unusual serrated or "deckle" border. A facsimile autograph appears on the obverse while the backs contain the card number and a "newspaper-clipping" design detailing a milestone in the player's career. This was a test set and uncut sheets are sometimes found. Card backs are either white or gray; the white back cards are slightly tougher to obtain. The wrapper is also considered collectible. Wrappers featured either Reggie Jackson or Tom Seaver and come with or without the phrase "With gum". Wrappers with the usual folds which are in Nr Mt condition have an approximate value of $20.

	NRMT	VG-E
COMPLETE SET (72)	3000.00	1350.00
COMMON CARD (1-72)	15.00	6.75

Card	NRMT	VG-E
☐ 1 Amos Otis	25.00	11.00
☐ 2 Darrell Evans	25.00	11.00
☐ 3 Bob Gibson	100.00	45.00
☐ 4 Dave Nelson	15.00	6.75
☐ 5 Steve Carlton	125.00	55.00
☐ 6 Jim Hunter	100.00	45.00
☐ 7 Thurman Munson	150.00	70.00
☐ 8 Bob Grich	25.00	11.00
☐ 9 Tom Seaver	200.00	90.00
☐ 10 Ted Simmons	25.00	11.00
☐ 11 Bobby Valentine	25.00	11.00
☐ 12 Don Sutton	50.00	22.00
☐ 13 Wilbur Wood	15.00	6.75
☐ 14 Doug Rader	15.00	6.75
☐ 15 Chris Chambliss	15.00	6.75
☐ 16 Pete Rose	175.00	80.00
☐ 17 John Hiller	15.00	6.75
☐ 18 Burt Hooton	15.00	6.75
☐ 19 Tim Foli	15.00	6.75
☐ 20 Lou Brock	100.00	45.00
☐ 21 Ron Bryant	15.00	6.75
☐ 22 Manny Sanguillen	15.00	6.75
☐ 23 Bob Tolan	15.00	6.75
☐ 24 Greg Luzinski	25.00	11.00
☐ 25 Brooks Robinson	125.00	55.00
☐ 26 Felix Millan	15.00	6.75
☐ 27 Luis Tiant	25.00	11.00
☐ 28 Willie McCovey	100.00	45.00
☐ 29 Chris Speier	15.00	6.75
☐ 30 George Scott	15.00	6.75
☐ 31 Willie Stargell	75.00	34.00
☐ 32 Rod Carew	125.00	55.00
☐ 33 Charlie Spikes	15.00	6.75
☐ 34 Nate Colbert	15.00	6.75
☐ 35 Rich Hebner	15.00	6.75
☐ 36 Bobby Bonds	25.00	11.00
☐ 37 Buddy Bell	25.00	11.00
☐ 38 Claude Osteen	15.00	6.75
☐ 39 Dick Allen	25.00	11.00
☐ 40 Bill Russell	15.00	6.75
☐ 41 Nolan Ryan	1000.00	450.00
☐ 42 Willie Davis	15.00	6.75
☐ 43 Carl Yastrzemski	125.00	55.00
☐ 44 Jon Matlack	15.00	6.75
☐ 45 Jim Palmer	100.00	45.00
☐ 46 Bert Campaneris	15.00	6.75
☐ 47 Bert Blyleven	25.00	11.00
☐ 48 Jeff Burroughs	15.00	6.75
☐ 49 Jim Colborn	15.00	6.75
☐ 50 Dave Johnson	25.00	11.00
☐ 51 John Mayberry	15.00	6.75
☐ 52 Don Kessinger	15.00	6.75
☐ 53 Joe Coleman	15.00	6.75
☐ 54 Tony Perez	75.00	34.00
☐ 55 Jose Cardenal	15.00	6.75
☐ 56 Paul Splittorff	15.00	6.75
☐ 57 Hank Aaron	150.00	70.00
☐ 58 Dave May	15.00	6.75
☐ 59 Fergie Jenkins	100.00	45.00
☐ 60 Ron Blomberg	15.00	6.75
☐ 61 Reggie Jackson	175.00	80.00
☐ 62 Tony Oliva	25.00	11.00
☐ 63 Bobby Murcer	25.00	11.00
☐ 64 Carlton Fisk	100.00	45.00
☐ 65 Steve Rogers	15.00	6.75
☐ 66 Frank Robinson	125.00	55.00
☐ 67 Joe Ferguson	15.00	6.75
☐ 68 Bill Melton	15.00	6.75
☐ 69 Bob Watson	15.00	6.75
☐ 70 Larry Bowa	25.00	11.00
☐ 71 Johnny Bench	150.00	70.00
☐ 72 Willie Horton	15.00	6.75

1975 Topps

The cards in the 1975 Topps set were issued in two different sizes: a regular standard size (2 1/2" by 3 1/2") and a mini size (2 1/2" by 3 1/8") which was issued as a test in certain areas of the country. The 660-card Topps baseball set for 1975 was radically different in appearance from sets of the preceding years. The most prominent change was the use of a two-color frame surrounding the picture area rather than a single, subdued color. A facsimile autograph appears on the picture, and the backs

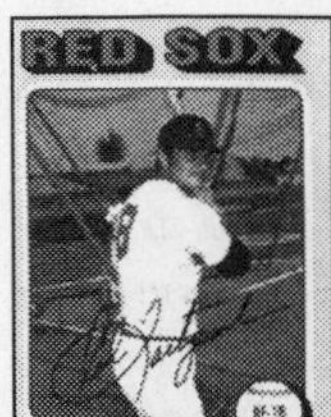

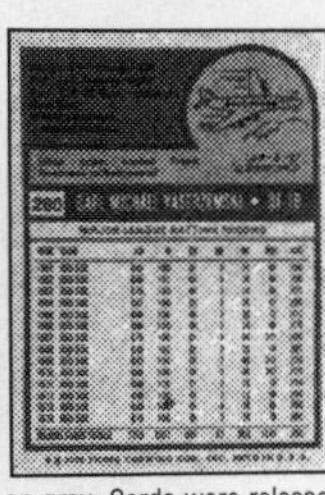

are printed in red and green on gray. Cards were released in ten-card wax packs as well as in 42-card rack packs. Cards 189-212 depict the MVP's of both leagues from 1951 through 1974. The first seven cards (1-7) feature players (listed in alphabetical order) breaking records or achieving milestones during the previous season. Cards 306-313 picture league leaders in various statistical categories. Cards 459-466 depict the results of post-season action. Team cards feature a checklist back for players on that team and show a small inset photo of the manager on the front. The following players' regular issue cards are explicitly denoted as All-Stars, 1, 50, 80, 140, 170, 180, 260, 320, 350, 390, 400, 420, 440, 470, 530, 570, and 600. This set is quite popular with collectors, at least in part due to the fact that the Rookie Cards of George Brett, Gary Carter, Keith Hernandez, Fred Lynn, Jim Rice and Robin Yount are all in the set. Topps minis have the same checklist and are valued approximately 1.5 times the prices listed below.

	NRMT	VG-E
COMPLETE SET (660)	800.00	350.00
COMMON CARD (1-660)	.50	.23
WRAPPER (15-CENT)	10.00	4.50
*MINIS 1.5X BASIC CARDS		
☐ 1 Hank Aaron RB	30.00	10.00
Sets Homer Mark		
☐ 2 Lou Brock RB	3.00	1.35
118 Stolen Bases		
☐ 3 Bob Gibson RB	3.00	1.35
3000th Strikeout		
☐ 4 Al Kaline RB	4.00	1.80
3000 Hit Club		
☐ 5 Nolan Ryan RB	30.00	13.50
Fans 300 for		
3rd Year in a Row		
☐ 6 Mike Marshall RB	1.00	.45
Hurls 106 Games		
☐ 7 Steve Busby HL	12.00	5.50
Dick Bosman		
Nolan Ryan		
☐ 8 Rogelio Moret	.50	.23
☐ 9 Frank Tepedino	.50	.23
☐ 10 Willie Davis	1.00	.45
☐ 11 Bill Melton	.50	.23
☐ 12 David Clyde	.50	.23
☐ 13 Gene Locklear	1.00	.45
☐ 14 Milt Wilcox	.50	.23
☐ 15 Jose Cardenal	1.00	.45
☐ 16 Frank Tanana	2.00	.90
☐ 17 Dave Concepcion	2.00	.90
☐ 18 Tigers: Team/Mgr.	2.00	.40
Ralph Houk		
(Checklist back)		
☐ 19 Jerry Koosman	1.00	.45
☐ 20 Thurman Munson	6.00	2.70
☐ 21 Rollie Fingers	3.00	1.35
☐ 22 Dave Cash	.50	.23
☐ 23 Bill Russell	1.00	.45
☐ 24 Al Fitzmorris	.50	.23
☐ 25 Lee May	1.00	.45
☐ 26 Dave McNally	1.00	.45
☐ 27 Ken Reitz	.50	.23
☐ 28 Tom Murphy	.50	.23
☐ 29 Dave Parker	4.00	1.80
☐ 30 Bert Blyleven	2.00	.90
☐ 31 Dave Rader	.50	.23
☐ 32 Reggie Cleveland	.50	.23
☐ 33 Dusty Baker	2.00	.90
☐ 34 Steve Renko	.50	.23
☐ 35 Ron Santo	1.00	.45
☐ 36 Joe Lovitto	.50	.23
☐ 37 Dave Freisleben	.50	.23
☐ 38 Buddy Bell	2.00	.90
☐ 39 Andre Thornton	1.00	.45
☐ 40 Bill Singer	.50	.23
☐ 41 Cesar Geronimo	1.00	.45
☐ 42 Joe Coleman	.50	.23
☐ 43 Cleon Jones	1.00	.45
☐ 44 Pat Dobson	.50	.23
☐ 45 Joe Rudi	1.00	.45
☐ 46 Phillies: Team/Mgr.	2.00	.40
Danny Ozark UER		
(Checklist back)		
(Terry Harmon listed as 339		
instead of 399)		
☐ 47 Tommy John	2.00	.90
☐ 48 Freddie Patek	1.00	.45
☐ 49 Larry Dierker	1.00	.45
☐ 50 Brooks Robinson	6.00	2.70
☐ 51 Bob Forsch	1.00	.45
☐ 52 Darrell Porter	1.00	.45
☐ 53 Dave Giusti	.50	.23
☐ 54 Eric Soderholm	.50	.23
☐ 55 Bobby Bonds	2.00	.90
☐ 56 Rick Wise	1.00	.45
☐ 57 Dave Johnson	1.00	.45
☐ 58 Chuck Taylor	.50	.23
☐ 59 Ken Henderson	.50	.23
☐ 60 Fergie Jenkins	3.00	1.35
☐ 61 Dave Winfield	40.00	18.00
☐ 62 Fritz Peterson	.50	.23
☐ 63 Steve Swisher	.50	.23
☐ 64 Dave Chalk	.50	.23
☐ 65 Don Gullett	1.00	.45
☐ 66 Willie Horton	1.00	.45
☐ 67 Tug McGraw	1.00	.45
☐ 68 Ron Blomberg	.50	.23
☐ 69 John Odom	.50	.23
☐ 70 Mike Schmidt	50.00	22.00
☐ 71 Charlie Hough	1.00	.45
☐ 72 Royals: Team/Mgr.	2.00	.40
Jack McKeon		
(Checklist back)		
☐ 73 J.R. Richard	1.00	.45
☐ 74 Mark Belanger	1.00	.45
☐ 75 Ted Simmons	2.00	.90
☐ 76 Ed Sprague	.50	.23
☐ 77 Richie Zisk	1.00	.45
☐ 78 Ray Corbin	.50	.23
☐ 79 Gary Matthews	1.00	.45
☐ 80 Carlton Fisk	10.00	4.50
☐ 81 Ron Reed	.50	.23
☐ 82 Pat Kelly	.50	.23
☐ 83 Jim Merritt	.50	.23
☐ 84 Enzo Hernandez	.50	.23
☐ 85 Bill Bonham	.50	.23
☐ 86 Joe Lis	.50	.23
☐ 87 George Foster	2.00	.90
☐ 88 Tom Egan	.50	.23
☐ 89 Jim Ray	.50	.23
☐ 90 Rusty Staub	2.00	.90
☐ 91 Dick Green	.50	.23
☐ 92 Cecil Upshaw	.50	.23
☐ 93 Dave Lopes	2.00	.90
☐ 94 Jim Lonborg	1.00	.45
☐ 95 John Mayberry	1.00	.45
☐ 96 Mike Cosgrove	.50	.23
☐ 97 Earl Williams	.50	.23
☐ 98 Rich Folkers	.50	.23
☐ 99 Mike Hegan	.50	.23
☐ 100 Willie Stargell	4.00	1.80
☐ 101 Expos: Team/Mgr.	2.00	.40
Gene Mauch		
(Checklist back)		
☐ 102 Joe Decker	.50	.23
☐ 103 Rick Miller	.50	.23
☐ 104 Bill Madlock	2.00	.90
☐ 105 Buzz Capra	.50	.23
☐ 106 Mike Hargrove	3.00	1.35
☐ 107 Jim Barr	.50	.23
☐ 108 Tom Hall	.50	.23
☐ 109 George Hendrick	1.00	.45
☐ 110 Wilbur Wood	.50	.23
☐ 111 Wayne Garrett	.50	.23
☐ 112 Larry Hardy	.50	.23
☐ 113 Elliott Maddox	.50	.23
☐ 114 Dick Lange	.50	.23
☐ 115 Joe Ferguson	.50	.23
☐ 116 Lerrin LaGrow	.50	.23
☐ 117 Orioles: Team/Mgr.	3.00	.60
Earl Weaver		
(Checklist back)		
☐ 118 Mike Anderson	.50	.23
☐ 119 Tommy Helms	.50	.23
☐ 120 Steve Busby UER	1.00	.45
(Photo actually		
Fran Healy)		
☐ 121 Bill North	.50	.23
☐ 122 Al Hrabosky	1.00	.45
☐ 123 Johnny Briggs	.50	.23
☐ 124 Jerry Reuss	1.00	.45
☐ 125 Ken Singleton	1.00	.45
☐ 126 Checklist 1-132	3.00	.60
☐ 127 Glenn Borgmann	.50	.23
☐ 128 Bill Lee	1.00	.45
☐ 129 Rick Monday	1.00	.45
☐ 130 Phil Niekro	3.00	1.35
☐ 131 Toby Harrah	1.00	.45
☐ 132 Randy Moffitt	.50	.23
☐ 133 Dan Driessen	1.00	.45
☐ 134 Ron Hodges	.50	.23
☐ 135 Charlie Spikes	.50	.23
☐ 136 Jim Mason	.50	.23
☐ 137 Terry Forster	1.00	.45
☐ 138 Del Unser	.50	.23
☐ 139 Horacio Pina	.50	.23
☐ 140 Steve Garvey	5.00	2.20
☐ 141 Mickey Stanley	1.00	.45
☐ 142 Bob Reynolds	.50	.23
☐ 143 Cliff Johnson	1.00	.45
☐ 144 Jim Wohlford	.50	.23
☐ 145 Ken Holtzman	1.00	.45
☐ 146 Padres: Team/Mgr.	2.00	.40
John McNamara		
(Checklist back)		
☐ 147 Pedro Garcia	.50	.23
☐ 148 Jim Rooker	.50	.23
☐ 149 Tim Foli	.50	.23
☐ 150 Bob Gibson	5.00	2.20
☐ 151 Steve Brye	.50	.23
☐ 152 Mario Guerrero	.50	.23
☐ 153 Rick Reuschel	1.00	.45
☐ 154 Mike Lum	.50	.23
☐ 155 Jim Bibby	.50	.23
☐ 156 Dave Kingman	2.00	.90
☐ 157 Pedro Borbon	1.00	.45
☐ 158 Jerry Grote	.50	.23
☐ 159 Steve Arlin	.50	.23
☐ 160 Graig Nettles	2.00	.90
☐ 161 Stan Bahnsen	.50	.23
☐ 162 Willie Montanez	.50	.23
☐ 163 Jim Brewer	.50	.23
☐ 164 Mickey Rivers	1.00	.45
☐ 165 Doug Rader	1.00	.45
☐ 166 Woodie Fryman	.50	.23
☐ 167 Rich Coggins	.50	.23
☐ 168 Bill Greif	.50	.23
☐ 169 Cookie Rojas	1.00	.45
☐ 170 Bert Campaneris	1.00	.45
☐ 171 Ed Kirkpatrick	.50	.23
☐ 172 Red Sox: Team/Mgr.	3.00	.60
Darrell Johnson		
(Checklist back)		
☐ 173 Steve Rogers	1.00	.45
☐ 174 Bake McBride	1.00	.45
☐ 175 Don Money	1.00	.45
☐ 176 Burt Hooton	1.00	.45
☐ 177 Vic Correll	.50	.23
☐ 178 Cesar Tovar	.50	.23
☐ 179 Tom Bradley	.50	.23
☐ 180 Joe Morgan	5.00	2.20
☐ 181 Fred Beene	.50	.23
☐ 182 Don Hahn	.50	.23
☐ 183 Mel Stottlemyre	1.00	.45
☐ 184 Jorge Orta	.50	.23
☐ 185 Steve Carlton	6.00	2.70
☐ 186 Willie Crawford	.50	.23
☐ 187 Denny Doyle	.50	.23
☐ 188 Tom Griffin	.50	.23
☐ 189 1951 MVP's	3.00	1.35
Larry (Yogi) Berra		
Roy Campanella		
(Campy never issued)		
☐ 190 1952 MVP's	2.00	.90
Bobby Shantz		
Hank Sauer		
☐ 191 1953 MVP's	2.00	.90
Al Rosen		
Roy Campanella		
☐ 192 1954 MVP's	4.00	1.80
Yogi Berra		
Willie Mays		
☐ 193 1955 MVP's UER	3.00	1.35
Yogi Berra		
Roy Campanella		
(Campy card never		
issued, pictured		
with LA cap)		
☐ 194 1956 MVP's	15.00	6.75
Mickey Mantle		
Don Newcombe		
☐ 195 1957 MVP's	25.00	11.00
Mickey Mantle		
Hank Aaron		
☐ 196 1958 MVP's	2.00	.90
Jackie Jensen		
Ernie Banks		
☐ 197 1959 MVP's	2.00	.90
Nellie Fox		
Ernie Banks		
☐ 198 1960 MVP's	2.00	.90
Roger Maris		
Dick Groat		
☐ 199 1961 MVP's	3.00	1.35
Roger Maris		
Frank Robinson		

☐ 200 1962 MVP's	15.00	6.75
Mickey Mantle		
Maury Wills		
(Wills never issued)		
☐ 201 1963 MVP's	2.00	.90
Elston Howard		
Sandy Koufax		
☐ 202 1964 MVP's	2.00	.90
Brooks Robinson		
Ken Boyer		
☐ 203 1965 MVP's	2.00	.90
Zoilo Versalles		
Willie Mays		
☐ 204 1966 MVP's	8.00	3.60
Frank Robinson		
Bob Clemente		
☐ 205 1967 MVP's	2.00	.90
Carl Yastrzemski		
Orlando Cepeda		
☐ 206 1968 MVP's	2.00	.90
Denny McLain		
Bob Gibson		
☐ 207 1969 MVP's	2.00	.90
Harmon Killebrew		
Willie McCovey		
☐ 208 1970 MVP's	2.00	.90
Boog Powell		
Johnny Bench		
☐ 209 1971 MVP's	2.00	.90
Vida Blue		
Joe Torre		
☐ 210 1972 MVP's	2.00	.90
Rich Allen		
Johnny Bench		
☐ 211 1973 MVP's	6.00	2.70
Reggie Jackson		
Pete Rose		
☐ 212 1974 MVP's	2.00	.90
Jeff Burroughs		
Steve Garvey		
☐ 213 Oscar Gamble	1.00	.45
☐ 214 Harry Parker	.50	.23
☐ 215 Bobby Valentine	1.00	.45
☐ 216 Giants: Team/Mgr.	2.00	.40
Wes Westrum		
(Checklist back)		
☐ 217 Lou Piniella	2.00	.90
☐ 218 Jerry Johnson	.50	.23
☐ 219 Ed Herrmann	.50	.23
☐ 220 Don Sutton	3.00	1.35
☐ 221 Aurelio Rodriguez	.50	.23
☐ 222 Dan Spillner	.50	.23
☐ 223 Robin Yount	100.00	45.00
☐ 224 Ramon Hernandez	.50	.23
☐ 225 Bob Grich	1.00	.45
☐ 226 Bill Campbell	.50	.23
☐ 227 Bob Watson	1.00	.45
☐ 228 George Brett	200.00	90.00
☐ 229 Barry Foote	.50	.23
☐ 230 Jim Hunter	3.00	1.35
☐ 231 Mike Tyson	.50	.23
☐ 232 Diego Segui	.50	.23
☐ 233 Billy Grabarkewitz	.50	.23
☐ 234 Tom Grieve	1.00	.45
☐ 235 Jack Billingham	1.00	.45
☐ 236 Angels: Team/Mgr.	2.00	.40
Dick Williams		
(Checklist back)		
☐ 237 Carl Morton	.50	.23
☐ 238 Dave Duncan	.50	.23
☐ 239 George Stone	.50	.23
☐ 240 Garry Maddox	1.00	.45
☐ 241 Dick Tidrow	.50	.23
☐ 242 Jay Johnstone	1.00	.45
☐ 243 Jim Kaat	2.00	.90
☐ 244 Bill Buckner	1.00	.45
☐ 245 Mickey Lolich	2.00	.90
☐ 246 Cardinals: Team/Mgr.	2.00	.40
Red Schoendienst		
(Checklist back)		
☐ 247 Enos Cabell	.50	.23
☐ 248 Randy Jones	2.00	.90
☐ 249 Danny Thompson	.50	.23
☐ 250 Ken Brett	.50	.23
☐ 251 Fran Healy	.50	.23
☐ 252 Fred Scherman	.50	.23
☐ 253 Jesus Alou	.50	.23
☐ 254 Mike Torrez	1.00	.45
☐ 255 Dwight Evans	2.00	.90
☐ 256 Billy Champion	.50	.23
☐ 257 Checklist: 133-264	3.00	.60
☐ 258 Dave LaRoche	.50	.23
☐ 259 Len Randle	.50	.23
☐ 260 Johnny Bench	12.00	5.50
☐ 261 Andy Hassler	.50	.23
☐ 262 Rowland Office	.50	.23
☐ 263 Jim Perry	1.00	.45
☐ 264 John Milner	.50	.23
☐ 265 Ron Bryant	.50	.23
☐ 266 Sandy Alomar	1.00	.45
☐ 267 Dick Ruthven	.50	.23
☐ 268 Hal McRae	1.00	.45
☐ 269 Doug Rau	.50	.23
☐ 270 Ron Fairly	1.00	.45
☐ 271 Gerry Moses	.50	.23
☐ 272 Lynn McGlothen	.50	.23
☐ 273 Steve Braun	.50	.23
☐ 274 Vicente Romo	.50	.23
☐ 275 Paul Blair	1.00	.45
☐ 276 White Sox Team/Mgr.	2.00	.40
Chuck Tanner		
(Checklist back)		
☐ 277 Frank Taveras	.50	.23
☐ 278 Paul Lindblad	.50	.23
☐ 279 Milt May	.50	.23
☐ 280 Carl Yastrzemski	6.00	2.70
☐ 281 Jim Slaton	.50	.23
☐ 282 Jerry Morales	.50	.23
☐ 283 Steve Foucault	.50	.23
☐ 284 Ken Griffey	4.00	1.80
☐ 285 Ellie Rodriguez	.50	.23
☐ 286 Mike Jorgensen	.50	.23
☐ 287 Roric Harrison	.50	.23
☐ 288 Bruce Ellingsen	.50	.23
☐ 289 Ken Rudolph	.50	.23
☐ 290 Jon Matlack	.50	.23
☐ 291 Bill Sudakis	.50	.23
☐ 292 Ron Schueler	.50	.23
☐ 293 Dick Sharon	.50	.23
☐ 294 Geoff Zahn	.50	.23
☐ 295 Vada Pinson	2.00	.90
☐ 296 Alan Foster	.50	.23
☐ 297 Craig Kusick	.50	.23
☐ 298 Johnny Grubb	.50	.23
☐ 299 Bucky Dent	2.00	.90
☐ 300 Reggie Jackson	15.00	6.75
☐ 301 Dave Roberts	.50	.23
☐ 302 Rick Burleson	1.00	.45
☐ 303 Grant Jackson	.50	.23
☐ 304 Pirates: Team/Mgr.	2.00	.40
Danny Murtaugh		
(Checklist back)		
☐ 305 Jim Colborn	.50	.23
☐ 306 Batting Leaders	2.00	.90
Rod Carew		
Ralph Garr		
☐ 307 Home Run Leaders	3.00	1.35
Dick Allen		
Mike Schmidt		
☐ 308 RBI Leaders	2.00	.90
Jeff Burroughs		
Johnny Bench		
☐ 309 Stolen Base Leaders	2.00	.90
Bill North		
Lou Brock		
☐ 310 Victory Leaders	2.00	.90
Jim Hunter		
Fergie Jenkins		
Andy Messersmith		
Phil Niekro		
☐ 311 ERA Leaders	2.00	.90
Jim Hunter		
Buzz Capra		
☐ 312 Strikeout Leaders	20.00	9.00
Nolan Ryan		
Steve Carlton		
☐ 313 Leading Firemen	1.00	.45
Terry Forster		
Mike Marshall		
☐ 314 Buck Martinez	.50	.23
☐ 315 Don Kessinger	1.00	.45
☐ 316 Jackie Brown	.50	.23
☐ 317 Joe Lahoud	.50	.23
☐ 318 Ernie McAnally	.50	.23
☐ 319 Johnny Oates	1.00	.45
☐ 320 Pete Rose	15.00	6.75
☐ 321 Rudy May	.50	.23
☐ 322 Ed Goodson	.50	.23
☐ 323 Fred Holdsworth	.50	.23
☐ 324 Ed Kranepool	1.00	.45
☐ 325 Tony Oliva	2.00	.90
☐ 326 Wayne Twitchell	.50	.23
☐ 327 Jerry Hairston	.50	.23
☐ 328 Sonny Siebert	.50	.23
☐ 329 Ted Kubiak	.50	.23
☐ 330 Mike Marshall	1.00	.45
☐ 331 Indians: Team/Mgr.	2.00	.40
Frank Robinson		
(Checklist back)		
☐ 332 Fred Kendall	.50	.23
☐ 333 Dick Drago	.50	.23
☐ 334 Greg Gross	.50	.23
☐ 335 Jim Palmer	5.00	2.20
☐ 336 Rennie Stennett	.50	.23
☐ 337 Kevin Kobel	.50	.23
☐ 338 Rich Stelmaszek	.50	.23
☐ 339 Jim Fregosi	1.00	.45
☐ 340 Paul Splittorff	.50	.23
☐ 341 Hal Breeden	.50	.23
☐ 342 Leroy Stanton	.50	.23
☐ 343 Danny Frisella	.50	.23
☐ 344 Ben Oglivie	1.00	.45
☐ 345 Clay Carroll	1.00	.45
☐ 346 Bobby Darwin	.50	.23
☐ 347 Mike Caldwell	.50	.23
☐ 348 Tony Muser	.50	.23
☐ 349 Ray Sadecki	.50	.23
☐ 350 Bobby Murcer	1.00	.45
☐ 351 Bob Boone	2.00	.90
☐ 352 Darold Knowles	.50	.23
☐ 353 Luis Melendez	.50	.23
☐ 354 Dick Bosman	.50	.23
☐ 355 Chris Cannizzaro	.50	.23
☐ 356 Rico Petrocelli	1.00	.45
☐ 357 Ken Forsch	.50	.23
☐ 358 Al Bumbry	1.00	.45
☐ 359 Paul Popovich	.50	.23
☐ 360 George Scott	1.00	.45
☐ 361 Dodgers: Team/Mgr.	2.00	.40
Walter Alston		
(Checklist back)		
☐ 362 Steve Hargan	.50	.23
☐ 363 Carmen Fanzone	.50	.23
☐ 364 Doug Bird	.50	.23
☐ 365 Bob Bailey	.50	.23
☐ 366 Ken Sanders	.50	.23
☐ 367 Craig Robinson	.50	.23
☐ 368 Vic Albury	.50	.23
☐ 369 Merv Rettenmund	.50	.23
☐ 370 Tom Seaver	12.00	5.50
☐ 371 Gates Brown	.50	.23
☐ 372 John D'Acquisto	.50	.23
☐ 373 Bill Sharp	.50	.23
☐ 374 Eddie Watt	.50	.23
☐ 375 Roy White	1.00	.45
☐ 376 Steve Yeager	1.00	.45
☐ 377 Tom Hilgendorf	.50	.23
☐ 378 Derrel Thomas	.50	.23
☐ 379 Bernie Carbo	.50	.23
☐ 380 Sal Bando	1.00	.45
☐ 381 John Curtis	.50	.23
☐ 382 Don Baylor	2.00	.90
☐ 383 Jim York	.50	.23
☐ 384 Brewers: Team/Mgr.	2.00	.40
Del Crandall		
(Checklist back)		
☐ 385 Dock Ellis	.50	.23
☐ 386 Checklist: 265-396	3.00	.60
☐ 387 Jim Spencer	.50	.23
☐ 388 Steve Stone	1.00	.45
☐ 389 Tony Solaita	.50	.23
☐ 390 Ron Cey	2.00	.90
☐ 391 Don DeMola	.50	.23
☐ 392 Bruce Bochte	1.00	.45
☐ 393 Gary Gentry	.50	.23
☐ 394 Larvell Blanks	.50	.23
☐ 395 Bud Harrelson	1.00	.45
☐ 396 Fred Norman	1.00	.45
☐ 397 Bill Freehan	1.00	.45
☐ 398 Elias Sosa	.50	.23
☐ 399 Terry Harmon	.50	.23
☐ 400 Dick Allen	2.00	.90
☐ 401 Mike Wallace	.50	.23
☐ 402 Bob Tolan	.50	.23
☐ 403 Tom Buskey	.50	.23
☐ 404 Ted Sizemore	.50	.23
☐ 405 John Montague	.50	.23
☐ 406 Bob Gallagher	.50	.23
☐ 407 Herb Washington	2.00	.90
☐ 408 Clyde Wright	.50	.23
☐ 409 Bob Robertson	.50	.23
☐ 410 Mike Cueller UER	1.00	.45
(Sic, Cuellar)		
☐ 411 George Mitterwald	.50	.23
☐ 412 Bill Hands	.50	.23
☐ 413 Marty Pattin	.50	.23
☐ 414 Manny Mota	1.00	.45
☐ 415 John Hiller	1.00	.45
☐ 416 Larry Lintz	.50	.23
☐ 417 Skip Lockwood	.50	.23
☐ 418 Leo Foster	.50	.23
☐ 419 Dave Goltz	.50	.23
☐ 420 Larry Bowa	2.00	.90
☐ 421 Mets: Team/Mgr.	3.00	.60
Yogi Berra		
(Checklist back)		
☐ 422 Brian Downing	1.00	.45
☐ 423 Clay Kirby	.50	.23
☐ 424 John Lowenstein	.50	.23
☐ 425 Tito Fuentes	.50	.23
☐ 426 George Medich	.50	.23

☐ 427 Clarence Gaston 1.00 .45
☐ 428 Dave Hamilton .50 .23
☐ 429 Jim Dwyer .50 .23
☐ 430 Luis Tiant 2.00 .90
☐ 431 Rod Gilbreath .50 .23
☐ 432 Ken Berry .50 .23
☐ 433 Larry Demery .50 .23
☐ 434 Bob Locker .50 .23
☐ 435 Dave Nelson .50 .23
☐ 436 Ken Frailing .50 .23
☐ 437 Al Cowens 1.00 .45
☐ 438 Don Carrithers .50 .23
☐ 439 Ed Brinkman .50 .23
☐ 440 Andy Messersmith 1.00 .45
☐ 441 Bobby Heise .50 .23
☐ 442 Maximino Leon .50 .23
☐ 443 Twins: Team/Mgr. 2.00 .40
Frank Quilici
(Checklist back)
☐ 444 Gene Garber 1.00 .45
☐ 445 Felix Millan .50 .23
☐ 446 Bart Johnson .50 .23
☐ 447 Terry Crowley .50 .23
☐ 448 Frank Duffy .50 .23
☐ 449 Charlie Williams .50 .23
☐ 450 Willie McCovey 5.00 2.20
☐ 451 Rick Dempsey 1.00 .45
☐ 452 Angel Mangual .50 .23
☐ 453 Claude Osteen 1.00 .45
☐ 454 Doug Griffin .50 .23
☐ 455 Don Wilson .50 .23
☐ 456 Bob Coluccio .50 .23
☐ 457 Mario Mendoza .50 .23
☐ 458 Ross Grimsley .50 .23
☐ 459 1974 AL Champs 1.00 .45
A's over Orioles
(Second base action
pictured)
☐ 460 Frank Taveras NLCS 2.00 .90
Steve Garvey
☐ 461 Reggie Jackson WS 4.00 1.80
☐ 462 World Series Game 2 1.00 .45
(Dodger dugout)
☐ 463 Rollie Fingers WS 2.00 .90
☐ 464 World Series Game 4 1.00 .45
(A's batter)
☐ 465 Joe Rudi WS 1.00 .45
☐ 466 World Series Summary 2.00 .90
A's do it again;
win third straight
(A's group picture)
☐ 467 Ed Halicki .50 .23
☐ 468 Bobby Mitchell .50 .23
☐ 469 Tom Dettore .50 .23
☐ 470 Jeff Burroughs 1.00 .45
☐ 471 Bob Stinson .50 .23
☐ 472 Bruce Dal Canton .50 .23
☐ 473 Ken McMullen .50 .23
☐ 474 Luke Walker .50 .23
☐ 475 Darrell Evans 1.00 .45
☐ 476 Ed Figueroa .50 .23
☐ 477 Tom Hutton .50 .23
☐ 478 Tom Burgmeier .50 .23
☐ 479 Ken Boswell .50 .23
☐ 480 Carlos May .50 .23
☐ 481 Will McEnaney 1.00 .45
☐ 482 Tom McCraw .50 .23
☐ 483 Steve Ontiveros .50 .23
☐ 484 Glenn Beckert 1.00 .45
☐ 485 Sparky Lyle 1.00 .45
☐ 486 Ray Fosse .50 .23
☐ 487 Astros: Team/Mgr. 2.00 .40
Preston Gomez
(Checklist back)
☐ 488 Bill Travers .50 .23
☐ 489 Cecil Cooper 2.00 .90
☐ 490 Reggie Smith 1.00 .45
☐ 491 Doyle Alexander 1.00 .45
☐ 492 Rich Hebner 1.00 .45
☐ 493 Don Stanhouse .50 .23
☐ 494 Pete LaCock .50 .23
☐ 495 Nelson Briles 1.00 .45
☐ 496 Pepe Frias .50 .23
☐ 497 Jim Nettles .50 .23
☐ 498 Al Downing .50 .23
☐ 499 Marty Perez .50 .23
☐ 500 Nolan Ryan 75.00 34.00
☐ 501 Bill Robinson 1.00 .45
☐ 502 Pat Bourque .50 .23
☐ 503 Fred Stanley .50 .23
☐ 504 Buddy Bradford .50 .23
☐ 505 Chris Speier .50 .23
☐ 506 Leron Lee .50 .23
☐ 507 Tom Carroll .50 .23
☐ 508 Bob Hansen .50 .23
☐ 509 Dave Hilton .50 .23
☐ 510 Vida Blue 1.00 .45
☐ 511 Rangers: Team/Mgr. 2.00 .40
Billy Martin
(Checklist back)
☐ 512 Larry Milbourne .50 .23
☐ 513 Dick Pole .50 .23
☐ 514 Jose Cruz 2.00 .90
☐ 515 Manny Sanguillen 1.00 .45
☐ 516 Don Hood .50 .23
☐ 517 Checklist: 397-528 3.00 .60
☐ 518 Leo Cardenas .50 .23
☐ 519 Jim Todd .50 .23
☐ 520 Amos Otis 1.00 .45
☐ 521 Dennis Blair .50 .23
☐ 522 Gary Sutherland .50 .23
☐ 523 Tom Paciorek 1.00 .45
☐ 524 John Doherty .50 .23
☐ 525 Tom House .50 .23
☐ 526 Larry Hisle 1.00 .45
☐ 527 Mac Scarce .50 .23
☐ 528 Eddie Leon .50 .23
☐ 529 Gary Thomasson .50 .23
☐ 530 Gaylord Perry 3.00 1.35
☐ 531 Reds: Team/Mgr. 4.00 .80
Sparky Anderson
(Checklist back)
☐ 532 Gorman Thomas 1.00 .45
☐ 533 Rudy Meoli .50 .23
☐ 534 Alex Johnson .50 .23
☐ 535 Gene Tenace 1.00 .45
☐ 536 Bob Moose .50 .23
☐ 537 Tommy Harper 1.00 .45
☐ 538 Duffy Dyer .50 .23
☐ 539 Jesse Jefferson .50 .23
☐ 540 Lou Brock 5.00 2.20
☐ 541 Roger Metzger .50 .23
☐ 542 Pete Broberg .50 .23
☐ 543 Larry Biittner .50 .23
☐ 544 Steve Mingori .50 .23
☐ 545 Billy Williams 3.00 1.35
☐ 546 John Knox .50 .23
☐ 547 Von Joshua .50 .23
☐ 548 Charlie Sands .50 .23
☐ 549 Bill Butler .50 .23
☐ 550 Ralph Garr 1.00 .45
☐ 551 Larry Christenson .50 .23
☐ 552 Jack Brohamer .50 .23
☐ 553 John Boccabella .50 .23
☐ 554 Rich Gossage 2.00 .90
☐ 555 Al Oliver 2.00 .90
☐ 556 Tim Johnson .50 .23
☐ 557 Larry Gura .50 .23
☐ 558 Dave Roberts .50 .23
☐ 559 Bob Montgomery .50 .23
☐ 560 Tony Perez 3.00 1.35
☐ 561 A's: Team/Mgr. 2.00 .40
Alvin Dark
(Checklist back)
☐ 562 Gary Nolan 1.00 .45
☐ 563 Wilbur Howard .50 .23
☐ 564 Tommy Davis 1.00 .45
☐ 565 Joe Torre 2.00 .90
☐ 566 Ray Burris .50 .23
☐ 567 Jim Sundberg 2.00 .90
☐ 568 Dale Murray .50 .23
☐ 569 Frank White 1.00 .45
☐ 570 Jim Wynn 1.00 .45
☐ 571 Dave Lemanczyk .50 .23
☐ 572 Roger Nelson .50 .23
☐ 573 Orlando Pena .50 .23
☐ 574 Tony Taylor 1.00 .45
☐ 575 Gene Clines .50 .23
☐ 576 Phil Roof .50 .23
☐ 577 John Morris .50 .23
☐ 578 Dave Tomlin .50 .23
☐ 579 Skip Pitlock .50 .23
☐ 580 Frank Robinson 6.00 2.70
☐ 581 Darrel Chaney .50 .23
☐ 582 Eduardo Rodriguez .50 .23
☐ 583 Andy Etchebarren .50 .23
☐ 584 Mike Garman .50 .23
☐ 585 Chris Chambliss 1.00 .45
☐ 586 Tim McCarver 2.00 .90
☐ 587 Chris Ward .50 .23
☐ 588 Rick Auerbach .50 .23
☐ 589 Braves: Team/Mgr. 2.00 .40
Clyde King
(Checklist back)
☐ 590 Cesar Cedeno 1.00 .45
☐ 591 Glenn Abbott .50 .23
☐ 592 Balor Moore .50 .23
☐ 593 Gene Lamont .50 .23
☐ 594 Jim Fuller .50 .23
☐ 595 Joe Niekro 1.00 .45
☐ 596 Ollie Brown .50 .23
☐ 597 Winston Llenas .50 .23
☐ 598 Bruce Kison .50 .23
☐ 599 Nate Colbert .50 .23
☐ 600 Rod Carew 5.00 2.20
☐ 601 Juan Beniquez .50 .23
☐ 602 John Vukovich .50 .23
☐ 603 Lew Krausse .50 .23
☐ 604 Oscar Zamora .50 .23
☐ 605 John Ellis .50 .23
☐ 606 Bruce Miller .50 .23
☐ 607 Jim Holt .50 .23
☐ 608 Gene Michael 1.00 .45
☐ 609 Elrod Hendricks .50 .23
☐ 610 Ron Hunt .50 .23
☐ 611 Yankees: Team/Mgr. 2.00 .40
Bill Virdon
(Checklist back)
☐ 612 Terry Hughes .50 .23
☐ 613 Bill Parsons .50 .23
☐ 614 Rookie Pitchers 1.00 .45
Jack Kucek
Dyar Miller
Vern Ruhle
Paul Siebert
☐ 615 Rookie Pitchers 2.00 .90
Pat Darcy
Dennis Leonard
Tom Underwood
Hank Webb
☐ 616 Rookie Outfielders 12.00 5.50
Dave Augustine
Pepe Mangual
Jim Rice
John Scott
☐ 617 Rookie Infielders 2.00 .90
Mike Cubbage
Doug DeCinces
Reggie Sanders
Manny Trillo
☐ 618 Rookie Pitchers 1.00 .45
Jamie Easterly
Tom Johnson
Scott McGregor
Rick Rhoden
☐ 619 Rookie Outfielders 1.00 .45
Benny Ayala
Nyls Nyman
Tommy Smith
Jerry Turner
☐ 620 Rookie Catcher/OF 20.00 9.00
Gary Carter
Marc Hill
Danny Meyer
Leon Roberts
☐ 621 Rookie Pitchers 2.00 .90
John Denny
Rawly Eastwick
Jim Kern
Juan Veintidos
☐ 622 Rookie Outfielders 6.00 2.70
Ed Armbrister
Fred Lynn
Tom Poquette
Terry Whitfield UER
(Listed as Ney York)
☐ 623 Rookie Infielders 6.00 2.70
Phil Garner
Keith Hernandez UER
(Sic, bats right)
Bob Sheldon
Tom Veryzer
☐ 624 Rookie Pitchers 1.00 .45
Doug Konieczny
Gary Lavelle
Jim Otten
Eddie Solomon
☐ 625 Boog Powell 2.00 .90
☐ 626 Larry Haney UER .50 .23
(Photo actually
Dave Duncan)
☐ 627 Tom Walker .50 .23
☐ 628 Ron LeFlore 1.00 .45
☐ 629 Joe Hoerner .50 .23
☐ 630 Greg Luzinski 2.00 .90
☐ 631 Lee Lacy .50 .23
☐ 632 Morris Nettles .50 .23
☐ 633 Paul Casanova .50 .23
☐ 634 Cy Acosta .50 .23
☐ 635 Chuck Dobson .50 .23
☐ 636 Charlie Moore .50 .23
☐ 637 Ted Martinez .50 .23
☐ 638 Cubs: Team/Mgr. 2.00 .40
Jim Marshall
(Checklist back)
☐ 639 Steve Kline .50 .23
☐ 640 Harmon Killebrew 5.00 2.20
☐ 641 Jim Northrup .50 .23
☐ 642 Mike Phillips .50 .23
☐ 643 Brent Strom .50 .23
☐ 644 Bill Fahey .50 .23

Card	NRMT	VG-E
☐ 645 Danny Cater	.50	.23
☐ 646 Checklist: 529-660	3.00	.60
☐ 647 Claudell Washington	2.00	.90
☐ 648 Dave Pagan	.50	.23
☐ 649 Jack Heidemann	.50	.23
☐ 650 Dave May	.50	.23
☐ 651 John Morlan	.50	.23
☐ 652 Lindy McDaniel	1.00	.45
☐ 653 Lee Richard UER (Listed as Richards on card front)	.50	.23
☐ 654 Jerry Terrell	.50	.23
☐ 655 Rico Carty	1.00	.45
☐ 656 Bill Plummer	.50	.23
☐ 657 Bob Oliver	.50	.23
☐ 658 Vic Harris	.50	.23
☐ 659 Bob Apodaca	.50	.23
☐ 660 Hank Aaron	30.00	9.00

1975 Topps Team Checklist Sheet

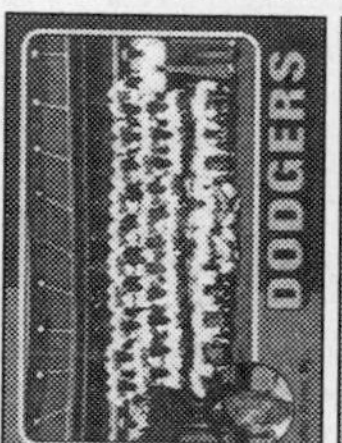

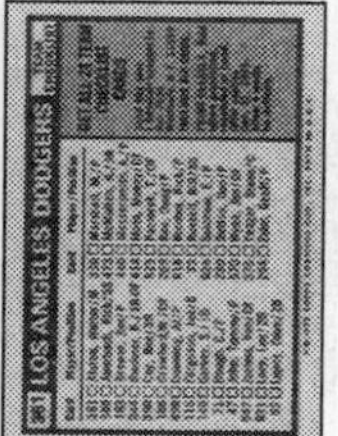

This uncut sheet of the 24 1975 Topps team checklists measures 10 1/2" by 20 1/8". The sheet was obtained by sending 40 cents plus one wrapper to Topps. When cut, each card measures the standard size.

	NRMT	VG-E
COMPLETE SET (1)	20.00	9.00
COMMON CARD	20.00	9.00
☐ 1 Topps Team CL Sheet	20.00	9.00

1976 Topps

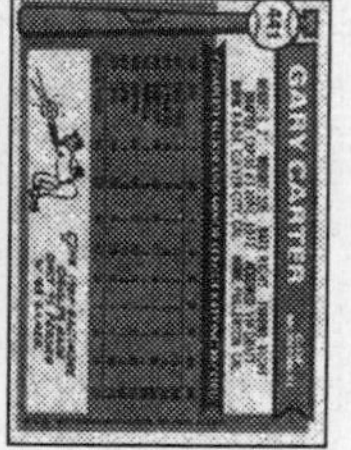

The 1976 Topps set of 660 standard-size cards is known for its sharp color photographs and interesting presentation of subjects. Team cards feature a checklist back for players on that team and show a small inset photo of the manager on the front. A "Father and Son" series (66-70) spotlights five Major Leaguers whose fathers also made the "Big Show." Other subseries include "All Time All Stars" (341-350), "Record Breakers" from the previous season (1-6), League Leaders (191-205), Post-season cards (461-462), and Rookie Prospects (589-599). The following players' regular issue cards are explicitly denoted as All-Stars, 10, 48, 60, 140, 150, 165, 169, 240, 300, 370, 380, 395, 400, 420, 475, 500, 580, and 650. Cards were issued in ten-card wax packs, 42-card rack packs as well as cello packs and other options. The key Rookie Cards in this set are Dennis Eckersley, Ron Guidry, and Willie Randolph.

	NRMT	VG-E
COMPLETE SET (660)	400.00	180.00
COMMON CARD (1-660)	.40	.18
☐ 1 Hank Aaron RB 2262 Career RBIs	15.00	4.70
☐ 2 Bobby Bonds RB Most leadoff HR's 32; plus three seasons 30 homers/30 steals	1.50	.70
☐ 3 Mickey Lolich RB Most Lefthanded Strikeouts: 2679	.75	.35
☐ 4 Dave Lopes RB Most Consecutive SB's: 38	.75	.35
☐ 5 Tom Seaver RB Most Consecutive seasons with 200 Strikeouts	4.00	1.80
☐ 6 Rennie Stennett RB 7 Hits in a 9 inning game	.75	.35
☐ 7 Jim Umbarger	.40	.18
☐ 8 Tito Fuentes	.40	.18
☐ 9 Paul Lindblad	.40	.18
☐ 10 Lou Brock	4.00	1.80
☐ 11 Jim Hughes	.40	.18
☐ 12 Richie Zisk	.75	.35
☐ 13 John Wockenfuss	.40	.18
☐ 14 Gene Garber	.75	.35
☐ 15 George Scott	.75	.35
☐ 16 Bob Apodaca	.40	.18
☐ 17 New York Yankees Team Card; Billy Martin MG (Checklist back)	1.50	.30
☐ 18 Dale Murray	.40	.18
☐ 19 George Brett	60.00	27.00
☐ 20 Bob Watson	.75	.35
☐ 21 Dave LaRoche	.40	.18
☐ 22 Bill Russell	.75	.35
☐ 23 Brian Downing	.40	.18
☐ 24 Cesar Geronimo	.75	.35
☐ 25 Mike Torrez	.75	.35
☐ 26 Andre Thornton	.75	.35
☐ 27 Ed Figueroa	.40	.18
☐ 28 Dusty Baker	1.50	.70
☐ 29 Rick Burleson	.75	.35
☐ 30 John Montefusco	.75	.35
☐ 31 Len Randle	.40	.18
☐ 32 Danny Frisella	.40	.18
☐ 33 Bill North	.40	.18
☐ 34 Mike Garman	.40	.18
☐ 35 Tony Oliva	1.50	.70
☐ 36 Frank Taveras	.40	.18
☐ 37 John Hiller	.75	.35
☐ 38 Garry Maddox	.75	.35
☐ 39 Pete Broberg	.40	.18
☐ 40 Dave Kingman	1.50	.70
☐ 41 Tippy Martinez	.75	.35
☐ 42 Barry Foote	.40	.18
☐ 43 Paul Splittorff	.40	.18
☐ 44 Doug Rader	.75	.35
☐ 45 Boog Powell	1.50	.70
☐ 46 Los Angeles Dodgers Team Card; Walter Alston MG (Checklist back)	1.50	.30
☐ 47 Jesse Jefferson	.40	.18
☐ 48 Dave Concepcion	1.50	.70
☐ 49 Dave Duncan	.75	.35
☐ 50 Fred Lynn	1.50	.70
☐ 51 Ray Burris	.40	.18
☐ 52 Dave Chalk	.40	.18
☐ 53 Mike Beard	.40	.18
☐ 54 Dave Rader	.40	.18
☐ 55 Gaylord Perry	2.50	1.10
☐ 56 Bob Tolan	.40	.18
☐ 57 Phil Garner	.75	.35
☐ 58 Ron Reed	.40	.18
☐ 59 Larry Hisle	.75	.35
☐ 60 Jerry Reuss	.75	.35
☐ 61 Ron LeFlore	.75	.35
☐ 62 Johnny Oates	.75	.35
☐ 63 Bobby Darwin	.40	.18
☐ 64 Jerry Koosman	.75	.35
☐ 65 Chris Chambliss	.75	.35
☐ 66 Gus Bell FS Buddy Bell	.75	.35
☐ 67 Ray Boone FS Bob Boone	.75	.35
☐ 68 Joe Coleman FS Joe Coleman Jr.	.40	.18
☐ 69 Jim Hegan FS Mike Hegan	.40	.18
☐ 70 Roy Smalley FS Roy Smalley Jr.	.75	.35
☐ 71 Steve Rogers	.75	.35
☐ 72 Hal McRae	.75	.35
☐ 73 Baltimore Orioles Team Card; Earl Weaver MG (Checklist back)	1.50	.30
☐ 74 Oscar Gamble	.75	.35
☐ 75 Larry Dierker	.75	.35
☐ 76 Willie Crawford	.40	.18
☐ 77 Pedro Borbon	.75	.35
☐ 78 Cecil Cooper	.75	.35
☐ 79 Jerry Morales	.40	.18
☐ 80 Jim Kaat	1.50	.70
☐ 81 Darrell Evans	.75	.35
☐ 82 Von Joshua	.40	.18
☐ 83 Jim Spencer	.40	.18
☐ 84 Brent Strom	.40	.18
☐ 85 Mickey Rivers	.75	.35
☐ 86 Mike Tyson	.40	.18
☐ 87 Tom Burgmeier	.40	.18
☐ 88 Duffy Dyer	.40	.18
☐ 89 Vern Ruhle	.40	.18
☐ 90 Sal Bando	.75	.35
☐ 91 Tom Hutton	.40	.18
☐ 92 Eduardo Rodriguez	.40	.18
☐ 93 Mike Phillips	.40	.18
☐ 94 Jim Dwyer	.40	.18
☐ 95 Brooks Robinson	5.00	2.20
☐ 96 Doug Bird	.40	.18
☐ 97 Wilbur Howard	.40	.18
☐ 98 Dennis Eckersley	40.00	18.00
☐ 99 Lee Lacy	.40	.18
☐ 100 Jim Hunter	2.50	1.10
☐ 101 Pete LaCock	.40	.18
☐ 102 Jim Willoughby	.40	.18
☐ 103 Biff Pocoroba	.40	.18
☐ 104 Cincinnati Reds Team Card; Sparky Anderson MG (Checklist back)	2.50	.50
☐ 105 Gary Lavelle	.40	.18
☐ 106 Tom Grieve	.75	.35
☐ 107 Dave Roberts	.40	.18
☐ 108 Don Kirkwood	.40	.18
☐ 109 Larry Lintz	.40	.18
☐ 110 Carlos May	.40	.18
☐ 111 Danny Thompson	.40	.18
☐ 112 Kent Tekulve	1.50	.70
☐ 113 Gary Sutherland	.40	.18
☐ 114 Jay Johnstone	.75	.35
☐ 115 Ken Holtzman	.75	.35
☐ 116 Charlie Moore	.40	.18
☐ 117 Mike Jorgensen	.40	.18
☐ 118 Boston Red Sox Team Card; Darrell Johnson MG (Checklist back)	1.50	.30
☐ 119 Checklist 1-132	1.50	.30
☐ 120 Rusty Staub	.75	.35
☐ 121 Tony Solaita	.40	.18
☐ 122 Mike Cosgrove	.40	.18
☐ 123 Walt Williams	.40	.18
☐ 124 Doug Rau	.40	.18
☐ 125 Don Baylor	1.50	.70
☐ 126 Tom Dettore	.40	.18
☐ 127 Larvell Blanks	.40	.18
☐ 128 Ken Griffey	2.50	1.10
☐ 129 Andy Etchebarren	.40	.18
☐ 130 Luis Tiant	1.50	.70
☐ 131 Bill Stein	.40	.18
☐ 132 Don Hood	.40	.18
☐ 133 Gary Matthews	.75	.35
☐ 134 Mike Ivie	.40	.18
☐ 135 Bake McBride	.75	.35
☐ 136 Dave Goltz	.40	.18
☐ 137 Bill Robinson	.75	.35
☐ 138 Lerrin LaGrow	.40	.18
☐ 139 Gorman Thomas	.75	.35
☐ 140 Vida Blue	.75	.35
☐ 141 Larry Parrish	1.50	.70
☐ 142 Dick Drago	.40	.18
☐ 143 Jerry Grote	.40	.18
☐ 144 Al Fitzmorris	.40	.18
☐ 145 Larry Bowa	.75	.35
☐ 146 George Medich	.40	.18
☐ 147 Houston Astros Team Card; Bill Virdon MG (Checklist back)	1.50	.30
☐ 148 Stan Thomas	.40	.18
☐ 149 Tommy Davis	.75	.35
☐ 150 Steve Garvey	4.00	1.80
☐ 151 Bill Bonham	.40	.18
☐ 152 Leroy Stanton	.40	.18
☐ 153 Buzz Capra	.40	.18
☐ 154 Bucky Dent	.75	.35
☐ 155 Jack Billingham	.75	.35
☐ 156 Rico Carty	.75	.35
☐ 157 Mike Caldwell	.40	.18
☐ 158 Ken Reitz	.40	.18
☐ 159 Jerry Terrell	.40	.18
☐ 160 Dave Winfield	15.00	6.75
☐ 161 Bruce Kison	.40	.18
☐ 162 Jack Pierce	.40	.18
☐ 163 Jim Slaton	.40	.18
☐ 164 Pepe Mangual	.40	.18
☐ 165 Gene Tenace	.75	.35
☐ 166 Skip Lockwood	.40	.18
☐ 167 Freddie Patek	.75	.35
☐ 168 Tom Hilgendorf	.40	.18
☐ 169 Graig Nettles	1.50	.70
☐ 170 Rick Wise	.40	.18
☐ 171 Greg Gross	.40	.18
☐ 172 Texas Rangers	1.50	.30

Card		
Team Card; Frank Lucchesi MG (Checklist back)		
☐ 173 Steve Swisher	.40	.18
☐ 174 Charlie Hough	.75	.35
☐ 175 Ken Singleton	.75	.35
☐ 176 Dick Lange	.40	.18
☐ 177 Marty Perez	.40	.18
☐ 178 Tom Buskey	.40	.18
☐ 179 George Foster	1.50	.70
☐ 180 Rich Gossage	1.50	.70
☐ 181 Willie Montanez	.40	.18
☐ 182 Harry Rasmussen	.40	.18
☐ 183 Steve Braun	.40	.18
☐ 184 Bill Greif	.40	.18
☐ 185 Dave Parker	1.50	.70
☐ 186 Tom Walker	.40	.18
☐ 187 Pedro Garcia	.40	.18
☐ 188 Fred Scherman	.40	.18
☐ 189 Claudell Washington	.75	.35
☐ 190 Jon Matlack	.40	.18
☐ 191 NL Batting Leaders	.75	.35
Bill Madlock		
Ted Simmons		
Manny Sanguillen		
☐ 192 AL Batting Leaders	2.50	1.10
Rod Carew		
Fred Lynn		
Thurman Munson		
☐ 193 NL Home Run Leaders	3.00	1.35
Mike Schmidt		
Dave Kingman		
Greg Luzinski		
☐ 194 AL Home Run Leaders	2.50	1.10
Reggie Jackson		
George Scott		
John Mayberry		
☐ 195 NL RBI Leaders	1.50	.70
Greg Luzinski		
Johnny Bench		
Tony Perez		
☐ 196 AL RBI Leaders	.75	.35
George Scott		
John Mayberry		
Fred Lynn		
☐ 197 NL Steals Leaders	1.50	.70
Dave Lopes		
Joe Morgan		
Lou Brock		
☐ 198 AL Steals Leaders	.75	.35
Mickey Rivers		
Claudell Washington		
Amos Otis		
☐ 199 NL Victory Leaders	1.50	.70
Tom Seaver		
Randy Jones		
Andy Messersmith		
☐ 200 AL Victory Leaders	1.50	.70
Jim Hunter		
Jim Palmer		
Vida Blue		
☐ 201 NL ERA Leaders	1.50	.70
Randy Jones		
Andy Messersmith		
Tom Seaver		
☐ 202 AL ERA Leaders	5.00	2.20
Jim Palmer		
Jim Hunter		
Dennis Eckersley		
☐ 203 NL Strikeout Leaders	1.50	.70
Tom Seaver		
John Montefusco		
Andy Messersmith		
☐ 204 AL Strikeout Leaders	.75	.35
Frank Tanana		
Bert Blyleven		
Gaylord Perry		
☐ 205 Leading Firemen	.75	.35
Al Hrabosky		
Rich Gossage		
☐ 206 Manny Trillo	.40	.18
☐ 207 Andy Hassler	.40	.18
☐ 208 Mike Lum	.40	.18
☐ 209 Alan Ashby	.75	.35
☐ 210 Lee May	.75	.35
☐ 211 Clay Carroll	.75	.35
☐ 212 Pat Kelly	.40	.18
☐ 213 Dave Heaverlo	.40	.18
☐ 214 Eric Soderholm	.40	.18
☐ 215 Reggie Smith	.75	.35
☐ 216 Montreal Expos	1.50	.30
Team Card; Karl Kuehl MG (Checklist back)		
☐ 217 Dave Freisleben	.40	.18
☐ 218 John Knox	.40	.18
☐ 219 Tom Murphy	.40	.18
☐ 220 Manny Sanguillen	.75	.35
☐ 221 Jim Todd	.40	.18
☐ 222 Wayne Garrett	.40	.18
☐ 223 Ollie Brown	.40	.18
☐ 224 Jim York	.40	.18
☐ 225 Roy White	.75	.35
☐ 226 Jim Sundberg	.75	.35
☐ 227 Oscar Zamora	.40	.18
☐ 228 John Hale	.40	.18
☐ 229 Jerry Remy	.40	.18
☐ 230 Carl Yastrzemski	5.00	2.20
☐ 231 Tom House	.40	.18
☐ 232 Frank Duffy	.40	.18
☐ 233 Grant Jackson	.40	.18
☐ 234 Mike Sadek	.40	.18
☐ 235 Bert Blyleven	1.50	.70
☐ 236 Kansas City Royals	1.50	.30
Team Card; Whitey Herzog MG (Checklist back)		
☐ 237 Dave Hamilton	.40	.18
☐ 238 Larry Biittner	.40	.18
☐ 239 John Curtis	.40	.18
☐ 240 Pete Rose	12.00	5.50
☐ 241 Hector Torres	.40	.18
☐ 242 Dan Meyer	.40	.18
☐ 243 Jim Rooker	.40	.18
☐ 244 Bill Sharp	.40	.18
☐ 245 Felix Millan	.40	.18
☐ 246 Cesar Tovar	.40	.18
☐ 247 Terry Harmon	.40	.18
☐ 248 Dick Tidrow	.40	.18
☐ 249 Cliff Johnson	.75	.35
☐ 250 Fergie Jenkins	2.50	1.10
☐ 251 Rick Monday	.75	.35
☐ 252 Tim Nordbrook	.40	.18
☐ 253 Bill Buckner	.75	.35
☐ 254 Rudy Meoli	.40	.18
☐ 255 Fritz Peterson	.40	.18
☐ 256 Rowland Office	.40	.18
☐ 257 Ross Grimsley	.40	.18
☐ 258 Nyls Nyman	.40	.18
☐ 259 Darrel Chaney	.40	.18
☐ 260 Steve Busby	.40	.18
☐ 261 Gary Thomasson	.40	.18
☐ 262 Checklist 133-264	1.50	.30
☐ 263 Lyman Bostock	1.50	.70
☐ 264 Steve Renko	.40	.18
☐ 265 Willie Davis	.75	.35
☐ 266 Alan Foster	.40	.18
☐ 267 Aurelio Rodriguez	.40	.18
☐ 268 Del Unser	.40	.18
☐ 269 Rick Austin	.40	.18
☐ 270 Willie Stargell	3.00	1.35
☐ 271 Jim Lonborg	.75	.35
☐ 272 Rick Dempsey	.75	.35
☐ 273 Joe Niekro	.75	.35
☐ 274 Tommy Harper	.75	.35
☐ 275 Rick Manning	.40	.18
☐ 276 Mickey Scott	.40	.18
☐ 277 Chicago Cubs	1.50	.30
Team Card; Jim Marshall MG (Checklist back)		
☐ 278 Bernie Carbo	.40	.18
☐ 279 Roy Howell	.40	.18
☐ 280 Burt Hooton	.75	.35
☐ 281 Dave May	.40	.18
☐ 282 Dan Osborn	.40	.18
☐ 283 Merv Rettenmund	.40	.18
☐ 284 Steve Ontiveros	.40	.18
☐ 285 Mike Cuellar	.75	.35
☐ 286 Jim Wohlford	.40	.18
☐ 287 Pete Mackanin	.40	.18
☐ 288 Bill Campbell	.40	.18
☐ 289 Enzo Hernandez	.40	.18
☐ 290 Ted Simmons	.75	.35
☐ 291 Ken Sanders	.40	.18
☐ 292 Leon Roberts	.40	.18
☐ 293 Bill Castro	.40	.18
☐ 294 Ed Kirkpatrick	.40	.18
☐ 295 Dave Cash	.40	.18
☐ 296 Pat Dobson	.40	.18
☐ 297 Roger Metzger	.40	.18
☐ 298 Dick Bosman	.40	.18
☐ 299 Champ Summers	.40	.18
☐ 300 Johnny Bench	8.00	3.60
☐ 301 Jackie Brown	.40	.18
☐ 302 Rick Miller	.40	.18
☐ 303 Steve Foucault	.40	.18
☐ 304 California Angels	1.50	.30
Team Card; Dick Williams MG (Checklist back)		
☐ 305 Andy Messersmith	.75	.35
☐ 306 Rod Gilbreath	.40	.18
☐ 307 Al Bumbry	.75	.35
☐ 308 Jim Barr	.40	.18
☐ 309 Bill Melton	.40	.18
☐ 310 Randy Jones	.75	.35
☐ 311 Cookie Rojas	.75	.35
☐ 312 Don Carrithers	.40	.18
☐ 313 Dan Ford	.40	.18
☐ 314 Ed Kranepool	.40	.18
☐ 315 Al Hrabosky	.75	.35
☐ 316 Robin Yount	30.00	13.50
☐ 317 John Candelaria	1.50	.70
☐ 318 Bob Boone	1.50	.70
☐ 319 Larry Gura	.40	.18
☐ 320 Willie Horton	.75	.35
☐ 321 Jose Cruz	1.50	.70
☐ 322 Glenn Abbott	.40	.18
☐ 323 Rob Sperring	.40	.18
☐ 324 Jim Bibby	.40	.18
☐ 325 Tony Perez	2.50	1.10
☐ 326 Dick Pole	.40	.18
☐ 327 Dave Moates	.40	.18
☐ 328 Carl Morton	.40	.18
☐ 329 Joe Ferguson	.40	.18
☐ 330 Nolan Ryan	65.00	29.00
☐ 331 San Diego Padres	1.50	.30
Team Card; John McNamara MG (Checklist back)		
☐ 332 Charlie Williams	.40	.18
☐ 333 Bob Coluccio	.40	.18
☐ 334 Dennis Leonard	.75	.35
☐ 335 Bob Grich	.75	.35
☐ 336 Vic Albury	.40	.18
☐ 337 Bud Harrelson	.75	.35
☐ 338 Bob Bailey	.40	.18
☐ 339 John Denny	.75	.35
☐ 340 Jim Rice	5.00	2.20
☐ 341 Lou Gehrig ATG	12.00	5.50
☐ 342 Rogers Hornsby ATG	3.00	1.35
☐ 343 Pie Traynor ATG	1.50	.70
☐ 344 Honus Wagner ATG	5.00	2.20
☐ 345 Babe Ruth ATG	15.00	6.75
☐ 346 Ty Cobb ATG	8.00	3.60
☐ 347 Ted Williams ATG	10.00	4.50
☐ 348 Mickey Cochrane ATG	1.50	.70
☐ 349 Walter Johnson ATG	3.00	1.35
☐ 350 Lefty Grove ATG	1.50	.70
☐ 351 Randy Hundley	.75	.35
☐ 352 Dave Giusti	.40	.18
☐ 353 Sixto Lezcano	.75	.35
☐ 354 Ron Blomberg	.40	.18
☐ 355 Steve Carlton	5.00	2.20
☐ 356 Ted Martinez	.40	.18
☐ 357 Ken Forsch	.40	.18
☐ 358 Buddy Bell	.75	.35
☐ 359 Rick Reuschel	.75	.35
☐ 360 Jeff Burroughs	.75	.35
☐ 361 Detroit Tigers	1.50	.30
Team Card; Ralph Houk MG (Checklist back)		
☐ 362 Will McEnaney	.75	.35
☐ 363 Dave Collins	.75	.35
☐ 364 Elias Sosa	.40	.18
☐ 365 Carlton Fisk	6.00	2.70
☐ 366 Bobby Valentine	.75	.35
☐ 367 Bruce Miller	.40	.18
☐ 368 Wilbur Wood	.40	.18
☐ 369 Frank White	.75	.35
☐ 370 Ron Cey	.75	.35
☐ 371 Elrod Hendricks	.40	.18
☐ 372 Rick Baldwin	.40	.18
☐ 373 Johnny Briggs	.40	.18
☐ 374 Dan Warthen	.40	.18
☐ 375 Ron Fairly	.75	.35
☐ 376 Rich Hebner	.75	.35
☐ 377 Mike Hegan	.40	.18
☐ 378 Steve Stone	.75	.35
☐ 379 Ken Boswell	.40	.18
☐ 380 Bobby Bonds	1.50	.70
☐ 381 Denny Doyle	.40	.18
☐ 382 Matt Alexander	.40	.18
☐ 383 John Ellis	.40	.18
☐ 384 Philadelphia Phillies	1.50	.30
Team Card; Danny Ozark MG (Checklist back)		
☐ 385 Mickey Lolich	.75	.35
☐ 386 Ed Goodson	.40	.18
☐ 387 Mike Miley	.40	.18
☐ 388 Stan Perzanowski	.40	.18
☐ 389 Glenn Adams	.40	.18
☐ 390 Don Gullett	.75	.35
☐ 391 Jerry Hairston	.40	.18
☐ 392 Checklist 265-396	1.50	.30
☐ 393 Paul Mitchell	.40	.18
☐ 394 Fran Healy	.40	.18
☐ 395 Jim Wynn	.75	.35
☐ 396 Bill Lee	.40	.18

☐ 397 Tim Foli .40 .18
☐ 398 Dave Tomlin .40 .18
☐ 399 Luis Melendez .40 .18
☐ 400 Rod Carew 4.00 1.80
☐ 401 Ken Brett .40 .18
☐ 402 Don Money .75 .35
☐ 403 Geoff Zahn .40 .18
☐ 404 Enos Cabell .40 .18
☐ 405 Rollie Fingers 2.50 1.10
☐ 406 Ed Herrmann .40 .18
☐ 407 Tom Underwood .40 .18
☐ 408 Charlie Spikes .40 .18
☐ 409 Dave Lemanczyk .40 .18
☐ 410 Ralph Garr .75 .35
☐ 411 Bill Singer .40 .18
☐ 412 Toby Harrah .75 .35
☐ 413 Pete Varney .40 .18
☐ 414 Wayne Garland .40 .18
☐ 415 Vada Pinson 1.50 .70
☐ 416 Tommy John 1.50 .70
☐ 417 Gene Clines .40 .18
☐ 418 Jose Morales .40 .18
☐ 419 Reggie Cleveland .40 .18
☐ 420 Joe Morgan 4.00 1.80
☐ 421 Oakland A's 1.50 .30
Team Card;
(No MG on front;
checklist back)
☐ 422 Johnny Grubb .40 .18
☐ 423 Ed Halicki .40 .18
☐ 424 Phil Roof .40 .18
☐ 425 Rennie Stennett .40 .18
☐ 426 Bob Forsch .40 .18
☐ 427 Kurt Bevacqua .40 .18
☐ 428 Jim Crawford .40 .18
☐ 429 Fred Stanley .40 .18
☐ 430 Jose Cardenal .75 .35
☐ 431 Dick Ruthven .40 .18
☐ 432 Tom Veryzer .40 .18
☐ 433 Rick Waits .40 .18
☐ 434 Morris Nettles .40 .18
☐ 435 Phil Niekro 2.50 1.10
☐ 436 Bill Fahey .40 .18
☐ 437 Terry Forster .40 .18
☐ 438 Doug DeCinces .75 .35
☐ 439 Rick Rhoden .75 .35
☐ 440 John Mayberry .75 .35
☐ 441 Gary Carter 5.00 2.20
☐ 442 Hank Webb .40 .18
☐ 443 San Francisco Giants 1.50 .30
Team Card;
(No MG on front;
checklist back)
☐ 444 Gary Nolan .75 .35
☐ 445 Rico Petrocelli .75 .35
☐ 446 Larry Haney .40 .18
☐ 447 Gene Locklear .75 .35
☐ 448 Tom Johnson .40 .18
☐ 449 Bob Robertson .40 .18
☐ 450 Jim Palmer 4.00 1.80
☐ 451 Buddy Bradford .40 .18
☐ 452 Tom Hausman .40 .18
☐ 453 Lou Piniella 1.50 .70
☐ 454 Tom Griffin .40 .18
☐ 455 Dick Allen 1.50 .70
☐ 456 Joe Coleman .40 .18
☐ 457 Ed Crosby .40 .18
☐ 458 Earl Williams .40 .18
☐ 459 Jim Brewer .40 .18
☐ 460 Cesar Cedeno .75 .35
☐ 461 NL and AL Champs .75 .35
Reds sweep Bucs,
Bosox surprise A's
☐ 462 '75 World Series .75 .35
Reds Champs
☐ 463 Steve Hargan .40 .18
☐ 464 Ken Henderson .40 .18
☐ 465 Mike Marshall .75 .35
☐ 466 Bob Stinson .40 .18
☐ 467 Woodie Fryman .40 .18
☐ 468 Jesus Alou .40 .18
☐ 469 Rawly Eastwick .75 .35
☐ 470 Bobby Murcer .75 .35
☐ 471 Jim Burton .40 .18
☐ 472 Bob Davis .40 .18
☐ 473 Paul Blair .75 .35
☐ 474 Ray Corbin .40 .18
☐ 475 Joe Rudi .75 .35
☐ 476 Bob Moose 1.50 .70
☐ 477 Cleveland Indians 1.50 .30
Team Card;
Frank Robinson MG
(Checklist back)
☐ 478 Lynn McGlothen .40 .18
☐ 479 Bobby Mitchell .40 .18
☐ 480 Mike Schmidt 25.00 11.00
☐ 481 Rudy May .40 .18

☐ 482 Tim Hosley .40 .18
☐ 483 Mickey Stanley .40 .18
☐ 484 Eric Raich .40 .18
☐ 485 Mike Hargrove .75 .35
☐ 486 Bruce Dal Canton .40 .18
☐ 487 Leron Lee .40 .18
☐ 488 Claude Osteen .75 .35
☐ 489 Skip Jutze .40 .18
☐ 490 Frank Tanana .75 .35
☐ 491 Terry Crowley .40 .18
☐ 492 Marty Pattin .40 .18
☐ 493 Derrel Thomas .40 .18
☐ 494 Craig Swan .75 .35
☐ 495 Nate Colbert .40 .18
☐ 496 Juan Beniquez .40 .18
☐ 497 Joe McIntosh .40 .18
☐ 498 Glenn Borgmann .40 .18
☐ 499 Mario Guerrero .40 .18
☐ 500 Reggie Jackson 12.00 5.50
☐ 501 Billy Champion .40 .18
☐ 502 Tim McCarver 1.50 .70
☐ 503 Elliott Maddox .40 .18
☐ 504 Pittsburgh Pirates 1.50 .30
Team Card;
Danny Murtaugh MG
(Checklist back)
☐ 505 Mark Belanger .75 .35
☐ 506 George Mitterwald .40 .18
☐ 507 Ray Bare .40 .18
☐ 508 Duane Kuiper .40 .18
☐ 509 Bill Hands .40 .18
☐ 510 Amos Otis .75 .35
☐ 511 Jamie Easterley .40 .18
☐ 512 Ellie Rodriguez .40 .18
☐ 513 Bart Johnson .40 .18
☐ 514 Dan Driessen .75 .35
☐ 515 Steve Yeager .75 .35
☐ 516 Wayne Granger .40 .18
☐ 517 John Milner .40 .18
☐ 518 Doug Flynn .40 .18
☐ 519 Steve Brye .40 .18
☐ 520 Willie McCovey 4.00 1.80
☐ 521 Jim Colborn .40 .18
☐ 522 Ted Sizemore .40 .18
☐ 523 Bob Montgomery .40 .18
☐ 524 Pete Falcone .40 .18
☐ 525 Billy Williams 2.50 1.10
☐ 526 Checklist 397-528 1.50 .30
☐ 527 Mike Anderson .40 .18
☐ 528 Dock Ellis .40 .18
☐ 529 Deron Johnson .75 .35
☐ 530 Don Sutton 2.50 1.10
☐ 531 New York Mets 1.50 .30
Team Card;
Joe Frazier MG
(Checklist back)
☐ 532 Milt May .40 .18
☐ 533 Lee Richard .40 .18
☐ 534 Stan Bahnsen .40 .18
☐ 535 Dave Nelson .40 .18
☐ 536 Mike Thompson .40 .18
☐ 537 Tony Muser .40 .18
☐ 538 Pat Darcy .40 .18
☐ 539 John Balaz .75 .35
☐ 540 Bill Freehan .75 .35
☐ 541 Steve Mingori .40 .18
☐ 542 Keith Hernandez 1.50 .70
☐ 543 Wayne Twitchell .40 .18
☐ 544 Pepe Frias .40 .18
☐ 545 Sparky Lyle .75 .35
☐ 546 Dave Rosello .40 .18
☐ 547 Roric Harrison .40 .18
☐ 548 Manny Mota .75 .35
☐ 549 Randy Tate .40 .18
☐ 550 Hank Aaron 25.00 11.00
☐ 551 Jerry DaVanon .40 .18
☐ 552 Terry Humphrey .40 .18
☐ 553 Randy Moffitt .40 .18
☐ 554 Ray Fosse .40 .18
☐ 555 Dyar Miller .40 .18
☐ 556 Minnesota Twins 1.50 .30
Team Card;
Gene Mauch MG
(Checklist back)
☐ 557 Dan Spillner .40 .18
☐ 558 Clarence Gaston .75 .35
☐ 559 Clyde Wright .40 .18
☐ 560 Jorge Orta .40 .18
☐ 561 Tom Carroll .40 .18
☐ 562 Adrian Garrett .40 .18
☐ 563 Larry Demery .40 .18
☐ 564 Bubble Gum Champ 1.50 .70
Kurt Bevacqua
☐ 565 Tug McGraw .75 .35
☐ 566 Ken McMullen .40 .18
☐ 567 George Stone .40 .18
☐ 568 Rob Andrews .40 .18

☐ 569 Nelson Briles .75 .35
☐ 570 George Hendrick .75 .35
☐ 571 Don DeMola .40 .18
☐ 572 Rich Coggins .40 .18
☐ 573 Bill Travers .40 .18
☐ 574 Don Kessinger .75 .35
☐ 575 Dwight Evans 1.50 .70
☐ 576 Maximino Leon .40 .18
☐ 577 Marc Hill .40 .18
☐ 578 Ted Kubiak .40 .18
☐ 579 Clay Kirby .40 .18
☐ 580 Bert Campaneris .75 .35
☐ 581 St. Louis Cardinals 1.50 .30
Team Card;
Red Schoendienst MG
(Checklist back)
☐ 582 Mike Kekich .40 .18
☐ 583 Tommy Helms .40 .18
☐ 584 Stan Wall .40 .18
☐ 585 Joe Torre 1.50 .70
☐ 586 Ron Schueler .40 .18
☐ 587 Leo Cardenas .40 .18
☐ 588 Kevin Kobel .40 .18
☐ 589 Rookie Pitchers 1.50 .70
Santo Alcala
Mike Flanagan
Joe Pactwa
Pablo Torrealba
☐ 590 Rookie Outfielders .75 .35
Henry Cruz
Chet Lemon
Ellis Valentine
Terry Whitfield
☐ 591 Rookie Pitchers .75 .35
Steve Grilli
Craig Mitchell
Jose Sosa
George Throop
☐ 592 Rookie Infielders 6.00 2.70
Willie Randolph
Dave McKay
Jerry Royster
Roy Staiger
☐ 593 Rookie Pitchers .75 .35
Larry Anderson
Ken Crosby
Mark Littell
Butch Metzger
☐ 594 Rookie Catchers/OF .75 .35
Andy Merchant
Ed Ott
Royle Stillman
Jerry White
☐ 595 Rookie Pitchers .75 .35
Art DeFillipis
Randy Lerch
Sid Monge
Steve Barr
☐ 596 Rookie Infielders .75 .35
Craig Reynolds
Lamar Johnson
Johnnie LeMaster
Jerry Manuel
☐ 597 Rookie Pitchers .75 .35
Don Aase
Jack Kucek
Frank LaCorte
Mike Pazik
☐ 598 Rookie Outfielders .75 .35
Hector Cruz
Jamie Quirk
Jerry Turner
Joe Wallis
☐ 599 Rookie Pitchers 6.00 2.70
Rob Dressler
Ron Guidry
Bob McClure
Pat Zachry
☐ 600 Tom Seaver 8.00 3.60
☐ 601 Ken Rudolph .40 .18
☐ 602 Doug Konieczny .40 .18
☐ 603 Jim Holt .40 .18
☐ 604 Joe Lovitto .40 .18
☐ 605 Al Downing .40 .18
☐ 606 Milwaukee Brewers 1.50 .30
Team Card;
Alex Grammas MG
(Checklist back)
☐ 607 Rich Hinton .40 .18
☐ 608 Vic Correll .40 .18
☐ 609 Fred Norman .75 .35
☐ 610 Greg Luzinski 1.50 .70
☐ 611 Rich Folkers .40 .18
☐ 612 Joe Lahoud .40 .18
☐ 613 Tim Johnson .40 .18
☐ 614 Fernando Arroyo .40 .18
☐ 615 Mike Cubbage .40 .18

	NRMT	VG-E
☐ 616 Buck Martinez	.40	.18
☐ 617 Darold Knowles	.40	.18
☐ 618 Jack Brohamer	.40	.18
☐ 619 Bill Butler	.40	.18
☐ 620 Al Oliver	.75	.35
☐ 621 Tom Hall	.40	.18
☐ 622 Rick Auerbach	.40	.18
☐ 623 Bob Allietta	.40	.18
☐ 624 Tony Taylor	.75	.35
☐ 625 J.R. Richard	.75	.35
☐ 626 Bob Sheldon	.40	.18
☐ 627 Bill Plummer	.40	.18
☐ 628 John D'Acquisto	.40	.18
☐ 629 Sandy Alomar	.75	.35
☐ 630 Chris Speier	.40	.18
☐ 631 Atlanta Braves Team Card; Dave Bristol MG (Checklist back)	1.50	.30
☐ 632 Rogelio Moret	.40	.18
☐ 633 John Stearns	.75	.35
☐ 634 Larry Christenson	.40	.18
☐ 635 Jim Fregosi	.75	.35
☐ 636 Joe Decker	.40	.18
☐ 637 Bruce Bochte	.40	.18
☐ 638 Doyle Alexander	.75	.35
☐ 639 Fred Kendall	.40	.18
☐ 640 Bill Madlock	1.50	.70
☐ 641 Tom Paciorek	.75	.35
☐ 642 Dennis Blair	.40	.18
☐ 643 Checklist 529-660	1.50	.30
☐ 644 Tom Bradley	.40	.18
☐ 645 Darrell Porter	.75	.35
☐ 646 John Lowenstein	.40	.18
☐ 647 Ramon Hernandez	.40	.18
☐ 648 Al Cowens	.40	.18
☐ 649 Dave Roberts	.40	.18
☐ 650 Thurman Munson	5.00	2.20
☐ 651 John Odom	.40	.18
☐ 652 Ed Armbrister	.40	.18
☐ 653 Mike Norris	.75	.35
☐ 654 Doug Griffin	.40	.18
☐ 655 Mike Vail	.40	.18
☐ 656 Chicago White Sox Team Card; Chuck Tanner MG (Checklist back)	1.50	.30
☐ 657 Roy Smalley	.75	.35
☐ 658 Jerry Johnson	.40	.18
☐ 659 Ben Oglivie	.75	.35
☐ 660 Dave Lopes	1.50	.30

1976 Topps Traded

The cards in this 44-card set measure 2 1/2" by 3 1/2". The 1976 Topps Traded set contains 43 players and one unnumbered checklist card. The individuals pictured were traded after the Topps regular set was printed. A "Sports Extra" heading design is found on each picture and is also used to introduce the biographical section of the reverse. Each card is numbered according to the player's regular 1976 card with the addition of "T" to indicate his new status. As in 1974, the cards were inserted in all packs toward the end of the production run. According to published reports at the time, they were not released until April, 1976. Because they were produced in large quantities, they are no scarcer than the basic cards. Reports at the time indicated that a dealer could make approximately 35 sets from a vending case. The vending cases included both regular and traded cards.

	NRMT	VG-E
COMPLETE SET (44)	20.00	9.00
COMMON CARD	.25	.11
☐ 27T Ed Figueroa	.25	.11
☐ 28T Dusty Baker	1.00	.45
☐ 44T Doug Rader	.50	.23
☐ 58T Ron Reed	.25	.11
☐ 74T Oscar Gamble	1.00	.45
☐ 80T Jim Kaat	1.00	.45
☐ 83T Jim Spencer	.25	.11
☐ 85T Mickey Rivers	.50	.23
☐ 99T Lee Lacy	.25	.11
☐ 120T Rusty Staub	.50	.23
☐ 127T Larvell Blanks	.25	.11
☐ 146T George Medich	.25	.11
☐ 158T Ken Reitz	.25	.11
☐ 208T Mike Lum	.25	.11
☐ 211T Clay Carroll	.25	.11
☐ 231T Tom House	.25	.11
☐ 250T Fergie Jenkins	2.50	1.10
☐ 259T Darrel Chaney	.25	.11
☐ 292T Leon Roberts	.25	.11
☐ 296T Pat Dobson	.25	.11
☐ 309T Bill Melton	.25	.11
☐ 338T Bob Bailey	.25	.11
☐ 380T Bobby Bonds	1.00	.45
☐ 383T John Ellis	.25	.11
☐ 385T Mickey Lolich	.50	.23
☐ 401T Ken Brett	.25	.11
☐ 410T Ralph Garr	.50	.23
☐ 411T Bill Singer	.25	.11
☐ 428T Jim Crawford	.25	.11
☐ 434T Morris Nettles	.25	.11
☐ 464T Ken Henderson	.25	.11
☐ 497T Joe McIntosh	.25	.11
☐ 524T Pete Falcone	.25	.11
☐ 527T Mike Anderson	.25	.11
☐ 528T Dock Ellis	.25	.11
☐ 532T Milt May	.25	.11
☐ 554T Ray Fosse	.25	.11
☐ 579T Clay Kirby	.25	.11
☐ 583T Tommy Helms	.25	.11
☐ 592T Willie Randolph	4.00	1.80
☐ 618T Jack Brohamer	.25	.11
☐ 632T Rogelio Moret	.25	.11
☐ 649T Dave Roberts	.25	.11
☐ NNO Traded Checklist	1.50	.30

1976 Topps Team Checklist Sheet

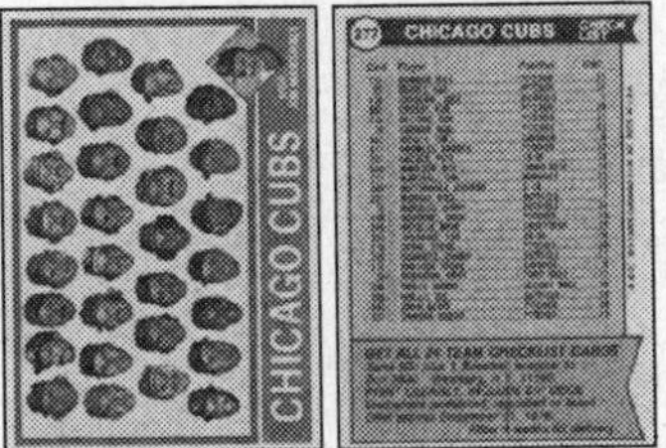

This uncut sheet of the 24 1976 Topps team checklists measures 10" by 21". The sheet was obtained by sending 50 cents plus one wrapper to Topps. When seperated, these cards measure the standard-size.

	NRMT	VG-E
COMPLETE SET (1)	15.00	6.75
COMMON CARD	15.00	6.75
☐ 1 Topps Team CL Sheet	15.00	6.75

1977 Topps

In 1977 for the fifth consecutive year, Topps produced a 660-card standard-size baseball set. Among other fashions, this set was released in 10-card wax packs as well as thirty-nine card rack packs. The player's name, team affiliation, and his position are compactly arranged over the picture area and a facsimile autograph appears on the photo. Team cards feature a checklist of that team's players in the set and a small picture of the manager on the front of the card. Appearing for the first time are the series "Brothers" (631-634) and "Turn Back the Clock" (433-437). Other subseries in the set are League Leaders (1-8), Record Breakers (231-234), Playoffs cards (276-277), World Series cards (411-413), and Rookie Prospects (472-479/487-494). The following players' regular issue cards are explicitly denoted as All-Stars, 30, 70, 100, 120, 170, 210, 240, 265, 301, 347, 400, 420, 450, 500, 521, 550, 560, and 580. The key Rookie Cards in the set are Jack Clark, Andre Dawson, Mark "The Bird" Fidrych, Dennis Martinez and Dale Murphy. Cards numbered 23 or lower, that feature Yankees and do not follow the numbering checklisted below, are not necessarily error cards. They are undoubtedly Burger King cards, a separate set with its own pricing and mass distribution. Burger King cards are indistinguishable from the corresponding Topps cards except for the card numbering difference and the fact that Burger King cards do not have a printing sheet designation (such as A through F like the regular Topps) anywhere on the card back in very small print. There was an aluminum version of the Dale Murphy rookie card number 476 produced (legally) in the early '80s; proceeds from the sales originally priced at 10.00) of this "card" went to the Huntington's Disease Foundation.

	NRMT	VG-E
COMPLETE SET (660)	350.00	160.00
COMMON CARD (1-660)	.30	.14
☐ 1 Batting Leaders George Brett Bill Madlock	8.00	2.30
☐ 2 Home Run Leaders Graig Nettles Mike Schmidt	2.00	.90
☐ 3 RBI Leaders Lee May George Foster	1.25	.55
☐ 4 Stolen Base Leaders Bill North Dave Lopes	.60	.25
☐ 5 Victory Leaders Jim Palmer Randy Jones	1.25	.55
☐ 6 Strikeout Leaders Nolan Ryan Tom Seaver	15.00	6.75
☐ 7 ERA Leaders Mark Fidrych John Denny	.60	.25
☐ 8 Leading Firemen Bill Campbell Rawly Eastwick	.60	.25
☐ 9 Doug Rader	.30	.14
☐ 10 Reggie Jackson	10.00	4.50
☐ 11 Rob Dressler	.30	.14
☐ 12 Larry Haney	.30	.14
☐ 13 Luis Gomez	.30	.14
☐ 14 Tommy Smith	.30	.14
☐ 15 Don Gullett	.60	.25
☐ 16 Bob Jones	.30	.14
☐ 17 Steve Stone	.60	.25
☐ 18 Indians Team/Mgr. Frank Robinson (Checklist back)	1.25	.25
☐ 19 John D'Acquisto	.30	.14
☐ 20 Graig Nettles	1.25	.55
☐ 21 Ken Forsch	.30	.14
☐ 22 Bill Freehan	.60	.25
☐ 23 Dan Driessen	.30	.14
☐ 24 Carl Morton	.30	.14
☐ 25 Dwight Evans	1.25	.55
☐ 26 Ray Sadecki	.30	.14
☐ 27 Bill Buckner	.60	.25
☐ 28 Woodie Fryman	.30	.14
☐ 29 Bucky Dent	.60	.25
☐ 30 Greg Luzinski	1.25	.55
☐ 31 Jim Todd	.30	.14
☐ 32 Checklist 1-132	1.25	.25
☐ 33 Wayne Garland	.30	.14
☐ 34 Angels Team/Mgr. Norm Sherry (Checklist back)	1.25	.25
☐ 35 Rennie Stennett	.30	.14
☐ 36 John Ellis	.30	.14
☐ 37 Steve Hargan	.30	.14
☐ 38 Craig Kusick	.30	.14
☐ 39 Tom Griffin	.30	.14
☐ 40 Bobby Murcer	.60	.25
☐ 41 Jim Kern	.30	.14
☐ 42 Jose Cruz	.60	.2
☐ 43 Ray Bare	.30	.1
☐ 44 Bud Harrelson	.60	.2
☐ 45 Rawly Eastwick	.30	.1
☐ 46 Buck Martinez	.30	.1
☐ 47 Lynn McGlothen	.30	.1
☐ 48 Tom Paciorek	.60	.2
☐ 49 Grant Jackson	.30	.1
☐ 50 Ron Cey	.60	.2
☐ 51 Brewers Team/Mgr. Alex Grammas	1.25	.2

(Checklist back)		
☐ 52 Ellis Valentine	.30	.14
☐ 53 Paul Mitchell	.30	.14
☐ 54 Sandy Alomar	.60	.25
☐ 55 Jeff Burroughs	.60	.25
☐ 56 Rudy May	.30	.14
☐ 57 Marc Hill	.30	.14
☐ 58 Chet Lemon	.60	.25
☐ 59 Larry Christenson	.30	.14
☐ 60 Jim Rice	2.00	.90
☐ 61 Manny Sanguillen	.60	.25
☐ 62 Eric Raich	.30	.14
☐ 63 Tito Fuentes	.30	.14
☐ 64 Larry Biittner	.30	.14
☐ 65 Skip Lockwood	.30	.14
☐ 66 Roy Smalley	.60	.25
☐ 67 Joaquin Andujar	.60	.25
☐ 68 Bruce Bochte	.30	.14
☐ 69 Jim Crawford	.30	.14
☐ 70 Johnny Bench	6.00	2.70
☐ 71 Dock Ellis	.30	.14
☐ 72 Mike Anderson	.30	.14
☐ 73 Charlie Williams	.30	.14
☐ 74 A's Team/Mgr.	1.25	.25
Jack McKeon		
(Checklist back)		
☐ 75 Dennis Leonard	.60	.25
☐ 76 Tim Foli	.30	.14
☐ 77 Dyar Miller	.30	.14
☐ 78 Bob Davis	.30	.14
☐ 79 Don Money	.60	.25
☐ 80 Andy Messersmith	.60	.25
☐ 81 Juan Beniquez	.30	.14
☐ 82 Jim Rooker	.30	.14
☐ 83 Kevin Bell	.30	.14
☐ 84 Ollie Brown	.30	.14
☐ 85 Duane Kuiper	.30	.14
☐ 86 Pat Zachry	.30	.14
☐ 87 Glenn Borgmann	.30	.14
☐ 88 Stan Wall	.30	.14
☐ 89 Butch Hobson	.60	.25
☐ 90 Cesar Cedeno	.60	.25
☐ 91 John Verhoeven	.30	.14
☐ 92 Dave Rosello	.30	.14
☐ 93 Tom Poquette	.30	.14
☐ 94 Craig Swan	.30	.14
☐ 95 Keith Hernandez	.60	.25
☐ 96 Lou Piniella	.60	.25
☐ 97 Dave Heaverlo	.30	.14
☐ 98 Milt May	.30	.14
☐ 99 Tom Hausman	.30	.14
☐ 100 Joe Morgan	3.00	1.35
☐ 101 Dick Bosman	.30	.14
☐ 102 Jose Morales	.30	.14
☐ 103 Mike Bacsik	.30	.14
☐ 104 Omar Moreno	.60	.25
☐ 105 Steve Yeager	.60	.25
☐ 106 Mike Flanagan	.60	.25
☐ 107 Bill Melton	.30	.14
☐ 108 Alan Foster	.30	.14
☐ 109 Jorge Orta	.30	.14
☐ 110 Steve Carlton	4.00	1.80
☐ 111 Rico Petrocelli	.60	.25
☐ 112 Bill Greif	.30	.14
☐ 113 Blue Jays Leaders	1.25	.25
Roy Hartsfield MG		
Don Leppert CO		
Bob Miller CO		
Jackie Moore CO		
Harry Warner CO		
(Checklist back)		
☐ 114 Bruce Dal Canton	.30	.14
☐ 115 Rick Manning	.30	.14
☐ 116 Joe Niekro	.60	.25
☐ 117 Frank White	.60	.25
☐ 118 Rick Jones	.30	.14
☐ 119 John Stearns	.30	.14
☐ 120 Rod Carew	3.00	1.35
☐ 121 Gary Nolan	.30	.14
☐ 122 Ben Oglivie	.60	.25
☐ 123 Fred Stanley	.30	.14
☐ 124 George Mitterwald	.30	.14
☐ 125 Bill Travers	.30	.14
☐ 126 Rod Gilbreath	.30	.14
☐ 127 Ron Fairly	.60	.25
☐ 128 Tommy John	1.25	.55
☐ 129 Mike Sadek	.30	.14
☐ 130 Al Oliver	.60	.25
☐ 131 Orlando Ramirez	.30	.14
☐ 132 Chip Lang	.30	.14
☐ 133 Ralph Garr	.60	.25
☐ 134 Padres Team/Mgr.	1.25	.25
John McNamara		
(Checklist back)		
☐ 135 Mark Belanger	.60	.25
☐ 136 Jerry Mumphrey	.60	.25
☐ 137 Jeff Terpko	.30	.14
☐ 138 Bob Stinson	.30	.14

☐ 139 Fred Norman	.30	.14
☐ 140 Mike Schmidt	15.00	6.75
☐ 141 Mark Littell	.30	.14
☐ 142 Steve Dillard	.30	.14
☐ 143 Ed Herrmann	.30	.14
☐ 144 Bruce Sutter	2.50	1.10
☐ 145 Tom Veryzer	.30	.14
☐ 146 Dusty Baker	1.25	.55
☐ 147 Jackie Brown	.30	.14
☐ 148 Fran Healy	.30	.14
☐ 149 Mike Cubbage	.30	.14
☐ 150 Tom Seaver	6.00	2.70
☐ 151 Johnny LeMaster	.30	.14
☐ 152 Gaylord Perry	2.00	.90
☐ 153 Ron Jackson	.30	.14
☐ 154 Dave Giusti	.30	.14
☐ 155 Joe Rudi	.60	.25
☐ 156 Pete Mackanin	.30	.14
☐ 157 Ken Brett	.30	.14
☐ 158 Ted Kubiak	.30	.14
☐ 159 Bernie Carbo	.30	.14
☐ 160 Will McEnaney	.30	.14
☐ 161 Garry Templeton	1.25	.55
☐ 162 Mike Cuellar	.60	.25
☐ 163 Dave Hilton	.30	.14
☐ 164 Tug McGraw	.60	.25
☐ 165 Jim Wynn	.60	.25
☐ 166 Bill Campbell	.30	.14
☐ 167 Rich Hebner	.60	.25
☐ 168 Charlie Spikes	.30	.14
☐ 169 Darold Knowles	.30	.14
☐ 170 Thurman Munson	4.00	1.80
☐ 171 Ken Sanders	.30	.14
☐ 172 John Milner	.30	.14
☐ 173 Chuck Scrivener	.30	.14
☐ 174 Nelson Briles	.60	.25
☐ 175 Butch Wynegar	.60	.25
☐ 176 Bob Robertson	.30	.14
☐ 177 Bart Johnson	.30	.14
☐ 178 Bombo Rivera	.30	.14
☐ 179 Paul Hartzell	.30	.14
☐ 180 Dave Lopes	.60	.25
☐ 181 Ken McMullen	.30	.14
☐ 182 Dan Spillner	.30	.14
☐ 183 Cardinals Team/Mgr.	1.25	.25
Vern Rapp		
(Checklist back)		
☐ 184 Bo McLaughlin	.30	.14
☐ 185 Sixto Lezcano	.30	.14
☐ 186 Doug Flynn	.30	.14
☐ 187 Dick Pole	.30	.14
☐ 188 Bob Tolan	.30	.14
☐ 189 Rick Dempsey	.60	.25
☐ 190 Ray Burris	.30	.14
☐ 191 Doug Griffin	.30	.14
☐ 192 Clarence Gaston	.60	.25
☐ 193 Larry Gura	.30	.14
☐ 194 Gary Matthews	.60	.25
☐ 195 Ed Figueroa	.30	.14
☐ 196 Len Randle	.30	.14
☐ 197 Ed Ott	.30	.14
☐ 198 Wilbur Wood	.30	.14
☐ 199 Pepe Frias	.30	.14
☐ 200 Frank Tanana	.60	.25
☐ 201 Ed Kranepool	.30	.14
☐ 202 Tom Johnson	.30	.14
☐ 203 Ed Armbrister	.30	.14
☐ 204 Jeff Newman	.30	.14
☐ 205 Pete Falcone	.30	.14
☐ 206 Boog Powell	1.25	.55
☐ 207 Glenn Abbott	.30	.14
☐ 208 Checklist 133-264	1.25	.25
☐ 209 Rob Andrews	.30	.14
☐ 210 Fred Lynn	.60	.12
☐ 211 Giants Team/Mgr.	1.25	.55
Joe Altobelli		
(Checklist back)		
☐ 212 Jim Mason	.30	.14
☐ 213 Maximino Leon	.30	.14
☐ 214 Darrell Porter	.60	.25
☐ 215 Butch Metzger	.30	.14
☐ 216 Doug DeCinces	.60	.25
☐ 217 Tom Underwood	.30	.14
☐ 218 John Wathan	.30	.14
☐ 219 Joe Coleman	.30	.14
☐ 220 Chris Chambliss	.60	.25
☐ 221 Bob Bailey	.30	.14
☐ 222 Francisco Barrios	.30	.14
☐ 223 Earl Williams	.30	.14
☐ 224 Rusty Torres	.30	.14
☐ 225 Bob Apodaca	.30	.14
☐ 226 Leroy Stanton	.60	.25
☐ 227 Joe Sambito	.30	.14
☐ 228 Twins Team/Mgr.	1.25	.25
Gene Mauch		
(Checklist back)		
☐ 229 Don Kessinger	.60	.25

☐ 230 Vida Blue	.60	.25
☐ 231 George Brett RB	12.00	5.50
Most consecutive games – 3 or more hits		
☐ 232 Minnie Minoso RB	.60	.25
Oldest to hit safely		
☐ 233 Jose Morales RB	.30	.14
Most pinch-hits season		
☐ 234 Nolan Ryan RB	20.00	9.00
Most seasons, 300 strikeouts		
☐ 235 Cecil Cooper	.60	.25
☐ 236 Tom Buskey	.30	.14
☐ 237 Gene Clines	.30	.14
☐ 238 Tippy Martinez	.60	.25
☐ 239 Bill Plummer	.30	.14
☐ 240 Ron LeFlore	.60	.25
☐ 241 Dave Tomlin	.30	.14
☐ 242 Ken Henderson	.30	.14
☐ 243 Ron Reed	.30	.14
☐ 244 John Mayberry	.60	.25
(Cartoon mentions T206 Wagner)		
☐ 245 Rick Rhoden	.60	.25
☐ 246 Mike Vail	.30	.14
☐ 247 Chris Knapp	.30	.14
☐ 248 Wilbur Howard	.30	.14
☐ 249 Pete Redfern	.30	.14
☐ 250 Bill Madlock	.60	.25
☐ 251 Tony Muser	.30	.14
☐ 252 Dale Murray	.30	.14
☐ 253 John Hale	.30	.14
☐ 254 Doyle Alexander	.30	.14
☐ 255 George Scott	.60	.25
☐ 256 Joe Hoerner	.30	.14
☐ 257 Mike Miley	.30	.14
☐ 258 Luis Tiant	.60	.25
☐ 259 Mets Team/Mgr.	1.25	.25
Joe Frazier		
(Checklist back)		
☐ 260 J.R. Richard	.60	.25
☐ 261 Phil Garner	.60	.25
☐ 262 Al Cowens	.30	.14
☐ 263 Mike Marshall	.60	.25
☐ 264 Tom Hutton	.30	.14
☐ 265 Mark Fidrych	4.00	1.80
☐ 266 Derrel Thomas	.30	.14
☐ 267 Ray Fosse	.30	.14
☐ 268 Rick Sawyer	.30	.14
☐ 269 Joe Lis	.30	.14
☐ 270 Dave Parker	1.25	.55
☐ 271 Terry Forster	.30	.14
☐ 272 Lee Lacy	.30	.14
☐ 273 Eric Soderholm	.30	.14
☐ 274 Don Stanhouse	.30	.14
☐ 275 Mike Hargrove	.60	.25
☐ 276 Chris Chambliss ALCS	1.25	.55
homer decides it		
☐ 277 Pete Rose NLCS	2.50	1.10
☐ 278 Danny Frisella	.30	.14
☐ 279 Joe Wallis	.30	.14
☐ 280 Jim Hunter	2.00	.90
☐ 281 Roy Staiger	.30	.14
☐ 282 Sid Monge	.30	.14
☐ 283 Jerry DaVanon	.30	.14
☐ 284 Mike Norris	.30	.14
☐ 285 Brooks Robinson	4.00	1.80
☐ 286 Johnny Grubb	.30	.06
☐ 287 Reds Team/Mgr.	1.25	.55
Sparky Anderson		
(Checklist back)		
☐ 288 Bob Montgomery	.30	.14
☐ 289 Gene Garber	.60	.25
☐ 290 Amos Otis	.60	.25
☐ 291 Jason Thompson	.60	.25
☐ 292 Rogelio Moret	.30	.14
☐ 293 Jack Brohamer	.30	.14
☐ 294 George Medich	.30	.14
☐ 295 Gary Carter	2.50	1.10
☐ 296 Don Hood	.30	.14
☐ 297 Ken Reitz	.30	.14
☐ 298 Charlie Hough	.60	.25
☐ 299 Otto Velez	.60	.25
☐ 300 Jerry Koosman	.60	.25
☐ 301 Toby Harrah	.60	.25
☐ 302 Mike Garman	.30	.14
☐ 303 Gene Tenace	.60	.25
☐ 304 Jim Hughes	.30	.14
☐ 305 Mickey Rivers	.60	.25
☐ 306 Rick Waits	.30	.14
☐ 307 Gary Sutherland	.30	.14
☐ 308 Gene Pentz	.30	.14
☐ 309 Red Sox Team/Mgr.	1.25	.25
Don Zimmer		
(Checklist back)		
☐ 310 Larry Bowa	.60	.25
☐ 311 Vern Ruhle	.30	.14
☐ 312 Rob Belloir	.30	.14

☐ 313 Paul Blair	.60	.25
☐ 314 Steve Mingori	.30	.14
☐ 315 Dave Chalk	.30	.14
☐ 316 Steve Rogers	.30	.14
☐ 317 Kurt Bevacqua	.30	.14
☐ 318 Duffy Dyer	.30	.14
☐ 319 Rich Gossage	1.25	.55
☐ 320 Ken Griffey	1.25	.55
☐ 321 Dave Goltz	.30	.14
☐ 322 Bill Russell	.60	.25
☐ 323 Larry Lintz	.30	.14
☐ 324 John Curtis	.30	.14
☐ 325 Mike Ivie	.30	.14
☐ 326 Jesse Jefferson	.30	.14
☐ 327 Astros Team/Mgr.	1.25	.25
Bill Virdon		
(Checklist back)		
☐ 328 Tommy Boggs	.30	.14
☐ 329 Ron Hodges	.30	.14
☐ 330 George Hendrick	.60	.25
☐ 331 Jim Colborn	.30	.14
☐ 332 Elliott Maddox	.30	.14
☐ 333 Paul Reuschel	.30	.14
☐ 334 Bill Stein	.30	.14
☐ 335 Bill Robinson	.60	.25
☐ 336 Denny Doyle	.30	.14
☐ 337 Ron Schueler	.30	.14
☐ 338 Dave Duncan	.30	.14
☐ 339 Adrian Devine	.30	.14
☐ 340 Hal McRae	.60	.25
☐ 341 Joe Kerrigan	.30	.14
☐ 342 Jerry Remy	.30	.14
☐ 343 Ed Halicki	.30	.14
☐ 344 Brian Downing	.60	.25
☐ 345 Reggie Smith	.60	.25
☐ 346 Bill Singer	.30	.14
☐ 347 George Foster	1.25	.55
☐ 348 Brent Strom	.30	.14
☐ 349 Jim Holt	.30	.14
☐ 350 Larry Dierker	.60	.25
☐ 351 Jim Sundberg	.60	.25
☐ 352 Mike Phillips	.30	.14
☐ 353 Stan Thomas	.30	.14
☐ 354 Pirates Team/Mgr.	1.25	.25
Chuck Tanner		
(Checklist back)		
☐ 355 Lou Brock	3.00	1.35
☐ 356 Checklist 265-396	1.25	.25
☐ 357 Tim McCarver	1.25	.55
☐ 358 Tom House	.30	.14
☐ 359 Willie Randolph	1.25	.55
☐ 360 Rick Monday	.60	.25
☐ 361 Eduardo Rodriguez	.30	.14
☐ 362 Tommy Davis	.60	.25
☐ 363 Dave Roberts	.30	.14
☐ 364 Vic Correll	.30	.14
☐ 365 Mike Torrez	.60	.25
☐ 366 Ted Sizemore	.30	.14
☐ 367 Dave Hamilton	.30	.14
☐ 368 Mike Jorgensen	.30	.14
☐ 369 Terry Humphrey	.30	.14
☐ 370 John Montefusco	.30	.14
☐ 371 Royals Team/Mgr.	1.25	.25
Whitey Herzog		
(Checklist back)		
☐ 372 Rich Folkers	.30	.14
☐ 373 Bert Campaneris	.60	.25
☐ 374 Kent Tekulve	.60	.25
☐ 375 Larry Hisle	.60	.25
☐ 376 Nino Espinosa	.30	.14
☐ 377 Dave McKay	.30	.14
☐ 378 Jim Umbarger	.30	.14
☐ 379 Larry Cox	.30	.14
☐ 380 Lee May	.60	.25
☐ 381 Bob Forsch	.30	.14
☐ 382 Charlie Moore	.30	.14
☐ 383 Stan Bahnsen	.30	.14
☐ 384 Darrel Chaney	.30	.14
☐ 385 Dave LaRoche	.30	.14
☐ 386 Manny Mota	.60	.25
☐ 387 Yankees Team/Mgr.	2.00	.40
Billy Martin		
(Checklist back)		
☐ 388 Terry Harmon	.30	.14
☐ 389 Ken Kravec	.30	.14
☐ 390 Dave Winfield	10.00	4.50
☐ 391 Dan Warthen	.30	.14
☐ 392 Phil Roof	.30	.14
☐ 393 John Lowenstein	.30	.14
☐ 394 Bill Laxton	.30	.14
☐ 395 Manny Trillo	.30	.14
☐ 396 Tom Murphy	.30	.14
☐ 397 Larry Herndon	.60	.25
☐ 398 Tom Burgmeier	.30	.14
☐ 399 Bruce Boisclair	.30	.14
☐ 400 Steve Garvey	2.00	.90
☐ 401 Mickey Scott	.30	.14
☐ 402 Tommy Helms	.30	.14
☐ 403 Tom Grieve	.60	.25
☐ 404 Eric Rasmussen	.30	.14
☐ 405 Claudell Washington	.60	.25
☐ 406 Tim Johnson	.30	.14
☐ 407 Dave Freisleben	.30	.14
☐ 408 Cesar Tovar	.30	.14
☐ 409 Pete Broberg	.30	.14
☐ 410 Willie Montanez	.30	.14
☐ 411 Joe Morgan WS	2.00	.90
Johnny Bench		
☐ 412 Johnny Bench WS	2.00	.90
☐ 413 World Series Summary	.60	.25
Cincy wins 2nd		
straight series		
☐ 414 Tommy Harper	.60	.25
☐ 415 Jay Johnstone	.60	.25
☐ 416 Chuck Hartenstein	.30	.14
☐ 417 Wayne Garrett	.30	.14
☐ 418 White Sox Team/Mgr.	1.25	.25
Bob Lemon		
(Checklist back)		
☐ 419 Steve Swisher	.30	.14
☐ 420 Rusty Staub	1.25	.55
☐ 421 Doug Rau	.30	.14
☐ 422 Freddie Patek	.60	.25
☐ 423 Gary Lavelle	.30	.14
☐ 424 Steve Brye	.30	.14
☐ 425 Joe Torre	1.25	.55
☐ 426 Dick Drago	.30	.14
☐ 427 Dave Rader	.30	.14
☐ 428 Rangers Team/Mgr.	1.25	.25
Frank Lucchesi		
(Checklist back)		
☐ 429 Ken Boswell	.30	.14
☐ 430 Fergie Jenkins	2.00	.90
☐ 431 Dave Collins UER	.60	.25
(Photo actually		
Bobby Jones)		
☐ 432 Buzz Capra	.30	.14
☐ 433 Nate Colbert TBC	.30	.14
(5 HR, 13 RBI)		
☐ 434 Carl Yastrzemski TBC	1.25	.55
'67 Triple Crown		
☐ 435 Maury Wills TBC	.60	.25
104 steals		
☐ 436 Bob Keegan TBC	.30	.14
Majors' only no-hitter		
☐ 437 Ralph Kiner TBC	1.25	.55
Leads NL in HR's		
7th straight year		
☐ 438 Marty Perez	.30	.14
☐ 439 Gorman Thomas	.60	.25
☐ 440 Jon Matlack	.30	.14
☐ 441 Larvell Blanks	.30	.14
☐ 442 Braves Team/Mgr.	1.25	.25
Dave Bristol		
(Checklist back)		
☐ 443 Lamar Johnson	.30	.14
☐ 444 Wayne Twitchell	.30	.14
☐ 445 Ken Singleton	.60	.25
☐ 446 Bill Bonham	.30	.14
☐ 447 Jerry Turner	.30	.14
☐ 448 Ellie Rodriguez	.30	.14
☐ 449 Al Fitzmorris	.30	.14
☐ 450 Pete Rose	10.00	4.50
☐ 451 Checklist 397-528	1.25	.25
☐ 452 Mike Caldwell	.30	.14
☐ 453 Pedro Garcia	.30	.14
☐ 454 Andy Etchebarren	.30	.14
☐ 455 Rick Wise	.30	.14
☐ 456 Leon Roberts	.30	.14
☐ 457 Steve Luebber	.30	.14
☐ 458 Leo Foster	.30	.14
☐ 459 Steve Foucault	.30	.14
☐ 460 Willie Stargell	2.50	1.10
☐ 461 Dick Tidrow	.30	.14
☐ 462 Don Baylor	1.25	.55
☐ 463 Jamie Quirk	.30	.14
☐ 464 Randy Moffitt	.30	.14
☐ 465 Rico Carty	.60	.25
☐ 466 Fred Holdsworth	.30	.14
☐ 467 Phillies Team/Mgr.	1.25	.25
Danny Ozark		
(Checklist back)		
☐ 468 Ramon Hernandez	.30	.14
☐ 469 Pat Kelly	.30	.14
☐ 470 Ted Simmons	.60	.25
☐ 471 Del Unser	.30	.14
☐ 472 Rookie Pitchers	.30	.14
Don Aase		
Bob McClure		
Gil Patterson		
Dave Wehrmeister		
☐ 473 Rookie Outfielders	40.00	18.00
Andre Dawson		
Gene Richards		
John Scott		
Denny Walling		
☐ 474 Rookie Shortstops	.60	.25
Bob Bailor		
Kiko Garcia		
Craig Reynolds		
Alex Taveras		
☐ 475 Rookie Pitchers	.60	.25
Chris Batton		
Rick Camp		
Scott McGregor		
Manny Sarmiento		
☐ 476 Rookie Catchers	20.00	9.00
Gary Alexander		
Rick Cerone		
Dale Murphy		
Kevin Pasley		
☐ 477 Rookie Infielders	.60	.25
Doug Ault		
Rich Dauer		
Orlando Gonzalez		
Phil Mankowski		
☐ 478 Rookie Pitchers	.60	.25
Jim Gideon		
Leon Hooten		
Dave Johnson		
Mark Lemongello		
☐ 479 Rookie Outfielders	.60	.25
Brian Asselstine		
Wayne Gross		
Sam Mejias		
Alvis Woods		
☐ 480 Carl Yastrzemski	4.00	1.80
☐ 481 Roger Metzger	.30	.14
☐ 482 Tony Solaita	.30	.14
☐ 483 Richie Zisk	.30	.14
☐ 484 Burt Hooton	.60	.25
☐ 485 Roy White	.60	.25
☐ 486 Ed Bane	.30	.14
☐ 487 Rookie Pitchers	.60	.25
Larry Anderson		
Ed Glynn		
Joe Henderson		
Greg Terlecky		
☐ 488 Rookie Outfielders	4.00	1.80
Jack Clark		
Ruppert Jones		
Lee Mazzilli		
Dan Thomas		
☐ 489 Rookie Pitchers	.60	.25
Len Barker		
Randy Lerch		
Greg Minton		
Mike Overy		
☐ 490 Rookie Shortstops	.60	.25
Billy Almon		
Mickey Klutts		
Tommy McMillan		
Mark Wagner		
☐ 491 Rookie Pitchers	4.00	1.80
Mike Dupree		
Dennis Martinez		
Craig Mitchell		
Bob Sykes		
☐ 492 Rookie Outfielders	.60	.25
Tony Armas		
Steve Kemp		
Carlos Lopez		
Gary Woods		
☐ 493 Rookie Pitchers	.60	.25
Mike Krukow		
Jim Otten		
Gary Wheelock		
Mike Willis		
☐ 494 Rookie Infielders	1.25	.55
Juan Bernhardt		
Mike Champion		
Jim Gantner		
Bump Wills		
☐ 495 Al Hrabosky	.30	.14
☐ 496 Gary Thomasson	.30	.14
☐ 497 Clay Carroll	.30	.14
☐ 498 Sal Bando	.60	.25
☐ 499 Pablo Torrealba	.30	.14
☐ 500 Dave Kingman	1.25	.55
☐ 501 Jim Bibby	.30	.14
☐ 502 Randy Hundley	.30	.14
☐ 503 Bill Lee	.30	.14
☐ 504 Dodgers Team/Mgr.	1.25	.25
Tom Lasorda		
(Checklist back)		
☐ 505 Oscar Gamble	.60	.25
☐ 506 Steve Grilli	.30	.14
☐ 507 Mike Hegan	.30	.14
☐ 508 Dave Pagan	.30	.14
☐ 509 Cookie Rojas	.60	.25
☐ 510 John Candelaria	.30	.14
☐ 511 Bill Fahey	.30	.14

☐ 512 Jack Billingham .30 .14
☐ 513 Jerry Terrell .30 .14
☐ 514 Cliff Johnson .30 .14
☐ 515 Chris Speier .30 .14
☐ 516 Bake McBride .60 .25
☐ 517 Pete Vuckovich .60 .25
☐ 518 Cubs Team/Mgr. 1.25 .25
Herman Franks
(Checklist back)
☐ 519 Don Kirkwood .30 .14
☐ 520 Garry Maddox .30 .14
☐ 521 Bob Grich .60 .25
☐ 522 Enzo Hernandez .30 .14
☐ 523 Rollie Fingers 2.00 .90
☐ 524 Rowland Office .30 .14
☐ 525 Dennis Eckersley 6.00 2.70
☐ 526 Larry Parrish .60 .25
☐ 527 Dan Meyer .60 .25
☐ 528 Bill Castro .30 .14
☐ 529 Jim Essian .30 .14
☐ 530 Rick Reuschel .60 .25
☐ 531 Lyman Bostock .60 .25
☐ 532 Jim Willoughby .30 .14
☐ 533 Mickey Stanley .30 .14
☐ 534 Paul Splittorff .30 .14
☐ 535 Cesar Geronimo .30 .14
☐ 536 Vic Albury .30 .14
☐ 537 Dave Roberts .30 .14
☐ 538 Frank Taveras .30 .14
☐ 539 Mike Wallace .30 .14
☐ 540 Bob Watson .60 .25
☐ 541 John Denny .60 .25
☐ 542 Frank Duffy .30 .14
☐ 543 Ron Blomberg .30 .14
☐ 544 Gary Ross .30 .14
☐ 545 Bob Boone .60 .25
☐ 546 Orioles Team/Mgr. 1.25 .25
Earl Weaver
(Checklist back)
☐ 547 Willie McCovey 3.00 1.35
☐ 548 Joel Youngblood .30 .14
☐ 549 Jerry Royster .30 .14
☐ 550 Randy Jones .30 .14
☐ 551 Bill North .30 .14
☐ 552 Pepe Mangual .30 .14
☐ 553 Jack Heidemann .30 .14
☐ 554 Bruce Kimm .30 .14
☐ 555 Dan Ford .30 .14
☐ 556 Doug Bird .30 .14
☐ 557 Jerry White .30 .14
☐ 558 Elias Sosa .30 .14
☐ 559 Alan Bannister .30 .14
☐ 560 Dave Concepcion 1.25 .55
☐ 561 Pete LaCock .30 .14
☐ 562 Checklist 529-660 1.25 .25
☐ 563 Bruce Kison .30 .14
☐ 564 Alan Ashby .60 .25
☐ 565 Mickey Lolich .60 .25
☐ 566 Rick Miller .30 .14
☐ 567 Enos Cabell .30 .14
☐ 568 Carlos May .30 .14
☐ 569 Jim Lonborg .60 .25
☐ 570 Bobby Bonds 1.25 .55
☐ 571 Darrell Evans .60 .25
☐ 572 Ross Grimsley .30 .14
☐ 573 Joe Ferguson .30 .14
☐ 574 Aurelio Rodriguez .30 .14
☐ 575 Dick Ruthven .30 .14
☐ 576 Fred Kendall .30 .14
☐ 577 Jerry Augustine .30 .14
☐ 578 Bob Randall .30 .14
☐ 579 Don Carrithers .30 .14
☐ 580 George Brett 30.00 13.50
☐ 581 Pedro Borbon .30 .14
☐ 582 Ed Kirkpatrick .30 .14
☐ 583 Paul Lindblad .30 .14
☐ 584 Ed Goodson .30 .14
☐ 585 Rick Burleson .60 .25
☐ 586 Steve Renko .30 .14
☐ 587 Rick Baldwin .30 .14
☐ 588 Dave Moates .30 .14
☐ 589 Mike Cosgrove .30 .14
☐ 590 Buddy Bell .60 .25
☐ 591 Chris Arnold .30 .14
☐ 592 Dan Briggs .30 .14
☐ 593 Dennis Blair .30 .14
☐ 594 Biff Pocoroba .30 .14
☐ 595 John Hiller .30 .14
☐ 596 Jerry Martin .30 .14
☐ 597 Mariners Leaders 1.25 .25
Darrell Johnson MG
Don Bryant CO
Jim Busby CO
Vada Pinson CO
Wes Stock CO
(Checklist back)
☐ 598 Sparky Lyle .60 .25
☐ 599 Mike Tyson .30 .14
☐ 600 Jim Palmer 3.00 1.35
☐ 601 Mike Lum .30 .14
☐ 602 Andy Hassler .30 .14
☐ 603 Willie Davis .60 .25
☐ 604 Jim Slaton .30 .14
☐ 605 Felix Millan .30 .14
☐ 606 Steve Braun .30 .14
☐ 607 Larry Demery .30 .14
☐ 608 Roy Howell .30 .14
☐ 609 Jim Barr .30 .14
☐ 610 Jose Cardenal .60 .25
☐ 611 Dave Lemanczyk .30 .14
☐ 612 Barry Foote .30 .14
☐ 613 Reggie Cleveland .30 .14
☐ 614 Greg Gross .30 .14
☐ 615 Phil Niekro 2.00 .90
☐ 616 Tommy Sandt .30 .14
☐ 617 Bobby Darwin .30 .14
☐ 618 Pat Dobson .30 .14
☐ 619 Johnny Oates .60 .25
☐ 620 Don Sutton 2.00 .90
☐ 621 Tigers Team/Mgr. 1.25 .25
Ralph Houk
(Checklist back)
☐ 622 Jim Wohlford .30 .14
☐ 623 Jack Kucek .30 .14
☐ 624 Hector Cruz .30 .14
☐ 625 Ken Holtzman .60 .25
☐ 626 Al Bumbry .60 .25
☐ 627 Bob Myrick .30 .14
☐ 628 Mario Guerrero .30 .14
☐ 629 Bobby Valentine .30 .14
☐ 630 Bert Blyleven 1.25 .55
☐ 631 George Brett 8.00 3.60
Ken Brett
☐ 632 Bob Forsch .60 .25
Ken Forsch
☐ 633 Lee May .60 .25
Carlos May
☐ 634 Paul Reuschel .60 .25
Rick Reuschel UER
(Photos switched)
☐ 635 Robin Yount 15.00 6.75
☐ 636 Santo Alcala .30 .14
☐ 637 Alex Johnson .30 .14
☐ 638 Jim Kaat 1.25 .55
☐ 639 Jerry Morales .30 .14
☐ 640 Carlton Fisk 5.00 2.20
☐ 641 Dan Larson .30 .14
☐ 642 Willie Crawford .30 .14
☐ 643 Mike Pazik .30 .14
☐ 644 Matt Alexander .30 .14
☐ 645 Jerry Reuss .60 .25
☐ 646 Andres Mora .30 .14
☐ 647 Expos Team/Mgr. 1.25 .25
Dick Williams
(Checklist back)
☐ 648 Jim Spencer .30 .14
☐ 649 Dave Cash .30 .14
☐ 650 Nolan Ryan 50.00 22.00
☐ 651 Von Joshua .30 .14
☐ 652 Tom Walker .30 .14
☐ 653 Diego Segui .60 .25
☐ 654 Ron Pruitt .30 .14
☐ 655 Tony Perez 2.00 .90
☐ 656 Ron Guidry 1.25 .55
☐ 657 Mick Kelleher .30 .14
☐ 658 Marty Pattin .30 .14
☐ 659 Merv Rettenmund .30 .14
☐ 660 Willie Horton 1.25 .25

1977 Topps Cloth Stickers

The "cards" in this 73-card set measure 2 1/2" by 3 1/2". The 1977 Cloth Stickers series was issued as a test set separately from the regular baseball series of that year. The packs of these cards contained two stickers as well as one "checklist puzzle" piece. The obverse pictures are identical to those appearing in the regular set, but the backs are completely different. There are 55 player cards and 18 unnumbered checklists, the latter bearing the title "Baseball Patches". The player cards are sequenced in alphabetical order. The checklists are puzzle pieces which, when properly arranged, form pictures of the A.L. and N.L. All-Star teams. Puzzle pieces are coded below by U (Upper), M (Middle), B (Bottom), L (left), C (Center), and R (Right). Cards marked with an SP in the checklist are in shorter supply than all others in the set.

	NRMT	VG-E
COMPLETE SET (73)	200.00	90.00
COMMON CARD (1-55)	.50	.23
COMMON SP PLAYER (1-55)	1.00	.45
COMMON PUZZLE (56-73)	.15	.07

☐ 1 Alan Ashby .50 .23
☐ 2 Buddy Bell SP 1.50 .70
☐ 3 Johnny Bench 8.00 3.60
☐ 4 Vida Blue 1.00 .45
☐ 5 Bert Blyleven 1.00 .45
☐ 6 Steve Braun SP 1.00 .45
☐ 7 George Brett 25.00 11.00
☐ 8 Lou Brock 5.00 2.20
☐ 9 Jose Cardenal .50 .23
☐ 10 Rod Carew SP 10.00 4.50
☐ 11 Steve Carlton 7.00 3.10
☐ 12 Dave Cash 1.00 .45
☐ 13 Cesar Cedeno SP 1.50 .70
☐ 14 Ron Cey 1.00 .45
☐ 15 Mark Fidrych 1.00 .45
☐ 16 Dan Ford .50 .23
☐ 17 Wayne Garland .50 .23
☐ 18 Ralph Garr .75 .35
☐ 19 Steve Garvey 4.00 1.80
☐ 20 Mike Hargrove 1.00 .45
☐ 21 Jim Hunter 3.00 1.35
☐ 22 Reggie Jackson 12.00 5.50
☐ 23 Randy Jones .50 .23
☐ 24 Dave Kingman SP 1.50 .70
☐ 25 Bill Madlock 1.00 .45
☐ 26 Lee May SP 1.50 .70
☐ 27 John Mayberry .50 .23
☐ 28 John(Andy)Messersmith .50 .23
☐ 29 Willie Montanez .50 .23
☐ 30 John Montefusco SP 1.00 .45
☐ 31 Joe Morgan 5.00 2.20
☐ 32 Thurman Munson 3.00 1.35
☐ 33 Bobby Murcer 1.00 .45
☐ 34 Al Oliver SP 1.50 .70
☐ 35 Dave Pagan .50 .23
☐ 36 Jim Palmer SP 10.00 4.50
☐ 37 Tony Perez 1.00 .45
☐ 38 Pete Rose SP 15.00 6.75
☐ 39 Joe Rudi .75 .35
☐ 40 Nolan Ryan SP 60.00 27.00
☐ 41 Mike Schmidt 20.00 9.00
☐ 42 Tom Seaver 10.00 4.50
☐ 43 Ted Simmons 1.00 .45
☐ 44 Bill Singer .50 .23
☐ 45 Willie Stargell 4.00 1.80
☐ 46 Rusty Staub 1.00 .45
☐ 47 Don Sutton 2.00 .90
☐ 48 Luis Tiant 1.00 .45
☐ 49 Bill Travers .50 .23
☐ 50 Claudell Washington 1.00 .45
☐ 51 Bob Watson 1.00 .45
☐ 52 Dave Winfield 12.00 5.50
☐ 53 Carl Yastrzemski 6.00 2.70
☐ 54 Robin Yount 12.00 5.50
☐ 55 Richie Zisk .50 .23
☐ 56 AL Puzzle UL .15 .07
(unnumbered)
☐ 57 AL Puzzle UC .15 .07
(unnumbered)
☐ 58 AL Puzzle UR .15 .07
(unnumbered)
☐ 59 AL Puzzle ML .15 .07
(unnumbered)
☐ 60 AL Puzzle MC .15 .07
(unnumbered)
☐ 61 AL Puzzle MR .15 .07
(unnumbered)
☐ 62 AL Puzzle BL SP .25 .11
(unnumbered)
☐ 63 AL Puzzle BC SP .25 .11
(unnumbered)
☐ 64 AL Puzzle BR SP .25 .11
(unnumbered)
☐ 65 NL Puzzle UL .15 .07
(unnumbered)
☐ 66 NL Puzzle UC .15 .07
(unnumbered)
☐ 67 NL Puzzle UR .15 .07
(unnumbered)
☐ 68 NL Puzzle ML .15 .07
(unnumbered)
☐ 69 NL Puzzle MC .15 .07
(unnumbered)
☐ 70 NL Puzzle MR .15 .07

Card	NRMT	VG-E
(unnumbered)		
☐ 71 NL Puzzle BL	.15	.07
(unnumbered)		
☐ 72 NL Puzzle BC	.15	.07
(unnumbered)		
☐ 73 NL Puzzle BR	.15	.07
(unnumbered)		

1978 Topps

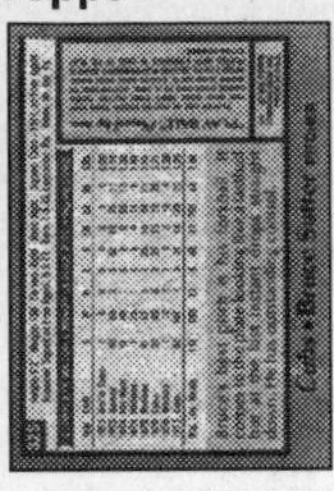

The cards in this 726-card set measure 2 1/2" by 3 1/2". The 1978 Topps set experienced an increase in number of cards from the previous five regular issue sets of 660. Card numbers 1 through 7 feature Record Breakers (RB) of the 1977 season. Other subsets within this set include League Leaders (201-208), Post-season cards (411-413), and Rookie Prospects (701-711). The key Rookie Cards in this set are the multi-player Rookie Card of Paul Molitor and Alan Trammell, Jack Morris, Eddie Murray, Lance Parrish, and Lou Whitaker. Almost all of the Molitor/Trammell cards are found with black printing smudges. The manager cards in the set feature a "then and now" format on the card front showing the manager as he looked during his playing days. While no scarcities exist, 66 of the cards are more abundant in supply, as they were "double printed." These 66 double-printed cards are noted in the checklist by DP. Team cards again feature a checklist of that team's players in the set on the back. As in previous years, this set was issued in many different ways: some of them include 14-card wax packs and 39-card rack packs. Cards numbered 23 or lower, that feature Astros, Rangers, Tigers, or Yankees and do not follow the numbering checklisted below, are not necessarily error cards. They are undoubtedly Burger King cards, a separate set with its own pricing and mass distribution. Burger King cards are indistinguishable from the corresponding Topps cards except for the card numbering difference and the fact that Burger King cards do not have a printing sheet designation (such as A through F like the regular Topps) anywhere on the card back in very small print.

	NRMT	VG-E
COMPLETE SET (726)	275.00	125.00
COMMON CARD (1-726)	.25	.11
COMMON CARD DP	.15	.07
☐ 1 Lou Brock RB	2.50	.75
Most lifetime steals		
☐ 2 Sparky Lyle RB	.50	.23
Most career games pure relief		
☐ 3 Willie McCovey RB	1.50	.70
Most times 2 HR's in inning		
☐ 4 Brooks Robinson RB	2.00	.90
Most consecutive seasons with one club		
☐ 5 Pete Rose RB	3.00	1.35
Most lifetime switch-hitter hits		
☐ 6 Nolan Ryan RB	15.00	6.75
Most games 10 or more strikeouts		
☐ 7 Reggie Jackson RB	3.00	1.35
Most homers, one World Series		
☐ 8 Mike Sadek	.25	.11
☐ 9 Doug DeCinces	.50	.23
☐ 10 Phil Niekro	1.50	.70
☐ 11 Rick Manning	.25	.11
☐ 12 Don Aase	.25	.11
☐ 13 Art Howe	.50	.23
☐ 14 Lerrin LaGrow	.25	.11
☐ 15 Tony Perez DP	1.00	.45
☐ 16 Roy White	.50	.23
☐ 17 Mike Krukow	.25	.11
☐ 18 Bob Grich	.50	.23
☐ 19 Darrell Porter	.50	.23
☐ 20 Pete Rose DP	5.00	2.20
☐ 21 Steve Kemp	.25	.11
☐ 22 Charlie Hough	.50	.23
☐ 23 Bump Wills	.25	.11
☐ 24 Don Money DP	.15	.07
☐ 25 Jon Matlack	.25	.11
☐ 26 Rich Hebner	.50	.23
☐ 27 Geoff Zahn	.25	.11
☐ 28 Ed Ott	.25	.11
☐ 29 Bob Lacey	.25	.11
☐ 30 George Hendrick	.50	.23
☐ 31 Glenn Abbott	.25	.11
☐ 32 Garry Templeton	.50	.23
☐ 33 Dave Lemanczyk	.25	.11
☐ 34 Willie McCovey	2.50	1.10
☐ 35 Sparky Lyle	.50	.23
☐ 36 Eddie Murray	120.00	55.00
☐ 37 Rick Waits	.25	.11
☐ 38 Willie Montanez	.25	.11
☐ 39 Floyd Bannister	.25	.11
☐ 40 Carl Yastrzemski	3.00	1.35
☐ 41 Burt Hooton	.50	.23
☐ 42 Jorge Orta	.25	.11
☐ 43 Bill Atkinson	.25	.11
☐ 44 Toby Harrah	.50	.23
☐ 45 Mark Fidrych	1.50	.70
☐ 46 Al Cowens	.25	.11
☐ 47 Jack Billingham	.25	.11
☐ 48 Don Baylor	1.00	.45
☐ 49 Ed Kranepool	.50	.23
☐ 50 Rick Reuschel	.50	.23
☐ 51 Charlie Moore DP	.15	.07
☐ 52 Jim Lonborg	.25	.11
☐ 53 Phil Garner DP	.25	.11
☐ 54 Tom Johnson	.25	.11
☐ 55 Mitchell Page	.25	.11
☐ 56 Randy Jones	.25	.11
☐ 57 Dan Meyer	.25	.11
☐ 58 Bob Forsch	.25	.11
☐ 59 Otto Velez	.25	.11
☐ 60 Thurman Munson	3.00	1.35
☐ 61 Larvell Blanks	.25	.11
☐ 62 Jim Barr	.25	.11
☐ 63 Don Zimmer MG	.50	.23
☐ 64 Gene Pentz	.25	.11
☐ 65 Ken Singleton	.50	.23
☐ 66 Chicago White Sox	1.00	.20
Team Card (Checklist back)		
☐ 67 Claudell Washington	.50	.23
☐ 68 Steve Foucault DP	.15	.07
☐ 69 Mike Vail	.25	.11
☐ 70 Rich Gossage	1.00	.45
☐ 71 Terry Humphrey	.25	.11
☐ 72 Andre Dawson	10.00	4.50
☐ 73 Andy Hassler	.25	.11
☐ 74 Checklist 1-121	1.00	.20
☐ 75 Dick Ruthven	.25	.11
☐ 76 Steve Ontiveros	.25	.11
☐ 77 Ed Kirkpatrick	.25	.11
☐ 78 Pablo Torrealba	.25	.11
☐ 79 Darrell Johnson DP MG	.15	.07
☐ 80 Ken Griffey	1.00	.45
☐ 81 Pete Redfern	.25	.11
☐ 82 San Francisco Giants	1.00	.20
Team Card (Checklist back)		
☐ 83 Bob Montgomery	.25	.11
☐ 84 Kent Tekulve	.50	.23
☐ 85 Ron Fairly	.50	.23
☐ 86 Dave Tomlin	.25	.11
☐ 87 John Lowenstein	.25	.11
☐ 88 Mike Phillips	.25	.11
☐ 89 Ken Clay	.25	.11
☐ 90 Larry Bowa	1.00	.45
☐ 91 Oscar Zamora	.25	.11
☐ 92 Adrian Devine	.25	.11
☐ 93 Bobby Cox DP	.25	.11
☐ 94 Chuck Scrivener	.25	.11
☐ 95 Jamie Quirk	.25	.11
☐ 96 Baltimore Orioles	1.00	.20
Team Card (Checklist back)		
☐ 97 Stan Bahnsen	.25	.11
☐ 98 Jim Essian	.50	.23
☐ 99 Willie Hernandez	1.00	.45
☐ 100 George Brett	20.00	9.00
☐ 101 Sid Monge	.25	.11
☐ 102 Matt Alexander	.25	.11
☐ 103 Tom Murphy	.25	.11
☐ 104 Lee Lacy	.25	.11
☐ 105 Reggie Cleveland	.25	.11
☐ 106 Bill Plummer	.25	.11
☐ 107 Ed Halicki	.25	.11
☐ 108 Von Joshua	.25	.11
☐ 109 Joe Torre MG	.50	.23
☐ 110 Richie Zisk	.25	.11
☐ 111 Mike Tyson	.25	.11
☐ 112 Houston Astros	1.00	.20
Team Card (Checklist back)		
☐ 113 Don Carrithers	.25	.11
☐ 114 Paul Blair	.50	.23
☐ 115 Gary Nolan	.25	.11
☐ 116 Tucker Ashford	.25	.11
☐ 117 John Montague	.25	.11
☐ 118 Terry Harmon	.25	.11
☐ 119 Dennis Martinez	1.50	.70
☐ 120 Gary Carter	1.50	.70
☐ 121 Alvis Woods	.25	.11
☐ 122 Dennis Eckersley	4.00	1.80
☐ 123 Manny Trillo	.25	.11
☐ 124 Dave Rozema	.25	.11
☐ 125 George Scott	.50	.23
☐ 126 Paul Moskau	.25	.11
☐ 127 Chet Lemon	.50	.23
☐ 128 Bill Russell	.50	.23
☐ 129 Jim Colborn	.25	.11
☐ 130 Jeff Burroughs	.50	.23
☐ 131 Bert Blyleven	1.00	.45
☐ 132 Enos Cabell	.25	.11
☐ 133 Jerry Augustine	.25	.11
☐ 134 Steve Henderson	.25	.11
☐ 135 Ron Guidry DP	1.00	.45
☐ 136 Ted Sizemore	.25	.11
☐ 137 Craig Kusick	.25	.11
☐ 138 Larry Demery	.25	.11
☐ 139 Wayne Gross	.25	.11
☐ 140 Rollie Fingers	1.50	.70
☐ 141 Ruppert Jones	.25	.11
☐ 142 John Montefusco	.25	.11
☐ 143 Keith Hernandez	.50	.23
☐ 144 Jesse Jefferson	.25	.11
☐ 145 Rick Monday	.50	.23
☐ 146 Doyle Alexander	.25	.11
☐ 147 Lee Mazzilli	.25	.11
☐ 148 Andre Thornton	.50	.23
☐ 149 Dale Murray	.25	.11
☐ 150 Bobby Bonds	1.00	.45
☐ 151 Milt Wilcox	.25	.11
☐ 152 Ivan DeJesus	.25	.11
☐ 153 Steve Stone	.50	.23
☐ 154 Cecil Cooper DP	.25	.11
☐ 155 Butch Hobson	.25	.11
☐ 156 Andy Messersmith	.50	.23
☐ 157 Pete LaCock DP	.15	.07
☐ 158 Joaquin Andujar	.50	.23
☐ 159 Lou Piniella	.50	.23
☐ 160 Jim Palmer	2.50	1.10
☐ 161 Bob Boone	1.00	.45
☐ 162 Paul Thormodsgard	.25	.11
☐ 163 Bill North	.25	.11
☐ 164 Bob Owchinko	.25	.11
☐ 165 Rennie Stennett	.25	.11
☐ 166 Carlos Lopez	.25	.11
☐ 167 Tim Foli	.25	.11
☐ 168 Reggie Smith	.50	.23
☐ 169 Jerry Johnson	.25	.11
☐ 170 Lou Brock	2.50	1.10
☐ 171 Pat Zachry	.25	.11
☐ 172 Mike Hargrove	.50	.23
☐ 173 Robin Yount UER	10.00	4.50
(Played for Newark in 1973, not 1971)		
☐ 174 Wayne Garland	.25	.11
☐ 175 Jerry Morales	.25	.11
☐ 176 Milt May	.25	.11
☐ 177 Gene Garber DP	.25	.11
☐ 178 Dave Chalk	.25	.11
☐ 179 Dick Tidrow	.25	.11
☐ 180 Dave Concepcion	1.00	.45
☐ 181 Ken Forsch	.25	.11
☐ 182 Jim Spencer	.25	.11
☐ 183 Doug Bird	.25	.11
☐ 184 Checklist 122-242	1.00	.20
☐ 185 Ellis Valentine	.25	.11
☐ 186 Bob Stanley DP	.25	.11
☐ 187 Jerry Royster DP	.15	.07
☐ 188 Al Bumbry	.50	.23
☐ 189 Tom Lasorda MG	1.50	.70
☐ 190 John Candelaria	.50	.23
☐ 191 Rodney Scott	.25	.11
☐ 192 San Diego Padres	1.00	.20
Team Card (Checklist back)		
☐ 193 Rich Chiles	.25	.11
☐ 194 Derrel Thomas	.25	.11
☐ 195 Larry Dierker	.50	.23
☐ 196 Bob Bailor	.25	.11
☐ 197 Nino Espinosa	.25	.11
☐ 198 Ron Pruitt	.25	.11
☐ 199 Craig Reynolds	.25	.11
☐ 200 Reggie Jackson	8.00	3.60
☐ 201 Batting Leaders	1.00	.45
Dave Parker		
Rod Carew		
☐ 202 Home Run Leaders DP	.50	.23
George Foster		
Jim Rice		
☐ 203 RBI Leaders	.50	.23

George Foster
Larry Hisle
☐ 204 Steals Leaders DP .25 .11
Frank Taveras
Freddie Patek
☐ 205 Victory Leaders 1.50 .70
Steve Carlton
Dave Goltz
Dennis Leonard
Jim Palmer
☐ 206 Strikeout Leaders DP 5.00 2.20
Phil Niekro
Nolan Ryan
☐ 207 ERA Leaders DP .50 .23
John Candelaria
Frank Tanana
☐ 208 Top Firemen 1.00 .45
Rollie Fingers
Bill Campbell
☐ 209 Dock Ellis .25 .11
☐ 210 Jose Cardenal .25 .11
☐ 211 Earl Weaver MG DP 1.00 .45
☐ 212 Mike Caldwell .25 .11
☐ 213 Alan Bannister .25 .11
☐ 214 California Angels 1.00 .20
Team Card
(Checklist back)
☐ 215 Darrell Evans .50 .23
☐ 216 Mike Paxton .25 .11
☐ 217 Rod Gilbreath .25 .11
☐ 218 Marty Pattin .25 .11
☐ 219 Mike Cubbage .25 .11
☐ 220 Pedro Borbon .25 .11
☐ 221 Chris Speier .25 .11
☐ 222 Jerry Martin .25 .11
☐ 223 Bruce Kison .25 .11
☐ 224 Jerry Tabb .25 .11
☐ 225 Don Gullett DP .25 .11
☐ 226 Joe Ferguson .25 .11
☐ 227 Al Fitzmorris .25 .11
☐ 228 Manny Mota DP .25 .11
☐ 229 Leo Foster .25 .11
☐ 230 Al Hrabosky .25 .11
☐ 231 Wayne Nordhagen .25 .11
☐ 232 Mickey Stanley .25 .11
☐ 233 Dick Pole .25 .11
☐ 234 Herman Franks MG .25 .11
☐ 235 Tim McCarver .50 .23
☐ 236 Terry Whitfield .25 .11
☐ 237 Rich Dauer .25 .11
☐ 238 Juan Beniquez .25 .11
☐ 239 Dyar Miller .25 .11
☐ 240 Gene Tenace .50 .23
☐ 241 Pete Vuckovich .50 .23
☐ 242 Barry Bonnell DP .15 .07
☐ 243 Bob McClure .25 .11
☐ 244 Montreal Expos .50 .10
Team Card DP
(Checklist back)
☐ 245 Rick Burleson .50 .23
☐ 246 Dan Driessen .25 .11
☐ 247 Larry Christenson .25 .11
☐ 248 Frank White DP .50 .23
☐ 249 Dave Goltz DP .15 .07
☐ 250 Graig Nettles DP .50 .23
☐ 251 Don Kirkwood .25 .11
☐ 252 Steve Swisher DP .15 .07
☐ 253 Jim Kern .25 .11
☐ 254 Dave Collins .50 .23
☐ 255 Jerry Reuss .50 .23
☐ 256 Joe Altobelli MG .25 .11
☐ 257 Hector Cruz .25 .11
☐ 258 John Hiller .25 .11
☐ 259 Los Angeles Dodgers 1.00 .20
Team Card
(Checklist back)
☐ 260 Bert Campaneris .50 .23
☐ 261 Tim Hosley .25 .11
☐ 262 Rudy May .25 .11
☐ 263 Danny Walton .25 .11
☐ 264 Jamie Easterly .25 .11
☐ 265 Sal Bando DP .50 .23
☐ 266 Bob Shirley .25 .11
☐ 267 Doug Ault .25 .11
☐ 268 Gil Flores .25 .11
☐ 269 Wayne Twitchell .25 .11
☐ 270 Carlton Fisk 3.00 1.35
☐ 271 Randy Lerch DP .15 .07
☐ 272 Royle Stillman .25 .11
☐ 273 Fred Norman .25 .11
☐ 274 Freddie Patek .50 .23
☐ 275 Dan Ford .25 .11
☐ 276 Bill Bonham DP .15 .07
☐ 277 Bruce Boisclair .25 .11
☐ 278 Enrique Romo .25 .11
☐ 279 Bill Virdon MG .25 .11
☐ 280 Buddy Bell .50 .23
☐ 281 Eric Rasmussen DP .15 .07
☐ 282 New York Yankees 1.50 .30
Team Card
(Checklist back)
☐ 283 Omar Moreno .25 .11
☐ 284 Randy Moffitt .25 .11
☐ 285 Steve Yeager DP .50 .23
☐ 286 Ben Oglivie .50 .23
☐ 287 Kiko Garcia .25 .11
☐ 288 Dave Hamilton .25 .11
☐ 289 Checklist 243-363 1.00 .20
☐ 290 Willie Horton .50 .23
☐ 291 Gary Ross .25 .11
☐ 292 Gene Richards .25 .11
☐ 293 Mike Willis .25 .11
☐ 294 Larry Parrish .50 .23
☐ 295 Bill Lee .25 .11
☐ 296 Biff Pocoroba .25 .11
☐ 297 Warren Brusstar DP .15 .07
☐ 298 Tony Armas .50 .23
☐ 299 Whitey Herzog MG .50 .23
☐ 300 Joe Morgan 2.50 1.10
☐ 301 Buddy Schultz .25 .11
☐ 302 Chicago Cubs 1.00 .20
Team Card
(Checklist back)
☐ 303 Sam Hinds .25 .11
☐ 304 John Milner .25 .11
☐ 305 Rico Carty .50 .23
☐ 306 Joe Niekro .50 .23
☐ 307 Glenn Borgmann .25 .11
☐ 308 Jim Rooker .25 .11
☐ 309 Cliff Johnson .25 .11
☐ 310 Don Sutton 1.50 .70
☐ 311 Jose Baez DP .15 .07
☐ 312 Greg Minton .25 .11
☐ 313 Andy Etchebarren .25 .11
☐ 314 Paul Lindblad .25 .11
☐ 315 Mark Belanger .50 .23
☐ 316 Henry Cruz DP .15 .07
☐ 317 Dave Johnson .25 .11
☐ 318 Tom Griffin .25 .11
☐ 319 Alan Ashby .25 .11
☐ 320 Fred Lynn .50 .23
☐ 321 Santo Alcala .25 .11
☐ 322 Tom Paciorek .50 .23
☐ 323 Jim Fregosi DP .25 .11
☐ 324 Vern Rapp MG .25 .11
☐ 325 Bruce Sutter 1.00 .45
☐ 326 Mike Lum DP .15 .07
☐ 327 Rick Langford DP .15 .07
☐ 328 Milwaukee Brewers 1.00 .20
Team Card
(Checklist back)
☐ 329 John Verhoeven .25 .11
☐ 330 Bob Watson .50 .23
☐ 331 Mark Littell .25 .11
☐ 332 Duane Kuiper .25 .11
☐ 333 Jim Todd .25 .11
☐ 334 John Stearns .25 .11
☐ 335 Bucky Dent .50 .23
☐ 336 Steve Busby .25 .11
☐ 337 Tom Grieve .50 .23
☐ 338 Dave Heaverlo .25 .11
☐ 339 Mario Guerrero .25 .11
☐ 340 Bake McBride .50 .23
☐ 341 Mike Flanagan .50 .23
☐ 342 Aurelio Rodriguez .25 .11
☐ 343 John Wathan DP .15 .07
☐ 344 Sam Ewing .25 .11
☐ 345 Luis Tiant .50 .23
☐ 346 Larry Biittner .25 .11
☐ 347 Terry Forster .25 .11
☐ 348 Del Unser .25 .11
☐ 349 Rick Camp DP .15 .07
☐ 350 Steve Garvey 1.50 .70
☐ 351 Jeff Torborg .50 .23
☐ 352 Tony Scott .25 .11
☐ 353 Doug Bair .25 .11
☐ 354 Cesar Geronimo .25 .11
☐ 355 Bill Travers .25 .11
☐ 356 New York Mets 1.00 .20
Team Card
(Checklist back)
☐ 357 Tom Poquette .25 .11
☐ 358 Mark Lemongello .25 .11
☐ 359 Marc Hill .25 .11
☐ 360 Mike Schmidt 12.00 5.50
☐ 361 Chris Knapp .25 .11
☐ 362 Dave May .25 .11
☐ 363 Bob Randall .25 .11
☐ 364 Jerry Turner .25 .11
☐ 365 Ed Figueroa .25 .11
☐ 366 Larry Milbourne DP .15 .07
☐ 367 Rick Dempsey .50 .23
☐ 368 Balor Moore .25 .11
☐ 369 Tim Nordbrook .25 .11
☐ 370 Rusty Staub 1.00 .45
☐ 371 Ray Burris .25 .11
☐ 372 Brian Asselstine .25 .11
☐ 373 Jim Willoughby .25 .11
☐ 374 Jose Morales .25 .11
☐ 375 Tommy John 1.00 .45
☐ 376 Jim Wohlford .25 .11
☐ 377 Manny Sarmiento .25 .11
☐ 378 Bobby Winkles MG .25 .11
☐ 379 Skip Lockwood .25 .11
☐ 380 Ted Simmons .50 .23
☐ 381 Philadelphia Phillies 1.00 .20
Team Card
(Checklist back)
☐ 382 Joe Lahoud .25 .11
☐ 383 Mario Mendoza .25 .11
☐ 384 Jack Clark 1.00 .45
☐ 385 Tito Fuentes .25 .11
☐ 386 Bob Gorinski .25 .11
☐ 387 Ken Holtzman .50 .23
☐ 388 Bill Fahey DP .15 .07
☐ 389 Julio Gonzalez .25 .11
☐ 390 Oscar Gamble .50 .23
☐ 391 Larry Haney .25 .11
☐ 392 Billy Almon .25 .11
☐ 393 Tippy Martinez .50 .23
☐ 394 Roy Howell DP .15 .07
☐ 395 Jim Hughes .25 .11
☐ 396 Bob Stinson DP .15 .07
☐ 397 Greg Gross .25 .11
☐ 398 Don Hood .25 .11
☐ 399 Pete Mackanin .25 .11
☐ 400 Nolan Ryan 40.00 18.00
☐ 401 Sparky Anderson MG .50 .23
☐ 402 Dave Campbell .25 .11
☐ 403 Bud Harrelson .50 .23
☐ 404 Detroit Tigers 1.00 .20
Team Card
(Checklist back)
☐ 405 Rawly Eastwick .25 .11
☐ 406 Mike Jorgensen .25 .11
☐ 407 Odell Jones .25 .11
☐ 408 Joe Zdeb .25 .11
☐ 409 Ron Schueler .25 .11
☐ 410 Bill Madlock .50 .23
☐ 411 Willie Randolph ALCS .50 .23
☐ 412 Davey Lopes NLCS .50 .23
☐ 413 Reggie Jackson WS 3.00 1.35
☐ 414 Darold Knowles DP .15 .07
☐ 415 Ray Fosse .25 .11
☐ 416 Jack Brohamer .25 .11
☐ 417 Mike Garman DP .15 .07
☐ 418 Tony Muser .25 .11
☐ 419 Jerry Garvin .25 .11
☐ 420 Greg Luzinski 1.00 .45
☐ 421 Junior Moore .25 .11
☐ 422 Steve Braun .25 .11
☐ 423 Dave Rosello .25 .11
☐ 424 Boston Red Sox 1.00 .20
Team Card
(Checklist back)
☐ 425 Steve Rogers DP .25 .11
☐ 426 Fred Kendall .25 .11
☐ 427 Mario Soto .50 .23
☐ 428 Joel Youngblood .25 .11
☐ 429 Mike Barlow .25 .11
☐ 430 Al Oliver .50 .23
☐ 431 Butch Metzger .25 .11
☐ 432 Terry Bulling .25 .11
☐ 433 Fernando Gonzalez .25 .11
☐ 434 Mike Norris .25 .11
☐ 435 Checklist 364-484 1.00 .20
☐ 436 Vic Harris DP .15 .07
☐ 437 Bo McLaughlin .25 .11
☐ 438 John Ellis .25 .11
☐ 439 Ken Kravec .25 .11
☐ 440 Dave Lopes .50 .23
☐ 441 Larry Gura .25 .11
☐ 442 Elliott Maddox .25 .11
☐ 443 Darrel Chaney .25 .11
☐ 444 Roy Hartsfield MG .25 .11
☐ 445 Mike Ivie .25 .11
☐ 446 Tug McGraw .50 .23
☐ 447 Leroy Stanton .25 .11
☐ 448 Bill Castro .25 .11
☐ 449 Tim Blackwell DP .15 .07
☐ 450 Tom Seaver 4.00 1.80
☐ 451 Minnesota Twins 1.00 .20
Team Card
(Checklist back)
☐ 452 Jerry Mumphrey .25 .11
☐ 453 Doug Flynn .25 .11
☐ 454 Dave LaRoche .25 .11
☐ 455 Bill Robinson .50 .23
☐ 456 Vern Ruhle .25 .11
☐ 457 Bob Bailey .25 .11
☐ 458 Jeff Newman .25 .11
☐ 459 Charlie Spikes .25 .11

☐ 460 Jim Hunter	1.50	.70
☐ 461 Rob Andrews DP	.15	.07
☐ 462 Rogelio Moret	.25	.11
☐ 463 Kevin Bell	.25	.11
☐ 464 Jerry Grote	.25	.11
☐ 465 Hal McRae	.50	.23
☐ 466 Dennis Blair	.25	.11
☐ 467 Alvin Dark MG	.50	.23
☐ 468 Warren Cromartie	.50	.23
☐ 469 Rick Cerone	.50	.23
☐ 470 J.R. Richard	.50	.23
☐ 471 Roy Smalley	.50	.23
☐ 472 Ron Reed	.25	.11
☐ 473 Bill Buckner	.50	.23
☐ 474 Jim Slaton	.25	.11
☐ 475 Gary Matthews	.50	.23
☐ 476 Bill Stein	.25	.11
☐ 477 Doug Capilla	.25	.11
☐ 478 Jerry Remy	.25	.11
☐ 479 St. Louis Cardinals Team Card (Checklist back)	1.00	.20
☐ 480 Ron LeFlore	.50	.23
☐ 481 Jackson Todd	.25	.11
☐ 482 Rick Miller	.25	.11
☐ 483 Ken Macha	.25	.11
☐ 484 Jim Norris	.25	.11
☐ 485 Chris Chambliss	.50	.23
☐ 486 John Curtis	.25	.11
☐ 487 Jim Tyrone	.25	.11
☐ 488 Dan Spillner	.25	.11
☐ 489 Rudy Meoli	.25	.11
☐ 490 Amos Otis	.50	.23
☐ 491 Scott McGregor	.50	.23
☐ 492 Jim Sundberg	.50	.23
☐ 493 Steve Renko	.25	.11
☐ 494 Chuck Tanner MG	.50	.23
☐ 495 Dave Cash	.25	.11
☐ 496 Jim Clancy DP	.15	.07
☐ 497 Glenn Adams	.25	.11
☐ 498 Joe Sambito	.25	.11
☐ 499 Seattle Mariners Team Card (Checklist back)	1.00	.20
☐ 500 George Foster	1.00	.45
☐ 501 Dave Roberts	.25	.11
☐ 502 Pat Rockett	.25	.11
☐ 503 Ike Hampton	.25	.11
☐ 504 Roger Freed	.25	.11
☐ 505 Felix Millan	.25	.11
☐ 506 Ron Blomberg	.25	.11
☐ 507 Willie Crawford	.25	.11
☐ 508 Johnny Oates	.50	.23
☐ 509 Brent Strom	.25	.11
☐ 510 Willie Stargell	2.00	.90
☐ 511 Frank Duffy	.25	.11
☐ 512 Larry Herndon	.25	.11
☐ 513 Barry Foote	.25	.11
☐ 514 Rob Sperring	.25	.11
☐ 515 Tim Corcoran	.25	.11
☐ 516 Gary Beare	.25	.11
☐ 517 Andres Mora	.25	.11
☐ 518 Tommy Boggs DP	.15	.07
☐ 519 Brian Downing	.50	.23
☐ 520 Larry Hisle	.25	.11
☐ 521 Steve Staggs	.25	.11
☐ 522 Dick Williams MG	.50	.23
☐ 523 Donnie Moore	.25	.11
☐ 524 Bernie Carbo	.25	.11
☐ 525 Jerry Terrell	.25	.11
☐ 526 Cincinnati Reds Team Card (Checklist back)	1.00	.20
☐ 527 Vic Correll	.25	.11
☐ 528 Rob Picciolo	.25	.11
☐ 529 Paul Hartzell	.25	.11
☐ 530 Dave Winfield	8.00	3.60
☐ 531 Tom Underwood	.25	.11
☐ 532 Skip Jutze	.25	.11
☐ 533 Sandy Alomar	.50	.23
☐ 534 Wilbur Howard	.25	.11
☐ 535 Checklist 485-605	1.00	.20
☐ 536 Roric Harrison	.25	.11
☐ 537 Bruce Bochte	.25	.11
☐ 538 Johnny LeMaster	.25	.11
☐ 539 Vic Davalillo DP	.15	.07
☐ 540 Steve Carlton	3.00	1.35
☐ 541 Larry Cox	.25	.11
☐ 542 Tim Johnson	.25	.11
☐ 543 Larry Harlow DP	.15	.07
☐ 544 Len Randle DP	.15	.07
☐ 545 Bill Campbell	.25	.11
☐ 546 Ted Martinez	.25	.11
☐ 547 John Scott	.25	.11
☐ 548 Billy Hunter DP MG	.15	.07
☐ 549 Joe Kerrigan	.25	.11
☐ 550 John Mayberry	.50	.23
☐ 551 Atlanta Braves Team Card (Checklist back)	1.00	.20
☐ 552 Francisco Barrios	.25	.11
☐ 553 Terry Puhl	.50	.23
☐ 554 Joe Coleman	.25	.11
☐ 555 Butch Wynegar	.25	.11
☐ 556 Ed Armbrister	.25	.11
☐ 557 Tony Solaita	.25	.11
☐ 558 Paul Mitchell	.25	.11
☐ 559 Phil Mankowski	.25	.11
☐ 560 Dave Parker	1.00	.45
☐ 561 Charlie Williams	.25	.11
☐ 562 Glenn Burke	.25	.11
☐ 563 Dave Rader	.25	.11
☐ 564 Mick Kelleher	.25	.11
☐ 565 Jerry Koosman	.50	.23
☐ 566 Merv Rettenmund	.25	.11
☐ 567 Dick Drago	.25	.11
☐ 568 Tom Hutton	.25	.11
☐ 569 Lary Sorensen	.25	.11
☐ 570 Dave Kingman	1.00	.45
☐ 571 Buck Martinez	.25	.11
☐ 572 Rick Wise	.25	.11
☐ 573 Luis Gomez	.25	.11
☐ 574 Bob Lemon MG	1.00	.45
☐ 575 Pat Dobson	.25	.11
☐ 576 Sam Mejias	.25	.11
☐ 577 Oakland A's Team Card (Checklist back)	1.00	.20
☐ 578 Buzz Capra	.25	.11
☐ 579 Rance Mulliniks	.25	.11
☐ 580 Rod Carew	2.50	1.10
☐ 581 Lynn McGlothen	.25	.11
☐ 582 Fran Healy	.25	.11
☐ 583 George Medich	.25	.11
☐ 584 John Hale	.25	.11
☐ 585 Woodie Fryman DP	.15	.07
☐ 586 Ed Goodson	.25	.11
☐ 587 John Urrea	.25	.11
☐ 588 Jim Mason	.25	.11
☐ 589 Bob Knepper	.25	.11
☐ 590 Bobby Murcer	.50	.23
☐ 591 George Zeber	.25	.11
☐ 592 Bob Apodaca	.25	.11
☐ 593 Dave Skaggs	.25	.11
☐ 594 Dave Freisleben	.25	.11
☐ 595 Sixto Lezcano	.25	.11
☐ 596 Gary Wheelock	.25	.11
☐ 597 Steve Dillard	.25	.11
☐ 598 Eddie Solomon	.25	.11
☐ 599 Gary Woods	.25	.11
☐ 600 Frank Tanana	.50	.23
☐ 601 Gene Mauch MG	.50	.23
☐ 602 Eric Soderholm	.25	.11
☐ 603 Will McEnaney	.25	.11
☐ 604 Earl Williams	.25	.11
☐ 605 Rick Rhoden	.50	.23
☐ 606 Pittsburgh Pirates Team Card (Checklist back)	1.00	.20
☐ 607 Fernando Arroyo	.25	.11
☐ 608 Johnny Grubb	.25	.11
☐ 609 John Denny	.25	.11
☐ 610 Garry Maddox	.50	.23
☐ 611 Pat Scanlon	.25	.11
☐ 612 Ken Henderson	.25	.11
☐ 613 Marty Perez	.25	.11
☐ 614 Joe Wallis	.25	.11
☐ 615 Clay Carroll	.25	.11
☐ 616 Pat Kelly	.25	.11
☐ 617 Joe Nolan	.25	.11
☐ 618 Tommy Helms	.25	.11
☐ 619 Thad Bosley DP	.15	.07
☐ 620 Willie Randolph	1.00	.45
☐ 621 Craig Swan DP	.15	.07
☐ 622 Champ Summers	.25	.11
☐ 623 Eduardo Rodriguez	.25	.11
☐ 624 Gary Alexander DP	.15	.07
☐ 625 Jose Cruz	.50	.23
☐ 626 Toronto Blue Jays Team Card DP (Checklist back)	1.00	.20
☐ 627 David Johnson	.25	.11
☐ 628 Ralph Garr	.50	.23
☐ 629 Don Stanhouse	.25	.11
☐ 630 Ron Cey	1.00	.45
☐ 631 Danny Ozark MG	.25	.11
☐ 632 Rowland Office	.25	.11
☐ 633 Tom Veryzer	.25	.11
☐ 634 Len Barker	.25	.11
☐ 635 Joe Rudi	.50	.23
☐ 636 Jim Bibby	.25	.11
☐ 637 Duffy Dyer	.25	.11
☐ 638 Paul Splittorff	.25	.11
☐ 639 Gene Clines	.25	.11
☐ 640 Lee May DP	.25	.11
☐ 641 Doug Rau	.25	.11
☐ 642 Denny Doyle	.25	.11
☐ 643 Tom House	.25	.11
☐ 644 Jim Dwyer	.25	.11
☐ 645 Mike Torrez	.50	.23
☐ 646 Rick Auerbach DP	.15	.07
☐ 647 Steve Dunning	.25	.11
☐ 648 Gary Thomasson	.25	.11
☐ 649 Moose Haas	.25	.11
☐ 650 Cesar Cedeno	.50	.23
☐ 651 Doug Rader	.25	.11
☐ 652 Checklist 606-726	1.00	.20
☐ 653 Ron Hodges DP	.15	.07
☐ 654 Pepe Frias	.25	.11
☐ 655 Lyman Bostock	.50	.23
☐ 656 Dave Garcia MG	.25	.11
☐ 657 Bombo Rivera	.25	.11
☐ 658 Manny Sanguillen	.50	.23
☐ 659 Texas Rangers Team Card (Checklist back)	1.00	.20
☐ 660 Jason Thompson	.50	.23
☐ 661 Grant Jackson	.25	.11
☐ 662 Paul Dade	.25	.11
☐ 663 Paul Reuschel	.25	.11
☐ 664 Fred Stanley	.25	.11
☐ 665 Dennis Leonard	.50	.23
☐ 666 Billy Smith	.25	.11
☐ 667 Jeff Byrd	.25	.11
☐ 668 Dusty Baker	1.00	.45
☐ 669 Pete Falcone	.25	.11
☐ 670 Jim Rice	1.00	.45
☐ 671 Gary Lavelle	.25	.11
☐ 672 Don Kessinger	.50	.23
☐ 673 Steve Brye	.25	.11
☐ 674 Ray Knight	1.50	.70
☐ 675 Jay Johnstone	.50	.23
☐ 676 Bob Myrick	.25	.11
☐ 677 Ed Herrmann	.25	.11
☐ 678 Tom Burgmeier	.25	.11
☐ 679 Wayne Garrett	.25	.11
☐ 680 Vida Blue	.50	.23
☐ 681 Rob Belloir	.25	.11
☐ 682 Ken Brett	.25	.11
☐ 683 Mike Champion	.25	.11
☐ 684 Ralph Houk MG	.50	.23
☐ 685 Frank Taveras	.25	.11
☐ 686 Gaylord Perry	1.50	.70
☐ 687 Julio Cruz	.25	.11
☐ 688 George Mitterwald	.25	.11
☐ 689 Cleveland Indians Team Card (Checklist back)	1.00	.20
☐ 690 Mickey Rivers	.50	.23
☐ 691 Ross Grimsley	.25	.11
☐ 692 Ken Reitz	.25	.11
☐ 693 Lamar Johnson	.25	.11
☐ 694 Elias Sosa	.25	.11
☐ 695 Dwight Evans	1.00	.45
☐ 696 Steve Mingori	.25	.11
☐ 697 Roger Metzger	.25	.11
☐ 698 Juan Bernhardt	.25	.11
☐ 699 Jackie Brown	.25	.11
☐ 700 Johnny Bench	4.00	1.80
☐ 701 Rookie Pitchers Tom Hume Larry Landreth Steve McCatty Bruce Taylor	.50	.23
☐ 702 Rookie Catchers Bill Nahorodny Kevin Pasley Rick Sweet Don Werner	.50	.23
☐ 703 Rookie Pitchers DP Larry Andersen Tim Jones Mickey Mahler Jack Morris	5.00	2.20
☐ 704 Rookie 2nd Basemen Garth Iorg Dave Oliver Sam Perlozzo Lou Whitaker	12.00	5.50
☐ 705 Rookie Outfielders Dave Bergman Miguel Dilone Clint Hurdle Willie Norwood	1.00	.45
☐ 706 Rookie 1st Basemen Wayne Cage Ted Cox Pat Putnam Dave Revering	.50	.23
☐ 707 Rookie Shortstops Mickey Klutts	100.00	45.00

Paul Molitor
Alan Trammell
U.L. Washington
☐ 708 Rookie Catchers 5.00 2.20
Bo Diaz
Dale Murphy
Lance Parrish
Ernie Whitt
☐ 709 Rookie Pitchers .50 .23
Steve Burke
Matt Keough
Lance Rautzhan
Dan Schatzeder
☐ 710 Rookie Outfielders 1.00 .45
Dell Alston
Rick Bosetti
Mike Easler
Keith Smith
☐ 711 Rookie Pitchers DP .25 .11
Cardell Camper
Dennis Lamp
Craig Mitchell
Roy Thomas
☐ 712 Bobby Valentine .50 .23
☐ 713 Bob Davis .25 .11
☐ 714 Mike Anderson .25 .11
☐ 715 Jim Kaat 1.00 .45
☐ 716 Clarence Gaston .50 .23
☐ 717 Nelson Briles .25 .11
☐ 718 Ron Jackson .25 .11
☐ 719 Randy Elliott .25 .11
☐ 720 Fergie Jenkins 1.50 .70
☐ 721 Billy Martin MG 1.00 .45
☐ 722 Pete Broberg .25 .11
☐ 723 John Wockenfuss .25 .11
☐ 724 Kansas City Royals 1.00 .20
Team Card
(Checklist back)
☐ 725 Kurt Bevacqua .25 .11
☐ 726 Wilbur Wood 1.00 .22

1978 Topps Team Checklist Sheet

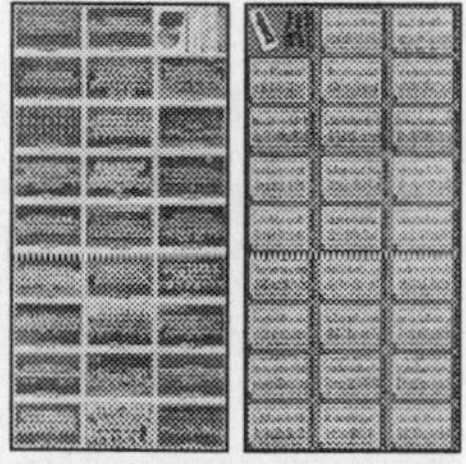

As part of a mail-away offer, Topps offered all 26 team checklist cards on an uncut sheet. These cards enabled the collector to have an easy reference for which card(s) he/she needed to finish their sets. When cut from the sheet, all cards measure the standard size.

	NRMT	VG-E
COMPLETE SET (1)	15.00	6.75
COMMON SHEET (1)	15.00	6.75

☐ 1 Team Checklist Sheet 15.00 6.75

1978 Topps Zest

This set of five standard-size cards is very similar to the 1978 Topps regular issue. Although the cards were produced by Topps, they were used in a promotion for Zest Soap. The sponsor of the set, Zest Soap, is not mentioned anywhere on the cards. The card numbers are different and the backs are written in English and Spanish. By the choice of players in this small set, Zest appears to have been targeting the Hispanic community. Each player's card number in the regular 1978 Topps set is also given. A different photo was used for Montanez, showing his head and shoulders as a New York Met rather than as an Atlanta Brave in a batting stance as shown on Willie's Topps regular card.

	NRMT	VG-E
COMPLETE SET (5)	6.00	2.70
COMMON CARD (1-5)	1.00	.45

☐ 1 Joaquin Andujar 1.50 .70
78T-158
☐ 2 Bert Campaneris 2.00 .90
78T-260
☐ 3 Ed Figueroa 1.00 .45
78T-365
☐ 4 Willie Montanez 1.50 .70
78T-38
(different pose)
(New York Mets)
☐ 5 Manny Mota 1.50 .70
78T-228

1979 Topps

The cards in this 726-card set measure 2 1/2" by 3 1/2". Topps continued with the same number of cards as in 1978. Various series spotlight League Leaders (1-8), "Season and Career Record Holders" (411-418), "Record Breakers" (201-206), and one "Prospects" card for each team (701-726). Team cards feature a checklist on back of that team's players in the set and a small picture of the manager on the front of the card. There are 66 cards that were double printed and these are noted in the checklist by the abbreviation DP. Bump Wills (369) was initially depicted in a Ranger uniform but with a Blue Jays affiliation; later printings correctly labeled him with Texas. The set price includes either Wills card. The key Rookie Cards in this set are Pedro Guerrero, Carney Lansford, Ozzie Smith, Bob Welch and Willie Wilson. As in previous years, this set was released in many different formats, among them are 12-card wax packs and 39-card rack packs. Cards numbered 23 or lower, which feature Phillies or Yankees and do not follow the numbering checklisted below, are not necessarily error cards. They are undoubtedly Burger King cards, separate sets for each team each with its own pricing and mass distribution. Burger King cards are indistinguishable from the corresponding Topps cards except for the card numbering difference and the fact that Burger King cards do not have a printing sheet designation (such as A through F like the regular Topps) anywhere on the card back in very small print.

	NRMT	VG-E
COMPLETE SET (726)	200.00	90.00
COMMON CARD (1-726)	.20	.09
COMMON CARD DP	.10	.05

☐ 1 Batting Leaders 2.50 .50
Rod Carew
Dave Parker
☐ 2 Home Run Leaders .75 .35
Jim Rice
George Foster
☐ 3 RBI Leaders .75 .35
Jim Rice
George Foster
☐ 4 Stolen Base Leaders .40 .18
Ron LeFlore
Omar Moreno
☐ 5 Victory Leaders .40 .18
Ron Guidry
Gaylord Perry
☐ 6 Strikeout Leaders 6.00 2.70
Nolan Ryan
J.R. Richard
☐ 7 ERA Leaders .40 .18
Ron Guidry
Craig Swan
☐ 8 Leading Firemen .75 .35
Rich Gossage
Rollie Fingers
☐ 9 Dave Campbell .20 .09
☐ 10 Lee May .40 .18
☐ 11 Marc Hill .20 .09
☐ 12 Dick Drago .20 .09
☐ 13 Paul Dade .20 .09
☐ 14 Rafael Landestoy .20 .09
☐ 15 Ross Grimsley .20 .09
☐ 16 Fred Stanley .20 .09
☐ 17 Donnie Moore .20 .09
☐ 18 Tony Solaita .20 .09
☐ 19 Larry Gura DP .10 .05
☐ 20 Joe Morgan DP 1.00 .45
☐ 21 Kevin Kobel .20 .09
☐ 22 Mike Jorgensen .20 .09
☐ 23 Terry Forster .20 .09
☐ 24 Paul Molitor 20.00 9.00
☐ 25 Steve Carlton 2.50 1.10
☐ 26 Jamie Quirk .20 .09
☐ 27 Dave Goltz .20 .09
☐ 28 Steve Brye .20 .09
☐ 29 Rick Langford .20 .09
☐ 30 Dave Winfield 6.00 2.70
☐ 31 Tom House DP .10 .05
☐ 32 Jerry Mumphrey .20 .09
☐ 33 Dave Rozema .20 .09
☐ 34 Rob Andrews .20 .09
☐ 35 Ed Figueroa .20 .09
☐ 36 Alan Ashby .20 .09
☐ 37 Joe Kerrigan DP .10 .05
☐ 38 Bernie Carbo .20 .09
☐ 39 Dale Murphy 4.00 1.80
☐ 40 Dennis Eckersley 2.00 .90
☐ 41 Twins Team/Mgr. .75 .15
Gene Mauch
(Checklist back)
☐ 42 Ron Blomberg .20 .09
☐ 43 Wayne Twitchell .20 .09
☐ 44 Kurt Bevacqua .20 .09
☐ 45 Al Hrabosky .20 .09
☐ 46 Ron Hodges .20 .09
☐ 47 Fred Norman .20 .09
☐ 48 Merv Rettenmund .20 .09
☐ 49 Vern Ruhle .20 .09
☐ 50 Steve Garvey DP .75 .35
☐ 51 Ray Fosse DP .10 .05
☐ 52 Randy Lerch .20 .09
☐ 53 Mick Kelleher .20 .09
☐ 54 Dell Alston DP .10 .05
☐ 55 Willie Stargell 1.50 .70
☐ 56 John Hale .20 .09
☐ 57 Eric Rasmussen .20 .09
☐ 58 Bob Randall DP .10 .05
☐ 59 John Denny DP .10 .05
☐ 60 Mickey Rivers .40 .18
☐ 61 Bo Diaz .20 .09
☐ 62 Randy Moffitt .20 .09
☐ 63 Jack Brohamer .20 .09
☐ 64 Tom Underwood .20 .09
☐ 65 Mark Belanger .35 .16
☐ 66 Tigers Team/Mgr. .75 .15
Les Moss
(Checklist back)
☐ 67 Jim Mason DP .10 .05
☐ 68 Joe Niekro DP .20 .09
☐ 69 Elliott Maddox .20 .09
☐ 70 John Candelaria .40 .18
☐ 71 Brian Downing .40 .18
☐ 72 Steve Mingori .20 .09
☐ 73 Ken Henderson .20 .09
☐ 74 Shane Rawley .20 .09
☐ 75 Steve Yeager .40 .18
☐ 76 Warren Cromartie .40 .18
☐ 77 Dan Briggs DP .10 .05
☐ 78 Elias Sosa .20 .09
☐ 79 Ted Cox .20 .09
☐ 80 Jason Thompson .40 .18
☐ 81 Roger Erickson .20 .09
☐ 82 Mets Team/Mgr. .75 .15
Joe Torre
(Checklist back)
☐ 83 Fred Kendall .20 .09
☐ 84 Greg Minton .20 .09
☐ 85 Gary Matthews .40 .18
☐ 86 Rodney Scott .20 .09
☐ 87 Pete Falcone .20 .09
☐ 88 Bob Molinaro .20 .09
☐ 89 Dick Tidrow .20 .09
☐ 90 Bob Boone .75 .35
☐ 91 Terry Crowley .20 .09
☐ 92 Jim Bibby .20 .09
☐ 93 Phil Mankowski .20 .09
☐ 94 Len Barker .20 .09
☐ 95 Robin Yount 8.00 3.60
☐ 96 Indians Team/Mgr. .75 .15
Jeff Torborg
(Checklist back)
☐ 97 Sam Mejias .20 .09

☐ 98 Ray Burris .20 .09
☐ 99 John Wathan .40 .18
☐ 100 Tom Seaver DP 2.00 .90
☐ 101 Roy Howell .20 .09
☐ 102 Mike Anderson .20 .09
☐ 103 Jim Todd .20 .09
☐ 104 Johnny Oates DP .20 .09
☐ 105 Rick Camp DP .10 .05
☐ 106 Frank Duffy .20 .09
☐ 107 Jesus Alou DP .10 .05
☐ 108 Eduardo Rodriguez .20 .09
☐ 109 Joel Youngblood .20 .09
☐ 110 Vida Blue .40 .18
☐ 111 Roger Freed .20 .09
☐ 112 Phillies Team/Mgr. .75 .15
Danny Ozark
(Checklist back)
☐ 113 Pete Redfern .20 .09
☐ 114 Cliff Johnson .20 .09
☐ 115 Nolan Ryan 30.00 13.50
☐ 116 Ozzie Smith 100.00 45.00
☐ 117 Grant Jackson .20 .09
☐ 118 Bud Harrelson .40 .18
☐ 119 Don Stanhouse .20 .09
☐ 120 Jim Sundberg .40 .18
☐ 121 Checklist 1-121 DP .40 .08
☐ 122 Mike Paxton .20 .09
☐ 123 Lou Whitaker 4.00 1.80
☐ 124 Dan Schatzeder .20 .09
☐ 125 Rick Burleson .20 .09
☐ 126 Doug Bair .20 .09
☐ 127 Thad Bosley .20 .09
☐ 128 Ted Martinez .20 .09
☐ 129 Marty Pattin DP .10 .05
☐ 130 Bob Watson DP .20 .09
☐ 131 Jim Clancy .20 .09
☐ 132 Rowland Office .20 .09
☐ 133 Bill Castro .20 .09
☐ 134 Alan Bannister .20 .09
☐ 135 Bobby Murcer .40 .18
☐ 136 Jim Kaat .40 .18
☐ 137 Larry Wolfe DP .10 .05
☐ 138 Mark Lee .20 .09
☐ 139 Luis Pujols .20 .09
☐ 140 Don Gullett .40 .18
☐ 141 Tom Paciorek .40 .18
☐ 142 Charlie Williams .20 .09
☐ 143 Tony Scott .20 .09
☐ 144 Sandy Alomar .40 .18
☐ 145 Rick Rhoden .20 .09
☐ 146 Duane Kuiper .20 .09
☐ 147 Dave Hamilton .20 .09
☐ 148 Bruce Boisclair .20 .09
☐ 149 Manny Sarmiento .20 .09
☐ 150 Wayne Cage .20 .09
☐ 151 John Hiller .20 .09
☐ 152 Rick Cerone .20 .09
☐ 153 Dennis Lamp .20 .09
☐ 154 Jim Gantner DP .20 .09
☐ 155 Dwight Evans .75 .35
☐ 156 Buddy Solomon .20 .09
☐ 157 U.L. Washington UER .20 .09
(Sic, bats left,
should be right)
☐ 158 Joe Sambito .20 .09
☐ 159 Roy White .40 .18
☐ 160 Mike Flanagan .75 .35
☐ 161 Barry Foote .20 .09
☐ 162 Tom Johnson .20 .09
☐ 163 Glenn Burke .20 .09
☐ 164 Mickey Lolich .40 .18
☐ 165 Frank Taveras .20 .09
☐ 166 Leon Roberts .20 .09
☐ 167 Roger Metzger DP .10 .05
☐ 168 Dave Freisleben .20 .09
☐ 169 Bill Nahorodny .20 .09
☐ 170 Don Sutton 1.25 .55
☐ 171 Gene Clines .20 .09
☐ 172 Mike Bruhert .20 .09
☐ 173 John Lowenstein .20 .09
☐ 174 Rick Auerbach .20 .09
☐ 175 George Hendrick .75 .35
☐ 176 Aurelio Rodriguez .20 .09
☐ 177 Ron Reed .20 .09
☐ 178 Alvis Woods .20 .09
☐ 179 Jim Beattie DP .20 .09
☐ 180 Larry Hisle .20 .09
☐ 181 Mike Garman .20 .09
☐ 182 Tim Johnson .20 .09
☐ 183 Paul Splittorff .20 .09
☐ 184 Darrel Chaney .20 .09
☐ 185 Mike Torrez .40 .18
☐ 186 Eric Soderholm .20 .09
☐ 187 Mark Lemongello .20 .09
☐ 188 Pat Kelly .20 .09
☐ 189 Eddie Whitson .20 .09
☐ 190 Ron Cey .40 .18
☐ 191 Mike Norris .20 .09
☐ 192 Cardinals Team/Mgr. .75 .15
Ken Boyer
(Checklist back)
☐ 193 Glenn Adams .20 .09
☐ 194 Randy Jones .20 .09
☐ 195 Bill Madlock .40 .18
☐ 196 Steve Kemp DP .20 .09
☐ 197 Bob Apodaca .20 .09
☐ 198 Johnny Grubb .20 .09
☐ 199 Larry Milbourne .20 .09
☐ 200 Johnny Bench DP 2.00 .90
☐ 201 Mike Edwards RB .20 .09
☐ 202 Ron Guidry RB .75 .35
☐ 203 J.R. Richard RB .20 .09
☐ 204 Pete Rose RB 2.00 .90
☐ 205 John Stearns RB .20 .09
☐ 206 Sammy Stewart RB .20 .09
☐ 207 Dave Lemanczyk .20 .09
☐ 208 Clarence Gaston .40 .18
☐ 209 Reggie Cleveland .20 .09
☐ 210 Larry Bowa .40 .18
☐ 211 Denny Martinez 1.25 .55
☐ 212 Carney Lansford 1.50 .70
☐ 213 Bill Travers .20 .09
☐ 214 Red Sox Team/Mgr. .75 .15
Don Zimmer
(Checklist back)
☐ 215 Willie McCovey 2.00 .90
☐ 216 Wilbur Wood .20 .09
☐ 217 Steve Dillard .20 .09
☐ 218 Dennis Leonard .40 .18
☐ 219 Roy Smalley .40 .18
☐ 220 Cesar Geronimo .20 .09
☐ 221 Jesse Jefferson .20 .09
☐ 222 Bob Beall .20 .09
☐ 223 Kent Tekulve .40 .18
☐ 224 Dave Revering .20 .09
☐ 225 Rich Gossage .75 .35
☐ 226 Ron Pruitt .20 .09
☐ 227 Steve Stone .40 .18
☐ 228 Vic Davalillo .20 .09
☐ 229 Doug Flynn .20 .09
☐ 230 Bob Forsch .20 .09
☐ 231 John Wockenfuss .20 .09
☐ 232 Jimmy Sexton .20 .09
☐ 233 Paul Mitchell .20 .09
☐ 234 Toby Harrah .40 .18
☐ 235 Steve Rogers .20 .09
☐ 236 Jim Dwyer .20 .09
☐ 237 Billy Smith .20 .09
☐ 238 Balor Moore .20 .09
☐ 239 Willie Horton .40 .18
☐ 240 Rick Reuschel .40 .18
☐ 241 Checklist 122-242 DP .40 .08
☐ 242 Pablo Torrealba .20 .09
☐ 243 Buck Martinez DP .10 .05
☐ 244 Pirates Team/Mgr. .75 .15
Chuck Tanner
(Checklist back)
☐ 245 Jeff Burroughs .40 .18
☐ 246 Darrell Jackson .20 .09
☐ 247 Tucker Ashford DP .10 .05
☐ 248 Pete LaCock .20 .09
☐ 249 Paul Thormodsgard .20 .09
☐ 250 Willie Randolph .40 .18
☐ 251 Jack Morris 2.00 .90
☐ 252 Bob Stinson .20 .09
☐ 253 Rick Wise .20 .09
☐ 254 Luis Gomez .20 .09
☐ 255 Tommy John .75 .35
☐ 256 Mike Sadek .20 .09
☐ 257 Adrian Devine .20 .09
☐ 258 Mike Phillips .20 .09
☐ 259 Reds Team/Mgr. .75 .15
Sparky Anderson
(Checklist back)
☐ 260 Richie Zisk .20 .09
☐ 261 Mario Guerrero .20 .09
☐ 262 Nelson Briles .20 .09
☐ 263 Oscar Gamble .40 .18
☐ 264 Don Robinson .20 .09
☐ 265 Don Money .20 .09
☐ 266 Jim Willoughby .20 .09
☐ 267 Joe Rudi .40 .18
☐ 268 Julio Gonzalez .20 .09
☐ 269 Woodie Fryman .20 .09
☐ 270 Butch Hobson .40 .18
☐ 271 Rawly Eastwick .20 .09
☐ 272 Tim Corcoran .20 .09
☐ 273 Jerry Terrell .20 .09
☐ 274 Willie Norwood .20 .09
☐ 275 Junior Moore .20 .09
☐ 276 Jim Colborn .20 .09
☐ 277 Tom Grieve .40 .18
☐ 278 Andy Messersmith .40 .18
☐ 279 Jerry Grote DP .10 .05
☐ 280 Andre Thornton .40 .18
☐ 281 Vic Correll DP .10 .05
☐ 282 Blue Jays Team/Mgr. .40 .08
Roy Hartsfield
(Checklist back)
☐ 283 Ken Kravec .20 .09
☐ 284 Johnnie LeMaster .20 .09
☐ 285 Bobby Bonds .75 .35
☐ 286 Duffy Dyer .20 .09
☐ 287 Andres Mora .20 .09
☐ 288 Milt Wilcox .20 .09
☐ 289 Jose Cruz .75 .35
☐ 290 Dave Lopes .40 .18
☐ 291 Tom Griffin .20 .09
☐ 292 Don Reynolds .20 .09
☐ 293 Jerry Garvin .20 .09
☐ 294 Pepe Frias .20 .09
☐ 295 Mitchell Page .20 .09
☐ 296 Preston Hanna .20 .09
☐ 297 Ted Sizemore .20 .09
☐ 298 Rich Gale .20 .09
☐ 299 Steve Ontiveros .20 .09
☐ 300 Rod Carew 2.00 .90
☐ 301 Tom Hume .20 .09
☐ 302 Braves Team/Mgr. .75 .15
Bobby Cox
(Checklist back)
☐ 303 Lary Sorensen DP .10 .05
☐ 304 Steve Swisher .20 .09
☐ 305 Willie Montanez .20 .09
☐ 306 Floyd Bannister .20 .09
☐ 307 Larvell Blanks .20 .09
☐ 308 Bert Blyleven .75 .35
☐ 309 Ralph Garr .40 .18
☐ 310 Thurman Munson 2.00 .90
☐ 311 Gary Lavelle .20 .09
☐ 312 Bob Robertson .20 .09
☐ 313 Dyar Miller .20 .09
☐ 314 Larry Harlow .20 .09
☐ 315 Jon Matlack .20 .09
☐ 316 Milt May .20 .09
☐ 317 Jose Cardenal .40 .18
☐ 318 Bob Welch 1.50 .70
☐ 319 Wayne Garrett .20 .09
☐ 320 Carl Yastrzemski 2.50 1.10
☐ 321 Gaylord Perry 1.25 .55
☐ 322 Danny Goodwin .20 .09
☐ 323 Lynn McGlothen .20 .09
☐ 324 Mike Tyson .20 .09
☐ 325 Cecil Cooper .40 .18
☐ 326 Pedro Borbon .20 .09
☐ 327 Art Howe DP .20 .09
☐ 328 Oakland A's Team/Mgr. .75 .15
Jack McKeon
(Checklist back)
☐ 329 Joe Coleman .20 .09
☐ 330 George Brett 15.00 6.75
☐ 331 Mickey Mahler .20 .09
☐ 332 Gary Alexander .20 .09
☐ 333 Chet Lemon .40 .18
☐ 334 Craig Swan .20 .09
☐ 335 Chris Chambliss .40 .18
☐ 336 Bobby Thompson .20 .09
☐ 337 John Montague .20 .09
☐ 338 Vic Harris .20 .09
☐ 339 Ron Jackson .20 .09
☐ 340 Jim Palmer 2.00 .90
☐ 341 Willie Upshaw .40 .18
☐ 342 Dave Roberts .20 .09
☐ 343 Ed Glynn .20 .09
☐ 344 Jerry Royster .20 .09
☐ 345 Tug McGraw .40 .18
☐ 346 Bill Buckner .40 .18
☐ 347 Doug Rau .20 .09
☐ 348 Andre Dawson 5.00 2.20
☐ 349 Jim Wright .20 .09
☐ 350 Garry Templeton .40 .18
☐ 351 Wayne Nordhagen DP .10 .05
☐ 352 Steve Renko .20 .09
☐ 353 Checklist 243-363 .75 .15
☐ 354 Bill Bonham .20 .09
☐ 355 Lee Mazzilli .20 .09
☐ 356 Giants Team/Mgr. .75 .15
Joe Altobelli
(Checklist back)
☐ 357 Jerry Augustine .20 .09
☐ 358 Alan Trammell 6.00 2.70
☐ 359 Dan Spillner DP .10 .05
☐ 360 Amos Otis .40 .18
☐ 361 Tom Dixon .20 .09
☐ 362 Mike Cubbage .20 .09
☐ 363 Craig Skok .20 .09
☐ 364 Gene Richards .20 .09
☐ 365 Sparky Lyle .40 .18
☐ 366 Juan Bernhardt .20 .09
☐ 367 Dave Skaggs .20 .09
☐ 368 Don Aase .20 .09

☐ 369A Bump Wills ERR	3.00	1.35
(Blue Jays)		
☐ 369B Bump Wills COR	3.00	1.35
(Rangers)		
☐ 370 Dave Kingman	.75	.35
☐ 371 Jeff Holly	.20	.09
☐ 372 Lamar Johnson	.20	.09
☐ 373 Lance Rautzhan	.20	.09
☐ 374 Ed Herrmann	.20	.09
☐ 375 Bill Campbell	.20	.09
☐ 376 Gorman Thomas	.40	.18
☐ 377 Paul Moskau	.20	.09
☐ 378 Rob Picciolo DP	.10	.05
☐ 379 Dale Murray	.20	.09
☐ 380 John Mayberry	.40	.18
☐ 381 Astros Team/Mgr.	.75	.15
Bill Virdon		
(Checklist back)		
☐ 382 Jerry Martin	.20	.09
☐ 383 Phil Garner	.40	.18
☐ 384 Tommy Boggs	.20	.09
☐ 385 Dan Ford	.20	.09
☐ 386 Francisco Barrios	.20	.09
☐ 387 Gary Thomasson	.20	.09
☐ 388 Jack Billingham	.20	.09
☐ 389 Joe Zdeb	.20	.09
☐ 390 Rollie Fingers	1.25	.55
☐ 391 Al Oliver	.40	.18
☐ 392 Doug Ault	.20	.09
☐ 393 Scott McGregor	.40	.18
☐ 394 Randy Stein	.20	.09
☐ 395 Dave Cash	.20	.09
☐ 396 Bill Plummer	.20	.09
☐ 397 Sergio Ferrer	.20	.09
☐ 398 Ivan DeJesus	.20	.09
☐ 399 David Clyde	.20	.09
☐ 400 Jim Rice	.75	.35
☐ 401 Ray Knight	.40	.18
☐ 402 Paul Hartzell	.20	.09
☐ 403 Tim Foli	.20	.09
☐ 404 White Sox Team/Mgr	.75	.15
Don Kessinger		
(Checklist back)		
☐ 405 Butch Wynegar DP	.10	.05
☐ 406 Joe Wallis DP	.10	.05
☐ 407 Pete Vuckovich	.40	.18
☐ 408 Charlie Moore DP	.10	.05
☐ 409 Willie Wilson	1.50	.70
☐ 410 Darrell Evans	.75	.35
☐ 411 George Sisler ATL	1.25	.55
Ty Cobb		
☐ 412 Hack Wilson ATL	1.25	.55
Hank Aaron		
☐ 413 Roger Maris ATL	1.50	.70
Hank Aaron		
☐ 414 Rogers Hornsby ATL	1.25	.55
Ty Cobb		
☐ 415 Lou Brock ATL	.75	.35
☐ 416 Jack Chesbro ATL	.40	.18
Cy Young		
☐ 417 Nolan Ryan ATL DP	4.00	1.80
Walter Johnson		
☐ 418 Dutch Leonard ATL DP	.20	.09
Walter Johnson		
☐ 419 Dick Ruthven	.20	.09
☐ 420 Ken Griffey	.40	.18
☐ 421 Doug DeCinces	.40	.18
☐ 422 Ruppert Jones	.20	.09
☐ 423 Bob Montgomery	.20	.09
☐ 424 Angels Team/Mgr.	.75	.15
Jim Fregosi		
(Checklist back)		
☐ 425 Rick Manning	.20	.09
☐ 426 Chris Speier	.20	.09
☐ 427 Andy Replogle	.20	.09
☐ 428 Bobby Valentine	.40	.18
☐ 429 John Urrea DP	.10	.05
☐ 430 Dave Parker	.40	.18
☐ 431 Glenn Borgmann	.20	.09
☐ 432 Dave Heaverlo	.20	.09
☐ 433 Larry Biittner	.20	.09
☐ 434 Ken Clay	.20	.09
☐ 435 Gene Tenace	.40	.18
☐ 436 Hector Cruz	.20	.09
☐ 437 Rick Williams	.20	.09
☐ 438 Horace Speed	.20	.09
☐ 439 Frank White	.40	.18
☐ 440 Rusty Staub	.75	.35
☐ 441 Lee Lacy	.20	.09
☐ 442 Doyle Alexander	.20	.09
☐ 443 Bruce Bochte	.20	.09
☐ 444 Aurelio Lopez	.20	.09
☐ 445 Steve Henderson	.20	.09
☐ 446 Jim Lonborg	.40	.18
☐ 447 Manny Sanguillen	.40	.18
☐ 448 Moose Haas	.20	.09
☐ 449 Bombo Rivera	.20	.09
☐ 450 Dave Concepcion	.75	.35
☐ 451 Royals Team/Mgr.	.75	.15
Whitey Herzog		
(Checklist back)		
☐ 452 Jerry Morales	.20	.09
☐ 453 Chris Knapp	.20	.09
☐ 454 Len Randle	.20	.09
☐ 455 Bill Lee DP	.10	.05
☐ 456 Chuck Baker	.20	.09
☐ 457 Bruce Sutter	.40	.18
☐ 458 Jim Essian	.20	.09
☐ 459 Sid Monge	.20	.09
☐ 460 Graig Nettles	.75	.35
☐ 461 Jim Barr DP	.10	.05
☐ 462 Otto Velez	.20	.09
☐ 463 Steve Comer	.20	.09
☐ 464 Joe Nolan	.20	.09
☐ 465 Reggie Smith	.40	.18
☐ 466 Mark Littell	.20	.09
☐ 467 Don Kessinger DP	.20	.09
☐ 468 Stan Bahnsen DP	.10	.05
☐ 469 Lance Parrish	.75	.35
☐ 470 Garry Maddox DP	.20	.09
☐ 471 Joaquin Andujar	.40	.18
☐ 472 Craig Kusick	.20	.09
☐ 473 Dave Roberts	.20	.09
☐ 474 Dick Davis	.20	.09
☐ 475 Dan Driessen	.20	.09
☐ 476 Tom Poquette	.20	.09
☐ 477 Bob Grich	.40	.18
☐ 478 Juan Beniquez	.20	.09
☐ 479 Padres Team/Mgr.	.75	.15
Roger Craig		
(Checklist back)		
☐ 480 Fred Lynn	.40	.18
☐ 481 Skip Lockwood	.20	.09
☐ 482 Craig Reynolds	.20	.09
☐ 483 Checklist 364-484 DP	.40	.08
☐ 484 Rick Waits	.20	.09
☐ 485 Bucky Dent	.40	.18
☐ 486 Bob Knepper	.20	.09
☐ 487 Miguel Dilone	.20	.09
☐ 488 Bob Owchinko	.20	.09
☐ 489 Larry Cox UER	.20	.09
(Photo actually		
Dave Rader)		
☐ 490 Al Cowens	.20	.09
☐ 491 Tippy Martinez	.20	.09
☐ 492 Bob Bailor	.20	.09
☐ 493 Larry Christenson	.20	.09
☐ 494 Jerry White	.20	.09
☐ 495 Tony Perez	1.25	.55
☐ 496 Barry Bonnell DP	.10	.05
☐ 497 Glenn Abbott	.20	.09
☐ 498 Rich Chiles	.20	.09
☐ 499 Rangers Team/Mgr.	.75	.15
Pat Corrales		
(Checklist back)		
☐ 500 Ron Guidry	.40	.18
☐ 501 Junior Kennedy	.20	.09
☐ 502 Steve Braun	.20	.09
☐ 503 Terry Humphrey	.20	.09
☐ 504 Larry McWilliams	.20	.09
☐ 505 Ed Kranepool	.40	.18
☐ 506 John D'Acquisto	.20	.09
☐ 507 Tony Armas	.40	.18
☐ 508 Charlie Hough	.40	.18
☐ 509 Mario Mendoza UER	.20	.09
(Career BA .278,		
should say .204)		
☐ 510 Ted Simmons	.75	.35
☐ 511 Paul Reuschel DP	.10	.05
☐ 512 Jack Clark	.40	.18
☐ 513 Dave Johnson	.40	.18
☐ 514 Mike Proly	.20	.09
☐ 515 Enos Cabell	.20	.09
☐ 516 Champ Summers DP	.10	.05
☐ 517 Al Bumbry	.40	.18
☐ 518 Jim Umbarger	.20	.09
☐ 519 Ben Oglivie	.40	.18
☐ 520 Gary Carter	1.25	.55
☐ 521 Sam Ewing	.20	.09
☐ 522 Ken Holtzman	.40	.18
☐ 523 John Milner	.20	.09
☐ 524 Tom Burgmeier	.20	.09
☐ 525 Freddie Patek	.20	.09
☐ 526 Dodgers Team/Mgr.	.75	.15
Tom Lasorda		
(Checklist back)		
☐ 527 Lerrin LaGrow	.20	.09
☐ 528 Wayne Gross DP	.10	.05
☐ 529 Brian Asselstine	.20	.09
☐ 530 Frank Tanana	.40	.18
☐ 531 Fernando Gonzalez	.20	.09
☐ 532 Buddy Schultz	.20	.09
☐ 533 Leroy Stanton	.20	.09
☐ 534 Ken Forsch	.20	.09
☐ 535 Ellis Valentine	.20	.09
☐ 536 Jerry Reuss	.40	.18
☐ 537 Tom Veryzer	.20	.09
☐ 538 Mike Ivie DP	.10	.05
☐ 539 John Ellis	.20	.09
☐ 540 Greg Luzinski	.40	.18
☐ 541 Jim Slaton	.20	.09
☐ 542 Rick Bosetti	.20	.09
☐ 543 Kiko Garcia	.20	.09
☐ 544 Fergie Jenkins	1.25	.55
☐ 545 John Stearns	.20	.09
☐ 546 Bill Russell	.40	.18
☐ 547 Clint Hurdle	.20	.09
☐ 548 Enrique Romo	.20	.09
☐ 549 Bob Bailey	.20	.09
☐ 550 Sal Bando	.40	.18
☐ 551 Cubs Team/Mgr.	.75	.15
Herman Franks		
(Checklist back)		
☐ 552 Jose Morales	.20	.09
☐ 553 Denny Walling	.20	.09
☐ 554 Matt Keough	.20	.09
☐ 555 Biff Pocoroba	.20	.09
☐ 556 Mike Lum	.20	.09
☐ 557 Ken Brett	.20	.09
☐ 558 Jay Johnstone	.40	.18
☐ 559 Greg Pryor	.20	.09
☐ 560 John Montefusco	.20	.09
☐ 561 Ed Ott	.20	.09
☐ 562 Dusty Baker	.75	.35
☐ 563 Roy Thomas	.20	.09
☐ 564 Jerry Turner	.20	.09
☐ 565 Rico Carty	.40	.18
☐ 566 Nino Espinosa	.20	.09
☐ 567 Richie Hebner	.40	.18
☐ 568 Carlos Lopez	.20	.09
☐ 569 Bob Sykes	.20	.09
☐ 570 Cesar Cedeno	.40	.18
☐ 571 Darrell Porter	.40	.18
☐ 572 Rod Gilbreath	.20	.09
☐ 573 Jim Kern	.20	.09
☐ 574 Claudell Washington	.40	.18
☐ 575 Luis Tiant	.40	.18
☐ 576 Mike Parrott	.20	.09
☐ 577 Brewers Team/Mgr.	.75	.15
George Bamberger		
(Checklist back)		
☐ 578 Pete Broberg	.20	.09
☐ 579 Greg Gross	.20	.09
☐ 580 Ron Fairly	.40	.18
☐ 581 Darold Knowles	.20	.09
☐ 582 Paul Blair	.40	.18
☐ 583 Julio Cruz	.20	.09
☐ 584 Jim Rooker	.20	.09
☐ 585 Hal McRae	.75	.35
☐ 586 Bob Horner	.75	.35
☐ 587 Ken Reitz	.20	.09
☐ 588 Tom Murphy	.20	.09
☐ 589 Terry Whitfield	.20	.09
☐ 590 J.R. Richard	.40	.18
☐ 591 Mike Hargrove	.40	.18
☐ 592 Mike Krukow	.20	.09
☐ 593 Rick Dempsey	.40	.18
☐ 594 Bob Shirley	.20	.09
☐ 595 Phil Niekro	1.25	.55
☐ 596 Jim Wohlford	.20	.09
☐ 597 Bob Stanley	.20	.09
☐ 598 Mark Wagner	.20	.09
☐ 599 Jim Spencer	.20	.09
☐ 600 George Foster	.40	.18
☐ 601 Dave LaRoche	.20	.09
☐ 602 Checklist 485-605	.75	.15
☐ 603 Rudy May	.20	.09
☐ 604 Jeff Newman	.20	.09
☐ 605 Rick Monday DP	.20	.09
☐ 606 Expos Team/Mgr.	.75	.15
Dick Williams		
(Checklist back)		
☐ 607 Omar Moreno	.20	.09
☐ 608 Dave McKay	.20	.09
☐ 609 Silvio Martinez	.20	.09
☐ 610 Mike Schmidt	8.00	3.60
☐ 611 Jim Norris	.20	.09
☐ 612 Rick Honeycutt	.40	.18
☐ 613 Mike Edwards	.20	.09
☐ 614 Willie Hernandez	.40	.18
☐ 615 Ken Singleton	.40	.18
☐ 616 Billy Almon	.20	.09
☐ 617 Terry Puhl	.20	.09
☐ 618 Jerry Remy	.20	.09
☐ 619 Ken Landreaux	.40	.18
☐ 620 Bert Campaneris	.40	.18
☐ 621 Pat Zachry	.20	.09
☐ 622 Dave Collins	.40	.18
☐ 623 Bob McClure	.20	.09
☐ 624 Larry Herndon	.20	.09
☐ 625 Mark Fidrych	1.25	.55

	NRMT	VG-E
☐ 626 Yankees Team/Mgr.	.75	.15
Bob Lemon		
(Checklist back)		
☐ 627 Gary Serum	.20	.09
☐ 628 Del Unser	.20	.09
☐ 629 Gene Garber	.40	.18
☐ 630 Bake McBride	.40	.18
☐ 631 Jorge Orta	.20	.09
☐ 632 Don Kirkwood	.20	.09
☐ 633 Rob Wilfong DP	.10	.05
☐ 634 Paul Lindblad	.20	.09
☐ 635 Don Baylor	.75	.35
☐ 636 Wayne Garland	.20	.09
☐ 637 Bill Robinson	.40	.18
☐ 638 Al Fitzmorris	.20	.09
☐ 639 Manny Trillo	.20	.09
☐ 640 Eddie Murray	20.00	9.00
☐ 641 Bobby Castillo	.20	.09
☐ 642 Wilbur Howard DP	.10	.05
☐ 643 Tom Hausman	.20	.09
☐ 644 Manny Mota	.40	.18
☐ 645 George Scott DP	.20	.09
☐ 646 Rick Sweet	.20	.09
☐ 647 Bob Lacey	.20	.09
☐ 648 Lou Piniella	.40	.18
☐ 649 John Curtis	.20	.09
☐ 650 Pete Rose	5.00	2.20
☐ 651 Mike Caldwell	.20	.09
☐ 652 Stan Papi	.20	.09
☐ 653 Warren Brusstar DP	.10	.05
☐ 654 Rick Miller	.20	.09
☐ 655 Jerry Koosman	.40	.18
☐ 656 Hosken Powell	.20	.09
☐ 657 George Medich	.20	.09
☐ 658 Taylor Duncan	.20	.09
☐ 659 Mariners Team/Mgr.	.75	.15
Darrell Johnson		
(Checklist back)		
☐ 660 Ron LeFlore DP	.20	.09
☐ 661 Bruce Kison	.20	.09
☐ 662 Kevin Bell	.20	.09
☐ 663 Mike Vail	.20	.09
☐ 664 Doug Bird	.20	.09
☐ 665 Lou Brock	2.00	.90
☐ 666 Rich Dauer	.20	.09
☐ 667 Don Hood	.20	.09
☐ 668 Bill North	.20	.09
☐ 669 Checklist 606-726	.75	.15
☐ 670 Jim Hunter DP	.75	.35
☐ 671 Joe Ferguson DP	.10	.05
☐ 672 Ed Halicki	.20	.09
☐ 673 Tom Hutton	.20	.09
☐ 674 Dave Tomlin	.20	.09
☐ 675 Tim McCarver	.75	.35
☐ 676 Johnny Sutton	.20	.09
☐ 677 Larry Parrish	.40	.18
☐ 678 Geoff Zahn	.20	.09
☐ 679 Derrel Thomas	.20	.09
☐ 680 Carlton Fisk	2.50	1.10
☐ 681 John Henry Johnson	.20	.09
☐ 682 Dave Chalk	.20	.09
☐ 683 Dan Meyer DP	.10	.05
☐ 684 Jamie Easterly DP	.10	.05
☐ 685 Sixto Lezcano	.20	.09
☐ 686 Ron Schueler DP	.10	.05
☐ 687 Rennie Stennett	.20	.09
☐ 688 Mike Willis	.20	.09
☐ 689 Orioles Team/Mgr.	.75	.15
Earl Weaver		
(Checklist back)		
☐ 690 Buddy Bell DP	.20	.09
☐ 691 Dock Ellis DP	.10	.05
☐ 692 Mickey Stanley	.20	.09
☐ 693 Dave Rader	.20	.09
☐ 694 Burt Hooton	.40	.18
☐ 695 Keith Hernandez	.75	.35
☐ 696 Andy Hassler	.20	.09
☐ 697 Dave Bergman	.20	.09
☐ 698 Bill Stein	.20	.09
☐ 699 Hal Dues	.20	.09
☐ 700 Reggie Jackson DP	2.00	.90
☐ 701 Orioles Prospects	.40	.18
Mark Corey		
John Flinn		
Sammy Stewart		
☐ 702 Red Sox Prospects	.40	.18
Joel Finch		
Garry Hancock		
Allen Ripley		
☐ 703 Angels Prospects	.40	.18
Jim Anderson		
Dave Frost		
Bob Slater		
☐ 704 White Sox Prospects	.40	.18
Ross Baumgarten		
Mike Colbern		
Mike Squires		
☐ 705 Indians Prospects	.75	.35
Alfredo Griffin		
Tim Norrid		
Dave Oliver		
☐ 706 Tigers Prospects	.40	.18
Dave Stegman		
Dave Tobik		
Kip Young		
☐ 707 Royals Prospects	.75	.35
Randy Bass		
Jim Gaudet		
Randy McGilberry		
☐ 708 Brewers Prospects	.75	.35
Kevin Bass		
Eddie Romero		
Ned Yost		
☐ 709 Twins Prospects	.40	.18
Sam Perlozzo		
Rick Sofield		
Kevin Stanfield		
☐ 710 Yankees Prospects	.40	.18
Brian Doyle		
Mike Heath		
Dave Rajsich		
☐ 711 A's Prospects	.75	.35
Dwayne Murphy		
Bruce Robinson		
Alan Wirth		
☐ 712 Mariners Prospects	.40	.18
Bud Anderson		
Greg Biercevicz		
Byron McLaughlin		
☐ 713 Rangers Prospects	.75	.35
Danny Darwin		
Pat Putnam		
Billy Sample		
☐ 714 Blue Jays Prospects	.40	.18
Victor Cruz		
Pat Kelly		
Ernie Whitt		
☐ 715 Braves Prospects	.75	.35
Bruce Benedict		
Glenn Hubbard		
Larry Whisenton		
☐ 716 Cubs Prospects	.40	.18
Dave Geisel		
Karl Pagel		
Scot Thompson		
☐ 717 Reds Prospects	.40	.18
Mike LaCoss		
Ron Oester		
Harry Spilman		
☐ 718 Astros Prospects	.40	.18
Bruce Bochy		
Mike Fischlin		
Don Pisker		
☐ 719 Dodgers Prospects	1.50	.70
Pedro Guerrero		
Rudy Law		
Joe Simpson		
☐ 720 Expos Prospects	.75	.35
Jerry Fry		
Jerry Pirtle		
Scott Sanderson		
☐ 721 Mets Prospects	.40	.18
Juan Berenguer		
Dwight Bernard		
Dan Norman		
☐ 722 Phillies Prospects	.75	.35
Jim Morrison		
Lonnie Smith		
Jim Wright		
☐ 723 Pirates Prospects	.40	.18
Dale Berra		
Eugenio Cotes		
Ben Wiltbank		
☐ 724 Cardinals Prospects	.75	.35
Tom Bruno		
George Frazier		
Terry Kennedy		
☐ 725 Padres Prospects	.40	.18
Jim Beswick		
Steve Mura		
Broderick Perkins		
☐ 726 Giants Prospects	.40	.08
Greg Johnston		
Joe Strain		
John Tamargo		

1979 Topps Comics

This 33 card (comic) set, which measures approximately 3" by 3 1/4", is rather plentiful in spite of the fact that it was originally touted as a limited edition "test" issue. This flimsy set has never been very popular with collectors. These waxy comics are numbered and are blank backed.

Each comic also features an "Inside Baseball" tip in the lower right corner.

	NRMT	VG-E
COMPLETE SET (33)	20.00	9.00
COMMON CARD (1-33)	.15	.07

	NRMT	VG-E
☐ 1 Eddie Murray	1.50	.70
☐ 2 Jim Rice	.50	.23
☐ 3 Carl Yastrzemski	.75	.35
☐ 4 Nolan Ryan	4.00	1.80
☐ 5 Chet Lemon	.15	.07
☐ 6 Andre Thornton	.15	.07
☐ 7 Rusty Staub	.25	.11
☐ 8 Ron LeFlore	.15	.07
☐ 9 George Brett	3.00	1.35
☐ 10 Larry Hisle	.15	.07
☐ 11 Rod Carew	1.00	.45
☐ 12 Reggie Jackson	2.00	.90
☐ 13 Ron Guidry	.25	.11
☐ 14 Mitchell Page	.15	.07
☐ 15 Leon Roberts	.15	.07
☐ 16 Al Oliver	.25	.11
☐ 17 John Mayberry	.15	.07
☐ 18 Bob Horner	.25	.11
☐ 19 Phil Niekro	.75	.35
☐ 20 Dave Kingman	.25	.11
☐ 21 Johnny Bench	1.00	.45
☐ 22 Tom Seaver	1.00	.45
☐ 23 J.R. Richard	.15	.07
☐ 24 Steve Garvey	.50	.23
☐ 25 Reggie Smith	.15	.07
☐ 26 Ross Grimsley	.15	.07
☐ 27 Craig Swan	.15	.07
☐ 28 Pete Rose	1.50	.70
☐ 29 Dave Parker	.25	.11
☐ 30 Ted Simmons	.25	.11
☐ 31 Dave Winfield	1.00	.45
☐ 32 Jack Clark	.25	.11
☐ 33 Vida Blue	.15	.07

1979 Topps Team Checklist Sheet

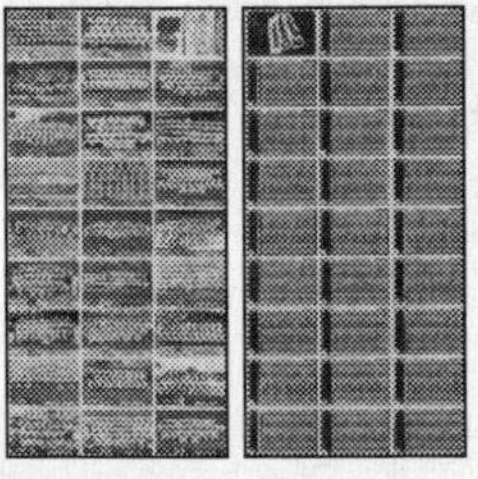

As part of a mail-away offer, Topps offered all 26 1979 team cards checklist cards on an uncut sheet. These cards enabled the collector to have an easy reference for which card(s) he/she needed to finish their sets. When cut from the sheet, all cards measure the standard size.

	NRMT	VG-E
COMPLETE SET (1)	15.00	6.75
COMMON SHEET (1)	15.00	6.75

	NRMT	VG-E
☐ 1 Team Checklist Sheet	15.00	6.75

1980 Topps

The cards in this 726-card set measure the standard size. In 1980 Topps released another set of the same size and number of cards as the previous two years. As with those sets, Topps again produced 66 double-printed cards in the set; they are noted by DP in the checklist below. The player's name appears over the picture and his position and team are found in pennant design. Every card carries a facsimile autograph. Team cards feature a team checklist of players in the set on the back and the manager's name on the front. Cards 1-6 show Highlights (HL) of the 1979 season, cards 201-207 are League Leaders, and cards 661-686 feature American and

National League rookie "Future Stars," one card for each team showing three young prospects. Ways this set was released include 15-card wax packs as well as 42-card rack packs. A special experiment in 1980 was the issuance of a 28-card cello pack with a three-pack of gum at the bottom so no cards would be damaged. The key Rookie Card in this set is Rickey Henderson; other Rookie Cards included in this set are Dan Quisenberry, Dave Stieb and Rick Sutcliffe.

	NRMT	VG-E
COMPLETE SET (726)	125.00	55.00
COMMON CARD (1-726)	.25	.11
COMMON CARD DP	.10	.05

Card	NRMT	VG-E
☐ 1 Lou Brock HL	3.00	.60
Carl Yastrzemski		
Enter 3000 hit circle		
☐ 2 Willie McCovey HL	2.50	1.10
512th homer sets new		
mark for NL lefties		
☐ 3 Manny Mota HL	.75	.35
All-time pinch-hits, 145		
☐ 4 Pete Rose HL	2.00	.90
Career Record 10th season		
with 200 or more hits		
☐ 5 Garry Templeton HL	.75	.35
First with 100 hits		
from each side of plate		
☐ 6 Del Unser HL	.75	.35
3 consecutive		
pinch homers		
☐ 7 Mike Lum	.25	.11
☐ 8 Craig Swan	.25	.11
☐ 9 Steve Braun	.25	.11
☐ 10 Dennis Martinez	1.50	.70
☐ 11 Jimmy Sexton	.25	.11
☐ 12 John Curtis DP	.10	.05
☐ 13 Ron Pruitt	.25	.11
☐ 14 Dave Cash	.25	.11
☐ 15 Bill Campbell	.25	.11
☐ 16 Jerry Narron	.25	.11
☐ 17 Bruce Sutter	.75	.35
☐ 18 Ron Jackson	.25	.11
☐ 19 Balor Moore	.25	.11
☐ 20 Dan Ford	.25	.11
☐ 21 Manny Sarmiento	.25	.11
☐ 22 Pat Putnam	.25	.11
☐ 23 Derrel Thomas	.25	.11
☐ 24 Jim Slaton	.25	.11
☐ 25 Lee Mazzilli	.75	.35
☐ 26 Marty Pattin	.25	.11
☐ 27 Del Unser	.25	.11
☐ 28 Bruce Kison	.25	.11
☐ 29 Mark Wagner	.25	.11
☐ 30 Vida Blue	1.50	.70
☐ 31 Jay Johnstone	.75	.35
☐ 32 Julio Cruz DP	.10	.05
☐ 33 Tony Scott	.25	.11
☐ 34 Jeff Newman DP	.10	.05
☐ 35 Luis Tiant	.75	.35
☐ 36 Rusty Torres	.25	.11
☐ 37 Kiko Garcia	.25	.11
☐ 38 Dan Spillner DP	.10	.05
☐ 39 Rowland Office	.25	.11
☐ 40 Carlton Fisk	2.00	.90
☐ 41 Rangers Team/Mgr.	1.50	.30
Pat Corrales		
(Checklist back)		
☐ 42 David Palmer	.25	.11
☐ 43 Bombo Rivera	.25	.11
☐ 44 Bill Fahey	.25	.11
☐ 45 Frank White	1.50	.70
☐ 46 Rico Carty	.75	.35
☐ 47 Bill Bonham DP	.10	.05
☐ 48 Rick Miller	.25	.11
☐ 49 Mario Guerrero	.25	.11
☐ 50 J.R. Richard	.75	.35
☐ 51 Joe Ferguson DP	.10	.05
☐ 52 Warren Brusstar	.25	.11
☐ 53 Ben Oglivie	.75	.35
☐ 54 Dennis Lamp	.25	.11
☐ 55 Bill Madlock	.75	.35
☐ 56 Bobby Valentine	.75	.35
☐ 57 Pete Vuckovich	.25	.11
☐ 58 Doug Flynn	.25	.11
☐ 59 Eddy Putman	.25	.11
☐ 60 Bucky Dent	.75	.35
☐ 61 Gary Serum	.25	.11
☐ 62 Mike Ivie	.25	.11
☐ 63 Bob Stanley	.25	.11
☐ 64 Joe Nolan	.25	.11
☐ 65 Al Bumbry	.75	.35
☐ 66 Royals Team/Mgr.	1.50	.30
Jim Frey		
(Checklist back)		
☐ 67 Doyle Alexander	.25	.11
☐ 68 Larry Harlow	.25	.11
☐ 69 Rick Williams	.25	.11
☐ 70 Gary Carter	2.50	1.10
☐ 71 John Milner DP	.10	.05
☐ 72 Fred Howard DP	.10	.05
☐ 73 Dave Collins	.25	.11
☐ 74 Sid Monge	.25	.11
☐ 75 Bill Russell	.75	.35
☐ 76 John Stearns	.25	.11
☐ 77 Dave Stieb	2.50	1.10
☐ 78 Ruppert Jones	.25	.11
☐ 79 Bob Owchinko	.25	.11
☐ 80 Ron LeFlore	.75	.35
☐ 81 Ted Sizemore	.25	.11
☐ 82 Astros Team/Mgr.	1.50	.30
Bill Virdon		
(Checklist back)		
☐ 83 Steve Trout	.25	.11
☐ 84 Gary Lavelle	.25	.11
☐ 85 Ted Simmons	.75	.35
☐ 86 Dave Hamilton	.25	.11
☐ 87 Pepe Frias	.25	.11
☐ 88 Ken Landreaux	.25	.11
☐ 89 Don Hood	.25	.11
☐ 90 Manny Trillo	.75	.35
☐ 91 Rick Dempsey	.75	.35
☐ 92 Rick Rhoden	.25	.11
☐ 93 Dave Roberts DP	.10	.05
☐ 94 Neil Allen	.75	.35
☐ 95 Cecil Cooper	.75	.35
☐ 96 A's Team/Mgr.	1.50	.30
Jim Marshall		
(Checklist back)		
☐ 97 Bill Lee	.75	.35
☐ 98 Jerry Terrell	.25	.11
☐ 99 Victor Cruz	.25	.11
☐ 100 Johnny Bench	3.00	1.35
☐ 101 Aurelio Lopez	.25	.11
☐ 102 Rich Dauer	.25	.11
☐ 103 Bill Caudill	.25	.11
☐ 104 Manny Mota	.75	.35
☐ 105 Frank Tanana	.75	.35
☐ 106 Jeff Leonard	1.50	.70
☐ 107 Francisco Barrios	.25	.11
☐ 108 Bob Horner	.75	.35
☐ 109 Bill Travers	.25	.11
☐ 110 Fred Lynn DP	.75	.35
☐ 111 Bob Knepper	.25	.11
☐ 112 White Sox Team/Mgr.	1.50	.30
Tony LaRussa		
(Checklist back)		
☐ 113 Geoff Zahn	.25	.11
☐ 114 Juan Beniquez	.25	.11
☐ 115 Sparky Lyle	.75	.35
☐ 116 Larry Cox	.25	.11
☐ 117 Dock Ellis	.25	.11
☐ 118 Phil Garner	.75	.35
☐ 119 Sammy Stewart	.25	.11
☐ 120 Greg Luzinski	.75	.35
☐ 121 Checklist 1-121	1.50	.30
☐ 122 Dave Rosello DP	.10	.05
☐ 123 Lynn Jones	.25	.11
☐ 124 Dave Lemanczyk	.25	.11
☐ 125 Tony Perez	2.50	1.10
☐ 126 Dave Tomlin	.25	.11
☐ 127 Gary Thomasson	.25	.11
☐ 128 Tom Burgmeier	.25	.11
☐ 129 Craig Reynolds	.25	.11
☐ 130 Amos Otis	.75	.35
☐ 131 Paul Mitchell	.25	.11
☐ 132 Biff Pocoroba	.25	.11
☐ 133 Jerry Turner	.25	.11
☐ 134 Matt Keough	.25	.11
☐ 135 Bill Buckner	.75	.35
☐ 136 Dick Ruthven	.25	.11
☐ 137 John Castino	.25	.11
☐ 138 Ross Baumgarten	.25	.11
☐ 139 Dane Iorg	.25	.11
☐ 140 Rich Gossage	1.50	.70
☐ 141 Gary Alexander	.25	.11
☐ 142 Phil Huffman	.25	.11
☐ 143 Bruce Bochte DP	.10	.05
☐ 144 Steve Comer	.25	.11
☐ 145 Darrell Evans	.75	.35
☐ 146 Bob Welch	.75	.35
☐ 147 Terry Puhl	.25	.11
☐ 148 Manny Sanguillen	.75	.35
☐ 149 Tom Hume	.25	.11
☐ 150 Jason Thompson	.25	.11
☐ 151 Tom Hausman DP	.10	.05
☐ 152 John Fulgham	.25	.11
☐ 153 Tim Blackwell	.25	.11
☐ 154 Lary Sorensen	.25	.11
☐ 155 Jerry Remy	.25	.11
☐ 156 Tony Brizzolara	.25	.11
☐ 157 Willie Wilson DP	.75	.35
☐ 158 Rob Picciolo DP	.10	.05
☐ 159 Ken Clay	.25	.11
☐ 160 Eddie Murray	12.00	5.50
☐ 161 Larry Christenson	.25	.11
☐ 162 Bob Randall	.25	.11
☐ 163 Steve Swisher	.25	.11
☐ 164 Greg Pryor	.25	.11
☐ 165 Omar Moreno	.25	.11
☐ 166 Glenn Abbott	.25	.11
☐ 167 Jack Clark	.75	.35
☐ 168 Rick Waits	.25	.11
☐ 169 Luis Gomez	.25	.11
☐ 170 Burt Hooton	.75	.35
☐ 171 Fernando Gonzalez	.25	.11
☐ 172 Ron Hodges	.25	.11
☐ 173 John Henry Johnson	.25	.11
☐ 174 Ray Knight	.75	.35
☐ 175 Rick Reuschel	.75	.35
☐ 176 Champ Summers	.25	.11
☐ 177 Dave Heaverlo	.25	.11
☐ 178 Tim McCarver	1.50	.70
☐ 179 Ron Davis	.25	.11
☐ 180 Warren Cromartie	.25	.11
☐ 181 Moose Haas	.25	.11
☐ 182 Ken Reitz	.25	.11
☐ 183 Jim Anderson DP	.10	.05
☐ 184 Steve Renko DP	.10	.05
☐ 185 Hal McRae	.75	.35
☐ 186 Junior Moore	.25	.11
☐ 187 Alan Ashby	.25	.11
☐ 188 Terry Crowley	.25	.11
☐ 189 Kevin Kobel	.25	.11
☐ 190 Buddy Bell	.75	.35
☐ 191 Ted Martinez	.25	.11
☐ 192 Braves Team/Mgr.	1.50	.30
Bobby Cox		
(Checklist back)		
☐ 193 Dave Goltz	.25	.11
☐ 194 Mike Easler	.25	.11
☐ 195 John Montefusco	.25	.11
☐ 196 Lance Parrish	.75	.35
☐ 197 Byron McLaughlin	.25	.11
☐ 198 Dell Alston DP	.10	.05
☐ 199 Mike LaCoss	.25	.11
☐ 200 Jim Rice	.75	.35
☐ 201 Batting Leaders	1.50	.70
Keith Hernandez		
Fred Lynn		
☐ 202 Home Run Leaders	1.50	.70
Dave Kingman		
Gorman Thomas		
☐ 203 RBI Leaders	2.50	1.10
Dave Winfield		
Don Baylor		
☐ 204 Stolen Base Leaders	.75	.35
Omar Moreno		
Willie Wilson		
☐ 205 Victory Leaders	1.50	.70
Joe Niekro		
Phil Niekro		
Mike Flanagan		
☐ 206 Strikeout Leaders	5.00	2.20
J.R. Richard		
Nolan Ryan		
☐ 207 ERA Leaders	1.50	.70
J.R. Richard		
Ron Guidry		
☐ 208 Wayne Cage	.25	.11
☐ 209 Von Joshua	.25	.11
☐ 210 Steve Carlton	2.00	.90
☐ 211 Dave Skaggs DP	.10	.05
☐ 212 Dave Roberts	.25	.11
☐ 213 Mike Jorgensen DP	.10	.05
☐ 214 Angels Team/Mgr.	1.50	.30
Jim Fregosi		
(Checklist back)		
☐ 215 Sixto Lezcano	.25	.11
☐ 216 Phil Mankowski	.25	.11
☐ 217 Ed Halicki	.25	.11
☐ 218 Jose Morales	.25	.11
☐ 219 Steve Mingori	.25	.11
☐ 220 Dave Concepcion	1.50	.70
☐ 221 Joe Cannon	.25	.11
☐ 222 Ron Hassey	.25	.11

☐ 223 Bob Sykes .25 .11
☐ 224 Willie Montanez .25 .11
☐ 225 Lou Piniella 1.50 .70
☐ 226 Bill Stein .25 .11
☐ 227 Len Barker .25 .11
☐ 228 Johnny Oates .75 .35
☐ 229 Jim Bibby .25 .11
☐ 230 Dave Winfield 5.00 2.20
☐ 231 Steve McCatty .25 .11
☐ 232 Alan Trammell 3.00 1.35
☐ 233 LaRue Washington .25 .11
☐ 234 Vern Ruhle .25 .11
☐ 235 Andre Dawson 3.00 1.35
☐ 236 Marc Hill .25 .11
☐ 237 Scott McGregor .75 .35
☐ 238 Rob Wilfong .25 .11
☐ 239 Don Aase .25 .11
☐ 240 Dave Kingman 1.50 .70
☐ 241 Checklist 122-242 1.50 .30
☐ 242 Lamar Johnson .25 .11
☐ 243 Jerry Augustine .25 .11
☐ 244 Cardinals Team/Mgr. 1.50 .30
Ken Boyer
(Checklist back)
☐ 245 Phil Niekro 2.50 1.10
☐ 246 Tim Foli DP .10 .05
☐ 247 Frank Riccelli .25 .11
☐ 248 Jamie Quirk .25 .11
☐ 249 Jim Clancy .25 .11
☐ 250 Jim Kaat 1.50 .70
☐ 251 Kip Young .25 .11
☐ 252 Ted Cox .25 .11
☐ 253 John Montague .25 .11
☐ 254 Paul Dade DP .10 .05
☐ 255 Dusty Baker DP .75 .35
☐ 256 Roger Erickson .25 .11
☐ 257 Larry Herndon .25 .11
☐ 258 Paul Moskau .25 .11
☐ 259 Mets Team/Mgr. 1.50 .30
Joe Torre
(Checklist back)
☐ 260 Al Oliver 1.50 .70
☐ 261 Dave Chalk .25 .11
☐ 262 Benny Ayala .25 .11
☐ 263 Dave LaRoche DP .10 .05
☐ 264 Bill Robinson .25 .11
☐ 265 Robin Yount 6.00 2.70
☐ 266 Bernie Carbo .25 .11
☐ 267 Dan Schatzeder .25 .11
☐ 268 Rafael Landestoy .25 .11
☐ 269 Dave Tobik .25 .11
☐ 270 Mike Schmidt DP 3.00 1.35
☐ 271 Dick Drago DP .10 .05
☐ 272 Ralph Garr .75 .35
☐ 273 Eduardo Rodriguez .25 .11
☐ 274 Dale Murphy 2.50 1.10
☐ 275 Jerry Koosman .75 .35
☐ 276 Tom Veryzer .25 .11
☐ 277 Rick Bosetti .25 .11
☐ 278 Jim Spencer .25 .11
☐ 279 Rob Andrews .25 .11
☐ 280 Gaylord Perry 2.50 1.10
☐ 281 Paul Blair .75 .35
☐ 282 Mariners Team/Mgr. 1.50 .30
Darrell Johnson
(Checklist back)
☐ 283 John Ellis .25 .11
☐ 284 Larry Murray DP .10 .05
☐ 285 Don Baylor 1.50 .70
☐ 286 Darold Knowles DP .10 .05
☐ 287 John Lowenstein .25 .11
☐ 288 Dave Rozema .25 .11
☐ 289 Bruce Bochy .25 .11
☐ 290 Steve Garvey 2.50 1.10
☐ 291 Randy Scarberry .25 .11
☐ 292 Dale Berra .25 .11
☐ 293 Elias Sosa .25 .11
☐ 294 Charlie Spikes .25 .11
☐ 295 Larry Gura .25 .11
☐ 296 Dave Rader .25 .11
☐ 297 Tim Johnson .25 .11
☐ 298 Ken Holtzman .75 .35
☐ 299 Steve Henderson .25 .11
☐ 300 Ron Guidry .75 .35
☐ 301 Mike Edwards .25 .11
☐ 302 Dodgers Team/Mgr. 1.50 .30
Tom Lasorda
(Checklist back)
☐ 303 Bill Castro .25 .11
☐ 304 Butch Wynegar .25 .11
☐ 305 Randy Jones .25 .11
☐ 306 Denny Walling .25 .11
☐ 307 Rick Honeycutt .75 .35
☐ 308 Mike Hargrove .75 .35
☐ 309 Larry McWilliams .25 .11
☐ 310 Dave Parker 1.50 .70
☐ 311 Roger Metzger .25 .11
☐ 312 Mike Barlow .25 .11
☐ 313 Johnny Grubb .25 .11
☐ 314 Tim Stoddard .25 .11
☐ 315 Steve Kemp .25 .11
☐ 316 Bob Lacey .25 .11
☐ 317 Mike Anderson DP .10 .05
☐ 318 Jerry Reuss .75 .35
☐ 319 Chris Speier .25 .11
☐ 320 Dennis Eckersley 1.50 .70
☐ 321 Keith Hernandez .75 .35
☐ 322 Claudell Washington .75 .35
☐ 323 Mick Kelleher .25 .11
☐ 324 Tom Underwood .25 .11
☐ 325 Dan Driessen .25 .11
☐ 326 Bo McLaughlin .25 .11
☐ 327 Ray Fosse DP .10 .05
☐ 328 Twins Team/Mgr. 1.50 .30
Gene Mauch
(Checklist back)
☐ 329 Bert Roberge .25 .11
☐ 330 Al Cowens .25 .11
☐ 331 Richie Hebner .75 .35
☐ 332 Enrique Romo .25 .11
☐ 333 Jim Norris DP .10 .05
☐ 334 Jim Beattie .25 .11
☐ 335 Willie McCovey 1.50 .70
☐ 336 George Medich .25 .11
☐ 337 Carney Lansford .75 .35
☐ 338 John Wockenfuss .25 .11
☐ 339 John D'Acquisto .25 .11
☐ 340 Ken Singleton .75 .35
☐ 341 Jim Essian .25 .11
☐ 342 Odell Jones .25 .11
☐ 343 Mike Vail .25 .11
☐ 344 Randy Lerch .25 .11
☐ 345 Larry Parrish .75 .35
☐ 346 Buddy Solomon .25 .11
☐ 347 Harry Chappas .25 .11
☐ 348 Checklist 243-363 1.50 .30
☐ 349 Jack Brohamer .25 .11
☐ 350 George Hendrick .75 .35
☐ 351 Bob Davis .25 .11
☐ 352 Dan Briggs .25 .11
☐ 353 Andy Hassler .25 .11
☐ 354 Rick Auerbach .25 .11
☐ 355 Gary Matthews .75 .35
☐ 356 Padres Team/Mgr. 1.50 .30
Jerry Coleman
(Checklist back)
☐ 357 Bob McClure .25 .11
☐ 358 Lou Whitaker 5.00 2.20
☐ 359 Randy Moffitt .25 .11
☐ 360 Darrell Porter DP .25 .11
☐ 361 Wayne Garland .25 .11
☐ 362 Danny Goodwin .25 .11
☐ 363 Wayne Gross .25 .11
☐ 364 Ray Burris .25 .11
☐ 365 Bobby Murcer .75 .35
☐ 366 Rob Dressler .25 .11
☐ 367 Billy Smith .25 .11
☐ 368 Willie Aikens .25 .11
☐ 369 Jim Kern .25 .11
☐ 370 Cesar Cedeno .75 .35
☐ 371 Jack Morris 1.50 .70
☐ 372 Joel Youngblood .25 .11
☐ 373 Dan Petry DP .25 .11
☐ 374 Jim Gantner .75 .35
☐ 375 Ross Grimsley .25 .11
☐ 376 Gary Allenson .25 .11
☐ 377 Junior Kennedy .25 .11
☐ 378 Jerry Mumphrey .25 .11
☐ 379 Kevin Bell .25 .11
☐ 380 Garry Maddox .75 .35
☐ 381 Cubs Team/Mgr. 1.50 .30
Preston Gomez
(Checklist back)
☐ 382 Dave Freisleben .25 .11
☐ 383 Ed Ott .25 .11
☐ 384 Joey McLaughlin .25 .11
☐ 385 Enos Cabell .25 .11
☐ 386 Darrell Jackson .25 .11
☐ 387A Fred Stanley YL 2.00 .90
☐ 387B Fred Stanley .25 .11
(Red name on front)
☐ 388 Mike Paxton .25 .11
☐ 389 Pete LaCock .25 .11
☐ 390 Fergie Jenkins 2.50 1.10
☐ 391 Tony Armas DP .25 .11
☐ 392 Milt Wilcox .25 .11
☐ 393 Ozzie Smith 20.00 9.00
☐ 394 Reggie Cleveland .25 .11
☐ 395 Ellis Valentine .25 .11
☐ 396 Dan Meyer .25 .11
☐ 397 Roy Thomas DP .10 .05
☐ 398 Barry Foote .25 .11
☐ 399 Mike Proly DP .10 .05
☐ 400 George Foster .75 .35
☐ 401 Pete Falcone .25 .11
☐ 402 Merv Rettenmund .25 .11
☐ 403 Pete Redfern DP .10 .05
☐ 404 Orioles Team/Mgr. 1.50 .30
Earl Weaver
(Checklist back)
☐ 405 Dwight Evans .75 .35
☐ 406 Paul Molitor 12.00 5.50
☐ 407 Tony Solaita .25 .11
☐ 408 Bill North .25 .11
☐ 409 Paul Splittorff .25 .11
☐ 410 Bobby Bonds 1.50 .70
☐ 411 Frank LaCorte .25 .11
☐ 412 Thad Bosley .25 .11
☐ 413 Allen Ripley .25 .11
☐ 414 George Scott .75 .35
☐ 415 Bill Atkinson .25 .11
☐ 416 Tom Brookens .25 .11
☐ 417 Craig Chamberlain DP .10 .05
☐ 418 Roger Freed DP .10 .05
☐ 419 Vic Correll .25 .11
☐ 420 Butch Hobson .75 .35
☐ 421 Doug Bird .25 .11
☐ 422 Larry Milbourne .25 .11
☐ 423 Dave Frost .25 .11
☐ 424 Yankees Team/Mgr. 1.50 .30
Dick Howser
(Checklist back)
☐ 425 Mark Belanger .75 .35
☐ 426 Grant Jackson .25 .11
☐ 427 Tom Hutton DP .10 .05
☐ 428 Pat Zachry .25 .11
☐ 429 Duane Kuiper .25 .11
☐ 430 Larry Hisle DP .10 .05
☐ 431 Mike Krukow .25 .11
☐ 432 Willie Norwood .25 .11
☐ 433 Rich Gale .25 .11
☐ 434 Johnnie LeMaster .25 .11
☐ 435 Don Gullett .75 .35
☐ 436 Billy Almon .25 .11
☐ 437 Joe Niekro .75 .35
☐ 438 Dave Revering .25 .11
☐ 439 Mike Phillips .25 .11
☐ 440 Don Sutton 2.50 1.10
☐ 441 Eric Soderholm .25 .11
☐ 442 Jorge Orta .25 .11
☐ 443 Mike Parrott .25 .11
☐ 444 Alvis Woods .25 .11
☐ 445 Mark Fidrych 2.50 1.10
☐ 446 Duffy Dyer .25 .11
☐ 447 Nino Espinosa .25 .11
☐ 448 Jim Wohlford .25 .11
☐ 449 Doug Bair .25 .11
☐ 450 George Brett 12.00 5.50
☐ 451 Indians Team/Mgr. .75 .15
Dave Garcia
(Checklist back)
☐ 452 Steve Dillard .25 .11
☐ 453 Mike Bacsik .25 .11
☐ 454 Tom Donohue .25 .11
☐ 455 Mike Torrez .25 .11
☐ 456 Frank Taveras .25 .11
☐ 457 Bert Blyleven 1.50 .70
☐ 458 Billy Sample .25 .11
☐ 459 Mickey Lolich DP .25 .11
☐ 460 Willie Randolph .75 .35
☐ 461 Dwayne Murphy .25 .11
☐ 462 Mike Sadek DP .10 .05
☐ 463 Jerry Royster .25 .11
☐ 464 John Denny .25 .11
☐ 465 Rick Monday .25 .11
☐ 466 Mike Squires .25 .11
☐ 467 Jesse Jefferson .25 .11
☐ 468 Aurelio Rodriguez .25 .11
☐ 469 Randy Niemann DP .10 .05
☐ 470 Bob Boone 1.50 .70
☐ 471 Hosken Powell DP .10 .05
☐ 472 Willie Hernandez .75 .35
☐ 473 Bump Wills .25 .11
☐ 474 Steve Busby .25 .11
☐ 475 Cesar Geronimo .25 .11
☐ 476 Bob Shirley .25 .11
☐ 477 Buck Martinez .25 .11
☐ 478 Gil Flores .25 .11
☐ 479 Expos Team/Mgr. 1.50 .30
Dick Williams
(Checklist back)
☐ 480 Bob Watson .75 .35
☐ 481 Tom Paciorek .75 .35
☐ 482 Rickey Henderson UER 40.00 18.00
(7 steals at Modesto,
should be at Fresno)
☐ 483 Bo Diaz .25 .11
☐ 484 Checklist 364-484 1.50 .30
☐ 485 Mickey Rivers .75 .35
☐ 486 Mike Tyson DP .10 .05
☐ 487 Wayne Nordhagen .25 .11

☐ 488 Roy Howell .25 .11
☐ 489 Preston Hanna DP .10 .05
☐ 490 Lee May .75 .35
☐ 491 Steve Mura DP .10 .05
☐ 492 Todd Cruz .25 .11
☐ 493 Jerry Martin .25 .11
☐ 494 Craig Minetto .25 .11
☐ 495 Bake McBride .25 .11
☐ 496 Silvio Martinez .25 .11
☐ 497 Jim Mason .25 .11
☐ 498 Danny Darwin .75 .35
☐ 499 Giants Team/Mgr. 1.50 .30
Dave Bristol
(Checklist back)
☐ 500 Tom Seaver 3.00 1.35
☐ 501 Rennie Stennett .25 .11
☐ 502 Rich Wortham DP .10 .05
☐ 503 Mike Cubbage .25 .11
☐ 504 Gene Garber .75 .35
☐ 505 Bert Campaneris .75 .35
☐ 506 Tom Buskey .25 .11
☐ 507 Leon Roberts .25 .11
☐ 508 U.L. Washington .25 .11
☐ 509 Ed Glynn .25 .11
☐ 510 Ron Cey 1.50 .70
☐ 511 Eric Wilkins .25 .11
☐ 512 Jose Cardenal .25 .11
☐ 513 Tom Dixon DP .10 .05
☐ 514 Steve Ontiveros .25 .11
☐ 515 Mike Caldwell UER .25 .11
1979 loss total reads
96 instead of 6#
☐ 516 Hector Cruz .25 .11
☐ 517 Don Stanhouse .25 .11
☐ 518 Nelson Norman .25 .11
☐ 519 Steve Nicosia .25 .11
☐ 520 Steve Rogers .25 .11
☐ 521 Ken Brett .25 .11
☐ 522 Jim Morrison .25 .11
☐ 523 Ken Henderson .25 .11
☐ 524 Jim Wright DP .10 .05
☐ 525 Clint Hurdle .25 .11
☐ 526 Phillies Team/Mgr. 1.50 .30
Dallas Green
(Checklist back)
☐ 527 Doug Rau DP .10 .05
☐ 528 Adrian Devine .25 .11
☐ 529 Jim Barr .25 .11
☐ 530 Jim Sundberg DP .25 .11
☐ 531 Eric Rasmussen .25 .11
☐ 532 Willie Horton .75 .35
☐ 533 Checklist 485-605 1.50 .30
☐ 534 Andre Thornton .75 .35
☐ 535 Bob Forsch .25 .11
☐ 536 Lee Lacy .25 .11
☐ 537 Alex Trevino .25 .11
☐ 538 Joe Strain .25 .11
☐ 539 Rudy May .25 .11
☐ 540 Pete Rose 3.00 1.35
☐ 541 Miguel Dilone .25 .11
☐ 542 Joe Coleman .25 .11
☐ 543 Pat Kelly .25 .11
☐ 544 Rick Sutcliffe 2.00 .90
☐ 545 Jeff Burroughs .75 .35
☐ 546 Rick Langford .25 .11
☐ 547 John Wathan .25 .11
☐ 548 Dave Rajsich .25 .11
☐ 549 Larry Wolfe .25 .11
☐ 550 Ken Griffey 1.50 .70
☐ 551 Pirates Team/Mgr. 1.50 .30
Chuck Tanner
(Checklist back)
☐ 552 Bill Nahorodny .25 .11
☐ 553 Dick Davis .25 .11
☐ 554 Art Howe .75 .35
☐ 555 Ed Figueroa .25 .11
☐ 556 Joe Rudi .75 .35
☐ 557 Mark Lee .25 .11
☐ 558 Alfredo Griffin .25 .11
☐ 559 Dale Murray .25 .11
☐ 560 Dave Lopes .75 .35
☐ 561 Eddie Whitson .25 .11
☐ 562 Joe Wallis .25 .11
☐ 563 Will McEnaney .25 .11
☐ 564 Rick Manning .25 .11
☐ 565 Dennis Leonard .75 .35
☐ 566 Bud Harrelson .75 .35
☐ 567 Skip Lockwood .25 .11
☐ 568 Gary Roenicke .75 .35
☐ 569 Terry Kennedy .75 .35
☐ 570 Roy Smalley .25 .11
☐ 571 Joe Sambito .25 .11
☐ 572 Jerry Morales DP .10 .05
☐ 573 Kent Tekulve .75 .35
☐ 574 Scot Thompson .25 .11
☐ 575 Ken Kravec .25 .11
☐ 576 Jim Dwyer .25 .11
☐ 577 Blue Jays Team/Mgr. 1.50 .30
Bobby Mattick
(Checklist back)
☐ 578 Scott Sanderson .75 .35
☐ 579 Charlie Moore .25 .11
☐ 580 Nolan Ryan 20.00 9.00
☐ 581 Bob Bailor .25 .11
☐ 582 Brian Doyle .25 .11
☐ 583 Bob Stinson .25 .11
☐ 584 Kurt Bevacqua .25 .11
☐ 585 Al Hrabosky .25 .11
☐ 586 Mitchell Page .25 .11
☐ 587 Garry Templeton .25 .11
☐ 588 Greg Minton .25 .11
☐ 589 Chet Lemon .75 .35
☐ 590 Jim Palmer 1.50 .70
☐ 591 Rick Cerone .25 .11
☐ 592 Jon Matlack .25 .11
☐ 593 Jesus Alou .25 .11
☐ 594 Dick Tidrow .25 .11
☐ 595 Don Money .25 .11
☐ 596 Rick Matula .25 .11
☐ 597 Tom Poquette .25 .11
☐ 598 Fred Kendall DP .10 .05
☐ 599 Mike Norris .25 .11
☐ 600 Reggie Jackson 3.00 1.35
☐ 601 Buddy Schultz .25 .11
☐ 602 Brian Downing .25 .11
☐ 603 Jack Billingham DP .10 .05
☐ 604 Glenn Adams .25 .11
☐ 605 Terry Forster .25 .11
☐ 606 Reds Team/Mgr. 1.50 .30
John McNamara
(Checklist back)
☐ 607 Woodie Fryman .25 .11
☐ 608 Alan Bannister .25 .11
☐ 609 Ron Reed .25 .11
☐ 610 Willie Stargell 1.25 .55
☐ 611 Jerry Garvin DP .10 .05
☐ 612 Cliff Johnson .25 .11
☐ 613 Randy Stein .25 .11
☐ 614 John Hiller .25 .11
☐ 615 Doug DeCinces .75 .35
☐ 616 Gene Richards .25 .11
☐ 617 Joaquin Andujar .75 .35
☐ 618 Bob Montgomery DP .10 .05
☐ 619 Sergio Ferrer .25 .11
☐ 620 Richie Zisk .25 .11
☐ 621 Bob Grich .75 .35
☐ 622 Mario Soto .25 .11
☐ 623 Gorman Thomas .75 .35
☐ 624 Lerrin LaGrow .25 .11
☐ 625 Chris Chambliss .75 .35
☐ 626 Tigers Team/Mgr. 1.50 .30
Sparky Anderson
(Checklist back)
☐ 627 Pedro Borbon .25 .11
☐ 628 Doug Capilla .25 .11
☐ 629 Jim Todd .25 .11
☐ 630 Larry Bowa .75 .35
☐ 631 Mark Littell .25 .11
☐ 632 Barry Bonnell .25 .11
☐ 633 Bob Apodaca .25 .11
☐ 634 Glenn Borgmann DP .10 .05
☐ 635 John Candelaria .75 .35
☐ 636 Toby Harrah .75 .35
☐ 637 Joe Simpson .25 .11
☐ 638 Mark Clear .25 .11
☐ 639 Larry Biittner .25 .11
☐ 640 Mike Flanagan .75 .35
☐ 641 Ed Kranepool .25 .11
☐ 642 Ken Forsch DP .10 .05
☐ 643 John Mayberry .75 .35
☐ 644 Charlie Hough .75 .35
☐ 645 Rick Burleson .25 .11
☐ 646 Checklist 606-726 1.50 .30
☐ 647 Milt May .25 .11
☐ 648 Roy White .25 .11
☐ 649 Tom Griffin .25 .11
☐ 650 Joe Morgan 1.50 .70
☐ 651 Rollie Fingers 2.50 1.10
☐ 652 Mario Mendoza .25 .11
☐ 653 Stan Bahnsen .25 .11
☐ 654 Bruce Boisclair DP .10 .05
☐ 655 Tug McGraw .75 .35
☐ 656 Larvell Blanks .25 .11
☐ 657 Dave Edwards .25 .11
☐ 658 Chris Knapp .25 .11
☐ 659 Brewers Team/Mgr. 1.50 .30
George Bamberger
(Checklist back)
☐ 660 Rusty Staub .75 .35
☐ 661 Orioles Rookies .75 .35
Mark Corey
Dave Ford
Wayne Krenchicki
☐ 662 Red Sox Rookies .75 .35
Joel Finch
Mike O'Berry
Chuck Rainey
☐ 663 Angels Rookies 1.50 .70
Ralph Botting
Bob Clark
Dickie Thon
☐ 664 White Sox Rookies .75 .35
Mike Colbern
Guy Hoffman
Dewey Robinson
☐ 665 Indians Rookies 1.50 .70
Larry Andersen
Bobby Cuellar
Sandy Wihtol
☐ 666 Tigers Rookies .75 .35
Mike Chris
Al Greene
Bruce Robbins
☐ 667 Royals Rookies 2.00 .90
Renie Martin
Bill Paschall
Dan Quisenberry
☐ 668 Brewers Rookies .75 .35
Danny Boitano
Willie Mueller
Lenn Sakata
☐ 669 Twins Rookies .75 .35
Dan Graham
Rick Sofield
Gary Ward
☐ 670 Yankees Rookies .75 .35
Bobby Brown
Brad Gulden
Darryl Jones
☐ 671 A's Rookies 2.50 1.10
Derek Bryant
Brian Kingman
Mike Morgan
☐ 672 Mariners Rookies .75 .35
Charlie Beamon
Rodney Craig
Rafael Vasquez
☐ 673 Rangers Rookies .75 .35
Brian Allard
Jerry Don Gleaton
Greg Mahlberg
☐ 674 Blue Jays Rookies .75 .35
Butch Edge
Pat Kelly
Ted Wilborn
☐ 675 Braves Rookies .75 .35
Bruce Benedict
Larry Bradford
Eddie Miller
☐ 676 Cubs Rookies .75 .35
Dave Geisel
Steve Macko
Karl Pagel
☐ 677 Reds Rookies .75 .35
Art DeFreites
Frank Pastore
Harry Spilman
☐ 678 Astros Rookies .75 .35
Reggie Baldwin
Alan Knicely
Pete Ladd
☐ 679 Dodgers Rookies 1.50 .70
Joe Beckwith
Mickey Hatcher
Dave Patterson
☐ 680 Expos Rookies 1.50 .70
Tony Bernazard
Randy Miller
John Tamargo
☐ 681 Mets Rookies 2.50 1.10
Dan Norman
Jesse Orosco
Mike Scott
☐ 682 Phillies Rookies .75 .35
Ramon Aviles
Dickie Noles
Kevin Saucier
☐ 683 Pirates Rookies .75 .35
Dorian Boyland
Alberto Lois
Harry Saferight
☐ 684 Cardinals Rookies 1.50 .70
George Frazier
Tom Herr
Dan O'Brien
☐ 685 Padres Rookies .75 .35
Tim Flannery
Brian Greer
Jim Wilhelm
☐ 686 Giants Rookies .75 .35
Greg Johnston
Dennis Littlejohn

Phil Nastu
☐ 687 Mike Heath DP .10 .05
☐ 688 Steve Stone .75 .35
☐ 689 Red Sox Team/Mgr. 1.50 .30
Don Zimmer
(Checklist back)
☐ 690 Tommy John 1.50 .70
☐ 691 Ivan DeJesus .25 .11
☐ 692 Rawly Eastwick DP .10 .05
☐ 693 Craig Kusick .25 .11
☐ 694 Jim Rooker .25 .11
☐ 695 Reggie Smith .75 .35
☐ 696 Julio Gonzalez .25 .11
☐ 697 David Clyde .25 .11
☐ 698 Oscar Gamble .75 .35
☐ 699 Floyd Bannister .25 .11
☐ 700 Rod Carew DP 1.00 .45
☐ 701 Ken Oberkfell .25 .11
☐ 702 Ed Farmer .25 .11
☐ 703 Otto Velez .25 .11
☐ 704 Gene Tenace .75 .35
☐ 705 Freddie Patek .25 .11
☐ 706 Tippy Martinez .75 .35
☐ 707 Elliott Maddox .25 .11
☐ 708 Bob Tolan .25 .11
☐ 709 Pat Underwood .25 .11
☐ 710 Graig Nettles 1.50 .70
☐ 711 Bob Galasso .25 .11
☐ 712 Rodney Scott .25 .11
☐ 713 Terry Whitfield .25 .11
☐ 714 Fred Norman .25 .11
☐ 715 Sal Bando .75 .35
☐ 716 Lynn McGlothen .25 .11
☐ 717 Mickey Klutts DP .10 .05
☐ 718 Greg Gross .25 .11
☐ 719 Don Robinson .75 .35
☐ 720 Carl Yastrzemski DP 1.50 .70
☐ 721 Paul Hartzell .25 .11
☐ 722 Jose Cruz .75 .35
☐ 723 Shane Rawley .25 .11
☐ 724 Jerry White .25 .11
☐ 725 Rick Wise .25 .11
☐ 726 Steve Yeager 1.50 .30

1980 Topps Super

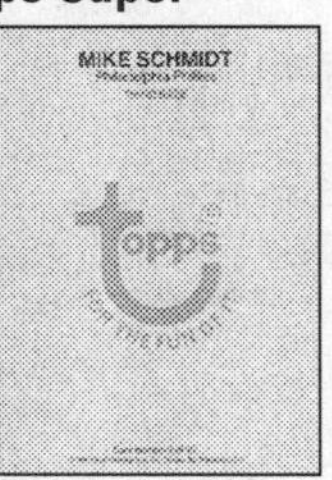

This 60-card set, measuring 4 7/8" by 6 7/8", consists primarily of star players. A player photo comprises the entire front with a facsimile signature at the lower portion of the photo. The backs contain a large Topps logo and the player's name. The cards were issued with either white or gray backs. The white backs have thicker card stock than the gray. White back cards were issued in three-card cellophane packs and gray back cards were issued through various promotional means. The prices below reflect those of the gray back. White backs are valued at 2.5 times these prices. There are a number of cards that were Triple Printed. They are indicated by below (TP).

	NRMT	VG-E
COMPLETE SET (60)	20.00	9.00
COMMON CARD (1-60)	.10	.05

☐ 1 Willie Stargell .50 .23
☐ 2 Mike Schmidt TP .75 .35
☐ 3 Johnny Bench .75 .35
☐ 4 Jim Palmer .50 .23
☐ 5 Jim Rice .25 .11
☐ 6 Reggie Jackson TP .75 .35
☐ 7 Ron Guidry .25 .11
☐ 8 Lee Mazzilli .25 .11
☐ 9 Don Baylor .50 .23
☐ 10 Fred Lynn .25 .11
☐ 11 Ken Singleton .25 .11
☐ 12 Rod Carew TP .50 .23
☐ 13 Steve Garvey TP .25 .11
☐ 14 George Brett TP 1.50 .70
☐ 15 Tom Seaver .75 .35
☐ 16 Dave Kingman .25 .11
☐ 17 Dave Parker TP .25 .11
☐ 18 Dave Winfield .75 .35
☐ 19 Pete Rose 1.00 .45
☐ 20 Nolan Ryan 3.00 1.35
☐ 21 Graig Nettles .25 .11
☐ 22 Carl Yastrzemski .75 .35
☐ 23 Tommy John .50 .23
☐ 24 George Foster .25 .11
☐ 25 J.R. Richard .10 .05
☐ 26 Keith Hernandez .25 .11
☐ 27 Bob Horner .10 .05
☐ 28 Eddie Murray 2.00 .90
☐ 29 Steve Kemp .10 .05
☐ 30 Gorman Thomas .10 .05
☐ 31 Sixto Lezcano .10 .05
☐ 32 Bruce Sutter .25 .11
☐ 33 Cecil Cooper .25 .11
☐ 34 Larry Bowa .25 .11
☐ 35 Al Oliver .50 .23
☐ 36 Ted Simmons .25 .11
☐ 37 Garry Templeton .10 .05
☐ 38 Jerry Koosman .25 .11
☐ 39 Darrell Porter .10 .05
☐ 40 Roy Smalley .10 .05
☐ 41 Craig Swan .10 .05
☐ 42 Jason Thompson .10 .05
☐ 43 Andre Thornton .10 .05
☐ 44 Rick Manning .10 .05
☐ 45 Kent Tekulve .10 .05
☐ 46 Phil Niekro .75 .35
☐ 47 Buddy Bell .25 .11
☐ 48 Randy Jones .10 .05
☐ 49 Brian Downing .10 .05
☐ 50 Amos Otis .10 .05
☐ 51 Rick Bosetti .10 .05
☐ 52 Gary Carter .50 .23
☐ 53 Larry Parrish .25 .11
☐ 54 Jack Clark .25 .11
☐ 55 Bruce Bochte .10 .05
☐ 56 Cesar Cedeno .10 .05
☐ 57 Chet Lemon .10 .05
☐ 58 Dave Revering .10 .05
☐ 59 Vida Blue .25 .11
☐ 60 Dave Lopes .25 .11

1980 Topps Team Checklist Sheet

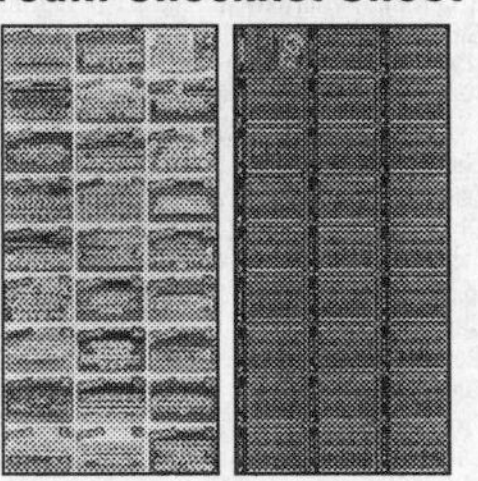

As part of a mail-away offer, Topps offered all 26 1980 team checklist cards on an uncut sheet. These cards enabled the collector to have an easy reference for which card(s) he/she needed to finish their sets. When cut from the sheet, all cards measure the standard size.

	NRMT	VG-E
COMPLETE SET (1)	15.00	6.75
COMMON SHEET (1)	15.00	6.75

☐ 1 Team Checklist Sheet 15.00 6.75

1981 Topps

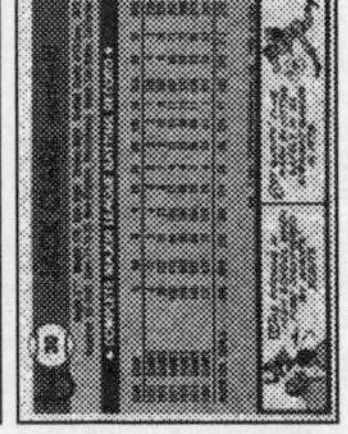

The cards in this 726-card set measure the standard size. League Leaders (1-8), Record Breakers (201-208), and Post-season cards (401-404) are the topical subsets. The team cards are all grouped together (661-686) and feature team checklist backs and a very small photo of the team's manager in the upper right corner of the obverse. The obverses carry the player's position and team in a baseball cap design, and the company name is printed in a small baseball. The backs are red and gray. The 66 double-printed cards are noted in the checklist by DP. This set was issued primarily in 15-card wax packs and 50-card rack packs. Notable Rookie Cards in the set include Harold Baines, Kirk Gibson, Tim Raines, Jeff Reardon, and Fernando Valenzuela.

	NRMT	VG-E
COMPLETE SET (726)	50.00	22.00
COMMON CARD (1-726)	.15	.07
COMMON CARD DP	.10	.05

☐ 1 Batting Leaders 2.50 1.10
George Brett
Bill Buckner
☐ 2 Home Run Leaders 1.50 .70
Reggie Jackson
Ben Oglivie
Mike Schmidt
☐ 3 RBI Leaders 1.50 .70
Cecil Cooper
Mike Schmidt
☐ 4 Stolen Base Leaders 1.50 .70
Rickey Henderson
Ron LeFlore
☐ 5 Victory Leaders 1.50 .70
Steve Stone
Steve Carlton
☐ 6 Strikeout Leaders 1.50 .70
Len Barker
Steve Carlton
☐ 7 ERA Leaders .75 .35
Rudy May
Don Sutton
☐ 8 Leading Firemen .75 .35
Dan Quisenberry
Rollie Fingers
Tom Hume
☐ 9 Pete LaCock DP .10 .05
☐ 10 Mike Flanagan .40 .18
☐ 11 Jim Wohlford DP .10 .05
☐ 12 Mark Clear .15 .07
☐ 13 Joe Charboneau 1.50 .70
☐ 14 John Tudor .40 .18
☐ 15 Larry Parrish .15 .07
☐ 16 Ron Davis .15 .07
☐ 17 Cliff Johnson .15 .07
☐ 18 Glenn Adams .15 .07
☐ 19 Jim Clancy .15 .07
☐ 20 Jeff Burroughs .15 .07
☐ 21 Ron Oester .15 .07
☐ 22 Danny Darwin .40 .18
☐ 23 Alex Trevino .15 .07
☐ 24 Don Stanhouse .15 .07
☐ 25 Sixto Lezcano .15 .07
☐ 26 U.L. Washington .15 .07
☐ 27 Champ Summers DP .10 .05
☐ 28 Enrique Romo .15 .07
☐ 29 Gene Tenace .40 .18
☐ 30 Jack Clark .40 .18
☐ 31 Checklist 1-121 DP .15 .07
☐ 32 Ken Oberkfell .15 .07
☐ 33 Rick Honeycutt .15 .07
☐ 34 Aurelio Rodriguez .15 .07
☐ 35 Mitchell Page .15 .07
☐ 36 Ed Farmer .15 .07
☐ 37 Gary Roenicke .15 .07
☐ 38 Win Remmerswaal .15 .07
☐ 39 Tom Veryzer .15 .07
☐ 40 Tug McGraw .40 .18
☐ 41 Ranger Rookies .15 .07
Bob Babcock
John Butcher
Jerry Don Gleaton
☐ 42 Jerry White DP .10 .05
☐ 43 Jose Morales .15 .07
☐ 44 Larry McWilliams .15 .07
☐ 45 Enos Cabell .15 .07
☐ 46 Rick Bosetti .15 .07
☐ 47 Ken Brett .15 .07
☐ 48 Dave Skaggs .15 .07
☐ 49 Bob Shirley .15 .07
☐ 50 Dave Lopes .40 .18
☐ 51 Bill Robinson DP .15 .07
☐ 52 Hector Cruz .15 .07
☐ 53 Kevin Saucier .15 .07
☐ 54 Ivan DeJesus .15 .07
☐ 55 Mike Norris .15 .07
☐ 56 Buck Martinez .15 .07
☐ 57 Dave Roberts .15 .07
☐ 58 Joel Youngblood .15 .07
☐ 59 Dan Petry .40 .18
☐ 60 Willie Randolph .40 .18
☐ 61 Butch Wynegar .15 .07
☐ 62 Joe Pettini .15 .07
☐ 63 Steve Renko DP .10 .05
☐ 64 Brian Asselstine .15 .07
☐ 65 Scott McGregor .15 .07

☐ 66 Royals Rookies	.15	.07
Manny Castillo		
Tim Ireland		
Mike Jones		
☐ 67 Ken Kravec	.15	.07
☐ 68 Matt Alexander DP	.10	.05
☐ 69 Ed Halicki	.15	.07
☐ 70 Al Oliver DP	.40	.18
☐ 71 Hal Dues	.15	.07
☐ 72 Barry Evans DP	.10	.05
☐ 73 Doug Bair	.15	.07
☐ 74 Mike Hargrove	.40	.18
☐ 75 Reggie Smith	.40	.18
☐ 76 Mario Mendoza	.15	.07
☐ 77 Mike Barlow	.15	.07
☐ 78 Steve Dillard	.15	.07
☐ 79 Bruce Robbins	.15	.07
☐ 80 Rusty Staub	.40	.18
☐ 81 Dave Stapleton	.15	.07
☐ 82 Astros Rookies DP	.15	.07
Danny Heep		
Alan Knicely		
Bobby Sprowl		
☐ 83 Mike Proly	.15	.07
☐ 84 Johnnie LeMaster	.15	.07
☐ 85 Mike Caldwell	.15	.07
☐ 86 Wayne Gross	.15	.07
☐ 87 Rick Camp	.15	.07
☐ 88 Joe Lefebvre	.15	.07
☐ 89 Darrell Jackson	.15	.07
☐ 90 Bake McBride	.15	.07
☐ 91 Tim Stoddard DP	.10	.05
☐ 92 Mike Easler	.15	.07
☐ 93 Ed Glynn DP	.10	.05
☐ 94 Harry Spilman DP	.10	.05
☐ 95 Jim Sundberg	.40	.18
☐ 96 A's Rookies	.15	.07
Dave Beard		
Ernie Camacho		
Pat Dempsey		
☐ 97 Chris Speier	.15	.07
☐ 98 Clint Hurdle	.15	.07
☐ 99 Eric Wilkins	.15	.07
☐ 100 Rod Carew	1.25	.55
☐ 101 Benny Ayala	.15	.07
☐ 102 Dave Tobik	.15	.07
☐ 103 Jerry Martin	.15	.07
☐ 104 Terry Forster	.15	.07
☐ 105 Jose Cruz	.40	.18
☐ 106 Don Money	.15	.07
☐ 107 Rich Wortham	.15	.07
☐ 108 Bruce Benedict	.15	.07
☐ 109 Mike Scott	.40	.18
☐ 110 Carl Yastrzemski	1.50	.70
☐ 111 Greg Minton	.15	.07
☐ 112 White Sox Rookies	.15	.07
Rusty Kuntz		
Fran Mullins		
Leo Sutherland		
☐ 113 Mike Phillips	.15	.07
☐ 114 Tom Underwood	.15	.07
☐ 115 Roy Smalley	.15	.07
☐ 116 Joe Simpson	.15	.07
☐ 117 Pete Falcone	.15	.07
☐ 118 Kurt Bevacqua	.15	.07
☐ 119 Tippy Martinez	.15	.07
☐ 120 Larry Bowa	.40	.18
☐ 121 Larry Harlow	.15	.07
☐ 122 John Denny	.15	.07
☐ 123 Al Cowens	.15	.07
☐ 124 Jerry Garvin	.15	.07
☐ 125 Andre Dawson	2.00	.90
☐ 126 Charlie Leibrandt	.75	.35
☐ 127 Rudy Law	.15	.07
☐ 128 Gary Allenson DP	.10	.05
☐ 129 Art Howe	.15	.07
☐ 130 Larry Gura	.15	.07
☐ 131 Keith Moreland	.40	.18
☐ 132 Tommy Boggs	.15	.07
☐ 133 Jeff Cox	.15	.07
☐ 134 Steve Mura	.15	.07
☐ 135 Gorman Thomas	.40	.18
☐ 136 Doug Capilla	.15	.07
☐ 137 Hosken Powell	.15	.07
☐ 138 Rich Dotson DP	.15	.07
☐ 139 Oscar Gamble	.15	.07
☐ 140 Bob Forsch	.15	.07
☐ 141 Miguel Dilone	.15	.07
☐ 142 Jackson Todd	.15	.07
☐ 143 Dan Meyer	.15	.07
☐ 144 Allen Ripley	.15	.07
☐ 145 Mickey Rivers	.40	.18
☐ 146 Bobby Castillo	.15	.07
☐ 147 Dale Berra	.15	.07
☐ 148 Randy Niemann	.15	.07
☐ 149 Joe Nolan	.15	.07
☐ 150 Mark Fidrych	1.50	.70
☐ 151 Claudell Washington	.40	.18
☐ 152 John Urrea	.15	.07
☐ 153 Tom Poquette	.15	.07
☐ 154 Rick Langford	.15	.07
☐ 155 Chris Chambliss	.40	.18
☐ 156 Bob McClure	.15	.07
☐ 157 John Wathan	.15	.07
☐ 158 Fergie Jenkins	1.50	.70
☐ 159 Brian Doyle	.15	.07
☐ 160 Garry Maddox	.15	.07
☐ 161 Dan Graham	.15	.07
☐ 162 Doug Corbett	.15	.07
☐ 163 Bill Almon	.15	.07
☐ 164 LaMarr Hoyt	.40	.18
☐ 165 Tony Scott	.15	.07
☐ 166 Floyd Bannister	.15	.07
☐ 167 Terry Whitfield	.15	.07
☐ 168 Don Robinson DP	.10	.05
☐ 169 John Mayberry	.15	.07
☐ 170 Ross Grimsley	.15	.07
☐ 171 Gene Richards	.15	.07
☐ 172 Gary Woods	.15	.07
☐ 173 Bump Wills	.15	.07
☐ 174 Doug Rau	.15	.07
☐ 175 Dave Collins	.15	.07
☐ 176 Mike Krukow	.15	.07
☐ 177 Rick Peters	.15	.07
☐ 178 Jim Essian DP	.10	.05
☐ 179 Rudy May	.15	.07
☐ 180 Pete Rose	2.00	.90
☐ 181 Elias Sosa	.15	.07
☐ 182 Bob Grich	.40	.18
☐ 183 Dick Davis DP	.10	.05
☐ 184 Jim Dwyer	.15	.07
☐ 185 Dennis Leonard	.15	.07
☐ 186 Wayne Nordhagen	.15	.07
☐ 187 Mike Parrott	.15	.07
☐ 188 Doug DeCinces	.40	.18
☐ 189 Craig Swan	.15	.07
☐ 190 Cesar Cedeno	.40	.18
☐ 191 Rick Sutcliffe	.40	.18
☐ 192 Braves Rookies	.40	.18
Terry Harper		
Ed Miller		
Rafael Ramirez		
☐ 193 Pete Vuckovich	.40	.18
☐ 194 Rod Scurry	.15	.07
☐ 195 Rich Murray	.15	.07
☐ 196 Duffy Dyer	.15	.07
☐ 197 Jim Kern	.15	.07
☐ 198 Jerry Dybzinski	.15	.07
☐ 199 Chuck Rainey	.15	.07
☐ 200 George Foster	.40	.18
☐ 201 Johnny Bench RB	1.50	.70
Most homers catchers		
☐ 202 Steve Carlton RB	1.50	.70
Most strikeouts,		
lefthander, lifetime		
☐ 203 Bill Gullickson RB	.75	.35
Most SO's, game, rookie		
☐ 204 Ron LeFlore RB	.40	.18
Rodney Scott RB		
Most stolen bases		
teammates, season		
☐ 205 Pete Rose RB	1.50	.70
Most cons. seasons		
600 or more at-bats		
☐ 206 Mike Schmidt RB	1.50	.70
Most homers, 3rd baseman, season		
☐ 207 Ozzie Smith RB	2.00	.90
Most assists,		
season, shortstop		
☐ 208 Willie Wilson RB	.40	.18
Most AB's season		
☐ 209 Dickie Thon DP	.40	.18
☐ 210 Jim Palmer	1.00	.45
☐ 211 Derrel Thomas	.15	.07
☐ 212 Steve Nicosia	.15	.07
☐ 213 Al Holland	.15	.07
☐ 214 Angels Rookies	.15	.07
Ralph Botting		
Jim Dorsey		
John Harris		
☐ 215 Larry Hisle	.15	.07
☐ 216 John Henry Johnson	.15	.07
☐ 217 Rich Hebner	.15	.07
☐ 218 Paul Splittorff	.15	.07
☐ 219 Ken Landreaux	.15	.07
☐ 220 Tom Seaver	2.00	.90
☐ 221 Bob Davis	.15	.07
☐ 222 Jorge Orta	.15	.07
☐ 223 Roy Lee Jackson	.15	.07
☐ 224 Pat Zachry	.15	.07
☐ 225 Ruppert Jones	.15	.07
☐ 226 Manny Sanguillen DP	.10	.05
☐ 227 Fred Martinez	.15	.07
☐ 228 Tom Paciorek	.40	.18
☐ 229 Rollie Fingers	1.50	.70
☐ 230 George Hendrick	.40	.18
☐ 231 Joe Beckwith	.15	.07
☐ 232 Mickey Klutts	.15	.07
☐ 233 Skip Lockwood	.15	.07
☐ 234 Lou Whitaker	1.50	.70
☐ 235 Scott Sanderson	.15	.07
☐ 236 Mike Ivie	.15	.07
☐ 237 Charlie Moore	.15	.07
☐ 238 Willie Hernandez	.40	.18
☐ 239 Rick Miller DP	.10	.05
☐ 240 Nolan Ryan	8.00	3.60
☐ 241 Checklist 122-242 DP	.15	.07
☐ 242 Chet Lemon	.15	.07
☐ 243 Sal Butera	.15	.07
☐ 244 Cardinals Rookies	.15	.07
Tito Landrum		
Al Olmsted		
Andy Rincon		
☐ 245 Ed Figueroa	.15	.07
☐ 246 Ed Ott DP	.10	.05
☐ 247 Glenn Hubbard DP	.10	.05
☐ 248 Joey McLaughlin	.15	.07
☐ 249 Larry Cox	.15	.07
☐ 250 Ron Guidry	.40	.18
☐ 251 Tom Brookens	.15	.07
☐ 252 Victor Cruz	.15	.07
☐ 253 Dave Bergman	.15	.07
☐ 254 Ozzie Smith	6.00	2.70
☐ 255 Mark Littell	.15	.07
☐ 256 Bombo Rivera	.15	.07
☐ 257 Rennie Stennett	.15	.07
☐ 258 Joe Price	.15	.07
☐ 259 Mets Rookies	1.50	.70
Juan Berenguer		
Hubie Brooks		
Mookie Wilson		
☐ 260 Ron Cey	.40	.18
☐ 261 Rickey Henderson	4.00	1.80
☐ 262 Sammy Stewart	.15	.07
☐ 263 Brian Downing	.40	.18
☐ 264 Jim Norris	.15	.07
☐ 265 John Candelaria	.40	.18
☐ 266 Tom Herr	.40	.18
☐ 267 Stan Bahnsen	.15	.07
☐ 268 Jerry Royster	.15	.07
☐ 269 Ken Forsch	.15	.07
☐ 270 Greg Luzinski	.40	.18
☐ 271 Bill Castro	.15	.07
☐ 272 Bruce Kimm	.15	.07
☐ 273 Stan Papi	.15	.07
☐ 274 Craig Chamberlain	.15	.07
☐ 275 Dwight Evans	.75	.35
☐ 276 Dan Spillner	.15	.07
☐ 277 Alfredo Griffin	.15	.07
☐ 278 Rick Sofield	.15	.07
☐ 279 Bob Knepper	.15	.07
☐ 280 Ken Griffey	.75	.35
☐ 281 Fred Stanley	.15	.07
☐ 282 Mariners Rookies	.15	.07
Rick Anderson		
Greg Biercevicz		
Rodney Craig		
☐ 283 Billy Sample	.15	.07
☐ 284 Brian Kingman	.15	.07
☐ 285 Jerry Turner	.15	.07
☐ 286 Dave Frost	.15	.07
☐ 287 Lenn Sakata	.15	.07
☐ 288 Bob Clark	.15	.07
☐ 289 Mickey Hatcher	.40	.18
☐ 290 Bob Boone DP	.40	.18
☐ 291 Aurelio Lopez	.15	.07
☐ 292 Mike Squires	.15	.07
☐ 293 Charlie Lea	.15	.07
☐ 294 Mike Tyson DP	.10	.05
☐ 295 Hal McRae	.75	.35
☐ 296 Bill Nahorodny DP	.10	.05
☐ 297 Bob Bailor	.15	.07
☐ 298 Buddy Solomon	.15	.07
☐ 299 Elliott Maddox	.15	.07
☐ 300 Paul Molitor	3.00	1.35
☐ 301 Matt Keough	.15	.07
☐ 302 Dodgers Rookies	3.00	1.35
Jack Perconte		
Mike Scioscia		
Fernando Valenzuela		
☐ 303 Johnny Oates	.40	.18
☐ 304 John Castino	.15	.07
☐ 305 Ken Clay	.15	.07
☐ 306 Juan Beniquez DP	.10	.05
☐ 307 Gene Garber	.15	.07
☐ 308 Rick Manning	.15	.07
☐ 309 Luis Salazar	.15	.07
☐ 310 Vida Blue DP	.15	.07
☐ 311 Freddie Patek	.15	.07
☐ 312 Rick Rhoden	.15	.07
☐ 313 Luis Pujols	.15	.07

☐ 314 Rich Dauer .15 .07
☐ 315 Kirk Gibson 3.00 1.35
☐ 316 Craig Minetto .15 .07
☐ 317 Lonnie Smith .40 .18
☐ 318 Steve Yeager .15 .07
☐ 319 Rowland Office .15 .07
☐ 320 Tom Burgmeier .15 .07
☐ 321 Leon Durham .40 .18
☐ 322 Neil Allen .15 .07
☐ 323 Jim Morrison DP .10 .05
☐ 324 Mike Willis .15 .07
☐ 325 Ray Knight .40 .18
☐ 326 Biff Pocoroba .15 .07
☐ 327 Moose Haas .15 .07
☐ 328 Twins Rookies .15 .07
Dave Engle
Greg Johnston
Gary Ward
☐ 329 Joaquin Andujar .40 .18
☐ 330 Frank White .40 .18
☐ 331 Dennis Lamp .15 .07
☐ 332 Lee Lacy DP .10 .05
☐ 333 Sid Monge .15 .07
☐ 334 Dane Iorg .15 .07
☐ 335 Rick Cerone .15 .07
☐ 336 Eddie Whitson .15 .07
☐ 337 Lynn Jones .15 .07
☐ 338 Checklist 243-363 .75 .35
☐ 339 John Ellis .15 .07
☐ 340 Bruce Kison .15 .07
☐ 341 Dwayne Murphy .15 .07
☐ 342 Eric Rasmussen DP .10 .05
☐ 343 Frank Taveras .15 .07
☐ 344 Byron McLaughlin .15 .07
☐ 345 Warren Cromartie .15 .07
☐ 346 Larry Christenson DP .10 .05
☐ 347 Harold Baines 2.50 1.10
☐ 348 Bob Sykes .15 .07
☐ 349 Glenn Hoffman .15 .07
☐ 350 J.R. Richard .40 .18
☐ 351 Otto Velez .15 .07
☐ 352 Dick Tidrow DP .10 .05
☐ 353 Terry Kennedy .15 .07
☐ 354 Mario Soto .15 .07
☐ 355 Bob Horner .40 .18
☐ 356 Padres Rookies .15 .07
George Stablein
Craig Stimac
Tom Tellmann
☐ 357 Jim Slaton .15 .07
☐ 358 Mark Wagner .15 .07
☐ 359 Tom Hausman .15 .07
☐ 360 Willie Wilson .40 .18
☐ 361 Joe Strain .15 .07
☐ 362 Bo Diaz .15 .07
☐ 363 Geoff Zahn .15 .07
☐ 364 Mike Davis .15 .07
☐ 365 Graig Nettles DP .40 .18
☐ 366 Mike Ramsey .15 .07
☐ 367 Dennis Martinez .75 .35
☐ 368 Leon Roberts .15 .07
☐ 369 Frank Tanana .40 .18
☐ 370 Dave Winfield 2.50 1.10
☐ 371 Charlie Hough .40 .18
☐ 372 Jay Johnstone .40 .18
☐ 373 Pat Underwood .15 .07
☐ 374 Tommy Hutton .15 .07
☐ 375 Dave Concepcion .40 .18
☐ 376 Ron Reed .15 .07
☐ 377 Jerry Morales .15 .07
☐ 378 Dave Rader .15 .07
☐ 379 Lary Sorensen .15 .07
☐ 380 Willie Stargell 1.50 .70
☐ 381 Cubs Rookies .15 .07
Carlos Lezcano
Steve Macko
Randy Martz
☐ 382 Paul Mirabella .15 .07
☐ 383 Eric Soderholm DP .10 .05
☐ 384 Mike Sadek .15 .07
☐ 385 Joe Sambito .15 .07
☐ 386 Dave Edwards .15 .07
☐ 387 Phil Niekro 1.50 .70
☐ 388 Andre Thornton .40 .18
☐ 389 Marty Pattin .15 .07
☐ 390 Cesar Geronimo .15 .07
☐ 391 Dave Lemanczyk DP .10 .05
☐ 392 Lance Parrish .40 .18
☐ 393 Broderick Perkins .15 .07
☐ 394 Woodie Fryman .15 .07
☐ 395 Scot Thompson .15 .07
☐ 396 Bill Campbell .15 .07
☐ 397 Julio Cruz .15 .07
☐ 398 Ross Baumgarten .15 .07
☐ 399 Orioles Rookies 1.50 .70
Mike Boddicker
Mark Corey
Floyd Rayford
☐ 400 Reggie Jackson 2.00 .90
☐ 401 George Brett ALCS 2.00 .90
☐ 402 NL Champs .75 .35
Phillies squeak
past Astros
(Phillies celebrating)
☐ 403 Larry Bowa WS .75 .35
☐ 404 Tug McGraw WS .75 .35
☐ 405 Nino Espinosa .15 .07
☐ 406 Dickie Noles .15 .07
☐ 407 Ernie Whitt .15 .07
☐ 408 Fernando Arroyo .15 .07
☐ 409 Larry Herndon .15 .07
☐ 410 Bert Campaneris .40 .18
☐ 411 Terry Puhl .15 .07
☐ 412 Britt Burns .15 .07
☐ 413 Tony Bernazard .15 .07
☐ 414 John Pacella DP .10 .05
☐ 415 Ben Oglivie .40 .18
☐ 416 Gary Alexander .15 .07
☐ 417 Dan Schatzeder .15 .07
☐ 418 Bobby Brown .15 .07
☐ 419 Tom Hume .15 .07
☐ 420 Keith Hernandez .40 .18
☐ 421 Bob Stanley .15 .07
☐ 422 Dan Ford .15 .07
☐ 423 Shane Rawley .15 .07
☐ 424 Yankees Rookies .15 .07
Tim Lollar
Bruce Robinson
Dennis Werth
☐ 425 Al Bumbry .40 .18
☐ 426 Warren Brusstar .15 .07
☐ 427 John D'Acquisto .15 .07
☐ 428 John Stearns .15 .07
☐ 429 Mick Kelleher .15 .07
☐ 430 Jim Bibby .15 .07
☐ 431 Dave Roberts .15 .07
☐ 432 Len Barker .15 .07
☐ 433 Rance Mulliniks .15 .07
☐ 434 Roger Erickson .15 .07
☐ 435 Jim Spencer .15 .07
☐ 436 Gary Lucas .15 .07
☐ 437 Mike Heath DP .10 .05
☐ 438 John Montefusco .15 .07
☐ 439 Denny Walling .15 .07
☐ 440 Jerry Reuss .40 .18
☐ 441 Ken Reitz .15 .07
☐ 442 Ron Pruitt .15 .07
☐ 443 Jim Beattie DP .10 .05
☐ 444 Garth Iorg .15 .07
☐ 445 Ellis Valentine .15 .07
☐ 446 Checklist 364-484 .75 .35
☐ 447 Junior Kennedy DP .10 .05
☐ 448 Tim Corcoran .15 .07
☐ 449 Paul Mitchell .15 .07
☐ 450 Dave Kingman DP .40 .18
☐ 451 Indians Rookies .15 .07
Chris Bando
Tom Brennan
Sandy Wihtol
☐ 452 Renie Martin .15 .07
☐ 453 Rob Wilfong DP .10 .05
☐ 454 Andy Hassler .15 .07
☐ 455 Rick Burleson .15 .07
☐ 456 Jeff Reardon 2.00 .90
☐ 457 Mike Lum .15 .07
☐ 458 Randy Jones .15 .07
☐ 459 Greg Gross .15 .07
☐ 460 Rich Gossage .75 .35
☐ 461 Dave McKay .15 .07
☐ 462 Jack Brohamer .15 .07
☐ 463 Milt May .15 .07
☐ 464 Adrian Devine .15 .07
☐ 465 Bill Russell .40 .18
☐ 466 Bob Molinaro .15 .07
☐ 467 Dave Stieb .40 .18
☐ 468 John Wockenfuss .15 .07
☐ 469 Jeff Leonard .40 .18
☐ 470 Manny Trillo .15 .07
☐ 471 Mike Vail .15 .07
☐ 472 Dyar Miller DP .10 .05
☐ 473 Jose Cardenal .15 .07
☐ 474 Mike LaCoss .15 .07
☐ 475 Buddy Bell .40 .18
☐ 476 Jerry Koosman .40 .18
☐ 477 Luis Gomez .15 .07
☐ 478 Juan Eichelberger .15 .07
☐ 479 Expos Rookies 3.00 1.35
Tim Raines
Roberto Ramos
Bobby Pate
☐ 480 Carlton Fisk 2.00 .90
☐ 481 Bob Lacey DP .10 .05
☐ 482 Jim Gantner .40 .18
☐ 483 Mike Griffin .15 .07
☐ 484 Max Venable DP .10 .05
☐ 485 Garry Templeton .15 .07
☐ 486 Marc Hill .15 .07
☐ 487 Dewey Robinson .15 .07
☐ 488 Damaso Garcia .15 .07
☐ 489 John Littlefield .15 .07
☐ 490 Eddie Murray 3.00 1.35
☐ 491 Gordy Pladson .15 .07
☐ 492 Barry Foote .15 .07
☐ 493 Dan Quisenberry .40 .18
☐ 494 Bob Walk .40 .18
☐ 495 Dusty Baker .75 .35
☐ 496 Paul Dade .15 .07
☐ 497 Fred Norman .15 .07
☐ 498 Pat Putnam .15 .07
☐ 499 Frank Pastore .15 .07
☐ 500 Jim Rice .40 .18
☐ 501 Tim Foli DP .10 .05
☐ 502 Giants Rookies .15 .07
Chris Bourjos
Al Hargesheimer
Mike Rowland
☐ 503 Steve McCatty .15 .07
☐ 504 Dale Murphy 1.50 .70
☐ 505 Jason Thompson .15 .07
☐ 506 Phil Huffman .15 .07
☐ 507 Jamie Quirk .15 .07
☐ 508 Rob Dressler .15 .07
☐ 509 Pete Mackanin .15 .07
☐ 510 Lee Mazzilli .15 .07
☐ 511 Wayne Garland .15 .07
☐ 512 Gary Thomasson .15 .07
☐ 513 Frank LaCorte .15 .07
☐ 514 George Riley .15 .07
☐ 515 Robin Yount 2.00 .90
☐ 516 Doug Bird .15 .07
☐ 517 Richie Zisk .15 .07
☐ 518 Grant Jackson .15 .07
☐ 519 John Tamargo DP .10 .05
☐ 520 Steve Stone .40 .18
☐ 521 Sam Mejias .15 .07
☐ 522 Mike Colbern .15 .07
☐ 523 John Fulgham .15 .07
☐ 524 Willie Aikens .15 .07
☐ 525 Mike Torrez .15 .07
☐ 526 Phillies Rookies .15 .07
Marty Bystrom
Jay Loviglio
Jim Wright
☐ 527 Danny Goodwin .15 .07
☐ 528 Gary Matthews .40 .18
☐ 529 Dave LaRoche .15 .07
☐ 530 Steve Garvey .75 .35
☐ 531 John Curtis .15 .07
☐ 532 Bill Stein .15 .07
☐ 533 Jesus Figueroa .15 .07
☐ 534 Dave Smith .40 .18
☐ 535 Omar Moreno .15 .07
☐ 536 Bob Owchinko DP .10 .05
☐ 537 Ron Hodges .15 .07
☐ 538 Tom Griffin .15 .07
☐ 539 Rodney Scott .15 .07
☐ 540 Mike Schmidt DP 2.00 .90
☐ 541 Steve Swisher .15 .07
☐ 542 Larry Bradford DP .10 .05
☐ 543 Terry Crowley .15 .07
☐ 544 Rich Gale .15 .07
☐ 545 Johnny Grubb .15 .07
☐ 546 Paul Moskau .15 .07
☐ 547 Mario Guerrero .15 .07
☐ 548 Dave Goltz .15 .07
☐ 549 Jerry Remy .15 .07
☐ 550 Tommy John .75 .35
☐ 551 Pirates Rookies 1.50 .70
Vance Law
Tony Pena
Pascual Perez
☐ 552 Steve Trout .15 .07
☐ 553 Tim Blackwell .15 .07
☐ 554 Bert Blyleven UER .75 .35
(1 is missing from
1980 on card back)
☐ 555 Cecil Cooper .40 .18
☐ 556 Jerry Mumphrey .15 .07
☐ 557 Chris Knapp .15 .07
☐ 558 Barry Bonnell .15 .07
☐ 559 Willie Montanez .15 .07
☐ 560 Joe Morgan 1.50 .70
☐ 561 Dennis Littlejohn .15 .07
☐ 562 Checklist 485-605 .75 .35
☐ 563 Jim Kaat .40 .18
☐ 564 Ron Hassey DP .10 .05
☐ 565 Burt Hooton .15 .07
☐ 566 Del Unser .15 .07
☐ 567 Mark Bomback .15 .07
☐ 568 Dave Revering .15 .07
☐ 569 Al Williams DP .10 .05
☐ 570 Ken Singleton .40 .18

☐ 571 Todd Cruz .15 .07
☐ 572 Jack Morris .75 .35
☐ 573 Phil Garner .40 .18
☐ 574 Bill Caudill .15 .07
☐ 575 Tony Perez 1.50 .70
☐ 576 Reggie Cleveland .15 .07
☐ 577 Blue Jays Rookies .15 .07
Luis Leal
Brian Milner
Ken Schrom
☐ 578 Bill Gullickson .75 .35
☐ 579 Tim Flannery .15 .07
☐ 580 Don Baylor .75 .35
☐ 581 Roy Howell .15 .07
☐ 582 Gaylord Perry 1.50 .70
☐ 583 Larry Milbourne .15 .07
☐ 584 Randy Lerch .15 .07
☐ 585 Amos Otis .40 .18
☐ 586 Silvio Martinez .15 .07
☐ 587 Jeff Newman .15 .07
☐ 588 Gary Lavelle .15 .07
☐ 589 Lamar Johnson .15 .07
☐ 590 Bruce Sutter .40 .18
☐ 591 John Lowenstein .15 .07
☐ 592 Steve Comer .15 .07
☐ 593 Steve Kemp .15 .07
☐ 594 Preston Hanna DP .10 .05
☐ 595 Butch Hobson .15 .07
☐ 596 Jerry Augustine .15 .07
☐ 597 Rafael Landestoy .15 .07
☐ 598 George Vukovich DP .10 .05
☐ 599 Dennis Kinney .15 .07
☐ 600 Johnny Bench 2.00 .90
☐ 601 Don Aase .15 .07
☐ 602 Bobby Murcer .40 .18
☐ 603 John Verhoeven .15 .07
☐ 604 Rob Picciolo .15 .07
☐ 605 Don Sutton 1.50 .70
☐ 606 Reds Rookies DP .15 .07
Bruce Berenyi
Geoff Combe
Paul Householder
☐ 607 David Palmer .15 .07
☐ 608 Greg Pryor .15 .07
☐ 609 Lynn McGlothen .15 .07
☐ 610 Darrell Porter .15 .07
☐ 611 Rick Matula DP .10 .05
☐ 612 Duane Kuiper .15 .07
☐ 613 Jim Anderson .15 .07
☐ 614 Dave Rozema .15 .07
☐ 615 Rick Dempsey .40 .18
☐ 616 Rick Wise .15 .07
☐ 617 Craig Reynolds .15 .07
☐ 618 John Milner .15 .07
☐ 619 Steve Henderson .15 .07
☐ 620 Dennis Eckersley 1.50 .70
☐ 621 Tom Donohue .15 .07
☐ 622 Randy Moffitt .15 .07
☐ 623 Sal Bando .40 .18
☐ 624 Bob Welch .40 .18
☐ 625 Bill Buckner .40 .18
☐ 626 Tigers Rookies .15 .07
Dave Steffen
Jerry Ujdur
Roger Weaver
☐ 627 Luis Tiant .40 .18
☐ 628 Vic Correll .15 .07
☐ 629 Tony Armas .40 .18
☐ 630 Steve Carlton 1.50 .70
☐ 631 Ron Jackson .15 .07
☐ 632 Alan Bannister .15 .07
☐ 633 Bill Lee .40 .18
☐ 634 Doug Flynn .15 .07
☐ 635 Bobby Bonds .40 .18
☐ 636 Al Hrabosky .15 .07
☐ 637 Jerry Narron .15 .07
☐ 638 Checklist 606-726 .75 .35
☐ 639 Carney Lansford .40 .18
☐ 640 Dave Parker .40 .18
☐ 641 Mark Belanger .40 .18
☐ 642 Vern Ruhle .15 .07
☐ 643 Lloyd Moseby .40 .18
☐ 644 Ramon Aviles DP .10 .05
☐ 645 Rick Reuschel .40 .18
☐ 646 Marvis Foley .15 .07
☐ 647 Dick Drago .15 .07
☐ 648 Darrell Evans .40 .18
☐ 649 Manny Sarmiento .15 .07
☐ 650 Bucky Dent .40 .18
☐ 651 Pedro Guerrero .75 .35
☐ 652 John Montague .15 .07
☐ 653 Bill Fahey .15 .07
☐ 654 Ray Burris .15 .07
☐ 655 Dan Driessen .15 .07
☐ 656 Jon Matlack .15 .07
☐ 657 Mike Cubbage DP .10 .05
☐ 658 Milt Wilcox .15 .07
☐ 659 Brewers Rookies .15 .07
John Flinn
Ed Romero
Ned Yost
☐ 660 Gary Carter 1.50 .70
☐ 661 Orioles Team/Mgr. .75 .35
Earl Weaver
(Checklist back)
☐ 662 Red Sox Team/Mgr. .75 .35
Ralph Houk
(Checklist back)
☐ 663 Angels Team/Mgr. .75 .35
Jim Fregosi
(Checklist back)
☐ 664 White Sox Team/Mgr. .75 .35
Tony LaRussa
(Checklist back)
☐ 665 Indians Team/Mgr. .75 .35
Dave Garcia
(Checklist back)
☐ 666 Tigers Team/Mgr. .75 .35
Sparky Anderson
(Checklist back)
☐ 667 Royals Team/Mgr. .75 .35
Jim Frey
(Checklist back)
☐ 668 Brewers Team/Mgr. .75 .35
Bob Rodgers
(Checklist back)
☐ 669 Twins Team/Mgr. .75 .35
John Goryl
(Checklist back)
☐ 670 Yankees Team/Mgr. .75 .35
Gene Michael
(Checklist back)
☐ 671 A's Team/Mgr. .75 .35
Billy Martin
(Checklist back)
☐ 672 Mariners Team/Mgr. .75 .35
Maury Wills
(Checklist back)
☐ 673 Rangers Team/Mgr. .75 .35
Don Zimmer
(Checklist back)
☐ 674 Blue Jays Team/Mgr. .75 .35
Bobby Mattick
(Checklist back)
☐ 675 Braves Team/Mgr. .75 .35
Bobby Cox
(Checklist back)
☐ 676 Cubs Team/Mgr. .75 .35
Joe Amalfitano
(Checklist back)
☐ 677 Reds Team/Mgr. .75 .35
John McNamara
(Checklist back)
☐ 678 Astros Team/Mgr. .75 .35
Bill Virdon
(Checklist back)
☐ 679 Dodgers Team/Mgr. .75 .35
Tom Lasorda
(Checklist back)
☐ 680 Expos Team/Mgr. .75 .35
Dick Williams
(Checklist back)
☐ 681 Mets Team/Mgr. .75 .35
Joe Torre
(Checklist back)
☐ 682 Phillies Team/Mgr. .75 .35
Dallas Green
(Checklist back)
☐ 683 Pirates Team/Mgr. .75 .35
Chuck Tanner
(Checklist back)
☐ 684 Cardinals Team/Mgr. .75 .35
Whitey Herzog
(Checklist back)
☐ 685 Padres Team/Mgr. .75 .35
Frank Howard
(Checklist back)
☐ 686 Giants Team/Mgr. .75 .35
Dave Bristol
(Checklist back)
☐ 687 Jeff Jones .15 .07
☐ 688 Kiko Garcia .15 .07
☐ 689 Red Sox Rookies 1.50 .70
Bruce Hurst
Keith MacWhorter
Reid Nichols
☐ 690 Bob Watson .40 .18
☐ 691 Dick Ruthven .15 .07
☐ 692 Lenny Randle .15 .07
☐ 693 Steve Howe .40 .18
☐ 694 Bud Harrelson DP .15 .07
☐ 695 Kent Tekulve .40 .18
☐ 696 Alan Ashby .15 .07
☐ 697 Rick Waits .15 .07
☐ 698 Mike Jorgensen .15 .07
☐ 699 Glenn Abbott .15 .07
☐ 700 George Brett 4.00 1.80
☐ 701 Joe Rudi .40 .18
☐ 702 George Medich .15 .07
☐ 703 Alvis Woods .15 .07
☐ 704 Bill Travers DP .10 .05
☐ 705 Ted Simmons .40 .18
☐ 706 Dave Ford .15 .07
☐ 707 Dave Cash .15 .07
☐ 708 Doyle Alexander .15 .07
☐ 709 Alan Trammell DP 1.50 .70
☐ 710 Ron LeFlore DP .15 .07
☐ 711 Joe Ferguson .15 .07
☐ 712 Bill Bonham .15 .07
☐ 713 Bill North .15 .07
☐ 714 Pete Redfern .15 .07
☐ 715 Bill Madlock .40 .18
☐ 716 Glenn Borgmann .15 .07
☐ 717 Jim Barr DP .10 .05
☐ 718 Larry Biittner .15 .07
☐ 719 Sparky Lyle .40 .18
☐ 720 Fred Lynn .40 .18
☐ 721 Toby Harrah .40 .18
☐ 722 Joe Niekro .40 .18
☐ 723 Bruce Bochte .15 .07
☐ 724 Lou Piniella .40 .18
☐ 725 Steve Rogers .15 .07
☐ 726 Rick Monday .40 .18

1981 Topps Traded

For the first time since 1976, Topps issued a 132-card factory boxed "traded" set in 1981, issued exclusively through hobby dealers. This set was sequentially numbered, alphabetically, from 727 to 858 and carries the same design as the regular issue 1981 Topps set. There are no key Rookie Cards in this set although Tim Raines, Jeff Reardon, and Fernando Valenzuela are depicted in their rookie year for cards. The key extended Rookie Card in the set is Danny Ainge.

	NRMT	VG-E
COMPLETE SET (132)	30.00	13.50
COMPLETE FACT.SET (132)	30.00	13.50
COMMON CARD (727-858)	.25	.11

☐ 727 Danny Ainge 5.00 2.20
☐ 728 Doyle Alexander .25 .11
☐ 729 Gary Alexander .25 .11
☐ 730 Bill Almon .25 .11
☐ 731 Joaquin Andujar 1.00 .45
☐ 732 Bob Bailor .25 .11
☐ 733 Juan Beniquez .25 .11
☐ 734 Dave Bergman .25 .11
☐ 735 Tony Bernazard .25 .11
☐ 736 Larry Biittner .25 .11
☐ 737 Doug Bird .25 .11
☐ 738 Bert Blyleven 3.00 1.35
☐ 739 Mark Bomback .25 .11
☐ 740 Bobby Bonds 1.00 .45
☐ 741 Rick Bosetti .25 .11
☐ 742 Hubie Brooks 1.00 .45
☐ 743 Rick Burleson .25 .11
☐ 744 Ray Burris .25 .11
☐ 745 Jeff Burroughs .25 .11
☐ 746 Enos Cabell .25 .11
☐ 747 Ken Clay .25 .11
☐ 748 Mark Clear .25 .11
☐ 749 Larry Cox .25 .11
☐ 750 Hector Cruz .25 .11
☐ 751 Victor Cruz .25 .11
☐ 752 Mike Cubbage .25 .11
☐ 753 Dick Davis .25 .11
☐ 754 Brian Doyle .25 .11
☐ 755 Dick Drago .25 .11
☐ 756 Leon Durham 1.00 .45
☐ 757 Jim Dwyer .25 .11
☐ 758 Dave Edwards UER .25 .11
No birthdate on card
☐ 759 Jim Essian .25 .11
☐ 760 Bill Fahey .25 .11
☐ 761 Rollie Fingers 3.00 1.35

☐ 762 Carlton Fisk	5.00	2.20
☐ 763 Barry Foote	.25	.11
☐ 764 Ken Forsch	.25	.11
☐ 765 Kiko Garcia	.25	.11
☐ 766 Cesar Geronimo	.25	.11
☐ 767 Gary Gray	.25	.11
☐ 768 Mickey Hatcher	1.00	.45
☐ 769 Steve Henderson	.25	.11
☐ 770 Marc Hill	.25	.11
☐ 771 Butch Hobson	.25	.11
☐ 772 Rick Honeycutt	.25	.11
☐ 773 Roy Howell	.25	.11
☐ 774 Mike Ivie	.25	.11
☐ 775 Roy Lee Jackson	.25	.11
☐ 776 Cliff Johnson	.25	.11
☐ 777 Randy Jones	.25	.11
☐ 778 Ruppert Jones	.25	.11
☐ 779 Mick Kelleher	.25	.11
☐ 780 Terry Kennedy	.25	.11
☐ 781 Dave Kingman	3.00	1.35
☐ 782 Bob Knepper	.25	.11
☐ 783 Ken Kravec	.25	.11
☐ 784 Bob Lacey	.25	.11
☐ 785 Dennis Lamp	.25	.11
☐ 786 Rafael Landestoy	.25	.11
☐ 787 Ken Landreaux	.25	.11
☐ 788 Carney Lansford	1.00	.45
☐ 789 Dave LaRoche	.25	.11
☐ 790 Joe Lefebvre	.25	.11
☐ 791 Ron LeFlore	1.00	.45
☐ 792 Randy Lerch	.25	.11
☐ 793 Sixto Lezcano	.25	.11
☐ 794 John Littlefield	.25	.11
☐ 795 Mike Lum	.25	.11
☐ 796 Greg Luzinski	1.00	.45
☐ 797 Fred Lynn	1.00	.45
☐ 798 Jerry Martin	.25	.11
☐ 799 Buck Martinez	.25	.11
☐ 800 Gary Matthews	1.00	.45
☐ 801 Mario Mendoza	.25	.11
☐ 802 Larry Milbourne	.25	.11
☐ 803 Rick Miller	.25	.11
☐ 804 John Montefusco	.25	.11
☐ 805 Jerry Morales	.25	.11
☐ 806 Jose Morales	.25	.11
☐ 807 Joe Morgan	4.00	1.80
☐ 808 Jerry Mumphrey	.25	.11
☐ 809 Gene Nelson	.25	.11
☐ 810 Ed Ott	.25	.11
☐ 811 Bob Owchinko	.25	.11
☐ 812 Gaylord Perry	4.00	1.80
☐ 813 Mike Phillips	.25	.11
☐ 814 Darrell Porter	.25	.11
☐ 815 Mike Proly	.25	.11
☐ 816 Tim Raines	6.00	2.70
☐ 817 Lenny Randle	.25	.11
☐ 818 Doug Rau	.25	.11
☐ 819 Jeff Reardon	3.00	1.35
☐ 820 Ken Reitz	.25	.11
☐ 821 Steve Renko	.25	.11
☐ 822 Rick Reuschel	1.00	.45
☐ 823 Dave Revering	.25	.11
☐ 824 Dave Roberts	.25	.11
☐ 825 Leon Roberts	.25	.11
☐ 826 Joe Rudi	1.00	.45
☐ 827 Kevin Saucier	.25	.11
☐ 828 Tony Scott	.25	.11
☐ 829 Bob Shirley	.25	.11
☐ 830 Ted Simmons	1.00	.45
☐ 831 Lary Sorensen	.25	.11
☐ 832 Jim Spencer	.25	.11
☐ 833 Harry Spilman	.25	.11
☐ 834 Fred Stanley	.25	.11
☐ 835 Rusty Staub	1.00	.45
☐ 836 Bill Stein	.25	.11
☐ 837 Joe Strain	.25	.11
☐ 838 Bruce Sutter	1.00	.45
☐ 839 Don Sutton	4.00	1.80
☐ 840 Steve Swisher	.25	.11
☐ 841 Frank Tanana	1.00	.45
☐ 842 Gene Tenace	1.00	.45
☐ 843 Jason Thompson	.25	.11
☐ 844 Dickie Thon	1.00	.45
☐ 845 Bill Travers	.25	.11
☐ 846 Tom Underwood	.25	.11
☐ 847 John Urrea	.25	.11
☐ 848 Mike Vail	.25	.11
☐ 849 Ellis Valentine	.25	.11
☐ 850 Fernando Valenzuela	6.00	2.70
☐ 851 Pete Vuckovich	1.00	.45
☐ 852 Mark Wagner	.25	.11
☐ 853 Bob Walk	1.00	.45
☐ 854 Claudell Washington	.25	.11
☐ 855 Dave Winfield	5.00	2.20
☐ 856 Geoff Zahn	.25	.11
☐ 857 Richie Zisk	.25	.11
☐ 858 Checklist 727-858	.25	.11

1981 Topps Scratchoffs

The cards in this 108-card set measure 1 13/16" by 3 1/4" in a three-card panel measuring 3 1/4" by 5 1/4". The 1981 Topps Scratch-Offs were issued in their own wrapper with bubble gum. The title "Scratch-Off" refers to the black dots of each card which, when rubbed or scraped with a hard edge, reveal a baseball game. While there are only 108 possible individual cards in the set, there are 144 possible panels combinations. The N.L. players appear with green backgrounds and A.L. players with red backgrounds. The numbering of the cards in the set is according to league with American Leaguers (1-54) and National Leaguers (55-108). Some cards are found without dots. An intact panel is worth 20 percent more than the sum of its individual cards.

	NRMT	VG-E
COMPLETE SET (108)	10.00	4.50
COMMON CARD (1-108)	.10	.05

☐ 1 George Brett	1.00	.45
☐ 2 Cecil Cooper	.15	.07
☐ 3 Reggie Jackson	.60	.25
☐ 4 Al Oliver	.15	.07
☐ 5 Fred Lynn	.15	.07
☐ 6 Tony Armas	.10	.05
☐ 7 Ben Oglivie	.10	.05
☐ 8 Tony Perez	.40	.18
☐ 9 Eddie Murray	.60	.25
☐ 10 Robin Yount	.40	.18
☐ 11 Steve Kemp	.10	.05
☐ 12 Joe Charboneau	.25	.11
☐ 13 Jim Rice	.25	.11
☐ 14 Lance Parrish	.15	.07
☐ 15 John Mayberry	.10	.05
☐ 16 Richie Zisk	.10	.05
☐ 17 Ken Singleton	.10	.05
☐ 18 Rod Carew	.40	.18
☐ 19 Rick Manning	.10	.05
☐ 20 Willie Wilson	.15	.07
☐ 21 Buddy Bell	.15	.07
☐ 22 Dave Revering	.10	.05
☐ 23 Tom Paciorek	.15	.07
☐ 24 Champ Summers	.10	.05
☐ 25 Carney Lansford	.15	.07
☐ 26 Lamar Johnson	.10	.05
☐ 27 Willie Aikens	.10	.05
☐ 28 Rick Cerone	.10	.05
☐ 29 Al Bumbry	.10	.05
☐ 30 Bruce Bochte	.10	.05
☐ 31 Mickey Rivers	.15	.07
☐ 32 Mike Hargrove	.15	.07
☐ 33 John Castino	.10	.05
☐ 34 Chet Lemon	.10	.05
☐ 35 Paul Molitor	.60	.25
☐ 36 Willie Randolph	.15	.07
☐ 37 Rick Burleson	.10	.05
☐ 38 Alan Trammell	.50	.23
☐ 39 Rickey Henderson	.60	.25
☐ 40 Dan Meyer	.10	.05
☐ 41 Ken Landreaux	.10	.05
☐ 42 Damaso Garcia	.10	.05
☐ 43 Roy Smalley	.10	.05
☐ 44 Otto Velez	.10	.05
☐ 45 Sixto Lezcano	.10	.05
☐ 46 Toby Harrah	.15	.07
☐ 47 Frank White	.15	.07
☐ 48 Dave Stapleton	.10	.05
☐ 49 Steve Stone	.10	.05
☐ 50 Jim Palmer	.40	.18
☐ 51 Larry Gura	.10	.05
☐ 52 Tommy John	.25	.11
☐ 53 Mike Norris	.10	.05
☐ 54 Ed Farmer	.10	.05
☐ 55 Bill Buckner	.15	.07
☐ 56 Steve Garvey	.25	.11
☐ 57 Reggie Smith	.15	.07
☐ 58 Bake McBride	.10	.05
☐ 59 Dave Parker	.15	.07
☐ 60 Mike Schmidt	.75	.35
☐ 61 Bob Horner	.10	.05
☐ 62 Pete Rose	.75	.35
☐ 63 Ted Simmons	.15	.07
☐ 64 Johnny Bench	.40	.18
☐ 65 George Foster	.15	.07
☐ 66 Gary Carter	.25	.11
☐ 67 Keith Hernandez	.15	.07
☐ 68 Ozzie Smith	.75	.35
☐ 69 Dave Kingman	.15	.07
☐ 70 Jack Clark	.15	.07
☐ 71 Dusty Baker	.15	.07
☐ 72 Dale Murphy	.40	.18
☐ 73 Ron Cey	.15	.07
☐ 74 Greg Luzinski	.15	.07
☐ 75 Lee Mazzilli	.10	.05
☐ 76 Gary Matthews	.10	.05
☐ 77 Cesar Cedeno	.10	.05
☐ 78 Warren Cromartie	.10	.05
☐ 79 Steve Henderson	.10	.05
☐ 80 Ellis Valentine	.10	.05
☐ 81 Mike Easler	.10	.05
☐ 82 Garry Templeton	.10	.05
☐ 83 Jose Cruz	.15	.07
☐ 84 Dave Collins	.10	.05
☐ 85 George Hendrick	.10	.05
☐ 86 Gene Richards	.10	.05
☐ 87 Terry Whitfield	.10	.05
☐ 88 Terry Puhl	.10	.05
☐ 89 Larry Parrish	.10	.05
☐ 90 Andre Dawson	.40	.18
☐ 91 Ken Griffey	.15	.07
☐ 92 Dave Lopes	.15	.07
☐ 93 Doug Flynn	.10	.05
☐ 94 Ivan DeJesus	.10	.05
☐ 95 Dave Concepcion	.15	.07
☐ 96 John Stearns	.10	.05
☐ 97 Jerry Mumphrey	.10	.05
☐ 98 Jerry Martin	.10	.05
☐ 99 Art Howe	.15	.07
☐ 100 Omar Moreno	.10	.05
☐ 101 Ken Reitz	.10	.05
☐ 102 Phil Garner	.15	.07
☐ 103 Jerry Reuss	.15	.07
☐ 104 Steve Carlton	.40	.18
☐ 105 Jim Bibby	.10	.05
☐ 106 Steve Rogers	.10	.05
☐ 107 Tom Seaver	.40	.18
☐ 108 Vida Blue	.15	.07

1981 Topps Stickers

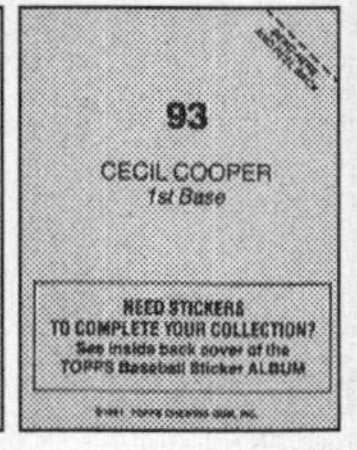

Made for Topps by Panini, an Italian company, these 262 stickers measure 1 15/16" by 2 9/16" and are numbered on both front and back. The set was the first of the Topps/O-Pee-Chee/Panini genre of sticker sets. The fronts feature white-bordered color player action shots. The backs carry the player's name and position. Team affiliations are not shown. An album onto which the stickers could be affixed was available at retail stores. The first 32 stickers depict 1980 major league pitching and batting leaders. Stickers 33-240 are arranged by teams as follows: Baltimore Orioles (33-40), Boston Red Sox (41-48), California Angels (49-56), Chicago White Sox (57-64), Cleveland Indians (65-72), Detroit Tigers (73-80), Kansas City Royals (81-88), Milwaukee Brewers (91-98), Minnesota Twins (99-106), New York Yankees (107-114), Oakland A's (115-122), Seattle Mariners (123-130), Texas Rangers (130-136), Toronto Blue Jays (137-143), Atlanta Braves (144-150), Chicago Cubs (151-158), Cincinnati Reds (159-166), Houston Astros (167-174), Los Angeles Dodgers (175-182), Montreal Expos (183-190), New York Mets (191-198), Philadelphia Phillies (199-208), Pittsburgh Pirates (209-216), St. Louis Cardinals (217-224), San Diego Padres (225-232) and San Francisco Giants (233-240). Stickers 241-262 have color photos of "All-Star" players printed on silver (AL) or gold (NL) foil.

	NRMT	VG-E
COMPLETE SET (262)	25.00	11.00
COMMON STICKER (1-240)	.05	.02
COMMON FOIL (241-262)	.10	.05

☐ 1 Steve Stone	.05	.02
☐ 2 Tommy John	.15	.07

Mike Norris		
☐ 3 Rudy May	.05	.02
☐ 4 Mike Norris	.05	.02
☐ 5 Len Barker	.05	.02
☐ 6 Mike Norris	.05	.02
☐ 7 Dan Quisenberry	.15	.07
☐ 8 Rich Gossage	.25	.11
☐ 9 George Brett	2.50	1.10
☐ 10 Cecil Cooper	.15	.07
☐ 11 Reggie Jackson	.40	.18
Ben Oglivie		
☐ 12 Gorman Thomas	.05	.02
☐ 13 Cecil Cooper	.15	.07
☐ 14 George Brett	1.25	.55
Ben Oglivie		
☐ 15 Rickey Henderson	2.50	1.10
☐ 16 Willie Wilson	.15	.07
☐ 17 Bill Buckner	.15	.07
☐ 18 Keith Hernandez	.15	.07
☐ 19 Mike Schmidt	1.50	.70
☐ 20 Bob Horner	.05	.02
☐ 21 Mike Schmidt	1.50	.70
☐ 22 George Hendrick	.05	.02
☐ 23 Ron LeFlore	.15	.07
☐ 24 Omar Moreno	.05	.02
☐ 25 Steve Carlton	.60	.25
☐ 26 Joe Niekro	.15	.07
☐ 27 Don Sutton	.25	.11
☐ 28 Steve Carlton	.60	.25
☐ 29 Steve Carlton	.60	.25
☐ 30 Nolan Ryan	3.00	1.35
☐ 31 Rollie Fingers	.15	.07
Tom Hume		
☐ 32 Bruce Sutter	.15	.07
☐ 33 Ken Singleton	.05	.02
☐ 34 Eddie Murray	2.00	.90
☐ 35 Al Bumbry	.05	.02
☐ 36 Rich Dauer	.05	.02
☐ 37 Scott McGregor	.05	.02
☐ 38 Rick Dempsey	.15	.07
☐ 39 Jim Palmer	.40	.18
☐ 40 Steve Stone	.05	.02
☐ 41 Jim Rice	.25	.11
☐ 42 Fred Lynn	.15	.07
☐ 43 Carney Lansford	.15	.07
☐ 44 Tony Perez	.25	.11
☐ 45 Carl Yastrzemski	.60	.25
☐ 46 Carlton Fisk	.75	.35
☐ 47 Dave Stapleton	.05	.02
☐ 48 Dennis Eckersley	.30	.14
☐ 49 Rod Carew	.60	.25
☐ 50 Brian Downing	.15	.07
☐ 51 Don Baylor	.25	.11
☐ 52 Rick Burleson	.05	.02
☐ 53 Bobby Grich	.15	.07
☐ 54 Butch Hobson	.05	.02
☐ 55 Andy Hassler	.05	.02
☐ 56 Frank Tanana	.15	.07
☐ 57 Chet Lemon	.05	.02
☐ 58 Lamar Johnson	.05	.02
☐ 59 Wayne Nordhagen	.05	.02
☐ 60 Jim Morrison	.05	.02
☐ 61 Bob Molinaro	.05	.02
☐ 62 Rich Dotson	.05	.02
☐ 63 Britt Burns	.05	.02
☐ 64 Ed Farmer	.05	.02
☐ 65 Toby Harrah	.15	.07
☐ 66 Joe Charboneau	.25	.11
☐ 67 Miguel Dilone	.05	.02
☐ 68 Mike Hargrove	.15	.07
☐ 69 Rick Manning	.05	.02
☐ 70 Andre Thornton	.15	.07
☐ 71 Ron Hassey	.05	.02
☐ 72 Len Barker	.05	.02
☐ 73 Lance Parrish	.15	.07
☐ 74 Steve Kemp	.05	.02
☐ 75 Alan Trammell	.75	.35
☐ 76 Champ Summers	.05	.02
☐ 77 Rick Peters	.05	.02
☐ 78 Kirk Gibson	1.25	.55
☐ 79 Johnny Wockenfuss	.05	.02
☐ 80 Jack Morris	.25	.11
☐ 81 Willie Wilson	.15	.07
☐ 82 George Brett	2.50	1.10
☐ 83 Frank White	.15	.07
☐ 84 Willie Aikens	.05	.02
☐ 85 Clint Hurdle	.05	.02
☐ 86 Hal McRae	.15	.07
☐ 87 Dennis Leonard	.05	.02
☐ 88 Larry Gura	.05	.02
☐ 89 AL Pennant Winner	.05	.02
☐ 90 AL Pennant Winner	.05	.02
☐ 91 Paul Molitor	1.50	.70
☐ 92 Ben Oglivie	.15	.07
☐ 93 Cecil Cooper	.15	.07
☐ 94 Ted Simmons	.15	.07
☐ 95 Robin Yount	.75	.35
☐ 96 Gorman Thomas	.05	.02
☐ 97 Mike Caldwell	.05	.02
☐ 98 Moose Haas	.05	.02
☐ 99 John Castino	.05	.02
☐ 100 Roy Smalley	.05	.02
☐ 101 Ken Landreaux	.05	.02
☐ 102 Butch Wynegar	.05	.02
☐ 103 Ron Jackson	.05	.02
☐ 104 Jerry Koosman	.15	.07
☐ 105 Roger Erickson	.05	.02
☐ 106 Doug Corbett	.05	.02
☐ 107 Reggie Jackson	.75	.35
☐ 108 Willie Randolph	.15	.07
☐ 109 Rick Cerone	.05	.02
☐ 110 Bucky Dent	.15	.07
☐ 111 Dave Winfield	.75	.35
☐ 112 Ron Guidry	.15	.07
☐ 113 Rich Gossage	.25	.11
☐ 114 Tommy John	.25	.11
☐ 115 Rickey Henderson	2.50	1.10
☐ 116 Tony Armas	.05	.02
☐ 117 Dave Revering	.05	.02
☐ 118 Wayne Gross	.05	.02
☐ 119 Dwayne Murphy	.05	.02
☐ 120 Jeff Newman	.05	.02
☐ 121 Rick Langford	.05	.02
☐ 122 Mike Norris	.05	.02
☐ 123 Bruce Bochte	.05	.02
☐ 124 Tom Paciorek	.05	.02
☐ 125 Dan Meyer	.05	.02
☐ 126 Julio Cruz	.05	.02
☐ 127 Richie Zisk	.05	.02
☐ 128 Floyd Bannister	.05	.02
☐ 129 Shane Rawley	.05	.02
☐ 130 Buddy Bell	.15	.07
☐ 131 Al Oliver	.15	.07
☐ 132 Mickey Rivers	.15	.07
☐ 133 Jim Sundberg	.15	.07
☐ 134 Bump Wills	.05	.02
☐ 135 Jon Matlack	.05	.02
☐ 136 Danny Darwin	.15	.07
☐ 137 Damaso Garcia	.05	.02
☐ 138 Otto Velez	.05	.02
☐ 139 John Mayberry	.05	.02
☐ 140 Alfredo Griffin	.05	.02
☐ 141 Alvis Woods	.05	.02
☐ 142 Dave Stieb	.15	.07
☐ 143 Jim Clancy	.05	.02
☐ 144 Gary Matthews	.15	.07
☐ 145 Bob Horner	.15	.07
☐ 146 Dale Murphy	.50	.23
☐ 147 Chris Chambliss	.15	.07
☐ 148 Phil Niekro	.25	.11
☐ 149 Glenn Hubbard	.05	.02
☐ 150 Rick Camp	.05	.02
☐ 151 Dave Kingman	.15	.07
☐ 152 Bill Caudill	.05	.02
☐ 153 Bill Buckner	.15	.07
☐ 154 Barry Foote	.05	.02
☐ 155 Mike Tyson	.05	.02
☐ 156 Ivan DeJesus	.05	.02
☐ 157 Rick Reuschel	.15	.07
☐ 158 Ken Reitz	.05	.02
☐ 159 George Foster	.15	.07
☐ 160 Johnny Bench	.75	.35
☐ 161 Dave Concepcion	.15	.07
☐ 162 Dave Collins	.05	.02
☐ 163 Ken Griffey	.15	.07
☐ 164 Dan Driessen	.05	.02
☐ 165 Tom Seaver	.75	.35
☐ 166 Tom Hume	.05	.02
☐ 167 Cesar Cedeno	.15	.07
☐ 168 Rafael Landestoy	.05	.02
☐ 169 Jose Cruz	.15	.07
☐ 170 Art Howe	.05	.02
☐ 171 Terry Puhl	.05	.02
☐ 172 Joe Sambito	.05	.02
☐ 173 Nolan Ryan	3.00	1.35
☐ 174 Joe Niekro	.15	.07
☐ 175 Dave Lopes	.15	.07
☐ 176 Steve Garvey	.25	.11
☐ 177 Ron Cey	.15	.07
☐ 178 Reggie Smith	.15	.07
☐ 179 Bill Russell	.15	.07
☐ 180 Burt Hooton	.05	.02
☐ 181 Jerry Reuss	.15	.07
☐ 182 Dusty Baker	.15	.07
☐ 183 Larry Parrish	.05	.02
☐ 184 Gary Carter	.30	.14
☐ 185 Rodney Scott	.05	.02
☐ 186 Ellis Valentine	.05	.02
☐ 187 Andre Dawson	.75	.35
☐ 188 Warren Cromartie	.05	.02
☐ 189 Chris Speier	.05	.02
☐ 190 Steve Rogers	.05	.02
☐ 191 Lee Mazzilli	.05	.02
☐ 192 Doug Flynn	.05	.02
☐ 193 Steve Henderson	.05	.02
☐ 194 John Stearns	.05	.02
☐ 195 Joel Youngblood	.05	.02
☐ 196 Frank Taveras	.05	.02
☐ 197 Pat Zachry	.05	.02
☐ 198 Neil Allen	.05	.02
☐ 199 Mike Schmidt	1.50	.70
☐ 200 Pete Rose	1.25	.55
☐ 201 Larry Bowa	.15	.07
☐ 202 Bake McBride	.05	.02
☐ 203 Bob Boone	.15	.07
☐ 204 Garry Maddox	.05	.02
☐ 205 Tug McGraw	.15	.07
☐ 206 Steve Carlton	.50	.23
☐ 207 NL Pennant Winner	.05	.02
(World Champions)		
☐ 208 NL Pennant Winner	.05	.02
(World Champions)		
☐ 209 Phil Garner	.15	.07
☐ 210 Dave Parker	.15	.07
☐ 211 Omar Moreno	.05	.02
☐ 212 Mike Easler	.05	.02
☐ 213 Bill Madlock	.15	.07
☐ 214 Ed Ott	.05	.02
☐ 215 Willie Stargell	.40	.18
☐ 216 Jim Bibby	.05	.02
☐ 217 Garry Templeton	.05	.02
☐ 218 Sixto Lezcano	.05	.02
☐ 219 Keith Hernandez	.15	.07
☐ 220 George Hendrick	.05	.02
☐ 221 Bruce Sutter	.15	.07
☐ 222 Ken Oberkfell	.05	.02
☐ 223 Tony Scott	.05	.02
☐ 224 Darrell Porter	.15	.07
☐ 225 Gene Richards	.05	.02
☐ 226 Broderick Perkins	.05	.02
☐ 227 Jerry Mumphrey	.05	.02
☐ 228 Luis Salazar	.05	.02
☐ 229 Jerry Turner	.05	.02
☐ 230 Ozzie Smith	2.50	1.10
☐ 231 John Curtis	.05	.02
☐ 232 Rick Wise	.05	.02
☐ 233 Terry Whitfield	.05	.02
☐ 234 Jack Clark	.15	.07
☐ 235 Darrell Evans	.15	.07
☐ 236 Larry Herndon	.05	.02
☐ 237 Milt May	.05	.02
☐ 238 Greg Minton	.05	.02
☐ 239 Vida Blue	.15	.07
☐ 240 Eddie Whitson	.05	.02
☐ 241 Cecil Cooper FOIL	.25	.11
☐ 242 Willie Randolph FOIL	.15	.07
☐ 243 George Brett FOIL	3.00	1.35
☐ 244 Robin Yount FOIL	1.00	.45
☐ 245 Reggie Jackson FOIL	1.00	.45
☐ 246 Al Oliver FOIL	.25	.11
☐ 247 Willie Wilson FOIL	.25	.11
☐ 248 Rick Cerone FOIL	.10	.05
☐ 249 Steve Stone FOIL	.10	.05
☐ 250 Tommy John FOIL	.25	.11
☐ 251 Rich Gossage FOIL	.25	.11
☐ 252 Steve Garvey FOIL	.25	.11
☐ 253 Phil Garner FOIL	.25	.11
☐ 254 Mike Schmidt FOIL	2.00	.90
☐ 255 Garry Templeton FOIL	.10	.05
☐ 256 George Hendrick FOIL	.10	.05
☐ 257 Dave Parker FOIL	.25	.11
☐ 258 Cesar Cedeno FOIL	.25	.11
☐ 259 Gary Carter FOIL	.40	.18
☐ 260 Jim Bibby FOIL	.10	.05
☐ 261 Steve Carlton FOIL	.75	.35
☐ 262 Tug McGraw FOIL	.25	.11
☐ xx Album	1.00	.45

1981 Topps Super Home Team

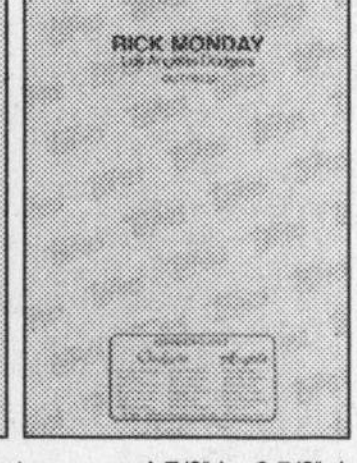

The cards in this 102-card set measure 4 7/8" by 6 7/8". In 1981 Topps issued an attractive series of photos of players from eleven AL and NL teams. The Phillies, Red Sox and Reds each were marketed in twelve-player subsets. Eighteen-player subsets were issued for the following areas: Chicago (nine White Sox and nine Cubs); New York (twelve Yankees and six Mets); Los Angeles (twelve Dodgers and six Angels); and Texas (six Rangers and six Astros). The cards of each subset contain a subset checklist on the reverse. Team sets could be obtained via a mail offer printed on the wrapper. These cards are often sold by the team or team pair. The checklist below is organized alphabetically by team(s); Boston (1-12), Chicago (13-30), Cincinnati (31-42), Los Angeles (43-60), New York (61-78), Philadelphia (79-90) and Texas (91-102).

	NRMT	VG-E
COMPLETE SET (102)	35.00	16.00
COMMON CARD (1-102)	.15	.07
☐ 1 Tom Burgmeier	.15	.07
☐ 2 Dennis Eckersley	.75	.35
☐ 3 Dwight Evans	.50	.23
☐ 4 Carlton Fisk	1.00	.45
☐ 5 Glenn Hoffman	.15	.07
☐ 6 Carney Lansford	.25	.11
☐ 7 Tony Perez	.75	.35
☐ 8 Jim Rice	.50	.23
☐ 9 Bob Stanley	.15	.07
☐ 10 Dave Stapleton	.15	.07
☐ 11 Frank Tanana	.25	.11
☐ 12 Carl Yastrzemski	1.00	.45
☐ 13 Britt Burns	.15	.07
☐ 14 Rich Dotson	.15	.07
☐ 15 Ed Farmer	.15	.07
☐ 16 Lamar Johnson	.15	.07
☐ 17 Ron LeFlore	.15	.07
☐ 18 Chet Lemon	.15	.07
☐ 19 Bob Molinaro	.15	.07
☐ 20 Jim Morrison	.15	.07
☐ 21 Wayne Nordhagen	.15	.07
☐ 22 Tim Blackwell	.15	.07
☐ 23 Bill Buckner	.25	.11
☐ 24 Ivan DeJesus	.15	.07
☐ 25 Leon Durham	.25	.11
☐ 26 Dave Kingman	.50	.23
☐ 27 Mike Krukow	.15	.07
☐ 28 Ken Reitz	.15	.07
☐ 29 Rick Reuschel	.25	.11
☐ 30 Mike Tyson	.15	.07
☐ 31 Johnny Bench	1.00	.45
☐ 32 Dave Collins	.15	.07
☐ 33 Dave Concepcion	.25	.11
☐ 34 Dan Driessen	.15	.07
☐ 35 George Foster	.25	.11
☐ 36 Ken Griffey	.25	.11
☐ 37 Tom Hume	.15	.07
☐ 38 Ray Knight	.25	.11
☐ 39 Joe Nolan	.15	.07
☐ 40 Ron Oester	.15	.07
☐ 41 Tom Seaver	1.00	.45
☐ 42 Mario Soto	.15	.07
☐ 43 Dusty Baker	.25	.11
☐ 44 Ron Cey	.25	.11
☐ 45 Steve Garvey	.50	.23
☐ 46 Burt Hooton	.15	.07
☐ 47 Steve Howe	.15	.07
☐ 48 Davey Lopes	.25	.11
☐ 49 Rick Monday	.25	.11
☐ 50 Jerry Reuss	.25	.11
☐ 51 Bill Russell	.25	.11
☐ 52 Reggie Smith	.25	.11
☐ 53 Bob Welch	.25	.11
☐ 54 Steve Yeager	.15	.07
☐ 55 Don Baylor	.50	.23
☐ 56 Rick Burleson	.15	.07
☐ 57 Rod Carew	1.00	.45
☐ 58 Bobby Grich	.25	.11
☐ 59 Butch Hobson	.15	.07
☐ 60 Fred Lynn	.25	.11
☐ 61 Rick Cerone	.15	.07
☐ 62 Bucky Dent	.25	.11
☐ 63 Rich Gossage	.50	.23
☐ 64 Ron Guidry	.25	.11
☐ 65 Reggie Jackson	1.00	.45
☐ 66 Tommy John	.50	.23
☐ 67 Ruppert Jones	.15	.07
☐ 68 Rudy May	.15	.07
☐ 69 Graig Nettles	.50	.23
☐ 70 Willie Randolph	.25	.11
☐ 71 Bob Watson	.50	.23
☐ 72 Dave Winfield	1.00	.45
☐ 73 Neil Allen	.15	.07
☐ 74 Doug Flynn	.15	.07
☐ 75 Lee Mazzilli	.15	.07
☐ 76 Rusty Staub	.25	.11
☐ 77 Frank Taveras	.15	.07
☐ 78 Alex Trevino	.15	.07
☐ 79 Bob Boone	.25	.11
☐ 80 Larry Bowa	.25	.11
☐ 81 Steve Carlton	1.00	.45
☐ 82 Greg Luzinski	.25	.11
☐ 83 Garry Maddox	.15	.07
☐ 84 Bake McBride	.15	.07
☐ 85 Tug McGraw	.25	.11
☐ 86 Pete Rose	1.25	.55
☐ 87 Dick Ruthven	.15	.07
☐ 88 Mike Schmidt	1.25	.55
☐ 89 Manny Trillo	.15	.07
☐ 90 Del Unser	.15	.07
☐ 91 Buddy Bell	.25	.11
☐ 92 Jon Matlack	.15	.07
☐ 93 Al Oliver	.25	.11
☐ 94 Mickey Rivers	.25	.11
☐ 95 Jim Sundberg	.25	.11
☐ 96 Bump Wills	.15	.07
☐ 97 Cesar Cedeno	.25	.11
☐ 98 Jose Cruz	.50	.23
☐ 99 Art Howe	.25	.11
☐ 100 Terry Puhl	.15	.07
☐ 101 Nolan Ryan	3.00	1.35
☐ 102 Don Sutton	.75	.35

1981 Topps Super National

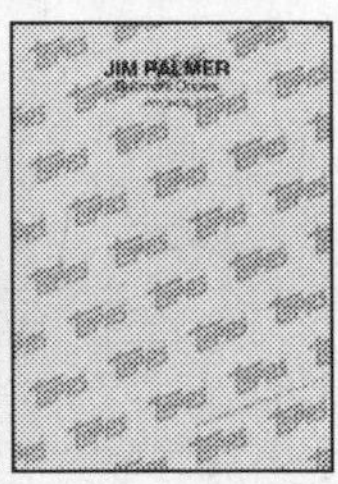

The cards in this 15-card set measure 4 7/8" by 6 7/8". In a format similar to the Home Team series of 1981 and the Super Star Photo set of 1980, these cards feature excellent photos of the top stars of 1981. The pictures of players appearing in both the regional Home Team and National sets are identical, but Brett, Cooper, Palmer, Parker and Simmons are unique to the latter and are indicated in the checklist below with an asterisk. The backs of the cards contain the player's name, team and position and a single copyright line.

	NRMT	VG-E
COMPLETE SET (15)	4.00	1.80
COMMON CARD (1-15)	.10	.05
☐ 1 Buddy Bell	.20	.09
☐ 2 Johnny Bench	.50	.23
☐ 3 George Brett	1.00	.45
☐ 4 Rod Carew	.40	.18
☐ 5 Cecil Cooper	.10	.05
☐ 6 Steve Garvey	.30	.14
☐ 7 Rich Gossage	.20	.09
☐ 8 Reggie Jackson	.50	.23
☐ 9 Jim Palmer	.40	.18
☐ 10 Dave Parker	.20	.09
☐ 11 Jim Rice	.20	.09
☐ 12 Pete Rose	.75	.35
☐ 13 Mike Schmidt	.75	.35
☐ 14 Tom Seaver	.50	.23
☐ 15 Ted Simmons	.20	.09

1981 Topps Team Checklist Sheet

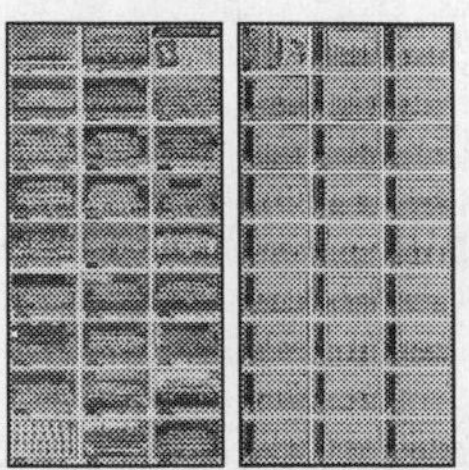

As part of a mail-away offer, Topps offered all 26 1981 team checklist cards on an uncut sheet. These cards enabled the collector to have an easy reference for which card(s) he/she needed to finish their sets. When cut form the sheet, all cards measure the standard size.

	NRMT	VG-E
COMPLETE SET (1)	15.00	6.75
COMMON SHEET (1)	15.00	6.75
☐ 1 Team Checklist Sheet	15.00	6.75

1982 Topps

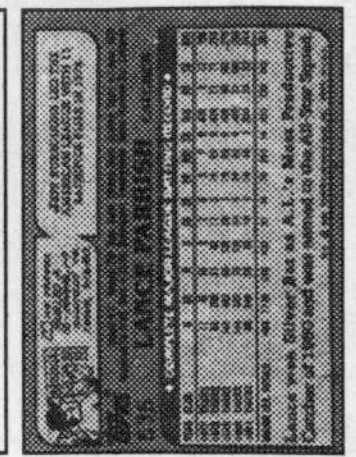

The cards in this 792-card set measure the standard size. The 1982 baseball series was the first of the largest sets Topps issued at one printing. The 66-card increase from the previous year's total eliminated the "double print" practice, that had occurred in every regular issue since 1978. Cards 1-6 depict Highlights of the strike-shortened 1981 season, cards 161-168 picture League Leaders, and there are subsets of AL (547-557) and NL (337-347) All-Stars (AS). The abbreviation "SA" in the checklist is given for the 40 "Super Action" cards introduced in this set. The team cards are actually Team Leader (TL) cards picturing the batting average and ERA leader for that team with a checklist back. All 26 of these cards were available from Topps on a perforated sheet through an offer on wax pack wrappers. Cards were primarily distributed in 15-card wax packs and 51-card rack packs. Notable Rookie Cards include Brett Butler, Chili Davis, Cal Ripken Jr., Lee Smith, and Dave Stewart. Be careful when purchasing blank-back Cal Ripken Jr. Rookie Cards. Those cards are undoubtedly counterfeit.

	NRMT	VG-E
COMPLETE SET (792)	120.00	55.00
COMMON CARD (1-792)	.15	.07
☐ 1 Steve Carlton HL Sets new NL strikeout record	1.00	.45
☐ 2 Ron Davis HL Fans 8 straight in relief	.30	.14
☐ 3 Tim Raines HL 71 steals as rookie	.60	.25
☐ 4 Pete Rose HL Sets NL hit mark	1.00	.45
☐ 5 Nolan Ryan HL Pitches fifth no-hitter	3.00	1.35
☐ 6 Fernando Valenzuela HL 8 shutouts as rookie	.30	.14
☐ 7 Scott Sanderson	.15	.07
☐ 8 Rich Dauer	.15	.07
☐ 9 Ron Guidry	.30	.14
☐ 10 Ron Guidry SA	.30	.14
☐ 11 Gary Alexander	.15	.07
☐ 12 Moose Haas	.15	.07
☐ 13 Lamar Johnson	.15	.07
☐ 14 Steve Howe	.15	.07
☐ 15 Ellis Valentine	.15	.07
☐ 16 Steve Comer	.15	.07
☐ 17 Darrell Evans	.30	.14
☐ 18 Fernando Arroyo	.15	.07
☐ 19 Ernie Whitt	.15	.07
☐ 20 Garry Maddox	.15	.07
☐ 21 Orioles Rookies Bob Bonner Cal Ripken Jeff Schneider	70.00	32.00
☐ 22 Jim Beattie	.15	.07
☐ 23 Willie Hernandez	.30	.14
☐ 24 Dave Frost	.15	.07
☐ 25 Jerry Remy	.15	.07
☐ 26 Jorge Orta	.15	.07
☐ 27 Tom Herr	.30	.14
☐ 28 John Urrea	.15	.07
☐ 29 Dwayne Murphy	.15	.07
☐ 30 Tom Seaver	1.50	.70
☐ 31 Tom Seaver SA	1.25	.55
☐ 32 Gene Garber	.15	.07
☐ 33 Jerry Morales	.15	.07
☐ 34 Joe Sambito	.15	.07
☐ 35 Willie Aikens	.15	.07
☐ 36 Rangers TL BA: Al Oliver Pitching: Doc Medich (Checklist on back)	.60	.25
☐ 37 Dan Graham	.15	.07
☐ 38 Charlie Lea	.15	.07
☐ 39 Lou Whitaker	1.25	.55
☐ 40 Dave Parker	.30	.14
☐ 41 Dave Parker SA	.30	.14
☐ 42 Rick Sofield	.15	.07
☐ 43 Mike Cubbage	.15	.07

☐ 44 Britt Burns .15 .07
☐ 45 Rick Cerone .15 .07
☐ 46 Jerry Augustine .15 .07
☐ 47 Jeff Leonard .15 .07
☐ 48 Bobby Castillo .15 .07
☐ 49 Alvis Woods .15 .07
☐ 50 Buddy Bell .30 .14
☐ 51 Cubs Rookies .60 .25
Jay Howell
Carlos Lezcano
Ty Waller
☐ 52 Larry Andersen .15 .07
☐ 53 Greg Gross .15 .07
☐ 54 Ron Hassey .15 .07
☐ 55 Rick Burleson .15 .07
☐ 56 Mark Littell .15 .07
☐ 57 Craig Reynolds .15 .07
☐ 58 John D'Acquisto .15 .07
☐ 59 Rich Gedman .30 .14
☐ 60 Tony Armas .15 .07
☐ 61 Tommy Boggs .15 .07
☐ 62 Mike Tyson .15 .07
☐ 63 Mario Soto .15 .07
☐ 64 Lynn Jones .15 .07
☐ 65 Terry Kennedy .15 .07
☐ 66 Astros TL 2.00 .90
BA: Art Howe
Pitching: Nolan Ryan
(Checklist on back)
☐ 67 Rich Gale .15 .07
☐ 68 Roy Howell .15 .07
☐ 69 Al Williams .15 .07
☐ 70 Tim Raines 1.25 .55
☐ 71 Roy Lee Jackson .15 .07
☐ 72 Rick Auerbach .15 .07
☐ 73 Buddy Solomon .15 .07
☐ 74 Bob Clark .15 .07
☐ 75 Tommy John .60 .25
☐ 76 Greg Pryor .15 .07
☐ 77 Miguel Dilone .15 .07
☐ 78 George Medich .15 .07
☐ 79 Bob Bailor .15 .07
☐ 80 Jim Palmer 1.25 .55
☐ 81 Jim Palmer SA .60 .25
☐ 82 Bob Welch .30 .14
☐ 83 Yankees Rookies .60 .25
Steve Balboni
Andy McGaffigan
Andre Robertson
☐ 84 Rennie Stennett .15 .07
☐ 85 Lynn McGlothen .15 .07
☐ 86 Dane Iorg .15 .07
☐ 87 Matt Keough .15 .07
☐ 88 Biff Pocoroba .15 .07
☐ 89 Steve Henderson .15 .07
☐ 90 Nolan Ryan 6.00 2.70
☐ 91 Carney Lansford .30 .14
☐ 92 Brad Havens .15 .07
☐ 93 Larry Hisle .15 .07
☐ 94 Andy Hassler .15 .07
☐ 95 Ozzie Smith 3.00 1.35
☐ 96 Royals TL 1.25 .55
BA: George Brett
Pitching: Larry Gura
(Checklist on back)
☐ 97 Paul Moskau .15 .07
☐ 98 Terry Bulling .15 .07
☐ 99 Barry Bonnell .15 .07
☐ 100 Mike Schmidt 1.50 .70
☐ 101 Mike Schmidt SA 1.50 .70
☐ 102 Dan Briggs .15 .07
☐ 103 Bob Lacey .15 .07
☐ 104 Rance Mulliniks .15 .07
☐ 105 Kirk Gibson 1.00 .45
☐ 106 Enrique Romo .15 .07
☐ 107 Wayne Krenchicki .15 .07
☐ 108 Bob Sykes .15 .07
☐ 109 Dave Revering .15 .07
☐ 110 Carlton Fisk 1.50 .70
☐ 111 Carlton Fisk SA 1.25 .55
☐ 112 Billy Sample .15 .07
☐ 113 Steve McCatty .15 .07
☐ 114 Ken Landreaux .15 .07
☐ 115 Gaylord Perry 1.25 .55
☐ 116 Jim Wohlford .15 .07
☐ 117 Rawly Eastwick .15 .07
☐ 118 Expos Rookies .30 .14
Terry Francona
Brad Mills
Bryn Smith
☐ 119 Joe Pittman .15 .07
☐ 120 Gary Lucas .15 .07
☐ 121 Ed Lynch .15 .07
☐ 122 Jamie Easterly UER .15 .07
(Photo actually
Reggie Cleveland)
☐ 123 Danny Goodwin .15 .07
☐ 124 Reid Nichols .15 .07
☐ 125 Danny Ainge 1.50 .70
☐ 126 Braves TL .60 .25
BA: Claudell Washington
Pitching: Rick Mahler
(Checklist on back)
☐ 127 Lonnie Smith .30 .14
☐ 128 Frank Pastore .15 .07
☐ 129 Checklist 1-132 .60 .25
☐ 130 Julio Cruz .15 .07
☐ 131 Stan Bahnsen .15 .07
☐ 132 Lee May .30 .14
☐ 133 Pat Underwood .15 .07
☐ 134 Dan Ford .15 .07
☐ 135 Andy Rincon .15 .07
☐ 136 Lenn Sakata .15 .07
☐ 137 George Cappuzzello .15 .07
☐ 138 Tony Pena .30 .14
☐ 139 Jeff Jones .15 .07
☐ 140 Ron LeFlore .30 .14
☐ 141 Indians Rookies .30 .14
Chris Bando
Tom Brennan
Von Hayes
☐ 142 Dave LaRoche .15 .07
☐ 143 Mookie Wilson .30 .14
☐ 144 Fred Breining .15 .07
☐ 145 Bob Horner .30 .14
☐ 146 Mike Griffin .15 .07
☐ 147 Denny Walling .15 .07
☐ 148 Mickey Klutts .15 .07
☐ 149 Pat Putnam .15 .07
☐ 150 Ted Simmons .30 .14
☐ 151 Dave Edwards .15 .07
☐ 152 Ramon Aviles .15 .07
☐ 153 Roger Erickson .15 .07
☐ 154 Dennis Werth .15 .07
☐ 155 Otto Velez .15 .07
☐ 156 Oakland A's TL .60 .25
BA: Rickey Henderson
Pitching: Steve McCatty
(Checklist on back)
☐ 157 Steve Crawford .15 .07
☐ 158 Brian Downing .15 .07
☐ 159 Larry Biittner .15 .07
☐ 160 Luis Tiant .30 .14
☐ 161 Batting Leaders .30 .14
Bill Madlock
Carney Lansford
☐ 162 Home Run Leaders 1.25 .55
Mike Schmidt
Tony Armas
Dwight Evans
Bobby Grich
Eddie Murray
☐ 163 RBI Leaders 1.25 .55
Mike Schmidt
Eddie Murray
☐ 164 Stolen Base Leaders 1.25 .55
Tim Raines
Rickey Henderson
☐ 165 Victory Leaders .60 .25
Tom Seaver
Denny Martinez
Steve McCatty
Jack Morris
Pete Vuckovich
☐ 166 Strikeout Leaders .30 .14
Fernando Valenzuela
Len Barker
☐ 167 ERA Leaders 2.00 .90
Nolan Ryan
Steve McCatty
☐ 168 Leading Firemen .60 .25
Bruce Sutter
Rollie Fingers
☐ 169 Charlie Leibrandt .15 .07
☐ 170 Jim Bibby .15 .07
☐ 171 Giants Rookies 2.00 .90
Bob Brenly
Chili Davis
Bob Tufts
☐ 172 Bill Gullickson .15 .07
☐ 173 Jamie Quirk .15 .07
☐ 174 Dave Ford .15 .07
☐ 175 Jerry Mumphrey .15 .07
☐ 176 Dewey Robinson .15 .07
☐ 177 John Ellis .15 .07
☐ 178 Dyar Miller .15 .07
☐ 179 Steve Garvey .60 .25
☐ 180 Steve Garvey SA .30 .14
☐ 181 Silvio Martinez .15 .07
☐ 182 Larry Herndon .15 .07
☐ 183 Mike Proly .15 .07
☐ 184 Mick Kelleher .15 .07
☐ 185 Phil Niekro 1.25 .55
☐ 186 Cardinals TL .60 .25
BA: Keith Hernandez
Pitching: Bob Forsch
(Checklist on back)
☐ 187 Jeff Newman .15 .07
☐ 188 Randy Martz .15 .07
☐ 189 Glenn Hoffman .15 .07
☐ 190 J.R. Richard .30 .14
☐ 191 Tim Wallach 1.25 .55
☐ 192 Broderick Perkins .15 .07
☐ 193 Darrell Jackson .15 .07
☐ 194 Mike Vail .15 .07
☐ 195 Paul Molitor 2.00 .90
☐ 196 Willie Upshaw .15 .07
☐ 197 Shane Rawley .15 .07
☐ 198 Chris Speier .15 .07
☐ 199 Don Aase .15 .07
☐ 200 George Brett 2.50 1.10
☐ 201 George Brett SA 2.50 1.10
☐ 202 Rick Manning .15 .07
☐ 203 Blue Jays Rookies .60 .25
Jesse Barfield
Brian Milner
Boomer Wells
☐ 204 Gary Roenicke .15 .07
☐ 205 Neil Allen .15 .07
☐ 206 Tony Bernazard .15 .07
☐ 207 Rod Scurry .15 .07
☐ 208 Bobby Murcer .30 .14
☐ 209 Gary Lavelle .15 .07
☐ 210 Keith Hernandez .30 .14
☐ 211 Dan Petry .15 .07
☐ 212 Mario Mendoza .15 .07
☐ 213 Dave Stewart 1.50 .70
☐ 214 Brian Asselstine .15 .07
☐ 215 Mike Krukow .15 .07
☐ 216 White Sox TL .60 .25
BA: Chet Lemon
Pitching: Dennis Lamp
(Checklist on back)
☐ 217 Bo McLaughlin .15 .07
☐ 218 Dave Roberts .15 .07
☐ 219 John Curtis .15 .07
☐ 220 Manny Trillo .15 .07
☐ 221 Jim Slaton .15 .07
☐ 222 Butch Wynegar .15 .07
☐ 223 Lloyd Moseby .15 .07
☐ 224 Bruce Bochte .15 .07
☐ 225 Mike Torrez .15 .07
☐ 226 Checklist 133-264 .60 .25
☐ 227 Ray Burris .15 .07
☐ 228 Sam Mejias .15 .07
☐ 229 Geoff Zahn .15 .07
☐ 230 Willie Wilson .30 .14
☐ 231 Phillies Rookies .60 .25
Mark Davis
Bob Dernier
Ozzie Virgil
☐ 232 Terry Crowley .15 .07
☐ 233 Duane Kuiper .15 .07
☐ 234 Ron Hodges .15 .07
☐ 235 Mike Easler .15 .07
☐ 236 John Martin .15 .07
☐ 237 Rusty Kuntz .15 .07
☐ 238 Kevin Saucier .15 .07
☐ 239 Jon Matlack .15 .07
☐ 240 Bucky Dent .30 .14
☐ 241 Bucky Dent SA .15 .07
☐ 242 Milt May .15 .07
☐ 243 Bob Owchinko .15 .07
☐ 244 Rufino Linares .15 .07
☐ 245 Ken Reitz .15 .07
☐ 246 New York Mets TL .60 .25
BA: Hubie Brooks
Pitching: Mike Scott
(Checklist on back)
☐ 247 Pedro Guerrero .30 .14
☐ 248 Frank LaCorte .15 .07
☐ 249 Tim Flannery .15 .07
☐ 250 Tug McGraw .30 .14
☐ 251 Fred Lynn .30 .14
☐ 252 Fred Lynn SA .30 .14
☐ 253 Chuck Baker .15 .07
☐ 254 Jorge Bell 1.25 .55
☐ 255 Tony Perez 1.25 .55
☐ 256 Tony Perez SA .60 .25
☐ 257 Larry Harlow .15 .07
☐ 258 Bo Diaz .15 .07
☐ 259 Rodney Scott .15 .07
☐ 260 Bruce Sutter .30 .14
☐ 261 Tigers Rookies UER .15 .07
Howard Bailey
Marty Castillo
Dave Rucker
(Rucker photo act-
ally Roger Weaver)
☐ 262 Doug Bair .15 .07
☐ 263 Victor Cruz .15 .07
☐ 264 Dan Quisenberry .30 .14

☐ 265 Al Bumbry .15 .07
☐ 266 Rick Leach .15 .07
☐ 267 Kurt Bevacqua .15 .07
☐ 268 Rickey Keeton .15 .07
☐ 269 Jim Essian .15 .07
☐ 270 Rusty Staub .30 .14
☐ 271 Larry Bradford .15 .07
☐ 272 Bump Wills .15 .07
☐ 273 Doug Bird .15 .07
☐ 274 Bob Ojeda .60 .25
☐ 275 Bob Watson .30 .14
☐ 276 Angels TL .60 .25
BA: Rod Carew
Pitching: Ken Forsch
(Checklist on back)
☐ 277 Terry Puhl .15 .07
☐ 278 John Littlefield .15 .07
☐ 279 Bill Russell .30 .14
☐ 280 Ben Oglivie .30 .14
☐ 281 John Verhoeven .15 .07
☐ 282 Ken Macha .15 .07
☐ 283 Brian Allard .15 .07
☐ 284 Bob Grich .30 .14
☐ 285 Sparky Lyle .30 .14
☐ 286 Bill Fahey .15 .07
☐ 287 Alan Bannister .15 .07
☐ 288 Garry Templeton .15 .07
☐ 289 Bob Stanley .15 .07
☐ 290 Ken Singleton .30 .14
☐ 291 Pirates Rookies .30 .14
Vance Law
Bob Long
Johnny Ray
☐ 292 David Palmer .15 .07
☐ 293 Rob Picciolo .15 .07
☐ 294 Mike LaCoss .15 .07
☐ 295 Jason Thompson .15 .07
☐ 296 Bob Walk .15 .07
☐ 297 Clint Hurdle .15 .07
☐ 298 Danny Darwin .15 .07
☐ 299 Steve Trout .15 .07
☐ 300 Reggie Jackson 1.50 .70
☐ 301 Reggie Jackson SA 1.25 .55
☐ 302 Doug Flynn .15 .07
☐ 303 Bill Caudill .15 .07
☐ 304 Johnnie LeMaster .15 .07
☐ 305 Don Sutton .60 .25
☐ 306 Don Sutton SA .30 .14
☐ 307 Randy Bass .15 .07
☐ 308 Charlie Moore .15 .07
☐ 309 Pete Redfern .15 .07
☐ 310 Mike Hargrove .30 .14
☐ 311 Dodgers TL .60 .25
BA: Dusty Baker
Pitching: Burt Hooton
(Checklist on back)
☐ 312 Lenny Randle .15 .07
☐ 313 John Harris .15 .07
☐ 314 Buck Martinez .15 .07
☐ 315 Burt Hooton .15 .07
☐ 316 Steve Braun .15 .07
☐ 317 Dick Ruthven .15 .07
☐ 318 Mike Heath .15 .07
☐ 319 Dave Rozema .15 .07
☐ 320 Chris Chambliss .30 .14
☐ 321 Chris Chambliss SA .15 .07
☐ 322 Garry Hancock .15 .07
☐ 323 Bill Lee .30 .14
☐ 324 Steve Dillard .15 .07
☐ 325 Jose Cruz .30 .14
☐ 326 Pete Falcone .15 .07
☐ 327 Joe Nolan .15 .07
☐ 328 Ed Farmer .15 .07
☐ 329 U.L. Washington .15 .07
☐ 330 Rick Wise .15 .07
☐ 331 Benny Ayala .15 .07
☐ 332 Don Robinson .15 .07
☐ 333 Brewers Rookies .15 .07
Frank DiPino
Marshall Edwards
Chuck Porter
☐ 334 Aurelio Rodriguez .15 .07
☐ 335 Jim Sundberg .30 .14
☐ 336 Mariners TL .60 .25
BA: Tom Paciorek
Pitching: Glenn Abbott
(Checklist on back)
☐ 337 Pete Rose AS 1.00 .45
☐ 338 Dave Lopes AS .30 .14
☐ 339 Mike Schmidt AS 1.25 .55
☐ 340 Dave Concepcion AS .30 .14
☐ 341 Andre Dawson AS .60 .25
☐ 342A George Foster AS .30 .14
(With autograph)
☐ 342B George Foster AS 1.25 .55
(W/o autograph)
☐ 343 Dave Parker AS .30 .14
☐ 344 Gary Carter AS .30 .14
☐ 345 Fernando Valenzuela AS .30 .14
☐ 346 Tom Seaver AS ERR 1.25 .55
("t ed")
☐ 346B Tom Seaver AS COR 1.25 .55
("tied")
☐ 347 Bruce Sutter AS .30 .14
☐ 348 Derrel Thomas .15 .07
☐ 349 George Frazier .15 .07
☐ 350 Thad Bosley .15 .07
☐ 351 Reds Rookies .15 .07
Scott Brown
Geoff Combe
Paul Householder
☐ 352 Dick Davis .15 .07
☐ 353 Jack O'Connor .15 .07
☐ 354 Roberto Ramos .15 .07
☐ 355 Dwight Evans .60 .25
☐ 356 Denny Lewallyn .15 .07
☐ 357 Butch Hobson .15 .07
☐ 358 Mike Parrott .15 .07
☐ 359 Jim Dwyer .15 .07
☐ 360 Len Barker .15 .07
☐ 361 Rafael Landestoy .15 .07
☐ 362 Jim Wright UER .15 .07
(Wrong Jim Wright
pictured)
☐ 363 Bob Molinaro .15 .07
☐ 364 Doyle Alexander .15 .07
☐ 365 Bill Madlock .30 .14
☐ 366 Padres TL .60 .25
BA: Luis Salazar
Pitching: Juan
Eichelberger
(Checklist on back)
☐ 367 Jim Kaat .30 .14
☐ 368 Alex Trevino .15 .07
☐ 369 Champ Summers .15 .07
☐ 370 Mike Norris .15 .07
☐ 371 Jerry Don Gleaton .15 .07
☐ 372 Luis Gomez .15 .07
☐ 373 Gene Nelson .15 .07
☐ 374 Tim Blackwell .15 .07
☐ 375 Dusty Baker .60 .25
☐ 376 Chris Welsh .15 .07
☐ 377 Kiko Garcia .15 .07
☐ 378 Mike Caldwell .15 .07
☐ 379 Rob Wilfong .15 .07
☐ 380 Dave Stieb .30 .14
☐ 381 Red Sox Rookies .30 .14
Bruce Hurst
Dave Schmidt
Julio Valdez
☐ 382 Joe Simpson .15 .07
☐ 383A Pascual Perez ERR 8.00 3.60
(No position
on front)
☐ 383B Pascual Perez COR .30 .14
☐ 384 Keith Moreland .15 .07
☐ 385 Ken Forsch .15 .07
☐ 386 Jerry White .15 .07
☐ 387 Tom Veryzer .15 .07
☐ 388 Joe Rudi .15 .07
☐ 389 George Vukovich .15 .07
☐ 390 Eddie Murray 2.00 .90
☐ 391 Dave Tobik .15 .07
☐ 392 Rick Bosetti .15 .07
☐ 393 Al Hrabosky .15 .07
☐ 394 Checklist 265-396 .60 .25
☐ 395 Omar Moreno .15 .07
☐ 396 Twins TL .60 .25
BA: John Castino
Pitching: Fernando
Arroyo
(Checklist on back)
☐ 397 Ken Brett .15 .07
☐ 398 Mike Squires .15 .07
☐ 399 Pat Zachry .15 .07
☐ 400 Johnny Bench 1.50 .70
☐ 401 Johnny Bench SA 1.25 .55
☐ 402 Bill Stein .15 .07
☐ 403 Jim Tracy .15 .07
☐ 404 Dickie Thon .15 .07
☐ 405 Rick Reuschel .30 .14
☐ 406 Al Holland .15 .07
☐ 407 Danny Boone .15 .07
☐ 408 Ed Romero .15 .07
☐ 409 Don Cooper .15 .07
☐ 410 Ron Cey .30 .14
☐ 411 Ron Cey SA .15 .07
☐ 412 Luis Leal .15 .07
☐ 413 Dan Meyer .15 .07
☐ 414 Elias Sosa .15 .07
☐ 415 Don Baylor .60 .25
☐ 416 Marty Bystrom .15 .07
☐ 417 Pat Kelly .15 .07
☐ 418 Rangers Rookies .15 .07
John Butcher
Bobby Johnson
Dave Schmidt
☐ 419 Steve Stone .30 .14
☐ 420 George Hendrick .15 .07
☐ 421 Mark Clear .15 .07
☐ 422 Cliff Johnson .15 .07
☐ 423 Stan Papi .15 .07
☐ 424 Bruce Benedict .15 .07
☐ 425 John Candelaria .15 .07
☐ 426 Orioles TL .60 .25
BA: Eddie Murray
Pitching: Sammy Stewart
(Checklist on back)
☐ 427 Ron Oester .15 .07
☐ 428 LaMarr Hoyt .15 .07
☐ 429 John Wathan .15 .07
☐ 430 Vida Blue .30 .14
☐ 431 Vida Blue SA .15 .07
☐ 432 Mike Scott .30 .14
☐ 433 Alan Ashby .15 .07
☐ 434 Joe Lefebvre .15 .07
☐ 435 Robin Yount 2.00 .90
☐ 436 Joe Strain .15 .07
☐ 437 Juan Berenguer .15 .07
☐ 438 Pete Mackanin .15 .07
☐ 439 Dave Righetti 1.25 .55
☐ 440 Jeff Burroughs .15 .07
☐ 441 Astros Rookies .15 .07
Danny Heep
Billy Smith
Bobby Sprowl
☐ 442 Bruce Kison .15 .07
☐ 443 Mark Wagner .15 .07
☐ 444 Terry Forster .15 .07
☐ 445 Larry Parrish .15 .07
☐ 446 Wayne Garland .15 .07
☐ 447 Darrell Porter .30 .14
☐ 448 Darrell Porter SA .15 .07
☐ 449 Luis Aguayo .15 .07
☐ 450 Jack Morris .30 .14
☐ 451 Ed Miller .15 .07
☐ 452 Lee Smith 4.00 1.80
☐ 453 Art Howe .15 .07
☐ 454 Rick Langford .15 .07
☐ 455 Tom Burgmeier .15 .07
☐ 456 Chicago Cubs TL .60 .25
BA: Bill Buckner
Pitching: Randy Martz
(Checklist on back)
☐ 457 Tim Stoddard .15 .07
☐ 458 Willie Montanez .15 .07
☐ 459 Bruce Berenyi .15 .07
☐ 460 Jack Clark .30 .14
☐ 461 Rich Dotson .15 .07
☐ 462 Dave Chalk .15 .07
☐ 463 Jim Kern .15 .07
☐ 464 Juan Bonilla .15 .07
☐ 465 Lee Mazzilli .15 .07
☐ 466 Randy Lerch .15 .07
☐ 467 Mickey Hatcher .15 .07
☐ 468 Floyd Bannister .15 .07
☐ 469 Ed Ott .15 .07
☐ 470 John Mayberry .15 .07
☐ 471 Royals Rookies .15 .07
Atlee Hammaker
Mike Jones
Darryl Motley
☐ 472 Oscar Gamble .15 .07
☐ 473 Mike Stanton .15 .07
☐ 474 Ken Oberkfell .15 .07
☐ 475 Alan Trammell 1.25 .55
☐ 476 Brian Kingman .15 .07
☐ 477 Steve Yeager .15 .07
☐ 478 Ray Searage .15 .07
☐ 479 Rowland Office .15 .07
☐ 480 Steve Carlton 1.25 .55
☐ 481 Steve Carlton SA 1.25 .55
☐ 482 Glenn Hubbard .15 .07
☐ 483 Gary Woods .15 .07
☐ 484 Ivan DeJesus .15 .07
☐ 485 Kent Tekulve .30 .14
☐ 486 Yankees TL .30 .14
BA: Jerry Mumphrey
Pitching: Tommy John
(Checklist on back)
☐ 487 Bob McClure .15 .07
☐ 488 Ron Jackson .15 .07
☐ 489 Rick Dempsey .30 .14
☐ 490 Dennis Eckersley 1.25 .55
☐ 491 Checklist 397-528 .60 .25
☐ 492 Joe Price .15 .07
☐ 493 Chet Lemon .15 .07
☐ 494 Hubie Brooks .30 .14
☐ 495 Dennis Leonard .15 .07
☐ 496 Johnny Grubb .15 .07
☐ 497 Jim Anderson .15 .07
☐ 498 Dave Bergman .15 .07

☐ 499 Paul Mirabella .15 .07
☐ 500 Rod Carew 1.00 .45
☐ 501 Rod Carew SA 1.25 .55
☐ 502 Braves Rookies 2.00 .90
Steve Bedrosian UER
(Photo actually
Larry Owen)
Brett Butler
Larry Owen
☐ 503 Julio Gonzalez .15 .07
☐ 504 Rick Peters .15 .07
☐ 505 Graig Nettles .30 .14
☐ 506 Graig Nettles SA .15 .07
☐ 507 Terry Harper .15 .07
☐ 508 Jody Davis .15 .07
☐ 509 Harry Spilman .15 .07
☐ 510 Fernando Valenzuela .60 .25
☐ 511 Ruppert Jones .15 .07
☐ 512 Jerry Dybzinski .15 .07
☐ 513 Rick Rhoden .15 .07
☐ 514 Joe Ferguson .15 .07
☐ 515 Larry Bowa .30 .14
☐ 516 Larry Bowa SA .15 .07
☐ 517 Mark Brouhard .15 .07
☐ 518 Garth Iorg .15 .07
☐ 519 Glenn Adams .15 .07
☐ 520 Mike Flanagan .30 .14
☐ 521 Bill Almon .15 .07
☐ 522 Chuck Rainey .15 .07
☐ 523 Gary Gray .15 .07
☐ 524 Tom Hausman .15 .07
☐ 525 Ray Knight .30 .14
☐ 526 Expos TL .60 .25
BA: Warren Cromartie
Pitching: Bill Gullickson
(Checklist on back)
☐ 527 John Henry Johnson .15 .07
☐ 528 Matt Alexander .15 .07
☐ 529 Allen Ripley .15 .07
☐ 530 Dickie Noles .15 .07
☐ 531 A's Rookies .15 .07
Rich Bordi
Mark Budaska
Kelvin Moore
☐ 532 Toby Harrah .30 .14
☐ 533 Joaquin Andujar .30 .14
☐ 534 Dave McKay .15 .07
☐ 535 Lance Parrish .60 .25
☐ 536 Rafael Ramirez .15 .07
☐ 537 Doug Capilla .15 .07
☐ 538 Lou Piniella .30 .14
☐ 539 Vern Ruhle .15 .07
☐ 540 Andre Dawson 1.25 .55
☐ 541 Barry Evans .15 .07
☐ 542 Ned Yost .15 .07
☐ 543 Bill Robinson .15 .07
☐ 544 Larry Christenson .15 .07
☐ 545 Reggie Smith .30 .14
☐ 546 Reggie Smith SA .15 .07
☐ 547 Rod Carew AS 1.25 .55
☐ 548 Willie Randolph AS .30 .14
☐ 549 George Brett AS 2.50 1.10
☐ 550 Bucky Dent AS .30 .14
☐ 551 Reggie Jackson AS 1.25 .55
☐ 552 Ken Singleton AS .30 .14
☐ 553 Dave Winfield AS 1.25 .55
☐ 554 Carlton Fisk AS .60 .25
☐ 555 Scott McGregor AS .15 .07
☐ 556 Jack Morris AS .30 .14
☐ 557 Rich Gossage AS .30 .14
☐ 558 John Tudor .15 .07
☐ 559 Indians TL .30 .14
BA: Mike Hargrove
Pitching: Bert Blyleven
(Checklist on back)
☐ 560 Doug Corbett .15 .07
☐ 561 Cardinals Rookies .15 .07
Glenn Brummer
Luis DeLeon
Gene Roof
☐ 562 Mike O'Berry .15 .07
☐ 563 Ross Baumgarten .15 .07
☐ 564 Doug DeCinces .30 .14
☐ 565 Jackson Todd .15 .07
☐ 566 Mike Jorgensen .15 .07
☐ 567 Bob Babcock .15 .07
☐ 568 Joe Pettini .15 .07
☐ 569 Willie Randolph .30 .14
☐ 570 Willie Randolph SA .30 .14
☐ 571 Glenn Abbott .15 .07
☐ 572 Juan Beniquez .15 .07
☐ 573 Rick Waits .15 .07
☐ 574 Mike Ramsey .15 .07
☐ 575 Al Cowens .15 .07
☐ 576 Giants TL .60 .25
BA: Milt May
Pitching: Vida Blue
(Checklist on back)
☐ 577 Rick Monday .15 .07
☐ 578 Shooty Babitt .15 .07
☐ 579 Rick Mahler .15 .07
☐ 580 Bobby Bonds .30 .14
☐ 581 Ron Reed .15 .07
☐ 582 Luis Pujols .15 .07
☐ 583 Tippy Martinez .15 .07
☐ 584 Hosken Powell .15 .07
☐ 585 Rollie Fingers 1.25 .55
☐ 586 Rollie Fingers SA .60 .25
☐ 587 Tim Lollar .15 .07
☐ 588 Dale Berra .15 .07
☐ 589 Dave Stapleton .15 .07
☐ 590 Al Oliver .30 .14
☐ 591 Al Oliver SA .15 .07
☐ 592 Craig Swan .15 .07
☐ 593 Billy Smith .15 .07
☐ 594 Renie Martin .15 .07
☐ 595 Dave Collins .15 .07
☐ 596 Damaso Garcia .15 .07
☐ 597 Wayne Nordhagen .15 .07
☐ 598 Bob Galasso .15 .07
☐ 599 White Sox Rookies .15 .07
Jay Loviglio
Reggie Patterson
Leo Sutherland
☐ 600 Dave Winfield 2.00 .90
☐ 601 Sid Monge .15 .07
☐ 602 Freddie Patek .15 .07
☐ 603 Rich Hebner .30 .14
☐ 604 Orlando Sanchez .15 .07
☐ 605 Steve Rogers .15 .07
☐ 606 Blue Jays TL .60 .25
BA: John Mayberry
Pitching: Dave Stieb
(Checklist on back)
☐ 607 Leon Durham .15 .07
☐ 608 Jerry Royster .15 .07
☐ 609 Rick Sutcliffe .30 .14
☐ 610 Rickey Henderson 2.50 1.10
☐ 611 Joe Niekro .30 .14
☐ 612 Gary Ward .15 .07
☐ 613 Jim Gantner .30 .14
☐ 614 Juan Eichelberger .15 .07
☐ 615 Bob Boone .30 .14
☐ 616 Bob Boone SA .15 .07
☐ 617 Scott McGregor .15 .07
☐ 618 Tim Foli .15 .07
☐ 619 Bill Campbell .15 .07
☐ 620 Ken Griffey .30 .14
☐ 621 Ken Griffey SA .30 .14
☐ 622 Dennis Lamp .15 .07
☐ 623 Mets Rookies .60 .25
Ron Gardenhire
Terry Leach
Tim Leary
☐ 624 Fergie Jenkins .60 .25
☐ 625 Hal McRae .30 .14
☐ 626 Randy Jones .15 .07
☐ 627 Enos Cabell .15 .07
☐ 628 Bill Travers .15 .07
☐ 629 John Wockenfuss .15 .07
☐ 630 Joe Charboneau .15 .07
☐ 631 Gene Tenace .30 .14
☐ 632 Bryan Clark .15 .07
☐ 633 Mitchell Page .15 .07
☐ 634 Checklist 529-660 .60 .25
☐ 635 Ron Davis .15 .07
☐ 636 Phillies TL 1.25 .55
BA: Pete Rose
Pitching: Steve Carlton
(Checklist on back)
☐ 637 Rick Camp .15 .07
☐ 638 John Milner .15 .07
☐ 639 Ken Kravec .15 .07
☐ 640 Cesar Cedeno .30 .14
☐ 641 Steve Mura .15 .07
☐ 642 Mike Scioscia .30 .14
☐ 643 Pete Vuckovich .15 .07
☐ 644 John Castino .15 .07
☐ 645 Frank White .30 .14
☐ 646 Frank White SA .15 .07
☐ 647 Warren Brusstar .15 .07
☐ 648 Jose Morales .15 .07
☐ 649 Ken Clay .15 .07
☐ 650 Carl Yastrzemski 1.25 .55
☐ 651 Carl Yastrzemski SA 1.25 .55
☐ 652 Steve Nicosia .15 .07
☐ 653 Angels Rookies .60 .25
Tom Brunansky
Luis Sanchez
Daryl Sconiers
☐ 654 Jim Morrison .15 .07
☐ 655 Joel Youngblood .15 .07
☐ 656 Eddie Whitson .15 .07
☐ 657 Tom Poquette .15 .07
☐ 658 Tito Landrum .15 .07
☐ 659 Fred Martinez .15 .07
☐ 660 Dave Concepcion .30 .14
☐ 661 Dave Concepcion SA .15 .07
☐ 662 Luis Salazar .15 .07
☐ 663 Hector Cruz .15 .07
☐ 664 Dan Spillner .15 .07
☐ 665 Jim Clancy .15 .07
☐ 666 Tigers TL .60 .25
BA: Steve Kemp
Pitching: Dan Petry
(Checklist on back)
☐ 667 Jeff Reardon .60 .25
☐ 668 Dale Murphy 1.25 .55
☐ 669 Larry Milbourne .15 .07
☐ 670 Steve Kemp .15 .07
☐ 671 Mike Davis .15 .07
☐ 672 Bob Knepper .15 .07
☐ 673 Keith Drumwright .15 .07
☐ 674 Dave Goltz .15 .07
☐ 675 Cecil Cooper .30 .14
☐ 676 Sal Butera .15 .07
☐ 677 Alfredo Griffin .15 .07
☐ 678 Tom Paciorek .15 .07
☐ 679 Sammy Stewart .15 .07
☐ 680 Gary Matthews .30 .14
☐ 681 Dodgers Rookies 1.25 .55
Mike Marshall
Ron Roenicke
Steve Sax
☐ 682 Jesse Jefferson .15 .07
☐ 683 Phil Garner .30 .14
☐ 684 Harold Baines 1.25 .55
☐ 685 Bert Blyleven .60 .25
☐ 686 Gary Allenson .15 .07
☐ 687 Greg Minton .15 .07
☐ 688 Leon Roberts .15 .07
☐ 689 Lary Sorensen .15 .07
☐ 690 Dave Kingman .30 .14
☐ 691 Dan Schatzeder .15 .07
☐ 692 Wayne Gross .15 .07
☐ 693 Cesar Geronimo .15 .07
☐ 694 Dave Wehrmeister .15 .07
☐ 695 Warren Cromartie .15 .07
☐ 696 Pirates TL .60 .25
BA: Bill Madlock
Pitching: Eddie Solomon
(Checklist on back)
☐ 697 John Montefusco .15 .07
☐ 698 Tony Scott .15 .07
☐ 699 Dick Tidrow .15 .07
☐ 700 George Foster .30 .14
☐ 701 George Foster SA .15 .07
☐ 702 Steve Renko .15 .07
☐ 703 Brewers TL .60 .25
BA: Cecil Cooper
Pitching: Pete Vuckovich
(Checklist on back)
☐ 704 Mickey Rivers .15 .07
☐ 705 Mickey Rivers SA .15 .07
☐ 706 Barry Foote .15 .07
☐ 707 Mark Bomback .15 .07
☐ 708 Gene Richards .15 .07
☐ 709 Don Money .15 .07
☐ 710 Jerry Reuss .30 .14
☐ 711 Mariners Rookies .60 .25
Dave Edler
Dave Henderson
Reggie Walton
☐ 712 Dennis Martinez .30 .14
☐ 713 Del Unser .15 .07
☐ 714 Jerry Koosman .30 .14
☐ 715 Willie Stargell 1.25 .55
☐ 716 Willie Stargell SA .30 .14
☐ 717 Rick Miller .15 .07
☐ 718 Charlie Hough .30 .14
☐ 719 Jerry Narron .15 .07
☐ 720 Greg Luzinski .30 .14
☐ 721 Greg Luzinski SA .15 .07
☐ 722 Jerry Martin .15 .07
☐ 723 Junior Kennedy .15 .07
☐ 724 Dave Rosello .15 .07
☐ 725 Amos Otis .30 .14
☐ 726 Amos Otis SA .15 .07
☐ 727 Sixto Lezcano .15 .07
☐ 728 Aurelio Lopez .15 .07
☐ 729 Jim Spencer .15 .07
☐ 730 Gary Carter 1.25 .55
☐ 731 Padres Rookies .15 .07
Mike Armstrong
Doug Gwosdz
Fred Kuhaulua
☐ 732 Mike Lum .15 .07
☐ 733 Larry McWilliams .15 .07
☐ 734 Mike Ivie .15 .07
☐ 735 Rudy May .15 .07
☐ 736 Jerry Turner .15 .07
☐ 737 Reggie Cleveland .15 .07

	NRMT	VG-E
☐ 738 Dave Engle	.15	.07
☐ 739 Joey McLaughlin	.15	.07
☐ 740 Dave Lopes	.30	.14
☐ 741 Dave Lopes SA	.15	.07
☐ 742 Dick Drago	.15	.07
☐ 743 John Stearns	.15	.07
☐ 744 Mike Witt	.30	.14
☐ 745 Bake McBride	.15	.07
☐ 746 Andre Thornton	.15	.07
☐ 747 John Lowenstein	.15	.07
☐ 748 Marc Hill	.15	.07
☐ 749 Bob Shirley	.15	.07
☐ 750 Jim Rice	.60	.25
☐ 751 Rick Honeycutt	.15	.07
☐ 752 Lee Lacy	.15	.07
☐ 753 Tom Brookens	.15	.07
☐ 754 Joe Morgan	1.25	.55
☐ 755 Joe Morgan SA	.30	.14
☐ 756 Reds TL BA: Ken Griffey Pitching: Tom Seaver (Checklist on back)	.60	.25
☐ 757 Tom Underwood	.15	.07
☐ 758 Claudell Washington	.15	.07
☐ 759 Paul Splittorff	.15	.07
☐ 760 Bill Buckner	.30	.14
☐ 761 Dave Smith	.15	.07
☐ 762 Mike Phillips	.15	.07
☐ 763 Tom Hume	.15	.07
☐ 764 Steve Swisher	.15	.07
☐ 765 Gorman Thomas	.30	.14
☐ 766 Twins Rookies Lenny Faedo Kent Hrbek Tim Laudner	1.50	.70
☐ 767 Roy Smalley	.15	.07
☐ 768 Jerry Garvin	.15	.07
☐ 769 Richie Zisk	.15	.07
☐ 770 Rich Gossage	.60	.25
☐ 771 Rich Gossage SA	.30	.14
☐ 772 Bert Campaneris	.30	.14
☐ 773 John Denny	.15	.07
☐ 774 Jay Johnstone	.30	.14
☐ 775 Bob Forsch	.15	.07
☐ 776 Mark Belanger	.30	.14
☐ 777 Tom Griffin	.15	.07
☐ 778 Kevin Hickey	.15	.07
☐ 779 Grant Jackson	.15	.07
☐ 780 Pete Rose	1.50	.70
☐ 781 Pete Rose SA	1.00	.45
☐ 782 Frank Taveras	.15	.07
☐ 783 Greg Harris	.15	.07
☐ 784 Milt Wilcox	.15	.07
☐ 785 Dan Driessen	.15	.07
☐ 786 Red Sox TL BA: Carney Lansford Pitching: Mike Torrez (Checklist on back)	.60	.25
☐ 787 Fred Stanley	.15	.07
☐ 788 Woodie Fryman	.15	.07
☐ 789 Checklist 661-792	.60	.25
☐ 790 Larry Gura	.15	.07
☐ 791 Bobby Brown	.15	.07
☐ 792 Frank Tanana	.30	.14

1982 Topps Sticker Variations

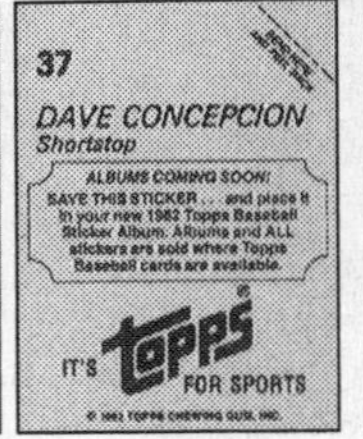

This 48-card (skip-numbered) set is actually a slightly different version of the 1982 Topps stickers. They are the same size (1 15/16" by 2 9/16") and are easily confused. They were produced for insertion into the regular packs of cards that year. They are distinguishable from the "other" sticker set by the fact that on their backs these say the Topps sticker album is "Coming Soon." There are no foils in this set. All of the stickers in this set depict a single player. Colored borders surround the posed color player photos on the fronts, blue for the NL and red for the AL. The player's name and position appear on the back. The stickers are numbered on the front and back. Choice of players for this small set appears to have been systematic, i.e., taking every fourth player between number 17 and number 109 and every fifth player between number 151 and number 251.

	NRMT	VG-E
COMPLETE SET (48)	4.00	1.80
COMMON STICKER	.05	.02

	NRMT	VG-E
☐ 17 Chris Chambliss	.05	.02
☐ 21 Bruce Benedict	.05	.02
☐ 25 Leon Durham	.05	.02
☐ 29 Bill Buckner	.10	.05
☐ 33 Dave Collins	.05	.02
☐ 37 Dave Concepcion	.10	.05
☐ 41 Nolan Ryan	2.00	.90
☐ 45 Bob Knepper	.05	.02
☐ 49 Ken Landreaux	.05	.02
☐ 53 Burt Hooton	.05	.02
☐ 57 Andre Dawson	.40	.18
☐ 61 Gary Carter	.25	.11
☐ 65 Joel Youngblood	.05	.02
☐ 69 Ellis Valentine	.05	.02
☐ 73 Garry Maddox	.05	.02
☐ 77 Bob Boone	.10	.05
☐ 81 Omar Moreno	.05	.02
☐ 85 Willie Stargell	.25	.11
☐ 89 Ken Oberkfell	.05	.02
☐ 93 Darrell Porter	.05	.02
☐ 97 Juan Eichelberger	.05	.02
☐ 101 Luis Salazar	.05	.02
☐ 105 Enos Cabell	.05	.02
☐ 109 Larry Herndon	.05	.02
☐ 143 Scott McGregor	.05	.02
☐ 148 Mike Flanagan	.10	.05
☐ 151 Mike Torrez	.05	.02
☐ 156 Carney Lansford	.10	.05
☐ 161 Fred Lynn	.10	.05
☐ 166 Rich Dotson	.05	.02
☐ 171 Tony Bernazard	.05	.02
☐ 176 Bo Diaz	.05	.02
☐ 181 Alan Trammell	.25	.11
☐ 186 Milt Wilcox	.05	.02
☐ 191 Dennis Leonard	.05	.02
☐ 196 Willie Aikens	.05	.02
☐ 201 Ted Simmons	.10	.05
☐ 206 Hosken Powell	.05	.02
☐ 211 Roger Erickson	.05	.02
☐ 215 Graig Nettles	.10	.05
☐ 216 Reggie Jackson	.50	.23
☐ 221 Rickey Henderson	.75	.35
☐ 226 Cliff Johnson	.05	.02
☐ 231 Jeff Burroughs	.05	.02
☐ 236 Tom Paciorek	.10	.05
☐ 241 Pat Putnam	.05	.02
☐ 246 Lloyd Moseby	.05	.02
☐ 251 Barry Bonnell	.05	.02

1982 Topps Team Checklist Sheet

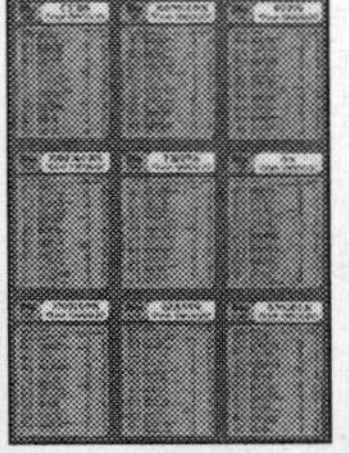

As part of a mail-away offer, Topps offered all 26 1982 team checklist cards on an uncut sheet. These cards enabled the collector to have an easy reference for which card(s) he/she needed to finish their sets. When cut from the sheet, all cards measure the standard-size.

	NRMT	VG-E
COMPLETE SET (1)	15.00	6.75
COMMON SHEET (1)	15.00	6.75

	NRMT	VG-E
☐ 1 Team Checklist Sheet	15.00	6.75

1982 Topps Traded

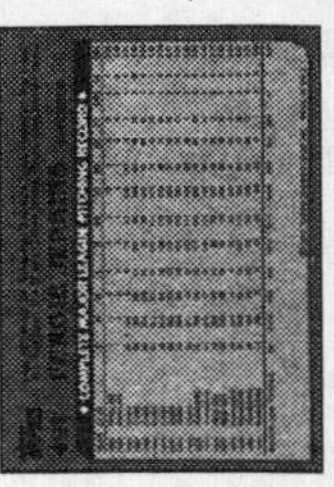

The cards in this 132-card set measure the standard size. The 1982 Topps Traded or extended series is distinguished by a "T" printed after the number (located on the reverse). This was the first time Topps began a tradition of newly numbering (and alphabetizing) their traded series from 1T to 132T. All 131 player photos used in the set are completely new. Of this total, 112 individuals are seen in the uniform of their new team, 11 youngsters have been elevated to single card status from multi-player "Future Stars" cards, and eight more are entirely new to the 1982 Topps lineup. The backs are almost completely red in color with black print. There are no key Rookie Cards in this set. Although the Cal Ripken card is this set's most valuable card, it is not his Rookie Card since he had already been included in the 1982 regular set, albeit on a multi-player card.

	NRMT	VG-E
COMP.FACT.SET (132)	300.00	135.00
COMMON CARD (1T-132T)	.50	.23

	NRMT	VG-E
☐ 1T Doyle Alexander	.50	.23
☐ 2T Jesse Barfield	1.00	.45
☐ 3T Ross Baumgarten	.50	.23
☐ 4T Steve Bedrosian	1.00	.45
☐ 5T Mark Belanger	1.00	.45
☐ 6T Kurt Bevacqua	.50	.23
☐ 7T Tim Blackwell	.50	.23
☐ 8T Vida Blue	1.00	.45
☐ 9T Bob Boone	1.00	.45
☐ 10T Larry Bowa	1.00	.45
☐ 11T Dan Briggs	.50	.23
☐ 12T Bobby Brown	.50	.23
☐ 13T Tom Brunansky	1.00	.45
☐ 14T Jeff Burroughs	.50	.23
☐ 15T Enos Cabell	.50	.23
☐ 16T Bill Campbell	.50	.23
☐ 17T Bobby Castillo	.50	.23
☐ 18T Bill Caudill	.50	.23
☐ 19T Cesar Cedeno	1.00	.45
☐ 20T Dave Collins	.50	.23
☐ 21T Doug Corbett	.50	.23
☐ 22T Al Cowens	.50	.23
☐ 23T Chili Davis	6.00	2.70
☐ 24T Dick Davis	.50	.23
☐ 25T Ron Davis	.50	.23
☐ 26T Doug DeCinces	1.00	.45
☐ 27T Ivan DeJesus	.50	.23
☐ 28T Bob Dernier	.50	.23
☐ 29T Bo Diaz	.50	.23
☐ 30T Roger Erickson	.50	.23
☐ 31T Jim Essian	.50	.23
☐ 32T Ed Farmer	.50	.23
☐ 33T Doug Flynn	.50	.23
☐ 34T Tim Foli	.50	.23
☐ 35T Dan Ford	.50	.23
☐ 36T George Foster	1.00	.45
☐ 37T Dave Frost	.50	.23
☐ 38T Rich Gale	.50	.23
☐ 39T Ron Gardenhire	.50	.23
☐ 40T Ken Griffey	1.00	.45
☐ 41T Greg Harris	.50	.23
☐ 42T Von Hayes	1.00	.45
☐ 43T Larry Herndon	.50	.23
☐ 44T Kent Hrbek	2.00	.90
☐ 45T Mike Ivie	.50	.23
☐ 46T Grant Jackson	.50	.23
☐ 47T Reggie Jackson	10.00	4.50
☐ 48T Ron Jackson	.50	.23
☐ 49T Fergie Jenkins	2.00	.90
☐ 50T Lamar Johnson	.50	.23
☐ 51T Randy Johnson	.50	.23
☐ 52T Jay Johnstone	1.00	.45
☐ 53T Mick Kelleher	.50	.23
☐ 54T Steve Kemp	.50	.23
☐ 55T Junior Kennedy	.50	.23
☐ 56T Jim Kern	.50	.23
☐ 57T Ray Knight	1.00	.45
☐ 58T Wayne Krenchicki	.50	.23
☐ 59T Mike Krukow	.50	.23
☐ 60T Duane Kuiper	.50	.23
☐ 61T Mike LaCoss	.50	.23
☐ 62T Chet Lemon	.50	.23
☐ 63T Sixto Lezcano	.50	.23
☐ 64T Dave Lopes	1.00	.45
☐ 65T Jerry Martin	.50	.23
☐ 66T Renie Martin	.50	.23
☐ 67T John Mayberry	.50	.23
☐ 68T Lee Mazzilli	.50	.23
☐ 69T Bake McBride	.50	.23
☐ 70T Dan Meyer	.50	.23
☐ 71T Larry Milbourne	.50	.23

	NRMT	VG-E
☐ 72T Eddie Milner	.50	.23
☐ 73T Sid Monge	.50	.23
☐ 74T John Montefusco	.50	.23
☐ 75T Jose Morales	.50	.23
☐ 76T Keith Moreland	.50	.23
☐ 77T Jim Morrison	.50	.23
☐ 78T Rance Mulliniks	.50	.23
☐ 79T Steve Mura	.50	.23
☐ 80T Gene Nelson	.50	.23
☐ 81T Joe Nolan	.50	.23
☐ 82T Dickie Noles	.50	.23
☐ 83T Al Oliver	1.00	.45
☐ 84T Jorge Orta	.50	.23
☐ 85T Tom Paciorek	1.00	.45
☐ 86T Larry Parrish	.50	.23
☐ 87T Jack Perconte	.50	.23
☐ 88T Gaylord Perry	2.00	.90
☐ 89T Rob Picciolo	.50	.23
☐ 90T Joe Pittman	.50	.23
☐ 91T Hosken Powell	.50	.23
☐ 92T Mike Proly	.50	.23
☐ 93T Greg Pryor	.50	.23
☐ 94T Charlie Puleo	.50	.23
☐ 95T Shane Rawley	.50	.23
☐ 96T Johnny Ray	1.00	.45
☐ 97T Dave Revering	.50	.23
☐ 98T Cal Ripken	250.00	110.00
☐ 99T Allen Ripley	.50	.23
☐ 100T Bill Robinson	.50	.23
☐ 101T Aurelio Rodriguez	.50	.23
☐ 102T Joe Rudi	.50	.23
☐ 103T Steve Sax	2.00	.90
☐ 104T Dan Schatzeder	.50	.23
☐ 105T Bob Shirley	.50	.23
☐ 106T Eric Show	1.00	.45
☐ 107T Roy Smalley	.50	.23
☐ 108T Lonnie Smith	1.00	.45
☐ 109T Ozzie Smith	25.00	11.00
☐ 110T Reggie Smith	1.00	.45
☐ 111T Lary Sorensen	.50	.23
☐ 112T Elias Sosa	.50	.23
☐ 113T Mike Stanton	.50	.23
☐ 114T Steve Stroughter	.50	.23
☐ 115T Champ Summers	.50	.23
☐ 116T Rick Sutcliffe	1.00	.45
☐ 117T Frank Tanana	1.00	.45
☐ 118T Frank Taveras	.50	.23
☐ 119T Garry Templeton	.50	.23
☐ 120T Alex Trevino	.50	.23
☐ 121T Jerry Turner	.50	.23
☐ 122T Ed VandeBerg	.50	.23
☐ 123T Tom Veryzer	.50	.23
☐ 124T Ron Washington	.50	.23
☐ 125T Bob Watson	1.00	.45
☐ 126T Dennis Werth	.50	.23
☐ 127T Eddie Whitson	.50	.23
☐ 128T Rob Wilfong	.50	.23
☐ 129T Bump Wills	.50	.23
☐ 130T Gary Woods	.50	.23
☐ 131T Butch Wynegar	.50	.23
☐ 132T Checklist: 1-132	.50	.23

1982 Topps/O-Pee-Chee Stickers

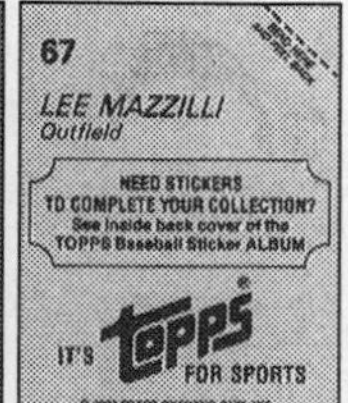

Made for Topps and O-Pee-Chee by Panini, an Italian company, these 260 stickers measure 1 15/16" by 2 9/16" and are numbered on both front and back. The fronts feature color player photos with color borders, blue for the NL and red for the AL. The backs carry the player's name and position and a bilingual ad for O-Pee-Chee. Team affiliations are not shown. The stickers were issued both as inserts in the regular 1982 issue and in individual gumless packs. An album onto which the stickers could be affixed was available at retail stores. The album and the sticker numbering are organized as follows: League Leaders (1-16), Atlanta Braves (17-24), Chicago Cubs (25-32), Cincinnati Reds (33-40), Houston Astros (41-48), Los Angeles Dodgers (49-56), Montreal Expos (57-65), New York Mets (66-72), Philadelphia Phillies (73-80), Pittsburgh Pirates (81-88), St. Louis Cardinals (89-96), San Diego Padres (97-104), San Francisco Giants (105-112), Highlights (113-120), NL Foil All-Stars (121-130), AL Foil All-Stars (131-140), Baltimore Orioles (141-148), Boston Red Sox (149-156), California Angels (157-164), Chicago White Sox (165-172) Cleveland Indians (173-180), Detroit Tigers (181-188), Kansas City Royals (189-196), Milwaukee Brewers (197-204), Minnesota Twins (205-212), New York Yankees (213-221), Oakland A's (222-228), Seattle Mariners (229-236), Texas Rangers (237-244), Toronto Blue Jays (245-252) and postseason games (253-260).

	NRMT	VG-E
COMPLETE SET (260)	15.00	6.75
COMMON STICKER (1-120)	.05	.02
COMMON FOIL (121-140)	.10	.05
COMMON STICKER (141-260)	.05	.02
*TOPPS AND OPC: SAME VALUE		

	NRMT	VG-E
☐ 1 Bill Madlock LL	.10	.05
☐ 2 Carney Lansford LL	.10	.05
☐ 3 Mike Schmidt LL	.60	.25
☐ 4 Tony Armas LL	.30	.14
Bobby Grich		
Dwight Evans		
Eddie Murray		
☐ 5 Mike Schmidt LL	.60	.25
☐ 6 Eddie Murray LL	.60	.25
☐ 7 Tim Raines LL	.15	.07
☐ 8 Rickey Henderson LL	.60	.25
☐ 9 Tom Seaver LL	.40	.18
☐ 10 Steve McCatty LL	.05	.02
Dennis Martinez		
Pete Vuckovich		
Jack Morris		
☐ 11 Fernando Valenzuela LL	.15	.07
☐ 12 Len Barker LL	.05	.02
☐ 13 Nolan Ryan LL	1.50	.70
☐ 14 Steve McCatty LL	.05	.02
☐ 15 Bruce Sutter LL	.10	.05
☐ 16 Rollie Fingers LL	.15	.07
☐ 17 Chris Chambliss	.05	.02
☐ 18 Bob Horner	.10	.05
☐ 19 Dale Murphy	.40	.18
☐ 20 Phil Niekro	.15	.07
☐ 21 Bruce Benedict	.05	.02
☐ 22 Claudell Washington	.05	.02
☐ 23 Glenn Hubbard	.05	.02
☐ 24 Rick Camp	.05	.02
☐ 25 Leon Durham	.10	.05
☐ 26 Ken Reitz	.05	.02
☐ 27 Dick Tidrow	.05	.02
☐ 28 Tim Blackwell	.05	.02
☐ 29 Bill Buckner	.10	.05
☐ 30 Steve Henderson	.05	.02
☐ 31 Mike Krukow	.05	.02
☐ 32 Ivan DeJesus	.05	.02
☐ 33 Dave Collins	.05	.02
☐ 34 Ron Oester	.05	.02
☐ 35 Johnny Bench	.75	.35
☐ 36 Tom Seaver	.75	.35
☐ 37 Dave Concepcion	.10	.05
☐ 38 Tom Hume	.05	.02
☐ 39 Ray Knight	.10	.05
☐ 40 George Foster	.10	.05
☐ 41 Nolan Ryan	3.00	1.35
☐ 42 Terry Puhl	.05	.02
☐ 43 Art Howe	.10	.05
☐ 44 Jose Cruz	.10	.05
☐ 45 Bob Knepper	.05	.02
☐ 46 Craig Reynolds	.05	.02
☐ 47 Cesar Cedeno	.10	.05
☐ 48 Alan Ashby	.05	.02
☐ 49 Ken Landreaux	.05	.02
☐ 50 Fernando Valenzuela	.40	.18
☐ 51 Ron Cey	.10	.05
☐ 52 Dusty Baker	.10	.05
☐ 53 Burt Hooton	.05	.02
☐ 54 Steve Garvey	.15	.07
☐ 55 Pedro Guerrero	.10	.05
☐ 56 Jerry Reuss	.10	.05
☐ 57 Andre Dawson	.60	.25
☐ 58 Chris Speier	.05	.02
☐ 59 Steve Rogers	.05	.02
☐ 60 Warren Cromartie	.05	.02
☐ 61 Gary Carter	.25	.11
☐ 62 Tim Raines	.40	.18
☐ 63 Scott Sanderson	.05	.02
☐ 64 Larry Parrish	.05	.02
☐ 65 Joel Youngblood	.05	.02
☐ 66 Neil Allen	.05	.02
☐ 67 Lee Mazzilli	.05	.02
☐ 68 Hubie Brooks	.10	.05
☐ 69 Ellis Valentine	.05	.02
☐ 70 Doug Flynn	.05	.02
☐ 71 Pat Zachry	.05	.02
☐ 72 Dave Kingman	.10	.05
☐ 73 Garry Maddox	.05	.02

	NRMT	VG-E
☐ 74 Mike Schmidt	1.25	.55
☐ 75 Steve Carlton	.60	.25
☐ 76 Manny Trillo	.05	.02
☐ 77 Bob Boone	.10	.05
☐ 78 Pete Rose	1.25	.55
☐ 79 Gary Matthews	.10	.05
☐ 80 Larry Bowa	.10	.05
☐ 81 Omar Moreno	.05	.02
☐ 82 Rick Rhoden	.05	.02
☐ 83 Bill Madlock	.10	.05
☐ 84 Mike Easler	.05	.02
☐ 85 Willie Stargell	.40	.18
☐ 86 Jim Bibby	.05	.02
☐ 87 Dave Parker	.10	.05
☐ 88 Tim Foli	.05	.02
☐ 89 Ken Oberkfell	.05	.02
☐ 90 Bob Forsch	.05	.02
☐ 91 George Hendrick	.05	.02
☐ 92 Keith Hernandez	.10	.05
☐ 93 Darrell Porter	.05	.02
☐ 94 Bruce Sutter	.10	.05
☐ 95 Sixto Lezcano	.05	.02
☐ 96 Garry Templeton	.05	.02
☐ 97 Juan Eichelberger	.05	.02
☐ 98 Broderick Perkins	.05	.02
☐ 99 Ruppert Jones	.05	.02
☐ 100 Terry Kennedy	.05	.02
☐ 101 Luis Salazar	.05	.02
☐ 102 Gary Lucas	.05	.02
☐ 103 Gene Richards	.05	.02
☐ 104 Ozzie Smith	2.00	.90
☐ 105 Enos Cabell	.05	.02
☐ 106 Jack Clark	.10	.05
☐ 107 Greg Minton	.05	.02
☐ 108 Johnnie LeMaster	.05	.02
☐ 109 Larry Herndon	.05	.02
☐ 110 Milt May	.05	.02
☐ 111 Vida Blue	.10	.05
☐ 112 Darrell Evans	.10	.05
☐ 113 Len Barker HL	.05	.02
☐ 114 Julio Cruz HL	.05	.02
☐ 115 Billy Martin MG HL	.10	.05
☐ 116 Tim Raines HL	.15	.07
☐ 117 Pete Rose HL	.60	.25
☐ 118 Bill Stein HL	.05	.02
☐ 119 Fern.Valenzuela HL	.15	.07
☐ 120 Carl Yastrzemski HL	.30	.14
☐ 121 Pete Rose FOIL	1.50	.70
☐ 122 Manny Trillo FOIL	.10	.05
☐ 123 Mike Schmidt FOIL	1.50	.70
☐ 124 Dave Concepcion FOIL	.15	.07
☐ 125 Andre Dawson FOIL	.75	.35
☐ 126 George Foster FOIL	.15	.07
☐ 127 Dave Parker FOIL	.25	.11
☐ 128 Gary Carter FOIL	.30	.14
☐ 129 Steve Carlton FOIL	.75	.35
☐ 130 Bruce Sutter FOIL	.15	.07
☐ 131 Rod Carew FOIL	.75	.35
☐ 132 Jerry Remy FOIL	.10	.05
☐ 133 George Brett FOIL	2.50	1.10
☐ 134 Rick Burleson FOIL	.10	.05
☐ 135 Dwight Evans FOIL	.15	.07
☐ 136 Ken Singleton FOIL	.10	.05
☐ 137 Dave Winfield FOIL	.75	.35
☐ 138 Carlton Fisk FOIL	.75	.35
☐ 139 Jack Morris FOIL	.25	.11
☐ 140 Rich Gossage FOIL	.15	.07
☐ 141 Al Bumbry	.10	.05
☐ 142 Doug DeCinces	.05	.02
☐ 143 Scott McGregor	.05	.02
☐ 144 Ken Singleton	.05	.02
☐ 145 Eddie Murray	1.50	.70
☐ 146 Jim Palmer	.40	.18
☐ 147 Rich Dauer	.05	.02
☐ 148 Mike Flanagan	.10	.05
☐ 149 Jerry Remy	.05	.02
☐ 150 Jim Rice	.10	.05
☐ 151 Mike Torrez	.05	.02
☐ 152 Tony Perez	.15	.07
☐ 153 Dwight Evans	.10	.05
☐ 154 Mark Clear	.05	.02
☐ 155 Carl Yastrzemski	.60	.25
☐ 156 Carney Lansford	.10	.05
☐ 157 Rick Burleson	.05	.02
☐ 158 Don Baylor	.15	.07
☐ 159 Ken Forsch	.05	.02
☐ 160 Rod Carew	.60	.25
☐ 161 Fred Lynn	.10	.05
☐ 162 Bob Grich	.10	.05
☐ 163 Dan Ford	.05	.02
☐ 164 Butch Hobson	.05	.02
☐ 165 Greg Luzinski	.10	.05
☐ 166 Rich Dotson	.05	.02
☐ 167 Billy Almon	.05	.02
☐ 168 Chet Lemon	.05	.02
☐ 169 Steve Trout	.05	.02
☐ 170 Carlton Fisk	.60	.25

☐ 171 Tony Bernazard .05 .02
☐ 172 Ron LeFlore .10 .05
☐ 173 Bert Blyleven .15 .07
☐ 174 Andre Thornton .05 .02
☐ 175 Jorge Orta .05 .02
☐ 176 Bo Diaz .05 .02
☐ 177 Toby Harrah .10 .05
☐ 178 Len Barker .05 .02
☐ 179 Rick Manning .05 .02
☐ 180 Mike Hargrove .10 .05
☐ 181 Alan Trammell .40 .18
☐ 182 Al Cowens .05 .02
☐ 183 Jack Morris .10 .05
☐ 184 Kirk Gibson .30 .14
☐ 185 Steve Kemp .05 .02
☐ 186 Milt Wilcox .05 .02
☐ 187 Lou Whitaker .30 .14
☐ 188 Lance Parrish .15 .07
☐ 189 Willie Wilson .05 .02
☐ 190 George Brett 2.00 .90
☐ 191 Dennis Leonard .05 .02
☐ 192 John Wathan .05 .02
☐ 193 Frank White .10 .05
☐ 194 Amos Otis .10 .05
☐ 195 Larry Gura .05 .02
☐ 196 Willie Aikens .05 .02
☐ 197 Ben Oglivie .10 .05
☐ 198 Rollie Fingers .30 .14
☐ 199 Cecil Cooper .10 .05
☐ 200 Paul Molitor .75 .35
☐ 201 Ted Simmons .10 .05
☐ 202 Pete Vuckovich .05 .02
☐ 203 Robin Yount .60 .25
☐ 204 Gorman Thomas .10 .05
☐ 205 Rob Wilfong .05 .02
☐ 206 Hosken Powell .05 .02
☐ 207 Roy Smalley .05 .02
☐ 208 Butch Wynegar .05 .02
☐ 209 John Castino .05 .02
☐ 210 Doug Corbett .05 .02
☐ 211 Roger Erickson .05 .02
☐ 212 Mickey Hatcher .05 .02
☐ 213 Dave Winfield .60 .25
☐ 214 Tommy John .15 .07
☐ 215 Graig Nettles .10 .05
☐ 216 Reggie Jackson .75 .35
☐ 217 Rich Gossage .15 .07
☐ 218 Rick Cerone .05 .02
☐ 219 Willie Randolph .10 .05
☐ 220 Jerry Mumphrey .05 .02
☐ 221 Rickey Henderson 1.25 .55
☐ 222 Mike Norris .05 .02
☐ 223 Jim Spencer .05 .02
☐ 224 Tony Armas .05 .02
☐ 225 Matt Keough .05 .02
☐ 226 Cliff Johnson .05 .02
☐ 227 Dwayne Murphy .05 .02
☐ 228 Steve McCatty .05 .02
☐ 229 Richie Zisk .05 .02
☐ 230 Lenny Randle .05 .02
☐ 231 Jeff Burroughs .05 .02
☐ 232 Bruce Bochte .05 .02
☐ 233 Gary Gray .05 .02
☐ 234 Floyd Bannister .05 .02
☐ 235 Julio Cruz .05 .02
☐ 236 Tom Paciorek .05 .02
☐ 237 Danny Darwin .10 .05
☐ 238 Buddy Bell .10 .05
☐ 239 Al Oliver .10 .05
☐ 240 Jim Sundberg .10 .05
☐ 241 Pat Putnam .05 .02
☐ 242 Steve Comer .05 .02
☐ 243 Mickey Rivers .05 .02
☐ 244 Bump Wills .05 .02
☐ 245 Damaso Garcia .05 .02
☐ 246 Lloyd Moseby .05 .02
☐ 247 Ernie Whitt .05 .02
☐ 248 John Mayberry .05 .02
☐ 249 Otto Velez .05 .02
☐ 250 Dave Stieb .10 .05
☐ 251 Barry Bonnell .05 .02
☐ 252 Alfredo Griffin .05 .02
☐ 253 Gary Carter PLAY .10 .05
☐ 254 1981 AL Playoffs .05 .02
(Action at plate)
☐ 255 Dodgers Team .10 .05
World Champions
(Left half photo)
☐ 256 Dodgers Team .10 .05
World Champions
(Right half photo)
☐ 257 Fernando Valenzuela WS .15 .07
☐ 258 Steve Garvey WS .10 .05
☐ 259 Jerry Reuss WS .10 .05
Steve Yeager
☐ 260 Pedro Guerrero WS .10 .05
☐ xx Album 1.00 .45

1983 Topps

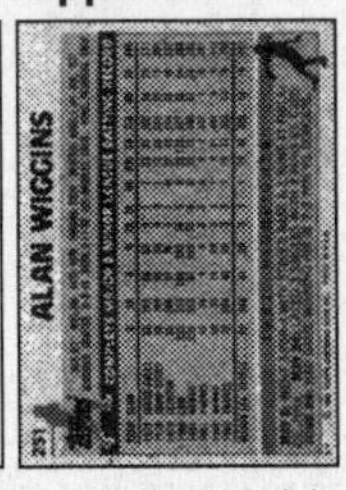

The cards in this 792-card set measure the standard size. Each player card front features a large action shot with a small cameo portrait at bottom right. There are special series for AL and NL All Stars (386-407), League Leaders (701-708), and Record Breakers (1-6). In addition, there are 34 "Super Veteran" (SV) cards and six numbered checklist cards. The Super Veteran cards are oriented horizontally and show two pictures of the featured player, a recent picture and a picture showing the player as a rookie. The team cards are actually Team Leader (TL) cards picturing the batting and pitching leader for that team with a checklist back. Cards were primarily issued in 15-card wax packs and 51-card rack packs. Notable Rookie Cards include Wade Boggs, Tony Gwynn and Ryne Sandberg.

	NRMT	VG-E
COMPLETE SET (792)	125.00	55.00
COMMON CARD (1-792)	.15	.07

☐ 1 Tony Armas RB .60 .25
☐ 2 Rickey Henderson RB 1.00 .45
Sets modern SB record
☐ 3 Greg Minton RB .15 .07
269 1/3 homerless
innings streak
☐ 4 Lance Parrish RB .30 .14
☐ 5 Manny Trillo RB .30 .14
479 consecutive
errorless chances,
second baseman
☐ 6 John Wathan RB .15 .07
ML catcher steals, season
☐ 7 Gene Richards .15 .07
☐ 8 Steve Balboni .15 .07
☐ 9 Joey McLaughlin .15 .07
☐ 10 Gorman Thomas .15 .07
☐ 11 Billy Gardner MG .15 .07
☐ 12 Paul Mirabella .15 .07
☐ 13 Larry Herndon .15 .07
☐ 14 Frank LaCorte .15 .07
☐ 15 Ron Cey .30 .14
☐ 16 George Vukovich .15 .07
☐ 17 Kent Tekulve .30 .14
☐ 18 Kent Tekulve SV .15 .07
☐ 19 Oscar Gamble .15 .07
☐ 20 Carlton Fisk 1.00 .45
☐ 21 Baltimore Orioles TL .60 .25
BA: Eddie Murray
ERA: Jim Palmer
(Checklist on back)
☐ 22 Randy Martz .15 .07
☐ 23 Mike Heath .15 .07
☐ 24 Steve Mura .15 .07
☐ 25 Hal McRae .30 .14
☐ 26 Jerry Royster .15 .07
☐ 27 Doug Corbett .15 .07
☐ 28 Bruce Bochte .15 .07
☐ 29 Randy Jones .15 .07
☐ 30 Jim Rice .30 .14
☐ 31 Bill Gullickson .30 .14
☐ 32 Dave Bergman .15 .07
☐ 33 Jack O'Connor .15 .07
☐ 34 Paul Householder .15 .07
☐ 35 Rollie Fingers 1.25 .55
☐ 36 Rollie Fingers SV .60 .25
☐ 37 Darrell Johnson MG .15 .07
☐ 38 Tim Flannery .15 .07
☐ 39 Terry Puhl .15 .07
☐ 40 Fernando Valenzuela 1.25 .55
☐ 41 Jerry Turner .15 .07
☐ 42 Dale Murray .15 .07
☐ 43 Bob Dernier .15 .07
☐ 44 Don Robinson .15 .07
☐ 45 John Mayberry .15 .07
☐ 46 Richard Dotson .15 .07
☐ 47 Dave McKay .15 .07
☐ 48 Lary Sorensen .15 .07
☐ 49 Willie McGee 1.25 .55
☐ 50 Bob Horner UER .15 .07
('82 RBI total 7)
☐ 51 Chicago Cubs TL .30 .14
BA: Leon Durham
ERA: Fergie Jenkins
(Checklist on back)
☐ 52 Onix Concepcion .15 .07
☐ 53 Mike Witt .15 .07
☐ 54 Jim Maler .15 .07
☐ 55 Mookie Wilson .30 .14
☐ 56 Chuck Rainey .15 .07
☐ 57 Tim Blackwell .15 .07
☐ 58 Al Holland .15 .07
☐ 59 Benny Ayala .15 .07
☐ 60 Johnny Bench 1.50 .70
☐ 61 Johnny Bench SV .60 .25
☐ 62 Bob McClure .15 .07
☐ 63 Rick Monday .15 .07
☐ 64 Bill Stein .15 .07
☐ 65 Jack Morris .30 .14
☐ 66 Bob Lillis MG .15 .07
☐ 67 Sal Butera .15 .07
☐ 68 Eric Show .15 .07
☐ 69 Lee Lacy .15 .07
☐ 70 Steve Carlton 1.00 .45
☐ 71 Steve Carlton SV .60 .25
☐ 72 Tom Paciorek .15 .07
☐ 73 Allen Ripley .15 .07
☐ 74 Julio Gonzalez .15 .07
☐ 75 Amos Otis .30 .14
☐ 76 Rick Mahler .15 .07
☐ 77 Hosken Powell .15 .07
☐ 78 Bill Caudill .15 .07
☐ 79 Mick Kelleher .15 .07
☐ 80 George Foster .30 .14
☐ 81 Yankees TL .30 .14
BA: Jerry Mumphrey
ERA: Dave Righetti
(Checklist on back)
☐ 82 Bruce Hurst .15 .07
☐ 83 Ryne Sandberg 25.00 11.00
☐ 84 Milt May .15 .07
☐ 85 Ken Singleton .30 .14
☐ 86 Tom Hume .15 .07
☐ 87 Joe Rudi .15 .07
☐ 88 Jim Gantner .30 .14
☐ 89 Leon Roberts .15 .07
☐ 90 Jerry Reuss .30 .14
☐ 91 Larry Milbourne .15 .07
☐ 92 Mike LaCoss .15 .07
☐ 93 John Castino .15 .07
☐ 94 Dave Edwards .15 .07
☐ 95 Alan Trammell 1.25 .55
☐ 96 Dick Howser MG .15 .07
☐ 97 Ross Baumgarten .15 .07
☐ 98 Vance Law .15 .07
☐ 99 Dickie Noles .15 .07
☐ 100 Pete Rose 1.50 .70
☐ 101 Pete Rose SV 1.00 .45
☐ 102 Dave Beard .15 .07
☐ 103 Darrell Porter .15 .07
☐ 104 Bob Walk .15 .07
☐ 105 Don Baylor .60 .25
☐ 106 Gene Nelson .15 .07
☐ 107 Mike Jorgensen .15 .07
☐ 108 Glenn Hoffman .15 .07
☐ 109 Luis Leal .15 .07
☐ 110 Ken Griffey .30 .14
☐ 111 Montreal Expos TL .30 .14
BA: Al Oliver
ERA: Steve Rogers
(Checklist on back)
☐ 112 Bob Shirley .15 .07
☐ 113 Ron Roenicke .15 .07
☐ 114 Jim Slaton .15 .07
☐ 115 Chili Davis 1.25 .55
☐ 116 Dave Schmidt .15 .07
☐ 117 Alan Knicely .15 .07
☐ 118 Chris Welsh .15 .07
☐ 119 Tom Brookens .15 .07
☐ 120 Len Barker .15 .07
☐ 121 Mickey Hatcher .15 .07
☐ 122 Jimmy Smith .15 .07
☐ 123 George Frazier .15 .07
☐ 124 Marc Hill .15 .07
☐ 125 Leon Durham .15 .07
☐ 126 Joe Torre MG .30 .14
☐ 127 Preston Hanna .15 .07
☐ 128 Mike Ramsey .15 .07
☐ 129 Checklist: 1-132 .30 .14
☐ 130 Dave Stieb .30 .14
☐ 131 Ed Ott .15 .07
☐ 132 Todd Cruz .15 .07
☐ 133 Jim Barr .15 .07
☐ 134 Hubie Brooks .30 .14
☐ 135 Dwight Evans .30 .14
☐ 136 Willie Aikens .15 .07
☐ 137 Woodie Fryman .15 .07
☐ 138 Rick Dempsey .30 .14

☐ 139 Bruce Berenyi	.15	.07
☐ 140 Willie Randolph	.30	.14
☐ 141 Indians TL	.30	.14
BA: Toby Harrah		
ERA: Rick Sutcliffe		
(Checklist on back)		
☐ 142 Mike Caldwell	.15	.07
☐ 143 Joe Pettini	.15	.07
☐ 144 Mark Wagner	.15	.07
☐ 145 Don Sutton	1.25	.55
☐ 146 Don Sutton SV	.60	.25
☐ 147 Rick Leach	.15	.07
☐ 148 Dave Roberts	.15	.07
☐ 149 Johnny Ray	.15	.07
☐ 150 Bruce Sutter	.30	.14
☐ 151 Bruce Sutter SV	.15	.07
☐ 152 Jay Johnstone	.30	.14
☐ 153 Jerry Koosman	.30	.14
☐ 154 Johnnie LeMaster	.15	.07
☐ 155 Dan Quisenberry	.30	.14
☐ 156 Billy Martin MG	.30	.14
☐ 157 Steve Bedrosian	.30	.14
☐ 158 Rob Wilfong	.15	.07
☐ 159 Mike Stanton	.15	.07
☐ 160 Dave Kingman	.60	.25
☐ 161 Dave Kingman SV	.30	.14
☐ 162 Mark Clear	.15	.07
☐ 163 Cal Ripken	15.00	6.75
☐ 164 David Palmer	.15	.07
☐ 165 Dan Driessen	.15	.07
☐ 166 John Pacella	.15	.07
☐ 167 Mark Brouhard	.15	.07
☐ 168 Juan Eichelberger	.15	.07
☐ 169 Doug Flynn	.15	.07
☐ 170 Steve Howe	.15	.07
☐ 171 Giants TL	.60	.25
BA: Joe Morgan		
ERA: Bill Laskey		
(Checklist on back)		
☐ 172 Vern Ruhle	.15	.07
☐ 173 Jim Morrison	.15	.07
☐ 174 Jerry Ujdur	.15	.07
☐ 175 Bo Diaz	.15	.07
☐ 176 Dave Righetti	.30	.14
☐ 177 Harold Baines	.60	.25
☐ 178 Luis Tiant	.30	.14
☐ 179 Luis Tiant SV	.15	.07
☐ 180 Rickey Henderson	1.50	.70
☐ 181 Terry Felton	.15	.07
☐ 182 Mike Fischlin	.15	.07
☐ 183 Ed VandeBerg	.15	.07
☐ 184 Bob Clark	.15	.07
☐ 185 Tim Lollar	.15	.07
☐ 186 Whitey Herzog MG	.30	.14
☐ 187 Terry Leach	.15	.07
☐ 188 Rick Miller	.15	.07
☐ 189 Dan Schatzeder	.15	.07
☐ 190 Cecil Cooper	.30	.14
☐ 191 Joe Price	.15	.07
☐ 192 Floyd Rayford	.15	.07
☐ 193 Harry Spilman	.15	.07
☐ 194 Cesar Geronimo	.15	.07
☐ 195 Bob Stoddard	.15	.07
☐ 196 Bill Fahey	.15	.07
☐ 197 Jim Eisenreich	1.25	.55
☐ 198 Kiko Garcia	.15	.07
☐ 199 Marty Bystrom	.15	.07
☐ 200 Rod Carew	.75	.35
☐ 201 Rod Carew SV	.60	.25
☐ 202 Blue Jays TL	.30	.14
BA: Damaso Garcia		
ERA: Dave Stieb		
(Checklist on back)		
☐ 203 Mike Morgan	.15	.07
☐ 204 Junior Kennedy	.15	.07
☐ 205 Dave Parker	.30	.14
☐ 206 Ken Oberkfell	.15	.07
☐ 207 Rick Camp	.15	.07
☐ 208 Dan Meyer	.15	.07
☐ 209 Mike Moore	.30	.14
☐ 210 Jack Clark	.30	.14
☐ 211 John Denny	.15	.07
☐ 212 John Stearns	.15	.07
☐ 213 Tom Burgmeier	.15	.07
☐ 214 Jerry White	.15	.07
☐ 215 Mario Soto	.15	.07
☐ 216 Tony LaRussa MG	.30	.14
☐ 217 Tim Stoddard	.15	.07
☐ 218 Roy Howell	.15	.07
☐ 219 Mike Armstrong	.15	.07
☐ 220 Dusty Baker	.30	.14
☐ 221 Joe Niekro	.30	.14
☐ 222 Damaso Garcia	.15	.07
☐ 223 John Montefusco	.15	.07
☐ 224 Mickey Rivers	.15	.07
☐ 225 Enos Cabell	.15	.07
☐ 226 Enrique Romo	.15	.07
☐ 227 Chris Bando	.15	.07
☐ 228 Joaquin Andujar	.15	.07
☐ 229 Phillies TL	.60	.25
BA: Bo Diaz		
ERA: Steve Carlton		
(Checklist on back)		
☐ 230 Fergie Jenkins	1.25	.55
☐ 231 Fergie Jenkins SV	.60	.25
☐ 232 Tom Brunansky	.60	.25
☐ 233 Wayne Gross	.15	.07
☐ 234 Larry Andersen	.15	.07
☐ 235 Claudell Washington	.15	.07
☐ 236 Steve Renko	.15	.07
☐ 237 Dan Norman	.15	.07
☐ 238 Bud Black	.30	.14
☐ 239 Dave Stapleton	.15	.07
☐ 240 Rich Gossage	.60	.25
☐ 241 Rich Gossage SV	.30	.14
☐ 242 Joe Nolan	.15	.07
☐ 243 Duane Walker	.15	.07
☐ 244 Dwight Bernard	.15	.07
☐ 245 Steve Sax	.30	.14
☐ 246 George Bamberger MG	.15	.07
☐ 247 Dave Smith	.15	.07
☐ 248 Bake McBride	.15	.07
☐ 249 Checklist: 133-264	.30	.14
☐ 250 Bill Buckner	.30	.14
☐ 251 Alan Wiggins	.15	.07
☐ 252 Luis Aguayo	.15	.07
☐ 253 Larry McWilliams	.15	.07
☐ 254 Rick Cerone	.15	.07
☐ 255 Gene Garber	.15	.07
☐ 256 Gene Garber SV	.15	.07
☐ 257 Jesse Barfield	.30	.14
☐ 258 Manny Castillo	.15	.07
☐ 259 Jeff Jones	.15	.07
☐ 260 Steve Kemp	.15	.07
☐ 261 Tigers TL	.30	.14
BA: Larry Herndon		
ERA: Dan Petry		
(Checklist on back)		
☐ 262 Ron Jackson	.15	.07
☐ 263 Renie Martin	.15	.07
☐ 264 Jamie Quirk	.15	.07
☐ 265 Joel Youngblood	.15	.07
☐ 266 Paul Boris	.15	.07
☐ 267 Terry Francona	.15	.07
☐ 268 Storm Davis	.15	.07
☐ 269 Ron Oester	.15	.07
☐ 270 Dennis Eckersley	1.25	.55
☐ 271 Ed Romero	.15	.07
☐ 272 Frank Tanana	.30	.14
☐ 273 Mark Belanger	.15	.07
☐ 274 Terry Kennedy	.15	.07
☐ 275 Ray Knight	.30	.14
☐ 276 Gene Mauch MG	.15	.07
☐ 277 Rance Mulliniks	.15	.07
☐ 278 Kevin Hickey	.15	.07
☐ 279 Greg Gross	.15	.07
☐ 280 Bert Blyleven	1.25	.55
☐ 281 Andre Robertson	.15	.07
☐ 282 Reggie Smith	1.25	.55
(Ryne Sandberg		
ducking back)		
☐ 283 Reggie Smith SV	.15	.07
☐ 284 Jeff Lahti	.15	.07
☐ 285 Lance Parrish	.30	.14
☐ 286 Rick Langford	.15	.07
☐ 287 Bobby Brown	.15	.07
☐ 288 Joe Cowley	.15	.07
☐ 289 Jerry Dybzinski	.15	.07
☐ 290 Jeff Reardon	.30	.14
☐ 291 Pirates TL	.30	.14
BA: Bill Madlock		
ERA: John Candelaria		
(Checklist on back)		
☐ 292 Craig Swan	.15	.07
☐ 293 Glenn Gulliver	.15	.07
☐ 294 Dave Engle	.15	.07
☐ 295 Jerry Remy	.15	.07
☐ 296 Greg Harris	.15	.07
☐ 297 Ned Yost	.15	.07
☐ 298 Floyd Chiffer	.15	.07
☐ 299 George Wright	.15	.07
☐ 300 Mike Schmidt	1.50	.70
☐ 301 Mike Schmidt SV	1.00	.45
☐ 302 Ernie Whitt	.15	.07
☐ 303 Miguel Dilone	.15	.07
☐ 304 Dave Rucker	.15	.07
☐ 305 Larry Bowa	.30	.14
☐ 306 Tom Lasorda MG	.60	.25
☐ 307 Lou Piniella	.30	.14
☐ 308 Jesus Vega	.15	.07
☐ 309 Jeff Leonard	.15	.07
☐ 310 Greg Luzinski	.30	.14
☐ 311 Glenn Brummer	.15	.07
☐ 312 Brian Kingman	.15	.07
☐ 313 Gary Gray	.15	.07
☐ 314 Ken Dayley	.15	.07
☐ 315 Rick Burleson	.15	.07
☐ 316 Paul Splittorff	.15	.07
☐ 317 Gary Rajsich	.15	.07
☐ 318 John Tudor	.15	.07
☐ 319 Lenn Sakata	.15	.07
☐ 320 Steve Rogers	.15	.07
☐ 321 Brewers TL	.60	.25
BA: Robin Yount		
ERA: Pete Vuckovich		
(Checklist on back)		
☐ 322 Dave Van Gorder	.15	.07
☐ 323 Luis DeLeon	.15	.07
☐ 324 Mike Marshall	.15	.07
☐ 325 Von Hayes	.30	.14
☐ 326 Garth Iorg	.15	.07
☐ 327 Bobby Castillo	.15	.07
☐ 328 Craig Reynolds	.15	.07
☐ 329 Randy Niemann	.15	.07
☐ 330 Buddy Bell	.30	.14
☐ 331 Mike Krukow	.15	.07
☐ 332 Glenn Wilson	.30	.14
☐ 333 Dave LaRoche	.15	.07
☐ 334 Dave LaRoche SV	.15	.07
☐ 335 Steve Henderson	.15	.07
☐ 336 Rene Lachemann MG	.15	.07
☐ 337 Tito Landrum	.15	.07
☐ 338 Bob Owchinko	.15	.07
☐ 339 Terry Harper	.15	.07
☐ 340 Larry Gura	.15	.07
☐ 341 Doug DeCinces	.30	.14
☐ 342 Atlee Hammaker	.15	.07
☐ 343 Bob Bailor	.15	.07
☐ 344 Roger LaFrancois	.15	.07
☐ 345 Jim Clancy	.15	.07
☐ 346 Joe Pittman	.15	.07
☐ 347 Sammy Stewart	.15	.07
☐ 348 Alan Bannister	.15	.07
☐ 349 Checklist: 265-396	.30	.14
☐ 350 Robin Yount	2.00	.90
☐ 351 Reds TL	.30	.14
BA: Cesar Cedeno		
ERA: Mario Soto		
(Checklist on back)		
☐ 352 Mike Scioscia	.30	.14
☐ 353 Steve Comer	.15	.07
☐ 354 Randy Johnson	.15	.07
☐ 355 Jim Bibby	.15	.07
☐ 356 Gary Woods	.15	.07
☐ 357 Len Matuszek	.15	.07
☐ 358 Jerry Garvin	.15	.07
☐ 359 Dave Collins	.15	.07
☐ 360 Nolan Ryan	6.00	2.70
☐ 361 Nolan Ryan SV	4.00	1.80
☐ 362 Bill Almon	.15	.07
☐ 363 John Stuper	.15	.07
☐ 364 Brett Butler	1.25	.55
☐ 365 Dave Lopes	.30	.14
☐ 366 Dick Williams MG	.15	.07
☐ 367 Bud Anderson	.15	.07
☐ 368 Richie Zisk	.15	.07
☐ 369 Jesse Orosco	.15	.07
☐ 370 Gary Carter	1.25	.55
☐ 371 Mike Richardt	.15	.07
☐ 372 Terry Crowley	.15	.07
☐ 373 Kevin Saucier	.15	.07
☐ 374 Wayne Krenchicki	.15	.07
☐ 375 Pete Vuckovich	.15	.07
☐ 376 Ken Landreaux	.15	.07
☐ 377 Lee May	.30	.14
☐ 378 Lee May SV	.15	.07
☐ 379 Guy Sularz	.15	.07
☐ 380 Ron Davis	.15	.07
☐ 381 Red Sox TL	.30	.14
BA: Jim Rice		
ERA: Bob Stanley		
(Checklist on back)		
☐ 382 Bob Knepper	.15	.07
☐ 383 Ozzie Virgil	.15	.07
☐ 384 Dave Dravecky	1.25	.55
☐ 385 Mike Easler	.15	.07
☐ 386 Rod Carew AS	1.25	.55
☐ 387 Bob Grich AS	.30	.14
☐ 388 George Brett AS	2.00	.90
☐ 389 Robin Yount AS	1.25	.55
☐ 390 Reggie Jackson AS	1.25	.55
☐ 391 Rickey Henderson AS	1.25	.55
☐ 392 Fred Lynn AS	.30	.14
☐ 393 Carlton Fisk AS	.60	.25
☐ 394 Pete Vuckovich AS	.15	.07
☐ 395 Larry Gura AS	.15	.07
☐ 396 Dan Quisenberry AS	.30	.14
☐ 397 Pete Rose AS	1.00	.45
☐ 398 Manny Trillo AS	.15	.07
☐ 399 Mike Schmidt AS	1.00	.45
☐ 400 Dave Concepcion AS	.30	.14

☐ 401 Dale Murphy AS 1.25 .55
☐ 402 Andre Dawson AS 1.25 .55
☐ 403 Tim Raines AS 1.25 .55
☐ 404 Gary Carter AS 1.25 .55
☐ 405 Steve Rogers AS .15 .07
☐ 406 Steve Carlton AS 1.25 .55
☐ 407 Bruce Sutter AS .30 .14
☐ 408 Rudy May .15 .07
☐ 409 Marvis Foley .15 .07
☐ 410 Phil Niekro 1.25 .55
☐ 411 Phil Niekro SV .60 .25
☐ 412 Rangers TL .30 .14
BA: Buddy Bell
ERA: Charlie Hough
(Checklist on back)
☐ 413 Matt Keough .15 .07
☐ 414 Julio Cruz .15 .07
☐ 415 Bob Forsch .15 .07
☐ 416 Joe Ferguson .15 .07
☐ 417 Tom Hausman .15 .07
☐ 418 Greg Pryor .15 .07
☐ 419 Steve Crawford .15 .07
☐ 420 Al Oliver .30 .14
☐ 421 Al Oliver SV .15 .07
☐ 422 George Cappuzzello .15 .07
☐ 423 Tom Lawless .15 .07
☐ 424 Jerry Augustine .15 .07
☐ 425 Pedro Guerrero .30 .14
☐ 426 Earl Weaver MG 1.25 .55
☐ 427 Roy Lee Jackson .15 .07
☐ 428 Champ Summers .15 .07
☐ 429 Eddie Whitson .15 .07
☐ 430 Kirk Gibson 1.25 .55
☐ 431 Gary Gaetti 1.00 .45
☐ 432 Porfirio Altamirano .15 .07
☐ 433 Dale Berra .15 .07
☐ 434 Dennis Lamp .15 .07
☐ 435 Tony Armas .15 .07
☐ 436 Bill Campbell .15 .07
☐ 437 Rick Sweet .15 .07
☐ 438 Dave LaPoint .15 .07
☐ 439 Rafael Ramirez .15 .07
☐ 440 Ron Guidry .30 .14
☐ 441 Astros TL .30 .14
BA: Ray Knight
ERA: Joe Niekro
(Checklist on back)
☐ 442 Brian Downing .15 .07
☐ 443 Don Hood .15 .07
☐ 444 Wally Backman .15 .07
☐ 445 Mike Flanagan .30 .14
☐ 446 Reid Nichols .15 .07
☐ 447 Bryn Smith .15 .07
☐ 448 Darrell Evans .30 .14
☐ 449 Eddie Milner .15 .07
☐ 450 Ted Simmons .30 .14
☐ 451 Ted Simmons SV .15 .07
☐ 452 Lloyd Moseby .15 .07
☐ 453 Lamar Johnson .15 .07
☐ 454 Bob Welch .30 .14
☐ 455 Sixto Lezcano .15 .07
☐ 456 Lee Elia MG .15 .07
☐ 457 Milt Wilcox .15 .07
☐ 458 Ron Washington .15 .07
☐ 459 Ed Farmer .15 .07
☐ 460 Roy Smalley .15 .07
☐ 461 Steve Trout .15 .07
☐ 462 Steve Nicosia .15 .07
☐ 463 Gaylord Perry 1.25 .55
☐ 464 Gaylord Perry SV .60 .25
☐ 465 Lonnie Smith .15 .07
☐ 466 Tom Underwood .15 .07
☐ 467 Rufino Linares .15 .07
☐ 468 Dave Goltz .15 .07
☐ 469 Ron Gardenhire .15 .07
☐ 470 Greg Minton .15 .07
☐ 471 Kansas City Royals TL .30 .14
BA: Willie Wilson
ERA: Vida Blue
(Checklist on back)
☐ 472 Gary Allenson .15 .07
☐ 473 John Lowenstein .15 .07
☐ 474 Ray Burris .15 .07
☐ 475 Cesar Cedeno .30 .14
☐ 476 Rob Picciolo .15 .07
☐ 477 Tom Niedenfuer .15 .07
☐ 478 Phil Garner .30 .14
☐ 479 Charlie Hough .30 .14
☐ 480 Toby Harrah .15 .07
☐ 481 Scot Thompson .15 .07
☐ 482 Tony Gwynn UER 50.00 22.00
(No Topps logo under
card number on back)
☐ 483 Lynn Jones .15 .07
☐ 484 Dick Ruthven .15 .07
☐ 485 Omar Moreno .15 .07
☐ 486 Clyde King MG .15 .07
☐ 487 Jerry Hairston .15 .07
☐ 488 Alfredo Griffin .15 .07
☐ 489 Tom Herr .25 .11
☐ 490 Jim Palmer 1.25 .55
☐ 491 Jim Palmer SV .60 .25
☐ 492 Paul Serna .15 .07
☐ 493 Steve McCatty .15 .07
☐ 494 Bob Brenly .15 .07
☐ 495 Warren Cromartie .15 .07
☐ 496 Tom Veryzer .15 .07
☐ 497 Rick Sutcliffe .30 .14
☐ 498 Wade Boggs 16.00 7.25
☐ 499 Jeff Little .15 .07
☐ 500 Reggie Jackson 1.50 .70
☐ 501 Reggie Jackson SV 1.25 .55
☐ 502 Atlanta Braves TL .30 .14
BA: Dale Murphy
ERA: Phil Niekro
(Checklist on back)
☐ 503 Moose Haas .15 .07
☐ 504 Don Werner .15 .07
☐ 505 Garry Templeton .15 .07
☐ 506 Jim Gott .15 .07
☐ 507 Tony Scott .15 .07
☐ 508 Tom Filer .15 .07
☐ 509 Lou Whitaker .60 .25
☐ 510 Tug McGraw .30 .14
☐ 511 Tug McGraw SV .15 .07
☐ 512 Doyle Alexander .15 .07
☐ 513 Fred Stanley .15 .07
☐ 514 Rudy Law .15 .07
☐ 515 Gene Tenace .30 .14
☐ 516 Bill Virdon MG .15 .07
☐ 517 Gary Ward .15 .07
☐ 518 Bill Laskey .15 .07
☐ 519 Terry Bulling .15 .07
☐ 520 Fred Lynn .30 .14
☐ 521 Bruce Benedict .15 .07
☐ 522 Pat Zachry .15 .07
☐ 523 Carney Lansford .30 .14
☐ 524 Tom Brennan .15 .07
☐ 525 Frank White .30 .14
☐ 526 Checklist: 397-528 .30 .14
☐ 527 Larry Biittner .15 .07
☐ 528 Jamie Easterly .15 .07
☐ 529 Tim Laudner .15 .07
☐ 530 Eddie Murray 1.50 .70
☐ 531 Oakland A's TL .60 .25
BA: Rickey Henderson
ERA: Rick Langford
(Checklist on back)
☐ 532 Dave Stewart .30 .14
☐ 533 Luis Salazar .15 .07
☐ 534 John Butcher .15 .07
☐ 535 Manny Trillo .15 .07
☐ 536 John Wockenfuss .15 .07
☐ 537 Rod Scurry .15 .07
☐ 538 Danny Heep .15 .07
☐ 539 Roger Erickson .15 .07
☐ 540 Ozzie Smith 2.50 1.10
☐ 541 Britt Burns .15 .07
☐ 542 Jody Davis .15 .07
☐ 543 Alan Fowlkes .15 .07
☐ 544 Larry Whisenton .15 .07
☐ 545 Floyd Bannister .15 .07
☐ 546 Dave Garcia MG .15 .07
☐ 547 Geoff Zahn .15 .07
☐ 548 Brian Giles .15 .07
☐ 549 Charlie Puleo .15 .07
☐ 550 Carl Yastrzemski 1.00 .45
☐ 551 Carl Yastrzemski SV 1.25 .55
☐ 552 Tim Wallach .30 .14
☐ 553 Dennis Martinez .30 .14
☐ 554 Mike Vail .15 .07
☐ 555 Steve Yeager .15 .07
☐ 556 Willie Upshaw .15 .07
☐ 557 Rick Honeycutt .15 .07
☐ 558 Dickie Thon .15 .07
☐ 559 Pete Redfern .15 .07
☐ 560 Ron LeFlore .30 .14
☐ 561 Cardinals TL .30 .14
BA: Lonnie Smith
ERA: Joaquin Andujar
(Checklist on back)
☐ 562 Dave Rozema .15 .07
☐ 563 Juan Bonilla .15 .07
☐ 564 Sid Monge .15 .07
☐ 565 Bucky Dent .30 .14
☐ 566 Manny Sarmiento .15 .07
☐ 567 Joe Simpson .15 .07
☐ 568 Willie Hernandez .30 .14
☐ 569 Jack Perconte .15 .07
☐ 570 Vida Blue .30 .14
☐ 571 Mickey Klutts .15 .07
☐ 572 Bob Watson .30 .14
☐ 573 Andy Hassler .15 .07
☐ 574 Glenn Adams .15 .07
☐ 575 Neil Allen .15 .07
☐ 576 Frank Robinson MG 1.25 .55
☐ 577 Luis Aponte .15 .07
☐ 578 David Green .15 .07
☐ 579 Rich Dauer .15 .07
☐ 580 Tom Seaver 1.50 .70
☐ 581 Tom Seaver SV 1.25 .55
☐ 582 Marshall Edwards .15 .07
☐ 583 Terry Forster .15 .07
☐ 584 Dave Hostetler .15 .07
☐ 585 Jose Cruz .30 .14
☐ 586 Frank Viola 1.25 .55
☐ 587 Ivan DeJesus .15 .07
☐ 588 Pat Underwood .15 .07
☐ 589 Alvis Woods .15 .07
☐ 590 Tony Pena .15 .07
☐ 591 White Sox TL .30 .14
BA: Greg Luzinski
ERA: LaMarr Hoyt
(Checklist on back)
☐ 592 Shane Rawley .15 .07
☐ 593 Broderick Perkins .15 .07
☐ 594 Eric Rasmussen .15 .07
☐ 595 Tim Raines 1.25 .55
☐ 596 Randy Johnson .15 .07
☐ 597 Mike Proly .15 .07
☐ 598 Dwayne Murphy .15 .07
☐ 599 Don Aase .15 .07
☐ 600 George Brett 2.50 1.10
☐ 601 Ed Lynch .15 .07
☐ 602 Rich Gedman .15 .07
☐ 603 Joe Morgan 1.25 .55
☐ 604 Joe Morgan SV 1.25 .55
☐ 605 Gary Roenicke .15 .07
☐ 606 Bobby Cox MG .30 .14
☐ 607 Charlie Leibrandt .15 .07
☐ 608 Don Money .15 .07
☐ 609 Danny Darwin .15 .07
☐ 610 Steve Garvey .60 .25
☐ 611 Bert Roberge .15 .07
☐ 612 Steve Swisher .15 .07
☐ 613 Mike Ivie .15 .07
☐ 614 Ed Glynn .15 .07
☐ 615 Garry Maddox .15 .07
☐ 616 Bill Nahorodny .15 .07
☐ 617 Butch Wynegar .15 .07
☐ 618 LaMarr Hoyt .30 .14
☐ 619 Keith Moreland .15 .07
☐ 620 Mike Norris .15 .07
☐ 621 New York Mets TL .30 .14
BA: Mookie Wilson
ERA: Craig Swan
(Checklist on back)
☐ 622 Dave Edler .15 .07
☐ 623 Luis Sanchez .15 .07
☐ 624 Glenn Hubbard .15 .07
☐ 625 Ken Forsch .15 .07
☐ 626 Jerry Martin .15 .07
☐ 627 Doug Bair .15 .07
☐ 628 Julio Valdez .15 .07
☐ 629 Charlie Lea .15 .07
☐ 630 Paul Molitor 1.50 .70
☐ 631 Tippy Martinez .15 .07
☐ 632 Alex Trevino .15 .07
☐ 633 Vicente Romo .15 .07
☐ 634 Max Venable .15 .07
☐ 635 Graig Nettles .30 .14
☐ 636 Graig Nettles SV .15 .07
☐ 637 Pat Corrales MG .15 .07
☐ 638 Dan Petry .15 .07
☐ 639 Art Howe .15 .07
☐ 640 Andre Thornton .15 .07
☐ 641 Billy Sample .15 .07
☐ 642 Checklist: 529-660 .30 .14
☐ 643 Bump Wills .15 .07
☐ 644 Joe Lefebvre .15 .07
☐ 645 Bill Madlock .30 .14
☐ 646 Jim Essian .15 .07
☐ 647 Bobby Mitchell .15 .07
☐ 648 Jeff Burroughs .15 .07
☐ 649 Tommy Boggs .15 .07
☐ 650 George Hendrick .15 .07
☐ 651 Angels TL .60 .25
BA: Rod Carew
ERA: Mike Witt
(Checklist on back)
☐ 652 Butch Hobson .15 .07
☐ 653 Ellis Valentine .15 .07
☐ 654 Bob Ojeda .15 .07
☐ 655 Al Bumbry .30 .14
☐ 656 Dave Frost .15 .07
☐ 657 Mike Gates .15 .07
☐ 658 Frank Pastore .15 .07
☐ 659 Charlie Moore .15 .07
☐ 660 Mike Hargrove .30 .14
☐ 661 Bill Russell .30 .14
☐ 662 Joe Sambito .15 .07

☐ 663 Tom O'Malley .15 .07
☐ 664 Bob Molinaro .15 .07
☐ 665 Jim Sundberg .30 .14
☐ 666 Sparky Anderson MG .30 .14
☐ 667 Dick Davis .15 .07
☐ 668 Larry Christenson .15 .07
☐ 669 Mike Squires .15 .07
☐ 670 Jerry Mumphrey .15 .07
☐ 671 Lenny Faedo .15 .07
☐ 672 Jim Kaat .60 .25
☐ 673 Jim Kaat SV .30 .14
☐ 674 Kurt Bevacqua .15 .07
☐ 675 Jim Beattie .15 .07
☐ 676 Biff Pocoroba .15 .07
☐ 677 Dave Revering .15 .07
☐ 678 Juan Beniquez .15 .07
☐ 679 Mike Scott .30 .14
☐ 680 Andre Dawson 1.25 .55
☐ 681 Dodgers Leaders .30 .14
BA: Pedro Guerrero
ERA: Fernando Valenzuela
(Checklist on back)
☐ 682 Bob Stanley .15 .07
☐ 683 Dan Ford .15 .07
☐ 684 Rafael Landestoy .15 .07
☐ 685 Lee Mazzilli .15 .07
☐ 686 Randy Lerch .15 .07
☐ 687 U.L. Washington .15 .07
☐ 688 Jim Wohlford .15 .07
☐ 689 Ron Hassey .15 .07
☐ 690 Kent Hrbek .60 .25
☐ 691 Dave Tobik .15 .07
☐ 692 Denny Walling .15 .07
☐ 693 Sparky Lyle .30 .14
☐ 694 Sparky Lyle SV .15 .07
☐ 695 Ruppert Jones .15 .07
☐ 696 Chuck Tanner MG .15 .07
☐ 697 Barry Foote .15 .07
☐ 698 Tony Bernazard .15 .07
☐ 699 Lee Smith 2.50 1.10
☐ 700 Keith Hernandez .30 .14
☐ 701 Batting Leaders .30 .14
AL: Willie Wilson
NL: Al Oliver
☐ 702 Home Run Leaders .60 .25
AL: Reggie Jackson
AL: Gorman Thomas
NL: Dave Kingman
☐ 703 RBI Leaders .30 .14
AL: Hal McRae
NL: Dale Murphy
NL: Al Oliver
☐ 704 SB Leaders 1.25 .55
AL: Rickey Henderson
NL: Tim Raines
☐ 705 Victory Leaders .60 .25
AL: LaMarr Hoyt
NL: Steve Carlton
☐ 706 Strikeout Leaders .60 .25
AL: Floyd Bannister
NL: Steve Carlton
☐ 707 ERA Leaders .30 .14
AL: Rick Sutcliffe
NL: Steve Rogers
☐ 708 Leading Firemen .30 .14
AL: Dan Quisenberry
NL: Bruce Sutter
☐ 709 Jimmy Sexton .15 .07
☐ 710 Willie Wilson .30 .14
☐ 711 Mariners TL .30 .14
BA: Bruce Bochte
ERA: Jim Beattie
(Checklist on back)
☐ 712 Bruce Kison .15 .07
☐ 713 Ron Hodges .15 .07
☐ 714 Wayne Nordhagen .15 .07
☐ 715 Tony Perez 1.25 .55
☐ 716 Tony Perez SV .60 .25
☐ 717 Scott Sanderson .15 .07
☐ 718 Jim Dwyer .15 .07
☐ 719 Rich Gale .15 .07
☐ 720 Dave Concepcion .30 .14
☐ 721 John Martin .15 .07
☐ 722 Jorge Orta .15 .07
☐ 723 Randy Moffitt .15 .07
☐ 724 Johnny Grubb .15 .07
☐ 725 Dan Spillner .15 .07
☐ 726 Harvey Kuenn MG .15 .07
☐ 727 Chet Lemon .15 .07
☐ 728 Ron Reed .15 .07
☐ 729 Jerry Morales .15 .07
☐ 730 Jason Thompson .15 .07
☐ 731 Al Williams .15 .07
☐ 732 Dave Henderson .30 .14
☐ 733 Buck Martinez .15 .07
☐ 734 Steve Braun .15 .07
☐ 735 Tommy John .60 .25
☐ 736 Tommy John SV .30 .14
☐ 737 Mitchell Page .15 .07
☐ 738 Tim Foli .15 .07
☐ 739 Rick Ownbey .15 .07
☐ 740 Rusty Staub .30 .14
☐ 741 Rusty Staub SV .15 .07
☐ 742 Padres TL .30 .14
BA: Terry Kennedy
ERA: Tim Lollar
(Checklist on back)
☐ 743 Mike Torrez .15 .07
☐ 744 Brad Mills .15 .07
☐ 745 Scott McGregor .15 .07
☐ 746 John Wathan .15 .07
☐ 747 Fred Breining .15 .07
☐ 748 Derrel Thomas .15 .07
☐ 749 Jon Matlack .15 .07
☐ 750 Ben Oglivie .15 .07
☐ 751 Brad Havens .15 .07
☐ 752 Luis Pujols .15 .07
☐ 753 Elias Sosa .15 .07
☐ 754 Bill Robinson .15 .07
☐ 755 John Candelaria .15 .07
☐ 756 Russ Nixon MG .15 .07
☐ 757 Rick Manning .15 .07
☐ 758 Aurelio Rodriguez .15 .07
☐ 759 Doug Bird .15 .07
☐ 760 Dale Murphy 1.25 .55
☐ 761 Gary Lucas .15 .07
☐ 762 Cliff Johnson .15 .07
☐ 763 Al Cowens .15 .07
☐ 764 Pete Falcone .15 .07
☐ 765 Bob Boone .30 .14
☐ 766 Barry Bonnell .15 .07
☐ 767 Duane Kuiper .15 .07
☐ 768 Chris Speier .15 .07
☐ 769 Checklist: 661-792 .30 .14
☐ 770 Dave Winfield 2.00 .90
☐ 771 Twins TL .30 .14
BA: Kent Hrbek
ERA: Bobby Castillo
(Checklist on back)
☐ 772 Jim Kern .15 .07
☐ 773 Larry Hisle .15 .07
☐ 774 Alan Ashby .15 .07
☐ 775 Burt Hooton .15 .07
☐ 776 Larry Parrish .15 .07
☐ 777 John Curtis .15 .07
☐ 778 Rich Hebner .30 .14
☐ 779 Rick Waits .15 .07
☐ 780 Gary Matthews .30 .14
☐ 781 Rick Rhoden .15 .07
☐ 782 Bobby Murcer .30 .14
☐ 783 Bobby Murcer SV .15 .07
☐ 784 Jeff Newman .15 .07
☐ 785 Dennis Leonard .15 .07
☐ 786 Ralph Houk MG .15 .07
☐ 787 Dick Tidrow .15 .07
☐ 788 Dane Iorg .15 .07
☐ 789 Bryan Clark .15 .07
☐ 790 Bob Grich .30 .14
☐ 791 Gary Lavelle .15 .07
☐ 792 Chris Chambliss .30 .14

1983 Topps Glossy Send-Ins

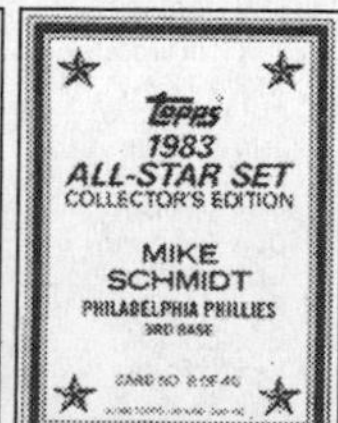

The cards in this 40-card set measure the standard size. The 1983 Topps "Collector's Edition" or "All-Star Set" (popularly known as "Glossies") consists of color ballplayer picture cards with shiny, glazed surfaces. The player's name appears in small print outside the frame line at bottom left. The backs contain no biography or record and list only the set titles, the player's name, team, position, and the card number.

	NRMT	VG-E
COMPLETE SET (40)	15.00	6.75
COMMON CARD (1-40)	.10	.05

☐ 1 Carl Yastrzemski 1.00 .45
☐ 2 Mookie Wilson .10 .05
☐ 3 Andre Thornton .10 .05
☐ 4 Keith Hernandez .20 .09
☐ 5 Robin Yount 1.00 .45
☐ 6 Terry Kennedy .10 .05
☐ 7 Dave Winfield 1.00 .45
☐ 8 Mike Schmidt 2.00 .90
☐ 9 Buddy Bell .20 .09
☐ 10 Fernando Valenzuela .35 .16
☐ 11 Rich Gossage .20 .09
☐ 12 Bob Horner .10 .05
☐ 13 Toby Harrah .10 .05
☐ 14 Pete Rose 2.00 .90
☐ 15 Cecil Cooper .20 .09
☐ 16 Dale Murphy .50 .23
☐ 17 Carlton Fisk 1.00 .45
☐ 18 Ray Knight .10 .05
☐ 19 Jim Palmer .75 .35
☐ 20 Gary Carter .35 .16
☐ 21 Richie Zisk .10 .05
☐ 22 Dusty Baker .20 .09
☐ 23 Willie Wilson .10 .05
☐ 24 Bill Buckner .20 .09
☐ 25 Dave Stieb .10 .05
☐ 26 Bill Madlock .10 .05
☐ 27 Lance Parrish .20 .09
☐ 28 Nolan Ryan 5.00 2.20
☐ 29 Rod Carew 1.00 .45
☐ 30 Al Oliver .20 .09
☐ 31 George Brett 2.50 1.10
☐ 32 Jack Clark .10 .05
☐ 33 Rickey Henderson 1.25 .55
☐ 34 Dave Concepcion .20 .09
☐ 35 Kent Hrbek .20 .09
☐ 36 Steve Carlton .75 .35
☐ 37 Eddie Murray 1.50 .70
☐ 38 Ruppert Jones .10 .05
☐ 39 Reggie Jackson 1.00 .45
☐ 40 Bruce Sutter .20 .09

1983 Topps Traded

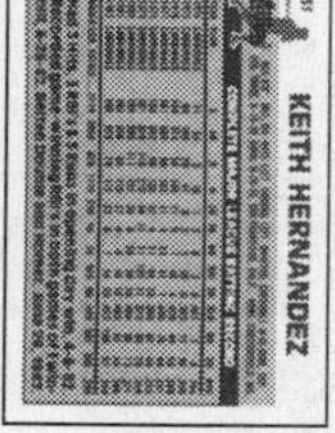

For the third year in a row, Topps issued a 132-card standard-size Traded (or extended) set featuring some of the year's top rookies and players who had changed teams during the year. The cards were available through hobby dealers only in factory set form and were printed in Ireland by the Topps affiliate in that country. The set is numbered alphabetically by player. The Darryl Strawberry card number 108 can be found with either one or two asterisks (in the lower left corner of the reverse). There is no difference in value for either version. The key (extended) Rookie Cards in this set include Julio Franco, Tony Phillips and Darryl Strawberry.

	NRMT	VG-E
COMP.FACT.SET (132)	40.00	18.00
COMMON CARD (1T-132T)	.25	.11

☐ 1T Neil Allen .25 .11
☐ 2T Bill Almon .25 .11
☐ 3T Joe Altobelli MG .25 .11
☐ 4T Tony Armas .25 .11
☐ 5T Doug Bair .25 .11
☐ 6T Steve Baker .25 .11
☐ 7T Floyd Bannister .25 .11
☐ 8T Don Baylor 2.00 .90
☐ 9T Tony Bernazard .25 .11
☐ 10T Larry Biittner .25 .11
☐ 11T Dann Bilardello .25 .11
☐ 12T Doug Bird .25 .11
☐ 13T Steve Boros MG .25 .11
☐ 14T Greg Brock .25 .11
☐ 15T Mike C. Brown .25 .11
☐ 16T Tom Burgmeier .25 .11
☐ 17T Randy Bush .25 .11
☐ 18T Bert Campaneris 1.00 .45
☐ 19T Ron Cey 1.00 .45
☐ 20T Chris Codiroli .25 .11
☐ 21T Dave Collins .25 .11
☐ 22T Terry Crowley .25 .11
☐ 23T Julio Cruz .25 .11
☐ 24T Mike Davis .25 .11
☐ 25T Frank DiPino .25 .11
☐ 26T Bill Doran 1.00 .45

☐ 27T Jerry Dybzinski .25 .11
☐ 28T Jamie Easterly .25 .11
☐ 29T Juan Eichelberger .25 .11
☐ 30T Jim Essian .25 .11
☐ 31T Pete Falcone .25 .11
☐ 32T Mike Ferraro MG .25 .11
☐ 33T Terry Forster .25 .11
☐ 34T Julio Franco 4.00 1.80
☐ 35T Rich Gale .25 .11
☐ 36T Kiko Garcia .25 .11
☐ 37T Steve Garvey 2.00 .90
☐ 38T Johnny Grubb .25 .11
☐ 39T Mel Hall 1.00 .45
☐ 40T Von Hayes 1.00 .45
☐ 41T Danny Heep .25 .11
☐ 42T Steve Henderson .25 .11
☐ 43T Keith Hernandez 2.00 .90
☐ 44T Leo Hernandez .25 .11
☐ 45T Willie Hernandez 1.00 .45
☐ 46T Al Holland .25 .11
☐ 47T Frank Howard MG 1.00 .45
☐ 48T Bobby Johnson .25 .11
☐ 49T Cliff Johnson .25 .11
☐ 50T Odell Jones .25 .11
☐ 51T Mike Jorgensen .25 .11
☐ 52T Bob Kearney .25 .11
☐ 53T Steve Kemp .25 .11
☐ 54T Matt Keough .25 .11
☐ 55T Ron Kittle 1.00 .45
☐ 56T Mickey Klutts .25 .11
☐ 57T Alan Knicely .25 .11
☐ 58T Mike Krukow .25 .11
☐ 59T Rafael Landestoy .25 .11
☐ 60T Carney Lansford 1.00 .45
☐ 61T Joe Lefebvre .25 .11
☐ 62T Bryan Little .25 .11
☐ 63T Aurelio Lopez .25 .11
☐ 64T Mike Madden .25 .11
☐ 65T Rick Manning .25 .11
☐ 66T Billy Martin MG 1.00 .45
☐ 67T Lee Mazzilli .25 .11
☐ 68T Andy McGaffigan .25 .11
☐ 69T Craig McMurtry .25 .11
☐ 70T John McNamara MG .25 .11
☐ 71T Orlando Mercado .25 .11
☐ 72T Larry Milbourne .25 .11
☐ 73T Randy Moffitt .25 .11
☐ 74T Sid Monge .25 .11
☐ 75T Jose Morales .25 .11
☐ 76T Omar Moreno .25 .11
☐ 77T Joe Morgan
☐ 78T Mike Morgan .25 .11
☐ 79T Dale Murray .25 .11
☐ 80T Jeff Newman .25 .11
☐ 81T Pete O'Brien 1.00 .45
☐ 82T Jorge Orta .25 .11
☐ 83T Alejandro Pena 1.00 .45
☐ 84T Pascual Perez .25 .11
☐ 85T Tony Perez
☐ 86T Broderick Perkins .25 .11
☐ 87T Tony Phillips 4.00 1.80
☐ 88T Charlie Puleo .25 .11
☐ 89T Pat Putnam .25 .11
☐ 90T Jamie Quirk .25 .11
☐ 91T Doug Rader MG .25 .11
☐ 92T Chuck Rainey .25 .11
☐ 93T Bobby Ramos .25 .11
☐ 94T Gary Redus 1.00 .45
☐ 95T Steve Renko .25 .11
☐ 96T Leon Roberts .25 .11
☐ 97T Aurelio Rodriguez .25 .11
☐ 98T Dick Ruthven .25 .11
☐ 99T Daryl Sconiers .25 .11
☐ 100T Mike Scott 1.00 .45
☐ 101T Tom Seaver 5.00 2.20
☐ 102T John Shelby .25 .11
☐ 103T Bob Shirley .25 .11
☐ 104T Joe Simpson .25 .11
☐ 105T Doug Sisk .25 .11
☐ 106T Mike Smithson .25 .11
☐ 107T Elias Sosa .25 .11
☐ 108T Darryl Strawberry 20.00 9.00
☐ 109T Tom Tellmann .25 .11
☐ 110T Gene Tenace 1.00 .45
☐ 111T Gorman Thomas .25 .11
☐ 112T Dick Tidrow .25 .11
☐ 113T Dave Tobik .25 .11
☐ 114T Wayne Tolleson .25 .11
☐ 115T Mike Torrez .25 .11
☐ 116T Manny Trillo .25 .11
☐ 117T Steve Trout .25 .11
☐ 118T Lee Tunnell .25 .11
☐ 119T Mike Vail .25 .11
☐ 120T Ellis Valentine .25 .11
☐ 121T Tom Veryzer .25 .11
☐ 122T George Vukovich .25 .11
☐ 123T Rick Waits .25 .11
☐ 124T Greg Walker 1.00 .45
☐ 125T Chris Welsh .25 .11
☐ 126T Len Whitehouse .25 .11
☐ 127T Eddie Whitson .25 .11
☐ 128T Jim Wohlford .25 .11
☐ 129T Matt Young .25 .11
☐ 130T Joel Youngblood .25 .11
☐ 131T Pat Zachry .25 .11
☐ 132T Checklist 1T-132T .25 .11

1983 Topps Foldouts

The cards in this 85-card (five folders with 17 photos in each folder) set measure 3 1/2" by 5 5/16". The 1983 Fold-Outs were an innovation by Topps featuring five sets of 17 postcard-size photos each. Each of the five sets had a theme of career leaders in a particular category. The five catagories -- batting leaders, home run leaders, stolen base leaders, pitching leaders and relief aces -- featured the 17 top active players in their respective categories. If a player were a leader in more than one category, he is pictured in more than one of the five sets. These foldout booklets are typically sold intact and are priced below at one price per complete panel. Each picture contains a facsimile autograph as well. The quality of the photos is very good. In the checklist below the leaders are listed in order of their career standing as shown on each foldout.

	NRMT	VG-E
COMPLETE SET (5)	5.00	2.20
COMMON PANEL (1-5)	1.00	.45

☐ 1 Career Wins 1.25 .55
Gaylord Perry, 307
Steve Carlton
Jim Kaat
Fergie Jenkins
Tom Seaver
Jim Palmer
Don Sutton
Phil Niekro
Tommy John
Nolan Ryan
Vida Blue
Jerry Koosman
Mike Torrez
Bert Blyleven
Joe Niekro
Jerry Reuss
Paul Splittorff

☐ 2 Home Run Leaders 1.50 .70
Reggie Jackson, 464
Carl Yastrzemski
Johnny Bench
Tony Perez
Mike Schmidt
Dave Kingman
Graig Nettles
Rusty Staub
Greg Luzinski
George Foster
John Mayberry
Bobby Murcer
Joe Morgan
Jim Rice
Rick Monday
Darrell Evans
Ron Cey

☐ 3 Batting Leaders 1.50 .70
Rod Carew, .331
George Brett
Bill Madlock
Lonnie Smith
Willie Wilson
Pete Rose
Dave Parker
Cecil Cooper
Jim Rice
Al Oliver
Pedro Guerrero
Ken Griffey
Fred Lynn
Steve Garvey
Bake McBride
Keith Hernandez
Dane Iorg

☐ 4 Relief Aces 1.00 .45
Rollie Fingers, 301
Bruce Sutter
Rich Gossage
Tug McGraw
Gene Garber
Kent Tekulve
Bill Campbell
Terry Forster
Tom Burgmeier
Greg Lavelle
Dan Quisenberry
Jim Kern
Randy Moffitt
Ron Reed
EliasSosa
Ed Farmer
Greg Minton

☐ 5 Steals Leaders 1.00 .45
Joe Morgan, 663
Cesar Cedeno
Ron LeFlore
Davey Lopes
Omar Moreno
Rod Carew
Amos Otis
Rickey Henderson
Larry Bowa
Willie Wilson
Don Baylor
Julio Cruz
Mickey Rivers
Dave Concepcion
Jose Cruz
Garry Maddox
Al Bumbry

1983 Topps Leader Sheet

The cards in this 8-player sheet measure 2 1/2" by 3 1/2". The full sheet is 7 1/2" by 10 1/2". The full sheet is typically kept intact as it has not been perforated. The cards are blank backed and feature the league statistical leaders from the previous season. The cards are unnumbered and are listed below in left to right order of appearance on the sheet.

	NRMT	VG-E
COMPLETE SHEET	2.00	.90
COMMON CARD	.25	.11

☐ 1 Willie Wilson .25 .11
AL Batting
.332 Batting Average

☐ 2 Reggie Jackson .50 .23
Gorman Thomas
AL Home Runs
39 Home Runs

☐ 3 Al Oliver .25 .11
NL Batting
.331 Batting Average

☐ 4 LaMarr Hoyt .25 .11
AL Victories
19 Victories

☐ 5 Steve Carlton .50 .23
NL Victories
23 Victories

☐ 6 Dan Quisenberry .25 .11
AL Saves
35 Saves

☐ 7 Dave Kingman .25 .11
NL Home Runs
37 Home Runs

☐ 8 Bruce Sutter .25 .11
NL Saves
36 Saves

1983 Topps/O-Pee-Chee Stickers

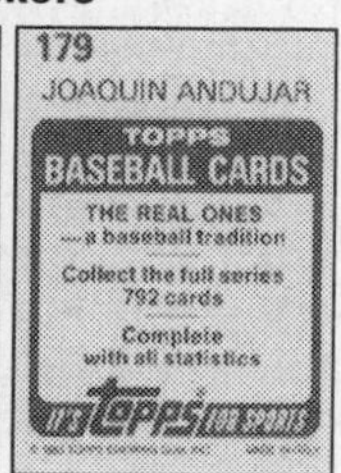

Made for Topps and O-Pee-Chee by Panini, an Italian company, these 330 stickers measure approximately 1 15/16" by 2 9/16" and are numbered on both front and back. The fronts feature white-bordered color player photos framed with a colored and a black line. The colored line is red for AL players and blue for NL players. The backs carry player names and a bilingual ad for the O-Pee-Chee sticker album. The album, onto which the stickers could be affixed, was available at retail stores. The album and the sticker numbering are organized as follows: Home Run Kings (1-14), AL Pitching and Batting Leaders (15-22), Baltimore Orioles (23-30), Boston Red Sox (31-38), California Angels (39-46), Chicago White Sox (47-54), Cleveland Indians (55-62), Detroit Tigers (63-70), Kansas City Royals (71-78), Milwaukee Brewers (79-86), Minnesota Twins (87-94), New York Yankees (95-102), Oakland A's (103-110), Seattle Mariners (111-118), Texas Rangers (119-126), Toronto Blue Jays (127-134), 1982 Record Breakers (135-146), 1982 Championship Series (147-158), AL and NL All-Stars (159-178), 1982 World Series (179-190), 1982 Record Breakers (191-202), NL Pitching and Batting Leaders (203-210), Atlanta Braves (211-218), Chicago Cubs (219-226), Cincinnati Reds (227-234), Houston Astros (235-242), Los Angeles Dodgers (243-250), Montreal Expos (251-258), New York Mets (259-266), Philadelphia Phillies (267-274), Pittsburgh Pirates (275-282), St. Louis Cardinals (283-290), San Diego Padres (291-298), San Francisco Giants (299-306), and Stars of the Future (307-330). Wade Boggs and Ryne Sandberg are featured during their Rookie Card year.

	NRMT	VG-E
COMPLETE SET (330)	15.00	6.75
COMMON STICKER (1-330)	.05	.02
COMMON FOIL	.10	.05
*OPC: 2X VALUES BELOW		
☐ 1 Hank Aaron FOIL	1.25	.55
☐ 2 Babe Ruth FOIL	3.00	1.35
☐ 3 Willie Mays FOIL	1.50	.70
☐ 4 Frank Robinson FOIL	.30	.14
☐ 5 Reggie Jackson	.50	.23
☐ 6 Carl Yastrzemski	.40	.18
☐ 7 Johnny Bench	.50	.23
☐ 8 Tony Perez	.15	.07
☐ 9 Lee May	.10	.05
☐ 10 Mike Schmidt	.60	.25
☐ 11 Dave Kingman	.10	.05
☐ 12 Reggie Smith	.10	.05
☐ 13 Graig Nettles	.10	.05
☐ 14 Rusty Staub	.10	.05
☐ 15 Willie Wilson	.05	.02
☐ 16 LaMarr Hoyt	.05	.02
☐ 17 Reggie Jackson and Gorman Thomas	.15	.07
☐ 18 Floyd Bannister	.05	.02
☐ 19 Hal McRae	.10	.05
☐ 20 Rick Sutcliffe	.05	.02
☐ 21 Rickey Henderson	.50	.23
☐ 22 Dan Quisenberry	.05	.02
☐ 23 Jim Palmer FOIL	.40	.18
☐ 24 John Lowenstein	.05	.02
☐ 25 Mike Flanagan	.10	.05
☐ 26 Cal Ripken	4.00	1.80
☐ 27 Rich Dauer	.05	.02
☐ 28 Ken Singleton	.10	.05
☐ 29 Eddie Murray	.50	.23
☐ 30 Rick Dempsey	.10	.05
☐ 31 Carl Yastrzemski FOIL	.60	.25
☐ 32 Carney Lansford	.10	.05
☐ 33 Jerry Remy	.05	.02
☐ 34 Dennis Eckersley	.15	.07
☐ 35 Dave Stapleton	.05	.02
☐ 36 Mark Clear	.05	.02
☐ 37 Jim Rice	.10	.05
☐ 38 Dwight Evans	.10	.05
☐ 39 Rod Carew	.40	.18
☐ 40 Don Baylor	.10	.05
☐ 41 Reggie Jackson FOIL	.75	.35
☐ 42 Geoff Zahn	.05	.02
☐ 43 Bobby Grich	.10	.05
☐ 44 Fred Lynn	.10	.05
☐ 45 Bob Boone	.10	.05
☐ 46 Doug DeCinces	.05	.02
☐ 47 Tom Paciorek	.05	.02
☐ 48 Britt Burns	.05	.02
☐ 49 Tony Bernazard	.05	.02
☐ 50 Steve Kemp	.05	.02
☐ 51 Greg Luzinski FOIL	.15	.07
☐ 52 Harold Baines	.10	.05
☐ 53 LaMarr Hoyt	.05	.02
☐ 54 Carlton Fisk	.30	.14
☐ 55 Andre Thornton FOIL	.10	.05
☐ 56 Mike Hargrove	.10	.05
☐ 57 Len Barker	.05	.02
☐ 58 Toby Harrah	.05	.02
☐ 59 Dan Spillner	.05	.02
☐ 60 Rick Manning	.05	.02
☐ 61 Rick Sutcliffe	.05	.02
☐ 62 Ron Hassey	.05	.02
☐ 63 Lance Parrish FOIL	.15	.07
☐ 64 John Wockenfuss	.05	.02
☐ 65 Lou Whitaker	.10	.05
☐ 66 Alan Trammell	.15	.07
☐ 67 Kirk Gibson	.15	.07
☐ 68 Larry Herndon	.05	.02
☐ 69 Jack Morris	.10	.05
☐ 70 Dan Petry	.05	.02
☐ 71 Frank White	.10	.05
☐ 72 Amos Otis	.10	.05
☐ 73 Willie Wilson FOIL	.10	.05
☐ 74 Dan Quisenberry	.05	.02
☐ 75 Hal McRae	.10	.05
☐ 76 George Brett	1.50	.70
☐ 77 Larry Gura	.05	.02
☐ 78 John Wathan	.05	.02
☐ 79 Rollie Fingers	.15	.07
☐ 80 Cecil Cooper	.10	.05
☐ 81 Robin Yount FOIL	.50	.23
☐ 82 Ben Oglivie	.05	.02
☐ 83 Paul Molitor	.40	.18
☐ 84 Gorman Thomas	.05	.02
☐ 85 Ted Simmons	.10	.05
☐ 86 Pete Vuckovich	.05	.02
☐ 87 Gary Gaetti	.25	.11
☐ 88 Kent Hrbek FOIL	.30	.14
☐ 89 John Castino	.05	.02
☐ 90 Tom Brunansky	.05	.02
☐ 91 Bobby Mitchell	.05	.02
☐ 92 Gary Ward	.05	.02
☐ 93 Tim Laudner	.05	.02
☐ 94 Ron Davis	.05	.02
☐ 95 Willie Randolph	.10	.05
☐ 96 Roy Smalley	.05	.02
☐ 97 Jerry Mumphrey	.05	.02
☐ 98 Ken Griffey	.10	.05
☐ 99 Dave Winfield FOIL	.50	.23
☐ 100 Rich Gossage	.10	.05
☐ 101 Butch Wynegar	.05	.02
☐ 102 Ron Guidry	.10	.05
☐ 103 Rickey Henderson FOIL	.75	.35
☐ 104 Mike Heath	.05	.02
☐ 105 Dave Lopes	.10	.05
☐ 106 Rick Langford	.05	.02
☐ 107 Dwayne Murphy	.05	.02
☐ 108 Tony Armas	.05	.02
☐ 109 Matt Keough	.05	.02
☐ 110 Danny Meyer	.05	.02
☐ 111 Bruce Bochte	.05	.02
☐ 112 Julio Cruz	.05	.02
☐ 113 Floyd Bannister	.05	.02
☐ 114 Gaylord Perry FOIL	.30	.14
☐ 115 Al Cowens	.05	.02
☐ 116 Richie Zisk	.05	.02
☐ 117 Jim Essian	.05	.02
☐ 118 Bill Caudill	.05	.02
☐ 119 Buddy Bell FOIL	.15	.07
☐ 120 Larry Parrish	.05	.02
☐ 121 Danny Darwin	.05	.02
☐ 122 Bucky Dent	.10	.05
☐ 123 Johnny Grubb	.05	.02
☐ 124 George Wright	.05	.02
☐ 125 Charlie Hough	.10	.05
☐ 126 Jim Sundberg	.05	.02
☐ 127 Dave Stieb FOIL	.10	.05
☐ 128 Willie Upshaw	.05	.02
☐ 129 Alfredo Griffin	.05	.02
☐ 130 Lloyd Moseby	.05	.02
☐ 131 Ernie Whitt	.05	.02
☐ 132 Jim Clancy	.05	.02
☐ 133 Barry Bonnell	.05	.02
☐ 134 Damaso Garcia	.05	.02
☐ 135 Jim Kaat RB	.10	.05
☐ 136 Jim Kaat RB	.10	.05
☐ 137 Greg Minton RB	.05	.02
☐ 138 Greg Minton RB	.05	.02
☐ 139 Paul Molitor RB	.15	.07
☐ 140 Paul Molitor RB	.15	.07
☐ 141 Manny Trillo RB	.05	.02
☐ 142 Manny Trillo RB	.05	.02
☐ 143 Joel Youngblood RB	.05	.02
☐ 144 Joel Youngblood RB	.05	.02
☐ 145 Robin Yount RB	.15	.07
☐ 146 Robin Yount RB	.15	.07
☐ 147 Willie McGee LCS	.10	.05
☐ 148 Darrell Porter LCS	.05	.02
☐ 149 Darrell Porter LCS	.05	.02
☐ 150 Robin Yount LCS	.15	.07
☐ 151 Bruce Benedict LCS	.05	.02
☐ 152 Bruce Benedict LCS	.05	.02
☐ 153 George Hendrick LCS	.05	.02
☐ 154 Bruce Benedict LCS	.05	.02
☐ 155 Doug DeCinces LCS	.05	.02
☐ 156 Paul Molitor LCS	.15	.07
☐ 157 Charlie Moore LCS	.05	.02
☐ 158 Fred Lynn LCS	.10	.05
☐ 159 Rickey Henderson	.50	.23
☐ 160 Dale Murphy	.15	.07
☐ 161 Willie Wilson	.05	.02
☐ 162 Jack Clark	.10	.05
☐ 163 Reggie Jackson	.50	.23
☐ 164 Andre Dawson	.25	.11
☐ 165 Dan Quisenberry	.05	.02
☐ 166 Bruce Sutter	.10	.05
☐ 167 Robin Yount	.30	.14
☐ 168 Ozzie Smith	.75	.35
☐ 169 Frank White	.10	.05
☐ 170 Phil Garner	.10	.05
☐ 171 Doug DeCinces	.05	.02
☐ 172 Mike Schmidt	.60	.25
☐ 173 Cecil Cooper	.10	.05
☐ 174 Al Oliver	.10	.05
☐ 175 Jim Palmer	.25	.11
☐ 176 Steve Carlton	.40	.18
☐ 177 Carlton Fisk	.30	.14
☐ 178 Gary Carter	.10	.05
☐ 179 Joaquin Andujar WS	.05	.02
☐ 180 Ozzie Smith WS	.25	.11
☐ 181 Cecil Cooper WS	.10	.05
☐ 182 Darrell Porter WS	.05	.02
☐ 183 Darrell Porter WS	.05	.02
☐ 184 Mike Caldwell WS	.05	.02
☐ 185 Mike Caldwell WS	.05	.02
☐ 186 Ozzie Smith WS	.25	.11
☐ 187 Bruce Sutter WS	.10	.05
☐ 188 Keith Hernandez WS	.10	.05
☐ 189 Dane Iorg WS	.05	.02
☐ 190 Dane Iorg WS	.05	.02
☐ 191 Tony Armas RB	.05	.02
☐ 192 Tony Armas RB	.05	.02
☐ 193 Lance Parrish RB	.10	.05
☐ 194 Lance Parrish RB	.10	.05
☐ 195 John Wathan RB	.05	.02
☐ 196 John Wathan RB	.05	.02
☐ 197 Rickey Henderson RB	.25	.11
☐ 198 Rickey Henderson RB	.25	.11
☐ 199 Rickey Henderson RB	.25	.11
☐ 200 Rickey Henderson RB	.25	.11
☐ 201 Rickey Henderson RB	.25	.11
☐ 202 Rickey Henderson RB	.25	.11
☐ 203 Steve Carlton	.40	.18
☐ 204 Steve Carlton	.40	.18
☐ 205 Al Oliver	.10	.05
☐ 206 Dale Murphy and Al Oliver	.15	.07
☐ 207 Dave Kingman	.10	.05
☐ 208 Steve Rogers	.05	.02
☐ 209 Bruce Sutter	.10	.05
☐ 210 Tim Raines	.15	.07
☐ 211 Dale Murphy FOIL	.30	.14
☐ 212 Chris Chambliss	.10	.05
☐ 213 Gene Garber	.05	.02
☐ 214 Bob Horner	.05	.02
☐ 215 Glenn Hubbard	.05	.02
☐ 216 Claudell Washington	.05	.02
☐ 217 Bruce Benedict	.05	.02
☐ 218 Phil Niekro	.15	.07
☐ 219 Leon Durham FOIL	.10	.05
☐ 220 Jay Johnstone	.10	.05
☐ 221 Larry Bowa	.10	.05
☐ 222 Keith Moreland	.05	.02
☐ 223 Bill Buckner	.10	.05
☐ 224 Fergie Jenkins	.15	.07
☐ 225 Dick Tidrow	.05	.02
☐ 226 Jody Davis	.05	.02
☐ 227 Dave Concepcion	.10	.05
☐ 228 Dan Driessen	.05	.02
☐ 229 Johnny Bench	.50	.23
☐ 230 Ron Oester	.05	.02
☐ 231 Cesar Cedeno	.10	.05

☐ 232 Alex Trevino	.05	.02
☐ 233 Tom Seaver	.50	.23
☐ 234 Mario Soto	.05	.02
☐ 235 Nolan Ryan FOIL	3.00	1.35
☐ 236 Art Howe	.10	.05
☐ 237 Phil Garner	.10	.05
☐ 238 Ray Knight	.10	.05
☐ 239 Terry Puhl	.05	.02
☐ 240 Joe Niekro	.10	.05
☐ 241 Alan Ashby	.05	.02
☐ 242 Jose Cruz	.10	.05
☐ 243 Steve Garvey	.15	.07
☐ 244 Ron Cey	.10	.05
☐ 245 Dusty Baker	.10	.05
☐ 246 Ken Landreaux	.05	.02
☐ 247 Jerry Reuss	.10	.05
☐ 248 Pedro Guerrero	.10	.05
☐ 249 Bill Russell	.10	.05
☐ 250 Fern.Valenzuela FOIL	.15	.07
☐ 251 Al Oliver FOIL	.15	.07
☐ 252 Andre Dawson	.25	.11
☐ 253 Tim Raines	.15	.07
☐ 254 Jeff Reardon	.10	.05
☐ 255 Gary Carter	.10	.05
☐ 256 Steve Rogers	.05	.02
☐ 257 Tim Wallach	.10	.05
☐ 258 Chris Speier	.05	.02
☐ 259 Dave Kingman	.10	.05
☐ 260 Bob Bailor	.05	.02
☐ 261 Hubie Brooks	.10	.05
☐ 262 Craig Swan	.05	.02
☐ 263 George Foster	.10	.05
☐ 264 John Stearns	.05	.02
☐ 265 Neil Allen	.05	.02
☐ 266 Mookie Wilson FOIL	.25	.11
☐ 267 Steve Carlton FOIL	.60	.25
☐ 268 Manny Trillo	.05	.02
☐ 269 Gary Matthews	.05	.02
☐ 270 Mike Schmidt	.60	.25
☐ 271 Ivan DeJesus	.05	.02
☐ 272 Pete Rose	.75	.35
☐ 273 Bo Diaz	.05	.02
☐ 274 Sid Monge	.05	.02
☐ 275 Bill Madlock FOIL	.15	.07
☐ 276 Jason Thompson	.05	.02
☐ 277 Don Robinson	.05	.02
☐ 278 Omar Moreno	.05	.02
☐ 279 Dale Berra	.05	.02
☐ 280 Dave Parker	.10	.05
☐ 281 Tony Pena	.05	.02
☐ 282 John Candelaria	.05	.02
☐ 283 Lonnie Smith	.05	.02
☐ 284 Bruce Sutter FOIL	.15	.07
☐ 285 George Hendrick	.05	.02
☐ 286 Tom Herr	.10	.05
☐ 287 Ken Oberkfell	.05	.02
☐ 288 Ozzie Smith	.75	.35
☐ 289 Bob Forsch	.05	.02
☐ 290 Keith Hernandez	.10	.05
☐ 291 Garry Templeton	.05	.02
☐ 292 Broderick Perkins	.05	.02
☐ 293 Terry Kennedy FOIL	.10	.05
☐ 294 Gene Richards	.05	.02
☐ 295 Ruppert Jones	.05	.02
☐ 296 Tim Lollar	.05	.02
☐ 297 John Montefusco	.05	.02
☐ 298 Sixto Lezcano	.05	.02
☐ 299 Greg Minton	.05	.02
☐ 300 Jack Clark FOIL	.15	.07
☐ 301 Milt May	.05	.02
☐ 302 Reggie Smith	.10	.05
☐ 303 Joe Morgan	.25	.11
☐ 304 John LeMaster	.05	.02
☐ 305 Darrell Evans	.10	.05
☐ 306 Al Holland	.05	.02
☐ 307 Jesse Barfield	.10	.05
☐ 308 Wade Boggs	3.00	1.35
☐ 309 Tom Brunansky	.05	.02
☐ 310 Storm Davis	.05	.02
☐ 311 Von Hayes	.05	.02
☐ 312 Dave Hostetler	.05	.02
☐ 313 Kent Hrbek	.10	.05
☐ 314 Tim Laudner	.05	.02
☐ 315 Cal Ripken	4.00	1.80
☐ 316 Andre Robertson	.05	.02
☐ 317 Ed VandeBerg	.05	.02
☐ 318 Glenn Wilson	.10	.05
☐ 319 Chili Davis	.10	.05
☐ 320 Bob Dernier	.05	.02
☐ 321 Terry Francona	.05	.02
☐ 322 Brian Giles	.05	.02
☐ 323 David Green	.05	.02
☐ 324 Atlee Hammaker	.05	.02
☐ 325 Bill Laskey	.05	.02
☐ 326 Willie McGee	.25	.11
☐ 327 Johnny Ray	.05	.02
☐ 328 Ryne Sandberg	4.00	1.80
☐ 329 Steve Sax	.10	.05
☐ 330 Eric Show	.05	.02
☐ xx Album	1.00	.45

1983 Topps Sticker Boxes

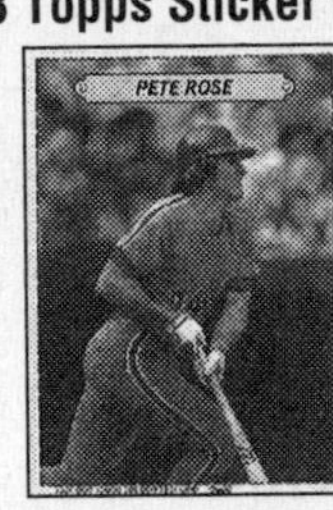

The cards in this eight (box) card set measure the standard size. The 1983 Topps baseball stickers were distributed in boxes which themselves contained a baseball card. In all there were eight different boxes each originally containing 30 stickers but no foils; hence, eight blank-backed cards comprise the box set. The box itself contained an offer for the sticker album and featured a Reggie Jackson photo. Stickers in the boxes came in six strips of five. The prices below reflect the value of the cards on the outside of the box only.

	NRMT	VG-E
COMPLETE SET (8)	10.00	4.50
COMMON CARD (1-8)	.75	.35
☐ 1 Fernando Valenzuela	.75	.35
☐ 2 Gary Carter	1.50	.70
☐ 3 Mike Schmidt	2.50	1.10
☐ 4 Reggie Jackson	2.00	.90
☐ 5 Jim Palmer	1.50	.70
☐ 6 Rollie Fingers	.75	.35
☐ 7 Pete Rose	2.50	1.10
☐ 8 Rickey Henderson	2.00	.90

1983 Topps Reprint 52

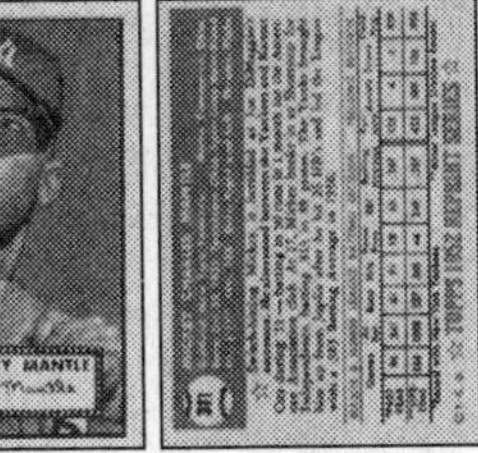

This 402 card standard-size set feature reprinted versions of the cards in the 52 Topps set. These sets were issued in complete form only available from Topps. Five players did not agree to be in this set, that is why the set only contains 402 cards. The five cards not in this set are Billy Loes (#20), Dom DiMaggio (#22), Saul Rogovin (#159), Solly Hemus (#196) and Tommy Holmes (#289).

	NRMT	VG-E
COMP. SET (402)	225.00	100.00
COMP. FACTORY SET (402)	275.00	125.00
COMMON CARD (1-407)	.50	.23
SEMISTARS	1.00	.45
STARS	2.00	.90
☐ 1 Andy Pafko	3.00	1.35
☐ 11 Phil Rizzuto	10.00	4.50
☐ 26 Monte Irvin	7.50	3.40
☐ 29 Ted Kluszewski	7.50	3.40
☐ 33 Warren Spahn	10.00	4.50
☐ 36 Gil Hodges	10.00	4.50
☐ 37 Duke Snider	15.00	6.75
☐ 59 Robin Roberts	10.00	4.50
☐ 65 Enos Slaughter	10.00	4.50
☐ 88 Bob Feller	15.00	6.75
☐ 91 Red Schoendienst	7.50	3.40
☐ 122 Jackie Jensen	5.00	2.20
☐ 129 Johnny Mize	7.50	3.40
☐ 175 Billy Martin	10.00	4.50
☐ 191 Yogi Berra	15.00	6.75
☐ 195 Minnie Minoso	7.50	3.40
☐ 216 Richie Ashburn	10.00	4.50
☐ 227 Joe Garagiola	5.00	2.20
☐ 243 Larry Doby	5.00	2.20
☐ 246 George Kell	7.50	3.40
☐ 261 Willie Mays	25.00	11.00
☐ 268 Bob Lemon	7.50	3.40
☐ 277 Early Wynn	7.50	3.40
☐ 311 Mickey Mantle	50.00	22.00
☐ 312 Jackie Robinson	25.00	11.00
☐ 313 Bobby Thomson	5.00	2.20
☐ 314 Roy Campanella	10.00	4.50
☐ 315 Leo Durocher MG	7.50	3.40
☐ 321 Joe Black	5.00	2.20
☐ 333 Pee Wee Reese	10.00	4.50
☐ 342 Clem Labine	5.00	2.20
☐ 369 Dick Groat	5.00	2.20
☐ 372 Gil McDougald	5.00	2.20
☐ 384 Frank Crosetti CO	5.00	2.20
☐ 392 Hoyt Wilhelm	7.50	3.40
☐ 394 Billy Herman CO	5.00	2.20
☐ 396 Dick Williams	5.00	2.20
☐ 400 Bill Dickey CO	7.50	3.40
☐ 407 Eddie Mathews	10.00	4.50

1984 Topps

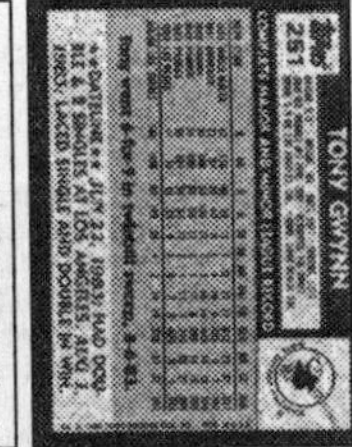

The cards in this 792-card set measure the standard size. For the second year in a row, Topps utilized a dual picture on the front of the card. A portrait is shown in a square insert and an action shot is featured in the main photo. Card numbers 1-6 feature 1983 Highlights (HL), cards 131-138 depict League Leaders, card numbers 386-407 feature All-Stars, and card numbers 701-718 feature active Major League career leaders in various statistical categories. Each team leader (TL) card features the team's leading hitter and pitcher pictured on the front with a team checklist back. There are six numerical checklist cards in the set. The player cards feature team logos in the upper right corner of the reverse. Cards were primarily distributed in 15-card wax packs and 54-card rack packs. The key Rookie Cards in this set are Don Mattingly and Darryl Strawberry. Topps tested a special send-in offer in Michigan and a few other states whereby collectors could obtain direct from Topps ten cards of their choice. Needless to say most people ordered the key (most valuable) players necessitating the printing of a special sheet to keep up with the demand. The special sheet had five cards of Darryl Strawberry, three cards of Don Mattingly, etc. The test was apparently a failure in Topps' eyes as they have never tried it again.

	NRMT	VG-E
COMPLETE SET (792)	40.00	18.00
COMMON CARD (1-792)	.10	.05
☐ 1 Steve Carlton HL	.60	.25
300th win and		
all-time SO king		
☐ 2 Rickey Henderson HL	.60	.25
100 stolen bases		
three times		
☐ 3 Dan Quisenberry HL	.10	.05
Sets save record		
☐ 4 Nolan Ryan HL	1.00	.45
Steve Carlton		
Gaylord Perry		
All surpass Johnson		
☐ 5 Dave Righetti HL	.20	.09
Bob Forsch		
Mike Warren		
All pitch no-hitters		
☐ 6 Johnny Bench HL	.60	.25
Gaylord Perry		
Carl Yastrzemski		
Superstars retire		
☐ 7 Gary Lucas	.10	.05
☐ 8 Don Mattingly	8.00	3.60
☐ 9 Jim Gott	.10	.05
☐ 10 Robin Yount	1.00	.45
☐ 11 Minnesota Twins TL	.20	.09
Kent Hrbek		
Ken Schrom		
(Checklist on back)		
☐ 12 Billy Sample	.10	.05
☐ 13 Scott Holman	.10	.05
☐ 14 Tom Brookens	.20	.09

☐ 15 Burt Hooton .10 .05
☐ 16 Omar Moreno .10 .05
☐ 17 John Denny .10 .05
☐ 18 Dale Berra .10 .05
☐ 19 Ray Fontenot .10 .05
☐ 20 Greg Luzinski .20 .09
☐ 21 Joe Altobelli MG .10 .05
☐ 22 Bryan Clark .10 .05
☐ 23 Keith Moreland .10 .05
☐ 24 John Martin .10 .05
☐ 25 Glenn Hubbard .10 .05
☐ 26 Bud Black .10 .05
☐ 27 Daryl Sconiers .10 .05
☐ 28 Frank Viola .40 .18
☐ 29 Danny Heep .10 .05
☐ 30 Wade Boggs 1.25 .55
☐ 31 Andy McGaffigan .10 .05
☐ 32 Bobby Ramos .10 .05
☐ 33 Tom Burgmeier .10 .05
☐ 34 Eddie Milner .10 .05
☐ 35 Don Sutton .60 .25
☐ 36 Denny Walling .10 .05
☐ 37 Texas Rangers TL .20 .09
Buddy Bell
Rick Honeycutt
(Checklist on back)
☐ 38 Luis DeLeon .10 .05
☐ 39 Garth Iorg .10 .05
☐ 40 Dusty Baker .40 .18
☐ 41 Tony Bernazard .10 .05
☐ 42 Johnny Grubb .10 .05
☐ 43 Ron Reed .10 .05
☐ 44 Jim Morrison .10 .05
☐ 45 Jerry Mumphrey .10 .05
☐ 46 Ray Smith .10 .05
☐ 47 Rudy Law .10 .05
☐ 48 Julio Franco .40 .18
☐ 49 John Stuper .10 .05
☐ 50 Chris Chambliss .10 .05
☐ 51 Jim Frey MG .10 .05
☐ 52 Paul Splittorff .10 .05
☐ 53 Juan Beniquez .10 .05
☐ 54 Jesse Orosco .10 .05
☐ 55 Dave Concepcion .20 .09
☐ 56 Gary Allenson .10 .05
☐ 57 Dan Schatzeder .10 .05
☐ 58 Max Venable .10 .05
☐ 59 Sammy Stewart .10 .05
☐ 60 Paul Molitor UER 1.00 .45
('83 stats .272, 613,
167; should be .270,
608, 164)
☐ 61 Chris Codiroli .10 .05
☐ 62 Dave Hostetler .10 .05
☐ 63 Ed VandeBerg .10 .05
☐ 64 Mike Scioscia .10 .05
☐ 65 Kirk Gibson .60 .25
☐ 66 Houston Astros TL 1.00 .45
Jose Cruz
Nolan Ryan
(Checklist on back)
☐ 67 Gary Ward .10 .05
☐ 68 Luis Salazar .10 .05
☐ 69 Rod Scurry .10 .05
☐ 70 Gary Matthews .10 .05
☐ 71 Leo Hernandez .10 .05
☐ 72 Mike Squires .10 .05
☐ 73 Jody Davis .10 .05
☐ 74 Jerry Martin .10 .05
☐ 75 Bob Forsch .10 .05
☐ 76 Alfredo Griffin .10 .05
☐ 77 Brett Butler .60 .25
☐ 78 Mike Torrez .10 .05
☐ 79 Rob Wilfong .10 .05
☐ 80 Steve Rogers .10 .05
☐ 81 Billy Martin MG .20 .09
☐ 82 Doug Bird .10 .05
☐ 83 Richie Zisk .10 .05
☐ 84 Lenny Faedo .10 .05
☐ 85 Atlee Hammaker .10 .05
☐ 86 John Shelby .10 .05
☐ 87 Frank Pastore .10 .05
☐ 88 Rob Picciolo .10 .05
☐ 89 Mike Smithson .10 .05
☐ 90 Pedro Guerrero .20 .09
☐ 91 Dan Spillner .10 .05
☐ 92 Lloyd Moseby .10 .05
☐ 93 Bob Knepper .10 .05
☐ 94 Mario Ramirez .10 .05
☐ 95 Aurelio Lopez .20 .09
☐ 96 Kansas City Royals TL .20 .09
Hal McRae
Larry Gura
(Checklist on back)
☐ 97 LaMarr Hoyt .10 .05
☐ 98 Steve Nicosia .10 .05
☐ 99 Craig Lefferts .10 .05
☐ 100 Reggie Jackson .75 .35
☐ 101 Porfirio Altamirano .10 .05
☐ 102 Ken Oberkfell .10 .05
☐ 103 Dwayne Murphy .10 .05
☐ 104 Ken Dayley .10 .05
☐ 105 Tony Armas .10 .05
☐ 106 Tim Stoddard .10 .05
☐ 107 Ned Yost .10 .05
☐ 108 Randy Moffitt .10 .05
☐ 109 Brad Wellman .10 .05
☐ 110 Ron Guidry .20 .09
☐ 111 Bill Virdon MG .10 .05
☐ 112 Tom Niedenfuer .10 .05
☐ 113 Kelly Paris .10 .05
☐ 114 Checklist 1-132 .20 .09
☐ 115 Andre Thornton .10 .05
☐ 116 George Bjorkman .10 .05
☐ 117 Tom Veryzer .10 .05
☐ 118 Charlie Hough .20 .09
☐ 119 John Wockenfuss .10 .05
☐ 120 Keith Hernandez .20 .09
☐ 121 Pat Sheridan .10 .05
☐ 122 Cecilio Guante .10 .05
☐ 123 Butch Wynegar .10 .05
☐ 124 Damaso Garcia .10 .05
☐ 125 Britt Burns .10 .05
☐ 126 Atlanta Braves TL .40 .18
Dale Murphy
Craig McMurtry
(Checklist on back)
☐ 127 Mike Madden .10 .05
☐ 128 Rick Manning .10 .05
☐ 129 Bill Laskey .10 .05
☐ 130 Ozzie Smith 1.00 .45
☐ 131 Batting Leaders .60 .25
Bill Madlock
Wade Boggs
☐ 132 Home Run Leaders .60 .25
Mike Schmidt
Jim Rice
☐ 133 RBI Leaders .60 .25
Dale Murphy
Cecil Cooper
Jim Rice
☐ 134 Stolen Base Leaders .60 .25
Tim Raines
Rickey Henderson
☐ 135 Victory Leaders .60 .25
John Denny
LaMarr Hoyt
☐ 136 Strikeout Leaders .60 .25
Steve Carlton
Jack Morris
☐ 137 ERA Leaders .20 .09
Atlee Hammaker
Rick Honeycutt
☐ 138 Leading Firemen .20 .09
Al Holland
Dan Quisenberry
☐ 139 Bert Campaneris .20 .09
☐ 140 Storm Davis .10 .05
☐ 141 Pat Corrales MG .10 .05
☐ 142 Rich Gale .10 .05
☐ 143 Jose Morales .10 .05
☐ 144 Brian Harper .20 .09
☐ 145 Gary Lavelle .10 .05
☐ 146 Ed Romero .10 .05
☐ 147 Dan Petry .20 .09
☐ 148 Joe Lefebvre .10 .05
☐ 149 Jon Matlack .10 .05
☐ 150 Dale Murphy .60 .25
☐ 151 Steve Trout .10 .05
☐ 152 Glenn Brummer .10 .05
☐ 153 Dick Tidrow .10 .05
☐ 154 Dave Henderson .20 .09
☐ 155 Frank White .20 .09
☐ 156 Oakland A's TL .60 .25
Rickey Henderson
Tim Conroy
(Checklist on back)
☐ 157 Gary Gaetti .40 .18
☐ 158 John Curtis .10 .05
☐ 159 Darryl Cias .10 .05
☐ 160 Mario Soto .10 .05
☐ 161 Junior Ortiz .10 .05
☐ 162 Bob Ojeda .10 .05
☐ 163 Lorenzo Gray .10 .05
☐ 164 Scott Sanderson .10 .05
☐ 165 Ken Singleton .10 .05
☐ 166 Jamie Nelson .10 .05
☐ 167 Marshall Edwards .10 .05
☐ 168 Juan Bonilla .10 .05
☐ 169 Larry Parrish .10 .05
☐ 170 Jerry Reuss .10 .05
☐ 171 Frank Robinson MG .40 .18
☐ 172 Frank DiPino .10 .05
☐ 173 Marvell Wynne .10 .05
☐ 174 Juan Berenguer .10 .05
☐ 175 Graig Nettles .20 .09
☐ 176 Lee Smith .60 .25
☐ 177 Jerry Hairston .10 .05
☐ 178 Bill Krueger .10 .05
☐ 179 Buck Martinez .10 .05
☐ 180 Manny Trillo .10 .05
☐ 181 Roy Thomas .10 .05
☐ 182 Darryl Strawberry 2.00 .90
☐ 183 Al Williams .10 .05
☐ 184 Mike O'Berry .10 .05
☐ 185 Sixto Lezcano .10 .05
☐ 186 Cardinal TL .20 .09
Lonnie Smith
John Stuper
(Checklist on back)
☐ 187 Luis Aponte .10 .05
☐ 188 Bryan Little .10 .05
☐ 189 Tim Conroy .10 .05
☐ 190 Ben Oglivie .10 .05
☐ 191 Mike Boddicker .10 .05
☐ 192 Nick Esasky .10 .05
☐ 193 Darrell Brown .10 .05
☐ 194 Domingo Ramos .10 .05
☐ 195 Jack Morris .20 .09
☐ 196 Don Slaught .20 .09
☐ 197 Garry Hancock .10 .05
☐ 198 Bill Doran .20 .09
☐ 199 Willie Hernandez .20 .09
☐ 200 Andre Dawson .60 .25
☐ 201 Bruce Kison .10 .05
☐ 202 Bobby Cox MG .20 .09
☐ 203 Matt Keough .10 .05
☐ 204 Bobby Meacham .10 .05
☐ 205 Greg Minton .10 .05
☐ 206 Andy Van Slyke .60 .25
☐ 207 Donnie Moore .10 .05
☐ 208 Jose Oquendo .20 .09
☐ 209 Manny Sarmiento .10 .05
☐ 210 Joe Morgan .60 .25
☐ 211 Rick Sweet .10 .05
☐ 212 Broderick Perkins .10 .05
☐ 213 Bruce Hurst .10 .05
☐ 214 Paul Householder .10 .05
☐ 215 Tippy Martinez .10 .05
☐ 216 White Sox TL .60 .25
Carlton Fisk
Richard Dotson
(Checklist on back)
☐ 217 Alan Ashby .10 .05
☐ 218 Rick Waits .10 .05
☐ 219 Joe Simpson .10 .05
☐ 220 Fernando Valenzuela .20 .09
☐ 221 Cliff Johnson .10 .05
☐ 222 Rick Honeycutt .10 .05
☐ 223 Wayne Krenchicki .10 .05
☐ 224 Sid Monge .10 .05
☐ 225 Lee Mazzilli .10 .05
☐ 226 Juan Eichelberger .10 .05
☐ 227 Steve Braun .10 .05
☐ 228 John Rabb .10 .05
☐ 229 Paul Owens MG .10 .05
☐ 230 Rickey Henderson 1.00 .45
☐ 231 Gary Woods .10 .05
☐ 232 Tim Wallach .20 .09
☐ 233 Checklist 133-264 .20 .09
☐ 234 Rafael Ramirez .10 .05
☐ 235 Matt Young .10 .05
☐ 236 Ellis Valentine .10 .05
☐ 237 John Castino .10 .05
☐ 238 Reid Nichols .10 .05
☐ 239 Jay Howell .10 .05
☐ 240 Eddie Murray 1.50 .70
☐ 241 Bill Almon .10 .05
☐ 242 Alex Trevino .10 .05
☐ 243 Pete Ladd .10 .05
☐ 244 Candy Maldonado .10 .05
☐ 245 Rick Sutcliffe .20 .09
☐ 246 New York Mets TL .60 .25
Mookie Wilson
Tom Seaver
(Checklist on back)
☐ 247 Onix Concepcion .10 .05
☐ 248 Bill Dawley .10 .05
☐ 249 Jay Johnstone .20 .09
☐ 250 Bill Madlock .20 .09
☐ 251 Tony Gwynn 4.00 1.80
☐ 252 Larry Christenson .10 .05
☐ 253 Jim Wohlford .10 .05
☐ 254 Shane Rawley .10 .05
☐ 255 Bruce Benedict .10 .05
☐ 256 Dave Geisel .10 .05
☐ 257 Julio Cruz .10 .05
☐ 258 Luis Sanchez .10 .05
☐ 259 Sparky Anderson MG .40 .18
☐ 260 Scott McGregor .10 .05
☐ 261 Bobby Brown .10 .05

☐ 262 Tom Candiotti .60 .25
☐ 263 Jack Fimple .10 .05
☐ 264 Doug Frobel .10 .05
☐ 265 Donnie Hill .10 .05
☐ 266 Steve Lubratich .10 .05
☐ 267 Carmelo Martinez .10 .05
☐ 268 Jack O'Connor .10 .05
☐ 269 Aurelio Rodriguez .10 .05
☐ 270 Jeff Russell .40 .18
☐ 271 Moose Haas .10 .05
☐ 272 Rick Dempsey .10 .05
☐ 273 Charlie Puleo .10 .05
☐ 274 Rick Monday .10 .05
☐ 275 Len Matuszek .10 .05
☐ 276 Angels TL .60 .25
Rod Carew
Geoff Zahn
(Checklist on back)
☐ 277 Eddie Whitson .10 .05
☐ 278 Jorge Bell .40 .18
☐ 279 Ivan DeJesus .10 .05
☐ 280 Floyd Bannister .10 .05
☐ 281 Larry Milbourne .10 .05
☐ 282 Jim Barr .10 .05
☐ 283 Larry Biittner .10 .05
☐ 284 Howard Bailey .10 .05
☐ 285 Darrell Porter .10 .05
☐ 286 Lary Sorensen .10 .05
☐ 287 Warren Cromartie .10 .05
☐ 288 Jim Beattie .10 .05
☐ 289 Randy Johnson .10 .05
☐ 290 Dave Dravecky .20 .09
☐ 291 Chuck Tanner MG .10 .05
☐ 292 Tony Scott .10 .05
☐ 293 Ed Lynch .10 .05
☐ 294 U.L. Washington .10 .05
☐ 295 Mike Flanagan .10 .05
☐ 296 Jeff Newman .10 .05
☐ 297 Bruce Berenyi .10 .05
☐ 298 Jim Gantner .20 .09
☐ 299 John Butcher .10 .05
☐ 300 Pete Rose .75 .35
☐ 301 Frank LaCorte .10 .05
☐ 302 Barry Bonnell .10 .05
☐ 303 Marty Castillo .10 .05
☐ 304 Warren Brusstar .10 .05
☐ 305 Roy Smalley .10 .05
☐ 306 Dodgers TL .20 .09
Pedro Guerrero
Bob Welch
(Checklist on back)
☐ 307 Bobby Mitchell .10 .05
☐ 308 Ron Hassey .10 .05
☐ 309 Tony Phillips 1.00 .45
☐ 310 Willie McGee .40 .18
☐ 311 Jerry Koosman .20 .09
☐ 312 Jorge Orta .10 .05
☐ 313 Mike Jorgensen .10 .05
☐ 314 Orlando Mercado .10 .05
☐ 315 Bob Grich .20 .09
☐ 316 Mark Bradley .10 .05
☐ 317 Greg Pryor .10 .05
☐ 318 Bill Gullickson .10 .05
☐ 319 Al Bumbry .20 .09
☐ 320 Bob Stanley .10 .05
☐ 321 Harvey Kuenn MG .20 .09
☐ 322 Ken Schrom .10 .05
☐ 323 Alan Knicely .10 .05
☐ 324 Alejandro Pena .20 .09
☐ 325 Darrell Evans .20 .09
☐ 326 Bob Kearney .10 .05
☐ 327 Ruppert Jones .10 .05
☐ 328 Vern Ruhle .10 .05
☐ 329 Pat Tabler .10 .05
☐ 330 John Candelaria .10 .05
☐ 331 Bucky Dent .20 .09
☐ 332 Kevin Gross .20 .09
☐ 333 Larry Herndon .20 .09
☐ 334 Chuck Rainey .10 .05
☐ 335 Don Baylor .40 .18
☐ 336 Seattle Mariners TL .20 .09
Pat Putnam
Matt Young
(Checklist on back)
☐ 337 Kevin Hagen .10 .05
☐ 338 Mike Warren .10 .05
☐ 339 Roy Lee Jackson .10 .05
☐ 340 Hal McRae .20 .09
☐ 341 Dave Tobik .10 .05
☐ 342 Tim Foli .10 .05
☐ 343 Mark Davis .10 .05
☐ 344 Rick Miller .10 .05
☐ 345 Kent Hrbek .20 .09
☐ 346 Kurt Bevacqua .10 .05
☐ 347 Allan Ramirez .10 .05
☐ 348 Toby Harrah .20 .09
☐ 349 Bob L. Gibson .10 .05

☐ 350 George Foster .20 .09
☐ 351 Russ Nixon MG .10 .05
☐ 352 Dave Stewart .20 .09
☐ 353 Jim Anderson .10 .05
☐ 354 Jeff Burroughs .10 .05
☐ 355 Jason Thompson .10 .05
☐ 356 Glenn Abbott .10 .05
☐ 357 Ron Cey .20 .09
☐ 358 Bob Dernier .10 .05
☐ 359 Jim Acker .10 .05
☐ 360 Willie Randolph .20 .09
☐ 361 Dave Smith .10 .05
☐ 362 David Green .10 .05
☐ 363 Tim Laudner .10 .05
☐ 364 Scott Fletcher .10 .05
☐ 365 Steve Bedrosian .10 .05
☐ 366 Padres TL .20 .09
Terry Kennedy
Dave Dravecky
(Checklist on back)
☐ 367 Jamie Easterly .10 .05
☐ 368 Hubie Brooks .10 .05
☐ 369 Steve McCatty .10 .05
☐ 370 Tim Raines .40 .18
☐ 371 Dave Gumpert .10 .05
☐ 372 Gary Roenicke .10 .05
☐ 373 Bill Scherrer .10 .05
☐ 374 Don Money .10 .05
☐ 375 Dennis Leonard .10 .05
☐ 376 Dave Anderson .10 .05
☐ 377 Danny Darwin .20 .09
☐ 378 Bob Brenly .10 .05
☐ 379 Checklist 265-396 .20 .09
☐ 380 Steve Garvey .40 .18
☐ 381 Ralph Houk MG .20 .09
☐ 382 Chris Nyman .10 .05
☐ 383 Terry Puhl .10 .05
☐ 384 Lee Tunnell .10 .05
☐ 385 Tony Perez .60 .25
☐ 386 George Hendrick AS .10 .05
☐ 387 Johnny Ray AS .10 .05
☐ 388 Mike Schmidt AS .50 .23
☐ 389 Ozzie Smith AS .75 .35
☐ 390 Tim Raines AS .60 .25
☐ 391 Dale Murphy AS .60 .25
☐ 392 Andre Dawson AS .60 .25
☐ 393 Gary Carter AS .60 .25
☐ 394 Steve Rogers AS .10 .05
☐ 395 Steve Carlton AS .60 .25
☐ 396 Jesse Orosco AS .10 .05
☐ 397 Eddie Murray AS .75 .35
☐ 398 Lou Whitaker AS .40 .18
☐ 399 George Brett AS 1.00 .45
☐ 400 Cal Ripken AS 2.00 .90
☐ 401 Jim Rice AS .20 .09
☐ 402 Dave Winfield AS .60 .25
☐ 403 Lloyd Moseby AS .10 .05
☐ 404 Ted Simmons AS .20 .09
☐ 405 LaMarr Hoyt AS .10 .05
☐ 406 Ron Guidry AS .20 .09
☐ 407 Dan Quisenberry AS .10 .05
☐ 408 Lou Piniella .20 .09
☐ 409 Juan Agosto .10 .05
☐ 410 Claudell Washington .10 .05
☐ 411 Houston Jimenez .10 .05
☐ 412 Doug Rader MG .10 .05
☐ 413 Spike Owen .20 .09
☐ 414 Mitchell Page .10 .05
☐ 415 Tommy John .40 .18
☐ 416 Dane Iorg .10 .05
☐ 417 Mike Armstrong .10 .05
☐ 418 Ron Hodges .10 .05
☐ 419 John Henry Johnson .10 .05
☐ 420 Cecil Cooper .20 .09
☐ 421 Charlie Lea .10 .05
☐ 422 Jose Cruz .20 .09
☐ 423 Mike Morgan .10 .05
☐ 424 Dann Bilardello .10 .05
☐ 425 Steve Howe .10 .05
☐ 426 Orioles TL 1.50 .70
Cal Ripken
Mike Boddicker
(Checklist on back)
☐ 427 Rick Leach .10 .05
☐ 428 Fred Breining .10 .05
☐ 429 Randy Bush .10 .05
☐ 430 Rusty Staub .20 .09
☐ 431 Chris Bando .10 .05
☐ 432 Charles Hudson .10 .05
☐ 433 Rich Hebner .10 .05
☐ 434 Harold Baines .40 .18
☐ 435 Neil Allen .10 .05
☐ 436 Rick Peters .10 .05
☐ 437 Mike Proly .10 .05
☐ 438 Biff Pocoroba .10 .05
☐ 439 Bob Stoddard .10 .05
☐ 440 Steve Kemp .10 .05

☐ 441 Bob Lillis MG .10 .05
☐ 442 Byron McLaughlin .10 .05
☐ 443 Benny Ayala .10 .05
☐ 444 Steve Renko .10 .05
☐ 445 Jerry Remy .10 .05
☐ 446 Luis Pujols .10 .05
☐ 447 Tom Brunansky .20 .09
☐ 448 Ben Hayes .10 .05
☐ 449 Joe Pettini .10 .05
☐ 450 Gary Carter .60 .25
☐ 451 Bob Jones .10 .05
☐ 452 Chuck Porter .10 .05
☐ 453 Willie Upshaw .10 .05
☐ 454 Joe Beckwith .10 .05
☐ 455 Terry Kennedy .10 .05
☐ 456 Chicago Cubs TL .40 .18
Keith Moreland
Fergie Jenkins
(Checklist on back)
☐ 457 Dave Rozema .10 .05
☐ 458 Kiko Garcia .10 .05
☐ 459 Kevin Hickey .10 .05
☐ 460 Dave Winfield 1.00 .45
☐ 461 Jim Maler .10 .05
☐ 462 Lee Lacy .10 .05
☐ 463 Dave Engle .10 .05
☐ 464 Jeff A. Jones .10 .05
☐ 465 Mookie Wilson .20 .09
☐ 466 Gene Garber .10 .05
☐ 467 Mike Ramsey .10 .05
☐ 468 Geoff Zahn .10 .05
☐ 469 Tom O'Malley .10 .05
☐ 470 Nolan Ryan 4.00 1.80
☐ 471 Dick Howser MG .10 .05
☐ 472 Mike G. Brown .10 .05
☐ 473 Jim Dwyer .10 .05
☐ 474 Greg Bargar .10 .05
☐ 475 Gary Redus .10 .05
☐ 476 Tom Tellmann .10 .05
☐ 477 Rafael Landestoy .10 .05
☐ 478 Alan Bannister .10 .05
☐ 479 Frank Tanana .20 .09
☐ 480 Ron Kittle .10 .05
☐ 481 Mark Thurmond .10 .05
☐ 482 Enos Cabell .10 .05
☐ 483 Fergie Jenkins .60 .25
☐ 484 Ozzie Virgil .10 .05
☐ 485 Rick Rhoden .10 .05
☐ 486 N.Y. Yankees TL .60 .25
Don Baylor
Ron Guidry
(Checklist on back)
☐ 487 Ricky Adams .10 .05
☐ 488 Jesse Barfield .20 .09
☐ 489 Dave Von Ohlen .10 .05
☐ 490 Cal Ripken 5.00 2.20
☐ 491 Bobby Castillo .10 .05
☐ 492 Tucker Ashford .10 .05
☐ 493 Mike Norris .10 .05
☐ 494 Chili Davis .40 .18
☐ 495 Rollie Fingers .60 .25
☐ 496 Terry Francona .10 .05
☐ 497 Bud Anderson .10 .05
☐ 498 Rich Gedman .10 .05
☐ 499 Mike Witt .10 .05
☐ 500 George Brett 1.25 .55
☐ 501 Steve Henderson .10 .05
☐ 502 Joe Torre MG .20 .09
☐ 503 Elias Sosa .10 .05
☐ 504 Mickey Rivers .10 .05
☐ 505 Pete Vuckovich .10 .05
☐ 506 Ernie Whitt .10 .0
☐ 507 Mike LaCoss .10 .0
☐ 508 Mel Hall .20 .0
☐ 509 Brad Havens .10 .0
☐ 510 Alan Trammell .60 .2
☐ 511 Marty Bystrom .10 .0
☐ 512 Oscar Gamble .10 .0
☐ 513 Dave Beard .10 .0
☐ 514 Floyd Rayford .10 .0
☐ 515 Gorman Thomas .10 .0
☐ 516 Montreal Expos TL .20 .0
Al Oliver
Charlie Lea
(Checklist on back)
☐ 517 John Moses .10 .0
☐ 518 Greg Walker .20 .0
☐ 519 Ron Davis .10 .0
☐ 520 Bob Boone .20 .0
☐ 521 Pete Falcone .10 .0
☐ 522 Dave Bergman .10 .0
☐ 523 Glenn Hoffman .10 .0
☐ 524 Carlos Diaz .10 .0
☐ 525 Willie Wilson .10 .0
☐ 526 Ron Oester .10 .0
☐ 527 Checklist 397-528 .20 .0
☐ 528 Mark Brouhard .10 .0

☐ 529 Keith Atherton	.10	.05
☐ 530 Dan Ford	.10	.05
☐ 531 Steve Boros MG	.10	.05
☐ 532 Eric Show	.10	.05
☐ 533 Ken Landreaux	.10	.05
☐ 534 Pete O'Brien	.20	.09
☐ 535 Bo Diaz	.10	.05
☐ 536 Doug Bair	.10	.05
☐ 537 Johnny Ray	.10	.05
☐ 538 Kevin Bass	.10	.05
☐ 539 George Frazier	.10	.05
☐ 540 George Hendrick	.10	.05
☐ 541 Dennis Lamp	.10	.05
☐ 542 Duane Kuiper	.10	.05
☐ 543 Craig McMurtry	.10	.05
☐ 544 Cesar Geronimo	.10	.05
☐ 545 Bill Buckner	.20	.09
☐ 546 Indians TL	.20	.09
Mike Hargrove		
Lary Sorensen		
(Checklist on back)		
☐ 547 Mike Moore	.10	.05
☐ 548 Ron Jackson	.10	.05
☐ 549 Walt Terrell	.10	.05
☐ 550 Jim Rice	.20	.09
☐ 551 Scott Ullger	.10	.05
☐ 552 Ray Burris	.10	.05
☐ 553 Joe Nolan	.10	.05
☐ 554 Ted Power	.10	.05
☐ 555 Greg Brock	.10	.05
☐ 556 Joey McLaughlin	.10	.05
☐ 557 Wayne Tolleson	.10	.05
☐ 558 Mike Davis	.10	.05
☐ 559 Mike Scott	.20	.09
☐ 560 Carlton Fisk	.75	.35
☐ 561 Whitey Herzog MG	.20	.09
☐ 562 Manny Castillo	.10	.05
☐ 563 Glenn Wilson	.20	.09
☐ 564 Al Holland	.10	.05
☐ 565 Leon Durham	.10	.05
☐ 566 Jim Bibby	.10	.05
☐ 567 Mike Heath	.10	.05
☐ 568 Pete Filson	.10	.05
☐ 569 Bake McBride	.10	.05
☐ 570 Dan Quisenberry	.10	.05
☐ 571 Bruce Bochy	.10	.05
☐ 572 Jerry Royster	.10	.05
☐ 573 Dave Kingman	.40	.18
☐ 574 Brian Downing	.10	.05
☐ 575 Jim Clancy	.10	.05
☐ 576 Giants TL	.20	.09
Jeff Leonard		
Atlee Hammaker		
(Checklist on back)		
☐ 577 Mark Clear	.10	.05
☐ 578 Lenn Sakata	.10	.05
☐ 579 Bob James	.10	.05
☐ 580 Lonnie Smith	.10	.05
☐ 581 Jose DeLeon	.10	.05
☐ 582 Bob McClure	.10	.05
☐ 583 Derrel Thomas	.10	.05
☐ 584 Dave Schmidt	.10	.05
☐ 585 Dan Driessen	.10	.05
☐ 586 Joe Niekro	.20	.09
☐ 587 Von Hayes	.10	.05
☐ 588 Milt Wilcox	.10	.05
☐ 589 Mike Easler	.10	.05
☐ 590 Dave Stieb	.10	.05
☐ 591 Tony LaRussa MG	.20	.09
☐ 592 Andre Robertson	.10	.05
☐ 593 Jeff Lahti	.10	.05
☐ 594 Gene Richards	.10	.05
☐ 595 Jeff Reardon	.20	.09
☐ 596 Ryne Sandberg	2.00	.90
☐ 597 Rick Camp	.10	.05
☐ 598 Rusty Kuntz	.10	.05
☐ 599 Doug Sisk	.10	.05
☐ 600 Rod Carew	.60	.25
☐ 601 John Tudor	.10	.05
☐ 602 John Wathan	.10	.05
☐ 603 Renie Martin	.10	.05
☐ 604 John Lowenstein	.10	.05
☐ 605 Mike Caldwell	.10	.05
☐ 606 Blue Jays TL	.20	.09
Lloyd Moseby		
Dave Stieb		
(Checklist on back)		
☐ 607 Tom Hume	.10	.05
☐ 608 Bobby Johnson	.10	.05
☐ 609 Dan Meyer	.10	.05
☐ 610 Steve Sax	.20	.09
☐ 611 Chet Lemon	.20	.09
☐ 612 Harry Spilman	.10	.05
☐ 613 Greg Gross	.10	.05
☐ 614 Len Barker	.10	.05
☐ 615 Garry Templeton	.10	.05
☐ 616 Don Robinson	.10	.05
☐ 617 Rick Cerone	.10	.05
☐ 618 Dickie Noles	.10	.05
☐ 619 Jerry Dybzinski	.10	.05
☐ 620 Al Oliver	.20	.09
☐ 621 Frank Howard MG	.20	.09
☐ 622 Al Cowens	.10	.05
☐ 623 Ron Washington	.10	.05
☐ 624 Terry Harper	.10	.05
☐ 625 Larry Gura	.10	.05
☐ 626 Bob Clark	.10	.05
☐ 627 Dave LaPoint	.10	.05
☐ 628 Ed Jurak	.10	.05
☐ 629 Rick Langford	.10	.05
☐ 630 Ted Simmons	.20	.09
☐ 631 Dennis Martinez	.20	.09
☐ 632 Tom Foley	.10	.05
☐ 633 Mike Krukow	.10	.05
☐ 634 Mike Marshall	.10	.05
☐ 635 Dave Righetti	.20	.09
☐ 636 Pat Putnam	.10	.05
☐ 637 Phillies TL	.20	.09
Gary Matthews		
John Denny		
(Checklist on back)		
☐ 638 George Vukovich	.10	.05
☐ 639 Rick Lysander	.10	.05
☐ 640 Lance Parrish	.20	.09
☐ 641 Mike Richardt	.10	.05
☐ 642 Tom Underwood	.10	.05
☐ 643 Mike C. Brown	.10	.05
☐ 644 Tim Lollar	.10	.05
☐ 645 Tony Pena	.10	.05
☐ 646 Checklist 529-660	.20	.09
☐ 647 Ron Roenicke	.10	.05
☐ 648 Len Whitehouse	.10	.05
☐ 649 Tom Herr	.20	.09
☐ 650 Phil Niekro	.60	.25
☐ 651 John McNamara MG	.10	.05
☐ 652 Rudy May	.10	.05
☐ 653 Dave Stapleton	.10	.05
☐ 654 Bob Bailor	.10	.05
☐ 655 Amos Otis	.20	.09
☐ 656 Bryn Smith	.10	.05
☐ 657 Thad Bosley	.10	.05
☐ 658 Jerry Augustine	.10	.05
☐ 659 Duane Walker	.10	.05
☐ 660 Ray Knight	.20	.09
☐ 661 Steve Yeager	.10	.05
☐ 662 Tom Brennan	.10	.05
☐ 663 Johnnie LeMaster	.10	.05
☐ 664 Dave Stegman	.10	.05
☐ 665 Buddy Bell	.20	.09
☐ 666 Detroit Tigers TL	.60	.25
Lou Whitaker		
Jack Morris		
(Checklist on back)		
☐ 667 Vance Law	.10	.05
☐ 668 Larry McWilliams	.10	.05
☐ 669 Dave Lopes	.20	.09
☐ 670 Rich Gossage	.60	.25
☐ 671 Jamie Quirk	.10	.05
☐ 672 Ricky Nelson	.10	.05
☐ 673 Mike Walters	.10	.05
☐ 674 Tim Flannery	.10	.05
☐ 675 Pascual Perez	.10	.05
☐ 676 Brian Giles	.10	.05
☐ 677 Doyle Alexander	.10	.05
☐ 678 Chris Speier	.10	.05
☐ 679 Art Howe	.10	.05
☐ 680 Fred Lynn	.20	.09
☐ 681 Tom Lasorda MG	.40	.18
☐ 682 Dan Morogiello	.10	.05
☐ 683 Marty Barrett	.20	.09
☐ 684 Bob Shirley	.10	.05
☐ 685 Willie Aikens	.10	.05
☐ 686 Joe Price	.10	.05
☐ 687 Roy Howell	.10	.05
☐ 688 George Wright	.10	.05
☐ 689 Mike Fischlin	.10	.05
☐ 690 Jack Clark	.20	.09
☐ 691 Steve Lake	.10	.05
☐ 692 Dickie Thon	.10	.05
☐ 693 Alan Wiggins	.10	.05
☐ 694 Mike Stanton	.10	.05
☐ 695 Lou Whitaker	.60	.25
☐ 696 Pirates TL	.20	.09
Bill Madlock		
Rick Rhoden		
(Checklist on back)		
☐ 697 Dale Murray	.10	.05
☐ 698 Marc Hill	.10	.05
☐ 699 Dave Rucker	.10	.05
☐ 700 Mike Schmidt	.75	.35
☐ 701 NL Active Batting	.60	.25
Bill Madlock		
Pete Rose		
Dave Parker		
☐ 702 NL Active Hits	.60	.25
Pete Rose		
Rusty Staub		
Tony Perez		
☐ 703 NL Active Home Run	.60	.25
Mike Schmidt		
Tony Perez		
Dave Kingman		
☐ 704 NL Active RBI	.60	.25
Tony Perez		
Rusty Staub		
Al Oliver		
☐ 705 NL Active Steals	.60	.25
Joe Morgan		
Cesar Cedeno		
Larry Bowa		
☐ 706 NL Active Victory	.60	.25
Steve Carlton		
Fergie Jenkins		
Tom Seaver		
☐ 707 NL Active Strikeout	1.50	.70
Steve Carlton		
Nolan Ryan		
Tom Seaver		
☐ 708 NL Active ERA	.60	.25
Tom Seaver		
Steve Carlton		
Steve Rogers		
☐ 709 NL Active Save	.20	.09
Bruce Sutter		
Tug McGraw		
Gene Garber		
☐ 710 AL Active Batting	.60	.25
Rod Carew		
George Brett		
Cecil Cooper		
☐ 711 AL Active Hits	.60	.25
Rod Carew		
Bert Campaneris		
Reggie Jackson		
☐ 712 AL Active Home Run	.60	.25
Reggie Jackson		
Graig Nettles		
Greg Luzinski		
☐ 713 AL Active RBI	.60	.25
Reggie Jackson		
Ted Simmons		
Graig Nettles		
☐ 714 AL Active Steals	.20	.09
Bert Campaneris		
Dave Lopes		
Omar Moreno		
☐ 715 AL Active Victory	.60	.25
Jim Palmer		
Don Sutton		
Tommy John		
☐ 716 AL Active Strikeout	.60	.25
Don Sutton		
Bert Blyleven		
Jerry Koosman		
☐ 717 AL Active ERA	.60	.25
Jim Palmer		
Rollie Fingers		
Ron Guidry		
☐ 718 AL Active Save	.60	.25
Rollie Fingers		
Rich Gossage		
Dan Quisenberry		
☐ 719 Andy Hassler	.10	.05
☐ 720 Dwight Evans	.20	.09
☐ 721 Del Crandall MG	.10	.05
☐ 722 Bob Welch	.10	.05
☐ 723 Rich Dauer	.10	.05
☐ 724 Eric Rasmussen	.10	.05
☐ 725 Cesar Cedeno	.20	.09
☐ 726 Brewers TL	.20	.09
Ted Simmons		
Moose Haas		
(Checklist on back)		
☐ 727 Joel Youngblood	.10	.05
☐ 728 Tug McGraw	.20	.09
☐ 729 Gene Tenace	.20	.09
☐ 730 Bruce Sutter	.20	.09
☐ 731 Lynn Jones	.10	.05
☐ 732 Terry Crowley	.10	.05
☐ 733 Dave Collins	.10	.05
☐ 734 Odell Jones	.10	.05
☐ 735 Rick Burleson	.10	.05
☐ 736 Dick Ruthven	.10	.05
☐ 737 Jim Essian	.10	.05
☐ 738 Bill Schroeder	.10	.05
☐ 739 Bob Watson	.20	.09
☐ 740 Tom Seaver	.75	.35
☐ 741 Wayne Gross	.10	.05
☐ 742 Dick Williams MG	.20	.09
☐ 743 Don Hood	.10	.05
☐ 744 Jamie Allen	.10	.05

☐ 745 Dennis Eckersley	.60	.25
☐ 746 Mickey Hatcher	.10	.05
☐ 747 Pat Zachry	.10	.05
☐ 748 Jeff Leonard	.10	.05
☐ 749 Doug Flynn	.10	.05
☐ 750 Jim Palmer	.60	.25
☐ 751 Charlie Moore	.10	.05
☐ 752 Phil Garner	.20	.09
☐ 753 Doug Gwosdz	.10	.05
☐ 754 Kent Tekulve	.20	.09
☐ 755 Garry Maddox	.10	.05
☐ 756 Reds TL	.20	.09
Ron Oester		
Mario Soto		
(Checklist on back)		
☐ 757 Larry Bowa	.20	.09
☐ 758 Bill Stein	.10	.05
☐ 759 Richard Dotson	.10	.05
☐ 760 Bob Horner	.10	.05
☐ 761 John Montefusco	.10	.05
☐ 762 Rance Mulliniks	.10	.05
☐ 763 Craig Swan	.10	.05
☐ 764 Mike Hargrove	.20	.09
☐ 765 Ken Forsch	.10	.05
☐ 766 Mike Vail	.10	.05
☐ 767 Carney Lansford	.20	.09
☐ 768 Champ Summers	.10	.05
☐ 769 Bill Caudill	.10	.05
☐ 770 Ken Griffey	.20	.09
☐ 771 Billy Gardner MG	.10	.05
☐ 772 Jim Slaton	.10	.05
☐ 773 Todd Cruz	.10	.05
☐ 774 Tom Gorman	.10	.05
☐ 775 Dave Parker	.20	.09
☐ 776 Craig Reynolds	.10	.05
☐ 777 Tom Paciorek	.20	.09
☐ 778 Andy Hawkins	.10	.05
☐ 779 Jim Sundberg	.20	.09
☐ 780 Steve Carlton	.75	.35
☐ 781 Checklist 661-792	.20	.09
☐ 782 Steve Balboni	.10	.05
☐ 783 Luis Leal	.10	.05
☐ 784 Leon Roberts	.10	.05
☐ 785 Joaquin Andujar	.10	.05
☐ 786 Red Sox TL	.60	.25
Wade Boggs		
Bob Ojeda		
(Checklist on back)		
☐ 787 Bill Campbell	.10	.05
☐ 788 Milt May	.10	.05
☐ 789 Bert Blyleven	.20	.09
☐ 790 Doug DeCinces	.10	.05
☐ 791 Terry Forster	.10	.05
☐ 792 Bill Russell	.20	.09

1984 Topps Tiffany

This 792 card standard-size set was issued by Topps as a parallel to their regular issue. Printed in their Ireland facility, these cards are differentiated from the regular cards by the glossy fronts and pure white stock. These sets were available only through Topps' dealer network and sold only in factory set form.

	NRMT	VG-E
COMPLETE SET (792)	200.00	90.00
COMMON CARD (1-792)	.25	.11
*STARS: 6X to 10X BASIC CARDS		
*ROOKIES: 4X to 8X BASIC CARDS		

1984 Topps Glossy All-Stars

The cards in this 22-card set measure the standard size. Unlike the 1983 Topps Glossy set which was not distributed with its regular baseball cards, the 1984 Topps Glossy set was distributed as inserts in Topps Rak-Paks. The set features the nine American and National League All-Stars who started in the 1983 All Star game in Chicago. The managers and team captains (Yastrzemski and Bench) complete the set. The cards are numbered on the back and are ordered by position within league (AL: 1-11 and NL: 12-22).

	NRMT	VG-E
COMPLETE SET (22)	5.00	2.20
COMMON CARD (1-22)	.05	.02
☐ 1 Harvey Kuenn MG	.05	.02
☐ 2 Rod Carew	.50	.23
☐ 3 Manny Trillo	.05	.02
☐ 4 George Brett	1.00	.45
☐ 5 Robin Yount	.50	.23
☐ 6 Jim Rice	.10	.05
☐ 7 Fred Lynn	.10	.05
☐ 8 Dave Winfield	.50	.23
☐ 9 Ted Simmons	.10	.05
☐ 10 Dave Stieb	.05	.02
☐ 11 Carl Yastrzemski CAPT	.50	.23
☐ 12 Whitey Herzog MG	.05	.02
☐ 13 Al Oliver	.10	.05
☐ 14 Steve Sax	.10	.05
☐ 15 Mike Schmidt	.75	.35
☐ 16 Ozzie Smith	1.00	.45
☐ 17 Tim Raines	.15	.07
☐ 18 Andre Dawson	.25	.11
☐ 19 Dale Murphy	.25	.11
☐ 20 Gary Carter	.15	.07
☐ 21 Mario Soto	.05	.02
☐ 22 Johnny Bench CAPT	.50	.23

1984 Topps Glossy Send-Ins

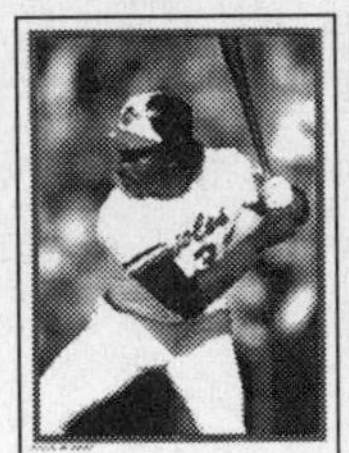

The cards in this 40-card set measure the standard size. Similar to last year's glossy set, this set was issued as a bonus prize to Topps All-Star Baseball Game cards found in wax packs. Twenty-five bonus runs from the game cards were necessary to obtain a five card subset of the series. There were eight different subsets of five cards. The cards are numbered and the set contains 20 stars from each league.

	NRMT	VG-E
COMPLETE SET (40)	12.50	5.50
COMMON CARD (1-40)	.10	.05
☐ 1 Pete Rose	2.00	.90
☐ 2 Lance Parrish	.20	.09
☐ 3 Steve Rogers	.10	.05
☐ 4 Eddie Murray	1.50	.70
☐ 5 Johnny Ray	.10	.05
☐ 6 Rickey Henderson	1.25	.55
☐ 7 Atlee Hammaker	.10	.05
☐ 8 Wade Boggs	1.50	.70
☐ 9 Gary Carter	.35	.16
☐ 10 Jack Morris	.20	.09
☐ 11 Darrell Evans	.20	.09
☐ 12 George Brett	2.50	1.10
☐ 13 Bob Horner	.10	.05
☐ 14 Ron Guidry	.20	.09
☐ 15 Nolan Ryan	5.00	2.20
☐ 16 Dave Winfield	1.00	.45
☐ 17 Ozzie Smith	2.50	1.10
☐ 18 Ted Simmons	.20	.09
☐ 19 Bill Madlock	.10	.05
☐ 20 Tony Armas	.10	.05
☐ 21 Al Oliver	.20	.09
☐ 22 Jim Rice	.20	.09
☐ 23 George Hendrick	.10	.05
☐ 24 Dave Stieb	.10	.05
☐ 25 Pedro Guerrero	.20	.09
☐ 26 Rod Carew	1.00	.45
☐ 27 Steve Carlton	.75	.35
☐ 28 Dave Righetti	.10	.05
☐ 29 Darryl Strawberry	.50	.23
☐ 30 Lou Whitaker	.20	.09
☐ 31 Dale Murphy	.35	.16
☐ 32 LaMarr Hoyt	.10	.05
☐ 33 Jesse Orosco	.10	.05
☐ 34 Cecil Cooper	.20	.09
☐ 35 Andre Dawson	.50	.23
☐ 36 Robin Yount	1.00	.45
☐ 37 Tim Raines	.35	.16
☐ 38 Dan Quisenberry	.10	.05
☐ 39 Mike Schmidt	2.00	.90
☐ 40 Carlton Fisk	1.00	.45

1984 Topps Traded

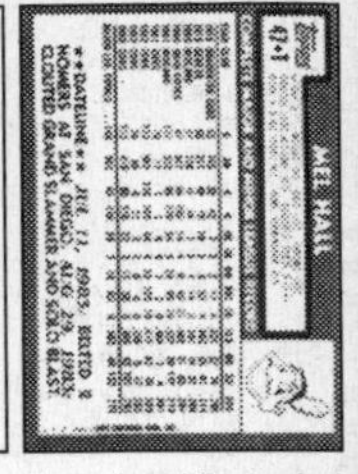

In now standard procedure, Topps issued its standard-size Traded (or extended) set for the fourth year in a row. Several of 1984's top rookies not contained in the regular set are pictured in the Traded set. Extended Rookie Cards in this set include Dwight Gooden, Jimmy Key, Mark Langston, Jose Rijo, and Bret Saberhagen. Again this year, the Topps affiliate in Ireland printed the cards, and the cards were available through hobby channels only in factory set form. The set numbering is in alphabetical order by player's name.

	NRMT	VG-E
COMP.FACT.SET (132)	40.00	18.00
COMMON CARD (1T-132T)	.25	.11
☐ 1T Willie Aikens	.25	.11
☐ 2T Luis Aponte	.25	.11
☐ 3T Mike Armstrong	.25	.11
☐ 4T Bob Bailor	.25	.11
☐ 5T Dusty Baker	1.25	.55
☐ 6T Steve Balboni	.25	.11
☐ 7T Alan Bannister	.25	.11
☐ 8T Dave Beard	.25	.11
☐ 9T Joe Beckwith	.25	.11
☐ 10T Bruce Berenyi	.25	.11
☐ 11T Dave Bergman	.25	.11
☐ 12T Tony Bernazard	.25	.11
☐ 13T Yogi Berra MG	2.00	.90
☐ 14T Barry Bonnell	.25	.11
☐ 15T Phil Bradley	1.00	.45
☐ 16T Fred Breining	.25	.11
☐ 17T Bill Buckner	1.00	.45
☐ 18T Ray Burris	.25	.11
☐ 19T John Butcher	.25	.11
☐ 20T Brett Butler	1.25	.55
☐ 21T Enos Cabell	.25	.11
☐ 22T Bill Campbell	.25	.11
☐ 23T Bill Caudill	.25	.11
☐ 24T Bob Clark	.25	.11
☐ 25T Bryan Clark	.25	.11
☐ 26T Jaime Cocanower	.25	.11
☐ 27T Ron Darling	1.50	.70
☐ 28T Alvin Davis	1.00	.45
☐ 29T Ken Dayley	.25	.11
☐ 30T Jeff Dedmon	.25	.11
☐ 31T Bob Dernier	.25	.11
☐ 32T Carlos Diaz	.25	.11
☐ 33T Mike Easler	.25	.11
☐ 34T Dennis Eckersley	2.00	.90
☐ 35T Jim Essian	.25	.11
☐ 36T Darrell Evans	1.00	.45
☐ 37T Mike Fitzgerald	.25	.11
☐ 38T Tim Foli	.25	.11
☐ 39T George Frazier	.25	.11
☐ 40T Rich Gale	.25	.11
☐ 41T Barbaro Garbey	.25	.11
☐ 42T Dwight Gooden	10.00	4.50
☐ 43T Rich Gossage	1.25	.55
☐ 44T Wayne Gross	.25	.11
☐ 45T Mark Gubicza	1.00	.45
☐ 46T Jackie Gutierrez	.25	.11
☐ 47T Mel Hall	1.00	.45
☐ 48T Toby Harrah	1.00	.45
☐ 49T Ron Hassey	.25	.11
☐ 50T Rich Hebner	.25	.11
☐ 51T Willie Hernandez	1.00	.45
☐ 52T Ricky Horton	.25	.11
☐ 53T Art Howe	.25	.11
☐ 54T Dane Iorg	.25	.11
☐ 55T Brook Jacoby	1.00	.45
☐ 56T Mike Jeffcoat	.25	.11
☐ 57T Dave Johnson MG	1.00	.45
☐ 58T Lynn Jones	.25	.11
☐ 59T Ruppert Jones	.25	.11
☐ 60T Mike Jorgensen	.25	.11
☐ 61T Bob Kearney	.25	.11
☐ 62T Jimmy Key	4.00	1.80
☐ 63T Dave Kingman	1.25	.55
☐ 64T Jerry Koosman	1.00	.45
☐ 65T Wayne Krenchicki	.25	.11
☐ 66T Rusty Kuntz	.25	.11

☐ 67T Rene Lachemann MG	.25	.11
☐ 68T Frank LaCorte	.25	.11
☐ 69T Dennis Lamp	.25	.11
☐ 70T Mark Langston	2.00	.90
☐ 71T Rick Leach	.25	.11
☐ 72T Craig Lefferts	1.00	.45
☐ 73T Gary Lucas	.25	.11
☐ 74T Jerry Martin	.25	.11
☐ 75T Carmelo Martinez	.25	.11
☐ 76T Mike Mason	.25	.11
☐ 77T Gary Matthews	1.00	.45
☐ 78T Andy McGaffigan	.25	.11
☐ 79T Larry Milbourne	.25	.11
☐ 80T Sid Monge	.25	.11
☐ 81T Jackie Moore MG	.25	.11
☐ 82T Joe Morgan	2.50	1.10
☐ 83T Graig Nettles	1.25	.55
☐ 84T Phil Niekro	1.50	.70
☐ 85T Ken Oberkfell	.25	.11
☐ 86T Mike O'Berry	.25	.11
☐ 87T Al Oliver	1.00	.45
☐ 88T Jorge Orta	.25	.11
☐ 89T Amos Otis	1.00	.45
☐ 90T Dave Parker	1.00	.45
☐ 91T Tony Perez	1.50	.70
☐ 92T Gerald Perry	1.00	.45
☐ 93T Gary Pettis	.25	.11
☐ 94T Rob Picciolo	.25	.11
☐ 95T Vern Rapp MG	.25	.11
☐ 96T Floyd Rayford	.25	.11
☐ 97T Randy Ready	1.00	.45
☐ 98T Ron Reed	.25	.11
☐ 99T Gene Richards	.25	.11
☐ 100T Jose Rijo	1.50	.70
☐ 101T Jeff D. Robinson	.25	.11
☐ 102T Ron Romanick	.25	.11
☐ 103T Pete Rose	5.00	2.20
☐ 104T Bret Saberhagen	2.00	.90
☐ 105T Juan Samuel	.40	.18
☐ 106T Scott Sanderson	.25	.11
☐ 107T Dick Schofield	1.00	.45
☐ 108T Tom Seaver	5.00	2.20
☐ 109T Jim Slaton	.25	.11
☐ 110T Mike Smithson	.25	.11
☐ 111T Lary Sorensen	.25	.11
☐ 112T Tim Stoddard	.25	.11
☐ 113T Champ Summers	.25	.11
☐ 114T Jim Sundberg	1.00	.45
☐ 115T Rick Sutcliffe	1.00	.45
☐ 116T Craig Swan	.25	.11
☐ 117T Tim Teufel	.25	.11
☐ 118T Derrel Thomas	.25	.11
☐ 119T Gorman Thomas	.25	.11
☐ 120T Alex Trevino	.25	.11
☐ 121T Manny Trillo	.25	.11
☐ 122T John Tudor	.25	.11
☐ 123T Tom Underwood	.25	.11
☐ 124T Mike Vail	.25	.11
☐ 125T Tom Waddell	.25	.11
☐ 126T Gary Ward	.25	.11
☐ 127T Curt Wilkerson	.25	.11
☐ 128T Frank Williams	.25	.11
☐ 129T Glenn Wilson	.25	.11
☐ 130T John Wockenfuss	.25	.11
☐ 131T Ned Yost	.25	.11
☐ 132T Checklist 1T-132T	.25	.11

1984 Topps Traded Tiffany

This 132-card standard-size set was issued by Topps as a premium parallel to their regular issue. This set was printed in the Topps Ireland factory and are differentiated from the regular cards by their glossy sheen and clean backs. These sets were only available through the Topps hobby distribution system.

	NRMT	VG-E
COMPLETE FACT.SET (132)	75.00	34.00
COMMON CARD (1T-132T)	.40	.18
*STARS: 1.5X BASIC CARDS		
*ROOKIES: 1.5X BASIC CARDS		

1984 Topps Cereal

The cards in this 33-card set measure the standard size. The cards are numbered both on the front and the back. The 1984 Topps Cereal Series is exactly the same as the Ralston-Purina issue of this year except for a Topps logo and the words "Cereal Series" on the tops of the fronts of the cards in place of the Ralston checkerboard background. The checkerboard background is absent from the reverse, and a Topps logo is on the reverse of the cereal cards. These cards were distributed in unmarked boxes of Ralston-Purina cereal with a pack of four cards (three players and a checklist) being inside random cereal boxes. The back of the checklist details an offer to obtain any twelve cards direct from the issuer for only 1.50.

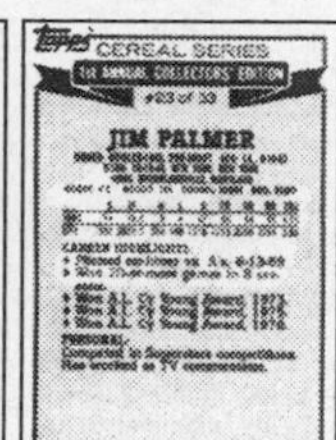

	NRMT	VG-E
COMPLETE SET (34)	12.50	5.50
COMMON CARD (1-33)	.10	.05
☐ 1 Eddie Murray	2.00	.90
☐ 2 Ozzie Smith	2.50	1.10
☐ 3 Ted Simmons	.20	.09
☐ 4 Pete Rose	1.50	.70
☐ 5 Greg Luzinski	.20	.09
☐ 6 Andre Dawson	.50	.23
☐ 7 Dave Winfield	1.00	.45
☐ 8 Tom Seaver	1.00	.45
☐ 9 Jim Rice	.20	.09
☐ 10 Fernando Valenzuela	.20	.09
☐ 11 Wade Boggs	1.25	.55
☐ 12 Dale Murphy	.35	.16
☐ 13 George Brett	2.50	1.10
☐ 14 Nolan Ryan	4.00	1.80
☐ 15 Rickey Henderson	1.00	.45
☐ 16 Steve Carlton	1.00	.45
☐ 17 Rod Carew	1.00	.45
☐ 18 Steve Garvey	.20	.09
☐ 19 Reggie Jackson	1.00	.45
☐ 20 Dave Concepcion	.20	.09
☐ 21 Robin Yount	1.00	.45
☐ 22 Mike Schmidt	1.50	.70
☐ 23 Jim Palmer	1.00	.45
☐ 24 Bruce Sutter	.20	.09
☐ 25 Dan Quisenberry	.10	.05
☐ 26 Bill Madlock	.10	.05
☐ 27 Cecil Cooper	.20	.09
☐ 28 Gary Carter	.50	.23
☐ 29 Fred Lynn	.20	.09
☐ 30 Pedro Guerrero	.20	.09
☐ 31 Ron Guidry	.20	.09
☐ 32 Keith Hernandez	.20	.09
☐ 33 Carlton Fisk	1.00	.45
☐ NNO Checklist Card	.10	.05

1984 Topps/O-Pee-Chee Stickers

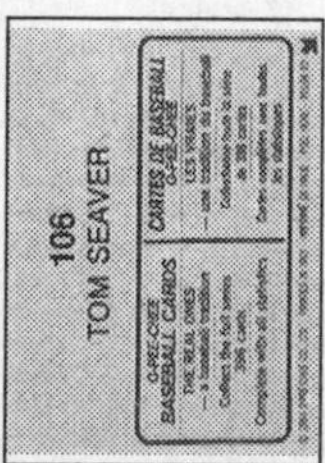

Made in Italy for Topps and O-Pee-Chee by Panini, these 386 stickers measure approximately 1 15/16" by 2 9/16" and are numbered on both front and back. The fronts feature white-bordered color player photos. The horizontal back carries the player's name and a bilingual ad for O-Pee-Chee in red lettering. The stickers were also issued boxes of seven strips of five stickers each. An album onto which the stickers could be affixed was available at retail stores. The album and the sticker numbering are organized as follows: 1983 Highlights (1-10), 1983 Championship Series (11-18), World Series (19-26), Atlanta Braves (27-38), Chicago Cubs (39-50), Cincinnati Reds (51-62), Houston Astros (63-74), Los Angeles Dodgers (75-86), Montreal Expos (87-98), 1983 Stat Leaders (99-102), New York Mets (103-114), Philadelphia Phillies (115-126), Pittsburgh Pirates (127-138), St. Louis Cardinals (139-150), San Diego Padres (151-162), San Francisco Giants (163-174), 1983 Stat Leaders (175-178), Foil All-Stars (179-198), 1983 Stat Leaders (199-202), Baltimore Orioles (203-214), Boston Red Sox (215-226), California Angels (227-238), Chicago White Sox (239-250), Cleveland Indians (251-262), Detroit Tigers (263-274), Kansas City Royals (275-286), 1983 Stat Leaders (287-290), Milwaukee Brewers (291-302), Minnesota Twins (303-314), New York Yankees (315-326), Oakland A's (327-338), Seattle Mariners (339-350), Texas Rangers (351-362), Toronto Blue Jays (363-374), and Stars of the Future (375-386). There were stickers issued which corresponded with Don Mattingly and Darryl Strawberry Rookie Year for cards.

	NRMT	VG-E
COMPLETE SET (386)	15.00	6.75
COMMON STICKER (1-178)	.05	.02
COMMON FOIL (179-198)	.10	.05
COMMON STICKER (199-386)	.05	.02
*TOPPS AND OPC: SAME VALUE		
☐ 1 Steve Carlton (Top half)	.15	.07
☐ 2 Steve Carlton (Bottom half)	.15	.07
☐ 3 Rickey Henderson (Top half)	.15	.07
☐ 4 Rickey Henderson (Bottom half)	.15	.07
☐ 5 Fred Lynn (Top half)	.10	.05
☐ 6 Fred Lynn (Bottom half)	.10	.05
☐ 7 Greg Luzinski (Top half)	.10	.05
☐ 8 Greg Luzinski (Bottom half)	.10	.05
☐ 9 Dan Quisenberry (Top half)	.05	.02
☐ 10 Dan Quisenberry (Bottom half)	.05	.02
☐ 11 LaMarr Hoyt LCS	.05	.02
☐ 12 Mike Flanagan LCS	.05	.02
☐ 13 Mike Boddicker LCS	.05	.02
☐ 14 Tito Landrum LCS	.05	.02
☐ 15 Steve Carlton LCS	.15	.07
☐ 16 Fern.Valenzuela LCS	.10	.05
☐ 17 Charlie Hudson LCS	.05	.02
☐ 18 Gary Matthews LCS	.05	.02
☐ 19 John Denny WS	.05	.02
☐ 20 John Lowenstein WS	.05	.02
☐ 21 Jim Palmer WS	.15	.07
☐ 22 Benny Ayala WS	.05	.02
☐ 23 Rick Dempsey WS	.05	.02
☐ 24 Cal Ripken WS	1.25	.55
☐ 25 Sammy Stewart WS	.05	.02
☐ 26 Eddie Murray WS	.15	.07
☐ 27 Dale Murphy	.15	.07
☐ 28 Chris Chambliss	.05	.02
☐ 29 Glenn Hubbard	.05	.02
☐ 30 Bob Horner	.05	.02
☐ 31 Phil Niekro	.15	.07
☐ 32 Claudell Washington	.05	.02
☐ 33 Rafael Ramirez (135)	.05	.02
☐ 34 Bruce Benedict (82)	.05	.02
☐ 35 Gene Garber (59)	.05	.02
☐ 36 Pascual Perez (347)	.05	.02
☐ 37 Jerry Royster (281)	.05	.02
☐ 38 Steve Bedrosian(283)	.05	.02
☐ 39 Keith Moreland	.05	.02
☐ 40 Leon Durham	.05	.02
☐ 41 Ron Cey	.10	.05
☐ 42 Bill Buckner	.10	.05
☐ 43 Jody Davis	.05	.02
☐ 44 Lee Smith	.30	.14
☐ 45 Ryne Sandberg (70)	1.25	.55
☐ 46 Larry Bowa (301)	.10	.05
☐ 47 Chuck Rainey (247)	.05	.02
☐ 48 Fergie Jenkins (170)	.15	.07
☐ 49 Dick Ruthven (333)	.05	.02
☐ 50 Jay Johnstone (298)	.05	.02
☐ 51 Mario Soto	.05	.02
☐ 52 Gary Redus	.05	.02
☐ 53 Ron Oester	.05	.02
☐ 54 Cesar Cedeno	.10	.05
☐ 55 Dan Driessen	.05	.02
☐ 56 Dave Concepcion	.10	.05
☐ 57 Dann Bilardello(147)	.05	.02
☐ 58 Joe Price (98)	.05	.02
☐ 59 Tom Hume (35)	.05	.02
☐ 60 Eddie Milner (84)	.05	.02
☐ 61 Paul Householder (226)	.05	.02
☐ 62 Bill Scherrer (269)	.05	.02
☐ 63 Phil Garner	.10	.05
☐ 64 Dickie Thon	.05	.02
☐ 65 Jose Cruz	.10	.05
☐ 66 Nolan Ryan	2.00	.90
☐ 67 Terry Puhl	.05	.02
☐ 68 Ray Knight	.10	.05
☐ 69 Joe Niekro (312)	.10	.05
☐ 70 Jerry Mumphrey (45)	.05	.02

☐ 71 Bill Dawley (314) .05 .02
☐ 72 Alan Ashby (162) .05 .02
☐ 73 Denny Walling (81) .05 .02
☐ 74 Frank DiPino (360) .05 .02
☐ 75 Pedro Guerrero .10 .05
☐ 76 Ken Landreaux .05 .02
☐ 77 Bill Russell .10 .05
☐ 78 Steve Sax .10 .05
☐ 79 Fernando Valenzuela .10 .05
☐ 80 Dusty Baker .10 .05
☐ 81 Jerry Reuss (73) .05 .02
☐ 82 Alejandro Pena (34) .10 .05
☐ 83 Rick Monday .05 .02
☐ 84 Rick Honeycutt (60) .05 .02
☐ 85 Mike Marshall (245) .05 .02
☐ 86 Steve Yeager (284) .05 .02
☐ 87 Al Oliver .10 .05
☐ 88 Steve Rogers .05 .02
☐ 89 Jeff Reardon .10 .05
☐ 90 Gary Carter .10 .05
☐ 91 Tim Raines .15 .07
☐ 92 Andre Dawson .15 .07
☐ 93 Manny Trillo (137) .05 .02
☐ 94 Tim Wallach (348) .10 .05
☐ 95 Chris Speier (172) .05 .02
☐ 96 Bill Gullickson(134) .05 .02
☐ 97 Doug Flynn (271) .05 .02
☐ 98 Charlie Lea (58) .05 .02
☐ 99 Bill Madlock .10 .05
(102B/288B)
☐ 100 Wade Boggs .60 .25
(200B/287B)
☐ 101 Mike Schmidt (176) .60 .25
☐ 102A Jim Rice (287A/177) .10 .05
☐ 102B Reggie Jackson .50 .23
(99/288B)
☐ 103 Hubie Brooks .05 .02
☐ 104 Jesse Orosco .05 .02
☐ 105 George Foster .10 .05
☐ 106 Tom Seaver .50 .23
☐ 107 Keith Hernandez .10 .05
☐ 108 Mookie Wilson .10 .05
☐ 109 Bob Bailor (122) .05 .02
☐ 110 Walt Terrell (209) .05 .02
☐ 111 Brian Giles (126) .05 .02
☐ 112 Jose Oquendo (372) .05 .02
☐ 113 Mike Torrez (258) .05 .02
☐ 114 Junior Ortiz (371) .05 .02
☐ 115 Pete Rose .75 .35
☐ 116 Joe Morgan .25 .11
☐ 117 Mike Schmidt .60 .25
☐ 118 Gary Matthews .05 .02
☐ 119 Steve Carlton .40 .18
☐ 120 Bo Diaz .05 .02
☐ 121 Ivan DeJesus (210) .05 .02
☐ 122 John Denny (109) .05 .02
☐ 123 Garry Maddox (335) .05 .02
☐ 124 Von Hayes (224) .05 .02
☐ 125 Al Holland (158) .05 .02
☐ 126 Tony Perez (111) .15 .07
☐ 127 John Candelaria .05 .02
☐ 128 Jason Thompson .05 .02
☐ 129 Tony Pena .05 .02
☐ 130 Dave Parker .10 .05
☐ 131 Bill Madlock .05 .02
☐ 132 Kent Tekulve .10 .05
☐ 133 Larry McWilliams .05 .02
(146)
☐ 134 Johnny Ray (96) .05 .02
☐ 135 Marvell Wynne (33) .05 .02
☐ 136 Dale Berra (299) .05 .02
☐ 137 Mike Easler (93) .05 .02
☐ 138 Lee Lacy (233) .05 .02
☐ 139 George Hendrick .05 .02
☐ 140 Lonnie Smith .05 .02
☐ 141 Willie McGee .15 .07
☐ 142 Tom Herr .10 .05
☐ 143 Darrell Porter .05 .02
☐ 144 Ozzie Smith .40 .18
☐ 145 Bruce Sutter (221) .10 .05
☐ 146 Dave LaPoint (133) .05 .02
☐ 147 Neil Allen (57) .05 .02
☐ 148 Ken Oberkfell (238) .05 .02
☐ 149 David Green (324) .05 .02
☐ 150 Andy Van Slyke (235) .25 .11
☐ 151 Garry Templeton .05 .02
☐ 152 Juan Bonilla .05 .02
☐ 153 Alan Wiggins .05 .02
☐ 154 Terry Kennedy .05 .02
☐ 155 Dave Dravecky .10 .05
☐ 156 Steve Garvey .15 .07
☐ 157 Bobby Brown (361) .05 .02
☐ 158 Ruppert Jones (125) .05 .02
☐ 159 Luis Salazar (214) .05 .02
☐ 160 Tony Gwynn (212) 2.50 1.10
☐ 161 Gary Lucas (211) .05 .02
☐ 162 Eric Show (72) .05 .02
☐ 163 Darrell Evans .10 .05
☐ 164 Gary Lavelle .05 .02
☐ 165 Atlee Hammaker .05 .02
☐ 166 Jeff Leonard .05 .02
☐ 167 Jack Clark .10 .05
☐ 168 Johnny LeMaster .05 .02
☐ 169 Duane Kuiper (260) .05 .02
☐ 170 Tom O'Malley (48) .05 .02
☐ 171 Chili Davis (311) .10 .05
☐ 172 Bill Laskey (95) .05 .02
☐ 173 Joel Youngblood(300) .05 .02
☐ 174 Bob Brenly (225) .05 .02
☐ 175 Atlee Hammaker(202) .05 .02
☐ 176 Rick Honeycutt (101) .05 .02
☐ 177 John Denny .05 .02
(102A/287A)
☐ 178 LaMarr Hoyt .05 .02
(200A/288A)
☐ 179 Tim Raines FOIL .15 .07
☐ 180 Dale Murphy FOIL .25 .11
☐ 181 Andre Dawson FOIL .25 .11
☐ 182 Steve Rogers FOIL .10 .05
☐ 183 Gary Carter FOIL .10 .05
☐ 184 Steve Carlton FOIL .50 .23
☐ 185 George Hendrick FOIL .10 .05
☐ 186 Johnny Ray FOIL .10 .05
☐ 187 Ozzie Smith FOIL .50 .23
☐ 188 Mike Schmidt FOIL .75 .35
☐ 189 Jim Rice FOIL .10 .05
☐ 190 Dave Winfield FOIL .40 .18
☐ 191 Lloyd Moseby FOIL .10 .05
☐ 192 LaMarr Hoyt FOIL .10 .05
☐ 193 Ted Simmons FOIL .10 .05
☐ 194 Ron Guidry FOIL .10 .05
☐ 195 Eddie Murray FOIL .50 .23
☐ 196 Lou Whitaker FOIL .10 .05
☐ 197 Cal Ripken FOIL 3.00 1.35
☐ 198 George Brett FOIL 1.25 .55
☐ 199 Dale Murphy (290) .15 .07
☐ 200A Cecil Cooper .10 .05
(288A/178)
☐ 200B Jim Rice (287B/100) .10 .05
☐ 201 Tim Raines (289) .15 .07
☐ 202 Rickey Henderson .40 .18
(175)
☐ 203 Eddie Murray .40 .18
☐ 204 Cal Ripken 2.50 1.10
☐ 205 Gary Roenicke .05 .02
☐ 206 Ken Singleton .05 .02
☐ 207 Scott McGregor .05 .02
☐ 208 Tippy Martinez .05 .02
☐ 209 John Lowenstein(110) .05 .02
☐ 210 Mike Flanagan (121) .05 .02
☐ 211 Jim Palmer (161) .25 .11
☐ 212 Dan Ford (160) .05 .02
☐ 213 Rick Dempsey (234) .05 .02
☐ 214 Rich Dauer (159) .05 .02
☐ 215 Jerry Remy .05 .02
☐ 216 Wade Boggs .60 .25
☐ 217 Jim Rice .10 .05
☐ 218 Tony Armas .05 .02
☐ 219 Dwight Evans .10 .05
☐ 220 Bob Stanley (370) .05 .02
☐ 221 Dave Stapleton (145) .05 .02
☐ 222 Rich Gedman .05 .02
☐ 223 Glenn Hoffman (272) .05 .02
☐ 224 Dennis Eckersley .15 .07
(124)
☐ 225 John Tudor (174) .05 .02
☐ 226 Bruce Hurst (61) .05 .02
☐ 227 Rod Carew .40 .18
☐ 228 Bobby Grich .10 .05
☐ 229 Doug DeCinces .05 .02
☐ 230 Fred Lynn .10 .05
☐ 231 Reggie Jackson .50 .23
☐ 232 Tommy John .10 .05
☐ 233 Luis Sanchez (138) .05 .02
☐ 234 Bob Boone (213) .10 .05
☐ 235 Bruce Kison (150) .05 .02
☐ 236 Brian Downing (262) .05 .02
☐ 237 Ken Forsch (246) .05 .02
☐ 238 Rick Burleson (148) .05 .02
☐ 239 Dennis Lamp .05 .02
☐ 240 LaMarr Hoyt .05 .02
☐ 241 Richard Dotson .05 .02
☐ 242 Harold Baines .10 .05
☐ 243 Carlton Fisk .30 .14
☐ 244 Greg Luzinski .10 .05
☐ 245 Rudy Law (85) .05 .02
☐ 246 Tom Paciorek (237) .05 .02
☐ 247 Floyd Bannister(47) .05 .02
☐ 248 Julio Cruz (369) .05 .02
☐ 249 Vance Law (358) .05 .02
☐ 250 Scott Fletcher(270) .05 .02
☐ 251 Toby Harrah .10 .05
☐ 252 Pat Tabler .05 .02
☐ 253 Gorman Thomas .05 .02
☐ 254 Rick Sutcliffe .10 .05
☐ 255 Andre Thornton .05 .02
☐ 256 Bake McBride .05 .02
☐ 257 Alan Bannister(313) .05 .02
☐ 258 Jamie Easterly(113) .05 .02
☐ 259 Lary Sorensen (285) .05 .02
☐ 260 Mike Hargrove (169) .10 .05
☐ 261 Bert Blyleven (346) .10 .05
☐ 262 Ron Hassey (236) .05 .02
☐ 263 Jack Morris .10 .05
☐ 264 Larry Herndon .05 .02
☐ 265 Lance Parrish .10 .05
☐ 266 Alan Trammell .15 .07
☐ 267 Lou Whitaker .10 .05
☐ 268 Aurelio Lopez .05 .02
☐ 269 Dan Petry (62) .05 .02
☐ 270 Glenn Wilson (250) .10 .05
☐ 271 Chet Lemon (97) .05 .02
☐ 272 Kirk Gibson (223) .15 .07
☐ 273 Enos Cabell (338) .05 .02
☐ 274 John Wockenfuss(321) .05 .02
☐ 275 George Brett 1.00 .45
☐ 276 Willie Aikens .05 .02
☐ 277 Frank White .10 .05
☐ 278 Hal McRae .10 .05
☐ 279 Dan Quisenberry .05 .02
☐ 280 Willie Wilson .05 .02
☐ 281 Paul Splittorff(281) .05 .02
☐ 282 U.L. Washington(322) .05 .02
☐ 283 Bud Black (38) .05 .02
☐ 284 John Wathan (86) .05 .02
☐ 285 Larry Gura (259) .05 .02
☐ 286 Pat Sheridan (323) .05 .02
☐ 287A Rusty Staub .10 .05
(102A/177)
☐ 287B Dave Righetti .05 .02
(100/200B)
☐ 288A Bob Forsch .05 .02
(178/200A)
☐ 288B Mike Warren .05 .02
(99/102B)
☐ 289 Al Holland (201) .05 .02
☐ 290 Dan Quisenberry(199) .05 .02
☐ 291 Cecil Cooper .10 .05
☐ 292 Moose Haas .05 .02
☐ 293 Ted Simmons .10 .05
☐ 294 Paul Molitor .30 .14
☐ 295 Robin Yount .30 .14
☐ 296 Ben Oglivie .05 .02
☐ 297 Tom Tellman (325) .05 .02
☐ 298 Jim Gantner (50) .10 .05
☐ 299 Rick Manning (136) .05 .02
☐ 300 Don Sutton (173) .15 .07
☐ 301 Charlie Moore (46) .05 .02
☐ 302 Jim Slaton (337) .05 .02
☐ 303 Gary Ward .05 .02
☐ 304 Tom Brunansky .10 .05
☐ 305 Kent Hrbek .10 .05
☐ 306 Gary Gaetti .15 .07
☐ 307 John Castino .05 .02
☐ 308 Ken Schrom .05 .02
☐ 309 Ron Davis (334) .05 .02
☐ 310 Lenny Faedo (336) .05 .02
☐ 311 Darrell Brown (171) .05 .02
☐ 312 Frank Viola (69) .15 .07
☐ 313 Dave Engle (257) .05 .02
☐ 314 Randy Bush (71) .05 .02
☐ 315 Dave Righetti .05 .02
☐ 316 Rich Gossage .10 .05
☐ 317 Ken Griffey .10 .05
☐ 318 Ron Guidry .10 .05
☐ 319 Dave Winfield .30 .14
☐ 320 Don Baylor .10 .05
☐ 321 Butch Wynegar (274) .05 .02
☐ 322 Omar Moreno (282) .05 .02
☐ 323 Andre Robertson(286) .05 .02
☐ 324 Willie Randolph(149) .10 .05
☐ 325 Don Mattingly (297) 5.00 2.20
☐ 326 Graig Nettles .10 .05
☐ 327 Rickey Henderson .40 .18
☐ 328 Carney Lansford .10 .05
☐ 329 Jeff Burroughs .05 .02
☐ 330 Chris Codiroli .05 .02
☐ 331 Dave Lopes .10 .05
☐ 332 Dwayne Murphy .05 .02
☐ 333 Wayne Gross (49) .05 .02
☐ 334 Bill Almon (309) .05 .02
☐ 335 Tom Underwood (123) .05 .02
☐ 336 Dave Beard (310) .05 .02
☐ 337 Mike Heath (302) .05 .02
☐ 338 Mike Davis (273) .05 .02
☐ 339 Pat Putnam .05 .02
☐ 340 Tony Bernazard .05 .02
☐ 341 Steve Henderson .05 .02
☐ 342 Richie Zisk .05 .02
☐ 343 Dave Henderson .10 .05
☐ 344 Al Cowens .05 .02

	NRMT	VG-E
☐ 345 Bill Caudill (359)	.05	.02
☐ 346 Jim Beattie (261)	.05	.02
☐ 347 Rick Nelson (36)	.05	.02
☐ 348 Roy Thomas (94)	.05	.02
☐ 349 Spike Owen (362)	.10	.05
☐ 350 Jamie Allen (373)	.05	.02
☐ 351 Buddy Bell	.10	.05
☐ 352 Billy Sample	.05	.02
☐ 353 George Wright	.05	.02
☐ 354 Larry Parrish	.05	.02
☐ 355 Jim Sundberg	.10	.05
☐ 356 Charlie Hough	.10	.05
☐ 357 Pete O'Brien	.05	.02
☐ 358 Wayne Tolleson(249)	.05	.02
☐ 359 Danny Darwin (345)	.05	.02
☐ 360 Dave Stewart (74)	.10	.05
☐ 361 Mickey Rivers (157)	.05	.02
☐ 362 Bucky Dent (349)	.10	.05
☐ 363 Willie Upshaw	.05	.02
☐ 364 Damaso Garcia	.05	.02
☐ 365 Lloyd Moseby	.05	.02
☐ 366 Cliff Johnson	.05	.02
☐ 367 Jim Clancy	.05	.02
☐ 368 Dave Stieb	.05	.02
☐ 369 Alfredo Griffin(248)	.05	.02
☐ 370 Barry Bonnell (222)	.05	.02
☐ 371 Luis Leal (114)	.05	.02
☐ 372 Jesse Barfield(112)	.05	.02
☐ 373 Ernie Whitt (350)	.05	.02
☐ 374 Rance Mulliniks(326)	.05	.02
☐ 375 Mike Boddicker	.05	.02
☐ 376 Greg Brock	.05	.02
☐ 377 Bill Doran	.10	.05
☐ 378 Nick Esasky	.05	.02
☐ 379 Julio Franco	.25	.11
☐ 380 Mel Hall	.05	.02
☐ 381 Bob Kearney	.05	.02
☐ 382 Ron Kittle	.05	.02
☐ 383 Carmelo Martinez	.05	.02
☐ 384 Craig McMurtry	.05	.02
☐ 385 Darryl Strawberry	1.25	.55
☐ 386 Matt Young	.05	.02
☐ xx Album	1.00	.45

1984 Topps Sticker Boxes

'he 24 cards in this set measure 2 1/2" by 3 1/2". For the second straight year, Topps issued blank-backed baseball ards on the boxes containing its stickers. Two cards per ox were issued featuring "24 Leaders in Batting Average n 1983 -- Righties, Lefties and Switch Hitters." Officially alled Super Bats Picture Cards, the player's name and 983 batting average were featured within the dotted line ut-out around the card. The team name and batting ide(s) of the player were on the outside of the dotted line. 'he price below includes only the cards on the box. Box 0 was not issued.

	NRMT	VG-E
:OMPLETE SET (12)	10.00	4.50
:OMMON PAIR (1-13)	.25	.11
] 1 Al Oliver Lou Whitaker	.75	.35
] 2 Ken Oberkfell Ted Simmons	.25	.11
] 3 Alan Wiggins Hal McRae	.50	.23
] 4 Tim Raines Lloyd Moseby	.75	.35
] 5 Lonnie Smith Willie Wilson	.25	.11
] 6 Keith Hernandez Robin Yount	.50	.23
] 7 Johnny Ray Wade Boggs	2.00	.90
] 8 Willie McGee Ken Singleton	.75	.35
] 9 Ray Knight Alan Trammell	.75	.35
] 11 George Hendrick Rod Carew	1.25	.55
☐ 12 Bill Madlock Eddie Murray	1.25	.55
☐ 13 Jose Cruz Cal Ripken	8.00	3.60

1984 Topps Rub Downs

The cards in this 112-player (32 different sheets) set measure 2 3/8" by 3 5/16". The Topps Rub Downs set was actually similar to earlier Topps tatoo or decal-type offerings. The full color photo could be transfered from the rub down to another surface by rubbing a coin over the paper backing. Distributed in packages of two rub down sheets, some contained two or three player action poses, others head shots and various pieces of player equipment. Players from all teams were included in the set. Although the sheets are unnumbered, they are numbered here in alphabetical order based on each card first being placed in alphabetical order.

	NRMT	VG-E
COMPLETE SET (32)	8.00	3.60
COMMON SHEET (1-32)	.10	.05
☐ 1 Tony Armas Harold Baines Lonnie Smith	.10	.05
☐ 2 Don Baylor George Hendrick Ron Kittle Johnnie LeMaster	.10	.05
☐ 3 Buddy Bell Ray Knight Lloyd Moseby	.15	.07
☐ 4 Bruce Benedict Atlee Hammaker Frank White	.10	.05
☐ 5 Wade Boggs Rick Dempsey Keith Hernandez	.75	.35
☐ 6 George Brett Andre Dawson Paul Molitor Alan Wiggins	1.50	.70
☐ 7 Tom Brunansky Pedro Guerrero Darryl Strawberry	.75	.35
☐ 8 Bill Buckner Rich Gossage Dave Stieb Rick Sutcliffe	.15	.07
☐ 9 Rod Carew Carlton Fisk Johnny Ray Matt Young	.75	.35
☐ 10 Steve Carlton Bob Horner Dan Quisenberry	.40	.18
☐ 11 Gary Carter Phil Garner Ron Guidry	.15	.07
☐ 12 Ron Cey Steve Kemp Greg Luzinski Kent Tekulve	.15	.07
☐ 13 Chris Chambliss Dwight Evans Julio Franco	.40	.18
☐ 14 Jack Clark Damaso Garcia Hal McRae Lance Parrish	.25	.11
☐ 15 Dave Concepcion Cecil Cooper Fred Lynn Jesse Orosco	.25	.11
☐ 16 Jose Cruz Gary Matthews Jack Morris Jim Rice	.25	.11
☐ 17 Ron Davis Kent Hrbek Tom Seaver	.60	.25
☐ 18 John Denny Carney Lansford Mario Soto Lou Whitaker	.15	.07
☐ 19 Leon Durham Dave Lopes Steve Sax	.10	.05
☐ 20 George Foster Gary Gaetti Bobby Grich Gary Redus	.25	.11
☐ 21 Steve Garvey Jerry Remy Bill Russell George Wright	.15	.07
☐ 22 Moose Haas Bruce Sutter Dickie Thon Andre Thornton	.10	.05
☐ 23 Toby Harrah Pat Putnam Tim Raines Mike Schmidt	.75	.35
☐ 24 Rickey Henderson Dave Righetti Pete Rose	1.25	.55
☐ 25 Steve Henderson Bill Madlock Alan Trammell	.25	.11
☐ 26 LaMarr Hoyt Larry Parrish Nolan Ryan	2.00	.90
☐ 27 Reggie Jackson Eric Show Jason Thompson	.50	.23
☐ 28 Tommy John Terry Kennedy Eddie Murray Ozzie Smith	1.00	.45
☐ 29 Jeff Leonard Dale Murphy Ken Singleton Dave Winfield	.50	.23
☐ 30 Craig McMurtry Cal Ripken Steve Rogers Willie Upshaw	2.50	1.10
☐ 31 Ben Oglivie Jim Palmer Darrell Porter	.25	.11
☐ 32 Tony Pena Fernando Valenzuela Robin Yount	.40	.18

1984 Topps Super

The cards in this 30-card set measure 4 7/8" by 6 7/8". The 1984 Topps Supers feature enlargements from the 1984 regular set. The cards differ from the corresponding cards of the regular set in size and number only. As one would expect, only those considered stars and superstars appear in this set.

	NRMT	VG-E
COMPLETE SET (30)	10.00	4.50
COMMON CARD (1-30)	.10	.05
☐ 1 Cal Ripken	4.00	1.80
☐ 2 Dale Murphy	1.00	.45
☐ 3 LaMarr Hoyt	.10	.05
☐ 4 John Denny	.10	.05
☐ 5 Jim Rice	.25	.11
☐ 6 Mike Schmidt	1.25	.55
☐ 7 Wade Boggs	1.50	.70
☐ 8 Bill Madlock	.10	.05
☐ 9 Dan Quisenberry	.10	.05
☐ 10 Al Holland	.10	.05
☐ 11 Ron Kittle	.10	.05
☐ 12 Darryl Strawberry	1.00	.45
☐ 13 George Brett	1.50	.70
☐ 14 Bill Buckner	.25	.11
☐ 15 Carlton Fisk	.50	.23
☐ 16 Steve Carlton	.75	.35

☐ 17 Ron Guidry .25 .11
☐ 18 Gary Carter .50 .23
☐ 19 Rickey Henderson .75 .35
☐ 20 Andre Dawson .50 .23
☐ 21 Reggie Jackson 1.00 .45
☐ 22 Steve Garvey .25 .11
☐ 23 Fred Lynn .25 .11
☐ 24 Pedro Guerrero .25 .11
☐ 25 Eddie Murray 1.25 .55
☐ 26 Keith Hernandez .25 .11
☐ 27 Dave Winfield .75 .35
☐ 28 Nolan Ryan 3.00 1.35
☐ 29 Robin Yount .50 .23
☐ 30 Fernando Valenzuela .25 .11

1985 Topps

The 1985 Topps set contains 792 standard-size full-color cards. Cards were primarily distributed in 15-card wax packs and 51-card rack packs. Full color card fronts feature both the Topps and team logos along with the team name, player's name, and his position. The first ten cards (1-10) are Record Breakers, cards 131-143 are Father and Sons, and cards 701 to 722 portray All-Star selections. Cards 271-282 represent "First Draft Picks" still active in professional baseball and cards 389-404 feature selected members of the 1984 U.S. Olympic Baseball Team. Rookie Cards include Roger Clemens, Eric Davis, Shawon Dunston, Dwight Gooden, Orel Hershiser, Jimmy Key, Mark Langston, Mark McGwire, Terry Pendleton, Kirby Puckett, Jose Rijo and Bret Saberhagen.

	NRMT	VG-E
COMPLETE SET (792)	50.00	22.00
COMMON CARD (1-792)	.10	.05

☐ 1 Carlton Fisk RB .60 .25
Longest game by catcher
☐ 2 Steve Garvey RB .60 .25
Consecutive error-less games, 1B
☐ 3 Dwight Gooden RB .60 .25
Most rookie strikeouts
☐ 4 Cliff Johnson RB .10 .05
Most pinch-hit homers
☐ 5 Joe Morgan RB .60 .25
Most homers 2B, lifetime
☐ 6 Pete Rose RB .40 .18
Most career singles
☐ 7 Nolan Ryan RB 1.50 .70
Most career strikeouts
☐ 8 Juan Samuel RB .10 .05
Most SB's, rookie season
☐ 9 Bruce Sutter RB .20 .09
Most NL season saves
☐ 10 Don Sutton RB .40 .18
Most seasons 100 or more K's
☐ 11 Ralph Houk MG .10 .05
(Checklist back)
☐ 12 Dave Lopes .20 .09
(Now with Cubs on card front)
☐ 13 Tim Lollar .10 .05
☐ 14 Chris Bando .10 .05
☐ 15 Jerry Koosman .10 .05
☐ 16 Bobby Meacham .10 .05
☐ 17 Mike Scott .10 .05
☐ 18 Mickey Hatcher .10 .05
☐ 19 George Frazier .10 .05
☐ 20 Chet Lemon .10 .05
☐ 21 Lee Tunnell .10 .05
☐ 22 Duane Kuiper .10 .05
☐ 23 Bret Saberhagen .60 .25
☐ 24 Jesse Barfield .10 .05
☐ 25 Steve Bedrosian .10 .05
☐ 26 Roy Smalley .10 .05
☐ 27 Bruce Berenyi .10 .05
☐ 28 Dann Bilardello .10 .05
☐ 29 Odell Jones .10 .05
☐ 30 Cal Ripken 3.00 1.35
☐ 31 Terry Whitfield .10 .05
☐ 32 Chuck Porter .10 .05
☐ 33 Tito Landrum .10 .05
☐ 34 Ed Nunez .10 .05
☐ 35 Graig Nettles .20 .09
☐ 36 Fred Breining .10 .05
☐ 37 Reid Nichols .10 .05
☐ 38 Jackie Moore MG .10 .05
(Checklist back)
☐ 39 John Wockenfuss .10 .05
☐ 40 Phil Niekro .60 .25
☐ 41 Mike Fischlin .10 .05
☐ 42 Luis Sanchez .10 .05
☐ 43 Andre David .10 .05
☐ 44 Dickie Thon .10 .05
☐ 45 Greg Minton .10 .05
☐ 46 Gary Woods .10 .05
☐ 47 Dave Rozema .10 .05
☐ 48 Tony Fernandez .20 .09
☐ 49 Butch Davis .10 .05
☐ 50 John Candelaria .10 .05
☐ 51 Bob Watson .20 .09
☐ 52 Jerry Dybzinski .10 .05
☐ 53 Tom Gorman .10 .05
☐ 54 Cesar Cedeno .20 .09
☐ 55 Frank Tanana .10 .05
☐ 56 Jim Dwyer .10 .05
☐ 57 Pat Zachry .10 .05
☐ 58 Orlando Mercado .10 .05
☐ 59 Rick Waits .10 .05
☐ 60 George Hendrick .10 .05
☐ 61 Curt Kaufman .10 .05
☐ 62 Mike Ramsey .10 .05
☐ 63 Steve McCatty .10 .05
☐ 64 Mark Bailey .10 .05
☐ 65 Bill Buckner .20 .09
☐ 66 Dick Williams MG .20 .09
(Checklist back)
☐ 67 Rafael Santana .10 .05
☐ 68 Von Hayes .10 .05
☐ 69 Jim Winn .10 .05
☐ 70 Don Baylor .40 .18
☐ 71 Tim Laudner .10 .05
☐ 72 Rick Sutcliffe .10 .05
☐ 73 Rusty Kuntz .10 .05
☐ 74 Mike Krukow .10 .05
☐ 75 Willie Upshaw .10 .05
☐ 76 Alan Bannister .10 .05
☐ 77 Joe Beckwith .10 .05
☐ 78 Scott Fletcher .10 .05
☐ 79 Rick Mahler .10 .05
☐ 80 Keith Hernandez .20 .09
☐ 81 Lenn Sakata .10 .05
☐ 82 Joe Price .10 .05
☐ 83 Charlie Moore .10 .05
☐ 84 Spike Owen .10 .05
☐ 85 Mike Marshall .10 .05
☐ 86 Don Aase .10 .05
☐ 87 David Green .10 .05
☐ 88 Bryn Smith .10 .05
☐ 89 Jackie Gutierrez .10 .05
☐ 90 Rich Gossage .20 .09
☐ 91 Jeff Burroughs .10 .05
☐ 92 Paul Owens MG .10 .05
(Checklist back)
☐ 93 Don Schulze .10 .05
☐ 94 Toby Harrah .10 .05
☐ 95 Jose Cruz .20 .09
☐ 96 Johnny Ray .10 .05
☐ 97 Pete Filson .10 .05
☐ 98 Steve Lake .10 .05
☐ 99 Milt Wilcox .10 .05
☐ 100 George Brett 1.25 .55
☐ 101 Jim Acker .10 .05
☐ 102 Tommy Dunbar .10 .05
☐ 103 Randy Lerch .10 .05
☐ 104 Mike Fitzgerald .10 .05
☐ 105 Ron Kittle .10 .05
☐ 106 Pascual Perez .10 .05
☐ 107 Tom Foley .10 .05
☐ 108 Darnell Coles .10 .05
☐ 109 Gary Roenicke .10 .05
☐ 110 Alejandro Pena .10 .05
☐ 111 Doug DeCinces .10 .05
☐ 112 Tom Tellmann .10 .05
☐ 113 Tom Herr .20 .09
☐ 114 Bob James .10 .05
☐ 115 Rickey Henderson .60 .25
☐ 116 Dennis Boyd .10 .05
☐ 117 Greg Gross .10 .05
☐ 118 Eric Show .10 .05
☐ 119 Pat Corrales MG .10 .05
(Checklist back)
☐ 120 Steve Kemp .10 .05
☐ 121 Checklist: 1-132 .20 .09
☐ 122 Tom Brunansky .20 .09
☐ 123 Dave Smith .10 .05
☐ 124 Rich Hebner .10 .05
☐ 125 Kent Tekulve .10 .05
☐ 126 Ruppert Jones .10 .05
☐ 127 Mark Gubicza .20 .09
☐ 128 Ernie Whitt .10 .05
☐ 129 Gene Garber .10 .05
☐ 130 Al Oliver .20 .09
☐ 131 Buddy Bell FS .20 .09
Gus Bell
☐ 132 Dale Berra FS .20 .09
Yogi Berra
☐ 133 Bob Boone FS .20 .09
Ray Boone
☐ 134 Terry Francona FS .20 .09
Tito Francona
☐ 135 Terry Kennedy FS .20 .09
Bob Kennedy
☐ 136 Jeff Kunkel FS .10 .05
Bill Kunkel
☐ 137 Vance Law FS .20 .09
Vern Law
☐ 138 Dick Schofield FS .10 .05
Dick Schofield
☐ 139 Joel Skinner FS .10 .05
Bob Skinner
☐ 140 Roy Smalley Jr. FS .20 .09
Roy Smalley
☐ 141 Mike Stenhouse FS .10 .05
Dave Stenhouse
☐ 142 Steve Trout FS .20 .09
Dizzy Trout
☐ 143 Ozzie Virgil FS .10 .05
Ossie Virgil
☐ 144 Ron Gardenhire .10 .05
☐ 145 Alvin Davis .20 .09
☐ 146 Gary Redus .10 .05
☐ 147 Bill Swaggerty .10 .05
☐ 148 Steve Yeager .10 .05
☐ 149 Dickie Noles .10 .05
☐ 150 Jim Rice .20 .09
☐ 151 Moose Haas .10 .05
☐ 152 Steve Braun .10 .05
☐ 153 Frank LaCorte .10 .05
☐ 154 Argenis Salazar .10 .05
☐ 155 Yogi Berra MG .40 .18
(Checklist back)
☐ 156 Craig Reynolds .10 .05
☐ 157 Tug McGraw .20 .09
☐ 158 Pat Tabler .10 .05
☐ 159 Carlos Diaz .10 .05
☐ 160 Lance Parrish .20 .09
☐ 161 Ken Schrom .10 .05
☐ 162 Benny Distefano .10 .05
☐ 163 Dennis Eckersley .60 .25
☐ 164 Jorge Orta .10 .05
☐ 165 Dusty Baker .20 .09
☐ 166 Keith Atherton .10 .05
☐ 167 Rufino Linares .10 .05
☐ 168 Garth Iorg .10 .05
☐ 169 Dan Spillner .10 .05
☐ 170 George Foster .20 .09
☐ 171 Bill Stein .10 .05
☐ 172 Jack Perconte .10 .05
☐ 173 Mike Young .10 .05
☐ 174 Rick Honeycutt .10 .05
☐ 175 Dave Parker .20 .09
☐ 176 Bill Schroeder .10 .05
☐ 177 Dave Von Ohlen .10 .05
☐ 178 Miguel Dilone .10 .05
☐ 179 Tommy John .40 .18
☐ 180 Dave Winfield .60 .25
☐ 181 Roger Clemens 8.00 3.60
☐ 182 Tim Flannery .10 .05
☐ 183 Larry McWilliams .10 .05
☐ 184 Carmen Castillo .10 .05
☐ 185 Al Holland .10 .05
☐ 186 Bob Lillis MG .10 .05
(Checklist back)
☐ 187 Mike Walters .10 .05
☐ 188 Greg Pryor .10 .05
☐ 189 Warren Brusstar .10 .05
☐ 190 Rusty Staub .20 .09
☐ 191 Steve Nicosia .10 .05
☐ 192 Howard Johnson .20 .09
☐ 193 Jimmy Key .75 .35
☐ 194 Dave Stegman .10 .05
☐ 195 Glenn Hubbard .10 .05
☐ 196 Pete O'Brien .10 .05
☐ 197 Mike Warren .10 .05
☐ 198 Eddie Milner .10 .05
☐ 199 Dennis Martinez .20 .09
☐ 200 Reggie Jackson .75 .35
☐ 201 Burt Hooton .10 .05
☐ 202 Gorman Thomas .10 .05
☐ 203 Bob McClure .10 .05
☐ 204 Art Howe .10 .05
☐ 205 Steve Rogers .10 .05
☐ 206 Phil Garner .10 .05

☐ 207 Mark Clear	.10	.05
☐ 208 Champ Summers	.10	.05
☐ 209 Bill Campbell	.10	.05
☐ 210 Gary Matthews	.10	.05
☐ 211 Clay Christiansen	.10	.05
☐ 212 George Vukovich	.10	.05
☐ 213 Billy Gardner MG (Checklist back)	.20	.09
☐ 214 John Tudor	.10	.05
☐ 215 Bob Brenly	.10	.05
☐ 216 Jerry Don Gleaton	.10	.05
☐ 217 Leon Roberts	.10	.05
☐ 218 Doyle Alexander	.10	.05
☐ 219 Gerald Perry	.10	.05
☐ 220 Fred Lynn	.20	.09
☐ 221 Ron Reed	.10	.05
☐ 222 Hubie Brooks	.10	.05
☐ 223 Tom Hume	.10	.05
☐ 224 Al Cowens	.10	.05
☐ 225 Mike Boddicker	.10	.05
☐ 226 Juan Beniquez	.10	.05
☐ 227 Danny Darwin	.10	.05
☐ 228 Dion James	.10	.05
☐ 229 Dave LaPoint	.10	.05
☐ 230 Gary Carter	.60	.25
☐ 231 Dwayne Murphy	.10	.05
☐ 232 Dave Beard	.10	.05
☐ 233 Ed Jurak	.10	.05
☐ 234 Jerry Narron	.10	.05
☐ 235 Garry Maddox	.10	.05
☐ 236 Mark Thurmond	.10	.05
☐ 237 Julio Franco	.20	.09
☐ 238 Jose Rijo	.40	.18
☐ 239 Tim Teufel	.10	.05
☐ 240 Dave Stieb	.20	.09
☐ 241 Jim Frey MG (Checklist back)	.10	.05
☐ 242 Greg Harris	.10	.05
☐ 243 Barbaro Garbey	.10	.05
☐ 244 Mike Jones	.10	.05
☐ 245 Chili Davis	.20	.09
☐ 246 Mike Norris	.10	.05
☐ 247 Wayne Tolleson	.10	.05
☐ 248 Terry Forster	.10	.05
☐ 249 Harold Baines	.20	.09
☐ 250 Jesse Orosco	.10	.05
☐ 251 Brad Gulden	.10	.05
☐ 252 Dan Ford	.10	.05
☐ 253 Sid Bream	.20	.09
☐ 254 Pete Vuckovich	.10	.05
☐ 255 Lonnie Smith	.10	.05
☐ 256 Mike Stanton	.10	.05
☐ 257 Bryan Little UER Name spelled Brian on front	.10	.05
☐ 258 Mike C. Brown	.10	.05
☐ 259 Gary Allenson	.10	.05
☐ 260 Dave Righetti	.20	.09
☐ 261 Checklist: 133-264	.20	.09
☐ 262 Greg Booker	.10	.05
☐ 263 Mel Hall	.10	.05
☐ 264 Joe Sambito	.10	.05
☐ 265 Juan Samuel	.10	.05
☐ 266 Frank Viola	.20	.09
☐ 267 Henry Cotto	.10	.05
☐ 268 Chuck Tanner MG (Checklist back)	.20	.09
☐ 269 Doug Baker	.10	.05
☐ 270 Dan Quisenberry	.20	.09
☐ 271 Tim Foli FDP68	.10	.05
☐ 272 Jeff Burroughs FDP69	.10	.05
☐ 273 Bill Almon FDP74	.10	.05
☐ 274 Floyd Bannister FDP76	.10	.05
☐ 275 Harold Baines FDP77	.20	.09
☐ 276 Bob Horner FDP78	.10	.05
☐ 277 Al Chambers FDP79	.10	.05
☐ 278 Darryl Strawberry FDP80	.40	.18
☐ 279 Mike Moore FDP81	.10	.05
☐ 280 Shawon Dunston FDP82	.60	.25
☐ 281 Tim Belcher FDP83	.60	.25
☐ 282 Shawn Abner FDP84	.10	.05
☐ 283 Fran Mullins	.10	.05
☐ 284 Marty Bystrom	.10	.05
☐ 285 Dan Driessen	.10	.05
☐ 286 Rudy Law	.10	.05
☐ 287 Walt Terrell	.10	.05
☐ 288 Jeff Kunkel	.10	.05
☐ 289 Tom Underwood	.10	.05
☐ 290 Cecil Cooper	.20	.09
☐ 291 Bob Welch	.10	.05
☐ 292 Brad Komminsk	.10	.05
☐ 293 Curt Young	.10	.05
☐ 294 Tom Nieto	.10	.05
☐ 295 Joe Niekro	.10	.05
☐ 296 Ricky Nelson	.10	.05
☐ 297 Gary Lucas	.10	.05
☐ 298 Marty Barrett	.10	.05
☐ 299 Andy Hawkins	.10	.05
☐ 300 Rod Carew	.60	.25
☐ 301 John Montefusco	.10	.05
☐ 302 Tim Corcoran	.10	.05
☐ 303 Mike Jeffcoat	.10	.05
☐ 304 Gary Gaetti	.20	.09
☐ 305 Dale Berra	.10	.05
☐ 306 Rick Reuschel	.10	.05
☐ 307 Sparky Anderson MG (Checklist back)	.20	.09
☐ 308 John Wathan	.10	.05
☐ 309 Mike Witt	.10	.05
☐ 310 Manny Trillo	.10	.05
☐ 311 Jim Gott	.10	.05
☐ 312 Marc Hill	.10	.05
☐ 313 Dave Schmidt	.10	.05
☐ 314 Ron Oester	.10	.05
☐ 315 Doug Sisk	.10	.05
☐ 316 John Lowenstein	.10	.05
☐ 317 Jack Lazorko	.10	.05
☐ 318 Ted Simmons	.20	.09
☐ 319 Jeff Jones	.10	.05
☐ 320 Dale Murphy	.60	.25
☐ 321 Ricky Horton	.10	.05
☐ 322 Dave Stapleton	.10	.05
☐ 323 Andy McGaffigan	.10	.05
☐ 324 Bruce Bochy	.10	.05
☐ 325 John Denny	.10	.05
☐ 326 Kevin Bass	.10	.05
☐ 327 Brook Jacoby	.10	.05
☐ 328 Bob Shirley	.10	.05
☐ 329 Ron Washington	.10	.05
☐ 330 Leon Durham	.10	.05
☐ 331 Bill Laskey	.10	.05
☐ 332 Brian Harper	.20	.09
☐ 333 Willie Hernandez	.10	.05
☐ 334 Dick Howser MG (Checklist back)	.20	.09
☐ 335 Bruce Benedict	.10	.05
☐ 336 Rance Mulliniks	.10	.05
☐ 337 Billy Sample	.10	.05
☐ 338 Britt Burns	.10	.05
☐ 339 Danny Heep	.10	.05
☐ 340 Robin Yount	.75	.35
☐ 341 Floyd Rayford	.10	.05
☐ 342 Ted Power	.10	.05
☐ 343 Bill Russell	.10	.05
☐ 344 Dave Henderson	.10	.05
☐ 345 Charlie Lea	.10	.05
☐ 346 Terry Pendleton	.60	.25
☐ 347 Rick Langford	.10	.05
☐ 348 Bob Boone	.20	.09
☐ 349 Domingo Ramos	.10	.05
☐ 350 Wade Boggs	.75	.35
☐ 351 Juan Agosto	.10	.05
☐ 352 Joe Morgan	.60	.25
☐ 353 Julio Solano	.10	.05
☐ 354 Andre Robertson	.10	.05
☐ 355 Bert Blyleven	.20	.09
☐ 356 Dave Meier	.10	.05
☐ 357 Rich Bordi	.10	.05
☐ 358 Tony Pena	.10	.05
☐ 359 Pat Sheridan	.10	.05
☐ 360 Steve Carlton	.40	.18
☐ 361 Alfredo Griffin	.10	.05
☐ 362 Craig McMurtry	.10	.05
☐ 363 Ron Hodges	.10	.05
☐ 364 Richard Dotson	.10	.05
☐ 365 Danny Ozark MG (Checklist back)	.10	.05
☐ 366 Todd Cruz	.10	.05
☐ 367 Keefe Cato	.10	.05
☐ 368 Dave Bergman	.10	.05
☐ 369 R.J. Reynolds	.10	.05
☐ 370 Bruce Sutter	.20	.09
☐ 371 Mickey Rivers	.10	.05
☐ 372 Roy Howell	.10	.05
☐ 373 Mike Moore	.10	.05
☐ 374 Brian Downing	.10	.05
☐ 375 Jeff Reardon	.20	.09
☐ 376 Jeff Newman	.10	.05
☐ 377 Checklist: 265-396	.20	.09
☐ 378 Alan Wiggins	.10	.05
☐ 379 Charles Hudson	.10	.05
☐ 380 Ken Griffey	.20	.09
☐ 381 Roy Smith	.10	.05
☐ 382 Denny Walling	.10	.05
☐ 383 Rick Lysander	.10	.05
☐ 384 Jody Davis	.10	.05
☐ 385 Jose DeLeon	.10	.05
☐ 386 Dan Gladden	.20	.09
☐ 387 Buddy Biancalana	.10	.05
☐ 388 Bert Roberge	.10	.05
☐ 389 Rod Dedeaux OLY CO	.20	.09
☐ 390 Sid Akins OLY	.10	.05
☐ 391 Flavio Alfaro OLY	.10	.05
☐ 392 Don August OLY	.10	.05
☐ 393 Scott Bankhead OLY	.20	.09
☐ 394 Bob Caffrey OLY	.10	.05
☐ 395 Mike Dunne OLY	.20	.09
☐ 396 Gary Green OLY	.20	.09
☐ 397 John Hoover OLY	.10	.05
☐ 398 Shane Mack OLY	.40	.18
☐ 399 John Marzano OLY	.20	.09
☐ 400 Oddibe McDowell OLY	.20	.09
☐ 401 Mark McGwire OLY	35.00	16.00
☐ 402 Pat Pacillo OLY	.20	.09
☐ 403 Cory Snyder OLY	.40	.18
☐ 404 Billy Swift OLY	.50	.23
☐ 405 Tom Veryzer	.10	.05
☐ 406 Len Whitehouse	.10	.05
☐ 407 Bobby Ramos	.10	.05
☐ 408 Sid Monge	.10	.05
☐ 409 Brad Wellman	.10	.05
☐ 410 Bob Horner	.10	.05
☐ 411 Bobby Cox MG (Checklist back)	.20	.09
☐ 412 Bud Black	.10	.05
☐ 413 Vance Law	.10	.05
☐ 414 Gary Ward	.10	.05
☐ 415 Ron Darling UER (No trivia answer)	.20	.09
☐ 416 Wayne Gross	.10	.05
☐ 417 John Franco	.40	.18
☐ 418 Ken Landreaux	.10	.05
☐ 419 Mike Caldwell	.10	.05
☐ 420 Andre Dawson	.60	.25
☐ 421 Dave Rucker	.10	.05
☐ 422 Carney Lansford	.20	.09
☐ 423 Barry Bonnell	.10	.05
☐ 424 Al Nipper	.10	.05
☐ 425 Mike Hargrove	.20	.09
☐ 426 Vern Ruhle	.10	.05
☐ 427 Mario Ramirez	.10	.05
☐ 428 Larry Andersen	.10	.05
☐ 429 Rick Cerone	.10	.05
☐ 430 Ron Davis	.10	.05
☐ 431 U.L. Washington	.10	.05
☐ 432 Thad Bosley	.10	.05
☐ 433 Jim Morrison	.10	.05
☐ 434 Gene Richards	.10	.05
☐ 435 Dan Petry	.10	.05
☐ 436 Willie Aikens	.10	.05
☐ 437 Al Jones	.10	.05
☐ 438 Joe Torre MG (Checklist back)	.40	.18
☐ 439 Junior Ortiz	.10	.05
☐ 440 Fernando Valenzuela	.20	.09
☐ 441 Duane Walker	.10	.05
☐ 442 Ken Forsch	.10	.05
☐ 443 George Wright	.10	.05
☐ 444 Tony Phillips	.10	.05
☐ 445 Tippy Martinez	.10	.05
☐ 446 Jim Sundberg	.10	.05
☐ 447 Jeff Lahti	.10	.05
☐ 448 Derrel Thomas	.10	.05
☐ 449 Phil Bradley	.20	.09
☐ 450 Steve Garvey	.40	.18
☐ 451 Bruce Hurst	.10	.05
☐ 452 John Castino	.10	.05
☐ 453 Tom Waddell	.10	.05
☐ 454 Glenn Wilson	.10	.05
☐ 455 Bob Knepper	.10	.05
☐ 456 Tim Foli	.10	.05
☐ 457 Cecilio Guante	.10	.05
☐ 458 Randy Johnson	.10	.05
☐ 459 Charlie Leibrandt	.10	.05
☐ 460 Ryne Sandberg	1.25	.55
☐ 461 Marty Castillo	.10	.05
☐ 462 Gary Lavelle	.10	.05
☐ 463 Dave Collins	.10	.05
☐ 464 Mike Mason	.10	.05
☐ 465 Bob Grich	.20	.09
☐ 466 Tony LaRussa MG (Checklist back)	.40	.18
☐ 467 Ed Lynch	.10	.05
☐ 468 Wayne Krenchicki	.10	.05
☐ 469 Sammy Stewart	.10	.05
☐ 470 Steve Sax	.20	.09
☐ 471 Pete Ladd	.10	.05
☐ 472 Jim Essian	.10	.05
☐ 473 Tim Wallach	.20	.09
☐ 474 Kurt Kepshire	.10	.05
☐ 475 Andre Thornton	.10	.05
☐ 476 Jeff Stone	.10	.05
☐ 477 Bob Ojeda	.10	.05
☐ 478 Kurt Bevacqua	.10	.05
☐ 479 Mike Madden	.10	.05
☐ 480 Lou Whitaker	.40	.18
☐ 481 Dale Murray	.10	.05
☐ 482 Harry Spilman	.10	.05
☐ 483 Mike Smithson	.10	.05
☐ 484 Larry Bowa	.20	.09
☐ 485 Matt Young	.10	.05

☐ 486 Steve Balboni	.10	.05
☐ 487 Frank Williams	.10	.05
☐ 488 Joel Skinner	.10	.05
☐ 489 Bryan Clark	.10	.05
☐ 490 Jason Thompson	.10	.05
☐ 491 Rick Camp	.10	.05
☐ 492 Dave Johnson MG (Checklist back)	.20	.09
☐ 493 Orel Hershiser	.75	.35
☐ 494 Rich Dauer	.10	.05
☐ 495 Mario Soto	.10	.05
☐ 496 Donnie Scott	.10	.05
☐ 497 Gary Pettis UER (Photo actually Gary's little brother Lynn)	.10	.05
☐ 498 Ed Romero	.10	.05
☐ 499 Danny Cox	.10	.05
☐ 500 Mike Schmidt	.75	.35
☐ 501 Dan Schatzeder	.10	.05
☐ 502 Rick Miller	.10	.05
☐ 503 Tim Conroy	.10	.05
☐ 504 Jerry Willard	.10	.05
☐ 505 Jim Beattie	.10	.05
☐ 506 Franklin Stubbs	.10	.05
☐ 507 Ray Fontenot	.10	.05
☐ 508 John Shelby	.10	.05
☐ 509 Milt May	.10	.05
☐ 510 Kent Hrbek	.20	.09
☐ 511 Lee Smith	.40	.18
☐ 512 Tom Brookens	.10	.05
☐ 513 Lynn Jones	.10	.05
☐ 514 Jeff Cornell	.10	.05
☐ 515 Dave Concepcion	.20	.09
☐ 516 Roy Lee Jackson	.10	.05
☐ 517 Jerry Martin	.10	.05
☐ 518 Chris Chambliss	.10	.05
☐ 519 Doug Rader MG (Checklist back)	.10	.05
☐ 520 LaMarr Hoyt	.10	.05
☐ 521 Rick Dempsey	.10	.05
☐ 522 Paul Molitor	.75	.35
☐ 523 Candy Maldonado	.10	.05
☐ 524 Rob Wilfong	.10	.05
☐ 525 Darrell Porter	.10	.05
☐ 526 David Palmer	.10	.05
☐ 527 Checklist: 397-528	.20	.09
☐ 528 Bill Krueger	.10	.05
☐ 529 Rich Gedman	.10	.05
☐ 530 Dave Dravecky	.20	.09
☐ 531 Joe Lefebvre	.10	.05
☐ 532 Frank DiPino	.10	.05
☐ 533 Tony Bernazard	.10	.05
☐ 534 Brian Dayett	.10	.05
☐ 535 Pat Putnam	.10	.05
☐ 536 Kirby Puckett	8.00	3.60
☐ 537 Don Robinson	.10	.05
☐ 538 Keith Moreland	.10	.05
☐ 539 Aurelio Lopez	.10	.05
☐ 540 Claudell Washington	.10	.05
☐ 541 Mark Davis	.10	.05
☐ 542 Don Slaught	.10	.05
☐ 543 Mike Squires	.10	.05
☐ 544 Bruce Kison	.10	.05
☐ 545 Lloyd Moseby	.10	.05
☐ 546 Brent Gaff	.10	.05
☐ 547 Pete Rose MG (Checklist back)	.50	.23
☐ 548 Larry Parrish	.10	.05
☐ 549 Mike Scioscia	.10	.05
☐ 550 Scott McGregor	.10	.05
☐ 551 Andy Van Slyke	.40	.18
☐ 552 Chris Codiroli	.10	.05
☐ 553 Bob Clark	.10	.05
☐ 554 Doug Flynn	.10	.05
☐ 555 Bob Stanley	.10	.05
☐ 556 Sixto Lezcano	.10	.05
☐ 557 Len Barker	.10	.05
☐ 558 Carmelo Martinez	.10	.05
☐ 559 Jay Howell	.10	.05
☐ 560 Bill Madlock	.10	.05
☐ 561 Darryl Motley	.10	.05
☐ 562 Houston Jimenez	.10	.05
☐ 563 Dick Ruthven	.10	.05
☐ 564 Alan Ashby	.10	.05
☐ 565 Kirk Gibson	.20	.09
☐ 566 Ed VandeBerg	.10	.05
☐ 567 Joel Youngblood	.10	.05
☐ 568 Cliff Johnson	.10	.05
☐ 569 Ken Oberkfell	.10	.05
☐ 570 Darryl Strawberry	.40	.18
☐ 571 Charlie Hough	.20	.09
☐ 572 Tom Paciorek	.10	.05
☐ 573 Jay Tibbs	.10	.05
☐ 574 Joe Altobelli MG (Checklist back)	.10	.05
☐ 575 Pedro Guerrero	.20	.09
☐ 576 Jaime Cocanower	.10	.05
☐ 577 Chris Speier	.10	.05
☐ 578 Terry Francona	.10	.05
☐ 579 Ron Romanick	.10	.05
☐ 580 Dwight Evans	.20	.09
☐ 581 Mark Wagner	.10	.05
☐ 582 Ken Phelps	.10	.05
☐ 583 Bobby Brown	.10	.05
☐ 584 Kevin Gross	.10	.05
☐ 585 Butch Wynegar	.10	.05
☐ 586 Bill Scherrer	.10	.05
☐ 587 Doug Frobel	.10	.05
☐ 588 Bobby Castillo	.10	.05
☐ 589 Bob Dernier	.10	.05
☐ 590 Ray Knight	.20	.09
☐ 591 Larry Herndon	.10	.05
☐ 592 Jeff D. Robinson	.10	.05
☐ 593 Rick Leach	.10	.05
☐ 594 Curt Wilkerson	.10	.05
☐ 595 Larry Gura	.10	.05
☐ 596 Jerry Hairston	.10	.05
☐ 597 Brad Lesley	.10	.05
☐ 598 Jose Oquendo	.10	.05
☐ 599 Storm Davis	.10	.05
☐ 600 Pete Rose	.75	.35
☐ 601 Tom Lasorda MG (Checklist back)	.40	.18
☐ 602 Jeff Dedmon	.10	.05
☐ 603 Rick Manning	.10	.05
☐ 604 Daryl Sconiers	.10	.05
☐ 605 Ozzie Smith	.75	.35
☐ 606 Rich Gale	.10	.05
☐ 607 Bill Almon	.10	.05
☐ 608 Craig Lefferts	.10	.05
☐ 609 Broderick Perkins	.10	.05
☐ 610 Jack Morris	.20	.09
☐ 611 Ozzie Virgil	.10	.05
☐ 612 Mike Armstrong	.10	.05
☐ 613 Terry Puhl	.10	.05
☐ 614 Al Williams	.10	.05
☐ 615 Marvell Wynne	.10	.05
☐ 616 Scott Sanderson	.10	.05
☐ 617 Willie Wilson	.10	.05
☐ 618 Pete Falcone	.10	.05
☐ 619 Jeff Leonard	.10	.05
☐ 620 Dwight Gooden	1.50	.70
☐ 621 Marvis Foley	.10	.05
☐ 622 Luis Leal	.10	.05
☐ 623 Greg Walker	.10	.05
☐ 624 Benny Ayala	.10	.05
☐ 625 Mark Langston	.60	.25
☐ 626 German Rivera	.10	.05
☐ 627 Eric Davis	.75	.35
☐ 628 Rene Lachemann MG (Checklist back)	.10	.05
☐ 629 Dick Schofield	.10	.05
☐ 630 Tim Raines	.20	.09
☐ 631 Bob Forsch	.10	.05
☐ 632 Bruce Bochte	.10	.05
☐ 633 Glenn Hoffman	.10	.05
☐ 634 Bill Dawley	.10	.05
☐ 635 Terry Kennedy	.10	.05
☐ 636 Shane Rawley	.10	.05
☐ 637 Brett Butler	.20	.09
☐ 638 Mike Pagliarulo	.10	.05
☐ 639 Ed Hodge	.10	.05
☐ 640 Steve Henderson	.10	.05
☐ 641 Rod Scurry	.10	.05
☐ 642 Dave Owen	.10	.05
☐ 643 Johnny Grubb	.10	.05
☐ 644 Mark Huismann	.10	.05
☐ 645 Damaso Garcia	.10	.05
☐ 646 Scot Thompson	.10	.05
☐ 647 Rafael Ramirez	.10	.05
☐ 648 Bob Jones	.10	.05
☐ 649 Sid Fernandez	.20	.09
☐ 650 Greg Luzinski	.20	.09
☐ 651 Jeff Russell	.10	.05
☐ 652 Joe Nolan	.10	.05
☐ 653 Mark Brouhard	.10	.05
☐ 654 Dave Anderson	.10	.05
☐ 655 Joaquin Andujar	.10	.05
☐ 656 Chuck Cottier MG (Checklist back)	.10	.05
☐ 657 Jim Slaton	.10	.05
☐ 658 Mike Stenhouse	.10	.05
☐ 659 Checklist: 529-660	.20	.09
☐ 660 Tony Gwynn	2.50	1.10
☐ 661 Steve Crawford	.10	.05
☐ 662 Mike Heath	.10	.05
☐ 663 Luis Aguayo	.10	.05
☐ 664 Steve Farr	.20	.09
☐ 665 Don Mattingly	2.00	.90
☐ 666 Mike LaCoss	.10	.05
☐ 667 Dave Engle	.10	.05
☐ 668 Steve Trout	.10	.05
☐ 669 Lee Lacy	.10	.05
☐ 670 Tom Seaver	.75	.35
☐ 671 Dane Iorg	.10	.05
☐ 672 Juan Berenguer	.10	.05
☐ 673 Buck Martinez	.10	.05
☐ 674 Atlee Hammaker	.10	.05
☐ 675 Tony Perez	.60	.25
☐ 676 Albert Hall	.10	.05
☐ 677 Wally Backman	.10	.05
☐ 678 Joey McLaughlin	.10	.05
☐ 679 Bob Kearney	.10	.05
☐ 680 Jerry Reuss	.10	.05
☐ 681 Ben Oglivie	.10	.05
☐ 682 Doug Corbett	.10	.05
☐ 683 Whitey Herzog MG (Checklist back)	.20	.09
☐ 684 Bill Doran	.10	.05
☐ 685 Bill Caudill	.10	.05
☐ 686 Mike Easler	.10	.05
☐ 687 Bill Gullickson	.10	.05
☐ 688 Len Matuszek	.10	.05
☐ 689 Luis DeLeon	.10	.05
☐ 690 Alan Trammell	.40	.18
☐ 691 Dennis Rasmussen	.10	.05
☐ 692 Randy Bush	.10	.05
☐ 693 Tim Stoddard	.10	.05
☐ 694 Joe Carter	2.00	.90
☐ 695 Rick Rhoden	.10	.05
☐ 696 John Rabb	.10	.05
☐ 697 Onix Concepcion	.10	.05
☐ 698 Jorge Bell	.20	.09
☐ 699 Donnie Moore	.10	.05
☐ 700 Eddie Murray	1.00	.45
☐ 701 Eddie Murray AS	.60	.25
☐ 702 Damaso Garcia AS	.10	.05
☐ 703 George Brett AS	.75	.35
☐ 704 Cal Ripken AS	1.50	.70
☐ 705 Dave Winfield AS	.60	.25
☐ 706 Rickey Henderson AS	.60	.25
☐ 707 Tony Armas AS	.10	.05
☐ 708 Lance Parrish AS	.20	.09
☐ 709 Mike Boddicker AS	.10	.05
☐ 710 Frank Viola AS	.20	.09
☐ 711 Dan Quisenberry AS	.10	.05
☐ 712 Keith Hernandez AS	.20	.09
☐ 713 Ryne Sandberg AS	.60	.25
☐ 714 Mike Schmidt AS	.40	.18
☐ 715 Ozzie Smith AS	.50	.23
☐ 716 Dale Murphy AS	.60	.25
☐ 717 Tony Gwynn AS	.75	.35
☐ 718 Jeff Leonard AS	.10	.05
☐ 719 Gary Carter AS	.60	.25
☐ 720 Rick Sutcliffe AS	.10	.05
☐ 721 Bob Knepper AS	.10	.05
☐ 722 Bruce Sutter AS	.20	.09
☐ 723 Dave Stewart	.20	.09
☐ 724 Oscar Gamble	.10	.05
☐ 725 Floyd Bannister	.10	.05
☐ 726 Al Bumbry	.10	.05
☐ 727 Frank Pastore	.10	.05
☐ 728 Bob Bailor	.10	.05
☐ 729 Don Sutton	.60	.25
☐ 730 Dave Kingman	.20	.09
☐ 731 Neil Allen	.10	.05
☐ 732 John McNamara MG (Checklist back)	.10	.05
☐ 733 Tony Scott	.10	.05
☐ 734 John Henry Johnson	.10	.05
☐ 735 Garry Templeton	.10	.05
☐ 736 Jerry Mumphrey	.10	.05
☐ 737 Bo Diaz	.10	.05
☐ 738 Omar Moreno	.10	.05
☐ 739 Ernie Camacho	.10	.05
☐ 740 Jack Clark	.20	.09
☐ 741 John Butcher	.10	.05
☐ 742 Ron Hassey	.10	.05
☐ 743 Frank White	.20	.09
☐ 744 Doug Bair	.10	.05
☐ 745 Buddy Bell	.20	.09
☐ 746 Jim Clancy	.10	.05
☐ 747 Alex Trevino	.10	.05
☐ 748 Lee Mazzilli	.10	.05
☐ 749 Julio Cruz	.10	.05
☐ 750 Rollie Fingers	.60	.25
☐ 751 Kelvin Chapman	.10	.05
☐ 752 Bob Owchinko	.10	.05
☐ 753 Greg Brock	.10	.05
☐ 754 Larry Milbourne	.10	.05
☐ 755 Ken Singleton	.10	.05
☐ 756 Rob Picciolo	.10	.05
☐ 757 Willie McGee	.20	.09
☐ 758 Ray Burris	.10	.05
☐ 759 Jim Fanning MG (Checklist back)	.10	.05
☐ 760 Nolan Ryan	3.00	1.35
☐ 761 Jerry Remy	.10	.05
☐ 762 Eddie Whitson	.10	.05
☐ 763 Kiko Garcia	.10	.05

	NRMT	VG-E
☐ 764 Jamie Easterly	.10	.05
☐ 765 Willie Randolph	.20	.09
☐ 766 Paul Mirabella	.10	.05
☐ 767 Darrell Brown	.10	.05
☐ 768 Ron Cey	.20	.09
☐ 769 Joe Cowley	.10	.05
☐ 770 Carlton Fisk	.60	.25
☐ 771 Geoff Zahn	.10	.05
☐ 772 Johnnie LeMaster	.10	.05
☐ 773 Hal McRae	.20	.09
☐ 774 Dennis Lamp	.10	.05
☐ 775 Mookie Wilson	.20	.09
☐ 776 Jerry Royster	.10	.05
☐ 777 Ned Yost	.10	.05
☐ 778 Mike Davis	.10	.05
☐ 779 Nick Esasky	.10	.05
☐ 780 Mike Flanagan	.10	.05
☐ 781 Jim Gantner	.10	.05
☐ 782 Tom Niedenfuer	.10	.05
☐ 783 Mike Jorgensen	.10	.05
☐ 784 Checklist: 661-792	.20	.09
☐ 785 Tony Armas	.10	.05
☐ 786 Enos Cabell	.10	.05
☐ 787 Jim Wohlford	.10	.05
☐ 788 Steve Comer	.10	.05
☐ 789 Luis Salazar	.10	.05
☐ 790 Ron Guidry	.20	.09
☐ 791 Ivan DeJesus	.10	.05
☐ 792 Darrell Evans	.20	.09

1985 Topps Tiffany

For the second year, Topps issued a special glossy set through their hobby dealers. This set is a direct parallel to the regular Topps issue. These 792 cards are differentiated from the regular issue by their glossy fronts and very clear backs. These sets were only available through Topps' hobby dealers. Within the hobby, it is highly believed that 10,000 of these sets were made by Topps.

	NRMT	VG-E
COMPLETE FACT.SET (792)	225.00	100.00
COMMON CARD (1-792)	.25	.11
*STARS: 4X to 8X BASIC CARDS		
*ROOKIES: 3X to 6X BASIC CARDS		

1985 Topps Glossy All-Stars

The cards in this 22-card set the standard size. Similar in design, both front and back, to last year's Glossy set, this edition features the managers, starting nine players and honorary captains of the National and American League teams in the 1984 All-Star game. The set is numbered on the reverse with players essentially ordered by position within league, NL: 1-11 and AL: 12-22.

	NRMT	VG-E
COMPLETE SET (22)	5.00	2.20
COMMON CARD (1-22)	.05	.02
☐ 1 Paul Owens MG	.05	.02
☐ 2 Steve Garvey	.15	.07
☐ 3 Ryne Sandberg	1.00	.45
☐ 4 Mike Schmidt	.75	.35
☐ 5 Ozzie Smith	1.00	.45
☐ 6 Tony Gwynn	1.25	.55
☐ 7 Dale Murphy	.25	.11
☐ 8 Darryl Strawberry	.10	.05
☐ 9 Gary Carter	.15	.07
☐ 10 Charlie Lea	.05	.02
☐ 11 Willie McCovey CAPT	.10	.05
☐ 12 Joe Altobelli MG	.05	.02
☐ 13 Rod Carew	.50	.23
☐ 14 Lou Whitaker	.10	.05
☐ 15 George Brett	1.00	.45
☐ 16 Cal Ripken	2.00	.90
☐ 17 Dave Winfield	.50	.23
☐ 18 Chet Lemon	.05	.02
☐ 19 Reggie Jackson	.50	.23
☐ 20 Lance Parrish	.05	.02
☐ 21 Dave Stieb	.05	.02
☐ 22 Hank Greenberg CAPT	.10	.05

1985 Topps Glossy Send-Ins

The cards in this 40-card set measure the standard size. Similar to last year's glossy set, this set was issued as a bonus prize to Topps All-Star Baseball Game cards found in wax packs. The set could be obtained by sending in the "Bonus Runs" from the "Winning Pitch" game insert cards. For 25 runs and 75 cents, a collector could send in for one of the eight different five card series plus automatically be entered in the Grand Prize Sweepstakes for a chance at a free trip to the All-Star game. The cards are numbered and contain 20 stars from each league.

	NRMT	VG-E
COMPLETE SET (40)	10.00	4.50
COMMON CARD (1-40)	.10	.05
☐ 1 Dale Murphy	.50	.23
☐ 2 Jesse Orosco	.10	.05
☐ 3 Bob Brenly	.10	.05
☐ 4 Mike Boddicker	.10	.05
☐ 5 Dave Kingman	.25	.11
☐ 6 Jim Rice	.25	.11
☐ 7 Frank Viola	.25	.11
☐ 8 Alvin Davis	.10	.05
☐ 9 Rick Sutcliffe	.10	.05
☐ 10 Pete Rose	1.50	.70
☐ 11 Leon Durham	.10	.05
☐ 12 Joaquin Andujar	.10	.05
☐ 13 Keith Hernandez	.25	.11
☐ 14 Dave Winfield	.75	.35
☐ 15 Reggie Jackson	.75	.35
☐ 16 Alan Trammell	.50	.23
☐ 17 Bert Blyleven	.25	.11
☐ 18 Tony Armas	.10	.05
☐ 19 Rich Gossage	.25	.11
☐ 20 Jose Cruz	.25	.11
☐ 21 Ryne Sandberg	2.50	1.10
☐ 22 Bruce Sutter	.10	.05
☐ 23 Mike Schmidt	1.50	.70
☐ 24 Cal Ripken	5.00	2.20
☐ 25 Dan Petry	.10	.05
☐ 26 Jack Morris	.25	.11
☐ 27 Don Mattingly	3.00	1.35
☐ 28 Eddie Murray	1.50	.70
☐ 29 Tony Gwynn	3.00	1.35
☐ 30 Charlie Lea	.10	.05
☐ 31 Juan Samuel	.10	.05
☐ 32 Phil Niekro	.75	.35
☐ 33 Alejandro Pena	.10	.05
☐ 34 Harold Baines	.25	.11
☐ 35 Dan Quisenberry	.10	.05
☐ 36 Gary Carter	.50	.23
☐ 37 Mario Soto	.10	.05
☐ 38 Dwight Gooden	.75	.35
☐ 39 Tom Brunansky	.10	.05
☐ 40 Dave Stieb	.10	.05

1985 Topps Traded

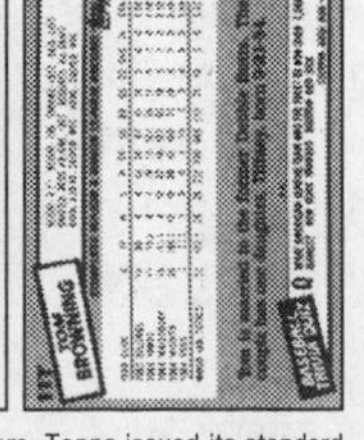

In its now standard procedure, Topps issued its standard-size Traded (or extended) set for the fifth year in a row. In addition to the typical factory set hobby distribution, Topps tested the limited issuance of these Traded cards in wax packs. Card design is identical to the regular-issue 1985 Topps set except for whiter card stock and T-suffixed numbering on back. The set numbering is in alphabetical order by player's name. The key extended Rookie Cards in this set include Vince Coleman, Mariano Duncan, Ozzie Guillen, and Mickey Tettleton.

	NRMT	VG-E
COMP.FACT.SET (132)	12.00	5.50
COMMON CARD (1T-132T)	.15	.07
☐ 1T Don Aase	.15	.07
☐ 2T Bill Almon	.15	.07
☐ 3T Benny Ayala	.15	.07
☐ 4T Dusty Baker	.40	.18
☐ 5T George Bamberger MG	.15	.07
☐ 6T Dale Berra	.15	.07
☐ 7T Rich Bordi	.15	.07
☐ 8T Daryl Boston	.15	.07
☐ 9T Hubie Brooks	.15	.07
☐ 10T Chris Brown	.15	.07
☐ 11T Tom Browning	.75	.35
☐ 12T Al Bumbry	.15	.07
☐ 13T Ray Burris	.15	.07
☐ 14T Jeff Burroughs	.15	.07
☐ 15T Bill Campbell	.15	.07
☐ 16T Don Carman	.15	.07
☐ 17T Gary Carter	.75	.35
☐ 18T Bobby Castillo	.15	.07
☐ 19T Bill Caudill	.15	.07
☐ 20T Rick Cerone	.15	.07
☐ 21T Bryan Clark	.15	.07
☐ 22T Jack Clark	.40	.18
☐ 23T Pat Clements	.15	.07
☐ 24T Vince Coleman	.75	.35
☐ 25T Dave Collins	.15	.07
☐ 26T Danny Darwin	.15	.07
☐ 27T Jim Davenport MG	.15	.07
☐ 28T Jerry Davis	.15	.07
☐ 29T Brian Dayett	.15	.07
☐ 30T Ivan DeJesus	.15	.07
☐ 31T Ken Dixon	.15	.07
☐ 32T Mariano Duncan	.75	.35
☐ 33T John Felske MG	.15	.07
☐ 34T Mike Fitzgerald	.15	.07
☐ 35T Ray Fontenot	.15	.07
☐ 36T Greg Gagne	.40	.18
☐ 37T Oscar Gamble	.15	.07
☐ 38T Scott Garrelts	.15	.07
☐ 39T Bob L. Gibson	.15	.07
☐ 40T Jim Gott	.15	.07
☐ 41T David Green	.15	.07
☐ 42T Alfredo Griffin	.15	.07
☐ 43T Ozzie Guillen	1.50	.70
☐ 44T Eddie Haas MG	.15	.07
☐ 45T Terry Harper	.15	.07
☐ 46T Toby Harrah	.15	.07
☐ 47T Greg Harris	.15	.07
☐ 48T Ron Hassey	.15	.07
☐ 49T Rickey Henderson	1.00	.45
☐ 50T Steve Henderson	.15	.07
☐ 51T George Hendrick	.15	.07
☐ 52T Joe Hesketh	.15	.07
☐ 53T Teddy Higuera	.40	.18
☐ 54T Donnie Hill	.15	.07
☐ 55T Al Holland	.15	.07
☐ 56T Burt Hooton	.15	.07
☐ 57T Jay Howell	.15	.07
☐ 58T Ken Howell	.15	.07
☐ 59T LaMarr Hoyt	.15	.07
☐ 60T Tim Hulett	.15	.07
☐ 61T Bob James	.15	.07
☐ 62T Steve Jeltz	.15	.07
☐ 63T Cliff Johnson	.15	.07
☐ 64T Howard Johnson	.40	.18
☐ 65T Ruppert Jones	.15	.07
☐ 66T Steve Kemp	.15	.07
☐ 67T Bruce Kison	.15	.07
☐ 68T Alan Knicely	.15	.07
☐ 69T Mike LaCoss	.15	.07
☐ 70T Lee Lacy	.15	.07
☐ 71T Dave LaPoint	.15	.07
☐ 72T Gary Lavelle	.15	.07
☐ 73T Vance Law	.15	.07
☐ 74T Johnnie LeMaster	.15	.07
☐ 75T Sixto Lezcano	.15	.07
☐ 76T Tim Lollar	.15	.07
☐ 77T Fred Lynn	.40	.18
☐ 78T Billy Martin MG	.40	.18
☐ 79T Ron Mathis	.15	.07
☐ 80T Len Matuszek	.15	.07
☐ 81T Gene Mauch MG	.40	.18
☐ 82T Oddibe McDowell	.40	.18
☐ 83T Roger McDowell	.40	.18
☐ 84T John McNamara MG	.15	.07
☐ 85T Donnie Moore	.15	.07
☐ 86T Gene Nelson	.15	.07
☐ 87T Steve Nicosia	.15	.07
☐ 88T Al Oliver	.40	.18
☐ 89T Joe Orsulak	.40	.18
☐ 90T Rob Picciolo	.15	.07

☐ 91T Chris Pittaro	.15	.07
☐ 92T Jim Presley	.40	.18
☐ 93T Rick Reuschel	.15	.07
☐ 94T Bert Roberge	.15	.07
☐ 95T Bob Rodgers MG	.15	.07
☐ 96T Jerry Royster	.15	.07
☐ 97T Dave Rozema	.15	.07
☐ 98T Dave Rucker	.15	.07
☐ 99T Vern Ruhle	.15	.07
☐ 100T Paul Runge	.15	.07
☐ 101T Mark Salas	.15	.07
☐ 102T Luis Salazar	.15	.07
☐ 103T Joe Sambito	.15	.07
☐ 104T Rick Schu	.15	.07
☐ 105T Donnie Scott	.15	.07
☐ 106T Larry Sheets	.15	.07
☐ 107T Don Slaught	.15	.07
☐ 108T Roy Smalley	.15	.07
☐ 109T Lonnie Smith	.15	.07
☐ 110T Nate Snell UER (Headings on back for a batter)	.15	.07
☐ 111T Chris Speier	.15	.07
☐ 112T Mike Stenhouse	.15	.07
☐ 113T Tim Stoddard	.15	.07
☐ 114T Jim Sundberg	.15	.07
☐ 115T Bruce Sutter	.40	.18
☐ 116T Don Sutton	.75	.35
☐ 117T Kent Tekulve	.15	.07
☐ 118T Tom Tellmann	.15	.07
☐ 119T Walt Terrell	.15	.07
☐ 120T Mickey Tettleton	1.00	.45
☐ 121T Derrel Thomas	.15	.07
☐ 122T Rich Thompson	.15	.07
☐ 123T Alex Trevino	.15	.07
☐ 124T John Tudor	.15	.07
☐ 125T Jose Uribe	.15	.07
☐ 126T Bobby Valentine MG	.15	.07
☐ 127T Dave Von Ohlen	.15	.07
☐ 128T U.L. Washington	.15	.07
☐ 129T Earl Weaver MG	.75	.35
☐ 130T Eddie Whitson	.15	.07
☐ 131T Herm Winningham	.15	.07
☐ 132T Checklist 1-132	.15	.07

1985 Topps Traded Tiffany

Just as in 1984, Topps issued an glossy update set. The 132-card standard-size set is a parallel to the Topps update issue. These sets were issued to the hobby through Topps dealer network and were printed in Ireland.

	NRMT	VG-E
COMPLETE FACT.SET (132)	50.00	22.00
COMMON CARD (1T-132T)	.40	.18
*STARS: 3X TO 6X BASIC CARDS		
*ROOKIES: 1.5X TO 3X BASIC CARDS		

1985 Topps 3-D

This innovative 30-card set was issued in packs of one. These large cards are very difficult to store (due to the 3-D effect) as they are not really stackable and are crumpled if placed in an album using plastic sheets. The cards are blank-backed except for two covered adhesive strips and measure approximately 4 1/4" by 5 7/8". Cards are numbered on the front and feature a prominent team logo on the front as well.

	NRMT	VG-E
COMPLETE SET (30)	15.00	6.75
COMMON CARD (1-30)	.10	.05

☐ 1 Mike Schmidt	1.25	.55
☐ 2 Eddie Murray	1.25	.55
☐ 3 Dale Murphy	.50	.23
☐ 4 George Brett	2.50	1.10
☐ 5 Pete Rose	1.00	.45
☐ 6 Jim Rice	.25	.11
☐ 7 Ryne Sandberg	2.50	1.10
☐ 8 Don Mattingly	3.00	1.35
☐ 9 Darryl Strawberry	.25	.11
☐ 10 Rickey Henderson	.75	.35
☐ 11 Keith Hernandez	.25	.11
☐ 12 Dave Kingman	.10	.05
☐ 13 Tony Gwynn	2.50	1.10
☐ 14 Reggie Jackson	.75	.35
☐ 15 Gary Carter	.50	.23
☐ 16 Cal Ripken	4.00	1.80
☐ 17 Tim Raines	.25	.11
☐ 18 Dave Winfield	.75	.35
☐ 19 Dwight Gooden	.50	.23
☐ 20 Dave Stieb	.10	.05
☐ 21 Fernando Valenzuela	.25	.11
☐ 22 Mark Langston	.25	.11
☐ 23 Bruce Sutter	.10	.05
☐ 24 Dan Quisenberry	.10	.05
☐ 25 Steve Carlton	.75	.35
☐ 26 Mike Boddicker	.10	.05
☐ 27 Rich Gossage	.25	.11
☐ 28 Jack Morris	.25	.11
☐ 29 Rick Sutcliffe	.10	.05
☐ 30 Tom Seaver	.75	.35

1985 Topps/O-Pee-Chee Stickers

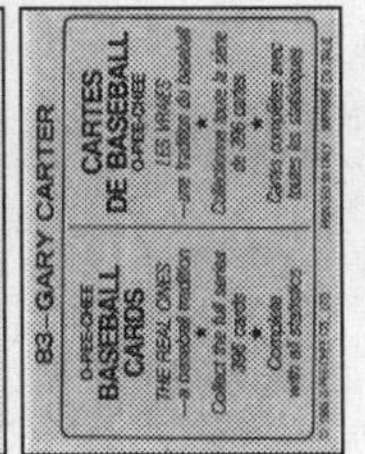

Made in Italy for Topps and O-Pee-Chee by Panini, these 376 stickers measure approximately 2 1/8" by 3" and are numbered on both front and back. Some stickers are player cutouts. The fronts feature white-bordered color player photos. The horizontal backs carry a bilingual ad for O-Pee-Chee in blue lettering. An album onto which the stickers could be affixed was available at retail stores. The album and the sticker numbering are organized as follows: 1984 Record Breakers (1-8), 1984 Championship Series (9-14), 1984 World Series (15-21), Atlanta Braves (22-33), Chicago Cubs (34-45), Cincinnati Reds (46-57), Houston Astros (58-69), Los Angeles Dodgers (70-81), Montreal Expos (82-93), 1984 Stat Leaders (94-97), New York Mets (98-109), Philadelphia Phillies (110-121), Pittsburgh Pirates (122-133), St. Louis Cardinals (134-145), San Diego Padres (146-157), San Francisco Giants (158-169), 1984 Stat Leaders (170-173), Foil All-Stars (174-191), 1984 Stat Leaders (192-195), Baltimore Orioles (196-207), Boston Red Sox (208-219), California Angels (220-231), Chicago White Sox (232-243), Cleveland Indians (244-255), Detroit Tigers (256-267), Kansas City Royals (268-279), 1984 Stat Leaders (280-283), Milwaukee Brewers (284-295), Minnesota Twins (296-307), New York Yankees (308-319), Oakland A's (320-331), Seattle Mariners (332-343), Texas Rangers (344-355), Toronto Blue Jays (356-367) and Future Stars (368-376). For those stickers featuring more than one player, the other numbers on that sticker are given below in parentheses. Kirby Puckett, Mark Langston and Dwight Gooden are featured in their Rookie Card year.

	NRMT	VG-E
COMPLETE SET (376)	15.00	6.75
COMMON STICKERS (1-376)	.05	.02
COMMON FOIL	.10	.05
*TOPPS AND OPC: SAME VALUE		

☐ 1 Steve Garvey FOIL (Top half)	.15	.07
☐ 2 Steve Garvey FOIL (Bottom half)	.15	.07
☐ 3 Dwight Gooden (Top half)	.50	.23
☐ 4 Dwight Gooden (Bottom half)	.50	.23
☐ 5 Joe Morgan (Top half)	.10	.05
☐ 6 Joe Morgan (Bottom half)	.10	.05
☐ 7 Don Sutton (Top half)	.10	.05
☐ 8 Don Sutton (Bottom half)	.10	.05
☐ 9 AL Championships (Jack Morris)	.10	.05
☐ 10 AL Championships (Milt Wilcox)	.05	.02
☐ 11 AL Championships (Kirk Gibson)	.10	.05
☐ 12 NL Championships (Cubs at plate)	.05	.02
☐ 13 NL Championships (Steve Garvey swings)	.10	.05
☐ 14 NL Championships (Steve Garvey)	.10	.05
☐ 15 World Series (Jack Morris)	.10	.05
☐ 16 World Series (Kurt Bevacqua)	.05	.02
☐ 17 World Series (Milt Wilcox)	.05	.02
☐ 18 World Series (Alan Trammell ready to throw)	.10	.05
☐ 19 World Series (Kirk Gibson)	.10	.05
☐ 20 World Series (Alan Trammell)	.10	.05
☐ 21 World Series (Chet Lemon back)	.05	.02
☐ 22 Dale Murphy	.15	.07
☐ 23 Steve Bedrosian	.05	.02
☐ 24 Bob Horner	.05	.02
☐ 25 Claudell Washington	.05	.02
☐ 26 Rick Mahler (212)	.05	.02
☐ 27 Rafael Ramirez (213)	.05	.02
☐ 28 Craig McMurtry (214)	.05	.02
☐ 29 Chris Chambliss(215)	.10	.05
☐ 30 Alex Trevino (216)	.05	.02
☐ 31 Bruce Benedict (217)	.05	.02
☐ 32 Ken Oberkfell (218)	.05	.02
☐ 33 Glenn Hubbard (219)	.05	.02
☐ 34 Ryne Sandberg	1.25	.55
☐ 35 Rick Sutcliffe	.05	.02
☐ 36 Leon Durham	.05	.02
☐ 37 Jody Davis	.05	.02
☐ 38 Bob Dernier (224)	.05	.02
☐ 39 Keith Moreland(225)	.05	.02
☐ 40 Scott Sanderson(226)	.05	.02
☐ 41 Lee Smith (227)	.25	.11
☐ 42 Ron Cey (228)	.10	.05
☐ 43 Steve Trout (229)	.05	.02
☐ 44 Gary Matthews(230)	.05	.02
☐ 45 Larry Bowa (231)	.10	.05
☐ 46 Mario Soto	.05	.02
☐ 47 Dave Parker	.10	.05
☐ 48 Dave Concepcion	.10	.05
☐ 49 Gary Redus	.05	.02
☐ 50 Ted Power (236)	.05	.02
☐ 51 Nick Esasky (237)	.05	.02
☐ 52 Duane Walker (238)	.05	.02
☐ 53 Eddie Milner (239)	.05	.02
☐ 54 Ron Oester (240)	.05	.02
☐ 55 Cesar Cedeno (241)	.10	.05
☐ 56 Joe Price (242)	.05	.02
☐ 57 Pete Rose (243)	.75	.35
☐ 58 Nolan Ryan	2.50	1.10
☐ 59 Jose Cruz	.10	.05
☐ 60 Jerry Mumphrey	.05	.02
☐ 61 Enos Cabell	.05	.02
☐ 62 Bob Knepper (248)	.05	.02
☐ 63 Dickie Thon (249)	.05	.02
☐ 64 Phil Garner (250)	.10	.05
☐ 65 Craig Reynolds (251)	.05	.02
☐ 66 Frank DiPino (252)	.05	.02
☐ 67 Terry Puhl (253)	.05	.02
☐ 68 Bill Doran (254)	.05	.02
☐ 69 Joe Niekro (255)	.05	.02
☐ 70 Pedro Guerrero	.10	.05
☐ 71 Fernando Valenzuela	.10	.05
☐ 72 Mike Marshall	.05	.02
☐ 73 Alejandro Pena	.05	.02
☐ 74 Orel Hershiser(260)	.75	.35
☐ 75 Ken Landreaux (261)	.05	.02
☐ 76 Bill Russell (262)	.10	.05
☐ 77 Steve Sax (263)	.10	.05
☐ 78 Rick Honeycutt(264)	.05	.02
☐ 79 Mike Scioscia (265)	.05	.02
☐ 80 Tom Niedenfuer(266)	.05	.02
☐ 81 Candy Maldonado(267)	.05	.02
☐ 82 Tim Raines	.10	.05
☐ 83 Gary Carter	.10	.05
☐ 84 Charlie Lea	.05	.02
☐ 85 Jeff Reardon	.10	.05
☐ 86 Andre Dawson (272)	.15	.07
☐ 87 Tim Wallach (273)	.10	.05
☐ 88 Terry Francona (274)	.10	.05
☐ 89 Steve Rogers (275)	.05	.02
☐ 90 Bryn Smith (276)	.05	.02
☐ 91 Bill Gullickson(277)	.05	.02
☐ 92 Dan Driessen (278)	.05	.02
☐ 93 Doug Flynn (279)	.05	.02
☐ 94 Mike Schmidt (170/192/280)	.60	.25

☐ 95 Tony Armas (171/193/281) .05 .02
☐ 96 Dale Murphy (172/194/282) .15 .07
☐ 97 Rick Sutcliffe (173/195/283) .05 .02
☐ 98 Keith Hernandez .10 .05
☐ 99 George Foster .10 .05
☐ 100 Darryl Strawberry .30 .14
☐ 101 Jesse Orosco .05 .02
☐ 102 Mookie Wilson (288) .10 .05
☐ 103 Doug Sisk (289) .05 .02
☐ 104 Hubie Brooks (290) .05 .02
☐ 105 Ron Darling (291) .10 .05
☐ 106 Wally Backman (292) .05 .02
☐ 107 Dwight Gooden (293) .75 .35
☐ 108 Mike Fitzgerald(294) .05 .02
☐ 109 Walt Terrell (295) .05 .02
☐ 110 Ozzie Virgil .05 .02
☐ 111 Mike Schmidt .60 .25
☐ 112 Steve Carlton .40 .18
☐ 113 Al Holland .05 .02
☐ 114 Juan Samuel (300) .05 .02
☐ 115 Von Hayes (301) .05 .02
☐ 116 Jeff Stone (302) .05 .02
☐ 117 Jerry Koosman (303) .10 .05
☐ 118 Al Oliver (304) .10 .05
☐ 119 John Denny (305) .05 .02
☐ 120 Charles Hudson (306) .05 .02
☐ 121 Garry Maddox (307) .05 .02
☐ 122 Bill Madlock .10 .05
☐ 123 John Candelaria .05 .02
☐ 124 Tony Pena .05 .02
☐ 125 Jason Thompson .05 .02
☐ 126 Lee Lacy (312) .05 .02
☐ 127 Rick Rhoden (313) .05 .02
☐ 128 Doug Frobel (314) .05 .02
☐ 129 Kent Tekulve (315) .05 .02
☐ 130 Johnny Ray (316) .05 .02
☐ 131 Marvell Wynne (317) .05 .02
☐ 132 Larry McWilliams (318) .05 .02
☐ 133 Dale Berra (319) .05 .02
☐ 134 George Hendrick .05 .02
☐ 135 Bruce Sutter .10 .05
☐ 136 Joaquin Andujar .05 .02
☐ 137 Ozzie Smith .40 .18
☐ 138 Andy Van Slyke (324) .15 .07
☐ 139 Lonnie Smith (325) .05 .02
☐ 140 Darrell Porter (326) .05 .02
☐ 141 Willie McGee (327) .10 .05
☐ 142 Tom Herr (328) .10 .05
☐ 143 Dave LaPoint (329) .05 .02
☐ 144 Neil Allen (330) .05 .02
☐ 145 David Green (331) .05 .02
☐ 146 Tony Gwynn 2.00 .90
☐ 147 Rich Gossage .10 .05
☐ 148 Terry Kennedy .05 .02
☐ 149 Steve Garvey .15 .07
☐ 150 Alan Wiggins (336) .05 .02
☐ 151 Garry Templeton(337) .05 .02
☐ 152 Ed Whitson (338) .05 .02
☐ 153 Tim Lollar (339) .05 .02
☐ 154 Dave Dravecky (340) .10 .05
☐ 155 Graig Nettles (341) .10 .05
☐ 156 Eric Show (342) .05 .02
☐ 157 Carmelo Martinez (343) .05 .02
☐ 158 Bob Brenly .05 .02
☐ 159 Gary Lavelle .05 .02
☐ 160 Jack Clark .10 .05
☐ 161 Jeff Leonard .05 .02
☐ 162 Chili Davis (348) .10 .05
☐ 163 Mike Krukow (349) .05 .02
☐ 164 Johnnie LeMaster (350) .05 .02
☐ 165 Atlee Hammaker (351) .05 .02
☐ 166 Dan Gladden (352) .05 .02
☐ 167 Greg Minton (353) .05 .02
☐ 168 Joel Youngblood(354) .05 .02
☐ 169 Frank Williams (355) .05 .02
☐ 170 Tony Gwynn (94/192/280) 1.50 .70
☐ 171 Don Mattingly (95/193/281) 2.00 .90
☐ 172 Bruce Sutter (96/194/282) .10 .05
☐ 173 Dan Quisenberry (97/195/283) .05 .02
☐ 174 Tony Gwynn FOIL 2.50 1.10
☐ 175 Ryne Sandberg FOIL 1.50 .70
☐ 176 Steve Garvey FOIL .30 .14
☐ 177 Dale Murphy FOIL .30 .14
☐ 179 Darryl Strawberry FOIL .50 .23
☐ 180 Gary Carter FOIL .30 .14
☐ 181 Ozzie Smith FOIL .60 .25
☐ 182 Charlie Lea FOIL .10 .05
☐ 183 Lou Whitaker FOIL .15 .07
☐ 184 Rod Carew FOIL .60 .25
☐ 185 Cal Ripken FOIL 3.00 1.35
☐ 186 Dave Winfield FOIL .50 .23
☐ 187 Reggie Jackson FOIL .75 .35
☐ 188 George Brett FOIL 1.25 .55
☐ 189 Lance Parrish FOIL .15 .07
☐ 190 Chet Lemon FOIL .10 .05
☐ 191 Dave Stieb FOIL .10 .05
☐ 192 Gary Carter (94/170/280) .10 .05
☐ 193 Mike Schmidt (95/171/281) .60 .25
☐ 194 Tony Armas (96/172/282) .05 .02
☐ 195 Mike Witt (97/173/283) .05 .02
☐ 196 Eddie Murray .40 .18
☐ 197 Cal Ripken 2.50 1.10
☐ 198 Scott McGregor .05 .02
☐ 199 Rick Dempsey .05 .02
☐ 200 Tippy Martinez (360) .05 .02
☐ 201 Ken Singleton (361) .05 .02
☐ 202 Mike Boddicker (362) .05 .02
☐ 203 Rich Dauer (363) .05 .02
☐ 204 John Shelby (364) .05 .02
☐ 205 Al Bumbry (365) .05 .02
☐ 206 John Lowenstein(366) .05 .02
☐ 207 Mike Flanagan (367) .05 .02
☐ 208 Jim Rice .10 .05
☐ 209 Tony Armas .05 .02
☐ 210 Wade Boggs .50 .23
☐ 211 Bruce Hurst .05 .02
☐ 212 Dwight Evans (26) .10 .05
☐ 213 Mike Easler (27) .05 .02
☐ 214 Bill Buckner (28) .10 .05
☐ 215 Bob Stanley (29) .05 .02
☐ 216 Jackie Gutierrez(30) .05 .02
☐ 217 Rich Gedman (31) .05 .02
☐ 218 Jerry Remy (32) .05 .02
☐ 219 Marty Barrett (33) .05 .02
☐ 220 Reggie Jackson .50 .23
☐ 221 Geoff Zahn .05 .02
☐ 222 Doug DeCinces .05 .02
☐ 223 Rod Carew .40 .18
☐ 224 Brian Downing (38) .10 .05
☐ 225 Fred Lynn (39) .10 .05
☐ 226 Gary Pettis (40) .05 .02
☐ 227 Mike Witt (41) .05 .02
☐ 228 Bob Boone (42) .10 .05
☐ 229 Tommy John (43) .15 .07
☐ 230 Bobby Grich (44) .10 .05
☐ 231 Ron Romanick (45) .05 .02
☐ 232 Ron Kittle .05 .02
☐ 233 Richard Dotson .05 .02
☐ 234 Harold Baines .10 .05
☐ 235 Tom Seaver .50 .23
☐ 236 Greg Walker (50) .05 .02
☐ 237 Roy Smalley (51) .05 .02
☐ 238 Greg Luzinski (52) .10 .05
☐ 239 Julio Cruz (53) .05 .02
☐ 240 Scott Fletcher (54) .05 .02
☐ 241 Rudy Law (55) .05 .02
☐ 242 Vance Law (56) .05 .02
☐ 243 Carlton Fisk (57) .30 .14
☐ 244 Andre Thornton .05 .02
☐ 245 Julio Franco .15 .07
☐ 246 Brett Butler .10 .05
☐ 247 Bert Blyleven .10 .05
☐ 248 Mike Hargrove (62) .10 .05
☐ 249 George Vukovich(63) .05 .02
☐ 250 Pat Tabler (64) .05 .02
☐ 251 Brook Jacoby (65) .05 .02
☐ 252 Tony Bernazard (66) .05 .02
☐ 253 Ernie Camacho (67) .05 .02
☐ 254 Mel Hall (68) .05 .02
☐ 255 Carmen Castillo (69) .05 .02
☐ 256 Jack Morris .10 .05
☐ 257 Willie Hernandez .05 .02
☐ 258 Alan Trammell .15 .07
☐ 259 Lance Parrish .10 .05
☐ 260 Chet Lemon (74) .05 .02
☐ 261 Lou Whitaker (75) .15 .07
☐ 262 Howard Johnson (76) .10 .05
☐ 263 Barbaro Garbey (77) .05 .02
☐ 264 Dan Petry (78) .05 .02
☐ 265 Aurelio Lopez (79) .05 .02
☐ 266 Larry Herndon (80) .05 .02
☐ 267 Kirk Gibson (81) .10 .05
☐ 268 George Brett .75 .35
☐ 269 Dan Quisenberry .05 .02
☐ 270 Hal McRae .10 .05
☐ 271 Steve Balboni .05 .02
☐ 272 Pat Sheridan (86) .05 .02
☐ 273 Jorge Orta (87) .05 .02
☐ 274 Frank White (88) .10 .05
☐ 275 Bud Black (89) .05 .02
☐ 276 Darryl Motley (90) .05 .02
☐ 277 Willie Wilson (91) .05 .02
☐ 278 Larry Gura (92) .05 .02
☐ 279 Don Slaught (93) .05 .02
☐ 280 Dwight Gooden (94/170/192) 1.50 .70
☐ 281 Mark Langston (95/171/193) .25 .11
☐ 282 Tim Raines (96/172/194) .10 .05
☐ 283 Rickey Henderson (97/173/195/283) .30 .14
☐ 284 Robin Yount .30 .14
☐ 285 Rollie Fingers .25 .11
☐ 286 Jim Sundberg .05 .02
☐ 287 Cecil Cooper .10 .05
☐ 288 Jamie Cocanower(102) .05 .02
☐ 289 Mike Caldwell (103) .05 .02
☐ 290 Don Sutton (104) .15 .07
☐ 291 Rick Manning (105) .05 .02
☐ 292 Ben Oglivie (106) .05 .02
☐ 293 Moose Haas (107) .05 .02
☐ 294 Ted Simmons (108) .10 .05
☐ 295 Jim Gantner (109) .05 .02
☐ 296 Kent Hrbek .10 .05
☐ 297 Ron Davis .05 .02
☐ 298 Dave Engle .05 .02
☐ 299 Tom Brunansky .10 .05
☐ 300 Frank Viola (114) .10 .05
☐ 301 Mike Smithson (115) .05 .02
☐ 302 Gary Gaetti (116) .10 .05
☐ 303 Tim Teufel (117) .05 .02
☐ 304 Mickey Hatcher(118) .05 .02
☐ 305 John Butcher (119) .05 .02
☐ 306 Darrell Brown (120) .05 .02
☐ 307 Kirby Puckett (121) 5.00 2.20
☐ 308 Dave Winfield .30 .14
☐ 309 Phil Niekro .15 .07
☐ 310 Don Mattingly 2.00 .90
☐ 311 Don Baylor .10 .05
☐ 312 Willie Randolph(126) .10 .05
☐ 313 Ron Guidry (127) .10 .05
☐ 314 Dave Righetti (128) .10 .05
☐ 315 Bobby Meacham (129) .05 .02
☐ 316 Butch Wynegar (130) .05 .02
☐ 317 Mike Pagliarulo(131) .05 .02
☐ 318 Joe Cowley (132) .05 .02
☐ 319 John Montefusco(133) .05 .02
☐ 320 Dave Kingman .10 .05
☐ 321 Rickey Henderson .30 .14
☐ 322 Bill Caudill .05 .02
☐ 323 Dwayne Murphy .05 .02
☐ 324 Steve McCatty (138) .05 .02
☐ 325 Joe Morgan (139) .25 .11
☐ 326 Mike Heath (140) .05 .02
☐ 327 Chris Codiroli (141) .05 .02
☐ 328 Ray Burris (142) .05 .02
☐ 329 Tony Phillips (143) .15 .07
☐ 330 Carney Lansford(144) .10 .05
☐ 331 Bruce Bochte (145) .05 .02
☐ 332 Alvin Davis .10 .05
☐ 333 Al Cowens .05 .02
☐ 334 Jim Beattie .05 .02
☐ 335 Bob Kearney .05 .02
☐ 336 Ed VandeBerg (150) .05 .02
☐ 337 Mark Langston (151) .25 .11
☐ 338 Dave Henderson (152) .10 .05
☐ 339 Spike Owen (153) .05 .02
☐ 340 Matt Young (154) .05 .02
☐ 341 Jack Perconte (155) .05 .02
☐ 342 Barry Bonnell (156) .05 .02
☐ 343 Mike Stanton (157) .05 .02
☐ 344 Pete O'Brien .05 .02
☐ 345 Charlie Hough .10 .05
☐ 346 Larry Parrish .05 .02
☐ 347 Buddy Bell .10 .05
☐ 348 Frank Tanana (162) .05 .02
☐ 349 Curt Wilkerson (163) .05 .02
☐ 350 Jeff Kunkel (164) .05 .02
☐ 351 Billy Sample (165) .05 .02
☐ 352 Danny Darwin (166) .05 .02
☐ 353 Gary Ward (167) .05 .02
☐ 354 Mike Mason (168) .05 .02
☐ 355 Mickey Rivers (169) .05 .02
☐ 356 Dave Stieb .05 .02
☐ 357 Damaso Garcia .05 .02
☐ 358 Willie Upshaw .05 .02
☐ 359 Lloyd Moseby .05 .02
☐ 360 George Bell (200) .10 .05
☐ 361 Luis Leal (201) .05 .02
☐ 362 Jesse Barfield (202) .05 .02
☐ 363 Dave Collins (203) .05 .02
☐ 364 Roy Lee Jackson(204) .05 .02
☐ 365 Doyle Alexander(205) .05 .02
☐ 366 Alfredo Griffin(206) .05 .02
☐ 367 Cliff Johnson (207) .05 .02
☐ 368 Alvin Davis .10 .05

☐ 369 Juan Samuel	.05	.02
☐ 370 Brook Jacoby	.05	.02
☐ 371 Mark Langston and Dwight Gooden	.25	.11
☐ 372 Mike Fitzgerald	.05	.02
☐ 373 Jackie Gutierrez	.05	.02
☐ 374 Dan Gladden	.05	.02
☐ 375 Carmelo Martinez	.05	.02
☐ 376 Kirby Puckett	5.00	2.20
☐ xx Album	1.00	.45

1985 Topps Rub Downs

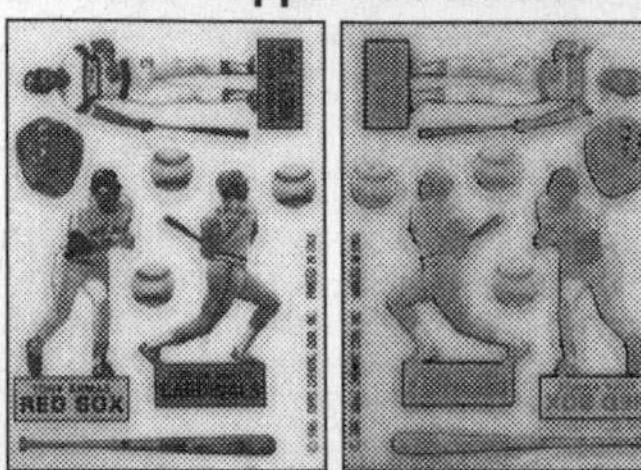

The cards in this 112 player (32 different sheets) set measure 2 3/8" by 3 5/16". The full color photo could be transfered from the rub down to another surface by rubbing a coin over the paper backing. Distributed in packages of two rub down sheets, some contained two or three player action poses, others head shots and various pieces of player equipment. Players from all teams were included in the set. Although the sheets are unnumbered, they are numbered here in alphabetical order based on each card first being placed in alphabetical order.

	NRMT	VG-E
COMPLETE SET (32)	10.00	4.50
COMMON SHEET (1-32)	.10	.05
☐ 1 Tony Armas	.10	.05
Harold Baines		
Lonnie Smith		
☐ 2 Don Baylor	.10	.05
George Hendrick		
Ron Kittle		
Johnnie LeMaster		
☐ 3 Buddy Bell	1.50	.70
Tony Gwynn		
Lloyd Moseby		
☐ 4 Bruce Benedict	.10	.05
Atlee Hammaker		
Frank White		
☐ 5 Mike Boddicker	.75	.35
Rod Carew		
Carlton Fisk		
Johnny Ray		
☐ 6 Wade Boggs	.60	.25
Rick Dempsey		
Keith Hernandez		
☐ 7 George Brett	1.25	.55
Andre Dawson		
Paul Molitor		
Alan Wiggins		
☐ 8 Tom Brunansky	.25	.11
Pedro Guerrero		
Darryl Strawberry		
☐ 9 Bill Buckner	1.50	.70
Tim Raines		
Ryne Sandberg		
Mike Schmidt		
☐ 10 Steve Carlton	.40	.18
Bob Horner		
Dan Quisenberry		
☐ 11 Gary Carter	.15	.07
Phil Garner		
Ron Guidry		
☐ 12 Jack Clark	.15	.07
Damaso Garcia		
Hal McRae		
Lance Parrish		
☐ 13 Dave Concepcion	.15	.07
Cecil Cooper		
Fred Lynn		
Jesse Orosco		
☐ 14 Jose Cruz	.25	.11
Jack Morris		
Jim Rice		
Rick Sutcliffe		
☐ 15 Alvin Davis	.15	.07
Steve Kemp		
Greg Luzinski		
Kent Tekulve		
☐ 16 Ron Davis	.10	.05
Kent Hrbek		
Juan Samuel		
☐ 17 John Denny	.10	.05
Carney Lansford		
Mario Soto		
Lou Whitaker		
☐ 18 Leon Durham	.10	.05
Willie Hernandez		
Steve Sax		
☐ 19 Dwight Evans	1.00	.45
Julio Franco		
Dwight Gooden		
☐ 20 George Foster	.15	.07
Gary Gaetti		
Bobby Grich		
Gary Redus		
☐ 21 Steve Garvey	.15	.07
Jerry Remy		
Bill Russell		
George Wright		
☐ 22 Kirk Gibson	2.00	.90
Rich Gossage		
Don Mattingly		
Dave Stieb		
☐ 23 Moose Haas	.10	.05
Bruce Sutter		
Dickie Thon		
Andre Thornton		
☐ 24 Rickey Henderson	1.00	.45
Dave Righetti		
Pete Rose		
☐ 25 Steve Henderson	.15	.07
Bill Madlock		
Alan Trammell		
☐ 26 LaMarr Hoyt	2.00	.90
Larry Parrish		
Nolan Ryan		
☐ 27 Reggie Jackson	.50	.23
Eric Show		
Jason Thompson		
☐ 28 Terry Kennedy	1.25	.55
Eddie Murray		
Tom Seaver		
Ozzie Smith		
☐ 29 Mark Langston	.50	.23
Ben Oglivie		
Darrell Porter		
☐ 30 Jeff Leonard	.50	.23
Gary Matthews		
Dale Murphy		
Dave Winfield		
☐ 31 Craig McMurtry	2.00	.90
Cal Ripken		
Steve Rogers		
Willie Upshaw		
☐ 32 Tony Pena	.40	.18
Fernando Valenzuela		
Robin Yount		

1985 Topps Super

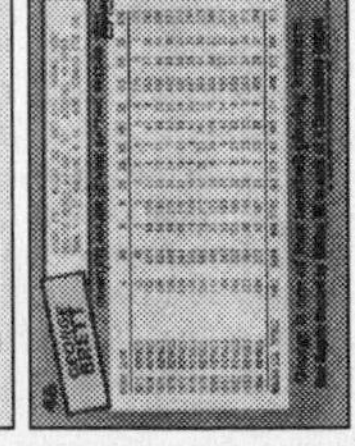

This 60-card set was issued in packs of three. These large cards measure 4 7/8" by 6 7/8". The fronts of the cards are merely a blow-up of the Topps regular issue. In fact, the cards differ from the corresponding cards of the regular set in size and number only. As one would expect, only those considered stars and superstars appear in this set. Backs are green with maroon printing. A checklist for the set is contained on the back of the wrapper. The back of the wrapper also gives details of Topps' offer to send your "missing" cards.

	NRMT	VG-E
COMPLETE SET (60)	10.00	4.50
COMMON CARD (1-60)	.10	.05
☐ 1 Ryne Sandberg	2.00	.90
☐ 2 Willie Hernandez	.10	.05
☐ 3 Rick Sutcliffe	.10	.05
☐ 4 Don Mattingly	3.00	1.35
☐ 5 Tony Gwynn	2.00	.90
☐ 6 Alvin Davis	.10	.05
☐ 7 Dwight Gooden	.75	.35
☐ 8 Dan Quisenberry	.10	.05
☐ 9 Bruce Sutter	.10	.05
☐ 10 Tony Armas	.10	.05
☐ 11 Dale Murphy	.50	.23
☐ 12 Mike Schmidt	.75	.35
☐ 13 Gary Carter	.50	.23
☐ 14 Rickey Henderson	.75	.35
☐ 15 Tim Raines	.25	.11
☐ 16 Mike Boddicker	.10	.05
☐ 17 Alejandro Pena	.10	.05
☐ 18 Eddie Murray	.75	.35
☐ 19 Gary Matthews	.10	.05
☐ 20 Mark Langston	.25	.11
☐ 21 Mario Soto	.10	.05
☐ 22 Dave Stieb	.10	.05
☐ 23 Nolan Ryan	3.00	1.35
☐ 24 Steve Carlton	.75	.35
☐ 25 Alan Trammell	.50	.23
☐ 26 Steve Garvey	.50	.23
☐ 27 Kirk Gibson	.25	.11
☐ 28 Juan Samuel	.10	.05
☐ 29 Reggie Jackson	.75	.35
☐ 30 Darryl Strawberry	.25	.11
☐ 31 Tom Seaver	.75	.35
☐ 32 Pete Rose	.75	.35
☐ 33 Dwight Evans	.25	.11
☐ 34 Jose Cruz	.25	.11
☐ 35 Bert Blyleven	.25	.11
☐ 36 Keith Hernandez	.25	.11
☐ 37 Robin Yount	.50	.23
☐ 38 Joaquin Andujar	.10	.05
☐ 39 Lloyd Moseby	.10	.05
☐ 40 Chili Davis	.25	.11
☐ 41 Kent Hrbek	.25	.11
☐ 42 Dave Parker	.25	.11
☐ 43 Jack Morris	.25	.11
☐ 44 Pedro Guerrero	.10	.05
☐ 45 Mike Witt	.10	.05
☐ 46 George Brett	1.50	.70
☐ 47 Ozzie Smith	1.50	.70
☐ 48 Cal Ripken	3.00	1.35
☐ 49 Rich Gossage	.25	.11
☐ 50 Jim Rice	.25	.11
☐ 51 Harold Baines	.25	.11
☐ 52 Fernando Valenzuela	.25	.11
☐ 53 Buddy Bell	.10	.05
☐ 54 Jesse Orosco	.10	.05
☐ 55 Lance Parrish	.10	.05
☐ 56 Jason Thompson	.10	.05
☐ 57 Tom Brunansky	.10	.05
☐ 58 Dave Righetti	.10	.05
☐ 59 Dave Kingman	.10	.05
☐ 60 Dave Winfield	.75	.35

1986 Topps

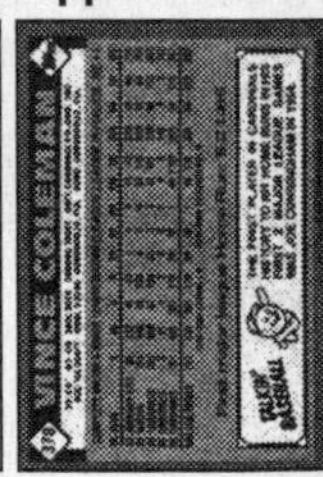

This set consists of 792 standard-size cards. Cards were primarily distributed in 15-card wax packs and 48-card rack packs. This was also the first year Topps offered a factory set to hobby dealers. Standard card fronts feature a black and white split border framing a color photo with team name on top and player name on bottom. Subsets include Pete Rose tribute (1-7), Record Breakers (201-207), Turn Back the Clock (401-405), All-Stars (701-722) and Team Leaders (seeded throughout the set). Manager cards feature the team checklist on the reverse. There are two uncorrected errors involving misnumbered cards; see card numbers 51, 57, 141, and 171 in the checklist below. The key Rookie Cards in this set are Darren Daulton, Len Dykstra, Cecil Fielder, and Mickey Tettleton.

	MINT	NRMT
COMPLETE SET (792)	20.00	9.00
COMP.FACT.SET (792)	25.00	11.00
COMMON CARD (1-792)	.05	.02
☐ 1 Pete Rose	.75	.35
☐ 2 Rose Special: '63-'66	.25	.11
☐ 3 Rose Special: '67-'70	.25	.11
☐ 4 Rose Special: '71-'74	.25	.11
☐ 5 Rose Special: '75-'78	.25	.11
☐ 6 Rose Special: '79-'82	.25	.11
☐ 7 Rose Special: '83-'85	.25	.11

☐ 8 Dwayne Murphy	.05	.02
☐ 9 Roy Smith	.05	.02
☐ 10 Tony Gwynn	1.00	.45
☐ 11 Bob Ojeda	.05	.02
☐ 12 Jose Uribe	.05	.02
☐ 13 Bob Kearney	.05	.02
☐ 14 Julio Cruz	.05	.02
☐ 15 Eddie Whitson	.05	.02
☐ 16 Rick Schu	.05	.02
☐ 17 Mike Stenhouse	.05	.02
☐ 18 Brent Gaff	.05	.02
☐ 19 Rich Hebner	.05	.02
☐ 20 Lou Whitaker	.10	.05
☐ 21 George Bamberger MG (Checklist back)	.05	.02
☐ 22 Duane Walker	.05	.02
☐ 23 Manny Lee	.05	.02
☐ 24 Len Barker	.05	.02
☐ 25 Willie Wilson	.05	.02
☐ 26 Frank DiPino	.05	.02
☐ 27 Ray Knight	.10	.05
☐ 28 Eric Davis	.20	.09
☐ 29 Tony Phillips	.05	.02
☐ 30 Eddie Murray	.50	.23
☐ 31 Jamie Easterly	.05	.02
☐ 32 Steve Yeager	.05	.02
☐ 33 Jeff Lahti	.05	.02
☐ 34 Ken Phelps	.05	.02
☐ 35 Jeff Reardon	.10	.05
☐ 36 Lance Parrish TL	.05	.02
☐ 37 Mark Thurmond	.05	.02
☐ 38 Glenn Hoffman	.05	.02
☐ 39 Dave Rucker	.05	.02
☐ 40 Ken Griffey	.10	.05
☐ 41 Brad Wellman	.05	.02
☐ 42 Geoff Zahn	.05	.02
☐ 43 Dave Engle	.05	.02
☐ 44 Lance McCullers	.05	.02
☐ 45 Damaso Garcia	.05	.02
☐ 46 Billy Hatcher	.05	.02
☐ 47 Juan Berenguer	.05	.02
☐ 48 Bill Almon	.05	.02
☐ 49 Rick Manning	.05	.02
☐ 50 Dan Quisenberry	.05	.02
☐ 51 Bobby Wine MG ERR (Checklist back) (Number of card on back is actually 57)	.05	.02
☐ 52 Chris Welsh	.05	.02
☐ 53 Len Dykstra	.75	.35
☐ 54 John Franco	.40	.18
☐ 55 Fred Lynn	.10	.05
☐ 56 Tom Niedenfuer	.05	.02
☐ 57 Bill Doran (See also 51)	.05	.02
☐ 58 Bill Krueger	.05	.02
☐ 59 Andre Thornton	.05	.02
☐ 60 Dwight Evans	.10	.05
☐ 61 Karl Best	.05	.02
☐ 62 Bob Boone	.10	.05
☐ 63 Ron Roenicke	.05	.02
☐ 64 Floyd Bannister	.05	.02
☐ 65 Dan Driessen	.05	.02
☐ 66 Bob Forsch TL	.10	.05
☐ 67 Carmelo Martinez	.05	.02
☐ 68 Ed Lynch	.05	.02
☐ 69 Luis Aguayo	.05	.02
☐ 70 Dave Winfield	.40	.18
☐ 71 Ken Schrom	.05	.02
☐ 72 Shawon Dunston	.05	.02
☐ 73 Randy O'Neal	.05	.02
☐ 74 Rance Mulliniks	.05	.02
☐ 75 Jose DeLeon	.05	.02
☐ 76 Dion James	.05	.02
☐ 77 Charlie Leibrandt	.05	.02
☐ 78 Bruce Benedict	.05	.02
☐ 79 Dave Schmidt	.05	.02
☐ 80 Darryl Strawberry	.40	.18
☐ 81 Gene Mauch MG (Checklist back)	.10	.05
☐ 82 Tippy Martinez	.05	.02
☐ 83 Phil Garner	.05	.02
☐ 84 Curt Young	.05	.02
☐ 85 Tony Perez (Eric Davis also shown on card)	.40	.18
☐ 86 Tom Waddell	.05	.02
☐ 87 Candy Maldonado	.05	.02
☐ 88 Tom Nieto	.05	.02
☐ 89 Randy St.Claire	.05	.02
☐ 90 Garry Templeton	.05	.02
☐ 91 Steve Crawford	.05	.02
☐ 92 Al Cowens	.05	.02
☐ 93 Scot Thompson	.05	.02
☐ 94 Rich Bordi	.05	.02
☐ 95 Ozzie Virgil	.05	.02
☐ 96 Jim Clancy TL	.10	.05

☐ 97 Gary Gaetti	.10	.05
☐ 98 Dick Ruthven	.05	.02
☐ 99 Buddy Biancalana	.05	.02
☐ 100 Nolan Ryan	1.50	.70
☐ 101 Dave Bergman	.05	.02
☐ 102 Joe Orsulak	.05	.02
☐ 103 Luis Salazar	.05	.02
☐ 104 Sid Fernandez	.10	.05
☐ 105 Gary Ward	.05	.02
☐ 106 Ray Burris	.05	.02
☐ 107 Rafael Ramirez	.05	.02
☐ 108 Ted Power	.05	.02
☐ 109 Len Matuszek	.05	.02
☐ 110 Scott McGregor	.05	.02
☐ 111 Roger Craig MG (Checklist back)	.10	.05
☐ 112 Bill Campbell	.05	.02
☐ 113 U.L. Washington	.05	.02
☐ 114 Mike C. Brown	.05	.02
☐ 115 Jay Howell	.05	.02
☐ 116 Brook Jacoby	.05	.02
☐ 117 Bruce Kison	.05	.02
☐ 118 Jerry Royster	.05	.02
☐ 119 Barry Bonnell	.05	.02
☐ 120 Steve Carlton	.40	.18
☐ 121 Nelson Simmons	.05	.02
☐ 122 Pete Filson	.05	.02
☐ 123 Greg Walker	.05	.02
☐ 124 Luis Sanchez	.05	.02
☐ 125 Dave Lopes	.10	.05
☐ 126 Mookie Wilson TL	.10	.05
☐ 127 Jack Howell	.05	.02
☐ 128 John Wathan	.05	.02
☐ 129 Jeff Dedmon	.05	.02
☐ 130 Alan Trammell	.40	.18
☐ 131 Checklist: 1-132	.10	.05
☐ 132 Razor Shines	.05	.02
☐ 133 Andy McGaffigan	.05	.02
☐ 134 Carney Lansford	.10	.05
☐ 135 Joe Niekro	.10	.05
☐ 136 Mike Hargrove	.10	.05
☐ 137 Charlie Moore	.05	.02
☐ 138 Mark Davis	.05	.02
☐ 139 Daryl Boston	.05	.02
☐ 140 John Candelaria	.05	.02
☐ 141 Chuck Cottier MG (Checklist back) (See also 171)	.05	.02
☐ 142 Bob Jones	.05	.02
☐ 143 Dave Van Gorder	.05	.02
☐ 144 Doug Sisk	.05	.02
☐ 145 Pedro Guerrero	.10	.05
☐ 146 Jack Perconte	.05	.02
☐ 147 Larry Sheets	.05	.02
☐ 148 Mike Heath	.05	.02
☐ 149 Brett Butler	.10	.05
☐ 150 Joaquin Andujar	.05	.02
☐ 151 Dave Stapleton	.05	.02
☐ 152 Mike Morgan	.05	.02
☐ 153 Ricky Adams	.05	.02
☐ 154 Bert Roberge	.05	.02
☐ 155 Bob Grich	.10	.05
☐ 156 Richard Dotson TL	.05	.02
☐ 157 Ron Hassey	.05	.02
☐ 158 Derrel Thomas	.05	.02
☐ 159 Orel Hershiser UER (82 Alburquerque)	.40	.18
☐ 160 Chet Lemon	.05	.02
☐ 161 Lee Tunnell	.05	.02
☐ 162 Greg Gagne	.05	.02
☐ 163 Pete Ladd	.05	.02
☐ 164 Steve Balboni	.05	.02
☐ 165 Mike Davis	.05	.02
☐ 166 Dickie Thon	.05	.02
☐ 167 Zane Smith	.05	.02
☐ 168 Jeff Burroughs	.05	.02
☐ 169 George Wright	.05	.02
☐ 170 Gary Carter	.40	.18
☐ 171 Bob Rodgers MG ERR (Checklist back) (Number of card on back actually 141)	.05	.02
☐ 172 Jerry Reed	.05	.02
☐ 173 Wayne Gross	.05	.02
☐ 174 Brian Snyder	.05	.02
☐ 175 Steve Sax	.05	.02
☐ 176 Jay Tibbs	.05	.02
☐ 177 Joel Youngblood	.05	.02
☐ 178 Ivan DeJesus	.05	.02
☐ 179 Stu Cliburn	.05	.02
☐ 180 Don Mattingly	.60	.25
☐ 181 Al Nipper	.05	.02
☐ 182 Bobby Brown	.05	.02
☐ 183 Larry Andersen	.05	.02
☐ 184 Tim Laudner	.05	.02
☐ 185 Rollie Fingers	.40	.18
☐ 186 Jose Cruz TL	.10	.05

☐ 187 Scott Fletcher	.05	.02
☐ 188 Bob Dernier	.05	.02
☐ 189 Mike Mason	.05	.02
☐ 190 George Hendrick	.05	.02
☐ 191 Wally Backman	.05	.02
☐ 192 Milt Wilcox	.05	.02
☐ 193 Daryl Sconiers	.05	.02
☐ 194 Craig McMurtry	.05	.02
☐ 195 Dave Concepcion	.10	.05
☐ 196 Doyle Alexander	.05	.02
☐ 197 Enos Cabell	.05	.02
☐ 198 Ken Dixon	.05	.02
☐ 199 Dick Howser MG (Checklist back)	.10	.05
☐ 200 Mike Schmidt	.50	.23
☐ 201 Vince Coleman RB Most SB's rookie season	.10	.05
☐ 202 Dwight Gooden RB Youngest 20 game winner	.40	.18
☐ 203 Keith Hernandez RB Most game-winning RBI's	.10	.05
☐ 204 Phil Niekro RB Oldest shutout pitcher	.40	.18
☐ 205 Tony Perez RB Oldest grand slammer	.40	.18
☐ 206 Pete Rose RB Most lifetime hits	.30	.14
☐ 207 Fernando Valenzuela RB Most cons. innings start of season, no earned runs	.10	.05
☐ 208 Ramon Romero	.05	.02
☐ 209 Randy Ready	.05	.02
☐ 210 Calvin Schiraldi	.05	.02
☐ 211 Ed Wojna	.05	.02
☐ 212 Chris Speier	.05	.02
☐ 213 Bob Shirley	.05	.02
☐ 214 Randy Bush	.05	.02
☐ 215 Frank White	.10	.05
☐ 216 Dwayne Murphy TL	.10	.05
☐ 217 Bill Scherrer	.05	.02
☐ 218 Randy Hunt	.05	.02
☐ 219 Dennis Lamp	.05	.02
☐ 220 Bob Horner	.05	.02
☐ 221 Dave Henderson	.05	.02
☐ 222 Craig Gerber	.05	.02
☐ 223 Atlee Hammaker	.05	.02
☐ 224 Cesar Cedeno	.10	.05
☐ 225 Ron Darling	.05	.02
☐ 226 Lee Lacy	.05	.02
☐ 227 Al Jones	.05	.02
☐ 228 Tom Lawless	.05	.02
☐ 229 Bill Gullickson	.05	.02
☐ 230 Terry Kennedy	.05	.02
☐ 231 Jim Frey MG (Checklist back)	.10	.05
☐ 232 Rick Rhoden	.05	.02
☐ 233 Steve Lyons	.05	.02
☐ 234 Doug Corbett	.05	.02
☐ 235 Butch Wynegar	.05	.02
☐ 236 Frank Eufemia	.05	.02
☐ 237 Ted Simmons	.10	.05
☐ 238 Larry Parrish	.05	.02
☐ 239 Joel Skinner	.05	.02
☐ 240 Tommy John	.20	.09
☐ 241 Tony Fernandez	.05	.02
☐ 242 Rich Thompson	.05	.02
☐ 243 Johnny Grubb	.05	.02
☐ 244 Craig Lefferts	.05	.02
☐ 245 Jim Sundberg	.05	.02
☐ 246 Steve Carlton TL	.20	.09
☐ 247 Terry Harper	.05	.02
☐ 248 Spike Owen	.05	.02
☐ 249 Rob Deer	.10	.05
☐ 250 Dwight Gooden	.40	.18
☐ 251 Rich Dauer	.05	.02
☐ 252 Bobby Castillo	.05	.02
☐ 253 Dann Bilardello	.05	.02
☐ 254 Ozzie Guillen	.40	.18
☐ 255 Tony Armas	.05	.02
☐ 256 Kurt Kepshire	.05	.02
☐ 257 Doug DeCinces	.05	.02
☐ 258 Tim Burke	.05	.02
☐ 259 Dan Pasqua	.05	.02
☐ 260 Tony Pena	.05	.02
☐ 261 Bobby Valentine MG (Checklist back)	.10	.05
☐ 262 Mario Ramirez	.05	.02
☐ 263 Checklist: 133-264	.10	.05
☐ 264 Darren Daulton	.75	.35
☐ 265 Ron Davis	.05	.02
☐ 266 Keith Moreland	.05	.02
☐ 267 Paul Molitor	.40	.18
☐ 268 Mike Scott	.05	.02
☐ 269 Dane Iorg	.05	.02
☐ 270 Jack Morris	.10	.05

☐ 271 Dave Collins .05 .02
☐ 272 Tim Tolman .05 .02
☐ 273 Jerry Willard .05 .02
☐ 274 Ron Gardenhire .05 .02
☐ 275 Charlie Hough .10 .05
☐ 276 Willie Randolph TL .10 .05
☐ 277 Jaime Cocanower .05 .02
☐ 278 Sixto Lezcano .05 .02
☐ 279 Al Pardo .05 .02
☐ 280 Tim Raines .10 .05
☐ 281 Steve Mura .05 .02
☐ 282 Jerry Mumphrey .05 .02
☐ 283 Mike Fischlin .05 .02
☐ 284 Brian Dayett .05 .02
☐ 285 Buddy Bell .10 .05
☐ 286 Luis DeLeon .05 .02
☐ 287 John Christensen .05 .02
☐ 288 Don Aase .05 .02
☐ 289 Johnnie LeMaster .05 .02
☐ 290 Carlton Fisk .40 .18
☐ 291 Tom Lasorda MG .20 .09
(Checklist back)
☐ 292 Chuck Porter .05 .02
☐ 293 Chris Chambliss .10 .05
☐ 294 Danny Cox .05 .02
☐ 295 Kirk Gibson .10 .05
☐ 296 Geno Petralli .05 .02
☐ 297 Tim Lollar .05 .02
☐ 298 Craig Reynolds .05 .02
☐ 299 Bryn Smith .05 .02
☐ 300 George Brett .75 .35
☐ 301 Dennis Rasmussen .05 .02
☐ 302 Greg Gross .05 .02
☐ 303 Curt Wardle .05 .02
☐ 304 Mike Gallego .10 .05
☐ 305 Phil Bradley .05 .02
☐ 306 Terry Kennedy TL .05 .02
☐ 307 Dave Sax .05 .02
☐ 308 Ray Fontenot .05 .02
☐ 309 John Shelby .05 .02
☐ 310 Greg Minton .05 .02
☐ 311 Dick Schofield .05 .02
☐ 312 Tom Filer .05 .02
☐ 313 Joe DeSa .05 .02
☐ 314 Frank Pastore .05 .02
☐ 315 Mookie Wilson .10 .05
☐ 316 Sammy Khalifa .05 .02
☐ 317 Ed Romero .05 .02
☐ 318 Terry Whitfield .05 .02
☐ 319 Rick Camp .05 .02
☐ 320 Jim Rice .10 .05
☐ 321 Earl Weaver MG .40 .18
(Checklist back)
☐ 322 Bob Forsch .05 .02
☐ 323 Jerry Davis .05 .02
☐ 324 Dan Schatzeder .05 .02
☐ 325 Juan Beniquez .05 .02
☐ 326 Kent Tekulve .05 .02
☐ 327 Mike Pagliarulo .05 .02
☐ 328 Pete O'Brien .05 .02
☐ 329 Kirby Puckett 1.50 .70
☐ 330 Rick Sutcliffe .05 .02
☐ 331 Alan Ashby .05 .02
☐ 332 Darryl Motley .05 .02
☐ 333 Tom Henke .10 .05
☐ 334 Ken Oberkfell .05 .02
☐ 335 Don Sutton .40 .18
☐ 336 Andre Thornton TL .10 .05
☐ 337 Darnell Coles .05 .02
☐ 338 Jorge Bell .10 .05
☐ 339 Bruce Berenyi .05 .02
☐ 340 Cal Ripken 1.50 .70
☐ 341 Frank Williams .05 .02
☐ 342 Gary Redus .05 .02
☐ 343 Carlos Diaz .05 .02
☐ 344 Jim Wohlford .05 .02
☐ 345 Donnie Moore .05 .02
☐ 346 Bryan Little .05 .02
☐ 347 Teddy Higuera .10 .05
☐ 348 Cliff Johnson .05 .02
☐ 349 Mark Clear .05 .02
☐ 350 Jack Clark .10 .05
☐ 351 Chuck Tanner MG .10 .05
(Checklist back)
☐ 352 Harry Spilman .05 .02
☐ 353 Keith Atherton .05 .02
☐ 354 Tony Bernazard .05 .02
☐ 355 Lee Smith .40 .18
☐ 356 Mickey Hatcher .05 .02
☐ 357 Ed VandeBerg .05 .02
☐ 358 Rick Dempsey .05 .02
☐ 359 Mike LaCoss .05 .02
☐ 360 Lloyd Moseby .05 .02
☐ 361 Shane Rawley .05 .02
☐ 362 Tom Paciorek .05 .02
☐ 363 Terry Forster .05 .02
☐ 364 Reid Nichols .05 .02
☐ 365 Mike Flanagan .05 .02
☐ 366 Dave Concepcion TL .10 .05
☐ 367 Aurelio Lopez .05 .02
☐ 368 Greg Brock .05 .02
☐ 369 Al Holland .05 .02
☐ 370 Vince Coleman .40 .18
☐ 371 Bill Stein .05 .02
☐ 372 Ben Oglivie .05 .02
☐ 373 Urbano Lugo .05 .02
☐ 374 Terry Francona .05 .02
☐ 375 Rich Gedman .05 .02
☐ 376 Bill Dawley .05 .02
☐ 377 Joe Carter 1.00 .45
☐ 378 Bruce Bochte .05 .02
☐ 379 Bobby Meacham .05 .02
☐ 380 LaMarr Hoyt .05 .02
☐ 381 Ray Miller MG .05 .02
(Checklist back)
☐ 382 Ivan Calderon .10 .05
☐ 383 Chris Brown .05 .02
☐ 384 Steve Trout .05 .02
☐ 385 Cecil Cooper .10 .05
☐ 386 Cecil Fielder 1.00 .45
☐ 387 Steve Kemp .05 .02
☐ 388 Dickie Noles .05 .02
☐ 389 Glenn Davis .10 .05
☐ 390 Tom Seaver .50 .23
☐ 391 Julio Franco .20 .09
☐ 392 John Russell .05 .02
☐ 393 Chris Pittaro .05 .02
☐ 394 Checklist: 265-396 .10 .05
☐ 395 Scott Garrelts .05 .02
☐ 396 Dwight Evans TL .10 .05
☐ 397 Steve Buechele .10 .05
☐ 398 Earnie Riles .05 .02
☐ 399 Bill Swift .05 .02
☐ 400 Rod Carew .40 .18
☐ 401 Fernando Valenzuela .10 .05
TBC '81
☐ 402 Tom Seaver TBC '76 .40 .18
☐ 403 Willie Mays TBC '71 .40 .18
☐ 404 Frank Robinson .40 .18
TBC '66
☐ 405 Roger Maris TBC '61 .40 .18
☐ 406 Scott Sanderson .05 .02
☐ 407 Sal Butera .05 .02
☐ 408 Dave Smith .05 .02
☐ 409 Paul Runge .05 .02
☐ 410 Dave Kingman .10 .05
☐ 411 Sparky Anderson MG .20 .09
(Checklist back)
☐ 412 Jim Clancy .05 .02
☐ 413 Tim Flannery .05 .02
☐ 414 Tom Gorman .05 .02
☐ 415 Hal McRae .10 .05
☐ 416 Dennis Martinez .10 .05
☐ 417 R.J. Reynolds .05 .02
☐ 418 Alan Knicely .05 .02
☐ 419 Frank Wills .05 .02
☐ 420 Von Hayes .05 .02
☐ 421 David Palmer .05 .02
☐ 422 Mike Jorgensen .05 .02
☐ 423 Dan Spillner .05 .02
☐ 424 Rick Miller .05 .02
☐ 425 Larry McWilliams .05 .02
☐ 426 Charlie Moore TL .10 .05
☐ 427 Joe Cowley .05 .02
☐ 428 Max Venable .05 .02
☐ 429 Greg Booker .05 .02
☐ 430 Kent Hrbek .10 .05
☐ 431 George Frazier .05 .02
☐ 432 Mark Bailey .05 .02
☐ 433 Chris Codiroli .05 .02
☐ 434 Curt Wilkerson .05 .02
☐ 435 Bill Caudill .05 .02
☐ 436 Doug Flynn .05 .02
☐ 437 Rick Mahler .05 .02
☐ 438 Clint Hurdle .05 .02
☐ 439 Rick Honeycutt .05 .02
☐ 440 Alvin Davis .05 .02
☐ 441 Whitey Herzog MG .20 .09
(Checklist back)
☐ 442 Ron Robinson .05 .02
☐ 443 Bill Buckner .10 .05
☐ 444 Alex Trevino .05 .02
☐ 445 Bert Blyleven .20 .09
☐ 446 Lenn Sakata .05 .02
☐ 447 Jerry Don Gleaton .05 .02
☐ 448 Herm Winningham .05 .02
☐ 449 Rod Scurry .05 .02
☐ 450 Graig Nettles .10 .05
☐ 451 Mark Brown .05 .02
☐ 452 Bob Clark .05 .02
☐ 453 Steve Jeltz .05 .02
☐ 454 Burt Hooton .05 .02
☐ 455 Willie Randolph .10 .05
☐ 456 Dale Murphy TL .40 .18
☐ 457 Mickey Tettleton .60 .25
☐ 458 Kevin Bass .05 .02
☐ 459 Luis Leal .05 .02
☐ 460 Leon Durham .05 .02
☐ 461 Walt Terrell .05 .02
☐ 462 Domingo Ramos .05 .02
☐ 463 Jim Gott .05 .02
☐ 464 Ruppert Jones .05 .02
☐ 465 Jesse Orosco .05 .02
☐ 466 Tom Foley .05 .02
☐ 467 Bob James .05 .02
☐ 468 Mike Scioscia .05 .02
☐ 469 Storm Davis .05 .02
☐ 470 Bill Madlock .05 .02
☐ 471 Bobby Cox MG .20 .09
(Checklist back)
☐ 472 Joe Hesketh .05 .02
☐ 473 Mark Brouhard .05 .02
☐ 474 John Tudor .05 .02
☐ 475 Juan Samuel .05 .02
☐ 476 Ron Mathis .05 .02
☐ 477 Mike Easler .05 .02
☐ 478 Andy Hawkins .05 .02
☐ 479 Bob Melvin .05 .02
☐ 480 Oddibe McDowell .05 .02
☐ 481 Scott Bradley .05 .02
☐ 482 Rick Lysander .05 .02
☐ 483 George Vukovich .05 .02
☐ 484 Donnie Hill .05 .02
☐ 485 Gary Matthews .05 .02
☐ 486 Bobby Grich TL .10 .05
☐ 487 Bret Saberhagen .20 .09
☐ 488 Lou Thornton .05 .02
☐ 489 Jim Winn .05 .02
☐ 490 Jeff Leonard .05 .02
☐ 491 Pascual Perez .05 .02
☐ 492 Kelvin Chapman .05 .02
☐ 493 Gene Nelson .05 .02
☐ 494 Gary Roenicke .05 .02
☐ 495 Mark Langston .05 .02
☐ 496 Jay Johnstone .10 .05
☐ 497 John Stuper .05 .02
☐ 498 Tito Landrum .05 .02
☐ 499 Bob L. Gibson .05 .02
☐ 500 Rickey Henderson .40 .18
☐ 501 Dave Johnson MG .10 .05
(Checklist back)
☐ 502 Glen Cook .05 .02
☐ 503 Mike Fitzgerald .05 .02
☐ 504 Denny Walling .05 .02
☐ 505 Jerry Koosman .10 .05
☐ 506 Bill Russell .10 .05
☐ 507 Steve Ontiveros .10 .05
☐ 508 Alan Wiggins .05 .02
☐ 509 Ernie Camacho .05 .02
☐ 510 Wade Boggs .40 .18
☐ 511 Ed Nunez .05 .02
☐ 512 Thad Bosley .05 .02
☐ 513 Ron Washington .05 .02
☐ 514 Mike Jones .05 .02
☐ 515 Darrell Evans .10 .05
☐ 516 Greg Minton TL .05 .02
☐ 517 Milt Thompson .10 .05
☐ 518 Buck Martinez .05 .02
☐ 519 Danny Darwin .05 .02
☐ 520 Keith Hernandez .10 .05
☐ 521 Nate Snell .05 .02
☐ 522 Bob Bailor .05 .02
☐ 523 Joe Price .05 .02
☐ 524 Darrell Miller .05 .02
☐ 525 Marvell Wynne .05 .02
☐ 526 Charlie Lea .05 .02
☐ 527 Checklist: 397-528 .10 .05
☐ 528 Terry Pendleton .20 .09
☐ 529 Marc Sullivan .05 .02
☐ 530 Rich Gossage .20 .09
☐ 531 Tony LaRussa MG .10 .05
(Checklist back)
☐ 532 Don Carman .05 .02
☐ 533 Billy Sample .05 .02
☐ 534 Jeff Calhoun .05 .02
☐ 535 Toby Harrah .05 .02
☐ 536 Jose Rijo .05 .02
☐ 537 Mark Salas .05 .02
☐ 538 Dennis Eckersley .40 .18
☐ 539 Glenn Hubbard .05 .02
☐ 540 Dan Petry .05 .02
☐ 541 Jorge Orta .05 .02
☐ 542 Don Schulze .05 .02
☐ 543 Jerry Narron .05 .02
☐ 544 Eddie Milner .05 .02
☐ 545 Jimmy Key .40 .18
☐ 546 Dave Henderson TL .10 .05
☐ 547 Roger McDowell .10 .05
☐ 548 Mike Young .05 .02
☐ 549 Bob Welch .05 .02
☐ 550 Tom Herr .05 .02

☐ 551 Dave LaPoint .05 .02
☐ 552 Marc Hill .05 .02
☐ 553 Jim Morrison .05 .02
☐ 554 Paul Householder .05 .02
☐ 555 Hubie Brooks .05 .02
☐ 556 John Denny .05 .02
☐ 557 Gerald Perry .05 .02
☐ 558 Tim Stoddard .05 .02
☐ 559 Tommy Dunbar .05 .02
☐ 560 Dave Righetti .05 .02
☐ 561 Bob Lillis MG .05 .02
(Checklist back)
☐ 562 Joe Beckwith .05 .02
☐ 563 Alejandro Sanchez .05 .02
☐ 564 Warren Brusstar .05 .02
☐ 565 Tom Brunansky .05 .02
☐ 566 Alfredo Griffin .05 .02
☐ 567 Jeff Barkley .05 .02
☐ 568 Donnie Scott .05 .02
☐ 569 Jim Acker .05 .02
☐ 570 Rusty Staub .10 .05
☐ 571 Mike Jeffcoat .05 .02
☐ 572 Paul Zuvella .05 .02
☐ 573 Tom Hume .05 .02
☐ 574 Ron Kittle .05 .02
☐ 575 Mike Boddicker .05 .02
☐ 576 Andre Dawson TL .40 .18
☐ 577 Jerry Reuss .05 .02
☐ 578 Lee Mazzilli .05 .02
☐ 579 Jim Slaton .05 .02
☐ 580 Willie McGee .10 .05
☐ 581 Bruce Hurst .05 .02
☐ 582 Jim Gantner .05 .02
☐ 583 Al Bumbry .05 .02
☐ 584 Brian Fisher .05 .02
☐ 585 Garry Maddox .05 .02
☐ 586 Greg Harris .05 .02
☐ 587 Rafael Santana .05 .02
☐ 588 Steve Lake .05 .02
☐ 589 Sid Bream .05 .02
☐ 590 Bob Knepper .05 .02
☐ 591 Jackie Moore MG .05 .02
(Checklist back)
☐ 592 Frank Tanana .05 .02
☐ 593 Jesse Barfield .05 .02
☐ 594 Chris Bando .05 .02
☐ 595 Dave Parker .10 .05
☐ 596 Onix Concepcion .05 .02
☐ 597 Sammy Stewart .05 .02
☐ 598 Jim Presley .05 .02
☐ 599 Rick Aguilera .40 .18
☐ 600 Dale Murphy .40 .18
☐ 601 Gary Lucas .05 .02
☐ 602 Mariano Duncan .40 .18
☐ 603 Bill Laskey .05 .02
☐ 604 Gary Pettis .05 .02
☐ 605 Dennis Boyd .05 .02
☐ 606 Hal McRae TL .05 .02
☐ 607 Ken Dayley .05 .02
☐ 608 Bruce Bochy .05 .02
☐ 609 Barbaro Garbey .05 .02
☐ 610 Ron Guidry .10 .05
☐ 611 Gary Woods .05 .02
☐ 612 Richard Dotson .05 .02
☐ 613 Roy Smalley .05 .02
☐ 614 Rick Waits .05 .02
☐ 615 Johnny Ray .05 .02
☐ 616 Glenn Brummer .05 .02
☐ 617 Lonnie Smith .05 .02
☐ 618 Jim Pankovits .05 .02
☐ 619 Danny Heep .05 .02
☐ 620 Bruce Sutter .10 .05
☐ 621 John Felske MG .05 .02
(Checklist back)
☐ 622 Gary Lavelle .05 .02
☐ 623 Floyd Rayford .05 .02
☐ 624 Steve McCatty .05 .02
☐ 625 Bob Brenly .05 .02
☐ 626 Roy Thomas .05 .02
☐ 627 Ron Oester .05 .02
☐ 628 Kirk McCaskill .10 .05
☐ 629 Mitch Webster .05 .02
☐ 630 Fernando Valenzuela .10 .05
☐ 631 Steve Braun .05 .02
☐ 632 Dave Von Ohlen .05 .02
☐ 633 Jackie Gutierrez .05 .02
☐ 634 Roy Lee Jackson .05 .02
☐ 635 Jason Thompson .05 .02
☐ 636 Lee Smith TL .15 .07
☐ 637 Rudy Law .05 .02
☐ 638 John Butcher .05 .02
☐ 639 Bo Diaz .05 .02
☐ 640 Jose Cruz .10 .05
☐ 641 Wayne Tolleson .05 .02
☐ 642 Ray Searage .05 .02
☐ 643 Tom Brookens .05 .02
☐ 644 Mark Gubicza .05 .02
☐ 645 Dusty Baker .10 .05
☐ 646 Mike Moore .05 .02
☐ 647 Mel Hall .05 .02
☐ 648 Steve Bedrosian .05 .02
☐ 649 Ronn Reynolds .05 .02
☐ 650 Dave Stieb .05 .02
☐ 651 Billy Martin MG .10 .05
(Checklist back)
☐ 652 Tom Browning .05 .02
☐ 653 Jim Dwyer .05 .02
☐ 654 Ken Howell .05 .02
☐ 655 Manny Trillo .05 .02
☐ 656 Brian Harper .05 .02
☐ 657 Juan Agosto .05 .02
☐ 658 Rob Wilfong .05 .02
☐ 659 Checklist: 529-660 .10 .05
☐ 660 Steve Garvey .20 .09
☐ 661 Roger Clemens 1.50 .70
☐ 662 Bill Schroeder .05 .02
☐ 663 Neil Allen .05 .02
☐ 664 Tim Corcoran .05 .02
☐ 665 Alejandro Pena .05 .02
☐ 666 Rangers Leaders .10 .05
Charlie Hough
☐ 667 Tim Teufel .05 .02
☐ 668 Cecilio Guante .05 .02
☐ 669 Ron Cey .10 .05
☐ 670 Willie Hernandez .05 .02
☐ 671 Lynn Jones .05 .02
☐ 672 Rob Picciolo .05 .02
☐ 673 Ernie Whitt .05 .02
☐ 674 Pat Tabler .05 .02
☐ 675 Claudell Washington .05 .02
☐ 676 Matt Young .05 .02
☐ 677 Nick Esasky .05 .02
☐ 678 Dan Gladden .05 .02
☐ 679 Britt Burns .05 .02
☐ 680 George Foster .10 .05
☐ 681 Dick Williams MG .10 .05
(Checklist back)
☐ 682 Junior Ortiz .05 .02
☐ 683 Andy Van Slyke .10 .05
☐ 684 Bob McClure .05 .02
☐ 685 Tim Wallach .05 .02
☐ 686 Jeff Stone .05 .02
☐ 687 Mike Trujillo .05 .02
☐ 688 Larry Herndon .05 .02
☐ 689 Dave Stewart .10 .05
☐ 690 Ryne Sandberg UER .50 .23
(No Topps logo
on front)
☐ 691 Mike Madden .05 .02
☐ 692 Dale Berra .05 .02
☐ 693 Tom Tellmann .05 .02
☐ 694 Garth Iorg .05 .02
☐ 695 Mike Smithson .05 .02
☐ 696 Bill Russell TL .10 .05
☐ 697 Bud Black .05 .02
☐ 698 Brad Komminsk .05 .02
☐ 699 Pat Corrales MG .05 .02
(Checklist back)
☐ 700 Reggie Jackson .50 .23
☐ 701 Keith Hernandez AS .10 .05
☐ 702 Tom Herr AS .05 .02
☐ 703 Tim Wallach AS .05 .02
☐ 704 Ozzie Smith AS .40 .18
☐ 705 Dale Murphy AS .40 .18
☐ 706 Pedro Guerrero AS .05 .02
☐ 707 Willie McGee AS .05 .02
☐ 708 Gary Carter AS .20 .09
☐ 709 Dwight Gooden AS .40 .18
☐ 710 John Tudor AS .05 .02
☐ 711 Jeff Reardon AS .05 .02
☐ 712 Don Mattingly AS .50 .23
☐ 713 Damaso Garcia AS .05 .02
☐ 714 George Brett AS .50 .23
☐ 715 Cal Ripken AS 1.00 .45
☐ 716 Rickey Henderson AS .40 .18
☐ 717 Dave Winfield AS .40 .18
☐ 718 George Bell AS .05 .02
☐ 719 Carlton Fisk AS .20 .09
☐ 720 Bret Saberhagen AS .05 .02
☐ 721 Ron Guidry AS .10 .05
☐ 722 Dan Quisenberry AS .05 .02
☐ 723 Marty Bystrom .05 .02
☐ 724 Tim Hulett .05 .02
☐ 725 Mario Soto .05 .02
☐ 726 Rick Dempsey TL .10 .05
☐ 727 David Green .05 .02
☐ 728 Mike Marshall .05 .02
☐ 729 Jim Beattie .05 .02
☐ 730 Ozzie Smith .50 .23
☐ 731 Don Robinson .05 .02
☐ 732 Floyd Youmans .05 .02
☐ 733 Ron Romanick .05 .02
☐ 734 Marty Barrett .05 .02
☐ 735 Dave Dravecky .10 .05
☐ 736 Glenn Wilson .05 .02
☐ 737 Pete Vuckovich .05 .02
☐ 738 Andre Robertson .05 .02
☐ 739 Dave Rozema .05 .02
☐ 740 Lance Parrish .10 .05
☐ 741 Pete Rose MG .20 .09
(Checklist back)
☐ 742 Frank Viola .10 .05
☐ 743 Pat Sheridan .05 .02
☐ 744 Lary Sorensen .05 .02
☐ 745 Willie Upshaw .05 .02
☐ 746 Denny Gonzalez .05 .02
☐ 747 Rick Cerone .05 .02
☐ 748 Steve Henderson .05 .02
☐ 749 Ed Jurak .05 .02
☐ 750 Gorman Thomas .05 .02
☐ 751 Howard Johnson .10 .05
☐ 752 Mike Krukow .05 .02
☐ 753 Dan Ford .05 .02
☐ 754 Pat Clements .05 .02
☐ 755 Harold Baines .20 .09
☐ 756 Rick Rhoden TL .05 .02
☐ 757 Darrell Porter .05 .02
☐ 758 Dave Anderson .05 .02
☐ 759 Moose Haas .05 .02
☐ 760 Andre Dawson .40 .18
☐ 761 Don Slaught .05 .02
☐ 762 Eric Show .05 .02
☐ 763 Terry Puhl .05 .02
☐ 764 Kevin Gross .05 .02
☐ 765 Don Baylor .20 .09
☐ 766 Rick Langford .05 .02
☐ 767 Jody Davis .05 .02
☐ 768 Vern Ruhle .05 .02
☐ 769 Harold Reynolds .40 .18
☐ 770 Vida Blue .10 .05
☐ 771 John McNamara MG .05 .02
(Checklist back)
☐ 772 Brian Downing .05 .02
☐ 773 Greg Pryor .05 .02
☐ 774 Terry Leach .05 .02
☐ 775 Al Oliver .10 .05
☐ 776 Gene Garber .05 .02
☐ 777 Wayne Krenchicki .05 .02
☐ 778 Jerry Hairston .05 .02
☐ 779 Rick Reuschel .05 .02
☐ 780 Robin Yount .40 .18
☐ 781 Joe Nolan .05 .02
☐ 782 Ken Landreaux .05 .02
☐ 783 Ricky Horton .05 .02
☐ 784 Alan Bannister .05 .02
☐ 785 Bob Stanley .05 .02
☐ 786 Mickey Hatcher TL .05 .02
☐ 787 Vance Law .05 .02
☐ 788 Marty Castillo .05 .02
☐ 789 Kurt Bevacqua .05 .02
☐ 790 Phil Niekro .40 .18
☐ 791 Checklist: 661-792 .10 .05
☐ 792 Charles Hudson .05 .02

1986 Topps Tiffany

These 792 cards form a parallel to the regular Topps set. These cards, available only through the Topps dealer network were issued in factory sealed boxes. These cards have a "glossy" front and a very clear back. These cards were printed in the Topps Ireland plant. Reports within the hobby indicate that it is believed that 5,000 of these sets were produced.

	MINT	NRMT
COMPLETE FACT.SET (792)	150.00	70.00
COMMON CARD (1-792)	.15	.07
*STARS: 5X to 10 X BASIC CARDS		
*ROOKIES: 4X to 8X BASIC CARDS		

1986 Topps Glossy All-Stars

This 22-card standard-size set was distributed as an insert, one card per rak pack. The players featured are the starting lineups of the 1985 All-Star Game played in Minnesota. The cards are very colorful and have a high gloss finish.

	MINT	NRMT
COMPLETE SET (22)	5.00	2.20
COMMON CARD (1-22)	.05	.02
☐ 1 Sparky Anderson MG	.05	.02
☐ 2 Eddie Murray	.75	.35
☐ 3 Lou Whitaker	.10	.05
☐ 4 George Brett	1.00	.45
☐ 5 Cal Ripken	2.00	.90
☐ 6 Jim Rice	.10	.05
☐ 7 Rickey Henderson	.40	.18
☐ 8 Dave Winfield	.50	.23
☐ 9 Carlton Fisk	.40	.18
☐ 10 Jack Morris	.10	.05
☐ 11 AL Team Photo	.05	.02
☐ 12 Dick Williams MG	.05	.02
☐ 13 Steve Garvey	.10	.05
☐ 14 Tom Herr	.05	.02
☐ 15 Graig Nettles	.10	.05
☐ 16 Ozzie Smith	1.00	.45
☐ 17 Tony Gwynn	1.25	.55
☐ 18 Dale Murphy	.25	.11
☐ 19 Darryl Strawberry	.10	.05
☐ 20 Terry Kennedy	.05	.02
☐ 21 LaMarr Hoyt	.05	.02
☐ 22 NL Team Photo	.05	.02

1986 Topps Glossy Send-Ins

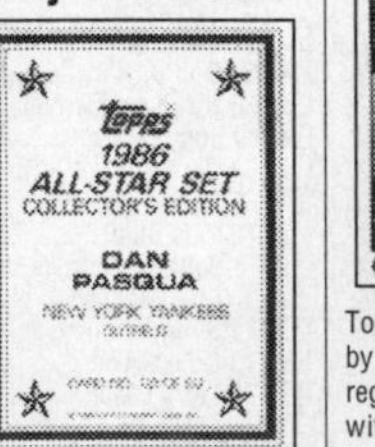

This 60-card glossy standard-size set was produced by Topps and distributed ten cards at a time based on the offer found on the wax packs. Each series of ten cards was available by sending in 1.00 plus six "special offer" cards inserted one per wax pack. The card backs are printed in red and blue on white card stock. The card fronts feature a white border and a green frame surrounding a full-color photo of the player.

	MINT	NRMT
COMPLETE SET (60)	12.50	5.50
COMMON CARD (1-60)	.10	.05
☐ 1 Oddibe McDowell	.10	.05
☐ 2 Reggie Jackson	.75	.35
☐ 3 Fernando Valenzuela	.20	.09
☐ 4 Jack Clark	.10	.05
☐ 5 Rickey Henderson	.60	.25
☐ 6 Steve Balboni	.10	.05
☐ 7 Keith Hernandez	.20	.09
☐ 8 Lance Parrish	.20	.09
☐ 9 Willie McGee	.20	.09
☐ 10 Chris Brown	.10	.05
☐ 11 Darryl Strawberry	.20	.09
☐ 12 Ron Guidry	.20	.09
☐ 13 Dave Parker	.20	.09
☐ 14 Cal Ripken	4.00	1.80
☐ 15 Tim Raines	.20	.09
☐ 16 Rod Carew	.75	.35
☐ 17 Mike Schmidt	1.25	.55
☐ 18 George Brett	2.00	.90
☐ 19 Joe Hesketh	.10	.05
☐ 20 Dan Pasqua	.10	.05
☐ 21 Vince Coleman	.20	.09
☐ 22 Tom Seaver	.50	.23
☐ 23 Gary Carter	.30	.14
☐ 24 Orel Hershiser	.20	.09
☐ 25 Pedro Guerrero	.10	.05
☐ 26 Wade Boggs	.75	.35
☐ 27 Bret Saberhagen	.20	.09
☐ 28 Carlton Fisk	.75	.35
☐ 29 Kirk Gibson	.20	.09
☐ 30 Brian Fisher	.10	.05
☐ 31 Don Mattingly	2.50	1.10
☐ 32 Tom Herr	.10	.05
☐ 33 Eddie Murray	1.25	.55
☐ 34 Ryne Sandberg	2.00	.90
☐ 35 Dan Quisenberry	.10	.05
☐ 36 Jim Rice	.20	.09
☐ 37 Dale Murphy	.30	.14
☐ 38 Steve Garvey	.20	.09
☐ 39 Roger McDowell	.10	.05
☐ 40 Earnie Riles	.10	.05
☐ 41 Dwight Gooden	.30	.14
☐ 42 Dave Winfield	.60	.25
☐ 43 Dave Stieb	.10	.05
☐ 44 Bob Horner	.10	.05
☐ 45 Nolan Ryan	4.00	1.80
☐ 46 Ozzie Smith	2.00	.90
☐ 47 George Bell	.10	.05
☐ 48 Gorman Thomas	.10	.05
☐ 49 Tom Browning	.10	.05
☐ 50 Larry Sheets	.10	.05
☐ 51 Pete Rose	1.25	.55
☐ 52 Brett Butler	.20	.09
☐ 53 John Tudor	.10	.05
☐ 54 Phil Bradley	.10	.05
☐ 55 Jeff Reardon	.20	.09
☐ 56 Rich Gossage	.20	.09
☐ 57 Tony Gwynn	2.50	1.10
☐ 58 Ozzie Guillen	.20	.09
☐ 59 Glenn Davis	.10	.05
☐ 60 Darrell Evans	.10	.05

1986 Topps Wax Box Cards

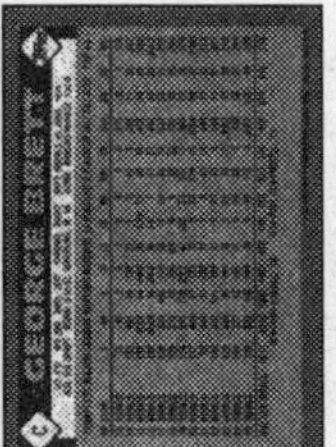

Topps printed cards (each measuring the standard 2 1/2" by 3 1/2") on the bottoms of their wax pack boxes for their regular issue cards; there are four different boxes, each with four cards. These sixteen cards ("numbered" A through P) are listed below; they are not considered an integral part of the regular set but are considered a separate set. The order of the set is alphabetical by player's name. These wax box cards are styled almost exactly like the 1986 Topps regular issue cards. Complete boxes would be worth an additional 25 percent premium over the prices below. The card lettering is sequenced in alphabetical order.

	MINT	NRMT
COMPLETE SET (16)	8.00	3.60
COMMON CARD (A-P)	.25	.11
☐ A George Bell	.25	.11
☐ B Wade Boggs	1.00	.45
☐ C George Brett	2.00	.90
☐ D Vince Coleman	.40	.18
☐ E Carlton Fisk	.75	.35
☐ F Dwight Gooden	.60	.25
☐ G Pedro Guerrero	.40	.18
☐ H Ron Guidry	.40	.18
☐ I Reggie Jackson	1.00	.45
☐ J Don Mattingly	2.00	.90
☐ K Oddibe McDowell	.25	.11
☐ L Willie McGee	.40	.18
☐ M Dale Murphy	.60	.25
☐ N Pete Rose	1.50	.70
☐ O Bret Saberhagen	.40	.18
☐ P Fernando Valenzuela	.40	.18

1986 Topps Traded

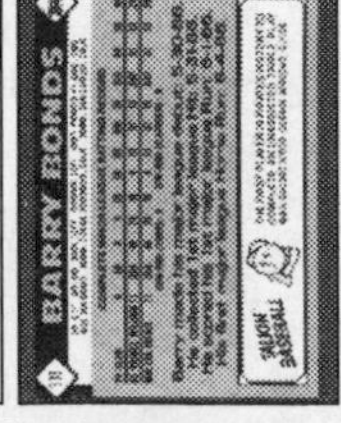

This 132-card standard-size Traded set was distributed in factory set form in a red and white box through hobby dealers. The cards are identical in style to regular-issue 1986 Topps cards except for whiter stock and t-suffixed numbering. The key extended Rookie Cards in this set are Barry Bonds, Bobby Bonilla, Jose Canseco, Will Clark, Andres Galarraga, Bo Jackson, Wally Joyner, John Kruk, and Kevin Mitchell.

	MINT	NRMT
COMP.FACT.SET (132)	8.00	3.60
COMMON CARD (1T-132T)	.05	.02
☐ 1T Andy Allanson	.05	.02
☐ 2T Neil Allen	.05	.02
☐ 3T Joaquin Andujar	.05	.02
☐ 4T Paul Assenmacher	.05	.02
☐ 5T Scott Bailes	.05	.02
☐ 6T Don Baylor	.20	.09
☐ 7T Steve Bedrosian	.05	.02
☐ 8T Juan Beniquez	.05	.02
☐ 9T Juan Berenguer	.05	.02
☐ 10T Mike Bielecki	.05	.02
☐ 11T Barry Bonds	3.00	1.35
☐ 12T Bobby Bonilla	.75	.35
☐ 13T Juan Bonilla	.05	.02
☐ 14T Rich Bordi	.05	.02
☐ 15T Steve Boros MG	.05	.02
☐ 16T Rick Burleson	.05	.02
☐ 17T Bill Campbell	.05	.02
☐ 18T Tom Candiotti	.05	.02
☐ 19T John Cangelosi	.05	.02
☐ 20T Jose Canseco	1.50	.70
☐ 21T Carmen Castillo	.05	.02
☐ 22T Rick Cerone	.05	.02
☐ 23T John Cerutti	.05	.02
☐ 24T Will Clark	1.25	.55
☐ 25T Mark Clear	.05	.02
☐ 26T Darnell Coles	.05	.02
☐ 27T Dave Collins	.05	.02
☐ 28T Tim Conroy	.05	.02
☐ 29T Joe Cowley	.05	.02
☐ 30T Joel Davis	.05	.02
☐ 31T Rob Deer	.05	.02
☐ 32T John Denny	.05	.02
☐ 33T Mike Easler	.05	.02
☐ 34T Mark Eichhorn	.05	.02
☐ 35T Steve Farr	.05	.02
☐ 36T Scott Fletcher	.05	.02
☐ 37T Terry Forster	.05	.02
☐ 38T Terry Francona	.05	.02
☐ 39T Jim Fregosi MG	.05	.02
☐ 40T Andres Galarraga	1.50	.70
☐ 41T Ken Griffey	.10	.05
☐ 42T Bill Gullickson	.05	.02
☐ 43T Jose Guzman	.05	.02
☐ 44T Moose Haas	.05	.02
☐ 45T Billy Hatcher	.05	.02
☐ 46T Mike Heath	.05	.02
☐ 47T Tom Hume	.05	.02
☐ 48T Pete Incaviglia	.40	.18
☐ 49T Dane Iorg	.05	.02
☐ 50T Bo Jackson	.75	.35
☐ 51T Wally Joyner	.40	.18
☐ 52T Charlie Kerfeld	.05	.02
☐ 53T Eric King	.05	.02
☐ 54T Bob Kipper	.05	.02
☐ 55T Wayne Krenchicki	.05	.02
☐ 56T John Kruk	.40	.18
☐ 57T Mike LaCoss	.05	.02
☐ 58T Pete Ladd	.05	.02
☐ 59T Mike Laga	.05	.02
☐ 60T Hal Lanier MG	.05	.02
☐ 61T Dave LaPoint	.05	.02
☐ 62T Rudy Law	.05	.02
☐ 63T Rick Leach	.05	.02
☐ 64T Tim Leary	.05	.02
☐ 65T Dennis Leonard	.05	.02
☐ 66T Jim Leyland MG	.05	.02
☐ 67T Steve Lyons	.05	.02
☐ 68T Mickey Mahler	.05	.02
☐ 69T Candy Maldonado	.05	.02
☐ 70T Roger Mason	.05	.02
☐ 71T Bob McClure	.05	.02
☐ 72T Andy McGaffigan	.05	.02
☐ 73T Gene Michael MG	.05	.02
☐ 74T Kevin Mitchell	.40	.18
☐ 75T Omar Moreno	.05	.02
☐ 76T Jerry Mumphrey	.05	.02
☐ 77T Phil Niekro	.40	.18
☐ 78T Randy Niemann	.05	.02
☐ 79T Juan Nieves	.05	.02
☐ 80T Otis Nixon	.40	.18
☐ 81T Bob Ojeda	.10	.05
☐ 82T Jose Oquendo	.05	.02
☐ 83T Tom Paciorek	.05	.02
☐ 84T David Palmer	.05	.02
☐ 85T Frank Pastore	.05	.02
☐ 86T Lou Piniella MG	.10	.05
☐ 87T Dan Plesac	.05	.02
☐ 88T Darrell Porter	.05	.02
☐ 89T Rey Quinones	.05	.02
☐ 90T Gary Redus	.05	.02
☐ 91T Bip Roberts	.40	.18
☐ 92T Billy Joe Robidoux	.05	.02
☐ 93T Jeff D. Robinson	.05	.02
☐ 94T Gary Roenicke	.05	.02

☐ 95T Ed Romero	.05	.02
☐ 96T Argenis Salazar	.05	.02
☐ 97T Joe Sambito	.05	.02
☐ 98T Billy Sample	.05	.02
☐ 99T Dave Schmidt	.05	.02
☐ 100T Ken Schrom	.05	.02
☐ 101T Tom Seaver	.50	.23
☐ 102T Ted Simmons	.10	.05
☐ 103T Sammy Stewart	.05	.02
☐ 104T Kurt Stillwell	.05	.02
☐ 105T Franklin Stubbs	.05	.02
☐ 106T Dale Sveum	.05	.02
☐ 107T Chuck Tanner MG	.05	.02
☐ 108T Danny Tartabull	.10	.05
☐ 109T Tim Teufel	.05	.02
☐ 110T Bob Tewksbury	.10	.05
☐ 111T Andres Thomas	.05	.02
☐ 112T Milt Thompson	.05	.02
☐ 113T Robby Thompson	.10	.05
☐ 114T Jay Tibbs	.05	.02
☐ 115T Wayne Tolleson	.05	.02
☐ 116T Alex Trevino	.05	.02
☐ 117T Manny Trillo	.05	.02
☐ 118T Ed VandeBerg	.05	.02
☐ 119T Ozzie Virgil	.05	.02
☐ 120T Bob Walk	.05	.02
☐ 121T Gene Walter	.05	.02
☐ 122T Claudell Washington	.05	.02
☐ 123T Bill Wegman	.05	.02
☐ 124T Dick Williams MG	.10	.05
☐ 125T Mitch Williams	.10	.05
☐ 126T Bobby Witt	.20	.09
☐ 127T Todd Worrell	.40	.18
☐ 128T George Wright	.05	.02
☐ 129T Ricky Wright	.05	.02
☐ 130T Steve Yeager	.05	.02
☐ 131T Paul Zuvella	.05	.02
☐ 132T Checklist 1T-132T	.05	.02

1986 Topps Traded Tiffany

For the third consecutive season, Topps issued a Tiffany Update issue to go with their regular issue. These 132 cards feature the same players as in the regular set but have a "glossy" front and very clear back. These cards, released through Topps hobby dealers, were sent out only if the dealer ordered the regular Tiffany set. These cards were printed in Topps' Ireland plant.

	MINT	NRMT
COMPLETE FACT.SET (132)	50.00	22.00
COMMON CARD (1T-132T)	.20	.09
*STARS: 4X to 8X BASIC CARDS		
*ROOKIES: 2X to 4X BASIC CARDS		

1986 Topps 3-D

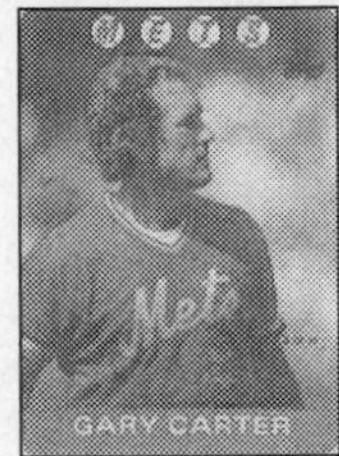

This set consists of 30 plastic-sculpted "cards" each measuring 4 3/8" by 6". Each card was individually wrapped in a red paper wrapper. The card back is blank except for two adhesive strips which could used for mounting the card. Cards are numbered on the front in the lower right corner above the name.

	MINT	NRMT
COMPLETE SET (30)	20.00	9.00
COMMON CARD (1-30)	.25	.11
☐ 1 Bert Blyleven	.25	.11
☐ 2 Gary Carter	.75	.35
☐ 3 Wade Boggs	2.00	.90
☐ 4 Dwight Gooden	.50	.23
☐ 5 George Brett	4.00	1.80
☐ 6 Rich Gossage	.50	.23
☐ 7 Darrell Evans	.25	.11
☐ 8 Pedro Guerrero	.25	.11
☐ 9 Ron Guidry	.50	.23
☐ 10 Keith Hernandez	.50	.23
☐ 11 Rickey Henderson	1.50	.70
☐ 12 Orel Hershiser	.50	.23
☐ 13 Reggie Jackson	1.50	.70
☐ 14 Willie McGee	.50	.23
☐ 15 Don Mattingly	5.00	2.20
☐ 16 Dale Murphy	.75	.35
☐ 17 Jack Morris	.50	.23
☐ 18 Dave Parker	.50	.23
☐ 19 Eddie Murray	2.00	.90
☐ 20 Jeff Reardon	.25	.11
☐ 21 Dan Quisenberry	.25	.11
☐ 22 Pete Rose	2.00	.90
☐ 23 Jim Rice	.50	.23
☐ 24 Mike Schmidt	2.00	.90
☐ 25 Bret Saberhagen	.50	.23
☐ 26 Darryl Strawberry	.50	.23
☐ 27 Dave Stieb	.25	.11
☐ 28 John Tudor	.25	.11
☐ 29 Dave Winfield	1.50	.70
☐ 30 Fernando Valenzuela	.50	.23

1986 Topps Mini Leaders

The 1986 Topps Mini set of Major League Leaders features 66 cards of leaders of the various statistical categories for the 1985 season. The cards are numbered on the back and measure approximately 2 1/8" by 2 15/16". They are very similar in design to the Team Leader "Dean" cards in the 1986 Topps regular issue. The order of the set numbering is alphabetical by player's name as well as alphabetical by team city name within league.

	MINT	NRMT
COMPLETE SET (66)	4.00	1.80
COMMON CARD (1-66)	.05	.02
☐ 1 Eddie Murray	.50	.23
☐ 2 Cal Ripken	1.50	.70
☐ 3 Wade Boggs	.40	.18
☐ 4 Dennis Boyd	.05	.02
☐ 5 Dwight Evans	.10	.05
☐ 6 Bruce Hurst	.05	.02
☐ 7 Gary Pettis	.05	.02
☐ 8 Harold Baines	.10	.05
☐ 9 Floyd Bannister	.05	.02
☐ 10 Britt Burns	.05	.02
☐ 11 Carlton Fisk	.30	.14
☐ 12 Brett Butler	.10	.05
☐ 13 Darrell Evans	.10	.05
☐ 14 Jack Morris	.10	.05
☐ 15 Lance Parrish	.05	.02
☐ 16 Walt Terrell	.05	.02
☐ 17 Steve Balboni	.05	.02
☐ 18 George Brett	.75	.35
☐ 19 Charlie Leibrandt	.05	.02
☐ 20 Bret Saberhagen	.10	.05
☐ 21 Lonnie Smith	.05	.02
☐ 22 Willie Wilson	.05	.02
☐ 23 Bert Blyleven	.10	.05
☐ 24 Mike Smithson	.05	.02
☐ 25 Frank Viola	.10	.05
☐ 26 Ron Guidry	.10	.05
☐ 27 Rickey Henderson	.30	.14
☐ 28 Don Mattingly	1.00	.45
☐ 29 Dave Winfield	.25	.11
☐ 30 Mike Moore	.05	.02
☐ 31 Gorman Thomas	.05	.02
☐ 32 Toby Harrah	.05	.02
☐ 33 Charlie Hough	.05	.02
☐ 34 Doyle Alexander	.05	.02
☐ 35 Jimmy Key	.15	.07
☐ 36 Dave Stieb	.05	.02
☐ 37 Dale Murphy	.15	.07
☐ 38 Keith Moreland	.05	.02
☐ 39 Ryne Sandberg	.75	.35
☐ 40 Tom Browning	.05	.02
☐ 41 Dave Parker	.10	.05
☐ 42 Mario Soto	.05	.02
☐ 43 Nolan Ryan	1.50	.70
☐ 44 Pedro Guerrero	.05	.02
☐ 45 Orel Hershiser	.15	.07
☐ 46 Mike Scioscia	.05	.02
☐ 47 Fernando Valenzuela	.10	.05
☐ 48 Bob Welch	.05	.02
☐ 49 Tim Raines	.10	.05
☐ 50 Gary Carter	.15	.07
☐ 51 Sid Fernandez	.05	.02
☐ 52 Dwight Gooden	.10	.05
☐ 53 Keith Hernandez	.10	.05
☐ 54 Juan Samuel	.05	.02
☐ 55 Mike Schmidt	.50	.23
☐ 56 Glenn Wilson	.05	.02
☐ 57 Rick Reuschel	.05	.02
☐ 58 Joaquin Andujar	.05	.02
☐ 59 Jack Clark	.05	.02
☐ 60 Vince Coleman	.10	.05
☐ 61 Danny Cox	.05	.02
☐ 62 Tom Herr	.05	.02
☐ 63 Willie McGee	.10	.05
☐ 64 John Tudor	.05	.02
☐ 65 Tony Gwynn	1.00	.45
☐ 66 Checklist Card	.05	.02

1986 Topps/O-Pee-Chee Stickers

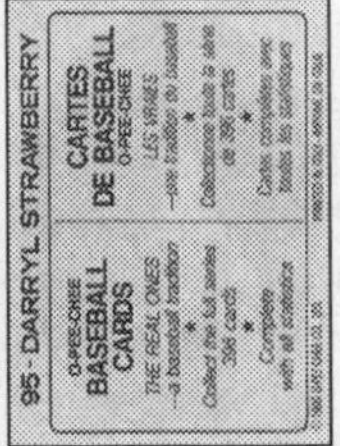

Made in Italy for O-Pee-Chee by Panini, these 315 stickers measure approximately 2 1/8" by 3" and are numbered on both front and back. The fronts feature white-bordered color player photos. The horizontal backs carry a bilingual ad for O-Pee-Chee. An album onto which the stickers could be affixed was available at retail stores. The album and the sticker numbering are organized as follows: 1985 Highlights (1-10), 1985 Championship Series (11-16), 1985 World Series (17-23), Houston Astros (24-33), Atlanta Braves (34-43), St. Louis Cardinals (44-53), Chicago Cubs (54-63), Los Angeles Dodgers (64-73), Montreal Expos (74-83), San Francisco Giants (84-93), New York Mets (94-103), San Diego Padres (104-113), Philadelphia Phillies (114-123), Pittsburgh Pirates (124-133), Cincinnati Reds (134-143), 1985 NL Stat Leaders (144, 145), Foil All-Stars (146-163), 1985 AL Stat Leaders (164, 165), Oakland A's (166-175), California Angels (176-185), Toronto Blue Jays (186-195), Milwaukee Brewers (196-205), Cleveland Indians (206-215), Seattle Mariners (216-225), Baltimore Orioles (226-235), Texas Rangers (236-245), Boston Red Sox (246-255), Kansas City Royals (256-265), Detroit Tigers (266-275), Minnesota Twins (276-285), Chicago White Sox (286-295), New York Yankees (296-305), and Future Stars (306-315). For those stickers featuring more than one player, the other numbers on that sticker are given below in parentheses. The Topps stickers contain offers on the back to obtain either a trip for four to Spring Training of the team of your choice or a complete set of Topps baseball cards directly from Topps.

	MINT	NRMT
COMPLETE SET (315)	15.00	6.75
COMMON STICKER (1-315)	.05	.02
COMMON FOIL PLAYER	.10	.05
*TOPPS AND OPC: SAME VALUE		
☐ 1 Pete Rose FOIL (Top half)	.60	.25
☐ 2 Pete Rose FOIL (Bottom half)	.60	.25
☐ 3 George Brett (175)	.75	.35
☐ 4 Rod Carew (178)	.40	.18
☐ 5 Vince Coleman (179)	.15	.07
☐ 6 Dwight Gooden (180)	.30	.14
☐ 7 Phil Niekro (181)	.15	.07
☐ 8 Tony Perez (182)	.15	.07
☐ 9 Nolan Ryan (183)	2.00	.90
☐ 10 Tom Seaver (184)	.50	.23
☐ 11 NL Championship (Ozzie Smith batting)	.15	.07
☐ 12 NL Championship (Bill Madlock)	.10	.05
☐ 13 NL Championship (Cardinals celebrate)	.10	.05
☐ 14 AL Championship (Al Oliver swings)	.10	.05
☐ 15 AL Championship (Jim Sundberg)	.05	.02
☐ 16 AL Championship (George Brett swings)	.75	.35
☐ 17 World Series	.10	.05

(Bret Saberhagen)
☐ 18 World Series .05 .02
(Dane Iorg swings)
☐ 19 World Series .05 .02
(Tito Landrum)
☐ 20 World Series .05 .02
(John Tudor)
☐ 21 World Series .05 .02
(Buddy Biancalana)
☐ 22 World Series .05 .02
(Darryl Motley)
☐ 23 World Series .30 .14
(George Brett and
Frank White)
☐ 24 Nolan Ryan 2.00 .90
☐ 25 Bill Doran .05 .02
☐ 26 Jose Cruz (185) .10 .05
☐ 27 Mike Scott (188) .05 .02
☐ 28 Kevin Bass (189) .05 .02
☐ 29 Glenn Davis (190) .10 .05
☐ 30 Mark Bailey (191) .05 .02
☐ 31 Dave Smith (192) .05 .02
☐ 32 Phil Garner (193) .05 .02
☐ 33 Dickie Thon (194) .05 .02
☐ 34 Bob Horner .05 .02
☐ 35 Dale Murphy .15 .07
☐ 36 Glenn Hubbard (195) .05 .02
☐ 37 Bruce Sutter (198) .10 .05
☐ 38 Ken Oberkfell (199) .05 .02
☐ 39 Claudell Washington .05 .02
(200)
☐ 40 Steve Bedrosian (201) .05 .02
☐ 41 Terry Harper (202) .05 .02
☐ 42 Rafael Ramirez (203) .05 .02
☐ 43 Rick Mahler (204) .05 .02
☐ 44 Joaquin Andujar .05 .02
☐ 45 Willie McGee .10 .05
☐ 46 Ozzie Smith (205) .40 .18
☐ 47 Vince Coleman (208) .15 .07
☐ 48 Danny Cox (209) .05 .02
☐ 49 Tom Herr (210) .05 .02
☐ 50 Jack Clark (211) .10 .05
☐ 51 Andy Van Slyke (212) .10 .05
☐ 52 John Tudor (213) .05 .02
☐ 53 Terry Pendleton(214) .15 .07
☐ 54 Keith Moreland .05 .02
☐ 55 Ryne Sandberg .60 .25
☐ 56 Lee Smith (215) .15 .07
☐ 57 Steve Trout (218) .05 .02
☐ 58 Jody Davis (219) .05 .02
☐ 59 Gary Matthews (220) .05 .02
☐ 60 Leon Durham (221) .05 .02
☐ 61 Rick Sutcliffe (222) .05 .02
☐ 62 Dennis Eckersley .15 .07
(223)
☐ 63 Bob Dernier (224) .05 .02
☐ 64 Fernando Valenzuela .10 .05
☐ 65 Pedro Guerrero .05 .02
☐ 66 Jerry Reuss (225) .05 .02
☐ 67 Greg Brock (228) .05 .02
☐ 68 Mike Scioscia (229) .05 .02
☐ 69 Ken Howell (230) .05 .02
☐ 70 Bill Madlock (231) .05 .02
☐ 71 Mike Marshall (232) .05 .02
☐ 72 Steve Sax (233) .05 .02
☐ 73 Orel Hershiser (234) .15 .07
☐ 74 Andre Dawson .15 .07
☐ 75 Tim Raines .10 .05
☐ 76 Jeff Reardon (235) .10 .05
☐ 77 Hubie Brooks (238) .05 .02
☐ 78 Bill Gullickson(239) .05 .02
☐ 79 Bryn Smith (240) .05 .02
☐ 80 Terry Francona (241) .05 .02
☐ 81 Vance Law (242) .05 .02
☐ 82 Tim Wallach (243) .05 .02
☐ 83 He.Winningham (244) .05 .02
☐ 84 Jeff Leonard .05 .02
☐ 85 Chris Brown .05 .02
☐ 86 Scott Garrelts (245) .05 .02
☐ 87 Jose Uribe (248) .05 .02
☐ 88 Manny Trillo (249) .05 .02
☐ 89 Dan Driessen (250) .05 .02
☐ 90 Dan Gladden (251) .05 .02
☐ 91 Mark Davis (252) .05 .02
☐ 92 Bob Brenly (253) .05 .02
☐ 93 Mike Krukow (254) .05 .02
☐ 94 Dwight Gooden .30 .14
☐ 95 Darryl Strawberry .15 .07
☐ 96 Gary Carter (255) .10 .05
☐ 97 Wally Backman (258) .05 .02
☐ 98 Ron Darling (259) .05 .02
☐ 99 Keith Hernandez(260) .10 .05
☐ 100 George Foster (261) .10 .05
☐ 101 Howard Johnson (262) .10 .05
☐ 102 Rafael Santana (263) .05 .02
☐ 103 Roger McDowell (264) .05 .02
☐ 104 Steve Garvey .15 .07
☐ 105 Tony Gwynn 1.00 .45
☐ 106 Graig Nettles (265) .10 .05
☐ 107 Rich Gossage (268) .10 .05
☐ 108 Andy Hawkins (269) .05 .02
☐ 109 Carmelo Martinez .05 .02
(270)
☐ 110 Garry Templeton(271) .05 .02
☐ 111 Terry Kennedy (272) .05 .02
☐ 112 Tim Flannery (273) .05 .02
☐ 113 LaMarr Hoyt (274) .05 .02
☐ 114 Mike Schmidt .60 .25
☐ 115 Ozzie Virgil .05 .02
☐ 116 Steve Carlton (275) .40 .18
☐ 117 Garry Maddox (278) .05 .02
☐ 118 Glenn Wilson (279) .05 .02
☐ 119 Kevin Gross (280) .05 .02
☐ 120 Von Hayes (281) .05 .02
☐ 121 Juan Samuel (282) .05 .02
☐ 122 Rick Schu (283) .05 .02
☐ 123 Shane Rawley (284) .05 .02
☐ 124 Johnny Ray .05 .02
☐ 125 Tony Pena .05 .02
☐ 126 Rick Reuschel (285) .05 .02
☐ 127 Sammy Khalifa (288) .05 .02
☐ 128 Marvell Wynne (289) .05 .02
☐ 129 Jason Thompson (290) .05 .02
☐ 130 Rick Rhoden (291) .05 .02
☐ 131 Bill Almon (292) .05 .02
☐ 132 Joe Orsulak (293) .05 .02
☐ 133 Jim Morrison (294) .05 .02
☐ 134 Pete Rose .75 .35
☐ 135 Dave Parker .10 .05
☐ 136 Mario Soto (295) .05 .02
☐ 137 Dave Concepcion(298) .10 .05
☐ 138 Ron Oester (299) .05 .02
☐ 139 Buddy Bell (300) .10 .05
☐ 140 Ted Power (301) .05 .02
☐ 141 Tom Browning (302) .05 .02
☐ 142 John Franco (303) .15 .07
☐ 143 Tony Perez (304) .15 .07
☐ 144 Willie McGee (305) .10 .05
☐ 145 Dale Murphy (306) .15 .07
☐ 146 Tony Gwynn FOIL 1.50 .70
☐ 147 Tom Herr FOIL .10 .05
☐ 148 Steve Garvey FOIL .30 .14
☐ 149 Dale Murphy FOIL .15 .07
☐ 150 Darryl Strawberry FOIL .30 .14
☐ 151 Graig Nettles FOIL .15 .07
☐ 152 Terry Kennedy FOIL .10 .05
☐ 153 Ozzie Smith FOIL .60 .25
☐ 154 LaMarr Hoyt FOIL .10 .05
☐ 155 Rickey Henderson FOIL .40 .18
☐ 156 Lou Whitaker FOIL .10 .05
☐ 157 George Brett FOIL 1.25 .55
☐ 158 Eddie Murray FOIL .50 .23
☐ 159 Cal Ripken FOIL 3.00 1.35
☐ 160 Dave Winfield FOIL .40 .18
☐ 161 Jim Rice FOIL .10 .05
☐ 162 Carlton Fisk FOIL .40 .18
☐ 163 Jack Morris FOIL .10 .05
☐ 164 Wade Boggs (307) .30 .14
☐ 165 Darrell Evans (308) .10 .05
☐ 166 Mike Davis .05 .02
☐ 167 Dave Kingman .10 .05
☐ 168 Alfredo Griffin(309) .05 .02
☐ 169 Carney Lansford(310) .10 .05
☐ 170 Bruce Bochte (311) .05 .02
☐ 171 Dwayne Murphy (312) .05 .02
☐ 172 Dave Collins (313) .05 .02
☐ 173 Chris Codiroli (314) .05 .02
☐ 174 Mike Heath (315) .05 .02
☐ 175 Jay Howell (3) .05 .02
☐ 176 Rod Carew .40 .18
☐ 177 Reggie Jackson .50 .23
☐ 178 Doug DeCinces (4) .05 .02
☐ 179 Bob Boone (5) .10 .05
☐ 180 Ron Romanick (6) .05 .02
☐ 181 Bob Grich (7) .10 .05
☐ 182 Donnie Moore (8) .05 .02
☐ 183 Brian Downing (9) .05 .02
☐ 184 Ruppert Jones (10) .05 .02
☐ 185 Juan Beniquez (26) .05 .02
☐ 186 Dave Stieb .05 .02
☐ 187 George Bell .05 .02
☐ 188 Willie Upshaw (27) .05 .02
☐ 189 Tom Henke (28) .10 .05
☐ 190 Damaso Garcia (29) .05 .02
☐ 191 Jimmy Key (30) .15 .07
☐ 192 Jesse Barfield (31) .05 .02
☐ 193 Dennis Lamp (32) .05 .02
☐ 194 Tony Fernandez (33) .05 .02
☐ 195 Lloyd Moseby (36) .05 .02
☐ 196 Cecil Cooper .10 .05
☐ 197 Robin Yount .15 .07
☐ 198 Rollie Fingers (37) .15 .07
☐ 199 Ted Simmons (38) .10 .05
☐ 200 Ben Oglivie (39) .05 .02
☐ 201 Moose Haas (40) .05 .02
☐ 202 Jim Gantner (41) .05 .02
☐ 203 Paul Molitor (42) .15 .07
☐ 204 Charlie Moore (43) .05 .02
☐ 205 Danny Darwin (46) .05 .02
☐ 206 Brett Butler .10 .05
☐ 207 Brook Jacoby .05 .02
☐ 208 Andre Thornton (47) .05 .02
☐ 209 Tom Waddell (48) .05 .02
☐ 210 Tony Bernazard (49) .05 .02
☐ 211 Julio Franco (50) .10 .05
☐ 212 Pat Tabler (51) .05 .02
☐ 213 Joe Carter (52) .30 .14
☐ 214 George Vukovich (53) .05 .02
☐ 215 Rich Thompson (56) .05 .02
☐ 216 Gorman Thomas .05 .02
☐ 217 Phil Bradley .05 .02
☐ 218 Alvin Davis (57) .05 .02
☐ 219 Jim Presley (58) .05 .02
☐ 220 Matt Young (59) .05 .02
☐ 221 Mike Moore (60) .05 .02
☐ 222 Dave Henderson (61) .05 .02
☐ 223 Ed Nunez (62) .05 .02
☐ 224 Spike Owen (63) .05 .02
☐ 225 Mark Langston (66) .10 .05
☐ 226 Cal Ripken 2.00 .90
☐ 227 Eddie Murray .30 .14
☐ 228 Fred Lynn (67) .10 .05
☐ 229 Lee Lacy (68) .05 .02
☐ 230 Scott McGregor (69) .05 .02
☐ 231 Storm Davis (70) .05 .02
☐ 232 Rick Dempsey (71) .10 .05
☐ 233 Mike Boddicker (72) .05 .02
☐ 234 Mike Young (73) .05 .02
☐ 235 Sammy Stewart (76) .05 .02
☐ 236 Pete O'Brien .05 .02
☐ 237 Oddibe McDowell .05 .02
☐ 238 Toby Harrah (77) .05 .02
☐ 239 Gary Ward (78) .05 .02
☐ 240 Larry Parrish (79) .05 .02
☐ 241 Charlie Hough (80) .10 .05
☐ 242 Burt Hooton (81) .05 .02
☐ 243 Don Slaught (82) .05 .02
☐ 244 Curt Wilkerson (83) .05 .02
☐ 245 Greg Harris (86) .05 .02
☐ 246 Jim Rice .10 .05
☐ 247 Wade Boggs .30 .14
☐ 248 Rich Gedman (87) .05 .02
☐ 249 Dennis Boyd (88) .05 .02
☐ 250 Marty Barrett (89) .05 .02
☐ 251 Dwight Evans (90) .10 .05
☐ 252 Bill Buckner (91) .10 .05
☐ 253 Bob Stanley (92) .05 .02
☐ 254 Tony Armas (93) .05 .02
☐ 255 Mike Easler (96) .05 .02
☐ 256 George Brett .75 .35
☐ 257 Dan Quisenberry .05 .02
☐ 258 Willie Wilson (97) .05 .02
☐ 259 Jim Sundberg (98) .05 .02
☐ 260 Bret Saberhagen (99) .15 .07
☐ 261 Bud Black (100) .05 .02
☐ 262 Charlie Leibrandt .05 .02
(101)
☐ 263 Frank White (102) .10 .05
☐ 264 Lonnie Smith (103) .05 .02
☐ 265 Steve Balboni (106) .05 .02
☐ 266 Kirk Gibson .10 .05
☐ 267 Alan Trammell .15 .07
☐ 268 Jack Morris (107) .10 .05
☐ 269 Darrell Evans (108) .10 .05
☐ 270 Dan Petry (109) .05 .02
☐ 271 Larry Herndon (110) .05 .02
☐ 272 Lou Whitaker (111) .10 .05
☐ 273 Lance Parrish (112) .10 .05
☐ 274 Chet Lemon (113) .05 .02
☐ 275 Willie Hernandez .05 .02
(116)
☐ 276 Tom Brunansky .05 .02
☐ 277 Kent Hrbek .10 .05
☐ 278 Mark Salas (117) .05 .02
☐ 279 Bert Blyleven (118) .10 .05
☐ 280 Tim Teufel (119) .05 .02
☐ 281 Ron Davis (120) .05 .02
☐ 282 Mike Smithson (121) .05 .02
☐ 283 Gary Gaetti (122) .10 .05
☐ 284 Frank Viola (123) .10 .05
☐ 285 Kirby Puckett (126) 1.50 .70
☐ 286 Carlton Fisk .30 .14
☐ 287 Tom Seaver .50 .23
☐ 288 Harold Baines (127) .10 .05
☐ 289 Ron Kittle (128) .05 .02
☐ 290 Bob James (129) .05 .02
☐ 291 Rudy Law (130) .05 .02
☐ 292 Britt Burns (131) .05 .02
☐ 293 Greg Walker (132) .05 .02
☐ 294 Ozzie Guillen (133) .15 .07
☐ 295 Tim Hulett (136) .05 .02
☐ 296 Don Mattingly 1.50 .70

Card	MINT	NRMT
☐ 297 Rickey Henderson	.25	.11
☐ 298 Dave Winfield (137)	.15	.07
☐ 299 Butch Wynegar (138)	.05	.02
☐ 300 Don Baylor (139)	.10	.05
☐ 301 Eddie Whitson (140)	.05	.02
☐ 302 Ron Guidry (141)	.10	.05
☐ 303 Dave Righetti (142)	.05	.02
☐ 304 Bobby Meacham (143)	.05	.02
☐ 305 Willie Randolph(144)	.10	.05
☐ 306 Vince Coleman (145)	.15	.07
☐ 307 Oddibe McDowell(164)	.05	.02
☐ 308 Larry Sheets (165)	.05	.02
☐ 309 Ozzie Guillen (168)	.15	.07
☐ 310 Ernie Riles (169)	.05	.02
☐ 311 Chris Brown (170)	.05	.02
☐ 312 Brian Fisher and	.05	.02
Roger McDowell (171)		
☐ 313 Tom Browning (172)	.05	.02
☐ 314 Glenn Davis (173)	.05	.02
☐ 315 Mark Salas (174)	.05	.02
☐ xx Album	1.00	.45

1986 Topps Super

This 60-card set actually consists of giant-sized versions of the Topps regular issue of some of the most popular players. The cards measure 4 7/8" by 6 7/8". Cards are very similar to the Topps regular issue; two exceptions are that on the back they are numbered differently and an additional line of type is printed at the bottom of the back noting an accomplishment of that player at the end of the 1985 season.

	MINT	NRMT
COMPLETE SET (60)	14.00	6.25
COMMON CARD (1-60)	.10	.05
☐ 1 Don Mattingly	2.50	1.10
☐ 2 Willie McGee	.20	.09
☐ 3 Bret Saberhagen	.20	.09
☐ 4 Dwight Gooden	.30	.14
☐ 5 Dan Quisenberry	.10	.05
☐ 6 Jeff Reardon	.10	.05
☐ 7 Ozzie Guillen	.10	.05
☐ 8 Vince Coleman	.20	.09
☐ 9 Harold Baines	.20	.09
☐ 10 Jorge Bell	.10	.05
☐ 11 Bert Blyleven	.20	.09
☐ 12 Wade Boggs	.75	.35
☐ 13 Phil Bradley	.10	.05
☐ 14 George Brett	1.25	.55
☐ 15 Hubie Brooks	.10	.05
☐ 16 Tom Browning	.10	.05
☐ 17 Bill Buckner	.10	.05
☐ 18 Brett Butler	.20	.09
☐ 19 Gary Carter	.30	.14
☐ 20 Cecil Cooper	.10	.05
☐ 21 Darrell Evans	.10	.05
☐ 22 Dwight Evans	.20	.09
☐ 23 Carlton Fisk	.30	.14
☐ 24 Steve Garvey	.30	.14
☐ 25 Kirk Gibson	.20	.09
☐ 26 Rich Gossage	.20	.09
☐ 27 Pedro Guerrero	.10	.05
☐ 28 Ron Guidry	.20	.09
☐ 29 Tony Gwynn	2.00	.90
☐ 30 Rickey Henderson	.60	.25
☐ 31 Keith Hernandez	.20	.09
☐ 32 Tom Herr	.10	.05
☐ 33 Orel Hershiser	.30	.14
☐ 34 Jay Howell	.10	.05
☐ 35 Reggie Jackson	.60	.25
☐ 36 Bob James	.10	.05
☐ 37 Charlie Leibrandt	.10	.05
☐ 38 Jack Morris	.20	.09
☐ 39 Dale Murphy	.30	.14
☐ 40 Eddie Murray	.75	.35
☐ 41 Dave Parker	.20	.09
☐ 42 Tim Raines	.20	.09
☐ 43 Jim Rice	.20	.09
☐ 44 Dave Righetti	.10	.05
☐ 45 Cal Ripken	3.00	1.35
☐ 46 Pete Rose	.75	.35
☐ 47 Nolan Ryan	3.00	1.35
☐ 48 Ryne Sandberg	1.50	.70
☐ 49 Mike Schmidt	.75	.35
☐ 50 Tom Seaver	.50	.23
☐ 51 Bryn Smith	.10	.05
☐ 52 Lee Smith	.30	.14
☐ 53 Ozzie Smith	1.50	.70
☐ 54 Dave Stieb	.10	.05
☐ 55 Darryl Strawberry	.30	.14
☐ 56 Gorman Thomas	.10	.05
☐ 57 John Tudor	.10	.05
☐ 58 Fernando Valenzuela	.20	.09
☐ 59 Willie Wilson	.10	.05
☐ 60 Dave Winfield	.60	.25

1987 Topps

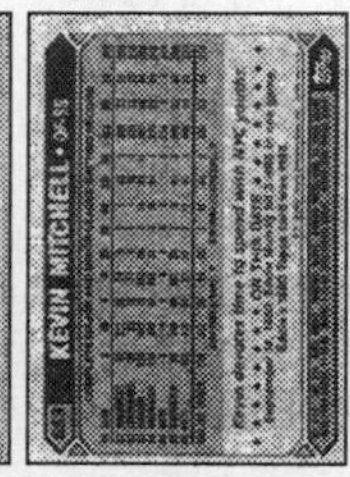

This set consists of 792 standard-size cards. Cards were primarily issued in 17-card wax packs, 50-card rack packs and factory sets. Card fronts feature wood grain borders encasing a color photo (reminiscent of Topps' classic 1962 baseball set). Subsets include Record Breakers (1-7), Turn Back the Clock (311-315), All-Star selections (595-616) and Team Leaders (scattered throughout the set). The manager cards contain a team checklist on back. The key Rookie Cards in this set are Barry Bonds, Bobby Bonilla, Will Clark, Mike Greenwell, Bo Jackson, Wally Joyner, John Kruk, Barry Larkin, Kevin Mitchell, Rafael Palmiero, Ruben Sierra, and Devon White.

	MINT	NRMT
COMPLETE SET (792)	12.00	5.50
COMP.FACT.SET (792)	15.00	6.75
COMMON CARD (1-792)	.05	.02
☐ 1 Roger Clemens RB	.15	.07
Most K's 9-inning game		
☐ 2 Jim Deshaies RB	.05	.02
Most cons. K's,		
start of game		
☐ 3 Dwight Evans RB	.10	.05
Earliest home run		
☐ 4 Davey Lopes RB	.05	.02
Most steals season,		
40-year-old		
☐ 5 Dave Righetti RB	.05	.02
Most saves season		
☐ 6 Ruben Sierra RB	.05	.02
Youngest player to		
switch hit HR's, game		
☐ 7 Todd Worrell RB	.10	.05
Most saves rookie season		
☐ 8 Terry Pendleton	.05	.02
☐ 9 Jay Tibbs	.05	.02
☐ 10 Cecil Cooper	.10	.05
☐ 11 Indians Team	.05	.02
(Mound conference)		
☐ 12 Jeff Sellers	.05	.02
☐ 13 Nick Esasky	.05	.02
☐ 14 Dave Stewart	.05	.02
☐ 15 Claudell Washington	.05	.02
☐ 16 Pat Clements	.05	.02
☐ 17 Pete O'Brien	.05	.02
☐ 18 Dick Howser MG	.10	.05
(Checklist back)		
☐ 19 Matt Young	.05	.02
☐ 20 Gary Carter	.20	.09
☐ 21 Mark Davis	.05	.02
☐ 22 Doug DeCinces	.05	.02
☐ 23 Lee Smith	.05	.02
☐ 24 Tony Walker	.05	.02
☐ 25 Bert Blyleven	.10	.05
☐ 26 Greg Brock	.05	.02
☐ 27 Joe Cowley	.05	.02
☐ 28 Rick Dempsey	.10	.05
☐ 29 Jimmy Key	.05	.02
☐ 30 Tim Raines	.10	.05
☐ 31 Braves Team	.05	.02
(Glenn Hubbard and		
Rafael Ramirez)		
☐ 32 Tim Leary	.05	.02
☐ 33 Andy Van Slyke	.10	.05
☐ 34 Jose Rijo	.05	.02
☐ 35 Sid Bream	.05	.02
☐ 36 Eric King	.05	.02
☐ 37 Marvell Wynne	.05	.02
☐ 38 Dennis Leonard	.05	.02
☐ 39 Marty Barrett	.05	.02
☐ 40 Dave Righetti	.05	.02
☐ 41 Bo Diaz	.05	.02
☐ 42 Gary Redus	.05	.02
☐ 43 Gene Michael MG	.05	.02
(Checklist back)		
☐ 44 Greg Harris	.05	.02
☐ 45 Jim Presley	.05	.02
☐ 46 Dan Gladden	.05	.02
☐ 47 Dennis Powell	.05	.02
☐ 48 Wally Backman	.05	.02
☐ 49 Terry Harper	.05	.02
☐ 50 Dave Smith	.05	.02
☐ 51 Mel Hall	.05	.02
☐ 52 Keith Atherton	.05	.02
☐ 53 Ruppert Jones	.05	.02
☐ 54 Bill Dawley	.05	.02
☐ 55 Tim Wallach	.05	.02
☐ 56 Brewers Team	.05	.02
(Mound conference)		
☐ 57 Scott Nielsen	.05	.02
☐ 58 Thad Bosley	.05	.02
☐ 59 Ken Dayley	.05	.02
☐ 60 Tony Pena	.05	.02
☐ 61 Bobby Thigpen	.10	.05
☐ 62 Bobby Meacham	.05	.02
☐ 63 Fred Toliver	.05	.02
☐ 64 Harry Spilman	.05	.02
☐ 65 Tom Browning	.05	.02
☐ 66 Marc Sullivan	.05	.02
☐ 67 Bill Swift	.05	.02
☐ 68 Tony LaRussa MG	.10	.05
(Checklist back)		
☐ 69 Lonnie Smith	.05	.02
☐ 70 Charlie Hough	.05	.02
☐ 71 Mike Aldrete	.10	.05
☐ 72 Walt Terrell	.05	.02
☐ 73 Dave Anderson	.05	.02
☐ 74 Dan Pasqua	.05	.02
☐ 75 Ron Darling	.05	.02
☐ 76 Rafael Ramirez	.05	.02
☐ 77 Bryan Oelkers	.05	.02
☐ 78 Tom Foley	.05	.02
☐ 79 Juan Nieves	.05	.02
☐ 80 Wally Joyner	.20	.09
☐ 81 Padres Team	.05	.02
(Andy Hawkins and		
Terry Kennedy)		
☐ 82 Rob Murphy	.05	.02
☐ 83 Mike Davis	.05	.02
☐ 84 Steve Lake	.05	.02
☐ 85 Kevin Bass	.05	.02
☐ 86 Nate Snell	.05	.02
☐ 87 Mark Salas	.05	.02
☐ 88 Ed Wojna	.05	.02
☐ 89 Ozzie Guillen	.10	.05
☐ 90 Dave Stieb	.05	.02
☐ 91 Harold Reynolds	.05	.02
☐ 92A Urbano Lugo	.20	.09
ERR (no trademark)		
☐ 92B Urbano Lugo COR	.05	.02
☐ 93 Jim Leyland MG	.10	.05
(Checklist back)		
☐ 94 Calvin Schiraldi	.05	.02
☐ 95 Oddibe McDowell	.05	.02
☐ 96 Frank Williams	.05	.02
☐ 97 Glenn Wilson	.05	.02
☐ 98 Bill Scherrer	.05	.02
☐ 99 Darryl Motley	.05	.02
(Now with Braves		
on card front)		
☐ 100 Steve Garvey	.20	.09
☐ 101 Carl Willis	.05	.02
☐ 102 Paul Zuvella	.05	.02
☐ 103 Rick Aguilera	.10	.05
☐ 104 Billy Sample	.05	.02
☐ 105 Floyd Youmans	.05	.02
☐ 106 Blue Jays Team	.05	.02
(George Bell and		
Jesse Barfield)		
☐ 107 John Butcher	.05	.02
☐ 108 Jim Gantner UER	.05	.02
(Brewers logo		
reversed)		
☐ 109 R.J. Reynolds	.05	.02
☐ 110 John Tudor	.05	.02
☐ 111 Alfredo Griffin	.05	.02
☐ 112 Alan Ashby	.05	.02
☐ 113 Neil Allen	.05	.02
☐ 114 Billy Beane	.05	.02
☐ 115 Donnie Moore	.05	.02
☐ 116 Bill Russell	.05	.02
☐ 117 Jim Beattie	.05	.02

☐ 118 Bobby Valentine MG	.05	.02
(Checklist back)		
☐ 119 Ron Robinson	.05	.02
☐ 120 Eddie Murray	.20	.09
☐ 121 Kevin Romine	.05	.02
☐ 122 Jim Clancy	.05	.02
☐ 123 John Kruk	.10	.05
☐ 124 Ray Fontenot	.05	.02
☐ 125 Bob Brenly	.05	.02
☐ 126 Mike Loynd	.05	.02
☐ 127 Vance Law	.05	.02
☐ 128 Checklist 1-132	.05	.02
☐ 129 Rick Cerone	.05	.02
☐ 130 Dwight Gooden	.20	.09
☐ 131 Pirates Team	.05	.02
(Sid Bream and		
Tony Pena)		
☐ 132 Paul Assenmacher	.05	.02
☐ 133 Jose Oquendo	.05	.02
☐ 134 Rich Yett	.05	.02
☐ 135 Mike Easler	.05	.02
☐ 136 Ron Romanick	.05	.02
☐ 137 Jerry Willard	.05	.02
☐ 138 Roy Lee Jackson	.05	.02
☐ 139 Devon White	.20	.09
☐ 140 Bret Saberhagen	.05	.02
☐ 141 Herm Winningham	.05	.02
☐ 142 Rick Sutcliffe	.05	.02
☐ 143 Steve Boros MG	.05	.02
(Checklist back)		
☐ 144 Mike Scioscia	.05	.02
☐ 145 Charlie Kerfeld	.05	.02
☐ 146 Tracy Jones	.05	.02
☐ 147 Randy Niemann	.05	.02
☐ 148 Dave Collins	.05	.02
☐ 149 Ray Searage	.05	.02
☐ 150 Wade Boggs	.20	.09
☐ 151 Mike LaCoss	.05	.02
☐ 152 Toby Harrah	.05	.02
☐ 153 Duane Ward	.10	.05
☐ 154 Tom O'Malley	.05	.02
☐ 155 Eddie Whitson	.05	.02
☐ 156 Mariners Team	.05	.02
(Mound conference)		
☐ 157 Danny Darwin	.05	.02
☐ 158 Tim Teufel	.05	.02
☐ 159 Ed Olwine	.05	.02
☐ 160 Julio Franco	.10	.05
☐ 161 Steve Ontiveros	.05	.02
☐ 162 Mike LaValliere	.05	.02
☐ 163 Kevin Gross	.05	.02
☐ 164 Sammy Khalifa	.05	.02
☐ 165 Jeff Reardon	.10	.05
☐ 166 Bob Boone	.10	.05
☐ 167 Jim Deshaies	.05	.02
☐ 168 Lou Piniella MG	.10	.05
(Checklist back)		
☐ 169 Ron Washington	.05	.02
☐ 170 Bo Jackson	.30	.14
☐ 171 Chuck Cary	.05	.02
☐ 172 Ron Oester	.05	.02
☐ 173 Alex Trevino	.05	.02
☐ 174 Henry Cotto	.05	.02
☐ 175 Bob Stanley	.05	.02
☐ 176 Steve Buechele	.05	.02
☐ 177 Keith Moreland	.05	.02
☐ 178 Cecil Fielder	.05	.02
☐ 179 Bill Wegman	.05	.02
☐ 180 Chris Brown	.05	.02
☐ 181 Cardinals Team	.05	.02
(Mound conference)		
☐ 182 Lee Lacy	.05	.02
☐ 183 Andy Hawkins	.05	.02
☐ 184 Bobby Bonilla	.30	.14
☐ 185 Roger McDowell	.05	.02
☐ 186 Bruce Benedict	.05	.02
☐ 187 Mark Huismann	.05	.02
☐ 188 Tony Phillips	.05	.02
☐ 189 Joe Hesketh	.05	.02
☐ 190 Jim Sundberg	.05	.02
☐ 191 Charles Hudson	.05	.02
☐ 192 Cory Snyder	.05	.02
☐ 193 Roger Craig MG	.10	.05
(Checklist back)		
☐ 194 Kirk McCaskill	.05	.02
☐ 195 Mike Pagliarulo	.05	.02
☐ 196 Randy O'Neal UER	.05	.02
(Wrong ML career		
W-L totals)		
☐ 197 Mark Bailey	.05	.02
☐ 198 Lee Mazzilli	.05	.02
☐ 199 Mariano Duncan	.05	.02
☐ 200 Pete Rose	.25	.11
☐ 201 John Cangelosi	.05	.02
☐ 202 Ricky Wright	.05	.02
☐ 203 Mike Kingery	.10	.05
☐ 204 Sammy Stewart	.05	.02
☐ 205 Graig Nettles	.10	.05
☐ 206 Twins Team	.05	.02
(Frank Viola and		
Tim Laudner)		
☐ 207 George Frazier	.05	.02
☐ 208 John Shelby	.05	.02
☐ 209 Rick Schu	.05	.02
☐ 210 Lloyd Moseby	.05	.02
☐ 211 John Morris	.05	.02
☐ 212 Mike Fitzgerald	.05	.02
☐ 213 Randy Myers	.20	.09
☐ 214 Omar Moreno	.05	.02
☐ 215 Mark Langston	.10	.05
☐ 216 B.J. Surhoff	.20	.09
☐ 217 Chris Codiroli	.05	.02
☐ 218 Sparky Anderson MG	.10	.05
(Checklist back)		
☐ 219 Cecilio Guante	.05	.02
☐ 220 Joe Carter	.20	.09
☐ 221 Vern Ruhle	.05	.02
☐ 222 Denny Walling	.05	.02
☐ 223 Charlie Leibrandt	.05	.02
☐ 224 Wayne Tolleson	.05	.02
☐ 225 Mike Smithson	.05	.02
☐ 226 Max Venable	.05	.02
☐ 227 Jamie Moyer	.10	.05
☐ 228 Curt Wilkerson	.05	.02
☐ 229 Mike Birkbeck	.05	.02
☐ 230 Don Baylor	.05	.02
☐ 231 Giants Team	.05	.02
(Bob Brenly and		
Jim Gott)		
☐ 232 Reggie Williams	.05	.02
☐ 233 Russ Morman	.05	.02
☐ 234 Pat Sheridan	.05	.02
☐ 235 Alvin Davis	.05	.02
☐ 236 Tommy John	.10	.05
☐ 237 Jim Morrison	.05	.02
☐ 238 Bill Krueger	.05	.02
☐ 239 Juan Espino	.05	.02
☐ 240 Steve Balboni	.05	.02
☐ 241 Danny Heep	.05	.02
☐ 242 Rick Mahler	.05	.02
☐ 243 Whitey Herzog MG	.10	.05
(Checklist back)		
☐ 244 Dickie Noles	.05	.02
☐ 245 Willie Upshaw	.05	.02
☐ 246 Jim Dwyer	.05	.02
☐ 247 Jeff Reed	.05	.02
☐ 248 Gene Walter	.05	.02
☐ 249 Jim Pankovits	.05	.02
☐ 250 Teddy Higuera	.05	.02
☐ 251 Rob Wilfong	.05	.02
☐ 252 Dennis Martinez	.10	.05
☐ 253 Eddie Milner	.05	.02
☐ 254 Bob Tewksbury	.10	.05
☐ 255 Juan Samuel	.05	.02
☐ 256 Royals Team	.05	.02
(George Brett and		
Frank White)		
☐ 257 Bob Forsch	.05	.02
☐ 258 Steve Yeager	.05	.02
☐ 259 Mike Greenwell	.20	.09
☐ 260 Vida Blue	.10	.05
☐ 261 Ruben Sierra	.20	.09
☐ 262 Jim Winn	.05	.02
☐ 263 Stan Javier	.05	.02
☐ 264 Checklist 133-264	.05	.02
☐ 265 Darrell Evans	.10	.05
☐ 266 Jeff Hamilton	.05	.02
☐ 267 Howard Johnson	.05	.02
☐ 268 Pat Corrales MG	.10	.05
(Checklist back)		
☐ 269 Cliff Speck	.05	.02
☐ 270 Jody Davis	.05	.02
☐ 271 Mike G. Brown	.05	.02
☐ 272 Andres Galarraga	.25	.11
☐ 273 Gene Nelson	.05	.02
☐ 274 Jeff Hearron UER	.05	.02
(Duplicate 1986		
stat line on back)		
☐ 275 LaMarr Hoyt	.05	.02
☐ 276 Jackie Gutierrez	.05	.02
☐ 277 Juan Agosto	.05	.02
☐ 278 Gary Pettis	.05	.02
☐ 279 Dan Plesac	.05	.02
☐ 280 Jeff Leonard	.05	.02
☐ 281 Reds Team	.20	.09
(Pete Rose, Bo Diaz,		
and Bill Gullickson)		
☐ 282 Jeff Calhoun	.05	.02
☐ 283 Doug Drabek	.20	.09
☐ 284 John Moses	.05	.02
☐ 285 Dennis Boyd	.05	.02
☐ 286 Mike Woodard	.05	.02
☐ 287 Dave Von Ohlen	.05	.02
☐ 288 Tito Landrum	.05	.02
☐ 289 Bob Kipper	.05	.02
☐ 290 Leon Durham	.05	.02
☐ 291 Mitch Williams	.10	.05
☐ 292 Franklin Stubbs	.05	.02
☐ 293 Bob Rodgers MG	.05	.02
(Checklist back,		
inconsistent design		
on card back)		
☐ 294 Steve Jeltz	.05	.02
☐ 295 Len Dykstra	.20	.09
☐ 296 Andres Thomas	.05	.02
☐ 297 Don Schulze	.05	.02
☐ 298 Larry Herndon	.05	.02
☐ 299 Joel Davis	.05	.02
☐ 300 Reggie Jackson	.25	.11
☐ 301 Luis Aquino UER	.05	.02
(No trademark,		
never corrected)		
☐ 302 Bill Schroeder	.05	.02
☐ 303 Juan Berenguer	.05	.02
☐ 304 Phil Garner	.05	.02
☐ 305 John Franco	.10	.05
☐ 306 Red Sox Team	.10	.05
(Tom Seaver,		
John McNamara MG,		
and Rich Gedman)		
☐ 307 Lee Guetterman	.05	.02
☐ 308 Don Slaught	.05	.02
☐ 309 Mike Young	.05	.02
☐ 310 Frank Viola	.05	.02
☐ 311 Rickey Henderson	.20	.09
TBC '82		
☐ 312 Reggie Jackson	.20	.09
TBC '77		
☐ 313 Roberto Clemente	.25	.11
TBC '72		
☐ 314 Carl Yastrzemski UER	.20	.09
TBC '67 (Sic, 112		
RBI's on back)		
☐ 315 Maury Wills TBC '62	.10	.05
☐ 316 Brian Fisher	.05	.02
☐ 317 Clint Hurdle	.05	.02
☐ 318 Jim Fregosi MG	.10	.05
(Checklist back)		
☐ 319 Greg Swindell	.20	.09
☐ 320 Barry Bonds	1.25	.55
☐ 321 Mike Laga	.05	.02
☐ 322 Chris Bando	.05	.02
☐ 323 Al Newman	.05	.02
☐ 324 David Palmer	.05	.02
☐ 325 Garry Templeton	.05	.02
☐ 326 Mark Gubicza	.05	.02
☐ 327 Dale Sveum	.05	.02
☐ 328 Bob Welch	.05	.02
☐ 329 Ron Roenicke	.05	.02
☐ 330 Mike Scott	.05	.02
☐ 331 Mets Team	.10	.05
(Gary Carter and		
Darryl Strawberry)		
☐ 332 Joe Price	.05	.02
☐ 333 Ken Phelps	.05	.02
☐ 334 Ed Correa	.05	.02
☐ 335 Candy Maldonado	.05	.02
☐ 336 Allan Anderson	.05	.02
☐ 337 Darrell Miller	.05	.02
☐ 338 Tim Conroy	.05	.02
☐ 339 Donnie Hill	.05	.02
☐ 340 Roger Clemens	.50	.23
☐ 341 Mike C. Brown	.05	.02
☐ 342 Bob James	.05	.02
☐ 343 Hal Lanier MG	.10	.05
(Checklist back)		
☐ 344A Joe Niekro	.05	.02
(Copyright inside		
righthand border)		
☐ 344B Joe Niekro	.05	.02
(Copyright outside		
righthand border)		
☐ 345 Andre Dawson	.20	.09
☐ 346 Shawon Dunston	.05	.02
☐ 347 Mickey Brantley	.05	.02
☐ 348 Carmelo Martinez	.05	.02
☐ 349 Storm Davis	.05	.02
☐ 350 Keith Hernandez	.10	.05
☐ 351 Gene Garber	.05	.02
☐ 352 Mike Felder	.05	.02
☐ 353 Ernie Camacho	.05	.02
☐ 354 Jamie Quirk	.05	.02
☐ 355 Don Carman	.05	.02
☐ 356 White Sox Team	.05	.02
(Mound conference)		
☐ 357 Steve Fireovid	.05	.02
☐ 358 Sal Butera	.05	.02
☐ 359 Doug Corbett	.05	.02
☐ 360 Pedro Guerrero	.10	.05
☐ 361 Mark Thurmond	.05	.02
☐ 362 Luis Quinones	.05	.02

☐ 363 Jose Guzman .05 .02
☐ 364 Randy Bush .05 .02
☐ 365 Rick Rhoden .05 .02
☐ 366 Mark McGwire 1.50 .70
☐ 367 Jeff Lahti .05 .02
☐ 368 John McNamara MG .05 .02
(Checklist back)
☐ 369 Brian Dayett .05 .02
☐ 370 Fred Lynn .10 .05
☐ 371 Mark Eichhorn .05 .02
☐ 372 Jerry Mumphrey .05 .02
☐ 373 Jeff Dedmon .05 .02
☐ 374 Glenn Hoffman .05 .02
☐ 375 Ron Guidry .10 .05
☐ 376 Scott Bradley .05 .02
☐ 377 John Henry Johnson .05 .02
☐ 378 Rafael Santana .05 .02
☐ 379 John Russell .05 .02
☐ 380 Rich Gossage .10 .05
☐ 381 Expos Team .05 .02
(Mound conference)
☐ 382 Rudy Law .05 .02
☐ 383 Ron Davis .05 .02
☐ 384 Johnny Grubb .05 .02
☐ 385 Orel Hershiser .10 .05
☐ 386 Dickie Thon .05 .02
☐ 387 T.R. Bryden .05 .02
☐ 388 Geno Petralli .05 .02
☐ 389 Jeff D. Robinson .05 .02
☐ 390 Gary Matthews .05 .02
☐ 391 Jay Howell .05 .02
☐ 392 Checklist 265-396 .05 .02
☐ 393 Pete Rose MG .25 .11
(Checklist back)
☐ 394 Mike Bielecki .05 .02
☐ 395 Damaso Garcia .05 .02
☐ 396 Tim Lollar .05 .02
☐ 397 Greg Walker .05 .02
☐ 398 Brad Havens .05 .02
☐ 399 Curt Ford .05 .02
☐ 400 George Brett .40 .18
☐ 401 Billy Joe Robidoux .05 .02
☐ 402 Mike Trujillo .05 .02
☐ 403 Jerry Royster .05 .02
☐ 404 Doug Sisk .05 .02
☐ 405 Brook Jacoby .05 .02
☐ 406 Yankees Team .20 .09
(Rickey Henderson and
Don Mattingly)
☐ 407 Jim Acker .05 .02
☐ 408 John Mizerock .05 .02
☐ 409 Milt Thompson .05 .02
☐ 410 Fernando Valenzuela .10 .05
☐ 411 Darnell Coles .05 .02
☐ 412 Eric Davis .05 .02
☐ 413 Moose Haas .05 .02
☐ 414 Joe Orsulak .05 .02
☐ 415 Bobby Witt .10 .05
☐ 416 Tom Nieto .05 .02
☐ 417 Pat Perry .05 .02
☐ 418 Dick Williams MG .10 .05
(Checklist back)
☐ 419 Mark Portugal .10 .05
☐ 420 Will Clark .60 .25
☐ 421 Jose DeLeon .05 .02
☐ 422 Jack Howell .05 .02
☐ 423 Jaime Cocanower .05 .02
☐ 424 Chris Speier .05 .02
☐ 425 Tom Seaver UER .20 .09
Earned Runs amount is wrong
For 86 Red Sox and Career
Also the ERA is wrong for 86 and career
☐ 426 Floyd Rayford .05 .02
☐ 427 Edwin Nunez .05 .02
☐ 428 Bruce Bochy .05 .02
☐ 429 Tim Pyznarski .05 .02
☐ 430 Mike Schmidt .25 .11
☐ 431 Dodgers Team .05 .02
(Mound conference)
☐ 432 Jim Slaton .05 .02
☐ 433 Ed Hearn .05 .02
☐ 434 Mike Fischlin .05 .02
☐ 435 Bruce Sutter .05 .02
☐ 436 Andy Allanson .05 .02
☐ 437 Ted Power .05 .02
☐ 438 Kelly Downs .05 .02
☐ 439 Karl Best .05 .02
☐ 440 Willie McGee .05 .02
☐ 441 Dave Leiper .05 .02
☐ 442 Mitch Webster .05 .02
☐ 443 John Felske MG .05 .02
(Checklist back)
☐ 444 Jeff Russell .05 .02
☐ 445 Dave Lopes .10 .05
☐ 446 Chuck Finley .20 .09
☐ 447 Bill Almon .05 .02
☐ 448 Chris Bosio .10 .05
☐ 449 Pat Dodson .05 .02
☐ 450 Kirby Puckett .50 .23
☐ 451 Joe Sambito .05 .02
☐ 452 Dave Henderson .05 .02
☐ 453 Scott Terry .05 .02
☐ 454 Luis Salazar .05 .02
☐ 455 Mike Boddicker .05 .02
☐ 456 A's Team .05 .02
(Mound conference)
☐ 457 Len Matuszek .05 .02
☐ 458 Kelly Gruber .05 .02
☐ 459 Dennis Eckersley .20 .09
☐ 460 Darryl Strawberry .10 .05
☐ 461 Craig McMurtry .05 .02
☐ 462 Scott Fletcher .05 .02
☐ 463 Tom Candiotti .05 .02
☐ 464 Butch Wynegar .05 .02
☐ 465 Todd Worrell .10 .05
☐ 466 Kal Daniels .05 .02
☐ 467 Randy St.Claire .05 .02
☐ 468 George Bamberger MG .10 .05
(Checklist back)
☐ 469 Mike Diaz .05 .02
☐ 470 Dave Dravecky .10 .05
☐ 471 Ronn Reynolds .05 .02
☐ 472 Bill Doran .05 .02
☐ 473 Steve Farr .05 .02
☐ 474 Jerry Narron .05 .02
☐ 475 Scott Garrelts .05 .02
☐ 476 Danny Tartabull .05 .02
☐ 477 Ken Howell .05 .02
☐ 478 Tim Laudner .05 .02
☐ 479 Bob Sebra .05 .02
☐ 480 Jim Rice .10 .05
☐ 481 Phillies Team .05 .02
(Glenn Wilson,
Juan Samuel and
Von Hayes)
☐ 482 Daryl Boston .05 .02
☐ 483 Dwight Lowry .05 .02
☐ 484 Jim Traber .05 .02
☐ 485 Tony Fernandez .05 .02
☐ 486 Otis Nixon .10 .05
☐ 487 Dave Gumpert .05 .02
☐ 488 Ray Knight .10 .05
☐ 489 Bill Gullickson .05 .02
☐ 490 Dale Murphy .20 .09
☐ 491 Ron Karkovice .10 .05
☐ 492 Mike Heath .05 .02
☐ 493 Tom Lasorda MG .10 .05
(Checklist back)
☐ 494 Barry Jones .05 .02
☐ 495 Gorman Thomas .05 .02
☐ 496 Bruce Bochte .05 .02
☐ 497 Dale Mohorcic .05 .02
☐ 498 Bob Kearney .05 .02
☐ 499 Bruce Ruffin .05 .02
☐ 500 Don Mattingly .30 .14
☐ 501 Craig Lefferts .05 .02
☐ 502 Dick Schofield .05 .02
☐ 503 Larry Andersen .05 .02
☐ 504 Mickey Hatcher .05 .02
☐ 505 Bryn Smith .05 .02
☐ 506 Orioles Team .05 .02
(Mound conference)
☐ 507 Dave L. Stapleton .05 .02
☐ 508 Scott Bankhead .05 .02
☐ 509 Enos Cabell .05 .02
☐ 510 Tom Henke .05 .02
☐ 511 Steve Lyons .05 .02
☐ 512 Dave Magadan .10 .05
☐ 513 Carmen Castillo .05 .02
☐ 514 Orlando Mercado .05 .02
☐ 515 Willie Hernandez .05 .02
☐ 516 Ted Simmons .10 .05
☐ 517 Mario Soto .05 .02
☐ 518 Gene Mauch MG .10 .05
(Checklist back)
☐ 519 Curt Young .05 .02
☐ 520 Jack Clark .10 .05
☐ 521 Rick Reuschel .05 .02
☐ 522 Checklist 397-528 .05 .02
☐ 523 Earnie Riles .05 .02
☐ 524 Bob Shirley .05 .02
☐ 525 Phil Bradley .05 .02
☐ 526 Roger Mason .05 .02
☐ 527 Jim Wohlford .05 .02
☐ 528 Ken Dixon .05 .02
☐ 529 Alvaro Espinoza .05 .02
☐ 530 Tony Gwynn .50 .23
☐ 531 Astros Team .10 .05
(Yogi Berra conference)
☐ 532 Jeff Stone .05 .02
☐ 533 Argenis Salazar .05 .02
☐ 534 Scott Sanderson .05 .02
☐ 535 Tony Armas .05 .02
☐ 536 Terry Mulholland .10 .05
☐ 537 Rance Mulliniks .05 .02
☐ 538 Tom Niedenfuer .05 .02
☐ 539 Reid Nichols .05 .02
☐ 540 Terry Kennedy .05 .02
☐ 541 Rafael Belliard .05 .02
☐ 542 Ricky Horton .05 .02
☐ 543 Dave Johnson MG .10 .05
(Checklist back)
☐ 544 Zane Smith .05 .02
☐ 545 Buddy Bell .10 .05
☐ 546 Mike Morgan .05 .02
☐ 547 Rob Deer .05 .02
☐ 548 Bill Mooneyham .05 .02
☐ 549 Bob Melvin .05 .02
☐ 550 Pete Incaviglia .10 .05
☐ 551 Frank Wills .05 .02
☐ 552 Larry Sheets .05 .02
☐ 553 Mike Maddux .05 .02
☐ 554 Buddy Biancalana .05 .02
☐ 555 Dennis Rasmussen .05 .02
☐ 556 Angels Team .05 .02
(Rene Lachemann CO,
Mike Witt, and
Bob Boone)
☐ 557 John Cerutti .05 .02
☐ 558 Greg Gagne .05 .02
☐ 559 Lance McCullers .05 .02
☐ 560 Glenn Davis .05 .02
☐ 561 Rey Quinones .05 .02
☐ 562 Bryan Clutterbuck .05 .02
☐ 563 John Stefero .05 .02
☐ 564 Larry McWilliams .05 .02
☐ 565 Dusty Baker .10 .05
☐ 566 Tim Hulett .05 .02
☐ 567 Greg Mathews .05 .02
☐ 568 Earl Weaver MG .20 .09
(Checklist back)
☐ 569 Wade Rowdon .05 .02
☐ 570 Sid Fernandez .05 .02
☐ 571 Ozzie Virgil .05 .02
☐ 572 Pete Ladd .05 .02
☐ 573 Hal McRae .10 .05
☐ 574 Manny Lee .05 .02
☐ 575 Pat Tabler .05 .02
☐ 576 Frank Pastore .05 .02
☐ 577 Dann Bilardello .05 .02
☐ 578 Billy Hatcher .05 .02
☐ 579 Rick Burleson .05 .02
☐ 580 Mike Krukow .05 .02
☐ 581 Cubs Team .05 .02
(Ron Cey and
Steve Trout)
☐ 582 Bruce Berenyi .05 .02
☐ 583 Junior Ortiz .05 .02
☐ 584 Ron Kittle .05 .02
☐ 585 Scott Bailes .05 .02
☐ 586 Ben Oglivie .05 .02
☐ 587 Eric Plunk .05 .02
☐ 588 Wallace Johnson .05 .02
☐ 589 Steve Crawford .05 .02
☐ 590 Vince Coleman .05 .02
☐ 591 Spike Owen .05 .02
☐ 592 Chris Welsh .05 .02
☐ 593 Chuck Tanner MG .10 .05
(Checklist back)
☐ 594 Rick Anderson .05 .02
☐ 595 Keith Hernandez AS .10 .05
☐ 596 Steve Sax AS .05 .02
☐ 597 Mike Schmidt AS .20 .09
☐ 598 Ozzie Smith AS .20 .09
☐ 599 Tony Gwynn AS .20 .09
☐ 600 Dave Parker AS .10 .05
☐ 601 Darryl Strawberry AS .10 .05
☐ 602 Gary Carter AS .10 .05
☐ 603A Dwight Gooden AS .20 .09
ERR (no trademark)
☐ 603B Dwight Gooden AS COR .20 .09
☐ 604 Fernando Valenzuela AS .10 .05
☐ 605 Todd Worrell AS .10 .05
☐ 606 Don Mattingly AS COR .20 .09
☐ 606A Don Mattingly AS .75 .35
ERR (no trademark)
☐ 607 Tony Bernazard AS .05 .02
☐ 608 Wade Boggs AS .20 .09
☐ 609 Cal Ripken AS .50 .23
☐ 610 Jim Rice AS .10 .05
☐ 611 Kirby Puckett AS .40 .18
☐ 612 George Bell AS .05 .02
☐ 613 Lance Parrish AS UER .10 .05
(Pitcher heading
on back)
☐ 614 Roger Clemens AS .15 .07
☐ 615 Teddy Higuera AS .05 .02
☐ 616 Dave Righetti AS .05 .02
☐ 617 Al Nipper .05 .02
☐ 618 Tom Kelly MG .10 .05
(Checklist back)

Card	MINT	NRMT
☐ 619 Jerry Reed	.05	.02
☐ 620 Jose Canseco	.40	.18
☐ 621 Danny Cox	.05	.02
☐ 622 Glenn Braggs	.05	.02
☐ 623 Kurt Stillwell	.05	.02
☐ 624 Tim Burke	.05	.02
☐ 625 Mookie Wilson	.10	.05
☐ 626 Joel Skinner	.05	.02
☐ 627 Ken Oberkfell	.05	.02
☐ 628 Bob Walk	.05	.02
☐ 629 Larry Parrish	.05	.02
☐ 630 John Candelaria	.05	.02
☐ 631 Tigers Team (Mound conference)	.05	.02
☐ 632 Rob Woodward	.05	.02
☐ 633 Jose Uribe	.05	.02
☐ 634 Rafael Palmeiro	.60	.25
☐ 635 Ken Schrom	.05	.02
☐ 636 Darren Daulton	.10	.05
☐ 637 Bip Roberts	.20	.09
☐ 638 Rich Bordi	.05	.02
☐ 639 Gerald Perry	.05	.02
☐ 640 Mark Clear	.05	.02
☐ 641 Domingo Ramos	.05	.02
☐ 642 Al Pulido	.05	.02
☐ 643 Ron Shepherd	.05	.02
☐ 644 John Denny	.05	.02
☐ 645 Dwight Evans	.10	.05
☐ 646 Mike Mason	.05	.02
☐ 647 Tom Lawless	.05	.02
☐ 648 Barry Larkin	.60	.25
☐ 649 Mickey Tettleton	.10	.05
☐ 650 Hubie Brooks	.05	.02
☐ 651 Benny Distefano	.05	.02
☐ 652 Terry Forster	.05	.02
☐ 653 Kevin Mitchell	.10	.05
☐ 654 Checklist 529-660	.10	.05
☐ 655 Jesse Barfield	.05	.02
☐ 656 Rangers Team (Bobby Valentine MG and Ricky Wright)	.05	.02
☐ 657 Tom Waddell	.05	.02
☐ 658 Robby Thompson	.10	.05
☐ 659 Aurelio Lopez	.05	.02
☐ 660 Bob Horner	.05	.02
☐ 661 Lou Whitaker	.10	.05
☐ 662 Frank DiPino	.05	.02
☐ 663 Cliff Johnson	.05	.02
☐ 664 Mike Marshall	.05	.02
☐ 665 Rod Scurry	.05	.02
☐ 666 Von Hayes	.05	.02
☐ 667 Ron Hassey	.05	.02
☐ 668 Juan Bonilla	.05	.02
☐ 669 Bud Black	.05	.02
☐ 670 Jose Cruz	.05	.02
☐ 671A Ray Soff ERR (No D* before copyright line)	.05	.02
☐ 671B Ray Soff COR (D* before copyright line)	.05	.02
☐ 672 Chili Davis	.10	.05
☐ 673 Don Sutton	.20	.09
☐ 674 Bill Campbell	.05	.02
☐ 675 Ed Romero	.05	.02
☐ 676 Charlie Moore	.05	.02
☐ 677 Bob Grich	.10	.05
☐ 678 Carney Lansford	.10	.05
☐ 679 Kent Hrbek	.10	.05
☐ 680 Ryne Sandberg	.25	.11
☐ 681 George Bell	.05	.02
☐ 682 Jerry Reuss	.05	.02
☐ 683 Gary Roenicke	.05	.02
☐ 684 Kent Tekulve	.05	.02
☐ 685 Jerry Hairston	.05	.02
☐ 686 Doyle Alexander	.05	.02
☐ 687 Alan Trammell	.05	.02
☐ 688 Juan Beniquez	.05	.02
☐ 689 Darrell Porter	.05	.02
☐ 690 Dane Iorg	.05	.02
☐ 691 Dave Parker	.10	.05
☐ 692 Frank White	.10	.05
☐ 693 Terry Puhl	.05	.02
☐ 694 Phil Niekro	.20	.09
☐ 695 Chico Walker	.05	.02
☐ 696 Gary Lucas	.05	.02
☐ 697 Ed Lynch	.05	.02
☐ 698 Ernie Whitt	.05	.02
☐ 699 Ken Landreaux	.05	.02
☐ 700 Dave Bergman	.05	.02
☐ 701 Willie Randolph	.10	.05
☐ 702 Greg Gross	.05	.02
☐ 703 Dave Schmidt	.05	.02
☐ 704 Jesse Orosco	.05	.02
☐ 705 Bruce Hurst	.05	.02
☐ 706 Rick Manning	.05	.02
☐ 707 Bob McClure	.05	.02
☐ 708 Scott McGregor	.05	.02
☐ 709 Dave Kingman	.10	.05
☐ 710 Gary Gaetti	.05	.02
☐ 711 Ken Griffey	.10	.05
☐ 712 Don Robinson	.05	.02
☐ 713 Tom Brookens	.05	.02
☐ 714 Dan Quisenberry	.05	.02
☐ 715 Bob Dernier	.05	.02
☐ 716 Rick Leach	.05	.02
☐ 717 Ed VandeBerg	.05	.02
☐ 718 Steve Carlton	.20	.09
☐ 719 Tom Hume	.05	.02
☐ 720 Richard Dotson	.05	.02
☐ 721 Tom Herr	.05	.02
☐ 722 Bob Knepper	.05	.02
☐ 723 Brett Butler	.10	.05
☐ 724 Greg Minton	.05	.02
☐ 725 George Hendrick	.05	.02
☐ 726 Frank Tanana	.05	.02
☐ 727 Mike Moore	.05	.02
☐ 728 Tippy Martinez	.05	.02
☐ 729 Tom Paciorek	.05	.02
☐ 730 Eric Show	.05	.02
☐ 731 Dave Concepcion	.10	.05
☐ 732 Manny Trillo	.05	.02
☐ 733 Bill Caudill	.05	.02
☐ 734 Bill Madlock	.05	.02
☐ 735 Rickey Henderson	.20	.09
☐ 736 Steve Bedrosian	.05	.02
☐ 737 Floyd Bannister	.05	.02
☐ 738 Jorge Orta	.05	.02
☐ 739 Chet Lemon	.05	.02
☐ 740 Rich Gedman	.05	.02
☐ 741 Paul Molitor	.20	.09
☐ 742 Andy McGaffigan	.05	.02
☐ 743 Dwayne Murphy	.05	.02
☐ 744 Roy Smalley	.05	.02
☐ 745 Glenn Hubbard	.05	.02
☐ 746 Bob Ojeda	.05	.02
☐ 747 Johnny Ray	.05	.02
☐ 748 Mike Flanagan	.05	.02
☐ 749 Ozzie Smith	.25	.11
☐ 750 Steve Trout	.05	.02
☐ 751 Garth Iorg	.05	.02
☐ 752 Dan Petry	.05	.02
☐ 753 Rick Honeycutt	.05	.02
☐ 754 Dave LaPoint	.05	.02
☐ 755 Luis Aguayo	.05	.02
☐ 756 Carlton Fisk	.20	.09
☐ 757 Nolan Ryan	.75	.35
☐ 758 Tony Bernazard	.05	.02
☐ 759 Joel Youngblood	.05	.02
☐ 760 Mike Witt	.05	.02
☐ 761 Greg Pryor	.05	.02
☐ 762 Gary Ward	.05	.02
☐ 763 Tim Flannery	.05	.02
☐ 764 Bill Buckner	.10	.05
☐ 765 Kirk Gibson	.10	.05
☐ 766 Don Aase	.05	.02
☐ 767 Ron Cey	.10	.05
☐ 768 Dennis Lamp	.05	.02
☐ 769 Steve Sax	.05	.02
☐ 770 Dave Winfield	.20	.09
☐ 771 Shane Rawley	.05	.02
☐ 772 Harold Baines	.10	.05
☐ 773 Robin Yount	.20	.09
☐ 774 Wayne Krenchicki	.05	.02
☐ 775 Joaquin Andujar	.05	.02
☐ 776 Tom Brunansky	.05	.02
☐ 777 Chris Chambliss	.05	.02
☐ 778 Jack Morris	.10	.05
☐ 779 Craig Reynolds	.05	.02
☐ 780 Andre Thornton	.05	.02
☐ 781 Atlee Hammaker	.05	.02
☐ 782 Brian Downing	.05	.02
☐ 783 Willie Wilson	.05	.02
☐ 784 Cal Ripken	.75	.35
☐ 785 Terry Francona	.05	.02
☐ 786 Jimy Williams MG (Checklist back)	.10	.05
☐ 787 Alejandro Pena	.05	.02
☐ 788 Tim Stoddard	.05	.02
☐ 789 Dan Schatzeder	.05	.02
☐ 790 Julio Cruz	.05	.02
☐ 791 Lance Parrish UER (No trademark, never corrected)	.10	.05
☐ 792 Checklist 661-792	.05	.02

1987 Topps Tiffany

These 792 standard-size cards were a parallel to the regular Topps issue. These cards feature "glossy" fronts and easy to read backs. These cards are in the same style as the regular Topps issue. This set was printed in Ireland and was issued only in factory set form. Unlike previous years, a significantly higher amount of these cards were produced. Therefore, the values of these cards are a much lower mulitplier to the regular cards than previous years.

	MINT	NRMT
COMPLETE FACT.SET (792)	25.00	11.00
COMMON CARD (1-792)	.10	.05
*STARS: 2X BASIC CARDS		
*ROOKIES: 2X BASIC CARDS		

1987 Topps Glossy All-Stars

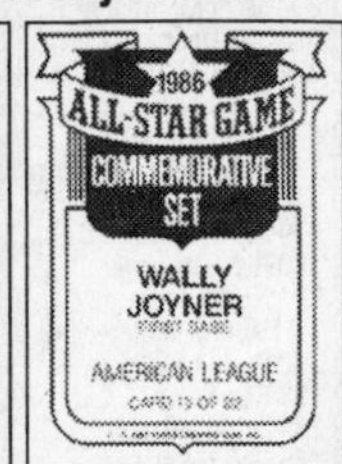

This set of 22 glossy cards was inserted one per rack pack. Players selected for the set are the starting players (plus manager and two pitchers) in the 1986 All-Star Game in Houston. Cards measure the standard size and the backs feature red and blue printing on a white card stock.

	MINT	NRMT
COMPLETE SET (22)	5.00	2.20
COMMON CARD (1-22)	.05	.02
☐ 1 Whitey Herzog MG	.05	.02
☐ 2 Keith Hernandez	.10	.05
☐ 3 Ryne Sandberg	1.00	.45
☐ 4 Mike Schmidt	.75	.35
☐ 5 Ozzie Smith	1.00	.45
☐ 6 Tony Gwynn	1.25	.55
☐ 7 Dale Murphy	.30	.14
☐ 8 Darryl Strawberry	.10	.05
☐ 9 Gary Carter	.20	.09
☐ 10 Dwight Gooden	.20	.09
☐ 11 Fernando Valenzuela	.10	.05
☐ 12 Dick Howser MG	.05	.02
☐ 13 Wally Joyner	.10	.05
☐ 14 Lou Whitaker	.10	.05
☐ 15 Wade Boggs	.50	.23
☐ 16 Cal Ripken	2.00	.90
☐ 17 Dave Winfield	.40	.18
☐ 18 Rickey Henderson	.40	.18
☐ 19 Kirby Puckett	1.25	.55
☐ 20 Lance Parrish	.05	.02
☐ 21 Roger Clemens	.75	.35
☐ 22 Teddy Higuera	.05	.02

1987 Topps Glossy Send-Ins

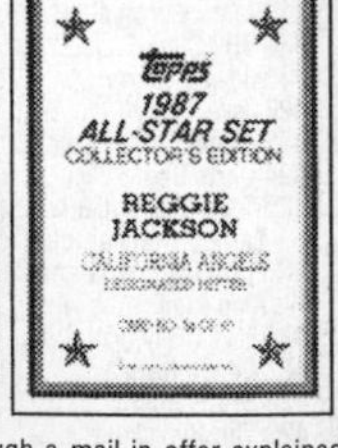

Topps issued this set through a mail-in offer explained and advertised on the wax packs. This 60-card set features glossy fronts with each card measuring the standard size. The offer provided your choice of any one of the six 10-card subsets (1-10, 11-20, etc.) for 1.00 plus six of the Special Offer ("Spring Fever Baseball") insert cards, which were found one per wax pack. The last two players (numerically) in each ten-card subset are actually "Hot Prospects."

	MINT	NRMT
COMPLETE SET (60)	12.50	5.50
COMMON CARD (1-60)	.10	.05
☐ 1 Don Mattingly	2.00	.90
☐ 2 Tony Gwynn	1.50	.70
☐ 3 Gary Gaetti	.20	.09
☐ 4 Glenn Davis	.10	.05
☐ 5 Roger Clemens	1.00	.45
☐ 6 Dale Murphy	.50	.23
☐ 7 Lou Whitaker	.20	.09
☐ 8 Roger McDowell	.10	.05

☐ 9 Cory Snyder	.10	.05
☐ 10 Todd Worrell	.10	.05
☐ 11 Gary Carter	.35	.16
☐ 12 Eddie Murray	1.00	.45
☐ 13 Bob Knepper	.10	.05
☐ 14 Harold Baines	.20	.09
☐ 15 Jeff Reardon	.20	.09
☐ 16 Joe Carter	.35	.16
☐ 17 Dave Parker	.20	.09
☐ 18 Wade Boggs	.60	.25
☐ 19 Danny Tartabull	.20	.09
☐ 20 Jim Deshaies	.10	.05
☐ 21 Rickey Henderson	.60	.25
☐ 22 Rob Deer	.10	.05
☐ 23 Ozzie Smith	1.25	.55
☐ 24 Dave Righetti	.10	.05
☐ 25 Kent Hrbek	.20	.09
☐ 26 Keith Hernandez	.20	.09
☐ 27 Don Baylor	.20	.09
☐ 28 Mike Schmidt	1.00	.45
☐ 29 Pete Incaviglia	.20	.09
☐ 30 Barry Bonds	2.50	1.10
☐ 31 George Brett	1.50	.70
☐ 32 Darryl Strawberry	.20	.09
☐ 33 Mike Witt	.10	.05
☐ 34 Kevin Bass	.10	.05
☐ 35 Jesse Barfield	.10	.05
☐ 36 Bob Ojeda	.10	.05
☐ 37 Cal Ripken	4.00	1.80
☐ 38 Vince Coleman	.10	.05
☐ 39 Wally Joyner	.50	.23
☐ 40 Robby Thompson	.10	.05
☐ 41 Pete Rose	1.00	.45
☐ 42 Jim Rice	.20	.09
☐ 43 Tony Bernazard	.10	.05
☐ 44 Eric Davis	.20	.09
☐ 45 George Bell	.10	.05
☐ 46 Hubie Brooks	.10	.05
☐ 47 Jack Morris	.20	.09
☐ 48 Tim Raines	.20	.09
☐ 49 Mark Eichhorn	.10	.05
☐ 50 Kevin Mitchell	.20	.09
☐ 51 Dwight Gooden	.20	.09
☐ 52 Doug DeCinces	.10	.05
☐ 53 Fernando Valenzuela	.20	.09
☐ 54 Reggie Jackson	.60	.25
☐ 55 Johnny Ray	.10	.05
☐ 56 Mike Pagliarulo	.10	.05
☐ 57 Kirby Puckett	2.00	.90
☐ 58 Lance Parrish	.20	.09
☐ 59 Jose Canseco	1.00	.45
☐ 60 Greg Mathews	.10	.05

1987 Topps Rookies

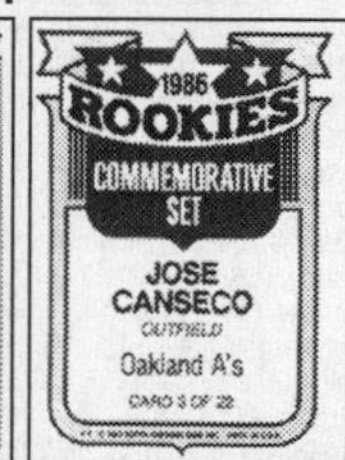

Inserted in each supermarket jumbo pack is a card from this series of 22 of 1986's best rookies as determined by Topps. Jumbo packs consisted of 100 (regular issue 1987 Topps baseball) cards with a stick of gum plus the insert "Rookie" card. The card fronts are in full color and measure the standard size. The card backs are printed in red and blue on white card stock and are numbered at the bottom essentially by alphabetical order.

	MINT	NRMT
COMPLETE SET (22)	10.00	4.50
COMMON CARD (1-22)	.10	.05
☐ 1 Andy Allanson	.10	.05
☐ 2 John Cangelosi	.10	.05
☐ 3 Jose Canseco	2.50	1.10
☐ 4 Will Clark	2.50	1.10
☐ 5 Mark Eichhorn	.10	.05
☐ 6 Pete Incaviglia	.20	.09
☐ 7 Wally Joyner	.50	.23
☐ 8 Eric King	.10	.05
☐ 9 Dave Magadan	.20	.09
☐ 10 John Morris	.10	.05
☐ 11 Juan Nieves	.10	.05
☐ 12 Rafael Palmeiro	2.00	.90
☐ 13 Billy Joe Robidoux	.10	.05
☐ 14 Bruce Ruffin	.10	.05
☐ 15 Ruben Sierra	.40	.18
☐ 16 Cory Snyder	.10	.05
☐ 17 Kurt Stillwell	.10	.05
☐ 18 Dale Sveum	.10	.05
☐ 19 Danny Tartabull	.20	.09
☐ 20 Andres Thomas	.10	.05
☐ 21 Robby Thompson	.20	.09
☐ 22 Todd Worrell	.30	.14

1987 Topps Wax Box Cards

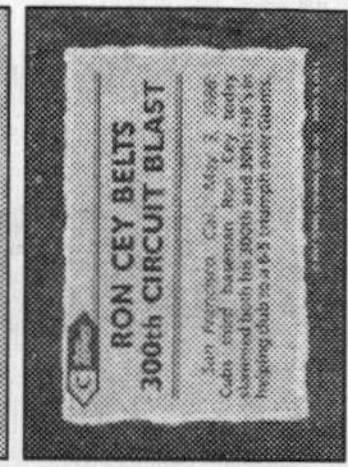

This set of eight cards is really four different sets of two smaller (approximately 2 1/8" by 3") cards which were printed on the side of the wax pack box; these eight cards are lettered A through H and are very similar in design to the Topps regular issue cards. The order of the set is alphabetical by player's name. Complete boxes would be worth an additional 25 percent premium over the prices below. The card backs are done in a newspaper headline style describing something about that player that happened the previous season. The card backs feature blue and yellow ink on gray card stock.

	MINT	NRMT
COMPLETE SET (8)	3.00	1.35
COMMON CARD (A-H)	.25	.11
☐ A Don Baylor	.40	.18
☐ B Steve Carlton	.75	.35
☐ C Ron Cey	.25	.11
☐ D Cecil Cooper	.25	.11
☐ E Rickey Henderson	1.00	.45
☐ F Jim Rice	.35	.16
☐ G Don Sutton	.60	.25
☐ H Dave Winfield	.75	.35

1987 Topps Traded

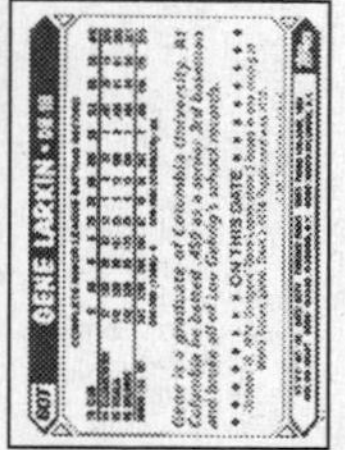

This 132-card standard-size Traded set was distributed exclusively in factory set form in a special green and white box through hobby dealers. The card fronts are identical in style to the Topps regular issue except for whiter stock and t-suffixed numbering on back. The cards are ordered alphabetically by player's last name. The key extended Rookie Cards in this set are Ellis Burks, David Cone, Greg Maddux, Fred McGriff and Matt Williams.

	MINT	NRMT
COMP.FACT.SET (132)	8.00	3.60
COMMON CARD (1T-132T)	.05	.02
☐ 1T Bill Almon	.05	.02
☐ 2T Scott Bankhead	.05	.02
☐ 3T Eric Bell	.05	.02
☐ 4T Juan Beniquez	.05	.02
☐ 5T Juan Berenguer	.05	.02
☐ 6T Greg Booker	.05	.02
☐ 7T Thad Bosley	.05	.02
☐ 8T Larry Bowa MG	.15	.07
☐ 9T Greg Brock	.05	.02
☐ 10T Bob Brower	.05	.02
☐ 11T Jerry Browne	.05	.02
☐ 12T Ralph Bryant	.05	.02
☐ 13T DeWayne Buice	.05	.02
☐ 14T Ellis Burks	.50	.23
☐ 15T Ivan Calderon	.05	.02
☐ 16T Jeff Calhoun	.05	.02
☐ 17T Casey Candaele	.05	.02
☐ 18T John Cangelosi	.05	.02
☐ 19T Steve Carlton	.30	.14
☐ 20T Juan Castillo	.05	.02
☐ 21T Rick Cerone	.05	.02
☐ 22T Ron Cey	.15	.07
☐ 23T John Christensen	.05	.02
☐ 24T David Cone	.50	.23
☐ 25T Chuck Crim	.05	.02
☐ 26T Storm Davis	.05	.02
☐ 27T Andre Dawson	.30	.14
☐ 28T Rick Dempsey	.15	.07
☐ 29T Doug Drabek	.30	.14
☐ 30T Mike Dunne	.05	.02
☐ 31T Dennis Eckersley	.30	.14
☐ 32T Lee Elia MG	.05	.02
☐ 33T Brian Fisher	.05	.02
☐ 34T Terry Francona	.05	.02
☐ 35T Willie Fraser	.05	.02
☐ 36T Billy Gardner MG	.05	.02
☐ 37T Ken Gerhart	.05	.02
☐ 38T Dan Gladden	.05	.02
☐ 39T Jim Gott	.05	.02
☐ 40T Cecilio Guante	.05	.02
☐ 41T Albert Hall	.05	.02
☐ 42T Terry Harper	.05	.02
☐ 43T Mickey Hatcher	.05	.02
☐ 44T Brad Havens	.05	.02
☐ 45T Neal Heaton	.05	.02
☐ 46T Mike Henneman	.30	.14
☐ 47T Donnie Hill	.05	.02
☐ 48T Guy Hoffman	.05	.02
☐ 49T Brian Holton	.05	.02
☐ 50T Charles Hudson	.05	.02
☐ 51T Danny Jackson	.05	.02
☐ 52T Reggie Jackson	.40	.18
☐ 53T Chris James	.05	.02
☐ 54T Dion James	.05	.02
☐ 55T Stan Jefferson	.05	.02
☐ 56T Joe Johnson	.05	.02
☐ 57T Terry Kennedy	.05	.02
☐ 58T Mike Kingery	.15	.07
☐ 59T Ray Knight	.15	.07
☐ 60T Gene Larkin	.05	.02
☐ 61T Mike LaValliere	.05	.02
☐ 62T Jack Lazorko	.05	.02
☐ 63T Terry Leach	.05	.02
☐ 64T Tim Leary	.05	.02
☐ 65T Jim Lindeman	.05	.02
☐ 66T Steve Lombardozzi	.05	.02
☐ 67T Bill Long	.05	.02
☐ 68T Barry Lyons	.05	.02
☐ 69T Shane Mack	.05	.02
☐ 70T Greg Maddux	5.00	2.20
☐ 71T Bill Madlock	.05	.02
☐ 72T Joe Magrane	.05	.02
☐ 73T Dave Martinez	.15	.07
☐ 74T Fred McGriff	.40	.18
☐ 75T Mark McLemore	.05	.02
☐ 76T Kevin McReynolds	.05	.02
☐ 77T Dave Meads	.05	.02
☐ 78T Eddie Milner	.05	.02
☐ 79T Greg Minton	.05	.02
☐ 80T John Mitchell	.05	.02
☐ 81T Kevin Mitchell	.30	.14
☐ 82T Charlie Moore	.05	.02
☐ 83T Jeff Musselman	.05	.02
☐ 84T Gene Nelson	.05	.02
☐ 85T Graig Nettles	.15	.07
☐ 86T Al Newman	.05	.02
☐ 87T Reid Nichols	.05	.02
☐ 88T Tom Niedenfuer	.05	.02
☐ 89T Joe Niekro	.05	.02
☐ 90T Tom Nieto	.05	.02
☐ 91T Matt Nokes	.15	.07
☐ 92T Dickie Noles	.05	.02
☐ 93T Pat Pacillo	.05	.02
☐ 94T Lance Parrish	.15	.07
☐ 95T Tony Pena	.05	.02
☐ 96T Luis Polonia	.15	.07
☐ 97T Randy Ready	.05	.02
☐ 98T Jeff Reardon	.15	.07
☐ 99T Gary Redus	.05	.02
☐ 100T Jeff Reed	.05	.02
☐ 101T Rick Rhoden	.05	.02
☐ 102T Cal Ripken Sr. MG	.05	.02
☐ 103T Wally Ritchie	.05	.02
☐ 104T Jeff M. Robinson	.05	.02
☐ 105T Gary Roenicke	.05	.02
☐ 106T Jerry Royster	.05	.02
☐ 107T Mark Salas	.05	.02
☐ 108T Luis Salazar	.05	.02
☐ 109T Benny Santiago	.15	.07
☐ 110T Dave Schmidt	.05	.02
☐ 111T Kevin Seitzer	.15	.07
☐ 112T John Shelby	.05	.02
☐ 113T Steve Shields	.05	.02
☐ 114T John Smiley	.15	.07
☐ 115T Chris Speier	.05	.02

☐ 116T Mike Stanley	.10	.05
☐ 117T Terry Steinbach	.25	.11
☐ 118T Les Straker	.05	.02
☐ 119T Jim Sundberg	.05	.02
☐ 120T Danny Tartabull	.15	.07
☐ 121T Tom Trebelhorn MG	.05	.02
☐ 122T Dave Valle	.05	.02
☐ 123T Ed VandeBerg	.05	.02
☐ 124T Andy Van Slyke	.15	.07
☐ 125T Gary Ward	.05	.02
☐ 126T Alan Wiggins	.05	.02
☐ 127T Bill Wilkinson	.05	.02
☐ 128T Frank Williams	.05	.02
☐ 129T Matt Williams	2.00	.90
☐ 130T Jim Winn	.05	.02
☐ 131T Matt Young	.05	.02
☐ 132T Checklist 1T-132T	.05	.02

1987 Topps Traded Tiffany

Since the update Tiffany cards were issued in the same quantities as the regular cards, again these cards are not valued as high as a multiplier as the previous years. These 132 standard-size cards parallel the regular cards but have glossy fronts and easy to read backs. These cards were issued in factory set form only.

	MINT	NRMT
COMPLETE FACT.SET (132)	15.00	6.75
COMMON CARD (1T-132T)	.10	.05
*STARS: 2X BASIC CARDS		
*ROOKIES: 2X BASIC CARDS		

1987 Topps Coins

This full-color set of 48 coins contains a full-color photo of the player with a scroll at the bottom containing the player's name, position and team. The backs contain the coin number and brief biographical data. Some of the coins have gold rims and some have silver rims. Each coin measures approximately 1 1/2" in diameter. The 1987 set is very similar to the 1988 set of the following year; the 1988 coins have gold stars on the name scroll on the front of the coin.

	MINT	NRMT
COMPLETE SET (48)	8.00	3.60
COMMON COIN (1-48)	.05	.02

☐ 1 Harold Baines	.10	.05
☐ 2 Jesse Barfield	.05	.02
☐ 3 George Bell	.05	.02
☐ 4 Wade Boggs	.40	.18
☐ 5 George Brett	.75	.35
☐ 6 Jose Canseco	.75	.35
☐ 7 Joe Carter	.25	.11
☐ 8 Roger Clemens	.50	.23
☐ 9 Alvin Davis	.05	.02
☐ 10 Rob Deer	.05	.02
☐ 11 Kirk Gibson	.10	.05
☐ 12 Rickey Henderson	.30	.14
☐ 13 Kent Hrbek	.10	.05
☐ 14 Pete Incaviglia	.10	.05
☐ 15 Reggie Jackson	.50	.23
☐ 16 Wally Joyner	.40	.18
☐ 17 Don Mattingly	1.00	.45
☐ 18 Jack Morris	.10	.05
☐ 19 Eddie Murray	.50	.23
☐ 20 Kirby Puckett	1.00	.45
☐ 21 Jim Rice	.10	.05
☐ 22 Dave Righetti	.05	.02
☐ 23 Cal Ripken	2.00	.90
☐ 24 Cory Snyder	.05	.02
☐ 25 Danny Tartabull	.05	.02
☐ 26 Dave Winfield	.25	.11
☐ 27 Hubie Brooks	.05	.02
☐ 28 Gary Carter	.15	.07
☐ 29 Vince Coleman	.05	.02
☐ 30 Eric Davis	.10	.05
☐ 31 Glenn Davis	.05	.02
☐ 32 Steve Garvey	.10	.05
☐ 33 Dwight Gooden	.10	.05
☐ 34 Tony Gwynn	1.00	.45
☐ 35 Von Hayes	.05	.02
☐ 36 Keith Hernandez	.10	.05
☐ 37 Dale Murphy	.15	.07
☐ 38 Dave Parker	.10	.05
☐ 39 Tony Pena	.05	.02
☐ 40 Nolan Ryan	2.00	.90
☐ 41 Ryne Sandberg	.75	.35
☐ 42 Steve Sax	.05	.02
☐ 43 Mike Schmidt	.60	.25
☐ 44 Mike Scott	.05	.02
☐ 45 Ozzie Smith	.75	.35
☐ 46 Darryl Strawberry	.10	.05
☐ 47 Fernando Valenzuela	.10	.05
☐ 48 Todd Worrell	.05	.02

1987 Topps Mini Leaders

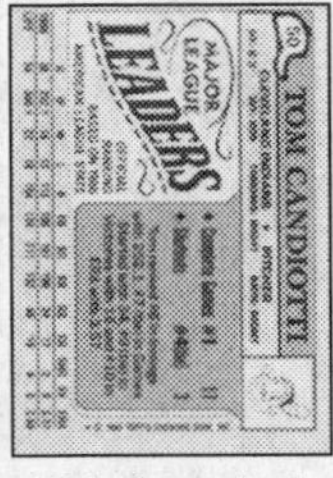

The 1987 Topps Mini set of Major League Leaders features 77 cards of leaders of the various statistical categories for the 1986 season. The cards are numbered on the back and measure approximately 2 5/32" by 3". The card backs are printed in orange and brown on white card stock. They are very similar in design to the Team Leader cards in the 1987 Topps regular issue. The cards were distributed as a separate issue in wax packs of seven for 30 cents. Eleven of the cards were double printed and are hence more plentiful; they are marked DP in the checklist below. The order of the set is alphabetical by player's name within team; the teams themselves are ordered alphabetically by city name within each league.

	MINT	NRMT
COMPLETE SET (77)	5.00	2.20
COMMON CARD (1-77)	.05	.02

☐ 1 Bob Horner DP	.05	.02
☐ 2 Dale Murphy	.25	.11
☐ 3 Lee Smith	.15	.07
☐ 4 Eric Davis	.10	.05
☐ 5 John Franco	.10	.05
☐ 6 Dave Parker	.10	.05
☐ 7 Kevin Bass	.05	.02
☐ 8 Glenn Davis DP	.05	.02
☐ 9 Bill Doran DP	.05	.02
☐ 10 Bob Knepper DP	.05	.02
☐ 11 Mike Scott	.05	.02
☐ 12 Dave Smith	.05	.02
☐ 13 Mariano Duncan	.05	.02
☐ 14 Orel Hershiser	.10	.05
☐ 15 Steve Sax DP	.05	.02
☐ 16 Fernando Valenzuela	.10	.05
☐ 17 Tim Raines	.10	.05
☐ 18 Jeff Reardon	.10	.05
☐ 19 Floyd Youmans	.05	.02
☐ 20 Gary Carter DP	.10	.05
☐ 21 Ron Darling	.05	.02
☐ 22 Sid Fernandez	.05	.02
☐ 23 Dwight Gooden	.15	.07
☐ 24 Keith Hernandez	.10	.05
☐ 25 Bob Ojeda	.05	.02
☐ 26 Darryl Strawberry	.10	.05
☐ 27 Steve Bedrosian	.05	.02
☐ 28 Von Hayes DP	.05	.02
☐ 29 Juan Samuel	.05	.02
☐ 30 Mike Schmidt	.50	.23
☐ 31 Rick Rhoden	.05	.02
☐ 32 Vince Coleman	.05	.02
☐ 33 Danny Cox	.05	.02
☐ 34 Todd Worrell	.05	.02
☐ 35 Tony Gwynn	1.00	.45
☐ 36 Mike Krukow	.05	.02
☐ 37 Candy Maldonado	.05	.02
☐ 38 Don Aase	.05	.02
☐ 39 Eddie Murray	.50	.23
☐ 40 Cal Ripken	1.50	.70
☐ 41 Wade Boggs	.30	.14
☐ 42 Roger Clemens	.50	.23
☐ 43 Bruce Hurst	.05	.02
☐ 44 Jim Rice	.10	.05
☐ 45 Wally Joyner	.25	.11
☐ 46 Donnie Moore	.05	.02
☐ 47 Gary Pettis	.05	.02
☐ 48 Mike Witt	.05	.02
☐ 49 John Cangelosi	.05	.02
☐ 50 Tom Candiotti	.05	.02
☐ 51 Joe Carter	.15	.07
☐ 52 Pat Tabler	.05	.02
☐ 53 Kirk Gibson DP	.10	.05
☐ 54 Willie Hernandez	.05	.02
☐ 55 Jack Morris	.10	.05
☐ 56 Alan Trammell DP	.15	.07
☐ 57 George Brett	.75	.35
☐ 58 Willie Wilson	.05	.02
☐ 59 Rob Deer	.05	.02
☐ 60 Teddy Higuera	.05	.02
☐ 61 Bert Blyleven DP	.05	.02
☐ 62 Gary Gaetti DP	.05	.02
☐ 63 Kirby Puckett	1.00	.45
☐ 64 Rickey Henderson	.30	.14
☐ 65 Don Mattingly	1.00	.45
☐ 66 Dennis Rasmussen	.05	.02
☐ 67 Dave Righetti	.05	.02
☐ 68 Jose Canseco	.60	.25
☐ 69 Dave Kingman	.05	.02
☐ 70 Phil Bradley	.05	.02
☐ 71 Mark Langston	.05	.02
☐ 72 Pete O'Brien	.05	.02
☐ 73 Jesse Barfield	.05	.02
☐ 74 George Bell	.05	.02
☐ 75 Tony Fernandez	.05	.02
☐ 76 Tom Henke	.05	.02
☐ 77 Checklist Card	.05	.02

1987 Topps/O-Pee-Chee Stickers

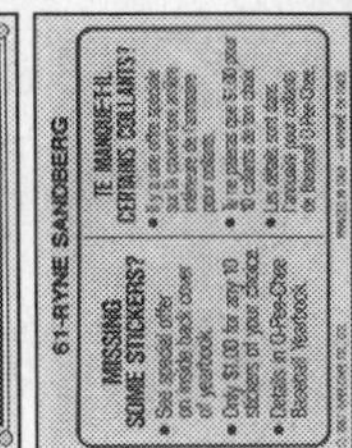

Made in Italy for Topps and O-Pee-Chee by Panini, these 313 stickers measure approximately 2 1/8" by 3" and are numbered on both front and back. The fronts feature white-bordered color player photos. The horizontal backs carry a bilingual ad for O-Pee-Chee. The Topps stickers contain offers on the back to obtain either a trip for four to Spring Training of the team of your choice or a complete set of Topps baseball cards directly from Topps. An album onto which the stickers could be affixed was available at retail stores. The album and the sticker numbering are organized as follows: 1986 Highlights (1-12), 1986 Championship Series (13-18), 1986 World Series (19-25), Houston Astros (26-35), Atlanta Braves (36-45), St. Louis Cardinals (46-55), Chicago Cubs (56-65), Los Angeles Dodgers (66-75), Montreal Expos (76-85), San Francisco Giants (86-95), New York Mets (96-105), San Diego Padres (106-115), Philadelphia Phillies (116-125), Pittsburgh Pirates (126-135), Cincinnati Reds (136-145), Foil All-Stars (146-163), Oakland A's (164-173), California Angels (174-183), Toronto Blue Jays (184-193), Milwaukee Brewers (194-203), Cleveland Indians (204-213), Seattle Mariners (214-223), Baltimore Orioles (224-233), Texas Rangers (234-243), Boston Red Sox (244-253), Kansas City Royals (254-263), Detroit Tigers (264-273), Minnesota Twins (274-283), Chicago White Sox (284-293), New York Yankees (294-303), and Future Stars (304-313). For those stickers featuring more than one player, the other numbers on that sticker are given below in parentheses. There was a variation of this set that was test-marketed by Topps. Its stickers had card backings (precursors of the Super Stars sticker backs) rather than the paper backing Topps had been using in previous years. Apparently the test was successful as both Topps and O-Pee-Chee switched to the home-printed, stiffer-backed stickers the following year. Will Clark and Barry Bonds are featured on stickers during their Rookie Card Year

	MINT	NRMT
COMPLETE SET (313)	15.00	6.75
COMMON STICKER (1-145)	.05	.02
COMMON FOIL (146-163)	.10	.05
COMMON STICKER (147-313)	.05	.02
*TOPPS AND OPC: SAME VALUE		

☐ 1 Jim Deshaies (172)	.05	.02
☐ 2 Roger Clemens (175) (Top half)	.15	.07
☐ 3 Roger Clemens (176)	.15	.07

(Bottom half)
4 Dwight Evans (177) | .10 | .05
5 Dwight Gooden (178) (Top half) | .15 | .07
6 Dwight Gooden (180) (Bottom half) | .15 | .07
7 Dave Lopes (181) | .10 | .05
8 Dave Righetti (182) (Top half) | .05 | .02
9 Dave Righetti (183) (Bottom half) | .05 | .02
10 Ruben Sierra (185) | .50 | .23
11 Todd Worrell (186) (Top half) | .05 | .02
12 Todd Worrell (187) (Bottom half) | .05 | .02
13 Len Dykstra LCS | .15 | .07
14 Gary Carter LCS | .10 | .05
15 Mike Scott LCS | .05 | .02
16 Gary Pettis LCS | .05 | .02
17 Jim Rice LCS | .10 | .05
18 Marty Barrett LCS | .05 | .02
19 Bruce Hurst WS | .05 | .02
20 Dwight Evans WS | .10 | .05
21 Len Dykstra WS | .15 | .07
22 Gary Carter WS | .10 | .05
23 Dave Henderson WS | .05 | .02
24 Ray Knight WS | .10 | .05
25 Mets Celebrate WS | .10 | .05
26 Glenn Davis | .05 | .02
27 Nolan Ryan (188) | 2.00 | .90
28 Charlie Kerfeld(189) | .05 | .02
29 Jose Cruz (190) | .10 | .05
30 Phil Garner (191) | .10 | .05
31 Bill Doran (192) | .05 | .02
32 Bob Knepper (195) | .05 | .02
33 Denny Walling (196) | .05 | .02
34 Kevin Bass (197) | .05 | .02
35 Mike Scott | .05 | .02
36 Dale Murphy | .15 | .07
37 Paul Assenmacher (198) | .05 | .02
38 Ken Oberkfell (200) | .05 | .02
39 Andres Thomas (201) | .05 | .02
40 Gene Garber (202) | .05 | .02
41 Bob Horner | .05 | .02
42 Rafael Ramirez (203) | .05 | .02
43 Rick Mahler (204) | .05 | .02
44 Omar Moreno (205) | .05 | .02
45 Dave Palmer (206) | .05 | .02
46 Ozzie Smith | .40 | .18
47 Bob Forsch (207) | .05 | .02
48 Willie McGee (209) | .05 | .02
49 Tom Herr (210) | .05 | .02
50 Vince Coleman (211) | .05 | .02
51 Andy Van Slyke (212) | .10 | .05
52 Jack Clark (215) | .10 | .05
53 John Tudor (216) | .05 | .02
54 Terry Pendleton(217) | .10 | .05
55 Todd Worrell | .10 | .05
56 Lee Smith | .15 | .07
57 Leon Durham (218) | .05 | .02
58 Jerry Mumphrey (219) | .05 | .02
59 Shawon Dunston (220) | .10 | .05
60 Scott Sanderson(221) | .05 | .02
61 Ryne Sandberg | .50 | .23
62 Gary Matthews (222) | .05 | .02
63 Dennis Eckersley (225) | .15 | .07
64 Jody Davis (226) | .05 | .02
65 Keith Moreland (227) | .05 | .02
66 Mike Marshall (228) | .05 | .02
67 Bill Madlock (229) | .10 | .05
68 Greg Brock (230) | .05 | .02
69 Pedro Guerrero (231) | .10 | .05
70 Steve Sax | .05 | .02
71 Rick Honeycutt (232) | .05 | .02
72 Franklin Stubbs(235) | .05 | .02
73 Mike Scioscia (236) | .05 | .02
74 Mariano Duncan (237) | .05 | .02
75 Fernando Valenzuela | .10 | .05
76 Hubie Brooks | .05 | .02
77 Andre Dawson (238) | .15 | .07
78 Tim Burke (240) | .05 | .02
79 Floyd Youmans (241) | .05 | .02
80 Tim Wallach (242) | .05 | .02
81 Jeff Reardon (243) | .10 | .05
82 Mitch Webster (244) | .05 | .02
83 Bryn Smith (245) | .05 | .02
84 Andres Galarraga (246) | .50 | .23
85 Tim Raines | .10 | .05
86 Chris Brown | .05 | .02
87 Bob Brenly (247) | .05 | .02
88 Will Clark (249) | 1.50 | .70
89 Scott Garrelts (250) | .05 | .02
90 Jeffrey Leonard(251) | .05 | .02
91 Robby Thompson (252) | .10 | .05
92 Mike Krukow (255) | .05 | .02
93 Danny Gladden (256) | .05 | .02
94 Candy Maldonado(257) | .05 | .02
95 Chili Davis | .10 | .05
96 Dwight Gooden | .15 | .07
97 Sid Fernandez (258) | .05 | .02
98 Len Dykstra (259) | .15 | .07
99 Bob Ojeda (260) | .05 | .02
100 Wally Backman (261) | .05 | .02
101 Gary Carter | .10 | .05
102 Keith Hernandez(262) | .10 | .05
103 Darryl Strawberry (265) | .15 | .07
104 Roger McDowell (266) | .05 | .02
105 Ron Darling (267) | .05 | .02
106 Tony Gwynn | .75 | .35
107 Dave Dravecky (268) | .10 | .05
108 Terry Kennedy (269) | .05 | .02
109 Rich Gossage (270) | .10 | .05
110 Garry Templeton(271) | .05 | .02
111 Lance McCullers(272) | .05 | .02
112 Eric Show (275) | .05 | .02
113 John Kruk (276) | .50 | .23
114 Tim Flannery (277) | .05 | .02
115 Steve Garvey | .15 | .07
116 Mike Schmidt | .60 | .25
117 Glenn Wilson (278) | .05 | .02
118 Kent Tekulve (280) | .05 | .02
119 Gary Redus (281) | .05 | .02
120 Shane Rawley (282) | .05 | .02
121 Von Hayes | .05 | .02
122 Don Carman (283) | .05 | .02
123 Bruce Ruffin (285) | .05 | .02
124 Steve Bedrosian(286) | .05 | .02
125 Juan Samuel (287) | .05 | .02
126 Sid Bream (288) | .05 | .02
127 Cecilio Guante (289) | .05 | .02
128 Rick Reuschel (290) | .05 | .02
129 Tony Pena (291) | .05 | .02
130 Rick Rhoden | .05 | .02
131 Barry Bonds (292) | 3.00 | 1.35
132 Joe Orsulak (295) | .05 | .02
133 Jim Morrison (296) | .05 | .02
134 R.J. Reynolds (297) | .05 | .02
135 Johnny Ray | .05 | .02
136 Eric Davis | .10 | .05
137 Tom Browning (298) | .05 | .02
138 John Franco (300) | .10 | .05
139 Pete Rose (301) | .75 | .35
140 Bill Gullickson(302) | .05 | .02
141 Ron Oester (303) | .05 | .02
142 Bo Diaz (304) | .05 | .02
143 Buddy Bell (305) | .10 | .05
144 Eddie Milner (306) | .05 | .02
145 Dave Parker | .10 | .05
146 Kirby Puckett FOIL | 1.25 | .55
147 Rickey Henderson FOIL | .40 | .18
148 Wade Boggs FOIL | .40 | .18
149 Lance Parrish FOIL | .15 | .07
150 Wally Joyner FOIL | .75 | .35
151 Cal Ripken FOIL | 3.00 | 1.35
152 Dave Winfield FOIL | .40 | .18
153 Lou Whitaker FOIL | .10 | .05
154 Roger Clemens FOIL | .60 | .25
155 Tony Gwynn FOIL | 1.25 | .55
156 Ryne Sandberg FOIL | .75 | .35
157 Keith Hernandez FOIL | .10 | .05
158 Gary Carter FOIL | .30 | .14
159 Darryl Strawberry FOIL | .15 | .07
160 Mike Schmidt FOIL | 1.00 | .45
161 Dale Murphy FOIL | .30 | .14
162 Ozzie Smith FOIL | .60 | .25
163 Dwight Gooden FOIL | .30 | .14
164 Jose Canseco | .75 | .35
165 Curt Young (307) | .05 | .02
166 Alfredo Griffin(308) | .05 | .02
167 Dave Stewart (309) | .10 | .05
168 Mike Davis (310) | .05 | .02
169 Bruce Bochte (311) | .05 | .02
170 Dwayne Murphy (312) | .05 | .02
171 Carney Lansford(313) | .10 | .05
172 Joaquin Andujar (1) | .05 | .02
173 Dave Kingman | .10 | .05
174 Wally Joyner | .50 | .23
175 Gary Pettis (2) | .05 | .02
176 Dick Schofield (3) | .05 | .02
177 Donnie Moore (4) | .05 | .02
178 Brian Downing (5) | .05 | .02
179 Mike Witt | .05 | .02
180 Bob Boone (6) | .10 | .05
181 Kirk McCaskill (7) | .05 | .02
182 Doug DeCinces (8) | .05 | .02
183 Don Sutton (9) | .15 | .07
184 Jesse Barfield | .05 | .02
185 Tom Henke (10) | .05 | .02
186 Willie Upshaw (11) | .05 | .02
187 Mark Eichhorn (12) | .05 | .02
188 Damaso Garcia (27) | .05 | .02
189 Jim Clancy (28) | .05 | .02
190 Lloyd Moseby (29) | .05 | .02
191 Tony Fernandez (30) | .05 | .02
192 Jimmy Key (31) | .10 | .05
193 George Bell | .05 | .02
194 Rob Deer | .05 | .02
195 Mark Clear (32) | .05 | .02
196 Robin Yount (33) | .25 | .11
197 Jim Gantner (34) | .05 | .02
198 Cecil Cooper (35) | .10 | .05
199 Teddy Higuera | .05 | .02
200 Paul Molitor (38) | .25 | .11
201 Dan Plesac (39) | .05 | .02
202 Billy Joe Robidoux (40) | .05 | .02
203 Earnie Riles (42) | .05 | .02
204 Ken Schrom (43) | .05 | .02
205 Pat Tabler (44) | .05 | .02
206 Mel Hall (45) | .05 | .02
207 Tony Bernazard (47) | .05 | .02
208 Joe Carter | .15 | .07
209 Ernie Camacho (48) | .05 | .02
210 Julio Franco (49) | .10 | .05
211 Tom Candiotti (50) | .05 | .02
212 Brook Jacoby (51) | .05 | .02
213 Cory Snyder | .05 | .02
214 Jim Presley | .05 | .02
215 Mike Moore (52) | .05 | .02
216 Harold Reynolds (53) | .10 | .05
217 Scott Bradley (54) | .05 | .02
218 Matt Young (57) | .05 | .02
219 Mark Langston (58) | .10 | .05
220 Alvin Davis (59) | .05 | .02
221 Phil Bradley (60) | .05 | .02
222 Ken Phelps (62) | .05 | .02
223 Danny Tartabull | .10 | .05
224 Eddie Murray | .30 | .14
225 Rick Dempsey (63) | .05 | .02
226 Fred Lynn (64) | .10 | .05
227 Mike Boddicker (65) | .05 | .02
228 Don Aase (66) | .05 | .02
229 Larry Sheets (67) | .05 | .02
230 Storm Davis (68) | .05 | .02
231 Lee Lacy (69) | .05 | .02
232 Jim Traber (71) | .05 | .02
233 Cal Ripken | 2.00 | .90
234 Larry Parrish | .05 | .02
235 Gary Ward (72) | .05 | .02
236 Pete Incaviglia (73) | .10 | .05
237 Scott Fletcher (74) | .05 | .02
238 Greg Harris (77) | .05 | .02
239 Pete O'Brien | .05 | .02
240 Charlie Hough (78) | .05 | .02
241 Don Slaught (79) | .05 | .02
242 Steve Buechele (80) | .05 | .02
243 Oddibe McDowell (81) | .05 | .02
244 Roger Clemens (82) | .40 | .18
245 Bob Stanley (83) | .05 | .02
246 Tom Seaver (84) | .50 | .23
247 Rich Gedman (87) | .05 | .02
248 Jim Rice | .10 | .05
249 Dennis Boyd (88) | .05 | .02
250 Bill Buckner (89) | .10 | .05
251 Dwight Evans (90) | .10 | .05
252 Don Baylor (91) | .10 | .05
253 Wade Boggs | .25 | .11
254 George Brett | .75 | .35
255 Steve Farr (92) | .05 | .02
256 Jim Sundberg (93) | .05 | .02
257 Dan Quisenberry (94) | .05 | .02
258 Charlie Leibrandt(97) | .05 | .02
259 Argenis Salazar (98) | .05 | .02
260 Frank White (99) | .10 | .05
261 Willie Wilson (100) | .05 | .02
262 Lonnie Smith (102) | .05 | .02
263 Steve Balboni | .05 | .02
264 Darrell Evans | .10 | .05
265 Johnny Grubb (103) | .05 | .02
266 Jack Morris (104) | .10 | .05
267 Lou Whitaker (105) | .10 | .05
268 Chet Lemon (107) | .05 | .02
269 Lance Parrish (108) | .10 | .05
270 Alan Trammell (109) | .15 | .07
271 Darnell Coles (110) | .05 | .02
272 Willie Hernandez (111) | .05 | .02
273 Kirk Gibson | .10 | .05
274 Kirby Puckett | .75 | .35
275 Mike Smithson (112) | .05 | .02
276 Mickey Hatcher (113) | .05 | .02
277 Frank Viola (114) | .05 | .02
278 Bert Blyleven (117) | .10 | .05
279 Gary Gaetti | .10 | .05
280 Tom Brunansky (118) | .05 | .02
281 Kent Hrbek (119) | .10 | .05
282 Roy Smalley (120) | .05 | .02

☐ 283 Greg Gagne (122) .05 .02
☐ 284 Harold Baines .10 .05
☐ 285 Ron Hassey (123) .05 .02
☐ 286 Floyd Bannister(124) .05 .02
☐ 287 Ozzie Guillen (125) .05 .02
☐ 288 Carlton Fisk (126) .25 .11
☐ 289 Tim Hulett (127) .05 .02
☐ 290 Joe Cowley (128) .05 .02
☐ 291 Greg Walker (129) .05 .02
☐ 292 Neil Allen (131) .05 .02
☐ 293 John Cangelosi .05 .02
☐ 294 Don Mattingly 1.00 .45
☐ 295 Mike Easler (132) .05 .02
☐ 296 Rickey Henderson(133) .25 .11
☐ 297 Dan Pasqua (134) .05 .02
☐ 298 Dave Winfield (137) .25 .11
☐ 299 Dave Righetti .05 .02
☐ 300 Mike Pagliarulo(138) .05 .02
☐ 301 Ron Guidry (139) .10 .05
☐ 302 Willie Randolph(140) .10 .05
☐ 303 Dennis Rasmussen (141) .05 .02
☐ 304 Jose Canseco (142) .75 .35
☐ 305 Andres Thomas (143) .05 .02
☐ 306 Danny Tartabull(144) .10 .05
☐ 307 Robby Thompson (165) .10 .05
☐ 308 Pete Incaviglia(166) .10 .05
☐ 309 Dale Sveum (167) .05 .02
☐ 310 Todd Worrell (168) .10 .05
☐ 311 Andy Allanson (169) .05 .02
☐ 312 Bruce Ruffin (170) .05 .02
☐ 313 Wally Joyner (171) .50 .23
☐ xx Album 1.00 .45

1988 Topps

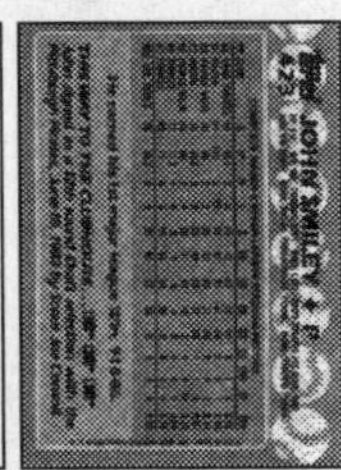

This set consists of 792 standard-size cards. The cards were primarily issued in 15-card wax packs, 42-card rack packs and factory sets. Card fronts feature white borders encasing a color photo with team name running across the top and player name diagonally across the bottom. Subsets include Record Breakers (1-7), All-Stars (386-407), Turn Back the Clock (661-665), and Team Leaders (scattered throughout the set). The manager cards contain a team checklist on back. The key Rookie Cards in this set are Ellis Burks, Ken Caminiti, Tom Glavine, Jeff Montgomery, and Matt Williams.

	MINT	NRMT
COMPLETE SET (792)	10.00	4.50
COMP.FACT.SET (792)	12.00	5.50
COMMON CARD (1-792)	.05	.02

☐ 1 Vince Coleman RB .05 .02
100 Steals for
Third Cons. Season
☐ 2 Don Mattingly RB .20 .09
Six Grand Slams
☐ 3 Mark McGwire RB .30 .14
Rookie Homer Record
(No white spot)
☐ 3A Mark McGwire RB .20 .09
Rookie Homer Record
(White spot behind
left foot)
☐ 4 Eddie Murray RB .20 .09
Switch Home Runs,
Two Straight Games
(No caption on front)
☐ 4A Eddie Murray RB .40 .18
Switch Home Runs,
Two Straight Games
(Caption in box
on card front)
☐ 5 Phil Niekro .10 .05
Joe Niekro RB
Brothers Win Record
☐ 6 Nolan Ryan RB .40 .18
11th 200 K's Season
☐ 7 Benito Santiago RB .05 .02
34-Game Hitting Streak
Rookie Record
☐ 8 Kevin Elster .10 .05
☐ 9 Andy Hawkins .05 .02
☐ 10 Ryne Sandberg .25 .11
☐ 11 Mike Young .05 .02
☐ 12 Bill Schroeder .05 .02
☐ 13 Andres Thomas .05 .02
☐ 14 Sparky Anderson MG .10 .05
(Checklist back)
☐ 15 Chili Davis .05 .02
☐ 16 Kirk McCaskill .05 .02
☐ 17 Ron Oester .05 .02
☐ 18A Al Leiter ERR .20 .09
(Photo actually
Steve George,
right ear visible)
☐ 18B Al Leiter COR .20 .09
(Left ear visible)
☐ 19 Mark Davidson .05 .02
☐ 20 Kevin Gross .05 .02
☐ 21 Red Sox TL .10 .05
Wade Boggs and
Spike Owen
☐ 22 Greg Swindell .05 .02
☐ 23 Ken Landreaux .05 .02
☐ 24 Jim Deshaies .05 .02
☐ 25 Andres Galarraga .20 .09
☐ 26 Mitch Williams .10 .05
☐ 27 R.J. Reynolds .05 .02
☐ 28 Jose Nunez .05 .02
☐ 29 Argenis Salazar .05 .02
☐ 30 Sid Fernandez .05 .02
☐ 31 Bruce Bochy .05 .02
☐ 32 Mike Morgan .05 .02
☐ 33 Rob Deer .05 .02
☐ 34 Ricky Horton .05 .02
☐ 35 Harold Baines .05 .02
☐ 36 Jamie Moyer .05 .02
☐ 37 Ed Romero .05 .02
☐ 38 Jeff Calhoun .05 .02
☐ 39 Gerald Perry .05 .02
☐ 40 Orel Hershiser .20 .09
☐ 41 Bob Melvin .05 .02
☐ 42 Bill Landrum .05 .02
☐ 43 Dick Schofield .05 .02
☐ 44 Lou Piniella MG .10 .05
(Checklist back)
☐ 45 Kent Hrbek .10 .05
☐ 46 Darnell Coles .05 .02
☐ 47 Joaquin Andujar .05 .02
☐ 48 Alan Ashby .05 .02
☐ 49 Dave Clark .05 .02
☐ 50 Hubie Brooks .05 .02
☐ 51 Orioles TL .40 .18
Eddie Murray and
Cal Ripken
☐ 52 Don Robinson .05 .02
☐ 53 Curt Wilkerson .05 .02
☐ 54 Jim Clancy .05 .02
☐ 55 Phil Bradley .05 .02
☐ 56 Ed Hearn .05 .02
☐ 57 Tim Crews .05 .02
☐ 58 Dave Magadan .05 .02
☐ 59 Danny Cox .05 .02
☐ 60 Rickey Henderson .20 .09
☐ 61 Mark Knudson .05 .02
☐ 62 Jeff Hamilton .05 .02
☐ 63 Jimmy Jones .05 .02
☐ 64 Ken Caminiti .75 .35
☐ 65 Leon Durham .05 .02
☐ 66 Shane Rawley .05 .02
☐ 67 Ken Oberkfell .05 .02
☐ 68 Dave Dravecky .10 .05
☐ 69 Mike Hart .05 .02
☐ 70 Roger Clemens .40 .18
☐ 71 Gary Pettis .05 .02
☐ 72 Dennis Eckersley .20 .09
☐ 73 Randy Bush .05 .02
☐ 74 Tom Lasorda MG .20 .09
(Checklist back)
☐ 75 Joe Carter .20 .09
☐ 76 Dennis Martinez .10 .05
☐ 77 Tom O'Malley .05 .02
☐ 78 Dan Petry .05 .02
☐ 79 Ernie Whitt .05 .02
☐ 80 Mark Langston .05 .02
☐ 81 Reds TL .05 .02
Ron Robinson
and John Franco
☐ 82 Darrel Akerfelds .05 .02
☐ 83 Jose Oquendo .05 .02
☐ 84 Cecilio Guante .05 .02
☐ 85 Howard Johnson .05 .02
☐ 86 Ron Karkovice .05 .02
☐ 87 Mike Mason .05 .02
☐ 88 Earnie Riles .05 .02
☐ 89 Gary Thurman .05 .02
☐ 90 Dale Murphy .20 .09
☐ 91 Joey Cora .25 .11
☐ 92 Len Matuszek .05 .02
☐ 93 Bob Sebra .05 .02
☐ 94 Chuck Jackson .05 .02
☐ 95 Lance Parrish .05 .02
☐ 96 Todd Benzinger .10 .05
☐ 97 Scott Garrelts .05 .02
☐ 98 Rene Gonzales .05 .02
☐ 99 Chuck Finley .10 .05
☐ 100 Jack Clark .10 .05
☐ 101 Allan Anderson .05 .02
☐ 102 Barry Larkin .30 .14
☐ 103 Curt Young .05 .02
☐ 104 Dick Williams MG .10 .05
(Checklist back)
☐ 105 Jesse Orosco .05 .02
☐ 106 Jim Walewander .05 .02
☐ 107 Scott Bailes .05 .02
☐ 108 Steve Lyons .05 .02
☐ 109 Joel Skinner .05 .02
☐ 110 Teddy Higuera .05 .02
☐ 111 Expos TL .05 .02
Hubie Brooks and
Vance Law
☐ 112 Les Lancaster .05 .02
☐ 113 Kelly Gruber .05 .02
☐ 114 Jeff Russell .05 .02
☐ 115 Johnny Ray .05 .02
☐ 116 Jerry Don Gleaton .05 .02
☐ 117 James Steels .05 .02
☐ 118 Bob Welch .05 .02
☐ 119 Robbie Wine .05 .02
☐ 120 Kirby Puckett .40 .18
☐ 121 Checklist 1-132 .05 .02
☐ 122 Tony Bernazard .05 .02
☐ 123 Tom Candiotti .05 .02
☐ 124 Ray Knight .10 .05
☐ 125 Bruce Hurst .05 .02
☐ 126 Steve Jeltz .05 .02
☐ 127 Jim Gott .05 .02
☐ 128 Johnny Grubb .05 .02
☐ 129 Greg Minton .05 .02
☐ 130 Buddy Bell .10 .05
☐ 131 Don Schulze .05 .02
☐ 132 Donnie Hill .05 .02
☐ 133 Greg Mathews .05 .02
☐ 134 Chuck Tanner MG .10 .05
(Checklist back)
☐ 135 Dennis Rasmussen .05 .02
☐ 136 Brian Dayett .05 .02
☐ 137 Chris Bosio .05 .02
☐ 138 Mitch Webster .05 .02
☐ 139 Jerry Browne .05 .02
☐ 140 Jesse Barfield .05 .02
☐ 141 Royals TL .20 .09
George Brett and
Bret Saberhagen
☐ 142 Andy Van Slyke .10 .05
☐ 143 Mickey Tettleton .10 .05
☐ 144 Don Gordon .05 .02
☐ 145 Bill Madlock .10 .05
☐ 146 Donell Nixon .05 .02
☐ 147 Bill Buckner .10 .05
☐ 148 Carmelo Martinez .05 .02
☐ 149 Ken Howell .05 .02
☐ 150 Eric Davis .05 .02
☐ 151 Bob Knepper .05 .02
☐ 152 Jody Reed .10 .05
☐ 153 John Habyan .05 .02
☐ 154 Jeff Stone .05 .02
☐ 155 Bruce Sutter .10 .05
☐ 156 Gary Matthews .05 .02
☐ 157 Atlee Hammaker .05 .02
☐ 158 Tim Hulett .05 .02
☐ 159 Brad Arnsberg .05 .02
☐ 160 Willie McGee .05 .02
☐ 161 Bryn Smith .05 .02
☐ 162 Mark McLemore .05 .02
☐ 163 Dale Mohorcic .05 .02
☐ 164 Dave Johnson MG .10 .05
(Checklist back)
☐ 165 Robin Yount .20 .09
☐ 166 Rick Rodriquez .05 .02
☐ 167 Rance Mulliniks .05 .02
☐ 168 Barry Jones .05 .02
☐ 169 Ross Jones .05 .02
☐ 170 Rich Gossage .05 .02
☐ 171 Cubs TL .05 .02
Shawon Dunston
and Manny Trillo
☐ 172 Lloyd McClendon .05 .02
☐ 173 Eric Plunk .05 .02
☐ 174 Phil Garner .05 .02
☐ 175 Kevin Bass .05 .02
☐ 176 Jeff Reed .05 .0
☐ 177 Frank Tanana .05 .02
☐ 178 Dwayne Henry .05 .02

☐ 179 Charlie Puleo	.05	.02
☐ 180 Terry Kennedy	.05	.02
☐ 181 David Cone	.20	.09
☐ 182 Ken Phelps	.05	.02
☐ 183 Tom Lawless	.05	.02
☐ 184 Ivan Calderon	.05	.02
☐ 185 Rick Rhoden	.05	.02
☐ 186 Rafael Palmeiro	.20	.09
☐ 187 Steve Kiefer	.05	.02
☐ 188 John Russell	.05	.02
☐ 189 Wes Gardner	.05	.02
☐ 190 Candy Maldonado	.05	.02
☐ 191 John Cerutti	.05	.02
☐ 192 Devon White	.10	.05
☐ 193 Brian Fisher	.05	.02
☐ 194 Tom Kelly MG	.10	.05
(Checklist back)		
☐ 195 Dan Quisenberry	.05	.02
☐ 196 Dave Engle	.05	.02
☐ 197 Lance McCullers	.05	.02
☐ 198 Franklin Stubbs	.05	.02
☐ 199 Dave Meads	.05	.02
☐ 200 Wade Boggs	.20	.09
☐ 201 Rangers TL	.05	.02
Bobby Valentine MG		
Pete O'Brien,		
Pete Incaviglia and		
Steve Buechele		
☐ 202 Glenn Hoffman	.05	.02
☐ 203 Fred Toliver	.05	.02
☐ 204 Paul O'Neill	.05	.02
☐ 205 Nelson Liriano	.05	.02
☐ 206 Domingo Ramos	.05	.02
☐ 207 John Mitchell	.05	.02
☐ 208 Steve Lake	.05	.02
☐ 209 Richard Dotson	.05	.02
☐ 210 Willie Randolph	.10	.05
☐ 211 Frank DiPino	.05	.02
☐ 212 Greg Brock	.05	.02
☐ 213 Albert Hall	.05	.02
☐ 214 Dave Schmidt	.05	.02
☐ 215 Von Hayes	.05	.02
☐ 216 Jerry Reuss	.05	.02
☐ 217 Harry Spilman	.05	.02
☐ 218 Dan Schatzeder	.05	.02
☐ 219 Mike Stanley	.10	.05
☐ 220 Tom Henke	.05	.02
☐ 221 Rafael Belliard	.05	.02
☐ 222 Steve Farr	.05	.02
☐ 223 Stan Jefferson	.05	.02
☐ 224 Tom Trebelhorn MG	.05	.02
(Checklist back)		
☐ 225 Mike Scioscia	.05	.02
☐ 226 Dave Lopes	.10	.05
☐ 227 Ed Correa	.05	.02
☐ 228 Wallace Johnson	.05	.02
☐ 229 Jeff Musselman	.05	.02
☐ 230 Pat Tabler	.05	.02
☐ 231 Pirates TL	.20	.09
Barry Bonds and		
Bobby Bonilla		
☐ 232 Bob James	.05	.02
☐ 233 Rafael Santana	.05	.02
☐ 234 Ken Dayley	.05	.02
☐ 235 Gary Ward	.05	.02
☐ 236 Ted Power	.05	.02
☐ 237 Mike Heath	.05	.02
☐ 238 Luis Polonia	.20	.09
☐ 239 Roy Smalley	.05	.02
☐ 240 Lee Smith	.20	.09
☐ 241 Damaso Garcia	.05	.02
☐ 242 Tom Niedenfuer	.05	.02
☐ 243 Mark Ryal	.05	.02
☐ 244 Jeff D. Robinson	.05	.02
☐ 245 Rich Gedman	.05	.02
☐ 246 Mike Campbell	.05	.02
☐ 247 Thad Bosley	.05	.02
☐ 248 Storm Davis	.05	.02
☐ 249 Mike Marshall	.05	.02
☐ 250 Nolan Ryan	.75	.35
☐ 251 Tom Foley	.05	.02
☐ 252 Bob Brower	.05	.02
☐ 253 Checklist 133-264	.05	.02
☐ 254 Lee Elia MG	.05	.02
(Checklist back)		
☐ 255 Mookie Wilson	.10	.05
☐ 256 Ken Schrom	.05	.02
☐ 257 Jerry Royster	.05	.02
☐ 258 Ed Nunez	.05	.02
☐ 259 Ron Kittle	.05	.02
☐ 260 Vince Coleman	.05	.02
☐ 261 Giants TL	.05	.02
(Five players)		
☐ 262 Drew Hall	.05	.02
☐ 263 Glenn Braggs	.05	.02
☐ 264 Les Straker	.05	.02
☐ 265 Do Diaz	.05	.02

☐ 266 Paul Assenmacher	.05	.02
☐ 267 Billy Bean	.05	.02
☐ 268 Bruce Ruffin	.05	.02
☐ 269 Ellis Burks	.30	.14
☐ 270 Mike Witt	.05	.02
☐ 271 Ken Gerhart	.05	.02
☐ 272 Steve Ontiveros	.05	.02
☐ 273 Garth Iorg	.05	.02
☐ 274 Junior Ortiz	.05	.02
☐ 275 Kevin Seitzer	.10	.05
☐ 276 Luis Salazar	.05	.02
☐ 277 Alejandro Pena	.05	.02
☐ 278 Jose Cruz	.05	.02
☐ 279 Randy St.Claire	.05	.02
☐ 280 Pete Incaviglia	.05	.02
☐ 281 Jerry Hairston	.05	.02
☐ 282 Pat Perry	.05	.02
☐ 283 Phil Lombardi	.05	.02
☐ 284 Larry Bowa MG	.10	.05
(Checklist back)		
☐ 285 Jim Presley	.05	.02
☐ 286 Chuck Crim	.05	.02
☐ 287 Manny Trillo	.05	.02
☐ 288 Pat Pacillo	.05	.02
(Chris Sabo in		
background of photo)		
☐ 289 Dave Bergman	.05	.02
☐ 290 Tony Fernandez	.05	.02
☐ 291 Astros TL	.05	.02
Billy Hatcher		
and Kevin Bass		
☐ 292 Carney Lansford	.10	.05
☐ 293 Doug Jones	.20	.09
☐ 294 Al Pedrique	.05	.02
☐ 295 Bert Blyleven	.10	.05
☐ 296 Floyd Rayford	.05	.02
☐ 297 Zane Smith	.05	.02
☐ 298 Milt Thompson	.05	.02
☐ 299 Steve Crawford	.05	.02
☐ 300 Don Mattingly	.30	.14
☐ 301 Bud Black	.05	.02
☐ 302 Jose Uribe	.05	.02
☐ 303 Eric Show	.05	.02
☐ 304 George Hendrick	.05	.02
☐ 305 Steve Sax	.05	.02
☐ 306 Billy Hatcher	.05	.02
☐ 307 Mike Trujillo	.05	.02
☐ 308 Lee Mazzilli	.05	.02
☐ 309 Bill Long	.05	.02
☐ 310 Tom Herr	.05	.02
☐ 311 Scott Sanderson	.05	.02
☐ 312 Joey Meyer	.05	.02
☐ 313 Bob McClure	.05	.02
☐ 314 Jimy Williams MG	.05	.02
(Checklist back)		
☐ 315 Dave Parker	.20	.09
☐ 316 Jose Rijo	.05	.02
☐ 317 Tom Nieto	.05	.02
☐ 318 Mel Hall	.05	.02
☐ 319 Mike Loynd	.05	.02
☐ 320 Alan Trammell	.05	.02
☐ 321 White Sox TL	.10	.05
Harold Baines and		
Carlton Fisk		
☐ 322 Vicente Palacios	.05	.02
☐ 323 Rick Leach	.05	.02
☐ 324 Danny Jackson	.05	.02
☐ 325 Glenn Hubbard	.05	.02
☐ 326 Al Nipper	.05	.02
☐ 327 Larry Sheets	.05	.02
☐ 328 Greg Cadaret	.05	.02
☐ 329 Chris Speier	.05	.02
☐ 330 Eddie Whitson	.05	.02
☐ 331 Brian Downing	.05	.02
☐ 332 Jerry Reed	.05	.02
☐ 333 Wally Backman	.05	.02
☐ 334 Dave LaPoint	.05	.02
☐ 335 Claudell Washington	.05	.02
☐ 336 Ed Lynch	.05	.02
☐ 337 Jim Gantner	.05	.02
☐ 338 Brian Holton UER	.05	.02
(1987 ERA .389,		
should be 3.89)		
☐ 339 Kurt Stillwell	.05	.02
☐ 340 Jack Morris	.05	.02
☐ 341 Carmen Castillo	.05	.02
☐ 342 Larry Andersen	.05	.02
☐ 343 Greg Gagne	.05	.02
☐ 344 Tony LaRussa MG	.10	.05
(Checklist back)		
☐ 345 Scott Fletcher	.05	.02
☐ 346 Vance Law	.05	.02
☐ 347 Joe Johnson	.05	.02
☐ 348 Jim Eisenreich	.20	.09
☐ 349 Bob Walk	.05	.02
☐ 350 Will Clark	.25	.11
☐ 351 Cardinals TL	.10	.05

Card		
Red Schoendienst CO		
and Tony Pena		
☐ 352 Billy Ripken	.10	.05
☐ 353 Ed Olwine	.05	.02
☐ 354 Marc Sullivan	.05	.02
☐ 355 Roger McDowell	.05	.02
☐ 356 Luis Aguayo	.05	.02
☐ 357 Floyd Bannister	.05	.02
☐ 358 Rey Quinones	.05	.02
☐ 359 Tim Stoddard	.05	.02
☐ 360 Tony Gwynn	.50	.23
☐ 361 Greg Maddux	1.25	.55
☐ 362 Juan Castillo	.05	.02
☐ 363 Willie Fraser	.05	.02
☐ 364 Nick Esasky	.05	.02
☐ 365 Floyd Youmans	.05	.02
☐ 366 Chet Lemon	.05	.02
☐ 367 Tim Leary	.05	.02
☐ 368 Gerald Young	.05	.02
☐ 369 Greg Harris	.05	.02
☐ 370 Jose Canseco	.20	.09
☐ 371 Joe Hesketh	.05	.02
☐ 372 Matt Williams	.60	.25
☐ 373 Checklist 265-396	.05	.02
☐ 374 Doc Edwards MG	.05	.02
(Checklist back)		
☐ 375 Tom Brunansky	.05	.02
☐ 376 Bill Wilkinson	.05	.02
☐ 377 Sam Horn	.05	.02
☐ 378 Todd Frohwirth	.05	.02
☐ 379 Rafael Ramirez	.05	.02
☐ 380 Joe Magrane	.05	.02
☐ 381 Angels TL	.10	.05
Wally Joyner and		
Jack Howell		
☐ 382 Keith A. Miller	.05	.02
☐ 383 Eric Bell	.05	.02
☐ 384 Neil Allen	.05	.02
☐ 385 Carlton Fisk	.20	.09
☐ 386 Don Mattingly AS	.20	.09
☐ 387 Willie Randolph AS	.05	.02
☐ 388 Wade Boggs AS	.20	.09
☐ 389 Alan Trammell AS	.10	.05
☐ 390 George Bell AS	.05	.02
☐ 391 Kirby Puckett AS	.20	.09
☐ 392 Dave Winfield AS	.20	.09
☐ 393 Matt Nokes AS	.05	.02
☐ 394 Roger Clemens AS	.20	.09
☐ 395 Jimmy Key AS	.10	.05
☐ 396 Tom Henke AS	.05	.02
☐ 397 Jack Clark AS	.05	.02
☐ 398 Juan Samuel AS	.05	.02
☐ 399 Tim Wallach AS	.05	.02
☐ 400 Ozzie Smith AS	.20	.09
☐ 401 Andre Dawson AS	.20	.09
☐ 402 Tony Gwynn AS	.20	.09
☐ 403 Tim Raines AS	.05	.02
☐ 404 Benny Santiago AS	.05	.02
☐ 405 Dwight Gooden AS	.10	.05
☐ 406 Shane Rawley AS	.05	.02
☐ 407 Steve Bedrosian AS	.05	.02
☐ 408 Dion James	.05	.02
☐ 409 Joel McKeon	.05	.02
☐ 410 Tony Pena	.05	.02
☐ 411 Wayne Tolleson	.05	.02
☐ 412 Randy Myers	.05	.02
☐ 413 John Christensen	.05	.02
☐ 414 John McNamara MG	.05	.02
(Checklist back)		
☐ 415 Don Carman	.05	.02
☐ 416 Keith Moreland	.05	.02
☐ 417 Mark Ciardi	.05	.02
☐ 418 Joel Youngblood	.05	.02
☐ 419 Scott McGregor	.05	.02
☐ 420 Wally Joyner	.20	.09
☐ 421 Ed VandeBerg	.05	.02
☐ 422 Dave Concepcion	.10	.05
☐ 423 John Smiley	.10	.05
☐ 424 Dwayne Murphy	.05	.02
☐ 425 Jeff Reardon	.10	.05
☐ 426 Randy Ready	.05	.02
☐ 427 Paul Kilgus	.05	.02
☐ 428 John Shelby	.05	.02
☐ 429 Tigers TL	.10	.05
Alan Trammell and		
Kirk Gibson		
☐ 430 Glenn Davis	.05	.02
☐ 431 Casey Candaele	.05	.02
☐ 432 Mike Moore	.05	.02
☐ 433 Bill Pecota	.05	.02
☐ 434 Rick Aguilera	.05	.02
☐ 435 Mike Pagliarulo	.05	.02
☐ 436 Mike Bielecki	.05	.02
☐ 437 Fred Manrique	.05	.02
☐ 438 Rob Ducey	.05	.02
☐ 439 Dave Martinez	.05	.02
☐ 440 Steve Bedrosian	.05	.02
☐ 441 Rick Manning	.05	.02

☐ 442 Tom Bolton .05 .02
☐ 443 Ken Griffey .05 .02
☐ 444 Cal Ripken Sr. MG .05 .02
(Checklist back)
UER (two copyrights)
☐ 445 Mike Krukow .05 .02
☐ 446 Doug DeCinces .05 .02
(Now with Cardinals
on card front)
☐ 447 Jeff Montgomery .20 .09
☐ 448 Mike Davis .05 .02
☐ 449 Jeff M. Robinson .05 .02
☐ 450 Barry Bonds .50 .23
☐ 451 Keith Atherton .05 .02
☐ 452 Willie Wilson .05 .02
☐ 453 Dennis Powell .05 .02
☐ 454 Marvell Wynne .05 .02
☐ 455 Shawn Hillegas .05 .02
☐ 456 Dave Anderson .05 .02
☐ 457 Terry Leach .05 .02
☐ 458 Ron Hassey .05 .02
☐ 459 Yankees TL .20 .09
Dave Winfield and
Willie Randolph
☐ 460 Ozzie Smith .25 .11
☐ 461 Danny Darwin .05 .02
☐ 462 Don Slaught .05 .02
☐ 463 Fred McGriff .20 .09
☐ 464 Jay Tibbs .05 .02
☐ 465 Paul Molitor .20 .09
☐ 466 Jerry Mumphrey .05 .02
☐ 467 Don Aase .05 .02
☐ 468 Darren Daulton .10 .05
☐ 469 Jeff Dedmon .05 .02
☐ 470 Dwight Evans .10 .05
☐ 471 Donnie Moore .05 .02
☐ 472 Robby Thompson .05 .02
☐ 473 Joe Niekro .05 .02
☐ 474 Tom Brookens .05 .02
☐ 475 Pete Rose MG .25 .11
(Checklist back)
☐ 476 Dave Stewart .10 .05
☐ 477 Jamie Quirk .05 .02
☐ 478 Sid Bream .05 .02
☐ 479 Brett Butler .05 .02
☐ 480 Dwight Gooden .10 .05
☐ 481 Mariano Duncan .05 .02
☐ 482 Mark Davis .05 .02
☐ 483 Rod Booker .05 .02
☐ 484 Pat Clements .05 .02
☐ 485 Harold Reynolds .05 .02
☐ 486 Pat Keedy .05 .02
☐ 487 Jim Pankovits .05 .02
☐ 488 Andy McGaffigan .05 .02
☐ 489 Dodgers TL .05 .02
Pedro Guerrero and
Fernando Valenzuela
☐ 490 Larry Parrish .05 .02
☐ 491 B.J. Surhoff .10 .05
☐ 492 Doyle Alexander .05 .02
☐ 493 Mike Greenwell .10 .05
☐ 494 Wally Ritchie .05 .02
☐ 495 Eddie Murray .20 .09
☐ 496 Guy Hoffman .05 .02
☐ 497 Kevin Mitchell .10 .05
☐ 498 Bob Boone .10 .05
☐ 499 Eric King .05 .02
☐ 500 Andre Dawson .20 .09
☐ 501 Tim Birtsas .05 .02
☐ 502 Dan Gladden .05 .02
☐ 503 Junior Noboa .05 .02
☐ 504 Bob Rodgers MG .05 .02
(Checklist back)
☐ 505 Willie Upshaw .05 .02
☐ 506 John Cangelosi .05 .02
☐ 507 Mark Gubicza .05 .02
☐ 508 Tim Teufel .05 .02
☐ 509 Bill Dawley .05 .02
☐ 510 Dave Winfield .20 .09
☐ 511 Joel Davis .05 .02
☐ 512 Alex Trevino .05 .02
☐ 513 Tim Flannery .05 .02
☐ 514 Pat Sheridan .05 .02
☐ 515 Juan Nieves .05 .02
☐ 516 Jim Sundberg .05 .02
☐ 517 Ron Robinson .05 .02
☐ 518 Greg Gross .05 .02
☐ 519 Mariners TL .05 .02
Harold Reynolds and
Phil Bradley
☐ 520 Dave Smith .05 .02
☐ 521 Jim Dwyer .05 .02
☐ 522 Bob Patterson .05 .02
☐ 523 Gary Roenicke .05 .02
☐ 524 Gary Lucas .05 .02
☐ 525 Marty Barrett .05 .02
☐ 526 Juan Berenguer .05 .02
☐ 527 Steve Henderson .05 .02
☐ 528A Checklist 397-528 .20 .09
ERR (455 S. Carlton)
☐ 528B Checklist 397-528 .10 .05
COR (455 S. Hillegas)
☐ 529 Tim Burke .05 .02
☐ 530 Gary Carter .20 .09
☐ 531 Rich Yett .05 .02
☐ 532 Mike Kingery .05 .02
☐ 533 John Farrell .05 .02
☐ 534 John Wathan MG .05 .02
(Checklist back)
☐ 535 Ron Guidry .05 .02
☐ 536 John Morris .05 .02
☐ 537 Steve Buechele .05 .02
☐ 538 Bill Wegman .05 .02
☐ 539 Mike LaValliere .05 .02
☐ 540 Bret Saberhagen .05 .02
☐ 541 Juan Beniquez .05 .02
☐ 542 Paul Noce .05 .02
☐ 543 Kent Tekulve .05 .02
☐ 544 Jim Traber .05 .02
☐ 545 Don Baylor .05 .02
☐ 546 John Candelaria .05 .02
☐ 547 Felix Fermin .05 .02
☐ 548 Shane Mack .05 .02
☐ 549 Braves TL .05 .02
Albert Hall,
Dale Murphy,
Ken Griffey
and Dion James
☐ 550 Pedro Guerrero .10 .05
☐ 551 Terry Steinbach .05 .02
☐ 552 Mark Thurmond .05 .02
☐ 553 Tracy Jones .05 .02
☐ 554 Mike Smithson .05 .02
☐ 555 Brook Jacoby .05 .02
☐ 556 Stan Clarke .05 .02
☐ 557 Craig Reynolds .05 .02
☐ 558 Bob Ojeda .05 .02
☐ 559 Ken Williams .05 .02
☐ 560 Tim Wallach .05 .02
☐ 561 Rick Cerone .05 .02
☐ 562 Jim Lindeman .05 .02
☐ 563 Jose Guzman .05 .02
☐ 564 Frank Lucchesi MG .05 .02
(Checklist back)
☐ 565 Lloyd Moseby .05 .02
☐ 566 Charlie O'Brien .05 .02
☐ 567 Mike Diaz .05 .02
☐ 568 Chris Brown .05 .02
☐ 569 Charlie Leibrandt .05 .02
☐ 570 Jeffrey Leonard .05 .02
☐ 571 Mark Williamson .05 .02
☐ 572 Chris James .05 .02
☐ 573 Bob Stanley .05 .02
☐ 574 Graig Nettles .05 .02
☐ 575 Don Sutton .20 .09
☐ 576 Tommy Hinzo .05 .02
☐ 577 Tom Browning .05 .02
☐ 578 Gary Gaetti .05 .02
☐ 579 Mets TL .10 .05
Gary Carter and
Kevin McReynolds
☐ 580 Mark McGwire .60 .25
☐ 581 Tito Landrum .05 .02
☐ 582 Mike Henneman .10 .05
☐ 583 Dave Valle .05 .02
☐ 584 Steve Trout .05 .02
☐ 585 Ozzie Guillen .05 .02
☐ 586 Bob Forsch .05 .02
☐ 587 Terry Puhl .05 .02
☐ 588 Jeff Parrett .05 .02
☐ 589 Geno Petralli .05 .02
☐ 590 George Bell .05 .02
☐ 591 Doug Drabek .05 .02
☐ 592 Dale Sveum .05 .02
☐ 593 Bob Tewksbury .05 .02
☐ 594 Bobby Valentine MG .10 .05
(Checklist back)
☐ 595 Frank White .10 .05
☐ 596 John Kruk .10 .05
☐ 597 Gene Garber .05 .02
☐ 598 Lee Lacy .05 .02
☐ 599 Calvin Schiraldi .05 .02
☐ 600 Mike Schmidt .25 .11
☐ 601 Jack Lazorko .05 .02
☐ 602 Mike Aldrete .05 .02
☐ 603 Rob Murphy .05 .02
☐ 604 Chris Bando .05 .02
☐ 605 Kirk Gibson .10 .05
☐ 606 Moose Haas .05 .02
☐ 607 Mickey Hatcher .05 .02
☐ 608 Charlie Kerfeld .05 .02
☐ 609 Twins TL .10 .05
Gary Gaetti and
Kent Hrbek
☐ 610 Keith Hernandez .10 .05
☐ 611 Tommy John .10 .05
☐ 612 Curt Ford .05 .02
☐ 613 Bobby Thigpen .05 .02
☐ 614 Herm Winningham .05 .02
☐ 615 Jody Davis .05 .02
☐ 616 Jay Aldrich .05 .02
☐ 617 Oddibe McDowell .05 .02
☐ 618 Cecil Fielder .20 .09
☐ 619 Mike Dunne .05 .02
(Inconsistent design,
black name on front)
☐ 620 Cory Snyder .05 .02
☐ 621 Gene Nelson .05 .02
☐ 622 Kal Daniels .05 .02
☐ 623 Mike Flanagan .05 .02
☐ 624 Jim Leyland MG .10 .05
(Checklist back)
☐ 625 Frank Viola .05 .02
☐ 626 Glenn Wilson .05 .02
☐ 627 Joe Boever .05 .02
☐ 628 Dave Henderson .05 .02
☐ 629 Kelly Downs .05 .02
☐ 630 Darrell Evans .10 .05
☐ 631 Jack Howell .05 .02
☐ 632 Steve Shields .05 .02
☐ 633 Barry Lyons .05 .02
☐ 634 Jose DeLeon .05 .02
☐ 635 Terry Pendleton .10 .05
☐ 636 Charles Hudson .05 .02
☐ 637 Jay Bell .25 .11
☐ 638 Steve Balboni .05 .02
☐ 639 Brewers TL .05 .02
Glenn Braggs
and Tony Muser CO
☐ 640 Garry Templeton .05 .02
(Inconsistent design,
green border)
☐ 641 Rick Honeycutt .05 .02
☐ 642 Bob Dernier .05 .02
☐ 643 Rocky Childress .05 .02
☐ 644 Terry McGriff .05 .02
☐ 645 Matt Nokes .05 .02
☐ 646 Checklist 529-660 .05 .02
☐ 647 Pascual Perez .05 .02
☐ 648 Al Newman .05 .02
☐ 649 DeWayne Buice .05 .02
☐ 650 Cal Ripken .75 .35
☐ 651 Mike Jackson .10 .05
☐ 652 Bruce Benedict .05 .02
☐ 653 Jeff Sellers .05 .02
☐ 654 Roger Craig MG .10 .05
(Checklist back)
☐ 655 Len Dykstra .10 .05
☐ 656 Lee Guetterman .05 .02
☐ 657 Gary Redus .05 .02
☐ 658 Tim Conroy .05 .02
(Inconsistent design,
name in white)
☐ 659 Bobby Meacham .05 .02
☐ 660 Rick Reuschel .05 .02
☐ 661 Nolan Ryan TBC '83 .35 .16
☐ 662 Jim Rice TBC '78 .10 .05
☐ 663 Ron Blomberg TBC '73 .05 .02
☐ 664 Bob Gibson TBC '68 .20 .09
☐ 665 Stan Musial TBC '63 .20 .09
☐ 666 Mario Soto .05 .02
☐ 667 Luis Quinones .05 .02
☐ 668 Walt Terrell .05 .02
☐ 669 Phillies TL .05 .02
Lance Parrish
and Mike Ryan CO
☐ 670 Dan Plesac .05 .02
☐ 671 Tim Laudner .05 .02
☐ 672 John Davis .05 .02
☐ 673 Tony Phillips .05 .02
☐ 674 Mike Fitzgerald .05 .02
☐ 675 Jim Rice .10 .05
☐ 676 Ken Dixon .05 .02
☐ 677 Eddie Milner .05 .02
☐ 678 Jim Acker .05 .02
☐ 679 Darrell Miller .05 .02
☐ 680 Charlie Hough .10 .05
☐ 681 Bobby Bonilla .05 .02
☐ 682 Jimmy Key .05 .02
☐ 683 Julio Franco .10 .05
☐ 684 Hal Lanier MG .05 .02
(Checklist back)
☐ 685 Ron Darling .05 .02
☐ 686 Terry Francona .05 .02
☐ 687 Mickey Brantley .05 .02
☐ 688 Jim Winn .05 .02
☐ 689 Tom Pagnozzi .10 .05
☐ 690 Jay Howell .05 .02
☐ 691 Dan Pasqua .05 .02
☐ 692 Mike Birkbeck .05 .02
☐ 693 Benito Santiago .05 .02

Card	MINT	NRMT
☐ 694 Eric Nolte	.05	.02
☐ 695 Shawon Dunston	.05	.02
☐ 696 Duane Ward	.05	.02
☐ 697 Steve Lombardozzi	.05	.02
☐ 698 Brad Havens	.05	.02
☐ 699 Padres TL Benito Santiago and Tony Gwynn	.10	.05
☐ 700 George Brett	.40	.18
☐ 701 Sammy Stewart	.05	.02
☐ 702 Mike Gallego	.05	.02
☐ 703 Bob Brenly	.05	.02
☐ 704 Dennis Boyd	.05	.02
☐ 705 Juan Samuel	.05	.02
☐ 706 Rick Mahler	.05	.02
☐ 707 Fred Lynn	.05	.02
☐ 708 Gus Polidor	.05	.02
☐ 709 George Frazier	.05	.02
☐ 710 Darryl Strawberry	.10	.05
☐ 711 Bill Gullickson	.05	.02
☐ 712 John Moses	.05	.02
☐ 713 Willie Hernandez	.05	.02
☐ 714 Jim Fregosi MG (Checklist back)	.05	.02
☐ 715 Todd Worrell	.05	.02
☐ 716 Lenn Sakata	.05	.02
☐ 717 Jay Baller	.05	.02
☐ 718 Mike Felder	.05	.02
☐ 719 Denny Walling	.05	.02
☐ 720 Tim Raines	.10	.05
☐ 721 Pete O'Brien	.05	.02
☐ 722 Manny Lee	.05	.02
☐ 723 Bob Kipper	.05	.02
☐ 724 Danny Tartabull	.05	.02
☐ 725 Mike Boddicker	.05	.02
☐ 726 Alfredo Griffin	.05	.02
☐ 727 Greg Booker	.05	.02
☐ 728 Andy Allanson	.05	.02
☐ 729 Blue Jays TL George Bell and Fred McGriff	.10	.05
☐ 730 John Franco	.10	.05
☐ 731 Rick Schu	.05	.02
☐ 732 David Palmer	.05	.02
☐ 733 Spike Owen	.05	.02
☐ 734 Craig Lefferts	.05	.02
☐ 735 Kevin McReynolds	.05	.02
☐ 736 Matt Young	.05	.02
☐ 737 Butch Wynegar	.05	.02
☐ 738 Scott Bankhead	.05	.02
☐ 739 Daryl Boston	.05	.02
☐ 740 Rick Sutcliffe	.05	.02
☐ 741 Mike Easler	.05	.02
☐ 742 Mark Clear	.05	.02
☐ 743 Larry Herndon	.05	.02
☐ 744 Whitey Herzog MG (Checklist back)	.10	.05
☐ 745 Bill Doran	.05	.02
☐ 746 Gene Larkin	.05	.02
☐ 747 Bobby Witt	.05	.02
☐ 748 Reid Nichols	.05	.02
☐ 749 Mark Eichhorn	.05	.02
☐ 750 Bo Jackson	.20	.09
☐ 751 Jim Morrison	.05	.02
☐ 752 Mark Grant	.05	.02
☐ 753 Danny Heep	.05	.02
☐ 754 Mike LaCoss	.05	.02
☐ 755 Ozzie Virgil	.05	.02
☐ 756 Mike Maddux	.05	.02
☐ 757 John Marzano	.05	.02
☐ 758 Eddie Williams	.10	.05
☐ 759 A's TL UER Mark McGwire and Jose Canseco (two copyrights)	.30	.14
☐ 760 Mike Scott	.05	.02
☐ 761 Tony Armas	.05	.02
☐ 762 Scott Bradley	.05	.02
☐ 763 Doug Sisk	.05	.02
☐ 764 Greg Walker	.05	.02
☐ 765 Neal Heaton	.05	.02
☐ 766 Henry Cotto	.05	.02
☐ 767 Jose Lind	.05	.02
☐ 768 Dickie Noles (Now with Tigers on card front)	.05	.02
☐ 769 Cecil Cooper	.10	.05
☐ 770 Lou Whitaker	.10	.05
☐ 771 Ruben Sierra	.05	.02
☐ 772 Sal Butera	.05	.02
☐ 773 Frank Williams	.05	.02
☐ 774 Gene Mauch MG (Checklist back)	.10	.05
☐ 775 Dave Stieb	.05	.02
☐ 776 Checklist 661-792	.05	.02
☐ 777 Lonnie Smith	.05	.02
☐ 778A Keith Comstock ERR (White "Padres")	2.00	.90
☐ 778B Keith Comstock COR (Blue "Padres")	.05	.02
☐ 779 Tom Glavine	.50	.23
☐ 780 Fernando Valenzuela	.10	.05
☐ 781 Keith Hughes	.05	.02
☐ 782 Jeff Ballard	.05	.02
☐ 783 Ron Roenicke	.05	.02
☐ 784 Joe Sambito	.05	.02
☐ 785 Alvin Davis	.05	.02
☐ 786 Joe Price (Inconsistent design, orange team name)	.05	.02
☐ 787 Bill Almon	.05	.02
☐ 788 Ray Searage	.05	.02
☐ 789 Indians' TL Joe Carter and Cory Snyder	.10	.05
☐ 790 Dave Righetti	.10	.05
☐ 791 Ted Simmons	.10	.05
☐ 792 John Tudor	.05	.02

1988 Topps Tiffany

This was the fifth year that Topps issued a "Tiffany" set. These 792 standard-size cards parallel the regular Topps cards. These cards were issued in factory set form only, produced in Topps Irish facility, and only available through Topps hobby dealers. These cards were again produced in relatively large quantities and the mulitplier value is reduced compared to pre-1987 levels.

	MINT	NRMT
COMPLETE FACT.SET (792)	40.00	18.00
COMMON CARD (1-792)	.10	.05
*STARS: 3X to 6X BASIC CARDS		
*ROOKIES: 2X to 4X BASIC CARDS		

1988 Topps Glossy All-Stars

This set of 22 glossy cards was inserted one per rack pack. Players selected for the set are the starting players (plus manager and honorary captain) in the 1987 All-Star Game in Oakland. Cards measure the standard size and the backs feature red and blue printing on a white card stock.

	MINT	NRMT
COMPLETE SET (22)	4.00	1.80
COMMON CARD (1-22)	.05	.02
☐ 1 John McNamara MG	.05	.02
☐ 2 Don Mattingly	1.00	.45
☐ 3 Willie Randolph	.05	.02
☐ 4 Wade Boggs	.50	.23
☐ 5 Cal Ripken	2.00	.90
☐ 6 George Bell	.05	.02
☐ 7 Rickey Henderson	.40	.18
☐ 8 Dave Winfield	.40	.18
☐ 9 Terry Kennedy	.05	.02
☐ 10 Bret Saberhagen	.05	.02
☐ 11 Jim Hunter CAPT	.10	.05
☐ 12 Dave Johnson MG	.05	.02
☐ 13 Jack Clark	.10	.05
☐ 14 Ryne Sandberg	1.00	.45
☐ 15 Mike Schmidt	.75	.35
☐ 16 Ozzie Smith	1.00	.45
☐ 17 Eric Davis	.10	.05
☐ 18 Andre Dawson	.25	.11
☐ 19 Darryl Strawberry	.10	.05
☐ 20 Gary Carter	.15	.07
☐ 21 Mike Scott	.05	.02
☐ 22 Billy Williams CAPT	.10	.05

1988 Topps Glossy Send-Ins

Topps issued this set through a mail-in offer explained and advertised on the wax packs. This 60-card set features glossy fronts with each card measuring the standard size. The offer provided your choice of any one of the six 10-card subsets (1-10, 11-20, etc.) for 1.25 plus six of the Special Offer ("Spring Fever Baseball") insert cards, which were found one per wax pack. One complete

set was obtainable by sending 7.50 plus 18 special offer cards. The last two players (numerically) in each ten-card subset are actually "Hot Prospects."

	MINT	NRMT
COMPLETE SET (60)	10.00	4.50
COMMON CARD (1-60)	.10	.05
☐ 1 Andre Dawson	.30	.14
☐ 2 Jesse Barfield	.10	.05
☐ 3 Mike Schmidt	1.00	.45
☐ 4 Ruben Sierra	.10	.05
☐ 5 Mike Scott	.10	.05
☐ 6 Cal Ripken	4.00	1.80
☐ 7 Gary Carter	.30	.14
☐ 8 Kent Hrbek	.20	.09
☐ 9 Kevin Seitzer	.20	.09
☐ 10 Mike Henneman	.20	.09
☐ 11 Don Mattingly	2.00	.90
☐ 12 Tim Raines	.20	.09
☐ 13 Roger Clemens	1.25	.55
☐ 14 Ryne Sandberg	1.25	.55
☐ 15 Tony Fernandez	.10	.05
☐ 16 Eric Davis	.20	.09
☐ 17 Jack Morris	.20	.09
☐ 18 Tim Wallach	.10	.05
☐ 19 Mike Dunne	.10	.05
☐ 20 Mike Greenwell	.20	.09
☐ 21 Dwight Evans	.20	.09
☐ 22 Darryl Strawberry	.20	.09
☐ 23 Cory Snyder	.10	.05
☐ 24 Pedro Guerrero	.10	.05
☐ 25 Rickey Henderson	.50	.23
☐ 26 Dale Murphy	.40	.18
☐ 27 Kirby Puckett	1.50	.70
☐ 28 Steve Bedrosian	.10	.05
☐ 29 Devon White	.10	.05
☐ 30 Benito Santiago	.10	.05
☐ 31 George Bell	.10	.05
☐ 32 Keith Hernandez	.20	.09
☐ 33 Dave Stewart	.10	.05
☐ 34 Dave Parker	.20	.09
☐ 35 Tom Henke	.10	.05
☐ 36 Willie McGee	.20	.09
☐ 37 Alan Trammell	.30	.14
☐ 38 Tony Gwynn	2.00	.90
☐ 39 Mark McGwire	2.00	.90
☐ 40 Joe Magrane	.10	.05
☐ 41 Jack Clark	.10	.05
☐ 42 Willie Randolph	.10	.05
☐ 43 Juan Samuel	.10	.05
☐ 44 Joe Carter	.40	.18
☐ 45 Shane Rawley	.10	.05
☐ 46 Dave Winfield	.50	.23
☐ 47 Ozzie Smith	1.25	.55
☐ 48 Wally Joyner	.20	.09
☐ 49 B.J. Surhoff	.20	.09
☐ 50 Ellis Burks	.60	.25
☐ 51 Wade Boggs	.60	.25
☐ 52 Howard Johnson	.10	.05
☐ 53 George Brett	2.00	.90
☐ 54 Dwight Gooden	.20	.09
☐ 55 Jose Canseco	1.00	.45
☐ 56 Lee Smith	.20	.09
☐ 57 Paul Molitor	.75	.35
☐ 58 Andres Galarraga	.50	.23
☐ 59 Matt Nokes	.10	.05
☐ 60 Casey Candaele	.10	.05

1988 Topps Rookies

Inserted in each supermarket jumbo pack is a card from this series of 22 of 1987's best rookies as determined by Topps. Jumbo packs consisted of 100 (regular issue 1988 Topps baseball) cards with a stick of gum plus the insert "Rookie" card. The card fronts are in full color and measure the standard size. The card backs are printed in red and blue on white card stock and are numbered at the bottom.

	MINT	NRMT
COMPLETE SET (22)	4.00	1.80
COMMON CARD (1-22)	.05	.02

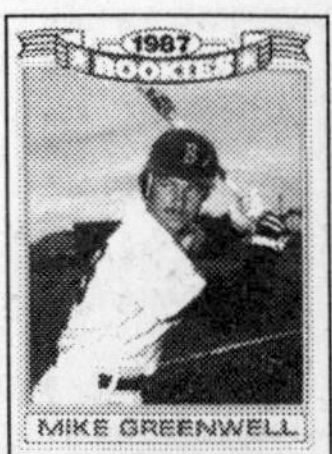

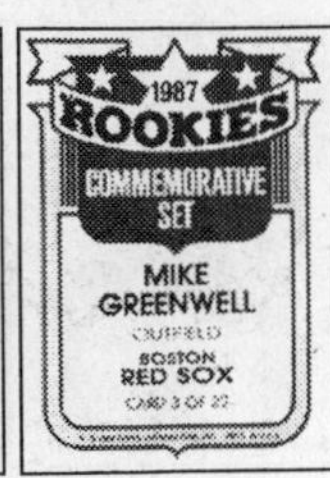

☐ 1 Billy Ripken	.05	.02
☐ 2 Ellis Burks	1.00	.45
☐ 3 Mike Greenwell	.20	.09
☐ 4 DeWayne Buice	.05	.02
☐ 5 Devon White	.40	.18
☐ 6 Fred Manrique	.05	.02
☐ 7 Mike Henneman	.10	.05
☐ 8 Matt Nokes	.05	.02
☐ 9 Kevin Seitzer	.10	.05
☐ 10 B.J. Surhoff	.20	.09
☐ 11 Casey Candaele	.05	.02
☐ 12 Randy Myers	.40	.18
☐ 13 Mark McGwire	2.00	.90
☐ 14 Luis Polonia	.10	.05
☐ 15 Terry Steinbach	.20	.09
☐ 16 Mike Dunne	.05	.02
☐ 17 Al Pedrique	.05	.02
☐ 18 Benito Santiago	.10	.05
☐ 19 Kelly Downs	.05	.02
☐ 20 Joe Magrane	.05	.02
☐ 21 Jerry Browne	.05	.02
☐ 22 Jeff Musselman	.05	.02

1988 Topps Wax Box Cards

The cards in this 16-card set measure the standard size. Cards have essentially the same design as the 1988 Topps regular issue set. The cards were printed on the bottoms of the regular issue wax pack boxes. These 16 cards, "lettered" A through P, are considered a separate set in their own right and are not typically included in a complete set of the regular issue 1988 Topps cards. The value of the panels uncut is slightly greater, perhaps by 25 percent greater, than the value of the individual cards cut up carefully. The card lettering is sequenced alphabetically by player's name.

	MINT	NRMT
COMPLETE SET (16)	5.00	2.20
COMMON CARD (A-P)	.10	.05
☐ A Don Baylor	.20	.09
☐ B Steve Bedrosian	.10	.05
☐ C Juan Beniquez	.10	.05
☐ D Bob Boone	.20	.09
☐ E Darrell Evans	.20	.09
☐ F Tony Gwynn	1.25	.55
☐ G John Kruk	.20	.09
☐ H Marvell Wynne	.10	.05
☐ I Joe Carter	.30	.14
☐ J Eric Davis	.20	.09
☐ K Howard Johnson	.10	.05
☐ L Darryl Strawberry	.20	.09
☐ M Rickey Henderson	.60	.25
☐ N Nolan Ryan	2.50	1.10
☐ O Mike Schmidt	1.00	.45
☐ P Kent Tekulve	.10	.05

1988 Topps Traded

This standard-size 132-card Traded set was distributed exclusively in factory set form in blue and white taped boxes through hobby dealers. The cards are identical in style to the Topps regular issue except for whiter stock and t-suffixed numbering on back. Cards are ordered alphabetically by player's last name. This set generated additional interest upon release due to the inclusion of

members of the 1988 U.S. Olympic baseball team. These Olympians are indicated in the checklist below by OLY. The key extended Rookie Cards in this set are Jim Abbott, Roberto Alomar, Brady Anderson, Andy Benes, Jay Buhner, Ron Gant, Mark Grace, Tino Martinez, Jack McDowell, Charles Nagy, Robin Ventura and Walt Weiss.

	MINT	NRMT
COMP.FACT.SET (132)	12.00	5.50
COMMON CARD (1T-132T)	.10	.05
☐ 1T Jim Abbott OLY	.40	.18
☐ 2T Juan Agosto	.10	.05
☐ 3T Luis Alicea	.20	.09
☐ 4T Roberto Alomar	3.00	1.35
☐ 5T Brady Anderson	1.50	.70
☐ 6T Jack Armstrong	.10	.05
☐ 7T Don August	.10	.05
☐ 8T Floyd Bannister	.10	.05
☐ 9T Bret Barberie OLY	.20	.09
☐ 10T Jose Bautista	.10	.05
☐ 11T Don Baylor	.30	.14
☐ 12T Tim Belcher	.20	.09
☐ 13T Buddy Bell	.20	.09
☐ 14T Andy Benes OLY	.75	.35
☐ 15T Damon Berryhill	.10	.05
☐ 16T Bud Black	.10	.05
☐ 17T Pat Borders	.20	.09
☐ 18T Phil Bradley	.10	.05
☐ 19T Jeff Branson OLY	.20	.09
☐ 20T Tom Brunansky	.10	.05
☐ 21T Jay Buhner	1.50	.70
☐ 22T Brett Butler	.20	.09
☐ 23T Jim Campanis OLY	.10	.05
☐ 24T Sil Campusano	.10	.05
☐ 25T John Candelaria	.10	.05
☐ 26T Jose Cecena	.10	.05
☐ 27T Rick Cerone	.10	.05
☐ 28T Jack Clark	.20	.09
☐ 29T Kevin Coffman	.10	.05
☐ 30T Pat Combs OLY	.10	.05
☐ 31T Henry Cotto	.10	.05
☐ 32T Chili Davis	.30	.14
☐ 33T Mike Davis	.10	.05
☐ 34T Jose DeLeon	.10	.05
☐ 35T Richard Dotson	.10	.05
☐ 36T Cecil Espy	.10	.05
☐ 37T Tom Filer	.10	.05
☐ 38T Mike Fiore OLY	.10	.05
☐ 39T Ron Gant	.50	.23
☐ 40T Kirk Gibson	.40	.18
☐ 41T Rich Gossage	.30	.14
☐ 42T Mark Grace	1.50	.70
☐ 43T Alfredo Griffin	.10	.05
☐ 44T Ty Griffin OLY	.10	.05
☐ 45T Bryan Harvey	.20	.09
☐ 46T Ron Hassey	.10	.05
☐ 47T Ray Hayward	.10	.05
☐ 48T Dave Henderson	.10	.05
☐ 49T Tom Herr	.10	.05
☐ 50T Bob Horner	.10	.05
☐ 51T Ricky Horton	.10	.05
☐ 52T Jay Howell	.10	.05
☐ 53T Glenn Hubbard	.10	.05
☐ 54T Jeff Innis	.10	.05
☐ 55T Danny Jackson	.10	.05
☐ 56T Darrin Jackson	.20	.09
☐ 57T Roberto Kelly	.40	.18
☐ 58T Ron Kittle	.10	.05
☐ 59T Ray Knight	.20	.09
☐ 60T Vance Law	.10	.05
☐ 61T Jeffrey Leonard	.10	.05
☐ 62T Mike Macfarlane	.20	.09
☐ 63T Scotti Madison	.10	.05
☐ 64T Kirt Manwaring	.20	.09
☐ 65T Mark Marquess OLY CO	.10	.05
☐ 66T Tino Martinez OLY	5.00	2.20
☐ 67T Billy Masse OLY	.10	.05
☐ 68T Jack McDowell	.40	.18
☐ 69T Jack McKeon MG	.10	.05
☐ 70T Larry McWilliams	.10	.05
☐ 71T Mickey Morandini OLY	.30	.14
☐ 72T Keith Moreland	.10	.05
☐ 73T Mike Morgan	.10	.05
☐ 74T Charles Nagy OLY	1.00	.45
☐ 75T Al Nipper	.10	.05
☐ 76T Russ Nixon MG	.10	.05
☐ 77T Jesse Orosco	.10	.05
☐ 78T Joe Orsulak	.10	.05
☐ 79T Dave Palmer	.10	.05
☐ 80T Mark Parent	.10	.05
☐ 81T Dave Parker	.30	.14
☐ 82T Dan Pasqua	.10	.05
☐ 83T Melido Perez	.10	.05
☐ 84T Steve Peters	.10	.05
☐ 85T Dan Petry	.10	.05
☐ 86T Gary Pettis	.10	.05
☐ 87T Jeff Pico	.10	.05
☐ 88T Jim Poole OLY	.20	.09
☐ 89T Ted Power	.10	.05
☐ 90T Rafael Ramirez	.10	.05
☐ 91T Dennis Rasmussen	.10	.05
☐ 92T Jose Rijo	.10	.05
☐ 93T Ernie Riles	.10	.05
☐ 94T Luis Rivera	.10	.05
☐ 95T Doug Robbins OLY	.10	.05
☐ 96T Frank Robinson MG	.30	.14
☐ 97T Cookie Rojas MG	.10	.05
☐ 98T Chris Sabo	.20	.09
☐ 99T Mark Salas	.10	.05
☐ 100T Luis Salazar	.10	.05
☐ 101T Rafael Santana	.10	.05
☐ 102T Nelson Santovenia	.10	.05
☐ 103T Mackey Sasser	.10	.05
☐ 104T Calvin Schiraldi	.10	.05
☐ 105T Mike Schooler	.10	.05
☐ 106T Scott Servais OLY	.20	.09
☐ 107T Dave Silvestri OLY	.10	.05
☐ 108T Don Slaught	.10	.05
☐ 109T Joe Slusarski OLY	.10	.05
☐ 110T Lee Smith	.40	.18
☐ 111T Pete Smith	.10	.05
☐ 112T Jim Snyder MG	.10	.05
☐ 113T Ed Sprague OLY	.75	.35
☐ 114T Pete Stanicek	.10	.05
☐ 115T Kurt Stillwell	.10	.05
☐ 116T Todd Stottlemyre	.40	.18
☐ 117T Bill Swift	.10	.05
☐ 118T Pat Tabler	.10	.05
☐ 119T Scott Terry	.10	.05
☐ 120T Mickey Tettleton	.20	.09
☐ 121T Dickie Thon	.10	.05
☐ 122T Jeff Treadway	.10	.05
☐ 123T Willie Upshaw	.10	.05
☐ 124T Robin Ventura OLY	1.50	.70
☐ 125T Ron Washington	.10	.05
☐ 126T Walt Weiss	.20	.09
☐ 127T Bob Welch	.10	.05
☐ 128T David Wells	.40	.18
☐ 129T Glenn Wilson	.10	.05
☐ 130T Ted Wood OLY	.20	.09
☐ 131T Don Zimmer MG	.20	.09
☐ 132T Checklist 1T-132T	.10	.05

1988 Topps Traded Tiffany

As a bonus for those dealers who ordered the regula Tiffany sets, they received an equivalent number of Tiffan update sets. These 132 standard-size cards parallel th regular traded issue. Again issued in the Topps Iris facility, these cards feature glossy fronts and easy to rea backs. These sets were only issued in complete factor form.

	MINT	NRM
COMPLETE FACT.SET (132)	30.00	13.5
COMMON CARD (1T-132T)	.10	.0

*STARS: 2.5X to 5X BASIC CARDS ....
*ROOKIES: 1.25X TO 2.5X BASIC CARDS

1988 Topps Big

This set of 264 cards was issued as three separate distributed series of 88 cards each. Cards were distribut in wax packs with seven cards for a suggested retail of cents. These cards are very reminiscent in style of t

1956 Topps card set. The cards measure approximately 2 5/8" by 3 3/4" and are oriented horizontally.

	MINT	NRMT
COMPLETE SET (264)	20.00	9.00
COMMON CARD (1-264)	.05	.02
☐ 1 Paul Molitor	1.00	.45
☐ 2 Milt Thompson	.05	.02
☐ 3 Billy Hatcher	.05	.02
☐ 4 Mike Witt	.05	.02
☐ 5 Vince Coleman	.05	.02
☐ 6 Dwight Evans	.10	.05
☐ 7 Tim Wallach	.05	.02
☐ 8 Alan Trammell	.15	.07
☐ 9 Will Clark	1.00	.45
☐ 10 Jeff Reardon	.10	.05
☐ 11 Dwight Gooden	.10	.05
☐ 12 Benito Santiago	.10	.05
☐ 13 Jose Canseco	.75	.35
☐ 14 Dale Murphy	.50	.23
☐ 15 George Bell	.05	.02
☐ 16 Ryne Sandberg	1.25	.55
☐ 17 Brook Jacoby	.05	.02
☐ 18 Fernando Valenzuela	.10	.05
☐ 19 Scott Fletcher	.05	.02
☐ 20 Eric Davis	.10	.05
☐ 21 Willie Wilson	.05	.02
☐ 22 B.J. Surhoff	.10	.05
☐ 23 Steve Bedrosian	.05	.02
☐ 24 Dave Winfield	.75	.35
☐ 25 Bobby Bonilla	.10	.05
☐ 26 Larry Sheets	.05	.02
☐ 27 Ozzie Guillen	.05	.02
☐ 28 Checklist 1-88	.05	.02
☐ 29 Nolan Ryan	3.00	1.35
☐ 30 Bob Boone	.10	.05
☐ 31 Tom Herr	.05	.02
☐ 32 Wade Boggs	.60	.25
☐ 33 Neal Heaton	.05	.02
☐ 34 Doyle Alexander	.05	.02
☐ 35 Candy Maldonado	.05	.02
☐ 36 Kirby Puckett	2.00	.90
☐ 37 Gary Carter	.15	.07
☐ 38 Lance McCullers	.05	.02
☐ 39A Terry Steinbach (Topps logo in black)	.10	.05
☐ 39B Terry Steinbach (Topps logo in white)	.10	.05
☐ 40 Gerald Perry	.05	.02
☐ 41 Tom Henke	.10	.05
☐ 42 Leon Durham	.05	.02
☐ 43 Cory Snyder	.05	.02
☐ 44 Dale Sveum	.05	.02
☐ 45 Lance Parrish	.05	.02
☐ 46 Steve Sax	.05	.02
☐ 47 Charlie Hough	.10	.05
☐ 48 Kal Daniels	.05	.02
☐ 49 Bo Jackson	.10	.05
☐ 50 Ron Guidry	.05	.02
☐ 51 Bill Doran	.05	.02
☐ 52 Wally Joyner	.15	.07
☐ 53 Terry Pendleton	.10	.05
☐ 54 Marty Barrett	.05	.02
☐ 55 Andres Galarraga	.60	.25
☐ 56 Larry Herndon	.05	.02
☐ 57 Kevin Mitchell	.10	.05
☐ 58 Greg Gagne	.05	.02
☐ 59 Keith Hernandez	.10	.05
☐ 60 John Kruk	.10	.05
☐ 61 Mike LaValliere	.05	.02
☐ 62 Cal Ripken	3.00	1.35
☐ 63 Ivan Calderon	.05	.02
☐ 64 Alvin Davis	.05	.02
☐ 65 Luis Polonia	.10	.05
☐ 66 Robin Yount	.50	.23
☐ 67 Juan Samuel	.05	.02
☐ 68 Andres Thomas	.05	.02
☐ 69 Jeff Musselman	.05	.02
☐ 70 Jerry Mumphrey	.05	.02
☐ 71 Joe Carter	.50	.23
☐ 72 Mike Scioscia	.05	.02
☐ 73 Pete Incaviglia	.05	.02
☐ 74 Barry Larkin	.75	.35
☐ 75 Frank White	.10	.05
☐ 76 Willie Randolph	.10	.05
☐ 77 Kevin Bass	.05	.02
☐ 78 Brian Downing	.05	.02
☐ 79 Willie McGee	.10	.05
☐ 80 Ellis Burks	.75	.35
☐ 81 Hubie Brooks	.05	.02
☐ 82 Darrell Evans	.10	.05
☐ 83 Robby Thompson	.05	.02
☐ 84 Kent Hrbek	.10	.05
☐ 85 Ron Darling	.05	.02
☐ 86 Stan Jefferson	.05	.02
☐ 87 Teddy Higuera	.05	.02
☐ 88 Mike Schmidt	.75	.35
☐ 89 Barry Bonds	1.00	.45
☐ 90 Jim Presley	.05	.02
☐ 91 Orel Hershiser	.10	.05
☐ 92 Jesse Barfield	.05	.02
☐ 93 Tom Candiotti	.05	.02
☐ 94 Bret Saberhagen	.10	.05
☐ 95 Jose Uribe	.05	.02
☐ 96 Tom Browning	.05	.02
☐ 97 Johnny Ray	.05	.02
☐ 98 Mike Morgan	.05	.02
☐ 99 Lou Whitaker	.10	.05
☐ 100 Jim Sundberg	.05	.02
☐ 101 Roger McDowell	.05	.02
☐ 102 Randy Ready	.05	.02
☐ 103 Mike Gallego	.05	.02
☐ 104 Steve Buechele	.05	.02
☐ 105 Greg Walker	.05	.02
☐ 106 Jose Lind	.05	.02
☐ 107 Steve Trout	.05	.02
☐ 108 Rick Rhoden	.05	.02
☐ 109 Jim Pankovits	.05	.02
☐ 110 Ken Griffey	.10	.05
☐ 111 Danny Cox	.05	.02
☐ 112 Franklin Stubbs	.05	.02
☐ 113 Lloyd Moseby	.05	.02
☐ 114 Mel Hall	.05	.02
☐ 115 Kevin Seitzer	.10	.05
☐ 116 Tim Raines	.10	.05
☐ 117 Juan Castillo	.05	.02
☐ 118 Roger Clemens	1.00	.45
☐ 119 Mike Aldrete	.05	.02
☐ 120 Mario Soto	.05	.02
☐ 121 Jack Howell	.05	.02
☐ 122 Rick Schu	.05	.02
☐ 123 Jeff D. Robinson	.05	.02
☐ 124 Doug Drabek	.10	.05
☐ 125 Henry Cotto	.05	.02
☐ 126 Checklist 89-176	.05	.02
☐ 127 Gary Gaetti	.10	.05
☐ 128 Rick Sutcliffe	.05	.02
☐ 129 Howard Johnson	.05	.02
☐ 130 Chris Brown	.05	.02
☐ 131 Dave Henderson	.05	.02
☐ 132 Curt Wilkerson	.05	.02
☐ 133 Mike Marshall	.05	.02
☐ 134 Kelly Gruber	.05	.02
☐ 135 Julio Franco	.10	.05
☐ 136 Kurt Stillwell	.05	.02
☐ 137 Donnie Hill	.05	.02
☐ 138 Mike Pagliarulo	.05	.02
☐ 139 Von Hayes	.05	.02
☐ 140 Mike Scott	.05	.02
☐ 141 Bob Kipper	.05	.02
☐ 142 Harold Reynolds	.10	.05
☐ 143 Bob Brenly	.05	.02
☐ 144 Dave Concepcion	.10	.05
☐ 145 Devon White	.10	.05
☐ 146 Jeff Stone	.05	.02
☐ 147 Chet Lemon	.05	.02
☐ 148 Ozzie Virgil	.05	.02
☐ 149 Todd Worrell	.10	.05
☐ 150 Mitch Webster	.05	.02
☐ 151 Rob Deer	.05	.02
☐ 152 Rich Gedman	.05	.02
☐ 153 Andre Dawson	.50	.23
☐ 154 Mike Davis	.05	.02
☐ 155 Nelson Liriano	.05	.02
☐ 156 Greg Swindell	.05	.02
☐ 157 George Brett	1.50	.70
☐ 158 Kevin McReynolds	.05	.02
☐ 159 Brian Fisher	.05	.02
☐ 160 Mike Kingery	.05	.02
☐ 161 Tony Gwynn	1.50	.70
☐ 162 Don Baylor	.10	.05
☐ 163 Jerry Browne	.05	.02
☐ 164 Dan Pasqua	.05	.02
☐ 165 Rickey Henderson	.75	.35
☐ 166 Brett Butler	.10	.05
☐ 167 Nick Esasky	.05	.02
☐ 168 Kirk McCaskill	.05	.02
☐ 169 Fred Lynn	.05	.02
☐ 170 Jack Morris	.10	.05
☐ 171 Pedro Guerrero	.05	.02
☐ 172 Dave Stieb	.05	.02
☐ 173 Pat Tabler	.05	.02
☐ 174 Floyd Bannister	.05	.02
☐ 175 Rafael Belliard	.05	.02
☐ 176 Mark Langston	.05	.02
☐ 177 Greg Mathews	.05	.02
☐ 178 Claudell Washington	.05	.02
☐ 179 Mark McGwire	2.00	.90
☐ 180 Bert Blyleven	.10	.05
☐ 181 Jim Rice	.15	.07
☐ 182 Mookie Wilson	.05	.02
☐ 183 Willie Fraser	.05	.02
☐ 184 Andy Van Slyke	.10	.05
☐ 185 Matt Nokes	.05	.02
☐ 186 Eddie Whitson	.05	.02
☐ 187 Tony Fernandez	.05	.02
☐ 188 Rick Reuschel	.10	.05
☐ 189 Ken Phelps	.05	.02
☐ 190 Juan Nieves	.05	.02
☐ 191 Kirk Gibson	.10	.05
☐ 192 Glenn Davis	.05	.02
☐ 193 Zane Smith	.05	.02
☐ 194 Jose DeLeon	.05	.02
☐ 195 Gary Ward	.05	.02
☐ 196 Pascual Perez	.05	.02
☐ 197 Carlton Fisk	.60	.25
☐ 198 Oddibe McDowell	.05	.02
☐ 199 Mark Gubicza	.05	.02
☐ 200 Glenn Hubbard	.05	.02
☐ 201 Frank Viola	.05	.02
☐ 202 Jody Reed	.10	.05
☐ 203 Len Dykstra	.10	.05
☐ 204 Dick Schofield	.05	.02
☐ 205 Sid Bream	.05	.02
☐ 206 Willie Hernandez	.05	.02
☐ 207 Keith Moreland	.05	.02
☐ 208 Mark Eichhorn	.05	.02
☐ 209 Rene Gonzales	.05	.02
☐ 210 Dave Valle	.05	.02
☐ 211 Tom Brunansky	.05	.02
☐ 212 Charles Hudson	.05	.02
☐ 213 John Farrell	.05	.02
☐ 214 Jeff Treadway	.05	.02
☐ 215 Eddie Murray	1.00	.45
☐ 216 Checklist 177-264	.05	.02
☐ 217 Greg Brock	.05	.02
☐ 218 John Shelby	.05	.02
☐ 219 Craig Reynolds	.05	.02
☐ 220 Dion James	.05	.02
☐ 221 Carney Lansford	.05	.02
☐ 222 Juan Berenguer	.05	.02
☐ 223 Luis Rivera	.05	.02
☐ 224 Harold Baines	.10	.05
☐ 225 Shawon Dunston	.05	.02
☐ 226 Luis Aguayo	.05	.02
☐ 227 Pete O'Brien	.05	.02
☐ 228 Ozzie Smith	1.25	.55
☐ 229 Don Mattingly	2.00	.90
☐ 230 Danny Tartabull	.05	.02
☐ 231 Andy Allanson	.05	.02
☐ 232 John Franco	.10	.05
☐ 233 Mike Greenwell	.10	.05
☐ 234 Bob Ojeda	.05	.02
☐ 235 Chili Davis	.10	.05
☐ 236 Mike Dunne	.05	.02
☐ 237 Jim Morrison	.05	.02
☐ 238 Carmelo Martinez	.05	.02
☐ 239 Ernie Whitt	.05	.02
☐ 240 Scott Garrelts	.05	.02
☐ 241 Mike Moore	.05	.02
☐ 242 Dave Parker	.10	.05
☐ 243 Tim Laudner	.05	.02
☐ 244 Bill Wegman	.05	.02
☐ 245 Bob Horner	.05	.02
☐ 246 Rafael Santana	.05	.02
☐ 247 Alfredo Griffin	.05	.02
☐ 248 Mark Bailey	.05	.02
☐ 249 Ron Gant	.50	.23
☐ 250 Bryn Smith	.05	.02
☐ 251 Lance Johnson	.40	.18
☐ 252 Sam Horn	.05	.02
☐ 253 Darryl Strawberry	.10	.05
☐ 254 Chuck Finley	.10	.05
☐ 255 Darnell Coles	.05	.02
☐ 256 Mike Henneman	.10	.05
☐ 257 Andy Hawkins	.05	.02
☐ 258 Jim Clancy	.05	.02
☐ 259 Atlee Hammaker	.05	.02
☐ 260 Glenn Wilson	.05	.02
☐ 261 Larry McWilliams	.05	.02
☐ 262 Jack Clark	.10	.05
☐ 263 Walt Weiss	.15	.07
☐ 264 Gene Larkin	.05	.02

1988 Topps Coins

This full-color set of 60 coins contains a full-color photo of the player with a gold-starred scroll at the bottom containing the player's name, position and team. The backs contain the coin number and brief biographical data. Some of the coins have gold rims and some have silver rims. Each coin measures approximately 1 1/2" in diameter. The 1988 set is very similar to the 1987 set of the previous year; the 1988 coins have gold stars on the name scroll on the front of the coin as well as a 1988 copyright at the bottom of the reverse.

	MINT	NRMT
COMPLETE SET (60)	8.00	3.60
COMMON COIN (1-60)	.05	.02
☐ 1 George Bell	.05	.02
☐ 2 Roger Clemens	.50	.23
☐ 3 Mark McGwire	1.00	.45
☐ 4 Wade Boggs	.40	.18
☐ 5 Harold Baines	.10	.05
☐ 6 Ivan Calderon	.05	.02
☐ 7 Jose Canseco	.50	.23
☐ 8 Joe Carter	.10	.05
☐ 9 Jack Clark	.05	.02
☐ 10 Alvin Davis	.05	.02
☐ 11 Dwight Evans	.10	.05
☐ 12 Tony Fernandez	.05	.02
☐ 13 Gary Gaetti	.05	.02
☐ 14 Mike Greenwell	.05	.02
☐ 15 Charlie Hough	.05	.02
☐ 16 Wally Joyner	.15	.07
☐ 17 Jimmy Key	.10	.05
☐ 18 Mark Langston	.05	.02
☐ 19 Don Mattingly	1.00	.45
☐ 20 Paul Molitor	.50	.23
☐ 21 Jack Morris	.10	.05
☐ 22 Eddie Murray	.50	.23
☐ 23 Kirby Puckett	1.00	.45
☐ 24 Cal Ripken	2.00	.90
☐ 25 Bret Saberhagen	.10	.05
☐ 26 Ruben Sierra	.05	.02
☐ 27 Cory Snyder	.05	.02
☐ 28 Terry Steinbach	.10	.05
☐ 29 Danny Tartabull	.05	.02
☐ 30 Alan Trammell	.15	.07
☐ 31 Devon White	.10	.05
☐ 32 Robin Yount	.25	.11
☐ 33 Andre Dawson	.10	.05
☐ 34 Steve Bedrosian	.05	.02
☐ 35 Benny Santiago	.05	.02
☐ 36 Tony Gwynn	1.00	.45
☐ 37 Bobby Bonilla	.15	.07
☐ 38 Will Clark	.50	.23
☐ 39 Eric Davis	.05	.02
☐ 40 Mike Dunne	.05	.02
☐ 41 John Franco	.10	.05
☐ 42 Dwight Evans	.10	.05
☐ 43 Pedro Guerrero	.05	.02
☐ 44 Dion James	.05	.02
☐ 45 John Kruk	.10	.05
☐ 46 Jeffrey Leonard	.05	.02
☐ 47 Carmelo Martinez	.05	.02
☐ 48 Dale Murphy	.25	.11
☐ 49 Tim Raines	.10	.05
☐ 50 Nolan Ryan	2.00	.90
☐ 51 Juan Samuel	.05	.02
☐ 52 Ryne Sandberg	.75	.35
☐ 53 Mike Schmidt	.60	.25
☐ 54 Mike Scott	.05	.02
☐ 55 Ozzie Smith	.75	.35
☐ 56 Darryl Strawberry	.10	.05
☐ 57 Rick Sutcliffe	.05	.02
☐ 58 Fernando Valenzuela	.10	.05
☐ 59 Tim Wallach	.05	.02
☐ 60 Todd Worrell	.10	.05

1988 Topps Mini Leaders

The 1988 Topps Mini set of Major League Leaders features 77 cards of leaders of the various statistical categories for the 1987 season. The cards are numbered on the back and measure approximately 2 1/8" by 3". The set numbering is alphabetical by player within team and the teams themselves are in alphabetical order as well. The card backs are printed in blue, red, and yellow on white card stock. The cards were distributed as a separate issue in wax packs.

	MINT	NRMT
COMPLETE SET (77)	5.00	2.20
COMMON CARD (1-77)	.05	.02
☐ 1 Wade Boggs	.30	.14
☐ 2 Roger Clemens	.50	.23
☐ 3 Dwight Evans	.10	.05
☐ 4 DeWayne Buice	.05	.02
☐ 5 Brian Downing	.05	.02
☐ 6 Wally Joyner	.10	.05
☐ 7 Ivan Calderon	.05	.02
☐ 8 Carlton Fisk	.30	.14
☐ 9 Gary Redus	.05	.02
☐ 10 Darrell Evans	.10	.05
☐ 11 Jack Morris	.10	.05
☐ 12 Alan Trammell	.15	.07
☐ 13 Lou Whitaker	.10	.05
☐ 14 Bret Saberhagen	.05	.02
☐ 15 Kevin Seitzer	.05	.02
☐ 16 Danny Tartabull	.05	.02
☐ 17 Willie Wilson	.05	.02
☐ 18 Teddy Higuera	.05	.02
☐ 19 Paul Molitor	.30	.14
☐ 20 Dan Plesac	.05	.02
☐ 21 Robin Yount	.25	.11
☐ 22 Kent Hrbek	.10	.05
☐ 23 Kirby Puckett	1.00	.45
☐ 24 Jeff Reardon	.10	.05
☐ 25 Frank Viola	.05	.02
☐ 26 Rickey Henderson	.30	.14
☐ 27 Don Mattingly	1.00	.45
☐ 28 Willie Randolph	.05	.02
☐ 29 Dave Righetti	.05	.02
☐ 30 Jose Canseco	.50	.23
☐ 31 Mark McGwire	1.00	.45
☐ 32 Dave Stewart	.05	.02
☐ 33 Phil Bradley	.05	.02
☐ 34 Mark Langston	.05	.02
☐ 35 Harold Reynolds	.10	.05
☐ 36 Charlie Hough	.10	.05
☐ 37 George Bell	.05	.02
☐ 38 Tom Henke	.05	.02
☐ 39 Jimmy Key	.10	.05
☐ 40 Dion James	.05	.02
☐ 41 Dale Murphy	.25	.11
☐ 42 Zane Smith	.05	.02
☐ 43 Andre Dawson	.15	.07
☐ 44 Lee Smith	.10	.05
☐ 45 Rick Sutcliffe	.05	.02
☐ 46 Eric Davis	.10	.05
☐ 47 John Franco	.10	.05
☐ 48 Dave Parker	.10	.05
☐ 49 Billy Hatcher	.05	.02
☐ 50 Nolan Ryan	1.50	.70
☐ 51 Mike Scott	.05	.02
☐ 52 Pedro Guerrero	.05	.02
☐ 53 Orel Hershiser	.10	.05
☐ 54 Fernando Valenzuela	.10	.05
☐ 55 Bob Welch	.05	.02
☐ 56 Andres Galarraga	.25	.11
☐ 57 Tim Raines	.10	.05
☐ 58 Tim Wallach	.05	.02
☐ 59 Len Dykstra	.10	.05
☐ 60 Dwight Gooden	.10	.05
☐ 61 Howard Johnson	.05	.02
☐ 62 Roger McDowell	.05	.02
☐ 63 Darryl Strawberry	.10	.05
☐ 64 Steve Bedrosian	.05	.02
☐ 65 Shane Rawley	.05	.02
☐ 66 Juan Samuel	.05	.02
☐ 67 Mike Schmidt	.50	.23
☐ 68 Mike Dunne	.05	.02
☐ 69 Jack Clark	.05	.02
☐ 70 Vince Coleman	.05	.02
☐ 71 Willie McGee	.10	.05
☐ 72 Ozzie Smith	.75	.35
☐ 73 Todd Worrell	.05	.02
☐ 74 Tony Gwynn	1.00	.45
☐ 75 John Kruk	.10	.05
☐ 76 Rick Reuschel	.10	.05
☐ 77 Checklist Card	.05	.02

1988 Topps/O-Pee-Chee Stickers

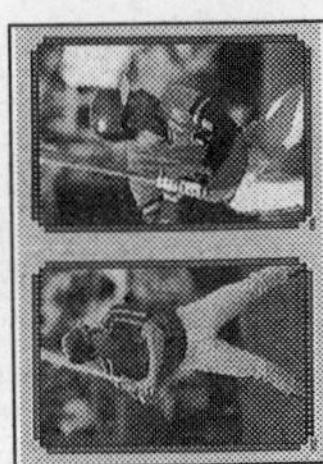

Printed in Canada, these 313 stickers measure approximately 2 1/8" by 3" and are numbered on their fronts. The sticker backs are actually cards (1988 O-Pee-Chee Super Stars) and are considered a separate set. The stickers feature yellow- and red-bordered color player photos. An album onto which the stickers could be affixed was available at retail stores. The album and the sticker numbering are organized as follows: 1987 Highlights (1-12), 1987 Championship Series (13-18), 1987 World Series (19-25), Houston Astros (26-35), Atlanta Braves (36-45), St. Louis Cardinals (46-55), Chicago Cubs (56-65), Los Angeles Dodgers (66-75), Montreal Expos (76-85), San Francisco Giants (86-95), New York Mets (96-105), San Diego Padres (106-115), Philadelphia Phillies (116-125), Pittsburgh Pirates (126-135), Cincinnati Reds (136-145), Foil All-Stars (146-163), Oakland A's (164-173), California Angels (174-183), Toronto Blue Jays (184-193), Milwaukee Brewers (194-203), Cleveland Indians (204-213), Seattle Mariners (214-223), Baltimore Orioles (224-233), Texas Rangers (234-243), Boston Red Sox (244-253), Kansas City Royals (254-263), Detroit Tigers (264-273), Minnesota Twins (274-283), Chicago White Sox (284-293), New York Yankees (294-303) and Future Stars (304-313). For those stickers featuring more than one player, the other numbers on that sticker are given below in parentheses. Although the prices listed below are for the stickers only, there are instances where having an especially desirable sticker card back (attached to that sticker) will increase the values listed below.

	MINT	NRMT
COMPLETE SET (313)	15.00	6.75
COMMON STICKER (1-145)	.05	.02
COMMON FOIL (146-163)	.10	.05
COMMON STICKER (164-313)	.05	.02
*TOPPS AND OPC: SAME VALUE		
☐ 1 Mark McGwire (263)	.75	.35
☐ 2 Benny Santiago (304)	.05	.02
☐ 3 Don Mattingly (187)	1.00	.45
☐ 4 Vince Coleman (223)	.05	.02
☐ 5 Bob Boone (272)	.10	.05
☐ 6 Steve Bedrosian(278)	.05	.02
☐ 7 Nolan Ryan (276)	2.00	.90
☐ 8 Darrell Evans (306)	.10	.05
☐ 9 Mike Schmidt (255)	.60	.25
☐ 10 Don Baylor (256)	.10	.05
☐ 11 Eddie Murray (145)	.50	.23
☐ 12 Juan Beniquez (237)	.05	.02
☐ 13 John Tudor	.05	.02
☐ 14 Jeff Reardon	.10	.05
☐ 15 Tom Brunansky	.05	.02
☐ 16 Jeffrey Leonard	.05	.02
☐ 17 Gary Gaetti	.10	.05
☐ 18 Jose Oquendo	.05	.02
☐ 19 Dan Gladden	.05	.02
☐ 20 Bert Blyleven	.10	.05
☐ 21 John Tudor	.05	.02
☐ 22 Tom Lawless	.05	.02
☐ 23 Curt Ford	.05	.02
☐ 24 Kent Hrbek	.10	.05
☐ 25 Frank Viola	.05	.02
☐ 26 Dave Smith (216)	.05	.02
☐ 27 Jim Deshaies (240)	.05	.02
☐ 28 Billy Hatcher (171)	.05	.02
☐ 29 Kevin Bass (196)	.05	.02
☐ 30 Mike Scott	.05	.02
☐ 31 Denny Walling (224)	.05	.02
☐ 32 Alan Ashby (185)	.05	.02
☐ 33 Ken Caminiti (292)	.75	.35
☐ 34 Bill Doran (245)	.05	.02
☐ 35 Glenn Davis	.05	.02
☐ 36 Ozzie Virgil	.05	.02
☐ 37 Ken Oberkfell (260)	.05	.02
☐ 38 Ken Griffey (183)	.10	.0
☐ 39 Albert Hall (287)	.05	.02
☐ 40 Zane Smith (310)	.05	.0
☐ 41 Andres Thomas (207)	.05	.0
☐ 42 Dion James (178)	.05	.0
☐ 43 Jim Acker (249)	.05	.0
☐ 44 Tom Glavine (226)	1.25	.5
☐ 45 Dale Murphy	.15	.0
☐ 46 Jack Clark	.10	.0
☐ 47 Vince Coleman (269)	.05	.0
☐ 48 Ricky Horton (221)	.05	.0
☐ 49 Terry Pendleton(303)	.10	.0
☐ 50 Tom Herr (271)	.05	.0
☐ 51 Joe Magrane (265)	.05	.0
☐ 52 Tony Pena (211)	.05	.0
☐ 53 Ozzie Smith (298)	.40	.1
☐ 54 Todd Worrell (109)	.05	.0
☐ 55 Willie McGee	.05	.0

☐ 56 Andre Dawson .10 .05
☐ 57 Ryne Sandberg (225) .50 .23
☐ 58 Keith Moreland (291) .05 .02
☐ 59 Greg Maddux (198) 3.00 1.35
☐ 60 Jody Davis (290) .05 .02
☐ 61 Rick Sutcliffe .05 .02
☐ 62 Jamie Moyer (295) .05 .02
☐ 63 Leon Durham (172) .05 .02
☐ 64 Lee Smith (313) .10 .05
☐ 65 Shawon Dunston (250) .05 .02
☐ 66 Franklin Stubbs(257) .05 .02
☐ 67 Mike Scioscia (235) .05 .02
☐ 68 Orel Hershiser (177) .10 .05
☐ 69 Mike Marshall (289) .05 .02
☐ 70 Fernando Valenzuela .10 .05
☐ 71 Mickey Hatcher (281) .05 .02
☐ 72 Matt Young (166) .05 .02
☐ 73 Bob Welch (236) .05 .02
☐ 74 Steve Sax (170) .05 .02
☐ 75 Pedro Guerrero .05 .02
☐ 76 Tim Raines .10 .05
☐ 77 Casey Candaele (252) .05 .02
☐ 78 Mike Fitzgerald(248) .05 .02
☐ 79 Andres Galarraga (301) .30 .14
☐ 80 Neal Heaton (212) .05 .02
☐ 81 Hubie Brooks (296) .05 .02
☐ 82 Floyd Youmans (258) .05 .02
☐ 83 Herm Winningham(201) .05 .02
☐ 84 Denny Martinez (307) .10 .05
☐ 85 Tim Wallach .05 .02
☐ 86 Jeffrey Leonard .05 .02
☐ 87 Will Clark (251) .40 .18
☐ 88 Kevin Mitchell (288) .10 .05
☐ 89 Mike Aldrete (267) .05 .02
☐ 90 Scott Garrelts (191) .05 .02
☐ 91 Jose Uribe (231) .05 .02
☐ 92 Bob Brenly (246) .05 .02
☐ 93 Robby Thompson (189) .05 .02
☐ 94 Don Robinson (217) .05 .02
☐ 95 Candy Maldonado .05 .02
☐ 96 Darryl Strawberry .10 .05
☐ 97 Keith Hernandez(192) .10 .05
☐ 98 Ron Darling (220) .05 .02
☐ 99 Howard Johnson (218) .05 .02
☐ 100 Roger McDowell (190) .05 .02
☐ 101 Dwight Gooden .10 .05
☐ 102 Kevin McReynolds (165) .05 .02
☐ 103 Sid Fernandez (275) .05 .02
☐ 104 Dave Magadan (241) .05 .02
☐ 105 Gary Carter (167) .10 .05
☐ 106 Carmelo Martinez (302) .05 .02
☐ 107 Eddie Whitson (205) .05 .02
☐ 108 Tim Flannery (180) .05 .02
☐ 109 Stan Jefferson (266) .05 .02
☐ 110 John Kruk .15 .07
☐ 111 Chris Brown (168) .05 .02
☐ 112 Benito Santiago (215) .05 .02
☐ 113 Garry Templeton(270) .05 .02
☐ 114 Lance McCullers(186) .05 .02
☐ 115 Tony Gwynn .75 .35
☐ 116 Steve Bedrosian .05 .02
☐ 117 Von Hayes (247) .05 .02
☐ 118 Kevin Gross (279) .05 .02
☐ 119 Bruce Ruffin (238) .05 .02
☐ 120 Juan Samuel (184) .05 .02
☐ 121 Shane Rawley (182) .05 .02
☐ 122 Chris James (222) .05 .02
☐ 123 Lance Parrish (199) .05 .02
☐ 124 Glenn Wilson (181) .05 .02
☐ 125 Mike Schmidt .60 .25
☐ 126 Andy Van Slyke .10 .05
☐ 127 Jose Lind (297) .10 .05
☐ 128 Al Pedrique (176) .05 .02
☐ 129 Bobby Bonilla (277) .15 .07
☐ 130 Sid Bream (175) .05 .02
☐ 131 Mike LaValliere(230) .05 .02
☐ 132 Mike Dunne (197) .05 .02
☐ 133 Jeff D. Robinson (232) .05 .02
☐ 134 Doug Drabek (195) .10 .05
☐ 135 Barry Bonds .75 .35
☐ 136 Dave Parker .10 .05
☐ 137 Nick Esasky (208) .05 .02
☐ 138 Buddy Bell (280) .10 .05
☐ 139 Kal Daniels (239) .05 .02
☐ 140 Barry Larkin (285) .50 .23
☐ 141 Eric Davis .05 .02
☐ 142 John Franco (227) .10 .05
☐ 143 Bo Diaz (229) .05 .02
☐ 144 Ron Oester (261) .05 .02
☐ 145 Dennis Rasmussen(11) .05 .02
☐ 146 Eric Davis FOIL .10 .05
☐ 147 Ryne Sandberg FOIL .75 .35
☐ 148 Andre Dawson FOIL .30 .14
☐ 149 Mike Schmidt FOIL 1.00 .45
☐ 150 Jack Clark FOIL .15 .07
☐ 151 Darryl Strawberry FOIL .15 .07
☐ 152 Gary Carter FOIL .30 .14
☐ 153 Ozzie Smith FOIL .60 .25
☐ 154 Mike Scott FOIL .10 .05
☐ 155 Rickey Henderson FOIL .40 .18
☐ 156 Don Mattingly FOIL 1.50 .70
☐ 157 Wade Boggs FOIL .40 .18
☐ 158 George Bell FOIL .05 .02
☐ 159 Dave Winfield FOIL .40 .18
☐ 160 Cal Ripken FOIL 3.00 1.35
☐ 161 Terry Kennedy FOIL .10 .05
☐ 162 Willie Randolph FOIL .15 .07
☐ 163 Bret Saberhagen FOIL .10 .05
☐ 164 Mark McGwire .75 .35
☐ 165 Tony Phillips (102) .10 .05
☐ 166 Jay Howell (72) .05 .02
☐ 167 Carney Lansford(105) .10 .05
☐ 168 Dave Stewart (111) .10 .05
☐ 169 Alfredo Griffin (54) .05 .02
☐ 170 Dennis Eckersley(74) .10 .05
☐ 171 Mike Davis (28) .05 .02
☐ 172 Luis Polonia (63) .10 .05
☐ 173 Jose Canseco .50 .23
☐ 174 Mike Witt .05 .02
☐ 175 Jack Howell (130) .05 .02
☐ 176 Greg Minton (128) .05 .02
☐ 177 Dick Schofield (68) .05 .02
☐ 178 Gary Pettis (42) .05 .02
☐ 179 Wally Joyner .15 .07
☐ 180 DeWayne Buice (108) .05 .02
☐ 181 Brian Downing (124) .05 .02
☐ 182 Bob Boone (121) .10 .05
☐ 183 Devon White (38) .15 .07
☐ 184 Jim Clancy (120) .05 .02
☐ 185 Willie Upshaw (32) .05 .02
☐ 186 Tom Henke (114) .05 .02
☐ 187 Ernie Whitt (3) .05 .02
☐ 188 George Bell .05 .02
☐ 189 Lloyd Moseby (93) .05 .02
☐ 190 Jimmy Key (100) .10 .05
☐ 191 Dave Stieb (90) .05 .02
☐ 192 Jesse Barfield (97) .05 .02
☐ 193 Tony Fernandez .05 .02
☐ 194 Paul Molitor .25 .11
☐ 195 Jim Gantner (134) .05 .02
☐ 196 Teddy Higuera (29) .05 .02
☐ 197 Glenn Braggs (132) .05 .02
☐ 198 Rob Deer (59) .05 .02
☐ 199 Dale Sveum (123) .05 .02
☐ 200 Bill Wegman (308) .05 .02
☐ 201 Robin Yount (83) .25 .11
☐ 202 B.J. Surhoff .10 .05
☐ 203 Dan Plesac .05 .02
☐ 204 Pat Tabler .05 .02
☐ 205 Mel Hall (107) .05 .02
☐ 206 Scott Bailes (305) .05 .02
☐ 207 Julio Franco (41) .10 .05
☐ 208 Cory Snyder (137) .05 .02
☐ 209 Chris Bando (312) .05 .02
☐ 210 Greg Swindell (311) .05 .02
☐ 211 Brook Jacoby (52) .05 .02
☐ 212 Brett Butler (80) .10 .05
☐ 213 Joe Carter .15 .07
☐ 214 Mark Langston .10 .05
☐ 215 Rey Quinones (112) .05 .02
☐ 216 Ed Nunez (16) .05 .02
☐ 217 Jim Presley (94) .05 .02
☐ 218 Phil Bradley (99) .05 .02
☐ 219 Alvin Davis .05 .02
☐ 220 Dave Valle (98) .05 .02
☐ 221 Harold Reynolds (48) .10 .05
☐ 222 Scott Bradley (122) .05 .02
☐ 223 Gary Matthews (4) .05 .02
☐ 224 Eric Bell (31) .05 .02
☐ 225 Terry Kennedy (57) .05 .02
☐ 226 Dave Schmidt (44) .05 .02
☐ 227 Billy Ripken (142) .05 .02
☐ 228 Cal Ripken 2.00 .90
☐ 229 Ray Knight (143) .10 .05
☐ 230 Larry Sheets (131) .05 .02
☐ 231 Mike Boddicker (91) .05 .02
☐ 232 Tom Niedenfuer (133) .05 .02
☐ 233 Eddie Murray .50 .23
☐ 234 Ruben Sierra .15 .07
☐ 235 Steve Buechele (67) .05 .02
☐ 236 Charlie Hough (73) .10 .05
☐ 237 Oddibe McDowell (12) .05 .02
☐ 238 Mike Stanley (119) .05 .02
☐ 239 Pete Incaviglia(139) .05 .02
☐ 240 Pete O'Brien (27) .05 .02
☐ 241 Scott Fletcher (104) .05 .02
☐ 242 Dale Mohorcic (300) .05 .02
☐ 243 Larry Parrish .05 .02
☐ 244 Wade Boggs .25 .11
☐ 245 Dwight Evans (34) .10 .05
☐ 246 Sam Horn (92) .05 .02
☐ 247 Jim Rice (117) .10 .05
☐ 248 Marty Barrett (78) .05 .02
☐ 249 Mike Greenwell (43) .10 .05
☐ 250 Ellis Burks (65) .30 .14
☐ 251 Roger Clemens (87) .25 .11
☐ 252 Rich Gedman (77) .05 .02
☐ 253 Bruce Hurst .05 .02
☐ 254 Bret Saberhagen .10 .05
☐ 255 Frank White (9) .10 .05
☐ 256 Dan Quisenberry (10) .05 .02
☐ 257 Danny Tartabull (66) .05 .02
☐ 258 Bo Jackson (82) .15 .07
☐ 259 George Brett .75 .35
☐ 260 Charlie Leibrandt(37) .05 .02
☐ 261 Kevin Seitzer (144) .10 .05
☐ 262 Mark Gubicza (282) .05 .02
☐ 263 Willie Wilson (1) .05 .02
☐ 264 Frank Tanana (286) .05 .02
☐ 265 Darrell Evans (51) .10 .05
☐ 266 Bill Madlock (109) .10 .05
☐ 267 Kirk Gibson (89) .10 .05
☐ 268 Jack Morris .10 .05
☐ 269 Matt Nokes (47) .05 .02
☐ 270 Lou Whitaker (113) .10 .05
☐ 271 Eric King (50) .05 .02
☐ 272 Jim Morrison (5) .05 .02
☐ 273 Alan Trammell .10 .05
☐ 274 Kent Hrbek .10 .05
☐ 275 Tom Brunansky (103) .05 .02
☐ 276 Bert Blyleven (7) .10 .05
☐ 277 Gary Gaetti (129) .10 .05
☐ 278 Tim Laudner (6) .05 .02
☐ 279 Gene Larkin (118) .10 .05
☐ 280 Jeff Reardon (138) .10 .05
☐ 281 Danny Gladden (71) .05 .02
☐ 282 Frank Viola (262) .05 .02
☐ 283 Kirby Puckett .50 .23
☐ 284 Ozzie Guillen .10 .05
☐ 285 Ivan Calderon (140) .05 .02
☐ 286 Donnie Hill (264) .05 .02
☐ 287 Ken Williams (39) .05 .02
☐ 288 Jim Winn (88) .05 .02
☐ 289 Bob James (69) .05 .02
☐ 290 Carlton Fisk (60) .25 .11
☐ 291 Richard Dotson (58) .05 .02
☐ 292 Greg Walker (33) .05 .02
☐ 293 Harold Baines .10 .05
☐ 294 Willie Randolph .10 .05
☐ 295 Mike Pagliarulo (62) .05 .02
☐ 296 Ron Guidry (81) .05 .02
☐ 297 Rickey Henderson(127) .25 .11
☐ 298 Rick Rhoden (53) .05 .02
☐ 299 Don Mattingly 1.00 .45
☐ 300 Dave Righetti (242) .05 .02
☐ 301 Clau.Washington (79) .05 .02
☐ 302 Dave Winfield (106) .25 .11
☐ 303 Gary Ward (49) .05 .02
☐ 304 Al Pedrique (2) .05 .02
☐ 305 Casey Candaele (206) .05 .02
☐ 306 Kevin Seitzer (8) .10 .05
☐ 307 Mike Dunne (84) .05 .02
☐ 308 Jeff Musselman (200) .05 .02
☐ 309 Mark McGwire .75 .35
☐ 310 Ellis Burks (40) .30 .14
☐ 311 Matt Nokes (210) .05 .02
☐ 312 Mike Greenwell (209) .10 .05
☐ 313 Devon White (64) .15 .07
☐ xx Album 1.00 .45

1988 Topps/O-Pee-Chee Sticker Backs

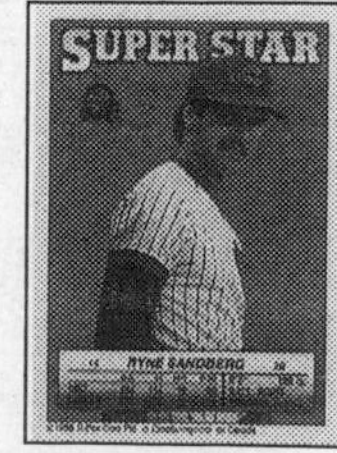

These 67 cards were actually the backs of the 1988 O-Pee-Chee Stickers. In previous years O-Pee-Chee had used a disposable peel-off sticker back. The 1988 Super Star sticker back was actually collectible and attractive. In fact, many collectors felt that the sticker backs were more desirable than the stickers. The white-bordered cards measure approximately 2 1/8" by 3" and have either a red (AL, 1-33) or blue (NL, 34-66) background behind the player's photo. The player's 1987 and career statistics were shown at the bottom of each card. The cards are numbered in the statistics box in small print. Three different front (sticker) combinations exist for each of the 66 players and checklist. The cards were retailed in cellophane wax packs at 25 cents for a stick of gum and five sticker cards.

	MINT	NRMT
COMPLETE SET (67)	6.00	2.70
COMMON CARD (1-67)	.05	.02

	MINT	NRMT
☐ 1 Jack Clark	.10	.05
☐ 2 Andres Galarraga	.25	.11
☐ 3 Keith Hernandez	.10	.05
☐ 4 Tom Herr	.05	.02
☐ 5 Juan Samuel	.05	.02
☐ 6 Ryne Sandberg	.50	.23
☐ 7 Terry Pendleton	.10	.05
☐ 8 Mike Schmidt	.50	.23
☐ 9 Tim Wallach	.05	.02
☐ 10 Hubie Brooks	.05	.02
☐ 11 Shawon Dunston	.05	.02
☐ 12 Ozzie Smith	.30	.14
☐ 13 Andre Dawson	.15	.07
☐ 14 Eric Davis	.10	.05
☐ 15 Pedro Guerrero	.05	.02
☐ 16 Tony Gwynn	.60	.25
☐ 17 Jeffrey Leonard	.05	.02
☐ 18 Dale Murphy	.25	.11
☐ 19 Dave Parker	.10	.05
☐ 20 Tim Raines	.10	.05
☐ 21 Darryl Strawberry	.10	.05
☐ 22 Gary Carter	.15	.07
☐ 23 Jody Davis	.05	.02
☐ 24 Ozzie Virgil	.05	.02
☐ 25 Dwight Gooden	.10	.05
☐ 26 Mike Scott	.05	.02
☐ 27 Rick Sutcliffe	.05	.02
☐ 28 Sid Fernandez	.05	.02
☐ 29 Neal Heaton	.05	.02
☐ 30 Fernando Valenzuela	.10	.05
☐ 31 Steve Bedrosian	.05	.02
☐ 32 John Franco	.10	.05
☐ 33 Lee Smith	.10	.05
☐ 34 Wally Joyner	.15	.07
☐ 35 Don Mattingly	.75	.35
☐ 36 Mark McGwire	.40	.18
☐ 37 Willie Randolph	.05	.02
☐ 38 Lou Whitaker	.10	.05
☐ 39 Frank White	.10	.05
☐ 40 Wade Boggs	.30	.14
☐ 41 George Brett	.60	.25
☐ 42 Paul Molitor	.25	.11
☐ 43 Tony Fernandez	.05	.02
☐ 44 Cal Ripken	1.50	.70
☐ 45 Alan Trammell	.15	.07
☐ 46 Jesse Barfield	.05	.02
☐ 47 George Bell	.05	.02
☐ 48 Jose Canseco	.40	.18
☐ 49 Joe Carter	.15	.07
☐ 50 Dwight Evans	.10	.05
☐ 51 Rickey Henderson	.30	.14
☐ 52 Kirby Puckett	.50	.23
☐ 53 Cory Snyder	.05	.02
☐ 54 Dave Winfield	.25	.11
☐ 55 Terry Kennedy	.05	.02
☐ 56 Matt Nokes	.05	.02
☐ 57 B.J. Surhoff	.10	.05
☐ 58 Roger Clemens	.75	.35
☐ 59 Jack Morris	.10	.05
☐ 60 Bret Saberhagen	.05	.02
☐ 61 Ron Guidry	.10	.05
☐ 62 Bruce Hurst	.05	.02
☐ 63 Mark Langston	.05	.02
☐ 64 Tom Henke	.05	.02
☐ 65 Dan Plesac	.05	.02
☐ 66 Dave Righetti	.05	.02
☐ 67 Checklist	.05	.02

1988 Topps Revco League Leaders

Topps produced this 33-card boxed standard-size set for Revco stores subtitled "League Leaders". The cards feature a high-gloss, full-color photo of the player inside a white border. The card backs are printed in red and black on white card stock. The statistics provided on the card backs cover only two lines, last season and Major League totals.

	MINT	NRMT
COMPLETE SET (33)	5.00	2.20
COMMON CARD (1-33)	.05	.02

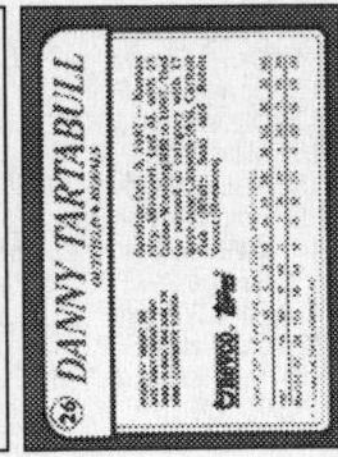

	MINT	NRMT
☐ 1 Tony Gwynn	1.00	.45
☐ 2 Andre Dawson	.25	.11
☐ 3 Vince Coleman	.05	.02
☐ 4 Jack Clark	.10	.05
☐ 5 Tim Raines	.10	.05
☐ 6 Tim Wallach	.05	.02
☐ 7 Juan Samuel	.05	.02
☐ 8 Nolan Ryan	2.00	.90
☐ 9 Rick Sutcliffe	.05	.02
☐ 10 Kent Tekulve	.05	.02
☐ 11 Steve Bedrosian	.05	.02
☐ 12 Orel Hershiser	.10	.05
☐ 13 Rick Reuschel	.05	.02
☐ 14 Fernando Valenzuela	.10	.05
☐ 15 Bob Welch	.05	.02
☐ 16 Wade Boggs	.30	.14
☐ 17 Mark McGwire	1.00	.45
☐ 18 George Bell	.05	.02
☐ 19 Harold Reynolds	.05	.02
☐ 20 Paul Molitor	.40	.18
☐ 21 Kirby Puckett	1.00	.45
☐ 22 Kevin Seitzer	.10	.05
☐ 23 Brian Downing	.05	.02
☐ 24 Dwight Evans	.10	.05
☐ 25 Willie Wilson	.05	.02
☐ 26 Danny Tartabull	.05	.02
☐ 27 Jimmy Key	.10	.05
☐ 28 Roger Clemens	.75	.35
☐ 29 Dave Stewart	.10	.05
☐ 30 Mark Eichhorn	.05	.02
☐ 31 Tom Henke	.05	.02
☐ 32 Charlie Hough	.05	.02
☐ 33 Mark Langston	.05	.02

1988 Topps Rite-Aid Team MVP's

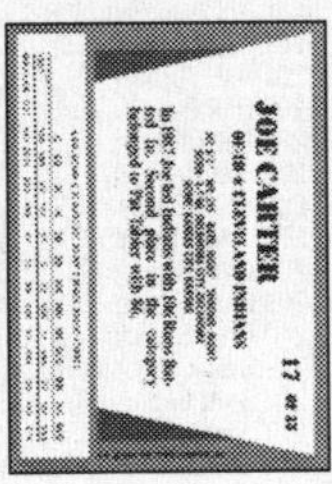

Topps produced this 33-card boxed standard-size set for Rite Aid Drug and Discount Stores subtitled "Team MVP's". The Rite Aid logo is at the top of every obverse. The cards feature a high-gloss, full-color photo of the player inside a red, white, and blue border. The card backs are printed in blue and black on white card stock. The checklist for the set is found on the back panel of the small collector box. The statistics provided on the card backs cover only two lines, last season and Major League totals.

	MINT	NRMT
COMPLETE SET (33)	4.00	1.80
COMMON CARD (1-33)	.05	.02

	MINT	NRMT
☐ 1 Dale Murphy	.25	.11
☐ 2 Andre Dawson	.25	.11
☐ 3 Eric Davis	.10	.05
☐ 4 Mike Scott	.05	.02
☐ 5 Pedro Guerrero	.05	.02
☐ 6 Tim Raines	.10	.05
☐ 7 Darryl Strawberry	.10	.05
☐ 8 Mike Schmidt	.60	.25
☐ 9 Mike Dunne	.05	.02
☐ 10 Jack Clark	.10	.05
☐ 11 Tony Gwynn	1.00	.45
☐ 12 Will Clark	.40	.18
☐ 13 Cal Ripken	2.00	.90
☐ 14 Wade Boggs	.30	.14
☐ 15 Wally Joyner	.10	.05
☐ 16 Harold Baines	.10	.05
☐ 17 Joe Carter	.25	.11
☐ 18 Alan Trammell	.15	.07
☐ 19 Kevin Seitzer	.10	.05
☐ 20 Paul Molitor	.40	.18
☐ 21 Kirby Puckett	1.00	.45
☐ 22 Don Mattingly	1.00	.45
☐ 23 Mark McGwire	1.00	.45
☐ 24 Alvin Davis	.05	.02
☐ 25 Ruben Sierra	.05	.02
☐ 26 George Bell	.05	.02
☐ 27 Jack Morris	.10	.05
☐ 28 Jeff Reardon	.05	.02
☐ 29 John Tudor	.05	.02
☐ 30 Rick Reuschel	.10	.05
☐ 31 Gary Gaetti	.10	.05
☐ 32 Jeffrey Leonard	.05	.02
☐ 33 Frank Viola	.05	.02

1988 Topps UK Minis

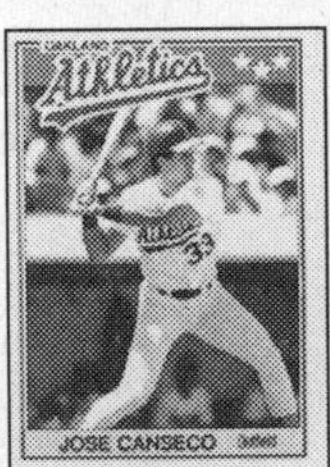

The 1988 Topps UK (United Kingdom) Mini set of "American Baseball" features 88 cards. The cards measure approximately 2 1/8" by 3". The card backs are printed in blue, red, and yellow on white card stock. The cards were distributed as a separate issue in packs. A custom black and yellow small set box was also available for holding a complete set; the box has a complete checklist on the back panel. The set player numbering is according to alphabetical order.

	MINT	NRMT
COMPLETE SET (88)	5.00	2.20
COMMON CARD (1-88)	.05	.02

	MINT	NRMT
☐ 1 Harold Baines	.05	.02
☐ 2 Steve Bedrosian	.05	.02
☐ 3 George Bell	.05	.02
☐ 4 Wade Boggs	.30	.14
☐ 5 Barry Bonds	.60	.25
☐ 6 Bob Boone	.10	.05
☐ 7 George Brett	.75	.35
☐ 8 Hubie Brooks	.05	.02
☐ 9 Ivan Calderon	.05	.02
☐ 10 Jose Canseco	.50	.23
☐ 11 Gary Carter	.15	.07
☐ 12 Joe Carter	.15	.07
☐ 13 Jack Clark	.05	.02
☐ 14 Will Clark	.40	.18
☐ 15 Roger Clemens	.75	.35
☐ 16 Vince Coleman	.05	.02
☐ 17 Alvin Davis	.05	.02
☐ 18 Eric Davis	.10	.05
☐ 19 Glenn Davis	.05	.02
☐ 20 Andre Dawson	.15	.07
☐ 21 Mike Dunne	.05	.02
☐ 22 Dwight Evans	.10	.05
☐ 23 Tony Fernandez	.05	.02
☐ 24 John Franco	.10	.05
☐ 25 Gary Gaetti	.10	.05
☐ 26 Kirk Gibson	.10	.05
☐ 27 Dwight Gooden	.10	.05
☐ 28 Pedro Guerrero	.05	.02
☐ 29 Tony Gwynn	1.00	.45
☐ 30 Billy Hatcher	.05	.02
☐ 31 Rickey Henderson	.30	.14
☐ 32 Tom Henke	.05	.02
☐ 33 Keith Hernandez	.10	.05
☐ 34 Orel Hershiser	.10	.05
☐ 35 Teddy Higuera	.05	.02
☐ 36 Charlie Hough	.05	.02
☐ 37 Kent Hrbek	.10	.05
☐ 38 Brook Jacoby	.05	.02
☐ 39 Dion James	.05	.02
☐ 40 Wally Joyner	.10	.05
☐ 41 John Kruk	.10	.05
☐ 42 Mark Langston	.05	.02
☐ 43 Jeffrey Leonard	.05	.02
☐ 44 Candy Maldonado	.05	.02
☐ 45 Don Mattingly	1.00	.45
☐ 46 Willie McGee	.05	.02
☐ 47 Mark McGwire	1.00	.45
☐ 48 Kevin Mitchell	.05	.02
☐ 49 Paul Molitor	.30	.14

□ 50 Jack Morris .10 .05
□ 51 Lloyd Moseby .05 .02
□ 52 Dale Murphy .25 .11
□ 53 Eddie Murray .50 .23
□ 54 Matt Nokes .05 .02
□ 55 Dave Parker .10 .05
□ 56 Larry Parrish .05 .02
□ 57 Kirby Puckett 1.00 .45
□ 58 Tim Raines .10 .05
□ 59 Willie Randolph .05 .02
□ 60 Harold Reynolds .05 .02
□ 61 Cal Ripken 1.50 .70
□ 62 Nolan Ryan 1.50 .70
□ 63 Bret Saberhagen .05 .02
□ 64 Juan Samuel .05 .02
□ 65 Ryne Sandberg .75 .35
□ 66 Benito Santiago .05 .02
□ 67 Mike Schmidt .50 .23
□ 68 Mike Scott .05 .02
□ 69 Kevin Seitzer .10 .05
□ 70 Larry Sheets .05 .02
□ 71 Ruben Sierra .05 .02
□ 72 Ozzie Smith .75 .35
□ 73 Zane Smith .05 .02
□ 74 Cory Snyder .05 .02
□ 75 Dave Stewart .05 .02
□ 76 Darryl Strawberry .10 .05
□ 77 Rick Sutcliffe .05 .02
□ 78 Danny Tartabull .05 .02
□ 79 Alan Trammell .15 .07
□ 80 Fernando Valenzuela .10 .05
□ 81 Andy Van Slyke .10 .05
□ 82 Frank Viola .05 .02
□ 83 Greg Walker .05 .02
□ 84 Tim Wallach .05 .02
□ 85 Dave Winfield .30 .14
□ 86 Mike Witt .05 .02
□ 87 Robin Yount .15 .07
□ 88 Checklist Card .05 .02

1988 Topps UK Minis Tiffany

This set parallels the regular UK mini set. These cards were issued in factory set form only and are valued at a multiple of the regular cards. These cards were issued only in complete factory set form.

	MINT	NRMT
COMPLETE SET (88)	25.00	11.00
COMMON CARD (1-88)	.25	.11
*STARS: 3X to 6X BASIC CARDS		

1989 Topps

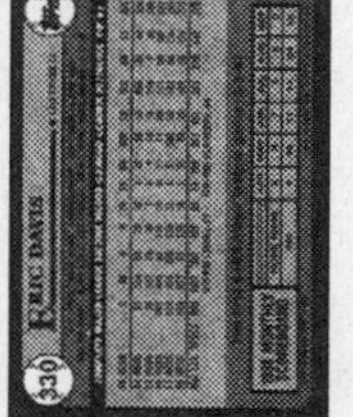

This set consists of 792 standard-size cards. Cards were primarily issued in 15-card wax packs, 42-card rack packs and factory sets. Subsets in the set include Record Breakers (1-7), Turn Back the Clock (661-665), All-Star selections (386-407) and First Draft Picks, Future Stars and Team Leaders (all scattered throughout the set). The manager cards contain a team checklist on back. The key Rookie Cards in this set are Jim Abbott, Sandy Alomar Jr., Brady Anderson, Steve Avery, Andy Benes, Dante Bichette, Craig Biggio, Randy Johnson, Ramon Martinez, Gary Sheffield, John Smoltz, and Robin Ventura.

	MINT	NRMT
COMPLETE SET (792)	10.00	4.50
COMP.FACT.SET (792)	12.00	5.50
COMMON CARD (1-792)	.05	.02

□ 1 George Bell RB .05 .02
Slams 3 Opening Day HR's
□ 2 Wade Boggs RB .20 .09
200 Hits 6th Straight Season
□ 3 Gary Carter RB .10 .05
Career Putouts Record
□ 4 Andre Dawson RB .10 .05
Logs Double Figures
in HR and SB
□ 5 Orel Hershiser RB .10 .05
59 Scoreless Innings
□ 6 Doug Jones RB UER .05 .02
Earns His 15th
Straight Save
(Photo actually
Chris Codiroli)
□ 7 Kevin McReynolds RB .05 .02
Steals 21 Without
Being Caught
□ 8 Dave Eiland .05 .02
□ 9 Tim Teufel .05 .02
□ 10 Andre Dawson .20 .09
□ 11 Bruce Sutter .05 .02
□ 12 Dale Sveum .05 .02
□ 13 Doug Sisk .05 .02
□ 14 Tom Kelly MG .05 .02
(Team checklist back)
□ 15 Robby Thompson .05 .02
□ 16 Ron Robinson .05 .02
□ 17 Brian Downing .05 .02
□ 18 Rick Rhoden .05 .02
□ 19 Greg Gagne .05 .02
□ 20 Steve Bedrosian .05 .02
□ 21 Chicago White Sox TL .05 .02
Greg Walker
□ 22 Tim Crews .05 .02
□ 23 Mike Fitzgerald .05 .02
□ 24 Larry Andersen .05 .02
□ 25 Frank White .10 .05
□ 26 Dale Mohorcic .05 .02
□ 27A Orestes Destrade .05 .02
(F* next to copyright)
□ 27B Orestes Destrade .05 .02
(E*F* next to
copyright)
□ 28 Mike Moore .05 .02
□ 29 Kelly Gruber .05 .02
□ 30 Dwight Gooden .10 .05
□ 31 Terry Francona .05 .02
□ 32 Dennis Rasmussen .05 .02
□ 33 B.J. Surhoff .20 .09
□ 34 Ken Williams .05 .02
□ 35 John Tudor UER .05 .02
(With Red Sox in '84,should be Pirates)
□ 36 Mitch Webster .05 .02
□ 37 Bob Stanley .05 .02
□ 38 Paul Runge .05 .02
□ 39 Mike Maddux .05 .02
□ 40 Steve Sax .05 .02
□ 41 Terry Mulholland .05 .02
□ 42 Jim Eppard .05 .02
□ 43 Guillermo Hernandez .05 .02
□ 44 Jim Snyder MG .05 .02
(Team checklist back)
□ 45 Kal Daniels .05 .02
□ 46 Mark Portugal .05 .02
□ 47 Carney Lansford .10 .05
□ 48 Tim Burke .05 .02
□ 49 Craig Biggio .50 .23
□ 50 George Bell .05 .02
□ 51 California Angels TL .05 .02
Mark McLemore
□ 52 Bob Brenly .05 .02
□ 53 Ruben Sierra .05 .02
□ 54 Steve Trout .05 .02
□ 55 Julio Franco .10 .05
□ 56 Pat Tabler .05 .02
□ 57 Alejandro Pena .05 .02
□ 58 Lee Mazzilli .05 .02
□ 59 Mark Davis .05 .02
□ 60 Tom Brunansky .05 .02
□ 61 Neil Allen .05 .02
□ 62 Alfredo Griffin .05 .02
□ 63 Mark Clear .05 .02
□ 64 Alex Trevino .05 .02
□ 65 Rick Reuschel .05 .02
□ 66 Manny Trillo .05 .02
□ 67 Dave Palmer .05 .02
□ 68 Darrell Miller .05 .02
□ 69 Jeff Ballard .05 .02
□ 70 Mark McGwire .40 .18
□ 71 Mike Boddicker .05 .02
□ 72 John Moses .05 .02
□ 73 Pascual Perez .05 .02
□ 74 Nick Leyva MG .05 .02
(Team checklist back)
□ 75 Tom Henke .05 .02
□ 76 Terry Blocker .05 .02
□ 77 Doyle Alexander .05 .02
□ 78 Jim Sundberg .05 .02
□ 79 Scott Bankhead .05 .02
□ 80 Cory Snyder .05 .02
□ 81 Montreal Expos TL .10 .05
Tim Raines
□ 82 Dave Leiper .05 .02
□ 83 Jeff Blauser .10 .05
□ 84 Bill Bene FDP .05 .02
□ 85 Kevin McReynolds .05 .02
□ 86 Al Nipper .05 .02
□ 87 Larry Owen .05 .02
□ 88 Darryl Hamilton .05 .02
□ 89 Dave LaPoint .05 .02
□ 90 Vince Coleman UER .05 .02
(Wrong birth year)
□ 91 Floyd Youmans .05 .02
□ 92 Jeff Kunkel .05 .02
□ 93 Ken Howell .05 .02
□ 94 Chris Speier .05 .02
□ 95 Gerald Young .05 .02
□ 96 Rick Cerone .05 .02
□ 97 Greg Mathews .05 .02
□ 98 Larry Sheets .05 .02
□ 99 Sherman Corbett .05 .02
□ 100 Mike Schmidt .25 .11
□ 101 Les Straker .05 .02
□ 102 Mike Gallego .05 .02
□ 103 Tim Birtsas .05 .02
□ 104 Dallas Green MG .05 .02
(Team checklist back)
□ 105 Ron Darling .05 .02
□ 106 Willie Upshaw .05 .02
□ 107 Jose DeLeon .05 .02
□ 108 Fred Manrique .05 .02
□ 109 Hipolito Pena .05 .02
□ 110 Paul Molitor .20 .09
□ 111 Cincinnati Reds TL .05 .02
Eric Davis
(Swinging bat)
□ 112 Jim Presley .05 .02
□ 113 Lloyd Moseby .05 .02
□ 114 Bob Kipper .05 .02
□ 115 Jody Davis .05 .02
□ 116 Jeff Montgomery .10 .05
□ 117 Dave Anderson .05 .02
□ 118 Checklist 1-132 .05 .02
□ 119 Terry Puhl .05 .02
□ 120 Frank Viola .05 .02
□ 121 Garry Templeton .05 .02
□ 122 Lance Johnson .10 .05
□ 123 Spike Owen .05 .02
□ 124 Jim Traber .05 .02
□ 125 Mike Krukow .05 .02
□ 126 Sid Bream .05 .02
□ 127 Walt Terrell .05 .02
□ 128 Milt Thompson .05 .02
□ 129 Terry Clark .05 .02
□ 130 Gerald Perry .05 .02
□ 131 Dave Otto .05 .02
□ 132 Curt Ford .05 .02
□ 133 Bill Long .05 .02
□ 134 Don Zimmer MG .05 .02
(Team checklist back)
□ 135 Jose Rijo .05 .02
□ 136 Joey Meyer .05 .02
□ 137 Geno Petralli .05 .02
□ 138 Wallace Johnson .05 .02
□ 139 Mike Flanagan .05 .02
□ 140 Shawon Dunston .05 .02
□ 141 Cleveland Indians TL .05 .02
Brook Jacoby
□ 142 Mike Diaz .05 .02
□ 143 Mike Campbell .05 .02
□ 144 Jay Bell 2.00 .90
□ 145 Dave Stewart .10 .05
□ 146 Gary Pettis .05 .02
□ 147 DeWayne Buice .05 .02
□ 148 Bill Pecota .05 .02
□ 149 Doug Dascenzo .05 .02
□ 150 Fernando Valenzuela .10 .05
□ 151 Terry McGriff .05 .02
□ 152 Mark Thurmond .05 .02
□ 153 Jim Pankovits .05 .02
□ 154 Don Carman .05 .02
□ 155 Marty Barrett .05 .02
□ 156 Dave Gallagher .05 .02
□ 157 Tom Glavine .25 .11
□ 158 Mike Aldrete .05 .02
□ 159 Pat Clements .05 .02
□ 160 Jeffrey Leonard .05 .02
□ 161 Gregg Olson FDP UER .20 .09
(Born Scribner, NE,
should be Omaha, NE)
□ 162 John Davis .05 .02
□ 163 Bob Forsch .05 .02
□ 164 Hal Lanier MG .05 .02
(Team checklist back)
□ 165 Mike Dunne .05 .02
□ 166 Doug Jennings .05 .02
□ 167 Steve Searcy FS .05 .02
□ 168 Willie Wilson .05 .02
□ 169 Mike Jackson .05 .02
□ 170 Tony Fernandez .05 .02
□ 171 Atlanta Braves TL .05 .02
Andres Thomas
□ 172 Frank Williams .05 .02
□ 173 Mel Hall .05 .02
□ 174 Todd Burns .05 .02

☐ 175 John Shelby .05 .02
☐ 176 Jeff Parrett .05 .02
☐ 177 Monty Fariss FDP .05 .02
☐ 178 Mark Grant .05 .02
☐ 179 Ozzie Virgil .05 .02
☐ 180 Mike Scott .05 .02
☐ 181 Craig Worthington .05 .02
☐ 182 Bob McClure .05 .02
☐ 183 Oddibe McDowell .05 .02
☐ 184 John Costello .05 .02
☐ 185 Claudell Washington .05 .02
☐ 186 Pat Perry .05 .02
☐ 187 Darren Daulton .10 .05
☐ 188 Dennis Lamp .05 .02
☐ 189 Kevin Mitchell .10 .05
☐ 190 Mike Witt .05 .02
☐ 191 Sil Campusano .05 .02
☐ 192 Paul Mirabella .05 .02
☐ 193 Sparky Anderson MG .10 .05
(Team checklist back)
UER (553 Salazer)
☐ 194 Greg W. Harris .05 .02
☐ 195 Ozzie Guillen .05 .02
☐ 196 Denny Walling .05 .02
☐ 197 Neal Heaton .05 .02
☐ 198 Danny Heep .05 .02
☐ 199 Mike Schooler .05 .02
☐ 200 George Brett .40 .18
☐ 201 Blue Jays TL .05 .02
Kelly Gruber
☐ 202 Brad Moore .05 .02
☐ 203 Rob Ducey .05 .02
☐ 204 Brad Havens .05 .02
☐ 205 Dwight Evans .10 .05
☐ 206 Roberto Alomar .30 .14
☐ 207 Terry Leach .05 .02
☐ 208 Tom Pagnozzi .05 .02
☐ 209 Jeff Bittiger .05 .02
☐ 210 Dale Murphy .20 .09
☐ 211 Mike Pagliarulo .05 .02
☐ 212 Scott Sanderson .05 .02
☐ 213 Rene Gonzales .05 .02
☐ 214 Charlie O'Brien .05 .02
☐ 215 Kevin Gross .05 .02
☐ 216 Jack Howell .05 .02
☐ 217 Joe Price .05 .02
☐ 218 Mike LaValliere .05 .02
☐ 219 Jim Clancy .05 .02
☐ 220 Gary Gaetti .05 .02
☐ 221 Cecil Espy .05 .02
☐ 222 Mark Lewis FDP .20 .09
☐ 223 Jay Buhner .25 .11
☐ 224 Tony LaRussa MG .10 .05
(Team checklist back)
☐ 225 Ramon Martinez .25 .11
☐ 226 Bill Doran .05 .02
☐ 227 John Farrell .05 .02
☐ 228 Nelson Santovenia .05 .02
☐ 229 Jimmy Key 2.00 .90
☐ 230 Ozzie Smith .25 .11
☐ 231 San Diego Padres TL .20 .09
Roberto Alomar
(Gary Carter at plate)
☐ 232 Ricky Horton .05 .02
☐ 233 Gregg Jefferies FS 2.00 .90
☐ 234 Tom Browning .05 .02
☐ 235 John Kruk .10 .05
☐ 236 Charles Hudson .05 .02
☐ 237 Glenn Hubbard .05 .02
☐ 238 Eric King .05 .02
☐ 239 Tim Laudner .05 .02
☐ 240 Greg Maddux .75 .35
☐ 241 Brett Butler .10 .05
☐ 242 Ed VandeBerg .05 .02
☐ 243 Bob Boone .10 .05
☐ 244 Jim Acker .05 .02
☐ 245 Jim Rice 2.00 .90
☐ 246 Rey Quinones .05 .02
☐ 247 Shawn Hillegas .05 .02
☐ 248 Tony Phillips .05 .02
☐ 249 Tim Leary .05 .02
☐ 250 Cal Ripken .75 .35
☐ 251 John Dopson .05 .02
☐ 252 Billy Hatcher .05 .02
☐ 253 Jose Alvarez .05 .02
☐ 254 Tom Lasorda MG .10 .05
(Team checklist back)
☐ 255 Ron Guidry .10 .05
☐ 256 Benny Santiago .05 .02
☐ 257 Rick Aguilera .10 .05
☐ 258 Checklist 133-264 .05 .02
☐ 259 Larry McWilliams .05 .02
☐ 260 Dave Winfield .20 .09
☐ 261 St.Louis Cardinals TL .05 .02
Tom Brunansky
(With Luis Alicea)
☐ 262 Jeff Pico .05 .02
☐ 263 Mike Felder .05 .02
☐ 264 Rob Dibble .10 .05
☐ 265 Kent Hrbek .10 .05
☐ 266 Luis Aquino .05 .02
☐ 267 Jeff M. Robinson .05 .02
☐ 268 N. Keith Miller .05 .02
☐ 269 Tom Bolton .05 .02
☐ 270 Wally Joyner .10 .05
☐ 271 Jay Tibbs .05 .02
☐ 272 Ron Hassey .05 .02
☐ 273 Jose Lind .05 .02
☐ 274 Mark Eichhorn .05 .02
☐ 275 Danny Tartabull UER .05 .02
(Born San Juan, PR
should be Miami, FL)
☐ 276 Paul Kilgus .05 .02
☐ 277 Mike Davis .05 .02
☐ 278 Andy McGaffigan .05 .02
☐ 279 Scott Bradley .05 .02
☐ 280 Bob Knepper .05 .02
☐ 281 Gary Redus .05 .02
☐ 282 Cris Carpenter .05 .02
☐ 283 Andy Allanson .05 .02
☐ 284 Jim Leyland MG .10 .05
(Team checklist back)
☐ 285 John Candelaria .05 .02
☐ 286 Darrin Jackson .05 .02
☐ 287 Juan Nieves .05 .02
☐ 288 Pat Sheridan .05 .02
☐ 289 Ernie Whitt .05 .02
☐ 290 John Franco .10 .05
☐ 291 New York Mets TL .10 .05
Darryl Strawberry
(With Keith Hernandez
and Kevin McReynolds)
☐ 292 Jim Corsi .05 .02
☐ 293 Glenn Wilson .05 .02
☐ 294 Juan Berenguer .05 .02
☐ 295 Scott Fletcher .05 .02
☐ 296 Ron Gant .10 .05
☐ 297 Oswald Peraza .05 .02
☐ 298 Chris James .05 .02
☐ 299 Steve Ellsworth .05 .02
☐ 300 Darryl Strawberry .10 .05
☐ 301 Charlie Leibrandt .05 .02
☐ 302 Gary Ward .05 .02
☐ 303 Felix Fermin .05 .02
☐ 304 Joel Youngblood .05 .02
☐ 305 Dave Smith .05 .02
☐ 306 Tracy Woodson .05 .02
☐ 307 Lance McCullers .05 .02
☐ 308 Ron Karkovice .05 .02
☐ 309 Mario Diaz .05 .02
☐ 310 Rafael Palmeiro .20 .09
☐ 311 Chris Bosio .05 .02
☐ 312 Tom Lawless .05 .02
☐ 313 Dennis Martinez .10 .05
☐ 314 Bobby Valentine MG .05 .02
(Team checklist back)
☐ 315 Greg Swindell .05 .02
☐ 316 Walt Weiss .05 .02
☐ 317 Jack Armstrong .05 .02
☐ 318 Gene Larkin .05 .02
☐ 319 Greg Booker .05 .02
☐ 320 Lou Whitaker .10 .05
☐ 321 Boston Red Sox TL .05 .02
Jody Reed
☐ 322 John Smiley .05 .02
☐ 323 Gary Thurman .05 .02
☐ 324 Bob Milacki .05 .02
☐ 325 Jesse Barfield .05 .02
☐ 326 Dennis Boyd .05 .02
☐ 327 Mark Lemke .20 .09
☐ 328 Rick Honeycutt .05 .02
☐ 329 Bob Melvin .05 .02
☐ 330 Eric Davis .10 .05
☐ 331 Curt Wilkerson .05 .02
☐ 332 Tony Armas .05 .02
☐ 333 Bob Ojeda .05 .02
☐ 334 Steve Lyons .05 .02
☐ 335 Dave Righetti .05 .02
☐ 336 Steve Balboni .05 .02
☐ 337 Calvin Schiraldi .05 .02
☐ 338 Jim Adduci .05 .02
☐ 339 Scott Bailes .05 .02
☐ 340 Kirk Gibson 2.00 .90
☐ 341 Jim Deshaies .05 .02
☐ 342 Tom Brookens .05 .02
☐ 343 Gary Sheffield FS .75 .35
☐ 344 Tom Trebelhorn MG .05 .02
(Team checklist back)
☐ 345 Charlie Hough .10 .05
☐ 346 Rex Hudler .05 .02
☐ 347 John Cerutti .05 .02
☐ 348 Ed Hearn .05 .02
☐ 349 Ron Jones .05 .02
☐ 350 Andy Van Slyke .10 .05
☐ 351 San Fran. Giants TL .05 .02
Bob Melvin
(With Bill Fahey CO)
☐ 352 Rick Schu .05 .02
☐ 353 Marvell Wynne .05 .02
☐ 354 Larry Parrish .05 .02
☐ 355 Mark Langston .05 .02
☐ 356 Kevin Elster .05 .02
☐ 357 Jerry Reuss .05 .02
☐ 358 Ricky Jordan .10 .05
☐ 359 Tommy John 2.00 .90
☐ 360 Ryne Sandberg .25 .11
☐ 361 Kelly Downs .05 .02
☐ 362 Jack Lazorko .05 .02
☐ 363 Rich Yett .05 .02
☐ 364 Rob Deer .05 .02
☐ 365 Mike Henneman .05 .02
☐ 366 Herm Winningham .05 .02
☐ 367 Johnny Paredes .05 .02
☐ 368 Brian Holton .05 .02
☐ 369 Ken Caminiti .25 .11
☐ 370 Dennis Eckersley .20 .09
☐ 371 Manny Lee .05 .02
☐ 372 Craig Lefferts .05 .02
☐ 373 Tracy Jones .05 .02
☐ 374 John Wathan MG .05 .02
(Team checklist back)
☐ 375 Terry Pendleton .10 .05
☐ 376 Steve Lombardozzi .05 .02
☐ 377 Mike Smithson .05 .02
☐ 378 Checklist 265-396 .05 .02
☐ 379 Tim Flannery .05 .02
☐ 380 Rickey Henderson .20 .09
☐ 381 Baltimore Orioles TL .05 .02
Larry Sheets
☐ 382 John Smoltz .50 .23
☐ 383 Howard Johnson .05 .02
☐ 384 Mark Salas .05 .02
☐ 385 Von Hayes .05 .02
☐ 386 Andres Galarraga AS .20 .09
☐ 387 Ryne Sandberg AS .20 .09
☐ 388 Bobby Bonilla AS .10 .05
☐ 389 Ozzie Smith AS .20 .09
☐ 390 Darryl Strawberry AS .10 .05
☐ 391 Andre Dawson AS .20 .09
☐ 392 Andy Van Slyke AS .05 .02
☐ 393 Gary Carter AS .20 .09
☐ 394 Orel Hershiser AS .10 .05
☐ 395 Danny Jackson AS .05 .02
☐ 396 Kirk Gibson AS .10 .05
☐ 397 Don Mattingly AS .20 .09
☐ 398 Julio Franco AS .05 .02
☐ 399 Wade Boggs AS .20 .09
☐ 400 Alan Trammell AS 2.00 .90
☐ 401 Jose Canseco AS .20 .09
☐ 402 Mike Greenwell AS .05 .02
☐ 403 Kirby Puckett AS .20 .09
☐ 404 Bob Boone AS .05 .02
☐ 405 Roger Clemens AS .20 .09
☐ 406 Frank Viola AS .05 .02
☐ 407 Dave Winfield AS .20 .09
☐ 408 Greg Walker .05 .02
☐ 409 Ken Dayley .05 .02
☐ 410 Jack Clark .10 .05
☐ 411 Mitch Williams .05 .02
☐ 412 Barry Lyons .05 .02
☐ 413 Mike Kingery .05 .02
☐ 414 Jim Fregosi MG .05 .02
(Team checklist back)
☐ 415 Rich Gossage 2.00 .90
☐ 416 Fred Lynn .05 .02
☐ 417 Mike LaCoss .05 .02
☐ 418 Bob Dernier .05 .02
☐ 419 Tom Filer .05 .02
☐ 420 Joe Carter .20 .09
☐ 421 Kirk McCaskill .05 .02
☐ 422 Bo Diaz .05 .02
☐ 423 Brian Fisher .05 .02
☐ 424 Luis Polonia UER .05 .02
(Wrong birthdate)
☐ 425 Jay Howell .05 .02
☐ 426 Dan Gladden .05 .02
☐ 427 Eric Show .05 .02
☐ 428 Craig Reynolds .05 .02
☐ 429 Minnesota Twins TL .05 .02
Greg Gagne
(Taking throw at 2nd)
☐ 430 Mark Gubicza .05 .02
☐ 431 Luis Rivera .05 .02
☐ 432 Chad Kreuter .05 .02
☐ 433 Albert Hall .05 .02
☐ 434 Ken Patterson .05 .02
☐ 435 Len Dykstra .05 .02
☐ 436 Bobby Meacham .05 .02
☐ 437 Andy Benes FDP .25 .11
☐ 438 Greg Gross .05 .02
☐ 439 Frank DiPino .05 .02

☐ 440 Bobby Bonilla	2.00	.90
☐ 441 Jerry Reed	.05	.02
☐ 442 Jose Oquendo	.05	.02
☐ 443 Rod Nichols	.05	.02
☐ 444 Moose Stubing MG (Team checklist back)	.05	.02
☐ 445 Matt Nokes	.05	.02
☐ 446 Rob Murphy	.05	.02
☐ 447 Donell Nixon	.05	.02
☐ 448 Eric Plunk	.05	.02
☐ 449 Carmelo Martinez	.05	.02
☐ 450 Roger Clemens	.40	.18
☐ 451 Mark Davidson	.05	.02
☐ 452 Israel Sanchez	.05	.02
☐ 453 Tom Prince	.05	.02
☐ 454 Paul Assenmacher	.05	.02
☐ 455 Johnny Ray	.05	.02
☐ 456 Tim Belcher	.05	.02
☐ 457 Mackey Sasser	.05	.02
☐ 458 Donn Pall	.05	.02
☐ 459 Seattle Mariners TL Dave Valle	.05	.02
☐ 460 Dave Stieb	.05	.02
☐ 461 Buddy Bell	.10	.05
☐ 462 Jose Guzman	.05	.02
☐ 463 Steve Lake	.05	.02
☐ 464 Bryn Smith	.05	.02
☐ 465 Mark Grace	.20	.09
☐ 466 Chuck Crim	.05	.02
☐ 467 Jim Walewander	.05	.02
☐ 468 Henry Cotto	.05	.02
☐ 469 Jose Bautista	.05	.02
☐ 470 Lance Parrish	.05	.02
☐ 471 Steve Curry	.05	.02
☐ 472 Brian Harper	.05	.02
☐ 473 Don Robinson	.05	.02
☐ 474 Bob Rodgers MG (Team checklist back)	.05	.02
☐ 475 Dave Parker	.10	.05
☐ 476 Jon Perlman	.05	.02
☐ 477 Dick Schofield	.05	.02
☐ 478 Doug Drabek	.05	.02
☐ 479 Mike Macfarlane	.10	.05
☐ 480 Keith Hernandez	.10	.05
☐ 481 Chris Brown	.05	.02
☐ 482 Steve Peters	.05	.02
☐ 483 Mickey Hatcher	.05	.02
☐ 484 Steve Shields	.05	.02
☐ 485 Hubie Brooks	.05	.02
☐ 486 Jack McDowell	.05	.02
☐ 487 Scott Lusader	.05	.02
☐ 488 Kevin Coffman Now with Cubs	.05	.02
☐ 489 Phila. Phillies TL Mike Schmidt	.10	.05
☐ 490 Chris Sabo	.05	.02
☐ 491 Mike Birkbeck	.05	.02
☐ 492 Alan Ashby	.05	.02
☐ 493 Todd Benzinger	.05	.02
☐ 494 Shane Rawley	.05	.02
☐ 495 Candy Maldonado	.05	.02
☐ 496 Dwayne Henry	.05	.02
☐ 497 Pete Stanicek	.05	.02
☐ 498 Dave Valle	.05	.02
☐ 499 Don Heinkel	.05	.02
☐ 500 Jose Canseco	.20	.09
☐ 501 Vance Law	.05	.02
☐ 502 Duane Ward	.05	.02
☐ 503 Al Newman	.05	.02
☐ 504 Bob Walk	.05	.02
☐ 505 Pete Rose MG (Team checklist back)	.25	.11
☐ 506 Kirt Manwaring	.05	.02
☐ 507 Steve Farr	.05	.02
☐ 508 Wally Backman	.05	.02
☐ 509 Bud Black	.05	.02
☐ 510 Bob Horner	.05	.02
☐ 511 Richard Dotson	.05	.02
☐ 512 Donnie Hill	.05	.02
☐ 513 Jesse Orosco	.05	.02
☐ 514 Chet Lemon	.05	.02
☐ 515 Barry Larkin	.20	.09
☐ 516 Eddie Whitson	.05	.02
☐ 517 Greg Brock	.05	.02
☐ 518 Bruce Ruffin	.05	.02
☐ 519 New York Yankees TL Willie Randolph	.05	.02
☐ 520 Rick Sutcliffe	.05	.02
☐ 521 Mickey Tettleton	.10	.05
☐ 522 Randy Kramer	.05	.02
☐ 523 Andres Thomas	.05	.02
☐ 524 Checklist 397-528	.05	.02
☐ 525 Chili Davis	.10	.05
☐ 526 Wes Gardner	.05	.02
☐ 527 Dave Henderson	.05	.02
☐ 528 Luis Medina (Lower left front has white triangle)	.05	.02
☐ 529 Tom Foley	.05	.02
☐ 530 Nolan Ryan	.75	.35
☐ 531 Dave Hengel	.05	.02
☐ 532 Jerry Browne	.05	.02
☐ 533 Andy Hawkins	.05	.02
☐ 534 Doc Edwards MG (Team checklist back)	.05	.02
☐ 535 Todd Worrell UER (4 wins in '88, should be 5)	.05	.02
☐ 536 Joel Skinner	.05	.02
☐ 537 Pete Smith	.05	.02
☐ 538 Juan Castillo	.05	.02
☐ 539 Barry Jones	.05	.02
☐ 540 Bo Jackson	.20	.09
☐ 541 Cecil Fielder	.10	.05
☐ 542 Todd Frohwirth	.05	.02
☐ 543 Damon Berryhill	.05	.02
☐ 544 Jeff Sellers	.05	.02
☐ 545 Mookie Wilson	.10	.05
☐ 546 Mark Williamson	.05	.02
☐ 547 Mark McLemore	.05	.02
☐ 548 Bobby Witt	.05	.02
☐ 549 Chicago Cubs TL Jamie Moyer (Pitching)	.05	.02
☐ 550 Orel Hershiser	.10	.05
☐ 551 Randy Ready	.05	.02
☐ 552 Greg Cadaret	.05	.02
☐ 553 Luis Salazar	.05	.02
☐ 554 Nick Esasky	.05	.02
☐ 555 Bert Blyleven	.10	.05
☐ 556 Bruce Fields	.05	.02
☐ 557 Keith A. Miller	.05	.02
☐ 558 Dan Pasqua	.05	.02
☐ 559 Juan Agosto	.05	.02
☐ 560 Tim Raines	.10	.05
☐ 561 Luis Aguayo	.05	.02
☐ 562 Danny Cox	.05	.02
☐ 563 Bill Schroeder	.05	.02
☐ 564 Russ Nixon MG (Team checklist back)	.05	.02
☐ 565 Jeff Russell	.05	.02
☐ 566 Al Pedrique	.05	.02
☐ 567 David Wells UER (Complete Pitching Recor)	.05	.02
☐ 568 Mickey Brantley	.05	.02
☐ 569 German Jimenez	.05	.02
☐ 570 Tony Gwynn UER ('88 average should be italicized as league leader)	.50	.23
☐ 571 Billy Ripken	.05	.02
☐ 572 Atlee Hammaker	.05	.02
☐ 573 Jim Abbott FDP	.20	.09
☐ 574 Dave Clark	.05	.02
☐ 575 Juan Samuel	.05	.02
☐ 576 Greg Minton	.05	.02
☐ 577 Randy Bush	.05	.02
☐ 578 John Morris	.05	.02
☐ 579 Houston Astros TL Glenn Davis (Batting stance)	.05	.02
☐ 580 Harold Reynolds	.05	.02
☐ 581 Gene Nelson	.05	.02
☐ 582 Mike Marshall	.05	.02
☐ 583 Paul Gibson	.05	.02
☐ 584 Randy Velarde UER (Signed 1935, should be 1985)	.05	.02
☐ 585 Harold Baines	.10	.05
☐ 586 Joe Boever	.05	.02
☐ 587 Mike Stanley	.05	.02
☐ 588 Luis Alicea	.05	.02
☐ 589 Dave Meads	.05	.02
☐ 590 Andres Galarraga	.20	.09
☐ 591 Jeff Musselman	.05	.02
☐ 592 John Cangelosi	.05	.02
☐ 593 Drew Hall	.05	.02
☐ 594 Jimy Williams MG (Team checklist back)	.05	.02
☐ 595 Teddy Higuera	.05	.02
☐ 596 Kurt Stillwell	.05	.02
☐ 597 Terry Taylor	.05	.02
☐ 598 Ken Gerhart	.05	.02
☐ 599 Tom Candiotti	.05	.02
☐ 600 Wade Boggs	.20	.09
☐ 601 Dave Dravecky	.10	.05
☐ 602 Devon White	.05	.02
☐ 603 Frank Tanana	.05	.02
☐ 604 Paul O'Neill	.10	.05
☐ 605A Bob Welch ERR (Missing line on back, "Complete M.L. Pitching Record")	2.00	.90
☐ 605B Bob Welch COR	.05	.02
☐ 606 Rick Dempsey	.05	.02
☐ 607 Willie Ansley FDP	.05	.02
☐ 608 Phil Bradley	.05	.02
☐ 609 Detroit Tigers TL Frank Tanana (With Alan Trammell and Mike Heath)	.05	.02
☐ 610 Randy Myers	.10	.05
☐ 611 Don Slaught	.05	.02
☐ 612 Dan Quisenberry	.05	.02
☐ 613 Gary Varsho	.05	.02
☐ 614 Joe Hesketh	.05	.02
☐ 615 Robin Yount	.20	.09
☐ 616 Steve Rosenberg	.05	.02
☐ 617 Mark Parent	.05	.02
☐ 618 Rance Mulliniks	.05	.02
☐ 619 Checklist 529-660	.05	.02
☐ 620 Barry Bonds	.40	.18
☐ 621 Rick Mahler	.05	.02
☐ 622 Stan Javier	.05	.02
☐ 623 Fred Toliver	.05	.02
☐ 624 Jack McKeon MG (Team checklist back)	.05	.02
☐ 625 Eddie Murray	.20	.09
☐ 626 Jeff Reed	.05	.02
☐ 627 Greg A. Harris	.05	.02
☐ 028 Matt Williams	.25	.11
☐ 629 Pete O'Brien	.05	.02
☐ 630 Mike Greenwell	.05	.02
☐ 631 Dave Bergman	.05	.02
☐ 632 Bryan Harvey	.10	.05
☐ 633 Daryl Boston	.05	.02
☐ 634 Marvin Freeman	.05	.02
☐ 635 Willie Randolph	.10	.05
☐ 636 Bill Wilkinson	.05	.02
☐ 637 Carmen Castillo	.05	.02
☐ 638 Floyd Bannister	.05	.02
☐ 639 Oakland A's TL Walt Weiss	.05	.02
☐ 640 Willie McGee	.05	.02
☐ 641 Curt Young	.05	.02
☐ 642 Argenis Salazar	.05	.02
☐ 643 Louie Meadows	.05	.02
☐ 644 Lloyd McClendon	.05	.02
☐ 645 Jack Morris	.10	.05
☐ 646 Kevin Bass	.05	.02
☐ 647 Randy Johnson	1.00	.45
☐ 648 Sandy Alomar FS	.50	.23
☐ 649 Stewart Cliburn	.05	.02
☐ 650 Kirby Puckett	.40	.18
☐ 651 Tom Niedenfuer	.05	.02
☐ 652 Rich Gedman	.05	.02
☐ 653 Tommy Barrett	.05	.02
☐ 654 Whitey Herzog MG (Team checklist back)	.10	.05
☐ 655 Dave Magadan	.05	.02
☐ 656 Ivan Calderon	.05	.02
☐ 657 Joe Magrane	.05	.02
☐ 658 R.J. Reynolds	.05	.02
☐ 659 Al Leiter	.20	.09
☐ 660 Will Clark	.20	.09
☐ 661 Dwight Gooden TBC84	.20	.09
☐ 662 Lou Brock TBC79	.20	.09
☐ 663 Hank Aaron TBC74	.20	.09
☐ 664 Gil Hodges TBC69	.20	.09
☐ 665A Tony Oliva TBC64 ERR (fabricated card is enlarged version of Oliva's 64T card; Topps copyright missing)	2.00	.90
☐ 665B Tony Oliva TBC64 COR (fabricated card)	.10	.05
☐ 666 Randy St.Claire	.05	.02
☐ 667 Dwayne Murphy	.05	.02
☐ 668 Mike Bielecki	.05	.02
☐ 669 L.A. Dodgers TL Orel Hershiser (Mound conference with Mike Scioscia)	.10	.05
☐ 670 Kevin Seitzer	.05	.02
☐ 671 Jim Gantner	.05	.02
☐ 672 Allan Anderson	.05	.02
☐ 673 Don Baylor	.20	.09
☐ 674 Otis Nixon	.05	.02
☐ 675 Bruce Hurst	.05	.02
☐ 676 Ernie Riles	.05	.02
☐ 677 Dave Schmidt	.05	.02
☐ 678 Dion James	.05	.02
☐ 679 Willie Fraser	.05	.02
☐ 680 Gary Carter	.20	.09
☐ 681 Jeff D. Robinson	.05	.02
☐ 682 Rick Leach	.05	.02
☐ 683 Jose Cecena	.05	.02
☐ 684 Dave Johnson MG (Team checklist back)	.05	.02

☐ 685 Jeff Treadway .05 .02
☐ 686 Scott Terry .05 .02
☐ 687 Alvin Davis .05 .02
☐ 688 Zane Smith .05 .02
☐ 689A Stan Jefferson .05 .02
(Pink triangle on front bottom left)
☐ 689B Stan Jefferson .05 .02
(Violet triangle on front bottom left)
☐ 690 Doug Jones .05 .02
☐ 691 Roberto Kelly UER .05 .02
(83 Oneonita)
☐ 692 Steve Ontiveros .05 .02
☐ 693 Pat Borders .10 .05
☐ 694 Les Lancaster .05 .02
☐ 695 Carlton Fisk .20 .09
☐ 696 Don August .05 .02
☐ 697A Franklin Stubbs .05 .02
(Team name on front in white)
☐ 697B Franklin Stubbs .05 .02
(Team name on front in gray)
☐ 698 Keith Atherton .05 .02
☐ 699 Pittsburgh Pirates TL .05 .02
Al Pedrique
(Tony Gwynn sliding)
☐ 700 Don Mattingly .30 .14
☐ 701 Storm Davis .05 .02
☐ 702 Jamie Quirk .05 .02
☐ 703 Scott Garrelts .05 .02
☐ 704 Carlos Quintana .05 .02
☐ 705 Terry Kennedy .05 .02
☐ 706 Pete Incaviglia .10 .05
☐ 707 Steve Jeltz .05 .02
☐ 708 Chuck Finley .10 .05
☐ 709 Tom Herr .05 .02
☐ 710 David Cone .20 .09
☐ 711 Candy Sierra .05 .02
☐ 712 Bill Swift .05 .02
☐ 713 Ty Griffin FDP .05 .02
☐ 714 Joe Morgan MG .05 .02
(Team checklist back)
☐ 715 Tony Pena .05 .02
☐ 716 Wayne Tolleson .05 .02
☐ 717 Jamie Moyer .05 .02
☐ 718 Glenn Braggs .05 .02
☐ 719 Danny Darwin .05 .02
☐ 720 Tim Wallach .05 .02
☐ 721 Ron Tingley .05 .02
☐ 722 Todd Stottlemyre .10 .05
☐ 723 Rafael Belliard .05 .02
☐ 724 Jerry Don Gleaton .05 .02
☐ 725 Terry Steinbach .10 .05
☐ 726 Dickie Thon .05 .02
☐ 727 Joe Orsulak .05 .02
☐ 728 Charlie Puleo .05 .02
☐ 729 Texas Rangers TL .05 .02
Steve Buechele
(Inconsistent design, team name on front surrounded by black, should be white)
☐ 730 Danny Jackson .05 .02
☐ 731 Mike Young .05 .02
☐ 732 Steve Buechele .05 .02
☐ 733 Randy Bockus .05 .02
☐ 734 Jody Reed .05 .02
☐ 735 Roger McDowell .05 .02
☐ 736 Jeff Hamilton .05 .02
☐ 737 Norm Charlton .10 .05
☐ 738 Darnell Coles .05 .02
☐ 739 Brook Jacoby .05 .02
☐ 740 Dan Plesac .05 .02
☐ 741 Ken Phelps .05 .02
☐ 742 Mike Harkey FS .05 .02
☐ 743 Mike Heath .05 .02
☐ 744 Roger Craig MG .05 .02
(Team checklist back)
☐ 745 Fred McGriff .20 .09
☐ 746 German Gonzalez UER .05 .02
(Wrong birthdate)
☐ 747 Wil Tejada .05 .02
☐ 748 Jimmy Jones .05 .02
☐ 749 Rafael Ramirez .05 .02
☐ 750 Bret Saberhagen .05 .02
☐ 751 Ken Oberkfell .05 .02
☐ 752 Jim Gott .05 .02
☐ 753 Jose Uribe .05 .02
☐ 754 Bob Brower .05 .02
☐ 755 Mike Scioscia .05 .02
☐ 756 Scott Medvin .05 .02
☐ 757 Brady Anderson .50 .23
☐ 758 Gene Walter .05 .02
☐ 759 Milwaukee Brewers TL .05 .02
Rob Deer
☐ 760 Lee Smith 2.00 .90
☐ 761 Dante Bichette .40 .18
☐ 762 Bobby Thigpen .05 .02
☐ 763 Dave Martinez .05 .02
☐ 764 Robin Ventura FDP .40 .18
☐ 765 Glenn Davis .05 .02
☐ 766 Cecilio Guante .05 .02
☐ 767 Mike Capel .05 .02
☐ 768 Bill Wegman .05 .02
☐ 769 Junior Ortiz .05 .02
☐ 770 Alan Trammell .10 .05
☐ 771 Ron Kittle .05 .02
☐ 772 Ron Oester .05 .02
☐ 773 Keith Moreland .05 .02
☐ 774 Frank Robinson MG .20 .09
(Team checklist back)
☐ 775 Jeff Reardon .10 .05
☐ 776 Nelson Liriano .05 .02
☐ 777 Ted Power .05 .02
☐ 778 Bruce Benedict .05 .02
☐ 779 Craig McMurtry .05 .02
☐ 780 Pedro Guerrero .10 .05
☐ 781 Greg Briley .05 .02
☐ 782 Checklist 661-792 .05 .02
☐ 783 Trevor Wilson .05 .02
☐ 784 Steve Avery FDP .10 .05
☐ 785 Ellis Burks 2.00 .90
☐ 786 Melido Perez .05 .02
☐ 787 Dave West .05 .02
☐ 788 Mike Morgan .05 .02
☐ 789 Kansas City Royals TL .20 .09
Bo Jackson
(Throwing)
☐ 790 Sid Fernandez .05 .02
☐ 791 Jim Lindeman .05 .02
☐ 792 Rafael Santana .05 .02

1989 Topps Tiffany

Again, Topps issed a standard-size "Glossy" parallel to their regular set. These cards, printed in the Topps Irish facility, have 792 standard-size cards and were issued in complete set form only. These cards have a "shiny" front as well as an easy to read back. These cards were issued only through Topps hobby dealers.

	MINT	NRMT
COMPLETE FACT.SET (792)	50.00	22.00
COMMON CARD (1-792)	.10	.05
*STARS: 3X to 6X BASIC CARDS		
*ROOKIES: 2X to 4X BASIC CARDS		

1989 Topps Batting Leaders

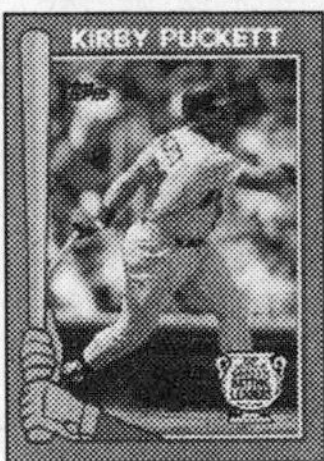

The 1989 Topps Batting Leaders set contains 22 standard-size glossy cards. The fronts are bright red. The set depicts the 22 veterans with the highest lifetime batting averages. The cards were distributed one per Topps blister pack. These blister packs were sold exclusively through K-Mart stores. The cards in the set were numbered by K-Mart essentially in order of highest active career batting average entering the 1989 season.

	MINT	NRMT
COMPLETE SET (22)	50.00	22.00
COMMON CARD (1-22)	.50	.23

☐ 1 Wade Boggs 4.00 1.80
☐ 2 Tony Gwynn 15.00 6.75
☐ 3 Don Mattingly 10.00 4.50
☐ 4 Kirby Puckett 12.50 5.50
☐ 5 George Brett 10.00 4.50
☐ 6 Pedro Guerrero .50 .23
☐ 7 Tim Raines 1.00 .45
☐ 8 Keith Hernandez 1.00 .45
☐ 9 Jim Rice 1.00 .45
☐ 10 Paul Molitor 5.00 2.20
☐ 11 Eddie Murray 5.00 2.20
☐ 12 Willie McGee .50 .23
☐ 13 Dave Parker 1.00 .45
☐ 14 Julio Franco 1.00 .45
☐ 15 Rickey Henderson 4.00 1.80
☐ 16 Kent Hrbek 1.00 .45
☐ 17 Willie Wilson .50 .23
☐ 18 Johnny Ray .50 .23
☐ 19 Pat Tabler .50 .23
☐ 20 Carney Lansford .50 .23
☐ 21 Robin Yount 2.00 .90
☐ 22 Alan Trammell 2.00 .90

1989 Topps Glossy All-Stars

These glossy cards were inserted with Topps rack packs and honor the starting line-ups, managers, and honorary captains of the 1988 National and American League All-Star teams. The standard size cards are very similar in design to what Topps has used since 1984. The backs are printed in red and blue on white card stock.

	MINT	NRMT
COMPLETE SET (22)	3.00	1.35
COMMON CARD (1-22)	.05	.02

☐ 1 Tom Kelly MG .05 .02
☐ 2 Mark McGwire .75 .35
☐ 3 Paul Molitor .40 .18
☐ 4 Wade Boggs .25 .11
☐ 5 Cal Ripken 1.50 .70
☐ 6 Jose Canseco .30 .14
☐ 7 Rickey Henderson .30 .14
☐ 8 Dave Winfield .30 .14
☐ 9 Terry Steinbach .10 .05
☐ 10 Frank Viola .05 .02
☐ 11 Bobby Doerr CAPT .10 .05
☐ 12 Whitey Herzog MG .05 .02
☐ 13 Will Clark .30 .14
☐ 14 Ryne Sandberg .50 .23
☐ 15 Bobby Bonilla .15 .07
☐ 16 Ozzie Smith .50 .23
☐ 17 Vince Coleman .05 .02
☐ 18 Andre Dawson .25 .11
☐ 19 Darryl Strawberry .10 .05
☐ 20 Gary Carter .15 .07
☐ 21 Dwight Gooden .10 .05
☐ 22 Willie Stargell CAPT .15 .07

1989 Topps Glossy Send-Ins

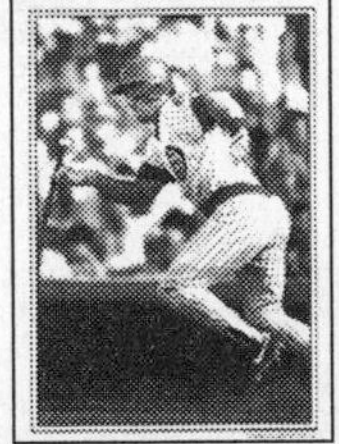

The 1989 Topps Glossy Send-In set contains 60 standard-size cards. The fronts have color photos with white borders; the backs are light blue. The cards were distributed through the mail by Topps in six groups of ten cards. The last two cards out of each group of ten are young players or prospects.

	MINT	NRMT
COMPLETE SET (60)	10.00	4.50
COMMON CARD (1-60)	.10	.05

☐ 1 Kirby Puckett 2.00 .90
☐ 2 Eric Davis .20 .09
☐ 3 Joe Carter .30 .14
☐ 4 Andy Van Slyke .20 .09
☐ 5 Wade Boggs .50 .23
☐ 6 David Cone .20 .09
☐ 7 Kent Hrbek .20 .09
☐ 8 Darryl Strawberry .20 .09
☐ 9 Jay Buhner .50 .23
☐ 10 Ron Gant .50 .23
☐ 11 Will Clark .50 .23
☐ 12 Jose Canseco .75 .35
☐ 13 Juan Samuel .10 .05

	MINT	NRMT
☐ 14 George Brett	1.50	.70
☐ 15 Benito Santiago	.10	.05
☐ 16 Dennis Eckersley	.30	.14
☐ 17 Gary Carter	.30	.14
☐ 18 Frank Viola	.10	.05
☐ 19 Roberto Alomar	1.50	.70
☐ 20 Paul Gibson	.10	.05
☐ 21 Dave Winfield	.40	.18
☐ 22 Howard Johnson	.10	.05
☐ 23 Roger Clemens	1.00	.45
☐ 24 Bobby Bonilla	.20	.09
☐ 25 Alan Trammell	.30	.14
☐ 26 Kevin McReynolds	.10	.05
☐ 27 George Bell	.10	.05
☐ 28 Bruce Hurst	.10	.05
☐ 29 Mark Grace	.75	.35
☐ 30 Tim Belcher	.10	.05
☐ 31 Mike Greenwell	.10	.05
☐ 32 Glenn Davis	.10	.05
☐ 33 Gary Gaetti	.10	.05
☐ 34 Ryne Sandberg	1.50	.70
☐ 35 Rickey Henderson	.50	.23
☐ 36 Dwight Evans	.20	.09
☐ 37 Dwight Gooden	.20	.09
☐ 38 Robin Yount	.30	.14
☐ 39 Damon Berryhill	.10	.05
☐ 40 Chris Sabo	.10	.05
☐ 41 Mark McGwire	1.50	.70
☐ 42 Ozzie Smith	1.50	.70
☐ 43 Paul Molitor	.50	.23
☐ 44 Andres Galarraga	.50	.23
☐ 45 Dave Stewart	.20	.09
☐ 46 Tom Browning	.10	.05
☐ 47 Cal Ripken	3.00	1.35
☐ 48 Orel Hershiser	.20	.09
☐ 49 Dave Gallagher	.10	.05
☐ 50 Walt Weiss	.10	.05
☐ 51 Don Mattingly	2.00	.90
☐ 52 Tony Fernandez	.10	.05
☐ 53 Tim Raines	.20	.09
☐ 54 Jeff Reardon	.20	.09
☐ 55 Kirk Gibson	.20	.09
☐ 56 Jack Clark	.10	.05
☐ 57 Danny Jackson	.10	.05
☐ 58 Tony Gwynn	2.00	.90
☐ 59 Cecil Espy	.10	.05
☐ 60 Jody Reed	.10	.05

1989 Topps Rookies

Inserted in each supermarket jumbo pack is a card from this series of 22 of 1988's best rookies as determined by Topps. Jumbo packs consisted of 100 (regular issue 1989 Topps baseball) cards with a stick of gum plus the insert "Rookie" card. The card fronts are in full color and measure the standard size. The card backs are printed in red and blue on white card stock and are numbered at the bottom. The order of the set is alphabetical by player's name.

	MINT	NRMT
COMPLETE SET (22)	6.00	2.70
COMMON CARD (1-22)	.05	.02
☐ 1 Roberto Alomar	1.50	.70
☐ 2 Brady Anderson	1.25	.55
☐ 3 Tim Belcher	.10	.05
☐ 4 Damon Berryhill	.05	.02
☐ 5 Jay Buhner	1.25	.55
☐ 6 Kevin Elster	.10	.05
☐ 7 Cecil Espy	.05	.02
☐ 8 Dave Gallagher	.05	.02
☐ 9 Ron Gant	.75	.35
☐ 10 Paul Gibson	.05	.02
☐ 11 Mark Grace	1.50	.70
☐ 12 Darrin Jackson	.05	.02
☐ 13 Gregg Jefferies	.10	.05
☐ 14 Ricky Jordan	.05	.02
☐ 15 Al Leiter	.10	.05
☐ 16 Melido Perez	.05	.02
☐ 17 Chris Sabo	.05	.02
☐ 18 Nelson Santovenia	.05	.02
☐ 19 Mackey Sasser	.05	.02
☐ 20 Gary Sheffield	1.50	.70
☐ 21 Walt Weiss	.05	.02
☐ 22 David Wells	.10	.05

1989 Topps Wax Box Cards

The cards in this 16-card set measure the standard size. Cards have essentially the same design as the 1989 Topps regular issue set. The cards were printed on the bottoms of the regular issue wax pack boxes. These 16 cards, "lettered" A through P, are considered a separate set in their own right and are not typically included in a complete set of the regular issue 1989 Topps cards. The order of the set is alphabetical by player's name. The value of the panels uncut is slightly greater, perhaps by 25 percent greater, than the value of the individual cards cut up carefully. The sixteen cards in this set honor players (and one manager) who reached career milestones during the 1988 season.

	MINT	NRMT
COMPLETE SET (16)	8.00	3.60
COMMON CARD (A-P)	.10	.05
☐ A George Brett (475th Double)	1.00	.45
☐ B Bill Buckner (2600th Hit)	.20	.09
☐ C Darrell Evans (400th Home Run)	.20	.09
☐ D Rich Gossage (300th Save)	.20	.09
☐ E Greg Gross (125th Pinch Hit)	.10	.05
☐ F Rickey Henderson (775th Stolen Base)	.60	.25
☐ G Keith Hernandez (125th Game-Winning RBI)	.20	.09
☐ H Tom Lasorda MG (1000th Managerial Win)	.35	.16
☐ I Jim Rice (1400th Run Batted In)	.20	.09
☐ J Cal Ripken (1000th Cons. Game)	2.50	1.10
☐ K Nolan Ryan (4700th Strikeout)	2.50	1.10
☐ L Mike Schmidt (1000th Long Hit)	.75	.35
☐ M Bruce Sutter (300th Save)	.20	.09
☐ N Don Sutton (750th Game Started)	.35	.16
☐ O Kent Tekulve (1000th Appearance)	.10	.05
☐ P Dave Winfield (1400th Run Batted In)	.50	.23

1989 Topps Traded

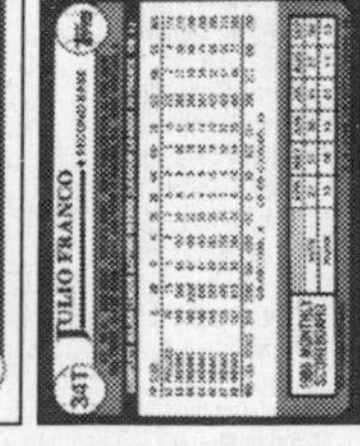

The 1989 Topps Traded set contains 132 standard-size cards. The cards were distributed exclusively in factory set form in red and white taped boxes through hobby dealers. The cards are identical to the 1989 Topps regular issue cards except for whiter stock and t-suffixed numbering on back. Rookie Cards in this set include Ken Griffey Jr., Ken Hill and Deion Sanders.

	MINT	NRMT
COMP.FACT.SET (132)	8.00	3.60
COMMON CARD (1T-132T)	.05	.02
☐ 1T Don Aase	.05	.02
☐ 2T Jim Abbott	.20	.09
☐ 3T Kent Anderson	.05	.02
☐ 4T Keith Atherton	.05	.02
☐ 5T Wally Backman	.05	.02
☐ 6T Steve Balboni	.05	.02
☐ 7T Jesse Barfield	.05	.02
☐ 8T Steve Bedrosian	.05	.02
☐ 9T Todd Benzinger	.05	.02
☐ 10T Geronimo Berroa	.10	.05
☐ 11T Bert Blyleven	.10	.05
☐ 12T Bob Boone	.10	.05
☐ 13T Phil Bradley	.05	.02
☐ 14T Jeff Brantley	.05	.02
☐ 15T Kevin Brown	.20	.09
☐ 16T Jerry Browne	.05	.02
☐ 17T Chuck Cary	.05	.02
☐ 18T Carmen Castillo	.05	.02
☐ 19T Jim Clancy	.05	.02
☐ 20T Jack Clark	.10	.05
☐ 21T Bryan Clutterbuck	.05	.02
☐ 22T Jody Davis	.05	.02
☐ 23T Mike Devereaux	.05	.02
☐ 24T Frank DiPino	.05	.02
☐ 25T Benny Distefano	.05	.02
☐ 26T John Dopson	.05	.02
☐ 27T Len Dykstra	.10	.05
☐ 28T Jim Eisenreich	.20	.09
☐ 29T Nick Esasky	.05	.02
☐ 30T Alvaro Espinoza	.05	.02
☐ 31T Darrell Evans UER (Stat headings on back are for a pitcher)	.10	.05
☐ 32T Junior Felix	.05	.02
☐ 33T Felix Fermin	.05	.02
☐ 34T Julio Franco	.10	.05
☐ 35T Terry Francona	.05	.02
☐ 36T Cito Gaston MG	.10	.05
☐ 37T Bob Geren UER (Photo actually Mike Fennell)	.05	.02
☐ 38T Tom Gordon	.20	.09
☐ 39T Tommy Gregg	.05	.02
☐ 40T Ken Griffey Sr.	.05	.02
☐ 41T Ken Griffey Jr.	6.00	2.70
☐ 42T Kevin Gross	.05	.02
☐ 43T Lee Guetterman	.05	.02
☐ 44T Mel Hall	.05	.02
☐ 45T Erik Hanson	.10	.05
☐ 46T Gene Harris	.05	.02
☐ 47T Andy Hawkins	.05	.02
☐ 48T Rickey Henderson	.20	.09
☐ 49T Tom Herr	.05	.02
☐ 50T Ken Hill	.40	.18
☐ 51T Brian Holman	.05	.02
☐ 52T Brian Holton	.05	.02
☐ 53T Art Howe MG	.05	.02
☐ 54T Ken Howell	.05	.02
☐ 55T Bruce Hurst	.05	.02
☐ 56T Chris James	.05	.02
☐ 57T Randy Johnson	1.00	.45
☐ 58T Jimmy Jones	.05	.02
☐ 59T Terry Kennedy	.05	.02
☐ 60T Paul Kilgus	.05	.02
☐ 61T Eric King	.05	.02
☐ 62T Ron Kittle	.05	.02
☐ 63T John Kruk	.10	.05
☐ 64T Randy Kutcher	.05	.02
☐ 65T Steve Lake	.05	.02
☐ 66T Mark Langston	.05	.02
☐ 67T Dave LaPoint	.05	.02
☐ 68T Rick Leach	.05	.02
☐ 69T Terry Leach	.05	.02
☐ 70T Jim Lefebvre MG	.05	.02
☐ 71T Al Leiter	.20	.09
☐ 72T Jeffrey Leonard	.05	.02
☐ 73T Derek Lilliquist	.05	.02
☐ 74T Rick Mahler	.05	.02
☐ 75T Tom McCarthy	.05	.02
☐ 76T Lloyd McClendon	.05	.02
☐ 77T Lance McCullers	.05	.02
☐ 78T Oddibe McDowell	.05	.02
☐ 79T Roger McDowell	.05	.02
☐ 80T Larry McWilliams	.05	.02
☐ 81T Randy Milligan	.05	.02
☐ 82T Mike Moore	.05	.02
☐ 83T Keith Moreland	.05	.02
☐ 84T Mike Morgan	.05	.02
☐ 85T Jamie Moyer	.05	.02
☐ 86T Rob Murphy	.05	.02
☐ 87T Eddie Murray	.20	.09
☐ 88T Pete O'Brien	.05	.0[illegible]
☐ 89T Gregg Olson	.10	.[illegible]
☐ 90T Steve Ontiveros	.05	[illegible]

	MINT	NRMT
☐ 91T Jesse Orosco	.05	.02
☐ 92T Spike Owen	.05	.02
☐ 93T Rafael Palmeiro	.20	.09
☐ 94T Clay Parker	.05	.02
☐ 95T Jeff Parrett	.05	.02
☐ 96T Lance Parrish	.05	.02
☐ 97T Dennis Powell	.05	.02
☐ 98T Rey Quinones	.05	.02
☐ 99T Doug Rader MG	.05	.02
☐ 100T Willie Randolph	.10	.05
☐ 101T Shane Rawley	.05	.02
☐ 102T Randy Ready	.05	.02
☐ 103T Bip Roberts	.10	.05
☐ 104T Kenny Rogers	.10	.05
☐ 105T Ed Romero	.05	.02
☐ 106T Nolan Ryan	1.50	.70
☐ 107T Luis Salazar	.05	.02
☐ 108T Juan Samuel	.05	.02
☐ 109T Alex Sanchez	.05	.02
☐ 110T Deion Sanders	.75	.35
☐ 111T Steve Sax	.05	.02
☐ 112T Rick Schu	.05	.02
☐ 113T Dwight Smith	.10	.05
☐ 114T Lonnie Smith	.05	.02
☐ 115T Billy Spiers	.05	.02
☐ 116T Kent Tekulve	.05	.02
☐ 117T Walt Terrell	.05	.02
☐ 118T Milt Thompson	.05	.02
☐ 119T Dickie Thon	.05	.02
☐ 120T Jeff Torborg MG	.05	.02
☐ 121T Jeff Treadway	.05	.02
☐ 122T Omar Vizquel	.40	.18
☐ 123T Jerome Walton	.20	.09
☐ 124T Gary Ward	.05	.02
☐ 125T Claudell Washington	.05	.02
☐ 126T Curt Wilkerson	.05	.02
☐ 127T Eddie Williams	.05	.02
☐ 128T Frank Williams	.05	.02
☐ 129T Ken Williams	.05	.02
☐ 130T Mitch Williams	.05	.02
☐ 131T Steve Wilson	.05	.02
☐ 132T Checklist 1T-132T	.05	.02

1989 Topps Traded Tiffany

For each set of regular Tiffany cards ordered, dealers received an update set. These 132 standard-size cards update the regular Topps issue. Again, these cards feature "glossy" fronts as well as easy to read backs. This set was issued only in complete form from the company. Again, the Topps Ireland printing facility produced these cards.

	MINT	NRMT
COMPLETE FACT.SET (132)	40.00	18.00
COMMON CARD (1T-132T)	.15	.07
*STARS: 3X to 6X BASIC CARDS		
*ROOKIES: 2X to 4X BASIC CARDS		

1989 Topps Ames 20/20 Club

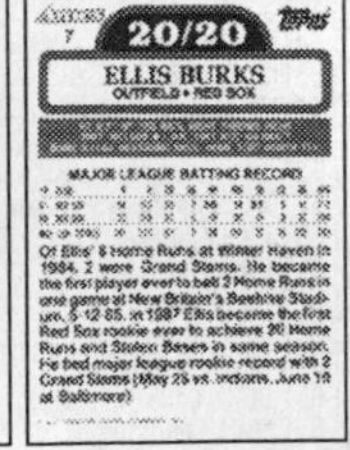

The 1989 (Topps) Ames 20/20 Club set contains 33 standard-size glossy cards. The fronts resemble plaques with gold and silver trim. The vertically oriented backs show career stats. The cards were distributed at Ames department stores as a boxed set. The set was produced by Topps for Ames; the Topps logo is also on the front of each card. The set includes active major leaguers who have had seasons of at least 20 home runs and 20 stolen bases. The backs include lifetime batting records with home run and stolen base totals for their 20/20 years highlighted. The subject list for the set is printed on the back panel of the set's custom box. These numbered cards are ordered alphabetically by player's name.

	MINT	NRMT
COMPLETE SET (33)	5.00	2.20
COMMON CARD (1-33)	.05	.02
☐ 1 Jesse Barfield	.05	.02
2 Kevin Bass	.05	.02
...on Baylor	.10	.05
...ge Bell	.05	.02
...onds	.60	.25

	MINT	NRMT
☐ 6 Phil Bradley	.05	.02
☐ 7 Ellis Burks	.25	.11
☐ 8 Jose Canseco	.40	.18
☐ 9 Joe Carter	.15	.07
☐ 10 Kal Daniels	.05	.02
☐ 11 Eric Davis	.10	.05
☐ 12 Mike Davis	.05	.02
☐ 13 Andre Dawson	.25	.11
☐ 14 Kirk Gibson	.15	.07
☐ 15 Pedro Guerrero	.05	.02
☐ 16 Rickey Henderson	.40	.18
☐ 17 Bo Jackson	.15	.07
☐ 18 Howard Johnson	.05	.02
☐ 19 Jeffrey Leonard	.05	.02
☐ 20 Kevin McReynolds	.05	.02
☐ 21 Dale Murphy	.15	.07
☐ 22 Dwayne Murphy	.05	.02
☐ 23 Dave Parker	.10	.05
☐ 24 Kirby Puckett	.75	.35
☐ 25 Juan Samuel	.05	.02
☐ 26 Ryne Sandberg	.60	.25
☐ 27 Mike Schmidt	.60	.25
☐ 28 Darryl Strawberry	.10	.05
☐ 29 Alan Trammell	.15	.07
☐ 30 Andy Van Slyke	.10	.05
☐ 31 Devon White	.05	.02
☐ 32 Dave Winfield	.30	.14
☐ 33 Robin Yount	.25	.11

1989 Topps Baseball Talk

The BB Talk Soundcards include action photos of players, complete player statistics, exclusive specially recorded baseball programs and player autographs. These cards were produced by Parker Brothers. The fronts of the cards feature oversized replicas of Topps cards.

	MINT	NRMT
COMPLETE SET (164)	125.00	55.00
COMMON CARD (1-164)	.25	.11
☐ 1 1975 World Series Game 6	1.50	.70
☐ 2 1986 World Series Game 6	1.00	.45
☐ 3 1986 A.L. Championship Game 5	1.00	.45
☐ 4 1956 World Series Game 5	1.00	.45
☐ 5 1986 N.L. Championship Game 6	1.00	.45
☐ 6 1969 World Series Game 5	1.00	.45
☐ 7 1984 World Series Game 5	1.00	.45
☐ 8 1988 World Series Game 1	1.50	.70
☐ 9 Reggie Jackson	2.50	1.10
☐ 10 Brooks Robinson	2.00	.90
☐ 11 Billy Williams	2.00	.90
☐ 12 Bobby Thomson	1.00	.45
☐ 13 Harmon Killebrew	2.00	.90
☐ 14 Johnny Bench	2.50	1.10
☐ 15 Tom Seaver	2.00	.90
☐ 16 Willie Stargell	2.00	.90
☐ 17 Ernie Banks	3.00	1.35
☐ 18 Gaylord Perry	1.50	.70
☐ 19 Bill Mazeroski	1.00	.45
☐ 20 Babe Ruth	7.50	3.40
☐ 21 Lou Gehrig	6.00	2.70
☐ 22 Ty Cobb	3.00	1.35
☐ 23 Bob Gibson	2.00	.90
☐ 24 Al Kaline	2.00	.90
☐ 25 Rod Carew	2.00	.90
☐ 26 Lou Brock	2.00	.90
☐ 27 Stan Musial	3.00	1.35
☐ 28 Joe L. Morgan	2.00	.90
☐ 29 Willie McCovey	2.00	.90
☐ 30 Duke Snider	2.00	.90
☐ 31 Whitey Ford	2.00	.90
☐ 32 Eddie Mathews	2.00	.90
☐ 33 Carl Yastrzemski	2.00	.90
☐ 34 Pete Rose	4.00	1.80
☐ 35 Hank Aaron	4.00	1.80
☐ 36 Ralph Kiner	1.50	.70
☐ 37 Steve Carlton	2.00	.90
☐ 38 Roberto Clemente	5.00	2.20
☐ 39 Don Drysdale	2.00	.90
☐ 40 Robin Roberts	1.50	.70
☐ 41 Hank Aaron	4.00	1.80
☐ 42 Dave Winfield	2.00	.90
☐ 43 Alan Trammell	1.00	.45
☐ 44 Darryl Strawberry	.50	.23
☐ 45 Ozzie Smith	6.00	2.70
☐ 46 Kirby Puckett	8.00	3.60
☐ 47 Will Clark	2.50	1.10
☐ 48 Keith Hernandez	.50	.23
☐ 49 Wally Joyner	.50	.23
☐ 50 Mike Scott	.25	.11
☐ 51 Eric Davis	.50	.23
☐ 52 George Brett	6.00	2.70
☐ 53 George Bell	.25	.11
☐ 54 Tommy Lasorda MG	1.50	.70
☐ 55 Rickey Henderson	2.50	1.10
☐ 56 Robin Yount	2.50	1.10
☐ 57 Wade Boggs	2.50	1.10
☐ 58 Roger Clemens	3.00	1.35
☐ 59 Alvin Davis	.25	.11
☐ 60 Jose Canseco	2.50	1.10
☐ 61 Fernando Valenzuela	.50	.23
☐ 62 Tony Gwynn	8.00	3.60
☐ 63 Dwight Gooden	.50	.23
☐ 64 Mark McGwire	8.00	3.60
☐ 65 Jack Clark	.25	.11
☐ 66 Dale Murphy	1.50	.70
☐ 67 Kirk Gibson	1.00	.45
☐ 68 Jack Morris	.50	.23
☐ 69 Ryne Sandberg	6.00	2.70
☐ 70 Nolan Ryan	15.00	6.75
☐ 71 John Tudor	.25	.11
☐ 72 Mike Schmidt	4.00	1.80
☐ 73 Dave Righetti	.25	.11
☐ 74 Pedro Guerrero	.50	.23
☐ 75 Rick Sutcliffe	.25	.11
☐ 76 Gary Carter	.50	.23
☐ 77 Cal Ripken	15.00	6.75
☐ 78 Andre Dawson	1.00	.45
☐ 79 Andy Van Slyke	.50	.23
☐ 80 Tim Raines	.50	.23
☐ 81 Frank Viola	.25	.11
☐ 82 Orel Hershiser	.50	.23
☐ 83 Rick Reuschel	.25	.11
☐ 84 Willie McGee	.50	.23
☐ 85 Mark Langston	.25	.11
☐ 86 Ron Darling	.25	.11
☐ 87 Gregg Jefferies	.50	.23
☐ 88 Harold Baines	.50	.23
☐ 89 Eddie Murray	4.00	1.80
☐ 90 Barry Larkin	2.50	1.10
☐ 91 Gary Gaetti	.50	.23
☐ 92 Bret Saberhagen	.25	.11
☐ 93 Roger McDowell	.25	.11
☐ 94 Joe Magrane	.25	.11
☐ 95 Juan Samuel	.25	.11
☐ 96 Bert Blyleven	.50	.23
☐ 97 Kal Daniels	.25	.11
☐ 98 Kevin Bass	.25	.11
☐ 99 Glenn Davis	.25	.11
☐ 100 Steve Sax	.25	.11
☐ 101 Rich Gossage	.50	.23
☐ 102 Roger Craig MG	.25	.11
☐ 103 Carney Lansford	.25	.11
☐ 104 Joe Carter	.50	.23
☐ 105 Bruce Sutter	.25	.11
☐ 106 Barry Bonds	4.00	1.80
☐ 107 Danny Jackson	.25	.11
☐ 108 Mike Flanagan	.25	.11
☐ 109 Dwight Evans	.50	.23
☐ 110 Ron Guidry	.25	.11
☐ 111 Bruce Hurst	.25	.11
☐ 112 Jim Rice	1.00	.45
☐ 113 Oddibe McDowell	.25	.11
☐ 114 Bobby Bonilla	1.00	.45
☐ 115 Bob Welch	.25	.11
☐ 116 Dave Parker	.50	.23
☐ 117 Tim Wallach	.25	.11
☐ 118 Tom Henke	.50	.23
☐ 119 Mike Greenwell	.25	.11
☐ 120 Kevin Seitzer	.25	.11
☐ 121 Randy Myers	.50	.23
☐ 122 Andres Galarraga	1.50	.70
☐ 123 Don Mattingly	8.00	3.60
☐ 124 Cory Snyder	.25	.11
☐ 125 Mike Witt	.25	.11
☐ 126 Mike LaValliere	.25	.11
☐ 127 Pete Incaviglia	.25	.11
☐ 128 Dennis Eckersley	1.00	.45
☐ 129 Jimmy Key	.50	.23
☐ 130 John Franco	.50	.23
☐ 131 Dan Plesac	.25	.11

☐ 132 Tony LaRussa MG .50 .23
☐ 133 Hubie Brooks .25 .11
☐ 134 Chili Davis .50 .23
☐ 135 Bob Boone .50 .23
☐ 136 Jeff Reardon .50 .23
☐ 137 Candy Maldonado .25 .11
☐ 138 Mike Marshall .25 .11
☐ 139 Tommy John .50 .23
☐ 140 Chris Sabo .25 .11
☐ 141 Vince Coleman .25 .11
☐ 142 Frank White .50 .23
☐ 143 Harold Reynolds .25 .11
☐ 144 Lee Smith .50 .23
☐ 145 John Kruk .50 .23
☐ 146 Tony Fernandez .25 .11
☐ 147 Steve Bedrosian .25 .11
☐ 148 Benito Santiago .25 .11
☐ 149 Ozzie Guillen .25 .11
☐ 150 Gerald Perry .25 .11
☐ 151 Carlton Fisk 1.50 .70
☐ 152 Tom Brunansky .25 .11
☐ 153 Paul Molitor 4.00 1.80
☐ 154 Todd Worrell .25 .11
☐ 155 Brett Butler .50 .23
☐ 156 Sparky Anderson MG .50 .23
☐ 157 Kent Hrbek .50 .23
☐ 158 Frank Tanana .25 .11
☐ 159 Kevin Mitchell .50 .23
☐ 160 Charlie Hough .50 .23
☐ 161 Doug Jones .25 .11
☐ 162 Lou Whitaker .50 .23
☐ 163 Fred Lynn .25 .11
☐ 164 Checklist .25 .11

1989 Topps Big

The 1989 Topps Big Baseball set contains 330 glossy cards measuring approximately 2 1/2" by 3 3/4". The fronts feature mug shots superimposed on action photos. The horizontally oriented backs have color cartoons and statistics for the player's previous season and total career. Team members for the United States Olympic team were also included in this set. The set was released in three series of 110 cards. The cards were distributed in seven-card packs marked with the series number.

	MINT	NRMT
COMPLETE SET (330)	25.00	11.00
COMMON CARD (1-330)	.05	.02

☐ 1 Orel Hershiser .10 .05
☐ 2 Harold Reynolds .10 .05
☐ 3 Jody Davis .05 .02
☐ 4 Greg Walker .05 .02
☐ 5 Barry Bonds 1.00 .45
☐ 6 Bret Saberhagen .05 .02
☐ 7 Johnny Ray .05 .02
☐ 8 Mike Fiore .05 .02
☐ 9 Juan Castillo .05 .02
☐ 10 Todd Burns .05 .02
☐ 11 Carmelo Martinez .05 .02
☐ 12 Geno Petralli .05 .02
☐ 13 Mel Hall .05 .02
☐ 14 Tom Browning .05 .02
☐ 15 Fred McGriff .50 .23
☐ 16 Kevin Elster .05 .02
☐ 17 Tim Leary .05 .02
☐ 18 Jim Rice .15 .07
☐ 19 Bret Barberie .05 .02
☐ 20 Jay Buhner .50 .23
☐ 21 Atlee Hammaker .05 .02
☐ 22 Lou Whitaker .10 .05
☐ 23 Paul Runge .05 .02
☐ 24 Carlton Fisk .50 .23
☐ 25 Jose Lind .05 .02
☐ 26 Mark Gubicza .05 .02
☐ 27 Billy Ripken .05 .02
☐ 28 Mike Pagliarulo .05 .02
☐ 29 Jim Deshaies .05 .02
☐ 30 Mark McLemore .05 .02
☐ 31 Scott Terry .05 .02
☐ 32 Franklin Stubbs .05 .02
☐ 33 Don August .05 .02
☐ 34 Mark McGwire 1.25 .55
☐ 35 Eric Show .05 .02
☐ 36 Cecil Espy .05 .02
☐ 37 Ron Tingley .05 .02
☐ 38 Mickey Brantley .05 .02
☐ 39 Paul O'Neill .10 .05
☐ 40 Ed Sprague .25 .11
☐ 41 Len Dykstra .10 .05
☐ 42 Roger Clemens .75 .35
☐ 43 Ron Gant .30 .14
☐ 44 Dan Pasqua .05 .02
☐ 45 Jeff D. Robinson .05 .02
☐ 46 George Brett 1.50 .70
☐ 47 Bryn Smith .05 .02
☐ 48 Mike Marshall .05 .02
☐ 49 Doug Robbins .05 .02
☐ 50 Don Mattingly 2.00 .90
☐ 51 Mike Scott .05 .02
☐ 52 Steve Jeltz .05 .02
☐ 53 Dick Schofield .05 .02
☐ 54 Tom Brunansky .05 .02
☐ 55 Gary Sheffield 2.00 .90
☐ 56 Dave Valle .05 .02
☐ 57 Carney Lansford .05 .02
☐ 58 Tony Gwynn 1.50 .70
☐ 59 Checklist 1-110 .05 .02
☐ 60 Damon Berryhill .05 .02
☐ 61 Jack Morris .10 .05
☐ 62 Brett Butler .10 .05
☐ 63 Mickey Hatcher .05 .02
☐ 64 Bruce Sutter .05 .02
☐ 65 Robin Ventura .75 .35
☐ 66 Junior Ortiz .05 .02
☐ 67 Pat Tabler .05 .02
☐ 68 Greg Swindell .05 .02
☐ 69 Jeff Branson .05 .02
☐ 70 Manny Lee .05 .02
☐ 71 Dave Magadan .05 .02
☐ 72 Rich Gedman .05 .02
☐ 73 Tim Raines .15 .07
☐ 74 Mike Maddux .05 .02
☐ 75 Jim Presley .05 .02
☐ 76 Chuck Finley .10 .05
☐ 77 Jose Oquendo .05 .02
☐ 78 Rob Deer .05 .02
☐ 79 Jay Howell .05 .02
☐ 80 Terry Steinbach .10 .05
☐ 81 Ed Whitson .05 .02
☐ 82 Ruben Sierra .05 .02
☐ 83 Bruce Benedict .05 .02
☐ 84 Fred Manrique .05 .02
☐ 85 John Smiley .05 .02
☐ 86 Mike Macfarlane .05 .02
☐ 87 Rene Gonzales .05 .02
☐ 88 Charles Hudson .05 .02
☐ 89 Glenn Davis .05 .02
☐ 90 Les Straker .05 .02
☐ 91 Carmen Castillo .05 .02
☐ 92 Tracy Woodson .05 .02
☐ 93 Tino Martinez .60 .25
☐ 94 Herm Winningham .05 .02
☐ 95 Kelly Gruber .05 .02
☐ 96 Terry Leach .05 .02
☐ 97 Jody Reed .05 .02
☐ 98 Nelson Santovenia .05 .02
☐ 99 Tony Armas .05 .02
☐ 100 Greg Brock .05 .02
☐ 101 Dave Stewart .10 .05
☐ 102 Roberto Alomar 1.25 .55
☐ 103 Jim Sundberg .05 .02
☐ 104 Albert Hall .05 .02
☐ 105 Steve Lyons .05 .02
☐ 106 Sid Bream .05 .02
☐ 107 Danny Tartabull .10 .05
☐ 108 Rick Dempsey .05 .02
☐ 109 Rich Renteria .05 .02
☐ 110 Ozzie Smith 1.25 .55
☐ 111 Steve Sax .05 .02
☐ 112 Kelly Downs .05 .02
☐ 113 Larry Sheets .05 .02
☐ 114 Andy Benes .50 .23
☐ 115 Pete O'Brien .05 .02
☐ 116 Kevin McReynolds .05 .02
☐ 117 Juan Berenguer .05 .02
☐ 118 Billy Hatcher .05 .02
☐ 119 Rick Cerone .05 .02
☐ 120 Andre Dawson .40 .18
☐ 121 Storm Davis .05 .02
☐ 122 Devon White .05 .02
☐ 123 Alan Trammell .15 .07
☐ 124 Vince Coleman .05 .02
☐ 125 Al Leiter .10 .05
☐ 126 Dale Sveum .05 .02
☐ 127 Pete Incaviglia .05 .02
☐ 128 Dave Stieb .05 .02
☐ 129 Kevin Mitchell .10 .05
☐ 130 Dave Schmidt .05 .02
☐ 131 Gary Redus .05 .02
☐ 132 Ron Robinson .05 .02
☐ 133 Darnell Coles .05 .02
☐ 134 Benito Santiago .05 .02
☐ 135 John Farrell .05 .02
☐ 136 Willie Wilson .05 .02
☐ 137 Steve Bedrosian .05 .02
☐ 138 Don Slaught .05 .02
☐ 139 Darryl Strawberry .10 .05
☐ 140 Frank Viola .05 .02
☐ 141 Dave Silvestri .05 .02
☐ 142 Carlos Quintana .05 .02
☐ 143 Vance Law .05 .02
☐ 144 Dave Parker .10 .05
☐ 145 Tim Belcher .05 .02
☐ 146 Will Clark .75 .35
☐ 147 Mark Williamson .05 .02
☐ 148 Ozzie Guillen .05 .02
☐ 149 Kirk McCaskill .05 .02
☐ 150 Pat Sheridan .05 .02
☐ 151 Terry Pendleton .10 .05
☐ 152 Roberto Kelly .05 .02
☐ 153 Joey Meyer .05 .02
☐ 154 Mark Grant .05 .02
☐ 155 Joe Carter .30 .14
☐ 156 Steve Buechele .05 .02
☐ 157 Tony Fernandez .05 .02
☐ 158 Jeff Reed .05 .02
☐ 159 Bobby Bonilla .15 .07
☐ 160 Henry Cotto .05 .02
☐ 161 Kurt Stillwell .05 .02
☐ 162 Mickey Morandini .10 .05
☐ 163 Robby Thompson .05 .02
☐ 164 Rick Schu .05 .02
☐ 165 Stan Jefferson .05 .02
☐ 166 Ron Darling .05 .02
☐ 167 Kirby Puckett 2.00 .90
☐ 168 Bill Doran .05 .02
☐ 169 Dennis Lamp .05 .02
☐ 170 Ty Griffin .05 .02
☐ 171 Ron Hassey .05 .02
☐ 172 Dale Murphy .50 .23
☐ 173 Andres Galarraga .50 .23
☐ 174 Tim Flannery .05 .02
☐ 175 Cory Snyder .05 .02
☐ 176 Checklist 111-220 .05 .02
☐ 177 Tommy Barrett .05 .02
☐ 178 Dan Petry .05 .02
☐ 179 Billy Masse .05 .02
☐ 180 Terry Kennedy .05 .02
☐ 181 Joe Orsulak .05 .02
☐ 182 Doyle Alexander .05 .02
☐ 183 Willie McGee .10 .05
☐ 184 Jim Gantner .05 .02
☐ 185 Keith Hernandez .10 .05
☐ 186 Greg Gagne .05 .02
☐ 187 Kevin Bass .05 .02
☐ 188 Mark Eichhorn .05 .02
☐ 189 Mark Grace .75 .35
☐ 190 Jose Canseco .60 .25
☐ 191 Bobby Witt .05 .02
☐ 192 Rafael Santana .05 .02
☐ 193 Dwight Evans .10 .05
☐ 194 Greg Booker .05 .02
☐ 195 Brook Jacoby .05 .02
☐ 196 Rafael Belliard .05 .02
☐ 197 Candy Maldonado .05 .02
☐ 198 Mickey Tettleton .10 .05
☐ 199 Barry Larkin .50 .23
☐ 200 Frank White .10 .05
☐ 201 Wally Joyner .10 .05
☐ 202 Chet Lemon .05 .02
☐ 203 Joe Magrane .05 .02
☐ 204 Glenn Braggs .05 .02
☐ 205 Scott Fletcher .05 .02
☐ 206 Gary Ward .05 .02
☐ 207 Nelson Liriano .05 .02
☐ 208 Howard Johnson .05 .02
☐ 209 Kent Hrbek .10 .05
☐ 210 Ken Caminiti .75 .35
☐ 211 Mike Greenwell .05 .02
☐ 212 Ryne Sandberg 1.25 .55
☐ 213 Joe Slusarski .05 .02
☐ 214 Donell Nixon .05 .02
☐ 215 Tim Wallach .05 .02
☐ 216 John Kruk .10 .05
☐ 217 Charles Nagy .50 .23
☐ 218 Alvin Davis .05 .02
☐ 219 Oswald Peraza .05 .02
☐ 220 Mike Schmidt .75 .35
☐ 221 Spike Owen .05 .0
☐ 222 Mike Smithson .05
☐ 223 Dion James .05
☐ 224 Ernie Whitt .05
☐ 225 Mike Davis .05
☐ 226 Gene Larkin .05
☐ 227 Pat Combs .05

Card	Mint	NrMt
☐ 228 Jack Howell	.05	.02
☐ 229 Ron Oester	.05	.02
☐ 230 Paul Gibson	.05	.02
☐ 231 Mookie Wilson	.10	.05
☐ 232 Glenn Hubbard	.05	.02
☐ 233 Shawon Dunston	.05	.02
☐ 234 Otis Nixon	.10	.05
☐ 235 Melido Perez	.05	.02
☐ 236 Jerry Browne	.05	.02
☐ 237 Rick Rhoden	.05	.02
☐ 238 Bo Jackson	.15	.07
☐ 239 Randy Velarde	.05	.02
☐ 240 Jack Clark	.05	.02
☐ 241 Wade Boggs	.60	.25
☐ 242 Lonnie Smith	.05	.02
☐ 243 Mike Flanagan	.05	.02
☐ 244 Willie Randolph	.10	.05
☐ 245 Oddibe McDowell	.05	.02
☐ 246 Ricky Jordan	.05	.02
☐ 247 Greg Briley	.05	.02
☐ 248 Rex Hudler	.05	.02
☐ 249 Robin Yount	.50	.23
☐ 250 Lance Parrish	.05	.02
☐ 251 Chris Sabo	.05	.02
☐ 252 Mike Henneman	.05	.02
☐ 253 Gregg Jefferies	.30	.14
☐ 254 Curt Young	.05	.02
☐ 255 Andy Van Slyke	.10	.05
☐ 256 Rod Booker	.05	.02
☐ 257 Rafael Palmeiro	.50	.23
☐ 258 Jose Uribe	.05	.02
☐ 259 Ellis Burks	.40	.18
☐ 260 John Smoltz	1.00	.45
☐ 261 Tom Foley	.05	.02
☐ 262 Lloyd Moseby	.05	.02
☐ 263 Jim Poole	.05	.02
☐ 264 Gary Gaetti	.10	.05
☐ 265 Bob Dernier	.05	.02
☐ 266 Harold Baines	.10	.05
☐ 267 Tom Candiotti	.05	.02
☐ 268 Rafael Ramirez	.05	.02
☐ 269 Bob Boone	.10	.05
☐ 270 Buddy Bell	.10	.05
☐ 271 Rickey Henderson	.60	.25
☐ 272 Willie Fraser	.05	.02
☐ 273 Eric Davis	.10	.05
☐ 274 Jeff M. Robinson	.05	.02
☐ 275 Damaso Garcia	.05	.02
☐ 276 Sid Fernandez	.10	.05
☐ 277 Stan Javier	.05	.02
☐ 278 Marty Barrett	.05	.02
☐ 279 Gerald Perry	.05	.02
☐ 280 Rob Ducey	.05	.02
☐ 281 Mike Scioscia	.05	.02
☐ 282 Randy Bush	.05	.02
☐ 283 Tom Herr	.05	.02
☐ 284 Glenn Wilson	.05	.02
☐ 285 Pedro Guerrero	.05	.02
☐ 286 Cal Ripken	3.00	1.35
☐ 287 Randy Johnson	1.25	.55
☐ 288 Julio Franco	.10	.05
☐ 289 Ivan Calderon	.05	.02
☐ 290 Rich Yett	.05	.02
☐ 291 Scott Servais	.05	.02
☐ 292 Bill Pecota	.05	.02
☐ 293 Ken Phelps	.05	.02
☐ 294 Chili Davis	.10	.05
☐ 295 Manny Trillo	.05	.02
☐ 296 Mike Boddicker	.05	.02
☐ 297 Geronimo Berroa	.05	.02
☐ 298 Todd Stottlemyre	.15	.07
☐ 299 Kirk Gibson	.15	.07
☐ 300 Wally Backman	.05	.02
☐ 301 Hubie Brooks	.05	.02
☐ 302 Von Hayes	.05	.02
☐ 303 Matt Nokes	.05	.02
☐ 304 Dwight Gooden	.10	.05
☐ 305 Walt Weiss	.05	.02
☐ 306 Mike LaValliere	.05	.02
☐ 307 Cris Carpenter	.05	.02
☐ 308 Ted Wood	.05	.02
☐ 309 Jeff Russell	.05	.02
☐ 310 Dave Gallagher	.05	.02
☐ 311 Andy Allanson	.05	.02
☐ 312 Craig Reynolds	.05	.02
☐ 313 Kevin Seitzer	.05	.02
☐ 314 Dave Winfield	.60	.25
☐ 315 Andy McGaffigan	.05	.02
☐ 316 Nick Esasky	.05	.02
[illegible] Jeff Blauser	.10	.05
[illegible] George Bell	.05	.02
[illegible]die Murray	1.00	.45
[illegible] Davidson	.05	.02
[illegible]muel	.05	.02
[illegible]tt	.10	.05
[illegible]	.05	.02
[illegible]	.05	.02
☐ 325 Gary Carter	.15	.07
☐ 326 Dave Henderson	.05	.02
☐ 327 Checklist 221-330	.05	.02
☐ 328 Garry Templeton	.05	.02
☐ 329 Pat Perry	.05	.02
☐ 330 Paul Molitor	.50	.23

1989 Topps Cap'n Crunch

The 1989 Topps Cap'n Crunch set contains 22 standard-size cards. The fronts have red, white and blue borders surrounding "mugshot" photos. The backs are horizontally oriented and show lifetime stats. The team logos have been airbrushed out. Two cards were included (in a cellophane wrapper with a piece of gum) in each specially marked Cap'n Crunch cereal box. The set was not available as a complete set as part of any mail-in offer.

	MINT	NRMT
COMPLETE SET (22)	12.00	5.50
COMMON CARD (1-22)	.25	.11
☐ 1 Jose Canseco	1.00	.45
☐ 2 Kirk Gibson	.40	.18
☐ 3 Orel Hershiser	.40	.18
☐ 4 Frank Viola	.25	.11
☐ 5 Tony Gwynn	1.50	.70
☐ 6 Cal Ripken	3.00	1.35
☐ 7 Darryl Strawberry	.40	.18
☐ 8 Don Mattingly	1.50	.70
☐ 9 George Brett	1.25	.55
☐ 10 Andre Dawson	.75	.35
☐ 11 Dale Murphy	.60	.25
☐ 12 Alan Trammell	.60	.25
☐ 13 Eric Davis	.25	.11
☐ 14 Jack Clark	.25	.11
☐ 15 Eddie Murray	.75	.35
☐ 16 Mike Schmidt	1.00	.45
☐ 17 Dwight Gooden	.40	.18
☐ 18 Roger Clemens	1.50	.70
☐ 19 Will Clark	1.00	.45
☐ 20 Kirby Puckett	1.50	.70
☐ 21 Robin Yount	.60	.25
☐ 22 Mark McGwire	1.50	.70

1989 Topps Coins

The 1989 Topps Coins set contains 60 coins, each measuring approximately 1 1/2" in diameter. The coins were issued in packs of three coins. The set is arranged by league order with the Most Valuable Player, Cy Young Award Winner, Rookie of the Year and Batting Leaders being first, then the rest of the league being arranged alphabetically within the league group. The National League players are 1-28 and the American League players are 29-60.

	MINT	NRMT
COMPLETE SET (60)	8.00	3.60
COMMON COIN (1-60)	.05	.02
☐ 1 Kirk Gibson	.15	.07
☐ 2 Orel Hershiser	.10	.05
☐ 3 Chris Sabo	.05	.02
☐ 4 Tony Gwynn	1.00	.45
☐ 5 Bobby Bonilla	.10	.05
☐ 6 Brett Butler	.10	.05
☐ 7 Jack Clark	.10	.05
☐ 8 Will Clark	.40	.18
☐ 9 Eric Davis	.10	.05
☐ 10 Glenn Davis	.05	.02
☐ 11 Andre Dawson	.15	.07
☐ 12 John Franco	.10	.05
☐ 13 Andres Galarraga	.30	.14
☐ 14 Dwight Gooden	.10	.05
☐ 15 Mark Grace	.40	.18
☐ 16 Pedro Guerrero	.05	.02
☐ 17 Ricky Jordan	.05	.02
☐ 18 Mike Marshall	.05	.02
☐ 19 Dale Murphy	.15	.07
☐ 20 Eddie Murray	.50	.23
☐ 21 Gerald Perry	.05	.02
☐ 22 Tim Raines	.10	.05
☐ 23 Juan Samuel	.05	.02
☐ 24 Benito Santiago	.05	.02
☐ 25 Ozzie Smith	.75	.35
☐ 26 Darryl Strawberry	.10	.05
☐ 27 Andy Van Slyke	.05	.02
☐ 28 Gerald Young	.05	.02
☐ 29 Jose Canseco	.30	.14
☐ 30 Frank Viola	.05	.02
☐ 31 Walt Weiss	.05	.02
☐ 32 Wade Boggs	.30	.14
☐ 33 Harold Baines	.10	.05
☐ 34 George Brett	1.00	.45
☐ 35 Jay Buhner	.50	.23
☐ 36 Joe Carter	.15	.07
☐ 37 Roger Clemens	.60	.25
☐ 38 Alvin Davis	.05	.02
☐ 39 Tony Fernandez	.05	.02
☐ 40 Carlton Fisk	.30	.14
☐ 41 Mike Greenwell	.05	.02
☐ 42 Kent Hrbek	.10	.05
☐ 43 Don Mattingly	1.00	.45
☐ 44 Fred McGriff	.25	.11
☐ 45 Mark McGwire	1.00	.45
☐ 46 Paul Molitor	.75	.35
☐ 47 Rafael Palmeiro	.30	.14
☐ 48 Kirby Puckett	1.00	.45
☐ 49 Johnny Ray	.05	.02
☐ 50 Cal Ripken	2.00	.90
☐ 51 Ruben Sierra	.05	.02
☐ 52 Pete Stanicek	.05	.02
☐ 53 Dave Stewart	.05	.02
☐ 54 Greg Swindell	.05	.02
☐ 55 Danny Tartabull	.05	.02
☐ 56 Alan Trammell	.15	.07
☐ 57 Lou Whitaker	.10	.05
☐ 58 Dave Winfield	.30	.14
☐ 59 Mike Witt	.05	.02
☐ 60 Robin Yount	.25	.11

1989 Topps Doubleheaders All-Stars

The 1989 Topps Doubleheaders were a novel idea from Topps to capitalize on the interest in rookie cards. The one side of the plastic holder shows a small color photo of the rookie card while the other side shows a photo of the current year Topps card on the other side. The holders measure 2" by 2 1/8". The set contains 24 holders, eight starting players, two starting pitchers, one reliever, and one DH from each league. They are unnumbered. Apparently the twelve from each league are considered by Topps as the "best" at each position.

	MINT	NRMT
COMPLETE SET (24)	15.00	6.75
COMMON CARD (1-24)	.25	.11
☐ 1 Don Mattingly	3.00	1.35
☐ 2 Julio Franco	.50	.23
☐ 3 Wade Boggs	1.25	.55
☐ 4 Alan Trammell	.75	.35
☐ 5 Jose Canseco	1.25	.55
☐ 6 Mike Greenwell	.25	.11
☐ 7 Kirby Puckett	3.00	1.35
☐ 8 Carlton Fisk	.75	.35
☐ 9 Roger Clemens	1.50	.70
☐ 10 Frank Viola	.25	.11
☐ 11 Dennis Eckersley	.75	.35
☐ 12 Mark McGwire	2.50	1.10
☐ 13 Will Clark	1.00	.45
☐ 14 Ryne Sandberg	3.00	1.35

	MINT	NRMT
☐ 15 Bobby Bonilla	.50	.23
☐ 16 Ozzie Smith	3.00	1.35
☐ 17 Andre Dawson	.75	.35
☐ 18 Darryl Strawberry	.50	.23
☐ 19 Andy Van Slyke	.50	.23
☐ 20 Alan Ashby	.25	.11
☐ 21 Orel Hershiser	.50	.23
☐ 22 Danny Jackson	.25	.11
☐ 23 John Franco	.50	.23
☐ 24 Kirk Gibson	.50	.23

1989 Topps Hills Team MVP's

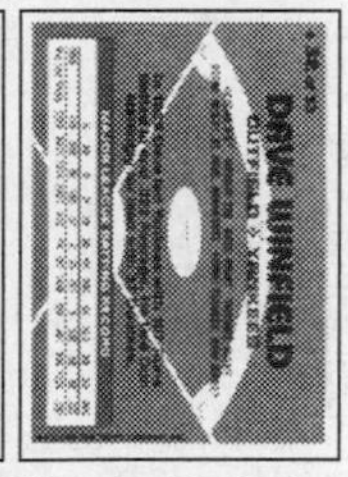

The 1989 Topps Hills Team MVP's set contains 33 glossy standard-size cards. The fronts and backs are yellow, red, white and navy. The horizontally oriented backs are green. The cards were distributed through Hills stores as a boxed set. The set was printed in Ireland. These numbered cards are ordered alphabetically by player's name.

	MINT	NRMT
COMPLETE SET (33)	5.00	2.20
COMMON CARD (1-33)	.05	.02
☐ 1 Harold Baines	.10	.05
☐ 2 Wade Boggs	.30	.14
☐ 3 George Brett	.75	.35
☐ 4 Tom Brunansky	.05	.02
☐ 5 Jose Canseco	.40	.18
☐ 6 Joe Carter	.15	.07
☐ 7 Will Clark	.40	.18
☐ 8 Roger Clemens	.60	.25
☐ 9 David Cone	.15	.07
☐ 10 Glenn Davis	.05	.02
☐ 11 Andre Dawson	.25	.11
☐ 12 Dennis Eckersley	.15	.07
☐ 13 Andres Galarraga	.25	.11
☐ 14 Kirk Gibson	.15	.07
☐ 15 Mike Greenwell	.05	.02
☐ 16 Tony Gwynn	.75	.35
☐ 17 Orel Hershiser	.10	.05
☐ 18 Danny Jackson	.05	.02
☐ 19 Mark Langston	.05	.02
☐ 20 Fred McGriff	.40	.18
☐ 21 Dale Murphy	.15	.07
☐ 22 Eddie Murray	.30	.14
☐ 23 Kirby Puckett	.75	.35
☐ 24 Johnny Ray	.05	.02
☐ 25 Juan Samuel	.05	.02
☐ 26 Ruben Sierra	.05	.02
☐ 27 Dave Stewart	.05	.02
☐ 28 Darryl Strawberry	.10	.05
☐ 29 Alan Trammell	.15	.07
☐ 30 Andy Van Slyke	.05	.02
☐ 31 Frank Viola	.05	.02
☐ 32 Dave Winfield	.40	.18
☐ 33 Robin Yount	.25	.11

1989 Topps Mini Leaders

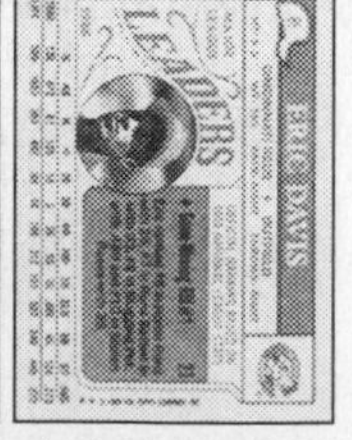

The 1989 Topps Mini League Leaders set contains 77 cards measuring approximately 2 1/8" by 3". The fronts have color photos with large white borders. The backs are yellow and feature 1988 and career stats. The cards were distributed in seven-card cello packs. These numbered cards are ordered alphabetically by player within team and the teams themselves are ordered alphabetically.

	MINT	NRMT
COMPLETE SET (77)	5.00	2.20
COMMON CARD (1-77)	.05	.02
☐ 1 Dale Murphy	.15	.07
☐ 2 Gerald Perry	.05	.02
☐ 3 Andre Dawson	.25	.11
☐ 4 Greg Maddux	1.50	.70
☐ 5 Rafael Palmeiro	.25	.11
☐ 6 Tom Browning	.05	.02
☐ 7 Kal Daniels	.05	.02
☐ 8 Eric Davis	.10	.05
☐ 9 John Franco	.10	.05
☐ 10 Danny Jackson	.05	.02
☐ 11 Barry Larkin	.30	.14
☐ 12 Jose Rijo	.05	.02
☐ 13 Chris Sabo	.05	.02
☐ 14 Nolan Ryan	1.50	.70
☐ 15 Mike Scott	.05	.02
☐ 16 Gerald Young	.05	.02
☐ 17 Kirk Gibson	.10	.05
☐ 18 Orel Hershiser	.10	.05
☐ 19 Steve Sax	.05	.02
☐ 20 John Tudor	.05	.02
☐ 21 Hubie Brooks	.05	.02
☐ 22 Andres Galarraga	.25	.11
☐ 23 Otis Nixon	.05	.02
☐ 24 David Cone	.10	.05
☐ 25 Sid Fernandez	.05	.02
☐ 26 Dwight Gooden	.10	.05
☐ 27 Kevin McReynolds	.05	.02
☐ 28 Darryl Strawberry	.10	.05
☐ 29 Juan Samuel	.05	.02
☐ 30 Bobby Bonilla	.15	.07
☐ 31 Sid Bream	.05	.02
☐ 32 Jim Gott	.05	.02
☐ 33 Andy Van Slyke	.05	.02
☐ 34 Vince Coleman	.05	.02
☐ 35 Jose DeLeon	.05	.02
☐ 36 Joe Magrane	.05	.02
☐ 37 Ozzie Smith	.75	.35
☐ 38 Todd Worrell	.10	.05
☐ 39 Tony Gwynn	1.00	.45
☐ 40 Brett Butler	.10	.05
☐ 41 Will Clark	.30	.14
☐ 42 Rick Reuschel	.10	.05
☐ 43 Checklist Card	.05	.02
☐ 44 Eddie Murray	.50	.23
☐ 45 Wade Boggs	.30	.14
☐ 46 Roger Clemens	.50	.23
☐ 47 Dwight Evans	.10	.05
☐ 48 Mike Greenwell	.05	.02
☐ 49 Bruce Hurst	.05	.02
☐ 50 Johnny Ray	.05	.02
☐ 51 Doug Jones	.05	.02
☐ 52 Greg Swindell	.05	.02
☐ 53 Gary Pettis	.05	.02
☐ 54 George Brett	.75	.35
☐ 55 Mark Gubicza	.05	.02
☐ 56 Willie Wilson	.05	.02
☐ 57 Teddy Higuera	.05	.02
☐ 58 Paul Molitor	.30	.14
☐ 59 Robin Yount	.15	.07
☐ 60 Allan Anderson	.05	.02
☐ 61 Gary Gaetti	.10	.05
☐ 62 Kirby Puckett	1.00	.45
☐ 63 Jeff Reardon	.10	.05
☐ 64 Frank Viola	.05	.02
☐ 65 Jack Clark	.05	.02
☐ 66 Rickey Henderson	.30	.14
☐ 67 Dave Winfield	.30	.14
☐ 68 Jose Canseco	.40	.18
☐ 69 Dennis Eckersley	.15	.07
☐ 70 Mark McGwire	1.00	.45
☐ 71 Dave Stewart	.05	.02
☐ 72 Alvin Davis	.05	.02
☐ 73 Mark Langston	.05	.02
☐ 74 Harold Reynolds	.05	.02
☐ 75 George Bell	.05	.02
☐ 76 Tony Fernandez	.05	.02
☐ 77 Fred McGriff	.40	.18

1989 Topps/O-Pee-Chee Stickers

Printed in Canada, these 326 stickers measure approximately 2 1/8" by 3" and feature white-bordered color player photos. The borders are highlighted by colored lines and baseball icons. The stickers are numbered at the lower right. The sticker backs are actually cards (1989 O-Pee-Chee Super Stars) and are considered a separate set. An album onto which the stickers could be affixed was available at retail stores. The album and the sticker numbering are organized as follows: 1988 Highlights (1-12), Houston Astros (13-23), Atlanta Braves (24-34), St. Louis Cardinals (35-45), Chicago Cubs (46-

56), Los Angeles Dodgers (57-67), Montreal Expos (68-78), San Francisco Giants (79-89), New York Mets (90-100), San Diego Padres (101-111), Philadelphia Phillies (112-122), Pittsburgh Pirates (123-133), Cincinnati Reds (134-144), Foil All-Stars (145-162), Oakland A's (163-173), California Angels (174-184), Toronto Blue Jays (185-195), Milwaukee Brewers (196-206), Cleveland Indians (207-217), Seattle Mariners (218-228), Baltimore Orioles (229-239), Texas Rangers (240-250), Boston Red Sox (251-261), Kansas City Royals (262-272), Detroit Tigers (273-283), Minnesota Twins (284-294), Chicago White Sox (295-305), New York Yankees (306-316) and Future Stars (317-326). For those stickers featuring more than one player, the other numbers on that sticker are given below in parentheses. Although the prices listed below are for the stickers only, there are instances where having an especially desirable sticker card back (attached to that sticker) will increase the values listed below.

	MINT	NRMT
COMPLETE SET (326)	15.00	6.75
COMMON STICKER (1-326)	.05	.02
*TOPPS AND OPC: SAME VALUE		
☐ 1 George Bell	.05	.02
☐ 2 Gary Carter	.15	.07
☐ 3 Doug Jones	.05	.02
☐ 4 John Franco	.10	.05
☐ 5 Andre Dawson	.15	.07
☐ 6 Pat Tabler	.05	.02
☐ 7 Tom Browning	.05	.02
☐ 8 Jeff Reardon	.10	.05
☐ 9 Wade Boggs	.30	.14
☐ 10 Kevin McReynolds	.05	.02
☐ 11 Jose Canseco	.30	.14
☐ 12 Orel Hershiser	.10	.05
☐ 13 Dave Smith	.05	.02
☐ 14 Kevin Bass	.05	.02
☐ 15 Mike Scott	.05	.02
☐ 16 Bill Doran	.05	.02
☐ 17 Rafael Ramirez	.05	.02
☐ 18 Buddy Bell	.10	.05
☐ 19 Billy Hatcher	.05	.02
☐ 20 Nolan Ryan	2.00	.90
☐ 21 Glenn Davis	.05	.02
☐ 22 Bob Knepper	.05	.02
☐ 23 Gerald Young	.05	.02
☐ 24 Dion James	.05	.02
☐ 25 Bruce Sutter	.05	.02
☐ 26 Andres Thomas	.05	.02
☐ 27 Zane Smith	.05	.02
☐ 28 Ozzie Virgil	.05	.02
☐ 29 Rick Mahler	.05	.02
☐ 30 Albert Hall	.05	.02
☐ 31 Pete Smith	.05	.02
☐ 32 Dale Murphy	.25	.11
☐ 33 Gerald Perry	.05	.02
☐ 34 Ron Gant	.25	.11
☐ 35 Bob Horner	.05	.02
☐ 36 Willie McGee	.10	.05
☐ 37 Luis Alicea	.05	.02
☐ 38 Tony Pena	.05	.02
☐ 39 Todd Worrell	.10	.05
☐ 40 Pedro Guerrero	.05	.02
☐ 41 Tom Brunansky	.05	.02
☐ 42 Terry Pendleton	.10	.05
☐ 43 Vince Coleman	.05	.02
☐ 44 Ozzie Smith	.50	.23
☐ 45 Jose Oquendo	.05	.02
☐ 46 Vance Law	.05	.02
☐ 47 Rafael Palmeiro	.25	.11
☐ 48 Greg Maddux	2.50	1.10
☐ 49 Shawon Dunston	.05	.02
☐ 50 Mark Grace	.40	.18
☐ 51 Damon Berryhill	.05	.02
☐ 52 Rick Sutcliffe	.05	[illegible]
☐ 53 Jamie Moyer	.05	[illegible]
☐ 54 Andre Dawson	.15	
☐ 55 Ryne Sandberg	.50	
☐ 56 Calvin Schiraldi	.05	
☐ 57 Steve Sax	.05	
☐ 58 Mike Scioscia	.05	
☐ 59 Alfredo Griffin	.05	

☐ 60 Fernando Valenzuela .10 .05
☐ 61 Jay Howell .05 .02
☐ 62 Tim Leary .05 .02
☐ 63 John Shelby .05 .02
☐ 64 John Tudor .05 .02
☐ 65 Orel Hershiser .10 .05
☐ 66 Kirk Gibson .15 .07
☐ 67 Mike Marshall .05 .02
☐ 68 Luis Rivera .05 .02
☐ 69 Tim Burke .05 .02
☐ 70 Tim Wallach .05 .02
☐ 71 Pascual Perez .05 .02
☐ 72 Hubie Brooks .05 .02
☐ 73 Jeff Parrett .05 .02
☐ 74 Denny Martinez .10 .05
☐ 75 Andy McGaffigan .05 .02
☐ 76 Andres Galarraga .25 .11
☐ 77 Tim Raines .10 .05
☐ 78 Nelson Santovenia .05 .02
☐ 79 Rick Reuschel .10 .05
☐ 80 Mike Aldrete .05 .02
☐ 81 Kelly Downs .05 .02
☐ 82 Jose Uribe .05 .02
☐ 83 Mike Krukow .05 .02
☐ 84 Kevin Mitchell .05 .02
☐ 85 Brett Butler .10 .05
☐ 86 Don Robinson .05 .02
☐ 87 Robby Thompson .05 .02
☐ 88 Will Clark .30 .14
☐ 89 Candy Maldonado .05 .02
☐ 90 Len Dykstra .10 .05
☐ 91 Howard Johnson .05 .02
☐ 92 Roger McDowell .05 .02
☐ 93 Keith Hernandez .10 .05
☐ 94 Gary Carter .15 .07
☐ 95 Kevin McReynolds .05 .02
☐ 96 Dave Cone .25 .11
☐ 97 Randy Myers .10 .05
☐ 98 Darryl Strawberry .10 .05
☐ 99 Dwight Gooden .10 .05
☐ 100 Ron Darling .05 .02
☐ 101 Benito Santiago .05 .02
☐ 102 John Kruk .10 .05
☐ 103 Chris Brown .05 .02
☐ 104 Roberto Alomar 1.00 .45
☐ 105 Keith Moreland .05 .02
☐ 106 Randy Ready .05 .02
☐ 107 Marvell Wynne .05 .02
☐ 108 Lance McCullers .05 .02
☐ 109 Tony Gwynn .75 .35
☐ 110 Mark Davis .05 .02
☐ 111 Andy Hawkins .05 .02
☐ 112 Steve Bedrosian .05 .02
☐ 113 Phil Bradley .05 .02
☐ 114 Steve Jeltz .05 .02
☐ 115 Von Hayes .05 .02
☐ 116 Kevin Gross .05 .02
☐ 117 Juan Samuel .05 .02
☐ 118 Shane Rawley .05 .02
☐ 119 Chris James .05 .02
☐ 120 Mike Schmidt .60 .25
☐ 121 Don Carman .05 .02
☐ 122 Bruce Ruffin .05 .02
☐ 123 Bob Walk .05 .02
☐ 124 John Smiley .05 .02
☐ 125 Sid Bream .05 .02
☐ 126 Jose Lind .05 .02
☐ 127 Barry Bonds .60 .25
☐ 128 Mike LaValliere .05 .02
☐ 129 Jeff D. Robinson .05 .02
☐ 130 Mike Dunne .05 .02
☐ 131 Bobby Bonilla .15 .07
☐ 132 Andy Van Slyke .10 .05
☐ 133 Rafael Belliard .05 .02
☐ 134 Nick Esasky .05 .02
☐ 135 Bo Diaz .05 .02
☐ 136 John Franco .10 .05
☐ 137 Barry Larkin .30 .14
☐ 138 Eric Davis .05 .02
☐ 139 Jeff Treadway .05 .02
☐ 140 Jose Rijo .05 .02
☐ 141 Tom Browning .05 .02
☐ 142 Chris Sabo .05 .02
☐ 143 Danny Jackson .05 .02
☐ 144 Kal Daniels .05 .02
☐ 145 Rickey Henderson AS .25 .11
☐ 146 Paul Molitor AS .25 .11
147 Wade Boggs AS .25 .11
[illegible]8 Jose Canseco AS .25 .11
[illegible] Dave Winfield AS .25 .11
[illegible]al Ripken AS 1.00 .45
[illegible]k McGwire AS .25 .11
[illegible] Steinbach AS .10 .05
[illegible]iola AS .05 .02
[illegible]eman AS .05 .02
[illegible]erg AS .25 .11
[illegible] AS .15 .07

☐ 157 Darryl Strawberry AS .10 .05
☐ 158 Bobby Bonilla AS .10 .05
☐ 159 Will Clark AS .15 .07
☐ 160 Gary Carter AS .15 .07
☐ 161 Ozzie Smith AS .25 .11
☐ 162 Dwight Gooden AS .10 .05
☐ 163 Dave Stewart .10 .05
☐ 164 Dave Henderson .05 .02
☐ 165 Terry Steinbach .10 .05
☐ 166 Bob Welch .10 .05
☐ 167 Dennis Eckersley .15 .07
☐ 168 Walt Weiss .05 .02
☐ 169 Dave Parker .10 .05
☐ 170 Carney Lansford .10 .05
☐ 171 Jose Canseco .30 .14
☐ 172 Mark McGwire .75 .35
☐ 173 Ron Hassey .05 .02
☐ 174 Dick Schofield .05 .02
☐ 175 Bob Boone .10 .05
☐ 176 Mike Witt .05 .02
☐ 177 Chili Davis .10 .05
☐ 178 Brian Downing .10 .05
☐ 179 Devon White .10 .05
☐ 180 Bryan Harvey .10 .05
☐ 181 Jack Howell .05 .02
☐ 182 Johnny Ray .05 .02
☐ 183 Wally Joyner .10 .05
☐ 184 Kirk McCaskill .05 .02
☐ 185 Fred McGriff .50 .23
☐ 186 Jimmy Key .10 .05
☐ 187 Kelly Gruber .05 .02
☐ 188 Lloyd Moseby .05 .02
☐ 189 Tony Fernandez .05 .02
☐ 190 Mike Flanagan .05 .02
☐ 191 Pat Borders .05 .02
☐ 192 Rance Mulliniks .05 .02
☐ 193 George Bell .05 .02
☐ 194 Dave Stieb .05 .02
☐ 195 Tom Henke .05 .02
☐ 196 Glenn Braggs .05 .02
☐ 197 Dan Plesac .05 .02
☐ 198 Teddy Higuera .05 .02
☐ 199 Jeffrey Leonard .05 .02
☐ 200 B.J. Surhoff .10 .05
☐ 201 Greg Brock .05 .02
☐ 202 Rob Deer .05 .02
☐ 203 Jim Gantner .05 .02
☐ 204 Paul Molitor .25 .11
☐ 205 Robin Yount .25 .11
☐ 206 Dale Sveum .05 .02
☐ 207 Andy Allanson .05 .02
☐ 208 Julio Franco .10 .05
☐ 209 Bud Black .05 .02
☐ 210 Cory Snyder .05 .02
☐ 211 Tom Candiotti .05 .02
☐ 212 Brook Jacoby .05 .02
☐ 213 Greg Swindell .05 .02
☐ 214 John Farrell .05 .02
☐ 215 Doug Jones .05 .02
☐ 216 Joe Carter .15 .07
☐ 217 Scott Bailes .05 .02
☐ 218 Henry Cotto .05 .02
☐ 219 Mickey Brantley .05 .02
☐ 220 Mike Moore .05 .02
☐ 221 Mark Langston .10 .05
☐ 222 Steve Balboni .05 .02
☐ 223 Jim Presley .05 .02
☐ 224 Rey Quinones .05 .02
☐ 225 Scott Bradley .05 .02
☐ 226 Harold Reynolds .10 .05
☐ 227 Alvin Davis .05 .02
☐ 228 Bill Swift .05 .02
☐ 229 Jose Bautista .05 .02
☐ 230 Jeff Ballard .05 .02
☐ 231 Mickey Tettleton .10 .05
☐ 232 Pete Stanicek .05 .02
☐ 233 Jim Traber .05 .02
☐ 234 Rene Gonzales .05 .02
☐ 235 Terry Kennedy .05 .02
☐ 236 Tom Niedenfuer .05 .02
☐ 237 Cal Ripken 2.00 .90
☐ 238 Eddie Murray .30 .14
☐ 239 Larry Sheets .05 .02
☐ 240 Cecil Espy .05 .02
☐ 241 Jose Guzman .05 .02
☐ 242 Ruben Sierra .05 .02
☐ 243 Jeff Russell .05 .02
☐ 244 Mike Stanley .05 .02
☐ 245 Charlie Hough .10 .05
☐ 246 Scott Fletcher .05 .02
☐ 247 Mitch Williams .05 .02
☐ 248 Pete O'Brien .05 .02
☐ 249 Pete Incaviglia .05 .02
☐ 250 Steve Buechele .05 .02
☐ 251 Lee Smith .10 .05
☐ 252 Dwight Evans .10 .05
☐ 253 Rich Gedman .05 .02

☐ 254 Ellis Burks .15 .07
☐ 255 Mike Greenwell .05 .02
☐ 256 Jim Rice .10 .05
☐ 257 Marty Barrett .05 .02
☐ 258 Bob Stanley .05 .02
☐ 259 Roger Clemens .50 .23
☐ 260 Wade Boggs .30 .14
☐ 261 Mike Boddicker .05 .02
☐ 262 Frank White .10 .05
☐ 263 Bret Saberhagen .05 .02
☐ 264 Kevin Seitzer .05 .02
☐ 265 Bo Jackson .15 .07
☐ 266 Kurt Stillwell .05 .02
☐ 267 Danny Tartabull .05 .02
☐ 268 Willie Wilson .05 .02
☐ 269 Floyd Bannister .05 .02
☐ 270 George Brett .75 .35
☐ 271 Mark Gubicza .05 .02
☐ 272 Steve Farr .05 .02
☐ 273 Mike Henneman .05 .02
☐ 274 Doyle Alexander .05 .02
☐ 275 Frank Tanana .05 .02
☐ 276 Luis Salazar .05 .02
☐ 277 Jack Morris .10 .05
☐ 278 Tom Brookens .05 .02
☐ 279 Gary Pettis .05 .02
☐ 280 Matt Nokes .05 .02
☐ 281 Alan Trammell .15 .07
☐ 282 Lou Whitaker .10 .05
☐ 283 Chet Lemon .05 .02
☐ 284 Jeff Reardon .10 .05
☐ 285 Bert Blyleven .10 .05
☐ 286 Danny Gladden .05 .02
☐ 287 Kent Hrbek .10 .05
☐ 288 Greg Gagne .05 .02
☐ 289 Gary Gaetti .10 .05
☐ 290 Tim Laudner .05 .02
☐ 291 Juan Berenguer .05 .02
☐ 292 Frank Viola .05 .02
☐ 293 Kirby Puckett .50 .23
☐ 294 Gene Larkin .05 .02
☐ 295 Dave Gallagher .05 .02
☐ 296 Melido Perez .05 .02
☐ 297 Ivan Calderon .05 .02
☐ 298 Steve Lyons .05 .02
☐ 299 Carlton Fisk .25 .11
☐ 300 Fred Manrique .05 .02
☐ 301 Dan Pasqua .05 .02
☐ 302 Jack McDowell .10 .05
☐ 303 Ozzie Guillen .05 .02
☐ 304 Harold Baines .10 .05
☐ 305 Bobby Thigpen .05 .02
☐ 306 John Candelaria .05 .02
☐ 307 Dave Righetti .05 .02
☐ 308 Jack Clark .10 .05
☐ 309 Willie Randolph .10 .05
☐ 310 Tommy John .10 .05
☐ 311 Mike Pagliarulo .05 .02
☐ 312 Rickey Henderson .30 .14
☐ 313 Rafael Santana .05 .02
☐ 314 Don Mattingly 1.00 .45
☐ 315 Dave Winfield .25 .11
☐ 316 Richard Dotson .05 .02
☐ 317 Tim Belcher .05 .02
☐ 318 Damon Berryhill .05 .02
☐ 319 Jay Buhner .40 .18
☐ 320 Cecil Espy .05 .02
☐ 321 Dave Gallagher .05 .02
☐ 322 Ron Gant .25 .11
☐ 323 Paul Gibson .05 .02
☐ 324 Mark Grace .40 .18
☐ 325 Chris Sabo ROY .05 .02
☐ 326 Walt Weiss ROY .10 .05
☐ xx Album 1.00 .45

1989 Topps/O-Pee-Chee Sticker Backs

These 67 cards were actually the backs of the 1989 O-Pee-Chee Stickers. The white-bordered cards measure approximately 2 1/8" by 3" and have colorful backgrounds behind the cut-out color player photos. Cards 1-33 feature NL players; cards 34-66 feature AL players. The player's name and position appear in a colored banner near the bottom of the photo. Below are player biography and statistics. The cards are numbered at the lower left.

	MINT	NRMT
COMPLETE SET (67)	6.00	2.70
COMMON CARD (1-67)	.05	.02
☐ 1 George Brett	.60	.25
☐ 2 Don Mattingly	.75	.35
☐ 3 Mark McGwire	.50	.23
☐ 4 Julio Franco	.10	.05
☐ 5 Harold Reynolds	.10	.05
☐ 6 Lou Whitaker	.10	.05
☐ 7 Wade Boggs	.30	.14
☐ 8 Gary Gaetti	.10	.05
☐ 9 Paul Molitor	.25	.11
☐ 10 Tony Fernandez	.05	.02
☐ 11 Cal Ripken	1.50	.70
☐ 12 Alan Trammell	.15	.07
☐ 13 Jose Canseco	.15	.07
☐ 14 Joe Carter	.10	.05
☐ 15 Dwight Evans	.10	.05
☐ 16 Mike Greenwell	.05	.02
☐ 17 Dave Henderson	.05	.02
☐ 18 Rickey Henderson	.30	.14
☐ 19 Kirby Puckett	.40	.18
☐ 20 Dave Winfield	.30	.14
☐ 21 Robin Yount	.15	.07
☐ 22 Bob Boone	.10	.05
☐ 23 Carlton Fisk	.25	.11
☐ 24 Geno Petralli	.05	.02
☐ 25 Roger Clemens	.40	.18
☐ 26 Mark Gubicza	.05	.02
☐ 27 Dave Stewart	.10	.05
☐ 28 Teddy Higuera	.05	.02
☐ 29 Bruce Hurst	.05	.02
☐ 30 Frank Viola	.05	.02
☐ 31 Dennis Eckersley	.15	.07
☐ 32 Doug Jones	.05	.02
☐ 33 Jeff Reardon	.10	.05
☐ 34 Will Clark	.25	.11
☐ 35 Glenn Davis	.05	.02
☐ 36 Andres Galarraga	.25	.11
☐ 37 Juan Samuel	.05	.02
☐ 38 Ryne Sandberg	.40	.18
☐ 39 Steve Sax	.05	.02
☐ 40 Bobby Bonilla	.10	.05
☐ 41 Howard Johnson	.05	.02
☐ 42 Vance Law	.05	.02
☐ 43 Shawon Dunston	.05	.02
☐ 44 Barry Larkin	.15	.07
☐ 45 Ozzie Smith	.30	.14
☐ 46 Barry Bonds	.50	.23
☐ 47 Eric Davis	.05	.02
☐ 48 Andre Dawson	.15	.07
☐ 49 Kirk Gibson	.10	.05
☐ 50 Tony Gwynn	.60	.25
☐ 51 Kevin McReynolds	.05	.02
☐ 52 Rafael Palmeiro	.15	.07
☐ 53 Darryl Strawberry	.10	.05
☐ 54 Andy Van Slyke	.10	.05
☐ 55 Gary Carter	.15	.07
☐ 56 Mike LaValliere	.05	.02
☐ 57 Benito Santiago	.05	.02
☐ 58 Dave Cone	.25	.11
☐ 59 Dwight Gooden	.10	.05
☐ 60 Orel Hershiser	.10	.05
☐ 61 Tom Browning	.05	.02
☐ 62 Danny Jackson	.05	.02
☐ 63 Bob Knepper	.05	.02
☐ 64 Mark Davis	.05	.02
☐ 65 John Franco	.10	.05
☐ 66 Randy Myers	.10	.05
☐ 67 Checklist	.05	.02

1989 Topps UK Minis

The 1989 Topps UK Minis baseball set contains 88 cards measuring approximately 2 1/8" by 3". The fronts are red, white and blue. The backs are yellow and red, and feature 1988 and career stats. The cards were distributed in five-card poly packs. The card set numbering is in alphabetical order by player's name.

	MINT	NRMT
COMPLETE SET (88)	12.00	5.50
COMMON CARD (1-88)	.10	.05
☐ 1 Brady Anderson	1.25	.55
☐ 2 Harold Baines	.20	.09
☐ 3 George Bell	.10	.05
☐ 4 Wade Boggs	.60	.25
☐ 5 Barry Bonds	1.25	.55
☐ 6 Bobby Bonilla	.20	.09
☐ 7 George Brett	1.50	.70
☐ 8 Hubie Brooks	.10	.05
☐ 9 Tom Brunansky	.10	.05
☐ 10 Jay Buhner	.60	.25
☐ 11 Brett Butler	.20	.09
☐ 12 Jose Canseco	.60	.25
☐ 13 Joe Carter	.35	.16
☐ 14 Jack Clark	.10	.05
☐ 15 Will Clark	.60	.25
☐ 16 Roger Clemens	1.00	.45
☐ 17 David Cone	.35	.16
☐ 18 Alvin Davis	.10	.05
☐ 19 Eric Davis	.20	.09
☐ 20 Glenn Davis	.10	.05
☐ 21 Andre Dawson	.50	.23
☐ 22 Bill Doran	.10	.05
☐ 23 Dennis Eckersley	.35	.16
☐ 24 Dwight Evans	.20	.09
☐ 25 Tony Fernandez	.10	.05
☐ 26 Carlton Fisk	.60	.25
☐ 27 John Franco	.20	.09
☐ 28 Andres Galarraga	.50	.23
☐ 29 Ron Gant	.35	.16
☐ 30 Kirk Gibson	.20	.09
☐ 31 Dwight Gooden	.20	.09
☐ 32 Mike Greenwell	.10	.05
☐ 33 Mark Gubicza	.10	.05
☐ 34 Pedro Guerrero	.10	.05
☐ 35 Ozzie Guillen	.10	.05
☐ 36 Tony Gwynn	2.00	.90
☐ 37 Rickey Henderson	.60	.25
☐ 38 Orel Hershiser	.20	.09
☐ 39 Teddy Higuera	.10	.05
☐ 40 Charlie Hough	.10	.05
☐ 41 Kent Hrbek	.10	.05
☐ 42 Bruce Hurst	.10	.05
☐ 43 Bo Jackson	.20	.09
☐ 44 Gregg Jefferies	.20	.09
☐ 45 Ricky Jordan	.10	.05
☐ 46 Wally Joyner	.10	.05
☐ 47 Mark Langston	.10	.05
☐ 48 Mike Marshall	.10	.05
☐ 49 Don Mattingly	2.00	.90
☐ 50 Fred McGriff	.50	.23
☐ 51 Mark McGwire	1.50	.70
☐ 52 Kevin McReynolds	.10	.05
☐ 53 Paul Molitor	.50	.23
☐ 54 Jack Morris	.20	.09
☐ 55 Dale Murphy	.35	.16
☐ 56 Eddie Murray	1.00	.45
☐ 57 Pete O'Brien	.10	.05
☐ 58 Rafael Palmeiro	.35	.16
☐ 59 Gerald Perry	.10	.05
☐ 60 Kirby Puckett	2.00	.90
☐ 61 Tim Raines	.20	.09
☐ 62 Johnny Ray	.10	.05
☐ 63 Rick Reuschel	.10	.05
☐ 64 Cal Ripken	4.00	1.80
☐ 65 Chris Sabo	.10	.05
☐ 66 Juan Samuel	.10	.05
☐ 67 Ryne Sandberg	1.50	.70
☐ 68 Benito Santiago	.10	.05
☐ 69 Steve Sax	.10	.05
☐ 70 Mike Schmidt	1.00	.45
☐ 71 Ruben Sierra	.10	.05
☐ 72 Ozzie Smith	1.50	.70
☐ 73 Cory Snyder	.10	.05
☐ 74 Dave Stewart	.10	.05
☐ 75 Darryl Strawberry	.20	.09
☐ 76 Greg Swindell	.10	.05
☐ 77 Alan Trammell	.35	.16
☐ 78 Fernando Valenzuela	.20	.09
☐ 79 Andy Van Slyke	.10	.05
☐ 80 Frank Viola	.10	.05
☐ 81 Claudell Washington	.10	.05
☐ 82 Walt Weiss	.10	.05
☐ 83 Lou Whitaker	.20	.09
☐ 84 Dave Winfield	.50	.23
☐ 85 Mike Witt	.10	.05
☐ 86 Gerald Young	.10	.05
☐ 87 Robin Yount	.35	.16
☐ 88 Checklist Card	.10	.05

1990 Topps

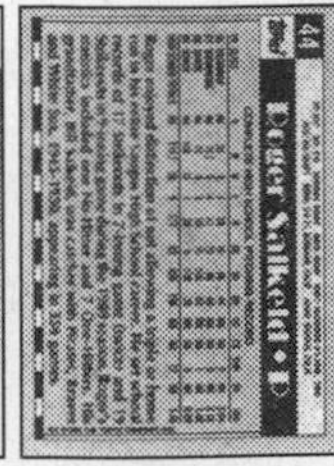

The 1990 Topps set contains 792 standard-size cards. Cards were issued primarily in wax packs, rack packs and hobby and retail factory sets. Card fronts feature various colored borders with the player's name at the bottom and team name at top. Subsets include All-Stars (385-407), Turn Back the Clock (661-665) and Draft Picks (scattered throughout the set). The key Rookie Cards in this set are Juan Gonzalez, Marquis Grissom, Ben McDonald, Sammy Sosa, Frank Thomas, Larry Walker and Bernie Williams. The Thomas card (414A) was printed without his name on front creating a scarce variation. The card is rarely seen and, for a newer issue, has experienced unprecedented growth as far as value. Be careful when purchasing this card as counterfeits have been produced.

	MINT	NRMT
COMPLETE SET (792)	12.00	5.50
COMP.FACT.SET (792)	15.00	6.75
COMMON CARD (1-792)	.05	.02
☐ 1 Nolan Ryan	.75	.35
☐ 2 Nolan Ryan Salute New York Mets	.40	.18
☐ 3 Nolan Ryan Salute California Angels	.40	.18
☐ 4 Nolan Ryan Salute Houston Astros	.40	.18
☐ 5 Nolan Ryan Salute Texas Rangers UER (Says Texas Stadium rather than Arlington Stadium)	.40	.18
☐ 6 Vince Coleman RB (50 consecutive SB's	.05	.02
☐ 7 Rickey Henderson RB (40 career leadoff HR's	.20	.09
☐ 8 Cal Ripken RB (20 or more homers for 8 consecutive years, record for shortstops)	.40	.18
☐ 9 Eric Plunk	.05	.02
☐ 10 Barry Larkin	.20	.09
☐ 11 Paul Gibson	.05	.02
☐ 12 Joe Girardi	.10	.05
☐ 13 Mark Williamson	.05	.02
☐ 14 Mike Fetters	.10	.05
☐ 15 Teddy Higuera	.05	.02
☐ 16 Kent Anderson	.05	.02
☐ 17 Kelly Downs	.05	.02
☐ 18 Carlos Quintana	.05	.02
☐ 19 Al Newman	.05	.02
☐ 20 Mark Gubicza	.05	.02
☐ 21 Jeff Torborg MG	.05	.02
☐ 22 Bruce Ruffin	.05	.02
☐ 23 Randy Velarde	.05	.02
☐ 24 Joe Hesketh	.05	.02
☐ 25 Willie Randolph	.10	.05
☐ 26 Don Slaught	.05	.02
☐ 27 Rick Leach	.05	.02
☐ 28 Duane Ward	.05	.02
☐ 29 John Cangelosi	.05	.02
☐ 30 David Cone	.20	.09
☐ 31 Henry Cotto	.05	.02
☐ 32 John Farrell	.05	.02
☐ 33 Greg Walker	.05	.02
☐ 34 Tony Fossas	.05	.02
☐ 35 Benito Santiago	.05	.02
☐ 36 John Costello	.05	.02
☐ 37 Domingo Ramos	.05	.02
☐ 38 Wes Gardner	.05	.02
☐ 39 Curt Ford	.05	.02
☐ 40 Jay Howell	.05	
☐ 41 Matt Williams	.20	
☐ 42 Jeff M. Robinson	.05	
☐ 43 Dante Bichette	.20	
☐ 44 Roger Salkeld FDP	.05	
☐ 45 Dave Parker UER (Born in Jackson, not Calhoun)	.10	

- ☐ 46 Rob Dibble .05 .02
- ☐ 47 Brian Harper .05 .02
- ☐ 48 Zane Smith .05 .02
- ☐ 49 Tom Lawless .05 .02
- ☐ 50 Glenn Davis .05 .02
- ☐ 51 Doug Rader MG .05 .02
- ☐ 52 Jack Daugherty .05 .02
- ☐ 53 Mike LaCoss .05 .02
- ☐ 54 Joel Skinner .05 .02
- ☐ 55 Darrell Evans UER .10 .05
  (HR total should be 414, not 424)
- ☐ 56 Franklin Stubbs .05 .02
- ☐ 57 Greg Vaughn .10 .05
- ☐ 58 Keith Miller .05 .02
- ☐ 59 Ted Power .05 .02
- ☐ 60 George Brett .40 .18
- ☐ 61 Deion Sanders .20 .09
- ☐ 62 Ramon Martinez .10 .05
- ☐ 63 Mike Pagliarulo .05 .02
- ☐ 64 Danny Darwin .05 .02
- ☐ 65 Devon White .10 .05
- ☐ 66 Greg Litton .05 .02
- ☐ 67 Scott Sanderson .05 .02
- ☐ 68 Dave Henderson .05 .02
- ☐ 69 Todd Frohwirth .05 .02
- ☐ 70 Mike Greenwell .05 .02
- ☐ 71 Allan Anderson .05 .02
- ☐ 72 Jeff Huson .05 .02
- ☐ 73 Bob Milacki .05 .02
- ☐ 74 Jeff Jackson FDP .05 .02
- ☐ 75 Doug Jones .05 .02
- ☐ 76 Dave Valle .05 .02
- ☐ 77 Dave Bergman .05 .02
- ☐ 78 Mike Flanagan .05 .02
- ☐ 79 Ron Kittle .05 .02
- ☐ 80 Jeff Russell .05 .02
- ☐ 81 Bob Rodgers MG .05 .02
- ☐ 82 Scott Terry .05 .02
- ☐ 83 Hensley Meulens .05 .02
- ☐ 84 Ray Searage .05 .02
- ☐ 85 Juan Samuel .05 .02
- ☐ 86 Paul Kilgus .05 .02
- ☐ 87 Rick Luecken .05 .02
- ☐ 88 Glenn Braggs .05 .02
- ☐ 89 Clint Zavaras .05 .02
- ☐ 90 Jack Clark .10 .05
- ☐ 91 Steve Frey .05 .02
- ☐ 92 Mike Stanley .05 .02
- ☐ 93 Shawn Hillegas .05 .02
- ☐ 94 Herm Winningham .05 .02
- ☐ 95 Todd Worrell .05 .02
- ☐ 96 Jody Reed .05 .02
- ☐ 97 Curt Schilling .20 .09
- ☐ 98 Jose Gonzalez .05 .02
- ☐ 99 Rich Monteleone .05 .02
- ☐ 100 Will Clark .20 .09
- ☐ 101 Shane Rawley .05 .02
- ☐ 102 Stan Javier .05 .02
- ☐ 103 Marvin Freeman .05 .02
- ☐ 104 Bob Knepper .05 .02
- ☐ 105 Randy Myers .10 .05
- ☐ 106 Charlie O'Brien .05 .02
- ☐ 107 Fred Lynn .05 .02
- ☐ 108 Rod Nichols .05 .02
- ☐ 109 Roberto Kelly .05 .02
- ☐ 110 Tommy Helms MG .05 .02
- ☐ 111 Ed Whited .05 .02
- ☐ 112 Glenn Wilson .05 .02
- ☐ 113 Manny Lee .05 .02
- ☐ 114 Mike Bielecki .05 .02
- ☐ 115 Tony Pena .05 .02
- ☐ 116 Floyd Bannister .05 .02
- ☐ 117 Mike Sharperson .05 .02
- ☐ 118 Erik Hanson .10 .05
- ☐ 119 Billy Hatcher .05 .02
- ☐ 120 John Franco .05 .02
- ☐ 121 Robin Ventura .20 .09
- ☐ 122 Shawn Abner .05 .02
- ☐ 123 Rich Gedman .05 .02
- ☐ 124 Dave Dravecky .10 .05
- ☐ 125 Kent Hrbek .10 .05
- ☐ 126 Randy Kramer .05 .02
- ☐ 127 Mike Devereaux .05 .02
- ☐ 128 Checklist 1 .05 .02
- ☐ 129 Ron Jones .05 .02
- ☐ 130 Bert Blyleven .10 .05
- 131 Matt Nokes .05 .02
- [illegible] Lance Blankenship .05 .02
- [illegible] Ricky Horton .05 .02
- [illegible]rl Cunningham FDP .05 .02
- [illegible] Magadan .05 .02
- [illegible] Brown .20 .09
- [illegible]evey .05 .02
- [illegible] .20 .09
- [illegible] .05 .02
- [illegible] .20 .09
- ☐ 141 John Hart MG .05 .02
- ☐ 142 Jeff Wetherby .05 .02
- ☐ 143 Rafael Belliard .05 .02
- ☐ 144 Bud Black .05 .02
- ☐ 145 Terry Steinbach .10 .05
- ☐ 146 Rob Richie .05 .02
- ☐ 147 Chuck Finley .10 .05
- ☐ 148 Edgar Martinez .20 .09
- ☐ 149 Steve Farr .05 .02
- ☐ 150 Kirk Gibson .20 .09
- ☐ 151 Rick Mahler .05 .02
- ☐ 152 Lonnie Smith .05 .02
- ☐ 153 Randy Milligan .05 .02
- ☐ 154 Mike Maddux .05 .02
- ☐ 155 Ellis Burks .10 .05
- ☐ 156 Ken Patterson .05 .02
- ☐ 157 Craig Biggio .20 .09
- ☐ 158 Craig Lefferts .05 .02
- ☐ 159 Mike Felder .05 .02
- ☐ 160 Dave Righetti .05 .02
- ☐ 161 Harold Reynolds .05 .02
- ☐ 162 Todd Zeile .10 .05
- ☐ 163 Phil Bradley .05 .02
- ☐ 164 Jeff Juden FDP .05 .02
- ☐ 165 Walt Weiss .05 .02
- ☐ 166 Bobby Witt .05 .02
- ☐ 167 Kevin Appier .20 .09
- ☐ 168 Jose Lind .05 .02
- ☐ 169 Richard Dotson .05 .02
- ☐ 170 George Bell .05 .02
- ☐ 171 Russ Nixon MG .05 .02
- ☐ 172 Tom Lampkin .05 .02
- ☐ 173 Tim Belcher .05 .02
- ☐ 174 Jeff Kunkel .05 .02
- ☐ 175 Mike Moore .05 .02
- ☐ 176 Luis Quinones .05 .02
- ☐ 177 Mike Henneman .05 .02
- ☐ 178 Chris James .05 .02
- ☐ 179 Brian Holton .05 .02
- ☐ 180 Tim Raines .10 .05
- ☐ 181 Juan Agosto .05 .02
- ☐ 182 Mookie Wilson .05 .02
- ☐ 183 Steve Lake .05 .02
- ☐ 184 Danny Cox .05 .02
- ☐ 185 Ruben Sierra .05 .02
- ☐ 186 Dave LaPoint .05 .02
- ☐ 187 Rick Wrona .05 .02
- ☐ 188 Mike Smithson .05 .02
- ☐ 189 Dick Schofield .05 .02
- ☐ 190 Rick Reuschel .05 .02
- ☐ 191 Pat Borders .05 .02
- ☐ 192 Don August .05 .02
- ☐ 193 Andy Benes .10 .05
- ☐ 194 Glenallen Hill .05 .02
- ☐ 195 Tim Burke .05 .02
- ☐ 196 Gerald Young .05 .02
- ☐ 197 Doug Drabek .05 .02
- ☐ 198 Mike Marshall .05 .02
- ☐ 199 Sergio Valdez .05 .02
- ☐ 200 Don Mattingly .30 .14
- ☐ 201 Cito Gaston MG .05 .02
- ☐ 202 Mike Macfarlane .05 .02
- ☐ 203 Mike Roesler .05 .02
- ☐ 204 Bob Dernier .05 .02
- ☐ 205 Mark Davis .05 .02
- ☐ 206 Nick Esasky .05 .02
- ☐ 207 Bob Ojeda .05 .02
- ☐ 208 Brook Jacoby .05 .02
- ☐ 209 Greg Mathews .05 .02
- ☐ 210 Ryne Sandberg .25 .11
- ☐ 211 John Cerutti .05 .02
- ☐ 212 Joe Orsulak .05 .02
- ☐ 213 Scott Bankhead .05 .02
- ☐ 214 Terry Francona .05 .02
- ☐ 215 Kirk McCaskill .05 .02
- ☐ 216 Ricky Jordan .05 .02
- ☐ 217 Don Robinson .05 .02
- ☐ 218 Wally Backman .05 .02
- ☐ 219 Donn Pall .05 .02
- ☐ 220 Barry Bonds .25 .11
- ☐ 221 Gary Mielke .05 .02
- ☐ 222 Kurt Stillwell UER .05 .02
  (Graduate misspelled as gradute)
- ☐ 223 Tommy Gregg .05 .02
- ☐ 224 Delino DeShields .20 .09
- ☐ 225 Jim Deshaies .05 .02
- ☐ 226 Mickey Hatcher .05 .02
- ☐ 227 Kevin Tapani .10 .05
- ☐ 228 Dave Martinez .05 .02
- ☐ 229 David Wells .05 .02
- ☐ 230 Keith Hernandez .10 .05
- ☐ 231 Jack McKeon MG .05 .02
- ☐ 232 Darnell Coles .05 .02
- ☐ 233 Ken Hill .20 .09
- ☐ 234 Mariano Duncan .05 .02
- ☐ 235 Jeff Reardon .10 .05
- ☐ 236 Hal Morris .10 .05
- ☐ 237 Kevin Ritz .05 .02
- ☐ 238 Felix Jose .05 .02
- ☐ 239 Eric Show .05 .02
- ☐ 240 Mark Grace .20 .09
- ☐ 241 Mike Krukow .05 .02
- ☐ 242 Fred Manrique .05 .02
- ☐ 243 Barry Jones .05 .02
- ☐ 244 Bill Schroeder .05 .02
- ☐ 245 Roger Clemens .40 .18
- ☐ 246 Jim Eisenreich .10 .05
- ☐ 247 Jerry Reed .05 .02
- ☐ 248 Dave Anderson .05 .02
- ☐ 249 Mike(Texas) Smith .05 .02
- ☐ 250 Jose Canseco .20 .09
- ☐ 251 Jeff Blauser .10 .05
- ☐ 252 Otis Nixon .10 .05
- ☐ 253 Mark Portugal .05 .02
- ☐ 254 Francisco Cabrera .05 .02
- ☐ 255 Bobby Thigpen .05 .02
- ☐ 256 Marvell Wynne .05 .02
- ☐ 257 Jose DeLeon .05 .02
- ☐ 258 Barry Lyons .05 .02
- ☐ 259 Lance McCullers .05 .02
- ☐ 260 Eric Davis .10 .05
- ☐ 261 Whitey Herzog MG .10 .05
- ☐ 262 Checklist 2 .05 .02
- ☐ 263 Mel Stottlemyre Jr. .05 .02
- ☐ 264 Bryan Clutterbuck .05 .02
- ☐ 265 Pete O'Brien .05 .02
- ☐ 266 German Gonzalez .05 .02
- ☐ 267 Mark Davidson .05 .02
- ☐ 268 Rob Murphy .05 .02
- ☐ 269 Dickie Thon .05 .02
- ☐ 270 Dave Stewart .10 .05
- ☐ 271 Chet Lemon .05 .02
- ☐ 272 Bryan Harvey .05 .02
- ☐ 273 Bobby Bonilla .10 .05
- ☐ 274 Mauro Gozzo .05 .02
- ☐ 275 Mickey Tettleton .10 .05
- ☐ 276 Gary Thurman .05 .02
- ☐ 277 Lenny Harris .05 .02
- ☐ 278 Pascual Perez .05 .02
- ☐ 279 Steve Buechele .05 .02
- ☐ 280 Lou Whitaker .10 .05
- ☐ 281 Kevin Bass .05 .02
- ☐ 282 Derek Lilliquist .05 .02
- ☐ 283 Joey Belle .50 .23
- ☐ 284 Mark Gardner .05 .02
- ☐ 285 Willie McGee .05 .02
- ☐ 286 Lee Guetterman .05 .02
- ☐ 287 Vance Law .05 .02
- ☐ 288 Greg Briley .05 .02
- ☐ 289 Norm Charlton .05 .02
- ☐ 290 Robin Yount .20 .09
- ☐ 291 Dave Johnson MG .10 .05
- ☐ 292 Jim Gott .05 .02
- ☐ 293 Mike Gallego .05 .02
- ☐ 294 Craig McMurtry .05 .02
- ☐ 295 Fred McGriff .20 .09
- ☐ 296 Jeff Ballard .05 .02
- ☐ 297 Tommy Herr .05 .02
- ☐ 298 Dan Gladden .05 .02
- ☐ 299 Adam Peterson .05 .02
- ☐ 300 Bo Jackson .20 .09
- ☐ 301 Don Aase .05 .02
- ☐ 302 Marcus Lawton .05 .02
- ☐ 303 Rick Cerone .05 .02
- ☐ 304 Marty Clary .05 .02
- ☐ 305 Eddie Murray .20 .09
- ☐ 306 Tom Niedenfuer .05 .02
- ☐ 307 Bip Roberts .05 .02
- ☐ 308 Jose Guzman .05 .02
- ☐ 309 Eric Yelding .05 .02
- ☐ 310 Steve Bedrosian .05 .02
- ☐ 311 Dwight Smith .05 .02
- ☐ 312 Dan Quisenberry .05 .02
- ☐ 313 Gus Polidor .05 .02
- ☐ 314 Donald Harris FDP .05 .02
- ☐ 315 Bruce Hurst .05 .02
- ☐ 316 Carney Lansford .10 .05
- ☐ 317 Mark Guthrie .05 .02
- ☐ 318 Wallace Johnson .05 .02
- ☐ 319 Dion James .05 .02
- ☐ 320 Dave Stieb .05 .02
- ☐ 321 Joe Morgan MG .05 .02
- ☐ 322 Junior Ortiz .05 .02
- ☐ 323 Willie Wilson .05 .02
- ☐ 324 Pete Harnisch .05 .02
- ☐ 325 Robby Thompson .05 .02
- ☐ 326 Tom McCarthy .05 .02
- ☐ 327 Ken Williams .05 .02
- ☐ 328 Curt Young .05 .02
- ☐ 329 Oddibe McDowell .05 .02
- ☐ 330 Ron Darling .05 .02
- ☐ 331 Juan Gonzalez 2.00 .90
- ☐ 332 Paul O'Neill .10 .05

☐ 333 Bill Wegman .05 .02
☐ 334 Johnny Ray .05 .02
☐ 335 Andy Hawkins .05 .02
☐ 336 Ken Griffey Jr. 1.50 .70
☐ 337 Lloyd McClendon .05 .02
☐ 338 Dennis Lamp .05 .02
☐ 339 Dave Clark .05 .02
☐ 340 Fernando Valenzuela .10 .05
☐ 341 Tom Foley .05 .02
☐ 342 Alex Trevino .05 .02
☐ 343 Frank Tanana .05 .02
☐ 344 George Canale .05 .02
☐ 345 Harold Baines .10 .05
☐ 346 Jim Presley .05 .02
☐ 347 Junior Felix .05 .02
☐ 348 Gary Wayne .05 .02
☐ 349 Steve Finley .20 .09
☐ 350 Bret Saberhagen .05 .02
☐ 351 Roger Craig MG .05 .02
☐ 352 Bryn Smith .05 .02
☐ 353 Sandy Alomar Jr. .20 .09
(Not listed as Jr.
on card front)
☐ 354 Stan Belinda .05 .02
☐ 355 Marty Barrett .05 .02
☐ 356 Randy Ready .05 .02
☐ 357 Dave West .05 .02
☐ 358 Andres Thomas .05 .02
☐ 359 Jimmy Jones .05 .02
☐ 360 Paul Molitor .20 .09
☐ 361 Randy McCament .05 .02
☐ 362 Damon Berryhill .05 .02
☐ 363 Dan Petry .05 .02
☐ 364 Rolando Roomes .05 .02
☐ 365 Ozzie Guillen .05 .02
☐ 366 Mike Heath .05 .02
☐ 367 Mike Morgan .05 .02
☐ 368 Bill Doran .05 .02
☐ 369 Todd Burns .05 .02
☐ 370 Tim Wallach .05 .02
☐ 371 Jimmy Key .10 .05
☐ 372 Terry Kennedy .05 .02
☐ 373 Alvin Davis .05 .02
☐ 374 Steve Cummings .05 .02
☐ 375 Dwight Evans .10 .05
☐ 376 Checklist 3 UER .05 .02
(Higuera misalphabet-
ized in Brewer list)
☐ 377 Mickey Weston .05 .02
☐ 378 Luis Salazar .05 .02
☐ 379 Steve Rosenberg .05 .02
☐ 380 Dave Winfield .20 .09
☐ 381 Frank Robinson MG .20 .09
☐ 382 Jeff Musselman .05 .02
☐ 383 John Morris .05 .02
☐ 384 Pat Combs .05 .02
☐ 385 Fred McGriff AS .20 .09
☐ 386 Julio Franco AS .05 .02
☐ 387 Wade Boggs AS .20 .09
☐ 388 Cal Ripken AS .40 .18
☐ 389 Robin Yount AS .20 .09
☐ 390 Ruben Sierra AS .05 .02
☐ 391 Kirby Puckett AS .20 .09
☐ 392 Carlton Fisk AS .10 .05
☐ 393 Bret Saberhagen AS .05 .02
☐ 394 Jeff Ballard AS .05 .02
☐ 395 Jeff Russell AS .05 .02
☐ 396 A.Bartlett Giamatti .20 .09
COMM MEM
☐ 397 Will Clark AS .20 .09
☐ 398 Ryne Sandberg AS .20 .09
☐ 399 Howard Johnson AS .05 .02
☐ 400 Ozzie Smith AS .20 .09
☐ 401 Kevin Mitchell AS .05 .02
☐ 402 Eric Davis AS .10 .05
☐ 403 Tony Gwynn AS .20 .09
☐ 404 Craig Biggio AS .20 .09
☐ 405 Mike Scott AS .05 .02
☐ 406 Joe Magrane AS .05 .02
☐ 407 Mark Davis AS .05 .02
☐ 408 Trevor Wilson .05 .02
☐ 409 Tom Brunansky .05 .02
☐ 410 Joe Boever .05 .02
☐ 411 Ken Phelps .05 .02
☐ 412 Jamie Moyer .05 .02
☐ 413 Brian DuBois .05 .02
☐ 414A Frank Thomas FDP 1500.00 700.00
ERR (Name missing
on card front)
☐ 414B Frank Thomas FDP COR 4.00 1.80
☐ 415 Shawon Dunston .05 .02
☐ 416 Dave Johnson (P) .05 .02
☐ 417 Jim Gantner .05 .02
☐ 418 Tom Browning .05 .02
☐ 419 Beau Allred .05 .02
☐ 420 Carlton Fisk .20 .09
☐ 421 Greg Minton .05 .02
☐ 422 Pat Sheridan .05 .02
☐ 423 Fred Toliver .05 .02
☐ 424 Jerry Reuss .05 .02
☐ 425 Bill Landrum .05 .02
☐ 426 Jeff Hamilton UER .05 .02
(Stats say he fanned
197 times in 1987, but
he only had 147 at bats)
☐ 427 Carmen Castillo .05 .02
☐ 428 Steve Davis .05 .02
☐ 429 Tom Kelly MG .05 .02
☐ 430 Pete Incaviglia .05 .02
☐ 431 Randy Johnson .30 .14
☐ 432 Damaso Garcia .05 .02
☐ 433 Steve Olin .10 .05
☐ 434 Mark Carreon .05 .02
☐ 435 Kevin Seitzer .05 .02
☐ 436 Mel Hall .05 .02
☐ 437 Les Lancaster .05 .02
☐ 438 Greg Myers .05 .02
☐ 439 Jeff Parrett .05 .02
☐ 440 Alan Trammell .10 .05
☐ 441 Bob Kipper .05 .02
☐ 442 Jerry Browne .05 .02
☐ 443 Cris Carpenter .05 .02
☐ 444 Kyle Abbott FDP .05 .02
☐ 445 Danny Jackson .05 .02
☐ 446 Dan Pasqua .05 .02
☐ 447 Atlee Hammaker .05 .02
☐ 448 Greg Gagne .05 .02
☐ 449 Dennis Rasmussen .05 .02
☐ 450 Rickey Henderson .20 .09
☐ 451 Mark Lemke .10 .05
☐ 452 Luis DeLosSantos .05 .02
☐ 453 Jody Davis .05 .02
☐ 454 Jeff King .10 .05
☐ 455 Jeffrey Leonard .05 .02
☐ 456 Chris Gwynn .05 .02
☐ 457 Gregg Jefferies .10 .05
☐ 458 Bob McClure .05 .02
☐ 459 Jim Lefebvre MG .05 .02
☐ 460 Mike Scott .05 .02
☐ 461 Carlos Martinez .05 .02
☐ 462 Denny Walling .05 .02
☐ 463 Drew Hall .05 .02
☐ 464 Jerome Walton .05 .02
☐ 465 Kevin Gross .05 .02
☐ 466 Rance Mulliniks .05 .02
☐ 467 Juan Nieves .05 .02
☐ 468 Bill Ripken .05 .02
☐ 469 John Kruk .10 .05
☐ 470 Frank Viola .05 .02
☐ 471 Mike Brumley .05 .02
☐ 472 Jose Uribe .05 .02
☐ 473 Joe Price .05 .02
☐ 474 Rich Thompson .05 .02
☐ 475 Bob Welch .05 .02
☐ 476 Brad Komminsk .05 .02
☐ 477 Willie Fraser .05 .02
☐ 478 Mike LaValliere .05 .02
☐ 479 Frank White .10 .05
☐ 480 Sid Fernandez .05 .02
☐ 481 Garry Templeton .05 .02
☐ 482 Steve Carter .05 .02
☐ 483 Alejandro Pena .05 .02
☐ 484 Mike Fitzgerald .05 .02
☐ 485 John Candelaria .05 .02
☐ 486 Jeff Treadway .05 .02
☐ 487 Steve Searcy .05 .02
☐ 488 Ken Oberkfell .05 .02
☐ 489 Nick Leyva MG .05 .02
☐ 490 Dan Plesac .05 .02
☐ 491 Dave Cochrane .05 .02
☐ 492 Ron Oester .05 .02
☐ 493 Jason Grimsley .05 .02
☐ 494 Terry Puhl .05 .02
☐ 495 Lee Smith .10 .05
☐ 496 Cecil Espy UER .05 .02
('88 stats have 3
SB's, should be 33)
☐ 497 Dave Schmidt .05 .02
☐ 498 Rick Schu .05 .02
☐ 499 Bill Long .05 .02
☐ 500 Kevin Mitchell .05 .02
☐ 501 Matt Young .05 .02
☐ 502 Mitch Webster .05 .02
☐ 503 Randy St.Claire .05 .02
☐ 504 Tom O'Malley .05 .02
☐ 505 Kelly Gruber .05 .02
☐ 506 Tom Glavine .20 .09
☐ 507 Gary Redus .05 .02
☐ 508 Terry Leach .05 .02
☐ 509 Tom Pagnozzi .05 .02
☐ 510 Dwight Gooden .10 .05
☐ 511 Clay Parker .05 .02
☐ 512 Gary Pettis .05 .02
☐ 513 Mark Eichhorn .05 .02
☐ 514 Andy Allanson .05 .02
☐ 515 Len Dykstra .10 .05
☐ 516 Tim Leary .05 .02
☐ 517 Roberto Alomar .25 .11
☐ 518 Bill Krueger .05 .02
☐ 519 Bucky Dent MG .05 .02
☐ 520 Mitch Williams .05 .02
☐ 521 Craig Worthington .05 .02
☐ 522 Mike Dunne .05 .02
☐ 523 Jay Bell .10 .05
☐ 524 Daryl Boston .05 .02
☐ 525 Wally Joyner .10 .05
☐ 526 Checklist 4 .05 .02
☐ 527 Ron Hassey .05 .02
☐ 528 Kevin Wickander UER .05 .02
(Monthly scoreboard
strikeout total was 2.2,
that was his innings
pitched total)
☐ 529 Greg A. Harris .05 .02
☐ 530 Mark Langston .05 .02
☐ 531 Ken Caminiti .20 .09
☐ 532 Cecilio Guante .05 .02
☐ 533 Tim Jones .05 .02
☐ 534 Louie Meadows .05 .02
☐ 535 John Smoltz .20 .09
☐ 536 Bob Geren .05 .02
☐ 537 Mark Grant .05 .02
☐ 538 Bill Spiers UER .05 .02
(Photo actually
George Canale)
☐ 539 Neal Heaton .05 .02
☐ 540 Danny Tartabull .05 .02
☐ 541 Pat Perry .05 .02
☐ 542 Darren Daulton .10 .05
☐ 543 Nelson Liriano .05 .02
☐ 544 Dennis Boyd .05 .02
☐ 545 Kevin McReynolds .05 .02
☐ 546 Kevin Hickey .05 .02
☐ 547 Jack Howell .05 .02
☐ 548 Pat Clements .05 .02
☐ 549 Don Zimmer MG .05 .02
☐ 550 Julio Franco .10 .05
☐ 551 Tim Crews .05 .02
☐ 552 Mike(Miss.) Smith .05 .02
☐ 553 Scott Scudder UER .05 .02
(Cedar Rap1ds)
☐ 554 Jay Buhner .20 .09
☐ 555 Jack Morris .10 .05
☐ 556 Gene Larkin .05 .02
☐ 557 Jeff Innis .05 .02
☐ 558 Rafael Ramirez .05 .02
☐ 559 Andy McGaffigan .05 .02
☐ 560 Steve Sax .05 .02
☐ 561 Ken Dayley .05 .02
☐ 562 Chad Kreuter .05 .02
☐ 563 Alex Sanchez .05 .02
☐ 564 Tyler Houston FDP .20 .09
☐ 565 Scott Fletcher .05 .02
☐ 566 Mark Knudson .05 .02
☐ 567 Ron Gant .10 .05
☐ 568 John Smiley .10 .05
☐ 569 Ivan Calderon .05 .02
☐ 570 Cal Ripken .75 .35
☐ 571 Brett Butler .10 .05
☐ 572 Greg W. Harris .05 .02
☐ 573 Danny Heep .05 .02
☐ 574 Bill Swift .05 .02
☐ 575 Lance Parrish .05 .02
☐ 576 Mike Dyer .05 .02
☐ 577 Charlie Hayes .10 .05
☐ 578 Joe Magrane .05 .02
☐ 579 Art Howe MG .05 .02
☐ 580 Joe Carter .20 .09
☐ 581 Ken Griffey Sr. .05 .02
☐ 582 Rick Honeycutt .05 .02
☐ 583 Bruce Benedict .05 .02
☐ 584 Phil Stephenson .05 .02
☐ 585 Kal Daniels .05 .02
☐ 586 Edwin Nunez .05 .02
☐ 587 Lance Johnson .10 .05
☐ 588 Rick Rhoden .05 .02
☐ 589 Mike Aldrete .05 .02
☐ 590 Ozzie Smith .25 .11
☐ 591 Todd Stottlemyre .05 .02
☐ 592 R.J. Reynolds .05 .02
☐ 593 Scott Bradley .05 .02
☐ 594 Luis Sojo .05 .02
☐ 595 Greg Swindell .05 .02
☐ 596 Jose DeJesus .05 [illegible]
☐ 597 Chris Bosio .05 [illegible]
☐ 598 Brady Anderson .20
☐ 599 Frank Williams .05
☐ 600 Darryl Strawberry .10
☐ 601 Luis Rivera .05
☐ 602 Scott Garrelts .05
☐ 603 Tony Armas .05

Card	Mint	NRMT
☐ 604 Ron Robinson	.05	.02
☐ 605 Mike Scioscia	.05	.02
☐ 606 Storm Davis	.05	.02
☐ 607 Steve Jeltz	.05	.02
☐ 608 Eric Anthony	.10	.05
☐ 609 Sparky Anderson MG	.10	.05
☐ 610 Pedro Guerrero	.05	.02
☐ 611 Walt Terrell	.05	.02
☐ 612 Dave Gallagher	.05	.02
☐ 613 Jeff Pico	.05	.02
☐ 614 Nelson Santovenia	.05	.02
☐ 615 Rob Deer	.05	.02
☐ 616 Brian Holman	.05	.02
☐ 617 Geronimo Berroa	.10	.05
☐ 618 Ed Whitson	.05	.02
☐ 619 Rob Ducey	.05	.02
☐ 620 Tony Castillo	.05	.02
☐ 621 Melido Perez	.05	.02
☐ 622 Sid Bream	.05	.02
☐ 623 Jim Corsi	.05	.02
☐ 624 Darrin Jackson	.05	.02
☐ 625 Roger McDowell	.05	.02
☐ 626 Bob Melvin	.05	.02
☐ 627 Jose Rijo	.05	.02
☐ 628 Candy Maldonado	.05	.02
☐ 629 Eric Hetzel	.05	.02
☐ 630 Gary Gaetti	.10	.05
☐ 631 John Wetteland	.20	.09
☐ 632 Scott Lusader	.05	.02
☐ 633 Dennis Cook	.05	.02
☐ 634 Luis Polonia	.05	.02
☐ 635 Brian Downing	.05	.02
☐ 636 Jesse Orosco	.05	.02
☐ 637 Craig Reynolds	.05	.02
☐ 638 Jeff Montgomery	.10	.05
☐ 639 Tony LaRussa MG	.10	.05
☐ 640 Rick Sutcliffe	.05	.02
☐ 641 Doug Strange	.05	.02
☐ 642 Jack Armstrong	.05	.02
☐ 643 Alfredo Griffin	.05	.02
☐ 644 Paul Assenmacher	.05	.02
☐ 645 Jose Oquendo	.05	.02
☐ 646 Checklist 5	.05	.02
☐ 647 Rex Hudler	.05	.02
☐ 648 Jim Clancy	.05	.02
☐ 649 Dan Murphy	.05	.02
☐ 650 Mike Witt	.05	.02
☐ 651 Rafael Santana	.05	.02
☐ 652 Mike Boddicker	.05	.02
☐ 653 John Moses	.05	.02
☐ 654 Paul Coleman FDP	.05	.02
☐ 655 Gregg Olson	.05	.02
☐ 656 Mackey Sasser	.05	.02
☐ 657 Terry Mulholland	.05	.02
☐ 658 Donell Nixon	.05	.02
☐ 659 Greg Cadaret	.05	.02
☐ 660 Vince Coleman	.05	.02
☐ 661 Dick Howser TBC'85 UER (Seaver's 300th on 7/11/85, should be 8/4/85)	.05	.02
☐ 662 Mike Schmidt TBC'80	.20	.09
☐ 663 Fred Lynn TBC'75	.05	.02
☐ 664 Johnny Bench TBC'70	.20	.09
☐ 665 Sandy Koufax TBC'65	.25	.11
☐ 666 Brian Fisher	.05	.02
☐ 667 Curt Wilkerson	.05	.02
☐ 668 Joe Oliver	.05	.02
☐ 669 Tom Lasorda MG	.20	.09
☐ 670 Dennis Eckersley	.20	.09
☐ 671 Bob Boone	.10	.05
☐ 672 Roy Smith	.05	.02
☐ 673 Joey Meyer	.05	.02
☐ 674 Spike Owen	.05	.02
☐ 675 Jim Abbott	.10	.05
☐ 676 Randy Kutcher	.05	.02
☐ 677 Jay Tibbs	.05	.02
☐ 678 Kirt Manwaring UER ('88 Phoenix stats repeated)	.05	.02
☐ 679 Gary Ward	.05	.02
☐ 680 Howard Johnson	.05	.02
☐ 681 Mike Schooler	.05	.02
☐ 682 Dann Bilardello	.05	.02
☐ 683 Kenny Rogers	.10	.05
☐ 684 Julio Machado	.05	.02
☐ 685 Tony Fernandez	.05	.02
[illegible]86 Carmelo Martinez	.05	.02
[illegible] Tim Birtsas	.05	.02
[illegible]ilt Thompson	.05	.02
[illegible]h Yett	.05	.02
[illegible] McGwire	.40	.18
[illegible]ary	.05	.02
[illegible]osa	.75	.35
[illegible]aldi	.05	.02
[illegible]	.10	.05
[illegible]	.05	.02
☐ 696 B.J. Surhoff	.10	.05
☐ 697 Mike Davis	.05	.02
☐ 698 Omar Vizquel	.20	.09
☐ 699 Jim Leyland MG	.05	.02
☐ 700 Kirby Puckett	.40	.18
☐ 701 Bernie Williams	.75	.35
☐ 702 Tony Phillips	.05	.02
☐ 703 Jeff Brantley	.10	.05
☐ 704 Chip Hale	.05	.02
☐ 705 Claudell Washington	.05	.02
☐ 706 Geno Petralli	.05	.02
☐ 707 Luis Aquino	.05	.02
☐ 708 Larry Sheets	.05	.02
☐ 709 Juan Berenguer	.05	.02
☐ 710 Von Hayes	.05	.02
☐ 711 Rick Aguilera	.10	.05
☐ 712 Todd Benzinger	.05	.02
☐ 713 Tim Drummond	.05	.02
☐ 714 Marquis Grissom	.40	.18
☐ 715 Greg Maddux	.60	.25
☐ 716 Steve Balboni	.05	.02
☐ 717 Ron Karkovice	.05	.02
☐ 718 Gary Sheffield	.25	.11
☐ 719 Wally Whitehurst	.05	.02
☐ 720 Andres Galarraga	.20	.09
☐ 721 Lee Mazzilli	.05	.02
☐ 722 Felix Fermin	.05	.02
☐ 723 Jeff D. Robinson	.05	.02
☐ 724 Juan Bell	.05	.02
☐ 725 Terry Pendleton	.10	.05
☐ 726 Gene Nelson	.05	.02
☐ 727 Pat Tabler	.05	.02
☐ 728 Jim Acker	.05	.02
☐ 729 Bobby Valentine MG	.05	.02
☐ 730 Tony Gwynn	.50	.23
☐ 731 Don Carman	.05	.02
☐ 732 Ernest Riles	.05	.02
☐ 733 John Dopson	.05	.02
☐ 734 Kevin Elster	.05	.02
☐ 735 Charlie Hough	.05	.02
☐ 736 Rick Dempsey	.05	.02
☐ 737 Chris Sabo	.05	.02
☐ 738 Gene Harris	.05	.02
☐ 739 Dale Sveum	.05	.02
☐ 740 Jesse Barfield	.05	.02
☐ 741 Steve Wilson	.05	.02
☐ 742 Ernie Whitt	.05	.02
☐ 743 Tom Candiotti	.05	.02
☐ 744 Kelly Mann	.05	.02
☐ 745 Hubie Brooks	.05	.02
☐ 746 Dave Smith	.05	.02
☐ 747 Randy Bush	.05	.02
☐ 748 Doyle Alexander	.05	.02
☐ 749 Mark Parent UER ('87 BA .80, should be .080)	.05	.02
☐ 750 Dale Murphy	.20	.09
☐ 751 Steve Lyons	.05	.02
☐ 752 Tom Gordon	.05	.02
☐ 753 Chris Speier	.05	.02
☐ 754 Bob Walk	.05	.02
☐ 755 Rafael Palmeiro	.20	.09
☐ 756 Ken Howell	.05	.02
☐ 757 Larry Walker	1.00	.45
☐ 758 Mark Thurmond	.05	.02
☐ 759 Tom Trebelhorn MG	.05	.02
☐ 760 Wade Boggs	.20	.09
☐ 761 Mike Jackson	.05	.02
☐ 762 Doug Dascenzo	.05	.02
☐ 763 Dennis Martinez	.10	.05
☐ 764 Tim Teufel	.05	.02
☐ 765 Chili Davis	.10	.05
☐ 766 Brian Meyer	.05	.02
☐ 767 Tracy Jones	.05	.02
☐ 768 Chuck Crim	.05	.02
☐ 769 Greg Hibbard	.05	.02
☐ 770 Cory Snyder	.05	.02
☐ 771 Pete Smith	.05	.02
☐ 772 Jeff Reed	.05	.02
☐ 773 Dave Leiper	.05	.02
☐ 774 Ben McDonald	.20	.09
☐ 775 Andy Van Slyke	.10	.05
☐ 776 Charlie Leibrandt	.05	.02
☐ 777 Tim Laudner	.05	.02
☐ 778 Mike Jeffcoat	.05	.02
☐ 779 Lloyd Moseby	.05	.02
☐ 780 Orel Hershiser	.10	.05
☐ 781 Mario Diaz	.05	.02
☐ 782 Jose Alvarez	.05	.02
☐ 783 Checklist 6	.05	.02
☐ 784 Scott Bailes	.05	.02
☐ 785 Jim Rice	.10	.05
☐ 786 Eric King	.05	.02
☐ 787 Rene Gonzales	.05	.02
☐ 788 Frank DiPino	.05	.02
☐ 789 John Wathan MG	.05	.02
☐ 790 Gary Carter	.20	.09
☐ 791 Alvaro Espinoza	.05	.02
☐ 792 Gerald Perry	.05	.02

1990 Topps Tiffany

For the seventh year, Topps issued through its hobby dealer network a special "Tiffany" set. These sets which parallel the regular cards consist of 792 standard-size cards. These cards were only issued in complete set form. Since less cards were ordered than in the previous three years, the multiple on these cards are slightly higher than the preceeding sets.

	MINT	NRMT
COMPLETE FACT.SET (792)	75.00	34.00
COMMON CARD (1-792)	.10	.05
*STARS: 4X to 8X BASIC CARDS		
* ROOKIES: 3X to 6X BASIC CARDS		

1990 Topps Batting Leaders

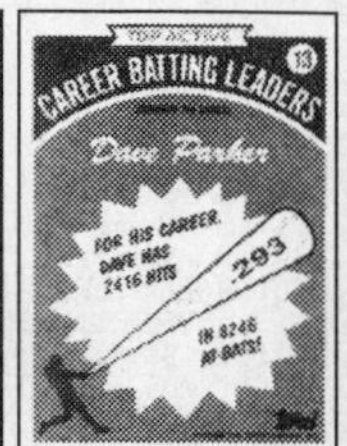

The 1990 Topps Batting Leaders set contains 22 standard-size cards. The front borders are emerald green, and the backs are white, blue and evergreen. This set, like the 1989 set of the same name, depicts the 22 major leaguers with the highest lifetime batting averages (minimum 765 games). The card numbers correspond to the player's rank in terms of career batting average. Many of the photos are the same as those from the 1989 set. The cards were distributed one per special Topps blister pack available only at K-Mart stores and were produced by Topps. The K-Mart logo does not appear anywhere on the cards themselves, although there is a Topps logo on the front and back of each card.

	MINT	NRMT
COMPLETE SET (22)	60.00	27.00
COMMON CARD (1-22)	.50	.23
☐ 1 Wade Boggs	4.00	1.80
☐ 2 Tony Gwynn	15.00	6.75
☐ 3 Kirby Puckett	12.50	5.50
☐ 4 Don Mattingly	10.00	4.50
☐ 5 George Brett	10.00	4.50
☐ 6 Pedro Guerrero	.50	.23
☐ 7 Tim Raines	1.00	.45
☐ 8 Paul Molitor	5.00	2.20
☐ 9 Jim Rice	1.00	.45
☐ 10 Keith Hernandez	1.00	.45
☐ 11 Julio Franco	1.00	.45
☐ 12 Carney Lansford	.50	.23
☐ 13 Dave Parker	1.00	.45
☐ 14 Willie McGee	.50	.23
☐ 15 Robin Yount	2.00	.90
☐ 16 Tony Fernandez	.50	.23
☐ 17 Eddie Murray	4.00	1.80
☐ 18 Johnny Ray	.50	.23
☐ 19 Lonnie Smith	.50	.23
☐ 20 Phil Bradley	.50	.23
☐ 21 Rickey Henderson	4.00	1.80
☐ 22 Kent Hrbek	1.00	.45

1990 Topps Glossy All-Stars

The 1990 Topps Glossy All-Star set contains 22 standard-size glossy cards. The front and back borders are white, and other design elements are red, blue and yellow. This set is almost identical to previous year sets of the same name. One card was included in each 1990 Topps rack pack. The players selected for the set were the starters, managers, and honorary captains in the previous year's All-Star Game.

	MINT	NRMT
COMPLETE SET (22)	3.00	1.35
COMMON CARD (1-22)	.05	.02

	MINT	NRMT
☐ 1 Tom Lasorda MG	.05	.02
☐ 2 Will Clark	.30	.14
☐ 3 Ryne Sandberg	.60	.25
☐ 4 Howard Johnson	.05	.02
☐ 5 Ozzie Smith	.60	.25
☐ 6 Kevin Mitchell	.05	.02
☐ 7 Eric Davis	.05	.02
☐ 8 Tony Gwynn	.75	.35
☐ 9 Benito Santiago	.05	.02
☐ 10 Rick Reuschel	.05	.02
☐ 11 Don Drysdale CAPT	.15	.07
☐ 12 Tony LaRussa MG	.05	.02
☐ 13 Mark McGwire	.50	.23
☐ 14 Julio Franco	.05	.02
☐ 15 Wade Boggs	.30	.14
☐ 16 Cal Ripken	1.50	.70
☐ 17 Bo Jackson	.10	.05
☐ 18 Kirby Puckett	.75	.35
☐ 19 Ruben Sierra	.05	.02
☐ 20 Terry Steinbach	.10	.05
☐ 21 Dave Stewart	.05	.02
☐ 22 Carl Yastrzemski CAPT	.25	.11

1990 Topps Glossy Send-Ins

The 1990 Topps Glossy 60 set was issued as a mailaway by Topps for the eighth straight year. This standard-size, 60-card set features two young players among every ten players as Topps again broke down these cards into six series of ten cards each.

	MINT	NRMT
COMPLETE SET (60)	10.00	4.50
COMMON CARD (1-60)	.10	.05

	MINT	NRMT
☐ 1 Ryne Sandberg	1.25	.55
☐ 2 Nolan Ryan	2.50	1.10
☐ 3 Glenn Davis	.10	.05
☐ 4 Dave Stewart	.20	.09
☐ 5 Barry Larkin	.35	.16
☐ 6 Carney Lansford	.20	.09
☐ 7 Darryl Strawberry	.20	.09
☐ 8 Steve Sax	.10	.05
☐ 9 Carlos Martinez	.10	.05
☐ 10 Gary Sheffield	1.00	.45
☐ 11 Don Mattingly	1.50	.70
☐ 12 Mark Grace	.75	.35
☐ 13 Bret Saberhagen	.10	.05
☐ 14 Mike Scott	.10	.05
☐ 15 Robin Yount	.35	.16
☐ 16 Ozzie Smith	1.25	.55
☐ 17 Jeff Ballard	.10	.05
☐ 18 Rick Reuschel	.10	.05
☐ 19 Greg Briley	.10	.05
☐ 20 Ken Griffey Jr.	4.00	1.80
☐ 21 Kevin Mitchell	.20	.09
☐ 22 Wade Boggs	.60	.25
☐ 23 Dwight Gooden	.20	.09
☐ 24 George Bell	.10	.05
☐ 25 Eric Davis	.20	.09
☐ 26 Ruben Sierra	.10	.05
☐ 27 Roberto Alomar	.60	.25
☐ 28 Gary Gaetti	.20	.09
☐ 29 Gregg Olson	.10	.05
☐ 30 Tom Gordon	.10	.05
☐ 31 Jose Canseco	.60	.25
☐ 32 Pedro Guerrero	.10	.05
☐ 33 Joe Carter	.35	.16
☐ 34 Mike Scioscia	.10	.05
☐ 35 Julio Franco	.20	.09
☐ 36 Joe Magrane	.10	.05
☐ 37 Rickey Henderson	.60	.25
☐ 38 Tim Raines	.20	.09
☐ 39 Jerome Walton	.10	.05
☐ 40 Bob Geren	.10	.05
☐ 41 Andre Dawson	.35	.16
☐ 42 Mark McGwire	1.25	.55
☐ 43 Howard Johnson	.10	.05
☐ 44 Bo Jackson	.20	.09
☐ 45 Shawon Dunston	.10	.05
☐ 46 Carlton Fisk	.35	.16
☐ 47 Mitch Williams	.10	.05
☐ 48 Kirby Puckett	1.50	.70
☐ 49 Craig Worthington	.10	.05
☐ 50 Jim Abbott	.20	.09
☐ 51 Cal Ripken	3.00	1.35
☐ 52 Will Clark	.35	.16
☐ 53 Dennis Eckersley	.35	.16
☐ 54 Craig Biggio	.50	.23
☐ 55 Fred McGriff	.35	.16
☐ 56 Tony Gwynn	2.00	.90
☐ 57 Mickey Tettleton	.10	.05
☐ 58 Mark Davis	.10	.05
☐ 59 Omar Vizquel	.20	.09
☐ 60 Gregg Jefferies	.20	.09

1990 Topps Rookies

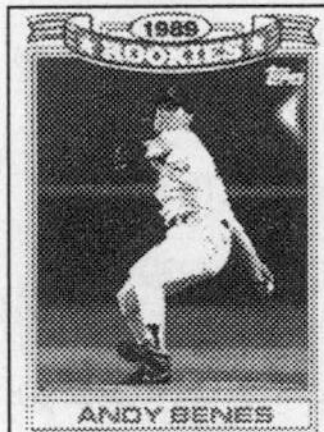

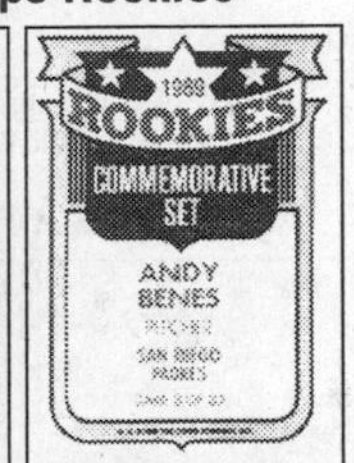

The 1990 Topps Jumbo Rookies set contains 33 standard-size glossy cards. The front and back borders are white, and other design elements are red, blue and yellow. This set is almost identical to previous year sets of the same name except that it contains 33 cards rather than only 22. One card was included in each 1990 Topps "jumbo" pack. The cards are numbered in alphabetical order. Sets of these cards were issued and stamped with various colors so Topps could test for colors of foil stamping.

	MINT	NRMT
COMPLETE SET (33)	5.00	2.20
COMMON CARD (1-33)	.05	.02

	MINT	NRMT
☐ 1 Jim Abbott	.10	.05
☐ 2 Joey Belle	1.00	.45
☐ 3 Andy Benes	.15	.07
☐ 4 Greg Briley	.05	.02
☐ 5 Kevin Brown	.25	.11
☐ 6 Mark Carreon	.05	.02
☐ 7 Mike Devereaux	.05	.02
☐ 8 Junior Felix	.05	.02
☐ 9 Bob Geren	.05	.02
☐ 10 Tom Gordon	.10	.05
☐ 11 Ken Griffey Jr.	3.00	1.35
☐ 12 Pete Harnisch	.05	.02
☐ 13 Greg W. Harris	.05	.02
☐ 14 Greg Hibbard	.05	.02
☐ 15 Ken Hill	.15	.07
☐ 16 Gregg Jefferies	.10	.05
☐ 17 Jeff King	.15	.07
☐ 18 Derek Lilliquist	.05	.02
☐ 19 Carlos Martinez	.05	.02
☐ 20 Ramon Martinez	.25	.11
☐ 21 Bob Milacki	.05	.02
☐ 22 Gregg Olson	.05	.02
☐ 23 Donn Pall	.05	.02
☐ 24 Kenny Rogers	.10	.05
☐ 25 Gary Sheffield	.75	.35
☐ 26 Dwight Smith	.05	.02
☐ 27 Billy Spiers	.05	.02
☐ 28 Omar Vizquel	.25	.11
☐ 29 Jerome Walton	.05	.02
☐ 30 Dave West	.05	.02
☐ 31 John Wetteland	.25	.11
☐ 32 Steve Wilson	.05	.02
☐ 33 Craig Worthington	.05	.02

1990 Topps Wax Box Cards

The 1990 Topps wax box cards comprise four different box bottoms with four cards each, for a total of 16 standard-size cards. The front borders are green. The vertically oriented backs are yellowish green. These cards depict various career milestones achieved during the 1989 season. The card numbers are actually the letters A through P. The card ordering is alphabetical by player's name.

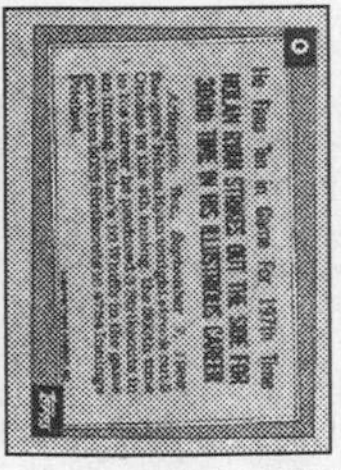

	MINT	NRMT
COMPLETE SET (16)	8.00	3.60
COMMON CARD (A-P)	.10	.05

	MINT	NRMT
☐ A Wade Boggs	.75	.35
☐ B George Brett	1.00	.45
☐ C Andre Dawson	.50	.23
☐ D Darrell Evans	.10	.05
☐ E Dwight Gooden	.25	.11
☐ F Rickey Henderson	.75	.35
☐ G Tom Lasorda MG	.50	.23
☐ H Fred Lynn	.10	.05
☐ I Mark McGwire	1.00	.45
☐ J Dave Parker	.25	.11
☐ K Jeff Reardon	.10	.05
☐ L Rick Reuschel	.10	.05
☐ M Jim Rice	.25	.11
☐ N Cal Ripken	2.50	1.10
☐ O Nolan Ryan	2.50	1.10
☐ P Ryne Sandberg	1.00	.45

1990 Topps Traded

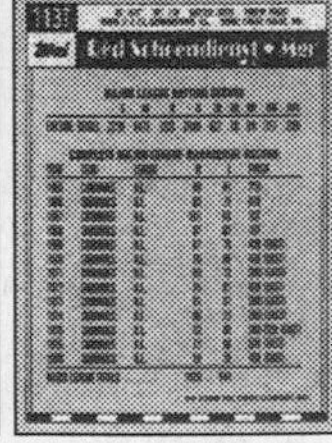

The 1990 Topps Traded Set was the tenth consecutive year Topps issued a 132-card standard-size set at the end of the year. For the first time, Topps not only issued the set in factory set form but also distributed (on a significant basis) the set via 7-card wax packs. Unlike the factory set cards (which feature the whiter paper stock typical of the previous years Traded sets), the wax pack cards feature gray paper stock. Gray and white stock cards are equally valued. This set was arranged alphabetically by player and includes a mix of traded players and rookies for whom Topps did not include a card in the regular set. The key Rookie Cards in this set are Carlos Baerga, Travis Fryman, Todd Hundley and Dave Justice.

	MINT	NRMT
COMPLETE SET (132)	3.00	1.35
COMPLETE FACT.SET (132)	3.00	1.35
COMMON CARD (1T-132T)	.05	.02

	MINT	NRMT
☐ 1T Darrel Akerfelds	.05	.02
☐ 2T Sandy Alomar Jr.	.20	.09
☐ 3T Brad Arnsberg	.05	.02
☐ 4T Steve Avery	.20	.09
☐ 5T Wally Backman	.05	.02
☐ 6T Carlos Baerga	.25	.11
☐ 7T Kevin Bass	.05	.02
☐ 8T Willie Blair	.05	.02
☐ 9T Mike Blowers	.20	.09
☐ 10T Shawn Boskie	.05	.02
☐ 11T Daryl Boston	.05	.02
☐ 12T Dennis Boyd	.05	.02
☐ 13T Glenn Braggs	.05	.02
☐ 14T Hubie Brooks	.05	.02
☐ 15T Tom Brunansky	.05	.02
☐ 16T John Burkett	.10	.05
☐ 17T Casey Candaele	.05	.0
☐ 18T John Candelaria	.05	
☐ 19T Gary Carter	.20	
☐ 20T Joe Carter	.10	
☐ 21T Rick Cerone	.05	
☐ 22T Scott Coolbaugh	.05	
☐ 23T Bobby Cox MG	.05	
☐ 24T Mark Davis	.05	
☐ 25T Storm Davis	.05	

Card	MINT	NRMT
☐ 26T Edgar Diaz	.05	.02
☐ 27T Wayne Edwards	.05	.02
☐ 28T Mark Eichhorn	.05	.02
☐ 29T Scott Erickson	.25	.11
☐ 30T Nick Esasky	.05	.02
☐ 31T Cecil Fielder	.10	.05
☐ 32T John Franco	.05	.02
☐ 33T Travis Fryman	.40	.18
☐ 34T Bill Gullickson	.05	.02
☐ 35T Darryl Hamilton	.05	.02
☐ 36T Mike Harkey	.05	.02
☐ 37T Bud Harrelson MG	.05	.02
☐ 38T Billy Hatcher	.05	.02
☐ 39T Keith Hernandez	.10	.05
☐ 40T Joe Hesketh	.05	.02
☐ 41T Dave Hollins	.20	.09
☐ 42T Sam Horn	.05	.02
☐ 43T Steve Howard	.05	.02
☐ 44T Todd Hundley	.40	.18
☐ 45T Jeff Huson	.05	.02
☐ 46T Chris James	.05	.02
☐ 47T Stan Javier	.05	.02
☐ 48T Dave Justice	.75	.35
☐ 49T Jeff Kaiser	.05	.02
☐ 50T Dana Kiecker	.05	.02
☐ 51T Joe Klink	.05	.02
☐ 52T Brent Knackert	.05	.02
☐ 53T Brad Komminsk	.05	.02
☐ 54T Mark Langston	.05	.02
☐ 55T Tim Layana	.05	.02
☐ 56T Rick Leach	.05	.02
☐ 57T Terry Leach	.05	.02
☐ 58T Tim Leary	.05	.02
☐ 59T Craig Lefferts	.05	.02
☐ 60T Charlie Leibrandt	.05	.02
☐ 61T Jim Leyritz	.20	.09
☐ 62T Fred Lynn	.05	.02
☐ 63T Kevin Maas	.10	.05
☐ 64T Shane Mack	.05	.02
☐ 65T Candy Maldonado	.05	.02
☐ 66T Fred Manrique	.05	.02
☐ 67T Mike Marshall	.05	.02
☐ 68T Carmelo Martinez	.05	.02
☐ 69T John Marzano	.05	.02
☐ 70T Ben McDonald	.10	.05
☐ 71T Jack McDowell	.20	.09
☐ 72T John McNamara MG	.05	.02
☐ 73T Orlando Mercado	.05	.02
☐ 74T Stump Merrill MG	.05	.02
☐ 75T Alan Mills	.05	.02
☐ 76T Hal Morris	.10	.05
☐ 77T Lloyd Moseby	.05	.02
☐ 78T Randy Myers	.10	.05
☐ 79T Tim Naehring	.20	.09
☐ 80T Junior Noboa	.05	.02
☐ 81T Matt Nokes	.05	.02
☐ 82T Pete O'Brien	.05	.02
☐ 83T John Olerud	.20	.09
☐ 84T Greg Olson	.05	.02
☐ 85T Junior Ortiz	.05	.02
☐ 86T Dave Parker	.10	.05
☐ 87T Rick Parker	.05	.02
☐ 88T Bob Patterson	.05	.02
☐ 89T Alejandro Pena	.05	.02
☐ 90T Tony Pena	.05	.02
☐ 91T Pascual Perez	.05	.02
☐ 92T Gerald Perry	.05	.02
☐ 93T Dan Petry	.05	.02
☐ 94T Gary Pettis	.05	.02
☐ 95T Tony Phillips	.05	.02
☐ 96T Lou Piniella MG	.10	.05
☐ 97T Luis Polonia	.05	.02
☐ 98T Jim Presley	.05	.02
☐ 99T Scott Radinsky	.05	.02
☐ 100T Willie Randolph	.10	.05
☐ 101T Jeff Reardon	.10	.05
☐ 102T Greg Riddoch MG	.05	.02
☐ 103T Jeff Robinson	.05	.02
☐ 104T Ron Robinson	.05	.02
☐ 105T Kevin Romine	.05	.02
☐ 106T Scott Ruskin	.05	.02
☐ 107T John Russell	.05	.02
☐ 108T Bill Sampen	.05	.02
☐ 109T Juan Samuel	.05	.02
☐ 110T Scott Sanderson	.05	.02
☐ 111T Jack Savage	.05	.02
112T Dave Schmidt	.05	.02
3T Red Schoendienst MG	.20	.09
Terry Shumpert	.05	.02
Matt Sinatro	.05	.02
Slaught	.05	.02
Smith	.05	.02
ith	.10	.05
ento	.20	.09
bbs UER	.05	.02
d has		
'89,		
'83 stats are missing)		
☐ 121T Russ Swan	.05	.02
☐ 122T Bob Tewksbury	.05	.02
☐ 123T Wayne Tolleson	.05	.02
☐ 124T John Tudor	.05	.02
☐ 125T Randy Veres	.05	.02
☐ 126T Hector Villanueva	.05	.02
☐ 127T Mitch Webster	.05	.02
☐ 128T Ernie Whitt	.05	.02
☐ 129T Frank Wills	.05	.02
☐ 130T Dave Winfield	.20	.09
☐ 131T Matt Young	.05	.02
☐ 132T Checklist 1T-132T	.05	.02

1990 Topps Traded Tiffany

Again, one of these sets were issued for each regular Tiffany set produced. These 132 standard-size cards parallel the regular Traded issue and feature Glossy fronts and clearer backs. These cards were issued in complete set form only and were distributed through Topps hobby network.

	MINT	NRMT
COMPLETE FACT.SET (132)	15.00	6.75
COMMON CARD (1T-132T)	.10	.05
*STARS: 4X to 8X BASIC CARDS		
*ROOKIES: 3X to 6X BASIC CARDS		

1990 Topps Ames All-Stars

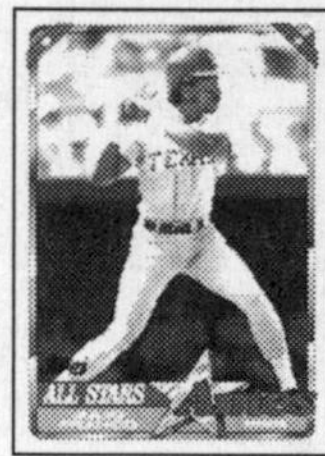

The 1990 Topps Ames All-Stars set was issued by Topps for the Ames department stores for the second straight year. This standard-size set featured 33 of the leading hitters active in major league baseball.

	MINT	NRMT
COMPLETE SET (33)	5.00	2.20
COMMON CARD (1-33)	.05	.02
☐ 1 Dave Winfield	.30	.14
☐ 2 George Brett	.75	.35
☐ 3 Jim Rice	.10	.05
☐ 4 Dwight Evans	.10	.05
☐ 5 Robin Yount	.25	.11
☐ 6 Dave Parker	.10	.05
☐ 7 Eddie Murray	.30	.14
☐ 8 Keith Hernandez	.10	.05
☐ 9 Andre Dawson	.25	.11
☐ 10 Fred Lynn	.05	.02
☐ 11 Dale Murphy	.15	.07
☐ 12 Jack Clark	.10	.05
☐ 13 Rickey Henderson	.50	.23
☐ 14 Paul Molitor	.40	.18
☐ 15 Cal Ripken	2.00	.90
☐ 16 Wade Boggs	.25	.11
☐ 17 Tim Raines	.10	.05
☐ 18 Don Mattingly	1.00	.45
☐ 19 Kent Hrbek	.10	.05
☐ 20 Kirk Gibson	.10	.05
☐ 21 Julio Franco	.10	.05
☐ 22 George Bell	.05	.02
☐ 23 Darryl Strawberry	.10	.05
☐ 24 Kirby Puckett	1.00	.45
☐ 25 Juan Samuel	.05	.02
☐ 26 Alvin Davis	.05	.02
☐ 27 Joe Carter	.10	.05
☐ 28 Eric Davis	.10	.05
☐ 29 Jose Canseco	.40	.18
☐ 30 Wally Joyner	.10	.05
☐ 31 Will Clark	.30	.14
☐ 32 Ruben Sierra	.05	.02
☐ 33 Danny Tartabull	.05	.02

1990 Topps Big

The 1990 Topps Big set contains 330 cards each measuring a slightly over-sized 2 5/8" by 3 3/4". In 1989 Topps had issued two oversize sets (Bigs and Bowmans), but in 1990 only the Topps Big were issued by Topps as an oversize set. The set was issued in three series of 110 cards. Some dealers believe the third series was distributed in far less quantity than the first two series.

	MINT	NRMT
COMPLETE SET (330)	20.00	9.00
COMMON CARD (1-330)	.05	.02
☐ 1 Dwight Evans	.10	.05
☐ 2 Kirby Puckett	2.50	1.10
☐ 3 Kevin Gross	.05	.02
☐ 4 Ron Hassey	.05	.02
☐ 5 Lloyd McClendon	.05	.02
☐ 6 Bo Jackson	.10	.05
☐ 7 Lonnie Smith	.05	.02
☐ 8 Alvaro Espinoza	.05	.02
☐ 9 Roberto Alomar	.50	.23
☐ 10 Glenn Braggs	.05	.02
☐ 11 David Cone	.15	.07
☐ 12 Claudell Washington	.05	.02
☐ 13 Pedro Guerrero	.05	.02
☐ 14 Todd Benzinger	.05	.02
☐ 15 Jeff Russell	.05	.02
☐ 16 Terry Kennedy	.05	.02
☐ 17 Kelly Gruber	.05	.02
☐ 18 Alfredo Griffin	.05	.02
☐ 19 Mark Grace	.60	.25
☐ 20 Dave Winfield	.60	.25
☐ 21 Bret Saberhagen	.10	.05
☐ 22 Roger Clemens	1.25	.55
☐ 23 Bob Walk	.05	.02
☐ 24 Dave Magadan	.05	.02
☐ 25 Spike Owen	.05	.02
☐ 26 Jody Davis	.05	.02
☐ 27 Kent Hrbek	.10	.05
☐ 28 Mark McGwire	1.50	.70
☐ 29 Eddie Murray	1.00	.45
☐ 30 Paul O'Neill	.10	.05
☐ 31 Jose DeLeon	.05	.02
☐ 32 Steve Lyons	.05	.02
☐ 33 Dan Plesac	.05	.02
☐ 34 Jack Howell	.05	.02
☐ 35 Greg Briley	.05	.02
☐ 36 Andy Hawkins	.05	.02
☐ 37 Cecil Espy	.05	.02
☐ 38 Rick Sutcliffe	.05	.02
☐ 39 Jack Clark	.05	.02
☐ 40 Dale Murphy	.50	.23
☐ 41 Mike Henneman	.05	.02
☐ 42 Rick Honeycutt	.05	.02
☐ 43 Willie Randolph	.10	.05
☐ 44 Marty Barrett	.05	.02
☐ 45 Willie Wilson	.05	.02
☐ 46 Wallace Johnson	.05	.02
☐ 47 Greg Brock	.05	.02
☐ 48 Tom Browning	.05	.02
☐ 49 Gerald Young	.05	.02
☐ 50 Dennis Eckersley	.15	.07
☐ 51 Scott Garrelts	.05	.02
☐ 52 Gary Redus	.05	.02
☐ 53 Al Newman	.05	.02
☐ 54 Daryl Boston	.05	.02
☐ 55 Ron Oester	.05	.02
☐ 56 Danny Tartabull	.10	.05
☐ 57 Gregg Jefferies	.10	.05
☐ 58 Tom Foley	.05	.02
☐ 59 Robin Yount	.25	.11
☐ 60 Pat Borders	.05	.02
☐ 61 Mike Greenwell	.10	.05
☐ 62 Shawon Dunston	.05	.02
☐ 63 Steve Buechele	.05	.02
☐ 64 Dave Stewart	.10	.05
☐ 65 Jose Oquendo	.05	.02
☐ 66 Ron Gant	.15	.07
☐ 67 Mike Scioscia	.05	.02
☐ 68 Randy Velarde	.05	.02
☐ 69 Von Hayes	.05	.02
☐ 70 Tim Wallach	.05	.02
☐ 71 Eric Show	.05	.02
☐ 72 Eric Davis	.10	.05
☐ 73 Mike Gallego	.05	.02
☐ 74 Rob Deer	.05	.02
☐ 75 Ryne Sandberg	1.50	.70
☐ 76 Kevin Seitzer	.10	.05
☐ 77 Wade Boggs	.60	.25
☐ 78 Greg Gagne	.05	.02
☐ 79 John Smiley	.05	.02

☐ 80 Ivan Calderon .05 .02
☐ 81 Pete Incaviglia .05 .02
☐ 82 Orel Hershiser .10 .05
☐ 83 Carney Lansford .05 .02
☐ 84 Mike Fitzgerald .05 .02
☐ 85 Don Mattingly 2.50 1.10
☐ 86 Chet Lemon .05 .02
☐ 87 Rolando Roomes .05 .02
☐ 88 Billy Spiers .05 .02
☐ 89 Pat Tabler .05 .02
☐ 90 Danny Heep .05 .02
☐ 91 Andre Dawson .50 .23
☐ 92 Randy Bush .05 .02
☐ 93 Tony Gwynn 2.50 1.10
☐ 94 Tom Brunansky .05 .02
☐ 95 Johnny Ray .05 .02
☐ 96 Matt Williams .60 .25
☐ 97 Barry Lyons .05 .02
☐ 98 Jeff Hamilton .05 .02
☐ 99 Tom Glavine .50 .23
☐ 100 Ken Griffey Sr. .10 .05
☐ 101 Tom Henke .10 .05
☐ 102 Dave Righetti .05 .02
☐ 103 Paul Molitor 1.00 .45
☐ 104 Mike LaValliere .05 .02
☐ 105 Frank White .10 .05
☐ 106 Bob Welch .10 .05
☐ 107 Ellis Burks .25 .11
☐ 108 Andres Galarraga .50 .23
☐ 109 Mitch Williams .05 .02
☐ 110 Checklist 1-110 .05 .02
☐ 111 Craig Biggio .40 .18
☐ 112 Dave Stieb .05 .02
☐ 113 Ron Darling .05 .02
☐ 114 Bert Blyleven .10 .05
☐ 115 Dickie Thon .05 .02
☐ 116 Carlos Martinez .05 .02
☐ 117 Jeff King .15 .07
☐ 118 Terry Steinbach .10 .05
☐ 119 Frank Tanana .05 .02
☐ 120 Mark Lemke .05 .02
☐ 121 Chris Sabo .05 .02
☐ 122 Glenn Davis .05 .02
☐ 123 Mel Hall .05 .02
☐ 124 Jim Gantner .05 .02
☐ 125 Benito Santiago .05 .02
☐ 126 Milt Thompson .05 .02
☐ 127 Rafael Palmeiro .50 .23
☐ 128 Barry Bonds .75 .35
☐ 129 Mike Bielecki .05 .02
☐ 130 Lou Whitaker .10 .05
☐ 131 Bob Ojeda .05 .02
☐ 132 Dion James .05 .02
☐ 133 Dennis Martinez .10 .05
☐ 134 Fred McGriff .50 .23
☐ 135 Terry Pendleton .10 .05
☐ 136 Pat Combs .05 .02
☐ 137 Kevin Mitchell .10 .05
☐ 138 Marquis Grissom .75 .35
☐ 139 Chris Bosio .05 .02
☐ 140 Omar Vizquel .15 .07
☐ 141 Steve Sax .05 .02
☐ 142 Nelson Liriano .05 .02
☐ 143 Kevin Elster .05 .02
☐ 144 Dan Pasqua .05 .02
☐ 145 Dave Smith .05 .02
☐ 146 Craig Worthington .05 .02
☐ 147 Dan Gladden .05 .02
☐ 148 Oddibe McDowell .05 .02
☐ 149 Bip Roberts .10 .05
☐ 150 Randy Ready .05 .02
☐ 151 Dwight Smith .05 .02
☐ 152 Eddie Whitson .05 .02
☐ 153 George Bell .05 .02
☐ 154 Tim Raines .15 .07
☐ 155 Sid Fernandez .05 .02
☐ 156 Henry Cotto .05 .02
☐ 157 Harold Baines .10 .05
☐ 158 Willie McGee .10 .05
☐ 159 Bill Doran .05 .02
☐ 160 Steve Balboni .05 .02
☐ 161 Pete Smith .05 .02
☐ 162 Frank Viola .05 .02
☐ 163 Gary Sheffield .75 .35
☐ 164 Bill Landrum .05 .02
☐ 165 Tony Fernandez .05 .02
☐ 166 Mike Heath .05 .02
☐ 167 Jody Reed .05 .02
☐ 168 Wally Joyner .10 .05
☐ 169 Robby Thompson .05 .02
☐ 170 Ken Caminiti .50 .23
☐ 171 Nolan Ryan 4.00 1.80
☐ 172 Ricky Jordan .05 .02
☐ 173 Lance Blankenship .05 .02
☐ 174 Dwight Gooden .10 .05
☐ 175 Ruben Sierra .05 .02
☐ 176 Carlton Fisk .50 .23
☐ 177 Garry Templeton .05 .02
☐ 178 Mike Devereaux .05 .02
☐ 179 Mookie Wilson .05 .02
☐ 180 Jeff Blauser .05 .02
☐ 181 Scott Bradley .05 .02
☐ 182 Luis Salazar .05 .02
☐ 183 Rafael Ramirez .05 .02
☐ 184 Vince Coleman .05 .02
☐ 185 Doug Drabek .05 .02
☐ 186 Darryl Strawberry .10 .05
☐ 187 Tim Burke .05 .02
☐ 188 Jesse Barfield .05 .02
☐ 189 Barry Larkin .50 .23
☐ 190 Alan Trammell .15 .07
☐ 191 Steve Lake .05 .02
☐ 192 Derek Lilliquist .05 .02
☐ 193 Don Robinson .05 .02
☐ 194 Kevin McReynolds .05 .02
☐ 195 Melido Perez .05 .02
☐ 196 Jose Lind .05 .02
☐ 197 Eric Anthony .05 .02
☐ 198 B.J. Surhoff .10 .05
☐ 199 John Olerud .75 .35
☐ 200 Mike Moore .05 .02
☐ 201 Mark Gubicza .05 .02
☐ 202 Phil Bradley .05 .02
☐ 203 Ozzie Smith 1.50 .70
☐ 204 Greg Maddux 2.50 1.10
☐ 205 Julio Franco .10 .05
☐ 206 Tom Herr .05 .02
☐ 207 Scott Fletcher .05 .02
☐ 208 Bobby Bonilla .10 .05
☐ 209 Bob Geren .05 .02
☐ 210 Junior Felix .05 .02
☐ 211 Dick Schofield .05 .02
☐ 212 Jim Deshaies .05 .02
☐ 213 Jose Uribe .05 .02
☐ 214 John Kruk .10 .05
☐ 215 Ozzie Guillen .10 .05
☐ 216 Howard Johnson .05 .02
☐ 217 Andy Van Slyke .10 .05
☐ 218 Tim Laudner .05 .02
☐ 219 Manny Lee .05 .02
☐ 220 Checklist 111-220 .05 .02
☐ 221 Cory Snyder .05 .02
☐ 222 Billy Hatcher .05 .02
☐ 223 Bud Black .05 .02
☐ 224 Will Clark .60 .25
☐ 225 Kevin Tapani .25 .11
☐ 226 Mike Pagliarulo .05 .02
☐ 227 Dave Parker .10 .05
☐ 228 Ben McDonald .25 .11
☐ 229 Carlos Baerga .40 .18
☐ 230 Roger McDowell .05 .02
☐ 231 Delino DeShields .25 .11
☐ 232 Mark Langston .05 .02
☐ 233 Wally Backman .05 .02
☐ 234 Jim Eisenreich .10 .05
☐ 235 Mike Schooler .05 .02
☐ 236 Kevin Bass .05 .02
☐ 237 John Farrell .05 .02
☐ 238 Kal Daniels .05 .02
☐ 239 Tony Phillips .05 .02
☐ 240 Todd Stottlemyre .05 .02
☐ 241 Greg Olson .05 .02
☐ 242 Charlie Hough .05 .02
☐ 243 Mariano Duncan .05 .02
☐ 244 Bill Ripken .05 .02
☐ 245 Joe Carter .40 .18
☐ 246 Tim Belcher .05 .02
☐ 247 Roberto Kelly .05 .02
☐ 248 Candy Maldonado .05 .02
☐ 249 Mike Scott .05 .02
☐ 250 Ken Griffey Jr. 6.00 2.70
☐ 251 Nick Esasky .05 .02
☐ 252 Tom Gordon .10 .05
☐ 253 John Tudor .05 .02
☐ 254 Gary Gaetti .10 .05
☐ 255 Neal Heaton .05 .02
☐ 256 Jerry Browne .05 .02
☐ 257 Jose Rijo .05 .02
☐ 258 Mike Boddicker .05 .02
☐ 259 Brett Butler .10 .05
☐ 260 Andy Benes .10 .05
☐ 261 Kevin Brown .10 .05
☐ 262 Hubie Brooks .05 .02
☐ 263 Randy Milligan .05 .02
☐ 264 John Franco .10 .05
☐ 265 Sandy Alomar Jr. .15 .07
☐ 266 Dave Valle .05 .02
☐ 267 Jerome Walton .05 .02
☐ 268 Bob Boone .10 .05
☐ 269 Ken Howell .05 .02
☐ 270 Jose Canseco .60 .25
☐ 271 Joe Magrane .05 .02
☐ 272 Brian DuBois .05 .02
☐ 273 Carlos Quintana .05 .02
☐ 274 Lance Johnson .05 .02
☐ 275 Steve Bedrosian .05 .02
☐ 276 Brook Jacoby .05 .02
☐ 277 Fred Lynn UER .10 .05
(Pirates logo
on card front)
☐ 278 Jeff Ballard .05 .02
☐ 279 Otis Nixon .10 .05
☐ 280 Chili Davis .10 .05
☐ 281 Joe Oliver .05 .02
☐ 282 Brian Holman .05 .02
☐ 283 Juan Samuel .05 .02
☐ 284 Rick Aguilera .10 .05
☐ 285 Jeff Reardon .10 .05
☐ 286 Sammy Sosa 1.50 .70
☐ 287 Carmelo Martinez .05 .02
☐ 288 Greg Swindell .05 .02
☐ 289 Erik Hanson .05 .02
☐ 290 Tony Pena .05 .02
☐ 291 Pascual Perez .05 .02
☐ 292 Rickey Henderson .75 .35
☐ 293 Kurt Stillwell .05 .02
☐ 294 Todd Zeile .10 .05
☐ 295 Bobby Thigpen .05 .02
☐ 296 Larry Walker 1.25 .55
☐ 297 Rob Murphy .05 .02
☐ 298 Mitch Webster .05 .02
☐ 299 Devon White .10 .05
☐ 300 Len Dykstra .10 .05
☐ 301 Keith Hernandez .10 .05
☐ 302 Gene Larkin .05 .02
☐ 303 Jeffrey Leonard .05 .02
☐ 304 Jim Presley .05 .02
☐ 305 Lloyd Moseby .05 .02
☐ 306 John Smoltz .50 .23
☐ 307 Sam Horn .05 .02
☐ 308 Greg Litton .05 .02
☐ 309 Dave Henderson .05 .02
☐ 310 Mark McLemore .05 .02
☐ 311 Gary Pettis .05 .02
☐ 312 Mark Davis .05 .02
☐ 313 Cecil Fielder .25 .11
☐ 314 Jack Armstrong .05 .02
☐ 315 Alvin Davis .05 .02
☐ 316 Doug Jones .05 .02
☐ 317 Eric Yelding .05 .02
☐ 318 Joe Orsulak .05 .02
☐ 319 Chuck Finley .10 .05
☐ 320 Glenn Wilson .05 .02
☐ 321 Harold Reynolds .10 .05
☐ 322 Teddy Higuera .05 .02
☐ 323 Lance Parrish .05 .02
☐ 324 Bruce Hurst .05 .02
☐ 325 Dave West .05 .02
☐ 326 Kirk Gibson .10 .05
☐ 327 Cal Ripken 4.00 1.80
☐ 328 Rick Reuschel .05 .02
☐ 329 Jim Abbott .10 .05
☐ 330 Checklist 221-330 .05 .02

1990 Topps Coins

The 1989 Topps Coins set contains 60 coins, each measuring approximately 1 1/2" in diameter. The coins were issued in packs of three coins. The set is arranged by league order with the Most Valuable Player, Cy Young Award Winner, Rookie of the Year and Batting Leaders being first, then the rest of the league being arranged alphabetically within the league group. The American League players are 1-32 and the National League players are 33-60.

	MINT	NRMT
COMPLETE SET (60)	8.00	3.60
COMMON COIN (1-60)	.05	.02

☐ 1 Robin Yount .25 .11
☐ 2 Bret Saberhagen .05 .02
☐ 3 Gregg Olson .05 .02
☐ 4 Kirby Puckett 1.50 .70
☐ 5 George Bell .05 .02
☐ 6 Wade Boggs .40 .18
☐ 7 Jerry Browne .05 .02
☐ 8 Ellis Burks .15 .07
☐ 9 Ivan Calderon .05 .02
☐ 10 Tom Candiotti .05 .02

Card	MINT	NRMT
☐ 11 Alvin Davis	.05	.02
☐ 12 Chili Davis	.10	.05
☐ 13 Chuck Finley	.05	.02
☐ 14 Gary Gaetti	.10	.05
☐ 15 Tom Gordon	.05	.02
☐ 16 Ken Griffey Jr.	3.00	1.35
☐ 17 Rickey Henderson	.40	.18
☐ 18 Kent Hrbek	.10	.05
☐ 19 Bo Jackson	.10	.05
☐ 20 Carlos Martinez	.05	.02
☐ 21 Don Mattingly	1.50	.70
☐ 22 Fred McGriff	.50	.23
☐ 23 Paul Molitor	.75	.35
☐ 24 Cal Ripken	2.50	1.10
☐ 25 Nolan Ryan	2.50	1.10
☐ 26 Steve Sax	.05	.02
☐ 27 Gary Sheffield	1.00	.45
☐ 28 Ruben Sierra	.05	.02
☐ 29 Dave Stewart	.05	.02
☐ 30 Mickey Tettleton	.05	.02
☐ 31 Alan Trammell	.15	.07
☐ 32 Lou Whitaker	.10	.05
☐ 33 Kevin Mitchell	.05	.02
☐ 34 Mark Davis	.05	.02
☐ 35 Jerome Walton	.05	.02
☐ 36 Tony Gwynn	1.50	.70
☐ 37 Roberto Alomar	.50	.23
☐ 38 Tim Belcher	.05	.02
☐ 39 Craig Biggio	.30	.14
☐ 40 Barry Bonds	.60	.25
☐ 41 Bobby Bonilla	.10	.05
☐ 42 Joe Carter	.10	.05
☐ 43 Will Clark	.40	.18
☐ 44 Eric Davis	.10	.05
☐ 45 Glenn Davis	.05	.02
☐ 46 Sid Fernandez	.05	.02
☐ 47 Pedro Guerrero	.05	.02
☐ 48 Von Hayes	.05	.02
☐ 49 Tom Herr	.05	.02
☐ 50 Howard Johnson	.05	.02
☐ 51 Barry Larkin	.40	.18
☐ 52 Joe Magrane	.05	.02
☐ 53 Dale Murphy	.25	.11
☐ 54 Tim Raines	.10	.05
☐ 55 Willie Randolph	.10	.05
☐ 56 Ryne Sandberg	1.00	.45
☐ 57 Dwight Smith	.05	.02
☐ 58 Lonnie Smith	.05	.02
☐ 59 Robby Thompson	.05	.02
☐ 60 Tim Wallach	.05	.02

1990 Topps Debut '89

The 1990 Topps Major League Debut Set is a 152-card, standard-size set arranged in alphabetical order by player's name. Each card front features the date of the player's first major league appearance. Strangely enough, even though the set commemorates the 1989 Major League debuts, the set was not issued until the 1990 season had almost begun. Key cards in this set include Joey (Albert) Belle, Juan Gonzalez, Ken Griffey, Jr., David Justice, Deion Sanders and Sammy Sosa

	MINT	NRMT
COMPLETE SET (152)	12.00	5.50
COMMON CARD (1-152)	.05	.02

Card	MINT	NRMT
☐ 1 Jim Abbott	.25	.11
☐ 2 Beau Allred	.05	.02
☐ 3 Wilson Alvarez	.50	.23
☐ 4 Kent Anderson	.05	.02
☐ 5 Eric Anthony	.05	.02
☐ 6 Kevin Appier	.50	.23
☐ 7 Larry Arndt	.05	.02
☐ 8 John Barfield	.05	.02
☐ 9 Billy Bates	.05	.02
☐ 10 Kevin Batiste	.05	.02
☐ 11 Blaine Beatty	.05	.02
☐ 12 Stan Belinda	.05	.02
☐ 13 Juan Bell	.05	.02
☐ 14 Joey Belle (Now known as Albert)	3.00	1.35
☐ 15 Andy Benes	.50	.23
☐ 16 Mike Benjamin	.05	.02
☐ 17 Geronimo Berroa	.25	.11
☐ 18 Mike Blowers	.10	.05
☐ 19 Brian Brady	.05	.02
☐ 20 Francisco Cabrera	.10	.05
☐ 21 George Canale	.05	.02
☐ 22 Jose Cano	.05	.02
☐ 23 Steve Carter	.05	.02
☐ 24 Pat Combs	.05	.02
☐ 25 Scott Coolbaugh	.05	.02
☐ 26 Steve Cummings	.05	.02
☐ 27 Pete Dalena	.05	.02
☐ 28 Jeff Datz	.05	.02
☐ 29 Bobby Davidson	.05	.02
☐ 30 Drew Denson	.05	.02
☐ 31 Gary DiSarcina	.25	.11
☐ 32 Brian DuBois	.05	.02
☐ 33 Mike Dyer	.05	.02
☐ 34 Wayne Edwards	.05	.02
☐ 35 Junior Felix	.05	.02
☐ 36 Mike Fetters	.05	.02
☐ 37 Steve Finley	.50	.23
☐ 38 Darrin Fletcher	.10	.05
☐ 39 LaVel Freeman	.05	.02
☐ 40 Steve Frey	.05	.02
☐ 41 Mark Gardner	.05	.02
☐ 42 Joe Girardi	.40	.18
☐ 43 Juan Gonzalez	3.00	1.35
☐ 44 Goose Gozzo	.05	.02
☐ 45 Tommy Greene	.05	.02
☐ 46 Ken Griffey Jr.	6.00	2.70
☐ 47 Jason Grimsley	.05	.02
☐ 48 Marquis Grissom	1.25	.55
☐ 49 Mark Guthrie	.05	.02
☐ 50 Chip Hale	.05	.02
☐ 51 Jack Hardy	.05	.02
☐ 52 Gene Harris	.05	.02
☐ 53 Mike Hartley	.05	.02
☐ 54 Scott Hemond	.05	.02
☐ 55 Xavier Hernandez	.05	.02
☐ 56 Eric Hetzel	.05	.02
☐ 57 Greg Hibbard	.05	.02
☐ 58 Mark Higgins	.05	.02
☐ 59 Glenallen Hill	.10	.05
☐ 60 Chris Hoiles	.40	.18
☐ 61 Shawn Holman	.05	.02
☐ 62 Dann Howitt	.05	.02
☐ 63 Mike Huff	.05	.02
☐ 64 Terry Jorgensen	.05	.02
☐ 65 Dave Justice	1.50	.70
☐ 66 Jeff King	.40	.18
☐ 67 Matt Kinzer	.05	.02
☐ 68 Joe Kraemer	.05	.02
☐ 69 Marcus Lawton	.05	.02
☐ 70 Derek Lilliquist	.05	.02
☐ 71 Scott Little	.05	.02
☐ 72 Greg Litton	.05	.02
☐ 73 Rick Luecken	.05	.02
☐ 74 Julio Machado	.05	.02
☐ 75 Tom Magrann	.05	.02
☐ 76 Kelly Mann	.05	.02
☐ 77 Randy McCament	.05	.02
☐ 78 Ben McDonald	.30	.14
☐ 79 Chuck McElroy	.05	.02
☐ 80 Jeff McKnight	.05	.02
☐ 81 Kent Mercker	.10	.05
☐ 82 Matt Merullo	.05	.02
☐ 83 Hensley Meulens	.05	.02
☐ 84 Kevin Mmahat	.05	.02
☐ 85 Mike Munoz	.05	.02
☐ 86 Dan Murphy	.05	.02
☐ 87 Jaime Navarro	.25	.11
☐ 88 Randy Nosek	.05	.02
☐ 89 John Olerud	.75	.35
☐ 90 Steve Olin	.10	.05
☐ 91 Joe Oliver	.10	.05
☐ 92 Francisco Oliveras	.05	.02
☐ 93 Gregg Olson	.10	.05
☐ 94 John Orton	.05	.02
☐ 95 Dean Palmer	.50	.23
☐ 96 Ramon Pena	.05	.02
☐ 97 Jeff Peterek	.05	.02
☐ 98 Marty Pevey	.05	.02
☐ 99 Rusty Richards	.05	.02
☐ 100 Jeff Richardson	.05	.02
☐ 101 Rob Richie	.05	.02
☐ 102 Kevin Ritz	.05	.02
☐ 103 Rosario Rodriguez	.05	.02
☐ 104 Mike Roesler	.05	.02
☐ 105 Kenny Rogers	.25	.11
☐ 106 Bobby Rose	.05	.02
☐ 107 Alex Sanchez	.05	.02
☐ 108 Deion Sanders	1.50	.70
☐ 109 Jeff Schaefer	.05	.02
☐ 110 Jeff Schulz	.05	.02
☐ 111 Mike Schwabe	.05	.02
☐ 112 Dick Scott	.05	.02
☐ 113 Scott Scudder	.05	.02
☐ 114 Rudy Seanez	.05	.02
☐ 115 Joe Skalski	.05	.02
☐ 116 Dwight Smith	.10	.05
☐ 117 Greg Smith	.05	.02
☐ 118 Mike Smith	.05	.02
☐ 119 Paul Sorrento	.50	.23
☐ 120 Sammy Sosa	1.50	.70
☐ 121 Billy Spiers	.05	.02
☐ 122 Mike Stanton	.05	.02
☐ 123 Phil Stephenson	.05	.02
☐ 124 Doug Strange	.05	.02
☐ 125 Russ Swan	.05	.02
☐ 126 Kevin Tapani	.25	.11
☐ 127 Stu Tate	.05	.02
☐ 128 Greg Vaughn	.30	.14
☐ 129 Robin Ventura	.50	.23
☐ 130 Randy Veres	.05	.02
☐ 131 Jose Vizcaino	.25	.11
☐ 132 Omar Vizquel	.50	.23
☐ 133 Larry Walker	1.50	.70
☐ 134 Jerome Walton	.10	.05
☐ 135 Gary Wayne	.05	.02
☐ 136 Lenny Webster	.05	.02
☐ 137 Mickey Weston	.05	.02
☐ 138 Jeff Wetherby	.05	.02
☐ 139 John Wetteland	.50	.23
☐ 140 Ed Whited	.05	.02
☐ 141 Wally Whitehurst	.05	.02
☐ 142 Kevin Wickander	.05	.02
☐ 143 Dean Wilkins	.05	.02
☐ 144 Dana Williams	.05	.02
☐ 145 Paul Wilmet	.05	.02
☐ 146 Craig Wilson	.05	.02
☐ 147 Matt Winters	.05	.02
☐ 148 Eric Yelding	.05	.02
☐ 149 Clint Zavaras	.05	.02
☐ 150 Todd Zeile	.25	.11
☐ 151 Checklist Card	.05	.02
☐ 152 Checklist Card	.05	.02

1990 Topps Doubleheaders

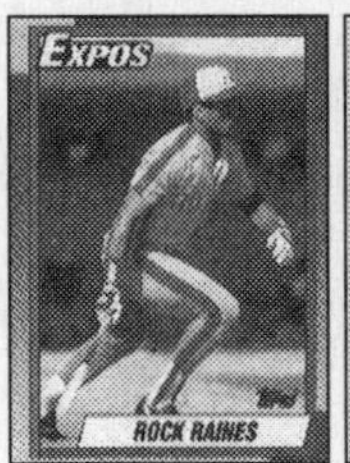

The 1990 Topps Double Headers set consists of 72 collectibles. Each Double Header consists of a clear plastic holder that contains a mini-reproduction of the player's 1990 card on one side and a mini-reproduction of his rookie card on the other side. The Double Headers were packaged in a paper pouch to conceal the player's identity prior to purchase. Three different checklists (A, B, and C) are printed on the outside of the packs, with the players listed in alphabetical order, and the double headers are checklisted below in alphabetcal order.

	MINT	NRMT
COMPLETE SET (72)	25.00	11.00
COMMON CARD (1-72)	.25	.11

Card	MINT	NRMT
☐ 1 Jim Abbott	.50	.23
☐ 2 Jeff Ballard	.25	.11
☐ 3 George Bell	.25	.11
☐ 4 Wade Boggs	1.50	.70
☐ 5 Barry Bonds	2.00	.90
☐ 6 Bobby Bonilla	.50	.23
☐ 7 Ellis Burks	1.00	.45
☐ 8 Jose Canseco	1.50	.70
☐ 9 Joe Carter	.75	.35
☐ 10 Will Clark	1.25	.55
☐ 11 Roger Clemens	4.00	1.80
☐ 12 Vince Coleman	.25	.11
☐ 13 Alvin Davis	.25	.11
☐ 14 Eric Davis	.50	.23
☐ 15 Glenn Davis	.25	.11
☐ 16 Mark Davis	.25	.11
☐ 17 Andre Dawson	.75	.35
☐ 18 Shawon Dunston	.25	.11
☐ 19 Dennis Eckersley	.75	.35
☐ 20 Sid Fernandez	.25	.11
☐ 21 Tony Fernandez	.25	.11
☐ 22 Chuck Finley	.25	.11
☐ 23 Carlton Fisk	.75	.35
☐ 24 Julio Franco	.50	.23

☐ 25 Gary Gaetti	.50	.23
☐ 26 Doc Gooden	.50	.23
☐ 27 Mark Grace	1.50	.70
☐ 28 Mike Greenwell	.25	.11
☐ 29 Ken Griffey Jr.	10.00	4.50
☐ 30 Pedro Guerrero	.25	.11
☐ 31 Tony Gwynn	5.00	2.20
☐ 32 Von Hayes	.25	.11
☐ 33 Rickey Henderson	1.50	.70
☐ 34 Orel Hershiser	.50	.23
☐ 35 Bo Jackson	.50	.23
☐ 36 Gregg Jefferies	.50	.23
☐ 37 Howard Johnson	.25	.11
☐ 38 Ricky Jordan	.25	.11
☐ 39 Carney Lansford	.25	.11
☐ 40 Barry Larkin	1.50	.70
☐ 41 Greg Maddux	6.00	2.70
☐ 42 Joe Magrane	.25	.11
☐ 43 Don Mattingly	4.00	1.80
☐ 44 Fred McGriff	1.00	.45
☐ 45 Mark McGwire	5.00	2.20
☐ 46 Kevin McReynolds	.25	.11
☐ 47 Kevin Mitchell	.25	.11
☐ 48 Gregg Olson	.25	.11
☐ 49 Kirby Puckett	4.00	1.80
☐ 50 Rock Raines	.50	.23
☐ 51 Harold Reynolds	.50	.23
☐ 52 Cal Ripken	8.00	3.60
☐ 53 Nolan Ryan	8.00	3.60
☐ 54 Bret Saberhagen	.25	.11
☐ 55 Ryne Sandberg	3.00	1.35
☐ 56 Benny Santiago	.25	.11
☐ 57 Steve Sax	.25	.11
☐ 58 Mike Scioscia	.25	.11
☐ 59 Mike Scott	.25	.11
☐ 60 Ruben Sierra	.25	.11
☐ 61 Lonnie Smith	.25	.11
☐ 62 Ozzie Smith	3.00	1.35
☐ 63 Dave Stewart	.25	.11
☐ 64 Darryl Strawberry	.50	.23
☐ 65 Greg Swindell	.25	.11
☐ 66 Alan Trammell	.75	.35
☐ 67 Frank Viola	.25	.11
☐ 68 Tim Wallach	.25	.11
☐ 69 Jerome Walton	.25	.11
☐ 70 Lou Whitaker	.50	.23
☐ 71 Mitch Williams	.25	.11
☐ 72 Robin Yount	1.00	.45

1990 Topps Heads Up

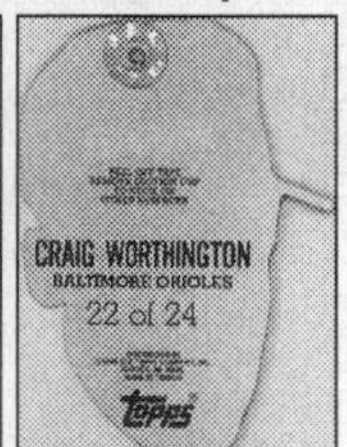

Though this collectible item made a limited appearance in 1989, the 1990 Topps set features 24 different Heads-Up pin-ups. Each item is a die-cut pin-up of a baseball star printed on thick white board, with a suction cup attached to the back. The die-cuts follow the contours of the player's hat and head, and they can be attached to any flat surface. The player's name and number appear on the back. The pin-ups are listed below according to the checklist printed on the back of each wrapper.

	MINT	NRMT
COMPLETE SET (24)	7.00	3.10
COMMON CARD (1-24)	.10	.05
☐ 1 Tony Gwynn	1.50	.70
☐ 2 Will Clark	.75	.35
☐ 3 Doc Gooden	.25	.11
☐ 4 Dennis Eckersley	.50	.23
☐ 5 Ken Griffey Jr.	3.00	1.35
☐ 6 Craig Biggio	.75	.35
☐ 7 Bret Saberhagen	.10	.05
☐ 8 Bo Jackson	.25	.11
☐ 9 Ryne Sandberg	1.00	.45
☐ 10 Gregg Olson	.10	.05
☐ 11 John Franco	.10	.05
☐ 12 Rafael Palmeiro	.50	.23
☐ 13 Gary Sheffield	1.00	.45
☐ 14 Mark McGwire	1.25	.55
☐ 15 Kevin Mitchell	.10	.05
☐ 16 Jim Abbott	.25	.11
☐ 17 Harold Reynolds	.10	.05
☐ 18 Jose Canseco	1.00	.45
☐ 19 Don Mattingly	1.00	.45
☐ 20 Kirby Puckett	1.25	.55
☐ 21 Tom Gordon	.10	.05
☐ 22 Craig Worthington	.10	.05
☐ 23 Dwight Smith	.10	.05
☐ 24 Jerome Walton	.10	.05

1990 Topps Hills Hit Men

The 1990 Topps Hit Men set is a standard-size 33-card set arranged in order of slugging percentage. The set was produced by Topps for Hills Department stores. Each card in the set has a glossy-coated front.

	MINT	NRMT
COMPLETE SET (33)	5.00	2.20
COMMON CARD (1-33)	.05	.02
☐ 1 Eric Davis	.10	.05
☐ 2 Will Clark	.40	.18
☐ 3 Don Mattingly	1.00	.45
☐ 4 Darryl Strawberry	.10	.05
☐ 5 Kevin Mitchell	.10	.05
☐ 6 Pedro Guerrero	.10	.05
☐ 7 Jose Canseco	.30	.14
☐ 8 Jim Rice	.10	.05
☐ 9 Danny Tartabull	.05	.02
☐ 10 George Brett	1.00	.45
☐ 11 Kent Hrbek	.10	.05
☐ 12 George Bell	.05	.02
☐ 13 Eddie Murray	.40	.18
☐ 14 Fred Lynn	.05	.02
☐ 15 Andre Dawson	.25	.11
☐ 16 Dale Murphy	.15	.07
☐ 17 Dave Winfield	.40	.18
☐ 18 Jack Clark	.10	.05
☐ 19 Wade Boggs	.30	.14
☐ 20 Ruben Sierra	.05	.02
☐ 21 Dave Parker	.10	.05
☐ 22 Glenn Davis	.05	.02
☐ 23 Dwight Evans	.10	.05
☐ 24 Jesse Barfield	.05	.02
☐ 25 Kirk Gibson	.10	.05
☐ 26 Alvin Davis	.05	.02
☐ 27 Kirby Puckett	1.00	.45
☐ 28 Joe Carter	.10	.05
☐ 29 Carlton Fisk	.40	.18
☐ 30 Harold Baines	.10	.05
☐ 31 Andres Galarraga	.50	.23
☐ 32 Cal Ripken	2.00	.90
☐ 33 Howard Johnson	.05	.02

1990 Topps Mini Leaders

The 1990 Topps League Leader Minis is an 88-card set with cards measuring approximately 2 1/8" by 3". The set features players who finished 1989 in the top five in any major hitting or pitching category. This set marked the fifth year that Topps issued their Mini set. The card numbering is alphabetical by player within team and the teams themselves are ordered alphabetically.

	MINT	NRMT
COMPLETE SET (88)	5.00	2.20
COMMON CARD (1-88)	.05	.02
☐ 1 Jeff Ballard	.05	.02
☐ 2 Phil Bradley	.05	.02
☐ 3 Wade Boggs	.30	.14
☐ 4 Roger Clemens	.50	.23
☐ 5 Nick Esasky	.05	.02
☐ 6 Jody Reed	.05	.02
☐ 7 Bert Blyleven	.10	.05
☐ 8 Chuck Finley	.10	.05
☐ 9 Kirk McCaskill	.05	.02
☐ 10 Devon White	.05	.02
☐ 11 Ivan Calderon	.05	.02
☐ 12 Bobby Thigpen	.05	.02
☐ 13 Joe Carter	.15	.07
☐ 14 Gary Pettis	.05	.02
☐ 15 Tom Gordon	.05	.02
☐ 16 Bo Jackson	.10	.05
☐ 17 Bret Saberhagen	.05	.02
☐ 18 Kevin Seitzer	.05	.02
☐ 19 Chris Bosio	.05	.02
☐ 20 Paul Molitor	.30	.14
☐ 21 Dan Plesac	.05	.02
☐ 22 Robin Yount	.15	.07
☐ 23 Kirby Puckett	1.00	.45
☐ 24 Don Mattingly	1.00	.45
☐ 25 Steve Sax	.05	.02
☐ 26 Storm Davis	.05	.02
☐ 27 Dennis Eckersley	.15	.07
☐ 28 Rickey Henderson	.30	.14
☐ 29 Carney Lansford	.05	.02
☐ 30 Mark McGwire	1.00	.45
☐ 31 Mike Moore	.05	.02
☐ 32 Dave Stewart	.05	.02
☐ 33 Alvin Davis	.05	.02
☐ 34 Harold Reynolds	.05	.02
☐ 35 Mike Schooler	.05	.02
☐ 36 Cecil Espy	.05	.02
☐ 37 Julio Franco	.10	.05
☐ 38 Jeff Russell	.05	.02
☐ 39 Nolan Ryan	2.00	.90
☐ 40 Ruben Sierra	.05	.02
☐ 41 George Bell	.05	.02
☐ 42 Tony Fernandez	.05	.02
☐ 43 Fred McGriff	.30	.14
☐ 44 Dave Stieb	.05	.02
☐ 45 Checklist Card	.05	.02
☐ 46 Lonnie Smith	.05	.02
☐ 47 John Smoltz	.40	.18
☐ 48 Mike Bielecki	.05	.02
☐ 49 Mark Grace	.50	.23
☐ 50 Greg Maddux	2.00	.90
☐ 51 Ryne Sandberg	.75	.35
☐ 52 Mitch Williams	.05	.02
☐ 53 Eric Davis	.10	.05
☐ 54 John Franco	.10	.05
☐ 55 Glenn Davis	.05	.02
☐ 56 Mike Scott	.05	.02
☐ 57 Tim Belcher	.05	.02
☐ 58 Orel Hershiser	.10	.05
☐ 59 Jay Howell	.05	.02
☐ 60 Eddie Murray	.40	.18
☐ 61 Tim Burke	.05	.02
☐ 62 Mark Langston	.05	.02
☐ 63 Tim Raines	.10	.05
☐ 64 Tim Wallach	.05	.02
☐ 65 David Cone	.15	.07
☐ 66 Sid Fernandez	.05	.02
☐ 67 Howard Johnson	.05	.02
☐ 68 Juan Samuel	.05	.02
☐ 69 Von Hayes	.05	.02
☐ 70 Barry Bonds	.50	.23
☐ 71 Bobby Bonilla	.10	.05
☐ 72 Andy Van Slyke	.05	.02
☐ 73 Vince Coleman	.05	.02
☐ 74 Jose DeLeon	.05	.02
☐ 75 Pedro Guerrero	.05	.02
☐ 76 Joe Magrane	.05	.02
☐ 77 Roberto Alomar	.50	.23
☐ 78 Jack Clark	.05	.02
☐ 79 Mark Davis	.05	.02
☐ 80 Tony Gwynn	1.25	.55
☐ 81 Bruce Hurst	.05	.02
☐ 82 Eddie Whitson	.05	.02
☐ 83 Brett Butler	.10	.05
☐ 84 Will Clark	.30	.14
☐ 85 Scott Garrelts	.05	.02
☐ 86 Kevin Mitchell	.05	.02
☐ 87 Rick Reuschel	.05	.02
☐ 88 Robby Thompson	.05	.02

1990 Topps Stickers

These 328 stickers measure approximately 2 1/8" by 3" and feature color player photos with white borders that have multicolored highlights. The stickers are numbered at the bottom right. The backs are actually cards from the 1990 Topps Super Stars and are considered a separate set. An album onto which the stickers could be affixed was available at retail stores. The album and the sticker numbering are organized as follows: 1989 Highlights (1-

12), Houston Astros (13-23), Atlanta Braves (24-34), St. Louis Cardinals (35-45), Chicago Cubs (46-56), Los Angeles Dodgers (57-67), Montreal Expos (68-78), San Francisco Giants (79-89), New York Mets (90-100), San Diego Padres (101-111), Philadelphia Phillies (112-122), Pittsburgh Pirates (123-133), Cincinnati Reds (134-144), Foil All-Stars (145-164), California Angels (165-175), Oakland A's (176-186), Toronto Blue Jays (187-197), Milwaukee Brewers (198-208), Cleveland Indians (209-219), Seattle Mariners (220-230), Baltimore Orioles (231-241), Texas Rangers (242-252), Boston Red Sox (253-263), Kansas City Royals (264-274), Detroit Tigers (275-285), Minnesota Twins (286-296), Chicago White Sox (297-307), New York Yankees (308-318) and Future Stars (319-328). For those stickers featuring more than one player, the other numbers on that sticker are given below in parentheses. Although the prices listed below are for the stickers only, there are instances where having an especially desirable sticker card back (attached to that sticker) will increase the values listed below.

	MINT	NRMT
COMPLETE SET (328)	15.00	6.75
COMMON STICKER (1-328)	.05	.02
☐ 1 Rick Cerone HL (321)	.05	.02
☐ 2 Kevin Elster HL (322)	.05	.02
☐ 3 Nolan Ryan HL (323)	1.00	.45
☐ 4 Vince Coleman HL (319)	.05	.02
☐ 5 Cal Ripken HL (240)	1.00	.45
☐ 6 Jeff Reardon HL (328)	.10	.05
☐ 7 Rickey Henderson HL (320)	.15	.07
☐ 8 Wade Boggs HL (324)	.15	.07
☐ 9 Barry Bonds HL (325)	.25	.11
☐ 10 Gregg Olson HL (236)	.05	.02
☐ 11 Tony Fernandez HL (327)	.05	.02
☐ 12 Ryne Sandberg HL (326)	.25	.11
☐ 13 Glenn Davis	.05	.02
☐ 14 Danny Darwin (316)	.05	.02
☐ 15 Bill Doran (298)	.05	.02
☐ 16 Dave Smith (255)	.05	.02
☐ 17 Kevin Bass (278)	.05	.02
☐ 18 Rafael Ramirez (177)	.05	.02
☐ 19 Mike Scott	.05	.02
☐ 20 Ken Caminiti (235)	.25	.11
☐ 21 Jim Deshaies (272)	.05	.02
☐ 22 Gerald Young (314)	.05	.02
☐ 23 Craig Biggio (186)	.30	.14
☐ 24 Lonnie Smith	.05	.02
☐ 25 Dale Murphy (210)	.25	.11
☐ 26 Tom Glavine	.25	.11
☐ 27 Gerald Perry (313)	.05	.02
☐ 28 Jeff Blauser (269)	.05	.02
☐ 29 Jeff Treadway (252)	.05	.02
☐ 30 John Smoltz (299)	.30	.14
☐ 31 Darrell Evans (295)	.10	.05
☐ 32 Oddibe McDowell (265)	.05	.02
☐ 33 Andres Thomas (304)	.05	.02
☐ 34 Joe Boever (191)	.05	.02
☐ 35 Pedro Guerrero	.05	.02
☐ 36 Ken Dayley (226)	.05	.02
☐ 37 Milt Thompson (188)	.05	.02
☐ 38 Jose DeLeon (180)	.05	.02
☐ 39 Vince Coleman (293)	.05	.02
☐ 40 Terry Pendleton (225)	.10	.05
☐ 41 Joe Magrane	.05	.02
☐ 42 Ozzie Smith (179)	.40	.18
☐ 43 Todd Worrell (195)	.05	.02
☐ 44 Jose Oquendo (238)	.05	.02
☐ 45 Tom Brunansky (287)	.05	.02
☐ 46 Ryne Sandberg	.50	.23
☐ 47 Andre Dawson (268)	.15	.07
☐ 48 Mitch Williams	.05	.02
☐ 49 Damon Berryhill (204)	.05	.02
☐ 50 Jerome Walton (274)	.05	.02
☐ 51 Greg Maddux (315)	2.00	.90
☐ 52 Dwight Smith (248)	.05	.02
☐ 53 Shawon Dunston (194)	.05	.02
☐ 54 Mike Bielecki (239)	.05	.02
☐ 55 Rick Sutcliffe (305)	.05	.02
☐ 56 Mark Grace (228)	.30	.14
☐ 57 Eddie Murray	.30	.14
☐ 58 Alfredo Griffin (197)	.05	.02
☐ 59 Fernando Valenzuela (277)	.10	.05
☐ 60 Kirk Gibson (201)	.10	.05
☐ 61 Ramon Martinez (190)	.15	.07
☐ 62 Mike Marshall (309)	.05	.02
☐ 63 Orel Hershiser	.10	.05
☐ 64 Mike Scioscia (271)	.05	.02
☐ 65 Jay Howell (279)	.05	.02
☐ 66 Willie Randolph (283)	.10	.05
☐ 67 Jeff Hamilton (280)	.05	.02

☐ 68 Denny Martinez	.10	.05
☐ 69 Tim Raines (184)	.10	.05
☐ 70 Mark Langston	.05	.02
☐ 71 Dave Martinez (301)	.05	.02
☐ 72 Tim Burke (258)	.05	.02
☐ 73 Spike Owen (232)	.05	.02
☐ 74 Tim Wallach (254)	.05	.02
☐ 75 Andres Galarraga (208)	.25	.11
☐ 76 Kevin Gross (234)	.05	.02
☐ 77 Hubie Brooks (263)	.05	.02
☐ 78 Bryn Smith (207)	.05	.02
☐ 79 Kevin Mitchell	.05	.02
☐ 80 Craig Lefferts (256)	.05	.02
☐ 81 Ernest Riles (247)	.05	.02
☐ 82 Scott Garrelts (185)	.05	.02
☐ 83 Robby Thompson (251)	.05	.02
☐ 84 Don Robinson (282)	.05	.02
☐ 85 Will Clark	.30	.14
☐ 86 Steve Bedrosian (183)	.05	.02
☐ 87 Brett Butler (284)	.10	.05
☐ 88 Matt Williams (227)	.40	.18
☐ 89 Rick Reuschel (291)	.05	.02
☐ 90 Howard Johnson	.05	.02
☐ 91 Darryl Strawberry (246)	.10	.05
☐ 92 Sid Fernandez	.05	.02
☐ 93 David Cone (189)	.15	.07
☐ 94 Kevin McReynolds (311)	.05	.02
☐ 95 Frank Viola (229)	.05	.02
☐ 96 Dwight Gooden (206)	.10	.05
☐ 97 Kevin Elster (267)	.05	.02
☐ 98 Ron Darling (289)	.05	.02
☐ 99 Dave Magadan (257)	.05	.02
☐ 100 Randy Myers (192)	.05	.02
☐ 101 Tony Gwynn	1.00	.45
☐ 102 Mark Davis (312)	.05	.02
☐ 103 Bip Roberts (212)	.05	.02
☐ 104 Jack Clark (205)	.10	.05
☐ 105 Chris James (211)	.05	.02
☐ 106 Mike Pagliarulo (199)	.05	.02
☐ 107 Eddie Whitson	.05	.02
☐ 108 Bruce Hurst (245)	.05	.02
☐ 109 Roberto Alomar (202)	.50	.23
☐ 110 Benito Santiago (224)	.05	.02
☐ 111 Eric Show (307)	.05	.02
☐ 112 Ricky Jordan	.05	.02
☐ 113 Steve Jeltz (203)	.05	.02
☐ 114 Von Hayes	.05	.02
☐ 115 Dickie Thon (182)	.05	.02
☐ 116 Ken Howell (213)	.05	.02
☐ 117 John Kruk (306)	.10	.05
☐ 118 Len Dykstra (302)	.10	.05
☐ 119 Jeff Parrett (300)	.05	.02
☐ 120 Randy Ready (230)	.05	.02
☐ 121 Roger McDowell (262)	.05	.02
☐ 122 Tom Herr (250)	.05	.02
☐ 123 Barry Bonds	.50	.23
☐ 124 Andy Van Slyke (219)	.10	.05
☐ 125 Bob Walk (216)	.05	.02
☐ 126 R.J. Reynolds (243)	.05	.02
☐ 127 Gary Redus (249)	.05	.02
☐ 128 Bill Landrum (276)	.05	.02
☐ 129 Bobby Bonilla	.10	.05
☐ 130 Doug Drabek (218)	.05	.02
☐ 131 Jose Lind (221)	.05	.02
☐ 132 John Smiley (241)	.05	.02
☐ 133 Mike LaValliere (214)	.05	.02
☐ 134 Eric Davis	.10	.05
☐ 135 Tom Browning (270)	.05	.02
☐ 136 Barry Larkin	.30	.14
☐ 137 Jose Rijo (318)	.05	.02
☐ 138 Todd Benzinger (292)	.05	.02
☐ 139 Rick Mahler (217)	.05	.02
☐ 140 Chris Sabo (196)	.05	.02
☐ 141 Paul O'Neill (175)	.10	.05
☐ 142 Danny Jackson (273)	.05	.02
☐ 143 Rolando Roomes (261)	.05	.02
☐ 144 John Franco (233)	.10	.05
☐ 145 Ozzie Smith AS	.25	.11
☐ 146 Tony Gwynn AS	.50	.23
☐ 147 Will Clark AS	.25	.11
☐ 148 Kevin Mitchell AS	.05	.02
☐ 149 Eric Davis AS	.10	.05
☐ 150 Howard Johnson AS	.05	.02
☐ 151 Pedro Guerrero AS	.05	.02
☐ 152 Ryne Sandberg AS	.25	.11
☐ 153 Benito Santiago AS	.05	.02
☐ 154 Rick Reuschel AS	.05	.02
☐ 155 Bo Jackson AS	.10	.05
☐ 156 Wade Boggs AS	.25	.11
☐ 157 Kirby Puckett AS	.40	.18
☐ 158 Harold Baines AS	.10	.05
☐ 159 Julio Franco AS	.10	.05
☐ 160 Cal Ripken AS	1.00	.45
☐ 161 Ruben Sierra AS	.05	.02
☐ 162 Mark McGwire AS	.20	.09
☐ 163 Terry Steinbach AS	.10	.05
☐ 164 Dave Stewart AS	.10	.05

☐ 165 Bert Blyleven	.10	.05
☐ 166 Wally Joyner (285)	.10	.05
☐ 167 Kirk McCaskill (290)	.05	.02
☐ 168 Devon White (223)	.05	.02
☐ 169 Brian Downing (294)	.05	.02
☐ 170 Lance Parrish (296)	.10	.05
☐ 171 Chuck Finley	.10	.05
☐ 172 Jim Abbott (317)	.10	.05
☐ 173 Chili Davis (181)	.10	.05
☐ 174 Johnny Ray (260)	.05	.02
☐ 175 Bryan Harvey (141)	.05	.02
☐ 176 Mark McGwire	.75	.35
☐ 177 Jose Canseco (18)	.30	.14
☐ 178 Mike Moore	.05	.02
☐ 179 Dave Parker (42)	.10	.05
☐ 180 Bob Welch (38)	.10	.05
☐ 181 Rickey Henderson (173)	.40	.18
☐ 182 Dennis Eckersley (115)	.15	.07
☐ 183 Carney Lansford (86)	.10	.05
☐ 184 Dave Henderson (69)	.05	.02
☐ 185 Dave Stewart (82)	.10	.05
☐ 186 Terry Steinbach (23)	.10	.05
☐ 187 Fred McGriff	.25	.11
☐ 188 Junior Felix (37)	.05	.02
☐ 189 Ernie Whitt (93)	.05	.02
☐ 190 Dave Smith (61)	.05	.02
☐ 191 Jimmy Key (34)	.05	.02
☐ 192 George Bell (100)	.05	.02
☐ 193 Kelly Gruber	.05	.02
☐ 194 Tony Fernandez (53)	.05	.02
☐ 195 John Cerutti (43)	.05	.02
☐ 196 Tom Henke (140)	.05	.02
☐ 197 Nelson Liriano (58)	.05	.02
☐ 198 Robin Yount	.25	.11
☐ 199 Paul Molitor (106)	.30	.14
☐ 200 Dan Plesac	.05	.02
☐ 201 Teddy Higuera (60)	.05	.02
☐ 202 Gary Sheffield (109)	.30	.14
☐ 203 B.J. Surhoff (113)	.10	.05
☐ 204 Rob Deer (49)	.05	.02
☐ 205 Chris Bosio (104)	.05	.02
☐ 206 Glenn Braggs (96)	.05	.02
☐ 207 Jim Gantner (78)	.05	.02
☐ 208 Greg Brock (75)	.05	.02
☐ 209 Joe Carter	.10	.05
☐ 210 Jerry Browne (25)	.05	.02
☐ 211 Cory Snyder (105)	.05	.02
☐ 212 Joey Belle (103)	2.00	.90
☐ 213 Bud Black (116)	.05	.02
☐ 214 Greg Swindell (133)	.05	.02
☐ 215 Doug Jones	.05	.02
☐ 216 Tom Candiotti (125)	.05	.02
☐ 217 John Farrell (217)	.05	.02
☐ 218 Pete O'Brien (130)	.05	.02
☐ 219 Brook Jacoby (124)	.05	.02
☐ 220 Alvin Davis	.05	.02
☐ 221 Harold Reynolds (131)	.10	.05
☐ 222 Scott Bankhead	.05	.02
☐ 223 Jeffrey Leonard (168)	.05	.02
☐ 224 Jim Presley (110)	.05	.02
☐ 225 Ken Griffey Jr. (40)	3.00	1.35
☐ 226 Greg Briley (36)	.05	.02
☐ 227 Darnell Coles (88)	.05	.02
☐ 228 Mike Schooler (56)	.05	.02
☐ 229 Scott Bradley (95)	.05	.02
☐ 230 Randy Johnson (120)	.50	.23
☐ 231 Cal Ripken	2.00	.90
☐ 232 Jeff Ballard (73)	.05	.02
☐ 233 Randy Milligan (144)	.05	.02
☐ 234 Joe Orsulak (76)	.05	.02
☐ 235 Billy Ripken (20)	.05	.02
☐ 236 Mark Williamson (10)	.05	.02
☐ 237 Mickey Tettleton	.05	.02
☐ 238 Gregg Olson (44)	.05	.02
☐ 239 Craig Worthington (54)	.05	.02
☐ 240 Bob Milacki (5)	.05	.02
☐ 241 Phil Bradley (132)	.05	.02
☐ 242 Nolan Ryan	2.00	.90
☐ 243 Julio Franco (126)	.10	.05
☐ 244 Ruben Sierra	.05	.02
☐ 245 Harold Baines (108)	.10	.05
☐ 246 Jeff Kunkel (91)	.05	.02
☐ 247 Pete Incaviglia (81)	.05	.02
☐ 248 Kevin Brown (52)	.15	.07
☐ 249 Cecil Espy (127)	.05	.02
☐ 250 Rafael Palmeiro (122)	.15	.07
☐ 251 Steve Buechele (83)	.05	.02
☐ 252 Jeff Russell (29)	.05	.02
☐ 253 Wade Boggs	.30	.14
☐ 254 Mike Greenwell (74)	.05	.02
☐ 255 Roger Clemens (16)	.50	.23
☐ 256 Marty Barrett (80)	.05	.02
☐ 257 Dwight Evans (99)	.10	.05
☐ 258 Mike Boddicker (72)	.05	.02
☐ 259 Ellis Burks	.15	.07
☐ 260 John Dopson (174)	.05	.02
☐ 261 Rob Murphy (143)	.05	.02

☐ 262 Lee Smith (121)	.10	.05
☐ 263 Nick Esasky (77)	.05	.02
☐ 264 Bo Jackson	.10	.05
☐ 265 George Brett (32)	.75	.35
☐ 266 Bret Saberhagen	.05	.02
☐ 267 Kevin Seitzer (97)	.05	.02
☐ 268 Tom Gordon (47)	.05	.02
☐ 269 Kurt Stillwell (28)	.05	.02
☐ 270 Steve Farr (135)	.05	.02
☐ 271 Jim Eisenreich (64)	.10	.05
☐ 272 Mark Gubicza (21)	.05	.02
☐ 273 Jeff Montgomery (142)	.05	.02
☐ 274 Danny Tartabull (50)	.05	.02
☐ 275 Lou Whitaker	.10	.05
☐ 276 Jack Morris (128)	.10	.05
☐ 277 Frank Tanana (59)	.05	.02
☐ 278 Chet Lemon (17)	.05	.02
☐ 279 Fred Lynn (65)	.10	.05
☐ 280 Mike Heath (67)	.05	.02
☐ 281 Alan Trammell	.15	.07
☐ 282 Mike Henneman (84)	.05	.02
☐ 283 Gary Pettis (66)	.05	.02
☐ 284 Jeff M. Robinson (87)	.05	.02
☐ 285 Dave Bergman (166)	.05	.02
☐ 286 Kirby Puckett	.50	.23
☐ 287 Kent Hrbek (45)	.10	.05
☐ 288 Gary Gaetti	.10	.05
☐ 289 Jeff Reardon (98)	.10	.05
☐ 290 Brian Harper (167)	.05	.02
☐ 291 Gene Larkin (89)	.05	.02
☐ 292 Dan Gladden (138)	.05	.02
☐ 293 Al Newman (39)	.05	.02
☐ 294 Randy Bush (169)	.05	.02
☐ 295 Greg Gagne (31)	.05	.02
☐ 296 Allan Anderson (170)	.05	.02
☐ 297 Bobby Thigpen	.05	.02
☐ 298 Ozzie Guillen (15)	.05	.02
☐ 299 Ivan Calderon (30)	.05	.02
☐ 300 Carlos Martinez (119)	.05	.02
☐ 301 Steve Lyons (71)	.05	.02
☐ 302 Ron Kittle (118)	.05	.02
☐ 303 Carlton Fisk	.30	.14
☐ 304 Melido Perez (33)	.05	.02
☐ 305 Dave Gallagher (55)	.05	.02
☐ 306 Dan Pasqua (117)	.05	.02
☐ 307 Scott Fletcher (111)	.05	.02
☐ 308 Don Mattingly	1.00	.45
☐ 309 Dan Pasqua (62)	.05	.02
☐ 310 Steve Sax	.05	.02
☐ 311 Alvaro Espinoza (94)	.05	.02
☐ 312 Roberto Kelly (102)	.05	.02
☐ 313 Mel Hall (27)	.05	.02
☐ 314 Jesse Barfield (22)	.05	.02
☐ 315 Chuck Cary (51)	.05	.02
☐ 316 Bob Geren (14)	.05	.02
☐ 317 Andy Hawkins (172)	.05	.02
☐ 318 Don Slaught (137)	.05	.02
☐ 319 Jim Abbott FS (4)	.10	.05
☐ 320 Greg Briley FS (7)	.05	.02
☐ 321 Bob Geren FS (1)	.05	.02
☐ 322 Tom Gordon FS (2)	.05	.02
☐ 323 Ken Griffey Jr. FS (3)	1.50	.70
☐ 324 Gregg Jefferies FS (8)	.05	.02
☐ 325 Carlos Martinez FS (9)	.05	.02
☐ 326 Gary Sheffield FS (12)	.25	.11
☐ 327 Jerome Walton FS (11)	.05	.02
☐ 328 Craig Worthington FS(6)	.05	.02
☐ xx Album	1.00	.45

1990 Topps TV All-Stars

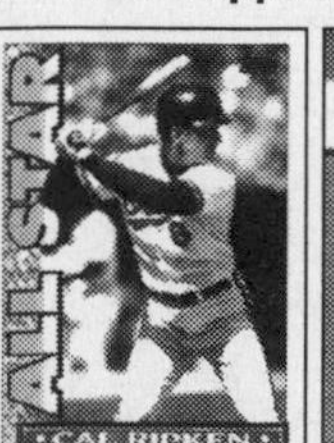

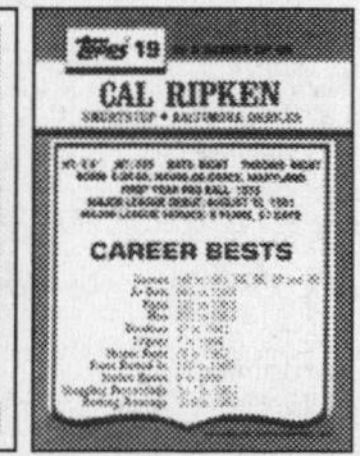

This All-Star team set contains 66 cards measuring the standard size. The fronts feature posed or action color player photos with a high gloss. In block lettering, the words "All-Star" are printed vertically in blue on the left side of the card. The player's name appears in a red plaque below the picture, and white borders round out the card face. The backs are printed in black lettering and have a red and white background. Inside a decal design, biographical information and career bests are superimposed on a blue, pink, and white background. These cards were offered only on television as a complete set for sale through an 800 number.

	MINT	NRMT
COMPLETE SET (66)	80.00	36.00
COMMON CARD (1-66)	.50	.23
☐ 1 Mark McGwire	5.00	2.20
☐ 2 Julio Franco	.50	.23
☐ 3 Ozzie Guillen	.50	.23
☐ 4 Carney Lansford	.50	.23
☐ 5 Bo Jackson	1.00	.45
☐ 6 Kirby Puckett	8.00	3.60
☐ 7 Ruben Sierra	1.00	.45
☐ 8 Carlton Fisk	1.50	.70
☐ 9 Nolan Ryan	15.00	6.75
☐ 10 Rickey Henderson	3.00	1.35
☐ 11 Jose Canseco	3.00	1.35
☐ 12 Mark Davis	.50	.23
☐ 13 Dennis Eckersley	2.00	.90
☐ 14 Chuck Finley	.50	.23
☐ 15 Bret Saberhagen	.50	.23
☐ 16 Dave Stewart	.50	.23
☐ 17 Don Mattingly	8.00	3.60
☐ 18 Steve Sax	.50	.23
☐ 19 Cal Ripken	15.00	6.75
☐ 20 Wade Boggs	3.00	1.35
☐ 21 George Bell	.50	.23
☐ 22 Mike Greenwell	.50	.23
☐ 23 Robin Yount	2.50	1.10
☐ 24 Mickey Tettleton	.50	.23
☐ 25 Roger Clemens	5.00	2.20
☐ 26 Fred McGriff	2.50	1.10
☐ 27 Jeff Ballard	.50	.23
☐ 28 Dwight Evans	1.00	.45
☐ 29 Paul Molitor	4.00	1.80
☐ 30 Gregg Olson	.50	.23
☐ 31 Dan Plesac	.50	.23
☐ 32 Greg Swindell	.50	.23
☐ 33 Tony LaRussa MG Cito Gaston MG	.50	.23
☐ 34 Will Clark	3.00	1.35
☐ 35 Roberto Alomar	3.00	1.35
☐ 36 Barry Larkin	2.50	1.10
☐ 37 Ken Caminiti	2.50	1.10
☐ 38 Eric Davis	1.00	.45
☐ 39 Tony Gwynn	8.00	3.60
☐ 40 Kevin Mitchell	.50	.23
☐ 41 Craig Biggio	2.50	1.10
☐ 42 Mike Scott	.50	.23
☐ 43 Joe Carter	2.00	.90
☐ 44 Jack Clark	.50	.23
☐ 45 Glenn Davis	.50	.23
☐ 46 Orel Hershiser	1.00	.45
☐ 47 Jay Howell	.50	.23
☐ 48 Bruce Hurst	.50	.23
☐ 49 Dave Smith	.50	.23
☐ 50 Pedro Guerrero	.50	.23
☐ 51 Ryne Sandberg	6.00	2.70
☐ 52 Ozzie Smith	6.00	2.70
☐ 53 Howard Johnson	.50	.23
☐ 54 Von Hayes	.50	.23
☐ 55 Tim Raines	1.00	.45
☐ 56 Darryl Strawberry	1.00	.45
☐ 57 Mike LaValliere	.50	.23
☐ 58 Dwight Gooden	1.00	.45
☐ 59 Bobby Bonilla	1.00	.45
☐ 60 Tim Burke	.50	.23
☐ 61 Sid Fernandez	.50	.23
☐ 62 Andres Galarraga	2.50	1.10
☐ 63 Mark Grace	3.00	1.35
☐ 64 Joe Magrane	.50	.23
☐ 65 Mitch Williams	.50	.23
☐ 66 Roger Craig MG and Don Zimmer MG	.50	.23

1990 Topps TV Cardinals

This Cardinals team set contains 66 cards measuring the standard size. The fronts feature posed or action color player photos with a high gloss. In block lettering, the team name is printed vertically in red and pink on the left side of the card. The player's name appears in a blue plaque below the picture, and white borders round out the card face. The backs are printed in black lettering and have a red and white background. Inside a decal design, player information and statistics are superimposed on an indistinct version of the same picture as on the front. Cards numbered 1-36 were with the parent club, while cards 37-66 were in the farm system.

	MINT	NRMT
COMPLETE SET (66)	50.00	22.00
COMMON CARD (1-66)	.25	.11
☐ 1 Whitey Herzog MG	.50	.23
☐ 2 Steve Braun CO	.25	.11
☐ 3 Rich Hacker CO	.25	.11
☐ 4 Dave Ricketts CO	.25	.11
☐ 5 Jim Riggleman CO	.25	.11
☐ 6 Mike Roarke CO	.25	.11
☐ 7 Cris Carpenter	.25	.11
☐ 8 John Costello	.25	.11
☐ 9 Danny Cox	.25	.11
☐ 10 Ken Dayley	.25	.11
☐ 11 Jose DeLeon	.25	.11
☐ 12 Frank DiPino	.25	.11
☐ 13 Ken Hill	1.50	.70
☐ 14 Howard Hilton	.25	.11
☐ 15 Ricky Horton	.25	.11
☐ 16 Joe Magrane	.25	.11
☐ 17 Greg Mathews	.25	.11
☐ 18 Bryn Smith	.25	.11
☐ 19 Scott Terry	.25	.11
☐ 20 Bob Tewksbury	.25	.11
☐ 21 John Tudor	.25	.11
☐ 22 Todd Worrell	.50	.23
☐ 23 Tom Pagnozzi	.25	.11
☐ 24 Todd Zeile	.50	.23
☐ 25 Pedro Guerrero	.50	.23
☐ 26 Tim Jones	.25	.11
☐ 27 Jose Oquendo	.25	.11
☐ 28 Terry Pendleton	1.50	.70
☐ 29 Ozzie Smith	25.00	11.00
☐ 30 Denny Walling	.25	.11
☐ 31 Tom Brunansky	.50	.23
☐ 32 Vince Coleman	.50	.23
☐ 33 Dave Collins	.25	.11
☐ 34 Willie McGee	1.00	.45
☐ 35 John Morris	.25	.11
☐ 36 Milt Thompson	.25	.11
☐ 37 Gibson Alba	.25	.11
☐ 38 Scott Arnold	.25	.11
☐ 39 Rod Brewer	.25	.11
☐ 40 Greg Carmona	.25	.11
☐ 41 Mark Clark	1.50	.70
☐ 42 Stan Clarke	.25	.11
☐ 43 Paul Coleman	.25	.11
☐ 44 Todd Crosby	.25	.11
☐ 45 Brad DuVall	.25	.11
☐ 46 John Ericks	.25	.11
☐ 47 Bien Figueroa	.25	.11
☐ 48 Terry Francona	.25	.11
☐ 49 Ed Fulton	.25	.11
☐ 50 Bernard Gilkey	3.00	1.35
☐ 51 Ernie Camacho	.25	.11
☐ 52 Mike Hinkle	.25	.11
☐ 53 Ray Lankford	6.00	2.70
☐ 54 Julian Martinez	.25	.11
☐ 55 Jesus Mendez	.25	.11
☐ 56 Mike Milchin	.25	.11
☐ 57 Mauricio Nunez	.25	.11
☐ 58 Omar Olivares	.25	.11
☐ 59 Geronimo Pena	.25	.11
☐ 60 Mike Perez	.25	.11
☐ 61 Gaylen Pitts MG	.25	.11
☐ 62 Mark Riggins CO	.25	.11
☐ 63 Tim Sherrill	.25	.11
☐ 64 Roy Silver	.25	.11
☐ 65 Ray Stephens	.25	.11
☐ 66 Craig Wilson	.25	.11

1990 Topps TV Cubs

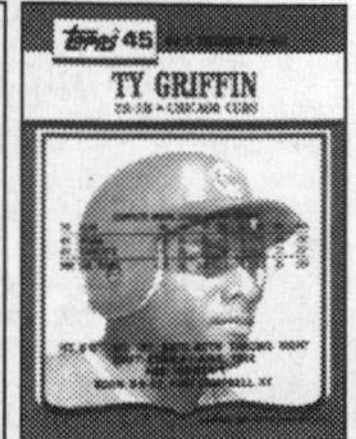

This Cubs team set contains 66 standard-size cards. The fronts feature posed or action color player photos with a high gloss. In block lettering, the team name is printed vertically in blue on the left side of the card. The player's name appears in a gold plaque below the picture, and white borders round out the card face. The backs are printed in black and have a red and white background. Inside a decal design, player information and statistics are superimposed on an indistinct version of the same picture as on the front. Cards numbered 1-35 were with the parent club, while cards 36-66 were in the farm system. The key card in this set is Greg Maddux

	MINT	NRMT
COMPLETE SET (66)	100.00	45.00
COMMON CARD (1-66)	.25	.11

	MINT	NRMT
☐ 1 Don Zimmer MG	.50	.23
☐ 2 Joe Altobelli CO	.25	.11
☐ 3 Chuck Cottier CO	.25	.11
☐ 4 Jose Martinez CO	.25	.11
☐ 5 Dick Pole CO	.25	.11
☐ 6 Phil Roof CO	.25	.11
☐ 7 Paul Assenmacher	.25	.11
☐ 8 Mike Bielecki	.25	.11
☐ 9 Mike Harkey	.25	.11
☐ 10 Joe Kraemer	.25	.11
☐ 11 Les Lancaster	.25	.11
☐ 12 Greg Maddux	50.00	22.00
☐ 13 Jose Nunez	.25	.11
☐ 14 Jeff Pico	.25	.11
☐ 15 Rick Sutcliffe	.50	.23
☐ 16 Dean Wilkins	.25	.11
☐ 17 Mitch Williams	.50	.23
☐ 18 Steve Wilson	.25	.11
☐ 19 Damon Berryhill	.25	.11
☐ 20 Joe Girardi	2.00	.90
☐ 21 Rick Wrona	.25	.11
☐ 22 Shawon Dunston	.50	.23
☐ 23 Mark Grace	20.00	9.00
☐ 24 Domingo Ramos	.25	.11
☐ 25 Luis Salazar	.25	.11
☐ 26 Ryne Sandberg	40.00	18.00
☐ 27 Greg Smith	.25	.11
☐ 28 Curtis Wilkerson	.25	.11
☐ 29 Dave Clark	.25	.11
☐ 30 Doug Dascenzo	.25	.11
☐ 31 Andre Dawson	5.00	2.20
☐ 32 Lloyd McClendon	.25	.11
☐ 33 Dwight Smith	.25	.11
☐ 34 Jerome Walton	.25	.11
☐ 35 Marvell Wynne	.25	.11
☐ 36 Alex Arias	.25	.11
☐ 37 Bob Bafia	.25	.11
☐ 38 Brad Bierley	.25	.11
☐ 39 Shawn Boskie	.25	.11
☐ 40 Danny Clay	.25	.11
☐ 41 Rusty Crockett	.25	.11
☐ 42 Earl Cunningham	.25	.11
☐ 43 Len Damian	.25	.11
☐ 44 Darrin Duffy	.25	.11
☐ 45 Ty Griffin	.25	.11
☐ 46 Brian Guinn	.25	.11
☐ 47 Phil Hannon	.25	.11
☐ 48 Phil Harrison	.25	.11
☐ 49 Jeff Hearron	.25	.11
☐ 50 Greg Kallevig	.25	.11
☐ 51 Ced Landrum	.25	.11
☐ 52 Bill Long	.25	.11
☐ 53 Derrick May	.50	.23
☐ 54 Ray Mullino	.25	.11
☐ 55 Erik Pappas	.25	.11
☐ 56 Steve Parker	.25	.11
☐ 57 Dave Pavlas	.25	.11
☐ 58 Laddie Renfroe	.25	.11
☐ 59 Jeff Small	.25	.11
☐ 60 Doug Strange	.25	.11
☐ 61 Gary Varsho	.25	.11
☐ 62 Hector Villanueva	.25	.11
☐ 63 Rick Wilkins	.50	.23
☐ 64 Dana Williams	.25	.11
☐ 65 Bill Wrona	.25	.11
☐ 66 Fernando Zarranz	.25	.11

1990 Topps TV Mets

This Mets team set contains 66 cards measuring the standard size. The fronts feature posed or action color player photos with a high gloss. In block lettering, the words "All Star" are printed vertically in orange and yellow on the left side of the card. The player's name appears in a red plaque below the picture, and white borders round out the card face. The backs are printed in black lettering and have a red and white background. Inside a decal design, player information and statistics are superimposed on an indistinct version of the same picture as on the front. Cards numbered 1-34 were with the parent club, while cards 35-66 were in the farm system.

	MINT	NRMT
COMPLETE SET (66)	20.00	9.00
COMMON CARD (1-66)	.25	.11

	MINT	NRMT
☐ 1 Dave Johnson MG	.50	.23
☐ 2 Mike Cubbage CO	.25	.11
☐ 3 Doc Edwards CO	.25	.11
☐ 4 Bud Harrelson CO	.25	.11
☐ 5 Greg Pavlick CO	.25	.11
☐ 6 Mel Stottlemyre CO	.25	.11
☐ 7 Blaine Beatty	.25	.11
☐ 8 David Cone	5.00	2.20
☐ 9 Ron Darling	.25	.11
☐ 10 Sid Fernandez	.25	.11
☐ 11 John Franco	1.50	.70
☐ 12 Dwight Gooden	4.00	1.80
☐ 13 Jeff Innis	.25	.11
☐ 14 Julio Machado	.25	.11
☐ 15 Jeff Musselman	.25	.11
☐ 16 Bob Ojeda	.25	.11
☐ 17 Alejandro Pena	.25	.11
☐ 18 Frank Viola	.50	.23
☐ 19 Wally Whitehurst	.25	.11
☐ 20 Barry Lyons	.25	.11
☐ 21 Orlando Mercado	.25	.11
☐ 22 Mackey Sasser	.25	.11
☐ 23 Kevin Elster	.25	.11
☐ 24 Gregg Jefferies	1.00	.45
☐ 25 Howard Johnson	.50	.23
☐ 26 Dave Magadan	.25	.11
☐ 27 Mike Marshall	.25	.11
☐ 28 Tom O'Malley	.25	.11
☐ 29 Tim Teufel	.25	.11
☐ 30 Mark Carreon	.25	.11
☐ 31 Kevin McReynolds	.25	.11
☐ 32 Keith Miller	.25	.11
☐ 33 Darryl Strawberry	3.00	1.35
☐ 34 Lou Thornton	.25	.11
☐ 35 Shawn Barton	.25	.11
☐ 36 Tim Bogar	.25	.11
☐ 37 Terry Bross	.25	.11
☐ 38 Kevin Brown	.25	.11
☐ 39 Mike DeButch	.25	.11
☐ 40 Alex Diaz	.25	.11
☐ 41 Chris Donnels	.25	.11
☐ 42 Jeff Gardner	.25	.11
☐ 43 Denny Gonzalez	.25	.11
☐ 44 Kenny Graves	.25	.11
☐ 45 Manny Hernandez	.25	.11
☐ 46 Keith Hughes	.25	.11
☐ 47 Todd Hundley	6.00	2.70
☐ 48 Chris Jelic	.25	.11
☐ 49 Dave Liddell	.25	.11
☐ 50 Terry McDaniel	.25	.11
☐ 51 Cesar Mejia	.25	.11
☐ 52 Scott Nielsen	.25	.11
☐ 53 Dale Plummer	.25	.11
☐ 54 Darren Reed	.25	.11
☐ 55 Gil Roca	.25	.11
☐ 56 Jaime Roseboro	.25	.11
☐ 57 Roger Samuels	.25	.11
☐ 58 Zoilo Sanchez	.25	.11
☐ 59 Pete Schourek	1.50	.70
☐ 60 Craig Shipley	.25	.11
☐ 61 Ray Soff	.25	.11
☐ 62 Steve Swisher MG	.25	.11
☐ 63 Kelvin Torve	.25	.11
☐ 64 Dave Trautwein	.25	.11
☐ 65 Julio Valera	.25	.11
☐ 66 Alan Zinter	.25	.11

1990 Topps TV Red Sox

This Red Sox team set contains 66 cards measuring the standard size. The fronts feature posed or action color player photos with a high gloss. In block lettering, the team name is printed vertically in red and yellow on the left side of the card. The player's name appears in a blue plaque below the picture, and white borders round out the card face. The backs are printed in black and have a red and white background. Inside a decal design, player information and statistics are superimposed over an

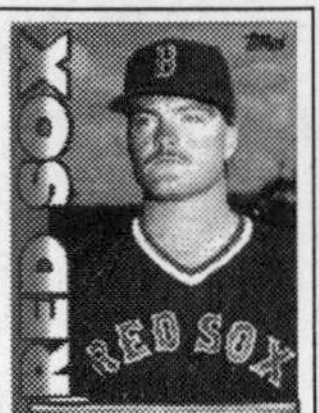

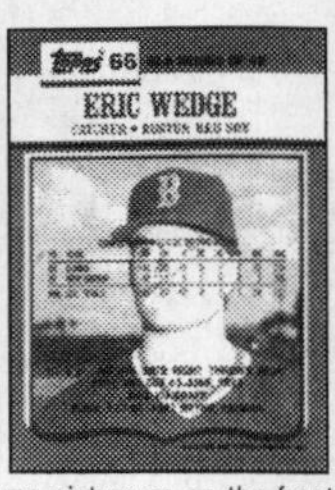

indistinct version of the same picture as on the front. Cards numbered 1-33 were with the parent club, while cards 34-66 were in the farm system. The set features an early card of Mo Vaughn.

	MINT	NRMT
COMPLETE SET (66)	35.00	16.00
COMMON CARD (1-66)	.25	.11

	MINT	NRMT
☐ 1 Joe Morgan MG	.25	.11
☐ 2 Dick Berardino CO	.25	.11
☐ 3 Al Bumbry CO	.25	.11
☐ 4 Bill Fischer CO	.25	.11
☐ 5 Richie Hebner CO	.25	.11
☐ 6 Rac Slider CO	.25	.11
☐ 7 Mike Boddicker	.25	.11
☐ 8 Roger Clemens	20.00	9.00
☐ 9 John Dopson	.25	.11
☐ 10 Wes Gardner	.25	.11
☐ 11 Greg A. Harris	.25	.11
☐ 12 Dana Kiecker	.25	.11
☐ 13 Dennis Lamp	.25	.11
☐ 14 Rob Murphy	.25	.11
☐ 15 Jeff Reardon	.50	.23
☐ 16 Mike Rochford	.25	.11
☐ 17 Lee Smith	2.00	.90
☐ 18 Rich Gedman	.25	.11
☐ 19 John Marzano	.25	.11
☐ 20 Tony Pena	.50	.23
☐ 21 Marty Barrett	.25	.11
☐ 22 Wade Boggs	10.00	4.50
☐ 23 Bill Buckner	.50	.23
☐ 24 Danny Heep	.25	.11
☐ 25 Jody Reed	.25	.11
☐ 26 Luis Rivera	.25	.11
☐ 27 Billy Joe Robidoux	.25	.11
☐ 28 Ellis Burks	2.00	.90
☐ 29 Dwight Evans	1.50	.70
☐ 30 Mike Greenwell	.50	.23
☐ 31 Randy Kutcher	.25	.11
☐ 32 Carlos Quintana	.25	.11
☐ 33 Kevin Romine	.25	.11
☐ 34 Ed Nottle MG	.25	.11
☐ 35 Mark Meleski CO	.25	.11
☐ 36 Steve Bast	.25	.11
☐ 37 Greg Blosser	.25	.11
☐ 38 Tom Bolton	.25	.11
☐ 39 Scott Cooper	.50	.23
☐ 40 Zach Crouch	.25	.11
☐ 41 Steve Curry	.25	.11
☐ 42 Mike Dalton	.25	.11
☐ 43 John Flaherty	.25	.11
☐ 44 Angel Gonzalez	.25	.11
☐ 45 Eric Hetzel	.25	.11
☐ 46 Daryl Irvine	.25	.11
☐ 47 Joe Johnson	.25	.11
☐ 48 Rick Lancellotti	.25	.11
☐ 49 John Leister	.25	.11
☐ 50 Derek Livernois	.25	.11
☐ 51 Josias Manzanillo	.25	.11
☐ 52 Kevin Morton	.25	.11
☐ 53 Julius McDougal	.25	.11
☐ 54 Tim Naehring	3.00	1.35
☐ 55 Jim Pankovits	.25	.11
☐ 56 Mickey Pina	.25	.11
☐ 57 Phil Plantier	.50	.23
☐ 58 Jerry Reed	.25	.11
☐ 59 Larry Shikles	.25	.11
☐ 60 Tito Stewart	.25	.11
☐ 61 Jeff Stone	.25	.11
☐ 62 John Trautwein	.25	.11
☐ 63 Gary Tremblay	.25	.11
☐ 64 Mo Vaughn	12.00	5.50
☐ 65 Scott Wade	.25	.11
☐ 66 Eric Wedge	.25	.11

1990 Topps TV Yankees

This Yankees team set contains 66 standard-size cards The fronts feature posed or action color player photos with a high gloss. In block lettering, the team name is printed vertically in light gray on the left side of the card The player's name appears in a gold plaque below the

picture, and white borders round out the card face. The backs are printed in black lettering and have a red and white background. Inside a decal design, player information and statistics are superimposed on an indistinct version of the same picture as on the front. Cards numbered 1-34 were with the parent club, while cards 35-66 were in the farm system. An early card of Deion Sanders is featured in this set.

	MINT	NRMT
COMPLETE SET (66)	75.00	34.00
COMMON CARD (1-66)	.25	.11
☐ 1 Bucky Dent MG	.50	.23
☐ 2 Mark Connor CO	.25	.11
☐ 3 Billy Connors CO	.25	.11
☐ 4 Mike Ferraro CO	.25	.11
☐ 5 Joe Sparks CO	.25	.11
☐ 6 Champ Summers CO	.25	.11
☐ 7 Greg Cadaret	.25	.11
☐ 8 Chuck Cary	.25	.11
☐ 9 Lee Guetterman	.25	.11
☐ 10 Andy Hawkins	.25	.11
☐ 11 Dave LaPoint	.25	.11
☐ 12 Tim Leary	.25	.11
☐ 13 Lance McCullers	.25	.11
☐ 14 Alan Mills	.25	.11
☐ 15 Clay Parker	.25	.11
☐ 16 Pascual Perez	.25	.11
☐ 17 Eric Plunk	.25	.11
☐ 18 Dave Righetti	.50	.23
☐ 19 Jeff D. Robinson	.25	.11
☐ 20 Rick Cerone	.25	.11
☐ 21 Bob Geren	.25	.11
☐ 22 Steve Balboni	.25	.11
☐ 23 Mike Blowers	1.50	.70
☐ 24 Alvaro Espinoza	.25	.11
☐ 25 Don Mattingly	50.00	22.00
☐ 26 Steve Sax	.50	.23
☐ 27 Wayne Tolleson	.25	.11
☐ 28 Randy Velarde	.50	.23
☐ 29 Jesse Barfield	.50	.23
☐ 30 Mel Hall	.25	.11
☐ 31 Roberto Kelly	.50	.23
☐ 32 Luis Polonia	.25	.11
☐ 33 Deion Sanders	7.50	3.40
☐ 34 Dave Winfield	7.50	3.40
☐ 35 Steve Adkins	.25	.11
☐ 36 Oscar Azocar	.25	.11
☐ 37 Bob Brower	.25	.11
☐ 38 Britt Burns	.25	.11
☐ 39 Bob Davidson	.25	.11
☐ 40 Brian Dorsett	.25	.11
☐ 41 Dave Eiland	.25	.11
☐ 42 John Fishel	.25	.11
☐ 43 Andy Fox	.25	.11
☐ 44 John Habyan	.25	.11
☐ 45 Cullen Hartzog	.25	.11
☐ 46 Sterling Hitchcock	1.50	.70
☐ 47 Brian Johnson	.25	.11
☐ 48 Jimmy Jones	.25	.11
☐ 49 Scott Kamieniecki	.50	.23
☐ 50 Jim Leyritz	1.50	.70
☐ 51 Mark Leiter	.25	.11
☐ 52 Jason Maas	.25	.11
☐ 53 Kevin Maas	.25	.11
☐ 54 Hensley Meulens	.25	.11
☐ 55 Kevin Mmahat	.25	.11
☐ 56 Rich Monteleone	.25	.11
☐ 57 Vince Phillips	.25	.11
☐ 58 Carlos Rodriguez	.25	.11
☐ 59 Dave Sax	.25	.11
☐ 60 Willie Smith	.25	.11
☐ 61 Van Snider	.25	.11
☐ 62 Andy Stankiewicz	.25	.11
☐ 63 Wade Taylor	.25	.11
☐ 64 Ricky Torres	.25	.11
☐ 65 Jim Walewander	.25	.11
☐ 66 Bernie Williams	10.00	4.50

1991 Topps

s set marks Topps tenth consecutive year of issuing a 2-card standard-size set. Cards were primarily issued in wax packs, rack packs and factory sets. The fronts feature a full color player photo with a white border. Topps also commemorated their fortieth anniversary by including a "Topps 40" logo on the front and back of each card. Virtually all of the cards have been discovered without the 40th logo on the back. Subsets include Record Breakers (2-8) and All-Stars (386-407). In addition, First Draft Picks and Future Stars subset cards are scattered throughout the set. The key Rookie Cards include Chipper Jones and Brian McRae. As a special promotion Topps inserted (randomly) into their wax packs one of every previous card they ever issued.

	MINT	NRMT
COMPLETE SET (792)	12.00	5.50
COMP.FACT.SET (792)	15.00	6.75
COMMON CARD (1-792)	.05	.02
☐ 1 Nolan Ryan	.75	.35
☐ 2 George Brett RB	.20	.09
Batting Title, 3 decades		
☐ 3 Carlton Fisk RB	.05	.02
Catcher HR Record		
☐ 4 Kevin Maas RB	.05	.02
Quickest to 10 HR's		
☐ 5 Cal Ripken RB	.40	.18
Most cons. errorless games		
☐ 6 Nolan Ryan RB	.40	.18
Oldest pitcher, no-hitter		
☐ 7 Ryne Sandberg RB	.20	.09
Most cons. errorless games		
☐ 8 Bobby Thigpen RB	.05	.02
Most saves, season		
☐ 9 Darrin Fletcher	.05	.02
☐ 10 Gregg Olson	.05	.02
☐ 11 Roberto Kelly	.05	.02
☐ 12 Paul Assenmacher	.05	.02
☐ 13 Mariano Duncan	.05	.02
☐ 14 Dennis Lamp	.05	.02
☐ 15 Von Hayes	.05	.02
☐ 16 Mike Heath	.05	.02
☐ 17 Jeff Brantley	.05	.02
☐ 18 Nelson Liriano	.05	.02
☐ 19 Jeff D. Robinson	.05	.02
☐ 20 Pedro Guerrero	.05	.02
☐ 21 Joe Morgan MG	.05	.02
☐ 22 Storm Davis	.05	.02
☐ 23 Jim Gantner	.05	.02
☐ 24 Dave Martinez	.05	.02
☐ 25 Tim Belcher	.05	.02
☐ 26 Luis Sojo UER	.05	.02
(Born in Barquisimento, not Carquis)		
☐ 27 Bobby Witt	.05	.02
☐ 28 Alvaro Espinoza	.05	.02
☐ 29 Bob Walk	.05	.02
☐ 30 Gregg Jefferies	.10	.05
☐ 31 Colby Ward	.05	.02
☐ 32 Mike Simms	.05	.02
☐ 33 Barry Jones	.05	.02
☐ 34 Atlee Hammaker	.05	.02
☐ 35 Greg Maddux	.60	.25
☐ 36 Donnie Hill	.05	.02
☐ 37 Tom Bolton	.05	.02
☐ 38 Scott Bradley	.05	.02
☐ 39 Jim Neidlinger	.05	.02
☐ 40 Kevin Mitchell	.10	.05
☐ 41 Ken Dayley	.05	.02
☐ 42 Chris Hoiles	.05	.02
☐ 43 Roger McDowell	.05	.02
☐ 44 Mike Felder	.05	.02
☐ 45 Chris Sabo	.05	.02
☐ 46 Tim Drummond	.05	.02
☐ 47 Brook Jacoby	.05	.02
☐ 48 Dennis Boyd	.05	.02
☐ 49A Pat Borders ERR	.20	.09
(40 steals at Kinston in '86)		
☐ 49B Pat Borders COR	.05	.02
(0 steals at Kinston in '86)		
☐ 50 Bob Welch	.05	.02
☐ 51 Art Howe MG	.05	.02
☐ 52 Francisco Oliveras	.05	.02
☐ 53 Mike Sharperson UER	.05	.02
(Born in 1961, not 1960)		
☐ 54 Gary Mielke	.05	.02
☐ 55 Jeffrey Leonard	.05	.02
☐ 56 Jeff Parrett	.05	.02
☐ 57 Jack Howell	.05	.02
☐ 58 Mel Stottlemyre Jr.	.05	.02
☐ 59 Eric Yelding	.05	.02
☐ 60 Frank Viola	.05	.02
☐ 61 Stan Javier	.05	.02
☐ 62 Lee Guetterman	.05	.02
☐ 63 Milt Thompson	.05	.02
☐ 64 Tom Herr	.05	.02
☐ 65 Bruce Hurst	.05	.02
☐ 66 Terry Kennedy	.05	.02
☐ 67 Rick Honeycutt	.05	.02
☐ 68 Gary Sheffield	.20	.09
☐ 69 Steve Wilson	.05	.02
☐ 70 Ellis Burks	.10	.05
☐ 71 Jim Acker	.05	.02
☐ 72 Junior Ortiz	.05	.02
☐ 73 Craig Worthington	.05	.02
☐ 74 Shane Andrews	.05	.02
☐ 75 Jack Morris	.10	.05
☐ 76 Jerry Browne	.05	.02
☐ 77 Drew Hall	.05	.02
☐ 78 Geno Petralli	.05	.02
☐ 79 Frank Thomas	1.50	.70
☐ 80A Fernando Valenzuela	.10	.05
ERR (104 earned runs in '90 tied for league lead)		
☐ 80B Fernando Valenzuela	.10	.05
COR (104 earned runs in '90 led league, 20 CG's in 1986 now italicized)		
☐ 81 Cito Gaston MG	.05	.02
☐ 82 Tom Glavine	.20	.09
☐ 83 Daryl Boston	.05	.02
☐ 84 Bob McClure	.05	.02
☐ 85 Jesse Barfield	.05	.02
☐ 86 Les Lancaster	.05	.02
☐ 87 Tracy Jones	.05	.02
☐ 88 Bob Tewksbury	.05	.02
☐ 89 Darren Daulton	.10	.05
☐ 90 Danny Tartabull	.05	.02
☐ 91 Greg Colbrunn	.05	.02
☐ 92 Danny Jackson	.05	.02
☐ 93 Ivan Calderon	.05	.02
☐ 94 John Dopson	.05	.02
☐ 95 Paul Molitor	.20	.09
☐ 96 Trevor Wilson	.05	.02
☐ 97A Brady Anderson ERR	.25	.11
(September, 2 RBI and 3 hits, should be 3 RBI and 14 hits		
☐ 97B Brady Anderson COR	.20	.09
☐ 98 Sergio Valdez	.05	.02
☐ 99 Chris Gwynn	.05	.02
☐ 100 Don Mattingly COR	.30	.14
(101 hits in 1990)		
☐ 100A Don Mattingly ERR	1.00	.45
(10 hits in 1990)		
☐ 101 Rob Ducey	.05	.02
☐ 102 Gene Larkin	.05	.02
☐ 103 Tim Costo	.05	.02
☐ 104 Don Robinson	.05	.02
☐ 105 Kevin McReynolds	.05	.02
☐ 106 Ed Nunez	.05	.02
☐ 107 Luis Polonia	.05	.02
☐ 108 Matt Young	.05	.02
☐ 109 Greg Riddoch MG	.05	.02
☐ 110 Tom Henke	.05	.02
☐ 111 Andres Thomas	.05	.02
☐ 112 Frank DiPino	.05	.02
☐ 113 Carl Everett	.15	.07
☐ 114 Lance Dickson	.05	.02
☐ 115 Hubie Brooks	.05	.02
☐ 116 Mark Davis	.05	.02
☐ 117 Dion James	.05	.02
☐ 118 Tom Edens	.05	.02
☐ 119 Carl Nichols	.05	.02
☐ 120 Joe Carter	.05	.02
☐ 121 Eric King	.05	.02
☐ 122 Paul O'Neill	.10	.05
☐ 123 Greg A. Harris	.05	.02
☐ 124 Randy Bush	.05	.02
☐ 125 Steve Bedrosian	.05	.02
☐ 126 Bernard Gilkey	.10	.05
☐ 127 Joe Price	.05	.02
☐ 128 Travis Fryman	.20	.09
(Front has SS back has SS-3B)		
☐ 129 Mark Eichhorn	.05	.02
☐ 130 Ozzie Smith	.25	.11

☐ 131A Checklist 1 ERR .20 .09
727 Phil Bradley
☐ 131B Checklist 1 COR .05 .02
717 Phil Bradley
☐ 132 Jamie Quirk .05 .02
☐ 133 Greg Briley .05 .02
☐ 134 Kevin Elster .05 .02
☐ 135 Jerome Walton .05 .02
☐ 136 Dave Schmidt .05 .02
☐ 137 Randy Ready .05 .02
☐ 138 Jamie Moyer .05 .02
☐ 139 Jeff Treadway .05 .02
☐ 140 Fred McGriff .20 .09
☐ 141 Nick Leyva MG .05 .02
☐ 142 Curt Wilkerson .05 .02
☐ 143 John Smiley .05 .02
☐ 144 Dave Henderson .05 .02
☐ 145 Lou Whitaker .05 .02
☐ 146 Dan Plesac .05 .02
☐ 147 Carlos Baerga .20 .09
☐ 148 Rey Palacios .05 .02
☐ 149 Al Osuna UER .05 .02
(Shown throwing right,
but bio says lefty)
☐ 150 Cal Ripken .75 .35
☐ 151 Tom Browning .05 .02
☐ 152 Mickey Hatcher .05 .02
☐ 153 Bryan Harvey .05 .02
☐ 154 Jay Buhner .20 .09
☐ 155A Dwight Evans ERR .20 .09
(Led league with
162 games in '82)
☐ 155B Dwight Evans COR .10 .05
(Tied for lead with
162 games in '82)
☐ 156 Carlos Martinez .05 .02
☐ 157 John Smoltz .20 .09
☐ 158 Jose Uribe .05 .02
☐ 159 Joe Boever .05 .02
☐ 160 Vince Coleman UER .05 .02
(Wrong birth year,
born 9/22/60)
☐ 161 Tim Leary .05 .02
☐ 162 Ozzie Canseco .05 .02
☐ 163 Dave Johnson .05 .02
☐ 164 Edgar Diaz .05 .02
☐ 165 Sandy Alomar Jr. .20 .09
☐ 166 Harold Baines .05 .02
☐ 167A Randy Tomlin ERR .20 .09
(Harriburg)
☐ 167B Randy Tomlin COR .05 .02
(Harrisburg)
☐ 168 John Olerud .10 .05
☐ 169 Luis Aquino .05 .02
☐ 170 Carlton Fisk .20 .09
☐ 171 Tony LaRussa MG .10 .05
☐ 172 Pete Incaviglia .05 .02
☐ 173 Jason Grimsley .05 .02
☐ 174 Ken Caminiti .20 .09
☐ 175 Jack Armstrong .05 .02
☐ 176 John Orton .05 .02
☐ 177 Reggie Harris .05 .02
☐ 178 Dave Valle .05 .02
☐ 179 Pete Harnisch .05 .02
☐ 180 Tony Gwynn .50 .23
☐ 181 Duane Ward .05 .02
☐ 182 Junior Noboa .05 .02
☐ 183 Clay Parker .05 .02
☐ 184 Gary Green .05 .02
☐ 185 Joe Magrane .05 .02
☐ 186 Rod Booker .05 .02
☐ 187 Greg Cadaret .05 .02
☐ 188 Damon Berryhill .05 .02
☐ 189 Daryl Irvine .05 .02
☐ 190 Matt Williams .20 .09
☐ 191 Willie Blair .05 .02
☐ 192 Rob Deer .05 .02
☐ 193 Felix Fermin .05 .02
☐ 194 Xavier Hernandez .05 .02
☐ 195 Wally Joyner .10 .05
☐ 196 Jim Vatcher .05 .02
☐ 197 Chris Nabholz .05 .02
☐ 198 R.J. Reynolds .05 .02
☐ 199 Mike Hartley .05 .02
☐ 200 Darryl Strawberry .10 .05
☐ 201 Tom Kelly MG .05 .02
☐ 202 Jim Leyritz .10 .05
☐ 203 Gene Harris .05 .02
☐ 204 Herm Winningham .05 .02
☐ 205 Mike Perez .05 .02
☐ 206 Carlos Quintana .05 .02
☐ 207 Gary Wayne .05 .02
☐ 208 Willie Wilson .05 .02
☐ 209 Ken Howell .05 .02
☐ 210 Lance Parrish .05 .02
☐ 211 Brian Barnes .05 .02
☐ 212 Steve Finley .05 .02
☐ 213 Frank Wills .05 .02
☐ 214 Joe Girardi .10 .05
☐ 215 Dave Smith .05 .02
☐ 216 Greg Gagne .05 .02
☐ 217 Chris Bosio .05 .02
☐ 218 Rick Parker .05 .02
☐ 219 Jack McDowell .10 .05
☐ 220 Tim Wallach .05 .02
☐ 221 Don Slaught .05 .02
☐ 222 Brian McRae .25 .11
☐ 223 Allan Anderson .05 .02
☐ 224 Juan Gonzalez .75 .35
☐ 225 Randy Johnson .25 .11
☐ 226 Alfredo Griffin .05 .02
☐ 227 Steve Avery UER .10 .05
(Pitched 13 games for
Durham in 1989, not 2)
☐ 228 Rex Hudler .05 .02
☐ 229 Rance Mulliniks .05 .02
☐ 230 Sid Fernandez .05 .02
☐ 231 Doug Rader MG .05 .02
☐ 232 Jose DeJesus .05 .02
☐ 233 Al Leiter .10 .05
☐ 234 Scott Erickson .05 .02
☐ 235 Dave Parker .10 .05
☐ 236A Frank Tanana ERR .10 .05
(Tied for lead with
269 K's in '75)
☐ 236B Frank Tanana COR .05 .02
(Led league with
269 K's in '75)
☐ 237 Rick Cerone .05 .02
☐ 238 Mike Dunne .05 .02
☐ 239 Darren Lewis .05 .02
☐ 240 Mike Scott .05 .02
☐ 241 Dave Clark UER .05 .02
(Career totals 19 HR
and 5 3B, should
be 22 and 3)
☐ 242 Mike LaCoss .05 .02
☐ 243 Lance Johnson .05 .02
☐ 244 Mike Jeffcoat .05 .02
☐ 245 Kal Daniels .05 .02
☐ 246 Kevin Wickander .05 .02
☐ 247 Jody Reed .05 .02
☐ 248 Tom Gordon .05 .02
☐ 249 Bob Melvin .05 .02
☐ 250 Dennis Eckersley .05 .02
☐ 251 Mark Lemke .05 .02
☐ 252 Mel Rojas .10 .05
☐ 253 Garry Templeton .05 .02
☐ 254 Shawn Boskie .05 .02
☐ 255 Brian Downing .05 .02
☐ 256 Greg Hibbard .05 .02
☐ 257 Tom O'Malley .05 .02
☐ 258 Chris Hammond .05 .02
☐ 259 Hensley Meulens .05 .02
☐ 260 Harold Reynolds .05 .02
☐ 261 Bud Harrelson MG .05 .02
☐ 262 Tim Jones .05 .02
☐ 263 Checklist 2 .05 .02
☐ 264 Dave Hollins .05 .02
☐ 265 Mark Gubicza .05 .02
☐ 266 Carmelo Castillo .05 .02
☐ 267 Mark Knudson .05 .02
☐ 268 Tom Brookens .05 .02
☐ 269 Joe Hesketh .05 .02
☐ 270 Mark McGwire COR .40 .18
(1987 Slugging Pctg.
listed as .618)
☐ 270A Mark McGwire ERR .50 .23
(1987 Slugging Pctg.
listed as 618)
☐ 271 Omar Olivares .05 .02
☐ 272 Jeff King .10 .05
☐ 273 Johnny Ray .05 .02
☐ 274 Ken Williams .05 .02
☐ 275 Alan Trammell .10 .05
☐ 276 Bill Swift .05 .02
☐ 277 Scott Coolbaugh .05 .02
☐ 278 Alex Fernandez UER .10 .05
(No '90 White Sox stats)
☐ 279A Jose Gonzalez ERR .05 .02
(Photo actually
Billy Bean)
☐ 279B Jose Gonzalez COR .05 .02
☐ 280 Bret Saberhagen .10 .05
☐ 281 Larry Sheets .05 .02
☐ 282 Don Carman .05 .02
☐ 283 Marquis Grissom .20 .09
☐ 284 Billy Spiers .05 .02
☐ 285 Jim Abbott .10 .05
☐ 286 Ken Oberkfell .05 .02
☐ 287 Mark Grant .05 .02
☐ 288 Derrick May .05 .02
☐ 289 Tim Birtsas .05 .02
☐ 290 Steve Sax .05 .02
☐ 291 John Wathan MG .05 .02
☐ 292 Bud Black .05 .02
☐ 293 Jay Bell .10 .05
☐ 294 Mike Moore .05 .02
☐ 295 Rafael Palmeiro .20 .09
☐ 296 Mark Williamson .05 .02
☐ 297 Manny Lee .05 .02
☐ 298 Omar Vizquel .20 .09
☐ 299 Scott Radinsky .05 .02
☐ 300 Kirby Puckett .40 .18
☐ 301 Steve Farr .05 .02
☐ 302 Tim Teufel .05 .02
☐ 303 Mike Boddicker .05 .02
☐ 304 Kevin Reimer .05 .02
☐ 305 Mike Scioscia .05 .02
☐ 306A Lonnie Smith ERR .20 .09
(136 games in '90)
☐ 306B Lonnie Smith COR .05 .02
(135 games in '90)
☐ 307 Andy Benes .10 .05
☐ 308 Tom Pagnozzi .05 .02
☐ 309 Norm Charlton .05 .02
☐ 310 Gary Carter .20 .09
☐ 311 Jeff Pico .05 .02
☐ 312 Charlie Hayes .05 .02
☐ 313 Ron Robinson .05 .02
☐ 314 Gary Pettis .05 .02
☐ 315 Roberto Alomar .20 .09
☐ 316 Gene Nelson .05 .02
☐ 317 Mike Fitzgerald .05 .02
☐ 318 Rick Aguilera .10 .05
☐ 319 Jeff McKnight .05 .02
☐ 320 Tony Fernandez .05 .02
☐ 321 Bob Rodgers MG .05 .02
☐ 322 Terry Shumpert .05 .02
☐ 323 Cory Snyder .05 .02
☐ 324A Ron Kittle ERR .20 .09
(Set another
standard ...)
☐ 324B Ron Kittle COR .05 .02
(Tied another
standard ...)
☐ 325 Brett Butler .05 .02
☐ 326 Ken Patterson .05 .02
☐ 327 Ron Hassey .05 .02
☐ 328 Walt Terrell .05 .02
☐ 329 Dave Justice UER .25 .11
(Drafted third round
on card, should say
fourth pick)
☐ 330 Dwight Gooden .10 .05
☐ 331 Eric Anthony .05 .02
☐ 332 Kenny Rogers .05 .02
☐ 333 Chipper Jones FDP 3.00 1.35
☐ 334 Todd Benzinger .05 .02
☐ 335 Mitch Williams .05 .02
☐ 336 Matt Nokes .05 .02
☐ 337A Keith Comstock ERR .20 .09
(Cubs logo on front)
☐ 337B Keith Comstock COR .05 .02
(Mariners logo on front)
☐ 338 Luis Rivera .05 .02
☐ 339 Larry Walker .30 .14
☐ 340 Ramon Martinez .10 .05
☐ 341 John Moses .05 .0
☐ 342 Mickey Morandini .05 .0
☐ 343 Jose Oquendo .05 .0
☐ 344 Jeff Russell .05 .0
☐ 345 Len Dykstra .10 .0
☐ 346 Jesse Orosco .05 .0
☐ 347 Greg Vaughn .05 .0
☐ 348 Todd Stottlemyre .05 .0
☐ 349 Dave Gallagher .05 .0
☐ 350 Glenn Davis .05 .0
☐ 351 Joe Torre MG .10 .0
☐ 352 Frank White .10 .0
☐ 353 Tony Castillo .05 .0
☐ 354 Sid Bream .05 .0
☐ 355 Chili Davis .05 .0
☐ 356 Mike Marshall .05 .0
☐ 357 Jack Savage .05 .0
☐ 358 Mark Parent .05 .0
☐ 359 Chuck Cary .05 .0
☐ 360 Tim Raines .10 .0
☐ 361 Scott Garrelts .05 .0
☐ 362 Hector Villenueva .05 .0
☐ 363 Rick Mahler .05 .0
☐ 364 Dan Pasqua .05 .0
☐ 365 Mike Schooler .05 .0
☐ 366A Checklist 3 ERR .20 .0
19 Carl Nichols
☐ 366B Checklist 3 COR .05 .0
119 Carl Nichols
☐ 367 Dave Walsh .05 .
☐ 368 Felix Jose .05 .
☐ 369 Steve Searcy .05 .
☐ 370 Kelly Gruber .05 .

☐ 371 Jeff Montgomery	.10	.05
☐ 372 Spike Owen	.05	.02
☐ 373 Darrin Jackson	.05	.02
☐ 374 Larry Casian	.05	.02
☐ 375 Tony Pena	.05	.02
☐ 376 Mike Harkey	.05	.02
☐ 377 Rene Gonzales	.05	.02
☐ 378A Wilson Alvarez ERR ('89 Port Charlotte and '90 Birmingham stat lines omitted)	.50	.23
☐ 378B Wilson Alvarez COR (Text still says 143 K's in 1988, whereas stats say 134)	.20	.09
☐ 379 Randy Velarde	.05	.02
☐ 380 Willie McGee	.05	.02
☐ 381 Jim Leyland MG	.05	.02
☐ 382 Mackey Sasser	.05	.02
☐ 383 Pete Smith	.05	.02
☐ 384 Gerald Perry	.05	.02
☐ 385 Mickey Tettleton	.10	.05
☐ 386 Cecil Fielder AS	.10	.05
☐ 387 Julio Franco AS	.05	.02
☐ 388 Kelly Gruber AS	.05	.02
☐ 389 Alan Trammell AS	.10	.05
☐ 390 Jose Canseco AS	.20	.09
☐ 391 Rickey Henderson AS	.20	.09
☐ 392 Ken Griffey Jr. AS	.75	.35
☐ 393 Carlton Fisk AS	.20	.09
☐ 394 Bob Welch AS	.05	.02
☐ 395 Chuck Finley AS	.05	.02
☐ 396 Bobby Thigpen AS	.05	.02
☐ 397 Eddie Murray AS	.20	.09
☐ 398 Ryne Sandberg AS	.20	.09
☐ 399 Matt Williams AS	.20	.09
☐ 400 Barry Larkin AS	.20	.09
☐ 401 Barry Bonds AS	.20	.09
☐ 402 Darryl Strawbery AS	.10	.05
☐ 403 Bobby Bonilla AS	.10	.05
☐ 404 Mike Scioscia AS	.05	.02
☐ 405 Doug Drabek AS	.05	.02
☐ 406 Frank Viola AS	.05	.02
☐ 407 John Franco AS	.05	.02
☐ 408 Earnie Riles	.05	.02
☐ 409 Mike Stanley	.05	.02
☐ 410 Dave Righetti	.05	.02
☐ 411 Lance Blankenship	.05	.02
☐ 412 Dave Bergman	.05	.02
☐ 413 Terry Mulholland	.05	.02
☐ 414 Sammy Sosa	.25	.11
☐ 415 Rick Sutcliffe	.05	.02
☐ 416 Randy Milligan	.05	.02
☐ 417 Bill Krueger	.05	.02
☐ 418 Nick Esasky	.05	.02
☐ 419 Jeff Reed	.05	.02
☐ 420 Bobby Thigpen	.05	.02
☐ 421 Alex Cole	.05	.02
☐ 422 Rick Reuschel	.05	.02
☐ 423 Rafael Ramirez UER (Born 1959, not 1958)	.05	.02
☐ 424 Calvin Schiraldi	.05	.02
☐ 425 Andy Van Slyke	.10	.05
☐ 426 Joe Grahe	.05	.02
☐ 427 Rick Dempsey	.05	.02
☐ 428 John Barfield	.05	.02
☐ 429 Stump Merrill MG	.05	.02
☐ 430 Gary Gaetti	.10	.05
☐ 431 Paul Gibson	.05	.02
☐ 432 Delino DeShields	.05	.02
☐ 433 Pat Tabler	.05	.02
☐ 434 Julio Machado	.05	.02
☐ 435 Kevin Maas	.05	.02
☐ 436 Scott Bankhead	.05	.02
☐ 437 Doug Dascenzo	.05	.02
☐ 438 Vicente Palacios	.05	.02
☐ 439 Dickie Thon	.05	.02
☐ 440 George Bell	.05	.02
☐ 441 Zane Smith	.05	.02
☐ 442 Charlie O'Brien	.05	.02
☐ 443 Jeff Innis	.05	.02
☐ 444 Glenn Braggs	.05	.02
☐ 445 Greg Swindell	.05	.02
☐ 446 Craig Grebeck	.05	.02
☐ 447 John Burkett	.05	.02
☐ 448 Craig Lefferts	.05	.02
☐ 449 Juan Berenguer	.05	.02
☐ 450 Wade Boggs	.20	.09
☐ 451 Neal Heaton	.05	.02
☐ 452 Bill Schroeder	.05	.02
☐ 453 Lenny Harris	.05	.02
☐ 454A Kevin Appier ERR ('90 Omaha stat line omitted)	.20	.09
☐ 454B Kevin Appier COR	.20	.09
☐ 455 Walt Weiss	.05	.02
☐ 456 Charlie Leibrandt	.05	.02
☐ 457 Todd Hundley	.20	.09
☐ 458 Brian Holman	.05	.02
☐ 459 Tom Trebelhorn MG UER (Pitching and batting columns switched)	.05	.02
☐ 460 Dave Stieb	.05	.02
☐ 461 Robin Ventura	.20	.09
☐ 462 Steve Frey	.05	.02
☐ 463 Dwight Smith	.05	.02
☐ 464 Steve Buechele	.05	.02
☐ 465 Ken Griffey Sr.	.05	.02
☐ 466 Charles Nagy	.20	.09
☐ 467 Dennis Cook	.05	.02
☐ 468 Tim Hulett	.05	.02
☐ 469 Chet Lemon	.05	.02
☐ 470 Howard Johnson	.05	.02
☐ 471 Mike Lieberthal	.15	.07
☐ 472 Kirt Manwaring	.05	.02
☐ 473 Curt Young	.05	.02
☐ 474 Phil Plantier	.10	.05
☐ 475 Teddy Higuera	.05	.02
☐ 476 Glenn Wilson	.05	.02
☐ 477 Mike Fetters	.05	.02
☐ 478 Kurt Stillwell	.05	.02
☐ 479 Bob Patterson UER (Has a decimal point between 7 and 9)	.05	.02
☐ 480 Dave Magadan	.05	.02
☐ 481 Eddie Whitson	.05	.02
☐ 482 Tino Martinez	.20	.09
☐ 483 Mike Aldrete	.05	.02
☐ 484 Dave LaPoint	.05	.02
☐ 485 Terry Pendleton	.10	.05
☐ 486 Tommy Greene	.05	.02
☐ 487 Rafael Belliard	.05	.02
☐ 488 Jeff Manto	.05	.02
☐ 489 Bobby Valentine MG	.05	.02
☐ 490 Kirk Gibson	.10	.05
☐ 491 Kurt Miller	.05	.02
☐ 492 Ernie Whitt	.05	.02
☐ 493 Jose Rijo	.05	.02
☐ 494 Chris James	.05	.02
☐ 495 Charlie Hough	.05	.02
☐ 496 Marty Barrett	.05	.02
☐ 497 Ben McDonald	.10	.05
☐ 498 Mark Salas	.05	.02
☐ 499 Melido Perez	.05	.02
☐ 500 Will Clark	.20	.09
☐ 501 Mike Bielecki	.05	.02
☐ 502 Carney Lansford	.10	.05
☐ 503 Roy Smith	.05	.02
☐ 504 Julio Valera	.05	.02
☐ 505 Chuck Finley	.10	.05
☐ 506 Darnell Coles	.05	.02
☐ 507 Steve Jeltz	.05	.02
☐ 508 Mike York	.05	.02
☐ 509 Glenallen Hill	.05	.02
☐ 510 John Franco	.05	.02
☐ 511 Steve Balboni	.05	.02
☐ 512 Jose Mesa	.10	.05
☐ 513 Jerald Clark	.05	.02
☐ 514 Mike Stanton	.05	.02
☐ 515 Alvin Davis	.05	.02
☐ 516 Karl Rhodes	.05	.02
☐ 517 Joe Oliver	.05	.02
☐ 518 Cris Carpenter	.05	.02
☐ 519 Sparky Anderson MG	.10	.05
☐ 520 Mark Grace	.20	.09
☐ 521 Joe Orsulak	.05	.02
☐ 522 Stan Belinda	.05	.02
☐ 523 Rodney McCray	.05	.02
☐ 524 Darrel Akerfelds	.05	.02
☐ 525 Willie Randolph	.10	.05
☐ 526A Moises Alou ERR (37 runs in 2 games for '90 Pirates)	.50	.23
☐ 526B Moises Alou COR (0 runs in 2 games for '90 Pirates)	.20	.09
☐ 527A Checklist 4 ERR 105 Keith Miller 719 Kevin McReynolds	.20	.09
☐ 527B Checklist 4 COR 105 Kevin McReynolds 719 Keith Miller	.05	.02
☐ 528 Denny Martinez	.10	.05
☐ 529 Marc Newfield	.15	.07
☐ 530 Roger Clemens	.40	.18
☐ 531 Dave Rohde	.05	.02
☐ 532 Kirk McCaskill	.05	.02
☐ 533 Oddibe McDowell	.05	.02
☐ 534 Mike Jackson	.05	.02
☐ 535 Ruben Sierra UER (Back reads 100 Runs amd 100 RBI's)	.05	.02
☐ 536 Mike Witt	.05	.02
☐ 537 Jose Lind	.05	.02
☐ 538 Bip Roberts	.05	.02
☐ 539 Scott Terry	.05	.02
☐ 540 George Brett	.40	.18
☐ 541 Domingo Ramos	.05	.02
☐ 542 Rob Murphy	.05	.02
☐ 543 Junior Felix	.05	.02
☐ 544 Alejandro Pena	.05	.02
☐ 545 Dale Murphy	.20	.09
☐ 546 Jeff Ballard	.05	.02
☐ 547 Mike Pagliarulo	.05	.02
☐ 548 Jaime Navarro	.05	.02
☐ 549 John McNamara MG	.05	.02
☐ 550 Eric Davis	.10	.05
☐ 551 Bob Kipper	.05	.02
☐ 552 Jeff Hamilton	.05	.02
☐ 553 Joe Klink	.05	.02
☐ 554 Brian Harper	.05	.02
☐ 555 Turner Ward	.05	.02
☐ 556 Gary Ward	.05	.02
☐ 557 Wally Whitehurst	.05	.02
☐ 558 Otis Nixon	.10	.05
☐ 559 Adam Peterson	.05	.02
☐ 560 Greg Smith	.05	.02
☐ 561 Tim McIntosh	.05	.02
☐ 562 Jeff Kunkel	.05	.02
☐ 563 Brent Knackert	.05	.02
☐ 564 Dante Bichette	.20	.09
☐ 565 Craig Biggio	.20	.09
☐ 566 Craig Wilson	.05	.02
☐ 567 Dwayne Henry	.05	.02
☐ 568 Ron Karkovice	.05	.02
☐ 569 Curt Schilling	.20	.09
☐ 570 Barry Bonds	.25	.11
☐ 571 Pat Combs	.05	.02
☐ 572 Dave Anderson	.05	.02
☐ 573 Rich Rodriguez UER (Stats say drafted 4th, but bio says 9th round)	.05	.02
☐ 574 John Marzano	.05	.02
☐ 575 Robin Yount	.20	.09
☐ 576 Jeff Kaiser	.05	.02
☐ 577 Bill Doran	.05	.02
☐ 578 Dave West	.05	.02
☐ 579 Roger Craig MG	.05	.02
☐ 580 Dave Stewart	.10	.05
☐ 581 Luis Quinones	.05	.02
☐ 582 Marty Clary	.05	.02
☐ 583 Tony Phillips	.05	.02
☐ 584 Kevin Brown	.05	.02
☐ 585 Pete O'Brien	.05	.02
☐ 586 Fred Lynn	.05	.02
☐ 587 Jose Offerman UER (Text says he signed 7/24/86, but bio says 1988)	.05	.02
☐ 588 Mark Whiten	.05	.02
☐ 589 Scott Ruskin	.05	.02
☐ 590 Eddie Murray	.20	.09
☐ 591 Ken Hill	.10	.05
☐ 592 B.J. Surhoff	.10	.05
☐ 593A Mike Walker ERR ('90 Canton-Akron stat line omitted)	.20	.09
☐ 593B Mike Walker COR	.05	.02
☐ 594 Rich Garces	.05	.02
☐ 595 Bill Landrum	.05	.02
☐ 596 Ronnie Walden	.05	.02
☐ 597 Jerry Don Gleaton	.05	.02
☐ 598 Sam Horn	.05	.02
☐ 599A Greg Myers ERR ('90 Syracuse stat line omitted)	.20	.09
☐ 599B Greg Myers COR	.05	.02
☐ 600 Bo Jackson	.05	.02
☐ 601 Bob Ojeda	.05	.02
☐ 602 Casey Candaele	.05	.02
☐ 603A Wes Chamberlain ERR (Photo actually Louie Meadows)	.20	.09
☐ 603B Wes Chamberlain COR	.05	.02
☐ 604 Billy Hatcher	.05	.02
☐ 605 Jeff Reardon	.10	.05
☐ 606 Jim Gott	.05	.02
☐ 607 Edgar Martinez	.20	.09
☐ 608 Todd Burns	.05	.02
☐ 609 Jeff Torborg MG	.05	.02
☐ 610 Andres Galarraga	.20	.09
☐ 611 Dave Eiland	.05	.02
☐ 612 Steve Lyons	.05	.02
☐ 613 Eric Show	.05	.02
☐ 614 Luis Salazar	.05	.02
☐ 615 Bert Blyleven	.10	.05
☐ 616 Todd Zeile	.10	.05
☐ 617 Bill Wegman	.05	.02
☐ 618 Sil Campusano	.05	.02
☐ 619 David Wells	.05	.02
☐ 620 Ozzie Guillen	.05	.02

☐ 621 Ted Power .05 .02
☐ 622 Jack Daugherty .05 .02
☐ 623 Jeff Blauser .05 .02
☐ 624 Tom Candiotti .05 .02
☐ 625 Terry Steinbach .10 .05
☐ 626 Gerald Young .05 .02
☐ 627 Tim Layana .05 .02
☐ 628 Greg Litton .05 .02
☐ 629 Wes Gardner .05 .02
☐ 630 Dave Winfield .20 .09
☐ 631 Mike Morgan .05 .02
☐ 632 Lloyd Moseby .05 .02
☐ 633 Kevin Tapani .05 .02
☐ 634 Henry Cotto .05 .02
☐ 635 Andy Hawkins .05 .02
☐ 636 Geronimo Pena .05 .02
☐ 637 Bruce Ruffin .05 .02
☐ 638 Mike Macfarlane .05 .02
☐ 639 Frank Robinson MG .05 .02
☐ 640 Andre Dawson .20 .09
☐ 641 Mike Henneman .05 .02
☐ 642 Hal Morris .05 .02
☐ 643 Jim Presley .05 .02
☐ 644 Chuck Crim .05 .02
☐ 645 Juan Samuel .05 .02
☐ 646 Andujar Cedeno .05 .02
☐ 647 Mark Portugal .05 .02
☐ 648 Lee Stevens .05 .02
☐ 649 Bill Sampen .05 .02
☐ 650 Jack Clark .10 .05
☐ 651 Alan Mills .05 .02
☐ 652 Kevin Romine .05 .02
☐ 653 Anthony Telford .05 .02
☐ 654 Paul Sorrento .10 .05
☐ 655 Erik Hanson .05 .02
☐ 656A Checklist 5 ERR .20 .09
348 Vicente Palacios
381 Jose Lind
537 Mike LaValliere
665 Jim Leyland
☐ 656B Checklist 5 ERR .20 .09
433 Vicente Palacios
(Palacios should be 438)
537 Jose Lind
665 Mike LaValliere
381 Jim Leyland
☐ 656C Checklist 5 COR .20 .09
438 Vicente Palacios
537 Jose Lind
665 Mike LaValliere
381 Jim Leyland
☐ 657 Mike Kingery .05 .02
☐ 658 Scott Aldred .05 .02
☐ 659 Oscar Azocar .05 .02
☐ 660 Lee Smith .10 .05
☐ 661 Steve Lake .05 .02
☐ 662 Ron Dibble .05 .02
☐ 663 Greg Brock .05 .02
☐ 664 John Farrell .05 .02
☐ 665 Mike LaValliere .05 .02
☐ 666 Danny Darwin .05 .02
☐ 667 Kent Anderson .05 .02
☐ 668 Bill Long .05 .02
☐ 669 Lou Piniella MG .10 .05
☐ 670 Rickey Henderson .20 .09
☐ 671 Andy McGaffigan .05 .02
☐ 672 Shane Mack .05 .02
☐ 673 Greg Olson UER .05 .02
(6 RBI in '88 at Tidewater
and 2 RBI in '87,
should be 48 and 15)
☐ 674A Kevin Gross ERR .20 .09
(89 BB with Phillies
in '88 tied for
league lead)
☐ 674B Kevin Gross COR .05 .02
(89 BB with Phillies
in '88 led league)
☐ 675 Tom Brunansky .05 .02
☐ 676 Scott Chiamparino .05 .02
☐ 677 Billy Ripken .05 .02
☐ 678 Mark Davidson .05 .02
☐ 679 Bill Bathe .05 .02
☐ 680 David Cone .10 .05
☐ 681 Jeff Schaefer .05 .02
☐ 682 Ray Lankford .20 .09
☐ 683 Derek Lilliquist .05 .02
☐ 684 Milt Cuyler .05 .02
☐ 685 Doug Drabek .05 .02
☐ 686 Mike Gallego .05 .02
☐ 687A John Cerutti ERR .20 .09
(4.46 ERA in '90)
☐ 687B John Cerutti COR .05 .02
(4.76 ERA in '90)
☐ 688 Rosario Rodriguez .05 .02
☐ 689 John Kruk .10 .05
☐ 690 Orel Hershiser .05 .02
☐ 691 Mike Blowers .05 .02
☐ 692A Efrain Valdez ERR .20 .09
(Born 6/11/66)
☐ 692B Efrain Valdez COR .05 .02
(Born 7/11/66 and two
lines of text added)
☐ 693 Francisco Cabrera .05 .02
☐ 694 Randy Veres .05 .02
☐ 695 Kevin Seitzer .05 .02
☐ 696 Steve Olin .05 .02
☐ 697 Shawn Abner .05 .02
☐ 698 Mark Guthrie .05 .02
☐ 699 Jim Lefebvre MG .05 .02
☐ 700 Jose Canseco .20 .09
☐ 701 Pascual Perez .05 .02
☐ 702 Tim Naehring .10 .05
☐ 703 Juan Agosto .05 .02
☐ 704 Devon White .10 .05
☐ 705 Robby Thompson .05 .02
☐ 706A Brad Arnsberg ERR .20 .09
(68.2 IP in '90)
☐ 706B Brad Arnsberg COR .05 .02
(62.2 IP in '90)
☐ 707 Jim Eisenreich .10 .05
☐ 708 John Mitchell .05 .02
☐ 709 Matt Sinatro .05 .02
☐ 710 Kent Hrbek .10 .05
☐ 711 Jose DeLeon .05 .02
☐ 712 Ricky Jordan .05 .02
☐ 713 Scott Scudder .05 .02
☐ 714 Marvell Wynne .05 .02
☐ 715 Tim Burke .05 .02
☐ 716 Bob Geren .05 .02
☐ 717 Phil Bradley .05 .02
☐ 718 Steve Crawford .05 .02
☐ 719 Keith Miller .05 .02
☐ 720 Cecil Fielder .10 .05
☐ 721 Mark Lee .05 .02
☐ 722 Wally Backman .05 .02
☐ 723 Candy Maldonado .05 .02
☐ 724 David Segui .10 .05
☐ 725 Ron Gant .10 .05
☐ 726 Phil Stephenson .05 .02
☐ 727 Mookie Wilson .05 .02
☐ 728 Scott Sanderson .05 .02
☐ 729 Don Zimmer MG .05 .02
☐ 730 Barry Larkin .20 .09
☐ 731 Jeff Gray .05 .02
☐ 732 Franklin Stubbs .05 .02
☐ 733 Kelly Downs .05 .02
☐ 734 John Russell .05 .02
☐ 735 Ron Darling .05 .02
☐ 736 Dick Schofield .05 .02
☐ 737 Tim Crews .05 .02
☐ 738 Mel Hall .05 .02
☐ 739 Russ Swan .05 .02
☐ 740 Ryne Sandberg .25 .11
☐ 741 Jimmy Key .10 .05
☐ 742 Tommy Gregg .05 .02
☐ 743 Bryn Smith .05 .02
☐ 744 Nelson Santovenia .05 .02
☐ 745 Doug Jones .05 .02
☐ 746 John Shelby .05 .02
☐ 747 Tony Fossas .05 .02
☐ 748 Al Newman .05 .02
☐ 749 Greg W. Harris .05 .02
☐ 750 Bobby Bonilla .10 .05
☐ 751 Wayne Edwards .05 .02
☐ 752 Kevin Bass .05 .02
☐ 753 Paul Marak UER .05 .02
(Stats say drafted in
Jan. but bio says May)
☐ 754 Bill Pecota .05 .02
☐ 755 Mark Langston .05 .02
☐ 756 Jeff Huson .05 .02
☐ 757 Mark Gardner .05 .02
☐ 758 Mike Devereaux .05 .02
☐ 759 Bobby Cox MG .10 .05
☐ 760 Benny Santiago .05 .02
☐ 761 Larry Andersen .05 .02
☐ 762 Mitch Webster .05 .02
☐ 763 Dana Kiecker .05 .02
☐ 764 Mark Carreon .05 .02
☐ 765 Shawon Dunston .05 .02
☐ 766 Jeff Robinson .05 .02
☐ 767 Dan Wilson .25 .11
☐ 768 Don Pall .05 .02
☐ 769 Tim Sherrill .05 .02
☐ 770 Jay Howell .05 .02
☐ 771 Gary Redus UER .05 .02
(Born in Tanner,
should say Athens)
☐ 772 Kent Mercker UER .05 .02
(Born in Indianapolis,
should say Dublin, Ohio)
☐ 773 Tom Foley .05 .02
☐ 774 Dennis Rasmussen .05 .02
☐ 775 Julio Franco .10 .05
☐ 776 Brent Mayne .05 .02
☐ 777 John Candelaria .05 .02
☐ 778 Dan Gladden .05 .02
☐ 779 Carmelo Martinez .05 .02
☐ 780A Randy Myers ERR .20 .09
(15 career losses)
☐ 780B Randy Myers COR .05 .02
(19 career losses)
☐ 781 Darryl Hamilton .05 .02
☐ 782 Jim Deshaies .05 .02
☐ 783 Joel Skinner .05 .02
☐ 784 Willie Fraser .05 .02
☐ 785 Scott Fletcher .05 .02
☐ 786 Eric Plunk .05 .02
☐ 787 Checklist 6 .05 .02
☐ 788 Bob Milacki .05 .02
☐ 789 Tom Lasorda MG .05 .02
☐ 790 Ken Griffey Jr. 1.50 .70
☐ 791 Mike Benjamin .05 .02
☐ 792 Mike Greenwell .05 .02

1991 Topps Desert Shield

These 792 standard-size cards are parallel to the regular Topps issue. These cards were issued in special packs available only to servicepeople serving in the Desert Shield (later to be Desert Storm) campaign. The cards are differentiated by a "Desert Shield" logo in the upper right corner. There were many different types of forgeries created for these cards so some caution is urged in purchasing any expensive cards from the set.

	MINT	NRMT
COMPLETE SET (792)	1500.00	700.00
COMMON CARD (1-792)	1.00	.45
*STARS: 40X to 80X BASIC CARDS		
*ROOKIES: 25X to 50X BASIC CARDS		

1991 Topps Micro

This 792 card set parallels the regular Topps issue. The cards are significantly smaller than the regular Topps cards and are valued at a percentage of the regular 1991 Topps cards.

	MINT	NRMT
COMPLETE FACT.SET (792)	10.00	4.50
COMMON CARD (1-792)	.05	.02
*STARS: .5X to 1X BASIC CARDS		

1991 Topps Tiffany

This 792 standard-size set proved to be the final time Topps issued their Tiffany sets. These cards again parallel the regular issue and have "glossy" fronts and easy to read backs. These cards were issued in complete set form only. Since a limited amount of these sets were produced, the multiplier is one of the highest for any of these Topps sets.

	MINT	NRMT
COMPLETE FACT.SET (792)	200.00	90.00
COMMON CARD (1-792)	.15	.07
*STARS: 15X to 30X BASIC CARDS		
*ROOKIES: 10X to 20X BASIC CARDS		

1991 Topps Rookies

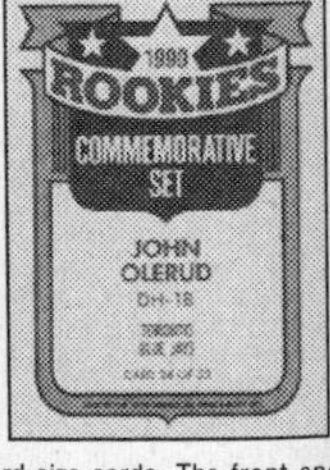

This set contains 33 standard-size cards. The front and back borders are white and other design elements are red, blue, and yellow. This set is identical to the previous year's set. Topps also commemorated its 40th anniversary by including a "Topps 40" logo on the front. The cards are unnumbered and checklisted below in alphabetical order.

	MINT	NRMT
COMPLETE SET (33)	12.00	5.50
COMMON CARD (1-33)	.10	.05

☐ 1 Sandy Alomar .20 .09
☐ 2 Kevin Appier .35 .16
☐ 3 Steve Avery .10 .05

☐ 4 Carlos Baerga	.20	.09
☐ 5 John Burkett	.10	.05
☐ 6 Alex Cole	.10	.05
☐ 7 Pat Combs	.10	.05
☐ 8 Delino DeShields	.20	.09
☐ 9 Travis Fryman	.35	.16
☐ 10 Marquis Grissom	.35	.16
☐ 11 Mike Harkey	.10	.05
☐ 12 Glenallen Hill	.10	.05
☐ 13 Jeff Huson	.10	.05
☐ 14 Felix Jose	.10	.05
☐ 15 Dave Justice	1.00	.45
☐ 16 Jim Leyritz	.10	.05
☐ 17 Kevin Maas	.10	.05
☐ 18 Ben McDonald	.10	.05
☐ 19 Kent Mercker	.10	.05
☐ 20 Hal Morris	.10	.05
☐ 21 Chris Nabholz	.10	.05
☐ 22 Tim Naehring	.35	.16
☐ 23 Jose Offerman	.10	.05
☐ 24 John Olerud	.50	.23
☐ 25 Scott Radinsky	.10	.05
☐ 26 Scott Ruskin	.10	.05
☐ 27 Kevin Tapani	.20	.09
☐ 28 Frank Thomas	6.00	2.70
☐ 29 Randy Tomlin	.10	.05
☐ 30 Greg Vaughn	.10	.05
☐ 31 Robin Ventura	.35	.16
☐ 32 Larry Walker	1.00	.45
☐ 33 Todd Zeile	.20	.09

1991 Topps Wax Box Cards

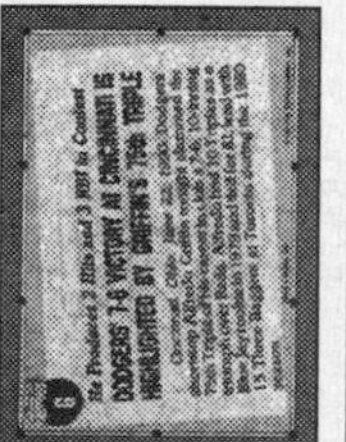

Topps again in 1991 issued cards on the bottom of their wax pack boxes. There are four different boxes, each with four cards and a checklist on the side. These standard-size cards have yellow borders rather than the white borders of the regular issue cards, and they have different photos of the players. The backs are printed in pink and blue on gray cardboard stock and feature outstanding achievements of the players. The cards are numbered by letter on the back. The cards have the typical Topps 1991 design on the front of the card. The set was ordered in alphabetical order and lettered A-P.

	MINT	NRMT
COMPLETE SET (16)	6.00	2.70
COMMON CARD (A-P)	.10	.05
☐ A Bert Blyleven	.20	.09
☐ B George Brett	1.00	.45
☐ C Brett Butler	.10	.05
☐ D Andre Dawson	.50	.23
☐ E Dwight Evans	.20	.09
☐ F Carlton Fisk	.35	.16
☐ G Alfredo Griffin	.10	.05
☐ H Rickey Henderson	.50	.23
☐ I Willie McGee	.10	.05
☐ J Dale Murphy	.35	.16
☐ K Eddie Murray	.60	.25
☐ L Dave Parker	.20	.09
☐ M Jeff Reardon	.10	.05
☐ N Nolan Ryan	2.50	1.10
☐ O Juan Samuel	.10	.05
☐ P Robin Yount	.35	.16

1991 Topps Traded

he 1991 Topps Traded set contains 132 standard-size ards. The cards were issued primarily in factory set form rough hobby dealers but were also made available on a nited basis in wax packs. The cards in the wax packs ray backs) and collated factory sets (white backs) are om different card stock. Both versions are valued ually. The card design is identical to the regular issue 91 Topps cards except for the whiter stock (for factory t cards) and T-suffixed numbering. The set is numbered alphabetical order. The set includes a Team U.S.A. bset, featuring 25 of America's top collegiate players. e key Rookie Cards in this set are Jeff Bagwell, Jason Giambi, Todd Greene, Charles Johnson and Ivan Rodriguez.

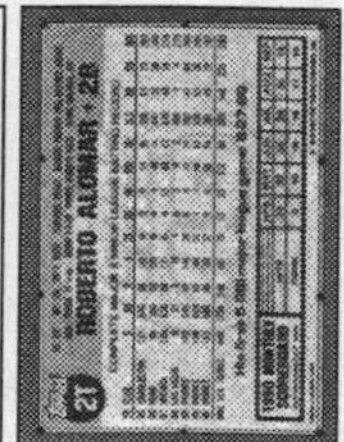

	MINT	NRMT
COMPLETE SET (132)	6.00	2.70
COMP.FACT.SET (132)	5.00	2.20
COMMON CARD (1T-132T)	.05	.02
☐ 1T Juan Agosto	.05	.02
☐ 2T Roberto Alomar	.20	.09
☐ 3T Wally Backman	.05	.02
☐ 4T Jeff Bagwell	2.50	1.10
☐ 5T Skeeter Barnes	.05	.02
☐ 6T Steve Bedrosian	.05	.02
☐ 7T Derek Bell	.20	.09
☐ 8T George Bell	.05	.02
☐ 9T Rafael Belliard	.05	.02
☐ 10T Dante Bichette	.20	.09
☐ 11T Bud Black	.05	.02
☐ 12T Mike Boddicker	.05	.02
☐ 13T Sid Bream	.05	.02
☐ 14T Hubie Brooks	.05	.02
☐ 15T Brett Butler	.15	.07
☐ 16T Ivan Calderon	.05	.02
☐ 17T John Candelaria	.05	.02
☐ 18T Tom Candiotti	.05	.02
☐ 19T Gary Carter	.20	.09
☐ 20T Joe Carter	.15	.07
☐ 21T Rick Cerone	.05	.02
☐ 22T Jack Clark	.10	.05
☐ 23T Vince Coleman	.05	.02
☐ 24T Scott Coolbaugh	.05	.02
☐ 25T Danny Cox	.05	.02
☐ 26T Danny Darwin	.05	.02
☐ 27T Chili Davis	.15	.07
☐ 28T Glenn Davis	.05	.02
☐ 29T Steve Decker	.05	.02
☐ 30T Rob Deer	.05	.02
☐ 31T Rich DeLucia	.05	.02
☐ 32T John Dettmer USA	.10	.05
☐ 33T Brian Downing	.05	.02
☐ 34T Darren Dreifort USA	.20	.09
☐ 35T Kirk Dressendorfer	.05	.02
☐ 36T Jim Essian MG	.05	.02
☐ 37T Dwight Evans	.10	.05
☐ 38T Steve Farr	.05	.02
☐ 39T Jeff Fassero	.15	.07
☐ 40T Junior Felix	.05	.02
☐ 41T Tony Fernandez	.05	.02
☐ 42T Steve Finley	.10	.05
☐ 43T Jim Fregosi MG	.05	.02
☐ 44T Gary Gaetti	.10	.05
☐ 45T Jason Giambi USA	1.00	.45
☐ 46T Kirk Gibson	.10	.05
☐ 47T Leo Gomez	.05	.02
☐ 48T Luis Gonzalez	.20	.09
☐ 49T Jeff Granger USA	.20	.09
☐ 50T Todd Greene USA	1.25	.55
☐ 51T Jeffrey Hammonds USA	.50	.23
☐ 52T Mike Hargrove MG	.05	.02
☐ 53T Pete Harnisch	.05	.02
☐ 54T Rick Helling USA UER (Misspelled Hellings on card back)	.10	.05
☐ 55T Glenallen Hill	.05	.02
☐ 56T Charlie Hough	.05	.02
☐ 57T Pete Incaviglia	.05	.02
☐ 58T Bo Jackson	.10	.05
☐ 59T Danny Jackson	.05	.02
☐ 60T Reggie Jefferson	.20	.09
☐ 61T Charles Johnson USA	2.00	.90
☐ 62T Jeff Johnson	.05	.02
☐ 63T Todd Johnson USA	.05	.02
☐ 64T Barry Jones	.05	.02
☐ 65T Chris Jones	.05	.02
☐ 66T Scott Kamieniecki	.05	.02
☐ 67T Pat Kelly	.05	.02
☐ 68T Darryl Kile	.20	.09
☐ 69T Chuck Knoblauch	.25	.11
☐ 70T Bill Krueger	.05	.02
☐ 71T Scott Leius	.05	.02
☐ 72T Donnie Leshnock USA	.05	.02
☐ 73T Mark Lewis	.05	.02
☐ 74T Candy Maldonado	.05	.02
☐ 75T Jason McDonald USA	.20	.09
☐ 76T Willie McGee	.05	.02
☐ 77T Fred McGriff	.20	.09
☐ 78T Billy McMillon USA	.20	.09
☐ 79T Hal McRae MG	.05	.02
☐ 80T Dan Melendez USA	.05	.02
☐ 81T Orlando Merced	.10	.05
☐ 82T Jack Morris	.20	.09
☐ 83T Phil Nevin USA	.20	.09
☐ 84T Otis Nixon	.10	.05
☐ 85T Johnny Oates MG	.05	.02
☐ 86T Bob Ojeda	.05	.02
☐ 87T Mike Pagliarulo	.05	.02
☐ 88T Dean Palmer	.20	.09
☐ 89T Dave Parker	.15	.07
☐ 90T Terry Pendleton	.10	.05
☐ 91T Tony Phillips (P) USA	.05	.02
☐ 92T Doug Piatt	.05	.02
☐ 93T Ron Polk USA CO	.05	.02
☐ 94T Tim Raines	.10	.05
☐ 95T Willie Randolph	.10	.05
☐ 96T Dave Righetti	.05	.02
☐ 97T Ernie Riles	.05	.02
☐ 98T Chris Roberts USA	.20	.09
☐ 99T Jeff D. Robinson	.05	.02
☐ 100T Jeff M. Robinson	.05	.02
☐ 101T Ivan Rodriguez	1.50	.70
☐ 102T Steve Rodriguez USA	.05	.02
☐ 103T Tom Runnells MG	.05	.02
☐ 104T Scott Sanderson	.05	.02
☐ 105T Bob Scanlan	.05	.02
☐ 106T Pete Schourek	.10	.05
☐ 107T Gary Scott	.05	.02
☐ 108T Paul Shuey USA	.20	.09
☐ 109T Doug Simons	.05	.02
☐ 110T Dave Smith	.05	.02
☐ 111T Cory Snyder	.05	.02
☐ 112T Luis Sojo	.05	.02
☐ 113T Kennie Steenstra USA	.05	.02
☐ 114T Darryl Strawberry	.10	.05
☐ 115T Franklin Stubbs	.05	.02
☐ 116T Todd Taylor USA	.05	.02
☐ 117T Wade Taylor	.05	.02
☐ 118T Garry Templeton	.05	.02
☐ 119T Mickey Tettleton	.10	.05
☐ 120T Tim Teufel	.05	.02
☐ 121T Mike Timlin	.05	.02
☐ 122T David Tuttle USA	.05	.02
☐ 123T Mo Vaughn	.40	.18
☐ 124T Jeff Ware USA	.05	.02
☐ 125T Devon White	.10	.05
☐ 126T Mark Whiten	.05	.02
☐ 127T Mitch Williams	.05	.02
☐ 128T Craig Wilson USA	.05	.02
☐ 129T Willie Wilson	.05	.02
☐ 130T Chris Wimmer USA	.05	.02
☐ 131T Ivan Zweig USA	.05	.02
☐ 132T Checklist 1T-132T	.05	.02

1991 Topps Traded Tiffany

In the final Tiffany relase, this 132-card standard-size set was released as a parallel issue to the regular Topps Traded issue. These cards were released in very limited quantities and the multiplier for these cards is higher than many previous Tiffany issues. These cards were issued in complete factory set form only.

	MINT	NRMT
COMPLETE FACT.SET (132)	40.00	18.00
COMMON CARD (1T-132T)	.15	.07

*STARS: 3X to 6X BASIC CARDS

*YOUNG STARS: 2.5X to 5X BASIC CARDS

*ROOKIES: 2X to 4X BASIC CARDS

1991 Topps Cracker Jack I

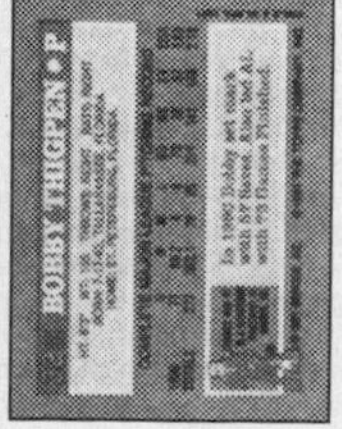

This 36-card set is the first of two 36-card series produced by Topps for Cracker Jack, and the cards were inserted inside specially marked packages of Cracker Jack. These cards were the "toy surprise" inside. The cards measure approximately one-fourth standard-size (1

1/4" by 1 3/4") and are frequently referenced as micro-cards. The micro-cards have color player photos with different color borders but are otherwise identical to the corresponding cards in the Topps regular issue. The horizontally oriented backs are printed in red, blue, and pink, and include biography, complete Major League batting record, career highlights, and the Cracker Jack sailor at the lower left corner. Standard-size cards featuring four micro-cards each were seen at shows but were not inserted inside the product. These were apparently test runs or uncut sheets. Although each mini-card is numbered on the back, the numbering of the four cards on any standard-size card is not consecutive.

	MINT	NRMT
COMPLETE SET (36)	10.00	4.50
COMMON CARD (1-36)	.10	.05

	MINT	NRMT
☐ 1 Nolan Ryan	2.50	1.10
☐ 2 Paul Molitor	.60	.25
☐ 3 Tim Raines	.20	.09
☐ 4 Frank Viola	.10	.05
☐ 5 Sandy Alomar Jr.	.20	.09
☐ 6 Ryne Sandberg	1.00	.45
☐ 7 Don Mattingly	1.25	.55
☐ 8 Pedro Guerrero	.10	.05
☐ 9 Jose Rijo	.10	.05
☐ 10 Jose Canseco	.60	.25
☐ 11 Dave Parker	.10	.05
☐ 12 Doug Drabek	.10	.05
☐ 13 Cal Ripken	2.50	1.10
☐ 14 Dave Justice	.50	.23
☐ 15 George Brett	1.00	.45
☐ 16 Eric Davis	.20	.09
☐ 17 Mark Langston	.10	.05
☐ 18 Rickey Henderson	.60	.25
☐ 19 Barry Bonds	.60	.25
☐ 20 Kevin Maas	.10	.05
☐ 21 Len Dykstra	.20	.09
☐ 22 Roger Clemens	1.00	.45
☐ 23 Robin Yount	.35	.16
☐ 24 Mark Grace	.60	.25
☐ 25 Bo Jackson	.20	.09
☐ 26 Tony Gwynn	1.25	.55
☐ 27 Mark McGwire	1.25	.55
☐ 28 Dwight Gooden	.20	.09
☐ 29 Wade Boggs	.50	.23
☐ 30 Kevin Mitchell	.10	.05
☐ 31 Cecil Fielder	.35	.16
☐ 32 Bobby Thigpen	.10	.05
☐ 33 Benito Santiago	.10	.05
☐ 34 Kirby Puckett	1.25	.55
☐ 35 Will Clark	.60	.25
☐ 36 Ken Griffey Jr.	3.00	1.35

1991 Topps Cracker Jack II

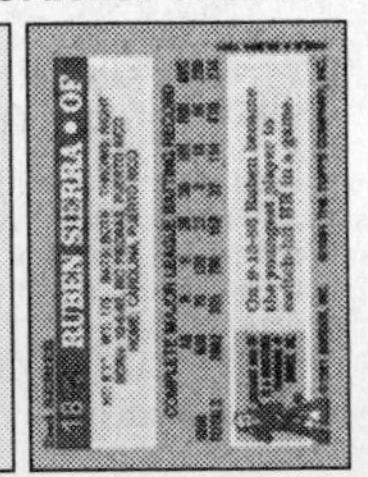

This 36-card set is the second of two different 36-card series produced by Topps for Cracker Jack, and the cards were inserted inside specially marked packages of Cracker Jack. These cards were the "toy surprise" inside. The cards measure approximately one-fourth standard-size (1 1/4" by 1 3/4") and are frequently referenced as micro-cards. The micro-cards have color player photos with different color borders but are otherwise identical to the corresponding cards in the Topps regular issue. The horizontally oriented backs are printed in red, blue, and pink, and include biography, complete Major League batting record, career highlights, and the Cracker Jack sailor at the lower left corner. Standard-size cards featuring four micro-cards each were seen at shows but were not inserted inside the product. These were apparently test runs or uncut sheets. Although each mini-card is numbered on the back, the numbering of the four cards on any standard-size card is not consecutive.

	MINT	NRMT
COMPLETE SET (36)	6.00	2.70
COMMON CARD (1-36)	.10	.05

	MINT	NRMT
☐ 1 Eddie Murray	.60	.25
☐ 2 Carlton Fisk	.35	.16
☐ 3 Eric Anthony	.10	.05
☐ 4 Kelly Gruber	.10	.05
☐ 5 Von Hayes	.10	.05
☐ 6 Ben McDonald	.10	.05
☐ 7 Andre Dawson	.50	.23
☐ 8 Ellis Burks	.20	.09
☐ 9 Matt Williams	.50	.23
☐ 10 Dave Stewart	.10	.05
☐ 11 Barry Larkin	.35	.16
☐ 12 Chuck Finley	.10	.05
☐ 13 Shane Andrews	.10	.05
☐ 14 Bret Saberhagen	.10	.05
☐ 15 Bobby Bonilla	.20	.09
☐ 16 Roberto Kelly	.10	.05
☐ 17 Orel Hershiser	.20	.09
☐ 18 Ruben Sierra	.10	.05
☐ 19 Ron Gant	.20	.09
☐ 20 Frank Thomas	3.00	1.35
☐ 21 Tim Wallach	.10	.05
☐ 22 Gregg Olson	.10	.05
☐ 23 Shawon Dunston	.10	.05
☐ 24 Kent Hrbek	.10	.05
☐ 25 Ramon Martinez	.35	.16
☐ 26 Alan Trammell	.35	.16
☐ 27 Ozzie Smith	1.00	.45
☐ 28 Bob Welch	.20	.09
☐ 29 Chris Sabo	.10	.05
☐ 30 Steve Sax	.10	.05
☐ 31 Bip Roberts	.10	.05
☐ 32 Dave Stieb	.10	.05
☐ 33 Howard Johnson	.10	.05
☐ 34 Mike Greenwell	.10	.05
☐ 35 Delino DeShields	.20	.09
☐ 36 Alex Fernandez	.35	.16

1991 Topps Debut '90

The 1991 Topps Major League Debut Set contains 171 standard-size cards. Although the checklist card is arranged chronologically in order of first major league appearance in 1990, the player cards are arranged alphabetically by the player's last name. The front design features mostly posed color player photos, with two different color stripes on the top and sides of the picture. The card face is white, and the player's name is given in the color stripe below the picture. The horizontally oriented backs have player information and statistics in blue lettering on a pink and white background. Carlos Baerga and Frank Thomas are among the more prominent players featured in this set.

	MINT	NRMT
COMPLETE SET (171)	20.00	9.00
COMMON CARD (1-171)	.05	.02

	MINT	NRMT
☐ 1 Paul Abbott	.05	.02
☐ 2 Steve Adkins	.05	.02
☐ 3 Scott Aldred	.05	.02
☐ 4 Gerald Alexander	.05	.02
☐ 5 Moises Alou	.75	.35
☐ 6 Steve Avery	.50	.23
☐ 7 Oscar Azocar	.05	.02
☐ 8 Carlos Baerga	.75	.35
☐ 9 Kevin Baez	.05	.02
☐ 10 Jeff Baldwin	.05	.02
☐ 11 Brian Barnes	.05	.02
☐ 12 Kevin Bearse	.05	.02
☐ 13 Kevin Belcher	.05	.02
☐ 14 Mike Bell	.05	.02
☐ 15 Sean Berry	.25	.11
☐ 16 Joe Bitker	.05	.02
☐ 17 Willie Blair	.05	.02
☐ 18 Brian Bohanon	.05	.02
☐ 19 Mike Bordick	.10	.05
☐ 20 Shawn Boskie	.10	.05
☐ 21 Rod Brewer	.05	.02
☐ 22 Kevin D. Brown	.05	.02
☐ 23 Dave Burba	.15	.07
☐ 24 Jim Campbell	.05	.02
☐ 25 Ozzie Canseco	.05	.02
☐ 26 Chuck Carr	.25	.11
☐ 27 Larry Casian	.05	.02
☐ 28 Andujar Cedeno	.05	.02
☐ 29 Wes Chamberlain	.05	.02
☐ 30 Scott Chiamparino	.05	.02
☐ 31 Steve Chitren	.05	.02
☐ 32 Pete Coachman	.05	.02
☐ 33 Alex Cole	.05	.02
☐ 34 Jeff Conine	3.00	1.35
☐ 35 Scott Cooper	.10	.05
☐ 36 Milt Cuyler	.05	.02
☐ 37 Steve Decker	.05	.02
☐ 38 Rich DeLucia	.05	.02
☐ 39 Delino DeShields	.25	.11
☐ 40 Mark Dewey	.05	.02
☐ 41 Carlos Diaz	.05	.02
☐ 42 Lance Dickson	.05	.02
☐ 43 Narciso Elvira	.05	.02
☐ 44 Luis Encarnacion	.05	.02
☐ 45 Scott Erickson	.40	.18
☐ 46 Paul Faries	.05	.02
☐ 47 Howard Farmer	.05	.02
☐ 48 Alex Fernandez	.50	.23
☐ 49 Travis Fryman	1.25	.55
☐ 50 Rich Garces	.05	.02
☐ 51 Carlos Garcia	.10	.05
☐ 52 Mike Gardiner	.05	.02
☐ 53 Bernard Gilkey	.40	.18
☐ 54 Tom Gilles	.05	.02
☐ 55 Jerry Goff	.05	.02
☐ 56 Leo Gomez	.05	.02
☐ 57 Luis Gonzalez	.25	.11
☐ 58 Joe Grahe	.05	.02
☐ 59 Craig Grebeck	.05	.02
☐ 60 Kip Gross	.05	.02
☐ 61 Eric Gunderson	.05	.02
☐ 62 Chris Hammond	.05	.02
☐ 63 Dave Hansen	.05	.02
☐ 64 Reggie Harris	.05	.02
☐ 65 Bill Haselman	.05	.02
☐ 66 Randy Hennis	.05	.02
☐ 67 Carlos Hernandez	.05	.02
☐ 68 Howard Hilton	.05	.02
☐ 69 Dave Hollins	.25	.11
☐ 70 Darren Holmes	.15	.07
☐ 71 John Hoover	.05	.02
☐ 72 Steve Howard	.05	.02
☐ 73 Thomas Howard	.05	.02
☐ 74 Todd Hundley	2.00	.90
☐ 75 Daryl Irvine	.05	.02
☐ 76 Chris Jelic	.05	.02
☐ 77 Dana Kiecker	.05	.02
☐ 78 Brent Knackert	.05	.02
☐ 79 Jimmy Kremers	.05	.02
☐ 80 Jerry Kutzler	.05	.02
☐ 81 Ray Lankford	3.00	1.35
☐ 82 Tim Layana	.05	.02
☐ 83 Terry Lee	.05	.02
☐ 84 Mark Leiter	.15	.07
☐ 85 Scott Leius	.15	.07
☐ 86 Mark Leonard	.05	.02
☐ 87 Darren Lewis	.10	.05
☐ 88 Scott Lewis	.05	.02
☐ 89 Jim Leyritz	.25	.11
☐ 90 Dave Liddell	.05	.02
☐ 91 Luis Lopez	.05	.02
☐ 92 Kevin Maas	.05	.02
☐ 93 Bob MacDonald	.05	.02
☐ 94 Carlos Maldonado	.05	.02
☐ 95 Chuck Malone	.05	.02
☐ 96 Ramon Manon	.05	.02
☐ 97 Jeff Manto	.05	.02
☐ 98 Paul Marak	.05	.02
☐ 99 Tino Martinez	2.00	.90
☐ 100 Derrick May	.10	.05
☐ 101 Brent Mayne	.10	.05
☐ 102 Paul McClellan	.05	.02
☐ 103 Rodney McCray	.05	.02
☐ 104 Tim McIntosh	.05	.02
☐ 105 Brian McRae	.50	.23
☐ 106 Jose Melendez	.05	.02
☐ 107 Orlando Merced	.30	.14
☐ 108 Alan Mills	.05	.02
☐ 109 Gino Minutelli	.05	.02
☐ 110 Mickey Morandini	.10	.05
☐ 111 Pedro Munoz	.10	.05
☐ 112 Chris Nabholz	.05	.02
☐ 113 Tim Naehring	.75	.35
☐ 114 Charles Nagy	.75	.35
☐ 115 Jim Neidlinger	.05	.02
☐ 116 Rafael Novoa	.05	.02
☐ 117 Jose Offerman	.25	.11
☐ 118 Omar Olivares	.05	.02
☐ 119 Javier Ortiz	.05	.02
☐ 120 Al Osuna	.05	.02
☐ 121 Rick Parker	.05	.02
☐ 122 Dave Pavlas	.05	.02
☐ 123 Geronimo Pena	.05	.02
☐ 124 Mike Perez	.05	.02

☐ 125 Phil Plantier	.15	.07
☐ 126 Jim Poole	.10	.05
☐ 127 Tom Quinlan	.05	.02
☐ 128 Scott Radinsky	.05	.02
☐ 129 Darren Reed	.05	.02
☐ 130 Karl Rhodes	.05	.02
☐ 131 Jeff Richardson	.05	.02
☐ 132 Rich Rodriguez	.05	.02
☐ 133 Dave Rohde	.05	.02
☐ 134 Mel Rojas	.30	.14
☐ 135 Vic Rosario	.05	.02
☐ 136 Rich Rowland	.05	.02
☐ 137 Scott Ruskin	.05	.02
☐ 138 Bill Sampen	.05	.02
☐ 139 Andres Santana	.05	.02
☐ 140 David Segui	.50	.23
☐ 141 Jeff Shaw	.05	.02
☐ 142 Tim Sherrill	.05	.02
☐ 143 Terry Shumpert	.05	.02
☐ 144 Mike Simms	.05	.02
☐ 145 Daryl Smith	.05	.02
☐ 146 Luis Sojo	.05	.02
☐ 147 Steve Springer	.05	.02
☐ 148 Ray Stephens	.05	.02
☐ 149 Lee Stevens	.05	.02
☐ 150 Mel Stottlemyre Jr.	.05	.02
☐ 151 Glenn Sutko	.05	.02
☐ 152 Anthony Telford	.05	.02
☐ 153 Frank Thomas	15.00	6.75
☐ 154 Randy Tomlin	.10	.05
☐ 155 Brian Traxler	.05	.02
☐ 156 Efrain Valdez	.05	.02
☐ 157 Rafael Valdez	.05	.02
☐ 158 Julio Valera	.05	.02
☐ 159 Jim Vatcher	.05	.02
☐ 160 Hector Villanueva	.05	.02
☐ 161 Hector Wagner	.05	.02
☐ 162 Dave Walsh	.05	.02
☐ 163 Steve Wapnick	.05	.02
☐ 164 Colby Ward	.05	.02
☐ 165 Turner Ward	.05	.02
☐ 166 Terry Wells	.05	.02
☐ 167 Mark Whiten	.10	.05
☐ 168 Mike York	.05	.02
☐ 169 Cliff Young	.05	.02
☐ 170 Checklist Card	.05	.02
☐ 171 Checklist Card	.05	.02

1991 Topps East Coast National

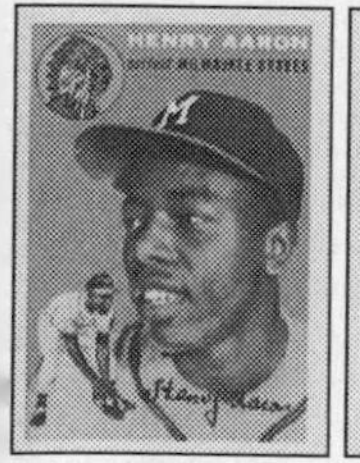

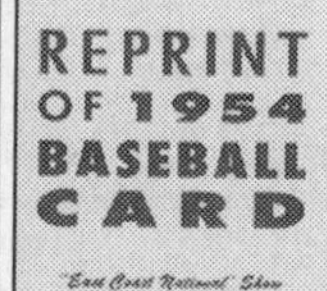

This four-card, standard-size set was included in the paid admission for the 1991 East Coast National Show (August 15-18). Each card is a reproduction of the player's first Topps card: Aaron, ('54 Topps) Mantle, ('52 Topps) Musial, ('58 Topps) and Robinson ('57 Topps). In blue print on white, the backs indicate that these cards are reprints. The cards are unnumbered and checklisted below in alphabetical order.

	MINT	NRMT
COMPLETE SET (4)	15.00	6.75
COMMON CARD (1-4)	2.50	1.10
☐ 1 Hank Aaron	5.00	2.20
☐ 2 Mickey Mantle	8.00	3.60
☐ 3 Stan Musial	4.00	1.80
☐ 4 Frank Robinson	2.50	1.10

1991 Topps Glossy All-Stars

These 22 glossy standard-size cards were inserted one per Topps rack packs and honor the starting lineup, managers and honorary captains of the 1990 National and American League All-Star teams. This would be the final year that this insert set was issued and the design is similar to what Topps produced each year since 1984.

	MINT	NRMT
COMPLETE SET (22)	8.00	3.60
COMMON CARD (1-22)	.10	.05

☐ 1 Tony LaRussa MG	.20	.09
☐ 2 Mark McGwire	1.00	.45
☐ 3 Steve Sax	.10	.05
☐ 4 Wade Boggs	.60	.25
☐ 5 Cal Ripken, Jr	2.00	.90
☐ 6 Rickey Henderson	.60	.25
☐ 7 Ken Griffey, Jr.	2.50	1.10
☐ 8 Jose Canseco	.60	.25
☐ 9 Sandy Alomar, Jr.	.35	.16
☐ 10 Bob Welch	.10	.05
☐ 11 Al Lopez CAPT	.20	.09
☐ 12 Roger Craig MG	.10	.05
☐ 13 Will Clark	.60	.25
☐ 14 Ryne Sandberg	.75	.35
☐ 15 Chris Sabo	.10	.05
☐ 16 Ozzie Smith	1.00	.45
☐ 17 Kevin Mitchell	.10	.05
☐ 18 Len Dykstra	.10	.05
☐ 19 Andre Dawson	.50	.23
☐ 20 Mike Scoscia	.10	.05
☐ 21 Jack Armstrong	.10	.05
☐ 22 Juan Marichal CAPT	.35	.16

1992 Topps Pre-Production Sheet

This 1992 Topps pre-production sample sheet measures approximately 7 3/4" by 10 3/4" and features nine player cards. The sheet is unperforated and if cut, the cards would measure the standard size. The fronts have glossy color action photos on a white card face, with different color borders overlaying the picture. In a horizontal format, the backs have biography and complete Major League statistics. Moreover, some of the backs display pictures of baseball stadiums, if the player's career length permits. The cards are numbered on the back with "1992 Pre-Production Sample" prominent. There are two different types of sheets issued. Either sheet has the same value.

	MINT	NRMT
COMPLETE SET (9)	5.00	2.20
COMMON CARD	.50	.23
☐ 3 Shawon Dunston	1.00	.45
☐ 16 Mike Heath	.50	.23
☐ 18 Todd Frohwirth	.50	.23
☐ 20 Bip Roberts	1.00	.45
☐ 131 Rob Dibble	.50	.23
☐ 174 Otis Nixon	.50	.23
☐ 273 Denny Martinez	1.00	.45
☐ 325 Brett Butler	1.00	.45
☐ 798 Tom Lasorda MG	1.00	.45

1992 Topps Gold Pre-Production Sheet

This 1992 Topps Gold pre-production sample sheet measures approximately 7 3/4" by 10 3/4" and features nine player cards. The sheet is unperforated and if cut, the cards would measure the standard size. The fronts have glossy color action photos on a white card face, with different color borders overlaying the picture. In a horizontal format, the backs have biography and complete Major League statistics. Moreover, some of the backs

display pictures of baseball stadiums, if the player's career length permits. The cards are numbered on the back with "1992 Pre-Production Sample" prominent.

	MINT	NRMT
COMPLETE SET (9)	25.00	11.00
COMMON CARD	1.00	.45
☐ 1 Nolan Ryan	10.00	4.50
☐ 15 Denny Martinez	1.50	.70
☐ 20 Bip Roberts	1.50	.70
☐ 40 Cal Ripken	10.00	4.50
☐ 261 Tom Lasorda MG	1.50	.70
☐ 370 Shawon Dunston	1.50	.70
☐ 512 Mike Heath	1.00	.45
☐ 655 Brett Butler	1.50	.70
☐ 757 Rob Dibble	1.00	.45

1992 Topps

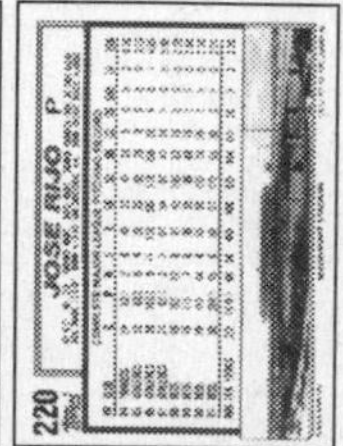

The 1992 Topps set contains 792 standard-size cards. Cards were distributed in plastic wrap packs, jumbo packs, rack packs and factory sets. The fronts have either posed or action color player photos on a white card face. Different color stripes frame the pictures, and the player's name and team name appear in two short color stripes respectively at the bottom. Special subsets included are Record Breakers (2-5), Prospects (58, 126, 179, 473, 551, 591, 618, 656, 676), and All-Stars (386-407). The key Rookie Cards in this set are Shawn Green, John Jaha and Manny Ramirez.

	MINT	NRMT
COMPLETE SET (792)	25.00	11.00
COMP.FACT.SET (802)	30.00	13.50
COMP.HOLIDAY SET (811)	35.00	16.00
COMMON CARD (1-792)	.05	.02
☐ 1 Nolan Ryan	.75	.35
☐ 2 Ricky Henderson RB Most career SB's (Some cards have print marks that show 1.991 on the front)	.05	.02
☐ 3 Jeff Reardon RB 10 seasons, 20 or more saves	.05	.02
☐ 4 Nolan Ryan RB 22 cons. 100 K seasons	.40	.18
☐ 5 Dave Winfield RB Oldest player, cycle	.05	.02
☐ 6 Brien Taylor	.10	.05
☐ 7 Jim Olander	.05	.02
☐ 8 Bryan Hickerson	.05	.02
☐ 9 Jon Farrell	.05	.02
☐ 10 Wade Boggs	.05	.02
☐ 11 Jack McDowell	.05	.02
☐ 12 Luis Gonzalez	.05	.02
☐ 13 Mike Scioscia	.05	.02
☐ 14 Wes Chamberlain	.05	.02
☐ 15 Dennis Martinez	.10	.05
☐ 16 Jeff Montgomery	.10	.05
☐ 17 Randy Milligan	.05	.02
☐ 18 Greg Cadaret	.05	.02
☐ 19 Jamie Quirk	.05	.02
☐ 20 Bip Roberts	.05	.02
☐ 21 Buck Rodgers MG	.05	.02
☐ 22 Bill Wegman	.05	.02
☐ 23 Chuck Knoblauch	.20	.09
☐ 24 Randy Myers	.10	.05

☐ 25 Ron Gant	.10	.05
☐ 26 Mike Bielecki	.05	.02
☐ 27 Juan Gonzalez	.60	.25
☐ 28 Mike Schooler	.05	.02
☐ 29 Mickey Tettleton	.05	.02
☐ 30 John Kruk	.10	.05
☐ 31 Bryn Smith	.05	.02
☐ 32 Chris Nabholz	.05	.02
☐ 33 Carlos Baerga	.10	.05
☐ 34 Jeff Juden	.05	.02
☐ 35 Dave Righetti	.05	.02
☐ 36 Scott Ruffcorn	.05	.02
☐ 37 Luis Polonia	.05	.02
☐ 38 Tom Candiotti	.05	.02
☐ 39 Greg Olson	.05	.02
☐ 40 Cal Ripken	2.00	.90
☐ 41 Craig Lefferts	.05	.02
☐ 42 Mike Macfarlane	.05	.02
☐ 43 Jose Lind	.05	.02
☐ 44 Rick Aguilera	.05	.02
☐ 45 Gary Carter	.20	.09
☐ 46 Steve Farr	.05	.02
☐ 47 Rex Hudler	.05	.02
☐ 48 Scott Scudder	.05	.02
☐ 49 Damon Berryhill	.05	.02
☐ 50 Ken Griffey Jr.	1.25	.55
☐ 51 Tom Runnells MG	.05	.02
☐ 52 Juan Bell	.05	.02
☐ 53 Tommy Gregg	.05	.02
☐ 54 David Wells	.05	.02
☐ 55 Rafael Palmeiro	.05	.02
☐ 56 Charlie O'Brien	.05	.02
☐ 57 Donn Pall	.05	.02
☐ 58 1992 Prospects C	.20	.09
Brad Ausmus		
Jim Campanis Jr.		
Dave Nilsson		
Doug Robbins		
☐ 59 Mo Vaughn	.30	.14
☐ 60 Tony Fernandez	.05	.02
☐ 61 Paul O'Neill	.10	.05
☐ 62 Gene Nelson	.05	.02
☐ 63 Randy Ready	.05	.02
☐ 64 Bob Kipper	.05	.02
☐ 65 Willie McGee	.05	.02
☐ 66 Scott Stahoviak	.10	.05
☐ 67 Luis Salazar	.05	.02
☐ 68 Marvin Freeman	.05	.02
☐ 69 Kenny Lofton	.75	.35
☐ 70 Gary Gaetti	.10	.05
☐ 71 Erik Hanson	.05	.02
☐ 72 Eddie Zosky	.05	.02
☐ 73 Brian Barnes	.05	.02
☐ 74 Scott Leius	.05	.02
☐ 75 Bret Saberhagen	.05	.02
☐ 76 Mike Gallego	.05	.02
☐ 77 Jack Armstrong	.05	.02
☐ 78 Ivan Rodriguez	.40	.18
☐ 79 Jesse Orosco	.05	.02
☐ 80 David Justice	.20	.09
☐ 81 Ced Landrum	.05	.02
☐ 82 Doug Simons	.05	.02
☐ 83 Tommy Greene	.05	.02
☐ 84 Leo Gomez	.05	.02
☐ 85 Jose DeLeon	.05	.02
☐ 86 Steve Finley	.10	.05
☐ 87 Bob MacDonald	.05	.02
☐ 88 Darrin Jackson	.05	.02
☐ 89 Neal Heaton	.05	.02
☐ 90 Robin Yount	.05	.02
☐ 91 Jeff Reed	.05	.02
☐ 92 Lenny Harris	.05	.02
☐ 93 Reggie Jefferson	.10	.05
☐ 94 Sammy Sosa	.20	.09
☐ 95 Scott Bailes	.05	.02
☐ 96 Tom McKinnon	.05	.02
☐ 97 Luis Rivera	.05	.02
☐ 98 Mike Harkey	.05	.02
☐ 99 Jeff Treadway	.05	.02
☐ 100 Jose Canseco	.05	.02
☐ 101 Omar Vizquel	.10	.05
☐ 102 Scott Kamieniecki	.05	.02
☐ 103 Ricky Jordan	.05	.02
☐ 104 Jeff Ballard	.05	.02
☐ 105 Felix Jose	.05	.02
☐ 106 Mike Boddicker	.05	.02
☐ 107 Dan Pasqua	.05	.02
☐ 108 Mike Timlin	.05	.02
☐ 109 Roger Craig MG	.05	.02
☐ 110 Ryne Sandberg	.25	.11
☐ 111 Mark Carreon	.05	.02
☐ 112 Oscar Azocar	.05	.02
☐ 113 Mike Greenwell	.05	.02
☐ 114 Mark Portugal	.05	.02
☐ 115 Terry Pendleton	.10	.05
☐ 116 Willie Randolph	.10	.05
☐ 117 Scott Terry	.05	.02
☐ 118 Chili Davis	.10	.05
☐ 119 Mark Gardner	.05	.02
☐ 120 Alan Trammell	.05	.02
☐ 121 Derek Bell	.10	.05
☐ 122 Gary Varsho	.05	.02
☐ 123 Bob Ojeda	.05	.02
☐ 124 Shawn Livsey	.05	.02
☐ 125 Chris Hoiles	.05	.02
☐ 126 1992 Prospects 1B	.40	.18
Ryan Klesko		
John Jaha		
Rico Brogna		
Dave Staton		
☐ 127 Carlos Quintana	.05	.02
☐ 128 Kurt Stillwell	.05	.02
☐ 129 Melido Perez	.05	.02
☐ 130 Alvin Davis	.05	.02
☐ 131 Checklist 1-132	.05	.02
☐ 132 Eric Show	.05	.02
☐ 133 Rance Mulliniks	.05	.02
☐ 134 Darryl Kile	.10	.05
☐ 135 Von Hayes	.05	.02
☐ 136 Bill Doran	.05	.02
☐ 137 Jeff D. Robinson	.05	.02
☐ 138 Monty Fariss	.05	.02
☐ 139 Jeff Innis	.05	.02
☐ 140 Mark Grace UER	.05	.02
(Home Calie., should		
be Calif.)		
☐ 141 Jim Leyland MG UER	.10	.05
(No closed parenthesis		
after East in 1991)		
☐ 142 Todd Van Poppel	.05	.02
☐ 143 Paul Gibson	.05	.02
☐ 144 Bill Swift	.05	.02
☐ 145 Danny Tartabull	.05	.02
☐ 146 Al Newman	.05	.02
☐ 147 Cris Carpenter	.05	.02
☐ 148 Anthony Young	.05	.02
☐ 149 Brian Bohanon	.05	.02
☐ 150 Roger Clemens UER	.40	.18
(League leading ERA in		
1990 not italicized)		
☐ 151 Jeff Hamilton	.05	.02
☐ 152 Charlie Leibrandt	.05	.02
☐ 153 Ron Karkovice	.05	.02
☐ 154 Hensley Meulens	.05	.02
☐ 155 Scott Bankhead	.05	.02
☐ 156 Manny Ramirez	1.25	.55
☐ 157 Keith Miller	.05	.02
☐ 158 Todd Frohwirth	.05	.02
☐ 159 Darrin Fletcher	.05	.02
☐ 160 Bobby Bonilla	.10	.05
☐ 161 Casey Candaele	.05	.02
☐ 162 Paul Faries	.05	.02
☐ 163 Dana Kiecker	.05	.02
☐ 164 Shane Mack	.05	.02
☐ 165 Mark Langston	.05	.02
☐ 166 Geronimo Pena	.05	.02
☐ 167 Andy Allanson	.05	.02
☐ 168 Dwight Smith	.05	.02
☐ 169 Chuck Crim	.05	.02
☐ 170 Alex Cole	.05	.02
☐ 171 Bill Plummer MG	.05	.02
☐ 172 Juan Berenguer	.05	.02
☐ 173 Brian Downing	.05	.02
☐ 174 Steve Frey	.05	.02
☐ 175 Orel Hershiser	.10	.05
☐ 176 Ramon Garcia	.05	.02
☐ 177 Dan Gladden	.05	.02
☐ 178 Jim Acker	.05	.02
☐ 179 1992 Prospects 2B	.05	.02
Bobby DeJardin		
Cesar Bernhardt		
Armando Moreno		
Andy Stankiewicz		
☐ 180 Kevin Mitchell	.05	.02
☐ 181 Hector Villanueva	.05	.02
☐ 182 Jeff Reardon	.10	.05
☐ 183 Brent Mayne	.05	.02
☐ 184 Jimmy Jones	.05	.02
☐ 185 Benito Santiago	.05	.02
☐ 186 Cliff Floyd	.20	.09
☐ 187 Ernie Riles	.05	.02
☐ 188 Jose Guzman	.05	.02
☐ 189 Junior Felix	.05	.02
☐ 190 Glenn Davis	.05	.02
☐ 191 Charlie Hough	.05	.02
☐ 192 Dave Fleming	.05	.02
☐ 193 Omar Olivares	.05	.02
☐ 194 Eric Karros	.05	.02
☐ 195 David Cone	.10	.05
☐ 196 Frank Castillo	.10	.05
☐ 197 Glenn Braggs	.05	.02
☐ 198 Scott Aldred	.05	.02
☐ 199 Jeff Blauser	.05	.02
☐ 200 Len Dykstra	.10	.05
☐ 201 Buck Showalter MG	.20	.09
☐ 202 Rick Honeycutt	.05	.02
☐ 203 Greg Myers	.05	.02
☐ 204 Trevor Wilson	.05	.02
☐ 205 Jay Howell	.05	.02
☐ 206 Luis Sojo	.05	.02
☐ 207 Jack Clark	.10	.05
☐ 208 Julio Machado	.05	.02
☐ 209 Lloyd McClendon	.05	.02
☐ 210 Ozzie Guillen	.05	.02
☐ 211 Jeremy Hernandez	.05	.02
☐ 212 Randy Velarde	.05	.02
☐ 213 Les Lancaster	.05	.02
☐ 214 Andy Mota	.05	.02
☐ 215 Rich Gossage	.10	.05
☐ 216 Brent Gates	.05	.02
☐ 217 Brian Harper	.05	.02
☐ 218 Mike Flanagan	.05	.02
☐ 219 Jerry Browne	.05	.02
☐ 220 Jose Rijo	.05	.02
☐ 221 Skeeter Barnes	.05	.02
☐ 222 Jaime Navarro	.05	.02
☐ 223 Mel Hall	.05	.02
☐ 224 Bret Barberie	.05	.02
☐ 225 Roberto Alomar	.20	.09
☐ 226 Pete Smith	.05	.02
☐ 227 Daryl Boston	.05	.02
☐ 228 Eddie Whitson	.05	.02
☐ 229 Shawn Boskie	.05	.02
☐ 230 Dick Schofield	.05	.02
☐ 231 Brian Drahman	.05	.02
☐ 232 John Smiley	.05	.02
☐ 233 Mitch Webster	.05	.02
☐ 234 Terry Steinbach	.10	.05
☐ 235 Jack Morris	.10	.05
☐ 236 Bill Pecota	.05	.02
☐ 237 Jose Hernandez	.05	.02
☐ 238 Greg Litton	.05	.02
☐ 239 Brian Holman	.05	.02
☐ 240 Andres Galarraga	.05	.02
☐ 241 Gerald Young	.05	.02
☐ 242 Mike Mussina	.30	.14
☐ 243 Alvaro Espinoza	.05	.02
☐ 244 Darren Daulton	.10	.05
☐ 245 John Smoltz	.05	.02
☐ 246 Jason Pruitt	.05	.02
☐ 247 Chuck Finley	.10	.05
☐ 248 Jim Gantner	.05	.02
☐ 249 Tony Fossas	.05	.02
☐ 250 Ken Griffey Sr.	.05	.02
☐ 251 Kevin Elster	.05	.02
☐ 252 Dennis Rasmussen	.05	.02
☐ 253 Terry Kennedy	.05	.02
☐ 254 Ryan Bowen	.05	.02
☐ 255 Robin Ventura	.10	.05
☐ 256 Mike Aldrete	.05	.02
☐ 257 Jeff Russell	.05	.02
☐ 258 Jim Lindeman	.05	.02
☐ 259 Ron Darling	.05	.02
☐ 260 Devon White	.05	.02
☐ 261 Tom Lasorda MG	.05	.02
☐ 262 Terry Lee	.05	.02
☐ 263 Bob Patterson	.05	.02
☐ 264 Checklist 133-264	.05	.02
☐ 265 Teddy Higuera	.05	.02
☐ 266 Roberto Kelly	.05	.02
☐ 267 Steve Bedrosian	.05	.02
☐ 268 Brady Anderson	.05	.02
☐ 269 Ruben Amaro Jr.	.05	.02
☐ 270 Tony Gwynn	.50	.23
☐ 271 Tracy Jones	.05	.02
☐ 272 Jerry Don Gleaton	.05	.02
☐ 273 Craig Grebeck	.05	.02
☐ 274 Bob Scanlan	.05	.02
☐ 275 Todd Zeile	.05	.02
☐ 276 Shawn Green	.25	.11
☐ 277 Scott Chiamparino	.05	.02
☐ 278 Darryl Hamilton	.05	.02
☐ 279 Jim Clancy	.05	.02
☐ 280 Carlos Martinez	.05	.02
☐ 281 Kevin Appier	.10	.05
☐ 282 John Wehner	.05	.02
☐ 283 Reggie Sanders	.10	.05
☐ 284 Gene Larkin	.05	.02
☐ 285 Bob Welch	.05	.02
☐ 286 Gilberto Reyes	.05	.02
☐ 287 Pete Schourek	.05	.02
☐ 288 Andujar Cedeno	.05	.02
☐ 289 Mike Morgan	.05	.02
☐ 290 Bo Jackson	.10	.05
☐ 291 Phil Garner MG	.05	.02
☐ 292 Ray Lankford	.20	.09
☐ 293 Mike Henneman	.05	.02
☐ 294 Dave Valle	.05	.02
☐ 295 Alonzo Powell	.05	.02
☐ 296 Tom Brunansky	.05	.02
☐ 297 Kevin Brown	.10	.05

☐ 298 Kelly Gruber	.05	.02
☐ 299 Charles Nagy	.10	.05
☐ 300 Don Mattingly	.30	.14
☐ 301 Kirk McCaskill	.05	.02
☐ 302 Joey Cora	.10	.05
☐ 303 Dan Plesac	.05	.02
☐ 304 Joe Oliver	.05	.02
☐ 305 Tom Glavine	.05	.02
☐ 306 Al Shirley	.10	.05
☐ 307 Bruce Ruffin	.05	.02
☐ 308 Craig Shipley	.05	.02
☐ 309 Dave Martinez	.05	.02
☐ 310 Jose Mesa	.10	.05
☐ 311 Henry Cotto	.05	.02
☐ 312 Mike LaValliere	.05	.02
☐ 313 Kevin Tapani	.05	.02
☐ 314 Jeff Huson (Shows Jose Canseco sliding into second)	.05	.02
☐ 315 Juan Samuel	.05	.02
☐ 316 Curt Schilling	.20	.09
☐ 317 Mike Bordick	.05	.02
☐ 318 Steve Howe	.05	.02
☐ 319 Tony Phillips	.10	.05
☐ 320 George Bell	.05	.02
☐ 321 Lou Piniella MG	.10	.05
☐ 322 Tim Burke	.05	.02
☐ 323 Milt Thompson	.05	.02
☐ 324 Danny Darwin	.05	.02
☐ 325 Joe Orsulak	.05	.02
☐ 326 Eric King	.05	.02
☐ 327 Jay Buhner	.05	.02
☐ 328 Joel Johnston	.05	.02
☐ 329 Franklin Stubbs	.05	.02
☐ 330 Will Clark	.05	.02
☐ 331 Steve Lake	.05	.02
☐ 332 Chris Jones	.05	.02
☐ 333 Pat Tabler	.05	.02
☐ 334 Kevin Gross	.05	.02
☐ 335 Dave Henderson	.05	.02
☐ 336 Greg Anthony	.05	.02
☐ 337 Alejandro Pena	.05	.02
☐ 338 Shawn Abner	.05	.02
☐ 339 Tom Browning	.05	.02
☐ 340 Otis Nixon	.10	.05
☐ 341 Bob Geren	.05	.02
☐ 342 Tim Spehr	.05	.02
☐ 343 John Vander Wal	.05	.02
☐ 344 Jack Daugherty	.05	.02
☐ 345 Zane Smith	.05	.02
☐ 346 Rheal Cormier	.05	.02
☐ 347 Kent Hrbek	.10	.05
☐ 348 Rick Wilkins	.05	.02
☐ 349 Steve Lyons	.05	.02
☐ 350 Gregg Olson	.05	.02
☐ 351 Greg Riddoch MG	.05	.02
☐ 352 Ed Nunez	.05	.02
☐ 353 Braulio Castillo	.05	.02
☐ 354 Dave Bergman	.05	.02
☐ 355 Warren Newson	.05	.02
☐ 356 Luis Quinones	.05	.02
☐ 357 Mike Witt	.05	.02
☐ 358 Ted Wood	.05	.02
☐ 359 Mike Moore	.05	.02
☐ 360 Lance Parrish	.05	.02
☐ 361 Barry Jones	.05	.02
☐ 362 Javier Ortiz	.05	.02
☐ 363 John Candelaria	.05	.02
☐ 364 Glenallen Hill	.05	.02
☐ 365 Duane Ward	.05	.02
☐ 366 Checklist 265-396	.05	.02
☐ 367 Rafael Belliard	.05	.02
☐ 368 Bill Krueger	.05	.02
☐ 369 Steve Whitaker	.05	.02
☐ 370 Shawon Dunston	.05	.02
☐ 371 Dante Bichette	.05	.02
☐ 372 Kip Gross	.05	.02
☐ 373 Don Robinson	.05	.02
☐ 374 Bernie Williams	.20	.09
☐ 375 Bert Blyleven	.10	.05
☐ 376 Chris Donnels	.05	.02
☐ 377 Bob Zupcic	.05	.02
☐ 378 Joel Skinner	.05	.02
☐ 379 Steve Chitren	.05	.02
☐ 380 Barry Bonds	.25	.11
☐ 381 Sparky Anderson MG	.10	.05
☐ 382 Sid Fernandez	.05	.02
☐ 383 Dave Hollins	.05	.02
☐ 384 Mark Lee	.05	.02
☐ 385 Tim Wallach	.05	.02
☐ 386 Will Clark AS	.05	.02
☐ 387 Ryne Sandberg AS	.20	.09
☐ 388 Howard Johnson AS	.05	.02
☐ 389 Barry Larkin AS	.05	.02
☐ 390 Barry Bonds AS	.10	.05
☐ 391 Ron Gant AS	.10	.05
☐ 392 Bobby Bonilla AS	.10	.05
☐ 393 Craig Biggio AS	.05	.02
☐ 394 Dennis Martinez AS	.05	.02
☐ 395 Tom Glavine AS	.10	.05
☐ 396 Lee Smith AS	.10	.05
☐ 397 Cecil Fielder AS	.10	.05
☐ 398 Julio Franco AS	.05	.02
☐ 399 Wade Boggs AS	.05	.02
☐ 400 Cal Ripken AS	.40	.18
☐ 401 Jose Canseco AS	.10	.05
☐ 402 Joe Carter AS	.10	.05
☐ 403 Ruben Sierra AS	.05	.02
☐ 404 Matt Nokes AS	.05	.02
☐ 405 Roger Clemens AS	.20	.09
☐ 406 Jim Abbott AS	.05	.02
☐ 407 Bryan Harvey AS	.05	.02
☐ 408 Bob Milacki	.05	.02
☐ 409 Geno Petralli	.05	.02
☐ 410 Dave Stewart	.10	.05
☐ 411 Mike Jackson	.05	.02
☐ 412 Luis Aquino	.05	.02
☐ 413 Tim Teufel	.05	.02
☐ 414 Jeff Ware	.05	.02
☐ 415 Jim Deshaies	.05	.02
☐ 416 Ellis Burks	.10	.05
☐ 417 Allan Anderson	.05	.02
☐ 418 Alfredo Griffin	.05	.02
☐ 419 Wally Whitehurst	.05	.02
☐ 420 Sandy Alomar Jr.	.10	.05
☐ 421 Juan Agosto	.05	.02
☐ 422 Sam Horn	.05	.02
☐ 423 Jeff Fassero	.10	.05
☐ 424 Paul McClellan	.05	.02
☐ 425 Cecil Fielder	.10	.05
☐ 426 Tim Raines	.10	.05
☐ 427 Eddie Taubensee	.05	.02
☐ 428 Dennis Boyd	.05	.02
☐ 429 Tony LaRussa MG	.10	.05
☐ 430 Steve Sax	.05	.02
☐ 431 Tom Gordon	.05	.02
☐ 432 Billy Hatcher	.05	.02
☐ 433 Cal Eldred	.05	.02
☐ 434 Wally Backman	.05	.02
☐ 435 Mark Eichhorn	.05	.02
☐ 436 Mookie Wilson	.05	.02
☐ 437 Scott Servais	.05	.02
☐ 438 Mike Maddux	.05	.02
☐ 439 Chico Walker	.05	.02
☐ 440 Doug Drabek	.05	.02
☐ 441 Rob Deer	.05	.02
☐ 442 Dave West	.05	.02
☐ 443 Spike Owen	.05	.02
☐ 444 Tyrone Hill	.05	.02
☐ 445 Matt Williams	.05	.02
☐ 446 Mark Lewis	.05	.02
☐ 447 David Segui	.05	.02
☐ 448 Tom Pagnozzi	.05	.02
☐ 449 Jeff Johnson	.05	.02
☐ 450 Mark McGwire	.40	.18
☐ 451 Tom Henke	.05	.02
☐ 452 Wilson Alvarez	.10	.05
☐ 453 Gary Redus	.05	.02
☐ 454 Darren Holmes	.05	.02
☐ 455 Pete O'Brien	.05	.02
☐ 456 Pat Combs	.05	.02
☐ 457 Hubie Brooks	.05	.02
☐ 458 Frank Tanana	.05	.02
☐ 459 Tom Kelly MG	.05	.02
☐ 460 Andre Dawson	.05	.02
☐ 461 Doug Jones	.05	.02
☐ 462 Rich Rodriguez	.05	.02
☐ 463 Mike Simms	.05	.02
☐ 464 Mike Jeffcoat	.05	.02
☐ 465 Barry Larkin	.10	.05
☐ 466 Stan Belinda	.05	.02
☐ 467 Lonnie Smith	.05	.02
☐ 468 Greg Harris	.05	.02
☐ 469 Jim Eisenreich	.05	.02
☐ 470 Pedro Guerrero	.05	.02
☐ 471 Jose DeJesus	.05	.02
☐ 472 Rich Rowland	.05	.02
☐ 473 1992 Prospects 3B UER Frank Bolick Craig Paquette Tom Redington Paul Russo (Line around top border)	.20	.09
☐ 474 Mike Rossiter	.05	.02
☐ 475 Robby Thompson	.05	.02
☐ 476 Randy Bush	.05	.02
☐ 477 Greg Hibbard	.05	.02
☐ 478 Dale Sveum	.05	.02
☐ 479 Chito Martinez	.05	.02
☐ 480 Scott Sanderson	.05	.02
☐ 481 Tino Martinez	.20	.09
☐ 482 Jimmy Key	.10	.05
☐ 483 Terry Shumpert	.05	.02
☐ 484 Mike Hartley	.05	.02
☐ 485 Chris Sabo	.05	.02
☐ 486 Bob Walk	.05	.02
☐ 487 John Cerutti	.05	.02
☐ 488 Scott Cooper	.05	.02
☐ 489 Bobby Cox MG	.10	.05
☐ 490 Julio Franco	.10	.05
☐ 491 Jeff Brantley	.05	.02
☐ 492 Mike Devereaux	.05	.02
☐ 493 Jose Offerman	.05	.02
☐ 494 Gary Thurman	.05	.02
☐ 495 Carney Lansford	.10	.05
☐ 496 Joe Grahe	.05	.02
☐ 497 Andy Ashby	.05	.02
☐ 498 Gerald Perry	.05	.02
☐ 499 Dave Otto	.05	.02
☐ 500 Vince Coleman	.05	.02
☐ 501 Rob Mallicoat	.05	.02
☐ 502 Greg Briley	.05	.02
☐ 503 Pascual Perez	.05	.02
☐ 504 Aaron Sele	.10	.05
☐ 505 Bobby Thigpen	.05	.02
☐ 506 Todd Benzinger	.05	.02
☐ 507 Candy Maldonado	.05	.02
☐ 508 Bill Gullickson	.05	.02
☐ 509 Doug Dascenzo	.05	.02
☐ 510 Frank Viola	.05	.02
☐ 511 Kenny Rogers	.05	.02
☐ 512 Mike Heath	.05	.02
☐ 513 Kevin Bass	.05	.02
☐ 514 Kim Batiste	.05	.02
☐ 515 Delino DeShields	.05	.02
☐ 516 Ed Sprague Jr.	.10	.05
☐ 517 Jim Gott	.05	.02
☐ 518 Jose Melendez	.05	.02
☐ 519 Hal McRae MG	.05	.02
☐ 520 Jeff Bagwell	.60	.25
☐ 521 Joe Hesketh	.05	.02
☐ 522 Milt Cuyler	.05	.02
☐ 523 Shawn Hillegas	.05	.02
☐ 524 Don Slaught	.05	.02
☐ 525 Randy Johnson	.20	.09
☐ 526 Doug Piatt	.05	.02
☐ 527 Checklist 397-528	.05	.02
☐ 528 Steve Foster	.05	.02
☐ 529 Joe Girardi	.05	.02
☐ 530 Jim Abbott	.05	.02
☐ 531 Larry Walker	.20	.09
☐ 532 Mike Huff	.05	.02
☐ 533 Mackey Sasser	.05	.02
☐ 534 Benji Gil	.10	.05
☐ 535 Dave Stieb	.05	.02
☐ 536 Willie Wilson	.05	.02
☐ 537 Mark Leiter	.05	.02
☐ 538 Jose Uribe	.05	.02
☐ 539 Thomas Howard	.05	.02
☐ 540 Ben McDonald	.05	.02
☐ 541 Jose Tolentino	.05	.02
☐ 542 Keith Mitchell	.05	.02
☐ 543 Jerome Walton	.05	.02
☐ 544 Cliff Brantley	.05	.02
☐ 545 Andy Van Slyke	.10	.05
☐ 546 Paul Sorrento	.05	.02
☐ 547 Herm Winningham	.05	.02
☐ 548 Mark Guthrie	.05	.02
☐ 549 Joe Torre MG	.10	.05
☐ 550 Darryl Strawberry	.10	.05
☐ 551 1992 Prospects SS UER Wilfredo Cordero Chipper Jones Manny Alexander Alex Arias (No line around top border)	1.50	.70
☐ 552 Dave Gallagher	.05	.02
☐ 553 Edgar Martinez	.05	.02
☐ 554 Donald Harris	.05	.02
☐ 555 Frank Thomas	1.00	.45
☐ 556 Storm Davis	.05	.02
☐ 557 Dickie Thon	.05	.02
☐ 558 Scott Garrelts	.05	.02
☐ 559 Steve Olin	.05	.02
☐ 560 Rickey Henderson	.05	.02
☐ 561 Jose Vizcaino	.05	.02
☐ 562 Wade Taylor	.05	.02
☐ 563 Pat Borders	.05	.02
☐ 564 Jimmy Gonzalez	.05	.02
☐ 565 Lee Smith	.10	.05
☐ 566 Bill Sampen	.05	.02
☐ 567 Dean Palmer	.05	.02
☐ 568 Bryan Harvey	.05	.02
☐ 569 Tony Pena	.05	.02
☐ 570 Lou Whitaker	.10	.05
☐ 571 Randy Tomlin	.05	.02
☐ 572 Greg Vaughn	.05	.02
☐ 573 Kelly Downs	.05	.02
☐ 574 Steve Avery UER (Should be 13 games	.05	.02

for Durham in 1989)
☐ 575 Kirby Puckett .40 .18
☐ 576 Heathcliff Slocumb .05 .02
☐ 577 Kevin Seitzer .05 .02
☐ 578 Lee Guetterman .05 .02
☐ 579 Johnny Oates MG .05 .02
☐ 580 Greg Maddux .60 .25
☐ 581 Stan Javier .05 .02
☐ 582 Vicente Palacios .05 .02
☐ 583 Mel Rojas .10 .05
☐ 584 Wayne Rosenthal .05 .02
☐ 585 Lenny Webster .05 .02
☐ 586 Rod Nichols .05 .02
☐ 587 Mickey Morandini .05 .02
☐ 588 Russ Swan .05 .02
☐ 589 Mariano Duncan .05 .02
☐ 590 Howard Johnson .05 .02
☐ 591 1992 Prospects OF .10 .05
Jeromy Burnitz
Jacob Brumfield
Alan Cockrell
D.J. Dozier
☐ 592 Denny Neagle .05 .02
☐ 593 Steve Decker .05 .02
☐ 594 Brian Barber .10 .05
☐ 595 Bruce Hurst .05 .02
☐ 596 Kent Mercker .05 .02
☐ 597 Mike Magnante .05 .02
☐ 598 Jody Reed .05 .02
☐ 599 Steve Searcy .05 .02
☐ 600 Paul Molitor .20 .09
☐ 601 Dave Smith .05 .02
☐ 602 Mike Fetters .05 .02
☐ 603 Luis Mercedes .05 .02
☐ 604 Chris Gwynn .05 .02
☐ 605 Scott Erickson .10 .05
☐ 606 Brook Jacoby .05 .02
☐ 607 Todd Stottlemyre .05 .02
☐ 608 Scott Bradley .05 .02
☐ 609 Mike Hargrove MG .10 .05
☐ 610 Eric Davis .10 .05
☐ 611 Brian Hunter .05 .02
☐ 612 Pat Kelly .05 .02
☐ 613 Pedro Munoz .05 .02
☐ 614 Al Osuna .05 .02
☐ 615 Matt Merullo .05 .02
☐ 616 Larry Andersen .05 .02
☐ 617 Junior Ortiz .05 .02
☐ 618 1992 Prospects OF .05 .02
Cesar Hernandez
Steve Hosey
Jeff McNeely
Dan Peltier
☐ 619 Danny Jackson .05 .02
☐ 620 George Brett .40 .18
☐ 621 Dan Gakeler .05 .02
☐ 622 Steve Buechele .05 .02
☐ 623 Bob Tewksbury .05 .02
☐ 624 Shawn Estes .40 .18
☐ 625 Kevin McReynolds .05 .02
☐ 626 Chris Haney .05 .02
☐ 627 Mike Sharperson .05 .02
☐ 628 Mark Williamson .05 .02
☐ 629 Wally Joyner .10 .05
☐ 630 Carlton Fisk .20 .09
☐ 631 Armando Reynoso .05 .02
☐ 632 Felix Fermin .05 .02
☐ 633 Mitch Williams .05 .02
☐ 634 Manuel Lee .05 .02
☐ 635 Harold Baines .10 .05
☐ 636 Greg Harris .05 .02
☐ 637 Orlando Merced .05 .02
☐ 638 Chris Bosio .05 .02
☐ 639 Wayne Housie .05 .02
☐ 640 Xavier Hernandez .05 .02
☐ 641 David Howard .05 .02
☐ 642 Tim Crews .05 .02
☐ 643 Rick Cerone .05 .02
☐ 644 Terry Leach .05 .02
☐ 645 Deion Sanders .20 .09
☐ 646 Craig Wilson .05 .02
☐ 647 Marquis Grissom .10 .05
☐ 648 Scott Fletcher .05 .02
☐ 649 Norm Charlton .05 .02
☐ 650 Jesse Barfield .05 .02
☐ 651 Joe Slusarski .05 .02
☐ 652 Bobby Rose .05 .02
☐ 653 Dennis Lamp .05 .02
☐ 654 Allen Watson .10 .05
☐ 655 Brett Butler .10 .05
☐ 656 1992 Prospects OF .20 .09
Rudy Pemberton
Henry Rodriguez
Lee Tinsley
Gerald Williams
☐ 657 Dave Johnson .05 .02
☐ 658 Checklist 529-660 .05 .02
☐ 659 Brian McRae .05 .02
☐ 660 Fred McGriff .05 .02
☐ 661 Bill Landrum .05 .02
☐ 662 Juan Guzman .05 .02
☐ 663 Greg Gagne .05 .02
☐ 664 Ken Hill .05 .02
☐ 665 Dave Haas .05 .02
☐ 666 Tom Foley .05 .02
☐ 667 Roberto Hernandez .10 .05
☐ 668 Dwayne Henry .05 .02
☐ 669 Jim Fregosi MG .05 .02
☐ 670 Harold Reynolds .05 .02
☐ 671 Mark Whiten .05 .02
☐ 672 Eric Plunk .05 .02
☐ 673 Todd Hundley .05 .02
☐ 674 Mo Sanford .05 .02
☐ 675 Bobby Witt .05 .02
☐ 676 1992 Prospects P .05 .02
Sam Militello
Pat Mahomes
Turk Wendell
Roger Salkeld
☐ 677 John Marzano .05 .02
☐ 678 Joe Klink .05 .02
☐ 679 Pete Incaviglia .05 .02
☐ 680 Dale Murphy .20 .09
☐ 681 Rene Gonzales .05 .02
☐ 682 Andy Benes .10 .05
☐ 683 Jim Poole .05 .02
☐ 684 Trever Miller .05 .02
☐ 685 Scott Livingstone .05 .02
☐ 686 Rich DeLucia .05 .02
☐ 687 Harvey Pulliam .05 .02
☐ 688 Tim Belcher .05 .02
☐ 689 Mark Lemke .05 .02
☐ 690 John Franco .05 .02
☐ 691 Walt Weiss .05 .02
☐ 692 Scott Ruskin .05 .02
☐ 693 Jeff King .10 .05
☐ 694 Mike Gardiner .05 .02
☐ 695 Gary Sheffield .05 .02
☐ 696 Joe Boever .05 .02
☐ 697 Mike Felder .05 .02
☐ 698 John Habyan .05 .02
☐ 699 Cito Gaston MG .05 .02
☐ 700 Ruben Sierra .05 .02
☐ 701 Scott Radinsky .05 .02
☐ 702 Lee Stevens .05 .02
☐ 703 Mark Wohlers .05 .02
☐ 704 Curt Young .05 .02
☐ 705 Dwight Evans .10 .05
☐ 706 Rob Murphy .05 .02
☐ 707 Gregg Jefferies .10 .05
☐ 708 Tom Bolton .05 .02
☐ 709 Chris James .05 .02
☐ 710 Kevin Maas .05 .02
☐ 711 Ricky Bones .05 .02
☐ 712 Curt Wilkerson .05 .02
☐ 713 Roger McDowell .05 .02
☐ 714 Calvin Reese .05 .02
☐ 715 Craig Biggio .05 .02
☐ 716 Kirk Dressendorfer .05 .02
☐ 717 Ken Dayley .05 .02
☐ 718 B.J. Surhoff .10 .05
☐ 719 Terry Mulholland .05 .02
☐ 720 Kirk Gibson .10 .05
☐ 721 Mike Pagliarulo .05 .02
☐ 722 Walt Terrell .05 .02
☐ 723 Jose Oquendo .05 .02
☐ 724 Kevin Morton .05 .02
☐ 725 Dwight Gooden .10 .05
☐ 726 Kirt Manwaring .05 .02
☐ 727 Chuck McElroy .05 .02
☐ 728 Dave Burba .05 .02
☐ 729 Art Howe MG .05 .02
☐ 730 Ramon Martinez .10 .05
☐ 731 Donnie Hill .05 .02
☐ 732 Nelson Santovenia .05 .02
☐ 733 Bob Melvin .05 .02
☐ 734 Scott Hatteberg .05 .02
☐ 735 Greg Swindell .05 .02
☐ 736 Lance Johnson .10 .05
☐ 737 Kevin Reimer .05 .02
☐ 738 Dennis Eckersley .05 .02
☐ 739 Rob Ducey .05 .02
☐ 740 Ken Caminiti .20 .09
☐ 741 Mark Gubicza .05 .02
☐ 742 Billy Spiers .05 .02
☐ 743 Darren Lewis .05 .02
☐ 744 Chris Hammond .05 .02
☐ 745 Dave Magadan .05 .02
☐ 746 Bernard Gilkey .10 .05
☐ 747 Willie Banks .05 .02
☐ 748 Matt Nokes .05 .02
☐ 749 Jerald Clark .05 .02
☐ 750 Travis Fryman .10 .05
☐ 751 Steve Wilson .05 .02
☐ 752 Billy Ripken .05 .02
☐ 753 Paul Assenmacher .05 .02
☐ 754 Charlie Hayes .05 .02
☐ 755 Alex Fernandez .10 .05
☐ 756 Gary Pettis .05 .02
☐ 757 Rob Dibble .05 .02
☐ 758 Tim Naehring .10 .05
☐ 759 Jeff Torborg MG .05 .02
☐ 760 Ozzie Smith .25 .11
☐ 761 Mike Fitzgerald .05 .02
☐ 762 John Burkett .10 .05
☐ 763 Kyle Abbott .05 .02
☐ 764 Tyler Green .10 .05
☐ 765 Pete Harnisch .05 .02
☐ 766 Mark Davis .05 .02
☐ 767 Kal Daniels .05 .02
☐ 768 Jim Thome .60 .25
☐ 769 Jack Howell .05 .02
☐ 770 Sid Bream .05 .02
☐ 771 Arthur Rhodes .05 .02
☐ 772 Garry Templeton UER .05 .02
(Stat heading in for pitchers)
☐ 773 Hal Morris .05 .02
☐ 774 Bud Black .05 .02
☐ 775 Ivan Calderon .05 .02
☐ 776 Doug Henry .05 .02
☐ 777 John Olerud .10 .05
☐ 778 Tim Leary .05 .02
☐ 779 Jay Bell .10 .05
☐ 780 Eddie Murray .20 .09
☐ 781 Paul Abbott .05 .02
☐ 782 Phil Plantier .05 .02
☐ 783 Joe Magrane .05 .02
☐ 784 Ken Patterson .05 .02
☐ 785 Albert Belle .25 .11
☐ 786 Royce Clayton .10 .05
☐ 787 Checklist 661-792 .05 .02
☐ 788 Mike Stanton .05 .02
☐ 789 Bobby Valentine MG .05 .02
☐ 790 Joe Carter .10 .05
☐ 791 Danny Cox .05 .02
☐ 792 Dave Winfield .05 .02

1992 Topps Gold

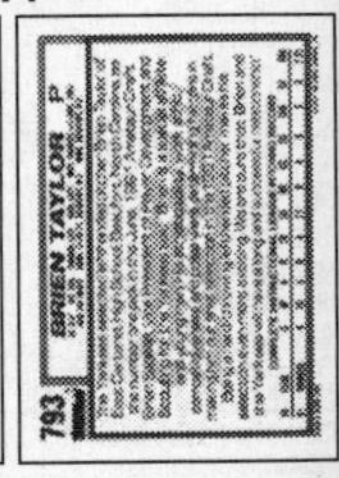

Topps produced a 792-card Topps Gold factory se packaged in a foil display box. Only this set contained ar additional card of Brien Taylor, numbered 793 and hanc signed by him. The production run was 12,000 sets. The Topps Gold cards were also available in regular series packs. According to Topps, on average collectors woulc find one Topps Gold card in every 36 wax packs, one ir every 18 cello packs, one in every 12 rak packs, five pe Vending box, one in every six jumbo packs, and ten pe regular factory set. The packs also featured "Match-the Stats" game cards in which the consumer could save "Runs". For 2.00 and every 100 Runs saved in this game the consumer could receive through a mail-in offer te Topps Gold cards. These particular Topps Gold card carry the word "Winner" in gold foil on the card front. Th checklist cards in the regular set were replaced with si individual Rookie player cards (131, 264, 366, 527, 658 787) in the gold set. There were a number of uncorrecte errors in the Gold set. Steve Finley (86) has gold ban indicating he is Mark Davidson of the Astros. Anduja Cedeno (288) is listed as a member of the New Yor Yankees. Mike Huff (532) is listed as a member of th Boston Red Sox. Barry Larkin (465) is listed as a membe of the Houston Astros but is correctly listed as a membe of the Cincinnati Reds on his Gold Winners cards Typically the individual cards are sold at a multiple of th player's respective value in the regular set.

	MINT	NRM
COMPLETE SET (792)	120.00	55.0
COMPLETE FACT.SET (793)	120.00	55.0
COMMON CARD (1-792)	.25	.1
*STARS: 7.5X to 15X BASIC CARDS		
*RC'S: 6X to 12X BASIC CARDS		

☐ 131 Terry Mathews .50 .2
(Replaces Checklist 1)

☐ 264 Rod Beck (Replaces Checklist 2)	1.00	.45
☐ 366 Tony Perezchica (Replaces Checklist 3)	.50	.23
☐ 527 Terry McDaniel (Replaces Checklist 4)	.50	.23
☐ 658 John Ramos (Replaces Checklist 5)	.50	.23
☐ 787 Brian Williams (Replaces Checklist 6)	.50	.23
☐ 793 Brien Taylor AU/12000	10.00	4.50

1992 Topps Gold Winners

The 1992 Topps baseball card packs featured "Match-the-Stats" game cards in which the consumer could save "Runs". For 2.00 and every 100 Runs saved in this game, the consumer could receive through a mail-in offer ten Topps Gold cards. These particular Topps Gold cards carry the word "Winner" in gold foil on the card front. The checklist cards in the regular set were replaced with six individual Rookie player cards (131, 264, 366, 527, 658, 787) in the gold set. Typically the individual cards are sold at a multiple of the player's respective value in the regular set.

	MINT	NRMT
COMPLETE SET (792)	60.00	27.00
COMMON CARD (1-792)	.10	.05
*STARS: 2X to 4X BASIC CARDS		
*ROOKIE CARD: 1.5X to 3X BASIC CARDS		

☐ 131 Terry Mathews (Replaces Checklist 1)	.15	.07
☐ 264 Rod Beck (Replaces Checklist 2)	.30	.14
☐ 366 Tony Perezchica (Replaces Checklist 3)	.15	.07
☐ 527 Terry McDaniel (Replaces Checklist 4)	.15	.07
☐ 658 John Ramos (Replaces Checklist 5)	.15	.07
☐ 787 Brian Williams (Replaces Checklist 6)	.15	.07

1992 Topps Micro

This 804 card parallel set was issued in factory set form only. The set is an exact replica of the regular issue 1992 Topps set (not including the Traded set).The cards, however, measure considerably smaller (1" by 1 3/8") than the regular cards. The set also includes 12 special gold foil parallel mini cards which are listed below. Please refer to the multipliers provided for values on the other singles.

	MINT	NRMT
COMPLETE FACT.SET (804)	12.50	5.50
COMMON CARD (1-792)	.05	.02
COMMON GOLD INSERT	.05	.02
*STARS: .5X BASIC CARDS		
*YOUNG STARS: .5X BASIC CARDS		

☐ G1 Nolan Ryan RB	1.50	.70
☐ G2 Rickey Henderson RB	.25	.11
☐ G10 Wade Boggs Gold	.25	.11
☐ G50 Ken Griffey Jr.	3.00	1.35
☐ G100 Jose Canseco	.25	.11
☐ G270 Tony Gwynn	.75	.35
☐ G300 Don Mattingly	.75	.35
☐ G380 Barry Bonds	.40	.18
☐ G397 Cecil Fielder AS	.10	.05
☐ G403 Ruben Sierra AS	.15	.07
☐ G460 Andre Dawson	.25	.11
☐ G725 Dwight Gooden	.15	.07

1992 Topps Traded

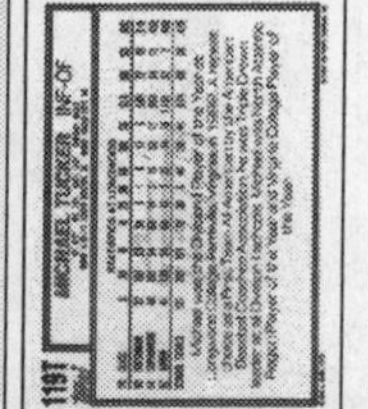

The 1992 Topps Traded set comprises 132 standard-size cards. The set was distributed exclusively in factory set form through hobby dealers. As in past editions, the set focuses on promising rookies, new managers, and players who changed teams. The set also includes a Team U.S.A. subset, featuring 25 of America's top college players and the Team U.S.A. coach. Card design is identical to the regular issue 1992 Topps cards except for the T-suffixed numbering. The cards are arranged in alphabetical order by player's last name. The key Rookie Cards in this set are Nomar Garciaparra, Brian Jordan and Michael Tucker.

	MINT	NRMT
COMP.FACT.SET (132)	35.00	16.00
COMMON CARD (1T-132T)	.10	.05

☐ 1T Willie Adams USA	.10	.05
☐ 2T Jeff Alkire USA	.10	.05
☐ 3T Felipe Alou MG	.10	.05
☐ 4T Moises Alou	.40	.18
☐ 5T Ruben Amaro	.10	.05
☐ 6T Jack Armstrong	.10	.05
☐ 7T Scott Bankhead	.10	.05
☐ 8T Tim Belcher	.10	.05
☐ 9T George Bell	.10	.05
☐ 10T Freddie Benavides	.10	.05
☐ 11T Todd Benzinger	.10	.05
☐ 12T Joe Boever	.10	.05
☐ 13T Ricky Bones	.10	.05
☐ 14T Bobby Bonilla	.20	.09
☐ 15T Hubie Brooks	.10	.05
☐ 16T Jerry Browne	.10	.05
☐ 17T Jim Bullinger	.10	.05
☐ 18T Dave Burba	.10	.05
☐ 19T Kevin Campbell	.10	.05
☐ 20T Tom Candiotti	.10	.05
☐ 21T Mark Carreon	.10	.05
☐ 22T Gary Carter	.20	.09
☐ 23T Archi Cianfrocco	.10	.05
☐ 24T Phil Clark	.10	.05
☐ 25T Chad Curtis	.40	.18
☐ 26T Eric Davis	.20	.09
☐ 27T Tim Davis USA	.10	.05
☐ 28T Gary DiSarcina	.10	.05
☐ 29T Darren Dreifort USA	.20	.09
☐ 30T Mariano Duncan	.10	.05
☐ 31T Mike Fitzgerald	.10	.05
☐ 32T John Flaherty	.10	.05
☐ 33T Darrin Fletcher	.10	.05
☐ 34T Scott Fletcher	.10	.05
☐ 35T Ron Fraser CO USA	.10	.05
☐ 36T Andres Galarraga	.20	.09
☐ 37T Dave Gallagher	.10	.05
☐ 38T Mike Gallego	.10	.05
☐ 39T Nomar Garciaparra USA	25.00	11.00
☐ 40T Jason Giambi USA	.75	.35
☐ 41T Danny Gladden	.10	.05
☐ 42T Rene Gonzales	.10	.05
☐ 43T Jeff Granger USA	.20	.09
☐ 44T Rick Greene USA	.10	.05
☐ 45T Jeffrey Hammonds USA	.40	.18
☐ 46T Charlie Hayes	.10	.05
☐ 47T Von Hayes	.10	.05
☐ 48T Rick Helling USA	.10	.05
☐ 49T Butch Henry	.10	.05
☐ 50T Carlos Hernandez	.10	.05
☐ 51T Ken Hill	.20	.09
☐ 52T Butch Hobson	.10	.05
☐ 53T Vince Horsman	.10	.05
☐ 54T Pete Incaviglia	.10	.05
☐ 55T Gregg Jefferies	.20	.09
☐ 56T Charles Johnson USA	1.00	.45
☐ 57T Doug Jones	.10	.05
☐ 58T Brian Jordan	.50	.23
☐ 59T Wally Joyner	.20	.09
☐ 60T Daron Kirkreit USA	.20	.09
☐ 61T Bill Krueger	.10	.05
☐ 62T Gene Lamont MG	.10	.05
☐ 63T Jim Lefebvre MG	.10	.05
☐ 64T Danny Leon	.10	.05
☐ 65T Pat Listach	.10	.05
☐ 66T Kenny Lofton	1.50	.70
☐ 67T Dave Martinez	.10	.05
☐ 68T Derrick May	.10	.05
☐ 69T Kirk McCaskill	.10	.05
☐ 70T Chad McConnell USA	.20	.09
☐ 71T Kevin McReynolds	.10	.05
☐ 72T Rusty Meacham	.10	.05
☐ 73T Keith Miller	.10	.05
☐ 74T Kevin Mitchell	.20	.09
☐ 75T Jason Moler USA	.10	.05
☐ 76T Mike Morgan	.10	.05
☐ 77T Jack Morris	.20	.09
☐ 78T Calvin Murray USA	.20	.09
☐ 79T Eddie Murray	.40	.18
☐ 80T Randy Myers	.20	.09
☐ 81T Denny Neagle	.20	.09
☐ 82T Phil Nevin USA	.20	.09
☐ 83T Dave Nilsson	.40	.18
☐ 84T Junior Ortiz	.10	.05
☐ 85T Donovan Osborne	.20	.09
☐ 86T Bill Pecota	.10	.05
☐ 87T Melido Perez	.10	.05
☐ 88T Mike Perez	.10	.05
☐ 89T Hipolito Pichardo	.10	.05
☐ 90T Willie Randolph	.20	.09
☐ 91T Darren Reed	.10	.05
☐ 92T Bip Roberts	.10	.05
☐ 93T Chris Roberts USA	.20	.09
☐ 94T Steve Rodriguez USA	.10	.05
☐ 95T Bruce Ruffin	.10	.05
☐ 96T Scott Ruskin	.10	.05
☐ 97T Bret Saberhagen	.10	.05
☐ 98T Rey Sanchez	.10	.05
☐ 99T Steve Sax	.10	.05
☐ 100T Curt Schilling	.40	.18
☐ 101T Dick Schofield	.10	.05
☐ 102T Gary Scott	.10	.05
☐ 103T Kevin Seitzer	.10	.05
☐ 104T Frank Seminara	.10	.05
☐ 105T Gary Sheffield	.40	.18
☐ 106T John Smiley	.10	.05
☐ 107T Cory Snyder	.10	.05
☐ 108T Paul Sorrento	.10	.05
☐ 109T Sammy Sosa	.40	.18
☐ 110T Matt Stairs	.10	.05
☐ 111T Andy Stankiewicz	.10	.05
☐ 112T Kurt Stillwell	.10	.05
☐ 113T Rick Sutcliffe	.10	.05
☐ 114T Bill Swift	.10	.05
☐ 115T Jeff Tackett	.10	.05
☐ 116T Danny Tartabull	.10	.05
☐ 117T Eddie Taubensee	.10	.05
☐ 118T Dickie Thon	.10	.05
☐ 119T Michael Tucker USA	1.00	.45
☐ 120T Scooter Tucker	.10	.05
☐ 121T Marc Valdes USA	.10	.05
☐ 122T Julio Valera	.10	.05
☐ 123T Jason Varitek USA	.50	.23
☐ 124T Ron Villone USA	.20	.09
☐ 125T Frank Viola	.10	.05
☐ 126T B.J. Wallace USA	.20	.09
☐ 127T Dan Walters	.10	.05
☐ 128T Craig Wilson USA	.10	.05
☐ 129T Chris Wimmer USA	.10	.05
☐ 130T Dave Winfield	.20	.09
☐ 131T Herm Winningham	.10	.05
☐ 132T Checklist 1T-132T	.10	.05

1992 Topps Traded Gold

This 132 card standard-size set parallels the regular 1992 Topps Traded set. It was only issued through the Topps dealer network. Six thousand of these sets were produced and the only player difference is that Kerry Woodson replaces the checklist card

	MINT	NRMT
COMPLETE FACT.SET (132)	50.00	22.00
COMMON CARDS (1T-132T)	.15	.07
*GOLD CARDS 1.5 BASIC CARDS		

☐ 132T Kerry Woodson Replaces Checklist	.40	.18

1992 Topps Dairy Queen Team USA

This 33-card standard size set was produced by Topps for Dairy Queen. The set was available in four-card packs with the purchase of a regular-sized sundae in a Team USA helmet during June and July 1992. The set features 16 Team USA players from the 1984 and 1988 teams who are now major league stars as well as 15 1992 Team USA prospects. Completing the set is a 1988 Gold Medal team celebration card and the 1992 Head Coach Ron Fraser. The front design features posed color player photos bordered in blue and red on a white background. The Team USA logo is printed in red and blue at the top. The Dairy Queen logo and the player's name overlay the bottom of the picture. The horizontally oriented backs feature Major League, Team USA tour, and Olympic statistics printed in red and blue on a light blue box.

	MINT	NRMT
COMPLETE SET (33)	15.00	6.75
COMMON CARD (1-33)	.25	.11
☐ 1 Mark McGwire	3.00	1.35
☐ 2 Will Clark	1.50	.70
☐ 3 John Marzano	.25	.11
☐ 4 Barry Larkin	1.50	.70
☐ 5 Bobby Witt	.50	.23
☐ 6 Scott Bankhead	.25	.11
☐ 7 B.J. Surhoff	.75	.35
☐ 8 Shane Mack	.25	.11
☐ 9 Jim Abbott	.50	.23
☐ 10 Ben McDonald	.25	.11
☐ 11 Robin Ventura	.50	.23
☐ 12 Charles Nagy	.50	.23
☐ 13 Andy Benes	.50	.23
☐ 14 Joe Slusarski	.25	.11
☐ 15 Ed Sprague	.25	.11
☐ 16 Bret Barberie	.25	.11
☐ 17 Team USA Strikes Gold	.50	.23
☐ 18 Jeff Granger	.25	.11
☐ 19 John Dettmer	.25	.11
☐ 20 Todd Greene	1.00	.45
☐ 21 Jeffrey Hammonds	1.00	.45
☐ 22 Dan Melendez	.25	.11
☐ 23 Kennie Steenstra	.25	.11
☐ 24 Todd Johnson	.25	.11
☐ 25 Chris Roberts	.50	.23
☐ 26 Steve Rodriguez	.25	.11
☐ 27 Charles Johnson	1.50	.70
☐ 28 Chris Wimmer	.25	.11
☐ 29 Tony Phillips P	.25	.11
☐ 30 Craig Wilson	.25	.11
☐ 31 Jason Giambi	2.00	.90
☐ 32 Paul Shuey	.50	.23
☐ 33 Ron Fraser CO	.25	.11

1992 Topps Debut '91

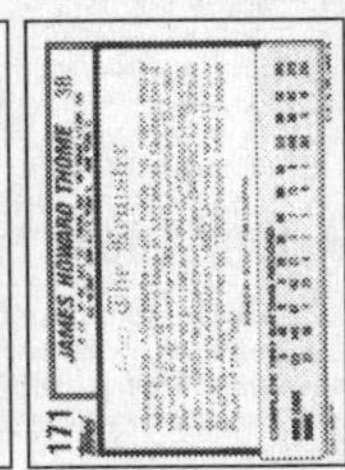

The 1991 Topps Debut '91 set contains 194 standard-size cards. The fronts feature a mix of either posed or action glossy color player photos, framed with two color border stripes on a white card face. The date of the player's first major league appearance is given in a color bar in the lower right corner. In addition to biography and 1991 batting record, the horizontally oriented backs present player profiles in the form of a newspaper article from The Register. Future MVP's Jeff Bagwell and Mo Vaughn are among the featured players in the set.

	MINT	NRMT
COMPLETE SET (194)	20.00	9.00
COMMON CARD (1-194)	.05	.02
☐ 1 Kyle Abbott	.05	.02
☐ 2 Dana Allison	.05	.02
☐ 3 Rich Amaral	.10	.05
☐ 4 Ruben Amaro Jr.	.05	.02
☐ 5 Andy Ashby	.25	.11
☐ 6 Jim Austin	.05	.02
☐ 7 Jeff Bagwell	5.00	2.20
☐ 8 Jeff Banister	.05	.02
☐ 9 Willie Banks	.05	.02
☐ 10 Bret Barberie	.05	.02
☐ 11 Kim Batiste	.05	.02
☐ 12 Chris Beasley	.05	.02
☐ 13 Rod Beck	.75	.35
☐ 14 Derek Bell	.30	.14
☐ 15 Esteban Beltre	.05	.02
☐ 16 Freddie Benavides	.05	.02
☐ 17 Ricky Bones	.10	.05
☐ 18 Denis Boucher	.05	.02
☐ 19 Ryan Bowen	.05	.02
☐ 20 Cliff Brantley	.05	.02
☐ 21 John Briscoe	.05	.02
☐ 22 Scott Brosius	.15	.07
☐ 23 Terry Bross	.05	.02
☐ 24 Jarvis Brown	.05	.02
☐ 25 Scott Bullett	.05	.02
☐ 26 Kevin Campbell	.05	.02
☐ 27 Amalio Carreno	.05	.02
☐ 28 Matias Carrillo	.05	.02
☐ 29 Jeff Carter	.05	.02
☐ 30 Vinny Castilla	1.50	.70
☐ 31 Braulio Castillo	.05	.02
☐ 32 Frank Castillo	.25	.11
☐ 33 Darrin Chapin	.05	.02
☐ 34 Mike Christopher	.05	.02
☐ 35 Mark Clark	.40	.18
☐ 36 Royce Clayton	.75	.35
☐ 37 Stu Cole	.05	.02
☐ 38 Gary Cooper	.05	.02
☐ 39 Archie Corbin	.05	.02
☐ 40 Rheal Cormier	.10	.05
☐ 41 Chris Cron	.05	.02
☐ 42 Mike Dalton	.05	.02
☐ 43 Mark Davis	.05	.02
☐ 44 Francisco DeLaRosa	.05	.02
☐ 45 Chris Donnels	.05	.02
☐ 46 Brian Drahman	.05	.02
☐ 47 Tom Drees	.05	.02
☐ 48 Kirk Dressendorfer	.05	.02
☐ 49 Bruce Egloff	.05	.02
☐ 50 Cal Eldred	.50	.23
☐ 51 Jose Escobar	.05	.02
☐ 52 Tony Eusebio	.25	.11
☐ 53 Hector Fajardo	.05	.02
☐ 54 Monty Fariss	.05	.02
☐ 55 Jeff Fassero	.40	.18
☐ 56 Dave Fleming	.10	.05
☐ 57 Kevin Flora	.05	.02
☐ 58 Steve Foster	.05	.02
☐ 59 Dan Gakeler	.05	.02
☐ 60 Ramon Garcia	.05	.02
☐ 61 Chris Gardner	.05	.02
☐ 62 Jeff Gardner	.05	.02
☐ 63 Chris George	.05	.02
☐ 64 Ray Giannelli	.05	.02
☐ 65 Tom Goodwin	.25	.11
☐ 66 Mark Grater	.05	.02
☐ 67 Johnny Guzman	.05	.02
☐ 68 Juan Guzman	.50	.23
☐ 69 Dave Haas	.05	.02
☐ 70 Chris Haney	.05	.02
☐ 71 Shawn Hare	.05	.02
☐ 72 Donald Harris	.05	.02
☐ 73 Doug Henry	.05	.02
☐ 74 Pat Hentgen	1.50	.70
☐ 75 Gil Heredia	.05	.02
☐ 76 Jeremy Hernandez	.05	.02
☐ 77 Jose Hernandez	.05	.02
☐ 78 Roberto Hernandez	.75	.35
☐ 79 Bryan Hickerson	.05	.02
☐ 80 Milt Hill	.05	.02
☐ 81 Vince Horsman	.05	.02
☐ 82 Wayne Housie	.05	.02
☐ 83 Chris Howard	.05	.02
☐ 84 David Howard	.05	.02
☐ 85 Mike Humphreys	.05	.02
☐ 86 Brian Hunter	.05	.02
☐ 87 Jim Hunter	.05	.02
☐ 88 Mike Ignasiak	.05	.02
☐ 89 Reggie Jefferson	.50	.23
☐ 90 Jeff Johnson	.05	.02
☐ 91 Joel Johnston	.05	.02
☐ 92 Calvin Jones	.05	.02
☐ 93 Chris Jones	.05	.02
☐ 94 Stacy Jones	.05	.02
☐ 95 Jeff Juden	.25	.11
☐ 96 Scott Kamieniecki	.10	.05
☐ 97 Eric Karros	2.00	.90
☐ 98 Pat Kelly	.10	.05
☐ 99 John Kiely	.05	.02
☐ 100 Darryl Kile	1.50	.70
☐ 101 Wayne Kirby	.05	.02
☐ 102 Garland Kiser	.05	.02
☐ 103 Chuck Knoblauch	3.00	1.35
☐ 104 Randy Knorr	.05	.02
☐ 105 Tom Kramer	.05	.02
☐ 106 Ced Landrum	.05	.02
☐ 107 Patrick Lennon	.05	.02
☐ 108 Jim Lewis	.05	.02
☐ 109 Mark Lewis	.30	.14
☐ 110 Doug Lindsey	.05	.02
☐ 111 Scott Livingstone	.05	.02
☐ 112 Kenny Lofton	5.00	2.20
☐ 113 Ever Magallanes	.05	.02
☐ 114 Mike Magnante	.05	.02
☐ 115 Barry Manuel	.05	.02
☐ 116 Josias Manzanillo	.05	.02
☐ 117 Chito Martinez	.05	.02
☐ 118 Terry Mathews	.05	.02
☐ 119 Rob Maurer	.05	.02
☐ 120 Tim Mauser	.05	.02
☐ 121 Terry McDaniel	.05	.02
☐ 122 Rusty Meacham	.05	.02
☐ 123 Luis Mercedes	.05	.02
☐ 124 Paul Miller	.05	.02
☐ 125 Keith Mitchell	.05	.02
☐ 126 Bobby Moore	.05	.02
☐ 127 Kevin Morton	.05	.02
☐ 128 Andy Mota	.05	.02
☐ 129 Jose Mota	.05	.02
☐ 130 Mike Mussina	4.00	1.80
☐ 131 Jeff Mutis	.05	.02
☐ 132 Denny Neagle	.75	.35
☐ 133 Warren Newson	.05	.02
☐ 134 Jim Olander	.05	.02
☐ 135 Erik Pappas	.05	.02
☐ 136 Jorge Pedre	.05	.02
☐ 137 Yorkis Perez	.05	.02
☐ 138 Mark Petkovsek	.10	.05
☐ 139 Doug Piatt	.05	.02
☐ 140 Jeff Plympton	.05	.02
☐ 141 Harvey Pulliam	.05	.02
☐ 142 John Ramos	.05	.02
☐ 143 Mike Remlinger	.05	.02
☐ 144 Laddie Renfroe	.05	.02
☐ 145 Armando Reynoso	.10	.05
☐ 146 Arthur Rhodes	.15	.07
☐ 147 Pat Rice	.05	.02
☐ 148 Nikco Riesgo	.05	.02
☐ 149 Carlos Rodriguez	.05	.02
☐ 150 Ivan Rodriguez	4.00	1.80
☐ 151 Wayne Rosenthal	.05	.02
☐ 152 Rico Rossy	.05	.02
☐ 153 Stan Royer	.05	.02
☐ 154 Rey Sanchez	.15	.07
☐ 155 Reggie Sanders	.50	.23
☐ 156 Mo Sanford	.05	.02
☐ 157 Bob Scanlan	.05	.02
☐ 158 Pete Schourek	.25	.11
☐ 159 Gary Scott	.05	.02
☐ 160 Tim Scott	.05	.02
☐ 161 Tony Scruggs	.05	.02
☐ 162 Scott Servais	.05	.02
☐ 163 Doug Simons	.05	.02
☐ 164 Heathcliff Slocumb	.40	.18
☐ 165 Joe Slusarski	.05	.02
☐ 166 Tim Spehr	.05	.02
☐ 167 Ed Sprague	.30	.14
☐ 168 Jeff Tackett	.05	.02
☐ 169 Eddie Taubensee	.25	.11
☐ 170 Wade Taylor	.05	.02
☐ 171 Jim Thome	4.00	1.80
☐ 172 Mike Timlin	.25	.11
☐ 173 Jose Tolentino	.05	.02
☐ 174 John Vander Wal	.05	.02
☐ 175 Todd Van Poppel	.05	.02
☐ 176 Mo Vaughn	4.00	1.80
☐ 177 Dave Wainhouse	.05	.02
☐ 178 Don Wakamatsu	.05	.02
☐ 179 Bruce Walton	.05	.02
☐ 180 Kevin Ward	.05	.02
☐ 181 Dave Weathers	.05	.02
☐ 182 Eric Wedge	.05	.02
☐ 183 John Wehner	.05	.02
☐ 184 Rick Wilkins	.10	.05
☐ 185 Bernie Williams	2.50	1.10
☐ 186 Brian Williams	.05	.02
☐ 187 Ron Witmeyer	.05	.02
☐ 188 Mark Wohlers	1.00	.45
☐ 189 Ted Wood	.05	.02
☐ 190 Anthony Young	.05	.02
☐ 191 Eddie Zosky	.05	.02
☐ 192 Bob Zupcic	.05	.02
☐ 193 Checklist 1	.05	.02
☐ 194 Checklist 2	.05	.02

1992 Topps Kids

This 132-card standard size set was packaged in seven card wax packs with a stick of bubble gum. The fron features action and posed player pictures that are part photo and part-cartoon on a brightly colored background The player's name is printed at the bottom in a variety o colors and styles. The backs carry a cartoon with a trivia fact and a "Fun Box" including trivia questions, puzzles quotable quotes, tips from the pros, or a "Did You Know feature. Statistical information is shown in a multi-colore grid at the bottom. The set numbering is arranged by teams in alphabetical order within division.

	MINT	NRMT
COMPLETE SET (132)	12.00	5.50
COMMON CARD (1-132)	.05	.02
☐ 1 Ryne Sandberg	.75	.35
☐ 2 Andre Dawson	.25	.11
☐ 3 George Bell	.05	.02
☐ 4 Mark Grace	.40	.18
☐ 5 Shawon Dunston	.05	.02
☐ 6 Tim Wallach	.05	.02
☐ 7 Ivan Calderon	.05	.02
☐ 8 Marquis Grissom	.15	.07
☐ 9 Delino DeShields	.05	.02
☐ 10 Dennis Martinez	.15	.07
☐ 11 Dwight Gooden	.15	.07
☐ 12 Howard Johnson	.05	.02
☐ 13 John Franco	.15	.07
☐ 14 Gregg Jefferies	.15	.07
☐ 15 Kevin McReynolds	.05	.02
☐ 16 David Cone	.15	.07
☐ 17 Len Dykstra	.15	.07
☐ 18 John Kruk	.15	.07
☐ 19 Von Hayes	.05	.02
☐ 20 Mitch Williams	.05	.02
☐ 21 Barry Bonds	.50	.23
☐ 22 Bobby Bonilla	.15	.07
☐ 23 Andy Van Slyke	.15	.07
☐ 24 Doug Drabek	.05	.02
☐ 25 Ozzie Smith	.75	.35
☐ 26 Pedro Guerrero	.05	.02
☐ 27 Todd Zeile	.05	.02
☐ 28 Lee Smith	.15	.07
☐ 29 Felix Jose	.05	.02
☐ 30 Jose DeLeon	.05	.02
☐ 31 David Justice	.40	.18
☐ 32 Ron Gant	.15	.07
☐ 33 Terry Pendleton	.15	.07
☐ 34 Tom Glavine	.25	.11
☐ 35 Otis Nixon	.05	.02
☐ 36 Steve Avery	.05	.02
☐ 37 Barry Larkin	.25	.11
☐ 38 Eric Davis	.15	.07
☐ 39 Chris Sabo	.05	.02
☐ 40 Rob Dibble	.05	.02
☐ 41 Paul O'Neill	.15	.07
☐ 42 Jose Rijo	.05	.02
☐ 43 Craig Biggio	.25	.11
☐ 44 Jeff Bagwell	1.00	.45
☐ 45 Ken Caminiti	.40	.18
☐ 46 Steve Finley	.25	.11
☐ 47 Darryl Strawberry	.15	.07
☐ 48 Ramon Martinez	.15	.07
☐ 49 Brett Butler	.15	.07
☐ 50 Eddie Murray	.50	.23
☐ 51 Kal Daniels	.05	.02
☐ 52 Orel Hershiser	.15	.07
☐ 53 Tony Gwynn	1.00	.45
☐ 54 Benito Santiago	.05	.02
☐ 55 Fred McGriff	.25	.11
☐ 56 Bip Roberts	.05	.02
☐ 57 Tony Fernandez	.05	.02
☐ 58 Will Clark	.40	.18
☐ 59 Kevin Mitchell	.15	.07
☐ 60 Matt Williams	.25	.11
☐ 61 Willie McGee	.15	.07
☐ 62 Dave Righetti	.05	.02
☐ 63 Cal Ripken	1.50	.70
☐ 64 Ben McDonald	.05	.02
☐ 65 Glenn Davis	.05	.02
☐ 66 Gregg Olson	.05	.02
☐ 67 Roger Clemens	.75	.35
☐ 68 Wade Boggs	.40	.18
☐ 69 Mike Greenwell	.05	.02
☐ 70 Ellis Burks	.25	.11
☐ 71 Sandy Alomar Jr.	.15	.07
☐ 72 Greg Swindell	.05	.02
☐ 73 Albert Belle	.75	.35
☐ 74 Mark Whiten	.05	.02
☐ 75 Alan Trammell	.25	.11
☐ 76 Cecil Fielder	.15	.07
☐ 77 Lou Whitaker	.15	.07
☐ 78 Travis Fryman	.15	.07
☐ 79 Tony Phillips	.05	.02
☐ 80 Robin Yount	.25	.11
☐ 81 Paul Molitor	.40	.18
☐ 82 B.J. Surhoff	.05	.02
☐ 83 Greg Vaughn	.05	.02
☐ 84 Don Mattingly	1.00	.45
☐ 85 Steve Sax	.05	.02
☐ 86 Kevin Maas	.05	.02
☐ 87 Mel Hall	.05	.02
☐ 88 Roberto Kelly	.05	.02
☐ 89 Joe Carter	.25	.11
☐ 90 Roberto Alomar	.40	.18
☐ 91 Dave Stieb	.05	.02
☐ 92 Kelly Gruber	.05	.02
☐ 93 Tom Henke	.05	.02
☐ 94 Chuck Finley	.05	.02
☐ 95 Wally Joyner	.05	.02
☐ 96 Dave Winfield	.40	.18
☐ 97 Jim Abbott	.15	.07
☐ 98 Mark Langston	.05	.02
☐ 99 Frank Thomas	2.00	.90
☐ 100 Ozzie Guillen	.05	.02
☐ 101 Bobby Thigpen	.05	.02
☐ 102 Robin Ventura	.15	.07
☐ 103 Bo Jackson	.15	.07
☐ 104 Tim Raines	.15	.07
☐ 105 George Brett	.75	.35
☐ 106 Danny Tartabull	.05	.02
☐ 107 Bret Saberhagen	.05	.02
☐ 108 Brian McRae	.05	.02
☐ 109 Kirby Puckett	1.00	.45
☐ 110 Scott Erickson	.05	.02
☐ 111 Kent Hrbek	.15	.07
☐ 112 Chuck Knoblauch	.60	.25
☐ 113 Chili Davis	.15	.07
☐ 114 Rick Aguilera	.15	.07
☐ 115 Jose Canseco	.50	.23
☐ 116 Dave Henderson	.05	.02
☐ 117 Dave Stewart	.05	.02
☐ 118 Rickey Henderson	.50	.23
☐ 119 Dennis Eckersley	.25	.11
☐ 120 Harold Baines	.05	.02
☐ 121 Mark McGwire	1.00	.45
☐ 122 Ken Griffey Jr.	2.50	1.10
☐ 123 Harold Reynolds	.15	.07
☐ 124 Erik Hanson	.05	.02
☐ 125 Edgar Martinez	.25	.11
☐ 126 Randy Johnson	.40	.18
☐ 127 Nolan Ryan	2.00	.90
☐ 128 Ruben Sierra	.05	.02
☐ 129 Julio Franco	.15	.07
☐ 130 Rafael Palmeiro	.25	.11
☐ 131 Juan Gonzalez	1.00	.45
☐ 132 Checklist Card	.05	.02

1992 Topps McDonald's

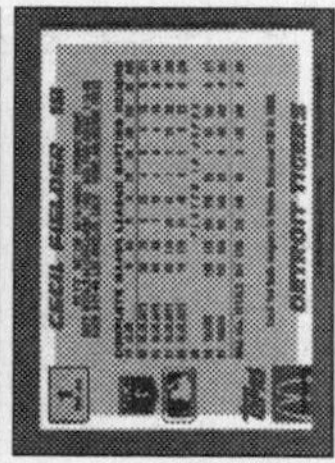

This 44-card standard-size set was produced by Topps for McDonald's and distributed in the New York, New Jersey, and Connecticut areas. The set was subtitled "McDonald's Baseball's Best". For 99 cents with the purchase of an Extra Value Meal or 1.79 with any other food purchase, the collector received a 5-card cello pack. The top card of each pack was always one of eleven different rookies (34-44) randomly packed with four other non-rookie cards. On the fronts, the color player photos are edged with canary yellow and black borders. The player's name and sponsor logo are gold foil stamped at the bottom. The backs are bordered in red and white and display biographical and statistical information on a orange-yellow background. The cards are numbered on the back.

	MINT	NRMT
COMPLETE SET (44)	30.00	13.50
COMMON CARD (1-44)	.25	.11
☐ 1 Cecil Fielder	.50	.23
☐ 2 Benny Santiago	.25	.11
☐ 3 Rickey Henderson	1.25	.55
☐ 4 Roberto Alomar	1.00	.45
☐ 5 Ryne Sandberg	2.00	.90
☐ 6 George Brett	2.00	.90
☐ 7 Terry Pendleton	.50	.23
☐ 8 Ken Griffey Jr.	6.00	2.70
☐ 9 Bobby Bonilla	.50	.23
☐ 10 Roger Clemens	2.50	1.10
☐ 11 Ozzie Smith	2.00	.90
☐ 12 Barry Bonds	1.25	.55
☐ 13 Cal Ripken	5.00	2.20
☐ 14 Ron Gant	.50	.23
☐ 15 Carlton Fisk	.75	.35
☐ 16 Steve Avery	.25	.11
☐ 17 Robin Yount	.75	.35
☐ 18 Will Clark	1.25	.55
☐ 19 Kirby Puckett	2.50	1.10
☐ 20 Jim Abbott	.25	.11
☐ 21 Barry Larkin	.75	.35
☐ 22 Jose Canseco	1.25	.55
☐ 23 Howard Johnson	.25	.11
☐ 24 Nolan Ryan	5.00	2.20
☐ 25 Frank Thomas	5.00	2.20
☐ 26 Danny Tartabull	.25	.11
☐ 27 Julio Franco	.25	.11
☐ 28 David Justice	1.00	.45
☐ 29 Joe Carter	.50	.23
☐ 30 Dale Murphy	1.00	.45
☐ 31 Andre Dawson	1.00	.45
☐ 32 Dwight Gooden	.50	.23
☐ 33 Bo Jackson	.50	.23
☐ 34 Jeff Bagwell	3.00	1.35
☐ 35 Chuck Knoblauch	1.00	.45
☐ 36 Derek Bell	.50	.23
☐ 37 Jim Thome	3.00	1.35
☐ 38 Royce Clayton	.25	.11
☐ 39 Ryan Klesko	2.00	.90
☐ 40 Chito Martinez	.25	.11
☐ 41 Ivan Rodriguez	2.00	.90
☐ 42 Todd Hundley	.75	.35
☐ 43 Eric Karros	1.00	.45
☐ 44 Todd Van Poppel	.25	.11

1993 Topps Pre-Production

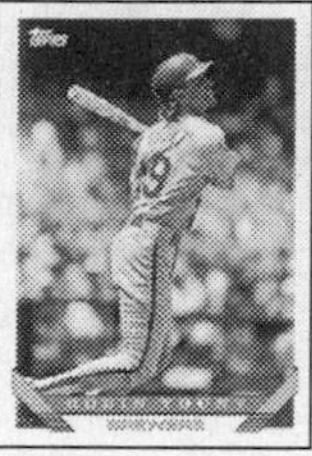
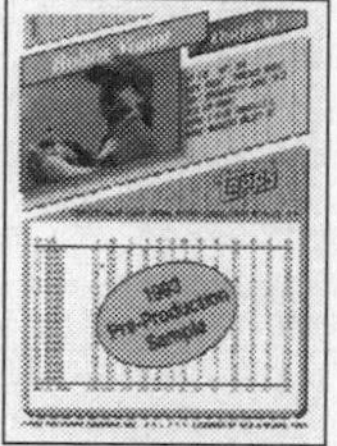

These nine pre-production cards were included in the 1992 Topps Holiday set as a special insert set. The cards are standard size and were done in the style of the 1993 Topps baseball cards. The fronts feature color action player photos bordered in white. A team color-coded horizontal bar and two short diagonal bars accent the pictures at the bottom. The backs carry a color close-up photo, biography, statistics, and (where space allows) a summary of the player's outstanding performance during a game. The cards say "1993 Pre-Production Sample" inside a gray in the middle of the card back.

	MINT	NRMT
COMPLETE SET (9)	8.00	3.60
COMMON CARD (1-250)	.25	.11
☐ 1 Robin Yount	.50	.23
☐ 2 Barry Bonds	1.25	.55
☐ 11 Eric Karros	.25	.11
☐ 32 Don Mattingly	1.50	.70
☐ 100 Mark McGwire	1.50	.70
☐ 150 Frank Thomas	3.00	1.35
☐ 179 Ken Griffey Jr.	4.00	1.80
☐ 230 Carlton Fisk	.50	.23
☐ 250 Chuck Knoblauch	1.00	.45

1993 Topps Pre-Production Sheet

The 1993 Topps Pre-Production sheet was sent out to give collectors a preview of the design of Topps' 1993 regular issue cards. The sheet measures 8" by 11" and features nine standard-size cards. The fronts feature color action player photos with white borders. The player's name appears in a stripe at the bottom of the picture, and this stripe and two short diagonal stripes at the bottom corners of the picture are team color-coded. The backs are colorful and carry a color head shot, biography, complete statistical information, with a career highlight if space permits. A gray circle with the message "1993 Pre-Production Sample: For General Look Only" is superimposed over the statistical section. The cards are all numbered "000" and are therefore checklisted below in alphabetical order.

	MINT	NRMT
COMPLETE SET (9)	7.00	3.10
COMMON CARD (1-9)	.25	.11
□ 1 Roberto Alomar	1.00	.45
□ 2 Bobby Bonilla	.50	.23
□ 3 Gary Carter	.75	.35
□ 4 Andre Dawson	.75	.35
□ 5 Dave Fleming	.25	.11
□ 6 Ken Griffey Jr.	4.00	1.80
□ 7 Pete Incaviglia	.25	.11
□ 8 Spike Owen	.25	.11
□ 9 Larry Walker	1.00	.45

1993 Topps

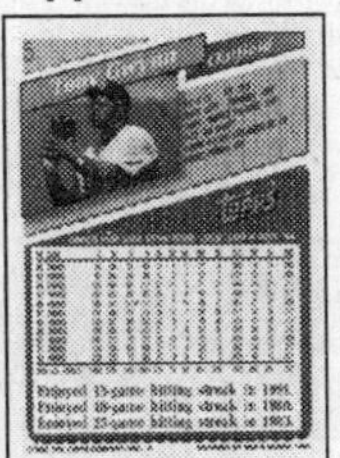

The 1993 Topps baseball set consists of two series, respectively, of 396 and 429 standard-size cards. A Topps Gold card was inserted in every 15-card pack, and Topps Black Gold cards were randomly inserted throughout the packs. The fronts feature color action player photos with white borders. The player's name appears in a stripe at the bottom of the picture, and this stripe and two short diagonal stripes at the bottom corners of the picture are team color-coded. The backs are colorful and carry a color head shot, biography, complete statistical information, with a career highlight if space permitted. Cards 401-411 comprise an All-Star subset. Rookie Cards in this set include Jim Edmonds, Derek Jeter and Jason Kendall.

	MINT	NRMT
COMPLETE SET (825)	30.00	13.50
COMP.RETAIL.SET (838)	40.00	18.00
COMP.HOBBY.SET (847)	40.00	18.00
COMPLETE SERIES 1 (396)	15.00	6.75
COMPLETE SERIES 2 (429)	15.00	6.75
COMMON CARD (1-825)	.10	.05
□ 1 Robin Yount	.10	.05
□ 2 Barry Bonds	.50	.23
□ 3 Ryne Sandberg	.50	.23
□ 4 Roger Clemens	.75	.35
□ 5 Tony Gwynn	1.00	.45
□ 6 Jeff Tackett	.10	.05
□ 7 Pete Incaviglia	.10	.05
□ 8 Mark Wohlers	.10	.05
□ 9 Kent Hrbek	.20	.09
□ 10 Will Clark	.10	.05
□ 11 Eric Karros	.20	.09
□ 12 Lee Smith	.20	.09
□ 13 Esteban Beltre	.10	.05
□ 14 Greg Briley	.10	.05
□ 15 Marquis Grissom	.20	.09
□ 16 Dan Plesac	.10	.05
□ 17 Dave Hollins	.10	.05
□ 18 Terry Steinbach	.20	.09
□ 19 Ed Nunez	.10	.05
□ 20 Tim Salmon	.50	.23
□ 21 Luis Salazar	.10	.05
□ 22 Jim Eisenreich	.20	.09
□ 23 Todd Stottlemyre	.10	.05
□ 24 Tim Naehring	.10	.05
□ 25 John Franco	.10	.05
□ 26 Skeeter Barnes	.10	.05
□ 27 Carlos Garcia	.10	.05
□ 28 Joe Orsulak	.10	.05
□ 29 Dwayne Henry	.10	.05
□ 30 Fred McGriff	.10	.05
□ 31 Derek Lilliquist	.10	.05
□ 32 Don Mattingly	.60	.25
□ 33 B.J. Wallace	.10	.05
□ 34 Juan Gonzalez	1.00	.45
□ 35 John Smoltz	.10	.05
□ 36 Scott Servais	.10	.05
□ 37 Lenny Webster	.10	.05
□ 38 Chris James	.10	.05
□ 39 Roger McDowell	.10	.05
□ 40 Ozzie Smith	.50	.23
□ 41 Alex Fernandez	.20	.09
□ 42 Spike Owen	.10	.05
□ 43 Ruben Amaro	.10	.05
□ 44 Kevin Seitzer	.10	.05
□ 45 Dave Fleming	.10	.05
□ 46 Eric Fox	.10	.05
□ 47 Bob Scanlan	.10	.05
□ 48 Bert Blyleven	.20	.09
□ 49 Brian McRae	.10	.05
□ 50 Roberto Alomar	.40	.18
□ 51 Mo Vaughn	.50	.23
□ 52 Bobby Bonilla	.20	.09
□ 53 Frank Tanana	.10	.05
□ 54 Mike LaValliere	.10	.05
□ 55 Mark McLemore	.10	.05
□ 56 Chad Mottola	.20	.09
□ 57 Norm Charlton	.10	.05
□ 58 Jose Melendez	.10	.05
□ 59 Carlos Martinez	.10	.05
□ 60 Roberto Kelly	.10	.05
□ 61 Gene Larkin	.10	.05
□ 62 Rafael Belliard	.10	.05
□ 63 Al Osuna	.10	.05
□ 64 Scott Chiamparino	.10	.05
□ 65 Brett Butler	.20	.09
□ 66 John Burkett	.10	.05
□ 67 Felix Jose	.10	.05
□ 68 Omar Vizquel	.20	.09
□ 69 John Vander Wal	.10	.05
□ 70 Roberto Hernandez	.20	.09
□ 71 Ricky Bones	.10	.05
□ 72 Jeff Grotewold	.10	.05
□ 73 Mike Moore	.10	.05
□ 74 Steve Buechele	.10	.05
□ 75 Juan Guzman	.20	.09
□ 76 Kevin Appier	.20	.09
□ 77 Junior Felix	.10	.05
□ 78 Greg W. Harris	.10	.05
□ 79 Dick Schofield	.10	.05
□ 80 Cecil Fielder	.20	.09
□ 81 Lloyd McClendon	.10	.05
□ 82 David Segui	.10	.05
□ 83 Reggie Sanders	.10	.05
□ 84 Kurt Stillwell	.10	.05
□ 85 Sandy Alomar	.20	.09
□ 86 John Habyan	.10	.05
□ 87 Kevin Reimer	.10	.05
□ 88 Mike Stanton	.10	.05
□ 89 Eric Anthony	.10	.05
□ 90 Scott Erickson	.10	.05
□ 91 Craig Colbert	.10	.05
□ 92 Tom Pagnozzi	.10	.05
□ 93 Pedro Astacio	.10	.05
□ 94 Lance Johnson	.20	.09
□ 95 Larry Walker	.40	.18
□ 96 Russ Swan	.10	.05
□ 97 Scott Fletcher	.10	.05
□ 98 Derek Jeter	4.00	1.80
□ 99 Mike Williams	.10	.05
□ 100 Mark McGwire	.75	.35
□ 101 Jim Bullinger	.10	.05
□ 102 Brian Hunter	.10	.05
□ 103 Jody Reed	.10	.05
□ 104 Mike Butcher	.10	.05
□ 105 Gregg Jefferies	.20	.09
□ 106 Howard Johnson	.10	.05
□ 107 John Kiely	.10	.05
□ 108 Jose Lind	.10	.05
□ 109 Sam Horn	.10	.05
□ 110 Barry Larkin	.10	.05
□ 111 Bruce Hurst	.10	.05
□ 112 Brian Barnes	.10	.05
□ 113 Thomas Howard	.10	.05
□ 114 Mel Hall	.10	.05
□ 115 Robby Thompson	.10	.05
□ 116 Mark Lemke	.10	.05
□ 117 Eddie Taubensee	.10	.05
□ 118 David Hulse	.10	.05
□ 119 Pedro Munoz	.10	.05
□ 120 Ramon Martinez	.20	.09
□ 121 Todd Worrell	.10	.05
□ 122 Joey Cora	.20	.09
□ 123 Moises Alou	.20	.09
□ 124 Franklin Stubbs	.10	.05
□ 125 Pete O'Brien	.10	.05
□ 126 Bob Ayrault	.10	.05
□ 127 Carney Lansford	.20	.09
□ 128 Kal Daniels	.10	.05
□ 129 Joe Grahe	.10	.05
□ 130 Jeff Montgomery	.20	.09
□ 131 Dave Winfield	.10	.05
□ 132 Preston Wilson	.50	.23
□ 133 Steve Wilson	.10	.05
□ 134 Lee Guetterman	.10	.05
□ 135 Mickey Tettleton	.10	.05
□ 136 Jeff King	.20	.09
□ 137 Alan Mills	.10	.05
□ 138 Joe Oliver	.10	.05
□ 139 Gary Gaetti	.20	.09
□ 140 Gary Sheffield	.40	.18
□ 141 Dennis Cook	.10	.05
□ 142 Charlie Hayes	.10	.05
□ 143 Jeff Huson	.10	.05
□ 144 Kent Mercker	.10	.05
□ 145 Eric Young	.40	.18
□ 146 Scott Leius	.10	.05
□ 147 Bryan Hickerson	.10	.05
□ 148 Steve Finley	.20	.09
□ 149 Rheal Cormier	.10	.05
□ 150 Frank Thomas UER (Categories leading league are italicized but not printed in red)	1.50	.70
□ 151 Archi Cianfrocco	.10	.05
□ 152 Rich DeLucia	.10	.05
□ 153 Greg Vaughn	.10	.05
□ 154 Wes Chamberlain	.10	.05
□ 155 Dennis Eckersley	.20	.09
□ 156 Sammy Sosa	.40	.18
□ 157 Gary DiSarcina	.10	.05
□ 158 Kevin Koslofski	.10	.05
□ 159 Doug Linton	.10	.05
□ 160 Lou Whitaker	.20	.09
□ 161 Chad McConnell	.10	.05
□ 162 Joe Hesketh	.10	.05
□ 163 Tim Wakefield	.20	.09
□ 164 Leo Gomez	.10	.05
□ 165 Jose Rijo	.10	.05
□ 166 Tim Scott	.10	.05
□ 167 Steve Olin UER (Born 10/4/65 should say 10/10/65)	.10	.05
□ 168 Kevin Maas	.10	.05
□ 169 Kenny Rogers	.10	.05
□ 170 David Justice	.40	.18
□ 171 Doug Jones	.10	.05
□ 172 Jeff Reboulet	.10	.05
□ 173 Andres Galarraga	.10	.05
□ 174 Randy Velarde	.10	.05
□ 175 Kirk McCaskill	.10	.05
□ 176 Darren Lewis	.10	.05
□ 177 Lenny Harris	.10	.05
□ 178 Jeff Fassero	.20	.09
□ 179 Ken Griffey Jr.	2.00	.90
□ 180 Darren Daulton	.20	.09
□ 181 John Jaha	.20	.09
□ 182 Ron Darling	.10	.05
□ 183 Greg Maddux	1.25	.55
□ 184 Damion Easley	.10	.05
□ 185 Jack Morris	.20	.09
□ 186 Mike Magnante	.10	.05
□ 187 John Dopson	.10	.05
□ 188 Sid Fernandez	.10	.05
□ 189 Tony Phillips	.10	.05
□ 190 Doug Drabek	.10	.05
□ 191 Sean Lowe	.10	.05
□ 192 Bob Milacki	.10	.05
□ 193 Steve Foster	.10	.05
□ 194 Jerald Clark	.10	.05
□ 195 Pete Harnisch	.10	.05
□ 196 Pat Kelly	.10	.05
□ 197 Jeff Frye	.10	.05
□ 198 Alejandro Pena	.10	.05
□ 199 Junior Ortiz	.10	.05
□ 200 Kirby Puckett	.75	.35
□ 201 Jose Uribe	.10	.05
□ 202 Mike Scioscia	.10	.05
□ 203 Bernard Gilkey	.20	.09
□ 204 Dan Pasqua	.10	.05
□ 205 Gary Carter	.10	.05
□ 206 Henry Cotto	.10	.05
□ 207 Paul Molitor	.40	.18
□ 208 Mike Hartley	.10	.05
□ 209 Jeff Parrett	.10	.05
□ 210 Mark Langston	.10	.05
□ 211 Doug Dascenzo	.10	.05
□ 212 Rick Reed	.10	.05
□ 213 Candy Maldonado	.10	.05
□ 214 Danny Darwin	.10	.05
□ 215 Pat Howell	.10	.05
□ 216 Mark Leiter	.10	.05
□ 217 Kevin Mitchell	.20	.09
□ 218 Ben McDonald	.10	.05
□ 219 Bip Roberts	.10	.05
□ 220 Benny Santiago	.10	.05
□ 221 Carlos Baerga	.20	.09
□ 222 Bernie Williams	.40	.18
□ 223 Roger Pavlik	.10	.05
□ 224 Sid Bream	.10	.05
□ 225 Matt Williams	.10	.05
□ 226 Willie Banks	.10	.05
□ 227 Jeff Bagwell	.75	.35

☐ 228 Tom Goodwin	.10	.05
☐ 229 Mike Perez	.10	.05
☐ 230 Carlton Fisk	.40	.18
☐ 231 John Wetteland	.20	.09
☐ 232 Tino Martinez	.40	.18
☐ 233 Rick Greene	.10	.05
☐ 234 Tim McIntosh	.10	.05
☐ 235 Mitch Williams	.10	.05
☐ 236 Kevin Campbell	.10	.05
☐ 237 Jose Vizcaino	.10	.05
☐ 238 Chris Donnels	.10	.05
☐ 239 Mike Boddicker	.10	.05
☐ 240 John Olerud	.10	.05
☐ 241 Mike Gardiner	.10	.05
☐ 242 Charlie O'Brien	.10	.05
☐ 243 Rob Deer	.10	.05
☐ 244 Denny Neagle	.20	.09
☐ 245 Chris Sabo	.10	.05
☐ 246 Gregg Olson	.10	.05
☐ 247 Frank Seminara UER	.10	.05
(Acquired 12/3/98)		
☐ 248 Scott Scudder	.10	.05
☐ 249 Tim Burke	.10	.05
☐ 250 Chuck Knoblauch	.40	.18
☐ 251 Mike Bielecki	.10	.05
☐ 252 Xavier Hernandez	.10	.05
☐ 253 Jose Guzman	.10	.05
☐ 254 Cory Snyder	.10	.05
☐ 255 Orel Hershiser	.20	.09
☐ 256 Wil Cordero	.10	.05
☐ 257 Luis Alicea	.10	.05
☐ 258 Mike Schooler	.10	.05
☐ 259 Craig Grebeck	.10	.05
☐ 260 Duane Ward	.10	.05
☐ 261 Bill Wegman	.10	.05
☐ 262 Mickey Morandini	.10	.05
☐ 263 Vince Horsman	.10	.05
☐ 264 Paul Sorrento	.10	.05
☐ 265 Andre Dawson	.40	.18
☐ 266 Rene Gonzales	.10	.05
☐ 267 Keith Miller	.10	.05
☐ 268 Derek Bell	.20	.09
☐ 269 Todd Steverson	.10	.05
☐ 270 Frank Viola	.10	.05
☐ 271 Wally Whitehurst	.10	.05
☐ 272 Kurt Knudsen	.10	.05
☐ 273 Dan Walters	.10	.05
☐ 274 Rick Sutcliffe	.10	.05
☐ 275 Andy Van Slyke	.20	.09
☐ 276 Paul O'Neill	.20	.09
☐ 277 Mark Whiten	.10	.05
☐ 278 Chris Nabholz	.10	.05
☐ 279 Todd Burns	.10	.05
☐ 280 Tom Glavine	.10	.05
☐ 281 Butch Henry	.10	.05
☐ 282 Shane Mack	.10	.05
☐ 283 Mike Jackson	.10	.05
☐ 284 Henry Rodriguez	.20	.09
☐ 285 Bob Tewksbury	.10	.05
☐ 286 Ron Karkovice	.10	.05
☐ 287 Mike Gallego	.10	.05
☐ 288 Dave Cochrane	.10	.05
☐ 289 Jesse Orosco	.10	.05
☐ 290 Dave Stewart	.20	.09
☐ 291 Tommy Greene	.10	.05
☐ 292 Rey Sanchez	.10	.05
☐ 293 Rob Ducey	.10	.05
☐ 294 Brent Mayne	.10	.05
☐ 295 Dave Stieb	.10	.05
☐ 296 Luis Rivera	.10	.05
☐ 297 Jeff Innis	.10	.05
☐ 298 Scott Livingstone	.10	.05
☐ 299 Bob Patterson	.10	.05
☐ 300 Cal Ripken	1.50	.70
☐ 301 Cesar Hernandez	.10	.05
☐ 302 Randy Myers	.20	.09
☐ 303 Brook Jacoby	.10	.05
☐ 304 Melido Perez	.10	.05
☐ 305 Rafael Palmeiro	.10	.05
☐ 306 Damon Berryhill	.10	.05
☐ 307 Dan Serafini	.30	.14
☐ 308 Darryl Kile	.20	.09
☐ 309 J.T. Bruett	.10	.05
☐ 310 Dave Righetti	.10	.05
☐ 311 Jay Howell	.10	.05
☐ 312 Geronimo Pena	.10	.05
☐ 313 Greg Hibbard	.10	.05
☐ 314 Mark Gardner	.10	.05
☐ 315 Edgar Martinez	.10	.05
☐ 316 Dave Nilsson	.20	.09
☐ 317 Kyle Abbott	.10	.05
☐ 318 Willie Wilson	.10	.05
☐ 319 Paul Assenmacher	.10	.05
☐ 320 Tim Fortugno	.10	.05
☐ 321 Rusty Meacham	.10	.05
☐ 322 Pat Borders	.10	.05
☐ 323 Mike Greenwell	.10	.05
☐ 324 Willie Randolph	.20	.09
☐ 325 Bill Gullickson	.10	.05
☐ 326 Gary Varsho	.10	.05
☐ 327 Tim Hulett	.10	.05
☐ 328 Scott Ruskin	.10	.05
☐ 329 Mike Maddux	.10	.05
☐ 330 Danny Tartabull	.10	.05
☐ 331 Kenny Lofton	.75	.35
☐ 332 Geno Petralli	.10	.05
☐ 333 Otis Nixon	.20	.09
☐ 334 Jason Kendall	.60	.25
☐ 335 Mark Portugal	.10	.05
☐ 336 Mike Pagliarulo	.10	.05
☐ 337 Kirt Manwaring	.10	.05
☐ 338 Bob Ojeda	.10	.05
☐ 339 Mark Clark	.10	.05
☐ 340 John Kruk	.20	.09
☐ 341 Mel Rojas	.20	.09
☐ 342 Erik Hanson	.10	.05
☐ 343 Doug Henry	.10	.05
☐ 344 Jack McDowell	.10	.05
☐ 345 Harold Baines	.20	.09
☐ 346 Chuck McElroy	.10	.05
☐ 347 Luis Sojo	.10	.05
☐ 348 Andy Stankiewicz	.10	.05
☐ 349 Hipolito Pichardo	.10	.05
☐ 350 Joe Carter	.10	.05
☐ 351 Ellis Burks	.20	.09
☐ 352 Pete Schourek	.10	.05
☐ 353 Bubby Groom	.10	.05
☐ 354 Jay Bell	.20	.09
☐ 355 Brady Anderson	.10	.05
☐ 356 Freddie Benavides	.10	.05
☐ 357 Phil Stephenson	.10	.05
☐ 358 Kevin Wickander	.10	.05
☐ 359 Mike Stanley	.10	.05
☐ 360 Ivan Rodriguez	.50	.23
☐ 361 Scott Bankhead	.10	.05
☐ 362 Luis Gonzalez	.10	.05
☐ 363 John Smiley	.10	.05
☐ 364 Trevor Wilson	.10	.05
☐ 365 Tom Candiotti	.10	.05
☐ 366 Craig Wilson	.10	.05
☐ 367 Steve Sax	.10	.05
☐ 368 Delino DeShields	.10	.05
☐ 369 Jaime Navarro	.10	.05
☐ 370 Dave Valle	.10	.05
☐ 371 Mariano Duncan	.10	.05
☐ 372 Rod Nichols	.10	.05
☐ 373 Mike Morgan	.10	.05
☐ 374 Julio Valera	.10	.05
☐ 375 Wally Joyner	.20	.09
☐ 376 Tom Henke	.10	.05
☐ 377 Herm Winningham	.10	.05
☐ 378 Orlando Merced	.10	.05
☐ 379 Mike Munoz	.10	.05
☐ 380 Todd Hundley	.10	.05
☐ 381 Mike Flanagan	.10	.05
☐ 382 Tim Belcher	.10	.05
☐ 383 Jerry Browne	.10	.05
☐ 384 Mike Benjamin	.10	.05
☐ 385 Jim Leyritz	.10	.05
☐ 386 Ray Lankford	.10	.05
☐ 387 Devon White	.10	.05
☐ 388 Jeremy Hernandez	.10	.05
☐ 389 Brian Harper	.10	.05
☐ 390 Wade Boggs	.40	.18
☐ 391 Derrick May	.10	.05
☐ 392 Travis Fryman	.20	.09
☐ 393 Ron Gant	.20	.09
☐ 394 Checklist 1-132	.10	.05
☐ 395 Checklist 133-264 UER	.10	.05
(Eckerlsey)		
☐ 396 Checklist 265-396	.10	.05
☐ 397 George Brett	.75	.35
☐ 398 Bobby Witt	.10	.05
☐ 399 Daryl Boston	.10	.05
☐ 400 Bo Jackson	.20	.09
☐ 401 Fred McGriff	.50	.23
Frank Thomas		
☐ 402 Ryne Sandberg	.20	.09
Carlos Baerga		
☐ 403 Gary Sheffield	.20	.09
Edgar Martinez		
☐ 404 Barry Larkin	.20	.09
Travis Fryman		
☐ 405 Andy Van Slyke	.50	.23
Ken Griffey Jr.		
☐ 406 Larry Walker	.40	.18
Kirby Puckett		
☐ 407 Barry Bonds	.20	.09
Joe Carter		
☐ 408 Darren Daulton	.20	.09
Brian Harper		
☐ 409 Greg Maddux	.40	.18
Roger Clemens		
☐ 410 Tom Glavine	.20	.09
Dave Fleming		
☐ 411 Lee Smith	.20	.09
Dennis Eckersley		
☐ 412 Jamie McAndrew	.10	.05
☐ 413 Pete Smith	.10	.05
☐ 414 Juan Guerrero	.10	.05
☐ 415 Todd Frohwirth	.10	.05
☐ 416 Randy Tomlin	.10	.05
☐ 417 B.J. Surhoff	.20	.09
☐ 418 Jim Gott	.10	.05
☐ 419 Mark Thompson	.10	.05
☐ 420 Kevin Tapani	.10	.05
☐ 421 Curt Schilling	.20	.09
☐ 422 J.T. Snow	.50	.23
☐ 423 1993 Prospects	.50	.23
Ryan Klesko		
Ivan Cruz		
Bubba Smith		
Larry Sutton		
☐ 424 John Valentin	.20	.09
☐ 425 Joe Girardi	.10	.05
☐ 426 Nigel Wilson	.10	.05
☐ 427 Bob MacDonald	.10	.05
☐ 428 Todd Zeile	.10	.05
☐ 429 Milt Cuyler	.10	.05
☐ 430 Eddie Murray	.40	.18
☐ 431 Rich Amaral	.10	.05
☐ 432 Pete Young	.10	.05
☐ 433 Roger Bailey and	.10	.05
Tom Schmidt		
☐ 434 Jack Armstrong	.10	.05
☐ 435 Willie McGee	.10	.05
☐ 436 Greg W. Harris	.10	.05
☐ 437 Chris Hammond	.10	.05
☐ 438 Ritchie Moody	.10	.05
☐ 439 Bryan Harvey	.10	.05
☐ 440 Ruben Sierra	.10	.05
☐ 441 Don Lemon and	.10	.05
Todd Pridy		
☐ 442 Kevin McReynolds	.10	.05
☐ 443 Terry Leach	.10	.05
☐ 444 David Nied	.10	.05
☐ 445 Dale Murphy	.10	.05
☐ 446 Luis Mercedes	.10	.05
☐ 447 Keith Shepherd	.10	.05
☐ 448 Ken Caminiti	.40	.18
☐ 449 James Austin	.10	.05
☐ 450 Darryl Strawberry	.20	.09
☐ 451 1993 Prospects	.20	.09
Ramon Caraballo		
Jon Shave		
Brent Gates		
Quinton McCracken		
☐ 452 Bob Wickman	.10	.05
☐ 453 Victor Cole	.10	.05
☐ 454 John Johnstone	.10	.05
☐ 455 Chili Davis	.20	.09
☐ 456 Scott Taylor	.10	.05
☐ 457 Tracy Woodson	.10	.05
☐ 458 David Wells	.10	.05
☐ 459 Derek Wallace	.10	.05
☐ 460 Randy Johnson	.40	.18
☐ 461 Steve Reed	.10	.05
☐ 462 Felix Fermin	.10	.05
☐ 463 Scott Aldred	.10	.05
☐ 464 Greg Colbrunn	.10	.05
☐ 465 Tony Fernandez	.10	.05
☐ 466 Mike Felder	.10	.05
☐ 467 Lee Stevens	.10	.05
☐ 468 Matt Whiteside	.10	.05
☐ 469 Dave Hansen	.10	.05
☐ 470 Rob Dibble	.10	.05
☐ 471 Dave Gallagher	.10	.05
☐ 472 Chris Gwynn	.10	.05
☐ 473 Dave Henderson	.10	.05
☐ 474 Ozzie Guillen	.10	.05
☐ 475 Jeff Reardon	.20	.09
☐ 476 Mark Voisard and	.10	.05
Will Scalzitti		
☐ 477 Jimmy Jones	.10	.05
☐ 478 Greg Cadaret	.10	.05
☐ 479 Todd Pratt	.10	.05
☐ 480 Pat Listach	.10	.05
☐ 481 Ryan Luzinski	.10	.05
☐ 482 Darren Reed	.10	.05
☐ 483 Brian Griffiths	.10	.05
☐ 484 John Wehner	.10	.05
☐ 485 Glenn Davis	.10	.05
☐ 486 Eric Wedge	.10	.05
☐ 487 Jesse Hollins	.10	.05
☐ 488 Manuel Lee	.10	.05
☐ 489 Scott Fredrickson	.10	.05
☐ 490 Omar Olivares	.10	.05
☐ 491 Shawn Hare	.10	.05
☐ 492 Tom Lampkin	.10	.05
☐ 493 Jeff Nelson	.10	.05
☐ 494 1993 Prospects	.20	.09
Kevin Young		

Adell Davenport
Eduardo Perez
Lou Lucca
☐ 495 Ken Hill .20 .09
☐ 496 Reggie Jefferson .10 .05
☐ 497 Matt Petersen and .10 .05
Willie Brown
☐ 498 Bud Black .10 .05
☐ 499 Chuck Crim .10 .05
☐ 500 Jose Canseco .15 .07
☐ 501 Johnny Oates MG .20 .09
Bobby Cox MG
☐ 502 Butch Hobson MG .10 .05
Jim Lefebvre MG
☐ 503 Buck Rodgers MG .20 .09
Tony Perez MG
☐ 504 Gene Lamont MG .20 .09
Don Baylor MG
☐ 505 Mike Hargrove MG .20 .09
Rene Lachemann MG
☐ 506 Sparky Anderson MG .20 .09
Art Howe MG
☐ 507 Hal McRae MG .20 .09
Tom Lasorda MG
☐ 508 Phil Garner MG .20 .09
Felipe Alou MG
☐ 509 Tom Kelly MG .10 .05
Jeff Torborg MG
☐ 510 Buck Showalter MG .20 .09
Jim Fregosi MG
☐ 511 Tony LaRussa MG .20 .09
Jim Leyland MG
☐ 512 Lou Piniella MG .20 .09
Joe Torre MG
☐ 513 Kevin Kennedy MG .10 .05
Jim Riggleman MG
☐ 514 Cito Gaston MG .20 .09
Dusty Baker MG
☐ 515 Greg Swindell .10 .05
☐ 516 Alex Arias .10 .05
☐ 517 Bill Pecota .10 .05
☐ 518 Benji Grigsby UER .10 .05
(Misspelled Bengi
on card front)
☐ 519 David Howard .10 .05
☐ 520 Charlie Hough .10 .05
☐ 521 Kevin Flora .10 .05
☐ 522 Shane Reynolds .10 .05
☐ 523 Doug Bochtler .10 .05
☐ 524 Chris Hoiles .10 .05
☐ 525 Scott Sanderson .10 .05
☐ 526 Mike Sharperson .10 .05
☐ 527 Mike Fetters .10 .05
☐ 528 Paul Quantrill .10 .05
☐ 529 1993 Prospects 2.00 .90
Dave Silvestri
Chipper Jones
Benji Gil
Jeff Patzke
☐ 530 Sterling Hitchcock .20 .09
☐ 531 Joe Millette .10 .05
☐ 532 Tom Brunansky .10 .05
☐ 533 Frank Castillo .10 .05
☐ 534 Randy Knorr .10 .05
☐ 535 Jose Oquendo .10 .05
☐ 536 Dave Haas .10 .05
☐ 537 Jason Hutchins and .10 .05
Ryan Turner
☐ 538 Jimmy Baron .10 .05
☐ 539 Kerry Woodson .10 .05
☐ 540 Ivan Calderon .10 .05
☐ 541 Denis Boucher .10 .05
☐ 542 Royce Clayton .10 .05
☐ 543 Reggie Williams .10 .05
☐ 544 Steve Decker .10 .05
☐ 545 Dean Palmer .20 .09
☐ 546 Hal Morris .10 .05
☐ 547 Ryan Thompson .10 .05
☐ 548 Lance Blankenship .10 .05
☐ 549 Hensley Meulens .10 .05
☐ 550 Scott Radinsky .10 .05
☐ 551 Eric Young .40 .18
☐ 552 Jeff Blauser .10 .05
☐ 553 Andujar Cedeno .10 .05
☐ 554 Arthur Rhodes .10 .05
☐ 555 Terry Mulholland .10 .05
☐ 556 Darryl Hamilton .10 .05
☐ 557 Pedro Martinez .40 .18
☐ 558 Ryan Whitman and .10 .05
Mark Skeels
☐ 559 Jamie Arnold .20 .09
☐ 560 Zane Smith .10 .05
☐ 561 Matt Nokes .10 .05
☐ 562 Bob Zupcic .10 .05
☐ 563 Shawn Boskie .10 .05
☐ 564 Mike Timlin .10 .05
☐ 565 Jerald Clark .10 .05
☐ 566 Rod Brewer .10 .05
☐ 567 Mark Carreon .10 .05
☐ 568 Andy Benes .20 .09
☐ 569 Shawn Barton .10 .05
☐ 570 Tim Wallach .10 .05
☐ 571 Dave Mlicki .10 .05
☐ 572 Trevor Hoffman .10 .05
☐ 573 John Patterson .10 .05
☐ 574 De Shawn Warren .10 .05
☐ 575 Monty Fariss .10 .05
☐ 576 1993 Prospects .20 .09
Darrell Sherman
Damon Buford
Cliff Floyd
Michael Moore
☐ 577 Tim Costo .10 .05
☐ 578 Dave Magadan .10 .05
☐ 579 Neil Garret and .20 .09
Jason Bates
☐ 580 Walt Weiss .10 .05
☐ 581 Chris Haney .10 .05
☐ 582 Shawn Abner .10 .05
☐ 583 Marvin Freeman .10 .05
☐ 584 Casey Candaele .10 .05
☐ 585 Ricky Jordan .10 .05
☐ 586 Jeff Tabaka .10 .05
☐ 587 Manny Alexander .10 .05
☐ 588 Mike Trombley .10 .05
☐ 589 Carlos Hernandez .10 .05
☐ 590 Cal Eldred .10 .05
☐ 591 Alex Cole .10 .05
☐ 592 Phil Plantier .10 .05
☐ 593 Brett Merriman .10 .05
☐ 594 Jerry Nielsen .10 .05
☐ 595 Shawon Dunston .10 .05
☐ 596 Jimmy Key .20 .09
☐ 597 Gerald Perry .10 .05
☐ 598 Rico Brogna .20 .09
☐ 599 Clemente Nunez and .20 .09
Daniel Robinson
☐ 600 Bret Saberhagen .10 .05
☐ 601 Craig Shipley .10 .05
☐ 602 Henry Mercedes .10 .05
☐ 603 Jim Thome .75 .35
☐ 604 Rod Beck .20 .09
☐ 605 Chuck Finley .10 .05
☐ 606 J. Owens .10 .05
☐ 607 Dan Smith .10 .05
☐ 608 Bill Doran .10 .05
☐ 609 Lance Parrish .10 .05
☐ 610 Denny Martinez .20 .09
☐ 611 Tom Gordon .10 .05
☐ 612 Byron Mathews .10 .05
☐ 613 Joel Adamson .10 .05
☐ 614 Brian Williams .10 .05
☐ 615 Steve Avery .10 .05
☐ 616 1993 Prospects .40 .18
Matt Mieske
Tracy Sanders
Midre Cummings
Ryan Freeburg
☐ 617 Craig Lefferts .10 .05
☐ 618 Tony Pena .10 .05
☐ 619 Billy Spiers .10 .05
☐ 620 Todd Benzinger .10 .05
☐ 621 Mike Kotarski and .10 .05
Greg Boyd
☐ 622 Ben Rivera .10 .05
☐ 623 Al Martin .20 .09
☐ 624 Sam Militello UER .10 .05
(Profile says drafted
in 1988, bio says
drafted in 1990)
☐ 625 Rick Aguilera .10 .05
☐ 626 Dan Gladden .10 .05
☐ 627 Andres Berumen .10 .05
☐ 628 Kelly Gruber .10 .05
☐ 629 Cris Carpenter .10 .05
☐ 630 Mark Grace .10 .05
☐ 631 Jeff Brantley .10 .05
☐ 632 Chris Widger .10 .05
☐ 633 Three Russians UER .20 .09
Rudolf Razjigaev
Eugneyi Puchkov
Ilya Bogatyrev
Bogatyrev is a shortstop,
card has pitching header
☐ 634 Mo Sanford .10 .05
☐ 635 Albert Belle .50 .23
☐ 636 Tim Teufel .10 .05
☐ 637 Greg Myers .10 .05
☐ 638 Brian Bohanon .10 .05
☐ 639 Mike Bordick .10 .05
☐ 640 Dwight Gooden .20 .09
☐ 641 Pat Leahy and .10 .05
Gavin Baugh
☐ 642 Milt Hill .10 .05
☐ 643 Luis Aquino .10 .05
☐ 644 Dante Bichette .10 .05
☐ 645 Bobby Thigpen .10 .05
☐ 646 Rich Scheid .10 .05
☐ 647 Brian Sackinsky .10 .05
☐ 648 Ryan Hawblitzel .10 .05
☐ 649 Tom Marsh .10 .05
☐ 650 Terry Pendleton .10 .05
☐ 651 Rafael Bournigal .10 .05
☐ 652 Dave West .10 .05
☐ 653 Steve Hosey .10 .05
☐ 654 Gerald Williams .10 .05
☐ 655 Scott Cooper .10 .05
☐ 656 Gary Scott .10 .05
☐ 657 Mike Harkey .10 .05
☐ 658 1993 Prospects .10 .05
Jeromy Burnitz
Melvin Nieves
Rich Becker
Shon Walker
☐ 659 Ed Sprague .10 .05
☐ 660 Alan Trammell .10 .05
☐ 661 Garvin Alston and .20 .09
Michael Case
☐ 662 Donovan Osborne .10 .05
☐ 663 Jeff Gardner .10 .05
☐ 664 Calvin Jones .10 .05
☐ 665 Darrin Fletcher .10 .05
☐ 666 Glenallen Hill .10 .05
☐ 667 Jim Rosenbohm .10 .05
☐ 668 Scott Lewis .10 .05
☐ 669 Kip Yaughn .10 .05
☐ 670 Julio Franco .20 .09
☐ 671 Dave Martinez .10 .05
☐ 672 Kevin Bass .10 .05
☐ 673 Todd Van Poppel .10 .05
☐ 674 Mark Gubicza .10 .05
☐ 675 Tim Raines .20 .09
☐ 676 Rudy Seanez .10 .05
☐ 677 Charlie Leibrandt .10 .05
☐ 678 Randy Milligan .10 .05
☐ 679 Kim Batiste .10 .05
☐ 680 Craig Biggio .10 .05
☐ 681 Darren Holmes .10 .05
☐ 682 John Candelaria .10 .05
☐ 683 Jerry Stafford and .20 .09
Eddie Christian
☐ 684 Pat Mahomes .10 .05
☐ 685 Bob Walk .10 .05
☐ 686 Russ Springer .10 .05
☐ 687 Tony Sheffield .10 .05
☐ 688 Dwight Smith .10 .05
☐ 689 Eddie Zosky .10 .05
☐ 690 Bien Figueroa .10 .05
☐ 691 Jim Tatum .10 .05
☐ 692 Chad Kreuter .10 .05
☐ 693 Rich Rodriguez .10 .05
☐ 694 Shane Turner .10 .05
☐ 695 Kent Bottenfield .10 .05
☐ 696 Jose Mesa .20 .09
☐ 697 Darrell Whitmore .10 .05
☐ 698 Ted Wood .10 .05
☐ 699 Chad Curtis .20 .09
☐ 700 Nolan Ryan 1.50 .70
☐ 701 1993 Prospects 2.00 .90
Mike Piazza
Brook Fordyce
Carlos Delgado
Donnie Leshnock
☐ 702 Tim Pugh .10 .05
☐ 703 Jeff Kent .20 .09
☐ 704 Jon Goodrich and .20 .09
Danny Figueroa
☐ 705 Bob Welch .10 .05
☐ 706 Sherard Clinkscales .10 .05
☐ 707 Donn Pall .10 .05
☐ 708 Greg Olson .10 .05
☐ 709 Jeff Juden .10 .05
☐ 710 Mike Mussina .40 .18
☐ 711 Scott Chiamparino .10 .05
☐ 712 Stan Javier .10 .05
☐ 713 John Doherty .10 .05
☐ 714 Kevin Gross .10 .05
☐ 715 Greg Gagne .10 .05
☐ 716 Steve Cooke .10 .05
☐ 717 Steve Farr .10 .05
☐ 718 Jay Buhner .10 .05
☐ 719 Butch Henry .10 .05
☐ 720 David Cone .20 .09
☐ 721 Rick Wilkins .10 .05
☐ 722 Chuck Carr .10 .05
☐ 723 Kenny Felder .10 .05
☐ 724 Guillermo Velasquez .10 .05
☐ 725 Billy Hatcher .10 .05
☐ 726 Mike Veneziale and .20 .09
Ken Kendrena
☐ 727 Jonathan Hurst .10 .05
☐ 728 Steve Frey .10 .05

☐ 729 Mark Leonard	.10	.05
☐ 730 Charles Nagy	.20	.09
☐ 731 Donald Harris	.10	.05
☐ 732 Travis Buckley	.10	.05
☐ 733 Tom Browning	.10	.05
☐ 734 Anthony Young	.10	.05
☐ 735 Steve Shifflett	.10	.05
☐ 736 Jeff Russell	.10	.05
☐ 737 Wilson Alvarez	.20	.09
☐ 738 Lance Painter	.10	.05
☐ 739 Dave Weathers	.10	.05
☐ 740 Len Dykstra	.20	.09
☐ 741 Mike Devereaux	.10	.05
☐ 742 1993 Prospects Rene Arocha Alan Embree Brien Taylor Tim Crabtree	.20	.09
☐ 743 Dave Landaker	.10	.05
☐ 744 Chris George	.10	.05
☐ 745 Eric Davis	.20	.09
☐ 746 Mark Strittmatter and Lamarr Rogers	.20	.09
☐ 747 Carl Willis	.10	.05
☐ 748 Stan Belinda	.10	.05
☐ 749 Scott Kamieniecki	.10	.05
☐ 750 Rickey Henderson	.10	.05
☐ 751 Eric Hillman	.10	.05
☐ 752 Pat Hentgen	.10	.05
☐ 753 Jim Corsi	.10	.05
☐ 754 Brian Jordan	.20	.09
☐ 755 Bill Swift	.10	.05
☐ 756 Mike Henneman	.10	.05
☐ 757 Harold Reynolds	.10	.05
☐ 758 Sean Berry	.10	.05
☐ 759 Charlie Hayes	.10	.05
☐ 760 Luis Polonia	.10	.05
☐ 761 Darrin Jackson	.10	.05
☐ 762 Mark Lewis	.10	.05
☐ 763 Rob Maurer	.10	.05
☐ 764 Willie Greene	.20	.09
☐ 765 Vince Coleman	.10	.05
☐ 766 Todd Revenig	.10	.05
☐ 767 Rich Ireland	.10	.05
☐ 768 Mike Macfarlane	.10	.05
☐ 769 Francisco Cabrera	.10	.05
☐ 770 Robin Ventura	.20	.09
☐ 771 Kevin Ritz	.10	.05
☐ 772 Chito Martinez	.10	.05
☐ 773 Cliff Brantley	.10	.05
☐ 774 Curtis Leskanic	.10	.05
☐ 775 Chris Bosio	.10	.05
☐ 776 Jose Offerman	.10	.05
☐ 777 Mark Guthrie	.10	.05
☐ 778 Don Slaught	.10	.05
☐ 779 Rich Monteleone	.10	.05
☐ 780 Jim Abbott	.20	.09
☐ 781 Jack Clark	.10	.05
☐ 782 Reynol Mendoza and Dan Roman	.20	.09
☐ 783 Heathcliff Slocumb	.10	.05
☐ 784 Jeff Branson	.10	.05
☐ 785 Kevin Brown	.20	.09
☐ 786 1993 Prospects Mike Christopher Ken Ryan Aaron Taylor Gus Gandarillas	.20	.09
☐ 787 Mike Matthews	.20	.09
☐ 788 Mackey Sasser	.10	.05
☐ 789 Jeff Conine UER (No inclusion of 1990 stats in career total)	.20	.09
☐ 790 George Bell	.10	.05
☐ 791 Pat Rapp	.10	.05
☐ 792 Joe Boever	.10	.05
☐ 793 Jim Poole	.10	.05
☐ 794 Andy Ashby	.20	.09
☐ 795 Deion Sanders	.40	.18
☐ 796 Scott Brosius	.10	.05
☐ 797 Brad Pennington	.10	.05
☐ 798 Greg Blosser	.10	.05
☐ 799 Jim Edmonds	1.00	.45
☐ 800 Shawn Jeter	.10	.05
☐ 801 Jesse Levis	.10	.05
☐ 802 Phil Clark UER (Word "a" is missing in sentence beginning with "In 1992 ...")	.10	.05
☐ 803 Ed Pierce	.10	.05
☐ 804 Jose Valentin	.25	.11
☐ 805 Terry Jorgensen	.10	.05
☐ 806 Mark Hutton	.10	.05
☐ 807 Troy Neel	.10	.05
☐ 808 Bret Boone	.20	.09
☐ 809 Cris Colon	.10	.05
☐ 810 Domingo Martinez	.10	.05
☐ 811 Javier Lopez	.40	.18
☐ 812 Matt Walbeck	.10	.05
☐ 813 Dan Wilson	.20	.09
☐ 814 Scooter Tucker	.10	.05
☐ 815 Billy Ashley	.10	.05
☐ 816 Tim Laker	.10	.05
☐ 817 Bobby Jones	.20	.09
☐ 818 Brad Brink	.10	.05
☐ 819 William Pennyfeather	.10	.05
☐ 820 Stan Royer	.10	.05
☐ 821 Doug Brocail	.10	.05
☐ 822 Kevin Rogers	.10	.05
☐ 823 Checklist 397-540	.10	.05
☐ 824 Checklist 541-691	.10	.05
☐ 825 Checklist 692-825	.10	.05

1993 Topps Gold

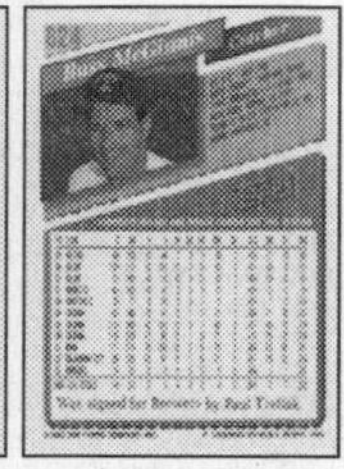

Several insertion schemes were devised for these 825 standard-size cards. Gold cards were inserted one per wax pack, three per rack pack, five per jumbo pack, and ten per factory set. The cards are identical to the regular-issue 1993 Topps baseball cards except that the gold-foil Topps Gold logo appears in an upper corner, and the team color-coded stripe at the bottom of the front, which carried the player's name, has been replaced with an embossed gold-foil stripe. The checklist cards (394-396, 823-825) have been replaced by player cards.

	MINT	NRMT
COMPLETE GOLD SET (825)	70.00	32.00
COMPLETE SERIES 1 (396)	40.00	18.00
COMPLETE SERIES 2 (429)	30.00	13.50
COMMON CARD (1G-825G)	.15	.07
*STARS: 2X to 4X BASIC CARDS		
*YOUNG STARS: 1.5X to 3X BASIC CARDS		
*ROOKIES: 1.25X to 2.5X BASIC CARDS		

☐ 394 Bernardo Brito Replaces Checklist 1	.25	.11
☐ 395 Jim McNamara Replaces Checklist 2	.25	.11
☐ 396 Rich Sauveur Replaces Checklist 3	.25	.11
☐ 823 Keith Brown Replaces Checklist 4	.25	.11
☐ 824 Russ McGinnis Replaces Checklist 5	.25	.11
☐ 825 Mike Walker UER (Card has 1993 Mariner stats, should be 1992) Replaces Checklist 6	.25	.11

1993 Topps Inaugural Marlins/Rockies

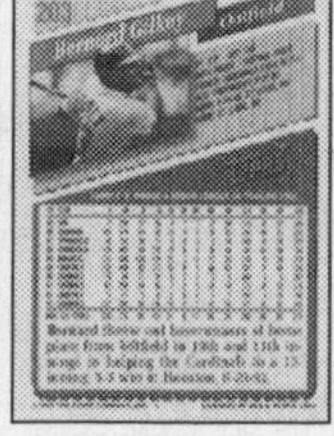

These 825-card standard-size sets were issued by Topps to commemorate the debut seasons of the Colorado Rockies and Florida Marlins. Gold foil Marlins or Rockies logos distinguish these from regular issue cards. These cards were only issued in factory set form. 5,000 Rockies sets and 4,000 Marlins sets were initially printed, but each team had the option of receiving a maximum of 10,000 sets. The Rockies sets were distributed through the four team-owned stores and at Mile High Stadium. The Marlins sets were distributed through FMI and Joe Robbie Stadium.

	MINT	NRMT
COMP. MARLINS FACT.SET (825)	150.00	70.00
COMP. ROCKIES FACT.SET (825)	120.00	55.00
COMMON CARD (1-825)	.15	.07
COMMON ROCKIES	.30	.14
COMMON MARLINS	.40	.18
*STARS: 3X to 6X BASIC CARDS		
*YOUNG STARS: 2X to 4X BASIC CARDS		
*ROOKIES: 2X to 4X BASIC CARDS		

1993 Topps Micro

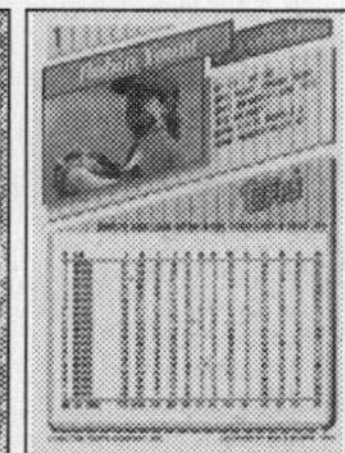

This set was only issued in factory set form. It was issued as a 837 card set with the regular 825 card as well as a special 12 card prism insert set. The cards measure 1" by 1 3/8" which is approximately 40 percent of the regular card size. Only the Prism inserts are listed below. Please refer to the multiplier for values on the other other cards. This was the final year Topps issued the Micro factory set.

	MINT	NRMT
COMPLETE FACT. SET (837)	15.00	6.75
COMMON CARD (1-825)	.05	.02
COMMON PRISM INSERT	.10	.05
*MICRO: 2X BASIC CARDS		

☐ P1 Robin Yount	.40	.18
☐ P20 Tim Salmon	.30	.14
☐ P32 Don Mattingly	.60	.25
☐ P50 Roberto Alomar	.25	.11
☐ P150 Frank Thomas	1.25	.55
☐ P155 Dennis Eckersley	.25	.11
☐ P179 Ken Griffey Jr.	1.25	.55
☐ P200 Kirby Puckett	.60	.25
☐ P397 George Brett	.50	.23
☐ P426 Nigel Wilson	.10	.05
☐ P444 David Nied	.10	.05
☐ P700 Nolan Ryan	1.00	.45

1993 Topps Black Gold

Topps Black Gold cards 1-22 were randomly inserted in series I packs while card numbers 23-44 were featured in series II packs. They were also inserted three per factory set. In the packs, the cards were inserted one evrery 72 hobby or retail packs; one every 12 jumbo packs and one every 24 rack packs. Hobbyists could obtain the set by collecting individual random insert cards or receive 11, 22, or 44 Black Gold cards by mail when they sent in special "You've Just Won" cards, which were randomly inserted in packs. Series I packs featured three different "You've Just Won" cards, entitling the holder to receive Group A (cards 1-11), Group B (cards 12-22), or Groups A and B (Cards 1-22). In a similar fashion, four "You've Just Won" cards were inserted in series II packs and entitled the holder to receive Group C (23-33), Group D (34-44), Groups C and D (23-44), or Groups A-D (1-44). By returning the "You've Just Won" card with 1.50 for postage and handling, the collector received not only the Black Gold cards won but also a special "You've Just Won" card and a congratulatory letter informing the collector that his/her name has been entered into a drawing for one of 500 uncut sheets of all 44 Topps Black Gold cards in a leatherette frame. These standard-size cards feature different color player photos than either the 1993 Topps regular issue or the Topps Gold issue. The player pictures are cut out and superimposed on a black gloss background. Inside white borders, gold refractory foil edges the top and bottom of the card face. On a black-and-gray pinstripe pattern inside white borders, the horizontal backs have a a second cut out player photo and a player profile on a blue panel. The player's name appears in gold foil lettering on a blue-and-gray geometric shape. The first 22 cards are National Leaguers while the second 22 cards are American Leaguers. Winner cards C and D were both originally produced erroneously and later corrected; the error versions show the players from Winner A and B on the respective fronts of Winner cards Cand D. There is no value difference in the variations at this time. The winner cards were redeemable until January 31, 1994.

	MINT	NRMT
COMPLETE SET (44)	10.00	4.50
COMPLETE SERIES 1 (22)	4.00	1.80
COMPLETE SERIES 2 (22)	6.00	2.70
COMMON CARD (1-44)	.10	.05

	MINT	NRMT
☐ 1 Barry Bonds	.75	.35
☐ 2 Will Clark	.40	.18
☐ 3 Darren Daulton	.25	.11
☐ 4 Andre Dawson	.40	.18
☐ 5 Delino DeShields	.25	.11
☐ 6 Tom Glavine	.40	.18
☐ 7 Marquis Grissom	.25	.11
☐ 8 Tony Gwynn	1.25	.55
☐ 9 Eric Karros	.25	.11
☐ 10 Ray Lankford	.40	.18
☐ 11 Barry Larkin	.40	.18
☐ 12 Greg Maddux	2.00	.90
☐ 13 Fred McGriff	.40	.18
☐ 14 Joe Oliver	.10	.05
☐ 15 Terry Pendleton	.25	.11
☐ 16 Bip Roberts	.25	.11
☐ 17 Ryne Sandberg	.75	.35
☐ 18 Gary Sheffield	.40	.18
☐ 19 Lee Smith	.25	.11
☐ 20 Ozzie Smith	.75	.35
☐ 21 Andy Van Slyke	.10	.05
☐ 22 Larry Walker	.60	.25
☐ 23 Roberto Alomar	.60	.25
☐ 24 Brady Anderson	.40	.18
☐ 25 Carlos Baerga	.25	.11
☐ 26 Joe Carter	.40	.18
☐ 27 Roger Clemens	.60	.25
☐ 28 Mike Devereaux	.10	.05
☐ 29 Dennis Eckersley	.40	.18
☐ 30 Cecil Fielder	.25	.11
☐ 31 Travis Fryman	.25	.11
☐ 32 Juan Gonzalez UER (No copyright or licensing on card)	1.50	.70
☐ 33 Ken Griffey Jr.	3.00	1.35
☐ 34 Brian Harper	.10	.05
☐ 35 Pat Listach	.10	.05
☐ 36 Kenny Lofton	1.25	.55
☐ 37 Edgar Martinez	.40	.18
☐ 38 Jack McDowell	.10	.05
☐ 39 Mark McGwire	1.00	.45
☐ 40 Kirby Puckett	1.25	.55
☐ 41 Mickey Tettleton	.10	.05
☐ 42 Frank Thomas UER (No copyright or licensing on card)	3.00	1.35
☐ 43 Robin Ventura	.25	.11
☐ 44 Dave Winfield	.60	.25
☐ A Winner A 1-11	.50	.23
☐ B Winner B 12-22	.50	.23
☐ C Winner C 23-33	.75	.35
☐ D Winner D 34-44	.75	.35
☐ AB Winner AB 1-22 UER (Numbers 10 and 11 have the 1 missing)	1.00	.45
☐ CD Winner C/D 23-44	1.50	.70
☐ ABCD Winner ABCD 1-44	2.50	1.10

1993 Topps Traded

This 132-card standard-size set focuses on promising rookies, new managers, free agents, and players who changed teams. The set also includes 22 members of Team USA. The set has the same design on the front as the regular 1993 Topps issue. The backs are also the same design and carry a head shot, biography, stats, and career highlights. Rookie Cards in this set include Todd Helton, A.J. Hinch, Dante Powell and Todd Walker.

	MINT	NRMT
COMP.FACT.SET (132)	18.00	8.00
COMMON CARD (1T-132T)	.10	.05

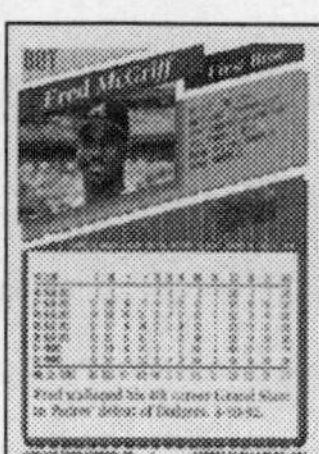

	MINT	NRMT
☐ 1T Barry Bonds	.50	.23
☐ 2T Rich Renteria	.10	.05
☐ 3T Aaron Sele	.20	.09
☐ 4T Carlton Loewer USA	.20	.09
☐ 5T Erik Pappas	.10	.05
☐ 6T Greg McMichael	.10	.05
☐ 7T Freddie Benavides	.10	.05
☐ 8T Kirk Gibson	.20	.09
☐ 9T Tony Fernandez	.10	.05
☐ 10T Jay Gainer	.10	.05
☐ 11T Orestes Destrade	.10	.05
☐ 12T A.J. Hinch USA	2.50	1.10
☐ 13T Bobby Munoz	.10	.05
☐ 14T Tom Henke	.10	.05
☐ 15T Rob Butler	.10	.05
☐ 16T Gary Wayne	.10	.05
☐ 17T David McCarty	.10	.05
☐ 18T Walt Weiss	.10	.05
☐ 19T Todd Helton USA	10.00	4.50
☐ 20T Mark Whiten	.10	.05
☐ 21T Ricky Gutierrez	.10	.05
☐ 22T Dustin Hermanson USA	.50	.23
☐ 23T Sherman Obando	.10	.05
☐ 24T Mike Piazza	2.00	.90
☐ 25T Jeff Russell	.10	.05
☐ 26T Jason Bere	.20	.09
☐ 27T Jack Voigt	.10	.05
☐ 28T Chris Bosio	.10	.05
☐ 29T Phil Hiatt	.10	.05
☐ 30T Matt Beaumont USA	.40	.18
☐ 31T Andres Galarraga	.30	.14
☐ 32T Greg Swindell	.10	.05
☐ 33T Vinny Castilla	.40	.18
☐ 34T Pat Clougherty USA	.10	.05
☐ 35T Greg Briley	.10	.05
☐ 36T Dallas Green MG Davey Johnson MG	.10	.05
☐ 37T Tyler Green	.10	.05
☐ 38T Craig Paquette	.10	.05
☐ 39T Danny Sheaffer	.10	.05
☐ 40T Jim Converse	.10	.05
☐ 41T Terry Harvey USA	.10	.05
☐ 42T Phil Plantier	.10	.05
☐ 43T Doug Saunders	.10	.05
☐ 44T Benny Santiago	.10	.05
☐ 45T Dante Powell USA	1.50	.70
☐ 46T Jeff Parrett	.10	.05
☐ 47T Wade Boggs	.40	.18
☐ 48T Paul Molitor	.40	.18
☐ 49T Turk Wendell	.10	.05
☐ 50T David Wells	.10	.05
☐ 51T Gary Sheffield	.40	.18
☐ 52T Kevin Young	.10	.05
☐ 53T Nelson Liriano	.10	.05
☐ 54T Greg Maddux	1.25	.55
☐ 55T Derek Bell	.20	.09
☐ 56T Matt Turner	.10	.05
☐ 57T Charlie Nelson USA	.10	.05
☐ 58T Mike Hampton	.30	.14
☐ 59T Troy O'Leary	.20	.09
☐ 60T Benji Gil	.10	.05
☐ 61T Mitch Lyden	.10	.05
☐ 62T J.T. Snow	.40	.18
☐ 63T Damon Buford	.10	.05
☐ 64T Gene Harris	.10	.05
☐ 65T Randy Myers	.20	.09
☐ 66T Felix Jose	.10	.05
☐ 67T Todd Dunn USA	.20	.09
☐ 68T Jimmy Key	.20	.09
☐ 69T Pedro Castellano	.10	.05
☐ 70T Mark Merila USA	.20	.09
☐ 71T Rich Rodriguez	.10	.05
☐ 72T Matt Mieske	.20	.09
☐ 73T Pete Incaviglia	.10	.05
☐ 74T Carl Everett	.20	.09
☐ 75T Jim Abbott	.10	.05
☐ 76T Luis Aquino	.10	.05
☐ 77T Rene Arocha	.10	.05
☐ 78T Jon Shave	.10	.05
☐ 79T Todd Walker USA	3.00	1.35
☐ 80T Jack Armstrong	.10	.05
☐ 81T Jeff Richardson	.10	.05
☐ 82T Blas Minor	.10	.05
☐ 83T Dave Winfield	.40	.18
☐ 84T Paul O'Neill	.20	.09
☐ 85T Steve Reich USA	.10	.05
☐ 86T Chris Hammond	.10	.05
☐ 87T Hilly Hathaway	.10	.05
☐ 88T Fred McGriff	.40	.18
☐ 89T Dave Telgheder	.10	.05
☐ 90T Richie Lewis	.10	.05
☐ 91T Brent Gates	.20	.09
☐ 92T Andre Dawson	.30	.14
☐ 93T Andy Barkett USA	.20	.09
☐ 94T Doug Drabek	.10	.05
☐ 95T Joe Klink	.10	.05
☐ 96T Willie Blair	.10	.05
☐ 97T Danny Graves USA	.20	.09
☐ 98T Pat Meares	.20	.09
☐ 99T Mike Lansing	.20	.09
☐ 100T Marcos Armas	.10	.05
☐ 101T Darren Grass USA	.10	.05
☐ 102T Chris Jones	.10	.05
☐ 103T Ken Ryan	.10	.05
☐ 104T Ellis Burks	.20	.09
☐ 105T Roberto Kelly	.10	.05
☐ 106T Dave Magadan	.10	.05
☐ 107T Paul Wilson USA	.75	.35
☐ 108T Rob Natal	.10	.05
☐ 109T Paul Wagner	.10	.05
☐ 110T Jeromy Burnitz	.10	.05
☐ 111T Monty Fariss	.10	.05
☐ 112T Kevin Mitchell	.20	.09
☐ 113T Scott Pose	.10	.05
☐ 114T Dave Stewart	.20	.09
☐ 115T Russ Johnson USA	.50	.23
☐ 116T Armando Reynoso	.10	.05
☐ 117T Geronimo Berroa	.20	.09
☐ 118T Woody Williams	.10	.05
☐ 119T Tim Bogar	.10	.05
☐ 120T Bob Scafa USA	.10	.05
☐ 121T Henry Cotto	.10	.05
☐ 122T Gregg Jefferies	.20	.09
☐ 123T Norm Charlton	.10	.05
☐ 124T Bret Wagner USA	.40	.18
☐ 125T David Cone	.20	.09
☐ 126T Daryl Boston	.10	.05
☐ 127T Tim Wallach	.10	.05
☐ 128T Mike Martin USA	.20	.09
☐ 129T John Cummings	.10	.05
☐ 130T Ryan Bowen	.10	.05
☐ 131T John Powell USA	.20	.09
☐ 132T Checklist 1-132	.10	.05

1993 Topps Commanders of the Hill

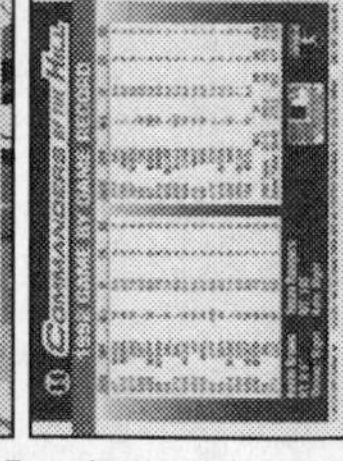

This 30-card set issued by Topps features pitchers of the American and National Leagues. The cards were available individually at commissary on military bases. The standard-size fronts display an action photo with a camouflage design border. The team name is printed vertically along the left edge in brown and outlined in yellow. A banner across the bottom of the picture carries the player's name and his achievement. The horizontal red, white and blue backs carry biography and 1992 game statistics.

	MINT	NRMT
COMPLETE SET (30)	12.00	5.50
COMMON CARD (1-30)	.10	.05

	MINT	NRMT
☐ 1 Dennis Eckersley	.40	.18
☐ 2 Mike Mussina	1.00	.45
☐ 3 Roger Clemens	1.00	.45
☐ 4 Jim Abbott	.10	.05
☐ 5 Jack McDowell	.10	.05
☐ 6 Charles Nagy	.25	.11
☐ 7 Bill Gullickson	.10	.05
☐ 8 Kevin Appier	.25	.11
☐ 9 Bill Wegman	.10	.05
☐ 10 John Smiley	.10	.05
☐ 11 Melido Perez	.10	.05
☐ 12 Dave Stewart	.10	.05

☐ 13 Dave Fleming	.10	.05
☐ 14 Kevin Brown	.25	.11
☐ 15 Juan Guzman	.10	.05
☐ 16 Randy Johnson	.60	.25
☐ 17 Greg Maddux	4.00	1.80
☐ 18 Tom Glavine	.25	.11
☐ 19 Greg Maddux	4.00	1.80
☐ 20 Jose Rijo	.10	.05
☐ 21 Pete Harnisch	.10	.05
☐ 22 Tom Candiotti	.10	.05
☐ 23 Denny Martinez	.25	.11
☐ 24 Sid Fernandez	.10	.05
☐ 25 Curt Schilling	.25	.11
☐ 26 Doug Drabek	.10	.05
☐ 27 Bob Tewksbury	.10	.05
☐ 28 Andy Benes	.25	.11
☐ 29 Bill Swift	.10	.05
☐ 30 John Smoltz	.40	.18

1993 Topps Full Shots

Issued as one-card inserts in retail re-packs containing a pack each of 1993 Topps Series I and II, and in specially marked jumbo boxes of 1993 Bowman, these 21 cards measure approximately 3 1/2" by 5" and feature on their fronts white-bordered color player action photos. The player's name appears in tan lettering at the top, his team name is printed vertically up one side in ghosted white lettering, and the set's name and logo also appear. The back carries another color player photo, with the player's name and position appearing in white lettering at the top within a brown stripe. The player's team name is shown at the bottom of the picture and below is the player's biography and stats. The set's name and logo round out the back. The cards are numbered on the back. In contrast to many of the oversized cards offered by other baseball card manufacturers, Full Shots were unique cards rather than enlarged versions of existing cards.

	MINT	NRMT
COMPLETE SET (21)	50.00	22.00
COMMON CARD (1-21)	.50	.23
☐ 1 Frank Thomas	10.00	4.50
☐ 2 Ken Griffey Jr.	10.00	4.50
☐ 3 Barry Bonds	2.50	1.10
☐ 4 Juan Gonzalez	5.00	2.20
☐ 5 Roberto Alomar	2.50	1.10
☐ 6 Mike Piazza	10.00	4.50
☐ 7 Tony Gwynn	5.00	2.20
☐ 8 Jeff Bagwell	4.00	1.80
☐ 9 Tim Salmon	2.50	1.10
☐ 10 John Olerud	.50	.23
☐ 11 Cal Ripken	8.00	3.60
☐ 12 David McCarty	.50	.23
☐ 13 Darren Daulton	1.00	.45
☐ 14 Carlos Baerga	1.00	.45
☐ 15 Roger Clemens	4.00	1.80
☐ 16 John Kruk	.50	.23
☐ 17 Barry Larkin	1.50	.70
☐ 18 Gary Sheffield	2.00	.90
☐ 19 Tom Glavine	1.00	.45
☐ 20 Andres Galarraga	2.00	.90
☐ 21 Fred McGriff	1.50	.70

1994 Topps Pre-Production

This nine-card standard-size set was issued by Topps for hobby dealers to preview the 1994 Topps regular-issue series. The cards feature glossy color player photos with white borders on the fronts. The player's name is in white cursive lettering at the bottom left, with the team name and player's position printed on a team color-coded bar. There is an inner multi-colored border along the left side that extends obliquely across the bottom. The horizontal backs carry an action shot of the player with biography, statistics, and highlights. The back of each card is identical to the player's regular issue 1994 Topps card back except for a diagonal white box across the statistics stating "PRE-PRODUCTION SAMPLE Design and Photo Selection Subject To Change." These cards were also

issued in some of the 1993 Topps factory sets. The factory set versions are worth about the same as the hobby versions. There is both a horizontal and vertical version of Ryan.

	MINT	NRMT
COMPLETE SET (9)	7.00	3.10
COMMON CARD	.25	.11
☐ 2 Barry Bonds	1.00	.45
☐ 6 Jeff Tackett	.25	.11
☐ 34 Juan Gonzalez	2.00	.90
☐ 225 Matt Williams	.75	.35
☐ 294 Carlos Quintana	.25	.11
☐ 331 Kenny Lofton	1.00	.45
☐ 390 Wade Boggs	1.00	.45
☐ 397 George Brett	1.25	.55
☐ 700 Nolan Ryan	3.00	1.35

1994 Topps

These 792 standard-size cards were issued in two series of 396. Two types of factory sets were also issued. One features the 792 basic cards, ten Topps Gold, three Black Gold and three Finest Pre-Production cards for a total of 808. The other factory set (Bakers Dozen) includes the 792 basic cards, ten Topps Gold, three Black Gold, ten 1995 Topps Pre-Production cards and a sample pack of three special Topps cards for a total of 818. The standard cards feature glossy color player photos with white borders on the fronts. The player's name is in white cursive lettering at the bottom left, with the team name and player's position printed on a team color-coded bar. There is an inner multicolored border along the left side that extends obliquely across the bottom. The horizontal backs carry an action shot of the player with biography, statistics and highlights. Subsets include Draft Picks (201-210/739-762), All-Stars (384-394) and Stat Twins (601-609). Rookie Cards include Alan Benes, Jeff D'Amico, Brooks Kieschnick, Kirk Presley and Pat Watkins.

	MINT	NRMT
COMPLETE SET (792)	30.00	13.50
COMP.FACT.SET (808)	50.00	22.00
COMP.BAKER SET (818)	50.00	22.00
COMPLETE SERIES 1 (396)	15.00	6.75
COMPLETE SERIES 2 (396)	15.00	6.75
COMMON CARD (1-792)	.10	.05
☐ 1 Mike Piazza	1.25	.55
☐ 2 Bernie Williams	.40	.18
☐ 3 Kevin Rogers	.10	.05
☐ 4 Paul Carey	.10	.05
☐ 5 Ozzie Guillen	.10	.05
☐ 6 Derrick May	.10	.05
☐ 7 Jose Mesa	.20	.09
☐ 8 Todd Hundley	.20	.09
☐ 9 Chris Haney	.10	.05
☐ 10 John Olerud	.20	.09
☐ 11 Andujar Cedeno	.10	.05
☐ 12 John Smiley	.10	.05
☐ 13 Phil Plantier	.10	.05
☐ 14 Willie Banks	.10	.05
☐ 15 Jay Bell	.20	.09
☐ 16 Doug Henry	.10	.05
☐ 17 Lance Blankenship	.10	.05
☐ 18 Greg W. Harris	.10	.05
☐ 19 Scott Livingstone	.10	.05
☐ 20 Bryan Harvey	.10	.05
☐ 21 Wil Cordero	.20	.09
☐ 22 Roger Pavlik	.10	.05
☐ 23 Mark Lemke	.10	.05
☐ 24 Jeff Nelson	.10	.05
☐ 25 Todd Zeile	.10	.05
☐ 26 Billy Hatcher	.10	.05
☐ 27 Joe Magrane	.10	.05
☐ 28 Tony Longmire	.10	.05
☐ 29 Omar Daal	.10	.05
☐ 30 Kirt Manwaring	.10	.05
☐ 31 Melido Perez	.10	.05
☐ 32 Tim Hulett	.10	.05
☐ 33 Jeff Schwartz	.10	.05
☐ 34 Nolan Ryan	1.50	.70
☐ 35 Jose Guzman	.10	.05
☐ 36 Felix Fermin	.10	.05
☐ 37 Jeff Innis	.10	.05
☐ 38 Brett Mayne	.10	.05
☐ 39 Huck Flener	.10	.05
☐ 40 Jeff Bagwell	.75	.35
☐ 41 Kevin Wickander	.10	.05
☐ 42 Ricky Gutierrez	.10	.05
☐ 43 Pat Mahomes	.10	.05
☐ 44 Jeff King	.20	.09
☐ 45 Cal Eldred	.10	.05
☐ 46 Craig Paquette	.10	.05
☐ 47 Richie Lewis	.10	.05
☐ 48 Tony Phillips	.10	.05
☐ 49 Armando Reynoso	.10	.05
☐ 50 Moises Alou	.20	.09
☐ 51 Manuel Lee	.10	.05
☐ 52 Otis Nixon	.20	.09
☐ 53 Billy Ashley	.10	.05
☐ 54 Mark Whiten	.10	.05
☐ 55 Jeff Russell	.10	.05
☐ 56 Chad Curtis	.10	.05
☐ 57 Kevin Stocker	.10	.05
☐ 58 Mike Jackson	.10	.05
☐ 59 Matt Nokes	.10	.05
☐ 60 Chris Bosio	.10	.05
☐ 61 Damon Buford	.10	.05
☐ 62 Tim Belcher	.10	.05
☐ 63 Glenallen Hill	.10	.05
☐ 64 Bill Wertz	.10	.05
☐ 65 Eddie Murray	.40	.18
☐ 66 Tom Gordon	.10	.05
☐ 67 Alex Gonzalez	.20	.09
☐ 68 Eddie Taubensee	.10	.05
☐ 69 Jacob Brumfield	.10	.05
☐ 70 Andy Benes	.20	.09
☐ 71 Rich Becker	.20	.09
☐ 72 Steve Cooke	.10	.05
☐ 73 Billy Spiers	.10	.05
☐ 74 Scott Brosius	.10	.05
☐ 75 Alan Trammell	.30	.14
☐ 76 Luis Aquino	.10	.05
☐ 77 Jerald Clark	.10	.05
☐ 78 Mel Rojas	.10	.05
☐ 79 Outfield Prospects Billy Masse Stanton Cameron Tim Clark Craig McClure	.30	.14
☐ 80 Jose Canseco	.30	.14
☐ 81 Greg McMichael	.10	.05
☐ 82 Brian Turang	.10	.05
☐ 83 Tom Urbani	.10	.05
☐ 84 Garret Anderson	.40	.18
☐ 85 Tony Pena	.10	.05
☐ 86 Ricky Jordan	.10	.05
☐ 87 Jim Gott	.10	.05
☐ 88 Pat Kelly	.10	.05
☐ 89 Bud Black	.10	.05
☐ 90 Robin Ventura	.20	.09
☐ 91 Rick Sutcliffe	.10	.05
☐ 92 Jose Bautista	.10	.05
☐ 93 Bob Ojeda	.10	.05
☐ 94 Phil Hiatt	.10	.05
☐ 95 Tim Pugh	.10	.05
☐ 96 Randy Knorr	.10	.05
☐ 97 Todd Jones	.10	.05
☐ 98 Ryan Thompson	.10	.05
☐ 99 Tim Mauser	.10	.05
☐ 100 Kirby Puckett	.75	.35
☐ 101 Mark Dewey	.10	.05
☐ 102 B.J. Surhoff	.10	.05
☐ 103 Sterling Hitchcock	.20	.09
☐ 104 Alex Arias	.10	.05
☐ 105 David Wells	.10	.05
☐ 106 Daryl Boston	.10	.05
☐ 107 Mike Stanton	.10	.05
☐ 108 Gary Redus	.10	.05
☐ 109 Delino DeShields	.10	.05
☐ 110 Lee Smith	.20	.09
☐ 111 Greg Litton	.10	.05
☐ 112 Frankie Rodriguez	.10	.05

☐ 113 Russ Springer	.10	.05
☐ 114 Mitch Williams	.10	.05
☐ 115 Eric Karros	.20	.09
☐ 116 Jeff Brantley	.10	.05
☐ 117 Jack Voigt	.10	.05
☐ 118 Jason Bere	.10	.05
☐ 119 Kevin Roberson	.10	.05
☐ 120 Jimmy Key	.20	.09
☐ 121 Reggie Jefferson	.20	.09
☐ 122 Jeromy Burnitz	.20	.09
☐ 123 Billy Brewer	.10	.05
☐ 124 Willie Canate	.10	.05
☐ 125 Greg Swindell	.10	.05
☐ 126 Hal Morris	.10	.05
☐ 127 Brad Ausmus	.10	.05
☐ 128 George Tsamis	.10	.05
☐ 129 Denny Neagle	.20	.09
☐ 130 Pat Listach	.10	.05
☐ 131 Steve Karsay	.10	.05
☐ 132 Bret Barberie	.10	.05
☐ 133 Mark Leiter	.10	.05
☐ 134 Greg Colbrunn	.10	.05
☐ 135 David Nied	.10	.05
☐ 136 Dean Palmer	.20	.09
☐ 137 Steve Avery	.10	.05
☐ 138 Bill Haselman	.10	.05
☐ 139 Tripp Cromer	.10	.05
☐ 140 Frank Viola	.10	.05
☐ 141 Rene Gonzales	.10	.05
☐ 142 Curt Schilling	.20	.09
☐ 143 Tim Wallach	.10	.05
☐ 144 Bobby Munoz	.10	.05
☐ 145 Brady Anderson	.30	.14
☐ 146 Rod Beck	.20	.09
☐ 147 Mike LaValliere	.10	.05
☐ 148 Greg Hibbard	.10	.05
☐ 149 Kenny Lofton	.50	.23
☐ 150 Doc Gooden	.20	.09
☐ 151 Greg Gagne	.10	.05
☐ 152 Ray McDavid	.10	.05
☐ 153 Chris Donnels	.10	.05
☐ 154 Dan Wilson	.20	.09
☐ 155 Todd Stottlemyre	.10	.05
☐ 156 David McCarty	.10	.05
☐ 157 Paul Wagner	.10	.05
☐ 158 Shortstop Prospects	1.50	.70
Orlando Miller		
Brandon Wilson		
Derek Jeter		
Mike Neal		
☐ 159 Mike Fetters	.10	.05
☐ 160 Scott Lydy	.10	.05
☐ 161 Darrell Whitmore	.10	.05
☐ 162 Bob MacDonald	.10	.05
☐ 163 Vinny Castilla	.30	.14
☐ 164 Denis Boucher	.10	.05
☐ 165 Ivan Rodriguez	.50	.23
☐ 166 Ron Gant	.20	.09
☐ 167 Tim Davis	.10	.05
☐ 168 Steve Dixon	.10	.05
☐ 169 Scott Fletcher	.10	.05
☐ 170 Terry Mulholland	.10	.05
☐ 171 Greg Myers	.10	.05
☐ 172 Brett Butler	.20	.09
☐ 173 Bob Wickman	.10	.05
☐ 174 Dave Martinez	.10	.05
☐ 175 Fernando Valenzuela	.20	.09
☐ 176 Craig Grebeck	.10	.05
☐ 177 Shawn Boskie	.10	.05
☐ 178 Albie Lopez	.10	.05
☐ 179 Butch Huskey	.20	.09
☐ 180 George Brett	.75	.35
☐ 181 Juan Guzman	.10	.05
☐ 182 Eric Anthony	.10	.05
☐ 183 Rob Dibble	.10	.05
☐ 184 Craig Shipley	.10	.05
☐ 185 Kevin Tapani	.10	.05
☐ 186 Marcus Moore	.10	.05
☐ 187 Graeme Lloyd	.10	.05
☐ 188 Mike Bordick	.10	.05
☐ 189 Chris Hammond	.10	.05
☐ 190 Cecil Fielder	.20	.09
☐ 191 Curtis Leskanic	.10	.05
☐ 192 Lou Frazier	.10	.05
☐ 193 Steve Dreyer	.10	.05
☐ 194 Javier Lopez	.30	.14
☐ 195 Edgar Martinez	.30	.14
☐ 196 Allen Watson	.10	.05
☐ 197 John Flaherty	.10	.05
☐ 198 Kurt Stillwell	.10	.05
☐ 199 Danny Jackson	.10	.05
☐ 200 Cal Ripken	1.50	.70
☐ 201 Mike Bell FDP	.40	.18
☐ 202 Alan Benes FDP	1.00	.45
☐ 203 Matt Farner FDP	.20	.09
☐ 204 Jeff Granger FDP	.20	.09
☐ 205 Brooks Kieschnick FDP	.30	.14
☐ 206 Jeremy Lee FDP	.30	.14
☐ 207 Charles Peterson FDP	.30	.14
☐ 208 Alan Rice FDP	.20	.09
☐ 209 Billy Wagner FDP	.75	.35
☐ 210 Kelly Wunsch FDP	.20	.09
☐ 211 Tom Candiotti	.10	.05
☐ 212 Domingo Jean	.10	.05
☐ 213 John Burkett	.10	.05
☐ 214 George Bell	.10	.05
☐ 215 Dan Plesac	.10	.05
☐ 216 Manny Ramirez	.50	.23
☐ 217 Mike Maddux	.10	.05
☐ 218 Kevin McReynolds	.10	.05
☐ 219 Pat Borders	.10	.05
☐ 220 Doug Drabek	.10	.05
☐ 221 Larry Luebbers	.10	.05
☐ 222 Trevor Hoffman	.20	.09
☐ 223 Pat Meares	.10	.05
☐ 224 Danny Miceli	.10	.05
☐ 225 Greg Vaughn	.10	.05
☐ 226 Scott Hemond	.10	.05
☐ 227 Pat Rapp	.10	.05
☐ 228 Kirk Gibson	.20	.09
☐ 229 Lance Painter	.10	.05
☐ 230 Larry Walker	.40	.18
☐ 231 Benji Gil	.10	.05
☐ 232 Mark Wohlers	.20	.09
☐ 233 Rich Amaral	.10	.05
☐ 234 Eric Pappas	.10	.05
☐ 235 Scott Cooper	.10	.05
☐ 236 Mike Butcher	.10	.05
☐ 237 Outfield Prospects	.20	.09
Curtis Pride		
Shawn Green		
Mark Sweeney		
Eddie Davis		
☐ 238 Kim Batiste	.10	.05
☐ 239 Paul Assenmacher	.10	.05
☐ 240 Will Clark	.30	.14
☐ 241 Jose Offerman	.10	.05
☐ 242 Todd Frohwirth	.10	.05
☐ 243 Tim Raines	.10	.05
☐ 244 Rick Wilkins	.10	.05
☐ 245 Bret Saberhagen	.10	.05
☐ 246 Thomas Howard	.10	.05
☐ 247 Stan Belinda	.10	.05
☐ 248 Rickey Henderson	.30	.14
☐ 249 Brian Williams	.10	.05
☐ 250 Barry Larkin	.30	.14
☐ 251 Jose Valentin	.20	.09
☐ 252 Lenny Webster	.10	.05
☐ 253 Blas Minor	.10	.05
☐ 254 Tim Teufel	.10	.05
☐ 255 Bobby Witt	.10	.05
☐ 256 Walt Weiss	.10	.05
☐ 257 Chad Kreuter	.10	.05
☐ 258 Roberto Mejia	.10	.05
☐ 259 Cliff Floyd	.20	.09
☐ 260 Julio Franco	.20	.09
☐ 261 Rafael Belliard	.10	.05
☐ 262 Marc Newfield	.20	.09
☐ 263 Gerald Perry	.10	.05
☐ 264 Ken Ryan	.10	.05
☐ 265 Chili Davis	.20	.09
☐ 266 Dave West	.10	.05
☐ 267 Royce Clayton	.20	.09
☐ 268 Pedro Martinez	.40	.18
☐ 269 Mark Hutton	.10	.05
☐ 270 Frank Thomas	1.50	.70
☐ 271 Brad Pennington	.10	.05
☐ 272 Mike Harkey	.10	.05
☐ 273 Sandy Alomar	.20	.09
☐ 274 Dave Gallagher	.10	.05
☐ 275 Wally Joyner	.20	.09
☐ 276 Ricky Trlicek	.10	.05
☐ 277 Al Osuna	.10	.05
☐ 278 Calvin Reese	.20	.09
☐ 279 Kevin Higgins	.10	.05
☐ 280 Rick Aguilera	.10	.05
☐ 281 Orlando Merced	.10	.05
☐ 282 Mike Mohler	.10	.05
☐ 283 John Jaha	.10	.05
☐ 284 Robb Nen	.20	.09
☐ 285 Travis Fryman	.20	.09
☐ 286 Mark Thompson	.10	.05
☐ 287 Mike Lansing	.20	.09
☐ 288 Craig Lefferts	.10	.05
☐ 289 Damon Berryhill	.10	.05
☐ 290 Randy Johnson	.40	.18
☐ 291 Jeff Reed	.10	.05
☐ 292 Danny Darwin	.10	.05
☐ 293 J.T. Snow	.30	.14
☐ 294 Tyler Green	.10	.05
☐ 295 Chris Hoiles	.10	.05
☐ 296 Roger McDowell	.10	.05
☐ 297 Spike Owen	.10	.05
☐ 298 Salomon Torres	.10	.05
☐ 299 Wilson Alvarez	.20	.09
☐ 300 Ryne Sandberg	.50	.23
☐ 301 Derek Lilliquist	.10	.05
☐ 302 Howard Johnson	.10	.05
☐ 303 Greg Cadaret	.10	.05
☐ 304 Pat Hentgen	.20	.09
☐ 305 Craig Biggio	.30	.14
☐ 306 Scott Service	.10	.05
☐ 307 Melvin Nieves	.20	.09
☐ 308 Mike Trombley	.10	.05
☐ 309 Carlos Garcia	.10	.05
☐ 310 Robin Yount UER	.30	.14
(listed with 111 triples in		
1988; should be 11)		
☐ 311 Marcos Armas	.10	.05
☐ 312 Rich Rodriguez	.10	.05
☐ 313 Justin Thompson	.40	.18
☐ 314 Danny Sheaffer	.10	.05
☐ 315 Ken Hill	.10	.05
☐ 316 Pitching Prospects	.40	.18
Chad Ogea		
Duff Brumley		
Terrell Wade		
Chris Michalak		
☐ 317 Cris Carpenter	.10	.05
☐ 318 Jeff Blauser	.10	.05
☐ 319 Ted Power	.10	.05
☐ 320 Ozzie Smith	.50	.23
☐ 321 John Dopson	.10	.05
☐ 322 Chris Turner	.10	.05
☐ 323 Pete Incaviglia	.10	.05
☐ 324 Alan Mills	.10	.05
☐ 325 Jody Reed	.10	.05
☐ 326 Rich Monteleone	.10	.05
☐ 327 Mark Carreon	.10	.05
☐ 328 Donn Pall	.10	.05
☐ 329 Matt Walbeck	.10	.05
☐ 330 Charles Nagy	.20	.09
☐ 331 Jeff McKnight	.10	.05
☐ 332 Jose Lind	.10	.05
☐ 333 Mike Timlin	.10	.05
☐ 334 Doug Jones	.10	.05
☐ 335 Kevin Mitchell	.10	.05
☐ 336 Luis Lopez	.10	.05
☐ 337 Shane Mack	.10	.05
☐ 338 Randy Tomlin	.10	.05
☐ 339 Matt Mieske	.10	.05
☐ 340 Mark McGwire	.75	.35
☐ 341 Nigel Wilson	.10	.05
☐ 342 Danny Gladden	.10	.05
☐ 343 Mo Sanford	.10	.05
☐ 344 Sean Berry	.10	.05
☐ 345 Kevin Brown	.20	.09
☐ 346 Greg Olson	.10	.05
☐ 347 Dave Magadan	.10	.05
☐ 348 Rene Arocha	.10	.05
☐ 349 Carlos Quintana	.10	.05
☐ 350 Jim Abbott	.10	.05
☐ 351 Gary DiSarcina	.10	.05
☐ 352 Ben Rivera	.10	.05
☐ 353 Carlos Hernandez	.10	.05
☐ 354 Darren Lewis	.10	.05
☐ 355 Harold Reynolds	.10	.05
☐ 356 Scott Ruffcorn	.10	.05
☐ 357 Mark Gubicza	.10	.05
☐ 358 Paul Sorrento	.10	.05
☐ 359 Anthony Young	.10	.05
☐ 360 Mark Grace	.30	.14
☐ 361 Rob Butler	.10	.05
☐ 362 Kevin Bass	.10	.05
☐ 363 Eric Helfand	.10	.05
☐ 364 Derek Bell	.20	.09
☐ 365 Scott Erickson	.10	.05
☐ 366 Al Martin	.10	.05
☐ 367 Ricky Bones	.10	.05
☐ 368 Jeff Branson	.10	.05
☐ 369 Third Base Prospects	.40	.18
Luis Ortiz		
David Bell		
Jason Giambi		
George Arias		
☐ 370 Benito Santiago	.10	.05
(See also 379)		
☐ 371 John Doherty	.10	.05
☐ 372 Joe Girardi	.10	.05
☐ 373 Tim Scott	.10	.05
☐ 374 Marvin Freeman	.10	.05
☐ 375 Deion Sanders	.40	.18
☐ 376 Roger Salkeld	.10	.05
☐ 377 Bernard Gilkey	.20	.09
☐ 378 Tony Fossas	.10	.05
☐ 379 Mark McLemore UER	.10	.05
(Card number is 370)		
☐ 380 Darren Daulton	.20	.09
☐ 381 Chuck Finley	.10	.05
☐ 382 Mitch Webster	.10	.05
☐ 383 Gerald Williams	.15	.07

☐ 384 Frank Thomas AS	.60	.25
Fred McGriff AS		
☐ 385 Roberto Alomar AS	.20	.09
Robby Thompson AS		
☐ 386 Wade Boggs AS	.30	.14
Matt Williams AS		
☐ 387 Cal Ripken AS	.50	.23
Jeff Blauser AS		
☐ 388 Ken Griffey Jr. AS	.50	.23
Len Dykstra AS		
☐ 389 Juan Gonzalez AS	.40	.18
David Justice AS		
☐ 390 George Belle AS	.20	.09
Bobby Bonds AS		
☐ 391 Mike Stanley AS	.40	.18
Mike Piazza AS		
☐ 392 Jack McDowell AS	.30	.14
Greg Maddux AS		
☐ 393 Jimmy Key AS	.20	.09
Tom Glavine AS		
☐ 394 Jeff Montgomery AS	.10	.05
Randy Myers AS		
☐ 395 Checklist 1-198	.10	.05
☐ 396 Checklist 199-396	.10	.05
☐ 397 Tim Salmon	.40	.18
☐ 398 Todd Benzinger	.10	.05
☐ 399 Frank Castillo	.10	.05
☐ 400 Ken Griffey Jr.	2.00	.90
☐ 401 John Kruk	.20	.09
☐ 402 Dave Telgheder	.10	.05
☐ 403 Gary Gaetti	.20	.09
☐ 404 Jim Edmonds	.40	.18
☐ 405 Don Slaught	.10	.05
☐ 406 Jose Oquendo	.10	.05
☐ 407 Bruce Ruffin	.10	.05
☐ 408 Phil Clark	.10	.05
☐ 409 Joe Klink	.10	.05
☐ 410 Lou Whitaker	.20	.09
☐ 411 Kevin Seitzer	.10	.05
☐ 412 Darrin Fletcher	.10	.05
☐ 413 Kenny Rogers	.10	.05
☐ 414 Bill Pecota	.10	.05
☐ 415 Dave Fleming	.10	.05
☐ 416 Luis Alicea	.10	.05
☐ 417 Paul Quantrill	.10	.05
☐ 418 Damion Easley	.10	.05
☐ 419 Wes Chamberlain	.10	.05
☐ 420 Harold Baines	.20	.09
☐ 421 Scott Radinsky	.10	.05
☐ 422 Rey Sanchez	.10	.05
☐ 423 Junior Ortiz	.10	.05
☐ 424 Jeff Kent	.10	.05
☐ 425 Brian McRae	.10	.05
☐ 426 Ed Sprague	.10	.05
☐ 427 Tom Edens	.10	.05
☐ 428 Willie Greene	.20	.09
☐ 429 Bryan Hickerson	.10	.05
☐ 430 Dave Winfield	.30	.14
☐ 431 Pedro Astacio	.10	.05
☐ 432 Mike Gallego	.10	.05
☐ 433 Dave Burba	.10	.05
☐ 434 Bob Walk	.10	.05
☐ 435 Darryl Hamilton	.10	.05
☐ 436 Vince Horsman	.10	.05
☐ 437 Bob Natal	.10	.05
☐ 438 Mike Henneman	.10	.05
☐ 439 Willie Blair	.10	.05
☐ 440 Denny Martinez	.20	.09
☐ 441 Dan Peltier	.10	.05
☐ 442 Tony Tarasco	.10	.05
☐ 443 John Cummings	.10	.05
☐ 444 Geronimo Pena	.10	.05
☐ 445 Aaron Sele	.10	.05
☐ 446 Stan Javier	.10	.05
☐ 447 Mike Williams	.10	.05
☐ 448 First Base Prospects	.30	.14
Greg Pirkl		
Roberto Petagine		
D.J.Boston		
Shawn Wooten		
☐ 449 Jim Poole	.10	.05
☐ 450 Carlos Baerga	.20	.09
☐ 451 Bob Scanlan	.10	.05
☐ 452 Lance Johnson	.10	.05
☐ 453 Eric Hillman	.10	.05
☐ 454 Keith Miller	.10	.05
☐ 455 Dave Stewart	.20	.09
☐ 456 Pete Harnisch	.10	.05
☐ 457 Roberto Kelly	.10	.05
☐ 458 Tim Worrell	.10	.05
☐ 459 Pedro Munoz	.10	.05
☐ 460 Orel Hershiser	.20	.09
☐ 461 Randy Velarde	.10	.05
☐ 462 Trevor Wilson	.10	.05
☐ 463 Jerry Goff	.10	.05
☐ 464 Bill Wegman	.10	.05
☐ 465 Dennis Eckersley	.30	.14
☐ 466 Jeff Conine	.20	.09
☐ 467 Joe Boever	.10	.05
☐ 468 Dante Bichette	.30	.14
☐ 469 Jeff Shaw	.10	.05
☐ 470 Rafael Palmeiro	.30	.14
☐ 471 Phil Leftwich	.10	.05
☐ 472 Jay Buhner	.30	.14
☐ 473 Bob Tewksbury	.10	.05
☐ 474 Tim Naehring	.10	.05
☐ 475 Tom Glavine	.30	.14
☐ 476 Dave Hollins	.10	.05
☐ 477 Arthur Rhodes	.10	.05
☐ 478 Joey Cora	.20	.09
☐ 479 Mike Morgan	.10	.05
☐ 480 Albert Belle	.50	.23
☐ 481 John Franco	.10	.05
☐ 482 Hipolito Pichardo	.10	.05
☐ 483 Duane Ward	.10	.05
☐ 484 Luis Gonzalez	.10	.05
☐ 485 Joe Oliver	.10	.05
☐ 486 Wally Whitehurst	.10	.05
☐ 487 Mike Benjamin	.10	.05
☐ 488 Eric Davis	.20	.09
☐ 489 Scott Kamieniecki	.10	.05
☐ 490 Kent Hrbek	.20	.09
☐ 491 John Hope	.10	.05
☐ 492 Jesse Orosco	.10	.05
☐ 493 Troy Neel	.10	.05
☐ 494 Ryan Bowen	.10	.05
☐ 495 Mickey Tettleton	.10	.05
☐ 496 Chris Jones	.10	.05
☐ 497 John Wetteland	.20	.09
☐ 498 David Hulse	.10	.05
☐ 499 Greg Maddux	1.25	.55
☐ 500 Bo Jackson	.20	.09
☐ 501 Donovan Osborne	.10	.05
☐ 502 Mike Greenwell	.10	.05
☐ 503 Steve Frey	.10	.05
☐ 504 Jim Eisenreich	.20	.09
☐ 505 Robby Thompson	.10	.05
☐ 506 Leo Gomez	.10	.05
☐ 507 Dave Staton	.10	.05
☐ 508 Wayne Kirby	.10	.05
☐ 509 Tim Bogar	.10	.05
☐ 510 David Cone	.20	.09
☐ 511 Devon White	.10	.05
☐ 512 Xavier Hernandez	.10	.05
☐ 513 Tim Costo	.10	.05
☐ 514 Gene Harris	.10	.05
☐ 515 Jack McDowell	.10	.05
☐ 516 Kevin Gross	.10	.05
☐ 517 Scott Leius	.10	.05
☐ 518 Lloyd McClendon	.10	.05
☐ 519 Alex Diaz	.10	.05
☐ 520 Wade Boggs	.40	.18
☐ 521 Bob Welch	.10	.05
☐ 522 Henry Cotto	.10	.05
☐ 523 Mike Moore	.10	.05
☐ 524 Tim Laker	.10	.05
☐ 525 Andres Galarraga	.30	.14
☐ 526 Jamie Moyer	.10	.05
☐ 527 Second Base Prospects	.20	.09
Norberto Martin		
Ruben Santana		
Jason Hardtke		
Chris Sexton		
☐ 528 Sid Bream	.10	.05
☐ 529 Erik Hanson	.10	.05
☐ 530 Ray Lankford	.30	.14
☐ 531 Rob Deer	.10	.05
☐ 532 Rod Correia	.10	.05
☐ 533 Roger Mason	.10	.05
☐ 534 Mike Devereaux	.10	.05
☐ 535 Jeff Montgomery	.20	.09
☐ 536 Dwight Smith	.10	.05
☐ 537 Jeremy Hernandez	.10	.05
☐ 538 Ellis Burks	.20	.09
☐ 539 Bobby Jones	.20	.09
☐ 540 Paul Molitor	.40	.18
☐ 541 Jeff Juden	.10	.05
☐ 542 Chris Sabo	.10	.05
☐ 543 Larry Casian	.10	.05
☐ 544 Jeff Gardner	.10	.05
☐ 545 Ramon Martinez	.20	.09
☐ 546 Paul O'Neill	.20	.09
☐ 547 Steve Hosey	.10	.05
☐ 548 Dave Nilsson	.20	.09
☐ 549 Ron Darling	.10	.05
☐ 550 Matt Williams	.30	.14
☐ 551 Jack Armstrong	.10	.05
☐ 552 Bill Krueger	.10	.05
☐ 553 Freddie Benavides	.10	.05
☐ 554 Jeff Fassero	.10	.05
☐ 555 Chuck Knoblauch	.40	.18
☐ 556 Guillermo Velasquez	.10	.05
☐ 557 Joel Johnston	.10	.05
☐ 558 Tom Lampkin	.10	.05
☐ 559 Todd Van Poppel	.10	.05
☐ 560 Gary Sheffield	.40	.18
☐ 561 Skeeter Barnes	.10	.05
☐ 562 Darren Holmes	.10	.05
☐ 563 John Vander Wal	.10	.05
☐ 564 Mike Ignasiak	.10	.05
☐ 565 Fred McGriff	.30	.14
☐ 566 Luis Polonia	.10	.05
☐ 567 Mike Perez	.10	.05
☐ 568 John Valentin	.20	.09
☐ 569 Mike Felder	.10	.05
☐ 570 Tommy Greene	.10	.05
☐ 571 David Segui	.10	.05
☐ 572 Roberto Hernandez	.20	.09
☐ 573 Steve Wilson	.10	.05
☐ 574 Willie McGee	.10	.05
☐ 575 Randy Myers	.10	.05
☐ 576 Darrin Jackson	.10	.05
☐ 577 Eric Plunk	.10	.05
☐ 578 Mike Macfarlane	.10	.05
☐ 579 Doug Brocail	.10	.05
☐ 580 Steve Finley	.20	.09
☐ 581 John Roper	.10	.05
☐ 582 Danny Cox	.10	.05
☐ 583 Chip Hale	.10	.05
☐ 584 Scott Bullett	.10	.05
☐ 585 Kevin Reimer	.10	.05
☐ 586 Brent Gates	.10	.05
☐ 587 Matt Turner	.10	.05
☐ 588 Rich Rowland	.10	.05
☐ 589 Kent Bottenfield	.10	.05
☐ 590 Marquis Grissom	.20	.09
☐ 591 Doug Strange	.10	.05
☐ 592 Jay Howell	.10	.05
☐ 593 Omar Vizquel	.20	.09
☐ 594 Rheal Cormier	.10	.05
☐ 595 Andre Dawson	.30	.14
☐ 596 Hilly Hathaway	.10	.05
☐ 597 Todd Pratt	.10	.05
☐ 598 Mike Mussina	.40	.18
☐ 599 Alex Fernandez	.20	.09
☐ 600 Don Mattingly	.60	.25
☐ 601 Frank Thomas ST	1.00	.45
☐ 602 Ryne Sandberg ST	.40	.18
☐ 603 Wade Boggs ST	.40	.18
☐ 604 Cal Ripken ST	.75	.35
☐ 605 Barry Bonds ST	.40	.18
☐ 606 Ken Griffey Jr. ST	1.00	.45
☐ 607 Kirby Puckett ST	.40	.18
☐ 608 Darren Daulton ST	.20	.09
☐ 609 Paul Molitor ST	.40	.18
☐ 610 Terry Steinbach	.20	.09
☐ 611 Todd Worrell	.10	.05
☐ 612 Jim Thome	.50	.23
☐ 613 Chuck McElroy	.10	.05
☐ 614 John Habyan	.10	.05
☐ 615 Sid Fernandez	.10	.05
☐ 616 Outfield Prospects	.30	.14
Eddie Zambrano		
Glenn Murray		
Chad Mottola		
Jermaine Allensworth		
☐ 617 Steve Bedrosian	.10	.05
☐ 618 Rob Ducey	.10	.05
☐ 619 Tom Browning	.10	.05
☐ 620 Tony Gwynn	1.00	.45
☐ 621 Carl Willis	.10	.05
☐ 622 Kevin Young	.10	.05
☐ 623 Rafael Novoa	.10	.05
☐ 624 Jerry Browne	.10	.05
☐ 625 Charlie Hough	.10	.05
☐ 626 Chris Gomez	.10	.05
☐ 627 Steve Reed	.10	.05
☐ 628 Kirk Rueter	.10	.05
☐ 629 Matt Whiteside	.10	.05
☐ 630 David Justice	.40	.18
☐ 631 Brad Holman	.10	.05
☐ 632 Brian Jordan	.20	.09
☐ 633 Scott Bankhead	.10	.05
☐ 634 Torey Lovullo	.10	.05
☐ 635 Len Dykstra	.20	.09
☐ 636 Ben McDonald	.10	.05
☐ 637 Steve Howe	.10	.05
☐ 638 Jose Vizcaino	.10	.05
☐ 639 Bill Swift	.10	.05
☐ 640 Darryl Strawberry	.20	.09
☐ 641 Steve Farr	.10	.05
☐ 642 Tom Kramer	.10	.05
☐ 643 Joe Orsulak	.10	.05
☐ 644 Tom Henke	.10	.05
☐ 645 Joe Carter	.30	.14
☐ 646 Ken Caminiti	.40	.18
☐ 647 Reggie Sanders	.10	.05
☐ 648 Andy Ashby	.10	.05
☐ 649 Derek Parks	.10	.05
☐ 650 Andy Van Slyke	.20	.09
☐ 651 Juan Bell	.10	.05

Card	MINT	NRMT
□ 652 Roger Smithberg	.10	.05
□ 653 Chuck Carr	.10	.05
□ 654 Bill Gullickson	.10	.05
□ 655 Charlie Hayes	.10	.05
□ 656 Chris Nabholz	.10	.05
□ 657 Karl Rhodes	.10	.05
□ 658 Pete Smith	.10	.05
□ 659 Bret Boone	.10	.05
□ 660 Gregg Jefferies	.20	.09
□ 661 Bob Zupcic	.10	.05
□ 662 Steve Sax	.10	.05
□ 663 Mariano Duncan	.10	.05
□ 664 Jeff Tackett	.10	.05
□ 665 Mark Langston	.10	.05
□ 666 Steve Buechele	.10	.05
□ 667 Candy Maldonado	.10	.05
□ 668 Woody Williams	.10	.05
□ 669 Tim Wakefield	.10	.05
□ 670 Danny Tartabull	.10	.05
□ 671 Charlie O'Brien	.10	.05
□ 672 Felix Jose	.10	.05
□ 673 Bobby Ayala	.10	.05
□ 674 Scott Servais	.10	.05
□ 675 Roberto Alomar	.40	.18
□ 676 Pedro Martinez	.40	.18
□ 677 Eddie Guardado	.10	.05
□ 678 Mark Lewis	.10	.05
□ 679 Jaime Navarro	.10	.05
□ 680 Ruben Sierra	.10	.05
□ 681 Rick Renteria	.10	.05
□ 682 Storm Davis	.10	.05
□ 683 Cory Snyder	.10	.05
□ 684 Ron Karkovice	.10	.05
□ 685 Juan Gonzalez	1.00	.45
□ 686 Catchers Prospects	.40	.18
Chris Howard		
Carlos Delgado		
Jason Kendall		
Paul Bako		
□ 687 John Smoltz	.30	.14
□ 688 Brian Dorsett	.10	.05
□ 689 Omar Olivares	.10	.05
□ 690 Mo Vaughn	.50	.23
□ 691 Joe Grahe	.10	.05
□ 692 Mickey Morandini	.10	.05
□ 693 Tino Martinez	.40	.18
□ 694 Brian Barnes	.10	.05
□ 695 Mike Stanley	.10	.05
□ 696 Mark Clark	.10	.05
□ 697 Dave Hansen	.10	.05
□ 698 Willie Wilson	.10	.05
□ 699 Pete Schourek	.10	.05
□ 700 Barry Bonds	.50	.23
□ 701 Kevin Appier	.20	.09
□ 702 Tony Fernandez	.10	.05
□ 703 Darryl Kile	.20	.09
□ 704 Archi Cianfrocco	.10	.05
□ 705 Jose Rijo	.10	.05
□ 706 Brian Harper	.10	.05
□ 707 Zane Smith	.10	.05
□ 708 Dave Henderson	.10	.05
□ 709 Angel Miranda UER	.10	.05
(no Topps logo on back)		
□ 710 Orestes Destrade	.10	.05
□ 711 Greg Gohr	.10	.05
□ 712 Eric Young	.20	.09
□ 713 Relief Pitchers	.20	.09
Prospects		
Todd Williams		
Ron Watson		
Kirk Bullinger		
Mike Welch		
□ 714 Tim Spehr	.10	.05
□ 715 Hank Aaron	.50	.23
□ 716 Nate Minchey	.10	.05
□ 717 Mike Blowers	.10	.05
□ 718 Kent Mercker	.10	.05
□ 719 Tom Pagnozzi	.10	.05
□ 720 Roger Clemens	.75	.35
□ 721 Eduardo Perez	.10	.05
□ 722 Milt Thompson	.10	.05
□ 723 Gregg Olson	.10	.05
□ 724 Kirk McCaskill	.10	.05
□ 725 Sammy Sosa	.40	.18
□ 726 Alvaro Espinoza	.10	.05
□ 727 Henry Rodriguez	.10	.05
□ 728 Jim Leyritz	.10	.05
□ 729 Steve Scarsone	.10	.05
□ 730 Bobby Bonilla	.20	.09
□ 731 Chris Gwynn	.10	.05
□ 732 Al Leiter	.10	.05
□ 733 Bip Roberts	.10	.05
□ 734 Mark Portugal	.10	.05
□ 735 Terry Pendleton	.20	.09
□ 736 Dave Valle	.10	.05
□ 737 Paul Kilgus	.10	.05
□ 738 Greg A. Harris	.10	.05
□ 739 Jon Ratliff DP	.20	.09
□ 740 Kirk Presley DP	.20	.09
□ 741 Josue Estrada DP	.20	.09
□ 742 Wayne Gomes DP	.20	.09
□ 743 Pat Watkins DP	.20	.09
□ 744 Jamey Wright DP	.40	.18
□ 745 Jay Powell DP	.20	.09
□ 746 Ryan McGuire DP	.30	.14
□ 747 Marc Barcelo DP	.20	.09
□ 748 Sloan Smith DP	.20	.09
□ 749 John Wasdin DP	.30	.14
□ 750 Marc Vlades DP	.20	.09
□ 751 Dan Ehler DP	.20	.09
□ 752 Andre King DP	.20	.09
□ 753 Greg Keagle DP	.10	.05
□ 754 Jason Myers DP	.20	.09
□ 755 Dax Winslett DP	.20	.09
□ 756 Casey Whitten DP	.20	.09
□ 757 Tony Fuduric DP	.20	.09
□ 758 Greg Norton DP	.20	.09
□ 759 Jeff D'Amico DP	.40	.18
□ 760 Ryan Hancock DP	.20	.09
□ 761 David Cooper DP	.20	.09
□ 762 Kevin Orie DP	.75	.35
□ 763 John O'Donoghue	.10	.05
Mike Oquist		
□ 764 Cory Bailey	.10	.05
Scott Hatteberg		
□ 765 Mark Holzemer	.10	.05
Paul Swingle		
□ 766 James Baldwin	.30	.14
Rod Bolton		
□ 767 Jerry Di Poto	.20	.09
Julian Tavarez		
□ 768 Danny Bautista	.20	.09
Sean Bergman		
□ 769 Bob Hamelin	.10	.05
Joe Vitiello		
□ 770 Mark Kiefer	.20	.09
Troy O'Leary		
□ 771 Denny Hocking	.20	.09
Oscar Munoz		
□ 772 Russ Davis	.20	.09
Brien Taylor		
□ 773 Kyle Abbott	.20	.09
Miguel Jimenez		
□ 774 Kevin King	.10	.05
Eric Plantenberg		
□ 775 Jon Shave	.10	.05
Desi Wilson		
□ 776 Domingo Cedeno	.10	.05
Paul Spoljaric		
□ 777 Chipper Jones	2.50	1.10
Ryan Klesko		
□ 778 Steve Trachsel	.20	.09
Turk Wendell		
□ 779 Johnny Ruffin	.10	.05
Jerry Spradlin		
□ 780 Jason Bates	.20	.09
John Burke		
□ 781 Carl Everett	.20	.09
Dave Weathers		
□ 782 Gary Mota	.20	.09
James Mouton		
□ 783 Raul Mondesi	.30	.14
Ben Van Ryn		
□ 784 Gabe White	.30	.14
Rondell White		
□ 785 Brook Fordyce	.20	.09
Bill Pulsipher		
□ 786 Kevin Foster	.10	.05
Gene Schall		
□ 787 Rich Aude	.10	.05
Midre Cummings		
□ 788 Brian Barber	.20	.09
Rich Batchelor		
□ 789 Brian Johnson	.10	.05
Scott Sanders		
□ 790 Ricky Faneyte	.10	.05
J.R. Phillips		
□ 791 Checklist 3	.10	.05
□ 792 Checklist 4	.10	.05

1994 Topps Gold

The 1994 Topps Gold set is parallel to the basic issue. They were inserted one per wax or mini pack, two per mini jumbo, three per rack pack, four per jumbo, five per jumbo rack and ten per factory set. The only difference between the Gold issue and the basic cards is gold foil on the player's name and the Topps logo. As in previous Gold Sets, player cards replace the Checklist cards.

	MINT	NRMT
COMPLETE SET (792)	80.00	36.00
COMPLETE SERIES 1 (396)	40.00	18.00
COMPLETE SERIES 2 (396)	40.00	18.00

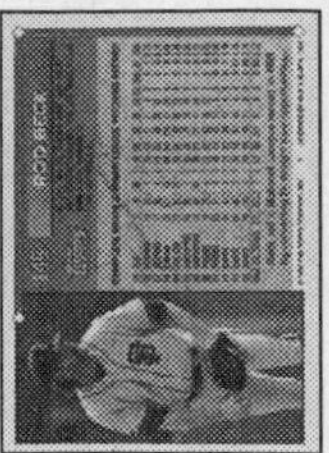

	MINT	NRMT
COMMON CARD (1-792)	.15	.07
SEMISTARS	.25	.11
*STARS: 2X to 4X BASIC CARDS		
*YOUNG STARS: 1.5X to 3X BASIC CARDS		

Card	MINT	NRMT
□ 395 Bill Brennan	.25	.11
Replaces Checklist 1		
□ 396 Jeff Bronkey	.25	.11
Replaces Checklist 2		
□ 791 Mike Cook	.25	.11
Replaces Checklist 3		
□ 792 Dan Pasqua	.25	.11
Replaces Checklist 4		

1994 Topps Spanish

Issued in complete factory set form only, these 792 standard-size cards parallel the regular Topps issue. These cards have the same front photos but are billingual. The factory set also contains the Topps Spanish Legends 10-card set. That set which is entitled "Topps Legends" features retired Latin players.

	MINT	NRMT
COMPLETE FACT.SET (802)	125.00	55.00
COMPLETE SET (792)	120.00	55.00
SPANISH LEGENDS SET (10)	5.00	2.20
COMMON CARD (1-792)	.20	.09
COMMON LEGENDS (L1-L10)	.25	.11
*STARS: 3X to 6X BASIC CARDS		
*YOUNG STARS: 2.5X to 5X BASIC CARDS		

Card	MINT	NRMT
□ L1 Felipe Alou	.60	.25
□ L2 Ruben Amaro	.25	.11
□ L3 Luis Aparicio	1.00	.45
□ L4 Rod Carew	1.00	.45
□ L5 Chico Carrasquel	.50	.23
□ L6 Orlando Cepeda	.75	.35
□ L7 Juan Marichal	1.00	.45
□ L8 Minnie Minoso	.75	.35
□ L9 Cookie Rojas	.25	.11
□ L10 Luis Tiant	.50	.23

1994 Topps Black Gold

Randomly inserted one in every 72 packs, this 44-card standard-size set was issued in two series of 22. Cards were also issued three per 1994 Topps factory set. Collectors had a chance, through redemption cards to receive all or part of the set. There are seven Winner redemption cards for a total 51 cards associated with this set. The set is considered complete with the 44 player cards. Card fronts feature color player action photos. The player's name at bottom and the team name at top are screened in gold foil. The backs contain a player photo and statistical rankings. The winner cards were redeemable until January 31, 1995

	MINT	NRMT
COMPLETE SET (44)	25.00	11.00
COMPLETE SERIES 1 (22)	15.00	6.75
COMPLETE SERIES 2 (22)	10.00	4.50
COMMON CARD (1-44)	.25	.11

☐ 1 Roberto Alomar	.75	.35
☐ 2 Carlos Baerga	.25	.11
☐ 3 Albert Belle	1.50	.70
☐ 4 Joe Carter	.40	.18
☐ 5 Cecil Fielder	.40	.18
☐ 6 Travis Fryman	.40	.18
☐ 7 Juan Gonzalez	2.00	.90
☐ 8 Ken Griffey Jr.	4.00	1.80
☐ 9 Chris Hoiles	.25	.11
☐ 10 Randy Johnson	.75	.35
☐ 11 Kenny Lofton	1.25	.55
☐ 12 Jack McDowell	.25	.11
☐ 13 Paul Molitor	.75	.35
☐ 14 Jeff Montgomery	.25	.11
☐ 15 John Olerud	.25	.11
☐ 16 Rafael Palmeiro	.40	.18
☐ 17 Kirby Puckett	1.50	.70
☐ 18 Cal Ripken	3.00	1.35
☐ 19 Tim Salmon	.75	.35
☐ 20 Mike Stanley	.25	.11
☐ 21 Frank Thomas	4.00	1.80
☐ 22 Robin Ventura	.40	.18
☐ 23 Jeff Bagwell	1.50	.70
☐ 24 Jay Bell	.25	.11
☐ 25 Craig Biggio	.40	.18
☐ 26 Jeff Blauser	.25	.11
☐ 27 Barry Bonds	1.00	.45
☐ 28 Darren Daulton	.40	.18
☐ 29 Len Dykstra	.40	.18
☐ 30 Andres Galarraga	.40	.18
☐ 31 Ron Gant	.40	.18
☐ 32 Tom Glavine	.40	.18
☐ 33 Mark Grace	.40	.18
☐ 34 Marquis Grissom	.40	.18
☐ 35 Gregg Jefferies	.25	.11
☐ 36 David Justice	.75	.35
☐ 37 John Kruk	.40	.18
☐ 38 Greg Maddux	2.50	1.10
☐ 39 Fred McGriff	.40	.18
☐ 40 Randy Myers	.25	.11
☐ 41 Mike Piazza	2.50	1.10
☐ 42 Sammy Sosa	.75	.35
☐ 43 Robby Thompson	.25	.11
☐ 44 Matt Williams	.75	.35
☐ A Winner A 1-11	1.00	.45
☐ B Winner B 12-22	1.00	.45
☐ C Winner C 23-33	1.00	.45
☐ D Winner D 34-44	1.00	.45
☐ AB Winner AB 1-22	2.00	.90
☐ CD Winner CD 23-44	2.00	.90
☐ ABCD Winner ABCD 1-44	4.00	1.80

1994 Topps Traded

his set consists of 132 standard-size cards featuring aded players in their new uniforms, rookies and draft hoices. Factory sets consisted of 140 cards including a et of eight Topps Finest cards. Card fronts feature a ayer photo with the player's name, team and position at e bottom. The horizontal backs have a player photo to e left with complete career statistics and highlights. The ards are numbered with a "T" suffix. Rookie Cards include rian Anderson, Rusty Greer, Ben Grieve, Paul Konerko, han Ho Park and Kevin Witt.

	MINT	NRMT
OMP.FACT.SET (140)	50.00	22.00
OMPLETE SET (132)	45.00	20.00
OMMON CARD (1T-132T)	.10	.05

☐ 1T Paul Wilson	.50	.23
☐ 2T Bill Taylor	.10	.05
☐ 3T Dan Wilson	.20	.09
☐ 4T Mark Smith	.10	.05
☐ 5T Toby Borland	.10	.05
☐ 6T Dave Clark	.10	.05
☐ 7T Denny Martinez	.20	.09
☐ 8T Dave Gallagher	.10	.05
☐ 9T Josias Manzanillo	.10	.05
☐ 10T Brian Anderson	.50	.23
☐ 11T Damon Berryhill	.10	.05
☐ 12T Alex Cole	.10	.05
☐ 13T Jacob Shumate	.20	.09
☐ 14T Oddibe McDowell	.10	.05
☐ 15T Willie Banks	.10	.05
☐ 16T Jerry Browne	.10	.05
☐ 17T Donnie Elliott	.10	.05
☐ 18T Ellis Burks	.20	.09
☐ 19T Chuck McElroy	.10	.05
☐ 20T Luis Polonia	.10	.05
☐ 21T Brian Harper	.10	.05
☐ 22T Mark Portugal	.10	.05
☐ 23T Dave Henderson	.10	.05
☐ 24T Mark Acre	.10	.05
☐ 25T Julio Franco	.20	.09
☐ 26T Darren Hall	.10	.05
☐ 27T Eric Anthony	.10	.05
☐ 28T Sid Fernandez	.10	.05
☐ 29T Rusty Greer	3.00	1.35
☐ 30T Riccardo Ingram	.10	.05
☐ 31T Gabe White	.10	.05
☐ 32T Tim Belcher	.10	.05
☐ 33T Terrence Long	1.00	.45
☐ 34T Mark Dalesandro	.10	.05
☐ 35T Mike Kelly	.10	.05
☐ 36T Jack Morris	.20	.09
☐ 37T Jeff Brantley	.10	.05
☐ 38T Larry Barnes	.20	.09
☐ 39T Brian R. Hunter	.10	.05
☐ 40T Otis Nixon	.10	.05
☐ 41T Bret Wagner	.20	.09
☐ 42T Pedro Martinez TR Delino Deshields	.30	.14
☐ 43T Heathcliff Slocumb	.20	.09
☐ 44T Ben Grieve	20.00	9.00
☐ 45T John Hudek	.10	.05
☐ 46T Shawon Dunston	.10	.05
☐ 47T Greg Colbrunn	.10	.05
☐ 48T Joey Hamilton	.30	.14
☐ 49T Marvin Freeman	.10	.05
☐ 50T Terry Mulholland	.10	.05
☐ 51T Keith Mitchell	.10	.05
☐ 52T Dwight Smith	.10	.05
☐ 53T Shawn Boskie	.10	.05
☐ 54T Kevin Witt	4.00	1.80
☐ 55T Ron Gant	.20	.09
☐ 56T 1994 Prospects Trenidad Hubbard Jason Schmidt Larry Sutton Stephen Larkin	.50	.23
☐ 57T Jody Reed	.10	.05
☐ 58T Rick Helling	.10	.05
☐ 59T John Powell	.20	.09
☐ 60T Eddie Murray	.40	.18
☐ 61T Joe Hall	.10	.05
☐ 62T Jorge Fabregas	.10	.05
☐ 63T Mike Mordecai	.10	.05
☐ 64T Ed Vosberg	.10	.05
☐ 65T Rickey Henderson	.30	.14
☐ 66T Tim Grieve	.10	.05
☐ 67T Jon Lieber	.10	.05
☐ 68T Chris Howard	.10	.05
☐ 69T Matt Walbeck	.10	.05
☐ 70T Chan Ho Park	3.00	1.35
☐ 71T Bryan Eversgerd	.10	.05
☐ 72T John Dettmer	.10	.05
☐ 73T Erik Hanson	.10	.05
☐ 74T Mike Thurman	.10	.05
☐ 75T Bobby Ayala	.10	.05
☐ 76T Rafael Palmeiro	.30	.14
☐ 77T Bret Boone	.20	.09
☐ 78T Paul Shuey	.10	.05
☐ 79T Kevin Foster	.10	.05
☐ 80T Dave Magadan	.10	.05
☐ 81T Bip Roberts	.10	.05
☐ 82T Howard Johnson	.10	.05
☐ 83T Xavier Hernandez	.10	.05
☐ 84T Ross Powell	.10	.05
☐ 85T Doug Million	.10	.05
☐ 86T Geronimo Berroa	.20	.09
☐ 87T Mark Farris	.20	.09
☐ 88T Butch Henry	.10	.05
☐ 89T Junior Felix	.10	.05
☐ 90T Bo Jackson	.20	.09
☐ 91T Hector Carrasco	.10	.05
☐ 92T Charlie O'Brien	.10	.05
☐ 93T Omar Vizquel	.20	.09
☐ 94T David Segui	.10	.05
☐ 95T Dustin Hermanson	.10	.05
☐ 96T Gar Finnvold	.10	.05
☐ 97T Dave Stevens	.10	.05
☐ 98T Corey Pointer	.20	.09
☐ 99T Felix Fermin	.10	.05
☐ 100T Lee Smith	.20	.09
☐ 101T Reid Ryan	.20	.09
☐ 102T Bobby Munoz	.10	.05
☐ 103T Deion Sanders TR Roberto Kelly	.30	.14
☐ 104T Turner Ward	.10	.05
☐ 105T W.VanLandingham	.10	.05
☐ 106T Vince Coleman	.10	.05
☐ 107T Stan Javier	.10	.05
☐ 108T Darrin Jackson	.10	.05
☐ 109T C.J. Nitkowski	.10	.05
☐ 110T Anthony Young	.10	.05
☐ 111T Kurt Miller	.10	.05
☐ 112T Paul Konerko	18.00	8.00
☐ 113T Walt Weiss	.10	.05
☐ 114T Daryl Boston	.10	.05
☐ 115T Will Clark	.30	.14
☐ 116T Matt Smith	.20	.09
☐ 117T Mark Leiter	.10	.05
☐ 118T Gregg Olson	.10	.05
☐ 119T Tony Pena	.10	.05
☐ 120T Jose Vizcaino	.10	.05
☐ 121T Rick White	.10	.05
☐ 122T Rich Rowland	.10	.05
☐ 123T Jeff Reboulet	.10	.05
☐ 124T Greg Hibbard	.10	.05
☐ 125T Chris Sabo	.10	.05
☐ 126T Doug Jones	.10	.05
☐ 127T Tony Fernandez	.10	.05
☐ 128T Carlos Reyes	.10	.05
☐ 129T Kevin Brown	.50	.23
☐ 130T Ryne Sandberg Farewell	1.00	.45
☐ 131T Ryne Sandberg Farewell	1.00	.45
☐ 132T Checklist 1-132	.10	.05

1994 Topps Traded Finest Inserts

Each Topps Traded factory set contained a complete 8-card set of Finest Inserts. These cards are numbered separately and designed differently the base cards. Each Finest Insert features a action shot of a player set against purple chrome background. The set highlights the top performers midway through the 1994 season, detailing their performances through July. The cards are numbered on back X of 8.

	MINT	NRMT
COMPLETE SET (8)	6.00	2.70
COMMON CARD (1-8)	.10	.05

☐ 1 Greg Maddux	1.25	.55
☐ 2 Mike Piazza	1.25	.55
☐ 3 Matt Williams	.10	.05
☐ 4 Raul Mondesi	.40	.18
☐ 5 Ken Griffey Jr.	2.00	.90
☐ 6 Kenny Lofton	.40	.18
☐ 7 Frank Thomas	1.50	.70
☐ 8 Manny Ramirez	.50	.23

1994 Topps Superstar Samplers

Sold only in retail outlets, each 1994 Topps Baker's Dozen factory set included a cello-wrapped 3-card sampler of a MLB player. Each player is represented by a Bowman, a Finest, and a Stadium Club card. These cards are identical to their regular issue counterparts except for a special "Topps Superstar Sampler" emblem on their backs. The prices listed below are for all three cards; the Finest card represents 50% of the value, while the Bowman or Stadium Club card are worth 25% each of the value. We have sequenced each player in alphabetical order.

	MINT	NRMT
COMPLETE SET (135)	1200.00	550.00
COMMON BAG (1-45)	6.00	2.70
☐ 1 Roberto Alomar	20.00	9.00
☐ 2 Carlos Baerga	10.00	4.50
☐ 3 Jeff Bagwell	60.00	27.00
☐ 4 Albert Belle	40.00	18.00
☐ 5 Barry Bonds	20.00	9.00
☐ 6 Bobby Bonilla	10.00	4.50
☐ 7 Jose Canseco	15.00	6.75
☐ 8 Joe Carter	10.00	4.50
☐ 9 Will Clark	15.00	6.75
☐ 10 Roger Clemens	40.00	18.00
☐ 11 Darren Daulton	10.00	4.50
☐ 12 Len Dykstra	10.00	4.50
☐ 13 Cecil Fielder	10.00	4.50
☐ 14 Cliff Floyd	6.00	2.70
☐ 15 Andres Galarraga	20.00	9.00
☐ 16 Tom Glavine	10.00	4.50
☐ 17 Juan Gonzalez	60.00	27.00
☐ 18 Mark Grace	15.00	6.75
☐ 19 Ken Griffey Jr.	120.00	55.00
☐ 20 Marquis Grissom	10.00	4.50
☐ 21 Tony Gwynn	60.00	27.00
☐ 22 Gregg Jefferies	6.00	2.70
☐ 23 Randy Johnson	20.00	9.00
☐ 24 David Justice	20.00	9.00
☐ 25 Barry Larkin	15.00	6.75
☐ 26 Greg Maddux	75.00	34.00
☐ 27 Don Mattingly	50.00	22.00
☐ 28 Jack McDowell	6.00	2.70
☐ 29 Fred McGriff	15.00	6.75
☐ 30 Paul Molitor	20.00	9.00
☐ 31 Raul Mondesi	20.00	9.00
☐ 32 John Olerud	6.00	2.70
☐ 33 Rafael Palmeiro	15.00	6.75
☐ 34 Mike Piazza	75.00	34.00
☐ 35 Kirby Puckett	50.00	22.00
☐ 36 Manny Ramirez	20.00	9.00
☐ 37 Cal Ripken	90.00	40.00
☐ 38 Tim Salmon	20.00	9.00
☐ 39 Ryne Sandberg	40.00	18.00
☐ 40 Gary Sheffield	20.00	9.00
☐ 41 Frank Thomas	100.00	45.00
☐ 42 Andy Van Slyke	6.00	2.70
☐ 43 Mo Vaughn	25.00	11.00
☐ 44 Larry Walker	20.00	9.00
☐ 45 Matt Williams	15.00	6.75

1995 Topps Pre-Production

Each 1994 Topps Baker's Dozen Factory set included a cello bag containing nine pre-production cards as well as one Spectralite version of one of those cards. The standard-size cards feature on their fronts color photos with ragged white borders and the player's name stamped in gold foil. The horizontal backs carry a color closeup photo, biography, major league batting or pitching record, and statistical highlights. The cards are easily distinguished from their regular issue counterparts not only by the "PP" number prefix but also by the words "Pre-Production Sample" printed across the 1994 stat line. The prices below are for the regular pre-production samples; the Spectralite versions are valued at 3X the values below.

	MINT	NRMT
COMPLETE SET (9)	9.00	4.00
COMMON CARD (PP1-PP9)	.25	.11
☐ PP1 Larry Walker	1.00	.45
☐ PP2 Mike Piazza	4.00	1.80
☐ PP3 Greg Vaughn	.25	.11
☐ PP4 Sandy Alomar	.50	.23
☐ PP5 Travis Fryman	.50	.23
☐ PP6 Ken Griffey Jr.	5.00	2.20
☐ PP7 Mike Devereaux	.25	.11
☐ PP8 Roberto Hernandez	.25	.11
☐ PP9 Alex Fernandez	.25	.11

1995 Topps

These 660 standard-size cards feature color action player photos with white borders on the fronts. This set was released in two series. The first series contained 396 cards while the second series had 264 cards. The player's name in gold-foil appears below the photo, with his position and team name underneath. The horizontal backs carry a color player close-up with a color player cut-out superimposed over it. Player biography, statistics and career highlights complete the backs. One "Own The Game" instant winner card has been inserted in every 120 packs. Rookie cards in this set include Karim Garcia and Rey Ordonez.

	MINT	NRMT
COMPLETE SET (660)	45.00	20.00
COMP.HOBBY SET (677)	60.00	27.00
COMP.RETAIL SET (677)	60.00	27.00
COMPLETE SERIES 1 (396)	25.00	11.00
COMPLETE SERIES 2 (264)	20.00	9.00
COMMON CARD (1-660)	.15	.07
☐ 1 Frank Thomas	2.50	1.10
☐ 2 Mickey Morandini	.15	.07
☐ 3 Babe Ruth 100th B-Day	2.00	.90
☐ 4 Scott Cooper	.15	.07
☐ 5 David Cone	.30	.14
☐ 6 Jacob Shumate	.30	.14
☐ 7 Trevor Hoffman	.30	.14
☐ 8 Shane Mack	.15	.07
☐ 9 Delino DeShields	.15	.07
☐ 10 Matt Williams	.40	.18
☐ 11 Sammy Sosa	.60	.25
☐ 12 Gary DiSarcina	.15	.07
☐ 13 Kenny Rogers	.15	.07
☐ 14 Jose Vizcaino	.15	.07
☐ 15 Lou Whitaker	.30	.14
☐ 16 Ron Darling	.15	.07
☐ 17 Dave Nilsson	.30	.14
☐ 18 Chris Hammond	.15	.07
☐ 19 Sid Bream	.15	.07
☐ 20 Denny Martinez	.30	.14
☐ 21 Orlando Merced	.15	.07
☐ 22 John Wetteland	.30	.14
☐ 23 Mike Devereaux	.15	.07
☐ 24 Rene Arocha	.15	.07
☐ 25 Jay Buhner	.40	.18
☐ 26 Darren Holmes	.15	.07
☐ 27 Hal Morris	.15	.07
☐ 28 Brian Buchanan	.30	.14
☐ 29 Keith Miller	.15	.07
☐ 30 Paul Molitor	.60	.25
☐ 31 Dave West	.15	.07
☐ 32 Tony Tarasco	.15	.07
☐ 33 Scott Sanders	.15	.07
☐ 34 Eddie Zambrano	.15	.07
☐ 35 Ricky Bones	.15	.07
☐ 36 John Valentin	.30	.14
☐ 37 Kevin Tapani	.15	.07
☐ 38 Tim Wallach	.15	.07
☐ 39 Darren Lewis	.15	.07
☐ 40 Travis Fryman	.30	.14
☐ 41 Mark Leiter	.15	.07
☐ 42 Jose Bautista	.15	.07
☐ 43 Pete Smith	.15	.07
☐ 44 Bret Barberie	.15	.07
☐ 45 Dennis Eckersley	.40	.18
☐ 46 Ken Hill	.15	.07
☐ 47 Chad Ogea	.15	.07
☐ 48 Pete Harnisch	.15	.07
☐ 49 James Baldwin	.30	.14
☐ 50 Mike Mussina	.40	.18
☐ 51 Al Martin	.30	.14
☐ 52 Mark Thompson	.30	.14
☐ 53 Matt Smith	.30	.14
☐ 54 Joey Hamilton	.30	.14
☐ 55 Edgar Martinez	.40	.18
☐ 56 John Smiley	.15	.07
☐ 57 Rey Sanchez	.15	.07
☐ 58 Mike Timlin	.15	.07
☐ 59 Ricky Bottalico	.30	.14
☐ 60 Jim Abbott	.15	.07
☐ 61 Mike Kelly	.15	.07
☐ 62 Brian Jordan	.30	.14
☐ 63 Ken Ryan	.15	.07
☐ 64 Matt Mieske	.30	.14
☐ 65 Rick Aguilera	.15	.07
☐ 66 Ismael Valdes	.30	.14
☐ 67 Royce Clayton	.15	.07
☐ 68 Junior Felix	.15	.07
☐ 69 Harold Reynolds	.15	.07
☐ 70 Juan Gonzalez	1.50	.70
☐ 71 Kelly Stinnett	.15	.07
☐ 72 Carlos Reyes	.15	.07
☐ 73 Dave Weathers	.15	.07
☐ 74 Mel Rojas	.15	.07
☐ 75 Doug Drabek	.15	.07
☐ 76 Charles Nagy	.30	.14
☐ 77 Tim Raines	.15	.07
☐ 78 Midre Cummings	.15	.07
☐ 79 First Base Prospects Gene Schall Scott Talanoa Harold Williams Ray Brown	.40	.18
☐ 80 Rafael Palmeiro	.40	.18
☐ 81 Charlie Hayes	.15	.07
☐ 82 Ray Lankford	.30	.14
☐ 83 Tim Davis	.15	.07
☐ 84 C.J. Nitkowski	.15	.07
☐ 85 Andy Ashby	.15	.07
☐ 86 Gerald Williams	.15	.07
☐ 87 Terry Shumpert	.15	.07
☐ 88 Heathcliff Slocumb	.15	.07
☐ 89 Domingo Cedeno	.15	.07
☐ 90 Mark Grace	.40	.18
☐ 91 Brad Woodall	.15	.07
☐ 92 Gar Finnvold	.15	.07
☐ 93 Jaime Navarro	.15	.07
☐ 94 Carlos Hernandez	.15	.07
☐ 95 Mark Langston	.15	.07
☐ 96 Chuck Carr	.15	.07
☐ 97 Mike Gardiner	.15	.07
☐ 98 Dave McCarty	.15	.07
☐ 99 Cris Carpenter	.15	.07
☐ 100 Barry Bonds	.75	.35
☐ 101 David Segui	.15	.07
☐ 102 Scott Brosius	.15	.07
☐ 103 Mariano Duncan	.15	.07
☐ 104 Kenny Lofton	.75	.35
☐ 105 Ken Caminiti	.60	.25
☐ 106 Darrin Jackson	.15	.07
☐ 107 Jim Poole	.15	.07
☐ 108 Wil Cordero	.15	.07
☐ 109 Danny Miceli	.15	.07
☐ 110 Walt Weiss	.15	.07
☐ 111 Tom Pagnozzi	.15	.07
☐ 112 Terrence Long	.60	.25
☐ 113 Bret Boone	.15	.07
☐ 114 Daryl Boston	.15	.07
☐ 115 Wally Joyner	.30	.14
☐ 116 Rob Butler	.15	.07
☐ 117 Rafael Belliard	.15	.07
☐ 118 Luis Lopez	.15	.07
☐ 119 Tony Fossas	.15	.07
☐ 120 Len Dykstra	.30	.14
☐ 121 Mike Morgan	.15	.07
☐ 122 Denny Hocking	.15	.07
☐ 123 Kevin Gross	.15	.07
☐ 124 Todd Benzinger	.15	.07
☐ 125 John Doherty	.15	.07
☐ 126 Eduardo Perez	.15	.07
☐ 127 Dan Smith	.15	.07
☐ 128 Joe Orsulak	.15	.07
☐ 129 Brent Gates	.15	.07
☐ 130 Jeff Conine	.30	.14
☐ 131 Doug Henry	.15	.07
☐ 132 Paul Sorrento	.15	.07
☐ 133 Mike Hampton	.30	.14
☐ 134 Tim Spehr	.15	.07
☐ 135 Julio Franco	.30	.14
☐ 136 Mike Dyer	.15	.07
☐ 137 Chris Sabo	.15	.07
☐ 138 Rheal Cormier	.15	.07
☐ 139 Paul Konerko	3.00	1.35

☐ 140 Dante Bichette	.40	.18
☐ 141 Chuck McElroy	.15	.07
☐ 142 Mike Stanley	.15	.07
☐ 143 Bob Hamelin	.15	.07
☐ 144 Tommy Greene	.15	.07
☐ 145 John Smoltz	.40	.18
☐ 146 Ed Sprague	.15	.07
☐ 147 Ray McDavid	.15	.07
☐ 148 Otis Nixon	.30	.14
☐ 149 Turk Wendell	.15	.07
☐ 150 Chris James	.15	.07
☐ 151 Derek Parks	.15	.07
☐ 152 Jose Offerman	.15	.07
☐ 153 Tony Clark	.75	.35
☐ 154 Chad Curtis	.15	.07
☐ 155 Mark Portugal	.15	.07
☐ 156 Bill Pulsipher	.30	.14
☐ 157 Troy Neel	.15	.07
☐ 158 Dave Winfield	.40	.18
☐ 159 Bill Wegman	.15	.07
☐ 160 Benito Santiago	.15	.07
☐ 161 Jose Mesa	.15	.07
☐ 162 Luis Gonzalez	.15	.07
☐ 163 Alex Fernandez	.30	.14
☐ 164 Freddie Benavides	.15	.07
☐ 165 Ben McDonald	.15	.07
☐ 166 Blas Minor	.15	.07
☐ 167 Bret Wagner	.30	.14
☐ 168 Mac Suzuki	.60	.25
☐ 169 Roberto Mejia	.15	.07
☐ 170 Wade Boggs	.40	.18
☐ 171 Calvin Reese	.15	.07
☐ 172 Hipolito Pichardo	.15	.07
☐ 173 Kim Batiste	.15	.07
☐ 174 Darren Hall	.15	.07
☐ 175 Tom Glavine	.40	.18
☐ 176 Phil Plantier	.15	.07
☐ 177 Chris Howard	.15	.07
☐ 178 Karl Rhodes	.15	.07
☐ 179 LaTroy Hawkins	.15	.07
☐ 180 Raul Mondesi	.40	.18
☐ 181 Jeff Reed	.15	.07
☐ 182 Milt Cuyler	.15	.07
☐ 183 Jim Edmonds	.60	.25
☐ 184 Hector Fajardo	.15	.07
☐ 185 Jeff Kent	.15	.07
☐ 186 Wilson Alvarez	.30	.14
☐ 187 Geronimo Berroa	.15	.07
☐ 188 Billy Spiers	.15	.07
☐ 189 Derek Lilliquist	.15	.07
☐ 190 Craig Biggio	.40	.18
☐ 191 Roberto Hernandez	.15	.07
☐ 192 Bob Natal	.15	.07
☐ 193 Bobby Ayala	.15	.07
☐ 194 Travis Miller	.30	.14
☐ 195 Bob Tewksbury	.15	.07
☐ 196 Rondell White	.40	.18
☐ 197 Steve Cooke	.15	.07
☐ 198 Jeff Branson	.15	.07
☐ 199 Derek Jeter	2.00	.90
☐ 200 Tim Salmon	.60	.25
☐ 201 Steve Frey	.15	.07
☐ 202 Kent Mercker	.15	.07
☐ 203 Randy Johnson	.60	.25
☐ 204 Todd Worrell	.15	.07
☐ 205 Mo Vaughn	.75	.35
☐ 206 Howard Johnson	.15	.07
☐ 207 John Wasdin	.30	.14
☐ 208 Eddie Williams	.15	.07
☐ 209 Tim Belcher	.15	.07
☐ 210 Jeff Montgomery	.30	.14
☐ 211 Kirt Manwaring	.15	.07
☐ 212 Ben Grieve	3.00	1.35
☐ 213 Pat Hentgen	.30	.14
☐ 214 Shawon Dunston	.15	.07
☐ 215 Mike Greenwell	.15	.07
☐ 216 Alex Diaz	.15	.07
☐ 217 Pat Mahomes	.15	.07
☐ 218 Dave Hansen	.15	.07
☐ 219 Kevin Rogers	.15	.07
☐ 220 Cecil Fielder	.30	.14
☐ 221 Andrew Lorraine	.15	.07
☐ 222 Jack Armstrong	.15	.07
☐ 223 Todd Hundley	.30	.14
☐ 224 Mark Acre	.15	.07
☐ 225 Darrell Whitmore	.15	.07
☐ 226 Randy Milligan	.15	.07
☐ 227 Wayne Kirby	.15	.07
☐ 228 Darryl Kile	.30	.14
☐ 229 Bob Zupcic	.15	.07
☐ 230 Jay Bell	.30	.14
☐ 231 Dustin Hermanson	.30	.14
☐ 232 Harold Baines	.30	.14
☐ 233 Alan Benes	.40	.18
☐ 234 Felix Fermin	.15	.07
☐ 235 Ellis Burks	.30	.14
☐ 236 Jeff Brantley	.15	.07
☐ 237 Outfield Prospects	1.50	.70
Brian Hunter		
Jose Malave		
Karim Garcia		
Shane Pullen		
☐ 238 Matt Nokes	.15	.07
☐ 239 Ben Rivera	.15	.07
☐ 240 Joe Carter	.40	.18
☐ 241 Jeff Granger	.15	.07
☐ 242 Terry Pendelton	.30	.14
☐ 243 Melvin Nieves	.30	.14
☐ 244 Frankie Rodriguez	.30	.14
☐ 245 Darryl Hamilton	.15	.07
☐ 246 Brooks Kieschnick	.30	.14
☐ 247 Todd Hollandsworth	.30	.14
☐ 248 Joe Rosselli	.15	.07
☐ 249 Bill Gullickson	.15	.07
☐ 250 Chuck Knoblauch	.60	.25
☐ 251 Kurt Miller	.15	.07
☐ 252 Bobby Jones	.30	.14
☐ 253 Lance Blankenship	.15	.07
☐ 254 Matt Whiteside	.15	.07
☐ 255 Darrin Fletcher	.15	.07
☐ 256 Eric Plunk	.15	.07
☐ 257 Shane Reynolds	.15	.07
☐ 258 Norberto Martin	.15	.07
☐ 259 Mike Thurman	.15	.07
☐ 260 Andy Van Slyke	.30	.14
☐ 261 Dwight Smith	.15	.07
☐ 262 Allen Watson	.15	.07
☐ 263 Dan Wilson	.30	.14
☐ 264 Brent Mayne	.15	.07
☐ 265 Bip Roberts	.15	.07
☐ 266 Sterling Hitchcock	.30	.14
☐ 267 Alex Gonzalez	.30	.14
☐ 268 Greg Harris	.15	.07
☐ 269 Ricky Jordan	.15	.07
☐ 270 Johnny Ruffin	.15	.07
☐ 271 Mike Stanton	.15	.07
☐ 272 Rich Rowland	.15	.07
☐ 273 Steve Trachsel	.15	.07
☐ 274 Pedro Munoz	.15	.07
☐ 275 Ramon Martinez	.30	.14
☐ 276 Dave Henderson	.15	.07
☐ 277 Chris Gomez	.15	.07
☐ 278 Joe Grahe	.15	.07
☐ 279 Rusty Greer	.60	.25
☐ 280 John Franco	.15	.07
☐ 281 Mike Bordick	.15	.07
☐ 282 Jeff D'Amico	.60	.25
☐ 283 Dave Magadan	.15	.07
☐ 284 Tony Pena	.15	.07
☐ 285 Greg Swindell	.15	.07
☐ 286 Doug Million	.15	.07
☐ 287 Gabe White	.15	.07
☐ 288 Trey Beamon	.30	.14
☐ 289 Arthur Rhodes	.15	.07
☐ 290 Juan Guzman	.15	.07
☐ 291 Jose Oquendo	.15	.07
☐ 292 Willie Blair	.15	.07
☐ 293 Eddie Taubensee	.15	.07
☐ 294 Steve Howe	.15	.07
☐ 295 Greg Maddux	2.00	.90
☐ 296 Mike Macfarlane	.15	.07
☐ 297 Curt Schilling	.15	.07
☐ 298 Phil Clark	.15	.07
☐ 299 Woody Williams	.15	.07
☐ 300 Jose Canseco	.40	.18
☐ 301 Aaron Sele	.15	.07
☐ 302 Carl Willis	.15	.07
☐ 303 Steve Buechele	.15	.07
☐ 304 Dave Burba	.15	.07
☐ 305 Orel Hershiser	.30	.14
☐ 306 Damion Easley	.15	.07
☐ 307 Mike Henneman	.15	.07
☐ 308 Josias Manzanillo	.15	.07
☐ 309 Kevin Seitzer	.15	.07
☐ 310 Ruben Sierra	.15	.07
☐ 311 Bryan Harvey	.15	.07
☐ 312 Jim Thome	.60	.25
☐ 313 Ramon Castro	.30	.14
☐ 314 Lance Johnson	.15	.07
☐ 315 Marquis Grissom	.30	.14
☐ 316 Starting Pitcher	.40	.18
Prospects		
Terrell Wade		
Juan Acevedo		
Matt Arrandale		
Eddie Priest		
☐ 317 Paul Wagner	.15	.07
☐ 318 Jamie Moyer	.15	.07
☐ 319 Todd Zeile	.15	.07
☐ 320 Chris Bosio	.15	.07
☐ 321 Steve Reed	.15	.07
☐ 322 Erik Hanson	.15	.07
☐ 323 Luis Polonia	.15	.07
☐ 324 Ryan Klesko	.40	.18
☐ 325 Kevin Appier	.30	.14
☐ 326 Jim Eisenreich	.30	.14
☐ 327 Randy Knorr	.15	.07
☐ 328 Craig Shipley	.15	.07
☐ 329 Tim Naehring	.15	.07
☐ 330 Randy Myers	.15	.07
☐ 331 Alex Cole	.15	.07
☐ 332 Jim Gott	.15	.07
☐ 333 Mike Jackson	.15	.07
☐ 334 John Flaherty	.15	.07
☐ 335 Chili Davis	.30	.14
☐ 336 Benji Gil	.15	.07
☐ 337 Jason Jacome	.15	.07
☐ 338 Stan Javier	.15	.07
☐ 339 Mike Fetters	.15	.07
☐ 340 Rich Renteria	.15	.07
☐ 341 Kevin Witt	.75	.35
☐ 342 Scott Servais	.15	.07
☐ 343 Craig Grebeck	.15	.07
☐ 344 Kirk Rueter	.15	.07
☐ 345 Don Slaught	.15	.07
☐ 346 Armando Benitez	.15	.07
☐ 347 Ozzie Smith	.75	.35
☐ 348 Mike Blowers	.15	.07
☐ 349 Armando Reynoso	.15	.07
☐ 350 Barry Larkin	.40	.18
☐ 351 Mike Williams	.15	.07
☐ 352 Scott Kamieniecki	.15	.07
☐ 353 Gary Gaetti	.30	.14
☐ 354 Todd Stottlemyre	.15	.07
☐ 355 Fred McGriff	.40	.18
☐ 356 Tim Mauser	.15	.07
☐ 357 Chris Gwynn	.15	.07
☐ 358 Frank Castillo	.15	.07
☐ 359 Jeff Reboulet	.15	.07
☐ 360 Roger Clemens	1.25	.55
☐ 361 Mark Carreon	.15	.07
☐ 362 Chad Kreuter	.15	.07
☐ 363 Mark Farris	.30	.14
☐ 364 Bob Welch	.15	.07
☐ 365 Dean Palmer	.15	.07
☐ 366 Jeromy Burnitz	.30	.14
☐ 367 B.J. Surhoff	.30	.14
☐ 368 Mike Butcher	.15	.07
☐ 369 Relief Pitcher	.30	.14
Prospects		
Brad Clontz		
Steve Phoenix		
Scott Gentile		
Bucky Buckles		
☐ 370 Eddie Murray	.60	.25
☐ 371 Orlando Miller	.15	.07
☐ 372 Ron Karkovice	.15	.07
☐ 373 Richie Lewis	.15	.07
☐ 374 Lenny Webster	.15	.07
☐ 375 Jeff Tackett	.15	.07
☐ 376 Tom Urbani	.15	.07
☐ 377 Tino Martinez	.60	.25
☐ 378 Mark Dewey	.15	.07
☐ 379 Charles O'Brien	.15	.07
☐ 380 Terry Mulholland	.15	.07
☐ 381 Thomas Howard	.15	.07
☐ 382 Chris Haney	.15	.07
☐ 383 Billy Hatcher	.15	.07
☐ 384 Jeff Bagwell AS	.60	.25
Frank Thomas AS		
☐ 385 Bret Boone AS	.15	.07
Carlos Baerga AS		
☐ 386 Matt Williams AS	.40	.18
Wade Boggs AS		
☐ 387 Wil Cordero AS	.60	.25
Cal Ripken AS		
☐ 388 Barry Bonds AS	.75	.35
Ken Griffey AS		
☐ 389 Tony Gwynn AS	.50	.23
Albert Belle AS		
☐ 390 Dante Bichette AS	.40	.18
Kirby Puckett AS		
☐ 391 Mike Piazza AS	.60	.25
Mike Stanley AS		
☐ 392 Greg Maddux AS	.60	.25
David Cone AS		
☐ 393 Danny Jackson AS	.15	.07
Jimmy Key AS		
☐ 394 John Franco AS	.15	.07
Lee Smith AS		
☐ 395 Checklist 1-198	.15	.07
☐ 396 Checklist 199-396	.15	.07
☐ 397 Ken Griffey Jr.	3.00	1.35
☐ 398 Rick Heiserman	.30	.14
☐ 399 Don Mattingly	1.00	.45
☐ 400 Henry Rodriguez	.15	.07
☐ 401 Lenny Harris	.15	.07
☐ 402 Ryan Thompson	.15	.07
☐ 403 Darren Oliver	.30	.14
☐ 404 Omar Vizquel	.30	.14
☐ 405 Jeff Bagwell	1.25	.55

- ☐ 406 Doug Webb .15 .07
- ☐ 407 Todd Van Poppel .15 .07
- ☐ 408 Leo Gomez .15 .07
- ☐ 409 Mark Whiten .15 .07
- ☐ 410 Pedro Martinez .60 .25
- ☐ 411 Reggie Sanders .15 .07
- ☐ 412 Kevin Foster .15 .07
- ☐ 413 Danny Tartabull .15 .07
- ☐ 414 Jeff Blauser .15 .07
- ☐ 415 Mike Magnante .15 .07
- ☐ 416 Tom Candiotti .15 .07
- ☐ 417 Rod Beck .15 .07
- ☐ 418 Jody Reed .15 .07
- ☐ 419 Vince Coleman .15 .07
- ☐ 420 Danny Jackson .15 .07
- ☐ 421 Ryan Nye .30 .14
- ☐ 422 Larry Walker .60 .25
- ☐ 423 Russ Johnson DP .30 .14
- ☐ 424 Pat Borders .15 .07
- ☐ 425 Lee Smith .30 .14
- ☐ 426 Paul O'Neill .30 .14
- ☐ 427 Devon White .15 .07
- ☐ 428 Jim Bullinger .15 .07
- ☐ 429 Starting Pitchers Prospects .30 .14
  - Greg Hansell
  - Brian Sackinsky
  - Carey Paige
  - Rob Welch
- ☐ 430 Steve Avery .15 .07
- ☐ 431 Tony Gwynn 1.50 .70
- ☐ 432 Pat Meares .15 .07
- ☐ 433 Bill Swift .15 .07
- ☐ 434 David Wells .15 .07
- ☐ 435 John Briscoe .15 .07
- ☐ 436 Roger Pavlik .15 .07
- ☐ 437 Jayson Peterson .30 .14
- ☐ 438 Roberto Alomar .60 .25
- ☐ 439 Billy Brewer .15 .07
- ☐ 440 Gary Sheffield .60 .25
- ☐ 441 Lou Frazier .15 .07
- ☐ 442 Terry Steinbach .30 .14
- ☐ 443 Jay Payton .40 .18
- ☐ 444 Jason Bere .15 .07
- ☐ 445 Denny Neagle .30 .14
- ☐ 446 Andres Galarraga .40 .18
- ☐ 447 Hector Carrasco .15 .07
- ☐ 448 Bill Risley .15 .07
- ☐ 449 Andy Benes .15 .07
- ☐ 450 Jim Leyritz .15 .07
- ☐ 451 Jose Oliva .15 .07
- ☐ 452 Greg Vaughn .15 .07
- ☐ 453 Rich Monteleone .15 .07
- ☐ 454 Tony Eusebio .15 .07
- ☐ 455 Chuck Finley .30 .14
- ☐ 456 Kevin Brown .30 .14
- ☐ 457 Joe Boever .15 .07
- ☐ 458 Bobby Munoz .15 .07
- ☐ 459 Bret Saberhagen .15 .07
- ☐ 460 Kurt Abbott .15 .07
- ☐ 461 Bobby Witt .15 .07
- ☐ 462 Cliff Floyd .30 .14
- ☐ 463 Mark Clark .15 .07
- ☐ 464 Andujar Cedeno .15 .07
- ☐ 465 Marvin Freeman .15 .07
- ☐ 466 Mike Piazza 2.00 .90
- ☐ 467 Willie Greene .15 .07
- ☐ 468 Pat Kelly .15 .07
- ☐ 469 Carlos Delgado .30 .14
- ☐ 470 Willie Banks .15 .07
- ☐ 471 Matt Walbeck .15 .07
- ☐ 472 Mark McGwire 1.25 .55
- ☐ 473 McKay Christensen .30 .14
- ☐ 474 Alan Trammell .40 .18
- ☐ 475 Tom Gordon .15 .07
- ☐ 476 Greg Colbrunn .15 .07
- ☐ 477 Darren Daulton .30 .14
- ☐ 478 Albie Lopez .15 .07
- ☐ 479 Robin Ventura .30 .14
- ☐ 480 Catcher Prospects .30 .14
  - Eddie Perez
  - Jason Kendall
  - Einar Diaz
  - Bret Hemphill
- ☐ 481 Bryan Eversgerd .15 .07
- ☐ 482 Dave Fleming .15 .07
- ☐ 483 Scott Livingstone .15 .07
- ☐ 484 Pete Schourek .15 .07
- ☐ 485 Bernie Williams .60 .25
- ☐ 486 Mark Lemke .15 .07
- ☐ 487 Eric Karros .30 .14
- ☐ 488 Scott Ruffcorn .15 .07
- ☐ 489 Billy Ashley .15 .07
- ☐ 490 Rico Brogna .15 .07
- ☐ 491 John Burkett .15 .07
- ☐ 492 Cade Gaspar .30 .14
- ☐ 493 Jorge Fabregas .15 .07
- ☐ 494 Greg Gagne .15 .07
- ☐ 495 Doug Jones .15 .07
- ☐ 496 Troy O'Leary .15 .07
- ☐ 497 Pat Rapp .15 .07
- ☐ 498 Butch Henry .15 .07
- ☐ 499 John Olerud .30 .14
- ☐ 500 John Hudek .15 .07
- ☐ 501 Jeff King .30 .14
- ☐ 502 Bobby Bonilla .30 .14
- ☐ 503 Albert Belle .75 .35
- ☐ 504 Rick Wilkins .15 .07
- ☐ 505 John Jaha .15 .07
- ☐ 506 Nigel Wilson .15 .07
- ☐ 507 Sid Fernandez .15 .07
- ☐ 508 Deion Sanders .60 .25
- ☐ 509 Gil Heredia .15 .07
- ☐ 510 Scott Elarton .75 .35
- ☐ 511 Melido Perez .15 .07
- ☐ 512 Greg McMichael .15 .07
- ☐ 513 Rusty Meacham .15 .07
- ☐ 514 Shawn Green .30 .14
- ☐ 515 Carlos Garcia .15 .07
- ☐ 516 Dave Stevens .15 .07
- ☐ 517 Eric Young .30 .14
- ☐ 518 Omar Daal .15 .07
- ☐ 519 Kirk Gibson .30 .14
- ☐ 520 Spike Owen .15 .07
- ☐ 521 Jacob Cruz 1.00 .45
- ☐ 522 Sandy Alomar Jr. .15 .07
- ☐ 523 Steve Bedrosian .15 .07
- ☐ 524 Ricky Gutierrez .15 .07
- ☐ 525 Dave Veres .15 .07
- ☐ 526 Gregg Jefferies .30 .14
- ☐ 527 Jose Valentin .30 .14
- ☐ 528 Robb Nen .15 .07
- ☐ 529 Jose Rijo .15 .07
- ☐ 530 Sean Berry .15 .07
- ☐ 531 Mike Gallego .15 .07
- ☐ 532 Roberto Kelly .15 .07
- ☐ 533 Kevin Stocker .15 .07
- ☐ 534 Kirby Puckett 1.25 .55
- ☐ 535 Chipper Jones 2.00 .90
- ☐ 536 Russ Davis .15 .07
- ☐ 537 Jon Lieber .15 .07
- ☐ 538 Trey Moore .30 .14
- ☐ 539 Joe Girardi .15 .07
- ☐ 540 Second Base Prospects .40 .18
  - Quilvio Veras
  - Arquimedez Pozo
  - Miguel Cairo
  - Jason Camilli
- ☐ 541 Tony Phillips .15 .07
- ☐ 542 Brian Anderson .15 .07
- ☐ 543 Ivan Rodriguez .75 .35
- ☐ 544 Jeff Cirillo .30 .14
- ☐ 545 Joey Cora .30 .14
- ☐ 546 Chris Hoiles .15 .07
- ☐ 547 Bernard Gilkey .30 .14
- ☐ 548 Mike Lansing .15 .07
- ☐ 549 Jimmy Key .30 .14
- ☐ 550 Mark Wohlers .30 .14
- ☐ 551 Chris Clemons .40 .18
- ☐ 552 Vinny Castilla .40 .18
- ☐ 553 Mark Guthrie .15 .07
- ☐ 554 Mike Lieberthal .15 .07
- ☐ 555 Tommy Davis .30 .14
- ☐ 556 Robby Thompson .15 .07
- ☐ 557 Danny Bautista .15 .07
- ☐ 558 Will Clark .40 .18
- ☐ 559 Rickey Henderson .40 .18
- ☐ 560 Todd Jones .15 .07
- ☐ 561 Jack McDowell .15 .07
- ☐ 562 Carlos Rodriguez .15 .07
- ☐ 563 Mark Eichhorn .15 .07
- ☐ 564 Jeff Nelson .15 .07
- ☐ 565 Eric Anthony .15 .07
- ☐ 566 Randy Velarde .15 .07
- ☐ 567 Javier Lopez .40 .18
- ☐ 568 Kevin Mitchell .30 .14
- ☐ 569 Steve Karsay .15 .07
- ☐ 570 Brian Meadows .30 .14
- ☐ 571 Rey Ordonez .60 .25
  - Mike Metcalfe
  - Kevin Orie
  - Ray Holbert
- ☐ 572 John Kruk .30 .14
- ☐ 573 Scott Leius .15 .07
- ☐ 574 John Patterson .15 .07
- ☐ 575 Kevin Brown .30 .14
- ☐ 576 Mike Moore .15 .07
- ☐ 577 Manny Ramirez .60 .25
- ☐ 578 Jose Lind .15 .07
- ☐ 579 Derrick May .15 .07
- ☐ 580 Cal Eldred .15 .07
- ☐ 581 Third Base Prospects .30 .14
  - David Bell
  - Joel Chelmis
  - Lino Diaz
  - Aaron Boone
- ☐ 582 J.T. Snow .30 .14
- ☐ 583 Luis Sojo .15 .07
- ☐ 584 Moises Alou .30 .14
- ☐ 585 Dave Clark .15 .07
- ☐ 586 Dave Hollins .15 .07
- ☐ 587 Nomar Garciaparra 4.00 1.80
- ☐ 588 Cal Ripken 2.50 1.10
- ☐ 589 Pedro Astacio .15 .07
- ☐ 590 J.R. Phillips .15 .07
- ☐ 591 Jeff Frye .15 .07
- ☐ 592 Bo Jackson .30 .14
- ☐ 593 Steve Ontiveros .15 .07
- ☐ 594 David Nied .15 .07
- ☐ 595 Brad Ausmus .15 .07
- ☐ 596 Carlos Baerga .30 .14
- ☐ 597 James Mouton .15 .07
- ☐ 598 Ozzie Guillen .15 .07
- ☐ 599 Outfield Prospects .60 .25
  - Ozzie Timmons
  - Curtis Goodwin
  - Johnny Damon
  - Jeff Abbott
- ☐ 600 Yorkis Perez .15 .07
- ☐ 601 Rich Rodriguez .15 .07
- ☐ 602 Mark McLemore .15 .07
- ☐ 603 Jeff Fassero .15 .07
- ☐ 604 John Roper .15 .07
- ☐ 605 Mark Johnson .30 .14
- ☐ 606 Wes Chamberlain .15 .07
- ☐ 607 Felix Jose .15 .07
- ☐ 608 Tony Longmire .15 .07
- ☐ 609 Duane Ward .15 .07
- ☐ 610 Brett Butler .30 .14
- ☐ 611 William VanLandingham .15 .07
- ☐ 612 Mickey Tettleton .15 .07
- ☐ 613 Brady Anderson .40 .18
- ☐ 614 Reggie Jefferson .30 .14
- ☐ 615 Mike Kingery .15 .07
- ☐ 616 Derek Bell .30 .14
- ☐ 617 Scott Erickson .15 .07
- ☐ 618 Bob Wickman .15 .07
- ☐ 619 Phil Leftwich .15 .07
- ☐ 620 David Justice .60 .25
- ☐ 621 Paul Wilson .30 .14
- ☐ 622 Pedro Martinez .60 .25
- ☐ 623 Terry Mathews .15 .07
- ☐ 624 Brian McRae .30 .14
- ☐ 625 Bruce Ruffin .15 .07
- ☐ 626 Steve Finley .30 .14
- ☐ 627 Ron Gant .30 .14
- ☐ 628 Rafael Bournigal .15 .07
- ☐ 629 Darryl Strawberry .30 .14
- ☐ 630 Luis Alicea .15 .07
- ☐ 631 Orioles Prospects .30 .14
  - Mark Smith
  - Scott Klingenbeck
- ☐ 632 Red Sox Prospects .30 .14
  - Cory Bailey
  - Scott Hatteberg
- ☐ 633 Angels Prospects .60 .25
  - Todd Greene
  - Troy Percival
- ☐ 634 White Sox Prospects .15 .07
  - Rod Bolton
  - Olmedo Saenz
- ☐ 635 Indians Prospects .30 .14
  - Steve Kline
  - Herb Perry
- ☐ 636 Tigers Prospects .30 .14
  - Sean Bergman
  - Shannon Penn
- ☐ 637 Royals Prospects .30 .14
  - Joe Randa
  - Joe Vitiello
- ☐ 638 Brewers Prospects .30 .14
  - Jose Mercedes
  - Duane Singleton
- ☐ 639 Twins Prospects .60 .25
  - Marc Barcelo
  - Marty Cordova
- ☐ 640 Yankees Prospects 1.25 .55
  - Andy Pettitte
  - Ruben Rivera
- ☐ 641 Athletics Prospects .30 .14
  - Willie Adams
  - Scott Spiezio
- ☐ 642 Mariners Prospects .30 .14
  - Eddy Diaz
  - Desi Relaford
- ☐ 643 Rangers Prospects .15 .07
  - Terrell Lowery
  - Jon Shave
- ☐ 644 Blue Jays Prospects .30 .14
  - Angel Martinez
  - Paul Spoljaric
- ☐ 645 Braves Prospects .60 .25

Tony Graffanino		
Damon Hollins		
☐ 646 Cubs Prospects	.30	.14
Darron Cox		
Doug Glanville		
☐ 647 Reds Prospects	.30	.14
Tim Belk		
Pat Watkins		
☐ 648 Rockies Propsects	.15	.07
Rod Pedraza		
Phil Schneider		
☐ 649 Marlins Prospects	.30	.14
Vic Darensbourg		
Marc Valdes		
☐ 650 Astros Prospects	.30	.14
Rick Huisman		
Roberto Petagine		
☐ 651 Dodgers Prospects	.60	.25
Roger Cedeno		
Ron Coomer		
☐ 652 Expos Prospects	.30	.14
Shane Andrews		
Carlos Perez		
☐ 653 Mets Prospects	.30	.14
Jason Isringhausen		
Chris Roberts		
☐ 654 Phillies Prospects	.30	.14
Wayne Gomes		
Kevin Jordan		
☐ 655 Pirates Prospects	.30	.14
Esteban Loiaza		
Steve Pegues		
☐ 656 Cardinals Prospects	.30	.14
Terry Bradshaw		
John Frascatore		
☐ 657 Padres Prospects	.30	.14
Andres Berumen		
Bryce Florie		
☐ 658 Giants Prospects	.30	.14
Dan Carlson		
Keith Williams		
☐ 659 Checklist	.15	.07
☐ 660 Checklist	.15	.07

1995 Topps Cyberstats

The 396-card Cyberstats insert set was issued one per pack and three per jumbo pack. Each 1995 Topps series had 198 Cyberstat cards. The idea was to present prorated statistics for the 1994 strike shortened season. The photos on front are the same as the basic issue. The difference is that the photo is given a glossy or metallic finish. The backs contain yearly and career statistics, including the prorated 1994 numbers.

	MINT	NRMT
COMPLETE SET (396)	80.00	36.00
COMPLETE SERIES 1 (198)	40.00	18.00
COMPLETE SERIES 2 (198)	40.00	18.00
COMMON CARD (1-396)	.25	.11

☐ 1 Frank Thomas	6.00	2.70
☐ 2 Mickey Morandini	.25	.11
☐ 3 Todd Worrell	.50	.23
☐ 4 David Cone	.50	.23
☐ 5 Trevor Hoffman	.50	.23
☐ 6 Shane Mack	.25	.11
☐ 7 Delino DeShields	.25	.11
☐ 8 Matt Williams	1.00	.45
☐ 9 Sammy Sosa	1.50	.70
☐ 10 Gary DiSarcina	.25	.11
☐ 11 Kenny Rogers	.25	.11
☐ 12 Jose Vizcaino	.25	.11
☐ 13 Lou Whitaker	.50	.23
☐ 14 Ron Darling	.25	.11
☐ 15 Dave Nilsson	.25	.11
☐ 16 Denny Martinez	.50	.23
☐ 17 Orlando Merced	.25	.11
☐ 18 John Wetteland	.50	.23
☐ 19 Mike Devereaux	.25	.11
☐ 20 Rene Arocha	.25	.11
☐ 21 Jay Buhner	1.00	.45
☐ 22 Hal Morris	.25	.11
☐ 23 Paul Molitor	1.50	.70
☐ 24 Dave West	.25	.11
☐ 25 Scott Sanders	.25	.11
☐ 26 Eddie Zambrano	.25	.11
☐ 27 Ricky Bones	.25	.11
☐ 28 John Valentin	.25	.11
☐ 29 Kevin Tapani	.25	.11
☐ 30 Tim Wallach	.25	.11
☐ 31 Darren Lewis	.25	.11
☐ 32 Travis Fryman	.50	.23
☐ 33 Bret Barberie	.25	.11
☐ 34 Dennis Eckersley	1.00	.45
☐ 35 Ken Hill	.25	.11
☐ 36 Pete Harnisch	.25	.11
☐ 37 Mike Mussina	1.50	.70
☐ 38 Dave Winfield	1.50	.70
☐ 39 Joey Hamilton	.50	.23
☐ 40 Edgar Martinez	1.00	.45
☐ 41 John Smiley	.25	.11
☐ 42 Jim Abbott	.25	.11
☐ 43 Mike Kelly	.25	.11
☐ 44 Brian Jordan	.50	.23
☐ 45 Ken Ryan	.25	.11
☐ 46 Matt Mieske	.25	.11
☐ 47 Rick Aguilera	.25	.11
☐ 48 Ismael Valdes	.50	.23
☐ 49 Royce Clayton	.25	.11
☐ 50 Juan Gonzalez	4.00	1.80
☐ 51 Mel Rojas	.25	.11
☐ 52 Doug Drabek	.25	.11
☐ 53 Charles Nagy	.50	.23
☐ 54 Tim Raines	.50	.23
☐ 55 Midre Cummings	.25	.11
☐ 56 Rafael Palmeiro	1.00	.45
☐ 57 Charlie Hayes	.25	.11
☐ 58 Ray Lankford	.50	.23
☐ 59 Tim Davis	.25	.11
☐ 60 Andy Ashby	.25	.11
☐ 61 Mark Grace	1.00	.45
☐ 62 Mark Langston	.25	.11
☐ 63 Chuck Carr	.25	.11
☐ 64 Barry Bonds	1.75	.80
☐ 65 David Segui	.25	.11
☐ 66 Mariano Duncan	.25	.11
☐ 67 Kenny Lofton	1.75	.80
☐ 68 Ken Caminiti	1.50	.70
☐ 69 Darrin Jackson	.25	.11
☐ 70 Wil Cordero	.25	.11
☐ 71 Walt Weiss	.25	.11
☐ 72 Tom Pagnozzi	.25	.11
☐ 73 Bret Boone	.25	.11
☐ 74 Wally Joyner	.50	.23
☐ 75 Luis Lopez	.25	.11
☐ 76 Len Dykstra	.50	.23
☐ 77 Pedro Munoz	.25	.11
☐ 78 Kevin Gross	.25	.11
☐ 79 Eduardo Perez	.25	.11
☐ 80 Brent Gates	.25	.11
☐ 81 Jeff Conine	.50	.23
☐ 82 Paul Sorrento	.25	.11
☐ 83 Julio Franco	.50	.23
☐ 84 Chris Sabo	.25	.11
☐ 85 Dante Bichette	1.00	.45
☐ 86 Mike Stanley	.25	.11
☐ 87 Bob Hamelin	.25	.11
☐ 88 Tommy Greene	.25	.11
☐ 89 Jeff Brantley	.25	.11
☐ 90 Ed Sprague	.25	.11
☐ 91 Otis Nixon	.50	.23
☐ 92 Chad Curtis	.25	.11
☐ 93 Chuck McElroy	.25	.11
☐ 94 Troy Neel	.25	.11
☐ 95 Benny Santiago	.25	.11
☐ 96 Jose Mesa	.50	.23
☐ 97 Luis Gonzalez	.25	.11
☐ 98 Alex Fernandez	.50	.23
☐ 99 Ben McDonald	.25	.11
☐ 100 Wade Boggs	1.50	.70
☐ 101 Tom Glavine	.50	.23
☐ 102 Phil Plantier	.25	.11
☐ 103 Raul Mondesi	1.50	.70
☐ 104 Jim Edmonds	1.50	.70
☐ 105 Jeff Kent	.25	.11
☐ 106 Wilson Alvarez	.25	.11
☐ 107 Geronimo Berroa	.25	.11
☐ 108 Craig Biggio	1.00	.45
☐ 109 Roberto Hernandez	.25	.11
☐ 110 Bobby Ayala	.25	.11
☐ 111 Bob Tewksbury	.25	.11
☐ 112 Rondell White	.50	.23
☐ 113 Steve Cooke	.25	.11
☐ 114 Tim Salmon	1.50	.70
☐ 115 Kent Mercker	.25	.11
☐ 116 Randy Johnson	1.50	.70
☐ 117 Mo Vaughn	2.00	.90
☐ 118 Eddie Williams	.25	.11
☐ 119 Jeff Montgomery	.25	.11
☐ 120 Kirt Manwaring	.25	.11
☐ 121 Pat Hentgen	.50	.23
☐ 122 Shawon Dunston	.25	.11
☐ 123 Tim Belcher	.25	.11
☐ 124 Cecil Fielder	.50	.23
☐ 125 Todd Hundley	.50	.23
☐ 126 Mark Acre	.25	.11
☐ 127 Darrell Whitmore	.25	.11
☐ 128 Darryl Kile	.50	.23
☐ 129 Jay Bell	.25	.11
☐ 130 Harold Baines	.25	.11
☐ 131 Felix Fermin	.25	.11
☐ 132 Ellis Burks	.50	.23
☐ 133 Joe Carter	.50	.23
☐ 134 Terry Pendleton	.25	.11
☐ 135 Junior Felix	.25	.11
☐ 136 Bill Gullickson	.25	.11
☐ 137 Melvin Nieves	.25	.11
☐ 138 Chuck Knoblauch	1.50	.70
☐ 139 Bobby Jones	.25	.11
☐ 140 Darrin Fletcher	.25	.11
☐ 141 Andy Van Slyke	.25	.11
☐ 142 Allen Watson	.25	.11
☐ 143 Dan Wilson	.25	.11
☐ 144 Bip Roberts	.25	.11
☐ 145 Sterling Hitchcock	.25	.11
☐ 146 Johnny Ruffin	.25	.11
☐ 147 Steve Trachsel	.25	.11
☐ 148 Ramon Martinez	.50	.23
☐ 149 Dave Henderson	.25	.11
☐ 150 Chris Gomez	.25	.11
☐ 151 Rusty Greer	1.00	.45
☐ 152 John Franco	.50	.23
☐ 153 Mike Bordick	.25	.11
☐ 154 Dave Magadan	.25	.11
☐ 155 Greg Swindell	.25	.11
☐ 156 Arthur Rhodes	.25	.11
☐ 157 Juan Guzman	.25	.11
☐ 158 Greg Maddux	5.00	2.20
☐ 159 Mike Macfarlane	.25	.11
☐ 160 Curt Schilling	.50	.23
☐ 161 Jose Canseco	1.00	.45
☐ 162 Aaron Sele	.25	.11
☐ 163 Steve Buechele	.25	.11
☐ 164 Orel Hershiser	.50	.23
☐ 165 Mike Henneman	.25	.11
☐ 166 Kevin Seitzer	.25	.11
☐ 167 Ruben Sierra	.25	.11
☐ 168 Alex Cole	.25	.11
☐ 169 Jim Thome	1.50	.70
☐ 170 Lance Johnson	.25	.11
☐ 171 Marquis Grissom	.50	.23
☐ 172 Jamie Moyer	.25	.11
☐ 173 Todd Zeile	.25	.11
☐ 174 Chris Bosio	.25	.11
☐ 175 Steve Howe	.25	.11
☐ 176 Luis Polonia	.25	.11
☐ 177 Ryan Klesko	1.50	.70
☐ 178 Kevin Appier	.50	.23
☐ 179 Tim Naehring	.25	.11
☐ 180 Randy Myers	.25	.11
☐ 181 Mike Jackson	.25	.11
☐ 182 Chili Davis	.50	.23
☐ 183 Jason Jacome	.25	.11
☐ 184 Stan Javier	.25	.11
☐ 185 Scott Servais	.25	.11
☐ 186 Kirk Rueter	.25	.11
☐ 187 Don Slaught	.25	.11
☐ 188 Ozzie Smith	2.00	.90
☐ 189 Barry Larkin	1.00	.45
☐ 190 Gary Gaetti	.50	.23
☐ 191 Fred McGriff	1.00	.45
☐ 192 Roger Clemens	3.00	1.35
☐ 193 Dean Palmer	.50	.23
☐ 194 Jeromy Burnitz	.25	.11
☐ 195 Scott Kamieniecki	.25	.11
☐ 196 Eddie Murray	1.50	.70
☐ 197 Ron Karkovice	.25	.11
☐ 198 Tino Martinez	1.50	.70
☐ 199 Ken Griffey Jr.	7.50	3.40
☐ 200 Don Mattingly	2.50	1.10
☐ 201 Henry Rodriguez	.25	.11
☐ 202 Lenny Harris	.25	.11
☐ 203 Ryan Thompson	.25	.11
☐ 204 Darren Oliver	.25	.11
☐ 205 Omar Vizquel	.50	.23
☐ 206 Jeff Bagwell	3.00	1.35
☐ 207 Todd Van Poppel	.25	.11
☐ 208 Leo Gomez	.25	.11
☐ 209 Mark Whiten	.25	.11
☐ 210 Pedro Martinez	1.50	.70
☐ 211 Reggie Sanders	.50	.23
☐ 212 Kevin Foster	.25	.11
☐ 213 Danny Tartabull	.25	.11
☐ 214 Jeff Blauser	.25	.11
☐ 215 Mike Magnante	.25	.11
☐ 216 Tom Candiotti	.25	.11

Card	MINT	NRMT
☐ 217 Rod Beck	.25	.11
☐ 218 Jody Reed	.25	.11
☐ 219 Vince Coleman	.25	.11
☐ 220 Danny Jackson	.25	.11
☐ 221 Larry Walker	1.50	.70
☐ 222 Pat Borders	.25	.11
☐ 223 Lee Smith	.50	.23
☐ 224 Paul O'Neill	.50	.23
☐ 225 Devon White	.25	.11
☐ 226 Jim Bullinger	.25	.11
☐ 227 Steve Avery	.25	.11
☐ 228 Tony Gwynn	4.00	1.80
☐ 229 Pat Meares	.25	.11
☐ 230 Bill Swift	.25	.11
☐ 231 David Wells	.25	.11
☐ 232 John Briscoe	.25	.11
☐ 233 Roger Pavlik	.25	.11
☐ 234 Roberto Alomar	1.50	.70
☐ 235 Billy Brewer	.25	.11
☐ 236 Gary Sheffield	1.50	.70
☐ 237 Lou Frazier	.25	.11
☐ 238 Terry Steinbach	.50	.23
☐ 239 Omar Daal	.25	.11
☐ 240 Jason Bere	.25	.11
☐ 241 Denny Neagle	.50	.23
☐ 242 Danny Bautista	.25	.11
☐ 243 Hector Carrasco	.25	.11
☐ 244 Bill Risley	.25	.11
☐ 245 Andy Benes	.50	.23
☐ 246 Jim Leyritz	.25	.11
☐ 247 Jose Oliva	.25	.11
☐ 248 Greg Vaughn	.25	.11
☐ 249 Rich Monteleone	.25	.11
☐ 250 Tony Eusebio	.25	.11
☐ 251 Chuck Finley	.25	.11
☐ 252 Joe Boever	.25	.11
☐ 253 Bobby Munoz	.25	.11
☐ 254 Bret Saberhagen	.25	.11
☐ 255 Kurt Abbott	.25	.11
☐ 256 Bobby Witt	.25	.11
☐ 257 Cliff Floyd	.25	.11
☐ 258 Mark Clark	.25	.11
☐ 259 Andujar Cedeno	.25	.11
☐ 260 Marvin Freeman	.25	.11
☐ 261 Mike Piazza	5.00	2.20
☐ 262 Pat Kelly	.25	.11
☐ 263 Carlos Delgado	.50	.23
☐ 264 Willie Banks	.25	.11
☐ 265 Matt Walbeck	.25	.11
☐ 266 Mark McGwire	3.00	1.35
☐ 267 Alan Trammell	1.00	.45
☐ 268 Tom Gordon	.25	.11
☐ 269 Greg Colbrunn	.25	.11
☐ 270 Darren Daulton	.50	.23
☐ 271 Albie Lopez	.25	.11
☐ 272 Robin Ventura	.50	.23
☐ 273 Bryan Eversgerd	.25	.11
☐ 274 Dave Fleming	.25	.11
☐ 275 Scott Livingstone	.25	.11
☐ 276 Pete Schourek	.25	.11
☐ 277 Bernie Williams	1.50	.70
☐ 278 Mark Lemke	.25	.11
☐ 279 Eric Karros	.50	.23
☐ 280 Billy Ashley	.25	.11
☐ 281 Rico Brogna	.25	.11
☐ 282 John Burkett	.25	.11
☐ 283 Jorge Fabregas	.25	.11
☐ 284 Greg Gagne	.25	.11
☐ 285 Doug Jones	.25	.11
☐ 286 Troy O'Leary	.25	.11
☐ 287 Pat Rapp	.25	.11
☐ 288 Butch Henry	.25	.11
☐ 289 John Olerud	.50	.23
☐ 290 John Hudek	.25	.11
☐ 291 Jeff King	.25	.11
☐ 292 Bobby Bonilla	.50	.23
☐ 293 Albert Belle	3.00	1.35
☐ 294 Rick Wilkins	.25	.11
☐ 295 John Jaha	.25	.11
☐ 296 Sid Fernandez	.25	.11
☐ 297 Deion Sanders	1.50	.70
☐ 298 Gil Heredia	.25	.11
☐ 299 Melido Perez	.25	.11
☐ 300 Greg McMichael	.25	.11
☐ 301 Rusty Meacham	.25	.11
☐ 302 Shawn Green	.50	.23
☐ 303 Carlos Garcia	.25	.11
☐ 304 Dave Stevens	.25	.11
☐ 305 Eric Young	.50	.23
☐ 306 Kirk Gibson	.50	.23
☐ 307 Spike Owen	.25	.11
☐ 308 Sandy Alomar Jr.	.25	.11
☐ 309 Ricky Gutierrez	.25	.11
☐ 310 Dave Veres	.25	.11
☐ 311 Gregg Jefferies	.50	.23
☐ 312 Jose Valentin	.25	.11
☐ 313 Robb Nen	.50	.23
☐ 314 Jose Rijo	.25	.11
☐ 315 Sean Berry	.25	.11
☐ 316 Mike Gallego	.25	.11
☐ 317 Roberto Kelly	.25	.11
☐ 318 Kevin Stocker	.25	.11
☐ 319 Kirby Puckett	3.00	1.35
☐ 320 Jon Lieber	.25	.11
☐ 321 Joe Girardi	.25	.11
☐ 322 Tony Phillips	.25	.11
☐ 323 Brian Anderson	.25	.11
☐ 324 Ivan Rodriguez	1.50	.70
☐ 325 Jeff Cirillo	.25	.11
☐ 326 Joey Cora	.50	.23
☐ 327 Chris Hoiles	.25	.11
☐ 328 Bernard Gilkey	.50	.23
☐ 329 Mike Lansing	.25	.11
☐ 330 Jimmy Key	.25	.11
☐ 331 Vinny Castilla	.50	.23
☐ 332 Mark Guthrie	.25	.11
☐ 333 Mike Lieberthal	.25	.11
☐ 334 Will Clark	1.00	.45
☐ 335 Rickey Henderson	1.00	.45
☐ 336 Todd Jones	.25	.11
☐ 337 Jack McDowell	.25	.11
☐ 338 Carlos Rodriguez	.25	.11
☐ 339 Mark Eichhorn	.25	.11
☐ 340 Jeff Nelson	.25	.11
☐ 341 Eric Anthony	.25	.11
☐ 342 Randy Velarde	.25	.11
☐ 343 Javier Lopez	.50	.23
☐ 344 Kevin Mitchell	.25	.11
☐ 345 Steve Bedrosian	.25	.11
☐ 346 John Kruk	.50	.23
☐ 347 Scott Leius	.25	.11
☐ 348 John Patterson	.25	.11
☐ 349 Kevin Brown	.50	.23
☐ 350 Mike Moore	.25	.11
☐ 351 Manny Ramirez	1.50	.70
☐ 352 Jose Lind	.25	.11
☐ 353 Derrick May	.25	.11
☐ 354 Cal Eldred	.25	.11
☐ 355 J.T. Snow	.50	.23
☐ 356 Luis Sojo	.25	.11
☐ 357 Moises Alou	.50	.23
☐ 358 Dave Clark	.25	.11
☐ 359 Dave Hollins	.25	.11
☐ 360 Cal Ripken UER Name spelled Ripkin	6.00	2.70
☐ 361 Pedro Astacio	.25	.11
☐ 362 Tony Longmire	.25	.11
☐ 363 Jeff Frye	.25	.11
☐ 364 Bo Jackson	.50	.23
☐ 365 Steve Ontiveros	.25	.11
☐ 366 David Nied	.25	.11
☐ 367 Brad Ausmus	.25	.11
☐ 368 Carlos Baerga	.50	.23
☐ 369 James Mouton	.25	.11
☐ 370 Ozzie Guillen	.25	.11
☐ 371 Yorkis Perez	.25	.11
☐ 372 Rich Rodriguez	.25	.11
☐ 373 Mark McLemore	.25	.11
☐ 374 Jeff Fassero	.25	.11
☐ 375 John Roper	.25	.11
☐ 376 Wes Chamberlain	.25	.11
☐ 377 Felix Jose	.25	.11
☐ 378 Brett Butler	.50	.23
☐ 379 William VanLandingham	.25	.11
☐ 380 Mickey Tettleton	.25	.11
☐ 381 Brady Anderson	1.00	.45
☐ 382 Reggie Jefferson	.50	.23
☐ 383 Mike Kingery	.25	.11
☐ 384 Derek Bell	.25	.11
☐ 385 Scott Erickson	.25	.11
☐ 386 Bob Wickman	.25	.11
☐ 387 Phil Leftwich	.25	.11
☐ 388 David Justice	1.50	.70
☐ 389 Pedro Martinez	1.50	.70
☐ 390 Terry Mathews	.25	.11
☐ 391 Brian McRae	.25	.11
☐ 392 Bruce Ruffin	.25	.11
☐ 393 Steve Finley	.50	.23
☐ 394 Rafael Bournigal	.25	.11
☐ 395 Darryl Strawberry	.50	.23
☐ 396 Luis Alicea	.25	.11

1995 Topps Cyber Season in Review

This seven-card set was distributed exclusively in 1995 Topps hobby factory sets. It continues the Cyberstats insert theme used in the regular issue product, which presented "what if" statistics to fill in the strike-shortened 1994 season. The Season in Review cards commemorate projected accomplishments including Barry Bonds' 61 home runs and Kenny Lofton's World Series MVP.

	MINT	NRMT
COMPLETE SET (7)	5.00	2.20
COMMON CARD (1-7)	.25	.11
☐ 1 Barry Bonds	1.00	.45
☐ 2 Jose Canseco	.75	.35
☐ 3 Juan Gonzalez	2.00	.90
☐ 4 Fred McGriff	.50	.23
☐ 5 Carlos Baerga	.25	.11
☐ 6 Ryan Klesko	.75	.35
☐ 7 Kenny Lofton	1.00	.45

1995 Topps Finest

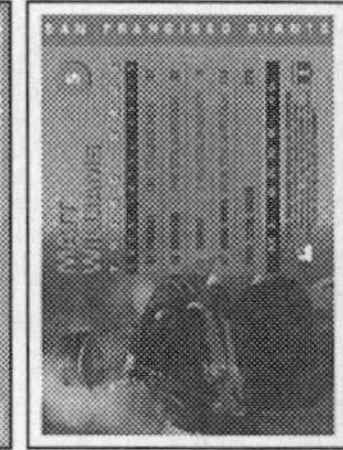

This 15-card standard-size set was inserted one every 36 Topps series two packs. This set featured the top 15 players in total bases from the 1994 season. The fronts feature a player photo, with his team identification and name on the bottom of the card. The horizontal backs feature another player photo along with a breakdown of how many of each type of hit each player got on the way to their season total. The set is sequenced in order of how they finished in the majors for the 1994 season.

	MINT	NRMT
COMPLETE SET (15)	70.00	32.00
COMMON CARD (1-15)	1.50	.70
☐ 1 Jeff Bagwell	8.00	3.60
☐ 2 Albert Belle	5.00	2.20
☐ 3 Ken Griffey Jr.	20.00	9.00
☐ 4 Frank Thomas	15.00	6.75
☐ 5 Matt Williams	3.00	1.35
☐ 6 Dante Bichette	3.00	1.35
☐ 7 Barry Bonds	5.00	2.20
☐ 8 Moises Alou	2.00	.90
☐ 9 Andres Galarraga	3.00	1.35
☐ 10 Kenny Lofton	5.00	2.20
☐ 11 Rafael Palmeiro	3.00	1.35
☐ 12 Tony Gwynn	8.00	3.60
☐ 13 Kirby Puckett	8.00	3.60
☐ 14 Jose Canseco	3.00	1.35
☐ 15 Jeff Conine	1.50	.70

1995 Topps League Leaders

Randomly inserted in jumbo packs at a rate of one in three and retail packs at a rate of one in six, this 50-card standard-size set showcases those that were among league leaders in various categories. Card fronts feature a player photo with a black background. The player's name appears in gold foil at the bottom and the category with which he led the league or was among the leaders is in yellow letters up the right side. The backs contain various graphs and where the player placed among the leaders.

	MINT	NRMT
COMPLETE SET (50)	50.00	22.00
COMPLETE SERIES 1 (25)	20.00	9.00
COMPLETE SERIES 2 (25)	30.00	13.50
COMMON CARD (LL1-LL50)	.50	.23

☐ LL1 Albert Belle	1.50	.70
☐ LL2 Kevin Mitchell	.50	.23
☐ LL3 Wade Boggs	1.25	.55
☐ LL4 Tony Gwynn	2.50	1.10
☐ LL5 Moises Alou	.75	.35
☐ LL6 Andres Galarraga	1.00	.45
☐ LL7 Matt Williams	1.00	.45
☐ LL8 Barry Bonds	1.50	.70
☐ LL9 Frank Thomas	5.00	2.20
☐ LL10 Jose Canseco	1.00	.45
☐ LL11 Jeff Bagwell	2.50	1.10
☐ LL12 Kirby Puckett	2.50	1.10
☐ LL13 Julio Franco	.75	.35
☐ LL14 Albert Belle	1.50	.70
☐ LL15 Fred McGriff	1.00	.45
☐ LL16 Kenny Lofton	1.50	.70
☐ LL17 Otis Nixon	.50	.23
☐ LL18 Brady Anderson	1.00	.45
☐ LL19 Deion Sanders	1.25	.55
☐ LL20 Chuck Carr	.50	.23
☐ LL21 Pat Hentgen	.75	.35
☐ LL22 Andy Benes	.75	.35
☐ LL23 Roger Clemens	2.50	1.10
☐ LL24 Greg Maddux	4.00	1.80
☐ LL25 Pedro Martinez	1.25	.55
☐ LL26 Paul O'Neill	.75	.35
☐ LL27 Jeff Bagwell	2.50	1.10
☐ LL28 Frank Thomas	6.00	2.70
☐ LL29 Hal Morris	.50	.23
☐ LL30 Kenny Lofton	1.50	.70
☐ LL31 Ken Griffey Jr.	6.00	2.70
☐ LL32 Jeff Bagwell	2.50	1.10
☐ LL33 Albert Belle	1.25	.55
☐ LL34 Fred McGriff	1.00	.45
☐ LL35 Cecil Fielder	.75	.35
☐ LL36 Matt Williams	1.00	.45
☐ LL37 Joe Carter	.75	.35
☐ LL38 Dante Bichette	1.00	.45
☐ LL39 Frank Thomas	5.00	2.20
☐ LL40 Mike Piazza	4.00	1.80
☐ LL41 Craig Biggio	1.00	.45
☐ LL42 Vince Coleman	.50	.23
☐ LL43 Marquis Grissom	.75	.35
☐ LL44 Chuck Knoblauch	1.25	.55
☐ LL45 Darren Lewis	.50	.23
☐ LL46 Randy Johnson	1.25	.55
☐ LL47 Jose Rijo	.50	.23
☐ LL48 Chuck Finley	.75	.35
☐ LL49 Bret Saberhagen	.50	.23
☐ LL50 Kevin Appier	.75	.35

1995 Topps Traded

This set contains 165 standard-size cards and was sold in 11-card packs for $1.29. The set features rookies, draft picks and players who had been traded. The fronts contain a photo with a white border. The backs have a player picture in a scoreboard and his statistics and information. All cards are numbered with a "T" prefix. Subsets featured are: At the Break (1T-10T) and All-Stars (156T-164T). Rookie Cards in this set include Ben Davis and Hideo Nomo.

	MINT	NRMT
COMPLETE SET (165)	20.00	9.00
COMMON CARD (1T-165T)	.15	.07

☐ 1T Frank Thomas ATB	1.25	.55
☐ 2T Ken Griffey Jr. ATB	1.50	.70
☐ 3T Barry Bonds ATB	.60	.25
☐ 4T Albert Belle ATB	.60	.25
☐ 5T Cal Ripken ATB	1.25	.55
☐ 6T Mike Piazza ATB	1.00	.45
☐ 7T Tony Gwynn ATB	.75	.35
☐ 8T Jeff Bagwell ATB	.60	.25
☐ 9T Mo Vaughn ATB	.60	.25
☐ 10T Matt Williams ATB	.40	.18
☐ 11T Ray Durham	.40	.18
☐ 12T Juan LeBron	1.00	.45
☐ 13T Shawn Green	.30	.14
☐ 14T Kevin Gross	.15	.07
☐ 15T Jon Nunnally	.30	.14
☐ 16T Brian Maxcy	.15	.07
☐ 17T Mark Kiefer	.15	.07
☐ 18T Carlos Beltran	.50	.23
☐ 19T Mike Mimbs	.30	.14
☐ 20T Larry Walker	.60	.25
☐ 21T Chad Curtis	.15	.07
☐ 22T Jeff Barry	.15	.07
☐ 23T Joe Oliver	.15	.07
☐ 24T Tomas Perez	.30	.14
☐ 25T Michael Barrett	.50	.23
☐ 26T Brian McRae	.15	.07
☐ 27T Derek Bell	.30	.14
☐ 28T Ray Durham	.30	.14
☐ 29T Todd Williams	.15	.07
☐ 30T Ryan Jaroncyk	.40	.18
☐ 31T Todd Steverson	.15	.07
☐ 32T Mike Devereaux	.15	.07
☐ 33T Rheal Cormier	.15	.07
☐ 34T Benny Santiago	.15	.07
☐ 35T Bobby Higginson	1.00	.45
☐ 36T Jack McDowell	.15	.07
☐ 37T Mike Macfarlane	.15	.07
☐ 38T Tony McKnight	.30	.14
☐ 39T Brian Hunter	.30	.14
☐ 40T Hideo Nomo	3.00	1.35
☐ 41T Brett Butler	.30	.14
☐ 42T Donovan Osborne	.15	.07
☐ 43T Scott Karl	.15	.07
☐ 44T Tony Phillips	.15	.07
☐ 45T Marty Cordova	.40	.18
☐ 46T Dave Mlicki	.15	.07
☐ 47T Bronson Arroyo	.50	.23
☐ 48T John Burkett	.15	.07
☐ 49T J.D. Smart	.15	.07
☐ 50T Mickey Tettleton	.15	.07
☐ 51T Todd Stottlemyre	.15	.07
☐ 52T Mike Perez	.15	.07
☐ 53T Terry Mulholland	.15	.07
☐ 54T Edgardo Alfonzo	.60	.25
☐ 55T Zane Smith	.15	.07
☐ 56T Jacob Brumfield	.15	.07
☐ 57T Andujar Cedeno	.15	.07
☐ 58T Jose Parra	.30	.14
☐ 59T Manny Alexander	.15	.07
☐ 60T Tony Tarasco	.15	.07
☐ 61T Orel Hershiser	.30	.14
☐ 62T Tim Scott	.15	.07
☐ 63T Felix Rodriguez	.30	.14
☐ 64T Ken Hill	.15	.07
☐ 65T Marquis Grissom	.30	.14
☐ 66T Lee Smith	.30	.14
☐ 67T Jason Bates	.15	.07
☐ 68T Felipe Lira	.15	.07
☐ 69T Alex Hernandez	.50	.23
☐ 70T Tony Fernandez	.15	.07
☐ 71T Scott Radinsky	.15	.07
☐ 72T Jose Canseco	.40	.18
☐ 73T Mark Grudzielanek	.50	.23
☐ 74T Ben Davis	1.25	.55
☐ 75T Jim Abbott	.15	.07
☐ 76T Roger Bailey	.15	.07
☐ 77T Gregg Jefferies	.30	.14
☐ 78T Erik Hanson	.15	.07
☐ 79T Brad Radke	.75	.35
☐ 80T Jaime Navarro	.15	.07
☐ 81T John Wetteland	.30	.14
☐ 82T Chad Fonville	.15	.07
☐ 83T John Mabry	.40	.18
☐ 84T Glenallen Hill	.15	.07
☐ 85T Ken Caminiti	.60	.25
☐ 86T Tom Goodwin	.15	.07
☐ 87T Darren Bragg	.30	.14
☐ 88T Pitching Prospects Pat Ahearne Gary Rath Larry Wimberly Robbie Bell	.50	.23
☐ 89T Jeff Russell	.15	.07
☐ 90T Dave Gallagher	.15	.07
☐ 91T Steve Finley	.30	.14
☐ 92T Vaughn Eshelman	.15	.07
☐ 93T Kevin Jarvis	.15	.07
☐ 94T Mark Gubicza	.15	.07
☐ 95T Tim Wakefield	.15	.07
☐ 96T Bob Tewksbury	.15	.07
☐ 97T Sid Roberson	.15	.07
☐ 98T Tom Henke	.15	.07
☐ 99T Michael Tucker	.30	.14
☐ 100T Jason Bates	.15	.07
☐ 101T Otis Nixon	.30	.14
☐ 102T Mark Whiten	.15	.07
☐ 103T Dilson Torres	.15	.07
☐ 104T Melvin Bunch	.15	.07
☐ 105T Terry Pendleton	.30	.14
☐ 106T Corey Jenkins	.60	.25
☐ 107T Glenn Dishman Rob Grable	.30	.14
☐ 108T Reggie Taylor	.50	.23
☐ 109T Curtis Goodwin	.15	.07
☐ 110T David Cone	.30	.14
☐ 111T Antonio Osuna	.15	.07
☐ 112T Paul Shuey	.15	.07
☐ 113T Doug Jones	.15	.07
☐ 114T Mark McLemore	.15	.07
☐ 115T Kevin Ritz	.15	.07
☐ 116T John Kruk	.30	.14
☐ 117T Trevor Wilson	.15	.07
☐ 118T Jerald Clark	.15	.07
☐ 119T Julian Tavarez	.15	.07
☐ 120T Tim Pugh	.15	.07
☐ 121T Todd Zeile	.15	.07
☐ 122T Prospects Mark Sweeney UER George Arias Richie Sexson Brian Schneider	.75	.35
☐ 123T Bobby Witt	.15	.07
☐ 124T Hideo Nomo	1.50	.70
☐ 125T Joey Cora	.30	.14
☐ 126T Jim Scharrer	.40	.18
☐ 127T Paul Quantrill	.15	.07
☐ 128T Chipper Jones ROY	1.50	.70
☐ 129T Kenny James	.15	.07
☐ 130T Lyle Mouton Mariano Rivera	.60	.25
☐ 131T Tyler Green	.15	.07
☐ 132T Brad Clontz	.15	.07
☐ 133T Jon Nunnally	.30	.14
☐ 134T Dave Magadan	.15	.07
☐ 135T Al Leiter	.15	.07
☐ 136T Bret Barberie	.15	.07
☐ 137T Bill Swift	.15	.07
☐ 138T Scott Cooper	.15	.07
☐ 139T Roberto Kelly	.15	.07
☐ 140T Charlie Hayes	.15	.07
☐ 141T Pete Harnisch	.15	.07
☐ 142T Rich Amaral	.15	.07
☐ 143T Rudy Seanez	.15	.07
☐ 144T Pat Listach	.15	.07
☐ 145T Quilvio Veras	.15	.07
☐ 146T Jose Olmeda	.15	.07
☐ 147T Roberto Petagine	.15	.07
☐ 148T Kevin Brown	.30	.14
☐ 149T Phil Plantier	.15	.07
☐ 150T Carlos Perez	.30	.14
☐ 151T Pat Borders	.15	.07
☐ 152T Tyler Green	.15	.07
☐ 153T Stan Belinda	.15	.07
☐ 154T Dave Stewart	.30	.14
☐ 155T Andre Dawson	.40	.18
☐ 156T Frank Thomas AS Fred McGriff UER (McGriff's team shown as Blue Jays)	.60	.25
☐ 157T Carlos Baerga AS Craig Biggio	.30	.14
☐ 158T Wade Boggs AS Matt Williams	.30	.14
☐ 159T Cal Ripken AS Ozzie Smith	.60	.25
☐ 160T Ken Griffey Jr. AS Tony Gwynn	.75	.35
☐ 161T Albert Belle AS Barry Bonds	.40	.18
☐ 162T Kirby Puckett Len Dykstra	.60	.25
☐ 163T Ivan Rodriguez AS Mike Piazza	.60	.25
☐ 164T Randy Johnson AS Hideo Nomo	.75	.35
☐ 165T Checklist	.15	.07

1995 Topps Traded Power Boosters

This 10-card standard-size set was inserted in packs at a rate of one in 36. The set is comprised of parallel cards for the first 10 cards of the regular Topps Traded set which was the "At the Break" subset. The cards are done on extra-thick stock. The fronts have an action photo on a "Power Boosted" background, which is similar to diffraction technology, with the words "at the break" on the left side. The backs have a head shot and player information including his mid-season statistics for 1995 and previous years.

	MINT	NRMT
COMPLETE SET (10)	120.00	55.00
COMMON CARD (1-10)	4.00	1.80
☐ 1 Frank Thomas	25.00	11.00
☐ 2 Ken Griffey Jr.	30.00	13.50
☐ 3 Barry Bonds	8.00	3.60
☐ 4 Albert Belle	8.00	3.60
☐ 5 Cal Ripken	25.00	11.00
☐ 6 Mike Piazza	20.00	9.00
☐ 7 Tony Gwynn	15.00	6.75
☐ 8 Jeff Bagwell	12.00	5.50
☐ 9 Mo Vaughn	8.00	3.60
☐ 10 Matt Williams	4.00	1.80

1996 Topps

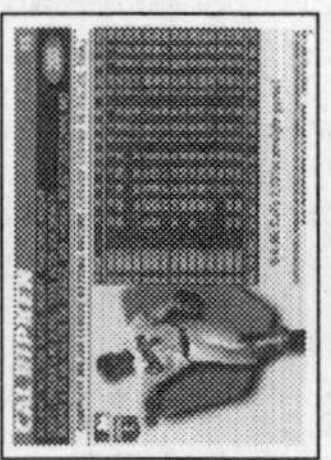

This set consists of 440 standard-size cards. These cards were issued in 12-card foil packs with a suggested retail price of $1.29. The fronts feature full-color photos surrounded by a white background. Information on the backs includes a player photo, season and career stats and text. First series subsets include Star Power (1-6, 8-12), Draft Picks (13-26), AAA Stars (101-104), and Future Stars (210-219). A special Mickey Mantle card was issued as card #7 (his uniform number) and became the last card to be issued as card #7 in the Topps brand set. Rookie Cards in this set include Sean Casey, Matt Morris and Ron Wright.

	MINT	NRMT
COMPLETE SET (440)	30.00	13.50
COMP.HOBBY SET (449)	50.00	22.00
COMP.CEREAL SET (444)	50.00	22.00
COMPLETE SERIES 1 (220)	15.00	6.75
COMPLETE SERIES 2 (220)	15.00	6.75
COMMON CARD (1-440)	.10	.05
☐ 1 Tony Gwynn STP	.60	.25
☐ 2 Mike Piazza STP	1.00	.45
☐ 3 Greg Maddux STP	1.00	.45
☐ 4 Jeff Bagwell STP	.40	.18
☐ 5 Larry Walker STP	.40	.18
☐ 6 Barry Larkin STP	.30	.14
☐ 7 Mickey Mantle	4.00	1.80
☐ 8 Tom Glavine STP UER	.20	.09
Won 21 games in June 95		
☐ 9 Craig Biggio STP	.30	.14
☐ 10 Barry Bonds STP	.40	.18
☐ 11 Heathcliff Slocumb STP	.10	.05
☐ 12 Matt Williams STP	.30	.14
☐ 13 Todd Helton	1.50	.70
☐ 14 Mark Redman	.20	.09
☐ 15 Michael Barrett	.10	.05
☐ 16 Ben Davis	.40	.18
☐ 17 Juan LeBron	.10	.05
☐ 18 Tony McKnight	.10	.05
☐ 19 Ryan Jaroncyk	.10	.05
☐ 20 Corey Jenkins	.20	.09
☐ 21 Jim Scharrer	.10	.05
☐ 22 Mark Bellhorn	.40	.18
☐ 23 Jarrod Washburn	.20	.09
☐ 24 Geoff Jenkins	.40	.18
☐ 25 Sean Casey	.75	.35
☐ 26 Brett Tomko	.10	.05
☐ 27 Tony Fernandez	.10	.05
☐ 28 Rich Becker	.10	.05
☐ 29 Andujar Cedeno	.10	.05
☐ 30 Paul Molitor	.40	.18
☐ 31 Brent Gates	.10	.05
☐ 32 Glenallen Hill	.10	.05
☐ 33 Mike Macfarlane	.10	.05
☐ 34 Manny Alexander	.10	.05
☐ 35 Todd Zeile	.10	.05
☐ 36 Joe Girardi	.10	.05
☐ 37 Tony Tarasco	.10	.05
☐ 38 Tim Belcher	.10	.05
☐ 39 Tom Goodwin	.10	.05
☐ 40 Orel Hershiser	.20	.09
☐ 41 Tripp Cromer	.10	.05
☐ 42 Sean Bergman	.10	.05
☐ 43 Troy Percival	.20	.09
☐ 44 Kevin Stocker	.10	.05
☐ 45 Albert Belle	.50	.23
☐ 46 Tony Eusebio	.10	.05
☐ 47 Sid Roberson	.10	.05
☐ 48 Todd Hollandsworth	.20	.09
☐ 49 Mark Wohlers	.20	.09
☐ 50 Kirby Puckett	.75	.35
☐ 51 Darren Holmes	.10	.05
☐ 52 Ron Karkovice	.10	.05
☐ 53 Al Martin	.10	.05
☐ 54 Pat Rapp	.10	.05
☐ 55 Mark Grace	.30	.14
☐ 56 Greg Gagne	.10	.05
☐ 57 Stan Javier	.10	.05
☐ 58 Scott Sanders	.10	.05
☐ 59 J.T. Snow	.30	.14
☐ 60 David Justice	.40	.18
☐ 61 Royce Clayton	.10	.05
☐ 62 Kevin Foster	.10	.05
☐ 63 Tim Naehring	.10	.05
☐ 64 Orlando Miller	.10	.05
☐ 65 Mike Mussina	.40	.18
☐ 66 Jim Eisenreich	.20	.09
☐ 67 Felix Fermin	.10	.05
☐ 68 Bernie Williams	.40	.18
☐ 69 Robb Nen	.10	.05
☐ 70 Ron Gant	.20	.09
☐ 71 Felipe Lira	.10	.05
☐ 72 Jacob Brumfield	.10	.05
☐ 73 John Mabry	.20	.09
☐ 74 Mark Carreon	.10	.05
☐ 75 Carlos Baerga	.20	.09
☐ 76 Jim Dougherty	.10	.05
☐ 77 Ryan Thompson	.10	.05
☐ 78 Scott Leius	.10	.05
☐ 79 Roger Pavlik	.10	.05
☐ 80 Gary Sheffield	.40	.18
☐ 81 Julian Tavarez	.10	.05
☐ 82 Andy Ashby	.10	.05
☐ 83 Mark Lemke	.10	.05
☐ 84 Omar Vizquel	.20	.09
☐ 85 Darren Daulton	.20	.09
☐ 86 Mike Lansing	.10	.05
☐ 87 Rusty Greer	.30	.14
☐ 88 Dave Stevens	.10	.05
☐ 89 Jose Offerman	.10	.05
☐ 90 Tom Henke	.20	.09
☐ 91 Troy O'Leary	.10	.05
☐ 92 Michael Tucker	.20	.09
☐ 93 Marvin Freeman	.10	.05
☐ 94 Alex Diaz	.10	.05
☐ 95 John Wetteland	.20	.09
☐ 96 Cal Ripken 2131	2.00	.90
☐ 97 Mike Mimbs	.10	.05
☐ 98 Bobby Higginson	.20	.09
☐ 99 Edgardo Alfonzo	.40	.18
☐ 100 Frank Thomas	1.50	.70
☐ 101 Steve Gibralter	.40	.18
Bob Abreu		
☐ 102 Brian Givens	.10	.05
T.J. Mathews		
☐ 103 Chris Pritchett	.10	.05
Trenidad Hubbard		
☐ 104 Eric Owens	.20	.09
Butch Huskey		
☐ 105 Doug Drabek	.10	.05
☐ 106 Tomas Perez	.10	.05
☐ 107 Mark Leiter	.10	.05
☐ 108 Joe Oliver	.10	.05
☐ 109 Tony Castillo	.10	.05
☐ 110 Checklist (1-110)	.10	.05
☐ 111 Kevin Seitzer	.10	.05
☐ 112 Pete Schourek	.10	.05
☐ 113 Sean Berry	.10	.05
☐ 114 Todd Stottlemyre	.10	.05
☐ 115 Joe Carter	.20	.09
☐ 116 Jeff King	.20	.09
☐ 117 Dan Wilson	.10	.05
☐ 118 Kurt Abbott	.10	.05
☐ 119 Lyle Mouton	.10	.05
☐ 120 Jose Rijo	.10	.05
☐ 121 Curtis Goodwin	.10	.05
☐ 122 Jose Valentin	.10	.05
☐ 123 Ellis Burks	.20	.09
☐ 124 David Cone	.20	.09
☐ 125 Eddie Murray	.40	.18
☐ 126 Brian Jordan	.20	.09
☐ 127 Darrin Fletcher	.10	.05
☐ 128 Curt Schilling	.20	.09
☐ 129 Ozzie Guillen	.10	.05
☐ 130 Kenny Rogers	.10	.05
☐ 131 Tom Pagnozzi	.10	.05
☐ 132 Garret Anderson	.20	.09
☐ 133 Bobby Jones	.10	.05
☐ 134 Chris Gomez	.10	.05
☐ 135 Mike Stanley	.10	.05
☐ 136 Hideo Nomo	1.00	.45
☐ 137 Jon Nunnally	.10	.05
☐ 138 Tim Wakefield	.10	.05
☐ 139 Steve Finley	.20	.09
☐ 140 Ivan Rodriguez	.50	.23
☐ 141 Quilvio Veras	.10	.05
☐ 142 Mike Fetters	.10	.05
☐ 143 Mike Greenwell	.10	.05
☐ 144 Bill Pulsipher	.10	.05
☐ 145 Mark McGwire	.75	.35
☐ 146 Frank Castillo	.10	.05
☐ 147 Greg Vaughn	.10	.05
☐ 148 Pat Hentgen	.20	.09
☐ 149 Walt Weiss	.10	.05
☐ 150 Randy Johnson	.40	.18
☐ 151 David Segui	.10	.05
☐ 152 Benji Gil	.10	.05
☐ 153 Tom Candiotti	.10	.05
☐ 154 Geronimo Berroa	.10	.05
☐ 155 John Franco	.20	.09
☐ 156 Jay Bell	.20	.09
☐ 157 Mark Gubicza	.10	.05
☐ 158 Hal Morris	.10	.05
☐ 159 Wilson Alvarez	.20	.09
☐ 160 Derek Bell	.10	.05
☐ 161 Ricky Bottalico	.20	.09
☐ 162 Bret Boone	.10	.05
☐ 163 Brad Radke	.20	.09
☐ 164 John Valentin	.20	.09
☐ 165 Steve Avery	.10	.05
☐ 166 Mark McLemore	.10	.05
☐ 167 Danny Jackson	.10	.05
☐ 168 Tino Martinez	.40	.18
☐ 169 Shane Reynolds	.10	.05
☐ 170 Terry Pendleton	.20	.09
☐ 171 Jim Edmonds	.40	.18
☐ 172 Esteban Loaiza	.10	.05
☐ 173 Ray Durham	.20	.09
☐ 174 Carlos Perez	.10	.05
☐ 175 Raul Mondesi	.30	.14
☐ 176 Steve Ontiveros	.10	.05
☐ 177 Chipper Jones	1.25	.55
☐ 178 Otis Nixon	.10	.05
☐ 179 John Burkett	.10	.05
☐ 180 Gregg Jefferies	.20	.09
☐ 181 Denny Martinez	.20	.09
☐ 182 Ken Caminiti	.40	.18
☐ 183 Doug Jones	.10	.05
☐ 184 Brian McRae	.10	.05
☐ 185 Don Mattingly	.60	.25
☐ 186 Mel Rojas	.10	.05
☐ 187 Marty Cordova	.20	.09
☐ 188 Vinny Castilla	.20	.09
☐ 189 John Smoltz	.20	.09
☐ 190 Travis Fryman	.20	.09
☐ 191 Chris Hoiles	.10	.05
☐ 192 Chuck Finley	.10	.05
☐ 193 Ryan Klesko	.30	.14
☐ 194 Alex Fernandez	.20	.09
☐ 195 Dante Bichette	.30	.14
☐ 196 Eric Karros	.20	.09
☐ 197 Roger Clemens	.75	.35
☐ 198 Randy Myers	.10	.05
☐ 199 Tony Phillips	.10	.05
☐ 200 Cal Ripken	1.50	.70
☐ 201 Rod Beck	.20	.09
☐ 202 Chad Curtis	.10	.05
☐ 203 Jack McDowell	.10	.05
☐ 204 Gary Gaetti	.20	.09
☐ 205 Ken Griffey Jr.	2.00	.90
☐ 206 Ramon Martinez	.20	.09
☐ 207 Jeff Kent	.10	.05
☐ 208 Brad Ausmus	.10	.05
☐ 209 Devon White	.10	.05
☐ 210 Jason Giambi	.20	.09
☐ 211 Nomar Garciaparra	1.50	.70
☐ 212 Billy Wagner	.20	.09
☐ 213 Todd Greene	.30	.14
☐ 214 Paul Wilson	.10	.05
☐ 215 Johnny Damon	.20	.09
☐ 216 Alan Benes	.20	.09
☐ 217 Karim Garcia	.20	.09
☐ 218 Dustin Hermanson	.10	.05
☐ 219 Derek Jeter	1.25	.55

☐ 220 Checklist (111-220)	.10	.05
☐ 221 Kirby Puckett STP	.40	.18
☐ 222 Cal Ripken STP	.75	.35
☐ 223 Albert Belle STP	.40	.18
☐ 224 Randy Johnson STP	.40	.18
☐ 225 Wade Boggs STP	.40	.18
☐ 226 Carlos Baerga STP	.10	.05
☐ 227 Ivan Rodriguez STP	.40	.18
☐ 228 Mike Mussina STP	.40	.18
☐ 229 Frank Thomas STP	1.00	.45
☐ 230 Ken Griffey Jr. STP	1.00	.45
☐ 231 Jose Mesa STP	.20	.09
☐ 232 Matt Morris	.60	.25
☐ 233 Craig Wilson	.25	.11
☐ 234 Alvie Shepherd	.10	.05
☐ 235 Randy Winn	.20	.09
☐ 236 David Yocum	.20	.09
☐ 237 Jason Brester	.25	.11
☐ 238 Shane Monahan	.25	.11
☐ 239 Brian McNichol	.20	.09
☐ 240 Reggie Taylor	.20	.09
☐ 241 Garrett Long	.20	.09
☐ 242 Jonathan Johnson	.40	.18
☐ 243 Jeff Liefer	.25	.11
☐ 244 Brian Powell	.20	.09
☐ 245 Brian Buchanan	.20	.09
☐ 246 Mike Piazza	1.25	.55
☐ 247 Edgar Martinez	.30	.14
☐ 248 Chuck Knoblauch	.40	.18
☐ 249 Andres Galarraga	.40	.18
☐ 250 Tony Gwynn	1.00	.45
☐ 251 Lee Smith	.20	.09
☐ 252 Sammy Sosa	.20	.09
☐ 253 Jim Thome	.40	.18
☐ 254 Frank Rodriguez	.10	.05
☐ 255 Charlie Hayes	.10	.05
☐ 256 Bernard Gilkey	.10	.05
☐ 257 John Smiley	.10	.05
☐ 258 Brady Anderson	.30	.14
☐ 259 Rico Brogna	.10	.05
☐ 260 Kirt Manwaring	.10	.05
☐ 261 Len Dykstra	.20	.09
☐ 262 Tom Glavine	.20	.09
☐ 263 Vince Coleman	.10	.05
☐ 264 John Olerud	.20	.09
☐ 265 Orlando Merced	.10	.05
☐ 266 Kent Mercker	.10	.05
☐ 267 Terry Steinbach	.20	.09
☐ 268 Brian L. Hunter	.20	.09
☐ 269 Jeff Fassero	.10	.05
☐ 270 Jay Buhner	.30	.14
☐ 271 Jeff Brantley	.10	.05
☐ 272 Tim Raines	.10	.05
☐ 273 Jimmy Key	.20	.09
☐ 274 Mo Vaughn	.50	.23
☐ 275 Andre Dawson	.30	.14
☐ 276 Jose Mesa	.20	.09
☐ 277 Brett Butler	.20	.09
☐ 278 Luis Gonzalez	.10	.05
☐ 279 Steve Sparks	.10	.05
☐ 280 Chili Davis	.20	.09
☐ 281 Carl Everett	.10	.05
☐ 282 Jeff Cirillo	.20	.09
☐ 283 Thomas Howard	.10	.05
☐ 284 Paul O'Neill	.20	.09
☐ 285 Pat Meares	.10	.05
☐ 286 Mickey Tettleton	.10	.05
☐ 287 Rey Sanchez	.10	.05
☐ 288 Bip Roberts	.10	.05
☐ 289 Roberto Alomar	.40	.18
☐ 290 Ruben Sierra	.10	.05
☐ 291 John Flaherty	.10	.05
☐ 292 Bret Saberhagen	.10	.05
☐ 293 Barry Larkin	.30	.14
☐ 294 Sandy Alomar	.20	.09
☐ 295 Ed Sprague	.10	.05
☐ 296 Gary DiSarcina	.10	.05
☐ 297 Marquis Grissom	.20	.09
☐ 298 John Frascatore	.10	.05
☐ 299 Will Clark	.20	.09
☐ 300 Barry Bonds	.50	.23
☐ 301 Ozzie Smith	.50	.23
☐ 302 Dave Nilsson	.10	.05
☐ 303 Pedro Martinez	.40	.18
☐ 304 Joey Cora	.20	.09
☐ 305 Rick Aguilera	.20	.09
☐ 306 Craig Biggio	.30	.14
☐ 307 Jose Vizcaino	.10	.05
☐ 308 Jeff Montgomery	.10	.05
☐ 309 Moises Alou	.20	.09
☐ 310 Robin Ventura	.20	.09
☐ 311 David Wells	.10	.05
☐ 312 Delino DeShields	.10	.05
☐ 313 Trevor Hoffman	.20	.09
☐ 314 Andy Benes	.20	.09
☐ 315 Deion Sanders	.40	.18
☐ 316 Jim Bullinger	.10	.05
☐ 317 John Jaha	.10	.05
☐ 318 Greg Maddux	1.25	.55
☐ 319 Tim Salmon	.40	.18
☐ 320 Ben McDonald	.10	.05
☐ 321 Sandy Martinez	.10	.05
☐ 322 Dan Miceli	.10	.05
☐ 323 Wade Boggs	.40	.18
☐ 324 Ismael Valdes	.20	.09
☐ 325 Juan Gonzalez	1.00	.45
☐ 326 Charles Nagy	.20	.09
☐ 327 Ray Lankford	.20	.09
☐ 328 Mark Portugal	.10	.05
☐ 329 Bobby Bonilla	.30	.14
☐ 330 Reggie Sanders	.10	.05
☐ 331 Jamie Brewington	.10	.05
☐ 332 Aaron Sele	.10	.05
☐ 333 Pete Harnisch	.10	.05
☐ 334 Cliff Floyd	.10	.05
☐ 335 Cal Eldred	.10	.05
☐ 336 Jason Bates	.10	.05
☐ 337 Tony Clark	.40	.18
☐ 338 Jose Herrera	.10	.05
☐ 339 Alex Ochoa	.10	.05
☐ 340 Mark Loretta	.10	.05
☐ 341 Donne Wall	.10	.05
☐ 342 Jason Kendall	.20	.09
☐ 343 Shannon Stewart	.20	.09
☐ 344 Brooks Kieschnick	.10	.05
☐ 345 Chris Snopek	.10	.05
☐ 346 Ruben Rivera	.20	.09
☐ 347 Jeff Suppan	.30	.14
☐ 348 Phil Nevin	.10	.05
☐ 349 John Wasdin	.10	.05
☐ 350 Jay Payton	.10	.05
☐ 351 Tim Crabtree	.10	.05
☐ 352 Rick Krivda	.10	.05
☐ 353 Bob Wolcott	.10	.05
☐ 354 Jimmy Haynes	.10	.05
☐ 355 Herb Perry	.10	.05
☐ 356 Ryne Sandberg	.50	.23
☐ 357 Harold Baines	.20	.09
☐ 358 Chad Ogea	.10	.05
☐ 359 Lee Tinsley	.10	.05
☐ 360 Matt Williams	.30	.14
☐ 361 Randy Velarde	.10	.05
☐ 362 Jose Canseco	.30	.14
☐ 363 Larry Walker	.40	.18
☐ 364 Kevin Appier	.10	.05
☐ 365 Darryl Hamilton	.10	.05
☐ 366 Jose Lima	.10	.05
☐ 367 Javy Lopez	.20	.09
☐ 368 Dennis Eckersley	.30	.14
☐ 369 Jason Isringhausen	.10	.05
☐ 370 Mickey Morandini	.10	.05
☐ 371 Scott Cooper	.10	.05
☐ 372 Jim Abbott	.20	.09
☐ 373 Paul Sorrento	.10	.05
☐ 374 Chris Hammond	.10	.05
☐ 375 Lance Johnson	.10	.05
☐ 376 Kevin Brown	.20	.09
☐ 377 Luis Alicea	.10	.05
☐ 378 Andy Pettitte	.50	.23
☐ 379 Dean Palmer	.20	.09
☐ 380 Jeff Bagwell	.75	.35
☐ 381 Jaime Navarro	.10	.05
☐ 382 Rondell White	.20	.09
☐ 383 Erik Hanson	.10	.05
☐ 384 Pedro Munoz	.10	.05
☐ 385 Heathcliff Slocumb	.10	.05
☐ 386 Wally Joyner	.10	.05
☐ 387 Bob Tewksbury	.10	.05
☐ 388 David Bell	.10	.05
☐ 389 Fred McGriff	.30	.14
☐ 390 Mike Henneman	.10	.05
☐ 391 Robby Thompson	.10	.05
☐ 392 Norm Charlton	.10	.05
☐ 393 Cecil Fielder	.20	.09
☐ 394 Benito Santiago	.10	.05
☐ 395 Rafael Palmeiro	.30	.14
☐ 396 Ricky Bones	.10	.05
☐ 397 Rickey Henderson	.30	.14
☐ 398 C.J. Nitkowski	.10	.05
☐ 399 Shawon Dunston	.10	.05
☐ 400 Manny Ramirez	.40	.18
☐ 401 Bill Swift	.10	.05
☐ 402 Chad Fonville	.10	.05
☐ 403 Joey Hamilton	.10	.05
☐ 404 Alex Gonzalez	.10	.05
☐ 405 Roberto Hernandez	.20	.09
☐ 406 Jeff Blauser	.10	.05
☐ 407 LaTroy Hawkins	.10	.05
☐ 408 Greg Colbrunn	.10	.05
☐ 409 Todd Hundley	.30	.14
☐ 410 Glenn Dishman	.10	.05
☐ 411 Joe Vitiello	.10	.05
☐ 412 Todd Worrell	.20	.09
☐ 413 Wil Cordero	.10	.05
☐ 414 Ken Hill	.10	.05
☐ 415 Carlos Garcia	.10	.05
☐ 416 Bryan Rekar	.10	.05
☐ 417 Shawn Green	.20	.09
☐ 418 Tyler Green	.10	.05
☐ 419 Mike Blowers	.10	.05
☐ 420 Kenny Lofton	.50	.23
☐ 421 Denny Neagle	.20	.09
☐ 422 Jeff Conine	.20	.09
☐ 423 Mark Langston	.10	.05
☐ 424 Steve Cox	1.00	.45
Jesse Ibarra		
Derrek Lee		
Ron Wright		
☐ 425 Jim Bonnici	.50	.23
Billy Owens		
Richie Sexson		
Daryle Ward		
☐ 426 Kevin Jordan	.30	.14
Bobby Morris		
Desi Relaford		
Adam Riggs		
☐ 427 Tim Harkrider	.20	.09
Rey Ordonez		
Neifi Perez		
Enrique Wilson		
☐ 428 Bartolo Colon	.20	.09
Doug Million		
Rafael Orellano		
Ray Ricken		
☐ 429 Jeff D'Amico	.20	.09
Marty Janzen		
Gary Rath		
Clint Sodowsky		
☐ 430 Matt Drews	.20	.09
Rich Hunter		
Matt Ruebel		
Bret Wagner		
☐ 431 Jaime Bluma	.30	.14
David Coggin		
Steve Montgomery		
Brandon Reed		
☐ 432 Mike Figga	1.00	.45
Raul Ibanez		
Paul Konerko		
Julio Mosquera		
☐ 433 Brian Barber	.20	.09
Marc Kroon		
Marc Valdes		
Don Wengert		
☐ 434 George Arias	1.50	.70
Chris Haas		
Scott Rolen		
Scott Spiezio		
☐ 435 Brian Banks	2.50	1.10
Vladimir Guerrero		
Andruw Jones		
Billy McMillon		
☐ 436 Roger Cedeno	1.25	.55
Derrick Gibson		
Ben Grieve		
Shane Spencer		
☐ 437 Anton French	.25	.11
Demond Smith		
DaRond Stovall		
Keith Williams		
☐ 438 Michael Coleman	.50	.23
Jacob Cruz		
Richard Hidalgo		
Charles Peterson		
☐ 439 Trey Beamon	.40	.18
Yamil Benitez		
Jermaine Dye		
Angel Echevarria		
☐ 440 Checklist	.10	.05
☐ F7 Mickey Mantle Last Day	12.00	5.50

1996 Topps Classic Confrontations

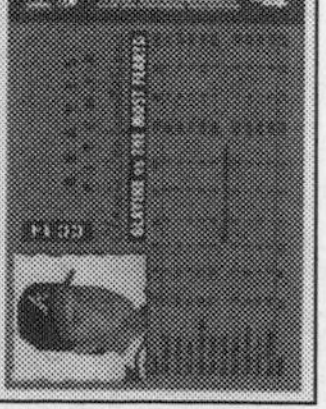

These cards were inserted at a rate of one in every 5-card Series 1 retail pack sold at Walmart. The first ten cards showcase hitters, while the last five cards feature pitchers. Inside white borders, the fronts show player cutouts on a brownish rock background featuring a shadow image of the player. The player's name is gold foil stamped across the bottom. The horizontal backs of the hitters' cards are aqua and present headshots and statistics. The backs of the pitchers cards are purple and present the same information.

	MINT	NRMT
COMPLETE SET (15)	6.00	2.70
COMMON CARD (CC1-CC15)	.10	.05

	MINT	NRMT
☐ CC1 Ken Griffey Jr.	1.50	.70
☐ CC2 Cal Ripken	1.25	.55
☐ CC3 Edgar Martinez	.40	.18
☐ CC4 Kirby Puckett	.60	.25
☐ CC5 Frank Thomas	1.25	.55
☐ CC6 Barry Bonds	.60	.25
☐ CC7 Reggie Sanders	.10	.05
☐ CC8 Andres Galarraga	.60	.25
☐ CC9 Tony Gwynn	.75	.35
☐ CC10 Mike Piazza	1.00	.45
☐ CC11 Randy Johnson	.60	.25
☐ CC12 Mike Mussina	.60	.25
☐ CC13 Roger Clemens	.75	.35
☐ CC14 Tom Glavine	.25	.11
☐ CC15 Greg Maddux	1.00	.45

1996 Topps Mantle

Randomly inserted in Series 1 packs, these cards are reprints of the original Mickey Mantle cards issued from 1951 through 1969. The fronts look the same except for a commemorative stamp, while the backs clearly state that they are "Mickey Mantle Commemorative" cards and have a 1996 copyright date. These cards honor Yankee great Mickey Mantle, who passed away in August 1995 after a gallant battle against cancer. Based on evidence from an uncut sheet auctioned off at the 1996 Kit Young Hawaii Trade Show, some collectors/dealers believe that cards 15 through 19 were slightly shorter printed in relation to the other 14 cards.

	MINT	NRMT
COMPLETE SET (19)	150.00	70.00
COMMON MANTLE (1-14)	8.00	3.60
COMMON MANTLE SP (15-19)	12.00	5.50
COMP.CASE SET (19)	1000.00	450.00
COMMON CASE (1-14)	50.00	22.00
COMMON CASE SP (15-19)	60.00	27.00
*'51-'53 CASE: 3X TO 6X LISTED CARDS		
COMP.FINEST SET (19)	150.00	70.00
COMMON FINEST (1-14)	8.00	3.60
COMMON FINEST SP (15-19)	12.00	5.50
*'51-'53 FINEST: .5X TO 1X LISTED CARDS		
COMP.REF.SET (19)	800.00	350.00
COMMON REF. (1-14)	40.00	18.00
COMMON REF.SP (15-19)	50.00	22.00
*'51-'53 REF: 2.5X TO 5X LISTED CARDS		
COMP.RDMP.SET (19)	300.00	135.00
COMMON RDMP. (1-19)	15.00	6.75
*'51-'53 RDMP: 1X TO 2X LISTED CARDS		

	MINT	NRMT
☐ 1 Mickey Mantle	15.00	6.75
1951 Bowman		
☐ 2 Mickey Mantle	20.00	9.00
1952 Topps		
☐ 3 Mickey Mantle	10.00	4.50
1953 Topps		
☐ 4 Mickey Mantle	8.00	3.60
1954 Bowman		
☐ 5 Mickey Mantle	8.00	3.60
1955 Bowman		
☐ 6 Mickey Mantle	8.00	3.60
1956 Topps		
☐ 7 Mickey Mantle	8.00	3.60
1957 Topps		
☐ 8 Mickey Mantle	8.00	3.60
1958 Topps		
☐ 9 Mickey Mantle	8.00	3.60
1959 Topps		
☐ 10 Mickey Mantle	8.00	3.60
1960 Topps		
☐ 11 Mickey Mantle	8.00	3.60
1961 Topps		
☐ 12 Mickey Mantle	8.00	3.60
1962 Topps		
☐ 13 Mickey Mantle	8.00	3.60
1963 Topps		
☐ 14 Mickey Mantle	8.00	3.60
1964 Topps		
☐ 15 Mickey Mantle	12.00	5.50
1965 Topps		
☐ 16 Mickey Mantle	12.00	5.50
1966 Topps		
☐ 17 Mickey Mantle	12.00	5.50
1967 Topps		
☐ 18 Mickey Mantle	12.00	5.50
1968 Topps		
☐ 19 Mickey Mantle	12.00	5.50
1969 Topps		

1996 Topps Masters of the Game

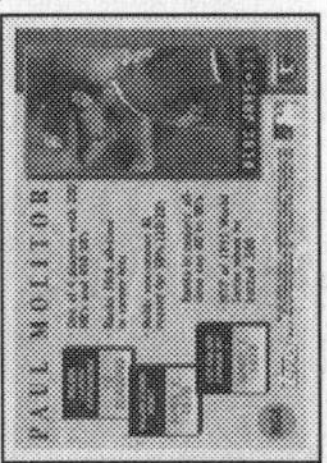

Cards from this 20-card standard-size set were randomly inserted into first-series hobby packs. In addition, every factory set contained two Masters of the Game cards. The horizontal fronts comprise of silver foil set against white borders. The left side of the card has a player photo. The words "Master of the Game" and the playerís name are printed on the right. The horizontal backs have a player photo, a brief write-up and some quick important dates in the playerís career. The cards are numbered with a "MG" prefix in the lower left corner.

	MINT	NRMT
COMPLETE SET (20)	30.00	13.50
COMMON CARD (1-20)	.75	.35

	MINT	NRMT
☐ 1 Dennis Eckersley	1.25	.55
☐ 2 Denny Martinez	.75	.35
☐ 3 Eddie Murray	1.50	.70
☐ 4 Paul Molitor	1.50	.70
☐ 5 Ozzie Smith	2.50	1.10
☐ 6 Rickey Henderson	1.25	.55
☐ 7 Tim Raines	.75	.35
☐ 8 Lee Smith	.75	.35
☐ 9 Cal Ripken	8.00	3.60
☐ 10 Chili Davis	.75	.35
☐ 11 Wade Boggs	1.50	.70
☐ 12 Tony Gwynn	5.00	2.20
☐ 13 Don Mattingly	4.00	1.80
☐ 14 Bret Saberhagen	.75	.35
☐ 15 Kirby Puckett	4.00	1.80
☐ 16 Joe Carter	1.00	.45
☐ 17 Roger Clemens	3.00	1.35
☐ 18 Barry Bonds	2.50	1.10
☐ 19 Greg Maddux	6.00	2.70
☐ 20 Frank Thomas	8.00	3.60

1996 Topps Mystery Finest

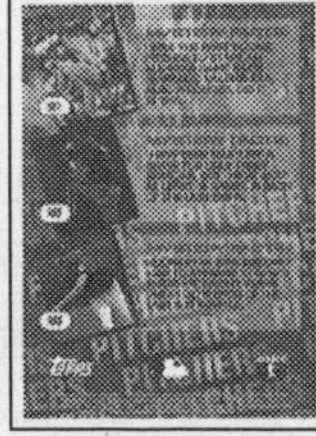

Randomly inserted in first-series packs, this 26-card standard-size set features a bit of a mystery. The fronts have opaque coating that must be removed before the player can be identified. After the opaque coating is removed, the fronts feature a player photo surrounded by silver borders. The backs feature a choice of players along with a corresponding mystery finest trivia fact. Some of these cards were also issued with refractor fronts.

	MINT	NRMT
COMPLETE SET (26)	150.00	70.00
COMMON CARD (M1-M26)	1.50	.70

	MINT	NRMT
☐ M1 Hideo Nomo	8.00	3.60
☐ M2 Greg Maddux	12.00	5.50
☐ M3 Randy Johnson	3.00	1.35
☐ M4 Chipper Jones	12.00	5.50
☐ M5 Marty Cordova	1.50	.70
☐ M6 Garret Anderson	2.00	.90
☐ M7 Cal Ripken	15.00	6.75
☐ M8 Kirby Puckett	8.00	3.60
☐ M9 Tony Gwynn	8.00	3.60
☐ M10 Manny Ramirez	3.00	1.35
☐ M11 Jim Edmonds	3.00	1.35
☐ M12 Mike Piazza	12.00	5.50
☐ M13 Barry Bonds	5.00	2.20
☐ M14 Raul Mondesi	2.50	1.10
☐ M15 Sammy Sosa	3.00	1.35
☐ M16 Ken Griffey Jr.	20.00	9.00
☐ M17 Albert Belle	8.00	3.60
☐ M18 Dante Bichette	2.00	.90
☐ M19 Mo Vaughn	5.00	2.20
☐ M20 Jeff Bagwell	8.00	3.60
☐ M21 Frank Thomas	15.00	6.75
☐ M22 Hideo Nomo	8.00	3.60
☐ M23 Cal Ripken	15.00	6.75
☐ M24 Mike Piazza	12.00	5.50
☐ M25 Ken Griffey Jr.	20.00	9.00
☐ M26 Frank Thomas	15.00	6.75

1996 Topps Power Boosters

Randomly inserted into packs, these cards are a metalli version of 25 of the first 26 cards from the basic Topp set. Card numbers 1-6 and 8-12 were issued in retai packs, while numbers 13-26 were issued in hobby packs Inserted in place of two basic cards, they are printed o 28 point stock and the fronts have prismatic foil printing Card number 7, which is Mickey Mantle in the regular se was not issued in a Power Booster form.

	MINT	NRM
COMPLETE SET (25)	90.00	40.0
COMP. STAR POWER SET (11)	50.00	22.0
COMP. DRAFT PICKS SET (14)	40.00	18.0
COMMON STAR POW. (1-6/8-12)	1.50	.7
COMMON DRAFT PICK (12-26)	2.00	.9

	MINT	NRM
☐ 1 Tony Gwynn	8.00	3.6
☐ 2 Mike Piazza	12.00	5.5
☐ 3 Greg Maddux	12.00	5.5
☐ 4 Jeff Bagwell	8.00	3.6
☐ 5 Larry Walker	2.50	1.1
☐ 6 Barry Larkin	2.50	1.1
☐ 8 Tom Glavine	2.00	.9
☐ 9 Craig Biggio	2.50	1.1
☐ 10 Barry Bonds	5.00	2.2
☐ 11 Heathcliff Slocumb	1.50	.7
☐ 12 Matt Williams	2.50	1.1
☐ 13 Todd Helton	15.00	6.7
☐ 14 Mark Redman	2.00	.9
☐ 15 Michael Barrett	2.00	.9
☐ 16 Ben Davis	6.00	2.7
☐ 17 Juan LeBron	5.00	2.2
☐ 18 Tony McKnight	2.00	.9
☐ 19 Ryan Jaroncyk	2.00	.9
☐ 20 Corey Jenkins	4.00	1.8
☐ 21 Jim Scharrer	2.00	.9
☐ 22 Mark Bellhorn	4.00	1.8
☐ 23 Jarrod Washburn	2.00	.9
☐ 24 Geoff Jenkins	4.00	1.8
☐ 25 Sean Casey	8.00	3.6
☐ 26 Brett Tomko	4.00	1.8

1996 Topps Profiles

Randomly inserted into Series 1 and 2 packs, this 20-ca standard-size set features 10 players from each leagu One card from each series was also included in all Top factory sets. Topps spokesmen Kirby Puckett (AL) a

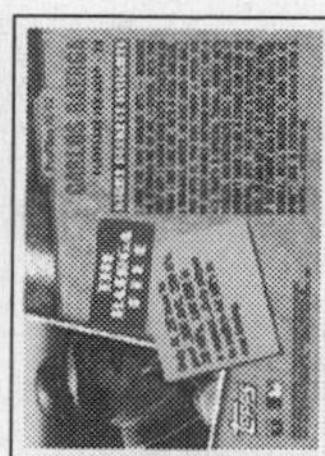

ony Gwynn (NL) give opinions on players within their eague. The fronts feature a player photo set against a ilver-foil background. The playerís name is on the ottom. A photo of either Gwynn or Puckett as well as the ords "Profiles by ..." is on the right. The backs feature a layer photo, some career data as well as Gwynn's or uckett's opinion about the featured player. The cards are umbered with either an "AL or NL" prefix on the back epending on the playerís league. The cards are equenced in alphabetical order within league.

	MINT	NRMT
OMPLETE SET (40)	40.00	18.00
OMPLETE SERIES 1 (20)	30.00	13.50
OMPLETE SERIES 2 (20)	10.00	4.50
OMMON CARD (AL1-NL20)	.50	.23
AL1 Roberto Alomar	1.00	.45
AL2 Carlos Baerga	.50	.23
AL3 Albert Belle	1.25	.55
AL4 Cecil Fielder	.60	.25
AL5 Ken Griffey Jr.	5.00	2.20
AL6 Randy Johnson	1.00	.45
AL7 Paul O'Neill	.60	.25
AL8 Cal Ripken	4.00	1.80
AL9 Frank Thomas	4.00	1.80
AL10 Mo Vaughn	1.25	.55
AL11 Jay Buhner	.75	.35
AL12 Marty Cordova	.50	.23
AL13 Jim Edmonds	1.00	.45
AL14 Juan Gonzalez	2.50	1.10
AL15 Kenny Lofton	1.25	.55
AL16 Edgar Martinez	.75	.35
AL17 Don Mattingly	2.00	.90
AL18 Mark McGwire	2.00	.90
AL19 Rafael Palmeiro	.75	.35
AL20 Tim Salmon	1.00	.45
NL1 Jeff Bagwell	2.00	.90
NL2 Derek Bell	.50	.23
NL3 Barry Bonds	1.25	.55
NL4 Greg Maddux	3.00	1.35
NL5 Fred McGriff	.75	.35
NL6 Raul Mondesi	.75	.35
NL7 Mike Piazza	3.00	1.35
NL8 Reggie Sanders	.50	.23
NL9 Sammy Sosa	1.00	.45
NL10 Larry Walker	1.00	.45
NL11 Dante Bichette	.60	.25
NL12 Andres Galarraga	1.00	.45
NL13 Ron Gant	.50	.23
NL14 Tom Glavine	.60	.25
NL15 Chipper Jones	3.00	1.35
NL16 David Justice	1.00	.45
NL17 Barry Larkin	.75	.35
NL18 Hideo Nomo	2.00	.90
NL19 Gary Sheffield	1.00	.45
NL20 Matt Williams	.75	.35

1996 Topps Road Warriors

; 20-card set was inserted only into Series 2 WalMart ks and featured leading hitters of the majors. The set equenced in alphabetical order.

	MINT	NRMT
IPLETE SET (20)	12.00	5.50
IMON CARD (RW1-RW20)	.25	.11
RW1 Derek Bell	.25	.11
RW2 Albert Belle	1.00	.45
☐ RW3 Craig Biggio	.50	.23
☐ RW4 Barry Bonds	1.00	.45
☐ RW5 Jay Buhner	.50	.23
☐ RW6 Jim Edmonds	.75	.35
☐ RW7 Gary Gaetti	.35	.16
☐ RW8 Ron Gant	.35	.16
☐ RW9 Edgar Martinez	.50	.23
☐ RW10 Tino Martinez	.75	.35
☐ RW11 Mark McGwire	1.50	.70
☐ RW12 Mike Piazza	3.00	1.35
☐ RW13 Manny Ramirez	.75	.35
☐ RW14 Tim Salmon	.75	.35
☐ RW15 Reggie Sanders	.25	.11
☐ RW16 Frank Thomas	4.00	1.80
☐ RW17 John Valentin	.25	.11
☐ RW18 Mo Vaughn	1.00	.45
☐ RW19 Robin Ventura	.35	.16
☐ RW20 Matt Williams	.50	.23

1996 Topps Wrecking Crew

Randomly inserted in Series 2 hobby packs, this 15-card set honors some of the hottest home run producers in the League. One card from this set was also inserted into Topps Hobby Factory sets. The cards feature color action player photos with foil stamping.

	MINT	NRMT
COMPLETE SET (15)	70.00	32.00
COMMON CARD (1-15)	1.50	.70
☐ WC1 Jeff Bagwell	8.00	3.60
☐ WC2 Albert Belle	5.00	2.20
☐ WC3 Barry Bonds	5.00	2.20
☐ WC4 Jose Canseco	2.50	1.10
☐ WC5 Joe Carter	2.00	.90
☐ WC6 Cecil Fielder	2.00	.90
☐ WC7 Ron Gant	1.50	.70
☐ WC8 Juan Gonzalez	10.00	4.50
☐ WC9 Ken Griffey Jr	20.00	9.00
☐ WC10 Fred McGriff	2.50	1.10
☐ WC11 Mark McGwire	8.00	3.60
☐ WC12 Mike Piazza	12.00	5.50
☐ WC13 Frank Thomas	15.00	6.75
☐ WC14 Mo Vaughn	5.00	2.20
☐ WC15 Matt Williams	2.50	1.10

1996 Topps Big Cards

This nine-card set measures approximately 3 1/2" by 5" and was distributed only by Walmart. One card was packed with the team set of the star player. The fronts feature oversized photos of the Topps cards. The cards are unnumbered and checklisted below in alphabetical order.

	MINT	NRMT
COMPLETE SET (9)	25.00	11.00
COMMON CARD (1-9)	2.00	.90
☐ 1 Albert Belle	2.00	.90
☐ 2 Juan Gonzalez	3.00	1.35
☐ 3 Ken Griffey Jr.	6.00	2.70
☐ 4 Derek Jeter	3.00	1.35
☐ 5 Greg Maddux	4.00	1.80
☐ 6 Hideo Nomo	3.00	1.35
☐ 7 Cal Ripken	5.00	2.20
☐ 8 Ryne Sandberg	3.00	1.35
☐ 9 Frank Thomas	5.00	2.20

1997 Topps

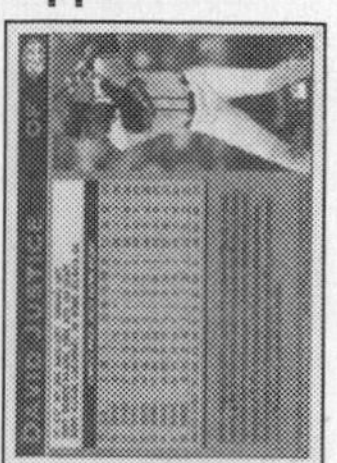

This 495-card set was primarily distributed in first and second series 11-card packs with a suggested retail price of $1.29. In addition, 8-card retail packs, 40-card jumbo packs and factory sets were made available. The card fronts feature a color action player photo with a gloss coating and a spot matte finish on the outside border with gold foil stamping. The backs carry another player photo, player information and statistics. The set includes the following subsets: Season Highlights (100-104, 462-466), Prospects (200-207, 487-494), the first ever expansion team cards of the Arizona Diamondbacks (249-251,468-469 and the Tampa Bay Devil Rays (252-253, 470-472) and Draft Picks (269-274, 477-483). Card 42 is a special Jackie Robinson tribute card commemorating the 50th anniversary of his contribution to baseball history and numbered for his Dodgers uniform number. Card #7 does not exist because it was retired in honor of Mickey Mantle. Card #84 does not exist because Mike Fetters' card was incorrectly numbered #61. Card #277 does not exist because Chipper Jones' card was incorrectly numbered #276. 1996 number one draft pick Kris Benson's first card highlights the wide selection of Rookie Cards available in the set.

	MINT	NRMT
COMPLETE SET (495)	30.00	13.50
COMPLETE SERIES 1 (275)	15.00	6.75
COMPLETE SERIES 2 (220)	15.00	6.75
COMMON CARD (1-496)	.10	.05
☐ 1 Barry Bonds	.50	.23
☐ 2 Tom Pagnozzi	.10	.05
☐ 3 Terrell Wade	.10	.05
☐ 4 Jose Valentin	.10	.05
☐ 5 Mark Clark	.10	.05
☐ 6 Brady Anderson	.30	.14
☐ 8 Wade Boggs	.40	.18
☐ 9 Scott Stahoviak	.10	.05
☐ 10 Andres Galarraga	.40	.18
☐ 11 Steve Avery	.10	.05
☐ 12 Rusty Greer	.20	.09
☐ 13 Derek Jeter	1.25	.55
☐ 14 Ricky Bottalico	.10	.05
☐ 15 Andy Ashby	.10	.05
☐ 16 Paul Shuey	.10	.05
☐ 17 F.P. Santangelo	.10	.05
☐ 18 Royce Clayton	.10	.05
☐ 19 Mike Mohler	.10	.05
☐ 20 Mike Piazza	1.25	.55
☐ 21 Jaime Navarro	.10	.05
☐ 22 Billy Wagner	.20	.09
☐ 23 Mike Timlin	.10	.05
☐ 24 Garret Anderson	.20	.09
☐ 25 Ben McDonald	.10	.05
☐ 26 Mel Rojas	.10	.05
☐ 27 John Burkett	.10	.05
☐ 28 Jeff King	.10	.05
☐ 29 Reggie Jefferson	.10	.05
☐ 30 Kevin Appier	.20	.09
☐ 31 Felipe Lira	.10	.05
☐ 32 Kevin Tapani	.10	.05
☐ 33 Mark Portugal	.10	.05
☐ 34 Carlos Garcia	.10	.05
☐ 35 Joey Cora	.20	.09
☐ 36 David Segui	.10	.05
☐ 37 Mark Grace	.30	.14
☐ 38 Erik Hanson	.10	.05
☐ 39 Jeff D'Amico	.20	.09
☐ 40 Jay Buhner	.30	.14
☐ 41 B.J. Surhoff	.20	.09
☐ 42 Jackie Robinson TRIB	2.00	.90
☐ 43 Roger Pavlik	.10	.05
☐ 44 Hal Morris	.10	.05
☐ 45 Mariano Duncan	.10	.05
☐ 46 Harold Baines	.10	.05
☐ 47 Jorge Fabregas	.10	.05
☐ 48 Jose Herrera	.10	.05
☐ 49 Jeff Cirillo	.20	.09
☐ 50 Tom Glavine	.20	.09
☐ 51 Pedro Astacio	.10	.05

☐ 52 Mark Gardner .10 .05
☐ 53 Arthur Rhodes .10 .05
☐ 54 Troy O'Leary .10 .05
☐ 55 Bip Roberts .10 .05
☐ 56 Mike Lieberthal .10 .05
☐ 57 Shane Andrews .10 .05
☐ 58 Scott Karl .10 .05
☐ 59 Gary DiSarcina .10 .05
☐ 60 Andy Pettitte .40 .18
☐ 61 Kevin Elster .10 .05
☐ 62 Mark McGwire .75 .35
☐ 63 Dan Wilson .10 .05
☐ 64 Mickey Morandini .10 .05
☐ 65 Chuck Knoblauch .40 .18
☐ 66 Tim Wakefield .10 .05
☐ 67 Raul Mondesi .30 .14
☐ 68 Todd Jones .10 .05
☐ 69 Albert Belle .50 .23
☐ 70 Trevor Hoffman .10 .05
☐ 71 Eric Young .20 .09
☐ 72 Robert Perez .10 .05
☐ 73 Butch Huskey .20 .09
☐ 74 Brian McRae .10 .05
☐ 75 Jim Edmonds .40 .18
☐ 76 Mike Henneman .10 .05
☐ 77 Frank Rodriguez .10 .05
☐ 78 Danny Tartabull .10 .05
☐ 79 Robb Nen .10 .05
☐ 80 Reggie Sanders .10 .05
☐ 81 Ron Karkovice .10 .05
☐ 82 Benito Santiago .10 .05
☐ 83 Mike Lansing .10 .05
☐ 84 Mike Fetters UER .10 .05
Card numbered 61
☐ 85 Craig Biggio .30 .14
☐ 86 Mike Bordick .10 .05
☐ 87 Ray Lankford .20 .09
☐ 88 Charles Nagy .20 .09
☐ 89 Paul Wilson .10 .05
☐ 90 John Wetteland .20 .09
☐ 91 Tom Candiotti .10 .05
☐ 92 Carlos Delgado .20 .09
☐ 93 Derek Bell .10 .05
☐ 94 Mark Lemke .10 .05
☐ 95 Edgar Martinez .30 .14
☐ 96 Rickey Henderson .30 .14
☐ 97 Greg Myers .10 .05
☐ 98 Jim Leyritz .10 .05
☐ 99 Mark Johnson .10 .05
☐ 100 Dwight Gooden HL .20 .09
☐ 101 Al Leiter HL .10 .05
☐ 102 John Mabry HL .10 .05
☐ 103 Alex Ochoa HL .10 .05
☐ 104 Mike Piazza HL 1.00 .45
☐ 105 Jim Thome .40 .18
☐ 106 Ricky Otero .10 .05
☐ 107 Jamey Wright .20 .09
☐ 108 Frank Thomas 1.50 .70
☐ 109 Jody Reed .10 .05
☐ 110 Orel Hershiser .20 .09
☐ 111 Terry Steinbach .20 .09
☐ 112 Mark Loretta .10 .05
☐ 113 Turk Wendell .10 .05
☐ 114 Marvin Benard .10 .05
☐ 115 Kevin Brown .20 .09
☐ 116 Robert Person .10 .05
☐ 117 Joey Hamilton .20 .09
☐ 118 Francisco Cordova .10 .05
☐ 119 John Smiley .10 .05
☐ 120 Travis Fryman .20 .09
☐ 121 Jimmy Key .20 .09
☐ 122 Tom Goodwin .10 .05
☐ 123 Mike Greenwell .10 .05
☐ 124 Juan Gonzalez 1.00 .45
☐ 125 Pete Harnisch .10 .05
☐ 126 Roger Cedeno .10 .05
☐ 127 Ron Gant .20 .09
☐ 128 Mark Langston .10 .05
☐ 129 Tim Crabtree .10 .05
☐ 130 Greg Maddux 1.25 .55
☐ 131 William VanLandingham .10 .05
☐ 132 Wally Joyner .10 .05
☐ 133 Randy Myers .10 .05
☐ 134 John Valentin .10 .05
☐ 135 Bret Boone .10 .05
☐ 136 Bruce Ruffin .10 .05
☐ 137 Chris Snopek .10 .05
☐ 138 Paul Molitor .40 .18
☐ 139 Mark McLemore .10 .05
☐ 140 Rafael Palmeiro .30 .14
☐ 141 Herb Perry .10 .05
☐ 142 Luis Gonzalez .10 .05
☐ 143 Doug Drabek .10 .05
☐ 144 Ken Ryan .10 .05
☐ 145 Todd Hundley .20 .09
☐ 146 Ellis Burks .20 .09
☐ 147 Ozzie Guillen .10 .05
☐ 148 Rich Becker .10 .05
☐ 149 Sterling Hitchcock .10 .05
☐ 150 Bernie Williams .40 .18
☐ 151 Mike Stanley .10 .05
☐ 152 Roberto Alomar .40 .18
☐ 153 Jose Mesa .20 .09
☐ 154 Steve Trachsel .10 .05
☐ 155 Alex Gonzalez .10 .05
☐ 156 Troy Percival .20 .09
☐ 157 John Smoltz .20 .09
☐ 158 Pedro Martinez .40 .18
☐ 159 Jeff Conine .20 .09
☐ 160 Bernard Gilkey .10 .05
☐ 161 Jim Eisenreich .20 .09
☐ 162 Mickey Tettleton .10 .05
☐ 163 Justin Thompson .20 .09
☐ 164 Jose Offerman .10 .05
☐ 165 Tony Phillips .10 .05
☐ 166 Ismael Valdes .20 .09
☐ 167 Ryne Sandberg .50 .23
☐ 168 Matt Mieske .10 .05
☐ 169 Geronimo Berroa .10 .05
☐ 170 Otis Nixon .10 .05
☐ 171 John Mabry .10 .05
☐ 172 Shawon Dunston .10 .05
☐ 173 Omar Vizquel .20 .09
☐ 174 Chris Hoiles .10 .05
☐ 175 Dwight Gooden .20 .09
☐ 176 Wilson Alvarez .10 .05
☐ 177 Todd Hollandsworth .20 .09
☐ 178 Roger Salkeld .10 .05
☐ 179 Rey Sanchez .10 .05
☐ 180 Rey Ordonez .10 .05
☐ 181 Denny Martinez .20 .09
☐ 182 Ramon Martinez .20 .09
☐ 183 Dave Nilsson .10 .05
☐ 184 Marquis Grissom .20 .09
☐ 185 Randy Velarde .10 .05
☐ 186 Ron Coomer .10 .05
☐ 187 Tino Martinez .40 .18
☐ 188 Jeff Brantley .10 .05
☐ 189 Steve Finley .20 .09
☐ 190 Andy Benes .10 .05
☐ 191 Terry Adams .10 .05
☐ 192 Mike Blowers .10 .05
☐ 193 Russ Davis .10 .05
☐ 194 Darryl Hamilton .10 .05
☐ 195 Jason Kendall .20 .09
☐ 196 Johnny Damon .20 .09
☐ 197 Dave Martinez .10 .05
☐ 198 Mike Macfarlane .10 .05
☐ 199 Norm Charlton .10 .05
☐ 200 Doug Million .25 .11
Damian Moss
Bobby Rodgers
☐ 201 Geoff Jenkins .20 .09
Raul Ibanez
Mike Cameron
☐ 202 Sean Casey .20 .09
Jim Bonnici
Dmitri Young
☐ 203 Jed Hansen .20 .09
Homer Bush
Feilipe Crespo
☐ 204 Kevin Orie .20 .09
Gabe Alvarez
Aaron Boone
☐ 205 Ben Davis .20 .09
Kevin Brown
Bobby Estalella
☐ 206 Billy McMillon .40 .18
Bubba Trammell
Dante Powell
☐ 207 Jarrod Washburn .20 .09
Marc Wilkins
Glendon Rusch
☐ 208 Brian Hunter .20 .09
☐ 209 Jason Giambi .20 .09
☐ 210 Henry Rodriguez .10 .05
☐ 211 Edgar Renteria .20 .09
☐ 212 Edgardo Alfonzo .20 .09
☐ 213 Fernando Vina .10 .05
☐ 214 Shawn Green .10 .05
☐ 215 Ray Durham .10 .05
☐ 216 Joe Randa .10 .05
☐ 217 Armando Reynoso .10 .05
☐ 218 Eric Davis .10 .05
☐ 219 Bob Tewksbury .10 .05
☐ 220 Jacob Cruz .10 .05
☐ 221 Glenallen Hill .10 .05
☐ 222 Gary Gaetti .20 .09
☐ 223 Donne Wall .10 .05
☐ 224 Brad Clontz .10 .05
☐ 225 Marty Janzen .10 .05
☐ 226 Todd Worrell .10 .05
☐ 227 John Franco .20 .09
☐ 228 David Wells .10 .05
☐ 229 Gregg Jefferies .20 .09
☐ 230 Tim Naehring .10 .05
☐ 231 Thomas Howard .10 .05
☐ 232 Roberto Hernandez .20 .09
☐ 233 Kevin Ritz .10 .05
☐ 234 Julian Tavarez .10 .05
☐ 235 Ken Hill .10 .05
☐ 236 Greg Gagne .10 .05
☐ 237 Bobby Chouinard .10 .05
☐ 238 Joe Carter .20 .09
☐ 239 Jermaine Dye .10 .05
☐ 240 Antonio Osuna .10 .05
☐ 241 Julio Franco .20 .09
☐ 242 Mike Grace .10 .05
☐ 243 Aaron Sele .10 .05
☐ 244 David Justice .40 .18
☐ 245 Sandy Alomar Jr. .20 .09
☐ 246 Jose Canseco .30 .14
☐ 247 Paul O'Neill .10 .05
☐ 248 Sean Berry .10 .05
☐ 249 Nick Bierbrodt .25 .11
Kevin Sweeney
☐ 250 Larry Rodriguez .25 .11
Vladimir Nunez
☐ 251 Ron Hartman .25 .11
David Hayman
☐ 252 Alex Sanchez .40 .18
Matthew Quatraro
☐ 253 Ronni Seberino .25 .11
Pablo Ortego
☐ 254 Rex Hudler .10 .05
☐ 255 Orlando Miller .10 .05
☐ 256 Mariano Rivera .20 .09
☐ 257 Brad Radke .10 .05
☐ 258 Bobby Higginson .20 .09
☐ 259 Jay Bell .10 .05
☐ 260 Mark Grudzielanek .10 .05
☐ 261 Lance Johnson .10 .05
☐ 262 Ken Caminiti .40 .18
☐ 263 J.T. Snow .20 .09
☐ 264 Gary Sheffield .40 .18
☐ 265 Darrin Fletcher .10 .05
☐ 266 Eric Owens .10 .05
☐ 267 Luis Castillo .20 .09
☐ 268 Scott Rolen 1.00 .45
☐ 269 Todd Noel .25 .11
John Oliver
☐ 270 Robert Stratton .25 .11
Corey Lee
☐ 271 Gil Meche .25 .11
Matt Halloran
☐ 272 Eric Milton 1.00 .45
Dermal Brown
☐ 273 Josh Garrett .25 .11
Chris Reitsma
☐ 274 A.J.Zapp .75 .35
Jason Marquis
☐ 275 Checklist .10 .05
☐ 276 Checklist .10 .05
☐ 277 Chipper Jones UER 1.25 .55
incorrectly numbered 276
☐ 278 Orlando Merced .10 .05
☐ 279 Ariel Prieto .10 .05
☐ 280 Al Leiter .10 .05
☐ 281 Pat Meares .10 .05
☐ 282 Darryl Strawberry .20 .09
☐ 283 Jamie Moyer .10 .05
☐ 284 Scott Servais .10 .05
☐ 285 Delino DeShields .10 .05
☐ 286 Danny Graves .10 .05
☐ 287 Gerald Williams .10 .05
☐ 288 Todd Greene .20 .0
☐ 289 Rico Brogna .10 .0
☐ 290 Derrick Gibson .40 .1
☐ 291 Joe Girardi .10 .0
☐ 292 Darren Lewis .10 .0
☐ 293 Nomar Garciaparra 1.25 .5
☐ 294 Greg Colbrunn .10 .0
☐ 295 Jeff Bagwell .75 .3
☐ 296 Brent Gates .10 .0
☐ 297 Jose Vizcaino .10 .0
☐ 298 Alex Ochoa .10 .0
☐ 299 Sid Fernandez .10 .0
☐ 300 Ken Griffey Jr. 2.00 .9
☐ 301 Chris Gomez .10 .0
☐ 302 Wendell Magee .10 .0
☐ 303 Darren Oliver .10 .0
☐ 304 Mel Nieves .10 .0
☐ 305 Sammy Sosa .40 .1
☐ 306 George Arias .10 .0
☐ 307 Jack McDowell .10 .0
☐ 308 Stan Javier .10 .0
☐ 309 Kimera Bartee .10 .0
☐ 310 James Baldwin .10 .0
☐ 311 Rocky Coppinger .20 .0
☐ 312 Keith Lockhart .10 .0
☐ 313 C.J. Nitkowski .10 .0

☐ 314 Allen Watson	.10	.05
☐ 315 Darryl Kile	.20	.09
☐ 316 Amaury Telemaco	.10	.05
☐ 317 Jason Isringhausen	.10	.05
☐ 318 Manny Ramirez	.40	.18
☐ 319 Terry Pendleton	.10	.05
☐ 320 Tim Salmon	.40	.18
☐ 321 Eric Karros	.20	.09
☐ 322 Mark Whiten	.10	.05
☐ 323 Rick Krivda	.10	.05
☐ 324 Brett Butler	.20	.09
☐ 325 Randy Johnson	.40	.18
☐ 326 Eddie Taubensee	.10	.05
☐ 327 Mark Leiter	.10	.05
☐ 328 Kevin Gross	.10	.05
☐ 329 Ernie Young	.10	.05
☐ 330 Pat Hentgen	.20	.09
☐ 331 Rondell White	.10	.05
☐ 332 Bobby Witt	.10	.05
☐ 333 Eddie Murray	.40	.18
☐ 334 Tim Raines	.20	.09
☐ 335 Jeff Fassero	.10	.05
☐ 336 Chuck Finley	.10	.05
☐ 337 Willie Adams	.10	.05
☐ 338 Chan Ho Park	.40	.18
☐ 339 Jay Powell	.10	.05
☐ 340 Ivan Rodriguez	.50	.23
☐ 341 Jermaine Allensworth	.10	.05
☐ 342 Jay Payton	.20	.09
☐ 343 T.J. Mathews	.10	.05
☐ 344 Tony Batista	.20	.09
☐ 345 Ed Sprague	.10	.05
☐ 346 Jeff Kent	.10	.05
☐ 347 Scott Erickson	.10	.05
☐ 348 Jeff Suppan	.20	.09
☐ 349 Pete Schourek	.10	.05
☐ 350 Kenny Lofton	.50	.23
☐ 351 Alan Benes	.20	.09
☐ 352 Fred McGriff	.30	.14
☐ 353 Charlie O'Brien	.10	.05
☐ 354 Darren Bragg	.10	.05
☐ 355 Alex Fernandez	.20	.09
☐ 356 Al Martin	.10	.05
☐ 357 Bob Wells	.10	.05
☐ 358 Chad Mottola	.10	.05
☐ 359 Devon White	.10	.05
☐ 360 David Cone	.20	.09
☐ 361 Bobby Jones	.10	.05
☐ 362 Scott Sanders	.10	.05
☐ 363 Karim Garcia	.40	.18
☐ 364 Kirt Manwaring	.10	.05
☐ 365 Chili Davis	.10	.05
☐ 366 Mike Hampton	.10	.05
☐ 367 Chad Ogea	.10	.05
☐ 368 Curt Schilling	.20	.09
☐ 369 Phil Nevin	.10	.05
☐ 370 Roger Clemens	.75	.35
☐ 371 Willie Greene	.20	.09
☐ 372 Kenny Rogers	.10	.05
☐ 373 Jose Rijo	.10	.05
☐ 374 Bobby Bonilla	.20	.09
☐ 375 Mike Mussina	.40	.18
☐ 376 Curtis Pride	.10	.05
☐ 377 Todd Walker	.10	.05
☐ 378 Jason Bere	.10	.05
☐ 379 Heathcliff Slocumb	.10	.05
☐ 380 Dante Bichette	.20	.09
☐ 381 Carlos Baerga	.20	.09
☐ 382 Livan Hernandez	.40	.18
☐ 383 Jason Schmidt	.20	.09
☐ 384 Kevin Stocker	.10	.05
☐ 385 Matt Williams	.30	.14
☐ 386 Bartolo Colon	.20	.09
☐ 387 Will Clark	.30	.14
☐ 388 Dennis Eckersley	.30	.14
☐ 389 Brooks Kieschnick	.20	.09
☐ 390 Ryan Klesko	.30	.14
☐ 391 Mark Carreon	.10	.05
☐ 392 Tim Worrell	.10	.05
☐ 393 Dean Palmer	.20	.09
☐ 394 Wil Cordero	.10	.05
☐ 395 Javy Lopez	.20	.09
☐ 396 Rich Aurilia	.10	.05
☐ 397 Greg Vaughn	.10	.05
☐ 398 Vinny Castilla	.20	.09
☐ 399 Jeff Montgomery	.20	.09
☐ 400 Cal Ripken	1.50	.70
☐ 401 Walt Weiss	.10	.05
☐ 402 Brad Ausmus	.10	.05
☐ 403 Ruben Rivera	.20	.09
☐ 404 Mark Wohlers	.10	.05
☐ 405 Rick Aguilera	.10	.05
☐ 406 Tony Clark	.40	.18
☐ 407 Lyle Mouton	.10	.05
☐ 408 Bill Pulsipher	.10	.05
☐ 409 Jose Rosado	.20	.09
☐ 410 Tony Gwynn	1.00	.45
☐ 411 Cecil Fielder	.20	.09
☐ 412 John Flaherty	.10	.05
☐ 413 Lenny Dykstra	.20	.09
☐ 414 Ugueth Urbina	.20	.09
☐ 415 Brian Jordan	.20	.09
☐ 416 Bob Abreu	.40	.18
☐ 417 Craig Paquette	.10	.05
☐ 418 Sandy Martinez	.10	.05
☐ 419 Jeff Blauser	.10	.05
☐ 420 Barry Larkin	.30	.14
☐ 421 Kevin Seitzer	.10	.05
☐ 422 Tim Belcher	.10	.05
☐ 423 Paul Sorrento	.10	.05
☐ 424 Cal Eldred	.10	.05
☐ 425 Robin Ventura	.20	.09
☐ 426 John Olerud	.20	.09
☐ 427 Bob Wolcott	.10	.05
☐ 428 Matt Lawton	.10	.05
☐ 429 Rod Beck	.10	.05
☐ 430 Shane Reynolds	.10	.05
☐ 431 Mike James	.10	.05
☐ 432 Steve Wojciechowski	.10	.05
☐ 433 Vladimir Guerrero	.75	.35
☐ 434 Dustin Hermanson	.10	.05
☐ 435 Marty Cordova	.20	.09
☐ 436 Marc Newfield	.10	.05
☐ 437 Todd Stottlemyre	.10	.05
☐ 438 Jeffrey Hammonds	.10	.05
☐ 439 Dave Stevens	.10	.05
☐ 440 Hideo Nomo	1.00	.45
☐ 441 Mark Thompson	.10	.05
☐ 442 Mark Lewis	.10	.05
☐ 443 Quinton McCracken	.10	.05
☐ 444 Cliff Floyd	.10	.05
☐ 445 Denny Neagle	.10	.05
☐ 446 John Jaha	.20	.09
☐ 447 Mike Sweeney	.20	.09
☐ 448 John Wasdin	.10	.05
☐ 449 Chad Curtis	.10	.05
☐ 450 Mo Vaughn	.50	.23
☐ 451 Donovan Osborne	.10	.05
☐ 452 Ruben Sierra	.10	.05
☐ 453 Michael Tucker	.10	.05
☐ 454 Kurt Abbott	.10	.05
☐ 455 Andruw Jones UER	1.00	.45
Birthdate is incorrectly listed as 1-22-67 should be 1-22-77		
☐ 456 Shannon Stewart	.20	.09
☐ 457 Scott Brosius	.10	.05
☐ 458 Juan Guzman	.10	.05
☐ 459 Ron Villone	.10	.05
☐ 460 Moises Alou	.20	.09
☐ 461 Larry Walker	.20	.09
☐ 462 Eddie Murray SH	.40	.18
☐ 463 Paul Molitor SH	.40	.18
☐ 464 Hideo Nomo SH	.40	.18
☐ 465 Barry Bonds SH	.40	.18
☐ 466 Todd Hundley SH	.20	.09
☐ 467 Rheal Cormier	.10	.05
☐ 468 Jason Conti	.40	.18
Jhensy Sandoval		
☐ 469 Rod Barajas	.25	.11
Jackie Rexrode		
☐ 470 Cedric Bowers	.40	.18
Jared Sandberg		
☐ 471 Chei Gunner	.50	.23
Paul Wilder		
☐ 472 Mike Decelle	.25	.11
Marcus McCain		
☐ 473 Todd Zeile	.10	.05
☐ 474 Neifi Perez	.20	.09
☐ 475 Jeromy Burnitz	.20	.09
☐ 476 Trey Beamon	.10	.05
☐ 477 Braden Looper	.25	.11
John Patterson		
☐ 478 Danny Peoples	.30	.14
Jake Westbrook		
☐ 479 Eric Chavez	1.25	.55
Adam Eaton		
☐ 480 Joe Lawrence	.25	.11
Pete Tucci		
☐ 481 Kris Benson	.75	.35
Billy Koch		
☐ 482 John Nicholson	.25	.11
Andy Prater		
☐ 483 Mark Johnson	1.00	.45
Mark Kotsay		
☐ 484 Armando Benitez	.10	.05
☐ 485 Mike Matheny	.10	.05
☐ 486 Jeff Reed	.10	.05
☐ 487 Mark Bellhorn	.10	.05
Russ Johnson		
Enrique Wilson		
☐ 488 Ben Grieve	.75	.35
Richard Hidalgo		
Scott Morgan		
☐ 489 Paul Konerko	.60	.25
Derrek Lee UER		
spelled Derek on back		
Ron Wright		
☐ 490 Wes Helms	.40	.18
Bill Mueller		
Brad Seitzer		
☐ 491 Jeff Abbott	.10	.05
Shane Monahan		
Edgard Velazquez		
☐ 492 Jimmy Anderson	.25	.11
Ron Blazier		
Gerald Witasick		
☐ 493 Darin Blood	.10	.05
Heath Murray		
Carl Pavano		
☐ 494 Nelson Figueroa	.25	.11
Mark Redman		
Mike Villano		
☐ 495 Checklist	.10	.05
☐ 496 Checklist	.10	.05
☐ NNO Derek Jeter AU	100.00	45.00

1997 Topps All-Stars

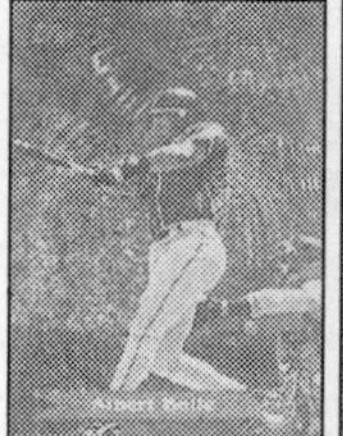

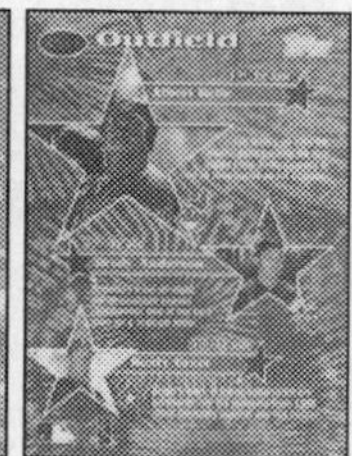

Randomly inserted in Series 1 packs at a rate of one in 18, this 22-card set printed on rainbow foilboard features the top 11 players from each league and from each position as voted by the Topps Sports Department. The fronts carry a photo of a "first team" all-star player while the backs carry a different photo of that player alongside the "second team" and "third team" selections. Only the "first team" players are checklisted listed below.

	MINT	NRMT
COMPLETE SET (22)	60.00	27.00
COMMON CARD (AS1-AS22)	1.50	.70
☐ AS1 Ivan Rodriguez	4.00	1.80
☐ AS2 Todd Hundley	2.00	.90
☐ AS3 Frank Thomas	12.00	5.50
☐ AS4 Andres Galarraga	3.00	1.35
☐ AS5 Chuck Knoblauch	3.00	1.35
☐ AS6 Eric Young	1.50	.70
☐ AS7 Jim Thome	3.00	1.35
☐ AS8 Chipper Jones	10.00	4.50
☐ AS9 Cal Ripken	12.00	5.50
☐ AS10 Barry Larkin	2.50	1.10
☐ AS11 Albert Belle	4.00	1.80
☐ AS12 Barry Bonds	4.00	1.80
☐ AS13 Ken Griffey Jr.	15.00	6.75
☐ AS14 Ellis Burks	2.00	.90
☐ AS15 Juan Gonzalez	8.00	3.60
☐ AS16 Gary Sheffield	3.00	1.35
☐ AS17 Andy Pettitte	3.00	1.35
☐ AS18 Tom Glavine	2.00	.90
☐ AS19 Pat Hentgen	2.00	.90
☐ AS20 John Smoltz	2.00	.90
☐ AS21 Roberto Hernandez	1.50	.70
☐ AS22 Mark Wohlers	1.50	.70

1997 Topps Awesome Impact

Randomly inserted in second series 11-card retail packs at a rate of 1:18, cards from this 20-card set feature a selection of top young stars and prospects. Each card front features a color player action shot cut out against a silver prismatic background.

	MINT	NRMT
COMPLETE SET (20)	100.00	45.00
COMMON CARD (AI1-AI20)	1.50	.70
☐ AI1 Jaime Bluma	1.50	.70
☐ AI2 Tony Clark	5.00	2.20
☐ AI3 Jermaine Dye	1.50	.70
☐ AI4 Nomar Garciaparra	15.00	6.75
☐ AI5 Vladimir Guerrero	10.00	4.50
☐ AI6 Todd Hollandsworth	2.00	.90
☐ AI7 Derek Jeter	15.00	6.75
☐ AI8 Andruw Jones	12.00	5.50
☐ AI9 Chipper Jones	15.00	6.75
☐ AI10 Jason Kendall	2.00	.90
☐ AI11 Brooks Kieschnick	2.00	.90
☐ AI12 Alex Ochoa	1.50	.70
☐ AI13 Rey Ordonez	1.50	.70
☐ AI14 Neifi Perez	2.00	.90
☐ AI15 Edgar Renteria	2.00	.90
☐ AI16 Mariano Rivera	2.00	.90
☐ AI17 Ruben Rivera	2.00	.90
☐ AI18 Scott Rolen	12.00	5.50
☐ AI19 Billy Wagner	5.00	2.20
☐ AI20 Todd Walker	1.50	.70

1997 Topps Hobby Masters

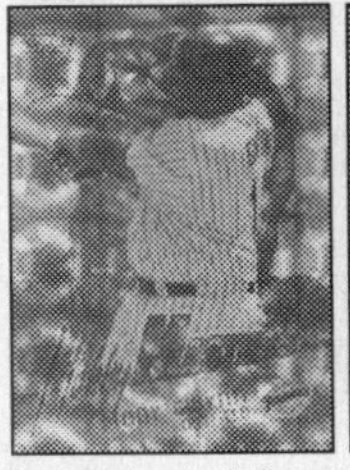

Randomly inserted in first and second series hobby packs at a rate of one in 36, cards from this 10-card set honor twenty players picked by hobby dealers from across the country as their all-time favorites. Cards 1-10 were issued in first series packs and 11-20 in second series. Printed on 28-point diffraction foilboard, one card replaces two regular cards when inserted in packs. The fronts feature borderless color player photos on a background of the player's profile. The backs carry player information.

	MINT	NRMT
COMPLETE SET (20)	110.00	50.00
COMPLETE SERIES 1 (10)	60.00	27.00
COMPLETE SERIES 2 (10)	50.00	22.00
COMMON CARD (HM1-HM20)	1.50	.70
☐ HM1 Ken Griffey Jr.	15.00	6.75
☐ HM2 Cal Ripken	12.00	5.50
☐ HM3 Greg Maddux	10.00	4.50
☐ HM4 Albert Belle	4.00	1.80
☐ HM5 Tony Gwynn	6.00	2.70
☐ HM6 Jeff Bagwell	6.00	2.70
☐ HM7 Randy Johnson	3.00	1.35
☐ HM8 Raul Mondesi	1.50	.70
☐ HM9 Juan Gonzalez	8.00	3.60
☐ HM10 Kenny Lofton	4.00	1.80
☐ HM11 Frank Thomas	12.00	5.50
☐ HM12 Mike Piazza	10.00	4.50
☐ HM13 Chipper Jones	10.00	4.50
☐ HM14 Brady Anderson	2.50	1.10
☐ HM15 Ken Caminiti	3.00	1.35
☐ HM16 Barry Bonds	4.00	1.80
☐ HM17 Mo Vaughn	4.00	1.80
☐ HM18 Derek Jeter	10.00	4.50
☐ HM19 Sammy Sosa	3.00	1.35
☐ HM20 Andres Galarraga	3.00	1.35

1997 Topps Inter-League Finest

Randomly inserted in Series 1 packs at a rate of one in 36, this 14-card set features top individual match-ups from inter-league rivalries. One player from each major league team is represented on each side of this double-sided set with a color photo and is covered with the patented Finest clear protector.

	MINT	NRMT
COMPLETE SET (14)	60.00	27.00
COMMON CARD (ILM1-ILM14)	3.00	1.35
COMP.REFRACTOR SET (14)	300.00	135.00
COMMON CARD (ILM1-ILM14)	15.00	6.75
*REFRACTORS: 2.5X TO 5X BASIC INTER-LEAGUE		
☐ ILM1 Mark McGwire	6.00	2.70
Barry Bonds		
☐ ILM2 Tim Salmon	10.00	4.50
Mike Piazza		

	MINT	NRMT
☐ ILM3 Ken Griffey Jr.	15.00	6.75
Dante Bichette		
☐ ILM4 Juan Gonzalez	10.00	4.50
Tony Gwynn		
☐ ILM5 Frank Thomas	12.00	5.50
Sammy Sosa		
☐ ILM6 Albert Belle	4.00	1.80
Barry Larkin		
☐ ILM7 Johnny Damon	3.00	1.35
Brian Jordan		
☐ ILM8 Paul Molitor	3.50	1.55
Jeff King		
☐ ILM9 John Jaha	5.00	2.20
Jeff Bagwell		
☐ ILM10 Bernie Williams	4.00	1.80
Todd Hundley		
☐ ILM11 Joe Carter	3.00	1.35
Henry Rodriguez		
☐ ILM12 Cal Ripken	10.00	4.50
Gregg Jefferies		
☐ ILM13 Mo Vaughn	10.00	4.50
Chipper Jones		
☐ ILM14 Travis Fryman	3.50	1.55
Gary Sheffield		

1997 Topps Mantle

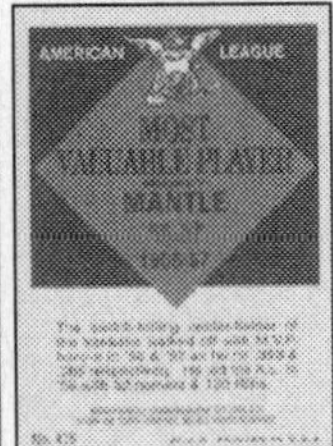

Randomly inserted at the rate of one in 12 Series 1 packs, this 16-card set features authentic reprints of Topps Mickey Mantle cards that were not reprinted last year. Each card is stamped with the commemorative gold foil logo.

	MINT	NRMT
COMPLETE SET (16)	125.00	55.00
COMMON MANTLE (21-36)	8.00	3.60
COMP.FINEST SET (16)	125.00	55.00
COMMON FINEST (21-36)	8.00	3.60
COMP.REF.SET (16)	600.00	275.00
COMMON REF. (21-36)	40.00	18.00
☐ 21 Mickey Mantle	8.00	3.60
Hank Bauer		
Yogi Berra		
1953 Bowman		
☐ 22 Mickey Mantle	8.00	3.60
1953 Bowman		
☐ 23 Mickey Mantle	8.00	3.60
Yogi Berra		
1957 Topps		
☐ 24 Mickey Mantle	8.00	3.60
Hank Aaron		
1958 Topps		
☐ 25 Mickey Mantle	8.00	3.60
1958 Topps AS		
☐ 26 Mickey Mantle	8.00	3.60
1959 Topps HL		
☐ 27 Mickey Mantle	8.00	3.60
1959 Topps AS		
☐ 28 Mickey Mantle	8.00	3.60
Ken Boyer		
1960 Topps		
☐ 29 Mickey Mantle	8.00	3.60
1960 Topps AS		
☐ 30 Mickey Mantle	8.00	3.60
1961 Topps HL		
☐ 31 Mickey Mantle	8.00	3.60
1961 Topps MVP		
☐ 32 Mickey Mantle	8.00	3.60
1961 Topps AS		
☐ 33 Mickey Mantle	8.00	3.60
Willie Mays		
1962 Topps		
Hank Aaron and Ernie Banks in background		
☐ 34 Mickey Mantle	8.00	3.60
1962 Topps IA		
☐ 35 Mickey Mantle	8.00	3.60
1962 AS		
☐ 36 Mickey Mantle	8.00	3.60
Roger Maris		
Al Kaline		
Norm Cash		
1964 Topps		

1997 Topps Mays

Randomly inserted at the rate of one in eight first series packs, cards from this 27-card set feature reprints of both the Topps and Bowman vintage Mays cards . Each card front is highlighted by a special commemorative gold foil stamp. Randomly inserted in first series hobby packs only (at the rate of one in 2,400) are personally signed cards. According to Topps, Mays signed about 65 each of the following cards: 51B, 52T, 53T, 55T, 57T, 58T, 60T, 60T AS, 61T, 61T AS, 63T, 64T, 65T, 66T, 69T, 70T, 72T, 73T. A special 4 1/4" by 5 3/4" jumbo reprint of the 1952 Topps Willie Mays card was made available exclusively in special series 1 Wal-Mart boxes. Each box (shaped much like a cereal box) contained ten 8-card retail packs and the aforementioned jumbo card and retailed for $10.

	MINT	NRMT
COMPLETE SET (27)	100.00	45.00
COMMON MAYS (1-27)	4.00	1.80
COMP.FINEST SET (27)	100.00	45.00
COMMON FINEST (1-27)	4.00	1.80
*'51-'52 FINEST: SAME VALUE AS REGULAR MAYS		
COMP.REF.SET (27)	400.00	180.00
COMMON REF. (1-27)	15.00	6.75
*'51-'52 REF: 4X REGULAR MAYS		
☐ 1 Willie Mays	8.00	3.60
1951 Bowman		
☐ 2 Willie Mays	6.00	2.70
1952 Topps		
☐ 3 Willie Mays	4.00	1.80
1953 Topps		
☐ 4 Willie Mays	4.00	1.80
1954 Bowman		
☐ 5 Willie Mays	4.00	1.80
1954 Topps		
☐ 6 Willie Mays	4.00	1.80
1955 Bowman		
☐ 7 Willie Mays	4.00	1.80
1955 Topps		
☐ 8 Willie Mays	4.00	1.80
1956 Topps		
☐ 9 Willie Mays	4.00	1.80
1957 Topps		
☐ 10 Willie Mays	4.00	1.80
1958 Topps		
☐ 11 Willie Mays	4.00	1.80
1959 Topps		
☐ 12 Willie Mays	4.00	1.80
1960 Topps		
☐ 13 Willie Mays	4.00	1.80
1960 Topps AS		
☐ 14 Willie Mays	4.00	1.80
1961 Topps		
☐ 15 Willie Mays	4.00	1.80
1961 Topps AS		
☐ 16 Willie Mays	4.00	1.80
1962 Topps		
☐ 17 Willie Mays	4.00	1.80
1963 Topps		
☐ 18 Willie Mays	4.00	1.80
1964 Topps		
☐ 19 Willie Mays	4.00	1.80
1965 Topps		
☐ 20 Willie Mays	4.00	1.80
1966 Topps		
☐ 21 Willie Mays	4.00	1.80

Card	MINT	NRMT
1967 Topps		
☐ 22 Willie Mays	4.00	1.80
1968 Topps		
☐ 23 Willie Mays	4.00	1.80
1969 Topps		
☐ 24 Willie Mays	4.00	1.80
1970 Topps		
☐ 25 Willie Mays	4.00	1.80
1971 Topps		
☐ 26 Willie Mays	4.00	1.80
1972 Topps		
☐ 27 Willie Mays	4.00	1.80
1973 Topps		
☐ J261 Willie Mays 1952 Jumbo	10.00	4.50
☐ NNO Willie Mays AU	100.00	45.00

1997 Topps Season's Best

This 25-card set was randomly inserted into Topps Series 2 packs and features five top players from each of the following five statistical categories: Leading Looters (top base stealers), Bleacher Reachers (top home run hitters), Hill Toppers (most wins), Number Crunchers (most RBI's), Kings of Swings (top slugging percentages). The fronts display color player photos printed on prismatic illusion foilboard. The backs carry another player photo and statistics.

	MINT	NRMT
COMPLETE SET (25)	25.00	11.00
COMMON CARD (1-25)	.50	.23
☐ SB1 Tony Gwynn	3.00	1.35
☐ SB2 Frank Thomas	6.00	2.70
☐ SB3 Ellis Burks	.75	.35
☐ SB4 Paul Molitor	1.25	.55
☐ SB5 Chuck Knoblauch	1.25	.55
☐ SB6 Mark McGwire	2.50	1.10
☐ SB7 Brady Anderson	.75	.35
☐ SB8 Ken Griffey Jr.	8.00	3.60
☐ SB9 Albert Belle	1.50	.70
☐ SB10 Andres Galarraga	1.25	.55
☐ SB11 Andres Galarraga	1.25	.55
☐ SB12 Albert Belle	1.50	.70
☐ SB13 Juan Gonzalez	4.00	1.80
☐ SB14 Mo Vaughn	2.00	.90
☐ SB15 Rafael Palmeiro	1.00	.45
☐ SB16 John Smoltz	.75	.35
☐ SB17 Andy Pettitte	1.25	.55
☐ SB18 Pat Hentgen	.75	.35
☐ SB19 Mike Mussina	1.25	.55
☐ SB20 Andy Benes	.50	.23
☐ SB21 Kenny Lofton	1.25	.55
☐ SB22 Tom Goodwin	.50	.23
☐ SB23 Otis Nixon	.50	.23
☐ SB24 Eric Young	.50	.23
☐ SB25 Lance Johnson	.50	.23

1997 Topps Sweet Strokes

his 15-card retail only set was randomly inserted in eries one packs at a rate of one in 12. Printed on ainbow foilboard, the set features color photos of some f Baseball's top hitters.

	MINT	NRMT
OMPLETE SET (15)	40.00	18.00
OMMON CARD (SS1-SS15)	1.00	.45
☐ SS1 Roberto Alomar	2.00	.90
☐ SS2 Jeff Bagwell	4.00	1.80
☐ SS3 Albert Belle	2.50	1.10
☐ SS4 Barry Bonds	2.50	1.10
☐ SS5 Mark Grace	1.50	.70
☐ SS6 Ken Griffey Jr.	10.00	4.50
☐ SS7 Tony Gwynn	4.00	1.80
☐ SS8 Chipper Jones	6.00	2.70
☐ SS9 Edgar Martinez	1.00	.45
☐ SS10 Mark McGwire	3.00	1.35
☐ SS11 Rafael Palmeiro	1.50	.70
☐ SS12 Mike Piazza	6.00	2.70
☐ SS13 Gary Sheffield	2.00	.90
☐ SS14 Frank Thomas	10.00	4.50
☐ SS15 Mo Vaughn	2.50	1.10

1997 Topps Team Timber

Randomly inserted into all second series packs at a rate of 1:36 and second series Hobby Collector packs at a rate of 1:8, cards from this 16-card set highlight a selection of baseball's top sluggers. Each card features a simulated wood-grain stock, but the fronts are UV-coated, making the cards bow noticeably.

	MINT	NRMT
COMPLETE SET (16)	70.00	32.00
COMMON CARD (TT1-TT16)	1.50	.70
☐ TT1 Ken Griffey Jr.	15.00	6.75
☐ TT2 Ken Caminiti	3.00	1.35
☐ TT3 Bernie Williams	3.00	1.35
☐ TT4 Jeff Bagwell	6.00	2.70
☐ TT5 Frank Thomas	12.00	5.50
☐ TT6 Andres Galarraga	3.00	1.35
☐ TT7 Barry Bonds	4.00	1.80
☐ TT8 Rafael Palmeiro	1.50	.70
☐ TT9 Brady Anderson	2.50	1.10
☐ TT10 Juan Gonzalez	8.00	3.60
☐ TT11 Mo Vaughn	4.00	1.80
☐ TT12 Mark McGwire	5.00	2.20
☐ TT13 Gary Sheffield	3.00	1.35
☐ TT14 Albert Belle	4.00	1.80
☐ TT15 Chipper Jones	10.00	4.50
☐ TT16 Mike Piazza	10.00	4.50

1997 Topps Dodgers Rookies of the Year

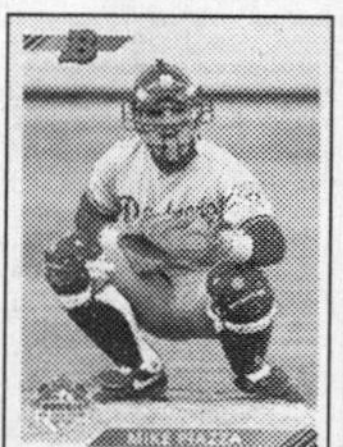

This six-card set honors five recent National League Rookies of the Year who have all been from the Los Angeles Dodgers. The fronts feature the player's rookie card reproduced on special foil board with the N.L. Rookie of the Year stamp. The backs carry player information. Jackie Robinson's 1952 Topps card with a Rookie of the Year designation has been reproduced to celebrate his being chosen as the very first Rookie of the Year recipient. The cards are listed below according to the year in which the player received the Rookie of the Year award.

	MINT	NRMT
COMPLETE SET (6)	40.00	18.00
COMMON CARD (1-6)	2.00	.90
☐ 1 Jackie Robinson	15.00	6.75
☐ 2 Eric Karros	4.00	1.80
☐ 3 Mike Piazza	12.00	5.50
☐ 4 Raul Mondesi	6.00	2.70
☐ 5 Hideo Nomo	10.00	4.50
☐ 6 Todd Hollandsworth	2.00	.90

1997-98 Topps Members Only 55

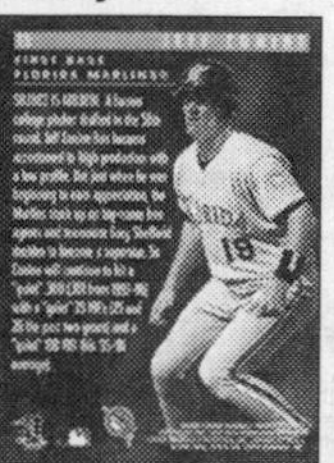

This 55-card set features color player photos of Topps' selection of 50 (#1-50) top American and National League players. The set includes five Finest Cards (#51-55) which represent Topps' selection of the top rookies from 1997. The backs carry information about the player. Each card displays the "Member Only" gold foil stamp.

	MINT	NRMT
COMPLETE SET (55)	20.00	9.00
COMMON CARD (1-55)	.10	.05
☐ 1 Brady Anderson	.30	.14
☐ 2 Carlos Baerga	.10	.05
☐ 3 Jeff Bagwell	1.25	.55
☐ 4 Albert Belle	.75	.35
☐ 5 Dante Bichette	.20	.09
☐ 6 Craig Biggio	.30	.14
☐ 7 Wade Boggs	.40	.18
☐ 8 Barry Bonds	.75	.35
☐ 9 Jay Buhner	.30	.14
☐ 10 Ellis Burks	.20	.09
☐ 11 Ken Caminiti	.30	.14
☐ 12 Jose Canseco	.30	.14
☐ 13 Joe Carter	.20	.09
☐ 14 Roger Clemens	1.00	.45
☐ 15 Jeff Conine	.20	.09
☐ 16 Andres Galarraga	.40	.18
☐ 17 Ron Gant	.20	.09
☐ 18 Juan Gonzalez	1.50	.70
☐ 19 Mark Grace	.30	.14
☐ 20 Ken Griffey Jr.	3.00	1.35
☐ 21 Tony Gwynn	1.50	.70
☐ 22 Pat Hentgen	.40	.18
☐ 23 Todd Hollandsworth	.10	.05
☐ 24 Todd Hundley	.20	.09
☐ 25 Derek Jeter	1.50	.70
☐ 26 Randy Johnson	.40	.18
☐ 27 Chipper Jones	1.50	.70
☐ 28 Ryan Klesko	.10	.05
☐ 29 Chuck Knoblauch	.40	.18
☐ 30 Barry Larkin	.20	.09
☐ 31 Kenny Lofton	.40	.18
☐ 32 Greg Maddux	2.00	.90
☐ 33 Mark McGwire	1.25	.55
☐ 34 Paul Molitor	.40	.18
☐ 35 Raul Mondesi	.30	.14
☐ 36 Hideo Nomo	1.50	.70
☐ 37 Rafael Palmeiro	.30	.14
☐ 38 Mike Piazza	2.00	.90
☐ 39 Manny Ramirez	.40	.18
☐ 40 Cal Ripken	2.50	1.10
☐ 41 Ivan Rodriguez	.40	.18
☐ 42 Tim Salmon	.40	.18
☐ 43 Gary Sheffield	.40	.18
☐ 44 John Smoltz	.20	.09
☐ 45 Sammy Sosa	.40	.18
☐ 46 Frank Thomas	2.50	1.10
☐ 47 Jim Thome	.40	.18
☐ 48 Mo Vaughn	.40	.18
☐ 49 Bernie Williams	.40	.18
☐ 50 Matt Williams	.30	.14
☐ 51 Darin Erstad	.30	.14
☐ 52 Vladimir Guerrero	.30	.14
☐ 53 Andruw Jones	.40	.18
☐ 54 Scott Rolen	1.50	.70
☐ 55 Todd Walker	.10	.05

1998 Topps Previews

This six-card set was a preview of the 1998 Topps set and features color action player photos in gold borders with gold foil printing. The backs carry another player photo with player information and career statistics with white borders.

	MINT	NRMT
COMPLETE SET (6)	12.00	5.50
COMMON CARD (PP1-PP6)	.50	.23
☐ PP1 Carlos Baerga	.50	.23
☐ PP2 Jeff Bagwell	4.00	1.80
☐ PP3 Marquis Grissom	1.00	.45
☐ PP4 Derek Jeter	3.00	1.35
☐ PP5 Randy Johnson	2.00	.90
☐ PP6 Mike Piazza	5.00	2.20

1998 Topps

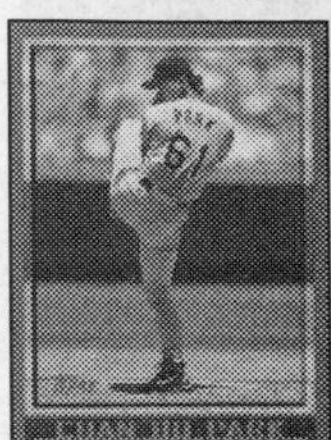

This 282-card set of Topps Series 1 was distributed in 11-card packs with a suggested retail price of $1.29. The fronts feature color action player photos printed on 16 pt. stock with player information and career statistics on the back. Card #7 was permanently retired in 1996 to honor Mickey Mantle. Series 1 contains the following subsets: Draft Picks (#245-249), Expansion Team Prospects (#250-253), and Prospects (#254-259). Hobby packs also included a redemption card program. Recipients of Memorabilia Madness and Wild Card inserts could win rare Clemente Memorabilia including game-used bats, game-worn jersey, autographed photos, signed checks, autographed vintage Clemente Topps trading cards, original, unautographed Clemente cards, including three rookie cards, Pirates jerseys bearing Clemente's name and number, and uncut sheets of 1998 Topps Baseball Minted in Cooperstown cards. A Wild Card was seeded in hobby packs at the rate of one in 72.

	MINT	NRMT
COMPLETE SERIES 1 (282)	20.00	9.00
COMMON CARD (1-283)	.10	.05
☐ 1 Tony Gwynn	1.00	.45
☐ 2 Larry Walker	.40	.18
☐ 3 Billy Wagner	.20	.09
☐ 4 Denny Neagle	.20	.09
☐ 5 Vladimir Guerrero	.60	.25
☐ 6 Kevin Brown	.20	.09
☐ 8 Mariano Rivera	.20	.09
☐ 9 Tony Clark	.40	.18
☐ 10 Deion Sanders	.40	.18
☐ 11 Francisco Cordova	.10	.05
☐ 12 Matt Williams	.30	.14
☐ 13 Carlos Baerga	.20	.09
☐ 14 Mo Vaughn	.50	.23
☐ 15 Bobby Witt	.10	.05
☐ 16 Matt Stairs	.10	.05
☐ 17 Chan Ho Park	.40	.18
☐ 18 Mike Bordick	.10	.05
☐ 19 Michael Tucker	.20	.09
☐ 20 Frank Thomas	1.50	.70
☐ 21 Roberto Clemente	1.00	.45
☐ 22 Dmitri Young	.10	.05
☐ 23 Steve Trachsel	.10	.05
☐ 24 Jeff Kent	.10	.05
☐ 25 Scott Rolen	1.00	.45
☐ 26 John Thomson	.10	.05
☐ 27 Joe Vitiello	.10	.05
☐ 28 Eddie Guardado	.10	.05
☐ 29 Charlie Hayes	.10	.05
☐ 30 Juan Gonzalez	1.00	.45
☐ 31 Garret Anderson	.20	.09
☐ 32 John Jaha	.10	.05
☐ 33 Omar Vizquel	.20	.09
☐ 34 Brian Hunter	.10	.05
☐ 35 Jeff Bagwell	.75	.35
☐ 36 Mark Lemke	.10	.05
☐ 37 Doug Glanville	.10	.05
☐ 38 Dan Wilson	.10	.05
☐ 39 Steve Cooke	.10	.05
☐ 40 Chili Davis	.20	.09
☐ 41 Mike Cameron	.20	.09
☐ 42 F.P. Santangelo	.10	.05
☐ 43 Brad Ausmus	.10	.05
☐ 44 Gary DiSarcina	.10	.05
☐ 45 Pat Hentgen	.20	.09
☐ 46 Wilton Guerrero	.10	.05
☐ 47 Devon White	.10	.05
☐ 48 Danny Patterson	.10	.05
☐ 49 Pat Meares	.10	.05
☐ 50 Rafael Palmeiro	.30	.14
☐ 51 Mark Gardner	.10	.05
☐ 52 Jeff Blauser	.10	.05
☐ 53 Dave Hollins	.10	.05
☐ 54 Carlos Garcia	.10	.05
☐ 55 Ben McDonald	.10	.05
☐ 56 John Mabry	.10	.05
☐ 57 Trevor Hoffman	.10	.05
☐ 58 Tony Fernandez	.10	.05
☐ 59 Rich Loiselle	.10	.05
☐ 60 Mark Leiter	.10	.05
☐ 61 Pat Kelly	.10	.05
☐ 62 John Flaherty	.10	.05
☐ 63 Roger Bailey	.10	.05
☐ 64 Tom Gordon	.10	.05
☐ 65 Ryan Klesko	.30	.14
☐ 66 Darryl Hamilton	.10	.05
☐ 67 Jim Eisenreich	.20	.09
☐ 68 Butch Huskey	.20	.09
☐ 69 Mark Grudzielanek	.10	.05
☐ 70 Marquis Grissom	.20	.09
☐ 71 Mark McLemore	.10	.05
☐ 72 Gary Gaetti	.20	.09
☐ 73 Greg Gagne	.10	.05
☐ 74 Lyle Mouton	.10	.05
☐ 75 Jim Edmonds	.40	.18
☐ 76 Shawn Green	.20	.09
☐ 77 Greg Vaughn	.10	.05
☐ 78 Terry Adams	.10	.05
☐ 79 Kevin Polcovich	.10	.05
☐ 80 Troy O'Leary	.10	.05
☐ 81 Jeff Shaw	.10	.05
☐ 82 Rich Becker	.10	.05
☐ 83 David Wells	.10	.05
☐ 84 Steve Karsay	.10	.05
☐ 85 Charles Nagy	.10	.05
☐ 86 B.J. Surhoff	.20	.09
☐ 87 Jamey Wright	.10	.05
☐ 88 James Baldwin	.10	.05
☐ 89 Edgardo Alfonzo	.20	.09
☐ 90 Jay Buhner	.30	.14
☐ 91 Brady Anderson	.30	.14
☐ 92 Scott Servais	.10	.05
☐ 93 Edgar Renteria	.10	.05
☐ 94 Mike Lieberthal	.10	.05
☐ 95 Rick Aguilera	.10	.05
☐ 96 Walt Weiss	.10	.05
☐ 97 Deivi Cruz	.10	.05
☐ 98 Kurt Abbott	.10	.05
☐ 99 Henry Rodriguez	.10	.05
☐ 100 Mike Piazza	1.25	.55
☐ 101 Bill Taylor	.10	.05
☐ 102 Todd Zeile	.10	.05
☐ 103 Rey Ordonez	.10	.05
☐ 104 Willie Greene	.20	.09
☐ 105 Tony Womack	.10	.05
☐ 106 Mike Sweeney	.10	.05
☐ 107 Jeffrey Hammonds	.20	.09
☐ 108 Kevin Orie	.10	.05
☐ 109 Alex Gonzalez	.10	.05
☐ 110 Jose Canseco	.30	.14
☐ 111 Paul Sorrento	.10	.05
☐ 112 Joey Hamilton	.10	.05
☐ 113 Brad Radke	.10	.05
☐ 114 Steve Avery	.10	.05
☐ 115 Esteban Loaiza	.10	.05
☐ 116 Stan Javier	.10	.05
☐ 117 Chris Gomez	.10	.05
☐ 118 Royce Clayton	.10	.05
☐ 119 Orlando Merced	.10	.05
☐ 120 Kevin Appier	.10	.05
☐ 121 Mel Nieves	.10	.05
☐ 122 Joe Girardi	.10	.05
☐ 123 Rico Brogna	.10	.05
☐ 124 Kent Mercker	.10	.05
☐ 125 Manny Ramirez	.40	.18
☐ 126 Jeromy Burnitz	.10	.05
☐ 127 Kevin Foster	.10	.05
☐ 128 Matt Morris	.10	.05
☐ 129 Jason Dickson	.10	.05
☐ 130 Tom Glavine	.10	.05
☐ 131 Wally Joyner	.10	.05
☐ 132 Rick Reed	.10	.05
☐ 133 Todd Jones	.10	.05
☐ 134 Dave Martinez	.10	.05
☐ 135 Sandy Alomar	.20	.09
☐ 136 Mike Lansing	.10	.05
☐ 137 Sean Berry	.10	.05
☐ 138 Doug Jones	.10	.05
☐ 139 Todd Stottlemyre	.10	.05
☐ 140 Jay Bell	.10	.05
☐ 141 Jaime Navarro	.10	.05
☐ 142 Chris Hoiles	.10	.05
☐ 143 Joey Cora	.20	.09
☐ 144 Scott Spiezio	.10	.05
☐ 145 Joe Carter	.20	.09
☐ 146 Jose Guillen	.40	.18
☐ 147 Damion Easley	.10	.05
☐ 148 Lee Stevens	.10	.05
☐ 149 Alex Fernandez	.10	.05
☐ 150 Randy Johnson	.40	.18
☐ 151 J.T. Snow	.10	.05
☐ 152 Chuck Finley	.10	.05
☐ 153 Bernard Gilkey	.10	.05
☐ 154 David Segui	.10	.05
☐ 155 Dante Bichette	.20	.09
☐ 156 Kevin Stocker	.10	.05
☐ 157 Carl Everett	.10	.05
☐ 158 Jose Valentin	.10	.05
☐ 159 Pokey Reese	.10	.05
☐ 160 Derek Jeter	1.00	.45
☐ 161 Roger Pavlik	.10	.05
☐ 162 Mark Wohlers	.10	.05
☐ 163 Ricky Bottalico	.10	.05
☐ 164 Ozzie Guillen	.10	.05
☐ 165 Mike Mussina	.40	.18
☐ 166 Gary Sheffield	.10	.05
☐ 167 Hideo Nomo	1.00	.45
☐ 168 Mark Grace	.30	.14
☐ 169 Aaron Sele	.10	.05
☐ 170 Darryl Kile	.20	.09
☐ 171 Shawn Estes	.20	.09
☐ 172 Vinny Castilla	.20	.09
☐ 173 Ron Coomer	.10	.05
☐ 174 Jose Rosado	.10	.05
☐ 175 Kenny Lofton	.50	.23
☐ 176 Jason Giambi	.10	.05
☐ 177 Hal Morris	.10	.05
☐ 178 Darren Bragg	.10	.05
☐ 179 Orel Hershiser	.20	.09
☐ 180 Ray Lankford	.20	.09
☐ 181 Hideki Irabu	.10	.05
☐ 182 Kevin Young	.10	.05
☐ 183 Javy Lopez	.10	.05
☐ 184 Jeff Montgomery	.10	.05
☐ 185 Mike Holtz	.10	.05
☐ 186 George Williams	.10	.05
☐ 187 Cal Eldred	.10	.05
☐ 188 Tom Candiotti	.10	.05
☐ 189 Glenallen Hill	.10	.05
☐ 190 Brian Giles	.10	.05
☐ 191 Dave Mlicki	.10	.05
☐ 192 Garrett Stephenson	.10	.05
☐ 193 Jeff Frye	.10	.05
☐ 194 Joe Oliver	.10	.05
☐ 195 Bob Hamelin	.10	.05
☐ 196 Luis Sojo	.10	.05
☐ 197 LaTroy Hawkins	.10	.05
☐ 198 Kevin Elster	.10	.05
☐ 199 Jeff Reed	.10	.05
☐ 200 Dennis Eckersley	.30	.14
☐ 201 Bill Mueller	.10	.05
☐ 202 Russ Davis	.10	.05
☐ 203 Armando Benitez	.10	.05
☐ 204 Quilvio Veras	.10	.05
☐ 205 Tim Naehring	.10	.05
☐ 206 Quinton McCracken	.10	.05
☐ 207 Raul Casanova	.10	.05
☐ 208 Matt Lawton	.10	.05
☐ 209 Luis Alicea	.10	.05
☐ 210 Luis Gonzalez	.10	.05
☐ 211 Allen Watson	.10	.05
☐ 212 Gerald Williams	.10	.05
☐ 213 David Bell	.10	.05
☐ 214 Todd Hollandsworth	.10	.05
☐ 215 Wade Boggs	.40	.18
☐ 216 Jose Mesa	.20	.09
☐ 217 Jamie Moyer	.10	.05
☐ 218 Darren Daulton	.20	.09
☐ 219 Mickey Morandini	.10	.05
☐ 220 Rusty Greer	.20	.09
☐ 221 Jim Bullinger	.10	.05
☐ 222 Jose Offerman	.10	.05
☐ 223 Matt Karchner	.10	.05
☐ 224 Woody Williams	.10	.05
☐ 225 Mark Loretta	.10	.05
☐ 226 Mike Hampton	.10	.05
☐ 227 Willie Adams	.10	.05
☐ 228 Scott Hatteberg	.10	.05
☐ 229 Rich Amaral	.10	.05
☐ 230 Terry Steinbach	.20	.09
☐ 231 Glendon Rusch	.10	.05
☐ 232 Bret Boone	.10	.05
☐ 233 Robert Person	.10	.05
☐ 234 Jose Hernandez	.10	.05
☐ 235 Doug Drabek	.10	.05
☐ 236 Jason McDonald	.10	.05
☐ 237 Chris Widger	.10	.05
☐ 238 Tom Martin	.10	.05
☐ 239 Dave Burba	.10	.05
☐ 240 Pete Rose Jr.	.20	.09
☐ 241 Bobby Ayala	.10	.05

☐ 242 Tim Wakefield	.10	.05
☐ 243 Dennis Springer	.10	.05
☐ 244 Tim Belcher	.10	.05
☐ 245 Jon Garland Geoff Goetz	.20	.09
☐ 246 Glenn Davis Lance Berkman	.20	.09
☐ 247 Vernon Wells Aaron Akin	.20	.09
☐ 248 Adam Kennedy Jason Romano	.20	.09
☐ 249 Jason Dellaero Troy Cameron	.20	.09
☐ 250 Alex Sanchez Jared Sandberg	.20	.09
☐ 251 Pablo Ortega James Manias	.20	.09
☐ 252 Jason Conti Mike Stoner	.40	.18
☐ 253 John Patterson Larry Rodriguez	.20	.09
☐ 254 Adrian Beltre Ryan Minor Aaron Boone	1.00	.45
☐ 255 Ben Grieve Brian Buchanan Dermal Brown	.75	.35
☐ 256 Carl Pavano Kerrry Wood Gil Meche	.20	.09
☐ 257 David Ortiz Daryle Ward Richie Sexson	.20	.09
☐ 258 Randy Winn Juan Encarnacion Andrew Vessel	.20	.09
☐ 259 Kris Benson Travis Smith Courtney Duncan	.30	.14
☐ 260 Chad Hermansen Brent Butler Warren Morris	.50	.23
☐ 261 Ben Davis Eli Marrero Ramon Hernandez	.20	.09
☐ 262 Eric Chavez Russell Branyan Russ Johnson	.50	.23
☐ 263 Todd Dunwoody John Barnes Ryan Jackson	.25	.11
☐ 264 Matt Clement Roy Halladay Brian Fuentes	.25	.11
☐ 265 Randy Johnson SH	.40	.18
☐ 266 Kevin Brown SH	.20	.09
☐ 267 Ricardo Rincon SH/Francisco Cordova	.10	.05
☐ 268 Nomar Garciaparra SH	.60	.25
☐ 269 Tino Martinez SH	.40	.18
☐ 270 Chuck Knoblauch IL	.40	.18
☐ 271 Pedro Martinez IL	.40	.18
☐ 272 Denny Neagle IL	.20	.09
☐ 273 Juan Gonzalez IL	.50	.23
☐ 274 Andres Galarraga IL	.40	.18
☐ 275 Checklist (1-195)	.10	.05
☐ 276 Checklist (196-283/inserts)	.10	.05
☐ 277 Moises Alou WS	.20	.09
☐ 278 Sandy Alomar WS	.20	.09
☐ 279 Gary Sheffield WS	.40	.18
☐ 280 Matt Williams WS	.30	.14
☐ 281 Livan Hernandez WS	.30	.14
☐ 282 Chad Ogea WS	.10	.05
☐ 283 Marlins Champs	.10	.05
☐ NNO Wild Card	5.00	2.20

1998 Topps Minted in Cooperstown

Randomly inserted in packs at the rate of one in eight, this 282 card set is a parallel version of the base set. The set is distinguished by the special "Minted in Cooperstown" logo stamped on each card. Card number 7 does not exist.

	MINT	NRMT
COMPLETE SET (282)	300.00	135.00
COMMON CARD (1-283)	1.00	.45
STARS: 6X TO 12X BASIC CARDS		
YOUNG STARS: 5X TO 10X BASIC CARDS		
ROOKIES: 4X TO 8X BASIC CARDS		

1998 Topps Baby Boomers

Randomly inserted in retail packs only at the rate of one in 36, this 15-card set features color photos of young players who have already made their mark in the game despite less than three years in the majors.

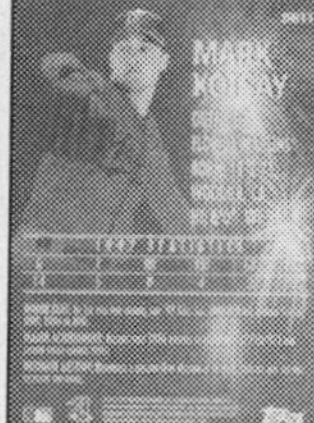

	MINT	NRMT
COMPLETE SET (15)	80.00	36.00
COMMON CARD (BB1-BB15)	2.00	.90
☐ BB1 Derek Jeter	10.00	4.50
☐ BB2 Scott Rolen	10.00	4.50
☐ BB3 Nomar Garciaparra	12.00	5.50
☐ BB4 Jose Cruz Jr.	15.00	6.75
☐ BB5 Darin Erstad	5.00	2.20
☐ BB6 Todd Helton	5.00	2.20
☐ BB7 Tony Clark	3.00	1.35
☐ BB8 Jose Guillen	4.00	1.80
☐ BB9 Andruw Jones	8.00	3.60
☐ BB10 Vladimir Guerrero	6.00	2.70
☐ BB11 Mark Kotsay	4.00	1.80
☐ BB12 Todd Greene	2.50	1.10
☐ BB13 Andy Pettitte	4.00	1.80
☐ BB14 Justin Thompson	2.50	1.10
☐ BB15 Alan Benes	2.00	.90

1998 Topps Clemente

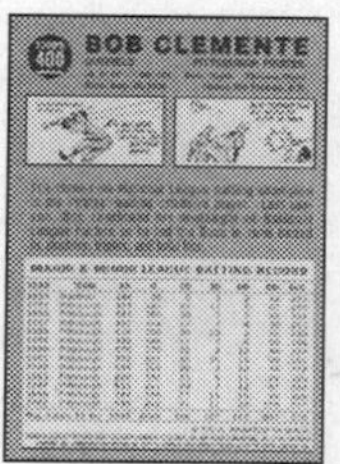

Randomly inserted in packs at the rate of one in 18, this 10-card set honors the memory of Roberto Clemente on the 25th anniversary of his untimely death with conventional reprints of his Topps cards that were originally printed in odd-numbered years (1955-1971). This set contains only odd-numbered cards.

	MINT	NRMT
COMPLETE SET (10)	50.00	22.00
COMMON CARD (1-19)	5.00	2.20
☐ 1 Roberto Clemente 1955	10.00	4.50
☐ 3 Roberto Clemente 1957	5.00	2.20
☐ 5 Roberto Clemente 1959	5.00	2.20
☐ 7 Roberto Clemente 1961	5.00	2.20
☐ 9 Roberto Clemente 1963	5.00	2.20
☐ 11 Roberto Clemente 1965	5.00	2.20
☐ 13 Roberto Clemente 1967	5.00	2.20
☐ 15 Roberto Clemente 1969	5.00	2.20
☐ 17 Roberto Clemente 1971	5.00	2.20
☐ 19 Roberto Clemente 1973	5.00	2.20

1998 Topps Clemente Finest

Randomly inserted in packs at the rate of one in 72, this nine-card set honors the memory of Roberto Clemente on the 25th anniversary of his untimely death with Finest reprints of his Topps cards that were originally printed in even-numbered years (1956-1972). This set contains only even-numbered cards.

	MINT	NRMT
COMPLETE SET (9)	80.00	36.00
COMMON CARD (2-18)	12.00	5.50
COMP.REF.SET (9)	200.00	90.00
*REFRACTORS: 2.5X FINEST		
☐ 2 Roberto Clemente 1956	12.00	5.50
☐ 4 Roberto Clemente 1958	12.00	5.50
☐ 6 Roberto Clemente 1960	12.00	5.50
☐ 8 Roberto Clemente 1962	12.00	5.50
☐ 10 Roberto Clemente 1964	12.00	5.50
☐ 12 Roberto Clemente 1966	12.00	5.50
☐ 14 Roberto Clemente 1968	12.00	5.50
☐ 16 Roberto Clemente 1970	12.00	5.50
☐ 18 Roberto Clemente 1972	12.00	5.50

1998 Topps Clemente Tribute

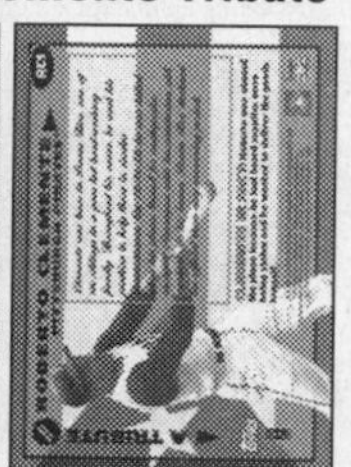

Randomly inserted in packs at the rate of one in 12, this five-card set honors the memory of Roberto Clemente on the 25th anniversary of his untimely death and features color photos printed on mirror foilboard on newly designed cards.

	MINT	NRMT
COMPLETE SET (5)	8.00	3.60
COMMON CARD (RC1-RC5)	2.00	.90
☐ RC1 Roberto Clemente Picking Bat from Rack	2.00	.90
☐ RC2 Roberto Clemente Posed batting shot	2.00	.90
☐ RC3 Roberto Clemente Follow through on swing	2.00	.90
☐ RC4 Roberto Clemente Portrait	2.00	.90
☐ RC5 Roberto Clemente	2.00	.90

1998 Topps Etch-A-Sketch

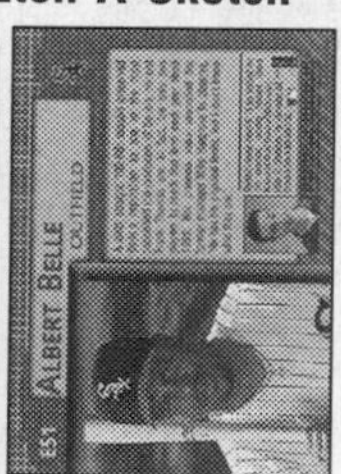

Randomly inserted in packs at the rate of one in 36, this nine-card set features drawings by artist George Vlosich III of some of baseball's hottest superstars using an Etch A Sketch as a canvas.

	MINT	NRMT
COMPLETE SET (9)	50.00	22.00
COMMON CARD (ES1-ES9)	3.00	1.35
☐ ES1 Albert Belle	3.00	1.35
☐ ES2 Barry Bonds	3.00	1.35
☐ ES3 Ken Griffey Jr.	12.00	5.50
☐ ES4 Greg Maddux	8.00	3.60
☐ ES5 Hideo Nomo	6.00	2.70
☐ ES6 Mike Piazza	8.00	3.60
☐ ES7 Cal Ripken	10.00	4.50
☐ ES8 Frank Thomas	10.00	4.50
☐ ES9 Mo Vaughn	3.00	1.35

1998 Topps Flashback

Randomly inserted in packs at the rate of one in 72, these two-sided cards of top players feature photographs of how they looked "then" as rookies on one side and how they look "now" as stars on the other.

	MINT	NRMT
COMPLETE SET (10)	80.00	36.00
COMMON CARD (FB1-FB10)	3.00	1.35

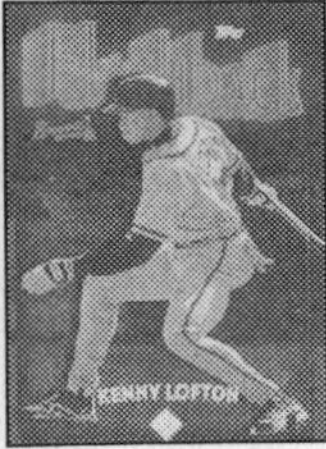

☐ FB1 Barry Bonds	8.00	3.60
☐ FB2 Ken Griffey Jr.	30.00	13.50
☐ FB3 Paul Molitor	6.00	2.70
☐ FB4 Randy Johnson	6.00	2.70
☐ FB5 Cal Ripken	25.00	11.00
☐ FB6 Tony Gwynn	15.00	6.75
☐ FB7 Kenny Lofton	8.00	3.60
☐ FB8 Gary Sheffield	6.00	2.70
☐ FB9 Deion Sanders	3.00	1.35
☐ FB10 Brady Anderson	4.00	1.80

1998 Topps HallBound

Randomly inserted in hobby packs only at the rate of one in 36, this 15-card set features color photos of top stars who are bound for the Hall of Fame printed on foil mirrorboard cards.

	MINT	NRMT
COMPLETE SET (15)	100.00	45.00
COMMON CARD (HB1-HB15)	2.00	.90
☐ HB1 Paul Molitor	2.00	.90
☐ HB2 Tony Gwynn	10.00	4.50
☐ HB3 Wade Boggs	2.50	1.10
☐ HB4 Roger Clemens	8.00	3.60
☐ HB5 Dennis Eckersley	2.00	.90
☐ HB6 Cal Ripken	15.00	6.75
☐ HB7 Greg Maddux	12.00	5.50
☐ HB8 Rickey Henderson	2.50	1.10
☐ HB9 Ken Griffey Jr.	20.00	9.00
☐ HB10 Frank Thomas	15.00	6.75
☐ HB11 Mark McGwire	10.00	4.50
☐ HB12 Barry Bonds	5.00	2.20
☐ HB13 Mike Piazza	12.00	5.50
☐ HB14 Juan Gonzalez	10.00	4.50
☐ HB15 Randy Johnson	4.00	1.80

1998 Topps Mystery Finest

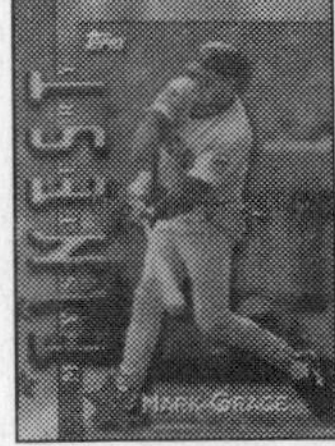

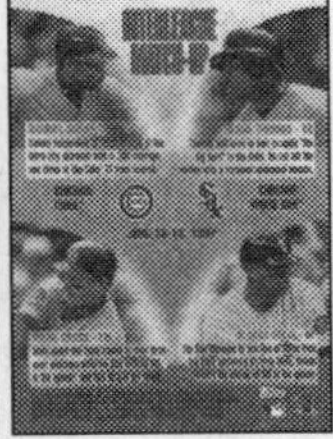

Randomly inserted in packs at the rate of one in 36, this 20-card set features color action player photos which showcase five of the 1997 season's most intriguing inter-league matchups.

	MINT	NRMT
COMPLETE SET (20)	150.00	70.00
COMMON CARD (ILM1-ILM20)	2.00	.90
COMP.REF.SET (20)	500.00	220.00
COMMON REF. (1-20)	6.00	2.70
*REFRACTORS: 1.5X TO 3X BASIC CARDS		
☐ ILM1 Chipper Jones	15.00	6.75
☐ ILM2 Cal Ripken	20.00	9.00
☐ ILM3 Greg Maddux	15.00	6.75
☐ ILM4 Rafael Palmeiro	2.50	1.10
☐ ILM5 Todd Hundley	2.00	.90
☐ ILM6 Derek Jeter	15.00	6.75
☐ ILM7 John Olerud	2.00	.90
☐ ILM8 Tino Martinez	5.00	2.20
☐ ILM9 Larry Walker	5.00	2.20
☐ ILM10 Ken Griffey Jr.	25.00	11.00
☐ ILM11 Andres Galarraga	5.00	2.20
☐ ILM12 Randy Johnson	5.00	2.20
☐ ILM13 Mike Piazza	15.00	6.75
☐ ILM14 Jim Edmonds	3.00	1.35
☐ ILM15 Eric Karros	2.00	.90
☐ ILM16 Tim Salmon	5.00	2.20
☐ ILM17 Sammy Sosa	5.00	2.20
☐ ILM18 Frank Thomas	20.00	9.00
☐ ILM19 Mark Grace	3.00	1.35
☐ ILM20 Albert Belle	6.00	2.70

1991 Topps Archives 1953

The 1953 Topps Archive set is a reprint of the original 274-card 1953 Topps set. The only card missing from the reprint set is that of Billy Loes (174), who did not give Topps permission to reprint his card. Moreover, the set has been extended by 57 cards, with cards honoring Mrs. Eleanor Engle, Hoyt Wilhelm (who had already been included in the set as card number 151), 1953 HOF inductees Dizzy Dean and Al Simmons, and "prospect" Hank Aaron. Although the original cards measured 2 5/8" by 3 3/4", the reprint cards measure the modern standard size. Production quantities were supposedly limited to not more than 18,000 cases.

	MINT	NRMT
COMPLETE SET (330)	40.00	18.00
COMMON CARD (1-220)	.10	.05
COMMON CARD (221-280)	.15	.07
COMMON CARD (281-337)	.20	.09
☐ 1 Jackie Robinson	6.00	2.70
☐ 2 Luke Easter	.15	.07
☐ 3 George Crowe	.10	.05
☐ 4 Ben Wade	.10	.05
☐ 5 Joe Dobson	.10	.05
☐ 6 Sam Jones	.10	.05
☐ 7 Bob Borkowski	.10	.05
☐ 8 Clem Koshorek	.10	.05
☐ 9 Joe Collins	.15	.07
☐ 10 Smoky Burgess	.15	.07
☐ 11 Sal Yvars	.10	.05
☐ 12 Howie Judson	.10	.05
☐ 13 Conrado Marrero	.10	.05
☐ 14 Clem Labine	.20	.09
☐ 15 Bobo Newsom	.15	.07
☐ 16 Peanuts Lowrey	.10	.05
☐ 17 Billy Hitchcock	.10	.05
☐ 18 Ted Lepcio	.10	.05
☐ 19 Mel Parnell	.10	.05
☐ 20 Hank Thompson	.10	.05
☐ 21 Billy Johnson	.10	.05
☐ 22 Howie Fox	.10	.05
☐ 23 Toby Atwell	.10	.05
☐ 24 Ferris Fain	.10	.05
☐ 25 Ray Boone	.10	.05
☐ 26 Dale Mitchell	.15	.07
☐ 27 Roy Campanella	2.50	1.10
☐ 28 Eddie Pellagrini	.10	.05
☐ 29 Hal Jeffcoat	.10	.05
☐ 30 Willard Nixon	.10	.05
☐ 31 Ewell Blackwell	.15	.07
☐ 32 Clyde Vollmer	.10	.05
☐ 33 Bob Kennedy	.10	.05
☐ 34 George Shuba	.15	.07
☐ 35 Irv Noren	.10	.05
☐ 36 Johnny Groth	.10	.05
☐ 37 Eddie Mathews	1.00	.45
☐ 38 Jim Hearn	.10	.05
☐ 39 Eddie Miksis	.10	.05
☐ 40 John Lipon	.10	.05
☐ 41 Enos Slaughter	.75	.35
☐ 42 Gus Zernial	.15	.07
☐ 43 Gil McDougald	.25	.11
☐ 44 Ellis Kinder	.10	.05
☐ 45 Grady Hatton	.10	.05
☐ 46 Johnny Klippstein	.10	.05
☐ 47 Bubba Church	.10	.05
☐ 48 Bob Del Greco	.10	.05
☐ 49 Faye Throneberry	.10	.05
☐ 50 Chuck Dressen MG	.15	.07
☐ 51 Frank Campos	.10	.05
☐ 52 Ted Gray	.10	.05
☐ 53 Sherm Lollar	.15	.07
☐ 54 Bob Feller	1.50	.70
☐ 55 Maurice McDermott	.10	.05
☐ 56 Gerry Staley	.10	.05
☐ 57 Carl Scheib	.10	.05
☐ 58 George Metkovich	.10	.05
☐ 59 Karl Drews	.10	.05
☐ 60 Cloyd Boyer	.10	.05
☐ 61 Early Wynn	.75	.35
☐ 62 Monte Irvin	.75	.35
☐ 63 Gus Niarhos	.10	.05
☐ 64 Dave Philley	.10	.05
☐ 65 Earl Harrist	.10	.05
☐ 66 Minnie Minoso	.50	.23
☐ 67 Roy Sievers	.15	.07
☐ 68 Del Rice	.10	.05
☐ 69 Dick Brodowski	.10	.05
☐ 70 Ed Yuhas	.10	.05
☐ 71 Tony Bartirome	.10	.05
☐ 72 Fred Hutchinson	.15	.07
☐ 73 Eddie Robinson	.10	.05
☐ 74 Joe Rossi	.10	.05
☐ 75 Mike Garcia	.15	.07
☐ 76 Pee Wee Reese	1.50	.70
☐ 77 Johnny Mize	.75	.35
☐ 78 Red Schoendienst	.75	.35
☐ 79 Johnny Wyrostek	.10	.05
☐ 80 Jim Hegan	.10	.05
☐ 81 Joe Black	.25	.11
☐ 82 Mickey Mantle	20.00	9.00
☐ 83 Howie Pollet	.10	.05
☐ 84 Bob Hooper	.10	.05
☐ 85 Bobby Morgan	.10	.05
☐ 86 Billy Martin	1.00	.45
☐ 87 Ed Lopat	.25	.11
☐ 88 Willie Jones	.10	.05
☐ 89 Chuck Stobbs	.10	.05
☐ 90 Hank Edwards	.10	.05
☐ 91 Ebba St.Claire	.10	.05
☐ 92 Paul Minner	.10	.05
☐ 93 Hal Rice	.10	.05
☐ 94 Bill Kennedy	.10	.05
☐ 95 Willard Marshall	.10	.05
☐ 96 Virgil Trucks	.10	.05
☐ 97 Don Kolloway	.10	.05
☐ 98 Cal Abrams	.10	.05
☐ 99 Dave Madison	.10	.05
☐ 100 Bill Miller	.10	.05
☐ 101 Ted Wilks	.10	.05
☐ 102 Connie Ryan	.10	.05
☐ 103 Joe Astroth	.10	.05
☐ 104 Yogi Berra	2.50	1.10
☐ 105 Joe Nuxhall	.15	.07
☐ 106 Johnny Antonelli	.15	.07
☐ 107 Danny O'Connell	.10	.05
☐ 108 Bob Porterfield	.10	.05
☐ 109 Alvin Dark	.15	.07
☐ 110 Herman Wehmeier	.10	.05
☐ 111 Hank Sauer	.15	.07
☐ 112 Ned Garver	.10	.05
☐ 113 Jerry Priddy	.10	.05
☐ 114 Phil Rizzuto	1.25	.55
☐ 115 George Spencer	.10	.05
☐ 116 Frank Smith	.10	.05
☐ 117 Sid Gordon	.10	.05
☐ 118 Gus Bell	.15	.07
☐ 119 Johnny Sain	.25	.11
☐ 120 Davey Williams	.10	.05
☐ 121 Walt Dropo	.10	.05
☐ 122 Elmer Valo	.10	.05
☐ 123 Tommy Byrne	.10	.05
☐ 124 Sibby Sisti	.10	.05
☐ 125 Dick Williams	.15	.07
☐ 126 Bill Connelly	.10	.05
☐ 127 Clint Courtney	.10	.05
☐ 128 Wilmer Mizell	.15	.07
☐ 129 Keith Thomas	.10	.05
☐ 130 Turk Lown	.10	.05
☐ 131 Harry Byrd	.10	.05
☐ 132 Tom Morgan	.10	.05
☐ 133 Gil Coan	.10	.05
☐ 134 Rube Walker	.10	.05
☐ 135 Al Rosen	.25	.11
☐ 136 Ken Heintzelman	.10	.05
☐ 137 John Rutherford	.10	.05
☐ 138 George Kell	.75	.35
☐ 139 Sammy White	.10	.05
☐ 140 Tommy Glaviano	.10	.05

☐ 141 Allie Reynolds .25 .11
☐ 142 Vic Wertz .15 .07
☐ 143 Billy Pierce .15 .07
☐ 144 Bob Schultz .10 .05
☐ 145 Harry Dorish .10 .05
☐ 146 Granny Hamner .15 .07
☐ 147 Warren Spahn 1.50 .70
☐ 148 Mickey Grasso .10 .05
☐ 149 Dom DiMaggio .50 .23
☐ 150 Harry Simpson .10 .05
☐ 151 Hoyt Wilhelm .75 .35
☐ 152 Bob Adams .10 .05
☐ 153 Andy Seminick .15 .07
☐ 154 Dick Groat .25 .11
☐ 155 Dutch Leonard .10 .05
☐ 156 Jim Rivera .10 .05
☐ 157 Bob Addis .10 .05
☐ 158 Johnny Logan .15 .07
☐ 159 Wayne Terwilliger .10 .05
☐ 160 Bob Young .10 .05
☐ 161 Vern Bickford .10 .05
☐ 162 Ted Kluszewski .50 .23
☐ 163 Fred Hatfield .10 .05
☐ 164 Frank Shea .10 .05
☐ 165 Billy Hoeft .10 .05
☐ 166 Billy Hunter .10 .05
☐ 167 Art Schult .10 .05
☐ 168 Willard Schmidt .10 .05
☐ 169 Dizzy Trout .10 .05
☐ 170 Bill Werle .10 .05
☐ 171 Bill Glynn .10 .05
☐ 172 Rip Repulski .10 .05
☐ 173 Preston Ward .10 .05
☐ 174 Billy Loes
(Not printed)
☐ 175 Ron Kline .10 .05
☐ 176 Don Hoak .15 .07
☐ 177 Jim Dyck .10 .05
☐ 178 Jim Waugh .10 .05
☐ 179 Gene Hermanski .10 .05
☐ 180 Virgil Stallcup .10 .05
☐ 181 Al Zarilla .10 .05
☐ 182 Bobby Hofman .10 .05
☐ 183 Stu Miller .10 .05
☐ 184 Hal Brown .10 .05
☐ 185 Jim Pendleton .10 .05
☐ 186 Charlie Bishop .10 .05
☐ 187 Jim Fridley .10 .05
☐ 188 Andy Carey .15 .07
☐ 189 Ray Jablonski .10 .05
☐ 190 Dixie Walker CO .15 .07
☐ 191 Ralph Kiner .75 .35
☐ 192 Wally Westlake .10 .05
☐ 193 Mike Clark .10 .05
☐ 194 Eddie Kazak .10 .05
☐ 195 Ed McGhee .10 .05
☐ 196 Bob Keegan .10 .05
☐ 197 Del Crandall .15 .07
☐ 198 Forrest Main .10 .05
☐ 199 Marion Fricano .10 .05
☐ 200 Gordon Goldsberry .10 .05
☐ 201 Paul LaPalme .10 .05
☐ 202 Carl Sawatski .10 .05
☐ 203 Cliff Fannin .10 .05
☐ 204 Dick Bokelman .10 .05
☐ 205 Vern Benson .10 .05
☐ 206 Ed Bailey .15 .07
☐ 207 Whitey Ford 1.50 .70
☐ 208 Jim Wilson .10 .05
☐ 209 Jim Greengrass .10 .05
☐ 210 Bob Cerv .10 .05
☐ 211 J.W. Porter .10 .05
☐ 212 Jack Dittmer .10 .05
☐ 213 Ray Scarborough .10 .05
☐ 214 Bill Bruton .15 .07
☐ 215 Gene Conley .10 .05
☐ 216 Jim Hughes .10 .05
☐ 217 Murray Wall .10 .05
☐ 218 Les Fusselman .10 .05
☐ 219 Pete Runnels UER .10 .05
(Photo actually
Don Johnson)
☐ 220 Satchel Paige UER 4.00 1.80
(Misspelled Satchell
on card front)
☐ 221 Bob Milliken .15 .07
☐ 222 Vic Janowicz .20 .09
☐ 223 Johnny O'Brien .20 .09
☐ 224 Lou Sleater .15 .07
☐ 225 Bobby Shantz .20 .09
☐ 226 Ed Erautt .15 .07
☐ 227 Morrie Martin .15 .07
☐ 228 Hal Newhouser 1.00 .45
☐ 229 Rocky Krsnich .15 .07
☐ 230 Johnny Lindell .15 .07
☐ 231 Solly Hemus .15 .07
☐ 232 Dick Kokos .15 .07

☐ 233 Al Aber .15 .07
☐ 234 Ray Murray .15 .07
☐ 235 John Hetki .15 .07
☐ 236 Harry Perkowski .15 .07
☐ 237 Bud Podbielan .15 .07
☐ 238 Cal Hogue .15 .07
☐ 239 Jim Delsing .15 .07
☐ 240 Fred Marsh .15 .07
☐ 241 Al Sima .15 .07
☐ 242 Charlie Silvera .20 .09
☐ 243 Carlos Bernier .15 .07
☐ 244 Willie Mays 12.00 5.50
☐ 245 Bill Norman CO .15 .07
☐ 246 Roy Face .30 .14
☐ 247 Mike Sandlock .15 .07
☐ 248 Gene Stephens .15 .07
☐ 249 Eddie O'Brien .20 .09
☐ 250 Bob Wilson .15 .07
☐ 251 Sid Hudson .15 .07
☐ 252 Hank Foiles .15 .07
☐ 253 Does not exist .07
☐ 254 Preacher Roe .35 .16
☐ 255 Dixie Howell .15 .07
☐ 256 Les Peden .15 .07
☐ 257 Bob Boyd .15 .07
☐ 258 Jim Gilliam .50 .23
☐ 259 Roy McMillan .20 .09
☐ 260 Sam Calderone .15 .07
☐ 261 Does not exist
☐ 262 Bob Oldis .15 .07
☐ 263 Johnny Podres .35 .16
☐ 264 Gene Woodling .30 .14
☐ 265 Jackie Jensen .35 .16
☐ 266 Bob Cain .15 .07
☐ 267 Does not exist
☐ 268 Does not exist
☐ 269 Duane Pillette .15 .07
☐ 270 Vern Stephens .20 .09
☐ 271 Does not exist
☐ 272 Bill Antonello .15 .07
☐ 273 Harvey Haddix .20 .09
☐ 274 John Riddle .15 .07
☐ 275 Does not exist
☐ 276 Ken Raffensberger .15 .07
☐ 277 Don Lund .15 .07
☐ 278 Willie Miranda .15 .07
☐ 279 Joe Coleman .15 .07
☐ 280 Milt Bolling .25 .11
☐ 281 Jimmie Dykes MG .25 .11
☐ 282 Ralph Houk .25 .11
☐ 283 Frank Thomas .25 .11
☐ 284 Bob Lemon .75 .35
☐ 285 Joe Adcock .25 .11
☐ 286 Jimmy Piersall .35 .16
☐ 287 Mickey Vernon .25 .11
☐ 288 Robin Roberts 1.00 .45
☐ 289 Rogers Hornsby MG .50 .23
☐ 290 Hank Bauer .25 .11
☐ 291 Hoot Evers .20 .09
☐ 292 Whitey Lockman .25 .11
☐ 293 Ralph Branca .25 .11
☐ 294 Wally Post .25 .11
☐ 295 Phil Cavarretta MG .25 .11
☐ 296 Gil Hodges 1.00 .45
☐ 297 Roy Smalley .20 .09
☐ 298 Bob Friend .25 .11
☐ 299 Dusty Rhodes .20 .09
☐ 300 Eddie Stanky .20 .09
☐ 301 Harvey Kuenn .35 .16
☐ 302 Marty Marion .25 .11
☐ 303 Sal Maglie .35 .16
☐ 304 Lou Boudreau MG .50 .23
☐ 305 Carl Furillo .35 .16
☐ 306 Bobo Holloman .20 .09
☐ 307 Steve O'Neill MG .20 .09
☐ 308 Carl Erskine .35 .16
☐ 309 Leo Durocher MG .75 .35
☐ 310 Lew Burdette .25 .11
☐ 311 Richie Ashburn 1.00 .45
☐ 312 Hoyt Wilhelm .75 .35
☐ 313 Bucky Harris MG .50 .23
☐ 314 Joe Garagiola .50 .23
☐ 315 Johnny Pesky .25 .11
☐ 316 Fred Haney MG .25 .11
☐ 317 Hank Aaron 10.00 4.50
☐ 318 Curt Simmons .25 .11
☐ 319 Ted Williams 10.00 4.50
☐ 320 Don Newcombe .50 .23
☐ 321 Charlie Grimm MG .25 .11
☐ 322 Paul Richards MG .25 .11
☐ 323 Wes Westrum .25 .11
☐ 324 Vern Law .20 .09
☐ 325 Casey Stengel MG .75 .35
☐ 326 Dizzy Dean and .50 .23
Al Simmons
(1953 HOF Inductees)
☐ 327 Duke Snider 2.50 1.10

☐ 328 Bill Rigney .25 .11
☐ 329 Al Lopez MG .50 .23
☐ 330 Bobby Thomson .30 .14
☐ 331 Nellie Fox 1.00 .45
☐ 332 Eleanor Engle 1.00 .45
☐ 333 Larry Doby .35 .16
☐ 334 Billy Goodman .25 .11
☐ 335 Checklist 1-140 .20 .09
☐ 336 Checklist 141-280 .20 .09
☐ 337 Checklist 281-337 .20 .09

1994 Topps Archives 1954

The 1954 Archives set includes 248 reprint cards from the original set, plus eight specially created prospect cards (Roberto Clemente, Harmon Killebrew, Bob Grim, Camilo Pascual, Herb Score, Elston Howard, Bill Virdon, and Don Zimmer). No factory sets were sold. Randomly inserted were 1,954 redemption cards good for actual 1954 Topps cards; 1,954 Hank Aaron autographed gold cards; and 1,954 redemption cards for full sets of ToppsGold Archives cards. Each 12-card pack contains 11 Archives cards plus one ToppsGold Archives card. A random insert card replaced the gold card in every 2,210 packs. Ted Williams' cards #1 and #250, as well as a new Mickey Mantle's card #259, were issued as inserts in the 1994 Upper Deck All-Time Heroes series. On a white-bordered color background, the fronts display a color closeup cutout, with the player's name, team name, and team logo across the top. A small black-and-white cutout is superposed next to the color closeup. A facsimile autograph is inscribed across the lower portion of the card. On a white background, the horizontal backs present biography, player profile and, on a green panel, minor league statistics and an "Inside Baseball" feature.

	MINT	NRMT
COMPLETE SET (256)	30.00	13.50
COMMON CARD (2-249)	.10	.05
COMMON CARD (251-258)	.15	.07

☐ 1 Not Issued
☐ 2 Gus Zernial .15 .07
☐ 3 Monte Irvin .50 .23
☐ 4 Hank Sauer .15 .07
☐ 5 Ed Lopat .15 .07
☐ 6 Pete Runnels .15 .07
☐ 7 Ted Kluszewski .20 .09
☐ 8 Bobby Young .10 .05
☐ 9 Harvey Haddix .15 .07
☐ 10 Jackie Robinson 4.00 1.80
☐ 11 Paul Smith .10 .05
☐ 12 Del Crandall .10 .05
☐ 13 Billy Martin .50 .23
☐ 14 Preacher Roe .15 .07
☐ 15 Al Rosen .20 .09
☐ 16 Vic Janowicz .20 .09
☐ 17 Phil Rizzuto .75 .35
☐ 18 Walt Dropo .10 .05
☐ 19 Johnny Lipon .10 .05
☐ 20 Warren Spahn .75 .35
☐ 21 Bobby Shantz .10 .05
☐ 22 Jim Greengrass .10 .05
☐ 23 Luke Easter .15 .07
☐ 24 Granny Hamner .15 .07
☐ 25 Harvey Kuenn .15 .07
☐ 26 Ray Jablonski .10 .05
☐ 27 Ferris Fain .10 .05
☐ 28 Paul Minner .10 .05
☐ 29 Jim Hegan .10 .05
☐ 30 Ed Mathews .75 .35
☐ 31 Johnny Klippstein .10 .05
☐ 32 Duke Snider 1.50 .70
☐ 33 Johnny Schmitz .10 .05
☐ 34 Jim Rivera .10 .05
☐ 35 Jim Gilliam .20 .09
☐ 36 Hoyt Wilhelm .50 .23
☐ 37 Whitey Ford .75 .35
☐ 38 Eddie Stanky MG .15 .07
☐ 39 Sherm Lollar .15 .07
☐ 40 Mel Parnell .10 .05

Card	MINT	NRMT
☐ 41 Willie Jones	.15	.07
☐ 42 Don Mueller	.10	.05
☐ 43 Dick Groat	.15	.07
☐ 44 Ned Garver	.10	.05
☐ 45 Richie Ashburn	.75	.35
☐ 46 Ken Raffensberger	.10	.05
☐ 47 Ellis Kinder	.10	.05
☐ 48 Billy Hunter	.10	.05
☐ 49 Ray Murray	.10	.05
☐ 50 Yogi Berra	1.50	.70
☐ 51 Johnny Lindell	.10	.05
☐ 52 Vic Power	.10	.05
☐ 53 Jack Dittmer	.10	.05
☐ 54 Vern Stephens	.15	.07
☐ 55 Phil Cavarretta MG	.15	.07
☐ 56 Willie Miranda	.10	.05
☐ 57 Luis Aloma	.10	.05
☐ 58 Bob Wilson	.10	.05
☐ 59 Gene Conley	.10	.05
☐ 60 Frank Baumholtz	.10	.05
☐ 61 Bob Cain	.10	.05
☐ 62 Eddie Robinson	.10	.05
☐ 63 Johnny Pesky	.15	.07
☐ 64 Hank Thompson	.10	.05
☐ 65 Bob Swift	.10	.05
☐ 66 Ted Lepcio	.10	.05
☐ 67 Jim Willis	.10	.05
☐ 68 Sammy Calderone	.10	.05
☐ 69 Bud Podbielan	.10	.05
☐ 70 Larry Doby	.20	.09
☐ 71 Frank Smith	.10	.05
☐ 72 Preston Ward	.10	.05
☐ 73 Wayne Terwilliger	.10	.05
☐ 74 Bill Taylor	.10	.05
☐ 75 Fred Haney MG	.10	.05
☐ 76 Bob Scheffing CO	.10	.05
☐ 77 Ray Boone	.10	.05
☐ 78 Ted Kazanski	.10	.05
☐ 79 Andy Pafko	.15	.07
☐ 80 Jackie Jensen	.15	.07
☐ 81 Dave Hoskins	.10	.05
☐ 82 Milt Bolling	.10	.05
☐ 83 Joe Collins	.15	.07
☐ 84 Dick Cole	.10	.05
☐ 85 Bob Turley	.15	.07
☐ 86 Billy Herman CO	.20	.09
☐ 87 Roy Face	.15	.07
☐ 88 Matt Batts	.10	.05
☐ 89 Howie Pollet	.10	.05
☐ 90 Willie Mays	6.00	2.70
☐ 91 Bob Oldis	.10	.05
☐ 92 Wally Westlake	.10	.05
☐ 93 Sid Hudson	.10	.05
☐ 94 Ernie Banks	3.00	1.35
☐ 95 Hal Rice	.10	.05
☐ 96 Charlie Silvera	.15	.07
☐ 97 Jerry Lane	.10	.05
☐ 98 Joe Black	.20	.09
☐ 99 Bob Hofman	.10	.05
☐ 100 Bob Keegan	.10	.05
☐ 101 Gene Woodling	.15	.07
☐ 102 Gil Hodges	.75	.35
☐ 103 Jim Lemon	.10	.05
☐ 104 Mike Sandlock	.10	.05
☐ 105 Andy Carey	.15	.07
☐ 106 Dick Kokos	.10	.05
☐ 107 Duane Pillette	.10	.05
☐ 108 Thornton Kipper	.10	.05
☐ 109 Bill Bruton	.15	.07
☐ 110 Harry Dorish	.10	.05
☐ 111 Jim Delsing	.10	.05
☐ 112 Bill Renna	.10	.05
☐ 113 Bob Boyd	.10	.05
☐ 114 Dean Stone	.10	.05
☐ 115 Rip Repulski	.10	.05
☐ 116 Steve Bilko	.10	.05
☐ 117 Solly Hemus	.10	.05
☐ 118 Carl Scheib	.10	.05
☐ 119 Johnny Antonelli	.15	.07
☐ 120 Roy McMillan	.15	.07
☐ 121 Clem Labine	.20	.09
☐ 122 Johnny Logan	.15	.07
☐ 123 Bobby Adams	.10	.05
☐ 124 Marion Fricano	.10	.05
☐ 125 Harry Perkowski	.10	.05
☐ 126 Ben Wade	.10	.05
☐ 127 Steve O'Neill MG	.10	.05
☐ 128 Henry Aaron	6.00	2.70
☐ 129 Forrest Jacobs	.10	.05
☐ 130 Hank Bauer	.20	.09
☐ 131 Reno Bertoia	.10	.05
☐ 132 Tom Lasorda	3.00	1.35
☐ 133 Del Baker CO	.10	.05
☐ 134 Cal Hogue	.10	.05
☐ 135 Joe Presko	.10	.05
☐ 136 Connie Ryan	.10	.05
☐ 137 Wally Moon	.15	.07
☐ 138 Bob Borkowski	.10	.05
☐ 139 Ed O'Brien	.15	.07
Johnny O'Brien		
☐ 140 Tom Wright	.10	.05
☐ 141 Joe Jay	.10	.05
☐ 142 Tom Poholsky	.10	.05
☐ 143 Rollie Hemsley CO	.10	.05
☐ 144 Bill Werle	.10	.05
☐ 145 Elmer Valo	.10	.05
☐ 146 Don Johnson	.10	.05
☐ 147 John Riddle CO	.10	.05
☐ 148 Bob Trice	.10	.05
☐ 149 Jim Robertson	.10	.05
☐ 150 Dick Kryhoski	.10	.05
☐ 151 Alex Grammas	.10	.05
☐ 152 Mike Blyzka	.10	.05
☐ 153 Rube Walker	.10	.05
☐ 154 Mike Fornieles	.10	.05
☐ 155 Bob Kennedy	.10	.05
☐ 156 Joe Coleman	.10	.05
☐ 157 Don Lenhardt	.10	.05
☐ 158 Peanuts Lowrey	.10	.05
☐ 159 Dave Philley	.10	.05
☐ 160 Red Kress CO	.10	.05
☐ 161 John Hetki	.10	.05
☐ 162 Herman Wehmeier	.10	.05
☐ 163 Frank House	.10	.05
☐ 164 Stu Miller	.10	.05
☐ 165 Jim Pendleton	.10	.05
☐ 166 Johnny Podres	.15	.07
☐ 167 Don Lund	.10	.05
☐ 168 Morrie Martin	.10	.05
☐ 169 Jim Hughes	.10	.05
☐ 170 Jim Rhodes	.10	.05
☐ 171 Leo Kiely	.10	.05
☐ 172 Hal Brown	.10	.05
☐ 173 Jack Harshman	.10	.05
☐ 174 Tom Qualters	.10	.05
☐ 175 Frank Leja	.10	.05
☐ 176 Bob Keely	.10	.05
☐ 177 Bob Milliken	.10	.05
☐ 178 Bill Glynn	.10	.05
☐ 179 Gair Allie	.10	.05
☐ 180 Wes Westrum	.10	.05
☐ 181 Mel Roach	.10	.05
☐ 182 Chuck Harmon	.10	.05
☐ 183 Earle Combs CO	.20	.09
☐ 184 Ed Bailey	.10	.05
☐ 185 Chuck Stobbs	.10	.05
☐ 186 Karl Olson	.10	.05
☐ 187 Heinie Manush CO	.20	.09
☐ 188 Dave Jolly	.10	.05
☐ 189 Bob Ross	.10	.05
☐ 190 Ray Herbert	.10	.05
☐ 191 Dick Schofield	.10	.05
☐ 192 Cot Deal CO	.10	.05
☐ 193 Johnny Hopp CO	.10	.05
☐ 194 Bill Sarni	.10	.05
☐ 195 Bill Consolo	.10	.05
☐ 196 Stan Jok	.10	.05
☐ 197 Schoolboy Rowe CO	.15	.07
☐ 198 Carl Sawatski	.10	.05
☐ 199 Rocky Nelson	.10	.05
☐ 200 Larry Jansen	.10	.05
☐ 201 Al Kaline	3.00	1.35
☐ 202 Bob Purkey	.10	.05
☐ 203 Harry Brecheen CO	.10	.05
☐ 204 Angel Scull	.10	.05
☐ 205 Johnny Sain	.15	.07
☐ 206 Ray Crone	.10	.05
☐ 207 Tom Oliver CO	.10	.05
☐ 208 Grady Hatton	.10	.05
☐ 209 Charlie Thompson	.10	.05
☐ 210 Bob Buhl	.10	.05
☐ 211 Don Hoak	.10	.05
☐ 212 Mickey Micelotta	.10	.05
☐ 213 John Fitzpatrick CO	.10	.05
☐ 214 Arnold Portocarrero	.10	.05
☐ 215 Ed McGhee	.10	.05
☐ 216 Al Sima	.10	.05
☐ 217 Paul Schreiber CO	.10	.05
☐ 218 Fred Marsh	.10	.05
☐ 219 Charlie Kress	.10	.05
☐ 220 Ruben Gomez	.10	.05
☐ 221 Dick Brodowski	.10	.05
☐ 222 Bill Wilson	.10	.05
☐ 223 Joe Haynes CO	.10	.05
☐ 224 Dick Weik	.10	.05
☐ 225 Don Liddle	.10	.05
☐ 226 Jehosie Heard	.10	.05
☐ 227 Buster Mills CO	.10	.05
☐ 228 Gene Hermanski	.10	.05
☐ 229 Bob Talbot	.10	.05
☐ 230 Bob Kuzava	.10	.05
☐ 231 Roy Smalley	.10	.05
☐ 232 Lou Limmer	.10	.05
☐ 233 Augie Galan	.10	.05
☐ 234 Jerry Lynch	.10	.05
☐ 235 Vern Law	.15	.07
☐ 236 Paul Penson	.10	.05
☐ 237 Mike Ryba	.10	.05
☐ 238 Al Aber	.10	.05
☐ 239 Bill Skowron	.20	.09
☐ 240 Sam Mele	.10	.05
☐ 241 Bob Miller	.10	.05
☐ 242 Curt Roberts	.10	.05
☐ 243 Ray Blades CO	.10	.05
☐ 244 Leroy Wheat	.10	.05
☐ 245 Roy Sievers	.15	.07
☐ 246 Howie Fox	.10	.05
☐ 247 Eddie Mayo CO	.10	.05
☐ 248 Al Smith	.10	.05
☐ 249 Wilmer Mizell	.15	.07
☐ 250 Not Issued		
☐ 251 Roberto Clemente	10.00	4.50
☐ 252 Bob Grim	.15	.07
☐ 253 Elston Howard	.25	.11
☐ 254 Harmon Killebrew	2.00	.90
☐ 255 Camilo Pascual	.15	.07
☐ 256 Herb Score	.20	.09
☐ 257 Bill Virdon	.15	.07
☐ 258 Don Zimmer	.20	.09
☐ NNO Hank Aaron AU	200.00	90.00
☐ NNO0 Gold Redemption Card Exp.	3.50	1.55

1994 Topps Archives 1954 Gold

This set parallels the 1994 Topps Archives 1954 reprint series. It has the same design as the regular issue reprint, except that the team logo and the facsimile autograph are gold-foil stamped on the fronts.

	MINT	NRMT
COMPLETE SET (256)	125.00	55.00
COMMON CARD (2-258)	.25	.11
*STARS: 2X TO 4X BASIC CARDS		

1995 Topps Archives Brooklyn Dodgers

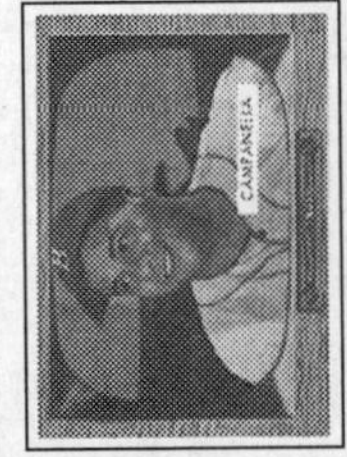

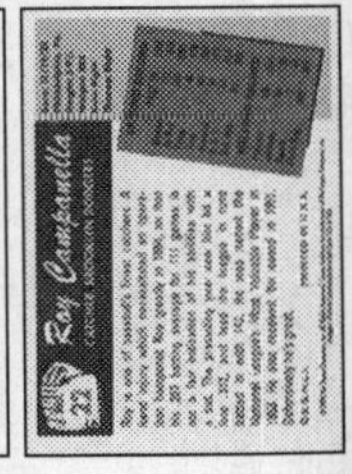

This 165-card set measures the standard size and is a single series release. The set honors the Brooklyn Dodgers teams of 1952-1956 and consists of 127 reprints of Topps and Bowman cards produced during that time. The cards "that never were" have been created for the players not featured on Topps and Bowman cards and replicate the design of the card for the year the player would have been pictured. Cards #117-120 commemorate the four games the Dodgers won for the 1955 World Series Championship. Though the cards are numbered as they were originally issued, Topps renumbered them as a complete set and they are checklisted below accordingly. A very limited amount of signed Sandy Koufax cards (#102) were signed and randomly inserted into packs.

	MINT	NRM
COMPLETE SET (165)	50.00	22.0
COMMON CARD (1-165)	.20	.0
☐ 1 Andy Pafko	.20	.0
☐ 2 Wayne Terwilliger	.20	.0
☐ 3 Billy Loes	.30	.1
☐ 4 Gil Hodges	1.00	.4
☐ 5 Duke Snider	1.00	.4
☐ 6 Jim Russell	.20	.0
☐ 7 Chris Van Cuyk	.20	.0
☐ 8 Preacher Roe	.40	.1
☐ 9 Johnny Schmitz	.20	.0
☐ 10 Bud Podbielan	.20	.0
☐ 11 Phil Haugstad	.20	.0
☐ 12 Clyde King	.20	.0
☐ 13 Billy Cox	.30	.1
☐ 14 Rocky Bridges	.20	.0
☐ 15 Carl Erskine	.40	.1
☐ 16 Erv Palica	.20	.0
☐ 17 Ralph Branca	.40	.1
☐ 18 Jackie Robinson	2.00	9

☐ 19 Roy Campanella	1.00	.45
☐ 20 Rube Walker	.20	.09
☐ 21 Johnny Rutherford	.20	.09
☐ 22 Joe Black	.30	.14
☐ 23 George Shuba	.20	.09
☐ 24 Pee Wee Reese	1.00	.45
☐ 25 Clem Labine	.40	.18
☐ 26 Bobby Morgan	.20	.09
☐ 27 Cookie Lavagetto CO	.20	.09
☐ 28 Chuck Dressen MG	.20	.09
☐ 29 Ben Wade	.20	.09
☐ 30 Rocky Nelson	.20	.09
☐ 31 Billy Herman CO	.30	.14
☐ 32 Jake Pitler CO	.20	.09
☐ 33 Dick Williams	.30	.14
☐ 34 Cal Abrams	.20	.09
☐ 35 Carl Furillo	.40	.18
☐ 36 Don Newcombe	.40	.18
☐ 37 Jackie Robinson	2.00	.90
☐ 38 Ben Wade	.20	.09
☐ 39 Clem Labine	.40	.18
☐ 40 Roy Campanella	1.00	.45
☐ 41 George Shuba	.20	.09
☐ 42 Chuck Dressen MG	.20	.09
☐ 43 Pee Wee Reese	1.00	.45
☐ 44 Joe Black	.30	.14
☐ 45 Bobby Morgan	.20	.09
☐ 46 Dick Williams	.30	.14
☐ 47 Rube Walker	.20	.09
☐ 48 Johnny Rutherford	.20	.09
☐ 49 Billy Loes	.30	.14
☐ 50 Don Hoak	.20	.09
☐ 51 Jim Hughes	.20	.09
☐ 52 Bob Milliken	.20	.09
☐ 53 Preacher Roe	.40	.18
☐ 54 Dixie Howell	.20	.09
☐ 55 Junior Gilliam	.40	.18
☐ 56 Johnny Podres	.40	.18
☐ 57 Bill Antonello	.20	.09
☐ 58 Ralph Branca	.40	.18
☐ 59 Gil Hodges	1.00	.45
☐ 60 Carl Furillo	.40	.18
☐ 61 Carl Erskine	.40	.18
☐ 62 Don Newcombe	.40	.18
☐ 63 Duke Snider	1.00	.45
☐ 64 Billy Cox	.30	.14
☐ 65 Russ Meyer	.20	.09
☐ 66 Jackie Robinson	2.00	.90
☐ 67 Preacher Roe	.40	.18
☐ 68 Duke Snider	1.00	.45
☐ 69 Junior Gilliam	.40	.18
☐ 70 Billy Herman CO	.30	.14
☐ 71 Joe Black	.30	.14
☐ 72 Gil Hodges	1.00	.45
☐ 73 Clem Labine	.40	.18
☐ 74 Ben Wade	.20	.09
☐ 75 Tom Lasorda	.75	.35
☐ 76 Rube Walker	.20	.09
☐ 77 Johnny Podres	.40	.18
☐ 78 Jim Hughes	.20	.09
☐ 79 Bob Milliken	.20	.09
☐ 80 Charlie Thompson	.20	.09
☐ 81 Don Hoak	.20	.09
☐ 82 Roberto Clemente	3.00	1.35
☐ 83 Don Zimmer	.30	.14
☐ 84 Roy Campanella	1.00	.45
☐ 85 Billy Cox	.30	.14
☐ 86 Carl Erskine	.40	.18
☐ 87 Carl Furillo	.40	.18
☐ 88 Don Newcombe	.40	.18
☐ 89 Pee Wee Reese	1.00	.45
☐ 90 George Shuba	.20	.09
☐ 91 Junior Gilliam	.40	.18
☐ 92 Billy Herman CO	.30	.14
☐ 93 Johnny Podres	.40	.18
☐ 94 Don Hoak	.20	.09
☐ 95 Jackie Robinson	2.00	.90
☐ 96 Jim Hughes	.20	.09
☐ 97 Sandy Amoros	.20	.09
☐ 98 Karl Spooner	.20	.09
☐ 99 Don Zimmer	.30	.14
☐ 100 Rube Walker	.20	.09
☐ 101 Bob Milliken	.20	.09
☐ 102 Sandy Koufax	3.00	1.35
☐ 103 Joe Black	.30	.14
☐ 104 Clem Labine	.40	.18
☐ 105 Gil Hodges	1.00	.45
☐ 106 Ed Roebuck	.20	.09
☐ 107 Bert Hamric	.20	.09
☐ 108 Duke Snider	1.00	.45
☐ 109 Walter Alston MG	.50	.23
☐ 110 Bob Borkowski	.20	.09
☐ 111 Roger Craig	.40	.18
☐ 112 Don Drysdale	1.50	.70
☐ 113 Dixie Howell	.20	.09
☐ 114 Frank Kellert	.20	.09
☐ 115 Tom Lasorda	.50	.23
☐ 116 Chuck Templeton	.20	.09
☐ 117 Jackie Robinson WS	1.00	.45
☐ 118 Gil Hodges WS	.50	.23
☐ 119 Duke Snider WS	.50	.23
☐ 120 Johnny Podres WS	.40	.18
☐ 121 Don Hoak	.30	.14
☐ 122 Roy Campanella	1.00	.45
☐ 123 Pee Wee Reese	1.00	.45
☐ 124 Bob Darnell	.20	.09
☐ 125 Don Zimmer	.40	.18
☐ 126 George Shuba	.20	.09
☐ 127 Johnny Podres	.50	.23
☐ 128 Junior Gilliam	.50	.23
☐ 129 Don Newcombe	.50	.23
☐ 130 Jim Hughes	.20	.09
☐ 131 Gil Hodges	1.00	.45
☐ 132 Carl Furillo	.50	.23
☐ 133 Carl Erskine	.50	.23
☐ 134 Erv Palica	.20	.09
☐ 135 Russ Meyer	.20	.09
☐ 136 Billy Loes	.40	.18
☐ 137 Walt Moryn	.20	.09
☐ 138 Chico Fernandez	.20	.09
☐ 139 Charlie Neal	.20	.09
☐ 140 Ken Lehman	.20	.09
☐ 141 Walter Alston MG	.50	.23
☐ 142 Jackie Robinson	2.00	.90
☐ 143 Sandy Amoros	.30	.14
☐ 144 Ed Roebuck	.20	.09
☐ 145 Roger Craig	.40	.18
☐ 146 Sandy Koufax	2.00	.90
☐ 147 Karl Spooner	.20	.09
☐ 148 Don Zimmer	.40	.18
☐ 149 Roy Campanella	1.00	.45
☐ 150 Gil Hodges	1.00	.45
☐ 151 Duke Snider	1.50	.70
☐ 152 Team Card	.40	.18
☐ 153 Johnny Podres	.50	.23
☐ 154 Don Bessent	.20	.09
☐ 155 Carl Furillo	.50	.23
☐ 156 Randy Jackson	.20	.09
☐ 157 Carl Erskine	.50	.23
☐ 158 Don Newcombe	.50	.23
☐ 159 Pee Wee Reese	1.00	.45
☐ 160 Billy Loes	.30	.14
☐ 161 Junior Gilliam	.50	.23
☐ 162 Clem Labine	.50	.23
☐ 163 Charlie Neal	.20	.09
☐ 164 Rube Walker	.20	.09
☐ 165 Checklist	.20	.09
☐ AU Sandy Koufax (Card 102)	600.00	275.00

1996 Topps Chrome

The 1996 Topps Chrome set was issued in one series totalling 165 cards and features the best old and new players from the 1996 Topps regular set. Each chromium card is a replica of its regular version with the exception of the Topps Chrome logo replacing the traditional logo. Inclued in the set is a Mickey Mantle #7 Commemorative card and a Cal Ripken Tribute card. The four-card packs retail for $3.00 each.

	MINT	NRMT
COMPLETE SET (165)	80.00	36.00
COMMON CARD (1-165)	.40	.18
☐ 1 Tony Gwynn STP	1.50	.70
☐ 2 Mike Piazza STP	2.50	1.10
☐ 3 Greg Maddux STP	2.50	1.10
☐ 4 Jeff Bagwell STP	1.50	.70
☐ 5 Larry Walker STP	1.50	.70
☐ 6 Barry Larkin STP	1.00	.45
☐ 7 Mickey Mantle COMM	10.00	4.50
☐ 8 Tom Glavine STP	.75	.35
☐ 9 Craig Biggio STP	1.00	.45
☐ 10 Barry Bonds STP	1.50	.70
☐ 11 Heathcliff Slocumb STP	.40	.18
☐ 12 Matt Williams STP	1.00	.45
☐ 13 Todd Helton	8.00	3.60
☐ 14 Paul Molitor	1.50	.70
☐ 15 Glenallen Hill	.40	.18
☐ 16 Troy Percival	.40	.18
☐ 17 Albert Belle	2.00	.90
☐ 18 Mark Wohlers	.75	.35
☐ 19 Kirby Puckett	3.00	1.35
☐ 20 Mark Grace	1.00	.45
☐ 21 J.T. Snow	.75	.35
☐ 22 David Justice	1.50	.70
☐ 23 Mike Mussina	1.50	.70
☐ 24 Bernie Williams	1.50	.70
☐ 25 Ron Gant	.75	.35
☐ 26 Carlos Baerga	.75	.35
☐ 27 Gary Sheffield	1.50	.70
☐ 28 Cal Ripken 2131	6.00	2.70
☐ 29 Frank Thomas	6.00	2.70
☐ 30 Kevin Seitzer	.40	.18
☐ 31 Joe Carter	.75	.35
☐ 32 Jeff King	.75	.35
☐ 33 David Cone	.75	.35
☐ 34 Eddie Murray	1.50	.70
☐ 35 Brian Jordan	.75	.35
☐ 36 Garret Anderson	.75	.35
☐ 37 Hideo Nomo	4.00	1.80
☐ 38 Steve Finley	.75	.35
☐ 39 Ivan Rodriguez	2.00	.90
☐ 40 Quilvio Veras	.40	.18
☐ 41 Mark McGwire	3.00	1.35
☐ 42 Greg Vaughn	.40	.18
☐ 43 Randy Johnson	1.50	.70
☐ 44 David Segui	.40	.18
☐ 45 Derek Bell	.40	.18
☐ 46 John Valentin	.75	.35
☐ 47 Steve Avery	.40	.18
☐ 48 Tino Martinez	1.50	.70
☐ 49 Shane Reynolds	.40	.18
☐ 50 Jim Edmonds	1.50	.70
☐ 51 Raul Mondesi	1.00	.45
☐ 52 Chipper Jones	5.00	2.20
☐ 53 Gregg Jefferies	.75	.35
☐ 54 Ken Caminiti	1.50	.70
☐ 55 Brian McRae	.40	.18
☐ 56 Don Mattingly	2.50	1.10
☐ 57 Marty Cordova	.40	.18
☐ 58 Vinny Castilla	.75	.35
☐ 59 John Smoltz	.75	.35
☐ 60 Travis Fryman	.75	.35
☐ 61 Ryan Klesko	1.00	.45
☐ 62 Alex Fernandez	.75	.35
☐ 63 Dante Bichette	.75	.35
☐ 64 Eric Karros	.75	.35
☐ 65 Roger Clemens	3.00	1.35
☐ 66 Randy Myers	.75	.35
☐ 67 Cal Ripken	6.00	2.70
☐ 68 Rod Beck	.75	.35
☐ 69 Jack McDowell	.40	.18
☐ 70 Ken Griffey Jr.	8.00	3.60
☐ 71 Ramon Martinez	.75	.35
☐ 72 Jason Giambi FS	1.00	.45
☐ 73 Nomar Garciaparra FS	6.00	2.70
☐ 74 Billy Wagner FS	1.00	.45
☐ 75 Todd Greene FS	1.00	.45
☐ 76 Paul Wilson FS	.40	.18
☐ 77 Johnny Damon FS	.75	.35
☐ 78 Alan Benes FS	.75	.35
☐ 79 Karim Garcia FS	.75	.35
☐ 80 Derek Jeter FS	5.00	2.20
☐ 81 Kirby Puckett STP	1.50	.70
☐ 82 Cal Ripken STP	3.00	1.35
☐ 83 Albert Belle STP	1.50	.70
☐ 84 Randy Johnson STP	1.50	.70
☐ 85 Wade Boggs STP	1.50	.70
☐ 86 Carlos Baerga STP	.75	.35
☐ 87 Ivan Rodriguez STP	1.50	.70
☐ 88 Mike Mussina STP	1.50	.70
☐ 89 Frank Thomas STP	4.00	1.80
☐ 90 Ken Griffey Jr. STP	4.00	1.80
☐ 91 Jose Mesa STP	.40	.18
☐ 92 Matt Morris	2.50	1.10
☐ 93 Mike Piazza	5.00	2.20
☐ 94 Edgar Martinez	1.50	.70
☐ 95 Chuck Knoblauch	1.50	.70
☐ 96 Andres Galarraga	1.50	.70
☐ 97 Tony Gwynn	4.00	1.80
☐ 98 Lee Smith	.75	.35
☐ 99 Sammy Sosa	1.50	.70
☐ 100 Jim Thome	1.50	.70
☐ 101 Bernard Gilkey	.75	.35
☐ 102 Brady Anderson	1.00	.45
☐ 103 Rico Brogna	.40	.18
☐ 104 Len Dykstra	.75	.35
☐ 105 Tom Glavine	.75	.35
☐ 106 John Olerud	.75	.35
☐ 107 Terry Steinbach	.75	.35
☐ 108 Brian Hunter	.75	.35
☐ 109 Jay Buhner	1.00	.45
☐ 110 Mo Vaughn	2.00	.90
☐ 111 Jose Mesa	.75	.35
☐ 112 Brett Butler	.75	.35

Card	MINT	NRMT
☐ 113 Chili Davis	.75	.35
☐ 114 Paul O'Neill	.75	.35
☐ 115 Roberto Alomar	1.50	.70
☐ 116 Barry Larkin	1.00	.45
☐ 117 Marquis Grissom	.75	.35
☐ 118 Will Clark	1.00	.45
☐ 119 Barry Bonds	2.00	.90
☐ 120 Ozzie Smith	2.00	.90
☐ 121 Pedro Martinez	1.50	.70
☐ 122 Craig Biggio	1.00	.45
☐ 123 Moises Alou	.75	.35
☐ 124 Robin Ventura	.75	.35
☐ 125 Greg Maddux	5.00	2.20
☐ 126 Tim Salmon	1.50	.70
☐ 127 Wade Boggs	1.50	.70
☐ 128 Ismael Valdes	.75	.35
☐ 129 Juan Gonzalez	4.00	1.80
☐ 130 Ray Lankford	.75	.35
☐ 131 Bobby Bonilla	.75	.35
☐ 132 Reggie Sanders	.40	.18
☐ 133 Alex Ochoa NOW	.40	.18
☐ 134 Mark Loretta NOW	.40	.18
☐ 135 Jason Kendall NOW	1.50	.70
☐ 136 Brooks Kieschnick NOW	.75	.35
☐ 137 Chris Snopek NOW	.40	.18
☐ 138 Ruben Rivera NOW	.75	.35
☐ 139 Jeff Suppan NOW	1.00	.45
☐ 140 John Wasdin NOW	.40	.18
☐ 141 Jay Payton NOW	.40	.18
☐ 142 Rick Krivda NOW	.40	.18
☐ 143 Jimmy Haynes NOW	.40	.18
☐ 144 Ryne Sandberg	2.00	.90
☐ 145 Matt Williams	1.00	.45
☐ 146 Jose Canseco	1.00	.45
☐ 147 Larry Walker	1.50	.70
☐ 148 Kevin Appier	.75	.35
☐ 149 Javy Lopez	.75	.35
☐ 150 Dennis Eckersley	1.00	.45
☐ 151 Jason Isringhausen	.40	.18
☐ 152 Dean Palmer	.75	.35
☐ 153 Jeff Bagwell	3.00	1.35
☐ 154 Rondell White	.75	.35
☐ 155 Wally Joyner	.40	.18
☐ 156 Fred McGriff	1.00	.45
☐ 157 Cecil Fielder	.75	.35
☐ 158 Rafael Palmeiro	1.00	.45
☐ 159 Rickey Henderson	1.00	.45
☐ 160 Shawon Dunston	.40	.18
☐ 161 Manny Ramirez	1.50	.70
☐ 162 Alex Gonzalez	.40	.18
☐ 163 Shawn Green	.75	.35
☐ 164 Kenny Lofton	2.00	.90
☐ 165 Jeff Conine	.75	.35

1996 Topps Chrome Refractors

Randomly inserted at the rate of one in every 12 packs, this 165-card set is parallel to the regular Chrome set. The difference in design is the refractive quality of the cards.

	MINT	NRMT
COMPLETE SET (165)	3000.00	1350.00
COMMON CARD (1-165)	8.00	3.60

*STARS: 10X TO 20X BASIC CARDS ..
*YOUNG STARS: 6X TO 12X BASIC CARDS

Card	MINT	NRMT
☐ 7 Mickey Mantle COMM	175.00	80.00
☐ 13 Todd Helton	60.00	27.00
☐ 19 Kirby Puckett	60.00	27.00
☐ 28 Cal Ripken TRIB	120.00	55.00
☐ 29 Frank Thomas	120.00	55.00
☐ 37 Hideo Nomo	80.00	36.00
☐ 41 Mark McGwire	60.00	27.00
☐ 52 Chipper Jones	80.00	36.00
☐ 65 Roger Clemens	60.00	27.00
☐ 67 Cal Ripken	120.00	55.00
☐ 70 Ken Griffey Jr.	150.00	70.00
☐ 73 Nomar Garciaparra	80.00	36.00
☐ 80 Derek Jeter FS	80.00	36.00
☐ 82 Cal Ripken STP	60.00	27.00
☐ 89 Frank Thomas STP	60.00	27.00
☐ 90 Ken Griffey Jr. STP	80.00	36.00
☐ 93 Mike Piazza	100.00	45.00
☐ 97 Tony Gwynn	80.00	36.00
☐ 125 Greg Maddux	100.00	45.00
☐ 129 Juan Gonzalez	80.00	36.00
☐ 153 Jeff Bagwell	60.00	27.00

1996 Topps Chrome Masters of the Game

Randomly inserted in packs at a rate of one in 12, this 20-card set honors players who are masters of their playing positions. The fronts feature color action photography with brilliant color metallization.

	MINT	NRMT
COMPLETE SET (20)	60.00	27.00
COMMON CARD (1-20)	1.50	.70
COMPLETE REFRACTOR SET (20)	200.00	90.00

*REFRACTORS: 1.25X TO 3X BASIC INSERTS

Card	MINT	NRMT
☐ 1 Dennis Eckersley	3.00	1.35
☐ 2 Denny Martinez	2.00	.90
☐ 3 Eddie Murray	4.00	1.80
☐ 4 Paul Molitor	4.00	1.80
☐ 5 Ozzie Smith	5.00	2.20
☐ 6 Rickey Henderson	3.00	1.35
☐ 7 Tim Raines	2.00	.90
☐ 8 Lee Smith	2.00	.90
☐ 9 Cal Ripken	15.00	6.75
☐ 10 Chili Davis	2.00	.90
☐ 11 Wade Boggs	4.00	1.80
☐ 12 Tony Gwynn	8.00	3.60
☐ 13 Don Mattingly	8.00	3.60
☐ 14 Bret Saberhagen	1.50	.70
☐ 15 Kirby Puckett	8.00	3.60
☐ 16 Joe Carter	2.00	.90
☐ 17 Roger Clemens	6.00	2.70
☐ 18 Barry Bonds	5.00	2.20
☐ 19 Greg Maddux	12.00	5.50
☐ 20 Frank Thomas	15.00	6.75

1996 Topps Chrome Wrecking Crew

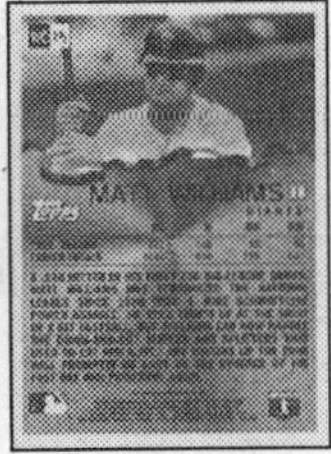

Randomly inserted in packs at a rate of one in 24, this 15-card set features baseball's top hitters and is printed in color action photography with brilliant color metallization.

	MINT	NRMT
COMPLETE SET (15)	80.00	36.00
COMMON CARD (WC1-WC15)	2.00	.90
COMPLETE REFRACTOR SET (20)	250.00	110.00

*REFRACTORS: 1.25X TO 3X BASIC INSERTS

Card	MINT	NRMT
☐ WC1 Jeff Bagwell	10.00	4.50
☐ WC2 Albert Belle	6.00	2.70
☐ WC3 Barry Bonds	6.00	2.70
☐ WC4 Jose Canseco	4.00	1.80
☐ WC5 Joe Carter	3.00	1.35
☐ WC6 Cecil Fielder	3.00	1.35
☐ WC7 Ron Gant	2.00	.90
☐ WC8 Juan Gonzalez	12.00	5.50
☐ WC9 Ken Griffey Jr.	25.00	11.00
☐ WC10 Fred McGriff	4.00	1.80
☐ WC11 Mark McGwire	8.00	3.60
☐ WC12 Mike Piazza	15.00	6.75
☐ WC13 Frank Thomas	20.00	9.00
☐ WC14 Mo Vaughn	6.00	2.70
☐ WC15 Matt Williams	4.00	1.80

1997 Topps Chrome

The 1997 Topps Chrome set was issued in one series totalling 165 cards and was distributed in four-card packs with a suggested retail price of $3.00. Using chromium technology to highlight the cards, this set features a metalized version of the cards of some of the best players from the 1997 regular Topps Series 1 , 2. An attractive 8 1/2" by 11" chrome promo sheet was sent to dealers advertising this set.

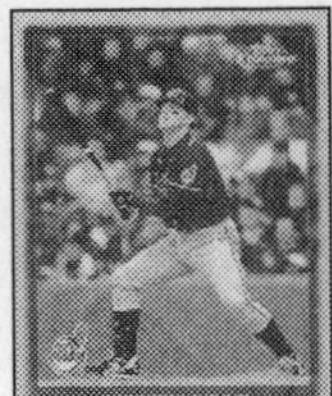

	MINT	NRMT
COMPLETE SET (165)	80.00	36.00
COMMON CARD (1-165)	.40	.18

Card	MINT	NRMT
☐ 1 Barry Bonds	2.00	.90
☐ 2 Jose Valentin	.40	.18
☐ 3 Brady Anderson	1.00	.45
☐ 4 Wade Boggs	1.50	.70
☐ 5 Andres Galarraga	1.00	.45
☐ 6 Rusty Greer	.75	.35
☐ 7 Derek Jeter	5.00	2.20
☐ 8 Ricky Bottalico	.40	.18
☐ 9 Mike Piazza	5.00	2.20
☐ 10 Garret Anderson	.75	.35
☐ 11 Jeff King	.75	.35
☐ 12 Kevin Appier	.75	.35
☐ 13 Mark Grace	1.00	.45
☐ 14 Jeff D'Amico	.40	.18
☐ 15 Jay Buhner	1.00	.45
☐ 16 Hal Morris	.40	.18
☐ 17 Harold Baines	.75	.35
☐ 18 Jeff Cirillo	.40	.18
☐ 19 Tom Glavine	.75	.35
☐ 20 Andy Pettitte	1.50	.70
☐ 21 Mark McGwire	3.00	1.35
☐ 22 Chuck Knoblauch	1.50	.70
☐ 23 Raul Mondesi	1.50	.70
☐ 24 Albert Belle	2.00	.90
☐ 25 Trevor Hoffman	.40	.18
☐ 26 Eric Young	.40	.18
☐ 27 Brian McRae	.40	.18
☐ 28 Jim Edmonds	1.50	.70
☐ 29 Robb Nen	.40	.18
☐ 30 Reggie Sanders	.40	.18
☐ 31 Mike Lansing	.40	.18
☐ 32 Craig Biggio	1.00	.45
☐ 33 Ray Lankford	.75	.35
☐ 34 Charles Nagy	.40	.18
☐ 35 Paul Wilson	.40	.18
☐ 36 John Wetteland	.40	.18
☐ 37 Derek Bell	.40	.18
☐ 38 Edgar Martinez	1.00	.45
☐ 39 Rickey Henderson	1.50	.70
☐ 40 Jim Thome	1.50	.70
☐ 41 Frank Thomas	6.00	2.70
☐ 42 Jackie Robinson	6.00	2.70
☐ 43 Terry Steinbach	.75	.35
☐ 44 Kevin Brown	.40	.18
☐ 45 Joey Hamilton	.40	.18
☐ 46 Travis Fryman	.75	.35
☐ 47 Juan Gonzalez	4.00	1.80
☐ 48 Ron Gant	.75	.35
☐ 49 Greg Maddux	5.00	2.20
☐ 50 Wally Joyner	.40	.18
☐ 51 John Valentin	.40	.18
☐ 52 Bret Boone	.40	.18
☐ 53 Paul Molitor	1.50	.70
☐ 54 Rafael Palmeiro	1.00	.45
☐ 55 Todd Hundley	.75	.35
☐ 56 Ellis Burks	.75	.35
☐ 57 Bernie Williams	1.50	.70
☐ 58 Roberto Alomar	1.50	.70
☐ 59 Jose Mesa	.75	.35
☐ 60 Troy Percival	.40	.18
☐ 61 John Smoltz	.75	.35
☐ 62 Jeff Conine	.75	.35
☐ 63 Bernard Gilkey	.40	.18
☐ 64 Mickey Tettleton	.40	.18
☐ 65 Justin Thompson	.40	.18
☐ 66 Tony Phillips	.40	.18
☐ 67 Ryne Sandberg	2.00	.90
☐ 68 Geronimo Berroa	.40	.18
☐ 69 Todd Hollandsworth	.75	.35
☐ 70 Rey Ordonez	.40	.18
☐ 71 Marquis Grissom	.75	.35
☐ 72 Tino Martinez	1.50	.70
☐ 73 Steve Finley	.75	.35
☐ 74 Andy Benes	.40	.18
☐ 75 Jason Kendall	.75	.35
☐ 76 Johnny Damon	.75	.35
☐ 77 Jason Giambi	.75	.35
☐ 78 Henry Rodriguez	.40	.18
☐ 79 Edgar Renteria	.75	.3

Card	MINT	NRMT
☐ 80 Ray Durham	.40	.18
☐ 81 Gregg Jefferies	.75	.35
☐ 82 Roberto Hernandez	.75	.35
☐ 83 Joe Carter	.75	.35
☐ 84 Jermaine Dye	.40	.18
☐ 85 Julio Franco	.75	.35
☐ 86 David Justice	1.50	.70
☐ 87 Jose Canseco	1.00	.45
☐ 88 Paul O'Neill	.75	.35
☐ 89 Mariano Rivera	.75	.35
☐ 90 Bobby Higginson	.75	.35
☐ 91 Mark Grudzielanek	.40	.18
☐ 92 Lance Johnson	.40	.18
☐ 93 Ken Caminiti	1.50	.70
☐ 94 Gary Sheffield	1.50	.70
☐ 95 Luis Castillo	.40	.18
☐ 96 Scott Rolen	4.00	1.80
☐ 97 Chipper Jones	5.00	2.20
☐ 98 Darryl Strawberry	.75	.35
☐ 99 Nomar Garciaparra	5.00	2.20
☐ 100 Jeff Bagwell	3.00	1.35
☐ 101 Ken Griffey Jr.	8.00	3.60
☐ 102 Sammy Sosa	1.50	.70
☐ 103 Jack McDowell	.40	.18
☐ 104 James Baldwin	.40	.18
☐ 105 Rocky Coppinger	.40	.18
☐ 106 Manny Ramirez	1.50	.70
☐ 107 Tim Salmon	1.50	.70
☐ 108 Eric Karros	.40	.18
☐ 109 Brett Butler	.75	.35
☐ 110 Randy Johnson	1.50	.70
☐ 111 Pat Hentgen	.75	.35
☐ 112 Rondell White	.75	.35
☐ 113 Eddie Murray	1.50	.70
☐ 114 Ivan Rodriguez	2.00	.90
☐ 115 Jermaine Allensworth	.40	.18
☐ 116 Ed Sprague	.40	.18
☐ 117 Kenny Lofton	2.00	.90
☐ 118 Alan Benes	.40	.18
☐ 119 Fred McGriff	1.00	.45
☐ 120 Alex Fernandez	.40	.18
☐ 121 Al Martin	.40	.18
☐ 122 Devon White	.40	.18
☐ 123 David Cone	.75	.35
☐ 124 Karim Garcia	.40	.18
☐ 125 Chili Davis	.75	.35
☐ 126 Roger Clemens	3.00	1.35
☐ 127 Bobby Bonilla	.75	.35
☐ 128 Mike Mussina	1.50	.70
☐ 129 Todd Walker	.40	.18
☐ 130 Dante Bichette	.75	.35
☐ 131 Carlos Baerga	.75	.35
☐ 132 Matt Williams	1.00	.45
☐ 133 Will Clark	1.00	.45
☐ 134 Dennis Eckersley	1.00	.45
☐ 135 Ryan Klesko	1.00	.45
☐ 136 Dean Palmer	.40	.18
☐ 137 Javy Lopez	.75	.35
☐ 138 Greg Vaughn	.40	.18
☐ 139 Vinny Castilla	.75	.35
☐ 140 Cal Ripken	6.00	2.70
☐ 141 Ruben Rivera	.40	.18
☐ 142 Mark Wohlers	.40	.18
☐ 143 Tony Clark	1.50	.70
☐ 144 Jose Rosado	.40	.18
☐ 145 Tony Gwynn	4.00	1.80
☐ 146 Cecil Fielder	.75	.35
☐ 147 Brian Jordan	.40	.18
☐ 148 Bob Abreu	.40	.18
☐ 149 Barry Larkin	.75	.35
☐ 150 Robin Ventura	.40	.18
☐ 151 John Olerud	.75	.35
☐ 152 Rod Beck	.40	.18
☐ 153 Vladimir Guerrero	3.00	1.35
☐ 154 Marty Cordova	.40	.18
☐ 155 Todd Stottlemyre	.40	.18
☐ 156 Hideo Nomo	4.00	1.80
☐ 157 Denny Neagle	.40	.18
☐ 158 John Jaha	.40	.18
☐ 159 Mo Vaughn	2.00	.90
☐ 160 Andruw Jones	4.00	1.80
☐ 161 Moises Alou	.75	.35
☐ 162 Larry Walker	1.50	.70
☐ 163 Eddie Murray SH	1.50	.70
☐ 164 Paul Molitor SH	1.50	.70
☐ 165 Checklist	.40	.18

1997 Topps Chrome Refractors

Randomly inserted in packs at a rate of one in 12, this 165-card set is a parallel version of the regular Topps Chrome set and is similar in design. The difference is found in the refractive quality of the cards.

	MINT	NRMT
COMPLETE SET (165)	2000.00	900.00
COMMON CARD (1-165)	6.00	2.70

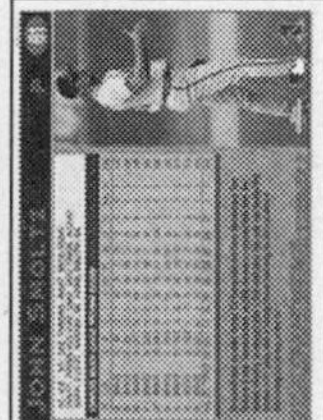

*STARS: 7.5X TO 15X BASE CARDS ..
*YOUNG STARS: 6X TO 12 X BASE CARDS

Card	MINT	NRMT
☐ 7 Derek Jeter	60.00	27.00
☐ 9 Mike Piazza	80.00	36.00
☐ 21 Mark McGwire	50.00	22.00
☐ 41 Frank Thomas	100.00	45.00
☐ 42 Jackie Robinson	100.00	45.00
☐ 47 Juan Gonzalez	60.00	27.00
☐ 49 Greg Maddux	80.00	36.00
☐ 96 Scott Rolen	50.00	22.00
☐ 97 Chipper Jones	80.00	36.00
☐ 99 Nomar Garciaparra	60.00	27.00
☐ 100 Jeff Bagwell	50.00	22.00
☐ 101 Ken Griffey Jr.	120.00	55.00
☐ 126 Roger Clemens	50.00	22.00
☐ 140 Cal Ripken	100.00	45.00
☐ 145 Tony Gwynn	60.00	27.00
☐ 153 Vladimir Guerrero	40.00	18.00
☐ 156 Hideo Nomo	60.00	27.00
☐ 160 Andruw Jones	50.00	22.00

1997 Topps Chrome All-Stars

Randomly inserted in packs at a rate of one in 24, this 22-card set features color player photos printed on rainbow foilboard. The set showcases the top three players from each position from both the American and National leagues as voted on by the Topps Sports Department.

	MINT	NRMT
COMPLETE SET (22)	120.00	55.00
COMMON CARD (AS1-AS22)	2.00	.90
COMP.REF.SET (22)	500.00	220.00

*REFRACTORS: 2X TO4 X BASIC CARDS

Card	MINT	NRMT
☐ AS1 Ivan Rodriguez	6.00	2.70
☐ AS2 Todd Hundley	3.00	1.35
☐ AS3 Frank Thomas	15.00	6.75
☐ AS4 Andres Galarraga	5.00	2.20
☐ AS5 Chuck Knoblauch	5.00	2.20
☐ AS6 Eric Young	2.00	.90
☐ AS7 Jim Thome	5.00	2.20
☐ AS8 Chipper Jones	15.00	6.75
☐ AS9 Cal Ripken	20.00	9.00
☐ AS10 Barry Larkin	4.00	1.80
☐ AS11 Albert Belle	6.00	2.70
☐ AS12 Barry Bonds	6.00	2.70
☐ AS13 Ken Griffey Jr.	25.00	11.00
☐ AS14 Ellis Burks	3.00	1.35
☐ AS15 Juan Gonzalez	12.00	5.50
☐ AS16 Gary Sheffield	5.00	2.20
☐ AS17 Andy Pettitte	5.00	2.20
☐ AS18 Tom Glavine	3.00	1.35
☐ AS19 Pat Hentgen	3.00	1.35
☐ AS20 John Smoltz	3.00	1.35
☐ AS21 Roberto Hernandez	2.00	.90
☐ AS22 Mark Wohlers	2.00	.90

1997 Topps Chrome Diamond Duos

Randomly inserted in packs at a rate of one in 36, this 10-card set features color player photos of two superstar teammates on double sided chromium cards.

	MINT	NRMT
COMPLETE SET (10)	100.00	45.00
COMMON CARD (DD1-DD10)	4.00	1.80
COMP.REF.SET (10)	400.00	180.00

*REFRACTORS: 2X TO 4X BASIC CARDS

Card	MINT	NRMT
☐ DD1 Chipper Jones / Andruw Jones	12.00	5.50
☐ DD2 Derek Jeter / Bernie Williams	10.00	4.50
☐ DD3 Ken Griffey Jr. / Jay Buhner	20.00	9.00
☐ DD4 Kenny Lofton / Manny Ramirez	5.00	2.20
☐ DD5 Jeff Bagwell / Craig Biggio	8.00	3.60
☐ DD6 Juan Gonzalez / Ivan Rodriguez	10.00	4.50
☐ DD7 Cal Ripken / Brady Anderson	15.00	6.75
☐ DD8 Mike Piazza / Hideo Nomo	15.00	6.75
☐ DD9 Andres Galarraga / Dante Bichette	4.00	1.80
☐ DD10 Frank Thomas / Albert Belle	15.00	6.75

1997 Topps Chrome Season's Best

Randomly inserted in packs at a rate of one in 18, this 25-card set features color player photos of the five top players from five statistical categories: most steals (Leading Looters), most home runs (Bleacher Reachers), most wins (Hill Toppers), most RBIs (Number Crunchers), and best slugging percentage (Kings of Swing).

	MINT	NRMT
COMPLETE SET (25)	100.00	45.00
COMMON CARD (1-25)	1.50	.70
COMP.REF.SET (25)	400.00	180.00

*REFRACTORS: 2X TO 4X BASIC CARDS

Card	MINT	NRMT
☐ 1 Tony Gwynn	10.00	4.50
☐ 2 Frank Thomas	15.00	6.75
☐ 3 Ellis Burks	2.00	.90
☐ 4 Paul Molitor	4.00	1.80
☐ 5 Chuck Knoblauch	4.00	1.80
☐ 6 Mark McGwire	8.00	3.60
☐ 7 Brady Anderson	3.00	1.35
☐ 8 Ken Griffey Jr.	20.00	9.00
☐ 9 Albert Belle	5.00	2.20
☐ 10 Andres Galarraga	4.00	1.80
☐ 11 Andres Galarraga	4.00	1.80
☐ 12 Albert Belle	5.00	2.20
☐ 13 Juan Gonzalez	10.00	4.50
☐ 14 Mo Vaughn	5.00	2.20
☐ 15 Rafael Palmeiro	3.00	1.35
☐ 16 John Smoltz	2.00	.90
☐ 17 Andy Pettitte	4.00	1.80
☐ 18 Pat Hentgen	2.00	.90
☐ 19 Mike Mussina	4.00	1.80
☐ 20 Andy Benes	1.50	.70
☐ 21 Kenny Lofton	5.00	2.20
☐ 22 Tom Goodwin	1.50	.70
☐ 23 Otis Nixon	1.50	.70
☐ 24 Eric Young	1.50	.70
☐ 25 Lance Johnson	1.50	.70

1997 Topps Chrome Jumbos

This six-card set contains jumbo versions of the six featured players' regular Topps Chrome cards and measures approximately 3 3/4" by 5 1/4". One of these cards was found in a special box with five Topps Chrome packs issued through Wal-Mart. The cards are numbered according to their corresponding number in the regular set.

	MINT	NRMT
COMPLETE SET (6)	12.00	5.50
COMMON CARD	1.00	.45

Card	MINT	NRMT
☐ 9 Mike Piazza	2.50	1.10
☐ 94 Gary Sheffield	1.00	.45

☐ 97 Chipper Jones	2.50	1.10
☐ 101 Ken Griffey Jr.	4.00	1.80
☐ 102 Sammy Sosa	1.00	.45
☐ 140 Cal Ripken Jr.	3.00	1.35

1995 Topps Embossed

This 140-card standard-size set was issued by Topps. The cards were issued in six-card packs with five regular cards and one parallel Golden Idols card in each pack. The suggested retail price of the packs was $3 with 24 packs per box. Each case contained four boxes. Cards 97-120 are a subset dedicated to active players who have won major awards. The cards are embossed on both sides. The fronts have an embossed player photo surrounded by a gray border. In addition, the TMB (Topps Embossed) logo is in an upper corner and the player's name at the bottom. The horizontal backs have an embossed player photo on the left, while vital statistics, seasonal and career statistics and some interesting facts about the player are on the right.

	MINT	NRMT
COMPLETE SET (140)	30.00	13.50
COMMON CARD (1-140)	.10	.05
☐ 1 Kenny Lofton	.75	.35
☐ 2 Gary Sheffield	.60	.25
☐ 3 Hal Morris	.25	.11
☐ 4 Cliff Floyd	.10	.05
☐ 5 Pat Hentgen	.60	.25
☐ 6 Tony Gwynn	1.50	.70
☐ 7 Jose Valentin	.10	.05
☐ 8 Jason Bere	.10	.05
☐ 9 Jeff Kent	.25	.11
☐ 10 John Valentin	.25	.11
☐ 11 Brian Anderson	.10	.05
☐ 12 Deion Sanders	.60	.25
☐ 13 Ryan Thompson	.10	.05
☐ 14 Ruben Sierra	.10	.05
☐ 15 Jay Bell	.10	.05
☐ 16 Chuck Carr	.10	.05
☐ 17 Brent Gates	.10	.05
☐ 18 Bret Boone	.10	.05
☐ 19 Paul Molitor	.60	.25
☐ 20 Chili Davis	.25	.11
☐ 21 Ryan Klesko	.75	.35
☐ 22 Will Clark	.40	.18
☐ 23 Greg Vaughn	.10	.05
☐ 24 Moises Alou	.25	.11
☐ 25 Ray Lankford	.25	.11
☐ 26 Jose Rijo	.10	.05
☐ 27 Bobby Jones	.10	.05
☐ 28 Rick Wilkins	.10	.05
☐ 29 Cal Eldred	.10	.05
☐ 30 Juan Gonzalez	1.50	.70
☐ 31 Royce Clayton	.25	.11
☐ 32 Bryan Harvey	.10	.05
☐ 33 Dave Nilsson	.10	.05
☐ 34 Chris Hoiles	.25	.11
☐ 35 David Nied	.10	.05
☐ 36 Javier Lopez	.40	.18
☐ 37 Tim Wallach	.10	.05
☐ 38 Bobby Bonilla	.25	.11
☐ 39 Danny Tartabull	.40	.18
☐ 40 Andy Benes	.25	.11
☐ 41 Dean Palmer	.25	.11
☐ 42 Chris Gomez	.10	.05
☐ 43 Kevin Appier	.25	.11
☐ 44 Brady Anderson	.40	.18
☐ 45 Alex Fernandez	.25	.11
☐ 46 Roberto Kelly	.10	.05
☐ 47 Dave Hollins	.10	.05
☐ 48 Chuck Finley	.10	.05
☐ 49 Wade Boggs	.60	.25
☐ 50 Travis Fryman	.25	.11
☐ 51 Ken Griffey Jr.	3.00	1.35
☐ 52 John Olerud	.25	.11
☐ 53 Delino DeShields	.25	.11
☐ 54 Ivan Rodriguez	.75	.35
☐ 55 Tommy Greene	.10	.05
☐ 56 Tom Pagnozzi	.10	.05
☐ 57 Bip Roberts	.10	.05
☐ 58 Luis Gonzalez	.10	.05
☐ 59 Rey Sanchez	.10	.05
☐ 60 Ken Ryan	.10	.05
☐ 61 Darren Daulton	.25	.11
☐ 62 Rick Aguilera	.25	.11
☐ 63 Wally Joyner	.25	.11
☐ 64 Mike Greenwell	.10	.05
☐ 65 Jay Buhner	.40	.18
☐ 66 Craig Biggio	.40	.18
☐ 67 Charles Nagy	.25	.11
☐ 68 Devon White	.10	.05
☐ 69 Randy Johnson	.60	.25
☐ 70 Shawon Dunston	.10	.05
☐ 71 Kirby Puckett	1.50	.70
☐ 72 Paul O'Neill	.25	.11
☐ 73 Tino Martinez	.60	.25
☐ 74 Carlos Garcia	.10	.05
☐ 75 Ozzie Smith	.75	.35
☐ 76 Cecil Fielder	.25	.11
☐ 77 Mike Stanley	.10	.05
☐ 78 Lance Johnson	.25	.11
☐ 79 Tony Phillips	.10	.05
☐ 80 Bobby Munoz	.10	.05
☐ 81 Kevin Tapani	.10	.05
☐ 82 William VanLandingham	.10	.05
☐ 83 Dante Bichette	.40	.18
☐ 84 Tom Candiotti	.10	.05
☐ 85 Wil Cordero	.10	.05
☐ 86 Jeff Conine	.25	.11
☐ 87 Joey Hamilton	.25	.11
☐ 88 Mark Whiten	.10	.05
☐ 89 Jeff Montgomery	.25	.11
☐ 90 Andres Galarraga	.60	.25
☐ 91 Roberto Alomar	.60	.25
☐ 92 Orlando Merced	.10	.05
☐ 93 Mike Mussina	.60	.25
☐ 94 Pedro Martinez	.60	.25
☐ 95 Carlos Baerga	.25	.11
☐ 96 Steve Trachsel	.10	.05
☐ 97 Lou Whitaker	.25	.11
☐ 98 David Cone	.25	.11
☐ 99 Chuck Knoblauch	.60	.25
☐ 100 Frank Thomas	2.50	1.10
☐ 101 David Justice	.60	.25
☐ 102 Raul Mondesi	.60	.25
☐ 103 Rickey Henderson	.40	.18
☐ 104 Doug Drabek	.10	.05
☐ 105 Sandy Alomar	.25	.11
☐ 106 Roger Clemens	1.25	.55
☐ 107 Mark McGwire	1.25	.55
☐ 108 Tim Salmon	.60	.25
☐ 109 Greg Maddux	2.00	.90
☐ 110 Mike Piazza	2.00	.90
☐ 111 Tom Glavine	.40	.18
☐ 112 Walt Weiss	.10	.05
☐ 113 Cal Ripken	2.50	1.10
☐ 114 Eddie Murray	.75	.35
☐ 115 Don Mattingly	1.25	.55
☐ 116 Ozzie Guillen	.10	.05
☐ 117 Bob Hamelin	.10	.05
☐ 118 Jeff Bagwell	1.50	.70
☐ 119 Eric Karros	.25	.11
☐ 120 Barry Bonds	.75	.35
☐ 121 Mickey Tettleton	.10	.05
☐ 122 Mark Langston	.10	.05
☐ 123 Robin Ventura	.25	.11
☐ 124 Bret Saberhagen	.10	.05
☐ 125 Albert Belle	1.00	.45
☐ 126 Rafael Palmeiro	.40	.18
☐ 127 Fred McGriff	.40	.18
☐ 128 Jimmy Key	.25	.11
☐ 129 Barry Larkin	.60	.25
☐ 130 Tim Raines	.25	.11
☐ 131 Len Dykstra	.25	.11
☐ 132 Todd Zeile	.10	.05
☐ 133 Joe Carter	.25	.11
☐ 134 Matt Williams	.40	.18
☐ 135 Terry Steinbach	.25	.11
☐ 136 Manny Ramirez	.75	.35
☐ 137 John Wetteland	.25	.11
☐ 138 Rod Beck	.25	.11
☐ 139 Mo Vaughn	.75	.35
☐ 140 Darren Lewis	.10	.05

1995 Topps Embossed Golden Idols

This 140-card parallel set was inserted one per Embossed pack. The only difference between these and the regular cards is the gold foil surrounding the front borders.

	MINT	NRMT
COMPLETE SET (140)	120.00	55.00
COMMON CARD (1-140)	.50	.23
*STARS: 2.5X to 4X BASIC CARDS		

1996 Topps Gallery

The 1996 Topps Gallery set was issued in one series totalling 180 cards. The eight-card packs retail for $3.00 each. The set is divided into 5 themes: Classics (1-90), New Editions (91-108), Modernists (109-126), Futurists (127-144) and Masters (145-180). Each theme features a different design on front, but the bulk of the set has full-bleed, color action shots.

	MINT	NRMT
COMPLETE SET (180)	40.00	18.00
COMMON CARD (1-180)	.25	.11
☐ 1 Tom Glavine	.50	.23
☐ 2 Carlos Baerga	.50	.23
☐ 3 Dante Bichette	.50	.23
☐ 4 Mark Langston	.25	.11
☐ 5 Ray Lankford	.50	.23
☐ 6 Moises Alou	.50	.23
☐ 7 Marquis Grissom	.50	.23
☐ 8 Ramon Martinez	.50	.23
☐ 9 Steve Finley	.50	.23
☐ 10 Todd Hundley	.50	.23
☐ 11 Brady Anderson	.75	.35
☐ 12 John Valentin	.50	.23
☐ 13 Heathcliff Slocumb	.25	.11
☐ 14 Ruben Sierra	.25	.11
☐ 15 Jeff Conine	.50	.23
☐ 16 Jay Buhner	.75	.35
☐ 17 Sammy Sosa	1.00	.45
☐ 18 Doug Drabek	.25	.11
☐ 19 Jose Mesa	.50	.23
☐ 20 Jeff King	.50	.23
☐ 21 Mickey Tettleton	.25	.11
☐ 22 Jeff Montgomery	.25	.11
☐ 23 Alex Fernandez	.50	.23
☐ 24 Greg Vaughn	.25	.11
☐ 25 Chuck Finley	.25	.11
☐ 26 Terry Steinbach	.50	.23
☐ 27 Rod Beck	.50	.23
☐ 28 Jack McDowell	.25	.11
☐ 29 Mark Wohlers	.50	.23
☐ 30 Len Dykstra	.50	.23
☐ 31 Bernie Williams	1.00	.45
☐ 32 Travis Fryman	.50	.23
☐ 33 Jose Canseco	.75	.35
☐ 34 Ken Caminiti	1.00	.45
☐ 35 Devon White	.25	.11
☐ 36 Bobby Bonilla	.50	.23
☐ 37 Paul Sorrento	.25	.11
☐ 38 Ryne Sandberg	1.25	.55
☐ 39 Derek Bell	.25	.11
☐ 40 Bobby Jones	.25	.11
☐ 41 J.T. Snow	.50	.23
☐ 42 Denny Neagle	.50	.23
☐ 43 Tim Wakefield	.25	.11
☐ 44 Andres Galarraga	1.00	.45
☐ 45 David Segui	.25	.11
☐ 46 Lee Smith	.50	.23
☐ 47 Mel Rojas	.25	.11
☐ 48 John Franco	.50	.23
☐ 49 Pete Schourek	.25	.11
☐ 50 John Wetteland	.50	.23
☐ 51 Paul Molitor	1.00	.45
☐ 52 Ivan Rodriguez	1.25	.55
☐ 53 Chris Hoiles	.25	.11
☐ 54 Mike Greenwell	.25	.11
☐ 55 Orel Hershiser	.50	.23
☐ 56 Brian McRae	.25	.11
☐ 57 Geronimo Berroa	.25	.11
☐ 58 Craig Biggio	.75	.35
☐ 59 David Justice	1.00	.45
☐ 60 Lance Johnson	.25	.11
☐ 61 Andy Ashby	.25	.11
☐ 62 Randy Myers	.25	.11
☐ 63 Gregg Jefferies	.50	.23
☐ 64 Kevin Appier	.50	.23
☐ 65 Rick Aguilera	.50	.23
☐ 66 Shane Reynolds	.25	.11
☐ 67 John Smoltz	.50	.23
☐ 68 Ron Gant	.50	.23
☐ 69 Eric Karros	.50	.23

Card	MINT	NRMT
☐ 70 Jim Thome	1.00	.45
☐ 71 Terry Pendleton	.50	.23
☐ 72 Kenny Rogers	.25	.11
☐ 73 Robin Ventura	.50	.23
☐ 74 Dave Nilsson	.50	.23
☐ 75 Brian Jordan	.50	.23
☐ 76 Glenallen Hill	.25	.11
☐ 77 Greg Colbrunn	.25	.11
☐ 78 Roberto Alomar	1.00	.45
☐ 79 Rickey Henderson	.75	.35
☐ 80 Carlos Garcia	.25	.11
☐ 81 Dean Palmer	.50	.23
☐ 82 Mike Stanley	.25	.11
☐ 83 Hal Morris	.25	.11
☐ 84 Wade Boggs	1.00	.45
☐ 85 Chad Curtis	.25	.11
☐ 86 Roberto Hernandez	.50	.23
☐ 87 John Olerud	.50	.23
☐ 88 Frank Castillo	.25	.11
☐ 89 Rafael Palmeiro	.75	.35
☐ 90 Trevor Hoffman	.50	.23
☐ 91 Marty Cordova	.50	.23
☐ 92 Hideo Nomo	2.50	1.10
☐ 93 Johnny Damon	.50	.23
☐ 94 Bill Pulsipher	.25	.11
☐ 95 Garret Anderson	.75	.35
☐ 96 Ray Durham	.50	.23
☐ 97 Ricky Bottalico	.50	.23
☐ 98 Carlos Perez	.25	.11
☐ 99 Troy Percival	.25	.11
☐ 100 Chipper Jones	3.00	1.35
☐ 101 Esteban Loaiza	.25	.11
☐ 102 John Mabry	.50	.23
☐ 103 Jon Nunnally	.25	.11
☐ 104 Andy Pettitte	1.25	.55
☐ 105 Lyle Mouton	.25	.11
☐ 106 Jason Isringhausen	.25	.11
☐ 107 Brian L.Hunter	.50	.23
☐ 108 Quilvio Veras	.25	.11
☐ 109 Jim Edmonds	1.00	.45
☐ 110 Ryan Klesko	.75	.35
☐ 111 Pedro Martinez	1.00	.45
☐ 112 Joey Hamilton	.50	.23
☐ 113 Vinny Castilla	.50	.23
☐ 114 Alex Gonzalez	.25	.11
☐ 115 Raul Mondesi	.75	.35
☐ 116 Rondell White	.50	.23
☐ 117 Dan Miceli	.25	.11
☐ 118 Tom Goodwin	.25	.11
☐ 119 Bret Boone	.25	.11
☐ 120 Shawn Green	.50	.23
☐ 121 Jeff Cirillo	.50	.23
☐ 122 Rico Brogna	.25	.11
☐ 123 Chris Gomez	.25	.11
☐ 124 Ismael Valdes	.50	.23
☐ 125 Javy Lopez	.50	.23
☐ 126 Manny Ramirez	1.00	.45
☐ 127 Paul Wilson	.25	.11
☐ 128 Billy Wagner	.75	.35
☐ 129 Eric Owens	.25	.11
☐ 130 Todd Greene	1.00	.45
☐ 131 Karim Garcia	.50	.23
☐ 132 Jimmy Haynes	.25	.11
☐ 133 Michael Tucker	.50	.23
☐ 134 John Wasdin	.25	.11
☐ 135 Brooks Kieschnick	.50	.23
☐ 136 Alex Ochoa	.25	.11
☐ 137 Ariel Prieto	.25	.11
☐ 138 Tony Clark	1.50	.70
☐ 139 Mark Loretta	.25	.11
☐ 140 Rey Ordonez	.50	.23
☐ 141 Chris Snopek	.25	.11
☐ 142 Roger Cedeno	.25	.11
☐ 143 Derek Jeter	3.00	1.35
☐ 144 Jeff Suppan	.75	.35
☐ 145 Greg Maddux	3.00	1.35
☐ 146 Ken Griffey Jr.	5.00	2.20
☐ 147 Tony Gwynn	2.50	1.10
☐ 148 Darren Daulton	.50	.23
☐ 149 Will Clark	.75	.35
☐ 150 Mo Vaughn	1.25	.55
☐ 151 Reggie Sanders	.25	.11
☐ 152 Kirby Puckett	2.00	.90
☐ 153 Paul O'Neill	.50	.23
☐ 154 Tim Salmon	1.00	.45
☐ 155 Mark McGwire	2.00	.90
☐ 156 Barry Bonds	1.25	.55
☐ 157 Albert Belle	1.25	.55
☐ 158 Edgar Martinez	.75	.35
☐ 159 Mike Mussina	1.00	.45
☐ 160 Cecil Fielder	.50	.23
☐ 161 Kenny Lofton	1.25	.55
☐ 162 Randy Johnson	1.00	.45
☐ 163 Juan Gonzalez	2.50	1.10
☐ 164 Jeff Bagwell	2.00	.90
☐ 165 Joe Carter	.50	.23
☐ 166 Mike Piazza	3.00	1.35
☐ 167 Eddie Murray	1.00	.45
☐ 168 Cal Ripken	4.00	1.80
☐ 169 Barry Larkin	.75	.35
☐ 170 Chuck Knoblauch	1.00	.45
☐ 171 Chili Davis	.25	.11
☐ 172 Fred McGriff	.75	.35
☐ 173 Matt Williams	.75	.35
☐ 174 Roger Clemens	2.00	.90
☐ 175 Frank Thomas	4.00	1.80
☐ 176 Dennis Eckersley	.75	.35
☐ 177 Gary Sheffield	1.00	.45
☐ 178 David Cone	.50	.23
☐ 179 Larry Walker	1.00	.45
☐ 180 Mark Grace	.75	.35
☐ NNO Mantle Masterpiece	20.00	9.00

1996 Topps Gallery Players Private Issue

Randomly inserted in packs at a rate of one in 12, this 180-card parallel is foil stamped. The backs are sequentially numbered 0-999, with the first 100 cards (#'s 0-99) sent to the players and the balance inserted in packs.

	MINT	NRMT
COMPLETE SET (180)	1000.00	450.00
COMMON CARD (1-180)	2.00	.90

*STARS: 7.5X TO 15X BASIC CARDS
*YOUNG STARS: 6X TO 12X BASIC CARDS

1996 Topps Gallery Expressionists

Randomly inserted in packs at a rate of one in 24, this 20-card set features 20 spiritual leaders printed on triple foil stamped and texture embossed cards. Card backs contain a second photo and narrative about the player.

	MINT	NRMT
COMPLETE SET (20)	120.00	55.00
COMMON CARD (1-20)	2.00	.90

Card	MINT	NRMT
☐ 1 Mike Piazza	20.00	9.00
☐ 2 J.T. Snow	3.00	1.35
☐ 3 Ken Griffey Jr.	30.00	13.50
☐ 4 Kirby Puckett	12.00	5.50
☐ 5 Carlos Baerga	3.00	1.35
☐ 6 Chipper Jones	20.00	9.00
☐ 7 Hideo Nomo	15.00	6.75
☐ 8 Mark McGwire	12.00	5.50
☐ 9 Gary Sheffield	6.00	2.70
☐ 10 Randy Johnson	6.00	2.70
☐ 11 Ray Lankford	3.00	1.35
☐ 12 Sammy Sosa	6.00	2.70
☐ 13 Denny Martinez	3.00	1.35
☐ 14 Jose Canseco	4.00	1.80
☐ 15 Tony Gwynn	15.00	6.75
☐ 16 Edgar Martinez	4.00	1.80
☐ 17 Reggie Sanders	2.00	.90
☐ 18 Andres Galarraga	6.00	2.70
☐ 19 Albert Belle	8.00	3.60
☐ 20 Barry Larkin	4.00	1.80

1996 Topps Gallery Photo Gallery

Randomly inserted in packs at a rate of one in 30, this 15-card set features top photography chronicling baseball's biggest stars and greatest moments from last year. Each double foil stamped card is printed on 24 pt. stock with customized designs to accentuate the photography.

	MINT	NRMT
COMPLETE SET (15)	100.00	45.00
COMMON CARD (PG1-PG15)	1.50	.70

Card	MINT	NRMT
☐ PG1 Eddie Murray	4.00	1.80
☐ PG2 Randy Johnson	4.00	1.80
☐ PG3 Cal Ripken	20.00	9.00
☐ PG4 Bret Boone	1.50	.70
☐ PG5 Frank Thomas	20.00	9.00
☐ PG6 Jeff Conine	2.00	.90
☐ PG7 Johnny Damon	2.00	.90
☐ PG8 Roger Clemens	8.00	3.60
☐ PG9 Albert Belle	5.00	2.20
☐ PG10 Ken Griffey Jr.	25.00	11.00
☐ PG11 Kirby Puckett	10.00	4.50
☐ PG12 David Justice	4.00	1.80
☐ PG13 Bobby Bonilla	2.00	.90
☐ PG14 Colorado Rockies	4.00	1.80
☐ PG15 Atlanta Braves	4.00	1.80

1997 Topps Gallery Promos

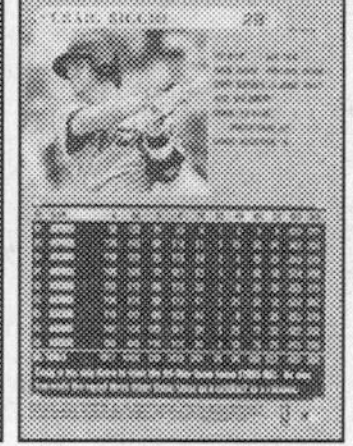

This four-card set was distributed as a promotion for the 1997 Topps Gallery set and features color player pictures in four different frame designs with a player portrait, biographical, and career statistics on the backs.

	MINT	NRMT
COMPLETE SET (4)	10.00	4.50
COMMON CARD (PP1-PP4)	1.00	.45

Card	MINT	NRMT
☐ PP1 Andruw Jones	2.00	.90
☐ PP2 Derek Jeter	3.00	1.35
☐ PP3 Mike Piazza	4.00	1.80
☐ PP4 Craig Biggio	1.00	.45

1997 Topps Gallery

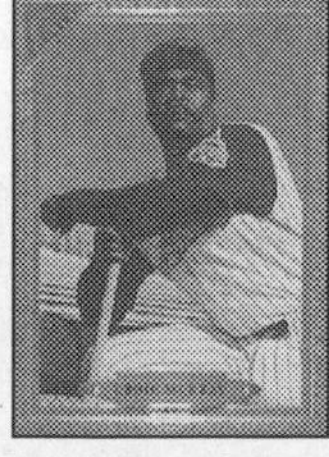

The 1997 Topps Gallery set was issued in one series totalling 180 cards. The eight-card packs retail for $4.00 each. This hobby only set is divided into four themes: Veterans, Prospects, Rising Stars and Young Stars. Printed on 24-point card stock with a high-gloss film and etch stamped with one or more foils, each theme features a different design on front with a variety of informative statistics and revealing player text on the back.

	MINT	NRMT
COMPLETE SET (180)	50.00	22.00
COMMON CARD (1-180)	.25	.11

Card	MINT	NRMT
☐ 1 Paul Molitor	1.00	.45
☐ 2 Devon White	.25	.11
☐ 3 Andres Galarraga	1.00	.45
☐ 4 Cal Ripken	4.00	1.80
☐ 5 Tony Gwynn	2.50	1.10
☐ 6 Mike Stanley	.25	.11
☐ 7 Orel Hershiser	.50	.23
☐ 8 Jose Canseco	.75	.35
☐ 9 Chili Davis	.50	.23
☐ 10 Harold Baines	.50	.23
☐ 11 Rickey Henderson	.75	.35

Card	MINT	NRMT
☐ 12 Darryl Strawberry	.50	.23
☐ 13 Todd Worrell	.25	.11
☐ 14 Cecil Fielder	.50	.23
☐ 15 Gary Gaetti	.50	.23
☐ 16 Bobby Bonilla	.50	.23
☐ 17 Will Clark	.75	.35
☐ 18 Kevin Brown	.50	.23
☐ 19 Tom Glavine	.50	.23
☐ 20 Wade Boggs	1.00	.45
☐ 21 Edgar Martinez	.75	.35
☐ 22 Lance Johnson	.25	.11
☐ 23 Gregg Jefferies	.50	.23
☐ 24 Bip Roberts	.25	.11
☐ 25 Tony Phillips	.25	.11
☐ 26 Greg Maddux	3.00	1.35
☐ 27 Mickey Tettleton	.25	.11
☐ 28 Terry Steinbach	.25	.11
☐ 29 Ryne Sandberg	1.25	.55
☐ 30 Wally Joyner	.25	.11
☐ 31 Joe Carter	.50	.23
☐ 32 Ellis Burks	.50	.23
☐ 33 Fred McGriff	.75	.35
☐ 34 Barry Larkin	.75	.35
☐ 35 John Franco	.50	.23
☐ 36 Rafael Palmeiro	.75	.35
☐ 37 Mark McGwire	2.00	.90
☐ 38 Ken Caminiti	1.00	.45
☐ 39 David Cone	.50	.23
☐ 40 Julio Franco	.50	.23
☐ 41 Roger Clemens	2.00	.90
☐ 42 Barry Bonds	1.25	.55
☐ 43 Dennis Eckersley	.75	.35
☐ 44 Eddie Murray	1.00	.45
☐ 45 Paul O'Neill	.50	.23
☐ 46 Craig Biggio	.75	.35
☐ 47 Roberto Alomar	1.00	.45
☐ 48 Mark Grace	.75	.35
☐ 49 Matt Williams	.75	.35
☐ 50 Jay Buhner	.75	.35
☐ 51 John Smoltz	.50	.23
☐ 52 Randy Johnson	1.00	.45
☐ 53 Ramon Martinez	.50	.23
☐ 54 Curt Schilling	.50	.23
☐ 55 Gary Sheffield	1.00	.45
☐ 56 Jack McDowell	.25	.11
☐ 57 Brady Anderson	.75	.35
☐ 58 Dante Bichette	.50	.23
☐ 59 Ron Gant	.25	.11
☐ 60 Alex Fernandez	.25	.11
☐ 61 Moises Alou	.25	.11
☐ 62 Travis Fryman	.50	.23
☐ 63 Dean Palmer	.25	.11
☐ 64 Todd Hundley	.50	.23
☐ 65 Jeff Brantley	.25	.11
☐ 66 Bernard Gilkey	.25	.11
☐ 67 Geronimo Berroa	.25	.11
☐ 68 John Wetteland	.25	.11
☐ 69 Robin Ventura	.25	.11
☐ 70 Ray Lankford	.25	.11
☐ 71 Kevin Appier	.25	.11
☐ 72 Larry Walker	1.00	.45
☐ 73 Juan Gonzalez	2.50	1.10
☐ 74 Jeff King	.25	.11
☐ 75 Greg Vaughn	.25	.11
☐ 76 Steve Finley	.50	.23
☐ 77 Brian McRae	.25	.11
☐ 78 Paul Sorrento	.25	.11
☐ 79 Ken Griffey Jr.	5.00	2.20
☐ 80 Omar Vizquel	.50	.23
☐ 81 Jose Mesa	.25	.11
☐ 82 Albert Belle	1.25	.55
☐ 83 Glenallen Hill	.25	.11
☐ 84 Sammy Sosa	1.00	.45
☐ 85 Andy Benes	.25	.11
☐ 86 David Justice	1.00	.45
☐ 87 Marquis Grissom	.50	.23
☐ 88 John Olerud	.50	.23
☐ 89 Tino Martinez	1.00	.45
☐ 90 Frank Thomas	4.00	1.80
☐ 91 Raul Mondesi	.75	.35
☐ 92 Steve Trachsel	.25	.11
☐ 93 Jim Edmonds	1.00	.45
☐ 94 Rusty Greer	.50	.23
☐ 95 Joey Hamilton	.25	.11
☐ 96 Ismael Valdes	.25	.11
☐ 97 Dave Nilsson	.25	.11
☐ 98 John Jaha	.25	.11
☐ 99 Alex Gonzalez	.25	.11
☐ 100 Javy Lopez	.50	.23
☐ 101 Ryan Klesko	.75	.35
☐ 102 Tim Salmon	1.00	.45
☐ 103 Bernie Williams	1.00	.45
☐ 104 Roberto Hernandez	.25	.11
☐ 105 Chuck Knoblauch	1.00	.45
☐ 106 Mike Lansing	.25	.11
☐ 107 Vinny Castilla	.50	.23
☐ 108 Reggie Sanders	.25	.11
☐ 109 Mo Vaughn	1.00	.45
☐ 110 Rondell White	.50	.23
☐ 111 Ivan Rodriguez	1.25	.55
☐ 112 Mike Mussina	1.00	.45
☐ 113 Carlos Baerga	.25	.11
☐ 114 Jeff Conine	.50	.23
☐ 115 Jim Thome	1.00	.45
☐ 116 Manny Ramirez	1.00	.45
☐ 117 Kenny Lofton	1.25	.55
☐ 118 Wilson Alvarez	.25	.11
☐ 119 Eric Karros	.25	.11
☐ 120 Robb Nen	.25	.11
☐ 121 Mark Wohlers	.25	.11
☐ 122 Ed Sprague	.25	.11
☐ 123 Pat Hentgen	.50	.23
☐ 124 Juan Guzman	.25	.11
☐ 125 Derek Bell	.25	.11
☐ 126 Jeff Bagwell	2.00	.90
☐ 127 Eric Young	.25	.11
☐ 128 John Valentin	.25	.11
☐ 129 Al Martin UER Picture of Javy Lopez	.25	.11
☐ 130 Trevor Hoffman	.50	.23
☐ 131 Henry Rodriguez	.25	.11
☐ 132 Pedro Martinez	.25	.11
☐ 133 Mike Piazza	3.00	1.35
☐ 134 Brian Jordan	.25	.11
☐ 135 Jose Valentin	.25	.11
☐ 136 Jeff Cirillo	.25	.11
☐ 137 Chipper Jones	3.00	1.35
☐ 138 Ricky Bottalico	.25	.11
☐ 139 Hideo Nomo	2.50	1.10
☐ 140 Troy Percival	.25	.11
☐ 141 Rey Ordonez	.25	.11
☐ 142 Edgar Renteria	.50	.23
☐ 143 Luis Castillo	.25	.11
☐ 144 Vladimir Guerrero	2.00	.90
☐ 145 Jeff D'Amico	.25	.11
☐ 146 Andruw Jones	2.50	1.10
☐ 147 Darin Erstad	1.50	.70
☐ 148 Bob Abreu	1.00	.45
☐ 149 Carlos Delgado	.50	.23
☐ 150 Jamey Wright	.25	.11
☐ 151 Nomar Garciaparra	3.00	1.35
☐ 152 Jason Kendall	.50	.23
☐ 153 Jermaine Allensworth	.25	.11
☐ 154 Scott Rolen	2.50	1.10
☐ 155 Rocky Coppinger	.25	.11
☐ 156 Paul Wilson	.25	.11
☐ 157 Garret Anderson	.50	.23
☐ 158 Mariano Rivera	.50	.23
☐ 159 Ruben Rivera	.50	.23
☐ 160 Andy Pettitte	1.00	.45
☐ 161 Derek Jeter	3.00	1.35
☐ 162 Neifi Perez	.50	.23
☐ 163 Ray Durham	.25	.11
☐ 164 James Baldwin	.25	.11
☐ 165 Marty Cordova	.25	.11
☐ 166 Tony Clark	1.00	.45
☐ 167 Michael Tucker	.25	.11
☐ 168 Mike Sweeney	.25	.11
☐ 169 Johnny Damon	.25	.11
☐ 170 Jermaine Dye	.25	.11
☐ 171 Alex Ochoa	.25	.11
☐ 172 Jason Isringhausen	.25	.11
☐ 173 Mark Grudzielanek	.25	.11
☐ 174 Jose Rosado	.25	.11
☐ 175 Todd Hollandsworth	.50	.23
☐ 176 Alan Benes	.25	.11
☐ 177 Jason Giambi	.25	.11
☐ 178 Billy Wagner	.50	.23
☐ 179 Justin Thompson	.50	.23
☐ 180 Todd Walker	.25	.11

1997 Topps Gallery Player's Private Issue

Randomly inserted in packs at a rate of one in 12, this 180-card set is a foil-stamped parallel version of the regular Topps Gallery set, limited to 250, with some of the cards sent to the players. The cards are spot UV coated on the photo only to allow for autographing.

	MINT	NRMT
COMPLETE SET (180)	2000.00	900.00
COMMON CARD (1-180)	6.00	2.70

*STARS: 15X TO 30X BASIC CARDS ..
*YOUNG STARS: 12.5X TO 25X BASIC CARDS

1997 Topps Gallery Gallery of Heroes

Randomly inserted in packs at a rate of one in 36, this 10-card set features color player photos designed to command the attention paid to works hanging in art museums. The backs carry player information.

	MINT	NRMT
COMPLETE SET (10)	180.00	80.00
COMMON CARD (GH1-GH10)	10.00	4.50
☐ GH1 Derek Jeter	20.00	9.00
☐ GH2 Chipper Jones	25.00	11.00
☐ GH3 Frank Thomas	30.00	13.50
☐ GH4 Ken Griffey Jr.	40.00	18.00
☐ GH5 Cal Ripken	30.00	13.50
☐ GH6 Mark McGwire	15.00	6.75
☐ GH7 Mike Piazza	25.00	11.00
☐ GH8 Jeff Bagwell	15.00	6.75
☐ GH9 Tony Gwynn	20.00	9.00
☐ GH10 Mo Vaughn	10.00	4.50

1997 Topps Gallery Peter Max Serigraphs

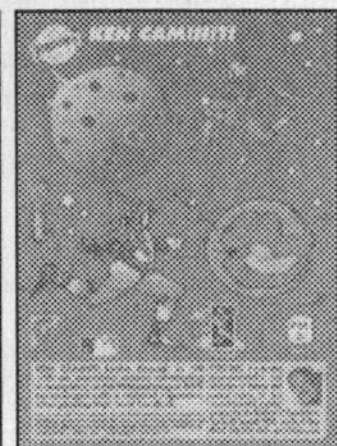

Randomly inserted in packs at a rate of one in 24, this 10-card set features painted renditions of ten superstars by the artist, Peter Max. The backs carry his commentary about the player.

	MINT	NRMT
COMPLETE SET (10)	100.00	45.00
COMMON CARD (1-10)	4.00	1.80

*AUTOGRAPHS: 15X TO 25X BASIC SERIGRAPHS

Card	MINT	NRMT
☐ 1 Derek Jeter	12.00	5.50
☐ 2 Albert Belle	6.00	2.70
☐ 3 Ken Caminiti	4.00	1.80
☐ 4 Chipper Jones	15.00	6.75
☐ 5 Ken Griffey Jr.	25.00	11.00
☐ 6 Frank Thomas	20.00	9.00
☐ 7 Cal Ripken	20.00	9.00
☐ 8 Mark McGwire	10.00	4.50
☐ 9 Barry Bonds	6.00	2.70
☐ 10 Mike Piazza	15.00	6.75

1997 Topps Gallery Photo Gallery

Randomly inserted in packs at a rate of one in 24, this 16-card set features color photos of some of baseball's hottest stars and their most memorable moments. Each card is enhanced by customized designs and double foil-stamping.

	MINT	NRMT
COMPLETE SET (16)	180.00	80.00
COMMON CARD (PG1-PG16)	3.00	1.35

☐ PG1 John Wetteland	3.00	1.35
☐ PG2 Paul Molitor	8.00	3.60
☐ PG3 Eddie Murray	8.00	3.60
☐ PG4 Ken Griffey Jr.	40.00	18.00
☐ PG5 Chipper Jones	25.00	11.00
☐ PG6 Derek Jeter	20.00	9.00
☐ PG7 Frank Thomas	30.00	13.50
☐ PG8 Mark McGwire	15.00	6.75
☐ PG9 Kenny Lofton	10.00	4.50
☐ PG10 Gary Sheffield	8.00	3.60
☐ PG11 Mike Piazza	25.00	11.00
☐ PG12 Vinny Castilla	4.00	1.80
☐ PG13 Andres Galarraga	8.00	3.60
☐ PG14 Andy Pettitte	8.00	3.60
☐ PG15 Robin Ventura	4.00	1.80
☐ PG16 Barry Larkin	5.00	2.20

1996 Topps Laser

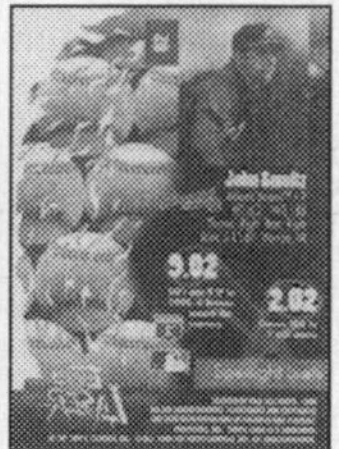

The 1996 Topps Laser contains 128 regular cards that are found on one of four perfected designs. Every card is etch foil-stamped and laser-cut. The four-card packs retail for $5.00 each.

	MINT	NRMT
COMPLETE SET (128)	120.00	55.00
COMPLETE SERIES 1 (64)	60.00	27.00
COMPLETE SERIES 2 (64)	60.00	27.00
COMMON CARD (1-128)	.50	.23

☐ 1 Moises Alou	1.00	.45
☐ 2 Derek Bell	.50	.23
☐ 3 Joe Carter	1.00	.45
☐ 4 Jeff Conine	1.00	.45
☐ 5 Darren Daulton	1.00	.45
☐ 6 Jim Edmonds	2.00	.90
☐ 7 Ron Gant	1.00	.45
☐ 8 Juan Gonzalez	5.00	2.20
☐ 9 Brian Jordan	1.00	.45
☐ 10 Ryan Klesko	1.50	.70
☐ 11 Paul Molitor	2.00	.90
☐ 12 Tony Phillips	.50	.23
☐ 13 Manny Ramirez	2.00	.90
☐ 14 Sammy Sosa	2.00	.90
☐ 15 Devon White	.50	.23
☐ 16 Bernie Williams	2.00	.90
☐ 17 Garrett Anderson	1.50	.70
☐ 18 Jay Bell	.50	.23
☐ 19 Craig Biggio	1.50	.70
☐ 20 Bobby Bonilla	1.00	.45
☐ 21 Ken Caminiti	2.00	.90
☐ 22 Shawon Dunston	.50	.23
☐ 23 Mark Grace	1.50	.70
☐ 24 Gregg Jefferies	1.00	.45
☐ 25 Jeff King	1.00	.45
☐ 26 Javy Lopez	1.00	.45
☐ 27 Edgar Martinez	1.50	.70
☐ 28 Dean Palmer	1.00	.45
☐ 29 J.T. Snow	1.00	.45
☐ 30 Mike Stanley	.50	.23
☐ 31 Terry Steinbach	1.00	.45
☐ 32 Robin Ventura	1.00	.45
☐ 33 Roberto Alomar	2.00	.90
☐ 34 Jeff Bagwell	4.00	1.80
☐ 35 Dante Bichette	1.00	.45
☐ 36 Wade Boggs	2.00	.90
☐ 37 Barry Bonds	2.50	1.10
☐ 38 Jose Canseco	1.50	.70
☐ 39 Vinny Castilla	1.00	.45
☐ 40 Will Clark	1.50	.70
☐ 41 Marty Cordova	.50	.23
☐ 42 Ken Griffey Jr.	10.00	4.50
☐ 43 Tony Gwynn	5.00	2.20
☐ 44 Rickey Henderson	1.50	.70
☐ 45 Chipper Jones	6.00	2.70
☐ 46 Mark McGwire	4.00	1.80
☐ 47 Brian McRae	.50	.23
☐ 48 Ryne Sandberg	2.50	1.10
☐ 49 Andy Ashby	.50	.23
☐ 50 Alan Benes	1.00	.45
☐ 51 Andy Benes	.50	.23
☐ 52 Roger Clemens	4.00	1.80
☐ 53 Doug Drabek	.50	.23
☐ 54 Dennis Eckersley	1.50	.70
☐ 55 Tom Glavine	1.00	.45
☐ 56 Randy Johnson	2.00	.90
☐ 57 Mark Langston	.50	.23
☐ 58 Denny Martinez	1.00	.45
☐ 59 Jack McDowell	.50	.23
☐ 60 Hideo Nomo	5.00	2.20
☐ 61 Shane Reynolds	.50	.23
☐ 62 John Smoltz	1.50	.70
☐ 63 Paul Wilson	.50	.23
☐ 64 Mark Wohlers	1.00	.45
☐ 65 Shawn Green	.50	.23
☐ 66 Marquis Grissom	1.00	.45
☐ 67 Dave Hollins	.50	.23
☐ 68 Todd Hundley	1.00	.45
☐ 69 David Justice	2.00	.90
☐ 70 Eric Karros	1.00	.45
☐ 71 Ray Lankford	1.00	.45
☐ 72 Fred McGriff	1.50	.70
☐ 73 Hal Morris	.50	.23
☐ 74 Eddie Murray	2.00	.90
☐ 75 Paul O'Neill	.50	.23
☐ 76 Rey Ordonez	1.00	.45
☐ 77 Reggie Sanders	.50	.23
☐ 78 Gary Sheffield	2.00	.90
☐ 79 Jim Thome	2.00	.90
☐ 80 Rondell White	1.00	.45
☐ 81 Travis Fryman	1.00	.45
☐ 82 Derek Jeter	6.00	2.70
☐ 83 Chuck Knoblauch	2.00	.90
☐ 84 Barry Larkin	1.50	.70
☐ 85 Tino Martinez	2.00	.90
☐ 86 Raul Mondesi	1.50	.70
☐ 87 John Olerud	.50	.23
☐ 88 Rafael Palmeiro	1.50	.70
☐ 89 Mike Piazza	6.00	2.70
☐ 90 Cal Ripken	8.00	3.60
☐ 91 Ivan Rodriguez	2.50	1.10
☐ 92 Frank Thomas	8.00	3.60
☐ 93 John Valentin	1.00	.45
☐ 94 Mo Vaughn	2.50	1.10
☐ 95 Quilvio Veras	.50	.23
☐ 96 Matt Williams	1.50	.70
☐ 97 Brady Anderson	1.50	.70
☐ 98 Carlos Baerga	1.00	.45
☐ 99 Albert Belle	2.50	1.10
☐ 100 Jay Buhner	1.50	.70
☐ 101 Johnny Damon	1.00	.45
☐ 102 Chili Davis	1.00	.45
☐ 103 Ray Durham	1.00	.45
☐ 104 Len Dykstra	1.00	.45
☐ 105 Cecil Fielder	1.00	.45
☐ 106 Andres Galarraga	2.00	.90
☐ 107 Brian L.Hunter	1.00	.45
☐ 108 Kenny Lofton	2.50	1.10
☐ 109 Kirby Puckett	4.00	1.80
☐ 110 Tim Salmon	2.00	.90
☐ 111 Greg Vaughn	.50	.23
☐ 112 Larry Walker	2.00	.90
☐ 113 Rick Aguilera	1.00	.45
☐ 114 Kevin Appier	1.00	.45
☐ 115 Kevin Brown	1.00	.45
☐ 116 David Cone	1.00	.45
☐ 117 Alex Fernandez	.50	.23
☐ 118 Chuck Finley	.50	.23
☐ 119 Joey Hamilton	1.00	.45
☐ 120 Jason Isringhausen	.50	.23
☐ 121 Greg Maddux	6.00	2.70
☐ 122 Pedro Martinez	2.00	.90
☐ 123 Jose Mesa	1.00	.45
☐ 124 Jeff Montgomery	.50	.23
☐ 125 Mike Mussina	2.00	.90
☐ 126 Randy Myers	1.00	.45
☐ 127 Kenny Rogers	.50	.23
☐ 128 Ismael Valdes	1.00	.45

1996 Topps Laser Bright Spots

Randomly inserted in packs at a rate of one in 20, this 16-card set highlights top young star players. The cards are printed on etched silver and gold diffraction foil.

	MINT	NRMT
COMPLETE SET (16)	100.00	45.00
COMPLETE SERIES 1 (8)	40.00	18.00
COMPLETE SERIES 2 (8)	60.00	27.00
COMMON CARD (1-16)	3.00	1.35

☐ 1 Brian L.Hunter	5.00	2.20
☐ 2 Derek Jeter	15.00	6.75
☐ 3 Jason Kendall	10.00	4.50
☐ 4 Brooks Kieschnick	5.00	2.20
☐ 5 Rey Ordonez	5.00	2.20
☐ 6 Jason Schmidt	5.00	2.20
☐ 7 Chris Snopek	3.00	1.35
☐ 8 Bob Wolcott	3.00	1.35
☐ 9 Alan Benes	5.00	2.20
☐ 10 Marty Cordova	3.00	1.35
☐ 11 Jimmy Haynes	3.00	1.35
☐ 12 Todd Hollandsworth	5.00	2.20
☐ 13 Derek Jeter	15.00	6.75
☐ 14 Chipper Jones	20.00	9.00
☐ 15 Hideo Nomo	15.00	6.75
☐ 16 Paul Wilson	3.00	1.35

1996 Topps Laser Power Cuts

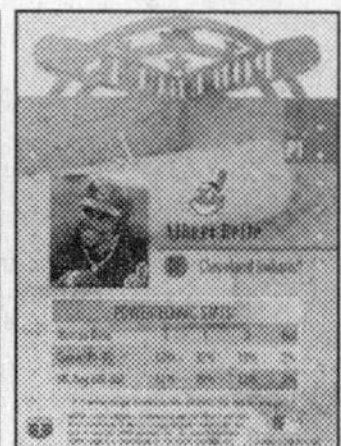

Randomly inserted in packs at a rate of one in 40, this 16-card set features baseball's biggest bats on laser-cut stock polished off with etched silver and gold diffraction foil.

	MINT	NRMT
COMPLETE SET (16)	160.00	70.00
COMPLETE SERIES 1 (8)	80.00	36.00
COMPLETE SERIES 2 (8)	80.00	36.00
COMMON CARD (1-16)	4.00	1.80

☐ 1 Albert Belle	10.00	4.50
☐ 2 Jay Buhner	5.00	2.20
☐ 3 Fred McGriff	5.00	2.20
☐ 4 Mike Piazza	25.00	11.00
☐ 5 Tim Salmon	8.00	3.60
☐ 6 Frank Thomas	30.00	13.50
☐ 7 Mo Vaughn	10.00	4.50
☐ 8 Matt Williams	5.00	2.20
☐ 9 Jeff Bagwell	15.00	6.75
☐ 10 Barry Bonds	10.00	4.50
☐ 11 Jose Canseco	5.00	2.20
☐ 12 Cecil Fielder	4.00	1.80
☐ 13 Juan Gonzalez	20.00	9.00
☐ 14 Ken Griffey Jr.	40.00	18.00
☐ 15 Sammy Sosa	8.00	3.60
☐ 16 Larry Walker	6.00	2.70

1996 Topps Laser Stadium Stars

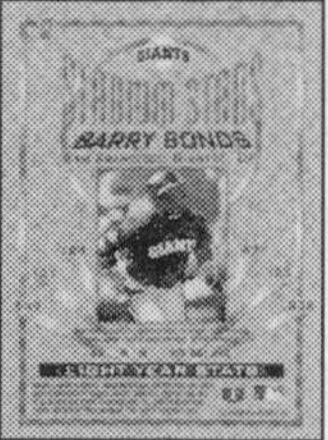

Randomly inserted in packs at a rate of one in 60, this 16-card set features the best and the brightest stars of the baseball diamond. Each highly detailed, laser-sculpted cover folds back to reveal striated silver and gold etched diffraction foil on every card.

	MINT	NRMT
COMPLETE SET (16)	240.00	110.00
COMPLETE SERIES 1 (8)	120.00	55.00
COMPLETE SERIES 2 (8)	120.00	55.00
COMMON CARD (1-16)	5.00	2.20

Card	MINT	NRMT
☐ 1 Carlos Baerga	5.00	2.20
☐ 2 Barry Bonds	12.00	5.50
☐ 3 Andres Galarraga	10.00	4.50
☐ 4 Ken Griffey Jr.	50.00	22.00
☐ 5 Barry Larkin	7.00	3.10
☐ 6 Raul Mondesi	7.00	3.10
☐ 7 Kirby Puckett	20.00	9.00
☐ 8 Cal Ripken	40.00	18.00
☐ 9 Will Clark	7.00	3.10
☐ 10 Roger Clemens	20.00	9.00
☐ 11 Tony Gwynn	25.00	11.00
☐ 12 Randy Johnson	12.00	5.50
☐ 13 Kenny Lofton	12.00	5.50
☐ 14 Edgar Martinez	7.00	3.10
☐ 15 Ryne Sandberg	12.00	5.50
☐ 16 Frank Thomas	40.00	18.00

1997 Topps Screenplays

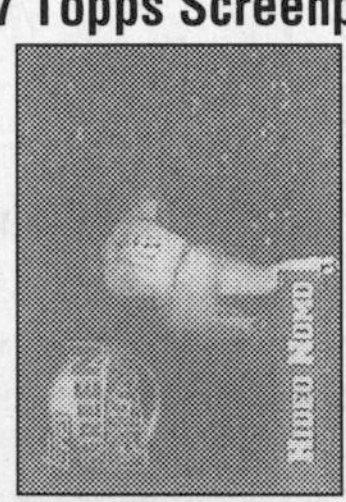

The 1997 Topps Screenplays set was issued in one series totalling 20 cards and distributed in one-card packs with a suggested retail price of 9.99. Each card displays 24 frames of actual game footage with the help of Kodak's revolutionary Kodamotion technology. The cards have a dura clear back. Each card is individually packaged in a fold metal finish collectible tin that resembles a movie reel canister and features a full-color image of the player inside.The tin contains a display stand for it and the card and includes player info, bio, and stats. The cards are unnumbered and checklisted below in alphabetical order. All values listed below are for a combination of the card and tin.

	MINT	NRMT
COMPLETE SET (20)	150.00	70.00
COMMON CARD (1-20)	3.00	1.35
☐ 1 Jeff Bagwell	10.00	4.50
☐ 2 Albert Belle	6.00	2.70
☐ 3 Barry Bonds	6.00	2.70
☐ 4 Andres Galarraga	5.00	2.20
☐ 5 Nomar Garciaparra	15.00	6.75
☐ 6 Juan Gonzalez	12.00	5.50
☐ 7 Ken Griffey Jr.	25.00	11.00
☐ 8 Tony Gwynn	12.00	5.50
☐ 9 Derek Jeter	15.00	6.75
☐ 10 Randy Johnson	5.00	2.20
☐ 11 Andruw Jones	12.00	5.50
☐ 12 Chipper Jones	15.00	6.75
☐ 13 Kenny Lofton	6.00	2.70
☐ 14 Mark McGwire	10.00	4.50
☐ 15 Paul Molitor	5.00	2.20
☐ 16 Hideo Nomo	12.00	5.50
☐ 17 Cal Ripken	20.00	9.00
☐ 18 Sammy Sosa	3.00	1.35
☐ 19 Frank Thomas	20.00	9.00
☐ 20 Jim Thome	5.00	2.20

1997 Topps Screenplays Premium Series

This six-card limited production set features six top stars from the regular base set in additional action shots. The cards were seeded at a rate of 1:21 packs. The cards are unnumbered and checklisted below in alphabetical order. The values listed below are for a combination of the card and the tin it was issued in.

	MINT	NRMT
COMPLETE SET (6)	300.00	135.00
COMMON CARD (1-6)	15.00	6.75
☐ 1 Ken Griffey Jr.	80.00	36.00
☐ 2 Chipper Jones	50.00	22.00
☐ 3 Mike Piazza	50.00	22.00
☐ 4 Cal Ripken	60.00	27.00
☐ 5 Frank Thomas	60.00	27.00
☐ 6 Larry Walker	15.00	6.75

1997 Topps Stars Promos

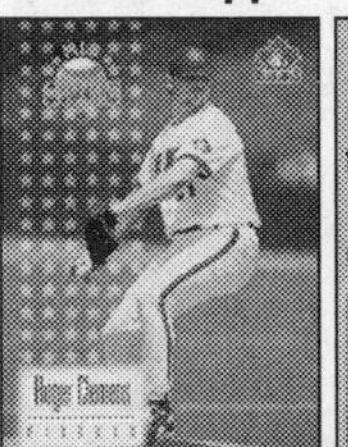

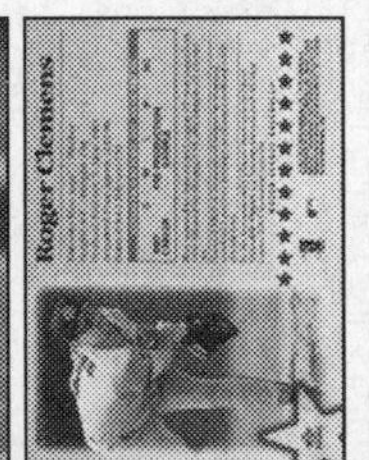

This three-card set features borderless color action photos of three top players printed on textured cards with six rows of stars running down one side of the front. The backs carry another player photo with player information and career statistics.

	MINT	NRMT
COMPLETE SET (3)	6.00	2.70
COMMON CARD (PP1-PP3)	1.00	.45
☐ PP1 Larry Walker	1.00	.45
☐ PP2 Roger Clemens	2.00	.90
☐ PP3 Frank Thomas	4.00	1.80

1997 Topps Stars

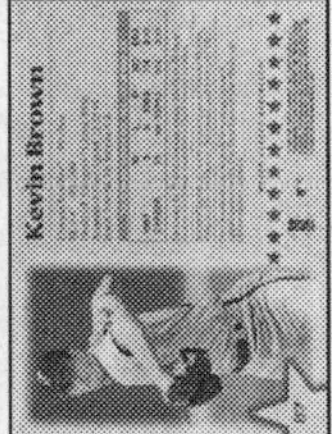

The 1997 Topps Stars set was issued in one series totalling 125 cards and was distributed in seven-card packs with a suggested retail price of $3. A checklisted card was added to every fifth pack as an extra card. The set was available exclusively to Home Team Advantage members and features color player photos printed on super-thick, 20-point stock with matte gold foil stamping and a textured matte laminate and spot UV coating. The backs carry another photo of the same player with biographical information and career statistics. Rookie cards include Lance Berkman, Mark Kotsay, Travis Lee and Kerry Wood.

	MINT	NRMT
COMPLETE SET (125)	40.00	18.00
COMMON CARD (1-125)	.15	.07
☐ 1 Larry Walker	.60	.25
☐ 2 Tino Martinez	.60	.25
☐ 3 Cal Ripken	2.50	1.10
☐ 4 Ken Griffey Jr.	3.00	1.35
☐ 5 Chipper Jones	2.00	.90
☐ 6 David Justice	.60	.25
☐ 7 Mike Piazza	2.00	.90
☐ 8 Jeff Bagwell	1.25	.55
☐ 9 Ron Gant	.30	.14
☐ 10 Sammy Sosa	.60	.25
☐ 11 Tony Gwynn	1.50	.70
☐ 12 Carlos Baerga	.30	.14
☐ 13 Frank Thomas	2.50	1.10
☐ 14 Moises Alou	.30	.14
☐ 15 Barry Larkin	.40	.18
☐ 16 Ivan Rodriguez	.75	.35
☐ 17 Greg Maddux	2.00	.90
☐ 18 Jim Edmonds	.60	.25
☐ 19 Jose Canseco	.40	.18
☐ 20 Rafael Palmeiro	.40	.18
☐ 21 Paul Molitor	.60	.25
☐ 22 Kevin Appier	.30	.14
☐ 23 Raul Mondesi	.60	.25
☐ 24 Lance Johnson	.15	.07
☐ 25 Edgar Martinez	.40	.18
☐ 26 Andres Galarraga	.60	.25
☐ 27 Mo Vaughn	.75	.35
☐ 28 Ken Caminiti	.60	.25
☐ 29 Cecil Fielder	.30	.14
☐ 30 Harold Baines	.30	.14
☐ 31 Roberto Alomar	.60	.25
☐ 32 Shawn Estes	.30	.14
☐ 33 Tom Glavine	.30	.14
☐ 34 Dennis Eckersley	.40	.18
☐ 35 Manny Ramirez	.60	.25
☐ 36 John Olerud	.30	.14
☐ 37 Juan Gonzalez	1.50	.70
☐ 38 Chuck Knoblauch	.60	.25
☐ 39 Albert Belle	.75	.35
☐ 40 Vinny Castilla	.30	.14
☐ 41 John Smoltz	.30	.14
☐ 42 Barry Bonds	.75	.35
☐ 43 Randy Johnson	.60	.25
☐ 44 Brady Anderson	.40	.18
☐ 45 Jeff Blauser	.15	.07
☐ 46 Craig Biggio	.40	.18
☐ 47 Jeff Conine	.30	.14
☐ 48 Marquis Grissom	.30	.14
☐ 49 Mark Grace	.40	.18
☐ 50 Roger Clemens	1.25	.55
☐ 51 Mark McGwire	1.25	.55
☐ 52 Fred McGriff	.40	.18
☐ 53 Gary Sheffield	.60	.25
☐ 54 Bobby Jones	.15	.07
☐ 55 Eric Young	.15	.07
☐ 56 Robin Ventura	.30	.14
☐ 57 Wade Boggs	.60	.25
☐ 58 Joe Carter	.30	.14
☐ 59 Ryne Sandberg	.75	.35
☐ 60 Matt Williams	.60	.25
☐ 61 Todd Hundley	.30	.14
☐ 62 Dante Bichette	.30	.14
☐ 63 Chili Davis	.30	.14
☐ 64 Kenny Lofton	.75	.35
☐ 65 Jay Buhner	.40	.18
☐ 66 Will Clark	.40	.18
☐ 67 Travis Fryman	.30	.14
☐ 68 Pat Hentgen	.30	.14
☐ 69 Ellis Burks	.30	.14
☐ 70 Mike Mussina	.60	.25
☐ 71 Hideo Nomo	1.50	.70
☐ 72 Sandy Alomar	.30	.14
☐ 73 Bobby Bonilla	.30	.14
☐ 74 Rickey Henderson	.40	.18
☐ 75 David Cone	.30	.14
☐ 76 Terry Steinbach	.15	.07
☐ 77 Pedro Martinez	.60	.25
☐ 78 Jim Thome	.60	.25
☐ 79 Rod Beck	.15	.07
☐ 80 Randy Myers	.15	.07
☐ 81 Charles Nagy	.15	.07
☐ 82 Mark Wohlers	.15	.07
☐ 83 Paul O'Neill	.30	.14
☐ 84 Curt Schilling	.30	.14
☐ 85 Joey Cora	.30	.14
☐ 86 John Franco	.30	.14
☐ 87 Kevin Brown	.15	.07
☐ 88 Benito Santiago	.15	.07
☐ 89 Ray Lankford	.30	.14
☐ 90 Bernie Williams	.60	.25
☐ 91 Jason Dickson	.15	.07
☐ 92 Jeff Cirillo	.30	.14
☐ 93 Nomar Garciaparra	2.00	.90
☐ 94 Mariano Rivera	.30	.14
☐ 95 Javy Lopez	.30	.14
☐ 96 Tony Womack	.75	.35
☐ 97 Jose Rosado	.15	.07
☐ 98 Denny Neagle	.30	.14
☐ 99 Darryl Kile	.30	.14
☐ 100 Justin Thompson	.30	.14
☐ 101 Juan Encarnacion	.40	.18
☐ 102 Brad Fullmer	.15	.07
☐ 103 Kris Benson	2.00	.90
☐ 104 Todd Helton	1.00	.45
☐ 105 Paul Konerko	1.00	.45
☐ 106 Travis Lee	8.00	3.60
☐ 107 Todd Greene	.30	.14
☐ 108 Mark Kotsay	2.50	1.10
☐ 109 Carl Pavano	.30	.14
☐ 110 Kerry Wood	2.50	1.10
☐ 111 Jason Romano	.50	.23
☐ 112 Geoff Goetz	.40	.18
☐ 113 Scott Hodges	.60	.25
☐ 114 Aaron Akin	.40	.18
☐ 115 Vernon Wells	2.00	.90
☐ 116 Chris Stowe	.40	.18
☐ 117 Brett Caradonna	.75	.35
☐ 118 Adam Kennedy	.60	.25
☐ 119 Jayson Werth	1.25	.55
☐ 120 Glenn Davis	.60	.25

	MINT	NRMT
☐ 121 Troy Cameron	1.50	.70
☐ 122 J.J. Davis	1.25	.55
☐ 123 Jason Dellaero	.60	.25
☐ 124 Jason Standridge	.40	.18
☐ 125 Lance Berkman	2.50	1.10
☐ NNO Checklist	.15	.07

1997 Topps Stars Always Mint

Randomly inserted in packs at the rate of one in 12, this 125-card set is parallel to the base set and is printed on double-chromed paper stock.

	MINT	NRMT
COMPLETE SET (125)	800.00	350.00
COMMON CARD (1-125)	2.50	1.10

*STARS: 7.5X TO 15X BASIC CARDS .
*YOUNG STARS: 6X TO 12X BASIC CARDS
*ROOKIES: 5X TO 10X BASIC CARDS

1997 Topps Stars '97 All-Stars

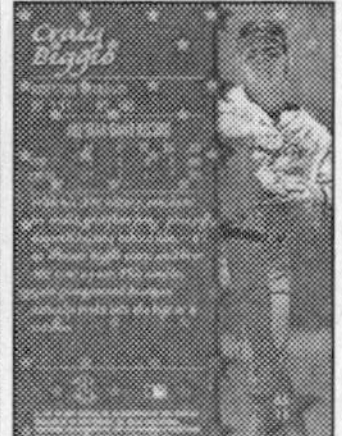

Randomly inserted in packs at the rate of one in 24, this 20-card set features color photos of players who represented their league in the 1997 All-Star Game in Cleveland and are printed on embossed uniluster.

	MINT	NRMT
COMPLETE SET (20)	300.00	135.00
COMMON CARD (AS1-AS20)	4.00	1.80
☐ AS1 Greg Maddux	40.00	18.00
☐ AS2 Randy Johnson	12.00	5.50
☐ AS3 Tino Martinez	12.00	5.50
☐ AS4 Jeff Bagwell	25.00	11.00
☐ AS5 Ivan Rodriguez	15.00	6.75
☐ AS6 Mike Piazza	40.00	18.00
☐ AS7 Cal Ripken	50.00	22.00
☐ AS8 Ken Caminiti	12.00	5.50
☐ AS9 Tony Gwynn	30.00	13.50
☐ AS10 Edgar Martinez	8.00	3.60
☐ AS11 Craig Biggio	8.00	3.60
☐ AS12 Roberto Alomar	12.00	5.50
☐ AS13 Larry Walker	12.00	5.50
☐ AS14 Brady Anderson	8.00	3.60
☐ AS15 Barry Bonds	15.00	6.75
☐ AS16 Ken Griffey Jr.	60.00	27.00
☐ AS17 Ray Lankford	6.00	2.70
☐ AS18 Paul O'Neill	6.00	2.70
☐ AS19 Jeff Blauser	4.00	1.80
☐ AS20 Sandy Alomar	6.00	2.70

1997 Topps Stars All-Star Memories

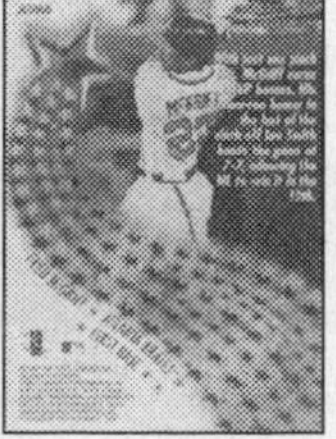

Randomly inserted in packs at the rate of one in 24, this 10-card set features color photos printed on laser-cut foilboard of the best performing all-star players.

	MINT	NRMT
COMPLETE SET (10)	80.00	36.00
COMMON CARD (ASM1-ASM10)	1.50	.70
☐ ASM1 Cal Ripken	20.00	9.00
☐ ASM2 Jeff Conine	1.50	.70
☐ ASM3 Mike Piazza	15.00	6.75
☐ ASM4 Randy Johnson	5.00	2.20
☐ ASM5 Ken Griffey Jr.	25.00	11.00
☐ ASM6 Fred McGriff	3.00	1.35
☐ ASM7 Moises Alou	2.00	.90
☐ ASM8 Hideo Nomo	12.00	5.50
☐ ASM9 Larry Walker	5.00	2.20
☐ ASM10 Sandy Alomar	2.00	.90

1997 Topps Stars Future All-Stars

Randomly inserted in packs at the rate of one in 12, this 15-card set features color photos printed on prismatic rainbow diffraction foilboard of players who are candidates to be next year's all-stars.

	MINT	NRMT
COMPLETE SET (15)	60.00	27.00
COMMON CARD (FAS1-FAS15)	1.00	.45
☐ FAS1 Derek Jeter	12.00	5.50
☐ FAS2 Andruw Jones	8.00	3.60
☐ FAS3 Vladimir Guerrero	6.00	2.70
☐ FAS4 Scott Rolen	8.00	3.60
☐ FAS5 Jose Guillen	4.00	1.80
☐ FAS6 Jose Cruz Jr.	25.00	11.00
☐ FAS7 Darin Erstad	5.00	2.20
☐ FAS8 Tony Clark	3.00	1.35
☐ FAS9 Scott Spiezio	1.50	.70
☐ FAS10 Kevin Orie	1.50	.70
☐ FAS11 Calvin Reese	1.00	.45
☐ FAS12 Billy Wagner	2.00	.90
☐ FAS13 Matt Morris	1.00	.45
☐ FAS14 Jeremi Gonzalez	1.50	.70
☐ FAS15 Hideki Irabu	3.00	1.35

1997 Topps Stars Rookie Reprints

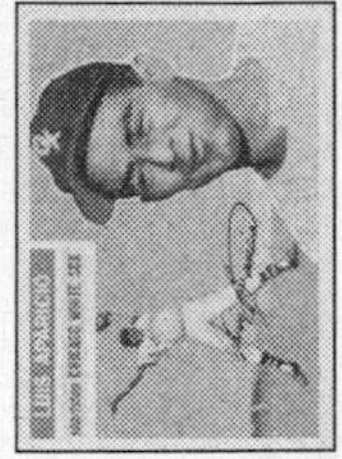

Randomly inserted in packs at the rate of one in six, this 15-card set features reprints of the rookie cards of 15 top Hall of Famers.

	MINT	NRMT
COMPLETE SET (15)	40.00	18.00
COMMON CARD (1-15)	3.00	1.35
☐ 1 Luis Aparicio	3.00	1.35
☐ 2 Richie Ashburn	3.00	1.35
☐ 3 Jim Bunning	3.00	1.35
☐ 4 Bob Feller	3.00	1.35
☐ 5 Rollie Fingers	2.50	1.10
☐ 6 Monte Irvin	3.00	1.35
☐ 7 Al Kaline	6.00	2.70
☐ 8 Ralph Kiner	3.00	1.35
☐ 9 Eddie Mathews	5.00	2.20
☐ 10 Hal Newhouser	3.00	1.35
☐ 11 Gaylord Perry	3.00	1.35
☐ 12 Robin Roberts	3.00	1.35
☐ 13 Brooks Robinson	5.00	2.20
☐ 14 Enos Slaughter	3.00	1.35
☐ 15 Earl Weaver	3.00	1.35

1997 Topps Stars Rookie Reprint Autographs

Randomly inserted in packs at the rate of one in 30, this 14-card set is an autographed parallel version of the regular Topps Stars Rookie Reprint set. The Topps

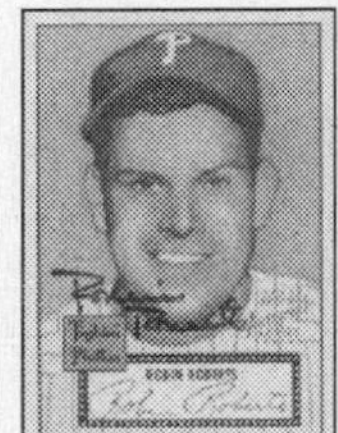

Certified Issue Autograph stamp is printed on each card. Card No. 2 does not exist.

	MINT	NRMT
COMPLETE SET (14)	350.00	160.00
COMMON CARD (1/3-15)	20.00	9.00
☐ 1 Luis Aparicio	30.00	13.50
☐ 3 Jim Bunning	30.00	13.50
☐ 4 Bob Feller	25.00	11.00
☐ 5 Rollie Fingers	20.00	9.00
☐ 6 Monte Irvin	20.00	9.00
☐ 7 Al Kaline	50.00	22.00
☐ 8 Ralph Kiner	30.00	13.50
☐ 9 Eddie Mathews	40.00	18.00
☐ 10 Hal Newhouser	20.00	9.00
☐ 11 Gaylord Perry	20.00	9.00
☐ 12 Robin Roberts	25.00	11.00
☐ 13 Brooks Robinson	40.00	18.00
☐ 14 Enos Slaughter	25.00	11.00
☐ 15 Earl Weaver	25.00	11.00

1987 Toys'R'Us Rookies

Topps produced this 33-card standard-size boxed set for Toys'R'Us stores. The set is subtitled "Baseball Rookies" and features predominantly younger players. The cards feature a high-gloss, full-color photo of the player inside a black border. The card backs are printed in orange and blue on white card stock. The set numbering is in alphabetical order by player's name.

	MINT	NRMT
COMPLETE SET (33)	7.50	3.40
COMMON CARD (1-33)	.10	.05
☐ 1 Andy Allanson	.10	.05
☐ 2 Paul Assenmacher	.20	.09
☐ 3 Scott Bailes	.10	.05
☐ 4 Barry Bonds	2.00	.90
☐ 5 Jose Canseco	.75	.35
☐ 6 John Cerutti	.10	.05
☐ 7 Will Clark	.75	.35
☐ 8 Kal Daniels	.10	.05
☐ 9 Jim Deshaies	.10	.05
☐ 10 Mark Eichhorn	.10	.05
☐ 11 Ed Hearn	.10	.05
☐ 12 Pete Incaviglia	.20	.09
☐ 13 Bo Jackson	.40	.18
☐ 14 Wally Joyner	.50	.23
☐ 15 Charlie Kerfeld	.10	.05
☐ 16 Eric King	.10	.05
☐ 17 John Kruk	.40	.18
☐ 18 Barry Larkin	1.00	.45
☐ 19 Mike LaValliere	.10	.05
☐ 20 Greg Mathews	.10	.05
☐ 21 Kevin Mitchell	.20	.09
☐ 22 Dan Plesac	.10	.05
☐ 23 Bruce Ruffin	.10	.05
☐ 24 Ruben Sierra	.40	.18
☐ 25 Cory Snyder	.10	.05
☐ 26 Kurt Stillwell	.10	.05
☐ 27 Dale Sveum	.10	.05
☐ 28 Danny Tartabull	.20	.09
☐ 29 Andres Thomas	.10	.05
☐ 30 Robby Thompson	.20	.09
☐ 31 Jim Traber	.10	.05
☐ 32 Mitch Williams	.20	.09
☐ 33 Todd Worrell	.20	.09

1988 Toys'R'Us Rookies

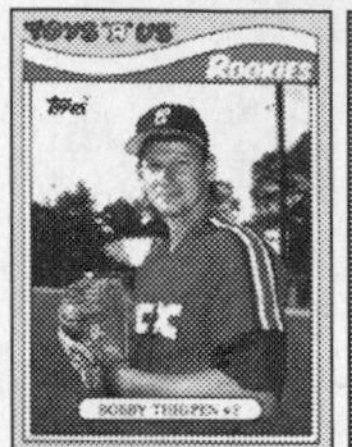
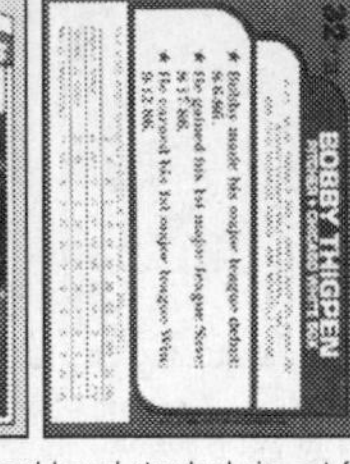

Topps produced this 33-card boxed standard-size set for Toys'R'Us stores. The set is subtitled "Baseball Rookies" and features predominantly younger players. The cards feature a high-gloss, full-color photo of the player inside a blue border. The card backs are printed in pink and blue on white card stock. The checklist for the set is found on the back panel of the small collector box. The statistics provided on the card backs cover only three lines, Minor League totals, last season, and Major League totals. The set numbering is in alphabetical order by player's name.

	MINT	NRMT
COMPLETE SET (33)	5.00	2.20
COMMON CARD (1-33)	.10	.05
☐ 1 Todd Benzinger	.10	.05
☐ 2 Bob Brower	.10	.05
☐ 3 Jerry Browne	.10	.05
☐ 4 DeWayne Buice	.10	.05
☐ 5 Ellis Burks	.50	.23
☐ 6 Ken Caminiti	1.00	.45
☐ 7 Casey Candaele	.10	.05
☐ 8 Dave Cone	.50	.23
☐ 9 Kelly Downs	.10	.05
☐ 10 Mike Dunne	.10	.05
☐ 11 Ken Gerhart	.10	.05
☐ 12 Mike Greenwell	.20	.09
☐ 13 Mike Henneman	.20	.09
☐ 14 Sam Horn	.10	.05
☐ 15 Joe Magrane	.10	.05
☐ 16 Fred Manrique	.10	.05
☐ 17 John Marzano	.10	.05
☐ 18 Fred McGriff	1.00	.45
☐ 19 Mark McGwire	1.50	.70
☐ 20 Jeff Musselman	.10	.05
☐ 21 Randy Myers	.20	.09
☐ 22 Matt Nokes	.10	.05
☐ 23 Al Pedrique	.10	.05
☐ 24 Luis Polonia	.20	.09
☐ 25 Billy Ripken	.10	.05
☐ 26 Benito Santiago	.20	.09
☐ 27 Kevin Seitzer	.20	.09
☐ 28 John Smiley	.10	.05
☐ 29 Mike Stanley	.20	.09
☐ 30 Terry Steinbach	.30	.14
☐ 31 B.J. Surhoff	.20	.09
☐ 32 Bobby Thigpen	.10	.05
☐ 33 Devon White	.30	.14

1989 Toys'R'Us Rookies

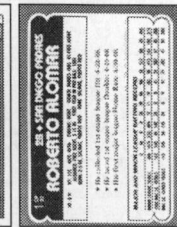

The 1989 Toys'R'Us Rookies set contains 33 standard-size glossy cards. The fronts are yellow and magenta. The horizontally oriented backs are sky blue and red, and feature 1988 and career stats. The cards were distributed through Toys'R'Us stores as a boxed set. The subjects are numbered alphabetically. The set checklist is printed on the back panel of the set's custom box.

	MINT	NRMT
COMPLETE SET (33)	4.00	1.80
COMMON CARD (1-33)	.10	.05
☐ 1 Roberto Alomar	.75	.35
☐ 2 Brady Anderson	.50	.23
☐ 3 Tim Belcher	.10	.05
☐ 4 Damon Berryhill	.10	.05
☐ 5 Jay Buhner	.50	.23
☐ 6 Sherman Corbett	.10	.05
☐ 7 Kevin Elster	.20	.09
☐ 8 Cecil Espy	.10	.05
☐ 9 Dave Gallagher	.10	.05
☐ 10 Ron Gant	.40	.18
☐ 11 Paul Gibson	.10	.05
☐ 12 Mark Grace	.60	.25
☐ 13 Bryan Harvey	.20	.09
☐ 14 Darrin Jackson	.10	.05
☐ 15 Gregg Jefferies	.20	.09
☐ 16 Ron Jones	.10	.05
☐ 17 Ricky Jordan	.10	.05
☐ 18 Roberto Kelly	.20	.09
☐ 19 Al Leiter	.20	.09
☐ 20 Jack McDowell	.20	.09
☐ 21 Melido Perez	.10	.05
☐ 22 Jeff Pico	.10	.05
☐ 23 Jody Reed	.10	.05
☐ 24 Chris Sabo	.10	.05
☐ 25 Nelson Santovenia	.10	.05
☐ 26 Mackey Sasser	.10	.05
☐ 27 Mike Schooler	.10	.05
☐ 28 Gary Sheffield	.75	.35
☐ 29 Pete Smith	.10	.05
☐ 30 Pete Stanicek	.10	.05
☐ 31 Jeff Treadway	.10	.05
☐ 32 Walt Weiss	.20	.09
☐ 33 Dave West	.10	.05

1990 Toys'R'Us Rookies

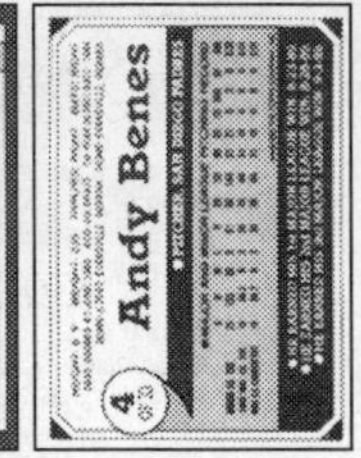

The 1990 Toys'R'Us Rookies set is a 33-card standard-size set of young prospects issued by Topps. For the fourth consecutive year Topps issued a rookie set for Toys'R'Us. There are several players in the set which were on Topps cards for the second time in 1990, i.e., not rookies even for the Topps Company. These players included Gregg Jefferies and Gregg Olson. This set might be more appropriately called the Young Stars set. The cards are numbered, with the numbering being essentially in alphabetical order by player's name. The set checklist is printed on the back panel of the set's custom box.

	MINT	NRMT
COMPLETE SET (33)	6.00	2.70
COMMON CARD (1-33)	.10	.05
☐ 1 Jim Abbott	.20	.09
☐ 2 Eric Anthony	.10	.05
☐ 3 Joey Belle	1.00	.45
☐ 4 Andy Benes	.20	.09
☐ 5 Greg Briley	.10	.05
☐ 6 Kevin Brown	.20	.09
☐ 7 Mark Carreon	.10	.05
☐ 8 Mike Devereaux	.10	.05
☐ 9 Junior Felix	.10	.05
☐ 10 Mark Gardner	.10	.05
☐ 11 Bob Geren	.10	.05
☐ 12 Tom Gordon	.20	.09
☐ 13 Ken Griffey Jr.	2.00	.90
☐ 14 Pete Harnisch	.10	.05
☐ 15 Ken Hill	.30	.14
☐ 16 Gregg Jefferies	.20	.09
☐ 17 Derek Lilliquist	.10	.05
☐ 18 Carlos Martinez	.10	.05
☐ 19 Ramon Martinez	.30	.14
☐ 20 Bob Milacki	.10	.05
☐ 21 Gregg Olson	.10	.05
☐ 22 Kenny Rogers	.20	.09
☐ 23 Alex Sanchez	.10	.05
☐ 24 Gary Sheffield	.50	.23
☐ 25 Dwight Smith	.20	.09
☐ 26 Billy Spiers	.10	.05
☐ 27 Greg Vaughn	.20	.09
☐ 28 Robin Ventura	.40	.18
☐ 29 Jerome Walton	.10	.05
☐ 30 Dave West	.10	.05
☐ 31 John Wetteland	.30	.14
☐ 32 Craig Worthington	.10	.05
☐ 33 Todd Zeile	.20	.09

1991 Toys'R'Us Rookies

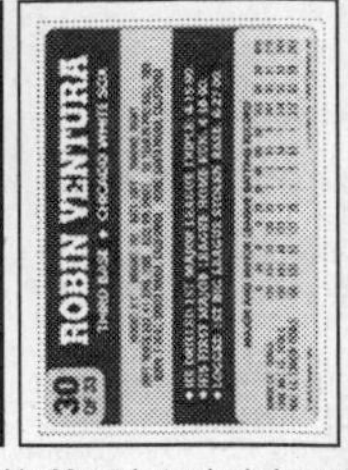

For the fifth year in a row this 33-card standard-size set was produced by Topps for Toys'R'Us, and the sponsor's logo adorns the top of the card front. The front design features glossy color action player photos with yellow borders on a black card face. The words "Topps 1991 Collectors' Edition" appear in a yellow stripe above the picture. The horizontally oriented backs are printed in brown and yellow, and present biographical information, career highlights, and statistics.

	MINT	NRMT
COMPLETE SET (33)	7.00	3.10
COMMON CARD (1-33)	.10	.05
☐ 1 Sandy Alomar Jr.	.20	.09
☐ 2 Kevin Appier	.20	.09
☐ 3 Steve Avery	.10	.05
☐ 4 Carlos Baerga	.20	.09
☐ 5 Alex Cole	.10	.05
☐ 6 Pat Combs	.10	.05
☐ 7 Delino DeShields	.20	.09
☐ 8 Travis Fryman	.50	.23
☐ 9 Marquis Grissom	.50	.23
☐ 10 Mike Harkey	.10	.05
☐ 11 Glenallen Hill	.20	.09
☐ 12 Jeff Huson	.10	.05
☐ 13 Felix Jose	.10	.05
☐ 14 Dave Justice	.75	.35
☐ 15 Dana Kiecker	.10	.05
☐ 16 Kevin Maas	.10	.05
☐ 17 Ben McDonald	.20	.09
☐ 18 Brian McRae	.20	.09
☐ 19 Kent Mercker	.10	.05
☐ 20 Hal Morris	.20	.09
☐ 21 Chris Nabholz	.10	.05
☐ 22 Tim Naehring	.20	.09
☐ 23 Jose Offerman	.10	.05
☐ 24 John Olerud	.20	.09
☐ 25 Scott Radinsky	.10	.05
☐ 26 Bill Sampen	.10	.05
☐ 27 Frank Thomas	2.00	.90
☐ 28 Randy Tomlin	.10	.05
☐ 29 Greg Vaughn	.10	.05
☐ 30 Robin Ventura	.40	.18
☐ 31 Larry Walker	.50	.23
☐ 32 Wally Whitehurst	.10	.05
☐ 33 Todd Zeile	.20	.09

1993 Toys'R'Us

This 100-card standard-size set produced by Topps Stadium Club for Toys'R'Us features 100 young stars, rookie stars, and future stars. The cards carry glossy, full-bleed color photos with the Toys'R'Us logo in an upper corner. In silver lettering on a blue bar near the bottom of the photo, are the words Future Star, Rookie Star, or Young Star. The player's name is printed on a red bar below. The horizontal backs display a player close-up superimposed on a blue sky with clouds background. Also included are player biography, statistics and some career highlights. The cards were distributed through Toys'R'Us in a molded plastic box designed to resemble a store. 7,500 cases of this product was produced.

	MINT	NRMT
COMPLETE SET (100)	10.00	4.50
COMMON CARD (1-100)	.05	.02

Card	MINT	NRMT
☐ 1 Ken Griffey Jr.	2.00	.90
☐ 2 Chad Curtis	.15	.07
☐ 3 Mike Bordick	.05	.02
☐ 4 Ryan Klesko	.50	.23
☐ 5 Pat Listach	.05	.02
☐ 6 Jim Bullinger	.05	.02
☐ 7 Tim Laker	.05	.02
☐ 8 Mike Devereaux	.05	.02
☐ 9 Kevin Young	.05	.02
☐ 10 John Valentin	.10	.05
☐ 11 Pat Mahomes	.05	.02
☐ 12 Todd Hundley	.10	.05
☐ 13 Roberto Alomar	.25	.11
☐ 14 David Justice	.25	.11
☐ 15 Mike Perez	.05	.02
☐ 16 Royce Clayton	.10	.05
☐ 17 Ryan Thompson	.05	.02
☐ 18 Dave Hollins	.05	.02
☐ 19 Brien Taylor	.05	.02
☐ 20 Melvin Nieves	.15	.07
☐ 21 Rheal Cormier	.05	.02
☐ 22 Mike Piazza	2.00	.90
☐ 23 Larry Walker	.40	.18
☐ 24 Tim Wakefield	.05	.02
☐ 25 Tim Costo	.05	.02
☐ 26 Pedro Munoz	.05	.02
☐ 27 Reggie Sanders	.10	.05
☐ 28 Arthur Rhodes	.05	.02
☐ 29 Scott Cooper	.05	.02
☐ 30 Marquis Grissom	.10	.05
☐ 31 Dave Nilsson	.10	.05
☐ 32 John Patterson	.05	.02
☐ 33 Ivan Rodriguez	.50	.23
☐ 34 Andy Stankiewicz	.05	.02
☐ 35 Bret Boone	.05	.02
☐ 36 Gerald Williams	.05	.02
☐ 37 Mike Mussina	.30	.14
☐ 38 Henry Rodriguez	.05	.02
☐ 39 Chuck Knoblauch	.40	.18
☐ 40 Bob Wickman	.05	.02
☐ 41 Donovan Osborne	.05	.02
☐ 42 Mike Timlin	.05	.02
☐ 43 Damion Easley	.05	.02
☐ 44 Pedro Astacio	.05	.02
☐ 45 David Segui	.05	.02
☐ 46 Willie Greene	.10	.05
☐ 47 Mike Trombley	.05	.02
☐ 48 Bernie Williams	.40	.18
☐ 49 Eric Anthony	.05	.02
☐ 50 Tim Naehring	.10	.05
☐ 51 Carlos Baerga	.10	.05
☐ 52 Brady Anderson	.15	.07
☐ 53 Mo Vaughn	.50	.23
☐ 54 Willie Banks	.05	.02
☐ 55 Mark Wohlers	.10	.05
☐ 56 Jeff Bagwell	.75	.35
☐ 57 Frank Seminara	.05	.02
☐ 58 Robin Ventura	.10	.05
☐ 59 Alan Embree	.05	.02
☐ 60 Rey Sanchez	.05	.02
☐ 61 Delino DeShields	.05	.02
☐ 62 Todd Van Poppel	.05	.02
☐ 63 Eric Karros	.25	.11
☐ 64 Gary Sheffield	.30	.14
☐ 65 Dan Wilson	.10	.05
☐ 66 Frank Thomas	2.00	.90
☐ 67 Tim Salmon	.50	.23
☐ 68 Dan Smith	.05	.02
☐ 69 Kenny Lofton	.50	.23
☐ 70 Carlos Garcia	.05	.02
☐ 71 Scott Livingstone	.05	.02
☐ 72 Sam Militello	.05	.02
☐ 73 Juan Guzman	.10	.05
☐ 74 Greg Colbrunn	.10	.05
☐ 75 David Hulse	.05	.02
☐ 76 Rusty Meacham	.05	.02
☐ 77 Dave Fleming	.05	.02
☐ 78 Rene Arocha	.05	.02
☐ 79 Derrick May	.05	.02
☐ 80 Cal Eldred	.05	.02
☐ 81 Bernard Gilkey	.10	.05
☐ 82 Deion Sanders	.25	.11
☐ 83 Reggie Jefferson	.10	.05
☐ 84 Jeff Kent	.10	.05
☐ 85 Juan Gonzalez	1.00	.45
☐ 86 Billy Ashley	.05	.02
☐ 87 Travis Fryman	.10	.05
☐ 88 Roberto Hernandez	.10	.05
☐ 89 Hipolito Pichardo	.05	.02
☐ 90 Wilfredo Cordero	.05	.02
☐ 91 John Jaha	.15	.07
☐ 92 Javier Lopez	.25	.11
☐ 93 Derek Bell	.10	.05
☐ 94 Jeff Juden	.05	.02
☐ 95 Steve Avery	.10	.05
☐ 96 Moises Alou	.10	.05
☐ 97 Brian Jordan	.15	.07
☐ 98 Brian Williams	.05	.02
☐ 99 Bob Zupcic	.05	.02
☐ 100 Ray Lankford	.25	.11

1993 Toys'R'Us Master Photos

This 12-card set of Stadium Club Master Photos was a bonus insert in the 1993 Toys'R'Us 100-card factory set. The photo cards measure approximately 5" by 7" with wide white borders with an inner prismatic gold-foil border. An action photo of the player is below a large colorful Toys 'R' Us logo with the words "Master Photo." The backs are blank, except for copyright symbols, licensing information, and MLBPA logo. The cards are unnumbered and checklisted below in alphabetical order.

	MINT	NRMT
COMPLETE SET (12)	5.00	2.20
COMMON CARD (1-12)	.10	.05
☐ 1 Moises Alou	.20	.09
☐ 2 Eric Anthony	.10	.05
☐ 3 Carlos Baerga	.20	.09
☐ 4 Willie Greene	.30	.14
☐ 5 Ken Griffey Jr.	2.50	1.10
☐ 6 Marquis Grissom	.20	.09
☐ 7 Chuck Knoblauch	.50	.23
☐ 8 Scott Livingstone	.10	.05
☐ 9 Sam Militello	.10	.05
☐ 10 Ivan Rodriguez	.50	.23
☐ 11 Gary Sheffield	.40	.18
☐ 12 Frank Thomas	2.00	.90

1992 Triple Play Previews

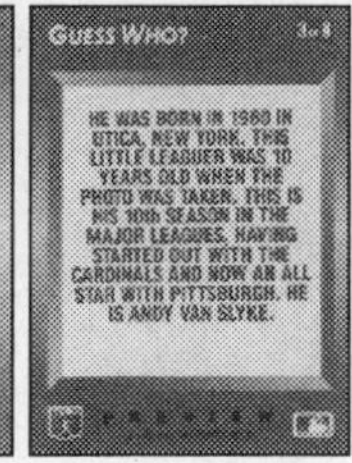

This eight-card standard-size set was issued by Donruss to preview the design of the 264-card 1992 Donruss Triple Play set. The front design and player photos are identical to those in the regular issue set; the only difference is the numbering and the word "preview" appearing across the bottom of the backs.

	MINT	NRMT
COMPLETE SET (8)	200.00	90.00
COMMON CARD (1-8)	5.00	2.20
☐ 1 Ken Griffey Jr.	70.00	32.00
☐ 2 Darryl Strawberry	8.00	3.60
☐ 3 Andy Van Slyke	8.00	3.60
☐ 4 Don Mattingly	35.00	16.00
☐ 5 Gary Carter Steve Finley Awesome Action	5.00	2.20
☐ 6 Frank Thomas	70.00	32.00
☐ 7 Kirby Puckett	40.00	18.00
☐ 8 David Cone John Franco Jeff Innis Fun at the Ballpark	5.00	2.20

1992 Triple Play

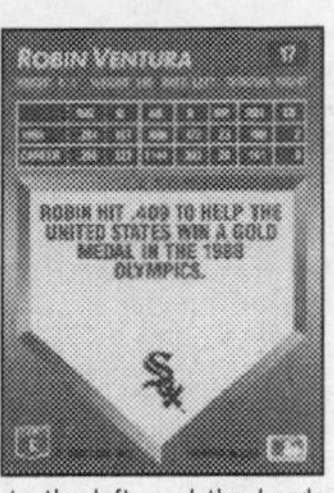

The 1992 Triple Play set contains 264 standard-size cards. Cards were distributed in 15-card foil packs and jumbo packs. Each 15-card foil pack came with one rub off game card. The Triple Play set was created especially for children ages 5-12, featuring bright color borders, player quotes, fun facts.The color action player photos on the fronts are slightly tilted to the left, and the border alternates shades from red to yellow and back to red again as one moves down the card face. Subsets include Little Hotshots (picturing some players when they were kids) and Awesome Action.

	MINT	NRMT
COMPLETE SET (264)	10.00	4.50
COMMON CARD (1-264)	.05	.02
☐ 1 SkyDome	.05	.02
☐ 2 Tom Foley	.05	.02
☐ 3 Scott Erickson	.05	.02
☐ 4 Matt Williams	.05	.02
☐ 5 David Valle	.05	.02
☐ 6 Andy Van Slyke LH	.05	.02
☐ 7 Tom Glavine	.05	.02
☐ 8 Kevin Appier	.05	.02
☐ 9 Pedro Guerrero	.05	.02
☐ 10 Terry Steinbach	.05	.02
☐ 11 Terry Mulholland	.05	.02
☐ 12 Mike Boddicker	.05	.02
☐ 13 Gregg Olson	.05	.02
☐ 14 Tim Burke	.05	.02
☐ 15 Candy Maldonado	.05	.02
☐ 16 Orlando Merced	.05	.02
☐ 17 Robin Ventura	.05	.02
☐ 18 Eric Anthony	.05	.02
☐ 19 Greg Maddux	.75	.35
☐ 20 Erik Hanson	.05	.02
☐ 21 Bobby Ojeda	.05	.02
☐ 22 Nolan Ryan	.75	.35
☐ 23 Dave Righetti	.05	.02
☐ 24 Reggie Jefferson	.05	.02
☐ 25 Jody Reed	.05	.02
☐ 26 Steve Finley and Gary Carter AA	.05	.02
☐ 27 Chili Davis	.05	.02
☐ 28 Hector Villanueva	.05	.02
☐ 29 Cecil Fielder	.05	.02
☐ 30 Hal Morris	.05	.02
☐ 31 Barry Larkin	.05	.02
☐ 32 Bobby Thigpen	.05	.02
☐ 33 Andy Benes	.05	.02
☐ 34 Harold Baines	.05	.02
☐ 35 David Cone	.05	.02
☐ 36 Mark Langston	.05	.02
☐ 37 Bryan Harvey	.05	.02
☐ 38 John Kruk	.05	.02
☐ 39 Scott Sanderson	.05	.02
☐ 40 Lonnie Smith	.05	.02
☐ 41 Rex Hudler AA	.05	.02
☐ 42 George Bell	.05	.02
☐ 43 Steve Finley	.05	.02
☐ 44 Mickey Tettleton	.05	.02
☐ 45 Robby Thompson	.05	.02
☐ 46 Pat Kelly	.05	.02
☐ 47 Marquis Grissom	.05	.02
☐ 48 Tony Pena	.05	.02
☐ 49 Alex Cole	.05	.02
☐ 50 Steve Buechele	.05	.02
☐ 51 Ivan Rodriguez	.40	.18
☐ 52 John Smiley	.05	.02
☐ 53 Gary Sheffield	.05	.02
☐ 54 Greg Olson	.05	.02
☐ 55 Ramon Martinez	.05	.02
☐ 56 B.J. Surhoff	.05	.02
☐ 57 Bruce Hurst	.05	.02
☐ 58 Todd Stottlemyre	.05	.02
☐ 59 Brett Butler	.05	.02
☐ 60 Glenn Davis	.05	.02
☐ 61 Glenn Braggs and Kirt Manwaring AA	.05	.02
☐ 62 Lee Smith	.05	.02
☐ 63 Rickey Henderson	.05	.02
☐ 64 Fun at the Ballpark Dave Cone Jeff Innis John Franco	.05	.02
☐ 65 Rick Aguilera	.05	.02
☐ 66 Kevin Elster	.05	.02
☐ 67 Dwight Evans	.05	.02
☐ 68 Andujar Cedeno	.05	.02
☐ 69 Brian McRae	.05	.02

☐ 70 Benito Santiago	.05	.02
☐ 71 Randy Johnson	.05	.02
☐ 72 Roberto Kelly	.05	.02
☐ 73 Juan Samuel AA	.05	.02
☐ 74 Alex Fernandez	.05	.02
☐ 75 Felix Jose	.05	.02
☐ 76 Brian Harper	.05	.02
☐ 77 Scott Sanderson LH	.05	.02
☐ 78 Ken Caminiti	.05	.02
☐ 79 Mo Vaughn	.40	.18
☐ 80 Roger McDowell	.05	.02
☐ 81 Robin Yount	.05	.02
☐ 82 Dave Magadan	.05	.02
☐ 83 Julio Franco	.05	.02
☐ 84 Roberto Alomar	.05	.02
☐ 85 Steve Avery	.05	.02
☐ 86 Travis Fryman	.05	.02
☐ 87 Fred McGriff	.05	.02
☐ 88 Dave Stewart	.05	.02
☐ 89 Larry Walker	.05	.02
☐ 90 Chris Sabo	.05	.02
☐ 91 Chuck Finley	.05	.02
☐ 92 Dennis Martinez	.05	.02
☐ 93 Jeff Johnson	.05	.02
☐ 94 Len Dykstra	.05	.02
☐ 95 Mark Whiten	.05	.02
☐ 96 Wade Taylor	.05	.02
☐ 97 Lance Dickson	.05	.02
☐ 98 Kevin Tapani	.05	.02
☐ 99 Luis Polonia and Tony Phillips AA	.05	.02
☐ 100 Milt Cuyler	.05	.02
☐ 101 Willie McGee	.05	.02
☐ 102 Tony Fernandez AA	.05	.02
☐ 103 Albert Belle	.50	.23
☐ 104 Todd Hundley	.05	.02
☐ 105 Ben McDonald	.05	.02
☐ 106 Doug Drabek	.05	.02
☐ 107 Tim Raines	.05	.02
☐ 108 Joe Carter	.05	.02
☐ 109 Reggie Sanders	.05	.02
☐ 110 John Olerud	.05	.02
☐ 111 Darren Lewis	.05	.02
☐ 112 Juan Gonzalez	.60	.25
☐ 113 Andre Dawson AA	.05	.02
☐ 114 Mark Grace	.05	.02
☐ 115 George Brett	.40	.18
☐ 116 Barry Bonds	.25	.11
☐ 117 Lou Whitaker	.05	.02
☐ 118 Jose Oquendo	.05	.02
☐ 119 Lee Stevens	.05	.02
☐ 120 Phil Plantier	.05	.02
☐ 121 Matt Merullo AA	.05	.02
☐ 122 Greg Vaughn	.05	.02
☐ 123 Royce Clayton	.05	.02
☐ 124 Bob Welch	.05	.02
☐ 125 Juan Samuel	.05	.02
☐ 126 Ron Gant	.05	.02
☐ 127 Edgar Martinez	.05	.02
☐ 128 Andy Ashby	.05	.02
☐ 129 Jack McDowell	.05	.02
☐ 130 Dave Henderson and Jerry Browne AA	.05	.02
☐ 131 Leo Gomez	.05	.02
☐ 132 Checklist 1-88	.05	.02
☐ 133 Phillie Phanatic	.05	.02
☐ 134 Bret Barberie	.05	.02
☐ 135 Kent Hrbek	.05	.02
☐ 136 Hall of Fame	.05	.02
☐ 137 Omar Vizquel	.05	.02
☐ 138 The Famous Chicken	.05	.02
☐ 139 Terry Pendleton	.05	.02
☐ 140 Jim Eisenreich	.05	.02
☐ 141 Todd Zeile	.05	.02
☐ 142 Todd Van Poppel	.05	.02
☐ 143 Darren Daulton	.05	.02
☐ 144 Mike Macfarlane	.05	.02
☐ 145 Luis Mercedes	.05	.02
☐ 146 Trevor Wilson	.05	.02
☐ 147 Dave Stieb	.05	.02
☐ 148 Andy Van Slyke	.05	.02
☐ 149 Carlton Fisk	.05	.02
☐ 150 Craig Biggio	.05	.02
☐ 151 Joe Girardi	.05	.02
☐ 152 Ken Griffey Jr.	1.50	.70
☐ 153 Jose Offerman	.05	.02
☐ 154 Bobby Witt	.05	.02
☐ 155 Will Clark	.05	.02
☐ 156 Steve Olin	.05	.02
☐ 157 Greg W. Harris	.05	.02
☐ 158 Dale Murphy LH	.05	.02
☐ 159 Don Mattingly	.50	.23
☐ 160 Shawon Dunston	.05	.02
☐ 161 Bill Gullickson	.05	.02
☐ 162 Paul O'Neill	.05	.02
☐ 163 Norm Charlton	.05	.02
☐ 164 Bo Jackson	.05	.02
☐ 165 Tony Fernandez	.05	.02
☐ 166 Dave Henderson	.05	.02
☐ 167 Dwight Gooden	.05	.02
☐ 168 Junior Felix	.05	.02
☐ 169 Lance Parrish	.05	.02
☐ 170 Pat Combs	.05	.02
☐ 171 Chuck Knoblauch	.05	.02
☐ 172 John Smoltz	.05	.02
☐ 173 Wrigley Field	.05	.02
☐ 174 Andre Dawson	.05	.02
☐ 175 Pete Harnisch	.05	.02
☐ 176 Alan Trammell	.15	.07
☐ 177 Kirk Dressendorfer	.05	.02
☐ 178 Matt Nokes	.05	.02
☐ 179 Wil Cordero	.05	.02
☐ 180 Scott Cooper	.05	.02
☐ 181 Glenallen Hill	.05	.02
☐ 182 John Franco	.05	.02
☐ 183 Rafael Palmeiro	.05	.02
☐ 184 Jay Bell	.05	.02
☐ 185 Bill Wegman	.05	.02
☐ 186 Deion Sanders	.05	.02
☐ 187 Darryl Strawberry	.05	.02
☐ 188 Jaime Navarro	.05	.02
☐ 189 Darrin Jackson	.05	.02
☐ 190 Eddie Zosky	.05	.02
☐ 191 Mike Scioscia	.05	.02
☐ 192 Chito Martinez	.05	.02
☐ 193 Pat Kelly and Ron Tingley AA	.05	.02
☐ 194 Ray Lankford	.05	.02
☐ 195 Dennis Eckersley	.05	.02
☐ 196 Ivan Calderon and Mike Maddux AA	.05	.02
☐ 197 Shane Mack	.05	.02
☐ 198 Checklist 89-176	.05	.02
☐ 199 Cal Ripken	.75	.35
☐ 200 Jeff Bagwell	.60	.25
☐ 201 Dave Howard	.05	.02
☐ 202 Kirby Puckett	.40	.18
☐ 203 Harold Reynolds	.05	.02
☐ 204 Jim Abbott	.05	.02
☐ 205 Mark Lewis	.05	.02
☐ 206 Frank Thomas	1.50	.70
☐ 207 Rex Hudler	.05	.02
☐ 208 Vince Coleman	.05	.02
☐ 209 Delino DeShields	.05	.02
☐ 210 Luis Gonzalez	.05	.02
☐ 211 Wade Boggs	.05	.02
☐ 212 Orel Hershiser	.05	.02
☐ 213 Cal Eldred	.05	.02
☐ 214 Jose Canseco	.05	.02
☐ 215 Jose Guzman	.05	.02
☐ 216 Roger Clemens	.20	.09
☐ 217 David Justice	.05	.02
☐ 218 Tony Phillips	.05	.02
☐ 219 Tony Gwynn	.40	.18
☐ 220 Mitch Williams	.05	.02
☐ 221 Bill Sampen	.05	.02
☐ 222 Billy Hatcher	.05	.02
☐ 223 Gary Gaetti	.05	.02
☐ 224 Tim Wallach	.05	.02
☐ 225 Kevin Maas	.05	.02
☐ 226 Kevin Brown	.05	.02
☐ 227 Sandy Alomar Jr.	.05	.02
☐ 228 John Habyan	.05	.02
☐ 229 Ryne Sandberg	.25	.11
☐ 230 Greg Gagne	.05	.02
☐ 231 Autographs (Mark McGwire)	.05	.02
☐ 232 Mike LaValliere	.05	.02
☐ 233 Mark Gubicza	.05	.02
☐ 234 Lance Parrish LH	.05	.02
☐ 235 Carlos Baerga	.05	.02
☐ 236 Howard Johnson	.05	.02
☐ 237 Mike Mussina	.30	.14
☐ 238 Ruben Sierra	.05	.02
☐ 239 Lance Johnson	.05	.02
☐ 240 Devon White	.05	.02
☐ 241 Dan Wilson	.05	.02
☐ 242 Kelly Gruber	.05	.02
☐ 243 Brett Butler LH	.05	.02
☐ 244 Ozzie Smith	.25	.11
☐ 245 Chuck McElroy	.05	.02
☐ 246 Shawn Boskie	.05	.02
☐ 247 Mark Davis	.05	.02
☐ 248 Bill Landrum	.05	.02
☐ 249 Frank Tanana	.05	.02
☐ 250 Darryl Hamilton	.05	.02
☐ 251 Gary DiSarcina	.05	.02
☐ 252 Mike Greenwell	.05	.02
☐ 253 Cal Ripken LH	.40	.18
☐ 254 Paul Molitor	.05	.02
☐ 255 Tim Teufel	.05	.02
☐ 256 Chris Hoiles	.05	.02
☐ 257 Rob Dibble	.05	.02
☐ 258 Sid Bream	.05	.02
☐ 259 Tino Martinez	.05	.02
☐ 260 Dale Murphy	.05	.02
☐ 261 Greg Hibbard	.05	.02
☐ 262 Mark McGwire	.30	.14
☐ 263 Oriole Park	.05	.02
☐ 264 Checklist 177-264	.05	.02

1992 Triple Play Gallery

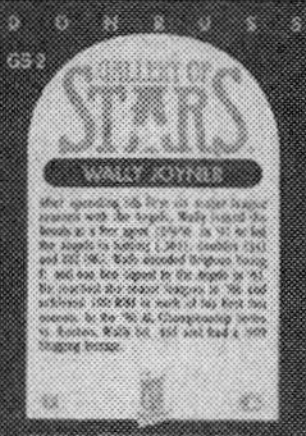

The 1992 Triple Play Gallery of Stars was an insert to the 1992 Triple Play baseball set. Randomly inserted into foil packs, the first six cards feature top players who changed teams in 1992 in their new uniforms. The second six cards were inserted one per jumbo pack. Each group of six cards is sequenced in alphabetical order. On bright-colored backgrounds, the fronts display color player portraits by noted sports artist Dick Perez. The words "Gallery of Stars" appear in a red and silver-foil stamped banner above the portrait, while the player's name appears in a similarly colored bar between two silver foil stars at the card bottom.

	MINT	NRMT
COMPLETE FOIL SET (6)	2.50	1.10
COMMON FOIL (GS1-GS6)	.50	.23
COMPLETE JUMBO SET (6)	18.00	8.00
COMMON JUMBO (GS7-GS12)	1.00	.45
☐ GS1 Bobby Bonilla	.60	.25
☐ GS2 Wally Joyner	.60	.25
☐ GS3 Jack Morris	.60	.25
☐ GS4 Steve Sax	.50	.23
☐ GS5 Danny Tartabull	.50	.23
☐ GS6 Frank Viola	.50	.23
☐ GS7 Jeff Bagwell	4.00	1.80
☐ GS8 Ken Griffey Jr.	6.00	2.70
☐ GS9 Dave Justice	1.00	.45
☐ GS10 Ryan Klesko	3.00	1.35
☐ GS11 Cal Ripken	5.00	2.20
☐ GS12 Frank Thomas	5.00	2.20

1993 Triple Play Previews

This 12-card set was issued by Donruss to preview the design of the 264-card 1993 Donruss Triple Play set. The front design and player photos are identical to those in the regular issue with the exception of the word "Preview" printed on the card.

	MINT	NRMT
COMPLETE SET (12)	100.00	45.00
COMMON CARD (1-12)	1.00	.45
☐ 1 Ken Griffey Jr.	50.00	22.00
☐ 2 Roberto Alomar	7.50	3.40
☐ 3 Cal Ripken	40.00	18.00
☐ 4 Eric Karros	3.00	1.35
☐ 5 Cecil Fielder	2.00	.90
☐ 6 Gary Sheffield	5.00	2.20
☐ 7 Darren Daulton	2.00	.90
☐ 8 Andy Van Slyke	1.00	.45
☐ 9 Dennis Eckersley	3.00	1.35
☐ 10 Ryne Sandberg	12.50	5.50
☐ 11 Mark Grace	5.00	2.20
☐ 12 David Segui Luis Polonia Awesome Action	1.00	.45

1993 Triple Play

The 1993 Donruss Triple Play baseball set consists of 264 standard-size cards. Approximately eight players from each of the 28 teams is represented in the set. Eack pack also included one of thirty Triple Play Action Baseball game cards. The fronts display color action player photos inside a red frame on a black card face. The player's last name appears in silver block lettering across the top of the picture. The team logo is placed at the lower right corner. The horizontal backs feature a color close-up photo, biography, and either trivia questions, fun facts, or player quotes. Scattered throughout the set are seven Little Hotshot (11, 77, 97, 143, 209, 229, 245) and eight

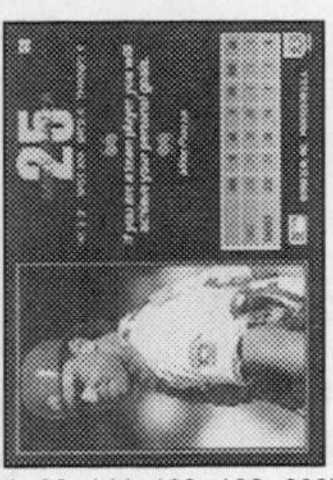

Awesome Action (12, 61, 64, 68, 144, 193, 196, 200) cards. There are no key Rookie Cards in this set, however the set does feature the first card of President Bill Clinton.

	MINT	NRMT
COMPLETE SET (264)	10.00	4.50
COMMON CARD (1-264)	.05	.02
☐ 1 Ken Griffey Jr.	2.00	.90
☐ 2 Roberto Alomar	.15	.07
☐ 3 Cal Ripken	1.50	.70
☐ 4 Eric Karros	.20	.09
☐ 5 Cecil Fielder	.20	.09
☐ 6 Gary Sheffield	.15	.07
☐ 7 Darren Daulton	.20	.09
☐ 8 Andy Van Slyke	.20	.09
☐ 9 Dennis Eckersley	.30	.14
☐ 10 Ryne Sandberg	.50	.23
☐ 11 Mark Grace LH	.30	.14
☐ 12 David Segui and	.05	.02
Luis Polonia AA		
☐ 13 Mike Mussina	.15	.07
☐ 14 Vince Coleman	.05	.02
☐ 15 Rafael Belliard	.05	.02
☐ 16 Ivan Rodriguez	.50	.23
☐ 17 Eddie Taubensee	.05	.02
☐ 18 Cal Eldred	.05	.02
☐ 19 Rick Wilkins	.05	.02
☐ 20 Edgar Martinez	.30	.14
☐ 21 Brian McRae	.05	.02
☐ 22 Darren Holmes	.05	.02
☐ 23 Mark Whiten	.05	.02
☐ 24 Todd Zeile	.05	.02
☐ 25 Scott Cooper	.05	.02
☐ 26 Frank Thomas	2.00	.90
☐ 27 Wil Cordero	.05	.02
☐ 28 Juan Guzman	.05	.02
☐ 29 Pedro Astacio	.05	.02
☐ 30 Steve Avery	.05	.02
☐ 31 Barry Larkin	.30	.14
☐ 32 Bill Clinton	1.00	.45
☐ 33 Scott Erickson	.05	.02
☐ 34 Mike Devereaux	.05	.02
☐ 35 Tino Martinez	.15	.07
☐ 36 Brent Mayne	.05	.02
☐ 37 Tim Salmon	.50	.23
☐ 38 Dave Hollins	.05	.02
☐ 39 Royce Clayton	.20	.09
☐ 40 Shawon Dunston	.05	.02
☐ 41 Eddie Murray	.15	.07
☐ 42 Larry Walker	.15	.07
☐ 43 Jeff Bagwell	.75	.35
☐ 44 Milt Cuyler	.05	.02
☐ 45 Mike Bordick	.05	.02
☐ 46 Mike Greenwell	.05	.02
☐ 47 Steve Sax	.05	.02
☐ 48 Chuck Knoblauch	.15	.07
☐ 49 Charles Nagy	.20	.09
☐ 50 Tim Wakefield	.20	.09
☐ 51 Tony Gwynn	.75	.35
☐ 52 Rob Dibble	.05	.02
☐ 53 Mickey Morandini	.05	.02
☐ 54 Steve Hosey	.05	.02
☐ 55 Mike Piazza	2.00	.90
☐ 56 Bill Wegman	.05	.02
☐ 57 Kevin Maas	.05	.02
☐ 58 Gary DiSarcina	.05	.02
☐ 59 Travis Fryman	.20	.09
☐ 60 Ruben Sierra	.05	.02
☐ 61 Ken Caminiti AA	.15	.07
☐ 62 Brian Jordan	.30	.14
☐ 63 Scott Chiamparino	.05	.02
☐ 64 George Brett and	.15	.07
Mike Bordick AA		
☐ 65 Carlos Garcia	.05	.02
☐ 66 Checklist	.05	.02
☐ 67 John Smoltz	.30	.14
☐ 68 Mark McGwire and	.15	.07
Brian Harper AA		
☐ 69 Kurt Stillwell	.05	.02
☐ 70 Chad Curtis	.20	.09
☐ 71 Rafael Palmeiro	.30	.14
☐ 72 Kevin Young	.05	.02
☐ 73 Glenn Davis	.05	.02
☐ 74 Dennis Martinez	.20	.09
☐ 75 Sam Militello	.05	.02
☐ 76 Mike Morgan	.05	.02
☐ 77 Frank Thomas LH	1.00	.45
☐ 78 Staying Fit	.05	.02
☐ 79 Steve Buechele	.05	.02
☐ 80 Carlos Baerga	.20	.09
☐ 81 Robby Thompson	.05	.02
☐ 82 Kirk McCaskill	.05	.02
☐ 83 Lee Smith	.20	.09
☐ 84 Gary Scott	.05	.02
☐ 85 Tony Pena	.05	.02
☐ 86 Howard Johnson	.05	.02
☐ 87 Mark McGwire	.60	.25
☐ 88 Bip Roberts	.05	.02
☐ 89 Devon White	.05	.02
☐ 90 John Franco	.05	.02
☐ 91 Tom Browning	.05	.02
☐ 92 Mickey Tettleton	.05	.02
☐ 93 Jeff Conine	.20	.09
☐ 94 Albert Belle	.75	.35
☐ 95 Fred McGriff	.30	.14
☐ 96 Nolan Ryan	1.50	.70
☐ 97 Paul Molitor LH	.20	.09
☐ 98 Juan Bell	.05	.02
☐ 99 Dave Fleming	.05	.02
☐ 100 Craig Biggio	.30	.14
☐ 101A Andy Stankiewicz ERR	.20	.09
(Name on front in white)		
☐ 101B Andy Stankiewicz ERR	.20	.09
(Name on front in red)		
☐ 102 Delino DeShields	.05	.02
☐ 103 Damion Easley	.05	.02
☐ 104 Kevin McReynolds	.05	.02
☐ 105 David Nied	.05	.02
☐ 106 Rick Sutcliffe	.05	.02
☐ 107 Will Clark	.30	.14
☐ 108 Tim Raines	.20	.09
☐ 109 Eric Anthony	.05	.02
☐ 110 Mike LaValliere	.05	.02
☐ 111 Dean Palmer	.20	.09
☐ 112 Eric Davis	.20	.09
☐ 113 Damon Berryhill	.05	.02
☐ 114 Felix Jose	.05	.02
☐ 115 Ozzie Guillen	.05	.02
☐ 116 Pat Listach	.05	.02
☐ 117 Tom Glavine	.30	.14
☐ 118 Roger Clemens	.40	.18
☐ 119 Dave Henderson	.05	.02
☐ 120 Don Mattingly	1.00	.45
☐ 121 Orel Hershiser	.20	.09
☐ 122 Ozzie Smith	.50	.23
☐ 123 Joe Carter	.20	.09
☐ 124 Bret Saberhagen	.05	.02
☐ 125 Mitch Williams	.05	.02
☐ 126 Jerald Clark	.05	.02
☐ 127 Mile High Stadium	.20	.09
☐ 128 Kent Hrbek	.20	.09
☐ 129 Equipment	.20	.09
Curt Schilling		
☐ 130 Gregg Jefferies	.20	.09
☐ 131 John Orton	.05	.02
☐ 132 Checklist	.05	.02
☐ 133 Bret Boone	.05	.02
☐ 134 Pat Borders	.05	.02
☐ 135 Gregg Olson	.05	.02
☐ 136 Brett Butler	.20	.09
☐ 137 Rob Deer	.05	.02
☐ 138 Darrin Jackson	.05	.02
☐ 139 John Kruk	.20	.09
☐ 140 Jay Bell	.20	.09
☐ 141 Bobby Witt	.05	.02
☐ 142 Dan Plesac	.05	.02
Randy Myers		
Jose Guzman		
New Cubs		
☐ 143 Wade Boggs LH	.15	.07
☐ 144 Ken Lofton AA	.15	.07
☐ 145 Ben McDonald	.05	.02
☐ 146 Dwight Gooden	.20	.09
☐ 147 Terry Pendleton	.20	.09
☐ 148 Julio Franco	.20	.09
☐ 149 Ken Caminiti	.30	.14
☐ 150 Greg Vaughn	.05	.02
☐ 151 Sammy Sosa	.15	.07
☐ 152 David Valle	.05	.02
☐ 153 Wally Joyner	.20	.09
☐ 154 Dante Bichette	.30	.14
☐ 155 Mark Lewis	.05	.02
☐ 156 Bob Tewksbury	.05	.02
☐ 157 Billy Hatcher	.05	.02
☐ 158 Jack McDowell	.05	.02
☐ 159 Marquis Grissom	.20	.09
☐ 160 Jack Morris	.20	.09
☐ 161 Ramon Martinez	.20	.09
☐ 162 Deion Sanders	.15	.07
☐ 163 Tim Belcher	.05	.02
☐ 164 Mascots	.05	.02
Pirate Parrot		
☐ 165 Scott Leius	.05	.02
☐ 166 Brady Anderson	.30	.14
☐ 167 Randy Johnson	.15	.07
☐ 168 Mark Gubicza	.05	.02
☐ 169 Chuck Finley	.05	.02
☐ 170 Terry Mulholland	.05	.02
☐ 171 Matt Williams	.30	.14
☐ 172 Dwight Smith	.05	.02
☐ 173 Bobby Bonilla	.20	.09
☐ 174 Ken Hill	.20	.09
☐ 175 Doug Jones	.05	.02
☐ 176 Tony Phillips	.05	.02
☐ 177 Terry Steinbach	.20	.09
☐ 178 Frank Viola	.05	.02
☐ 179 Robin Ventura	.20	.09
☐ 180 Shane Mack	.05	.02
☐ 181 Kenny Lofton	.75	.35
☐ 182 Jeff King	.20	.09
☐ 183 Tim Teufel	.05	.02
☐ 184 Chris Sabo	.05	.02
☐ 185 Len Dykstra	.20	.09
☐ 186 Trevor Wilson	.05	.02
☐ 187 Darryl Strawberry	.20	.09
☐ 188 Robin Yount	.30	.14
☐ 189 Bob Wickman	.05	.02
☐ 190 Luis Polonia	.05	.02
☐ 191 Alan Trammell	.30	.14
☐ 192 Bob Welch	.05	.02
☐ 193 Omar Vizquel AA	.20	.09
☐ 194 Tom Pagnozzi	.05	.02
☐ 195 Bret Barberie	.05	.02
☐ 196 Mike Scioscia AA	.05	.02
☐ 197 Randy Tomlin	.05	.02
☐ 198 Checklist	.05	.02
☐ 199 Ron Gant	.20	.09
☐ 200 Roberto Alomar AA	.30	.14
☐ 201 Andy Benes	.20	.09
☐ 202 Six Pirates Playing	.05	.02
Pepper		
☐ 203 Steve Finley	.20	.09
☐ 204 Steve Olin	.05	.02
☐ 205 Chris Hoiles	.05	.02
☐ 206 John Wetteland	.20	.09
☐ 207 Danny Tartabull	.05	.02
☐ 208 Bernard Gilkey	.20	.09
☐ 209 Tom Glavine LH	.30	.14
☐ 210 Benito Santiago	.05	.02
☐ 211 Mark Grace	.30	.14
☐ 212 Glenallen Hill	.05	.02
☐ 213 Jeff Brantley	.05	.02
☐ 214 George Brett	.75	.35
☐ 215 Mark Lemke	.05	.02
☐ 216 Ron Karkovice	.05	.02
☐ 217 Tom Brunansky	.05	.02
☐ 218 Todd Hundley	.30	.14
☐ 219 Rickey Henderson	.30	.14
☐ 220 Joe Oliver	.05	.02
☐ 221 Juan Gonzalez	1.00	.45
☐ 222 John Olerud	.05	.02
☐ 223 Hal Morris	.05	.02
☐ 224 Lou Whitaker	.20	.09
☐ 225 Bryan Harvey	.05	.02
☐ 226 Mike Gallego	.05	.02
☐ 227 Willie McGee	.05	.02
☐ 228 Jose Oquendo	.05	.02
☐ 229 Darren Daulton LH	.20	.09
☐ 230 Curt Schilling	.20	.09
☐ 231 Jay Buhner	.30	.14
☐ 232 Doug Drabek	.05	.02
Greg Swindell		
New Astros		
☐ 233 Jaime Navarro	.05	.02
☐ 234 Kevin Appier	.20	.09
☐ 235 Mark Langston	.05	.02
☐ 236 Jeff Montgomery	.20	.09
☐ 237 Joe Girardi	.05	.02
☐ 238 Ed Sprague	.05	.02
☐ 239 Dan Walters	.05	.02
☐ 240 Kevin Tapani	.05	.02
☐ 241 Pete Harnisch	.05	.02
☐ 242 Al Martin	.20	.09
☐ 243 Jose Canseco	.30	.14
☐ 244 Moises Alou	.20	.09
☐ 245 Mark McGwire LH	.15	.07
☐ 246 Luis Rivera	.05	.02
☐ 247 George Bell	.05	.02
☐ 248 B.J. Surhoff	.20	.09
☐ 249 David Justice	.15	.07
☐ 250 Brian Harper	.05	.02
☐ 251 Sandy Alomar Jr.	.20	.09
☐ 252 Kevin Brown	.20	.09
☐ 253 Tim Wallach	.05	.02
Todd Worrell		
Jody Reed		
New Dodgers		

	MINT	NRMT
☐ 254 Ray Lankford	.30	.14
☐ 255 Derek Bell	.20	.09
☐ 256 Joe Grahe	.05	.02
☐ 257 Charlie Hayes	.05	.02
☐ 258 Wade Boggs Jim Abbott New Yankees	.15	.07
☐ 259A Joe Robbie Stadium ERR (Misnumbered 129)	.20	.09
☐ 259B Joe Robbie Stadium COR	.20	.09
☐ 260 Kirby Puckett	.75	.35
☐ 261 Jay Bell Fun at the Ballpark	.05	.02
☐ 262 Bill Swift	.05	.02
☐ 263 Roger McDowell Fun at the Ballpark	.05	.02
☐ 264 Checklist	.05	.02

1993 Triple Play Action

The 1993 Triple Play Action set was inserted one per pack of Triple Play. The cards were designed to serve as a game card with a scratch-off section inside beside a baseball diamond design. The cards are printed on a lighter weight card stock. When unfolded the cards measure approximately 5" by 3 1/2", however when folded they measure the standard size. The front of the folded card features a color action player shot with a wide vertical gray border across the top. Within the upper border are the set title and the words "Action Baseball" printed in black. The player pictured on the card front is not named. Two team logos are superimposed across the photo at the bottom indicating which teams are paired up to play the scratch-off game inside. The inner portion of the card has six game rules printed on the upper left side followed by 32 scratch-off boxes. On the inner right side is a scoreboard printed above a green background baseball diamond. The backs are silver with the Leaf logo printed at the bottom.

	MINT	NRMT
COMPLETE SET (30)	10.00	4.50
COMMON CARD (1-30)	.10	.05
☐ 1 Andy Van Slyke	.10	.05
☐ 2 Bobby Bonilla	.20	.09
☐ 3 Ozzie Smith	.50	.23
☐ 4 Ryne Sandberg	.50	.23
☐ 5 Darren Daulton	.20	.09
☐ 6 Larry Walker	.40	.18
☐ 7 Eric Karros	.20	.09
☐ 8 Barry Larkin	.30	.14
☐ 9 Deion Sanders	.40	.18
☐ 10 Gary Sheffield	.40	.18
☐ 11 Will Clark	.30	.14
☐ 12 Jeff Bagwell	.75	.35
☐ 13 Roberto Alomar	.40	.18
☐ 14 Roger Clemens	.40	.18
☐ 15 Cecil Fielder	.20	.09
☐ 16 Robin Yount	.30	.14
☐ 17 Cal Ripken	1.50	.70
☐ 18 Carlos Baerga	.10	.05
☐ 19 Don Mattingly	1.00	.45
☐ 20 Kirby Puckett	.75	.35
☐ 21 Frank Thomas	2.00	.90
☐ 22 Juan Gonzalez	1.00	.45
☐ 23 Mark McGwire	.60	.25
☐ 24 Ken Griffey Jr.	2.00	.90
☐ 25 Wally Joyner	.20	.09
☐ 26 Chad Curtis	.10	.05
☐ 27 Rockies Vs. Marlins	.10	.05
☐ 28 Juan Guzman	.10	.05
☐ 29 David Justice	.40	.18
☐ 30 Joe Carter	.30	.14

1993 Triple Play Gallery

A one per pack insert in 1993 Donruss Triple Play jumbo packs, these ten standard-size cards have fronts that feature color player portraits by noted sports artist Dick

Perez. The words "Gallery of Stars" printed in gold foil appear near the top, and the player's name, also in gold foil, rests at the bottom. The backs have a gray-bordered, white rectangle with rounded corners that carries the player's career highlights and team logo. The set name appears above in yellow lettering. The cards are numbered on the back with a "GS" prefix.

	MINT	NRMT
COMPLETE SET (10)	20.00	9.00
COMMON CARD (GS1-GS10)	1.50	.70
☐ GS1 Barry Bonds	5.00	2.20
☐ GS2 Andre Dawson	2.50	1.10
☐ GS3 Wade Boggs	3.00	1.35
☐ GS4 Greg Maddux	12.00	5.50
☐ GS5 Dave Winfield	2.50	1.10
☐ GS6 Paul Molitor	4.00	1.80
☐ GS7 Jim Abbott	1.50	.70
☐ GS8 J.T. Snow	3.00	1.35
☐ GS9 Benito Santiago	1.50	.70
☐ GS10 David Nied	1.50	.70

1993 Triple Play League Leaders

Randomly inserted in magazine distributor packs only, the six standard-size cards comprising this set feature borderless color action player shots on both sides. A National League leader appears on one side, an American League leader is on the other. The player's league appears in gold-foil lettering across the top. The player's name in white cursive lettering is displayed near the bottom within the set logo, which has a simulated black marble plaque design. The cards are numbered on the American League side with an "L" prefix.

	MINT	NRMT
COMPLETE SET (6)	35.00	16.00
COMMON PAIR (L1-L6)	3.00	1.35
☐ L1 Barry Bonds Dennis Eckersley	6.00	2.70
☐ L2 Greg Maddux Dennis Eckersley	15.00	6.75
☐ L3 Eric Karros Pat Listach	3.00	1.35
☐ L4 Fred McGriff Juan Gonzalez	15.00	6.75
☐ L5 Darren Daulton Cecil Fielder	4.00	1.80
☐ L6 Gary Sheffield Edgar Martinez	5.00	2.20

1993 Triple Play Nicknames

Randomly inserted in foil packs only, this ten-card standard-size set is a new insert set featuring popular player's nicknames. The borderless fronts feature color player action shots. The player's name appears at the bottom, within an irregular red stripe that simulates a stroke of a paintbrush. His nickname appears in large prismatic-foil lettering at the top of the photo. The white back shades to red near the bottom and carries the player's last name in large purplish letters at the top. His first name appears in smaller white cursive lettering superposed upon his last name. The player's biography,

set off by thin black lines, is shown below. A color player action shot appears beneath on the left side, and his career highlights are shown alongside on the right. The player's team logo at the bottom rounds out the card.

	MINT	NRMT
COMPLETE SET (10)	35.00	16.00
COMMON CARD (1-10)	1.00	.45
☐ 1 Frank Thomas Big Hurt	8.00	3.60
☐ 2 Roger Clemens Rocket	3.00	1.35
☐ 3 Ryne Sandberg Ryno	3.00	1.35
☐ 4 Will Clark Thrill	1.25	.55
☐ 5 Ken Griffey Jr. Junior	10.00	4.50
☐ 6 Dwight Gooden	1.00	.45
☐ 7 Nolan Ryan Express	8.00	3.60
☐ 8 Deion Sanders Prime Time	2.00	.90
☐ 9 Ozzie Smith Wizard	3.00	1.35
☐ 10 Fred McGriff Crime Dog	1.50	.70

1994 Triple Play Promos

These ten standard-size promos feature on their fronts color player-action shots that are borderless, except at the bottom, where the player's name appears within a colored stripe. The horizontal back carries a posed color player photo on the left side. On the right, beneath the player's name and position, appear biography, statistics, and career highlights on a white background highlighted by his team's ghosted logo. The "Promotional Sample" disclaimer is stenciled obliquely across the front and back.

	MINT	NRMT
COMPLETE SET (10)	15.00	6.75
COMMON CARD (1-10)	.50	.23
☐ 1 Juan Gonzalez	2.00	.90
☐ 2 Frank Thomas	3.00	1.35
☐ 3 Barry Bonds	1.00	.45
☐ 4 Ken Griffey Jr.	4.00	1.80
☐ 5 Paul Molitor	.75	.35
☐ 6 Mike Piazza	2.50	1.10
☐ 7 Tim Salmon	1.00	.45
☐ 8 Lenny Dykstra	.50	.23
☐ 9 Don Mattingly	1.50	.70
☐ 10 Greg Maddux	2.50	1.10

1994 Triple Play

The 1994 Triple Play set consists of 300 standard-size cards, featuring ten players from each team along with a 17-card Rookie Review set. The fronts have color player action shots that are borderless, except at the bottom, where the player's name appears within a colored stripe. The horizontal back carries a posed color player photo on the left side. On the right, beneath the player's name and position, appear biography, statistics, and career highlights on a white background highlighted by his

team's ghosted logo. Triple Play game cards, reedemable for various prizes, were inserted one per pack.

	MINT	NRMT
COMPLETE SET (300)	15.00	6.75
COMMON CARD (1-300)	.05	.02

Card	MINT	NRMT
☐ 1 Mike Bordick	.05	.02
☐ 2 Dennis Eckersley	.30	.14
☐ 3 Brent Gates	.05	.02
☐ 4 Rickey Henderson	.30	.14
☐ 5 Mark McGwire	.60	.25
☐ 6 Troy Neel	.05	.02
☐ 7 Craig Paquette	.05	.02
☐ 8 Ruben Sierra	.05	.02
☐ 9 Terry Steinbach	.20	.09
☐ 10 Bobby Witt	.05	.02
☐ 11 Chad Curtis	.05	.02
☐ 12 Chili Davis	.20	.09
☐ 13 Gary DiSarcina	.05	.02
☐ 14 Damion Easley	.05	.02
☐ 15 Chuck Finley	.05	.02
☐ 16 Joe Grahe	.05	.02
☐ 17 Mark Langston	.05	.02
☐ 18 Eduardo Perez	.05	.02
☐ 19 Tim Salmon	.40	.18
☐ 20 J.T. Snow	.20	.09
☐ 21 Jeff Bagwell	.75	.35
☐ 22 Craig Biggio	.30	.14
☐ 23 Ken Caminiti	.40	.18
☐ 24 Andujar Cedeno	.05	.02
☐ 25 Doug Drabek	.05	.02
☐ 26 Steve Finley	.20	.09
☐ 27 Luis Gonzalez	.05	.02
☐ 28 Pete Harnisch	.05	.02
☐ 29 Darryl Kile	.20	.09
☐ 30 Mitch Williams	.05	.02
☐ 31 Roberto Alomar	.40	.18
☐ 32 Joe Carter	.20	.09
☐ 33 Juan Guzman	.05	.02
☐ 34 Pat Hentgen	.20	.09
☐ 35 Paul Molitor	.40	.18
☐ 36 John Olerud	.20	.09
☐ 37 Ed Sprague	.05	.02
☐ 38 Dave Stewart	.20	.09
☐ 39 Duane Ward	.05	.02
☐ 40 Devon White	.05	.02
☐ 41 Steve Avery	.05	.02
☐ 42 Jeff Blauser	.05	.02
☐ 43 Ron Gant	.20	.09
☐ 44 Tom Glavine	.30	.14
☐ 45 David Justice	.40	.18
☐ 46 Greg Maddux	1.25	.55
☐ 47 Fred McGriff	.30	.14
☐ 48 Terry Pendleton	.20	.09
☐ 49 Deion Sanders	.40	.18
☐ 50 John Smoltz	.30	.14
☐ 51 Ricky Bones	.05	.02
☐ 52 Cal Eldred	.05	.02
☐ 53 Darryl Hamilton	.05	.02
☐ 54 John Jaha	.05	.02
☐ 55 Pat Listach	.05	.02
☐ 56 Jaime Navarro	.05	.02
☐ 57 Dave Nilsson	.20	.09
☐ 58 B.J. Surhoff	.05	.02
☐ 59 Greg Vaughn	.05	.02
☐ 60 Robin Yount	.30	.14
☐ 61 Bernard Gilkey	.20	.09
☐ 62 Gregg Jefferies	.20	.09
☐ 63 Brian Jordan	.20	.09
☐ 64 Ray Lankford	.30	.14
☐ 65 Tom Pagnozzi	.05	.02
☐ 66 Ozzie Smith	.50	.23
☐ 67 Bob Tewksbury	.05	.02
☐ 68 Allen Watson	.05	.02
☐ 69 Mark Whiten	.05	.02
☐ 70 Todd Zeile	.05	.02
☐ 71 Steve Buechele	.05	.02
☐ 72 Mark Grace	.30	.14
☐ 73 Jose Guzman	.05	.02
☐ 74 Derrick May	.05	.02
☐ 75 Mike Morgan	.05	.02
☐ 76 Randy Myers	.05	.02
☐ 77 Ryne Sandberg	.50	.23
☐ 78 Sammy Sosa	.40	.18
☐ 79 Jose Vizcaino	.05	.02
☐ 80 Rick Wilkins	.05	.02
☐ 81 Pedro Astacio	.05	.02
☐ 82 Brett Butler	.20	.09
☐ 83 Delino DeShields	.05	.02
☐ 84 Orel Hershiser	.20	.09
☐ 85 Eric Karros	.20	.09
☐ 86 Ramon Martinez	.20	.09
☐ 87 Jose Offerman	.05	.02
☐ 88 Mike Piazza	1.25	.55
☐ 89 Darryl Strawberry	.20	.09
☐ 90 Tim Wallach	.05	.02
☐ 91 Moises Alou	.20	.09
☐ 92 Wil Cordero	.05	.02
☐ 93 Jeff Fassero	.05	.02
☐ 94 Darrin Fletcher	.05	.02
☐ 95 Marquis Grissom	.20	.09
☐ 96 Ken Hill	.05	.02
☐ 97 Mike Lansing	.20	.09
☐ 98 Kirk Rueter	.05	.02
☐ 99 Larry Walker	.40	.18
☐ 100 John Wetteland	.20	.09
☐ 101 Rod Beck	.20	.09
☐ 102 Barry Bonds	.50	.23
☐ 103 John Burkett	.05	.02
☐ 104 Royce Clayton	.20	.09
☐ 105 Darren Lewis	.05	.02
☐ 106 Kirt Manwaring	.05	.02
☐ 107 Willie McGee	.05	.02
☐ 108 Bill Swift	.05	.02
☐ 109 Robby Thompson	.05	.02
☐ 110 Matt Williams	.30	.14
☐ 111 Sandy Alomar Jr.	.20	.09
☐ 112 Carlos Baerga	.20	.09
☐ 113 Albert Belle	.75	.35
☐ 114 Wayne Kirby	.05	.02
☐ 115 Kenny Lofton	.60	.25
☐ 116 Jose Mesa	.20	.09
☐ 117 Eddie Murray	.40	.18
☐ 118 Charles Nagy	.20	.09
☐ 119 Paul Sorrento	.05	.02
☐ 120 Jim Thome	.50	.23
☐ 121 Rich Amaral	.05	.02
☐ 122 Eric Anthony	.05	.02
☐ 123 Mike Blowers	.05	.02
☐ 124 Chris Bosio	.05	.02
☐ 125 Jay Buhner	.30	.14
☐ 126 Dave Fleming	.05	.02
☐ 127 Ken Griffey Jr.	2.00	.90
☐ 128 Randy Johnson	.40	.18
☐ 129 Edgar Martinez	.30	.14
☐ 130 Tino Martinez	.40	.18
☐ 131 Bret Barberie	.05	.02
☐ 132 Ryan Bowen	.05	.02
☐ 133 Chuck Carr	.05	.02
☐ 134 Jeff Conine	.20	.09
☐ 135 Orestes Destrade	.05	.02
☐ 136 Chris Hammond	.05	.02
☐ 137 Bryan Harvey	.05	.02
☐ 138 Dave Magadan	.05	.02
☐ 139 Benito Santiago	.05	.02
☐ 140 Gary Sheffield	.40	.18
☐ 141 Bobby Bonilla	.20	.09
☐ 142 Jeromy Burnitz	.20	.09
☐ 143 Dwight Gooden	.20	.09
☐ 144 Todd Hundley	.20	.09
☐ 145 Bobby Jones	.20	.09
☐ 146 Jeff Kent	.05	.02
☐ 147 Joe Orsulak	.05	.02
☐ 148 Bret Saberhagen	.05	.02
☐ 149 Pete Schourek	.05	.02
☐ 150 Ryan Thompson	.05	.02
☐ 151 Brady Anderson	.30	.14
☐ 152 Harold Baines	.20	.09
☐ 153 Mike Devereaux	.05	.02
☐ 154 Chris Hoiles	.05	.02
☐ 155 Ben McDonald	.05	.02
☐ 156 Mark McLemore	.05	.02
☐ 157 Mike Mussina	.30	.14
☐ 158 Rafael Palmeiro	.30	.14
☐ 159 Cal Ripken	1.50	.70
☐ 160 Chris Sabo	.05	.02
☐ 161 Brad Ausmus	.05	.02
☐ 162 Derek Bell	.20	.09
☐ 163 Andy Benes	.20	.09
☐ 164 Doug Brocail	.05	.02
☐ 165 Archi Cianfrocco	.05	.02
☐ 166 Ricky Gutierrez	.05	.02
☐ 167 Tony Gwynn	.75	.35
☐ 168 Gene Harris	.05	.02
☐ 169 Pedro Martinez	.05	.02
☐ 170 Phil Plantier	.05	.02
☐ 171 Darren Daulton	.20	.09
☐ 172 Mariano Duncan	.05	.02
☐ 173 Lenny Dykstra	.20	.09
☐ 174 Tommy Greene	.05	.02
☐ 175 Dave Hollins	.05	.02
☐ 176 Danny Jackson	.05	.02
☐ 177 John Kruk	.20	.09
☐ 178 Terry Mulholland	.05	.02
☐ 179 Curt Schilling	.20	.09
☐ 180 Kevin Stocker	.05	.02
☐ 181 Jay Bell	.20	.09
☐ 182 Steve Cooke	.05	.02
☐ 183 Carlos Garcia	.05	.02
☐ 184 Joel Johnston	.05	.02
☐ 185 Jeff King	.20	.09
☐ 186 Al Martin	.05	.02
☐ 187 Orlando Merced	.05	.02
☐ 188 Don Slaught	.05	.02
☐ 189 Andy Van Slyke	.20	.09
☐ 190 Kevin Young	.05	.02
☐ 191 Kevin Brown	.20	.09
☐ 192 Jose Canseco	.30	.14
☐ 193 Will Clark	.30	.14
☐ 194 Juan Gonzalez	1.00	.45
☐ 195 Tom Henke	.05	.02
☐ 196 David Hulse	.05	.02
☐ 197 Dean Palmer	.20	.09
☐ 198 Roger Pavlik	.05	.02
☐ 199 Ivan Rodriguez	.50	.23
☐ 200 Kenny Rogers	.05	.02
☐ 201 Roger Clemens	.40	.18
☐ 202 Scott Cooper	.05	.02
☐ 203 Andre Dawson	.30	.14
☐ 204 Mike Greenwell	.05	.02
☐ 205 BIlly Hatcher	.05	.02
☐ 206 Jeff Russell	.05	.02
☐ 207 Aaron Sele	.05	.02
☐ 208 John Valentin	.20	.09
☐ 209 Mo Vaughn	.50	.23
☐ 210 Frank Viola	.05	.02
☐ 211 Rob Dibble	.05	.02
☐ 212 Willie Greene	.20	.09
☐ 213 Roberto Kelly	.05	.02
☐ 214 Barry Larkin	.30	.14
☐ 215 Kevin Mitchell	.05	.02
☐ 216 Hal Morris	.05	.02
☐ 217 Joe Oliver	.05	.02
☐ 218 Jose Rijo	.05	.02
☐ 219 Reggie Sanders	.05	.02
☐ 220 John Smiley	.05	.02
☐ 221 Dante Bichette	.30	.14
☐ 222 Ellis Burks	.20	.09
☐ 223 Andres Galarraga	.30	.14
☐ 224 Joe Girardi	.05	.02
☐ 225 Charlie Hayes	.05	.02
☐ 226 Darren Holmes	.05	.02
☐ 227 Howard Johnson	.05	.02
☐ 228 Roberto Mejia	.05	.02
☐ 229 David Nied	.05	.02
☐ 230 Armando Reynoso	.05	.02
☐ 231 Kevin Appier	.20	.09
☐ 232 David Cone	.20	.09
☐ 233 Greg Gagne	.05	.02
☐ 234 Tom Gordon	.05	.02
☐ 235 Felix Jose	.05	.02
☐ 236 Wally Joyner	.20	.09
☐ 237 Jose Lind	.05	.02
☐ 238 Brian McRae	.05	.02
☐ 239 Mike Macfarliane	.05	.02
☐ 240 Jeff Montgomery	.20	.09
☐ 241 Eric Davis	.20	.09
☐ 242 John Doherty	.05	.02
☐ 243 Cecil Fielder	.20	.09
☐ 244 Travis Fryman	.20	.09
☐ 245 Bill Gullickson	.05	.02
☐ 246 Mike Henneman	.05	.02
☐ 247 Tony Phillips	.05	.02
☐ 248 Mickey Tettleton	.05	.02
☐ 249 Alan Trammell	.30	.14
☐ 250 Lou Whitaker	.20	.09
☐ 251 Rick Aguilera	.05	.02
☐ 252 Scott Erickson	.05	.02
☐ 253 Kent Hrbek	.20	.09
☐ 254 Chuck Knoblauch	.40	.18
☐ 255 Shane Mack	.05	.02
☐ 256 Dave McCarty	.05	.02
☐ 257 Pat Meares	.05	.02
☐ 258 Kirby Puckett	.75	.35
☐ 259 Kevin Tapani	.05	.02
☐ 260 Dave Winfield	.30	.14
☐ 261 Wilson Alvarez	.20	.09
☐ 262 Jason Bere	.05	.02
☐ 263 Alex Fernandez	.20	.09
☐ 264 Ozzie Guillen	.05	.02
☐ 265 Roberto Hernandez	.20	.09
☐ 266 Lance Johnson	.05	.02
☐ 267 Jack McDowell	.05	.02
☐ 268 Tim Raines	.05	.02
☐ 269 Frank Thomas	2.00	.90
☐ 270 Robin Ventura	.20	.09
☐ 271 Jim Abbott	.05	.02

		MINT	NRMT
☐	272 Wade Boggs	.40	.18
☐	273 Mike Gallego	.05	.02
☐	274 Pat Kelly	.05	.02
☐	275 Jimmy Key	.20	.09
☐	276 Don Mattingly	1.00	.45
☐	277 Paul O'Neill	.20	.09
☐	278 Mike Stanley	.05	.02
☐	279 Danny Tartabull	.05	.02
☐	280 Bernie Williams	.40	.18
☐	281 Chipper Jones	1.50	.70
☐	282 Ryan Klesko	.30	.14
☐	283 Javier Lopez	.30	.14
☐	284 Jeffrey Hammonds	.20	.09
☐	285 Jeff McNeely	.05	.02
☐	286 Manny Ramirez	.60	.25
☐	287 Billy Ashley	.05	.02
☐	288 Raul Mondesi	.30	.14
☐	289 Cliff Floyd	.20	.09
☐	290 Rondell White	.30	.14
☐	291 Steve Karsay	.05	.02
☐	292 Midre Cummings	.05	.02
☐	293 Salomon Torres	.05	.02
☐	294 J.R. Phillips	.05	.02
☐	295 Marc Newfield	.20	.09
☐	296 Carlos Delgado	.30	.14
☐	297 Butch Huskey	.20	.09
☐	298 Checklist	.05	.02
☐	299 Checklist	.05	.02
☐	300 Checklist	.05	.02

1994 Triple Play Bomb Squad

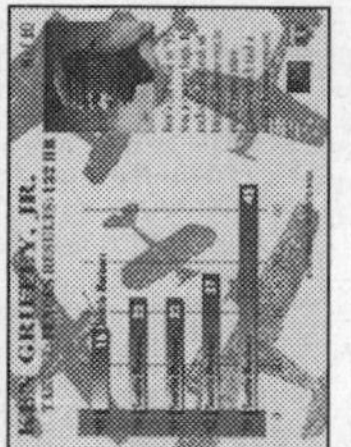

Randomly inserted in regular (one in 18) and jumbo (one in 8) packs, this ten-card standard-size set focuses on the top home run hitters in the majors. Card fronts feature a brown border surrounding a black and white photo. The Bomb Squad logo which includes a pair of wings is at the top. The player's name is at the bottom. Horizontal backs offer more color including a bar graph on yearly home run production with drawings of fighter planes serving as a background.

		MINT	NRMT
	COMPLETE SET (10)	40.00	18.00
	COMMON CARD (1-10)	1.00	.45
☐	1 Frank Thomas	10.00	4.50
☐	2 Cecil Fielder	1.50	.70
☐	3 Juan Gonzalez	6.00	2.70
☐	4 Barry Bonds	3.00	1.35
☐	5 David Justice	2.50	1.10
☐	6 Fred McGriff	2.00	.90
☐	7 Ron Gant	1.00	.45
☐	8 Ken Griffey Jr.	12.00	5.50
☐	9 Albert Belle	3.00	1.35
☐	10 Matt Williams	2.00	.90

1994 Triple Play Medalists

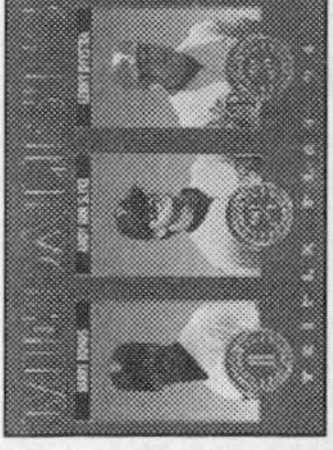

Randomly inserted in regular (one in 12) and jumbo packs (one in six), this 15-card standard-size set features the top three players in each league at their position. The players included were determined by statistical rankings over the past two seasons. Each card is horizontally designed with gold, silver and bronze foil on front with three player photos. There are also three player photos and brief highlights on back.

		MINT	NRMT
	COMPLETE SET (15)	35.00	16.00
	COMMON CARD (1-15)	1.00	.45
☐	1 Chris Hoiles Mickey Tettleton Brian Harper	1.00	.45
☐	2 Darren Daulton Rick Wilkins Kirt Manwaring	1.25	.55
☐	3 Frank Thomas Rafael Palmeiro John Olerud	8.00	3.60
☐	4 Mark Grace Fred McGriff Jeff Bagwell	3.00	1.35
☐	5 Roberto Alomar Carlos Baerga Lou Whitaker	1.25	.55
☐	6 Ryne Sandberg Craig Biggio Roggie Thompson	2.00	.90
☐	7 Tony Fernandez Cal Ripken Alan Trammell	6.00	2.70
☐	8 Barry Larkin Jay Bell Jeff Blauser	1.25	.55
☐	9 Robin Ventura Travis Fryman Wade Boggs	1.50	.70
☐	10 Terry Pendleton Dave Hollins Gary Sheffield	1.00	.45
☐	11 Ken Griffey Jr. Kirby Puckett Albert Belle	10.00	4.50
☐	12 Barry Bonds Andy Van Slyke Len Dykstra	2.00	.90
☐	13 Jack McDowell Kevin Brown Randy Johnson	1.00	.45
☐	14 Greg Maddux Jose Rijo Bill Swift	5.00	2.20
☐	15 Paul Molitor Dave Winfield Harold Baines	1.50	.70

1994 Triple Play Nicknames

Randomly inserted in regular (one in 36) and jumbo packs (one in 12), this eight-card standard-size set features players with a photo depicting the team name and mascot in the background. The back of each card describes how the team got its nickname as well as a player photo.

		MINT	NRMT
	COMPLETE SET (8)	40.00	18.00
	COMMON CARD (1-8)	2.00	.90
☐	1 Cecil Fielder	3.00	1.35
☐	2 Ryne Sandberg	8.00	3.60
☐	3 Gary Sheffield	6.00	2.70
☐	4 Joe Carter	3.00	1.35
☐	5 John Olerud	2.00	.90
☐	6 Cal Ripken	25.00	11.00
☐	7 Mark McGwire	10.00	4.50
☐	8 Gregg Jefferies	2.00	.90

1986 True Value

The 1986 True Value set consists of 30 cards, each measuring 2 1/2" by 3 1/2", which were printed as panels of four although one of the cards in the panel only pictures a featured product. The complete panel measures approximately 10 3/8" by 3 1/2". The True Value logo is in the upper left corner of the obverse of each card. Supposedly the cards were distributed to customers purchasing 5.00 or more at the store. Cards are frequently found with perforations intact and still in the closed form

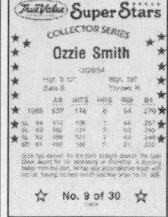

where only the top card in the folded panel is visible. The card number appears at the bottom of the reverse. Team logos have been surgically removed (airbrushed) from the photos.

		MINT	NRMT
	COMPLETE SET (30)	15.00	6.75
	COMMON CARD (1-30)	.25	.11
☐	1 Pedro Guerrero	.25	.11
☐	2 Steve Garvey	.50	.23
☐	3 Eddie Murray	1.00	.45
☐	4 Pete Rose	1.25	.55
☐	5 Don Mattingly	2.50	1.10
☐	6 Fernando Valenzuela	.50	.23
☐	7 Jim Rice	.50	.23
☐	8 Kirk Gibson	.50	.23
☐	9 Ozzie Smith	2.00	.90
☐	10 Dale Murphy	.75	.35
☐	11 Robin Yount	.75	.35
☐	12 Tom Seaver	1.00	.45
☐	13 Reggie Jackson	1.00	.45
☐	14 Ryne Sandberg	2.00	.90
☐	15 Bruce Sutter	.25	.11
☐	16 Gary Carter	.75	.35
☐	17 George Brett	2.50	1.10
☐	18 Rick Sutcliffe	.25	.11
☐	19 Dave Stieb	.25	.11
☐	20 Buddy Bell	.25	.11
☐	21 Alvin Davis	.25	.11
☐	22 Cal Ripken	4.00	1.80
☐	23 Bill Madlock	.25	.11
☐	24 Kent Hrbek	.50	.23
☐	25 Lou Whitaker	.50	.23
☐	26 Nolan Ryan	4.00	1.80
☐	27 Dwayne Murphy	.25	.11
☐	28 Mike Schmidt	1.25	.55
☐	29 Andre Dawson	.75	.35
☐	30 Wade Boggs	1.00	.45

1995 UC3

This 147-card standard-size set was issued by Pinnacle Brands. The cards were issued in 16-box cases with 36 packs per box and five cards per pack. The fronts feature a mix of horizontal and vertical designs. The player's photo is shown against a computer generated background. According to Pinnacle, this is the first set issued as an all-3D product. The key Rookie Card in this set is Hideo Nomo.

		MINT	NRMT
	COMPLETE SET (147)	20.00	9.00
	COMMON CARD (1-147)	.15	.07
☐	1 Frank Thomas	2.50	1.10
☐	2 Wil Cordero	.15	.07
☐	3 John Olerud	.30	.14
☐	4 Deion Sanders	.60	.25
☐	5 Mike Mussina	.60	.25
☐	6 Mo Vaughn	.75	.35
☐	7 Will Clark	.40	.18
☐	8 Chili Davis	.30	.14
☐	9 Jimmy Key	.30	.14
☐	10 John Valentin	.30	.14
☐	11 Tony Tarasco	.15	.07
☐	12 Alan Trammell	.40	.18
☐	13 David Cone	.30	.14
☐	14 Tim Salmon	.60	.25
☐	15 Danny Tartabull	.15	.07

	MINT	NRMT
☐ 16 Aaron Sele	.15	.07
☐ 17 Alex Fernandez	.30	.14
☐ 18 Barry Bonds	.75	.35
☐ 19 Andres Galarraga	.40	.18
☐ 20 Don Mattingly	1.00	.45
☐ 21 Kevin Appier	.30	.14
☐ 22 Paul Molitor	.60	.25
☐ 23 Omar Vizquel	.30	.14
☐ 24 Andy Benes	.15	.07
☐ 25 Rafael Palmeiro	.40	.18
☐ 26 Barry Larkin	.40	.18
☐ 27 Bernie Williams	.60	.25
☐ 28 Gary Sheffield	.40	.18
☐ 29 Wally Joyner	.30	.14
☐ 30 Wade Boggs	.60	.25
☐ 31 Rico Brogna	.15	.07
☐ 32 Ken Caminiti	.60	.25
☐ 33 Kirby Puckett	1.25	.55
☐ 34 Bobby Bonilla	.30	.14
☐ 35 Hal Morris	.15	.07
☐ 36 Moises Alou	.30	.14
☐ 37 Jim Thome	.60	.25
☐ 38 Chuck Knoblauch	.60	.25
☐ 39 Mike Piazza	2.00	.90
☐ 40 Travis Fryman	.30	.14
☐ 41 Rickey Henderson	.40	.18
☐ 42 Jack McDowell	.15	.07
☐ 43 Carlos Baerga	.15	.07
☐ 44 Gregg Jefferies	.30	.14
☐ 45 Kirk Gibson	.30	.14
☐ 46 Bret Saberhagen	.15	.07
☐ 47 Cecil Fielder	.30	.14
☐ 48 Manny Ramirez	.60	.25
☐ 49 Marquis Grissom	.30	.14
☐ 50 Dave Winfield	.40	.18
☐ 51 Mark McGwire	1.25	.55
☐ 52 Dennis Eckersley	.40	.18
☐ 53 Robin Ventura	.30	.14
☐ 54 Ryan Klesko	.40	.18
☐ 55 Jeff Bagwell	1.25	.55
☐ 56 Ozzie Smith	.75	.35
☐ 57 Brian McRae	.15	.07
☐ 58 Albert Belle	.75	.35
☐ 59 Darren Daulton	.30	.14
☐ 60 Jose Canseco	.40	.18
☐ 61 Greg Maddux	2.00	.90
☐ 62 Ben McDonald	.15	.07
☐ 63 Lenny Dykstra	.30	.14
☐ 64 Randy Johnson	.60	.25
☐ 65 Fred McGriff	.40	.18
☐ 66 Ray Lankford	.40	.18
☐ 67 Dave Justice	.60	.25
☐ 68 Paul O'Neill	.30	.14
☐ 69 Tony Gwynn	1.50	.70
☐ 70 Matt Williams	.40	.18
☐ 71 Dante Bichette	.40	.18
☐ 72 Craig Biggio	.40	.18
☐ 73 Ken Griffey Jr.	3.00	1.35
☐ 74 Juan Gonzalez	1.50	.70
☐ 75 Cal Ripken	2.50	1.10
☐ 76 Jay Bell	.30	.14
☐ 77 Joe Carter	.40	.18
☐ 78 Roberto Alomar	.60	.25
☐ 79 Mark Langston	.15	.07
☐ 80 Dave Hollins	.15	.07
☐ 81 Tom Glavine	.40	.18
☐ 82 Ivan Rodriguez	.75	.35
☐ 83 Mark Whiten	.15	.07
☐ 84 Raul Mondesi	.40	.18
☐ 85 Kenny Lofton	.75	.35
☐ 86 Ruben Sierra	.15	.07
☐ 87 Mark Grace	.40	.18
☐ 88 Royce Clayton	.15	.07
☐ 89 Billy Ashley	.15	.07
☐ 90 Larry Walker	.60	.25
☐ 91 Sammy Sosa	.60	.25
☐ 92 Jason Bere	.15	.07
☐ 93 Bob Hamelin	.15	.07
☐ 94 Greg Vaughn	.15	.07
☐ 95 Roger Clemens	1.25	.55
☐ 96 Scott Ruffcorn	.15	.07
☐ 97 Hideo Nomo	3.00	1.35
☐ 98 Michael Tucker	.40	.18
☐ 99 J.R. Phillips	.15	.07
☐ 100 Roberto Petagine	.15	.07
☐ 101 Chipper Jones	2.00	.90
☐ 102 Armando Benitez	.15	.07
☐ 103 Orlando Miller	.15	.07
☐ 104 Carlos Delgado	.40	.18
☐ 105 Jeff Cirillo	.30	.14
☐ 106 Shawn Green	.30	.14
☐ 107 Joe Randa	.15	.07
☐ 108 Vaughn Eshelman	.15	.07
☐ 109 Frank Rodriguez	.30	.14
☐ 110 Russ Davis	.15	.07
☐ 111 Todd Hollandsworth	.30	.14
☐ 112 Mark Grudzielanek	.50	.23
☐ 113 Jose Oliva	.15	.07
☐ 114 Ray Durham	.40	.18
☐ 115 Alex Rodriguez	2.50	1.10
☐ 116 Alex Gonzalez	.15	.07
☐ 117 Midre Cummings	.15	.07
☐ 118 Marty Cordova	.40	.18
☐ 119 John Mabry	.40	.18
☐ 120 Jason Jacome	.15	.07
☐ 121 Joe Vitiello	.15	.07
☐ 122 Charles Johnson	.40	.18
☐ 123 Cal Ripken ID	1.25	.55
☐ 124 Ken Griffey Jr. ID	1.50	.70
☐ 125 Frank Thomas ID	1.50	.70
☐ 126 Mike Piazza ID	1.00	.45
☐ 127 Matt Williams ID	.40	.18
☐ 128 Barry Bonds ID	.60	.25
☐ 129 Greg Maddux ID	1.00	.45
☐ 130 Randy Johnson ID	.60	.25
☐ 131 Albert Belle ID	.60	.25
☐ 132 Will Clark ID	.40	.18
☐ 133 Tony Gwynn ID	.60	.25
☐ 134 Manny Ramirez ID	.30	.14
☐ 135 Raul Mondesi ID	.40	.18
☐ 136 Mo Vaughn ID	.60	.25
☐ 137 Mark McGwire ID	.60	.25
☐ 138 Kirby Puckett ID	.60	.25
☐ 139 Don Mattingly ID	.60	.25
☐ 140 Carlos Baerga ID	.30	.14
☐ 141 Roger Clemens ID	.60	.25
☐ 142 Fred McGriff ID	.40	.18
☐ 143 Kenny Lofton ID	.60	.25
☐ 144 Jeff Bagwell ID	.60	.25
☐ 145 Larry Walker ID	.60	.25
☐ 146 Joe Carter ID	.40	.18
☐ 147 Rafael Palmeiro ID	.40	.18

1995 UC3 Artist's Proofs

This 147-card standard-size set is a parallel to the regular UC3 set. These cards were inserted one per UC3 box. The only difference between these and the regular UC3 cards is the words "Artist's Proof" in a circle in a bottom corner.

	MINT	NRMT
COMPLETE SET (147)	800.00	350.00
COMMON CARD (1-147)	2.50	1.10

*STARS: 10X TO 25X BASIC CARDS
*YOUNG STARS: 8X TO 20X BASIC CARDS

1995 UC3 Clear Shots

This 12-card standard-size set was inserted approximately one in every 24 packs. The fronts have two photos that alternate when the card is tilted slightly. One photo is a portrait while the other is an action shot. Along with the two photos changing are the words "Clear Shots," and a "UC3 1995" logo which changes with the player's team logo. The backs are opaque, but do have the card number in the upper left corner with a "CS" prefix.

	MINT	NRMT
COMPLETE SET (12)	60.00	27.00
COMMON CARD (CS1-CS12)	1.00	.45
☐ CS1 Alex Rodriguez	20.00	9.00
☐ CS2 Shawn Green	1.50	.70
☐ CS3 Hideo Nomo	15.00	6.75
☐ CS4 Charles Johnson	2.50	1.10
☐ CS5 Orlando Miller	1.00	.45
☐ CS6 Billy Ashley	1.00	.45
☐ CS7 Carlos Delgado	2.50	1.10
☐ CS8 Cliff Floyd	1.00	.45
☐ CS9 Chipper Jones	15.00	6.75
☐ CS10 Alex Gonzalez	1.00	.45
☐ CS11 J.R. Phillips	1.00	.45
☐ CS12 Michael Tucker	2.50	1.10
☐ PCS8 Cliff Floyd Promo	1.00	.45

1995 UC3 Cyclone Squad

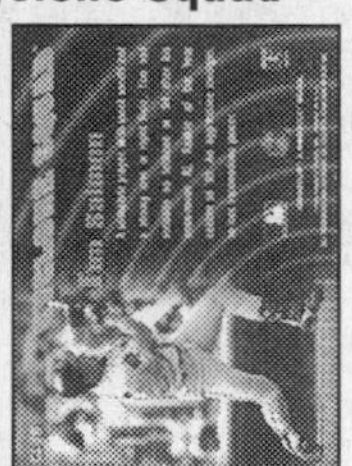

This 20-card standard-size set was inserted approximately one in every four packs. The front features a player photo against a background of two circular objects. The "UC3" logo is in the upper left. The bottom has the words "Cyclone Squad" and the player's name and team. The horizontal backs contain a black and white player photo along with some information. The cards are numbered in the upper left with a "CS" prefix.

	MINT	NRMT
COMPLETE SET (20)	20.00	9.00
COMMON CARD (CS1-CS20)	.50	.23
☐ CS1 Frank Thomas	4.00	1.80
☐ CS2 Ken Griffey Jr.	4.00	1.80
☐ CS3 Jeff Bagwell	1.50	.70
☐ CS4 Cal Ripken	3.00	1.35
☐ CS5 Barry Bonds	1.00	.45
☐ CS6 Mike Piazza	2.50	1.10
☐ CS7 Matt Williams	.75	.35
☐ CS8 Kirby Puckett	1.50	.70
☐ CS9 Jose Canseco	.75	.35
☐ CS10 Will Clark	.75	.35
☐ CS11 Don Mattingly	2.00	.90
☐ CS12 Albert Belle	1.50	.70
☐ CS13 Tony Gwynn	1.50	.70
☐ CS14 Raul Mondesi	.75	.35
☐ CS15 Bobby Bonilla	.50	.23
☐ CS16 Rafael Palmeiro	.75	.35
☐ CS17 Fred McGriff	.75	.35
☐ CS18 Tim Salmon	.75	.35
☐ CS19 Kenny Lofton	1.00	.45
☐ CS20 Joe Carter	.75	.35

1995 UC3 In Motion

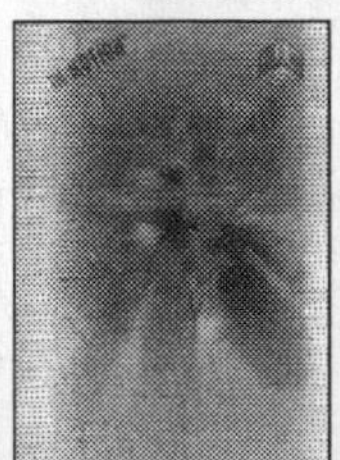

This 10-card standard-size set was inserted approximately one in every 18 packs. The fronts feature a player photo that compresses into many pieces when the card is tilted slightly. The upper left features the words "In Motion 95" with the UC3 logo in the upper right and the player's name in the lower left. The horizontal back features two color photos along with a short informational blurb. The cards are numbered with an "IM" prefix in the upper right corner.

	MINT	NRMT
COMPLETE SET (10)	40.00	18.00
COMMON CARD (IM1-IM10)	.75	.35
☐ IM1 Cal Ripken	6.00	2.70
☐ IM2 Ken Griffey Jr.	8.00	3.60
☐ IM3 Frank Thomas	8.00	3.60
☐ IM4 Mike Piazza	5.00	2.20
☐ IM5 Barry Bonds	2.00	.90
☐ IM6 Matt Williams	.75	.35
☐ IM7 Kirby Puckett	3.00	1.35
☐ IM8 Greg Maddux	5.00	2.20

☐ IM9 Don Mattingly	4.00	1.80
☐ IM10 Will Clark	1.25	.55

1991 Ultra

This 400-card standard-size set marked Fleer's first entry into the premium card market. The cards were distributed exclusively in foil-wrapped packs. Fleer claimed in their original press release that there would only be 15 percent the amount of Ultra issued as there was of the regular issue. The cards feature full color action photography on the fronts and three full-color photos on the backs. Fleer also issued the sets in their now traditional alphabetical order as well as the teams in alphabetical order. Subsets include Major League Prospects (373-390), Elite Performance (391-396), and Checklists (397-400). The key Rookie Cards in this set are Jeff Conine, Eric Karros and Brian McRae, Denny Neagle and Henry Rodriguez.

	MINT	NRMT
COMPLETE SET (400)	20.00	9.00
COMMON CARD (1-400)	.10	.05
☐ 1 Steve Avery	.20	.09
☐ 2 Jeff Blauser	.10	.05
☐ 3 Francisco Cabrera	.10	.05
☐ 4 Ron Gant	.20	.09
☐ 5 Tom Glavine	.40	.18
☐ 6 Tommy Gregg	.10	.05
☐ 7 Dave Justice	.50	.23
☐ 8 Oddibe McDowell	.10	.05
☐ 9 Greg Olson	.10	.05
☐ 10 Terry Pendleton	.20	.09
☐ 11 Lonnie Smith	.10	.05
☐ 12 John Smoltz	.40	.18
☐ 13 Jeff Treadway	.10	.05
☐ 14 Glenn Davis	.10	.05
☐ 15 Mike Devereaux	.10	.05
☐ 16 Leo Gomez	.10	.05
☐ 17 Chris Hoiles	.10	.05
☐ 18 Dave Johnson	.10	.05
☐ 19 Ben McDonald	.20	.09
☐ 20 Randy Milligan	.10	.05
☐ 21 Gregg Olson	.10	.05
☐ 22 Joe Orsulak	.10	.05
☐ 23 Bill Ripken	.10	.05
☐ 24 Cal Ripken	1.50	.70
☐ 25 David Segui	.20	.09
☐ 26 Craig Worthington	.10	.05
☐ 27 Wade Boggs	.40	.18
☐ 28 Tom Bolton	.10	.05
☐ 29 Tom Brunansky	.10	.05
☐ 30 Ellis Burks	.20	.09
☐ 31 Roger Clemens	.75	.35
☐ 32 Mike Greenwell	.10	.05
☐ 33 Greg A. Harris	.10	.05
☐ 34 Daryl Irvine	.10	.05
☐ 35 Mike Marshall UER (1990 in stats is shown as 990)	.10	.05
☐ 36 Tim Naehring	.20	.09
☐ 37 Tony Pena	.10	.05
☐ 38 Phil Plantier	.20	.09
☐ 39 Carlos Quintana	.10	.05
☐ 40 Jeff Reardon	.20	.09
☐ 41 Jody Reed	.10	.05
☐ 42 Luis Rivera	.10	.05
☐ 43 Jim Abbott	.20	.09
☐ 44 Chuck Finley	.20	.09
☐ 45 Bryan Harvey	.10	.05
☐ 46 Donnie Hill	.10	.05
☐ 47 Jack Howell	.10	.05
☐ 48 Wally Joyner	.20	.09
☐ 49 Mark Langston	.10	.05
☐ 50 Kirk McCaskill	.10	.05
☐ 51 Lance Parrish	.10	.05
☐ 52 Dick Schofield	.10	.05
☐ 53 Lee Stevens	.10	.05
☐ 54 Dave Winfield	.40	.18
☐ 55 George Bell	.10	.05
☐ 56 Damon Berryhill	.10	.05
☐ 57 Mike Bielecki	.10	.05
☐ 58 Andre Dawson	.40	.18
☐ 59 Shawon Dunston	.10	.05
☐ 60 Joe Girardi UER (Bats right, LH hitter shown is Doug Dascenzo)	.20	.09
☐ 61 Mark Grace	.40	.18
☐ 62 Mike Harkey	.10	.05
☐ 63 Les Lancaster	.10	.05
☐ 64 Greg Maddux	1.25	.55
☐ 65 Derrick May	.10	.05
☐ 66 Ryne Sandberg	.50	.23
☐ 67 Luis Salazar	.10	.05
☐ 68 Dwight Smith	.10	.05
☐ 69 Hector Villanueva	.10	.05
☐ 70 Jerome Walton	.10	.05
☐ 71 Mitch Williams	.10	.05
☐ 72 Carlton Fisk	.40	.18
☐ 73 Scott Fletcher	.10	.05
☐ 74 Ozzie Guillen	.10	.05
☐ 75 Greg Hibbard	.10	.05
☐ 76 Lance Johnson	.10	.05
☐ 77 Steve Lyons	.10	.05
☐ 78 Jack McDowell	.10	.05
☐ 79 Dan Pasqua	.10	.05
☐ 80 Melido Perez	.10	.05
☐ 81 Tim Raines	.20	.09
☐ 82 Sammy Sosa	.50	.23
☐ 83 Cory Snyder	.10	.05
☐ 84 Bobby Thigpen	.10	.05
☐ 85 Frank Thomas (Card says he is an outfielder)	3.00	1.35
☐ 86 Robin Ventura	.40	.18
☐ 87 Todd Benzinger	.10	.05
☐ 88 Glenn Braggs	.10	.05
☐ 89 Tom Browning UER (Front photo actually Norm Charlton)	.10	.05
☐ 90 Norm Charlton	.10	.05
☐ 91 Eric Davis	.20	.09
☐ 92 Rob Dibble	.10	.05
☐ 93 Bill Doran	.10	.05
☐ 94 Mariano Duncan UER (Right back photo is Billy Hatcher)	.10	.05
☐ 95 Billy Hatcher	.10	.05
☐ 96 Barry Larkin	.40	.18
☐ 97 Randy Myers	.20	.09
☐ 98 Hal Morris	.10	.05
☐ 99 Joe Oliver	.10	.05
☐ 100 Paul O'Neill	.20	.09
☐ 101 Jeff Reed (See also 104)	.10	.05
☐ 102 Jose Rijo	.10	.05
☐ 103 Chris Sabo (See also 106)	.10	.05
☐ 104 Beau Allred UER (Card number is 101)	.10	.05
☐ 105 Sandy Alomar Jr.	.40	.18
☐ 106 Carlos Baerga UER (Card number is 103)	.30	.14
☐ 107 Albert Belle	.60	.25
☐ 108 Jerry Browne	.10	.05
☐ 109 Tom Candiotti	.10	.05
☐ 110 Alex Cole	.10	.05
☐ 111 John Farrell (See also 114)	.10	.05
☐ 112 Felix Fermin	.10	.05
☐ 113 Brook Jacoby	.10	.05
☐ 114 Chris James UER (Card number is 111)	.10	.05
☐ 115 Doug Jones	.10	.05
☐ 116 Steve Olin (See also 119)	.10	.05
☐ 117 Greg Swindell	.10	.05
☐ 118 Turner Ward	.10	.05
☐ 119 Mitch Webster UER (Card number is 116)	.10	.05
☐ 120 Dave Bergman	.10	.05
☐ 121 Cecil Fielder	.20	.09
☐ 122 Travis Fryman	.40	.18
☐ 123 Mike Henneman	.10	.05
☐ 124 Lloyd Moseby	.10	.05
☐ 125 Dan Petry	.10	.05
☐ 126 Tony Phillips	.10	.05
☐ 127 Mark Salas	.10	.05
☐ 128 Frank Tanana	.10	.05
☐ 129 Alan Trammell	.40	.18
☐ 130 Lou Whitaker	.30	.14
☐ 131 Eric Anthony	.10	.05
☐ 132 Craig Biggio	.40	.18
☐ 133 Ken Caminiti	.40	.18
☐ 134 Casey Candaele	.10	.05
☐ 135 Andujar Cedeno	.10	.05
☐ 136 Mark Davidson	.10	.05
☐ 137 Jim Deshaies	.10	.05
☐ 138 Mark Portugal	.10	.05
☐ 139 Rafael Ramirez	.10	.05
☐ 140 Mike Scott	.10	.05
☐ 141 Eric Yelding	.10	.05
☐ 142 Gerald Young	.10	.05
☐ 143 Kevin Appier	.40	.18
☐ 144 George Brett	.75	.35
☐ 145 Jeff Conine	.50	.23
☐ 146 Jim Eisenreich	.20	.09
☐ 147 Tom Gordon	.10	.05
☐ 148 Mark Gubicza	.10	.05
☐ 149 Bo Jackson	.30	.14
☐ 150 Brent Mayne	.10	.05
☐ 151 Mike Macfarlane	.10	.05
☐ 152 Brian McRae	.40	.18
☐ 153 Jeff Montgomery	.20	.09
☐ 154 Bret Saberhagen	.20	.09
☐ 155 Kevin Seitzer	.10	.05
☐ 156 Terry Shumpert	.10	.05
☐ 157 Kurt Stillwell	.10	.05
☐ 158 Danny Tartabull	.10	.05
☐ 159 Tim Belcher	.10	.05
☐ 160 Kal Daniels	.10	.05
☐ 161 Alfredo Griffin	.10	.05
☐ 162 Lenny Harris	.10	.05
☐ 163 Jay Howell	.10	.05
☐ 164 Ramon Martinez	.30	.14
☐ 165 Mike Morgan	.10	.05
☐ 166 Eddie Murray	.40	.18
☐ 167 Jose Offerman	.10	.05
☐ 168 Juan Samuel	.10	.05
☐ 169 Mike Scioscia	.10	.05
☐ 170 Mike Sharperson	.10	.05
☐ 171 Darryl Strawberry	.20	.09
☐ 172 Greg Brock	.10	.05
☐ 173 Chuck Crim	.10	.05
☐ 174 Jim Gantner	.10	.05
☐ 175 Ted Higuera	.10	.05
☐ 176 Mark Knudson	.10	.05
☐ 177 Tim McIntosh	.10	.05
☐ 178 Paul Molitor	.40	.18
☐ 179 Dan Plesac	.10	.05
☐ 180 Gary Sheffield	.40	.18
☐ 181 Bill Spiers	.10	.05
☐ 182 B.J. Surhoff	.20	.09
☐ 183 Greg Vaughn	.10	.05
☐ 184 Robin Yount	.40	.18
☐ 185 Rick Aguilera	.20	.09
☐ 186 Greg Gagne	.10	.05
☐ 187 Dan Gladden	.10	.05
☐ 188 Brian Harper	.10	.05
☐ 189 Kent Hrbek	.20	.09
☐ 190 Gene Larkin	.10	.05
☐ 191 Shane Mack	.10	.05
☐ 192 Pedro Munoz	.10	.05
☐ 193 Al Newman	.10	.05
☐ 194 Junior Ortiz	.10	.05
☐ 195 Kirby Puckett	.75	.35
☐ 196 Kevin Tapani	.10	.05
☐ 197 Dennis Boyd	.10	.05
☐ 198 Tim Burke	.10	.05
☐ 199 Ivan Calderon	.10	.05
☐ 200 Delino DeShields	.10	.05
☐ 201 Mike Fitzgerald	.10	.05
☐ 202 Steve Frey	.10	.05
☐ 203 Andres Galarraga	.40	.18
☐ 204 Marquis Grissom	.40	.18
☐ 205 Dave Martinez	.10	.05
☐ 206 Dennis Martinez	.20	.09
☐ 207 Junior Noboa	.10	.05
☐ 208 Spike Owen	.10	.05
☐ 209 Scott Ruskin	.10	.05
☐ 210 Tim Wallach	.10	.05
☐ 211 Daryl Boston	.10	.05
☐ 212 Vince Coleman	.10	.05
☐ 213 David Cone	.20	.09
☐ 214 Ron Darling	.10	.05
☐ 215 Kevin Elster	.10	.05
☐ 216 Sid Fernandez	.10	.05
☐ 217 John Franco	.10	.05
☐ 218 Dwight Gooden	.20	.09
☐ 219 Tom Herr	.10	.05
☐ 220 Todd Hundley	.40	.18
☐ 221 Gregg Jefferies	.20	.09
☐ 222 Howard Johnson	.10	.05
☐ 223 Dave Magadan	.10	.05
☐ 224 Kevin McReynolds	.10	.05
☐ 225 Keith Miller	.10	.05
☐ 226 Mackey Sasser	.10	.05
☐ 227 Frank Viola	.10	.05
☐ 228 Jesse Barfield	.10	.05
☐ 229 Greg Cadaret	.10	.05
☐ 230 Alvaro Espinoza	.10	.05
☐ 231 Bob Geren	.10	.05
☐ 232 Lee Guetterman	.10	.05
☐ 233 Mel Hall	.10	.05
☐ 234 Andy Hawkins UER (Back center photo is not him)	.10	.05

☐ 235 Roberto Kelly .10 .05
☐ 236 Tim Leary .10 .05
☐ 237 Jim Leyritz .20 .09
☐ 238 Kevin Maas .10 .05
☐ 239 Don Mattingly .60 .25
☐ 240 Hensley Meulens .10 .05
☐ 241 Eric Plunk .10 .05
☐ 242 Steve Sax .10 .05
☐ 243 Todd Burns .10 .05
☐ 244 Jose Canseco .40 .18
☐ 245 Dennis Eckersley .30 .14
☐ 246 Mike Gallego .10 .05
☐ 247 Dave Henderson .10 .05
☐ 248 Rickey Henderson .40 .18
☐ 249 Rick Honeycutt .10 .05
☐ 250 Carney Lansford .20 .09
☐ 251 Mark McGwire .75 .35
☐ 252 Mike Moore .10 .05
☐ 253 Terry Steinbach .20 .09
☐ 254 Dave Stewart .20 .09
☐ 255 Walt Weiss .10 .05
☐ 256 Bob Welch .10 .05
☐ 257 Curt Young .10 .05
☐ 258 Wes Chamberlain .10 .05
☐ 259 Pat Combs .10 .05
☐ 260 Darren Daulton .20 .09
☐ 261 Jose DeJesus .10 .05
☐ 262 Len Dykstra .20 .09
☐ 263 Charlie Hayes .10 .05
☐ 264 Von Hayes .10 .05
☐ 265 Ken Howell .10 .05
☐ 266 John Kruk .20 .09
☐ 267 Roger McDowell .10 .05
☐ 268 Mickey Morandini .10 .05
☐ 269 Terry Mulholland .10 .05
☐ 270 Dale Murphy .40 .18
☐ 271 Randy Ready .10 .05
☐ 272 Dickie Thon .10 .05
☐ 273 Stan Belinda .10 .05
☐ 274 Jay Bell .20 .09
☐ 275 Barry Bonds .50 .23
☐ 276 Bobby Bonilla .30 .14
☐ 277 Doug Drabek .10 .05
☐ 278 Carlos Garcia .20 .09
☐ 279 Neal Heaton .10 .05
☐ 280 Jeff King .20 .09
☐ 281 Bill Landrum .10 .05
☐ 282 Mike LaValliere .10 .05
☐ 283 Jose Lind .10 .05
☐ 284 Orlando Merced .20 .09
☐ 285 Gary Redus .10 .05
☐ 286 Don Slaught .10 .05
☐ 287 Andy Van Slyke .20 .09
☐ 288 Jose DeLeon .10 .05
☐ 289 Pedro Guerrero .10 .05
☐ 290 Ray Lankford .40 .18
☐ 291 Joe Magrane .10 .05
☐ 292 Jose Oquendo .10 .05
☐ 293 Tom Pagnozzi .10 .05
☐ 294 Bryn Smith .10 .05
☐ 295 Lee Smith .20 .09
☐ 296 Ozzie Smith UER .50 .23
(Born 12-26, 54, should have hyphen)
☐ 297 Milt Thompson .10 .05
☐ 298 Craig Wilson .10 .05
☐ 299 Todd Zeile .20 .09
☐ 300 Shawn Abner .10 .05
☐ 301 Andy Benes .20 .09
☐ 302 Paul Faries .10 .05
☐ 303 Tony Gwynn 1.00 .45
☐ 304 Greg W. Harris .10 .05
☐ 305 Thomas Howard .10 .05
☐ 306 Bruce Hurst .10 .05
☐ 307 Craig Lefferts .10 .05
☐ 308 Fred McGriff .40 .18
☐ 309 Dennis Rasmussen .10 .05
☐ 310 Bip Roberts .10 .05
☐ 311 Benito Santiago .10 .05
☐ 312 Garry Templeton .10 .05
☐ 313 Ed Whitson .10 .05
☐ 314 Dave Anderson .10 .05
☐ 315 Kevin Bass .10 .05
☐ 316 Jeff Brantley .10 .05
☐ 317 John Burkett .20 .09
☐ 318 Will Clark .40 .18
☐ 319 Steve Decker .10 .05
☐ 320 Scott Garrelts .10 .05
☐ 321 Terry Kennedy .10 .05
☐ 322 Mark Leonard .10 .05
☐ 323 Darren Lewis .10 .05
☐ 324 Greg Litton .10 .05
☐ 325 Willie McGee .10 .05
☐ 326 Kevin Mitchell .20 .09
☐ 327 Don Robinson .10 .05
☐ 328 Andres Santana .10 .05
☐ 329 Robby Thompson .10 .05
☐ 330 Jose Uribe .10 .05
☐ 331 Matt Williams .40 .18
☐ 332 Scott Bradley .10 .05
☐ 333 Henry Cotto .10 .05
☐ 334 Alvin Davis .10 .05
☐ 335 Ken Griffey Sr. .10 .05
☐ 336 Ken Griffey Jr. 3.00 1.35
☐ 337 Erik Hanson .10 .05
☐ 338 Brian Holman .10 .05
☐ 339 Randy Johnson .50 .23
☐ 340 Edgar Martinez UER .40 .18
(Listed as playing SS)
☐ 341 Tino Martinez .40 .18
☐ 342 Pete O'Brien .10 .05
☐ 343 Harold Reynolds .10 .05
☐ 344 Dave Valle .10 .05
☐ 345 Omar Vizquel .40 .18
☐ 346 Brad Arnsberg .10 .05
☐ 347 Kevin Brown .20 .09
☐ 348 Julio Franco .20 .09
☐ 349 Jeff Huson .10 .05
☐ 350 Rafael Palmeiro .40 .18
☐ 351 Geno Petralli .10 .05
☐ 352 Gary Pettis .10 .05
☐ 353 Kenny Rogers .10 .05
☐ 354 Jeff Russell .10 .05
☐ 355 Nolan Ryan 1.50 .70
☐ 356 Ruben Sierra .10 .05
☐ 357 Bobby Witt .10 .05
☐ 358 Roberto Alomar .40 .18
☐ 359 Pat Borders .10 .05
☐ 360 Joe Carter UER .20 .09
(Reverse negative on back photo)
☐ 361 Kelly Gruber .10 .05
☐ 362 Tom Henke .10 .05
☐ 363 Glenallen Hill .10 .05
☐ 364 Jimmy Key .20 .09
☐ 365 Manny Lee .10 .05
☐ 366 Rance Mulliniks .10 .05
☐ 367 John Olerud UER .20 .09
(Throwing left on card; back has throws right; he does throw lefty)
☐ 368 Dave Stieb .10 .05
☐ 369 Duane Ward .10 .05
☐ 370 David Wells .10 .05
☐ 371 Mark Whiten .10 .05
☐ 372 Mookie Wilson .10 .05
☐ 373 Willie Banks MLP .10 .05
☐ 374 Steve Carter MLP .10 .05
☐ 375 Scott Chiamparino MLP .10 .05
☐ 376 Steve Chitren MLP .10 .05
☐ 377 Darrin Fletcher MLP .10 .05
☐ 378 Rich Garces MLP .10 .05
☐ 379 Reggie Jefferson MLP .40 .18
☐ 380 Eric Karros MLP .75 .35
☐ 381 Pat Kelly MLP .10 .05
☐ 382 Chuck Knoblauch MLP .50 .23
☐ 383 Denny Neagle MLP 1.25 .55
☐ 384 Dan Opperman MLP .10 .05
☐ 385 John Ramos MLP .10 .05
☐ 386 Henry Rodriguez MLP .60 .25
☐ 387 Mo Vaughn MLP .75 .35
☐ 388 Gerald Williams MLP .10 .05
☐ 389 Mike York MLP .10 .05
☐ 390 Eddie Zosky MLP .10 .05
☐ 391 Barry Bonds EP .40 .18
☐ 392 Cecil Fielder EP .20 .09
☐ 393 Rickey Henderson EP .40 .18
☐ 394 Dave Justice EP .40 .18
☐ 395 Nolan Ryan EP .75 .35
☐ 396 Bobby Thigpen EP .10 .05
☐ 397 Gregg Jefferies CL .10 .05
☐ 398 Von Hayes CL .10 .05
☐ 399 Terry Kennedy CL .10 .05
☐ 400 Nolan Ryan CL .40 .18

1991 Ultra Gold

This ten-card standard-size set presents Fleer's 1991 Ultra Team. These cards were randomly inserted into Ultra packs. On a gold background that fades as one moves toward the bottom of the card, the front design has a color head shot, with two cut-out action shots below. Player information is given in a dark blue strip at the bottom of the card face. In blue print on white background with gold borders, the back highlights the player's outstanding achievements. The set is sequenced in alphabetical order.

	MINT	NRMT
COMPLETE SET (10)	10.00	4.50
COMMON CARD (1-10)	.25	.11

☐ 1 Barry Bonds 1.00 .45
☐ 2 Will Clark .75 .35
☐ 3 Doug Drabek .25 .11
☐ 4 Ken Griffey Jr. 6.00 2.70
☐ 5 Rickey Henderson .75 .35
☐ 6 Bo Jackson .50 .23
☐ 7 Ramon Martinez .35 .16
☐ 8 Kirby Puckett UER 1.50 .70
(Boggs won 1988 batting title, so Puckett didn't win consecutive titles)
☐ 9 Chris Sabo .25 .11
☐ 10 Ryne Sandberg UER 1.00 .45
(Johnson and Hornsby didn't hit 40 homers in 1990, Fielder did hit 51 in '90)

1991 Ultra Update

The 120-card set was distributed exclusively in factory set form along with 20 team logo stickers through hobby dealers. The set includes the year's hottest rookies and important veteran players traded after the original Ultra series was produced. Card design is identical to regular issue 1991 cards except for the U-prefixed numbering on back. Cards are ordered alphabetically within and according to teams for each league. Rookie Cards in this set include Jeff Bagwell, Juan Guzman, Mike Mussina, and Ivan Rodriguez.

	MINT	NRMT
COMP.FACT.SET (120)	30.00	13.50
COMMON CARD (1-120)	.25	.11

☐ 1 Dwight Evans .50 .23
☐ 2 Chito Martinez .25 .11
☐ 3 Bob Melvin .25 .11
☐ 4 Mike Mussina 6.00 2.70
☐ 5 Jack Clark .50 .23
☐ 6 Dana Kiecker .25 .11
☐ 7 Steve Lyons .25 .11
☐ 8 Gary Gaetti .50 .23
☐ 9 Dave Gallagher .25 .11
☐ 10 Dave Parker .50 .23
☐ 11 Luis Polonia .25 .11
☐ 12 Luis Sojo .25 .11
☐ 13 Wilson Alvarez 1.00 .45
☐ 14 Alex Fernandez 2.00 .90
☐ 15 Craig Grebeck .25 .11
☐ 16 Ron Karkovice .25 .11
☐ 17 Warren Newson .25 .11
☐ 18 Scott Radinsky .25 .11
☐ 19 Glenallen Hill .25 .11
☐ 20 Charles Nagy 1.00 .45
☐ 21 Mark Whiten .25 .11
☐ 22 Milt Cuyler .25 .11
☐ 23 Paul Gibson .25 .11
☐ 24 Mickey Tettleton .50 .23
☐ 25 Todd Benzinger .25 .11
☐ 26 Storm Davis .25 .11
☐ 27 Kirk Gibson .50 .23
☐ 28 Bill Pecota .25 .11
☐ 29 Gary Thurman .25 .11
☐ 30 Darryl Hamilton .25 .11
☐ 31 Jaime Navarro .25 .11
☐ 32 Willie Randolph .50 .23
☐ 33 Bill Wegman .25 .11
☐ 34 Randy Bush .25 .11
☐ 35 Chili Davis .50 .23

☐ 36 Scott Erickson	1.25	.55
☐ 37 Chuck Knoblauch	4.00	1.80
☐ 38 Scott Leius	.25	.11
☐ 39 Jack Morris	.50	.23
☐ 40 John Habyan	.25	.11
☐ 41 Pat Kelly	.25	.11
☐ 42 Matt Nokes	.25	.11
☐ 43 Scott Sanderson	.25	.11
☐ 44 Bernie Williams	4.00	1.80
☐ 45 Harold Baines	.75	.35
☐ 46 Brook Jacoby	.25	.11
☐ 47 Earnest Riles	.25	.11
☐ 48 Willie Wilson	.25	.11
☐ 49 Jay Buhner	1.00	.45
☐ 50 Rich DeLucia	.25	.11
☐ 51 Mike Jackson	.25	.11
☐ 52 Bill Krueger	.25	.11
☐ 53 Bill Swift	.25	.11
☐ 54 Brian Downing	.25	.11
☐ 55 Juan Gonzalez	15.00	6.75
☐ 56 Dean Palmer	1.25	.55
☐ 57 Kevin Reimer	.25	.11
☐ 58 Ivan Rodriguez	8.00	3.60
☐ 59 Tom Candiotti	.25	.11
☐ 60 Juan Guzman	.75	.35
☐ 61 Bob MacDonald	.25	.11
☐ 62 Greg Myers	.25	.11
☐ 63 Ed Sprague	.50	.23
☐ 64 Devon White	.25	.11
☐ 65 Rafael Belliard	.25	.11
☐ 66 Juan Berenguer	.25	.11
☐ 67 Brian R. Hunter	.25	.11
☐ 68 Kent Mercker	.25	.11
☐ 69 Otis Nixon	.50	.23
☐ 70 Danny Jackson	.25	.11
☐ 71 Chuck McElroy	.25	.11
☐ 72 Gary Scott	.25	.11
☐ 73 Heathcliff Slocumb	1.00	.45
☐ 74 Chico Walker	.25	.11
☐ 75 Rick Wilkins	.25	.11
☐ 76 Chris Hammond	.25	.11
☐ 77 Luis Quinones	.25	.11
☐ 78 Herm Winningham	.25	.11
☐ 79 Jeff Bagwell	15.00	6.75
☐ 80 Jim Corsi	.25	.11
☐ 81 Steve Finley	1.00	.45
☐ 82 Luis Gonzalez	.75	.35
☐ 83 Pete Harnisch	.25	.11
☐ 84 Darryl Kile	2.00	.90
☐ 85 Brett Butler	.75	.35
☐ 86 Gary Carter	1.00	.45
☐ 87 Tim Crews	.25	.11
☐ 88 Orel Hershiser	.50	.23
☐ 89 Bob Ojeda	.25	.11
☐ 90 Bret Barberie	.25	.11
☐ 91 Barry Jones	.25	.11
☐ 92 Gilberto Reyes	.25	.11
☐ 93 Larry Walker	2.00	.90
☐ 94 Hubie Brooks	.25	.11
☐ 95 Tim Burke	.25	.11
☐ 96 Rick Cerone	.25	.11
☐ 97 Jeff Innis	.25	.11
☐ 98 Wally Backman	.25	.11
☐ 99 Tommy Greene	.25	.11
☐ 100 Ricky Jordan	.25	.11
☐ 101 Mitch Williams	.25	.11
☐ 102 John Smiley	.25	.11
☐ 103 Randy Tomlin	.25	.11
☐ 104 Gary Varsho	.25	.11
☐ 105 Cris Carpenter	.25	.11
☐ 106 Ken Hill	.75	.35
☐ 107 Felix Jose	.25	.11
☐ 108 Omar Olivares	.25	.11
☐ 109 Gerald Perry	.25	.11
☐ 110 Jerald Clark	.25	.11
☐ 111 Tony Fernandez	.25	.11
☐ 112 Darrin Jackson	.25	.11
☐ 113 Mike Maddux	.25	.11
☐ 114 Tim Teufel	.25	.11
☐ 115 Bud Black	.25	.11
☐ 116 Kelly Downs	.25	.11
☐ 117 Mike Felder	.25	.11
☐ 118 Willie McGee	.25	.11
☐ 119 Trevor Wilson	.25	.11
☐ 120 Checklist 1-120	.25	.11

1992 Ultra

Consisting of 600 standard-size cards, the 1992 Fleer Ultra set was issued in two series of 300 cards each. Cards were distributed exclusively in foil packs. The glossy color action player photos on the fronts are full-bleed except at the bottom where a diagonal gold-foil stripe edges a green marbleized border. The player's name and team appear on the marble-colored area in bars that are color-coded by team. The cards are numbered on

the back and ordered below alphabetically within and according to teams for each league with AL preceding NL. There are no notable Rookie Cards in the set. Some cards have been found without the word Fleer on the front.

	MINT	NRMT
COMPLETE SET (600)	30.00	13.50
COMPLETE SERIES 1 (300)	20.00	9.00
COMPLETE SERIES 2 (300)	10.00	4.50
COMMON CARD (1-600)	.10	.05

Card	MINT	NRMT
☐ 1 Glenn Davis	.10	.05
☐ 2 Mike Devereaux	.10	.05
☐ 3 Dwight Evans	.20	.09
☐ 4 Leo Gomez	.10	.05
☐ 5 Chris Hoiles	.10	.05
☐ 6 Sam Horn	.10	.05
☐ 7 Chito Martinez	.10	.05
☐ 8 Randy Milligan	.10	.05
☐ 9 Mike Mussina	.60	.25
☐ 10 Billy Ripken	.10	.05
☐ 11 Cal Ripken	1.50	.70
☐ 12 Tom Brunansky	.10	.05
☐ 13 Ellis Burks	.20	.09
☐ 14 Jack Clark	.20	.09
☐ 15 Roger Clemens	.75	.35
☐ 16 Mike Greenwell	.10	.05
☐ 17 Joe Hesketh	.10	.05
☐ 18 Tony Pena	.10	.05
☐ 19 Carlos Quintana	.10	.05
☐ 20 Jeff Reardon	.20	.09
☐ 21 Jody Reed	.10	.05
☐ 22 Luis Rivera	.10	.05
☐ 23 Mo Vaughn	.60	.25
☐ 24 Gary DiSarcina	.10	.05
☐ 25 Chuck Finley	.10	.05
☐ 26 Gary Gaetti	.20	.09
☐ 27 Bryan Harvey	.10	.05
☐ 28 Lance Parrish	.10	.05
☐ 29 Luis Polonia	.10	.05
☐ 30 Dick Schofield	.10	.05
☐ 31 Luis Sojo	.10	.05
☐ 32 Wilson Alvarez	.30	.14
☐ 33 Carlton Fisk	.40	.18
☐ 34 Craig Grebeck	.10	.05
☐ 35 Ozzie Guillen	.10	.05
☐ 36 Greg Hibbard	.10	.05
☐ 37 Charlie Hough	.10	.05
☐ 38 Lance Johnson	.10	.05
☐ 39 Ron Karkovice	.10	.05
☐ 40 Jack McDowell	.10	.05
☐ 41 Donn Pall	.10	.05
☐ 42 Melido Perez	.10	.05
☐ 43 Tim Raines	.20	.09
☐ 44 Frank Thomas	2.00	.90
☐ 45 Sandy Alomar Jr.	.20	.09
☐ 46 Carlos Baerga	.20	.09
☐ 47 Albert Belle	.50	.23
☐ 48 Jerry Browne UER (Reversed negative on card back)	.10	.05
☐ 49 Felix Fermin	.10	.05
☐ 50 Reggie Jefferson UER (Born 1968, not 1966)	.20	.09
☐ 51 Mark Lewis	.10	.05
☐ 52 Carlos Martinez	.10	.05
☐ 53 Steve Olin	.10	.05
☐ 54 Jim Thome	1.25	.55
☐ 55 Mark Whiten	.10	.05
☐ 56 Dave Bergman	.10	.05
☐ 57 Milt Cuyler	.10	.05
☐ 58 Rob Deer	.10	.05
☐ 59 Cecil Fielder	.20	.09
☐ 60 Travis Fryman	.20	.09
☐ 61 Scott Livingstone	.10	.05
☐ 62 Tony Phillips	.10	.05
☐ 63 Mickey Tettleton	.10	.05
☐ 64 Alan Trammell	.30	.14
☐ 65 Lou Whitaker	.20	.09
☐ 66 Kevin Appier	.20	.09
☐ 67 Mike Boddicker	.10	.05
☐ 68 George Brett	.75	.35
☐ 69 Jim Eisenreich	.20	.09
☐ 70 Mark Gubicza	.10	.05
☐ 71 David Howard	.10	.05
☐ 72 Joel Johnson	.10	.05
☐ 73 Mike Macfarlane	.10	.05
☐ 74 Brent Mayne	.10	.05
☐ 75 Brian McRae	.10	.05
☐ 76 Jeff Montgomery	.20	.09
☐ 77 Danny Tartabull	.10	.05
☐ 78 Don August	.10	.05
☐ 79 Dante Bichette	.30	.14
☐ 80 Ted Higuera	.10	.05
☐ 81 Paul Molitor	.40	.18
☐ 82 Jaime Navarro	.10	.05
☐ 83 Gary Sheffield	.40	.18
☐ 84 Bill Spiers	.10	.05
☐ 85 B.J. Surhoff	.20	.09
☐ 86 Greg Vaughn	.10	.05
☐ 87 Robin Yount	.30	.14
☐ 88 Rick Aguilera	.10	.05
☐ 89 Chili Davis	.20	.09
☐ 90 Scott Erickson	.20	.09
☐ 91 Brian Harper	.10	.05
☐ 92 Kent Hrbek	.20	.09
☐ 93 Chuck Knoblauch	.40	.18
☐ 94 Scott Leius	.10	.05
☐ 95 Shane Mack	.10	.05
☐ 96 Mike Pagliarulo	.10	.05
☐ 97 Kirby Puckett	.75	.35
☐ 98 Kevin Tapani	.10	.05
☐ 99 Jesse Barfield	.10	.05
☐ 100 Alvaro Espinoza	.10	.05
☐ 101 Mel Hall	.10	.05
☐ 102 Pat Kelly	.10	.05
☐ 103 Roberto Kelly	.10	.05
☐ 104 Kevin Maas	.10	.05
☐ 105 Don Mattingly	.60	.25
☐ 106 Hensley Meulens	.10	.05
☐ 107 Matt Nokes	.10	.05
☐ 108 Steve Sax	.10	.05
☐ 109 Harold Baines	.20	.09
☐ 110 Jose Canseco	.30	.14
☐ 111 Ron Darling	.10	.05
☐ 112 Mike Gallego	.10	.05
☐ 113 Dave Henderson	.10	.05
☐ 114 Rickey Henderson	.30	.14
☐ 115 Mark McGwire	.75	.35
☐ 116 Terry Steinbach	.20	.09
☐ 117 Dave Stewart	.20	.09
☐ 118 Todd Van Poppel	.10	.05
☐ 119 Bob Welch	.10	.05
☐ 120 Greg Briley	.10	.05
☐ 121 Jay Buhner	.30	.14
☐ 122 Rick DeLucia	.10	.05
☐ 123 Ken Griffey Jr.	2.50	1.10
☐ 124 Erik Hanson	.10	.05
☐ 125 Randy Johnson	.40	.18
☐ 126 Edgar Martinez	.30	.14
☐ 127 Tino Martinez	.40	.18
☐ 128 Pete O'Brien	.10	.05
☐ 129 Harold Reynolds	.10	.05
☐ 130 Dave Valle	.10	.05
☐ 131 Julio Franco	.20	.09
☐ 132 Juan Gonzalez	1.25	.55
☐ 133 Jeff Huson (Shows Jose Canseco sliding into second)	.20	.09
☐ 134 Mike Jeffcoat	.10	.05
☐ 135 Terry Mathews	.10	.05
☐ 136 Rafael Palmeiro	.30	.14
☐ 137 Dean Palmer	.20	.09
☐ 138 Geno Petralli	.10	.05
☐ 139 Ivan Rodriguez	.75	.35
☐ 140 Jeff Russell	.10	.05
☐ 141 Nolan Ryan	1.50	.70
☐ 142 Ruben Sierra	.10	.05
☐ 143 Roberto Alomar	.40	.18
☐ 144 Pat Borders	.10	.05
☐ 145 Joe Carter	.30	.14
☐ 146 Kelly Gruber	.10	.05
☐ 147 Jimmy Key	.20	.09
☐ 148 Manny Lee	.10	.05
☐ 149 Rance Mulliniks	.10	.05
☐ 150 Greg Myers	.10	.05
☐ 151 John Olerud	.20	.09
☐ 152 Dave Stieb	.10	.05
☐ 153 Todd Stottlemyre	.10	.05
☐ 154 Duane Ward	.10	.05
☐ 155 Devon White	.10	.05
☐ 156 Eddie Zosky	.10	.05
☐ 157 Steve Avery	.10	.05
☐ 158 Rafael Belliard	.10	.05
☐ 159 Jeff Blauser	.10	.05
☐ 160 Sid Bream	.10	.05
☐ 161 Ron Gant	.20	.09
☐ 162 Tom Glavine	.30	.14
☐ 163 Brian Hunter	.10	.05
☐ 164 Dave Justice	.40	.18
☐ 165 Mark Lemke	.10	.05

☐ 166 Greg Olson .10 .05
☐ 167 Terry Pendleton .20 .09
☐ 168 Lonnie Smith .10 .05
☐ 169 John Smoltz .30 .14
☐ 170 Mike Stanton .10 .05
☐ 171 Jeff Treadway .10 .05
☐ 172 Paul Assenmacher .10 .05
☐ 173 George Bell .10 .05
☐ 174 Shawon Dunston .10 .05
☐ 175 Mark Grace .30 .14
☐ 176 Danny Jackson .10 .05
☐ 177 Les Lancaster .10 .05
☐ 178 Greg Maddux 1.25 .55
☐ 179 Luis Salazar .10 .05
☐ 180 Rey Sanchez .10 .05
☐ 181 Ryne Sandberg .50 .23
☐ 182 Jose Vizcaino .10 .05
☐ 183 Chico Walker .10 .05
☐ 184 Jerome Walton .10 .05
☐ 185 Glenn Braggs .10 .05
☐ 186 Tom Browning .10 .05
☐ 187 Rob Dibble .10 .05
☐ 188 Bill Doran .10 .05
☐ 189 Chris Hammond .10 .05
☐ 190 Billy Hatcher .10 .05
☐ 191 Barry Larkin .30 .14
☐ 192 Hal Morris .10 .05
☐ 193 Joe Oliver .10 .05
☐ 194 Paul O'Neill .20 .09
☐ 195 Jeff Reed .10 .05
☐ 196 Jose Rijo .10 .05
☐ 197 Chris Sabo .10 .05
☐ 198 Jeff Bagwell 1.25 .55
☐ 199 Craig Biggio .30 .14
☐ 200 Ken Caminiti .40 .18
☐ 201 Andujar Cedeno .10 .05
☐ 202 Steve Finley .20 .09
☐ 203 Luis Gonzalez .10 .05
☐ 204 Pete Harnisch .10 .05
☐ 205 Xavier Hernandez .10 .05
☐ 206 Darryl Kile .20 .09
☐ 207 Al Osuna .10 .05
☐ 208 Curt Schilling .30 .14
☐ 209 Brett Butler .20 .09
☐ 210 Kal Daniels .10 .05
☐ 211 Lenny Harris .10 .05
☐ 212 Stan Javier .10 .05
☐ 213 Ramon Martinez .10 .05
☐ 214 Roger McDowell .10 .05
☐ 215 Jose Offerman .10 .05
☐ 216 Juan Samuel .10 .05
☐ 217 Mike Scioscia .10 .05
☐ 218 Mike Sharperson .10 .05
☐ 219 Darryl Strawberry .20 .09
☐ 220 Delino DeShields .10 .05
☐ 221 Tom Foley .10 .05
☐ 222 Steve Frey .10 .05
☐ 223 Dennis Martinez .20 .09
☐ 224 Spike Owen .10 .05
☐ 225 Gilberto Reyes .10 .05
☐ 226 Tim Wallach .10 .05
☐ 227 Daryl Boston .10 .05
☐ 228 Tim Burke .10 .05
☐ 229 Vince Coleman .10 .05
☐ 230 David Cone .20 .09
☐ 231 Kevin Elster .10 .05
☐ 232 Dwight Gooden .20 .09
☐ 233 Todd Hundley .30 .14
☐ 234 Jeff Innis .10 .05
☐ 235 Howard Johnson .10 .05
☐ 236 Dave Magadan .10 .05
☐ 237 Mackey Sasser .10 .05
☐ 238 Anthony Young .10 .05
☐ 239 Wes Chamberlain .10 .05
☐ 240 Darren Daulton .20 .09
☐ 241 Len Dykstra .20 .09
☐ 242 Tommy Greene .10 .05
☐ 243 Charlie Hayes .10 .05
☐ 244 Dave Hollins .10 .05
☐ 245 Ricky Jordan .10 .05
☐ 246 John Kruk .20 .09
☐ 247 Mickey Morandini .10 .05
☐ 248 Terry Mulholland .10 .05
☐ 249 Dale Murphy .30 .14
☐ 250 Jay Bell .20 .09
☐ 251 Barry Bonds .50 .23
☐ 252 Steve Buechele .10 .05
☐ 253 Doug Drabek .10 .05
☐ 254 Mike LaValliere .10 .05
☐ 255 Jose Lind .10 .05
☐ 256 Lloyd McClendon .10 .05
☐ 257 Orlando Merced .10 .05
☐ 258 Don Slaught .10 .05
☐ 259 John Smiley .10 .05
☐ 260 Zane Smith .10 .05
☐ 261 Randy Tomlin .10 .05
☐ 262 Andy Van Slyke .20 .09
☐ 263 Pedro Guerrero .10 .05
☐ 264 Felix Jose .10 .05
☐ 265 Ray Lankford .30 .14
☐ 266 Omar Olivares .10 .05
☐ 267 Jose Oquendo .10 .05
☐ 268 Tom Pagnozzi .10 .05
☐ 269 Bryn Smith .10 .05
☐ 270 Lee Smith UER .20 .09
(1991 record listed
as 61-61)
☐ 271 Ozzie Smith UER .50 .23
(Comma before year of
birth on card back)
☐ 272 Milt Thompson .10 .05
☐ 273 Todd Zeile .10 .05
☐ 274 Andy Benes .20 .09
☐ 275 Jerald Clark .10 .05
☐ 276 Tony Fernandez .10 .05
☐ 277 Tony Gwynn 1.00 .45
☐ 278 Greg W. Harris .10 .05
☐ 279 Thomas Howard .10 .05
☐ 280 Bruce Hurst .10 .05
☐ 281 Mike Maddux .10 .05
☐ 282 Fred McGriff .30 .14
☐ 283 Benito Santiago .10 .05
☐ 284 Kevin Bass .10 .05
☐ 285 Jeff Brantley .10 .05
☐ 286 John Burkett .10 .05
☐ 287 Will Clark .30 .14
☐ 288 Royce Clayton .10 .05
☐ 289 Steve Decker .10 .05
☐ 290 Kelly Downs .10 .05
☐ 291 Mike Felder .10 .05
☐ 292 Darren Lewis .10 .05
☐ 293 Kirt Manwaring .10 .05
☐ 294 Willie McGee .10 .05
☐ 295 Robby Thompson .10 .05
☐ 296 Matt Williams .30 .14
☐ 297 Trevor Wilson .10 .05
☐ 298 Checklist 1-100 .10 .05
☐ 299 Checklist 101-200 .10 .05
☐ 300 Checklist 201-300 .10 .05
☐ 301 Brady Anderson .30 .14
☐ 302 Todd Frohwirth .10 .05
☐ 303 Ben McDonald .10 .05
☐ 304 Mark McLemore .10 .05
☐ 305 Jose Mesa .20 .09
☐ 306 Bob Milacki .10 .05
☐ 307 Gregg Olson .10 .05
☐ 308 David Segui .10 .05
☐ 309 Rick Sutcliffe .10 .05
☐ 310 Jeff Tackett .10 .05
☐ 311 Wade Boggs .40 .18
☐ 312 Scott Cooper .10 .05
☐ 313 John Flaherty .10 .05
☐ 314 Wayne Housie .10 .05
☐ 315 Peter Hoy .10 .05
☐ 316 John Marzano .10 .05
☐ 317 Tim Naehring .20 .09
☐ 318 Phil Plantier .10 .05
☐ 319 Frank Viola .10 .05
☐ 320 Matt Young .10 .05
☐ 321 Jim Abbott .10 .05
☐ 322 Hubie Brooks .10 .05
☐ 323 Chad Curtis .30 .14
☐ 324 Alvin Davis .10 .05
☐ 325 Junior Felix .10 .05
☐ 326 Von Hayes .10 .05
☐ 327 Mark Langston .10 .05
☐ 328 Scott Lewis .10 .05
☐ 329 Don Robinson .10 .05
☐ 330 Bobby Rose .10 .05
☐ 331 Lee Stevens .10 .05
☐ 332 George Bell .10 .05
☐ 333 Esteban Beltre .10 .05
☐ 334 Joey Cora .20 .09
☐ 335 Alex Fernandez .20 .09
☐ 336 Roberto Hernandez .20 .09
☐ 337 Mike Huff .10 .05
☐ 338 Kirk McCaskill .10 .05
☐ 339 Dan Pasqua .10 .05
☐ 340 Scott Radinsky .10 .05
☐ 341 Steve Sax .10 .05
☐ 342 Bobby Thigpen .10 .05
☐ 343 Robin Ventura .20 .09
☐ 344 Jack Armstrong .10 .05
☐ 345 Alex Cole .10 .05
☐ 346 Dennis Cook .10 .05
☐ 347 Glenallen Hill .10 .05
☐ 348 Thomas Howard .10 .05
☐ 349 Brook Jacoby .10 .05
☐ 350 Kenny Lofton 1.50 .70
☐ 351 Charles Nagy .20 .09
☐ 352 Rod Nichols .10 .05
☐ 353 Junior Ortiz .10 .05
☐ 354 Dave Otto .10 .05
☐ 355 Tony Perezchica .10 .05
☐ 356 Scott Scudder .10 .05
☐ 357 Paul Sorrento .10 .05
☐ 358 Skeeter Barnes .10 .05
☐ 359 Mark Carreon .10 .05
☐ 360 John Doherty .10 .05
☐ 361 Dan Gladden .10 .05
☐ 362 Bill Gullickson .10 .05
☐ 363 Shawn Hare .10 .05
☐ 364 Mike Henneman .10 .05
☐ 365 Chad Kreuter .10 .05
☐ 366 Mark Leiter .10 .05
☐ 367 Mike Munoz .10 .05
☐ 368 Kevin Ritz .10 .05
☐ 369 Mark Davis .10 .05
☐ 370 Tom Gordon .10 .05
☐ 371 Chris Gwynn .10 .05
☐ 372 Gregg Jefferies .20 .09
☐ 373 Wally Joyner .20 .09
☐ 374 Kevin McReynolds .10 .05
☐ 375 Keith Miller .10 .05
☐ 376 Rico Rossy .10 .05
☐ 377 Curtis Wilkerson .10 .05
☐ 378 Ricky Bones .10 .05
☐ 379 Chris Bosio .10 .05
☐ 380 Cal Eldred .10 .05
☐ 381 Scott Fletcher .10 .05
☐ 382 Jim Gantner .10 .05
☐ 383 Darryl Hamilton .10 .05
☐ 384 Doug Henry .10 .05
☐ 385 Pat Listach .10 .05
☐ 386 Tim McIntosh .10 .05
☐ 387 Edwin Nunez .10 .05
☐ 388 Dan Plesac .10 .05
☐ 389 Kevin Seitzer .10 .05
☐ 390 Franklin Stubbs .10 .05
☐ 391 William Suero .10 .05
☐ 392 Bill Wegman .10 .05
☐ 393 Willie Banks .10 .05
☐ 394 Jarvis Brown .10 .05
☐ 395 Greg Gagne .10 .05
☐ 396 Mark Guthrie .10 .05
☐ 397 Bill Krueger .10 .05
☐ 398 Pat Mahomes .10 .05
☐ 399 Pedro Munoz .10 .05
☐ 400 John Smiley .10 .05
☐ 401 Gary Wayne .10 .05
☐ 402 Lenny Webster .10 .05
☐ 403 Carl Willis .10 .05
☐ 404 Greg Cadaret .10 .05
☐ 405 Steve Farr .10 .05
☐ 406 Mike Gallego .10 .05
☐ 407 Charlie Hayes .10 .05
☐ 408 Steve Howe .10 .05
☐ 409 Dion James .10 .05
☐ 410 Jeff Johnson .10 .05
☐ 411 Tim Leary .10 .05
☐ 412 Jim Leyritz .10 .05
☐ 413 Melido Perez .10 .05
☐ 414 Scott Sanderson .10 .05
☐ 415 Andy Stankiewicz .10 .05
☐ 416 Mike Stanley .10 .05
☐ 417 Danny Tartabull .10 .05
☐ 418 Lance Blankenship .10 .05
☐ 419 Mike Bordick .10 .05
☐ 420 Scott Brosius .10 .05
☐ 421 Dennis Eckersley .20 .09
☐ 422 Scott Hemond .10 .05
☐ 423 Carney Lansford .10 .05
☐ 424 Henry Mercedes .10 .05
☐ 425 Mike Moore .10 .05
☐ 426 Gene Nelson .10 .05
☐ 427 Randy Ready .10 .05
☐ 428 Bruce Walton .10 .05
☐ 429 Willie Wilson .10 .05
☐ 430 Rich Amaral .10 .05
☐ 431 Dave Cochrane .10 .05
☐ 432 Henry Cotto .10 .05
☐ 433 Calvin Jones .10 .05
☐ 434 Kevin Mitchell .20 .09
☐ 435 Clay Parker .10 .05
☐ 436 Omar Vizquel .20 .09
☐ 437 Floyd Bannister .10 .05
☐ 438 Kevin Brown .20 .09
☐ 439 John Cangelosi .10 .05
☐ 440 Brian Downing .10 .05
☐ 441 Monty Fariss .10 .05
☐ 442 Jose Guzman .10 .05
☐ 443 Donald Harris .10 .05
☐ 444 Kevin Reimer .10 .05
☐ 445 Kenny Rogers .10 .05
☐ 446 Wayne Rosenthal .10 .05
☐ 447 Dickie Thon .10 .05
☐ 448 Derek Bell .20 .09
☐ 449 Juan Guzman .20 .09
☐ 450 Tom Henke .10 .05
☐ 451 Candy Maldonado .10 .05
☐ 452 Jack Morris .20 .09

☐ 453 David Wells	.10	.05
☐ 454 Dave Winfield	.30	.14
☐ 455 Juan Berenguer	.10	.05
☐ 456 Damon Berryhill	.10	.05
☐ 457 Mike Bielecki	.10	.05
☐ 458 Marvin Freeman	.10	.05
☐ 459 Charlie Leibrandt	.10	.05
☐ 460 Kent Mercker	.10	.05
☐ 461 Otis Nixon	.10	.05
☐ 462 Alejandro Pena	.10	.05
☐ 463 Ben Rivera	.10	.05
☐ 464 Deion Sanders	.40	.18
☐ 465 Mark Wohlers	.20	.09
☐ 466 Shawn Boskie	.10	.05
☐ 467 Frank Castillo	.10	.05
☐ 468 Andre Dawson	.30	.14
☐ 469 Joe Girardi	.10	.05
☐ 470 Chuck McElroy	.10	.05
☐ 471 Mike Morgan	.10	.05
☐ 472 Ken Patterson	.10	.05
☐ 473 Bob Scanlan	.10	.05
☐ 474 Gary Scott	.10	.05
☐ 475 Dave Smith	.10	.05
☐ 476 Sammy Sosa	.40	.18
☐ 477 Hector Villanueva	.10	.05
☐ 478 Scott Bankhead	.10	.05
☐ 479 Tim Belcher	.10	.05
☐ 480 Freddie Benavides	.10	.05
☐ 481 Jacob Brumfield	.10	.05
☐ 482 Norm Charlton	.10	.05
☐ 483 Dwayne Henry	.10	.05
☐ 484 Dave Martinez	.10	.05
☐ 485 Bip Roberts	.10	.05
☐ 486 Reggie Sanders	.20	.09
☐ 487 Greg Swindell	.10	.05
☐ 488 Ryan Bowen	.10	.05
☐ 489 Casey Candaele	.10	.05
☐ 490 Juan Guerrero UER (photo on front is Andujar Cedeno	.10	.05
☐ 491 Pete Incaviglia	.10	.05
☐ 492 Jeff Juden	.10	.05
☐ 493 Rob Murphy	.10	.05
☐ 494 Mark Portugal	.10	.05
☐ 495 Rafael Ramirez	.10	.05
☐ 496 Scott Servais	.10	.05
☐ 497 Ed Taubensee	.10	.05
☐ 498 Brian Williams	.10	.05
☐ 499 Todd Benzinger	.10	.05
☐ 500 John Candelaria	.10	.05
☐ 501 Tom Candiotti	.10	.05
☐ 502 Tim Crews	.10	.05
☐ 503 Eric Davis	.20	.09
☐ 504 Jim Gott	.10	.05
☐ 505 Dave Hansen	.10	.05
☐ 506 Carlos Hernandez	.10	.05
☐ 507 Orel Hershiser	.20	.09
☐ 508 Eric Karros	.30	.14
☐ 509 Bob Ojeda	.10	.05
☐ 510 Steve Wilson	.10	.05
☐ 511 Moises Alou	.20	.09
☐ 512 Bret Barberie	.10	.05
☐ 513 Ivan Calderon	.10	.05
☐ 514 Gary Carter	.40	.18
☐ 515 Archi Cianfrocco	.10	.05
☐ 516 Jeff Fassero	.10	.05
☐ 517 Darrin Fletcher	.10	.05
☐ 518 Marquis Grissom	.20	.09
☐ 519 Chris Haney	.10	.05
☐ 520 Ken Hill	.20	.09
☐ 521 Chris Nabholz	.10	.05
☐ 522 Bill Sampen	.10	.05
☐ 523 John Vander Wal	.10	.05
☐ 524 Dave Wainhouse	.10	.05
☐ 525 Larry Walker	.40	.18
☐ 526 John Wetteland	.20	.09
☐ 527 Bobby Bonilla	.20	.09
☐ 528 Sid Fernandez	.10	.05
☐ 529 John Franco	.10	.05
☐ 530 Dave Gallagher	.10	.05
☐ 531 Paul Gibson	.10	.05
☐ 532 Eddie Murray	.40	.18
☐ 533 Junior Noboa	.10	.05
☐ 534 Charlie O'Brien	.10	.05
☐ 535 Bill Pecota	.10	.05
☐ 536 Willie Randolph	.20	.09
☐ 537 Bret Saberhagen	.10	.05
☐ 538 Dick Schofield	.10	.05
☐ 539 Pete Schourek	.10	.05
☐ 540 Ruben Amaro	.10	.05
☐ 541 Andy Ashby	.10	.05
☐ 542 Kim Batiste	.10	.05
☐ 543 Cliff Brantley	.10	.05
☐ 544 Mariano Duncan	.10	.05
☐ 545 Jeff Grotewold	.10	.05
☐ 546 Barry Jones	.10	.05
☐ 547 Julio Peguero	.10	.05
☐ 548 Curt Schilling	.40	.18
☐ 549 Mitch Williams	.10	.05
☐ 550 Stan Belinda	.10	.05
☐ 551 Scott Bullett	.10	.05
☐ 552 Cecil Espy	.10	.05
☐ 553 Jeff King	.20	.09
☐ 554 Roger Mason	.10	.05
☐ 555 Paul Miller	.10	.05
☐ 556 Denny Neagle	.30	.14
☐ 557 Vicente Palacios	.10	.05
☐ 558 Bob Patterson	.10	.05
☐ 559 Tom Prince	.10	.05
☐ 560 Gary Redus	.10	.05
☐ 561 Gary Varsho	.10	.05
☐ 562 Juan Agosto	.10	.05
☐ 563 Cris Carpenter	.10	.05
☐ 564 Mark Clark	.10	.05
☐ 565 Jose DeLeon	.10	.05
☐ 566 Rich Gedman	.10	.05
☐ 567 Bernard Gilkey	.20	.09
☐ 568 Rex Hudler	.10	.05
☐ 569 Tim Jones	.10	.05
☐ 570 Donovan Osborne	.10	.05
☐ 571 Mike Perez	.10	.05
☐ 572 Gerald Perry	.10	.05
☐ 573 Bob Tewksbury	.10	.05
☐ 574 Todd Worrell	.10	.05
☐ 575 Dave Eiland	.10	.05
☐ 576 Jeremy Hernandez	.10	.05
☐ 577 Craig Lefferts	.10	.05
☐ 578 Jose Melendez	.10	.05
☐ 579 Randy Myers	.20	.09
☐ 580 Gary Pettis	.10	.05
☐ 581 Rich Rodriguez	.10	.05
☐ 582 Gary Sheffield	.40	.18
☐ 583 Craig Shipley	.10	.05
☐ 584 Kurt Stillwell	.10	.05
☐ 585 Tim Teufel	.10	.05
☐ 586 Rod Beck	.40	.18
☐ 587 Dave Burba	.10	.05
☐ 588 Craig Colbert	.10	.05
☐ 589 Bryan Hickerson	.10	.05
☐ 590 Mike Jackson	.10	.05
☐ 591 Mark Leonard	.10	.05
☐ 592 Jim McNamara	.10	.05
☐ 593 John Patterson	.10	.05
☐ 594 Dave Righetti	.10	.05
☐ 595 Cory Snyder	.10	.05
☐ 596 Bill Swift	.10	.05
☐ 597 Ted Wood	.10	.05
☐ 598 Checklist 301-400	.10	.05
☐ 599 Checklist 401-500	.10	.05
☐ 600 Checklist 501-600	.10	.05

1992 Ultra All-Rookies

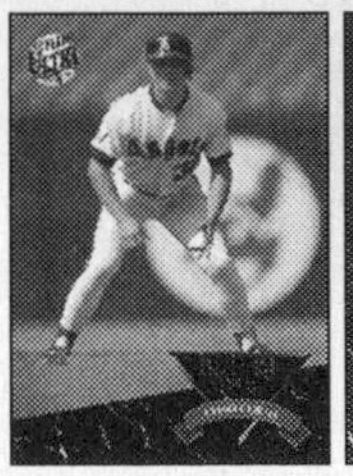
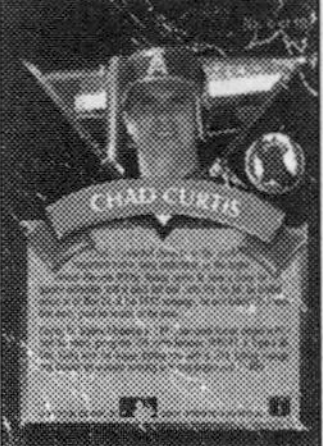

Cards from this ten-card standard-size set highlighting a selection of top rookies were randomly inserted in 1992 Ultra II foil packs. The fronts feature borderless color action player photos except at the bottom where they are edged by a marbleized black wedge. The words "All-Rookie Team" in gold foil lettering appear in a black marbleized inverted triangle at the lower right corner, with the player's name on a color banner.

	MINT	NRMT
COMPLETE SET (10)	12.00	5.50
COMMON CARD (1-10)	.50	.23
☐ 1 Eric Karros	2.00	.90
☐ 2 Andy Stankiewicz	.50	.23
☐ 3 Gary DiSarcina	.50	.23
☐ 4 Archi Cianfrocco	.50	.23
☐ 5 Jim McNamara	.50	.23
☐ 6 Chad Curtis	1.50	.70
☐ 7 Kenny Lofton	10.00	4.50
☐ 8 Reggie Sanders	1.00	.45
☐ 9 Pat Mahomes	.50	.23
☐ 10 Donovan Osborne	.50	.23

1992 Ultra All-Stars

Featuring many of the 1992 season's stars, cards from this 20-card standard-size set were randomly inserted in

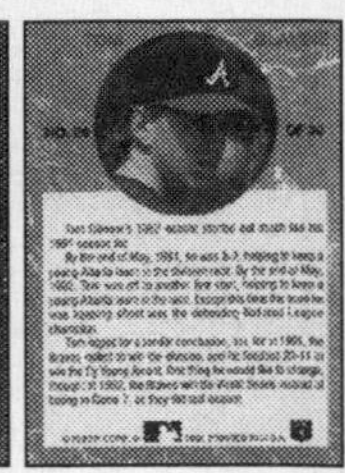

1992 Ultra II foil packs. The front design displays color action player photos enclosed by black marbleized borders. The word "All-Star" and the player's name are printed in gold foil lettering in the bottom border.

	MINT	NRMT
COMPLETE SET (20)	25.00	11.00
COMMON CARD (1-20)	.50	.23
☐ 1 Mark McGwire	3.00	1.35
☐ 2 Roberto Alomar	1.50	.70
☐ 3 Cal Ripken Jr.	6.00	2.70
☐ 4 Wade Boggs	1.00	.45
☐ 5 Mickey Tettleton	.50	.23
☐ 6 Ken Griffey Jr.	8.00	3.60
☐ 7 Roberto Kelly	.50	.23
☐ 8 Kirby Puckett	2.50	1.10
☐ 9 Frank Thomas	6.00	2.70
☐ 10 Jack McDowell	.50	.23
☐ 11 Will Clark	1.00	.45
☐ 12 Ryne Sandberg	2.00	.90
☐ 13 Barry Larkin	1.00	.45
☐ 14 Gary Sheffield	1.50	.70
☐ 15 Tom Pagnozzi	.50	.23
☐ 16 Barry Bonds	2.00	.90
☐ 17 Deion Sanders	1.50	.70
☐ 18 Darryl Strawberry	.75	.35
☐ 19 David Cone	.75	.35
☐ 20 Tom Glavine	1.00	.45

1992 Ultra Award Winners

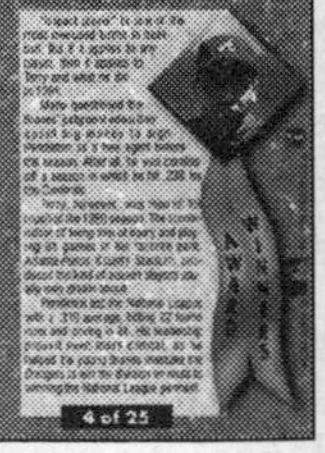

This 25-card standard-size set features 18 Gold Glove winners, both Cy Young Award winners, both Rookies of the Year, both league MVP's, and the World Series MVP. The cards were randomly inserted in 1992 Fleer Ultra I packs. The fronts carry full-bleed color player photos that have a diagonal blue marbleized border at the bottom. The player's name appears in this bottom border, and a diamond-shaped gold foil seal signifying the award the player won is superimposed at the lower right corner.

	MINT	NRMT
COMPLETE SET (25)	50.00	22.00
COMMON CARD (1-25)	.75	.35
☐ 1 Jack Morris	1.00	.45
☐ 2 Chuck Knoblauch	2.00	.90
☐ 3 Jeff Bagwell	8.00	3.60
☐ 4 Terry Pendleton	1.00	.45
☐ 5 Cal Ripken	10.00	4.50
☐ 6 Roger Clemens	4.00	1.80
☐ 7 Tom Glavine	1.50	.70
☐ 8 Tom Pagnozzi	.75	.35
☐ 9 Ozzie Smith	2.50	1.10
☐ 10 Andy Van Slyke	.75	.35
☐ 11 Barry Bonds	2.50	1.10
☐ 12 Tony Gwynn	4.00	1.80
☐ 13 Matt Williams	1.50	.70
☐ 14 Will Clark	1.50	.70
☐ 15 Robin Ventura	1.00	.45
☐ 16 Mark Langston	.75	.35
☐ 17 Tony Pena	.75	.35
☐ 18 Devon White	.75	.35
☐ 19 Don Mattingly	4.00	1.80
☐ 20 Roberto Alomar	2.00	.90
☐ 21A Cal Ripken ERR (Reversed negative on card back)	15.00	6.75

Card	MINT	NRMT
☐ 21B Cal Ripken COR	10.00	4.50
☐ 22 Ken Griffey Jr.	12.00	5.50
☐ 23 Kirby Puckett	4.00	1.80
☐ 24 Greg Maddux	8.00	3.60
☐ 25 Ryne Sandberg	2.50	1.10

1992 Ultra Gwynn

Tony Gwynn served as a spokesperson for Ultra during 1992 and was the exclusive subject of this 12-card standard-size set. The first ten cards of this set were randomly inserted in 1992 Ultra I packs. More than 2,000 of these cards were personaly autographed by Gwynn. The fronts display color posed and action shots of Gwynn framed by green marbled borders. The player's name and the words "Commemorative Series" appear in gold-foil lettering in the bottom border. On a green marbled background, the backs features a color head shot, career summary, and highlights. These insert cards are numbered on the back "No. X of 10." An additional special two-card subset was available through a mail-in offer for ten 1992 Ultra baseball wrappers plus 1.00 for shipping and handling. This offer was good through October 31st and, according to Fleer, over 100,000 sets were produced. The standard-size cards display action shots of Gwynn framed by green marbled borders. The player's name and the words "Commemorative Series" appear in gold-foil lettering in the bottom border. On a green marbled background, the backs features a color head shot and either a player profile (Special No. 1 on the card back) or Gwynn's comments about other players or the game itself (Special No. 2 on the card back).

	MINT	NRMT
COMPLETE SET (10)	10.00	4.50
COMMON GWYNN (1-10)	1.00	.45
COMMON SEND-OFF (S1/S2)	1.00	.45

Card	MINT	NRMT
☐ 1 Tony Gwynn (Leaping and catching ball at outfield wall)	1.00	.45
☐ 2 Tony Gwynn (Batting stance, brown Padres' uniform)	1.00	.45
☐ 3 Tony Gwynn (Awaiting flyball, glove above head)	1.00	.45
☐ 4 Tony Gwynn (Follow-through on swing)	1.00	.45
☐ 5 Tony Gwynn (Leading off base; crouching at the knees)	1.00	.45
☐ 6 Tony Gwynn (Posed with silver bat and Gold Glove trophy)	1.00	.45
☐ 7 Tony Gwynn (Bunting)	1.00	.45
☐ 8 Tony Gwynn (Full body shot; swinging)	1.00	.45
☐ 9 Tony Gwynn (Taking off for first)	1.00	.45
☐ 10 Tony Gwynn (Batting, following through, sunglasses on)	1.00	.45
☐ S1 Tony Gwynn (Batting)	1.00	.45
☐ S2 Tony Gwynn (Fielding)	1.00	.45
☐ AU0 Tony Gwynn AU (Autographed with certified signature)	175.00	80.00

1993 Ultra

The 1993 Ultra baseball set was issued in two series and totaled 650 standard-size cards. The full-bleed color-enhanced action photos are edged at the bottom by a gold foil stripe and a fawn-colored border that is streaked with white for a marbleized effect. On a dimensionalized ball park background, the horizontal backs have an action shot, a portrait, last season statistics, and the player's entire professional career totals. The cards are numbered on the back, grouped alphabetically within teams, with NL preceding AL. The first series closes with checklist cards (298-300). The second series features 83 Ultra Rookies, 51 Rockies and Marlins, traded veteran players, and other major league veterans not included in the first series. The Rookie cards show a gold foil stamped Rookie "flag" as part of the card design. The key Rookie Card in this set is Jim Edmonds.

	MINT	NRMT
COMPLETE SET (650)	30.00	13.50
COMPLETE SERIES 1 (300)	15.00	6.75
COMPLETE SERIES 2 (350)	15.00	6.75
COMMON CARD (1-650)	.15	.07

Card	MINT	NRMT
☐ 1 Steve Avery	.15	.07
☐ 2 Rafael Belliard	.15	.07
☐ 3 Damon Berryhill	.15	.07
☐ 4 Sid Bream	.15	.07
☐ 5 Ron Gant	.30	.14
☐ 6 Tom Glavine	.40	.18
☐ 7 Ryan Klesko	.75	.35
☐ 8 Mark Lemke	.15	.07
☐ 9 Javier Lopez	.60	.25
☐ 10 Greg Olson	.15	.07
☐ 11 Terry Pendleton	.30	.14
☐ 12 Deion Sanders	.60	.25
☐ 13 Mike Stanton	.15	.07
☐ 14 Paul Assenmacher	.15	.07
☐ 15 Steve Buechele	.15	.07
☐ 16 Frank Castillo	.15	.07
☐ 17 Shawon Dunston	.15	.07
☐ 18 Mark Grace	.40	.18
☐ 19 Derrick May	.15	.07
☐ 20 Chuck McElroy	.15	.07
☐ 21 Mike Morgan	.15	.07
☐ 22 Bob Scanlan	.15	.07
☐ 23 Dwight Smith	.15	.07
☐ 24 Sammy Sosa	.60	.25
☐ 25 Rick Wilkins	.15	.07
☐ 26 Tim Belcher	.15	.07
☐ 27 Jeff Branson	.15	.07
☐ 28 Bill Doran	.15	.07
☐ 29 Chris Hammond	.15	.07
☐ 30 Barry Larkin	.40	.18
☐ 31 Hal Morris	.15	.07
☐ 32 Joe Oliver	.15	.07
☐ 33 Jose Rijo	.15	.07
☐ 34 Bip Roberts	.15	.07
☐ 35 Chris Sabo	.15	.07
☐ 36 Reggie Sanders	.30	.14
☐ 37 Craig Biggio	.40	.18
☐ 38 Ken Caminiti	.60	.25
☐ 39 Steve Finley	.30	.14
☐ 40 Luis Gonzalez	.15	.07
☐ 41 Juan Guerrero	.15	.07
☐ 42 Pete Harnisch	.15	.07
☐ 43 Xavier Hernandez	.15	.07
☐ 44 Doug Jones	.15	.07
☐ 45 Al Osuna	.15	.07
☐ 46 Eddie Taubensee	.15	.07
☐ 47 Scooter Tucker	.15	.07
☐ 48 Brian Williams	.15	.07
☐ 49 Pedro Astacio	.15	.07
☐ 50 Rafael Bournigal	.15	.07
☐ 51 Brett Butler	.30	.14
☐ 52 Tom Candiotti	.15	.07
☐ 53 Eric Davis	.30	.14
☐ 54 Lenny Harris	.15	.07
☐ 55 Orel Hershiser	.30	.14
☐ 56 Eric Karros	.30	.14
☐ 57 Pedro Martinez	.60	.25
☐ 58 Roger McDowell	.15	.07
☐ 59 Jose Offerman	.15	.07
☐ 60 Mike Piazza	3.00	1.35
☐ 61 Moises Alou	.30	.14
☐ 62 Kent Bottenfield	.15	.07
☐ 63 Archi Cianfrocco	.15	.07
☐ 64 Greg Colbrunn	.15	.07
☐ 65 Wil Cordero	.15	.07
☐ 66 Delino DeShields	.15	.07
☐ 67 Darrin Fletcher	.15	.07
☐ 68 Ken Hill	.30	.14
☐ 69 Chris Nabholz	.15	.07
☐ 70 Mel Rojas	.30	.14
☐ 71 Larry Walker	.60	.25
☐ 72 Sid Fernandez	.15	.07
☐ 73 John Franco	.15	.07
☐ 74 Dave Gallagher	.15	.07
☐ 75 Todd Hundley	.40	.18
☐ 76 Howard Johnson	.15	.07
☐ 77 Jeff Kent	.30	.14
☐ 78 Eddie Murray	.60	.25
☐ 79 Bret Saberhagen	.15	.07
☐ 80 Chico Walker	.15	.07
☐ 81 Anthony Young	.15	.07
☐ 82 Kyle Abbott	.15	.07
☐ 83 Ruben Amaro	.15	.07
☐ 84 Juan Bell	.15	.07
☐ 85 Wes Chamberlain	.15	.07
☐ 86 Darren Daulton	.30	.14
☐ 87 Mariano Duncan	.15	.07
☐ 88 Dave Hollins	.15	.07
☐ 89 Ricky Jordan	.15	.07
☐ 90 John Kruk	.30	.14
☐ 91 Mickey Morandini	.15	.07
☐ 92 Terry Mulholland	.15	.07
☐ 93 Ben Rivera	.15	.07
☐ 94 Mike Williams	.15	.07
☐ 95 Stan Belinda	.15	.07
☐ 96 Jay Bell	.30	.14
☐ 97 Jeff King	.30	.14
☐ 98 Mike LaValliere	.15	.07
☐ 99 Lloyd McClendon	.15	.07
☐ 100 Orlando Merced	.15	.07
☐ 101 Zane Smith	.15	.07
☐ 102 Randy Tomlin	.15	.07
☐ 103 Andy Van Slyke	.30	.14
☐ 104 Tim Wakefield	.30	.14
☐ 105 John Wehner	.15	.07
☐ 106 Bernard Gilkey	.30	.14
☐ 107 Brian Jordan	.30	.14
☐ 108 Ray Lankford	.30	.14
☐ 109 Donovan Osborne	.15	.07
☐ 110 Tom Pagnozzi	.15	.07
☐ 111 Mike Perez	.15	.07
☐ 112 Lee Smith	.30	.14
☐ 113 Ozzie Smith	.75	.35
☐ 114 Bob Tewksbury	.15	.07
☐ 115 Todd Zeile	.15	.07
☐ 116 Andy Benes	.30	.14
☐ 117 Greg W. Harris	.15	.07
☐ 118 Darrin Jackson	.15	.07
☐ 119 Fred McGriff	.40	.18
☐ 120 Rich Rodriguez	.15	.07
☐ 121 Frank Seminara	.15	.07
☐ 122 Gary Sheffield	.60	.25
☐ 123 Craig Shipley	.15	.07
☐ 124 Kurt Stillwell	.15	.07
☐ 125 Dan Walters	.15	.07
☐ 126 Rod Beck	.30	.14
☐ 127 Mike Benjamin	.15	.07
☐ 128 Jeff Brantley	.15	.07
☐ 129 John Burkett	.15	.07
☐ 130 Will Clark	.40	.18
☐ 131 Royce Clayton	.30	.14
☐ 132 Steve Hosey	.15	.07
☐ 133 Mike Jackson	.15	.07
☐ 134 Darren Lewis	.15	.07
☐ 135 Kirt Manwaring	.15	.07
☐ 136 Bill Swift	.15	.07
☐ 137 Robby Thompson	.15	.07
☐ 138 Brady Anderson	.40	.18
☐ 139 Glenn Davis	.15	.07
☐ 140 Leo Gomez	.15	.07
☐ 141 Chito Martinez	.15	.07
☐ 142 Ben McDonald	.15	.07
☐ 143 Alan Mills	.15	.07
☐ 144 Mike Mussina	.60	.25
☐ 145 Gregg Olson	.15	.07
☐ 146 David Segui	.15	.07
☐ 147 Jeff Tackett	.15	.07
☐ 148 Jack Clark	.15	.07
☐ 149 Scott Cooper	.15	.07
☐ 150 Danny Darwin	.15	.07
☐ 151 John Dopson	.15	.07
☐ 152 Mike Greenwell	.15	.07
☐ 153 Tim Naehring	.15	.07
☐ 154 Tony Pena	.15	.07
☐ 155 Paul Quantrill	.15	.07
☐ 156 Mo Vaughn	.75	.35
☐ 157 Frank Viola	.15	.07
☐ 158 Bob Zupcic	.15	.07
☐ 159 Chad Curtis	.30	.14
☐ 160 Gary DiSarcina	.15	.07
☐ 161 Damion Easley	.15	.07
☐ 162 Chuck Finley	.15	.07
☐ 163 Tim Fortugno	.15	.07
☐ 164 Rene Gonzales	.15	.07

☐	165 Joe Grahe	.15	.07
☐	166 Mark Langston	.15	.07
☐	167 John Orton	.15	.07
☐	168 Luis Polonia	.15	.07
☐	169 Julio Valera	.15	.07
☐	170 Wilson Alvarez	.30	.14
☐	171 George Bell	.15	.07
☐	172 Joey Cora	.30	.14
☐	173 Alex Fernandez	.30	.14
☐	174 Lance Johnson	.15	.07
☐	175 Ron Karkovice	.15	.07
☐	176 Jack McDowell	.15	.07
☐	177 Scott Radinsky	.15	.07
☐	178 Tim Raines	.30	.14
☐	179 Steve Sax	.15	.07
☐	180 Bobby Thigpen	.15	.07
☐	181 Frank Thomas	2.50	1.10
☐	182 Sandy Alomar	.30	.14
☐	183 Carlos Baerga	.30	.14
☐	184 Felix Fermin	.15	.07
☐	185 Thomas Howard	.15	.07
☐	186 Mark Lewis	.15	.07
☐	187 Derek Lilliquist	.15	.07
☐	188 Carlos Martinez	.15	.07
☐	189 Charles Nagy	.30	.14
☐	190 Scott Scudder	.15	.07
☐	191 Paul Sorrento	.15	.07
☐	192 Jim Thome	1.25	.55
☐	193 Mark Whiten	.15	.07
☐	194 Milt Cuyler UER (Reversed negative on card front)	.15	.07
☐	195 Rob Deer	.15	.07
☐	196 John Doherty	.15	.07
☐	197 Travis Fryman	.30	.14
☐	198 Dan Gladden	.15	.07
☐	199 Mike Henneman	.15	.07
☐	200 John Kiely	.15	.07
☐	201 Chad Kreuter	.15	.07
☐	202 Scott Livingstone	.15	.07
☐	203 Tony Phillips	.15	.07
☐	204 Alan Trammell	.40	.18
☐	205 Mike Boddicker	.15	.07
☐	206 George Brett	1.25	.55
☐	207 Tom Gordon	.15	.07
☐	208 Mark Gubicza	.15	.07
☐	209 Gregg Jefferies	.30	.14
☐	210 Wally Joyner	.30	.14
☐	211 Kevin Koslofski	.15	.07
☐	212 Brent Mayne	.15	.07
☐	213 Brian McRae	.15	.07
☐	214 Kevin McReynolds	.15	.07
☐	215 Rusty Meacham	.15	.07
☐	216 Steve Shifflett	.15	.07
☐	217 James Austin	.15	.07
☐	218 Cal Eldred	.15	.07
☐	219 Darryl Hamilton	.15	.07
☐	220 Doug Henry	.15	.07
☐	221 John Jaha	.30	.14
☐	222 Dave Nilsson	.30	.14
☐	223 Jesse Orosco	.15	.07
☐	224 B.J. Surhoff	.30	.14
☐	225 Greg Vaughn	.15	.07
☐	226 Bill Wegman	.15	.07
☐	227 Robin Yount UER (Born in Illinois, not in Virginia)	.40	.18
☐	228 Rick Aguilera	.15	.07
☐	229 J.T. Bruett	.15	.07
☐	230 Scott Erickson	.15	.07
☐	231 Kent Hrbek	.30	.14
☐	232 Terry Jorgensen	.15	.07
☐	233 Scott Leius	.15	.07
☐	234 Pat Mahomes	.15	.07
☐	235 Pedro Munoz	.15	.07
☐	236 Kirby Puckett	1.25	.55
☐	237 Kevin Tapani	.15	.07
☐	238 Lenny Webster	.15	.07
☐	239 Carl Willis	.15	.07
☐	240 Mike Gallego	.15	.07
☐	241 John Habyan	.15	.07
☐	242 Pat Kelly	.15	.07
☐	243 Kevin Maas	.15	.07
☐	244 Don Mattingly	1.00	.45
☐	245 Hensley Meulens	.15	.07
☐	246 Sam Militello	.15	.07
☐	247 Matt Nokes	.15	.07
☐	248 Melido Perez	.15	.07
☐	249 Andy Stankiewicz	.15	.07
☐	250 Randy Velarde	.15	.07
☐	251 Bob Wickman	.15	.07
☐	252 Bernie Williams	.60	.25
☐	253 Lance Blankenship	.15	.07
☐	254 Mike Bordick	.15	.07
☐	255 Jerry Browne	.15	.07
☐	256 Ron Darling	.15	.07
☐	257 Dennis Eckersley	.30	.14
☐	258 Rickey Henderson	.40	.18
☐	259 Vince Horsman	.15	.07
☐	260 Troy Neel	.15	.07
☐	261 Jeff Parrett	.15	.07
☐	262 Terry Steinbach	.30	.14
☐	263 Bob Welch	.15	.07
☐	264 Bobby Witt	.15	.07
☐	265 Rich Amaral	.15	.07
☐	266 Bret Boone	.15	.07
☐	267 Jay Buhner	.40	.18
☐	268 Dave Fleming	.15	.07
☐	269 Randy Johnson	.60	.25
☐	270 Edgar Martinez	.40	.18
☐	271 Mike Schooler	.15	.07
☐	272 Russ Swan	.15	.07
☐	273 Dave Valle	.15	.07
☐	274 Omar Vizquel	.30	.14
☐	275 Kerry Woodson	.15	.07
☐	276 Kevin Brown	.30	.14
☐	277 Julio Franco	.30	.14
☐	278 Jeff Frye	.15	.07
☐	279 Juan Gonzalez	1.50	.70
☐	280 Jeff Huson	.15	.07
☐	281 Rafael Palmeiro	.40	.18
☐	282 Dean Palmer	.30	.14
☐	283 Roger Pavlik	.15	.07
☐	284 Ivan Rodriguez	.75	.35
☐	285 Kenny Rogers	.15	.07
☐	286 Derek Bell	.30	.14
☐	287 Pat Borders	.15	.07
☐	288 Joe Carter	.40	.18
☐	289 Bob MacDonald	.15	.07
☐	290 Jack Morris	.30	.14
☐	291 John Olerud	.30	.14
☐	292 Ed Sprague	.15	.07
☐	293 Todd Stottlemyre	.30	.14
☐	294 Mike Timlin	.15	.07
☐	295 Duane Ward	.15	.07
☐	296 David Wells	.15	.07
☐	297 Devon White	.15	.07
☐	298 Ray Lankford CL	.30	.14
☐	299 Bobby Witt CL	.15	.07
☐	300 Mike Piazza CL	.60	.25
☐	301 Steve Bedrosian	.15	.07
☐	302 Jeff Blauser	.15	.07
☐	303 Francisco Cabrera	.15	.07
☐	304 Marvin Freeman	.15	.07
☐	305 Brian Hunter	.15	.07
☐	306 David Justice	.60	.25
☐	307 Greg Maddux	2.00	.90
☐	308 Greg McMichael	.15	.07
☐	309 Kent Mercker	.15	.07
☐	310 Otis Nixon	.30	.14
☐	311 Pete Smith	.15	.07
☐	312 John Smoltz	.40	.18
☐	313 Jose Guzman	.15	.07
☐	314 Mike Harkey	.15	.07
☐	315 Greg Hibbard	.15	.07
☐	316 Candy Maldonado	.15	.07
☐	317 Randy Myers	.30	.14
☐	318 Dan Plesac	.15	.07
☐	319 Rey Sanchez	.15	.07
☐	320 Ryne Sandberg	.75	.35
☐	321 Tommy Shields	.15	.07
☐	322 Jose Vizcaino	.15	.07
☐	323 Matt Walbeck	.15	.07
☐	324 Willie Wilson	.15	.07
☐	325 Tom Browning	.15	.07
☐	326 Tim Costo	.15	.07
☐	327 Rob Dibble	.15	.07
☐	328 Steve Foster	.15	.07
☐	329 Roberto Kelly	.15	.07
☐	330 Randy Milligan	.15	.07
☐	331 Kevin Mitchell	.30	.14
☐	332 Tim Pugh	.15	.07
☐	333 Jeff Reardon	.30	.14
☐	334 John Roper	.15	.07
☐	335 Juan Samuel	.15	.07
☐	336 John Smiley	.15	.07
☐	337 Dan Wilson	.30	.14
☐	338 Scott Aldred	.15	.07
☐	339 Andy Ashby	.15	.07
☐	340 Freddie Benavides	.15	.07
☐	341 Dante Bichette	.40	.18
☐	342 Willie Blair	.15	.07
☐	343 Daryl Boston	.15	.07
☐	344 Vinny Castilla	.60	.25
☐	345 Jerald Clark	.15	.07
☐	346 Alex Cole	.15	.07
☐	347 Andres Galarraga	.40	.18
☐	348 Joe Girardi	.15	.07
☐	349 Ryan Hawblitzel	.15	.07
☐	350 Charlie Hayes	.15	.07
☐	351 Butch Henry	.15	.07
☐	352 Darren Holmes	.15	.07
☐	353 Dale Murphy	.60	.25
☐	354 David Nied	.15	.07
☐	355 Jeff Parrett	.15	.07
☐	356 Steve Reed	.15	.07
☐	357 Bruce Ruffin	.15	.07
☐	358 Danny Sheaffer	.15	.07
☐	359 Bryn Smith	.15	.07
☐	360 Jim Tatum	.15	.07
☐	361 Eric Young	.60	.25
☐	362 Gerald Young	.15	.07
☐	363 Luis Aquino	.15	.07
☐	364 Alex Arias	.15	.07
☐	365 Jack Armstrong	.15	.07
☐	366 Bret Barberie	.15	.07
☐	367 Ryan Bowen	.15	.07
☐	368 Greg Briley	.15	.07
☐	369 Cris Carpenter	.15	.07
☐	370 Chuck Carr	.15	.07
☐	371 Jeff Conine	.30	.14
☐	372 Steve Decker	.15	.07
☐	373 Orestes Destrade	.15	.07
☐	374 Monty Fariss	.15	.07
☐	375 Junior Felix	.15	.07
☐	376 Chris Hammond	.15	.07
☐	377 Bryan Harvey	.15	.07
☐	378 Trevor Hoffman	.40	.18
☐	379 Charlie Hough	.15	.07
☐	380 Joe Klink	.15	.07
☐	381 Richie Lewis	.15	.07
☐	382 Dave Magadan	.15	.07
☐	383 Bob McClure	.15	.07
☐	384 Scott Pose	.15	.07
☐	385 Rich Renteria	.15	.07
☐	386 Benito Santiago	.15	.07
☐	387 Walt Weiss	.15	.07
☐	388 Nigel Wilson	.15	.07
☐	389 Eric Anthony	.15	.07
☐	390 Jeff Bagwell	1.25	.55
☐	391 Andujar Cedeno	.15	.07
☐	392 Doug Drabek	.15	.07
☐	393 Darryl Kile	.30	.14
☐	394 Mark Portugal	.15	.07
☐	395 Karl Rhodes	.15	.07
☐	396 Scott Servais	.15	.07
☐	397 Greg Swindell	.15	.07
☐	398 Tom Goodwin	.15	.07
☐	399 Kevin Gross	.15	.07
☐	400 Carlos Hernandez	.15	.07
☐	401 Ramon Martinez	.30	[illegible]
☐	402 Raul Mondesi	.75	[illegible]
☐	403 Jody Reed	.15	[illegible]
☐	404 Mike Sharperson	.15	[illegible]
☐	405 Cory Snyder	.15	[illegible]
☐	406 Darryl Strawberry	.30	[illegible]
☐	407 Rick Trlicek	.15	[illegible]
☐	408 Tim Wallach	.15	[illegible]
☐	409 Todd Worrell	.15	[illegible]
☐	410 Tavo Alvarez	.15	[illegible]
☐	411 Sean Berry	.15	[illegible]
☐	412 Frank Bolick	.15	[illegible]
☐	413 Cliff Floyd	.30	[illegible]
☐	414 Mike Gardiner	.15	[illegible]
☐	415 Marquis Grissom	.30	[illegible]
☐	416 Tim Laker	.15	[illegible]
☐	417 Mike Lansing	.30	[illegible]
☐	418 Dennis Martinez	.30	[illegible]
☐	419 John Vander Wal	.15	[illegible]
☐	420 John Wetteland	.30	[illegible]
☐	421 Rondell White	.40	[illegible]
☐	422 Bobby Bonilla	.30	[illegible]
☐	423 Jeromy Burnitz	.15	[illegible]
☐	424 Vince Coleman	.15	[illegible]
☐	425 Mike Draper	.15	[illegible]
☐	426 Tony Fernandez	.15	[illegible]
☐	427 Dwight Gooden	.30	[illegible]
☐	428 Jeff Innis	.15	[illegible]
☐	429 Bobby Jones	.30	[illegible]
☐	430 Mike Maddux	.15	[illegible]
☐	431 Charlie O'Brien	.15	[illegible]
☐	432 Joe Orsulak	.15	[illegible]
☐	433 Pete Schourek	.15	[illegible]
☐	434 Frank Tanana	.15	[illegible]
☐	435 Ryan Thompson	.15	[illegible]
☐	436 Kim Batiste	.15	[illegible]
☐	437 Mark Davis	.15	[illegible]
☐	438 Jose DeLeon	.15	[illegible]
☐	439 Len Dykstra	.30	[illegible]
☐	440 Jim Eisenreich	.30	[illegible]
☐	441 Tommy Greene	.15	[illegible]
☐	442 Pete Incaviglia	.15	[illegible]
☐	443 Danny Jackson	.15	[illegible]
☐	444 Todd Pratt	.15	[illegible]
☐	445 Curt Schilling	.30	[illegible]
☐	446 Milt Thompson	.15	[illegible]
☐	447 David West	.15	[illegible]
☐	448 Mitch Williams	.15	[illegible]
☐	449 Steve Cooke	.15	[illegible]
☐	450 Carlos Garcia	.15	[illegible]
☐	451 Al Martin	.30	[illegible]

Card		MINT	NRMT
☐ 452 Blas Minor		.15	.07
☐ 453 Dennis Moeller		.15	.07
☐ 454 Denny Neagle		.30	.14
☐ 455 Don Slaught		.15	.07
☐ 456 Lonnie Smith		.15	.07
☐ 457 Paul Wagner		.15	.07
☐ 458 Bob Walk		.15	.07
☐ 459 Kevin Young		.15	.07
☐ 460 Rene Arocha		.15	.07
☐ 461 Brian Barber		.15	.07
☐ 462 Rheal Cormier		.15	.07
☐ 463 Gregg Jefferies		.30	.14
☐ 464 Joe Magrane		.15	.07
☐ 465 Omar Olivares		.15	.07
☐ 466 Geronimo Pena		.15	.07
☐ 467 Allen Watson		.15	.07
☐ 468 Mark Whiten		.15	.07
☐ 469 Derek Bell		.30	.14
☐ 470 Phil Clark		.15	.07
☐ 471 Pat Gomez		.15	.07
☐ 472 Tony Gwynn		1.50	.70
☐ 473 Jeremy Hernandez		.15	.07
☐ 474 Bruce Hurst		.15	.07
☐ 475 Phil Plantier		.15	.07
☐ 476 Scott Sanders		.15	.07
☐ 477 Tim Scott		.15	.07
☐ 478 Darrell Sherman		.15	.07
☐ 479 Guillermo Velasquez		.15	.07
☐ 480 Tim Worrell		.15	.07
☐ 481 Todd Benzinger		.15	.07
☐ 482 Bud Black		.15	.07
☐ 483 Barry Bonds		.75	.35
☐ 484 Dave Burba		.15	.07
☐ 485 Bryan Hickerson		.15	.07
☐ 486 Dave Martinez		.15	.07
☐ 487 Willie McGee		.15	.07
☐ 488 Jeff Reed		.15	.07
☐ 489 Kevin Rogers		.15	.07
☐ 490 Matt Williams		.40	.18
☐ 491 Trevor Wilson		.15	.07
☐ 492 Harold Baines		.30	.14
☐ 493 Mike Devereaux		.15	.07
☐ 494 Todd Frohwirth		.15	.07
☐ 495 Chris Hoiles		.15	.07
☐ 496 Luis Mercedes		.15	.07
☐ 497 Sherman Obando		.15	.07
☐ 498 Brad Pennington		.15	.07
☐ 499 Harold Reynolds		.15	.07
☐ 500 Arthur Rhodes		.15	.07
☐ 501 Cal Ripken		2.50	1.10
☐ 502 Rick Sutcliffe		.15	.07
☐ 503 Fernando Valenzuela		.30	.14
☐ 504 Mark Williamson		.15	.07
☐ 505 Scott Bankhead		.15	.07
☐ 506 Greg Blosser		.15	.07
☐ 507 Ivan Calderon		.15	.07
☐ 508 Roger Clemens		1.25	.55
☐ 509 Andre Dawson		.40	.18
☐ 510 Scott Fletcher		.15	.07
☐ 511 Greg A. Harris		.15	.07
☐ 512 Billy Hatcher		.15	.07
☐ 513 Bob Melvin		.15	.07
☐ 514 Carlos Quintana		.15	.07
☐ 515 Luis Rivera		.15	.07
☐ 516 Jeff Russell		.15	.07
☐ 517 Ken Ryan		.15	.07
☐ 518 Chili Davis		.30	.14
☐ 519 Jim Edmonds		1.50	.70
☐ 520 Gary Gaetti		.30	.14
☐ 521 Torey Lovullo		.15	.07
☐ 522 Troy Percival		.40	.18
☐ 523 Tim Salmon		.75	.35
☐ 524 Scott Sanderson		.15	.07
☐ 525 J.T. Snow		.75	.35
☐ 526 Jerome Walton		.15	.07
☐ 527 Jason Bere		.30	.14
☐ 528 Rod Bolton		.15	.07
☐ 529 Ellis Burks		.30	.14
☐ 530 Carlton Fisk		.60	.25
☐ 531 Craig Grebeck		.15	.07
☐ 532 Ozzie Guillen		.15	.07
☐ 533 Roberto Hernandez		.30	.14
☐ 534 Bo Jackson		.30	.14
☐ 535 Kirk McCaskill		.15	.07
☐ 536 Dave Stieb		.15	.07
☐ 537 Robin Ventura		.30	.14
☐ 538 Albert Belle		.75	.35
☐ 539 Mike Bielecki		.15	.07
☐ 540 Glenallen Hill		.15	.07
☐ 541 Reggie Jefferson		.30	.14
☐ 542 Kenny Lofton		1.25	.55
☐ 543 Jeff Mutis		.15	.07
☐ 544 Junior Ortiz		.15	.07
☐ 545 Manny Ramirez		1.25	.55
☐ 546 Jeff Treadway		.15	.07
☐ 547 Kevin Wickander		.15	.07
☐ 548 Cecil Fielder		.30	.14
☐ 549 Kirk Gibson		.30	.14
☐ 550 Greg Gohr		.15	.07
☐ 551 David Haas		.15	.07
☐ 552 Bill Krueger		.15	.07
☐ 553 Mike Moore		.15	.07
☐ 554 Mickey Tettleton		.15	.07
☐ 555 Lou Whitaker		.30	.14
☐ 556 Kevin Appier		.30	.14
☐ 557 Billy Brewer		.15	.07
☐ 558 David Cone		.30	.14
☐ 559 Greg Gagne		.15	.07
☐ 560 Mark Gardner		.15	.07
☐ 561 Phil Hiatt		.15	.07
☐ 562 Felix Jose		.15	.07
☐ 563 Jose Lind		.15	.07
☐ 564 Mike Macfarlane		.15	.07
☐ 565 Keith Miller		.15	.07
☐ 566 Jeff Montgomery		.30	.14
☐ 567 Hipolito Pichardo		.15	.07
☐ 568 Ricky Bones		.15	.07
☐ 569 Tom Brunansky		.15	.07
☐ 570 Joe Kmak		.15	.07
☐ 571 Pat Listach		.15	.07
☐ 572 Graeme Lloyd		.15	.07
☐ 573 Carlos Maldonado		.15	.07
☐ 574 Josias Manzanillo		.15	.07
☐ 575 Matt Mieske		.30	.14
☐ 576 Kevin Reimer		.15	.07
☐ 577 Bill Spiers		.15	.07
☐ 578 Dickie Thon		.15	.07
☐ 579 Willie Banks		.15	.07
☐ 580 Jim Deshaies		.15	.07
☐ 581 Mark Guthrie		.15	.07
☐ 582 Brian Harper		.15	.07
☐ 583 Chuck Knoblauch		.60	.25
☐ 584 Gene Larkin		.15	.07
☐ 585 Shane Mack		.15	.07
☐ 586 David McCarty		.15	.07
☐ 587 Mike Pagliarulo		.15	.07
☐ 588 Mike Trombley		.15	.07
☐ 589 Dave Winfield		.40	.18
☐ 590 Jim Abbott		.15	.07
☐ 591 Wade Boggs		.60	.25
☐ 592 Russ Davis		.40	.18
☐ 593 Steve Farr		.15	.07
☐ 594 Steve Howe		.15	.07
☐ 595 Mike Humphreys		.15	.07
☐ 596 Jimmy Key		.30	.14
☐ 597 Jim Leyritz		.15	.07
☐ 598 Bobby Munoz		.15	.07
☐ 599 Paul O'Neill		.30	.14
☐ 600 Spike Owen		.15	.07
☐ 601 Mike Stanley		.15	.07
☐ 602 Danny Tartabull		.15	.07
☐ 603 Scott Brosius		.15	.07
☐ 604 Storm Davis		.15	.07
☐ 605 Eric Fox		.15	.07
☐ 606 Rich Gossage		.30	.14
☐ 607 Scott Hemond		.15	.07
☐ 608 Dave Henderson		.15	.07
☐ 609 Mark McGwire		1.25	.55
☐ 610 Mike Mohler		.15	.07
☐ 611 Edwin Nunez		.15	.07
☐ 612 Kevin Seitzer		.15	.07
☐ 613 Ruben Sierra		.15	.07
☐ 614 Chris Bosio		.15	.07
☐ 615 Norm Charlton		.15	.07
☐ 616 Jim Converse		.15	.07
☐ 617 John Cummings		.15	.07
☐ 618 Mike Felder		.15	.07
☐ 619 Ken Griffey Jr.		3.00	1.35
☐ 620 Mike Hampton		.40	.18
☐ 621 Erik Hanson		.15	.07
☐ 622 Bill Haselman		.15	.07
☐ 623 Tino Martinez		.60	.25
☐ 624 Lee Tinsley		.30	.14
☐ 625 Fernando Vina		.15	.07
☐ 626 David Wainhouse		.15	.07
☐ 627 Jose Canseco		.60	.25
☐ 628 Benji Gil		.15	.07
☐ 629 Tom Henke		.15	.07
☐ 630 David Hulse		.15	.07
☐ 631 Manuel Lee		.15	.07
☐ 632 Craig Lefferts		.15	.07
☐ 633 Robb Nen		.40	.18
☐ 634 Gary Redus		.15	.07
☐ 635 Bill Ripken		.15	.07
☐ 636 Nolan Ryan		2.50	1.10
☐ 637 Dan Smith		.15	.07
☐ 638 Matt Whiteside		.15	.07
☐ 639 Roberto Alomar		.60	.25
☐ 640 Juan Guzman		.15	.07
☐ 641 Pat Hentgen		.40	.18
☐ 642 Darrin Jackson		.15	.07
☐ 643 Randy Knorr		.15	.07
☐ 644 Domingo Martinez		.15	.07
☐ 645 Paul Molitor		.60	.25
☐ 646 Dick Schofield		.15	.07
☐ 647 Dave Stewart		.30	.14
☐ 648 Rey Sanchez CL		.15	.07
☐ 649 Jeremy Hernandez CL		.15	.07
☐ 650 Junior Ortiz CL		.15	.07

1993 Ultra All-Rookies

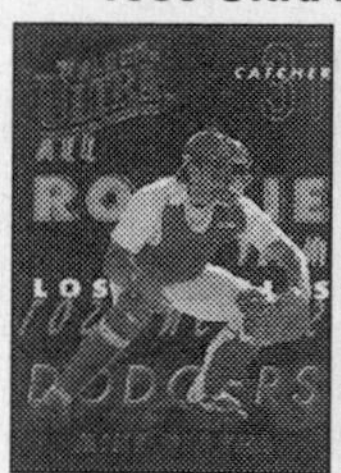

Inserted into series II packs at a rate of one in 18, this ten-card standard-size set features cutout color player action shots that are superposed upon a black background, which carries the player's uniform number, position, team name, and the set's title in multicolored lettering. The player's name appears in gold foil at the bottom. A posed color cutout player shot adorns the back, and is also projected upon a black background. The set's title appears at the top printed in gold foil and red lettering, and the player's name in gold foil precedes his career highlights, printed in white. The set is sequenced in alphabetical order. The key cards in this set are Mike Piazza and Tim Salmon.

	MINT	NRMT
COMPLETE SET (10)	15.00	6.75
COMMON CARD (1-10)	.50	.23
☐ 1 Rene Arocha	.50	.23
☐ 2 Jeff Conine	.75	.35
☐ 3 Phil Hiatt	.50	.23
☐ 4 Mike Lansing	.75	.35
☐ 5 Al Martin	.75	.35
☐ 6 David Nied	.50	.23
☐ 7 Mike Piazza	12.00	5.50
☐ 8 Tim Salmon	4.00	1.80
☐ 9 J.T. Snow	2.00	.90
☐ 10 Kevin Young	.50	.23

1993 Ultra All-Stars

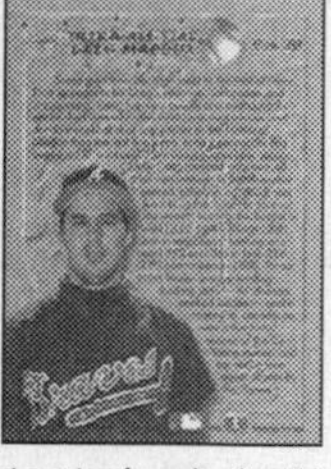

Inserted into series II packs at a rate of one in nine, this 20-card standard-size set features National League (1-10) and American League (11-20) All-Stars. The gray-bordered fronts carry color player action shots that are cutout and superposed upon their original, but faded and shifted, backgrounds. The player's name and the set's title are printed in gold foil upon simulated flames that issue from a baseball icon in the lower right. That same design of the player's name, the set's title, and flaming baseball icon appears again at the top of the gray-bordered back. The player's career highlights follow below.

	MINT	NRMT
COMPLETE SET (20)	40.00	18.00
COMMON CARD (1-20)	.75	.35
☐ 1 Darren Daulton	1.00	.45
☐ 2 Will Clark	1.50	.70
☐ 3 Ryne Sandberg	3.00	1.35
☐ 4 Barry Larkin	1.00	.45
☐ 5 Gary Sheffield	2.00	.90
☐ 6 Barry Bonds	3.00	1.35
☐ 7 Ray Lankford	1.50	.70
☐ 8 Larry Walker	2.00	.90
☐ 9 Greg Maddux	8.00	3.60
☐ 10 Lee Smith	1.00	.45
☐ 11 Ivan Rodriguez	3.00	1.35
☐ 12 Mark McGwire	4.00	1.80
☐ 13 Carlos Baerga	.75	.35

☐ 14 Cal Ripken	10.00	4.50
☐ 15 Edgar Martinez	1.50	.70
☐ 16 Juan Gonzalez	6.00	2.70
☐ 17 Ken Griffey Jr.	12.00	5.50
☐ 18 Kirby Puckett	5.00	2.20
☐ 19 Frank Thomas	10.00	4.50
☐ 20 Mike Mussina	2.00	.90

1993 Ultra Award Winners

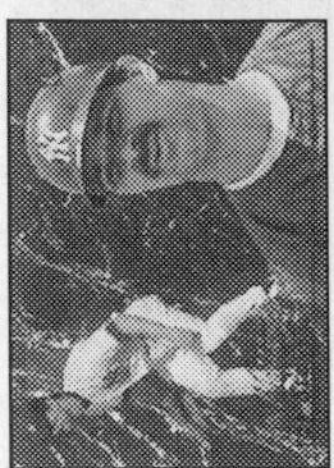
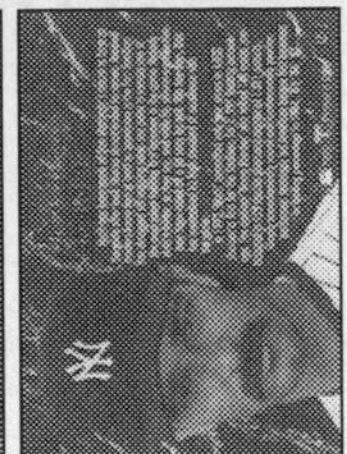

Randomly inserted in first series packs, this first series of 1993 Ultra Award Winners presents the Top Glove for the National (1-9) and American (10-18) Leagues and other major award winners (19-25). The 25 standard-size cards comprising this set feature horizontal black-marbleized card designs and carry two color player photos: an action shot on the left and a posed photo on the right. The player's name appears in gold-foil cursive lettering near the bottom left. The category of award is shown in gold foil below. A gold-foil line highlights the card's lower edge. The horizontal and black-marbleized design continues on the back. A color player head shot appears on the left side. The player's name reappears in gold-foil cursive lettering near the top. Below is the player's award category in gold foil above a gold-foil underline. The player's career highlights are shown in white lettering below.

	MINT	NRMT
COMPLETE SET (25)	40.00	18.00
COMMON CARD (1-25)	.75	.35
☐ 1 Greg Maddux	8.00	3.60
☐ 2 Tom Pagnozzi	.75	.35
☐ 3 Mark Grace	1.50	.70
☐ 4 Jose Lind	.75	.35
☐ 5 Terry Pendleton	1.00	.45
☐ 6 Ozzie Smith	3.00	1.35
☐ 7 Barry Bonds	3.00	1.35
☐ 8 Andy Van Slyke	.75	.35
☐ 9 Larry Walker	2.00	.90
☐ 10 Mark Langston	.75	.35
☐ 11 Ivan Rodriguez	3.00	1.35
☐ 12 Don Mattingly	6.00	2.70
☐ 13 Roberto Alomar	2.00	.90
☐ 14 Robin Ventura	1.00	.45
☐ 15 Cal Ripken	10.00	4.50
☐ 16 Ken Griffey	12.00	5.50
☐ 17 Kirby Puckett	5.00	2.20
☐ 18 Devon White	.75	.35
☐ 19 Pat Listach	.75	.35
☐ 20 Eric Karros	1.50	.70
☐ 21 Pat Borders	.75	.35
☐ 22 Greg Maddux	8.00	3.60
☐ 23 Dennis Eckersley	1.50	.70
☐ 24 Barry Bonds	3.00	1.35
☐ 25 Gary Sheffield	2.00	.90

1993 Ultra Eckersley

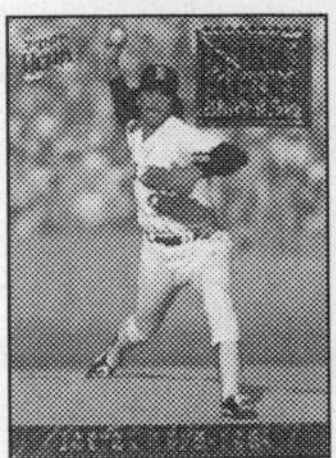
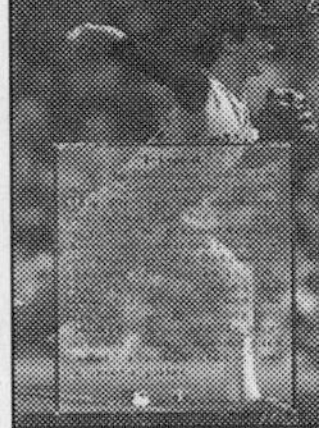

Randomly inserted in first series foil packs, this 10-card (cards 11 and 12 were mail-aways) standard-size set salutes one of baseball's greatest relief pitchers, Dennis Eckersley. The color action player photos on the fronts are full-bleed except at the bottom where a black marbleized border carries the team and years in silver foil lettering. A silver foil "Dennis Eckersley Career Highlights" emblem rounds out the front. On the back, a full-bleed color photo provides the background for a transparent pastel purple panel presenting career highlights in silver foil lettering. The cards are numbered on the back. Two additional cards (11 and 12) were available through a mail-in offer for ten 1993 Fleer Ultra baseball wrappers plus 1.00 for postage and handling. The expiration for this offer was September 30, 1993. Eckersley personally autographed more than 2,000 of these cards. The cards feature silver foil stamping on both sides.

	MINT	NRMT
COMPLETE SET (10)	4.00	1.80
COMMON ECK (1-10)	.50	.23
COMMON SEND-OFF (11-12)	1.00	.45
☐ 1 Dennis Eckersley Perfection	.50	.23
☐ 2 Dennis Eckersley The Kid	.50	.23
☐ 3 Dennis Eckersley The Warrior	.50	.23
☐ 4 Dennis Eckersley Beantown Blazer	.50	.23
☐ 5 Dennis Eckersley Eckspeak	.50	.23
☐ 6 Dennis Eckersley Down to Earth	.50	.23
☐ 7 Dennis Eckersley Wrigley Bound	.50	.23
☐ 8 Dennis Eckersley No Relief	.50	.23
☐ 9 Dennis Eckersley In Control	.50	.23
☐ 10 Dennis Eckersley Simply the Best	.50	.23
☐ 11 Dennis Eckersley Reign of Perfection	1.00	.45
☐ 12 Dennis Eckersley Leaving His Mark	1.00	.45
☐ P1 Dennis Eckersley Promo with Paul Mullan	4.00	1.80
☐ AU0 Dennis Eckersley AU (Certified autograph)	50.00	22.00

1993 Ultra Home Run Kings

Randomly inserted into all 1993 Ultra packs, this ten-card standard-size set features the best long ball hitters in baseball. The borderless cards carry cutout color action player photos that are superposed upon an outer space scene, which includes a baseball "planet" and background stars. The player's name and team, along with the set's logo, are printed in gold foil and rest at the bottom. The horizontal black-and-stellar back carries a color player close-up on the left side, and the player's name, nickname, and career highlights in white lettering on the right side. The set's logo, printed in gold foil at the upper right, rounds out the card.

	MINT	NRMT
COMPLETE SET (10)	15.00	6.75
COMMON CARD (1-10)	1.00	.45
☐ 1 Juan Gonzalez	8.00	3.60
☐ 2 Mark McGwire	5.00	2.20
☐ 3 Cecil Fielder	1.50	.70
☐ 4 Fred McGriff	1.50	.70
☐ 5 Albert Belle	6.00	2.70
☐ 6 Barry Bonds	4.00	1.80
☐ 7 Joe Carter	1.50	.70
☐ 8 Gary Sheffield	2.50	1.10
☐ 9 Darren Daulton	1.50	.70
☐ 10 Dave Hollins	1.00	.45

1993 Ultra Performers

This ten-card standard-size set could only be ordered directly from Fleer by sending in 9.95, five Fleer/Fleer Ultra baseball wrappers, and an order blank found in hobby and sports periodicals. Each borderless front features a color player action shot superposed upon four

other player photos, which are ghosted and color-screened. The player's name and the set name, both stamped in gold foil, appear at the bottom. The Ultra Performers set logo, a gold-foil-rimmed baseball icon with a blue trail, lies just above. The gold-foil Fleer Ultra logo appears in an upper corner. The back features a borderless color player action photo that is ghosted and color-screened on one side, where the player's name and career highlights appear. The set logo and gold-foil-stamped name appear below. The set's production number (out of 150,000 produced) rests within a ghosted rectangle at the bottom. The set is sequenced in alphabetical order.

	MINT	NRMT
COMPLETE SET (10)	25.00	11.00
COMMON CARD (1-10)	.50	.23
☐ 1 Barry Bonds	2.00	.90
☐ 2 Juan Gonzalez	4.00	1.80
☐ 3 Ken Griffey Jr.	10.00	4.50
☐ 4 Eric Karros	1.00	.45
☐ 5 Pat Listach	.50	.23
☐ 6 Greg Maddux	6.00	2.70
☐ 7 David Nied	.50	.23
☐ 8 Gary Sheffield	1.50	.70
☐ 9 J.T. Snow	1.50	.70
☐ 10 Frank Thomas	8.00	3.60

1993 Ultra Strikeout Kings

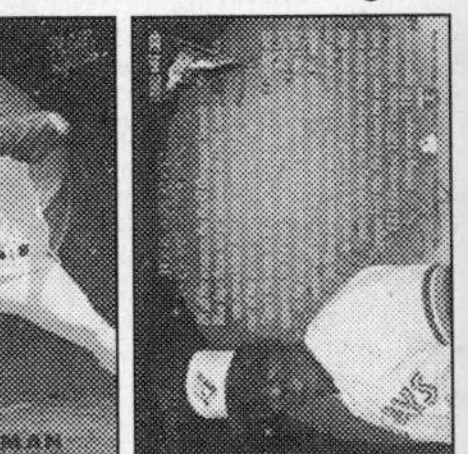

Inserted into series II packs at a rate of one in 37, this five-card standard-size showcases outstanding pitchers from both leagues. The color cutout action player photo on the front of each card shows a pitcher on the mound superposed upon a background of stars and a metallic baseball. The player's name appears in gold foil at the bottom. The gold foil-stamped set logo also appears on the front. Upon a metallic-baseball-and-stellar background, the horizontal back carries a posed color player photo on the left side, and the player's career highlights in yellow lettering on the right side. The player's name and team, as well as the set's logo, appear in gold foil at the top. The set is sequenced in alphabetical order.

	MINT	NRM
COMPLETE SET (5)	20.00	9.0
COMMON CARD (1-5)	1.00	.4
☐ 1 Roger Clemens	5.00	2.2
☐ 2 Juan Guzman	1.00	.4
☐ 3 Randy Johnson	2.00	.9
☐ 4 Nolan Ryan	15.00	6.7
☐ 5 John Smoltz	1.50	.7

1994 Ultra

The 1994 Ultra baseball set consists of 600 standard-size cards that were issued in two series of 300. Each pac[k] contains at least one insert card, while "Hot Packs" hav[e] nothing but insert cards in them. The front features a full-bleed color action player photo except at the bottom where a gold foil strip edges the picture. The player's name, his position, team name, and company logo a[re] gold foil stamped across the bottom of the front. Th[e] horizontal back has a montage of three different play[er]

cutouts on a action scene with a team color-coded border. Biography and statistics on a thin panel toward the bottom round out the back. The cards are numbered on the back, grouped alphabetically within teams, and checklisted below alphabetically according to teams for each league with AL preceding NL. Rookie Cards include Ray Durham and Chan Ho Park.

	MINT	NRMT
COMPLETE SET (600)	40.00	18.00
COMPLETE SERIES 1 (300)	20.00	9.00
COMPLETE SERIES 2 (300)	20.00	9.00
COMMON CARD (1-600)	.15	.07

Card	MINT	NRMT
☐ 1 Jeffrey Hammonds	.30	.14
☐ 2 Chris Hoiles	.15	.07
☐ 3 Ben McDonald	.15	.07
☐ 4 Mark McLemore	.15	.07
☐ 5 Alan Mills	.15	.07
☐ 6 Jamie Moyer	.15	.07
☐ 7 Brad Pennington	.15	.07
☐ 8 Jim Poole	.15	.07
☐ 9 Cal Ripken Jr.	2.50	1.10
☐ 10 Jack Voigt	.15	.07
☐ 11 Roger Clemens	1.25	.55
☐ 12 Danny Darwin	.15	.07
☐ 13 Andre Dawson	.40	.18
☐ 14 Scott Fletcher	.15	.07
☐ 15 Greg A Harris	.15	.07
☐ 16 Billy Hatcher	.15	.07
☐ 17 Jeff Russell	.15	.07
☐ 18 Aaron Sele	.15	.07
☐ 19 Mo Vaughn	.75	.35
☐ 20 Mike Butcher	.15	.07
☐ 21 Rod Correia	.15	.07
☐ 22 Steve Frey	.15	.07
☐ 23 Phil Leftwich	.15	.07
☐ 24 Torey Lovullo	.15	.07
☐ 25 Ken Patterson	.15	.07
☐ 26 Eduardo Perez UER (listed as a Twin instead of Angel)	.15	.07
☐ 27 Tim Salmon	.60	.25
☐ 28 J.T. Snow	.30	.14
☐ 29 Chris Turner	.15	.07
☐ 30 Wilson Alvarez	.30	.14
☐ 31 Jason Bere	.15	.07
☐ 32 Joey Cora	.30	.14
☐ 33 Alex Fernandez	.30	.14
☐ 34 Roberto Hernandez	.30	.14
☐ 35 Lance Johnson	.15	.07
☐ 36 Ron Karkovice	.15	.07
☐ 37 Kirk McCaskill	.15	.07
☐ 38 Jeff Schwarz	.15	.07
☐ 39 Frank Thomas	2.50	1.10
☐ 40 Sandy Alomar Jr.	.30	.14
☐ 41 Albert Belle	.75	.35
☐ 42 Felix Fermin	.15	.07
☐ 43 Wayne Kirby	.15	.07
☐ 44 Tom Kramer	.15	.07
☐ 45 Kenny Lofton	.75	.35
☐ 46 Jose Mesa	.30	.14
☐ 47 Eric Plunk	.15	.07
☐ 48 Paul Sorrento	.15	.07
☐ 49 Jim Thome	.75	.35
☐ 50 Bill Wertz	.15	.07
☐ 51 John Doherty	.15	.07
☐ 52 Cecil Fielder	.30	.14
☐ 53 Travis Fryman	.30	.14
☐ 54 Chris Gomez	.15	.07
☐ 55 Mike Henneman	.15	.07
☐ 56 Chad Kreuter	.15	.07
☐ 57 Bob MacDonald	.15	.07
☐ 58 Mike Moore	.15	.07
☐ 59 Tony Phillips	.15	.07
☐ 60 Lou Whitaker	.30	.14
☐ 61 Kevin Appier	.30	.14
☐ 62 Greg Gagne	.15	.07
☐ 63 Chris Gwynn	.15	.07
☐ 64 Bob Hamelin	.15	.07
☐ 65 Chris Haney	.15	.07
☐ 66 Phil Hiatt	.15	.07
☐ 67 Felix Jose	.15	.07
☐ 68 Jose Lind	.15	.07
☐ 69 Mike Macfarlane	.15	.07
☐ 70 Jeff Montgomery	.30	.14
☐ 71 Hipolito Pichardo	.15	.07
☐ 72 Juan Bell	.15	.07
☐ 73 Cal Eldred	.15	.07
☐ 74 Darryl Hamilton	.15	.07
☐ 75 Doug Henry	.15	.07
☐ 76 Mike Ignasiak	.15	.07
☐ 77 John Jaha	.15	.07
☐ 78 Graeme Lloyd	.15	.07
☐ 79 Angel Miranda	.15	.07
☐ 80 Dave Nilsson	.30	.14
☐ 81 Troy O'Leary	.15	.07
☐ 82 Kevin Reimer	.15	.07
☐ 83 Willie Banks	.15	.07
☐ 84 Larry Casian	.15	.07
☐ 85 Scott Erickson	.15	.07
☐ 86 Eddie Guardado	.15	.07
☐ 87 Kent Hrbek	.30	.14
☐ 88 Terry Jorgensen	.15	.07
☐ 89 Chuck Knoblauch	.60	.25
☐ 90 Pat Meares	.15	.07
☐ 91 Mike Trombley	.15	.07
☐ 92 Dave Winfield	.40	.18
☐ 93 Wade Boggs	.60	.25
☐ 94 Scott Kamieniecki	.15	.07
☐ 95 Pat Kelly	.15	.07
☐ 96 Jimmy Key	.30	.14
☐ 97 Jim Leyritz	.15	.07
☐ 98 Bobby Munoz	.15	.07
☐ 99 Paul O'Neill	.30	.14
☐ 100 Melido Perez	.15	.07
☐ 101 Mike Stanley	.15	.07
☐ 102 Danny Tartabull	.15	.07
☐ 103 Bernie Williams	.60	.25
☐ 104 Kurt Abbott	.30	.14
☐ 105 Mike Bordick	.15	.07
☐ 106 Ron Darling	.15	.07
☐ 107 Brent Gates	.15	.07
☐ 108 Miguel Jimenez	.15	.07
☐ 109 Steve Karsay	.15	.07
☐ 110 Scott Lydy	.15	.07
☐ 111 Mark McGwire	1.25	.55
☐ 112 Troy Neel	.15	.07
☐ 113 Craig Paquette	.15	.07
☐ 114 Bob Welch	.15	.07
☐ 115 Bobby Witt	.15	.07
☐ 116 Rich Amaral	.15	.07
☐ 117 Mike Blowers	.15	.07
☐ 118 Jay Buhner	.40	.18
☐ 119 Dave Fleming	.15	.07
☐ 120 Ken Griffey Jr.	3.00	1.35
☐ 121 Tino Martinez	.60	.25
☐ 122 Marc Newfield	.30	.14
☐ 123 Ted Power	.15	.07
☐ 124 Mackey Sasser	.15	.07
☐ 125 Omar Vizquel	.30	.14
☐ 126 Kevin Brown	.30	.14
☐ 127 Juan Gonzalez	1.50	.70
☐ 128 Tom Henke	.15	.07
☐ 129 David Hulse	.15	.07
☐ 130 Dean Palmer	.30	.14
☐ 131 Roger Pavlik	.15	.07
☐ 132 Ivan Rodriguez	.75	.35
☐ 133 Kenny Rogers	.15	.07
☐ 134 Doug Strange	.15	.07
☐ 135 Pat Borders	.15	.07
☐ 136 Joe Carter	.40	.18
☐ 137 Darnell Coles	.15	.07
☐ 138 Pat Hentgen	.30	.14
☐ 139 Al Leiter	.15	.07
☐ 140 Paul Molitor	.60	.25
☐ 141 John Olerud	.30	.14
☐ 142 Ed Sprague	.15	.07
☐ 143 Dave Stewart	.30	.14
☐ 144 Mike Timlin	.15	.07
☐ 145 Duane Ward	.15	.07
☐ 146 Devon White	.15	.07
☐ 147 Steve Avery	.15	.07
☐ 148 Steve Bedrosian	.15	.07
☐ 149 Damon Berryhill	.15	.07
☐ 150 Jeff Blauser	.15	.07
☐ 151 Tom Glavine	.40	.18
☐ 152 Chipper Jones	2.00	.90
☐ 153 Mark Lemke	.15	.07
☐ 154 Fred McGriff	.40	.18
☐ 155 Greg McMichael	.15	.07
☐ 156 Deion Sanders	.60	.25
☐ 157 John Smoltz	.40	.18
☐ 158 Mark Wohlers	.30	.14
☐ 159 Jose Bautista	.15	.07
☐ 160 Steve Buechele	.15	.07
☐ 161 Mike Harkey	.15	.07
☐ 162 Greg Hibbard	.15	.07
☐ 163 Chuck McElroy	.15	.07
☐ 164 Mike Morgan	.15	.07
☐ 165 Kevin Roberson	.15	.07
☐ 166 Ryne Sandberg	.75	.35
☐ 167 Jose Vizcaino	.15	.07
☐ 168 Rick Wilkins	.15	.07
☐ 169 Willie Wilson	.15	.07
☐ 170 Willie Greene	.30	.14
☐ 171 Roberto Kelly	.15	.07
☐ 172 Larry Luebbers	.15	.07
☐ 173 Kevin Mitchell	.30	.14
☐ 174 Joe Oliver	.15	.07
☐ 175 John Roper	.15	.07
☐ 176 Johnny Ruffin	.15	.07
☐ 177 Reggie Sanders	.15	.07
☐ 178 John Smiley	.15	.07
☐ 179 Jerry Spradlin	.15	.07
☐ 180 Freddie Benavides	.15	.07
☐ 181 Dante Bichette	.40	.18
☐ 182 Willie Blair	.15	.07
☐ 183 Kent Bottenfield	.15	.07
☐ 184 Jerald Clark	.15	.07
☐ 185 Joe Girardi	.15	.07
☐ 186 Roberto Mejia	.15	.07
☐ 187 Steve Reed	.15	.07
☐ 188 Armando Reynoso	.15	.07
☐ 189 Bruce Ruffin	.15	.07
☐ 190 Eric Young	.30	.14
☐ 191 Luis Aquino	.15	.07
☐ 192 Bret Barberie	.15	.07
☐ 193 Ryan Bowen	.15	.07
☐ 194 Chuck Carr	.15	.07
☐ 195 Orestes Destrade	.15	.07
☐ 196 Richie Lewis	.15	.07
☐ 197 Dave Magadan	.15	.07
☐ 198 Bob Natal	.15	.07
☐ 199 Gary Sheffield	.60	.25
☐ 200 Matt Turner	.15	.07
☐ 201 Darrell Whitmore	.15	.07
☐ 202 Eric Anthony	.15	.07
☐ 203 Jeff Bagwell	1.25	.55
☐ 204 Andujar Cedeno	.15	.07
☐ 205 Luis Gonzalez	.15	.07
☐ 206 Xavier Hernandez	.15	.07
☐ 207 Doug Jones	.15	.07
☐ 208 Darryl Kile	.30	.14
☐ 209 Scott Servais	.15	.07
☐ 210 Greg Swindell	.15	.07
☐ 211 Brian Williams	.15	.07
☐ 212 Pedro Astacio	.15	.07
☐ 213 Brett Butler	.30	.14
☐ 214 Omar Daal	.15	.07
☐ 215 Jim Gott	.15	.07
☐ 216 Raul Mondesi	.40	.18
☐ 217 Jose Offerman	.15	.07
☐ 218 Mike Piazza	2.00	.90
☐ 219 Cory Snyder	.15	.07
☐ 220 Tim Wallach	.15	.07
☐ 221 Todd Worrell	.15	.07
☐ 222 Moises Alou	.30	.14
☐ 223 Sean Berry	.15	.07
☐ 224 Wil Cordero	.30	.14
☐ 225 Jeff Fassero	.15	.07
☐ 226 Darrin Fletcher	.15	.07
☐ 227 Cliff Floyd	.40	.18
☐ 228 Marquis Grissom	.30	.14
☐ 229 Ken Hill	.15	.07
☐ 230 Mike Lansing	.30	.14
☐ 231 Kirk Rueter	.15	.07
☐ 232 John Wetteland	.30	.14
☐ 233 Rondell White	.40	.18
☐ 234 Tim Bogar	.15	.07
☐ 235 Jeromy Burnitz	.30	.14
☐ 236 Dwight Gooden	.30	.14
☐ 237 Todd Hundley	.30	.14
☐ 238 Jeff Kent	.15	.07
☐ 239 Josias Manzanillo	.15	.07
☐ 240 Joe Orsulak	.15	.07
☐ 241 Ryan Thompson	.15	.07
☐ 242 Kim Batiste	.15	.07
☐ 243 Darren Daulton	.30	.14
☐ 244 Tommy Greene	.15	.07
☐ 245 Dave Hollins	.15	.07
☐ 246 Pete Incaviglia	.15	.07
☐ 247 Danny Jackson	.15	.07
☐ 248 Ricky Jordan	.15	.07
☐ 249 John Kruk	.30	.14
☐ 250 Mickey Morandini	.15	.07
☐ 251 Terry Mulholland	.15	.07
☐ 252 Ben Rivera	.15	.07
☐ 253 Kevin Stocker	.15	.07
☐ 254 Jay Bell	.30	.14
☐ 255 Steve Cooke	.15	.07
☐ 256 Jeff King	.30	.14
☐ 257 Al Martin	.15	.07
☐ 258 Danny Miceli	.15	.07
☐ 259 Blas Minor	.15	.07
☐ 260 Don Slaught	.15	.07
☐ 261 Paul Wagner	.15	.07
☐ 262 Tim Wakefield	.15	.07

☐ 263 Kevin Young .15 .07
☐ 264 Rene Arocha .15 .07
☐ 265 Richard Batchelor .15 .07
☐ 266 Gregg Jefferies .30 .14
☐ 267 Brian Jordan .30 .14
☐ 268 Jose Oquendo .15 .07
☐ 269 Donovan Osborne .15 .07
☐ 270 Erik Pappas .15 .07
☐ 271 Mike Perez .15 .07
☐ 272 Bob Tewksbury .15 .07
☐ 273 Mark Whiten .15 .07
☐ 274 Todd Zeile .15 .07
☐ 275 Andy Ashby .15 .07
☐ 276 Brad Ausmus .15 .07
☐ 277 Phil Clark .15 .07
☐ 278 Jeff Gardner .15 .07
☐ 279 Ricky Gutierrez .15 .07
☐ 280 Tony Gwynn 1.50 .70
☐ 281 Tim Mauser .15 .07
☐ 282 Scott Sanders .15 .07
☐ 283 Frank Seminara .15 .07
☐ 284 Wally Whitehurst .15 .07
☐ 285 Rod Beck .30 .14
☐ 286 Barry Bonds .75 .35
☐ 287 Dave Burba .15 .07
☐ 288 Mark Carreon .15 .07
☐ 289 Royce Clayton .30 .14
☐ 290 Mike Jackson .15 .07
☐ 291 Darren Lewis .15 .07
☐ 292 Kirt Manwaring .15 .07
☐ 293 Dave Martinez .15 .07
☐ 294 Billy Swift .15 .07
☐ 295 Salomon Torres .15 .07
☐ 296 Matt Williams .40 .18
☐ 297 Checklist 1-75 .15 .07
☐ 298 Checklist 76-150 .15 .07
☐ 299 Checklist 151-225 .15 .07
☐ 300 Checklist 226-300 .15 .07
☐ 301 Brady Anderson .40 .18
☐ 302 Harold Baines .30 .14
☐ 303 Damon Buford .15 .07
☐ 304 Mike Devereaux .15 .07
☐ 305 Sid Fernandez .15 .07
☐ 306 Rick Krivda .15 .07
☐ 307 Mike Mussina .60 .25
☐ 308 Rafael Palmeiro .40 .18
☐ 309 Arthur Rhodes .15 .07
☐ 310 Chris Sabo .15 .07
☐ 311 Lee Smith .30 .14
☐ 312 Gregg Zaun .15 .07
☐ 313 Scott Cooper .15 .07
☐ 314 Mike Greenwell .15 .07
☐ 315 Tim Naehring .15 .07
☐ 316 Otis Nixon .30 .14
☐ 317 Paul Quantrill .15 .07
☐ 318 John Valentin .30 .14
☐ 319 Dave Valle .15 .07
☐ 320 Frank Viola .15 .07
☐ 321 Brian Anderson .30 .14
☐ 322 Garret Anderson .60 .25
☐ 323 Chad Curtis .15 .07
☐ 324 Chili Davis .30 .14
☐ 325 Gary DiSarcina .15 .07
☐ 326 Damion Easley .15 .07
☐ 327 Jim Edmonds .60 .25
☐ 328 Chuck Finley .15 .07
☐ 329 Joe Grahe .15 .07
☐ 330 Bo Jackson .30 .14
☐ 331 Mark Langston .15 .07
☐ 332 Harold Reynolds .15 .07
☐ 333 James Baldwin .30 .14
☐ 334 Ray Durham .75 .35
☐ 335 Julio Franco .30 .14
☐ 336 Craig Grebeck .15 .07
☐ 337 Ozzie Guillen .15 .07
☐ 338 Joe Hall .15 .07
☐ 339 Darrin Jackson .15 .07
☐ 340 Jack McDowell .15 .07
☐ 341 Tim Raines .15 .07
☐ 342 Robin Ventura .30 .14
☐ 343 Carlos Baerga .30 .14
☐ 344 Derek Lilliquist .15 .07
☐ 345 Dennis Martinez .30 .14
☐ 346 Jack Morris .30 .14
☐ 347 Eddie Murray .60 .25
☐ 348 Chris Nabholz .15 .07
☐ 349 Charles Nagy .30 .14
☐ 350 Chad Ogea .15 .07
☐ 351 Manny Ramirez .75 .35
☐ 352 Omar Vizquel .30 .14
☐ 353 Tim Belcher .15 .07
☐ 354 Eric Davis .30 .14
☐ 355 Kirk Gibson .30 .14
☐ 356 Rick Greene .15 .07
☐ 357 Mickey Tettleton .15 .07
☐ 358 Alan Trammell .40 .18
☐ 359 David Wells .15 .07
☐ 360 Stan Belinda .15 .07
☐ 361 Vince Coleman .15 .07
☐ 362 David Cone .30 .14
☐ 363 Gary Gaetti .30 .14
☐ 364 Tom Gordon .15 .07
☐ 365 Dave Henderson .15 .07
☐ 366 Wally Joyner .30 .14
☐ 367 Brent Mayne .15 .07
☐ 368 Brian McRae .15 .07
☐ 369 Michael Tucker .40 .18
☐ 370 Ricky Bones .15 .07
☐ 371 Brian Harper .15 .07
☐ 372 Tyrone Hill .15 .07
☐ 373 Mark Kiefer .15 .07
☐ 374 Pat Listach .15 .07
☐ 375 Mike Matheny .15 .07
☐ 376 Jose Mercedes .15 .07
☐ 377 Jody Reed .15 .07
☐ 378 Kevin Seitzer .15 .07
☐ 379 B.J. Surhoff .15 .07
☐ 380 Greg Vaughn .15 .07
☐ 381 Turner Ward .15 .07
☐ 382 Wes Weger .15 .07
☐ 383 Bill Wegman .15 .07
☐ 384 Rick Aguilera .15 .07
☐ 385 Rich Becker .30 .14
☐ 386 Alex Cole .15 .07
☐ 387 Steve Dunn .15 .07
☐ 388 Keith Garagozzo .15 .07
☐ 389 LaTroy Hawkins .15 .07
☐ 390 Shane Mack .15 .07
☐ 391 David McCarty .15 .07
☐ 392 Pedro Munoz .15 .07
☐ 393 Derek Parks .15 .07
☐ 394 Kirby Puckett 1.25 .55
☐ 395 Kevin Tapani .15 .07
☐ 396 Matt Walbeck .15 .07
☐ 397 Jim Abbott .15 .07
☐ 398 Mike Gallego .15 .07
☐ 399 Xavier Hernandez .15 .07
☐ 400 Don Mattingly 1.00 .45
☐ 401 Terry Mulholland .15 .07
☐ 402 Matt Nokes .15 .07
☐ 403 Luis Polonia .15 .07
☐ 404 Bob Wickman .15 .07
☐ 405 Mark Acre .15 .07
☐ 406 Fausto Cruz .15 .07
☐ 407 Dennis Eckersley .40 .18
☐ 408 Rickey Henderson .40 .18
☐ 409 Stan Javier .15 .07
☐ 410 Carlos Reyes .15 .07
☐ 411 Ruben Sierra .15 .07
☐ 412 Terry Steinbach .30 .14
☐ 413 Bill Taylor .15 .07
☐ 414 Todd Van Poppel .15 .07
☐ 415 Eric Anthony .15 .07
☐ 416 Bobby Ayala .15 .07
☐ 417 Chris Bosio .15 .07
☐ 418 Tim Davis .15 .07
☐ 419 Randy Johnson .60 .25
☐ 420 Kevin King .15 .07
☐ 421 Anthony Manahan .15 .07
☐ 422 Edgar Martinez .40 .18
☐ 423 Keith Mitchell .15 .07
☐ 424 Roger Salkeld .15 .07
☐ 425 Mac Suzuki .60 .25
☐ 426 Dan Wilson .30 .14
☐ 427 Duff Brumley .15 .07
☐ 428 Jose Canseco .40 .18
☐ 429 Will Clark .40 .18
☐ 430 Steve Dreyer .15 .07
☐ 431 Rick Helling .15 .07
☐ 432 Chris James .15 .07
☐ 433 Matt Whiteside .15 .07
☐ 434 Roberto Alomar .60 .25
☐ 435 Scott Brow .15 .07
☐ 436 Domingo Cedeno .15 .07
☐ 437 Carlos Delgado .60 .25
☐ 438 Juan Guzman .15 .07
☐ 439 Paul Spoljaric .15 .07
☐ 440 Todd Stottlemyre .15 .07
☐ 441 Woody Williams .15 .07
☐ 442 David Justice .60 .25
☐ 443 Mike Kelly .15 .07
☐ 444 Ryan Klesko .40 .18
☐ 445 Javier Lopez .40 .18
☐ 446 Greg Maddux 2.00 .90
☐ 447 Kent Mercker .15 .07
☐ 448 Charlie O'Brien .15 .07
☐ 449 Terry Pendleton .30 .14
☐ 450 Mike Stanton .15 .07
☐ 451 Tony Tarasco .15 .07
☐ 452 Terrell Wade .60 .25
☐ 453 Willie Banks .15 .07
☐ 454 Shawon Dunston .15 .07
☐ 455 Mark Grace .40 .18
☐ 456 Jose Guzman .15 .07
☐ 457 Jose Hernandez .15 .07
☐ 458 Glenallen Hill .15 .07
☐ 459 Blaise Ilsley .15 .07
☐ 460 Brooks Kieschnick .40 .18
☐ 461 Derrick May .15 .07
☐ 462 Randy Myers .15 .07
☐ 463 Karl Rhodes .15 .07
☐ 464 Sammy Sosa .60 .25
☐ 465 Steve Trachsel .15 .07
☐ 466 Anthony Young .15 .07
☐ 467 Eddie Zambrano .15 .07
☐ 468 Bret Boone .15 .07
☐ 469 Tom Browning .15 .07
☐ 470 Hector Carrasco .15 .07
☐ 471 Rob Dibble .15 .07
☐ 472 Erik Hanson .15 .07
☐ 473 Thomas Howard .15 .07
☐ 474 Barry Larkin .40 .18
☐ 475 Hal Morris .15 .07
☐ 476 Jose Rijo .15 .07
☐ 477 John Burke .15 .07
☐ 478 Ellis Burks .30 .14
☐ 479 Marvin Freeman .15 .07
☐ 480 Andres Galarraga .40 .18
☐ 481 Greg W. Harris .15 .07
☐ 482 Charlie Hayes .15 .07
☐ 483 Darren Holmes .15 .07
☐ 484 Howard Johnson .15 .07
☐ 485 Marcus Moore .15 .07
☐ 486 David Nied .15 .07
☐ 487 Mark Thompson .15 .07
☐ 488 Walt Weiss .15 .07
☐ 489 Kurt Abbott .15 .07
☐ 490 Matias Carrillo .15 .07
☐ 491 Jeff Conine .30 .14
☐ 492 Chris Hammond .15 .07
☐ 493 Bryan Harvey .15 .07
☐ 494 Charlie Hough .15 .07
☐ 495 Yorkis Perez .15 .07
☐ 496 Pat Rapp .15 .07
☐ 497 Benito Santiago .15 .07
☐ 498 David Weathers .15 .07
☐ 499 Craig Biggio .40 .18
☐ 500 Ken Caminiti .60 .25
☐ 501 Doug Drabek .15 .07
☐ 502 Tony Eusebio .15 .07
☐ 503 Steve Finley .30 .14
☐ 504 Pete Harnisch .15 .07
☐ 505 Brian L.Hunter .30 .14
☐ 506 Domingo Jean .15 .07
☐ 507 Todd Jones .15 .07
☐ 508 Orlando Miller .15 .07
☐ 509 James Mouton .30 .14
☐ 510 Roberto Petagine .15 .07
☐ 511 Shane Reynolds .15 .07
☐ 512 Mitch Williams .15 .07
☐ 513 Billy Ashley .15 .07
☐ 514 Tom Candiotti .15 .07
☐ 515 Delino DeShields .15 .07
☐ 516 Kevin Gross .15 .07
☐ 517 Orel Hershiser .30 .14
☐ 518 Eric Karros .30 .14
☐ 519 Ramon Martinez .30 .14
☐ 520 Chan Ho Park 2.00 .90
☐ 521 Henry Rodriguez .15 .07
☐ 522 Joey Eischen .15 .07
☐ 523 Rod Henderson .15 .07
☐ 524 Pedro J. Martinez .60 .25
☐ 525 Mel Rojas .15 .07
☐ 526 Larry Walker .60 .25
☐ 527 Gabe White .15 .07
☐ 528 Bobby Bonilla .30 .14
☐ 529 Jonathan Hurst .15 .07
☐ 530 Bobby Jones .30 .14
☐ 531 Kevin McReynolds .15 .07
☐ 532 Bill Pulsipher .15 .07
☐ 533 Bret Saberhagen .15 .07
☐ 534 David Segui .15 .07
☐ 535 Pete Smith .15 .07
☐ 536 Kelly Stinnett .15 .07
☐ 537 Dave Telgheder .15 .07
☐ 538 Quilvio Veras .30 .1
☐ 539 Jose Vizcaino .15 .0
☐ 540 Pete Walker .15 .0
☐ 541 Ricky Bottalico .60 .2
☐ 542 Wes Chamberlain .15 .07
☐ 543 Mariano Duncan .15 .0
☐ 544 Lenny Dykstra .30 .1
☐ 545 Jim Eisenreich .30 .1
☐ 546 Phil Geisler .15 .0
☐ 547 Wayne Gomes .30 .1
☐ 548 Doug Jones .15 .0
☐ 549 Jeff Juden .15 .0
☐ 550 Mike Lieberthal .15 .0
☐ 551 Tony Longmire .15 .0
☐ 552 Tom Marsh .15 .0
☐ 553 Bobby Munoz .15 .0

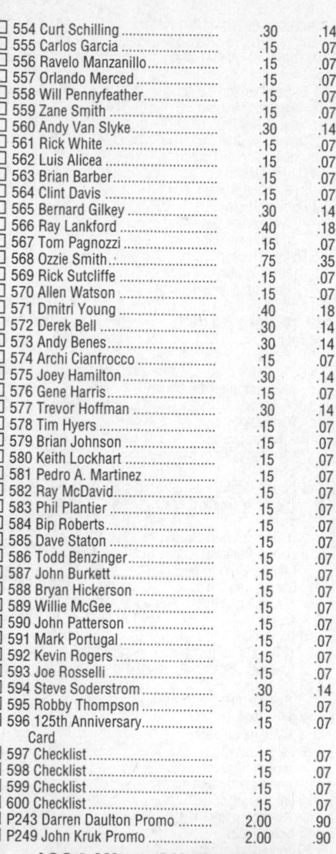

☐ 554 Curt Schilling	.30	.14
☐ 555 Carlos Garcia	.15	.07
☐ 556 Ravelo Manzanillo	.15	.07
☐ 557 Orlando Merced	.15	.07
☐ 558 Will Pennyfeather	.15	.07
☐ 559 Zane Smith	.15	.07
☐ 560 Andy Van Slyke	.30	.14
☐ 561 Rick White	.15	.07
☐ 562 Luis Alicea	.15	.07
☐ 563 Brian Barber	.15	.07
☐ 564 Clint Davis	.15	.07
☐ 565 Bernard Gilkey	.30	.14
☐ 566 Ray Lankford	.40	.18
☐ 567 Tom Pagnozzi	.15	.07
☐ 568 Ozzie Smith	.75	.35
☐ 569 Rick Sutcliffe	.15	.07
☐ 570 Allen Watson	.15	.07
☐ 571 Dmitri Young	.40	.18
☐ 572 Derek Bell	.30	.14
☐ 573 Andy Benes	.30	.14
☐ 574 Archi Cianfrocco	.15	.07
☐ 575 Joey Hamilton	.30	.14
☐ 576 Gene Harris	.15	.07
☐ 577 Trevor Hoffman	.30	.14
☐ 578 Tim Hyers	.15	.07
☐ 579 Brian Johnson	.15	.07
☐ 580 Keith Lockhart	.15	.07
☐ 581 Pedro A. Martinez	.15	.07
☐ 582 Ray McDavid	.15	.07
☐ 583 Phil Plantier	.15	.07
☐ 584 Bip Roberts	.15	.07
☐ 585 Dave Staton	.15	.07
☐ 586 Todd Benzinger	.15	.07
☐ 587 John Burkett	.15	.07
☐ 588 Bryan Hickerson	.15	.07
☐ 589 Willie McGee	.15	.07
☐ 590 John Patterson	.15	.07
☐ 591 Mark Portugal	.15	.07
☐ 592 Kevin Rogers	.15	.07
☐ 593 Joe Rosselli	.15	.07
☐ 594 Steve Soderstrom	.30	.14
☐ 595 Robby Thompson	.15	.07
☐ 596 125th Anniversary Card	.15	.07
☐ 597 Checklist	.15	.07
☐ 598 Checklist	.15	.07
☐ 599 Checklist	.15	.07
☐ 600 Checklist	.15	.07
☐ P243 Darren Daulton Promo	2.00	.90
☐ P249 John Kruk Promo	2.00	.90

1994 Ultra All-Rookies

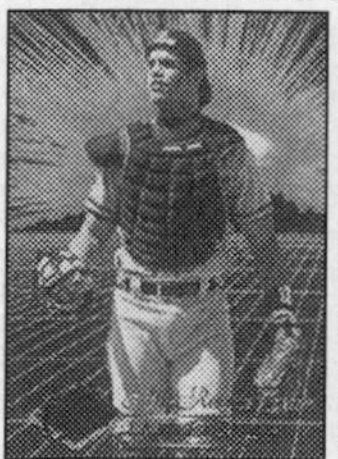

This 10-card standard-size set features top rookies of 1994 and were randomly inserted in second series jumbo and foil packs at a rate of one in 10. Card fronts have a color player photo cut-out over a computer generated background that resembles volcanic activity. The player's name and All-Rookie Team logo appear in gold foil at the bottom. On the backs, the player cut-out appears toward the right with text on the left. The background is much the same as the front. The set is sequenced in alphabetical order. Every second series Ultra hobby case included this set in jumbo (3 1/2" by 5") form.

	MINT	NRMT
COMPLETE SET (10)	10.00	4.50
COMMON CARD (1-10)	.50	.23
*JUMBOS: 1X TO 2X BASIC CARDS		
☐ 1 Kurt Abbott	.50	.23
☐ 2 Carlos Delgado	1.50	.70
☐ 3 Cliff Floyd	1.00	.45
☐ 4 Jeffrey Hammonds	1.00	.45
☐ 5 Ryan Klesko	1.25	.55
☐ 6 Javier Lopez	1.50	.70
☐ 7 Raul Mondesi	2.00	.90
☐ 8 James Mouton	.50	.23
☐ 9 Chan Ho Park	1.25	.55
☐ 10 Dave Staton	.50	.23

1994 Ultra All-Stars

Randomly inserted in second series foil and jumbo packs at a rate of one in three, this 20-card standard-size set

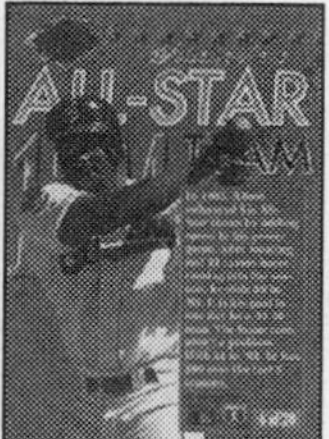

contains top major league stars. The fronts have a color player photo superimposed over a bright red (American League players) or dark blue (National League) background. The backs are much the same except they include highlights from 1993.

	MINT	NRMT
COMPLETE SET (20)	18.00	8.00
COMMON CARD (1-20)	.25	.11
☐ 1 Chris Hoiles	.25	.11
☐ 2 Frank Thomas	4.00	1.80
☐ 3 Roberto Alomar	1.00	.45
☐ 4 Cal Ripken Jr.	4.00	1.80
☐ 5 Robin Ventura	.50	.23
☐ 6 Albert Belle	1.25	.55
☐ 7 Juan Gonzalez	2.50	1.10
☐ 8 Ken Griffey Jr.	5.00	2.20
☐ 9 John Olerud	.25	.11
☐ 10 Jack McDowell	.25	.11
☐ 11 Mike Piazza	3.00	1.35
☐ 12 Fred McGriff	.75	.35
☐ 13 Ryne Sandberg	1.25	.55
☐ 14 Jay Bell	.25	.11
☐ 15 Matt Williams	.75	.35
☐ 16 Barry Bonds	1.25	.55
☐ 17 Lenny Dykstra	.50	.23
☐ 18 David Justice	1.00	.45
☐ 19 Tom Glavine	.75	.35
☐ 20 Greg Maddux	3.00	1.35

1994 Ultra Award Winners

Randomly inserted in all first series packs at a rate of one in three, this 25-card standard-size set features three MVP's, two Rookies of the Year, and 18 Top Glove defensive standouts. The set is divided into American League Top Gloves (1-9), National League Top Gloves (10-18), and Award Winners (19-25). A horizontal design includes a color player cut-out over a gold background on front. Also on front, is a gold foil logo that indicates the honor. The backs have a small photo and text.

	MINT	NRMT
COMPLETE SET (25)	15.00	6.75
COMMON CARD (1-25)	.25	.11
☐ 1 Ivan Rodriguez	1.25	.55
☐ 2 Don Mattingly	2.50	1.10
☐ 3 Roberto Alomar	1.00	.45
☐ 4 Robin Ventura	.50	.23
☐ 5 Omar Vizquel	.50	.23
☐ 6 Ken Griffey Jr.	5.00	2.20
☐ 7 Kenny Lofton	1.25	.55
☐ 8 Devon White	.25	.11
☐ 9 Mark Langston	.25	.11
☐ 10 Kirt Manwaring	.25	.11
☐ 11 Mark Grace	.75	.35
☐ 12 Robby Thompson	.25	.11
☐ 13 Matt Williams	.75	.35
☐ 14 Jay Bell	.25	.11
☐ 15 Barry Bonds	1.25	.55
☐ 16 Marquis Grissom	.50	.23
☐ 17 Larry Walker	1.00	.45
☐ 18 Greg Maddux	3.00	1.35
☐ 19 Frank Thomas	4.00	1.80
☐ 20 Barry Bonds	1.25	.55
☐ 21 Paul Molitor	1.00	.45
☐ 22 Jack McDowell	.25	.11
☐ 23 Greg Maddux	3.00	1.35
☐ 24 Tim Salmon	1.00	.45
☐ 25 Mike Piazza	3.00	1.35

1994 Ultra Career Achievement

Randomly inserted in all second series packs at a rate of one in 21, this five card standard-size set highlights veteran stars and milestones they have reached during their brilliant careers. Horizontally designed cards have fronts that feature a color player photo superimposed over solid color background that contains another player photo. A photo of the player earlier in his career is on back along with text. The cards are sequenced in alphabetical order.

	MINT	NRMT
COMPLETE SET (5)	12.00	5.50
COMMON CARD (1-5)	1.00	.45
☐ 1 Joe Carter	1.00	.45
☐ 2 Paul Molitor	2.00	.90
☐ 3 Cal Ripken Jr.	8.00	3.60
☐ 4 Ryne Sandberg	2.50	1.10
☐ 5 Dave Winfield	1.50	.70

1994 Ultra Firemen

Randomly inserted in all first series packs at a rate of one in 11, this ten-card standard-size set features ten of baseball's top relief pitchers. The fronts feature color player action cutouts superimposed upon borderless backgrounds consisting of pictures of fire-fighting equipment. The player's name appears in gold foil at the bottom. The horizontal back carries a color player head shot on one side, and career highlights inside a ghosted panel on the other, all on a borderless fire-fighting equipment background. The set is arranged according to American League (1-5) and National League (6-10) players.

	MINT	NRMT
COMPLETE SET (10)	5.00	2.20
COMMON CARD (1-10)	.50	.23
☐ 1 Jeff Montgomery	.50	.23
☐ 2 Duane Ward	.50	.23
☐ 3 Tom Henke	.60	.25
☐ 4 Roberto Hernandez	.50	.23
☐ 5 Dennis Eckersley	1.00	.45
☐ 6 Randy Myers	.50	.23
☐ 7 Rod Beck	.60	.25
☐ 8 Bryan Harvey	.50	.23
☐ 9 John Wetteland	.75	.35
☐ 10 Mitch Williams	.50	.23

1994 Ultra Hitting Machines

Randomly inserted in all second series packs at a rate of one in five, this 10-card horizontally designed standard-size set features top hitters from 1993. The fronts have a color player cut-out over a "Hitting Machines" background. The back has a smaller player cut-out and text. The set is sequenced in alphabetical order.

	MINT	NRMT
COMPLETE SET (10)	15.00	6.75
COMMON CARD (1-10)	.50	.23

☐ 1 Roberto Alomar	1.00	.45
☐ 2 Carlos Baerga	.50	.23
☐ 3 Barry Bonds	1.25	.55
☐ 4 Andres Galarraga	.75	.35
☐ 5 Juan Gonzalez	2.50	1.10
☐ 6 Tony Gwynn	2.00	.90
☐ 7 Paul Molitor	1.00	.45
☐ 8 John Olerud	.50	.23
☐ 9 Mike Piazza	3.00	1.35
☐ 10 Frank Thomas	4.00	1.80

1994 Ultra Home Run Kings

Randomly inserted exclusively in first series foil packs at a rate of one in 36, these 12 standard-size cards highlight home run hitters by an etched metalized look. Cards 1-6 feature American League Home Run Kings while cards 7-12 present National League Home Run Kings.

	MINT	NRMT
COMPLETE SET (12)	80.00	36.00
COMMON CARD (1-12)	2.00	.90
☐ 1 Juan Gonzalez	12.00	5.50
☐ 2 Ken Griffey Jr.	25.00	11.00
☐ 3 Frank Thomas	20.00	9.00
☐ 4 Albert Belle	6.00	2.70
☐ 5 Rafael Palmeiro	4.00	1.80
☐ 6 Joe Carter	4.00	1.80
☐ 7 Barry Bonds	6.00	2.70
☐ 8 David Justice	5.00	2.20
☐ 9 Matt Williams	4.00	1.80
☐ 10 Fred McGriff	4.00	1.80
☐ 11 Ron Gant	2.00	.90
☐ 12 Mike Piazza	15.00	6.75

1994 Ultra League Leaders

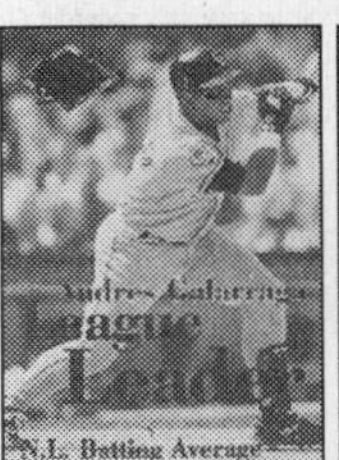
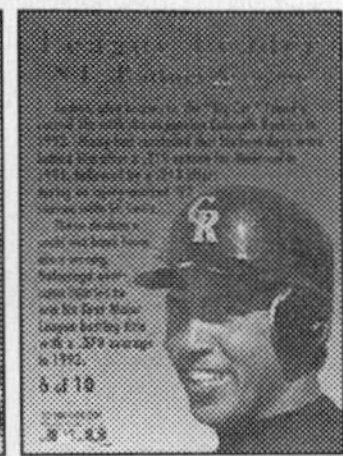

Randomly inserted in all first series packs at a rate of one in 11, this ten-card standard-size set features ten of 1993's leading players. The fronts feature borderless color player action shots, with a color-screening that shades from being imperceptible at the top to washing out the photos' true colors at the bottom. The player's name in gold foil appears across the card face. The borderless back carries a color player head shot in a lower corner with his career highlights appearing above, all on a monochrome background that shades from dark to light, from top to bottom. The set is arranged according to American League (1-5) and National League (6-10) players.

	MINT	NRMT
COMPLETE SET (10)	5.00	2.20
COMMON CARD (1-10)	.25	.11
☐ 1 John Olerud	.25	.11
☐ 2 Rafael Palmeiro	1.00	.45
☐ 3 Kenny Lofton	2.00	.90
☐ 4 Jack McDowell	.25	.11
☐ 5 Randy Johnson	1.50	.70
☐ 6 Andres Galarraga	1.00	.45
☐ 7 Lenny Dykstra	.75	.35
☐ 8 Chuck Carr	.25	.11
☐ 9 Tom Glavine	1.00	.45
☐ 10 Jose Rijo	.25	.11

1994 Ultra On-Base Leaders

Randomly inserted in second series jumbo packs at a rate of one in 36, this 12-card standard-size set features those that were among the Major League leaders in on-base percentage. Card fronts have the player superimposed over a metallic background that simulates statistics from a sports page. The backs have a player cut-out and text over a statistical background that is not metallic. The set is sequenced in alphabetical order.

	MINT	NRMT
COMPLETE SET (12)	150.00	70.00
COMMON CARD (1-12)	4.00	1.80
☐ 1 Roberto Alomar	12.00	5.50
☐ 2 Barry Bonds	15.00	6.75
☐ 3 Lenny Dykstra	6.00	2.70
☐ 4 Andres Galarraga	8.00	3.60
☐ 5 Mark Grace	8.00	3.60
☐ 6 Ken Griffey Jr.	60.00	27.00
☐ 7 Gregg Jefferies	4.00	1.80
☐ 8 Orlando Merced	4.00	1.80
☐ 9 Paul Molitor	12.00	5.50
☐ 10 John Olerud	6.00	2.70
☐ 11 Tony Phillips	4.00	1.80
☐ 12 Frank Thomas	50.00	22.00

1994 Ultra Phillies Finest

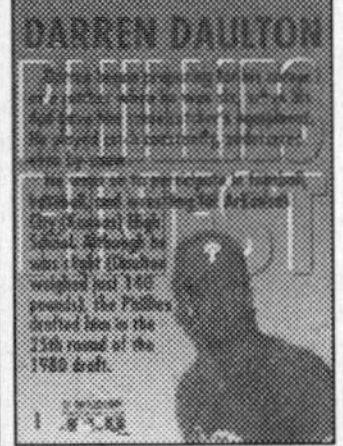

As the "Highlight Series" insert set, this 20-card standard-size set features Darren Daulton and John Kruk of the 1993 National League champion Philadelphia Phillies. The cards were inserted at a rate of one in six first series and one in 10 second series packs. Ten cards spotlight each player's career. Daulton and Kruk each signed more than 1,000 of their cards for random insertion. Moreover, the collector could receive four more cards (two of each player) through a mail-in offer by sending in ten 1994 series I wrappers plus 1.50 for postage and handling. The expiration for this redemption was September 30, 1994. The fronts feature borderless color player action shots. Behind the player, in "transparent" block lettering, the words "Phillies Finest" appear, followed by the player's name. His name also appears in gold foil in a lower corner. The back carries a color player head shot in a lower corner, with career highlights appearing above, all on a borderless red background.

	MINT	NRMT
COMPLETE SET (20)	10.00	4.50
COMPLETE SERIES 1 (10)	5.00	2.20
COMPLETE SERIES 2 (10)	5.00	2.20
COMMON DAULTON (1-5/11-15)	.50	.23
COMMON KRUK (6-10/16-20)	.50	.23
COMMON MAIL-IN (M1-M4)	1.00	.45
☐ 1 Darren Daulton (Standing behind home plate)	.50	.23
☐ 2 Darren Daulton (Swinging at a pitch)	.50	.23
☐ 3 Darren Daulton (Blocking home plate)	.50	.23
☐ 4 Darren Daulton (Just completed swing and is headed for fisrt)	.50	.23
☐ 5 Darren Daulton (Looking skyward after connecting with a pitch)	.50	.23
☐ 6 John Kruk (Swinging at a pitch)	.50	.23
☐ 7 John Kruk (Fielding)	.50	.23
☐ 8 John Kruk (Just completed a swing)	.50	.23
☐ 9 John Kruk (On deck)	.50	.23
☐ 10 John Kruk (Breaking out of batters box)	.50	.23
☐ 11 Darren Daulton (Looking skyward after swing)	.50	.23
☐ 12 Darren Daulton	.50	.23
☐ 13 Darren Daulton (Anticipating throw home)	.50	.23
☐ 14 Darren Daulton (Standing at home with ball in hand)	.50	.23
☐ 15 Darren Daulton (Running up first base line with in catching gear)	.50	.23
☐ 16 John Kruk (Follow through of swing)	.50	.23
☐ 17 John Kruk (Waiting on deck)	.50	.23
☐ 18 John Kruk (Follow through from first base dugout angle)	.50	.23
☐ 19 John Kruk (Swinging at pitch) chest high)	.50	.23
☐ 20 John Kruk (Looking out toward left field afer swinging)	.50	.23
☐ M1 Darren Daulton (About to throw down to second base)	1.00	.45
☐ M2 John Kruk (Fielding position)	1.00	.45
☐ M3 Darren Daulton (Awaiting pitch)	1.00	.45
☐ M4 John Kruk (Running)	1.00	.45
☐ AU1 Darren Daulton Certified Autograph	40.00	18.00
☐ AU2 John Kruk Certified Autograph	40.00	18.00

1994 Ultra RBI Kings

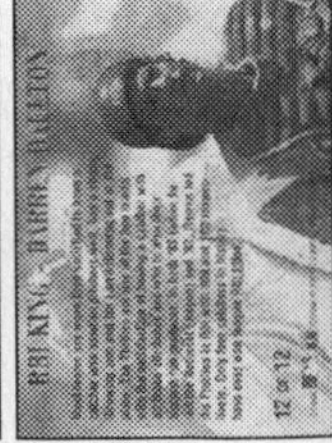

Randomly inserted in first series jumbo packs at a rate o one in 36, this 12-card standard-size set features RB leaders. These horizontal, metallized cards have a colo player photo on front that superimposes a playe image.The backs have a write-up and a small color playe photo. Cards 1-6 feature American League RBI King while cards 7-12 present National League RBI Kings.

	MINT	NRMT
COMPLETE SET (12)	150.00	70.0
COMMON CARD (1-12)	4.00	1.8
☐ 1 Albert Belle	15.00	6.7
☐ 2 Frank Thomas	50.00	22.0

☐ 3 Joe Carter	8.00	3.60
☐ 4 Juan Gonzalez	30.00	13.50
☐ 5 Cecil Fielder	6.00	2.70
☐ 6 Carlos Baerga	4.00	1.80
☐ 7 Barry Bonds	15.00	6.75
☐ 8 David Justice	12.00	5.50
☐ 9 Ron Gant	4.00	1.80
☐ 10 Mike Piazza	40.00	18.00
☐ 11 Matt Williams	8.00	3.60
☐ 12 Darren Daulton	6.00	2.70

1994 Ultra Rising Stars

Randomly inserted in second series foil packs and jumbo packs at a rate of one in 36, this 12-card set spotlights top young major league stars. Metallic fronts have the player superimposed over icons resembling outer space. The backs feature the player in the same format along with text. The set is sequenced in alphabetical order.

	MINT	NRMT
COMPLETE SET (12)	120.00	55.00
COMMON CARD (1-12)	4.00	1.80
☐ 1 Carlos Baerga	4.00	1.80
☐ 2 Jeff Bagwell	25.00	11.00
☐ 3 Albert Belle	15.00	6.75
☐ 4 Cliff Floyd	4.00	1.80
☐ 5 Travis Fryman	6.00	2.70
☐ 6 Marquis Grissom	6.00	2.70
☐ 7 Kenny Lofton	15.00	6.75
☐ 8 John Olerud	4.00	1.80
☐ 9 Mike Piazza	40.00	18.00
☐ 10 Kirk Rueter	4.00	1.80
☐ 11 Tim Salmon	12.00	5.50
☐ 12 Aaron Sele	4.00	1.80

1994 Ultra Second Year Standouts

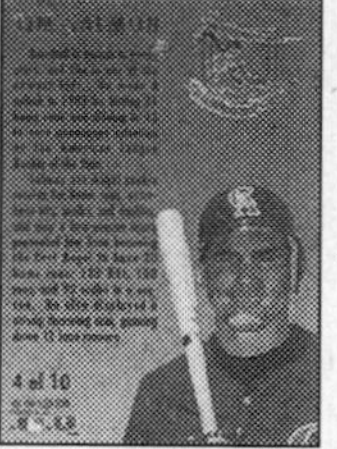

Randomly inserted in all first series packs at a rate of one in 11, this 10-card standard-size set included 10 1993 outstanding rookies who are destined to become future stars. The fronts feature two color playe action cutouts superimposed upon borderless team-colored backgrounds. The player's name appears in gold foil at the bottom. The back carries a color player head shot in a lower corner with his career highlights appearing alongside, all on a borderless team color-coded background. The set is arranged in alphabetical order according to American League (1-5) and National League (6-10) players.

	MINT	NRMT
COMPLETE SET (10)	15.00	6.75
COMMON CARD (1-10)	.50	.23
☐ 1 Jason Bere	.50	.23
☐ 2 Brent Gates	.50	.23
☐ 3 Jeffrey Hammonds	1.00	.45
☐ 4 Tim Salmon	3.00	1.35
☐ 5 Aaron Sele	.50	.23
☐ 6 Chuck Carr	.50	.23
☐ 7 Jeff Conine	1.00	.45
☐ 8 Greg McMichael	.50	.23
☐ 9 Mike Piazza	12.00	5.50
☐ 10 Kevin Stocker	.50	.23

1994 Ultra Strikeout Kings

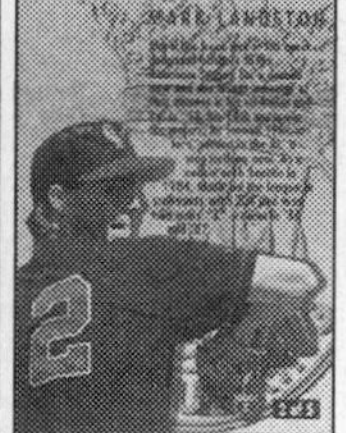

Randomly inserted in all second series packs at a rate of one in seven, this five-card standard-size set features top strikeout artists. Full-bleed fronts offer triple exposure photos and a gold foil Strikeout King logo. The backs contain a photo and write-up with the Strikeout King logo as background. The set is sequenced in alphabetical order.

	MINT	NRMT
COMPLETE SET (5)	5.00	2.20
COMMON CARD (1-5)	.25	.11
☐ 1 Randy Johnson	1.00	.45
☐ 2 Mark Langston	.25	.11
☐ 3 Greg Maddux	3.00	1.35
☐ 4 Jose Rijo	.25	.11
☐ 5 John Smoltz	.75	.35

1995 Ultra

This 450-card standard-size set was issued in two series. The first series contained 250 cards while the second series consisted of 200 cards. They were issued in 12-card packs (either hobby or retail) with a suggested retail price of $1.99. Also, 15-card pre-priced packs with a suggested retail of $2.69. Each pack contained two inserts: one is a Gold Medallion parallel while the other is from one of Ultra's many insert sets. "Hot Packs" contain nothing but insert cards. The full-bleed fronts feature the player's photo with the team name and player's name at the bottom. The "95 Fleer Ultra" logo is in the upper right corner. The backs have a two-photo design; one of which is a full-size duotone shot with the other being a full-color action shot. Personal bio, seasonal and career information are also included on the back. In each series the cards were grouped alphabetically within teams and checklisted alphabetically according to teams for each league with AL preceding NL. There are no key Rookie Cards in this set.

	MINT	NRMT
COMPLETE SET (450)	30.00	13.50
COMPLETE SERIES 1 (250)	18.00	8.00
COMPLETE SERIES 2 (200)	12.00	5.50
COMMON CARD (1-450)	.15	.07
☐ 1 Brady Anderson	.40	.18
☐ 2 Sid Fernandez	.15	.07
☐ 3 Jeffrey Hammonds	.30	.14
☐ 4 Chris Hoiles	.15	.07
☐ 5 Ben McDonald	.15	.07
☐ 6 Mike Mussina	.60	.25
☐ 7 Rafael Palmeiro	.40	.18
☐ 8 Jack Voigt	.15	.07
☐ 9 Wes Chamberlain	.15	.07
☐ 10 Roger Clemens	1.25	.55
☐ 11 Chris Howard	.15	.07
☐ 12 Tim Naehring	.15	.07
☐ 13 Otis Nixon	.30	.14
☐ 14 Rich Rowland	.15	.07
☐ 15 Ken Ryan	.15	.07
☐ 16 John Valentin	.30	.14
☐ 17 Mo Vaughn	.75	.35
☐ 18 Brian Anderson	.15	.07
☐ 19 Chili Davis	.30	.14
☐ 20 Damion Easley	.15	.07
☐ 21 Jim Edmonds	.60	.25
☐ 22 Mark Langston	.15	.07
☐ 23 Tim Salmon	.60	.25
☐ 24 J.T. Snow	.30	.14
☐ 25 Chris Turner	.15	.07
☐ 26 Wilson Alvarez	.30	.14
☐ 27 Joey Cora	.30	.14
☐ 28 Alex Fernandez	.30	.14
☐ 29 Roberto Hernandez	.15	.07
☐ 30 Lance Johnson	.30	.14
☐ 31 Ron Karkovice	.15	.07
☐ 32 Kirk McCaskill	.15	.07
☐ 33 Tim Raines	.15	.07
☐ 34 Frank Thomas	2.50	1.10
☐ 35 Sandy Alomar Jr.	.15	.07
☐ 36 Albert Belle	.75	.35
☐ 37 Mark Clark	.15	.07
☐ 38 Kenny Lofton	.75	.35
☐ 39 Eddie Murray	.60	.25
☐ 40 Eric Plunk	.15	.07
☐ 41 Manny Ramirez	.60	.25
☐ 42 Jim Thome	.60	.25
☐ 43 Omar Vizquel	.30	.14
☐ 44 Danny Bautista	.15	.07
☐ 45 Junior Felix	.15	.07
☐ 46 Cecil Fielder	.30	.14
☐ 47 Chris Gomez	.15	.07
☐ 48 Chad Kreuter	.15	.07
☐ 49 Mike Moore	.15	.07
☐ 50 Tony Phillips	.15	.07
☐ 51 Alan Trammell	.30	.14
☐ 52 David Wells	.15	.07
☐ 53 Kevin Appier	.30	.14
☐ 54 Billy Brewer	.15	.07
☐ 55 David Cone	.30	.14
☐ 56 Greg Gagne	.15	.07
☐ 57 Bob Hamelin	.15	.07
☐ 58 Jose Lind	.15	.07
☐ 59 Brent Mayne	.15	.07
☐ 60 Brian McRae	.15	.07
☐ 61 Terry Shumpert	.15	.07
☐ 62 Ricky Bones	.15	.07
☐ 63 Mike Fetters	.15	.07
☐ 64 Darryl Hamilton	.15	.07
☐ 65 John Jaha	.15	.07
☐ 66 Graeme Lloyd	.15	.07
☐ 67 Matt Mieske	.30	.14
☐ 68 Kevin Seitzer	.15	.07
☐ 69 Jose Valentin	.30	.14
☐ 70 Turner Ward	.15	.07
☐ 71 Rick Aguilera	.15	.07
☐ 72 Rich Becker	.15	.07
☐ 73 Alex Cole	.15	.07
☐ 74 Scott Leius	.15	.07
☐ 75 Pat Meares	.15	.07
☐ 76 Kirby Puckett	1.25	.55
☐ 77 Dave Stevens	.15	.07
☐ 78 Kevin Tapani	.15	.07
☐ 79 Matt Walbeck	.15	.07
☐ 80 Wade Boggs	.60	.25
☐ 81 Scott Kamieniecki	.15	.07
☐ 82 Pat Kelly	.15	.07
☐ 83 Jimmy Key	.30	.14
☐ 84 Paul O'Neill	.30	.14
☐ 85 Luis Polonia	.15	.07
☐ 86 Mike Stanley	.15	.07
☐ 87 Danny Tartabull	.15	.07
☐ 88 Bob Wickman	.15	.07
☐ 89 Mark Acre	.15	.07
☐ 90 Geronimo Berroa	.15	.07
☐ 91 Mike Bordick	.15	.07
☐ 92 Ron Darling	.15	.07
☐ 93 Stan Javier	.15	.07
☐ 94 Mark McGwire	1.25	.55
☐ 95 Troy Neel	.15	.07
☐ 96 Ruben Sierra	.15	.07
☐ 97 Terry Steinbach	.30	.14
☐ 98 Eric Anthony	.15	.07
☐ 99 Chris Bosio	.15	.07
☐ 100 Dave Fleming	.15	.07
☐ 101 Ken Griffey Jr.	3.00	1.35
☐ 102 Reggie Jefferson	.30	.14
☐ 103 Randy Johnson	.60	.25
☐ 104 Edgar Martinez	.40	.18
☐ 105 Bill Risley	.15	.07
☐ 106 Dan Wilson	.30	.14
☐ 107 Cris Carpenter	.15	.07
☐ 108 Will Clark	.40	.18
☐ 109 Juan Gonzalez	1.50	.70
☐ 110 Rusty Greer	.60	.25
☐ 111 David Hulse	.15	.07
☐ 112 Roger Pavlik	.15	.07
☐ 113 Ivan Rodriguez	.75	.35
☐ 114 Doug Strange	.15	.07
☐ 115 Matt Whiteside	.15	.07
☐ 116 Roberto Alomar	.60	.25
☐ 117 Brad Cornett	.15	.07
☐ 118 Carlos Delgado	.30	.14

☐ 119 Alex Gonzalez	.30	.14
☐ 120 Darren Hall	.15	.07
☐ 121 Pat Hentgen	.30	.14
☐ 122 Paul Molitor	.60	.25
☐ 123 Ed Sprague	.15	.07
☐ 124 Devon White	.30	.14
☐ 125 Tom Glavine	.40	.18
☐ 126 David Justice	.60	.25
☐ 127 Roberto Kelly	.15	.07
☐ 128 Mark Lemke	.15	.07
☐ 129 Greg Maddux	2.00	.90
☐ 130 Greg McMichael	.15	.07
☐ 131 Kent Mercker	.15	.07
☐ 132 Charlie O'Brien	.15	.07
☐ 133 John Smoltz	.40	.18
☐ 134 Willie Banks	.15	.07
☐ 135 Steve Buechele	.15	.07
☐ 136 Kevin Foster	.15	.07
☐ 137 Glenallen Hill	.15	.07
☐ 138 Rey Sanchez	.15	.07
☐ 139 Sammy Sosa	.60	.25
☐ 140 Steve Trachsel	.15	.07
☐ 141 Rick Wilkins	.15	.07
☐ 142 Jeff Brantley	.15	.07
☐ 143 Hector Carrasco	.15	.07
☐ 144 Kevin Jarvis	.15	.07
☐ 145 Barry Larkin	.40	.18
☐ 146 Chuck McElroy	.15	.07
☐ 147 Jose Rijo	.15	.07
☐ 148 Johnny Ruffin	.15	.07
☐ 149 Deion Sanders	.60	.25
☐ 150 Eddie Taubensee	.15	.07
☐ 151 Dante Bichette	.40	.18
☐ 152 Ellis Burks	.30	.14
☐ 153 Joe Girardi	.15	.07
☐ 154 Charlie Hayes	.15	.07
☐ 155 Mike Kingery	.15	.07
☐ 156 Steve Reed	.15	.07
☐ 157 Kevin Ritz	.15	.07
☐ 158 Bruce Ruffin	.15	.07
☐ 159 Eric Young	.30	.14
☐ 160 Kurt Abbott	.15	.07
☐ 161 Chuck Carr	.15	.07
☐ 162 Chris Hammond	.15	.07
☐ 163 Bryan Harvey	.15	.07
☐ 164 Terry Mathews	.15	.07
☐ 165 Yorkis Perez	.15	.07
☐ 166 Pat Rapp	.15	.07
☐ 167 Gary Sheffield	.60	.25
☐ 168 Dave Weathers	.15	.07
☐ 169 Jeff Bagwell	1.25	.55
☐ 170 Ken Caminiti	.60	.25
☐ 171 Doug Drabek	.15	.07
☐ 172 Steve Finley	.30	.14
☐ 173 John Hudek	.15	.07
☐ 174 Todd Jones	.15	.07
☐ 175 James Mouton	.15	.07
☐ 176 Shane Reynolds	.15	.07
☐ 177 Scott Servais	.15	.07
☐ 178 Tom Candiotti	.15	.07
☐ 179 Omar Daal	.15	.07
☐ 180 Darren Dreifort	.15	.07
☐ 181 Eric Karros	.30	.14
☐ 182 Ramon J.Martinez	.30	.14
☐ 183 Raul Mondesi	.40	.18
☐ 184 Henry Rodriguez	.15	.07
☐ 185 Todd Worrell	.15	.07
☐ 186 Moises Alou	.30	.14
☐ 187 Sean Berry	.15	.07
☐ 188 Wil Cordero	.15	.07
☐ 189 Jeff Fassero	.15	.07
☐ 190 Darrin Fletcher	.15	.07
☐ 191 Butch Henry	.15	.07
☐ 192 Ken Hill	.15	.07
☐ 193 Mel Rojas	.15	.07
☐ 194 John Wetteland	.30	.14
☐ 195 Bobby Bonilla	.30	.14
☐ 196 Rico Brogna	.15	.07
☐ 197 Bobby Jones	.30	.14
☐ 198 Jeff Kent	.15	.07
☐ 199 Josias Manzanillo	.15	.07
☐ 200 Kelly Stinnett	.15	.07
☐ 201 Ryan Thompson	.15	.07
☐ 202 Jose Vizcaino	.15	.07
☐ 203 Lenny Dykstra	.30	.14
☐ 204 Jim Eisenreich	.30	.14
☐ 205 Dave Hollins	.15	.07
☐ 206 Mike Lieberthal	.15	.07
☐ 207 Mickey Morandini	.15	.07
☐ 208 Bobby Munoz	.15	.07
☐ 209 Curt Schilling	.30	.14
☐ 210 Heathcliff Slocumb	.15	.07
☐ 211 David West	.15	.07
☐ 212 Dave Clark	.15	.07
☐ 213 Steve Cooke	.15	.07
☐ 214 Midre Cummings	.15	.07
☐ 215 Carlos Garcia	.15	.07
☐ 216 Jeff King	.30	.14
☐ 217 Jon Lieber	.15	.07
☐ 218 Orlando Merced	.15	.07
☐ 219 Don Slaught	.15	.07
☐ 220 Rick White	.15	.07
☐ 221 Rene Arocha	.15	.07
☐ 222 Bernard Gilkey	.30	.14
☐ 223 Brian Jordan	.30	.14
☐ 224 Tom Pagnozzi	.15	.07
☐ 225 Vicente Palacios	.15	.07
☐ 226 Geronimo Pena	.15	.07
☐ 227 Ozzie Smith	.75	.35
☐ 228 Allen Watson	.15	.07
☐ 229 Mark Whiten	.15	.07
☐ 230 Brad Ausmus	.15	.07
☐ 231 Derek Bell	.30	.14
☐ 232 Andy Benes	.15	.07
☐ 233 Tony Gwynn	1.50	.70
☐ 234 Joey Hamilton	.30	.14
☐ 235 Luis Lopez	.15	.07
☐ 236 Pedro A.Martinez	.15	.07
☐ 237 Scott Sanders	.15	.07
☐ 238 Eddie Williams	.15	.07
☐ 239 Rod Beck	.15	.07
☐ 240 Dave Burba	.15	.07
☐ 241 Darren Lewis	.15	.07
☐ 242 Kirt Manwaring	.15	.07
☐ 243 Mark Portugal	.15	.07
☐ 244 Darryl Strawberry	.30	.14
☐ 245 Robby Thompson	.15	.07
☐ 246 Wm.VanLandingham	.15	.07
☐ 247 Matt Williams	.40	.18
☐ 248 Checklist	.15	.07
☐ 249 Checklist	.15	.07
☐ 250 Checklist	.15	.07
☐ 251 Harold Baines	.30	.14
☐ 252 Bret Barberie	.15	.07
☐ 253 Armando Benitez	.15	.07
☐ 254 Mike Devereaux	.15	.07
☐ 255 Leo Gomez	.15	.07
☐ 256 Jamie Moyer	.15	.07
☐ 257 Arthur Rhodes	.15	.07
☐ 258 Cal Ripken	2.50	1.10
☐ 259 Luis Alicea	.15	.07
☐ 260 Jose Canseco	.40	.18
☐ 261 Scott Cooper	.15	.07
☐ 262 Andre Dawson	.40	.18
☐ 263 Mike Greenwell	.15	.07
☐ 264 Aaron Sele	.15	.07
☐ 265 Garret Anderson	.40	.18
☐ 266 Chad Curtis	.15	.07
☐ 267 Gary DiSarcina	.15	.07
☐ 268 Chuck Finley	.30	.14
☐ 269 Rex Hudler	.15	.07
☐ 270 Andrew Lorraine	.30	.14
☐ 271 Spike Owen	.15	.07
☐ 272 Lee Smith	.30	.14
☐ 273 Jason Bere	.15	.07
☐ 274 Ozzie Guillen	.15	.07
☐ 275 Norberto Martin	.15	.07
☐ 276 Scott Ruffcorn	.15	.07
☐ 277 Robin Ventura	.30	.14
☐ 278 Carlos Baerga	.30	.14
☐ 279 Jason Grimsley	.15	.07
☐ 280 Dennis Martinez	.30	.14
☐ 281 Charles Nagy	.30	.14
☐ 282 Paul Sorrento	.15	.07
☐ 283 Dave Winfield	.40	.18
☐ 284 John Doherty	.15	.07
☐ 285 Travis Fryman	.30	.14
☐ 286 Kirk Gibson	.30	.14
☐ 287 Lou Whitaker	.30	.14
☐ 288 Gary Gaetti	.30	.14
☐ 289 Tom Gordon	.15	.07
☐ 290 Mark Gubicza	.15	.07
☐ 291 Wally Joyner	.30	.14
☐ 292 Mike Macfarlane	.15	.07
☐ 293 Jeff Montgomery	.30	.14
☐ 294 Jeff Cirillo	.30	.14
☐ 295 Cal Eldred	.15	.07
☐ 296 Pat Listach	.15	.07
☐ 297 Jose Mercedes	.15	.07
☐ 298 Dave Nilsson	.30	.14
☐ 299 Duane Singleton	.15	.07
☐ 300 Greg Vaughn	.15	.07
☐ 301 Scott Erickson	.15	.07
☐ 302 Denny Hocking	.15	.07
☐ 303 Chuck Knoblauch	.60	.25
☐ 304 Pat Mahomes	.15	.07
☐ 305 Pedro Munoz	.15	.07
☐ 306 Erik Schullstrom	.15	.07
☐ 307 Jim Abbott	.15	.07
☐ 308 Tony Fernandez	.15	.07
☐ 309 Sterling Hitchcock	.30	.14
☐ 310 Jim Leyritz	.15	.07
☐ 311 Don Mattingly	1.00	.45
☐ 312 Jack McDowell	.15	.07
☐ 313 Melido Perez	.15	.07
☐ 314 Bernie Williams	.60	.25
☐ 315 Scott Brosius	.15	.07
☐ 316 Dennis Eckersley	.30	.14
☐ 317 Brent Gates	.15	.07
☐ 318 Rickey Henderson	.40	.18
☐ 319 Steve Karsay	.15	.07
☐ 320 Steve Ontiveros	.15	.07
☐ 321 Bill Taylor	.15	.07
☐ 322 Todd Van Poppel	.15	.07
☐ 323 Bob Welch	.15	.07
☐ 324 Bobby Ayala	.15	.07
☐ 325 Mike Blowers	.15	.07
☐ 326 Jay Buhner	.40	.18
☐ 327 Felix Fermin	.15	.07
☐ 328 Tino Martinez	.60	.25
☐ 329 Marc Newfield	.30	.14
☐ 330 Greg Pirkl	.15	.07
☐ 331 Alex Rodriguez	2.50	1.10
☐ 332 Kevin Brown	.30	.14
☐ 333 John Burkett	.15	.07
☐ 334 Jeff Frye	.15	.07
☐ 335 Kevin Gross	.15	.07
☐ 336 Dean Palmer	.30	.14
☐ 337 Joe Carter	.40	.18
☐ 338 Shawn Green	.30	.14
☐ 339 Juan Guzman	.15	.07
☐ 340 Mike Huff	.15	.07
☐ 341 Al Leiter	.15	.07
☐ 342 John Olerud	.30	.14
☐ 343 Dave Stewart	.30	.14
☐ 344 Todd Stottlemyre	.15	.07
☐ 345 Steve Avery	.15	.07
☐ 346 Jeff Blauser	.15	.07
☐ 347 Chipper Jones	2.00	.90
☐ 348 Mike Kelly	.15	.07
☐ 349 Ryan Klesko	.40	.18
☐ 350 Javier Lopez	.40	.18
☐ 351 Fred McGriff	.40	.18
☐ 352 Jose Oliva	.15	.07
☐ 353 Terry Pendleton	.30	.14
☐ 354 Mike Stanton	.15	.07
☐ 355 Tony Tarasco	.15	.07
☐ 356 Mark Wohlers	.30	.14
☐ 357 Jim Bullinger	.15	.07
☐ 358 Shawon Dunston	.15	.07
☐ 359 Mark Grace	.40	.18
☐ 360 Derrick May	.15	.07
☐ 361 Randy Myers	.15	.07
☐ 362 Karl Rhodes	.15	.07
☐ 363 Bret Boone	.15	.07
☐ 364 Brian Dorsett	.15	.07
☐ 365 Ron Gant	.30	.14
☐ 366 Brian R.Hunter	.15	.07
☐ 367 Hal Morris	.15	.07
☐ 368 Jack Morris	.30	.14
☐ 369 John Roper	.15	.07
☐ 370 Reggie Sanders	.15	.07
☐ 371 Pete Schourek	.15	.07
☐ 372 John Smiley	.15	.07
☐ 373 Marvin Freeman	.15	.07
☐ 374 Andres Galarraga	.40	.18
☐ 375 Mike Munoz	.15	.07
☐ 376 David Nied	.15	.07
☐ 377 Walt Weiss	.15	.07
☐ 378 Greg Colbrunn	.15	.07
☐ 379 Jeff Conine	.30	.14
☐ 380 Charles Johnson	.30	.14
☐ 381 Kurt Miller	.15	.07
☐ 382 Robb Nen	.15	.07
☐ 383 Benito Santiago	.15	.07
☐ 384 Craig Biggio	.40	.18
☐ 385 Tony Eusebio	.15	.07
☐ 386 Luis Gonzalez	.15	.07
☐ 387 Brian L.Hunter	.30	.14
☐ 388 Darryl Kile	.30	.14
☐ 389 Orlando Miller	.15	.07
☐ 390 Phil Plantier	.15	.07
☐ 391 Greg Swindell	.15	.07
☐ 392 Billy Ashley	.15	.07
☐ 393 Pedro Astacio	.15	.07
☐ 394 Brett Butler	.30	.14
☐ 395 Delino DeShields	.15	.07
☐ 396 Orel Hershiser	.30	.14
☐ 397 Garey Ingram	.15	.07
☐ 398 Chan Ho Park	.60	.25
☐ 399 Mike Piazza	2.00	.90
☐ 400 Ismael Valdes	.30	.14
☐ 401 Tim Wallach	.15	.07
☐ 402 Cliff Floyd	.30	.14
☐ 403 Marquis Grissom	.30	.14
☐ 404 Mike Lansing	.15	.07
☐ 405 Pedro J.Martinez	.60	.25
☐ 406 Kirk Rueter	.15	.07
☐ 407 Tim Scott	.15	.07
☐ 408 Jeff Shaw	.15	.07
☐ 409 Larry Walker	.60	.25

	MINT	NRMT
☐ 410 Rondell White	.40	.18
☐ 411 John Franco	.30	.14
☐ 412 Todd Hundley	.30	.14
☐ 413 Jason Jacome	.15	.07
☐ 414 Joe Orsulak	.15	.07
☐ 415 Bret Saberhagen	.15	.07
☐ 416 David Segui	.15	.07
☐ 417 Darren Daulton	.30	.14
☐ 418 Mariano Duncan	.15	.07
☐ 419 Tommy Greene	.15	.07
☐ 420 Gregg Jefferies	.30	.14
☐ 421 John Kruk	.30	.14
☐ 422 Kevin Stocker	.15	.07
☐ 423 Jay Bell	.30	.14
☐ 424 Al Martin	.30	.14
☐ 425 Denny Neagle	.30	.14
☐ 426 Zane Smith	.15	.07
☐ 427 Andy Van Slyke	.30	.14
☐ 428 Paul Wagner	.15	.07
☐ 429 Tom Henke	.15	.07
☐ 430 Danny Jackson	.15	.07
☐ 431 Ray Lankford	.40	.18
☐ 432 John Mabry	.40	.18
☐ 433 Bob Tewksbury	.15	.07
☐ 434 Todd Zeile	.15	.07
☐ 435 Andy Ashby	.15	.07
☐ 436 Andujar Cedeno	.15	.07
☐ 437 Donnie Elliott	.15	.07
☐ 438 Bryce Florie	.15	.07
☐ 439 Trevor Hoffman	.30	.14
☐ 440 Melvin Nieves	.15	.07
☐ 441 Bip Roberts	.15	.07
☐ 442 Barry Bonds	.75	.35
☐ 443 Royce Clayton	.15	.07
☐ 444 Mike Jackson	.15	.07
☐ 445 John Patterson	.15	.07
☐ 446 J.R. Phillips	.15	.07
☐ 447 Bill Swift	.15	.07
☐ 448 Checklist	.15	.07
☐ 449 Checklist	.15	.07
☐ 450 Checklist	.15	.07

1995 Ultra Gold Medallion

This 450-card parallels the regular Ultra issue. These cards were issued one per pack and are differentiated from the regular cards by the Ultra logo being replaced by the "Ultra Gold Medallion Edition logo."

	MINT	NRMT
COMPLETE SET (450)	110.00	50.00
COMPLETE SERIES 1 (250)	60.00	27.00
COMPLETE SERIES 2 (200)	50.00	22.00
COMMON CARD (1-450)	.30	.14

*STARS: 1.5X to 4X BASIC CARDS ....
*YOUNG STARS: 1.25X to 3X BASIC CARDS

1995 Ultra All-Rookies

This 10-card standard-size set features rookies who emerged with an impact in 1994. These cards were inserted one in every five second series packs. The fronts feature a player's photo in the middle of the card with each corner devoted to a close-up of part of that action shot. The horizontal backs feature some player information as well as a photo. That same photo is also included in the background as a duotone photo as well. The cards are numbered in the lower left as "X" of 10 and are sequenced in alphabetical order.

	MINT	NRMT
COMPLETE SET (10)	6.00	2.70
COMMON CARD (1-10)	.25	.11

*GOLD MEDAL: 2X TO 5X BASIC CARDS

	MINT	NRMT
☐ 1 Cliff Floyd	.50	.23
☐ 2 Chris Gomez	.25	.11
☐ 3 Rusty Greer	1.25	.55
☐ 4 Bob Hamelin	.25	.11
☐ 5 Joey Hamilton	.50	.23
☐ 6 John Hudek	.25	.11
☐ 7 Ryan Klesko	.75	.35
☐ 8 Raul Mondesi	.75	.35
☐ 9 Manny Ramirez	2.00	.90
☐ 10 Steve Trachsel	.25	.11

1995 Ultra All-Stars

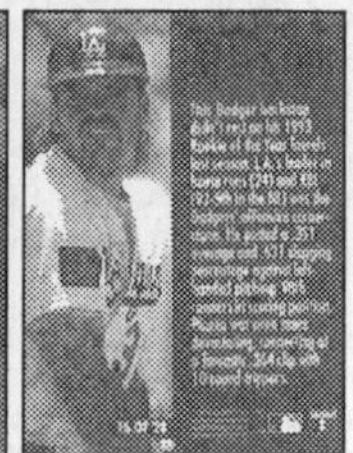

This 20-card standard-size set feature players who are considered to be the top players in the game. Cards were inserted one in every four second series packs. The fronts feature two photos. One photo is in full-color while the other is a shaded black and white shot. The playerís name, "All-Star" and his team name are at the bottom. The back is split between a player photo and career highlights. The cards are numbered in the bottom left as "X" of 20 and are sequenced in alphabetical order.

	MINT	NRMT
COMPLETE SET (20)	20.00	9.00
COMMON CARD (1-20)	.25	.11

*GOLD MEDAL: 1.25X TO 3X BASIC CARDS

	MINT	NRMT
☐ 1 Moises Alou	.25	.11
☐ 2 Albert Belle	1.25	.55
☐ 3 Craig Biggio	.75	.35
☐ 4 Wade Boggs	1.00	.45
☐ 5 Barry Bonds	1.25	.55
☐ 6 David Cone	.50	.23
☐ 7 Ken Griffey Jr.	5.00	2.20
☐ 8 Tony Gwynn	2.00	.90
☐ 9 Chuck Knoblauch	1.00	.45
☐ 10 Barry Larkin	.75	.35
☐ 11 Kenny Lofton	1.25	.55
☐ 12 Greg Maddux	3.00	1.35
☐ 13 Fred McGriff	.75	.35
☐ 14 Paul O'Neill	.50	.23
☐ 15 Mike Piazza	3.00	1.35
☐ 16 Kirby Puckett	2.00	.90
☐ 17 Cal Ripken	4.00	1.80
☐ 18 Ivan Rodriguez	1.25	.55
☐ 19 Frank Thomas	4.00	1.80
☐ 20 Matt Williams	.75	.35

1995 Ultra Award Winners

Featuring players who won major awards in 1994, this 25-card standard-size set was inserted one in every four first series packs. The horizontal fronts feature a full-color photo as well as a "stretched" duotone photo. The award the player won is indicated at the top while the player's name is on the bottom. The backs feature two more photos as well as reasons for the player winning the given award. The cards are numbered as "X" of 25.

	MINT	NRMT
COMPLETE SET (25)	20.00	9.00
COMMON CARD (1-25)	.25	.11

*GOLD MEDAL: 1.25X TO 3X BASIC CARDS

	MINT	NRMT
☐ 1 Ivan Rodriguez	1.25	.55
☐ 2 Don Mattingly	2.00	.90
☐ 3 Roberto Alomar	1.00	.45
☐ 4 Wade Boggs	1.00	.45
☐ 5 Omar Vizquel	.35	.16
☐ 6 Ken Griffey Jr.	5.00	2.20
☐ 7 Kenny Lofton	1.25	.55
☐ 8 Devon White	.25	.11
☐ 9 Mark Langston	.25	.11
☐ 10 Tom Pagnozzi	.25	.11
☐ 11 Jeff Bagwell	2.00	.90
☐ 12 Craig Biggio	.60	.25
☐ 13 Matt Williams	.60	.25
☐ 14 Barry Larkin	.60	.25
☐ 15 Barry Bonds	1.25	.55
☐ 16 Marquis Grissom	.35	.16
☐ 17 Darren Lewis	.25	.11
☐ 18 Greg Maddux	3.00	1.35
☐ 19 Frank Thomas	4.00	1.80
☐ 20 Jeff Bagwell	2.00	.90
☐ 21 David Cone	.35	.16
☐ 22 Greg Maddux	3.00	1.35
☐ 23 Bob Hamelin	.25	.11
☐ 24 Raul Mondesi	.60	.25
☐ 25 Moises Alou	.35	.16

1995 Ultra Gold Medallion Rookies

This 20-card standard-size set was available through a mail-in wrapper offer that expired 9/30/95. These players featured were all rookies in 1995 and were not included in the regular Ultra set. The design is essentially the same as the corresponding basic cards save for the medallion in the upper left-hand corner. The cards are numbered with an "M" prefix. The set is sequenced in alphabetical order.

	MINT	NRMT
COMPLETE SET (20)	12.00	5.50
COMMON CARD (M1-M20)	.25	.11

	MINT	NRMT
☐ M1 Manny Alexander	.25	.11
☐ M2 Edgardo Alfonzo	1.00	.45
☐ M3 Jason Bates	.25	.11
☐ M4 Andres Berumen	.25	.11
☐ M5 Darren Bragg	.25	.11
☐ M6 Jamie Brewington	.25	.11
☐ M7 Jason Christiansen	.25	.11
☐ M8 Brad Clontz	.25	.11
☐ M9 Marty Cordova	.50	.23
☐ M10 Johnny Damon	.35	.16
☐ M11 Vaughn Eshelman	.25	.11
☐ M12 Chad Fonville	.25	.11
☐ M13 Curtis Goodwin	.25	.11
☐ M14 Tyler Green	.25	.11
☐ M15 Bob Higginson	2.00	.90
☐ M16 Jason Isringhausen	.25	.11
☐ M17 Hideo Nomo	6.00	2.70
☐ M18 Jon Nunnally	.25	.11
☐ M19 Carlos Perez	.25	.11
☐ M20 Julian Tavarez	.25	.11

1995 Ultra Golden Prospects

Inserted one every eight first series hobby packs, this 10-card standard-size set features potential impact players. The horizontal fronts feature the same photo with multiple viewpoints giving the impression the photo has been "cut up" into various parts. The words "Golden Prospect" as well as the player's name and team are across the bottom. The horizontal backs have information about his career as well as a normal full-color photo. The cards are numbered as "X" of 10 and are sequenced alphabetically.

	MINT	NRMT
COMPLETE SET (10)	10.00	4.50
COMMON CARD (1-10)	.50	.23

*GOLD MEDAL: 1X TO 2X BASIC CARDS

☐ 1 James Baldwin	.75	.35
☐ 2 Alan Benes	1.00	.45
☐ 3 Armando Benitez	.50	.23
☐ 4 Ray Durham	1.00	.45
☐ 5 LaTroy Hawkins	.50	.23
☐ 6 Brian L.Hunter	1.00	.45
☐ 7 Derek Jeter	5.00	2.20
☐ 8 Charles Johnson	1.00	.45
☐ 9 Alex Rodriguez	6.00	2.70
☐ 10 Michael Tucker	1.00	.45

1995 Ultra Hitting Machines

This 10-card standard-size set features some of baseball's leading batters. Inserted one in every eight second-series retail packs, these horizontal cards have the player's photo against a background of the words "Hitting Machine." The player's name and team are identified on the bottom. The horizontal backs feature another player photo and reasons why they are great batters. The cards are numbered as "X" of 10 in the upper right and are sequenced in alphabetical order.

	MINT	NRMT
COMPLETE SET (10)	15.00	6.75
COMMON CARD (1-10)	.50	.23

*GOLD MEDAL: 1.25X TO 3X BASIC CARDS

☐ 1 Jeff Bagwell	2.00	.90
☐ 2 Albert Belle	1.25	.55
☐ 3 Dante Bichette	.75	.35
☐ 4 Barry Bonds	1.25	.55
☐ 5 Jose Canseco	.50	.23
☐ 6 Ken Griffey Jr.	5.00	2.20
☐ 7 Tony Gwynn	2.00	.90
☐ 8 Fred McGriff	.75	.35
☐ 9 Mike Piazza	3.00	1.35
☐ 10 Frank Thomas	4.00	1.80

1995 Ultra Home Run Kings

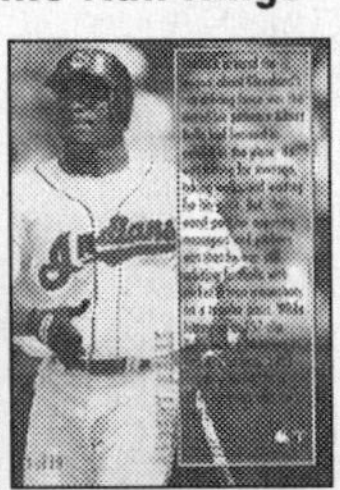

This 10-card standard-size set featured the five leading home run hitters in each league. These cards were issued one every eight first series retail packs. These cards have a player photo on one side with the letters HRK on the other side. The player is identified vertically in the middle. The backs have information about the playerís home run prowess as well as another action photo. The cards are numbered as "X" of 10 and are sequenced by league according to 1994's home rum standings.

	MINT	NRMT
COMPLETE SET (10)	30.00	13.50
COMMON CARD (1-10)	1.00	.45

*GOLD MEDAL: 3X TO 8X BASIC CARDS

☐ 1 Ken Griffey Jr.	12.00	5.50
☐ 2 Frank Thomas	10.00	4.50
☐ 3 Albert Belle	3.00	1.35
☐ 4 Jose Canseco	2.00	.90
☐ 5 Cecil Fielder	1.00	.45
☐ 6 Matt Williams	2.00	.90
☐ 7 Jeff Bagwell	5.00	2.20
☐ 8 Barry Bonds	3.00	1.35
☐ 9 Fred McGriff	2.00	.90
☐ 10 Andres Galarraga	2.00	.90

1995 Ultra League Leaders

This 10-card standard-size set was inserted one in three first series packs. The horizontal fronts feature a player photo against a background of his leagueís logo. The player is identified in one corner and the category he led the league in is featured in the other corner. The horizontal backs have a player photo as well as explaining more about the stat with which he paced the field.

	MINT	NRMT
COMPLETE SET (10)	8.00	3.60
COMMON CARD (1-10)	.25	.11

*GOLD MEDAL: 1.25X TO 3X BASIC CARDS

☐ 1 Paul O'Neill	.35	.16
☐ 2 Kenny Lofton	1.25	.55
☐ 3 Jimmy Key	.35	.16
☐ 4 Randy Johnson		
☐ 5 Lee Smith	.35	.16
☐ 6 Tony Gwynn	2.00	.90
☐ 7 Craig Biggio		
☐ 8 Greg Maddux	3.00	1.35
☐ 9 Andy Benes	.25	.11
☐ 10 John Franco	.25	.11

1995 Ultra On-Base Leaders

This 10-card standard-size set features ten players who are constantly reaching base safely. These cards were inserted one in every eight pre-priced second series jumbo packs. The fronts have an action photo against a background of several smaller action photos. The words "On-Base Leaders" are featured in the upper right corner along with the player's name. The horizontal backs contain the player's team, some information on how often they get on base and a player photo. The cards are numbered in the upper right corner as "X" of 10 and are sequenced in alphabetical order.

	MINT	NRMT
COMPLETE SET (10)	40.00	18.00
COMMON CARD (1-10)	2.50	1.10

*GOLD MEDAL: 5X TO 12X BASIC CARDS

☐ 1 Jeff Bagwell	8.00	3.60
☐ 2 Albert Belle	8.00	3.60
☐ 3 Craig Biggio	3.50	1.55
☐ 4 Wade Boggs	4.00	1.80
☐ 5 Barry Bonds	5.00	2.20
☐ 6 Will Clark	3.50	1.55
☐ 7 Tony Gwynn	8.00	3.60
☐ 8 David Justice	4.00	1.80
☐ 9 Paul O'Neill	2.50	1.10
☐ 10 Frank Thomas	20.00	9.00

1995 Ultra Power Plus

This six-card standard-size set was inserted one in every 37 first series packs. The six players portrayed are not only sluggers, but also excel at another part of the game. Unlike the 1995 Ultra cards and the other insert sets, these cards are 100 percent foil. The fronts have a player photo against a background that has the words "Power Plus" spelled in various size letters. The player and his team are identified on the bottom in gold foil. The backs have a player photo and some player information. The

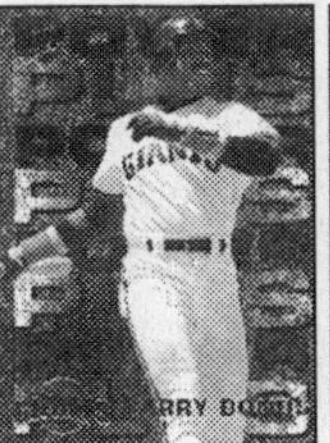

cards are numbered on the bottom right as "X" of 6 and are sequenced in alphabetical order by league.

	MINT	NRMT
COMPLETE SET (6)	50.00	22.00
COMMON CARD (1-6)	2.50	1.10

*GOLD MEDAL: 5X TO 12X BASIC CARDS

☐ 1 Albert Belle	5.00	2.20
☐ 2 Ken Griffey Jr.	20.00	9.00
☐ 3 Frank Thomas	15.00	6.75
☐ 4 Jeff Bagwell	8.00	3.60
☐ 5 Barry Bonds	5.00	2.20
☐ 6 Matt Williams	2.50	1.10

1995 Ultra RBI Kings

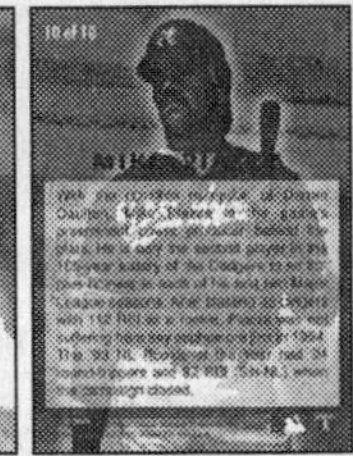

This 10-card standard-size set was inserted into series one jumbo packs at a rate of one every 11. The cards feature a player photo against a multi-colored background. The player's name, the words "RBI King" as well as his team identity are printed in gold foil in the middle. The backs have a player photo as well as some information about the players batting prowess. The cards are numbered in the upper left as "X" of 10 and are sequenced in order by league.

	MINT	NRMT
COMPLETE SET (10)	50.00	22.00
COMMON CARD (1-10)	1.50	.70

*GOLD MEDAL: 5X TO 12X BASIC CARDS

☐ 1 Kirby Puckett	8.00	3.60
☐ 2 Joe Carter	2.50	1.10
☐ 3 Albert Belle	4.00	1.80
☐ 4 Frank Thomas	15.00	6.75
☐ 5 Julio Franco	1.50	.70
☐ 6 Jeff Bagwell	8.00	3.60
☐ 7 Matt Williams	2.50	1.10
☐ 8 Dante Bichette	2.50	1.10
☐ 9 Fred McGriff	2.50	1.10
☐ 10 Mike Piazza	12.00	5.50

1995 Ultra Rising Stars

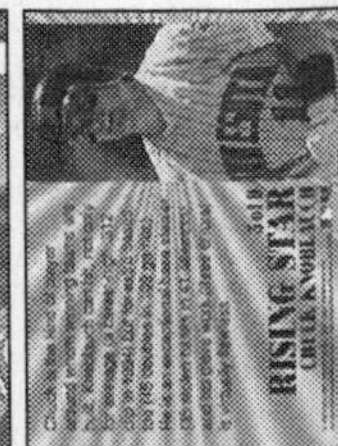

This nine-card standard-size set was inserted one every 37 second series packs. Horizontal fronts feature two photos with the words "Rising Stars" as well as the player's name and team on the bottom left. This front design is set against a shiny background. The backs contain player information as well as a player photo. The cards are numbered "X" of 9 and are sequenced in alphabetical order.

	MINT	NRMT
COMPLETE SET (9)	80.00	36.00
COMMON CARD (1-9)	2.00	.90

*GOLD MEDAL: 8X TO 20X BASIC CARDS

	MINT	NRMT
☐ 1 Moises Alou	2.00	.90
☐ 2 Jeff Bagwell	12.00	5.50
☐ 3 Albert Belle	8.00	3.60
☐ 4 Juan Gonzalez	15.00	6.75
☐ 5 Chuck Knoblauch	5.00	2.20
☐ 6 Kenny Lofton	8.00	3.60
☐ 7 Raul Mondesi	4.00	1.80
☐ 8 Mike Piazza	20.00	9.00
☐ 9 Frank Thomas	25.00	11.00

1995 Ultra Second Year Standouts

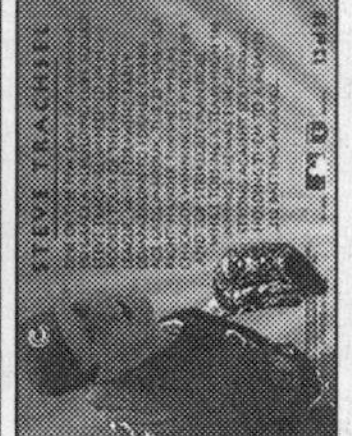

This 15-card standard-size set was inserted into first series packs at a rate of not greater than one in six packs. The players in this set were all rookies in 1994 whom big things were expected from in 1995. The horizontal fronts feature the player's photo against a yellowish background. The player, his team's identification as well as the team logo are all printed in gold foil in the middle. The horizontal backs have another player photo as well as information about the player's 1994 season. The cards are numbered in the lower right as "X" of 15 and are sequenced in alphabetical order.

	MINT	NRMT
COMPLETE SET (15)	10.00	4.50
COMMON CARD (1-15)	.50	.23

*GOLD MEDAL: 3X TO 8X BASIC CARDS

	MINT	NRMT
☐ 1 Cliff Floyd	1.00	.45
☐ 2 Chris Gomez	.50	.23
☐ 3 Rusty Greer	2.00	.90
☐ 4 Darren Hall	.50	.23
☐ 5 Bob Hamelin	.50	.23
☐ 6 Joey Hamilton	1.00	.45
☐ 7 Jeffrey Hammonds	1.00	.45
☐ 8 John Hudek	.50	.23
☐ 9 Ryan Klesko	1.50	.70
☐ 10 Raul Mondesi	1.50	.70
☐ 11 Manny Ramirez	3.00	1.35
☐ 12 Bill Risley	.50	.23
☐ 13 Steve Trachsel	.50	.23
☐ 14 W.VanLandingham	.50	.23
☐ 15 Rondell White	1.50	.70

1995 Ultra Strikeout Kings

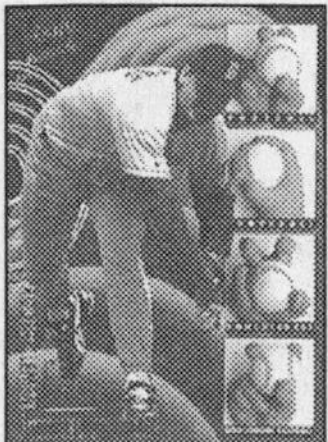

This six-card standard-size set was inserted one every five second series packs. The fronts have a player photo as well as photos of grips for four major pitches. The player's name as well as the words "Strikeout King" is printed in a bottom corner. The horizontal backs feature a player photo, a brief blurb as well as a team logo. The cards are numbered as "X" of 6 and are sequenced in alphabetical order.

	MINT	NRMT
COMPLETE SET (6)	5.00	2.20
COMMON CARD (1-6)	.25	.11

*GOLD MEDAL: 1X TO 2X BASIC CARDS

	MINT	NRMT
☐ 1 Andy Benes	.75	.35
☐ 2 Roger Clemens	1.50	.70
☐ 3 Randy Johnson	1.00	.45
☐ 4 Greg Maddux	3.00	1.35
☐ 5 Pedro Martinez	1.00	.45
☐ 6 Jose Rijo	.25	.11

1996 Ultra Promos

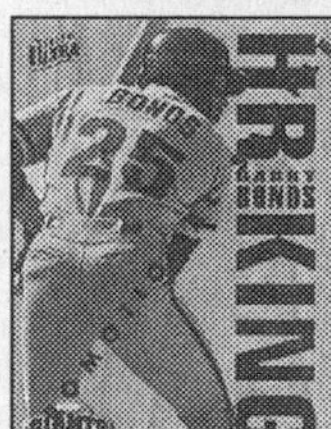

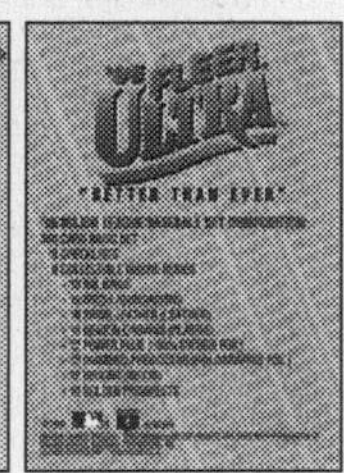

This 3-card standard-size set previews the 1996 Ultra series. The Griffey card represents the basic set and has the same front and back as its regular issue counterpart. The other two cards are from insert series and carry advertisements on their backs. Each card has the disclaimer "PROMOTIONAL SAMPLE" stamped diagonally across it. Since the cards are unnumbered, they are checklisted below in alphabetical order.

	MINT	NRMT
COMPLETE SET (3)	5.00	2.20
COMMON CARD (1-3)	1.00	.45

	MINT	NRMT
☐ 1 Barry Bonds HR King	1.00	.45
☐ 2 Ken Griffey Jr.	2.00	.90
☐ 3 Cal Ripken Prime Leather	2.00	.90

1996 Ultra

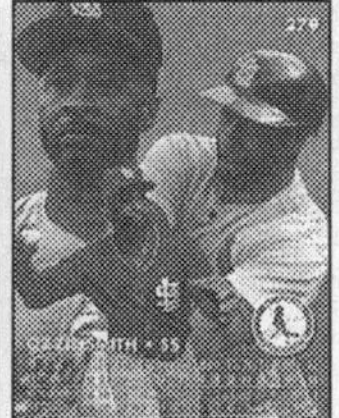

The 1996 Ultra set, produced by Fleer, contains 600 standard-size cards. The cards were distributed in packs that included two inserts. One insert is a Gold Medallion parallel while the other insert comes from one of the many Ultra insert sets. The cards are thicker than their 1995 counterparts and the fronts feature the player in an action shot in full-bleed color. Player's name and team are emblazoned across the bottom in silver foil. Backs show the players in two action shots and one pose. The backs are full-bleed color and include biography and player 1995 statistics in gold print across the bottom. The cards are sequenced in alphabetical order within league and team order.

	MINT	NRMT
COMPLETE SET (600)	60.00	27.00
COMPLETE SERIES 1 (300)	30.00	13.50
COMPLETE SERIES 2 (300)	30.00	13.50
COMMON CARD (1-600)	.15	.07

	MINT	NRMT
☐ 1 Manny Alexander	.15	.07
☐ 2 Brady Anderson	.40	.18
☐ 3 Bobby Bonilla	.30	.14
☐ 4 Scott Erickson	.15	.07
☐ 5 Curtis Goodwin	.15	.07
☐ 6 Chris Hoiles	.15	.07
☐ 7 Doug Jones	.15	.07
☐ 8 Jeff Manto	.15	.07
☐ 9 Mike Mussina	.60	.25
☐ 10 Rafael Palmeiro	.40	.18
☐ 11 Cal Ripken	2.50	1.10
☐ 12 Rick Aguilera	.15	.07
☐ 13 Luis Alicea	.15	.07
☐ 14 Stan Belinda	.15	.07
☐ 15 Jose Canseco	.40	.18
☐ 16 Roger Clemens	1.25	.55
☐ 17 Mike Greenwell	.15	.07
☐ 18 Mike Macfarlane	.15	.07
☐ 19 Tim Naehring	.30	.14
☐ 20 Troy O'Leary	.15	.07
☐ 21 John Valentin	.30	.14
☐ 22 Mo Vaughn	.75	.35
☐ 23 Tim Wakefield	.15	.07
☐ 24 Brian Anderson	.15	.07
☐ 25 Garret Anderson	.40	.18
☐ 26 Chili Davis	.15	.07
☐ 27 Gary DiSarcina	.15	.07
☐ 28 Jim Edmonds	.60	.25
☐ 29 Jorge Fabregas	.15	.07
☐ 30 Chuck Finley	.15	.07
☐ 31 Mark Langston	.15	.07
☐ 32 Troy Percival	.30	.14
☐ 33 Tim Salmon	.60	.25
☐ 34 Lee Smith	.30	.14
☐ 35 Wilson Alvarez	.30	.14
☐ 36 Ray Durham	.30	.14
☐ 37 Alex Fernandez	.30	.14
☐ 38 Ozzie Guillen	.15	.07
☐ 39 Roberto Hernandez	.30	.14
☐ 40 Lance Johnson	.15	.07
☐ 41 Ron Karkovice	.15	.07
☐ 42 Lyle Mouton	.15	.07
☐ 43 Tim Raines	.15	.07
☐ 44 Frank Thomas	2.50	1.10
☐ 45 Carlos Baerga	.30	.14
☐ 46 Albert Belle	.75	.35
☐ 47 Orel Hershiser	.30	.14
☐ 48 Kenny Lofton	.75	.35
☐ 49 Dennis Martinez	.30	.14
☐ 50 Jose Mesa	.30	.14
☐ 51 Eddie Murray	.60	.25
☐ 52 Chad Ogea	.15	.07
☐ 53 Manny Ramirez	.60	.25
☐ 54 Jim Thome	.60	.25
☐ 55 Omar Vizquel	.30	.14
☐ 56 Dave Winfield	.40	.18
☐ 57 Chad Curtis	.15	.07
☐ 58 Cecil Fielder	.30	.14
☐ 59 John Flaherty	.15	.07
☐ 60 Travis Fryman	.30	.14
☐ 61 Chris Gomez	.15	.07
☐ 62 Bob Higginson	.40	.18
☐ 63 Felipe Lira	.15	.07
☐ 64 Brian Maxcy	.15	.07
☐ 65 Alan Trammell	.40	.18
☐ 66 Lou Whitaker	.30	.14
☐ 67 Kevin Appier	.30	.14
☐ 68 Gary Gaetti	.30	.14
☐ 69 Tom Goodwin	.15	.07
☐ 70 Tom Gordon	.15	.07
☐ 71 Jason Jacome	.15	.07
☐ 72 Wally Joyner	.15	.07
☐ 73 Brent Mayne	.15	.07
☐ 74 Jeff Montgomery	.15	.07
☐ 75 Jon Nunnally	.15	.07
☐ 76 Joe Vitiello	.15	.07
☐ 77 Ricky Bones	.15	.07
☐ 78 Jeff Cirillo	.30	.14
☐ 79 Mike Fetters	.15	.07
☐ 80 Darryl Hamilton	.15	.07
☐ 81 David Hulse	.15	.07
☐ 82 Dave Nilsson	.30	.14
☐ 83 Kevin Seitzer	.15	.07
☐ 84 Steve Sparks	.15	.07
☐ 85 B.J. Surhoff	.30	.14
☐ 86 Jose Valentin	.15	.07
☐ 87 Greg Vaughn	.15	.07
☐ 88 Marty Cordova	.15	.07
☐ 89 Chuck Knoblauch	.60	.25
☐ 90 Pat Meares	.15	.07
☐ 91 Pedro Munoz	.15	.07
☐ 92 Kirby Puckett	1.25	.55
☐ 93 Brad Radke	.30	.14
☐ 94 Scott Stahoviak	.15	.07
☐ 95 Dave Stevens	.15	.07
☐ 96 Mike Trombley	.15	.07
☐ 97 Matt Walbeck	.15	.07
☐ 98 Wade Boggs	.60	.25
☐ 99 Russ Davis	.15	.07
☐ 100 Jim Leyritz	.15	.07
☐ 101 Don Mattingly	1.00	.45
☐ 102 Jack McDowell	.15	.07
☐ 103 Paul O'Neill	.30	.14
☐ 104 Andy Pettitte	.75	.35
☐ 105 Mariano Rivera	.60	.25
☐ 106 Ruben Sierra	.15	.07
☐ 107 Darryl Strawberry	.30	.14
☐ 108 John Wetteland	.30	.14
☐ 109 Bernie Williams	.60	.25
☐ 110 Geronimo Berroa	.15	.07
☐ 111 Scott Brosius	.15	.07
☐ 112 Dennis Eckersley	.40	.18
☐ 113 Brent Gates	.15	.07
☐ 114 Rickey Henderson	.40	.18
☐ 115 Mark McGwire	1.25	.55

☐ 116 Ariel Prieto	.15	.07
☐ 117 Terry Steinbach	.30	.14
☐ 118 Todd Stottlemyre	.15	.07
☐ 119 Todd Van Poppel	.15	.07
☐ 120 Steve Wojciechowski	.15	.07
☐ 121 Rich Amaral	.15	.07
☐ 122 Bobby Ayala	.15	.07
☐ 123 Mike Blowers	.15	.07
☐ 124 Chris Bosio	.15	.07
☐ 125 Joey Cora	.30	.14
☐ 126 Ken Griffey Jr.	3.00	1.35
☐ 127 Randy Johnson	.60	.25
☐ 128 Edgar Martinez	.40	.18
☐ 129 Tino Martinez	.60	.25
☐ 130 Alex Rodriguez	2.50	1.10
☐ 131 Dan Wilson	.15	.07
☐ 132 Will Clark	.40	.18
☐ 133 Jeff Frye	.15	.07
☐ 134 Benji Gil	.15	.07
☐ 135 Juan Gonzalez	1.50	.70
☐ 136 Rusty Greer	.60	.25
☐ 137 Mark McLemore	.15	.07
☐ 138 Roger Pavlik	.15	.07
☐ 139 Ivan Rodriguez	.75	.35
☐ 140 Kenny Rogers	.15	.07
☐ 141 Mickey Tettleton	.15	.07
☐ 142 Roberto Alomar	.60	.25
☐ 143 Joe Carter	.30	.14
☐ 144 Tony Castillo	.15	.07
☐ 145 Alex Gonzalez	.15	.07
☐ 146 Shawn Green	.30	.14
☐ 147 Pat Hentgen	.30	.14
☐ 148 Sandy Martinez	.15	.07
☐ 149 Paul Molitor	.60	.25
☐ 150 John Olerud	.30	.14
☐ 151 Ed Sprague	.15	.07
☐ 152 Jeff Blauser	.15	.07
☐ 153 Brad Clontz	.15	.07
☐ 154 Tom Glavine	.30	.14
☐ 155 Marquis Grissom	.30	.14
☐ 156 Chipper Jones	2.00	.90
☐ 157 David Justice	.60	.25
☐ 158 Ryan Klesko	.40	.18
☐ 159 Javier Lopez	.30	.14
☐ 160 Greg Maddux	2.00	.90
☐ 161 John Smoltz	.30	.14
☐ 162 Mark Wohlers	.30	.14
☐ 163 Jim Bullinger	.15	.07
☐ 164 Frank Castillo	.15	.07
☐ 165 Shawon Dunston	.15	.07
☐ 166 Kevin Foster	.15	.07
☐ 167 Luis Gonzalez	.15	.07
☐ 168 Mark Grace	.40	.18
☐ 169 Rey Sanchez	.15	.07
☐ 170 Scott Servais	.15	.07
☐ 171 Sammy Sosa	.60	.25
☐ 172 Ozzie Timmons	.15	.07
☐ 173 Steve Trachsel	.15	.07
☐ 174 Bret Boone	.15	.07
☐ 175 Jeff Branson	.15	.07
☐ 176 Jeff Brantley	.15	.07
☐ 177 Dave Burba	.15	.07
☐ 178 Ron Gant	.30	.14
☐ 179 Barry Larkin	.40	.18
☐ 180 Darren Lewis	.15	.07
☐ 181 Mark Portugal	.15	.07
☐ 182 Reggie Sanders	.15	.07
☐ 183 Pete Schourek	.15	.07
☐ 184 John Smiley	.15	.07
☐ 185 Jason Bates	.15	.07
☐ 186 Dante Bichette	.30	.14
☐ 187 Ellis Burks	.30	.14
☐ 188 Vinny Castilla	.30	.14
☐ 189 Andres Galarraga	.60	.25
☐ 190 Darren Holmes	.15	.07
☐ 191 Armando Reynoso	.15	.07
☐ 192 Kevin Ritz	.15	.07
☐ 193 Bill Swift	.15	.07
☐ 194 Larry Walker	.60	.25
☐ 195 Kurt Abbott	.15	.07
☐ 196 John Burkett	.15	.07
☐ 197 Greg Colbrunn	.15	.07
☐ 198 Jeff Conine	.30	.14
☐ 199 Andre Dawson	.40	.18
☐ 200 Chris Hammond	.15	.07
☐ 201 Charles Johnson	.30	.14
☐ 202 Robb Nen	.15	.07
☐ 203 Terry Pendleton	.30	.14
☐ 204 Quilvio Veras	.15	.07
☐ 205 Jeff Bagwell	1.25	.55
☐ 206 Derek Bell	.15	.07
☐ 207 Doug Drabek	.15	.07
☐ 208 Tony Eusebio	.15	.07
☐ 209 Mike Hampton	.15	.07
☐ 210 Brian L. Hunter	.30	.14
☐ 211 Todd Jones	.15	.07
☐ 212 Orlando Miller	.15	.07
☐ 213 James Mouton	.15	.07
☐ 214 Shane Reynolds	.15	.07
☐ 215 Dave Veres	.15	.07
☐ 216 Billy Ashley	.15	.07
☐ 217 Brett Butler	.15	.07
☐ 218 Chad Fonville	.15	.07
☐ 219 Todd Hollandsworth	.30	.14
☐ 220 Eric Karros	.30	.14
☐ 221 Ramon Martinez	.30	.14
☐ 222 Raul Mondesi	.40	.18
☐ 223 Hideo Nomo	1.50	.70
☐ 224 Mike Piazza	2.00	.90
☐ 225 Kevin Tapani	.15	.07
☐ 226 Ismael Valdes	.30	.14
☐ 227 Todd Worrell	.30	.14
☐ 228 Moises Alou	.30	.14
☐ 229 Wil Cordero	.15	.07
☐ 230 Jeff Fassero	.15	.07
☐ 231 Darrin Fletcher	.15	.07
☐ 232 Mike Lansing	.15	.07
☐ 233 Pedro J.Martinez	.60	.25
☐ 234 Carlos Perez	.15	.07
☐ 235 Mel Rojas	.15	.07
☐ 236 David Segui	.15	.07
☐ 237 Tony Tarasco	.15	.07
☐ 238 Rondell White	.30	.14
☐ 239 Edgardo Alfonzo	.60	.25
☐ 240 Rico Brogna	.15	.07
☐ 241 Carl Everett	.15	.07
☐ 242 Todd Hundley	.30	.14
☐ 243 Butch Huskey	.30	.14
☐ 244 Jason Isringhausen	.15	.07
☐ 245 Bobby Jones	.15	.07
☐ 246 Jeff Kent	.15	.07
☐ 247 Bill Pulsipher	.15	.07
☐ 248 Jose Vizcaino	.15	.07
☐ 249 Ricky Bottalico	.30	.14
☐ 250 Darren Daulton	.30	.14
☐ 251 Jim Eisenreich	.30	.14
☐ 252 Tyler Green	.15	.07
☐ 253 Charlie Hayes	.15	.07
☐ 254 Gregg Jefferies	.30	.14
☐ 255 Tony Longmire	.15	.07
☐ 256 Michael Mimbs	.15	.07
☐ 257 Mickey Morandini	.15	.07
☐ 258 Paul Quantrill	.15	.07
☐ 259 Heathcliff Slocumb	.15	.07
☐ 260 Jay Bell	.30	.14
☐ 261 Jacob Brumfield	.15	.07
☐ 262 Angelo Encarnacion	.15	.07
☐ 263 John Ericks	.15	.07
☐ 264 Mark Johnson	.15	.07
☐ 265 Esteban Loaiza	.15	.07
☐ 266 Al Martin	.15	.07
☐ 267 Orlando Merced	.15	.07
☐ 268 Dan Miceli	.15	.07
☐ 269 Denny Neagle	.30	.14
☐ 270 Brian Barber	.15	.07
☐ 271 Scott Cooper	.15	.07
☐ 272 Tripp Cromer	.15	.07
☐ 273 Bernard Gilkey	.30	.14
☐ 274 Tom Henke	.30	.14
☐ 275 Brian Jordan	.30	.14
☐ 276 John Mabry	.30	.14
☐ 277 Tom Pagnozzi	.15	.07
☐ 278 Mark Petkovsek	.15	.07
☐ 279 Ozzie Smith	.75	.35
☐ 280 Andy Ashby	.15	.07
☐ 281 Brad Ausmus	.15	.07
☐ 282 Ken Caminiti	.60	.25
☐ 283 Glenn Dishman	.15	.07
☐ 284 Tony Gwynn	1.50	.70
☐ 285 Joey Hamilton	.30	.14
☐ 286 Trevor Hoffman	.30	.14
☐ 287 Phil Plantier	.15	.07
☐ 288 Jody Reed	.15	.07
☐ 289 Eddie Williams	.15	.07
☐ 290 Barry Bonds	.75	.35
☐ 291 Jamie Brewington	.15	.07
☐ 292 Mark Carreon	.15	.07
☐ 293 Royce Clayton	.15	.07
☐ 294 Glenallen Hill	.15	.07
☐ 295 Mark Leiter	.15	.07
☐ 296 Kirt Manwaring	.15	.07
☐ 297 J.R. Phillips	.15	.07
☐ 298 Deion Sanders	.60	.25
☐ 299 Wm. VanLandingham	.15	.07
☐ 300 Matt Williams	.40	.18
☐ 301 Roberto Alomar	.60	.25
☐ 302 Armando Benitez	.15	.07
☐ 303 Mike Devereaux	.15	.07
☐ 304 Jeffrey Hammonds	.15	.07
☐ 305 Jimmy Haynes	.15	.07
☐ 306 Scott McClain	.15	.07
☐ 307 Kent Mercker	.15	.07
☐ 308 Randy Myers	.15	.07
☐ 309 B.J. Surhoff	.15	.07
☐ 310 Tony Tarasco	.15	.07
☐ 311 David Wells	.15	.07
☐ 312 Wil Cordero	.15	.07
☐ 313 Alex Delgado	.15	.07
☐ 314 Tom Gordon	.15	.07
☐ 315 Dwayne Hosey	.15	.07
☐ 316 Jose Malave	.15	.07
☐ 317 Kevin Mitchell	.15	.07
☐ 318 Jamie Moyer	.15	.07
☐ 319 Aaron Sele	.15	.07
☐ 320 Heathcliff Slocumb	.15	.07
☐ 321 Mike Stanley	.15	.07
☐ 322 Jeff Suppan	.40	.18
☐ 323 Jim Abbott	.30	.14
☐ 324 George Arias	.15	.07
☐ 325 Todd Greene	.60	.25
☐ 326 Bryan Harvey	.15	.07
☐ 327 J.T. Snow	.30	.14
☐ 328 Randy Velarde	.15	.07
☐ 329 Tim Wallach	.15	.07
☐ 330 Harold Baines	.30	.14
☐ 331 Jason Bere	.15	.07
☐ 332 Darren Lewis	.15	.07
☐ 333 Norberto Martin	.15	.07
☐ 334 Tony Phillips	.15	.07
☐ 335 Bill Simas	.15	.07
☐ 336 Chris Snopek	.15	.07
☐ 337 Kevin Tapani	.15	.07
☐ 338 Danny Tartabull	.15	.07
☐ 339 Robin Ventura	.30	.14
☐ 340 Sandy Alomar Jr.	.30	.14
☐ 341 Julio Franco	.30	.14
☐ 342 Jack McDowell	.15	.07
☐ 343 Charles Nagy	.30	.14
☐ 344 Julian Tavarez	.15	.07
☐ 345 Kimera Bartee	.15	.07
☐ 346 Greg Keagle	.15	.07
☐ 347 Mark Lewis	.15	.07
☐ 348 Jose Lima	.15	.07
☐ 349 Melvin Nieves	.15	.07
☐ 350 Mark Parent	.15	.07
☐ 351 Eddie Williams	.15	.07
☐ 352 Johnny Damon	.30	.14
☐ 353 Sal Fasano	.15	.07
☐ 354 Mark Gubicza	.15	.07
☐ 355 Bob Hamelin	.15	.07
☐ 356 Chris Haney	.15	.07
☐ 357 Keith Lockhart	.15	.07
☐ 358 Mike Macfarlane	.15	.07
☐ 359 Jose Offerman	.15	.07
☐ 360 Bip Roberts	.15	.07
☐ 361 Michael Tucker	.30	.14
☐ 362 Chuck Carr	.15	.07
☐ 363 Bobby Hughes	.15	.07
☐ 364 John Jaha	.15	.07
☐ 365 Mark Loretta	.15	.07
☐ 366 Mike Matheny	.15	.07
☐ 367 Ben McDonald	.15	.07
☐ 368 Matt Mieske	.15	.07
☐ 369 Angel Miranda	.15	.07
☐ 370 Fernando Vina	.15	.07
☐ 371 Rick Aguilera	.15	.07
☐ 372 Rich Becker	.15	.07
☐ 373 LaTroy Hawkins	.15	.07
☐ 374 Dave Hollins	.15	.07
☐ 375 Roberto Kelly	.15	.07
☐ 376 Matt Lawton	.15	.07
☐ 377 Paul Molitor	.60	.25
☐ 378 Dan Naulty	.15	.07
☐ 379 Rich Robertson	.15	.07
☐ 380 Frank Rodriguez	.15	.07
☐ 381 David Cone	.30	.14
☐ 382 Mariano Duncan	.15	.07
☐ 383 Andy Fox	.15	.07
☐ 384 Joe Girardi	.15	.07
☐ 385 Dwight Gooden	.30	.14
☐ 386 Derek Jeter	2.00	.90
☐ 387 Pat Kelly	.15	.07
☐ 388 Jimmy Key	.30	.14
☐ 389 Matt Luke	.15	.07
☐ 390 Tino Martinez	.60	.25
☐ 391 Jeff Nelson	.15	.07
☐ 392 Melido Perez	.15	.07
☐ 393 Tim Raines	.15	.07
☐ 394 Ruben Rivera	.30	.14
☐ 395 Kenny Rogers	.15	.07
☐ 396 Tony Batista	.40	.18
☐ 397 Allen Battle	.15	.07
☐ 398 Mike Bordick	.15	.07
☐ 399 Steve Cox	.15	.07
☐ 400 Jason Giambi	.40	.18
☐ 401 Doug Johns	.15	.07
☐ 402 Pedro Munoz	.15	.07
☐ 403 Phil Plantier	.15	.07
☐ 404 Scott Spiezio	.60	.25
☐ 405 George Williams	.15	.07
☐ 406 Ernie Young	.15	.07

Card	MINT	NRMT
☐ 407 Darren Bragg	.15	.07
☐ 408 Jay Buhner	.40	.18
☐ 409 Norm Charlton	.15	.07
☐ 410 Russ Davis	.15	.07
☐ 411 Sterling Hitchcock	.15	.07
☐ 412 Edwin Hurtado	.15	.07
☐ 413 Raul Ibanez	.15	.07
☐ 414 Mike Jackson	.15	.07
☐ 415 Luis Sojo	.15	.07
☐ 416 Paul Sorrento	.15	.07
☐ 417 Bob Wolcott	.15	.07
☐ 418 Damon Buford	.15	.07
☐ 419 Kevin Gross	.15	.07
☐ 420 Darryl Hamilton UER	.15	.07
☐ 421 Mike Henneman	.15	.07
☐ 422 Ken Hill	.15	.07
☐ 423 Dean Palmer	.30	.14
☐ 424 Bobby Witt	.15	.07
☐ 425 Tilson Brito	.15	.07
☐ 426 Giovanni Carrara	.15	.07
☐ 427 Domingo Cedeno	.15	.07
☐ 428 Felipe Crespo	.15	.07
☐ 429 Carlos Delgado	.30	.14
☐ 430 Juan Guzman	.15	.07
☐ 431 Erik Hanson	.15	.07
☐ 432 Marty Janzen	.15	.07
☐ 433 Otis Nixon	.15	.07
☐ 434 Robert Perez	.15	.07
☐ 435 Paul Quantrill	.15	.07
☐ 436 Bill Risley	.15	.07
☐ 437 Steve Avery	.15	.07
☐ 438 Jermaine Dye	.15	.07
☐ 439 Mark Lemke	.15	.07
☐ 440 Marty Malloy	.15	.07
☐ 441 Fred McGriff	.40	.18
☐ 442 Greg McMichael	.15	.07
☐ 443 Wonderful Monds	.15	.07
☐ 444 Eddie Perez	.15	.07
☐ 445 Jason Schmidt	.40	.18
☐ 446 Terrell Wade	.15	.07
☐ 447 Terry Adams	.15	.07
☐ 448 Scott Bullett	.15	.07
☐ 449 Robin Jennings	.15	.07
☐ 450 Doug Jones	.15	.07
☐ 451 Brooks Kieschnick	.30	.14
☐ 452 Dave Magadan	.15	.07
☐ 453 Jason Maxwell	.15	.07
☐ 454 Brian McRae	.15	.07
☐ 455 Rodney Myers	.15	.07
☐ 456 Jaime Navarro	.15	.07
☐ 457 Ryne Sandberg	.40	.18
☐ 458 Vince Coleman	.15	.07
☐ 459 Eric Davis	.30	.14
☐ 460 Steve Gibralter	.15	.07
☐ 461 Thomas Howard	.15	.07
☐ 462 Mike Kelly	.15	.07
☐ 463 Hal Morris	.15	.07
☐ 464 Eric Owens	.15	.07
☐ 465 Jose Rijo	.15	.07
☐ 466 Chris Sabo	.15	.07
☐ 467 Eddie Taubensee	.15	.07
☐ 468 Trenidad Hubbard	.15	.07
☐ 469 Curt Leskanic	.15	.07
☐ 470 Quinton McCracken	.15	.07
☐ 471 Jayhawk Owens	.15	.07
☐ 472 Steve Reed	.15	.07
☐ 473 Bryan Rekar	.15	.07
☐ 474 Bruce Ruffin	.15	.07
☐ 475 Bret Saberhagen	.15	.07
☐ 476 Walt Weiss	.15	.07
☐ 477 Eric Young	.30	.14
☐ 478 Kevin Brown	.30	.14
☐ 479 Al Leiter	.15	.07
☐ 480 Pat Rapp	.15	.07
☐ 481 Gary Sheffield	.60	.25
☐ 482 Devon White	.15	.07
☐ 483 Bob Abreu	.60	.25
☐ 484 Sean Berry	.15	.07
☐ 485 Craig Biggio	.40	.18
☐ 486 Jim Dougherty	.15	.07
☐ 487 Richard Hidalgo	.60	.25
☐ 488 Darryl Kile	.30	.14
☐ 489 Derrick May	.15	.07
☐ 490 Greg Swindell	.15	.07
☐ 491 Rick Wilkins	.15	.07
☐ 492 Mike Blowers	.15	.07
☐ 493 Tom Candiotti	.15	.07
☐ 494 Roger Cedeno	.30	.14
☐ 495 Delino DeShields	.15	.07
☐ 496 Greg Gagne	.15	.07
☐ 497 Karim Garcia	.30	.14
☐ 498 Wilton Guerrero	.60	.25
☐ 499 Chan Ho Park	.60	.25
☐ 500 Isreal Alcantara	.15	.07
☐ 501 Shane Andrews	.15	.07
☐ 502 Yamil Benitez	.40	.18
☐ 503 Cliff Floyd	.15	.07
☐ 504 Mark Grudzielanek	.30	.14
☐ 505 Ryan McGuire	.15	.07
☐ 506 Sherman Obando	.15	.07
☐ 507 Jose Paniagua	.15	.07
☐ 508 Henry Rodriguez	.15	.07
☐ 509 Kirk Rueter	.15	.07
☐ 510 Juan Acevedo	.15	.07
☐ 511 John Franco	.30	.14
☐ 512 Bernard Gilkey	.30	.14
☐ 513 Lance Johnson	.15	.07
☐ 514 Rey Ordonez	.30	.14
☐ 515 Robert Person	.15	.07
☐ 516 Paul Wilson	.15	.07
☐ 517 Toby Borland	.15	.07
☐ 518 David Doster	.15	.07
☐ 519 Lenny Dykstra	.30	.14
☐ 520 Sid Fernandez	.15	.07
☐ 521 Mike Grace	.15	.07
☐ 522 Rich Hunter	.15	.07
☐ 523 Benito Santiago	.15	.07
☐ 524 Gene Schall	.15	.07
☐ 525 Curt Schilling	.30	.14
☐ 526 Kevin Sefcik	.15	.07
☐ 527 Lee Tinsley	.15	.07
☐ 528 David West	.15	.07
☐ 529 Mark Whiten	.15	.07
☐ 530 Todd Zeile	.15	.07
☐ 531 Carlos Garcia	.15	.07
☐ 532 Charlie Hayes	.15	.07
☐ 533 Jason Kendall	.60	.25
☐ 534 Jeff King	.30	.14
☐ 535 Mike Kingery	.15	.07
☐ 536 Nelson Liriano	.15	.07
☐ 537 Dan Plesac	.15	.07
☐ 538 Paul Wagner	.15	.07
☐ 539 Luis Alicea	.15	.07
☐ 540 David Bell	.15	.07
☐ 541 Alan Benes	.30	.14
☐ 542 Andy Benes	.15	.07
☐ 543 Mike Busby	.15	.07
☐ 544 Royce Clayton	.15	.07
☐ 545 Dennis Eckersley	.40	.18
☐ 546 Gary Gaetti	.30	.14
☐ 547 Ron Gant	.30	.14
☐ 548 Aaron Holbert	.15	.07
☐ 549 Ray Lankford	.30	.14
☐ 550 T.J. Mathews	.15	.07
☐ 551 Willie McGee	.15	.07
☐ 552 Miguel Mejia	.40	.18
☐ 553 Todd Stottlemyre	.15	.07
☐ 554 Sean Bergman	.15	.07
☐ 555 Willie Blair	.15	.07
☐ 556 Andujar Cedeno	.15	.07
☐ 557 Steve Finley	.30	.14
☐ 558 Rickey Henderson	.40	.18
☐ 559 Wally Joyner	.15	.07
☐ 560 Scott Livingstone	.15	.07
☐ 561 Marc Newfield	.15	.07
☐ 562 Bob Tewksbury	.15	.07
☐ 563 Fernando Valenzuela	.30	.14
☐ 564 Rod Beck	.30	.14
☐ 565 Doug Creek	.15	.07
☐ 566 Shawon Dunston	.15	.07
☐ 567 Osvaldo Fernandez	.30	.14
☐ 568 Stan Javier	.15	.07
☐ 569 Marcus Jensen	.15	.07
☐ 570 Steve Scarsone	.15	.07
☐ 571 Robby Thompson	.15	.07
☐ 572 Allen Watson	.15	.07
☐ 573 Roberto Alomar STA	.60	.25
☐ 574 Jeff Bagwell STA	.60	.25
☐ 575 Albert Belle STA	.60	.25
☐ 576 Wade Boggs STA	.60	.25
☐ 577 Barry Bonds STA	.60	.25
☐ 578 Juan Gonzalez STA	.75	.35
☐ 579 Ken Griffey Jr. STA	1.50	.70
☐ 580 Tony Gwynn STA	.60	.25
☐ 581 Randy Johnson STA	.60	.25
☐ 582 Chipper Jones STA	1.00	.45
☐ 583 Barry Larkin STA	.40	.18
☐ 584 Kenny Lofton STA	.60	.25
☐ 585 Greg Maddux STA	1.00	.45
☐ 586 Raul Mondesi STA	.40	.18
☐ 587 Mike Piazza STA	1.00	.45
☐ 588 Cal Ripken STA	1.25	.55
☐ 589 Tim Salmon STA	.60	.25
☐ 590 Frank Thomas STA	1.50	.70
☐ 591 Mo Vaughn STA	.60	.25
☐ 592 Matt Williams STA	.40	.18
☐ 593 Marty Cordova RAW	.15	.07
☐ 594 Jim Edmonds RAW	.60	.25
☐ 595 Cliff Floyd RAW	.15	.07
☐ 596 Chipper Jones RAW	1.00	.45
☐ 597 Ryan Klesko RAW	.40	.18
☐ 598 Raul Mondesi RAW	.40	.18
☐ 599 Manny Ramirez RAW	.60	.25
☐ 600 Ruben Rivera RAW	.15	.07

1996 Ultra Gold Medallion

The 1996 Ultra Gold Medallion is a parallel to the regular Ultra issue. The cards were inserted one per pack in both first and second series. The card consists of a full gold foil paper with a full-color player cut out on top. Backs are identical to the regular cards.

	MINT	NRMT
COMPLETE SET (600)	200.00	90.00
COMPLETE SERIES 1 (300)	100.00	45.00
COMPLETE SERIES 2 (300)	100.00	45.00
COMMON CARD (1-600)	.25	.11
*STARS: 2X to 4X BASIC CARDS		
*YOUNG STARS: 1.5X to 3X BASIC CARS		

1996 Ultra Call to the Hall

Randomly inserted in packs at a rate of one in 24, this ten-card set features original illustrations of possible future Hall of Famers. The backs state why the player is a possible HOF.

	MINT	NRMT
COMPLETE SET (10)	80.00	36.00
COMMON CARD (1-10)	2.00	.90
*GOLD MEDAL: 1X TO 2X BASIC CARDS		
☐ 1 Barry Bonds	5.00	2.20
☐ 2 Ken Griffey Jr.	20.00	9.00
☐ 3 Tony Gwynn	8.00	3.60
☐ 4 Rickey Henderson	3.00	1.35
☐ 5 Greg Maddux	12.00	5.50
☐ 6 Eddie Murray	2.00	.90
☐ 7 Cal Ripken	15.00	6.75
☐ 8 Ryne Sandberg	5.00	2.20
☐ 9 Ozzie Smith	5.00	2.20
☐ 10 Frank Thomas	15.00	6.75

1996 Ultra Checklists

Randomly inserted in packs, this set of 10 standard-size cards features superstars of the game. Fronts are full-bleed color action photos of players with "Checklist" written in gold foil across the card. The horizontal backs are numbered and show the different card sets that are included in the Ultra line. The cards are sequenced in alphabetical order. A gold medallion parallel version of each card was issued.

	MINT	NRMT
COMPLETE SERIES 1 (10)	10.00	4.50
COMPLETE SERIES 2 (10)	10.00	4.50
COMMON CARD (A1-B10)	.50	.23
*GOLD MEDAL: 1X TO 2.5X BASIC CARDS		
☐ A1 Jeff Bagwell	1.50	.70
☐ A2 Barry Bonds	1.00	.45
☐ A3 Juan Gonzalez	2.00	.90
☐ A4 Ken Griffey Jr.	4.00	1.80
☐ A5 Chipper Jones	2.50	1.10
☐ A6 Mike Piazza	2.50	1.10
☐ A7 Manny Ramirez	.75	.35
☐ A8 Cal Ripken	3.00	1.35
☐ A9 Frank Thomas	3.00	1.35
☐ A10 Matt Williams	.75	.35
☐ B1 Albert Belle	1.00	.45
☐ B2 Cecil Fielder	.50	.23
☐ B3 Ken Griffey Jr.	4.00	1.80

Card	MINT	NRMT
☐ B4 Tony Gwynn	1.50	.70
☐ B5 Derek Jeter	2.50	1.10
☐ B6 Jason Kendall	.50	.23
☐ B7 Ryan Klesko	.75	.35
☐ B8 Greg Maddux	2.50	1.10
☐ B9 Cal Ripken	3.00	1.35
☐ B10 Frank Thomas	3.00	1.35

1996 Ultra Diamond Producers

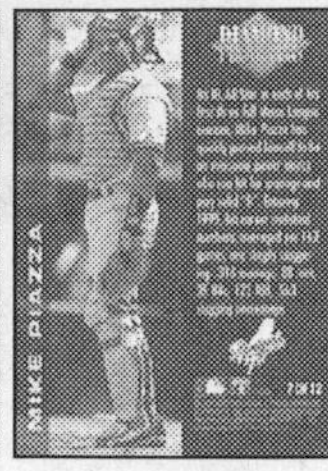

This 12-card standard-size set highlights the achievements of Major League stars. The cards were randomly inserted at a rate of one in 20. The horizontal fronts show the player close-up and an action photo on a metallic-silver paper. "Diamond Producers" and the player's name are printed in silver foil at the bottom of the card. The backs feature the player in an action shot on the left half and a white on black description of the player's career achievements. The cards are sequenced in alphabetical order and there are also gold medallion versions of these cards.

	MINT	NRMT
COMPLETE SET (12)	60.00	27.00
COMMON CARD (1-12)	2.00	.90

*GOLD MEDAL: 1X TO 2X BASIC CARDS

Card	MINT	NRMT
☐ 1 Albert Belle	4.00	1.80
☐ 2 Barry Bonds	4.00	1.80
☐ 3 Ken Griffey Jr.	15.00	6.75
☐ 4 Tony Gwynn	6.00	2.70
☐ 5 Greg Maddux	10.00	4.50
☐ 6 Hideo Nomo	6.00	2.70
☐ 7 Mike Piazza	10.00	4.50
☐ 8 Kirby Puckett	6.00	2.70
☐ 9 Cal Ripken	12.00	5.50
☐ 10 Frank Thomas	12.00	5.50
☐ 11 Mo Vaughn	4.00	1.80
☐ 12 Matt Williams	2.00	.90

1996 Ultra Fresh Foundations

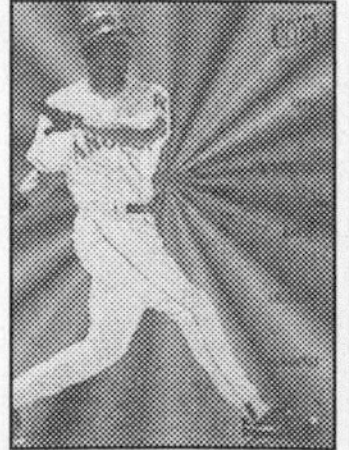

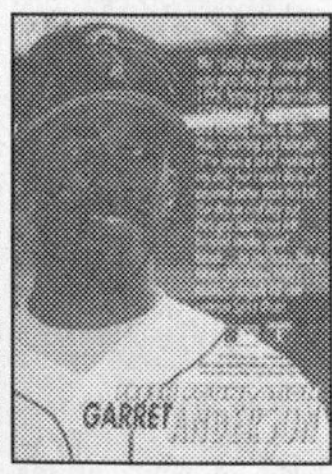

Randomly inserted one every three packs, this 10-card standard-size set highlights the play of hot young players. The fronts feature the player in a full-color action cut-out with a red prismatic background. The Ultra seal, card title, player name and team are printed in silver-foil down the left side of the card. Backs are full-bleed color action shots with player information. The cards are sequenced in alphabetical order and there are also gold medallion versions of these cards.

	MINT	NRMT
COMPLETE SET (10)	4.00	1.80
COMMON CARD (1-10)	.15	.07

*GOLD MEDAL: .75X TO 2X BASIC CARDS

Card	MINT	NRMT
☐ 1 Garret Anderson	.40	.18
☐ 2 Marty Cordova	.15	.07
☐ 3 Jim Edmonds	.60	.25
☐ 4 Brian L.Hunter	.25	.11
☐ 5 Chipper Jones	2.00	.90
☐ 6 Ryan Klesko	.40	.18
☐ 7 Raul Mondesi	.40	.18
☐ 8 Hideo Nomo	1.00	.45
☐ 9 Manny Ramirez	.60	.25
☐ 10 Rondell White	.25	.11

1996 Ultra Golden Prospects

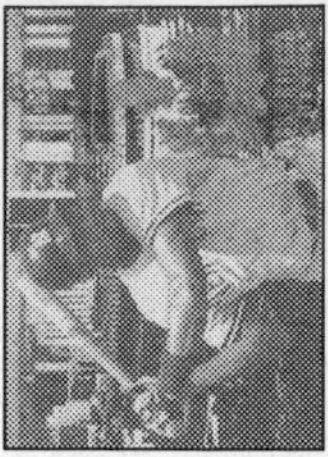

Randomly inserted at a rate of one in five hobby packs, this 10-card standard-size set features players who are likely to make it as major leaguers. The full-bleed fronts have team color-coded tinting over a stadium background. The player is featured in a horizontal action shot with the player's name and team name printed in gold foil. The horizontal backs also feature the minor leaguer in action and player information printed in white type. The cards are sequenced in alphabetical order and there are also gold medallion versions of these cards.

	MINT	NRMT
COMPLETE SET (10)	5.00	2.20
COMMON CARD (1-10)	.25	.11

*GOLD MEDAL: 1X TO 2X BASIC CARDS

Card	MINT	NRMT
☐ 1 Yamil Benitez	1.00	.45
☐ 2 Alberto Castillo	.25	.11
☐ 3 Roger Cedeno	.50	.23
☐ 4 Johnny Damon	.50	.23
☐ 5 Micah Franklin	.25	.11
☐ 6 Jason Giambi	1.00	.45
☐ 7 Jose Herrera	.25	.11
☐ 8 Derek Jeter	5.00	2.20
☐ 9 Kevin Jordan	.25	.11
☐ 10 Ruben Rivera	.50	.23

1996 Ultra Golden Prospects Hobby

Randomly inserted in hobby packs only at a rate of one in 72, this 15-card set is printed on crystal card stock and showcases players awaiting their Major League debut. The backs carry some of their accomplishments in the Minor League.

	MINT	NRMT
COMPLETE SET (15)	100.00	45.00
COMMON CARD (1-15)	6.00	2.70

*GOLD MEDAL: 1X TO 2X BASIC CARDS

Card	MINT	NRMT
☐ 1 Bob Abreu	8.00	3.60
☐ 2 Israel Alcantara	6.00	2.70
☐ 3 Tony Batista	7.50	3.40
☐ 4 Mike Cameron	20.00	9.00
☐ 5 Steve Cox	6.00	2.70
☐ 6 Jermaine Dye	6.00	2.70
☐ 7 Wilton Guerrero	10.00	4.50
☐ 8 Richard Hidalgo	15.00	6.75
☐ 9 Raul Ibanez	6.00	2.70
☐ 10 Marty Janzen	6.00	2.70
☐ 11 Robin Jennings	6.00	2.70
☐ 12 Jason Maxwell	6.00	2.70
☐ 13 Scott McClain	6.00	2.70
☐ 14 Wonderful Monds	6.00	2.70
☐ 15 Chris Singleton	6.00	2.70

1996 Ultra Hitting Machines

Randomly inserted in second series packs at a rate of one in 288, this 10-card set features players who hit the ball hard and often. The fronts display color action player photos on a die-cut machine gear background. The backs carry a color player portrait and player information.

	MINT	NRMT
COMPLETE SET (10)	400.00	180.00
COMMON CARD (1-10)	15.00	6.75

*GOLD MEDAL: 1X TO 2X BASIC CARDS

Card	MINT	NRMT
☐ 1 Albert Belle	30.00	13.50
☐ 2 Barry Bonds	30.00	13.50
☐ 3 Juan Gonzalez	60.00	27.00
☐ 4 Ken Griffey Jr.	120.00	55.00
☐ 5 Edgar Martinez	25.00	11.00
☐ 6 Rafael Palmeiro	25.00	11.00
☐ 7 Mike Piazza	80.00	36.00
☐ 8 Tim Salmon	30.00	13.50
☐ 9 Frank Thomas	100.00	45.00
☐ 10 Matt Williams	15.00	6.75

1996 Ultra Home Run Kings

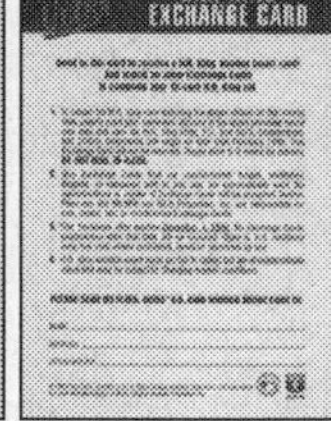

This 12-card standard-size set features leading power hitters. These cards were randomly inserted at a rate of one in 75 packs. The card fronts are thin wood with a color cut out of the player and HR KING printed diagonally in copper foil down the left side. The Fleer company was not happy with the final look of the card because of the transfer of the copper foil. Therefore all cards were made redemption cards. Backs of the cards have information about how to redeem the cards for replacement. The exchange offer expired on December 1, 1996. The cards are sequenced in alphabetical order.

	MINT	NRMT
COMPLETE SET (12)	60.00	27.00
COMMON CARD (1-12)	2.50	1.10

*GOLD MEDAL: 6X TO 10X BASIC CARDS
*REDEMPTION: .5X TO 1X BASIC CARDS

Card	MINT	NRMT
☐ 1 Albert Belle	5.00	2.20
☐ 2 Dante Bichette	2.50	1.10
☐ 3 Barry Bonds	5.00	2.20
☐ 4 Jose Canseco	3.50	1.55
☐ 5 Juan Gonzalez	10.00	4.50
☐ 6 Ken Griffey Jr.	20.00	9.00
☐ 7 Mark McGwire	6.00	2.70
☐ 8 Manny Ramirez	4.00	1.80
☐ 9 Tim Salmon	4.00	1.80
☐ 10 Frank Thomas	15.00	6.75
☐ 11 Mo Vaughn	5.00	2.20
☐ 12 Matt Williams	3.50	1.55

1996 Ultra On-Base Leaders

Randomly inserted in second series packs at a rate of one in four, this 10-card set features players with consistently high on-base percentage. The fronts display a color action player image on a black-and-white player background photo with images of bases along the side. The backs carry a color player portrait and player information.

	MINT	NRMT
COMPLETE SET (10)	6.00	2.70
COMMON CARD (1-10)	.50	.23
*GOLD MEDAL: 1X TO 2.5X BASIC CARDS		
☐ 1 Wade Boggs	.75	.35
☐ 2 Barry Bonds	1.00	.45
☐ 3 Tony Gwynn	1.50	.70
☐ 4 Rickey Henderson	.60	.25
☐ 5 Chuck Knoblauch	.75	.35
☐ 6 Edgar Martinez	.50	.23
☐ 7 Mike Piazza	2.50	1.10
☐ 8 Tim Salmon	.75	.35
☐ 9 Frank Thomas	3.00	1.35
☐ 10 Jim Thome	.75	.35

1996 Ultra Power Plus

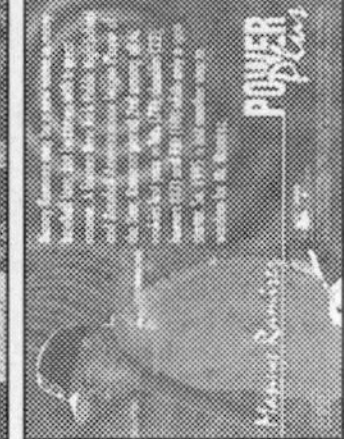

Randomly inserted at a rate of one in ten packs, this 12-card standard-size set features top all-around players. The horizontal fronts feature the player in two cut-out action photos against a multi-colored prismatic wheel background. The player's name and "Power Plus" are stamped in foil across the bottom. The backs are split between a full-color close-up shot of the player and player information printed in white type against a multi-colored circular background. The cards are sequenced in alphabetical order and gold medallion versions of these cards were also issued.

	MINT	NRMT
COMPLETE SET (12)	25.00	11.00
COMMON CARD (1-12)	1.00	.45
*GOLD MEDAL: 3X TO 6X BASIC CARDS		
☐ 1 Jeff Bagwell	4.00	1.80
☐ 2 Barry Bonds	2.50	1.10
☐ 3 Ken Griffey Jr.	10.00	4.50
☐ 4 Raul Mondesi	1.50	.70
☐ 5 Rafael Palmeiro	1.50	.70
☐ 6 Mike Piazza	6.00	2.70
☐ 7 Manny Ramirez	2.00	.90
☐ 8 Tim Salmon	2.00	.90
☐ 9 Reggie Sanders	1.00	.45
☐ 10 Frank Thomas	8.00	3.60
☐ 11 Larry Walker	2.00	.90
☐ 12 Matt Williams	1.50	.70

1996 Ultra Prime Leather

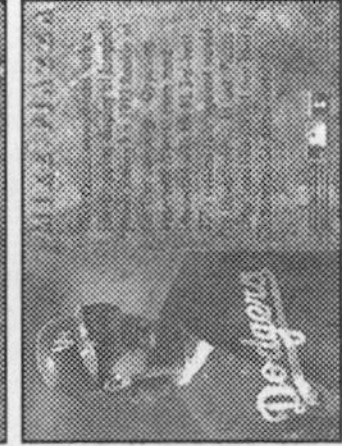

Eighteen outstanding defensive players are featured in this standard-size set which is inserted approximately one in every eight packs. The horizontal fronts feature a color cut-out shot of the player against an embossed leather-like background. The player's name and team are embossed across the bottom with a black shadow effect. The backs have player's achievements noted in black type with a red outline against a glossy leather background. The other half of the back is a full color shot of the player. The cards are sequenced in alphabetical order and gold medallion versions of these cards were also issued.

	MINT	NRMT
COMPLETE SET (18)	25.00	11.00
COMMON CARD (1-18)	1.00	.45
*GOLD MEDAL: 3X TO 6X BASIC CARDS		
☐ 1 Ivan Rodriguez	2.50	1.10
☐ 2 Will Clark	1.50	.70
☐ 3 Roberto Alomar	2.00	.90
☐ 4 Cal Ripken	8.00	3.60
☐ 5 Wade Boggs	2.00	.90
☐ 6 Ken Griffey Jr.	10.00	4.50
☐ 7 Kenny Lofton	2.50	1.10
☐ 8 Kirby Puckett	4.00	1.80
☐ 9 Tim Salmon	2.00	.90
☐ 10 Mike Piazza	6.00	2.70
☐ 11 Mark Grace	1.50	.70
☐ 12 Craig Biggio	1.50	.70
☐ 13 Barry Larkin	1.50	.70
☐ 14 Matt Williams	1.50	.70
☐ 15 Barry Bonds	2.50	1.10
☐ 16 Tony Gwynn	4.00	1.80
☐ 17 Brian McRae	1.00	.45
☐ 18 Raul Mondesi	1.50	.70

1996 Ultra Rawhide

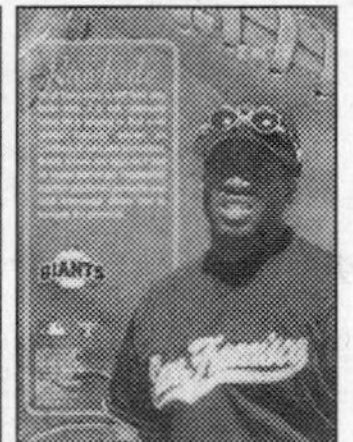

Randomly inserted in second series packs at a rate of one in 8, this 10-card set features leading defensive players. The embossed cards feature the Ultra logo, the word "Rawhide" and the players name against a background of a glove. The back gives a description of the player's defensive abilities.

	MINT	NRMT
COMPLETE SET (10)	15.00	6.75
COMMON CARD (1-10)	.50	.23
*GOLD MEDAL: 2X BASIC CARDS		
☐ 1 Roberto Alomar	1.25	.55
☐ 2 Barry Bonds	1.50	.70
☐ 3 Mark Grace	1.00	.45
☐ 4 Ken Griffey Jr.	6.00	2.70
☐ 5 Kenny Lofton	1.50	.70
☐ 6 Greg Maddux	4.00	1.80
☐ 7 Raul Mondesi	.50	.23
☐ 8 Mike Piazza	4.00	1.80
☐ 9 Cal Ripken	5.00	2.20
☐ 10 Matt Williams	1.00	.45

1996 Ultra RBI Kings

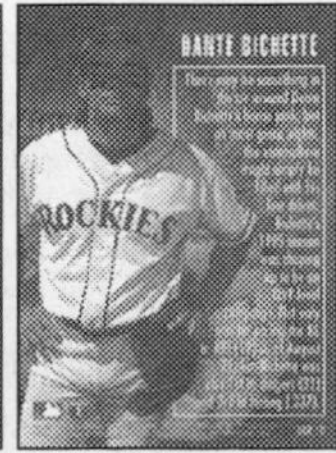

This 10-card standard-size set was randomly inserted at a rate of one in five retail packs. This set features top run producers. The full-color, full-bleed fronts feature player cutouts set against a background of baseballs. The player's name and team logo are printed in silver foil across the bottom. The backs show the players on a full-bleed surface with baseballs in the background and player name and accomplishments printed in white with a white box surrounding the type. The cards are sequenced in alphabetical order and gold medallion versions of these cards were also issued.

	MINT	NRMT
COMPLETE SET (10)	30.00	13.50
COMMON CARD (1-10)	2.50	1.10
*GOLD MEDAL: 1X TO 2X BASIC CARDS		
☐ 1 Derek Bell	2.50	1.10
☐ 2 Albert Belle	6.00	2.70
☐ 3 Dante Bichette	3.00	1.35
☐ 4 Barry Bonds	6.00	2.70
☐ 5 Jim Edmonds	4.00	1.80
☐ 6 Manny Ramirez	4.00	1.80
☐ 7 Reggie Sanders	2.50	1.10
☐ 8 Sammy Sosa	4.00	1.80
☐ 9 Frank Thomas	20.00	9.00
☐ 10 Mo Vaughn	6.00	2.70

1996 Ultra Respect

Randomly inserted in second series packs at a rate of one in 18, this 10-card set features players who are well regarded by their peers for both on and off field activies. The fronts consist of a player photo with the word "Respect" as well as his name and the Ultra logo on the right. The back has another player photo as well as reasons why the player has earned his reputation.

	MINT	NRMT
COMPLETE SET (10)	60.00	27.00
COMMON CARD (1-10)	1.50	.70
*GOLD MEDAL: 1X TO 2X BASIC CARDS		
☐ 1 Joe Carter	1.50	.70
☐ 2 Ken Griffey Jr.	15.00	6.75
☐ 3 Tony Gwynn	6.00	2.70
☐ 4 Greg Maddux	10.00	4.50
☐ 5 Eddie Murray	3.00	1.35
☐ 6 Kirby Puckett	6.00	2.70
☐ 7 Cal Ripken	12.00	5.50
☐ 8 Ryne Sandberg	4.00	1.80
☐ 9 Frank Thomas	12.00	5.50
☐ 10 Mo Vaughn	4.00	1.80

1996 Ultra Rising Stars

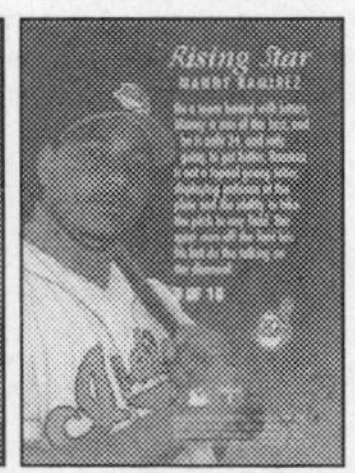

Randomly inserted in second series packs at a rate of one in four, this 10-card set features leadgin players of tomorrow. The fronts have a player photo superimposed on a stadium background. The words "Rising Star" as well as the player's name and the Ultra logo are in the middle of the front. The back has another player photo and informaton on the future of these young stars.

	MINT	NRMT
COMPLETE SET (10)	4.00	1.80
COMMON CARD (1-10)	.25	.11
*GOLD MEDAL: 1X BASIC CARDS		
☐ 1 Garret Anderson	.35	.16
☐ 2 Marty Cordova	.25	.11
☐ 3 Jim Edmonds	.75	.35
☐ 4 Cliff Floyd	.25	.11
☐ 5 Brian L.Hunter	.35	.16
☐ 6 Chipper Jones	2.50	1.10
☐ 7 Ryan Klesko	.50	.23
☐ 8 Hideo Nomo	1.50	.70
☐ 9 Manny Ramirez	.75	.35
☐ 10 Rondell White	.35	.16

1996 Ultra Season Crowns

This set features ten award winners and stat leaders. The cards were randomly inserted at a rate of one in ten. The clear acetate cards feature a full-color player cutout against a background of colored foliage and laurels. Backs include the player's 1995 statistics and other facts on a multi-colored background. The cards are sequenced in alphabetical order and gold medallion versions of these cards were also issued.

	MINT	NRMT
COMPLETE SET (10)	35.00	16.00
COMMON CARD (1-10)	.50	.23
*GOLD MEDAL: 1X TO 2X BASIC CARDS		

	MINT	NRMT
☐ 1 Barry Bonds	2.50	1.10
☐ 2 Tony Gwynn	4.00	1.80
☐ 3 Randy Johnson	2.00	.90
☐ 4 Kenny Lofton	2.50	1.10
☐ 5 Greg Maddux	6.00	2.70
☐ 6 Edgar Martinez	1.50	.70
☐ 7 Hideo Nomo	4.00	1.80
☐ 8 Cal Ripken	8.00	3.60
☐ 9 Frank Thomas	8.00	3.60
☐ 10 Tim Wakefield	.50	.23

1996 Ultra Thunderclap

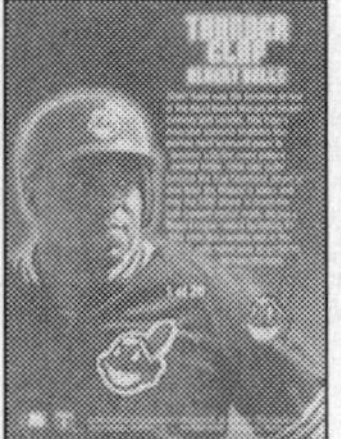

Randomly inserted one in 72 retail packs, these cards feature the leading power hitters. The player's photo is against a background of thunder and lightning and the words "Thunder Clap" and the player's name are on the bottom. The back consists of another player photo as well as a biography as to the player's power skills.

	MINT	NRMT
COMPLETE SET (20)	500.00	220.00
COMMON CARD (1-20)	12.00	5.50
*GOLD MEDAL: 3X BASIC CARDS		

	MINT	NRMT
☐ 1 Albert Belle	25.00	11.00
☐ 2 Barry Bonds	25.00	11.00
☐ 3 Bobby Bonilla	12.00	5.50
☐ 4 Jose Canseco	15.00	6.75
☐ 5 Joe Carter	12.00	5.50
☐ 6 Will Clark	15.00	6.75
☐ 7 Andre Dawson	15.00	6.75
☐ 8 Cecil Fielder	12.00	5.50
☐ 9 Andres Galarraga	20.00	9.00
☐ 10 Juan Gonzalez	50.00	22.00
☐ 11 Ken Griffey Jr.	100.00	45.00
☐ 12 Fred McGriff	15.00	6.75
☐ 13 Mark McGwire	40.00	18.00
☐ 14 Eddie Murray	25.00	11.00
☐ 15 Rafael Palmeiro	15.00	6.75
☐ 16 Kirby Puckett	50.00	22.00
☐ 17 Cal Ripken	80.00	36.00
☐ 18 Ryne Sandberg	30.00	13.50
☐ 19 Frank Thomas	80.00	36.00
☐ 20 Matt Williams	15.00	6.75

1997 Ultra

The 1997 Ultra was issued in two series totalling 553 cards. The first series consisted of 300 cards with the second containing 253. The 10-card packs had a suggested retail price of 2.49 each. Each pack had two

insert cards, with one insert being a gold medallion parallel and the other insert being from one of serveral other insert sets. The fronts features borderless color action player photos with career statistics on the backs. As in most Fleer produced sets, the cards are arranged in alphabetical order by league, player and team. Second series retail packs contained only cards 301-450 while second series hobby packs contained all cards from 301-553. Rookie Cards include Jose Cruz Jr. and Fernando Tatis.

	MINT	NRMT
COMPLETE SET (553)	60.00	27.00
COMPLETE SERIES 1 (300)	30.00	13.50
COMPLETE SERIES 2 (253)	30.00	13.50
COMMON CARD (1-450)	.15	.07
COMMON CARD (451-553)	.20	.09

	MINT	NRMT
☐ 1 Roberto Alomar	.60	.25
☐ 2 Brady Anderson	.40	.18
☐ 3 Rocky Coppinger	.30	.14
☐ 4 Jeffrey Hammonds	.30	.14
☐ 5 Chris Hoiles	.15	.07
☐ 6 Eddie Murray	.60	.25
☐ 7 Mike Mussina	.60	.25
☐ 8 Jimmy Myers	.15	.07
☐ 9 Randy Myers	.30	.14
☐ 10 Arthur Rhodes	.15	.07
☐ 11 Cal Ripken	2.50	1.10
☐ 12 Jose Canseco	.40	.18
☐ 13 Roger Clemens	1.25	.55
☐ 14 Tom Gordon	.15	.07
☐ 15 Jose Malave	.15	.07
☐ 16 Tim Naehring	.15	.07
☐ 17 Troy O'Leary	.15	.07
☐ 18 Bill Selby	.15	.07
☐ 19 Heathcliff Slocumb	.15	.07
☐ 20 Mike Stanley	.15	.07
☐ 21 Mo Vaughn	.75	.35
☐ 22 Garret Anderson	.30	.14
☐ 23 George Arias	.15	.07
☐ 24 Chili Davis	.15	.07
☐ 25 Jim Edmonds	.60	.25
☐ 26 Darin Erstad	1.00	.45
☐ 27 Chuck Finley	.15	.07
☐ 28 Todd Greene	.30	.14
☐ 29 Troy Percival	.15	.07
☐ 30 Tim Salmon	.60	.25
☐ 31 Jeff Schmidt	.15	.07
☐ 32 Randy Velarde	.15	.07
☐ 33 Shad Williams	.15	.07
☐ 34 Wilson Alvarez	.15	.07
☐ 35 Harold Baines	.30	.14
☐ 36 James Baldwin	.15	.07
☐ 37 Mike Cameron	.60	.25
☐ 38 Ray Durham	.15	.07
☐ 39 Ozzie Guillen	.15	.07
☐ 40 Roberto Hernandez	.15	.07
☐ 41 Darren Lewis	.15	.07
☐ 42 Jose Munoz	.15	.07
☐ 43 Tony Phillips	.15	.07
☐ 44 Frank Thomas	2.50	1.10
☐ 45 Sandy Alomar Jr.	.30	.14
☐ 46 Albert Belle	.75	.35
☐ 47 Mark Carreon	.15	.07
☐ 48 Julio Franco	.15	.07
☐ 49 Orel Hershiser	.30	.14
☐ 50 Kenny Lofton	.75	.35
☐ 51 Jack McDowell	.15	.07
☐ 52 Jose Mesa	.15	.07
☐ 53 Charles Nagy	.30	.14
☐ 54 Manny Ramirez	.60	.25
☐ 55 Julian Tavarez	.15	.07
☐ 56 Omar Vizquel	.30	.14
☐ 57 Raul Casanova	.15	.07
☐ 58 Tony Clark	.60	.25
☐ 59 Travis Fryman	.30	.14
☐ 60 Bob Higginson	.30	.14
☐ 61 Melvin Nieves	.15	.07
☐ 62 Curtis Pride	.15	.07
☐ 63 Justin Thompson	.30	.14
☐ 64 Alan Trammell	.40	.18
☐ 65 Kevin Appier	.30	.14
☐ 66 Johnny Damon	.15	.07
☐ 67 Keith Lockhart	.15	.07
☐ 68 Jeff Montgomery	.15	.07
☐ 69 Jose Offerman	.15	.07
☐ 70 Bip Roberts	.15	.07
☐ 71 Jose Rosado	.30	.14
☐ 72 Chris Stynes	.15	.07
☐ 73 Mike Sweeney	.30	.14
☐ 74 Jeff Cirillo	.30	.14
☐ 75 Jeff D'Amico	.30	.14
☐ 76 John Jaha	.15	.07
☐ 77 Scott Karl	.15	.07
☐ 78 Mike Matheny	.15	.07
☐ 79 Ben McDonald	.15	.07
☐ 80 Matt Mieske	.15	.07
☐ 81 Marc Newfield	.15	.07
☐ 82 Dave Nilsson	.15	.07
☐ 83 Jose Valentin	.15	.07
☐ 84 Fernando Vina	.15	.07
☐ 85 Rick Aguilera	.15	.07
☐ 86 Marty Cordova	.30	.14
☐ 87 Chuck Knoblauch	.60	.25
☐ 88 Matt Lawton	.15	.07
☐ 89 Pat Meares	.15	.07
☐ 90 Paul Molitor	.60	.25
☐ 91 Greg Myers	.15	.07
☐ 92 Dan Naulty	.15	.07
☐ 93 Kirby Puckett	1.25	.55
☐ 94 Frank Rodriguez	.15	.07
☐ 95 Wade Boggs	.60	.25
☐ 96 Cecil Fielder	.30	.14
☐ 97 Joe Girardi	.15	.07
☐ 98 Dwight Gooden	.30	.14
☐ 99 Derek Jeter	2.00	.90
☐ 100 Tino Martinez	.60	.25
☐ 101 Ramiro Mendoza	.40	.18
☐ 102 Andy Pettitte	.75	.35
☐ 103 Mariano Rivera	.30	.14
☐ 104 Ruben Rivera	.30	.14
☐ 105 Kenny Rogers	.15	.07
☐ 106 Darryl Strawberry	.30	.14
☐ 107 Bernie Williams	.60	.25
☐ 108 Tony Batista	.40	.18
☐ 109 Geronimo Berroa	.15	.07
☐ 110 Bobby Chouinard	.15	.07
☐ 111 Brent Gates	.15	.07
☐ 112 Jason Giambi	.30	.14
☐ 113 Damon Mashore	.15	.07
☐ 114 Mark McGwire	1.25	.55
☐ 115 Scott Spiezio	.30	.14
☐ 116 John Wasdin	.15	.07
☐ 117 Steve Wojciechowski	.15	.07
☐ 118 Ernie Young	.15	.07
☐ 119 Norm Charlton	.15	.07
☐ 120 Joey Cora	.30	.14
☐ 121 Ken Griffey Jr.	3.00	1.35
☐ 122 Sterling Hitchcock	.15	.07
☐ 123 Raul Ibanez	.15	.07
☐ 124 Randy Johnson	.60	.25
☐ 125 Edgar Martinez	.40	.18
☐ 126 Alex Rodriguez	2.50	1.10
☐ 127 Matt Wagner	.15	.07
☐ 128 Bob Wells	.15	.07
☐ 129 Dan Wilson	.15	.07
☐ 130 Will Clark	.40	.18
☐ 131 Kevin Elster	.15	.07
☐ 132 Juan Gonzalez	1.50	.70
☐ 133 Rusty Greer	.30	.14
☐ 134 Darryl Hamilton	.15	.07
☐ 135 Mike Henneman	.15	.07
☐ 136 Ken Hill	.15	.07
☐ 137 Mark McLemore	.15	.07
☐ 138 Dean Palmer	.15	.07
☐ 139 Roger Pavlik	.15	.07
☐ 140 Ivan Rodriguez	.75	.35
☐ 141 Joe Carter	.30	.14
☐ 142 Carlos Delgado	.30	.14
☐ 143 Alex Gonzalez	.15	.07
☐ 144 Juan Guzman	.15	.07
☐ 145 Pat Hentgen	.30	.14
☐ 146 Marty Janzen	.15	.07
☐ 147 Otis Nixon	.15	.07
☐ 148 Charlie O'Brien	.15	.07
☐ 149 John Olerud	.15	.07
☐ 150 Robert Perez	.15	.07
☐ 151 Jermaine Dye	.15	.07
☐ 152 Tom Glavine	.30	.14
☐ 153 Andruw Jones	1.50	.70
☐ 154 Chipper Jones	2.00	.90
☐ 155 Ryan Klesko	.40	.18
☐ 156 Javier Lopez	.30	.14
☐ 157 Greg Maddux	2.00	.90
☐ 158 Fred McGriff	.40	.18
☐ 159 Wonderful Monds	.15	.07
☐ 160 John Smoltz	.30	.14
☐ 161 Terrell Wade	.15	.07
☐ 162 Mark Wohlers	.15	.07

☐ 163 Brant Brown .15 .07
☐ 164 Mark Grace .40 .18
☐ 165 Tyler Houston .15 .07
☐ 166 Robin Jennings .15 .07
☐ 167 Jason Maxwell .15 .07
☐ 168 Ryne Sandberg .75 .35
☐ 169 Sammy Sosa .60 .25
☐ 170 Amaury Telemaco .15 .07
☐ 171 Steve Trachsel .15 .07
☐ 172 Pedro Valdes .15 .07
☐ 173 Tim Belk .15 .07
☐ 174 Bret Boone .15 .07
☐ 175 Jeff Brantley .15 .07
☐ 176 Eric Davis .15 .07
☐ 177 Barry Larkin .40 .18
☐ 178 Chad Mottola .15 .07
☐ 179 Mark Portugal .15 .07
☐ 180 Reggie Sanders .15 .07
☐ 181 John Smiley .15 .07
☐ 182 Eddie Taubensee .15 .07
☐ 183 Dante Bichette .30 .14
☐ 184 Ellis Burks .30 .14
☐ 185 Andres Galarraga .60 .25
☐ 186 Curt Leskanic .15 .07
☐ 187 Quinton McCracken .15 .07
☐ 188 Jeff Reed .15 .07
☐ 189 Kevin Ritz .15 .07
☐ 190 Walt Weiss .15 .07
☐ 191 Jamey Wright .30 .14
☐ 192 Eric Young .30 .14
☐ 193 Kevin Brown .30 .14
☐ 194 Luis Castillo .30 .14
☐ 195 Jeff Conine .30 .14
☐ 196 Andre Dawson .30 .14
☐ 197 Charles Johnson .15 .07
☐ 198 Al Leiter .15 .07
☐ 199 Ralph Milliard .15 .07
☐ 200 Robb Nen .15 .07
☐ 201 Edgar Renteria .30 .14
☐ 202 Gary Sheffield .60 .25
☐ 203 Bob Abreu .60 .25
☐ 204 Jeff Bagwell 1.25 .55
☐ 205 Derek Bell .15 .07
☐ 206 Sean Berry .15 .07
☐ 207 Richard Hidalgo .60 .25
☐ 208 Todd Jones .15 .07
☐ 209 Darryl Kile .30 .14
☐ 210 Orlando Miller .15 .07
☐ 211 Shane Reynolds .15 .07
☐ 212 Billy Wagner .30 .14
☐ 213 Donne Wall .15 .07
☐ 214 Roger Cedeno .15 .07
☐ 215 Greg Gagne .15 .07
☐ 216 Karim Garcia .30 .14
☐ 217 Wilton Guerrero .30 .14
☐ 218 Todd Hollandsworth .30 .14
☐ 219 Ramon Martinez .30 .14
☐ 220 Raul Mondesi .30 .14
☐ 221 Hideo Nomo 1.50 .70
☐ 222 Chan Ho Park .60 .25
☐ 223 Mike Piazza 2.00 .90
☐ 224 Ismael Valdes .30 .14
☐ 225 Moises Alou .30 .14
☐ 226 Derek Aucoin .15 .07
☐ 227 Yamil Benitez .15 .07
☐ 228 Jeff Fassero .15 .07
☐ 229 Darrin Fletcher .15 .07
☐ 230 Mark Grudzielanek .15 .07
☐ 231 Barry Manuel .15 .07
☐ 232 Pedro Martinez .60 .25
☐ 233 Henry Rodriguez .15 .07
☐ 234 Ugueth Urbina .30 .14
☐ 235 Rondell White .30 .14
☐ 236 Carlos Baerga .30 .14
☐ 237 John Franco .30 .14
☐ 238 Bernard Gilkey .15 .07
☐ 239 Todd Hundley .30 .14
☐ 240 Butch Huskey .30 .14
☐ 241 Jason Isringhausen .15 .07
☐ 242 Lance Johnson .15 .07
☐ 243 Bobby Jones .15 .07
☐ 244 Alex Ochoa .15 .07
☐ 245 Rey Ordonez .15 .07
☐ 246 Paul Wilson .15 .07
☐ 247 Ron Blazier .15 .07
☐ 248 David Doster .15 .07
☐ 249 Jim Eisenreich .30 .14
☐ 250 Mike Grace .15 .07
☐ 251 Mike Lieberthal .15 .07
☐ 252 Wendell Magee .30 .14
☐ 253 Mickey Morandini .15 .07
☐ 254 Ricky Otero .15 .07
☐ 255 Scott Rolen 1.50 .70
☐ 256 Curt Schilling .30 .14
☐ 257 Todd Zeile .15 .07
☐ 258 Jermaine Allensworth .30 .14
☐ 259 Trey Beamon .15 .07
☐ 260 Carlos Garcia .15 .07
☐ 261 Mark Johnson .15 .07
☐ 262 Jason Kendall .30 .14
☐ 263 Jeff King .15 .07
☐ 264 Al Martin .15 .07
☐ 265 Denny Neagle .15 .07
☐ 266 Matt Ruebel .15 .07
☐ 267 Marc Wilkins .15 .07
☐ 268 Alan Benes .15 .07
☐ 269 Dennis Eckersley .40 .18
☐ 270 Ron Gant .30 .14
☐ 271 Aaron Holbert .15 .07
☐ 272 Brian Jordan .30 .14
☐ 273 Ray Lankford .30 .14
☐ 274 John Mabry .15 .07
☐ 275 T.J. Mathews .15 .07
☐ 276 Ozzie Smith .75 .35
☐ 277 Todd Stottlemyre .15 .07
☐ 278 Mark Sweeney .15 .07
☐ 279 Andy Ashby .15 .07
☐ 280 Steve Finley .30 .14
☐ 281 John Flaherty .15 .07
☐ 282 Chris Gomez .15 .07
☐ 283 Tony Gwynn 1.50 .70
☐ 284 Joey Hamilton .30 .14
☐ 285 Rickey Henderson .40 .18
☐ 286 Trevor Hoffman .30 .14
☐ 287 Jason Thompson .15 .07
☐ 288 Fernando Valenzuela .30 .14
☐ 289 Greg Vaughn .15 .07
☐ 290 Barry Bonds .75 .35
☐ 291 Jay Canizaro .15 .07
☐ 292 Jacob Cruz .15 .07
☐ 293 Shawon Dunston .15 .07
☐ 294 Shawn Estes .15 .07
☐ 295 Mark Gardner .15 .07
☐ 296 Marcus Jensen .15 .07
☐ 297 Bill Mueller .15 .07
☐ 298 Chris Singleton .15 .07
☐ 299 Allen Watson .15 .07
☐ 300 Matt Williams .40 .18
☐ 301 Rod Beck .30 .14
☐ 302 Jay Bell .15 .07
☐ 303 Shawon Dunston .15 .07
☐ 304 Reggie Jefferson .30 .14
☐ 305 Darren Oliver .15 .07
☐ 306 Benito Santiago .15 .07
☐ 307 Gerald Williams .15 .07
☐ 308 Damon Buford .15 .07
☐ 309 Jeromy Burnitz .15 .07
☐ 310 Sterling Hitchcock .15 .07
☐ 311 Dave Hollins .15 .07
☐ 312 Mel Rojas .15 .07
☐ 313 Robin Ventura .15 .07
☐ 314 David Wells .15 .07
☐ 315 Cal Eldred .15 .07
☐ 316 Gary Gaetti .30 .14
☐ 317 John Hudek .15 .07
☐ 318 Brian Johnson .15 .07
☐ 319 Denny Neagle .15 .07
☐ 320 Larry Walker .60 .25
☐ 321 Russ Davis .15 .07
☐ 322 Delino DeShields .15 .07
☐ 323 Charlie Hayes .15 .07
☐ 324 Jermaine Dye .15 .07
☐ 325 John Ericks .15 .07
☐ 326 Jeff Fassero .15 .07
☐ 327 Nomar Garciaparra 2.00 .90
☐ 328 Willie Greene .30 .14
☐ 329 Greg McMichael .15 .07
☐ 330 Damion Easley .15 .07
☐ 331 Ricky Bones .15 .07
☐ 332 John Burkett .15 .07
☐ 333 Royce Clayton .15 .07
☐ 334 Greg Colbrunn .15 .07
☐ 335 Tony Eusebio .15 .07
☐ 336 Gregg Jefferies .15 .07
☐ 337 Wally Joyner .15 .07
☐ 338 Jim Leyritz .15 .07
☐ 339 Paul O'Neill .30 .14
☐ 340 Bruce Ruffin .15 .07
☐ 341 Michael Tucker .15 .07
☐ 342 Andy Benes .15 .07
☐ 343 Craig Biggio .40 .18
☐ 344 Rex Hudler .15 .07
☐ 345 Brad Radke .30 .14
☐ 346 Deion Sanders .60 .25
☐ 347 Moises Alou .30 .14
☐ 348 Brad Ausmus .15 .07
☐ 349 Armando Benitez .15 .07
☐ 350 Mark Gubicza .15 .07
☐ 351 Terry Steinbach .15 .07
☐ 352 Mark Whiten .15 .07
☐ 353 Ricky Bottalico .15 .07
☐ 354 Brian Giles .15 .07
☐ 355 Eric Karros .15 .07
☐ 356 Jimmy Key .30 .14
☐ 357 Carlos Perez .15 .07
☐ 358 Alex Fernandez .15 .07
☐ 359 J.T. Snow .30 .14
☐ 360 Bobby Bonilla .30 .14
☐ 361 Scott Brosius .15 .07
☐ 362 Greg Swindell .15 .07
☐ 363 Jose Vizcaino .15 .07
☐ 364 Matt Williams .40 .18
☐ 365 Darren Daulton .30 .14
☐ 366 Shane Andrews .15 .07
☐ 367 Jim Eisenreich .30 .14
☐ 368 Ariel Prieto .15 .07
☐ 369 Bob Tewksbury .15 .07
☐ 370 Mike Bordick .15 .07
☐ 371 Rheal Cormier .15 .07
☐ 372 Cliff Floyd .15 .07
☐ 373 David Justice .60 .25
☐ 374 John Wetteland .15 .07
☐ 375 Mike Blowers .15 .07
☐ 376 Jose Canseco .40 .18
☐ 377 Roger Clemens 1.25 .55
☐ 378 Kevin Mitchell .15 .07
☐ 379 Todd Zeile .15 .07
☐ 380 Jim Thome .60 .25
☐ 381 Turk Wendell .15 .07
☐ 382 Rico Brogna .15 .07
☐ 383 Eric Davis .15 .07
☐ 384 Mike Lansing .15 .07
☐ 385 Devon White .15 .07
☐ 386 Marquis Grissom .30 .14
☐ 387 Todd Worrell .30 .14
☐ 388 Jeff Kent .15 .07
☐ 389 Mickey Tettleton .15 .07
☐ 390 Steve Avery .15 .07
☐ 391 David Cone .30 .14
☐ 392 Scott Cooper .15 .07
☐ 393 Lee Stevens .15 .07
☐ 394 Kevin Elster .15 .07
☐ 395 Tom Goodwin .15 .07
☐ 396 Shawn Green .15 .07
☐ 397 Pete Harnisch .15 .07
☐ 398 Eddie Murray .60 .25
☐ 399 Joe Randa .15 .07
☐ 400 Scott Sanders .15 .07
☐ 401 John Valentin .15 .07
☐ 402 Todd Jones .15 .07
☐ 403 Terry Adams .15 .07
☐ 404 Brian Hunter .15 .07
☐ 405 Pat Listach .15 .07
☐ 406 Kenny Lofton .75 .35
☐ 407 Hal Morris .15 .07
☐ 408 Ed Sprague .15 .07
☐ 409 Rich Becker .15 .07
☐ 410 Edgardo Alfonzo .30 .14
☐ 411 Albert Belle .75 .35
☐ 412 Jeff King .15 .07
☐ 413 Kirt Manwaring .15 .07
☐ 414 Jason Schmidt .15 .07
☐ 415 Allen Watson .15 .07
☐ 416 Lee Tinsley .15 .07
☐ 417 Brett Butler .30 .14
☐ 418 Carlos Garcia .15 .07
☐ 419 Mark Lemke .15 .07
☐ 420 Jaime Navarro .15 .07
☐ 421 David Segui .15 .07
☐ 422 Ruben Sierra .15 .07
☐ 423 B.J. Surhoff .15 .07
☐ 424 Julian Tavarez .15 .07
☐ 425 Billy Taylor .15 .07
☐ 426 Ken Caminiti .60 .25
☐ 427 Chuck Carr .15 .07
☐ 428 Benji Gil .15 .07
☐ 429 Terry Mulholland .15 .07
☐ 430 Mike Stanton .15 .07
☐ 431 Wil Cordero .15 .07
☐ 432 Chili Davis .30 .14
☐ 433 Mariano Duncan .15 .07
☐ 434 Orlando Merced .15 .07
☐ 435 Kent Mercker .15 .07
☐ 436 John Olerud .30 .14
☐ 437 Quilvio Veras .15 .07
☐ 438 Mike Fetters .15 .07
☐ 439 Glenallen Hill .15 .07
☐ 440 Bill Swift .15 .07
☐ 441 Tim Wakefield .15 .07
☐ 442 Pedro Astacio .15 .07
☐ 443 Vinny Castilla .30 .14
☐ 444 Doug Drabek .15 .07
☐ 445 Alan Embree .15 .07
☐ 446 Lee Smith .30 .14
☐ 447 Darryl Hamilton .15 .07
☐ 448 Brian McRae .15 .07
☐ 449 Mike Timlin .15 .07
☐ 450 Bob Wickman .15 .07
☐ 451 Jason Dickson .15 .07
☐ 452 Chad Curtis .15 .07
☐ 453 Mark Leiter .15 .07

☐ 454 Damon Berryhill	.15	.07
☐ 455 Kevin Orie	.30	.14
☐ 456 Dave Burba	.15	.07
☐ 457 Chris Holt	.15	.07
☐ 458 Ricky Ledee	1.50	.70
☐ 459 Mike Devereaux	.15	.07
☐ 460 Pokey Reese	.15	.07
☐ 461 Tim Raines	.15	.07
☐ 462 Ryan Jones	.15	.07
☐ 463 Shane Mack	.15	.07
☐ 464 Darren Dreifort	.15	.07
☐ 465 Mark Parent	.15	.07
☐ 466 Mark Portugal	.15	.07
☐ 467 Dante Powell	.15	.07
☐ 468 Craig Grebeck	.15	.07
☐ 469 Ron Villone	.15	.07
☐ 470 Dmitri Young	.30	.14
☐ 471 Shannon Stewart	.30	.14
☐ 472 Rick Helling	.15	.07
☐ 473 Bill Haselman	.15	.07
☐ 474 Albie Lopez	.15	.07
☐ 475 Glendon Rusch	.15	.07
☐ 476 Derrick May	.15	.07
☐ 477 Chad Ogea	.15	.07
☐ 478 Kirk Rueter	.15	.07
☐ 479 Chris Hammond	.15	.07
☐ 480 Russ Johnson	.15	.07
☐ 481 James Mouton	.15	.07
☐ 482 Mike Macfarlane	.15	.07
☐ 483 Scott Ruffcorn	.15	.07
☐ 484 Jeff Frye	.15	.07
☐ 485 Richie Sexson	.15	.07
☐ 486 Emil Brown	.50	.23
☐ 487 Desi Wilson	.15	.07
☐ 488 Brent Gates	.15	.07
☐ 489 Tony Graffanino	.15	.07
☐ 490 Dan Miceli	.15	.07
☐ 491 Orlando Cabrera	.50	.23
☐ 492 Tony Womack	.60	.25
☐ 493 Jerome Walton	.15	.07
☐ 494 Mark Thompson	.15	.07
☐ 495 Jose Guillen	1.00	.45
☐ 496 Willie Blair	.15	.07
☐ 497 T.J. Staton	.50	.23
☐ 498 Scott Kamieniecki	.15	.07
☐ 499 Vince Coleman	.15	.07
☐ 500 Jeff Abbott	.15	.07
☐ 501 Chris Widger	.15	.07
☐ 502 Kevin Tapani	.15	.07
☐ 503 Carlos Castillo	.50	.23
☐ 504 Luis Gonzalez	.15	.07
☐ 505 Tim Belcher	.15	.07
☐ 506 Armando Reynoso	.15	.07
☐ 507 Jamie Moyer	.15	.07
☐ 508 Randall Simon	1.50	.70
☐ 509 Vladimir Guerrero	1.50	.70
☐ 510 Wady Almonte	.60	.25
☐ 511 Dustin Hermanson	.15	.07
☐ 512 Deivi Cruz	.50	.23
☐ 513 Luis Alicea	.15	.07
☐ 514 Felix Heredia	.15	.07
☐ 515 Don Slaught	.15	.07
☐ 516 Shigetoshi Hasegawa	.50	.23
☐ 517 Matt Walbeck	.15	.07
☐ 518 David Arias-Ortiz	1.00	.45
☐ 519 Brady Raggio	.15	.07
☐ 520 Rudy Pemberton	.15	.07
☐ 521 Wayne Kirby	.15	.07
☐ 522 Calvin Maduro	.15	.07
☐ 523 Mark Lewis	.15	.07
☐ 524 Mike Jackson	.15	.07
☐ 525 Sid Fernandez	.15	.07
☐ 526 Mike Bielecki	.15	.07
☐ 527 Bubba Trammell	.75	.35
☐ 528 Brent Brede	.15	.07
☐ 529 Matt Morris	.15	.07
☐ 530 Joe Borowski	.15	.07
☐ 531 Orlando Miller	.15	.07
☐ 532 Jim Bullinger	.15	.07
☐ 533 Robert Person	.15	.07
☐ 534 Doug Glanville	.15	.07
☐ 535 Terry Pendleton	.15	.07
☐ 536 Jorge Posada	.15	.07
☐ 537 Marc Sagmoen	.15	.07
☐ 538 Fernando Tatis	2.00	.90
☐ 539 Aaron Sele	.15	.07
☐ 540 Brian Banks	.15	.07
☐ 541 Derrek Lee	.15	.07
☐ 542 John Wasdin	.15	.07
☐ 543 Justin Towle	.60	.25
☐ 544 Pat Cline	.15	.07
☐ 545 Dave Magadan	.15	.07
☐ 546 Jeff Blauser	.15	.07
☐ 547 Phil Nevin	.15	.07
☐ 548 Todd Walker	.15	.07
☐ 549 Eli Marrero	.15	.07
☐ 550 Bartolo Colon	.15	.07
☐ 551 Jose Cruz Jr.	8.00	3.60
☐ 552 Todd Dunwoody	.30	.14
☐ 553 Hideki Irabu	1.00	.45
☐ P11 Cal Ripken Promo Three Card Strip	.15	.07

1997 Ultra Gold Medallion

This 553-card set is a gold-holofoil-stamped parallel version of the regular Ultra set and was inserted one per pack of both series 1 and series 2 cards. Unlike previous Gold Medallion sets, the 1997 edition features different photos than the corresponding regular cards.

	MINT	NRMT
COMPLETE SET (553)	275.00	125.00
COMPLETE SERIES 1 (300)	150.00	70.00
COMPLETE SERIES 2 (253)	125.00	55.00
COMMON CARD (1-300)	.25	.11
COMMON CARD (451-553)	.30	.14

*STARS: 2X to 4X BASIC CARDS
*YOUNG STARS: 1.5 X to 3X BASIC CARDS
*ROOKIES: 1X TO 2X BASIC CARDS

1997 Ultra Platinum Medallion

This 553-card set is a parallel to the regular Ultra and was inserted one per 100 packs of both series 1 and series 2 cards. Sparkling platinum lettering on front differentiates these cards from their far more common regular issue brethren. No set price is provided due to scarcity. As with the 1997 Gold Medallion set, the Platinum Medallion set features different photos than the corresponding regular cards.

	MINT	NRMT
COMPLETE SET (553)	8000.00	3600.00
COMPLETE SERIES 1 (300)	5000.00	2200.00
COMPLETE SERIES 2 (253)	3000.00	1350.00
COMMON CARD (1-553)	12.00	5.50

*STARS: 40X TO 80X BASIC CARDS
*YOUNG STARS: 30X TO 60X BASIC CARDS
*ROOKIES: 12.5X TO 25X BASIC CARDS

1997 Ultra Autographstix Emeralds

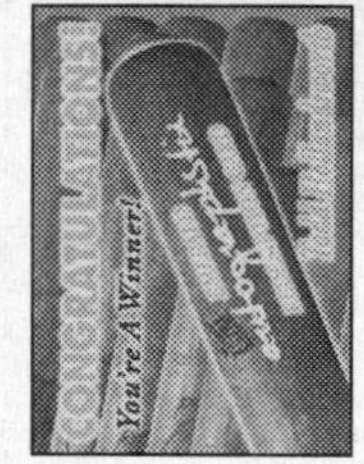

This six-card hobby exclusive Series 2 insert set consists of individually numbered Redemption cards for autographed bats from the players checklisted below. Only 25 of each card was produced. The deadline to exchange cards was July 1st, 1998.

	MINT	NRMT
COMPLETE SET (6)	1500.00	700.00
COMMON CARD (1-6)	60.00	27.00
☐ 1 Alex Ochoa	60.00	27.00
☐ 2 Todd Walker	100.00	45.00
☐ 3 Scott Rolen	400.00	180.00
☐ 4 Darin Erstad	300.00	135.00
☐ 5 Alex Rodriguez	800.00	350.00
☐ 6 Todd Hollandsworth	80.00	36.00

1997 Ultra Checklists

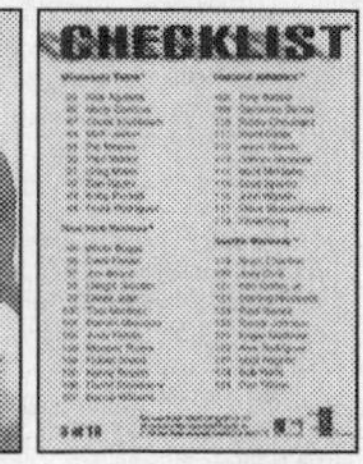

Randomly inserted in all first and second series packs at a rate of one in four, this 20-card set features borderless player photos on the front along with the word "Checklist", the player's name as well as the "ultra" logo at the bottom. The backs are checklists. The checklists for Series 1 are listed below with an "A" prefix and for Series 2 with a "B" prefix.

	MINT	NRMT
COMPLETE SERIES 1 (10)	10.00	4.50
COMPLETE SERIES 2 (10)	15.00	6.75
COMMON CARD (A1-B10)	.25	.11
☐ A1 Dante Bichette	.40	.18
☐ A2 Barry Bonds	.50	.23
☐ A3 Ken Griffey Jr.	2.00	.90
☐ A4 Greg Maddux	1.25	.55
☐ A5 Mark McGwire	.60	.25
☐ A6 Mike Piazza	1.25	.55
☐ A7 Cal Ripken	1.50	.70
☐ A8 John Smoltz	.25	.11
☐ A9 Sammy Sosa	.50	.23
☐ A10 Frank Thomas	2.00	.90
☐ B1 Andruw Jones	1.25	.55
☐ B2 Ken Griffey Jr.	2.00	.90
☐ B3 Frank Thomas	1.50	.70
☐ B4 Alex Rodriguez	1.25	.55
☐ B5 Cal Ripken	1.50	.70
☐ B6 Mike Piazza	1.25	.55
☐ B7 Greg Maddux	1.25	.55
☐ B8 Chipper Jones	1.00	.45
☐ B9 Derek Jeter	1.00	.45
☐ B10 Juan Gonzalez	1.00	.45

1997 Ultra Diamond Producers

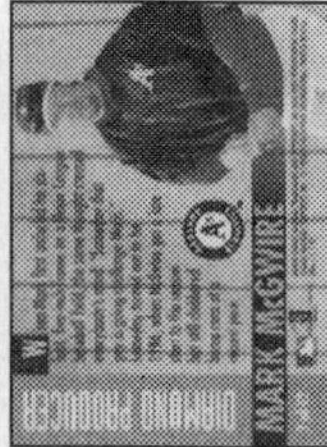

Randomly inserted in all first series packs at a rate of one in 288, this 12-card set features "flannel" material mounted on card stock and attempt to look and feel like actual uniforms.

	MINT	NRMT
COMPLETE SET (12)	600.00	275.00
COMMON CARD (1-12)	12.00	5.50
☐ 1 Jeff Bagwell	40.00	18.00
☐ 2 Barry Bonds	25.00	11.00
☐ 3 Ken Griffey Jr.	100.00	45.00
☐ 4 Chipper Jones	60.00	27.00
☐ 5 Kenny Lofton	25.00	11.00
☐ 6 Greg Maddux	60.00	27.00
☐ 7 Mark McGwire	40.00	18.00
☐ 8 Mike Piazza	60.00	27.00
☐ 9 Cal Ripken	80.00	36.00
☐ 10 Alex Rodriguez	60.00	27.00
☐ 11 Frank Thomas	80.00	36.00
☐ 12 Matt Williams	12.00	5.50

1997 Ultra Double Trouble

Randomly inserted in series 1 packs at a rate of one in four, this 20-card set features two players from each team. The horizontal cards feature players photos with their names in silver foil on the bottom and the words "double trouble" on the top. The backs feature information on what the players contributed to their team in 1996

	MINT	NRMT
COMPLETE SET (20)	12.00	5.50
COMMON CARD (1-20)	.40	.18

☐ 1 Roberto Alomar	2.00	.90
Cal Ripken		
☐ 2 Mo Vaughn	.60	.25
Jose Canseco		
☐ 3 Jim Edmonds	1.00	.45
Tim Salmon		
☐ 4 Harold Baines	2.00	.90
Frank Thomas		
☐ 5 Albert Belle	.75	.35
Kenny Lofton		
☐ 6 Marty Cordova	.50	.23
Chuck Knoblauch		
☐ 7 Derek Jeter	1.50	.70
Andy Pettitte		
☐ 8 Jason Giambi	1.00	.45
Mark McGwire		
☐ 9 Ken Griffey Jr.	4.00	1.80
Alex Rodriguez		
☐ 10 Juan Gonzalez	1.25	.55
Will Clark		
☐ 11 Greg Maddux	2.00	.90
Chipper Jones		
☐ 12 Mark Grace	1.00	.45
Sammy Sosa		
☐ 13 Dante Bichette	1.00	.45
Andres Galarraga		
☐ 14 Jeff Bagwell	1.00	.45
Derek Bell		
☐ 15 Hideo Nomo	2.00	.90
Mike Piazza		
☐ 16 Henry Rodriguez	.40	.18
Moises Alou		
☐ 17 Rey Ordonez	.40	.18
Alex Ochoa		
☐ 18 Ray Lankford	.40	.18
Ron Gant		
☐ 19 Tony Gwynn	1.25	.55
Rickey Henderson		
☐ 20 Barry Bonds	.60	.25
Matt Williams		

1997 Ultra Fame Game

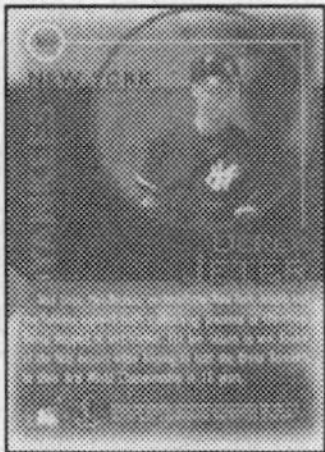

Randomly inserted in Series 2 hobby packs only at a rate of one in eight, this 18-card set features color photos of players who have displayed Hall of Fame potential on an elegant card design.

	MINT	NRMT
COMPLETE SET (18)	70.00	32.00
COMMON CARD (1-18)	2.50	1.10

☐ 1 Ken Griffey Jr.	12.00	5.50
☐ 2 Frank Thomas	10.00	4.50
☐ 3 Alex Rodriguez	10.00	4.50
☐ 4 Cal Ripken	10.00	4.50
☐ 5 Mike Piazza	8.00	3.60
☐ 6 Greg Maddux	8.00	3.60
☐ 7 Derek Jeter	8.00	3.60
☐ 8 Jeff Bagwell	5.00	2.20
☐ 9 Juan Gonzalez	6.00	2.70
☐ 10 Albert Belle	3.00	1.35
☐ 11 Tony Gwynn	6.00	2.70
☐ 12 Mark McGwire	5.00	2.20
☐ 13 Andy Pettitte	2.50	1.10
☐ 14 Kenny Lofton	3.00	1.35
☐ 15 Roberto Alomar	2.50	1.10
☐ 16 Ryne Sandberg	3.00	1.35
☐ 17 Barry Bonds	3.00	1.35
☐ 18 Eddie Murray	2.50	1.10

1997 Ultra Fielder's Choice

Randomly inserted in series 1 packs at a rate of one in 144, this 18-card set uses leather and gold foil to honor leading defensive players. The horizontal cards also include a player photo on the front as well as the big bold words "97 Fleer Ultra", "Fielder's Choice" and the player's name. The horizontal backs have another player photo as well as information about their defensive prowess.

	MINT	NRMT
COMPLETE SET (18)	300.00	135.00
COMMON CARD (1-18)	8.00	3.60

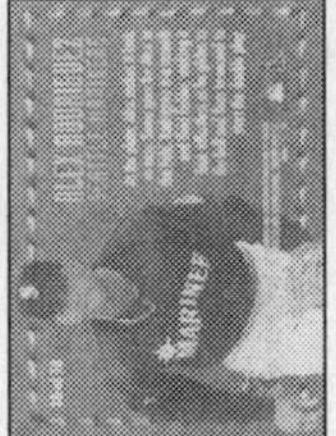

☐ 1 Roberto Alomar	15.00	6.75
☐ 2 Jeff Bagwell	30.00	13.50
☐ 3 Wade Boggs	15.00	6.75
☐ 4 Barry Bonds	20.00	9.00
☐ 5 Mark Grace	10.00	4.50
☐ 6 Ken Griffey Jr.	80.00	36.00
☐ 7 Marquis Grissom	8.00	3.60
☐ 8 Charles Johnson	9.00	4.00
☐ 9 Chuck Knoblauch	12.00	5.50
☐ 10 Barry Larkin	10.00	4.50
☐ 11 Kenny Lofton	20.00	9.00
☐ 12 Greg Maddux	50.00	22.00
☐ 13 Raul Mondesi	10.00	4.50
☐ 14 Rey Ordonez	8.00	3.60
☐ 15 Cal Ripken	60.00	27.00
☐ 16 Alex Rodriguez	50.00	22.00
☐ 17 Ivan Rodriguez	20.00	9.00
☐ 18 Matt Williams	10.00	4.50

1997 Ultra Golden Prospects

Randomly inserted in Series 2 hobby packs only at a rate of one in four, this 10-card set features color action player images on a gold baseball background with commentary on what makes these players so promising.

	MINT	NRMT
COMPLETE SET (10)	6.00	2.70
COMMON CARD (1-10)	.25	.11

☐ 1 Andruw Jones	2.50	1.10
☐ 2 Vladimir Guerrero	2.00	.90
☐ 3 Todd Walker	.25	.11
☐ 4 Karim Garcia	.35	.16
☐ 5 Kevin Orie	.35	.16
☐ 6 Brian Giles	.25	.11
☐ 7 Jason Dickson	.25	.11
☐ 8 Jose Guillen	1.00	.45
☐ 9 Ruben Rivera	.35	.16
☐ 10 Derrek Lee	.35	.16

1997 Ultra Hitting Machines

Randomly inserted in Series 2 hobby packs only at a rate of one in 36, this 18-card set features color action player images of the MLB's most productive hitters in "machine-style" die-cut settings.

	MINT	NRMT
COMPLETE SET (18)	200.00	90.00
COMMON CARD (1-18)	5.00	2.20

☐ 1 Andruw Jones	12.00	5.50
☐ 2 Ken Griffey Jr.	30.00	13.50
☐ 3 Frank Thomas	25.00	11.00
☐ 4 Alex Rodriguez	20.00	9.00
☐ 5 Cal Ripken	25.00	11.00
☐ 6 Mike Piazza	20.00	9.00
☐ 7 Derek Jeter	15.00	6.75
☐ 8 Albert Belle	8.00	3.60
☐ 9 Tony Gwynn	15.00	6.75
☐ 10 Jeff Bagwell	12.00	5.50
☐ 11 Mark McGwire	12.00	5.50
☐ 12 Kenny Lofton	8.00	3.60
☐ 13 Manny Ramirez	7.00	3.10
☐ 14 Roberto Alomar	7.00	3.10
☐ 15 Ryne Sandberg	8.00	3.60
☐ 16 Eddie Murray	7.00	3.10
☐ 17 Sammy Sosa	5.00	2.20
☐ 18 Ken Caminiti	7.00	3.10

1997 Ultra Leather Shop

Randomly inserted in Series 2 hobby packs only at a rate of one in six, this 12-card set features color player images of some of the best fielders in the game highlighted by simulated leather backgrounds.

	MINT	NRMT
COMPLETE SET (12)	20.00	9.00
COMMON CARD (1-12)	.75	.35

☐ 1 Ken Griffey Jr.	6.00	2.70
☐ 2 Alex Rodriguez	5.00	2.20
☐ 3 Cal Ripken	5.00	2.20
☐ 4 Derek Jeter	4.00	1.80
☐ 5 Juan Gonzalez	3.00	1.35
☐ 6 Tony Gwynn	3.00	1.35
☐ 7 Jeff Bagwell	2.50	1.10
☐ 8 Roberto Alomar	1.25	.55
☐ 9 Ryne Sandberg	1.50	.70
☐ 10 Ken Caminiti	1.25	.55
☐ 11 Kenny Lofton	1.25	.55
☐ 12 John Smoltz	.75	.35

1997 Ultra Home Run Kings

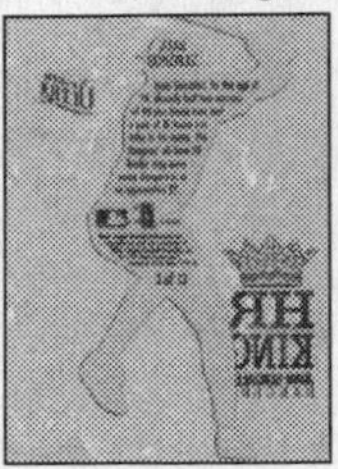

Randomly inserted in series 1 hobby packs only at a rate of one in 36, this 12-card set feaures ultra crystal cards with transparent refractive holo-foil technology. The players pictured are all leading power hitters.

	MINT	NRMT
COMPLETE SET (12)	100.00	45.00
COMMON CARD (1-12)	2.50	1.10

☐ 1 Albert Belle	6.00	2.70
☐ 2 Barry Bonds	6.00	2.70
☐ 3 Juan Gonzalez	12.00	5.50
☐ 4 Ken Griffey Jr.	25.00	11.00
☐ 5 Todd Hundley	2.50	1.10
☐ 6 Ryan Klesko	3.50	1.55
☐ 7 Mark McGwire	10.00	4.50
☐ 8 Mike Piazza	15.00	6.75
☐ 9 Sammy Sosa	4.00	1.80
☐ 10 Frank Thomas	20.00	9.00
☐ 11 Mo Vaughn	6.00	2.70
☐ 12 Matt Williams	3.50	1.55

1997 Ultra Power Plus

Randomly inserted in Series 1 packs at a rate of one in 24 and Series 2 hobby only packs at the rate of one in eight, this 12-card set utilizes silver rainbow holo-foil and

features players who not only hit with power but also excel at other parts of the game. The cards in the Series 1 insert set have an "A" prefix while the cards in the Series 2 insert set carry a "B" prefix in the checklist below.

	MINT	NRMT
COMPLETE SERIES 1 (12)	100.00	45.00
COMMON CARD (A1-A12)	2.50	1.10
COMPLETE SERIES 2 (12)	30.00	13.50
COMMON CARD (B1-B12)	2.00	.90

	MINT	NRMT
☐ A1 Jeff Bagwell	8.00	3.60
☐ A2 Barry Bonds	5.00	2.20
☐ A3 Juan Gonzalez	10.00	4.50
☐ A4 Ken Griffey Jr.	20.00	9.00
☐ A5 Chipper Jones	12.00	5.50
☐ A6 Mark McGwire	8.00	3.60
☐ A7 Mike Piazza	12.00	5.50
☐ A8 Cal Ripken	15.00	6.75
☐ A9 Alex Rodriguez	12.00	5.50
☐ A10 Sammy Sosa	4.00	1.80
☐ A11 Frank Thomas	15.00	6.75
☐ A12 Matt Williams	2.50	1.10
☐ B1 Ken Griffey Jr.	20.00	9.00
☐ B2 Frank Thomas	15.00	6.75
☐ B3 Alex Rodriguez	12.00	5.50
☐ B4 Cal Ripken	15.00	6.75
☐ B5 Mike Piazza	12.00	5.50
☐ B6 Chipper Jones	12.00	5.50
☐ B7 Albert Belle	2.50	1.10
☐ B8 Juan Gonzalez	10.00	4.50
☐ B9 Jeff Bagwell	8.00	3.60
☐ B10 Mark McGwire	8.00	3.60
☐ B11 Mo Vaughn	2.00	.90
☐ B12 Barry Bonds	2.00	.90

1997 Ultra RBI Kings

Randomly inserted in Series 1 packs at a rate of one in 18, this 10-card set features 100 percent etched-foil cards. The cards feature players who drive in many runs. The horizontal backs contain player information and another player photo.

	MINT	NRMT
COMPLETE SET (10)	50.00	22.00
COMMON CARD (1-10)	2.00	.90

	MINT	NRMT
☐ 1 Jeff Bagwell	6.00	2.70
☐ 2 Albert Belle	6.00	2.70
☐ 3 Dante Bichette	2.00	.90
☐ 4 Barry Bonds	4.00	1.80
☐ 5 Jay Buhner	2.50	1.10
☐ 6 Juan Gonzalez	8.00	3.60
☐ 7 Ken Griffey Jr.	15.00	6.75
☐ 8 Sammy Sosa	2.50	1.10
☐ 9 Frank Thomas	15.00	6.75
☐ 10 Mo Vaughn	4.00	1.80

1997 Ultra Rookie Reflections

Randomly inserted in series 1 packs at a rate of one in four, this 10-card set uses a silver foil design to feature young players. The horizontal backs contain player information as well as another player photo.

	MINT	NRMT
COMPLETE SET (10)	4.00	1.80
COMMON CARD (1-10)	.25	.11

	MINT	NRMT
☐ 1 James Baldwin	.25	.11
☐ 2 Jermaine Dye	.25	.11
☐ 3 Darin Erstad	1.50	.70
☐ 4 Todd Hollandsworth	.50	.23
☐ 5 Derek Jeter	2.50	1.10
☐ 6 Jason Kendall	.50	.23
☐ 7 Alex Ochoa	.25	.11
☐ 8 Rey Ordonez	.50	.23
☐ 9 Edgar Renteria	.50	.23
☐ 10 Scott Rolen	2.00	.90

1997 Ultra Season Crowns

Randomly inserted in series 1 packs at a rate of one in eight, this 12-card set features color photos of baseball's top stars with etched foil backgrounds.

	MINT	NRMT
COMPLETE SET (12)	15.00	6.75
COMMON CARD (1-12)	.75	.35

	MINT	NRMT
☐ 1 Albert Belle	2.00	.90
☐ 2 Dante Bichette	1.00	.45
☐ 3 Barry Bonds	1.50	.70
☐ 4 Kenny Lofton	1.50	.70
☐ 5 Edgar Martinez	1.00	.45
☐ 6 Mark McGwire	2.50	1.10
☐ 7 Andy Pettitte	1.25	.55
☐ 8 Mike Piazza	4.00	1.80
☐ 9 Alex Rodriguez	5.00	2.20
☐ 10 John Smoltz	.75	.35
☐ 11 Sammy Sosa	1.25	.55
☐ 12 Frank Thomas	6.00	2.70

1997 Ultra Starring Role

Randomly inserted in Series 2 hobby packs only at a rate of one in 288, this 12-card set featues color photos of tried-and-true clutch performers on die-cut plastic cards with foil stamping.

	MINT	NRMT
COMPLETE SET (12)	600.00	275.00
COMMON CARD (1-12)	25.00	11.00

	MINT	NRMT
☐ 1 Andruw Jones	40.00	18.00
☐ 2 Ken Griffey Jr.	100.00	45.00
☐ 3 Frank Thomas	80.00	36.00
☐ 4 Alex Rodriguez	60.00	27.00
☐ 5 Cal Ripken	80.00	36.00
☐ 6 Mike Piazza	60.00	27.00
☐ 7 Greg Maddux	60.00	27.00
☐ 8 Chipper Jones	60.00	27.00
☐ 9 Derek Jeter	50.00	22.00
☐ 10 Juan Gonzalez	50.00	22.00
☐ 11 Albert Belle	25.00	11.00
☐ 12 Tony Gwynn	50.00	22.00

1997 Ultra Thunderclap

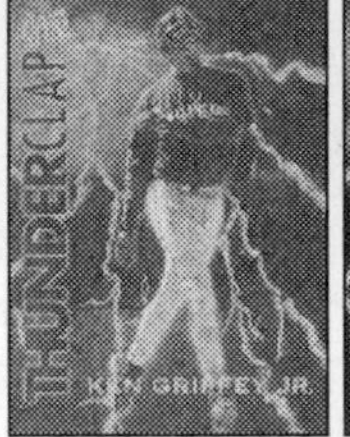

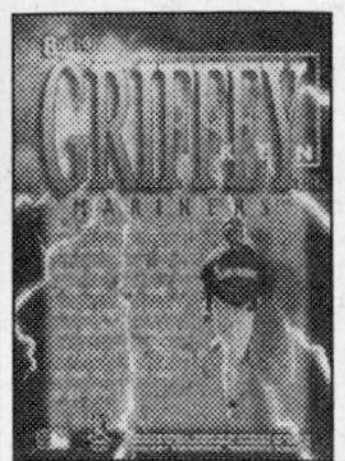

Randomly inserted in Series 2 hobby packs only at a rate of one in 18, this 10-card set features color images of superstars who are feared by opponents for their ability to totally dominate a game on a background displaying lightning from a thunderstorm.

	MINT	NRMT
COMPLETE SET (10)	80.00	36.00
COMMON CARD (1-10)	4.00	1.80

	MINT	NRMT
☐ 1 Barry Bonds	4.00	1.80
☐ 2 Mo Vaughn	4.00	1.80
☐ 3 Mark McGwire	6.00	2.70
☐ 4 Jeff Bagwell	6.00	2.70
☐ 5 Juan Gonzalez	8.00	3.60
☐ 6 Alex Rodriguez	12.00	5.50
☐ 7 Chipper Jones	10.00	4.50
☐ 8 Ken Griffey Jr.	15.00	6.75
☐ 9 Mike Piazza	10.00	4.50
☐ 10 Frank Thomas	12.00	5.50

1997 Ultra Top 30

Randomly inserted one in every Ultra series 2 retail packs only, this 30-card set features color action player images of top stars with a "Top 30" circle in the team-colored background. The backs carry another player image with his team logo the backsground circle.

	MINT	NRMT
COMPLETE SET (30)	30.00	13.50
COMMON CARD (1-30)	.40	.18
COMP.G.MED.SET (30)	300.00	135.00
COMMON G.MED. (1-30)	5.00	2.20

*GOLD MEDALLION: 6X TO 12X BASIC CARDS
G.MED SER.2 STATED ODDS 1:18 RETAIL

	MINT	NRMT
☐ 1 Andruw Jones	2.50	1.10
☐ 2 Ken Griffey	4.00	1.80
☐ 3 Frank Thomas	3.00	1.35
☐ 4 Alex Rodriguez	3.00	1.35
☐ 5 Cal Ripken	3.00	1.35
☐ 6 Mike Piazza	2.50	1.10
☐ 7 Greg Maddux	2.50	1.10
☐ 8 Chipper Jones	2.50	1.10
☐ 9 Derek Jeter	2.50	1.10
☐ 10 Juan Gonzalez	2.00	.90
☐ 11 Albert Belle	1.25	.55
☐ 12 Tony Gwynn	2.00	.90
☐ 13 Jeff Bagwell	1.50	.70
☐ 14 Mark McGwire	1.50	.70
☐ 15 Andy Pettitte	.75	.35
☐ 16 Mo Vaughn	1.00	.45
☐ 17 Kenny Lofton	1.00	.45
☐ 18 Manny Ramirez	.75	.35
☐ 19 Roberto Alomar	.75	.35
☐ 20 Ryne Sandberg	1.00	.45
☐ 21 Hideo Nomo	1.50	.70
☐ 22 Barry Bonds	1.00	.45
☐ 23 Eddie Murray	.75	.35
☐ 24 Ken Caminiti	.75	.35
☐ 25 John Smoltz	.50	.23

☐ 26 Pat Hentgen	.50	.23
☐ 27 Todd Hollandsworth	.40	.18
☐ 28 Matt Williams	.60	.25
☐ 29 Bernie Williams	.75	.35
☐ 30 Brady Anderson	.60	.25

1998 Ultra

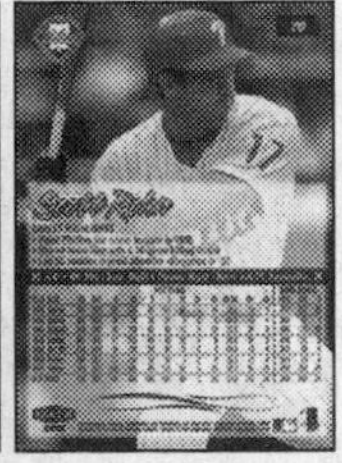

The 1998 Ultra Series 1 set features 250 cards and was distributed in 10-card packs with a suggested retail price of $2.59. The fronts carry UV coated color action player photos printed on 20 pt. card stock. The backs display another player photo with player information and career statistics. The set contains the following subsets: Season's Crown (211-220) seeded 1:12 packs, Prospects (221-245) seeded 1:4 packs, and Checklists (246-250) seeded 1:4 packs. Also seeded one in every pack, was one of 50 Million Dollar Moment cards which pictured some of the greatest moments in baseball histroy and gave the collector a chance to win a million dollars.

	MINT	NRMT
COMPLETE SERIES 1 (250)	100.00	45.00
COMP.SER.1 w/o SP's (210)	15.00	6.75
COMMON CARD (1-250)	.15	.07

☐ 1 Ken Griffey Jr.	3.00	1.35
☐ 2 Matt Morris	.15	.07
☐ 3 Roger Clemens	1.25	.55
☐ 4 Matt Williams	.40	.18
☐ 5 Roberto Hernandez	.30	.14
☐ 6 Rondell White	.30	.14
☐ 7 Tim Salmon	.60	.25
☐ 8 Brad Radke	.30	.14
☐ 9 Brett Butler	.30	.14
☐ 10 Carl Everett	.15	.07
☐ 11 Chili Davis	.30	.14
☐ 12 Chuck Finley	.15	.07
☐ 13 Darryl Kile	.30	.14
☐ 14 Deivi Cruz	.15	.07
☐ 15 Gary Gaetti	.30	.14
☐ 16 Matt Stairs	.15	.07
☐ 17 Pat Meares	.15	.07
☐ 18 Will Cunnane	.15	.07
☐ 19 Steve Woodard	.15	.07
☐ 20 Andy Ashby	.15	.07
☐ 21 Bobby Higginson	.30	.14
☐ 22 Brian Jordan	.15	.07
☐ 23 Craig Biggio	.40	.18
☐ 24 Jim Edmonds	.60	.25
☐ 25 Ryan McGuire	.15	.07
☐ 26 Scott Hatteberg	.15	.07
☐ 27 Willie Greene	.30	.14
☐ 28 Albert Belle	.75	.35
☐ 29 Ellis Burks	.30	.14
☐ 30 Hideo Nomo	1.50	.70
☐ 31 Jeff Bagwell	1.25	.55
☐ 32 Kevin Brown	.30	.14
☐ 33 Nomar Garciaparra	2.00	.90
☐ 34 Pedro Martinez	.60	.25
☐ 35 Raul Mondesi	.40	.18
☐ 36 Ricky Bottalico	.15	.07
☐ 37 Shawn Estes	.15	.07
☐ 38 Otis Nixon	.15	.07
☐ 39 Terry Steinbach	.15	.07
☐ 40 Tom Glavine	.30	.14
☐ 41 Todd Dunwoody	.30	.14
☐ 42 Deion Sanders	.60	.25
☐ 43 Gary Sheffield	.60	.25
☐ 44 Mike Lansing	.15	.07
☐ 45 Mike Lieberthal	.15	.07
☐ 46 Paul Sorrento	.15	.07
☐ 47 Paul O'Neill	.30	.14
☐ 48 Tom Goodwin	.15	.07
☐ 49 Andruw Jones	1.25	.55
☐ 50 Barry Bonds	.75	.35
☐ 51 Bernie Williams	.60	.25
☐ 52 Jeremi Gonzalez	.30	.14
☐ 53 Mike Piazza	2.00	.90
☐ 54 Russ Davis	.15	.07
☐ 55 Vinny Castilla	.30	.14
☐ 56 Rod Beck	.30	.14
☐ 57 Andres Galarraga	.60	.25
☐ 58 Ben McDonald	.15	.07
☐ 59 Billy Wagner	.30	.14
☐ 60 Charles Johnson	.30	.14
☐ 61 Fred McGriff	.40	.18
☐ 62 Dean Palmer	.15	.07
☐ 63 Frank Thomas	2.50	1.10
☐ 64 Ismael Valdes	.15	.07
☐ 65 Mark Bellhorn	.15	.07
☐ 66 Jeff King	.15	.07
☐ 67 John Wetteland	.30	.14
☐ 68 Mark Grace	.40	.18
☐ 69 Mark Kotsay	.60	.25
☐ 70 Scott Rolen	1.50	.70
☐ 71 Todd Hundley	.30	.14
☐ 72 Todd Worrell	.15	.07
☐ 73 Wilson Alvarez	.30	.14
☐ 74 Bobby Jones	.15	.07
☐ 75 Jose Canseco	.40	.18
☐ 76 Kevin Appier	.15	.07
☐ 77 Neifi Perez	.15	.07
☐ 78 Paul Molitor	.60	.25
☐ 79 Quilvio Veras	.15	.07
☐ 80 Randy Johnson	.60	.25
☐ 81 Glendon Rusch	.15	.07
☐ 82 Curt Schilling	.30	.14
☐ 83 Alex Rodriguez	2.00	.90
☐ 84 Rey Ordonez	.15	.07
☐ 85 Jeff Juden	.15	.07
☐ 86 Mike Cameron	.30	.14
☐ 87 Ryan Klesko	.40	.18
☐ 88 Trevor Hoffman	.30	.14
☐ 89 Chuck Knoblauch	.60	.25
☐ 90 Larry Walker	.60	.25
☐ 91 Mark McLemore	.15	.07
☐ 92 B.J. Surhoff	.30	.14
☐ 93 Darren Daulton	.30	.14
☐ 94 Ray Durham	.15	.07
☐ 95 Sammy Sosa	.60	.25
☐ 96 Eric Young	.15	.07
☐ 97 Gerald Williams	.15	.07
☐ 98 Javy Lopez	.30	.14
☐ 99 John Smiley	.15	.07
☐ 100 Juan Gonzalez	1.50	.70
☐ 101 Shawn Green	.15	.07
☐ 102 Charles Nagy	.15	.07
☐ 103 David Justice	.60	.25
☐ 104 Joey Hamilton	.15	.07
☐ 105 Pat Hentgen	.30	.14
☐ 106 Raul Casanova	.15	.07
☐ 107 Tony Phillips	.15	.07
☐ 108 Tony Gwynn	1.50	.70
☐ 109 Will Clark	.40	.18
☐ 110 Jason Giambi	.15	.07
☐ 111 Jay Bell	.15	.07
☐ 112 Johnny Damon	.15	.07
☐ 113 Alan Benes	.15	.07
☐ 114 Jeff Suppan	.15	.07
☐ 115 Kevin Polcovich	.15	.07
☐ 116 Shigetoshi Hasegawa	.30	.14
☐ 117 Steve Finley	.30	.14
☐ 118 Tony Clark	.60	.25
☐ 119 David Cone	.30	.14
☐ 120 Jose Guillen	.60	.25
☐ 121 Kevin Millwood	.60	.25
☐ 122 Greg Maddux	2.00	.90
☐ 123 Dave Nilsson	.15	.07
☐ 124 Hideki Irabu	.40	.18
☐ 125 Jason Kendall	.30	.14
☐ 126 Jim Thome	.60	.25
☐ 127 Delino DeShields	.15	.07
☐ 128 Edgar Renteria	.30	.14
☐ 129 Edgardo Alfonzo	.30	.14
☐ 130 J.T. Snow	.30	.14
☐ 131 Jeff Abbott	.15	.07
☐ 132 Jeffrey Hammonds	.30	.14
☐ 133 Todd Greene	.30	.14
☐ 134 Vladimir Guerrero	1.00	.45
☐ 135 Jay Buhner	.40	.18
☐ 136 Jeff Cirillo	.15	.07
☐ 137 Jeromy Burnitz	.15	.07
☐ 138 Mickey Morandini	.15	.07
☐ 139 Tino Martinez	.60	.25
☐ 140 Jeff Shaw	.15	.07
☐ 141 Rafael Palmeiro	.40	.18
☐ 142 Bobby Bonilla	.30	.14
☐ 143 Cal Ripken	2.50	1.10
☐ 144 Chad Fox	.15	.07
☐ 145 Dante Bichette	.30	.14
☐ 146 Dennis Eckersley	.40	.18
☐ 147 Mariano Rivera	.30	.14
☐ 148 Mo Vaughn	.75	.35
☐ 149 Reggie Sanders	.15	.07
☐ 150 Derek Jeter	1.50	.70
☐ 151 Rusty Greer	.30	.14
☐ 152 Brady Anderson	.30	.14
☐ 153 Brett Tomko	.15	.07
☐ 154 Jaime Navarro	.15	.07
☐ 155 Kevin Orie	.15	.07
☐ 156 Roberto Alomar	.60	.25
☐ 157 Edgar Martinez	.40	.18
☐ 158 John Olerud	.30	.14
☐ 159 John Smoltz	.30	.14
☐ 160 Ryne Sandberg	.75	.35
☐ 161 Billy Taylor	.15	.07
☐ 162 Chris Holt	.15	.07
☐ 163 Damion Easley	.15	.07
☐ 164 Darin Erstad	.75	.35
☐ 165 Joe Carter	.30	.14
☐ 166 Kelvim Escobar	.15	.07
☐ 167 Ken Caminiti	.60	.25
☐ 168 Pokey Reese	.15	.07
☐ 169 Ray Lankford	.30	.14
☐ 170 Livan Hernandez	.40	.18
☐ 171 Steve Kline	.15	.07
☐ 172 Tom Gordon	.15	.07
☐ 173 Travis Fryman	.30	.14
☐ 174 Al Martin	.15	.07
☐ 175 Andy Pettitte	.60	.25
☐ 176 Jeff Kent	.15	.07
☐ 177 Jimmy Key	.30	.14
☐ 178 Mark Grudzielanek	.15	.07
☐ 179 Tony Saunders	.15	.07
☐ 180 Barry Larkin	.40	.18
☐ 181 Bubba Trammell	.15	.07
☐ 182 Carlos Delgado	.30	.14
☐ 183 Carlos Baerga	.30	.14
☐ 184 Derek Bell	.15	.07
☐ 185 Henry Rodriguez	.15	.07
☐ 186 Jason Dickson	.15	.07
☐ 187 Ron Gant	.30	.14
☐ 188 Tony Womack	.15	.07
☐ 189 Justin Thompson	.15	.07
☐ 190 Fernando Tatis	.60	.25
☐ 191 Mark Wohlers	.15	.07
☐ 192 Takashi Kashiwada	.30	.14
☐ 193 Garret Anderson	.30	.14
☐ 194 Jose Cruz Jr.	2.50	1.10
☐ 195 Ricardo Rincon	.15	.07
☐ 196 Tim Naehring	.15	.07
☐ 197 Moises Alou	.30	.14
☐ 198 Eric Karros	.15	.07
☐ 199 John Jaha	.15	.07
☐ 200 Marty Cordova	.15	.07
☐ 201 Ken Hill	.15	.07
☐ 202 Chipper Jones	2.00	.90
☐ 203 Kenny Lofton	.75	.35
☐ 204 Mike Mussina	.60	.25
☐ 205 Manny Ramirez	.60	.25
☐ 206 Todd Hollandsworth	.15	.07
☐ 207 Cecil Fielder	.30	.14
☐ 208 Mark McGwire	1.50	.70
☐ 209 Jim Leyritz	.15	.07
☐ 210 Ivan Rodriguez	.75	.35
☐ 211 Jeff Bagwell SC	5.00	2.20
☐ 212 Barry Bonds SC	3.00	1.35
☐ 213 Roger Clemens SC	5.00	2.20
☐ 214 Nomar Garciaparra SC	8.00	3.60
☐ 215 Ken Griffey Jr. SC	12.00	5.50
☐ 216 Tony Gwynn SC	6.00	2.70
☐ 217 Randy Johnson SC	2.50	1.10
☐ 218 Mark McGwire SC	6.00	2.70
☐ 219 Scott Rolen SC	6.00	2.70
☐ 220 Frank Thomas SC	10.00	4.50
☐ 221 Matt Perisho PROS	.75	.35
☐ 222 Wes Helms PROS	1.50	.70
☐ 223 Dave Dellucci PROS	.75	.35
☐ 224 Todd Helton PROS	4.00	1.80
☐ 225 Brian Rose PROS	2.00	.90
☐ 226 Aaron Boone PROS	.75	.35
☐ 227 Keith Foulke PROS	.75	.35
☐ 228 Homer Bush PROS	.75	.35
☐ 229 Shannon Stewart PROS	1.00	.45
☐ 230 Richard Hidalgo PROS	1.50	.70
☐ 231 Russ Johnson PROS	.75	.35
☐ 232 Henry Blanco PROS	.75	.35
☐ 233 Paul Konerko PROS	5.00	2.20
☐ 234 Antone Williamson PROS	.75	.35
☐ 235 Shane Bowers PROS	.75	.35
☐ 236 Jose Vidro PROS	.75	.35
☐ 237 Derek Wallace PROS	.75	.35
☐ 238 Ricky Ledee PROS	2.50	1.10
☐ 239 Ben Grieve PROS	6.00	2.70
☐ 240 Lou Collier PROS	.75	.35
☐ 241 Derrek Lee PROS	2.00	.90
☐ 242 Ruben Rivera PROS	1.50	.70
☐ 243 Jorge Velandia PROS	.75	.35
☐ 244 Andrew Vessel PROS	.75	.35
☐ 245 Chris Carpenter PROS	.75	.35
☐ 246 Ken Griffey Jr. CL	1.50	.70
☐ 247 Alex Rodriguez CL	1.25	.55
☐ 248 Diamond Ink CL	.15	.07
☐ 249 Frank Thomas CL	1.25	.55
☐ 250 Cal Ripken CL	1.25	.55

1998 Ultra Gold Medallion

Randomly inserted one in every hobby only pack, this 250-card set is parallel to the base set and feature a gold metallic foil background.

	MINT	NRMT
COMPLETE SERIES 1 (250)	120.00	55.00
COMMON CARD (1-250)	.50	.23

*G.MED.STARS: 2X TO 4X BASIC CARDS
*G.MED.YOUNG STARS: 1.5X TO 3X BASIC CARDS
*G.MED.SEASON CROWNS: .6X TO 1.2X BASIC CARDS
*G.MED.PROSPECTS: .6X TO 1.2X BASIC CARDS
*G.MED.CHECKLISTS: 2X TO 4X BASIC CARDS

1998 Ultra Masterpieces

Randomly inserted in hobby packs only, this 250-card set is parallel to the base set. Only one of each of these cards were produced. With so few cards produced; we will not have pricing available. However, key cards will be tracked and information will be printed in upcoming issues of Beckett Baseball Card Monthly.

	MINT	NRMT
COMMON CARD (1-250)	200.00	90.00

1998 Ultra Platinum Medallion

Randomly inserted in hobby only packs at the rate of one in 100, this 250-card set is parallel to the base set. Only 100 of this set were produced and are serially numbered. Ten exchange cards good for a complete Platinum set were inserted into packs. Since there are so few of these cards issued and almost no market information -- no price is provided.

	MINT	NRMT
COMMON CARD (1-250)	20.00	9.00
MINOR STARS	30.00	13.50
SEMISTARS	50.00	22.00
UNLISTED STARS	80.00	36.00
☐ 1 Ken Griffey Jr.	400.00	180.00
☐ 3 Roger Clemens	150.00	70.00
☐ 28 Albert Belle	100.00	45.00
☐ 30 Hideo Nomo	250.00	110.00
☐ 31 Jeff Bagwell	150.00	70.00
☐ 33 Nomar Garciaparra	200.00	90.00
☐ 49 Andruw Jones	120.00	55.00
☐ 50 Barry Bonds	100.00	45.00
☐ 53 Mike Piazza	250.00	110.00
☐ 63 Frank Thomas	300.00	135.00
☐ 70 Scott Rolen	150.00	70.00
☐ 83 Alex Rodriguez	250.00	110.00
☐ 100 Juan Gonzalez	200.00	90.00
☐ 108 Tony Gwynn	200.00	90.00
☐ 122 Greg Maddux	250.00	110.00
☐ 134 Vladimir Guerrero	100.00	45.00
☐ 143 Cal Ripken	300.00	135.00
☐ 148 Mo Vaughn	100.00	45.00
☐ 150 Derek Jeter	200.00	90.00
☐ 160 Ryne Sandberg	100.00	45.00
☐ 194 Jose Cruz Jr.	200.00	90.00
☐ 202 Chipper Jones	200.00	90.00
☐ 203 Kenny Lofton	100.00	45.00
☐ 208 Mark McGwire	200.00	90.00
☐ 210 Ivan Rodriguez	100.00	45.00
☐ 211 Jeff Bagwell SC	100.00	45.00
☐ 213 Roger Clemens SC	100.00	45.00
☐ 214 Nomar Garciaparra SC	120.00	55.00
☐ 215 Ken Griffey Jr. SC	250.00	110.00
☐ 216 Tony Gwynn SC	120.00	55.00
☐ 218 Mark McGwire SC	120.00	55.00
☐ 219 Scott Rolen SC	100.00	45.00
☐ 220 Frank Thomas SC	200.00	90.00
☐ 233 Paul Konerko PROS	100.00	45.00
☐ 239 Ben Grieve PROS	120.00	55.00
☐ 246 Ken Griffey Jr. CL	200.00	90.00
☐ 247 Alex Rodriguez CL	120.00	55.00
☐ 249 Frank Thomas CL	150.00	70.00
☐ 250 Cal Ripken CL	150.00	70.00

1998 Ultra Artistic Talents

Randomly inserted in Series 1 packs at the rate of one in eight, this 18-card set features color pictures of top players on art enhanced cards.

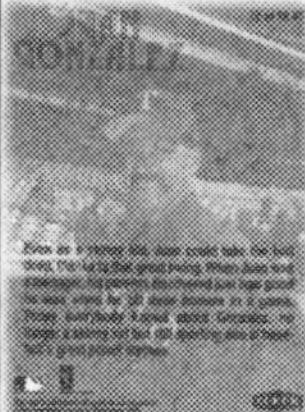

	MINT	NRMT
COMPLETE SET (18)	80.00	36.00
COMMON CARD (1-18)	2.50	1.10
☐ 1 Ken Griffey Jr.	10.00	4.50
☐ 2 Andruw Jones	4.00	1.80
☐ 3 Alex Rodriguez	6.00	2.70
☐ 4 Frank Thomas	8.00	3.60
☐ 5 Cal Ripken	8.00	3.60
☐ 6 Derek Jeter	5.00	2.20
☐ 7 Chipper Jones	6.00	2.70
☐ 8 Greg Maddux	6.00	2.70
☐ 9 Mike Piazza	6.00	2.70
☐ 10 Albert Belle	2.50	1.10
☐ 11 Darin Erstad	2.50	1.10
☐ 12 Juan Gonzalez	5.00	2.20
☐ 13 Jeff Bagwell	4.00	1.80
☐ 14 Tony Gwynn	5.00	2.20
☐ 15 Mark McGwire	5.00	2.20
☐ 16 Scott Rolen	5.00	2.20
☐ 17 Barry Bonds	2.50	1.10
☐ 18 Kenny Lofton	2.50	1.10

1998 Ultra Back to the Future

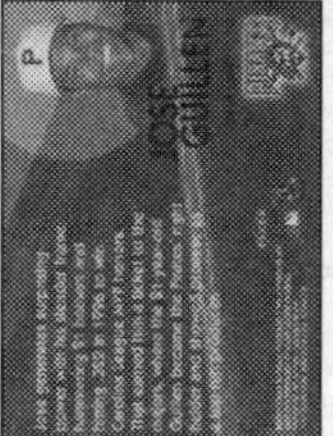

Randomly inserted in Series 1 packs at the rate of one in six, this 15-card set features color photos of top Rookies. The backs carry player information.

	MINT	NRMT
COMPLETE SET (15)	25.00	11.00
COMMON CARD (1-15)	.75	.35
☐ 1 Andruw Jones	2.50	1.10
☐ 2 Alex Rodriguez	4.00	1.80
☐ 3 Derek Jeter	3.00	1.35
☐ 4 Darin Erstad	1.50	.70
☐ 5 Mike Cameron	.75	.35
☐ 6 Scott Rolen	3.00	1.35
☐ 7 Nomar Garciaparra	4.00	1.80
☐ 8 Hideki Irabu	.75	.35
☐ 9 Jose Cruz Jr.	5.00	2.20
☐ 10 Vladimir Guerrero	2.00	.90
☐ 11 Mark Kotsay	1.25	.55
☐ 12 Tony Womack	.75	.35
☐ 13 Jason Dickson	.75	.35
☐ 14 Jose Guillen	1.25	.55
☐ 15 Tony Clark	1.25	.55

1998 Ultra Big Shots

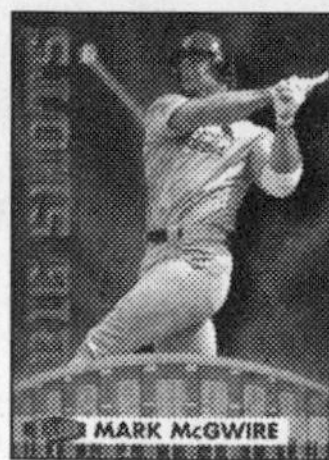

Randomly inserted in Series 1 packs at the rate of one in four, this 15-card set features color photos of players who hit the longest home runs in the 1997 season.

	MINT	NRMT
COMPLETE SET (15)	12.00	5.50
COMMON CARD (1-15)	.50	.23
☐ 1 Ken Griffey Jr.	4.00	1.80
☐ 2 Frank Thomas	3.00	1.35
☐ 3 Chipper Jones	2.50	1.10
☐ 4 Albert Belle	1.00	.45
☐ 5 Juan Gonzalez	2.00	.90
☐ 6 Jeff Bagwell	1.50	.70
☐ 7 Mark McGwire	2.00	.90
☐ 8 Barry Bonds	1.00	.45
☐ 9 Manny Ramirez	.75	.35
☐ 10 Mo Vaughn	1.00	.45
☐ 11 Matt Williams	.50	.23
☐ 12 Jim Thome	.75	.35
☐ 13 Tino Martinez	.50	.23
☐ 14 Mike Piazza	2.50	1.10
☐ 15 Tony Clark	.50	.23

1998 Ultra Diamond Producers

Randomly inserted in Series 1 packs at the rate of one in 288, this 15-card set features color photos of Major League Baseball's top players.

	MINT	NRMT
COMPLETE SET (15)	1000.00	450.00
COMMON CARD (1-15)	30.00	13.50
☐ 1 Ken Griffey Jr.	120.00	55.00
☐ 2 Andruw Jones	40.00	18.00
☐ 3 Alex Rodriguez	80.00	36.00
☐ 4 Frank Thomas	100.00	45.00
☐ 5 Cal Ripken	100.00	45.00
☐ 6 Derek Jeter	60.00	27.00
☐ 7 Chipper Jones	80.00	36.00
☐ 8 Greg Maddux	80.00	36.00
☐ 9 Mike Piazza	80.00	36.00
☐ 10 Juan Gonzalez	60.00	27.00
☐ 11 Jeff Bagwell	50.00	22.00
☐ 12 Tony Gwynn	60.00	27.00
☐ 13 Mark McGwire	60.00	27.00
☐ 14 Barry Bonds	30.00	13.50
☐ 15 Jose Cruz Jr.	80.00	36.00

1998 Ultra Double Trouble

Randonly inserted in Series 1 packs at the rate of one in four, this 20-card set features color photos of two star players per card.

	MINT	NRMT
COMPLETE SET (20)	12.00	5.50
COMMON CARD (1-20)	.50	.23
☐ 1 Ken Griffey Jr. Alex Rodriguez	5.00	2.20
☐ 2 Vladimir Guerrero Pedro Martinez	.75	.35
☐ 3 Andruw Jones Kenny Lofton	1.50	.70
☐ 4 Chipper Jones Greg Maddux	3.00	1.35
☐ 5 Derek Jeter Tino Martinez	1.50	.70
☐ 6 Frank Thomas Albert Belle	3.00	1.35
☐ 7 Cal Ripken Roberto Alomar	3.00	1.35
☐ 8 Mike Piazza Hideo Nomo	3.00	1.35
☐ 9 Darin Erstad Jason Dickson	.75	.35
☐ 10 Juan Gonzalez Ivan Rodriguez	2.00	.90
☐ 11 Jeff Bagwell Darryl Kile	1.25	.55

	MINT	NRMT
☐ 12 Tony Gwynn / Steve Finley	1.50	.70
☐ 13 Mark McGwire / Ray Lankford	1.25	.55
☐ 14 Barry Bonds / Jeff Kent	.75	.35
☐ 15 Andy Pettitte / Bernie Williams	.50	.23
☐ 16 Mo Vaughn / Nomar Garciaparra	2.00	.90
☐ 17 Matt Williams / Jim Thome	.50	.23
☐ 18 Hideki Irabu / Mariano Rivera	.50	.23
☐ 19 Roger Clemens / Jose Cruz Jr.	2.50	1.10
☐ 20 Manny Ramirez / David Justice	.50	.23

1998 Ultra Fall Classics

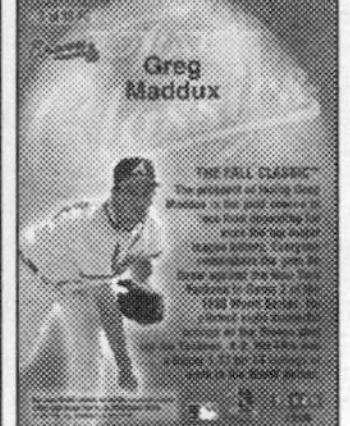

Randomly inserted in Series 1 packs at the rate of one in 18, this 15-card set features color photos of the top potential postseason heroes. The backs carry player information.

	MINT	NRMT
COMPLETE SET (15)	120.00	55.00
COMMON CARD (1-15)	5.00	2.20
☐ 1 Ken Griffey Jr.	20.00	9.00
☐ 2 Andruw Jones	6.00	2.70
☐ 3 Alex Rodriguez	12.00	5.50
☐ 4 Frank Thomas	15.00	6.75
☐ 5 Cal Ripken	15.00	6.75
☐ 6 Derek Jeter	10.00	4.50
☐ 7 Chipper Jones	12.00	5.50
☐ 8 Greg Maddux	12.00	5.50
☐ 9 Mike Piazza	12.00	5.50
☐ 10 Albert Belle	5.00	2.20
☐ 11 Juan Gonzalez	10.00	4.50
☐ 12 Jeff Bagwell	8.00	3.60
☐ 13 Tony Gwynn	10.00	4.50
☐ 14 Mark McGwire	10.00	4.50
☐ 15 Barry Bonds	5.00	2.20

1998 Ultra Kid Gloves

Radomly inserted in Series 1 packs at the rate of one in eight, this 12-card set features color photos of top young defensive players. The backs carry player information.

	MINT	NRMT
COMPLETE SET (12)	20.00	9.00
COMMON CARD (1-12)	.50	.23
☐ 1 Andruw Jones	2.50	1.10
☐ 2 Alex Rodriguez	4.00	1.80
☐ 3 Derek Jeter	3.00	1.35
☐ 4 Chipper Jones	4.00	1.80
☐ 5 Darin Erstad	1.50	.70
☐ 6 Todd Walker	1.00	.45
☐ 7 Scott Rolen	3.00	1.35
☐ 8 Nomar Garciaparra	4.00	1.80
☐ 9 Jose Cruz Jr.	5.00	2.20
☐ 10 Charles Johnson	1.00	.45
☐ 11 Rey Ordonez	.50	.23
☐ 12 Vladimir Guerrero	2.00	.90

1998 Ultra Power Plus

Randomly inserted in Series 1 packs at the rate of one in 36, this 10-card set features color action photos of top young and veteran players. The backs carry player information.

	MINT	NRMT
COMPLETE SET (10)	120.00	55.00
COMMON CARD (1-10)	8.00	3.60
☐ 1 Ken Griffey	30.00	13.50
☐ 2 Andruw Jones	10.00	4.50
☐ 3 Alex Rodriguez	20.00	9.00
☐ 4 Frank Thomas	25.00	11.00
☐ 5 Mike Piazza	20.00	9.00
☐ 6 Albert Belle	8.00	3.60
☐ 7 Juan Gonzalez	15.00	6.75
☐ 8 Jeff Bagwell	12.00	5.50
☐ 9 Barry Bonds	8.00	3.60
☐ 10 Jose Cruz Jr.	20.00	9.00

1998 Ultra Prime Leather

Randomly inserted in Series 1 packs at the rate of one in 144, this 18-card set features color photos of young and veteran players considered to be good glove men. The backs carry player information.

	MINT	NRMT
COMPLETE SET (18)	600.00	275.00
COMMON CARD (1-18)	15.00	6.75
☐ 1 Ken Griffey Jr.	80.00	36.00
☐ 2 Andruw Jones	25.00	11.00
☐ 3 Alex Rodriguez	50.00	22.00
☐ 4 Frank Thomas	60.00	27.00
☐ 5 Cal Ripken	60.00	27.00
☐ 6 Derek Jeter	40.00	18.00
☐ 7 Chipper Jones	50.00	22.00
☐ 8 Greg Maddux	50.00	22.00
☐ 9 Mike Piazza	50.00	22.00
☐ 10 Albert Belle	20.00	9.00
☐ 11 Darin Erstad	15.00	6.75
☐ 12 Juan Gonzalez	40.00	18.00
☐ 13 Jeff Bagwell	30.00	13.50
☐ 14 Tony Gwynn	40.00	18.00
☐ 15 Roberto Alomar	15.00	6.75
☐ 16 Barry Bonds	20.00	9.00
☐ 17 Kenny Lofton	20.00	9.00
☐ 18 Jose Cruz Jr.	50.00	22.00

1988 Upper Deck Promos

The first two cards were test issues given away as samples during the summer of 1988 in anticipation of Upper Deck obtaining licenses from Major League Baseball and the Major League Baseball Players Association. Not many were produced (probably less than 25,000 of each) but few were thrown away as they were distributed basically only to those who would hold on to them. There are three versions based on where the hologram is located. Type A, the most common variety, has a hologram on the bottom that extends as far as the photo. On Type B, the hologram is on the bottom but extends to the edge of the card. Type C, by far the scarcest, has the hologram at the top. Joyner and Buice were supposedly interested in investing in Upper Deck

(conflict of interest prohibited them) and apparently were helpful in getting Upper Deck the necessary licenses. Cards were passed out freely to every dealer at the National Sports Collectors Convention in Atlantic City, New Jersey in August 1988.

	MINT	NRMT
COMPLETE SET (6)	275.00	125.00
COMPLETE TYPE A SET (2)	35.00	16.00
COMPLETE TYPE B SET (2)	70.00	32.00
COMPLETE TYPE C SET (2)	175.00	80.00
☐ A1 DeWayne Buice	10.00	4.50
☐ A700 Wally Joyner	30.00	13.50
☐ B1 DeWayne Buice	20.00	9.00
☐ B700 Wally Joyner	60.00	27.00
☐ C1 DeWayne Buice	50.00	22.00
☐ C700 Wally Joyner	150.00	70.00

1989 Upper Deck

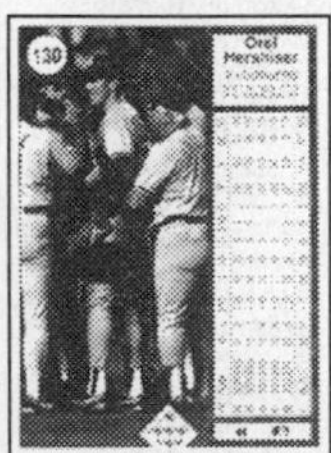

This attractive 800-card standard-size set was introduced in 1989 as the premier issue by the then-fledgling Upper Deck company. Unlike other 1989 releases, this set was issued in two separate series - a low series numbered 1-700 and a high series numbered 701-800. Cards were primarily issued in fin-wrapped low and high series foil packs, complete 800-card factory sets and 100-card high series factory sets. High series packs contained a mixture of both low and high series cards. Collectors should also note that many dealers consider that Upper Deck's "planned" production of 1,000,000 of each player was increased (perhaps even doubled) later in the year due to the explosion in popularity of the product. The cards feature slick paper stock, full color on both the front and the back and carry a hologram on the reverse to protect against counterfeiting. Subsets include Rookie Stars (1-26) and Collector's Choice art cards (668-693). The more significant variations involving changed photos or changed type are listed below. According to the company, the Murphy and Sheridan cards were corrected very early, after only two percent of the cards had been produced. Similarly, the Sheffield was corrected after 15 percent had been printed; Varsho, Gallego, and Schroeder were corrected after 20 percent; and Holton, Manrique, and Winningham were corrected 30 percent of the way through. Rookie Cards in the set include Jim Abbott, Sandy Alomar Jr., Dante Bichette, Craig Biggio, Steve Finley, Ken Griffey Jr., Erik Hanson, Charlie Hayes, Randy Johnson, Ramon Martinez, Gary Sheffield, John Smoltz and Todd Zeile. Cards with missing or duplicate holograms appear to be relatively common and are generally considered to be flawed copies that sell for substantial discounts.

	MINT	NRMT
COMPLETE SET (800)	120.00	55.00
COMP.FACT.SET (800)	120.00	55.00
COMPLETE LO SET (700)	110.00	50.00
COMPLETE HI SET (100)	10.00	4.50
COMPLETE HI FACT.SET (100)	8.00	3.60
COMMON CARD (1-800)	.20	.09
☐ 1 Ken Griffey Jr.	100.00	45.00
☐ 2 Luis Medina	.20	.09
☐ 3 Tony Chance	.20	.09
☐ 4 Dave Otto	.20	.09

☐ 5 Sandy Alomar Jr. UER (Born 6/16/66, should be 6/18/66)	2.50	1.10
☐ 6 Rolando Roomes	.20	.09
☐ 7 Dave West	.20	.09
☐ 8 Cris Carpenter	.20	.09
☐ 9 Gregg Jefferies	.50	.23
☐ 10 Doug Dascenzo	.20	.09
☐ 11 Ron Jones	.20	.09
☐ 12 Luis DeLosSantos	.20	.09
☐ 13 Gary Sheffield COR	4.00	1.80
☐ 13A Gary Sheffield ERR (SS upside down on card front)	4.00	1.80
☐ 14 Mike Harkey	.20	.09
☐ 15 Lance Blankenship	.20	.09
☐ 16 William Brennan	.20	.09
☐ 17 John Smoltz	2.50	1.10
☐ 18 Ramon Martinez	1.00	.45
☐ 19 Mark Lemke	.50	.23
☐ 20 Juan Bell	.20	.09
☐ 21 Rey Palacios	.20	.09
☐ 22 Felix Jose	.20	.09
☐ 23 Van Snider	.20	.09
☐ 24 Dante Bichette	2.00	.90
☐ 25 Randy Johnson	6.00	2.70
☐ 26 Carlos Quintana	.20	.09
☐ 27 Star Rookie CL	.20	.09
☐ 28 Mike Schooler	.20	.09
☐ 29 Randy St.Claire	.20	.09
☐ 30 Jerald Clark	.20	.09
☐ 31 Kevin Gross	.20	.09
☐ 32 Dan Firova	.20	.09
☐ 33 Jeff Calhoun	.20	.09
☐ 34 Tommy Hinzo	.20	.09
☐ 35 Ricky Jordan	.40	.18
☐ 36 Larry Parrish	.20	.09
☐ 37 Bret Saberhagen UER (Hit total 931, should be 1031)	.20	.09
☐ 38 Mike Smithson	.20	.09
☐ 39 Dave Dravecky	.40	.18
☐ 40 Ed Romero	.20	.09
☐ 41 Jeff Musselman	.20	.09
☐ 42 Ed Hearn	.20	.09
☐ 43 Rance Mulliniks	.20	.09
☐ 44 Jim Eisenreich	.75	.35
☐ 45 Sil Campusano	.20	.09
☐ 46 Mike Krukow	.20	.09
☐ 47 Paul Gibson	.20	.09
☐ 48 Mike LaCoss	.20	.09
☐ 49 Larry Herndon	.20	.09
☐ 50 Scott Garrelts	.20	.09
☐ 51 Dwayne Henry	.20	.09
☐ 52 Jim Acker	.20	.09
☐ 53 Steve Sax	.20	.09
☐ 54 Pete O'Brien	.20	.09
☐ 55 Paul Runge	.20	.09
☐ 56 Rick Rhoden	.20	.09
☐ 57 John Dopson	.20	.09
☐ 58 Casey Candaele UER (No stats for Astros for '88 season)	.20	.09
☐ 59 Dave Righetti	.20	.09
☐ 60 Joe Hesketh	.20	.09
☐ 61 Frank DiPino	.20	.09
☐ 62 Tim Laudner	.20	.09
☐ 63 Jamie Moyer	.20	.09
☐ 64 Fred Toliver	.20	.09
☐ 65 Mitch Webster	.20	.09
☐ 66 John Tudor	.20	.09
☐ 67 John Cangelosi	.20	.09
☐ 68 Mike Devereaux	.20	.09
☐ 69 Brian Fisher	.20	.09
☐ 70 Mike Marshall	.20	.09
☐ 71 Zane Smith	.20	.09
☐ 72A Brian Holton ERR (Photo actually Shawn Hillegas)	1.00	.45
☐ 72B Brian Holton COR	.40	.18
☐ 73 Jose Guzman	.20	.09
☐ 74 Rick Mahler	.20	.09
☐ 75 John Shelby	.20	.09
☐ 76 Jim Deshaies	.20	.09
☐ 77 Bobby Meacham	.20	.09
☐ 78 Bryn Smith	.20	.09
☐ 79 Joaquin Andujar	.20	.09
☐ 80 Richard Dotson	.20	.09
☐ 81 Charlie Lea	.20	.09
☐ 82 Calvin Schiraldi	.20	.09
☐ 83 Les Straker	.20	.09
☐ 84 Les Lancaster	.20	.09
☐ 85 Allan Anderson	.20	.09
☐ 86 Junior Ortiz	.20	.09
☐ 87 Jesse Orosco	.20	.09
☐ 88 Felix Fermin	.20	.09
☐ 89 Dave Anderson	.20	.09
☐ 90 Rafael Belliard UER (Born '61, not '51)	.20	.09
☐ 91 Franklin Stubbs	.20	.09
☐ 92 Cecil Espy	.20	.09
☐ 93 Albert Hall	.20	.09
☐ 94 Tim Leary	.20	.09
☐ 95 Mitch Williams	.20	.09
☐ 96 Tracy Jones	.20	.09
☐ 97 Danny Darwin	.20	.09
☐ 98 Gary Ward	.20	.09
☐ 99 Neal Heaton	.20	.09
☐ 100 Jim Pankovits	.20	.09
☐ 101 Bill Doran	.20	.09
☐ 102 Tim Wallach	.20	.09
☐ 103 Joe Magrane	.20	.09
☐ 104 Ozzie Virgil	.20	.09
☐ 105 Alvin Davis	.20	.09
☐ 106 Tom Brookens	.20	.09
☐ 107 Shawon Dunston	.20	.09
☐ 108 Tracy Woodson	.20	.09
☐ 109 Nelson Liriano	.20	.09
☐ 110 Devon White UER (Doubles total 46, should be 56)	.20	.09
☐ 111 Steve Balboni	.20	.09
☐ 112 Buddy Bell	.40	.18
☐ 113 German Jimenez	.20	.09
☐ 114 Ken Dayley	.20	.09
☐ 115 Andres Galarraga	.75	.35
☐ 116 Mike Scioscia	.20	.09
☐ 117 Gary Pettis	.20	.09
☐ 118 Ernie Whitt	.20	.09
☐ 119 Bob Boone	.40	.18
☐ 120 Ryne Sandberg	1.00	.45
☐ 121 Bruce Benedict	.20	.09
☐ 122 Hubie Brooks	.20	.09
☐ 123 Mike Moore	.20	.09
☐ 124 Wallace Johnson	.20	.09
☐ 125 Bob Horner	.20	.09
☐ 126 Chili Davis	.50	.23
☐ 127 Manny Trillo	.20	.09
☐ 128 Chet Lemon	.20	.09
☐ 129 John Cerutti	.20	.09
☐ 130 Orel Hershiser	.40	.18
☐ 131 Terry Pendleton	.20	.09
☐ 132 Jeff Blauser	.40	.18
☐ 133 Mike Fitzgerald	.20	.09
☐ 134 Henry Cotto	.20	.09
☐ 135 Gerald Young	.20	.09
☐ 136 Luis Salazar	.20	.09
☐ 137 Alejandro Pena	.20	.09
☐ 138 Jack Howell	.20	.09
☐ 139 Tony Fernandez	.20	.09
☐ 140 Mark Grace	.75	.35
☐ 141 Ken Caminiti	1.00	.45
☐ 142 Mike Jackson	.20	.09
☐ 143 Larry McWilliams	.20	.09
☐ 144 Andres Thomas	.20	.09
☐ 145 Nolan Ryan 3X	3.00	1.35
☐ 146 Mike Davis	.20	.09
☐ 147 DeWayne Buice	.20	.09
☐ 148 Jody Davis	.20	.09
☐ 149 Jesse Barfield	.20	.09
☐ 150 Matt Nokes	.20	.09
☐ 151 Jerry Reuss	.20	.09
☐ 152 Rick Cerone	.20	.09
☐ 153 Storm Davis	.20	.09
☐ 154 Marvell Wynne	.20	.09
☐ 155 Will Clark	.75	.35
☐ 156 Luis Aguayo	.20	.09
☐ 157 Willie Upshaw	.20	.09
☐ 158 Randy Bush	.20	.09
☐ 159 Ron Darling	.20	.09
☐ 160 Kal Daniels	.20	.09
☐ 161 Spike Owen	.20	.09
☐ 162 Luis Polonia	.20	.09
☐ 163 Kevin Mitchell UER ('88/total HR's 18/52, should be 19/53)	.40	.18
☐ 164 Dave Gallagher	.20	.09
☐ 165 Benito Santiago	.20	.09
☐ 166 Greg Gagne	.20	.09
☐ 167 Ken Phelps	.20	.09
☐ 168 Sid Fernandez	.20	.09
☐ 169 Bo Diaz	.20	.09
☐ 170 Cory Snyder	.20	.09
☐ 171 Eric Show	.20	.09
☐ 172 Robby Thompson	.20	.09
☐ 173 Marty Barrett	.20	.09
☐ 174 Dave Henderson	.20	.09
☐ 175 Ozzie Guillen	.20	.09
☐ 176 Barry Lyons	.20	.09
☐ 177 Kelvin Torve	.20	.09
☐ 178 Don Slaught	.20	.09
☐ 179 Steve Lombardozzi	.20	.09
☐ 180 Chris Sabo	.20	.09
☐ 181 Jose Uribe	.20	.09
☐ 182 Shane Mack	.20	.09
☐ 183 Ron Karkovice	.20	.09
☐ 184 Todd Benzinger	.20	.09
☐ 185 Dave Stewart	.40	.18
☐ 186 Julio Franco	.40	.18
☐ 187 Ron Robinson	.20	.09
☐ 188 Wally Backman	.20	.09
☐ 189 Randy Velarde	.20	.09
☐ 190 Joe Carter	.75	.35
☐ 191 Bob Welch	.20	.09
☐ 192 Kelly Paris	.20	.09
☐ 193 Chris Brown	.20	.09
☐ 194 Rick Reuschel	.20	.09
☐ 195 Roger Clemens	1.50	.70
☐ 196 Dave Concepcion	.40	.18
☐ 197 Al Newman	.20	.09
☐ 198 Brook Jacoby	.20	.09
☐ 199 Mookie Wilson	.40	.18
☐ 200 Don Mattingly	1.25	.55
☐ 201 Dick Schofield	.20	.09
☐ 202 Mark Gubicza	.20	.09
☐ 203 Gary Gaetti	.20	.09
☐ 204 Dan Pasqua	.20	.09
☐ 205 Andre Dawson	.75	.35
☐ 206 Chris Speier	.20	.09
☐ 207 Kent Tekulve	.20	.09
☐ 208 Rod Scurry	.20	.09
☐ 209 Scott Bailes	.20	.09
☐ 210 Rickey Henderson UER (Throws Right)	.75	.35
☐ 211 Harold Baines	.50	.23
☐ 212 Tony Armas	.20	.09
☐ 213 Kent Hrbek	.40	.18
☐ 214 Darrin Jackson	.20	.09
☐ 215 George Brett	1.50	.70
☐ 216 Rafael Santana	.20	.09
☐ 217 Andy Allanson	.20	.09
☐ 218 Brett Butler	.50	.23
☐ 219 Steve Jeltz	.20	.09
☐ 220 Jay Buhner	1.00	.45
☐ 221 Bo Jackson	.75	.35
☐ 222 Angel Salazar	.20	.09
☐ 223 Kirk McCaskill	.20	.09
☐ 224 Steve Lyons	.20	.09
☐ 225 Bert Blyleven	.40	.18
☐ 226 Scott Bradley	.20	.09
☐ 227 Bob Melvin	.20	.09
☐ 228 Ron Kittle	.20	.09
☐ 229 Phil Bradley	.20	.09
☐ 230 Tommy John	.50	.23
☐ 231 Greg Walker	.20	.09
☐ 232 Juan Berenguer	.20	.09
☐ 233 Pat Tabler	.20	.09
☐ 234 Terry Clark	.20	.09
☐ 235 Rafael Palmeiro	.75	.35
☐ 236 Paul Zuvella	.20	.09
☐ 237 Willie Randolph	.40	.18
☐ 238 Bruce Fields	.20	.09
☐ 239 Mike Aldrete	.20	.09
☐ 240 Lance Parrish	.20	.09
☐ 241 Greg Maddux	4.00	1.80
☐ 242 John Moses	.20	.09
☐ 243 Melido Perez	.20	.09
☐ 244 Willie Wilson	.20	.09
☐ 245 Mark McLemore	.20	.09
☐ 246 Von Hayes	.20	.09
☐ 247 Matt Williams	1.00	.45
☐ 248 John Candelaria UER (Listed as Yankee for part of '87, should be Mets)	.20	.09
☐ 249 Harold Reynolds	.20	.09
☐ 250 Greg Swindell	.20	.09
☐ 251 Juan Agosto	.20	.09
☐ 252 Mike Felder	.20	.09
☐ 253 Vince Coleman	.20	.09
☐ 254 Larry Sheets	.20	.09
☐ 255 George Bell	.20	.09
☐ 256 Terry Steinbach	.40	.18
☐ 257 Jack Armstrong	.20	.09
☐ 258 Dickie Thon	.20	.09
☐ 259 Ray Knight	.20	.09
☐ 260 Darryl Strawberry	.40	.18
☐ 261 Doug Sisk	.20	.09
☐ 262 Alex Trevino	.20	.09
☐ 263 Jeffrey Leonard	.20	.09
☐ 264 Tom Henke	.20	.09
☐ 265 Ozzie Smith	1.00	.45
☐ 266 Dave Bergman	.20	.09
☐ 267 Tony Phillips	.20	.09
☐ 268 Mark Davis	.20	.09
☐ 269 Kevin Elster	.20	.09
☐ 270 Barry Larkin	.75	.35
☐ 271 Manny Lee	.20	.09
☐ 272 Tom Brunansky	.20	.09
☐ 273 Craig Biggio	2.50	1.10
☐ 274 Jim Gantner	.20	.09

☐ 275 Eddie Murray .75 .35
☐ 276 Jeff Reed .20 .09
☐ 277 Tim Teufel .20 .09
☐ 278 Rick Honeycutt .20 .09
☐ 279 Guillermo Hernandez .20 .09
☐ 280 John Kruk .40 .18
☐ 281 Luis Alicea .20 .09
☐ 282 Jim Clancy .20 .09
☐ 283 Billy Ripken .20 .09
☐ 284 Craig Reynolds .20 .09
☐ 285 Robin Yount .75 .35
☐ 286 Jimmy Jones .20 .09
☐ 287 Ron Oester .20 .09
☐ 288 Terry Leach .20 .09
☐ 289 Dennis Eckersley .75 .35
☐ 290 Alan Trammell .50 .23
☐ 291 Jimmy Key .50 .23
☐ 292 Chris Bosio .20 .09
☐ 293 Jose DeLeon .20 .09
☐ 294 Jim Traber .20 .09
☐ 295 Mike Scott .20 .09
☐ 296 Roger McDowell .20 .09
☐ 297 Garry Templeton .20 .09
☐ 298 Doyle Alexander .20 .09
☐ 299 Nick Esasky .20 .09
☐ 300 Mark McGwire UER 1.50 .70
(Doubles total 52,
should be 51)
☐ 301 Darryl Hamilton .20 .09
☐ 302 Dave Smith .20 .09
☐ 303 Rick Sutcliffe .20 .09
☐ 304 Dave Stapleton .20 .09
☐ 305 Alan Ashby .20 .09
☐ 306 Pedro Guerrero .40 .18
☐ 307 Ron Guidry .20 .09
☐ 308 Steve Farr .20 .09
☐ 309 Curt Ford .20 .09
☐ 310 Claudell Washington .20 .09
☐ 311 Tom Prince .20 .09
☐ 312 Chad Kreuter .20 .09
☐ 313 Ken Oberkfell .20 .09
☐ 314 Jerry Browne .20 .09
☐ 315 R.J. Reynolds .20 .09
☐ 316 Scott Bankhead .20 .09
☐ 317 Milt Thompson .20 .09
☐ 318 Mario Diaz .20 .09
☐ 319 Bruce Ruffin .20 .09
☐ 320 Dave Valle .20 .09
☐ 321A Gary Varsho ERR 2.00 .90
(Back photo actually
Mike Bielecki bunting)
☐ 321B Gary Varsho COR .20 .09
(In road uniform)
☐ 322 Paul Mirabella .20 .09
☐ 323 Chuck Jackson .20 .09
☐ 324 Drew Hall .20 .09
☐ 325 Don August .20 .09
☐ 326 Israel Sanchez .20 .09
☐ 327 Denny Walling .20 .09
☐ 328 Joel Skinner .20 .09
☐ 329 Danny Tartabull .20 .09
☐ 330 Tony Pena .20 .09
☐ 331 Jim Sundberg .20 .09
☐ 332 Jeff D. Robinson .20 .09
☐ 333 Oddibe McDowell .20 .09
☐ 334 Jose Lind .20 .09
☐ 335 Paul Kilgus .20 .09
☐ 336 Juan Samuel .20 .09
☐ 337 Mike Campbell .20 .09
☐ 338 Mike Maddux .20 .09
☐ 339 Darnell Coles .20 .09
☐ 340 Bob Dernier .20 .09
☐ 341 Rafael Ramirez .20 .09
☐ 342 Scott Sanderson .20 .09
☐ 343 B.J. Surhoff .75 .35
☐ 344 Billy Hatcher .20 .09
☐ 345 Pat Perry .20 .09
☐ 346 Jack Clark .40 .18
☐ 347 Gary Thurman .20 .09
☐ 348 Tim Jones .20 .09
☐ 349 Dave Winfield .75 .35
☐ 350 Frank White .40 .18
☐ 351 Dave Collins .20 .09
☐ 352 Jack Morris .40 .18
☐ 353 Eric Plunk .20 .09
☐ 354 Leon Durham .20 .09
☐ 355 Ivan DeJesus .20 .09
☐ 356 Brian Holman .20 .09
☐ 357A Dale Murphy ERR 15.00 6.75
(Front has
reverse negative)
☐ 357B Dale Murphy COR .75 .35
☐ 358 Mark Portugal .20 .09
☐ 359 Andy McGaffigan .20 .09
☐ 360 Tom Glavine 1.00 .45
☐ 361 Keith Moreland .20 .09
☐ 362 Todd Stottlemyre .40 .18
☐ 363 Dave Leiper .20 .09
☐ 364 Cecil Fielder .50 .23
☐ 365 Carmelo Martinez .20 .09
☐ 366 Dwight Evans .40 .18
☐ 367 Kevin McReynolds .20 .09
☐ 368 Rich Gedman .20 .09
☐ 369 Len Dykstra .40 .18
☐ 370 Jody Reed .20 .09
☐ 371 Jose Canseco UER .75 .35
(Strikeout total 391,
should be 491)
☐ 372 Rob Murphy .20 .09
☐ 373 Mike Henneman .20 .09
☐ 374 Walt Weiss .20 .09
☐ 375 Rob Dibble .40 .18
☐ 376 Kirby Puckett 1.50 .70
(Mark McGwire
in background)
☐ 377 Dennis Martinez .40 .18
☐ 378 Ron Gant .40 .18
☐ 379 Brian Harper .20 .09
☐ 380 Nelson Santovenia .20 .09
☐ 381 Lloyd Moseby .20 .09
☐ 382 Lance McCullers .20 .09
☐ 383 Dave Stieb .20 .09
☐ 384 Tony Gwynn 2.00 .90
☐ 385 Mike Flanagan .20 .09
☐ 386 Bob Ojeda .20 .09
☐ 387 Bruce Hurst .20 .09
☐ 388 Dave Magadan .20 .09
☐ 389 Wade Boggs .75 .35
☐ 390 Gary Carter .75 .35
☐ 391 Frank Tanana .20 .09
☐ 392 Curt Young .20 .09
☐ 393 Jeff Treadway .20 .09
☐ 394 Darrell Evans .40 .18
☐ 395 Glenn Hubbard .20 .09
☐ 396 Chuck Cary .20 .09
☐ 397 Frank Viola .20 .09
☐ 398 Jeff Parrett .20 .09
☐ 399 Terry Blocker .20 .09
☐ 400 Dan Gladden .20 .09
☐ 401 Louie Meadows .20 .09
☐ 402 Tim Raines .40 .18
☐ 403 Joey Meyer .20 .09
☐ 404 Larry Andersen .20 .09
☐ 405 Rex Hudler .20 .09
☐ 406 Mike Schmidt 1.00 .45
☐ 407 John Franco .40 .18
☐ 408 Brady Anderson 2.50 1.10
☐ 409 Don Carman .20 .09
☐ 410 Eric Davis .40 .18
☐ 411 Bob Stanley .20 .09
☐ 412 Pete Smith .20 .09
☐ 413 Jim Rice .50 .23
☐ 414 Bruce Sutter .20 .09
☐ 415 Oil Can Boyd .20 .09
☐ 416 Ruben Sierra .20 .09
☐ 417 Mike LaValliere .20 .09
☐ 418 Steve Buechele .20 .09
☐ 419 Gary Redus .20 .09
☐ 420 Scott Fletcher .20 .09
☐ 421 Dale Sveum .20 .09
☐ 422 Bob Knepper .20 .09
☐ 423 Luis Rivera .20 .09
☐ 424 Ted Higuera .20 .09
☐ 425 Kevin Bass .20 .09
☐ 426 Ken Gerhart .20 .09
☐ 427 Shane Rawley .20 .09
☐ 428 Paul O'Neill .40 .18
☐ 429 Joe Orsulak .20 .09
☐ 430 Jackie Gutierrez .20 .09
☐ 431 Gerald Perry .20 .09
☐ 432 Mike Greenwell .20 .09
☐ 433 Jerry Royster .20 .09
☐ 434 Ellis Burks .50 .23
☐ 435 Ed Olwine .20 .09
☐ 436 Dave Rucker .20 .09
☐ 437 Charlie Hough .40 .18
☐ 438 Bob Walk .20 .09
☐ 439 Bob Brower .20 .09
☐ 440 Barry Bonds 1.50 .70
☐ 441 Tom Foley .20 .09
☐ 442 Rob Deer .20 .09
☐ 443 Glenn Davis .20 .09
☐ 444 Dave Martinez .20 .09
☐ 445 Bill Wegman .20 .09
☐ 446 Lloyd McClendon .20 .09
☐ 447 Dave Schmidt .20 .09
☐ 448 Darren Daulton .40 .18
☐ 449 Frank Williams .20 .09
☐ 450 Don Aase .20 .09
☐ 451 Lou Whitaker .40 .18
☐ 452 Goose Gossage .50 .23
☐ 453 Ed Whitson .20 .09
☐ 454 Jim Walewander .20 .09
☐ 455 Damon Berryhill .20 .09
☐ 456 Tim Burke .20 .09
☐ 457 Barry Jones .20 .09
☐ 458 Joel Youngblood .20 .09
☐ 459 Floyd Youmans .20 .09
☐ 460 Mark Salas .20 .09
☐ 461 Jeff Russell .20 .09
☐ 462 Darrell Miller .20 .09
☐ 463 Jeff Kunkel .20 .09
☐ 464 Sherman Corbett .20 .09
☐ 465 Curtis Wilkerson .20 .09
☐ 466 Bud Black .20 .09
☐ 467 Cal Ripken 3.00 1.35
☐ 468 John Farrell .20 .09
☐ 469 Terry Kennedy .20 .09
☐ 470 Tom Candiotti .20 .09
☐ 471 Roberto Alomar 1.25 .55
☐ 472 Jeff M. Robinson .20 .09
☐ 473 Vance Law .20 .09
☐ 474 Randy Ready UER .20 .09
(Strikeout total 136,
should be 115)
☐ 475 Walt Terrell .20 .09
☐ 476 Kelly Downs .20 .09
☐ 477 Johnny Paredes .20 .09
☐ 478 Shawn Hillegas .20 .09
☐ 479 Bob Brenly .20 .09
☐ 480 Otis Nixon .20 .09
☐ 481 Johnny Ray .20 .09
☐ 482 Geno Petralli .20 .09
☐ 483 Stu Cliburn .20 .09
☐ 484 Pete Incaviglia .20 .09
☐ 485 Brian Downing .20 .09
☐ 486 Jeff Stone .20 .09
☐ 487 Carmen Castillo .20 .09
☐ 488 Tom Niedenfuer .20 .09
☐ 489 Jay Bell .40 .18
☐ 490 Rick Schu .20 .09
☐ 491 Jeff Pico .20 .09
☐ 492 Mark Parent .20 .09
☐ 493 Eric King .20 .09
☐ 494 Al Nipper .20 .09
☐ 495 Andy Hawkins .20 .09
☐ 496 Daryl Boston .20 .09
☐ 497 Ernie Riles .20 .09
☐ 498 Pascual Perez .20 .09
☐ 499 Bill Long UER .20 .09
(Games started total
70, should be 44)
☐ 500 Kirt Manwaring .20 .09
☐ 501 Chuck Crim .20 .09
☐ 502 Candy Maldonado .20 .09
☐ 503 Dennis Lamp .20 .09
☐ 504 Glenn Braggs .20 .09
☐ 505 Joe Price .20 .09
☐ 506 Ken Williams .20 .09
☐ 507 Bill Pecota .20 .09
☐ 508 Rey Quinones .20 .09
☐ 509 Jeff Bittiger .20 .09
☐ 510 Kevin Seitzer .20 .09
☐ 511 Steve Bedrosian .20 .09
☐ 512 Todd Worrell .40 .18
☐ 513 Chris James .20 .09
☐ 514 Jose Oquendo .20 .09
☐ 515 David Palmer .20 .09
☐ 516 John Smiley .20 .09
☐ 517 Dave Clark .20 .09
☐ 518 Mike Dunne .20 .09
☐ 519 Ron Washington .20 .09
☐ 520 Bob Kipper .20 .09
☐ 521 Lee Smith .50 .23
☐ 522 Juan Castillo .20 .09
☐ 523 Don Robinson .20 .09
☐ 524 Kevin Romine .20 .09
☐ 525 Paul Molitor .75 .35
☐ 526 Mark Langston .20 .09
☐ 527 Donnie Hill .20 .09
☐ 528 Larry Owen .20 .09
☐ 529 Jerry Reed .20 .09
☐ 530 Jack McDowell .20 .09
☐ 531 Greg Mathews .20 .09
☐ 532 John Russell .20 .09
☐ 533 Dan Quisenberry .20 .09
☐ 534 Greg Gross .20 .09
☐ 535 Danny Cox .20 .09
☐ 536 Terry Francona .20 .09
☐ 537 Andy Van Slyke .40 .18
☐ 538 Mel Hall .20 .09
☐ 539 Jim Gott .20 .09
☐ 540 Doug Jones .20 .09
☐ 541 Craig Lefferts .20 .09
☐ 542 Mike Boddicker .20 .09
☐ 543 Greg Brock .20 .09
☐ 544 Atlee Hammaker .20 .09
☐ 545 Tom Bolton .20 .09
☐ 546 Mike Macfarlane .40 .18
☐ 547 Rich Renteria .20 .09
☐ 548 John Davis .20 .09

☐ 549 Floyd Bannister	.20	.09
☐ 550 Mickey Brantley	.20	.09
☐ 551 Duane Ward	.20	.09
☐ 552 Dan Petry	.20	.09
☐ 553 Mickey Tettleton UER	.40	.18
(Walks total 175,		
should be 136)		
☐ 554 Rick Leach	.20	.09
☐ 555 Mike Witt	.20	.09
☐ 556 Sid Bream	.20	.09
☐ 557 Bobby Witt	.20	.09
☐ 558 Tommy Herr	.20	.09
☐ 559 Randy Milligan	.20	.09
☐ 560 Jose Cecena	.20	.09
☐ 561 Mackey Sasser	.20	.09
☐ 562 Carney Lansford	.40	.18
☐ 563 Rick Aguilera	.40	.18
☐ 564 Ron Hassey	.20	.09
☐ 565 Dwight Gooden	.40	.18
☐ 566 Paul Assenmacher	.20	.09
☐ 567 Neil Allen	.20	.09
☐ 568 Jim Morrison	.20	.09
☐ 569 Mike Pagliarulo	.20	.09
☐ 570 Ted Simmons	.40	.18
☐ 571 Mark Thurmond	.20	.09
☐ 572 Fred McGriff	.75	.35
☐ 573 Wally Joyner	.40	.18
☐ 574 Jose Bautista	.20	.09
☐ 575 Kelly Gruber	.20	.09
☐ 576 Cecilio Guante	.20	.09
☐ 577 Mark Davidson	.20	.09
☐ 578 Bobby Bonilla UER	.75	.35
(Total steals 2 in '87,		
should be 3)		
☐ 579 Mike Stanley	.20	.09
☐ 580 Gene Larkin	.20	.09
☐ 581 Stan Javier	.20	.09
☐ 582 Howard Johnson	.20	.09
☐ 583A Mike Gallego ERR	1.00	.45
(Front reversed		
negative)		
☐ 583B Mike Gallego COR	.75	.35
☐ 584 David Cone	.75	.35
☐ 585 Doug Jennings	.20	.09
☐ 586 Charles Hudson	.20	.09
☐ 587 Dion James	.20	.09
☐ 588 Al Leiter	.75	.35
☐ 589 Charlie Puleo	.20	.09
☐ 590 Roberto Kelly	.20	.09
☐ 591 Thad Bosley	.20	.09
☐ 592 Pete Stanicek	.20	.09
☐ 593 Pat Borders	.40	.18
☐ 594 Bryan Harvey	.40	.18
☐ 595 Jeff Ballard	.20	.09
☐ 596 Jeff Reardon	.40	.18
☐ 597 Doug Drabek	.20	.09
☐ 598 Edwin Correa	.20	.09
☐ 599 Keith Atherton	.20	.09
☐ 600 Dave LaPoint	.20	.09
☐ 601 Don Baylor	.50	.23
☐ 602 Tom Pagnozzi	.20	.09
☐ 603 Tim Flannery	.20	.09
☐ 604 Gene Walter	.20	.09
☐ 605 Dave Parker	.40	.18
☐ 606 Mike Diaz	.20	.09
☐ 607 Chris Gwynn	.20	.09
☐ 608 Odell Jones	.20	.09
☐ 609 Carlton Fisk	.75	.35
☐ 610 Jay Howell	.20	.09
☐ 611 Tim Crews	.20	.09
☐ 612 Keith Hernandez	.40	.18
☐ 613 Willie Fraser	.20	.09
☐ 614 Jim Eppard	.20	.09
☐ 615 Jeff Hamilton	.20	.09
☐ 616 Kurt Stillwell	.20	.09
☐ 617 Tom Browning	.20	.09
☐ 618 Jeff Montgomery	.40	.18
☐ 619 Jose Rijo	.20	.09
☐ 620 Jamie Quirk	.20	.09
☐ 621 Willie McGee	.20	.09
☐ 622 Mark Grant UER	.20	.09
(Glove on wrong hand)		
☐ 623 Bill Swift	.20	.09
☐ 624 Orlando Mercado	.20	.09
☐ 625 John Costello	.20	.09
☐ 626 Jose Gonzalez	.20	.09
☐ 627A Bill Schroeder ERR	1.00	.45
(Back photo actually		
Ronn Reynolds buckling		
shin guards)		
☐ 627B Bill Schroeder COR	.75	.35
☐ 628A Fred Manrique ERR	.75	.35
(Back photo actually		
Ozzie Guillen throwing)		
☐ 628B Fred Manrique COR	.20	.09
(Swinging bat on back)		
☐ 629 Ricky Horton	.20	.09
☐ 630 Dan Plesac	.20	.09
☐ 631 Alfredo Griffin	.20	.09
☐ 632 Chuck Finley	.40	.18
☐ 633 Kirk Gibson	.50	.23
☐ 634 Randy Myers	.40	.18
☐ 635 Greg Minton	.20	.09
☐ 636A Herm Winningham	.75	.35
ERR (W1nningham		
on back)		
☐ 636B Herm Winningham COR	.20	.09
☐ 637 Charlie Leibrandt	.20	.09
☐ 638 Tim Birtsas	.20	.09
☐ 639 Bill Buckner	.40	.18
☐ 640 Danny Jackson	.20	.09
☐ 641 Greg Booker	.20	.09
☐ 642 Jim Presley	.20	.09
☐ 643 Gene Nelson	.20	.09
☐ 644 Rod Booker	.20	.09
☐ 645 Dennis Rasmussen	.20	.09
☐ 646 Juan Nieves	.20	.09
☐ 647 Bobby Thigpen	.20	.09
☐ 648 Tim Belcher	.20	.09
☐ 649 Mike Young	.20	.09
☐ 650 Ivan Calderon	.20	.09
☐ 651 Oswaldo Peraza	.20	.09
☐ 652A Pat Sheridan ERR	5.00	2.20
(No position on front)		
☐ 652B Pat Sheridan COR	.20	.09
☐ 653 Mike Morgan	.20	.09
☐ 654 Mike Heath	.20	.09
☐ 655 Jay Tibbs	.20	.09
☐ 656 Fernando Valenzuela	.40	.18
☐ 657 Lee Mazzilli	.20	.09
☐ 658 Frank Viola AL CY	.20	.09
☐ 659A Jose Canseco AL MVP	.75	.35
(Eagle logo in black)		
☐ 659B Jose Canseco AL MVP	.75	.35
(Eagle logo in blue)		
☐ 660 Walt Weiss AL ROY	.20	.09
☐ 661 Orel Hershiser NL CY	.40	.18
☐ 662 Kirk Gibson NL MVP	.50	.23
☐ 663 Chris Sabo NL ROY	.20	.09
☐ 664 Dennis Eckersley	.40	.18
ALCS MVP		
☐ 665 Orel Hershiser	.40	.18
NLCS MVP		
☐ 666 Kirk Gibson WS	.75	.35
☐ 667 Orel Hershiser WS MVP	.40	.18
☐ 668 Wally Joyner TC	.40	.18
☐ 669 Nolan Ryan TC	1.00	.45
☐ 670 Jose Canseco TC	.75	.35
☐ 671 Fred McGriff TC	.75	.35
☐ 672 Dale Murphy TC	.75	.35
☐ 673 Paul Molitor TC	.75	.35
☐ 674 Ozzie Smith TC	.75	.35
☐ 675 Ryne Sandberg TC	.75	.35
☐ 676 Kirk Gibson TC	.75	.35
☐ 677 Andres Galarraga TC	.75	.35
☐ 678 Will Clark TC	.75	.35
☐ 679 Cory Snyder TC	.20	.09
☐ 680 Alvin Davis TC	.20	.09
☐ 681 Darryl Strawberry TC	.40	.18
☐ 682 Cal Ripken TC	1.00	.45
☐ 683 Tony Gwynn TC	.75	.35
☐ 684 Mike Schmidt TC	.75	.35
☐ 685 Andy Van Slyke TC UER	.40	.18
(96 Junior Ortiz)		
☐ 686 Ruben Sierra TC	.20	.09
☐ 687 Wade Boggs TC	.75	.35
☐ 688 Eric Davis TC	.40	.18
☐ 689 George Brett TC	.75	.35
☐ 690 Alan Trammell TC	.40	.18
☐ 691 Frank Viola TC	.20	.09
☐ 692 Harold Baines TC	.40	.18
☐ 693 Don Mattingly TC	.75	.35
☐ 694 Checklist 1-100	.20	.09
☐ 695 Checklist 101-200	.20	.09
☐ 696 Checklist 201-300	.20	.09
☐ 697 Checklist 301-400	.20	.09
☐ 698 Checklist 401-500 UER	.20	.09
(467 Cal Ripkin Jr.)		
☐ 699 Checklist 501-600 UER	.20	.09
(543 Greg Booker)		
☐ 700 Checklist 601-700	.20	.09
☐ 701 Checklist 701-800	.20	.09
☐ 702 Jesse Barfield	.20	.09
☐ 703 Walt Terrell	.20	.09
☐ 704 Dickie Thon	.20	.09
☐ 705 Al Leiter	.75	.35
☐ 706 Dave LaPoint	.20	.09
☐ 707 Charlie Hayes	.75	.35
☐ 708 Andy Hawkins	.20	.09
☐ 709 Mickey Hatcher	.20	.09
☐ 710 Lance McCullers	.20	.09
☐ 711 Ron Kittle	.20	.09
☐ 712 Bert Blyleven	.40	.18
☐ 713 Rick Dempsey	.20	.09
☐ 714 Ken Williams	.20	.09
☐ 715 Steve Rosenberg	.20	.09
☐ 716 Joe Skalski	.20	.09
☐ 717 Spike Owen	.20	.09
☐ 718 Todd Burns	.20	.09
☐ 719 Kevin Gross	.20	.09
☐ 720 Tommy Herr	.20	.09
☐ 721 Rob Ducey	.20	.09
☐ 722 Gary Green	.20	.09
☐ 723 Gregg Olson	.75	.35
☐ 724 Greg W. Harris	.20	.09
☐ 725 Craig Worthington	.20	.09
☐ 726 Tom Howard	.20	.09
☐ 727 Dale Mohorcic	.20	.09
☐ 728 Rich Yett	.20	.09
☐ 729 Mel Hall	.20	.09
☐ 730 Floyd Youmans	.20	.09
☐ 731 Lonnie Smith	.20	.09
☐ 732 Wally Backman	.20	.09
☐ 733 Trevor Wilson	.20	.09
☐ 734 Jose Alvarez	.20	.09
☐ 735 Bob Milacki	.20	.09
☐ 736 Tom Gordon	.75	.35
☐ 737 Wally Whitehurst	.20	.09
☐ 738 Mike Aldrete	.20	.09
☐ 739 Keith Miller	.20	.09
☐ 740 Randy Milligan	.20	.09
☐ 741 Jeff Parrett	.20	.09
☐ 742 Steve Finley	1.00	.45
☐ 743 Junior Felix	.20	.09
☐ 744 Pete Harnisch	.40	.18
☐ 745 Bill Spiers	.20	.09
☐ 746 Hensley Meulens	.20	.09
☐ 747 Juan Bell	.20	.09
☐ 748 Steve Sax	.20	.09
☐ 749 Phil Bradley	.20	.09
☐ 750 Rey Quinones	.20	.09
☐ 751 Tommy Gregg	.20	.09
☐ 752 Kevin Brown	.75	.35
☐ 753 Derek Lilliquist	.20	.09
☐ 754 Todd Zeile	.75	.35
☐ 755 Jim Abbott	.75	.35
(Triple exposure)		
☐ 756 Ozzie Canseco	.20	.09
☐ 757 Nick Esasky	.20	.09
☐ 758 Mike Moore	.20	.09
☐ 759 Rob Murphy	.20	.09
☐ 760 Rick Mahler	.20	.09
☐ 761 Fred Lynn	.20	.09
☐ 762 Kevin Blankenship	.20	.09
☐ 763 Eddie Murray	.75	.35
☐ 764 Steve Searcy	.20	.09
☐ 765 Jerome Walton	.75	.35
☐ 766 Erik Hanson	.40	.18
☐ 767 Bob Boone	.40	.18
☐ 768 Edgar Martinez	.75	.35
☐ 769 Jose DeJesus	.20	.09
☐ 770 Greg Briley	.20	.09
☐ 771 Steve Peters	.20	.09
☐ 772 Rafael Palmeiro	.75	.35
☐ 773 Jack Clark	.40	.18
☐ 774 Nolan Ryan	3.00	1.35
(Throwing football)		
☐ 775 Lance Parrish	.20	.09
☐ 776 Joe Girardi	.75	.35
☐ 777 Willie Randolph	.40	.18
☐ 778 Mitch Williams	.20	.09
☐ 779 Dennis Cook	.20	.09
☐ 780 Dwight Smith	.40	.18
☐ 781 Lenny Harris	.20	.09
☐ 782 Torey Lovullo	.20	.09
☐ 783 Norm Charlton	.40	.18
☐ 784 Chris Brown	.20	.09
☐ 785 Todd Benzinger	.20	.09
☐ 786 Shane Rawley	.20	.09
☐ 787 Omar Vizquel	2.00	.90
☐ 788 LaVel Freeman	.20	.09
☐ 789 Jeffrey Leonard	.20	.09
☐ 790 Eddie Williams	.20	.09
☐ 791 Jamie Moyer	.20	.09
☐ 792 Bruce Hurst UER	.20	.09
(Workd Series)		
☐ 793 Julio Franco	.40	.18
☐ 794 Claudell Washington	.20	.09
☐ 795 Jody Davis	.20	.09
☐ 796 Oddibe McDowell	.20	.09
☐ 797 Paul Kilgus	.20	.09
☐ 798 Tracy Jones	.20	.09
☐ 799 Steve Wilson	.20	.09
☐ 800 Pete O'Brien	.20	.09

1990 Upper Deck

The 1990 Upper Deck set contains 800 standard-size cards issued in two series, low numbers (1-700) and high numbers (701-800). Cards were distributed in fin-

wrapped low and high series foil packs, complete 800-card factory sets and 100-card high series factory sets. High series foil packs contained a mixture of low and high series cards. The front and back borders are white, and both sides feature full-color photos. The horizontally oriented backs have recent stats and anti-counterfeiting holograms. Team checklist cards are mixed in with the first 100 cards of the set. Rookie Cards in the set include Wilson Alvarez, Carlos Baerga, Juan Gonzalez, Marquis Grissom, Todd Hundley, David Justice, Ray Lankford, Ben McDonald, Dean Palmer, Sammy Sosa and Larry Walker. The high series contains a Nolan Ryan variation; all cards produced before August 12th only discuss Ryan's sixth no-hitter while the later-issue cards include a stripe honoring Ryan's 300th victory. Card 702 (Rookie Threats) was originally scheduled to be Mike Witt. A few Witt cards with 702 on back and checklist cards showing Witt as 702 escaped into early packs; they are characterized by a black rectangle covering much of the card's back.

	MINT	NRMT
COMPLETE SET (800)	20.00	9.00
COMPLETE FACT.SET (800)	20.00	9.00
COMPLETE LO SET (700)	16.00	7.25
COMPLETE HI SET (100)	4.00	1.80
COMPLETE HI FACT.SET (100)	4.00	1.80
COMMON CARD (1-800)	.10	.05

Card	MINT	NRMT
☐ 1 Star Rookie Checklist	.10	.05
☐ 2 Randy Nosek	.10	.05
☐ 3 Tom Drees UER	.10	.05
(11th line, hulred, should be hurled)		
☐ 4 Curt Young	.10	.05
☐ 5 Devon White TC	.10	.05
☐ 6 Luis Salazar	.10	.05
☐ 7 Von Hayes TC	.10	.05
☐ 8 Jose Bautista	.10	.05
☐ 9 Marquis Grissom	.75	.35
☐ 10 Orel Hershiser TC	.20	.09
☐ 11 Rick Aguilera	.20	.09
☐ 12 Benito Santiago TC	.10	.05
☐ 13 Deion Sanders	.40	.18
☐ 14 Marvell Wynne	.10	.05
☐ 15 Dave West	.10	.05
☐ 16 Bobby Bonilla TC	.20	.09
☐ 17 Sammy Sosa	1.50	.70
☐ 18 Steve Sax TC	.10	.05
☐ 19 Jack Howell	.10	.05
☐ 20 Mike Schmidt Special UER (Suprising, should be surprising)	.50	.23
☐ 21 Robin Ventura UER	.40	.18
(Samta Maria)		
☐ 22 Brian Meyer	.10	.05
☐ 23 Blaine Beatty	.10	.05
☐ 24 Ken Griffey Jr. TC	1.00	.45
☐ 25 Greg Vaughn UER	.40	.18
(Association misspelled as assiocation)		
☐ 26 Xavier Hernandez	.10	.05
☐ 27 Jason Grimsley	.10	.05
☐ 28 Eric Anthony UER	.20	.09
(Ashville, should be Asheville)		
☐ 29 Tim Raines TC UER	.20	.09
(Wallach listed before Walker)		
☐ 30 David Wells	.10	.05
☐ 31 Hal Morris	.20	.09
☐ 32 Bo Jackson TC	.20	.09
☐ 33 Kelly Mann	.10	.05
☐ 34 Nolan Ryan Special	.75	.35
☐ 35 Scott Service UER	.10	.05
(Born Cincinatti on 7/27/67, should be Cincinnati 2/27)		
☐ 36 Mark McGwire TC	.40	.18
☐ 37 Tino Martinez	.75	.35
☐ 38 Chili Davis	.20	.09
☐ 39 Scott Sanderson	.10	.05
☐ 40 Kevin Mitchell TC	.10	.05
☐ 41 Lou Whitaker TC	.20	.09
☐ 42 Scott Coolbaugh UER	.10	.05
(Definately)		
☐ 43 Jose Cano UER	.10	.05
(Born 9/7/62, should be 3/7/62)		
☐ 44 Jose Vizcaino	.40	.18
☐ 45 Bob Hamelin	.40	.18
☐ 46 Jose Offerman UER	.40	.18
(Posesses)		
☐ 47 Kevin Blankenship	.10	.05
☐ 48 Kirby Puckett TC	.40	.18
☐ 49 Tommy Greene UER	.10	.05
(Livest, should be liveliest)		
☐ 50 Will Clark Special UER (Perenial, should be perennial)	.40	.18
☐ 51 Rob Nelson	.10	.05
☐ 52 Chris Hammond UER	.10	.05
(Chatanooga)		
☐ 53 Joe Carter TC	.20	.09
☐ 54A Ben McDonald ERR	5.00	2.20
(No Rookie designation on card front)		
☐ 54B Ben McDonald COR	.40	.18
☐ 55 Andy Benes UER	.40	.18
(Whichita)		
☐ 56 John Olerud	.40	.18
☐ 57 Roger Clemens TC	.40	.18
☐ 58 Tony Armas	.10	.05
☐ 59 George Canale	.10	.05
☐ 60A Mickey Tettleton TC ERR (683 Jamie Weston)	2.00	.90
☐ 60B Mickey Tettleton TC COR (683 Mickey Weston)	.10	.05
☐ 61 Mike Stanton	.20	.09
☐ 62 Dwight Gooden TC	.20	.09
☐ 63 Kent Mercker UER	.20	.09
(Albuguerque)		
☐ 64 Francisco Cabrera	.10	.05
☐ 65 Steve Avery UER	.30	.14
(Born NJ, should be MI, Merker should be Mercker)		
☐ 66 Jose Canseco	.40	.18
☐ 67 Matt Merullo	.10	.05
☐ 68 Vince Coleman TC UER	.10	.05
(Guererro)		
☐ 69 Ron Karkovice	.10	.05
☐ 70 Kevin Maas	.20	.09
☐ 71 Dennis Cook UER	.10	.05
(Shown with righty glove on card back)		
☐ 72 Juan Gonzalez UER	4.00	1.80
(135 games for Tulsa in '89, should be 133)		
☐ 73 Andre Dawson TC	.40	.18
☐ 74 Dean Palmer UER	.50	.23
(Permanent misspelled as perminant)		
☐ 75 Bo Jackson Special UER (Monsterous, should be monstrous)	.40	.18
☐ 76 Rob Richie	.10	.05
☐ 77 Bobby Rose UER	.10	.05
(Pickin, should be pick in)		
☐ 78 Brian DuBois UER	.10	.05
(Commiting)		
☐ 79 Ozzie Guillen TC	.10	.05
☐ 80 Gene Nelson	.10	.05
☐ 81 Bob McClure	.10	.05
☐ 82 Julio Franco TC	.10	.05
☐ 83 Greg Minton	.10	.05
☐ 84 John Smoltz TC UER	.40	.18
(Oddibe not Odibbe)		
☐ 85 Willie Fraser	.10	.05
☐ 86 Neal Heaton	.10	.05
☐ 87 Kevin Tapani UER	.20	.09
(24th line has excpet, should be except)		
☐ 88 Mike Scott TC	.10	.05
☐ 89A Jim Gott ERR	2.50	1.10
(Photo actually Rick Reed)		
☐ 89B Jim Gott COR	.10	.05
☐ 90 Lance Johnson	.20	.09
☐ 91 Robin Yount TC UER	.40	.18
(Checklist on back has 178 Rob Deer and 176 Mike Felder)		
☐ 92 Jeff Parrett	.10	.05
☐ 93 Julio Machado UER	.10	.05
(Valenzuelan, should be Venezuelan)		
☐ 94 Ron Jones	.10	.05
☐ 95 George Bell TC	.10	.05
☐ 96 Jerry Reuss	.10	.05
☐ 97 Brian Fisher	.10	.05
☐ 98 Kevin Ritz UER	.10	.05
(Amercian)		
☐ 99 Barry Larkin TC	.40	.18
☐ 100 Checklist 1-100	.10	.05
☐ 101 Gerald Perry	.10	.05
☐ 102 Kevin Appier	.40	.18
☐ 103 Julio Franco	.20	.09
☐ 104 Craig Biggio	.40	.18
☐ 105 Bo Jackson UER	.40	.18
('89 BA wrong, should be .256)		
☐ 106 Junior Felix	.10	.05
☐ 107 Mike Harkey	.10	.05
☐ 108 Fred McGriff	.40	.18
☐ 109 Rick Sutcliffe	.10	.05
☐ 110 Pete O'Brien	.10	.05
☐ 111 Kelly Gruber	.10	.05
☐ 112 Dwight Evans	.20	.09
☐ 113 Pat Borders	.10	.05
☐ 114 Dwight Gooden	.20	.09
☐ 115 Kevin Batiste	.10	.05
☐ 116 Eric Davis	.20	.09
☐ 117 Kevin Mitchell UER	.20	.09
(Career HR total 99, should be 100)		
☐ 118 Ron Oester	.10	.05
☐ 119 Brett Butler	.20	.09
☐ 120 Danny Jackson	.10	.05
☐ 121 Tommy Gregg	.10	.05
☐ 122 Ken Caminiti	.40	.18
☐ 123 Kevin Brown	.40	.18
☐ 124 George Brett UER	.75	.35
(133 runs, should be 1300)		
☐ 125 Mike Scott	.10	.05
☐ 126 Cory Snyder	.10	.05
☐ 127 George Bell	.10	.05
☐ 128 Mark Grace	.40	.18
☐ 129 Devon White	.10	.05
☐ 130 Tony Fernandez	.10	.05
☐ 131 Don Aase	.10	.05
☐ 132 Rance Mulliniks	.10	.05
☐ 133 Marty Barrett	.10	.05
☐ 134 Nelson Liriano	.10	.05
☐ 135 Mark Carreon	.10	.05
☐ 136 Candy Maldonado	.10	.05
☐ 137 Tim Birtsas	.10	.05
☐ 138 Tom Brookens	.10	.05
☐ 139 John Franco	.10	.05
☐ 140 Mike LaCoss	.10	.05
☐ 141 Jeff Treadway	.10	.05
☐ 142 Pat Tabler	.10	.05
☐ 143 Darrell Evans	.20	.09
☐ 144 Rafael Ramirez	.10	.05
☐ 145 Oddibe McDowell UER	.10	.05
(Misspelled Odibbe)		
☐ 146 Brian Downing	.10	.05
☐ 147 Curt Wilkerson	.10	.05
☐ 148 Ernie Whitt	.10	.05
☐ 149 Bill Schroeder	.10	.05
☐ 150 Domingo Ramos UER	.10	.05
(Says throws right, but shows him throwing lefty)		
☐ 151 Rick Honeycutt	.10	.05
☐ 152 Don Slaught	.10	.05
☐ 153 Mitch Webster	.10	.05
☐ 154 Tony Phillips	.10	.05
☐ 155 Paul Kilgus	.10	.05
☐ 156 Ken Griffey Jr. UER	4.00	1.80
(Simultaniously)		
☐ 157 Gary Sheffield	.50	.23
☐ 158 Wally Backman	.10	.05
☐ 159 B.J. Surhoff	.20	.09
☐ 160 Louie Meadows	.10	.05
☐ 161 Paul O'Neill	.20	.09
☐ 162 Jeff McKnight	.10	.05
☐ 163 Alvaro Espinoza	.10	.05
☐ 164 Scott Scudder	.10	.05
☐ 165 Jeff Reed	.10	.05
☐ 166 Gregg Jefferies	.20	.09
☐ 167 Barry Larkin	.40	.18
☐ 168 Gary Carter	.30	.14
☐ 169 Robby Thompson	.10	.05
☐ 170 Rolando Roomes	.10	.05
☐ 171 Mark McGwire UER	.75	.35
(Total games 427 and hits 479, should be 467 and 427)		
☐ 172 Steve Sax	.10	.05
☐ 173 Mark Williamson	.10	.05
☐ 174 Mitch Williams	.10	.05
☐ 175 Brian Holton	.10	.05
☐ 176 Rob Deer	.10	.05
☐ 177 Tim Raines	.20	.09
☐ 178 Mike Felder	.10	.05
☐ 179 Harold Reynolds	.10	.05
☐ 180 Terry Francona	.10	.05
☐ 181 Chris Sabo	.10	.05

☐ 182 Darryl Strawberry .20 .09
☐ 183 Willie Randolph .20 .09
☐ 184 Bill Ripken .10 .05
☐ 185 Mackey Sasser .10 .05
☐ 186 Todd Benzinger .10 .05
☐ 187 Kevin Elster UER .10 .05
(16 homers in 1989, should be 10)
☐ 188 Jose Uribe .10 .05
☐ 189 Tom Browning .10 .05
☐ 190 Keith Miller .10 .05
☐ 191 Don Mattingly .60 .25
☐ 192 Dave Parker .20 .09
☐ 193 Roberto Kelly UER .10 .05
(96 RBI, should be 62)
☐ 194 Phil Bradley .10 .05
☐ 195 Ron Hassey .10 .05
☐ 196 Gerald Young .10 .05
☐ 197 Hubie Brooks .10 .05
☐ 198 Bill Doran .10 .05
☐ 199 Al Newman .10 .05
☐ 200 Checklist 101-200 .10 .05
☐ 201 Terry Puhl .10 .05
☐ 202 Frank DiPino .10 .05
☐ 203 Jim Clancy .10 .05
☐ 204 Bob Ojeda .10 .05
☐ 205 Alex Trevino .10 .05
☐ 206 Dave Henderson .10 .05
☐ 207 Henry Cotto .10 .05
☐ 208 Rafael Belliard UER .10 .05
(Born 1961, not 1951)
☐ 209 Stan Javier .10 .05
☐ 210 Jerry Reed .10 .05
☐ 211 Doug Dascenzo .10 .05
☐ 212 Andres Thomas .10 .05
☐ 213 Greg Maddux 1.25 .55
☐ 214 Mike Schooler .10 .05
☐ 215 Lonnie Smith .10 .05
☐ 216 Jose Rijo .10 .05
☐ 217 Greg Gagne .10 .05
☐ 218 Jim Gantner .10 .05
☐ 219 Allan Anderson .10 .05
☐ 220 Rick Mahler .10 .05
☐ 221 Jim Deshaies .10 .05
☐ 222 Keith Hernandez .20 .09
☐ 223 Vince Coleman .10 .05
☐ 224 David Cone .40 .18
☐ 225 Ozzie Smith .50 .23
☐ 226 Matt Nokes .10 .05
☐ 227 Barry Bonds .50 .23
☐ 228 Felix Jose .10 .05
☐ 229 Dennis Powell .10 .05
☐ 230 Mike Gallego .10 .05
☐ 231 Shawon Dunston UER .10 .05
('89 stats are Andre Dawson's)
☐ 232 Ron Gant .20 .09
☐ 233 Omar Vizquel .40 .18
☐ 234 Derek Lilliquist .10 .05
☐ 235 Erik Hanson .20 .09
☐ 236 Kirby Puckett UER .75 .35
(824 games, should be 924)
☐ 237 Bill Spiers .10 .05
☐ 238 Dan Gladden .10 .05
☐ 239 Bryan Clutterbuck .10 .05
☐ 240 John Moses .10 .05
☐ 241 Ron Darling .10 .05
☐ 242 Joe Magrane .10 .05
☐ 243 Dave Magadan .10 .05
☐ 244 Pedro Guerrero UER .10 .05
(Misspelled Guererro)
☐ 245 Glenn Davis .10 .05
☐ 246 Terry Steinbach .20 .09
☐ 247 Fred Lynn .10 .05
☐ 248 Gary Redus .10 .05
☐ 249 Ken Williams .10 .05
☐ 250 Sid Bream .10 .05
☐ 251 Bob Welch UER .10 .05
(2587 career strike-outs, should be 1587)
☐ 252 Bill Buckner .10 .05
☐ 253 Carney Lansford .20 .09
☐ 254 Paul Molitor .40 .18
☐ 255 Jose DeJesus .10 .05
☐ 256 Orel Hershiser .20 .09
☐ 257 Tom Brunansky .10 .05
☐ 258 Mike Davis .10 .05
☐ 259 Jeff Ballard .10 .05
☐ 260 Scott Terry .10 .05
☐ 261 Sid Fernandez .10 .05
☐ 262 Mike Marshall .10 .05
☐ 263 Howard Johnson UER .10 .05
(192 SO, should be 592)
☐ 264 Kirk Gibson UER .20 .09
(659 runs, should be 669)
☐ 265 Kevin McReynolds .10 .05
☐ 266 Cal Ripken 1.50 .70
☐ 267 Ozzie Guillen UER .10 .05
(Career triples 27, should be 29)
☐ 268 Jim Traber .10 .05
☐ 269 Bobby Thigpen UER .10 .05
(31 saves in 1989, should be 34)
☐ 270 Joe Orsulak .10 .05
☐ 271 Bob Boone .20 .09
☐ 272 Dave Stewart UER .20 .09
(Totals wrong due to omission of '86 stats)
☐ 273 Tim Wallach .10 .05
☐ 274 Luis Aquino UER .10 .05
(Says throws lefty, but shows him throwing righty)
☐ 275 Mike Moore .10 .05
☐ 276 Tony Pena .10 .05
☐ 277 Eddie Murray UER .40 .18
(Several typos in career total stats)
☐ 278 Milt Thompson .10 .05
☐ 279 Alejandro Pena .10 .05
☐ 280 Ken Dayley .10 .05
☐ 281 Carmen Castillo .10 .05
☐ 282 Tom Henke .10 .05
☐ 283 Mickey Hatcher .10 .05
☐ 284 Roy Smith .10 .05
☐ 285 Manny Lee .10 .05
☐ 286 Dan Pasqua .10 .05
☐ 287 Larry Sheets .10 .05
☐ 288 Garry Templeton .10 .05
☐ 289 Eddie Williams .10 .05
☐ 290 Brady Anderson UER .40 .18
(Home: Silver Springs, not Siver Springs)
☐ 291 Spike Owen .10 .05
☐ 292 Storm Davis .10 .05
☐ 293 Chris Bosio .10 .05
☐ 294 Jim Eisenreich .20 .09
☐ 295 Don August .10 .05
☐ 296 Jeff Hamilton .10 .05
☐ 297 Mickey Tettleton .20 .09
☐ 298 Mike Scioscia .10 .05
☐ 299 Kevin Hickey .10 .05
☐ 300 Checklist 201-300 .10 .05
☐ 301 Shawn Abner .10 .05
☐ 302 Kevin Bass .10 .05
☐ 303 Bip Roberts .10 .05
☐ 304 Joe Girardi .20 .09
☐ 305 Danny Darwin .10 .05
☐ 306 Mike Heath .10 .05
☐ 307 Mike Macfarlane .10 .05
☐ 308 Ed Whitson .10 .05
☐ 309 Tracy Jones .10 .05
☐ 310 Scott Fletcher .10 .05
☐ 311 Darnell Coles .10 .05
☐ 312 Mike Brumley .10 .05
☐ 313 Bill Swift .10 .05
☐ 314 Charlie Hough .10 .05
☐ 315 Jim Presley .10 .05
☐ 316 Luis Polonia .10 .05
☐ 317 Mike Morgan .10 .05
☐ 318 Lee Guetterman .10 .05
☐ 319 Jose Oquendo .10 .05
☐ 320 Wayne Tolleson .10 .05
☐ 321 Jody Reed .10 .05
☐ 322 Damon Berryhill .10 .05
☐ 323 Roger Clemens .75 .35
☐ 324 Ryne Sandberg .50 .23
☐ 325 Benito Santiago UER .10 .05
(Misspelled Santago on card back)
☐ 326 Bret Saberhagen UER .10 .05
(1140 hits, should be 1240; 56 CG, should be 52)
☐ 327 Lou Whitaker .20 .09
☐ 328 Dave Gallagher .10 .05
☐ 329 Mike Pagliarulo .10 .05
☐ 330 Doyle Alexander .10 .05
☐ 331 Jeffrey Leonard .10 .05
☐ 332 Torey Lovullo .10 .05
☐ 333 Pete Incaviglia .10 .05
☐ 334 Rickey Henderson .40 .18
☐ 335 Rafael Palmeiro .40 .18
☐ 336 Ken Hill .40 .18
☐ 337 Dave Winfield UER .40 .18
(1418 RBI, should be 1438)
☐ 338 Alfredo Griffin .10 .05
☐ 339 Andy Hawkins .10 .05
☐ 340 Ted Power .10 .05
☐ 341 Steve Wilson .10 .05
☐ 342 Jack Clark UER .20 .09
(916 BB, should be 1006; 1142 SO, should be 1130)
☐ 343 Ellis Burks .30 .14
☐ 344 Tony Gwynn UER 1.00 .45
(Doubles stats on card back are wrong)
☐ 345 Jerome Walton UER .10 .05
(Total At Bats 476, should be 475)
☐ 346 Roberto Alomar UER .50 .23
(61 doubles, should be 51)
☐ 347 Carlos Martinez UER .10 .05
(Born 8/11/64, should be 8/11/65)
☐ 348 Chet Lemon .10 .05
☐ 349 Willie Wilson .10 .05
☐ 350 Greg Walker .10 .05
☐ 351 Tom Bolton .10 .05
☐ 352 German Gonzalez .10 .05
☐ 353 Harold Baines .30 .14
☐ 354 Mike Greenwell .10 .05
☐ 355 Ruben Sierra .10 .05
☐ 356 Andres Galarraga .40 .18
☐ 357 Andre Dawson .40 .18
☐ 358 Jeff Brantley .20 .09
☐ 359 Mike Bielecki .10 .05
☐ 360 Ken Oberkfell .10 .05
☐ 361 Kurt Stillwell .10 .05
☐ 362 Brian Holman .10 .05
☐ 363 Kevin Seitzer UER .10 .05
(Career triples total does not add up)
☐ 364 Alvin Davis .10 .05
☐ 365 Tom Gordon .20 .09
☐ 366 Bobby Bonilla UER .20 .09
(Two steals in 1987, should be 3)
☐ 367 Carlton Fisk .40 .18
☐ 368 Steve Carter UER .10 .05
(Charlotesville)
☐ 369 Joel Skinner .10 .05
☐ 370 John Cangelosi .10 .05
☐ 371 Cecil Espy .10 .05
☐ 372 Gary Wayne .10 .05
☐ 373 Jim Rice .40 .18
☐ 374 Mike Dyer .10 .05
☐ 375 Joe Carter .40 .18
☐ 376 Dwight Smith .10 .05
☐ 377 John Wetteland .40 .18
☐ 378 Earnie Riles .10 .05
☐ 379 Otis Nixon .10 .05
☐ 380 Vance Law .10 .05
☐ 381 Dave Bergman .10 .05
☐ 382 Frank White .20 .09
☐ 383 Scott Bradley .10 .05
☐ 384 Israel Sanchez UER .10 .05
(Totals don't include '89 stats)
☐ 385 Gary Pettis .10 .05
☐ 386 Donn Pall .10 .05
☐ 387 John Smiley .20 .09
☐ 388 Tom Candiotti .10 .05
☐ 389 Junior Ortiz .10 .05
☐ 390 Steve Lyons .10 .05
☐ 391 Brian Harper .10 .05
☐ 392 Fred Manrique .10 .05
☐ 393 Lee Smith .20 .09
☐ 394 Jeff Kunkel .10 .05
☐ 395 Claudell Washington .10 .05
☐ 396 John Tudor .10 .05
☐ 397 Terry Kennedy UER .10 .05
(Career totals all wrong)
☐ 398 Lloyd McClendon .10 .05
☐ 399 Craig Lefferts .10 .05
☐ 400 Checklist 301-400 .10 .05
☐ 401 Keith Moreland .10 .05
☐ 402 Rich Gedman .10 .05
☐ 403 Jeff D. Robinson .10 .05
☐ 404 Randy Ready .10 .05
☐ 405 Rick Cerone .10 .05
☐ 406 Jeff Blauser .20 .09
☐ 407 Larry Andersen .10 .05
☐ 408 Joe Boever .10 .05
☐ 409 Felix Fermin .10 .05
☐ 410 Glenn Wilson .10 .05
☐ 411 Rex Hudler .10 .05
☐ 412 Mark Grant .10 .05
☐ 413 Dennis Martinez .20 .09
☐ 414 Darrin Jackson .10 .05
☐ 415 Mike Aldrete .10 .05
☐ 416 Roger McDowell .10 .05
☐ 417 Jeff Reardon .20 .09
☐ 418 Darren Daulton .20 .09

☐ 419 Tim Laudner .10 .05
☐ 420 Don Carman .10 .05
☐ 421 Lloyd Moseby .10 .05
☐ 422 Doug Drabek .10 .05
☐ 423 Lenny Harris UER .10 .05
(Walks 2 in '89,
should be 20)
☐ 424 Jose Lind .10 .05
☐ 425 Dave Johnson (P) .10 .05
☐ 426 Jerry Browne .10 .05
☐ 427 Eric Yelding .10 .05
☐ 428 Brad Komminsk .10 .05
☐ 429 Jody Davis .10 .05
☐ 430 Mariano Duncan .10 .05
☐ 431 Mark Davis .10 .05
☐ 432 Nelson Santovenia .10 .05
☐ 433 Bruce Hurst .10 .05
☐ 434 Jeff Huson .10 .05
☐ 435 Chris James .10 .05
☐ 436 Mark Guthrie .10 .05
☐ 437 Charlie Hayes .20 .09
☐ 438 Shane Rawley .10 .05
☐ 439 Dickie Thon .10 .05
☐ 440 Juan Berenguer .10 .05
☐ 441 Kevin Romine .10 .05
☐ 442 Bill Landrum .10 .05
☐ 443 Todd Frohwirth .10 .05
☐ 444 Craig Worthington .10 .05
☐ 445 Fernando Valenzuela .20 .09
☐ 446 Joey Belle 1.00 .45
☐ 447 Ed Whited UER .10 .05
(Ashville, should
be Asheville)
☐ 448 Dave Smith .10 .05
☐ 449 Dave Clark .10 .05
☐ 450 Juan Agosto .10 .05
☐ 451 Dave Valle .10 .05
☐ 452 Kent Hrbek .20 .09
☐ 453 Von Hayes .10 .05
☐ 454 Gary Gaetti .20 .09
☐ 455 Greg Briley .10 .05
☐ 456 Glenn Braggs .10 .05
☐ 457 Kirt Manwaring .10 .05
☐ 458 Mel Hall .10 .05
☐ 459 Brook Jacoby .10 .05
☐ 460 Pat Sheridan .10 .05
☐ 461 Rob Murphy .10 .05
☐ 462 Jimmy Key .30 .14
☐ 463 Nick Esasky .10 .05
☐ 464 Rob Ducey .10 .05
☐ 465 Carlos Quintana UER .10 .05
(Internatinoal)
☐ 466 Larry Walker 2.00 .90
☐ 467 Todd Worrell .10 .05
☐ 468 Kevin Gross .10 .05
☐ 469 Terry Pendleton .20 .09
☐ 470 Dave Martinez .10 .05
☐ 471 Gene Larkin .10 .05
☐ 472 Len Dykstra UER .20 .09
('89 and total runs
understated by 10)
☐ 473 Barry Lyons .10 .05
☐ 474 Terry Mulholland .10 .05
☐ 475 Chip Hale .10 .05
☐ 476 Jesse Barfield .10 .05
☐ 477 Dan Plesac .10 .05
☐ 478A Scott Garrelts ERR 2.00 .90
(Photo actually
Bill Bathe)
☐ 478B Scott Garrelts COR .10 .05
☐ 479 Dave Righetti .10 .05
☐ 480 Gus Polidor UER .10 .05
(Wearing 14 on front,
but 10 on back)
☐ 481 Mookie Wilson .10 .05
☐ 482 Luis Rivera .10 .05
☐ 483 Mike Flanagan .10 .05
☐ 484 Dennis Boyd .10 .05
☐ 485 John Cerutti .10 .05
☐ 486 John Costello .10 .05
☐ 487 Pascual Perez .10 .05
☐ 488 Tommy Herr .10 .05
☐ 489 Tom Foley .10 .05
☐ 490 Curt Ford .10 .05
☐ 491 Steve Lake .10 .05
☐ 492 Tim Teufel .10 .05
☐ 493 Randy Bush .10 .05
☐ 494 Mike Jackson .10 .05
☐ 495 Steve Jeltz .10 .05
☐ 496 Paul Gibson .10 .05
☐ 497 Steve Balboni .10 .05
☐ 498 Bud Black .10 .05
☐ 499 Dale Sveum .10 .05
☐ 500 Checklist 401-500 .10 .05
☐ 501 Tim Jones .10 .05
☐ 502 Mark Portugal .10 .05
☐ 503 Ivan Calderon .10 .05
☐ 504 Rick Rhoden .10 .05
☐ 505 Willie McGee .10 .05
☐ 506 Kirk McCaskill .10 .05
☐ 507 Dave LaPoint .10 .05
☐ 508 Jay Howell .10 .05
☐ 509 Johnny Ray .10 .05
☐ 510 Dave Anderson .10 .05
☐ 511 Chuck Crim .10 .05
☐ 512 Joe Hesketh .10 .05
☐ 513 Dennis Eckersley .40 .18
☐ 514 Greg Brock .10 .05
☐ 515 Tim Burke .10 .05
☐ 516 Frank Tanana .10 .05
☐ 517 Jay Bell .20 .09
☐ 518 Guillermo Hernandez .10 .05
☐ 519 Randy Kramer UER .10 .05
(Codiroli misspelled
as Codoroli)
☐ 520 Charles Hudson .10 .05
☐ 521 Jim Corsi .10 .05
(Word "originally" is
misspelled on back)
☐ 522 Steve Rosenberg .10 .05
☐ 523 Cris Carpenter .10 .05
☐ 524 Matt Winters .10 .05
☐ 525 Melido Perez .10 .05
☐ 526 Chris Gwynn UER .10 .05
(Albeguergue)
☐ 527 Bert Blyleven UER .20 .09
(Games career total is
wrong, should be 644)
☐ 528 Chuck Cary .10 .05
☐ 529 Daryl Boston .10 .05
☐ 530 Dale Mohorcic .10 .05
☐ 531 Geronimo Berroa .20 .09
☐ 532 Edgar Martinez .40 .18
☐ 533 Dale Murphy .40 .18
☐ 534 Jay Buhner .40 .18
☐ 535 John Smoltz UER .40 .18
(HEA Stadium)
☐ 536 Andy Van Slyke .20 .09
☐ 537 Mike Henneman .10 .05
☐ 538 Miguel Garcia .10 .05
☐ 539 Frank Williams .10 .05
☐ 540 R.J. Reynolds .10 .05
☐ 541 Shawn Hillegas .10 .05
☐ 542 Walt Weiss .10 .05
☐ 543 Greg Hibbard .10 .05
☐ 544 Nolan Ryan 1.50 .70
☐ 545 Todd Zeile .20 .09
☐ 546 Hensley Meulens .10 .05
☐ 547 Tim Belcher .10 .05
☐ 548 Mike Witt .10 .05
☐ 549 Greg Cadaret UER .10 .05
(Aquiring, should
be Acquiring)
☐ 550 Franklin Stubbs .10 .05
☐ 551 Tony Castillo .10 .05
☐ 552 Jeff M. Robinson .10 .05
☐ 553 Steve Olin .20 .09
☐ 554 Alan Trammell .30 .14
☐ 555 Wade Boggs 4X .40 .18
(Bo Jackson
in background)
☐ 556 Will Clark .40 .18
☐ 557 Jeff King .20 .09
☐ 558 Mike Fitzgerald .10 .05
☐ 559 Ken Howell .10 .05
☐ 560 Bob Kipper .10 .05
☐ 561 Scott Bankhead .10 .05
☐ 562A Jeff Innis ERR 2.00 .90
(Photo actually
David West)
☐ 562B Jeff Innis COR .10 .05
☐ 563 Randy Johnson .60 .25
☐ 564 Wally Whitehurst .10 .05
☐ 565 Gene Harris .10 .05
☐ 566 Norm Charlton .10 .05
☐ 567 Robin Yount UER .40 .18
(7602 career hits,
should be 2606)
☐ 568 Joe Oliver UER .10 .05
(Fl.orida)
☐ 569 Mark Parent .10 .05
☐ 570 John Farrell UER .10 .05
(Loss total added wrong)
☐ 571 Tom Glavine .40 .18
☐ 572 Rod Nichols .10 .05
☐ 573 Jack Morris .20 .09
☐ 574 Greg Swindell .10 .05
☐ 575 Steve Searcy .10 .05
☐ 576 Ricky Jordan .10 .05
☐ 577 Matt Williams .40 .18
☐ 578 Mike LaValliere .10 .05
☐ 579 Bryn Smith .10 .05
☐ 580 Bruce Ruffin .10 .05
☐ 581 Randy Myers .20 .09
☐ 582 Rick Wrona .10 .05
☐ 583 Juan Samuel .10 .05
☐ 584 Les Lancaster .10 .05
☐ 585 Jeff Musselman .10 .05
☐ 586 Rob Dibble .10 .05
☐ 587 Eric Show .10 .05
☐ 588 Jesse Orosco .10 .05
☐ 589 Herm Winningham .10 .05
☐ 590 Andy Allanson .10 .05
☐ 591 Dion James .10 .05
☐ 592 Carmelo Martinez .10 .05
☐ 593 Luis Quinones .10 .05
☐ 594 Dennis Rasmussen .10 .05
☐ 595 Rich Yett .10 .05
☐ 596 Bob Walk .10 .05
☐ 597A Andy McGaffigan ERR .20 .09
(Photo actually
Rich Thompson)
☐ 597B Andy McGaffigan COR .10 .05
☐ 598 Billy Hatcher .10 .05
☐ 599 Bob Knepper .10 .05
☐ 600 Checklist 501-600 UER .10 .05
(599 Bob Kneppers)
☐ 601 Joey Cora .40 .18
☐ 602 Steve Finley .40 .18
☐ 603 Kal Daniels UER .10 .05
(12 hits in '87, should
be 123; 335 runs,
should be 235)
☐ 604 Gregg Olson .10 .05
☐ 605 Dave Stieb .10 .05
☐ 606 Kenny Rogers .20 .09
(Shown catching
football)
☐ 607 Zane Smith .10 .05
☐ 608 Bob Geren UER .10 .05
(Origionally)
☐ 609 Chad Kreuter .10 .05
☐ 610 Mike Smithson .10 .05
☐ 611 Jeff Wetherby .10 .05
☐ 612 Gary Mielke .10 .05
☐ 613 Pete Smith .10 .05
☐ 614 Jack Daugherty UER .10 .05
(Born 7/30/60, should
be 7/3/60)
☐ 615 Lance McCullers .10 .05
☐ 616 Don Robinson .10 .05
☐ 617 Jose Guzman .10 .05
☐ 618 Steve Bedrosian .10 .05
☐ 619 Jamie Moyer .10 .05
☐ 620 Atlee Hammaker .10 .05
☐ 621 Rick Luecken UER .10 .05
(Innings pitched wrong)
☐ 622 Greg W. Harris .10 .05
☐ 623 Pete Harnisch .10 .05
☐ 624 Jerald Clark .10 .05
☐ 625 Jack McDowell UER .10 .05
(Career totals for Games
and GS don't include
1987 season)
☐ 626 Frank Viola .10 .05
☐ 627 Teddy Higuera .10 .05
☐ 628 Marty Pevey .10 .05
☐ 629 Bill Wegman .10 .05
☐ 630 Eric Plunk .10 .05
☐ 631 Drew Hall .10 .05
☐ 632 Doug Jones .10 .05
☐ 633 Geno Petralli UER .10 .05
(Sacremento)
☐ 634 Jose Alvarez .10 .05
☐ 635 Bob Milacki .10 .05
☐ 636 Bobby Witt .10 .05
☐ 637 Trevor Wilson .10 .05
☐ 638 Jeff Russell UER .10 .05
(Shutout stats wrong)
☐ 639 Mike Krukow .10 .05
☐ 640 Rick Leach .10 .05
☐ 641 Dave Schmidt .10 .05
☐ 642 Terry Leach .10 .05
☐ 643 Calvin Schiraldi .10 .05
☐ 644 Bob Melvin .10 .05
☐ 645 Jim Abbott .20 .09
☐ 646 Jaime Navarro .10 .05
☐ 647 Mark Langston UER .10 .05
(Several errors in
stats totals)
☐ 648 Juan Nieves .10 .05
☐ 649 Damaso Garcia .10 .05
☐ 650 Charlie O'Brien .10 .05
☐ 651 Eric King .10 .05
☐ 652 Mike Boddicker .10 .05
☐ 653 Duane Ward .10 .05
☐ 654 Bob Stanley .10 .05
☐ 655 Sandy Alomar Jr. .40 .18
☐ 656 Danny Tartabull UER .10 .05
(395 BB, should be 295)
☐ 657 Randy McCament .10 .05

☐ 658 Charlie Leibrandt .10 .05
☐ 659 Dan Quisenberry .10 .05
☐ 660 Paul Assenmacher .10 .05
☐ 661 Walt Terrell .10 .05
☐ 662 Tim Leary .10 .05
☐ 663 Randy Milligan .10 .05
☐ 664 Bo Diaz .10 .05
☐ 665 Mark Lemke UER .20 .09
(Richmond misspelled as Richomond)
☐ 666 Jose Gonzalez .10 .05
☐ 667 Chuck Finley UER .20 .09
(Born 11/16/62, should be 11/26/62)
☐ 668 John Kruk .20 .09
☐ 669 Dick Schofield .10 .05
☐ 670 Tim Crews .10 .05
☐ 671 John Dopson .10 .05
☐ 672 John Orton .10 .05
☐ 673 Eric Hetzel .10 .05
☐ 674 Lance Parrish .10 .05
☐ 675 Ramon Martinez .20 .09
☐ 676 Mark Gubicza .10 .05
☐ 677 Greg Litton .10 .05
☐ 678 Greg Mathews .10 .05
☐ 679 Dave Dravecky .20 .09
☐ 680 Steve Farr .10 .05
☐ 681 Mike Devereaux .10 .05
☐ 682 Ken Griffey Sr. .10 .05
☐ 683A Mickey Weston ERR 2.00 .90
(Listed as Jamie on card)
☐ 683B Mickey Weston COR .10 .05
(Technically still an error as birthdate is listed as 3/26/81)
☐ 684 Jack Armstrong .10 .05
☐ 685 Steve Buechele .10 .05
☐ 686 Bryan Harvey .10 .05
☐ 687 Lance Blankenship .10 .05
☐ 688 Dante Bichette .40 .18
☐ 689 Todd Burns .10 .05
☐ 690 Dan Petry .10 .05
☐ 691 Kent Anderson .10 .05
☐ 692 Todd Stottlemyre .20 .09
☐ 693 Wally Joyner UER .20 .09
(Several stats errors)
☐ 694 Mike Rochford .10 .05
☐ 695 Floyd Bannister .10 .05
☐ 696 Rick Reuschel .10 .05
☐ 697 Jose DeLeon .10 .05
☐ 698 Jeff Montgomery .20 .09
☐ 699 Kelly Downs .10 .05
☐ 700A Checklist 601-700 2.00 .90
(683 Jamie Weston)
☐ 700B Checklist 601-700 .10 .05
(683 Mickey Weston)
☐ 701 Jim Gott .10 .05
☐ 702 Rookie Threats .50 .23
Delino DeShields
Marquis Grissom
Larry Walker
☐ 703 Alejandro Pena .10 .05
☐ 704 Willie Randolph .20 .09
☐ 705 Tim Leary .10 .05
☐ 706 Chuck McElroy .10 .05
☐ 707 Gerald Perry .10 .05
☐ 708 Tom Brunansky .10 .05
☐ 709 John Franco .10 .05
☐ 710 Mark Davis .10 .05
☐ 711 David Justice 1.50 .70
☐ 712 Storm Davis .10 .05
☐ 713 Scott Ruskin .10 .05
☐ 714 Glenn Braggs .10 .05
☐ 715 Kevin Bearse .10 .05
☐ 716 Jose Nunez .10 .05
☐ 717 Tim Layana .10 .05
☐ 718 Greg Myers .10 .05
☐ 719 Pete O'Brien .10 .05
☐ 720 John Candelaria .10 .05
☐ 721 Craig Grebeck .10 .05
☐ 722 Shawn Boskie .10 .05
☐ 723 Jim Leyritz .40 .18
☐ 724 Bill Sampen .10 .05
☐ 725 Scott Radinsky .10 .05
☐ 726 Todd Hundley .75 .35
☐ 727 Scott Hemond .10 .05
☐ 728 Lenny Webster .10 .05
☐ 729 Jeff Reardon .20 .09
☐ 730 Mitch Webster .10 .05
☐ 731 Brian Bohanon .10 .05
☐ 732 Rick Parker .10 .05
☐ 733 Terry Shumpert .10 .05
☐ 734A Ryan's 6th No-Hitter 2.50 1.10
(No stripe on front)
☐ 734B Ryan's 6th No-Hitter .75 .35
(stripe added on card front for 300th win)
☐ 735 John Burkett .20 .09
☐ 736 Derrick May .20 .09
☐ 737 Carlos Baerga .50 .23
☐ 738 Greg Smith .10 .05
☐ 739 Scott Sanderson .10 .05
☐ 740 Joe Kraemer .10 .05
☐ 741 Hector Villanueva .10 .05
☐ 742 Mike Fetters .20 .09
☐ 743 Mark Gardner .10 .05
☐ 744 Matt Nokes .10 .05
☐ 745 Dave Winfield .40 .18
☐ 746 Delino DeShields .40 .18
☐ 747 Dann Howitt .10 .05
☐ 748 Tony Pena .10 .05
☐ 749 Oil Can Boyd .10 .05
☐ 750 Mike Benjamin .10 .05
☐ 751 Alex Cole .20 .09
☐ 752 Eric Gunderson .10 .05
☐ 753 Howard Farmer .10 .05
☐ 754 Joe Carter .20 .09
☐ 755 Ray Lankford 1.00 .45
☐ 756 Sandy Alomar Jr. .40 .18
☐ 757 Alex Sanchez .10 .05
☐ 758 Nick Esasky .10 .05
☐ 759 Stan Belinda .10 .05
☐ 760 Jim Presley .10 .05
☐ 761 Gary DiSarcina .40 .18
☐ 762 Wayne Edwards .10 .05
☐ 763 Pat Combs .10 .05
☐ 764 Mickey Pina .10 .05
☐ 765 Wilson Alvarez .50 .23
☐ 766 Dave Parker .20 .09
☐ 767 Mike Blowers .40 .18
☐ 768 Tony Phillips .10 .05
☐ 769 Pascual Perez .10 .05
☐ 770 Gary Pettis .10 .05
☐ 771 Fred Lynn .10 .05
☐ 772 Mel Rojas .40 .18
☐ 773 David Segui .40 .18
☐ 774 Gary Carter .40 .18
☐ 775 Rafael Valdez .10 .05
☐ 776 Glenallen Hill .20 .09
☐ 777 Keith Hernandez .20 .09
☐ 778 Billy Hatcher .10 .05
☐ 779 Marty Clary .10 .05
☐ 780 Candy Maldonado .10 .05
☐ 781 Mike Marshall .10 .05
☐ 782 Billy Joe Robidoux .10 .05
☐ 783 Mark Langston .10 .05
☐ 784 Paul Sorrento .40 .18
☐ 785 Dave Hollins .40 .18
☐ 786 Cecil Fielder .20 .09
☐ 787 Matt Young .10 .05
☐ 788 Jeff Huson .10 .05
☐ 789 Lloyd Moseby .10 .05
☐ 790 Ron Kittle .10 .05
☐ 791 Hubie Brooks .10 .05
☐ 792 Craig Lefferts .10 .05
☐ 793 Kevin Bass .10 .05
☐ 794 Bryn Smith .10 .05
☐ 795 Juan Samuel .10 .05
☐ 796 Sam Horn .10 .05
☐ 797 Randy Myers .20 .09
☐ 798 Chris James .10 .05
☐ 799 Bill Gullickson .10 .05
☐ 800 Checklist 701-800 .10 .05

1990 Upper Deck Jackson Heroes

This ten-card standard-size set was issued as an insert in 1990 Upper Deck High Number packs as part of the Upper Deck promotional giveaway of 2,500 officially signed and personally numbered Reggie Jackson cards. Signed cards ending with 00 have the words "Mr. October" added to the autograph. These cards cover Jackson's major league career. The complete set price refers only to the unautographed card set of ten. One-card packs of over-sized (3 1/2" by 5") versions of these cards were later inserted into retail blister repacks containing one foil pack each of 1993 Upper Deck Series I and II. These cards were later inserted into various forms of repackaging. The larger cards are also distinguishable by the Upper Deck Fifth Anniversary logo and "1993 Hall of Fame Inductee" logo on the front of the card. These over-sized cards were a limited edition of 10,000 numbered cards and have no extra value than the basic cards.

	MINT	NRMT
COMPLETE SET (10)	15.00	6.75
COMMON REGGIE (1-9)	1.50	.70

☐ 1 Reggie Jackson 1.50 .70
1969 Emerging Superstar
☐ 2 Reggie Jackson 1.50 .70
1973 An MVP Year
☐ 3 Reggie Jackson 1.50 .70
1977 Mr. October
☐ 4 Reggie Jackson 1.50 .70
1978 vs. Bob Welch
☐ 5 Reggie Jackson 1.50 .70
1982 Under the Halo
☐ 6 Reggie Jackson 1.50 .70
1984 500 Homers
☐ 7 Reggie Jackson 1.50 .70
1986 Moving Up the List
☐ 8 Reggie Jackson 1.50 .70
1987 A Great Career Ends
☐ 9 Jackson Heroes art/CL 1.50 .70
☐ AU1 Reggie Jackson AU 300.00 135.00
(Signed and Numbered out of 2500)
☐ NNO0 Reggie Jackson 4.00 1.80
Header Card

1991 Upper Deck

This set marked the third year Upper Deck issued a 800-card standard-size set in two separate series of 700 and 100 cards respectively. Cards were distributed in low and high series foil packs and factory sets. The 100-card extended or high-number series was issued by Upper Deck several months after the release of their first series. For the first time in Upper Deck's three-year history, they did not issue a factory Extended set. The basic cards are made on the typical Upper Deck slick, white card stock and features full-color photos on both the front and the back. Subsets include Star Rookies (1-26), Team Cards (28-34, 43-49, 77-82, 95-99) and Top Prospects (50-76). Several other special achievement cards are seeded throughout the set. The team checklist (TC) cards in the set feature an attractive Vernon Wells drawing of a featured player for that particular team. Rookie Cards in this set include Jeff Bagwell, Jeff Conine, Chipper Jones, Eric Karros, Brian McRae, Mike Mussina and Reggie Sanders. A special Michael Jordan card (numbered SP1) was randomly included in packs on a somewhat limited basis. The Hank Aaron hologram card was randomly inserted in the 1991 Upper Deck high number foil packs. Neither card is included in the price of the regular issue set.

	MINT	NRMT
COMPLETE SET (800)	20.00	9.00
COMP.FACT.SET (800)	20.00	9.00
COMPLETE LO SET (700)	16.00	7.25
COMPLETE HI SET (100)	4.00	1.80
COMMON CARD (1-800)	.05	.02

☐ 1 Star Rookie Checklist .05 .02
☐ 2 Phil Plantier .10 .05
☐ 3 D.J. Dozier .05 .02
☐ 4 Dave Hansen .05 .02
☐ 5 Maurice Vaughn .40 .18
☐ 6 Leo Gomez .05 .02
☐ 7 Scott Aldred .05 .02
☐ 8 Scott Chiamparino .05 .02
☐ 9 Lance Dickson .05 .02
☐ 10 Sean Berry .10 .05
☐ 11 Bernie Williams .25 .11
☐ 12 Brian Barnes UER .05 .02
(Photo either not him

or in wrong jersey)		
☐ 13 Narciso Elvira	.05	.02
☐ 14 Mike Gardiner	.05	.02
☐ 15 Greg Colbrunn	.05	.02
☐ 16 Bernard Gilkey	.10	.05
☐ 17 Mark Lewis	.05	.02
☐ 18 Mickey Morandini	.05	.02
☐ 19 Charles Nagy	.20	.09
☐ 20 Geronimo Pena	.05	.02
☐ 21 Henry Rodriguez	.40	.18
☐ 22 Scott Cooper	.05	.02
☐ 23 Andujar Cedeno UER	.05	.02
(Shown batting left, back says right)		
☐ 24 Eric Karros	.50	.23
☐ 25 Steve Decker UER	.05	.02
(Lewis-Clark State College, not Lewis and Clark)		
☐ 26 Kevin Belcher	.05	.02
☐ 27 Jeff Conine	.25	.11
☐ 28 Dave Stewart TC	.10	.05
☐ 29 Carlton Fisk TC	.20	.09
☐ 30 Rafael Palmeiro TC	.20	.09
☐ 31 Chuck Finley TC	.05	.02
☐ 32 Harold Reynolds TC	.05	.02
☐ 33 Bret Saberhagen TC	.05	.02
☐ 34 Gary Gaetti TC	.05	.02
☐ 35 Scott Leius	.05	.02
☐ 36 Neal Heaton	.05	.02
☐ 37 Terry Lee	.05	.02
☐ 38 Gary Redus	.05	.02
☐ 39 Barry Jones	.05	.02
☐ 40 Chuck Knoblauch	.25	.11
☐ 41 Larry Andersen	.05	.02
☐ 42 Darryl Hamilton	.05	.02
☐ 43 Mike Greenwell TC	.05	.02
☐ 44 Kelly Gruber TC	.05	.02
☐ 45 Jack Morris TC	.10	.05
☐ 46 Sandy Alomar Jr. TC	.15	.07
☐ 47 Gregg Olson TC	.05	.02
☐ 48 Dave Parker TC	.10	.05
☐ 49 Roberto Kelly TC	.05	.02
☐ 50 Top Prospect Checklist	.05	.02
☐ 51 Kyle Abbott	.05	.02
☐ 52 Jeff Juden	.05	.02
☐ 53 Todd Van Poppel UER	.05	.02
(Born Arlington and attended John Martin HS, should say Hinsdale and James Martin HS)		
☐ 54 Steve Karsay	.10	.05
☐ 55 Chipper Jones	4.00	1.80
☐ 56 Chris Johnson UER	.05	.02
(Called Tim on back)		
☐ 57 John Ericks	.05	.02
☐ 58 Gary Scott	.05	.02
☐ 59 Kiki Jones	.05	.02
☐ 60 Wil Cordero	.05	.02
☐ 61 Royce Clayton	.20	.09
☐ 62 Tim Costo	.05	.02
☐ 63 Roger Salkeld	.05	.02
☐ 64 Brook Fordyce	.05	.02
☐ 65 Mike Mussina	1.25	.55
☐ 66 Dave Staton	.05	.02
☐ 67 Mike Lieberthal	.15	.07
☐ 68 Kurt Miller	.05	.02
☐ 69 Dan Peltier	.05	.02
☐ 70 Greg Blosser	.05	.02
☐ 71 Reggie Sanders	.25	.11
☐ 72 Brent Mayne	.05	.02
☐ 73 Rico Brogna	.10	.05
☐ 74 Willie Banks	.05	.02
☐ 75 Len Brutcher	.05	.02
☐ 76 Pat Kelly	.05	.02
☐ 77 Chris Sabo TC	.05	.02
☐ 78 Ramon Martinez TC	.15	.07
☐ 79 Matt Williams TC	.10	.05
☐ 80 Roberto Alomar TC	.20	.09
☐ 81 Glenn Davis TC	.05	.02
☐ 82 Ron Gant TC	.10	.05
☐ 83 Cecil Fielder FEAT	.10	.05
☐ 84 Orlando Merced	.10	.05
☐ 85 Domingo Ramos	.05	.02
☐ 86 Tom Bolton	.05	.02
☐ 87 Andres Santana	.05	.02
☐ 88 John Dopson	.05	.02
☐ 89 Kenny Williams	.05	.02
☐ 90 Marty Barrett	.05	.02
☐ 91 Tom Pagnozzi	.05	.02
☐ 92 Carmelo Martinez	.05	.02
☐ 93 Bobby Thigpen SAVE	.05	.02
☐ 94 Barry Bonds TC	.20	.09
☐ 95 Gregg Jefferies TC	.05	.02
☐ 96 Tim Wallach TC	.05	.02
☐ 97 Len Dykstra TC	.10	.05
☐ 98 Pedro Guerrero TC	.05	.02
☐ 99 Mark Grace TC	.20	.09
☐ 100 Checklist 1-100	.05	.02
☐ 101 Kevin Elster	.05	.02
☐ 102 Tom Brookens	.05	.02
☐ 103 Mackey Sasser	.05	.02
☐ 104 Felix Fermin	.05	.02
☐ 105 Kevin McReynolds	.05	.02
☐ 106 Dave Stieb	.05	.02
☐ 107 Jeffrey Leonard	.05	.02
☐ 108 Dave Henderson	.05	.02
☐ 109 Sid Bream	.05	.02
☐ 110 Henry Cotto	.05	.02
☐ 111 Shawon Dunston	.05	.02
☐ 112 Mariano Duncan	.05	.02
☐ 113 Joe Girardi	.10	.05
☐ 114 Billy Hatcher	.05	.02
☐ 115 Greg Maddux	.60	.25
☐ 116 Jerry Browne	.05	.02
☐ 117 Juan Samuel	.05	.02
☐ 118 Steve Olin	.05	.02
☐ 119 Alfredo Griffin	.05	.02
☐ 120 Mitch Webster	.05	.02
☐ 121 Joel Skinner	.05	.02
☐ 122 Frank Viola	.05	.02
☐ 123 Cory Snyder	.05	.02
☐ 124 Howard Johnson	.05	.02
☐ 125 Carlos Baerga	.10	.05
☐ 126 Tony Fernandez	.05	.02
☐ 127 Dave Stewart	.10	.05
☐ 128 Jay Buhner	.20	.09
☐ 129 Mike LaValliere	.05	.02
☐ 130 Scott Bradley	.05	.02
☐ 131 Tony Phillips	.05	.02
☐ 132 Ryne Sandberg	.25	.11
☐ 133 Paul O'Neill	.10	.05
☐ 134 Mark Grace	.20	.09
☐ 135 Chris Sabo	.05	.02
☐ 136 Ramon Martinez	.10	.05
☐ 137 Brook Jacoby	.05	.02
☐ 138 Candy Maldonado	.05	.02
☐ 139 Mike Scioscia	.05	.02
☐ 140 Chris James	.05	.02
☐ 141 Craig Worthington	.05	.02
☐ 142 Manny Lee	.05	.02
☐ 143 Tim Raines	.10	.05
☐ 144 Sandy Alomar Jr.	.15	.07
☐ 145 John Olerud	.10	.05
☐ 146 Ozzie Canseco	.10	.05
(With Jose)		
☐ 147 Pat Borders	.05	.02
☐ 148 Harold Reynolds	.05	.02
☐ 149 Tom Henke	.05	.02
☐ 150 R.J. Reynolds	.05	.02
☐ 151 Mike Gallego	.05	.02
☐ 152 Bobby Bonilla	.10	.05
☐ 153 Terry Steinbach	.10	.05
☐ 154 Barry Bonds	.25	.11
☐ 155 Jose Canseco	.20	.09
☐ 156 Gregg Jefferies	.10	.05
☐ 157 Matt Williams	.20	.09
☐ 158 Craig Biggio	.20	.09
☐ 159 Daryl Boston	.05	.02
☐ 160 Ricky Jordan	.05	.02
☐ 161 Stan Belinda	.05	.02
☐ 162 Ozzie Smith	.25	.11
☐ 163 Tom Brunansky	.05	.02
☐ 164 Todd Zeile	.10	.05
☐ 165 Mike Greenwell	.05	.02
☐ 166 Kal Daniels	.05	.02
☐ 167 Kent Hrbek	.10	.05
☐ 168 Franklin Stubbs	.05	.02
☐ 169 Dick Schofield	.05	.02
☐ 170 Junior Ortiz	.05	.02
☐ 171 Hector Villanueva	.05	.02
☐ 172 Dennis Eckersley	.20	.09
☐ 173 Mitch Williams	.05	.02
☐ 174 Mark McGwire	.40	.18
☐ 175 Fernando Valenzuela 3X	.10	.05
☐ 176 Gary Carter	.20	.09
☐ 177 Dave Magadan	.05	.02
☐ 178 Robby Thompson	.05	.02
☐ 179 Bob Ojeda	.05	.02
☐ 180 Ken Caminiti	.20	.09
☐ 181 Don Slaught	.05	.02
☐ 182 Luis Rivera	.05	.02
☐ 183 Jay Bell	.10	.05
☐ 184 Jody Reed	.05	.02
☐ 185 Wally Backman	.05	.02
☐ 186 Dave Martinez	.05	.02
☐ 187 Luis Polonia	.05	.02
☐ 188 Shane Mack	.05	.02
☐ 189 Spike Owen	.05	.02
☐ 190 Scott Bailes	.05	.02
☐ 191 John Russell	.05	.02
☐ 192 Walt Weiss	.05	.02
☐ 193 Jose Oquendo	.05	.02
☐ 194 Carney Lansford	.10	.05
☐ 195 Jeff Huson	.05	.02
☐ 196 Keith Miller	.05	.02
☐ 197 Eric Yelding	.05	.02
☐ 198 Ron Darling	.05	.02
☐ 199 John Kruk	.10	.05
☐ 200 Checklist 101-200	.05	.02
☐ 201 John Shelby	.05	.02
☐ 202 Bob Geren	.05	.02
☐ 203 Lance McCullers	.05	.02
☐ 204 Alvaro Espinoza	.05	.02
☐ 205 Mark Salas	.05	.02
☐ 206 Mike Pagliarulo	.05	.02
☐ 207 Jose Uribe	.05	.02
☐ 208 Jim Deshaies	.05	.02
☐ 209 Ron Karkovice	.05	.02
☐ 210 Rafael Ramirez	.05	.02
☐ 211 Donnie Hill	.05	.02
☐ 212 Brian Harper	.05	.02
☐ 213 Jack Howell	.05	.02
☐ 214 Wes Gardner	.05	.02
☐ 215 Tim Burke	.05	.02
☐ 216 Doug Jones	.05	.02
☐ 217 Hubie Brooks	.05	.02
☐ 218 Tom Candiotti	.05	.02
☐ 219 Gerald Perry	.05	.02
☐ 220 Jose DeLeon	.05	.02
☐ 221 Wally Whitehurst	.05	.02
☐ 222 Alan Mills	.05	.02
☐ 223 Alan Trammell	.20	.09
☐ 224 Dwight Gooden	.10	.05
☐ 225 Travis Fryman	.20	.09
☐ 226 Joe Carter	.20	.09
☐ 227 Julio Franco	.10	.05
☐ 228 Craig Lefferts	.05	.02
☐ 229 Gary Pettis	.05	.02
☐ 230 Dennis Rasmussen	.05	.02
☐ 231A Brian Downing ERR	.05	.02
(No position on front)		
☐ 231B Brian Downing COR	.15	.07
(DH on front)		
☐ 232 Carlos Quintana	.05	.02
☐ 233 Gary Gaetti	.10	.05
☐ 234 Mark Langston	.05	.02
☐ 235 Tim Wallach	.05	.02
☐ 236 Greg Swindell	.05	.02
☐ 237 Eddie Murray	.20	.09
☐ 238 Jeff Manto	.05	.02
☐ 239 Lenny Harris	.05	.02
☐ 240 Jesse Orosco	.05	.02
☐ 241 Scott Lusader	.05	.02
☐ 242 Sid Fernandez	.05	.02
☐ 243 Jim Leyritz	.10	.05
☐ 244 Cecil Fielder	.10	.05
☐ 245 Darryl Strawberry	.10	.05
☐ 246 Frank Thomas UER	1.50	.70
(Comiskey Park misspelled Comisky)		
☐ 247 Kevin Mitchell	.10	.05
☐ 248 Lance Johnson	.10	.05
☐ 249 Rick Reuschel	.05	.02
☐ 250 Mark Portugal	.05	.02
☐ 251 Derek Lilliquist	.05	.02
☐ 252 Brian Holman	.05	.02
☐ 253 Rafael Valdez UER	.05	.02
(Born 4/17/68, should be 12/17/67)		
☐ 254 B.J. Surhoff	.10	.05
☐ 255 Tony Gwynn	.50	.23
☐ 256 Andy Van Slyke	.10	.05
☐ 257 Todd Stottlemyre	.05	.02
☐ 258 Jose Lind	.05	.02
☐ 259 Greg Myers	.05	.02
☐ 260 Jeff Ballard	.05	.02
☐ 261 Bobby Thigpen	.05	.02
☐ 262 Jimmy Kremers	.05	.02
☐ 263 Robin Ventura	.20	.09
☐ 264 John Smoltz	.20	.09
☐ 265 Sammy Sosa	.25	.11
☐ 266 Gary Sheffield	.20	.09
☐ 267 Len Dykstra	.10	.05
☐ 268 Bill Spiers	.05	.02
☐ 269 Charlie Hayes	.05	.02
☐ 270 Brett Butler	.15	.07
☐ 271 Bip Roberts	.05	.02
☐ 272 Rob Deer	.05	.02
☐ 273 Fred Lynn	.05	.02
☐ 274 Dave Parker	.15	.07
☐ 275 Andy Benes	.10	.05
☐ 276 Glenallen Hill	.05	.02
☐ 277 Steve Howard	.05	.02
☐ 278 Doug Drabek	.05	.02
☐ 279 Joe Oliver	.05	.02
☐ 280 Todd Benzinger	.05	.02
☐ 281 Eric King	.05	.02
☐ 282 Jim Presley	.05	.02
☐ 283 Ken Patterson	.05	.02
☐ 284 Jack Daugherty	.05	.02
☐ 285 Ivan Calderon	.05	.02

☐ 286 Edgar Diaz .05 .02
☐ 287 Kevin Bass .05 .02
☐ 288 Don Carman .05 .02
☐ 289 Greg Brock .05 .02
☐ 290 John Franco .05 .02
☐ 291 Joey Cora .15 .07
☐ 292 Bill Wegman .05 .02
☐ 293 Eric Show .05 .02
☐ 294 Scott Bankhead .05 .02
☐ 295 Garry Templeton .05 .02
☐ 296 Mickey Tettleton .10 .05
☐ 297 Luis Sojo .05 .02
☐ 298 Jose Rijo .05 .02
☐ 299 Dave Johnson .05 .02
☐ 300 Checklist 201-300 .05 .02
☐ 301 Mark Grant .05 .02
☐ 302 Pete Harnisch .05 .02
☐ 303 Greg Olson .05 .02
☐ 304 Anthony Telford .05 .02
☐ 305 Lonnie Smith .05 .02
☐ 306 Chris Hoiles .05 .02
☐ 307 Bryn Smith .05 .02
☐ 308 Mike Devereaux .05 .02
☐ 309A Milt Thompson ERR .20 .09
(Under yr information
has print dot)
☐ 309B Milt Thompson COR .05 .02
(Under yr information
says 86)
☐ 310 Bob Melvin .05 .02
☐ 311 Luis Salazar .05 .02
☐ 312 Ed Whitson .05 .02
☐ 313 Charlie Hough .05 .02
☐ 314 Dave Clark .05 .02
☐ 315 Eric Gunderson .05 .02
☐ 316 Dan Petry .05 .02
☐ 317 Dante Bichette UER .20 .09
(Assists misspelled
as assissts)
☐ 318 Mike Heath .05 .02
☐ 319 Damon Berryhill .05 .02
☐ 320 Walt Terrell .05 .02
☐ 321 Scott Fletcher .05 .02
☐ 322 Dan Plesac .05 .02
☐ 323 Jack McDowell .05 .02
☐ 324 Paul Molitor .20 .09
☐ 325 Ozzie Guillen .05 .02
☐ 326 Gregg Olson .05 .02
☐ 327 Pedro Guerrero .05 .02
☐ 328 Bob Milacki .05 .02
☐ 329 John Tudor UER .05 .02
('90 Cardinals,
should be '90 Dodgers)
☐ 330 Steve Finley UER .10 .05
(Born 3/12/65,
should be 5/12)
☐ 331 Jack Clark .10 .05
☐ 332 Jerome Walton .05 .02
☐ 333 Andy Hawkins .05 .02
☐ 334 Derrick May .05 .02
☐ 335 Roberto Alomar .20 .09
☐ 336 Jack Morris .15 .07
☐ 337 Dave Winfield .20 .09
☐ 338 Steve Searcy .05 .02
☐ 339 Chili Davis .10 .05
☐ 340 Larry Sheets .05 .02
☐ 341 Ted Higuera .05 .02
☐ 342 David Segui .10 .05
☐ 343 Greg Cadaret .05 .02
☐ 344 Robin Yount .20 .09
☐ 345 Nolan Ryan .75 .35
☐ 346 Ray Lankford .20 .09
☐ 347 Cal Ripken .75 .35
☐ 348 Lee Smith .15 .07
☐ 349 Brady Anderson .20 .09
☐ 350 Frank DiPino .05 .02
☐ 351 Hal Morris .05 .02
☐ 352 Deion Sanders .20 .09
☐ 353 Barry Larkin .20 .09
☐ 354 Don Mattingly .30 .14
☐ 355 Eric Davis .10 .05
☐ 356 Jose Offerman .05 .02
☐ 357 Mel Rojas .15 .07
☐ 358 Rudy Seanez .05 .02
☐ 359 Oil Can Boyd .05 .02
☐ 360 Nelson Liriano .05 .02
☐ 361 Ron Gant .10 .05
☐ 362 Howard Farmer .05 .02
☐ 363 David Justice .25 .11
☐ 364 Delino DeShields .05 .02
☐ 365 Steve Avery .10 .05
☐ 366 David Cone .15 .07
☐ 367 Lou Whitaker .15 .07
☐ 368 Von Hayes .05 .02
☐ 369 Frank Tanana .05 .02
☐ 370 Tim Teufel .05 .02
☐ 371 Randy Myers .10 .05

☐ 372 Roberto Kelly .05 .02
☐ 373 Jack Armstrong .05 .02
☐ 374 Kelly Gruber .05 .02
☐ 375 Kevin Maas .05 .02
☐ 376 Randy Johnson .25 .11
☐ 377 David West .05 .02
☐ 378 Brent Knackert .05 .02
☐ 379 Rick Honeycutt .05 .02
☐ 380 Kevin Gross .05 .02
☐ 381 Tom Foley .05 .02
☐ 382 Jeff Blauser .05 .02
☐ 383 Scott Ruskin .05 .02
☐ 384 Andres Thomas .05 .02
☐ 385 Dennis Martinez .10 .05
☐ 386 Mike Henneman .05 .02
☐ 387 Felix Jose .05 .02
☐ 388 Alejandro Pena .05 .02
☐ 389 Chet Lemon .05 .02
☐ 390 Craig Wilson .05 .02
☐ 391 Chuck Crim .05 .02
☐ 392 Mel Hall .05 .02
☐ 393 Mark Knudson .05 .02
☐ 394 Norm Charlton .05 .02
☐ 395 Mike Felder .05 .02
☐ 396 Tim Layana .05 .02
☐ 397 Steve Frey .05 .02
☐ 398 Bill Doran .05 .02
☐ 399 Dion James .05 .02
☐ 400 Checklist 301-400 .05 .02
☐ 401 Ron Hassey .05 .02
☐ 402 Don Robinson .05 .02
☐ 403 Gene Nelson .05 .02
☐ 404 Terry Kennedy .05 .02
☐ 405 Todd Burns .05 .02
☐ 406 Roger McDowell .05 .02
☐ 407 Bob Kipper .05 .02
☐ 408 Darren Daulton .10 .05
☐ 409 Chuck Cary .05 .02
☐ 410 Bruce Ruffin .05 .02
☐ 411 Juan Berenguer .05 .02
☐ 412 Gary Ward .05 .02
☐ 413 Al Newman .05 .02
☐ 414 Danny Jackson .05 .02
☐ 415 Greg Gagne .05 .02
☐ 416 Tom Herr .05 .02
☐ 417 Jeff Parrett .05 .02
☐ 418 Jeff Reardon .10 .05
☐ 419 Mark Lemke .05 .02
☐ 420 Charlie O'Brien .05 .02
☐ 421 Willie Randolph .10 .05
☐ 422 Steve Bedrosian .05 .02
☐ 423 Mike Moore .05 .02
☐ 424 Jeff Brantley .05 .02
☐ 425 Bob Welch .05 .02
☐ 426 Terry Mulholland .05 .02
☐ 427 Willie Blair .05 .02
☐ 428 Darrin Fletcher .05 .02
☐ 429 Mike Witt .05 .02
☐ 430 Joe Boever .05 .02
☐ 431 Tom Gordon .05 .02
☐ 432 Pedro Munoz .05 .02
☐ 433 Kevin Seitzer .05 .02
☐ 434 Kevin Tapani .05 .02
☐ 435 Bret Saberhagen .10 .05
☐ 436 Ellis Burks .10 .05
☐ 437 Chuck Finley .10 .05
☐ 438 Mike Boddicker .05 .02
☐ 439 Francisco Cabrera .05 .02
☐ 440 Todd Hundley .20 .09
☐ 441 Kelly Downs .05 .02
☐ 442 Dann Howitt .05 .02
☐ 443 Scott Garrelts .05 .02
☐ 444 Rickey Henderson 3X .20 .09
☐ 445 Will Clark .20 .09
☐ 446 Ben McDonald .10 .05
☐ 447 Dale Murphy .20 .09
☐ 448 Dave Righetti .05 .02
☐ 449 Dickie Thon .05 .02
☐ 450 Ted Power .05 .02
☐ 451 Scott Coolbaugh .05 .02
☐ 452 Dwight Smith .05 .02
☐ 453 Pete Incaviglia .05 .02
☐ 454 Andre Dawson .20 .09
☐ 455 Ruben Sierra .05 .02
☐ 456 Andres Galarraga .20 .09
☐ 457 Alvin Davis .05 .02
☐ 458 Tony Castillo .05 .02
☐ 459 Pete O'Brien .05 .02
☐ 460 Charlie Leibrandt .05 .02
☐ 461 Vince Coleman .05 .02
☐ 462 Steve Sax .05 .02
☐ 463 Omar Olivares .05 .02
☐ 464 Oscar Azocar .05 .02
☐ 465 Joe Magrane .05 .02
☐ 466 Karl Rhodes .05 .02
☐ 467 Benito Santiago .05 .02
☐ 468 Joe Klink .05 .02

☐ 469 Sil Campusano .05 .02
☐ 470 Mark Parent .05 .02
☐ 471 Shawn Boskie UER .05 .02
(Depleted misspelled
as depleated)
☐ 472 Kevin Brown .15 .07
☐ 473 Rick Sutcliffe .05 .02
☐ 474 Rafael Palmeiro .20 .09
☐ 475 Mike Harkey .05 .02
☐ 476 Jaime Navarro .05 .02
☐ 477 Marquis Grissom UER .20 .09
(DeShields misspelled
as DeSheilds)
☐ 478 Marty Clary .05 .02
☐ 479 Greg Briley .05 .02
☐ 480 Tom Glavine .20 .09
☐ 481 Lee Guetterman .05 .02
☐ 482 Rex Hudler .05 .02
☐ 483 Dave LaPoint .05 .02
☐ 484 Terry Pendleton .10 .05
☐ 485 Jesse Barfield .05 .02
☐ 486 Jose DeJesus .05 .02
☐ 487 Paul Abbott .05 .02
☐ 488 Ken Howell .05 .02
☐ 489 Greg W. Harris .05 .02
☐ 490 Roy Smith .05 .02
☐ 491 Paul Assenmacher .05 .02
☐ 492 Geno Petralli .05 .02
☐ 493 Steve Wilson .05 .02
☐ 494 Kevin Reimer .05 .02
☐ 495 Bill Long .05 .02
☐ 496 Mike Jackson .05 .02
☐ 497 Oddibe McDowell .05 .02
☐ 498 Bill Swift .05 .02
☐ 499 Jeff Treadway .05 .02
☐ 500 Checklist 401-500 .05 .02
☐ 501 Gene Larkin .05 .02
☐ 502 Bob Boone .10 .05
☐ 503 Allan Anderson .05 .02
☐ 504 Luis Aquino .05 .02
☐ 505 Mark Guthrie .05 .02
☐ 506 Joe Orsulak .05 .02
☐ 507 Dana Kiecker .05 .02
☐ 508 Dave Gallagher .05 .02
☐ 509 Greg A. Harris .05 .02
☐ 510 Mark Williamson .05 .02
☐ 511 Casey Candaele .05 .02
☐ 512 Mookie Wilson .05 .02
☐ 513 Dave Smith .05 .02
☐ 514 Chuck Carr .05 .02
☐ 515 Glenn Wilson .05 .02
☐ 516 Mike Fitzgerald .05 .02
☐ 517 Devon White .05 .02
☐ 518 Dave Hollins .05 .02
☐ 519 Mark Eichhorn .05 .02
☐ 520 Otis Nixon .05 .02
☐ 521 Terry Shumpert .05 .02
☐ 522 Scott Erickson .10 .05
☐ 523 Danny Tartabull .05 .02
☐ 524 Orel Hershiser .10 .05
☐ 525 George Brett .40 .18
☐ 526 Greg Vaughn .05 .02
☐ 527 Tim Naehring .10 .05
☐ 528 Curt Schilling .20 .09
☐ 529 Chris Bosio .05 .02
☐ 530 Sam Horn .05 .02
☐ 531 Mike Scott .05 .02
☐ 532 George Bell .05 .02
☐ 533 Eric Anthony .05 .02
☐ 534 Julio Valera .05 .02
☐ 535 Glenn Davis .05 .02
☐ 536 Larry Walker UER .30 .14
(Should have comma
after Expos in text)
☐ 537 Pat Combs .05 .0
☐ 538 Chris Nabholz .05 .0
☐ 539 Kirk McCaskill .05 .0
☐ 540 Randy Ready .05 .0
☐ 541 Mark Gubicza .05 .0
☐ 542 Rick Aguilera .10 .0
☐ 543 Brian McRae .20 .0
☐ 544 Kirby Puckett .40 .1
☐ 545 Bo Jackson .15 .0
☐ 546 Wade Boggs .20 .0
☐ 547 Tim McIntosh .05 .0
☐ 548 Randy Milligan .05 .0
☐ 549 Dwight Evans .10 .0
☐ 550 Billy Ripken .05 .0
☐ 551 Erik Hanson .05 .0
☐ 552 Lance Parrish .05 .0
☐ 553 Tino Martinez .20 .0
☐ 554 Jim Abbott .10 .0
☐ 555 Ken Griffey Jr. UER 1.50 .
(Second most votes for
1991 All-Star Game)
☐ 556 Milt Cuyler .05 .0
☐ 557 Mark Leonard .05 .0

☐ 558 Jay Howell	.05	.02
☐ 559 Lloyd Moseby	.05	.02
☐ 560 Chris Gwynn	.05	.02
☐ 561 Mark Whiten	.05	.02
☐ 562 Harold Baines	.10	.05
☐ 563 Junior Felix	.05	.02
☐ 564 Darren Lewis	.05	.02
☐ 565 Fred McGriff	.20	.09
☐ 566 Kevin Appier	.20	.09
☐ 567 Luis Gonzalez	.15	.07
☐ 568 Frank White	.10	.05
☐ 569 Juan Agosto	.05	.02
☐ 570 Mike Macfarlane	.05	.02
☐ 571 Bert Blyleven	.10	.05
☐ 572 Ken Griffey Sr. Ken Griffey Jr.	.50	.23
☐ 573 Lee Stevens	.05	.02
☐ 574 Edgar Martinez	.20	.09
☐ 575 Wally Joyner	.10	.05
☐ 576 Tim Belcher	.05	.02
☐ 577 John Burkett	.05	.02
☐ 578 Mike Morgan	.05	.02
☐ 579 Paul Gibson	.05	.02
☐ 580 Jose Vizcaino	.05	.02
☐ 581 Duane Ward	.05	.02
☐ 582 Scott Sanderson	.05	.02
☐ 583 David Wells	.05	.02
☐ 584 Willie McGee	.05	.02
☐ 585 John Cerutti	.05	.02
☐ 586 Danny Darwin	.05	.02
☐ 587 Kurt Stillwell	.05	.02
☐ 588 Rich Gedman	.05	.02
☐ 589 Mark Davis	.05	.02
☐ 590 Bill Gullickson	.05	.02
☐ 591 Matt Young	.05	.02
☐ 592 Bryan Harvey	.05	.02
☐ 593 Omar Vizquel	.20	.09
☐ 594 Scott Lewis	.05	.02
☐ 595 Dave Valle	.05	.02
☐ 596 Tim Crews	.05	.02
☐ 597 Mike Bielecki	.05	.02
☐ 598 Mike Sharperson	.05	.02
☐ 599 Dave Bergman	.05	.02
☐ 600 Checklist 501-600	.05	.02
☐ 601 Steve Lyons	.05	.02
☐ 602 Bruce Hurst	.05	.02
☐ 603 Donn Pall	.05	.02
☐ 604 Jim Vatcher	.05	.02
☐ 605 Dan Pasqua	.05	.02
☐ 606 Kenny Rogers	.05	.02
☐ 607 Jeff Schulz	.05	.02
☐ 608 Brad Arnsberg	.05	.02
☐ 609 Willie Wilson	.05	.02
☐ 610 Jamie Moyer	.05	.02
☐ 611 Ron Oester	.05	.02
☐ 612 Dennis Cook	.05	.02
☐ 613 Rick Mahler	.05	.02
☐ 614 Bill Landrum	.05	.02
☐ 615 Scott Scudder	.05	.02
☐ 616 Tom Edens	.05	.02
☐ 617 1917 Revisited (White Sox in vintage uniforms)	.10	.05
☐ 618 Jim Gantner	.05	.02
☐ 619 Darrel Akerfelds	.05	.02
☐ 620 Ron Robinson	.05	.02
☐ 621 Scott Radinsky	.05	.02
☐ 622 Pete Smith	.05	.02
☐ 623 Melido Perez	.05	.02
☐ 624 Jerald Clark	.05	.02
☐ 625 Carlos Martinez	.05	.02
☐ 626 Wes Chamberlain	.05	.02
☐ 627 Bobby Witt	.05	.02
☐ 628 Ken Dayley	.05	.02
☐ 629 John Barfield	.05	.02
☐ 630 Bob Tewksbury	.05	.02
☐ 631 Glenn Braggs	.05	.02
☐ 632 Jim Neidlinger	.05	.02
☐ 633 Tom Browning	.05	.02
☐ 634 Kirk Gibson	.10	.05
☐ 635 Rob Dibble	.05	.02
☐ 636 Rickey Henderson SB Lou Brock May 1, 1991 on front)	.30	.14
☐ 636A Rickey Henderson SB Lou Brock no date on card)	.20	.09
☐ 637 Jeff Montgomery	.10	.05
☐ 638 Mike Schooler	.05	.02
☐ 639 Storm Davis	.05	.02
☐ 640 Rich Rodriguez	.05	.02
☐ 641 Phil Bradley	.05	.02
☐ 642 Kent Mercker	.05	.02
☐ 643 Carlton Fisk	.20	.09
☐ 644 Mike Bell	.05	.02
☐ 645 Alex Fernandez	.15	.07
☐ 646 Juan Gonzalez	.75	.35
☐ 647 Ken Hill	.10	.05
☐ 648 Jeff Russell	.05	.02
☐ 649 Chuck Malone	.05	.02
☐ 650 Steve Buechele	.05	.02
☐ 651 Mike Benjamin	.05	.02
☐ 652 Tony Pena	.05	.02
☐ 653 Trevor Wilson	.05	.02
☐ 654 Alex Cole	.05	.02
☐ 655 Roger Clemens	.40	.18
☐ 656 Mark McGwire BASH	.20	.09
☐ 657 Joe Grahe	.05	.02
☐ 658 Jim Eisenreich	.10	.05
☐ 659 Dan Gladden	.05	.02
☐ 660 Steve Farr	.05	.02
☐ 661 Bill Sampen	.05	.02
☐ 662 Dave Rohde	.05	.02
☐ 663 Mark Gardner	.05	.02
☐ 664 Mike Simms	.05	.02
☐ 665 Moises Alou	.20	.09
☐ 666 Mickey Hatcher	.05	.02
☐ 667 Jimmy Key	.10	.05
☐ 668 John Wetteland	.20	.09
☐ 669 John Smiley	.05	.02
☐ 670 Jim Acker	.05	.02
☐ 671 Pascual Perez	.05	.02
☐ 672 Reggie Harris UER (Opportunity misspelled as oppurtinty)	.05	.02
☐ 673 Matt Nokes	.05	.02
☐ 674 Rafael Novoa	.05	.02
☐ 675 Hensley Meulens	.05	.02
☐ 676 Jeff M. Robinson	.05	.02
☐ 677 Ground Breaking (New Comiskey Park; Carlton Fisk and Robin Ventura)	.10	.05
☐ 678 Johnny Ray	.05	.02
☐ 679 Greg Hibbard	.05	.02
☐ 680 Paul Sorrento	.10	.05
☐ 681 Mike Marshall	.05	.02
☐ 682 Jim Clancy	.05	.02
☐ 683 Rob Murphy	.05	.02
☐ 684 Dave Schmidt	.05	.02
☐ 685 Jeff Gray	.05	.02
☐ 686 Mike Hartley	.05	.02
☐ 687 Jeff King	.10	.05
☐ 688 Stan Javier	.05	.02
☐ 689 Bob Walk	.05	.02
☐ 690 Jim Gott	.05	.02
☐ 691 Mike LaCoss	.05	.02
☐ 692 John Farrell	.05	.02
☐ 693 Tim Leary	.05	.02
☐ 694 Mike Walker	.05	.02
☐ 695 Eric Plunk	.05	.02
☐ 696 Mike Fetters	.05	.02
☐ 697 Wayne Edwards	.05	.02
☐ 698 Tim Drummond	.05	.02
☐ 699 Willie Fraser	.05	.02
☐ 700 Checklist 601-700	.05	.02
☐ 701 Mike Heath	.05	.02
☐ 702 Rookie Threats Luis Gonzalez Karl Rhodes Jeff Bagwell	.75	.35
☐ 703 Jose Mesa	.10	.05
☐ 704 Dave Smith	.05	.02
☐ 705 Danny Darwin	.05	.02
☐ 706 Rafael Belliard	.05	.02
☐ 707 Rob Murphy	.05	.02
☐ 708 Terry Pendleton	.10	.05
☐ 709 Mike Pagliarulo	.05	.02
☐ 710 Sid Bream	.05	.02
☐ 711 Junior Felix	.05	.02
☐ 712 Dante Bichette	.20	.09
☐ 713 Kevin Gross	.05	.02
☐ 714 Luis Sojo	.05	.02
☐ 715 Bob Ojeda	.05	.02
☐ 716 Julio Machado	.05	.02
☐ 717 Steve Farr	.05	.02
☐ 718 Franklin Stubbs	.05	.02
☐ 719 Mike Boddicker	.05	.02
☐ 720 Willie Randolph	.10	.05
☐ 721 Willie McGee	.05	.02
☐ 722 Chili Davis	.10	.05
☐ 723 Danny Jackson	.05	.02
☐ 724 Cory Snyder	.05	.02
☐ 725 MVP Lineup Andre Dawson George Bell Ryne Sandberg	.20	.09
☐ 726 Rob Deer	.05	.02
☐ 727 Rich DeLucia	.05	.02
☐ 728 Mike Perez	.05	.02
☐ 729 Mickey Tettleton	.10	.05
☐ 730 Mike Blowers	.05	.02
☐ 731 Gary Gaetti	.10	.05
☐ 732 Brett Butler	.10	.05
☐ 733 Dave Parker	.10	.05
☐ 734 Eddie Zosky	.05	.02
☐ 735 Jack Clark	.10	.05
☐ 736 Jack Morris	.10	.05
☐ 737 Kirk Gibson	.10	.05
☐ 738 Steve Bedrosian	.05	.02
☐ 739 Candy Maldonado	.05	.02
☐ 740 Matt Young	.05	.02
☐ 741 Rich Garces	.05	.02
☐ 742 George Bell	.05	.02
☐ 743 Deion Sanders	.20	.09
☐ 744 Bo Jackson	.10	.05
☐ 745 Luis Mercedes	.05	.02
☐ 746 Reggie Jefferson UER (Throwing left on card; back has throws right)	.20	.09
☐ 747 Pete Incaviglia	.05	.02
☐ 748 Chris Hammond	.05	.02
☐ 749 Mike Stanton	.05	.02
☐ 750 Scott Sanderson	.05	.02
☐ 751 Paul Faries	.05	.02
☐ 752 Al Osuna	.05	.02
☐ 753 Steve Chitren	.05	.02
☐ 754 Tony Fernandez	.05	.02
☐ 755 Jeff Bagwell UER (Strikeout and walk totals reversed)	2.50	1.10
☐ 756 Kirk Dressendorfer	.05	.02
☐ 757 Glenn Davis	.05	.02
☐ 758 Gary Carter	.20	.09
☐ 759 Zane Smith	.05	.02
☐ 760 Vance Law	.05	.02
☐ 761 Denis Boucher	.05	.02
☐ 762 Turner Ward	.05	.02
☐ 763 Roberto Alomar	.20	.09
☐ 764 Albert Belle	.30	.14
☐ 765 Joe Carter	.20	.09
☐ 766 Pete Schourek	.10	.05
☐ 767 Heathcliff Slocumb	.20	.09
☐ 768 Vince Coleman	.05	.02
☐ 769 Mitch Williams	.05	.02
☐ 770 Brian Downing	.05	.02
☐ 771 Dana Allison	.05	.02
☐ 772 Pete Harnisch	.05	.02
☐ 773 Tim Raines	.10	.05
☐ 774 Darryl Kile	.20	.09
☐ 775 Fred McGriff	.20	.09
☐ 776 Dwight Evans	.10	.05
☐ 777 Joe Slusarski	.05	.02
☐ 778 Dave Righetti	.05	.02
☐ 779 Jeff Hamilton	.05	.02
☐ 780 Ernest Riles	.05	.02
☐ 781 Ken Dayley	.05	.02
☐ 782 Eric King	.05	.02
☐ 783 Devon White	.10	.05
☐ 784 Beau Allred	.05	.02
☐ 785 Mike Timlin	.05	.02
☐ 786 Ivan Calderon	.05	.02
☐ 787 Hubie Brooks	.05	.02
☐ 788 Juan Agosto	.05	.02
☐ 789 Barry Jones	.05	.02
☐ 790 Wally Backman	.05	.02
☐ 791 Jim Presley	.05	.02
☐ 792 Charlie Hough	.05	.02
☐ 793 Larry Andersen	.05	.02
☐ 794 Steve Finley	.10	.05
☐ 795 Shawn Abner	.05	.02
☐ 796 Jeff M. Robinson	.05	.02
☐ 797 Joe Bitker	.05	.02
☐ 798 Eric Show	.05	.02
☐ 799 Bud Black	.05	.02
☐ 800 Checklist 701-800	.05	.02
☐ HH1 Hank Aaron Hologram	1.50	.70
☐ SP1 Michael Jordan SP (Shown batting in White Sox uniform)	15.00	6.75
☐ SP2 Rickey Henderson Nolan Ryan May 1, 1991 Records	1.50	.70

1991 Upper Deck Aaron Heroes

These standard-size cards were issued in honor of Hall of Famer Hank Aaron and inserted in Upper Deck high number wax packs. The fronts have color player photos superimposed over a circular shot. Inside a red border stripe, a tan background fills in the rest of the card face. The Baseball Heroes logo adorns the card face. The backs have a similar design, except with an extended caption presented on a light gray background. Aaron autographed 2,500 of card number 27, which featured his portrait by noted sports artist Vernon Wells. The cards are numbered on the back in continuation of the Baseball Heroes set.

	MINT	NRMT
COMPLETE SET (10)	5.00	2.20
COMMON AARON (19-27)	.50	.23

	MINT	NRMT
☐ 19 Hank Aaron 1954 Rookie Year	.50	.23
☐ 20 Hank Aaron 1957 MVP	.50	.23
☐ 21 Hank Aaron 1966 Move to Atlanta	.50	.23
☐ 22 Hank Aaron 1970 3,000 Hits	.50	.23
☐ 23 Hank Aaron 1974 715 Homers	.50	.23
☐ 24 Hank Aaron 1975 Return to Milwaukee	.50	.23
☐ 25 Hank Aaron 1976 755 Homers	.50	.23
☐ 26 Hank Aaron 1982 Hall of Fame	.50	.23
☐ 27 Checklist 19-27	.50	.23
☐ AU3 Hank Aaron AU (Signed and Numbered out of 2500)	300.00	135.00
☐ NNO0 Title/Header card SP	1.00	.45

1991 Upper Deck Heroes of Baseball

These standard-size cards were randomly inserted in Upper Deck Baseball Heroes wax packs. On a white card face, the fronts of the first three cards have sepia-toned player photos, with red, gold, and blue border stripes. The player's name appears in a gold border stripe beneath the picture, with the Upper Deck "Heroes of Baseball" logo in the lower right corner. The backs have a similar design to the fronts, except with a career summary and an advertisement for Upper Deck "Heroes of Baseball" games that will be played prior to regularly scheduled Major League games. The fourth card features a color portrait of the three players by noted sports artist Vernon Wells.

	MINT	NRMT
COMPLETE SET (4)	25.00	11.00
COMMON CARD (H1-H4)	8.00	3.60

	MINT	NRMT
☐ H1 Harmon Killebrew	8.00	3.60
☐ H2 Gaylord Perry	8.00	3.60
☐ H3 Ferguson Jenkins	8.00	3.60
☐ H4 Harmon Killebrew DRAW Ferguson Jenkins Gaylord Perry	8.00	3.60
☐ AU1 Harmon Killebrew AU/3000	75.00	34.00
☐ AU2 Gaylord Perry AU/3000	75.00	34.00
☐ AU3 Ferguson Jenkins AU/3000	75.00	34.00

1991 Upper Deck Ryan Heroes

This nine-card standard-size set was included in first series 1991 Upper Deck packs. The set which honors Nolan Ryan and is numbered as a continuation of the Baseball Heroes set which began with Reggie Jackson in 1990. This set honors Ryan's long career and his place in Baseball History. Card number 18 features the artwork of Vernon Wells while the other cards are photos. The complete set price below does not include the signed

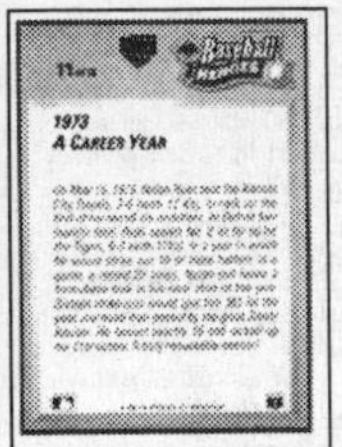

Ryan card of which only 2500 were made. Signed cards ending with 00 have the expression "Strikeout King" added. These Ryan cards were apparently issued on 100-card sheets with the following configuration: ten each of the nine Ryan Baseball Heroes cards, five Michael Jordan cards and five Baseball Heroes header cards. The Baseball Heroes header card is a standard size card which explains the continuation of the Baseball Heroes series on the back while the front just says Baseball Heroes.

	MINT	NRMT
COMPLETE SET (10)	5.00	2.20
COMMON RYAN (10-18)	.50	.23

	MINT	NRMT
☐ 10 Nolan Ryan Tom Seaver Jerry Koosman 1968 Victory 1	.50	.23
☐ 11 Nolan Ryan 1973 A Career Year	.50	.23
☐ 12 Nolan Ryan 1975 Double Milestone	.50	.23
☐ 13 Nolan Ryan 1979 Back Home	.50	.23
☐ 14 Nolan Ryan 1981 All Time Leader	.50	.23
☐ 15 Nolan Ryan 1989 5,000 K's	.50	.23
☐ 16 Nolan Ryan 1990 6th No-Hitter	.50	.23
☐ 17 Nolan Ryan 1990 And Still Counting	.50	.23
☐ 18 NBlan Ryan Checklist Card Vernon Wells drawing with 5 poses of Ryan including each team he played for	.50	.23
☐ AU2 Nolan Ryan AU (Signed and Numbered out of 2500)	600.00	275.00
☐ NNO0 Baseball Heroes SP (Header card)	1.00	.45

1991 Upper Deck Silver Sluggers

The Upper Deck Silver Slugger set features nine players from each league, representing the nine batting positions on the team. The cards were issued one per 1991 Upper Deck jumbo pack. The cards measure the standard size. The fronts have glossy color action player photos, with white borders on three sides and a "Silver Slugger" bat serving as the border on the left side. The player's name appears in a tan stripe below the picture, with the team logo superimposed at the lower right corner. The card back is dominated by another color action photo with career highlights in a horizontally oriented rectangle to the left of the picture. The cards are numbered on the back with an SS prefix.

	MINT	NRMT
COMPLETE SET (18)	15.00	6.75
COMMON CARD (SS1-SS18)	.50	.23

	MINT	NRMT
☐ SS1 Julio Franco	.75	.35
☐ SS2 Alan Trammell	1.00	.45
☐ SS3 Rickey Henderson	1.25	.55
☐ SS4 Jose Canseco	1.25	.55
☐ SS5 Barry Bonds	2.00	.90
☐ SS6 Eddie Murray	1.25	.55
☐ SS7 Kelly Gruber	.50	.23
☐ SS8 Ryne Sandberg	2.00	.90
☐ SS9 Darryl Strawberry	.75	.35
☐ SS10 Ellis Burks	.75	.35
☐ SS11 Lance Parrish	.50	.23
☐ SS12 Cecil Fielder	.75	.35
☐ SS13 Matt Williams	1.25	.55
☐ SS14 Dave Parker	.75	.35
☐ SS15 Bobby Bonilla	.75	.35
☐ SS16 Don Robinson	.50	.23
☐ SS17 Benito Santiago	.50	.23
☐ SS18 Barry Larkin	1.25	.55

1991 Upper Deck Final Edition

The 1991 Upper Deck Final Edition boxed set contains 100 standard-size cards and showcases players who made major contributions during their team's late-season pennant drive. In addition to the late season traded and impact rookie cards (22-78), the set includes two special subsets: Diamond Skills cards (1-21), depicting the best Minor League prospects, and All-Star cards (80-99). Six assorted team logo hologram cards were issued with each set. The basic card fronts feature posed or action color player photos on a white card face, with the upper left corner of the picture cut out to provide space for the Upper Deck logo. The pictures are bordered in green on the left, with the player's name in a tan border below the picture. The cards are numbered on the back with an F suffix. Among the outstanding Rookie Cards in this set are Ryan Klesko, Kenny Lofton, Pedro Martinez, Ivan Rodriguez, Jim Thome, Rondell White, and Dmitri Young.

	MINT	NRMT
COMPLETE SET (100)	5.00	2.20
COMMON CARD (1F-100F)	.05	.02

	MINT	NRMT
☐ 1F Ryan Klesko CL Reggie Sanders	.20	.09
☐ 2F Pedro Martinez	1.00	.45
☐ 3F Lance Dickson	.05	.02
☐ 4F Royce Clayton	.10	.05
☐ 5F Scott Bryant	.05	.02
☐ 6F Dan Wilson	.25	.11
☐ 7F Dmitri Young	.25	.11
☐ 8F Ryan Klesko	.75	.35
☐ 9F Tom Goodwin	.10	.05
☐ 10F Rondell White	.30	.14
☐ 11F Reggie Sanders	.25	.11
☐ 12F Todd Van Poppel	.05	.02
☐ 13F Arthur Rhodes	.10	.05
☐ 14F Eddie Zosky	.05	.02
☐ 15F Gerald Williams	.05	.02
☐ 16F Robert Eenhoorn	.05	.02
☐ 17F Jim Thome	1.25	.55
☐ 18F Marc Newfield	.15	.07
☐ 19F Kerwin Moore	.05	.02
☐ 20F Jeff McNeely	.05	.02
☐ 21F Frankie Rodriguez	.20	.09
☐ 22F Andy Mota	.05	.02
☐ 23F Chris Haney	.05	.02
☐ 24F Kenny Lofton	1.50	.7
☐ 25F Dave Nilsson	.20	.0
☐ 26F Derek Bell	.10	.0
☐ 27F Frank Castillo	.10	.0
☐ 28F Candy Maldonado	.05	.0
☐ 29F Chuck McElroy	.05	.0
☐ 30F Chito Martinez	.05	.0
☐ 31F Steve Howe	.05	.0
☐ 32F Freddie Benavides	.05	.0
☐ 33F Scott Kamieniecki	.05	.0
☐ 34F Denny Neagle	.60	.2
☐ 35F Mike Humphreys	.05	.0
☐ 36F Mike Remlinger	.05	.0
☐ 37F Scott Coolbaugh	.05	.0
☐ 38F Darren Lewis	.05	.0
☐ 39F Thomas Howard	.05	.0
☐ 40F John Candelaria	.05	.0
☐ 41F Todd Benzinger	.05	.0

☐ 42F Wilson Alvarez	.20	.09
☐ 43F Patrick Lennon	.05	.02
☐ 44F Rusty Meacham	.05	.02
☐ 45F Ryan Bowen	.05	.02
☐ 46F Rick Wilkins	.05	.02
☐ 47F Ed Sprague	.10	.05
☐ 48F Bob Scanlan	.05	.02
☐ 49F Tom Candiotti	.05	.02
☐ 50F Dennis Martinez	.10	.05
(Perfecto)		
☐ 51F Oil Can Boyd	.05	.02
☐ 52F Glenallen Hill	.05	.02
☐ 53F Scott Livingstone	.05	.02
☐ 54F Brian R. Hunter	.05	.02
☐ 55F Ivan Rodriguez	1.50	.70
☐ 56F Keith Mitchell	.05	.02
☐ 57F Roger McDowell	.05	.02
☐ 58F Otis Nixon	.10	.05
☐ 59F Juan Bell	.05	.02
☐ 60F Bill Krueger	.05	.02
☐ 61F Chris Donnels	.05	.02
☐ 62F Tommy Greene	.05	.02
☐ 63F Doug Simons	.05	.02
☐ 64F Andy Ashby	.20	.09
☐ 65F Anthony Young	.05	.02
☐ 66F Kevin Morton	.05	.02
☐ 67F Bret Barberie	.05	.02
☐ 68F Scott Servais	.05	.02
☐ 69F Ron Darling	.05	.02
☐ 70F Tim Burke	.05	.02
☐ 71F Vicente Palacios	.05	.02
☐ 72F Gerald Alexander	.05	.02
☐ 73F Reggie Jefferson	.20	.09
☐ 74F Dean Palmer	.20	.09
☐ 75F Mark Whiten	.05	.02
☐ 76F Randy Tomlin	.05	.02
☐ 77F Mark Wohlers	.15	.07
☐ 78F Brook Jacoby	.05	.02
☐ 79F Ken Griffey Jr. CL	.40	.18
Ryne Sandberg		
☐ 80F Jack Morris AS	.10	.05
☐ 81F Sandy Alomar Jr. AS	.15	.07
☐ 82F Cecil Fielder AS	.10	.05
☐ 83F Roberto Alomar AS	.20	.09
☐ 84F Wade Boggs AS	.20	.09
☐ 85F Cal Ripken AS	.40	.18
☐ 86F Rickey Henderson AS	.20	.09
☐ 87F Ken Griffey Jr. AS	.75	.35
☐ 88F Dave Henderson AS	.05	.02
☐ 89F Danny Tartabull AS	.05	.02
☐ 90F Tom Glavine AS	.20	.09
☐ 91F Benito Santiago AS	.05	.02
☐ 92F Will Clark AS	.20	.09
☐ 93F Ryne Sandberg AS	.20	.09
☐ 94F Chris Sabo AS	.05	.02
☐ 95F Ozzie Smith AS	.10	.05
☐ 96F Ivan Calderon AS	.05	.02
☐ 97F Tony Gwynn AS	.25	.11
☐ 98F Andre Dawson AS	.20	.09
☐ 99F Bobby Bonilla AS	.10	.05
☐ 100F Checklist 1-100	.05	.02

1992 Upper Deck

he 1992 Upper Deck set contains 800 standard-size ards issued in two separate series of 700 and 100 cards espectively. The cards were distributed in low and high eries foil packs in addition to factory sets. Factory sets eature a unique gold-foil hologram on the card backs (in ontrast to the silver hologram on foil pack cards). The asic issue card fronts features shadow-bordered action olor player photos on a white card face. The player's ame appears above the photo, with the team name uperimposed at the lower right corner. Special subsets cluded in the set are Star Rookies (1-27), Team hecklists (29-40/86-99), with player portraits by Vernon ells; Top Prospects (52-77); Bloodlines (79-85), amond Skills (640-650/711-721) and Diamond Debuts 71-780). Rookie Cards in the set include Shawn Green, ey Hamilton, Brian Jordan and Manny Ramirez. A ecial card picturing Tom Selleck and Frank Thomas, commemorating the forgettable movie "Mr. Baseball", was randomly inserted into high series packs. A standard-size Ted Williams hologram card was randomly inserted into low series packs. By mailing in 15 low series foil wrappers, a completed order form, and a handling fee, the collector could receive an 8 1/2" by 11" numbered, black and white lithograph picturing Ted Williams in his batting swing.

	MINT	NRMT
COMPLETE SET (800)	15.00	6.75
COMP.FACT.SET (800)	20.00	9.00
COMPLETE LO SET (700)	12.00	5.50
COMPLETE HI SET (100)	3.00	1.35
COMMON CARD (1-800)	.05	.02

Card		
☐ 1 Ryan Klesko CL	.40	.18
Jim Thome		
☐ 2 Royce Clayton SR	.10	.05
☐ 3 Brian Jordan SR	.25	.11
☐ 4 Dave Fleming SR	.05	.02
☐ 5 Jim Thome SR	.60	.25
☐ 6 Jeff Juden SR	.05	.02
☐ 7 Roberto Hernandez SR	.10	.05
☐ 8 Kyle Abbott SR	.05	.02
☐ 9 Chris George SR	.05	.02
☐ 10 Rob Maurer SR	.05	.02
☐ 11 Donald Harris SR	.05	.02
☐ 12 Ted Wood SR	.05	.02
☐ 13 Patrick Lennon SR	.05	.02
☐ 14 Willie Banks SR	.05	.02
☐ 15 Roger Salkeld SR UER	.05	.02
(Bill was his grand-		
father, not his father)		
☐ 16 Wil Cordero SR	.05	.02
☐ 17 Arthur Rhodes SR	.05	.02
☐ 18 Pedro Martinez SR	.40	.18
☐ 19 Andy Ashby SR	.05	.02
☐ 20 Tom Goodwin SR	.05	.02
☐ 21 Braulio Castillo SR	.05	.02
☐ 22 Todd Van Poppel SR	.05	.02
☐ 23 Brian Williams SR	.05	.02
☐ 24 Ryan Klesko SR	.40	.18
☐ 25 Kenny Lofton SR	.75	.35
☐ 26 Derek Bell SR	.10	.05
☐ 27 Reggie Sanders SR	.10	.05
☐ 28 Dave Winfield's 400th	.15	.07
☐ 29 David Justice TC	.10	.05
☐ 30 Rob Dibble TC	.05	.02
☐ 31 Craig Biggio TC	.15	.07
☐ 32 Eddie Murray TC	.20	.09
☐ 33 Fred McGriff TC	.10	.05
☐ 34 Willie McGee TC	.05	.02
☐ 35 Shawon Dunston TC	.05	.02
☐ 36 Delino DeShields TC	.05	.02
☐ 37 Howard Johnson TC	.05	.02
☐ 38 John Kruk TC	.05	.02
☐ 39 Doug Drabek TC	.05	.02
☐ 40 Todd Zeile TC	.05	.02
☐ 41 Steve Avery	.05	.02
Playoff Perfection		
☐ 42 Jeremy Hernandez	.05	.02
☐ 43 Doug Henry	.05	.02
☐ 44 Chris Donnels	.05	.02
☐ 45 Mo Sanford	.05	.02
☐ 46 Scott Kamieniecki	.05	.02
☐ 47 Mark Lemke	.05	.02
☐ 48 Steve Farr	.05	.02
☐ 49 Francisco Oliveras	.05	.02
☐ 50 Ced Landrum	.05	.02
☐ 51 Rondell White CL	.20	.09
Mark Newfield		
☐ 52 Eduardo Perez TP	.05	.02
☐ 53 Tom Nevers TP	.05	.02
☐ 54 David Zancanaro TP	.05	.02
☐ 55 Shawn Green TP	.25	.11
☐ 56 Mark Wohlers TP	.15	.07
☐ 57 Dave Nilsson TP	.15	.07
☐ 58 Dmitri Young TP	.20	.09
☐ 59 Ryan Hawblitzel TP	.05	.02
☐ 60 Raul Mondesi TP	.40	.18
☐ 61 Rondell White TP	.20	.09
☐ 62 Steve Hosey TP	.05	.02
☐ 63 Manny Ramirez TP	1.25	.55
☐ 64 Marc Newfield TP	.15	.07
☐ 65 Jeromy Burnitz TP	.10	.05
☐ 66 Mark Smith TP	.05	.02
☐ 67 Joey Hamilton TP	.40	.18
☐ 68 Tyler Green TP	.05	.02
☐ 69 Jon Farrell TP	.05	.02
☐ 70 Kurt Miller TP	.05	.02
☐ 71 Jeff Plympton TP	.05	.02
☐ 72 Dan Wilson TP	.10	.05
☐ 73 Joe Vitiello TP	.05	.02
☐ 74 Rico Brogna TP	.10	.05
☐ 75 David McCarty TP	.05	.02
☐ 76 Bob Wickman TP	.05	.02
☐ 77 Carlos Rodriguez TP	.05	.02
☐ 78 Jim Abbott	.05	.02
Stay In School		
☐ 79 Ramon Martinez	.20	.09
Pedro Martinez		
☐ 80 Kevin Mitchell	.05	.02
Keith Mitchell		
☐ 81 Sandy Alomar Jr.	.20	.09
Roberto Alomar		
☐ 82 Cal Ripken	.50	.23
Billy Ripken		
☐ 83 Tony Gwynn	.20	.09
Chris Gwynn		
☐ 84 Dwight Gooden	.15	.07
Gary Sheffield		
☐ 85 Ken Griffey Sr.	.60	.25
Ken Griffey Jr.		
Craig Griffey		
☐ 86 Jim Abbott TC	.05	.02
☐ 87 Frank Thomas TC	.75	.35
☐ 88 Danny Tartabull TC	.05	.02
☐ 89 Scott Erickson TC	.05	.02
☐ 90 Rickey Henderson TC	.15	.07
☐ 91 Edgar Martinez TC	.10	.05
☐ 92 Nolan Ryan TC	.40	.18
☐ 93 Ben McDonald TC	.05	.02
☐ 94 Ellis Burks TC	.10	.05
☐ 95 Greg Swindell TC	.05	.02
☐ 96 Cecil Fielder TC	.10	.05
☐ 97 Greg Vaughn TC	.05	.02
☐ 98 Kevin Maas TC	.05	.02
☐ 99 Dave Stieb TC	.05	.02
☐ 100 Checklist 1-100	.05	.02
☐ 101 Joe Oliver	.05	.02
☐ 102 Hector Villanueva	.05	.02
☐ 103 Ed Whitson	.05	.02
☐ 104 Danny Jackson	.05	.02
☐ 105 Chris Hammond	.05	.02
☐ 106 Ricky Jordan	.05	.02
☐ 107 Kevin Bass	.05	.02
☐ 108 Darrin Fletcher	.05	.02
☐ 109 Junior Ortiz	.05	.02
☐ 110 Tom Bolton	.05	.02
☐ 111 Jeff King	.10	.05
☐ 112 Dave Magadan	.05	.02
☐ 113 Mike LaValliere	.05	.02
☐ 114 Hubie Brooks	.05	.02
☐ 115 Jay Bell	.10	.05
☐ 116 David Wells	.05	.02
☐ 117 Jim Leyritz	.05	.02
☐ 118 Manuel Lee	.05	.02
☐ 119 Alvaro Espinoza	.05	.02
☐ 120 B.J. Surhoff	.10	.05
☐ 121 Hal Morris	.05	.02
☐ 122 Shawon Dawson	.05	.02
☐ 123 Chris Sabo	.05	.02
☐ 124 Andre Dawson	.15	.07
☐ 125 Eric Davis	.10	.05
☐ 126 Chili Davis	.10	.05
☐ 127 Dale Murphy	.15	.07
☐ 128 Kirk McCaskill	.05	.02
☐ 129 Terry Mulholland	.05	.02
☐ 130 Rick Aguilera	.05	.02
☐ 131 Vince Coleman	.05	.02
☐ 132 Andy Van Slyke	.10	.05
☐ 133 Gregg Jefferies	.10	.05
☐ 134 Barry Bonds	.25	.11
☐ 135 Dwight Gooden	.10	.05
☐ 136 Dave Stieb	.05	.02
☐ 137 Albert Belle	.25	.11
☐ 138 Teddy Higuera	.05	.02
☐ 139 Jesse Barfield	.05	.02
☐ 140 Pat Borders	.05	.02
☐ 141 Bip Roberts	.05	.02
☐ 142 Rob Dibble	.05	.02
☐ 143 Mark Grace	.15	.07
☐ 144 Barry Larkin	.15	.07
☐ 145 Ryne Sandberg	.25	.11
☐ 146 Scott Erickson	.10	.05
☐ 147 Luis Polonia	.05	.02
☐ 148 John Burkett	.05	.02
☐ 149 Luis Sojo	.05	.02
☐ 150 Dickie Thon	.05	.02
☐ 151 Walt Weiss	.05	.02
☐ 152 Mike Scioscia	.05	.02
☐ 153 Mark McGwire	.40	.18
☐ 154 Matt Williams	.15	.07
☐ 155 Rickey Henderson	.15	.07
☐ 156 Sandy Alomar Jr.	.10	.05
☐ 157 Brian McRae	.05	.02
☐ 158 Harold Baines	.10	.05
☐ 159 Kevin Appier	.10	.05
☐ 160 Felix Fermin	.05	.02
☐ 161 Leo Gomez	.05	.02
☐ 162 Craig Biggio	.15	.07
☐ 163 Ben McDonald	.05	.02
☐ 164 Randy Johnson	.20	.09
☐ 165 Cal Ripken	.75	.35

☐ 166 Frank Thomas	1.00	.45
☐ 167 Delino DeShields	.05	.02
☐ 168 Greg Gagne	.05	.02
☐ 169 Ron Karkovice	.05	.02
☐ 170 Charlie Leibrandt	.05	.02
☐ 171 Dave Righetti	.05	.02
☐ 172 Dave Henderson	.05	.02
☐ 173 Steve Decker	.05	.02
☐ 174 Darryl Strawberry	.10	.05
☐ 175 Will Clark	.15	.07
☐ 176 Ruben Sierra	.05	.02
☐ 177 Ozzie Smith	.25	.11
☐ 178 Charles Nagy	.10	.05
☐ 179 Gary Pettis	.05	.02
☐ 180 Kirk Gibson	.10	.05
☐ 181 Randy Milligan	.05	.02
☐ 182 Dave Valle	.05	.02
☐ 183 Chris Hoiles	.05	.02
☐ 184 Tony Phillips	.05	.02
☐ 185 Brady Anderson	.15	.07
☐ 186 Scott Fletcher	.05	.02
☐ 187 Gene Larkin	.05	.02
☐ 188 Lance Johnson	.10	.05
☐ 189 Greg Olson	.05	.02
☐ 190 Melido Perez	.05	.02
☐ 191 Lenny Harris	.05	.02
☐ 192 Terry Kennedy	.05	.02
☐ 193 Mike Gallego	.05	.02
☐ 194 Willie McGee	.05	.02
☐ 195 Juan Samuel	.05	.02
☐ 196 Jeff Huson (Shows Jose Canseco sliding into second)	.10	.05
☐ 197 Alex Cole	.05	.02
☐ 198 Ron Robinson	.05	.02
☐ 199 Joel Skinner	.05	.02
☐ 200 Checklist 101-200	.05	.02
☐ 201 Kevin Reimer	.05	.02
☐ 202 Stan Belinda	.05	.02
☐ 203 Pat Tabler	.05	.02
☐ 204 Jose Guzman	.05	.02
☐ 205 Jose Lind	.05	.02
☐ 206 Spike Owen	.05	.02
☐ 207 Joe Orsulak	.05	.02
☐ 208 Charlie Hayes	.05	.02
☐ 209 Mike Devereaux	.05	.02
☐ 210 Mike Fitzgerald	.05	.02
☐ 211 Willie Randolph	.10	.05
☐ 212 Rod Nichols	.05	.02
☐ 213 Mike Boddicker	.05	.02
☐ 214 Bill Spiers	.05	.02
☐ 215 Steve Olin	.05	.02
☐ 216 David Howard	.05	.02
☐ 217 Gary Varsho	.05	.02
☐ 218 Mike Harkey	.05	.02
☐ 219 Luis Aquino	.05	.02
☐ 220 Chuck McElroy	.05	.02
☐ 221 Doug Drabek	.05	.02
☐ 222 Dave Winfield	.15	.07
☐ 223 Rafael Palmeiro	.15	.07
☐ 224 Joe Carter	.15	.07
☐ 225 Bobby Bonilla	.15	.07
☐ 226 Ivan Calderon	.05	.02
☐ 227 Gregg Olson	.05	.02
☐ 228 Tim Wallach	.05	.02
☐ 229 Terry Pendleton	.10	.05
☐ 230 Gilberto Reyes	.05	.02
☐ 231 Carlos Baerga	.10	.05
☐ 232 Greg Vaughn	.05	.02
☐ 233 Bret Saberhagen	.05	.02
☐ 234 Gary Sheffield	.20	.09
☐ 235 Mark Lewis	.05	.02
☐ 236 George Bell	.05	.02
☐ 237 Danny Tartabull	.05	.02
☐ 238 Willie Wilson	.05	.02
☐ 239 Doug Dascenzo	.05	.02
☐ 240 Bill Pecota	.05	.02
☐ 241 Julio Franco	.10	.05
☐ 242 Ed Sprague	.05	.02
☐ 243 Juan Gonzalez	.60	.25
☐ 244 Chuck Finley	.05	.02
☐ 245 Ivan Rodriguez	.40	.18
☐ 246 Len Dykstra	.10	.05
☐ 247 Deion Sanders	.20	.09
☐ 248 Dwight Evans	.10	.05
☐ 249 Larry Walker	.20	.09
☐ 250 Billy Ripken	.05	.02
☐ 251 Mickey Tettleton	.05	.02
☐ 252 Tony Pena	.05	.02
☐ 253 Benito Santiago	.05	.02
☐ 254 Kirby Puckett	.40	.18
☐ 255 Cecil Fielder	.10	.05
☐ 256 Howard Johnson	.05	.02
☐ 257 Andujar Cedeno	.05	.02
☐ 258 Jose Rijo	.05	.02
☐ 259 Al Osuna	.05	.02
☐ 260 Todd Hundley	.15	.07
☐ 261 Orel Hershiser	.10	.05
☐ 262 Ray Lankford	.20	.09
☐ 263 Robin Ventura	.10	.05
☐ 264 Felix Jose	.05	.02
☐ 265 Eddie Murray	.20	.09
☐ 266 Kevin Mitchell	.10	.05
☐ 267 Gary Carter	.15	.07
☐ 268 Mike Benjamin	.05	.02
☐ 269 Dick Schofield	.05	.02
☐ 270 Jose Uribe	.05	.02
☐ 271 Pete Incaviglia	.05	.02
☐ 272 Tony Fernandez	.05	.02
☐ 273 Alan Trammell	.10	.05
☐ 274 Tony Gwynn	.50	.23
☐ 275 Mike Greenwell	.05	.02
☐ 276 Jeff Bagwell	.60	.25
☐ 277 Frank Viola	.05	.02
☐ 278 Randy Myers	.10	.05
☐ 279 Ken Caminiti	.20	.09
☐ 280 Bill Doran	.05	.02
☐ 281 Dan Pasqua	.05	.02
☐ 282 Alfredo Griffin	.05	.02
☐ 283 Jose Oquendo	.05	.02
☐ 284 Kal Daniels	.05	.02
☐ 285 Bobby Thigpen	.05	.02
☐ 286 Robby Thompson	.05	.02
☐ 287 Mark Eichhorn	.05	.02
☐ 288 Mike Felder	.05	.02
☐ 289 Dave Gallagher	.05	.02
☐ 290 Dave Anderson	.05	.02
☐ 291 Mel Hall	.05	.02
☐ 292 Jerald Clark	.05	.02
☐ 293 Al Newman	.05	.02
☐ 294 Rob Deer	.05	.02
☐ 295 Matt Nokes	.05	.02
☐ 296 Jack Armstrong	.05	.02
☐ 297 Jim Deshaies	.05	.02
☐ 298 Jeff Innis	.05	.02
☐ 299 Jeff Reed	.05	.02
☐ 300 Checklist 201-300	.05	.02
☐ 301 Lonnie Smith	.05	.02
☐ 302 Jimmy Key	.10	.05
☐ 303 Junior Felix	.05	.02
☐ 304 Mike Heath	.05	.02
☐ 305 Mark Langston	.05	.02
☐ 306 Greg W. Harris	.05	.02
☐ 307 Brett Butler	.10	.05
☐ 308 Luis Rivera	.05	.02
☐ 309 Bruce Ruffin	.05	.02
☐ 310 Paul Faries	.05	.02
☐ 311 Terry Leach	.05	.02
☐ 312 Scott Brosius	.05	.02
☐ 313 Scott Leius	.05	.02
☐ 314 Harold Reynolds	.05	.02
☐ 315 Jack Morris	.10	.05
☐ 316 David Segui	.05	.02
☐ 317 Bill Gullickson	.05	.02
☐ 318 Todd Frohwirth	.05	.02
☐ 319 Mark Leiter	.05	.02
☐ 320 Jeff M. Robinson	.05	.02
☐ 321 Gary Gaetti	.10	.05
☐ 322 John Smoltz	.15	.07
☐ 323 Andy Benes	.10	.05
☐ 324 Kelly Gruber	.05	.02
☐ 325 Jim Abbott	.05	.02
☐ 326 John Kruk	.10	.05
☐ 327 Kevin Seitzer	.05	.02
☐ 328 Darrin Jackson	.05	.02
☐ 329 Kurt Stillwell	.05	.02
☐ 330 Mike Maddux	.05	.02
☐ 331 Dennis Eckersley	.15	.07
☐ 332 Dan Gladden	.05	.02
☐ 333 Jose Canseco	.15	.07
☐ 334 Kent Hrbek	.10	.05
☐ 335 Ken Griffey Sr.	.05	.02
☐ 336 Greg Swindell	.05	.02
☐ 337 Trevor Wilson	.05	.02
☐ 338 Sam Horn	.05	.02
☐ 339 Mike Henneman	.05	.02
☐ 340 Jerry Browne	.05	.02
☐ 341 Glenn Braggs	.05	.02
☐ 342 Tom Glavine	.15	.07
☐ 343 Wally Joyner	.10	.05
☐ 344 Fred McGriff	.15	.07
☐ 345 Ron Gant	.10	.05
☐ 346 Ramon Martinez	.10	.05
☐ 347 Wes Chamberlain	.05	.02
☐ 348 Terry Shumpert	.05	.02
☐ 349 Tim Teufel	.05	.02
☐ 350 Wally Backman	.05	.02
☐ 351 Joe Girardi	.05	.02
☐ 352 Devon White	.05	.02
☐ 353 Greg Maddux	.60	.25
☐ 354 Ryan Bowen	.05	.02
☐ 355 Roberto Alomar	.20	.09
☐ 356 Don Mattingly	.30	.14
☐ 357 Pedro Guerrero	.05	.02
☐ 358 Steve Sax	.05	.02
☐ 359 Joey Cora	.10	.05
☐ 360 Jim Gantner	.05	.02
☐ 361 Brian Barnes	.05	.02
☐ 362 Kevin McReynolds	.05	.02
☐ 363 Bret Barberie	.05	.02
☐ 364 David Cone	.10	.05
☐ 365 Dennis Martinez	.10	.05
☐ 366 Brian Hunter	.05	.02
☐ 367 Edgar Martinez	.15	.07
☐ 368 Steve Finley	.10	.05
☐ 369 Greg Briley	.05	.02
☐ 370 Jeff Blauser	.05	.02
☐ 371 Todd Stottlemyre	.05	.02
☐ 372 Luis Gonzalez	.05	.02
☐ 373 Rick Wilkins	.05	.02
☐ 374 Darryl Kile	.10	.05
☐ 375 John Olerud	.10	.05
☐ 376 Lee Smith	.10	.05
☐ 377 Kevin Maas	.05	.02
☐ 378 Dante Bichette	.15	.07
☐ 379 Tom Pagnozzi	.05	.02
☐ 380 Mike Flanagan	.05	.02
☐ 381 Charlie O'Brien	.05	.02
☐ 382 Dave Martinez	.05	.02
☐ 383 Keith Miller	.05	.02
☐ 384 Scott Ruskin	.05	.02
☐ 385 Kevin Elster	.05	.02
☐ 386 Alvin Davis	.05	.02
☐ 387 Casey Candaele	.05	.02
☐ 388 Pete O'Brien	.05	.02
☐ 389 Jeff Treadway	.05	.02
☐ 390 Scott Bradley	.05	.02
☐ 391 Mookie Wilson	.05	.02
☐ 392 Jimmy Jones	.05	.02
☐ 393 Candy Maldonado	.05	.02
☐ 394 Eric Yelding	.05	.02
☐ 395 Tom Henke	.05	.02
☐ 396 Franklin Stubbs	.05	.02
☐ 397 Milt Thompson	.05	.02
☐ 398 Mark Carreon	.05	.02
☐ 399 Randy Velarde	.05	.02
☐ 400 Checklist 301-400	.05	.02
☐ 401 Omar Vizquel	.10	.05
☐ 402 Joe Boever	.05	.02
☐ 403 Bill Krueger	.05	.02
☐ 404 Jody Reed	.05	.02
☐ 405 Mike Schooler	.05	.02
☐ 406 Jason Grimsley	.05	.02
☐ 407 Greg Myers	.05	.02
☐ 408 Randy Ready	.05	.02
☐ 409 Mike Timlin	.05	.02
☐ 410 Mitch Williams	.05	.02
☐ 411 Garry Templeton	.05	.02
☐ 412 Greg Cadaret	.05	.02
☐ 413 Donnie Hill	.05	.02
☐ 414 Wally Whitehurst	.05	.02
☐ 415 Scott Sanderson	.05	.02
☐ 416 Thomas Howard	.05	.02
☐ 417 Neal Heaton	.05	.02
☐ 418 Charlie Hough	.05	.02
☐ 419 Jack Howell	.05	.02
☐ 420 Greg Hibbard	.05	.02
☐ 421 Carlos Quintana	.05	.02
☐ 422 Kim Batiste	.05	.02
☐ 423 Paul Molitor	.20	.09
☐ 424 Ken Griffey Jr.	1.25	.55
☐ 425 Phil Plantier	.05	.02
☐ 426 Denny Neagle	.15	.07
☐ 427 Von Hayes	.05	.02
☐ 428 Shane Mack	.05	.02
☐ 429 Darren Daulton	.10	.05
☐ 430 Dwayne Henry	.05	.02
☐ 431 Lance Parrish	.05	.02
☐ 432 Mike Humphreys	.05	.02
☐ 433 Tim Burke	.05	.02
☐ 434 Bryan Harvey	.05	.02
☐ 435 Pat Kelly	.05	.02
☐ 436 Ozzie Guillen	.05	.02
☐ 437 Bruce Hurst	.05	.02
☐ 438 Sammy Sosa	.20	.09
☐ 439 Dennis Rasmussen	.05	.02
☐ 440 Ken Patterson	.05	.02
☐ 441 Jay Buhner	.15	.07
☐ 442 Pat Combs	.05	.02
☐ 443 Wade Boggs	.20	.0
☐ 444 George Brett	.40	.1
☐ 445 Mo Vaughn	.30	.1
☐ 446 Chuck Knoblauch	.20	.0
☐ 447 Tom Candiotti	.05	.0
☐ 448 Mark Portugal	.05	.0
☐ 449 Mickey Morandini	.05	.0
☐ 450 Duane Ward	.05	.0
☐ 451 Otis Nixon	.10	.0
☐ 452 Bob Welch	.05	.0
☐ 453 Rusty Meacham	.05	.0
☐ 454 Keith Mitchell	.05	.0

- ☐ 455 Marquis Grissom .10 .05
- ☐ 456 Robin Yount .15 .07
- ☐ 457 Harvey Pulliam .05 .02
- ☐ 458 Jose DeLeon .05 .02
- ☐ 459 Mark Gubicza .05 .02
- ☐ 460 Darryl Hamilton .05 .02
- ☐ 461 Tom Browning .05 .02
- ☐ 462 Monty Fariss .05 .02
- ☐ 463 Jerome Walton .05 .02
- ☐ 464 Paul O'Neill .10 .05
- ☐ 465 Dean Palmer .10 .05
- ☐ 466 Travis Fryman .10 .05
- ☐ 467 John Smiley .05 .02
- ☐ 468 Lloyd Moseby .05 .02
- ☐ 469 John Wehner .05 .02
- ☐ 470 Skeeter Barnes .05 .02
- ☐ 471 Steve Chitren .05 .02
- ☐ 472 Kent Mercker .05 .02
- ☐ 473 Terry Steinbach .10 .05
- ☐ 474 Andres Galarraga .15 .07
- ☐ 475 Steve Avery .05 .02
- ☐ 476 Tom Gordon .05 .02
- ☐ 477 Cal Eldred .05 .02
- ☐ 478 Omar Olivares .05 .02
- ☐ 479 Julio Machado .05 .02
- ☐ 480 Bob Milacki .05 .02
- ☐ 481 Les Lancaster .05 .02
- ☐ 482 John Candelaria .05 .02
- ☐ 483 Brian Downing .05 .02
- ☐ 484 Roger McDowell .05 .02
- ☐ 485 Scott Scudder .05 .02
- ☐ 486 Zane Smith .05 .02
- ☐ 487 John Cerutti .05 .02
- ☐ 488 Steve Buechele .05 .02
- ☐ 489 Paul Gibson .05 .02
- ☐ 490 Curtis Wilkerson .05 .02
- ☐ 491 Marvin Freeman .05 .02
- ☐ 492 Tom Foley .05 .02
- ☐ 493 Juan Berenguer .05 .02
- ☐ 494 Ernest Riles .05 .02
- ☐ 495 Sid Bream .05 .02
- ☐ 496 Chuck Crim .05 .02
- ☐ 497 Mike Macfarlane .05 .02
- ☐ 498 Dale Sveum .05 .02
- ☐ 499 Storm Davis .05 .02
- ☐ 500 Checklist 401-500 .05 .02
- ☐ 501 Jeff Reardon .10 .05
- ☐ 502 Shawn Abner .05 .02
- ☐ 503 Tony Fossas .05 .02
- ☐ 504 Cory Snyder .05 .02
- ☐ 505 Matt Young .05 .02
- ☐ 506 Allan Anderson .05 .02
- ☐ 507 Mark Lee .05 .02
- ☐ 508 Gene Nelson .05 .02
- ☐ 509 Mike Pagliarulo .05 .02
- ☐ 510 Rafael Belliard .05 .02
- ☐ 511 Jay Howell .05 .02
- ☐ 512 Bob Tewksbury .05 .02
- ☐ 513 Mike Morgan .05 .02
- ☐ 514 John Franco .05 .02
- ☐ 515 Kevin Gross .05 .02
- ☐ 516 Lou Whitaker .10 .05
- ☐ 517 Orlando Merced .05 .02
- ☐ 518 Todd Benzinger .05 .02
- ☐ 519 Gary Redus .05 .02
- ☐ 520 Walt Terrell .05 .02
- ☐ 521 Jack Clark .10 .05
- ☐ 522 Dave Parker .10 .05
- ☐ 523 Tim Naehring .10 .05
- ☐ 524 Mark Whiten .05 .02
- ☐ 525 Ellis Burks .10 .05
- ☐ 526 Frank Castillo .10 .05
- ☐ 527 Brian Harper .05 .02
- ☐ 528 Brook Jacoby .05 .02
- ☐ 529 Rick Sutcliffe .05 .02
- ☐ 530 Joe Klink .05 .02
- ☐ 531 Terry Bross .05 .02
- ☐ 532 Jose Offerman .05 .02
- ☐ 533 Todd Zeile .05 .02
- ☐ 534 Eric Karros .15 .07
- ☐ 535 Anthony Young .05 .02
- ☐ 536 Milt Cuyler .05 .02
- ☐ 537 Randy Tomlin .05 .02
- ☐ 538 Scott Livingstone .05 .02
- ☐ 539 Jim Eisenreich .10 .05
- ☐ 540 Don Slaught .05 .02
- ☐ 541 Scott Cooper .05 .02
- ☐ 542 Joe Grahe .05 .02
- ☐ 543 Tom Brunansky .05 .02
- ☐ 544 Eddie Zosky .05 .02
- ☐ 545 Roger Clemens .40 .18
- ☐ 546 David Justice .20 .09
- ☐ 547 Dave Stewart .10 .05
- ☐ 548 David West .05 .02
- ☐ 549 Dave Smith .05 .02
- ☐ 550 Dan Plesac .05 .02
- ☐ 551 Alex Fernandez .10 .05
- ☐ 552 Bernard Gilkey .10 .05
- ☐ 553 Jack McDowell .05 .02
- ☐ 554 Tino Martinez .20 .09
- ☐ 555 Bo Jackson .10 .05
- ☐ 556 Bernie Williams .15 .07
- ☐ 557 Mark Gardner .05 .02
- ☐ 558 Glenallen Hill .05 .02
- ☐ 559 Oil Can Boyd .05 .02
- ☐ 560 Chris James .05 .02
- ☐ 561 Scott Servais .05 .02
- ☐ 562 Rey Sanchez .05 .02
- ☐ 563 Paul McClellan .05 .02
- ☐ 564 Andy Mota .05 .02
- ☐ 565 Darren Lewis .05 .02
- ☐ 566 Jose Melendez .05 .02
- ☐ 567 Tommy Greene .05 .02
- ☐ 568 Rich Rodriguez .05 .02
- ☐ 569 Heathcliff Slocumb .05 .02
- ☐ 570 Joe Hesketh .05 .02
- ☐ 571 Carlton Fisk .20 .09
- ☐ 572 Erik Hanson .05 .02
- ☐ 573 Wilson Alvarez .10 .05
- ☐ 574 Rheal Cormier .05 .02
- ☐ 575 Tim Raines .10 .05
- ☐ 576 Bobby Witt .05 .02
- ☐ 577 Roberto Kelly .05 .02
- ☐ 578 Kevin Brown .10 .05
- ☐ 579 Chris Nabholz .05 .02
- ☐ 580 Jesse Orosco .05 .02
- ☐ 581 Jeff Brantley .05 .02
- ☐ 582 Rafael Ramirez .05 .02
- ☐ 583 Kelly Downs .05 .02
- ☐ 584 Mike Simms .05 .02
- ☐ 585 Mike Remlinger .05 .02
- ☐ 586 Dave Hollins .05 .02
- ☐ 587 Larry Andersen .05 .02
- ☐ 588 Mike Gardiner .05 .02
- ☐ 589 Craig Lefferts .05 .02
- ☐ 590 Paul Assenmacher .05 .02
- ☐ 591 Bryn Smith .05 .02
- ☐ 592 Donn Pall .05 .02
- ☐ 593 Mike Jackson .05 .02
- ☐ 594 Scott Radinsky .05 .02
- ☐ 595 Brian Holman .05 .02
- ☐ 596 Geronimo Pena .05 .02
- ☐ 597 Mike Jeffcoat .05 .02
- ☐ 598 Carlos Martinez .05 .02
- ☐ 599 Geno Petralli .05 .02
- ☐ 600 Checklist 501-600 .05 .02
- ☐ 601 Jerry Don Gleaton .05 .02
- ☐ 602 Adam Peterson .05 .02
- ☐ 603 Craig Grebeck .05 .02
- ☐ 604 Mark Guthrie .05 .02
- ☐ 605 Frank Tanana .05 .02
- ☐ 606 Hensley Meulens .05 .02
- ☐ 607 Mark Davis .05 .02
- ☐ 608 Eric Plunk .05 .02
- ☐ 609 Mark Williamson .05 .02
- ☐ 610 Lee Guetterman .05 .02
- ☐ 611 Bobby Rose .05 .02
- ☐ 612 Bill Wegman .05 .02
- ☐ 613 Mike Hartley .05 .02
- ☐ 614 Chris Beasley .05 .02
- ☐ 615 Chris Bosio .05 .02
- ☐ 616 Henry Cotto .05 .02
- ☐ 617 Chico Walker .05 .02
- ☐ 618 Russ Swan .05 .02
- ☐ 619 Bob Walk .05 .02
- ☐ 620 Billy Swift .05 .02
- ☐ 621 Warren Newson .05 .02
- ☐ 622 Steve Bedrosian .05 .02
- ☐ 623 Ricky Bones .05 .02
- ☐ 624 Kevin Tapani .05 .02
- ☐ 625 Juan Guzman .10 .05
- ☐ 626 Jeff Johnson .05 .02
- ☐ 627 Jeff Montgomery .10 .05
- ☐ 628 Ken Hill .10 .05
- ☐ 629 Gary Thurman .05 .02
- ☐ 630 Steve Howe .05 .02
- ☐ 631 Jose DeJesus .05 .02
- ☐ 632 Kirk Dressendorfer .05 .02
- ☐ 633 Jaime Navarro .05 .02
- ☐ 634 Lee Stevens .05 .02
- ☐ 635 Pete Harnisch .05 .02
- ☐ 636 Bill Landrum .05 .02
- ☐ 637 Rich DeLucia .05 .02
- ☐ 638 Luis Salazar .05 .02
- ☐ 639 Rob Murphy .05 .02
- ☐ 640 Jose Canseco CL .20 .09
  Rickey Henderson
- ☐ 641 Roger Clemens DS .20 .09
- ☐ 642 Jim Abbott DS .05 .02
- ☐ 643 Travis Fryman DS .10 .05
- ☐ 644 Jesse Barfield DS .05 .02
- ☐ 645 Cal Ripken DS .40 .18
- ☐ 646 Wade Boggs DS .15 .07
- ☐ 647 Cecil Fielder DS .10 .05
- ☐ 648 Rickey Henderson DS .15 .07
- ☐ 649 Jose Canseco DS .10 .05
- ☐ 650 Ken Griffey Jr. DS .75 .35
- ☐ 651 Kenny Rogers .05 .02
- ☐ 652 Luis Mercedes .05 .02
- ☐ 653 Mike Stanton .05 .02
- ☐ 654 Glenn Davis .05 .02
- ☐ 655 Nolan Ryan .75 .35
- ☐ 656 Reggie Jefferson .10 .05
- ☐ 657 Javier Ortiz .05 .02
- ☐ 658 Greg A. Harris .05 .02
- ☐ 659 Mariano Duncan .05 .02
- ☐ 660 Jeff Shaw .05 .02
- ☐ 661 Mike Moore .05 .02
- ☐ 662 Chris Haney .05 .02
- ☐ 663 Joe Slusarski .05 .02
- ☐ 664 Wayne Housie .05 .02
- ☐ 665 Carlos Garcia .05 .02
- ☐ 666 Bob Ojeda .05 .02
- ☐ 667 Bryan Hickerson .05 .02
- ☐ 668 Tim Belcher .05 .02
- ☐ 669 Ron Darling .05 .02
- ☐ 670 Rex Hudler .05 .02
- ☐ 671 Sid Fernandez .05 .02
- ☐ 672 Chito Martinez .05 .02
- ☐ 673 Pete Schourek .05 .02
- ☐ 674 Armando Reynoso .05 .02
- ☐ 675 Mike Mussina .30 .14
- ☐ 676 Kevin Morton .05 .02
- ☐ 677 Norm Charlton .05 .02
- ☐ 678 Danny Darwin .05 .02
- ☐ 679 Eric King .05 .02
- ☐ 680 Ted Power .05 .02
- ☐ 681 Barry Jones .05 .02
- ☐ 682 Carney Lansford .10 .05
- ☐ 683 Mel Rojas .10 .05
- ☐ 684 Rick Honeycutt .05 .02
- ☐ 685 Jeff Fassero .05 .02
- ☐ 686 Cris Carpenter .05 .02
- ☐ 687 Tim Crews .05 .02
- ☐ 688 Scott Terry .05 .02
- ☐ 689 Chris Gwynn .05 .02
- ☐ 690 Gerald Perry .05 .02
- ☐ 691 John Barfield .05 .02
- ☐ 692 Bob Melvin .05 .02
- ☐ 693 Juan Agosto .05 .02
- ☐ 694 Alejandro Pena .05 .02
- ☐ 695 Jeff Russell .05 .02
- ☐ 696 Carmelo Martinez .05 .02
- ☐ 697 Bud Black .05 .02
- ☐ 698 Dave Otto .05 .02
- ☐ 699 Billy Hatcher .05 .02
- ☐ 700 Checklist 601-700 .05 .02
- ☐ 701 Clemente Nunez .10 .05
- ☐ 702 Rookie Threats .05 .02
  Mark Clark
  Donovan Osborne
  Brian Jordan
- ☐ 703 Mike Morgan .05 .02
- ☐ 704 Keith Miller .05 .02
- ☐ 705 Kurt Stillwell .05 .02
- ☐ 706 Damon Berryhill .05 .02
- ☐ 707 Von Hayes .05 .02
- ☐ 708 Rick Sutcliffe .05 .02
- ☐ 709 Hubie Brooks .05 .02
- ☐ 710 Ryan Turner .05 .02
- ☐ 711 Barry Bonds CL .10 .05
  Andy Van Slyke
- ☐ 712 Jose Rijo DS .05 .02
- ☐ 713 Tom Glavine DS .10 .05
- ☐ 714 Shawon Dunston DS .05 .02
- ☐ 715 Andy Van Slyke DS .05 .02
- ☐ 716 Ozzie Smith DS .20 .09
- ☐ 717 Tony Gwynn DS .20 .09
- ☐ 718 Will Clark DS .15 .07
- ☐ 719 Marquis Grissom DS .10 .05
- ☐ 720 Howard Johnson DS .05 .02
- ☐ 721 Barry Bonds DS .20 .09
- ☐ 722 Kirk McCaskill .05 .02
- ☐ 723 Sammy Sosa .20 .09
- ☐ 724 George Bell .05 .02
- ☐ 725 Gregg Jefferies .10 .05
- ☐ 726 Gary DiSarcina .05 .02
- ☐ 727 Mike Bordick .10 .05
- ☐ 728 Eddie Murray .20 .09
  400 Home Run Club
- ☐ 729 Rene Gonzales .05 .02
- ☐ 730 Mike Bielecki .05 .02
- ☐ 731 Calvin Jones .05 .02
- ☐ 732 Jack Morris .10 .05
- ☐ 733 Frank Viola .05 .02
- ☐ 734 Dave Winfield .15 .07
- ☐ 735 Kevin Mitchell .10 .05
- ☐ 736 Bill Swift .05 .02
- ☐ 737 Dan Gladden .05 .02
- ☐ 738 Mike Jackson .05 .02
- ☐ 739 Mark Carreon .05 .02

☐ 740 Kirt Manwaring	.05	.02
☐ 741 Randy Myers	.10	.05
☐ 742 Kevin McReynolds	.05	.02
☐ 743 Steve Sax	.05	.02
☐ 744 Wally Joyner	.10	.05
☐ 745 Gary Sheffield	.20	.09
☐ 746 Danny Tartabull	.05	.02
☐ 747 Julio Valera	.05	.02
☐ 748 Denny Neagle	.15	.07
☐ 749 Lance Blankenship	.05	.02
☐ 750 Mike Gallego	.05	.02
☐ 751 Bret Saberhagen	.05	.02
☐ 752 Ruben Amaro	.05	.02
☐ 753 Eddie Murray	.20	.09
☐ 754 Kyle Abbott	.05	.02
☐ 755 Bobby Bonilla	.10	.05
☐ 756 Eric Davis	.10	.05
☐ 757 Eddie Taubensee	.05	.02
☐ 758 Andres Galarraga	.20	.09
☐ 759 Pete Incaviglia	.05	.02
☐ 760 Tom Candiotti	.05	.02
☐ 761 Tim Belcher	.05	.02
☐ 762 Ricky Bones	.05	.02
☐ 763 Bip Roberts	.05	.02
☐ 764 Pedro Munoz	.05	.02
☐ 765 Greg Swindell	.05	.02
☐ 766 Kenny Lofton	.75	.35
☐ 767 Gary Carter	.20	.09
☐ 768 Charlie Hayes	.05	.02
☐ 769 Dickie Thon	.05	.02
☐ 770 Donovan Osborne DD CL	.05	.02
☐ 771 Bret Boone DD	.10	.05
☐ 772 Archi Cianfrocco DD	.05	.02
☐ 773 Mark Clark DD	.05	.02
☐ 774 Chad Curtis DD	.20	.09
☐ 775 Pat Listach DD	.05	.02
☐ 776 Pat Mahomes DD	.05	.02
☐ 777 Donovan Osborne DD	.05	.02
☐ 778 John Patterson DD	.05	.02
☐ 779 Andy Stankiewicz DD	.05	.02
☐ 780 Turk Wendell DD	.10	.05
☐ 781 Bill Krueger	.05	.02
☐ 782 Rickey Henderson Grand Theft	.15	.07
☐ 783 Kevin Seitzer	.05	.02
☐ 784 Dave Martinez	.05	.02
☐ 785 John Smiley	.05	.02
☐ 786 Matt Stairs	.05	.02
☐ 787 Scott Scudder	.05	.02
☐ 788 John Wetteland	.10	.05
☐ 789 Jack Armstrong	.05	.02
☐ 790 Ken Hill	.10	.05
☐ 791 Dick Schofield	.05	.02
☐ 792 Mariano Duncan	.05	.02
☐ 793 Bill Pecota	.05	.02
☐ 794 Mike Kelly	.05	.02
☐ 795 Willie Randolph	.10	.05
☐ 796 Butch Henry	.05	.02
☐ 797 Carlos Hernandez	.05	.02
☐ 798 Doug Jones	.05	.02
☐ 799 Melido Perez	.05	.02
☐ 800 Checklist 701-800	.05	.02
☐ HH2 Ted Williams Hologram (Top left corner says 91 Upper Deck 92)	2.00	.90
☐ SP3 Deion Sanders FB/BB	1.00	.45
☐ SP4 Tom Selleck Frank Thomas SP (Mr. Baseball)	3.00	1.35

1992 Upper Deck Bench/Morgan Heroes

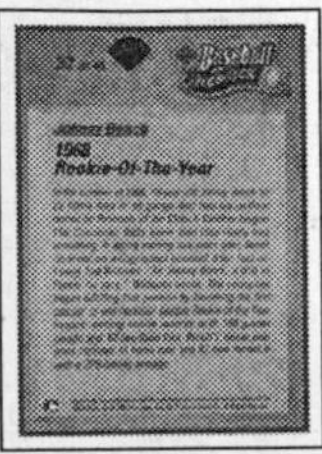

This standard size 10-card set was randomly inserted in 1992 Upper Deck high number packs. Both Bench and Morgan autographed 2,500 of card number 45, which displays a portrait by sports artist Vernon Wells. The fronts feature color photos of Bench (37-39), Morgan (40-42), or both (43-44) at various stages of their baseball careers. These pictures are partially contained within a blue and white bordered circle. The photos rest on a parchment card face trimmed with a brick red and white border. The Upper Deck Baseball Heroes logo appears in the lower right corner. The back design displays career highlights on a gray plaque resting on the same parchment background as on the front.

	MINT	NRMT
COMPLETE SET (10)	10.00	4.50
COMMON BENCH/MORG (37-45)	1.00	.45
☐ 37 Johnny Bench 1968 Rookie-of-the-Year	1.00	.45
☐ 38 Johnny Bench 1968-77 Ten Straight Gold Gloves	1.00	.45
☐ 39 Johnny Bench 1970 and 1972 MVP	1.00	.45
☐ 40 Joe Morgan 1965 Rookie Year	1.00	.45
☐ 41 Joe Morgan 1975-76 Back-to-Back MVP	1.00	.45
☐ 42 Johnny Bench 1980-83 The Golden Years	1.00	.45
☐ 43 Johnny Bench Joe Morgan 1972-79 Big Red Machine	1.00	.45
☐ 44 Johnny Bench Joe Morgan 1989 and 1990 Hall of Fame	1.00	.45
☐ 45 Checklist-Heroes 37-45	1.00	.45
☐ AU5 Johnny Bench and Joe Morgan AU (Signed and Numbered of 2500)	150.00	70.00
☐ NNO0 Baseball Heroes SP (Header card)	2.50	1.10

1992 Upper Deck College POY Holograms

This three-card standard-size set was randomly inserted in 1992 Upper Deck high series foil packs. This set features College Player of the Year winners for 1989 through 1991. The full-bleed fronts display two action player holographic photos. The player's name is superimposed at the bottom edge over a team color-coded bar. The backs carry a second action player shot on the right side with the player's name and the year he made POY printed on a color-coded bar along the left side. In a vertical format, the player's career summary is printed on the left. The cards are numbered on the back with the prefix "CP".

	MINT	NRMT
COMPLETE SET (3)	2.00	.90
COMMON CARD (CP1-CP3)	.75	.35
☐ CP1 David McCarty	.75	.35
☐ CP2 Mike Kelly	.75	.35
☐ CP3 Ben McDonald	.75	.35

1992 Upper Deck Heroes of Baseball

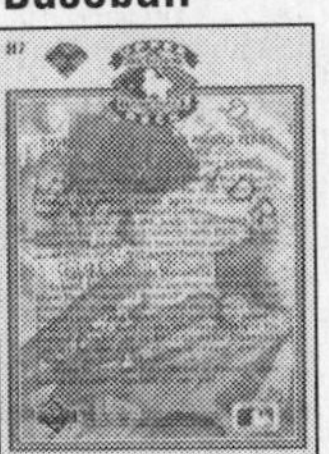

Continuing a popular insert set introduced the previous year, Upper Deck produced four new commemorative cards, including three player cards and one portrait card by sports artist Vernon Wells. These cards were randomly inserted in 1992 Upper Deck baseball low number foil packs. Three thousand of each card were personally numbered and autographed by each player. On a white card face, the fronts carry sepia-tone player photos with red, gold, and blue border stripes. The player's name appears in a gold border stripe beneath the picture, with the Upper Deck "Heroes of Baseball" logo in the lower right corner.

	MINT	NRMT
COMPLETE SET (4)	8.00	3.60
COMMON CARD (H5-H8)	1.00	.45
☐ H5 Vida Blue	1.00	.45
☐ H6 Lou Brock	4.00	1.80
☐ H7 Rollie Fingers	2.00	.90
☐ H8 Vida Blue ART Lou Brock Rollie Fingers	3.00	1.35
☐ AU5 Vida Blue AU/3000	15.00	6.75
☐ AU6 Lou Brock AU/3000	60.00	27.00
☐ AU7 R.Fingers AU/3000	30.00	13.50

1992 Upper Deck Heroes Highlights

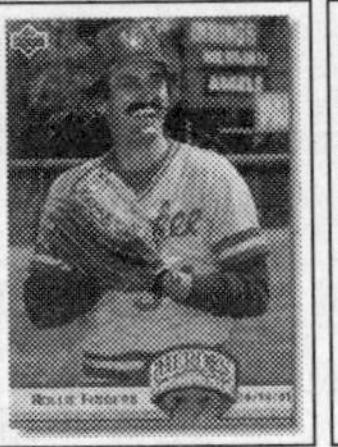

To dealers participating in Heroes of Baseball Collectors shows, Upper Deck made available this ten-card insert standard-size set, which commemorates one of the greatest moments in the careers of ten of baseball's all-time players. The cards were primarily randomly inserted in high number packs sold at these shows. However at the first Heroes show in Anaheim, the cards were inserted into low number packs. The fronts feature color player photos with a shadowed strip for a three-dimensional effect. The player's name and the date of the great moment in the hero's career appear with a "Heroes Highlights" logo in a bottom border of varying shades of brown and blue-green. The backs have white borders and display a blue-green and brown bordered monument design accented with baseballs. The major portion of the design is parchment-textured and contains text highlighting a special moment in the player's career. The cards are numbered on the back with an "HI" prefix. The card numbering follows alphabetical order by player's name.

	MINT	NRMT
COMPLETE SET (10)	20.00	9.00
COMMON CARD (HI1-HI10)	1.00	.45
☐ HI1 Bobby Bonds	1.00	.45
☐ HI2 Lou Brock	4.00	1.80
☐ HI3 Rollie Fingers	2.50	1.10
☐ HI4 Bob Gibson	4.00	1.80
☐ HI5 Reggie Jackson	6.00	2.70
☐ HI6 Gaylord Perry	2.50	1.10
☐ HI7 Robin Roberts	2.50	1.10
☐ HI8 Brooks Robinson	5.00	2.20
☐ HI9 Billy Williams	2.50	1.10
☐ HI10 Ted Williams	8.00	3.60

1992 Upper Deck Home Run Heroes

This 26-card standard-size set was inserted one per pac into 1992 Upper Deck low series jumbo packs. The se spotlights the 1991 home run leaders from each of the 2 Major League teams. The fronts display color actio player photos with a shadow strip around the picture for three-dimensional effect. A gold bat icon runs verticall down the left side and contains the words "Homeru Heroes" printed in white.

	MINT	NRM
COMPLETE SET (26)	12.00	5.5
COMMON CARD (HR1-HR26)	.25	.1

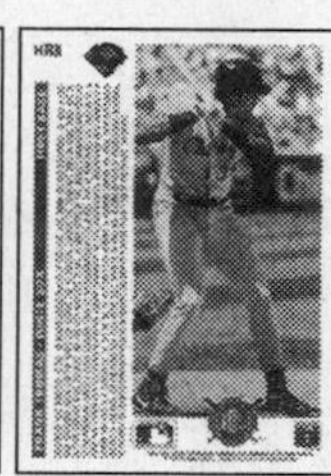

	MINT	NRMT
☐ HR1 Jose Canseco	.50	.23
☐ HR2 Cecil Fielder	.35	.16
☐ HR3 Howard Johnson	.25	.11
☐ HR4 Cal Ripken	4.00	1.80
☐ HR5 Matt Williams	.50	.23
☐ HR6 Joe Carter	.50	.23
☐ HR7 Ron Gant	.35	.16
☐ HR8 Frank Thomas	4.00	1.80
☐ HR9 Andre Dawson	.50	.23
☐ HR10 Fred McGriff	.50	.23
☐ HR11 Danny Tartabull	.25	.11
☐ HR12 Chili Davis	.35	.16
☐ HR13 Albert Belle	1.25	.55
☐ HR14 Jack Clark	.25	.11
☐ HR15 Paul O'Neill	.35	.16
☐ HR16 Darryl Strawberry	.35	.16
☐ HR17 Dave Winfield	.50	.23
☐ HR18 Jay Buhner	.50	.23
☐ HR19 Juan Gonzalez	1.50	.70
☐ HR20 Greg Vaughn	.25	.11
☐ HR21 Barry Bonds	.75	.35
☐ HR22 Matt Nokes	.25	.11
☐ HR23 John Kruk	.35	.16
☐ HR24 Ivan Calderon	.25	.11
☐ HR25 Jeff Bagwell	2.00	.90
☐ HR26 Todd Zeile	.25	.11

1992 Upper Deck Scouting Report

serted one per high series jumbo pack, cards from this -card standard-size set feature outstanding prospects in seball. The fronts carry color action player photos that e full-bleed on the top and right, bordered below by a ck stripe with the player's name, and by a black jagged t border that resembles torn paper. The words couting Report" are printed vertically in silver lettering in left border.

	MINT	NRMT
MPLETE SET (25)	15.00	6.75
MMON CARD (SR1-SR25)	.50	.23

	MINT	NRMT
SR1 Andy Ashby	.50	.23
SR2 Willie Banks	.50	.23
SR3 Kim Batiste	.50	.23
SR4 Derek Bell	1.00	.45
SR5 Archi Cianfrocco	.50	.23
SR6 Royce Clayton	1.00	.45
SR7 Gary DiSarcina	.50	.23
SR8 Dave Fleming	.50	.23
SR9 Butch Henry	.50	.23
SR10 Todd Hundley	1.25	.55
SR11 Brian Jordan	1.50	.70
SR12 Eric Karros	1.25	.55
SR13 Pat Listach	.50	.23
SR14 Scott Livingstone	.50	.23
SR15 Kenny Lofton	8.00	3.60
SR16 Pat Mahomes	.50	.23
SR17 Denny Neagle	1.50	.70
SR18 Dave Nilsson	1.00	.45
SR19 Donovan Osborne	.50	.23
SR20 Reggie Sanders	1.00	.45
SR21 Andy Stankiewicz	.50	.23
SR22 Jim Thome	6.00	2.70
SR23 Julio Valera	.50	.23
SR24 Mark Wohlers	1.25	.55
SR25 Anthony Young	.50	.23

1992 Upper Deck Williams Best

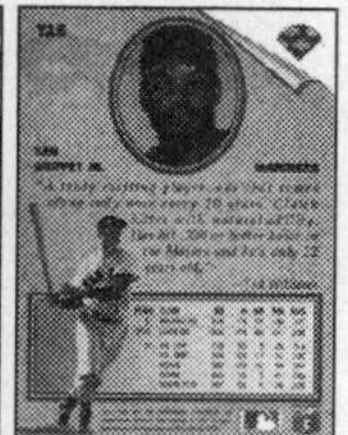

This 20-card standard-size set contains Ted Williams' choices of best current and future hitters in the game. The cards were randomly inserted in Upper Deck high number foil packs. The fronts feature full-bleed color action photos with the player's name in a black field separated from the picture by Ted Williams' gold-stamped signature.

	MINT	NRMT
COMPLETE SET (20)	25.00	11.00
COMMON CARD (T1-T20)	.50	.23

	MINT	NRMT
☐ T1 Wade Boggs	1.00	.45
☐ T2 Barry Bonds	1.50	.70
☐ T3 Jose Canseco	1.00	.45
☐ T4 Will Clark	1.00	.45
☐ T5 Cecil Fielder	.75	.35
☐ T6 Tony Gwynn	2.50	1.10
☐ T7 Rickey Henderson	1.00	.45
☐ T8 Fred McGriff	1.00	.45
☐ T9 Kirby Puckett	2.00	.90
☐ T10 Ruben Sierra	.50	.23
☐ T11 Roberto Alomar	1.25	.55
☐ T12 Jeff Bagwell	3.00	1.35
☐ T13 Albert Belle	1.50	.70
☐ T14 Juan Gonzalez	4.00	1.80
☐ T15 Ken Griffey Jr.	8.00	3.60
☐ T16 Chris Hoiles	.50	.23
☐ T17 David Justice	1.25	.55
☐ T18 Phil Plantier	.50	.23
☐ T19 Frank Thomas	6.00	2.70
☐ T20 Robin Ventura	.75	.35

1992 Upper Deck Williams Heroes

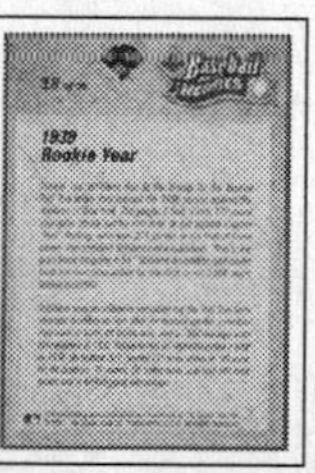

This standard-size ten-card set was randomly inserted in 1992 Upper Deck low number foil packs. Williams autographed 2,500 of card 36, which displays his portrait by sports artist Vernon Wells. The fronts features sepia-tone photos of Williams in various stages of his career that are partially contained within a blue and white bordered circle. The photos rest on a parchment card face trimmed with a brick red and white border. The Upper Deck Baseball Heroes logo appears in the lower right corner. The back design displays career highlights on a gray plaque resting on the same parchment background as on the front. The cards are numbered on the back in continuation of the Upper Deck heroes series.

	MINT	NRMT
COMPLETE SET (10)	6.00	2.70
COMMON WILLIAMS (28-36)	.50	.23

	MINT	NRMT
☐ 28 Ted Williams 1939 Rookie Year	.50	.23
☐ 29 Ted Williams 1941 .406 BA	.50	.23
☐ 30 Ted Williams 1942 Triple Crown Year	.50	.23
☐ 31 Ted Williams 1946 and 1949 MVP	.50	.23
☐ 32 Ted Williams 1947 2nd Triple Crown	.50	.23
☐ 33 Ted Williams 1950s Player of the Decade	.50	.23
☐ 34 Ted Williams 1960 500 Home Run Club	.50	.23
☐ 35 Ted Williams 1966 Hall of Fame	.50	.23
☐ 36 Baseball Heroes CL	.50	.23
☐ AU4 Ted Williams (Signed and Numbered of 2500)	500.00	220.00
☐ NNO0 Baseball Heroes SP (Header card)	2.00	.90

1992 Upper Deck Williams Wax Boxes

These eight oversized "cards," measuring approximately 5 1/4" by 7 1/4", were featured on the bottom panels of 1992 Upper Deck low series wax boxes. They are identical in design to the Williams Heroes insert cards, displaying color player photos in an oval frame. The backs are blank and they are unnumbered. We have checklisted them below according to the numbering of the Heroes cards.

	MINT	NRMT
COMPLETE SET (8)	3.00	1.35
COMMON CARD (28-35)	.50	.23

	MINT	NRMT
☐ 28 Ted Williams 1939 Rookie Year	.50	.23
☐ 29 Ted Williams 1941 .406	.50	.23
☐ 30 Ted Williams 1942 Triple Crown Year	.50	.23
☐ 31 Ted Williams 1946 and 1949 MVP	.50	.23
☐ 32 Ted Williams 1947 2nd Triple Crown	.50	.23
☐ 33 Ted Williams 1950s Player of the Decade	.50	.23
☐ 34 Ted Williams 1900 500 Home Run Club	.50	.23
☐ 35 Ted Williams 1966 Hall of Fame	.50	.23

1992 Upper Deck FanFest

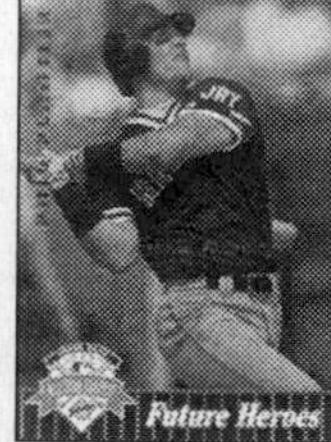

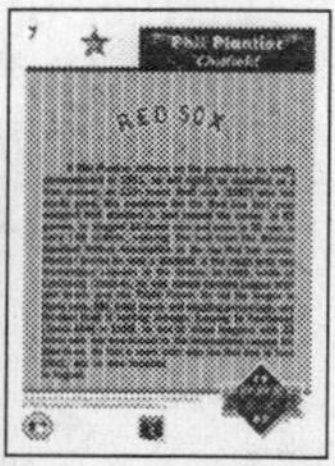

As a title sponsor of the 1992 All-Star FanFest in San Diego, Upper Deck produced this 54-card standard size set to commemorate past, present, and future All-Stars Heroes of Major League Baseball. Sixty sets were packaged in a case, and each case had at least one gold foil set. Cards 1-10 feature ten Future Heroes that are, in Upper Deck's opinion, sure bets to make an upcoming team; cards 11-44 present active All-Star alumni; and cards 45-54 salute All-Star Heroes of the past with ten fan favorites. The glossy action color photos on the front are borderless except for a pinstripe-patterned bottom border and an All-Star FanFest insignia superimposed at the lower left corner. The bottom border on the ten Future Heroes cards is navy blue and silver while the bottom border on the All-Star Heroes is silver and white. The player's name is superimposed on the photo in silver and runs vertically down the left edge of the card. The backs display the team name and career and personal information on a gray and white pinstripe panel. The player's name and position appear in a navy bar in the upper right corner.

	MINT	NRMT
COMPLETE SET (54)	10.00	4.50
COMMON CARD (1-54)	.10	.05
*GOLD: 15X VALUE		
☐ 1 Steve Avery	.10	.05
☐ 2 Ivan Rodriguez	.60	.25
☐ 3 Jeff Bagwell	1.25	.55
☐ 4 Delino DeShields	.10	.05
☐ 5 Royce Clayton	.10	.05
☐ 6 Robin Ventura	.20	.09
☐ 7 Phil Plantier	.10	.05
☐ 8 Ray Lankford	.40	.18
☐ 9 Juan Gonzalez	1.50	.70
☐ 10 Frank Thomas	2.50	1.10
☐ 11 Roberto Alomar	.40	.18
☐ 12 Sandy Alomar Jr.	.20	.09
☐ 13 Wade Boggs	.40	.18
☐ 14 Barry Bonds	.60	.25
☐ 15 Bobby Bonilla	.20	.09
☐ 16 George Brett	.75	.35
☐ 17 Jose Canseco	.30	.14
☐ 18 Will Clark	.30	.14
☐ 19 Roger Clemens	1.00	.45
☐ 20 Eric Davis	.20	.09
☐ 21 Rob Dibble	.10	.05
☐ 22 Cecil Fielder	.20	.09
☐ 23 Dwight Gooden	.20	.09
☐ 24 Ken Griffey Jr.	3.00	1.35
☐ 25 Tony Gwynn	1.25	.55
☐ 26 Bryan Harvey	.10	.05
☐ 27 Rickey Henderson	.40	.18
☐ 28 Howard Johnson	.10	.05
☐ 29 Wally Joyner	.20	.09
☐ 30 Barry Larkin	.30	.14
☐ 31 Don Mattingly	1.25	.55
☐ 32 Mark McGwire	1.25	.55
☐ 33 Dale Murphy	.30	.14
☐ 34 Rafael Palmeiro	.30	.14
☐ 35 Kirby Puckett	1.00	.45
☐ 36 Cal Ripken	2.50	1.10
☐ 37 Nolan Ryan	2.50	1.10
☐ 38 Chris Sabo	.10	.05
☐ 39 Ryne Sandberg	.75	.35
☐ 40 Benito Santiago	.10	.05
☐ 41 Ruben Sierra	.10	.05
☐ 42 Ozzie Smith	.75	.35
☐ 43 Darryl Strawberry	.20	.09
☐ 44 Robin Yount	.40	.18
☐ 45 Rollie Fingers	.20	.09
☐ 46 Reggie Jackson	.50	.23
☐ 47 Billy Williams	.20	.09
☐ 48 Lou Brock	.40	.18
☐ 49 Gaylord Perry	.20	.09
☐ 50 Ted Williams	1.00	.45
☐ 51 Brooks Robinson	.40	.18
☐ 52 Bob Gibson	.40	.18
☐ 53 Bobby Bonds	.10	.05
☐ 54 Robin Roberts	.20	.09

1992 Upper Deck Team MVP Holograms

The 54 hologram cards in this standard size set feature the top offensive player and pitcher from each Major League team plus two checklist cards. Only 216,000 number sets were produced, and each set was packaged in a custom-designed box with protective sleeve and included a numbered certificate. To display the set, Upper Deck also made available a custom album through a mail-in offer for 10.00. The horizontally oriented fronts display the players in action and close-up in three-dimensional form. The player's name appears at the bottom in a striped border. In the lower right corner, a baseball image on a black home plate design radiates streaks of light up into the picture. The backs are also horizontally oriented and show the player in action in a full-color picture. A green-bordered pale yellow panel contains a career summary. Cards 1-2 feature the AL and NL MVPs (with checklists) while cards 3-54 are arranged in alphabetical order.

	MINT	NRMT
COMPLETE SET (54)	20.00	9.00
COMMON CARD (1-54)	.10	.05
☐ 1 Cal Ripken MVP CL	1.50	.70
☐ 2 Terry Pendleton MVP CL	.25	.11
☐ 3 Jim Abbott	.10	.05
☐ 4 Roberto Alomar	.75	.35
☐ 5 Kevin Appier	.25	.11
☐ 6 Steve Avery	.10	.05
☐ 7 Jeff Bagwell	1.50	.70
☐ 8 Albert Belle	1.00	.45
☐ 9 Andy Benes	.25	.11
☐ 10 Wade Boggs	.75	.35
☐ 11 Barry Bonds	.75	.35
☐ 12 George Brett	1.50	.70
☐ 13 Ivan Calderon	.10	.05
☐ 14 Jose Canseco	.50	.23
☐ 15 Will Clark	.50	.23
☐ 16 Roger Clemens	1.00	.45
☐ 17 David Cone	.25	.11
☐ 18 Doug Drabek	.10	.05
☐ 19 Dennis Eckersley	.50	.23
☐ 20 Scott Erickson	.10	.05
☐ 21 Cecil Fielder	.25	.11
☐ 22 Ken Griffey Jr.	4.00	1.80
☐ 23 Bill Gullickson	.10	.05
☐ 24 Juan Guzman	.10	.05
☐ 25 Pete Harnisch	.10	.05
☐ 26 Howard Johnson	.10	.05
☐ 27 Randy Johnson	.75	.35
☐ 28 John Kruk	.25	.11
☐ 29 Barry Larkin	.50	.23
☐ 30 Greg Maddux	2.50	1.10
☐ 31 Dennis Martinez	.25	.11
☐ 32 Ramon Martinez	.25	.11
☐ 33 Don Mattingly	1.50	.70
☐ 34 Jack McDowell	.10	.05
☐ 35 Fred McGriff	.50	.23
☐ 36 Paul Molitor	.75	.35
☐ 37 Charles Nagy	.25	.11
☐ 38 Gregg Olson	.10	.05
☐ 39 Terry Pendleton	.25	.11
☐ 40 Luis Polonia	.10	.05
☐ 41 Kirby Puckett	1.50	.70
☐ 42 Dave Righetti	.10	.05
☐ 43 Jose Rijo	.10	.05
☐ 44 Cal Ripken	3.00	1.35
☐ 45 Nolan Ryan	3.00	1.35
☐ 46 Ryne Sandberg	1.25	.55
☐ 47 Scott Sanderson	.10	.05
☐ 48 Ruben Sierra	.10	.05
☐ 49 Lee Smith	.25	.11
☐ 50 Ozzie Smith	1.25	.55
☐ 51 Darryl Strawberry	.25	.11
☐ 52 Frank Thomas	3.00	1.35
☐ 53 Bill Wegman	.10	.05
☐ 54 Mitch Williams	.10	.05

1993 Upper Deck

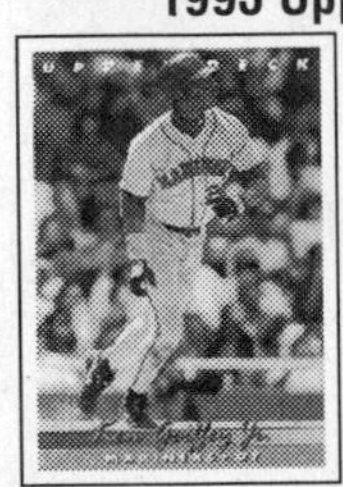

The 1993 Upper Deck set consists of two series of 420 standard-size cards. A special card (SP5) was randomly inserted in first series packs to commemorate the 3,000th hit of George Brett and Robin Yount. A special card (SP6) commemorating Nolan Ryan's last season was randomly inserted into second series packs. Both SP cards were inserted at a rate of one every 72 packs. The front designs features color action player photos bordered in white. The company name is printed along the photo surface of the card top. The player's name appears in script in a color stripe cutting across the bottom of the picture while the team name and his position appear in another color stripe immediately below. The backs have a color close-up photo on the upper portion and biography, statistics, and career higlights on the lower portion. Special subsets featured include Star Rookies (1-29), Community Heroes (30-40), and American League Teammates (41-55), Top Prospects (421-449), Inside the Numbers (450-470), Team Stars (471-485), Award Winners (486-499), and Diamond Debuts (500-510). Derek Jeter is the only notable Rookie Card in this set.

	MINT	NRMT
COMPLETE SET (840)	30.00	13.50
COMP.FACT.SET (840)	40.00	18.00
COMPLETE SERIES 1 (420)	15.00	6.75
COMPLETE SERIES 2 (420)	15.00	6.75
COMMON CARD (1-840)	.10	.05
COMP.GOLD FACT.SET (840)	80.00	36.00
COMMON GOLD HOLO. (1-840)	.25	.11
*GOLD HOLOGRAM: 1X TO 2.5X BASIC CARDS		
☐ 1 Tim Salmon CL	.40	.18
☐ 2 Mike Piazza SR	2.00	.90
☐ 3 Rene Arocha SR	.10	.05
☐ 4 Willie Greene SR	.20	.09
☐ 5 Manny Alexander SR	.10	.05
☐ 6 Dan Wilson SR	.20	.09
☐ 7 Dan Smith SR	.10	.05
☐ 8 Kevin Rogers SR	.10	.05
☐ 9 Kurt Miller SR	.10	.05
☐ 10 Joe Vitko SR	.10	.05
☐ 11 Tim Costo SR	.10	.05
☐ 12 Alan Embree SR	.10	.05
☐ 13 Jim Tatum SR	.10	.05
☐ 14 Cris Colon SR	.10	.0[illegible]
☐ 15 Steve Hosey SR	.10	.0[illegible]
☐ 16 Sterling Hitchcock SR	.20	.0[illegible]
☐ 17 Dave Mlicki SR	.10	.0[illegible]
☐ 18 Jessie Hollins SR	.10	.0[illegible]
☐ 19 Bobby Jones SR	.20	.0[illegible]
☐ 20 Kurt Miller SR	.10	.0[illegible]
☐ 21 Melvin Nieves SR	.20	.0[illegible]
☐ 22 Billy Ashley SR	.10	.0[illegible]
☐ 23 J.T. Snow SR	.50	.2[illegible]
☐ 24 Chipper Jones SR	2.00	.9[illegible]
☐ 25 Tim Salmon SR	.50	.2[illegible]
☐ 26 Tim Pugh SR	.10	.0[illegible]
☐ 27 David Nied SR	.10	.0[illegible]
☐ 28 Mike Trombley SR	.10	.0[illegible]
☐ 29 Javier Lopez SR	.40	.1[illegible]
☐ 30 Jim Abbott CL	.10	.0[illegible]
☐ 31 Jim Abbott CH	.10	.0[illegible]
☐ 32 Dale Murphy CH	.30	.1[illegible]
☐ 33 Tony Pena CH	.10	.0[illegible]
☐ 34 Kirby Puckett CH	.40	.1[illegible]
☐ 35 Harold Reynolds CH	.10	.0[illegible]
☐ 36 Cal Ripken CH	.75	.3[illegible]
☐ 37 Nolan Ryan CH	.75	[illegible]
☐ 38 Ryne Sandberg CH	.40	[illegible]
☐ 39 Dave Stewart CH	.10	[illegible]
☐ 40 Dave Winfield CH	.30	[illegible]
☐ 41 Joe Carter CL Mark McGwire	.40	[illegible]
☐ 42 Blockbuster Trade Joe Carter Roberto Alomar	.40	[illegible]
☐ 43 Brew Crew Paul Molitor Pat Listach Robin Yount	.40	[illegible]
☐ 44 Iron and Steel Cal Ripken Brady Anderson	.40	[illegible]
☐ 45 Youthful Tribe Albert Belle Sandy Alomar Jr. Jim Thome Carlos Baerga Kenny Lofton	.20	[illegible]
☐ 46 Motown Mashers Cecil Fielder Mickey Tettleton	.20	[illegible]
☐ 47 Yankee Pride Roberto Kelly Don Mattingly	.20	[illegible]
☐ 48 Boston Cy Sox Frank Viola Roger Clemens	.20	[illegible]
☐ 49 Bash Brothers Ruben Sierra Mark McGwire	.20	[illegible]
☐ 50 Twin Titles Kent Hrbek Kirby Puckett	.40	[illegible]
☐ 51 Southside Sluggers Robin Ventura Frank Thomas	.40	[illegible]
☐ 52 Latin Stars Juan Gonzalez Jose Canseco Ivan Rodriguez Rafael Palmeiro	.50	[illegible]
☐ 53 Lethal Lefties Mark Langston Jim Abbott Chuck Finley	.10	[illegible]
☐ 54 Royal Family Wally Joyner Gregg Jefferies	.10	[illegible]

George Brett
☐ 55 Pacific Sock Exchange .50 .23
Kevin Mitchell
Ken Griffey Jr.
Jay Buhner
☐ 56 George Brett .75 .35
☐ 57 Scott Cooper .10 .05
☐ 58 Mike Maddux .10 .05
☐ 59 Rusty Meacham .10 .05
☐ 60 Wil Cordero .10 .05
☐ 61 Tim Teufel .10 .05
☐ 62 Jeff Montgomery .20 .09
☐ 63 Scott Livingstone .10 .05
☐ 64 Doug Dascenzo .10 .05
☐ 65 Bret Boone .10 .05
☐ 66 Tim Wakefield .20 .09
☐ 67 Curt Schilling .20 .09
☐ 68 Frank Tanana .10 .05
☐ 69 Len Dykstra .20 .09
☐ 70 Derek Lilliquist .10 .05
☐ 71 Anthony Young .10 .05
☐ 72 Hipolito Pichardo .10 .05
☐ 73 Rod Beck .20 .09
☐ 74 Kent Hrbek .20 .09
☐ 75 Tom Glavine .30 .14
☐ 76 Kevin Brown .20 .09
☐ 77 Chuck Finley .10 .05
☐ 78 Bob Walk .10 .05
☐ 79 Rheal Cormier UER .10 .05
(Born in New Brunswick,
not British Columbia)
☐ 80 Rick Sutcliffe .10 .05
☐ 81 Harold Baines .20 .09
☐ 82 Lee Smith .20 .09
☐ 83 Geno Petralli .10 .05
☐ 84 Jose Oquendo .10 .05
☐ 85 Mark Gubicza .10 .05
☐ 86 Mickey Tettleton .10 .05
☐ 87 Bobby Witt .10 .05
☐ 88 Mark Lewis .10 .05
☐ 89 Kevin Appier .20 .09
☐ 90 Mike Stanton .10 .05
☐ 91 Rafael Belliard .10 .05
☐ 92 Kenny Rogers .10 .05
☐ 93 Randy Velarde .10 .05
☐ 94 Luis Sojo .10 .05
☐ 95 Mark Leiter .10 .05
☐ 96 Jody Reed .10 .05
☐ 97 Pete Harnisch .10 .05
☐ 98 Tom Candiotti .10 .05
☐ 99 Mark Portugal .10 .05
☐ 100 Dave Valle .10 .05
☐ 101 Shawon Dunston .10 .05
☐ 102 B.J. Surhoff .20 .09
☐ 103 Jay Bell .20 .09
☐ 104 Sid Bream .10 .05
☐ 105 Frank Thomas CL .40 .18
☐ 106 Mike Morgan .10 .05
☐ 107 Bill Doran .10 .05
☐ 108 Lance Blankenship .10 .05
☐ 109 Mark Lemke .10 .05
☐ 110 Brian Harper .10 .05
☐ 111 Brady Anderson .30 .14
☐ 112 Bip Roberts .10 .05
☐ 113 Mitch Williams .10 .05
☐ 114 Craig Biggio .30 .14
☐ 115 Eddie Murray .40 .18
☐ 116 Matt Nokes .10 .05
☐ 117 Lance Parrish .10 .05
☐ 118 Bill Swift .10 .05
☐ 119 Jeff Innis .10 .05
☐ 120 Mike LaValliere .10 .05
☐ 121 Hal Morris .10 .05
☐ 122 Walt Weiss .10 .05
☐ 123 Ivan Rodriguez .50 .23
☐ 124 Andy Van Slyke .20 .09
☐ 125 Roberto Alomar .40 .18
☐ 126 Robby Thompson .10 .05
☐ 127 Sammy Sosa .40 .18
☐ 128 Mark Langston .10 .05
☐ 129 Jerry Browne .10 .05
☐ 130 Chuck McElroy .10 .05
☐ 131 Frank Viola .10 .05
☐ 132 Leo Gomez .10 .05
☐ 133 Ramon Martinez .20 .09
☐ 134 Don Mattingly .60 .25
☐ 135 Roger Clemens .75 .35
☐ 136 Rickey Henderson .40 .18
☐ 137 Darren Daulton .20 .09
☐ 138 Ken Hill .20 .09
☐ 139 Ozzie Guillen .10 .05
☐ 140 Jerald Clark .10 .05
☐ 141 Dave Fleming .10 .05
☐ 142 Delino DeShields .10 .05
☐ 143 Matt Williams .30 .14
☐ 144 Larry Walker .40 .18
☐ 145 Ruben Sierra .10 .05
☐ 146 Ozzie Smith .50 .23

☐ 147 Chris Sabo .10 .05
☐ 148 Carlos Hernandez .10 .05
☐ 149 Pat Borders .10 .05
☐ 150 Orlando Merced .10 .05
☐ 151 Royce Clayton .20 .09
☐ 152 Kurt Stillwell .10 .05
☐ 153 Dave Hollins .10 .05
☐ 154 Mike Greenwell .10 .05
☐ 155 Nolan Ryan 1.50 .70
☐ 156 Felix Jose .10 .05
☐ 157 Junior Felix .10 .05
☐ 158 Derek Bell .20 .09
☐ 159 Steve Buechele .10 .05
☐ 160 John Burkett .10 .05
☐ 161 Pat Howell .10 .05
☐ 162 Milt Cuyler .10 .05
☐ 163 Terry Pendleton .20 .09
☐ 164 Jack Morris .20 .09
☐ 165 Tony Gwynn 1.00 .45
☐ 166 Deion Sanders .40 .18
☐ 167 Mike Devereaux .10 .05
☐ 168 Ron Darling .10 .05
☐ 169 Orel Hershiser .20 .09
☐ 170 Mike Jackson .10 .05
☐ 171 Doug Jones .10 .05
☐ 172 Dan Walters .10 .05
☐ 173 Darren Lewis .10 .05
☐ 174 Carlos Baerga .20 .09
☐ 175 Ryne Sandberg .50 .23
☐ 176 Gregg Jefferies .20 .09
☐ 177 John Jaha .20 .09
☐ 178 Luis Polonia .10 .05
☐ 179 Kirt Manwaring .10 .05
☐ 180 Mike Magnante .10 .05
☐ 181 Billy Ripken .10 .05
☐ 182 Mike Moore .10 .05
☐ 183 Eric Anthony .10 .05
☐ 184 Lenny Harris .10 .05
☐ 185 Tony Pena .10 .05
☐ 186 Mike Felder .10 .05
☐ 187 Greg Olson .10 .05
☐ 188 Rene Gonzales .10 .05
☐ 189 Mike Bordick .10 .05
☐ 190 Mel Rojas .20 .09
☐ 191 Todd Frohwirth .10 .05
☐ 192 Darryl Hamilton .10 .05
☐ 193 Mike Fetters .10 .05
☐ 194 Omar Olivares .10 .05
☐ 195 Tony Phillips .10 .05
☐ 196 Paul Sorrento .10 .05
☐ 197 Trevor Wilson .10 .05
☐ 198 Kevin Gross .10 .05
☐ 199 Ron Karkovice .10 .05
☐ 200 Brook Jacoby .10 .05
☐ 201 Mariano Duncan .10 .05
☐ 202 Dennis Cook .10 .05
☐ 203 Daryl Boston .10 .05
☐ 204 Mike Perez .10 .05
☐ 205 Manuel Lee .10 .05
☐ 206 Steve Olin .10 .05
☐ 207 Charlie Hough .10 .05
☐ 208 Scott Scudder .10 .05
☐ 209 Charlie O'Brien .10 .05
☐ 210 Barry Bonds CL .40 .18
☐ 211 Jose Vizcaino .10 .05
☐ 212 Scott Leius .10 .05
☐ 213 Kevin Mitchell .20 .09
☐ 214 Brian Barnes .10 .05
☐ 215 Pat Kelly .10 .05
☐ 216 Chris Hammond .10 .05
☐ 217 Rob Deer .10 .05
☐ 218 Cory Snyder .10 .05
☐ 219 Gary Carter .30 .14
☐ 220 Danny Darwin .10 .05
☐ 221 Tom Gordon .10 .05
☐ 222 Gary Sheffield .40 .18
☐ 223 Joe Carter .30 .14
☐ 224 Jay Buhner .30 .14
☐ 225 Jose Offerman .10 .05
☐ 226 Jose Rijo .10 .05
☐ 227 Mark Whiten .10 .05
☐ 228 Randy Milligan .10 .05
☐ 229 Bud Black .10 .05
☐ 230 Gary DiSarcina .10 .05
☐ 231 Steve Finley .20 .09
☐ 232 Dennis Martinez .20 .09
☐ 233 Mike Mussina .40 .18
☐ 234 Joe Oliver .10 .05
☐ 235 Chad Curtis .20 .09
☐ 236 Shane Mack .10 .05
☐ 237 Jaime Navarro .10 .05
☐ 238 Brian McRae .10 .05
☐ 239 Chili Davis .20 .09
☐ 240 Jeff King .20 .09
☐ 241 Dean Palmer .20 .09
☐ 242 Danny Tartabull .10 .05
☐ 243 Charles Nagy .20 .09

☐ 244 Ray Lankford .30 .14
☐ 245 Barry Larkin .30 .14
☐ 246 Steve Avery .10 .05
☐ 247 John Kruk .20 .09
☐ 248 Derrick May .10 .05
☐ 249 Stan Javier .10 .05
☐ 250 Roger McDowell .10 .05
☐ 251 Dan Gladden .10 .05
☐ 252 Wally Joyner .20 .09
☐ 253 Pat Listach .10 .05
☐ 254 Chuck Knoblauch .40 .18
☐ 255 Sandy Alomar Jr. .20 .09
☐ 256 Jeff Bagwell .75 .35
☐ 257 Andy Stankiewicz .10 .05
☐ 258 Darrin Jackson .10 .05
☐ 259 Brett Butler .20 .09
☐ 260 Joe Orsulak .10 .05
☐ 261 Andy Benes .20 .09
☐ 262 Kenny Lofton .75 .35
☐ 263 Robin Ventura .20 .09
☐ 264 Ron Gant .20 .09
☐ 265 Ellis Burks .20 .09
☐ 266 Juan Guzman .10 .05
☐ 267 Wes Chamberlain .10 .05
☐ 268 John Smiley .10 .05
☐ 269 Franklin Stubbs .10 .05
☐ 270 Tom Browning .10 .05
☐ 271 Dennis Eckersley .30 .14
☐ 272 Carlton Fisk .40 .18
☐ 273 Lou Whitaker .20 .09
☐ 274 Phil Plantier .10 .05
☐ 275 Bobby Bonilla .20 .09
☐ 276 Ben McDonald .10 .05
☐ 277 Bob Zupcic .10 .05
☐ 278 Terry Steinbach .20 .09
☐ 279 Terry Mulholland .10 .05
☐ 280 Lance Johnson .10 .05
☐ 281 Willie McGee .10 .05
☐ 282 Bret Saberhagen .20 .09
☐ 283 Randy Myers .20 .09
☐ 284 Randy Tomlin .10 .05
☐ 285 Mickey Morandini .10 .05
☐ 286 Brian Williams .10 .05
☐ 287 Tino Martinez .40 .18
☐ 288 Jose Melendez .10 .05
☐ 289 Jeff Huson .10 .05
☐ 290 Joe Grahe .10 .05
☐ 291 Mel Hall .10 .05
☐ 292 Otis Nixon .10 .05
☐ 293 Todd Hundley .30 .14
☐ 294 Casey Candaele .10 .05
☐ 295 Kevin Seitzer .10 .05
☐ 296 Eddie Taubensee .10 .05
☐ 297 Moises Alou .20 .09
☐ 298 Scott Radinsky .10 .05
☐ 299 Thomas Howard .10 .05
☐ 300 Kyle Abbott .10 .05
☐ 301 Omar Vizquel .20 .09
☐ 302 Keith Miller .10 .05
☐ 303 Rick Aguilera .10 .05
☐ 304 Bruce Hurst .10 .05
☐ 305 Ken Caminiti .40 .18
☐ 306 Mike Pagliarulo .10 .05
☐ 307 Frank Seminara .10 .05
☐ 308 Andre Dawson .30 .14
☐ 309 Jose Lind .10 .05
☐ 310 Joe Boever .10 .05
☐ 311 Jeff Parrett .10 .05
☐ 312 Alan Mills .10 .05
☐ 313 Kevin Tapani .10 .05
☐ 314 Daryl Kile .20 .09
☐ 315 Will Clark CL .20 .09
☐ 316 Mike Sharperson .10 .05
☐ 317 John Orton .10 .05
☐ 318 Bob Tewksbury .10 .05
☐ 319 Xavier Hernandez .10 .05
☐ 320 Paul Assenmacher .10 .05
☐ 321 John Franco .10 .05
☐ 322 Mike Timlin .10 .05
☐ 323 Jose Guzman .10 .05
☐ 324 Pedro Martinez .40 .18
☐ 325 Bill Spiers .10 .05
☐ 326 Melido Perez .10 .05
☐ 327 Mike Macfarlane .10 .05
☐ 328 Ricky Bones .10 .05
☐ 329 Scott Bankhead .10 .05
☐ 330 Rich Rodriguez .10 .05
☐ 331 Geronimo Pena .10 .05
☐ 332 Bernie Williams .40 .18
☐ 333 Paul Molitor .40 .18
☐ 334 Carlos Garcia .10 .05
☐ 335 David Cone .20 .09
☐ 336 Randy Johnson .40 .18
☐ 337 Pat Mahomes .10 .05
☐ 338 Erik Hanson .10 .05
☐ 339 Duane Ward .10 .05
☐ 340 Al Martin .20 .09

341	Pedro Munoz	.10	.05
342	Greg Colbrunn	.10	.05
343	Julio Valera	.10	.05
344	John Olerud	.10	.05
345	George Bell	.10	.05
346	Devon White	.10	.05
347	Donovan Osborne	.10	.05
348	Mark Gardner	.10	.05
349	Zane Smith	.10	.05
350	Wilson Alvarez	.20	.09
351	Kevin Koslofski	.10	.05
352	Roberto Hernandez	.20	.09
353	Glenn Davis	.10	.05
354	Reggie Sanders	.20	.09
355	Ken Griffey Jr.	2.00	.90
356	Marquis Grissom	.20	.09
357	Jack McDowell	.10	.05
358	Jimmy Key	.20	.09
359	Stan Belinda	.10	.05
360	Gerald Williams	.10	.05
361	Sid Fernandez	.10	.05
362	Alex Fernandez	.20	.09
363	John Smoltz	.30	.14
364	Travis Fryman	.20	.09
365	Jose Canseco	.30	.14
366	David Justice	.30	.14
367	Pedro Astacio	.10	.05
368	Tim Belcher	.10	.05
369	Steve Sax	.10	.05
370	Gary Gaetti	.20	.09
371	Jeff Frye	.10	.05
372	Bob Wickman	.10	.05
373	Ryan Thompson	.10	.05
374	David Hulse	.10	.05
375	Cal Eldred	.10	.05
376	Ryan Klesko	.50	.23
377	Damion Easley	.10	.05
378	John Kiely	.10	.05
379	Jim Bullinger	.10	.05
380	Brian Bohanon	.10	.05
381	Rod Brewer	.10	.05
382	Fernando Ramsey	.10	.05
383	Sam Militello	.10	.05
384	Arthur Rhodes	.10	.05
385	Eric Karros	.20	.09
386	Rico Brogna	.20	.09
387	John Valentin	.20	.09
388	Kerry Woodson	.10	.05
389	Ben Rivera	.10	.05
390	Matt Whiteside	.10	.05
391	Henry Rodriguez	.20	.09
392	John Wetteland	.20	.09
393	Kent Mercker	.10	.05
394	Bernard Gilkey	.20	.09
395	Doug Henry	.10	.05
396	Mo Vaughn	.50	.23
397	Scott Erickson	.10	.05
398	Bill Gullickson	.10	.05
399	Mark Guthrie	.10	.05
400	Dave Martinez	.10	.05
401	Jeff Kent	.20	.09
402	Chris Hoiles	.10	.05
403	Mike Henneman	.10	.05
404	Chris Nabholz	.10	.05
405	Tom Pagnozzi	.10	.05
406	Kelly Gruber	.10	.05
407	Bob Welch	.10	.05
408	Frank Castillo	.10	.05
409	John Dopson	.10	.05
410	Steve Farr	.10	.05
411	Henry Cotto	.10	.05
412	Bob Patterson	.10	.05
413	Todd Stottlemyre	.10	.05
414	Greg A. Harris	.10	.05
415	Denny Neagle	.20	.09
416	Bill Wegman	.10	.05
417	Willie Wilson	.10	.05
418	Terry Leach	.10	.05
419	Willie Randolph	.20	.09
420	Mark McGwire CL	.40	.18
421	Calvin Murray CL	.10	.05
422	Pete Janicki TP	.10	.05
423	Todd Jones TP	.20	.09
424	Mike Neill TP	.10	.05
425	Carlos Delgado TP	.40	.18
426	Jose Oliva TP	.10	.05
427	Tyrone Hill TP	.10	.05
428	Dmitri Young TP	.40	.18
429	Derek Wallace TP	.10	.05
430	Michael Moore TP	.10	.05
431	Cliff Floyd TP	.20	.09
432	Calvin Murray TP	.10	.05
433	Manny Ramirez TP	.75	.35
434	Marc Newfield TP	.20	.09
435	Charles Johnson TP	.40	.18
436	Butch Huskey TP	.40	.18
437	Brad Pennington TP	.10	.05
438	Ray McDavid TP	.10	.05
439	Chad McConnell TP	.10	.05
440	Midre Cummings TP	.10	.05
441	Benji Gil TP	.10	.05
442	Frankie Rodriguez TP	.10	.05
443	Chad Mottola TP	.10	.05
444	John Burke TP	.10	.05
445	Michael Tucker TP	.40	.18
446	Rick Greene TP	.10	.05
447	Rich Becker TP	.20	.09
448	Mike Robertson TP	.10	.05
449	Derek Jeter TP	4.00	1.80
450	Ivan Rodriguez CL	.20	.09
	David McCarty		
451	Jim Abbott IN	.10	.05
452	Jeff Bagwell IN	.40	.18
453	Jason Bere IN	.10	.05
454	Delino DeShields IN	.10	.05
455	Travis Fryman IN	.20	.09
456	Alex Gonzalez IN	.40	.18
457	Phil Hiatt IN	.10	.05
458	Dave Hollins IN	.10	.05
459	Chipper Jones IN	1.25	.55
460	David Justice IN	.20	.09
461	Ray Lankford IN	.20	.09
462	David McCarty IN	.10	.05
463	Mike Mussina IN	.30	.14
464	Jose Offerman IN	.10	.05
465	Dean Palmer IN	.10	.05
466	Geronimo Pena IN	.10	.05
467	Eduardo Perez IN	.10	.05
468	Ivan Rodriguez IN	.40	.18
469	Reggie Sanders IN	.10	.05
470	Bernie Williams IN	.40	.18
471	Barry Bonds CL	.40	.18
	Matt Williams		
	Will Clark		
472	Strike Force	.40	.18
	Greg Maddux		
	Steve Avery		
	John Smoltz		
	Tom Glavine		
473	Red October	.10	.05
	Jose Rijo		
	Rob Dibble		
	Roberto Kelly		
	Reggie Sanders		
	Barry Larkin		
474	Four Corners	.30	.14
	Gary Sheffield		
	Phil Plantier		
	Tony Gwynn		
	Fred McGriff		
475	Shooting Stars	.10	.05
	Doug Drabek		
	Craig Biggio		
	Jeff Bagwell		
476	Giant Sticks	.30	.14
	Will Clark		
	Barry Bonds		
	Matt Williams		
477	Boyhood Friends	.20	.09
	Eric Davis		
	Darryl Strawberry		
478	Rock Solid Foundation	.30	.14
	Dante Bichette		
	David Nied		
	Andres Galarraga		
479	Inaugural Catch	.10	.05
	Dave Magadan		
	Orestes Destrade		
	Bret Barberie		
	Jeff Conine		
480	Steel City Champions	.10	.05
	Tim Wakefield		
	Andy Van Slyke		
	Jay Bell		
481	Les Grandes Etoiles	.20	.09
	Marquis Grissom		
	Delino DeShields		
	Dennis Martinez		
	Larry Walker		
482	Runnin' Redbirds	.20	.09
	Geronimo Pena		
	Ray Lankford		
	Ozzie Smith		
	Bernard Gilkey		
483	Ivy Leaguers	.20	.09
	Randy Myers		
	Ryne Sandberg		
	Mark Grace		
484	Big Apple Power Switch	.20	.09
	Eddie Murray		
	Howard Johnson		
	Bobby Bonilla		
485	Hammers and Nails	.10	.05
	John Kruk		
	Dave Hollins		
	Darren Daulton		
	Len Dykstra		
486	Barry Bonds AW	.40	.18
487	Dennis Eckersley AW	.20	.09
488	Greg Maddux AW	.60	.25
489	Dennis Eckersley AW	.20	.09
490	Eric Karros AW	.10	.05
491	Pat Listach AW	.10	.05
492	Gary Sheffield AW	.40	.18
493	Mark McGwire AW	.40	.18
494	Gary Sheffield AW	.40	.18
495	Edgar Martinez AW	.30	.14
496	Fred McGriff AW	.20	.09
497	Juan Gonzalez AW	.50	.23
498	Darren Daulton AW	.10	.05
499	Cecil Fielder AW	.10	.05
500	Brent Gates CL	.10	.05
501	Tavo Alvarez DD	.10	.05
502	Rod Bolton DD	.10	.05
503	John Cummings DD	.10	.05
504	Brent Gates DD	.20	.09
505	Tyler Green DD	.10	.05
506	Jose Martinez DD	.10	.05
507	Troy Percival DD	.20	.09
508	Kevin Stocker DD	.10	.05
509	Matt Walbeck DD	.10	.05
510	Rondell White DD	.20	.09
511	Billy Ripken	.10	.05
512	Mike Moore	.10	.05
513	Jose Lind	.10	.05
514	Chito Martinez	.10	.05
515	Jose Guzman	.10	.05
516	Kim Batiste	.10	.05
517	Jeff Tackett	.10	.05
518	Charlie Hough	.10	.05
519	Marvin Freeman	.10	.05
520	Carlos Martinez	.10	.05
521	Eric Young	.30	.14
522	Pete Incaviglia	.10	.05
523	Scott Fletcher	.10	.05
524	Orestes Destrade	.10	.05
525	Ken Griffey Jr. CL	.40	.18
526	Ellis Burks	.20	.09
527	Juan Samuel	.10	.05
528	Dave Magadan	.10	.05
529	Jeff Parrett	.10	.05
530	Bill Krueger	.10	.05
531	Frank Bolick	.10	.05
532	Alan Trammell	.30	.14
533	Walt Weiss	.10	.05
534	David Cone	.20	.09
535	Greg Maddux	1.25	.55
536	Kevin Young	.10	.05
537	Dave Hansen	.10	.05
538	Alex Cole	.10	.05
539	Greg Hibbard	.10	.05
540	Gene Larkin	.10	.05
541	Jeff Reardon	.20	.09
542	Felix Jose	.10	.05
543	Jimmy Key	.20	.09
544	Reggie Jefferson	.20	.09
545	Gregg Jefferies	.20	.09
546	Dave Stewart	.20	.09
547	Tim Wallach	.10	.05
548	Spike Owen	.10	.05
549	Tommy Greene	.10	.05
550	Fernando Valenzuela	.20	.09
551	Rich Amaral	.10	.05
552	Bret Barberie	.10	.05
553	Edgar Martinez	.30	.14
554	Jim Abbott	.10	.05
555	Frank Thomas	1.50	.70
556	Wade Boggs	.40	.18
557	Tom Henke	.10	.05
558	Milt Thompson	.10	.05
559	Lloyd McClendon	.10	.05
560	Vinny Castilla	.40	.18
561	Ricky Jordan	.10	.05
562	Andujar Cedeno	.10	.05
563	Greg Vaughn	.10	.05
564	Cecil Fielder	.20	.09
565	Kirby Puckett	.75	.35
566	Mark McGwire	1.00	.45
567	Barry Bonds	.50	.23
568	Jody Reed	.10	.05
569	Todd Zeile	.10	.05
570	Mark Carreon	.10	.05
571	Joe Girardi	.10	.05
572	Luis Gonzalez	.10	.05
573	Mark Grace	.30	.14
574	Rafael Palmeiro	.30	.14
575	Darryl Strawberry	.20	.09
576	Will Clark	.30	.14
577	Fred McGriff	.30	.14
578	Kevin Reimer	.10	.05
579	Dave Righetti	.10	.05
580	Juan Bell	.10	.05

☐ 581 Jeff Brantley .10 .05
☐ 582 Brian Hunter .10 .05
☐ 583 Tim Naehring .10 .05
☐ 584 Glenallen Hill .10 .05
☐ 585 Cal Ripken 1.50 .70
☐ 586 Albert Belle .50 .23
☐ 587 Robin Yount .30 .14
☐ 588 Chris Bosio .10 .05
☐ 589 Pete Smith .10 .05
☐ 590 Chuck Carr .10 .05
☐ 591 Jeff Blauser .10 .05
☐ 592 Kevin McReynolds .10 .05
☐ 593 Andres Galarraga .30 .14
☐ 594 Kevin Maas .10 .05
☐ 595 Eric Davis .20 .09
☐ 596 Brian Jordan .20 .09
☐ 597 Tim Raines .20 .09
☐ 598 Rick Wilkins .10 .05
☐ 599 Steve Cooke .10 .05
☐ 600 Mike Gallego .10 .05
☐ 601 Mike Munoz .10 .05
☐ 602 Luis Rivera .10 .05
☐ 603 Junior Ortiz .10 .05
☐ 604 Brent Mayne .10 .05
☐ 605 Luis Alicea .10 .05
☐ 606 Damon Berryhill .10 .05
☐ 607 Dave Henderson .10 .05
☐ 608 Kirk McCaskill .10 .05
☐ 609 Jeff Fassero .10 .05
☐ 610 Mike Harkey .10 .05
☐ 611 Francisco Cabrera .10 .05
☐ 612 Rey Sanchez .10 .05
☐ 613 Scott Servais .10 .05
☐ 614 Darrin Fletcher .10 .05
☐ 615 Felix Fermin .10 .05
☐ 616 Kevin Seitzer .10 .05
☐ 617 Bob Scanlan .10 .05
☐ 618 Billy Hatcher .10 .05
☐ 619 John Vander Wal .10 .05
☐ 620 Joe Hesketh .10 .05
☐ 621 Hector Villanueva .10 .05
☐ 622 Randy Milligan .10 .05
☐ 623 Tony Tarasco .10 .05
☐ 624 Russ Swan .10 .05
☐ 625 Willie Wilson .10 .05
☐ 626 Frank Tanana .10 .05
☐ 627 Pete O'Brien .10 .05
☐ 628 Lenny Webster .10 .05
☐ 629 Mark Clark .10 .05
☐ 630 Roger Clemens CL .40 .18
☐ 631 Alex Arias .10 .05
☐ 632 Chris Gwynn .10 .05
☐ 633 Tom Bolton .10 .05
☐ 634 Greg Briley .10 .05
☐ 635 Kent Bottenfield .10 .05
☐ 636 Kelly Downs .10 .05
☐ 637 Manuel Lee .10 .05
☐ 638 Al Leiter .20 .09
☐ 639 Jeff Gardner .10 .05
☐ 640 Mike Gardiner .10 .05
☐ 641 Mark Gardner .10 .05
☐ 642 Jeff Branson .10 .05
☐ 643 Paul Wagner .10 .05
☐ 644 Sean Berry .10 .05
☐ 645 Phil Hiatt .10 .05
☐ 646 Kevin Mitchell .20 .09
☐ 647 Charlie Hayes .10 .05
☐ 648 Jim Deshaies .10 .05
☐ 649 Dan Pasqua .10 .05
☐ 650 Mike Maddux .10 .05
☐ 651 Domingo Martinez .10 .05
☐ 652 Greg McMichael .10 .05
☐ 653 Eric Wedge .10 .05
☐ 654 Mark Whiten .10 .05
☐ 655 Roberto Kelly .10 .05
☐ 656 Julio Franco .20 .09
☐ 657 Gene Harris .10 .05
☐ 658 Pete Schourek .10 .05
☐ 659 Mike Bielecki .10 .05
☐ 660 Ricky Gutierrez .10 .05
☐ 661 Chris Hammond .10 .05
☐ 662 Tim Scott .10 .05
☐ 663 Norm Charlton .10 .05
☐ 664 Doug Drabek .10 .05
☐ 665 Dwight Gooden .20 .09
☐ 666 Jim Gott .10 .05
☐ 667 Randy Myers .20 .09
☐ 668 Darren Holmes .10 .05
☐ 669 Tim Spehr .10 .05
☐ 670 Bruce Ruffin .10 .05
☐ 671 Bobby Thigpen .10 .05
☐ 672 Tony Fernandez .10 .05
☐ 673 Darrin Jackson .10 .05
☐ 674 Gregg Olson .10 .05
☐ 675 Rob Dibble .10 .05
☐ 676 Howard Johnson .10 .05
☐ 677 Mike Lansing .20 .09
☐ 678 Charlie Leibrandt .10 .05
☐ 679 Kevin Bass .10 .05
☐ 680 Hubie Brooks .10 .05
☐ 681 Scott Brosius .10 .05
☐ 682 Randy Knorr .10 .05
☐ 683 Dante Bichette .30 .14
☐ 684 Bryan Harvey .10 .05
☐ 685 Greg Gohr .10 .05
☐ 686 Willie Banks .10 .05
☐ 687 Robb Nen .30 .14
☐ 688 Mike Sciosia .10 .05
☐ 689 John Farrell .10 .05
☐ 690 John Candelaria .10 .05
☐ 691 Damon Buford .10 .05
☐ 692 Todd Worrell .10 .05
☐ 693 Pat Hentgen .30 .14
☐ 694 John Smiley .10 .05
☐ 695 Greg Swindell .10 .05
☐ 696 Derek Bell .20 .09
☐ 697 Terry Jorgensen .10 .05
☐ 698 Jimmy Jones .10 .05
☐ 699 David Wells .10 .05
☐ 700 Dave Martinez .10 .05
☐ 701 Steve Bedrosian .10 .05
☐ 702 Jeff Russell .10 .05
☐ 703 Joe Magrane .10 .05
☐ 704 Matt Mieske .20 .09
☐ 705 Paul Molitor .40 .18
☐ 706 Dale Murphy .30 .14
☐ 707 Steve Howe .10 .05
☐ 708 Greg Gagne .10 .05
☐ 709 Dave Eiland .10 .05
☐ 710 David West .10 .05
☐ 711 Luis Aquino .10 .05
☐ 712 Joe Orsulak .10 .05
☐ 713 Eric Plunk .10 .05
☐ 714 Mike Felder .10 .05
☐ 715 Joe Klink .10 .05
☐ 716 Lonnie Smith .10 .05
☐ 717 Monty Fariss .10 .05
☐ 718 Craig Lefferts .10 .05
☐ 719 John Habyan .10 .05
☐ 720 Willie Blair .10 .05
☐ 721 Darnell Coles .10 .05
☐ 722 Mark Williamson .10 .05
☐ 723 Bryn Smith .10 .05
☐ 724 Greg W. Harris .10 .05
☐ 725 Graeme Lloyd .10 .05
☐ 726 Cris Carpenter .10 .05
☐ 727 Chico Walker .10 .05
☐ 728 Tracy Woodson .10 .05
☐ 729 Jose Uribe .10 .05
☐ 730 Stan Javier .10 .05
☐ 731 Jay Howell .10 .05
☐ 732 Freddie Benavides .10 .05
☐ 733 Jeff Reboulet .10 .05
☐ 734 Scott Sanderson .10 .05
☐ 735 Ryne Sandberg CL .40 .18
☐ 736 Archi Cianfrocco .10 .05
☐ 737 Daryl Boston .10 .05
☐ 738 Craig Grebeck .10 .05
☐ 739 Doug Dascenzo .10 .05
☐ 740 Gerald Young .10 .05
☐ 741 Candy Maldonado .10 .05
☐ 742 Joey Cora .20 .09
☐ 743 Don Slaught .10 .05
☐ 744 Steve Decker .10 .05
☐ 745 Blas Minor .10 .05
☐ 746 Storm Davis .10 .05
☐ 747 Carlos Quintana .10 .05
☐ 748 Vince Coleman .10 .05
☐ 749 Todd Burns .10 .05
☐ 750 Steve Frey .10 .05
☐ 751 Ivan Calderon .10 .05
☐ 752 Steve Reed .10 .05
☐ 753 Danny Jackson .10 .05
☐ 754 Jeff Conine .20 .09
☐ 755 Juan Gonzalez 1.00 .45
☐ 756 Mike Kelly .10 .05
☐ 757 John Doherty .10 .05
☐ 758 Jack Armstrong .10 .05
☐ 759 John Wehner .10 .05
☐ 760 Scott Bankhead .10 .05
☐ 761 Jim Tatum .10 .05
☐ 762 Scott Pose .10 .05
☐ 763 Andy Ashby .10 .05
☐ 764 Ed Sprague .10 .05
☐ 765 Harold Baines .20 .09
☐ 766 Kirk Gibson .20 .09
☐ 767 Troy Neel .10 .05
☐ 768 Dick Schofield .10 .05
☐ 769 Dickie Thon .10 .05
☐ 770 Butch Henry .10 .05
☐ 771 Junior Felix .10 .05
☐ 772 Ken Ryan .10 .05
☐ 773 Trevor Hoffman .30 .14
☐ 774 Phil Plantier .10 .05
☐ 775 Bo Jackson .20 .09
☐ 776 Benito Santiago .10 .05
☐ 777 Andre Dawson .30 .14
☐ 778 Bryan Hickerson .10 .05
☐ 779 Dennis Moeller .10 .05
☐ 780 Ryan Bowen .10 .05
☐ 781 Eric Fox .10 .05
☐ 782 Joe Kmak .10 .05
☐ 783 Mike Hampton .30 .14
☐ 784 Darrell Sherman .10 .05
☐ 785 J.T. Snow .40 .18
☐ 786 Dave Winfield .30 .14
☐ 787 Jim Austin .10 .05
☐ 788 Craig Shipley .10 .05
☐ 789 Greg Myers .10 .05
☐ 790 Todd Benzinger .10 .05
☐ 791 Cory Snyder .10 .05
☐ 792 David Segui .10 .05
☐ 793 Armando Reynoso .10 .05
☐ 794 Chili Davis .20 .09
☐ 795 Dave Nilsson .20 .09
☐ 796 Paul O'Neill .20 .09
☐ 797 Jerald Clark .10 .05
☐ 798 Jose Mesa .20 .09
☐ 799 Brain Holman .10 .05
☐ 800 Jim Eisenreich .20 .09
☐ 801 Mark McLemore .10 .05
☐ 802 Luis Sojo .10 .05
☐ 803 Harold Reynolds .10 .05
☐ 804 Dan Plesac .10 .05
☐ 805 Dave Stieb .10 .05
☐ 806 Tom Brunansky .10 .05
☐ 807 Kelly Gruber .10 .05
☐ 808 Bob Ojeda .10 .05
☐ 809 Dave Burba .10 .05
☐ 810 Joe Boever .10 .05
☐ 811 Jeremy Hernandez .10 .05
☐ 812 Tim Salmon TC .30 .14
☐ 813 Jeff Bagwell TC .40 .18
☐ 814 Dennis Eckersley TC .20 .09
☐ 815 Roberto Alomar TC .20 .09
☐ 816 Steve Avery TC .10 .05
☐ 817 Pat Listach TC .10 .05
☐ 818 Gregg Jefferies TC .20 .09
☐ 819 Sammy Sosa TC .40 .18
☐ 820 Darryl Strawberry TC .20 .09
☐ 821 Dennis Martinez TC .10 .05
☐ 822 Robby Thompson TC .10 .05
☐ 823 Albert Belle TC .40 .18
☐ 824 Randy Johnson TC .30 .14
☐ 825 Nigel Wilson TC .10 .05
☐ 826 Bobby Bonilla TC .20 .09
☐ 827 Glenn Davis TC .10 .05
☐ 828 Gary Sheffield TC .40 .18
☐ 829 Darren Daulton TC .20 .09
☐ 830 Jay Bell TC .10 .05
☐ 831 Juan Gonzalez TC .50 .23
☐ 832 Andre Dawson TC .30 .14
☐ 833 Hal Morris TC .10 .05
☐ 834 David Nied TC .10 .05
☐ 835 Felix Jose TC .10 .05
☐ 836 Travis Fryman TC .20 .09
☐ 837 Shane Mack TC .10 .05
☐ 838 Robin Ventura TC .20 .09
☐ 839 Danny Tartabull TC .10 .05
☐ 840 Roberto Alomar CL .40 .18
☐ SP5 George Brett 1.50 .70
Robin Yount
3,000th Hit
☐ SP6 Nolan Ryan 3.00 1.35

1993 Upper Deck Clutch Performers

These 20 standard-size cards were inserted one every nine series II retail foil packs, as well as inserted one per series II retail jumbo packs. The fronts feature color player action shots that are borderless, except at the bottom, where a black stripe is set off by a gold-foil line and carries the set's title and Reggie Jackson's gold-foil signature. The player's name printed in white lettering rests at the bottom of the photo. The back carries a color player action shot below a black bar at the top that carries the player's name in gold-colored lettering. Below the picture appears a small black-and-white head shot of Reggie Jackson alongside his comments on the player. A player stat table appears below. The cards are numbered on the back with an "R" prefix and appear in alphabetical order. These 20 cards represent Reggie Jackson's selection of players who have come through under pressure.

	MINT	NRMT
COMPLETE SET (20)	20.00	9.00
COMMON CARD (R1-R20)	.25	.11

	MINT	NRMT
☐ R1 Roberto Alomar		
☐ R2 Wade Boggs	.75	.35
☐ R3 Barry Bonds	1.25	.55
☐ R4 Jose Canseco	.75	.35
☐ R5 Joe Carter	.75	.35
☐ R6 Will Clark	.75	.35
☐ R7 Roger Clemens	1.50	.70
☐ R8 Dennis Eckersley	.50	.23
☐ R9 Cecil Fielder	.50	.23
☐ R10 Juan Gonzalez	2.50	1.10
☐ R11 Ken Griffey Jr.	5.00	2.20
☐ R12 Rickey Henderson	.75	.35
☐ R13 Barry Larkin	.75	.35
☐ R14 Don Mattingly	2.00	.90
☐ R15 Fred McGriff	.75	.35
☐ R16 Terry Pendleton	.25	.11
☐ R17 Kirby Puckett	2.00	.90
☐ R18 Ryne Sandberg	1.25	.55
☐ R19 John Smoltz	.75	.35
☐ R20 Frank Thomas	4.00	1.80

1993 Upper Deck Fifth Anniversary

This 15-card standard-size set celebrates Upper Deck's five years in the sports card business.The cards are essentially reprinted versions of some of Upper Deck's most popular cards in the last five years. These cards were inserted one every nine second series hobby packs. The black-bordered fronts feature player photos that previously appeared on an Upper Deck card. The Five-Year Anniversary logo is located in one of the corners and the player's name is printed in gold-foil along the lower black border. The black backs carry a picture of the original card on the left side with narrative historical information on Upper Deck and a brief career summary of the player. The gold-colored year of issue of the original card is prominently displayed in the middle of the text. The cards are numbered on the back with an "A" prefix. One over-sized (3 1/2" by 5") version of each of these cards was initially inserted into retail blister repacks, which contained one foil pack each of 1993 Upper Deck Series I and II. These cards are individually numbered out of 10,000 and were later inserted into various forms of repackaging.

	MINT	NRMT
COMPLETE SET (15)	20.00	9.00
COMMON CARD (A1-A15)	.25	.11
*JUMBO CARDS: 2X VALUE		

	MINT	NRMT
☐ A1 Ken Griffey Jr.	8.00	3.60
☐ A2 Gary Sheffield	1.00	.45
☐ A3 Roberto Alomar	1.00	.45
☐ A4 Jim Abbott	.50	.23
☐ A5 Nolan Ryan	6.00	2.70
☐ A6 Juan Gonzalez	4.00	1.80
☐ A7 David Justice	1.00	.45
☐ A8 Carlos Baerga	.50	.23
☐ A9 Reggie Jackson	1.00	.45
☐ A10 Eric Karros	.50	.23
☐ A11 Chipper Jones	5.00	2.20
☐ A12 Ivan Rodriguez	1.25	.55
☐ A13 Pat Listach	.25	.11
☐ A14 Frank Thomas	6.00	2.70
☐ A15 Tim Salmon	1.50	.70

1993 Upper Deck Future Heroes

Inserted in second series foil packs at a rate of one every nine pack; this set continues the Heroes insert set begun in the 1990 Upper Deck high-number set, this ten-card standard-size set features eight different "Future Heroes" along with a checklist and header card. The fronts feature borderless color player action shots that bear the player's simulated autograph in gold foil in an upper corner. The player's name appears within a black stripe formed by the simulated tearing away of a piece of the photo. The player's team appears below. The back carries the player's name vertically within a black "tear-away" stripe along the right edge. Career highlights are displayed within a white, gray, and tan panel on the left.

	MINT	NRMT
COMPLETE SET (10)	12.00	5.50
COMMON CARD (55-63)	.50	.23

	MINT	NRMT
☐ 55 Roberto Alomar	1.00	.45
☐ 56 Barry Bonds	1.25	.55
☐ 57 Roger Clemens	1.50	.70
☐ 58 Juan Gonzalez	2.50	1.10
☐ 59 Ken Griffey Jr.	5.00	2.20
☐ 60 Mark McGwire	2.00	.90
☐ 61 Kirby Puckett	2.00	.90
☐ 62 Frank Thomas	4.00	1.80
☐ 63 Checklist	.50	.23
☐ NNO Header Card SP	.75	.35

1993 Upper Deck Home Run Heroes

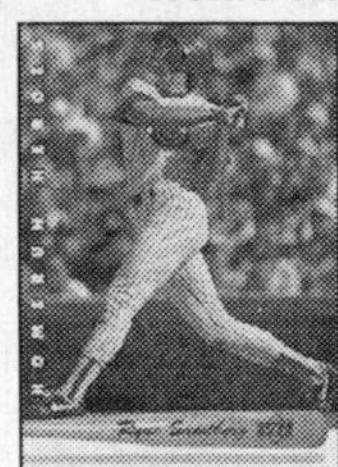

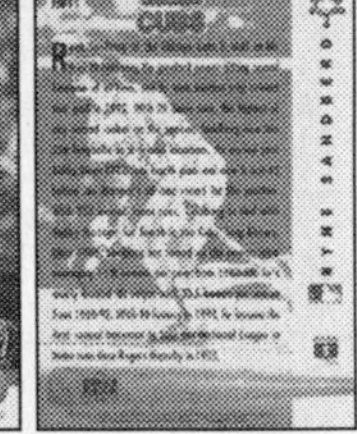

This 28-card standard-size set features the home run leader from each Major League team. Each 1993 first series 27-card jumbo pack contained one of these cards. The cards feature action color player photos with a three-dimensional baseball bat design at the bottom. Featuring embossed printing, the bat looks and feels as if it stands off the card, and a shadow design below it adds to the effect. The words "Homerun Heroes" are printed vertically down the left. The backs show a team color-coded photo as the background for player information. The player's name appears in a white border on the right. The baseball bat design is repeated at the bottom. The cards are numbered on the back with an "HR" prefix and the set is arranged in descending order according to the number of home runs.

	MINT	NRMT
COMPLETE SET (28)	15.00	6.75
COMMON CARD (HR1-HR28)	.25	.11

	MINT	NRMT
☐ HR1 Juan Gonzalez	2.50	1.10
☐ HR2 Mark McGwire	1.50	.70
☐ HR3 Cecil Fielder	.35	.16
☐ HR4 Fred McGriff	.50	.23
☐ HR5 Albert Belle	1.00	.45
☐ HR6 Barry Bonds	1.00	.45
☐ HR7 Joe Carter	.50	.23
☐ HR8 Darren Daulton	.35	.16
☐ HR9 Ken Griffey Jr.	5.00	2.20
☐ HR10 Dave Hollins	.25	.11
☐ HR11 Ryne Sandberg	1.25	.55
☐ HR12 George Bell	.25	.11
☐ HR13 Danny Tartabull	.25	.11
☐ HR14 Mike Devereaux	.25	.11
☐ HR15 Greg Vaughn	.25	.11
☐ HR16 Larry Walker	.75	.35
☐ HR17 David Justice	.35	.16
☐ HR18 Terry Pendleton	.25	.11
☐ HR19 Eric Karros	.35	.16
☐ HR20 Ray Lankford	.50	.23
☐ HR21 Matt Williams	.50	.23
☐ HR22 Eric Anthony	.25	.11
☐ HR23 Bobby Bonilla	.35	.16
☐ HR24 Kirby Puckett	2.00	.90
☐ HR25 Mike Macfarlane	.25	.11
☐ HR26 Tom Brunansky	.25	.11
☐ HR27 Paul O'Neill	.35	.16
☐ HR28 Gary Gaetti	.35	.16

1993 Upper Deck Iooss Collection

This 27-card standard-size set spotlights the work of famous sports photographer Walter Iooss Jr. by presenting 26 of the game's current greats in a candid photo set. The cards were inserted in series I retail foil packs at a rate of one every nine packs. They were also in retail jumbo packs at a rate of one in five packs. The posed color player photos on the fronts are full-bleed and either horizontally or vertically oriented. The words "The Upper Deck Iooss Collection" are printed in gold foil. The back carries a quote from Iooss about the shoot and the player's career highlights. The text blocks on the card backs are separated by a gradated bars of varying colors. The cards are numbered on the back with a "WI" prefix. One over-sized version of each of these cards were initially inserted into retail blister repacks containing one foil pack each of 1993 Upper Deck Series I and II. These over-sized (3 1/2" by 5") cards are individually numbered out of 10,000 and were later inserted in various forms of repackaging.

	MINT	NRMT
COMPLETE SET (27)	25.00	11.00
COMMON CARD (WI1-WI26)	.30	.14
*JUMBO CARDS: 2X VALUE		

	MINT	NRMT
☐ WI1 Tim Salmon	1.25	.55
☐ WI2 Jeff Bagwell	2.50	1.10
☐ WI3 Mark McGwire	2.00	.90
☐ WI4 Roberto Alomar	1.00	.45
☐ WI5 Steve Avery	.30	.14
☐ WI6 Paul Molitor	1.00	.45
☐ WI7 Ozzie Smith	1.50	.70
☐ WI8 Mark Grace	.75	.35
☐ WI9 Eric Karros	.50	.23
☐ WI10 Delino DeShields	.30	.14
☐ WI11 Will Clark	.75	.35
☐ WI12 Albert Belle	1.25	.55
☐ WI13 Ken Griffey Jr.	6.00	2.70
☐ WI14 Howard Johnson	.30	.14
☐ WI15 Cal Ripken Jr.	5.00	2.20
☐ WI16 Fred McGriff	.75	.35
☐ WI17 Darren Daulton	.50	.23
☐ WI18 Andy Van Slyke	.30	.14
☐ WI19 Nolan Ryan	5.00	2.20
☐ WI20 Wade Boggs	1.00	.45
☐ WI21 Barry Larkin	.75	.35
☐ WI22 George Brett	2.50	1.10
☐ WI23 Cecil Fielder	.50	.23
☐ WI24 Kirby Puckett	2.50	1.10
☐ WI25 Frank Thomas	5.00	2.20
☐ WI26 Don Mattingly	2.50	1.10
☐ NNO Title Card Iooss Header	.50	.23

1993 Upper Deck Mays Heroes

This standard-size ten-card set was randomly inserted in 1993 Upper Deck first series foil packs. The fronts feature color photos of Mays at various stages of his career that are partially contained within a black bordered circle. The

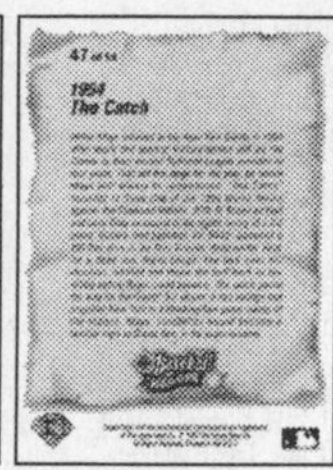

photos rest on a rough-edged sports page from a newspaper. The Upper Deck Baseball Heroes logo appears in the lower right corner. The back design displays career highlights on a blank newspaper page. The cards are numbered in continuation of Upper Deck's Heroes series.

	MINT	NRMT
COMPLETE SET (10)	3.00	1.35
COMMON MAYS (46-54)	.50	.23
☐ 46 Willie Mays 1951 Rookie-of-the-Year	.50	.23
☐ 47 Willie Mays 1954 The Catch	.50	.23
☐ 48 Willie Mays 1956-57 30-30 Club	.50	.23
☐ 49 Willie Mays 1961 Four-Homer Game	.50	.23
☐ 50 Willie Mays 1965 Most Valuable Player	.50	.23
☐ 51 Willie Mays 1969 600-Home Run Club	.50	.23
☐ 52 Willie Mays 1972 New York Homecoming	.50	.23
☐ 53 Willie Mays 1979 Hall of Fame	.50	.23
☐ 54 Baseball Heroes CL Vernon Wells Portrait	.50	.23
☐ NNO0 Baseball Heroes SP (Header card)	.50	.23

1993 Upper Deck On Deck

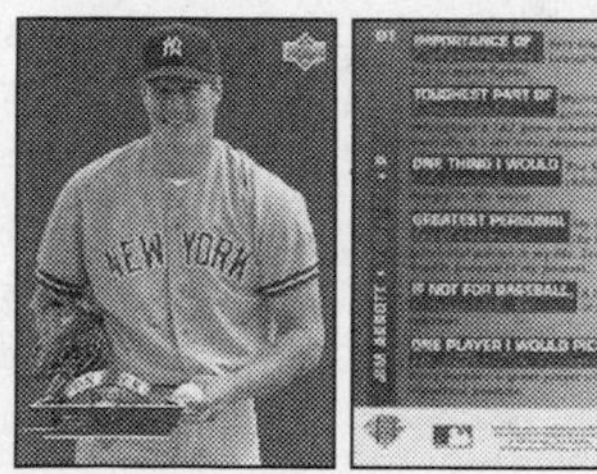

Inserted one per series II jumbo packs, these 25 standard-size cards profile baseball's top players. The fronts feature borderless color player photos, some action, others posed, and carry the player's simulated gold-foil signature within a team color-coded stripe that appears as part of the set's logo. The gradated-tan-colored back carries the player's name, position, and team vertically within a team color-coded stripe near the left edge. The player's answers to personal questions rounds out the back. The cards are numbered on the back with a "D" prefix in alphabetical order by name.

	MINT	NRMT
COMPLETE SET (25)	20.00	9.00
COMMON CARD (D1-D25)	.25	.11
☐ D1 Jim Abbott	.50	.23
☐ D2 Roberto Alomar	1.00	.45
☐ D3 Carlos Baerga	.25	.11
☐ D4 Albert Belle	1.25	.55
☐ D5 Wade Boggs	1.00	.45
☐ D6 George Brett	2.00	.90
☐ D7 Jose Canseco	.75	.35
☐ D8 Will Clark	.75	.35
☐ D9 Roger Clemens	1.50	.70
☐ D10 Dennis Eckersley	.50	.23
☐ D11 Cecil Fielder	.50	.23
☐ D12 Juan Gonzalez	2.50	1.10
☐ D13 Ken Griffey Jr.	5.00	2.20
☐ D14 Tony Gwynn	2.00	.90
☐ D15 Bo Jackson	.50	.23
☐ D16 Chipper Jones	4.00	1.80
☐ D17 Eric Karros	.50	.23
☐ D18 Mark McGwire	2.00	.90
☐ D19 Kirby Puckett	2.00	.90
☐ D20 Nolan Ryan	4.00	1.80
☐ D21 Tim Salmon	1.25	.55
☐ D22 Ryne Sandberg	1.25	.55
☐ D23 Darryl Strawberry	.50	.23
☐ D24 Frank Thomas	4.00	1.80
☐ D25 Andy Van Slyke	.25	.11

1993 Upper Deck Season Highlights

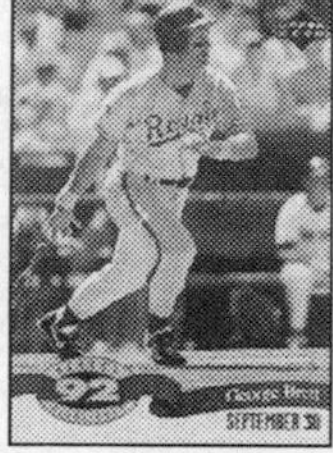

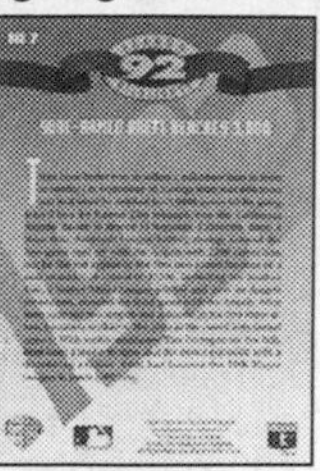

This 20-card standard-size insert set captures great moments of the 1992 Major League Baseball season. The cards were exclusively distributed in specially marked cases that were available only at Upper Deck Heroes of Baseball Card Shows and through the purchase of a specified quantity of second series cases. In these packs, the cards were inserted at a rate of one every nine. The fronts display a full-bleed color action photo with a special "'92 Season Highlights" logo running across the bottom. The ribbon intersecting the logo is blue on the American League cards and red on the National League. The date of the player's outstanding achievement is gold-foil stamped at the lower right. On backs that fade from the league color to white, a description of the achievement is presented. The year 1992 is printed diagonally across the backs. The cards are numbered on the back with an "HI" prefix in alphabetical order by player's name.

	MINT	NRMT
COMPLETE SET (20)	150.00	70.00
COMMON CARD (HI1-HI20)	2.50	1.10
MINOR STARS	4.00	1.80
SEMISTARS	5.00	2.20
UNLISTED STARS	10.00	4.50
☐ HI1 Roberto Alomar	10.00	4.50
☐ HI2 Steve Avery	2.50	1.10
☐ HI3 Harold Baines	4.00	1.80
☐ HI4 Damon Berryhill	2.50	1.10
☐ HI5 Barry Bonds	12.00	5.50
☐ HI6 Bret Boone	2.50	1.10
☐ HI7 George Brett	20.00	9.00
☐ HI8 Francisco Cabrera	2.50	1.10
☐ HI9 Ken Griffey Jr.	50.00	22.00
☐ HI10 Rickey Henderson	5.00	2.20
☐ HI11 Kenny Lofton	15.00	6.75
☐ HI12 Mickey Morandini	2.50	1.10
☐ HI13 Eddie Murray	12.00	5.50
☐ HI14 David Nied	2.50	1.10
☐ HI15 Jeff Reardon	4.00	1.80
☐ HI16 Bip Roberts	2.50	1.10
☐ HI17 Nolan Ryan	50.00	22.00
☐ HI18 Ed Sprague	2.50	1.10
☐ HI19 Dave Winfield	5.00	2.20
☐ HI20 Robin Yount	5.00	2.20

1993 Upper Deck Then And Now

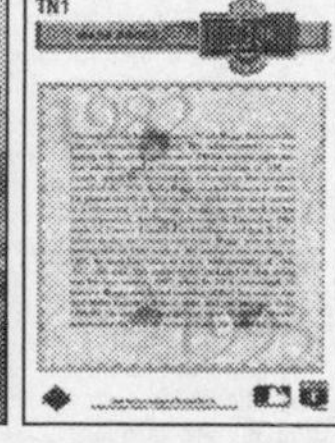

This 18-card, standard-size hologram set highlights veteran stars in their rookie year and today, reflecting on how they and the game have changed. Cards 1-9 were randomly inserted in series I foil packs; cards 10-18 were randomly inserted in series II foil packs. In either series, the cards were inserted one every 27 packs. The nine lithogram cards in the second series feature one card each of Hall of Famers Reggie Jackson, Mickey Mantle, and Willie Mays, as well as six active players. The horizontal fronts have a color close-up photo cutout and superimposed at the left corner of a full-bleed hologram portraying the player in an action scene. The skyline of the player's city serves as the background for the holograms. The player's name and the manufacturer's name form a right angle at the upper right corner. At the upper left corner, a "Then And Now" logo which includes the length of the player's career in years rounds out the front. On a sand-colored panel that resembles a postage stamp, the backs present career summary. The cards are numbered on the back with a "TN" prefix and arranged alphabetically within subgroup according to player's last name.

	MINT	NRMT
COMPLETE SET (18)	50.00	22.00
COMPLETE SERIES 1 (9)	20.00	9.00
COMPLETE SERIES 2 (9)	30.00	13.50
COMMON CARD (TN1-TN18)	.50	.23
☐ TN1 Wade Boggs	1.00	.45
☐ TN2 George Brett	4.00	1.80
☐ TN3 Rickey Henderson	1.00	.45
☐ TN4 Cal Ripken	8.00	3.60
☐ TN5 Nolan Ryan	8.00	3.60
☐ TN6 Ryne Sandberg	2.50	1.10
☐ TN7 Ozzie Smith	2.50	1.10
☐ TN8 Darryl Strawberry	.75	.35
☐ TN9 Dave Winfield	1.00	.45
☐ TN10 Dennis Eckersley	.75	.35
☐ TN11 Tony Gwynn	4.00	1.80
☐ TN12 Howard Johnson	.50	.23
☐ TN13 Don Mattingly	4.00	1.80
☐ TN14 Eddie Murray	1.50	.70
☐ TN15 Robin Yount	1.00	.45
☐ TN16 Reggie Jackson	2.50	1.10
☐ TN17 Mickey Mantle	15.00	6.75
☐ TN18 Willie Mays	8.00	3.60

1993 Upper Deck Triple Crown

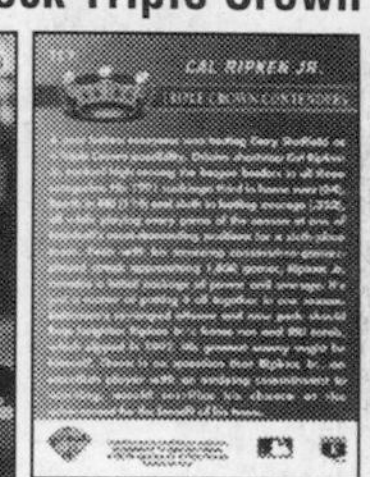

This ten-card, standard-size insert set highlights ten players who were selected by Upper Deck as having the best shot at winning Major League Baseball's Triple Crown. The cards were randomly inserted in series I hobby foil packs at a rate of one in 15. The fronts display glossy full-bleed color player photos. At the bottom, a purple ribbon edged in gold foil carries the words "Triple Crown Contenders," while the player's name appears in gold foil lettering immediately below on a gradated black background. A crown overlays the ribbon at the lower left corner and rounds out the front. On a gradated black background, the backs summarize the player's performance in home runs, RBIs, and batting average. The cards are numbered on the back with a "TC" prefix and arranged alphabetically by player's last name.

	MINT	NRMT
COMPLETE SET (10)	30.00	13.50
COMMON CARD (TC1-TC10)	1.00	.45
☐ TC1 Barry Bonds	2.50	1.10
☐ TC2 Jose Canseco	1.50	.70
☐ TC3 Will Clark	1.50	.70
☐ TC4 Ken Griffey Jr.	10.00	4.50
☐ TC5 Fred McGriff	1.00	.45
☐ TC6 Kirby Puckett	4.00	1.80
☐ TC7 Cal Ripken Jr.	8.00	3.60
☐ TC8 Gary Sheffield	2.00	.90
☐ TC9 Frank Thomas	8.00	3.60
☐ TC10 Larry Walker	2.00	.90

1993 Upper Deck All-Time Heroes Preview

This four-card boxed preview set was distributed to herald the release of the 165-card main set. The cards are patterned after the T-202 Hassan Triple Folders cards which first appeared in 1912. The cards measur approximately 2 1/4" by 5 1/4" and feature two side pane

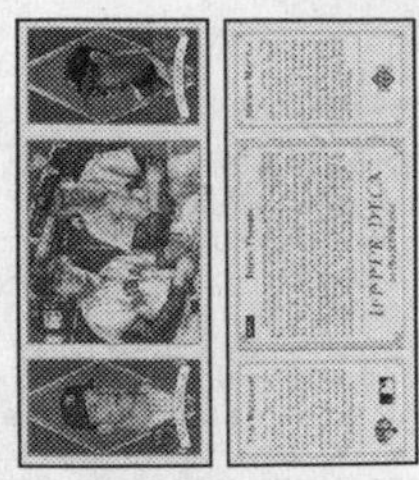

and a larger middle panel. The fronts feature two-player color drawings by Todd Reigle in their middle panels. The side panels feature photos of the two players. The white backs include player biographies and career highlights printed in red lettering. The cards are numbered on the back with an "HOB" prefix.

	MINT	NRMT
COMPLETE SET (4)	5.00	2.20
COMMON CARD (1-4)	1.50	.70
☐ 1 Ted Williams	1.50	.70
Mickey Mantle		
☐ 2 Reggie Jackson	1.50	.70
Mickey Mantle		
☐ 3 Ted Williams	1.50	.70
Reggie Jackson		
☐ 4 Reggie Jackson	1.50	.70
Mickey Mantle		
Ted Williams		

1993 Upper Deck All-Time Heroes

This 165-card set of All-Time Heroes of Baseball is patterned after the T-202 Hassan Triple Folders cards, which first appeared in 1912. The cards measure approximately 2 1/4" by 5 1/4" and feature two side panels and a larger middle panel. The set consists of 130 regular cards and the Classic Combinations subset (131-165). The fronts feature candid or action photos of the featured player on the center panel, along with a portrait on one of the side panels and the B.A.T. (Baseball Assistance Team) logo on the other. The backs include player biographies and career highlights, as well as an explanation of the B.A.T. cause. The Classic Combinations subset have center panels that feature either artwork by Todd Reigle or a photograph of multiple greats. The side panels feature photos of two players. The backs include player biographies on the side panels, with the center panel detailing the association between the players. Cards from the ten-card T202 Reprints set were randomly inserted in 1993 Upper Deck All-Time Heroes of Baseball foil packs. The foil packs contained 12 cards per pack. Each card is holographically enhanced. The stated odds (on the box) of finding a T202 Reprint insert card were one in five packs. Reggie Jackson and Mickey Mantle were the spokespersons for this set and they are featured prominently on the front of the box. The grand prize for the set's mail-in contest was an actual, original set of T202 Hassan Triplefolders, which Upper Deck had purchased in the open hobby market expressly for the promotion.

	MINT	NRMT
COMPLETE SET (165)	20.00	9.00
COMMON CARD (1-165)	.10	.05
☐ 1 Hank Aaron	1.50	.70
☐ 2 Tommie Agee	.10	.05
☐ 3 Bob Allison	.10	.05
☐ 4 Matty Alou	.10	.05
☐ 5 Sal Bando	.10	.05
☐ 6 Hank Bauer	.10	.05
☐ 7 Don Baylor	.15	.07
☐ 8 Glenn Beckert	.10	.05
☐ 9 Yogi Berra	.75	.35
☐ 10 Buddy Biancalana	.10	.05
☐ 11 Jack Billingham	.10	.05
☐ 12 Joe Black	.15	.07
☐ 13 Paul Blair	.10	.05
☐ 14 Steve Blass	.10	.05
☐ 15 Ray Boone	.10	.05
☐ 16 Lou Boudreau	.20	.09
☐ 17 Ken Brett	.10	.05
☐ 18 Nellie Briles	.10	.05
☐ 19 Bobby Brown	.15	.07
☐ 20 Bill Buckner	.15	.07
☐ 21 Don Buford	.10	.05
☐ 22 Al Bumbry	.10	.05
☐ 23 Lew Burdette	.15	.07
☐ 24 Jeff Burroughs	.10	.05
☐ 25 Johnny Callison	.10	.05
☐ 26 Bert Campaneris	.10	.05
☐ 27 Rico Carty	.10	.05
☐ 28 Dave Cash	.10	.05
☐ 29 Cesar Cedeno	.15	.07
☐ 30 Frank Chance	.20	.09
☐ 31 Joe Charboneau	.15	.07
☐ 32 Ty Cobb	1.50	.70
☐ 33 Jerry Coleman	.10	.05
☐ 34 Cecil Cooper	.10	.05
☐ 35 Frankie Crosetti	.10	.05
☐ 36 Alvin Dark	.10	.05
☐ 37 Tommy Davis	.10	.05
☐ 38 Dizzy Dean	.30	.14
☐ 39 Doug DeCinces	.10	.05
☐ 40 Bucky Dent	.10	.05
☐ 41 Larry Dierker	.10	.05
☐ 42 Larry Doby	.15	.07
☐ 43 Moe Drabowsky	.10	.05
☐ 44 Dave Dravecky	.10	.05
☐ 45 Del Ennis	.10	.05
☐ 46 Carl Erskine	.15	.07
☐ 47 Johnny Evers	.20	.09
☐ 48 Elroy Face	.10	.05
☐ 49 Rick Ferrell	.20	.09
☐ 50 Mark Fidrych	.15	.07
☐ 51 Curt Flood	.15	.07
☐ 52 Whitey Ford	.60	.25
☐ 53 George Foster	.15	.07
☐ 54 Jimmie Foxx	.40	.18
☐ 55 Jim Fregosi	.15	.07
☐ 56 Phil Garner	.10	.05
☐ 57 Ralph Garr	.10	.05
☐ 58 Lou Gehrig	2.00	.90
☐ 59 Bobby Grich	.15	.07
☐ 60 Jerry Grote	.10	.05
☐ 61 Harvey Haddix	.10	.05
☐ 62 Toby Harrah	.10	.05
☐ 63 Bud Harrelson	.15	.07
☐ 64 Jim Hegan	.10	.05
☐ 65 Gil Hodges	.25	.11
☐ 66 Ken Holtzman	.10	.05
☐ 67 Bob Horner	.10	.05
☐ 68 Rogers Hornsby	.40	.18
☐ 69 Carl Hubbell	.20	.09
☐ 70 Ron Hunt	.10	.05
☐ 71 Monte Irvin	.20	.09
☐ 72 Reggie Jackson	.75	.35
☐ 73 Larry Jansen	.10	.05
☐ 74 Ferguson Jenkins	.20	.09
☐ 75 Tommy John	.15	.07
☐ 76 Cliff Johnson	.10	.05
☐ 77 Davey Johnson	.15	.07
☐ 78 Walter Johnson	.40	.18
☐ 79 George Kell	.20	.09
☐ 80 Don Kessinger	.10	.05
☐ 81 Vern Law	.10	.05
☐ 82 Dennis Leonard	.10	.05
☐ 83 Johnny Logan	.10	.05
☐ 84 Mickey Lolich	.15	.07
☐ 85 Jim Lonborg	.10	.05
☐ 86 Bill Madlock	.10	.05
☐ 87 Mickey Mantle	3.00	1.35
☐ 88 Billy Martin	.20	.09
☐ 89 Christy Mathewson	.40	.18
☐ 90 Lee May	.10	.05
☐ 91 Willie Mays	1.50	.70
☐ 92 Bill Mazeroski	.15	.07
☐ 93 Gil McDougald	.15	.07
☐ 94 Sam McDowell	.10	.05
☐ 95 Minnie Minoso	.15	.07
☐ 96 Johnny Mize	.20	.09
☐ 97 Rick Monday	.10	.05
☐ 98 Wally Moon	.10	.05
☐ 99 Manny Mota	.10	.05
☐ 100 Bobby Murcer	.10	.05
☐ 101 Ron Necciai	.10	.05
☐ 102 Al Oliver	.15	.07
☐ 103 Mel Ott	.20	.09
☐ 104 Mel Parnell	.10	.05
☐ 105 Jimmy Piersall	.15	.07
☐ 106 Johnny Podres	.10	.05
☐ 107 Bobby Richardson	.15	.07
☐ 108 Robin Roberts	.20	.09
☐ 109 Al Rosen	.15	.07
☐ 110 Babe Ruth	3.00	1.35
☐ 111 Joe Sambito	.10	.05
☐ 112 Manny Sanguillen	.10	.05
☐ 113 Ron Santo	.15	.07
☐ 114 Bill Skowron	.10	.05
☐ 115 Enos Slaughter	.20	.09
☐ 116 Warren Spahn	.20	.09
☐ 117 Tris Speaker	.20	.09
☐ 118 Frank Thomas	.10	.05
☐ 119 Bobby Thomson	.15	.07
☐ 120 Andre Thornton	.10	.05
☐ 121 Marv Throneberry	.10	.05
☐ 122 Luis Tiant	.15	.07
☐ 123 Joe Tinker	.20	.09
☐ 124 Honus Wagner	.40	.18
☐ 125 Bill White	.15	.07
☐ 126 Ted Williams	2.00	.90
☐ 127 Earl Wilson	.10	.05
☐ 128 Joe Wood	.15	.07
☐ 129 Cy Young	.20	.09
☐ 130 Richie Zisk	.10	.05
☐ 131 Babe Ruth	1.50	.70
Lou Gehrig		
☐ 132 Ted Williams	.75	.35
Rogers Hornsby		
☐ 133 Lou Gehrig	1.50	.70
Babe Ruth		
☐ 134 Babe Ruth	1.50	.70
Mickey Mantle		
☐ 135 Mickey Mantle	1.00	.45
Reggie Jackson		
☐ 136 Mel Ott	.15	.07
Carl Hubbell		
☐ 137 Mickey Mantle	1.25	.55
Willie Mays		
☐ 138 Cy Young	.20	.09
Walter Johnson		
☐ 139 Honus Wagner	.20	.09
Rogers Hornsby		
☐ 140 Mickey Mantle	1.00	.45
Whitey Ford		
☐ 141 Mickey Mantle	1.00	.45
Billy Martin		
☐ 142 Cy Young	.20	.09
Walter Johnson		
☐ 143 Christy Mathewson	.20	.09
Walter Johnson		
☐ 144 Warren Spahn	.20	.09
Christy Mathewson		
☐ 145 Honus Wagner	.75	.35
Ty Cobb		
☐ 146 Babe Ruth	1.50	.70
Ty Cobb		
☐ 147 Joe Tinker	.20	.09
Johnny Evers		
☐ 148 Johnny Evers	.20	.09
Frank Chance		
☐ 149 Hank Aaron	1.50	.70
Babe Ruth		
☐ 150 Willie Mays	1.00	.45
Hank Aaron		
☐ 151 Babe Ruth	1.50	.70
Willie Mays		
☐ 152 Babe Ruth	1.00	.45
Whitey Ford		
☐ 153 Larry Doby	.10	.05
Minnie Minoso		
☐ 154 Joe Black	.15	.07
Monte Irvin		
☐ 155 Joe Wood	.15	.07
Christy Mathewson		
☐ 156 Christy Mathewson	.20	.09
Cy Young		
☐ 157 Cy Young	.15	.07
Joe Wood		
☐ 158 Cy Young	.15	.07
Whitey Ford		
☐ 159 Cy Young	.15	.07
Ferguson Jenkins		
☐ 160 Ty Cobb	.75	.35
Rogers Hornsby		
☐ 161 Tris Speaker	.75	.35
Ted Williams		
☐ 162 Rogers Hornsby	.75	.35
Ted Williams		
☐ 163 Willie Mays	.60	.25
Monte Irvin		
☐ 164 Willie Mays	.60	.25
Bobby Thomson		
☐ 165 Reggie Jackson	1.25	.55
Mickey Mantle		

1993 Upper Deck T202 Reprints

Randomly inserted in 1993 Upper Deck All-Time Heroes of Baseball foil packs, this ten-card set of reprints feature players from the 1912 Hassan "Triplefolders. The Hassan cigarette ads were replaced by the Upper Deck hologram and their designation of "T202" comes from their assignment in the American Card Catalog. The reprints are unnumbered and appear alphabetically

	MINT	NRMT
COMPLETE SET (10)	15.00	6.75
COMMON CARD (1-10)	1.00	.45
☐ 1 Art Devlin Christy Mathewson	1.00	.45
☐ 2 Hugh Jennings Ty Cobb	2.50	1.10
☐ 3 John Kling Cy Young	1.00	.45
☐ 4 Jack Knight Walter Johnson	1.00	.45
☐ 5 John McGraw Hugh Jennings	1.50	.70
☐ 6 George Moriarty Ty Cobb	2.00	.90
☐ 7 Charles O'Leary Ty Cobb	2.00	.90
☐ 8 Charles O'Leary Ty Cobb	2.00	.90
☐ 9 Joe Tinker Frank Chance	2.50	1.10
☐ 10 Joe Wood Tris Speaker	1.00	.45

1993 Upper Deck Clark Reggie Jackson

Issued to promote the reintroduction of the Reggie bar by the Clark Candy Co., these three standard-size cards highlight Jackson's career and feature on their fronts white-bordered color photos of Jackson as an Athletic and as a Yankee, with all team logos airbrushed out. Jackson's name and achievement appear in a bar at the bottom that shades from blue to black left to right. The Clark logo appears in the upper left and the Upper Deck logo rests in the lower right. Within a white rectangle superposed upon a photo of pintstripes, baseballs, bats, and a cap and glove, the white-bordered back recounts Jackson's achievement cited on the front. The Upper Deck hologram in the lower left rounds out the back. The cards are numbered on the back with a "C" prefix. One card was inserted in each Reggie bar and Jackson autographed 200 cards that were randomly inserted into the candy bar packages.

	MINT	NRMT
COMPLETE SET (3)	5.00	2.20
COMMON CARD (C1-C3)	2.00	.90
☐ C1 Reggie Jackson Inducted into HOF, 1993	2.00	.90
☐ C2 Reggie Jackson Mr. October, 1977	2.00	.90
☐ C3 Reggie Jackson AL MVP, 1973	2.00	.90

1993 Upper Deck Diamond Gallery

This 38-card standard-size boxed set features two player action photos on its horizontal fronts. One is a hologram, the other is a color action shot of the player, which is displayed on the left side projecting from a baseball diamond design. In the hologram, the player's uniform number appears behind him. The front is borderless on the sides and has oblique team-colored borders on the top and bottom, which contain the player's name and team, respectively. The back features another player action photo. This photo is borderless at the top, and ghosted in the oblique side borders and at the bottom of the photo, where the player's biography, stats and highlights appear. The cards are numbered on the back, with cards 29-31 belonging to the Gallery Heroes subset, and cards 32-36 belonging to the Diamonds in the Rough subset. Also included in the set are the checklist bearing the production number out of 123,600 sets produced, and a mail-away card for the Diamond Gallery card album.

	MINT	NRMT
COMPLETE SET (38)	18.00	8.00
COMMON CARD (1-36)	.10	.05
☐ 1 Tim Salmon	1.00	.45
☐ 2 Jeff Bagwell	1.50	.70
☐ 3 Mark McGwire	1.50	.70
☐ 4 Roberto Alomar	.75	.35
☐ 5 Terry Pendleton	.10	.05
☐ 6 Robin Yount	.50	.23
☐ 7 Ray Lankford	.25	.11
☐ 8 Ryne Sandberg	1.00	.45
☐ 9 Darryl Strawberry	.25	.11
☐ 10 Marquis Grissom	.25	.11
☐ 11 Barry Bonds	.75	.35
☐ 12 Carlos Baerga	.10	.05
☐ 13 Ken Griffey Jr.	4.00	1.80
☐ 14 Benito Santiago	.10	.05
☐ 15 Dwight Gooden	.25	.11
☐ 16 Cal Ripken	3.00	1.35
☐ 17 Tony Gwynn	2.00	.90
☐ 18 Dave Hollins	.10	.05
☐ 19 Andy Van Slyke	.10	.05
☐ 20 Juan Gonzalez	2.00	.90
☐ 21 Roger Clemens	1.25	.55
☐ 22 Barry Larkin	.50	.23
☐ 23 David Nied	.10	.05
☐ 24 George Brett	1.25	.55
☐ 25 Travis Fryman	.25	.11
☐ 26 Kirby Puckett	1.50	.70
☐ 27 Frank Thomas	3.00	1.35
☐ 28 Don Mattingly	1.50	.70
☐ 29 Rickey Henderson	.50	.23
☐ 30 Nolan Ryan	3.00	1.35
☐ 31 Ozzie Smith	1.00	.45
☐ 32 Wil Cordero	.10	.05
☐ 33 Phil Hiatt	.10	.05
☐ 34 Mike Piazza	3.00	1.35
☐ 35 J.T. Snow	.75	.35
☐ 36 Kevin Young	.10	.05
☐ NNO Checklist Card	.10	.05
☐ NNO Album Offer Card	.10	.05

1994 Upper Deck

The 1994 Upper Deck set was issued in two series of 280 and 270 standard-size cards for a total of 550. Card fronts feature a color photo of the player with a smaller version of the same photo along the left-hand border. The player's name appears in a black box in the upper left-hand corner. There are number of topical subsets including Star Rookies (1-30), Fantasy Team (31-40), The Future is Now (41-55), Home Field Advantage (267-294), Upper Deck Classic Alumni (295-299), Diamond Debuts (511-522) and Top Prospects (523-550). Three autograph cards

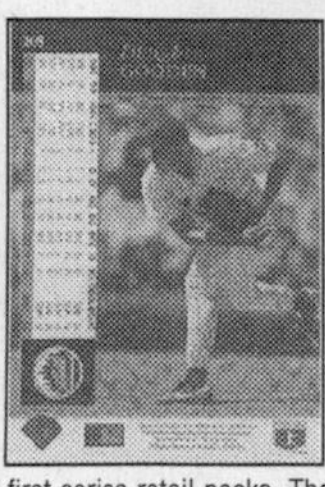

were randomly inserted into first series retail packs. They are Ken Griffey Jr. (KG), Mickey Mantle (MM) and a combo card with Griffey and Mantle (GM). An Alex Rodriguez (298A) autograph card was randomly inserted into second series retail packs. Rookie Cards include Alan Benes, Michael Jordan, Derrek Lee, Chan Ho Park, Alex Rodriguez and Billy Wagner. Many cards have been found with a significant variation on the back. The player's name, the horizontal bar containing the biographical information and the vertical bar containing the stats header are normally printed in copper-gold color. On the variation cards, these areas are printed in silver. It is not known exactly how many of the 550 cards have silver versions, nor has any premium been established for them. Also, all of the American League Home Field Advantage subset cards (#281-294) are minor uncorrected errors because the Upper Deck logos on the front are missing the year "1994".

	MINT	EXC
COMPLETE SET (550)	50.00	22.00
COMPLETE SERIES 1 (280)	30.00	13.50
COMPLETE SERIES 2 (270)	20.00	9.00
COMMON CARD (1-550)	.15	.07
☐ 1 Brian Anderson	.40	.18
☐ 2 Shane Andrews	.15	.07
☐ 3 James Baldwin	.30	.14
☐ 4 Rich Becker	.30	.14
☐ 5 Greg Blosser	.15	.07
☐ 6 Ricky Bottalico	.60	.25
☐ 7 Midre Cummings	.15	.07
☐ 8 Carlos Delgado	.40	.18
☐ 9 Steve Dreyer	.15	.07
☐ 10 Joey Eischen	.15	.07
☐ 11 Carl Everett	.15	.07
☐ 12 Cliff Floyd UER (text indicates he throws left; should be right)	.30	.14
☐ 13 Alex Gonzalez	.30	.14
☐ 14 Jeff Granger	.30	.14
☐ 15 Shawn Green	.30	.14
☐ 16 Brian L. Hunter	.60	.25
☐ 17 Butch Huskey	.30	.14
☐ 18 Mark Hutton	.15	.07
☐ 19 Michael Jordan	10.00	4.50
☐ 20 Steve Karsay	.15	.07
☐ 21 Jeff McNeely	.15	.07
☐ 22 Marc Newfield	.30	.14
☐ 23 Manny Ramirez	.75	.35
☐ 24 Alex Rodriguez	8.00	3.60
☐ 25 Scott Ruffcorn UER (photo on back is Robert Ellis)	.15	.07
☐ 26 Paul Spoljaric UER (Expos logo on back)	.15	.07
☐ 27 Salomon Torres	.15	.07
☐ 28 Steve Trachsel	.15	.07
☐ 29 Chris Turner	.15	.07
☐ 30 Gabe White	.15	.07
☐ 31 Randy Johnson FT	.60	.25
☐ 32 John Wetteland FT	.30	.14
☐ 33 Mike Piazza FT	1.00	.45
☐ 34 Rafael Palmeiro FT	.40	.18
☐ 35 Roberto Alomar FT	.60	.25
☐ 36 Matt Williams FT	.40	.18
☐ 37 Travis Fryman FT	.30	.14
☐ 38 Barry Bonds FT	.60	.25
☐ 39 Marquis Grissom FT	.30	.14
☐ 40 Albert Belle FT	.60	.25
☐ 41 Steve Avery FUT	.15	.07
☐ 42 Jason Bere FUT	.15	.07
☐ 43 Alex Fernandez FUT	.30	.14
☐ 44 Mike Mussina FUT	.60	.25
☐ 45 Aaron Sele FUT	.15	.07
☐ 46 Rod Beck FUT	.15	.07
☐ 47 Mike Piazza FUT	1.00	.45
☐ 48 John Olerud FUT	.15	[illegible]
☐ 49 Carlos Baerga FUT	.15	[illegible]
☐ 50 Gary Sheffield FUT	.60	[illegible]
☐ 51 Travis Fryman FUT	.30	[illegible]
☐ 52 Juan Gonzalez FUT	.75	[illegible]
☐ 53 Ken Griffey Jr. FUT	1.50	[illegible]
☐ 54 Tim Salmon FUT	.60	[illegible]

☐ 55 Frank Thomas FUT	1.50	.70
☐ 56 Tony Phillips	.15	.07
☐ 57 Julio Franco	.30	.14
☐ 58 Kevin Mitchell	.15	.07
☐ 59 Raul Mondesi	.40	.18
☐ 60 Rickey Henderson	.40	.18
☐ 61 Jay Buhner	.40	.18
☐ 62 Bill Swift	.15	.07
☐ 63 Brady Anderson	.40	.18
☐ 64 Ryan Klesko	.40	.18
☐ 65 Darren Daulton	.30	.14
☐ 66 Damion Easley	.15	.07
☐ 67 Mark McGwire	1.25	.55
☐ 68 John Roper	.15	.07
☐ 69 Dave Telgheder	.15	.07
☐ 70 Dave Nied	.15	.07
☐ 71 Mo Vaughn	.75	.35
☐ 72 Tyler Green	.15	.07
☐ 73 Dave Magadan	.15	.07
☐ 74 Chili Davis	.30	.14
☐ 75 Archi Cianfrocco	.15	.07
☐ 76 Joe Girardi	.15	.07
☐ 77 Chris Hoiles	.15	.07
☐ 78 Ryan Bowen	.15	.07
☐ 79 Greg Gagne	.15	.07
☐ 80 Aaron Sele	.30	.14
☐ 81 Dave Winfield	.40	.18
☐ 82 Chad Curtis	.15	.07
☐ 83 Andy Van Slyke	.30	.14
☐ 84 Kevin Stocker	.15	.07
☐ 85 Deion Sanders	.60	.25
☐ 86 Bernie Williams	.60	.25
☐ 87 John Smoltz	.40	.18
☐ 88 Ruben Santana	.15	.07
☐ 89 Dave Stewart	.30	.14
☐ 90 Don Mattingly	1.00	.45
☐ 91 Joe Carter	.40	.18
☐ 92 Ryne Sandberg	.75	.35
☐ 93 Chris Gomez	.15	.07
☐ 94 Tino Martinez	.60	.25
☐ 95 Terry Pendleton	.30	.14
☐ 96 Andre Dawson	.40	.18
☐ 97 Wil Cordero	.30	.14
☐ 98 Kent Hrbek	.30	.14
☐ 99 John Olerud	.30	.14
☐ 100 Kirt Manwaring	.15	.07
☐ 101 Tim Bogar	.15	.07
☐ 102 Mike Mussina	.60	.25
☐ 103 Nigel Wilson	.15	.07
☐ 104 Ricky Gutierrez	.15	.07
☐ 105 Roberto Mejia	.15	.07
☐ 106 Tom Pagnozzi	.15	.07
☐ 107 Mike Macfarlane	.15	.07
☐ 108 Jose Bautista	.15	.07
☐ 109 Luis Ortiz	.15	.07
☐ 110 Brent Gates	.15	.07
☐ 111 Tim Salmon	.60	.25
☐ 112 Wade Boggs	.60	.25
☐ 113 Tripp Cromer	.15	.07
☐ 114 Denny Hocking	.15	.07
☐ 115 Carlos Baerga	.30	.14
☐ 116 J.R. Phillips	.15	.07
☐ 117 Bo Jackson	.30	.14
☐ 118 Lance Johnson	.30	.14
☐ 119 Bobby Jones	.30	.14
☐ 120 Bobby Witt	.15	.07
☐ 121 Ron Karkovice	.15	.07
☐ 122 Jose Vizcaino	.15	.07
☐ 123 Danny Darwin	.15	.07
☐ 124 Eduardo Perez	.15	.07
☐ 125 Brian Looney	.15	.07
☐ 126 Pat Hentgen	.30	.14
☐ 127 Frank Viola	.15	.07
☐ 128 Darren Holmes	.15	.07
☐ 129 Wally Whitehurst	.15	.07
☐ 130 Matt Walbeck	.15	.07
☐ 131 Albert Belle	.75	.35
☐ 132 Steve Cooke	.15	.07
☐ 133 Kevin Appier	.30	.14
☐ 134 Joe Oliver	.15	.07
☐ 135 Benji Gil	.15	.07
☐ 136 Steve Buechele	.15	.07
☐ 137 Devon White	.15	.07
☐ 138 Sterling Hitchcock UER (two losses for career; should be four)	.30	.14
☐ 139 Phil Leftwich	.15	.07
☐ 140 Jose Canseco	.40	.18
☐ 141 Rick Aguilera	.15	.07
☐ 142 Rod Beck	.30	.14
☐ 143 Jose Rijo	.15	.07
144 Tom Glavine	.40	.18
145 Phil Plantier	.15	.07
146 Jason Bere	.15	.07
47 Jamie Moyer	.15	.07
48 Wes Chamberlain	.15	.07
49 Glenallen Hill	.15	.07
☐ 150 Mark Whiten	.15	.07
☐ 151 Bret Barberie	.15	.07
☐ 152 Chuck Knoblauch	.60	.25
☐ 153 Trevor Hoffman	.30	.14
☐ 154 Rick Wilkins	.15	.07
☐ 155 Juan Gonzalez	1.50	.70
☐ 156 Ozzie Guillen	.15	.07
☐ 157 Jim Eisenreich	.30	.14
☐ 158 Pedro Astacio	.15	.07
☐ 159 Joe Magrane	.15	.07
☐ 160 Ryan Thompson	.15	.07
☐ 161 Jose Lind	.15	.07
☐ 162 Jeff Conine	.30	.14
☐ 163 Todd Benzinger	.15	.07
☐ 164 Roger Salkeld	.15	.07
☐ 165 Gary DiSarcina	.15	.07
☐ 166 Kevin Gross	.15	.07
☐ 167 Charlie Hayes	.15	.07
☐ 168 Tim Costo	.15	.07
☐ 169 Wally Joyner	.30	.14
☐ 170 Johnny Ruffin	.15	.07
☐ 171 Kirk Rueter	.15	.07
☐ 172 Lenny Dykstra	.30	.14
☐ 173 Ken Hill	.15	.07
☐ 174 Mike Bordick	.15	.07
☐ 175 Billy Hall	.15	.07
☐ 176 Rob Butler	.15	.07
☐ 177 Jay Bell	.30	.14
☐ 178 Jeff Kent	.15	.07
☐ 179 David Wells	.15	.07
☐ 180 Dean Palmer	.30	.14
☐ 181 Mariano Duncan	.15	.07
☐ 182 Orlando Merced	.15	.07
☐ 183 Brett Butler	.30	.14
☐ 184 Milt Thompson	.15	.07
☐ 185 Chipper Jones	2.00	.90
☐ 186 Paul O'Neill	.30	.14
☐ 187 Mike Greenwell	.15	.07
☐ 188 Harold Baines	.30	.14
☐ 189 Todd Stottlemyre	.15	.07
☐ 190 Jeromy Burnitz	.30	.14
☐ 191 Rene Arocha	.15	.07
☐ 192 Jeff Fassero	.15	.07
☐ 193 Robby Thompson	.15	.07
☐ 194 Greg W. Harris	.15	.07
☐ 195 Todd Van Poppel	.15	.07
☐ 196 Jose Guzman	.15	.07
☐ 197 Shane Mack	.15	.07
☐ 198 Carlos Garcia	.15	.07
☐ 199 Kevin Roberson	.15	.07
☐ 200 David McCarty	.15	.07
☐ 201 Alan Trammell	.40	.18
☐ 202 Chuck Carr	.15	.07
☐ 203 Tommy Greene	.15	.07
☐ 204 Wilson Alvarez	.30	.14
☐ 205 Dwight Gooden	.30	.14
☐ 206 Tony Tarasco	.15	.07
☐ 207 Darren Lewis	.15	.07
☐ 208 Eric Karros	.30	.14
☐ 209 Chris Hammond	.15	.07
☐ 210 Jeffrey Hammonds	.30	.14
☐ 211 Rich Amaral	.15	.07
☐ 212 Danny Tartabull	.15	.07
☐ 213 Jeff Russell	.15	.07
☐ 214 Dave Staton	.15	.07
☐ 215 Kenny Lofton	.75	.35
☐ 216 Manuel Lee	.15	.07
☐ 217 Brian Koelling	.15	.07
☐ 218 Scott Lydy	.15	.07
☐ 219 Tony Gwynn	1.50	.70
☐ 220 Cecil Fielder	.30	.14
☐ 221 Royce Clayton	.30	.14
☐ 222 Reggie Sanders	.15	.07
☐ 223 Brian Jordan	.30	.14
☐ 224 Ken Griffey Jr.	3.00	1.35
☐ 225 Fred McGriff	.40	.18
☐ 226 Felix Jose	.15	.07
☐ 227 Brad Pennington	.15	.07
☐ 228 Chris Bosio	.15	.07
☐ 229 Mike Stanley	.15	.07
☐ 230 Willie Greene	.30	.14
☐ 231 Alex Fernandez	.30	.14
☐ 232 Brad Ausmus	.15	.07
☐ 233 Darrell Whitmore	.15	.07
☐ 234 Marcus Moore	.15	.07
☐ 235 Allen Watson	.15	.07
☐ 236 Jose Offerman	.15	.07
☐ 237 Rondell White	.40	.18
☐ 238 Jeff King	.30	.14
☐ 239 Luis Alicea	.15	.07
☐ 240 Dan Wilson	.30	.14
☐ 241 Ed Sprague	.15	.07
☐ 242 Todd Hundley	.30	.14
☐ 243 Al Martin	.15	.07
☐ 244 Mike Lansing	.30	.14
☐ 245 Ivan Rodriguez	.75	.35
☐ 246 Dave Fleming	.15	.07
☐ 247 John Doherty	.15	.07
☐ 248 Mark McLemore	.15	.07
☐ 249 Bob Hamelin	.15	.07
☐ 250 Curtis Pride	.30	.14
☐ 251 Zane Smith	.15	.07
☐ 252 Eric Young	.30	.14
☐ 253 Brian McRae	.15	.07
☐ 254 Tim Raines	.15	.07
☐ 255 Javier Lopez	.40	.18
☐ 256 Melvin Nieves	.30	.14
☐ 257 Randy Myers	.15	.07
☐ 258 Willie McGee	.15	.07
☐ 259 Jimmy Key UER (birthdate missing on back)	.30	.14
☐ 260 Tom Candiotti	.15	.07
☐ 261 Eric Davis	.30	.14
☐ 262 Craig Paquette	.15	.07
☐ 263 Robin Ventura	.30	.14
☐ 264 Pat Kelly	.15	.07
☐ 265 Gregg Jefferies	.30	.14
☐ 266 Cory Snyder	.15	.07
☐ 267 David Justice HFA	.40	.18
☐ 268 Sammy Sosa HFA	.60	.25
☐ 269 Barry Larkin HFA	.40	.18
☐ 270 Andres Galarraga HFA	.40	.18
☐ 271 Gary Sheffield HFA	.60	.25
☐ 272 Jeff Bagwell HFA	.60	.25
☐ 273 Mike Piazza HFA	1.00	.45
☐ 274 Larry Walker HFA	.60	.25
☐ 275 Bobby Bonilla HFA	.30	.14
☐ 276 John Kruk HFA	.15	.07
☐ 277 Jay Bell HFA	.15	.07
☐ 278 Ozzie Smith HFA	.60	.25
☐ 279 Tony Gwynn HFA	.60	.25
☐ 280 Barry Bonds HFA	.40	.18
☐ 281 Cal Ripken Jr. HFA	1.25	.55
☐ 282 Mo Vaughn HFA	.60	.25
☐ 283 Tim Salmon HFA	.60	.25
☐ 284 Frank Thomas HFA	1.50	.70
☐ 285 Albert Belle HFA	.60	.25
☐ 286 Cecil Fielder HFA	.30	.14
☐ 287 Wally Joyner HFA	.15	.07
☐ 288 Greg Vaughn HFA	.15	.07
☐ 289 Kirby Puckett HFA	.60	.25
☐ 290 Don Mattingly HFA	.60	.25
☐ 291 Terry Steinbach HFA	.15	.07
☐ 292 Ken Griffey Jr. HFA	1.50	.70
☐ 293 Juan Gonzalez HFA	.75	.35
☐ 294 Paul Molitor HFA	.60	.25
☐ 295 Tavo Alvarez UDC	.15	.07
☐ 296 Matt Brunson UDC	.30	.14
☐ 297 Shawn Green UDC	.30	.14
☐ 298 Alex Rodriguez UDC	3.00	1.35
☐ 299 Shannon Stewart UDC	.30	.14
☐ 300 Frank Thomas	2.50	1.10
☐ 301 Mickey Tettleton	.15	.07
☐ 302 Pedro Munoz	.15	.07
☐ 303 Jose Valentin	.30	.14
☐ 304 Orestes Destrade	.15	.07
☐ 305 Pat Listach	.15	.07
☐ 306 Scott Brosius	.15	.07
☐ 307 Kurt Miller	.15	.07
☐ 308 Rob Dibble	.15	.07
☐ 309 Mike Blowers	.15	.07
☐ 310 Jim Abbott	.15	.07
☐ 311 Mike Jackson	.15	.07
☐ 312 Craig Biggio	.40	.18
☐ 313 Kurt Abbott	.30	.14
☐ 314 Chuck Finley	.15	.07
☐ 315 Andres Galarraga	.40	.18
☐ 316 Mike Moore	.15	.07
☐ 317 Doug Strange	.15	.07
☐ 318 Pedro J. Martinez	.60	.25
☐ 319 Kevin McReynolds	.15	.07
☐ 320 Greg Maddux	2.00	.90
☐ 321 Mike Henneman	.15	.07
☐ 322 Scott Leius	.15	.07
☐ 323 John Franco	.15	.07
☐ 324 Jeff Blauser	.15	.07
☐ 325 Kirby Puckett	1.25	.55
☐ 326 Darryl Hamilton	.15	.07
☐ 327 John Smiley	.15	.07
☐ 328 Derrick May	.15	.07
☐ 329 Jose Vizcaino	.15	.07
☐ 330 Randy Johnson	.60	.25
☐ 331 Jack Morris	.30	.14
☐ 332 Graeme Lloyd	.15	.07
☐ 333 Dave Valle	.15	.07
☐ 334 Greg Myers	.15	.07
☐ 335 John Wetteland	.30	.14
☐ 336 Jim Gott	.15	.07
☐ 337 Tim Naehring	.15	.07
☐ 338 Mike Kelly	.15	.07
☐ 339 Jeff Montgomery	.30	.14
☐ 340 Rafael Palmeiro	.40	.18
☐ 341 Eddie Murray	.60	.25
☐ 342 Xavier Hernandez	.15	.07

☐ 343 Bobby Munoz	.15	.07
☐ 344 Bobby Bonilla	.30	.14
☐ 345 Travis Fryman	.30	.14
☐ 346 Steve Finley	.30	.14
☐ 347 Chris Sabo	.15	.07
☐ 348 Armando Reynoso	.15	.07
☐ 349 Ramon Martinez	.30	.14
☐ 350 Will Clark	.40	.18
☐ 351 Moises Alou	.30	.14
☐ 352 Jim Thome	.75	.35
☐ 353 Bob Tewksbury	.15	.07
☐ 354 Andujar Cedeno	.15	.07
☐ 355 Orel Hershiser	.30	.14
☐ 356 Mike Devereaux	.15	.07
☐ 357 Mike Perez	.15	.07
☐ 358 Dennis Martinez	.30	.14
☐ 359 Dave Nilsson	.30	.14
☐ 360 Ozzie Smith	.75	.35
☐ 361 Eric Anthony	.15	.07
☐ 362 Scott Sanders	.15	.07
☐ 363 Paul Sorrento	.15	.07
☐ 364 Tim Belcher	.15	.07
☐ 365 Dennis Eckersley	.40	.18
☐ 366 Mel Rojas	.15	.07
☐ 367 Tom Henke	.15	.07
☐ 368 Randy Tomlin	.15	.07
☐ 369 B.J. Surhoff	.15	.07
☐ 370 Larry Walker	.60	.25
☐ 371 Joey Cora	.30	.14
☐ 372 Mike Harkey	.15	.07
☐ 373 John Valentin	.30	.14
☐ 374 Doug Jones	.15	.07
☐ 375 David Justice	.60	.25
☐ 376 Vince Coleman	.15	.07
☐ 377 David Hulse	.15	.07
☐ 378 Kevin Seitzer	.15	.07
☐ 379 Pete Harnisch	.15	.07
☐ 380 Ruben Sierra	.15	.07
☐ 381 Mark Lewis	.15	.07
☐ 382 Bip Roberts	.15	.07
☐ 383 Paul Wagner	.15	.07
☐ 384 Stan Javier	.15	.07
☐ 385 Barry Larkin	.40	.18
☐ 386 Mark Portugal	.15	.07
☐ 387 Roberto Kelly	.15	.07
☐ 388 Andy Benes	.30	.14
☐ 389 Felix Fermin	.15	.07
☐ 390 Marquis Grissom	.30	.14
☐ 391 Troy Neel	.15	.07
☐ 392 Chad Kreuter	.15	.07
☐ 393 Gregg Olson	.15	.07
☐ 394 Charles Nagy	.30	.14
☐ 395 Jack McDowell	.15	.07
☐ 396 Luis Gonzalez	.15	.07
☐ 397 Benito Santiago	.15	.07
☐ 398 Chris James	.15	.07
☐ 399 Terry Mulholland	.15	.07
☐ 400 Barry Bonds	.75	.35
☐ 401 Joe Grahe	.15	.07
☐ 402 Duane Ward	.15	.07
☐ 403 John Burkett	.15	.07
☐ 404 Scott Servais	.15	.07
☐ 405 Bryan Harvey	.15	.07
☐ 406 Bernard Gilkey	.30	.14
☐ 407 Greg McMichael	.15	.07
☐ 408 Tim Wallach	.15	.07
☐ 409 Ken Caminiti	.60	.25
☐ 410 John Kruk	.30	.14
☐ 411 Darrin Jackson	.15	.07
☐ 412 Mike Gallego	.15	.07
☐ 413 David Cone	.30	.14
☐ 414 Lou Whitaker	.30	.14
☐ 415 Sandy Alomar Jr.	.30	.14
☐ 416 Bill Wegman	.15	.07
☐ 417 Pat Borders	.15	.07
☐ 418 Roger Pavlik	.15	.07
☐ 419 Pete Smith	.15	.07
☐ 420 Steve Avery	.15	.07
☐ 421 David Segui	.15	.07
☐ 422 Rheal Cormier	.15	.07
☐ 423 Harold Reynolds	.15	.07
☐ 424 Edgar Martinez	.40	.18
☐ 425 Cal Ripken Jr.	2.50	1.10
☐ 426 Jaime Navarro	.15	.07
☐ 427 Sean Berry	.15	.07
☐ 428 Bret Saberhagen	.15	.07
☐ 429 Bob Welch	.15	.07
☐ 430 Juan Guzman	.15	.07
☐ 431 Cal Eldred	.15	.07
☐ 432 Dave Hollins	.15	.07
☐ 433 Sid Fernandez	.15	.07
☐ 434 Willie Banks	.15	.07
☐ 435 Darryl Kile	.30	.14
☐ 436 Henry Rodriguez	.15	.07
☐ 437 Tony Fernandez	.15	.07
☐ 438 Walt Weiss	.15	.07
☐ 439 Kevin Tapani	.15	.07
☐ 440 Mark Grace	.40	.18
☐ 441 Brian Harper	.15	.07
☐ 442 Kent Mercker	.15	.07
☐ 443 Anthony Young	.15	.07
☐ 444 Todd Zeile	.15	.07
☐ 445 Greg Vaughn	.15	.07
☐ 446 Ray Lankford	.30	.14
☐ 447 Dave Weathers	.15	.07
☐ 448 Bret Boone	.15	.07
☐ 449 Charlie Hough	.15	.07
☐ 450 Roger Clemens	1.25	.55
☐ 451 Mike Morgan	.15	.07
☐ 452 Doug Drabek	.15	.07
☐ 453 Danny Jackson	.15	.07
☐ 454 Dante Bichette	.40	.18
☐ 455 Roberto Alomar	.60	.25
☐ 456 Ben McDonald	.15	.07
☐ 457 Kenny Rogers	.15	.07
☐ 458 Bill Gullickson	.15	.07
☐ 459 Darrin Fletcher	.15	.07
☐ 460 Curt Schilling	.15	.07
☐ 461 Billy Hatcher	.15	.07
☐ 462 Howard Johnson	.15	.07
☐ 463 Mickey Morandini	.15	.07
☐ 464 Frank Castillo	.15	.07
☐ 465 Delino DeShields	.15	.07
☐ 466 Gary Gaetti	.30	.14
☐ 467 Steve Farr	.15	.07
☐ 468 Roberto Hernandez	.30	.14
☐ 469 Jack Armstrong	.15	.07
☐ 470 Paul Molitor	.60	.25
☐ 471 Melido Perez	.15	.07
☐ 472 Greg Hibbard	.15	.07
☐ 473 Jody Reed	.15	.07
☐ 474 Tom Gordon	.15	.07
☐ 475 Gary Sheffield	.60	.25
☐ 476 John Jaha	.15	.07
☐ 477 Shawon Dunston	.15	.07
☐ 478 Reggie Jefferson	.30	.14
☐ 479 Don Slaught	.15	.07
☐ 480 Jeff Bagwell	1.25	.55
☐ 481 Tim Pugh	.15	.07
☐ 482 Kevin Young	.15	.07
☐ 483 Ellis Burks	.30	.14
☐ 484 Greg Swindell	.15	.07
☐ 485 Mark Langston	.15	.07
☐ 486 Omar Vizquel	.30	.14
☐ 487 Kevin Brown	.30	.14
☐ 488 Terry Steinbach	.30	.14
☐ 489 Mark Lemke	.15	.07
☐ 490 Matt Williams	.40	.18
☐ 491 Pete Incaviglia	.15	.07
☐ 492 Karl Rhodes	.15	.07
☐ 493 Shawn Green	.30	.14
☐ 494 Hal Morris	.15	.07
☐ 495 Derek Bell	.30	.14
☐ 496 Luis Polonia	.15	.07
☐ 497 Otis Nixon	.30	.14
☐ 498 Ron Darling	.15	.07
☐ 499 Mitch Williams	.15	.07
☐ 500 Mike Piazza	2.00	.90
☐ 501 Pat Meares	.15	.07
☐ 502 Scott Cooper	.15	.07
☐ 503 Scott Erickson	.15	.07
☐ 504 Jeff Juden	.15	.07
☐ 505 Lee Smith	.30	.14
☐ 506 Bobby Ayala	.15	.07
☐ 507 Dave Henderson	.15	.07
☐ 508 Erik Hanson	.15	.07
☐ 509 Bob Wickman	.15	.07
☐ 510 Sammy Sosa	.60	.25
☐ 511 Hector Carrasco DD	.15	.07
☐ 512 Tim Davis DD	.15	.07
☐ 513 Joey Hamilton DD	.30	.14
☐ 514 Robert Eenhoorn DD	.15	.07
☐ 515 Jorge Fabregas DD	.15	.07
☐ 516 Tim Hyers DD	.15	.07
☐ 517 John Hudek DD	.15	.07
☐ 518 James Mouton DD	.30	.14
☐ 519 Herbert Perry DD	.15	.07
☐ 520 Chan Ho Park DD	2.00	.90
☐ 521 W.Van Landingham DD	.15	.07
☐ 522 Paul Shuey DD	.15	.07
☐ 523 Ryan Hancock TP	.30	.14
☐ 524 Billy Wagner TP	1.25	.55
☐ 525 Jason Giambi	.60	.25
☐ 526 Jose Silva TP	.30	.14
☐ 527 Terrell Wade TP	.60	.25
☐ 528 Todd Dunn TP	.15	.07
☐ 529 Alan Benes TP	1.50	.70
☐ 530 Brooks Kieschnick TP	.60	.25
☐ 531 Todd Hollandsworth TP	.40	.18
☐ 532 Brad Fullmer TP	1.50	.70
☐ 533 Steve Soderstrom TP	.30	.14
☐ 534 Daron Kirkreit TP	.30	.14
☐ 535 Arquimedez Pozo TP	.40	.18
☐ 536 Charles Johnson TP	.60	.25
☐ 537 Preston Wilson TP	.60	.25
☐ 538 Alex Ochoa TP	.15	.07
☐ 539 Derrek Lee TP	2.00	.90
☐ 540 Wayne Gomes TP	.30	.14
☐ 541 Jermaine Allensworth TP	.75	.35
☐ 542 Mike Bell TP	.60	.25
☐ 543 Trot Nixon TP	.40	.18
☐ 544 Pokey Reese TP	.30	.14
☐ 545 Neifi Perez TP	1.25	.55
☐ 546 Johnny Damon TP	.60	.25
☐ 547 Matt Brunson TP	.30	.14
☐ 548 LaTroy Hawkins TP	.30	.14
☐ 549 Eddie Pearson TP	.40	.18
☐ 550 Derek Jeter TP	2.50	1.10
☐ A298 Alex Rodriguez AU	150.00	70.00
☐ P224 Ken Griffey Jr. Promo	3.00	1.35
☐ GM1 Ken Griffey Jr. AU Mickey Mantle AU/1000	1200.00	550.00
☐ KG1 Ken Griffey Jr. AU1000	250.00	110.00
☐ MM1 Mickey Mantle AU1000	600.00	275.00

1994 Upper Deck Electric Diamond

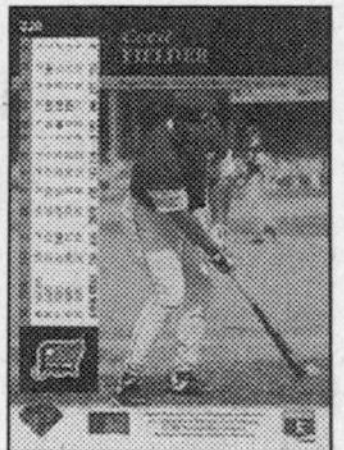

This 550-card set is a parallel issue to the basic 1994 Upper Deck cards. The cards were issued one per foil pack and two per mini jumbo. The only differences between these and the basic cards is the "Electric Diamond" in silver foil toward the bottom and the player's name is also in silver foil.

	MINT	NRMT
COMPLETE SET (550)	125.00	55.00
COMPLETE SERIES 1 (280)	75.00	34.00
COMPLETE SERIES 2 (270)	50.00	22.00
COMMON CARD (1-550)	.20	.09
*STARS: 1.5X to 4X BASIC CARDS		
*YOUNG STARS: 1.25X to 3X BASIC CARDS		
*ROOKIES: 1X to 2.5X BASIC CARDS.		

1994 Upper Deck Diamond Collection

This 30-card standard-size set was inserted regionally in first series hobby packs at a rate of one in 18. The three regions are Central (C1-C10), East (E1-E10) and West (W1-W10). While each card has the same horizontal format, the color scheme differs by region. The Central cards have a blue background, the East green and the West a deep shade of red. Color player photos are superimposed over the backgrounds. Each card has, "The Upper Deck Diamond Collection" as part of the background. The backs have a small photo and career highlights.

	MINT	NRMT
COMPLETE SET (30)	300.00	135.00
COMPLETE CENTRAL (10)	140.00	65.00
COMPLETE EAST (10)	60.00	27.00
COMPLETE WEST (10)	100.00	45.00
COMMON CARD	2.50	1.10
☐ C1 Jeff Bagwell	15.00	6.75
☐ C2 Michael Jordan	50.00	22.00
☐ C3 Barry Larkin	5.00	2.20
☐ C4 Kirby Puckett	15.00	6.75

☐ C5 Manny Ramirez	10.00	4.50
☐ C6 Ryne Sandberg	10.00	4.50
☐ C7 Ozzie Smith	10.00	4.50
☐ C8 Frank Thomas	30.00	13.50
☐ C9 Andy Van Slyke	2.50	1.10
☐ C10 Robin Yount	5.00	2.20
☐ E1 Roberto Alomar	8.00	3.60
☐ E2 Roger Clemens	15.00	6.75
☐ E3 Lenny Dykstra	4.00	1.80
☐ E4 Cecil Fielder	4.00	1.80
☐ E5 Cliff Floyd	2.50	1.10
☐ E6 Dwight Gooden	4.00	1.80
☐ E7 David Justice	8.00	3.60
☐ E8 Don Mattingly	12.00	5.50
☐ E9 Cal Ripken Jr.	30.00	13.50
☐ E10 Gary Sheffield	8.00	3.60
☐ W1 Barry Bonds	10.00	4.50
☐ W2 Andres Galarraga	5.00	2.20
☐ W3 Juan Gonzalez	20.00	9.00
☐ W4 Ken Griffey Jr.	40.00	18.00
☐ W5 Tony Gwynn	20.00	9.00
☐ W6 Rickey Henderson	5.00	2.20
☐ W7 Bo Jackson	4.00	1.80
☐ W8 Mark McGwire	15.00	6.75
☐ W9 Mike Piazza	25.00	11.00
☐ W10 Tim Salmon	8.00	3.60

1994 Upper Deck Griffey Jumbos

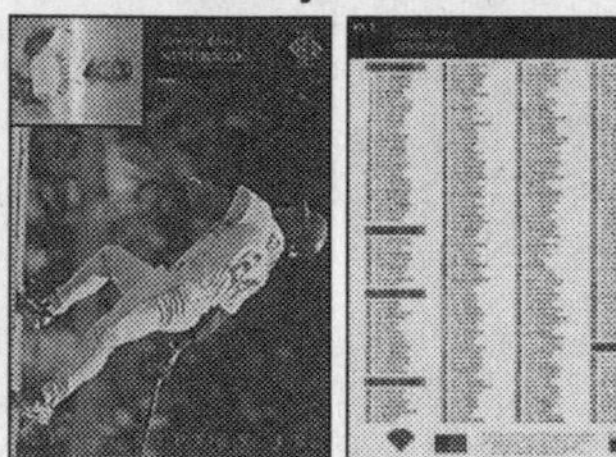

Measuring 4 7/8" by 6 13/16", these four Griffey cards serve as checklists for first series Upper Deck issues. They were issued one per first series hobby foil box. Card fronts have a full color photo with a small Griffey hologram. The first three cards provide a numerical, alphabetical and team organized checklist for the basic set. The fourth card is a checklist of inserts. Each card was printed in different quantities with CL1 the most plentiful and CL4 the more scarce. The backs are numbered with a CL prefix.

	MINT	NRMT
COMPLETE SET (4)	20.00	9.00
COMMON GRIFFEY (CL1-CL4)	4.00	1.80
☐ CL1 Numerical CL TP	4.00	1.80
☐ CL2 Alphabetical CL DP	5.00	2.20
☐ CL3 Team CL	6.00	2.70
☐ CL4 Insert CL SP	8.00	3.60

1994 Upper Deck Mantle Heroes

Randomly inserted in second series packs at a rate of one in 20, this 10-card standard-size set looks at various moments from The Mick's career. Metallic fronts feature a vintage photo with the card title at the bottom. The backs contain career highlights with a small scrapbook like photo. The numbering (64-72) is a continuation from previous Heroes sets.

	MINT	NRMT
COMPLETE SET (10)	100.00	45.00
COMMON MANTLE (64-72)	12.00	5.50
☐ 64 Mickey Mantle 1951 The Early Years	12.00	5.50
☐ 65 Mickey Mantle 1953 Tape-Measure Home Runs	12.00	5.50
☐ 66 Mickey Mantle 1956 Triple Crown Season	12.00	5.50
☐ 67 Mickey Mantle 1957 Second Consecutive MVP	12.00	5.50
☐ 68 Mickey Mantle 1961 Chasing the Babe	12.00	5.50
☐ 69 Mickey Mantle 1964 Series Home Run Record	12.00	5.50
☐ 70 Mickey Mantle 1967 500th Home Run	12.00	5.50
☐ 71 Mickey Mantle 1974 Hall of Fame	12.00	5.50
☐ 72 Mickey Mantle Checklist	12.00	5.50
☐ NNO0 Mickey Mantle Header Card	12.00	5.50

1994 Upper Deck Mantle's Long Shots

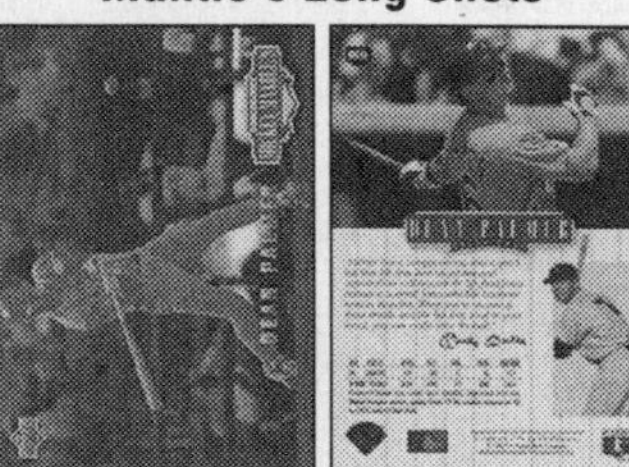

Randomly inserted in first series retail packs at a rate of one in 18, this 21-card silver foil standard-size set features top longball hitters as selected by Mickey Mantle. Card fronts are horizontal with a color player photo standing out from a dulled holographic image. The backs have a vertical format with a player photo at the top, a small photo of Mickey Mantle, a quote from The Mick and career power numbers. The cards are numbered on the back with a "MM" prefix and sequenced in alphabetical order. Two trade cards, were also random inserts and were redeemable (expiration: December 31, 1994) for either the basic silver foil set version (Silver Trade card) or the Electric Diamond version (blue Trade card).

	MINT	NRMT
COMPLETE SET (21)	50.00	22.00
COMMON CARD (MM1-MM21)	.50	.23
COMP.ELEC.DIAM.SET (21)	60.00	27.00
*ELEC.DIAMOND VERSIONS: 1.5X TO 4X BASIC CARDS		
☐ MM1 Jeff Bagwell	4.00	1.80
☐ MM2 Albert Belle	4.00	1.80
☐ MM3 Barry Bonds	2.50	1.10
☐ MM4 Jose Canseco	1.25	.55
☐ MM5 Joe Carter	1.25	.55
☐ MM6 Carlos Delgado	.75	.35
☐ MM7 Cecil Fielder	.75	.35
☐ MM8 Cliff Floyd	.50	.23
☐ MM9 Juan Gonzalez	5.00	2.20
☐ MM10 Ken Griffey Jr.	10.00	4.50
☐ MM11 David Justice	2.00	.90
☐ MM12 Fred McGriff	1.25	.55
☐ MM13 Mark McGwire	3.00	1.35
☐ MM14 Dean Palmer	.75	.35
☐ MM15 Mike Piazza	6.00	2.70
☐ MM16 Manny Ramirez	3.00	1.35
☐ MM17 Tim Salmon	2.00	.90
☐ MM18 Frank Thomas	10.00	4.50
☐ MM19 Mo Vaughn	2.50	1.10
☐ MM20 Matt Williams	1.25	.55
☐ MM21 Mickey Mantle	15.00	6.75
☐ NNO M.Mantle Blue ED Trade	12.00	5.50
☐ NNO M.Mantle Silver Trade	6.00	2.70

1994 Upper Deck Next Generation

Randomly inserted in second series retail packs at a rate of one in 20, this 18-card standard-size set spotlights young established stars and promising prospects. The set is sequenced in alphabetical order. Metallic fronts feature a color player photo on solid background. A small player hologram is halfway up the card on the right and comes between the player's first and last name. The Next

Generation logo is at bottom left. Horizontal backs contain statistical comparisons, where applicable, to Hall of Famers and brief write-up noting the comparisons. A Next Generation Electric Diamond Trade Card and a Next Generation Trade Card were seeded randomly in second series hobby packs. Each card could be redeemed for that set. Expiration date for redemption was October 31, 1994.

	MINT	NRMT
COMPLETE SET (18)	140.00	65.00
COMMON CARD (1-18)	2.00	.90
COMP.ELEC.DIAM.SET (18)	175.00	80.00
*ELEC.DIAMOND: 1.25X BASIC CARDS		
☐ 1 Roberto Alomar	6.00	2.70
☐ 2 Carlos Delgado	3.00	1.35
☐ 3 Cliff Floyd	2.00	.90
☐ 4 Alex Gonzalez	2.00	.90
☐ 5 Juan Gonzalez	15.00	6.75
☐ 6 Ken Griffey Jr.	30.00	13.50
☐ 7 Jeffrey Hammonds	3.00	1.35
☐ 8 Michael Jordan	40.00	18.00
☐ 9 David Justice	6.00	2.70
☐ 10 Ryan Klesko	4.00	1.80
☐ 11 Javier Lopez	4.00	1.80
☐ 12 Raul Mondesi	4.00	1.80
☐ 13 Mike Piazza	20.00	9.00
☐ 14 Kirby Puckett	12.00	5.50
☐ 15 Manny Ramirez	6.00	2.70
☐ 16 Alex Rodriguez	30.00	13.50
☐ 17 Tim Salmon	6.00	2.70
☐ 18 Gary Sheffield	6.00	2.70
☐ NNO Expired NG Trade Card	4.00	1.80
☐ NNO Expired NG Trade Card	4.00	1.80

1994 Upper Deck All-Star Jumbos

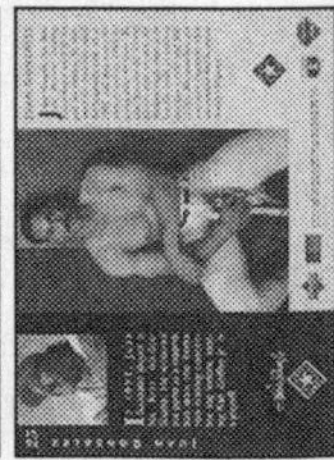

This 48-card boxed set captures the photography of Walter Iooss Jr. Iooss shot 42 of the 49 cards in the set. The set included an order form for an album. The cards are oversized, measuring 3 1/2" by 5 1/4". The full-bleed color player photos are edged on one side by a green stripe carrying the player's name. A special green foil All-Star logo appears in one of the lower corners. One set per 40-box case uses gold foil in place of green. The horizontal back has a thick black stripe carrying a small color photo and Iooss' comments on the left, with a career summary and another closeup photo on the remainder of the back. The set closes with six cards commemorating historic events during the 125-year history of baseball (43-48). Some dealers believe that gold production was limited to 1,200 sets.

	MINT	NRMT
COMPLETE SET (48)	18.00	8.00
COMMON CARD (1-48)	.10	.05
*GOLD CARDS: 10X VALUE		
☐ 1 Ken Griffey Jr.	2.50	1.10
☐ 2 Ruben Sierra Todd Van Poppel	.10	.05
☐ 3 Bryan Harvey Gary Sheffield	.20	.09
☐ 4 Gregg Jefferies Brian Jordan	.20	.09
☐ 5 Ryne Sandberg	1.00	.45
☐ 6 Matt Williams	.30	.14

Card	MINT	NRMT
John Burkett		
☐ 7 Darren Daulton	.20	.09
John Kruk		
☐ 8 Don Mattingly	1.25	.55
Wade Boggs		
☐ 9 Pat Listach	.10	.05
Greg Vaughn		
☐ 10 Tim Salmon	.40	.18
Eduardo Perez		
☐ 11 Fred McGriff	.50	.23
Tom Glavine		
☐ 12 Mo Vaughn	.60	.25
Andre Dawson		
☐ 13 Brian McRae	.10	.05
Kevin Appier		
☐ 14 Kirby Puckett	1.25	.55
Kent Hrbek		
☐ 15 Cal Ripken	2.50	1.10
☐ 16 Roberto Alomar	1.00	.45
Paul Molitor		
☐ 17 Tony Gwynn	1.00	.45
Phil Plantier		
☐ 18 Greg Maddux	2.00	.90
Steve Avery		
☐ 19 Mike Mussina	.40	.18
Chris Hoiles		
☐ 20 Randy Johnson	.60	.25
☐ 21 Roger Clemens	.50	.23
Aaron Sele		
☐ 22 Will Clark	.30	.14
Dean Palmer		
☐ 23 Cecil Fielder	.20	.09
Travis Fryman		
☐ 24 John Olerud	.20	.09
Joe Carter		
☐ 25 Juan Gonzalez	1.25	.55
☐ 26 Jose Rijo	.30	.14
Barry Larkin		
☐ 27 Andy Van Slyke	.10	.05
Jeff King		
☐ 28 Larry Walker	.50	.23
Marquis Grissom		
☐ 29 Kenny Lofton	1.25	.55
Albert Belle		
☐ 30 Mark Grace	.60	.25
Sammy Sosa		
☐ 31 Mike Piazza	2.00	.90
☐ 32 Ramon Martinez	.20	.09
Pedro Martinez		
Orel Hershiser		
☐ 33 David Justice	.30	.14
Terry Pendleton		
☐ 34 Ivan Rodriguez	.60	.25
Jose Canseco		
☐ 35 Barry Bonds	.60	.25
☐ 36 Jeff Bagwell	1.00	.45
Craig Biggio		
☐ 37 Jay Bell	.10	.05
Orlando Merced		
☐ 38 Jeff Kent	.10	.05
Dwight Gooden		
☐ 39 Andres Galarraga	.30	.14
Charlie Hayes		
☐ 40 Frank Thomas	2.50	1.10
☐ 41 Bobby Bonilla	.20	.09
☐ 42 Jack McDowell	.10	.05
Tim Raines		
☐ 43 1869 Red Stockings	.10	.05
☐ 44 Ty Cobb 25th Ann.	.60	.25
☐ 45 Babe Ruth 50th Ann.	1.25	.55
☐ 46 Mickey Mantle 75th Ann.	2.50	1.10
☐ 47 Hank Aaron 100th Ann.	.60	.25
☐ 48 Ken Griffey Jr. 125th Ann.	2.50	1.10
☐ P48 Ken Griffey Jr. Promo	5.00	2.20

1994 Upper Deck All-Time Heroes

This set consists of 225 standard-size cards. According to Upper Deck, production was limited to 4,015 numbered cases. Mantle and three other superstars (Reggie Jackson, Tom Seaver, and George Brett) each autographed 1,000 cards that were randomly inserted into packs. (Nolan Ryan had been expected to sign cards for this product but did not. Instead, Brett signed an additional 1,000 cards). According to Upper Deck, a signed card would be found in one of every 385 packs. Also cards from the parallel and gold foil-highlighted version of the All-Time Heroes set were inserted at a rate on one card per pack. The fronts feature black-and-white player photos with black borders above and below. The player's name, team name, and position appear at the lower left. A second photo "pops out" of a baseball diamond icon at the lower right. The backs include a small player photo, biography, and statistics. Special subsets featured are Off The Wire (1-18), All-Time Heroes (101-125), Diamond Legends (151-177), and Heroes of Baseball (208-224).

	MINT	NRMT
COMPLETE SET (225)	12.00	5.50
COMMON CARD (1-225)	.05	.02

Card	MINT	NRMT
☐ 1 Ted Williams	.50	.23
☐ 2 Johnny Vander Meer	.05	.02
☐ 3 Lou Brock	.10	.05
☐ 4 Lou Gehrig	1.00	.45
☐ 5 Hank Aaron	.25	.11
☐ 6 Tommie Agee	.05	.02
☐ 7 Mickey Mantle	.50	.23
☐ 8 Bill Mazeroski	.10	.05
☐ 9 Reggie Jackson	.25	.11
☐ 10 Willie Mays	1.00	.45
Mickey Mantle		
☐ 11 Roy Campanella	.15	.07
☐ 12 Harvey Haddix	.05	.02
☐ 13 Jimmy Piersall	.05	.02
☐ 14 Enos Slaughter	.10	.05
☐ 15 Nolan Ryan	.50	.23
☐ 16 Bobby Thomson	.05	.02
☐ 17 Willie Mays	.25	.11
☐ 18 Bucky Dent	.05	.02
☐ 19 Joe Garagiola	.10	.05
☐ 20 George Brett	.50	.23
☐ 21 Cecil Cooper	.05	.02
☐ 22 Ray Boone	.05	.02
☐ 23 King Kelly	.10	.05
☐ 24 Willie Mays	.50	.23
☐ 25 Napoleon Lajoie	.15	.07
☐ 26 Gil McDougald	.05	.02
☐ 27 Nelson Briles	.05	.02
☐ 28 Bucky Dent	.05	.02
☐ 29 Manny Sanguillen	.05	.02
☐ 30 Ty Cobb	.50	.23
☐ 31 Jim Grant	.05	.02
☐ 32 Del Ennis	.05	.02
☐ 33 Ron Hunt	.05	.02
☐ 34 Nolan Ryan	1.00	.45
☐ 35 Christy Mathewson	.15	.07
☐ 36 Robin Roberts	.15	.07
☐ 37 Frank Crosetti	.05	.02
☐ 38 Johnny Vander Meer	.05	.02
☐ 39 Virgil Trucks	.05	.02
☐ 40 Lou Gehrig	1.00	.45
☐ 41 Luke Appling	.10	.05
☐ 42 Rico Petrocelli	.05	.02
☐ 43 Harry Walker	.05	.02
☐ 44 Reggie Jackson	.40	.18
☐ 45 Mel Ott	.15	.07
☐ 46 Phil Cavarretta	.05	.02
☐ 47 Larry Doby	.10	.05
☐ 48 Johnny Mize	.10	.05
☐ 49 Ralph Kiner	.15	.07
☐ 50 Ted Williams	1.00	.45
☐ 51 Bobby Thomson	.10	.05
☐ 52 Joe Black	.05	.02
☐ 53 Monte Irvin	.10	.05
☐ 54 Bill Virdon	.05	.02
☐ 55 Honus Wagner	.15	.07
☐ 56 Herb Score	.05	.02
☐ 57 Jerry Coleman	.05	.02
☐ 58 Jimmie Foxx	.10	.05
☐ 59 Elroy Face	.05	.02
☐ 60 Babe Ruth	1.00	.45
☐ 61 Jimmy Piersall	.05	.02
☐ 62 Ed Charles	.05	.02
☐ 63 Johnny Podres	.05	.02
☐ 64 Charlie Neal	.05	.02
☐ 65 Bill White	.10	.05
☐ 66 Bill Skowron	.05	.02
☐ 67 Al Rosen	.05	.02
☐ 68 Eddie Lopat	.05	.02
☐ 69 Bud Harrelson	.05	.02
☐ 70 Steve Carlton	.25	.11
☐ 71 Vida Blue	.05	.02
☐ 72 Don Newcombe	.05	.02
☐ 73 Al Bumbry	.05	.02
☐ 74 Bill Madlock	.05	.02
☐ 75 Hank Aaron CL	.10	.05
☐ 76 Bill Mazeroski	.10	.05
☐ 77 Ron Cey	.05	.02
☐ 78 Tommy John	.10	.05
☐ 79 Lou Brock	.15	.07
☐ 80 Walter Johnson	.15	.07
☐ 81 Harvey Haddix	.05	.02
☐ 82 Al Oliver	.05	.02
☐ 83 Johnny Logan	.05	.02
☐ 84 Dave Dravecky	.05	.02
☐ 85 Tony Oliva	.10	.05
☐ 86 Dave Kingman	.05	.02
☐ 87 Luis Tiant	.05	.02
☐ 88 Sal Bando	.05	.02
☐ 89 Cesar Cedeno	.05	.02
☐ 90 Warren Spahn	.15	.07
☐ 91 Mickey Lolich	.05	.02
☐ 92 Lew Burdette	.05	.02
☐ 93 Hank Bauer	.05	.02
☐ 94 Marv Throneberry	.05	.02
☐ 95 Willie Stargell	.15	.07
☐ 96 George Kell	.10	.05
☐ 97 Ferguson Jenkins	.10	.05
☐ 98 Al Kaline	.15	.07
☐ 99 Billy Martin	.10	.05
☐ 100 Mickey Mantle	1.00	.45
☐ 101 1869 Red Stockings	.05	.02
☐ 102 King Kelly	.10	.05
☐ 103 Nap Lajoie	.10	.05
☐ 104 Christy Mathewson	.10	.05
☐ 105 Cy Young	.10	.05
☐ 106 Ty Cobb	.25	.11
☐ 107 Reggie Jackson CL	.10	.05
☐ 108 Rogers Hornsby	.10	.05
☐ 109 Walter Johnson	.10	.05
☐ 110 Babe Ruth	.50	.23
☐ 111 Hack Wilson	.10	.05
☐ 112 Lou Gehrig	.50	.23
☐ 113 Ted Williams	.50	.23
☐ 114 Yogi Berra	.10	.05
☐ 115 Bobby Thomson	.10	.05
☐ 116 Mickey Mantle	.50	.23
☐ 117 Willie Mays	.25	.11
☐ 118 Bill Mazeroski	.10	.05
☐ 119 Bob Gibson	.10	.05
☐ 120 1969 Miracle Mets	.40	.18
Nolan Ryan		
Tom Seaver		
Tommie Agee		
☐ 121 Hank Aaron	.25	.11
☐ 122 Reggie Jackson	.25	.11
☐ 123 George Brett	.25	.11
☐ 124 Steve Carlton	.15	.07
☐ 125 Nolan Ryan	.50	.23
☐ 126 Frank Thomas	.05	.02
☐ 127 Sam McDowell	.05	.02
☐ 128 Jim Lonborg	.05	.02
☐ 129 Bert Campaneris	.05	.02
☐ 130 Bob Gibson	.15	.07
☐ 131 Bobby Richardson	.10	.05
☐ 132 Bobby Grich	.05	.02
☐ 133 Billy Pierce	.05	.02
☐ 134 Enos Slaughter	.10	.05
☐ 135 Mickey Mantle CL	.25	.11
☐ 136 Orlando Cepeda	.10	.05
☐ 137 Rennie Stennett	.05	.02
☐ 138 Gene Alley	.05	.02
☐ 139 Manny Mota	.05	.02
☐ 140 Rogers Hornsby	.25	.11
☐ 141 Joe Charboneau	.05	.02
☐ 142 Rick Ferrell	.10	.05
☐ 143 Toby Harrah	.05	.02
☐ 144 Hank Aaron	.50	.23
☐ 145 Yogi Berra	.25	.11
☐ 146 Whitey Ford	.25	.11
☐ 147 Roy Campanella	.25	.11
☐ 148 Graig Nettles	.10	.05
☐ 149 Bobby Brown	.05	.02
☐ 150 Willie Mays CL	.10	.05
☐ 151 Cy Young	.10	.05
☐ 152 Walter Johnson	.10	.05
☐ 153 Christy Mathewson	.10	.05
☐ 154 Warren Spahn	.10	.05
☐ 155 Steve Carlton	.15	.07
☐ 156 Bob Gibson	.10	.05
☐ 157 Whitey Ford	.10	.05
☐ 158 Yogi Berra	.10	.05
☐ 159 Roy Campanella	.10	.05
☐ 160 Lou Gehrig	.50	.2[illegible]
☐ 161 Johnny Mize	.10	.0[illegible]
☐ 162 Rogers Hornsby	.10	[illegible]
☐ 163 Honus Wagner	.10	[illegible]
☐ 164 Hank Aaron	.25	[illegible]
☐ 165 Babe Ruth	.50	[illegible]
☐ 166 Willie Mays	.25	[illegible]
☐ 167 Reggie Jackson	.25	[illegible]
☐ 168 Mickey Mantle	.50	[illegible]

☐ 169 Jimmie Foxx	.10	.05
☐ 170 Ted Williams	.50	.23
☐ 171 Mel Ott	.10	.05
☐ 172 Willie Stargell	.10	.05
☐ 173 Al Kaline	.10	.05
☐ 174 Ty Cobb	.25	.11
☐ 175 Napoleon Lajoie	.10	.05
☐ 176 Lou Brock	.10	.05
☐ 177 Tom Seaver	.15	.07
☐ 178 Mark Fidrych	.10	.05
☐ 179 Don Baylor	.05	.02
☐ 180 Tom Seaver	.25	.11
☐ 181 Jerry Grote	.05	.02
☐ 182 George Foster	.05	.02
☐ 183 Buddy Bell	.05	.02
☐ 184 Ralph Garr	.05	.02
☐ 185 Steve Garvey	.10	.05
☐ 186 Joe Torre	.05	.02
☐ 187 Carl Erskine	.05	.02
☐ 188 Tommy Davis	.05	.02
☐ 189 Bill Buckner	.05	.02
☐ 190 Hack Wilson	.10	.05
☐ 191 Steve Blass	.05	.02
☐ 192 Ken Brett	.05	.02
☐ 193 Lee May	.05	.02
☐ 194 Bob Horner	.05	.02
☐ 195 Boog Powell	.10	.05
☐ 196 Darrell Evans	.05	.02
☐ 197 Paul Blair	.05	.02
☐ 198 Johnny Callison	.05	.02
☐ 199 Jimmie Reese	.05	.02
☐ 200 Cy Young	.15	.07
☐ 201 Ron Santo	.10	.05
☐ 202 Rico Carty	.05	.02
☐ 203 Ron Necciai	.05	.02
☐ 204 Lou Boudreau	.10	.05
☐ 205 Minnie Minoso	.10	.05
☐ 206 Eddie Yost	.05	.02
☐ 207 Tommie Agee	.05	.02
☐ 208 Dave Kingman	.05	.02
☐ 209 Tony Oliva	.10	.05
☐ 210 Reggie Jackson	.25	.11
☐ 211 Paul Blair	.05	.02
☐ 212 Ferguson Jenkins	.10	.05
☐ 213 Steve Garvey	.10	.05
☐ 214 Bert Campaneris	.05	.02
☐ 215 Orlando Cepeda	.10	.05
☐ 216 Bill Madlock	.05	.02
☐ 217 Rennie Stennett	.05	.02
☐ 218 Frank Thomas	.05	.02
☐ 219 Bob Gibson	.10	.05
☐ 220 Lou Brock	.10	.05
☐ 221 Rico Carty	.05	.02
☐ 222 Mickey Mantle	.50	.23
☐ 223 Robin Roberts	.10	.05
☐ 224 Manny Sanguillen	.05	.02
☐ 225 Mickey Mantle CL	.50	.23
☐ P44 Reggie Jackson Promo	3.00	1.35
☐ AU1 George Brett (2,000)	125.00	55.00
☐ AU2 Reggie Jackson (1,000)	100.00	45.00
☐ AU3 Mickey Mantle (1,000)	325.00	145.00
☐ AU4 Tom Seaver (1,000)	75.00	34.00

1994 Upper Deck All-Time Heroes 125th

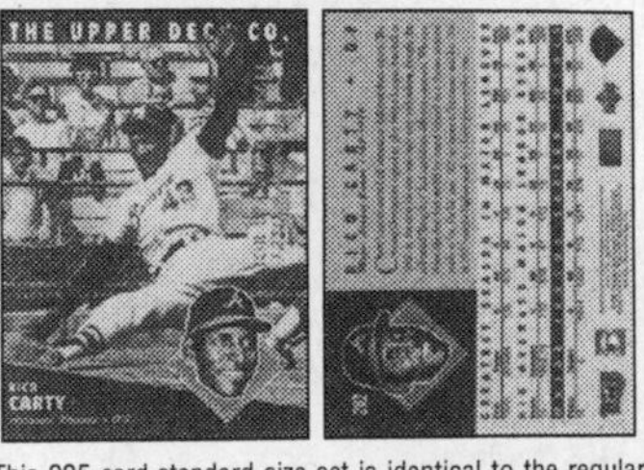

This 225-card standard-size set is identical to the regular issue 1994 Upper Deck All-Time Heroes of Baseball series, except that each card has on its front "Major League Baseball" and "125th Anniversary" stamped in bronze foil along the right edge. Every pack contained one 125th Anniversary gold card.

	MINT	NRMT
COMPLETE SET (225)	40.00	18.00
COMMON CARD (1-225)	.20	.09
STARS: 2X to 4X BASIC CARDS		

1994 Upper Deck All-Time Heroes 1954 Archives

Measuring the standard-size, these three chase cards were randomly inserted in the foil packs at a ratio of one card per 30 ten-card foil packs. Cards #1 and #250 of Ted Williams, which are similar in design to the two that were originally issued by Topps in 1954, were not included in that company's 1954 Archives edition due to the terms of his contract with Upper Deck. Like Williams, Mickey Mantle had an exclusive agreement with Upper Deck that precluded his appearance in the 1954 Topps Archives set. Mantle didn't even appear in the original 1954 Topps set due to his then exclusive contract with Bowman. This "card that never was" is similar to the original 1954 set design.

	MINT	NRMT
COMPLETE SET (3)	70.00	32.00
COMMON CARD	20.00	9.00
☐ 1 Ted Williams	20.00	9.00
☐ 250 Ted Williams	20.00	9.00
☐ 259 Mickey Mantle	40.00	18.00

1994 Upper Deck All-Time Heroes Next In Line

Capturing up and coming Minor League stars, this 20-card standard-size set was randomly inserted at a ratio of one in every 39 packs. Production was limited to 2,500 of each card. The fronts have a metallic finish with a color player cutout on the left, silhouetted by a blue-foil line. A black border on the right features the words "Next In Line," a color player headshot, and the player's name. The backs carry another color player photo, player information, and 1993 statistics. The cards are numbered on the back as "X of 20".

	MINT	NRMT
COMPLETE SET (20)	125.00	55.00
COMMON CARD (1-20)	3.00	1.35
☐ 1 Mike Bell	6.00	2.70
☐ 2 Alan Benes	10.00	4.50
☐ 3 D.J. Boston	3.00	1.35
☐ 4 Johnny Damon	12.00	5.50
☐ 5 Brad Fullmer	3.00	1.35
☐ 6 LaTroy Hawkins	3.00	1.35
☐ 7 Derek Jeter	30.00	13.50
☐ 8 Daron Kirkreit	3.00	1.35
☐ 9 Trot Nixon	5.00	2.20
☐ 10 Alex Ochoa	4.00	1.80
☐ 11 Kirk Presley	3.00	1.35
☐ 12 Jose Silva	3.00	1.35
☐ 13 Terrell Wade	3.00	1.35
☐ 14 Billy Wagner	6.00	2.70
☐ 15 Glenn Williams	4.00	1.80
☐ 16 Preston Wilson	6.00	2.70
☐ 17 Wayne Gomes	3.00	1.35
☐ 18 Ben Grieve	25.00	11.00
☐ 19 Dustin Hermanson	4.00	1.80
☐ 20 Paul Wilson	4.00	1.80

1994 Upper Deck: The American Epic

This 80-card boxed standard-size set recounts the story behind the PBS documentary "Baseball: The American Epic," produced by Ken Burns and sponsored by GM. The suggested retail price for the set, including the storage container, was 19.95. It was available from leading retail stores, the QVC television network, direct mail solicitation, and the Upper Deck Authenticated catalog. The fronts display full-bleed, color-tinted black-and-white player photos. The year celebrated and the player's name are printed in white lettering along the edges. The upper panel of the backs is either brown, purple, or green; the lower panel on all cards is white. The upper presents player profile while the lower records biography and career highlights. Like the documentary, the set is divided into "nine innings" and arranged chronologically as follows: 1st Inning (the 19th century [1-10]), 2nd Inning (the 1900s [11-20]), 3rd Inning (the 1910s [21-29]), 4th Inning (the 1920s [30-39]), 5th Inning (the 1930s [40-49]), 6th Inning (the 1940s [50-56]), 7th Inning (the 1950s [57-64]), 8th Inning (the 1960s [65-71]), and 9th Inning (1970-present [72-80]). Three insert cards were included with the set. A Michael Jordan card was available for direct mail customers, a Babe Ruth card for retail customers and a Mickey Mantle card for QVC customers. These cards are horizontal, full-bleed cards with black and white player photos. The backs are black and white with player information. The set price applies to either of the three versions and includes either of the three inserts.

	MINT	NRMT
COMPLETE SET (81)	15.00	6.75
COMMON CARD (1-80)	.05	.02
☐ 1 Our Game 1800s	.05	.02
☐ 2 Alexander Cartwright 1845	.10	.05
☐ 3 Henry Chadwick 1857	.05	.02
☐ 4 The Fair Sex 1866	.05	.02
☐ 5 Harry Wright 1869	.05	.02
☐ 6 Albert Goodwill Spalding 1876	.10	.05
☐ 7 Cap Anson 1883	.15	.07
☐ 8 Moses Fleetwood Walker 1884	.10	.05
☐ 9 King Kelly 1886	.10	.05
☐ 10 John Montgomery Ward 1890	.10	.05
☐ 11 Ty Cobb 1909	1.00	.45
☐ 12 John McGraw 1904	.15	.07
☐ 13 Rube Waddell 1904	.10	.05
☐ 14 Christy Mathewson 1905	.25	.11
☐ 15 Walter Johnson 1907	.30	.14
☐ 16 Alta Weiss 1908	.05	.02
☐ 17 Fred Merkle 1908	.05	.02
☐ 18 Take Me Out To The Ballgame	.05	.02
☐ 19 John Henry(Pop) Lloyd 1909	.10	.05
☐ 20 Honus Wagner 1909	.60	.25
☐ 21 Woodrow Wilson 1915	.10	.05
☐ 22 Nap Lajoie 1910	.10	.05

☐ 23 Addie Joss .10 .05
1911
☐ 24 Joe Wood .15 .07
1912
☐ 25 Royal Rooters .05 .02
1912
☐ 26 Ebbets Field .05 .02
1913
☐ 27 Johnny Evers .10 .05
1914
☐ 28 World War I .05 .02
1918
☐ 29 Joe Jackson .75 .35
1919
☐ 30 Babe Ruth 2.00 .90
1927
☐ 31 George(Rube) Foster .05 .02
1920
☐ 32 Ray Chapman .05 .02
1920
☐ 33 Kenesaw M. Landis .10 .05
1921
☐ 34 Yankee Stadium .05 .02
1923
☐ 35 Rogers Hornsby .30 .14
1923
☐ 36 Warren G. Harding .05 .02
1924
☐ 37 Lou Gehrig 2.00 .90
1925
☐ 38 Grover C. Alexander .10 .05
1926
☐ 39 House of David .05 .02
1929
☐ 40 Satchel Paige .60 .25
1933
☐ 41 Lefty Grove .10 .05
1931
☐ 42 Jimmie Foxx .15 .07
1932
☐ 43 Connie Mack .15 .07
1932
☐ 44 Josh Gibson .25 .11
1937
☐ 45 Dizzy Dean .10 .05
1934
☐ 46 Carl Hubbell .10 .05
1934
☐ 47 Franklin D. Roosevelt .15 .07
1937
☐ 48 Bob Feller .10 .05
1938
☐ 49 Cool Papa Bell .10 .05
1939
☐ 50 Jackie Robinson 1.50 .70
1947
☐ 51 Ted Williams 2.00 .90
1941
☐ 52 Sym-phony Band .05 .02
1941
☐ 53 Annabel Lee .05 .02
1944
☐ 54 Hank Greenberg .10 .05
1945
☐ 55 Branch Rickey .10 .05
1947
☐ 56 Harry S. Truman .15 .07
1948
☐ 57 Casey Stengel .25 .11
1953
☐ 58 Bobby Thomson .10 .05
1951
☐ 59 Dwight D. Eisenhower .10 .05
1952
☐ 60 Mario Cuomo .10 .05
1952
☐ 61 Buck O'Neil .10 .05
1945
☐ 62 Yogi Berra .40 .18
1955
☐ 63 Mickey Mantle 2.50 1.10
1956
☐ 64 Don Larsen .10 .05
1956
☐ 65 John F. Kennedy .75 .35
1960
☐ 66 Bill Mazeroski .10 .05
1960
☐ 67 Roger Maris .25 .11
1961
☐ 68 Frank Robinson .10 .05
1966
☐ 69 Bob Gibson .10 .05
1968
☐ 70 Tom Seaver .30 .14
1969
☐ 71 Curt Flood .05 .02
1969
☐ 72 Roberto Clemente 1.50 .70
1972
☐ 73 Luis Tiant .05 .02
1975
☐ 74 Marvin Miller .05 .02
1975
☐ 75 Reggie Jackson .40 .18
1977
☐ 76 Willie(Pops) Stargell .10 .05
1979
☐ 77 Pete Rose .50 .23
1985
☐ 78 Bill Clinton .75 .35
1988
☐ 79 Nolan Ryan 2.00 .90
1991
☐ 80 George Brett 1.00 .45
1993
☐ BC1 Babe Ruth 5.00 2.20
(Retail insert)
☐ BC2 Michael Jordan 5.00 2.20
(Direct mail insert)
☐ BC3 Mickey Mantle 5.00 2.20
(Home shopping insert)

1994 Upper Deck: The American Epic GM

This 9-card set recounts part of the story behind the PBS documentary "Baseball: The American Epic," produced by Ken Burns and sponsored by GM. A GM Merchandise and Memorabilia Catalog was based on the American Epic series and available at GM dealers. The catalog included an offer for this 9-card set for 1.00. The fronts display full-bleed, color-tinted black-and-white player photos. The year celebrated and the player's name are printed in white lettering along the edges. The GM logo appears in the lower right corner. The upper panel of the backs is either brown, purple, or green; the lower panel on all cards is white. The upper presents player profile while the lower records biography and career highlights.

	MINT	NRMT
COMPLETE SET (9)	4.00	1.80
COMMON CARD (1-9)	.10	.05

☐ 1 Hank Aaron .50 .23
1974
☐ 2 Roberto Clemente 1.00 .45
1972
☐ 3 Ty Cobb .50 .23
1909
☐ 4 Hank Greenberg .10 .05
1945
☐ 5 Mickey Mantle 1.25 .55
1956
☐ 6 Satchel Paige .25 .11
1941
☐ 7 Jackie Robinson .75 .35
1947
☐ 8 Babe Ruth 1.25 .55
1927
☐ 9 Ted Williams 1.00 .45
1941

1994 Upper Deck: The American Epic Little Debbies

This 15-card set recounts part of the story behind the PBS documentary "Baseball: The American Epic," produced by Ken Burns. The cards could be ordered through an on-pack offer on Little Debbies cakes for 3.99. The fronts display full-bleed, color-tinted black-and-white player photos. The year celebrated and the player's name are printed in white lettering along the edges. The upper panel of the backs is either brown, purple, or green; the lower panel on all cards is white. The upper presents player profile while the lower records biography and career

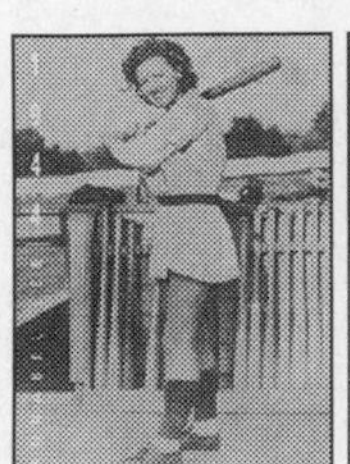

highlights. The Little Debbies logo appears on the bottom of the checklist card.

	MINT	NRMT
COMPLETE SET (15)	5.00	2.20
COMMON CARD (LD1-LD15)	.10	.05

☐ LD1 Our Game CL .10 .05
☐ LD2 Alexander Cartwright .10 .05
1845
☐ LD3 King Kelly .10 .05
1886
☐ LD4 John McGraw .20 .09
1904
☐ LD5 Christy Mathewson .20 .09
1905
☐ LD6 Walter Johnson .40 .18
1907
☐ LD7 Ted Williams 1.50 .70
1941
☐ LD8 Annabel Lee .10 .05
1944
☐ LD9 Jackie Robinson 1.00 .45
1947
☐ LD10 Bobby Thomson .20 .09
1951
☐ LD11 Buck O'Neil .20 .09
1954
☐ LD12 Mickey Mantle 1.50 .70
1956
☐ LD13 Bob Gibson .40 .18
1968
☐ LD14 Curt Flood .10 .05
1969
☐ LD15 Reggie Jackson .60 .25
1977

1995 Upper Deck

The 1995 Upper Deck baseball set was issued in two series of 225 cards for a total of 450. The cards were distributed in 12-card packs (36 per box) with a suggested retail price of $1.99. The fronts display full-bleed color action photos, with the player's name in copper foil across the bottom. The backs carry another photo, biography, and season and career statistics. Subsets include Top Prospect (1-15, 251-265), 90's Midpoint (101-110), Star Rookie (211-240), and Diamond Debuts (241-250). Rookie Cards in this set include Karim Garcia and Hideo Nomo. Five randomly inserted Trade Cards were each redeemable for nine updated cards of new rookies or players who changed teams, comprising a 45-card Trade Redemption set. The Trade cards expired Feb 1, 1996. Autographed jumbo cards (Roger Clemens for series one, Alex Rodriguez for either series) were available through a wrapper redemption offer.

	MINT	NRMT
COMPLETE SET (450)	60.00	27.00
COMPLETE SERIES 1 (225)	30.00	13.50
COMPLETE SERIES 2 (225)	30.00	13.50
COMMON CARD (1-450)	.15	.07
COMP.TRADE SET (45)	20.00	9.00
COMMON TRADE (451T-495T)	.25	.11

☐ 1 Ruben Rivera .60 .2
☐ 2 Bill Pulsipher .30 .1
☐ 3 Ben Grieve 3.00 1.
☐ 4 Curtis Goodwin .15

☐ 5 Damon Hollins	.30	.14
☐ 6 Todd Greene	.60	.25
☐ 7 Glenn Williams	.30	.14
☐ 8 Bret Wagner	.30	.14
☐ 9 Karim Garcia	1.50	.70
☐ 10 Nomar Garciaparra	4.00	1.80
☐ 11 Raul Casanova	.50	.23
☐ 12 Matt Smith	.30	.14
☐ 13 Paul Wilson	.30	.14
☐ 14 Jason Isringhausen	.30	.14
☐ 15 Reid Ryan	.60	.25
☐ 16 Lee Smith	.30	.14
☐ 17 Chili Davis	.30	.14
☐ 18 Brian Anderson	.15	.07
☐ 19 Gary DiSarcina	.15	.07
☐ 20 Bo Jackson	.30	.14
☐ 21 Chuck Finley	.30	.14
☐ 22 Darryl Kile	.30	.14
☐ 23 Shane Reynolds	.15	.07
☐ 24 Tony Eusebio	.15	.07
☐ 25 Craig Biggio	.40	.18
☐ 26 Doug Drabek	.15	.07
☐ 27 Brian L. Hunter	.30	.14
☐ 28 James Mouton	.15	.07
☐ 29 Geronimo Berroa	.15	.07
☐ 30 Rickey Henderson	.40	.18
☐ 31 Steve Karsay	.15	.07
☐ 32 Steve Ontiveros	.15	.07
☐ 33 Ernie Young	.15	.07
☐ 34 Dennis Eckersley	.40	.18
☐ 35 Mark McGwire	1.25	.55
☐ 36 Dave Stewart	.30	.14
☐ 37 Pat Hentgen	.30	.14
☐ 38 Carlos Delgado	.40	.18
☐ 39 Joe Carter	.40	.18
☐ 40 Roberto Alomar	.60	.25
☐ 41 John Olerud	.30	.14
☐ 42 Devon White	.30	.14
☐ 43 Roberto Kelly	.15	.07
☐ 44 Jeff Blauser	.15	.07
☐ 45 Fred McGriff	.40	.18
☐ 46 Tom Glavine	.40	.18
☐ 47 Mike Kelly	.15	.07
☐ 48 Javier Lopez	.40	.18
☐ 49 Greg Maddux	2.00	.90
☐ 50 Matt Mieske	.30	.14
☐ 51 Troy O'Leary	.15	.07
☐ 52 Jeff Cirillo	.30	.14
☐ 53 Cal Eldred	.15	.07
☐ 54 Pat Listach	.15	.07
☐ 55 Jose Valentin	.30	.14
☐ 56 John Mabry	.40	.18
☐ 57 Bob Tewksbury	.15	.07
☐ 58 Brian Jordan	.30	.14
☐ 59 Gregg Jefferies	.30	.14
☐ 60 Ozzie Smith	.75	.35
☐ 61 Geronimo Pena	.15	.07
☐ 62 Mark Whiten	.15	.07
☐ 63 Rey Sanchez	.15	.07
☐ 64 Willie Banks	.15	.07
☐ 65 Mark Grace	.40	.18
☐ 66 Randy Myers	.15	.07
☐ 67 Steve Trachsel	.15	.07
☐ 68 Derrick May	.15	.07
☐ 69 Brett Butler	.30	.14
☐ 70 Eric Karros	.30	.14
☐ 71 Tim Wallach	.15	.07
☐ 72 Delino DeShields	.15	.07
☐ 73 Darren Dreifort	.15	.07
☐ 74 Orel Hershiser	.30	.14
☐ 75 Billy Ashley	.15	.07
☐ 76 Sean Berry	.15	.07
☐ 77 Ken Hill	.15	.07
☐ 78 John Wetteland	.30	.14
☐ 79 Moises Alou	.30	.14
☐ 80 Cliff Floyd	.30	.14
☐ 81 Marquis Grissom	.30	.14
☐ 82 Larry Walker	.60	.25
☐ 83 Rondell White	.40	.18
☐ 84 William VanLandingham	.15	.07
☐ 85 Matt Williams	.40	.18
☐ 86 Rod Beck	.15	.07
☐ 87 Darren Lewis	.15	.07
☐ 88 Robby Thompson	.15	.07
☐ 89 Darryl Strawberry	.30	.14
☐ 90 Kenny Lofton	.75	.35
☐ 91 Charles Nagy	.30	.14
☐ 92 Sandy Alomar Jr.	.15	.07
☐ 93 Mark Clark	.15	.07
☐ 94 Dennis Martinez	.30	.14
☐ 95 Dave Winfield	.40	.18
☐ 96 Jim Thome	.60	.25
☐ 97 Manny Ramirez	.60	.25
☐ 98 Goose Gossage	.30	.14
99 Tino Martinez	.60	.25
100 Ken Griffey Jr.	3.00	1.35
101 Greg Maddux ANA	1.00	.45

☐ 102 Randy Johnson ANA	.60	.25
☐ 103 Barry Bonds ANA	.40	.18
☐ 104 Juan Gonzalez ANA	.60	.25
☐ 105 Frank Thomas ANA	1.50	.70
☐ 106 Matt Williams ANA	.40	.18
☐ 107 Paul Molitor ANA	.60	.25
☐ 108 Fred McGriff ANA	.40	.18
☐ 109 Carlos Baerga ANA	.30	.14
☐ 110 Ken Griffey Jr. ANA	1.50	.70
☐ 111 Reggie Jefferson	.30	.14
☐ 112 Randy Johnson	.60	.25
☐ 113 Marc Newfield	.30	.14
☐ 114 Robb Nen	.15	.07
☐ 115 Jeff Conine	.30	.14
☐ 116 Kurt Abbott	.15	.07
☐ 117 Charlie Hough	.15	.07
☐ 118 Dave Weathers	.15	.07
☐ 119 Juan Castillo	.15	.07
☐ 120 Bret Saberhagen	.15	.07
☐ 121 Rico Brogna	.15	.07
☐ 122 John Franco	.30	.14
☐ 123 Todd Hundley	.30	.14
☐ 124 Jason Jacome	.15	.07
☐ 125 Bobby Jones	.30	.14
☐ 126 Bret Barberie	.15	.07
☐ 127 Ben McDonald	.15	.07
☐ 128 Harold Baines	.30	.14
☐ 129 Jeffrey Hammonds	.30	.14
☐ 130 Mike Mussina	.60	.25
☐ 131 Chris Hoiles	.15	.07
☐ 132 Brady Anderson	.40	.18
☐ 133 Eddie Williams	.15	.07
☐ 134 Andy Benes	.15	.07
☐ 135 Tony Gwynn	1.50	.70
☐ 136 Bip Roberts	.15	.07
☐ 137 Joey Hamilton	.30	.14
☐ 138 Luis Lopez	.15	.07
☐ 139 Ray McDavid	.15	.07
☐ 140 Lenny Dykstra	.30	.14
☐ 141 Mariano Duncan	.15	.07
☐ 142 Fernando Valenzuela	.30	.14
☐ 143 Bobby Munoz	.15	.07
☐ 144 Kevin Stocker	.15	.07
☐ 145 John Kruk	.30	.14
☐ 146 Jon Lieber	.15	.07
☐ 147 Zane Smith	.15	.07
☐ 148 Steve Cooke	.15	.07
☐ 149 Andy Van Slyke	.30	.14
☐ 150 Jay Bell	.30	.14
☐ 151 Carlos Garcia	.15	.07
☐ 152 John Dettmer	.15	.07
☐ 153 Darren Oliver	.30	.14
☐ 154 Dean Palmer	.30	.14
☐ 155 Otis Nixon	.30	.14
☐ 156 Rusty Greer	.60	.25
☐ 157 Rick Helling	.15	.07
☐ 158 Jose Canseco	.40	.18
☐ 159 Roger Clemens	1.25	.55
☐ 160 Andre Dawson	.40	.18
☐ 161 Mo Vaughn	.75	.35
☐ 162 Aaron Sele	.15	.07
☐ 163 John Valentin	.30	.14
☐ 164 Brian R. Hunter	.15	.07
☐ 165 Bret Boone	.15	.07
☐ 166 Hector Carrasco	.15	.07
☐ 167 Pete Schourek	.15	.07
☐ 168 Willie Greene	.30	.14
☐ 169 Kevin Mitchell	.15	.07
☐ 170 Deion Sanders	.60	.25
☐ 171 John Roper	.15	.07
☐ 172 Charlie Hayes	.15	.07
☐ 173 David Nied	.15	.07
☐ 174 Ellis Burks	.30	.14
☐ 175 Dante Bichette	.40	.18
☐ 176 Marvin Freeman	.15	.07
☐ 177 Eric Young	.30	.14
☐ 178 David Cone	.30	.14
☐ 179 Greg Gagne	.15	.07
☐ 180 Bob Hamelin	.15	.07
☐ 181 Wally Joyner	.30	.14
☐ 182 Jeff Montgomery	.30	.14
☐ 183 Jose Lind	.15	.07
☐ 184 Chris Gomez	.15	.07
☐ 185 Travis Fryman	.30	.14
☐ 186 Kirk Gibson	.30	.14
☐ 187 Mike Moore	.15	.07
☐ 188 Lou Whitaker	.30	.14
☐ 189 Sean Bergman	.15	.07
☐ 190 Shane Mack	.15	.07
☐ 191 Rick Aguilera	.15	.07
☐ 192 Denny Hocking	.15	.07
☐ 193 Chuck Knoblauch	.60	.25
☐ 194 Kevin Tapani	.15	.07
☐ 195 Kent Hrbek	.30	.14
☐ 196 Ozzie Guillen	.15	.07
☐ 197 Wilson Alvarez	.30	.14
☐ 198 Tim Raines	.15	.07

☐ 199 Scott Ruffcorn	.15	.07
☐ 200 Michael Jordan	3.00	1.35
☐ 201 Robin Ventura	.30	.14
☐ 202 Jason Bere	.15	.07
☐ 203 Darrin Jackson	.15	.07
☐ 204 Russ Davis	.15	.07
☐ 205 Jimmy Key	.30	.14
☐ 206 Jack McDowell	.15	.07
☐ 207 Jim Abbott	.15	.07
☐ 208 Paul O'Neill	.30	.14
☐ 209 Bernie Williams	.60	.25
☐ 210 Don Mattingly	1.00	.45
☐ 211 Orlando Miller	.15	.07
☐ 212 Alex Gonzalez	.15	.07
☐ 213 Terrell Wade	.15	.07
☐ 214 Jose Oliva	.15	.07
☐ 215 Alex Rodriguez	2.50	1.10
☐ 216 Garret Anderson	.40	.18
☐ 217 Alan Benes	.40	.18
☐ 218 Armando Benitez	.15	.07
☐ 219 Dustin Hermanson	.30	.14
☐ 220 Charles Johnson	.40	.18
☐ 221 Julian Tavarez	.15	.07
☐ 222 Jason Giambi	.40	.18
☐ 223 LaTroy Hawkins	.15	.07
☐ 224 Todd Hollandsworth	.30	.14
☐ 225 Derek Jeter	2.00	.90
☐ 226 Hideo Nomo	3.00	1.35
☐ 227 Tony Clark	.75	.35
☐ 228 Roger Cedeno	.30	.14
☐ 229 Scott Stahoviak	.15	.07
☐ 230 Michael Tucker	.40	.18
☐ 231 Joe Rosselli	.15	.07
☐ 232 Antonio Osuna	.15	.07
☐ 233 Bobby Higginson	1.00	.45
☐ 234 Mark Grudzielanek	.50	.23
☐ 235 Ray Durham	.40	.18
☐ 236 Frank Rodriguez	.15	.07
☐ 237 Quilvio Veras	.15	.07
☐ 238 Darren Bragg	.30	.14
☐ 239 Ugueth Urbina	.30	.14
☐ 240 Jason Bates	.15	.07
☐ 241 David Bell	.15	.07
☐ 242 Ron Villone	.15	.07
☐ 243 Joe Randa	.15	.07
☐ 244 Carlos Perez	.30	.14
☐ 245 Brad Clontz	.15	.07
☐ 246 Steve Rodriguez	.15	.07
☐ 247 Joe Vitiello	.15	.07
☐ 248 Ozzie Timmons	.15	.07
☐ 249 Rudy Pemberton	.15	.07
☐ 250 Marty Cordova	.40	.18
☐ 251 Tony Graffanino	.15	.07
☐ 252 Mark Johnson	.15	.07
☐ 253 Tomas Perez	.30	.14
☐ 254 Jimmy Hurst	.30	.14
☐ 255 Edgardo Alfonzo	.60	.25
☐ 256 Jose Malave	.15	.07
☐ 257 Brad Radke	.75	.35
☐ 258 Jon Nunnally	.30	.14
☐ 259 Dilson Torres	.15	.07
☐ 260 Esteban Loaiza	.15	.07
☐ 261 Freddy Garcia	.30	.14
☐ 262 Don Wengert	.15	.07
☐ 263 Robert Person	.15	.07
☐ 264 Tim Unroe	.15	.07
☐ 265 Juan Acevedo	.15	.07
☐ 266 Eduardo Perez	.15	.07
☐ 267 Tony Phillips	.15	.07
☐ 268 Jim Edmonds	.60	.25
☐ 269 Jorge Fabregas	.15	.07
☐ 270 Tim Salmon	.60	.25
☐ 271 Mark Langston	.15	.07
☐ 272 J.T. Snow	.30	.14
☐ 273 Phil Plantier	.15	.07
☐ 274 Derek Bell	.30	.14
☐ 275 Jeff Bagwell	1.25	.55
☐ 276 Luis Gonzalez	.15	.07
☐ 277 John Hudek	.15	.07
☐ 278 Todd Stottlemyre	.15	.07
☐ 279 Mark Acre	.15	.07
☐ 280 Ruben Sierra	.15	.07
☐ 281 Mike Bordick	.15	.07
☐ 282 Ron Darling	.15	.07
☐ 283 Brent Gates	.15	.07
☐ 284 Todd Van Poppel	.15	.07
☐ 285 Paul Molitor	.60	.25
☐ 286 Ed Sprague	.15	.07
☐ 287 Juan Guzman	.15	.07
☐ 288 David Cone	.30	.14
☐ 289 Shawn Green	.30	.14
☐ 290 Marquis Grissom	.30	.14
☐ 291 Kent Mercker	.15	.07
☐ 292 Steve Avery	.15	.07
☐ 293 Chipper Jones	2.00	.90
☐ 294 John Smoltz	.40	.18
☐ 295 David Justice	.60	.25

Card	MINT	NRMT
☐ 296 Ryan Klesko	.40	.18
☐ 297 Joe Oliver	.15	.07
☐ 298 Ricky Bones	.15	.07
☐ 299 John Jaha	.15	.07
☐ 300 Greg Vaughn	.15	.07
☐ 301 Dave Nilsson	.30	.14
☐ 302 Kevin Seitzer	.15	.07
☐ 303 Bernard Gilkey	.30	.14
☐ 304 Allen Battle	.15	.07
☐ 305 Ray Lankford	.40	.18
☐ 306 Tom Pagnozzi	.15	.07
☐ 307 Allen Watson	.15	.07
☐ 308 Danny Jackson	.15	.07
☐ 309 Ken Hill	.15	.07
☐ 310 Todd Zeile	.15	.07
☐ 311 Kevin Roberson	.15	.07
☐ 312 Steve Buechele	.15	.07
☐ 313 Rick Wilkins	.15	.07
☐ 314 Kevin Foster	.15	.07
☐ 315 Sammy Sosa	.60	.25
☐ 316 Howard Johnson	.15	.07
☐ 317 Greg Hansell	.15	.07
☐ 318 Pedro Astacio	.15	.07
☐ 319 Rafael Bournigal	.15	.07
☐ 320 Mike Piazza	2.00	.90
☐ 321 Ramon Martinez	.30	.14
☐ 322 Raul Mondesi	.40	.18
☐ 323 Ismael Valdes	.30	.14
☐ 324 Wil Cordero	.15	.07
☐ 325 Tony Tarasco	.15	.07
☐ 326 Roberto Kelly	.15	.07
☐ 327 Jeff Fassero	.15	.07
☐ 328 Mike Lansing	.15	.07
☐ 329 Pedro J. Martinez	.60	.25
☐ 330 Kirk Rueter	.15	.07
☐ 331 Glenallen Hill	.15	.07
☐ 332 Kirt Manwaring	.15	.07
☐ 333 Royce Clayton	.15	.07
☐ 334 J.R. Phillips	.15	.07
☐ 335 Barry Bonds	.75	.35
☐ 336 Mark Portugal	.15	.07
☐ 337 Terry Mulholland	.15	.07
☐ 338 Omar Vizquel	.30	.14
☐ 339 Carlos Baerga	.30	.14
☐ 340 Albert Belle	.75	.35
☐ 341 Eddie Murray	.60	.25
☐ 342 Wayne Kirby	.15	.07
☐ 343 Chad Ogea	.15	.07
☐ 344 Tim Davis	.15	.07
☐ 345 Jay Buhner	.40	.18
☐ 346 Bobby Ayala	.15	.07
☐ 347 Mike Blowers	.15	.07
☐ 348 Dave Fleming	.15	.07
☐ 349 Edgar Martinez	.60	.25
☐ 350 Andre Dawson	.40	.18
☐ 351 Darrell Whitmore	.15	.07
☐ 352 Chuck Carr	.15	.07
☐ 353 John Burkett	.15	.07
☐ 354 Chris Hammond	.15	.07
☐ 355 Gary Sheffield	.60	.25
☐ 356 Pat Rapp	.15	.07
☐ 357 Greg Colbrunn	.15	.07
☐ 358 David Segui	.15	.07
☐ 359 Jeff Kent	.15	.07
☐ 360 Bobby Bonilla	.30	.14
☐ 361 Pete Harnisch	.15	.07
☐ 362 Ryan Thompson	.15	.07
☐ 363 Jose Vizcaino	.15	.07
☐ 364 Brett Butler	.30	.14
☐ 365 Cal Ripken Jr.	2.50	1.10
☐ 366 Rafael Palmeiro	.40	.18
☐ 367 Leo Gomez	.15	.07
☐ 368 Andy Van Slyke	.30	.14
☐ 369 Arthur Rhodes	.15	.07
☐ 370 Ken Caminiti	.40	.18
☐ 371 Steve Finley	.30	.14
☐ 372 Melvin Nieves	.15	.07
☐ 373 Andujar Cedeno	.15	.07
☐ 374 Trevor Hoffman	.30	.14
☐ 375 Fernando Valenzuela	.30	.14
☐ 376 Ricky Bottalico	.30	.14
☐ 377 Dave Hollins	.15	.07
☐ 378 Charlie Hayes	.15	.07
☐ 379 Tommy Greene	.15	.07
☐ 380 Darren Daulton	.30	.14
☐ 381 Curt Schilling	.30	.14
☐ 382 Midre Cummings	.15	.07
☐ 383 Al Martin	.30	.14
☐ 384 Jeff King	.30	.14
☐ 385 Orlando Merced	.15	.07
☐ 386 Denny Neagle	.30	.14
☐ 387 Don Slaught	.15	.07
☐ 388 Dave Clark	.15	.07
☐ 389 Kevin Gross	.15	.07
☐ 390 Will Clark	.40	.18
☐ 391 Ivan Rodriguez	.75	.35
☐ 392 Benji Gil	.15	.07
☐ 393 Jeff Frye	.15	.07
☐ 394 Kenny Rogers	.15	.07
☐ 395 Juan Gonzalez	1.50	.70
☐ 396 Mike Macfarlane	.15	.07
☐ 397 Lee Tinsley	.15	.07
☐ 398 Tim Naehring	.15	.07
☐ 399 Tim Vanegmond	.15	.07
☐ 400 Mike Greenwell	.15	.07
☐ 401 Ken Ryan	.15	.07
☐ 402 John Smiley	.15	.07
☐ 403 Tim Pugh	.15	.07
☐ 404 Reggie Sanders	.15	.07
☐ 405 Barry Larkin	.40	.18
☐ 406 Hal Morris	.15	.07
☐ 407 Jose Rijo	.15	.07
☐ 408 Lance Painter	.15	.07
☐ 409 Joe Girardi	.15	.07
☐ 410 Andres Galarraga	.40	.18
☐ 411 Mike Kingery	.15	.07
☐ 412 Roberto Mejia	.15	.07
☐ 413 Walt Weiss	.15	.07
☐ 414 Bill Swift	.15	.07
☐ 415 Larry Walker	.60	.25
☐ 416 Billy Brewer	.15	.07
☐ 417 Pat Borders	.15	.07
☐ 418 Tom Gordon	.15	.07
☐ 419 Kevin Appier	.30	.14
☐ 420 Gary Gaetti	.30	.14
☐ 421 Greg Gohr	.15	.07
☐ 422 Felipe Lira	.15	.07
☐ 423 John Doherty	.15	.07
☐ 424 Chad Curtis	.15	.07
☐ 425 Cecil Fielder	.30	.14
☐ 426 Alan Trammell	.40	.18
☐ 427 David McCarty	.15	.07
☐ 428 Scott Erickson	.15	.07
☐ 429 Pat Mahomes	.15	.07
☐ 430 Kirby Puckett	1.25	.55
☐ 431 Dave Stevens	.15	.07
☐ 432 Pedro Munoz	.15	.07
☐ 433 Chris Sabo	.15	.07
☐ 434 Alex Fernandez	.30	.14
☐ 435 Frank Thomas	2.50	1.10
☐ 436 Roberto Hernandez	.15	.07
☐ 437 Lance Johnson	.30	.14
☐ 438 Jim Abbott	.15	.07
☐ 439 John Wetteland	.30	.14
☐ 440 Melido Perez	.15	.07
☐ 441 Tony Fernandez	.15	.07
☐ 442 Pat Kelly	.15	.07
☐ 443 Mike Stanley	.15	.07
☐ 444 Danny Tartabull	.15	.07
☐ 445 Wade Boggs	.60	.25
☐ 446 Robin Yount	.40	.18
☐ 447 Ryne Sandberg	.75	.35
☐ 448 Nolan Ryan	2.50	1.10
☐ 449 George Brett	1.00	.45
☐ 450 Mike Schmidt	.75	.35
☐ 451 Jim Abbott TRADE	.25	.11
☐ 452 Danny Tartabull TRADE	.25	.11
☐ 453 Ariel Prieto TRADE	.35	.16
☐ 454 Scott Cooper TRADE	.25	.11
☐ 455 Tom Henke TRADE	.35	.16
☐ 456 Todd Zeile TRADE	.25	.11
☐ 457 Brian McRae TRADE	.25	.11
☐ 458 Luis Gonzalez TRADE	.25	.11
☐ 459 Jaime Navarro TRADE	.25	.11
☐ 460 Todd Worrell TRADE	.35	.16
☐ 461 Roberto Kelly TRADE	.25	.11
☐ 462 Chad Fonville TRADE	.25	.11
☐ 463 Shane Andrews TRADE	.25	.11
☐ 464 David Segui TRADE	.25	.11
☐ 465 Deion Sanders TRADE	.75	.35
☐ 466 Orel Hershiser TRADE	.35	.16
☐ 467 Ken Hill TRADE	.25	.11
☐ 468 Andy Benes TRADE	.35	.16
☐ 469 Terry Pendleton TRADE	.35	.16
☐ 470 Bobby Bonilla TRADE	.35	.16
☐ 471 Scott Erickson TRADE	.25	.11
☐ 472 Kevin Brown TRADE	.35	.16
☐ 473 Glenn Dishman TRADE	.35	.16
☐ 474 Phil Plantier TRADE	.25	.11
☐ 475 Gregg Jefferies TRADE	.35	.16
☐ 476 Tyler Green TRADE	.25	.11
☐ 477 Heathcliff Slocumb TRADE	.25	.11
☐ 478 Mark Whiten TRADE	.25	.11
☐ 479 Mickey Tettleton TRADE	.25	.11
☐ 480 Tim Wakefield TRADE	.25	.11
☐ 481 Vaughn Eshelman TRADE	.25	.11
☐ 482 Rick Aguilera TRADE	.35	.16
☐ 483 Erik Hanson TRADE	.25	.11
☐ 484 Willie McGee TRADE	.35	.16
☐ 485 Troy O'Leary TRADE	.25	.11
☐ 486 Benito Santiago TRADE	.25	.11
☐ 487 Darren Lewis TRADE	.25	.11
☐ 488 Dave Burba TRADE	.25	.11
☐ 489 Ron Gant TRADE	.35	.16
☐ 490 Bret Saberhagen TRADE	.25	.11
☐ 491 Vinny Castilla TRADE	.50	.23
☐ 492 Frank Rodriguez TRADE	.35	.16
☐ 493 Andy Pettitte TRADE	6.00	2.70
☐ 494 Ruben Sierra TRADE	.25	.11
☐ 495 David Cone TRADE	.35	.16
☐ J159 R. Clemens Jumbo AU	40.00	18.00
☐ J215 A. Rodriguez Jumbo AU	80.00	36.00
☐ P100 Ken Griffey Jr. Promo	3.00	1.35
☐ TC1 Orel Hershiser	1.00	.45
☐ TC2 Terry Pendleton	1.00	.45
☐ TC3 Benito Santiago	1.00	.45
☐ TC4 Kevin Brown	1.00	.45
☐ TC5 Gregg Jefferies	1.00	.45

1995 Upper Deck Electric Diamond

This 450-card parallel set was inserted one per retail pack or two per mini-jumbo pack. These cards are distinguished from their regular issue counterparts in that they are printed on a heavier cardstock and use a special foil treatment.

	MINT	NRMT
COMPLETE SET (450)	110.00	50.00
COMPLETE SERIES 1 (225)	50.00	22.00
COMPLETE SERIES 2 (225)	60.00	27.00
COMMON CARD (1-450)	.25	.11

*STARS: 2X to 4X BASIC CARDS
*YOUNG STARS: 1.5X to 3X BASIC CARDS

1995 Upper Deck Electric Diamond Gold

This 450-card parallel standard-size set was randomly inserted in retail and mini-jumbo packs. These cards are identical to the Electric Diamond series except for the special gold foil treatment.

	MINT	NRMT
COMPLETE SET (450)	2000.00	900.00
COMPLETE SERIES 1 (225)	1000.00	450.00
COMPLETE SERIES 2 (225)	1000.00	450.00
COMMON CARD (1-450)	3.00	1.35

*STARS: 12.5X TO 30X BASIC CARDS
*YOUNG STARS: 8X TO 20X BASIC CARDS

1995 Upper Deck Autographs

Trade cards to redeem these autographed issues were randomly seeded into second series packs. The actual signed cards share the same front design as the basic issue 1995 Upper Deck cards. The cards are unnumbered on back and therefore we have sequenced them in alphabetical order.

	MINT	NRMT
COMPLETE SET (5)	225.00	100.00
COMMON CARD	40.00	18.00
☐ 1 Roger Clemens	50.00	22.00
☐ 2 Reggie Jackson	40.00	18.00
☐ 3 Willie Mays	80.00	36.00
☐ 4 Raul Mondesi	40.00	18.00
☐ 5 Frank Robinson	40.00	18.00

1995 Upper Deck Checklists

Each of these 10 cards features a star player(s) on front and a checklist on the back. The cards w randomly inserted in hobby and retail packs at a ra one in 17. The horizontal fronts feature a player along with a sentence about the 1994 highlight. The are numbered as "X" of 5 in the upper left.

	MINT
COMPLETE SET (5)	25.00
COMPLETE SERIES 1 (5)	10.00
COMPLETE SERIES 2 (5)	15.00
COMMON CARD (1A-5B)	.75

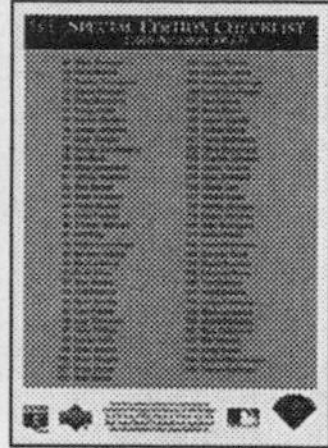

Card	MINT	NRMT
☐ 1A Montreal Expos	.75	.35
☐ 2A Fred McGriff	1.25	.55
☐ 3A John Valentin	.75	.35
☐ 4A Kenny Rogers	.75	.35
☐ 5A Greg Maddux	6.00	2.70
☐ 1B Cecil Fielder	1.00	.45
☐ 2B Tony Gwynn	4.00	1.80
☐ 3B Greg Maddux	6.00	2.70
☐ 4B Randy Johnson	1.25	.55
☐ 5B Mike Schmidt	2.50	1.10

1995 Upper Deck Predictor Award Winners

This set was inserted in hobby packs at a rate of approximately one in 30. This 40-card standard-size set features nine players and a Long Shot in each league for each of two categories -- MVP and Rookie of the Year. If the player pictured on the card won his category, the card was redeemable for a special foil version of all 20 Hobby Predictor cards. Fronts are full-color player action photos. Backs include the rules of the contest. These cards were redeemable until December 31, 1995. The cards are numbered in the upper left with an "H" prefix.

	MINT	NRMT
COMPLETE SET (40)	100.00	45.00
COMPLETE SERIES 1 (20)	60.00	27.00
COMPLETE SERIES 2 (20)	40.00	18.00
COMMON CARD (H1-H40)	1.00	.45
COMP.SER.1 EXCH.SET (20)	15.00	6.75
COMP.SER.2 EXCH.SET (20)	10.00	4.50

*AW EXCH.CARDS: .4X BASIC CARDS

Card	MINT	NRMT
☐ H1 Albert Belle MVP	2.50	1.10
☐ H2 Juan Gonzalez MVP	5.00	2.20
☐ H3 Ken Griffey Jr. MVP	10.00	4.50
☐ H4 Kirby Puckett MVP	4.00	1.80
☐ H5 Frank Thomas MVP	8.00	3.60
☐ H6 Jeff Bagwell MVP	4.00	1.80
☐ H7 Barry Bonds MVP	2.50	1.10
☐ H8 Mike Piazza MVP	6.00	2.70
☐ H9 Matt Williams MVP	1.50	.70
☐ H10 MVP Wild Card	1.00	.45
☐ H11 Armando Benitez ROY	1.00	.45
☐ H12 Alex Gonzalez ROY	1.25	.55
☐ H13 Shawn Green ROY	1.25	.55
☐ H14 Derek Jeter ROY	6.00	2.70
☐ H15 Alex Rodriguez ROY	10.00	4.50
☐ H16 Alan Benes ROY	1.50	.70
☐ H17 Brian L.Hunter ROY	1.25	.55
☐ H18 Charles Johnson ROY	1.50	.70
☐ H19 Jose Oliva ROY	1.00	.45
H20 ROY Wild Card	1.00	.45
H21 Cal Ripken MVP	8.00	3.60
H22 Don Mattingly MVP	4.00	1.80
23 Roberto Alomar MVP	2.00	.90
24 Kenny Lofton MVP	2.50	1.10
5 Will Clark MVP	1.50	.70
6 Mark McGwire MVP	4.00	1.80
Greg Maddux MVP	6.00	2.70
Fred McGriff MVP	1.50	.70
Andres Galarraga MVP	1.50	.70
ose Canseco MVP	1.50	.70
ay Durham ROY	1.25	.55
ark Grudzielanek ROY	1.50	.70
ott Ruffcorn ROY	1.00	.45
hael Tucker ROY	1.50	.70

Card	MINT	NRMT
☐ H35 Garret Anderson ROY	1.50	.70
☐ H36 Darren Bragg ROY	1.25	.55
☐ H37 Quilvio Veras ROY	1.00	.45
☐ H38 Hideo Nomo ROY W	6.00	2.70
☐ H39 Chipper Jones ROY	6.00	2.70
☐ H40 Marty Cordova ROY W	2.00	.90

1995 Upper Deck Predictor League Leaders

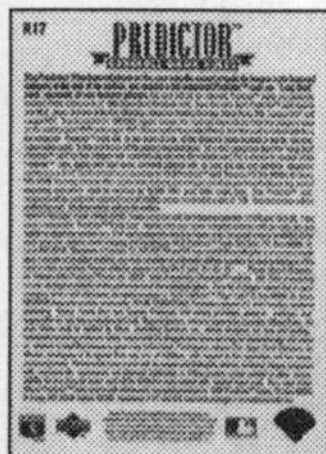

This 60-card standard-size insert set was available only in retail packs. The set included nine players and a Long Shot in each league for each of three categories -- Batting Average Leader, Home Run Leader and Runs Batted In Leader. If the player pictured on the card won his category, the card was redeemable for a special foil version of all 60 Retail Predictor cards. These cards were redeemable until December 31, 1995. Card fronts are full-color action photos of the player emerging from a marble diamond. Backs list the rules of the game. The cards are numbered in the upper left with an "R" prefix.

	MINT	NRMT
COMPLETE SET (60)	130.00	57.50
COMPLETE SERIES 1 (30)	80.00	36.00
COMPLETE SERIES 2 (30)	50.00	22.00
COMMON CARD (R1-R60)	1.00	.45
COMP.SER.1 EXCH.SET (30)	20.00	9.00
COMP.SER.2 EXCH.SET (30)	12.00	5.50

*LL EXCH.CARDS: .4X BASIC CARDS

Card	MINT	NRMT
☐ R1 Albert Belle HR W	2.50	1.10
☐ R2 Jose Canseco HR	1.50	.70
☐ R3 Juan Gonzalez HR	5.00	2.20
☐ R4 Ken Griffey Jr. HR	10.00	4.50
☐ R5 Frank Thomas HR	8.00	3.60
☐ R6 Jeff Bagwell HR	4.00	1.80
☐ R7 Barry Bonds HR	2.50	1.10
☐ R8 Fred McGriff HR	1.50	.70
☐ R9 Matt Williams HR	1.50	.70
☐ R10 HR Wild Card W (Bichette)	1.00	.45
☐ R11 Albert Belle RBI W	2.50	1.10
☐ R12 Joe Carter RBI	1.25	.55
☐ R13 Cecil Fielder RBI	1.25	.55
☐ R14 Kirby Puckett RBI	4.00	1.80
☐ R15 Frank Thomas RBI	8.00	3.60
☐ R16 Jeff Bagwell RBI	4.00	1.80
☐ R17 Barry Bonds RBI	2.50	1.10
☐ R18 Mike Piazza RBI	6.00	2.70
☐ R19 Matt Williams RBI	1.50	.70
☐ R20 RBI Wild Card W (M.Vaughn).	1.00	.45
☐ R21 Wade Boggs BAT	2.00	.90
☐ R22 Kenny Lofton BAT	2.50	1.10
☐ R23 Paul Molitor BAT	2.00	.90
☐ R24 Paul O'Neill BAT	1.25	.55
☐ R25 Frank Thomas BAT	8.00	3.60
☐ R26 Jeff Bagwell BAT	4.00	1.80
☐ R27 Tony Gwynn BAT W	4.00	1.80
☐ R28 Gregg Jefferies BAT	1.00	.45
☐ R29 Hal Morris BAT	1.00	.45
☐ R30 Batting Wild Card W (E.Martinez)	1.00	.45
☐ R31 Joe Carter HR	1.50	.70
☐ R32 Cecil Fielder HR	1.25	.55
☐ R33 Rafael Palmeiro HR	1.50	.70
☐ R34 Larry Walker HR	2.00	.90
☐ R35 Manny Ramirez HR	2.00	.90
☐ R36 Tim Salmon HR	2.00	.90
☐ R37 Mike Piazza HR	6.00	2.70
☐ R38 Andres Galarraga HR	1.50	.70
☐ R39 David Justice HR	2.00	.90
☐ R40 Gary Sheffield HR	2.00	.90
☐ R41 Juan Gonzalez RBI	5.00	2.20
☐ R42 Jose Canseco RBI	1.50	.70
☐ R43 Will Clark RBI	1.50	.70
☐ R44 Rafael Palmeiro RBI	1.50	.70
☐ R45 Ken Griffey Jr. RBI	10.00	4.50
☐ R46 Ruben Sierra RBI	1.00	.45
☐ R47 Larry Walker RBI	2.00	.90
☐ R48 Fred McGriff RBI	1.50	.70
☐ R49 Dante Bichette RBI W	1.50	.70
☐ R50 Darren Daulton RBI	1.25	.55
☐ R51 Will Clark BAT	1.50	.70
☐ R52 Ken Griffey Jr. BAT	10.00	4.50
☐ R53 Don Mattingly BAT	4.00	1.80
☐ R54 John Olerud BAT	1.00	.45
☐ R55 Kirby Puckett BAT	4.00	1.80
☐ R56 Raul Mondesi BAT	1.50	.70
☐ R57 Moises Alou BAT	1.00	.45
☐ R58 Bret Boone BAT	1.00	.45
☐ R59 Albert Belle BAT	2.50	1.10
☐ R60 Mike Piazza BAT	6.00	2.70

1995 Upper Deck Ruth Heroes

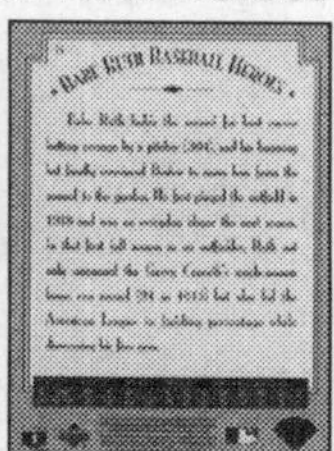

Randomly inserted in second series packs, this set of 10 standard-size cards celebrates the achievements of one of baseball's all-time greats. The set was issued on the Centennial of Ruth's birth. The fronts have silver foil paper and feature the Bambino in colorized action photos on a sepia-tone background. Backs highlight interesting moments from Ruth's career and statistics from separate years are featured at the bottom. The numbering (73-81) is a continuation from previous Heroes sets.

	MINT	NRMT
COMPLETE SET (10)	120.00	55.00
COMMON RUTH (73-81)	15.00	6.75

Card	MINT	NRMT
☐ 73 Babe Ruth 1914-18 Pitching Career	15.00	6.75
☐ 74 Babe Ruth 1919 Move to Outfield	15.00	6.75
☐ 75 Babe Ruth 1920 Renaissance Man	15.00	6.75
☐ 76 Babe Ruth 1923 House that Ruth Built	15.00	6.75
☐ 77 Babe Ruth 1927 60-home run Season	15.00	6.75
☐ 78 Babe Ruth 1928 Three Homers in Game 4	15.00	6.75
☐ 79 Babe Ruth 1932 The Called Shot	15.00	6.75
☐ 80 Babe Ruth 1930-35 Milestones	15.00	6.75
☐ 81 Babe Ruth 1935 The Last Hurrah	15.00	6.75
☐ NNO Babe Ruth Header Card An American Hero	15.00	6.75

1995 Upper Deck Special Edition

Inserted at a rate of one per pack, this 270 standard-size card set features full color action shots of players on a silver foil background. The back highlights the player's previous performance, including 1994 and career statistics. Another player photo is also featured on the back.

	MINT	NRMT
COMPLETE SET (270)	200.00	90.00
COMPLETE SERIES 1 (135)	80.00	36.00
COMPLETE SERIES 2 (135)	120.00	55.00
COMMON CARD (1-270)	.25	.11
COMP.SE GOLD SET (270)	2000.00	900.00
COMP.SE GOLD SER.1 (135)	800.00	350.00
COMP.SE GOLD SER.2 (135)	1200.00	550.00
COMMON SE GOLD (1-270)	2.00	.90

*SE GOLD STARS: 4X TO 10X BASIC SE

*SE GOLD YOUNG STARS: 3X TO 8X BASIC SE
*SE GOLD ROOKIES: 3X TO 8X BASIC SE

☐ 1 Cliff Floyd .50 .23
☐ 2 Wil Cordero .25 .11
☐ 3 Pedro J. Martinez 2.00 .90
☐ 4 Larry Walker 2.00 .90
☐ 5 Derek Jeter 6.00 2.70
☐ 6 Mike Stanley .25 .11
☐ 7 Melido Perez .25 .11
☐ 8 Jim Leyritz .25 .11
☐ 9 Danny Tartabull .25 .11
☐ 10 Wade Boggs 2.00 .90
☐ 11 Ryan Klesko 1.00 .45
☐ 12 Steve Avery .25 .11
☐ 13 Damon Hollins .50 .23
☐ 14 Chipper Jones 6.00 2.70
☐ 15 David Justice 2.00 .90
☐ 16 Glenn Williams .50 .23
☐ 17 Jose Oliva .25 .11
☐ 18 Terrell Wade .25 .11
☐ 19 Alex Fernandez .50 .23
☐ 20 Frank Thomas 8.00 3.60
☐ 21 Ozzie Guillen .50 .23
☐ 22 Roberto Hernandez .50 .23
☐ 23 Albie Lopez .25 .11
☐ 24 Eddie Murray 2.00 .90
☐ 25 Albert Belle 2.50 1.10
☐ 26 Omar Vizquel .50 .23
☐ 27 Carlos Baerga .50 .23
☐ 28 Jose Rijo .25 .11
☐ 29 Hal Morris .25 .11
☐ 30 Reggie Sanders .25 .11
☐ 31 Jack Morris .50 .23
☐ 32 Raul Mondesi 1.00 .45
☐ 33 Karim Garcia 5.00 2.20
☐ 34 Todd Hollandsworth .50 .23
☐ 35 Mike Piazza 6.00 2.70
☐ 36 Chan Ho Park 2.00 .90
☐ 37 Ramon Martinez .50 .23
☐ 38 Kenny Rogers .25 .11
☐ 39 Will Clark 1.00 .45
☐ 40 Juan Gonzalez 5.00 2.20
☐ 41 Ivan Rodriguez 2.50 1.10
☐ 42 Orlando Miller .25 .11
☐ 43 John Hudek .25 .11
☐ 44 Luis Gonzalez .25 .11
☐ 45 Jeff Bagwell 4.00 1.80
☐ 46 Cal Ripken 8.00 3.60
☐ 47 Mike Oquist .25 .11
☐ 48 Armando Benitez .25 .11
☐ 49 Ben McDonald .25 .11
☐ 50 Rafael Palmeiro 1.00 .45
☐ 51 Curtis Goodwin .25 .11
☐ 52 Vince Coleman .25 .11
☐ 53 Tom Gordon .25 .11
☐ 54 Mike Macfarlane .25 .11
☐ 55 Brian McRae .25 .11
☐ 56 Matt Smith .25 .11
☐ 57 David Segui .25 .11
☐ 58 Paul Wilson .50 .23
☐ 59 Bill Pulsipher .25 .11
☐ 60 Bobby Bonilla .50 .23
☐ 61 Jeff Kent .50 .23
☐ 62 Ryan Thompson .25 .11
☐ 63 Jason Isringhausen .50 .23
☐ 64 Ed Sprague .25 .11
☐ 65 Paul Molitor 2.00 .90
☐ 66 Juan Guzman .25 .11
☐ 67 Alex Gonzalez .25 .11
☐ 68 Shawn Green .50 .23
☐ 69 Mark Portugal .25 .11
☐ 70 Barry Bonds 2.50 1.10
☐ 71 Robby Thompson .25 .11
☐ 72 Royce Clayton .50 .23
☐ 73 Ricky Bottalico .50 .23
☐ 74 Doug Jones .25 .11
☐ 75 Darren Daulton .50 .23
☐ 76 Gregg Jefferies 1.00 .45
☐ 77 Scott Cooper .25 .11
☐ 78 Nomar Garciaparra 10.00 4.50
☐ 79 Ken Ryan .25 .11
☐ 80 Mike Greenwell .50 .23
☐ 81 LaTroy Hawkins .25 .11
☐ 82 Rich Becker .50 .23
☐ 83 Scott Erickson .50 .23
☐ 84 Pedro Munoz .25 .11
☐ 85 Kirby Puckett 4.00 1.80
☐ 86 Orlando Merced .25 .11
☐ 87 Jeff King .50 .23
☐ 88 Midre Cummings .25 .11
☐ 89 Bernard Gilkey .50 .23
☐ 90 Ray Lankford 1.00 .45
☐ 91 Todd Zeile .50 .23
☐ 92 Alan Benes .50 .23
☐ 93 Bret Wagner .25 .11
☐ 94 Rene Arocha .25 .11
☐ 95 Cecil Fielder .50 .23
☐ 96 Alan Trammell 1.00 .45
☐ 97 Tony Phillips .25 .11
☐ 98 Junior Felix .25 .11
☐ 99 Brian Harper .25 .11
☐ 100 Greg Vaughn .25 .11
☐ 101 Ricky Bones .25 .11
☐ 102 Walt Weiss .25 .11
☐ 103 Lance Painter .25 .11
☐ 104 Roberto Mejia .25 .11
☐ 105 Andres Galarraga 1.00 .45
☐ 106 Todd Van Poppel .25 .11
☐ 107 Ben Grieve 8.00 3.60
☐ 108 Brent Gates .25 .11
☐ 109 Jason Giambi 1.00 .45
☐ 110 Ruben Sierra .25 .11
☐ 111 Terry Steinbach .50 .23
☐ 112 Chris Hammond .25 .11
☐ 113 Charles Johnson 1.00 .45
☐ 114 Jesus Tavarez .25 .11
☐ 115 Gary Sheffield 2.00 .90
☐ 116 Chuck Carr .25 .11
☐ 117 Bobby Ayala .25 .11
☐ 118 Randy Johnson 2.00 .90
☐ 119 Edgar Martinez 1.00 .45
☐ 120 Alex Rodriguez 8.00 3.60
☐ 121 Kevin Foster .25 .11
☐ 122 Kevin Roberson .25 .11
☐ 123 Sammy Sosa 2.00 .90
☐ 124 Steve Trachsel .25 .11
☐ 125 Eduardo Perez .25 .11
☐ 126 Tim Salmon 2.00 .90
☐ 127 Todd Greene 2.00 .90
☐ 128 Jorge Fabregas .25 .11
☐ 129 Mark Langston .25 .11
☐ 130 Mitch Williams .50 .23
☐ 131 Raul Casanova 2.00 .90
☐ 132 Mel Nieves .50 .23
☐ 133 Andy Benes .50 .23
☐ 134 Dustin Hermanson .25 .11
☐ 135 Trevor Hoffman .50 .23
☐ 136 Mark Grudzielanek 2.00 .90
☐ 137 Ugueth Urbina .50 .23
☐ 138 Moises Alou .50 .23
☐ 139 Roberto Kelly .25 .11
☐ 140 Rondell White 1.00 .45
☐ 141 Paul O'Neill .50 .23
☐ 142 Jimmy Key .50 .23
☐ 143 Jack McDowell .25 .11
☐ 144 Ruben Rivera 2.00 .90
☐ 145 Don Mattingly 3.00 1.35
☐ 146 John Wetteland .50 .23
☐ 147 Tom Glavine 1.00 .45
☐ 148 Marquis Grissom .50 .23
☐ 149 Javier Lopez 1.00 .45
☐ 150 Fred McGriff 1.00 .45
☐ 151 Greg Maddux 6.00 2.70
☐ 152 Chris Sabo .25 .11
☐ 153 Ray Durham 1.00 .45
☐ 154 Robin Ventura .50 .23
☐ 155 Jim Abbott .25 .11
☐ 156 Jimmy Hurst .25 .11
☐ 157 Tim Raines .25 .11
☐ 158 Dennis Martinez .50 .23
☐ 159 Kenny Lofton 2.50 1.10
☐ 160 Dave Winfield 1.00 .45
☐ 161 Manny Ramirez 2.00 .90
☐ 162 Jim Thome 2.00 .90
☐ 163 Barry Larkin 1.00 .45
☐ 164 Bret Boone .25 .11
☐ 165 Deion Sanders 2.00 .90
☐ 166 Ron Gant .50 .23
☐ 167 Benito Santiago .50 .23
☐ 168 Hideo Nomo 8.00 3.60
☐ 169 Billy Ashley .25 .11
☐ 170 Roger Cedeno .50 .23
☐ 171 Ismael Valdes .50 .23
☐ 172 Eric Karros .50 .23
☐ 173 Rusty Greer 2.00 .90
☐ 174 Rick Helling .25 .11
☐ 175 Nolan Ryan 8.00 3.60
☐ 176 Dean Palmer .50 .23
☐ 177 Phil Plantier .25 .11
☐ 178 Darryl Kile .50 .23
☐ 179 Derek Bell .50 .23
☐ 180 Doug Drabek .25 .11
☐ 181 Craig Biggio 1.00 .45
☐ 182 Kevin Brown .50 .23
☐ 183 Harold Baines .50 .23
☐ 184 Jeffrey Hammonds .50 .23
☐ 185 Chris Hoiles .50 .23
☐ 186 Mike Mussina 1.00 .45
☐ 187 Bob Hamelin .25 .11
☐ 188 Jeff Montgomery .50 .23
☐ 189 Michael Tucker 1.00 .45
☐ 190 George Brett 4.00 1.80
☐ 191 Edgardo Alfonzo 2.00 .90
☐ 192 Brett Butler .50 .23
☐ 193 Bobby Jones .50 .23
☐ 194 Todd Hundley .50 .23
☐ 195 Bret Saberhagen .25 .11
☐ 196 Pat Hentgen .50 .23
☐ 197 Roberto Alomar 2.00 .90
☐ 198 David Cone .50 .23
☐ 199 Carlos Delgado .50 .23
☐ 200 Joe Carter 1.00 .45
☐ 201 Wm. VanLandingham .25 .11
☐ 202 Rod Beck .50 .23
☐ 203 J.R. Phillips .25 .11
☐ 204 Darren Lewis .25 .11
☐ 205 Matt Williams 1.00 .45
☐ 206 Lenny Dykstra .50 .23
☐ 207 Dave Hollins .25 .11
☐ 208 Mike Schmidt 2.50 1.10
☐ 209 Charlie Hayes .25 .11
☐ 210 Mo Vaughn 2.50 1.10
☐ 211 Jose Malave .25 .11
☐ 212 Roger Clemens 4.00 1.80
☐ 213 Jose Canseco 1.00 .45
☐ 214 Mark Whiten .25 .11
☐ 215 Marty Cordova 1.00 .45
☐ 216 Rick Aguilera .50 .23
☐ 217 Kevin Tapani .50 .23
☐ 218 Chuck Knoblauch 2.00 .90
☐ 219 Al Martin .50 .23
☐ 220 Jay Bell .50 .23
☐ 221 Carlos Garcia .25 .11
☐ 222 Freddy Garcia .25 .11
☐ 223 Jon Lieber .25 .11
☐ 224 Danny Jackson .25 .11
☐ 225 Ozzie Smith 2.50 1.10
☐ 226 Brian Jordan .50 .23
☐ 227 Ken Hill .25 .11
☐ 228 Scott Cooper .25 .11
☐ 229 Chad Curtis .50 .23
☐ 230 Lou Whitaker .50 .23
☐ 231 Kirk Gibson .50 .23
☐ 232 Travis Fryman .50 .23
☐ 233 Jose Valentin .50 .23
☐ 234 Dave Nilsson .50 .23
☐ 235 Cal Eldred .25 .11
☐ 236 Matt Mieske .50 .23
☐ 237 Bill Swift .25 .11
☐ 238 Marvin Freeman .25 .11
☐ 239 Jason Bates .25 .11
☐ 240 Larry Walker 2.00 .90
☐ 241 Dave Nied .25 .11
☐ 242 Dante Bichette 1.00 .45
☐ 243 Dennis Eckersley 1.00 .45
☐ 244 Todd Stottlemyre .50 .23
☐ 245 Rickey Henderson 1.00 .45
☐ 246 Geronimo Berroa .25 .11
☐ 247 Mark McGwire 4.00 1.80
☐ 248 Quilvio Veras .25 .11
☐ 249 Terry Pendleton .50 .23
☐ 250 Andre Dawson 1.00 .45
☐ 251 Jeff Conine .50 .23
☐ 252 Kurt Abbott .25 .11
☐ 253 Jay Buhner 1.00 .45
☐ 254 Darren Bragg .25 .11
☐ 255 Ken Griffey Jr. 10.00 4.50
☐ 256 Tino Martinez 2.00 .90
☐ 257 Mark Grace 1.00 .45
☐ 258 Ryne Sandberg 2.50 1.10
☐ 259 Randy Myers .50 .23
☐ 260 Howard Johnson .50 .23
☐ 261 Lee Smith .50 .23
☐ 262 J.T. Snow .25 .11
☐ 263 Chili Davis .50 .23
☐ 264 Chuck Finley .50 .23
☐ 265 Eddie Williams .25 .11
☐ 266 Joey Hamilton .50 .23
☐ 267 Ken Caminiti 2.00 .90
☐ 268 Andujar Cedeno .25 .11
☐ 269 Steve Finley .50 .23
☐ 270 Tony Gwynn 5.00 2.20

1995 Upper Deck Steal of a Deal

This set was inserted in hobby and retail packs at a rate o approximately one in 34. This 15-card standard-size se focuses on players who were acquired through, accordi to Upper Deck, "astute trades" or low round draft pic The horizontal fronts feature a player cutout on a gr background with a bronze seal. Backs feature informa of how the player was acquired and past performa The cards are numbered in the upper left with ar prefix.

	MINT
COMPLETE SET (15)	100.00
COMMON CARD (SD1-SD15)	2.00

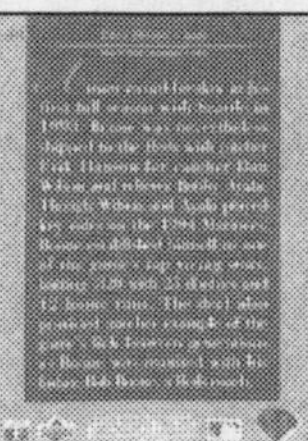

Card	MINT	NRMT
☐ SD1 Mike Piazza	20.00	9.00
☐ SD2 Fred McGriff	4.00	1.80
☐ SD3 Kenny Lofton	8.00	3.60
☐ SD4 Jose Oliva	2.00	.90
☐ SD5 Jeff Bagwell	12.00	5.50
☐ SD6 Roberto Alomar Joe Carter	6.00	2.70
☐ SD7 Steve Karsay	2.00	.90
☐ SD8 Ozzie Smith	8.00	3.60
☐ SD9 Dennis Eckersley	4.00	1.80
☐ SD10 Jose Canseco	4.00	1.80
☐ SD11 Carlos Baerga	2.00	.90
☐ SD12 Cecil Fielder	3.00	1.35
☐ SD13 Don Mattingly	12.00	5.50
☐ SD14 Bret Boone	2.00	.90
☐ SD15 Michael Jordan	30.00	13.50

1995 Upper Deck Sonic Heroes of Baseball

These standard-size cards were given out in three-card cello packs to customers who purchased a combo meal at participating Sonic Restaurants. The fronts feature black-and-white player photos with white borders. The words "Exclusive Edition" are printed in a blue bar at the top, with the player's name in a red bar directly below. The team name and the player's position appear on the bottom. The backs carry stats, career highlights, and sponsor and producer logos.

	MINT	NRMT
COMPLETE SET (20)	8.00	3.60
COMMON CARD (1-20)	.20	.09

Card	MINT	NRMT
☐ 1 Whitey Ford	.40	.18
☐ 2 Cy Young	.50	.23
☐ 3 Babe Ruth	1.25	.55
☐ 4 Lou Gehrig	.75	.35
☐ 5 Mike Schmidt	.75	.35
☐ 6 Nolan Ryan	1.00	.45
☐ 7 Robin Yount	.30	.14
☐ 8 Gary Carter	.30	.14
☐ 9 Tom Seaver	.40	.18
☐ 10 Reggie Jackson	.40	.18
☐ 11 Bob Gibson	.30	.14
☐ 12 Gil Hodges	.40	.18
☐ 13 Monte Irvin	.20	.09
☐ 14 Minnie Minoso	.20	.09
☐ 15 Willie Stargell	.30	.14
☐ 16 Al Kaline	.30	.14
☐ 17 Joe Jackson	.75	.35
☐ 18 Walter Johnson	.50	.23
☐ 19 Ty Cobb	.75	.35
☐ 20 Satchel Paige	.50	.23

1996 Upper Deck

…e 1996 Upper Deck set was issued in two series of 240 …rds, and a 30 card update set, for a total of 510 cards. … cards were distributed in 10-card packs with a …gested retail price of $1.99, and 28 packs were …ained in each box. The attractive fronts feature a full- … photo above a bronze foil bar that includes the …'s name, team and position in a white oval. Subsets … Young at Heart (100-117), Beat the Odds (145- …Postseason Checklist (218-222), Best of a

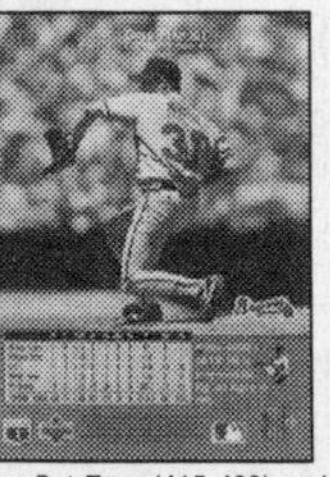

Generation (370-387), Strange But True (415-423) and Managerial Salute Checklists (476-480). The only Rookie Card of note is Livan Hernandez.

	MINT	NRMT
COMPLETE SET (480)	65.00	29.00
COMP.FACT.SET (510)	80.00	36.00
COMPLETE SERIES 1 (240)	35.00	16.00
COMPLETE SERIES 2 (240)	30.00	13.50
COMMON CARD (1-480)	.15	.07
COMP.UPDATE SET (30)	10.00	4.50
COMMON UPDATE (481U-510U)	.25	.11

Card	MINT	NRMT
☐ 1 Cal Ripken 2131	4.00	1.80
☐ 2 Eddie Murray 3000 Hits	.60	.25
☐ 3 Mark Wohlers	.30	.14
☐ 4 David Justice	.60	.25
☐ 5 Chipper Jones	2.00	.90
☐ 6 Javier Lopez	.30	.14
☐ 7 Mark Lemke	.15	.07
☐ 8 Marquis Grissom	.30	.14
☐ 9 Tom Glavine	.30	.14
☐ 10 Greg Maddux	2.00	.90
☐ 11 Manny Alexander	.15	.07
☐ 12 Curtis Goodwin	.15	.07
☐ 13 Scott Erickson	.15	.07
☐ 14 Chris Hoiles	.15	.07
☐ 15 Rafael Palmeiro	.40	.18
☐ 16 Rick Krivda	.15	.07
☐ 17 Jeff Manto	.15	.07
☐ 18 Mo Vaughn	.75	.35
☐ 19 Tim Wakefield	.15	.07
☐ 20 Roger Clemens	1.25	.55
☐ 21 Tim Naehring	.15	.07
☐ 22 Troy O'Leary	.15	.07
☐ 23 Mike Greenwell	.15	.07
☐ 24 Stan Belinda	.15	.07
☐ 25 John Valentin	.30	.14
☐ 26 J.T. Snow	.30	.14
☐ 27 Gary DiSarcina	.15	.07
☐ 28 Mark Langston	.15	.07
☐ 29 Brian Anderson	.15	.07
☐ 30 Jim Edmonds	.60	.25
☐ 31 Garret Anderson	.40	.18
☐ 32 Orlando Palmeiro	.15	.07
☐ 33 Brian McRae	.15	.07
☐ 34 Kevin Foster	.15	.07
☐ 35 Sammy Sosa	.60	.25
☐ 36 Todd Zeile	.15	.07
☐ 37 Jim Bullinger	.15	.07
☐ 38 Luis Gonzalez	.15	.07
☐ 39 Lyle Mouton	.15	.07
☐ 40 Ray Durham	.30	.14
☐ 41 Ozzie Guillen	.15	.07
☐ 42 Alex Fernandez	.30	.14
☐ 43 Brian Keyser	.15	.07
☐ 44 Robin Ventura	.30	.14
☐ 45 Reggie Sanders	.15	.07
☐ 46 Pete Schourek	.15	.07
☐ 47 John Smiley	.15	.07
☐ 48 Jeff Brantley	.15	.07
☐ 49 Thomas Howard	.15	.07
☐ 50 Bret Boone	.15	.07
☐ 51 Kevin Jarvis	.15	.07
☐ 52 Jeff Branson	.15	.07
☐ 53 Carlos Baerga	.30	.14
☐ 54 Jim Thome	.60	.25
☐ 55 Manny Ramirez	.60	.25
☐ 56 Omar Vizquel	.30	.14
☐ 57 Jose Mesa	.30	.14
☐ 58 Julian Tavarez UER	.15	.07
☐ 59 Orel Hershiser	.30	.14
☐ 60 Larry Walker	.60	.25
☐ 61 Bret Saberhagen	.15	.07
☐ 62 Vinny Castilla	.30	.14
☐ 63 Eric Young	.30	.14
☐ 64 Bryan Rekar	.15	.07
☐ 65 Andres Galarraga	.60	.25
☐ 66 Steve Reed	.15	.07
☐ 67 Chad Curtis	.15	.07
☐ 68 Bobby Higginson	.30	.14
☐ 69 Phil Nevin	.15	.07
☐ 70 Cecil Fielder	.30	.14
☐ 71 Felipe Lira	.15	.07
☐ 72 Chris Gomez	.15	.07
☐ 73 Charles Johnson	.30	.14
☐ 74 Quilvio Veras	.15	.07
☐ 75 Jeff Conine	.30	.14
☐ 76 John Burkett	.15	.07
☐ 77 Greg Colbrunn	.15	.07
☐ 78 Terry Pendleton	.15	.07
☐ 79 Shane Reynolds	.15	.07
☐ 80 Jeff Bagwell	1.25	.55
☐ 81 Orlando Miller	.15	.07
☐ 82 Mike Hampton	.15	.07
☐ 83 James Mouton	.15	.07
☐ 84 Brian L. Hunter	.30	.14
☐ 85 Derek Bell	.15	.07
☐ 86 Kevin Appier	.30	.14
☐ 87 Joe Vitiello	.15	.07
☐ 88 Wally Joyner	.15	.07
☐ 89 Michael Tucker	.30	.14
☐ 90 Johnny Damon	.30	.14
☐ 91 Jon Nunnally	.15	.07
☐ 92 Jason Jacome	.15	.07
☐ 93 Chad Fonville	.15	.07
☐ 94 Chan Ho Park	.60	.25
☐ 95 Hideo Nomo	1.50	.70
☐ 96 Ismael Valdes	.30	.14
☐ 97 Greg Gagne	.15	.07
☐ 98 Diamondbacks-Devil Rays	.60	.25
☐ 99 Raul Mondesi	.40	.18
☐ 100 Dave Winfield YH	.40	.18
☐ 101 Dennis Eckersley YH	.40	.18
☐ 102 Andre Dawson YH	.40	.18
☐ 103 Dennis Martinez YH	.30	.14
☐ 104 Lance Parrish YH	.30	.14
☐ 105 Eddie Murray YH	.60	.25
☐ 106 Alan Trammell YH	.40	.18
☐ 107 Lou Whitaker YH	.30	.14
☐ 108 Ozzie Smith YH	.60	.25
☐ 109 Paul Molitor YH	.60	.25
☐ 110 Rickey Henderson YH	.40	.18
☐ 111 Tim Raines YH	.30	.14
☐ 112 Harold Baines YH	.30	.14
☐ 113 Lee Smith YH	.30	.14
☐ 114 Fernando Valenzuela YH	.30	.14
☐ 115 Cal Ripken YH	1.25	.55
☐ 116 Tony Gwynn YH	.60	.25
☐ 117 Wade Boggs	.60	.25
☐ 118 Todd Hollandsworth	.30	.14
☐ 119 Dave Nilsson	.30	.14
☐ 120 Jose Valentin	.15	.07
☐ 121 Steve Sparks	.15	.07
☐ 122 Chuck Carr	.15	.07
☐ 123 John Jaha	.15	.07
☐ 124 Scott Karl	.15	.07
☐ 125 Chuck Knoblauch	.60	.25
☐ 126 Brad Radke	.30	.14
☐ 127 Pat Meares	.15	.07
☐ 128 Ron Coomer	.15	.07
☐ 129 Pedro Munoz	.15	.07
☐ 130 Kirby Puckett	1.25	.55
☐ 131 David Segui	.15	.07
☐ 132 Mark Grudzielanek	.30	.14
☐ 133 Mike Lansing	.15	.07
☐ 134 Sean Berry	.15	.07
☐ 135 Rondell White	.30	.14
☐ 136 Pedro J. Martinez	.60	.25
☐ 137 Carl Everett	.15	.07
☐ 138 Dave Mlicki	.15	.07
☐ 139 Bill Pulsipher	.15	.07
☐ 140 Jason Isringhausen	.15	.07
☐ 141 Rico Brogna	.15	.07
☐ 142 Edgardo Alfonzo	.60	.25
☐ 143 Jeff Kent	.15	.07
☐ 144 Andy Pettitte	.75	.35
☐ 145 Mike Piazza BO	1.00	.45
☐ 146 Cliff Floyd BO	.15	.07
☐ 147 Jason Isringhausen BO	.15	.07
☐ 148 Tim Wakefield BO	.15	.07
☐ 149 Chipper Jones BO	1.00	.45
☐ 150 Hideo Nomo BO	.50	.23
☐ 151 Mark McGwire BO	.60	.25
☐ 152 Ron Gant BO	.15	.07
☐ 153 Gary Gaetti BO	.15	.07
☐ 154 Don Mattingly	1.00	.45
☐ 155 Paul O'Neill	.30	.14
☐ 156 Derek Jeter	2.00	.90
☐ 157 Joe Girardi	.15	.07
☐ 158 Ruben Sierra	.15	.07
☐ 159 Jorge Posada	.15	.07
☐ 160 Geronimo Berroa	.15	.07
☐ 161 Steve Ontiveros	.15	.07
☐ 162 George Williams	.15	.07
☐ 163 Doug Johns	.15	.07
☐ 164 Ariel Prieto	.15	.07
☐ 165 Scott Brosius	.15	.07
☐ 166 Mike Bordick	.15	.07
☐ 167 Tyler Green	.15	.07
☐ 168 Mickey Morandini	.15	.07

☐ 169 Darren Daulton .30 .14
☐ 170 Gregg Jefferies .30 .14
☐ 171 Jim Eisenreich .30 .14
☐ 172 Heathcliff Slocumb .15 .07
☐ 173 Kevin Stocker .15 .07
☐ 174 Esteban Loaiza .15 .07
☐ 175 Jeff King .30 .14
☐ 176 Mark Johnson .15 .07
☐ 177 Denny Neagle .30 .14
☐ 178 Orlando Merced .15 .07
☐ 179 Carlos Garcia .15 .07
☐ 180 Brian Jordan .30 .14
☐ 181 Mike Morgan .15 .07
☐ 182 Mark Petkovsek .15 .07
☐ 183 Bernard Gilkey .30 .14
☐ 184 John Mabry .30 .14
☐ 185 Tom Henke .30 .14
☐ 186 Glenn Dishman .15 .07
☐ 187 Andy Ashby .15 .07
☐ 188 Bip Roberts .15 .07
☐ 189 Melvin Nieves .15 .07
☐ 190 Ken Caminiti .60 .25
☐ 191 Brad Ausmus .15 .07
☐ 192 Deion Sanders .60 .25
☐ 193 Jamie Brewington .15 .07
☐ 194 Glenallen Hill .15 .07
☐ 195 Barry Bonds .75 .35
☐ 196 Wm. Van Landingham .15 .07
☐ 197 Mark Carreon .15 .07
☐ 198 Royce Clayton .15 .07
☐ 199 Joey Cora .30 .14
☐ 200 Ken Griffey Jr. 3.00 1.35
☐ 201 Jay Buhner .40 .18
☐ 202 Alex Rodriguez 2.50 1.10
☐ 203 Norm Charlton .15 .07
☐ 204 Andy Benes .15 .07
☐ 205 Edgar Martinez .40 .18
☐ 206 Juan Gonzalez 1.50 .70
☐ 207 Will Clark .40 .18
☐ 208 Kevin Gross .15 .07
☐ 209 Roger Pavlik .15 .07
☐ 210 Ivan Rodriguez .75 .35
☐ 211 Rusty Greer .60 .25
☐ 212 Angel Martinez .15 .07
☐ 213 Tomas Perez .15 .07
☐ 214 Alex Gonzalez .15 .07
☐ 215 Joe Carter .30 .14
☐ 216 Shawn Green .15 .07
☐ 217 Edwin Hurtado .15 .07
☐ 218 Edgar Martinez .30 .14
Tony Pena CL
☐ 219 Chipper Jones .75 .35
Barry Larkin CL
☐ 220 Orel Hershiser CL .15 .07
☐ 221 Mike Devereaux CL .15 .07
☐ 222 Tom Glavine CL .30 .14
☐ 223 Karim Garcia .30 .14
☐ 224 Arquimedez Pozo .15 .07
☐ 225 Billy Wagner .40 .18
☐ 226 John Wasdin .15 .07
☐ 227 Jeff Suppan .40 .18
☐ 228 Steve Gibralter .15 .07
☐ 229 Jimmy Haynes .15 .07
☐ 230 Ruben Rivera .30 .14
☐ 231 Chris Snopek .15 .07
☐ 232 Alex Ochoa .15 .07
☐ 233 Shannon Stewart .15 .07
☐ 234 Quinton McCracken .15 .07
☐ 235 Trey Beamon .15 .07
☐ 236 Billy McMillon .15 .07
☐ 237 Steve Cox .15 .07
☐ 238 George Arias .15 .07
☐ 239 Jose Herrera .15 .07
☐ 240 Todd Greene .60 .25
☐ 241 Jason Kendall .60 .25
☐ 242 Brooks Kieschnick .30 .14
☐ 243 Osvaldo Fernandez .30 .14
☐ 244 Livan Hernandez 1.50 .70
☐ 245 Rey Ordonez .30 .14
☐ 246 Mike Grace .15 .07
☐ 247 Jay Canizaro .15 .07
☐ 248 Bob Wolcott .15 .07
☐ 249 Jermaine Dye .15 .07
☐ 250 Jason Schmidt .30 .14
☐ 251 Mike Sweeney .60 .25
☐ 252 Marcus Jensen .15 .07
☐ 253 Mendy Lopez .30 .14
☐ 254 Wilton Guerrero .60 .25
☐ 255 Paul Wilson .15 .07
☐ 256 Edgar Renteria .40 .18
☐ 257 Richard Hidalgo .60 .25
☐ 258 Bob Abreu .60 .25
☐ 259 Robert Smith .40 .18
☐ 260 Sal Fasano .15 .07
☐ 261 Enrique Wilson .40 .18
☐ 262 Rich Hunter .15 .07
☐ 263 Sergio Nunez .30 .14
☐ 264 Dan Serafini .15 .07
☐ 265 David Doster .15 .07
☐ 266 Ryan McGuire .15 .07
☐ 267 Scott Spiezio .40 .18
☐ 268 Rafael Orellano .15 .07
☐ 269 Steve Avery .15 .07
☐ 270 Fred McGriff .40 .18
☐ 271 John Smoltz .30 .14
☐ 272 Ryan Klesko .40 .18
☐ 273 Jeff Blauser .15 .07
☐ 274 Brad Clontz .15 .07
☐ 275 Roberto Alomar .60 .25
☐ 276 B.J. Surhoff .30 .14
☐ 277 Jeffrey Hammonds .30 .14
☐ 278 Brady Anderson .40 .18
☐ 279 Bobby Bonilla .30 .14
☐ 280 Cal Ripken 2.50 1.10
☐ 281 Mike Mussina .60 .25
☐ 282 Wil Cordero .15 .07
☐ 283 Mike Stanley .15 .07
☐ 284 Aaron Sele .15 .07
☐ 285 Jose Canseco .40 .18
☐ 286 Tom Gordon .15 .07
☐ 287 Heathcliff Slocumb .15 .07
☐ 288 Lee Smith .30 .14
☐ 289 Troy Percival .30 .14
☐ 290 Tim Salmon .60 .25
☐ 291 Chuck Finley .15 .07
☐ 292 Jim Abbott .30 .14
☐ 293 Chili Davis .15 .07
☐ 294 Steve Trachsel .15 .07
☐ 295 Mark Grace .30 .14
☐ 296 Rey Sanchez .15 .07
☐ 297 Scott Servais .15 .07
☐ 298 Jaime Navarro .15 .07
☐ 299 Frank Castillo .15 .07
☐ 300 Frank Thomas 2.50 1.10
☐ 301 Jason Bere .15 .07
☐ 302 Danny Tartabull .15 .07
☐ 303 Darren Lewis .15 .07
☐ 304 Roberto Hernandez .30 .14
☐ 305 Tony Phillips .15 .07
☐ 306 Wilson Alvarez .30 .14
☐ 307 Jose Rijo .15 .07
☐ 308 Hal Morris .15 .07
☐ 309 Mark Portugal .15 .07
☐ 310 Barry Larkin .40 .18
☐ 311 Dave Burba .15 .07
☐ 312 Ed Taubensee .15 .07
☐ 313 Sandy Alomar Jr. .30 .14
☐ 314 Dennis Martinez .30 .14
☐ 315 Albert Belle .75 .35
☐ 316 Eddie Murray .60 .25
☐ 317 Charles Nagy .30 .14
☐ 318 Chad Ogea .15 .07
☐ 319 Kenny Lofton .75 .35
☐ 320 Dante Bichette .30 .14
☐ 321 Armando Reynoso .15 .07
☐ 322 Walt Weiss .15 .07
☐ 323 Ellis Burks .30 .14
☐ 324 Kevin Ritz .15 .07
☐ 325 Bill Swift .15 .07
☐ 326 Jason Bates .15 .07
☐ 327 Tony Clark .60 .25
☐ 328 Travis Fryman .30 .14
☐ 329 Mark Parent .15 .07
☐ 330 Alan Trammell .40 .18
☐ 331 C.J. Nitkowski .15 .07
☐ 332 Jose Lima .15 .07
☐ 333 Phil Plantier .15 .07
☐ 334 Kurt Abbott .15 .07
☐ 335 Andre Dawson .40 .18
☐ 336 Chris Hammond .15 .07
☐ 337 Robb Nen .15 .07
☐ 338 Pat Rapp .15 .07
☐ 339 Al Leiter .15 .07
☐ 340 Gary Sheffield UER .60 .25
(HR total says 17
☐ 341 Todd Jones .15 .07
☐ 342 Doug Drabek .15 .07
☐ 343 Greg Swindell .15 .07
☐ 344 Tony Eusebio .15 .07
☐ 345 Craig Biggio .40 .18
☐ 346 Darryl Kile .30 .14
☐ 347 Mike Macfarlane .15 .07
☐ 348 Jeff Montgomery .15 .07
☐ 349 Chris Haney .15 .07
☐ 350 Bip Roberts .15 .07
☐ 351 Tom Goodwin .15 .07
☐ 352 Mark Gubicza .15 .07
☐ 353 Joe Randa .15 .07
☐ 354 Ramon Martinez .30 .14
☐ 355 Eric Karros .30 .14
☐ 356 Delino DeShields .15 .07
☐ 357 Brett Butler .30 .14
☐ 358 Todd Worrell .30 .14
☐ 359 Mike Blowers .15 .07
☐ 360 Mike Piazza 2.00 .90
☐ 361 Ben McDonald .15 .07
☐ 362 Ricky Bones .15 .07
☐ 363 Greg Vaughn .15 .07
☐ 364 Matt Mieske .15 .07
☐ 365 Kevin Seitzer .15 .07
☐ 366 Jeff Cirillo .30 .14
☐ 367 LaTroy Hawkins .15 .07
☐ 368 Frank Rodriguez .15 .07
☐ 369 Rick Aguilera .30 .14
☐ 370 Roberto Alomar BG .60 .25
☐ 371 Albert Belle BG .60 .25
☐ 372 Wade Boggs BG .60 .25
☐ 373 Barry Bonds BG .60 .25
☐ 374 Roger Clemens BG .60 .25
☐ 375 Dennis Eckersley BG .40 .18
☐ 376 Ken Griffey Jr. BG 1.50 .70
☐ 377 Tony Gwynn BG .60 .25
☐ 378 Rickey Henderson BG .40 .18
☐ 379 Greg Maddux BG 1.00 .45
☐ 380 Fred McGriff BG .40 .18
☐ 381 Paul Molitor BG .60 .25
☐ 382 Eddie Murray BG .60 .25
☐ 383 Mike Piazza BG 1.00 .45
☐ 384 Kirby Puckett BG .60 .25
☐ 385 Cal Ripken BG 1.25 .55
☐ 386 Ozzie Smith BG .60 .25
☐ 387 Frank Thomas BG 1.50 .70
☐ 388 Matt Walbeck .15 .07
☐ 389 Dave Stevens .15 .07
☐ 390 Marty Cordova .15 .07
☐ 391 Darrin Fletcher .15 .07
☐ 392 Cliff Floyd .15 .07
☐ 393 Mel Rojas .15 .07
☐ 394 Shane Andrews .15 .07
☐ 395 Moises Alou .30 .14
☐ 396 Carlos Perez .15 .07
☐ 397 Jeff Fassero .15 .07
☐ 398 Bobby Jones .15 .07
☐ 399 Todd Hundley .30 .14
☐ 400 John Franco .30 .14
☐ 401 Jose Vizcaino .15 .07
☐ 402 Bernard Gilkey .30 .14
☐ 403 Pete Harnisch .15 .07
☐ 404 Pat Kelly .15 .07
☐ 405 David Cone .30 .14
☐ 406 Bernie Williams .60 .25
☐ 407 John Wetteland .30 .14
☐ 408 Scott Kamieniecki .15 .07
☐ 409 Tim Raines .15 .07
☐ 410 Wade Boggs .60 .25
☐ 411 Terry Steinbach .30 .14
☐ 412 Jason Giambi .40 .18
☐ 413 Todd Van Poppel .15 .07
☐ 414 Pedro Munoz .15 .07
☐ 415 Eddie Murray SBT .60 .25
☐ 416 Dennis Eckersley SBT .40 .18
☐ 417 Bip Roberts SBT .15 .07
☐ 418 Glenallen Hill SBT .15 .07
☐ 419 John Hudek SBT .15 .07
☐ 420 Derek Bell SBT .15 .07
☐ 421 Larry Walker SBT .60 .25
☐ 422 Greg Maddux SBT 1.00 .45
☐ 423 Ken Caminiti SBT .60 .25
☐ 424 Brent Gates .15 .07
☐ 425 Mark McGwire 1.25 .55
☐ 426 Mark Whiten .15 .07
☐ 427 Sid Fernandez .15 .07
☐ 428 Ricky Bottalico .15 .07
☐ 429 Mike Mimbs .15 .07
☐ 430 Lenny Dykstra .30 .14
☐ 431 Todd Zeile .15 .07
☐ 432 Benito Santiago .15 .07
☐ 433 Danny Miceli .15 .07
☐ 434 Al Martin .15 .07
☐ 435 Jay Bell .30 .14
☐ 436 Charlie Hayes .15 .07
☐ 437 Mike Kingery .15 .07
☐ 438 Paul Wagner .15 .07
☐ 439 Tom Pagnozzi .15 .07
☐ 440 Ozzie Smith .75 .35
☐ 441 Ray Lankford .30 .14
☐ 442 Dennis Eckersley .40 .18
☐ 443 Ron Gant .30 .14
☐ 444 Alan Benes .30 .14
☐ 445 Rickey Henderson .40 .18
☐ 446 Jody Reed .15 .07
☐ 447 Trevor Hoffman .30 .1[illegible]
☐ 448 Andujar Cedeno .15 .0[illegible]
☐ 449 Steve Finley .30 .[illegible]
☐ 450 Tony Gwynn 1.50
☐ 451 Joey Hamilton .30
☐ 452 Mark Leiter .15
☐ 453 Rod Beck .15
☐ 454 Kirt Manwaring .15
☐ 455 Matt Williams .40
☐ 456 Robby Thompson .15

☐ 457 Shawon Dunston	.15	.07
☐ 458 Russ Davis	.15	.07
☐ 459 Paul Sorrento	.15	.07
☐ 460 Randy Johnson	.60	.25
☐ 461 Chris Bosio	.15	.07
☐ 462 Luis Sojo	.15	.07
☐ 463 Sterling Hitchcock	.15	.07
☐ 464 Benji Gil	.15	.07
☐ 465 Mickey Tettleton	.15	.07
☐ 466 Mark McLemore	.15	.07
☐ 467 Darryl Hamilton	.15	.07
☐ 468 Ken Hill	.15	.07
☐ 469 Dean Palmer	.30	.14
☐ 470 Carlos Delgado	.30	.14
☐ 471 Ed Sprague	.15	.07
☐ 472 Otis Nixon	.15	.07
☐ 473 Pat Hentgen	.30	.14
☐ 474 Juan Guzman	.15	.07
☐ 475 John Olerud	.30	.14
☐ 476 Buck Showalter CL	.15	.07
☐ 477 Bobby Cox CL	.15	.07
☐ 478 Tommy Lasorda CL	.60	.25
☐ 479 Buck Showalter CL	.15	.07
☐ 480 Sparky Anderson CL	.60	.25
☐ 481U Randy Myers	.50	.23
☐ 482U Kent Mercker	.25	.11
☐ 483U David Wells	.25	.11
☐ 484U Kevin Mitchell	.25	.11
☐ 485U Randy Velarde	.25	.11
☐ 486U Ryne Sandberg	1.50	.70
☐ 487U Doug Jones	.25	.11
☐ 488U Terry Adams	.25	.11
☐ 489U Kevin Tapani	.25	.11
☐ 490U Harold Baines	.50	.23
☐ 491U Eric Davis	.50	.23
☐ 492U Julio Franco	.50	.23
☐ 493U Jack McDowell	.25	.11
☐ 494U Devon White	.25	.11
☐ 495U Kevin Brown	.50	.23
☐ 496U Rick Wilkins	.25	.11
☐ 497U Sean Berry	.25	.11
☐ 498U Keith Lockhart	.25	.11
☐ 499U Mark Loretta	.25	.11
☐ 500U Paul Molitor	1.25	.55
☐ 501U Roberto Kelly	.25	.11
☐ 502U Lance Johnson	.25	.11
☐ 503U Tino Martinez	.50	.23
☐ 504U Kenny Rogers	.25	.11
☐ 505U Todd Stottlemyre	.25	.11
☐ 506U Gary Gaetti	.50	.23
☐ 507U Royce Clayton	.25	.11
☐ 508U Andy Benes	.50	.23
☐ 509U Wally Joyner	.25	.11
☐ 510U Erik Hanson	.25	.11

1996 Upper Deck Blue Chip Prospects

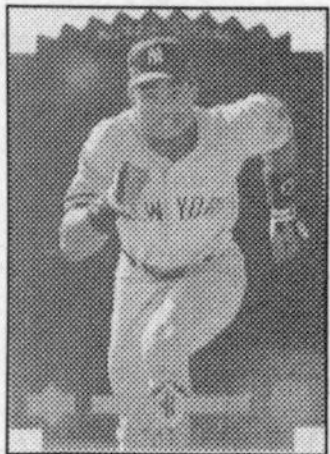

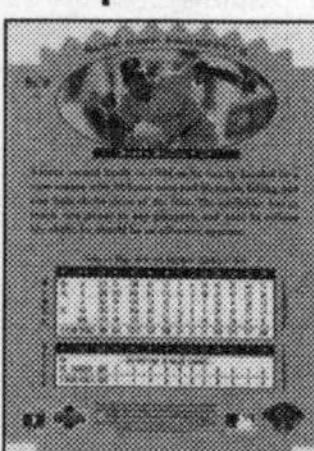

Randomly inserted in retail packs at a rate of one in 72, this 20-card set, diecut on the top and bottom, features some of the best young stars in the majors against a bluish background.

	MINT	NRMT
COMPLETE SET (20)	200.00	90.00
COMMON CARD (BC1-BC20)	5.00	2.20
☐ BC1 Hideo Nomo	30.00	13.50
☐ BC2 Johnny Damon	6.00	2.70
☐ BC3 Jason Isringhausen	5.00	2.20
☐ BC4 Bill Pulsipher	5.00	2.20
☐ BC5 Marty Cordova	5.00	2.20
☐ BC6 Michael Tucker	6.00	2.70
☐ BC7 John Wasdin	5.00	2.20
☐ BC8 Karim Garcia	6.00	2.70
☐ BC9 Ruben Rivera	6.00	2.70
☐ BC10 Chipper Jones	40.00	18.00
☐ BC11 Billy Wagner	8.00	3.60
☐ BC12 Brooks Kieschnick	6.00	2.70
☐ BC13 Alan Benes	6.00	2.70
☐ BC14 Roger Cedeno	5.00	2.20
☐ BC15 Alex Rodriguez	40.00	18.00
☐ BC16 Jason Schmidt	6.00	2.70
☐ BC17 Derek Jeter	30.00	13.50
☐ BC18 Brian L.Hunter	6.00	2.70
☐ BC19 Garret Anderson	8.00	3.60
☐ BC20 Manny Ramirez	12.00	5.50

1996 Upper Deck Diamond Destiny

Issued one per WalMark pack, these 40 cards feature leading players of baseball. The cards have two photos on the front with the player's name listed on the bottom. The backs have another photo along with biographical information. The cards are numbered with a "DD" prefix.

	MINT	NRMT
COMPLETE SET (40)	150.00	70.00
COMMON CARD (DD1-DD40)	1.50	.70
COMP.GOLD DD SET (40)	1500.00	700.00
COMMON GOLD (DD1-DD40)	20.00	9.00
*GOLD DD: 6X TO 12X BASIC CARDS		
COMP.SILVER DD SET (40)	500.00	220.00
COMMON SILVER (DD1-DD40)	6.00	2.70
*SILVER DD: 2X TO 4X BASIC CARDS		
☐ DD1 Chipper Jones	10.00	4.50
☐ DD2 Fred McGriff	2.50	1.10
☐ DD3 John Smoltz	2.00	.90
☐ DD4 Ryan Klesko	2.50	1.10
☐ DD5 Greg Maddux	10.00	4.50
☐ DD6 Cal Ripken	12.00	5.50
☐ DD7 Roberto Alomar	3.00	1.35
☐ DD8 Eddie Murray	3.00	1.35
☐ DD9 Brady Anderson	2.50	1.10
☐ DD10 Mo Vaughn	4.00	1.80
☐ DD11 Roger Clemens	4.00	1.80
☐ DD12 Darin Erstad	8.00	3.60
☐ DD13 Sammy Sosa	3.00	1.35
☐ DD14 Frank Thomas	12.00	5.50
☐ DD15 Barry Larkin	2.50	1.10
☐ DD16 Albert Belle	4.00	1.80
☐ DD17 Manny Ramirez	3.00	1.35
☐ DD18 Kenny Lofton	4.00	1.80
☐ DD19 Dante Bichette	2.00	.90
☐ DD20 Gary Sheffield	2.50	1.10
☐ DD21 Jeff Bagwell	6.00	2.70
☐ DD22 Hideo Nomo	6.00	2.70
☐ DD23 Mike Piazza	10.00	4.50
☐ DD24 Kirby Puckett	6.00	2.70
☐ DD25 Paul Molitor	3.00	1.35
☐ DD26 Chuck Knoblauch	3.00	1.35
☐ DD27 Wade Boggs	3.00	1.35
☐ DD28 Derek Jeter	10.00	4.50
☐ DD29 Rey Ordonez	1.50	.70
☐ DD30 Mark McGwire	6.00	2.70
☐ DD31 Ozzie Smith	4.00	1.80
☐ DD32 Tony Gwynn	6.00	2.70
☐ DD33 Barry Bonds	4.00	1.80
☐ DD34 Matt Williams	2.50	1.10
☐ DD35 Ken Griffey Jr.	15.00	6.75
☐ DD36 Jay Buhner	2.50	1.10
☐ DD37 Randy Johnson	3.00	1.35
☐ DD38 Alex Rodriguez	12.00	5.50
☐ DD39 Juan Gonzalez	8.00	3.60
☐ DD40 Joe Carter	2.00	.90

1996 Upper Deck Future Stock Prospects

Randomly inserted in packs at a rate of one in 6, this 20-card set highlights the top prospects who made their major league debuts in 1995. The cards are diecut at the top and feature a purple border surrounding the player's picture.

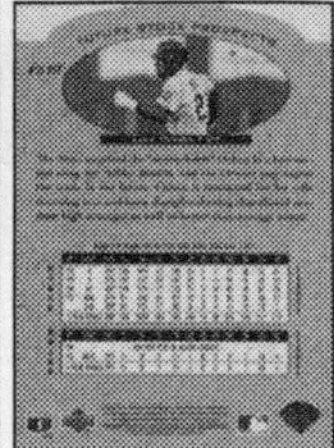

	MINT	NRMT
COMPLETE SET (20)	12.00	5.50
COMMON CARD (FS1-FS20)	1.00	.45
☐ FS1 George Arias	1.00	.45
☐ FS2 Brian Barber	1.00	.45
☐ FS3 Trey Beamon	1.00	.45
☐ FS4 Yamil Benitez	2.00	.90
☐ FS5 Jamie Brewington	1.00	.45
☐ FS6 Tony Clark	3.00	1.35
☐ FS7 Steve Cox	1.00	.45
☐ FS8 Carlos Delgado	1.50	.70
☐ FS9 Chad Fonville	1.00	.45
☐ FS10 Alex Ochoa	1.00	.45
☐ FS11 Curtis Goodwin	1.00	.45
☐ FS12 Todd Greene	2.00	.90
☐ FS13 Jimmy Haynes	1.00	.45
☐ FS14 Quinton McCracken	1.00	.45
☐ FS15 Billy McMillon	1.00	.45
☐ FS16 Chan Ho Park	2.00	.90
☐ FS17 Arquimedez Pozo	1.00	.45
☐ FS18 Chris Snopek	1.00	.45
☐ FS19 Shannon Stewart	1.00	.45
☐ FS20 Jeff Suppan	2.00	.90

1996 Upper Deck Gameface

These Gameface cards were seeded at a rate of one per Upper Deck and Collector's Choice Wal Mart retail pack. The Upper Deck packs contained eight cards and the Collector's Choice packs contained sixteen cards. Both packs carried a suggested retail price of $1.50. The card fronts feature the player's photo surrounded by a "cloudy" white border along with a Gameface logo at the bottom.

	MINT	NRMT
COMPLETE SET (10)	12.00	5.50
COMMON CARD (GF1-GF10)	.30	.14
☐ GF1 Ken Griffey Jr.	3.00	1.35
☐ GF2 Frank Thomas	2.50	1.10
☐ GF3 Barry Bonds	.75	.35
☐ GF4 Albert Belle	.75	.35
☐ GF5 Cal Ripken	2.50	1.10
☐ GF6 Mike Piazza	2.00	.90
☐ GF7 Chipper Jones	2.00	.90
☐ GF8 Matt Williams	.30	.14
☐ GF9 Hideo Nomo	1.50	.70
☐ GF10 Greg Maddux	2.00	.90

1996 Upper Deck Hot Commodities

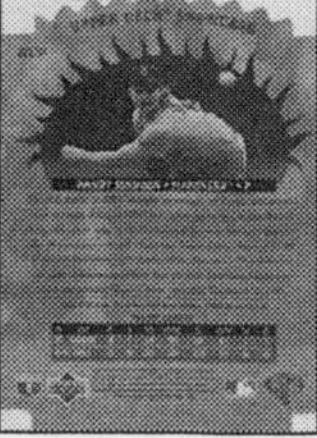

Cards from this 20 card set double die-cut set were randomly inserted into series two Upper Deck packs at a rate of one in 37. The set features some of baseball's most popular players.

	MINT	NRMT
OMPLETE SET (20)	150.00	70.00
OMMON CARD (HC1-HC20)	4.00	1.80
☐ HC1 Ken Griffey Jr.	30.00	13.50
☐ HC2 Hideo Nomo	15.00	6.75
☐ HC3 Roberto Alomar	6.00	2.70
☐ HC4 Paul Wilson	4.00	1.80
☐ HC5 Albert Belle	8.00	3.60
☐ HC6 Manny Ramirez	6.00	2.70
☐ HC7 Kirby Puckett	12.00	5.50
☐ HC8 Johnny Damon	5.00	2.20
☐ HC9 Randy Johnson	6.00	2.70
☐ HC10 Greg Maddux	20.00	9.00
☐ HC11 Chipper Jones	20.00	9.00
☐ HC12 Barry Bonds	8.00	3.60
☐ HC13 Mo Vaughn	8.00	3.60
☐ HC14 Mike Piazza	20.00	9.00
☐ HC15 Cal Ripken	25.00	11.00
☐ HC16 Tim Salmon	6.00	2.70
☐ HC17 Sammy Sosa	6.00	2.70
☐ HC18 Kenny Lofton	8.00	3.60
☐ HC19 Tony Gwynn	15.00	6.75
☐ HC20 Frank Thomas	25.00	11.00

1996 Upper Deck V.J. Lovero Showcase

pper Deck utilized photos from the files of V.J. Lovero to oduce this set. The cards feature the photos along with story of how Lovero took the photos. The cards are mbered with a "VJ" prefix.

	MINT	NRMT
MPLETE SET (19)	25.00	11.00
MMON CARD (VJ1-VJ19)	.50	.23
VJ1 Jim Abbott	.50	.23
VJ2 Hideo Nomo	3.00	1.35
VJ3 Derek Jeter	5.00	2.20
VJ4 Barry Bonds	2.00	.90
VJ5 Greg Maddux	5.00	2.20
VJ6 Mark McGwire	3.00	1.35
VJ7 Jose Canseco	1.00	.45
VJ8 Ken Caminiti	1.50	.70
VJ9 Raul Mondesi	1.00	.45
VJ10 Ken Griffey Jr.	8.00	3.60
VJ11 Jay Buhner	1.00	.45
VJ12 Randy Johnson	1.50	.70
VJ13 Roger Clemens	2.00	.90
VJ14 Brady Anderson	1.00	.45
VJ15 Frank Thomas	5.00	2.20
VJ16 Garret Anderson Jim Edmonds Tim Salmon	1.50	.70
VJ17 Mike Piazza	5.00	2.20
VJ18 Dante Bichette	.75	.35
VJ19 Tony Gwynn	3.00	1.35

1996 Upper Deck Nomo Highlights

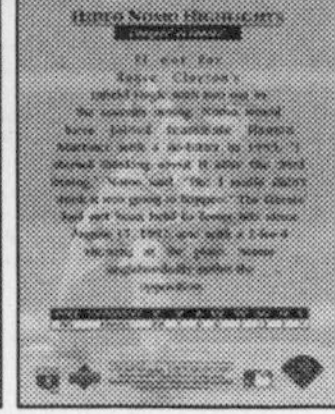

s Angeles Dodgers star pitcher and Upper Deck okesperson Hideo Nomo was featured in this special e card set. The cards were randomly seeded into cond series packs at a rate of one in 24 and feature game action as well as descriptions of some of Nomo's key 1995 games.

	MINT	NRMT
COMPLETE SET (5)	20.00	9.00
COMMON CARD (1-5)	5.00	2.20
☐ 1 Hideo Nomo Dodgers at Giants First Career Start	5.00	2.20
☐ 2 Hideo Nomo	5.00	2.20
☐ 3 Hideo Nomo 1995 All-Star Game	5.00	2.20
☐ 4 Hideo Nomo Dodgers at Giants One-Hitter	5.00	2.20
☐ 5 Hideo Nomo Dodgers at Padres Season-Ending Performance	5.00	2.20

1996 Upper Deck Power Driven

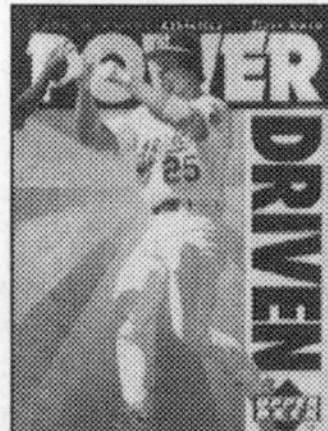

Randomly inserted in first series packs at a rate of one in 36, this 20-card set consists of embossed rainbow foil inserts of baseball's top power hitters.

	MINT	NRMT
COMPLETE SET (20)	120.00	55.00
COMMON CARD (PD1-PD20)	2.50	1.10
☐ PD1 Albert Belle	8.00	3.60
☐ PD2 Barry Bonds	8.00	3.60
☐ PD3 Jay Buhner	4.00	1.80
☐ PD4 Jose Canseco	4.00	1.80
☐ PD5 Cecil Fielder	3.00	1.35
☐ PD6 Juan Gonzalez	15.00	6.75
☐ PD7 Ken Griffey Jr.	30.00	13.50
☐ PD8 Eric Karros	3.00	1.35
☐ PD9 Fred McGriff	4.00	1.80
☐ PD10 Mark McGwire	12.00	5.50
☐ PD11 Rafael Palmeiro	4.00	1.80
☐ PD12 Mike Piazza	20.00	9.00
☐ PD13 Manny Ramirez	6.00	2.70
☐ PD14 Tim Salmon	6.00	2.70
☐ PD15 Reggie Sanders	2.50	1.10
☐ PD16 Sammy Sosa	6.00	2.70
☐ PD17 Frank Thomas	25.00	11.00
☐ PD18 Mo Vaughn	8.00	3.60
☐ PD19 Larry Walker	6.00	2.70
☐ PD20 Matt Williams	4.00	1.80

1996 Upper Deck Predictor Hobby

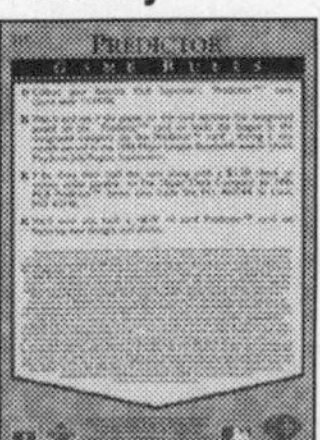

Randomly inserted in both series hobby packs at a rate of one in 12, this 60-card predictor set offers unique prizes as Major League Baseball players compete for monthly milestones and awards. The fronts feature a cutout player photo against a pinstriped background surrounded by a gray marble border.

	MINT	NRMT
COMPLETE SET (60)	110.00	50.00
COMPLETE SERIES 1 (30)	60.00	27.00
COMPLETE SERIES 2 (30)	50.00	22.00
COMMON CARD (H1-H60)	1.00	.45
COMP.AL PLAY.EXCH.SET (10)	20.00	9.00
COMP.AL PITCH.EXCH.SET (10)	6.00	2.70
COMP.AL ROOK.EXCH.SET (10)	8.00	3.60
COMP.NL PLAY.EXCH.SET (10)	12.00	5.50
COMP.NL PITCH.EXCH.SET (10)	8.00	3.60
COMP.NL ROOK.EXCH.SET (10)	6.00	2.70
*EXCH.CARDS: .6X TO 1.5X BASIC CARDS		
☐ H1 Albert Belle	2.50	1.10
☐ H2 Kenny Lofton	2.50	1.10
☐ H3 Rafael Palmeiro	1.50	.70
☐ H4 Ken Griffey Jr.	10.00	4.50
☐ H5 Tim Salmon	2.00	.90
☐ H6 Cal Ripken	8.00	3.60
☐ H7 Mark McGwire W	4.00	1.80
☐ H8 Frank Thomas W	8.00	3.60
☐ H9 Mo Vaughn W	2.50	1.10
☐ H10 Player of Month Longshot	1.00	.45
☐ H11 Roger Clemens	3.00	1.35
☐ H12 David Cone	1.25	.55
☐ H13 Jose Mesa	1.00	.45
☐ H14 Randy Johnson	2.00	.90
☐ H15 Chuck Finley	1.00	.45
☐ H16 Mike Mussina	2.00	.90
☐ H17 Kevin Appier	1.25	.55
☐ H18 Kenny Rogers	1.00	.45
☐ H19 Lee Smith	1.25	.55
☐ H20 Pitcher of Month Longshot W	1.00	.45
☐ H21 George Arias	1.00	.45
☐ H22 Jose Herrera	1.00	.45
☐ H23 Tony Clark	2.00	.90
☐ H24 Todd Greene	2.00	.90
☐ H25 Derek Jeter W	6.00	2.70
☐ H26 Arquimedez Pozo	1.00	.45
☐ H27 Matt Lawton	1.00	.45
☐ H28 Shannon Stewart	1.00	.45
☐ H29 Chris Snopek	1.00	.45
☐ H30 Most Rookie Hits Longshot	1.00	.45
☐ H31 Jeff Bagwell W	4.00	1.80
☐ H32 Dante Bichette	1.25	.55
☐ H33 Barry Bonds W	2.50	1.10
☐ H34 Tony Gwynn	4.00	1.80
☐ H35 Chipper Jones	6.00	2.70
☐ H36 Eric Karros	1.25	.55
☐ H37 Barry Larkin	1.50	.70
☐ H38 Mike Piazza	6.00	2.70
☐ H39 Matt Williams	1.50	.70
☐ H40 Long Shot Card	1.00	.45
☐ H41 Osvaldo Fernandez	1.00	.45
☐ H42 Tom Glavine	1.25	.55
☐ H43 Jason Isringhausen	1.00	.45
☐ H44 Greg Maddux	6.00	2.70
☐ H45 Pedro Martinez	2.00	.90
☐ H46 Hideo Nomo	4.00	1.80
☐ H47 Pete Schourek	1.00	.45
☐ H48 Paul Wilson	1.00	.45
☐ H49 Mark Wohlers	1.25	.55
☐ H50 Long Shot Card	1.00	.45
☐ H51 Bob Abreu	2.00	.90
☐ H52 Trey Beamon	1.00	.45
☐ H53 Yamil Benitez	1.50	.70
☐ H54 Roger Cedeno	1.00	.45
☐ H55 Todd Hollandsworth	1.25	.55
☐ H56 Marvin Benard	1.00	.45
☐ H57 Jason Kendall	2.00	.90
☐ H58 Brooks Kieschnick	1.25	.55
☐ H59 Rey Ordonez W	2.00	.90
☐ H60 Long Shot Card	1.00	.45

1996 Upper Deck Predictor Retail

Randomly inserted in both series retail packs at a rate of one in 12, this 60-card predictor set offers unique prizes as Major League Baseball players compete for "monthly milestones and awards." The fronts feature a "cutout" player photo against a pinstriped background surrounded by a gray marble border.

	MINT	NRMT
COMPLETE SET (60)	150.00	70.00
COMPLETE SERIES 1 (30)	100.00	45.00
COMPLETE SERIES 2 (30)	50.00	22.0

COMMON CARD (R1-R60)	1.00	.45
COMP.AL HR EXCH.SET (10)	20.00	9.00
COMP.AL RBI EXCH.SET (10)	15.00	6.75
COMP.AL AVG.EXCH.SET (10)	15.00	6.75
COMP.NL HR EXCH.SET (10)	10.00	4.50
COMP.NL RBI EXCH.SET (10)	8.00	3.60
COMP.NL AVG.EXCH.SET (10)	10.00	4.50

*EXCHANGE CARDS: .6X TO 1.5X BASIC CARDS

☐ R1 Albert Belle W	2.50	1.10
☐ R2 Jay Buhner W	1.50	.70
☐ R3 Juan Gonzalez	5.00	2.20
☐ R4 Ken Griffey Jr.	10.00	4.50
☐ R5 Mark McGwire W	4.00	1.80
☐ R6 Rafael Palmeiro	1.50	.70
☐ R7 Tim Salmon	2.00	.90
☐ R8 Frank Thomas	8.00	3.60
☐ R9 Mo Vaughn W	2.50	1.10
☐ R10 Monthly HR Ldr Longshot W	1.00	.45
☐ R11 Albert Belle W	2.50	1.10
☐ R12 Jay Buhner	1.50	.70
☐ R13 Jim Edmonds	2.00	.90
☐ R14 Cecil Fielder	1.25	.55
☐ R15 Ken Griffey Jr.	10.00	4.50
☐ R16 Edgar Martinez	1.50	.70
☐ R17 Manny Ramirez	2.00	.90
☐ R18 Frank Thomas	8.00	3.60
☐ R19 Mo Vaughn W	2.50	1.10
☐ R20 Monthly RBI Ldr Longshot	1.00	.45
☐ R21 Roberto Alomar W	2.00	.90
☐ R22 Carlos Baerga	1.25	.55
☐ R23 Wade Boggs	2.00	.90
☐ R24 Ken Griffey Jr.	10.00	4.50
☐ R25 Chuck Knoblauch	2.00	.90
☐ R26 Kenny Lofton	2.50	1.10
☐ R27 Edgar Martinez	1.50	.70
☐ R28 Tim Salmon	2.00	.90
☐ R29 Frank Thomas	8.00	3.60
☐ R30 Monthly Hits Ldr Longshot W	1.00	.45
☐ R31 Dante Bichette	1.50	.70
☐ R32 Barry Bonds W	2.50	1.10
☐ R33 Ron Gant	1.25	.55
☐ R34 Chipper Jones	6.00	2.70
☐ R35 Fred McGriff	1.50	.70
☐ R36 Mike Piazza	6.00	2.70
☐ R37 Sammy Sosa	2.00	.90
☐ R38 Larry Walker	2.00	.90
☐ R39 Matt Williams	1.50	.70
☐ R40 Long Shot Card	1.00	.45
☐ R41 Jeff Bagwell W	4.00	1.80
☐ R42 Dante Bichette	1.25	.55
☐ R43 Barry Bonds W	2.50	1.10
☐ R44 Jeff Conine	1.25	.55
☐ R45 Andres Galarraga	2.00	.90
☐ R46 Mike Piazza	6.00	2.70
☐ R47 Reggie Sanders	1.00	.45
☐ R48 Sammy Sosa	2.00	.90
☐ R49 Matt Williams	1.50	.70
☐ R50 Long Shot Card	1.00	.45
☐ R51 Jeff Bagwell	4.00	1.80
☐ R52 Derek Bell	1.00	.45
☐ R53 Dante Bichette	1.25	.55
☐ R54 Craig Biggio	1.50	.70
☐ R55 Barry Bonds	2.50	1.10
☐ R56 Bret Boone	1.00	.45
☐ R57 Tony Gwynn	4.00	1.80
☐ R58 Barry Larkin	1.50	.70
☐ R59 Mike Piazza W	6.00	2.70
☐ R60 Long Shot Card	1.00	.45

1996 Upper Deck Ripken Collection

This 23 card set was issued across all the various Upper Deck brands. The cards were issued to commemorate Cal Ripken's career, which had been capped the previous season by the breaking of the consecutive game streak ong held by Lou Gehrig. The cards were inserted at the ollowing ratios: Cards 1-4 were in Collector Choice first eries packs at a rate of one in 12. Cards 5-8 were serted into Upper Deck series one packs at a rate of one in 24. Cards 9-12 were placed into second series Collector Choice packs at a rate of one in 12. Cards 13-17 were in second series Upper Deck packs at a rate of one in 24. And Cards 18-22 were in SP Packs at a rate of one in 45. The header card (#23) was also inserted into only Collector Choice packs.

	MINT	NRMT
COMPLETE SET (23)	120.00	55.00
COMP.COLC SER.1 (5)	15.00	6.75
COMP.UD SER.1 (4)	25.00	11.00
COMP.COLC SER.2 (4)	12.00	5.50
COMP.UD SER.2 (5)	25.00	11.00
COMPLETE SP SET (5)	50.00	22.00
COMMON COLC (1-4/9-12)	4.00	1.80
COMMON UD (5-8/13-17)	6.00	2.70
COMMON SP (18-22)	12.00	5.50

☐ 1 Cal Ripken COLC After playing in 2,131 consecutive games	4.00	1.80
☐ 2 Cal Ripken COLC Barry Bonds 1995 All-Star Game	4.00	1.80
☐ 3 Cal Ripken COLC 300th home run	4.00	1.80
☐ 4 Cal Ripken COLC Chasing Pop-up 1994	4.00	1.80
☐ 5 Cal Ripken UD Running to first 1995	6.00	2.70
☐ 6 Cal Ripken UD Brian McRae sliding into second 1992	6.00	2.70
☐ 7 Cal Ripken UD 1992 Roberto Clemente Award	6.00	2.70
☐ 8 Cal Ripken UD Batting pose 1991	6.00	2.70
☐ 9 Cal Ripken COLC Batting follow-through 1991	4.00	1.80
☐ 10 Cal Ripken COLC 1991 1st Gold Glove	4.00	1.80
☐ 11 Cal Ripken COLC Midway through swing 1991	4.00	1.80
☐ 12 Cal Ripken COLC Fielding and throwing Ball 1990	4.00	1.80
☐ 13 Cal Ripken UD Black uniform top in field 1990	6.00	2.70
☐ 14 Cal Ripken UD Batting follow-through 1987	6.00	2.70
☐ 15 Cal Ripken UD In Backswing 1986	6.00	2.70
☐ 16 Cal Ripken UD Midway through swing 1984	6.00	2.70
☐ 17 Cal Ripken UD Ball about to enter glove 1983	6.00	2.70
☐ 18 Cal Ripken SP Throwing 1983	12.00	5.50
☐ 19 Cal Ripken SP Batting, Orange Uniform 1983	12.00	5.50
☐ 20 Cal Ripken SP Batting follow-through 1982	12.00	5.50
☐ 21 Cal Ripken SP Fielding at third Mark Belanger in background 1981	12.00	5.50
☐ 22 Cal Ripken SP Eddie Murray 1981	12.00	5.50
☐ NNO Cal Ripken Header COLC	4.00	1.80

1996 Upper Deck Run Producers

This 20 card set was randomly inserted into series two packs at a rate of one every 71 packs. The cards are thermographically printed, which gives the card a rubber surface texture. The cards are double die-cut and are foil stamped. These cards are designed to show off the technology of the Upper Deck cards.

	MINT	NRMT
COMPLETE SET (20)	200.00	90.00
COMMON CARD (RP1-RP20)	4.00	1.80

☐ RP1 Albert Belle	10.00	4.50
☐ RP2 Dante Bichette	4.00	1.80
☐ RP3 Barry Bonds	10.00	4.50
☐ RP4 Jay Buhner	6.00	2.70
☐ RP5 Jose Canseco	6.00	2.70
☐ RP6 Juan Gonzalez	20.00	9.00
☐ RP7 Ken Griffey Jr.	40.00	18.00
☐ RP8 Tony Gwynn	20.00	9.00
☐ RP9 Kenny Lofton	10.00	4.50
☐ RP10 Edgar Martinez	6.00	2.70
☐ RP11 Fred McGriff	6.00	2.70
☐ RP12 Mark McGwire	15.00	6.75
☐ RP13 Rafael Palmeiro	6.00	2.70
☐ RP14 Mike Piazza	25.00	11.00
☐ RP15 Manny Ramirez	10.00	4.50
☐ RP16 Tim Salmon	8.00	3.60
☐ RP17 Sammy Sosa	8.00	3.60
☐ RP18 Frank Thomas	30.00	13.50
☐ RP19 Mo Vaughn	10.00	4.50
☐ RP20 Matt Williams	6.00	2.70

1996 Upper Deck All-Stars

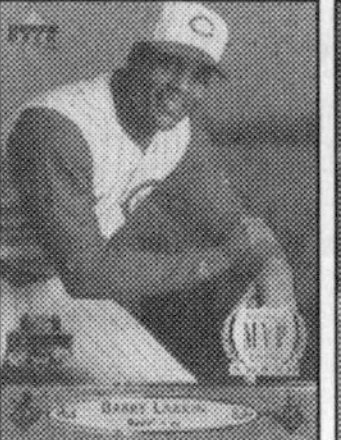

This 18-card set measures approximately 3 1/2" by 5" with a suggested retail price of $19.95 a set. The fronts feature borderless color player photos and are foil stamped with the official 1996 Major League Baseball All-Star game logo. The backs carry another player photo with player information and statistics. The cards are checklisted below in alphabetical order.

	MINT	NRMT
COMPLETE SET (18)	20.00	9.00
COMMON CARD (1-18)	.25	.11

☐ 1 Roberto Alomar	1.00	.45
☐ 2 Sandy Alomar Jr.	.25	.11
☐ 3 Jeff Bagwell	2.00	.90
☐ 4 Albert Belle	1.50	.70
☐ 5 Dante Bichette	.50	.23
☐ 6 Craig Biggio	.75	.35
☐ 7 Wade Boggs	1.00	.45
☐ 8 Barry Bonds	1.00	.45
☐ 9 Ken Griffey Jr.	5.00	2.20
☐ 10 Tony Gwynn	2.00	.90
☐ 11 Barry Larkin	.75	.35
☐ 12 Kenny Lofton	1.00	.45
☐ 13 Charles Nagy	.50	.23
☐ 14 Mike Piazza	3.00	1.35
☐ 15 Cal Ripken Jr.	4.00	1.80
☐ 16 John Smoltz	.50	.23
☐ 17 Frank Thomas	4.00	1.80
☐ 18 Matt Williams	.75	.35

1996 Upper Deck Ripken Collection Jumbos

With a suggested retail price of $19.95, cards from thi 22-card boxed set measures approximately 3 1/2" by 5 and features color borderless photos of Cal Ripken J with a gold foil facsimile autograph. The cards parallel th standard Ripken Collection inserted into various 199 Upper Deck Baseball products. The backs carr information about the player.

	MINT	NRM
COMPLETE SET (22)	20.00	9.0
COMMON CARD (1-22)	1.00	.4

☐ 1 Cal Ripken COLC 2.00 .90
after playing in 2131 consecutive games
☐ 2 Cal Ripken COLC 1.00 .45
Barry Bonds
1995 All-Star Game
☐ 3 Cal Ripken COLC 1.00 .45
300th home run
☐ 4 Cal Ripken COLC 1.00 .45
Chasing Pop-up
1994
☐ 5 Cal Ripken UD 1.00 .45
Running to first
1995
☐ 6 Cal Ripken UD 1.00 .45
Brian McRae sliding into second
1992
☐ 7 Cal Ripken UD 1.00 .45
1992 Roberto Clemente Award
☐ 8 Cal Ripken UD 1.00 .45
Batting pose
1991
☐ 9 Cal Ripken COLC 1.00 .45
Batting follow through
1991
☐ 10 Cal Ripken COLC 1.00 .45
1991 1st Gold Glove
☐ 11 Cal Ripken COLC 1.00 .45
Midway through swing
1991
☐ 12 Cal Ripken COLC 1.00 .45
Fielding and throwing ball
1990
☐ 13 Cal Ripken UD 1.00 .45
Black uniform top in field
1990
☐ 14 Cal Ripken UD 1.00 .45
Batting follow through
1987
☐ 15 Cal Ripken UD 1.00 .45
in Backswing
1986
☐ 16 Cal Ripken UD 1.00 .45
Midway through swing
1984
☐ 17 Cal Ripken UD 1.00 .45
Ball about to enter glove
1983
☐ 18 Cal Ripken SP 1.00 .45
Throwing
1983
☐ 19 Cal Ripken SP 1.00 .45
Batting. Orange uniform
1983
☐ 20 Cal Ripken SP 1.00 .45
Batting follow-through
1982
☐ 21 Cal Ripken SP 1.00 .45
Fielding at third
Mark Belanger in background
1981
☐ 22 Cal Ripken SP 1.00 .45
Eddie Murray
1981

1997 Upper Deck

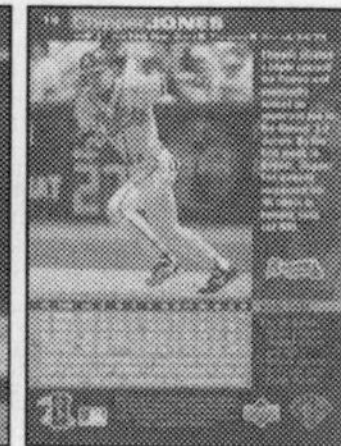

e 1997 Upper Deck set was issued in two series (series e 1-240, series two 271-520). The 12-card packs ailed for $2.49 each. Many cards have dates on the nt to identify when, and when possible, what significant ent is pictured. The backs include a player photo, stats d a brief blurb to go with vital statistics. Subsets ude Jackie Robinson Tribute (1-9), Strike Force (64-, Defensive Gems (136-153), Global Impact (181-207), ason Highlight Checklists (214-222/316-324), Star okies (223-240/271-288), Capture the Flag (370-387), ffey's Hot List (415-424) and Diamond Debuts (470-). It's critical to note that the Griffey's Hot List subset ds (in an unannounced move by the manufacturer) re shortprinted (about 1:7 packs) in relation to other ds in the series two set. The comparatively low print run on these cards created a dramatic surge in demand amongst set collectors and the cards soared in value on the secondary market. A 30-card first series Update set (numbered 241-270) was available to collectors that mailed in 10 series one wrappers along with $3 for postage and handling. The Series One Update set is composed primarily of 1996 post-season highlights. An additional 30-card series two Trade set (numbered 521-550) was also released around the end of the season. It too was available to collectors that mailed in ten series two wrappers along with $3 for postage and handling. The Series Two Trade set is composed primarily of traded players pictured in their new uniforms and a dynamic selection of rookies and prospects highlighted by the inclusion of Jose Cruz Jr. and Hideki Irabu.

	MINT	NRMT
COMP.MASTER SET (550)	185.00	85.00
COMPLETE SET (490)	120.00	55.00
COMPLETE SERIES 1 (240)	30.00	13.50
COMPLETE SERIES 2 (250)	90.00	40.00
COMP.SER.2 w/o GHL (240)	15.00	6.75
COMMON (1-240/271-520)	.15	.07
COMP.UPDATE SET (30)	45.00	20.00
COMMON UPDATE (241-270)	.50	.23
COMP.TRADE SET (30)	20.00	9.00
COMMON TRADE (521-550)	.25	.11

☐ 1 Jackie Robinson .50 .23
The Beginnings
☐ 2 Jackie Robinson .50 .23
Breaking the Barrier
☐ 3 Jackie Robinson .50 .23
The MVP Season, 1949
☐ 4 Jackie Robinson .50 .23
1951 season
☐ 5 Jackie Robinson .50 .23
1952 and 1953 seasons
☐ 6 Jackie Robinson .50 .23
1954 season
☐ 7 Jackie Robinson .50 .23
1955 season
☐ 8 Jackie Robinson .50 .23
1956 season
☐ 9 Jackie Robinson .50 .23
Hall of Fame
☐ 10 Chipper Jones 2.00 .90
☐ 11 Marquis Grissom .30 .14
☐ 12 Jermaine Dye .15 .07
☐ 13 Mark Lemke .15 .07
☐ 14 Terrell Wade .15 .07
☐ 15 Fred McGriff .40 .18
☐ 16 Tom Glavine .40 .18
☐ 17 Mark Wohlers .15 .07
☐ 18 Randy Myers .15 .07
☐ 19 Roberto Alomar .60 .25
☐ 20 Cal Ripken 2.50 1.10
☐ 21 Rafael Palmeiro .40 .18
☐ 22 Mike Mussina .60 .25
☐ 23 Brady Anderson .40 .18
☐ 24 Jose Canseco .40 .18
☐ 25 Mo Vaughn .75 .35
☐ 26 Roger Clemens 1.25 .55
☐ 27 Tim Naehring .15 .07
☐ 28 Jeff Suppan .30 .14
☐ 29 Troy Percival .15 .07
☐ 30 Sammy Sosa .60 .25
☐ 31 Amaury Telemaco .15 .07
☐ 32 Rey Sanchez .15 .07
☐ 33 Scott Servais .15 .07
☐ 34 Steve Trachsel .15 .07
☐ 35 Mark Grace .40 .18
☐ 36 Wilson Alvarez .15 .07
☐ 37 Harold Baines .30 .14
☐ 38 Tony Phillips .15 .07
☐ 39 James Baldwin .15 .07
☐ 40 Frank Thomas UER 2.50 1.10
Bio information is Ken Griffey Jr.'s
☐ 41 Lyle Mouton .15 .07
☐ 42 Chris Snopek .15 .07
☐ 43 Hal Morris .15 .07
☐ 44 Eric Davis .15 .07
☐ 45 Barry Larkin .40 .18
☐ 46 Reggie Sanders .15 .07
☐ 47 Pete Schourek .15 .07
☐ 48 Lee Smith .30 .14
☐ 49 Charles Nagy .30 .14
☐ 50 Albert Belle .75 .35
☐ 51 Julio Franco .30 .14
☐ 52 Kenny Lofton .75 .35
☐ 53 Orel Hershiser .30 .14
☐ 54 Omar Vizquel .30 .14
☐ 55 Eric Young .15 .07
☐ 56 Curtis Leskanic .15 .07
☐ 57 Quinton McCracken .15 .07
☐ 58 Kevin Ritz .15 .07
☐ 59 Walt Weiss .15 .07
☐ 60 Dante Bichette .40 .18
☐ 61 Mark Lewis .15 .07
☐ 62 Tony Clark .60 .25
☐ 63 Travis Fryman .30 .14
☐ 64 John Smoltz SF .30 .14
☐ 65 Greg Maddux SF .60 .25
☐ 66 Tom Glavine SF .30 .14
☐ 67 Mike Mussina SF .60 .25
☐ 68 Andy Pettitte SF .60 .25
☐ 69 Mariano Rivera SF .30 .14
☐ 70 Hideo Nomo SF .60 .25
☐ 71 Kevin Brown SF .30 .14
☐ 72 Randy Johnson SF .30 .14
☐ 73 Felipe Lira .15 .07
☐ 74 Kimera Bartee .15 .07
☐ 75 Alan Trammell .40 .18
☐ 76 Kevin Brown .30 .14
☐ 77 Edgar Renteria .30 .14
☐ 78 Al Leiter .15 .07
☐ 79 Charles Johnson .30 .14
☐ 80 Andre Dawson .40 .18
☐ 81 Billy Wagner .30 .14
☐ 82 Donne Wall .15 .07
☐ 83 Jeff Bagwell 1.25 .55
☐ 84 Keith Lockhart .15 .07
☐ 85 Jeff Montgomery .15 .07
☐ 86 Tom Goodwin .15 .07
☐ 87 Tim Belcher .15 .07
☐ 88 Mike Macfarlane .15 .07
☐ 89 Joe Randa .15 .07
☐ 90 Brett Butler .30 .14
☐ 91 Todd Worrell .30 .14
☐ 92 Todd Hollandsworth .30 .14
☐ 93 Ismael Valdes .30 .14
☐ 94 Hideo Nomo 1.50 .70
☐ 95 Mike Piazza 2.00 .90
☐ 96 Jeff Cirillo .15 .07
☐ 97 Ricky Bones .15 .07
☐ 98 Fernando Vina .15 .07
☐ 99 Ben McDonald .15 .07
☐ 100 John Jaha .15 .07
☐ 101 Mark Loretta .15 .07
☐ 102 Paul Molitor .60 .25
☐ 103 Rick Aguilera .30 .14
☐ 104 Marty Cordova .30 .14
☐ 105 Kirby Puckett 1.25 .55
☐ 106 Dan Naulty .15 .07
☐ 107 Frank Rodriguez .15 .07
☐ 108 Shane Andrews .15 .07
☐ 109 Henry Rodriguez .15 .07
☐ 110 Mark Grudzielanek .15 .07
☐ 111 Pedro Martinez .60 .25
☐ 112 Ugueth Urbina .30 .14
☐ 113 David Segui .15 .07
☐ 114 Rey Ordonez .15 .07
☐ 115 Bernard Gilkey .15 .07
☐ 116 Butch Huskey .30 .14
☐ 117 Paul Wilson .15 .07
☐ 118 Alex Ochoa .15 .07
☐ 119 John Franco .30 .14
☐ 120 Dwight Gooden .30 .14
☐ 121 Ruben Rivera .30 .14
☐ 122 Andy Pettitte .60 .25
☐ 123 Tino Martinez .60 .25
☐ 124 Bernie Williams .60 .25
☐ 125 Wade Boggs .60 .25
☐ 126 Paul O'Neill .30 .14
☐ 127 Scott Brosius .15 .07
☐ 128 Ernie Young .15 .07
☐ 129 Doug Johns .15 .07
☐ 130 Geronimo Berroa .15 .07
☐ 131 Jason Giambi .30 .14
☐ 132 John Wasdin .15 .07
☐ 133 Jim Eisenreich .30 .14
☐ 134 Ricky Otero .15 .07
☐ 135 Ricky Bottalico .15 .07
☐ 136 Mark Langston DG .15 .07
☐ 137 Greg Maddux DG .60 .25
☐ 138 Ivan Rodriguez DG .60 .25
☐ 139 Charles Johnson DG .15 .07
☐ 140 J.T. Snow DG .15 .07
☐ 141 Mark Grace DG .30 .14
☐ 142 Roberto Alomar DG .60 .25
☐ 143 Craig Biggio DG .40 .18
☐ 144 Ken Caminiti DG .60 .25
☐ 145 Matt Williams DG .30 .14
☐ 146 Omar Vizquel DG .30 .14
☐ 147 Cal Ripken DG 1.25 .55
☐ 148 Ozzie Smith DG .60 .25
☐ 149 Rey Ordonez DG .15 .07
☐ 150 Ken Griffey Jr. DG 1.50 .70
☐ 151 Devon White DG .15 .07
☐ 152 Barry Bonds DG .60 .25
☐ 153 Kenny Lofton DG .60 .25
☐ 154 Mickey Morandini .15 .07
☐ 155 Gregg Jefferies .15 .07
☐ 156 Curt Schilling .30 .14

☐ 157 Jason Kendall .30 .14
☐ 158 Francisco Cordova .15 .07
☐ 159 Dennis Eckersley .40 .18
☐ 160 Ron Gant .30 .14
☐ 161 Ozzie Smith .75 .35
☐ 162 Brian Jordan .30 .14
☐ 163 John Mabry .15 .07
☐ 164 Andy Ashby .15 .07
☐ 165 Steve Finley .30 .14
☐ 166 Fernando Valenzuela .30 .14
☐ 167 Archi Cianfrocco .15 .07
☐ 168 Wally Joyner .15 .07
☐ 169 Greg Vaughn .15 .07
☐ 170 Barry Bonds .75 .35
☐ 171 William VanLandingham .15 .07
☐ 172 Marvin Benard .15 .07
☐ 173 Rich Aurilia .15 .07
☐ 174 Jay Canizaro .15 .07
☐ 175 Ken Griffey Jr. 3.00 1.35
☐ 176 Bob Wells .15 .07
☐ 177 Jay Buhner .40 .18
☐ 178 Sterling Hitchcock .15 .07
☐ 179 Edgar Martinez .40 .18
☐ 180 Rusty Greer .30 .14
☐ 181 Dave Nilsson GI .15 .07
☐ 182 Larry Walker GI .60 .25
☐ 183 Edgar Renteria GI .30 .14
☐ 184 Rey Ordonez GI .15 .07
☐ 185 Rafael Palmeiro GI .40 .18
☐ 186 Osvaldo Fernandez GI .15 .07
☐ 187 Raul Mondesi GI .40 .18
☐ 188 Manny Ramirez GI .60 .25
☐ 189 Sammy Sosa GI .60 .25
☐ 190 Robert Eenhoorn GI .15 .07
☐ 191 Devon White GI .15 .07
☐ 192 Hideo Nomo GI .60 .25
☐ 193 Mac Suzuki GI .30 .14
☐ 194 Chan Ho Park GI .60 .25
☐ 195 Fernando Valenzuela GI .30 .14
☐ 196 Andruw Jones GI .60 .25
☐ 197 Vinny Castilla GI .30 .14
☐ 198 Dennis Martinez GI .30 .14
☐ 199 Ruben Rivera GI .30 .14
☐ 200 Juan Gonzalez GI .60 .25
☐ 201 Roberto Alomar GI .60 .25
☐ 202 Edgar Martinez GI .40 .18
☐ 203 Ivan Rodriguez GI .60 .25
☐ 204 Carlos Delgado GI .30 .14
☐ 205 Andres Galarraga GI .60 .25
☐ 206 Ozzie Guillen GI .15 .07
☐ 207 Midre Cummings GI .15 .07
☐ 208 Roger Pavlik .15 .07
☐ 209 Darren Oliver .15 .07
☐ 210 Dean Palmer .15 .07
☐ 211 Ivan Rodriguez .75 .35
☐ 212 Otis Nixon .15 .07
☐ 213 Pat Hentgen .30 .14
☐ 214 Ozzie Smith .60 .25
Andre Dawson
Kirby Puckett
HL/CL (1-27)
☐ 215 Barry Bonds .60 .25
Gary Sheffield
Brady Anderson
HL/CL (28-54)
☐ 216 Ken Caminiti HL/CL .60 .25
☐ 217 John Smoltz HL/CL .15 .07
☐ 218 Eric Young HL/CL .15 .07
☐ 219 Juan Gonzalez HL/CL .60 .25
☐ 220 Eddie Murray HL/CL .60 .25
☐ 221 Tommy Lasorda HL/CL .60 .25
☐ 222 Paul Molitor HL/CL .60 .25
☐ 223 Luis Castillo .40 .18
☐ 224 Justin Thompson .30 .14
☐ 225 Rocky Coppinger .30 .14
☐ 226 Jermaine Allensworth .15 .07
☐ 227 Jeff D'Amico .30 .14
☐ 228 Jamey Wright .30 .14
☐ 229 Scott Rolen 1.50 .70
☐ 230 Darin Erstad 1.00 .45
☐ 231 Marty Janzen .15 .07
☐ 232 Jacob Cruz .15 .07
☐ 233 Raul Ibanez .15 .07
☐ 234 Nomar Garciaparra 2.00 .90
☐ 235 Todd Walker .15 .07
☐ 236 Brian Giles .15 .07
☐ 237 Matt Beech .15 .07
☐ 238 Mike Cameron .30 .14
☐ 239 Jose Paniagua .15 .07
☐ 240 Andruw Jones 1.50 .70
☐ 241 Brant Brown UPD .50 .23
☐ 242 Robin Jennings UPD .50 .23
☐ 243 Willie Adams UPD .50 .23
☐ 244 Ken Caminiti UPD 2.00 .90
☐ 245 Brian Jordan UPD 1.00 .45
☐ 246 Chipper Jones UPD 6.00 2.70
☐ 247 Juan Gonzalez UPD 5.00 2.20
☐ 248 Bernie Williams UPD 2.00 .90
☐ 249 Roberto Alomar UPD 2.00 .90
☐ 250 Bernie Williams UPD 2.00 .90
☐ 251 David Wells UPD .50 .23
☐ 252 Cecil Fielder UPD 1.00 .45
☐ 253 Darryl Strawberry UPD 1.00 .45
☐ 254 Andy Pettitte UPD 2.00 .90
☐ 255 Javier Lopez UPD 1.00 .45
☐ 256 Gary Gaetti UPD .50 .23
☐ 257 Ron Gant UPD 1.00 .45
☐ 258 Brian Jordan UPD 1.00 .45
☐ 259 John Smoltz UPD 1.00 .45
☐ 260 Greg Maddux UPD 6.00 2.70
☐ 261 Tom Glavine UPD 1.00 .45
☐ 262 Andruw Jones UPD 5.00 2.20
☐ 263 Greg Maddux UPD 6.00 2.70
☐ 264 David Cone UPD 1.00 .45
☐ 265 Jim Leyritz UPD .50 .23
☐ 266 Andy Pettitte UPD 2.00 .90
☐ 267 John Wetteland UPD 1.00 .45
☐ 268 Dario Veras UPD .50 .23
☐ 269 Neifi Perez UPD 1.00 .45
☐ 270 Bill Mueller UPD .50 .23
☐ 271 Vladimir Guerrero 1.25 .55
☐ 272 Dmitri Young .15 .07
☐ 273 Nerio Rodriguez .30 .14
☐ 274 Kevin Orie .30 .14
☐ 275 Felipe Crespo .15 .07
☐ 276 Danny Graves .15 .07
☐ 277 Rod Myers .15 .07
☐ 278 Felix Heredia .30 .14
☐ 279 Ralph Milliard .15 .07
☐ 280 Greg Norton .15 .07
☐ 281 Derek Wallace .15 .07
☐ 282 Trot Nixon .15 .07
☐ 283 Bobby Chouinard .15 .07
☐ 284 Jay Witasick .15 .07
☐ 285 Travis Miller .15 .07
☐ 286 Brian Bevil .15 .07
☐ 287 Bobby Estalella .30 .14
☐ 288 Steve Soderstrom .15 .07
☐ 289 Mark Langston .15 .07
☐ 290 Tim Salmon .60 .25
☐ 291 Jim Edmonds .60 .25
☐ 292 Garret Anderson .30 .14
☐ 293 George Arias .15 .07
☐ 294 Gary DiSarcina .15 .07
☐ 295 Chuck Finley .15 .07
☐ 296 Todd Greene .30 .14
☐ 297 Randy Velarde .15 .07
☐ 298 David Justice .60 .25
☐ 299 Ryan Klesko .40 .18
☐ 300 John Smoltz .30 .14
☐ 301 Javier Lopez .30 .14
☐ 302 Greg Maddux 2.00 .90
☐ 303 Denny Neagle .30 .14
☐ 304 B.J. Surhoff .30 .14
☐ 305 Chris Hoiles .15 .07
☐ 306 Eric Davis .30 .14
☐ 307 Scott Erickson .30 .14
☐ 308 Mike Bordick .15 .07
☐ 309 John Valentin .15 .07
☐ 310 Heathcliff Slocumb .15 .07
☐ 311 Tom Gordon .15 .07
☐ 312 Mike Stanley .15 .07
☐ 313 Reggie Jefferson .30 .14
☐ 314 Darren Bragg .15 .07
☐ 315 Troy O'Leary .15 .07
☐ 316 John Mabry SH CL .15 .07
☐ 317 Mark Whiten SH CL .15 .07
☐ 318 Edgar Martinez SH CL .40 .18
☐ 319 Alex Rodriguez SH CL 1.25 .55
☐ 320 Mark McGwire SH CL .60 .25
☐ 321 Hideo Nomo SH CL .60 .25
☐ 322 Todd Hundley SH CL .30 .14
☐ 323 Barry Bonds SH CL .60 .25
☐ 324 Andruw Jones SH CL .60 .25
☐ 325 Ryne Sandberg .75 .35
☐ 326 Brian McRae .15 .07
☐ 327 Frank Castillo .15 .07
☐ 328 Shawon Dunston .15 .07
☐ 329 Ray Durham .15 .07
☐ 330 Robin Ventura .30 .14
☐ 331 Ozzie Guillen .15 .07
☐ 332 Roberto Hernandez .15 .07
☐ 333 Albert Belle .75 .35
☐ 334 Dave Martinez .15 .07
☐ 335 Willie Greene .30 .14
☐ 336 Jeff Brantley .15 .07
☐ 337 Kevin Jarvis .15 .07
☐ 338 John Smiley .15 .07
☐ 339 Eddie Taubensee .15 .07
☐ 340 Bret Boone .15 .07
☐ 341 Kevin Seitzer .15 .07
☐ 342 Jack McDowell .15 .07
☐ 343 Sandy Alomar Jr. .30 .14
☐ 344 Chad Curtis .15 .07
☐ 345 Manny Ramirez .60 .25
☐ 346 Chad Ogea .15 .07
☐ 347 Jim Thome .60 .25
☐ 348 Mark Thompson .15 .07
☐ 349 Ellis Burks .15 .07
☐ 350 Andres Galarraga .60 .25
☐ 351 Vinny Castilla .30 .14
☐ 352 Kirt Manwaring .15 .07
☐ 353 Larry Walker .60 .25
☐ 354 Omar Olivares .15 .07
☐ 355 Bobby Higginson .30 .14
☐ 356 Melvin Nieves .15 .07
☐ 357 Brian Johnson .15 .07
☐ 358 Devon White .15 .07
☐ 359 Jeff Conine .15 .07
☐ 360 Gary Sheffield .60 .25
☐ 361 Robb Nen .15 .07
☐ 362 Mike Hampton .15
☐ 363 Bob Abreu .60
☐ 364 Luis Gonzalez .15
☐ 365 Derek Bell .15
☐ 366 Sean Berry .15
☐ 367 Craig Biggio .40
☐ 368 Darryl Kile .30
☐ 369 Shane Reynolds .15
☐ 370 Jeff Bagwell CF .60
☐ 371 Ron Gant CF .15
☐ 372 Andy Benes CF .15
☐ 373 Gary Gaetti CF .15
☐ 374 Ramon Martinez CF .15
☐ 375 Raul Mondesi CF .40
☐ 376 Steve Finley CF .15
☐ 377 Ken Caminiti CF .60
☐ 378 Tony Gwynn CF .60
☐ 379 Dario Veras .40
☐ 380 Andy Pettitte CF .60
☐ 381 Ruben Rivera CF .15
☐ 382 David Cone CF .30
☐ 383 Roberto Alomar CF .60
☐ 384 Edgar Martinez CF .40
☐ 385 Ken Griffey Jr. CF 1.50
☐ 386 Mark McGwire CF .60
☐ 387 Rusty Greer CF .30
☐ 388 Jose Rosado .15
☐ 389 Kevin Appier .30
☐ 390 Johnny Damon .15
☐ 391 Jose Offerman .15
☐ 392 Michael Tucker .15
☐ 393 Craig Paquette .15
☐ 394 Bip Roberts .15
☐ 395 Ramon Martinez .15
☐ 396 Greg Gagne .15
☐ 397 Chan Ho Park .60
☐ 398 Karim Garcia .30
☐ 399 Wilton Guerrero .15
☐ 400 Eric Karros .30
☐ 401 Raul Mondesi .40
☐ 402 Matt Mieske .15
☐ 403 Mike Fetters .15
☐ 404 Dave Nilsson .15
☐ 405 Jose Valentin .15
☐ 406 Scott Karl .15
☐ 407 Marc Newfield .15
☐ 408 Cal Eldred .15
☐ 409 Rich Becker .15
☐ 410 Terry Steinbach .15
☐ 411 Chuck Knoblauch .60
☐ 412 Pat Meares .15
☐ 413 Brad Radke .15
☐ 414 Kirby Puckett UER 1.25
Card numbered 415
☐ 415 Andruw Jones GHL SP 6.00
☐ 416 Chipper Jones GHL SP 8.00
☐ 417 Mo Vaughn GHL SP 3.00
☐ 418 Frank Thomas GHL SP 12.00
☐ 419 Albert Belle GHL SP 3.00
☐ 420 Mark McGwire GHL SP 5.00
☐ 421 Derek Jeter GHL SP 8.00
☐ 422 Alex Rodriguez GHL SP 10.00
☐ 423 Juan Gonzalez GHL SP 6.00
☐ 424 Ken Griffey Jr. GHL SP 15.00
☐ 425 Rondell White .30
☐ 426 Darrin Fletcher .15
☐ 427 Cliff Floyd .15
☐ 428 Mike Lansing .15
☐ 429 F.P. Santangelo .15
☐ 430 Todd Hundley .30
☐ 431 Mark Clark .15
☐ 432 Pete Harnisch .15
☐ 433 Jason Isringhausen .15
☐ 434 Bobby Jones .15
☐ 435 Lance Johnson .15
☐ 436 Carlos Baerga .15
☐ 437 Mariano Duncan .15
☐ 438 David Cone .30
☐ 439 Mariano Rivera .30
☐ 440 Derek Jeter 2.00

☐ 441 Joe Girardi	.15	.07
☐ 442 Charlie Hayes	.15	.07
☐ 443 Tim Raines	.15	.07
☐ 444 Darryl Strawberry	.30	.14
☐ 445 Cecil Fielder	.30	.14
☐ 446 Ariel Prieto	.15	.07
☐ 447 Tony Batista	.15	.07
☐ 448 Brent Gates	.15	.07
☐ 449 Scott Spiezio	.15	.07
☐ 450 Mark McGwire	1.25	.55
☐ 451 Don Wengert	.15	.07
☐ 452 Mike Lieberthal	.15	.07
☐ 453 Lenny Dykstra	.30	.14
☐ 455 Darren Daulton	.30	.14
☐ 456 Kevin Stocker	.15	.07
☐ 457 Trey Beamon	.15	.07
☐ 458 Midre Cummings	.15	.07
☐ 459 Mark Johnson	.15	.07
☐ 460 Al Martin	.15	.07
☐ 461 Kevin Elster	.15	.07
☐ 462 Jon Lieber	.15	.07
☐ 463 Jason Schmidt	.15	.07
☐ 464 Paul Wagner	.15	.07
☐ 465 Andy Benes	.15	.07
☐ 466 Alan Benes	.15	.07
☐ 467 Royce Clayton	.15	.07
☐ 468 Gary Gaetti	.30	.14
☐ 469 Curt Lyons	.30	.14
☐ 470 Eugene Kingsale DD	.15	.07
☐ 471 Damian Jackson DD	.15	.07
☐ 472 Wendell Magee DD	.15	.07
☐ 473 Kevin L. Brown DD	.15	.07
☐ 474 Raul Casanova DD	.15	.07
☐ 475 Ramiro Mendoza	.40	.18
☐ 476 Todd Dunn DD	.15	.07
☐ 477 Chad Mottola DD	.15	.07
☐ 478 Andy Larkin DD	.15	.07
☐ 479 Jaime Bluma DD	.15	.07
☐ 480 Mac Suzuki DD	.30	.14
☐ 481 Brian Banks DD	.15	.07
☐ 482 Desi Wilson DD	.15	.07
☐ 483 Einar Diaz DD	.15	.07
☐ 484 Tom Pagnozzi	.15	.07
☐ 485 Ray Lankford	.15	.07
☐ 486 Todd Stottlemyre	.15	.07
☐ 487 Donovan Osborne	.15	.07
☐ 488 Trevor Hoffman	.15	.07
☐ 489 Chris Gomez	.15	.07
☐ 490 Ken Caminiti	.60	.25
☐ 491 John Flaherty	.15	.07
☐ 492 Tony Gwynn	1.50	.70
☐ 493 Joey Hamilton	.15	.07
☐ 494 Rickey Henderson	.40	.18
☐ 495 Glenallen Hill	.15	.07
☐ 496 Rod Beck	.15	.07
☐ 497 Osvaldo Fernandez	.15	.07
☐ 498 Rick Wilkins	.15	.07
☐ 499 Joey Cora	.30	.14
☐ 500 Alex Rodriguez	2.50	1.10
☐ 501 Randy Johnson	.60	.25
☐ 502 Paul Sorrento	.15	.07
☐ 503 Dan Wilson	.15	.07
☐ 504 Jamie Moyer	.15	.07
☐ 505 Will Clark	.40	.18
☐ 506 Mickey Tettleton	.15	.07
☐ 507 John Burkett	.15	.07
☐ 508 Ken Hill	.15	.07
☐ 509 Mark McLemore	.15	.07
☐ 510 Juan Gonzalez	1.50	.70
☐ 511 Bobby Witt	.15	.07
☐ 512 Carlos Delgado	.15	.07
☐ 513 Alex Gonzalez	.15	.07
☐ 514 Shawn Green	.15	.07
☐ 515 Joe Carter	.30	.14
☐ 516 Juan Guzman	.15	.07
☐ 517 Charlie O'Brien	.15	.07
☐ 518 Ed Sprague	.15	.07
☐ 519 Mike Timlin	.15	.07
☐ 520 Roger Clemens	1.25	.55
☐ 521 Eddie Murray TRADE	1.00	.45
☐ 522 Jason Dickson TRADE	.50	.23
☐ 523 Jim Leyritz TRADE	.25	.11
☐ 524 Michael Tucker TRADE	.50	.23
☐ 525 Kenny Lofton TRADE	1.25	.55
☐ 526 Jimmy Key TRADE	.50	.23
☐ 527 Mel Rojas TRADE	.25	.11
☐ 528 Deion Sanders TRADE	1.00	.45
☐ 529 Bartolo Colon TRADE	.50	.23
☐ 530 Matt Williams TRADE	.75	.35
☐ 531 Marquis Grissom TRADE	.50	.23
☐ 532 David Justice TRADE	1.00	.45
☐ 533 Bubba Trammell TRADE	1.00	.45
☐ 534 Moises Alou TRADE	.50	.23
☐ 535 Bobby Bonilla TRADE	.50	.23
☐ 536 Alex Fernandez TRADE	.50	.23
☐ 537 Jay Bell TRADE	.50	.23
☐ 538 Chili Davis TRADE	.50	.23
☐ 539 Jeff King TRADE	.25	.11
☐ 540 Todd Zeile TRADE	.25	.11
☐ 541 John Olerud TRADE	.50	.23
☐ 542 Jose Guillen TRADE	1.25	.55
☐ 543 Derrek Lee TRADE	.50	.23
☐ 544 Dante Powell TRADE	.25	.11
☐ 545 J.T. Snow TRADE	.50	.23
☐ 546 Jeff Kent TRADE	.25	.11
☐ 547 Jose Cruz Jr. TRADE	10.00	4.50
☐ 548 John Wetteland TRADE	.50	.23
☐ 549 Orlando Merced TRADE	.25	.11
☐ 550 Hideki Irabu TRADE	1.25	.55

1997 Upper Deck Amazing Greats

Randomly inserted in all first series packs at a rate of one in 138, this 20-card set features a horizontal design along with two player photos on the front. The cards feature translucent player images against a real wood grain stock.

	MINT	NRMT
COMPLETE SET (20)	600.00	275.00
COMMON CARD (AG1-AG20)	10.00	4.50
☐ AG1 Ken Griffey Jr.	80.00	36.00
☐ AG2 Roberto Alomar	15.00	6.75
☐ AG3 Alex Rodriguez	50.00	22.00
☐ AG4 Paul Molitor	15.00	6.75
☐ AG5 Chipper Jones	50.00	22.00
☐ AG6 Tony Gwynn	40.00	18.00
☐ AG7 Kenny Lofton	20.00	9.00
☐ AG8 Albert Belle	20.00	9.00
☐ AG9 Matt Williams	10.00	4.50
☐ AG10 Frank Thomas	60.00	27.00
☐ AG11 Greg Maddux	50.00	22.00
☐ AG12 Sammy Sosa	15.00	6.75
☐ AG13 Kirby Puckett	30.00	13.50
☐ AG14 Jeff Bagwell	30.00	13.50
☐ AG15 Cal Ripken	60.00	27.00
☐ AG16 Manny Ramirez	15.00	6.75
☐ AG17 Barry Bonds	20.00	9.00
☐ AG18 Mo Vaughn	20.00	9.00
☐ AG19 Eddie Murray	15.00	6.75
☐ AG20 Mike Piazza	50.00	22.00

1997 Upper Deck Blue Chip Prospects

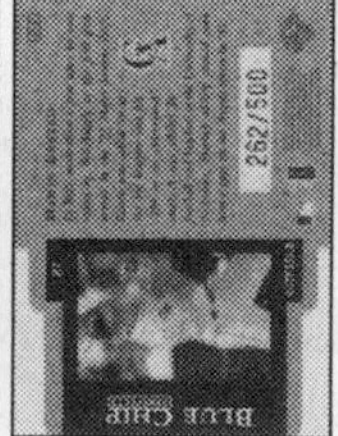

This rare 20-card set, randomly inserted into series two packs, features color photos of high expectation prospects who are likely to have a big impact on Major League Baseball. Only 500 of this crash numbered, limited edition set was produced.

	MINT	NRMT
COMPLETE SET (20)	500.00	220.00
COMMON CARD (BC1-BC20)	8.00	3.60
☐ BC1 Andruw Jones	60.00	27.00
☐ BC2 Derek Jeter	80.00	36.00
☐ BC3 Scott Rolen	60.00	27.00
☐ BC4 Manny Ramirez	25.00	11.00
☐ BC5 Todd Walker	10.00	4.50
☐ BC6 Rocky Coppinger	8.00	3.60
☐ BC7 Nomar Garciaparra	80.00	36.00
☐ BC8 Darin Erstad	40.00	18.00
☐ BC9 Jermaine Dye	8.00	3.60
☐ BC10 Vladimir Guerrero	50.00	22.00
☐ BC11 Edgar Renteria	10.00	4.50
☐ BC12 Bob Abreu	25.00	11.00
☐ BC13 Karim Garcia	10.00	4.50
☐ BC14 Jeff D'Amico	8.00	3.60
☐ BC15 Chipper Jones	80.00	36.00
☐ BC16 Todd Hollandsworth	10.00	4.50
☐ BC17 Andy Pettitte	25.00	11.00
☐ BC18 Ruben Rivera	10.00	4.50
☐ BC19 Jason Kendall	10.00	4.50
☐ BC20 Alex Rodriguez	80.00	36.00

1997 Upper Deck Game Jersey

Randomly inserted in all first series packs at a rate of one in 800, this 3-card set feaures swatches of real game-worn jerseys cut up and placed on the cards.

	MINT	NRMT
COMPLETE SET (3)	900.00	400.00
COMMON CARD (GJ1-GJ3)	80.00	36.00
☐ GJ1 Ken Griffey Jr.	600.00	275.00
☐ GJ2 Tony Gwynn	300.00	135.00
☐ GJ3 Rey Ordonez	80.00	36.00

1997 Upper Deck Hot Commodities

Randomly inserted in series two packs at a rate of one in 13, this 20-card set features color player images on a flame background in a black border. The backs carry a player head photo, statistics, and a commentary by ESPN sportscarster Dan Patrick.

	MINT	NRMT
COMPLETE SET (20)	120.00	55.00
COMMON CARD (HC1-HC20)	1.50	.70
☐ HC1 Alex Rodriguez	10.00	4.50
☐ HC2 Andruw Jones	8.00	3.60
☐ HC3 Derek Jeter	8.00	3.60
☐ HC4 Frank Thomas	10.00	4.50
☐ HC5 Ken Griffey Jr.	12.00	5.50
☐ HC6 Chipper Jones	8.00	3.60
☐ HC7 Juan Gonzalez	6.00	2.70
☐ HC8 Cal Ripken	10.00	4.50
☐ HC9 John Smoltz	1.50	.70
☐ HC10 Mark McGwire	5.00	2.20
☐ HC11 Barry Bonds	3.00	1.35
☐ HC12 Albert Belle	3.00	1.35
☐ HC13 Mike Piazza	8.00	3.60
☐ HC14 Manny Ramirez	2.50	1.10
☐ HC15 Mo Vaughn	3.00	1.35
☐ HC16 Tony Gwynn	6.00	2.70
☐ HC17 Vladimir Guerrero	6.00	2.70
☐ HC18 Hideo Nomo	6.00	2.70
☐ HC19 Greg Maddux	10.00	4.50
☐ HC20 Kirby Puckett	5.00	2.20

1997 Upper Deck Long Distance Connection

Randomly inserted in series two packs at a rate of one in 35, this 20-card set features color player images of some of the League's top power hitters on backgrounds utilizing

Light/FX technology. The backs carry the pictured player's statistics.

	MINT	NRMT
COMPLETE SET (20)	200.00	90.00
COMMON CARD (LD1-LD20)	8.00	3.60

☐ LD1 Mark McGwire	15.00	6.75
☐ LD2 Brady Anderson	8.00	3.60
☐ LD3 Ken Griffey Jr.	40.00	18.00
☐ LD4 Albert Belle	10.00	4.50
☐ LD5 Juan Gonzalez	20.00	9.00
☐ LD6 Andres Galarraga	8.00	3.60
☐ LD7 Jay Buhner	8.00	3.60
☐ LD8 Mo Vaughn	8.00	3.60
☐ LD9 Barry Bonds	8.00	3.60
☐ LD10 Gary Sheffield	8.00	3.60
☐ LD11 Todd Hundley	8.00	3.60
☐ LD12 Frank Thomas	30.00	13.50
☐ LD13 Sammy Sosa	8.00	3.60
☐ LD14 Rafael Palmeiro	8.00	3.60
☐ LD15 Alex Rodriguez	25.00	11.00
☐ LD16 Mike Piazza	25.00	11.00
☐ LD17 Ken Caminiti	8.00	3.60
☐ LD18 Chipper Jones	25.00	11.00
☐ LD19 Manny Ramirez	8.00	3.60
☐ LD20 Andruw Jones	15.00	6.75

1997 Upper Deck Memorable Moments

Cards from this set were distributed exclusively in 6-card retail Collector's Choice series one packs. Each pack contained one of ten different Memorable Moments inserts. The set features a selection of top stars captured in highlights of season's gone by. Each card features wave-like die cut top and bottom borders wth gold foil.

	MINT	NRMT
COMPLETE SET (20)	15.00	6.75
COMMON CARD (1-20)	.60	.25

☐ 1A Andruw Jones	2.00	.90
☐ 2A Chipper Jones	2.00	.90
☐ 2B Albert Belle	.75	.35
☐ 3A Cal Ripken	2.50	1.10
☐ 3B Derek Jeter	2.00	.90
☐ 4A Frank Thomas	2.50	1.10
☐ 4B Greg Maddux	2.00	.90
☐ 5A Manny Ramirez	.60	.25
☐ 5B Tony Gwynn	1.50	.70
☐ 6A Mike Piazza	2.00	.90
☐ 6B Ryne Sandberg	1.00	.45
☐ 7A Mark McGwire	1.25	.55
☐ 7B Juan Gonzalez	1.50	.70
☐ 8A Barry Bonds	.75	.35
☐ 8B Roger Clemens	1.00	.45
☐ 9A Ken Griffey Jr.	3.00	1.35
☐ 9B Jose Cruz Jr.	3.00	1.35
☐ 10A Alex Rodriguez	2.50	1.10
☐ 10B Mo Vaughn	.60	.25

1997 Upper Deck Power Package

Randomly inserted in all first series packs at a rate of one in 24, this 20-card set feaures some of the best longball hitters. The die cut cards feature some of baseball's

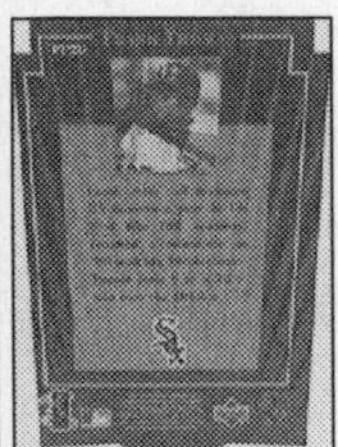

leading power hitters. Non-die cut jumbo (5 x 7) versions were distributed one per 1997 Series 1 Upper Deck retail Sam's box on the bottom of the box under the packs.

	MINT	NRMT
COMPLETE SET (20)	125.00	55.00
COMMON CARD (PP1-PP20)	3.00	1.35

*JUMBOS: .25X TO .5X BASIC POWER

☐ PP1 Ken Griffey Jr.	30.00	13.50
☐ PP2 Joe Carter	3.50	1.55
☐ PP3 Rafael Palmeiro	4.00	1.80
☐ PP4 Jay Buhner	4.00	1.80
☐ PP5 Sammy Sosa	6.00	2.70
☐ PP6 Fred McGriff	4.00	1.80
☐ PP7 Jeff Bagwell	12.00	5.50
☐ PP8 Albert Belle	8.00	3.60
☐ PP9 Matt Williams	4.00	1.80
☐ PP10 Mark McGwire	12.00	5.50
☐ PP11 Gary Sheffield	6.00	2.70
☐ PP12 Tim Salmon	6.00	2.70
☐ PP13 Ryan Klesko	4.00	1.80
☐ PP14 Manny Ramirez	6.00	2.70
☐ PP15 Mike Piazza	20.00	9.00
☐ PP16 Barry Bonds	8.00	3.60
☐ PP17 Mo Vaughn	8.00	3.60
☐ PP18 Jose Canseco	4.00	1.80
☐ PP19 Juan Gonzalez	15.00	6.75
☐ PP20 Frank Thomas	25.00	11.00

1997 Upper Deck Predictor

Randomly inserted in series two packs at a rate of one in five, this 30-card set featues a color player photo alongside a series of bats. The collector could activate the card by scratching off one of the bats to predict the performance of the pictured player during a single game. If the player matches or exceeds the predicted performance, the card could be mailed in with $2 to receive a Totally Virtual high-tech cel-card of the player pictured on the front. The backs carry the rules of the game. The deadline to redeem these cards was November 22nd, 1997.

	MINT	NRMT
COMPLETE SET (30)	30.00	13.50
COMMON CARD (1-30)	.50	.23

*SCRATCHED LOSER: .25X TO .5X UNSCRATCHED

☐ 1 Andruw Jones L	2.00	.90
☐ 2 Chipper Jones L	2.50	1.10
☐ 3 Greg Maddux W Complete Game Shutout	2.50	1.10
☐ 4 Fred McGriff W 4 Hits/2HR/3B	.50	.23
☐ 5 John Smoltz W Complete Game Shutout	.50	.23
☐ 6 Brady Anderson W Leadoff HR	.50	.23
☐ 7 Cal Ripken W Grand Slam	3.00	1.35
☐ 8 Mo Vaughn W 3HR/6RBI	1.00	.45
☐ 9 Sammy Sosa L	.50	.23
☐ 10 Albert Belle W Grand Slam/9th HR	1.00	.45
☐ 11 Frank Thomas L	3.00	1.35
☐ 12 Kenny Lofton W 5 Hits	1.00	.45
☐ 13 Jim Thome L	.75	.35
☐ 14 Dante Bichette W 6RBI's	.50	.23
☐ 15 Andres Galarraga L	.75	.35
☐ 16 Gary Sheffield L	.75	.35
☐ 17 Hideo Nomo W Base Hit	2.00	.90
☐ 18 Mike Piazza W Steal/9th HR	2.50	1.10
☐ 19 Derek Jeter W 2HR	2.50	1.10
☐ 20 Bernie Williams L	.75	.35
☐ 21 Mark McGwire W Grand Slam/4HR	1.50	.70
☐ 22 Ken Caminiti W 5RBI's	.50	.23
☐ 23 Tony Gwynn W 2 2B/3RBI	2.00	.90
☐ 24 Barry Bonds W 5RBI's	1.00	.45
☐ 25 Jay Buhner W 5RBI's	.50	.23
☐ 26 Ken Griffey Jr. W 3HR's	4.00	1.80
☐ 27 Alex Rodriguez W Cycle	2.50	1.10
☐ 28 Juan Gonzalez W 5RBI's/4 Hits	2.00	.90
☐ 29 Dean Palmer W 2HR's/5RBI's	.50	.23
☐ 30 Roger Clemens W Complete Game Shutout	1.50	.70

1997 Upper Deck Predictor Exchange

This 30-card set features color player photos printed on a totally virtual high-tech cel-card. The set could be obtained through a game promotion whose rules were printed on the backs of the Upper Deck Predictor cards. These cards have a totally different design from the regular Upper Deck predictor cards.

	MINT	NRMT
COMPLETE SET (30)	120.00	55.00
COMMON CARD (1-30)	2.00	.90

*STARS: 2X TO 4X BASIC PREDICTORS

1997 Upper Deck Rock Solid Foundation

Randomly inserted in all first series packs at a rate of one in seven, this 20-card set features players 25 and under who have made an impact in the majors. The fronts feature a player photo against a "silver" type background. The backs give player information as well as another player photo and are numbered with a "RS" prefix.

	MINT	NRMT
COMPLETE SET (20)	50.00	22.00
COMMON CARD (RS1-RS20)	1.00	.45

☐ RS1 Alex Rodriguez	15.00	6.75
☐ RS2 Rey Ordonez	1.00	.45
☐ RS3 Derek Jeter	10.00	4.50
☐ RS4 Darin Erstad	8.00	3.60
☐ RS5 Chipper Jones	10.00	4.50

	MINT	NRMT
☐ RS6 Johnny Damon	1.50	.70
☐ RS7 Ryan Klesko	2.00	.90
☐ RS8 Charles Johnson	1.50	.70
☐ RS9 Andy Pettitte	2.50	1.10
☐ RS10 Manny Ramirez	2.50	1.10
☐ RS11 Ivan Rodriguez	4.00	1.80
☐ RS12 Jason Kendall	1.50	.70
☐ RS13 Rondell White	1.50	.70
☐ RS14 Alex Ochoa	1.00	.45
☐ RS15 Javier Lopez	1.50	.70
☐ RS16 Pedro Martinez	2.50	1.10
☐ RS17 Carlos Delgado	1.50	.70
☐ RS18 Paul Wilson	1.00	.45
☐ RS19 Alan Benes	1.00	.45
☐ RS20 Raul Mondesi	2.00	.90

1997 Upper Deck Run Producers

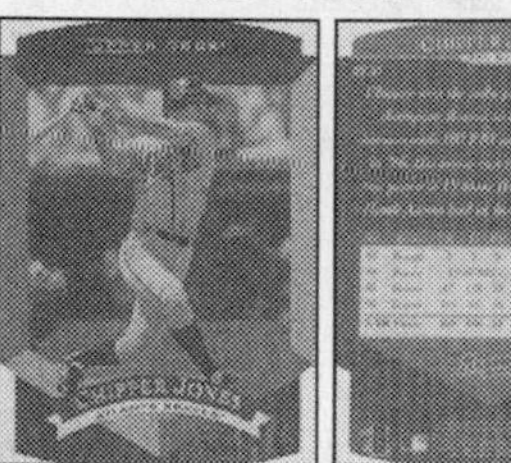

Randomly inserted in series two packs at a rate of one in 69, this 24-card set features color player images on die-cut cards that actually look and feel like home plate. The backs carry player information and career statistics.

	MINT	NRMT
COMPLETE SET (24)	350.00	160.00
COMMON CARD (RP1-RP24)	8.00	3.60
☐ RP1 Ken Griffey Jr.	60.00	27.00
☐ RP2 Barry Bonds	15.00	6.75
☐ RP3 Albert Belle	15.00	6.75
☐ RP4 Mark McGwire	25.00	11.00
☐ RP5 Frank Thomas	50.00	22.00
☐ RP6 Juan Gonzalez	30.00	13.50
☐ RP7 Brady Anderson	12.00	5.50
☐ RP8 Andres Galarraga	12.00	5.50
☐ RP9 Rafael Palmeiro	8.00	3.60
☐ RP10 Alex Rodriguez	40.00	18.00
☐ RP11 Jay Buhner	12.00	5.50
☐ RP12 Gary Sheffield	12.00	5.50
☐ RP13 Sammy Sosa	12.00	5.50
☐ RP14 Dante Bichette	12.00	5.50
☐ RP15 Mike Piazza	40.00	18.00
☐ RP16 Manny Ramirez	12.00	5.50
☐ RP17 Kenny Lofton	15.00	6.75
☐ RP18 Mo Vaughn	15.00	6.75
☐ RP19 Tim Salmon	12.00	5.50
☐ RP20 Chipper Jones	40.00	18.00
☐ RP21 Jim Thome	12.00	5.50
☐ RP22 Ken Caminiti	12.00	5.50
☐ RP23 Jeff Bagwell	25.00	11.00
☐ RP24 Paul Molitor	12.00	5.50

1997 Upper Deck Star Attractions

hese 20 cards were issued one per pack in special Upper eck Memorabilia Madness packs. The Memorabilia adness packs included various redemptions for signed 8 10 photos with the grand prize being a grouping of Ken riffey Jr. signed jersey, baseball and 8 by 10 photo. The cut cards feature the words "Star Attraction" on the top th the player and team identification on the sides. The cks have a photo and a brief blurb on the player. Cards -10 were inserted in Upper Deck packs while cards 1-20 were in Collectors Choice packs.

	MINT	NRMT
COMPLETE SET (20)	30.00	13.50
COMMON CARD (1-20)	.75	.35
☐ 1 Ken Griffey Jr.	4.00	1.80
☐ 2 Barry Bonds	1.00	.45
☐ 3 Jeff Bagwell	1.50	.70
☐ 4 Nomar Garciaparra	2.50	1.10
☐ 5 Tony Gwynn	2.00	.90
☐ 6 Roger Clemens	1.50	.70
☐ 7 Chipper Jones	2.50	1.10
☐ 8 Tino Martinez	.75	.35
☐ 9 Albert Belle	1.00	.45
☐ 10 Kenny Lofton	1.00	.45
☐ 11 Alex Rodriguez	2.50	1.10
☐ 12 Mark McGwire	1.50	.70
☐ 13 Cal Ripken Jr.	3.00	1.35
☐ 14 Larry Walker	.75	.35
☐ 15 Mike Piazza	2.50	1.10
☐ 16 Frank Thomas	3.00	1.35
☐ 17 Juan Gonzalez	2.00	.90
☐ 18 Greg Maddux	2.50	1.10
☐ 19 Jose Cruz Jr.	4.00	1.80
☐ 20 Mo Vaughn	1.00	.45

1997 Upper Deck Ticket To Stardom

Randomly inserted in all first series packs at a rate of one in 34, this 20-card set is designed in the form of a ticket and are designed to be matched. The horizontal fronts feature two player photos as well as using "light f/x technology and embossed player images.

	MINT	NRMT
COMPLETE SET (20)	120.00	55.00
COMMON CARD (TS1-TS20)	3.00	1.35
☐ TS1 Chipper Jones	25.00	11.00
☐ TS2 Jermaine Dye	3.00	1.35
☐ TS3 Rey Ordonez	4.00	1.80
☐ TS4 Alex Ochoa	3.00	1.35
☐ TS5 Derek Jeter	20.00	9.00
☐ TS6 Ruben Rivera	4.00	1.80
☐ TS7 Billy Wagner	5.00	2.20
☐ TS8 Jason Kendall	4.00	1.80
☐ TS9 Darin Erstad	12.00	5.50
☐ TS10 Alex Rodriguez	25.00	11.00
☐ TS11 Bob Abreu	8.00	3.60
☐ TS12 Richard Hidalgo	8.00	3.60
☐ TS13 Karim Garcia	4.00	1.80
☐ TS14 Andruw Jones	20.00	9.00
☐ TS15 Carlos Delgado	4.00	1.80
☐ TS16 Rocky Coppinger	3.00	1.35
☐ TS17 Jeff D'Amico	4.00	1.80
☐ TS18 Johnny Damon	3.00	1.35
☐ TS19 John Wasdin	3.00	1.35
☐ TS20 Manny Ramirez	8.00	3.60

1997 Upper Deck Award Winner Jumbos

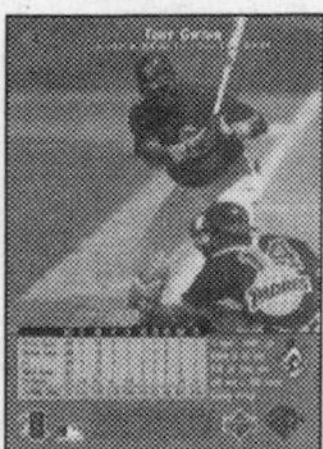

This 23-card set measures approximately 3 1/2" by 5" and features borderless color player photos with gold and silver foil highlights of both American and National League award winners. The backs carry another player photo and statistics with a sentence about winning his award. The set was issued through retail outlets and television promotions with a suggested retail set price of $19.95.

	MINT	NRMT
COMPLETE SET (23)	2.00	.90
COMMON CARD (1-23)	.50	.23
☐ 1 Alex Rodriguez American League Batting Leader	5.00	2.20
☐ 2 Tony Gwynn National League Batting Leader	3.00	1.35
☐ 3 Mark McGwire American League HR Leader	2.00	.90
☐ 4 Andres Galarraga National League HR Leader	1.50	.70
☐ 5 Albert Belle American League RBI Leader	1.50	.70
☐ 6 Andres Galarraga Nation League RBI Leader	1.50	.70
☐ 7 Kenny Lofton American League SB Leader	1.50	.70
☐ 8 Eric Young National League SB Leader	.50	.23
☐ 9 Andy Pettitte American League WIN Leader	1.50	.70
☐ 10 John Smoltz National League WIN Leader	.75	.35
☐ 11 Roger Clemens American League K Leader	2.00	.90
☐ 12 John Smoltz National League K Leader	.75	.35
☐ 13 Juan Guzman American League ERA Leader	.50	.23
☐ 14 Kevin Brown National League ERA Leader	.50	.23
☐ 15 John Wetteland American League SAVE Leader	.75	.35
☐ 16 Jeff Brantley National League SAVE Co-Leader	.50	.23
☐ 17 Todd Worrell National League SAVE Co-Leader	.75	.35
☐ 18 Derek Jeter American League ROY Leader	3.00	1.35
☐ 19 Todd Hollandsworth National League ROY Leader	.50	.23
☐ 20 Juan Gonzalez American League MVP Leader	3.00	1.35
☐ 21 Ken Caminiti National League MVP Leader	1.50	.70
☐ 22 Pat Hentgen American League CY Young Leader	1.50	.70
☐ 23 John Smoltz National League CY Young Leader	.75	.35

1997 Upper Deck Home Team Heroes

This 12-card set measures approximately 5" by 3 1/2" and features two color action embossed images of top players from the same team printed on a die-cut card with silver foil enhancements. The backs carry two small color action player photos with player information in paragraph form.

	MINT	NRMT
COMPLETE SET (12)	20.00	9.00
COMMON CARD (HT1-HT12)	1.00	.45
☐ HT1 Alex Rodriguez Ken Griffey Jr.	4.00	1.80
☐ HT2 Bernie Williams Derek Jeter	1.50	.70
☐ HT3 Bernard Gilkey Todd Hundley	1.00	.45
☐ HT4 Hideo Nomo Mike Piazza	2.50	1.10
☐ HT5 Andruw Jones Chipper Jones	2.50	1.10
☐ HT6 John Smoltz Greg Maddux	2.00	.90
☐ HT7 Mike Mussina Cal Ripken Jr.	3.00	1.35
☐ HT8 Andres Galarraga Dante Bichette	1.00	.45
☐ HT9 Juan Gonzalez	2.00	.90

Ivan Rodriguez		
☐ HT10 Albert Belle	2.50	1.10
Frank Thomas		
☐ HT11 Kenny Lofton	1.50	.70
Manny Ramirez		
☐ HT12 Ken Caminiti	2.00	.90
Tony Gwynn		

1997 Upper Deck Ken Griffey Jr. Highlight Reels

This five-card hi-tech Diamond Vision set features actual MLB video footage of Ken Griffey Jr.'s most unbelievable plays. Each card was distributed in clamshell packaging for a suggested retail price of $9.99. The cards measure approximately 3.5" by 5" with each card containing over 20 frames of actual video footage of the player.

	MINT	NRMT
COMPLETE SET (5)	50.00	22.00
COMMON CARD (1-5)	10.00	4.50
☐ 1 Ken Griffey Jr.	10.00	4.50
Record Setter		
☐ 2 Ken Griffey Jr.	10.00	4.50
Long Distance Connection		
☐ 3 Ken Griffey Jr.	10.00	4.50
Home Run Derby		
☐ 4 Ken Griffey Jr.	10.00	4.50
Swing for the Ages		
☐ 5 Ken Griffey Jr.	10.00	4.50
Postseason Power		

1997 Upper Deck Mariners Pepsi

Produced by Upper Deck and sponsored by the Pepsi-Cola Company, this set features borderless color player photos of the Seattle Mariners. The player's name and position are printed in a silver oval inside a blue foil bar at the bottom. The backs carry another player photo with player information and statistics below.

	MINT	NRMT
COMPLETE SET (21)	15.00	6.75
COMMON CARD (P1-P20)	.25	.11
☐ P1 Joey Cora	.75	.35
☐ P2 Ken Griffey Jr.	5.00	2.20
☐ P3 Jay Buhner	1.50	.70
☐ P4 Alex Rodriguez	4.00	1.80
☐ P5 Norm Charlton	.25	.11
☐ P6 Edgar Martinez	1.00	.45
☐ P7 Paul Sorrento	.25	.11
☐ P8 Randy Johnson	1.50	.70
☐ P9 Rich Amaral	.25	.11
☐ P10 Russ Davis	.50	.23
☐ P11 Greg McCarthy	.25	.11
☐ P12 Jamie Moyer	.25	.11
☐ P13 Jeff Fassero	.25	.11
☐ P14 Scott Sanders	.25	.11
☐ P15 Dan Wilson	.75	.35
☐ P16 Mike Blowers	.25	.11
☐ P17 Bobby Ayala	.25	.11
☐ P18 Brent Gates	.25	.11
☐ P19 John Marzano	.25	.11
☐ P20 Lou Piniella MG	.50	.23
☐ NNO Sponsor Card	.25	.11
Pepsi-Cola Co.		
Coupon		

1998 Upper Deck

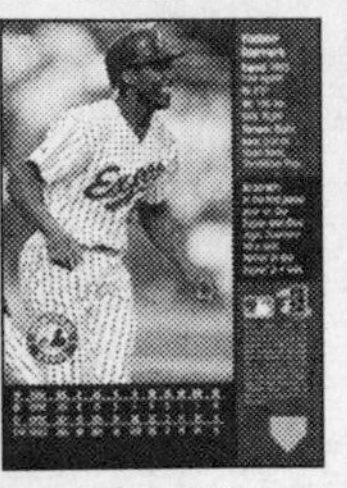

The 1998 Upper Deck Series 1 set consisted of 270 cards and was distributed in 12-card packs with a suggested retail price of $2.49. The fronts feature game dated photographs of some of the Season's most unforgettable moments with the pictured player. The set contains the following subsets: History in the Making (1-8), Griffey's Hot List (9-18), Define the Game (136-153), Season Highlights (244-252), and Star Rookie (253-270).

	MINT	NRMT
COMPLETE SERIES 1 (270)	30.00	13.50
COMMON CARD (1-270)	.15	.07
☐ 1 Tino Martinez HIST	.60	.25
☐ 2 Jimmy Key HIST	.30	.14
☐ 3 Jay Buhner HIST	.40	.18
☐ 4 Mark Gardner HIST	.15	.07
☐ 5 Greg Maddux HIST	1.00	.45
☐ 6 Pedro Martinez HIST	.60	.25
☐ 7 Hideo Nomo HIST	.75	.35
☐ 8 Sammy Sosa HIST	.60	.25
☐ 9 Mark McGwire GHL	1.50	.70
☐ 10 Ken Griffey Jr. GHL	3.00	1.35
☐ 11 Larry Walker GHL	.60	.25
☐ 12 Tino Martinez GHL	.60	.25
☐ 13 Mike Piazza GHL	2.00	.90
☐ 14 Jose Cruz Jr. GHL	2.50	1.10
☐ 15 Tony Gwynn GHL	1.50	.70
☐ 16 Greg Maddux GHL	2.00	.90
☐ 17 Roger Clemens GHL	1.25	.55
☐ 18 Alex Rodriguez GHL	2.00	.90
☐ 19 Shigetoshi Hasegawa	.30	.14
☐ 20 Eddie Murray	.60	.25
☐ 21 Jason Dickson	.15	.07
☐ 22 Darin Erstad	.75	.35
☐ 23 Chuck Finley	.15	.07
☐ 24 Dave Hollins	.15	.07
☐ 25 Garret Anderson	.30	.14
☐ 26 Michael Tucker	.30	.14
☐ 27 Kenny Lofton	.75	.35
☐ 28 Javier Lopez	.30	.14
☐ 29 Fred McGriff	.40	.18
☐ 30 Greg Maddux	2.00	.90
☐ 31 Jeff Blauser	.15	.07
☐ 32 John Smoltz	.30	.14
☐ 33 Mark Wohlers	.15	.07
☐ 34 Scott Erickson	.15	.07
☐ 35 Jimmy Key	.30	.14
☐ 36 Harold Baines	.30	.14
☐ 37 Randy Myers	.30	.14
☐ 38 B.J. Surhoff	.30	.14
☐ 39 Eric Davis	.30	.14
☐ 40 Rafael Palmeiro	.40	.18
☐ 41 Jeffrey Hammonds	.30	.14
☐ 42 Mo Vaughn	.75	.35
☐ 43 Tom Gordon	.15	.07
☐ 44 Tim Naehring	.15	.07
☐ 45 Darren Bragg	.15	.07
☐ 46 Aaron Sele	.15	.07
☐ 47 Troy O'Leary	.15	.07
☐ 48 John Valentin	.15	.07
☐ 49 Doug Glanville	.15	.07
☐ 50 Ryne Sandberg	.75	.35
☐ 51 Steve Trachsel	.15	.07
☐ 52 Mark Grace	.40	.18
☐ 53 Kevin Foster	.15	.07
☐ 54 Kevin Tapani	.15	.07
☐ 55 Kevin Orie	.15	.07
☐ 56 Lyle Mouton	.15	.07
☐ 57 Ray Durham	.15	.07
☐ 58 Jaime Navarro	.15	.07
☐ 59 Mike Cameron	.30	.14
☐ 60 Albert Belle	.75	.35
☐ 61 Doug Drabek	.15	.07
☐ 62 Chris Snopek	.15	.07
☐ 63 Ed Taubensee	.15	.07
☐ 64 Terry Pendleton	.15	.07
☐ 65 Barry Larkin	.40	.18
☐ 66 Willie Greene	.30	.14
☐ 67 Deion Sanders	.60	.25
☐ 68 Pokey Reese	.15	.07
☐ 69 Jeff Shaw	.15	.07
☐ 70 Jim Thome	.60	.25
☐ 71 Orel Hershiser	.30	.14
☐ 72 Omar Vizquel	.30	.14
☐ 73 Brian Giles	.15	.07
☐ 74 David Justice	.60	.25
☐ 75 Bartolo Colon	.15	.07
☐ 76 Sandy Alomar Jr.	.30	.14
☐ 77 Neifi Perez	.15	.07
☐ 78 Dante Bichette	.30	.14
☐ 79 Vinny Castilla	.30	.14
☐ 80 Eric Young	.15	.07
☐ 81 Quinton McCracken	.15	.07
☐ 82 Jamey Wright	.15	.07
☐ 83 John Thomson	.15	.07
☐ 84 Damion Easley	.15	.07
☐ 85 Justin Thompson	.30	.14
☐ 86 Willie Blair	.15	.07
☐ 87 Raul Casanova	.15	.07
☐ 88 Bobby Higginson	.30	.14
☐ 89 Bubba Trammell	.15	.07
☐ 90 Tony Clark	.60	.25
☐ 91 Livan Hernandez	.40	.18
☐ 92 Charles Johnson	.30	.14
☐ 93 Edgar Renteria	.30	.14
☐ 94 Alex Fernandez	.15	.07
☐ 95 Gary Sheffield	.60	.25
☐ 96 Moises Alou	.30	.14
☐ 97 Tony Saunders	.15	.07
☐ 98 Robb Nen	.15	.07
☐ 99 Darryl Kile	.30	.14
☐ 100 Craig Biggio	.40	.18
☐ 101 Chris Holt	.15	.07
☐ 102 Bob Abreu	.40	.18
☐ 103 Luis Gonzalez	.15	.07
☐ 104 Billy Wagner	.30	.14
☐ 105 Brad Ausmus	.15	.07
☐ 106 Chili Davis	.30	.14
☐ 107 Tim Belcher	.15	.07
☐ 108 Dean Palmer	.30	.14
☐ 109 Jeff King	.15	.07
☐ 110 Jose Rosado	.15	.07
☐ 111 Mike Macfarlane	.15	.07
☐ 112 Jay Bell	.15	.07
☐ 113 Todd Worrell	.15	.07
☐ 114 Chan Ho Park	.60	.25
☐ 115 Raul Mondesi	.40	.18
☐ 116 Brett Butler	.30	.14
☐ 117 Greg Gagne	.15	.07
☐ 118 Hideo Nomo	1.50	.70
☐ 119 Todd Zeile	.15	.07
☐ 120 Eric Karros	.15	.07
☐ 121 Cal Eldred	.15	.07
☐ 122 Jeff D'Amico	.15	.07
☐ 123 Antone Williamson	.15	.07
☐ 124 Doug Jones	.15	.07
☐ 125 Dave Nilsson	.15	.07
☐ 126 Gerald Williams	.15	.07
☐ 127 Fernando Vina	.15	.07
☐ 128 Ron Coomer	.15	.07
☐ 129 Matt Lawton	.15	.07
☐ 130 Paul Molitor	.60	.25
☐ 131 Todd Walker	.15	.07
☐ 132 Rick Aguilera	.30	.14
☐ 133 Brad Radke	.30	.14
☐ 134 Bob Tewksbury	.15	.07
☐ 135 Vladimir Guerrero	1.00	.45
☐ 136 Tony Gwynn DG	.75	.35
☐ 137 Roger Clemens DG	.60	.25
☐ 138 Dennis Eckersley DG	.30	.14
☐ 139 Brady Anderson DG	.30	.14
☐ 140 Ken Griffey Jr. DG	1.50	.70
☐ 141 Derek Jeter DG	.75	.35
☐ 142 Ken Caminiti DG	.30	.14
☐ 143 Frank Thomas DG	1.25	.55
☐ 144 Barry Bonds DG	.60	.25
☐ 145 Cal Ripken DG	1.25	.55
☐ 146 Alex Rodriguez DG	1.00	.45
☐ 147 Greg Maddux DG	1.00	.45
☐ 148 Kenny Lofton DG	.60	.25
☐ 149 Mike Piazza DG	1.00	.45
☐ 150 Mark McGwire DG	.60	.25
☐ 151 Andruw Jones DG	.75	.35
☐ 152 Rusty Greer DG	.30	.14
☐ 153 F.P. Santangelo DG	.15	.07
☐ 154 Mike Lansing	.15	.07
☐ 155 Lee Smith	.30	.14
☐ 156 Carlos Perez	.15	.07
☐ 157 Pedro Martinez	.60	.25
☐ 158 Ryan McGuire	.15	.07
☐ 159 F.P. Santangelo	.15	.07
☐ 160 Rondell White	.30	.14
☐ 161 Takashi Kashiwada	.60	.25

Card	MINT	NRMT
☐ 162 Butch Huskey	.30	.14
☐ 163 Edgardo Alfonzo	.30	.14
☐ 164 John Franco	.30	.14
☐ 165 Todd Hundley	.30	.14
☐ 166 Rey Ordonez	.15	.07
☐ 167 Armando Reynoso	.15	.07
☐ 168 John Olerud	.30	.14
☐ 169 Bernie Williams	.60	.25
☐ 170 Andy Pettitte	.60	.25
☐ 171 Wade Boggs	.60	.25
☐ 172 Paul O'Neill	.30	.14
☐ 173 Cecil Fielder	.30	.14
☐ 174 Charlie Hayes	.15	.07
☐ 175 David Cone	.30	.14
☐ 176 Hideki Irabu	.40	.18
☐ 177 Mark Bellhorn	.15	.07
☐ 178 Steve Karsay	.15	.07
☐ 179 Damon Mashore	.15	.07
☐ 180 Jason McDonald	.15	.07
☐ 181 Scott Spiezio	.15	.07
☐ 182 Ariel Prieto	.15	.07
☐ 183 Jason Giambi	.15	.07
☐ 184 Wendell Magee	.15	.07
☐ 185 Rico Brogna	.15	.07
☐ 186 Garrett Stephenson	.15	.07
☐ 187 Wayne Gomes	.15	.07
☐ 188 Ricky Bottalico	.15	.07
☐ 189 Mickey Morandini	.15	.07
☐ 190 Mike Lieberthal	.15	.07
☐ 191 Kevin Polcovich	.15	.07
☐ 192 Francisco Cordova	.15	.07
☐ 193 Kevin Young	.15	.07
☐ 194 Jon Lieber	.15	.07
☐ 195 Kevin Elster	.15	.07
☐ 196 Tony Womack	.15	.07
☐ 197 Lou Collier	.15	.07
☐ 198 Mike Difelice	.15	.07
☐ 199 Gary Gaetti	.30	.14
☐ 200 Dennis Eckersley	.40	.18
☐ 201 Alan Benes	.15	.07
☐ 202 Willie McGee	.30	.14
☐ 203 Ron Gant	.30	.14
☐ 204 Fernando Valenzuela	.30	.14
☐ 205 Mark McGwire	1.50	.70
☐ 206 Archi Cianfrocco	.15	.07
☐ 207 Andy Ashby	.15	.07
☐ 208 Steve Finley	.30	.14
☐ 209 Quilvio Veras	.15	.07
☐ 210 Ken Caminiti	.60	.25
☐ 211 Rickey Henderson	.40	.18
☐ 212 Joey Hamilton	.15	.07
☐ 213 Derrek Lee	.30	.14
☐ 214 Bill Mueller	.15	.07
☐ 215 Shawn Estes	.30	.14
☐ 216 J.T. Snow	.30	.14
☐ 217 Mark Gardner	.15	.07
☐ 218 Terry Mulholland	.15	.07
☐ 219 Dante Powell	.15	.07
☐ 220 Jeff Kent	.15	.07
☐ 221 Jamie Moyer	.15	.07
☐ 222 Joey Cora	.30	.14
☐ 223 Jeff Fassero	.15	.07
☐ 224 Dennis Martinez	.30	.14
☐ 225 Ken Griffey Jr.	3.00	1.35
☐ 226 Edgar Martinez	.40	.18
☐ 227 Russ Davis	.15	.07
☐ 228 Dan Wilson	.15	.07
☐ 229 Will Clark	.40	.18
☐ 230 Ivan Rodriguez	.75	.35
☐ 231 Benji Gil	.15	.07
☐ 232 Lee Stevens	.15	.07
☐ 233 Mickey Tettleton	.15	.07
☐ 234 Julio Santana	.15	.07
☐ 235 Rusty Greer	.30	.14
☐ 236 Bobby Witt	.15	.07
☐ 237 Ed Sprague	.15	.07
☐ 238 Pat Hentgen	.30	.14
☐ 239 Kelvim Escobar	.15	.07
☐ 240 Joe Carter	.30	.14
☐ 241 Carlos Delgado	.30	.14
☐ 242 Shannon Stewart	.30	.14
☐ 243 Benito Santiago	.15	.07
☐ 244 Tino Martinez SH	.60	.25
☐ 245 Ken Griffey Jr. SH	1.50	.70
☐ 246 Kevin Brown SH	.15	.07
☐ 247 Ryne Sandberg SH	.60	.25
☐ 248 Mo Vaughn SH	.60	.25
☐ 249 Darryl Hamilton SH	.15	.07
☐ 250 Randy Johnson SH	.60	.25
☐ 251 Steve Finley SH	.15	.07
☐ 252 Bobby Higginson SH	.15	.07
☐ 253 Brett Tomko	.30	.14
☐ 254 Mark Kotsay	.60	.25
☐ 255 Jose Guillen	.60	.25
☐ 256 Eli Marrero	.30	.14
☐ 257 Dennis Reyes	.15	.07
☐ 258 Richie Sexson	.15	.07
☐ 259 Pat Cline	.15	.07
☐ 260 Todd Helton	.75	.35
☐ 261 Juan Melo	.15	.07
☐ 262 Matt Morris	.30	.14
☐ 263 Jeremi Gonzalez	.30	.14
☐ 264 Jeff Abbott	.15	.07
☐ 265 Aaron Boone	.15	.07
☐ 266 Todd Dunwoody	.30	.14
☐ 267 Jaret Wright	1.50	.70
☐ 268 Derrick Gibson	.30	.14
☐ 269 Mario Valdez	.15	.07
☐ 270 Fernando Tatis	.60	.25

1998 Upper Deck 10th Anniversary Preview

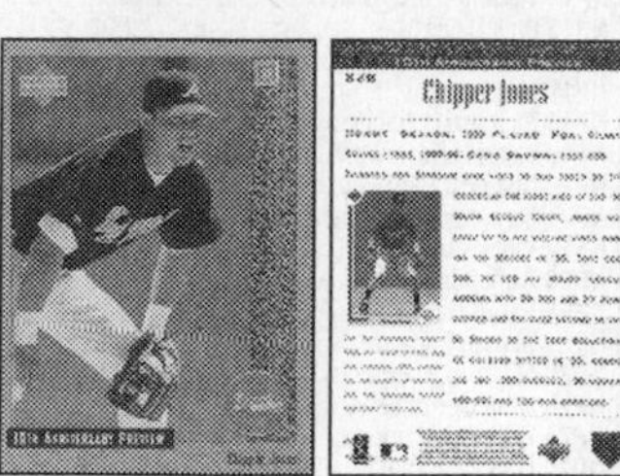

Randomly inserted in Series 1 packs at the rate of one in five, this 60-card set features color player photos in a design similar to the inaugural 1989 Upper Deck series. The backs carry a photo of that player's previous Upper Deck card. A 10th Anniversary Ballot Card was inserted one in four packs which allowed the collector to vote for the players they wanted to see in the 1999 Upper Deck tenth anniversary series.

	MINT	NRMT
COMPLETE SET (60)	120.00	55.00
COMMON CARD (1-60)	.75	.35
☐ 1 Greg Maddux	8.00	3.60
☐ 2 Mike Mussina	2.50	1.10
☐ 3 Roger Clemens	5.00	2.20
☐ 4 Hideo Nomo	6.00	2.70
☐ 5 David Cone	1.50	.70
☐ 6 Tom Glavine	1.50	.70
☐ 7 Andy Pettitte	2.50	1.10
☐ 8 Jimmy Key	1.50	.70
☐ 9 Randy Johnson	2.50	1.10
☐ 10 Dennis Eckersley	2.00	.90
☐ 11 Lee Smith	1.50	.70
☐ 12 John Franco	1.50	.70
☐ 13 Randy Myers	1.50	.70
☐ 14 Mike Piazza	8.00	3.60
☐ 15 Ivan Rodriguez	3.00	1.35
☐ 16 Todd Hundley	1.50	.70
☐ 17 Sandy Alomar Jr.	1.50	.70
☐ 18 Frank Thomas	10.00	4.50
☐ 19 Rafael Palmeiro	2.00	.90
☐ 20 Mark McGwire	6.00	2.70
☐ 21 Mo Vaughn	3.00	1.35
☐ 22 Fred McGriff	2.00	.90
☐ 23 Andres Galarraga	2.50	1.10
☐ 24 Mark Grace	2.00	.90
☐ 25 Jeff Bagwell	5.00	2.20
☐ 26 Roberto Alomar	2.50	1.10
☐ 27 Chuck Knoblauch	2.50	1.10
☐ 28 Ryne Sandberg	3.00	1.35
☐ 29 Eric Young	.75	.35
☐ 30 Craig Biggio	2.00	.90
☐ 31 Carlos Baerga	1.50	.70
☐ 32 Robin Ventura	1.50	.70
☐ 33 Matt Williams	2.00	.90
☐ 34 Wade Boggs	2.50	1.10
☐ 35 Dean Palmer	1.50	.70
☐ 36 Chipper Jones	8.00	3.60
☐ 37 Vinny Castilla	1.50	.70
☐ 38 Ken Caminiti	2.50	1.10
☐ 39 Omar Vizquel	1.50	.70
☐ 40 Cal Ripken	10.00	4.50
☐ 41 Derek Jeter	6.00	2.70
☐ 42 Alex Rodriguez	8.00	3.60
☐ 43 Barry Larkin	2.00	.90
☐ 44 Mark Grudzielanek	.75	.35
☐ 45 Albert Belle	3.00	1.35
☐ 46 Manny Ramirez	2.50	1.10
☐ 47 Jose Canseco	2.00	.90
☐ 48 Ken Griffey Jr.	12.00	5.50
☐ 49 Juan Gonzalez	6.00	2.70
☐ 50 Kenny Lofton	3.00	1.35
☐ 51 Sammy Sosa	2.50	1.10
☐ 52 Larry Walker	2.50	1.10
☐ 53 Gary Sheffield	2.50	1.10
☐ 54 Rickey Henderson	2.00	.90
☐ 55 Tony Gwynn	6.00	2.70
☐ 56 Barry Bonds	3.00	1.35
☐ 57 Paul Molitor	2.50	1.10
☐ 58 Edgar Martinez	2.00	.90
☐ 59 Chili Davis	1.50	.70
☐ 60 Eddie Murray	2.50	1.10

1998 Upper Deck 10th Anniversary Preview Retail

This 60 card set is a parallel to the 10th anniversary preview set inserted into 1998 Upper Deck. This set was only available as part of a retail package which also included 200 better 1997 Collectors Choice cards. The difference between these cards and the pack inserts are the gold foil printed on the card along with the words "Preview Edition" printed on the side. The box which contained all these cards had a SRP of $19.99.

	MINT	NRMT
COMPLETE SET (60)	20.00	9.00
COMMON CARD (1-60)	.10	.05
*:STARS: ,2X BASIC CARDS		

1998 Upper Deck A Piece of the Action

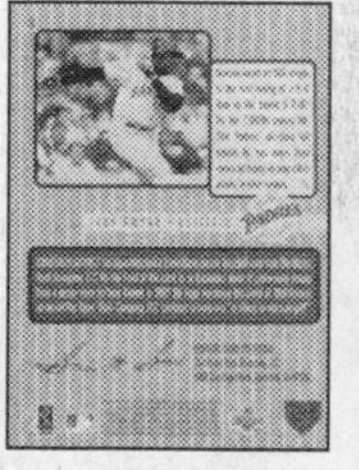

Randomly inserted in Series 1 packs at the rate of one in 2,500, this 10-card set features color photos of top players with pieces of actual game worn jerseys and game used bats embedded in the cards. The cards are unnumbered and checklisted below in alphabetical order.

	MINT	NRMT
COMPLETE SET (10)	2000.00	900.00
COMMON CARD (1-10)	80.00	36.00
☐ 1 Jay Buhner Bat	100.00	45.00
☐ 2 Tony Gwynn Bat	250.00	110.00
☐ 3 Tony Gwynn Jersey	300.00	135.00
☐ 4 Todd Hollandsworth Bat	80.00	36.00
☐ 5 Todd Hollandsworth Jersey	100.00	45.00
☐ 6 Greg Maddux Jersey	400.00	180.00
☐ 7 Alex Rodriguez Bat	300.00	135.00
☐ 8 Alex Rodriguez Jersey	400.00	180.00
☐ 9 Gary Sheffield Bat	100.00	45.00
☐ 10 Gary Sheffield Jersey	120.00	55.00

1998 Upper Deck Amazing Greats

Randomly inserted in Series 1 packs, this 30-card set features color photos of amazing players printed on a hi-tech plastic card. Only 2000 of this set were produced and are crash numbered.

	MINT	NRMT
COMPLETE SET (30)	800.00	350.00
COMMON CARD (AG1-AG30)	12.00	5.50
COMP.DIE CUT SET (30)	2500.00	1100.00
COMMON DIE CUT (AG1-AG30)	35.00	16.00
*DIE CUT STARS: 1.5X TO 3X BASIC CARDS		

☐ AG1 Ken Griffey Jr.	80.00	36.00
☐ AG2 Derek Jeter	40.00	18.00
☐ AG3 Alex Rodriguez	50.00	22.00
☐ AG4 Paul Molitor	15.00	6.75
☐ AG5 Jeff Bagwell	30.00	13.50
☐ AG6 Larry Walker	15.00	6.75
☐ AG7 Kenny Lofton	20.00	9.00
☐ AG8 Cal Ripken Jr.	60.00	27.00
☐ AG9 Juan Gonzalez	40.00	18.00
☐ AG10 Chipper Jones	50.00	22.00
☐ AG11 Greg Maddux	50.00	22.00
☐ AG12 Roberto Alomar	15.00	6.75
☐ AG13 Mike Piazza	50.00	22.00
☐ AG14 Andres Galarraga	12.00	5.50
☐ AG15 Barry Bonds	20.00	9.00
☐ AG16 Andy Pettitte	15.00	6.75
☐ AG17 Nomar Garciaparra	40.00	18.00
☐ AG18 Tino Martinez	12.00	5.50
☐ AG19 Tony Gwynn	40.00	18.00
☐ AG20 Frank Thomas	60.00	27.00
☐ AG21 Roger Clemens	30.00	13.50
☐ AG22 Sammy Sosa	12.00	5.50
☐ AG23 Jose Cruz Jr.	50.00	22.00
☐ AG24 Manny Ramirez	15.00	6.75
☐ AG25 Mark McGwire	40.00	18.00
☐ AG26 Randy Johnson	15.00	6.75
☐ AG27 Mo Vaughn	20.00	9.00
☐ AG28 Gary Sheffield	12.00	5.50
☐ AG29 Andruw Jones	25.00	11.00
☐ AG30 Albert Belle	20.00	9.00

1998 Upper Deck Griffey Home Run Chronicles

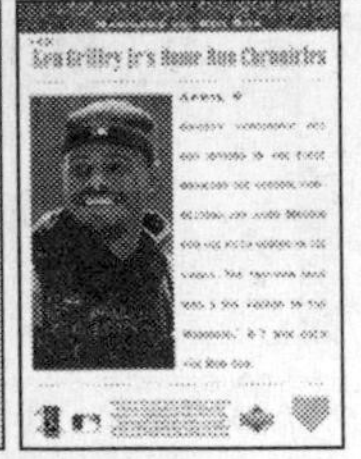

Randomly inserted in Series 1 packs at the rate of one in nine, this 30-card set features color photos of Ken Griffey Jr.'s first 30 home runs of the 1997 season.

	MINT	NRMT
COMPLETE SERIES 1 (30)	100.00	45.00
COMMON GRIFFEY (1-30)	4.00	1.80

1998 Upper Deck National Pride

Randomly inserted in Series 1 packs at the rate of one in 23, this 42-card set features color photos of some of the league's great players from countries other than the United States printed on die-cut ranbow foil cards. The backs carry player information.

	MINT	NRMT
COMPLETE SET (42)	350.00	160.00
COMMON CARD (NP1-NP42)	2.50	1.10
☐ NP1 Dave Nilsson	2.50	1.10
☐ NP2 Larry Walker	10.00	4.50
☐ NP3 Edgar Renteria	5.00	2.20
☐ NP4 Jose Canseco	8.00	3.60
☐ NP5 Rey Ordonez	2.50	1.10
☐ NP6 Rafael Palmeiro	8.00	3.60
☐ NP7 Livan Hernandez	10.00	4.50
☐ NP8 Andruw Jones	15.00	6.75
☐ NP9 Manny Ramirez	10.00	4.50
☐ NP10 Sammy Sosa	8.00	3.60
☐ NP11 Raul Mondesi	10.00	4.50
☐ NP12 Moises Alou	5.00	2.20
☐ NP13 Pedro Martinez	10.00	4.50
☐ NP14 Vladimir Guerrero	12.00	5.50
☐ NP15 Chili Davis	2.50	1.10
☐ NP16 Hideo Nomo	25.00	11.00
☐ NP17 Hideki Irabu	5.00	2.20
☐ NP18 Shigetoshi Hasegawa	5.00	2.20
☐ NP19 Takashi Kashiwada	5.00	2.20
☐ NP20 Chan Ho Park	10.00	4.50
☐ NP21 Fernando Valenzuela	5.00	2.20
☐ NP22 Vinny Castilla	5.00	2.20
☐ NP23 Armando Reynoso	2.50	1.10
☐ NP24 Karim Garcia	5.00	2.20
☐ NP25 Marvin Benard	2.50	1.10
☐ NP26 Mariano Rivera	5.00	2.20
☐ NP27 Juan Gonzalez	25.00	11.00
☐ NP28 Roberto Alomar	10.00	4.50
☐ NP29 Ivan Rodriguez	12.00	5.50
☐ NP30 Carlos Delgado	5.00	2.20
☐ NP31 Bernie Williams	10.00	4.50
☐ NP32 Edgar Martinez	8.00	3.60
☐ NP33 Frank Thomas	40.00	18.00
☐ NP34 Barry Bonds	12.00	5.50
☐ NP35 Mike Piazza	30.00	13.50
☐ NP36 Chipper Jones	30.00	13.50
☐ NP37 Cal Ripken Jr.	40.00	18.00
☐ NP38 Alex Rodriguez	30.00	13.50
☐ NP39 Ken Griffey Jr.	50.00	22.00
☐ NP40 Andres Galarraga	10.00	4.50
☐ NP41 Omar Vizquel	5.00	2.20
☐ NP42 Ozzie Guillen	2.50	1.10

1998 Upper Deck Power Deck Audio Griffey

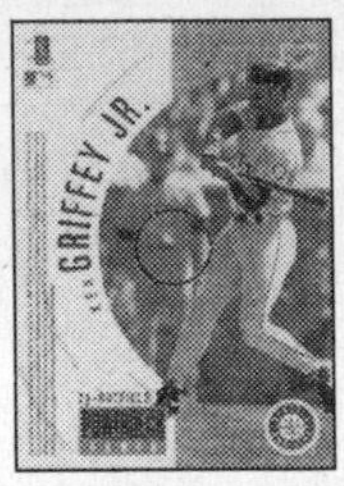

In an effort to premier their new Power Deck Audio technology, Upper Deck created three special Ken Griffey Jr. cards (blue, green and silver backgrounds), each of which contained the same five minute interview with the Mariner's superstar. These cards were randomly seeded exclusively into test packs comprising only 10% of the total first series 1998 Upper Deck print run. The seeding ratios are as follows: Blue 1:8, Green 1:100 and Silver 1:2400. Each test issue box contained a clear CD disc for which the card could be placed upon for playing on any common CD player. To play the card, the center hole had to be punched out. Prices below are for Mint unpunched cards. Punched out cards trade at twenty-five percent of the listed values.

	MINT	NRMT
COMPLETE SET (3)	100.00	45.00
COMMON GRIFFEY CD	5.00	2.20
☐ 1 Ken Griffey Jr. Blue	5.00	2.20
☐ 2 Ken Griffey Jr. Green	30.00	13.50
☐ 3 Ken Griffey Jr. Silver	80.00	36.00

1997 Upper Deck UD3

This 60-card standard-size super premium set was released by Upper Deck exclusively to retail outlets in mid-April,1997. The set is broken up into three distinct 20-card subsets: Homerun Heroes (1-20) featuring Electric Wood technology, Pro-Motion (21-40) featuring Light F/X technology and Future Impact (41-60) featuring

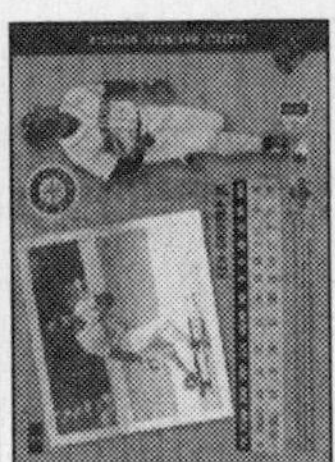

Cel Chrome technology. Packs carried a suggested retail price of $3.99. Each pack contained three cards, one from each of the subsets. Boxes contained 24 packs.

	MINT	NRMT
COMPLETE SET (60)	60.00	27.00
COMMON CARD (1-60)	.50	.23
☐ 1 Mark McGwire	2.50	1.10
☐ 2 Brady Anderson	1.00	.45
☐ 3 Ken Griffey Jr.	6.00	2.70
☐ 4 Albert Belle	1.50	.70
☐ 5 Andres Galarraga	1.25	.55
☐ 6 Juan Gonzalez	3.00	1.35
☐ 7 Jay Buhner	1.00	.45
☐ 8 Mo Vaughn	1.50	.70
☐ 9 Barry Bonds	1.50	.70
☐ 10 Gary Sheffield	1.25	.55
☐ 11 Todd Hundley	.75	.35
☐ 12 Ellis Burks	.75	.35
☐ 13 Ken Caminiti	1.25	.55
☐ 14 Vinny Castilla	.75	.35
☐ 15 Sammy Sosa	1.25	.55
☐ 16 Frank Thomas	5.00	2.20
☐ 17 Rafael Palmeiro	1.00	.45
☐ 18 Mike Piazza	4.00	1.80
☐ 19 Matt Williams	1.00	.45
☐ 20 Eddie Murray	1.25	.55
☐ 21 Roger Clemens	2.50	1.10
☐ 22 Tim Salmon	1.25	.55
☐ 23 Robin Ventura	.75	.35
☐ 24 Ron Gant	.50	.23
☐ 25 Cal Ripken	5.00	2.20
☐ 26 Bernie Williams	1.25	.55
☐ 27 Hideo Nomo	3.00	1.35
☐ 28 Ivan Rodriguez	1.50	.70
☐ 29 John Smoltz	.75	.35
☐ 30 Paul Molitor	1.25	.55
☐ 31 Greg Maddux	4.00	1.80
☐ 32 Raul Mondesi	1.25	.55
☐ 33 Roberto Alomar	1.25	.55
☐ 34 Barry Larkin	1.00	.45
☐ 35 Tony Gwynn	3.00	1.35
☐ 36 Jim Thome	1.25	.55
☐ 37 Kenny Lofton	1.50	.70
☐ 38 Jeff Bagwell	2.50	1.10
☐ 39 Ozzie Smith	1.50	.70
☐ 40 Kirby Puckett	2.50	1.10
☐ 41 Andruw Jones	3.00	1.35
☐ 42 Vladimir Guerrero	2.50	1.10
☐ 43 Edgar Renteria	.75	.35
☐ 44 Luis Castillo	.50	.23
☐ 45 Darin Erstad	2.00	.90
☐ 46 Nomar Garciaparra	4.00	1.80
☐ 47 Todd Greene	.75	.35
☐ 48 Jason Kendall	.75	.35
☐ 49 Rey Ordonez	.50	.23
☐ 50 Alex Rodriguez	5.00	2.20
☐ 51 Manny Ramirez	1.25	.55
☐ 52 Todd Walker	.50	.23
☐ 53 Ruben Rivera	.75	.35
☐ 54 Andy Pettitte	1.25	.55
☐ 55 Derek Jeter	4.00	1.80
☐ 56 Todd Hollandsworth	.75	.35
☐ 57 Rocky Coppinger	.50	.23
☐ 58 Scott Rolen	3.00	1.35
☐ 59 Jermaine Dye	.50	.23
☐ 60 Chipper Jones	4.00	1.80

1997 Upper Deck UD3 Generation Next

Randomly seeded into one in every 11 packs, cards from this 20-card set feature a selection of the game's top prospects. The horizontal card fronts feature a full-color cut-out player photo set against a metallized background with another picture of the player in action. Card backs include 1996 season statistics, a rarity for insert issues.

	MINT	NRMT
COMPLETE SET (20)	120.00	55.00
COMMON CARD (1-20)	2.00	.90

☐ GN1 Alex Rodriguez	15.00	6.75
☐ GN2 Vladimir Guerrero	10.00	4.50
☐ GN3 Luis Castillo	2.00	.90
☐ GN4 Rey Ordonez	3.00	1.35
☐ GN5 Andruw Jones	12.00	5.50
☐ GN6 Darin Erstad	8.00	3.60
☐ GN7 Edgar Renteria	3.00	1.35
☐ GN8 Jason Kendall	3.00	1.35
☐ GN9 Jermaine Dye	2.00	.90
☐ GN10 Chipper Jones	15.00	6.75
☐ GN11 Rocky Coppinger	2.00	.90
☐ GN12 Andy Pettitte	5.00	2.20
☐ GN13 Todd Greene	3.00	1.35
☐ GN14 Todd Hollandsworth	3.00	1.35
☐ GN15 Derek Jeter	15.00	6.75
☐ GN16 Ruben Rivera	3.00	1.35
☐ GN17 Todd Walker	2.00	.90
☐ GN18 Nomar Garciaparra	15.00	6.75
☐ GN19 Scott Rolen	12.00	5.50
☐ GN20 Manny Ramirez	5.00	2.20

1997 Upper Deck UD3 Marquee Attraction

Randomly seed into one in every 144 packs, cards from this 10-card set feature a selection of the game's top veteran stars. Horizontal card fronts feature a small color action player photo set against a bold diamond-shaped holographic image of the player. Card backs feature silver foil, statistics, another photo and text.

	MINT	NRMT
COMPLETE SET (10)	500.00	220.00
COMMON CARD (MA1-MA10)	25.00	11.00
☐ MA1 Ken Griffey Jr.	100.00	45.00
☐ MA2 Mark McGwire	40.00	18.00
☐ MA3 Juan Gonzalez	50.00	22.00
☐ MA4 Barry Bonds	25.00	11.00
☐ MA5 Frank Thomas	80.00	36.00
☐ MA6 Albert Belle	25.00	11.00
☐ MA7 Mike Piazza	60.00	27.00
☐ MA8 Cal Ripken	80.00	36.00
☐ MA9 Mo Vaughn	25.00	11.00
☐ MA10 Alex Rodriguez	60.00	27.00

1997 Upper Deck UD3 Superb Signatures

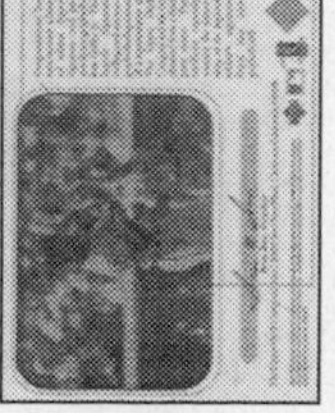

Randomly seeded into one in every 1,500 packs, cards from this four-card set feature actual autographs from some of baseball's top stars. Horizontal wood-cel card fronts feature a rectangular clear plastic player photo, statistics on height, weight, date of birth and hometown, plus of course a real autograph at the base of the card. Card backs feature text congratulating the bearer of the card plus the signature of Upper Deck's president Brian Burr.

	MINT	NRMT
COMPLETE SET (4)	1100.00	500.00
COMMON CARD	100.00	45.00
☐ 1 Ken Caminiti	100.00	45.00
☐ 2 Ken Griffey Jr.	600.00	275.00
☐ 3 Vladimir Guerrero	150.00	70.00
☐ 4 Derek Jeter	250.00	110.00

1954 Wilson

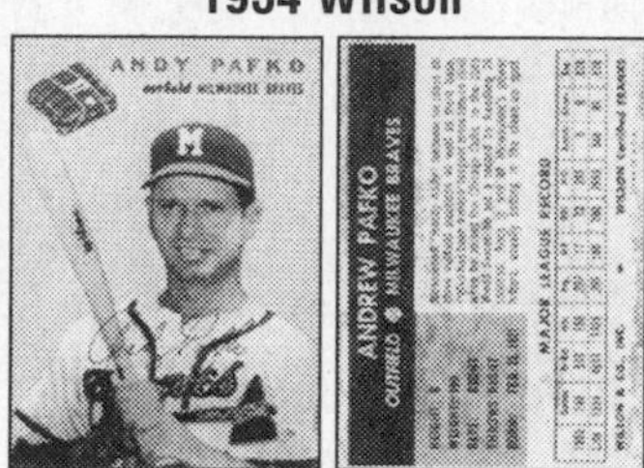

The cards in this 20-card set measure approximately 2 5/8" by 3 3/4". The 1954 "Wilson Wieners" set contains 20 full color, unnumbered cards. The obverse design of a package of hot dogs appearing to fly through the air is a distinctive feature of this set. Uncut sheets have been seen. Cards are numbered below alphabetically by player's name.

	NRMT	VG-E
COMPLETE SET (20)	7500.00	3400.00
COMMON CARD (1-20)	150.00	70.00
☐ 1 Roy Campanella	750.00	350.00
☐ 2 Del Ennis	175.00	80.00
☐ 3 Carl Erskine	175.00	80.00
☐ 4 Ferris Fain	150.00	70.00
☐ 5 Bob Feller	500.00	220.00
☐ 6 Nellie Fox	350.00	160.00
☐ 7 Johnny Groth	150.00	70.00
☐ 8 Stan Hack MG	150.00	70.00
☐ 9 Gil Hodges	400.00	180.00
☐ 10 Ray Jablonski	150.00	70.00
☐ 11 Harvey Kuenn	175.00	80.00
☐ 12 Roy McMillan	150.00	70.00
☐ 13 Andy Pafko	150.00	70.00
☐ 14 Paul Richards MG	150.00	70.00
☐ 15 Hank Sauer	150.00	70.00
☐ 16 Red Schoendienst	350.00	160.00
☐ 17 Enos Slaughter	350.00	160.00
☐ 18 Vern Stephens	150.00	70.00
☐ 19 Sammy White	150.00	70.00
☐ 20 Ted Williams	3000.00	1350.00

1990 Wonder Bread Stars

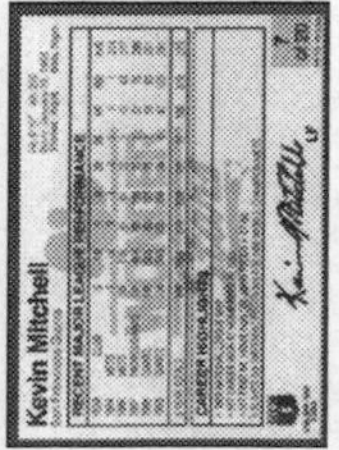

The 1990 Wonder Bread set was issued in 1990 by MSA (Michael Schechter Associates) in conjunction with Wonder Bread. One card was issued inside each specially marked package of Wonder Bread. Cards were available in grocery stores through June 15, 1990. The card was sealed in a pouch in the bread wrapper. This standard-size card set was issued without logos like many of the sets produced by MSA. Cards were printed on thin stock and hence were easily creased during bread handling making the set more difficult to put together one card at a time for condition-conscious collectors. Cards are numbered on the back in the lower right corner. Wonder Bread also offered sets in uncut sheet form to collectors mailing in with 3.00 and five proofs of purchase.

	MINT	NRMT
COMPLETE SET (20)	20.00	9.00
COMMON CARD (1-20)	.25	.11
☐ 1 Bo Jackson	.50	.23
☐ 2 Roger Clemens	1.25	.55
☐ 3 Jim Abbott	.25	.11
☐ 4 Orel Hershiser	.50	.23
☐ 5 Ozzie Smith	2.00	.90
☐ 6 Don Mattingly	2.50	1.10
☐ 7 Kevin Mitchell	.25	.11
☐ 8 Jerome Walton	.25	.11
☐ 9 Kirby Puckett	2.50	1.10
☐ 10 Darryl Strawberry	.50	.23
☐ 11 Robin Yount	.75	.35
☐ 12 Tony Gwynn	2.50	1.10
☐ 13 Alan Trammell	.75	.35
☐ 14 Jose Canseco	.75	.35
☐ 15 Greg Swindell	.25	.11
☐ 16 Nolan Ryan	4.00	1.80
☐ 17 Howard Johnson	.25	.11
☐ 18 Ken Griffey Jr.	5.00	2.20
☐ 19 Will Clark	.75	.35
☐ 20 Ryne Sandberg	2.00	.90

1985 Woolworth's

This 44-card standard-size set features color as well as black and white cards of All Time Record Holders. The cards are printed with blue ink on an orange and white back. The set was produced for Woolworth's by Topps and was packaged in a colorful box which contained a checklist of the cards in the set on the back panel. The numerical order of the cards coincides alphabetically with the player's name.

	NRMT	VG-E
COMPLETE SET (44)	4.00	1.80
COMMON CARD (1-44)	.05	.02
☐ 1 Hank Aaron	.75	.35
☐ 2 Grover C. Alexander	.25	.11
☐ 3 Ernie Banks	.25	.11
☐ 4 Yogi Berra	.25	.11
☐ 5 Lou Brock	.15	.07
☐ 6 Steve Carlton	.25	.11
☐ 7 Jack Chesbro	.05	.02
☐ 8 Ty Cobb	.75	.35
☐ 9 Sam Crawford	.15	.07
☐ 10 Rollie Fingers	.15	.07
☐ 11 Whitey Ford	.25	.11
☐ 12 John Frederick	.05	.02
☐ 13 Frankie Frisch	.15	.07
☐ 14 Lou Gehrig	.75	.35
☐ 15 Jim Gentile	.05	.02
☐ 16 Dwight Gooden	.50	.23
☐ 17 Rickey Henderson	.35	.16
☐ 18 Rogers Hornsby	.25	.11
☐ 19 Frank Howard	.10	.05
☐ 20 Cliff Johnson	.05	.02
☐ 21 Walter Johnson	.25	.11
☐ 22 Hub Leonard	.05	.02
☐ 23 Mickey Mantle	1.00	.45
☐ 24 Roger Maris	.50	.23
☐ 25 Christy Mathewson	.25	.11
☐ 26 Willie Mays	.75	.35
☐ 27 Stan Musial	.50	.23
☐ 28 Dan Quisenberry	.05	.02
☐ 29 Frank Robinson	.25	.11
☐ 30 Pete Rose	.50	.23
☐ 31 Babe Ruth	1.00	.45
☐ 32 Nolan Ryan	1.00	.45
☐ 33 George Sisler	.25	.11
☐ 34 Tris Speaker	.25	.11
☐ 35 Ed Walsh	.15	.07
☐ 36 Lloyd Waner	.15	.07
☐ 37 Earl Webb	.05	.02
☐ 38 Ted Williams	.75	.35
☐ 39 Maury Wills	.10	.05
☐ 40 Hack Wilson	.15	.07
☐ 41 Owen Wilson	.05	.02
☐ 42 Willie Wilson	.05	.02
☐ 43 Rudy York	.05	.02
☐ 44 Cy Young	.25	.11

1986 Woolworth's

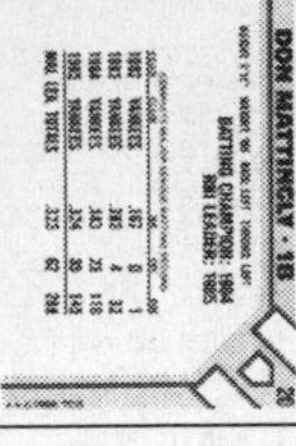

This boxed set of 33 standard-size cards was produced by Topps for Woolworth's variety stores. The set features players who hold or have held hitting, home run or RBI titles. The cards have a glossy finish. The card fronts are bordered in yellow with the subtitle "Topps Collectors' Series" across the top. The card backs are printed in green and blue ink on white card stock. The custom box gives the set checklist on the back.

	MINT	NRMT
COMPLETE SET (33)	4.00	1.80
COMMON CARD (1-33)	.05	.02

	MINT	NRMT
☐ 1 Tony Armas	.05	.02
☐ 2 Don Baylor	.10	.05
☐ 3 Wade Boggs	.30	.14
☐ 4 George Brett	1.00	.45
☐ 5 Bill Buckner	.05	.02
☐ 6 Rod Carew	.30	.14
☐ 7 Gary Carter	.15	.07
☐ 8 Cecil Cooper	.10	.05
☐ 9 Darrell Evans	.05	.02
☐ 10 Dwight Evans	.10	.05
☐ 11 George Foster	.10	.05
☐ 12 Bob Grich	.05	.02
☐ 13 Tony Gwynn	1.00	.45
☐ 14 Keith Hernandez	.10	.05
☐ 15 Reggie Jackson	.40	.18
☐ 16 Dave Kingman	.05	.02
☐ 17 Carney Lansford	.05	.02
☐ 18 Fred Lynn	.10	.05
☐ 19 Bill Madlock	.05	.02
☐ 20 Don Mattingly	1.50	.70
☐ 21 Willie McGee	.10	.05
☐ 22 Hal McRae	.05	.02
☐ 23 Dale Murphy	.25	.11
☐ 24 Eddie Murray	.50	.23
☐ 25 Ben Oglivie	.05	.02
☐ 26 Al Oliver	.05	.02
☐ 27 Dave Parker	.10	.05
☐ 28 Jim Rice	.10	.05
☐ 29 Pete Rose	.75	.35
☐ 30 Mike Schmidt	.75	.35
☐ 31 Gorman Thomas	.05	.02
☐ 32 Willie Wilson	.05	.02
☐ 33 Dave Winfield	.40	.18

1987 Woolworth's

Topps produced this 33-card standard-size set for Woolworth's stores. The set is subtitled "Topps Collectors Series Baseball Highlights" and consists of high gloss card fronts with full-color photos. The cards show and describe highlights of the previous season. The card backs are printed in gold and purple and are numbered. The set was sold nationally in Woolworth's for a 1.99 suggested retail price.

	MINT	NRMT
COMPLETE SET (33)	4.00	1.80
COMMON CARD (1-33)	.05	.02

	MINT	NRMT
☐ 1 Steve Carlton	.25	.11
☐ 2 Cecil Cooper	.10	.05
☐ 3 Rickey Henderson	.30	.14
☐ 4 Reggie Jackson	.40	.18
☐ 5 Jim Rice	.10	.05
☐ 6 Don Sutton	.25	.11
☐ 7 Roger Clemens	.75	.35
☐ 8 Mike Schmidt	.60	.25
☐ 9 Jesse Barfield	.05	.02
☐ 10 Wade Boggs	.30	.14
☐ 11 Tim Raines	.10	.05
☐ 12 Jose Canseco	.75	.35
☐ 13 Todd Worrell	.10	.05
☐ 14 Dave Righetti	.05	.02
☐ 15 Don Mattingly	1.00	.45
☐ 16 Tony Gwynn	1.00	.45
☐ 17 Marty Barrett	.05	.02
☐ 18 Mike Scott	.05	.02
☐ 19 Bruce Hurst	.05	.02
☐ 20 Calvin Schiraldi	.05	.02
☐ 21 Dwight Evans	.10	.05
☐ 22 Dave Henderson	.05	.02
☐ 23 Len Dykstra	.15	.07
☐ 24 Bob Ojeda	.05	.02
☐ 25 Gary Carter	.10	.05
☐ 26 Ron Darling	.05	.02
☐ 27 Jim Rice	.10	.05
☐ 28 Bruce Hurst	.05	.02
☐ 29 Darryl Strawberry	.10	.05
☐ 30 Ray Knight	.05	.02
☐ 31 Keith Hernandez	.10	.05
☐ 32 Mets Celebration	.05	.02
☐ 33 Ray Knight	.05	.02

1988 Woolworth's

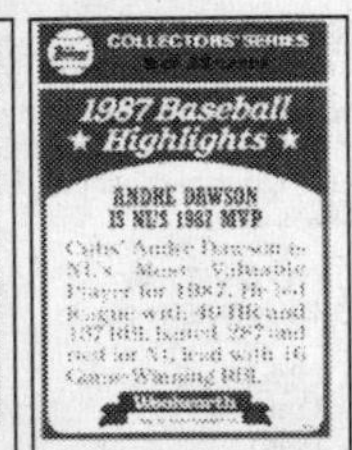

Topps produced this 33-card standard-size set for Woolworth's stores. The set is subtitled "Topps Collectors' Series Baseball Highlights" and consists of high gloss card fronts with full-color photos. The cards show and describe highlights of the previous season. Cards 19-33 commemorate the World Series with highlights and key players of each game in the series. The card backs are printed in red and blue on white card stock and are numbered. The set was sold nationally in Woolworth's for a 1.99 suggested retail price.

	MINT	NRMT
COMPLETE SET (33)	4.00	1.80
COMMON CARD (1-33)	.05	.02

	MINT	NRMT
☐ 1 Don Baylor	.10	.05
☐ 2 Vince Coleman	.05	.02
☐ 3 Darrell Evans	.05	.02
☐ 4 Don Mattingly	1.00	.45
☐ 5 Eddie Murray	.40	.18
☐ 6 Nolan Ryan	2.00	.90
☐ 7 Mike Schmidt	.50	.23
☐ 8 Andre Dawson	.25	.11
☐ 9 George Bell	.05	.02
☐ 10 Steve Bedrosian	.05	.02
☐ 11 Roger Clemens	.75	.35
☐ 12 Tony Gwynn	1.00	.45
☐ 13 Wade Boggs	.20	.09
☐ 14 Benito Santiago	.05	.02
☐ 15 Mark McGwire UER (Referenced on card back as NL ROY, sic)	1.00	.45
☐ 16 Dave Righetti	.05	.02
☐ 17 Jeffrey Leonard	.05	.02
☐ 18 Gary Gaetti	.05	.02
☐ 19 Frank Viola WS1	.05	.02
☐ 20 Dan Gladden WS1	.05	.02
☐ 21 Bert Blyleven WS2	.10	.05
☐ 22 Gary Gaetti WS2	.10	.05
☐ 23 John Tudor WS3	.05	.02
☐ 24 Todd Worrell WS3	.10	.05
☐ 25 Tom Lawless WS4	.05	.02
☐ 26 Willie McGee WS4	.10	.05
☐ 27 Danny Cox WS5	.05	.02
☐ 28 Curt Ford WS5	.05	.02
☐ 29 Don Baylor WS6	.10	.05
☐ 30 Kent Hrbek WS6	.10	.05
☐ 31 Kirby Puckett WS7	1.00	.45
☐ 32 Greg Gagne WS7	.05	.02
☐ 33 Frank Viola WS-MVP	.05	.02

1989 Woolworth's

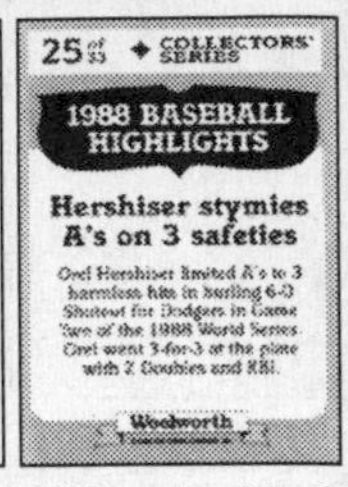

The 1989 Woolworth's Highlights set contains 33 standard-size glossy cards. The fronts have red and white borders. The vertically oriented backs are yellow and red, and describe highlights from the 1988 season including the World Series. The cards were distributed through Woolworth stores as a boxed set.

	MINT	NRMT
COMPLETE SET (33)	3.00	1.35
COMMON CARD (1-33)	.05	.02

	MINT	NRMT
☐ 1 Jose Canseco MVP	.50	.23
☐ 2 Kirk Gibson MVP	.15	.07
☐ 3 Frank Viola CY	.05	.02
☐ 4 Orel Hershiser CY	.10	.05
☐ 5 Walt Weiss ROY	.05	.02
☐ 6 Chris Sabo ROY	.05	.02
☐ 7 George Bell	.05	.02
☐ 8 Wade Boggs	.30	.14
☐ 9 Tom Browning	.05	.02
☐ 10 Gary Carter	.15	.07
☐ 11 Andre Dawson	.25	.11
☐ 12 John Franco	.10	.05
☐ 13 Randy Johnson	1.00	.45
☐ 14 Doug Jones	.05	.02
☐ 15 Kevin McReynolds	.05	.02
☐ 16 Gene Nelson	.05	.02
☐ 17 Jeff Reardon	.05	.02
☐ 18 Pat Tabler	.05	.02
☐ 19 Tim Belcher	.05	.02
☐ 20 Dennis Eckersley	.15	.07
☐ 21 Orel Hershiser	.10	.05
☐ 22 Gregg Jefferies	.10	.05
☐ 23 Jose Canseco	.50	.23
☐ 24 Kirk Gibson	.15	.07
☐ 25 Orel Hershiser	.10	.05
☐ 26 Mike Marshall	.05	.02
☐ 27 Mark McGwire	1.00	.45
☐ 28 Rick Honeycutt	.05	.02
☐ 29 Tim Belcher	.05	.02
☐ 30 Jay Howell	.05	.02
☐ 31 Mickey Hatcher	.05	.02
☐ 32 Mike Davis	.05	.02
☐ 33 Orel Hershiser	.10	.05

1990 Woolworth's

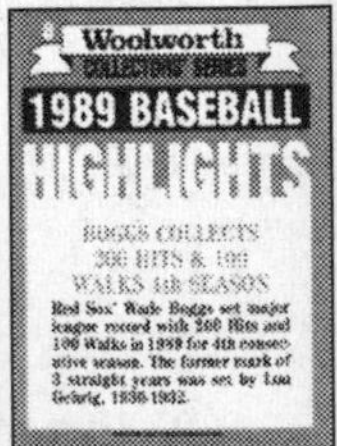

The 1990 Woolworth set is a 33-card standard-size set highlighting some of the more important events of the 1989 season. This set is broken down between major award winners, career highlights, and post-season heroes. The first six cards of the set feature the award winners while the last 11 cards of the set feature post-season heroes.

	MINT	NRMT
COMPLETE SET (33)	5.00	2.20
COMMON CARD (1-33)	.05	.02

	MINT	NRMT
☐ 1 Robin Yount MVP	.25	.11
☐ 2 Kevin Mitchell MVP	.05	.02
☐ 3 Bret Saberhagen CY	.05	.02
☐ 4 Mark Davis CY	.05	.02
☐ 5 Gregg Olson ROY	.05	.02
☐ 6 Jerome Walton ROY	.05	.02
☐ 7 Bert Blyleven	.10	.05
☐ 8 Wade Boggs	.30	.14

☐ 9 George Brett	1.00	.45
☐ 10 Vince Coleman	.05	.02
☐ 11 Andre Dawson	.25	.11
☐ 12 Dwight Evans	.05	.02
☐ 13 Carlton Fisk	.25	.11
☐ 14 Rickey Henderson	.40	.18
☐ 15 Dale Murphy	.20	.09
☐ 16 Eddie Murray	.30	.14
☐ 17 Jeff Reardon	.05	.02
☐ 18 Rick Reuschel	.05	.02
☐ 19 Cal Ripken	2.00	.90
☐ 20 Nolan Ryan	2.00	.90
☐ 21 Ryne Sandberg	.75	.35
☐ 22 Robin Yount	.25	.11
☐ 23 Rickey Henderson	.40	.18
☐ 24 Will Clark	.50	.23
☐ 25 Dave Stewart	.05	.02
☐ 26 Walt Weiss	.05	.02
☐ 27 Mike Moore	.05	.02
☐ 28 Terry Steinbach	.10	.05
☐ 29 Dave Henderson	.05	.02
☐ 30 Matt Williams	.50	.23
☐ 31 Rickey Henderson	.40	.18
☐ 32 Kevin Mitchell	.05	.02
☐ 33 Dave Stewart	.05	.02

1991 Woolworth's

Topps produced this 33-card boxed standard-size set for Woolworth stores. The cards feature glossy color player photos on the fronts, with yellow borders on a white card face. The backs are printed in red, black, and white, and commemorate outstanding achievements of the players featured on the cards. The set can be subdivided as follows: MVPs (1-2), Cy Young winners (3-4), ROYs (5-6), '90 highlights in alphabetical order (7-22), playoff MVPs (23-24), and World Series action in chronological order (25-33).

	MINT	NRMT
COMPLETE SET (33)	5.00	2.20
COMMON CARD (1-33)	.05	.02
☐ 1 Barry Bonds	.50	.23
☐ 2 Rickey Henderson (Bat on shoulder)	.30	.14
☐ 3 Doug Drabek	.05	.02
☐ 4 Bob Welch	.05	.02
☐ 5 David Justice	.30	.14
☐ 6 Sandy Alomar Jr.	.10	.05
☐ 7 Bert Blyleven	.10	.05
☐ 8 George Brett	1.00	.45
☐ 9 Andre Dawson	.25	.11
☐ 10 Dwight Evans	.05	.02
☐ 11 Alex Fernandez	.15	.07
☐ 12 Carlton Fisk	.25	.11
☐ 13 Kevin Maas	.05	.02
☐ 14 Dale Murphy	.20	.09
☐ 15 Eddie Murray	.30	.14
☐ 16 Dave Parker	.10	.05
☐ 17 Jeff Reardon	.05	.02
☐ 18 Cal Ripken	2.00	.90
☐ 19 Nolan Ryan	2.00	.90
☐ 20 Ryne Sandberg	.75	.35
☐ 21 Bobby Thigpen	.05	.02
☐ 22 Robin Yount	.25	.11
☐ 23 Rob Dibble and Randy Myers	.05	.02
☐ 24 Dave Stewart	.05	.02
☐ 25 Eric Davis	.05	.02
☐ 26 Rickey Henderson (Running bases)	.30	.14
☐ 27 Billy Hatcher	.05	.02
☐ 28 Joe Oliver	.05	.02
☐ 29 Chris Sabo	.05	.02
☐ 30 Barry Larkin	.25	.11
☐ 31 Jose Rijo (Pitching Game 4)	.05	.02
☐ 32 Reds Celebrate (1990 World Champions)	.05	.02
☐ 33 Jose Rijo World Series MVP	.05	.02

1936 World Wide Gum V355

The cards in this 135-card set measure approximately 2 1/2" by 3". The 1936 Canadian Goudey set was issued by World Wide Gum Company and contains black and white cards. This issue is the most difficult to obtain of the Canadian Goudeys. The fronts feature player photos with white borders. The bilingual (French and English) backs carry player biography and career highlights. The World Wide Gum Company has its location listed as Granby, Quebec on these cards (as opposed to Montreal on earlier issues). The cards are numbered on both sides.

	EX-MT	VG-E
COMPLETE SET (135)	16000.00	7200.00
COMMON CARD (1-135)	60.00	27.00
☐ 1 Jimmy Dykes	75.00	34.00
☐ 2 Paul Waner	125.00	55.00
☐ 3 Cy Blanton	60.00	27.00
☐ 4 Sam Leslie	60.00	27.00
☐ 5 Johnny Vergez	60.00	27.00
☐ 6 Arky Vaughan	125.00	55.00
☐ 7 Bill Terry	150.00	70.00
☐ 8 Joe Moore	60.00	27.00
☐ 9 Gus Mancuso	60.00	27.00
☐ 10 Fred Marberry	60.00	27.00
☐ 11 George Selkirk	75.00	34.00
☐ 12 Spud Davis	60.00	27.00
☐ 13 Chuck Klein	75.00	34.00
☐ 14 Fred Fitzsimmons	75.00	34.00
☐ 15 Bill DeLancey	60.00	27.00
☐ 16 Billy Herman	125.00	55.00
☐ 17 George Davis	60.00	27.00
☐ 18 Rip Collins	60.00	27.00
☐ 19 Dizzy Dean	350.00	160.00
☐ 20 Roy Parmelee	60.00	27.00
☐ 21 Vic Sorrell	60.00	27.00
☐ 22 Harry Danning	60.00	27.00
☐ 23 Hal Schumacher	75.00	34.00
☐ 24 Cy Perkins	60.00	27.00
☐ 25 Leo Durocher	200.00	90.00
☐ 26 Glenn Myatt	60.00	27.00
☐ 27 Bob Seeds	60.00	27.00
☐ 28 Jimmy Ripple	60.00	27.00
☐ 29 Al Schacht	75.00	34.00
☐ 30 Pete Fox	60.00	27.00
☐ 31 Del Baker	60.00	27.00
☐ 32 Herman(Flea) Clifton	60.00	27.00
☐ 33 Tommy Bridges	75.00	34.00
☐ 34 Bill Dickey	200.00	90.00
☐ 35 Wally Berger	75.00	34.00
☐ 36 Slick Castleman	60.00	27.00
☐ 37 Dick Bartell	75.00	34.00
☐ 38 Red Rolfe	75.00	34.00
☐ 39 Waite Hoyt	125.00	55.00
☐ 40 Wes Ferrell	75.00	34.00
☐ 41 Hank Greenberg	200.00	90.00
☐ 42 Charlie Gehringer	150.00	70.00
☐ 43 Goose Goslin	125.00	55.00
☐ 44 Schoolboy Rowe	75.00	34.00
☐ 45 Mickey Cochrane MG	150.00	70.00
☐ 46 Joe Cronin	150.00	70.00
☐ 47 Jimmie Foxx	300.00	135.00
☐ 48 Jerry Walker	60.00	27.00
☐ 49 Charlie Gelbert	60.00	27.00
☐ 50 Ray Hayworth	60.00	27.00
☐ 51 Joe DiMaggio	3500.00	1600.00
☐ 52 Billy Rogell	60.00	27.00
☐ 53 John McCarthy	60.00	27.00
☐ 54 Phil Cavarretta	75.00	34.00
☐ 55 KiKi Cuyler	125.00	55.00
☐ 56 Lefty Gomez	150.00	70.00
☐ 57 Gabby Hartnett	125.00	55.00
☐ 58 John Marcum	60.00	27.00
☐ 59 Burgess Whitehead	60.00	27.00
☐ 60 Whitey Whitehill	60.00	27.00
☐ 61 Bucky Walters	75.00	34.00
☐ 62 Luke Sewell	75.00	34.00
☐ 63 Joe Kuhel	60.00	27.00
☐ 64 Lou Finney	60.00	27.00
☐ 65 Fred Lindstrom	125.00	55.00
☐ 66 Paul Derringer	75.00	34.00
☐ 67 Steve O'Neill MG	75.00	34.00
☐ 68 Mule Haas	60.00	27.00
☐ 69 Marv Owen	60.00	27.00
☐ 70 Bill Hallahan	60.00	27.00
☐ 71 Billy Urbanski	60.00	27.00
☐ 72 Dan Taylor	60.00	27.00
☐ 73 Heinie Manush	125.00	55.00
☐ 74 Jo Jo White	60.00	27.00
☐ 75 Joe Medwick	150.00	70.00
☐ 76 Joe Vosmik	60.00	27.00
☐ 77 Al Simmons	150.00	70.00
☐ 78 Shaug Shaughnessy	60.00	27.00
☐ 79 Harry Smythe	60.00	27.00
☐ 80 Bennie Tate	60.00	27.00
☐ 81 Billy Rheil	60.00	27.00
☐ 82 Lauri Myllykangas	60.00	27.00
☐ 83 Ben Sankey	60.00	27.00
☐ 84 Crip Polli	60.00	27.00
☐ 85 Jim Bottomley	125.00	55.00
☐ 86 Watson Clark	60.00	27.00
☐ 87 Ossie Bluege	75.00	34.00
☐ 88 Lefty Grove	200.00	90.00
☐ 89 Charlie Grimm MG	75.00	34.00
☐ 90 Ben Chapman	75.00	34.00
☐ 91 Frank Crosetti	100.00	45.00
☐ 92 John Pomorski	60.00	27.00
☐ 93 Jess Haines	125.00	55.00
☐ 94 Chick Hafey	125.00	55.00
☐ 95 Tony Piet	60.00	27.00
☐ 96 Lou Gehrig	2500.00	1100.00
☐ 97 Billy Jurges	75.00	34.00
☐ 98 Smead Jolley	75.00	34.00
☐ 99 Jimmy Wilson	75.00	34.00
☐ 100 Lon Warneke	75.00	34.00
☐ 101 Vito Tamulis	60.00	27.00
☐ 102 Red Ruffing	125.00	55.00
☐ 103 Earl Grace	60.00	27.00
☐ 104 Rox Lawson	60.00	27.00
☐ 105 Stan Hack	75.00	34.00
☐ 106 Augie Galan	60.00	27.00
☐ 107 Frank Frisch MG	125.00	55.00
☐ 108 Bill McKechnie MG	125.00	55.00
☐ 109 Bill Lee	75.00	34.00
☐ 110 Connie Mack MG	150.00	70.00
☐ 111 Frank Reiber	60.00	27.00
☐ 112 Zeke Bonura	75.00	34.00
☐ 113 Luke Appling	125.00	55.00
☐ 114 Monte Pearson	60.00	27.00
☐ 115 Bob O'Farrell	60.00	27.00
☐ 116 Marvin Duke	60.00	27.00
☐ 117 Paul Florence	60.00	27.00
☐ 118 John Berley	60.00	27.00
☐ 119 Tom Oliver	60.00	27.00
☐ 120 Norman Kies	60.00	27.00
☐ 121 Hal King	60.00	27.00
☐ 122 Tom Abernathy	60.00	27.00
☐ 123 Phil Hensich	60.00	27.00
☐ 124 Ray Schalk	125.00	55.00
☐ 125 Paul Dunlap	60.00	27.00
☐ 126 Benny Bates	60.00	27.00
☐ 127 George Puccinelli	60.00	27.00
☐ 128 Stevie Stevenson	60.00	27.00
☐ 129 Rabbit Maranville MG	125.00	55.00
☐ 130 Bucky Harris MG	125.00	55.00
☐ 131 Al Lopez	125.00	55.00
☐ 132 Buddy Myer	75.00	34.00
☐ 133 Cliff Bolton	60.00	27.00
☐ 134 Estel Crabtree	60.00	27.00
☐ 135 Phil Weintraub	60.00	27.00

1977 Yankees Burger King

The cards in this 24-card set measure 2 1/2" by 3 1/2". The cards in this set marked with an asterisk have different poses than those cards in the regular 1977 Topps set. The checklist card is unnumbered and the Piniella card was issued subsequent to the original printing. The complete set price below refers to all 24 cards listed, including Piniella.

	NRMT	VG-E
COMPLETE SET (24)	40.00	18.00
COMMON CARD (1-23)	.25	.11

☐ 1 Yankees Team	1.50	.70
Billy Martin MG		
☐ 2 Thurman Munson * UER	8.00	3.60
(Facsimile autograph misspelled)		
☐ 3 Fran Healy	.25	.11
☐ 4 Jim Hunter	2.50	1.10
☐ 5 Ed Figueroa	.25	.11
☐ 6 Don Gullett *	.50	.23
(Mouth closed)		
☐ 7 Mike Torrez *	.50	.23
(Shown as A's in 1977 Topps)		
☐ 8 Ken Holtzman	.50	.23
☐ 9 Dick Tidrow	.25	.11
☐ 10 Sparky Lyle	.50	.23
☐ 11 Ron Guidry	.75	.35
☐ 12 Chris Chambliss	.50	.23
☐ 13 Willie Randolph *	.75	.35
(No rookie trophy)		
☐ 14 Bucky Dent *	.50	.23
(Shown as White Sox in 1977 Topps)		
☐ 15 Graig Nettles *	1.50	.70
(Closer photo than in 1977 Topps)		
☐ 16 Fred Stanley	.25	.11
☐ 17 Reggie Jackson *	12.50	5.50
(Looking up with bat)		
☐ 18 Mickey Rivers	.50	.23
☐ 19 Roy White	.50	.23
☐ 20 Jim Wynn *	.75	.35
(Shown as Brave in 1977 Topps)		
☐ 21 Paul Blair *	.75	.35
(Shown as Oriole in 1977 Topps)		
☐ 22 Carlos May *	.50	.23
(Shown as White Sox in 1977 Topps)		
☐ 23 Lou Piniella SP	20.00	9.00
☐ NNO Checklist Card TP	.25	.11

1978 Yankees Burger King

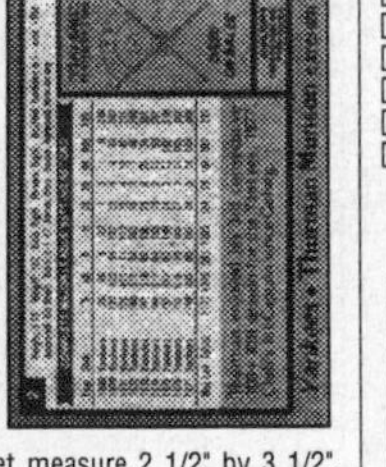

The cards in this 23-card set measure 2 1/2" by 3 1/2". These cards were distributed in packs of three players plus a checklist at Burger King's New York area outlets. Cards with an asterisk have different poses than those in the Topps regular issue.

	NRMT	VG-E
COMPLETE SET (23)	12.00	5.50
COMMON CARD (1-22)	.25	.11

☐ 1 Billy Martin MG	.75	.35
☐ 2 Thurman Munson	4.00	1.80
☐ 3 Cliff Johnson	.25	.11
☐ 4 Ron Guidry	1.25	.55
☐ 5 Ed Figueroa	.25	.11
☐ 6 Dick Tidrow	.25	.11
☐ 7 Jim Hunter	2.50	1.10
☐ 8 Don Gullett	.25	.11
☐ 9 Sparky Lyle	.50	.23
☐ 10 Rich Gossage *	1.25	.55
☐ 11 Rawly Eastwick *	.25	.11
☐ 12 Chris Chambliss	.50	.23
☐ 13 Willie Randolph	.50	.23
☐ 14 Graig Nettles	.75	.35
☐ 15 Bucky Dent	.50	.23
☐ 16 Jim Spencer *	.25	.11
☐ 17 Fred Stanley	.25	.11
☐ 18 Lou Piniella	1.00	.45
☐ 19 Roy White	.50	.23
☐ 20 Mickey Rivers	.50	.23
☐ 21 Reggie Jackson	4.00	1.80
☐ 22 Paul Blair	.25	.11
☐ NNO Checklist Card TP	.15	.07

1979 Yankees Burger King

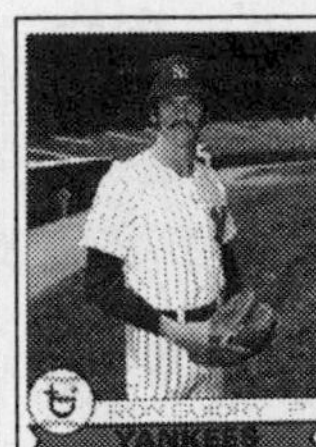

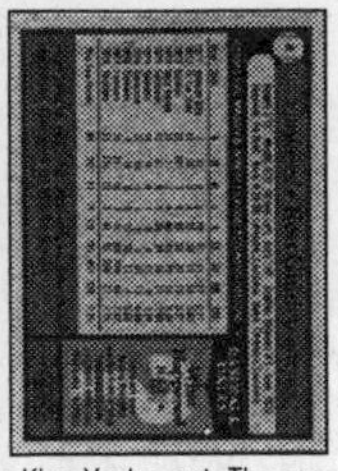

The cards in this 23-card set measure 2 1/2" by 3 1/2". There are 22 numbered cards and one unnumbered checklist in the 1979 Burger King Yankee set. The poses of Guidry, Tiant, John and Beniquez, each marked with an asterisk below, are different from their poses appearing in the regular Topps issue. The team card has a picture of Lemon rather than Martin.

	NRMT	VG-E
COMPLETE SET (23)	10.00	4.50
COMMON CARD (1-22)	.25	.11

☐ 1 Yankees Team:	.75	.35
Bob Lemon MG *		
☐ 2 Thurman Munson	4.00	1.80
☐ 3 Cliff Johnson	.25	.11
☐ 4 Ron Guidry *	.35	.16
☐ 5 Jay Johnstone	.35	.16
☐ 6 Jim Hunter	2.50	1.10
☐ 7 Jim Beattie	.25	.11
☐ 8 Luis Tiant *	.75	.35
(Shown as Red Sox in 1979 Topps)		
☐ 9 Tommy John *	1.25	.55
(Shown as Dodgers in 1979 Topps)		
☐ 10 Rich Gossage	.75	.35
☐ 11 Ed Figueroa	.25	.11
☐ 12 Chris Chambliss	.50	.23
☐ 13 Willie Randolph	.75	.35
☐ 14 Bucky Dent	.50	.23
☐ 15 Graig Nettles	.75	.35
☐ 16 Fred Stanley	.25	.11
☐ 17 Jim Spencer	.25	.11
☐ 18 Lou Piniella	1.00	.45
☐ 19 Roy White	.50	.23
☐ 20 Mickey Rivers	.50	.23
☐ 21 Reggie Jackson	4.00	1.80
☐ 22 Juan Beniquez *	.35	.16
☐ NNO Checklist Card TP	.15	.07

1989 Yankees Score Nat West

The 1989 Score National Westminster Bank New York Yankees set features 33 standard-size cards. The fronts and backs are navy; the backs have color mug shots, 1988 and career stats. The set was given away at a 1989 Yankees' home game.

	MINT	NRMT
COMPLETE SET (33)	20.00	9.00
COMMON CARD (1-33)	.25	.11

☐ 1 Don Mattingly	8.00	3.60
☐ 2 Steve Sax	.75	.35
☐ 3 Alvaro Espinoza	.25	.11
☐ 4 Luis Polonia	1.00	.45
☐ 5 Jesse Barfield	.25	.11
☐ 6 Dave Righetti	.50	.23
☐ 7 Dave Winfield	4.00	1.80
☐ 8 John Candelaria	.25	.11
☐ 9 Wayne Tolleson	.25	.11
☐ 10 Ken Phelps	.25	.11
☐ 11 Rafael Santana	.25	.11
☐ 12 Don Slaught	.25	.11
☐ 13 Mike Pagliarulo	.25	.11
☐ 14 Lance McCullers	.25	.11
☐ 15 Dave LaPoint	.25	.11
☐ 16 Dale Mohorcic	.25	.11
☐ 17 Steve Balboni	.25	.11
☐ 18 Roberto Kelly	.50	.23
☐ 19 Andy Hawkins	.25	.11
☐ 20 Mel Hall	.25	.11
☐ 21 Tom Brookens	.25	.11
☐ 22 Deion Sanders	5.00	2.20
☐ 23 Richard Dotson	.25	.11
☐ 24 Lee Guetterman	.25	.11
☐ 25 Bob Geren	.25	.11
☐ 26 Jimmy Jones	.25	.11
☐ 27 Chuck Cary	.25	.11
☐ 28 Ron Guidry	1.00	.45
☐ 29 Hal Morris	.75	.35
☐ 30 Clay Parker	.25	.11
☐ 31 Dallas Green MG	.50	.23
☐ 32 Thurman Munson MEM	5.00	2.20
☐ 33 Yankees Team Card	.50	.23

1990 Yankees Score Nat West

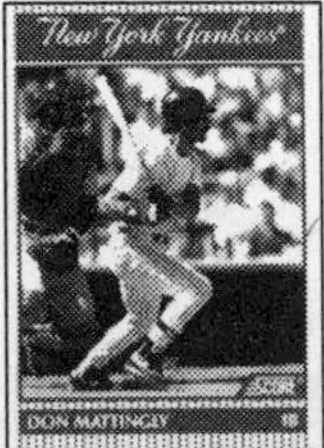

1990 Score National Westminster Bank Yankees is a 32-card, standard-size set featuring members of the 1990 New York Yankees. This set also has a special Billy Martin memorial card which honored the late Yankee manager who died in a truck accident on 12/25/89.

	MINT	NRMT
COMPLETE SET (32)	15.00	6.75
COMMON CARD (1-32)	.25	.11

☐ 1 Stump Merrill MG	.25	.11
☐ 2 Don Mattingly	7.50	3.40
☐ 3 Steve Sax	.50	.23
☐ 4 Alvaro Espinoza	.25	.11
☐ 5 Jesse Barfield	.50	.23
☐ 6 Roberto Kelly	.50	.23
☐ 7 Mel Hall	.25	.11
☐ 8 Claudell Washington	.50	.23
☐ 9 Bob Geren	.25	.11
☐ 10 Jim Leyritz	1.50	.70
☐ 11 Pascual Perez	.25	.11
☐ 12 Dave LaPoint	.25	.11
☐ 13 Tim Leary	.25	.11
☐ 14 Mike Witt	.25	.11
☐ 15 Chuck Cary	.25	.11
☐ 16 Dave Righetti	.50	.23
☐ 17 Lee Guetterman	.25	.11
☐ 18 Andy Hawkins	.25	.11
☐ 19 Greg Cadaret	.25	.11
☐ 20 Eric Plunk	.25	.11
☐ 21 Jimmy Jones	.25	.11
☐ 22 Deion Sanders	2.50	1.10
☐ 23 Jeff D. Robinson	.25	.11
☐ 24 Matt Nokes	.25	.11
☐ 25 Steve Balboni	.25	.11
☐ 26 Wayne Tolleson	.25	.11
☐ 27 Randy Velarde	.25	.11
☐ 28 Rick Cerone	.25	.11
☐ 29 Alan Mills	.25	.11
☐ 30 Billy Martin MEM	2.50	1.10
☐ 31 Stadium Card	.50	.23
☐ 32 All-Time Yankee Record	.50	.23

1993 Yoo-Hoo

This standard-size 20-card set was issued by Yoo-Hoo Chocolate Beverage Corporation and celebrates some of baseball's legends. The fronts and backs are bright yellow and carry a posed or action color photo that is edged in red. The Yoo-Hoo logo is in the upper left and the player's name is printed in red on a white bar in the lower left. The

Baseball Legends Limited Edition logo is in the lower right. The backs contain biography, player position, and career statistics. The cards are unnumbered and checklisted below in alphabetical order.

	MINT	NRMT
COMPLETE SET (20)	10.00	4.50
COMMON CARD (1-20)	.40	.18
☐ 1 Johnny Bench	.75	.35
☐ 2 Yogi Berra	1.00	.45
☐ 3 Lou Brock	.75	.35
☐ 4 Rod Carew	.75	.35
☐ 5 Bob Feller	1.00	.45
☐ 6 Whitey Ford	.75	.35
☐ 7 Steve Garvey	.40	.18
☐ 8 Al Kaline	1.00	.45
☐ 9 Willie McCovey	.60	.25
☐ 10 Joe Morgan	.60	.25
☐ 11 Stan Musial	1.25	.55
☐ 12 Gaylord Perry	.60	.25
☐ 13 Graig Nettles	.40	.18
☐ 14 Jim Rice	.40	.18
☐ 15 Phil Rizzuto	.75	.35
☐ 16 Brooks Robinson	1.00	.45
☐ 17 Pete Rose	1.25	.55
☐ 18 Tom Seaver	1.00	.45
☐ 19 Duke Snider	1.00	.45
☐ 20 Willie Stargell	.60	.25

1994 Yoo-Hoo

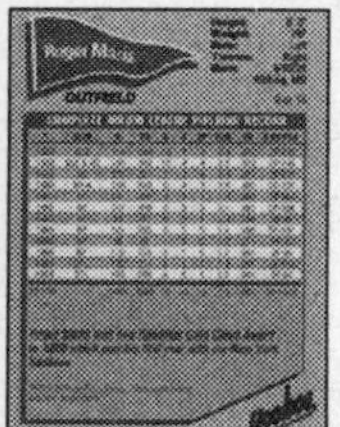

Issued in conjunction with Rawlings in two ten-card sets, each set consisting of eight player cards and two fact cards, this 20-card set features past winners of Rawlings Gold Glove Award. The first series was introduced in May, while the second series was released in August. The entire set could be received for proofs-of-purchase as well as postage and handling; a toll free number on Yoo-Hoo products could be called to obtain the details of the offer. The standard-size cards feature color player photos on their yellow-bordered fronts. Team logo have been airbrushed out. The player's name appears in white lettering within a red banner at the lower left. The yellow-bordered back carries the player's name in white lettering in a red banner at the top left, with biography appearing alongside on the right and statistics below. The Fact Cards are numbered 1-4 on their fronts and backs, and have been arbitrarily assigned an "F" prefix below to distinguish them from the player cards.

	MINT	NRMT
COMPLETE SET (20)	10.00	4.50
COMMON CARD (1-16)	.50	.23
☐ 1 Luis Aparicio	.75	.35
☐ 2 Bobby Bonds	.50	.23
☐ 3 Bob Boone	.75	.35
☐ 4 Steve Carlton	1.00	.45
☐ 5 Roberto Clemente	2.50	1.10
☐ 6 Bob Gibson	1.00	.45
☐ 7 Keith Hernandez	.75	.35
☐ 8 Jim Kaat	.75	.35
☐ 9 Roger Maris	1.50	.70
☐ 10 Don Mattingly	1.50	.70
☐ 11 Thurman Munson	.75	.35
☐ 12 Phil Rizzuto	1.00	.45
☐ 13 Brooks Robinson	1.00	.45
☐ 14 Ryne Sandberg	1.50	.70
☐ 15 Mike Schmidt	1.00	.45
☐ 16 Carl Yastrzemski	1.00	.45
☐ F1 Fact Card 1	.25	.11
☐ F2 Fact Card 2	.25	.11
☐ F3 Fact Card 3	.25	.11
☐ F4 Fact Card 4	.25	.11

1995 Zenith

The complete 1995 Zenith set consists of 150 standard-size cards. The cards are made of thick stock and are borderless. The fronts have an action photo with a pyramid design serving as background. The player's name

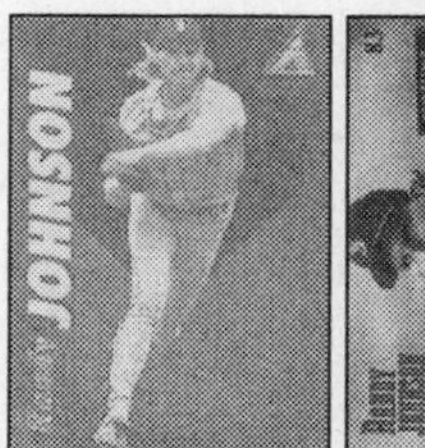

appears vertically up the left side with the Pinnacle logo in the upper right corner. The backs have a head shot and statistical information such as pitcherís strike frequency and what part of the field batters have the tendency to go to most. Included is a subset of 50 Rookies (111-150). The regular issued cards are in alphabetical order by first name. Rookie Cards in this set include Bobby Higginson and Hideo Nomo.

	MINT	NRMT
COMPLETE SET (150)	40.00	18.00
COMMON CARD (1-150)	.25	.11
☐ 1 Albert Belle	1.25	.55
☐ 2 Alex Fernandez	.50	.23
☐ 3 Andy Benes	.25	.11
☐ 4 Barry Larkin	.50	.23
☐ 5 Barry Bonds	1.25	.55
☐ 6 Ben McDonald	.25	.11
☐ 7 Bernard Gilkey	.50	.23
☐ 8 Billy Ashley	.25	.11
☐ 9 Bobby Bonilla	.50	.23
☐ 10 Bret Saberhagen	.25	.11
☐ 11 Brian Jordan	.50	.23
☐ 12 Cal Ripken	4.00	1.80
☐ 13 Carlos Baerga	.50	.23
☐ 14 Carlos Delgado	.75	.35
☐ 15 Cecil Fielder	.50	.23
☐ 16 Chili Davis	.50	.23
☐ 17 Chuck Knoblauch	1.00	.45
☐ 18 Craig Biggio	.75	.35
☐ 19 Danny Tartabull	.25	.11
☐ 20 Dante Bichette	.75	.35
☐ 21 Darren Daulton	.50	.23
☐ 22 David Justice	1.00	.45
☐ 23 Dave Winfield	.75	.35
☐ 24 David Cone	.50	.23
☐ 25 Dean Palmer	.50	.23
☐ 26 Deion Sanders	1.00	.45
☐ 27 Dennis Eckersley	.75	.35
☐ 28 Derek Bell	.50	.23
☐ 29 Don Mattingly	1.50	.70
☐ 30 Edgar Martinez	.75	.35
☐ 31 Eric Karros	.50	.23
☐ 32 James Mouton	.25	.11
☐ 33 Frank Thomas	4.00	1.80
☐ 34 Fred McGriff	.75	.35
☐ 35 Gary Sheffield	.75	.35
☐ 36 Gary Gaetti	.50	.23
☐ 37 Greg Maddux	3.00	1.35
☐ 38 Gregg Jefferies	.50	.23
☐ 39 Ivan Rodriguez	1.25	.55
☐ 40 Kenny Rogers	.25	.11
☐ 41 J.T. Snow	.50	.23
☐ 42 Hal Morris	.25	.11
☐ 43 Eddie Murray 3000th Hit	1.00	.45
☐ 44 Javier Lopez	.75	.35
☐ 45 Jay Bell	.50	.23
☐ 46 Jeff Conine	.50	.23
☐ 47 Jeff Bagwell	2.00	.90
☐ 48 Hideo Nomo Japanese	5.00	2.20
☐ 49 Jeff Kent	.25	.11
☐ 50 Jeff King	.50	.23
☐ 51 Jim Thome	1.00	.45
☐ 52 Jimmy Key	.50	.23
☐ 53 Joe Carter	.75	.35
☐ 54 John Valentin	.50	.23
☐ 55 John Olerud	.50	.23
☐ 56 Jose Canseco	.75	.35
☐ 57 Jose Rijo	.25	.11
☐ 58 Jose Offerman	.25	.11
☐ 59 Juan Gonzalez	2.50	1.10
☐ 60 Ken Caminiti	1.00	.45
☐ 61 Ken Griffey Jr.	5.00	2.20
☐ 62 Kenny Lofton	1.25	.55
☐ 63 Kevin Appier	.50	.23
☐ 64 Kevin Seitzer	.25	.11
☐ 65 Kirby Puckett	2.00	.90
☐ 66 Kirk Gibson	.50	.23
☐ 67 Larry Walker	1.00	.45
☐ 68 Lenny Dykstra	.50	.23
☐ 69 Manny Ramirez	1.00	.45
☐ 70 Mark Grace	.75	.35
☐ 71 Mark McGwire	2.00	.90
☐ 72 Marquis Grissom	.50	.23
☐ 73 Jim Edmonds	1.00	.45
☐ 74 Matt Williams	.75	.35
☐ 75 Mike Mussina	1.00	.45
☐ 76 Mike Piazza	3.00	1.35
☐ 77 Mo Vaughn	1.25	.55
☐ 78 Moises Alou	.50	.23
☐ 79 Ozzie Smith	1.25	.55
☐ 80 Paul O'Neill	.50	.23
☐ 81 Paul Molitor	1.00	.45
☐ 82 Rafael Palmeiro	.75	.35
☐ 83 Randy Johnson	1.00	.45
☐ 84 Raul Mondesi	.75	.35
☐ 85 Ray Lankford	.50	.23
☐ 86 Reggie Sanders	.50	.23
☐ 87 Rickey Henderson	.75	.35
☐ 88 Rico Brogna	.25	.11
☐ 89 Roberto Alomar	1.00	.45
☐ 90 Robin Ventura	.50	.23
☐ 91 Roger Clemens	2.00	.90
☐ 92 Ron Gant	.50	.23
☐ 93 Rondell White	.75	.35
☐ 94 Royce Clayton	.25	.11
☐ 95 Ruben Sierra	.25	.11
☐ 96 Rusty Greer	1.00	.45
☐ 97 Ryan Klesko	.75	.35
☐ 98 Sammy Sosa	1.00	.45
☐ 99 Shawon Dunston	.25	.11
☐ 100 Steve Ontiveros	.25	.11
☐ 101 Tim Naehring	.25	.11
☐ 102 Tim Salmon	1.00	.45
☐ 103 Tino Martinez	1.00	.45
☐ 104 Tony Gwynn	2.50	1.10
☐ 105 Travis Fryman	.50	.23
☐ 106 Vinny Castilla	.75	.35
☐ 107 Wade Boggs	1.00	.45
☐ 108 Wally Joyner	.50	.23
☐ 109 Wil Cordero	.25	.11
☐ 110 Will Clark	.75	.35
☐ 111 Chipper Jones	3.00	1.35
☐ 112 Armando Benitez	.25	.11
☐ 113 Curtis Goodwin	.25	.11
☐ 114 Gabe White	.25	.11
☐ 115 Vaughn Eshelman	.25	.11
☐ 116 Marty Cordova	.75	.35
☐ 117 Dustin Hermanson	.50	.23
☐ 118 Rich Becker	.25	.11
☐ 119 Ray Durham	.50	.23
☐ 120 Shane Andrews	.25	.11
☐ 121 Scott Ruffcorn	.25	.11
☐ 122 Mark Grudzielanek	.75	.35
☐ 123 James Baldwin	.50	.23
☐ 124 Carlos Perez	.50	.23
☐ 125 Julian Tavarez	.25	.11
☐ 126 Joe Vitiello	.25	.11
☐ 127 Jason Bates	.25	.11
☐ 128 Edgardo Alfonzo	1.00	.45
☐ 129 Juan Acevedo	.25	.11
☐ 130 Bill Pulsipher	.50	.23
☐ 131 Bob Higginson	1.50	.70
☐ 132 Russ Davis	.25	.11
☐ 133 Charles Johnson	.75	.35
☐ 134 Derek Jeter	3.00	1.35
☐ 135 Orlando Miller	.25	.11
☐ 136 LaTroy Hawkins	.25	.11
☐ 137 Brian L.Hunter	.50	.23
☐ 138 Roberto Petagine	.25	.11
☐ 139 Midre Cummings	.25	.11
☐ 140 Garret Anderson	.75	.35
☐ 141 Ugueth Urbina	.50	.23
☐ 142 Antonio Osuna	.25	.11
☐ 143 Michael Tucker	.75	.35
☐ 144 Benji Gil	.25	.11
☐ 145 Jon Nunnally	.50	.23
☐ 146 Alex Rodriguez	4.00	1.80
☐ 147 Todd Hollandsworth	.50	.23
☐ 148 Alex Gonzalez	.25	.11
☐ 149 Hideo Nomo	5.00	2.20
☐ 150 Shawn Green	.50	.23

1995 Zenith All-Star Salute

This 18-card set was randomly inserted in packs at a rate of one in six. The set commemorates many of the memorable plays of the 1995 All-Star Game played in Arlington, TX. The fronts have an action photo set out against the background of the game giving it a 3D look. The words "All-Star Salute" are in gold on the left with the player's name at the bottom. The backs have a color photo with personal All-Star Game tidbits. The cards are numbered "X of 18."

	MINT	NRMT
COMPLETE SET (18)	60.00	27.00
COMMON CARD (1-18)	1.00	.45

☐ 1 Cal Ripken	8.00	3.60
☐ 2 Frank Thomas	10.00	4.50
☐ 3 Mike Piazza	6.00	2.70
☐ 4 Kirby Puckett	4.00	1.80
☐ 5 Manny Ramirez		
☐ 6 Tony Gwynn	4.00	1.80
☐ 7 Hideo Nomo	6.00	2.70
☐ 8 Matt Williams		
☐ 9 Randy Johnson		
☐ 10 Raul Mondesi		
☐ 11 Albert Belle	4.00	1.80
☐ 12 Ivan Rodriguez	2.50	1.10
☐ 13 Barry Bonds	2.50	1.10
☐ 14 Carlos Baerga	1.00	.45
☐ 15 Ken Griffey Jr.	10.00	4.50
☐ 16 Jeff Conine	1.00	.45
☐ 17 Frank Thomas	10.00	4.50
☐ 18 Cal Ripken Barry Bonds	6.00	2.70

1995 Zenith Rookie Roll Call

This 18-card, Dufex-designed standard-size set was randomly inserted in packs at a rate of one in 24. The set is comprised of 18 top rookies from 1995. The fronts have two photos and a colorful star in the background with which rays of color emanate. The backs are laid out horizontally with a color photo on a multi-color foil background. Player information of previous accomplishments is also on the back and the cards are numbered "X of 18."

	MINT	NRMT
COMPLETE SET (18)	225.00	100.00
COMMON CARD (1-18)	8.00	3.60

☐ 1 Alex Rodriguez	60.00	27.00
☐ 2 Derek Jeter	50.00	22.00
☐ 3 Chipper Jones	50.00	22.00
☐ 4 Shawn Green	10.00	4.50
☐ 5 Todd Hollandsworth	10.00	4.50
☐ 6 Bill Pulsipher	8.00	3.60
☐ 7 Hideo Nomo	50.00	22.00
☐ 8 Ray Durham	8.00	3.60
☐ 9 Curtis Goodwin	8.00	3.60
☐ 10 Brian L.Hunter	10.00	4.50
☐ 11 Julian Tavarez	8.00	3.60
☐ 12 Marty Cordova UER Kevin Maas pictured	10.00	4.50
☐ 13 Michael Tucker	12.00	5.50
☐ 14 Edgardo Alfonzo	12.00	5.50
☐ 15 LaTroy Hawkins	8.00	3.60
☐ 16 Carlos Perez	8.00	3.60
☐ 17 Charles Johnson	12.00	5.50
☐ 18 Benji Gil	8.00	3.60

1995 Zenith Z-Team

This 18-card standard-size set was randomly inserted in packs at a rate of one in 72. The set is comprised of the best players in baseball and is done in 3-D Dufex. The fronts have a player action photo positioned on home plate which has the words "Z Team". There are multi-colored rays coming out of the card background. The back is laid out horizontally with a color head shot and a stadium crowd background. The back also has player information and a "Z Team" emblem.

	MINT	NRMT
COMPLETE SET (18)	400.00	180.00
COMMON CARD (1-18)	8.00	3.60

☐ 1 Cal Ripken	50.00	22.00
☐ 2 Ken Griffey Jr.	60.00	27.00
☐ 3 Frank Thomas	50.00	22.00
☐ 4 Matt Williams	10.00	4.50
☐ 5 Mike Piazza UER (Card says started at first base Piazza is a catcher)	40.00	18.00
☐ 6 Barry Bonds	15.00	6.75
☐ 7 Raul Mondesi	10.00	4.50
☐ 8 Greg Maddux	40.00	18.00
☐ 9 Jeff Bagwell	25.00	11.00
☐ 10 Manny Ramirez	12.00	5.50
☐ 11 Larry Walker	12.00	5.50
☐ 12 Tony Gwynn	30.00	13.50
☐ 13 Will Clark	10.00	4.50
☐ 14 Albert Belle	15.00	6.75
☐ 15 Kenny Lofton	15.00	6.75
☐ 16 Rafael Palmeiro	10.00	4.50
☐ 17 Don Mattingly	20.00	9.00
☐ 18 Carlos Baerga	8.00	3.60

1996 Zenith

This 1996 Zenith set was issued in one series totalling 150 cards. The six-card packs retail for $3.99 each. The set contains the subset: Honor Roll (131-150). The fronts feature a color player cutout over an arrangement of baseball bats on a black background. The backs carry a hit location chart and player statistics. The only notable Rookie Card is of Darin Erstad.

	MINT	NRMT
COMPLETE SET (150)	40.00	18.00
COMMON CARD (1-150)	.20	.09

☐ 1 Ken Griffey Jr.	4.00	1.80
☐ 2 Ozzie Smith	1.00	.45
☐ 3 Greg Maddux	2.50	1.10
☐ 4 Rondell White	.40	.18
☐ 5 Mark McGwire	1.00	.45
☐ 6 Jim Thome	.75	.35
☐ 7 Ivan Rodriguez	1.00	.45
☐ 8 Marc Newfield	.20	.09
☐ 9 Travis Fryman	.40	.18
☐ 10 Fred McGriff	.60	.25
☐ 11 Shawn Green	.20	.09
☐ 12 Mike Piazza	2.50	1.10
☐ 13 Dante Bichette	.40	.18
☐ 14 Tino Martinez	.75	.35
☐ 15 Sterling Hitchcock	.20	.09
☐ 16 Ryne Sandberg	1.00	.45
☐ 17 Rico Brogna	.20	.09
☐ 18 Roberto Alomar	.75	.35
☐ 19 Barry Larkin	.60	.25
☐ 20 Bernie Williams	.75	.35
☐ 21 Gary Sheffield	.75	.35
☐ 22 Frank Thomas	3.00	1.35
☐ 23 Gregg Jefferies	.40	.18
☐ 24 Jeff Bagwell	1.50	.70
☐ 25 Marty Cordova	.40	.18
☐ 26 Jim Edmonds	.75	.35
☐ 27 Jay Bell	.40	.18
☐ 28 Ben McDonald	.20	.09
☐ 29 Barry Bonds	1.00	.45
☐ 30 Mo Vaughn	1.00	.45
☐ 31 Johnny Damon	.40	.18
☐ 32 Dean Palmer	.40	.18
☐ 33 Ismael Valdes	.40	.18
☐ 34 Manny Ramirez	.75	.35
☐ 35 Edgar Martinez	.60	.25
☐ 36 Cecil Fielder	.40	.18
☐ 37 Ryan Klesko	.60	.25
☐ 38 Ray Lankford	.40	.18
☐ 39 Tim Salmon	.75	.35
☐ 40 Joe Carter	.40	.18
☐ 41 Jason Isringhausen	.20	.09
☐ 42 Rickey Henderson	.60	.25
☐ 43 Lenny Dykstra	.40	.18
☐ 44 Andre Dawson	.60	.25
☐ 45 Paul O'Neill	.40	.18
☐ 46 Ray Durham	.20	.09
☐ 47 Raul Mondesi	.60	.25
☐ 48 Jay Buhner	.60	.25
☐ 49 Eddie Murray	.75	.35
☐ 50 Henry Rodriguez	.20	.09
☐ 51 Hal Morris	.20	.09
☐ 52 Mike Mussina	.75	.35
☐ 53 Wally Joyner	.20	.09
☐ 54 Will Clark	.60	.25
☐ 55 Chipper Jones	2.50	1.10
☐ 56 Brian Jordan	.40	.18
☐ 57 Larry Walker	.75	.35
☐ 58 Wade Boggs	.75	.35
☐ 59 Melvin Nieves	.20	.09
☐ 60 Charles Johnson	.40	.18
☐ 61 Juan Gonzalez	2.00	.90
☐ 62 Carlos Delgado	.40	.18
☐ 63 Reggie Sanders	.20	.09
☐ 64 Brian L.Hunter	.40	.18
☐ 65 Edgardo Alfonzo	.75	.35
☐ 66 Kenny Lofton	1.00	.45
☐ 67 Paul Molitor	.75	.35
☐ 68 Mike Bordick	.20	.09
☐ 69 Garret Anderson	.60	.25
☐ 70 Orlando Merced	.20	.09
☐ 71 Craig Biggio	.60	.25
☐ 72 Chuck Knoblauch	.75	.35
☐ 73 Mark Grace	.60	.25
☐ 74 Jack McDowell	.20	.09
☐ 75 Randy Johnson	.75	.35
☐ 76 Cal Ripken	3.00	1.35
☐ 77 Matt Williams	.60	.25
☐ 78 Benji Gil	.20	.09
☐ 79 Moises Alou	.40	.18
☐ 80 Robin Ventura	.40	.18
☐ 81 Greg Vaughn	.20	.09
☐ 82 Carlos Baerga	.40	.18
☐ 83 Roger Clemens	1.50	.70
☐ 84 Hideo Nomo	2.00	.90
☐ 85 Pedro Martinez	.75	.35
☐ 86 John Valentin	.40	.18
☐ 87 Andres Galarraga	.75	.35
☐ 88 Andy Pettitte	1.00	.45
☐ 89 Derek Bell	.20	.09
☐ 90 Kirby Puckett	1.50	.70
☐ 91 Tony Gwynn	2.00	.90
☐ 92 Brady Anderson	.60	.25
☐ 93 Derek Jeter	2.50	1.10
☐ 94 Michael Tucker	.40	.18
☐ 95 Albert Belle	1.00	.45
☐ 96 David Cone	.40	.18
☐ 97 J.T. Snow	.40	.18
☐ 98 Tom Glavine	.40	.18
☐ 99 Alex Rodriguez	3.00	1.35
☐ 100 Sammy Sosa	.75	.35
☐ 101 Karim Garcia	.40	.18
☐ 102 Alan Benes	.40	.18
☐ 103 Chad Mottola	.20	.09
☐ 104 Robin Jennings	.20	.09
☐ 105 Bob Abreu	.75	.35
☐ 106 Tony Clark	.75	.35
☐ 107 George Arias	.20	.09
☐ 108 Jermaine Dye	.20	.09
☐ 109 Jeff Suppan	.60	.25
☐ 110 Ralph Milliard	.20	.09
☐ 111 Ruben Rivera	.40	.18
☐ 112 Billy Wagner	.60	.25
☐ 113 Jason Kendall	.75	.35
☐ 114 Mike Grace	.20	.09
☐ 115 Edgar Renteria	.75	.35
☐ 116 Jason Schmidt	.40	.18
☐ 117 Paul Wilson	.20	.09
☐ 118 Rey Ordonez	.20	.09
☐ 119 Rocky Coppinger	.40	.18
☐ 120 Wilton Guerrero	.75	.35
☐ 121 Brooks Kieschnick	.40	.18
☐ 122 Raul Casanova	.20	.09
☐ 123 Alex Ochoa	.20	.09
☐ 124 Chan Ho Park	.75	.35
☐ 125 John Wasdin	.20	.09
☐ 126 Eric Owens	.20	.09
☐ 127 Justin Thompson	.60	.25

☐ 128 Chris Snopek	.20	.09
☐ 129 Terrell Wade	.20	.09
☐ 130 Darin Erstad	4.00	1.80
☐ 131 Albert Belle HON	.75	.35
☐ 132 Cal Ripken HON	1.50	.70
☐ 133 Frank Thomas HON	2.00	.90
☐ 134 Greg Maddux HON	1.25	.55
☐ 135 Ken Griffey Jr. HON	2.00	.90
☐ 136 Mo Vaughn HON	.75	.35
☐ 137 Chipper Jones HON	1.25	.55
☐ 138 Mike Piazza HON	1.25	.55
☐ 139 Ryan Klesko HON	.60	.25
☐ 140 Hideo Nomo HON	.60	.25
☐ 141 Roberto Alomar HON	.75	.35
☐ 142 Manny Ramirez HON	.75	.35
☐ 143 Gary Sheffield HON	.75	.35
☐ 144 Barry Bonds HON	.75	.35
☐ 145 Matt Williams HON	.60	.25
☐ 146 Jim Edmonds HON	.75	.35
☐ 147 Derek Jeter HON	1.25	.55
☐ 148 Sammy Sosa HON	.75	.35
☐ 149 Kirby Puckett HON	.75	.35
☐ 150 Tony Gwynn HON	.75	.35

1996 Zenith Artist's Proofs

Randomly inserted in packs at a rate of one in 35, this 150-card set is parallel to the regular Zenith set. The cards are distinguished from the regular set by the "Artist's Proof" all-gold, rainbow holographic foil stamp on the front.

	MINT	NRMT
COMPLETE SET (150)	2000.00	900.00
COMMON CARD (1-150)	3.00	1.35

*STARS: 10X TO 25X BASIC CARDS ..
*YOUNG STARS: 8X TO 20X BASIC CARDS

1996 Zenith Diamond Club

Randomly inserted in packs at a rate of one in 24, cards from this 20-card set honor top performers on a Spectroetch card design printed on thick foil stock with etched highlights. The fronts feature an above-the-waist color action player cutout over a diamond-shaped opening on a grass-green background. The backs carry player information.

	MINT	NRMT
COMPLETE SET (20)	250.00	110.00
COMMON CARD (1-20)	2.00	.90

*REAL DIAMONDS: 3X TO 6X BASIC DIAM.CLUB

☐ 1 Albert Belle	8.00	3.60
☐ 2 Mo Vaughn	8.00	3.60
☐ 3 Ken Griffey Jr.	30.00	13.50
☐ 4 Mike Piazza	20.00	9.00
☐ 5 Cal Ripken	25.00	11.00
☐ 6 Jermaine Dye	2.00	.90
☐ 7 Jeff Bagwell	12.00	5.50
☐ 8 Frank Thomas	25.00	11.00
☐ 9 Alex Rodriguez	20.00	9.00
☐ 10 Ryan Klesko	4.00	1.80
☐ 11 Roberto Alomar	6.00	2.70
☐ 12 Sammy Sosa	6.00	2.70
☐ 13 Matt Williams	4.00	1.80
☐ 14 Gary Sheffield	6.00	2.70
☐ 15 Ruben Rivera	5.00	2.20
☐ 16 Darin Erstad	20.00	9.00
☐ 17 Randy Johnson	6.00	2.70
☐ 18 Greg Maddux	20.00	9.00
☐ 19 Karim Garcia	5.00	2.20
☐ 20 Chipper Jones	20.00	9.00

1996 Zenith Mozaics

Randomly inserted in packs at a rate of one in 10, this 25-card set features three-player image cards of the hottest superstars. The fronts display multiple player images representing the core of each of the 28 teams and are printed on rainbow holographic foil.

	MINT	NRMT
COMPLETE SET (25)	200.00	90.00
COMMON CARD (1-25)	3.00	1.35

☐ 1 Greg Maddux Chipper Jones Ryan Klesko	20.00	9.00
☐ 2 Juan Gonzalez Will Clark Ivan Rodriguez	12.00	5.50
☐ 3 Frank Thomas Robin Ventura Ray Durham	20.00	9.00
☐ 4 Matt Williams Barry Bonds Osvaldo Fernandez	6.00	2.70
☐ 5 Ken Griffey Jr. Randy Johnson Alex Rodriguez	30.00	13.50
☐ 6 Sammy Sosa Ryne Sandberg Mark Grace	6.00	2.70
☐ 7 Jim Edmonds Tim Salmon Garret Anderson	3.00	1.35
☐ 8 Cal Ripken Roberto Alomar Mike Mussina	20.00	9.00
☐ 9 Mo Vaughn Roger Clemens John Valentin	10.00	4.50
☐ 10 Barry Larkin Reggie Sanders Hal Morris	3.00	1.35
☐ 11 Ray Lankford Brian Jordan Ozzie Smith	3.00	1.35
☐ 12 Dante Bichette Larry Walker Andres Galarraga	3.00	1.35
☐ 13 Mike Piazza Hideo Nomo Raul Mondesi	20.00	9.00
☐ 14 Ben McDonald Greg Vaughn Kevin Seitzer	3.00	1.35
☐ 15 Joe Carter Carlos Delgado Alex Gonzalez	3.00	1.35
☐ 16 Gary Sheffield Charles Johnson Jeff Conine	3.00	1.35
☐ 17 Rondell White Moises Alou Henry Rodriguez	3.00	1.35
☐ 18 Albert Belle Manny Ramirez Carlos Baerga	6.00	2.70
☐ 19 Kirby Puckett Paul Molitor Chuck Knoblauch	10.00	4.50
☐ 20 Tony Gwynn Rickey Henderson Wally Joyner	12.00	5.50
☐ 21 Mark McGwire Mike Bordick Scott Brosius	10.00	4.50
☐ 22 Paul O'Neill Bernie Williams Wade Boggs	3.00	1.35
☐ 23 Jay Bell Orlando Merced Jason Kendall	3.00	1.35
☐ 24 Rico Brogna Paul Wilson Jason Isringhausen	3.00	1.35
☐ 25 Jeff Bagwell Craig Biggio Derek Bell	10.00	4.50

1996 Zenith Z-Team

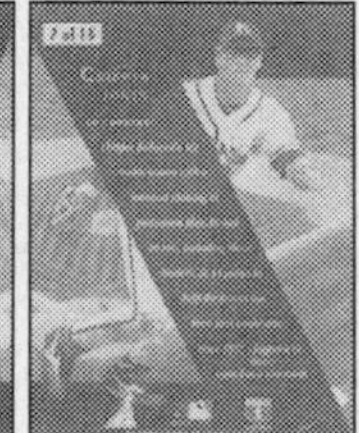

Randomly inserted in packs at a rate of one in 72, this 18-card set features a color action player cutout on a clear micro-etched design with a gold foil Z-Team logo and a see-through green baseball field background. The backs carry player information printed on the back of the Z.

	MINT	NRMT
COMPLETE SET (18)	500.00	220.00
COMMON CARD (1-18)	10.00	4.50

☐ 1 Ken Griffey Jr.	80.00	36.00
☐ 2 Albert Belle	20.00	9.00
☐ 3 Cal Ripken	60.00	27.00
☐ 4 Frank Thomas	60.00	27.00
☐ 5 Greg Maddux	50.00	22.00
☐ 6 Mo Vaughn	20.00	9.00
☐ 7 Chipper Jones	50.00	22.00
☐ 8 Mike Piazza	50.00	22.00
☐ 9 Ryan Klesko	12.00	5.50
☐ 10 Hideo Nomo	40.00	18.00
☐ 11 Roberto Alomar	15.00	6.75
☐ 12 Manny Ramirez	15.00	6.75
☐ 13 Gary Sheffield	12.00	5.50
☐ 14 Barry Bonds	20.00	9.00
☐ 15 Matt Williams	10.00	4.50
☐ 16 Jim Edmonds	10.00	4.50
☐ 17 Kirby Puckett	30.00	13.50
☐ 18 Sammy Sosa	12.00	5.50

1997 Zenith

The 1997 Zenith set was issued in one series totalling 50 cards and was distributed in packs containing five standard-size cards and two 8" by 10" cards with a suggested retail price of $9.99. The fronts feature borderless color action player photos. The backs carry a black-and-white player photo with career statistics. The set contains 42 established player cards and eight rookie cards (43-50).

	MINT	NRMT
COMPLETE SET (50)	50.00	22.00
COMMON CARD (1-50)	.25	.11

☐ 1 Frank Thomas	4.00	1.80
☐ 2 Tony Gwynn	2.50	1.10
☐ 3 Jeff Bagwell	2.00	.90
☐ 4 Paul Molitor	1.00	.45
☐ 5 Roberto Alomar	1.00	.45
☐ 6 Mike Piazza	3.00	1.35
☐ 7 Albert Belle	1.25	.55
☐ 8 Greg Maddux	3.00	1.35
☐ 9 Barry Larkin	.75	.35
☐ 10 Tony Clark	1.00	.45
☐ 11 Larry Walker	1.00	.45
☐ 12 Chipper Jones	3.00	1.35
☐ 13 Juan Gonzalez	2.50	1.10

☐ 14 Barry Bonds	1.25	.55
☐ 15 Ivan Rodriguez	1.25	.55
☐ 16 Sammy Sosa	1.00	.45
☐ 17 Derek Jeter	3.00	1.35
☐ 18 Hideo Nomo	2.50	1.10
☐ 19 Roger Clemens	2.00	.90
☐ 20 Ken Griffey Jr.	5.00	2.20
☐ 21 Andy Pettitte	1.00	.45
☐ 22 Alex Rodriguez	4.00	1.80
☐ 23 Tino Martinez	1.00	.45
☐ 24 Bernie Williams	1.00	.45
☐ 25 Ken Caminiti	1.00	.45
☐ 26 John Smoltz	.50	.23
☐ 27 Javier Lopez	.50	.23
☐ 28 Mark McGwire	2.00	.90
☐ 29 Gary Sheffield	1.00	.45
☐ 30 David Justice	1.00	.45
☐ 31 Randy Johnson	1.00	.45
☐ 32 Chuck Knoblauch	1.00	.45
☐ 33 Mike Mussina	1.00	.45
☐ 34 Deion Sanders	1.00	.45
☐ 35 Cal Ripken	4.00	1.80
☐ 36 Darin Erstad	1.50	.70
☐ 37 Kenny Lofton	1.25	.55
☐ 38 Jay Buhner	.75	.35
☐ 39 Brady Anderson	.75	.35
☐ 40 Edgar Martinez	1.00	.45
☐ 41 Mo Vaughn	1.25	.55
☐ 42 Ryne Sandberg	1.25	.55
☐ 43 Andruw Jones	2.50	1.10
☐ 44 Nomar Garciaparra	3.00	1.35
☐ 45 Hideki Irabu	1.25	.55
☐ 46 Wilton Guerrero	.25	.11
☐ 47 Jose Cruz Jr.	8.00	3.60
☐ 48 Vladimir Guerrero	2.00	.90
☐ 49 Scott Rolen	2.50	1.10
☐ 50 Jose Guillen	1.25	.55

1997 Zenith 8x10

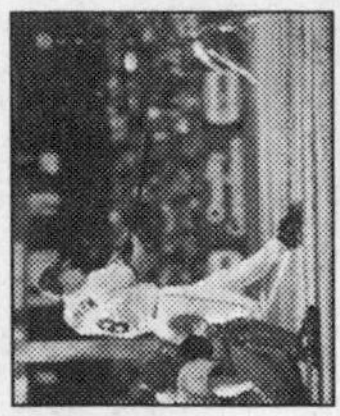

Randomly inserted one in every pack, this 24-card set features 8" by 10" versions of the base set cards of the players listed below.

	MINT	NRMT
COMPLETE SET (24)	50.00	22.00
COMMON CARD (1-24)	1.25	.55
COMP.DUFEX SET (24)	100.00	45.00
COMMON DUFEX (1-24)	4.00	1.80
*DUFEX: 1X TO 2.5X BASIC CARDS		
☐ 1 Frank Thomas	6.00	2.70
☐ 2 Tony Gwynn	4.00	1.80
☐ 3 Jeff Bagwell	3.00	1.35
☐ 4 Ken Griffey Jr.	8.00	3.60
☐ 5 Mike Piazza	5.00	2.20
☐ 6 Greg Maddux	5.00	2.20
☐ 7 Ken Caminiti	1.25	.55
☐ 8 Albert Belle	2.50	1.10
☐ 9 Ivan Rodriguez	2.00	.90
☐ 10 Sammy Sosa	1.25	.55
☐ 11 Mark McGwire	3.00	1.35
☐ 12 Roger Clemens	3.00	1.35
☐ 13 Alex Rodriguez	6.00	2.70
☐ 14 Chipper Jones	5.00	2.20
☐ 15 Juan Gonzalez	4.00	1.80
☐ 16 Barry Bonds	2.00	.90
☐ 17 Derek Jeter	5.00	2.20
☐ 18 Hideo Nomo	3.00	1.35
☐ 19 Cal Ripken	6.00	2.70
☐ 20 Hideki Irabu	3.00	1.35
☐ 21 Andruw Jones	5.00	2.20
☐ 22 Nomar Garciaparra	5.00	2.20
☐ 23 Vladimir Guerrero	4.00	1.80
☐ 24 Scott Rolen	4.00	1.80

1997 Zenith the Big Picture

These six 8" by 10" photos were released as promos to demonstrate what the 1997 Zenith 8 by 10's would look like. They have the notation the Big Picture at the bottom of the card. The cards are skip-numbered and share the same number as the regular cards

	MINT	NRMT
COMPLETE SET (6)	75.00	34.00
COMMON CARD	10.00	4.50
☐ 1 Frank Thomas	15.00	6.75
☐ 4 Ken Griffey Jr.	20.00	9.00
☐ 5 Mike Piazza	15.00	6.75
☐ 13 Alex Rodriguez	15.00	6.75
☐ 17 Derek Jeter	10.00	4.50
☐ 19 Cal Ripken Jr.	15.00	6.75

1997 Zenith V-2

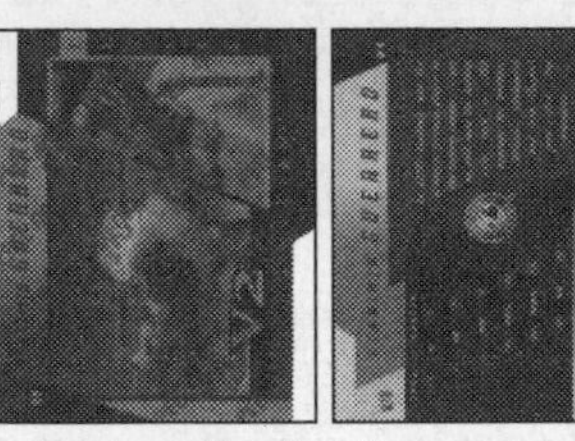

Randomly inserted in packs at the rate of one in 47, this eight-card set features color action player photos produced with motion technology and state-of-the-art foil printing.

	MINT	NRMT
COMPLETE SET (8)	400.00	180.00
COMMON CARD (1-8)	30.00	13.50
☐ 1 Ken Griffey Jr.	80.00	36.00
☐ 2 Andruw Jones	30.00	13.50
☐ 3 Frank Thomas	60.00	27.00
☐ 4 Mike Piazza	50.00	22.00
☐ 5 Alex Rodriguez	50.00	22.00
☐ 6 Cal Ripken	60.00	27.00
☐ 7 Derek Jeter	40.00	18.00
☐ 8 Vladimir Guerrero	25.00	11.00

1997 Zenith Z-Team

Randomly inserted in packs, cards from this nine-card set feature color action photos of top players printed on full Mirror Gold Holographic Mylar foil card stock. Only 1,000 sets were produced and each card is sequentially numbered on back.

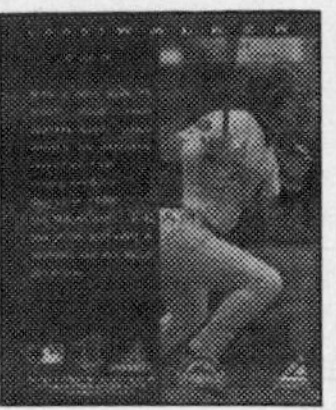

	MINT	NRMT
COMPLETE SET (9)	600.00	275.00
COMMON CARD (1-9)	25.00	11.00
☐ 1 Ken Griffey Jr.	120.00	55.00
☐ 2 Larry Walker	25.00	11.00
☐ 3 Frank Thomas	100.00	45.00
☐ 4 Alex Rodriguez	80.00	36.00
☐ 5 Mike Piazza	80.00	36.00
☐ 6 Cal Ripken	100.00	45.00
☐ 7 Derek Jeter	60.00	27.00
☐ 8 Andruw Jones	50.00	22.00
☐ 9 Roger Clemens	50.00	22.00

1992 Ziploc

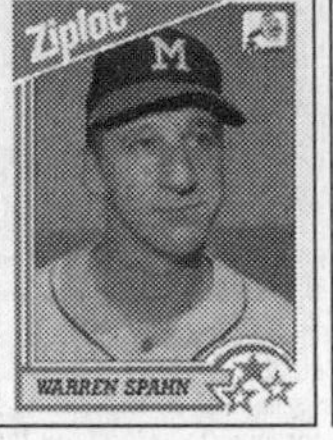

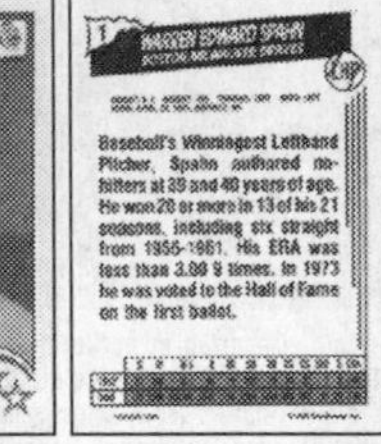

This 11-card standard-size set features posed player photos of many of the game's all-time greats. The Ziploc logo appears diagonally in the upper left corner, while the player's name is printed in black in a bright-yellow stripe accented with red and blue stars at the bottom. The team logo is superimposed over the photo at the upper right. The back design displays the player's full name and team in a slightly diagonal red stripe at the top. A biography, career summary, and statistics are printed in medium blue on a white background. The set was available via a mail-in offer for 50 cents and two UPC's from Ziploc sandwich bags. Individual cards were found one per specially marked package.

	MINT	NRMT
COMPLETE SET (11)	10.00	4.50
COMMON CARD (1-11)	.75	.35
☐ 1 Warren Spahn	1.00	.45
☐ 2 Bob Gibson	1.00	.45
☐ 3 Rollie Fingers	.75	.35
☐ 4 Carl Yastrzemski	1.25	.55
☐ 5 Brooks Robinson	1.50	.70
☐ 6 Pee Wee Reese	1.00	.45
☐ 7 Willie McCovey	1.00	.45
☐ 8 Willie Mays	2.00	.90
☐ 9 Nellie Fox	.75	.35
☐ 10 Yogi Berra	1.50	.70
☐ 11 Hank Aaron	2.00	.90

Acknowledgments

Each year we refine the process of developing the most accurate and up-to-date information for this book. I believe this year's Price Guide is our best yet. Thanks again to all the contributors nationwide (listed below) as well as our staff here in Dallas.

Those who have worked closely with us on this and many other books have again proven themselves invaluable: Levi Bleam and Jim Fleck (707 Sportscards), Peter Brennan, Ray Bright, Card Collectors Co., Cartophilium (Andrew Pywowarczuk), Dwisht Chapin, Barry Colla, Bill and Diane Dodge, Donruss/Leaf (Eric Tijerina), David Festberg, Fleer/SkyBox (Rich Bradley, Doug Drotman), Steve Freedman, Gervise Ford, Larry and Jeff Fritsch, Tony Galovich, Georgia Music and Sports (Dick DeCourcey), Dick Gilkeson, Steve Gold (AU Sports), Bill Goodwin (St. Louis Baseball Cards), Mike and Howard Gordon, George Grauer, John Greenwald, Greg's Cards, Wayne Grove, Bill Henderson, Jerry and Etta Hersh, Mike Hersh, Neil Hoppenworth, Jay and Mary Kasper, David Kohler (SportsCards Plus), Tom Leon, Paul Lewicki, Lew Lipset, Mike Livingston (University Trading Cards), Mark Macrae, Bill Madden, Bill Mastro, Michael McDonald (The Sports Page), Mid-Atlantic Sports Cards (Bill Bossert), Gary Mills, Brian Morris, Mike Mosier (Columbia City Collectibles Co.), B.A. Murry, Ralph Nozaki, Mike O'Brien, Oldies and Goodies (Nigel Spill), Pacific Trading Cards (Mike Cramer and Mike Monson), Pinnacle (Laurie Goldberg), Jack Pollard, Jeff Prillaman, Pat Quinn, Jerald Reichstein (Fabulous Cardboard), Gavin Riley, Clifton Rouse, John Rumierz, Kevin Savage (Sports Gallery), Gary Sawatski, Mike Schechter, Scoreboard (Brian Cahill), Barry Sloate, John E. Spalding, Phil Spector, Frank Steele, Murvin Sterling, Lee Temanson, Topps (Sy Berger and Brian Parkinson), Treat (Harold Anderson), Ed Twombly (New England Bullpen), Upper Deck (Steve Ryan, Marilyn Van Dyke, Terry Melia), Wayne Varner, Bill Vizas, Bill Wesslund (Portland Sports Card Co.), Kit Young and Bob Ivanjack (Kit Young Cards), Rick Young, Ted Zanidakis, Robert Zanze (Z-Cards and Sports), and Bill Zimpleman. Finally we give a special acknowledgment to the late Dennis W. Eckes, "Mr. Sport Americana." The success of the Beckett Price Guides has always been the result of a team effort.

It is very difficult to be "accurate" -- one can only do one's best. But this job is especially difficult since we're shooting at a moving target: Prices are fluctuating all the time. Having several full-time pricing experts has definitely proven to be better than just one, and I thank all of them for working together to provide you, our readers, with the most accurate prices possible.

Many people have provided price input, illustrative material, checklist verifications, errata, and/or background information. We should like to individually thank AbD Cards (Dale Wesolewski), Action Card Sales, Jerry Adamic, Johnny and Sandy Adams, Alex's MVP Cards & Comics, Doug Allen (Round Tripper Sportscards), Will Allison, Dennis Anderson, Ed Anderson, Shane Anderson, Bruce W. Andrews, Ellis Anmuth, Tom Antonowicz, Alan Applegate, Ric Apter, Jason Arasate, Clyde Archer, Randy Archer, Matt Argento, Burl Armstrong, Neil Armstrong (World Series Cards), Todd Armstrong, Ara Arzoumanian, B and J Sportscards, Shawn Bailey, Ball Four Cards (Frank and Steve Pemper), Frank and Vivian Barning, Bob Bartosz, Nathan Basford, Carl Berg, David Berman, Beulah Sports (Jeff Blatt), Brian Bigelow, George Birsic, B.J. Sportscollectables, David Boedicker (The Wild Pitch Inc.), Bob Boffa, Louis Bollman, Tim Bond (Tim's Cards & Comics), Andrew Bosarge, Brian W. Bottles, Bill Brandt, Jeff Breitenfield, John Brigandi, John Broggi, Chuck Brooks, Dan Bruner, Lesha Bundrick, Michael Bunker, John E. Burick, Ed Burkey Jr., Bubba Burnett, Virgil Burns, California Card Co., Capital Cards, Danny Cariseo, Carl Carlson (C.T.S.), Jim Carr, Patrick Carroll, Ira Cetron, Don Chaffee, Michael Chan, Sandy Chan, Ric Chandgie, Ray Cherry, Bigg Wayne Christian, Josh Chidester, Dick Cianciotto, Michael and Abe Citron, Dr. Jeffrey Clair, Derrick F. Clark, Bill Cochran, Don Coe, Michael Cohen, Tom Cohoon (Cardboard Dreams), Collection de Sport AZ (Ronald Villaneuve), Gary Collett, Andrew T. Collier, Charles A. Collins, Curt Cooter, Steven Cooter, Pedro Cortes, Rick Cosmen (RC Card Co.), Lou Costanzo (Champion Sports), Mike Coyne, Paul and Ryan Crabb, Tony Craig (T.C. Card Co.), Kevin Crane, Taylor Crane, Chad Cripe, Brian Cunningham, Allen Custer, Donald L. Cutler, Eugene C. Dalager, Dave Dame, Brett Daniel, Tony Daniele III, Scott Dantio, Roy Datema, John Davidson, Travis Deaton, Dee's Baseball Cards (Dee Robinson), Joe Delgrippo, Tim DelVecchio, Steve Dempski, John Derossett, Mark Diamond, Gilberto Diaz Jr., Ken Dinerman (California Cruizers), Cliff Dolgins, Discount Dorothy, Walter J. Dodds Sr., Bill Dodson, Richard Dolloff (Dolloff Coin Center), Ron Dorsey, Double Play Baseball Cards, Richard Duglin (Baseball Cards-N-More), The Dugout, Kyle Dunbar, B.M. Dungan, Ken Edick (Home Plate of Utah), Randall Edwards, Rick Einhorn, Mark Ely, Todd Entenman, Doak Ewing, Bryan Failing, R.J. Faletti, Terry Falkner, Mike and Chris

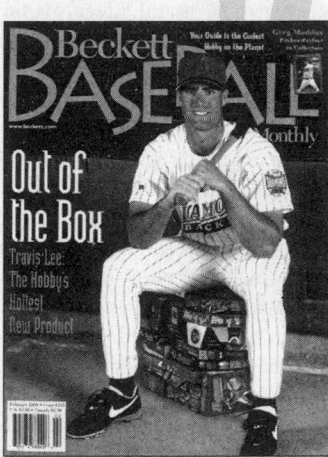

Fanning, John Fedak, Stephen A. Ferradino, Tom Ferrara, Dick Fields, Louis Fineberg, Jay Finglass, L.V. Fischer, Bob Flitter, Fremont Fong, Perry Fong, Craig Frank, Mark Franke, Walter Franklin, Paul Franzetti, Tom Freeman, Bob Frye, Chris Gala, Richard Galasso, Ray Garner, David Garza, David Gaumer, Georgetown Card Exchange, Richard Gibson Jr., Glenn A. Giesey, David Giove, Dick Goddard, Alvin Goldblum, Brian Goldner, Jeff Goldstein, Ron Gomez, Rich Gove, Joseph Griffin, Mike Grimm, Neil Gubitz (What-A-Card), Berry Guenther. Hall's Nostalgia, Hershell Hanks, Gregg Hara, Zac Hargis, Floyd Haynes (H and H Baseball Cards), Ben Heckert, Kevin Heffner, Kevin Heimbigner, Dennis Heitland, Joel Hellman, Arthur W. Henkel, Kevin Hense, Hit and Run Cards (Jon, David, and Kirk Peterson), Gary Holcomb, Lyle Holcomb, Rich Hovorka, John Howard, Mark Hromalik, H.P. Hubert, Dennis Hughes, Harold Hull, Johnny Hustle Card Co., Tom Imboden, Chris Imbriaco, Vern Isenberg, Dale Jackson, Marshall Jackson, Mike Jardina, Hal Jarvis, Paul Jastrzembski, Jeff's Sports Cards, David Jenkins, Donn Jennings Cards, George Johnson, Robe Johnson, Stephen Jones, Al Julian, Chuck Juliana, Dave Jurgensmeier, John Just, Robert Just, Nick Kardoulias, Scott Kashner, Frank J. Katen, Jerry Katz (Bottom of the Ninth), Mark Kauffman, Allan Kaye, Rick Keplinger, Sam Kessler, Kevin's Kards, Larry B. Killian, Kingdom Collectibles, Inc., John Klassnik, Philip C. Klutts, Don Knutsen, Steven Koenigsberg, Bob & Bryan Kornfield, Blake Krier, Neil Krohn, Scott Ku, Thomas Kunnecke, Gary Lambert, Matthew Lancaster (MC's Card and Hobby), Jason Lassic, Allan Latawiec, Howard Lau, Gerald A. Lavelle, Dan Lavin, Richard S. Lawrence, William Lawrence, Brent Lee, W.H. Lee, Morley Leeking, Ronald Lenhardt, Brian Lentz, Leo's Sports Collectibles, Irv Lerner, Larry and Sally Levine, Lisa Licitra, James Litopoulos, Larry Loeschen (A and J Sportscards), Neil Lopez, Allan Lowenberg, Kendall Loyd (Orlando Sportscards South), Robert Luce, David Macaray, Jim Macie, Joe Maddigan, David Madison, Rob Maerten, Frank Magaha, Pierre Marceau, Paul Marchant, Jim Marsh, Rich Markus, Bob Marquette, Brad L. Marten, Ronald L. Martin, Scott Martinez, Frank J. Masi, Duane Matthes, James S. Maxwell Jr., Dr. William McAvoy, Michael McCormick, Paul McCormick, McDag Productions Inc., Tony McLaughlin, Mendal Mearkle, Carlos Medina, Ken Melanson, William Mendel, Eric Meredith, Blake Meyer (Lone Star Sportscards), Tim Meyer, Joe Michalowicz, Lee Milazzo, Jimmy Milburn, Cary S. Miller, David (Otis) Miller, Eldon Miller, George Miller, Wayne Miller, Dick Millerd, Mitchell's Baseball Cards, Perry Miyashita, Douglas Mo, John Morales, William Munn, Mark Murphy, John Musacchio, Robert Nappe, National Sportscard Exchange, Roger Neufeldt, Bud Obermeyer, Francisco Ochoa, John O'Hara, Glenn Olson, Mike Orth, Ron Oser, Luther Owen, Earle Parrish, Clay Pasternack, Mickey Payne, Michael Perrotta, Doug and Zachary Perry, Tom Pfirrmann, Bob Pirro, George Pollitt, Don Prestia, Coy Priest, Loran Pulver, Bob Ragonese, Richard H. Ranck, Bryan Rappaport, Robert M. Ray, R.W. Ray, Phil Regli, Tom Reid, Glenn Renick, Rob Resnick, John Revell, Carson Ritchey, Bill Rodman, Craig Roehrig, David H. Rogers, Michael H. Rosen, Martin Rotunno, Michael Runyan, Mark Rush, George Rusnak, Mark Russell, Terry Sack, Joe Sak, Jennifer Salems, Barry Sanders, Everett Sands, Jon Sands, Tony Scarpa, John Schad, Dave Schau (Baseball Cards), Bruce M. Schwartz, Keith A. Schwartz, Charlie Seaver, Tom Shanyfelt, Steven C. Sharek, Eddie Silard, Art Smith, Ben Smith, Michael Smith, Jerry Sorice, Don Spagnolo, Carl Specht, Sports Card Fan-Attic, The Sport Hobbyist, Dauer Stackpole, Norm Stapleton, Bill Steinberg, Bob Stern, Lisa Stellato, Jason Stern, Andy Stoltz, Bill Stone, Tim Strandberg (East Texas Sports Cards), Edward Strauss, Strike Three, Richard Strobino, Superior Sport Card, Dr. Richard Swales, Paul Taglione, George Tahinos, Ian Taylor, Lyle Telfer, The Thirdhand Shoppe, Scott A. Thomas, Paul Thornton, Carl N. Thrower, Jim Thurtell, John Tomko, Bud Tompkins (Minnesota Connection), Philip J. Tremont, Ralph Triplette, Mike Trotta, Umpire's Choice Inc., Eric Unglaub, Hoyt Vanderpool, Rob Veres, Nathan Voss, Steven Wagman, Jonathan Waldman, Terry Walker, T. Wall, Gary A. Walter, Mark Weber, Joe and John Weisenburger (The Wise Guys), Brian and Mike Wentz, Richard West, Mike Wheat, Richard Wiercinski, Don Williams (Robin's Nest of Dolls), Jeff Williams, John Williams, Kent Williams, Craig Williamson, Opry Winston, Brandon Witz, Rich Wojtasick, John Wolf Jr., Jay Wolt (Cavalcade of Sports), Carl Womack, Pete Wooten, Peter Yee, Wes Young, Dean Zindler, Mark Zubrensky and Tim Zwick.

Every year we make active solicitations for expert input. We are particularly appreciative of help (however extensive or cursory) provided for this volume. We receive many inquiries, comments and questions regarding material within this book. In fact, each and every one is read and digested. Time constraints, however, prevent us from personally replying. But keep sharing your knowledge. Your letters and input are part of the "big picture" of hobby information we can pass along to readers in our books and magazines. Even though we cannot respond to each letter, you are making significant contributions to the hobby through your interest and comments.

The effort to continually refine and improve this book also involves a growing number of people and types of expertise on our home team. Our company boasts a substantial Sports Data Publishing team, which strengthens our ability to provide comprehensive analysis of the marketplace. SDP capably handled numerous technical details and provided able assistance in the preparation of this edition.

Our baseball analysts played a major part in compiling this year's book, traveling thousands of miles during the past year to attend sports card shows and visit card shops around the United States and Canada. The Beckett baseball specialists are, Mark Anderson, Mike Jaspersen, Rich Klein and Grant Sandground (Senior Price Guide Editor). Their pricing analysis and careful proofreading were key contributions to the accuracy of this annual.

Grant Sandground's coordination and reconciling of prices as Beckett Baseball Card Monthly Price Guide Editor helped immeasurably. Rich Klein, as research analyst, contributed detailed pricing analysis and hours of proofing. They were ably assisted by Jeany Finch and Beverly Mills, who helped enter new sets and pricing information, and ably handled administration of our contributor Price Guide surveys. Card librarian Gabriel Rangel handled the ever-growing quantity of cards we need organized for efforts such as this.

The effort was led by the Manager of Technical Services Dan Hitt. They were ably assisted by the rest of the Price Guide analysts: Pat Blandford, Theo Chen, Steven Judd, Lon Levitan, Rob Springs and Bill Sutherland.

The price gathering and analytical talents of this fine group of hobbyists have helped make our Beckett team stronger, while making this guide and its companion monthly Price Guide more widely recognized as the hobby's most reliable and relied upon sources of pricing information.

The Beckett Interactive Department, ably headed by Mark Harwell, played a critical role in technology. Working with software designed by assistant manager Eric Best, they spent countless hours programming, testing, and implementing it to simplify the handling of thousands of prices that must be checked and updated for each edition.

In the Production Department, Paul Kerutis and Marlon DePaula were responsible for the typesetting and for the card photos you see throughout the book.

Don Pendergraft spent tireless hours on the phone attending to the wishes of our dealer advertisers. Once the ad specifications were delivered to our offices, Phaedra Strecher used her computer skills to turn raw copy into attractive display advertisements.

In the years since this guide debuted, Beckett Publications has grown beyond any rational expectation. A great many talented and hard working individuals have been instrumental in this growth and success. Our whole team is to be congratulated for what we together have accomplished. Our Beckett Publications team is led by President Jeff Amano, Vice Presidents Claire Backus and Joe Galindo, Directors Jeff Anthony, C.R.Conant, Beth Harwell and Margaret Steele. They are ably assisted by Pete Adauto, Dana Alecknavage, John Ayres, Joel Brown, Kaye Ball, Airey Baringer, Rob Barry, Therese Bellar, Julie Binion, Louise Bird, Amy Brougher, Bob Brown, Angie Calandro, Allen Christopherson, Randall Calvert, Cara Carmichael, Susan Catka, Albert Chavez, Marty Click, Amy Duret, Von Daniel, Deniel Derrick, Aaron Derr, Ryan Duckworth, Mitchell Dyson, Eric Evans, Kandace Elmore, Craig Ferris, Gean Paul Figari, Carol Fowler, Mary Gonzalez-Davis, Rosanna Gonzalez-Oleachea, Jeff Greer, Mary Gregory, Robert Gregory, Jenifer Grellhesl, Julie Grove, Barry HackerTracy Hackler, Patti Harris, Mark Hartley, Joanna Hayden, Chris Hellem, Pepper Hastings, Bob Johnson, Doug Kale, Kevin King, Justin Kanoya, Edie Kelly, Gayle Klancnik, Rudy J. Klancnik, Tom Layberger, Jane Ann Layton, Sara Leeman, Benedito Leme, Lori Lindsey, Stanley Lira, Louis Marroquin, John Marshall, Mike McAllister, Teri McGahey, Matt McGuire, Omar Mediano, Sherry Monday, Mila Morante, Daniel Moscoso Jr., Allan Muir, Hugh Murphy, Shawn Murphy, Mike Obert, Stacy Olivieri, Andrea Paul, Clark Palomino, Don Pendergraft, Missy Patton, Mike Pagel, Wendy Pallugna, Laura Patterson, Mike Payne, Tim Polzer, Bob Richardson, Lisa Runyon, Wade Rugenstein, Susan Sainz, Christine Seibert, Brett Setter, Len Shelton, Dave Sliepka, Judi Smalling, Sheri Smith, Jeff Stanton, Marcia Stoesz, Mark Stokes, Dawn Sturgeon, Margie Swoyer, Tina Tackett, Doree Tate, Jim Tereschuk, Jim Thompson, Doug Williams, Steve Wilson, Ed Wornson, David Yandry, Bryan Winstead, Jay Zwerner and Mark Zeske. The whole Beckett Publications team has my thanks for jobs well done. Thank you, everyone.

I also thank my family, especially my wife, Patti, and our daughters, Christina, Rebecca, and Melissa, for putting up with me again.

Notes

Notes

Notes